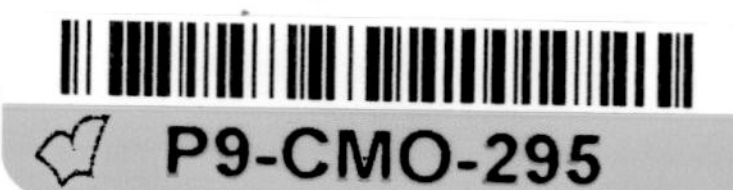

LINCOLN CHRISTIAN COLLEGE AND SEMINARY

CANNOT BE CHECKED OUT

Presented to

BY

ON

Your word is a lamp to my feet and
a light for my path. Psalm 119:105

This certifies that

AND

WERE UNITED IN

Holy Matrimony

ON ______________________ THE ______________________

DAY OF ______________________ A.D. ______________________

AT ______________________

IN ACCORDANCE WITH THE LAWS OF ______________________

OFFICIATING ______________________

WITNESS ______________________

WITNESS ______________________

A MAN WILL . . . BE UNITED TO HIS WIFE
AND THEY WILL BECOME ONE FLESH. GENESIS 2:24

MARRIAGES

HUSBAND

WIFE

PLACE DATE

HUSBAND

WIFE

PLACE DATE

HUSBAND

WIFE

PLACE DATE

HUSBAND

WIFE

PLACE DATE

HUSBAND

WIFE

PLACE DATE

HUSBAND

WIFE

PLACE DATE

LOVE IS PATIENT, LOVE IS KIND . . .
LOVE NEVER FAILS. 1 CORINTHIANS 13:4,8

BIRTHS

NAME

BORN TO DATE

NAME

BORN TO DATE

NAME

BORN TO DATE

NAME

BORN TO DATE

NAME

BORN TO DATE

NAME

BORN TO DATE

NAME

BORN TO DATE

NAME

BORN TO DATE

YOU KNIT ME TOGETHER IN MY MOTHER'S WOMB. PSALM 139:13

BAPTISMS

NAME

MINISTER

PLACE DATE

NAME

MINISTER

PLACE DATE

NAME

MINISTER

PLACE DATE

NAME

MINISTER

PLACE DATE

NAME

MINISTER

PLACE DATE

NAME

MINISTER

PLACE DATE

MAKE DISCIPLES OF ALL NATIONS, BAPTIZING THEM. MATTHEW 28:19

Special events

EVENT

PLACE DATE

EVENT

PLACE DATE

EVENT

PLACE DATE

EVENT

PLACE DATE

EVENT

PLACE DATE

EVENT

PLACE DATE

The Lord reigns,
let the earth be glad. Psalm 97:1

Church Record

EVENT

MINISTER

CHURCH DATE

EVENT

MINISTER

CHURCH DATE

EVENT

MINISTER

CHURCH DATE

EVENT

MINISTER

CHURCH DATE

EVENT

MINISTER

CHURCH DATE

EVENT

MINISTER

CHURCH DATE

You are . . . members of God's household. Ephesians 2:19

DEATHS

NAME

DATE

NAME

DATE

NAME

DATE

NAME

DATE

NAME

DATE

NAME

DATE

NAME

DATE

NAME

DATE

FOR TO ME, TO LIVE IS CHRIST
AND TO DIE IS GAIN. PHILIPPIANS 1:21

Old Testament Chronology

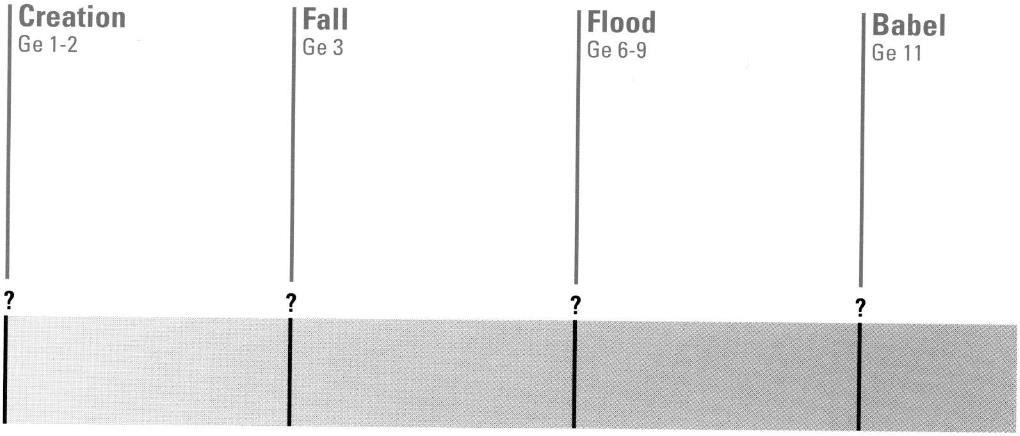

Creation
Ge 1-2

Fall
Ge 3

Flood
Ge 6-9

Babel
Ge 11

? ? ? ?

©1985 The Zondervan Corporation

Old Testament Chronology

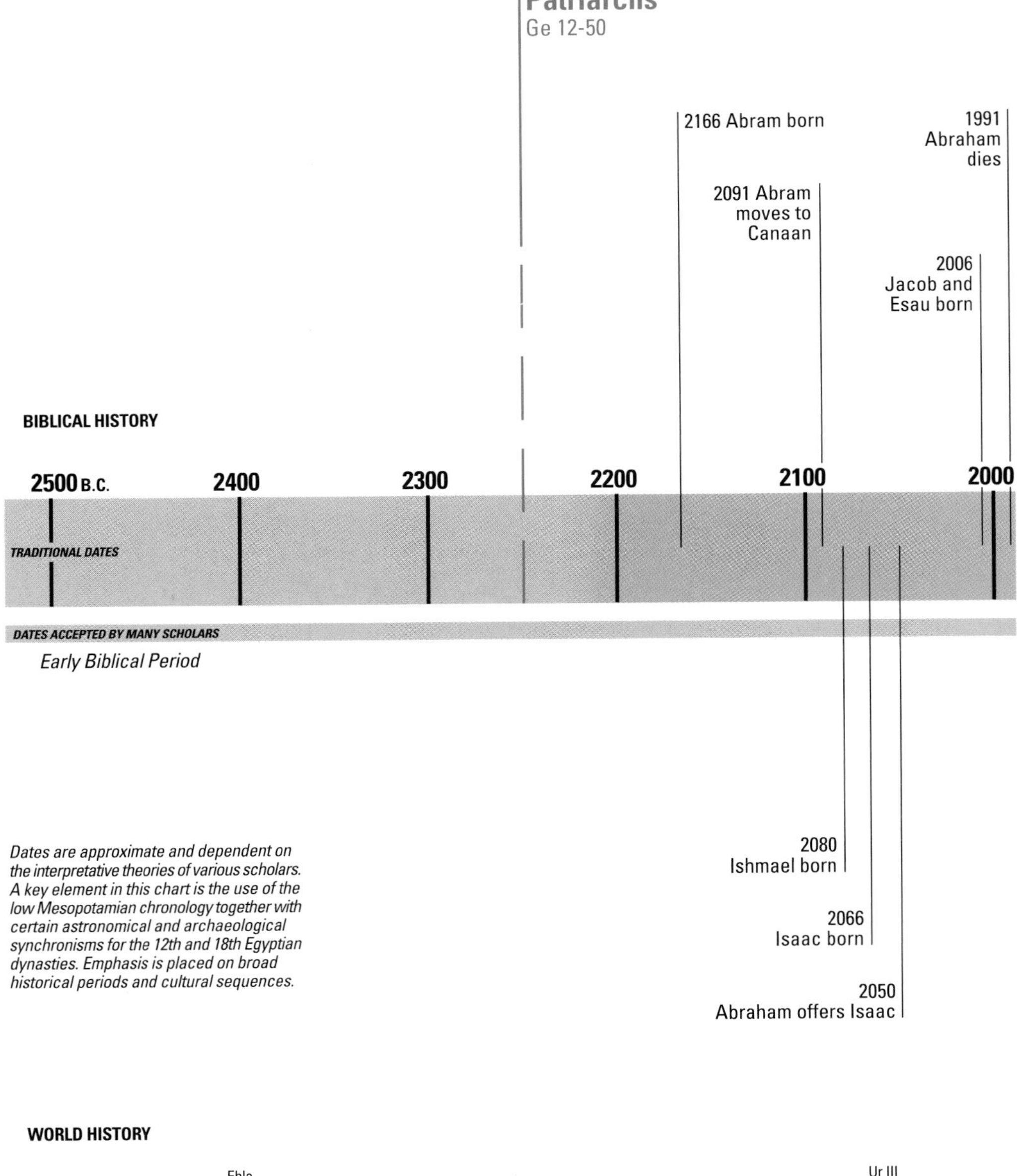

Patriarchs
Ge 12-50
2166 Abram born
1991 Abraham dies
2091 Abram moves to Canaan
2006 Jacob and Esau born
BIBLICAL HISTORY
2500 B.C.
2400
2300
2200
2100
2000
TRADITIONAL DATES
DATES ACCEPTED BY MANY SCHOLARS
Early Biblical Period
2080 Ishmael born
2066 Isaac born
2050 Abraham offers Isaac

Dates are approximate and dependent on the interpretative theories of various scholars. A key element in this chart is the use of the low Mesopotamian chronology together with certain astronomical and archaeological synchronisms for the 12th and 18th Egyptian dynasties. Emphasis is placed on broad historical periods and cultural sequences.

WORLD HISTORY

	2500 B.C.	Ebla texts 2400	2300	2200	2100 Ur III texts	2000
S. MESOPOTAMIA / N. MESOPOTAMIA	Early Dynastic Period		Akkadian Period		Neo-Sumerian Period	
EGYPT	Old Kingdom				1st Intermediate Period	
SYRIA-PALESTINE	Ebla					
ANATOLIA	Hattian Kingdoms					
CRETE	Early Minoan Period					
PERSIA	Elamite Dynasties					
GREECE	Early Helladic Period					
ITALY						

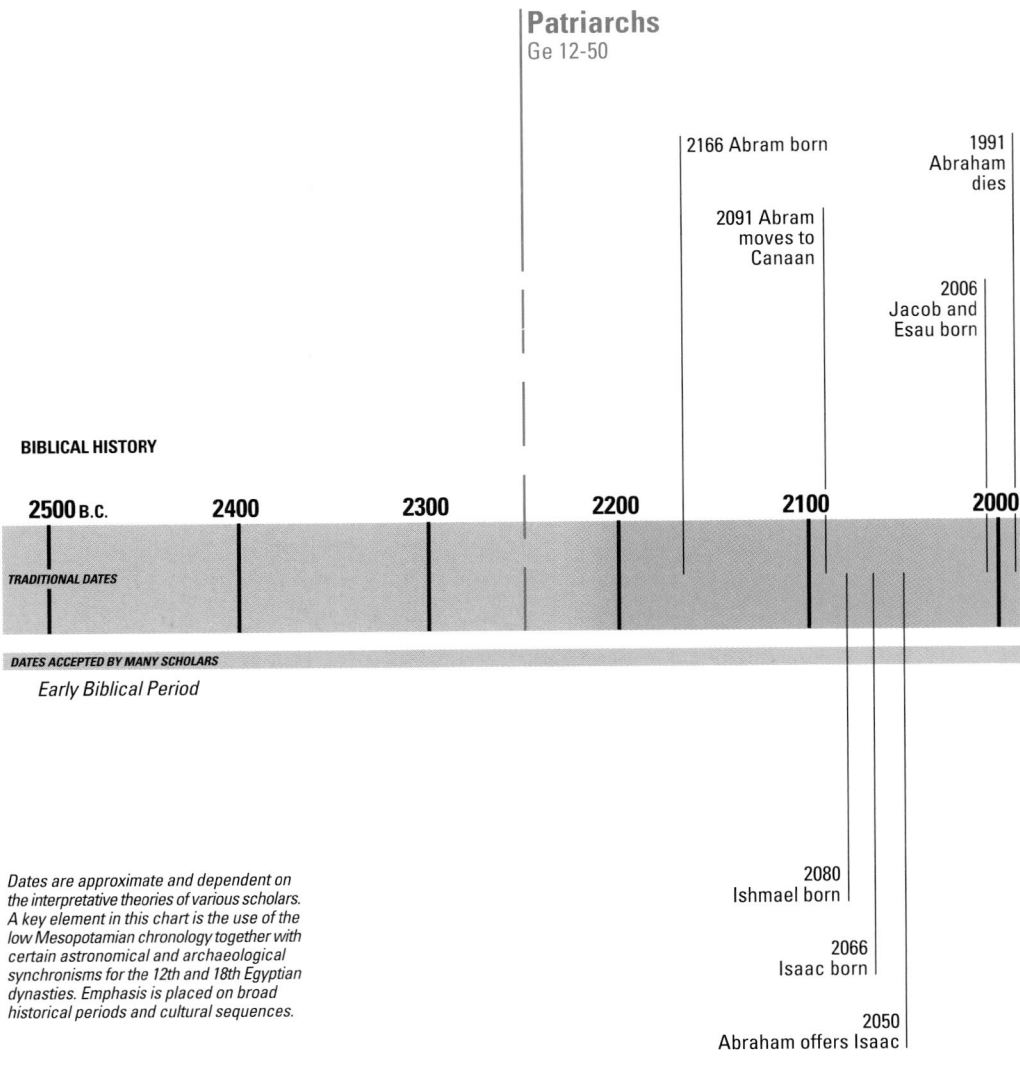

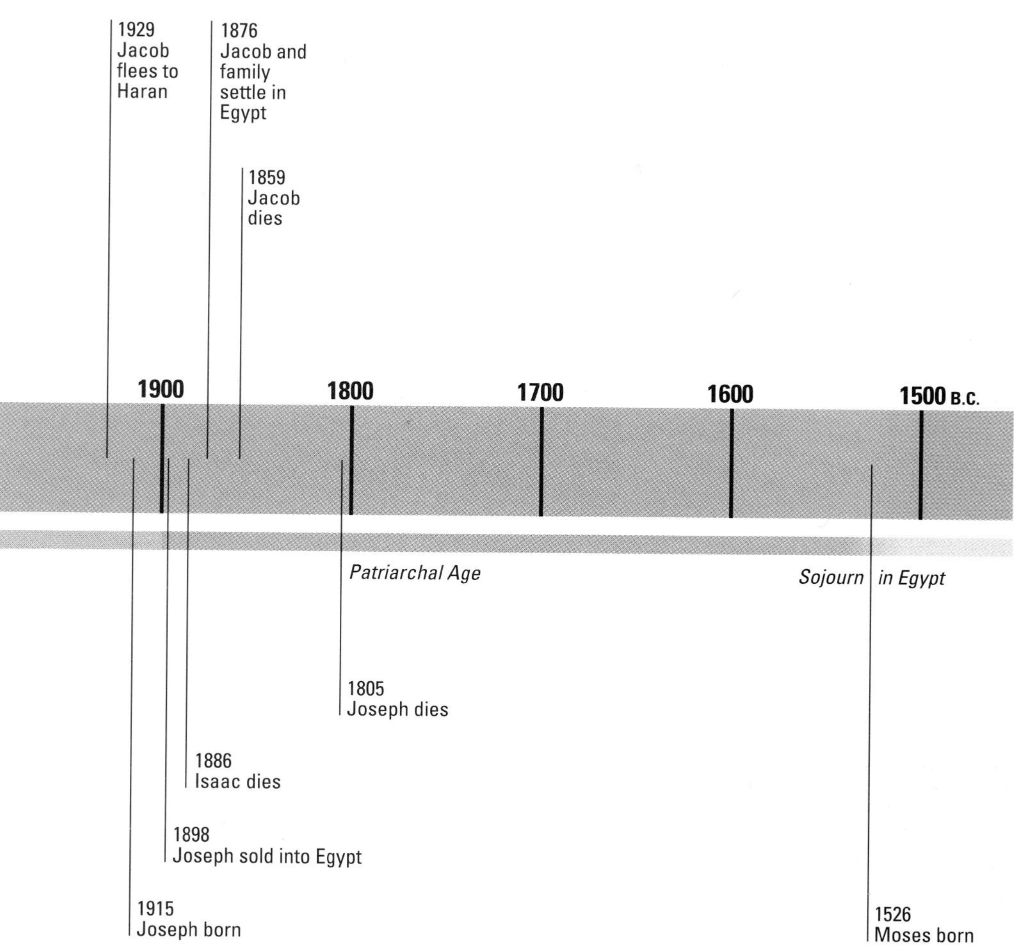
1929
Jacob flees to Haran
1876
Jacob and family settle in Egypt
1859
Jacob dies
1900
1800
1700
1600
1500 B.C.
Patriarchal Age
Sojourn in Egypt
1805
Joseph dies
1886
Isaac dies
1898
Joseph sold into Egypt
1915
Joseph born
1526
Moses born

Cappadocian texts
Mari texts
Hammurapi texts
1900
1800
1700
1600
1500 B.C.
Isin-Larsa Period
Old Babylonian Period
Middle Kingdom
2nd Intermediate (Hyksos) Period
New Kingdom
Amorite Period
Hyksos Period
Late Canaanite Period
Hittite Old Kingdom
Middle Minoan Period
Middle Helladic Period

©1985 The Zondervan Corporation

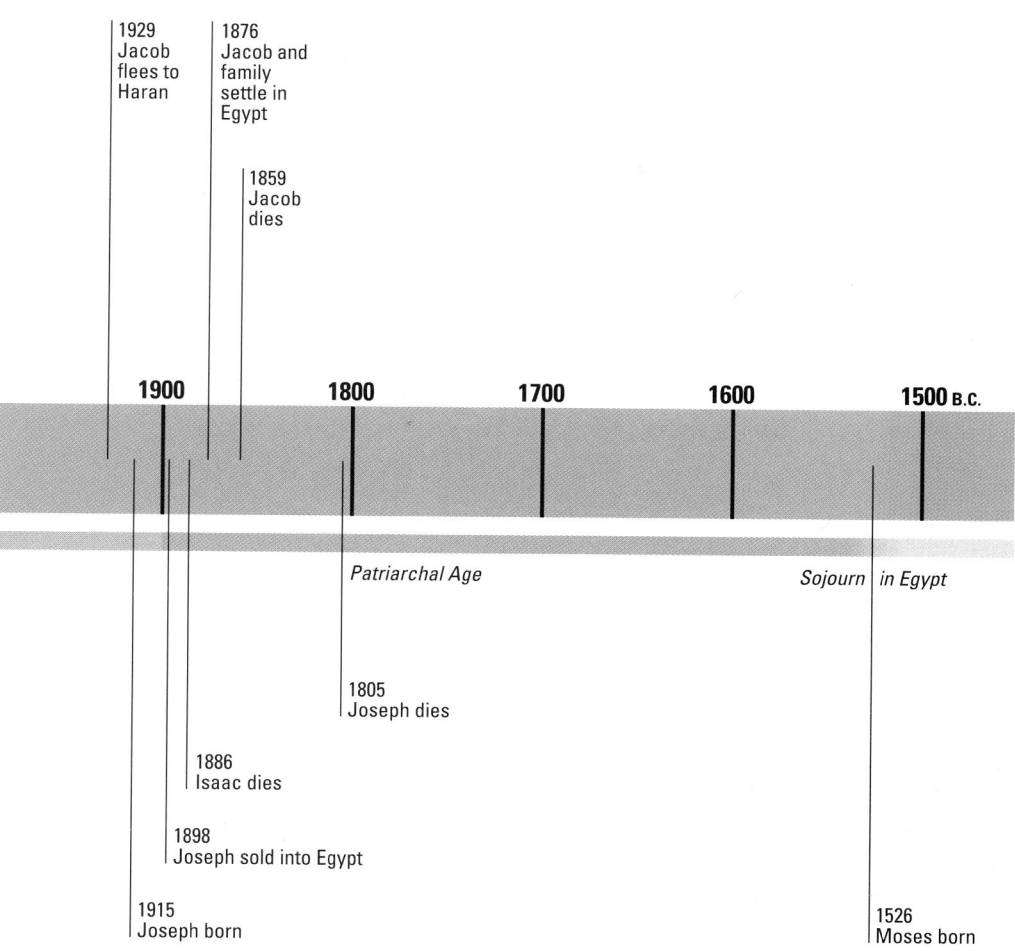

Old Testament Chronology

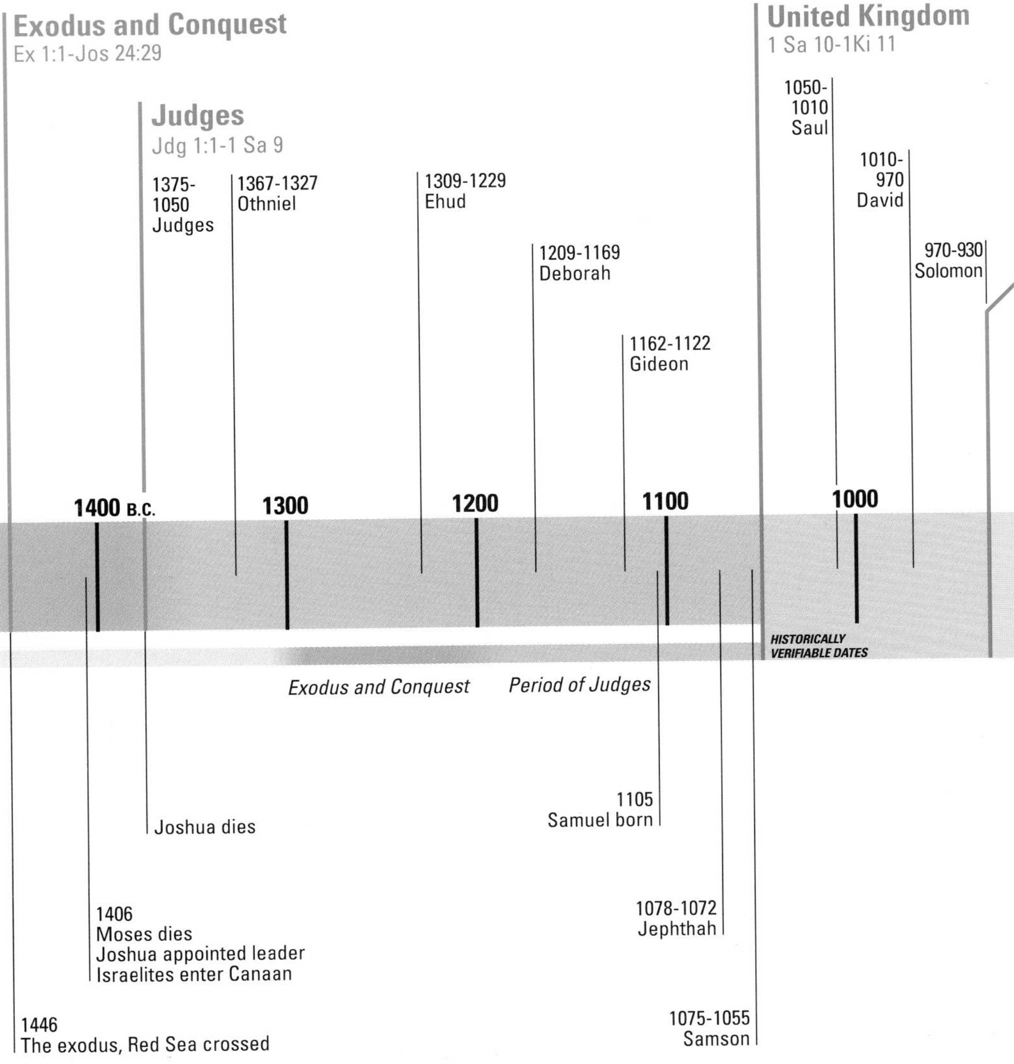

Exodus and Conquest
Ex 1:1-Jos 24:29
Judges
Jdg 1:1-1 Sa 9
1375-1050 Judges
1367-1327 Othniel
1309-1229 Ehud
1209-1169 Deborah
1162-1122 Gideon
United Kingdom
1 Sa 10-1Ki 11
1050-1010 Saul
1010-970 David
970-930 Solomon
1400 B.C.
1300
1200
1100
1000
HISTORICALLY VERIFIABLE DATES
Exodus and Conquest
Period of Judges
Joshua dies
1105 Samuel born
1406
Moses dies
Joshua appointed leader
Israelites enter Canaan
1078-1072 Jephthah
1446
The exodus, Red Sea crossed
1075-1055 Samson

Nuzi texts | Amarna texts | Ugaritic texts | Merneptah inscription | Medinet Habu inscriptions | Shishak inscription

	1400 B.C.	1300	1200	1100	1000
S. MESOPOTAMIA	Kassite Period				
N. MESOPOTAMIA	← Mitannian Kingdom		Middle Assyrian Period		
EGYPT	New Kingdom				
SYRIA-PALESTINE	Late Canaanite Period		Sea Peoples		Phoenician,
ANATOLIA	Hittite Empire		Phrygian Period		
CRETE	Late Minoan Period				Dorian States
PERSIA					
GREECE	Late Helladic (Mycenean) Period				Dorian States
ITALY					

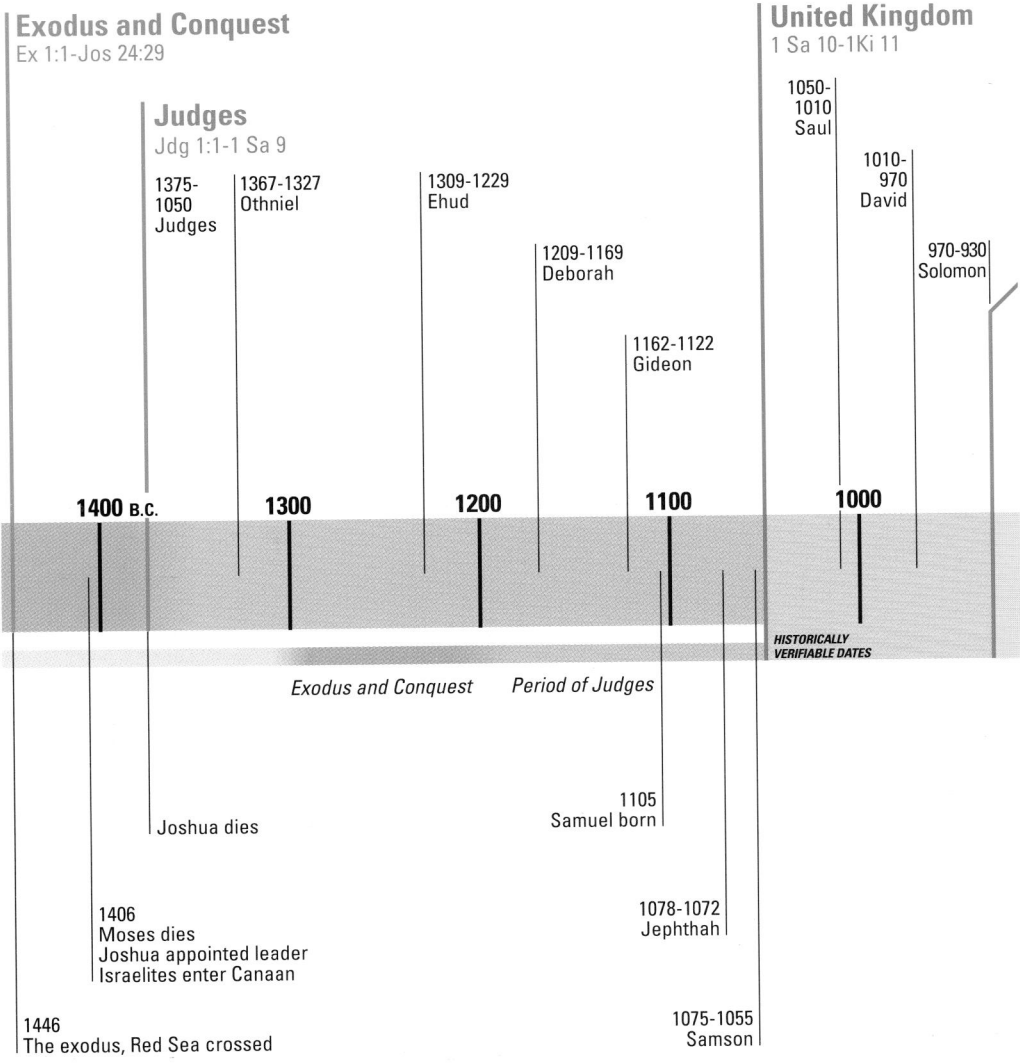

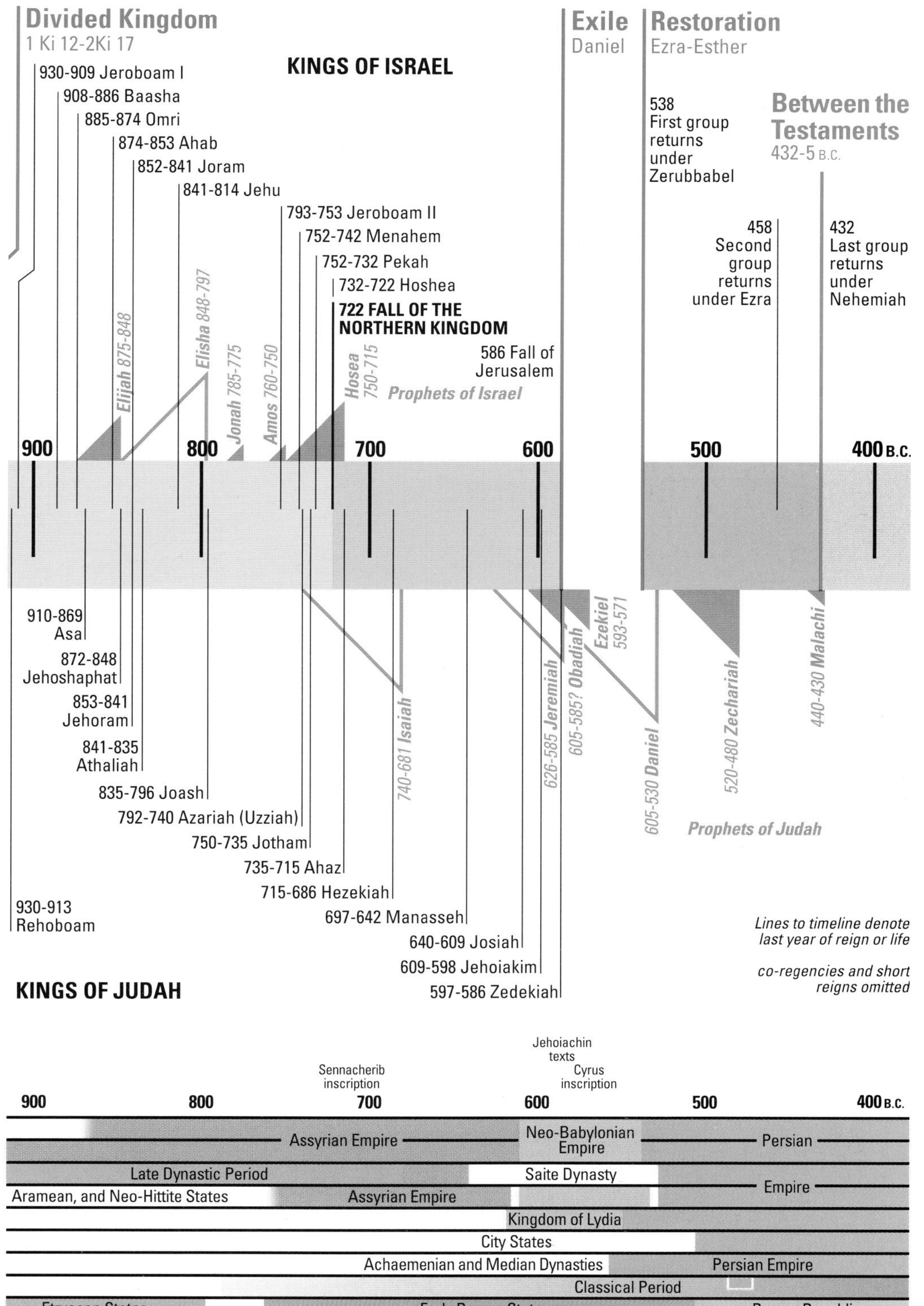

Divided Kingdom
1 Ki 12-2Ki 17
KINGS OF ISRAEL
930-909 Jeroboam I
908-886 Baasha
885-874 Omri
874-853 Ahab
852-841 Joram
841-814 Jehu
793-753 Jeroboam II
752-742 Menahem
752-732 Pekah
732-722 Hoshea
722 FALL OF THE NORTHERN KINGDOM
586 Fall of Jerusalem
Exile
Daniel
Restoration
Ezra-Esther
538 First group returns under Zerubbabel
Between the Testaments
432-5 B.C.
458 Second group returns under Ezra
432 Last group returns under Nehemiah
Elijah 875-848
Elisha 848-797
Jonah 785-775
Amos 760-750
Hosea 750-715
Prophets of Israel
900
800
700
600
500
400 B.C.
910-869 Asa
872-848 Jehoshaphat
853-841 Jehoram
841-835 Athaliah
835-796 Joash
792-740 Azariah (Uzziah)
750-735 Jotham
735-715 Ahaz
715-686 Hezekiah
697-642 Manasseh
640-609 Josiah
609-598 Jehoiakim
597-586 Zedekiah
930-913 Rehoboam
KINGS OF JUDAH
740-681 Isaiah
626-585 Jeremiah
605-585? Obadiah
Ezekiel 593-571
605-530 Daniel
520-480 Zechariah
440-430 Malachi
Prophets of Judah
Lines to timeline denote last year of reign or life
co-regencies and short reigns omitted
Sennacherib inscription
Jehoiachin texts
Cyrus inscription
900
800
700
600
500
400 B.C.
Assyrian Empire
Neo-Babylonian Empire
Persian
Late Dynastic Period
Saite Dynasty
Empire
Aramean, and Neo-Hittite States
Assyrian Empire
Kingdom of Lydia
City States
Achaemenian and Median Dynasties
Persian Empire
Classical Period
Etruscan States
Early Roman State
Roman Republic

©1985 The Zondervan Corporation

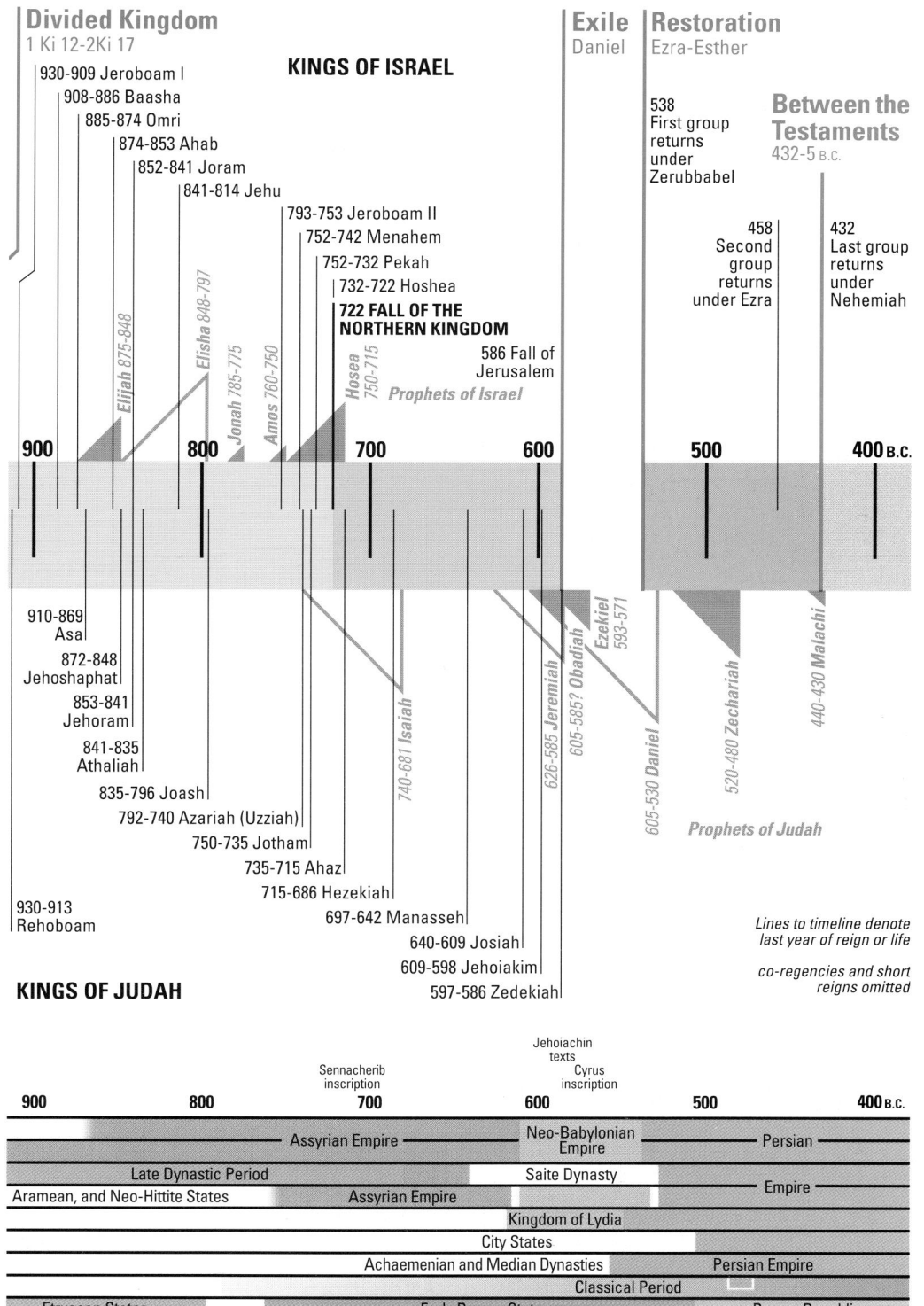

New Testament Chronology

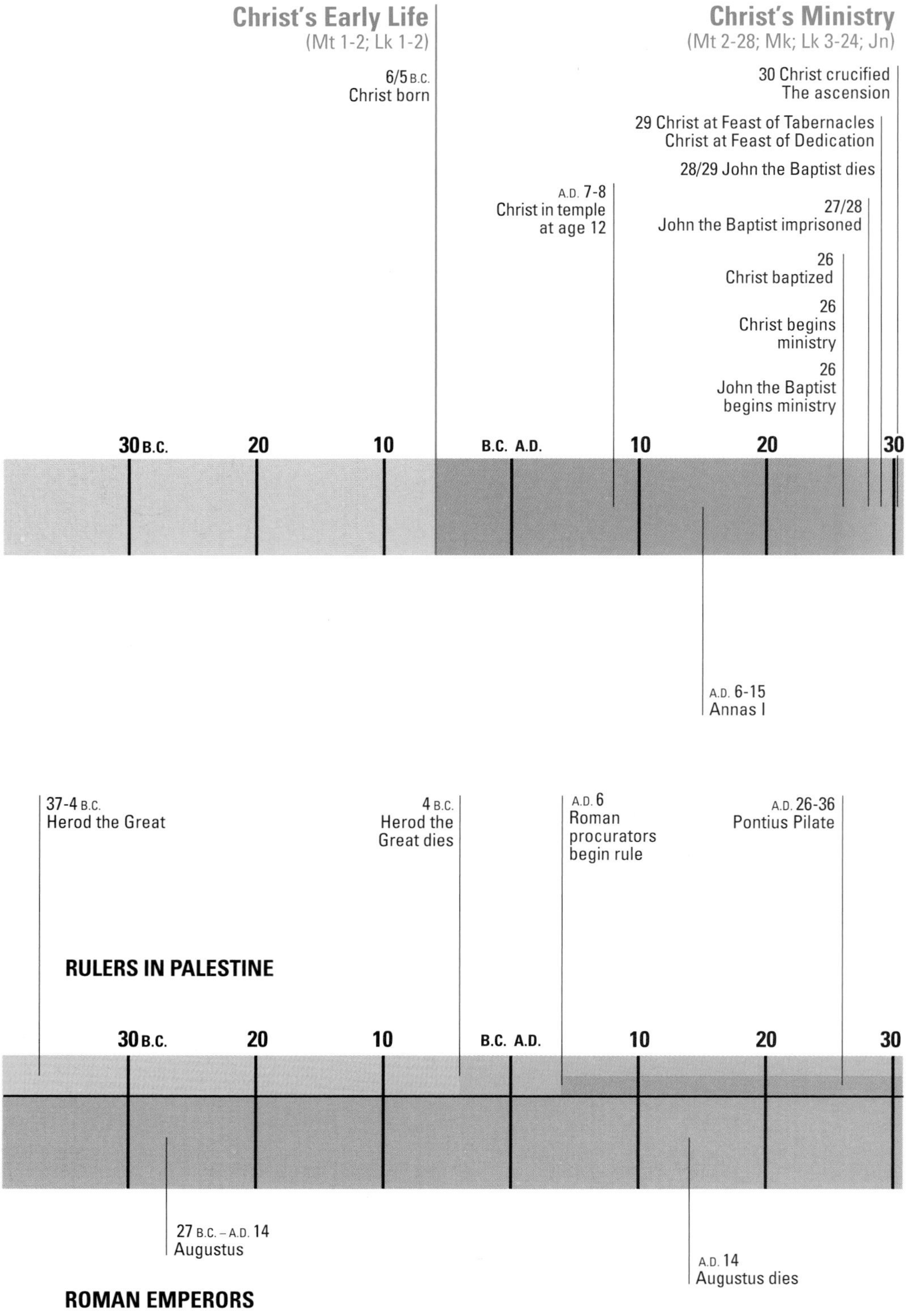

Christ's Early Life
(Mt 1-2; Lk 1-2)

6/5 B.C.
Christ born

Christ's Ministry
(Mt 2-28; Mk; Lk 3-24; Jn)

30 Christ crucified
The ascension

29 Christ at Feast of Tabernacles
Christ at Feast of Dedication

28/29 John the Baptist dies

A.D. 7-8
Christ in temple
at age 12

27/28
John the Baptist imprisoned

26
Christ baptized

26
Christ begins
ministry

26
John the Baptist
begins ministry

30 B.C. 20 10 B.C. A.D. 10 20 30

A.D. 6-15
Annas I

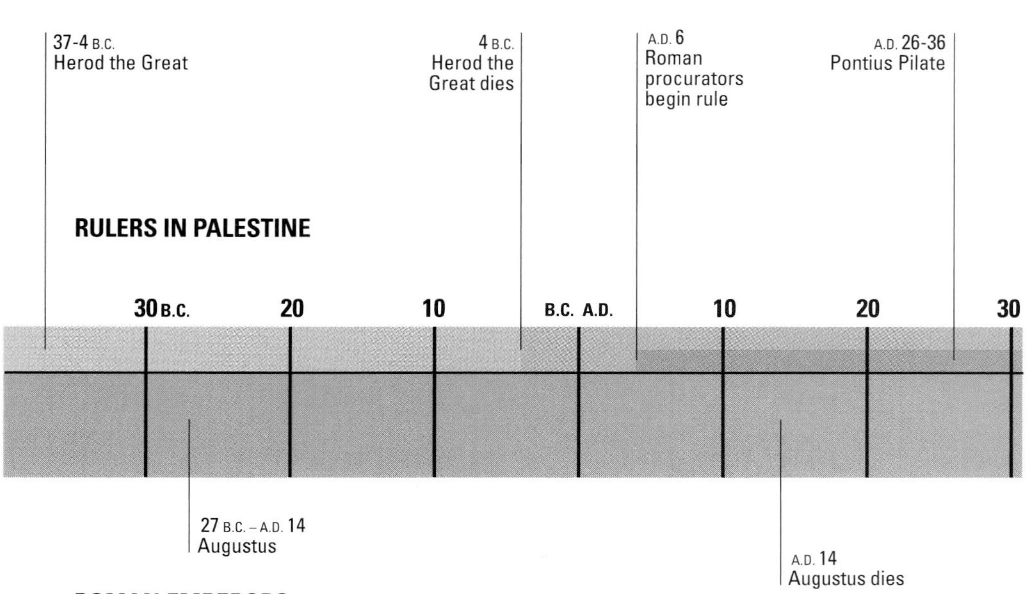

37-4 B.C.
Herod the Great
4 B.C.
Herod the
Great dies
A.D. 6
Roman
procurators
begin rule
A.D. 26-36
Pontius Pilate
RULERS IN PALESTINE
30 B.C.
20
10
B.C. A.D.
10
20
30
27 B.C. – A.D. 14
Augustus
A.D. 14
Augustus dies
ROMAN EMPERORS

The Early Church

(Acts-Revelation)

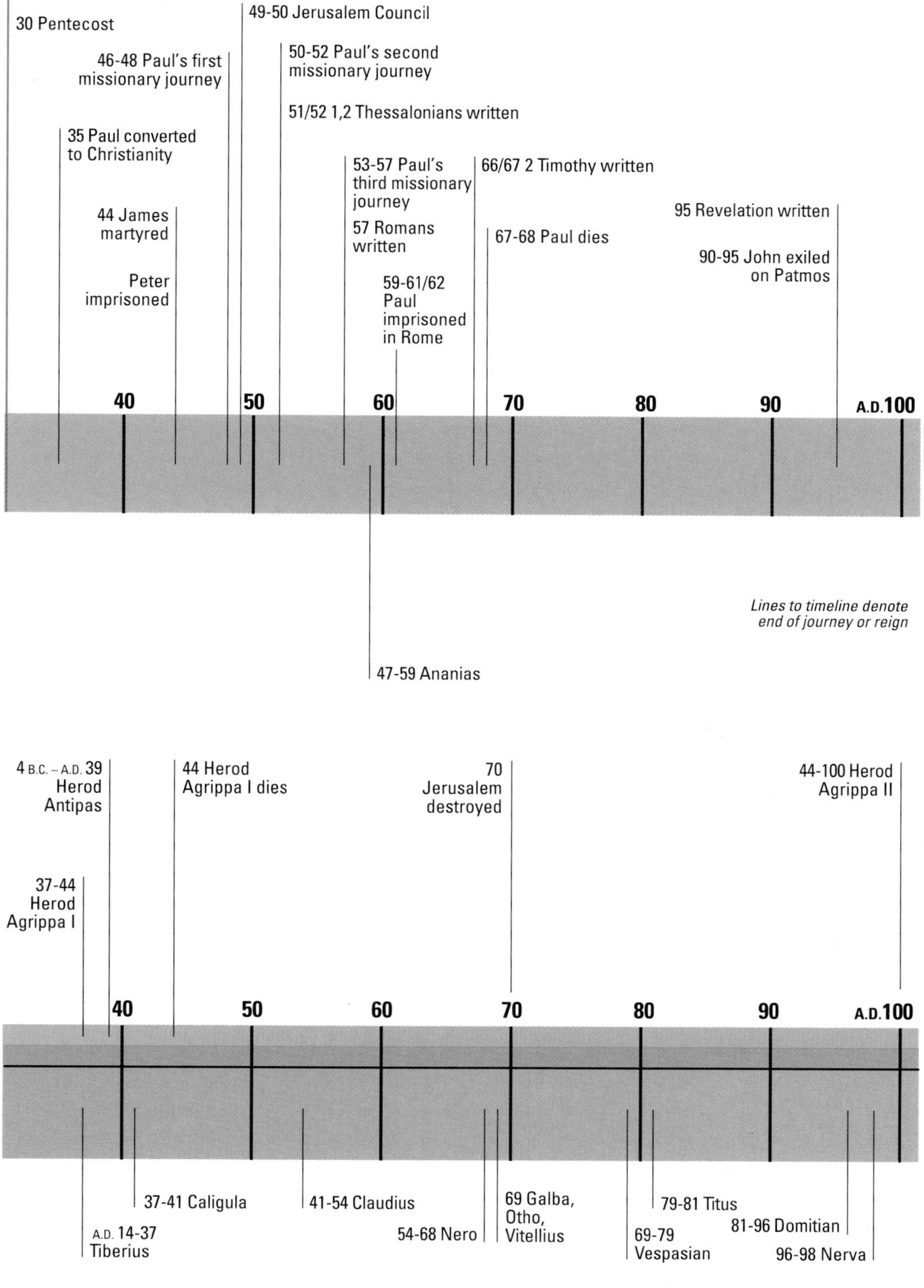

30 Pentecost

35 Paul converted to Christianity

44 James martyred

Peter imprisoned

46-48 Paul's first missionary journey

49-50 Jerusalem Council

50-52 Paul's second missionary journey

51/52 1,2 Thessalonians written

53-57 Paul's third missionary journey

57 Romans written

59-61/62 Paul imprisoned in Rome

66/67 2 Timothy written

67-68 Paul dies

90-95 John exiled on Patmos

95 Revelation written

40 50 60 70 80 90 A.D.100

47-59 Ananias

Lines to timeline denote end of journey or reign

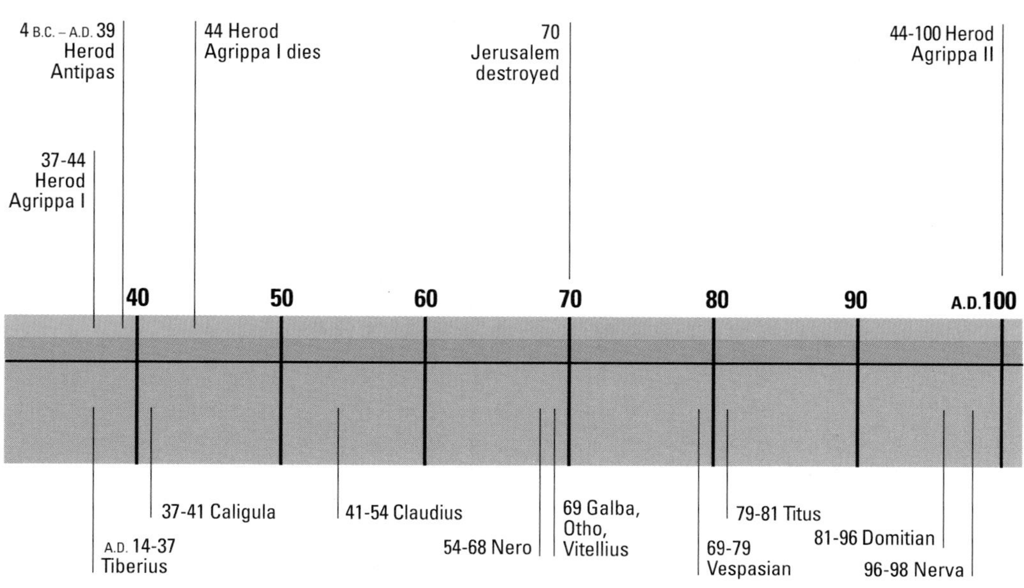
4 B.C. – A.D. 39 Herod Antipas
37-44 Herod Agrippa I
44 Herod Agrippa I dies
70 Jerusalem destroyed
44-100 Herod Agrippa II
40
50
60
70
80
90
A.D.100
A.D. 14-37 Tiberius
37-41 Caligula
41-54 Claudius
54-68 Nero
69 Galba, Otho, Vitellius
69-79 Vespasian
79-81 Titus
81-96 Domitian
96-98 Nerva

©1985 The Zondervan Corporation

ZONDERVAN
NASB
STUDY
BIBLE
UPDATED
NASB
The Most Literal Is
Now More Readable

GENERAL EDITOR
KENNETH BARKER

ASSOCIATE EDITORS
DONALD BURDICK   JOHN STEK
WALTER WESSEL   RONALD YOUNGBLOOD

NASB NOTES ADAPTATION
KENNETH BOA

ZondervanPublishingHouse
Grand Rapids, Michigan 49530, USA

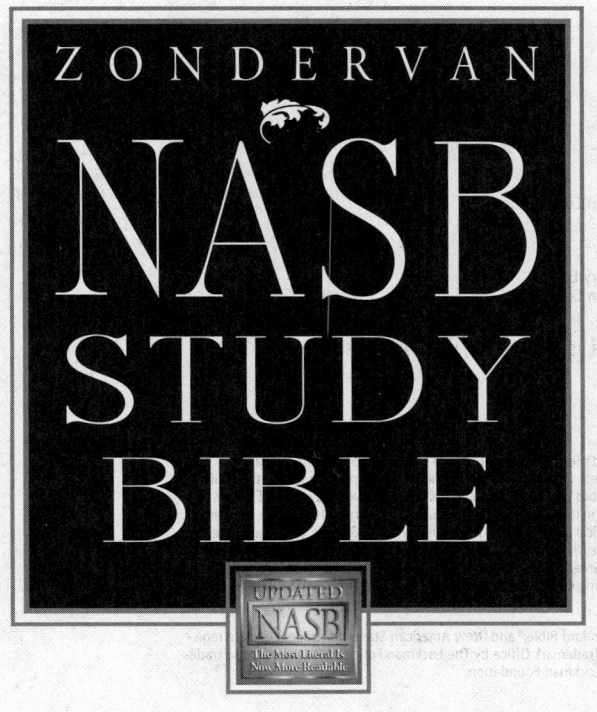

The Zondervan NASB Study Bible
Copyright © 1999 by the Zondervan Corporation
All rights reserved.

Adapted from
The NIV Study Bible, 10th Anniversary Edition
Copyright © 1995 by the Zondervan Corporation

NEW AMERICAN STANDARD BIBLE
Copyright © 1960, 1962, 1963, 1968, 1971, 1972, 1973, 1975, 1977, 1995
by THE LOCKMAN FOUNDATION
A Corporation Not for Profit
LA HABRA, CA
All Rights Reserved

The Tabernacle, Solomon's Temple, Herod's Temple, © 1981 by Hugh Claycombe; Solomon's Jerusalem, Jerusalem During the Time of the Prophets, Jerusalem of the Returning Exiles, Jerusalem During the Ministry of Jesus, Passion Week, The City of the Jebusites, David's Jerusalem, © 1982 by Hugh Claycombe. Ezekiel's Temple, plan adapted from the design given in the *Zondervan Pictorial Bible Dictionary*, © 1975 by the Zondervan Corporation, used by permission. "Analytical Outline for the NIV Harmony of the Gospels" (adapted to the NASB for this edition) pp. 15–23 from *The NIV Harmony of the Gospels* by Robert L. Thomas and Stanley N. Gundry, © 1988 by the authors, and reprinted by permission of HarperCollins Publishers, Inc. Color maps and index, © 1983 by Carta Map and Publishing Company. All other maps and charts are © 1985 by The Zondervan Corporation.

The "NASB," "NAS," "New American Standard Bible," and "New American Standard" trademarks are registered in the United States Patent and Trademark Office by The Lockman Foundation. Use of these trademarks requires the permission of The Lockman Foundation.

PERMISSION TO QUOTE
The text of the New American Standard Bible® may be quoted and/or reprinted up to and inclusive of five hundred (500) verses without express written permission of The Lockman Foundation, providing the verses do not amount to a complete book of the Bible nor do the verses quoted account for more than 25% of the total work in which they are quoted.

Notice of copyright must appear on the title or copyright page of the work as follows:

"Scripture taken from the NEW AMERICAN STANDARD BIBLE®, Copyright © 1960, 1962, 1963, 1968, 1971, 1972, 1973, 1975, 1977, 1995 by The Lockman Foundation. Used by permission."

When quotations from the NASB® text are used in not-for-sale media, such as church bulletins, orders of service, posters, transparencies or similar media, the abbreviation (NASB) may be used at the end of the quotation.

This permission to quote is limited to material which is wholly manufactured in compliance with the provisions of the copyright laws of the United States of America. The Lockman Foundation may terminate this permission at any time.

Quotations and/or reprints in excess of the above limitations, or other permission requests, must be directed to and approved in writing by The Lockman Foundation, PO Box 2279, La Habra, CA 90632-2279 (714)879-3055. http://www.lockman.org

Library of Congress Catalog Card Number 99071067

Published by Zondervan Publishing House
Grand Rapids, Michigan 49530, U.S.A.
http://www.zondervan.com

Printed in the United States of America

Interior Design: Sharon Wright, Belmont, MI
Typesetting: Blue Heron Bookcraft, Battle Ground, WA

2 3 4 5 6 7 8 9 / 05 04 03 02 01 00

RRD-C

GUARANTEE
Zondervan Publishing House guarantees leather Bibles unconditionally against manufacturing defects for a lifetime and hardcover and softcover Bibles for four years. This guarantee does not apply to normal wear. Contact Zondervan Customer Service, 800-727-1309, for replacement instructions.

Table of Contents

THE OLD TESTAMENT

THE NEW TESTAMENT

STUDY HELPS

MAPS

Foreword

SCRIPTURAL PROMISE

"The grass withers, the flower fades,
but the word of our God stands forever."
—Isaiah 40:8

The New American Standard Bible has been produced with the conviction that the words of Scripture as originally penned in the Hebrew, Aramaic, and Greek were inspired by God. Since they are the eternal Word of God, the Holy Scriptures speak with fresh power to each generation, to give wisdom that leads to salvation, that men may serve Christ to the glory of God.

The purpose of the Editorial Board in making this translation was to adhere as closely as possible to the original languages of the Holy Scriptures, and to make the translation in a fluent and readable style according to current English usage.

THE FOURFOLD AIM OF THE LOCKMAN FOUNDATION

1. These publications shall be true to the original Hebrew, Aramaic, and Greek.
2. They shall be grammatically correct.
3. They shall be understandable.
4. They shall give the Lord Jesus Christ His proper place, the place which the Word gives Him; therefore, no work will ever be personalized.

Preface to the New American Standard Bible

In the history of English Bible translations, the King James Version is the most prestigious. This time-honored version of 1611, itself a revision of the Bishops' Bible of 1568, became the basis for the English Revised Version appearing in 1881 (New Testament) and 1885 (Old Testament). The American counterpart of this last work was published in 1901 as the American Standard Version. The ASV, a product of both British and American scholarship, has been highly regarded for its scholarship and accuracy. Recognizing the values of the American Standard Version, The Lockman Foundation felt an urgency to preserve these and other lasting values of the ASV by incorporating recent discoveries of Hebrew and Greek textual sources and by rendering it into more current English. Therefore, in 1959 a new translation project was launched, based on the time-honored principles of translation of the ASV and KJV. The result is the New American Standard Bible.

Translation work for the NASB was begun in 1959. In the preparation of this work numerous other translations have been consulted along with the linguistic tools and literature of biblical scholarship. Decisions about English renderings were made by consensus of a team composed of educators and pastors. Subsequently, review and evaluation by other Hebrew and Greek scholars outside the Editorial Board were sought and carefully considered.

The Editorial Board has continued to function since publication of the complete Bible in 1971. This edition of the NASB represents revisions and refinements recommended over the last several years as well as thorough research based on modern English usage.

Principles of Translation

MODERN ENGLISH USAGE: The attempt has been made to render the grammar and terminology in contemporary English. When it was felt that the word-for-word literalness was unacceptable to the modern reader, a change was made in the direction of a more current English idiom. In the instances where this has been done, the more literal rendering has been indicated in the notes. There are a few exceptions to this procedure. In particular, frequently "And" is not translated at the beginning of sentences because of differences in style between ancient and modern writing. Punctuation is a relatively modern invention, and ancient writers often linked most of their sentences with "and" or other connectives. Also, the Hebrew idiom "answered and said" is sometimes reduced to "answered" or "said" as demanded by the context. For current English the idiom "it came about that" has not been translated in the New Testament except when a major transition is needed.

ALTERNATIVE READINGS: In addition to the more literal renderings, notations have been made to include alternate translations, reading of variant manuscripts and explanatory equivalents of the text. Only such notations have been used as have been felt justified in assisting the reader's comprehension of the terms used by the original author.

HEBREW TEXT: In the present translation the latest edition of Rudolf Kittel's BIBLIA HEBRAICA has been employed together with the most recent light from lexicography, cognate languages, and the Dead Sea Scrolls.

HEBREW TENSES: Consecution of tenses in Hebrew remains a puzzling factor in translation. The translators have been guided by the requirements of a literal translation, the sequence of tenses, and the immediate and broad contexts.

THE PROPER NAME OF GOD IN THE OLD TESTAMENT: In the Scriptures, the name of God is most significant and understandably so. It is inconceivable to think of spiritual matters without a proper designation for the Supreme Deity. Thus the most common name for the Deity is God, a translation of the original *Elohim*. One of the titles for God is Lord, a translation of *Adonai*. There is yet another name which is particularly assigned to God as His special or proper name, that is, the four letters YHWH (Exodus 3:14 and Isaiah 42:8). This name has not been pronounced by the Jews because of reverence for the great sacredness of the divine name. Therefore, it has been consistently translated LORD. The only exception to this translation of YHWH is when it occurs in immediate proximity to the word Lord, that is, *Adonai*. In that case it is regularly translated GOD in order to avoid confusion.

It is known that for many years YHWH has been transliterated as Yahweh, however no complete certainty attaches to this pronunciation.

GREEK TEXT: Consideration was given to the latest available manuscripts with a view to determining the best Greek text. In most instances the 26th edition of Eberhard Nestle's NOVUM TESTAMENTUM GRAECE was followed.

GREEK TENSES: A careful distinction has been made in the treatment of the Greek aorist tense (usually translated as the English past, "He did") and the Greek imperfect tense (normally rendered either as English past progressive, "He was doing"; or, if inceptive, as "He began to do" or "He started to do"; or else if customary past, as "He used to do"). "Began" is italicized if it renders an imperfect tense, in order to distinguish it from the Greek verb for "begin." In some contexts the difference between the Greek imperfect and the English past is conveyed better by the choice of vocabulary or by other words in the context, and in such cases the Greek imperfect may be rendered as a simple past tense (e.g. "had an illness for many years" would be preferable to "was having an illness for many years" and would be understood in the same way).

On the other hand, not all aorists have been rendered as English pasts ("He did"), for some of them are clearly to be rendered as English perfects ("He has done"), or even as past perfects ("He had done"), judging from the context in which they occur. Such aorists have been rendered as perfects or past perfects in this translation.

As for the distinction between aorist and present imperatives, the translators have usually rendered these imperatives in the customary manner, rather than attempting any such fine distinction as "Begin to do!" (for the aorist imperative), or, "Continually do!" (for the present imperative).

As for sequence of tenses, the translators took care to follow English rules rather than Greek in translating Greek presents, imperfects and aorists. Thus, where English says, "We knew that he was doing," Greek puts it, "We knew that he does"; similarly, "We knew that he had done" is the Greek, "We knew that he did." Likewise, the English, "When he had come, they met him," is represented in Greek by, "When he came, they met him." In all cases a consistent transfer has been made from the Greek tense in the subordinate clause to the appropriate tense in English.

In the rendering of negative questions introduced by the particle *mē* (which always expects the answer "No") the wording has been altered from a mere, "Will he not do this?" to a more accurate, "He will not do this, will he?"

THE LOCKMAN FOUNDATION

Introduction

ABOUT THE ZONDERVAN NASB STUDY BIBLE

The Zondervan NASB Study Bible is the work of a transdenominational team of Biblical scholars. All confess the authority of the Bible as God's infallible word to humanity. They have sought to clarify understanding of, develop appreciation for, and provide insight into that word.

But why a study Bible when the text itself is clearly written? Surely there is no substitute for the reading of the text itself; nothing people write *about* God's word can be on a level with the word itself. Further, it is the Holy Spirit alone—not fallible human beings—who can open the human mind to the divine message.

However, the Spirit also uses people to explain God's word to others. It was the Spirit who led Philip to the Ethiopian eunuch's chariot, where he asked, "Do you understand what you are reading?" (Ac 8:30). "How could I," the Ethiopian replied, "unless someone guides me?" Philip then showed him how an Old Testament passage in Isaiah related to the good news of Jesus.

This interrelationship of the Scriptures—so essential to understanding the complete Biblical message—is a major theme of the notes in *The Zondervan NASB Study Bible.*

Doctrinally, *The Zondervan NASB Study Bible* reflects traditional evangelical theology. Where editors were aware of significant differences of opinion on key passages or doctrines, they tried to follow an evenhanded approach by indicating those differences (e.g., see note on Rev 20:2). In finding solutions to problems mentioned in the book introductions, they went only as far as evidence (Biblical and non-Biblical) could carry them.

The result is a study Bible that can be used profitably by all Christians who want to be serious Bible students.

FEATURES OF THE ZONDERVAN NASB STUDY BIBLE

The Zondervan NASB Study Bible features the text of the New American Standard Bible, study notes keyed to and listed with Bible verses, introductions and outlines to books of the Bible, text notes, a cross-reference system (tens of thousands of entries), parallel passages, a concordance (nearly 20,000 references), charts, maps, essays and comprehensive indexes.

The text of the NASB, which is presented in verse-by-verse format, is organized into sections with headings.

Study Notes

The outstanding feature of this study Bible is that it contains nearly 20,000 study notes located on the same pages as the verses and passages they explain.

The study notes provide new information to supplement that found in the NASB text notes. Among other things, they

1. explain important words and concepts (see note on Lev 11:44 about "holiness");
2. interpret "difficult verses" (see notes on Mal 1:3 and Luke 14:26 for the concept of "hating" your parents);
3. draw parallels between specific people and events (see note on Ex 32:30 for the parallels between Moses and Christ as mediators);
4. describe historical and textual contexts of passages (see note on 1 Cor 8:1 for the practice of eating meat sacrificed to idols); and
5. demonstrate how one passage sheds light on another (see note on Ps 26:8 for how the presence of God's glory marked his presence in the tabernacle, in the temple, and finally in Jesus Christ himself).

Some elements of style should be noted:

1. Study notes on a *passage* precede notes on individual verses within that passage.
2. When a book of the Bible is referred to within a note on that book, the book name is not repeated. For example, a reference to 2 Timothy 2:18 within the notes on 2 Timothy is written 2:18, not 2 Tim 2:18.
3. In lists of references within a note, references from the book under discussion are placed first. The rest appear in Biblical order.

Introductions to Books of the Bible

Each introduction to each book of the Bible is different. Introductions vary in length and reflect both the nature of the material itself and the strengths and interests of contributing editors.

An introduction frequently reports on a book's title, author, and date of writing. It details the book's background and purpose, explores themes and theological significance, and points out special problems and distinctive literary features. Where appropriate, such as in Paul's letters to the churches, it describes the original recipients of a book and the city in which they lived.

A complete outline of the book's content is provided in each introduction (except for the introduction to Psalms). For Genesis, two outlines—a literary and a thematic—are given. Pairs of books that were originally one literary work, such as 1 and 2 Samuel, 1 and 2 Kings, and 1 and 2 Chronicles, are outlined together.

Marginal Notes

The NASB translation's extensive text notes appear within the center-column reference system. They examine such things as alternate translations, meanings of Hebrew and Greek terms, Old Testament quotations and variant readings in ancient Biblical manuscripts.

Cross-Reference System

Marginal notes and cross references appear in the center column on each page of Scripture. They are listed under the verse numbers to which they refer. Superior *numbers* refer to literal renderings, alternate translations, or explanations. Superior *letters* refer to cross-references.

Genesis 1:1–2 provides a good example of the resources of this cross-reference system.

The three lists of references in 1:1 all relate to creation, but each takes a different perspective. Note *a* takes up the time of creation: "in the beginning," and directs the reader to four other instances where this time is discussed. Note *b* addresses God's activity in creation, as well as His preexistence and His wondrous power. Note *c* focuses on "the heavens and the earth" as God's creation, and leads the reader to other references that deal with the created physical world.

The Creation

1 [a]In the beginning [b]God [c]created the heavens and the earth.
2 The earth was [1a]formless and void, and
[b]darkness was over the [2]surface of the deep,
and [c]the Spirit of God [d]was [3]moving over the
[2]surface of the waters.
3 Then [a]God said, "Let there be light";
and there was light.
4 God saw that the light was [a]good; and
God [b]separated the light from the darkness.
5 [a]God called the light day, and the dark-

1:1 [a]Ps 102:25; Is 40:21; John 1:1, 2; Heb 1:10 [b]Ps 89:11; 90:2; Acts 17:24; Rom 1:20; Heb 11:3 [c]Job 38:4; Is 42:5; 45:18; Rev 4:11
2 [1]Or *a waste and emptiness* [2]Lit *face of* [3]Or *hovering* [a]Jer 4:23 [b]Job 38:9 [c]Ps 104:30; Is 40:13, 14 [d]Deut 32:11; Is 31:5
3 [a]Ps 33:6, 9; 2 Cor 4:6

Genesis 1:2 provides an example of how the NASB marginal notes work in tandem with the cross references. Note that the superscript numbers refer to notes that can be found in the center column. These literal renderings, alternate translations or explanations always come first under the verse heading in the center column, despite their relative position in the note. The note's cross-references appear after the notes indicated by the superscript numbers.

Parallel Passages

Cross references that appear in italics denote parallel passages. Such parallel passages are especially common in Matthew, Mark, Luke and John, and in the historical books of Samuel, Kings and Chronicles.

Concordance

The concordance is designed as a quick-reference tool to enhance Bible study. By looking up key words, you can find verses for which you remember a word or two but not their location. For example, to find the verse that says, "Your word is a lamp to my feet And a light to my path," you could look in the concordance under either "word," "lamp," "light" or "path."

Maps

The Zondervan NASB Study Bible includes 59 maps: 13 full-color and 46 black-and-white. The 13 full-color maps at the end of this Bible cover nearly 4,000 years of history, from the patriarchs to Christianity in the world today.

Strategically placed throughout the text are almost four dozen black-and-white maps. The Contents: Maps page contains a complete list of the topics covered.

The cities of Jerusalem, Damascus, Rome, Corinth, Ephesus and Philippi have been reconstructed as they might have been in ancient times. These recreations allow Bible students to visualize David's city and, in the New Testament, the places through which Paul traveled on his missionary journeys.

Charts

Complementing the study notes are 35 charts, diagrams and drawings. Two full-color time lines, located in the front of this Bible, pinpoint significant dates in the Old and New Testaments. Other charts, carefully placed within the text, give detailed information about ancient, non-Biblical texts; about Old Testament covenants, sacrifices, and feast days; about Jewish sects; and about major archaeological finds relating to the New Testament.

Essays

Five brief essays provide additional information on specific sections of the Bible: Wisdom Literature, the Minor Prophets, the Synoptic Gospels, the Pastoral Letters, and the General Letters.

A sixth essay confronts the ethical question of war, and a seventh details the history, literature and social developments of the 400 years between the Old and New Testaments.

Subject, Notes and Map Indexes

The subject index contains references to key Biblical information and important topics. The notes index pinpoints other references to persons, places, events and topics mentioned in *The Zondervan NASB Study Bible* notes.

Two map indexes help in locating place-names on a map.

Harmony of the Gospels

As an additional study tool for the Gospels and the life of Christ, this Bible contains a portion of *The NIV Harmony of the Gospels* by Robert L. Thomas and Stanley N. Gundry.

Acknowledgments

The *Zondervan NASB Study Bible* is an adaptation of *The NIV Study Bible*. The following acknowledgments recognize the contributions of those individuals involved in the development of *The NIV Study Bible*.

My greatest debt of gratitude is owed to God for giving me the privilege of serving as General Editor of *The NIV Study Bible.* Special thanks go to the four Associate Editors: Donald W. Burdick, John H. Stek, Walter W. Wessel, and Ronald Youngblood. Without their help, it would have been impossible to complete this project in a little over seven years.

In addition, grateful acknowledgment is given to all those listed on the Contributors page. Obviously the editors and contributors have profited immensely from the labors of others. We feel deeply indebted to all the commentaries and other sources we have used in our work.

I should also thank the following individuals for rendering help in various ways (though I fear that I have inadvertently omitted a few names): Caroline Blauwkamp, David R. Douglass, Stanley N. Gundry, N. David Hill, Betty Hockenberry, Charles E. Hummel, Alan F. Johnson, Janet Johnston, Donald H. Madvig, Frances Steenwyk, and Edward Viening.

Nehemiah 8:7–8, 12 says:

The Levites . . . instructed the people in the Law while the people were standing there. They read from the Book of the Law of God, making it clear and giving the meaning so that the people could understand what was being read. . . . Then all the people went away . . . to celebrate with great joy, because they now understood the words that had been made known to them.

My associates and I will feel amply rewarded if those who use this study Bible have an experience similar to that of God's people in Nehemiah's time.

Kenneth L. Barker
General Editor
The NIV Study Bible

Tribute to Edwin H. Palmer

Edwin H. Palmer, who had served so capably as Executive Secretary of the NIV Committee on Bible Translation and as coordinator of all translation work on the NIV, was appointed general editor of *The NIV Study Bible* by Zondervan Bible Publishers in 1979. On September 16, 1980, he departed this life to "be with Christ, which is better by far" (Philippians 1:23, NIV). Before his death, however, he had laid most of the plans for *The NIV Study Bible,* had recruited the majority of the contributors, and had done some editorial work on the first manuscripts submitted. We gratefully acknowledge his significant contributions to the earliest stages of this project.

Contributors

General Editor: Kenneth L. Barker

Associate Editors: Donald W. Burdick, Walter W. Wessel, John H. Stek, Ronald Youngblood

NASB Adaptation: Kenneth Boa, William Kruidenier

The Zondervan NASB Study Bible is adapted from *The NIV Study Bible.*

The individuals named below contributed and/or reviewed material for *The NIV Study Bible.* However, since the General Editor and the Associate Editors extensively edited the notes on most books, they alone are responsible for their final form and content.

The chief contributors of original material to *The NIV Study Bible* are listed first. Where the Associate Editors and General Editor contributed an unusually large number of notes on certain books, their names are also listed.

Genesis	Ronald Youngblood
Exodus	Ronald Youngblood Walter C. Kaiser, Jr.
Leviticus	R. Laird Harris Ronald Youngblood
Numbers	Ronald B. Allen Kenneth L. Barker
Deuteronomy	Earl S. Kalland Kenneth L. Barker
Joshua	Arthur Lewis
Judges	John J. Davis Herbert Wolf
Ruth	Marvin R. Wilson John H. Stek
1,2 Samuel	J. Robert Vannoy
1,2 Kings	J. Robert Vannoy
1,2 Chronicles	Raymond Dillard
Ezra	Edwin Yamauchi Ronald Youngblood
Nehemiah	Edwin Yamauchi Ronald Youngblood
Esther	Raymond Dillard Edwin Yamauchi
Job	Elmer B. Smick Ronald Youngblood
Psalms	John H. Stek
Proverbs	Herbert Wolf
Ecclesiastes	Derek Kidner
Song of Songs	John H. Stek
Isaiah	Herbert Wolf John H. Stek
Jeremiah	Ronald Youngblood
Lamentations	Ronald Youngblood
Ezekiel	Mark Hillmer
Daniel	Gleason L. Archer, Jr. Ronald Youngblood
Hosea	Jack P. Lewis
Joel	Jack P. Lewis
Amos	Alan R. Millard John H. Stek
Obadiah	John M. Zinkand
Jonah	Marvin R. Wilson John H. Stek
Micah	Allan A. MacRae Thomas E. McComiskey
Nahum	G. Herbert Livingston Kenneth L. Barker
Habakkuk	Roland K. Harrison William C. Williams
Zephaniah	Roland K. Harrison
Haggai	Herbert Wolf
Zechariah	Kenneth L. Barker Larry L. Walker
Malachi	Herbert Wolf John H. Stek
Matthew	Ralph Earle Walter W. Wessel
Mark	Walter W. Wessel William L. Lane
Luke	Lewis Foster
John	Leon Morris
Acts	Lewis Foster
Romans	Walter W. Wessel
1 Corinthians	W. Harold Mare
2 Corinthians	Philip E. Hughes
Galatians	Robert Mounce
Ephesians	Walter L. Liefeld
Philippians	Richard B. Gaffin, Jr.
Colossians	Gerald F. Hawthorne Wilber B. Wallis
1,2 Thessalonians	Leon Morris
1,2 Timothy	Walter W. Wessel George W. Knight, III
Titus	D. Edmond Hiebert
Philemon	John Werner
Hebrews	Philip E. Hughes Donald W. Burdick
James	Donald W. Burdick
1,2 Peter	Donald W. Burdick John H. Skilton
1,2,3 John	Donald W. Burdick
Jude	Donald W. Burdick John H. Skilton
Revelation	Robert Mounce
"The Time between the Testaments" (essay)	David O'Brien

Explanation of General Format

NOTES AND CROSS REFERENCES are placed in a column adjoining the text on the page and listed under verse numbers to which they refer. Superior numbers refer to literal renderings, alternate translations, or explanations. Superior letters refer to cross references. Cross references in italics are parallel passages.

PARAGRAPHS are designated by bold face verse numbers or letters.

QUOTATION MARKS are used in the text in accordance with modern English usage.

"THOU," "THEE" AND "THY" are not used in this edition and have been rendered as "YOU" and "YOUR."

PERSONAL PRONOUNS are capitalized when pertaining to Deity.

ITALICS are used in the text to indicate words which are not found in the original Hebrew, Aramaic, or Greek but implied by it. Italics are used in the marginal notes to signify alternate readings for the text. Roman text in the marginal alternate readings is the same as italics in the Bible text.

SMALL CAPS in the New Testament are used in the text to indicate Old Testament quotations or obvious references to Old Testament texts. Variations of Old Testament wording are found in New Testament citations depending on whether the New Testament writer translated from a Hebrew text, used existing Greek or Aramaic translations, or paraphrased the material. It should be noted that modern rules for the indication of direct quotation were not used in biblical times; thus, the ancient writer would use exact quotations or references to quotation without specific indication of such.

ASTERISKS are used to mark verbs that are historical presents in the Greek which have been translated with an English past tense in order to conform to modern usage. The translators recognized that in some contexts the present tense seems more unexpected and unjustified to the English reader than a past tense would have been. But Greek authors frequently used the present tense for the sake of heightened vividness, thereby transporting their readers in imagination to the actual scene at the time of occurrence. However, the translators felt that it would be wise to change these historical presents to English past tenses.

Abbreviations and Special Markings

GENERAL

Aram	*Aramaic*
DSS	*Dead Sea Scrolls*
Gr	*Greek translation of O.T. (Septuagint or LXX) or Greek text of N.T.*
Heb	*Hebrew text, usually Masoretic*
Lat	*Latin*
M.T.	*Masoretic text*
Syr	*Syriac*
Lit	*A literal translation*
Or	*An alternate translation justified by the Hebrew, Aramaic, or Greek*
[ ]	*In text, brackets indicate words probably not in the original writings*
[ ]	*In margin, brackets indicate references to a name, place or thing similar to, but not identical with that in the text*
cf	*compare*
f, ff	*following verse or verses*
mg	*Refers to a marginal reading on another verse*
ms, mss	*manuscript, manuscripts*
v, vv	*verse, verses*

BOOKS OF THE BIBLE

The Old Testament

Genesis	Gen
Exodus	Ex
Leviticus	Lev
Numbers	Num
Deuteronomy	Deut
Joshua	Josh
Judges	Judg
Ruth	Ruth
First Samuel	1 Sam
Second Samuel	2 Sam
First Kings	1 Kin
Second Kings	2 Kin
First Chronicles	1 Chr
Second Chronicles	2 Chr
Ezra	Ezra
Nehemiah	Neh
Esther	Esth
Job	Job
Psalms	Ps
Proverbs	Prov
Ecclesiastes	Eccl
Song of Solomon	Song
Isaiah	Is
Jeremiah	Jer
Lamentations	Lam
Ezekiel	Ezek
Daniel	Dan
Hosea	Hos
Joel	Joel
Amos	Amos
Obadiah	Obad
Jonah	Jon
Micah	Mic
Nahum	Nah
Habakkuk	Hab
Zephaniah	Zeph
Haggai	Hag
Zechariah	Zech
Malachi	Mal

The New Testament

Matthew	Matt
Mark	Mark
Luke	Luke
John	John
Acts	Acts
Romans	Rom
First Corinthians	1 Cor
Second Corinthians	2 Cor
Galatians	Gal
Ephesians	Eph
Philippians	Phil
Colossians	Col
First Thessalonians	1 Thess
Second Thessalonians	2 Thess
First Timothy	1 Tim
Second Timothy	2 Tim
Titus	Titus
Philemon	Philem
Hebrews	Heb
James	James
First Peter	1 Pet
Second Peter	2 Pet
First John	1 John
Second John	2 John
Third John	3 John
Jude	Jude
Revelation	Rev

Transliterations

A simplified system has been used for transliterating words from ancient Biblical languages into English. The only transliterations calling for comment are these:

TRANSLITERATION	PRONUNCIATION
ʼ	Glottal stop
ḥ	Similar to the "ch" in the German word *Buch*
ṭ	Similar to the "t" in the verb "tear"
ʻ	Similar to the glottal stop
ṣ	Similar to the "ts" in "hits"
ś	Similar to the "s" in "sing"

Ancient Texts Relating to the Old Testament

Major representative examples of ancient Near Eastern non-Biblical documents that provide parallels to or shed light on various OT passages.

AMARNA LETTERS **Canaanite Akkadian** *14th century B.C.*	Hundreds of letters, written primarily by Canaanite scribes, illuminate social, political and religious relationships between Canaan and Egypt during the reigns of Amunhotep III and Akhenaten.
AMENEMOPE'S WISDOM **Egyptian** *Early 1st millennium B.C.*	Thirty chapters of wisdom instruction are similar to Prov 22:17-24:22 and provide the closest external parallels to OT wisdom literature.
ATRAHASIS EPIC **Akkadian** *Early 2nd millennium B.C.*	A cosmological epic depicts creation and early human history, including the flood (cf. Gen 1-9).
BABYLONIAN THEODICY **Akkadian** *Early 1st millennium B.C.*	A sufferer and his friend dialogue with each other (cf. Job).
CYRUS CYLINDER **Akkadian** *6th century B.C.*	King Cyrus of Persia records the conquest of Babylon (cf. Dan 5:30; 6:28) and boasts of his generous policies toward his new subjects and their gods.
DEAD SEA SCROLLS **Hebrew, Aramaic, Greek** *3rd century B.C. to 1st century A.D.*	Several hundred scrolls and fragments include the oldest copies of OT books and passages.
EBLA TABLETS **Sumerian, Eblaite** *Mid-3rd millennium B.C.*	Thousands of commercial, legal, literary and epistolary texts describe the cultural vitality and political power of a pre-patriarchal civilization in northern Syria.
ELEPHANTINE PAPYRI **Aramaic** *Late 5th century B.C.*	Contracts and letters document life among Jews who fled to southern Egypt after Jerusalem was destroyed in 586 B.C.
ENUMA ELISH **Akkadian** *Early 2nd millennium B.C.*	Marduk, the Babylonian god of cosmic order, is elevated to the supreme position in the pantheon. The 7-tablet epic contains an account of creation (cf. Gen 1–2).
GEZER CALENDAR **Hebrew** *10th century B.C.*	A schoolboy from west-central Israel describes the seasons, crops and farming activity of the agricultural year.
GILGAMESH EPIC **Akkadian** *Early 2nd millennium B.C.*	Gilgamesh, ruler of Uruk, experiences numerous adventures, including a meeting with Utnapishtim, the only survivor of a great deluge (cf. Gen 6–9).
HAMMURAPI'S CODE **Akkadian** *18th century B.C.*	Together with similar law codes that preceded and followed it, the Code of Hammurapi exhibits close parallels to numerous passages in the Mosaic legislation of the OT.
HYMN TO THE ATEN **Egyptian** *14th century B.C.*	The poem praises the beneficence and universality of the sun in language somewhat similar to that used in Ps 104.
ISHTAR'S DESCENT **Akkadian** *1st millennium B.C.*	The goddess Ishtar temporarily descends to the nether world, which is pictured in terms reminiscent of OT descriptions of Sheol.
JEHOIACHIN'S RATION DOCKETS **Akkadian** *Early 6th century B.C.*	Brief texts from the reign of Nebuchadnezzar II refer to rations allotted to Judah's exiled king Jehoiachin and his sons (cf. 2 Kin 25:27-30).
KING LISTS **Sumerian** *Late 3rd millennium B.C.*	The reigns of Sumerian kings before the flood are described as lasting for thousands of years, reminding us of the longevity of the preflood patriarchs in Gen 5.
LACHISH LETTERS **Hebrew** *Early 6th century B.C.*	Inscriptions on pottery fragments vividly portray the desperate days preceding the Babylonian siege of Jerusalem in 588-586 B.C. (cf. Jer 34:7).
LAMENTATION OVER THE DESTRUCTION OF UR **Sumerian** *Early 2nd millennium B.C.*	The poem mourns the destruction of the city of Ur at the hands of the Elamites (cf. the OT book of Lamentations).
LUDLUL BEL NEMEQI **Akkadian** *Late 2nd millennium B.C.*	A suffering Babylonian nobleman describes his distress in terms faintly reminiscent of the experiences of Job.

MARI TABLETS **Akkadian** *18th century B.C.*	Letters and administrative texts provide detailed information regarding customs, language and personal names that reflect the culture of the OT patriarchs.
MERNEPTAH STELE **Egyptian** *13th century B.C.*	Pharaoh Merneptah figuratively describes his victory over various peoples in western Asia, including "Israel."
MESHA STELE (MOABITE STONE) **Moabite** *9th century B.C.*	Mesha, king of Moab (see 2 Kin 3:4), rebels against a successor of Israel's king Omri.
MURASHU TABLETS **Akkadian** *5th century B.C.*	Commercial documents describe financial transactions engaged in by Murashu and Sons, a Babylonian firm that did business with Jews and other exiles.
MURSILIS'S TREATY WITH DUPPI-TESSUB **Hittite** *Mid-2nd millennium B.C.*	King Mursilis imposes a suzerainty treaty on King Duppi-tessub. The literary outline of this and other Hittite treaties is strikingly paralleled in OT covenants established by God with his people.
NABONIDUS CHRONICLE **Akkadian** *Mid-6th century B.C.*	The account describes the absence of King Nabonidus from Babylon. His son Belshazzar is therefore the regent in charge of the kingdom (cf. Dan 5:29-30).
NEBUCHADNEZZAR CHRONICLE **Akkadian** *Early 6th century B.C.*	A chronicle from the reign of Nebuchadnezzar II includes the Babylonian account of the siege of Jerusalem in 597 B.C. (see 2 Kin 24:10-17).
NUZI TABLETS **Akkadian** *Mid-2nd millennium B.C.*	Adoption, birthright-sale and other legal documents graphically illustrate OT patriarchal customs current centuries earlier.
PESSIMISTIC DIALOGUE **Akkadian** *Early 1st millennium B.C.*	A master and his servant discuss the pros and cons of various activities (cf. Eccl 1-2).
RAS SHAMRA TABLETS **Ugaritic** *15th century B.C.*	Canaanite deities and rulers experience adventures in epics that enrich our understanding of Canaanite mythology and religion and of OT poetry.
SARGON LEGEND **Akkadian** *1st millennium B.C.*	Sargon I (the Great), ruler of Akkad in the late 3rd millennium B.C., claims to have been rescued as an infant from a reed basket found floating in a river (cf. Ex 2).
SARGON'S DISPLAY INSCRIPTION **Akkadian** *8th century B.C.*	Sargon II takes credit for the conquest of Samaria in 722/721 B.C. and states that he captured and exiled 27,290 Israelites.
SENNACHERIB'S PRISM **Akkadian** *Early 7th century B.C.*	Sennacherib vividly describes his siege of Jerusalem in 701 B.C., making Hezekiah a prisoner in his own royal city (but cf. 2 Kin 19:35-37).
SEVEN LEAN YEARS TRADITION **Egyptian** *2nd century B.C.*	Egypt experiences 7 years of low Niles and famine, which, by a contractual agreement between Pharaoh Djoser (28th century B.C.) and a god, will be followed by prosperity (cf. Gen 41).
SHALMANESER'S BLACK OBELISK **Akkadian** *9th century B.C.*	Israel's king Jehu (or his servant) presents tribute to Assyria's king Shalmaneser III. Additional Assyrian and Babylonian texts refer to other kings of Israel and Judah.
SHISHAK'S GEOGRAPHICAL LIST **Egyptian** *10th century B.C.*	Pharaoh Shishak lists the cities that he captured or made tributary during his campaign in Judah and Israel (cf. 1 Kin 14:25-26).
SILOAM INSCRIPTION **Hebrew** *Late 8th century B.C.*	A Judahite workman describes the construction of an underground conduit to guarantee Jerusalem's water supply during Hezekiah's reign (cf. 2 Kin 20:20; 2 Chr 32:30).
SINUHE'S STORY **Egyptian** *20th-19th centuries B.C.*	An Egyptian official of the 12th dynasty goes into voluntary exile in Syria and Canaan during the OT patriarchal period.
TALE OF TWO BROTHERS **Egyptian** *13th century B.C.*	A young man rejects the amorous advances of his older brother's wife (cf. Gen 39).
WENAMUN'S JOURNEY **Egyptian** *11th century B.C.*	An official of the Temple of Amun at Thebes in Egypt is sent to Byblos in Canaan to buy lumber for the ceremonial barge of his god.

The Old Testament

Genesis

INTRODUCTION

Title

The first phrase in the Hebrew text of 1:1 is *bereshith* ("in [the] beginning"), which is also the Hebrew title of the book (books in ancient times customarily were named after their first word or two). The English title, Genesis, is Greek in origin and comes from the word *geneseos,* which appears in the Greek translation (Septuagint) of 2:4; 5:1. Depending on its context, the word can mean "birth," "genealogy," or "history of origin." In both its Hebrew and Greek forms, then, the title of Genesis appropriately describes its contents, since it is primarily a book of beginnings.

Background

Chs. 1—38 reflect a great deal of what we know from other sources about ancient Mesopotamian life and culture. Creation, genealogies, destructive floods, geography and mapmaking, construction techniques, migrations of peoples, sale and purchase of land, legal customs and procedures, sheepherding and cattle-raising—all these subjects and many others were matters of vital concern to the peoples of Mesopotamia during this time. They were also of interest to the individuals, families and tribes of whom we read in the first 38 chapters of Genesis. The author appears to locate Eden, man's first home, in or near Mesopotamia; the tower of Babel was built there; Abram was born there; Isaac took a wife from there; and Jacob lived there for 20 years. Although these patriarchs settled in Canaan, their original homeland was Mesopotamia.

The closest ancient literary parallels to Gen 1—38 also come from Mesopotamia. *Enuma elish,* the story of the god Marduk's rise to supremacy in the Babylonian pantheon, is similar in some respects (though thoroughly mythical and polytheistic) to the Gen 1 creation account. Some of the features of certain king lists from Sumer bear striking resemblance to the genealogy in Gen 5. The 11th tablet of the *Gilgamesh* epic is quite similar in outline to the flood narrative in Gen 6—8. Several of the major events of Gen 1—8 are narrated in the same order as similar events in the *Atrahasis* epic. In fact, the latter features the same basic motif of creation-rebellion-flood as the Biblical account. Clay tablets found recently at the ancient (c. 2500–2300 B.C.) site of Ebla (modern Tell Mardikh) in northern Syria may also contain some intriguing parallels (see chart, p. xix).

Two other important sets of documents demonstrate the reflection of Mesopotamia in the first 38 chapters of Genesis. From the Mari letters (see chart, p. xix), dating from the patriarchal period, we learn that the names of the patriarchs (including especially Abram, Jacob and Job) were typical of that time. The letters also clearly illustrate the freedom of travel that was possible between various parts of the Amorite world in which the patriarchs lived. The Nuzi tablets (see chart, p. xix), though a few centuries later than the patriarchal period, shed light on patriarchal customs, which tended to survive virtually intact for many centuries. The inheritance right of an adopted household member or slave (see 15:1–4), the obligation of a barren wife to furnish her husband with sons through a servant girl (see 16:2–4), strictures against expelling such a servant girl and her son (see 21:10–11), the authority of oral statements in ancient Near Eastern law, such as the deathbed bequest (see 27:1–4,22–23,33)—these and other legal customs, social contracts and provisions are graphically illustrated in Mesopotamian documents.

As Gen 1—38 is Mesopotamian in character and background, so chs. 39—50 reflect Egyptian influence—though in not quite so direct a way. Examples of such influence are: Egyptian grape cultivation (40:9–11), the riverside scene (ch. 41), Egypt as Canaan's breadbasket (ch. 42), Canaan as the source of numerous products for Egyptian consumption (ch. 43), Egyptian religious and social customs (the end of chs. 43; 46), Egyptian administrative procedures (ch. 47), Egyptian funerary practices (ch. 50) and several Egyptian words and names used throughout these chapters. The closest specific literary parallel from Egypt is the *Tale of Two Broth-*

ers, which bears some resemblance to the story of Joseph and Potiphar's wife (ch. 39). Egyptian autobiographical narratives (such as the *Story of Sinuhe* and the *Report of Wenamun*) and certain historical legends offer more general literary parallels.

Author and Date of Writing

Historically, Jews and Christians alike have held that Moses was the author/compiler of the first five books of the OT. These books, known also as the Pentateuch (meaning "five-volumed book"), were referred to in Jewish tradition as the five fifths of the law (of Moses). The Bible itself suggests Mosaic authorship of Genesis, since Ac 15:1 refers to circumcision as "the custom of Moses," an allusion to Gen 17. However, a certain amount of later editorial updating does appear to be indicated (see, e.g., notes on 14:14; 36:31; 47:11).

The historical period during which Moses lived seems to be fixed with a fair degree of accuracy by 1 Kings. We are told that "the fourth year of Solomon's reign over Israel" was the same as "the four hundred and eightieth year after the sons of Israel came out of the land of Egypt" (1Ki 6:1). Since the former was c. 966 B.C., the latter — and thus the date of the exodus — was c. 1446 (assuming that the 480 in 1Ki 6:1 is to be taken literally; see Introduction to Judges: Background). The 40-year period of Israel's wanderings in the desert, which lasted from c. 1446 to c. 1406, would have been the most likely time for Moses to write the bulk of what is today known as the Pentateuch.

During the last three centuries many scholars have claimed to find in the Pentateuch four underlying sources. The presumed documents, allegedly dating from the tenth to the fifth centuries B.C., are called J (for Jahweh/Yahweh, the personal OT name for God), E (for Elohim, a generic name for God), D (for Deuteronomic) and P (for Priestly). Each of these documents is claimed to have its own characteristics and its own theology, which often contradicts that of the other documents. The Pentateuch is thus depicted as a patchwork of stories, poems and laws. However, this view is not supported by conclusive evidence, and intensive archaeological and literary research has tended to undercut many of the arguments used to challenge Mosaic authorship.

Theme and Message

Genesis speaks of beginnings — of the heavens and the earth, of light and darkness, of seas and skies, of land and vegetation, of sun and moon and stars, of sea and air and land animals, of human beings (made in God's own image, the climax of His creative activity), of sin and redemption, of blessing and cursing, of society and civilization, of marriage and family, of art and craft and industry. The list could go on and on. A key word in Genesis is the Hebrew word for "account," or "records," which also serves to divide the book into its ten major parts (see Literary Features and Literary Outline) and which includes such concepts as birth, genealogy and history.

The book of Genesis is foundational to the understanding of the rest of the Bible. Its message is rich and complex, and listing its main elements gives a succinct outline of the Biblical message as a whole. It is supremely a book of relationships, highlighting those between God and nature, God and man, and man and man. It is thoroughly monotheistic, taking for granted that there is only one God worthy of the name and opposing the ideas that there are many gods (polytheism), that there is no god at all (atheism) and that everything is divine (pantheism). It clearly teaches that the one true God is sovereign over all that exists (i.e., His entire creation), and that by divine election He often exercises His unlimited freedom to overturn human customs, traditions and plans. It introduces us to the way in which God initiates and makes covenants with His chosen people, pledging His love and faithfulness to them and calling them to promise theirs to Him. It establishes sacrifice as the substitution of life for life (ch. 22). It gives us the first hint of God's provision for redemption from the forces of evil (compare 3:15 with Ro 16:17 – 20) and contains the oldest and most profound definition of faith (15:6). More than half of Heb 11 — the NT roll of the faithful — refers to characters in Genesis.

Literary Features

The message of a book is often enhanced by its literary structure and characteristics. Genesis is divided into ten main sections, most of which begin with the Hebrew word for "account" or "generations" (see 2:4 [account]; 5:1 [generations]; 6:9; 10:1; 11:10; 11:27; 25:12; 25:19; 36:1 — repeated for emphasis at 36:9 — and 37:2). The first five sections can be grouped together and, along with the introduction to the book as a whole (1:1 — 2:3), can be appropriately called "primeval history" (1:1 — 11:26), sketching the period from Adam to

Abraham. The last five sections constitute a much longer (but equally unified) account, and relate the story of God's dealings with Abraham, Isaac, Jacob and Joseph and their families—a section often called "patriarchal history" (11:27—50:26). This section is in turn composed of three narrative cycles (Abraham-Isaac, 11:27—25:11; Isaac-Jacob, 25:19—35:29; 37:1; Jacob-Joseph, 37:2—50:26), interspersed by the genealogies of Ishmael (25:12–18) and Esau (ch. 36).

The narrative frequently concentrates on the life of a later son in preference to the firstborn: Seth over Cain, Isaac over Ishmael, Jacob over Esau, Judah and Joseph over their brothers, and Ephraim over Manasseh. Such emphasis on divinely chosen men and their families is perhaps the most obvious literary and theological characteristic of the book of Genesis as a whole. It strikingly underscores the fact that the people of God are not the product of natural human developments, but are the result of God's sovereign and gracious intrusion in human history. He brings out of the fallen human race a new humanity consecrated to Himself, called and destined to be the people of His kingdom and the channel of His blessing to the whole earth.

Numbers with symbolic significance figure prominently in Genesis. The number ten, in addition to being the number of sections into which Genesis is divided, is also the number of names appearing in the genealogies of chs. 5 and 11 (see note on 5:5). The number seven also occurs frequently. The Hebrew text of 1:1 consists of exactly seven words and that of 1:2 of exactly 14 (twice seven). There are seven days of creation, seven names in the genealogy of ch. 4 (see note on 4:17–18; see also 4:15,24; 5:31), various sevens in the flood story, 70 descendants of Noah's sons (ch. 10), a sevenfold promise to Abram (12:2–3), seven years of abundance and then seven of famine in Egypt (ch. 41), and 70 descendants of Jacob (ch. 46). Other significant numbers, such as 12 and 40, are used with similar frequency.

The book of Genesis is basically prose narrative, punctuated here and there by brief poems (the longest is the so-called Blessing of Jacob in 49:2–27). Much of the prose has a lyrical quality and uses the full range of figures of speech and other devices that characterize the world's finest epic literature. Vertical and horizontal parallelism between the two sets of three days in the creation account (see note on 1:11); the ebb and flow of sin and judgment in ch. 3 (the serpent and woman and man sin successively; then God questions them in reverse order; then he judges them in the original order); the powerful monotony of "and he died" at the end of paragraphs in ch. 5; the climactic hinge effect of the phrase "But God remembered Noah" (8:1) at the midpoint of the flood story; the hourglass structure of the account of the tower of Babel in 11:1–9 (narrative in vv. 1–2,8–9; discourse in vv. 3–4,6–7; v. 5 acting as transition); the macabre pun in 40:19 (see 40:13); the alternation between brief accounts about firstborn sons and lengthy accounts about younger sons—these and numerous other literary devices add interest to the narrative and provide interpretive signals to which the reader should pay close attention.

It is no coincidence that many of the subjects and themes of the first three chapters of Genesis are reflected in the last three chapters of Revelation. We can only marvel at the superintending influence of the Lord Himself, who assures us that "all Scripture is inspired by God" (2 Tim 3:16) and that men "moved by the Holy Spirit spoke from God" (2 Pet 1:21).

Outlines

Literary Outline:

I. Introduction (1:1—2:3)
II. Body (2:4—50:26)
   A. "The account of the heavens and the earth" (2:4—4:26)
   B. "The book of the generations of Adam" (5:1—6:8)
   C. "The records of the generations of Noah" (6:9—9:29)
   D. "The records of the generations of Shem, Ham and Japheth" (10:1—11:9)
   E. "The records of the generations of Shem" (11:10–26)
   F. "The records of the generations of Terah" (11:27—25:11)
   G. "The records of the generations of Abraham's son Ishmael" (25:12–18)
   H. "The records of the generations of Abraham's son Isaac" (25:19—35:29)
   I. "The records of the generations of Esau" (36:1—37:1)
   J. "The records of the generations of Jacob" (37:2—50:26)

Thematic Outline:

- I. Primeval History (1:1—11:26)
  - A. Creation (1:1—2:3)
    - 1. Introduction (1:1–2)
    - 2. Body (1:3–31)
    - 3. Conclusion (2:1–3)
  - B. Adam and Eve in Eden (2:4–25)
  - C. The Fall and Its Consequences (ch. 3)
  - D. The Rapid "Progress" of Sin (4:1–16)
  - E. Two Genealogies (4:17—5:32)
    - 1. The genealogy of pride (4:17–24)
    - 2. The genealogy of death (4:25—5:32)
  - F. The Extent of Sin before the Flood (6:1–8)
  - G. The Great Flood (6:9—9:29)
    - 1. Preparing for the flood (6:9—7:10)
    - 2. Judgment and redemption (7:11—8:19)
      - a. The rising of the waters (7:11–24)
      - b. The receding of the waters (8:1–19)
    - 3. The flood's aftermath (8:20—9:29)
      - a. A new promise (8:20–22)
      - b. New ordinances (9:1–7)
      - c. A new relationship (9:8–17)
      - d. A new temptation (9:18–23)
      - e. A final word (9:24–29)
  - H. The Spread of the Nations (10:1—11:26)
    - 1. The diffusion of nations (ch. 10)
    - 2. The confusion of tongues (11:1–9)
    - 3. The first Semitic genealogy (11:10–26)
- II. Patriarchal History (11:27—50:26)
  - A. The Life of Abraham (11:27—25:11)
    - 1. Abraham's background (11:27–32)
    - 2. Abraham's land (chs. 12—14)
    - 3. Abraham's people (chs. 15—24)
    - 4. Abraham's last days (25:1–11)
  - B. The Descendants of Ishmael (25:12–18)
  - C. The Life of Jacob (25:19—35:29)
    - 1. Jacob at home (25:19—27:46)
    - 2. Jacob abroad (chs. 28—30)
    - 3. Jacob at home again (chs. 31—35)
  - D. The Descendants of Esau (36:1—37:1)
  - E. The Life of Joseph (37:2—50:26)
    - 1. Joseph's career (37:2—41:57)
    - 2. Jacob's migration (chs. 42—47)
    - 3. Jacob's last days (48:1—50:14)
    - 4. Joseph's last days (50:15–26)

The Creation

1 [a]In the beginning [b]God [c]created the heavens and the earth.
2 The earth was [1a]formless and void, and
[b]darkness was over the [2]surface of the deep,
and [c]the Spirit of God [d]was [3]moving over the
[2]surface of the waters.
3 Then [a]God said, "Let there be light";
and there was light.
4 God saw that the light was [a]good; and
God [b]separated the light from the darkness.
5 [a]God called the light day, and the darkness He called night. And [b]there was evening
and there was morning, one day.
6 Then God said, "Let there be [1]an
[a]expanse in the midst of the waters, and let
it separate the waters from the waters."
7 God made the [1]expanse, and separated
[a]the waters which were below the [1]expanse
from the waters [b]which were above the
[1]expanse; and it was so.
8 God called the [1]expanse heaven. And
there was evening and there was morning, a
second day.
9 Then God said, "[a]Let the waters below
the heavens be gathered into one place, and
let [b]the dry land appear"; and it was so.
10 God called the dry land earth, and the
[a]gathering of the waters He called seas; and
God saw that it was good.
11 Then God said, "Let the earth sprout
[1a]vegetation: [2]plants yielding seed, *and* fruit
trees on the earth bearing fruit after [3]their
kind [4]with seed in them"; and it was so.
12 The earth brought forth [1]vegetation,
[2]plants yielding seed after [3]their kind, and
trees bearing fruit [4]with seed in them, after
[3]their kind; and God saw that it was good.
13 There was evening and there was
morning, a third day.
14 Then God said, "Let there be [1a]lights in
the [2b]expanse of the heavens to separate the
day from the night, and let them be for [c]signs
and for [d]seasons and for days and years;

1:1 [a]Ps 102:25; Is 40:21; John 1:1, 2; Heb 1:10 [b]Ps 89:11; 90:2; Acts 17:24; Rom 1:20; Heb 11:3 [c]Job 38:4; Is 42:5; 45:18; Rev 4:11
2 [1]Or *a waste and emptiness* [2]Lit *face of* [3]Or *hovering* [a]Jer 4:23 [b]Job 38:9 [c]Ps 104:30; Is 40:13, 14 [d]Deut 32:11; Is 31:5
3 [a]Ps 33:6, 9; 2 Cor 4:6
4 [a]Ps 145:9, 10 [b]Is 45:7
5 [a]Ps 74:16 [b]Ps 65:8
6 [1]Or *a firmament* [a]Is 40:22; Jer 10:12; 2 Pet 3:5
7 [1]Or *firmament* [a]Job 38:8-11 [b]Ps 148:4
8 [1]Or *firmament*
9 [a]Ps 104:6-9; Jer 5:22; 2 Pet 3:5 [b]Ps 24:1, 2; 95:5
10 [a]Ps 33:7; 95:5; 146:6 **11** [1]Or *grass* [2]Or *herbs* [3]Lit *its* [4]Lit *in which is its seed* [a]Ps 65:9-13; 104:14; Heb 6:7 **12** [1]Or *grass* [2]Or *herbs* [3]Lit *its* [4]Lit *in which is its seed* **14** [1]Or *luminaries, light-bearers* [2]Or *firmament* [a]Ps 74:16; 136:7 [b]Ps 19:1; 150:1 [c]Jer 10:2 [d]Ps 104:19

1:1 A summary statement introducing the six days of creative activity. The truth of this majestic verse was joyfully affirmed by poet (Ps 102:25) and prophet (Is 40:21). *In the beginning God.* The Bible always assumes, and never argues, God's existence. Although everything else had a beginning, God has always been (Ps 90:2). *In the beginning.* John 1:1–10, which stresses the work of Christ in creation, opens with the same phrase. *God created.* The Hebrew noun *Elohim* is plural but the verb is singular, a normal usage in the OT when reference is to the one true God. This use of the plural expresses intensification rather than number and has been called the plural of majesty, or of potentiality. In the OT the Hebrew verb for "create" is used only of divine, never of human, activity. *the heavens and the earth.* "All things" (Is 44:24). That God created everything is also taught in Eccl 11:5; Jer 10:16; John 1:3; Col 1:16; Heb 1:2. The positive, life-oriented teaching of v. 1 is beautifully summarized in Is 45:18.

1:2 *earth.* The focus of this account. *formless and void.* The phrase, which appears elsewhere only in Jer 4:23, gives structure to the rest of the chapter (see note on v. 11). God's "separating" and "gathering" on days 1–3 gave form, and His "making" and "filling" on days 4–6 removed the void. *darkness . . . the waters.* Completes the picture of a world awaiting God's light-giving, order-making and life-creating word. *and.* Or "but." The awesome (and, for ancient man, fearful) picture of the original state of the visible creation is relieved by the majestic announcement that the mighty Spirit of God hovers over creation. The announcement anticipates God's creative words that follow. *Spirit of God.* He was active in creation, and His creative power continues today (see Job 33:4; Ps 104:30). *moving over.* Like a bird that provides for and protects its young (see Deut 32:11; Is 31:5). The imagery may also suggest the winged sun disk, which throughout the ancient Near East was a symbol of divine majesty.

1:3 *God said.* Merely by speaking, God brought all things into being (Ps 33:6,9; 148:5; Heb 11:3). *Let there be light.* God's first creative word called forth light in the midst of the primeval darkness. Light is necessary for making God's creative works visible and life possible. In the OT it is also symbolic of life and blessing (see 2 Sam 22:29; Job 3:20; 30:26; 33:30; Ps 49:19; 56:13; 97:11; 112:4; Is 53:11; 58:8,10; 59:9; 60:1,3). Paul uses this word to illustrate God's re-creating work in sin-darkened hearts (2 Cor 4:6).

1:4 Everything God created is good (see vv. 10,12,18,21,25); in fact, the conclusion declares it to be "very good" (v. 31). The creation, as fashioned and ordered by God, had no lingering traces of disorder and no dark and threatening forces arrayed against God or man. Even darkness and the deep were given benevolent functions in a world fashioned to bless and sustain life (see Ps 104:19–26; 127:2).

1:5 *called.* See vv. 8,10. In ancient times, to name something or someone implied having dominion or ownership (see 17:5,15; 41:45; 2 Kin 23:34; 24:17; Dan 1:7). Both day and night belong to the Lord (Ps 74:16). *one day.* Some say that the creation days were 24-hour days, others that they were indefinite periods.

1:6 *expanse.* The atmosphere, or "heaven" (v. 8), as seen from the earth. "Strong as a molten mirror" (Job 37:18) and "like a curtain" (Is 40:22) are among the many pictorial phrases used to describe it.

1:7 *and it was so.* The only possible outcome, whether stated (vv. 9,11,15,24,30) or implied, to God's "Let there be."

1:9 *one place.* A picturesque way of referring to the "seas" (v. 10) that surround the dry ground on all sides and into which the waters of the lakes and rivers flow. The earth was "formed out of water" (2 Pet 3:5) and "founded . . . upon the seas" (Ps 24:2), and the waters are not to cross the boundaries set for them (Ps 104:7–9; Jer 5:22).

1:11 *God said.* This phrase is used twice on the third day (vv. 9,11) and three times (vv. 24,26,29) on the sixth day. These two days are climactic, as the following structure of ch. 1 reveals (see note on v. 2 regarding "formless and void"):

Days of forming	*Days of filling*
1. "light" (v. 3)	4. "lights" (v. 14)
2. "waters below the expanse . . . waters above the expanse" (v. 7)	5. "every living creature that moves, with which the waters swarmed . . . every winged bird" (v. 21)
3a. "dry land" (v. 9)	$6a_1$. "cattle and creeping things and beasts of the earth" (v. 24)
	$6a_2$. "man" (v. 26)
b. "vegetation" (v. 11)	b. "every green plant for food" (v. 30)

Both the horizontal and vertical relationships between the days demonstrate the literary beauty of the chapter and stress the orderliness and symmetry of God's creative activity. *kind.* See vv. 12,21,24–25. Both creation and reproduction are orderly.

1:14 *be for signs.* In the ways mentioned here, not in any astrological or other such sense.

15 and let them be for [1]lights in the [2]expanse of the heavens to give light on the earth"; and it was so.

16 God made the two [1]great lights, the [a]greater [2]light [3]to govern the day, and the lesser [2]light [3]to govern the night; *He made* [b]the stars also.

17 [a]God placed them in the [1]expanse of the heavens to give light on the earth,

18 and [1]to [a]govern the day and the night, and to separate the light from the darkness; and God saw that it was good.

19 There was evening and there was morning, a fourth day.

20 Then God said, "Let the waters [1]teem with swarms of living creatures, and let birds fly above the earth [2]in the open [3]expanse of the heavens."

21 God created [a]the great sea monsters and every living creature that moves, with which the waters swarmed after their kind, and every winged bird after its kind; and God saw that it was good.

22 God blessed them, saying, "Be fruitful and multiply, and fill the waters in the seas, and let birds multiply on the earth."

23 There was evening and there was morning, a fifth day.

24 [a]Then God said, "Let the earth bring forth living creatures after [1]their kind: cattle and creeping things and beasts of the earth after [1]their kind"; and it was so.

25 God made the [a]beasts of the earth after [1]their kind, and the cattle after [1]their kind, and everything that creeps on the ground after its kind; and God saw that it was good.

26 Then God said, "Let [a]Us make [b]man in Our image, according to Our likeness; and let them [c]rule over the fish of the sea and over the birds of the [1]sky and over the cattle and over all the earth, and over every creeping thing that creeps on the earth."

27 God created man [a]in His own image, in the image of God He created him; [b]male and female He created them.

28 God blessed them; and God said to them, "[a]Be fruitful and multiply, and fill the earth, and subdue it; and rule over the fish of the sea and over the birds of the [1]sky and over every living thing that [2]moves on the earth."

29 Then God said, "Behold, [a]I have given you every plant yielding seed that is on the [1]surface of all the earth, and every tree [2]which has fruit yielding seed; it shall be food for you;

30 and [a]to every beast of the earth and to every bird of the [1]sky and to every thing that [2]moves on the earth [3]which has life, *I have given* every green plant for food"; and it was so.

31 God saw all that He had made, and behold, it was very [a]good. And there was evening and there was morning, the sixth day.

15 [1]Or *luminaries, light-bearers* [2]Or *firmament*
16 [1]Or *luminaries, light-bearers* [2]Or *luminary, light-bearer* [3]Lit *for the dominion of* [a]Ps 136:8, 9 [b]Job 38:7; Ps 8:3; Is 40:26
17 [1]Or *firmament* [a]Jer 33:20, 25
18 [1]Lit *for the dominion of* [a]Jer 31:35
20 [1]Or *swarm* [2]Lit *on the face of* [3]Or *firmament*
21 [a]Ps 104:25-28
24 [1]Lit *its* [a]Gen 2:19; 6:20; 7:14; 8:19
25 [1]Lit *its* [a]Gen 7:21, 22; Jer 27:5
26 [1]Lit *heavens* [a]Gen 3:22; 11:7 [b]Gen 5:1; 9:6; 1 Cor 11:7; Eph 4:24; James 3:9 [c]Ps 8:6-8
27 [a]Gen 5:1f; 1 Cor 11:7; Eph 4:24; Col 3:10 [b]Matt 19:4; Mark 10:6
28 [1]Lit *heavens* [2]Or *creeps* [a]Gen 9:1, 7; Lev 26:9; Ps 127:3, 5
29 [1]Lit *face of* [2]Lit *in which is the fruit of a tree yielding seed* [a]Ps 104:14; 136:25
30 [1]Lit *heavens* [2]Or *creeps* [3]Lit *in which is a living soul* [a]Ps 145:15, 16; 147:9
31 [a]Ps 104:24, 28; 119:68; 1 Tim 4:4

1:16 *two great lights.* The words "sun" and "moon" seem to be avoided deliberately here, since both were used as proper names for the pagan deities associated with these heavenly bodies. They are light-givers to be appreciated, not powers to be feared, because the one true God made them (see Is 40:26). Perhaps because of the emphasis on the greater light and lesser light, the stars seem to be mentioned almost as an afterthought. But Ps 136:9 indicates that the stars help the moon "rule by night." *to govern.* The great Creator-King assigns subordinate regulating roles to certain of His creatures (see vv. 26,28).

1:17–18 The three main functions of the heavenly bodies.

1:21 *sea monsters.* The Hebrew word underlying this phrase was used in Canaanite mythology to name a dreaded sea monster. He is often referred to figuratively in OT poetry as one of God's most powerful opponents. He is pictured as national (Babylon, Jer 51:34; Egypt, Is 51:9; Ezek 29:3; 32:2) or cosmic (Job 7:12; Ps 74:13; Is 27:1, though some take the latter as a reference to Egypt). In Genesis, however, the creatures of the sea are portrayed not as enemies to be feared but as part of God's good creation to be appreciated. *winged bird.* The term denotes anything that flies, including insects (see Deut 14:19–20).

1:22 *Be fruitful and multiply.* God's benediction on living things that inhabit the water and that fly in the air. By His blessing they flourish and fill both realms with life (see note on v. 28). God's rule over His created realm promotes and blesses life.

1:26 *Us . . . Our . . . Our.* God speaks as the Creator-King, announcing His crowning work to the members of His heavenly court (see 3:22; 11:7; Is 6:8; see also 1 Kin 22:19–23; Job 15:8; Jer 23:18). *image . . . likeness.* No distinction should be made between "image" and "likeness," which are synonyms in both the OT (5:1; 9:6) and the NT (1 Cor 11:7; Col 3:10; James 3:9). Since man is made in God's image, every human being is worthy of honor and respect; he is neither to be murdered (9:6) nor cursed (James 3:9). "Image" includes such characteristics as "righteousness and holiness" (Eph 4:24) and "knowledge" (Col 3:10). Believers are to be "conformed to the image" of Christ (Rom 8:29) and will someday be "like Him" (1 John 3:2). *rule.* Man is the climax of God's creative activity, and God has crowned him "with glory and majesty" and made him "to rule" over the rest of His creation (Ps 8:5–8). Since man was created in the image of the divine King, delegated sovereignty (kingship) was bestowed on him. (For redeemed man's ultimate kingship see notes on Heb 2:5–9.)

1:27 This highly significant verse is the first occurrence of poetry in the OT (which is about 40 percent poetry). *created.* The word is used here three times to describe the central divine act of the sixth day (see note on v. 1). *male and female.* Alike they bear the image of God, and together they share in the divine benediction that follows.

1:28 *God blessed them . . . fill . . . subdue . . . rule.* Man goes forth under this divine benediction—flourishing, filling the earth with his kind, and exercising dominion over the other earthly creatures (see v. 26; 2:15; Ps 8:6–8). Human culture, accordingly, is not anti-God (though fallen man often has turned his efforts into proud rebellion against God). Rather, it is the expression of man's bearing the image of his Creator and sharing, as God's servant, in God's kingly rule. As God's representative in the creaturely realm, he is steward of God's creatures. He is not to exploit, waste or despoil them, but to care for them and use them in the service of God and man.

1:29–30 People and animals seem to be portrayed as originally vegetarian (see 9:3).

1:31 *very good.* See note on v. 4. *the sixth day.* Perhaps to stress the finality and importance of this day, in the Hebrew text the definite article is first used here in regard to the creation days.

The Creation of Man and Woman

2 Thus the heavens and the earth were completed, and all [a]their hosts.

2 By [a]the seventh day God completed His work which He had done, and [b]He rested on the seventh day from all His work which He had done.

3 Then God blessed the seventh day and sanctified it, because in it He rested from all His work which God had created [1]and made.

4 [1a]This is the account of the heavens and the earth when they were created, in [b]the day that the LORD God made earth and heaven.

5 [a]Now no shrub of the field was yet in the earth, and no plant of the field had yet sprouted, [b]for the LORD God had not sent rain upon the earth, and there was no man to [1]cultivate the ground.

6 But a [1]mist used to rise from the earth and water the whole [2]surface of the ground.

7 Then the LORD God formed man of [a]dust from the ground, and breathed into his nostrils the breath of life; and [b]man became a living [1]being.

8 The LORD God planted a [a]garden toward the east, in Eden; and there He placed the man whom He had formed.

9 Out of the ground the LORD God caused to grow [a]every tree that is pleasing to the sight and good for food; [b]the tree of life also in the midst of the garden, and the tree of the knowledge of good and evil.

10 Now a [a]river [1]flowed out of Eden to water the garden; and from there it divided and became four [2]rivers.

11 The name of the first is Pishon; it [1]flows around the whole land of [a]Havilah, where there is gold.

12 The gold of that land is good; the bdellium and the onyx stone are there.

13 The name of the second river is Gihon; it [1]flows around the whole land of Cush.

14 The name of the third river is [1a]Tigris; it [2]flows east of Assyria. And the fourth river is the [3b]Euphrates.

15 Then the LORD God took the man and put him into the garden of Eden to cultivate it and keep it.

16 The LORD God [a]commanded the man, saying, "From any tree of the garden you may eat freely;

2:1 [a]Deut 4:19; 17:3
2 [a]Ex 20:8-11; 31:17 [b]Heb 4:4, 10
3 [1]Lit *to make*
4 [1]Lit *These are the generations* [a]Job 38:4-11 [b]Gen 1:3-31
5 [1]Lit *work, serve* [a]Gen 1:11 [b]Ps 65:9, 10; Jer 10:12, 13
6 [1]Or *flow* [2]Lit *face of*
7 [1]Lit *soul* [a]Gen 3:19 [b]1 Cor 15:45
8 [a]Gen 13:10; Is 51:3; Ezek 28:13
9 [a]Ezek 47:12 [b]Gen 3:22; Rev 2:7; 22:2, 14
10 [1]Lit *was going out* [2]Lit *heads* [a]Ps 46:4
11 [1]Lit *surrounds* [a]Gen 25:18
13 [1]Lit *is the one surrounding*
14 [1]Heb *Hiddekel* [2]Lit *is the one going* [3]Heb *Perath* [a]Dan 10:4 [b]Gen 15:18
16 [a]Gen 3:2, 3

2:2 *completed . . . rested.* God ceased on the seventh day, not because He was weary, but because nothing formless or empty remained. His creative work was completed—and it was totally effective, absolutely perfect, "very good" (1:31). It did not have to be repeated, repaired or revised, and the Creator rested to commemorate it.

2:3 *God blessed the seventh day and sanctified it . . . rested.* Although the word "Sabbath" is not used here, the Hebrew verb translated "rested" (see v. 2) is the origin of the noun "Sabbath." Ex 20:11 quotes the first half of v. 3, but substitutes "Sabbath" for "seventh," clearly equating the two. The first record of obligatory Sabbath observance is of Israel on her way from Egypt to Sinai (Ex 16), and according to Neh 9:13–14 the Sabbath was not an official covenant obligation until the giving of the law at Mount Sinai.

2:4 *account.* The Hebrew word for "account" or "generations" occurs ten times in Genesis—at the beginning of each main section (see Introduction: Literary Features). *the heavens and the earth.* See note on 1:1. The phrase "the account of the heavens and the earth" introduces the record of what happened to God's creation. The blight of sin and rebellion brought a threefold curse that darkens the story of Adam and Eve in God's good and beautiful garden: (1) on Satan (3:14); (2) on the ground, because of man (3:17); and (3) on Cain (4:11). 1:1–2:3 is a general account of creation, while 2:4–4:26 focuses on the beginning of human history. *LORD God.* "LORD" (Hebrew *YHWH,* "Yahweh") is the personal and covenant name of God (see note on Ex 3:15), emphasizing His role as Israel's Redeemer and covenant Lord (see note on Ex 6:6), while "God" (Hebrew *Elohim*) is a general term. Both names occur thousands of times in the OT, and often, as here, they appear together—clearly indicating that they refer to the same one and only God.

2:7 *formed.* The Hebrew for this verb commonly referred to the work of a potter (see Is 45:9; Jer 18:6), who fashions vessels from clay (see Job 33:6). "Make" (1:26), "created" (1:27) and "form" are used to describe God's creation of both man and animals (v. 19; 1:21,25). *man.* The Hebrew for "man" (*adam*) sounds like and may be related to the Hebrew for "ground" (*adamah*); it is also the name Adam (see 2:20). *breath of life.* Humans and animals alike have the breath of life in them (see 1:30; Job 33:4). *man became a living being.* The Hebrew phrase here translated "living being" is translated "living creatures" in 1:20,24. The words of 2:7 therefore imply that people, at least physically, have affinity with the animals. The great difference is that man is made "in the image of God" (1:27) and has an absolutely unique relation both to God as His servant and to the other creatures as their divinely appointed steward (Ps 8:5–8).

2:8 *toward the east.* From the standpoint of the author of Genesis. The garden was perhaps near where the Tigris and Euphrates rivers (see v. 14) meet, in what is today southern Iraq. *Eden.* A name synonymous with "paradise" and related to either (1) a Hebrew word meaning "bliss" or "delight" or (2) a Mesopotamian word meaning "a plain." Perhaps the author subtly suggests both.

2:9 *tree of life.* Signifying and giving life, without death, to those who eat its fruit (see 3:22; Rev 2:7; 22:2,14). *tree of the knowledge of good and evil.* Signifying and giving knowledge of good and evil, leading ultimately to death, to those who eat its fruit (v. 17; 3:3). "Knowledge of good and evil" refers to moral knowledge or ethical discernment (see Deut 1:39; Is 7:15–16). Adam and Eve possessed both life and moral discernment as they came from the hand of God. Their access to the fruit of the tree of life showed that God's will and intention for them was life. Ancient pagans believed that the gods intended for man always to be mortal. In eating the fruit of the tree of the knowledge of good and evil, Adam and Eve sought a creaturely source of discernment in order to be morally independent of God.

2:11 *Pishon.* Location unknown. The Hebrew word may be a common noun meaning "gusher." *Havilah.* Location unknown; perhaps mentioned again in 10:29. It is probably to be distinguished from the Havilah of 10:7, which was in Egypt.

2:13 *Gihon.* Location unknown. The Hebrew word may be a common noun meaning "spurter." Both the Pishon and the Gihon may have been streams in Lower Mesopotamia near the Persian Gulf. The names were those current when Moses wrote.

2:14 *Assyria.* Lit. "Asshur," an ancient capital city of Assyria ("Assyria" and "Asshur" are related words). *Euphrates.* Often called simply "the River" (1 Kin 4:21,24) because of its size and importance.

2:15 *cultivate . . . keep.* See note on 1:28. Man is now charged to govern the earth responsibly under God's sovereignty.

2:16 *any tree.* Including the tree of life (v. 9).

17 but from the tree of the knowledge of
good and evil you shall not [1]eat, for in the
day that you eat from it [a]you will surely die."
18 Then the LORD God said, "It is not good
for the man to be alone; [a]I will make him a
helper [1]suitable for him."
19 [a]Out of the ground the LORD God
formed every beast of the field and every
bird of the [1]sky, and [b]brought *them* to the
man to see what he would call them; and
whatever the man called a living creature,
that was its name.
20 The man gave names to all the cattle,
and to the birds of the [1]sky, and to every
beast of the field, but for [2]Adam there was
not found [a]a helper [3]suitable for him.
21 So the LORD God caused a [a]deep sleep
to fall upon the man, and he slept; then He
took one of his ribs and closed up the flesh
at that place.
22 The LORD God [1]fashioned into a
woman [a]the rib which He had taken from
the man, and brought her to the man.
23 The man said,
"[a]This is now bone of my bones,
And flesh of my flesh;
[1]She shall be called [2]Woman,
Because [1]she was taken out of [3]Man."
24 [a]For this reason a man shall leave his
father and his mother, and be joined to his
wife; and they shall become one flesh.
25 [a]And the man and his wife were both
naked and were not ashamed.

The Fall of Man

3 Now [a]the serpent was more crafty than
any beast of the field which the LORD God
had made. And he said to the woman,
"Indeed, has God said, 'You shall not eat
from [1]any tree of the garden'?"
2 The woman said to the serpent, "[a]From
the fruit of the trees of the garden we may
eat;
3 but from the fruit of the tree which is in
the middle of the garden, God has said, 'You
shall not eat from it or touch it, or you will
die.' "
4 [a]The serpent said to the woman, "You
surely will not die!
5 "For God knows that in the day you eat
from it your eyes will be opened, and [a]you
will be like God, knowing good and evil."
6 [a]When the woman saw that the tree
was good for food, and that it was a delight
to the eyes, and that the tree was desirable to
make *one* wise, she took from its fruit and
ate; and she gave also to her husband with
her, and he ate.
7 Then the eyes of both of them were
opened, and they [a]knew that they were
naked; and they sewed fig leaves together
and made themselves [1]loin coverings.
8 They heard the sound of [a]the LORD God
walking in the garden in the [1]cool of the day,
[b]and the man and his wife hid themselves
from the presence of the LORD God among
the trees of the garden.
9 Then the LORD God called to the man,
and said to him, "[a]Where are you?"
10 He said, "[a]I heard the sound of You in
the garden, and I was afraid because I was
naked; so I hid myself."
11 And He said, "Who told you that you
were naked? Have you eaten from the tree of
which I commanded you not to eat?"
12 [a]The man said, "The woman whom

17 [1]Lit *eat from it* [a]Deut 30:15, 19, 20; Rom 6:23; 1 Tim 5:6; James 1:15
18 [1]Lit *corresponding to* [a]1 Cor 11:9
19 [1]Lit *heavens* [a]Gen 1:24 [b]Gen 1:26
20 [1]Lit *heavens* [2]Or *man* [3]Lit *corresponding to* [a]Gen 2:18
21 [a]Gen 15:12
22 [1]Lit *built* [a]1 Cor 11:8, 9
23 [1]Lit *This one* [2]Heb *Ishshah* [3]Heb *Ish* [a]Gen 29:14; Eph 5:28, 29
24 [a]Matt 19:5; Mark 10:7, 8; 1 Cor 6:16; Eph 5:31
25 [a]Gen 3:7, 10, 11
3:1 [1]Or *every* [a]2 Cor 11:3; Rev 12:9; 20:2
2 [a]Gen 2:16, 17
4 [a]John 8:44; 2 Cor 11:3
5 [a]Is 14:14; Ezek 28:2, 12-17
6 [a]Rom 5:12-19; 1 Tim 2:14; James 1:14, 15; 1 John 2:16
7 [1]Or *girdles* [a]Is 47:3; Lam 1:8
8 [1]Lit *wind, breeze* [a]Gen 18:33; Lev 26:12; Deut 23:14 [b]Job 31:33; Ps 139:1-12; Hos 10:8; Amos 9:3; Rev 6:15-17
9 [a]Gen 4:9; 18:9
10 [a]Ex 20:18, 19; Deut 5:25
12 [a]Job 31:33; Prov 28:13

2:17 *surely die.* Despite the serpent's denial (3:4), disobeying God ultimately results in death.
2:18–25 The only full account of the creation of woman in ancient Near Eastern literature.
2:18 *not good . . . to be alone.* Without female companionship and a partner in reproduction, the man could not fully realize his humanity.
2:19 *call them.* His first act of dominion over the creatures around him (see note on 1:5).
2:24 *leave his father and his mother.* Instead of remaining under the protective custody of his parents a man leaves them and, with his wife, establishes a new family unit. *joined . . . one flesh.* The divine intention for husband and wife was monogamy. Together they were to form an inseparable union, of which "one flesh" is both a sign and an expression.
2:25 *naked . . . not ashamed.* Freedom from shame, signifying moral innocence, would soon be lost as a result of sin (see 3:7).
3:1 *serpent.* The great deceiver clothed himself as a serpent, one of God's good creatures. He insinuated a falsehood and portrayed rebellion as clever, but essentially innocent, self-interest. Therefore "the devil, or Satan," is later referred to as "the serpent of old" (Rev 12:9; 20:2). *crafty.* The Hebrew words for "crafty" and "naked" are almost identical. Though naked, the man and his wife felt no shame (2:25). The craftiness of the serpent led them to sin, and they then became ashamed of their nakedness (see v. 7). *Indeed, has God said . . . ?* The question and the response changed the course of human history. By causing the woman to doubt God's word, Satan brought evil into the world. Here the deceiver undertook to alienate man from God. In Job 1–2 he, as the accuser, acted to alienate God from man (see also Zech 3:1).
3:3 *You shall not . . . touch it.* The woman adds to God's word, distorting His directive and demonstrating that the serpent's subtle challenge was working its poison.
3:4 *You surely will not die!* The blatant denial of a specific divine pronouncement (see 2:17).
3:5 *God knows.* Satan accuses God of having unworthy motives. In Job 1:9–11; 2:4–5 he accuses the righteous man of the same. *your eyes will be opened, and you will be like God.* The statement is only half true. Their eyes were opened, to be sure (see v. 7), but the result was quite different from what the serpent had promised. *knowing good and evil.* See note on 2:9.
3:6 *good for food . . . a delight to the eyes . . . desirable to make one wise.* Three aspects of temptation. Cf. 1 John 2:16; Luke 4:3,5,9.
3:7 *they knew that they were naked.* No longer innocent like children, they had a new awareness of themselves and of each other in their nakedness and shame. *they . . . made . . . coverings.* Their own feeble and futile attempt to hide their shame, which only God could cover (see note on v. 21).
3:8 *the garden.* Once a place of joy and fellowship with God, it became a place of fear and of hiding from God.
3:9 *Where are you?* A rhetorical question (see 4:9).
3:12 *The woman whom You gave . . . gave me.* The man blames God and the woman—anyone but himself—for his sin.

You gave *to be* with me, she gave me from
the tree, and I ate."
13 Then the LORD God said to the woman,
"What is this you have done?" And the
woman said, "[a]The serpent deceived me,
and I ate."
14 The LORD God said to the serpent,
"[a]Because you have done this,
Cursed are you more than all cattle,
And more than every beast of the field;
On your belly you will go,
And [b]dust you will eat
All the days of your life;
15 And I will put [a]enmity
Between you and the woman,
And between your seed and her seed;
[b]He shall [1]bruise you on the head,
And you shall bruise him on the heel."
16 To the woman He said,
"I will greatly multiply
Your pain [1]in childbirth,
In pain you will [a]bring forth children;
Yet your desire will be for your
husband,
And [b]he will rule over you."
17 Then to Adam He said, "Because you
have listened to the voice of your wife, and
have eaten from the tree about which I commanded you, saying, 'You shall not eat from
it';
[a]Cursed is the ground because of you;
[b]In [1]toil you will eat of it
All the days of your life.
18 "Both thorns and thistles it shall grow
for you;
And you will eat the [1]plants of the field;
19 By the sweat of your face
You will eat bread,

13 [a]2 Cor 11:3; 1 Tim 2:14
14 [a]Deut 28:15-20 [b]Is 65:25; Mic 7:17
15 [1]Or *crush* [a]Rev 12:17 [b]Rom 16:20
16 [1]Lit *and your pregnancy, conception* [a]John 16:21; 1 Tim 2:15 [b]1 Cor 14:34
17 [1]Or *sorrow* [a]Gen 5:29; Rom 8:20-22; Heb 6:8 [b]Job 5:7; 14:1; Eccl 2:23
18 [1]Lit *plant*
19 [a]Ps 90:3; 104:29; Eccl 12:7 [b]Gen 2:7
20 [1]I.e. living; or life [a]2 Cor 11:3; 1 Tim 2:13
22 [a]Gen 1:26 [b]Gen 2:9; Rev 22:14
24 [a]Ezek 31:11 [b]Gen 2:8 [c]Ex 25:18-22; Ps 104:4; Ezek 10:1-20; Heb 1:7 [d]Gen 2:9
4:1 [1]Lit *knew* [2]I.e. gotten one [3]Or *man, the* LORD
2 [a]Luke 11:50, 51 [b]Gen 46:32; 47:3
3 [1]Lit *at the end of days*
4 [a]Heb 11:4 [b]1 Sam 15:22

Till you [a]return to the ground,
Because [b]from it you were taken;
For you are dust,
And to dust you shall return."
20 Now the man called his wife's name
[1a]Eve, because she was the mother of all *the*
living.
21 The LORD God made garments of skin
for Adam and his wife, and clothed them.
22 Then the LORD God said, "Behold, the
man has become like one of [a]Us, knowing
good and evil; and now, he might stretch out
his hand, and take also from [b]the tree of life,
and eat, and live forever"—
23 therefore the LORD God sent him out
from the garden of Eden, to cultivate the
ground from which he was taken.
24 So [a]He drove the man out; and at the
[b]east of the garden of Eden He stationed the
[c]cherubim and the flaming sword which
turned every direction to guard the way to
[d]the tree of life.

Cain and Abel

4 Now the man [1]had relations with his wife
Eve, and she conceived and gave birth to
[2]Cain, and she said, "I have gotten a [3]man-
child with *the help of* the LORD."
2 Again, she gave birth to his brother
Abel. And [a]Abel was [b]a keeper of flocks, but
Cain was a tiller of the ground.
3 So it came about [1]in the course of time
that Cain brought an offering to the LORD of
the fruit of the ground.
4 [a]Abel, on his part also brought of the
firstlings of his flock and of their fat portions.
And [b]the LORD had regard for Abel and for
his offering;

3:13 *The serpent deceived me.* The woman blames the serpent rather than herself.

3:14 *Cursed.* The serpent, the woman and the man were all judged, but only the serpent and the ground were cursed—the latter because of Adam (v. 17). *dust.* The symbol of death itself (v. 19) would be the serpent's food.

3:15 *He shall bruise you on the head, And you shall bruise him on the heel.* The antagonism between people and snakes is used to symbolize the outcome of the titanic struggle between God and the evil one, a struggle played out in the hearts and history of mankind. The offspring of the woman would eventually crush the serpent's head, a promise fulfilled in Christ's victory over Satan—a victory in which all believers will share (see Rom 16:20).

3:16 *pain in childbirth.* Her judgment fell on what was most uniquely hers as a woman and as a "helper suitable" (2:20) for her husband. Similarly, the man's "toil" (v. 17) was a judgment on him as worker of the soil. Some believe that the Hebrew root underlying "pain" and "toil" should here be understood in the sense of burdensome labor (see Prov 5:10, "hard-earned"; 14:23, "labor"). *bring forth children.* As a sign of grace in the midst of judgment, the human race would continue. *desire . . . rule.* Her sexual attraction for the man, and his headship over her, will become intimate aspects of her life in which she experiences trouble and anguish rather than unalloyed joy and blessing.

3:17–19 *you will eat.* Though he would have to work hard and long (judgment), the man would be able to produce food that would sustain life (grace).

3:19 *return to the ground . . . to dust you shall return.* Man's labor would not be able to stave off death. The origin of his body (see 2:7) and the source of his food (see v. 17) became a symbol of his eventual death.

3:21 *clothed them.* God graciously provided Adam and Eve with more effective clothing (cf. v. 7) to cover their shame (cf. v. 10).

3:22 *Us.* See note on 1:26. *knowing good and evil.* In a terribly perverted way, Satan's prediction (v. 5) came true. *live forever.* Sin, which always results in death (Rom 6:23; James 1:14–15), cuts the sinner off from God's gift of eternal life.

3:23 *sent him out from the garden of Eden, to cultivate the ground.* Before he sinned, man had worked in a beautiful and pleasant garden (2:15). Now he would have to work hard ground cursed with thorns and thistles (v. 18).

3:24 *cherubim.* Similar to the statues of winged figures that stood guard at the entrances to palaces and temples in ancient Mesopotamia (see note on Ex 25:18). *to guard.* The sword of God's judgment stood between fallen man and God's garden. The reason is given in v. 22. Only through God's redemption in Christ does man have access again to the tree of life (see Rev 2:7; 22:2,14,19).

4:1 *with the help of the LORD.* Eve acknowledged that God is the ultimate source of life (see Acts 17:25).

4:2 *Abel.* The name means "breath" or "temporary" or "meaningless" (the translation of the same basic Hebrew word that is in Eccl 1:2; 12:8) and hints at the shortness of Abel's life.

4:3–4 *Cain brought . . . fruit . . . Abel . . . brought of the firstlings of his flock and of their fat portions.* The contrast is not between an offer-

5 but [a]for Cain and for his offering He
had no regard. So [b]Cain became very angry
and his countenance fell.
6 Then the LORD said to Cain, "[a]Why are
you angry? And why has your countenance
fallen?
7 "[a]If you do well, [1]will not *your counte-*
nance be lifted up? [b]And if you do not do
well, sin is crouching at the door; and its
desire is for you, [c]but you must master it."
8 Cain [1]told Abel his brother. And it
came about when they were in the field, that
Cain rose up against Abel his brother and
[a]killed him.
9 Then the LORD said to Cain, "[a]Where is
Abel your brother?" And he said, "I do not
know. Am I my brother's keeper?"
10 He said, "What have you done? [a]The
voice of your brother's blood is crying to Me
from the ground.
11 "Now [a]you are cursed from the ground,
which has opened its mouth to receive your
brother's blood from your hand.
12 "[a]When you cultivate the ground, it will
no longer yield its strength to you; [b]you will
be a vagrant and a wanderer on the earth."
13 Cain said to the LORD, "My punishment
is too great to bear!
14 "Behold, You have [a]driven me this day
from the face of the ground; and from Your
face I will be hidden, and [b]I will be a vagrant
and a wanderer on the earth, and [c]whoever
finds me will kill me."
15 So the LORD said to him, "Therefore
whoever kills Cain, vengeance will be taken
on him [a]sevenfold." And the LORD [1][b]appoint-
ed a sign for Cain, so that no one finding him
would slay him.
16 Then Cain went out from the presence
[a]of the LORD, and [1]settled in the land of
[2]Nod, east of Eden.
17 Cain [1]had relations with his wife and
she conceived, and gave birth to Enoch; and
he built a city, and called the name of the
city Enoch, after the name of his son.
18 Now to Enoch was born Irad, and Irad
[1]became the father of Mehujael, and Mehujael [1]became the father of Methushael, and
Methushael [1]became the father of Lamech.
19 Lamech took to himself [a]two wives:
the name of the one was Adah, and the
name of the other, Zillah.
20 Adah gave birth to Jabal; he was the
father of those who dwell in tents and *have*
livestock.
21 His brother's name was Jubal; he was

5 [a]1 Sam 16:7 [b]Is 3:9; Jude 11
6 [a]Jon 4:4
7 [1]Or *surely you will be accepted* [a]Jer 3:12; Mic 7:18 [b]Num 32:23 [c]Job 11:14, 15; Rom 6:12, 16
8 [1]Lit *said to* [a]Matt 23:35; Luke 11:51; 1 John 3:12-15; Jude 11
9 [a]Gen 3:9
10 [a]Num 35:33; Deut 21:1-9; Heb 12:24; Rev 6:9, 10
11 [a]Gen 3:14; Deut 28:15-20; Gal 3:10
12 [a]Deut 28:15-24; Joel 1:10-20 [b]Lev 26:17, 36
14 [a]Gen 3:24; Jer 52:3 [b]Deut 28:64-67 [c]Num 35:19
15 [1]Or *set a mark on* [a]Gen 4:24 [b]Ezek 9:4, 6
16 [1]Lit *dwelt* [2]I.e. wandering [a]2 Kin 24:20; Jer 23:39; 52:3
17 [1]Lit *knew*
18 [1]Lit *begot*
19 [a]Gen 2:24

ing of plant life and an offering of animal life, but between a careless, thoughtless offering and a choice, generous offering (cf. Lev 3:16). Motivation and heart attitude are all-important, and God looked with favor on Abel and his offering because of Abel's faith (Heb 11:4). *firstlings.* Indicative of the recognition that all the productivity of the flock is from the Lord and all of it belongs to Him.

4:5 *angry.* God did not look with favor on Cain and his offering, and Cain (whose motivation and attitude were bad from the outset) reacted predictably.

4:7 *sin is crouching at the door.* The Hebrew word for "crouching" is the same as an ancient Babylonian word referring to an evil demon crouching at the door of a building to threaten the people inside. Sin may thus be pictured here as just such a demon, waiting to pounce on Cain—it desires to have him. He may already have been plotting his brother's murder. *its desire is for you.* In Hebrew, the same expression as that for "Your desire will be for [your husband]" in 3:16 (see also Song 7:10).

4:8 *rose up against . . . his brother and killed him.* The first murder was especially monstrous because it was committed against a brother (see vv. 9–11; 1 John 3:12) and against a good man (Matt 23:35; Heb 11:4)—a striking illustration of the awful consequences of the fall.

4:9 *Where . . . ?* A rhetorical question (see 3:9). *I do not know.* An outright lie. *Am I my brother's keeper?* A statement of callous indifference—all too common through the whole course of human history.

4:10 *your brother's blood is crying to Me.* Abel, in one sense a prophet (Luke 11:50–51), still speaks, though dead (Heb 11:4), for his spilled blood continues to cry out to God against all those who do violence to their human brothers. But the blood of Christ "speaks better than the blood of Abel" (Heb 12:24).

4:11 *cursed.* The ground had been cursed because of human sin (3:17), and now Cain himself is cursed. Formerly he had worked the ground, and it had produced life for him (vv. 2–3). Now the ground, soaked with his brother's blood, would symbolize death and would no longer yield for him its produce (v. 12).

4:12 *wanderer.* Estranged from his fellowman and finding even the ground inhospitable, he became a wanderer in the land of wandering (see note on v. 16).

4:13 *My punishment is too great to bear!* Confronted with his crime and its resulting curse, Cain responded not with remorse but with self-pity. His sin was virtually uninterrupted: impiety (v. 3), anger (v. 5), jealousy, deception and murder (v. 8), falsehood (v. 9) and self-seeking (v. 13). The final result was alienation from God Himself (vv. 14,16).

4:14–15 *whoever . . . whoever . . . no one.* These words seem to imply the presence of substantial numbers of people outside Cain's immediate family, but perhaps they only anticipate the future rapid growth of the race.

4:15 *sign.* A warning sign to protect him from an avenger. For the time being, the life of the murderer is spared (but see 6:7; 9:6). For a possible parallel see Ezek 9:4.

4:16 *Nod.* Location unknown. Nod means "wandering" (see vv. 12, 14).

4:17–18 *Cain . . . Enoch . . . Irad . . . Mehujael . . . Methushael . . . Lamech.* Together with that of Adam, these names add up to a total of seven, a number often signifying completeness (see v. 15). Each of the six names listed here is paralleled by a similar or identical name in the genealogy of Seth in ch. 5 as follows: Kenan (5:12), Enoch (5:21), Jared (5:18), Mahalalel (5:15), Methuselah (5:25), Lamech (5:28). The similarity between the two sets of names is striking and may suggest the selective nature of such genealogies (see note on 5:5). See also Introduction to 1 Chronicles: Genealogies.

4:17 *city.* The Hebrew for this word can refer to any permanent settlement, however small. Cain tried to redeem himself from his wandering state by the activity of his own hands—in the land of wandering he builds a city.

4:19 *took to himself two wives.* Polygamy entered history. Haughty Lamech, the seventh from Adam in the line of Cain, perhaps sought to attain the benefits of God's primeval blessing (see 1:28 and note) by his own device—multiplying his wives. Monogamy, however, was the original divine intention (see 2:23–24).

4:20–22 *Jabal . . . Jubal . . . Tubal-cain.* Lamech's three sons had

the father of all those who play the lyre and pipe.

22 As for Zillah, she also gave birth to Tubal-cain, the forger of all implements of bronze and iron; and the sister of Tubal-cain was Naamah.

23 Lamech said to his wives,

"Adah and Zillah,
Listen to my voice,
You wives of Lamech,
Give heed to my speech,
[a]For I [1]have killed a man for
wounding me;
And a boy for striking me;

24 If Cain is avenged [a]sevenfold,
Then Lamech seventy-sevenfold."

25 [a]Adam [1]had relations with his wife again; and she gave birth to a son, and named him [2]Seth, for, *she said*, "God [3]has appointed me another [4]offspring in place of Abel, [b]for Cain killed him."

26 To Seth, to him also [a]a son was born; and he called his name Enosh. Then *men* began [b]to call [1]upon the name of the LORD.

Descendants of Adam

5 This is the book of the generations of Adam. In the day when God created man, He made him [a]in the likeness of God.

2 He created them [a]male and female, and He [b]blessed them and named them [1]Man in the day when they were created.

3 When Adam had lived one hundred and thirty years, he [1]became the father of *a son* in his own likeness, according to his image, and named him Seth.

4 Then the days of Adam after he became the father of Seth were eight hundred years, and he had *other* sons and daughters.

5 So all the days that Adam lived were nine hundred and thirty years, and he died.

6 Seth lived one hundred and five years, and became the father of Enosh.

7 Then Seth lived eight hundred and seven years after he became the father of Enosh, and he had *other* sons and daughters.

8 So all the days of Seth were nine hundred and twelve years, and he died.

9 Enosh lived ninety years, and became the father of Kenan.

10 Then Enosh lived eight hundred and fifteen years after he became the father of Kenan, and he had *other* sons and daughters.

11 So all the days of Enosh were nine hundred and five years, and he died.

12 Kenan lived seventy years, and became the father of Mahalalel.

13 Then Kenan lived eight hundred and forty years after he became the father of Mahalalel, and he had *other* sons and daughters.

14 So all the days of Kenan were nine hundred and ten years, and he died.

15 Mahalalel lived sixty-five years, and became the father of Jared.

16 Then Mahalalel lived eight hundred and thirty years after he became the father of Jared, and he had *other* sons and daughters.

17 So all the days of Mahalalel were eight hundred and ninety-five years, and he died.

18 Jared lived one hundred and sixty-two years, and became the father of Enoch.

19 Then Jared lived eight hundred years after he became the father of Enoch, and he had *other* sons and daughters.

20 So all the days of Jared were nine hundred and sixty-two years, and he died.

21 Enoch lived sixty-five years, and became the father of Methuselah.

23 [1]Or *kill* [a]Ex 20:13; Lev 19:18; Deut 32:35; Ps 94:1
24 [a]Gen 4:15
25 [1]Lit *knew* [2]Heb *Sheth* [3]Heb *shath* [4]Lit *seed* [a]Gen 5:3 [b]Gen 4:8
26 [1]Or *by* [a]Luke 3:38 [b]Gen 12:8; 26:25; 1 Kin 18:24; Ps 116:17; Joel 2:32; Zeph 3:9; 1 Cor 1:2
5:1 [a]Gen 1:26, 27; Eph 4:24; Col 3:10
2 [1]Lit *Adam* [a]Matt 19:4; Mark 10:6 [b]Gen 1:28
3 [1]Lit *begot,* and so throughout the ch

similar names, each derived from a Hebrew verb meaning "to bring, carry, lead," and emphasizing activity. Tubal-cain's name was especially appropriate, since "Cain" means "metalsmith."

4:22 *implements.* For agriculture and construction, but they were also weapons.

4:23 *killed a man for wounding me.* Violent and wanton destruction of human life by one who proclaimed his complete independence from God by taking vengeance with his own hands (see Deut 32:35). Lamech proudly claimed to be master of his own destiny, thinking that he and his sons, by their own achievements, would redeem themselves from the curse on the line of Cain. This titanic claim climaxes the catalog of sins that began with Cain's prideful selfishness at the beginning of the chapter.

4:24 *seventy-sevenfold.* Lamech's vicious announcement of personal revenge found its counterpoint in Jesus' response to Peter's question about forgiveness in Matt 18:21–22.

4:25 *again . . . another offspring.* Abel was dead, and Cain was alienated; so Adam and Eve were granted a third son to carry on the family line.

4:26 *Enosh.* The name, like "Adam" (see note on 2:7), means "man." *began to call upon the name of the LORD.* Lamech's proud self-reliance, so characteristic of the line of Cain, is contrasted with dependence on God found in the line of Seth.

5:1 *generations.* See note on 2:4. *likeness.* See note on 1:26.

5:2 *male and female.* See note on 1:27. *blessed them.* See 1:28 and note. *named them.* See note on 1:5. *Man.* Often refers to both sexes (mankind) in the early chapters of Genesis (see, e.g., 3:22–24).

5:3 *his own likeness . . . his image.* See note on 1:26. As God created man in His own perfect image, so now sinful Adam has a son in his own imperfect image.

5:5 *nine hundred and thirty years.* See notes on v. 27; 6:3. Whether the large numbers describing human longevity in the early chapters of Genesis are literal or have a conventional literary function—or both—is uncertain. Some believe that several of the numbers have symbolic significance, such as Enoch's 365 (v. 23) years (365 being the number of days in a year, thus a full life) and Lamech's 777 (v. 31) years (777 being an expansion and multiple of seven, the number of completeness; cf. the "seventy-seven times" of Lamech's namesake in 4:24). The fact that there are exactly ten names in the Gen 5 list (as in the genealogy of 11:10–26) makes it likely that it includes gaps, the lengths of which may be summarized in the large numbers. Other ancient genealogies outside the Bible exhibit similarly large figures. For example, three kings in a Sumerian list (which also contains exactly ten names) are said to have reigned 72,000 years each—obviously exaggerated time spans. *and he died.* Repeated as a sad refrain throughout the chapter, the only exception being Enoch (see note on v. 24). The phrase is a stark reminder of God's judgment on sin resulting from Adam's fall.

22 Then Enoch [a]walked with God three hundred years after he became the father of Methuselah, and he had *other* sons and daughters.

23 So all the days of Enoch were three hundred and sixty-five years.

24 [a]Enoch walked with God; and he was not, for God [b]took him.

25 Methuselah lived one hundred and eighty-seven years, and became the father of Lamech.

26 Then Methuselah lived seven hundred and eighty-two years after he became the father of Lamech, and he had *other* sons and daughters.

27 So all the days of Methuselah were nine hundred and sixty-nine years, and he died.

28 Lamech lived one hundred and eighty-two years, and became the father of a son.

29 Now he called his name Noah, saying, "This one will [1]give us rest from our work and from the toil of our hands *arising* from [a]the ground which the LORD has cursed."

30 Then Lamech lived five hundred and ninety-five years after he became the father of Noah, and he had *other* sons and daughters.

31 So all the days of Lamech were seven hundred and seventy-seven years, and he died.

32 Noah was [a]five hundred years old, and Noah became the father of Shem, Ham, and Japheth.

22 [a]Gen 6:9; 17:1; 24:40; 48:15; Mic 6:8; Mal 2:6; 1 Thess 2:12
24 [a]2 Kin 2:11; Jude 14 [b]2 Kin 2:10; Ps 49:15; 73:24; Heb 11:5
29 [1]Lit *comfort us in* [a]Gen 3:17-19; 4:11
32 [a]Gen 7:6

The Corruption of Mankind

6 Now it came about, when men began to multiply on the face of the land, and daughters were born to them,

2 that the sons of God saw that the daughters of men were [1]beautiful; and they took wives for themselves, whomever they chose.

3 Then the LORD said, "[a]My Spirit shall not [1]strive with man forever, [2b]because he also is flesh; [3]nevertheless his days shall be one hundred and twenty years."

4 The [a]Nephilim were on the earth in those days, and also afterward, when the sons of God came in to the daughters of men, and they bore *children* to them. Those were the mighty men who *were* of old, men of renown.

5 Then the LORD saw that the wickedness of man was great on the earth, and that [a]every intent of the thoughts of his heart was only evil continually.

6 [a]The LORD was sorry that He had made man on the earth, and He was [b]grieved [1]in His heart.

7 The LORD said, "[a]I will blot out man whom I have created from the face of the land, from man to animals to creeping things and to birds of the [1]sky; for [b]I am sorry that I have made them."

8 But [a]Noah [b]found favor in the eyes of the LORD.

6:2 [1]Lit *good*
3 [1]Or *rule in;* some ancient versions read *abide in* [2]Or *in his going astray he is flesh* [3]Or *therefore* [a]Gal 5:16, 17; 1 Pet 3:20 [b]Ps 78:39
4 [a]Num 13:33
5 [a]Gen 8:21; Ps 14:1-3; Prov 6:18; Matt 15:19; Rom 1:28-32
6 [1]Lit *to* [a]Gen 6:7; Jer 18:7-10 [b]Is 63:10; Eph 4:30
7 [1]Lit *heavens* [a]Deut 28:63; 29:20 [b]Gen 6:6; Amos 7:3, 6
8 [a]Matt 24:37; Luke 17:26; 1 Pet 3:20 [b]Gen 19:19; Ex 33:17; Luke 1:30

5:22 *walked with God.* The phrase replaces the word "lived" in the other paragraphs of the chapter and reminds us that there is a difference between walking with God and merely living.

5:24 *and he was not, for God took him.* The phrase replaces "and he died" in the other paragraphs of the chapter. Like Elijah, who was "taken" (2 Kin 2:10) to heaven, Enoch was taken away (cf. Ps 49:15; 73:24) to the presence of God without experiencing death (Heb 11:5). Lamech, the seventh from Adam in the genealogy of Cain, was evil personified. But "Enoch, in the seventh generation from Adam" (Jude 14) in the genealogy of Seth, "obtained the witness . . . that he was pleasing to God" (Heb 11:5).

5:27 *nine hundred and sixty-nine years.* Only Noah and his family survived the flood. If the figures concerning life spans are literal, Methuselah died in the year of the flood (the figures in vv. 25,28 and 7:6 add up to exactly 969).

6:1 *multiply.* See note on 1:22.

6:2 *sons of God saw . . . daughters of men . . . and they took wives.* See v. 4. The phrase "sons of God" here has been interpreted to refer either to angels or to human beings. In such places as Job 1:6; 2:1 it refers to angels, and perhaps also in Ps 29:1 (where it is translated "sons of the mighty"). Some interpreters also appeal to Jude 6–7 (as well as to Jewish literature) in referring the phrase here to angels.

Others, however, maintain that intermarriage and cohabitation between angels and human beings, though commonly mentioned in ancient mythologies, are surely excluded by the very nature of the created order (ch. 1; Mark 12:25). Elsewhere, expressions equivalent to "sons of God" often refer to human beings, though in contexts quite different from the present one (see Deut 14:1; 32:5; Ps 73:15; Is 43:6; Hos 1:10; 11:1; Luke 3:38; 1 John 3:1–2,10). "Sons of God" (vv. 2,4) possibly refers to godly men, and "daughters of men" to sinful women (significantly, they are not called "daughters of God"), probably from the wicked line of Cain. If so, the context suggests that vv. 1–2 describe the intermarriage of the Sethites ("sons of God") of ch. 5 with the Cainites ("daughters of men") of ch. 4, indicating a breakdown in the separation of the two groups.

Another plausible suggestion is that the "sons of God" refers to royal figures (kings were closely associated with gods in the ancient Near East) who proudly perpetuated and aggravated the corrupt life-style of Lamech son of Cain (virtually a royal figure) and established for themselves royal harems.

6:3 Two key phrases in the Hebrew of this verse are obscure: the one rendered "strive with" (which could be translated "remain in") and the one rendered "is flesh" (which could be translated "is corrupt"). The verse seems to announce that the period of grace between God's declaration of judgment and its arrival would be 120 years (cf. 1 Pet 3:20). But if "remain in" is accepted, the verse announces that man's life span would henceforth be limited to 120 years (but see 11:10–26).

6:4 *Nephilim.* People of great size and strength (see Num 13:31–33). The Hebrew word means "fallen ones." In men's eyes they were "the mighty men . . . of old, men of renown," but in God's eyes they were sinners ("fallen ones") ripe for judgment.

6:5 One of the Bible's most vivid descriptions of total depravity. And because man's nature remained unchanged, things were no better after the flood (8:21).

6:6 *The LORD was sorry . . . He was grieved in His heart.* Man's sin is God's sorrow (see Eph 4:30).

6:7 *I will blot out man . . . from the face of the land.* The period of grace (see v. 3 and note) was coming to an end. *animals . . . creeping things . . . birds.* Though morally innocent, the animal world, as creatures under man's corrupted rule, shared in his judgment.

6:8–9 *found favor . . . righteous . . . blameless . . . walked with God.* See note on 5:22. Noah's godly life was a powerful contrast to the wicked lives of his contemporaries (see v. 5 and note; see also v. 12). This description of Noah does not imply sinless perfection.

9 These are *the records of* the generations of Noah. Noah was a [a]righteous man, [1][b]blameless in his [2]time; Noah [c]walked with God.

10 Noah [1]became the father of three sons: Shem, Ham, and Japheth.

11 Now the earth was [a]corrupt in the sight of God, and the earth was [b]filled with violence.

12 God looked on the earth, and behold, it was corrupt; for [a]all flesh had corrupted their way upon the earth.

13 Then God said to Noah, "[a]The end of all flesh has come before Me; for the earth is filled with violence because of them; and behold, I am about to destroy them with the earth.

14 "Make for yourself an ark of gopher wood; you shall make the ark with rooms, and shall [1]cover it inside and out with pitch.

15 "This is how you shall make it: the length of the ark three hundred [1]cubits, its breadth fifty [1]cubits, and its height thirty [1]cubits.

16 "You shall make a [1]window for the ark, and finish it to a cubit from [2]the top; and set the door of the ark in the side of it; you shall make it with lower, second, and third decks.

17 "Behold, [a]I, even I am bringing the flood of water upon the earth, to destroy all flesh in which is the breath of life, from under heaven; everything that is on the earth shall perish.

18 "But I will establish [a]My covenant with you; and [b]you shall enter the ark—you and your sons and your wife, and your sons' wives with you.

19 "[a]And of every living thing of all flesh, you shall bring two of every *kind* into the ark, to keep *them* alive with you; they shall be male and female.

20 "[a]Of the birds after their kind, and of the animals after their kind, of every creeping thing of the ground after its kind, two of every *kind* will come to you to keep *them* alive.

21 "As for you, take for yourself some of all [a]food which is edible, and gather *it* to yourself; and it shall be for food for you and for them."

22 [a]Thus Noah did; according to all that God had commanded him, so he did.

The Flood

7 Then the LORD said to Noah, "Enter the ark, you and all your household, for you *alone* I have seen *to be* [a]righteous before Me in this [1]time.

2 "You shall take [1]with you of every [a]clean animal [2]by sevens, a male and his female; and of the animals that are not clean two, a male and his female;

3 also of the birds of the [1]sky, [2]by sevens, male and female, to keep [3]offspring alive on the face of all the earth.

4 "For after [a]seven more days, I will send rain on the earth [b]forty days and forty nights; and I will blot out from the face of the land [c]every living thing that I have made."

5 [a]Noah did according to all that the LORD had commanded him.

6 Now Noah was [a]six hundred years old when the flood of water [1]came upon the earth.

9 [1]Lit *complete, perfect;* or *having integrity* [2]Lit *generations* [a]Ps 37:39; 2 Pet 2:5 [b]Gen 17:1; Deut 18:13; Job 1:1 [c]Gen 5:24
10 [1]Lit *begot*
11 [a]Deut 31:29; Judg 2:19 [b]Ezek 8:17
12 [a]Ps 14:1-3
13 [a]Is 34:1-4; Ezek 7:2, 3; Amos 8:2; 1 Pet 4:7
14 [1]Or *pitch*
15 [1]I.e. One cubit equals approx 18 in.
16 [1]Or *roof* [2]Lit *above*
17 [a]2 Pet 2:5
18 [a]Gen 9:9-16; 17:7 [b]Gen 7:7
19 [a]Gen 7:2, 14, 15
20 [a]Gen 7:3
21 [a]Gen 1:29, 30
22 [a]Gen 7:5; Heb 11:7
7:1 [1]Lit *generation* [a]Gen 6:9
2 [1]Lit *to* [2]Lit *seven seven* [a]Lev 11:1-31; Deut 14:3-20
3 [1]Lit *heavens* [2]Lit *seven seven* [3]Lit *seed*
4 [a]Gen 7:10 [b]Gen 7:12, 17 [c]Gen 6:7, 13
5 [a]Gen 6:22
6 [1]Lit *was* [a]Gen 5:32

6:9 *generations.* See note on 2:4. *righteous.* See note on Ps 1:5.
6:14 *ark.* The Hebrew for this word is used elsewhere only in reference to the basket that saved the baby Moses (Ex 2:3,5). *cover it . . . with pitch.* Moses' mother made his basket watertight in the same way (see Ex 2:3).
6:17 *flood of water upon the earth, to destroy all flesh . . . under heaven.* Some believe that the deluge was worldwide, partly because of the apparently universal terms of the text—both here and elsewhere (vv. 7,12–13; 7:4,19, 21–23; 8:21; 9:11,15). Others argue that nothing in the narrative of chs. 6–9 prevents the flood from being understood as regional—destroying everything in its wake, but of relatively limited scope and universal only from the standpoint of Moses' geographic knowledge. "Earth," e.g., may be defined in the more restricted sense of "land." "All flesh . . . under heaven" may mean all life within the range of Noah's perception. (See the universal language used to describe the drought and famine in the time of Joseph—41:54,57; see also note on 41:57.) Since the purpose of the floodwaters was to destroy sinful mankind (see v. 13), and since the writer possibly had in mind only the inhabitants of the ancient Near East, this flood may not have had to be worldwide to destroy them. The apostle Peter, however, seems to assume that the flood and its devastation were universal and total, except for Noah and his family (2 Pet 3:6; but see note there).
6:18 *covenant.* See note on 9:9. Noah would understand the full implications of God's covenant with him only after the floodwaters had dried up (see 9:8–17). *enter the ark.* The story of Noah's salvation from the flood illustrates God's redemption of His children (see Heb 11:7; 2 Pet 2:5) and typifies baptism (see 1 Pet 3:20–21). *your sons and your wife, and your sons' wives with you.* God extends His loving concern to the whole family of righteous Noah—a consistent pattern in God's dealings with His people, underscoring the moral and responsible relationship of parents to their children (see 17:7–27; 18:19; Deut 30:19; Ps 78:1–7; 102:28; 103:17–18; 112:1–2; Acts 2:38–39; 16:31; 1 Cor 7:14).
6:19 *two of every kind . . . to keep them alive.* Most animals were doomed to die in the flood (see note on v. 7), but at least one pair of each kind was preserved to restock the earth after the waters subsided.
6:20 *kind.* See note on 1:11.
6:22 *according to all that God had commanded him, so he did.* The account stresses Noah's obedience (see 7:5,9,16).
7:1 *Enter the ark.* The beginning of God's final word to Noah before the flood. God's first word to Noah after the flood begins similarly: "Go out of the ark" (8:16). *righteous.* See note on 6:8–9. As a "preacher of righteousness" (2 Pet 2:5), Noah warned his contemporaries of coming judgment and testified to the vitality of his own faith (see Heb 11:7).
7:2 *every clean animal by sevens . . . and of the . . . not clean two.* The ceremonially unclean animals would only have to reproduce themselves after the flood, but ceremonially clean animals would be needed also for the burnt offerings that Noah would sacrifice (see 8:20) and for food (see 9:3).
7:4 *forty days and forty nights.* A length of time often characterizing a critical period in redemptive history (see v. 12; Deut 9:11; Matt 4:1–11).

7 Then [a]Noah and his sons and his wife and his sons' wives with him entered the ark because of the water of the flood.

8 [a]Of clean animals and animals that are not clean and birds and everything that creeps on the ground,

9 there went into the ark to Noah [1]by twos, male and female, as God had commanded Noah.

10 It came about after [a]the seven days, that the water of the flood [1]came upon the earth.

11 In the [a]six hundredth year of Noah's life, in the second month, on the seventeenth day of the month, on the same day all [b]the fountains of the great deep burst open, and the [1]floodgates of the sky were opened.

12 [a]The rain [1]fell upon the earth for forty days and forty nights.

13 On the very same day [a]Noah and Shem and Ham and Japheth, the sons of Noah, and Noah's wife and the three wives of his sons with them, entered the ark,

14 they and every beast after its kind, and all the cattle after [1]their kind, and every creeping thing that creeps on the earth after its kind, and every bird after its kind, [2]all sorts of birds.

15 So they went into the ark to Noah, [a]by twos of all flesh in which was the breath of life.

16 Those that entered, male and female of all flesh, entered as God had commanded him; and the LORD closed *it* behind him.

17 Then the flood [1]came upon the earth for [a]forty days, and the water increased and lifted up the ark, so that it rose above the earth.

18 The water prevailed and increased greatly upon the earth, and the ark [1]floated on the [2]surface of the water.

19 The water prevailed more and more upon the earth, so that all the high mountains [1]everywhere under the heavens were covered.

20 The water prevailed fifteen [1]cubits higher, [a]and the mountains were covered.

21 [a]All flesh that [1]moved on the earth perished, birds and cattle and beasts and every swarming thing that swarms upon the earth, and all mankind;

22 of all that was on the dry land, all [a]in whose nostrils was the breath of the spirit of life, died.

23 Thus He blotted out [1]every living thing that was upon the face of the land, from man to animals to creeping things and to birds of the [2]sky, and they were blotted out from the earth; and only [a]Noah was left, together with those that were with him in the ark.

24 [a]The water prevailed upon the earth one hundred and fifty days.

The Flood Subsides

8 But [a]God remembered Noah and all the beasts and all the cattle that were with him in the ark; and [b]God caused a wind to pass over the earth, and the water subsided.

2 Also [a]the fountains of the deep and the [1]floodgates of the sky were closed, and [b]the rain from the sky was restrained;

3 and the water receded steadily from the earth, and at the end [a]of one hundred and fifty days the water decreased.

4 In the seventh month, on the seventeenth day of the month, [a]the ark rested upon the mountains of Ararat.

5 The water decreased steadily until the tenth month; in the tenth month, on the first day of the month, the tops of the mountains became visible.

6 Then it came about at the end of forty days, that Noah opened the [a]window of the ark which he had made;

7 and he sent out a raven, and it [1]flew here and there until the water was dried up [2]from the earth.

8 Then he sent out a dove from him, to see if the water was abated from the face of the land;

7 [a]Gen 6:18; 7:13; Matt 24:38f; Luke 17:27
8 [a]Gen 6:19, 20; 7:2, 3
9 [1]Lit *two two*
10 [1]Lit *were* [a]Gen 7:4
11 [1]Or *windows of the heavens* [a]Gen 7:6 [b]Gen 8:2
12 [1]Lit *was* [a]Gen 7:4, 17
13 [a]Gen 6:18; 7:7
14 [1]Lit *its* [2]Lit *every bird, every wing*
15 [a]Gen 6:19; 7:9
17 [1]Lit *was* [a]Gen 7:4
18 [1]Lit *went* [2]Lit *face*
19 [1]Lit *which were under all the heavens*
20 [1]I.e. One cubit equals approx 18 in. [a]Gen 8:4
21 [1]Or *crept* [a]Gen 6:7, 13, 17; 7:4
22 [a]Gen 2:7
23 [1]Lit *all existence* [2]Lit *heavens* [a]Matt 24:38, 39; Luke 17:26, 27; Heb 11:7; 1 Pet 3:20; 2 Pet 2:5
24 [a]Gen 8:3
8:1 [a]Gen 19:29; Ex 2:24; 1 Sam 1:19; Ps 105:42 [b]Ex 14:21; 15:10; Job 12:15; Ps 29:10; Is 44:27; Nah 1:4
2 [1]Or *windows of the heavens* [a]Gen 7:11 [b]Gen 7:4, 12
3 [a]Gen 7:24
4 [a]Gen 7:20
6 [a]Gen 6:16
7 [1]Lit *went out, going and returning* [2]Lit *from upon*

7:7 *entered the ark because of the water.* Noah and his family were saved, but life as usual continued for everyone else until it was too late (see Matt 24:37–39).

7:13 *Noah and . . . the sons of Noah, and Noah's wife and the three wives of his sons.* "A few persons, that is, eight" (1 Pet 3:20; see 2 Pet 2:5), survived the flood.

7:14 *every beast . . . all the cattle . . . every creeping thing that creeps on the earth . . . every bird.* Four of the five categories of animate life mentioned in 1:21–25. The fifth category—sea creatures—could remain alive outside the ark.

7:16 *God had commanded him . . . the LORD closed it behind him.* "God" gave the command, but in His role as redeeming "LORD" (see notes on 2:4; Ex 6:6) He closed the door of the ark behind Noah and his family. Neither divine name is mentioned in the rest of ch. 7, as the full fury of the flood was unleashed on sinful mankind.

7:20 *prevailed fifteen cubits higher, and the mountains were covered.* The ark was 30 cubits high (6:15), so the water was deep enough to keep it from running aground.

7:22 *breath of the spirit of life.* God's gift at creation (see 1:30; 2:7) was taken away because of sin.

8:1 So far the flood narrative has been an account of judgment; from this point on it is a story of redemption. *God remembered Noah.* Though He had not been mentioned since 7:16 or heard from for 150 days (see 7:24), God had not forgotten Noah and his family. To "remember" in the Bible is not merely to recall to mind; it is to express concern for someone, to act with loving care for him. When God remembers His people, He does so "with favor" (Neh 5:19; 13:31). *wind.* The Hebrew word translated "Spirit" in 1:2 is here rendered "wind," and introduces a series of parallels between the events of chs. 8–9 and those of ch. 1 in their literary order: Compare 8:2 with 1:7; 8:5 with 1:9; 8:7 with 1:20; 8:17 with 1:25; 9:1 with 1:28a; 9:2 with 1:28b; 9:3 with 1:30. Ch. 1 describes the original beginning, while chs. 8–9 describe a new beginning after the flood.

8:4 *mountains.* The word is plural and refers to a range of mountains. *Ararat.* The name is related to Assyrian Urartu, which became an extensive and mountainous kingdom (see Jer 51:27; see also Is 37:38), including much of the territory north of Mesopotamia and east of modern Turkey. The ark's landfall was probably in southern Urartu.

9 but the dove found no resting place for the sole of her foot, so she returned to him into the ark, for the water was on the [1]surface of all the earth. Then he put out his hand and took her, and brought her into the ark to himself.

10 So he waited yet another seven days; and again he sent out the dove from the ark.

11 The dove came to him toward [1]evening, and behold, in her [2]beak was a freshly picked olive leaf. So Noah knew that the water was abated from the earth.

12 Then he waited yet another seven days, and sent out [a]the dove; but she did not return to him again.

13 Now it came about in the [a]six hundred and first year, in the first *month,* on the first of the month, the water was dried up [1]from the earth. Then Noah removed the covering of the ark, and looked, and behold, the [2]surface of the ground was dried up.

14 In the second month, on the twenty-seventh day of the month, the earth was dry.

15 Then God spoke to Noah, saying,

16 “Go out of the ark, you and your wife and your sons and your sons’ wives with you.

17 “Bring out with you every living thing of all flesh that is with you, birds and animals and every creeping thing that creeps on the earth, that they may [1a]breed abundantly on the earth, and be fruitful and multiply on the earth.”

18 So Noah went out, and his sons and his wife and his sons’ wives with him.

19 Every beast, every creeping thing, and every bird, everything that moves on the earth, went out [1]by their families from the ark.

20 Then Noah built [a]an altar to the LORD, and took of every [b]clean animal and of every clean bird and offered [c]burnt offerings on the altar.

21 The LORD [a]smelled the soothing aroma; and the LORD said [1]to Himself, “I will never again [b]curse the ground on account of man, for [c]the [2]intent of man’s heart is evil from his youth; [d]and I will never again [3]destroy every living thing, as I have done.

22 “While the earth remains,
Seedtime and harvest,
And cold and heat,
And [a]summer and winter,
And [b]day and night
Shall not cease.”

Covenant of the Rainbow

9 And God blessed Noah and his sons and said to them, “[a]Be fruitful and multiply, and fill the earth.

2 “The fear of you and the terror of you will be on every beast of the earth and on every bird of the [1]sky; with everything that creeps on the ground, and all the fish of the sea, into your hand they are given.

3 “Every moving thing that is alive shall be food for you; I give all to you, [a]as *I gave* the green plant.

4 “Only you shall not eat flesh with its life, *that is,* [a]its blood.

5 “Surely I will require [1a]your lifeblood; [2b]from every beast I will require it. And

9 [1]Lit *face*
11 [1]Lit *the time of evening* [2]Lit *mouth*
12 [a]Jer 48:28
13 [1]Lit *from upon* [2]Lit *face* [a]Gen 7:6
17 [1]Or *swarm* [a]Gen 1:22, 28
19 [1]Or *according to their kind*
20 [a]Gen 12:7, 8; 13:18; 22:9 [b]Gen 7:2; Lev 11:1-47 [c]Gen 22:2; Ex 10:25
21 [1]Lit *to His heart* [2]Or *inclination* [3]Lit *smite* [a]Ex 29:18, 25 [b]Gen 3:17; 6:7, 13, 17; Is 54:9 [c]Gen 6:5; Ps 51:5; Jer 17:9; Rom 1:21; 3:23; Eph 2:1-3 [d]Gen 9:11, 15
22 [a]Ps 74:17 [b]Jer 33:20, 25
9:1 [a]Gen 1:28; 9:7
2 [1]Lit *heavens*
3 [a]Gen 1:29
4 [a]Lev 7:26f; 17:10-16; 19:26; Deut 12:16, 23; 15:23; 1 Sam 14:34; Acts 15:20, 29
5 [1]Lit *your blood of your lives* [2]Lit *from the hand of* [a]Ex 20:13; 21:12 [b]Ex 21:28, 29

8:11 *the dove came to him . . . in her beak was a freshly plucked olive leaf.* Olives do not grow at high elevations, and the fresh leaf was a sign to Noah that the water had receded from the earth. The modern symbol of peace represented by a dove carrying an olive branch in its beak has its origin in this story.

8:13 *in the six hundred and first year, in the first month, on the first of the month.* The date formula signals mankind's new beginning after the flood.

8:14 *In the second month, on the twenty-seventh day of the month.* More than a year after the flood began (see 7:11).

8:16 *Go out of the ark.* See note on 7:1.

8:17 *breed abundantly . . . be fruitful . . . multiply.* See 1:22 and note. The animals and birds could now repopulate their former habitats.

8:20 LORD. Since worship is a very personal matter, it is to God as "the LORD" (see note on 2:4) that Noah brought his sacrifice (see 4:4). *burnt offerings.* See Lev 1:3–4 and notes.

8:21 *smelled the soothing aroma.* A figurative way of saying that the Lord takes delight in His children's worship of Him (see Eph 5:2; Phil 4:18). *curse the ground.* Although the Hebrew here has a different word for "curse," the reference appears to be to the curse of 3:17. It may be that the Lord here pledged never to add curse upon curse as He had in regard to Cain (4:12). *for the intent of man's heart is evil.* For almost identical phraseology see 6:5. Because of man's extreme wickedness, God had destroyed him (6:7) by means of a flood (6:17). Although righteous Noah and his family had been saved, he and his offspring were descendants of Adam and carried in their hearts the inheritance of sin. God graciously promises never again to deal with sin by sending such a devastating deluge (see 9:11,15). Human history is held open for God's dealing with sin in a new and redemptive way—the way that was prepared for by God's action at Babel (see notes on 11:6,8) and that begins to unfold with the call of Abram (12:1). *from his youth.* The phrase replaces "continually" in 6:5 and emphasizes the truth that sin infects a person's life from his conception and birth (Ps 51:5; 58:3).

8:22 Times and seasons, created by God in the beginning (see 1:14), will never cease till the end of history.

9:1–7 At this new beginning, God renewed His original benediction (1:28) and His provision for man's food (cf. v. 3; 1:29–30). But because sin had brought violence into man's world and because God now appointed meat as a part of man's food (v. 3), further divine provisions and stipulations are added (vv. 4–6). Yet God's benediction dominates and encloses the whole (see v. 7).

9:2 *into your hand they are given.* God reaffirmed that mankind would rule over all creation, including the animals (see note on 1:26).

9:3 *Every moving thing that is alive shall be food.* Meat would now supplement mankind's diet.

9:4 *you shall not eat flesh with its life, that is, its blood.* Lev 17:14 stresses the intimate relationship between blood and life by twice declaring that "the life of all flesh is its blood." Life is the precious and mysterious gift of God, and man is not to seek to preserve it or increase the life-force within him by eating "life" that is "in the blood" (Lev 17:11)—as many pagan peoples throughout history have thought they could do.

9:5 *I will require your lifeblood; from every beast I will require it.* God Himself is the great defender of human life (see 4:9–12), which is precious to Him because man was created in His image (v. 6) and because man is the earthly representative and focal point

Major Covenants in the Old Testament

COVENANTS	REFERENCE	TYPE	PARTICIPANT	DESCRIPTION
NOAHIC	Gen 9:8-17	Royal Grant	Made with "righteous" (6:9) Noah (and his descendants and every living thing on earth—all life that is subject to man's jurisdiction)	An unconditional divine promise never to destroy all earthly life with some natural catastrophe; the covenant "sign" being the rainbow in the storm cloud
ABRAHAMIC A	Gen 15:9-21	Royal (land) Grant	Made with "righteous" (his faith was "reckoned to him as righteousness," v. 6) Abram (and his descendants, v. 16)	An unconditional divine promise to fulfill the grant of the land; a self-maledictory oath symbolically enacted it (v. 17)
ABRAHAMIC B	Gen 17	Suzerain-vassal	Made with Abraham as patriarchal head of his household	A conditional divine pledge to be Abraham's God and the God of his descendants (cf. "As for Me," v. 4; "as for you," v. 9); the condition: total consecration to the Lord as symbolized by circumcision
SINAITIC	Ex 19-24	Suzerain-vassal	Made with Israel as the descendants of Abraham, Isaac and Jacob and as the people the Lord has redeemed from bondage to an earthly power	A conditional divine pledge to be Israel's God (as her Protector and the Guarantor of her blessed destiny); the condition: Israel's total consecration to the Lord as His people (His kingdom) who live by His rule and serve His purposes in history
PHINEHAS	Num 25:10-13	Royal Grant	Made with the zealous priest Phinehas	An unconditional divine promise to maintain the family of Phinehas in a "perpetual priesthood" (implicitly a pledge to Israel to provide her forever with a faithful priesthood)
DAVIDIC	2 Sam 7:5-16	Royal Grant	Made with faithful King David after his devotion to God as Israel's king and the Lord's anointed vassal had come to special expression (v. 2)	An unconditional divine promise to establish and maintain the Davidic dynasty on the throne of Israel (implicitly a pledge to Israel) to provide her forever with a godly king like David and through that dynasty to do for her what He had done through David—bring her into rest in the promised land (1 Kin 4:20-21; 5:3-4)
NEW	Jer 31:31-34	Royal Grant	Promised to rebellious Israel as she is about to be expelled from the promised land in actualization of the most severe covenant curse (Lev 26:27-39; Deut 28:36-37, 45-68)	An unconditional divine promise to unfaithful Israel to forgive her sins and establish His relationship with her on a new basis by writing His law "on their heart"—a covenant of pure grace

Major Types of Royal Covenants/Treaties in the Ancient Near East

ROYAL GRANT (UNCONDITIONAL)
A king's grant (of land or some other benefit) to a loyal servant for faithful or exceptional service. The grant was normally perpetual and unconditional, but the servant's heirs benefited from it only as they continued their father's loyalty and service. (Cf. 1 Sam 8:14; 22:7; 27:6; Esth 8:1.)

PARITY
A covenant between equals, binding them to mutual friendship or at least to mutual respect for each other's spheres and interests. Participants called each other "brothers." (Cf. Gen 21:27; 26:31; 31:44-54; 1 Kin 5:12; 15:19; 20:32-34; Amos 1:9.)

SUZERAIN-VASSAL (CONDITIONAL)
A covenant regulating the relationship between a great king and one of his subject kings. The great king claimed absolute right of sovereignty, demanded total loyalty and service (the vassal must "love" his suzerain) and pledged protection of the subject's realm and dynasty, conditional on the vassal's faithfulness and loyalty to him. The vassal pledged absolute loyalty to his suzerain—whatever service his suzerain demanded—and exclusive reliance on the suzerain's protection. Participants called each other "lord" and "servant" or "father" and "son." (Cf. Josh 9:6,8; Ezek 17:13-18; Hosea 12:1.)

Commitments made in these covenants were accompanied by self-maledictory oaths (made orally, ceremonially or both). The gods were called upon to witness the covenants and implement the curses of the oaths if the covenants were violated.

[2]from *every* man, [2]from every man's brother
I will require the life of man.

6 "[a]Whoever sheds man's blood,
By man his blood shall be shed,
For [b]in the image of God
He made man.

7 "As for you, [a]be fruitful and multiply;
[1]Populate the earth abundantly and
multiply in it."

8 Then God spoke to Noah and to his
sons with him, saying,
9 "Now behold, [a]I Myself do establish My
covenant with you, and with your [1]descen-
dants after you;
10 and with every living creature that is
with you, the birds, the cattle, and every
beast of the earth with you; of all that comes
out of the ark, even every beast of the earth.
11 "I establish My covenant with you; and
all flesh shall [a]never again be cut off by the
water of the flood, [b]neither shall there again
be a flood to destroy the earth."
12 God said, "This is [a]the sign of the covenant which I am making between Me and
you and every living creature that is with
you, for [1]all successive generations;
13 I set My [a]bow in the cloud, and it shall
be for a sign of a covenant between Me and
the earth.
14 "It shall come about, when I bring a
cloud over the earth, that the bow will be
seen in the cloud,
15 and [a]I will remember My covenant,
which is between Me and you and every living creature of all flesh; and [b]never again
shall the water become a flood to destroy all
flesh.
16 "When the bow is in the cloud, then I
will look upon it, to remember the [a]everlast-
ing covenant between God and every living
creature of all flesh that is on the earth."
17 And God said to Noah, "This is the sign
of the covenant which I have established
between Me and all flesh that is on the earth."
18 Now the sons of Noah who came out of
the ark were Shem and Ham and Japheth;
and [a]Ham was the father of Canaan.
19 These three *were* the sons of Noah, and
[a]from these the whole earth was [1]populated.
20 Then Noah began [1]farming and planted a vineyard.
21 He drank of the wine and [a]became
drunk, and uncovered himself inside his
tent.
22 Ham, the father of Canaan, [a]saw the
nakedness of his father, and told his two
brothers outside.
23 But Shem and Japheth took a garment
and laid it upon both their shoulders and
walked backward and covered the nakedness
of their father; and their faces were [1]turned
away, so that they did not see their father's
nakedness.
24 When Noah awoke from his wine, he
knew what his youngest son had done to
him.
25 So he said,

"[a]Cursed be Canaan;
[1b]A servant of servants
He shall be to his brothers."

26 He also said,

"[a]Blessed be the LORD,
The God of Shem;
And let Canaan be [1]his servant.

5 [2]Lit *from the hand of*
6 [a]Ex 21:12-14; Lev 24:17; Num 35:33; Matt 26:52 [b]Gen 1:26, 27
7 [1]Lit *Swarm in the earth* [a]Gen 9:1
9 [1]Lit *seed* [a]Gen 6:18
11 [a]Gen 8:21 [b]Is 54:9
12 [1]Or *everlasting generations* [a]Gen 9:13, 17; 17:11
13 [a]Ezek 1:28
15 [a]Lev 26:42, 45; Deut 7:9; Ezek 16:60 [b]Gen 9:11
16 [a]Gen 17:13, 19; 2 Sam 23:5
18 [a]Gen 9:25-27; 10:6
19 [1]Lit *scattered* [a]Gen 9:1, 7; 10:32; 1 Chr 1:4
20 [1]Lit to be *a farmer*
21 [a]Prov 20:1
22 [a]Hab 2:15
23 [1]Lit *backward*
25 [1]I.e. The lowest of servants [a]Deut 27:16 [b]Josh 9:23
26 [1]Or *their* [a]Gen 14:20; 24:27

of God's kingdom. In the theocracy (kingdom of God) established at Sinai, a domestic animal that had taken human life was to be stoned to death (Ex 21:28–32).

9:6 *Whoever sheds man's blood, By man his blood shall be shed.* In the later theocracy, those guilty of premeditated murder were to be executed (see Ex 21:12–14; Num 35:16–32; see also Rom 13:3–4; 1 Pet 2:13–14). *For in the image of God He made man.* See 1:26 and note. In killing a human being, a murderer demonstrates his contempt for God as well as for his fellowman.

9:9 *Now . . . I Myself do establish My covenant.* God sovereignly promised in this covenant to Noah, to Noah's descendants and to all other living things (as a kind of gracious reward to righteous Noah, the new father of the human race—see 6:18) never again to destroy man and the earth until His purposes for His creation are fully realized ("while the earth remains," 8:22). For similar commitments by God see His covenants with Abram (15:18–20), Phinehas (Num 25:10–13) and David (2 Sam 7). See chart, p. 16.

9:11 *all flesh shall never again be cut off by the water of the flood.* A summary of the provisions of the Lord's covenant with Noah—an eternal covenant, as seen in such words and phrases as "never again" (vv. 11,15), "for all successive generations" (v. 12) and "everlasting" (v. 16).

9:12 *sign.* A covenant sign was a visible seal and reminder of covenant commitments. Circumcision would become the sign of the covenant with Abraham (see 17:11), and the Sabbath would be the sign of the covenant with Israel at Sinai (see Ex 31:16–17).

9:13 *bow.* Rain and the rainbow doubtless existed long before the time of Noah's flood, but after the flood the rainbow took on new meaning as the sign of the Noahic covenant.

9:19 *populated.* Thus anticipating the table of nations (see note on 11:8).

9:20 *began farming.* Noah, like his father Lamech (see 5:29), was a farmer.

9:21 *He drank of the wine and became drunk.* The first reference to wine connects it with drunkenness. *uncovered himself inside his tent.* Excessive use of wine led, among other things, to immodest behavior (see 19:30–35).

9:22 *father of Canaan.* Mentioned here because Ham, in acting as he did, showed himself to be the true father of Canaan (i.e., of the Canaanites; see note on 15:16). *told his two brothers.* He broadcast, rather than covered, his father's immodesty.

9:23 *faces were turned . . . so that they did not see.* They wanted to avoid further disgrace to their father.

9:24 *from his wine.* From the drunkenness caused by the wine.

9:25 *Cursed be Canaan.* Some maintain that Ham's son (see vv. 18,22) was to be punished because of his father's sin (see Ex 20:5), but Ex 20 restricts such punishment to "those who hate Me." It is probably better to hold that Canaan and his descendants were to be punished because they were going to be even worse than Ham (Lev 18:2–3,6–30). *servant of servants.* Joshua's subjection of the Gibeonites (Josh 9:27) is one of the fulfillments (see also Josh 16:10; Judg 1:28,30,33,35; 1 Kin 9:20–21). Noah's prophecy cannot be used to justify the enslavement of blacks, since those cursed here were Canaanites, who were Caucasian.

9:26 *Blessed be the LORD.* The Lord (instead of Shem) is blessed (praised) because He is the source of Shem's blessing. He is also

27 "[a]May God enlarge Japheth,
And let him dwell in the tents of Shem;
And let Canaan be [1]his servant."
28 Noah lived three hundred and fifty
years after the flood.
29 So all the days of Noah were nine hundred and fifty years, and he died.

Descendants of Noah

10 Now these are *the records of* the generations of Shem, Ham, and Japheth, the
sons of Noah; and sons were born to them
after the flood.
2 [a]The sons of Japheth *were* [b]Gomer and
Magog and [c]Madai and [d]Javan and Tubal
and [e]Meshech and Tiras.
3 The sons of Gomer *were* [a]Ashkenaz
and [1]Riphath and [b]Togarmah.
4 The sons of Javan *were* Elishah and
[a]Tarshish, Kittim and [1]Dodanim.
5 From these the coastlands of the
nations [1]were separated into their lands,
every one according to his language, according to their families, into their nations.

6 [a]The sons of Ham *were* Cush and Mizraim and Put and Canaan.
7 The sons of Cush *were* [a]Seba and Havilah and Sabtah and [b]Raamah and Sabteca; and
the sons of Raamah *were* [b]Sheba and [c]Dedan.
8 Now Cush [1]became the father of Nimrod; he [2]became a mighty one on the earth.
9 He was a mighty hunter before the
LORD; therefore it is said, "Like Nimrod a
mighty hunter before the LORD."
10 The beginning of his kingdom was
[1a]Babel and Erech and Accad and Calneh, in
the land of [b]Shinar.
11 From that land he went forth [a]into
Assyria, and built Nineveh and Rehoboth-Ir
and Calah,
12 and Resen between Nineveh and
Calah; that is the great city.
13 Mizraim [1]became the father of [a]Ludim
and Anamim and Lehabim and Naphtuhim
14 and [a]Pathrusim and Casluhim (from
which came the Philistines) and Caphtorim.
15 Canaan [1]became the father of [a]Sidon,
his firstborn, and [b]Heth

27 [1]Or *their* [a]Gen 10:2-5; Is 66:19
10:2 [a]1 Chr 1:5-7 [b]Ezek 38:2, 6 [c]2 Kin 17:6 [d]Is 66:19 [e]Ezek 38:2
3 [1]I.e. In 1 Chr 1:6, *Diphath* [a]Jer 51:27 [b]Ezek 27:14
4 [1]I.e. In 1 Chr 1:7, *Rodanim* [a]Ezek 27:12, 25
5 [1]Or *separated themselves*
6 [a]1 Chr 1:8-10
7 [a]Is 43:3 [b]Ezek 27:22 [c]Ezek 27:15, 20
8 [1]Lit *begot* [2]Lit *began to be*
10 [1]Or *Babylon* [a]Gen 11:9 [b]Gen 11:2; 14:1
11 [a]Mic 5:6
13 [1]Lit *begot* [a]Jer 46:9
14 [a]1 Chr 1:12
15 [1]Lit *begot* [a]1 Chr 1:13; Jer 47:4 [b]Gen 23:3

the "God of Shem" (and his descendants, the Semites—which included the Israelites) in a special sense.

9:27 *dwell in the tents of Shem.* Share in the blessings bestowed on Shem.

9:29 *and he died.* See note on 5:5. As the tenth and last member of the genealogy of Seth (5:3–32), Noah had an obituary that ends like those of his worthy ancestors.

10:1 *generations.* See note on 2:4. The links affirmed here may not all be based on strictly physical descent, but may include geographical, historical and linguistic associations (see note on v. 5.) For example, the Hebrew for "sons" can mean "descendants" or "successors" or "nations," and the Hebrew for "father" can mean "ancestor" or "predecessor" or "founder." See also Introduction to 1 Chronicles: Genealogies.

10:2 *Japheth.* As the least involved in the Biblical narrative and perhaps also as the oldest of Noah's sons (see note on v. 21), his descendants or successors are listed first. The genealogy of Shem, the chosen line, appears last in the chapter (see vv. 21–31; see also 11:10–26). The 14 nations that came from Japheth plus the 30 from Ham and the 26 from Shem add up to 70 (the multiple of 10 and 7, both numbers signifying completeness; see note on 5:5), perhaps in anticipation of the 70 members of Jacob's family in Egypt (see 46:27; Ex 1:5; also Deut 32:8). The Japhethites lived generally north and west of Canaan in Eurasia. *Gomer.* The people of Gomer (the later Cimmerians) and related nations (see v. 3) lived near the Black Sea. *Magog.* Possibly the father of a Scythian people who inhabited the Caucasus and adjacent regions southeast of the Black Sea. *Madai.* The later Medes. *Javan.* Ionia (southern Greece) and perhaps western Asia Minor. *Tubal, Meshech.* Not related to Tobolsk and Moscow in modern Russia. Together with Magog they are mentioned in later Assyrian inscriptions. See also Ezek 38:2. Probably Tubal was in Pontus, and Meshech was in the Moschian Mountains. Their movement was from eastern Asia Minor north to the Black Sea. *Tiras.* Possibly the Thrace of later times.

10:3 *Ashkenaz.* The later Scythians. All three names in this verse refer to peoples located in the upper Euphrates region.

10:4 *Elishah.* Either Alashia (an ancient name for Cyprus) or a reference to Sicily and southern Italy. *Tarshish.* Probably southern Spain. *Kittim.* A people living on Cyprus. *Dodanim.* Some manuscripts have "Rodanim" (see NASB marg.), a people whose name is perhaps reflected in Rhodes (a Greek isle).

10:5 See vv. 20,31. *lands . . . language . . . families . . . nations.* Geographic, ethnic, political and linguistic terms, respectively. These several criteria were used to differentiate the various groups of people.

10:6 *Ham.* The Hamites were located in southwestern Asia and northeast Africa. *Cush.* The upper Nile region, south of Egypt. *Mizraim.* Means "two Egypts," a reference to Upper and Lower Egypt. *Put.* Either Libya (see note on v. 13) or the land the ancient Egyptians called Punt (modern Somalia). *Canaan.* The name means "land of purple" (as does Phoenicia, the Greek name for the same general region)—so called because Canaan was a major producer and exporter of purple dye, highly prized by royalty. The territory was much later called Palestine after the Philistines (see v. 14).

10:7 *sons of Cush.* The seven Cushite nations here mentioned were all in Arabia. Sheba and Dedan (or their namesakes) reappear as two of Abraham's grandsons (see 25:3). Together with Raamah they are mentioned in Ezek 27:20–22.

10:8 *Cush.* Probably not the same as that in vv. 6–7. Located in Mesopotamia, its name may be related to that of the later Kassites. *Nimrod.* Possibly the Hebrew name of Sargon I, an early ruler of Akkad (see v. 10).

10:10 *Erech.* The Hebrew name for Uruk (modern Warka), one of the important cities in ancient Mesopotamia.

10:12 *great city.* Possibly a reference to Calah (or even Resen), but most likely to Nineveh (see Jon 1:2; 3:2; 4:11), either alone or including the surrounding urban areas.

10:13 *Ludim.* Perhaps the Lydians in Asia Minor (see note on v. 22). *Anamim.* Located in north Africa, west of Egypt, near Cyrene. *Lehabim.* Perhaps the Libyan desert tribes (see note on v. 6). *Naphtuhim.* People of Lower Egypt.

10:14 *Pathrusim.* The inhabitants of Upper Egypt (see note on v. 6). *Caphtorim.* Crete, known as Caphtor in ancient times, was for a while the homeland of various Philistine groups (see Jer 47:4; Amos 9:7). The Philistines themselves were a vigorous Indo-European maritime people who invaded Egypt early in the 12th century B.C. After being driven out, they migrated in large numbers to southwest Canaan, later extending their influence over most of the land. The Philistines of the patriarchal period (see 21:32,34; 26:1,8,14–15,18) no doubt had earlier settled in Canaan more peacefully and in smaller numbers.

10:15 *Sidon.* An important commercial city on the northwest coast of Canaan. *Heth.* The progenitor of the Hittites, a powerful

16 and [a]the Jebusite and the Amorite and
the Girgashite
17 and the Hivite and the Arkite and the
Sinite
18 and the Arvadite and the Zemarite and
the Hamathite; and afterward the families of
the Canaanite were spread abroad.
19 [a]The territory of the Canaanite [1]extended
from Sidon as you go toward Gerar, as far
as Gaza; as you go toward [b]Sodom and
Gomorrah and Admah and Zeboiim, as far as
Lasha.
20 These are the sons of Ham, according
to their families, according to their languages,
by their lands, by their nations.
21 Also to Shem, the father of all the children
of Eber, *and* the [1]older brother of
Japheth, children were born.

16 [a]Gen 15:19-21
19 [1]Lit *was* [a]Num 34:2-12 [b]Gen 14:2, 3
21 [1]Or *the brother of Japheth the elder*
22 [a]1 Chr 1:17 [b]Gen 14:1, 9 [c]Gen 11:10 [d]Is 66:19
23 [a]Job 1:1; Jer 25:20
24 [1]Lit *begot* [a]Gen 11:12; Luke 3:35
25 [1]I.e. division [a]1 Chr 1:19
26 [1]Lit *begot*
28 [1]I.e. Ebal in 1 Chr 1:22, *Ebal*

22 [a]The sons of Shem *were* [b]Elam and
Asshur and [c]Arpachshad and [d]Lud and
Aram.
23 The sons of Aram *were* [a]Uz and Hul
and Gether and Mash.
24 Arpachshad [1]became the father of
[a]Shelah; and Shelah [1]became the father of
Eber.
25 [a]Two sons were born to Eber; the name
of the one *was* [1]Peleg, for in his days the
earth was divided; and his brother's name
was Joktan.
26 Joktan [1]became the father of Almodad
and Sheleph and Hazarmaveth and Jerah
27 and Hadoram and Uzal and Diklah
28 and [1]Obal and Abimael and Sheba
29 and Ophir and Havilah and Jobab; all
these were the sons of Joktan.

people, centered in Asia Minor, who dominated much of Canaan from c. 1800 to c. 1200 B.C.
10:16 *Jebusite.* Inhabited Jerusalem at the time of Israel's conquest of Canaan. Jerusalem was also known as Jebus during part of its history (see Judg 19:10–11; 1 Chr 11:4). *Amorite.* The name comes from an Akkadian word meaning "westerner" (west from the Babylonian perspective). Amorites lived in the hill country of Canaan at the time of the Israelite conquest.
10:17–18 Together with the Girgashites (v. 16), these groups inhabited small city-states for the most part.
10:19 *Sodom and Gomorrah and Admah and Zeboiim.* See 14:2,8 (see also note on 13:10); probably located east and/or southeast of the Dead Sea.
10:21 *Also to Shem . . . children were born.* The descendants of Shem were called Shemites (later modified to Semites). *Eber.* Though a distant descendant of Shem (see vv. 24–25; 11:14–17), Eber's importance as the ancestor of the Hebrews ("Eber" is the origin of the Hebrew word for "Hebrew") is already hinted at here. The Ebla tablets (see Introduction: Background) frequently refer to a king named Ebrium, who ruled Ebla for 28 years. It is possible that Ebrium and Eber were the same person.
10:22 *Elam.* The Elamites lived east of Mesopotamia. *Asshur.* An early name for Assyria (see note on 2:14) in northern Mesopotamia. *Arpachshad.* See also 11:10–13; perhaps a compound form of the Hebrew word for Chaldea, in southern Mesopotamia. *Lud.* Probably the Lydians of Asia Minor (see note on v. 13). *Aram.* Located northeast of Canaan, the area known today as Syria.
10:24 *Shelah.* See 11:12–15.
10:25 *Peleg.* Peleg means "division" (see 11:16–19).
10:26 *Joktan.* The predecessor of numerous south Arabian kingdoms.
10:28 *Sheba.* In southwest Arabia (roughly the area of Yemen). A later queen of Sheba made a memorable visit to King Solomon in the tenth century B.C. (see 1 Kin 10:1–13).
10:29 *Ophir.* The source of much of King Solomon's gold (see 1 Kin 9:28; 10:11). Its location seems to have been south of Canaan, perhaps somewhere in Africa or south Arabia (but see note on 1 Kin 9:28).

Table of Nations

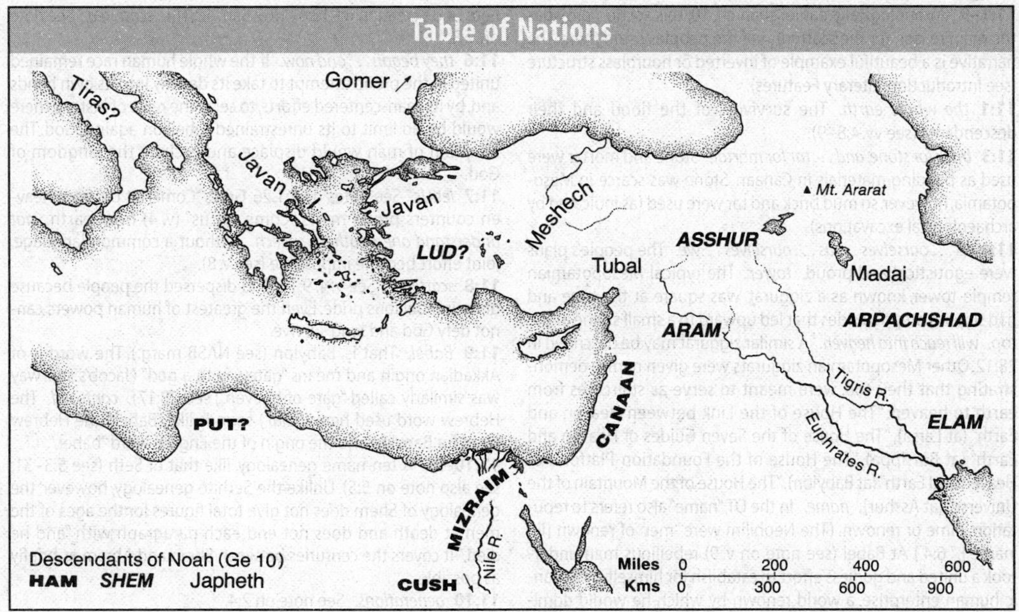

30 Now their [1]settlement [2]extended from
Mesha as you go toward Sephar, the hill
country of the east.
31 These are the sons of Shem, according
to their families, according to their languages,
by their lands, according to their nations.
32 These are the families of the sons of
Noah, according to their genealogies, by
their nations; and [a]out of these the nations
were separated on the earth after the flood.

Universal Language, Babel, Confusion

11 Now the whole earth [1]used the same
language and [2]the same words.
2 It came about as they journeyed east,
that they found a plain in the land [a]of Shinar
and [1]settled there.
3 They said to one another, "Come, let us
make bricks and burn *them* thoroughly."
And they used brick for stone, and they used
[a]tar for mortar.
4 They said, "Come, let us build for ourselves a city, and a tower whose top [a]*will
reach* into heaven, and let us make for ourselves [b]a name, otherwise we [c]will be scattered abroad over the face of the whole
earth."
5 [a]The LORD came down to see the city
and the tower which the sons of men had
built.
6 The LORD said, "Behold, they are one
people, and they all have [1a]the same language. And this is what they began to do,
and now nothing which they purpose to do
will be [2]impossible for them.
7 "Come, [a]let Us go down and there [b]con-
fuse their [1]language, so that they will not
understand one another's [1]speech."

30 [1]Lit *dwelling* [2]Lit *was* **32** [a]Gen 9:19 **11:1** [1]Lit *was one lip* [2]Or *few* or *one* set of *words* **2** [1]Lit *dwelt* [a]Gen 10:10; 14:1; Dan 1:2 **3** [a]Gen 14:10 **4** [a]Deut 1:28; 9:1; Ps 107:26 [b]Gen 6:4; 2 Sam 8:13 [c]Deut 4:27 **5** [a]Gen 18:21; Ex 3:8; 19:11, 18, 20 **6** [1]Lit *one lip* [2]Lit *withheld from* [a]Gen 11:1 **7** [1]Lit *lip* [a]Gen 1:26 [b]Gen 42:23; Ex 4:11; Deut 28:49; Is 33:19; Jer 5:15

8 [a]Gen 11:4; Ps 92:9; Luke 1:51 **9** [1]Or *Babylon;* cf Heb *balal,* confuse [2]Lit *lip* [a]Gen 10:10 **10** [1]Lit *begot,* and so throughout the ch [a]Gen 10:22-25

8 So the LORD [a]scattered them abroad
from there over the face of the whole earth;
and they stopped building the city.
9 Therefore its name was called [1a]Babel,
because there the LORD confused the [2]lan-
guage of the whole earth; and from there the
LORD scattered them abroad over the face of
the whole earth.

Descendants of Shem

10 [a]These are *the records of* the generations of Shem. Shem was one hundred years
old, and [1]became the father of Arpachshad
two years after the flood;
11 and Shem lived five hundred years
after he became the father of Arpachshad,
and he had *other* sons and daughters.
12 Arpachshad lived thirty-five years, and
became the father of Shelah;
13 and Arpachshad lived four hundred
and three years after he became the father of
Shelah, and he had *other* sons and daughters.
14 Shelah lived thirty years, and became
the father of Eber;
15 and Shelah lived four hundred and
three years after he became the father of
Eber, and he had *other* sons and daughters.
16 Eber lived thirty-four years, and
became the father of Peleg;
17 and Eber lived four hundred and thirty
years after he became the father of Peleg,
and he had *other* sons and daughters.
18 Peleg lived thirty years, and became the
father of Reu;
19 and Peleg lived two hundred and nine
years after he became the father of Reu, and
he had *other* sons and daughters.

11:1–9 Chronologically earlier than ch. 10, this section provides the main reason for the scattering of the peoples listed there. The narrative is a beautiful example of inverted or hourglass structure (see Introduction: Literary Features).

11:1 *the whole earth.* The survivors of the flood and their descendants (see vv. 4,8–9).

11:3 *brick for stone, and . . . tar for mortar.* Stone and mortar were used as building materials in Canaan. Stone was scarce in Mesopotamia, however, so mud brick and tar were used (as indicated by archaeological excavations).

11:4 *us . . . ourselves . . . us . . . ourselves . . . we.* The people's plans were egotistical and proud. *tower.* The typical Mesopotamian temple-tower, known as a ziggurat, was square at the base and had sloping, stepped sides that led upward to a small shrine at the top. *will reach into heaven.* A similar ziggurat may be described in 28:12. Other Mesopotamian ziggurats were given names demonstrating that they, too, were meant to serve as staircases from earth to heaven: "The House of the Link between Heaven and Earth" (at Larsa), "The House of the Seven Guides of Heaven and Earth" (at Borsippa), "The House of the Foundation-Platform of Heaven and Earth" (at Babylon), "The House of the Mountain of the Universe" (at Asshur). *name.* In the OT, "name" also refers to reputation, fame or renown. (The Nephilim were "men of renown [lit. 'name']," 6:4.) At Babel (see note on v. 9) rebellious man undertook a united and godless effort to establish for himself, by a titanic human enterprise, a world renown by which he would dominate God's creation (cf. 10:8–12; 2 Sam 18:18). *scattered.* See note on v. 8.

11:6 *they began . . . and now.* If the whole human race remained united in the proud attempt to take its destiny into its own hands and, by its man-centered efforts, to seize the reins of history, there would be no limit to its unrestrained rebellion against God. The kingdom of man would displace and exclude the kingdom of God.

11:7 *let Us.* See notes on 1:1,26. God's "Come, let Us" from heaven counters proud man's "Come, let us" (v. 4) from earth. *not understand one another's speech.* Without a common language, joint effort became impossible (see v. 8).

11:8 *scattered.* See v. 4; 9:19. God dispersed the people because of their rebellious pride. Even the greatest of human powers cannot defy God and long survive.

11:9 *Babel.* That is, Babylon (see NASB marg.). The word is of Akkadian origin and means "gateway to a god" (Jacob's stairway was similarly called "gate of heaven"; see 28:17). *confused.* The Hebrew word used here (*balal*) sounds like "Babel," the Hebrew word for Babylon and the origin of the English word "babel."

11:10–26 A ten-name genealogy, like that of Seth (see 5:3–31; see also note on 5:5). Unlike the Sethite genealogy, however, the genealogy of Shem does not give total figures for the ages of the men at death and does not end each paragraph with "and he died." It covers the centuries between Shem and Abram as briefly as possible.

11:10 *generations.* See note on 2:4.

20 Reu lived thirty-two years, and became
the father of Serug;
21 and Reu lived two hundred and seven
years after he became the father of Serug,
and he had *other* sons and daughters.
22 Serug lived thirty years, and became
the father of Nahor;
23 and Serug lived two hundred years
after he became the father of Nahor, and he
had *other* sons and daughters.
24 Nahor lived twenty-nine years, and
became the father of [a]Terah;
25 and Nahor lived one hundred and nineteen years after he became the father of
Terah, and he had *other* sons and daughters.
26 Terah lived seventy years, and became
[a]the father of Abram, Nahor and Haran.
27 Now these are *the records of* the generations of Terah. Terah became the father of
Abram, Nahor and Haran; and [a]Haran
became the father of [b]Lot.
28 Haran died [1]in the presence of his
father Terah in the land of his birth, in [a]Ur of
the Chaldeans.
29 Abram and [a]Nahor took wives for
themselves. The name of Abram's wife was
[b]Sarai; and the name of Nahor's wife was
[c]Milcah, the daughter of Haran, the father of
Milcah [1]and Iscah.
30 [a]Sarai was barren; she had no child.
31 Terah took Abram his son, and Lot the
son of Haran, his grandson, and Sarai his
daughter-in-law, his son Abram's wife; and
they went out [1]together from [a]Ur of the
Chaldeans in order to enter the land of
Canaan; and they went as far as Haran, and
[2]settled there.
32 The days of Terah were two hundred
and five years; and Terah died in Haran.

Abram Journeys to Egypt

12 Now [a]the LORD said to Abram,
"[1]Go forth from your country,
And from your relatives
And from your father's house,
To the land which I will show you;
2 And [a]I will make you a great nation,
And [b]I will bless you,
And make your name great;
And so [1c]you shall be a blessing;
3 And [a]I will bless those who bless
you,
And the one who [1]curses you I will
[2]curse.
[b]And in you all the families of the
earth will be blessed."
4 So Abram went forth as the LORD had
spoken to him; and [a]Lot went with him.
Now Abram was seventy-five years old when
he departed from Haran.
5 Abram took Sarai his wife and Lot his
nephew, and all their [a]possessions which
they had accumulated, and [b]the [1]persons
which they had acquired in Haran, and they
[2]set out for the land of Canaan; [c]thus they
came to the land of Canaan.
6 Abram passed through the land as far
as the site of [a]Shechem, to the [1]oak of
Moreh. Now the Canaanite *was* then in the
land.
7 The LORD [a]appeared to Abram and
said, "[b]To your [1]descendants I will give this
land." So he built [c]an altar there to the LORD
who had appeared to him.

24 [a]Josh 24:2
26 [a]Josh 24:2
27 [a]Gen 11:31; 12:4 [b]Gen 13:10; 14:12; 19:1, 29
28 [1]Or *during the lifetime of* [a]Gen 11:31
29 [1]Lit *and the father of* [a]Gen 24:10 [b]Gen 17:15; 20:12 [c]Gen 22:20, 23; 24:15
30 [a]Gen 16:1
31 [1]Lit *with them* [2]Lit *dwelt* [a]Gen 15:7; Neh 9:7; Acts 7:4

12:1 [1]Lit *Go for yourself* [a]Gen 15:7; Acts 7:3; Heb 11:8
2 [1]Lit *be a blessing* [a]Gen 17:4-6; 18:18; 46:3; Deut 26:5 [b]Gen 22:17 [c]Zech 8:13
3 [1]Or *reviles* [2]Or *bind under a curse* [a]Gen 24:35; 27:29; Num 24:9 [b]Gen 22:18; 26:4; 28:14; Acts 3:25; Gal 3:8
4 [a]Gen 11:27, 31
5 [1]Lit *souls* [2]Lit *went forth to go to* [a]Gen 13:6 [b]Gen 14:14; Lev 22:11 [c]Gen 11:31; Heb 11:8
6 [1]Or *terebinth* [a]Gen 35:4; Deut 11:30
7 [1]Lit *seed* [a]Gen 17:1; 18:1 [b]Gen 13:15; 15:18; Deut 34:4; Ps 105: 9-12; Acts 7:5; Gal 3:16 [c]Gen 13:4, 18; 22:9

11:26 *Terah . . . became the father of Abram, Nahor and Haran.* As in the case of Shem, Ham and Japheth, the names of the three sons may not be in chronological order by age (see 9:24; see also 10:21). Haran died while his father was still alive (see v. 28).
11:27 *generations.* See note on 2:4.
11:28 *Ur of the Chaldeans.* Possibly in northern Mesopotamia, but more likely the site on the Euphrates in southern Iraq excavated by Leonard Woolley between 1922 and 1934. Ruins and artifacts from Ur reveal a civilization and culture that reached high levels before Abram's time. King Ur-Nammu, who may have been Abram's contemporary, is famous for his law code.
11:30 *Sarai was barren.* The sterility of Abram's wife (see 15:2–3; 17:17) emphasized the fact that God's people would not come by natural generation from the post-Babel peoples. God was bringing a new humanity into being, of whom Abram was father (17:5), just as Adam and Noah were fathers of the fallen human race.
11:31 *they went as far as Haran.* In Hebrew the name of the town is spelled differently from that of Abram's brother (v. 26). The moon-god was worshiped at both Ur and Haran, and since Terah was an idolater (see Josh 24:2) he probably felt at home in either place. Haran was a flourishing caravan city in the 19th century B.C. In the 18th century it was ruled by Amorites (see note on 10:16).
12:1 *said.* God had spoken to Abram "when he was in Mesopotamia, before he lived in Haran" (Acts 7:2). *Go forth . . . show you.* Abram must leave the settled world of the post-Babel nations and begin a pilgrimage with God to a better world of God's making (see 24:7).
12:2–3 God's promise to Abram has a sevenfold structure: (1) "I will make you a great nation," (2) "I will bless you," (3) "and make your name great," (4) "you shall be a blessing," (5) "I will bless those who bless you," (6) "the one who curses you I will curse," and (7) "in you all the families of the earth will be blessed." God's original blessing on all mankind (1:28) would be restored and fulfilled through Abram and his offspring. In various ways and degrees, these promises were reaffirmed to Abram (v. 7; 15:5–21; 17:4–8; 18:18–19; 22:17–18), to Isaac (26:2–4), to Jacob (28:13–15; 35:11–12; 46:3) and to Moses (Ex 3:6–8; 6:2–8). The seventh promise is quoted in Acts 3:25 with reference to Peter's Jewish listeners (see Acts 3:12)—Abram's physical descendants—and in Gal 3:8 with reference to Paul's Gentile listeners—Abram's spiritual descendants.
12:4 *Abram went forth as the LORD had spoken to him.* See Heb 11:8. Prompt obedience grounded in faith characterized this patriarch throughout his life (see 17:23; 21:14; 22:3). *Lot went with him.* See 13:1,5. Lot at first was little more than Abram's ward. *seventy-five years old.* Although advanced in age at the time of his call, Abram would live for another full century (see 25:7; see also note on 5:5).
12:5 *persons which they had acquired.* Wealthy people in that ancient world always had servants to help them with their flocks and herds (see 15:3; 24:2). Not all servants were slaves; many were voluntarily employed.
12:6 *site of Shechem, to the oak of Moreh.* See perhaps 35:4; Judg 9:6,37. A famous sanctuary was located at Shechem in central Canaan, and a large tree was often a conspicuous feature at such holy places. But Abram worshiped the Lord there, not the local deity.
12:7 *The LORD appeared.* The Lord frequently appeared visibly to Abram and to others, but not in all His glory (see Ex 33:18–20; John 1:18). *an altar.* The first of several that Abram built at places

8 Then he proceeded from there to the
mountain on the east of Bethel, and pitched
his tent, with [a]Bethel on the west and Ai on
the east; and there he built an altar to the
LORD and [b]called upon the name of the LORD.
9 Abram journeyed on, continuing
toward [a]the [1]Negev.
10 Now there was [a]a famine in the land;
so Abram went down to Egypt to sojourn
there, for the famine was [b]severe in the land.
11 It came about when he [1]came near to
Egypt, that he said to Sarai his wife, "See now,
I know that you are a [2a]beautiful woman;
12 [a]and when the Egyptians see you, they
will say, 'This is his wife'; and they will kill
me, but they will let you live.
13 "Please say that you are [a]my sister so
that it may go well with me because of you,
and that [1b]I may live on account of you."
14 It came about when Abram came into
Egypt, the Egyptians [1]saw that the woman
was very beautiful.
15 Pharaoh's officials saw her and praised
her to Pharaoh; and [a]the woman was taken
into Pharaoh's house.
16 Therefore [a]he treated Abram well for
her sake; and [1b]gave him sheep and oxen
and donkeys and male and female servants
and female donkeys and camels.
17 But the LORD [a]struck Pharaoh and his
house with great plagues because of Sarai,
Abram's wife.
18 Then Pharaoh called Abram and said,
"[a]What is this you have done to me? Why
did you not tell me that she was your wife?
19 "Why did you say, 'She is my sister,' so
that I took her for my wife? Now then, [1]here
is your wife, take her and go."
20 Pharaoh commanded *his* men concern-

8 [a]Josh 8:9, 12 [b]Gen 4:26; 21:33
9 [1]I.e. South country [a]Gen 13:1, 3; 20:1; 24:62
10 [a]Gen 26:1 [b]Gen 43:1
11 [1]Lit *drew near to enter* [2]Lit *woman of beautiful appearance* [a]Gen 26:7; 29:17
12 [a]Gen 20:11
13 [1]Lit *my soul* [a]Gen 20:2, 5, 12; 26:7 [b]Jer 38:17, 20
14 [1]Lit *saw the woman that she was*
15 [a]Gen 20:2
16 [1]Lit *he had* [a]Gen 20:14 [b]Gen 13:2
17 [a]Gen 20:18; 1 Chr 16:21; Ps 105:14
18 [a]Gen 20:9, 10; 26:10
19 [1]Or *behold*
20 [1]Lit *sent*
13:1 [1]I.e. South country [a]Gen 12:9
2 [a]Gen 24:35
3 [1]Lit *by his stages* [2]I.e. South country [a]Gen 12:8
4 [a]Gen 12:7, 8
5 [a]Gen 12:5
6 [1]Lit *bear* [2]Lit *to dwell* [a]Gen 36:7 [b]Gen 12:5, 16; 13:2
7 [a]Gen 26:20 [b]Gen 12:6; 15:20, 21
8 [a]Prov 15:18; 20:3
10 [1]Lit *circle* [a]Gen 19:17-29; Deut 34:3 [b]Gen 19:24

ing him; and they [1]escorted him away, with
his wife and all that belonged to him.

Abram and Lot

13 So Abram went up from Egypt to [a]the
[1]Negev, he and his wife and all that
belonged to him, and Lot with him.
2 Now Abram was [a]very rich in livestock, in silver and in gold.
3 He went [1]on his journeys from the
[2]Negev as far as Bethel, to the place where
his tent had been at the beginning, [a]between
Bethel and Ai,
4 to the place of the [a]altar which he had
made there formerly; and there Abram called
on the name of the LORD.
5 Now [a]Lot, who went with Abram, also
had flocks and herds and tents.
6 And [a]the land could not [1]sustain them
[2]while dwelling together, [b]for their possessions were so great that they were not able to
remain together.
7 [a]And there was strife between the
herdsmen of Abram's livestock and the
herdsmen of Lot's livestock. Now [b]the
Canaanite and the Perizzite were dwelling
then in the land.
8 [a]So Abram said to Lot, "Please let there
be no strife between you and me, nor
between my herdsmen and your herdsmen,
for we are brothers.
9 "Is not the whole land before you?
Please separate from me; if *to* the left, then I
will go to the right; or if *to* the right, then I
will go to the left."
10 Lot lifted up his eyes and saw all the
[1a]valley of the Jordan, that it was well
watered everywhere—*this was* before the
LORD [b]destroyed Sodom and Gomorrah—like

where he had memorable spiritual experiences (see v. 8; 13:18; 22:9). He acknowledged that the land of Canaan belonged to the Lord in a special way (see Ex 20:24; Josh 22:19).

12:8 *Bethel.* Just north of Jerusalem, it was an important town in the religious history of God's ancient people (see, e.g., 28:10–22; 35:1–8; 1 Kin 12:26–29). Only Jerusalem is mentioned more often in the OT.

12:9 *Negev.* The dry wasteland stretching southward from Beersheba. The same Hebrew word is translated "southward" in 13:14.

12:10 *went down to Egypt . . . for the famine was severe.* Egypt's food supply was usually plentiful because the Nile's water supply was normally dependable.

12:11 *beautiful.* See v. 14. She was 65 at the time (see v. 4; 17:17). The Genesis Apocryphon (one of the Dead Sea Scrolls) praises Sarai's beauty. Abram's experience in this episode foreshadows Israel's later experience in Egypt, as the author of Genesis, writing after the exodus, was very much aware. Abram was truly the "father" of Israel.

12:13 *say that you are my sister.* If Pharaoh were to add Sarai to his harem while knowing that she was Abram's wife, he would have to kill Abram first.

12:15 *Pharaoh.* See note on Ex 1:11.

12:16 Livestock was an important measure of wealth in ancient times (see 13:2). *male and female servants.* See note on v. 5. *camels.* Although camels were not widely used until much later (see, e.g., Judg 6:5), archaeology has confirmed their occasional domestication as early as the patriarchal period.

12:19 *Why did you say, 'She is my sister' . . . ?* Egyptian ethics emphasized the importance of absolute truthfulness, and Abram was put in the uncomfortable position of being exposed as a liar.

12:20 *Pharaoh commanded his men.* See Ex 12:31–32.

13:2 *very rich.* Abram left Egypt with greater wealth than he had before—even as Israel would later leave Egypt laden with wealth from the Egyptians (Ex 3:22; 12:36).

13:4 *Abram called on the name of the LORD.* As he had done earlier at the same place (see 12:8).

13:6 *the land could not sustain them.* Livestock made up the greater part of their possessions, and the region around Bethel and Ai did not have enough water or pasture for such large flocks and herds (see v. 10; 26:17–22,32; 36:7).

13:7 *the Perizzite.* May refer to rural inhabitants in contrast to city dwellers.

13:8 *brothers.* Relatives (as often in the Bible).

13:9 Abram, always generous, gave his young nephew the opportunity to choose the land he wanted. He himself would not obtain wealth except by the Lord's blessing (see 14:22–24).

13:10 *valley.* The Hebrew for this word picturesquely describes this section of the Jordan Valley as oval in shape. *like the land of Egypt.* Because of its abundant and dependable water supply (see note on 12:10), Egypt came the closest to matching Eden's ideal conditions (see 2:10). *the LORD destroyed Sodom and Gomorrah.* See especially 18:16–19:29. The names of Sodom and Gomorrah became proverbial for vile wickedness and for divine judgment on

[c]the garden of the LORD, [d]like the land of
Egypt as you go to [e]Zoar.
11 So Lot chose for himself all the [1]valley
of the Jordan, and Lot journeyed eastward.
Thus they separated from each other.
12 Abram [1]settled in the land of Canaan,
while Lot [1]settled in [a]the cities of the [2]valley,
and moved his tents as far as Sodom.
13 Now [a]the men of Sodom were wicked
[1]exceedingly and [b]sinners against the LORD.
14 The LORD said to Abram, after Lot had
separated from him, "[a]Now lift up your eyes
and look from the place where you are,
[b]northward and southward and eastward
and westward;
15 [a]for all the land which you see, [b]I will
give it to you and to your [1]descendants forever.
16 "I will make your [1]descendants [a]as the
dust of the earth, so that if anyone can number the dust of the earth, then your [1]descen-
dants can also be numbered.
17 "Arise, [a]walk about the land through its
length and breadth; for [b]I will give it to you."
18 Then Abram moved his tent and came
and dwelt by the [1a]oaks of Mamre, which are
in Hebron, and there he built [b]an altar to the
LORD.

War of the Kings

14 And it came about in the days of Amraphel king of [a]Shinar, Arioch king of
Ellasar, Chedorlaomer king of [b]Elam, and
Tidal king of [1]Goiim,
2 *that* they made war with Bera king of
Sodom, and with Birsha king of Gomorrah,
Shinab king of [a]Admah, and Shemeber king
of [b]Zeboiim, and the king of Bela (that is,
[c]Zoar).
3 All these [1]came as allies to [a]the valley
of Siddim (that is, [b]the Salt Sea).

10 [c]Gen 2:8, 10 [d]Gen 47:6 [e]Gen 14:2, 8; 19:22; Deut 34:3
11 [1]Lit *circle*
12 [1]Lit *dwelt* [2]Lit *circle* [a]Gen 14:2; 19:24, 25, 29
13 [1]Lit *wicked and sinners exceedingly* [a]Gen 18:20; Ezek 16:49 [b]Gen 39:9; Num 32:23; 2 Pet 2:7, 8
14 [a]Deut 3:27; 34:1-4; Is 49:18 [b]Gen 28:14
15 [1]Lit *seed* [a]Gen 12:7 [b]Gen 13:17; 15:7; 17:8; 2 Chr 20:7; Acts 7:5
16 [1]Lit *seed* [a]Gen 16:10; 28:14; Num 23:10
17 [a]Num 13:17-24 [b]Gen 13:15
18 [1]Or *terebinths* [a]Gen 14:13 [b]Gen 8:20; 12:7, 8
14:1 [1]Or *nations* [a]Gen 10:10; 11:2 [b]Gen 10:22; Is 11:11; Dan 8:2
2 [a]Gen 10:19 [b]Deut 29:23 [c]Gen 13:10; 19:22
3 [1]Lit *joined together* [a]Gen 14:8, 10 [b]Num 34:12; Deut 3:17; Josh 3:16
5 [1]Lit *smote* [2]Or *the plain of Kiriathaim* [a]Deut 3:11, 13 [b]Deut 1:4; Josh 9:10 [c]Num 32:37
6 [a]Gen 36:20; Deut 2:12, 22 [b]Gen 21:21; Num 10:12
7 [1]Lit *smote* [a]Num 13:26 [b]2 Chr 20:2

4 Twelve years they had served Chedorlaomer, but the thirteenth year they rebelled.
5 In the fourteenth year Chedorlaomer
and the kings that were with him, came and
[1]defeated the [a]Rephaim in [b]Ashteroth-karna-
im and the Zuzim in Ham and the Emim in
[2c]Shaveh-kiriathaim,
6 and the [a]Horites in their Mount Seir, as
far as [b]El-paran, which is by the wilderness.
7 Then they turned back and came to En-
mishpat (that is, [a]Kadesh), and [1]conquered
all the country of the Amalekites, and also
the Amorites, who lived in [b]Hazazon-tamar.
8 And the king of Sodom and the king of
Gomorrah and the king of Admah and the
king of Zeboiim and the king of Bela (that is,
Zoar) came out; and they arrayed for battle
against them in [a]the valley of Siddim,
9 against Chedorlaomer king of Elam and
Tidal king of [1]Goiim and Amraphel king of
Shinar and Arioch king of Ellasar—four
kings against five.
10 Now the valley of Siddim was full of tar
pits; and [a]the kings of Sodom and Gomorrah
fled, and they fell [1]into them. But those who
survived fled to the [b]hill country.
11 Then they took all the goods of Sodom
and Gomorrah and all their food supply, and
departed.
12 They also took Lot, [a]Abram's nephew,
and his possessions and departed, [b]for he
was living in Sodom.
13 Then [1]a fugitive came and told Abram
the [a]Hebrew. Now he was [2]living by the
[3b]oaks of Mamre the Amorite, brother of
Eshcol and brother of Aner, and these were
[4c]allies with Abram.

8 [a]Gen 14:3 **9** [1]Or *nations* **10** [1]Lit *there* [a]Gen 14:17, 21, 22 [b]Gen 19:17 **12** [a]Gen 11:27 [b]Gen 13:12 **13** [1]Lit *the* [2]Lit *abiding* [3]Or *terebinths* [4]Lit *possessors of the covenant* [a]Gen 40:15; Ex 3:18 [b]Gen 13:18; 14:24 [c]Gen 21:27, 32

---

sin. Archaeology has confirmed that, prior to this catastrophe, the now dry area east and southeast of the Dead Sea (see note on 10:19) had ample water and was well populated.

13:12 *Lot . . . moved his tents as far as Sodom.* Since the men of Sodom were known to be wicked (see v. 13), Lot was flirting with temptation by choosing to live near them. Contrast the actions of Abram (v. 18).

13:14 *Lift up your eyes and look.* See Deut 34:1–4. Lot and Abram are a study in contrasts. The former looked selfishly and coveted (v. 10); the latter looked as God commanded and was blessed.

13:16 *as the dust of the earth.* A simile (common in the ancient Near East) for the large number of Abram's offspring (see 28:14; 2 Chr 1:9; see also Num 23:10). Similar phrases are: "as the stars of the heavens" and "as the sand which is on the seashore" (22:17).

13:17 *walk about the land through its length and breadth.* Either to inspect it or to exercise authority over it, demonstrating the promised ownership.

13:18 *oaks.* See note on 12:6. *Mamre.* A town named after one of Abram's allies (see 14:13). *Hebron.* Kiriath-arba (see note on 23:2). *altar.* See note on 12:7.

14:1 *Amraphel king of Shinar.* Not the great Babylonian king Hammurapi, as once thought. *Elam.* See note on 10:22. *Goiim.* The Hebrew word means "Gentile nations" and may be a common noun here (as in Is 9:1).

14:3 *Salt Sea.* The Dead Sea, whose water contains a 25 percent concentration of chloride and bromide salts, making it the densest large body of water on earth.

14:6 *Horites.* Formerly thought to be cave dwellers (the Hebrew word *ḥor* means "cave"), they are now known to have been the Hurrians, a non-Semitic people widely dispersed throughout the ancient Near East.

14:7 *En-mishpat.* Another name for Kadesh, it means "spring of judgment/justice." It is called Meribah-kadesh, "quarreling/litigation at Kadesh," in Deut 32:51 (see Num 27:14). *Kadesh.* Located in the southwest Negev (see note on 12:9), it was later called Kadesh-barnea (see Num 32:8). *Amalekites.* A tribal people living in the Negev and in the Sinai peninsula. *Amorites.* See note on 10:16.

14:10 *tar pits.* Lumps of asphalt are often seen even today floating in the southern end of the Dead Sea. *hill country.* The Dead Sea, the lowest body of water on earth (about 1,300 feet below sea level), is flanked by hills on both sides.

14:12 *Lot . . . was living in Sodom.* He moved into the town and was living among its wicked people (see 2 Pet 2:8). Though Lot was "righteous," he was now in danger of imitating the "sensual conduct of unprincipled men" (2 Pet 2:7).

14:13 *Hebrew.* Abram, the father of the Hebrew people, is the first Biblical character to be called a Hebrew (see "Eber" in note on 10:21). Usually an ethnic term in the Bible, it was normally used by non-Isra-

14 When Abram heard that [a]his [1]relative
had been taken captive, he [2]led out his trained
men, [b]born in his house, three hundred and
eighteen, and went in pursuit as far as [c]Dan.
15 [a]He divided [1]his forces against them by
night, he and his servants, and [2]defeated
them, and pursued them as far as Hobah,
which is [3]north of [b]Damascus.
16 He [a]brought back all the goods, and
also brought back [b]his [1]relative Lot with his
possessions, and also the women, and the
people.

God's Promise to Abram

17 Then after his return from the [1]defeat
of Chedorlaomer and the kings who were
with him, [a]the king of Sodom went out to
meet him at the valley of Shaveh (that is,
[b]the King's Valley).
18 And [a]Melchizedek king of Salem
brought out [b]bread and wine; now he was a
[c]priest of [1]God Most High.
19 He blessed him and said,
"Blessed be Abram of [1]God Most High,
[2a]Possessor of heaven and earth;
20 And blessed be [1]God Most High,
Who has delivered your enemies into
your hand."
[a]He gave him a tenth of all.
21 The king of Sodom said to Abram,
"Give the [1]people to me and take the goods
for yourself."

14 [1]Lit *brother* [2]Or *mustered* [a]Gen 14:12 [b]Gen 12:5; 15:3; 17:27; Eccl 2:7 [c]Deut 34:1; Judg 18:29; 1 Kin 15:20
15 [1]Lit *himself* [2]Lit *smote* [3]Lit *on the left* [a]Judg 7:16 [b]Gen 15:2
16 [1]Lit *brother* [a]1 Sam 30:8, 18, 19 [b]Gen 14:12, 14
17 [1]Lit *smiting* [a]Gen 14:10 [b]2 Sam 18:18
18 [1]Heb *El Elyon* [a]Heb 7:1-10 [b]Ps 104:15 [c]Ps 110:4; Heb 5:6, 10
19 [1]Heb *El Elyon* [2]Or *Creator* [a]Gen 14:22
20 [1]Heb *El Elyon* [a]Heb 7:4
21 [1]Lit *soul*
22 [1]Lit *lifted up my hand* [2]Heb *El Elyon* [3]Or *Creator* [a]Gen 14:19 [b]Ps 24:1
23 [a]2 Kin 5:16
24 [1]Lit *Not to me except* [a]Gen 14:13
15:1 [1]Or *Your very great reward* [a]Gen 15:4; 46:2; 1 Sam 15:10 [b]Gen 21:17; 26:24; Is 41:10 [c]Deut 33:29

22 Abram said to the king of Sodom, "I
have [1]sworn to the LORD [2a]God Most High,
[3b]possessor of heaven and earth,
23 that [a]I will not take a thread or a sandal
thong or anything that is yours, for fear you
would say, 'I have made Abram rich.'
24 "[1]I will take nothing except what the
young men have eaten, and the share of the
men who went with me, [a]Aner, Eshcol, and
Mamre; let them take their share."

Abram Promised a Son

15 After these things [a]the word of the
LORD came to Abram in a vision, saying,
"[b]Do not fear, Abram,
I am [c]a shield to you;
[1]Your [d]reward shall be very great."
2 Abram said, "O Lord [1]GOD, what will
You give me, since I [2]am childless, and the
[3]heir of my house is Eliezer of Damascus?"
3 And Abram said, "[1]Since You have giv-
en no [2]offspring to me, [3]one [a]born in my
house is my heir."
4 Then behold, the word of the LORD
came to him, saying, "This man will not be
your heir; [a]but one who will come forth from
your own [1]body, he shall be your heir."
5 And He took him outside and said,

[d]Num 18:20; Ps 58:11 **2** [1]Heb *YHWH,* usually rendered *LORD* [2]Lit *go* [3]Lit *son of acquisition* **3** [1]Lit *Behold* [2]Lit *seed* [3]Lit *and behold, a son of* [a]Gen 14:14 **4** [1]Lit *inward parts* [a]Gal 4:28

---

elites in a disparaging sense (see, e.g., 39:17). Outside the Bible, people known as the Habiru/Apiru (a word probably related to Hebrew) are referred to as a propertyless, dependent, immigrant (foreign) social class rather than as a specific ethnic group. Negative descriptions of them are given in the Amarna letters (clay tablets found in Egypt). *Mamre.* A town was named after him (see 13:18 and note).

14:14 *his trained men, born in his house, three hundred and eighteen.* A clear indication of Abram's great wealth. The Hebrew for "trained men" is found only here in the Bible. A related word used elsewhere in very ancient texts means "armed retainers." *Dan.* This well-known city in the north was not given the name "Dan" until the days of the judges (see Judg 18:29). The designation here is thus an editorial updating subsequent to Moses' time.

14:17 *King's Valley.* Near Jerusalem, probably to the east (see 2 Sam 18:18).

14:18 *Melchizedek king of Salem . . . priest.* See Heb 7:1. In ancient times, particularly in non-Israelite circles, kingly and priestly duties were often performed by the same individual. "Melchizedek" means "My king is righteousness" or "king of righteousness" (see Heb 7:2). "Salem" is a shortened form of "Jerusalem" (see Ps 76:2) and is related to the Hebrew word for "peace" (see Heb 7:2). The name of Adoni-zedek, another king of Jerusalem (see Josh 10:1), is very similar to that of Melchizedek and means "My lord is righteousness" or "lord of righteousness." *bread and wine.* An ordinary meal (see Judg 19:19), in no way related to the NT ordinance of communion. Melchizedek offered the food and drink as a show of friendship and hospitality.

14:19 *God Most High, Possessor of heaven and earth.* The titles "most high," "lord of heaven" and "creator of earth" (see NASB marg.) were frequently applied to the chief Canaanite deity in ancient times. Terminology and location (Jerusalem was in central Canaan) thus indicate that Melchizedek was probably a Canaanite king-priest. But Abram, by identifying Melchizedek's "God Most High" with "the LORD" (see v. 22), bore testimony to the one true God, whom Melchizedek had come to know.

14:20 *He gave him a tenth of all.* Although Melchizedek's view of God was no doubt deficient, Abram's response to his blessing seems to indicate that he recognized that Melchizedek served the same God as he (see v. 18). So Abram took the occasion to offer him a tithe of his spoils for God Most High. A tenth was the king's share (see 1 Sam 8:15,17). Melchizedek is later spoken of as a type or prefiguration of Jesus, our "great high priest" (Heb 4:14), whose priesthood is therefore in "the order of Melchizedek," not "according to the order of Aaron" (Heb 7:11; see Ps 110:4).

14:22 *I have sworn.* Lit. "I have raised my hand." The raising of the hand when making an oath was common practice in ancient times (see Deut 32:40; Rev 10:5–6).

14:23 *I will not take . . . anything that is yours.* Cf. 2 Kin 5:16. Abram refused to let himself become obligated to anyone but the Lord. Had he done so, this Canaanite king might later have claimed the right of kingship over Abram.

15:1 *I am a shield to you.* Whether "shield" or "sovereign" is meant (it can be translated either way), the reference is to the Lord as Abram's King. As elsewhere, "shield" stands for king (e.g., Deut 33:29; 2 Sam 22:3; Ps 7:10; 84:9). *Your reward shall be very great.* Though Abram was quite rich (13:2), God Himself was Abram's greatest treasure (cf. Deut 10:9).

15:2 *Eliezer of Damascus.* A servant probably acquired by Abram on his journey southward from Haran (see 12:5). He may also be the unnamed "servant" of 24:2.

15:3–4 Ancient documents uncovered at Nuzi (see chart, p. xix) near Kirkuk on a branch of the Tigris River, as well as at other places, demonstrate that a childless man could adopt one of his own male servants to be heir and guardian of his estate. Abram apparently contemplated doing this with Eliezer, or perhaps had already done so.

"Now look toward the heavens, and [a]count
the stars, if you are able to count them." And
He said to him, "[b]So shall your [1]descendants
be."
6 [a]Then he believed in the LORD; and He
reckoned it to him as righteousness.
7 And He said to him, "I am the LORD
who brought you out of [a]Ur of the Chaldeans, to [b]give you this land to [1]possess it."
8 He said, "O Lord [1]GOD, [a]how may I
know that I will [2]possess it?"
9 So He said to him, "[1]Bring Me a three
year old heifer, and a three year old female
goat, and a three year old ram, and a turtledove, and a young pigeon."
10 Then he [1]brought all these to Him and
[a]cut them [2]in two, and laid each half opposite the other; but he [b]did not cut the birds.
11 The birds of prey came down upon the
carcasses, and Abram drove them away.
12 Now when the sun was going down, [a]a
deep sleep fell upon Abram; and behold,
[1]terror *and* great darkness fell upon him.
13 *God* said to Abram, "Know for certain
that [a]your [1]descendants will be strangers in
a land that is not theirs, [2]where [b]they will be
enslaved and oppressed [c]four hundred years.
14 "But I will also judge the nation whom
they will serve, and afterward they will come
out [a]with [1]many possessions.
15 "As for you, [a]you shall go to your
fathers in peace; you will be buried at a good
old age.
16 "Then in [a]the fourth generation they
will return here, for [b]the iniquity of the Amorite is not yet complete."
17 It came about when the sun had set,
that it was very dark, and behold, *there
appeared* a smoking oven and a flaming
torch which [a]passed between these pieces.
18 On that day the LORD made a covenant
with Abram, saying,
"[a]To your [1]descendants I have given
this land,
From [b]the river of Egypt as far as the
great river, the river Euphrates:
19 [a]the Kenite and the Kenizzite and the
Kadmonite
20 and the Hittite and the Perizzite and
the Rephaim
21 and the Amorite and the Canaanite and
the Girgashite and the Jebusite."

5 [1]Lit *seed* [a]Gen 22:17; 26:4; Deut 1:10 [b]Ex 32:13; Rom 4:18; Heb 11:12
6 [a]Rom 4:3, 20-22; Gal 3:6; James 2:23
7 [1]Or *inherit* [a]Gen 11:31 [b]Gen 13:15, 17
8 [1]Heb *YHWH,* usually rendered LORD [2]Or *inherit* [a]Judg 6:36-40; Luke 1:18
9 [1]Lit *Take*
10 [1]Lit *took* [2]Lit *in the midst* [a]Gen 15:17 [b]Lev 1:17
12 [1]Or *a terror of great darkness* [a]Gen 2:21; 28:11; Job 33:15
13 [1]Lit *seed* [2]Lit *and shall serve them; and they shall afflict them* [a]Acts 7:6, 17 [b]Ex 1:11; Deut 5:15 [c]Ex 12:40; Gal 3:17
14 [1]Lit *great* [a]Ex 12:32-38
15 [a]Gen 25:8; 47:30
16 [a]Gen 15:13 [b]Lev 18:24-28
17 [a]Jer 34:18, 19
18 [1]Lit *seed* [a]Gen 17:8; Josh 21:43; Acts 7:5 [b]Ex 23:31; Num 34:1-15; Deut 1:7, 8
19 [a]Ex 3:17; 23:28; Josh 24:11; Neh 9:8

Sarai and Hagar

16 Now [a]Sarai, Abram's wife had borne
him no *children,* and she had [b]an Egyptian maid whose name was Hagar.
2 So Sarai said to Abram, "Now behold,
the LORD has prevented me from bearing
children. [a]Please go in to my maid; perhaps
I will [1]obtain children through her." And
Abram listened to the voice of Sarai.
3 After Abram had [1]lived [a]ten years in
the land of Canaan, Abram's wife Sarai took

16:1 [a]Gen 11:30 [b]Gen 12:16 **2** [1]Lit *be built from her* [a]Gen 30:3, 4, 9, 10 **3** [1]Lit *dwelt* [a]Gen 12:4

15:5 *count the stars, if you are able.* See 22:17. More than 8,000 stars are clearly visible in the darkness of a Near Eastern night. *So shall your descendants be.* The promise was initially fulfilled in Egypt (see Ex 1; see also Deut 1:10; Heb 11:12). Ultimately, all who belong to Christ are Abram's offspring (see Gal 3:29).

15:6 Abram is the "father of all who believe" (Rom 4:11), and this verse is the first specific reference to faith in God's promises. It also teaches that God graciously responds to a man's faith by crediting righteousness to him (see Heb 11:7).

15:7 *I am the LORD who brought you out.* Ancient royal covenants often began with (1) the self-identification of the king and (2) a brief historical prologue, as here (see Ex 20:2).

15:8 *how may I know . . . ?* Cf. Luke 1:18. Abram believed God's promise of a son, but he asked for a guarantee of the promise of the land.

15:9 *three year old.* The prime age for most sacrificial animals (see 1 Sam 1:24).

15:10 *he did not cut the birds.* Perhaps because they were too small (see Lev 1:17).

15:13 *land that is not theirs.* Egypt (see 46:3–4). *four hundred years.* A round number. According to Ex 12:40 Israel spent 430 years in Egypt.

15:15 The fulfillment is recorded in 25:8.

15:16 *in the fourth generation.* That is, after 400 years (see v. 13). A "generation" was the age of a man when his first son (from the legal standpoint) was born—in Abram's case, 100 years (see 21:5). *the iniquity of the Amorite is not yet complete.* Just how sinful many Canaanite religious practices were is now known from archaeological artifacts and from their own epic literature, discovered at Ras Shamra (ancient Ugarit) on the north Syrian coast beginning in 1929 (see chart, p. xix). Their "worship" was polytheistic and included child sacrifice, idolatry, religious prostitution and divination (cf. Deut 18:9–12). God was patient in judgment, even with the wicked Canaanites.

15:17 *smoking oven and a flaming torch.* Symbolizing the presence of God (see Ex 3:2; 14:24; 19:18; 1 Kin 18:38; Acts 2:3–4). *passed between these pieces.* Of the slaughtered animals (v. 10). In ancient times the parties solemnized a covenant by walking down an aisle flanked by the pieces of slaughtered animals (see Jer 34:18–19). The practice signified a self-maledictory oath: "May it be so done to me if I do not keep my oath and pledge." Having credited Abram's faith as righteousness, God now graciously ministered to his need for assurance concerning the land. He granted Abram a promissory covenant, as He had to Noah (see 9:9 and note; see also chart, p. 16).

15:18 *made a covenant.* Lit. "cut a covenant," referring to the slaughtering of the animals (the same Hebrew verb is translated "made" and "cut" in Jer 34:18). *I have given this land.* The Lord initially fulfilled this covenant through Joshua (see Josh 1:2–9; 21:43; see also 1 Kin 4:20–21). *river of Egypt.* Probably the modern Wadi el-Arish in northeastern Sinai.

15:19–21 A similar list of ten peoples is found in 10:15–18 (see notes there). The number ten signifies completeness.

16:1 *no children.* See note on 11:30. *Egyptian.* Perhaps Hagar was acquired while Abram and Sarai were in Egypt (see 12:10–20).

16:2 *The LORD has prevented me from bearing children.* Some time had passed since the revelation of 15:4 (see 16:3), and Sarai impatiently implied that God was not keeping His promise. *go in to my maid.* An ancient custom, illustrated in Old Assyrian marriage contracts, the Code of Hammurapi and the Nuzi tablets (see note on 15:3–4), to ensure the birth of a male heir. Sarai would herself solve the problem of her barrenness.

16:3 *ten years.* Abram was now 85 years old (see 12:4; 16:16).

Hagar the Egyptian, her maid, and gave her to her husband Abram as his wife.

4 He went in to Hagar, and she conceived; and when she saw that she had conceived, her mistress was despised in her sight.

5 And Sarai said to Abram, "[a]May the wrong done me be upon you. I gave my maid into your [1]arms, but when she saw that she had conceived, I was despised in her [2]sight. [b]May the LORD judge between [3]you and me."

6 But Abram said to Sarai, "Behold, your maid is in your [1]power; do to her what is good in your [2]sight." So Sarai treated her harshly, and [a]she fled from her presence.

7 Now [a]the angel of the LORD found her by a spring of water in the wilderness, by the spring on the way to [b]Shur.

8 He said, "Hagar, Sarai's maid, [a]where have you come from and where are you going?" And she said, "I am fleeing from the presence of my mistress Sarai."

9 Then the angel of the LORD said to her, "Return to your mistress, and submit yourself [1]to her authority."

10 Moreover, the [a]angel of the LORD said to her, "[b]I will greatly multiply your [1]descendants so that [2]they will be too many to count."

11 The angel of the LORD said to her further,

"Behold, you are with child,
And you will bear a son;
And you shall call his name [1]Ishmael,
Because [a]the LORD [2]has given heed to
your affliction.

12 "He will be a [a]wild donkey of a man,
His hand *will be* against everyone,
And everyone's hand *will be* against
him;
And he will [1]live [2b]to the east of all
his brothers."

13 Then she called the name of the LORD who spoke to her, "[1]You are [2]a God who sees"; for she said, "[a]Have I even [3]remained alive here after seeing Him?"

14 Therefore the well was called [1]Beer-lahai-roi; behold, it is between [a]Kadesh and Bered.

15 So Hagar bore Abram a son; and Abram called the name of his son, whom Hagar bore, Ishmael.

16 Abram was [a]eighty-six years old when Hagar bore Ishmael to [1]him.

Abraham and the Covenant of Circumcision

17 Now when Abram was ninety-nine years old, [a]the LORD appeared to Abram and said to him,

"I am [1]God [b]Almighty;
Walk before Me, and be [2c]blameless.

2 "I will [1]establish My [a]covenant
between Me and you,
And I will [b]multiply you exceedingly."

3 Abram [a]fell on his face, and God talked with him, saying,

4 "As for Me, behold, My covenant is
with you,
And you will be the father of a
[a]multitude of nations.

5 [1]Lit *bosom* [2]Lit *eyes* [3]Lit *me and you* [a]Jer 51:35 [b]Gen 31:53; Ex 5:21
6 [1]Lit *hand* [2]Lit *eyes* [a]Gen 16:9
7 [a]Gen 21:17, 18; 22:11, 15; 31:11 [b]Gen 20:1; 25:18
8 [a]Gen 3:9; 1 Kin 19:9, 13
9 [1]Lit *under her hands*
10 [1]Lit *seed* [2]Or *it shall not be counted for multitude* [a]Gen 22:15-18 [b]Gen 17:20
11 [1]I.e. God hears [2]Lit *has heard* [a]Ex 2:23, 24; 3:7, 9
12 [1]Lit *dwell* [2]Lit *before the face of;* or *in defiance of* [a]Job 24:5; 39:5-8 [b]Gen 25:18
13 [1]Or *You, God, see me* [2]Heb *Elroi* [3]Lit *seen here after the one who saw me* [a]Gen 32:30; Ps 139:1-12
14 [1]I.e. the well of the living one who sees me [a]Gen 14:7
16 [1]Lit *Abram* [a]Gen 12:4; 16:3
17:1 [1]Heb *El Shaddai* [2]Lit *complete, perfect;* or *having integrity* [a]Gen 12:7; 18:1 [b]Gen 28:3; 35:11 [c]Gen 6:9; Deut 18:13
2 [1]Lit *give* [a]Gen 15:18 [b]Gen 13:16; 15:5 **3** [a]Gen 17:17; 18:2 **4** [a]Gen 35:11; 48:19

16:4 *mistress was despised.* Peninnah acted similarly toward Hannah (see 1 Sam 1:6).

16:5 *May the LORD judge between you and me.* An expression of hostility or suspicion (see 31:53; see also 31:49).

16:7 *the angel of the LORD.* Since the angel of the Lord speaks for God in the first person (v. 10) and Hagar is said to name "the LORD who spoke to her, 'You are a God who sees' " (v. 13), the angel appears to be both distinguished from the Lord (in that he is called "messenger"—the Hebrew for "angel" means "messenger") and identified with Him. Similar distinction and identification can be found in 19:1,21; 31:11,13; Ex 3:2,4; Judg 2:1–5; 6:11–12,14; 13:3,6,8–11,13,15–17,20–23; Zech 3:1–6; 12:8. Traditional Christian interpretation has held that this "angel" was a preincarnate manifestation of Christ as God's Messenger-Servant. It may be, however, that, as the Lord's personal messenger who represented Him and bore His credentials, the angel could speak on behalf of (and so be identified with) the One who sent him (see especially 19:21; cf. 18:2,22; 19:2). Whether this "angel" was the second person of the Trinity remains therefore uncertain. *Shur.* Located east of Egypt (see 25:18; 1 Sam 15:7).

16:8 *I am fleeing from the presence of my mistress.* Not yet knowing exactly where she was going, Hagar answered only the first of the angel's questions.

16:10 A promise reaffirmed in 17:20 and fulfilled in 25:13–16.

16:11 *Ishmael.* See 17:20.

16:12 *wild donkey.* Away from human settlements, Ishmael would roam the desert like a wild donkey (see Job 24:5; Hos 8:9). *to the east of.* If the marginal rendering is correct ("in defiance of"), the hostility would be that between Sarai and Hagar (see vv. 4–6), which was passed on to their descendants (see 25:18).

16:13 *Have I even remained alive here after seeing Him?* Cf. Ex 33:23; to see God's face was believed to bring death (see 32:30; Ex 33:20).

16:14 *Beer-lahai-roi.* See NASB marg.; another possible translation that fits the context equally well is: "well of the one who sees me and who lives." *Kadesh.* See note on 14:7.

17:1 *ninety-nine years old.* Thirteen years had passed since Ishmael's birth (see 16:16; 17:24–25). *appeared.* See note on 12:7. *I am.* See note on 15:7. *God Almighty.* The Hebrew (*El-Shaddai*) perhaps means "God, the Mountain One," either highlighting the invincible power of God or referring to the mountains as God's symbolic home (see Ps 121:1). It was the special name by which God revealed Himself to the patriarchs (see Ex 6:3). *Shaddai* occurs 31 times in the book of Job and 17 times in the rest of the Bible. *Walk before Me, and be blameless.* Perhaps equivalent to "Walk with Me, and be blameless" (see notes on 5:22; 6:8–9). After Abram's and Sarai's attempt to obtain the promised offspring by using a surrogate mother, God appeared to Abram. The Lord made it clear that, if Abram was to receive God's promised and covenanted benefits, he must be God's faithful and obedient servant. His faith must be accompanied by the "obedience of faith" (Rom 1:5; see ch. 22).

17:2 *My covenant.* See 12:2–3; 13:14–16; 15:4–5. The covenant is God's. God calls it "My covenant" nine times in vv. 2–21, and He initiates (see 15:18), confirms (v. 2) and establishes (v. 7) it. *multiply you.* See 13:16 and note. Earlier God had covenanted to keep His promise concerning the land (ch. 15); here He broadens His covenant to include the promised offspring. See chart, p. 16.

5 "No longer shall your name be called
[1]Abram,
But [a]your name shall be
[2]Abraham;
For [b]I will make you the father of a
multitude of nations.

6 "I will make you exceedingly fruitful, and I will make nations of you, and [a]kings will come forth from you.

7 "I will establish My covenant between Me and you and your [1]descendants after you throughout their generations for an [a]everlasting covenant, [b]to be God to you and [c]to your [1]descendants after you.

8 "[a]I will give to you and to your [1]descendants after you, the land of your sojournings, all the land of Canaan, for an everlasting possession; and [b]I will be their God."

9 God said further to Abraham, "Now as for you, [a]you shall keep My covenant, you and your [1]descendants after you throughout their generations.

10 "[a]This is My covenant, which you shall keep, between Me and you and your [1]descendants after you: every male among you shall be circumcised.

11 "And [a]you shall be circumcised in the flesh of your foreskin, and it shall be the sign of the covenant between Me and you.

12 "And every male among you who is [a]eight days old shall be circumcised throughout your generations, a *servant* who is born in the house or who is bought with money from any foreigner, who is not of your [1]descendants.

13 "A *servant* who is born in your house or [a]who is bought with your money shall surely be circumcised; thus shall My covenant be in your flesh for an everlasting covenant.

14 "But an uncircumcised male who is not circumcised in the flesh of his foreskin, that person shall be [a]cut off from his people; he has broken My covenant."

15 Then God said to Abraham, "As for Sarai your wife, you shall not call her name Sarai, but [1]Sarah *shall be* her name.

16 "I will bless her, and indeed I will give you [a]a son by her. Then I will bless her, and she shall be *a mother of* nations; [b]kings of peoples will [1]come from her."

17 Then Abraham [a]fell on his face and laughed, and said in his heart, "Will a child be born to a man one hundred years old? And [b]will Sarah, who is ninety years old, bear *a child?*"

18 And Abraham said to God, "Oh that Ishmael might live before You!"

19 But God said, "No, but Sarah your wife will bear you [a]a son, and you shall call his name [1]Isaac; and [b]I will establish My covenant with him for an everlasting covenant for his [2]descendants after him.

5 [1]I.e. exalted father [2]I.e. father of a multitude [a]Neh 9:7 [b]Rom 4:17
6 [a]Gen 17:16; 35:11
7 [1]Lit *seed* [a]Gen 17:13, 19; Ps 105:9, 10; Luke 1:55 [b]Gen 26:24; Lev 11:45; 26:12, 45; Heb 11:16 [c]Gen 28:13; Gal 3:16
8 [1]Lit *seed* [a]Gen 12:7; 13:15, 17; Acts 7:5 [b]Ex 6:7; 29:45; Lev 26:12; Deut 29:13; Rev 21:7
9 [1]Lit *seed* [a]Ex 19:5
10 [1]Lit *seed* [a]John 7:22; Acts 7:8; Rom 4:11
11 [a]Ex 12:48; Deut 10:16; Acts 7:8; Rom 4:11
12 [a]Lev 12:3

12 [1]Lit *seed*
13 [a]Ex 12:44
14 [a]Ex 4:24-26
15 [1]I.e. princess
16 [1]Lit *be* [a]Gen 18:10 [b]Gen 17:6; 36:31
17 [a]Gen 17:3; 18:12; 21:6 [b]Gen 21:7
19 [1]I.e. he laughs [2]Lit *seed* [a]Gen 17:16; 18:10; 21:2 [b]Gen 26:2-5

17:5 *Abram . . . Abraham.* The first name means "Exalted Father," probably in reference to God (i.e., "[God is] Exalted Father"); the second means "father of many," in reference to Abraham. *your name shall be.* By giving Abram a new name (see Neh 9:7) God marked him in a special way as His servant (see notes on 1:5; 2:19).

17:6 *nations . . . kings.* This promise came also to Sarah (v. 16) and was renewed to Jacob (35:11; see 48:19). It referred to the proliferation of Abraham's offspring, who, like the descendants of Noah (see ch. 10), would someday become many nations and spread over the earth. Ultimately it finds fulfillment in such passages as Rom 4:16–18; 15:8–12; Gal 3:29; Rev 7:9; 21:24.

17:7 *everlasting.* From God's standpoint (see vv. 13,19), but capable of being broken from man's standpoint (see v. 14; cf. Is 24:5; Jer 31:32). *to be God to you.* The heart of God's covenant promise, repeated over and over in the OT (see, e.g., v. 8; Jer 24:7; 31:33; Ezek 34:30–31; Hos 2:23; Zech 8:8). This is God's pledge to be the protector of His people and the One who provides for their well-being and guarantees their future blessing (see 15:1).

17:8 *land.* See 12:7; 15:18; Acts 7:5. *everlasting possession.* The land, though an everlasting possession given by God, could be temporarily lost because of disobedience (see Deut 28:62–63; 30:1–10).

17:9 *as for you.* Balances the "As for Me" of v. 4. Having reviewed His covenanted commitment to Abraham (see 15:8–21), and having broadened it to include the promise of offspring, God now called upon Abraham to make a covenanted commitment to Him—to "Walk before Me, and be blameless" (v. 1). *keep My covenant.* Participation in the blessings of the Abrahamic covenant was conditioned on obedience (see 18:19; 22:18; 26:4–5).

17:10 *circumcised.* Circumcision was God's appointed "sign of the covenant" (v. 11), which signified Abraham's covenanted commitment to the Lord—that the Lord alone would be his God, whom he would trust and serve. It symbolized a self-maledictory oath (analogous to the oath to which God had submitted Himself; see note on 15:17): "If I am not loyal in faith and obedience to the Lord, may the sword of the Lord cut off me and my offspring (see v. 14) as I have cut off my foreskin." Thus Abraham was to place himself under the rule of the Lord as his King, consecrating himself, his offspring and all he possessed to the service of the Lord. For circumcision as signifying consecration to the Lord see Ex 6:12; Lev 19:23; 26:41; Deut 10:16; 30:6; Jer 4:4; 6:10; 9:25–26; Ezek 44:7,9. Other nations also practiced circumcision (see Jer 9:25–26; Ezek 32:18–19), but not for the covenant reasons that Israel did.

17:11 *sign of the covenant.* See notes on 9:12; 15:17. As the covenant sign, circumcision also (see note on v. 10) marked Abraham as the one to whom God had made covenant commitment (15:7–21) in response to Abraham's faith, which He "reckoned . . . to him as righteousness" (15:6). Paul comments on this aspect of the covenant sign in Rom 4:11.

17:12 *eight days old.* See 21:4 and Acts 7:8 (Isaac); Luke 1:59 (John the Baptist); 2:21 (Jesus); Phil 3:5 (Paul). Abraham was 99 years old when the newly initiated rite of circumcision was performed on him (see v. 24). The Arabs, who consider themselves descendants of Ishmael, are circumcised at the age of 13 (see v. 25). For them, as for other peoples, it serves as a rite of transition from childhood to manhood, thus into full participation in the community.

17:14 *cut off from his people.* Removed from the covenant people by divine judgment (see note on v. 10).

17:15 *Sarai . . . Sarah.* Both names evidently mean "princess." The renaming stressed that she was to be the mother of nations and kings (see v. 16) and thus to serve the Lord's purpose (see note on v. 5).

17:16 *son.* Fulfilled in Isaac (see 21:2–3).

17:17 *laughed.* In temporary disbelief (see 18:12; cf. Rom 4:19–21). The verb is a pun on the name "Isaac," which means "he laughs" (see v. 19; 18:12–15; 21:3,6).

20 "As for Ishmael, I have heard you; behold, I will bless him, and [a]will make him fruitful and will multiply him exceedingly. [b]He shall [1]become the father of twelve princes, and I will make him a [c]great nation.

21 "But My covenant I will establish with [a]Isaac, whom [b]Sarah will bear to you at this season next year."

22 When He finished talking with him, [a]God went up from Abraham.

23 Then Abraham took Ishmael his son, and all *the servants* who were [a]born in his house and all who were bought with his money, every male among the men of Abraham's household, and circumcised the flesh of their foreskin in the very same day, [b]as God had said to him.

24 Now Abraham was ninety-nine years old when [a]he was circumcised in the flesh of his foreskin.

25 And [a]Ishmael his son was thirteen years old when he was circumcised in the flesh of his foreskin.

26 In the very same day Abraham was circumcised, and Ishmael his son.

27 All the men of his household, who were [a]born in the house or bought with money from a foreigner, were circumcised with him.

Birth of Isaac Promised

18 Now [a]the LORD appeared to him by the [1b]oaks of Mamre, while he was sitting at the tent door in the heat of the day.

2 When he lifted up his eyes and looked, behold, three [a]men were standing opposite him; and when he saw *them,* he ran from the tent door to meet them and bowed himself to the earth,

3 and said, "[1]My lord, if now I have found favor in your sight, please do not [2]pass your servant by.

4 "Please let a little water be brought and [a]wash your feet, and [1]rest yourselves under the tree;

5 and I will [1a]bring a piece of bread, that you may [2]refresh yourselves; after that you may go on, since you have [3]visited your servant." And they said, "So do, as you have said."

6 So Abraham hurried into the tent to Sarah, and said, "[1]Quickly, prepare three [2]measures of fine flour, knead *it* and make bread cakes."

7 Abraham also ran to the herd, and took a tender and [1]choice calf and gave *it* to the servant, and he hurried to prepare it.

8 He took curds and milk and the calf which he had prepared, and placed *it* before them; and he was standing by them under the tree [1]as they ate.

9 Then they said to him, "Where is Sarah your wife?" And he said, "There, in the tent."

10 He said, "[a]I will surely return to you [1]at this time next year; and behold, Sarah your wife will have a son." And Sarah was listening at the tent door, which was behind him.

11 Now [a]Abraham and Sarah were old, advanced in age; Sarah was [b]past [1]childbearing.

12 Sarah laughed [1]to herself, saying, "[a]After I have become old, shall I have pleasure, my [b]lord being old also?"

13 And the LORD said to Abraham, "Why did Sarah laugh, saying, 'Shall I indeed [1]bear *a child,* when I am *so* old?'

14 "[a]Is anything too [1]difficult for the LORD? At the [b]appointed time I will return to you, [2]at this time next year, and Sarah will have a son."

15 Sarah denied *it* however, saying, "I did not laugh"; for she was afraid. And He said, "No, but you did laugh."

16 Then [a]the men rose up from there, and looked down toward Sodom; and Abraham was walking with them to send them off.

17 [a]The LORD said, "Shall I hide from Abraham [b]what I am about to do,

20 [1]Lit *beget twelve princes* [a]Gen 16:10 [b]Gen 25:12-16 [c]Gen 21:18
21 [a]Gen 17:19; 18:10, 14 [b]Gen 21:2
22 [a]Gen 18:33; 35:13
23 [a]Gen 14:14 [b]Gen 17:9-11
24 [a]Rom 4:11
25 [a]Gen 16:16
27 [a]Gen 14:14
18:1 [1]Or *terebinths* [a]Gen 12:7; 17:1 [b]Gen 13:18; 14:13
2 [a]Gen 18:16, 22; 32:24; Josh 5:13; Judg 13:6-11; Heb 13:2
3 [1]Or *O Lord* [2]Lit *pass away from your servant*
4 [1]Lit *support* [a]Gen 19:2; 24:32; 43:24
5 [1]Lit *take* [2]Lit *sustain your heart* [3]Lit *come to* [a]Judg 6:18, 19; 13:15, 16
6 [1]Lit *Hasten three measures* [2]Heb *seah;* i.e. one seah equals approx eleven qts
7 [1]Lit *good*
8 [1]Lit *and*
10 [1]Lit *when the time revives* [a]Gen 21:2; Rom 9:9
11 [1]Lit *the manner of women* [a]Gen 17:17; Rom 4:19 [b]Heb 11:11
12 [1]Lit *within* [a]Gen 17:17; Luke 1:18 [b]1 Pet 3:6
13 [1]Lit *surely bear*
14 [1]Or *wonderful* [2]Lit *when the time revives* [a]Jer 32:17, 27; Zech 8:6; Matt 19:26; Luke 1:37; Rom 4:21 [b]Gen 17:21; 18:10
16 [a]Gen 18:2, 22; 19:1 **17** [a]Gen 18:22, 26, 33; Amos 3:7 [b]Gen 18:21; 19:24

17:20 *multiply him.* See note on 13:16. *father of twelve princes.* Fulfilled in 25:16.

17:21 Paul cites the choice of Isaac (and not Ishmael) as one proof of God's sovereign right to choose to save by grace alone (see Rom 9:6–13). *at this season next year.* See 21:2.

17:22 *God went up from Abraham.* A solemn conclusion to the conversation.

17:23 *in the very same day.* Abraham was characterized by prompt obedience (see note on 12:4).

18:1 *appeared.* See note on 12:7. *oaks.* See note on 12:6. *Mamre.* See note on 13:18. *the heat of the day.* Early afternoon.

18:2 *three men.* At least two of the "men" were angels (see 19:1; see also note on 16:7). The third may have been the Lord Himself (see vv. 1,13,17,20,26,33; see especially v. 22). *ran.* The story in vv. 2–8 illustrates Near Eastern hospitality in several ways: 1. Abraham gave prompt attention to the needs of his guests (vv. 2,6–7). 2. He bowed low to the ground (v. 2). 3. He politely addressed one of his guests as "my lord" and called himself "your servant" (vv. 3,5), a common way of speaking when addressing a superior (see, e.g., 19:2,18–19). 4. He acted as if it would be a favor to him if they allowed him to serve them (vv. 3–5). 5. He asked that water be brought to wash their feet (see v. 4), an act of courtesy to refresh a traveler in a hot, dusty climate (see 19:2; 24:32; 43:24). 6. He prepared a lavish meal for them (vv. 5–8; a similar lavish offering was presented to a divine messenger in Judg 6:18–19; 13:15–16). 7. He stood nearby (v. 8), assuming the posture of a servant (see v. 22), to meet their every wish. Heb 13:2 is probably a reference to vv. 2–8 and 19:1–3.

18:6 *bread cakes.* Probably round, thin loaves.

18:10 See 17:21. Paul quotes this promise of Isaac's birth (see v. 14) in Rom 9:9 and relates it to Abraham's spiritual offspring (see Rom 9:7–8).

18:12 *laughed.* In disbelief, as also Abraham had at first (see note on 17:17).

18:14 *Is anything too difficult for the LORD?* The answer is no, for Sarah as well as for her descendants Mary and Elizabeth (see Luke 1:34–37). Nothing within God's will, including creation (see Jer 32:17) and redemption (see Matt 19:25–26), is impossible for Him.

18:16 *Sodom.* See notes on 10:19; 13:10.

18:17 Abraham was God's friend (see v. 19; 2 Chr 20:7; James 2:23; see also Is 41:8, but see note there). And because he was now

18 since Abraham will surely become a
great and [1]mighty nation, and in him [a]all the
nations of the earth will be blessed?
19 "For I have [1a]chosen him, so that he
may [b]command his children and his household after him to [c]keep the way of the LORD
by doing righteousness and justice, so that
the LORD may bring upon Abraham [d]what He
has spoken about him."
20 And the LORD said, "[a]The outcry of
Sodom and Gomorrah is indeed great, and
their sin is exceedingly grave.
21 "I will [a]go down now, and see if they
have done entirely according to its outcry,
which has come to Me; and if not, I will
know."
22 Then [a]the men turned away from there
and went toward Sodom, while Abraham
was still standing before [b]the LORD.
23 Abraham came near and said, "[a]Will
You indeed sweep away the righteous with
the wicked?
24 "Suppose there are fifty righteous within
the city; will You indeed sweep *it* away and
not [1]spare the place for the sake of the fifty
righteous who are in it?
25 "Far be it from You to do [1]such a thing,
to slay the righteous with the wicked, so that
the righteous and the wicked are *treated*
alike. Far be it from You! Shall not [a]the Judge
of all the earth [2]deal justly?"
26 So the LORD said, "[a]If I find in Sodom
fifty righteous within the city, then I will
[1]spare the whole place on their account."
27 And Abraham replied, "Now behold, I
have [1]ventured to speak to the Lord,
although I am *but* [a]dust and ashes.
28 "Suppose the fifty righteous are lacking
five, will You destroy the whole city because
of five?" And He said, "I will not destroy *it* if
I find forty-five there."
29 He spoke to Him yet again and said,
"Suppose forty are found there?" And He
said, "I will not do *it* on account of the
forty."
30 Then he said, "Oh may the Lord not be
angry, and I shall speak; suppose thirty are
found there?" And He said, "I will not do *it* if
I find thirty there."
31 And he said, "Now behold, I have
[1]ventured to speak to the Lord; suppose
twenty are found there?" And He said, "I will
not destroy *it* on account of the twenty."
32 Then he said, "[a]Oh may the Lord not
be angry, and I shall speak only this once;
suppose ten are found there?" And He said,
"I will not destroy *it* on account of the ten."
33 As soon as He had finished speaking to
Abraham [a]the LORD departed, and Abraham
returned to his place.

The Doom of Sodom

19 Now the [a]two angels came to Sodom in
the evening as Lot was sitting in the
gate of Sodom. When [b]Lot saw *them,* he rose
to meet them and [1]bowed down *with his* face
to the ground.
2 And he said, "Now behold, my lords,
please turn aside into your servant's house,
and spend the night, and wash your feet;
then you may rise early and go on your
way." They said however, "No, but we shall
spend the night in the square."
3 Yet he urged them strongly, so they
turned aside to him and entered his house;

18 [1]Or *populous* [a]Gen 12:3; 22:18; Acts 3:25; Gal 3:8
19 [1]Lit *known* [a]Neh 9:7; Amos 3:2 [b]Deut 6:6, 7 [c]Gen 17:9 [d]Gen 12:2, 3
20 [a]Gen 19:13; Ezek 16:49, 50
21 [a]Gen 11:5; Ex 3:8; Ps 14:2
22 [a]Gen 18:16; 19:1 [b]Gen 18:1, 17
23 [a]Ex 23:7; Num 16:22; 2 Sam 24:17; Ps 11:4-7
24 [1]Or *forgive*
25 [1]Lit *after this manner* [2]Lit *do justice* [a]Deut 1:16, 17; 32:4; Job 8:3, 20; Ps 58:11; 94:2; Is 3:10, 11; Rom 3:5, 6
26 [1]Or *forgive* [a]Jer 5:1
27 [1]Lit *undertaken* [a]Gen 3:19; Job 30:19; 42:6
31 [1]Lit *undertaken*
32 [a]Judg 6:39
33 [a]Gen 17:22; 35:13
19:1 [1]Lit *bowed himself* [a]Gen 18:2, 22 [b]Gen 18:2-5

God's covenant friend (see Job 29:4), God convened His heavenly council (see note on 1:26) at Abraham's tent. There He announced His purpose for Abraham (v. 10) and for the wicked of the plain (vv. 20–21)—redemption and judgment. He thus even gave Abraham opportunity to speak in His court and to intercede for the righteous in Sodom and Gomorrah. Abraham was later called a prophet (20:7). Here, in Abraham, is exemplified the great privilege of God's covenant people throughout the ages: God has revealed His purposes to them and allows their voice to be heard (in intercession) in the court of heaven.

18:18 *a great and mighty nation . . . will be blessed.* See note on 12:2–3.

18:19 *chosen.* Lit. "known." In Hebrew usage, "to know" sometimes connotes "to choose" (see, e.g., Amos 3:2).

18:20 *outcry.* A cry of righteous indignation (cf. the blood of Abel, 4:10) that became one of the reasons for the destruction of the cities (see 19:13). *Gomorrah.* See notes on 10:19; 13:10. *sin is exceedingly grave.* The sin of Sodom (and probably of Gomorrah as well) was already proverbial (see 13:13) and remained so for centuries (see Ezek 16:49–50).

18:21 *I will go down.* The result would be judgment (as in 11:5–9), but God also comes down to redeem (as in Ex 3:8). *see.* Not a denial of God's infinite knowledge but a figurative way of stating that He does not act out of ignorance or on the basis of mere complaints.

18:22 *Abraham was still standing before the LORD.* Illustrates the mutual accessibility that existed between God and His servant.

18:23 The second time Abraham intervened for his relatives and for Sodom (see 14:14–16).

18:25 *Judge of all the earth.* Abraham based his plea on the justice and authority ("Judge" could be translated "Ruler") of God, confident that God would do what was right (see Deut 32:4).

18:27 *Lord.* Abraham used the title "Lord," not the intimate name "LORD," throughout his prayer. He was appealing to God as "Judge of all the earth." *dust and ashes.* In contrast to God's exalted position, Abraham described himself as insignificant (see Job 30:19; 42:6).

18:32 *only this once.* Abraham's questioning in vv. 23–32 did not arise from a spirit of haggling but of compassion for his relatives and of wanting to know God's ways. *ten.* Perhaps Abraham stopped at ten because he had been counting while praying: Lot, his wife, possibly two sons (see 19:12), at least two married daughters and their husbands (see 19:14), and two unmarried daughters (see 19:8).

18:33 *his place.* Mamre (see v. 1). The next morning Abraham went back to see what God had done (see 19:27).

19:1–3 See note on 18:2.

19:1 *the two angels.* See notes on 16:7; 18:2. *Lot was sitting in the gate of Sodom.* Lot had probably become a member of Sodom's ruling council, since a city gateway served as the administrative and judicial center where legal matters were discussed and prosecuted (see Ruth 4:1–12).

19:2 *square.* A large open space near the main city gateway (see 2 Chr 32:6) where public gatherings were held. Important cities like Jerusalem could have two or more squares (see Neh 8:16).

[a]and he prepared a feast for them, and baked unleavened bread, and they ate.

4 Before they lay down, [a]the men of the city, the men of Sodom, surrounded the house, both young and old, all the people [1]from every quarter;

5 and they called to Lot and said to him, "[a]Where are the men who came to you tonight? Bring them out to us that we may [1]have relations with them."

6 But Lot went out to them at the doorway, and shut the door behind him,

7 and said, "Please, my brothers, do not act wickedly.

8 "Now behold, [a]I have two daughters who have not [1]had relations with man; please let me bring them out to you, and do to them [2]whatever you like; only do nothing to these men, inasmuch as they have come under the [3]shelter of my roof."

9 But they said, "Stand aside." Furthermore, they said, "This one came in [1]as an alien, and already [a]he is acting like a judge; now we will treat you worse than them." So they pressed hard against [2]Lot and came near to break the door.

10 But [a]the men reached out their [1]hands and brought Lot into the house [2]with them, and shut the door.

11 [a]They [1]struck the men who were at the doorway of the house with blindness, both small and great, so that they wearied *themselves trying* to find the doorway.

12 Then the *two* men said to Lot, "Whom else have you here? A son-in-law, and your sons, and your daughters, and whomever you have in the city, bring *them* out of the place;

13 for we are about to destroy this place, because [a]their outcry has become so great before the LORD that [b]the LORD has sent us to destroy it."

14 Lot went out and spoke to his sons-in-law, who [1]were to marry his daughters, and said, "Up, [a]get out of this place, for the LORD will destroy the city." [b]But he appeared to his sons-in-law [2]to be jesting.

15 When morning dawned, the angels urged Lot, saying, "Up, take your wife and your two daughters who are here, or you will be swept away in the [1]punishment of the city."

16 But he hesitated. So the men [a]seized his hand and the hand of his wife and the [1]hands of his two daughters, for [b]the compassion of the LORD *was* upon him; and they brought him out, and put him outside the city.

17 When they had brought them outside, [1]one said, "[a]Escape for your life! [b]Do not look behind you, and do not stay [2]anywhere in the [c]valley; escape to [d]the [3]mountains, or you will be swept away."

18 But Lot said to them, "Oh no, my lords!

19 "Now behold, your servant has found favor in your sight, and you have magnified your lovingkindness, which you have shown me by saving my life; but I cannot escape to the [1]mountains, for the disaster will overtake me and I will die;

20 now behold, this town is near *enough* to flee to, and it is small. Please, let me escape there (is it not small?) [1]that my life may be saved."

21 He said to him, "Behold, I grant you this [1]request also, not to overthrow the town of which you have spoken.

22 "Hurry, escape there, for I cannot do anything until you arrive there." Therefore the name of the town was called [1][a]Zoar.

23 The sun had risen over the earth when Lot came to Zoar.

24 Then the LORD [a]rained on Sodom and Gomorrah brimstone and fire from the LORD out of heaven,

25 and [a]He overthrew those cities, and all the [1]valley, and all the inhabitants of the cities, and what grew on the ground.

26 But his wife, from behind him, [a]looked *back*, and she became a pillar of salt.

27 Now Abraham arose early in the morning *and went* to [a]the place where he had stood before the LORD;

28 and he looked down toward Sodom and Gomorrah, and toward all the land of the [1]valley, and he saw, and behold, [a]the smoke of the land ascended like the smoke of a [2]furnace.

29 Thus it came about, when God destroyed the cities of the [1]valley, that [a]God remembered Abraham, and [b]sent Lot out of

3 [a]Gen 18:6-8
4 [1]Or *without exception;* lit *from every end* [a]Gen 13:13; 18:20
5 [1]I.e. have intercourse [a]Lev 18:22; Judg 19:22
8 [1]I.e. had intercourse [2]Lit *as is good in your sight* [3]Lit *shadow* [a]Judg 19:24
9 [1]Lit *to sojourn* [2]Lit *the man, against Lot* [a]Ex 2:14
10 [1]Lit *hand* [2]Lit *to* [a]Gen 19:1
11 [1]Lit *smote* [a]Deut 28:28, 29; 2 Kin 6:18; Acts 13:11
13 [a]Gen 18:20 [b]Lev 26:30-33; Deut 4:26; 28:45; 1 Chr 21:15
14 [1]Or *had married;* lit *were taking* [2]Lit *like one who was jesting* [a]Num 16:21, 45; Rev 18:4 [b]Jer 43:1, 2
15 [1]Or *iniquity*
16 [1]Lit *hand* [a]Deut 5:15; 6:21; 7:8; 2 Pet 2:7 [b]Ex 34:7; Ps 32:10; 33:18, 19
17 [1]Lit *he* [2]Lit *in all the circle* [3]Lit *mountain* [a]Jer 48:6 [b]Gen 19:26 [c]Gen 13:10 [d]Gen 14:10
19 [1]Lit *mountain*
20 [1]Lit *and my soul will live*
21 [1]Lit *thing*
22 [1]I.e. small [a]Gen 13:10; 14:2
24 [a]Deut 29:23; Ps 11:6; Is 13:19; Ezek 16:49, 50; Luke 17:29; Jude 7
25 [1]Lit *circle* [a]Deut 29:23; Ps 107:34; Is 13:19; Lam 4:6; 2 Pet 2:6
26 [a]Gen 19:17; Luke 17:32
27 [a]Gen 18:22
28 [1]Lit *circle* [2]Lit *kiln* [a]Rev 9:2; 18:9
29 [1]Lit *circle* [a]Deut 7:8; 9:5, 27 [b]2 Pet 2:7

19:3 *unleavened bread.* So that it could be baked quickly (see 18:6; Ex 12:39).

19:4–9 See Judg 19:22–25.

19:5 *have relations with them.* Homosexuality was so characteristic of the men of Sodom (see Jude 7) that it is still often called sodomy.

19:8 *under the shelter of my roof.* Ancient hospitality obliged a host to protect his guests in every situation.

19:9 *This one came in as an alien, and already he is acting like a judge.* Centuries later, Moses was also considered an outsider and accused of setting himself up as a judge (see Ex 2:14; Acts 7:27).

19:13 *we are about to destroy this place.* Sodom's wickedness had made it ripe for destruction (see Is 3:9; Jer 23:14; Lam 4:6; Zeph 2:8–9; 2 Pet 2:6; Jude 7).

19:14 *he appeared to his sons-in-law to be jesting.* Lot apparently had lost his power of moral persuasion even among his family members.

19:16 *hesitated.* Perhaps because of reluctance to leave his material possessions. *his hand and the hand of his wife and the hands of his two daughters.* The ten righteous people required to save Sodom (see 18:32) had now been reduced to four. *the compassion of the LORD was upon him.* Deliverance is due to divine mercy, not to human righteousness (cf. Titus 3:5).

19:24 *rained . . . brimstone and fire.* Perhaps from a violent earthquake spewing up asphalt, such as is still found in this region.

19:26 *his wife . . . looked back, and she became a pillar of salt.* Her disobedient hesitation (see v. 17) became proverbial in later generations (see Luke 17:32). Even today, grotesque salt formations near the southern end of the Dead Sea are reminders of her folly.

19:29 *God remembered Abraham.* See note on 8:1. *God . . . sent*

the midst of the overthrow, when He overthrew the cities in which Lot lived.

Lot Is Debased

30 Lot went up from Zoar, and [1][a]stayed in
the [2]mountains, and his two daughters with
him; for he was afraid to [3]stay in Zoar; and he
[1]stayed in a cave, he and his two daughters.
31 Then the firstborn said to the younger,
"Our father is old, and there is not a man [1]on
earth to [a]come in to us after the manner of
the earth.
32 "Come, [a]let us make our father drink
wine, and let us lie with him that we may
preserve [1]our family through our father."
33 So they made their father drink wine
that night, and the firstborn went in and lay
with her father; and he did not know when
she lay down or when she arose.
34 On the following day, the firstborn said
to the younger, "Behold, I lay last night with
my father; let us make him drink wine
tonight also; then you go in and lie with him,
that we may preserve [1]our family through
our father."
35 So they made their father drink wine
that night also, and the younger arose and
lay with him; and he did not know when she
lay down or when she arose.
36 Thus both the daughters of Lot were
with child by their father.
37 The firstborn bore a son, and called his
name [a]Moab; he is the father of the Moabites
to this day.
38 As for the younger, she also bore a son,
and called his name Ben-ammi; he is the
father of the [1]sons of [a]Ammon to this day.

Abraham's Treachery

20 Now Abraham journeyed from [a]there
toward the land of [b]the [1]Negev, and
[2]settled between Kadesh and Shur; then he
sojourned in [c]Gerar.
2 Abraham said of Sarah his wife, "[a]She
is my sister." So [b]Abimelech king of Gerar
sent and took Sarah.
3 [a]But God came to Abimelech in a
dream of the night, and said to him,
"Behold, [b]you are a dead man because of the
woman whom you have taken, for she is
[1]married."
4 Now Abimelech had not come near
her; and he said, "Lord, [a]will You slay a
nation, even *though* [1]blameless?
5 "Did he not himself say to me, 'She is
my sister'? And she [a]herself said, 'He is my
brother.' In [b]the integrity of my heart and the
innocence of my [1]hands I have done this."
6 Then God said to him in the dream,
"Yes, I know that in the integrity of your
heart you have done this, and I also [1][a]kept
you from sinning against Me; therefore I did
not let you touch her.
7 "Now therefore, restore the man's wife,
for [a]he is a prophet, and he will pray for you
and you will live. But if you do not restore
her, know that you shall surely die, you and
all who are yours."
8 So Abimelech arose early in the morning and called all his servants and told all
these things in their hearing; and the men
were greatly frightened.
9 [a]Then Abimelech called Abraham and
said to him, "What have you done to us?
And [1]how have I sinned against you, that
you have brought on me and on my kingdom
[b]a great sin? You have done to me [2]things
that ought not to be done."
10 And Abimelech said to Abraham,
"What have you [1]encountered, that you have
done this thing?"
11 Abraham said, "Because I thought,
surely there is no [a]fear of God in this place,
and [b]they will kill me because of my wife.
12 "Besides, she actually is my sister, the
daughter of my father, but not the daughter
of my mother, and she became my wife;
13 and it came about, when [a]God caused
me to wander from my father's house, that I
said to her, 'This is [1]the kindness which you
will show to me: [2]everywhere we go, [b]say of
me, "He is my brother." ' "
14 [a]Abimelech then took sheep and oxen
and male and female servants, and gave
them to Abraham, and restored his wife Sarah to him.
15 Abimelech said, "[a]Behold, my land is
before you; [1]settle wherever [2]you please."

30 [1]Lit *dwelt* [2]Lit *mountain* [3]Lit *dwell* [a]Gen 19:17, 19
31 [1]Or *in the land* [a]Gen 16:2, 4; 38:8; Deut 25:5
32 [1]Lit *seed from our father* [a]Luke 21:34
34 [1]Lit *seed from our father*
37 [a]Deut 2:9
38 [1]Heb *Bene-Ammon* [a]Deut 2:19
20:1 [1]I.e. South country [2]Lit *dwelt* [a]Gen 18:1 [b]Gen 12:9 [c]Gen 26:1, 6
2 [a]Gen 12:11-13; 20:12; 26:7 [b]Gen 12:15
3 [a]Gen 12:17, 18 [b]Gen 20:7
3 [1]Lit *married to a husband*
4 [1]Lit *righteous* [a]Gen 18:23-25
5 [1]Lit *palms* [a]Gen 20:13 [b]1 Kin 9:4; Ps 7:8; 26:6
6 [1]Lit *restrained* [a]1 Sam 25:26, 34
7 [a]1 Sam 7:5; 2 Kin 5:11; Job 42:8
9 [1]Lit *what* [2]Lit *deeds* [a]Gen 12:18 [b]Gen 39:9
10 [1]Lit *seen*
11 [a]Neh 5:15; Prov 16:6 [b]Gen 12:12; 26:7
13 [1]Lit *your* [2]Lit *at every place where* [a]Gen 12:1-9 [b]Gen 12:13; 20:5
14 [a]Gen 12:16
15 [1]Lit *dwell* [2]Lit *it is good in your sight* [a]Gen 13:9; 34:10; 47:6

Lot out of the midst of the overthrow. Lot's deliverance was the main concern of Abraham's prayer (18:23–32), which God now answered.

19:33 *they made their father drink wine . . . and the firstborn went in and lay with her father.* Though Lot's role was somewhat passive, he bore the basic responsibility for the drunkenness and incest that eventually resulted in his two daughters' becoming pregnant by him (see v. 36).

19:36–38 The sons born to Lot's daughters were the ancestors of the Moabites and Ammonites (see Deut 2:9,19), two nations that were to become bitter enemies of Abraham's descendants (see, e.g., 1 Sam 14:47; 2 Chr 20:1).

20:1 *between Kadesh and Shur.* See notes on 14:7; 16:7. *Gerar.* Located at the edge of Philistine territory, about halfway between Gaza on the Mediterranean coast and Beersheba in the northern Negev.

20:2 *Abimelech.* Probably the father or grandfather of the later king who bore the same name (see 26:1).

20:3 *dream.* Once again God intervened to spare the mother of the promised offspring. Dreams were a frequent mode of revelation in the OT (see 28:12; 31:10–11; 37:5–9; 40:5; 41:1; Num 12:6; Judg 7:13; 1 Kin 3:5; Dan 2:3; 4:5; 7:1).

20:7 *prophet.* See note on 18:17. Abraham was the first man to bear this title (see Ps 105:15).

20:11 *fear of God.* A conventional phrase equivalent to "true religion." "Fear" in this phrase has the sense of reverential trust in God that includes commitment to His revealed will (word).

20:12 *she actually is my sister, the daughter of my father, but not the daughter of my mother.* Abraham's half-truth was a sinful deception, not a legitimate explanation.

20:14–16 Abimelech's generosity was a strong contrast to Abraham's fearfulness and deception.

16 To Sarah he said, "Behold, I have given your [a]brother a thousand pieces of silver; behold, it is [1]your vindication before all who are with you, and before all men you are cleared."

17 [a]Abraham prayed to God, and God healed Abimelech and his wife and his maids, so that they bore *children*.

18 [a]For the LORD had closed fast all the wombs of the household of Abimelech because of Sarah, Abraham's wife.

Isaac Is Born

21 [a]Then the LORD took note of Sarah as He had said, and the LORD did for Sarah as He had [1]promised.

2 [a]So Sarah conceived and bore a son to Abraham in his old age, at [b]the appointed time of which God had spoken to him.

3 Abraham called the name of his son who was born to him, whom Sarah bore to him, [a]Isaac.

4 Then Abraham circumcised his son Isaac when he was [a]eight days old, as God had commanded him.

5 Now Abraham was [a]one hundred years old when his son Isaac was born to him.

6 Sarah said, "God has made [a]laughter for me; everyone who hears will laugh [1]with me."

7 And she said, "[a]Who would have said to Abraham that Sarah would nurse children? Yet I have borne him a son in his old age."

8 The child grew and was weaned, and Abraham made a great feast on the day that Isaac was weaned.

Sarah Turns against Hagar

9 Now Sarah saw [a]the son of Hagar the Egyptian, whom she had borne to Abraham, [1b]mocking.

10 Therefore she said to Abraham, "[a]Drive out this maid and her son, for the son of this maid shall not be an heir with my son [1]Isaac."

11 [a]The matter [1]distressed Abraham greatly because of his son.

12 But God said to Abraham, "[1]Do not be distressed because of the lad and your maid; whatever Sarah tells you, listen to her, for [a]through Isaac [2]your descendants shall be named.

13 "And of [a]the son of the maid I will make a nation also, because he is your [1]descendant."

14 So Abraham rose early in the morning and took bread and a [1]skin of water and gave *them* to Hagar, putting *them* on her shoulder, and *gave her* the boy, and sent her away. And she departed and wandered about in the wilderness of Beersheba.

15 When the water in the skin was used up, she [1]left the boy under one of the bushes.

16 Then she went and sat down opposite him, about a bowshot away, for she said, "Do not let me [1]see the boy die." And she sat opposite him, and [a]lifted up her voice and wept.

17 God [a]heard the lad crying; and the angel of God called to Hagar from heaven and said to her, "What is the matter with you, Hagar? [b]Do not fear, for God has heard the voice of the lad where he is.

18 "Arise, lift up the lad, and hold him by [1]the hand, [a]for I will make a great nation of him."

19 Then God [a]opened her eyes and she saw [b]a well of water; and she went and filled the [1]skin with water and gave the lad a drink.

20 [a]God was with the lad, and he grew; and he [1]lived in the wilderness and became an archer.

21 [a]He [1]lived in the wilderness of Paran, and his mother took a wife for him from the land of Egypt.

Covenant with Abimelech

22 Now it came about at that time that [a]Abimelech and Phicol, the commander of

16 [1]Lit *for you a covering of the eyes* [a]Gen 20:5
17 [a]Num 12:13; 21:7; James 5:16
18 [a]Gen 12:17
21:1 [1]Lit *spoken* [a]Gen 17:16, 21; 18:10, 14; Gal 4:23
2 [a]Acts 7:8; Gal 4:22; Heb 11:11 [b]Gen 17:21; 18:10, 14
3 [a]Gen 17:19, 21
4 [a]Gen 17:12; Acts 7:8
5 [a]Gen 17:17
6 [1]Lit *for* [a]Gen 18:13; Ps 126:2; Is 54:1
7 [a]Gen 18:11, 13
9 [1]Or *playing* [a]Gen 16:1, 4, 15 [b]Gal 4:29
10 [1]Lit *with Isaac* [a]Gal 4:30
11 [1]Lit *was very grievous in Abraham's sight* [a]Gen 17:18
12 [1]Lit *Do not let it be grievous in your sight* [2]Lit *your seed will be called* [a]Rom 9:7; Heb 11:18
13 [1]Lit *seed* [a]Gen 16:10; 21:18; 25:12-18
14 [1]I.e. a skin used as a bottle
15 [1]Lit *cast*
16 [1]Lit *look upon the death of the child* [a]Jer 6:26; Amos 8:10
17 [a]Ex 3:7; Deut 26:7; Ps 6:8 [b]Gen 26:24
18 [1]Lit *your* [a]Gen 16:10; 21:13; 25:12-16
19 [1]V 14, note 1 [a]Num 22:31; 2 Kin 6:17 [b]Gen 16:7, 14
20 [1]Lit *dwelt* [a]Gen 28:15; 39:2, 3, 21
21 [1]Lit *dwelt* [a]Gen 25:18
22 [a]Gen 20:2, 14; 26:26

20:16 *pieces.* That is, shekels. Originally the shekel was only a weight, not a coin, since coinage was not invented till the seventh century B.C.
21:1 *took note of Sarah as He had said.* See 17:16. *did for Sarah as He had promised.* See Gal 4:22–23,28.
21:3 *Isaac.* See note on 17:17.
21:4 See notes on 17:10,12.
21:5 Abraham, in fulfillment of the promise made to him (see 17:16), miraculously became a father at the age of 100 years (see 17:17).
21:6 *laughter . . . laugh.* See note on 17:17.
21:8 *weaned.* At age two or three, as was customary in the ancient Near East.
21:9 *the son of Hagar the Egyptian, whom she had borne.* Ishmael, who was in his late teens at this time (see 16:15–16). *mocking.* Or "at play." In either case, Sarah saw Ishmael as a potential threat to Isaac's inheritance (v. 10).
21:10 *Drive out this maid and her son.* See Gal 4:21–31. Driving them out would have had the effect of disinheriting Ishmael.
21:11 *The matter distressed Abraham.* Both love and legal custom played a part in Abraham's anguish. He knew that the customs of his day, illustrated later in the Nuzi tablets (see chart, p. xix), prohibited the arbitrary expulsion of a servant girl's son (whose legal status was relatively weak in any case).
21:12 *whatever Sarah tells you, listen to her.* God overruled in this matter (as He had done earlier; see 15:4), promising Abraham that both Isaac and Ishmael would have numerous descendants. *through Isaac your descendants shall be named.* See Rom 9:6–8 and Heb 11:17–19 for broader spiritual applications of this statement.
21:14 *early in the morning.* Though Abraham would now be separated from Ishmael for the first time, he responded to God's command with prompt obedience (see note on 12:4). *Beersheba.* See note on v. 31.
21:15 *one of the bushes.* See note on v. 33.
21:17 *God heard . . . God has heard.* A pun on the name "Ishmael," which means "God hears" (see 16:11; 17:20).
21:21 *wilderness of Paran.* Located in north central Sinai. *his mother took a wife for him from the land of Egypt.* Parents often arranged their children's marriages (see ch. 24).
21:22 *Abimelech.* See 20:2 and note. *Phicol.* Either a family

his army, spoke to Abraham, saying, "[b]God
is with you in all that you do;
23 now therefore, [a]swear to me here by
God that you will not deal falsely with me or
with my offspring or with my posterity, but
according to the kindness that I have shown
to you, you shall show to me and to the land
in which you have sojourned."
24 Abraham said, "I swear it."
25 But Abraham [1]complained to Abimelech because of the well of water which the
servants of Abimelech [a]had seized.
26 And Abimelech said, "I do not know
who has done this thing; you did not tell me,
nor did I hear of it [1]until today."
27 Abraham took sheep and oxen and
gave them to Abimelech, and [a]the two of
them made a covenant.
28 Then Abraham set seven ewe lambs of
the flock by themselves.
29 Abimelech said to Abraham, "What do
these seven ewe lambs mean, which you
have set by themselves?"
30 He said, "You shall take these seven
ewe lambs from my hand so that it may be a
[a]witness to me, that I dug this well."
31 Therefore he called that place [a]Beer-
sheba, because there the two of them took
an oath.
32 So they made a covenant at Beersheba;
and Abimelech and Phicol, the commander
of his army, arose and returned to the land of
the Philistines.
33 *Abraham* planted a tamarisk tree at
Beersheba, and there [a]he called on the name
of the LORD, the [b]Everlasting God.
34 And Abraham sojourned [a]in the land of
the Philistines for many days.

The Offering of Isaac

22 Now it came about after these things,
that [a]God tested Abraham, and said to
him, "[b]Abraham!" And he said, "Here I am."
2 He said, "Take now [a]your son, your
only son, whom you love, Isaac, and go to
the land of [b]Moriah, and offer him there as a
[c]burnt offering on one of the mountains of
which I will tell you."
3 So Abraham rose early in the morning
and saddled his donkey, and took two of his
young men with him and Isaac his son; and
he split wood for the burnt offering, and
arose and went to the place of which God
had told him.
4 On the third day Abraham raised his
eyes and saw the place from a distance.
5 Abraham said to his young men, "Stay
here with the donkey, and I and the lad will
go over there; and we will worship and
return to you."
6 Abraham took the wood of the burnt
offering and [a]laid it on Isaac his son, and he
took in his hand the fire and the knife. So
the two of them walked on together.
7 Isaac spoke to Abraham his father and
said, "My father!" And he said, "Here I am,
my son." And he said, "Behold, the fire and
the wood, but where is the [a]lamb for the
burnt offering?"

22 [b]Gen 26:28; Is 8:10
23 [a]Josh 2:12; 1 Sam 24:21
25 [1]Lit *reproved* [a]Gen 26:15, 18, 20-22
26 [1]Lit *except*
27 [a]Gen 26:31
30 [a]Gen 31:48
31 [a]Gen 21:14; 26:33
33 [a]Gen 12:8 [b]Ex 15:18; Deut 32:40; Ps 90:2; 93:2; Is 40:28; Jer 10:10; Hab 1:12; Heb 13:8
34 [a]Gen 22:19
22:1 [a]Deut 8:2, 16; Heb 11:17; James 1:12-14 [b]Gen 22:11
2 [a]Gen 22:12, 16; John 3:16; 1 John 4:9 [b]2 Chr 3:1 [c]Gen 8:20
6 [a]John 19:17
7 [a]Ex 29:38-42; John 1:29, 36; Rev 13:8

name or an official title, since it reappears over 60 years later (25:26) in a similar context (26:26).

21:23 *swear to me . . . by God . . . the kindness that I have shown . . . show to me.* Phrases commonly used when making covenants or treaties (see vv. 27,32). "Kindness" as used here refers to acts of friendship (cf. v. 27; 20:14). Such covenants always involved oaths.

21:27 *sheep and oxen.* Probably to be used in the treaty ceremony (see 15:10).

21:31 *Beersheba, because there the two of them took an oath.* Beersheba can mean "well of seven" or "well of the oath." For a similar pun on the name see 26:33. Beersheba, an important town in the northern Negev, marked the southernmost boundary of the Israelite monarchy in later times (see, e.g., 2 Sam 17:11). An ancient well there is still pointed out as "Abraham's well" (see v. 25), but its authenticity is not certain.

21:32 *Philistines.* See note on 10:14.

21:33 *tamarisk.* A shrub or small tree that thrives in arid regions. Its leafy branches provide welcome shade, and it is probably the unidentified bush under which Hagar put Ishmael in v. 15. *Everlasting God.* Hebrew *El Olam*, a phrase unique to this passage. It is one of a series of names that include *El*, "God," as an element (see 14:19 and note; 17:1 and note; 33:20; 35:7).

22:1 *after these things.* Isaac had grown into adolescence or young manhood, as implied also by 21:34 ("for many days"). *tested.* Not "tempted," for God does not tempt (James 1:13). Satan tempts us (see 1 Cor 7:5) in order to make us fall; God tests us in order to confirm our faith (Ex 20:20) or prove our commitment (Deut 8:2). See note on Matt 4:1. *Here I am.* Abraham answered with the response of a servant, as did Moses and Samuel when God called them by name (see Ex 3:4; 1 Sam 3:4,6,8).

22:2 *your son, your only son, whom you love, Isaac.* Isaac is placed last in this sequence in order to heighten the effect. He was the "only son" of the promise (21:12). *land of Moriah.* The author of Chronicles identifies the area as the temple mount in Jerusalem (2 Chr 3:1). Today "Mount Moriah" is occupied by the Dome of the Rock, an impressive Muslim structure erected in A.D. 691. A large outcropping of rock inside the building is still pointed to as the traditional site of the intended sacrifice of Isaac. *offer him there as a burnt offering.* Abraham had committed himself by covenant to be obedient to the Lord and had consecrated his son Isaac to the Lord by circumcision. The Lord put His servant's faith and loyalty to the supreme test, thereby instructing Abraham, Isaac and their descendants as to the kind of total consecration the Lord's covenant requires. The test also foreshadowed the perfect consecration in sacrifice that another offspring of Abraham would undergo (see note on v. 16) in order to wholly consecrate Abraham and his spiritual descendants to God and to fulfill the covenant promises.

22:3 *early in the morning.* Prompt obedience, even under such trying circumstances, characterized Abraham's response to God (see note on 12:4).

22:4 *third day.* Three days would be necessary for the journey from Beersheba (see v. 19) to Jerusalem.

22:5 *lad.* See v. 12. The Hebrew for this word has a wide range of meaning, from an infant (see Ex 2:6) to a young man of military age (see 1 Chr 12:28). *we will . . . return to you.* Abraham, the man of faith and "the father of all who believe" (Rom 4:11), "considered that God is able to raise people even from the dead" (Heb 11:19) if that were necessary to fulfill His promise.

8 Abraham said, "God will [1]provide for
Himself the lamb for the burnt offering, my
son." So the two of them walked on together.
9 Then they came to [a]the place of which
God had told him; and Abraham built [b]the
altar there and arranged the wood, and
bound his son Isaac and [c]laid him on the
altar, on top of the wood.
10 Abraham stretched out his hand and
took the knife to slay his son.
11 But [a]the angel of the LORD called to him
from heaven and said, "Abraham, Abraham!" And he said, "Here I am."
12 He said, "Do not stretch out your hand
against the lad, and do nothing to him; for
now [a]I know that you [1]fear God, since you
have not withheld [b]your son, your only son,
from Me."
13 Then Abraham raised his eyes and
looked, and behold, behind *him* a ram caught
in the thicket by his horns; and Abraham
went and took the ram and offered him up
for a burnt offering in the place of his son.
14 Abraham called the name of that place
[1]The LORD Will Provide, as it is said to this
day, "In the mount of the LORD [a]it will [2]be
provided."
15 Then the angel of the LORD called to
Abraham a second time from heaven,
16 and said, "[a]By Myself I have sworn,
declares the LORD, because you have done
this thing and have not withheld your son,
your only son,
17 indeed I will greatly bless you, and I
will greatly [a]multiply your [1]seed as the stars
of the heavens and as [b]the sand which is on
the seashore; and [c]your [1]seed shall possess
the gate of [2]their enemies.
18 "[a]In your [1]seed all the nations of the
earth shall [2]be blessed, because you have
[b]obeyed My voice."
19 [a]So Abraham returned to his young
men, and they arose and went together to
Beersheba; and Abraham lived at Beersheba.
20 Now it came about after these things,
that it was told Abraham, saying, "Behold,
[a]Milcah [1]also has borne children to your
brother Nahor:
21 Uz his firstborn and Buz his brother
and Kemuel the father of Aram
22 and Chesed and Hazo and Pildash and
Jidlaph and Bethuel."
23 Bethuel [1]became the father of [a]Rebek-
ah; these eight Milcah bore to Nahor, Abraham's brother.
24 His concubine, whose name was Reu-
mah, [1]also bore Tebah and Gaham and
Tahash and Maacah.

Death and Burial of Sarah

23 Now [1]Sarah lived one hundred and
twenty-seven years; *these were* the
years of the life of Sarah.
2 Sarah died in [a]Kiriath-arba (that is,
Hebron) in the land of Canaan; and Abraham [1]went in to mourn for Sarah and to
weep for her.
3 Then Abraham rose from before his
dead, and spoke to the [a]sons of Heth, saying,
4 "I am [a]a stranger and a sojourner among
you; [b]give me [1]a [c]burial site among you that
I may bury my dead out of my sight."
5 The sons of Heth answered Abraham,
saying to him,
6 "Hear us, my lord, you are a [1a]mighty
prince among us; bury your dead in the
choicest of our graves; none of us will refuse
you his grave for burying your dead."

8 [1]Lit *see*
9 [a]Gen 22:2 [b]Gen 12:7, 8; 13:18 [c]Heb 11:17-19; James 2:21
11 [a]Gen 16:7-11; 21:17, 18
12 [1]Or *reverence;* lit *are a fearer of God* [a]James 2:21, 22 [b]Gen 22:2, 16
14 [1]Heb *YHWH-jireh* [2]Lit *be seen* [a]Gen 22:8
16 [a]Ps 105:9; Luke 1:73; Heb 6:13, 14
17 [1]Or *descendants* [2]Lit *his* [a]Gen 15:5; 26:4; Jer 33:22; Heb 11:12 [b]Gen 32:12 [c]Gen 24:60
18 [1]Or *descendants* [2]Or *bless themselves* [a]Gen 12:3; 18:18; Acts 3:25; Gal 3:8, 16 [b]Gen 18:19; 22:3, 10; 26:5
19 [a]Gen 22:5
20 [1]Lit *she also* [a]Gen 11:29
23 [1]Lit *begot* [a]Gen 24:15
24 [1]Lit *she also*
23:1 [1]Lit *the life of Sarah was*
2 [1]Or *proceeded* [a]Josh 14:15; 15:13; 21:11
3 [a]Gen 10:15; 15:20
4 [1]Lit *possession of a grave* [a]Gen 17:8; Lev 25:23; 1 Chr 29:15; Ps 39:12; 105:12; 119:19; Heb 11:9, 13 [b]Acts 7:16 [c]Gen 49:30
6 [1]Lit *prince of God* [a]Gen 14:14; 20:7

22:8 *God will provide for Himself the lamb.* The immediate fulfillment of Abraham's trusting response was the ram of v. 13, but its ultimate fulfillment is the Lamb of God (John 1:29,36).
22:9 *laid him on the altar, on top of the wood.* Isaac is here a type (prefiguration) of Christ (see note on v. 16).
22:11 *angel of the LORD.* See note on 16:7. *Abraham, Abraham!* The repetition of the name indicates urgency (see 46:2; Ex 3:4; 1 Sam 3:10; Acts 9:4). *Here I am.* See note on v. 1.
22:12 *fear God.* See note on 20:11. *you have not withheld your son, your only son, from Me .* See v. 16. Abraham's "faith was perfected" by what he did (James 2:21–22).
22:13 *in the place of.* Substitutionary sacrifice of one life for another is here mentioned for the first time. As the ram died in Isaac's place, so also Jesus gave His life as a ransom "for" (lit. "instead of") many (Mark 10:45).
22:14 *mount of the LORD.* During the Israelite monarchy the phrase referred to the temple mount in Jerusalem (see Ps 24:3; Is 2:3; 30:29; Zech 8:3).
22:16 *By Myself I have sworn.* There is no greater name in which the Lord can take an oath (see Heb 6:13). *you . . . have not withheld your son, your only son.* Abraham's devotion is paralleled by God's love to us in Christ as reflected in John 3:16 and Rom 8:32, which may allude to this verse.
22:17 *multiply your seed as the stars of the heavens.* See 13:16; 15:5 and notes. *sand which is on the seashore.* Fulfilled, at least in part, during Solomon's reign (see 1 Kin 4:20). *gate.* Taking possession of the gate of a city was tantamount to occupying the city itself (see 24:60).
22:18 *all the nations of the earth shall be blessed.* See note on 12:2–3. *because you have obeyed My voice.* See note on 17:9.
22:23–24 Abraham's brother Nahor (see 11:26) became the father of eight sons by his wife and four by his concubine (see note on 25:6). They would later become the ancestors of 12 Aramean (see v. 21) tribes, just as Abraham's grandson Jacob would become the ancestor of the 12 tribes of Israel (see 49:28).
23:2 *Kiriath-arba.* Means "the town of Arba" (Arba was the most prominent member of a tribe living in the Hebron area [see Josh 14:15]). It can also mean "the town of four," referring to the place where Anak (see Josh 15:13–14; 21:11) and his three sons lived (see Judg 1:10,20). *went.* Either from Beersheba to Hebron or into where Sarah's body was lying.
23:3 *sons of Heth.* See note on 10:15. They were apparently in control of the Hebron area at this time.
23:4 *a stranger and a sojourner.* This and similar phrases were used often by the patriarchs and their descendants in reference to themselves (see 1 Chr 29:15; Ps 39:12; see also Heb 11:13). On this earth Abraham was "dwelling in tents" (Heb 11:9), the most temporary of dwellings. But he looked forward to the more permanent home promised him, which the author of Hebrews calls "the city which has foundations, whose architect and builder is God" (Heb 11:10).
23:6 *you are a mighty prince.* Probably intended as words of flattery.

7 So Abraham rose and bowed to the people of the land, the sons of Heth.

8 And he spoke with them, saying, "If it is your [1]wish *for me* to bury my dead out of my sight, hear me, and approach [a]Ephron the son of Zohar for me,

9 that he may give me the cave of Machpelah which he owns, which is at the end of his field; for the full price let him give it to me in [1]your presence for [2]a burial site."

10 Now Ephron was sitting among the sons of Heth; and Ephron the Hittite answered Abraham in the hearing of the sons of Heth; *even* [a]of all who went in at the gate of his city, saying,

11 "No, my lord, hear me; [a]I give you the field, and I give you the cave that is in it. In the presence of the sons of my people I give it to you; bury your dead."

12 And Abraham bowed before the people of the land.

13 He spoke to Ephron in the hearing of the people of the land, saying, "If you will only please listen to me; I will give the price of the field, accept *it* from me that I may bury my dead there."

14 Then Ephron answered Abraham, saying to him,

15 "My lord, listen to me; a piece of land worth four hundred [a]shekels of silver, what is that between me and you? So bury your dead."

16 Abraham listened to Ephron; and Abraham [a]weighed out for Ephron the silver which he had named in the [1]hearing of the sons of Heth, four hundred shekels of silver, [2]commercial standard.

17 So [a]Ephron's field, which was in Machpelah, which faced Mamre, the field and cave which was in it, and all the trees which were in the field, that were [1]within all the confines of its border, [2]were deeded over

8 [1]Lit *soul* [a]Gen 25:9
9 [1]Lit *the midst of you* [2]Lit *possession of a burial place*
10 [a]Gen 23:18; 34:20, 24; Ruth 4:1, 11
11 [a]2 Sam 24:21-24
15 [a]Ex 30:13; Ezek 45:12
16 [1]Lit *ears* [2]Lit *current according to the merchant* [a]2 Sam 14:26; Jer 32:9, 10; Zech 11:12
17 [1]Lit *in all its border around* [2]Or *were ratified* [a]Gen 25:9; 49:29, 30; 50:13
18 [a]Gen 23:10
20 [1]Or *were ratified* [2]Lit *possession of a burial place* [a]Jer 32:10-14
24:1 [a]Gen 18:11 [b]Gen 12:2; 13:2; 24:35; Gal 3:9
2 [a]Gen 39:4-6 [b]Gen 24:9; 47:29
3 [a]Gen 14:19, 22 [b]Deut 7:3; 2 Cor 6:14-17 [c]Gen 10:15-19; 26:34, 35; 28:1, 8
4 [a]Gen 12:1; Heb 11:15
6 [a]Gen 24:8
7 [1]Lit *seed* [a]Gen 24:3 [b]Gen 12:7; 13:15; 15:18; Ex 32:13 [c]Gen 16:7; 21:17; 22:11; Ex 23:20, 23

18 to Abraham for a possession [a]in the presence of the sons of Heth, before all who went in at the gate of his city.

19 After this, Abraham buried Sarah his wife in the cave of the field at Machpelah facing Mamre (that is, Hebron) in the land of Canaan.

20 So the field and the cave that is in it, [1]were [a]deeded over to Abraham for [2]a burial site by the sons of Heth.

A Bride for Isaac

24 Now [a]Abraham was old, advanced in age; and the LORD had [b]blessed Abraham in every way.

2 Abraham said to his servant, the oldest of his household, who had [a]charge of all that he owned, "[b]Please place your hand under my thigh,

3 and I will make you swear by the LORD, [a]the God of heaven and the God of earth, that you [b]shall not take a wife for my son from the daughters of [c]the Canaanites, among whom I live,

4 but you will go to [a]my country and to my relatives, and take a wife for my son Isaac."

5 The servant said to him, "Suppose the woman is not willing to follow me to this land; should I take your son back to the land from where you came?"

6 Then Abraham said to him, "[a]Beware that you do not take my son back there!

7 "[a]The LORD, the God of heaven, who took me from my father's house and from the land of my birth, and who spoke to me and who swore to me, saying, '[b]To your [1]descendants I will give this land,' He will send [c]His angel before you, and you will take a wife for my son from there.

8 "But if the woman is not willing to fol-

23:9 *cave of Machpelah.* Though inaccessible today, the tombs of several patriarchs and their wives—Abraham and Sarah, Isaac and Rebekah, Jacob and Leah (see v. 19; 25:8–10; 49:30–31; 50:12–13)—are, according to tradition, located in a large cave deep beneath the Mosque of Abraham, a Muslim shrine in Hebron. *end of his field.* Because buying the entire field would have made Abraham responsible for certain additional financial and social obligations, he wanted to buy only a small part of it. Hittite laws stipulated that when a landowner sold only part of his property to someone else, the original and principal landowner had to continue paying all dues on the land. But if the landowner disposed of an entire tract, the new owner had to pay the dues.

23:10 *in the hearing of the sons of Heth . . . who went in at the gate.* The main gateway of a city was usually the place where legal matters were transacted and attested (see v. 18; see also note on 19:1).

23:11 *my lord.* Perhaps intended to flatter Abraham (see v. 15). *give.* Or "sell."

23:15 *four hundred shekels of silver, what is that between me and you?* See note on 20:16. Despite Ephron's pretense of generosity, 400 shekels of silver was an exorbitant price for a field (see, e.g., Jer 32:9). Ephron was taking advantage of Abraham during a time of grief and bereavement. He knew that Abraham had to deal quickly in order to have a place to bury Sarah, so he insisted that Abraham buy the entire lot and assume responsibility for the dues as well.

23:16 *commercial standard.* Subject to more variation and therefore greater dishonesty than the later royal standard (see 2 Sam 14:26), which was carefully regulated and more precise.

23:17 *the field and cave which was in it, and all the trees.* In order to be free of all obligations relating to the field in which the cave of Machpelah was located, Ephron had held out for the sale of the entire field and its contents (see note on v. 9).

23:19 *buried Sarah his wife . . . in the land of Canaan.* In that culture, people had a strong desire to be buried "with their fathers" (see note on 25:8) in their native land. By purchasing a burial place in Canaan, Abraham indicated his unswerving commitment to the Lord's promise. Canaan was his new homeland.

24:2 *his servant, the oldest in his household.* Probably Eliezer of Damascus (see note on 15:2). *place your hand under my thigh.* Near the organ of procreation, probably because this oath was related to the continuation of Abraham's line through Isaac (see 47:29).

24:3 *the LORD, the God of heaven and the God of earth.* See v. 7. For a similar majestic title used by Abraham in an oath see 14:22.

24:4 *my country.* Mesopotamia (see note on v. 10). *take a wife for my son.* See note on 21:21.

24:7 *To your descendants I will give this land.* Repeats the promise of 12:7. *His angel.* See note on 16:7.

low you, then you will [a]be free from this my oath; [b]only do not take my son back there."

9 So the servant [a]placed his hand under the thigh of Abraham his master, and swore to him concerning this matter.

10 Then the servant took ten camels from the camels of his master, and set out with a variety of [a]good things of his master's in his hand; and he arose and went to [1]Mesopotamia, to [b]the city of Nahor.

11 He made the camels kneel down outside the city by [a]the well of water at evening time, [b]the time when women go out to draw water.

12 He said, "[a]O LORD, the God of my master Abraham, please [1][b]grant me success today, and show lovingkindness to my master Abraham.

13 "Behold, [a]I am standing by the [1]spring, and the daughters of the men of the city are coming out to draw water;

14 now may it be that the girl to whom I say, 'Please let down your jar so that I may drink,' and [1]who answers, 'Drink, and I will water your camels also'—*may* she *be the one* whom You have appointed for Your servant Isaac; and by this I will know that You have shown lovingkindness to my master."

Rebekah Is Chosen

15 [a]Before he had finished speaking, behold, [b]Rebekah who was born to Bethuel the son of [c]Milcah, the wife of Abraham's brother Nahor, came out with her jar on her shoulder.

16 The girl was [a]very beautiful, a virgin, and no man had [1]had relations with her; and she went down to the spring and filled her jar and came up.

17 Then the servant ran to meet her, and said, "[a]Please let me drink a little water from your jar."

18 [a]She said, "Drink, my lord"; and she quickly lowered her jar to her hand, and gave him a drink.

19 Now when she had finished giving him a drink, [a]she said, "I will draw also for your camels until they have finished drinking."

20 So she quickly emptied her jar into the trough, and ran back to the well to draw, and she drew for all his camels.

8 [a]Josh 2:17-20 [b]Gen 24:6
9 [a]Gen 24:2
10 [1]Heb *Aram-naharaim, Aram of the two rivers* [a]Gen 24:22, 53 [b]Gen 11:31, 32
11 [a]Gen 24:42 [b]Ex 2:16; 1 Sam 9:11
12 [1]Lit *cause to occur for me* [a]Gen 24:27, 42, 48; 26:24; Ex 3:6, 15 [b]Gen 27:20
13 [1]Lit *fountain of water* [a]Gen 24:43
14 [1]Lit *she will say*
15 [a]Gen 24:45 [b]Gen 22:20, 23 [c]Gen 11:29
16 [1]Lit *known* [a]Gen 12:11; 26:7; 29:17
17 [a]John 4:7
18 [a]Gen 24:14, 46
19 [a]Gen 24:14
21 [1]Lit *keeping silent* [a]Gen 24:12-14, 27, 52
22 [1]Lit *hands* [a]Gen 24:47; Ex 32:2, 3
24 [a]Gen 24:15
26 [a]Gen 24:48, 52; Ex 4:31
27 [a]Gen 24:12, 42, 48; Ex 18:10; Ruth 4:14; 1 Sam 25:32; 2 Sam 18:28; Luke 1:68 [b]Gen 32:10; Ps 98:3 [c]Gen 24:21, 48
28 [a]Gen 29:12
29 [a]Gen 29:5, 13
30 [1]Lit *hands* [2]Lit *Thus the man*
31 [a]Gen 29:13 [b]Gen 26:29; Ruth 3:10; Ps 115:15 [c]Gen 18:3-5; 19:2, 3
32 [1]Lit *he* [a]Gen 43:24; Judg 19:21
34 [a]Gen 24:2
35 [1]Lit *great* [a]Gen 24:1 [b]Gen 13:2

21 [a]Meanwhile, the man was gazing at her [1]in silence, to know whether the LORD had made his journey successful or not.

22 When the camels had finished drinking, the man took a [a]gold ring weighing a half-shekel and two bracelets for her [1]wrists weighing ten shekels in gold,

23 and said, "Whose daughter are you? Please tell me, is there room for us to lodge in your father's house?"

24 She said to him, "[a]I am the daughter of Bethuel, the son of Milcah, whom she bore to Nahor."

25 Again she said to him, "We have plenty of both straw and feed, and room to lodge in."

26 Then the man [a]bowed low and worshiped the LORD.

27 He said, "[a]Blessed be the LORD, the God of my master Abraham, who has not forsaken [b]His lovingkindness and His truth toward my master; as for me, [c]the LORD has guided me in the way to the house of my master's brothers."

28 Then [a]the girl ran and told her mother's household about these things.

29 Now Rebekah had a brother whose name was [a]Laban; and Laban ran outside to the man at the spring.

30 When he saw the ring and the bracelets on his sister's [1]wrists, and when he heard the words of Rebekah his sister, saying, "[2]This is what the man said to me," he went to the man; and behold, he was standing by the camels at the spring.

31 And he said, "[a]Come in, [b]blessed of the LORD! Why do you stand outside since [c]I have prepared the house, and a place for the camels?"

32 So the man entered the house. Then [1][a]Laban unloaded the camels, and he gave straw and feed to the camels, and water to wash his feet and the feet of the men who were with him.

33 But when *food* was set before him to eat, he said, "I will not eat until I have told my business." And he said, "Speak on."

34 So he said, "I am [a]Abraham's servant.

35 "The LORD has greatly [a]blessed my master, so that he has become [1]rich; and He has given him [b]flocks and herds, and silver and

---

24:10 *camels.* See note on 12:16. *Mesopotamia.* Hebrew *Aram-naharaim,* meaning "Aram of the two rivers"—the Euphrates and the Tigris. Aram (see note on 10:22) Naharaim was the northern part of the area called later by the Greeks "Mesopotamia," meaning "between the rivers." *city of Nahor.* Perhaps named after Abraham's brother (see v. 15; 11:26). It is mentioned in clay tablets excavated by the French beginning in 1933 at the ancient city of Mari on the Euphrates (see chart, p. xix). Nahor was located in the Haran (see note on 11:31) district and was ruled by an Amorite prince in the 18th century B.C.

24:11 *at evening time, the time the women go out to draw water.* The coolest time of day.

24:14 *by this I will know.* Like his master Abraham, the servant asked God for a sign to validate his errand (see note on 15:8). *lovingkindness.* See v. 27; probably a reference to God's covenant with Abraham, which had promised numerous descendants through Isaac (see 17:19; 21:12).

24:15 *Before he had finished speaking.* God had already begun to answer. *Rebekah . . . was born to Bethuel the son of . . . the wife of Abraham's brother.* Isaac would thus be marrying his father's grandniece (see v. 48).

24:22 *half-shekel.* See note on 20:16; see also Ex 38:26.

24:32–33 See note on 18:2.

24:34–49 The servant explained his mission to Rebekah's family. His speech, which summarizes the narrative of the earlier part of the chapter, is an excellent example of the ancient storyteller's art, which was designed to fix the details of a story in the hearer's memory.

gold, and servants and maids, and camels
and donkeys.
36 "Now [a]Sarah my master's wife bore a
son to my master [1]in her old age, and [b]he
has given him all that he has.
37 "[a]My master made me swear, saying,
'You shall not take a wife for my son from
the daughters of the Canaanites, in whose
land I [1]live;
38 but you shall go to my father's house
and to my relatives, and take a wife for my
son.'
39 "[a]I said to my master, 'Suppose the
woman does not follow me.'
40 "He said to me, '[a]The LORD, before
whom I have [b]walked, will send [c]His angel
with you to make your journey successful,
and you will take a wife for my son from my
relatives and from my father's house;
41 [a]then you will be free from my oath,
when you come to my relatives; and if they
do not give her to you, you will be free from
my oath.'
42 "So [a]I came today to the spring, and
said, 'O LORD, the God of my master Abraham, if now You will make my journey on
which I go [b]successful;
43 behold, [a]I am standing by the [1]spring,
and may it be that the maiden who comes
out to draw, and to whom I say, "[b]Please let
me drink a little water from your jar";
44 and she will say to me, "You drink, and
I will draw for your camels also"; let her be
the woman whom the LORD has appointed
for my master's son.'
45 "Before I had finished [a]speaking in my
heart, behold, [b]Rebekah came out with her
jar on her shoulder, and went down to the
spring and drew, and [c]I said to her, 'Please
let me drink.'
46 "She quickly lowered her jar from her
shoulder, and said, '[a]Drink, and I will water
your camels also'; so I drank, and she
watered the camels also.
47 "[a]Then I asked her, and said, 'Whose
daughter are you?' And she said, 'The
daughter of Bethuel, Nahor's son, whom
Milcah bore to him'; and I put the [b]ring on
her nose, and the bracelets on her [1]wrists.
48 "And I [a]bowed low and worshiped the
LORD, and blessed the LORD, the God of my
master Abraham, [b]who had guided me in the
right way to take the daughter of my master's [1]kinsman for his son.
49 "So now if you are going to [1a]deal kindly and truly with my master, tell me; and if
not, let me know, that I may turn to the right
hand or the left."
50 Then Laban and Bethuel replied, "[a]The
matter comes from the LORD; [b]*so* we cannot
speak to you bad or good.
51 "Here is Rebekah before you, take *her*
and go, and let her be the wife of your master's son, as the LORD has spoken."
52 When Abraham's servant heard their
words, he [a]bowed himself to the ground
[1]before the LORD.
53 The servant brought out [a]articles of silver and articles of gold, and garments, and
gave them to Rebekah; he also gave precious
things to her brother and to her mother.
54 Then he and the men who were with
him ate and drank and spent the night.
When they arose in the morning, he said,
"[a]Send me away to my master."
55 But her brother and her mother said,
"[a]Let the girl stay with us *a few* days, say
ten; afterward she may go."
56 He said to them, "Do not delay me,
since [a]the LORD has prospered my way. Send
me away that I may go to my master."
57 And they said, "We will call the girl
and [1]consult her wishes."
58 Then they called Rebekah and said to
her, "Will you go with this man?" And she
said, "I will go."
59 Thus they sent away their sister Rebekah and [a]her nurse with Abraham's servant
and his men.
60 They blessed Rebekah and said to her,
"May you, our sister,
[a]Become thousands of ten thousands,
And may [b]your [1]descendants possess
The gate of those who hate them."
61 Then Rebekah arose with her maids,
and they mounted the camels and followed
the man. So the servant took Rebekah and
departed.

Isaac Marries Rebekah

62 Now Isaac had come from going to
[a]Beer-lahai-roi; for he [1]was living in [b]the
[2]Negev.
63 Isaac went out [a]to [1]meditate in the
field toward evening; and [b]he lifted up his
eyes and looked, and behold, camels were
coming.
64 Rebekah lifted up her eyes, and when
she saw Isaac she dismounted from the
camel.
65 She said to the servant, "Who is that
man walking in the field to meet us?" And
the servant said, "He is my master." Then
she took her [1]veil and covered herself.
66 The servant told Isaac all the things
that he had done.
67 Then Isaac brought her into his mother
Sarah's tent, and [a]he took Rebekah, and she

36 [1]Lit *after she was old* [a]Gen 21:1-7 [b]Gen 25:5
37 [1]Lit *dwell* [a]Gen 24:2-4
39 [a]Gen 24:5
40 [a]Gen 24:7 [b]Gen 5:22, 24; 17:1 [c]Ex 23:20
41 [a]Gen 24:8
42 [a]Gen 24:11, 12 [b]Neh 1:11
43 [1]Lit *fountain of water* [a]Gen 24:13 [b]Gen 24:14
45 [a]1 Sam 1:13 [b]Gen 24:15 [c]Gen 24:17
46 [a]Gen 24:18, 19
47 [1]Lit *hands* [a]Gen 24:23, 24 [b]Ezek 16:11, 12
48 [1]Lit *brother* [a]Gen 24:26, 52 [b]Gen 24:27; Ps 32:8; 48:14; Is 48:17
49 [1]Lit *show lovingkindness and truth* [a]Gen 47:29; Josh 2:14
50 [a]Ps 118:23; Mark 12:11
50 [b]Gen 31:24, 29
52 [1]Lit *to* [a]Gen 24:26, 48
53 [a]Gen 24:10, 22; Ex 3:22; 11:2; 12:35
54 [a]Gen 24:56, 59; 30:25
55 [a]Judg 19:4
56 [a]Gen 24:40
57 [1]Lit *ask her mouth*
59 [a]Gen 35:8
60 [1]Lit *seed* [a]Gen 17:16 [b]Gen 22:17
62 [1]Lit *was dwelling* [2]I.e. South country [a]Gen 16:14; 25:11 [b]Gen 20:1
63 [1]Or *stroll;* meaning uncertain [a]Josh 1:8; Ps 1:2; 77:12; 119:15, 27, 48; 143:5; 145:5 [b]Gen 18:2
65 [1]Or *shawl*
67 [a]Gen 25:20

24:40 *before whom I have walked.* See notes on 5:22; 6:8–9; 17:1.
24:53 The rich gifts bestowed on Rebekah and her family indicated the wealth of the household into which she was being asked to marry—far from her loved ones and homeland.
24:60 See 22:17 and note.
24:62 *Beer-lahai-roi.* See note on 16:14.
24:65 *she took her veil and covered herself.* Apparently a sign that she was unmarried (cf. 38:14,19).
24:67 *tent.* Often used as a bridal chamber (see Ps 19:4–5).

became his wife, and [b]he loved her; thus
Isaac was comforted after [c]his mother's
death.

Abraham's Death

25 Now Abraham took another wife,
[1]whose name was Keturah.
2 [a]She bore to him Zimran and Jokshan
and Medan and Midian and Ishbak and
Shuah.
3 Jokshan [1]became the father of Sheba
and Dedan. And the sons of Dedan were
Asshurim and Letushim and Leummim.
4 The sons of Midian *were* Ephah and
Epher and Hanoch and Abida and Eldaah.
All these *were* the sons of Keturah.
5 [a]Now Abraham gave all that he had to
Isaac;
6 but to the sons of [1]his concubines,
Abraham gave gifts while he was still living,
and [a]sent them away from his son Isaac eastward, to the land of the east.
7 These are [1]all the years of Abraham's
life that he lived, [a]one hundred and seventy-
five years.
8 Abraham breathed his last and died [a]in
a [1]ripe old age, an old man and satisfied *with
life;* and he was [b]gathered to his people.
9 Then his sons Isaac and Ishmael buried
him in [a]the cave of Machpelah, in the field of
Ephron the son of Zohar the Hittite, facing
Mamre,
10 [a]the field which Abraham purchased
from the sons of Heth; there Abraham was
buried with Sarah his wife.
11 It came about after the death of Abraham, that [a]God blessed his son Isaac; and
Isaac [1]lived by [b]Beer-lahai-roi.

Descendants of Ishmael

12 Now these are *the records of* the generations of [a]Ishmael, Abraham's son, whom
Hagar the Egyptian, Sarah's maid, bore to
Abraham;
13 and these are the names of [a]the sons of
Ishmael, by their names, [1]in the order of
their birth: Nebaioth, the firstborn of Ishmael, and Kedar and Adbeel and Mibsam
14 and Mishma and Dumah and Massa,
15 Hadad and Tema, Jetur, Naphish and
Kedemah.
16 These are the sons of Ishmael and
these are their names, by their villages, and
by their camps; [a]twelve princes according to
their [1]tribes.
17 These are the years of the life of Ishmael, [a]one hundred and thirty-seven years;
and he breathed his last and died, and was
[b]gathered to his people.
18 They [1]settled from [a]Havilah to [b]Shur
which is [2]east of Egypt [3]as one goes toward
Assyria; [c]he [4]settled in defiance of all his
[5]relatives.

Isaac's Sons

19 Now these are *the records of* [a]the generations of Isaac, Abraham's son: Abraham
[1]became the father of Isaac;
20 and Isaac was forty years old when he
took [a]Rebekah, the [b]daughter of Bethuel the
[1]Aramean of Paddan-aram, the [c]sister of
Laban the [1]Aramean, to be his wife.
21 Isaac prayed to the LORD on behalf of
his wife, because she was barren; and [a]the
LORD [1]answered him and Rebekah his wife
[b]conceived.
22 But the children struggled together
within her; and she said, "If it is so, why
then am I *this way?*" So she went to [a]inquire
of the LORD.
23 The LORD said to her,
"[a]Two nations are in your womb;
[b]And two peoples will be separated
from your body;
And one people shall be stronger than
the other;
And [c]the older shall serve the
younger."

67 [b]Gen 29:18 [c]Gen 23:1, 2
25:1 [1]Lit *and her name*
2 [a]1 Chr 1:32, 33
3 [1]Lit *begot*
5 [a]Gen 24:35, 36
6 [1]Lit *concubines which belonged to Abraham* [a]Gen 21:14
7 [1]Lit *the days of* [a]Gen 12:4
8 [1]Lit *good* [a]Gen 15:15; 47:8, 9 [b]Gen 25:17; 35:29; 49:29, 33
9 [a]Gen 23:17, 18; 49:29, 30; 50:13
10 [a]Gen 23:3-16
11 [1]Lit *dwelt* [a]Gen 12:2, 3; 22:17; 26:3 [b]Gen 16:14; 24:62
12 [a]Gen 16:15
13 [1]Lit *in regard to their generations* [a]1 Chr 1:29-31
16 [1]Or *peoples* [a]Gen 17:20
17 [a]Gen 16:16 [b]Gen 25:8; 49:33
18 [1]Lit *dwelt* [2]Lit *before* [3]Lit *as you go* [4]Lit *fell over against* [5]Lit *brothers* [a]1 Sam 15:7 [b]Gen 20:1 [c]Gen 16:12
19 [1]Lit *begot* [a]Matt 1:2
20 [1]I.e. Syrian [a]Gen 24:15, 29, 67 [b]Gen 22:23 [c]Gen 24:29
21 [1]Lit *was entreated of him* [a]1 Sam 1:17; 1 Chr 5:20; 2 Chr 33:13; Ezra 8:23; Ps 127:3 [b]Rom 9:10
22 [a]1 Sam 9:9; 10:22
23 [a]Gen 17:4-6, 16; Num 20:14; Deut 2:4, 8 [b]Gen 27:29 [c]Gen 27:40; Mal 1:2, 3; Rom 9:12

25:1 *took another wife.* Or "married another woman"—his "concubine" (1 Chr 1:32). *took.* Or "had taken", since Abraham would have been 140 years old at this time if the order is chronological.
25:5 *gave all that he had to Isaac.* The law of primogeniture provided that at least a double share of the father's property be given to the firstborn son when the father died (Deut 21:15–17). Parallels to this practice come from Nuzi, from Larsa in the Old Babylonian period and from Assyria in the Middle Assyrian period. Isaac was Abraham's firstborn son according to law.
25:6 *gifts.* These doubtless represented the inheritance left to Abraham's other sons. *concubines.* Secondary wives; polygamy was practiced even by godly men in ancient times, though it was not the original divine intention (see note on 4:19).
25:7 *one hundred and seventy-five years.* Abraham lived for a full century after "he departed from Haran" (12:4).
25:8 *died in a ripe old age.* As God had promised (see 15:15). *an old man and satisfied with life.* A phrase used also of the patriarch Job (see Job 42:17). *was gathered to his people.* Joined his ancestors and/or deceased relatives in death (see 2 Kin 22:20; 2 Chr 34:28).
25:9 *Isaac and Ishmael.* Isaac, legally the firstborn (see note on v. 5), is listed first.
25:11 *Beer-lahai-roi.* See note on 16:14.
25:12 *generations.* See note on 2:4.
25:13 *names of the sons of Ishmael.* Many are Arab names, giving credence to the Arab tradition that Ishmael is their ancestor.
25:16 *twelve princes.* Twelve major tribes descended from Abraham's son Ishmael (as predicted in 17:20)—as was also true of Abraham's brother Nahor (see note on 22:23–24).
25:18 *in defiance of.* See note on 16:12; or possibly "to the east of" (see also 25:6).
25:19 *generations.* See note on 2:4.
25:20 *Paddan-aram.* Means "plain of Aram," another name for Aram-naharaim (Northwest Mesopotamia; see note on 24:10).
25:22 *struggled together.* The struggle between Jacob and Esau began in the womb (see also v. 26). *went.* Perhaps to a nearby place of worship.
25:23 *the older shall serve the younger.* The ancient law of primogeniture (see note on v. 5) provided that, under ordinary circumstances, the younger of two sons would be subservient to the older. God's election of the younger son highlights the fact that God's people are the product not of natural or worldly development but of His sovereign intervention in the affairs of men (see

24 When her days to be delivered were fulfilled, behold, there were twins in her womb.
25 Now the first came forth red, [a]all over
like a hairy garment; and they named him
Esau.
26 Afterward his brother came forth with
[a]his hand holding on to Esau's heel, so [b]his
name was called [1]Jacob; and Isaac was [c]six-
ty years old when she gave birth to them.
27 When the boys grew up, Esau became
a skillful hunter, a man of the field, but
Jacob was a [1]peaceful man, [2a]living in tents.
28 Now Isaac loved Esau, because [1]he had
[a]a taste for game, [b]but Rebekah loved Jacob.
29 When Jacob had cooked [a]stew, Esau
came in from the field and he was [1]famished;
30 and Esau said to Jacob, "Please let me
have a swallow of [1]that red stuff there, for I
am [2]famished." Therefore his name was
called [3]Edom.
31 But Jacob said, "[1]First sell me your
[a]birthright."
32 Esau said, "Behold, I am about to die;
so of what *use* then is the birthright to me?"
33 And Jacob said, "[1]First swear to me";
so he swore to him, and [a]sold his birthright
to Jacob.
34 Then Jacob gave Esau bread and lentil
stew; and he ate and drank, and rose and
went on his way. Thus Esau despised his
birthright.

Isaac Settles in Gerar

26 Now there was [a]a famine in the land,
besides the previous famine that had
occurred in the days of Abraham. So Isaac

25 [a]Gen 27:11
26 [1]I.e. one who takes by the heel or supplants [a]Hos 12:3 [b]Gen 27:36 [c]Gen 25:20
27 [1]Lit *complete* [2]Lit *dwelling* [a]Heb 11:9
28 [1]Lit *game was in his mouth* [a]Gen 27:19 [b]Gen 27:6-10
29 [1]Lit *weary* [a]2 Kin 4:38
30 [1]Lit *the red, this red* [2]Lit *weary* [3]I.e. red
31 [1]Lit *Today* [a]Deut 21:16, 17; 1 Chr 5:1, 2
33 [1]Lit *Today* [a]Heb 12:16
26:1 [a]Gen 12:10 [b]Gen 20:1, 2
2 [1]Lit *dwell* [a]Gen 12:7; 17:1; 18:1 [b]Gen 12:1
3 [1]Lit *seed* [a]Gen 26:24; 28:15; 31:3 [b]Gen 12:2 [c]Gen 12:7; 13:15; 15:18 [d]Gen 22:16-18; Ps 105:9
4 [1]Lit *seed* [2]Or *bless themselves* [a]Gen 15:5; 22:17; Ex 32:13 [b]Gen 22:18; Gal 3:8
5 [1]Lit *hearkened to My voice* [a]Gen 22:16
6 [1]Lit *dwelt*
7 [1]Lit *lest... place* [a]Gen 12:13; 20:2, 12 [b]Prov 29:25 [c]Gen 12:11; 24:16; 29:17
10 [a]Gen 20:9

went to Gerar, to [b]Abimelech king of the Philistines.
2 The LORD [a]appeared to him and said,
"Do not go down to Egypt; [1b]stay in the land
of which I shall tell you.
3 "Sojourn in this land and [a]I will be with
you and [b]bless you, for [c]to you and to your
[1]descendants I will give all these lands, and
I will establish [d]the oath which I swore to
your father Abraham.
4 "[a]I will multiply your [1]descendants as
the stars of heaven, and will give your
[1]descendants all these lands; and [b]by your
[1]descendants all the nations of the earth
[2]shall be blessed;
5 because Abraham [1a]obeyed Me and
kept My charge, My commandments, My
statutes and My laws."
6 So Isaac [1]lived in Gerar.
7 When the men of the place asked about
his wife, he said, "[a]She is my sister," for he
was [b]afraid to say, "my wife," *thinking,*
"[1]the men of the place might kill me on
account of Rebekah, for she is [c]beautiful."
8 It came about, when he had been there
a long time, that Abimelech king of the Philistines looked out through a window, and
saw, and behold, Isaac was caressing his
wife Rebekah.
9 Then Abimelech called Isaac and said,
"Behold, certainly she is your wife! How
then did you say, 'She is my sister'?" And
Isaac said to him, "Because I said, 'I might
die on account of her.' "
10 [a]Abimelech said, "What is this you
have done to us? One of the people might

note on 11:30). Part of this verse is quoted in Rom 9:10–12 as an example of God's sovereign right to do "whatever He pleases" (Ps 115:3)—not in an arbitrary way (see Rom 9:14), but according to His own perfect will.

25:24–26 For another unusual birth of twin boys see 38:27–30.

25:25 *red.* A pun on Edom, one of Esau's other names (Esau may mean "hairy").

25:26 *his hand holding on to Esau's heel.* Hostility between the Israelites (Jacob's descendants) and Edomites (Esau's descendants) became the rule rather than the exception (see, e.g., Num 20:14–21; Obad 9–10). *Jacob.* The name became proverbial for the unsavory quality of deceptiveness (see Jer 9:4).

25:31 *sell me your birthright.* In ancient times the birthright included the inheritance rights of the firstborn (see Heb 12:16; see also note on v. 5). Jacob was ever the schemer, seeking by any means to gain advantage over others. But it was by God's appointment and care, not Jacob's wits, that he came into the blessing.

25:33 *First swear to me.* A verbal oath was all that was required to make the transaction legal.

25:34 *lentil.* A small pea-like annual plant, the pods of which turn reddish-brown when boiled. It grows well even in bad soil and has provided an important source of nourishment in the Near East since ancient times (see 2 Sam 17:28; 23:11; Ezek 4:9). *Esau despised his birthright.* In so doing, he proved himself to be "godless" (Heb 12:16), since at the heart of the birthright were the covenant promises that Isaac had inherited from Abraham.

26:1–33 The events of some of these verses (e.g., vv. 1–11) occurred before the birth of Esau and Jacob. Verses 1–11 are placed here to highlight the fact that the birthright and blessing Jacob struggled to obtain from his father (see 25:22,31–33; 27:5–29) involved the covenant inheritance of Abraham that Isaac had received.

26:1 *the previous famine . . . in the days of Abraham.* See 12:10. *Gerar.* See note on 20:1. *Abimelech.* Probably the son or grandson of the earlier king who bore the same name (see 20:2). *Philistines.* See note on 10:14.

26:2 *appeared.* See note on 12:7.

26:3 *I will be with you.* God's promise to be a sustainer and protector of His people is repeated often (see, e.g., v. 24; 28:15; 31:3; Josh 1:5; Is 41:10; Jer 1:8,19; Matt 28:20; Acts 18:10; see also Gen 17:7 and note). *the oath which I swore to your father Abraham.* See 22:16–18.

26:4 *descendants as the stars of heaven.* See 13:16; 15:5 and notes. *by your descendants all the nations of the earth shall be blessed.* See note on 12:2–3.

26:5 *because Abraham obeyed Me.* See note on 17:9. *charge . . . commandments . . . statutes . . . laws.* Legal language describing various aspects of the divine regulations that God's people were expected to keep (see Lev 26:14–15,46; Deut 11:1). Addressing Israel after the covenant at Sinai, the author of Genesis used language that strictly applied only to that covenant. But he emphasized to Israel that their father Abraham had been obedient to God's will in his time and that they must follow his example if they were to receive the covenant promises.

26:7 *for she is beautiful.* See 12:11,14.

26:8 *caressing.* The word in Hebrew (a form of the verb translated "laugh" in 17:17; 18:12–13,15; 21:6 and "mock" in 21:9) is yet another pun on Isaac's name.

easily have lain with your wife, and you would have brought guilt upon us."

11 So Abimelech charged all the people, saying, "He who [a]touches this man or his wife shall surely be put to death."

12 Now Isaac sowed in that land and [1]reaped in the same year a hundredfold. And [a]the LORD blessed him,

13 and the man [a]became rich, and continued to grow [1]richer until he became very [1]wealthy;

14 for [a]he had possessions of flocks [1]and herds and a great household, so that the Philistines envied him.

15 Now [a]all the wells which his father's servants had dug in the days of Abraham his father, the Philistines stopped up [1]by filling them with earth.

16 Then Abimelech said to Isaac, "Go away from us, for you are [1a]too powerful for us."

17 And Isaac departed from there and camped in the valley of Gerar, and [1]settled there.

Quarrel over the Wells

18 Then Isaac dug again the wells of water which [1]had been dug in the days of his father Abraham, for the Philistines had stopped them up after the death of Abraham; and he [2]gave them the same names which his father had [3]given them.

19 But when Isaac's servants dug in the valley and found there a well of [1]flowing water,

20 the herdsmen of Gerar [a]quarreled with the herdsmen of Isaac, saying, "The water is ours!" So he named the well [1]Esek, because they contended with him.

21 Then they dug another well, and they quarreled over it too, so he named it [1]Sitnah.

22 He moved away from there and dug another well, and they did not quarrel over it; so he named it [1]Rehoboth, for he said, "[2a]At last the LORD has made [3]room for us, and we will be [b]fruitful in the land."

23 Then he went up from there to [a]Beersheba.

24 The LORD [a]appeared to him the same night and said,

"[b]I am the God of your father Abraham;
[c]Do not fear, for I am with you.
I [d]will bless you, and multiply your
[1]descendants,
For the sake of My servant Abraham."

25 So he built an [a]altar there and called upon the name of the LORD, and pitched his tent there; and there Isaac's servants dug a well.

Covenant with Abimelech

26 Then [a]Abimelech came to him from Gerar [1]with his adviser Ahuzzath and Phicol the commander of his army.

27 Isaac said to them, "[a]Why have you come to me, since you hate me and have sent me away from you?"

28 They said, "We see plainly [a]that the LORD has been with you; so we said, 'Let there now be an oath between us, *even* between [1]you and us, and let us make a covenant with you,

29 that you will do us no harm, just as we have not touched you [1]and have done to you nothing but good and have sent you away in peace. You are now the [a]blessed of the LORD.' "

30 Then [a]he made them a feast, and they ate and drank.

31 In the morning they arose early and [1a]exchanged oaths; then Isaac sent them away and they departed from him in peace.

32 Now it came about on the same day, that Isaac's servants came in and told him about the well which they had dug, and said to him, "We have found water."

33 So he called it Shibah; therefore the name of the city is [a]Beersheba to this day.

34 When Esau was forty years old [a]he [1]married Judith the daughter of Beeri the Hittite, and Basemath the daughter of Elon the Hittite;

35 and [a]they [1]brought grief to Isaac and Rebekah.

Jacob's Deception

27 Now it came about, when Isaac was old and [a]his eyes were too dim to see, that he called his [b]older son Esau and said to him, "My son." And he said to him, "Here I am."

11 [a]Ps 105:15
12 [1]Lit *found* [a]Gen 24:1; 26:3; Job 42:12; Prov 10:22
13 [1]Lit *great* [a]Prov 10:22
14 [1]Lit *and possessions of herds* [a]Gen 24:35; 25:5
15 [1]Lit *and filled them* [a]Gen 21:25, 30
16 [1]Lit *much mightier than we* [a]Ex 1:9
17 [1]Lit *dwelt*
18 [1]Lit *they had dug* [2]Lit *called their names as the names* [3]Lit *called*
19 [1]Lit *living*
20 [1]I.e. contention [a]Gen 21:25
21 [1]I.e. enmity
22 [1]I.e. broad places [2]Lit *Truly now* [3]Or *broad* [a]Ps 4:1; Is 54:2, 3 [b]Gen 17:6; Ex 1:7
23 [a]Gen 22:19
24 [a]Gen 26:2 [b]Gen 17:7, 8; 24:12; Ex 3:6; Acts 7:32
24 [1]Lit *seed* [c]Gen 15:1 [d]Gen 22:17; 26:3, 4
25 [a]Gen 12:7, 8; 13:4, 18; Ps 116:17
26 [1]Lit *and his confidential friend* [a]Gen 21:22
27 [a]Judg 11:7
28 [1]Lit *us and you* [a]Gen 21:22, 23
29 [1]Lit *and just as we* [a]Gen 24:31; Ps 115:15
30 [a]Gen 19:3
31 [1]Lit *swore one to another* [a]Gen 21:31
33 [a]Gen 21:31
34 [1]Lit *took as wife* [a]Gen 28:8; 36:2
35 [1]Lit *were a bitterness of spirit to* [a]Gen 27:46
27:1 [a]Gen 48:10; 1 Sam 3:2 [b]Gen 25:25, 33, 34

26:16 *you are too powerful for us.* An indication that the covenant promises were being fulfilled. Already in the days of the patriarchs, the presence of God's people in the land was seen as a threat by the peoples of the world. As the world's people pursued their own godless living, God's people aroused their hostility. A similar complaint was voiced by an Egyptian pharaoh hundreds of years later (Ex 1:9).

26:20 *The water is ours!* In those arid regions, disputes over water rights and pasturelands were common (see 13:6–11; 21:25; 36:7).

26:25 *built an altar.* See note on 12:7. *called upon the name of the LORD.* See 4:26 and note.

26:26 *Phicol.* See note on 21:22.

26:30 *made them a feast.* Covenants were often concluded with a shared meal, signifying the bond of friendship (see 31:54; Ex 24:11).

26:33 *the name of the city is Beersheba.* See note on 21:31.

26:34 *When Esau was forty years old he married.* As had his father Isaac (see 25:20). Forty years was roughly equivalent to a generation in later times (see Num 32:13). *Judith . . . Basemath.* In addition to these two wives, Esau also married Mahalath, who was the sister of Nebaioth and daughter of Ishmael (28:9). The Esau genealogy of ch. 36 also mentions three wives, but they are identified as "Adah the daughter of Elon the Hittite," "Oholibamah the daughter of Anah . . . the Hivite" and "Basemath, Ishmael's daughter, the sister of Nebaioth" (36:2–3). Possibly the lists have suffered in transmission, or perhaps alternate names or nicknames are used. It may also be that Esau married more than three wives.

26:35 *They brought grief.* Isaac and Rebekah were determined not to allow Jacob to make the same mistake of marrying Hittite or Canaanite women (see 27:46–28:2).

27:1 *his eyes were too dim to see.* In ancient times, blindness and near blindness were common among elderly people (see 48:10; 1 Sam 4:15). *Here I am.* See note on 22:1.

2 [1][a]Isaac said, "Behold now, I am old *and* I do not know the day of my death.

3 "Now then, please take your gear, your quiver and your bow, and go out to the field and [a]hunt game for me;

4 and prepare a savory dish for me such as I love, and bring it to me that I may eat, so that [a]my soul may bless you before I die."

5 Rebekah was listening while Isaac spoke to his son Esau. So when Esau went to the field to hunt for game to bring *home*,

6 [a]Rebekah said to her son Jacob, "Behold, I heard your father speak to your brother Esau, saying,

7 'Bring me *some* game and prepare a savory dish for me, that I may eat, and bless you in the presence of the LORD before my death.'

8 "Now therefore, my son, [a]listen to [1]me [2]as I command you.

9 "Go now to the flock and [1]bring me two choice [2]young goats from there, that I may prepare them *as* a savory dish for your father, such as he loves.

10 "Then you shall bring *it* to your father, that he may eat, so that he may bless you before his death."

11 Jacob [1]answered his mother Rebekah, "Behold, Esau my brother is a [a]hairy man and I am a smooth man.

12 "[a]Perhaps my father will feel me, then I will be as a [1]deceiver in his sight, and I will bring upon myself a curse and not a blessing."

13 But his mother said to him, "Your curse be on me, my son; only [a]obey my voice, and go, get *them* for me."

14 So he went and got *them*, and brought *them* to his mother; and his mother made savory food such as his father loved.

15 Then Rebekah took the [1]best [a]garments of Esau her elder son, which were with her in the house, and put them on Jacob her younger son.

16 And she put the skins of the [1]young goats on his hands and on the smooth part of his neck.

17 She also gave the savory food and the bread, which she had made, [1]to her son Jacob.

18 Then he came to his father and said, "My father." And he said, "Here I am. Who are you, my son?"

19 Jacob said to his father, "I am Esau your firstborn; I have done as you told me. [a]Get up, please, sit and eat of my game, that [1][b]you may bless me."

20 Isaac said to his son, "How is it that you have *it* so quickly, my son?" And he said, "[a]Because the LORD your God caused *it* to happen to me."

21 Then Isaac said to Jacob, "Please come close, that [a]I may feel you, my son, whether you are really my son Esau or not."

22 So Jacob came close to Isaac his father, and he felt him and said, "The voice is the voice of Jacob, but the hands are the hands of Esau."

23 He did not recognize him, because his hands were [a]hairy like his brother Esau's hands; so he blessed him.

24 And he said, "Are you really my son Esau?" And he said, "I am."

25 So he said, "Bring *it* to me, and I will eat of my son's game, that [1][a]I may bless you." And he brought *it* to him, and he ate; he also brought him wine and he drank.

26 Then his father Isaac said to him, "Please come close and kiss me, my son."

27 So he came close and kissed him; and when he smelled the smell of his garments, he [a]blessed him and said,

"See, [b]the smell of my son
Is like the smell of a field [c]which the
LORD has blessed;

28 Now may [a]God give you of the dew of
heaven,
And of the [b]fatness of the earth,
And an abundance of grain and new
wine;

29 [a]May peoples serve you,
And nations bow down to you;
[b]Be master of your brothers,
[c]And may your mother's sons bow
down to you.
[d]Cursed be those who curse you,
And blessed be those who bless you."

The Stolen Blessing

30 Now it came about, as soon as Isaac had finished blessing Jacob, and Jacob had hardly gone out from the presence of Isaac

2 [1]Lit *He* [a]Gen 47:29
3 [a]Gen 25:28
4 [a]Gen 27:19, 25, 31; 48:9, 15, 16; Deut 33:1; Heb 11:20
6 [a]Gen 25:28
8 [1]Lit *my voice* [2]Lit *according to what* [a]Gen 27:13, 43
9 [1]Lit *take* [2]Lit *kids of goats*
11 [1]Lit *said to* [a]Gen 25:25
12 [1]Lit *mocker* [a]Gen 27:21, 22
13 [a]Gen 27:8
15 [1]Lit *desirable;* or *choice* [a]Gen 27:27
16 [1]Lit *kids of the goats*
17 [1]Lit *into the hand of*
19 [1]Lit *your soul* [a]Gen 27:31 [b]Gen 27:4
20 [a]Gen 24:12
21 [a]Gen 27:12
23 [a]Gen 27:16
25 [1]Lit *my soul* [a]Gen 27:4
27 [a]Heb 11:20 [b]Song 4:11 [c]Ps 65:10
28 [a]Gen 27:39; Deut 33:13, 28; Prov 3:20; Zech 8:12 [b]Num 18:12
29 [a]Gen 25:23; Is 45:14; 49:7, 23; 60:12, 14 [b]Gen 9:26, 27; 27:37 [c]Gen 37:7, 10 [d]Gen 12:3; Num 24:9

27:4 *a savory dish . . . such as I love.* Rebekah and Jacob took advantage of Isaac's love for a certain kind of food (see vv. 9,14). *my soul may bless you before I die.* Oral statements, including deathbed bequests (see 49:28–33), had legal force in ancient Near Eastern law. *bless.* See note on v. 36.

27:5 *listening.* Eavesdropping.

27:6 *Rebekah.* Throughout the Jacob story the author develops a wordplay on "birthright" (*bekorah*) and "blessing" (*berakah*), both of which Jacob seeks to obtain; and Rebekah (*ribqah*) does her best to further the cause of her favorite son. *said to her son Jacob.* The parental favoritism mentioned in 25:28 is about to bear its poisonous fruit.

27:8 *my son, listen to me as I command you.* Rebekah proves to be just as deceitful as Jacob, whose very name signifies deceit (see v. 36; 25:26 and note).

27:13 *Your curse be on me.* Cf. the similar self-imprecation in Matt 27:25.

27:20 *your God.* Consistent with Jacob's language elsewhere (31:5,42; 32:9). Not until his safe return from Haran did he speak of the Lord as his own God (cf. 28:20–22; 33:18–20).

27:24 *Are you really my son Esau?* To the very end of the charade, Isaac remained suspicious.

27:27 *kissed him.* In his attempt to obtain the covenant blessing, Jacob the father of Israel betrayed with a kiss. Jesus the great Son of Israel, who ultimately obtained the blessing for Israel, was betrayed with a kiss (Matt 26:48–49; Luke 22:48).

27:29 *Be master of your brothers.* Isaac was unwittingly blessing Jacob and thus fulfilling God's promise to Rebekah in 25:23.

his father, that Esau his brother came in from
his hunting.
31 Then he also made savory food, and
brought it to his father; and he said to his
father, "[a]Let my father arise and eat of his
son's game, that [1][b]you may bless me."
32 Isaac his father said to him, "[a]Who are
you?" And he said, "I am your son, [b]your
firstborn, Esau."
33 Then Isaac [1]trembled violently, and
said, "[a]Who was he then that hunted game
and brought *it* to me, so that I ate of all *of it*
before you came, and blessed him? [b]Yes, and
he shall be blessed."
34 When Esau heard the words of his
father, [a]he cried out with an exceedingly
great and bitter cry, and said to his father,
"Bless me, *even* me also, O my father!"
35 And he said, "[a]Your brother came deceitfully and has taken away your blessing."
36 Then he said, "[1]Is he not rightly named
[a]Jacob, for he has supplanted me these two
times? He took away my birthright, and
behold, now he has taken away my blessing." And he said, "Have you not reserved a
blessing for me?"
37 But Isaac replied to Esau, "Behold, I
have made him [a]your master, and all his [1]rel-
atives I have given to him [2]as servants; and
with grain and new wine I have sustained
him. Now as for you then, what can I do, my
son?"
38 Esau said to his father, "Do you have
only one blessing, my father? Bless me, *even*
me also, O my father." So Esau lifted his
voice and [a]wept.
39 Then [a]Isaac his father answered and
said to him,

"Behold, [1][b]away from the [2]fertility of
the earth shall be your dwelling,
And [1]away from the dew of heaven
from above.
40 "By your sword you shall live,
And your brother [a]you shall serve;
But it shall come about [b]when you
become restless,
That you will [1]break his yoke from
your neck."

31 [1]Lit *your soul* [a]Gen 27:19 [b]Gen 27:4
32 [a]Gen 27:18 [b]Gen 25:33, 34
33 [1]Lit *trembled with a very great trembling* [a]Gen 27:35 [b]Gen 25:23; 28:3, 4; Num 23:20
34 [a]Heb 12:17
35 [a]Gen 27:19
36 [1]Or *Was he then named Jacob that he has* [a]Gen 25:26, 32-34
37 [1]Lit *brothers* [2]Lit *for* [a]Gen 27:28, 29
38 [a]Heb 12:17
39 [1]Or *of* [2]Lit *fatness* [a]Heb 11:20 [b]Gen 27:28; Deut 33:13, 28
40 [1]Lit *tear off* [a]Gen 25:23; 27:29 [b]2 Kin 8:20-22

41 So Esau [a]bore a grudge against Jacob
because of the blessing with which his father
had blessed him; and Esau said [1]to himself,
"[b]The days of mourning for my father are
near; then I will kill my brother Jacob."
42 Now when the words of her elder son
Esau were reported to Rebekah, she sent and
called her younger son Jacob, and said to
him, "Behold your brother Esau is consoling
himself concerning you *by planning* to kill
you.
43 "Now therefore, my son, [a]obey my
voice, and arise, [1]flee to [b]Haran, to my brother [c]Laban!
44 "Stay with him [a]a few days, until your
brother's fury [1]subsides,
45 until your brother's anger [1]against you
subsides and he forgets [a]what you did to
him. Then I will send and get you from
there. Why should I be bereaved of you both
in one day?"
46 Rebekah said to Isaac, "I am tired of
[1]living because of [a]the daughters of Heth; [b]if
Jacob takes a wife from the daughters of
Heth, like these, from the daughters of the
land, what good will my life be to me?"

Jacob Is Sent Away

28 So Isaac called Jacob and [a]blessed him
and charged him, and said to him,
"[b]You shall not take a wife from the daughters of Canaan.
2 "Arise, go to Paddan-aram, to the house
of [a]Bethuel your mother's father; and from
there take to yourself a wife from the daughters of Laban your mother's brother.
3 "May [1][a]God Almighty [b]bless you and
[c]make you fruitful and [d]multiply you, that
you may become a [e]company of peoples.
4 "May He also give you the [a]blessing of
Abraham, to you and to your [1]descendants
with you, that you may [b]possess the land of
your [c]sojournings, which God gave to Abraham."
5 Then [a]Isaac sent Jacob away, and he
went to Paddan-aram to Laban, son of
Bethuel the Aramean, the brother of Rebekah, the mother of Jacob and Esau.

41 [1]Lit *in his heart* [a]Gen 32:3-11; 37:4, 8 [b]Gen 50:2-4, 10
43 [1]Lit *flee for yourself* [a]Gen 27:8, 13 [b]Gen 11:31 [c]Gen 24:29
44 [1]Lit *turns away* [a]Gen 31:41
45 [1]Lit *turns away from you* [a]Gen 27:12, 19, 35
46 [1]Lit *my life* [a]Gen 26:34, 35; 28:8 [b]Gen 24:3
28:1 [a]Gen 27:33 [b]Gen 24:3, 4
2 [a]Gen 25:20
3 [1]Heb *El Shaddai* [a]Gen 17:1; 35:11; 48:3 [b]Gen 22:17 [c]Gen 17:6, 20 [d]Gen 17:2; 26:4, 24 [e]Gen 35:11; 48:4
4 [1]Lit *seed* [a]Gen 12:2; 22:17 [b]Gen 15:7, 8; 17:8 [c]1 Chr 29:15; Ps 39:12
5 [a]Gen 27:43

27:33 *Yes, and he shall be blessed.* The ancient world believed that blessings and curses had a kind of magical power to accomplish what they pronounced. But Isaac, as heir and steward of God's covenant blessing, acknowledged that he had solemnly transmitted that heritage to Jacob by way of a legally binding bequest (see note on v. 4).

27:34 *exceedingly great and bitter cry.* Esau's tears provided "no place for repentance" (Heb 12:17).

27:36 *Is he not rightly named Jacob . . . ?* Jacob means "he grasps the heel" (figuratively, "he deceives"); see 25:26 and note. *He took away my birthright . . . now he has taken away my blessing.* The Hebrew for "birthright" is *bekorah,* and for "blessing" it is *berakah* (see note on v. 6). Though Esau tried to separate birthright from blessing, the former led inevitably to the latter, since both involved the inheritance of the firstborn (see Heb 12:16–17).

27:39 *away from the fertility of the earth . . . away from the dew of heaven.* Cf. v. 28. Isaac's secondary blessing of Esau could be only a parody of his primary blessing of Jacob.

27:40 See 25:23 and notes on 25:22,26.

27:43 *obey my voice.* Bad advice earlier (see vv. 8,13), but sensible counsel this time.

27:44 *a few days.* Twenty years, as it turned out (see 31:38,41).

27:45 *you both.* Either Jacob and Isaac or Jacob and Esau, who would become a target for blood revenge if he killed Jacob (cf. 2 Sam 14:6–7).

27:46 See note on 26:35.

28:2 *Paddan-aram.* Means "plain of Aram," another name for Aram-naharaim (see note on 24:10). *from there take to yourself a wife.* See 24:3–4.

28:3 *God Almighty.* See note on 17:1.

28:4 *the blessing of Abraham.* For Paul's application of this phrase to Christian believers see Gal 3:14.

28:5 See map, p. 47.

6 Now Esau saw that Isaac had blessed Jacob and sent him away to Paddan-aram to take to himself a wife from there, *and that* when he blessed him he charged him, saying, "[a]You shall not take a wife from the daughters of Canaan,"

7 and that Jacob had obeyed his father and his mother and had gone to Paddan-aram.

8 So Esau saw that [a]the daughters of Canaan displeased [1]his father Isaac;

9 and Esau went to Ishmael, and [1]married, [a]besides the wives that he had, Mahalath the daughter of Ishmael, Abraham's son, the sister of Nebaioth.

Jacob's Dream

10 Then Jacob departed from [a]Beersheba and went toward [b]Haran.

11 He [1]came to [2]a [a]certain place and spent the night there, because the sun had set; and he took one of the stones of the place and put it [3]under his head, and lay down in that place.

12 [a]He had a dream, and behold, a ladder was set on the earth with its top reaching to heaven; and behold, [b]the angels of God were ascending and descending on it.

13 And behold, [a]the LORD stood [1]above it and said, "I am the LORD, [b]the God of your father Abraham and the God of Isaac; the land on which you lie, I will give it [c]to you and to [d]your [2]descendants.

14 "Your [1]descendants will also be like [a]the dust of the earth, and you will [2]spread out [b]to the west and to the east and to the north and to the south; and [c]in you and in your [1]descendants shall all the families of the earth be blessed.

15 "Behold, [a]I am with you and [b]will keep you wherever you go, and [c]will bring you back to this land; for [d]I will not leave you until I have done what I have [1]promised you."

16 Then Jacob [a]awoke from his sleep and said, "[b]Surely the LORD is in this place, and I did not know it."

17 He was afraid and said, "[a]How awesome is this place! This is none other than the house of God, and this is the gate of heaven."

18 So Jacob rose early in the morning, and took [a]the stone that he had put [1]under his head and set it up as a pillar and poured oil on its top.

19 He called the name of that place [1a]Bethel; however, [2]previously the name of the city had been [b]Luz.

20 Then Jacob [a]made a vow, saying, "[b]If God will be with me and will keep me on this journey that I [1]take, and will give me [2c]food to eat and garments to wear,

21 and [a]I return to my father's house in [1]safety, [b]then the LORD will be my God.

22 "This stone, which I have set up as a pillar, [a]will be God's house, and [b]of all that You give me I will surely give a tenth to You."

Jacob Meets Rachel

29 Then Jacob [1]went on his journey, and came to the land of [a]the sons of the east.

2 He looked, and [1]saw [a]a well in the field, and behold, three flocks of sheep were lying there beside it, for from that well they watered the flocks. Now the stone on the mouth of the well was large.

3 When all the flocks were gathered there, they would then roll the stone from the mouth of the well and water the sheep, and put the stone back in its place on the mouth of the well.

4 Jacob said to them, "My brothers, where are you from?" And they said, "We are from [a]Haran."

5 He said to them, "Do you know Laban the [a]son of Nahor?" And they said, "We know *him.*"

6 And he said to them, "Is it well with him?" And they said, "It is well, and here is [a]Rachel his daughter coming with the sheep."

6 [a]Gen 28:1
8 [1]Lit *in the eyes of his* [a]Gen 24:3; 26:34, 35; 27:46
9 [1]Lit *took for his wife* [a]Gen 26:34; 36:2
10 [a]Gen 26:23 [b]Gen 12:4, 5; 27:43
11 [1]Lit *lighted on* [2]Lit *the place* [3]Lit *at his head-place* [a]Gen 28:19
12 [a]Gen 41:1; Num 12:6 [b]John 1:51
13 [1]Or *beside him* [2]Lit *seed* [a]Gen 35:1; Amos 7:7 [b]Gen 26:3, 24 [c]Gen 13:15, 17; 26:3 [d]Gen 12:7; 15:18
14 [1]Lit *seed* [2]Lit *break through* [a]Gen 13:16; 22:17 [b]Gen 13:14, 15 [c]Gen 12:3; 18:18; 22:18; 26:4
15 [1]Lit *spoken to* [a]Gen 26:3, 24; 31:3 [b]Num 6:24; Ps 121:5, 7, 8 [c]Gen 48:21; Deut 30:3 [d]Num 23:19; Deut 7:9; 31:6, 8
16 [a]1 Kin 3:15; Jer 31:26 [b]Ex 3:4-6; Josh 5:13-15; Ps 139:7-12
17 [a]Ps 68:35
18 [1]Lit *at his head-place* [a]Gen 28:11; 35:14
19 [1]I.e. the house of God [2]Lit *at the first* [a]Judg 1:23 [b]Gen 35:6; 48:3
20 [1]Lit *go* [2]Lit *bread* [a]Gen 31:13; Judg 11:30; 2 Sam 15:8 [b]Gen 28:15 [c]1 Tim 6:8
21 [1]Lit *peace* [a]Judg 11:31 [b]Deut 26:17
22 [a]Gen 35:7 [b]Lev 27:30; Deut 14:22
29:1 [1]Lit *lifted up his feet* [a]Judg 6:3, 33

2 [1]Lit *behold* [a]Gen 24:10, 11; Ex 2:15, 16 **4** [a]Gen 28:10
5 [a]Gen 24:24, 29 **6** [a]Ex 2:16

28:9 *besides the wives that he had.* See 26:34 and note.

28:11 *one of the stones . . . under his head.* In ancient times headrests (e.g., in Egypt) were often quite hard, sometimes being made of metal. People were used to sleeping on the ground.

28:12 *ladder.* Not a ladder with rungs, it was more likely a stairway such as mounted the sloping side of a ziggurat (see note on 11:4). *angels of God were ascending and descending on it.* A sign that the Lord offered to be Jacob's God. Jesus told a disciple that he would "see the heavens opened and the angels of God ascending and descending on the Son of Man" (John 1:51). Jesus Himself is the bridge between heaven and earth (see John 14:6), the only "mediator . . . between God and men" (1 Tim 2:5).

28:13 *the LORD stood above it.* Mesopotamian ziggurats were topped with a small shrine where worshipers prayed to their gods.

28:14 *like the dust of the earth.* See note on 13:16. *in you . . . shall all the families of the earth be blessed.* Repeats the blessing of 12:3.

28:15 *I am with you.* See note on 26:3. *I will not leave you.* Unlike the gods of pagan religions, in which the gods were merely local deities who gave protection only within their own territories, the one true God assured Jacob that He would always be with him wherever he went.

28:17 *house of God . . . gate of heaven.* Phrases that related Jacob's stairway to the Mesopotamian ziggurats (see notes on 11:4,9).

28:18 *pillar.* A memorial of worship or of communion between man and God, common in ancient times. *poured oil on its top.* To consecrate it (see Ex 30:25–29).

28:21 *return . . . in safety.* Partially fulfilled in 33:18. *the LORD will be my God.* For the first time Jacob considered (conditionally: "If . . .") acknowledging the God of Abraham and Isaac (see v. 13; 27:20) as his own. His full acknowledgment came only after his safe return from Haran (see 33:20 and note).

28:22 *This stone . . . will be God's house.* In the sense that it would memorialize Jacob's meeting with God at Bethel (Bethel means "house of God"). *of all that You give me I will surely give a tenth to You.* A way of acknowledging the Lord as his God and King (see note on 14:20).

29:5 *son.* Or "grandson" (see note on 10:1; see also 24:15,29).

7 He said, "Behold, it is still high day; it is not time for the livestock to be gathered. Water the sheep, and go, pasture them."

8 But they said, "We cannot, until all the flocks are gathered, and they roll the stone from the mouth of the well; then we water the sheep."

9 While he was still speaking with them, Rachel came with her father's sheep, for she was a shepherdess.

10 When Jacob saw Rachel the daughter of Laban his mother's brother, and the sheep of Laban his mother's brother, Jacob went up and rolled the stone from the mouth of the well and watered the flock of Laban his mother's brother.

11 Then Jacob [a]kissed Rachel, and lifted his voice and wept.

12 Jacob told Rachel that he was a [1a]relative of her father and that he was Rebekah's son, and [b]she ran and told her father.

13 So when [a]Laban heard the news of Jacob his sister's son, he ran to meet him, and [b]embraced him and kissed him and brought him to his house. Then he related to Laban all these things.

14 Laban said to him, "Surely you are [a]my bone and my flesh." And he stayed with him a month.

15 Then Laban said to Jacob, "Because you are my [1]relative, should you therefore serve me for nothing? Tell me, what shall [a]your wages be?"

16 Now Laban had two daughters; the name of the older was Leah, and the name of the younger was Rachel.

17 And Leah's eyes were weak, but Rachel was [a]beautiful of form and [1]face.

18 Now Jacob [a]loved Rachel, so he said, "[b]I will serve you seven years for your younger daughter Rachel."

19 Laban said, "It is better that I give her to you than to give her to another man; stay with me."

20 So Jacob served seven years for Rachel and they seemed to him but a few days [a]because of his love for her.

11 [a]Gen 33:4 **12** [1]Lit *brother* [a]Gen 28:5 [b]Gen 24:28 **13** [a]Gen 24:29-31 [b]Gen 33:4 **14** [a]Gen 2:23; Judg 9:2; 2 Sam 5:1; 19:12, 13 **15** [1]Lit *brother* [a]Gen 31:41 **17** [1]Lit *beautiful of appearance* [a]Gen 12:11, 14; 26:7 **18** [a]Gen 24:67 [b]Hos 12:12 **20** [a]Song 8:7

Laban's Treachery

21 Then Jacob said to Laban, "Give *me* my wife, for my [1]time is completed, that I may [a]go in to her."

22 Laban gathered all the men of the place and made a feast.

23 Now in the evening he took his daughter Leah, and brought her to him; and *Jacob* went in to her.

24 Laban also gave his maid Zilpah to his daughter Leah as a maid.

25 So it came about in the morning that, behold, it was Leah! And he said to Laban, "[a]What is this you have done to me? Was it not for Rachel that I served with you? Why then have you [b]deceived me?"

26 But Laban said, "It is not [1]the practice in our place to [2]marry off the younger before the firstborn.

27 "Complete the week of this one, and we will give you the other also for the service which [a]you shall serve with me for another seven years."

28 Jacob did so and completed her week, and he gave him his daughter Rachel as his wife.

29 Laban also gave his maid Bilhah to his daughter Rachel as her maid.

30 So *Jacob* went in to Rachel also, and indeed [a]he loved Rachel more than Leah, and he served with [1]Laban for [b]another seven years.

31 Now the LORD saw that Leah was [1]unloved, and He opened her womb, but Rachel was barren.

32 Leah conceived and bore a son and named him [1]Reuben, for she said, "Because the LORD has [2a]seen my affliction; surely now my husband will love me."

33 Then she conceived again and bore a son and said, "[a]Because the LORD has [1]heard that I am [2]unloved, He has therefore given me this *son* also." So she named him Simeon.

34 She conceived again and bore a son and said, "Now this time my husband will become [1]attached to me, because I have borne him three sons." Therefore he was named [a]Levi.

21 [1]Lit *days are* [a]Judg 15:1 **25** [a]Gen 12:18; 20:9; 26:10 [b]1 Sam 28:12 **26** [1]Lit *done thus in* [2]Lit *give* **27** [a]Gen 31:41 **30** [1]Lit *him* [a]Gen 29:17, 18 [b]Gen 31:41 **31** [1]Lit *hated* **32** [1]I.e. see, a son [2]Lit *looked upon* [a]Gen 16:11; 31:42; Ex 3:7; 4:31; Deut 26:7; Ps 25:18 **33** [1]Heb *shama*, related to Simeon [2]Lit *hated* [a]Deut 21:15 **34** [1]Heb *lavah*, related to Levi [a]Gen 49:5

29:9 *shepherdess.* The task of caring for sheep and goats in the Middle East was shared by men and women.

29:10 *rolled the stone.* A feat of unusual strength for one man, because the stone was large (see v. 2).

29:11 *wept.* For joy.

29:14 *my bone and my flesh.* A Hebrew phrase that stresses blood kinship (see, e.g., 2:23).

29:16 *Leah . . . Rachel.* The names mean "cow" and "ewe" respectively, appropriate in a herdsman's family.

29:21 *my wife.* If Jacob had said "Rachel," Laban would have had no excuse for giving him Leah.

29:22 *feast.* A wedding feast was usually seven days long (see vv. 27–28; Judg 14:10,12).

29:23 *in the evening . . . Jacob went in to her.* The darkness, or perhaps a veil (see 24:65), may have concealed Leah's identity.

29:24 See v. 29; a wedding custom documented in Old Babylonian marriage contracts.

29:25 *you deceived me.* Jacob, the deceiver in name (see note on 25:26) as well as in behavior (see 27:36), had himself been deceived. The one who had tried everything to obtain the benefits of the firstborn had now, against his will, received the firstborn (vv. 16,26).

29:28 *he gave him his daughter Rachel.* Before Jacob worked another seven years (see v. 30).

29:30 *Jacob . . . loved Rachel more than Leah.* Not only because Rachel had been his choice from the beginning but also, no doubt, because Laban had tricked Jacob into marrying Leah.

29:31–35 Leah, though unloved, nevertheless became the mother of Jacob's first four sons, including Levi (ancestor of the Aaronic priestly line) and Judah (ancestor of David and his royal line, and ultimately of Jesus).

29:32 *named him Reuben . . . Because the LORD has seen my affliction.* Ishmael had received his name in similar circumstances (see 16:11).

35 And she conceived again and bore a
son and said, "This time I will [1]praise the
LORD." Therefore she named him [2a]Judah.
Then she stopped bearing.

The Sons of Jacob

30 Now when Rachel saw that [a]she bore
Jacob no children, [1]she became jealous
of her sister; and she said to Jacob, "[b]Give
me children, or else I die."
2 Then Jacob's anger burned against
Rachel, and he said, "Am I in the place of
God, who has [a]withheld from you the fruit
of the womb?"
3 She said, "[a]Here is my maid Bilhah, go
in to her that she may [b]bear on my knees,
that [1a]through her I too may have children."
4 So [a]she gave him her maid Bilhah as a
wife, and Jacob went in to her.
5 Bilhah conceived and bore Jacob a son.
6 Then Rachel said, "God has [1a]vindicat-
ed me, and has indeed heard my voice and
has given me a son." Therefore she named
him [2]Dan.
7 Rachel's maid Bilhah conceived again
and bore Jacob a second son.
8 So Rachel said, "With [1]mighty
wrestlings I have [2]wrestled with my sister,
and I have indeed prevailed." And she
named him Naphtali.
9 When Leah saw that she had stopped
bearing, she took her maid Zilpah and gave
her to Jacob as a wife.
10 Leah's maid Zilpah bore Jacob a son.
11 Then Leah said, "[1]How fortunate!" So
she named him [2]Gad.
12 Leah's maid Zilpah bore Jacob a second son.
13 Then Leah said, "[1]Happy am I! For
women [a]will call me happy." So she named
him [2]Asher.
14 Now in the days of wheat harvest Reuben went and found [a]mandrakes in the field,
and brought them to his mother Leah. Then
Rachel said to Leah, "Please give me some of
your son's mandrakes."
15 But she said to her, "Is it a small matter
for you to take my husband? And would you
take my son's mandrakes also?" So Rachel
said, "Therefore he may lie with you tonight
in return for your son's mandrakes."
16 When Jacob came in from the field in
the evening, then Leah went out to meet him
and said, "You must come in to me, for I
have surely hired you with my son's mandrakes." So he lay with her that night.
17 God gave heed to Leah, and she conceived and bore Jacob a fifth son.
18 Then Leah said, "God has given me my
[1]wages because I gave my maid to my husband." So she named him Issachar.
19 Leah conceived again and bore a sixth
son to Jacob.
20 Then Leah said, "God has endowed me
with a good gift; now my husband [1]will
dwell with me, because I have borne him six
sons." So she named him Zebulun.
21 Afterward she bore a daughter and
named her Dinah.
22 Then [a]God remembered Rachel, and
God gave heed to her and [b]opened her
womb.
23 So she conceived and bore a son and
said, "God has [a]taken away my reproach."
24 She named him Joseph, saying, "[a]May
the LORD [1]give me another son."

Jacob Prospers

25 Now it came about when Rachel had
borne Joseph, that Jacob said to Laban,
"[a]Send me away, that I may go to my own
place and to my own country.
26 "Give *me* my wives and my children [a]for
whom I have served you, and let me depart;
for you yourself know my service which I
have [1]rendered you."
27 But Laban said to him, "If now [1]it
pleases you, *stay with me;* I have divined

35 [1]Heb *Judah,* related to Judah [2]Heb *Jehudah* [a]Gen 49:8; Matt 1:2
30:1 [1]Lit *Rachel* [a]Gen 29:31 [b]1 Sam 1:5, 6
2 [a]Gen 20:18; 29:31
3 [1]Lit *from her I too may be built* [a]Gen 16:2 [b]Gen 50:23; Job 3:12
4 [a]Gen 16:3, 4
6 [1]Lit *judged* [2]I.e. He judged [a]Ps 35:24; 43:1; Lam 3:59
8 [1]Lit *wrestlings of God* [2]Heb *niphtal,* related to Naphtali
11 [1]Lit *With fortune!* Some versions read *Fortune has come* [2]I.e. Fortune
13 [1]Lit *With my happiness!* [2]I.e. happy [a]Luke 1:48
14 [a]Song 7:13
18 [1]Heb *sachar,* related to Issachar
20 [1]Heb *zabal,* related to Zebulun. Some translate *will honor*
22 [a]1 Sam 1:19, 20 [b]Gen 29:31
23 [a]Is 4:1; Luke 1:25
24 [1]Lit *add to me;* Heb *Joseph* [a]Gen 35:17
25 [a]Gen 24:54, 56
26 [1]Lit *served* [a]Gen 29:18, 20, 27; Hos 12:12
27 [1]Lit *I have found favor in your eyes*

30:1 *she became jealous of her sister.* As Jacob was of his older brother. *Give me children, or else I die.* Tragically prophetic words (see 35:16–19).
30:2 *Am I in the place of God . . . ?* Jacob was forever trying to secure the blessing by his own efforts. Here he has to acknowledge that the blessing of offspring could come only from God (see 31:7–13 for the blessing of flocks). Joseph later echoed these words (see 50:19).
30:3 *go in to her.* See v. 9; see also 16:2 and note. *on my knees.* Apparently an expression symbolic of adoption (see 48:10–16) and meaning "as though my own" (see note on 50:23).
30:4 *as a wife.* As a concubine (see 35:22).
30:5–12 Jacob's fifth, sixth, seventh and eighth sons were born to him through his maidservant concubines.
30:14 *give me some of your son's mandrakes.* The mandrake has fleshy, forked roots that resemble the lower part of a human body and were therefore superstitiously thought to induce pregnancy when eaten (see Song 7:13). Rachel, like Jacob (vv. 37–43), tried to obtain what she wanted by magical means.
30:16 *hired.* The Hebrew for this word is a pun on the name Issachar. (Issachar sounds like the Hebrew for "reward.")
30:17–20 Jacob's ninth and tenth sons were born through Leah, who was thus the mother of half of Jacob's 12 sons (see note on 29:31–35).
30:20 *endowed . . . gift.* The Hebrew terms for these words are puns on the name Zebulun. (Zebulun probably means "honor.")
30:21 *Dinah.* See ch. 34.
30:22 *God remembered Rachel.* See note on 8:1.
30:23 *reproach.* Barrenness was considered to be shameful, a mark of divine disfavor (see 16:2; 30:2).
30:24 *May the LORD give me another son.* The fulfillment of Rachel's wish would bring about her death (see 35:16–19).
30:27 *divined.* The attempt to discover hidden knowledge through mechanical means (see 44:5), the interpretation of omens (see Ezek 21:21) or the aid of supernatural powers (see Acts 16:16). It was strictly forbidden to Israel (Lev 19:26; Deut 18:10,14) because it reflected a pagan concept of the world controlled by evil forces, and therefore obviously not under the sovereign rule of the Lord. *the LORD has blessed me on your account.* Cf. 21:22; 26:28–29. The offspring of Abraham were a source of blessing (see 12:2).

[a]that the LORD has blessed me on your account."

28 He [1]continued, "[a]Name me your wages, and I will give it."

29 But he said to him, "[a]You yourself know how I have served you and how your cattle have [1]fared with me.

30 "For you had little before [1]I came and it has [2]increased to a multitude, and the LORD has blessed you [3]wherever I turned. But now, when shall I provide for my own household also?"

31 So he said, "What shall I give you?" And Jacob said, "You shall not give me anything. If you will do this *one* thing for me, I will again pasture *and* keep your flock:

32 let me pass through your entire flock today, removing from there every [a]speckled and spotted sheep and every black [1]one among the lambs and the spotted and speckled among the goats; and *such* shall be my wages.

33 "So my [1]honesty will answer for me later, when you come concerning my [2]wages. Every one that is not speckled and spotted among the goats and black among the lambs, *if found* with me, will be considered stolen."

34 Laban said, "[1]Good, let it be according to your word."

35 So he removed on that day the striped and spotted male goats and all the speckled and spotted female goats, every one with white in it, and all the black ones among the sheep, and gave them into the [1]care of his sons.

36 And he put *a distance of* three days' journey between himself and Jacob, and Jacob fed the rest of Laban's flocks.

37 Then Jacob [1]took fresh rods of poplar and almond and plane trees, and peeled white stripes in them, exposing the white which *was* [2]in the rods.

38 He set the rods which he had peeled in front of the flocks in the gutters, *even* in the watering troughs, where the flocks came to drink; and they [1]mated when they came to drink.

39 So the flocks [1]mated by the rods, and the flocks brought forth striped, speckled, and spotted.

40 Jacob separated the lambs, and [1]made the flocks face toward the striped and all the black in the flock of Laban; and he put his own herds apart, and did not put them with Laban's flock.

41 Moreover, whenever the [1]stronger of the flock [2]were mating, Jacob would place the rods in the sight of the flock in the gutters, so that they might [3]mate by the rods;

42 but when the flock was feeble, he did not put *them* in; so the feebler were Laban's and the [1]stronger Jacob's.

43 So [a]the man [1]became exceedingly prosperous, and had large flocks and female and male servants and camels and donkeys.

Jacob Leaves Secretly for Canaan

31 Now [1]Jacob heard the words of Laban's sons, saying, "Jacob has taken away all that was our father's, and from what belonged to our father he has made all this [2]wealth."

2 Jacob saw the [1]attitude of Laban, and behold, it was not *friendly* toward him as formerly.

3 Then the LORD said to Jacob, "[a]Return to the land of your fathers and to your relatives, and [b]I will be with you."

4 So Jacob sent and called Rachel and Leah to his flock in the field,

5 and said to them, "[a]I see your father's [1]attitude, that it is not *friendly* toward me as formerly, but [b]the God of my father has been with me.

6 "[a]You know that I have served your father with all my strength.

7 "Yet your father has [a]cheated me and [b]changed my wages ten times; however, [c]God did not allow him to hurt me.

8 "If [a]he spoke thus, 'The speckled shall be your wages,' then all the flock brought forth speckled; and if he spoke thus, 'The striped shall be your wages,' then all the flock brought forth striped.

9 "Thus God has [a]taken away your father's livestock and given *them* to me.

10 "And it came about at the time when the flock were [1]mating that I lifted up my eyes and saw in a dream, and behold, the male goats which were [2]mating *were* striped, speckled, and mottled.

11 "Then [a]the angel of God said to me in the dream, 'Jacob,' and I said, 'Here I am.'

27 [a]Gen 26:24; 39:3, 5; Is 61:9
28 [1]Lit *said* [a]Gen 29:15; 31:7, 41
29 [1]Lit *been* [a]Gen 31:6
30 [1]Lit *me* [2]Lit *broken forth* [3]Lit *at my foot*
32 [1]Lit *sheep* [a]Gen 31:8
33 [1]Lit *righteousness* [2]Lit *wages which are before you*
34 [1]Lit *Behold, would that it might be*
35 [1]Lit *hand*
37 [1]Lit *took to himself* [2]Lit *on*
38 [1]Or *conceived*
39 [1]Or *conceived*
40 [1]Lit *set the faces*
41 [1]Lit *bound ones;* i.e. firm and compact [2]Or *conceived* [3]Or *conceive*
42 [1]Lit *bound ones;* i.e. firm and compact
43 [1]Lit *broke forth* [a]Gen 12:16; 13:2; 24:35; 26:13, 14; 30:30
31:1 [1]Lit *he* [2]Lit *glory*
2 [1]Lit *face*
3 [a]Gen 32:9 [b]Gen 28:15
5 [1]Lit *face* [a]Gen 31:2 [b]Gen 21:22; 28:13, 15; 31:29, 42, 53; Is 41:10; Heb 13:5
6 [a]Gen 30:29
7 [a]Gen 29:25 [b]Gen 31:41 [c]Gen 15:1; 31:29
8 [a]Gen 30:32
9 [a]Gen 31:1, 16
10 [1]Or *conceiving* [2]Lit *leaping upon the flock*
11 [a]Gen 16:7-11; 22:11, 15; 31:13; 48:16

30:35 *he removed.* Secretly and without telling Jacob.

30:37 *poplar . . . white.* The Hebrew terms for these words are puns on the name Laban. As Jacob had gotten the best of Esau (whose other name, Edom, means "red"; see note on 25:25) by means of red stew (25:30), so he now tries to get the best of Laban (whose name means "white") by means of white branches. In effect, Jacob was using Laban's own tactic (deception) against him.

30:39 The scheme worked—but only because of God's intervention (see Jacob's own admission in 31:9), not because of Jacob's superstition.

30:43 *the man became exceedingly prosperous.* Over a period of six years (see 31:41). While in Haran Jacob obtained both family and wealth.

31:3 *Return to the land of your fathers.* Every sign Jacob was getting—from his wives (see vv. 14–16), from Laban (see v. 2), from Laban's sons (see v. 1) and now from God Himself—told him that it was time to return to Canaan. *I will be with you.* See note on 26:3.

31:4 *Rachel and Leah.* At long last (see v. 14) Rachel, the younger, has been given precedence over Leah—but she will soon become a deceiver like her husband Jacob (see vv. 31,35).

31:7 *ten times.* See v. 41. "Ten" here probably signifies completeness. In effect, Jacob accused Laban of cheating him at every turn.

31:9 See note on 30:39.

31:11 *angel of God.* See note on 16:7. *Here I am.* See note on 22:1.

12 "He said, 'Lift up now your eyes and see *that* all the male goats which are [1]mating are striped, speckled, and mottled; for [a]I have seen all that Laban has been doing to you.
13 'I am [a]the God *of* Bethel, where you [b]anointed a pillar, where you made a vow to Me; now arise, [1]leave this land, and [c]return to the land of your birth.' "
14 Rachel and Leah said to him, "Do we still have any portion or inheritance in our father's house?
15 "Are we not reckoned by him as foreigners? For [a]he has sold us, and has also [1]entirely consumed [2]our purchase price.
16 "Surely all the wealth which God has taken away from our father belongs to us and our children; now then, do whatever God has said to you."
17 Then Jacob arose and put his children and his wives upon camels;
18 and he drove away all his livestock and all his property which he had gathered, his acquired livestock which he had gathered in Paddan-aram, [a]to go to the land of Canaan to his father Isaac.
19 When Laban had gone to shear his flock, then Rachel stole the [1a]household idols that were her father's.
20 And Jacob [1]deceived Laban the Aramean by not telling him that he was fleeing.
21 So he fled with all that he had; and he arose and crossed the *Euphrates* River, and set his face toward the hill country of [a]Gilead.

12 [1]Lit *leaping upon the flock* [a]Ex 3:7
13 [1]Lit *go out from* [a]Gen 28:13, 19 [b]Gen 28:18, 20 [c]Gen 28:15; 32:9
15 [1]I.e. enjoyed the benefit of [2]Lit *our money* [a]Gen 29:20, 23, 27
18 [a]Gen 35:27
19 [1]Heb *teraphim* [a]Gen 31:30, 34; 35:2; Judg 17:5; 1 Sam 19:13; Hos 3:4
20 [1]Lit *stole the heart of*
21 [a]Gen 37:25

31:13 *Bethel, where you anointed a pillar.* See note on 28:18.
31:18 *Paddan-aram.* Means "plain of Aram," another name for Aram-naharaim (see note on 24:10). See map below.
31:19 *household idols.* Small portable idols, which Rachel probably stole because she thought they would bring her protection and blessing. Or perhaps she wanted to have something tangible to worship on the long journey ahead, a practice referred to much later in the writings of Josephus, a first-century Jewish historian. In any case, Rachel was not yet free of her pagan background (see 35:2; Josh 24:2).
31:21 *So he fled.* As he had fled earlier from Esau (27:42–43). Jacob's devious dealings produced only hostility from which he had to flee. *Gilead.* A fertile region southeast of the Sea of Galilee.

Jacob's Journeys

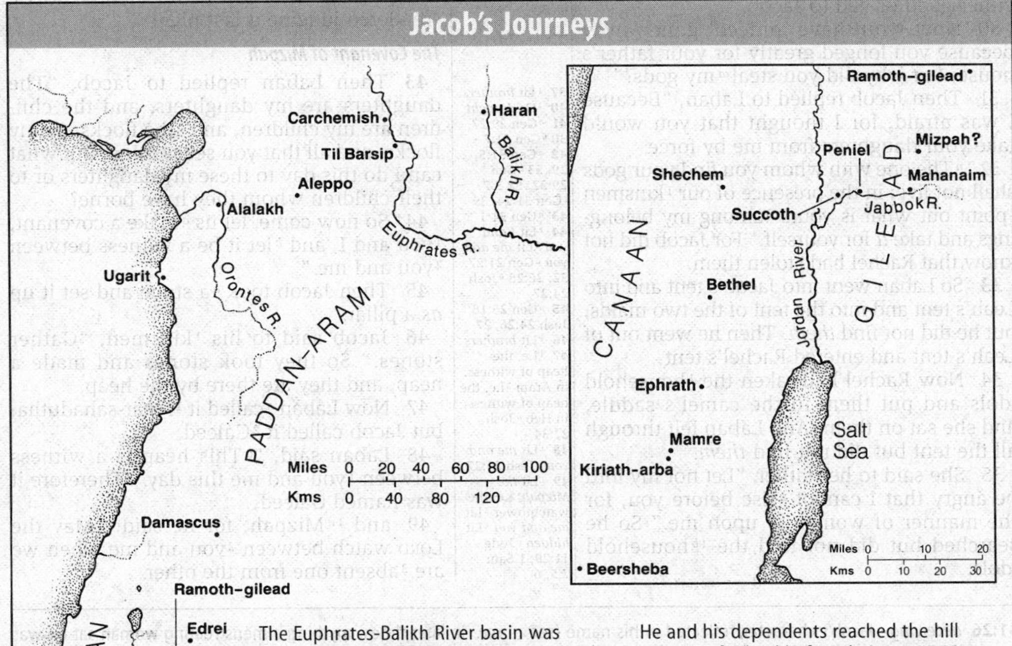

The Euphrates-Balikh River basin was Jacob's destination as he fled from Esau, ultimately reaching the home of his maternal uncle (Laban) near Haran.

His lengthy sojourn ended in a dispute with Laban and another flight—this time back to Canaan. His route likely took him toward Aleppo, then to Damascus and Edrei before reaching Peniel on the Jabbok River.

He and his dependents reached the hill country of Gilead before their caravan was overtaken by Laban. The covenant at Mizpah was celebrated on one of the hills later used as a border station between Aramean and Israelite territories.

Jacob tarried at Succoth, entered Canaan and proceeded to Shechem, where he erected an altar to the Lord.

Laban Pursues Jacob

22 When it was told Laban on the third
day that Jacob had fled,
23 then he took his [1]kinsmen with him
and pursued him *a distance of* seven days'
journey, and he overtook him in the hill
country of Gilead.
24 [a]God came to Laban the Aramean in a
[b]dream of the night and said to him, "[1c]Be
careful that you do not speak to Jacob either
good or bad."
25 Laban caught up with Jacob. Now
Jacob had pitched his tent in the hill country,
and Laban with his [1]kinsmen camped in the
hill country of Gilead.
26 Then Laban said to Jacob, "What have
you done [1]by deceiving me and carrying away
my daughters like captives of the sword?
27 "Why did you flee secretly and [1]deceive
me, and did not tell me so that I might have
sent you away with joy and with songs, with
[a]timbrel and with [b]lyre;
28 and did not allow me [a]to kiss my sons
and my daughters? Now you have done foolishly.
29 "It is in [1]my power to do you harm, but
[a]the God of your father spoke to me last
night, saying, '[2b]Be careful not to speak
either good or bad to Jacob.'
30 "Now you have indeed gone away
because you longed greatly for your father's
house; *but* why did you steal [a]my gods?"
31 Then Jacob replied to Laban, "Because
I was afraid, for I thought that you would
take your daughters from me by force.
32 "[a]The one with whom you find your gods
shall not live; in the presence of our [1]kinsmen
[2]point out what is yours [3]among my belong-
ings and take *it* for yourself." For Jacob did not
know that Rachel had stolen them.
33 So Laban went into Jacob's tent and into
Leah's tent and into the tent of the two maids,
but he did not find *them.* Then he went out of
Leah's tent and entered Rachel's tent.
34 Now Rachel had taken the [1]household
idols and put them in the camel's saddle,
and she sat on them. And Laban felt through
all the tent but did not find *them.*
35 She said to her father, "Let not my lord
be angry that I cannot [a]rise before you, for
the manner of women is upon me." So he
searched but did not find the [1b]household
idols.

23 [1]Lit *brothers*
24 [1]Lit *Take heed to yourself* [a]Gen 20:3; 31:29 [b]Gen 20:3, 6; 31:11 [c]Gen 24:50; 31:7, 29
25 [1]Lit *brothers*
26 [1]Lit *and you have stolen my heart*
27 [1]Lit *steal me* [a]Ex 15:20 [b]Gen 4:21
28 [a]Gen 31:55
29 [1]Lit *the power of my hand* [2]Lit *Take heed to yourself* [a]Gen 31:5, 24, 42, 53 [b]Gen 31:24
30 [a]Gen 31:19; Josh 24:2; Judg 18:24
32 [1]Lit *brothers* [2]Lit *recognize* [3]Lit *with me* [a]Gen 44:9
34 [1]Heb *teraphim*
35 [1]Heb *teraphim* [a]Lev 19:32 [b]Gen 31:19

36 Then Jacob became angry and contended with Laban; and Jacob said to Laban,
"What is my transgression? What is my sin
that you have hotly pursued me?
37 "Though you have felt through all my
goods, what have you found of all your
household goods? Set *it* here before my
[1]kinsmen and your [1]kinsmen, that they may
decide between us two.
38 "These twenty years I *have been* with
you; your ewes and your female goats have
not miscarried, nor have I eaten the rams of
your flocks.
39 "That which was torn *of beasts* I did not
bring to you; I bore the loss of it myself. You
required it of my hand *whether* stolen by day
or stolen by night.
40 "*Thus* I was: by day the [1]heat consumed
me and the frost by night, and my sleep fled
from my eyes.
41 "These twenty years I have been in your
house; [a]I served you fourteen years for your
two daughters and six years for your flock,
and you [b]changed my wages ten times.
42 "If [a]the God of my father, the God of
Abraham, and the fear of Isaac, had not been
for me, surely now you would have sent me
away empty-handed. [b]God has seen my
affliction and the toil of my hands, so He
[c]rendered judgment last night."

The Covenant of Mizpah

43 Then Laban replied to Jacob, "The
daughters are my daughters, and the children are my children, and [a]the flocks are my
flocks, and all that you see is mine. But what
can I do this day to these my daughters or to
their children whom they have borne?
44 "So now come, let us [a]make a covenant,
[1]you and I, and [b]let it be a witness between
[2]you and me."
45 Then Jacob took [a]a stone and set it up
as a pillar.
46 Jacob said to his [1]kinsmen, "Gather
stones." So they took stones and made a
heap, and they ate there by the heap.
47 Now Laban [a]called it [1]Jegar-sahadutha,
but Jacob called it [2]Galeed.
48 Laban said, "[a]This heap is a witness
between [1]you and me this day." Therefore it
was named Galeed,
49 and [1a]Mizpah, for he said, "May the
LORD watch between [2]you and me when we
are [3]absent one from the other.

37 [1]Lit *brothers*
40 [1]Or *drought*
41 [a]Gen 29:27, 30 [b]Gen 31:7
42 [a]Gen 31:5, 29, 53 [b]Gen 29:32; Ex 3:7 [c]Gen 31:24, 29
43 [a]Gen 31:1
44 [1]Lit *I and you* [2]Lit *me and you* [a]Gen 21:27, 32; 26:28 [b]Josh 24:27
45 [a]Gen 28:18; Josh 24:26, 27
46 [1]Lit *brothers*
47 [1]I.e. the heap of witness, in Aram [2]I.e. the heap of witness, in Heb [a]Josh 22:34
48 [1]Lit *me and you* [a]Josh 24:27
49 [1]Lit *the Mizpah;* i.e. the watchtower [2]Lit *me and you* [3]Lit *hidden* [a]Judg 11:29; 1 Sam 7:5, 6

31:26 *deceiving.* Jacob's character, reflected in his name (see note on 25:26; see also 27:36), is emphasized in the narrative again and again.

31:27 *lyre.* Much smaller, and with fewer strings (usually 6 to 12), than a modern harp.

31:32 *The one with whom you find your gods shall not live.* Cf. 44:7–12. Though he made the offer in all innocence, Jacob almost lost his beloved Rachel. He had now been deceived even by his wife.

31:34 *in the camel's saddle . . . sat on them.* Indicating the small size and powerlessness of the household gods.

31:35 *I cannot rise before you, for the manner of women is upon me.* In later times, anything a menstruating woman sat on was considered ritually unclean (Lev 15:20). Rachel, too, had become a deceiver.

31:42 *fear.* Here a surrogate for God. Or perhaps the Hebrew for this word means "Kinsman," stressing the intimacy of God's relationship to the patriarch.

31:46 *ate.* See note on 26:30.

31:48 For the naming of an altar under similar circumstances see Josh 22:10–12,34.

31:49 *May . . . other.* The so-called Mizpah benediction, which in context is in fact a denunciation or curse.

50 "If you mistreat my daughters, or if you take wives besides my daughters, *although* no man is with us, see, [a]God is witness between [1]you and me."

51 Laban said to Jacob, "Behold this heap and behold the pillar which I have set between [1]you and me.

52 "This heap is a witness, and the pillar is a witness, that I will not pass by this heap to you for harm, and you will not pass by this heap and this pillar to me, for harm.

53 "[a]The God of Abraham and the God of Nahor, the God of their father, [b]judge between us." So Jacob swore by [c]the fear of his father Isaac.

54 Then Jacob [a]offered a sacrifice on the mountain, and called his [1]kinsmen to [2]the meal; and they ate [3]the meal and spent the night on the mountain.

55 [1]Early in the morning Laban arose, and [a]kissed his sons and his daughters and blessed them. Then Laban departed and returned to his place.

Jacob's Fear of Esau

32 Now as Jacob went on his way, [a]the angels of God met him.

2 Jacob said when he saw them, "This is God's [1]camp." So he named that place [2a]Mahanaim.

3 Then Jacob [a]sent messengers before him to his brother Esau in the land of [b]Seir, the [1]country of [c]Edom.

4 He also commanded them saying, "Thus you shall say to my lord Esau: 'Thus says your servant Jacob, "I have sojourned with Laban, and [a]stayed until now;

5 [a]I have oxen and donkeys *and* flocks and male and female servants; and I have sent to tell my lord, [b]that I may find favor in your sight." ' "

6 The messengers returned to Jacob, saying, "We came to your brother Esau, and furthermore [a]he is coming to meet you, and four hundred men are with him."

7 Then Jacob was [a]greatly afraid and distressed; and he divided the people who were with him, and the flocks and the herds and the camels, into two companies;

8 for he said, "If Esau comes to the one company and [1]attacks it, then the company which is left will escape."

9 Jacob said, "O [a]God of my father Abraham and God of my father Isaac, O LORD, who said to me, '[b]Return to your country and to your relatives, and I will [1]prosper you,'

10 [1]I am unworthy [a]of all the lovingkindness and of all the [2]faithfulness which You have shown to Your servant; for with my staff *only* I crossed this Jordan, and now I have become two companies.

11 "[a]Deliver me, I pray, [b]from the hand of my brother, from the hand of Esau; for I fear him, that he will come and [1]attack me *and* the [c]mothers with the children.

12 "For You said, '[a]I will surely [1]prosper you and [b]make your [2]descendants as the sand of the sea, which is too great to be numbered.' "

13 So he spent the night there. Then he [1]selected from what [2]he had with him a [a]present for his brother Esau:

14 two hundred female goats and twenty male goats, two hundred ewes and twenty rams,

15 thirty milking camels and their colts, forty cows and ten bulls, twenty female donkeys and ten male donkeys.

16 He delivered *them* into the hand of his servants, every drove by itself, and said to his servants, "Pass on before me, and put a space between droves."

17 He commanded the [1]one in front, saying,

50 [1]Lit *me and you* [a]Jer 29:23; 42:5
51 [1]Lit *me and you*
53 [a]Gen 28:13 [b]Gen 16:5 [c]Gen 31:42
54 [1]Lit *brothers* [2]Lit *eat bread* [3]Lit *bread* [a]Ex 18:12
55 [1]Ch 32:1 in Heb [a]Gen 31:28, 43
32:1 [a]2 Kin 6:16, 17; Ps 34:7
2 [1]Or *company* [2]I.e. Two Camps, or Two Companies [a]Josh 21:38; 2 Sam 2:8
3 [1]Lit *field* [a]Gen 27:41, 42; 32:7, 11 [b]Gen 14:6; 33:14 [c]Gen 25:30; 36:8, 9
4 [a]Gen 31:41
5 [a]Gen 30:43 [b]Gen 33:8
6 [a]Gen 33:1
7 [a]Gen 32:11
8 [1]Lit *smites*
9 [1]Lit *do good with you* [a]Gen 28:13; 31:42 [b]Gen 28:15; 31:3, 13
10 [1]Lit *I am less than all* [2]Or *truth* [a]Gen 24:27
11 [1]Lit *smite* [a]Ps 59:1, 2 [b]Gen 27:41, 42; 33:4 [c]Hos 10:14
12 [1]Lit *do good with* [2]Lit *seed* [a]Gen 28:14 [b]Gen 22:17
13 [1]Lit *took* [2]Lit *had come to his hand* [a]Gen 43:11
17 [1]Lit *first*

31:51 *heap . . . pillar . . . between you and me.* Boundary markers between Laban's territory and Jacob's territory. Galeed, Jacob's name for the heap, is a pun on Gilead (see v. 47, where Aramaic *Jegar-sahadutha* means "witness heap"; *Galeed* also means "witness heap").

31:53 *God of their father.* Or possibly "gods of their father [i.e., Terah]," reflecting Laban's polytheistic background (see Josh 24:2). *fear of his father Isaac.* See note on v. 42. Jacob had met the "God of Isaac" (28:13) at Bethel 20 years earlier.

31:54 *sacrifice . . . meal.* Two important aspects of the covenant-making (see v. 44) process (see Ex 24:5–8,11). *kinsmen.* Those with whom he had now entered into a covenant. The common meal indicated mutual acceptance (see note on 26:30).

31:55 *blessed.* Or "said farewell to" (see 47:10).

32:1 *angels of God met him.* Jacob had just left the region of the hostile Laban and is about to enter the region of the hostile Esau. He was met by the angels of God, whom he had seen at Bethel when he was fleeing from Esau to go to Laban (28:12). Thus God was with Jacob, as He had promised (see 28:15; 31:3; see also note on 26:3).

32:2 *Mahanaim.* Means "two camps" and is located in Gilead (see note on 31:21) east of the Jordan and north of the Jabbok (see note on v. 22). Two camps had just met in hostility and separated in peace. Two camps were again about to meet (in hostility, Jacob thought) and separate in peace. But Jacob called this crucial place "two camps" after seeing the angelic encampment, suggesting that he saw God's encampment as a divine assurance. God's host had come to escort him safely to Canaan (see 33:12,15). Yet he also feared meeting with Esau, so he divided his household into two camps (see vv. 7,10), still trying to protect himself by his own devices.

32:3 *Seir . . . Edom.* Far to the south of Jacob's ultimate destination, but he assumed that Esau would come seeking revenge as soon as he heard that Jacob was on his way back.

32:4 *your servant.* A phrase suggesting both courtesy and humility.

32:6 *four hundred.* A round number for a sizable unit of fighting men (see 1 Sam 22:2; 25:13; 30:10).

32:9 *Jacob said.* His first recorded prayer since leaving Bethel.

32:11 *mothers with the children.* Jacob was afraid that Esau's wrath would extend to Jacob's family as well.

32:12 *your descendants as the sand of the sea.* A reference to God's promise in 28:14 (see 22:17 and note).

32:13 *present.* Probably a wordplay: Out of his "two companies" (Hebrew *maḥanayim,* v. 2; see vv. 7–8,10) Jacob selects a "present" (*minḥah*) for his brother.

ing, "When my brother Esau meets you and asks you, saying, 'To whom do you belong, and where are you going, and to whom do these *animals* in front of you belong?'

18 then you shall say, '*These* belong to your servant Jacob; it is a present sent to my lord Esau. And behold, he also is behind us.' "

19 Then he commanded also the second and the third, and all those who followed the droves, saying, "After this manner you shall speak to Esau when you find him;

20 and you shall say, 'Behold, your servant Jacob also is behind us.' " For he said, "I will appease him with the present that goes before me. Then afterward I will see his face; perhaps he will accept me."

21 So the present passed on before him, while he himself spent that night in the camp.

22 Now he arose that same night and took his two wives and his two maids and his eleven children, and crossed the ford of the [a]Jabbok.

23 He took them and sent them across the stream. And he sent across whatever he had.

Jacob Wrestles

24 Then Jacob was left alone, and a man [a]wrestled with him until daybreak.

25 When he saw that he had not prevailed against him, he touched the socket of his thigh; so the socket of Jacob's thigh was dislocated while he wrestled with him.

26 Then he said, "Let me go, for the dawn is breaking." But he said, "[a]I will not let you go unless you bless me."

27 So he said to him, "What is your name?" And he said, "Jacob."

28 [a]He said, "Your name shall no longer be Jacob, but [1]Israel; for you have striven with God and with men and have prevailed."

29 Then [a]Jacob asked him and said, "Please tell me your name." But he said, "Why is it that you ask my name?" And he blessed him there.

30 So Jacob named the place [1]Peniel, for *he said,* "[a]I have seen God face to face, yet my [2]life has been preserved."

31 Now the sun rose upon him just as he crossed over [a]Penuel, and he was limping on his thigh.

32 Therefore, to this day the sons of Israel do not eat the sinew of the hip which is on the socket of the thigh, because he touched the socket of Jacob's thigh in the sinew of the hip.

Jacob Meets Esau

33 Then Jacob lifted his eyes and looked, and behold, [a]Esau was coming, and four hundred men with him. So he divided the children [1]among Leah and Rachel and the two maids.

2 He put the maids and their children [1]in front, and Leah and her children [2]next, and Rachel and Joseph [2]last.

3 But he himself passed on ahead of them and [a]bowed down to the ground seven times, until he came near to his brother.

4 Then Esau ran to meet him and embraced him, and [a]fell on his neck and kissed him, and they wept.

5 He lifted his eyes and saw the women and the children, and said, "[1]Who are these with you?" So he said, "[a]The children whom God has graciously given your servant."

6 Then the maids came near [1]with their children, and they bowed down.

7 Leah likewise came near with her children, and they bowed down; and afterward Joseph came near with Rachel, and they bowed down.

8 And he said, "What do you mean by [a]all this company which I have met?" And he said, "[b]To find favor in the sight of my lord."

22 [a]Deut 3:16; Josh 12:2
24 [a]Hos 12:3, 4
26 [a]Hos 12:4
28 [1]I.e. he who strives with God; or God strives [a]Gen 35:10; 1 Kin 18:31
29 [a]Judg 13:17, 18
30 [1]I.e. the face of God [2]Lit *soul* [a]Gen 16:13; Ex 24:10, 11; 33:20; Num 12:8; Judg 6:22; 13:22
31 [a]Judg 8:8
33:1 [1]Or *to* [a]Gen 32:6
2 [1]Lit *first* [2]Lit *behind*
3 [a]Gen 42:6; 43:26
4 [a]Gen 45:14, 15
5 [1]Or *What relation are these to you?* [a]Gen 48:9; Ps 127:3; Is 8:18
6 [1]Lit *they and*
8 [a]Gen 32:13-16 [b]Gen 32:5

32:22 *Jabbok.* Today called the Wadi Zerqa, flowing westward into the Jordan about 20 miles north of the Dead Sea.
32:24 *left alone.* As he had been at Bethel (28:10–22). *a man.* God Himself (as Jacob eventually realized; see v. 30) in the form of an angel (see Hos 12:3–4 and note on Gen 16:7). *wrestled.* God wrestled (*ye'abeq*) with Jacob (*ya'aqob*) by the Jabbok (*yabboq*)—the author delighted in wordplay. Jacob had struggled all his life to prevail, first with Esau, then with Laban. Now, as he was about to reenter Canaan, he was shown that it was with God that he must "wrestle." It was God who held his destiny in His hands.
32:25 *had not prevailed against him . . . touched the socket.* God came to him in such a form that Jacob could wrestle with Him successfully, yet He showed Jacob that He could disable him at will.
32:26 *I will not let you go.* Jacob's persistence was soon rewarded (v. 29). *unless you bless me.* Jacob finally acknowledged that the blessing must come from God.
32:28 *Your name shall no longer be Jacob.* Now that Jacob had acknowledged God as the source of blessing and was about to reenter the promised land, the Lord acknowledged Jacob as His servant by changing his name (see 17:5 and note). *Israel.* Means "he struggles with God." Here in Father Jacob/Israel, the nation of Israel got her name and her characterization: the people who struggle with God (memorialized in the name Israel) and with men (memorialized in the name Jacob) and overcome. God later confirmed Jacob's new name (35:10).
32:29 *Why is it that you ask my name?* Such a request of God is both unworthy and impossible to fulfill (see Judg 13:17–18).
32:30 *I have seen God face to face, yet my life has been preserved.* See note on 16:13; see also Judg 6:22–23; 13:22. Only God's "back" (see Ex 33:23) or "feet" (see Ex 24:10) or "form" (see Num 12:8), in a symbolic sense, may be seen.
32:32 *do not eat the sinew.* Probably the sciatic muscle. Mentioned nowhere else in the Bible, this dietary prohibition is found in the later writings of Judaism. Jacob retained in his body, and Israel retained in her dietary practice, a perpetual reminder of this fateful encounter with God.
33:2 *Rachel and Joseph last.* Jacob wanted to keep his favorite wife and child farthest away from potential harm.
33:3 *bowed down to the ground seven times.* A sign of total submission, documented also in texts found at Tell el-Amarna in Egypt and dating to the 14th century B.C. (see chart, p. xix).
33:4 All Jacob's fears proved unfounded. God had been at work and had so blessed Esau (v. 9) that he no longer held a grudge against Jacob.

9 But Esau said, "[a]I have plenty, my
brother; let what you have be your own."
10 Jacob said, "No, please, if now I have
found favor in your sight, then take my present from my hand, [1]for I see your face as one
sees the face of God, and you have received
me favorably.
11 "Please take my [1][a]gift which has been
brought to you, [b]because God has dealt graciously with me and because I have [2]plenty."
Thus he urged him and he took *it*.
12 Then [1]Esau said, "Let us take our journey and go, and I will go before you."
13 But he said to him, "My lord knows
that the children are frail and that the flocks
and herds which are nursing are [1]a care to
me. And if they are driven hard one day, all
the flocks will die.
14 "Please let my lord pass on before his
servant, and I will proceed at my leisure,
according to the pace of the cattle that are
before me and according to the pace of the
children, until I come to my lord at [a]Seir."
15 Esau said, "Please let me leave with
you some of the people who are with me."
But he said, "[1]What need is there? [a]Let me
find favor in the sight of my lord."
16 So Esau returned that day on his way to
Seir.
17 Jacob journeyed to [1][a]Succoth, and built
for himself a house and made booths for his
livestock; therefore the place is named Succoth.

Jacob Settles in Shechem

18 Now Jacob came safely to the city of
[a]Shechem, which is in the land of Canaan,
when he came from [b]Paddan-aram, and
camped before the city.
19 [a]He bought the piece of land where he
had pitched his tent from the hand of the
sons of Hamor, Shechem's father, for one
hundred [1]pieces of money.
20 Then he erected there an altar and
called it [1]El-Elohe-Israel.

9 [a]Gen 27:39, 40
10 [1]Lit *for therefore I have seen your face like seeing God's face*
11 [1]Lit *blessing* [2]Lit *all* [a]1 Sam 25:27 [b]Gen 30:43
12 [1]Lit *he*
13 [1]Lit *upon me*
14 [a]Gen 32:3
15 [1]Lit *Why this?* [a]Ruth 2:13
17 [1]I.e. booths [a]Josh 13:27; Judg 8:5, 14; Ps 60:6
18 [a]Gen 12:6; Josh 24:1; Judg 9:1 [b]Gen 25:20; 28:2
19 [1]Heb *qesitah* [a]Josh 24:32; John 4:5
20 [1]I.e. God, the God of Israel

The Treachery of Jacob's Sons

34 Now [a]Dinah the daughter of Leah,
whom she had borne to Jacob, went
out to [1]visit the daughters of the land.
2 When Shechem the son of Hamor [a]the
Hivite, the prince of the land, saw her, he
took her and lay with her [1]by force.
3 [1]He was deeply attracted to Dinah the
daughter of Jacob, and he loved the girl and
[2]spoke tenderly to her.
4 So Shechem [a]spoke to his father Hamor,
saying, "Get me this young girl for a wife."
5 Now Jacob heard that he had defiled
Dinah his daughter; but his sons were with
his livestock in the field, so Jacob kept silent
until they came in.
6 Then Hamor the father of Shechem
went out to Jacob to speak with him.
7 Now the sons of Jacob came in from
the field when they heard *it*; and the men
were grieved, and they were very angry
because he had done a [1][a]disgraceful thing in
Israel [2]by lying with Jacob's daughter, for
such a thing ought not to be done.
8 But Hamor spoke with them, saying,
"The soul of my son Shechem longs for your
daughter; please give her to him [1]in marriage.
9 "Intermarry with us; give your daughters to us and take our daughters for yourselves.
10 "Thus you shall [1]live with us, and [a]the
land shall be *open* before you; [1]live and
[b]trade in it and [c]acquire property in it."
11 Shechem also said to her father and to
her brothers, "If I find favor in your sight,
then I will give whatever you say to me.
12 "Ask me ever so much bridal payment
and gift, and I will give according as you say
to me; but give me the girl [1]in marriage."
13 But Jacob's sons answered Shechem
and his father Hamor with deceit, because
he had defiled Dinah their sister.
14 They said to them, "We cannot do this

34:1 [1]Lit *see* [a]Gen 30:21
2 [1]Lit *and humbled her* [a]Gen 34:30
3 [1]Lit *His soul clung* [2]Lit *spoke to the heart of the girl*
4 [a]Judg 14:2
7 [1]Lit *senseless* [2]Lit *to lie* [a]Deut 22:20-30; Judg 20:6; 2 Sam 13:12
8 [1]Lit *for a wife*
10 [1]Lit *dwell* [a]Gen 13:9; 20:15 [b]Gen 42:34 [c]Gen 47:27
12 [1]Lit *for a wife*

33:9 *my brother.* Esau's generous and loving response was in contrast to Jacob's cautious and fearful "my lord" (v. 8).

33:11 *gift.* The Hebrew for "gift" is the same as that used for "blessing" in 27:35. The author of Genesis was conscious of the irony that Jacob now acknowledged that the blessing he had struggled for was from God. In his last attempt to express reconciliation with Esau, Jacob in a sense gave back the "blessing" he had stolen from his brother, doing so from the blessings the Lord had given him.

33:14 *until I come to my lord at Seir.* But Jacob, still the deceiver, had no intention of following Esau all the way to Seir.

33:18 *Paddan-aram.* Means "plain of Aram," another name for Aram-naharaim (see note on 24:10). *came safely.* The answer to Jacob's prayer of 20 years earlier (see 28:21). *Shechem.* An important city in central Canaan, first built and inhabited during the patriarchal period. Jacob followed in the footsteps of Father Abraham (see 12:6). Jacob dug a well there (see John 4:5–6) that can still be seen today.

33:19 *pieces of money.* The Hebrew word translated by this phrase (*qesitah*, a unit of money of unknown weight and value) is always found in patriarchal contexts (see Josh 24:32; Job 42:11).

33:20 *erected there an altar.* See note on 12:7. *called it El-Elohe-Israel.* Jacob formally acknowledged the God of his fathers as his God also (see 28:21). But he lingered at Shechem and did not return to Bethel (see 35:1), and that meant trouble (see ch. 34).

34:1–31 The name of God ends ch. 33 and begins ch. 35, but it is completely absent from this sordid chapter (see note on 7:16).

34:2 *Shechem.* See 33:19. He was probably named after the city.

34:4 *Get me this young girl for a wife.* See note on 21:21.

34:7 *Israel.* The clan of Israel. *such a thing ought not to be done.* Cf. Tamar's plea to Amnon in a similar situation (2 Sam 13:12).

34:9 *Intermarry with us.* The Canaanites wanted to absorb Israel (see v. 16) in order to benefit from the blessings Jacob had received from the Lord (both his offspring and his possessions—vv. 21–23). This was a danger Israel constantly faced from other peoples and nations—either absorption or hostility, both of which are perpetual threats to the people of God.

34:12 *bridal payment and gift.* For a specific example of this marriage custom see 24:53.

34:13 *Jacob's sons answered . . . with deceit.* Like father, like son (see 27:24; see also note on 25:26).

thing, to give our sister to [a]one who is uncircumcised, for that would be a disgrace to us.
15 "Only on this *condition* will we consent
to you: if you will become like us, in that
every male of you be circumcised,
16 then we will give our daughters to you,
and we will take your daughters for ourselves,
and we will [1]live with you and become one
people.
17 "But if you will not listen to us to be circumcised, then we will take our daughter
and go."
18 Now their words seemed [1]reasonable
to Hamor and Shechem, Hamor's son.
19 The young man did not delay to do the
thing, because he was delighted with Jacob's
daughter. Now he was more respected than
all the household of his father.
20 So Hamor and his son Shechem came
to the [a]gate of their city and spoke to the
men of their city, saying,
21 "These men are [1]friendly with us; therefore let them [2]live in the land and trade in it,
for behold, the land is [3]large enough for
them. Let us take their daughters [4]in marriage, and give our daughters to them.
22 "Only on this *condition* will the men
consent to us to [1]live with us, to become one
people: that every male among us be circumcised as they are circumcised.
23 "Will not their livestock and their property and all their animals be ours? Only let us
consent to them, and they will [1]live with
us."
24 [a]All who went out of the gate of his
city listened to Hamor and to his son Shechem, and every male was circumcised, all
who went out of the gate of his city.
25 Now it came about on the third day,
when they were in pain, that two of Jacob's
sons, [a]Simeon and Levi, Dinah's brothers,
each took his sword and came upon the city
unawares, and killed every male.
26 They killed Hamor and his son Shechem with the edge of the sword, and took
Dinah from Shechem's house, and went
forth.
27 Jacob's sons came upon the slain and
looted the city, because they had defiled
their sister.
28 They took their flocks and their herds
and their donkeys, and that which was in the
city and that which was in the field;
29 and they captured and looted all their
wealth and all their little ones and their
wives, even all that *was* in the houses.
30 Then Jacob said to Simeon and Levi,
"You have [a]brought trouble on me by [b]mak-
ing me odious among the inhabitants of the
land, among [c]the Canaanites and the Perizzites; and [1d]my men being few in number,
they will gather together against me and
[2]attack me and I will be destroyed, I and my
household."
31 But they said, "Should he [1]treat our sister as a harlot?"

Jacob Moves to Bethel

35 Then God said to Jacob, "Arise, go up
to [a]Bethel and [1]live there, and make an
altar there to [b]God, who appeared to you
[c]when you fled [2]from your brother Esau."
2 So Jacob said to his [a]household and to
all who were with him, "Put away [b]the foreign gods which are among you, and [c]purify
yourselves and change your garments;
3 and let us arise and go up to Bethel,
and I will make [a]an altar there to God, [b]who
answered me in the day of my distress and
[c]has been with me [1]wherever I have gone."
4 So they gave to Jacob all the foreign
gods which [1]they had and the rings which
were in their ears, and Jacob hid them under
the [2]oak which was near Shechem.
5 As they journeyed, there was [1a]a great
terror upon the cities which were around
them, and they did not pursue the sons of
Jacob.
6 So Jacob came to [a]Luz (that is, Bethel),
which is in the land of Canaan, he and all
the people who were with him.
7 [a]He built an altar there, and called the
place [1]El-bethel, because there God had
revealed Himself to him when he fled [2]from
his brother.
8 Now [a]Deborah, Rebekah's nurse, died,
and she was buried below Bethel under the
oak; it was named [1]Allon-bacuth.

Jacob Is Named Israel

9 Then God appeared to Jacob again

14 [a]Gen 17:14
16 [1]Lit *dwell*
18 [1]Lit *good*
20 [a]Ruth 4:1; 2 Sam 15:2
21 [1]Lit *peaceful* [2]Lit *dwell* [3]Lit *wide of hands before them* [4]Lit *to us for wives*
22 [1]Lit *dwell*
23 [1]Lit *dwell*
24 [a]Gen 23:10
25 [a]Gen 49:5-7
30 [1]Lit *I, few in number* [2]Lit *smite* [a]Josh 7:25 [b]Ex 5:21; 1 Sam 13:4; 2 Sam 10:6 [c]Gen 13:7; 34:2 [d]Gen 46:26, 27; Deut 4:27; 1 Chr 16:19; Ps 105:12
31 [1]Or *make*
35:1 [1]Lit *dwell* [2]Lit *from the face of* [a]Gen 28:19 [b]Gen 28:13 [c]Gen 27:43
2 [a]Gen 18:19; Josh 24:15 [b]Gen 31:19, 30, 34 [c]Ex 19:10, 14
3 [1]Lit *in the way which* [a]Gen 28:20-22 [b]Ps 107:6 [c]Gen 28:15; 31:3, 42
4 [1]Lit *were in their hand* [2]Or *terebinth*
5 [1]Or *a terror of God* [a]Ex 15:16; 23:27; Deut 2:25
6 [a]Gen 28:19; 48:3
7 [1]I.e. the God of Bethel [2]Lit *from the face of* [a]Gen 35:3
8 [1]I.e. oak of weeping [a]Gen 24:59

34:15 Using a sacred ceremony for a sinful purpose (see vv. 24–25).
34:20 *gate of their city.* See notes on 19:1; 23:10.
34:23 The greed of the men of Shechem led to their destruction.
34:24 The Canaanites were even willing to submit to Israel's covenant rite in order to attain their purposes.
34:25 *Simeon and Levi.* Because they slaughtered the men of Shechem, their own descendants would be scattered far and wide (see note on 49:7). *Dinah's brothers.* All three were children of Leah (29:33–34; 30:21). *killed every male.* Shechem's crime, serious as it was, hardly warranted such brutal and extensive retaliation (see vv. 27–29).
34:30 *Perizzites.* See note on 13:7.
35:1 *God . . . appeared to you when you fled.* See v. 7; 28:13.
35:2 *foreign gods which are among you.* See note on 31:19 (see also Josh 24:23).
35:3 *God . . . has been with me.* See 28:15; see also note on 26:3.
35:4 *rings.* Worn as amulets or charms; a pagan religious custom (cf. Hos 2:13). *the oak . . . near Shechem.* Obviously a well-known tree, perhaps the "oak" mentioned in 12:6 (see Josh 24:26).
35:5 *a great terror.* God protected His servant.
35:7 *built an altar.* See note on 12:7.
35:8 *Deborah, Rebekah's nurse, died.* After long years of faithful service (see 24:59). *the oak.* Again probably a well-known tree (see note on v. 4), perhaps the "oak" mentioned in 1 Sam 10:3. *below.* Either "lower than" or "to the south of."
35:9 *Jacob . . . when he came.* See map, p. 47. *Paddan-aram.*

when he came from Paddan-aram, and He [a]blessed him.

10 [a]God said to him,

"Your name is Jacob;
[1]You shall no longer be called Jacob,
But Israel shall be your name."

Thus He called [2]him Israel.

11 God also said to him,

"I am [1][a]God Almighty;
[b]Be fruitful and multiply;
A nation and a [c]company of nations
shall [2]come from you,
And [d]kings shall [2]come forth from
[3]you.

12 "[a]The land which I gave to Abraham
and Isaac,
I will give it to you,
And I will give the land to your
[1]descendants after you."

13 Then [a]God went up from him in the place where He had spoken with him.

14 Jacob set up [a]a pillar in the place where He had spoken with him, a pillar of stone, and he poured out a drink offering on it; he also poured oil on it.

15 So Jacob named the place where God had spoken with him, [1][a]Bethel.

16 Then they journeyed from Bethel; and when there was still some distance to go to [a]Ephrath, Rachel began to give birth and she [1]suffered severe labor.

17 When she was in severe labor the midwife said to her, "Do not fear, for now [a]you have another son."

18 It came about as her soul was departing (for she died), that she named him [1]Benoni; but his father called him [2]Benjamin.

19 So [a]Rachel died and was buried on the way to [b]Ephrath (that is, Bethlehem).

20 Jacob set up a pillar over her grave; that is the [a]pillar of Rachel's grave to this day.

21 Then Israel journeyed on and pitched his tent beyond the [1][a]tower of [2]Eder.

22 It came about while Israel was dwelling in that land, that [a]Reuben went and lay with Bilhah his father's concubine, and Israel heard *of it*.

The Sons of Israel

Now there were twelve sons of Jacob—

23 [a]the sons of Leah: Reuben, Jacob's firstborn, then Simeon and Levi and Judah and Issachar and Zebulun;

24 [a]the sons of Rachel: Joseph and Benjamin;

25 and [a]the sons of Bilhah, Rachel's maid: Dan and Naphtali;

26 and [a]the sons of Zilpah, Leah's maid: Gad and Asher. These are the sons of Jacob who were born to him in Paddan-aram.

27 Jacob came to his father Isaac at [a]Mamre of [b]Kiriath-arba (that is, Hebron), where Abraham and Isaac had sojourned.

28 Now the days of Isaac were [a]one hundred and eighty years.

29 Isaac breathed his last and died and was [a]gathered to his people, an [b]old man [1]of ripe age; and [c]his sons Esau and Jacob buried him.

Esau Moves

36 Now these are *the records of* the generations of [a]Esau (that is, Edom).

2 Esau [a]took his wives from the daughters of Canaan: Adah the daughter of Elon

9 [a]Gen 32:29
10 [1]Lit *Your name* [2]Lit *his name* [a]Gen 17:5; 32:28
11 [1]Heb *El Shaddai* [2]Or *come into being* [3]Lit *your loins* [a]Gen 17:1; 28:3; Ex 6:3 [b]Gen 9:1, 7 [c]Gen 48:4 [d]Gen 17:6, 16; 36:31
12 [1]Lit *seed* [a]Gen 12:7; 13:15; 26:3, 4; 28:13; Ex 32:13
13 [a]Gen 17:22; 18:33
14 [a]Gen 28:18, 19; 31:45
15 [1]I.e. the house of God [a]Gen 28:19
16 [1]Lit *had difficulty in her giving birth* [a]Gen 35:19; 48:7; Ruth 4:11; Mic 5:2
17 [a]Gen 30:24
18 [1]I.e. the son of my sorrow [2]I.e. the son of the right hand
19 [a]Gen 48:7 [b]Ruth 1:2; 4:11; Mic 5:2
20 [a]1 Sam 10:2
21 [1]Heb *Migdal-eder* [2]Or *flock* [a]Mic 4:8
22 [a]Gen 49:4; 1 Chr 5:1
23 [a]Gen 29:31-35; 30:18-20; 46:8; Ex 1:1-4
24 [a]Gen 30:22-24; 35:18
25 [a]Gen 30:5-8
26 [a]Gen 30:10-13
27 [a]Gen 13:18; 18:1; 23:19 [b]Josh 14:15
28 [a]Gen 25:26
29 [1]Lit *and satisfied with days* [a]Gen 25:8; 49:33 [b]Gen 15:15 [c]Gen 25:9 **36:1** [a]Gen 25:30 **2** [a]Gen 28:9

Means "plain of Aram," another name for Aram-naharaim (see note on 24:10).
35:10 *Jacob . . . Israel.* The previous assignment of an additional name (see 32:28) is here confirmed. For similar examples compare 21:31 with 26:33, and 28:19 with 35:15.
35:11–12 This event climaxes the Isaac-Jacob cycle (see Introduction: Literary Features). Now that Jacob was at last back at Bethel, where God had begun His direct relationship with him, God confirmed to this chosen son of Isaac the covenant promises made to Abraham (17:1–8; see 28:3). His words echo His original benediction pronounced on man in the beginning (1:28) and renewed after the flood (9:1,7). God's blessing on mankind would be fulfilled in and through Jacob and his offspring. See also 47:27; Ex 1:7.
35:13 See note on 17:22.
35:14 See 28:18 and note. *drink offering.* A liquid poured out as a sacrifice to a deity.
35:15 See 28:19; see also note on v. 10.
35:16 *Ephrath.* The older name for Bethlehem (see v. 19) in Judah (see Ruth 1:2; Mic 5:2).
35:17 *another son.* An echo of Rachel's own plea at the time of Joseph's birth (see 30:24).
35:18 *Benjamin.* The name can mean "son of the right hand" or "son of the south"—in distinction from the other sons, who were born in the north. One set of Hebrew terms for indicating direction was based on facing east, so south was on the right.
35:19 *Rachel died.* In childbirth (see note on 30:1).
35:20 *Rachel's grave.* See 1 Sam 10:2. The traditional, though not authentic, site is near Bethlehem.
35:21 *tower of Eder.* Means "tower of the flock," doubtless referring to a watchtower built to discourage thieves from stealing sheep and other animals (see, e.g., 2 Chr 26:10). The same Hebrew phrase is used figuratively in Mic 4:8, where "flock" refers to the people of Judah (see Mic 4:6–7).
35:22 Reuben's act was an arrogant and premature claim to the rights of the firstborn—here the right to inherit his father's concubine. For this he would lose his legal status as firstborn (see 49:3–4; 1 Chr 5:1; see also note on 37:21).
35:26 *sons of Jacob . . . born to him in Paddan-aram.* Obviously a summary statement since Benjamin was born in Canaan (see vv. 16–18).
35:27 *Mamre of Kiriath-arba (that is, Hebron).* See notes on 13:18; 23:2.
35:29 See note on 25:8. *buried him.* In the family tomb, the cave of Machpelah (49:30–31).
36:1 *generations.* See note on 2:4. Though repeated in v. 9, the word does not mark the start of a new main section there since the information in vv. 9–43 is merely an expansion of that in vv. 1–8. *Esau (that is, Edom).* See note on 25:25. Reddish rock formations, primarily sandstone, are conspicuous in the territory of the Edomites, located south and southeast of the Dead Sea.
36:2–3 See note on 26:34.

the Hittite, and [b]Oholibamah the daughter of Anah and the [c]granddaughter of Zibeon the Hivite;

3 also Basemath, Ishmael's daughter, the sister of Nebaioth.

4 Adah bore [a]Eliphaz to Esau, and Basemath bore Reuel,

5 and Oholibamah bore Jeush and Jalam and Korah. These are the sons of Esau who were born to him in the land of Canaan.

6 [a]Then Esau took his wives and his sons and his daughters and all [1]his household, and his livestock and all his cattle and all his goods which he had acquired in the land of Canaan, and went to *another* land away from his brother Jacob.

7 [a]For their property had become too great for them to [1]live together, and the [b]land where they [c]sojourned could not sustain them because of their livestock.

8 So Esau lived in the hill country of [a]Seir; Esau is [b]Edom.

Descendants of Esau

9 These then are *the records of* the generations of Esau the father of [1]the Edomites in the hill country of Seir.

10 These are the names of Esau's sons: Eliphaz the son of Esau's wife Adah, Reuel the son of Esau's wife Basemath.

11 The sons of Eliphaz were Teman, Omar, [1]Zepho and Gatam and Kenaz.

12 Timna was a concubine of Esau's son Eliphaz and she bore [a]Amalek to Eliphaz. These are the sons of Esau's wife Adah.

13 These are the sons of Reuel: Nahath and Zerah, Shammah and Mizzah. These were the sons of Esau's wife Basemath.

14 These were the sons of Esau's wife Oholibamah, the daughter of Anah and the [1]granddaughter of Zibeon: [2]she bore to Esau, Jeush and Jalam and Korah.

15 These are the chiefs of the sons of Esau. The sons of Eliphaz, the firstborn of Esau, are chief Teman, chief Omar, chief Zepho, chief Kenaz,

16 chief Korah, chief Gatam, chief Amalek. These are the chiefs [1]descended from Eliphaz in the land of Edom; these are the sons of Adah.

17 These are the sons of Reuel, Esau's son: chief Nahath, chief Zerah, chief Shammah, chief Mizzah. These are the chiefs [1]descended from Reuel in the land of Edom; these are the sons of Esau's wife Basemath.

18 These are the sons of Esau's wife Oholibamah: chief Jeush, chief Jalam, chief Korah. These are the chiefs [1]descended from Esau's wife Oholibamah, the daughter of Anah.

19 These are the sons of Esau (that is, Edom), and these are their chiefs.

20 These are the sons of Seir [a]the Horite, the inhabitants of the land: Lotan and Shobal and Zibeon and Anah,

21 and Dishon and Ezer and Dishan. These are the chiefs [1]descended from the Horites, the sons of Seir in the land of Edom.

22 The sons of Lotan were Hori and [1]Hemam; and Lotan's sister was Timna.

23 These are the sons of Shobal: [1]Alvan and Manahath and Ebal, [2]Shepho and Onam.

24 These are the sons of Zibeon: Aiah and Anah—he is the Anah who found the hot springs in the wilderness when he was pasturing the donkeys of his father Zibeon.

25 These are the children of Anah: Dishon, and Oholibamah, the daughter of Anah.

26 These are the sons of [1a]Dishon: [2]Hemdan and Eshban and Ithran and Cheran.

27 These are the sons of Ezer: Bilhan and Zaavan and [1]Akan.

28 These are the sons of Dishan: Uz and Aran.

29 These are the chiefs [1]descended from the Horites: chief Lotan, chief Shobal, chief Zibeon, chief Anah,

30 chief Dishon, chief Ezer, chief Dishan. These are the chiefs [1]descended from the Horites, according to their *various* chiefs in the land of Seir.

31 Now these are the kings who reigned in the land of Edom before any [a]king reigned over the sons of Israel.

32 [1a]Bela the son of Beor reigned in Edom, and the name of his city was Dinhabah.

33 Then Bela died, and Jobab the son of Zerah of Bozrah became king in his place.

34 Then Jobab died, and Husham of the land of the Temanites became king in his place.

35 Then Husham died, and Hadad the son of Bedad, who [1]defeated Midian in the field of Moab, became king in his place; and the name of his city was Avith.

36 Then Hadad died, and Samlah of Masrekah became king in his place.

37 Then Samlah died, and Shaul of Rehoboth on the *Euphrates* River became king in his place.

2 [b]Gen 36:25 [c]Gen 36:24
4 [a]1 Chr 1:35
6 [1]Lit *the souls of his house* [a]Gen 12:5
7 [1]Lit *dwell* [a]Gen 13:6 [b]Gen 17:8; Heb 11:9 [c]1 Chr 29:15; Ps 39:12
8 [a]Gen 32:3 [b]Gen 36:1, 19
9 [1]Lit *Edom*
11 [1]In 1 Chr 1:36, *Zephi*
12 [a]Ex 17:8-16; Num 24:20; Deut 25:17-19; 1 Sam 15:2, 3
14 [1]Gr *son* [2]Lit *and she*
16 [1]Lit *of Eliphaz*
17 [1]Lit *of Reuel*
18 [1]Lit *of Oholibamah, Esau's wife*
20 [a]Gen 14:6; Deut 2:12, 22; 1 Chr 1:38-42
21 [1]Lit *of the Horites*
22 [1]In 1 Chr 1:39, *Homam*
23 [1]In 1 Chr 1:40, *Alian* [2]In 1 Chr 1:40, *Shephi*
26 [1]Heb *Dishan* [2]In 1 Chr 1:41, *Hamran* [a]1 Chr 1:41
27 [1]In 1 Chr 1:42, *Jaakan*
29 [1]Lit *of the Horites*
30 [1]Lit *of the Horites*
31 [a]Gen 17:6, 16; 35:11; 1 Chr 1:43
32 [1]Lit *And Bela* [a]1 Chr 1:43
35 [1]Or *smote*

36:7 See 13:6; see also 26:20 and note.

36:8 *Seir.* Another name for Edom. The word itself is related to the Hebrew word meaning "hair," a possible meaning also for the name "Esau" (see note on 25:25). Esau's clan must have driven away the original Horite (see v. 20) inhabitants of Seir (see 14:6 and note). The descendants of Seir are listed in vv. 20–28.

36:10–14 The same list of Esau's descendants (see 1 Chr 1:35–37) is repeated in vv. 15–19 as a list of tribal chieftains.

36:11 *Eliphaz . . . Teman.* One of Job's friends was named Eliphaz the Temanite (Job 2:11), and Job himself was from the land of Uz (Job 1:1). Thus Job probably lived in Edom (see vv. 28,34).

36:12 *Amalek.* See note on 14:7.

36:20–28 See note on v. 8. The same list of Seir's descendants (see 1 Chr 1:38–42) is repeated in abbreviated form in vv. 29–30 as a list of tribal chieftains.

36:31 *before any king reigned over the sons of Israel.* Presupposes the later Israelite monarchy and is therefore an editorial updating subsequent to Moses' time (see note on 14:14).

38 Then Shaul died, and Baal-hanan the son of Achbor became king in his place.

39 Then Baal-hanan the son of Achbor died, and [1]Hadar became king in his place; and the name of his city was [2]Pau; and his wife's name was Mehetabel, the daughter of Matred, daughter of Mezahab.

40 Now these are the names of the chiefs [1]descended from Esau, according to their families *and* their localities, by their names: chief Timna, chief [2]Alvah, chief Jetheth,

41 chief Oholibamah, chief Elah, chief Pinon,

42 chief Kenaz, chief Teman, chief Mibzar,

43 chief Magdiel, chief Iram. These are the chiefs of Edom (that is, Esau, the father of [1]the Edomites), according to their habitations in the land of their possession.

Joseph's Dream

37 Now Jacob lived in [a]the land [1]where his father had sojourned, in the land of Canaan.

2 These are *the records of* the generations of Jacob.

Joseph, when [a]seventeen years of age, was pasturing the flock with his brothers while he was *still* a youth, along with [b]the sons of Bilhah and the sons of Zilpah, his father's wives. And Joseph brought back a [c]bad report about them to their father.

3 Now Israel loved Joseph more than all his sons, because he was [a]the son of his old age; and he made him a [1b]varicolored tunic.

4 His brothers saw that their father loved him more than all his brothers; and *so* they [a]hated him and could not speak to him [1]on friendly terms.

5 Then Joseph [1a]had a dream, and when he told it to his brothers, they hated him even more.

6 He said to them, "Please listen to this dream which I have [1]had;

7 for behold, we were binding sheaves in the field, and lo, my sheaf rose up and also stood erect; and behold, your sheaves gathered around and [a]bowed down to my sheaf."

8 Then his brothers said to him, "[a]Are you actually going to reign over us? Or are you really going to rule over us?" So they hated him even more for his dreams and for his words.

9 Now he [1]had still another dream, and related it to his brothers, and said, "Lo, I have [1]had still another dream; and behold, the sun and the moon and eleven stars were bowing down to me."

10 He related *it* to his father and to his brothers; and his father rebuked him and said to him, "What is this dream that you have [1]had? Shall I and your mother and [a]your brothers actually come to bow ourselves down before you to the ground?"

11 [a]His brothers were jealous of him, but his father [b]kept the saying *in mind.*

12 Then his brothers went to pasture their father's flock in Shechem.

13 Israel said to Joseph, "Are not your brothers pasturing *the flock* in [a]Shechem? Come, and I will send you to them." And he said to him, "[1]I will go."

14 Then he said to him, "Go now and see about the welfare of your brothers and the welfare of the flock, and bring word back to me." So he sent him from the valley of [a]Hebron, and he came to Shechem.

15 A man found him, and behold, he was wandering in the field; and the man asked him, "[1]What are you looking for?"

16 He said, "I am looking for my brothers; please tell me where they are pasturing *the flock.*"

39 [1]In 1 Chr 1:50, *Hadad* [2]In 1 Chr 1:50, *Pai*
40 [1]Lit *of Esau* [2]In 1 Chr 1:51, *Aliah*
43 [1]Heb *Edom*
37:1 [1]Lit *of his father's sojournings* [a]Gen 17:8; 28:4
2 [a]Gen 41:46 [b]Gen 35:25, 26 [c]1 Sam 2:22-24
3 [1]Or *full-length robe* [a]Gen 44:20 [b]Gen 37:23, 32
4 [1]Lit *in peace* [a]Gen 27:41; 1 Sam 17:28
5 [1]Lit *dreamed* [a]Gen 28:12; 31:10, 11, 24
6 [1]Lit *dreamed*
7 [a]Gen 42:6, 9; 43:26; 44:14
8 [a]Gen 49:26; Deut 33:16
9 [1]Lit *dreamed*
10 [1]Lit *dreamed* [a]Gen 27:29
11 [a]Acts 7:9 [b]Dan 7:28; Luke 2:19, 51
13 [1]Lit *Behold me* [a]Gen 33:18-20
14 [a]Gen 13:18; 23:2, 19; 35:27; Josh 14:14, 15; Judg 1:10
15 [1]Lit *saying, "What...?"*

36:43 *These . . . possession.* A summary statement for the whole chapter (just as v. 1 is a title for the whole chapter).

37:1 *Canaan.* Jacob made the promised land his homeland and was later buried there (49:29–30; 50:13). His son Joseph also insisted on being buried in Canaan, which he recognized as the land the Lord had promised to Israel (50:24–25). The Jacob-Joseph cycle (see Introduction: Literary Features) begins and ends with references to the land of promise.

37:2 *generations.* See note on 2:4. The word here introduces the tenth and final main section of Genesis. *Joseph.* The author immediately introduces Joseph, on whom the last cycle of the patriarchal narrative centers. In his generation, he, more than any other, represented Israel—as a people who struggled with God and with men and overcame (see note on 32:28) and as a source of blessing to the nations (see 12:2–3). It is, moreover, through the life of Joseph that the covenant family in Canaan becomes an emerging nation in Egypt, thus setting the stage for the exodus. The story of God's dealings with the patriarchs foreshadows the subsequent Biblical account of God's purpose with Israel. It begins with the election and calling out of Abram from the post-Babel nations and ends with Israel in Egypt (in the person of Joseph) preserving the life of the nations (see 41:57; 50:20). So God would deliver Israel out of the nations (the exodus), eventually to send them on a mission of life to the nations (cf. Matt 28:18–20; Acts 1:8). *a bad report about them.* Doubtless about all his brothers (as the later context indicates), not just the sons of his father's concubines.

37:3 *varicolored tunic.* A mark of Jacob's favoritism, "for in this manner the virgin daughters of the king dressed themselves in robes" (2 Sam 13:18).

37:5 *dream.* See note on 20:3.

37:7 *bowed down.* Joseph's dream would later come true (42:6; 43:26; 44:14).

37:8 *are you really going to rule over us?* Joseph would later become the "the one distinguished among his brothers" (Deut 33:16) and receive "the birthright" (1 Chr 5:2), at least the double portion of the inheritance (see note on 25:5), since his father adopted his two sons (48:5).

37:10 *your mother.* Jacob possibly refers to Leah, since Rachel has already died (see 35:19). *bow ourselves down before you.* An unsettling echo of a hope expressed earlier to Jacob by his father Isaac (see 27:29).

37:11 *kept the saying in mind.* A hint that Jacob later recalled Joseph's dreams when events brought about their fulfillment. Cf. Mary's equally sensitive response to events during Jesus' boyhood days (Luke 2:19,51).

37:12 *Shechem.* See note on 33:18.

17 Then the man said, "They have moved from here; for I heard *them* say, 'Let us go to [a]Dothan.' " So Joseph went after his brothers and found them at Dothan.

The Plot against Joseph

18 [1]When they saw him from a distance and before he came close to them, they [a]plotted against him to put him to death.

19 They said to one another, "[1]Here comes this dreamer!

20 "Now then, come and let us kill him and throw him into one of the pits; and [a]we will say, 'A wild beast devoured him.' Then let us see what will become of his dreams!"

21 But [a]Reuben heard *this* and rescued him out of their hands and said, "Let us not [1]take his life."

22 Reuben further said to them, "Shed no blood. Throw him into this pit that is in the wilderness, but do not lay hands on him"—that he might rescue him out of their hands, to restore him to his father.

23 So it came about, when Joseph [1]reached his brothers, that they stripped Joseph of his [2]tunic, the varicolored tunic that was on him;

24 and they took him and threw him into the pit. Now the pit was empty, without any water in it.

25 Then they sat down to eat [1]a meal. And as they raised their eyes and looked, behold, a caravan of [a]Ishmaelites was coming from Gilead, with their camels bearing [2][b]aromatic gum and [3][c]balm and [4]myrrh, [5]on their way to bring *them* down to Egypt.

26 Judah said to his brothers, "What profit is it for us to kill our brother and [a]cover up his blood?

27 "[a]Come and let us sell him to the Ishmaelites and not lay our hands on him, for he is our brother, our *own* flesh." And his brothers listened *to him.*

28 Then some [a]Midianite traders passed by, so they pulled *him* up and lifted Joseph out of the pit, and [b]sold [1]him to the Ishmaelites for twenty *shekels* of silver. Thus [c]they brought Joseph into Egypt.

29 Now Reuben returned to the pit, and behold, Joseph was not in the pit; so he [a]tore his garments.

30 He returned to his brothers and said, "[a]The boy is not *there;* as for me, where am I to go?"

31 So [a]they took Joseph's tunic, and slaughtered a male goat and dipped the tunic in the blood;

32 and they sent the varicolored tunic and brought it to their father and said, "We found this; please [1]examine *it* to *see* whether it is your son's tunic or not."

33 Then he [1]examined it and said, "It is my son's tunic. [a]A wild beast has devoured him; [b]Joseph has surely been torn to pieces!"

34 So Jacob [a]tore his clothes, and put sackcloth on his loins and mourned for his son many days.

35 Then all his sons and all his daughters arose to comfort him, but he refused to be comforted. And he said, "Surely I will [a]go down to Sheol in mourning for my son." So his father wept for him.

36 Meanwhile, the [1]Midianites [a]sold him in Egypt to Potiphar, Pharaoh's officer, the captain of the bodyguard.

Judah and Tamar

38 And it came about at that time, that Judah [1]departed from his brothers and

17 [a]2 Kin 6:13
18 [1]Or *And* [a]Ps 31:13; 37:12, 32; Mark 14:1; John 11:53; Acts 23:12
19 [1]Lit *Behold, this master of dreams comes*
20 [a]Gen 37:32, 33
21 [1]Lit *smite his soul* [a]Gen 42:22
23 [1]Lit *came to* [2]Or *full-length robe*
25 [1]Lit *bread* [2]Or *ladanum spice* [3]Or *mastic* [4]Or *resinous bark* [5]Lit *going* [a]Gen 16:11, 12; 37:28; 39:1 [b]Gen 43:11 [c]Jer 8:22; 46:11
26 [a]Gen 37:20
27 [a]Gen 42:21
28 [1]Lit *Joseph* [a]Gen 37:25; Judg 6:1-3; 8:22, 24 [b]Gen 45:4, 5; Ps 105:17; Acts 7:9 [c]Gen 39:1
29 [a]Gen 37:34; 44:13
30 [a]Gen 42:13, 36
31 [a]Gen 37:3, 23
32 [1]Or *recognize*
33 [1]Or *recognized* [a]Gen 37:20 [b]Gen 44:28
34 [a]Gen 37:29
35 [a]Gen 25:8; 35:29; 42:38; 44:29, 31
36 [1]Lit *Medanites* [a]Gen 39:1
38:1 [1]Lit *went down*

37:17 *Dothan.* Located about 13 miles north of Shechem, Dothan was already an ancient city by this time.

37:19 *dreamer.* The Hebrew for this word means "master of dreams" or "dream expert" and is here used with obvious sarcasm.

37:21 *Reuben . . . rescued him.* As Jacob's firstborn, he felt responsible for Joseph. He would later remind his brothers of this day (42:22). Initially Reuben's attempts to influence events seemed successful (30:14–17). But after his arrogant incest with Bilhah (see 35:22 and note) his efforts were always ineffective (see 42:37–38)—demonstrating his loss of the status of firstborn (see 49:3–4). Effective leadership passed to Judah (see vv. 26–27; 43:3–5,8–10; 44:14–34; 46:28; 49:8–12).

37:23–24 Similarly, in Egypt Joseph (though innocent of any wrongdoing) would be stripped of his position of privilege and thrown into prison—also as a result of domestic intrigue (ch. 39). His cloak also would be torn from him and shown to Potiphar, but he would be rescued (41:14).

37:25 *Ishmaelites.* Also called Midianites (v. 28; see Judg 8:22,24,26) and Medanites (the literal Hebrew for "Midianites" in v. 36). These various tribal groups were interrelated, since Midian and Medan, like Ishmael, were also sons of Abraham (25:2). *Gilead.* See note on 31:21. *balm.* An oil or gum, with healing properties (see Jer 51:8), exuded by the fruit or stems of one or more kinds of small trees. The balm of Gilead was especially effective (see Jer 8:22; 46:11). *myrrh.* Probably to be identified with labdanum, an aromatic gum (see Ps 45:8; Prov 7:17; Song 3:6; 5:13) exuded from the leaves of the cistus rose. Its oil was used in beauty treatments (see Esth 2:12), and it was sometimes mixed with wine and drunk to relieve pain (see Mark 15:23). As a gift fit for a king, myrrh was brought to Jesus after His birth (Matt 2:11) and applied to His body after His death (John 19:39–40).

37:28 *twenty shekels of silver.* In later times, this amount was the value of a male of Joseph's age who had been dedicated to the Lord (see Lev 27:5).

37:31–33 Again a slaughtered goat figures prominently in an act of deception (see 27:5–13).

37:34 *tore his clothes.* See v. 29. *put sackcloth on.* Wearing coarse and uncomfortable sackcloth instead of ordinary clothes was a sign of mourning.

37:35 *daughters.* The term can include daughters-in-law (e.g., a daughter-in-law of Jacob is mentioned in 38:2). *Sheol.* The grave. According to some, the Hebrew word *Sheol* can also refer in a more general way to the realm of the dead, the netherworld, where, it was thought, departed spirits live (for a description of *Sheol* see, e.g., Job 3:13–19).

37:36 *sold.* "As a slave" (Ps 105:17). The peoples of the Arabian Desert were long involved in international slave trade (cf. Amos 1:6,9). *bodyguard.* The Hebrew for this word can mean "executioners" (the captain of whom was in charge of the royal prisoners; see 40:4), or it can mean "butchers" (the captain of whom was the chief cook in the royal court; cf. 1 Sam 9:23–24).

38:1–30 The unsavory events of this chapter illustrate the dan-

[2]visited a certain [a]Adullamite, whose name
was Hirah.
2 Judah saw there a daughter of a certain
Canaanite whose name was [a]Shua; and he
took her and went in to her.
3 So she conceived and bore a son and
he named him [a]Er.
4 Then she conceived again and bore a
son and named him [a]Onan.
5 She bore still another son and named
him [a]Shelah; and it was at Chezib [1]that she
bore him.
6 Now Judah took a wife for Er his firstborn, and her name *was* Tamar.
7 But [a]Er, Judah's firstborn, was evil in
the sight of the LORD, so the LORD took his life.
8 Then Judah said to Onan, "[a]Go in to
your brother's wife, and perform your duty
as a brother-in-law to her, and raise up [1]off-
spring for your brother."
9 Onan knew that the [1a]offspring would
not be his; so when he went in to his brother's wife, he [2]wasted his seed on the ground
in order not to give [1]offspring to his brother.
10 But what he did was displeasing in the
sight of the LORD; so He [a]took his life also.
11 Then Judah said to his daughter-in-law
Tamar, "[a]Remain a widow in your father's
house until my son Shelah grows up"; for he
[1]thought, "*I am afraid* that he too may die
like his brothers." So Tamar went and lived
in her father's house.
12 Now [1]after a considerable time Shua's
daughter, the wife of Judah, died; and when
[2]the time of mourning was ended, Judah
went up to his sheepshearers at [a]Timnah, he
and his friend Hirah the Adullamite.
13 It was told to Tamar, "[1]Behold, your
father-in-law is going up to [a]Timnah to shear
his sheep."
14 So she [1]removed her widow's garments
and [a]covered *herself* with a [2]veil, and
wrapped herself, and sat in the gateway of
[3]Enaim, which is on the road to Timnah; for
she saw that Shelah had grown up, and [b]she
had not been given to him as a wife.
15 When Judah saw her, he thought she
was a harlot, for she had covered her face.
16 So he turned aside to her by the road,
and said, "[1]Here now, let me come in to
you"; for he did not know that she was his
daughter-in-law. And she said, "What will
you give me, that you may come in to me?"
17 He said, therefore, "I will send you a
[1]young goat from the flock." She said, moreover, "Will you give a pledge until you send
it?"
18 He said, "What pledge shall I give
you?" And she said, "[a]Your seal and your
cord, and your staff that is in your hand." So
he gave *them* to her and went in to her, and
she conceived by him.
19 Then she arose and departed, and
[1]removed her [2]veil and put on her widow's
garments.
20 When Judah sent the [1]young goat by
his friend the Adullamite, to receive the
pledge from the woman's hand, he did not
find her.
21 He asked the men of her place, saying,
"Where is the temple prostitute who was by
the road at Enaim?" But they said, "There
has been no temple prostitute here."
22 So he returned to Judah, and said, "I
did not find her; and furthermore, the men of
the place said, 'There has been no temple
prostitute here.'"
23 Then Judah said, "Let her [1]keep them,
otherwise we will become a laughingstock.
[2]After all, I sent this young goat, but you did
not find her."
24 Now it was about three months later

38:1 [2]Lit *turned aside to* [a]Josh 15:35; 1 Sam 22:1
2 [a]1 Chr 2:3
3 [a]Gen 46:12; Num 26:19
4 [a]Gen 46:12
5 [1]Lit *when* [a]Num 26:20
7 [a]Gen 46:12; Num 26:19; 1 Chr 2:3
8 [1]Lit *seed* [a]Deut 25:5, 6; Matt 22:24
9 [1]Lit *seed* [2]Lit *spilled on the ground* [a]Deut 25:6
10 [a]Gen 46:12; Num 26:19
11 [1]Lit *said* [a]Ruth 1:12, 13
12 [1]Lit *the days became many and* [2]Lit *Judah was comforted, he* [a]Josh 15:10, 57
13 [1]Lit *saying, Behold* [a]Josh 15:10, 57; Judg 14:1
14 [1]Lit *removed from herself*
14 [2]Or *shawl* [3]In Josh 15:34, *Enam* [a]Gen 24:65 [b]Gen 38:11, 26
16 [1]Or *Come, now*
17 [1]Lit *kid of goats*
18 [a]Gen 38:25; 41:42
19 [1]Lit *removed from herself* [2]Or *shawl*
20 [1]Lit *kid of goats by the hand of*
23 [1]Lit *take for herself* [2]Lit *Behold*

ger that Israel as God's separated people faced if they remained among the Canaanites (see 15:16 and note). In Egypt the Israelites were kept separate because the Egyptians despised them (43:32; 46:34). While there, God's people were able to develop into a nation without losing their identity. Judah's actions contrasted with those of Joseph (ch. 39)—demonstrating the moral superiority of Joseph, to whom leadership in Israel fell in his generation (see 37:5–9).

38:1 *departed from his brothers.* Joseph was separated from his brothers by force, but Judah voluntarily separated himself to seek his fortune among the Canaanites. *Adullamite.* Adullam was a town southwest of Jerusalem (see 2 Chr 11:5,7).

38:3–4 *Er . . . Onan.* The names also appear as designations of tribes in Mesopotamian documents of this time.

38:5 *Chezib.* Probably the same as Achzib (Josh 15:44), three miles west of Adullam. The "men of Cozeba" (another form of the same word) were descendants of Shelah son of Judah (see 1 Chr 4:21–22). The Hebrew root of the name means "deception" (see Mic 1:14 and note), a theme running throughout the story of Jacob and his sons.

38:6 *Judah took a wife for Er.* See note on 21:21.

38:8 A concise description of the custom known as "levirate marriage" (Latin *levir* means "brother-in-law"). Details of the practice are given in Deut 25:5–6, where it is laid down as a legal obligation within Israel (cf. Matt 22:24). The custom is illustrated in Ruth 4:5, though there it is extended to the nearest living relative (see Ruth 3:12 and note on Ruth 2:20), since neither Boaz nor the nearer kinsman was a brother-in-law.

38:9 *knew that the offspring would not be his.* Similarly, Ruth's nearest kinsman was fearful that if he married Ruth he would endanger his own estate (Ruth 4:5–6). *wasted his seed on the ground.* A means of birth control sometimes called "onanism" (after Onan).

38:10 *what he did.* His refusal to perform his levirate duty.

38:11 *he thought, ". . . he too may die like his brothers."* Thus Judah had no intention of giving Shelah to Tamar (see v. 14).

38:12 *Timnah.* Exact location unknown, but somewhere in the hill country of Judah (see Josh 15:48,57).

38:14 *sat . . . the road.* Prostitutes (see v. 15) customarily stationed themselves by the roadside (Jer 3:2). *Enaim.* Means "two springs"; probably the same as Enam in the western foothills of Judah (see Josh 15:33–34).

38:18 *seal and your cord.* Probably a small cylinder seal of the type used to sign clay documents by rolling them over the clay. The owner wore it around his neck on a cord threaded through a hole drilled lengthwise through it.

38:21 *temple prostitute.* The Hebrew here differs from that used for "harlot" in v. 15. Judah's friend perhaps deliberately used the

that Judah was informed, "[1]Your daughter-
in-law Tamar has played the harlot, and
behold, she is also with child by harlotry."
Then Judah said, "Bring her out and [a]let her
be burned!"
25 It was while she was being brought out
that she sent to her father-in-law, saying, "I
am with child by the man to whom these
things belong." And she said, "[a]Please examine and see, whose signet ring and cords and
staff are these?"
26 Judah recognized *them*, and said,
"[a]She is more righteous than I, inasmuch as
[b]I did not give her to my son Shelah." And
he did not [1]have relations with her again.
27 It came about at the time she was giving birth, that behold, there were [a]twins in
her womb.
28 Moreover, it took place while she was
giving birth, one put out a hand, and the
midwife took and tied a scarlet *thread* on his
hand, saying, "This one came out first."
29 But it came about as he drew back his
hand, that behold, his brother came out.
Then she said, "What a breach you have
made for yourself!" So he was named
[1a]Perez.
30 Afterward his brother came out who
had the scarlet *thread* on his hand; and he
was named [1a]Zerah.

Joseph's Success in Egypt

39 Now Joseph had been taken down to
Egypt; and Potiphar, an Egyptian officer of Pharaoh, the captain of the bodyguard, bought him [1]from the [a]Ishmaelites,
who had taken him down there.
2 [a]The LORD was with Joseph, so he
became a [1]successful man. And he was in
the house of his master, the Egyptian.
3 Now his master [a]saw that the LORD was
with him and *how* the LORD [b]caused all that
he did to prosper in his hand.
4 So Joseph [a]found favor in his sight and
[1]became his personal servant; and he made
him overseer over his house, and [b]all that he
owned he put in his [2]charge.
5 It came about that from the time he
made him overseer in his house and over all
that he owned, the LORD [a]blessed the Egyptian's house on account of Joseph; thus [b]the
LORD's blessing was upon all that he owned,
in the house and in the field.
6 So he left everything he owned in
Joseph's [1]charge; and with him *there* he did
not [2]concern himself with anything except
the [3]food which he [4]ate.
Now Joseph was [a]handsome in form and
appearance.
7 It came about after these events [a]that
his master's wife [1]looked with desire at
Joseph, and she said, "[b]Lie with me."
8 But [a]he refused and said to his master's
wife, "Behold, with me *here*, my master
[1]does not concern himself with anything in
the house, and he has put all that he owns in
my [2]charge.
9 "[1a]There is no one greater in this house
than I, and he has withheld nothing from me
except you, because you are his wife. How
then could I do this great evil and [b]sin
against God?"
10 As she spoke to Joseph day after day,
he did not listen to her to lie beside her *or* be
with her.
11 Now it happened [1]one day that he
went into the house to do his work, and
none of the men of the household was there
inside.
12 She caught him by his garment, saying,
"Lie with me!" And he left his garment in
her hand and fled, and went outside.

24 [1]Lit *saying, Your* [a]Lev 21:9
25 [a]Gen 37:32
26 [1]Lit *know her yet again* [a]1 Sam 24:17 [b]Gen 38:14
27 [a]Gen 25:24-26
29 [1]I.e. a breach [a]Gen 46:12; Ruth 4:12
30 [1]I.e. a dawning or brightness [a]1 Chr 2:4
39:1 [1]Lit *from the hand of* [a]Gen 37:25, 28, 36; Ps 105:17
2 [1]Or *prosperous* [a]Gen 39:3, 21, 23; Acts 7:9
3 [a]Gen 21:22; 26:28
3 [b]Ps 1:3
4 [1]Or *ministered to him* [2]Lit *hand* [a]Gen 18:3; 19:19 [b]Gen 24:2; 39:8, 22
5 [a]Gen 30:27 [b]Deut 28:3, 4, 11
6 [1]Lit *hand* [2]Lit *know* [3]Lit *bread* [4]Or *used to eat* [a]Gen 29:17; 1 Sam 16:12
7 [1]Lit *lifted up her eyes at* [a]Prov 7:15-20 [b]2 Sam 13:11
8 [1]Lit *does not know what is in the house* [2]Lit *hand* [a]Prov 6:23, 24
9 [1]Or *He is not greater* [a]Gen 41:40 [b]Gen 20:6; 42:18; 2 Sam 12:13; Ps 51:4
11 [1]Lit *about this day*

---

more acceptable term, since ritual prostitutes enjoyed a higher social status in Canaan than did ordinary prostitutes.

38:24 *let her be burned.* In later times, burning was the legal penalty for prostitution (see Lev 21:9).

38:27–30 For a similarly unusual birth of twin boys see 25:24–26.

38:29 *Perez.* Became the head of the leading clan in Judah and the ancestor of David (see Ruth 4:18–22) and ultimately of Christ (see Matt 1:1–6).

39:1 See 37:36. *taken down to Egypt.* Joseph's experiences in Egypt, as well as those of his youth in Canaan (see note on 37:23–24), are similar to Israel's national experiences in Egypt. Initially, because of God's blessing, Joseph attains a position of honor (in Potiphar's house); he is then unjustly thrown into prison, his only crime being his attractiveness and moral integrity; and finally he is raised up among the Egyptians as the one who, because God is with him, holds their lives in his hands. Similarly Israel was first received with honor in Egypt (because of Joseph); then she was subjected to cruel bondage, her only crime being God's evident blessings upon her; and finally God raised her up in the eyes of the Egyptians (through the ministry of Moses) as they came fearfully to recognize that these people and their God did indeed hold their lives in their hands. The author of Genesis knew the events of the exodus and shows how the history of God and the patriarchs moved forward to and foreshadowed that event (see also 15:13–16; 48:21–22; 50:24–25). *Ishmaelites.* See note on 37:25.

39:2–6 See vv. 20–23. Though Joseph's situation changed drastically, God's relationship to him remained the same.

39:2 *The LORD was with Joseph.* See note on 26:3. This fact, mentioned several times here (vv. 3,21,23), is stressed also by Stephen (Acts 7:9).

39:5 *the LORD blessed the Egyptian's house on account of Joseph.* The offspring of Abraham are becoming a blessing to the nations (see 12:2–3; 30:27).

39:6 *left everything he owned in Joseph's charge.* Joseph had full responsibility for the welfare of Potiphar's house, as later he would have full responsibility in prison (vv. 22–23) and later still in all Egypt (41:41). Always this Israelite came to hold the welfare of his "world" in his hands—but always by the blessing and overruling of God, never by his own wits, as his father Jacob had so long attempted. In the role that he played in Israel's history and in the manner in which he lived it, Joseph was a true representative of Israel.

39:7 *looked with desire at.* The phrase is used in the same sense in Akkadian in Section 25 of the Code of Hammurapi.

39:9 *sin against God.* All sin is against God, first and foremost (see Ps 51:4).

39:10 *As she spoke to Joseph day after day, he did not listen.* Samson twice succumbed under similar pressure (Judg 14:17; 16:16–17).

13 [1]When she saw that he had left his garment in her hand and had fled outside,

14 she called to the men of her household and said to them, "See, he has brought in a [1]Hebrew to us to make sport of us; he came in to me to lie with me, and I [2]screamed.

15 "When he heard that I raised my voice and [1]screamed, he left his garment beside me and fled and went outside."

16 So she [1]left his garment beside her until his master came home.

17 Then she [a]spoke to him [1]with these words, "[2]The Hebrew slave, whom you brought to us, came in to me to make sport of me;

18 and as I raised my voice and [1]screamed, he left his garment beside me and fled outside."

Joseph Imprisoned

19 Now when his master heard the words of his wife, which she spoke to him, saying, "[1]This is what your slave did to me," [a]his anger burned.

20 So Joseph's master took him and [a]put him into the jail, the place where the king's prisoners were confined; and he was there in the jail.

21 But [a]the LORD was with Joseph and extended kindness to him, and [b]gave him favor in the sight of the chief jailer.

22 The chief jailer [a]committed to Joseph's [1]charge all the prisoners who were in the jail; so that whatever was done there, he was [2]responsible *for it.*

23 [a]The chief jailer did not supervise anything under [1]Joseph's charge because [b]the LORD was with him; and whatever he did, [c]the LORD made to prosper.

Joseph Interprets a Dream

40 Then it came about after these things, [a]the cupbearer and the baker for the king of Egypt offended their lord, the king of Egypt.

2 Pharaoh was [a]furious with his two officials, the chief cupbearer and the chief baker.

3 So he put them in confinement in the house of the [a]captain of the bodyguard, in the jail, the *same* place where Joseph was imprisoned.

4 The captain of the bodyguard put Joseph in charge of them, and he [1]took care of them; and they were in confinement for [2]some time.

5 Then the cupbearer and the baker for the king of Egypt, who were confined in jail, both had a dream the same night, each man with his *own* dream *and* each dream with its *own* interpretation.

6 [1]When Joseph came to them in the morning and observed them, [2]behold, they were dejected.

7 He asked Pharaoh's officials who were with him in confinement in his master's house, "[1][a]Why are your faces so sad today?"

8 Then they said to him, "[a]We have [1]had a dream and there is no one to interpret it." Then Joseph said to them, "[b]Do not interpretations belong to God? Tell *it* to me, please."

9 So the chief cupbearer told his dream to Joseph, and said to him, "In my dream, [1]behold, *there was* a vine in front of me;

10 and on the vine *were* three branches. And as it was budding, its blossoms came out, *and* its clusters produced ripe grapes.

11 "Now Pharaoh's cup was in my hand; so I took the grapes and squeezed them into Pharaoh's cup, and I put the cup into Pharaoh's [1]hand."

12 Then Joseph said to him, "This is the [a]interpretation of it: the three branches are three days;

13 within three more days Pharaoh will [1]lift up your head and restore you to your [2]office; and you will put Pharaoh's cup into his hand according to your former custom when you were his cupbearer.

14 "Only [1]keep me in mind when it goes well with you, and please [a]do me a kindness [2]by mentioning me to Pharaoh and get me out of this house.

15 "For [a]I was in fact kidnapped from the land of the Hebrews, and even here I have done nothing that they should have put me into the [1]dungeon."

16 When the chief baker saw that he had interpreted favorably, he said to Joseph, "I

13 [1]Lit *And it came about when*
14 [1]Lit *Hebrew man* [2]Lit *called with a great voice*
15 [1]Lit *called out*
16 [1]Lit *let...lie beside*
17 [1]Lit *according to* [2]Lit *saying, "The* [a]Ex 23:1; Prov 26:28
18 [1]Lit *called out*
19 [1]Lit *According to these things your slave* [a]Prov 6:34
20 [a]Gen 40:3; Ps 105:18
21 [a]Gen 39:2; Ps 105:19; Acts 7:9 [b]Ex 3:21; 11:3; 12:36
22 [1]Lit *hand* [2]Lit *the doer* [a]Gen 39:4; 40:3, 4
23 [1]Lit *his hand* [a]Gen 39:3, 8 [b]Gen 39:2, 3 [c]Gen 39:3
40:1 [a]Gen 40:11, 13; Neh 1:11
2 [a]Prov 16:14
3 [a]Gen 39:1, 20
4 [1]Lit *ministered to* [2]Lit *days*
6 [1]Or *And* [2]Lit *and behold*
7 [1]Lit *saying, Why* [a]Neh 2:2
8 [1]Lit *dreamed* [a]Gen 41:15 [b]Gen 41:16; Dan 2:27, 28
9 [1]Lit *and behold*
11 [1]Lit *palm*
12 [a]Dan 2:36; 4:18, 19
13 [1]Or possibly *forgive you* [2]Lit *place*
14 [1]Lit *remember me with yourself* [2]Lit *and mention* [a]Josh 2:12; 1 Sam 20:14; 1 Kin 2:7
15 [1]Or *pit* [a]Gen 37:26-28

39:14 *a Hebrew.* See v. 17; see also note on 14:13.
39:20–23 See note on vv. 2–6.
39:20 *the place where the king's prisoners were confined.* Though understandably angry (see v. 19), Potiphar put Joseph in the "house of the captain of the bodyguard" (40:3)—certainly not the worst prison available.
40:2 *chief cupbearer.* Would be the divinely appointed agent for introducing Joseph to Pharaoh (see 41:9–14).
40:5 *each dream with its own interpretation.* Throughout the ancient Near East it was believed that dreams had specific meanings and that proper interpretation of them could help the dreamer predict his future (see note on 20:3). God was beginning to prepare the way for Joseph's rise in Egypt.
40:8 *interpretations belong to God.* Only God can interpret dreams properly and accurately (see 41:16,25,28; Dan 2:28). *Tell it to me.* Joseph presents himself as God's agent through whom God will make known the revelation contained in their dreams—Israel is God's prophetic people through whom God's revelation comes to the nations (see 18:17 and note; 41:16,28,32).
40:13 *lift up your head and restore you to your office.* See Ps 3:3; 27:6. For this meaning of the idiom "lift up one's head" see 2 Kin 25:27 and Jer 52:31, where the Hebrew for "released" in the context of freeing a prisoner means lit. "lifted up the head of."
40:14 *keep me in mind when it goes well with you.* Unfortunately, the cupbearer "did not remember Joseph" (v. 23) until two full years later (see 41:1,9–13).
40:15 *dungeon.* Probably hyperbole to reflect Joseph's despair (see note on 39:20). Since the same Hebrew word is translated "pit" in 37:24, the author of Genesis has established a link with Joseph's earlier experience at the hands of his brothers.

also *saw* in my dream, and behold, *there were* three baskets of white bread on my head;

17 and in the top basket *there were* some of all [1]sorts of baked food for Pharaoh, and the birds were eating them out of the basket on my head."

18 Then Joseph answered and said, "This is its interpretation: the three baskets are three days;

19 within three more days Pharaoh will lift up your head from you and will hang you on a tree, and the birds will eat your flesh off you."

20 Thus it came about on the third day, *which was* [a]Pharaoh's birthday, that he made a feast for all his servants; [b]and he lifted up the head of the chief cupbearer and the head of the chief baker among his servants.

21 He restored the chief cupbearer to his [1]office, and [a]he put the cup into Pharaoh's [2]hand;

22 but [a]he hanged the chief baker, just as Joseph had interpreted to them.

23 Yet the chief cupbearer did not remember Joseph, but [a]forgot him.

Pharaoh's Dream

41 Now it happened at the end of two full years that Pharaoh had a dream, and behold, he was standing by the Nile.

2 And lo, from the Nile there came up seven cows, sleek and [1]fat; and they grazed in the [a]marsh grass.

3 Then behold, seven other cows came up after them from the Nile, ugly and [1]gaunt, and they stood by the *other* cows on the bank of the Nile.

4 The ugly and [1]gaunt cows ate up the seven sleek and fat cows. Then Pharaoh awoke.

5 He fell asleep and dreamed a second time; and behold, seven ears of grain came up on a single stalk, plump and good.

6 Then behold, seven ears, thin and scorched by the east wind, sprouted up after them.

7 The thin ears swallowed up the seven plump and full ears. Then Pharaoh awoke, and behold, *it was* a dream.

8 Now in the morning [a]his spirit was troubled, so he sent and called for all the [1b]magicians of Egypt, and all its [c]wise men. And Pharaoh told them his [2]dreams, but [d]there was no one who could interpret them to Pharaoh.

9 Then the chief cupbearer spoke to Pharaoh, saying, "I would make mention today of [a]my *own* [1]offenses.

10 "Pharaoh was [a]furious with his servants, and [b]he put me in confinement in the house of the captain of the bodyguard, *both* me and the chief baker.

11 "[a]We had a dream [1]on the same night, [2]he and I; each of us dreamed according to the interpretation of his *own* dream.

12 "Now a Hebrew youth *was* with us there, a [a]servant of the captain of the bodyguard, and we related *them* to him, and [b]he interpreted our dreams for us. To each one he interpreted according to his *own* dream.

13 "And just [a]as he interpreted for us, so it happened; he restored me in my [1]office, but he hanged him."

Joseph Interprets

14 Then Pharaoh sent and [a]called for Joseph, and they [b]hurriedly brought him out of the dungeon; and when he had shaved himself and changed his clothes, he came to Pharaoh.

15 Pharaoh said to Joseph, "I have had a dream, [a]but no one can interpret it; and [b]I have heard [1]it said about you, that [2]when you hear a dream you can interpret it."

16 Joseph then answered Pharaoh, saying, "[1a]It is not in me; [b]God will [2]give Pharaoh a favorable answer."

17 So Pharaoh spoke to Joseph, "In my dream, behold, I was standing on the bank of the Nile;

18 and behold, seven cows, [1]fat and sleek came up out of the Nile, and they grazed in the marsh grass.

19 "Lo, seven other cows came up after them, poor and very ugly and [1]gaunt, such as I had never seen for [2]ugliness in all the land of Egypt;

20 and the lean and [1]ugly cows ate up the first seven fat cows.

21 "Yet when they had [1]devoured them, it could not be [2]detected that they had [1]devoured them, [3]for they were just as ugly as [4]before. Then I awoke.

22 "I saw also in my dream, and behold, seven ears, full and good, came up on a single stalk;

17 [1]Lit *food for Pharaoh made by a baker*
20 [a]Matt 14:6 [b]2 Kin 25:27; Jer 52:31
21 [1]Lit *wine-pouring* [2]Lit *palm* [a]Gen 40:13
22 [a]Gen 40:19; Esth 7:10
23 [a]Job 19:14; Ps 31:12; Eccl 9:15
41:2 [1]Lit *fat of flesh* [a]Job 8:11; Is 19:6, 7
3 [1]Lit *lean of flesh*
4 [1]Lit *lean of flesh*
8 [1]Or *soothsayer priests* [2]Lit *dream* [a]Dan 2:1, 3 [b]Ex 7:11, 22; Dan 1:20; 2:2 [c]Matt 2:1
8 [d]Dan 2:27; 4:7
9 [1]Or *sins* [a]Gen 40:14, 23
10 [a]Gen 40:2, 3 [b]Gen 39:20
11 [1]Lit *one night* [2]Lit *I and he* [a]Gen 40:5
12 [a]Gen 37:36 [b]Gen 40:12
13 [1]Lit *place* [a]Gen 40:21, 22
14 [a]Ps 105:20 [b]Dan 2:25
15 [1]Lit *about you, saying* [2]Lit *you hear a dream to interpret it* [a]Gen 41:8 [b]Dan 5:16
16 [1]Lit *Apart from me* [2]Lit *answer the peace of Pharaoh* [a]Dan 2:30; Zech 4:6; Acts 3:12; 2 Cor 3:5 [b]Gen 40:8; 41:25, 28, 32; Deut 29:29; Dan 2:22, 28, 47
18 [1]Lit *fat of flesh*
19 [1]Lit *lean of flesh* [2]Lit *badness*
20 [1]Lit *bad*
21 [1]Lit *entered their inward parts* [2]Or *known* [3]Lit *and* [4]Lit *in the beginning*

40:19 *lift up your head.* A grisly pun based on the same idiom used in v. 13.
40:20 *Pharaoh's birthday.* Centuries later, the birthday of Herod the tetrarch would become the occasion for another beheading (see Matt 14:6–10).
41:2 *from the Nile there came up seven cows.* Cattle often submerged themselves up to their necks in the Nile to escape sun and insects.
41:6 *scorched by the east wind.* The Palestinian sirocco (in Egypt the khamsin), which blows in from the desert (see Hos 13:15) in late spring and early fall, often withers vegetation (see Is 40:7; Ezek 17:10).
41:8 *his spirit was troubled.* See 40:6–7. *magicians.* Probably priests who claimed to possess occult knowledge. *no one who could interpret them to Pharaoh.* See Dan 2:10–11.
41:13 *just as he interpreted.* Because his words were from the Lord (see Ps 105:19).
41:14 *Pharaoh sent and called for Joseph.* Effecting his permanent release from prison (see Ps 105:20). *shaved.* Egyptians were normally smooth-shaven, while Palestinians wore beards (see 2 Sam 10:5; Jer 41:5).
41:16 *It is not in me; God will give Pharaoh a favorable answer.* See 40:8; Dan 2:27–28,30; 2 Cor 3:5.

23 and lo, seven ears, withered, thin, *and* scorched by the east wind, sprouted up after them;
24 and the thin ears swallowed the seven good ears. Then [a]I told it to the [1]magicians, but there was no one who could explain it to me."
25 Now Joseph said to Pharaoh, "Pharaoh's [1]dreams are one *and the same;* [a]God has told to Pharaoh what He is about to do.
26 "The seven good cows are seven years; and the seven good ears are seven years; the [1]dreams are one *and the same.*
27 "The seven lean and ugly cows that came up after them are seven years, and the seven thin ears scorched by the east wind [a]will be seven years of famine.
28 "[1]It is as I have spoken to Pharaoh: [a]God has shown to Pharaoh what He is about to do.
29 "Behold, [a]seven years of great abundance are coming in all the land of Egypt;
30 and after them [a]seven years of famine will [1]come, and all the abundance will be forgotten in the land of Egypt, and the famine will [2]ravage the land.
31 "So the abundance will be unknown in the land because of that subsequent famine; for it *will be* very severe.
32 "Now as for the repeating of the dream to Pharaoh twice, *it means* that [a]the matter is determined by God, and God will quickly bring it about.
33 "Now let Pharaoh look for a man [a]discerning and wise, and set him over the land of Egypt.
34 "Let Pharaoh take action to appoint overseers [1]in charge of the land, and let him exact a fifth *of the produce* of the land of Egypt in the seven years of abundance.
35 "Then let them [a]gather all the food of these good years that are coming, and store up the grain for food in the cities under Pharaoh's authority, and let them guard *it.*
36 "Let the food become as a reserve for the land for the seven years of famine which will occur in the land of Egypt, so that the land will not perish during the famine."
37 Now the [1]proposal seemed good [2]to Pharaoh and [2]to all his servants.

Joseph Is Made a Ruler of Egypt

38 Then Pharaoh said to his servants, "Can we find a man like this, [a]in whom is a divine spirit?"
39 So Pharaoh said to Joseph, "Since God has informed you of all this, there is no one so [a]discerning and wise as you are.
40 "[a]You shall be over my house, and according to your [1]command all my people shall [2]do homage; only in the throne I will be greater than you."
41 Pharaoh said to Joseph, "See, I have set you [a]over all the land of Egypt."
42 Then Pharaoh [a]took off his signet ring from his hand and put it on Joseph's hand, and clothed him in garments of fine linen and [b]put the gold necklace around his neck.
43 He had him ride in [1]his second chariot; and they proclaimed before him, "[2]Bow the knee!" And he set him over all the land of Egypt.
44 Moreover, Pharaoh said to Joseph, "*Though* I am Pharaoh, yet [a]without [1]your permission no one shall raise his hand or foot in all the land of Egypt."
45 Then Pharaoh named Joseph [1]Zaphenath-paneah; and he gave him Asenath, the daughter of Potiphera priest of [2][a]On, as his wife. And Joseph went forth over the land of Egypt.
46 Now Joseph was [a]thirty years old when he [1]stood before Pharaoh, king of Egypt. And Joseph went out from the presence of Pharaoh and went through all the land of Egypt.
47 During the seven years of plenty the land brought forth [1]abundantly.
48 So he gathered all the food of *these* sev-

24 [1]Or *soothsayer priests* [a]Is 8:19; Dan 4:7
25 [1]Lit *dream is* [a]Gen 41:28, 32; Dan 2:28, 29, 45
26 [1]Lit *dream is*
27 [a]2 Kin 8:1
28 [1]Lit *That is the thing which I spoke* [a]Gen 41:25, 32
29 [a]Gen 41:47
30 [1]Lit *arise* [2]Lit *destroy* [a]Gen 41:54, 56; 47:13; Ps 105:16
32 [a]Gen 41:25, 28
33 [a]Gen 41:39
34 [1]Lit *over*
35 [a]Gen 41:48
37 [1]Lit *word* [2]Lit *in the sight of*
38 [a]Job 32:8; Dan 4:8, 9, 18; 5:11, 14
39 [a]Gen 41:33
40 [1]Lit *mouth* [2]Lit *kiss* [a]Ps 105:21; Acts 7:10
41 [a]Gen 42:6; Ps 105:21; Dan 6:3; Acts 7:10
42 [a]Esth 3:10; 8:2 [b]Dan 5:7, 16, 29
43 [1]Lit *the second...which was his* [2]Heb *Abreck: Attention* or *Make way*
44 [1]Lit *you no one* [a]Ps 105:22
45 [1]Probably Egyptian for "God speaks; he lives" [2]Or *Heliopolis* [a]Jer 43:13; Ezek 30:17
46 [1]Or *entered the service of* [a]Gen 37:2
47 [1]Lit *by handfuls*

41:27 *seven years of famine.* See Acts 7:11. Long famines were rare in Egypt because of the regularity of the annual overflow of the Nile, but not uncommon elsewhere (see 2 Kin 8:1). According to the NT, the great famine in the time of Elijah lasted three and a half years (James 5:17), thus half of seven years; it had been cut short by Elijah's intercession (1 Kin 18:42; James 5:18).

41:32 Repetition of a divine revelation was often used for emphasis (see 37:5–9; Amos 7:1–6,7–9; 8:1–3).

41:38 *a divine spirit.* Lit. "a spirit of God (or of the gods)." The word "spirit" should probably not be capitalized in such passages, since reference to the Holy Spirit would be out of character in statements by pagan rulers.

41:40 *You shall be over my house.* Pharaoh took Joseph's advice (see v. 33) and decided that Joseph himself should be "governor over Egypt" (Acts 7:10; see also Ps 105:21). *according to your command all my people shall do homage.* More lit. "at your command all my people are to kiss (you)"—i.e., kiss your hands or feet in an act of homage and submission (see Ps 2:12 and note).

41:42 Three symbols of transfer and/or sharing of royal authority, referred to also in Esth 3:10 (signet ring); Esth 6:11 (robe); and Dan 5:7,16,29 (gold necklace).

41:43 *He had him ride in his second chariot.* The position was probably that of vizier, the highest executive office below that of the king himself. *Bow the knee!* The Hebrew here may be an Egyptian imperative of a Semitic loanword.

41:45 *named Joseph Zaphenath-paneah.* As a part of assigning Joseph an official position within his royal administration (see note on 1:5). Pharaoh presumed to use this marvelously endowed servant of the Lord for his own royal purposes—as a later Pharaoh would attempt to use divinely blessed Israel for the enrichment of Egypt (Ex 1). He did not recognize that Joseph served a Higher Power, whose kingdom and redemptive purposes are being advanced. (The meaning of Joseph's Egyptian name is uncertain.) *Asenath.* The name is Egyptian and probably means "She belongs to (the goddess) Neith." *Potiphera.* Not the same person as "Potiphar" (37:36; 39:1); the name (also Egyptian) means "he whom (the sun-god) Ra has given." *On.* Located ten miles northeast of modern Cairo, it was called Heliopolis ("city of the sun") by the Greeks and was an important center for the worship of Ra, who had a temple there. Potiphera therefore bore an appropriate name.

41:46 *thirty years old.* In just 13 years (see 37:2), Joseph had become second-in-command (v. 43) in Egypt.

en years which occurred in the land of Egypt and placed the food in the cities; he placed in every city the food from its own surrounding fields.

49 Thus Joseph stored up grain [1]in great abundance like the sand of the sea, until he stopped [2]measuring *it,* for it was [3]beyond measure.

The Sons of Joseph

50 Now before the year of famine came, [a]two sons were born to Joseph, whom Asenath, the daughter of Potiphera priest of [1]On, bore to him.

51 Joseph named the firstborn [1]Manasseh, "For," *he said,* "God has made me forget all my trouble and all my father's household."

52 He named the second [1]Ephraim, "For," *he said,* "[a]God has made me fruitful in the land of my affliction."

53 When the seven years of plenty which had been in the land of Egypt came to an end,

54 and [a]the seven years of famine began to come, just as Joseph had said, then there was famine in all the lands, but in all the land of Egypt there was bread.

55 So when all the land of Egypt was famished, the people cried out to Pharaoh for bread; and Pharaoh said to all the Egyptians, "Go to Joseph; [a]whatever he says to you, you shall do."

56 When the famine was *spread* over all the face of the earth, then Joseph opened all [1]the storehouses, and sold to the Egyptians; and the famine was severe in the land of Egypt.

57 *The people of* all the earth came to Egypt to buy grain from Joseph, because [a]the famine was severe in all the earth.

Joseph's Brothers Sent to Egypt

42 Now [a]Jacob saw that there was grain in Egypt, and Jacob said to his sons, "Why are you staring at one another?"

2 He said, "Behold, [a]I have heard that there is grain in Egypt; go down there and buy *some* for us [1]from that place, [b]so that we may live and not die."

3 Then ten brothers of Joseph went down to buy grain from Egypt.

4 But Jacob did not send Joseph's brother [a]Benjamin with his brothers, for he said, "[b]I am afraid that harm may befall him."

5 So the sons of Israel came to buy grain among those who were coming, [a]for the famine was in the land of Canaan *also.*

6 Now [a]Joseph was the ruler over the land; he was the one who sold to all the people of the land. And Joseph's brothers came and [b]bowed down to him with *their* faces to the ground.

7 When Joseph saw his brothers he recognized them, but he disguised himself to them and [a]spoke to them harshly. And he said to them, "Where have you come from?" And they said, "From the land of Canaan, to buy food."

8 But Joseph had recognized his brothers, although [a]they did not recognize him.

9 Joseph [a]remembered the dreams which he [1]had about them, and said to them, "You are spies; you have come to look at the [2]undefended parts of our land."

10 Then they said to him, "No, [a]my lord, but your servants have come to buy food.

11 "We are all sons of one man; we are [a]honest men, your servants are not spies."

12 Yet he said to them, "No, but you have come to look at the [1]undefended parts of our land!"

13 But they said, "Your servants are twelve brothers *in all,* the sons of one man in the land of Canaan; and behold, the youngest is with [a]our father today, and [b]one is no longer alive."

14 Joseph said to them, "It is as I said [1]to you, you are spies;

15 by this you will be tested: [a]by the life of Pharaoh, you shall not go from this place unless your youngest brother comes here!

49 [1]Lit *very much* [2]Lit *numbering* [3]Or *without number*
50 [1]Or *Heliopolis* [a]Gen 48:5
51 [1]I.e. making to forget
52 [1]I.e. fruitfulness [a]Gen 17:6; 28:3; 49:22
54 [a]Gen 41:30; Ps 105:16; Acts 7:11
55 [a]John 2:5
56 [1]Lit *that which was in them*
57 [a]Gen 12:10
42:1 [a]Acts 7:12
2 [a]Acts 7:12
2 [1]Lit *from there* [b]Gen 43:8; Ps 33:18, 19
4 [a]Gen 35:24 [b]Gen 42:38
5 [a]Gen 12:10; 26:1; 41:57; Acts 7:11
6 [a]Gen 41:41, 55 [b]Gen 37:7-10; 41:43; Is 60:14
7 [a]Gen 42:30
8 [a]Gen 37:2; 41:46
9 [1]Lit *had dreamed* [2]Lit *nakedness of the land* [a]Gen 37:6-9
10 [a]Gen 37:8
11 [a]Gen 42:16, 19, 31, 34
12 [1]Lit *nakedness of the land*
13 [a]Gen 43:7 [b]Gen 37:30; 42:32; 44:20
14 [1]Lit *to you, saying*
15 [a]1 Sam 17:55

41:49 *like the sand of the sea.* A simile also for the large number of offspring promised to Abraham and Jacob (see 22:17; 32:12).

41:52 *Ephraim.* The wordplay on the name (Ephraim sounds like the Hebrew for "twice fruitful") reflects the fact that God gave Joseph "two" (see v. 50) sons.

41:57 *all the earth.* The known world from the writer's perspective (the Middle East). This description of the famine in the time of Joseph echoes the author's description of the flood in the time of Noah. God saved only Noah and his family from the flood, so that Noah became the new (after Adam) father of the race. With the call of Abram out of the post-flood and post-Babel nations, God once more singled out one man, now to be the father of His special people. God promised that, through this man and his descendants, "all the families of the earth will be blessed" (12:3). The author highlights the fact that in this new crisis hope rested with one of these descendants.

42:2–3 Stephen refers to this incident (Acts 7:12).

42:4 *did not send Joseph's brother Benjamin.* Their mother Rachel had died (35:19), and Jacob thought Joseph also was dead (37:33). Jacob did not want to lose Benjamin, the remaining son of his beloved Rachel.

42:5 *famine was in the land of Canaan also.* As in the time of Abram (see 12:10 and note).

42:6 *bowed down to him.* In fulfillment of Joseph's dreams (see 37:7,9).

42:8 *Joseph had recognized his brothers.* Although at least 20 years had passed since he had last seen them (see 37:2; 41:46,53–54), they had been adults at the time and their appearance had not changed much. *they did not recognize him.* Joseph, a teenager at the time of his enslavement, was now an adult in an unexpected position of authority, wearing Egyptian clothes and speaking to his brothers through an interpreter (see v. 23). He was, moreover, shaven in the Egyptian manner (see note on 41:14).

42:10 *my lord . . . your servants.* Unwittingly, Joseph's brothers again fulfilled his dreams and their own scornful fears (see 37:8).

42:15 *by the life of Pharaoh.* The most solemn oaths were pronounced in the name of the reigning monarch (as here) or of the

16 "Send one of you that he may get your brother, while you remain confined, that your words may be tested, whether there is [a]truth in you. But if not, by the life of Pharaoh, surely you are spies."

17 So he put them all together in [a]prison for three days.

18 Now Joseph said to them on the third day, "Do this and live, for [a]I fear God:

19 if you are honest men, let one of your brothers be confined in [1]your prison; but as for *the rest of* you, go, carry grain for the famine of your households,

20 and [a]bring your youngest brother to me, so your words may be verified, and you will not die." And they did so.

21 Then they said to one another, "[a]Truly we are guilty concerning our brother, because we saw the distress of his soul when he pleaded with us, yet we would not listen; therefore this distress has come upon us."

22 Reuben answered them, saying, "[a]Did I not tell [1]you, 'Do not sin against the boy'; and you would not listen? [2b]Now comes the reckoning for his blood."

23 They did not know, however, that Joseph understood, for there was an interpreter between them.

24 He turned away from them and [a]wept. But when he returned to them and spoke to them, he [b]took Simeon from them and bound him before their eyes.

25 [a]Then Joseph gave orders to fill their bags with grain and to restore every man's money in his sack, and to give them provisions for the journey. And thus it was done for them.

26 So they loaded their donkeys with their grain and departed from there.

27 As one *of them* opened his sack to give his donkey fodder at the lodging place, he saw his [a]money; and behold, it was in the mouth of his sack.

28 Then he said to his brothers, "My money has been returned, and behold, it is even in my sack." And their hearts [1]sank, and they *turned* [2]trembling to one another, saying, "[a]What is this that God has done to us?"

Simeon Is Held Hostage

29 When they came to their father Jacob in the land of Canaan, they told him all that had happened to them, saying,

30 "The man, the lord of the land, [a]spoke harshly with us, and took us for spies of the country.

31 "But we said to him, 'We are [a]honest men; we are not spies.

32 'We are twelve brothers, sons of our father; one is no longer alive, and the youngest is with our father today in the land of Canaan.'

33 "The man, the lord of the land, said to us, '[a]By this I will know that you are honest men: leave one of your brothers with me and take *grain for* the famine of your households, and go.

34 'But bring your youngest brother to me that I may know that you are not spies, but [1]honest men. I will give your brother to you, and you may [a]trade in the land.' "

35 Now it came about as they were emptying their sacks, that behold, [a]every man's bundle of money *was* in his sack; and when they and their father saw their bundles of money, they were dismayed.

36 Their father Jacob said to them, "You have [a]bereaved me of my children: Joseph is no more, and Simeon is no more, and you would take Benjamin; all these things are against me."

37 Then Reuben spoke to his father, saying, "You may put my two sons to death if I do not bring him *back* to you; put him in my [1]care, and I will return him to you."

38 But [1]Jacob said, "My son shall not go down with you; for his [a]brother is dead, and he alone is left. [b]If harm should befall him on the journey [2]you are taking, then you will [c]bring my gray hair down to Sheol in sorrow."

The Return to Egypt

43 [a]Now the famine was severe in the land.

2 So it came about when they had finished eating the grain which they had brought from Egypt, that their father said to them, "Go back, buy us a little food."

3 Judah spoke to him, however, saying, "[a]The man solemnly warned [1]us, 'You shall not see my face unless your brother is with you.'

4 "If you send our brother with us, we will go down and buy you food.

5 "But if you do not send *him,* we will not go down; for the man said to us, 'You will not see my face unless your brother is with you.' "

6 Then Israel said, "Why did you treat

16 [a]Gen 42:11 **17** [a]Gen 40:4, 7 **18** [a]Gen 39:9; Lev 25:43; Neh 5:15 **19** [1]Lit *the house of your prison* **20** [a]Gen 42:34; 43:5; 44:23 **21** [a]Gen 37:26-28; 45:3; Hos 5:15 **22** [1]Lit *you saying* [2]Lit *And behold, his blood also is required* [a]Gen 37:21, 22 [b]Gen 9:5, 6; 1 Kin 2:32; 2 Chr 24:22; Ps 9:12 **24** [a]Gen 43:30; 45:14, 15 [b]Gen 43:14, 23 **25** [a]Gen 44:1; Rom 12:17, 20, 21; 1 Pet 3:9 **27** [a]Gen 43:21, 22 **28** [1]Lit *went out* [2]Lit *trembled* [a]Gen 43:23 **30** [a]Gen 42:7

31 [a]Gen 42:11 **33** [a]Gen 42:19, 20 **34** [1]Lit *you are honest* [a]Gen 34:10 **35** [a]Gen 43:12, 15, 21 **36** [a]Gen 43:14 **37** [1]Lit *hand* **38** [1]Lit *he* [2]Lit *on which you are going* [a]Gen 37:33, 34; 42:13; 44:27, 28 [b]Gen 42:4 [c]Gen 37:35; 44:29, 31 **43:1** [a]Gen 12:10; 26:1; 41:56, 57 **3** [1]Lit *us, saying* [a]Gen 43:5; 44:23

speaker's deities (Ps 16:4; Amos 8:14) or of the Lord Himself (Judg 8:19; 1 Sam 14:39,45; 19:6).

42:21 *distress of his soul . . . distress has come upon us.* The brothers realized they were beginning to reap what they had sown (see Gal 6:7).

42:22 See 37:21–22 and note on 37:21.

42:24 *he took Simeon.* Jacob's second son (see 29:32–33) is imprisoned instead of the firstborn Reuben, perhaps because the latter had saved Joseph's life years earlier (37:21–22).

42:37 *my two sons.* Reuben's generous offer as security for Benjamin's safety (see note on 37:21).

43:3 *Judah spoke to him.* From this point on, Judah became the spokesman for his brothers (see vv. 8–10; 44:14–34; 46:28). His tribe would become preeminent among the 12 (see 49:8–10), and he would be an ancestor of Jesus (see Matt 1:2,17; Luke 3:23,33).

me so badly [1]by telling the man whether you still had *another* brother?"

7 But they said, "The man questioned particularly about us and our relatives, saying, '[a]Is your father still alive? Have you *another* brother?' So we [1]answered his questions. Could we possibly know that he would say, 'Bring your brother down'?"

8 Judah said to his father Israel, "Send the lad with me and we will arise and go, [a]that we may live and not die, we as well as you and our little ones.

9 "[a]I myself will be surety for him; [1]you may hold me responsible for him. If I do not bring him *back* to you and set him before you, then [2]let me bear the blame before you forever.

10 "For if we had not delayed, surely by now we could have returned twice."

11 Then their father Israel said to them, "If *it must be* so, then do this: take some of the best products of the land in your [1]bags, and carry down to the man [a]as a present, a little [2b]balm and a little honey, [3]aromatic gum and [4]myrrh, pistachio nuts and almonds.

12 "Take double *the* money in your hand, and take back in your hand [a]the money that was returned in the mouth of your sacks; perhaps it was a mistake.

13 "Take your brother also, and arise, return to the man;

14 and may [1a]God Almighty [b]grant you compassion in the sight of the man, so that he will release to you [c]your other brother and Benjamin. And as for me, [d]if I am bereaved of my children, I am bereaved."

15 So the men took [a]this present, and they took double *the* money in their hand, and Benjamin; then they arose and went down to Egypt and stood before Joseph.

Joseph Sees Benjamin

16 When Joseph saw Benjamin with them, he said to his [a]house steward, "Bring the men into the house, and slay an animal and make ready; for the men are to dine with me at noon."

17 So the man did as Joseph said, and [1]brought the men to Joseph's house.

18 Now the men were afraid, because they were brought to Joseph's house; and they said, "*It is* because of the money that was returned in our sacks the first time that we are being brought in, that he may [1]seek occasion against us and fall upon us, and take us for slaves with our donkeys."

19 So they came near to Joseph's house steward, and spoke to him at the entrance of the house,

20 and said, "Oh, my lord, we indeed came down the first time to buy food,

21 and it came about when we came to the lodging place, that we opened our sacks, and behold, [a]each man's money was in the mouth of his sack, our money in [1]full. So [b]we have brought it back in our hand.

22 "We have also brought down other money in our hand to buy food; we do not know who put our money in our sacks."

23 He said, "[1]Be at ease, do not be afraid. [a]Your God and the God of your father has given you treasure in your sacks; [2]I had your money." Then [b]he brought Simeon out to them.

24 Then the man brought the men into Joseph's house and [a]gave them water, and they [b]washed their feet; and he gave their donkeys fodder.

25 So they prepared [a]the present [1]for Joseph's coming at noon; for they had heard that they were to eat [2]a meal there.

26 When Joseph came home, they brought into the house to him the present which was in their hand and [a]bowed to the ground before him.

27 Then he asked them about their welfare, and said, "[a]Is your old father well, of whom you spoke? Is he still alive?"

28 They said, "Your servant our father is well; he is still alive." [a]They bowed down [1]in homage.

29 As he lifted his eyes and saw his brother Benjamin, his mother's son, he said, "Is this [a]your youngest brother, of whom you spoke to me?" And he said, "[b]May God be gracious to you, my son."

30 Joseph hurried *out* for [1a]he was deeply stirred over his brother, and he sought *a place* to weep; and he entered his chamber and [b]wept there.

31 Then he washed his face and came out; and he [a]controlled himself and said, "[1]Serve the meal."

32 So they served him by himself, and them

6 [1]Lit *to tell*
7 [1]Lit *told him according to these words* [a]Gen 42:13; 43:27
8 [a]Gen 42:2
9 [1]Lit *from my hand you may require him* [2]Lit *I shall have sinned before you all the days* [a]Gen 42:37; 44:32; Philem 18, 19
11 [1]Or *vessels* [2]Or *mastic* [3]Or *ladanum spice* [4]Or *resinous bark* [a]Gen 32:20; 43:25, 26 [b]Gen 37:25; Jer 8:22; Ezek 27:17
12 [a]Gen 42:25, 35; 43:21, 22
14 [1]Heb *El Shaddai* [a]Gen 17:1; 28:3; 35:11 [b]Ps 106:46 [c]Gen 42:24 [d]Gen 42:36
15 [a]Gen 43:11
16 [a]Gen 44:1
17 [1]Lit *the man brought*
18 [1]Lit *roll himself upon us*
21 [1]Lit *its weight* [a]Gen 42:27, 35 [b]Gen 43:12, 15
23 [1]Lit *Peace be to you* [2]Lit *your money had come to me* [a]Gen 42:28 [b]Gen 42:24
24 [a]Gen 18:4; 19:2; 24:32 [b]Luke 7:44; John 13:5; 1 Tim 5:10
25 [1]Lit *until* [2]Lit *bread* [a]Gen 43:11, 15
26 [a]Gen 37:7, 10
27 [a]Gen 43:7; 45:3
28 [1]Lit *and prostrated themselves* [a]Gen 37:7, 10
29 [a]Gen 42:13 [b]Num 6:25; Ps 67:1
30 [1]Lit *his compassion grew warm* [a]1 Kin 3:26 [b]Gen 42:24; 45:2, 14, 15; 46:29
31 [1]Lit *Set on bread* [a]Gen 45:1

43:9 Judah offered himself as security for Benjamin's safety—an even more generous gesture than that of Reuben (see 42:37 and note).

43:11 *carry . . . as a present.* A customary practice when approaching one's superior, whether political (see 1 Sam 16:20), military (see 1 Sam 17:18) or religious (see 2 Kin 5:15). *balm . . . myrrh.* See 37:25 and note. *honey.* Either that produced by bees, or an inferior substitute made by boiling grape or date juice down to a thick syrup. *pistachio nuts.* Mentioned only here in the Bible; the fruit of a small, broad-crowned tree that is native to Asia Minor, Syria and Canaan but not to Egypt.

43:14 *God Almighty.* See note on 17:1. *if I am bereaved . . . I am bereaved.* Cf. Esther's similar phrase of resignation in Esth 4:16.

43:21 The brothers' statement to Joseph's steward compressed the details (see 42:27,35).

43:23 *Your God . . . has given you treasure.* The steward spoke better than he knew.

43:24 See note on 18:2.

43:26 *bowed to the ground.* Additional fulfillment of Joseph's dreams (37:7,9; see also 42:6; 43:28).

43:29 *Benjamin, his mother's son.* Joseph's special relationship to Benjamin is clear. *God be gracious to you.* Later blessings and benedictions would echo these words (see Num 6:25; Ps 67:1).

43:30 *Joseph . . . wept.* Both emotional and sensitive, he wept often (see 42:24; 45:2,14–15; 46:29).

43:32 *Egyptians could not eat bread with the Hebrews.* The taboo

by themselves, and the Egyptians who ate
with him by themselves, because the Egyptians could not eat bread with the Hebrews,
for that is [1][a]loathsome to the Egyptians.
33 Now they [1]were seated before him,
[a]the firstborn according to his birthright and
the youngest according to his youth, and the
men looked at one another in astonishment.
34 He took portions to them from [1]his
own table, [a]but Benjamin's portion was five
times as much as any of theirs. So they feasted and drank freely with him.

The Brothers Are Brought Back

44 [a]Then he commanded his house steward, saying, "Fill the men's sacks with
food, as much as they can carry, and put
each man's money in the mouth of his sack.
2 "Put my cup, the silver cup, in the
mouth of the sack of the youngest, and his
money for the grain." And he did [1]as Joseph
had told *him*.
3 [1]As soon as it was light, the men were
sent away, they with their donkeys.
4 They had *just* gone out of [a]the city, *and*
were not far off, when Joseph said to his
house steward, "Up, follow the men; and
when you overtake them, say to them, 'Why
have you repaid evil for good?
5 'Is not this the one from which my lord
drinks and which he indeed uses for [a]divina-
tion? You have done wrong in doing this.' "
6 So he overtook them and spoke these
words to them.
7 They said to him, "Why does my lord
speak such words as these? Far be it from
your servants to do such a thing.
8 "Behold, [a]the money which we found in
the mouth of our sacks we have brought
back to you from the land of Canaan. How
then could we steal silver or gold from your
lord's house?
9 " [a]With whomever of your servants it is
found, let him die, and we also will be my
lord's [b]slaves."
10 So he said, "Now let it also be according to your words; he with whom it is found
shall be my slave, and *the rest of* you shall be
innocent."
11 Then they hurried, each man lowered
his sack to the ground, and each man
opened his sack.
12 He searched, beginning with the oldest
and ending with the youngest, and [a]the cup
was found in Benjamin's sack.
13 Then they [a]tore their clothes, and
when each man loaded his donkey, they
returned to [b]the city.
14 When Judah and his brothers came to
Joseph's house, he was still there, and [a]they
fell to the ground before him.
15 Joseph said to them, "What is this deed
that you have done? Do you not know that
such a man as I can indeed practice [a]divina-
tion?"
16 So Judah said, "What can we say to my
lord? What can we speak? And how can we
justify ourselves? God has found out the
iniquity of your servants; behold, we are my
lord's [a]slaves, both we and the one in whose
[1]possession the cup has been found."
17 But he said, "Far be it from me to do
this. The man in whose [1]possession the cup
has been found, he shall be my slave; but as
for you, go up in peace to your father."
18 Then Judah approached him, and said,
"Oh my lord, may your servant please speak
a word in my lord's ears, and [1][a]do not be
angry with your servant; for [b]you are equal
to Pharaoh.
19 " [a]My lord asked his servants, saying,
'Have you a father or a brother?'
20 "We said to my lord, 'We have an old
father and [a]a little child of *his* old age. Now
[b]his brother is dead, so he alone is left of his
mother, and his father loves him.'
21 "Then you said to your servants, '[a]Bring
him down to me that I may set my eyes on
him.'
22 "But we said to my lord, 'The lad cannot
leave his father, for if he should leave his
father, [1]his father would die.'
23 "You said to your servants, however,
'[a]Unless your youngest brother comes down
with you, you will not see my face again.'
24 "Thus it came about when we went up
to your servant my father, we told him the
words of my lord.
25 " [a]Our father said, 'Go back, buy us a little food.'
26 "But we said, 'We cannot go down. If
our youngest brother is with us, then we will
go down; for we cannot see the man's face
unless our youngest brother is with us.'

32 [1]Lit *an abomination* [a]Gen 46:34; Ex 8:26
33 [1]Lit *sat* [a]Gen 42:7
34 [1]Lit *his face* [a]Gen 35:24; 45:22
44:1 [a]Gen 42:25
2 [1]Or *according to the word*
3 [1]Lit *The morning was light*
4 [a]Gen 44:13
5 [a]Gen 30:27; 44:15; Lev 19:26; Deut 18:10-14
8 [a]Gen 43:21
9 [a]Gen 31:32 [b]Gen 44:16
12 [a]Gen 44:2
13 [a]Gen 37:29, 34; Num 14:6; 2 Sam 1:11 [b]Gen 44:4
14 [a]Gen 37:7, 10
15 [a]Gen 44:5
16 [1]Lit *hand* [a]Gen 44:9
17 [1]Lit *hand*
18 [1]Lit *let not your anger burn against* [a]Gen 18:30, 32; Ex 32:22 [b]Gen 37:7, 8; 41:40-44
19 [a]Gen 43:7
20 [a]Gen 37:3; 43:8; 44:30 [b]Gen 37:33; 42:13, 38
21 [a]Gen 42:15, 20
22 [1]Lit *he would*
23 [a]Gen 43:3, 5
25 [a]Gen 43:2

was probably based on ritual or religious reasons (see Ex 8:26), unlike the Egyptian refusal to associate with shepherds (see 46:34), which was probably based on social custom.

43:34 *Benjamin's portion was five times as much.* Again reflecting his special status with Joseph (see note on v. 29; see also 45:22).

44:4 *the city.* Identity unknown, though Memphis (about 13 miles south of modern Cairo) and Zoan (in the eastern delta region) have been suggested.

44:5 *divination.* See v. 15; see also note on 30:27.

44:9 *With whomever of your servants it is found, let him die.* Years earlier, Jacob had given Laban a similar rash response (see 31:32 and note).

44:10 The steward softened the penalty contained in the brothers' proposal.

44:12 *beginning with the oldest and ending with the youngest.* For a similar building up of suspense see 31:33.

44:13 *tore their clothes.* A sign of distress and grief (see 37:29).

44:14 *fell to the ground before him.* Further fulfillment of Joseph's dreams in 37:7,9 (see 42:6; 43:26,28).

44:16 *God has found out the iniquity of your servants.* Like Joseph's steward (see note on 43:23), Judah spoke better than he knew—or perhaps his words had a double meaning (see 42:21).

44:18 *Judah . . . said.* See note on 43:3. *lord . . . servant.* See note on 42:10. *you are equal to Pharaoh.* Words more flattering than true (see 41:40,43).

27 "Your servant my father said to us, 'You
know that [a]my wife bore me two sons;
28 and the one went out from me, and [a]I
said, "Surely he is torn in pieces," and I have
not seen him since.
29 'If you take this one also from [1]me, and
harm befalls him, you will [a]bring my gray
hair down to Sheol in [2]sorrow.'
30 "Now, therefore, when I come to your
servant my father, and the lad is not with us,
since [1][a]his life is bound up in the lad's life,
31 when he sees that the lad is not *with*
us, he will die. Thus your servants will
[a]bring the gray hair of your servant our
father down to Sheol in sorrow.
32 "For your servant [a]became surety for the
lad to my father, saying, 'If I do not bring
him *back* to you, then [1]let me bear the blame
before my father forever.'
33 "Now, therefore, please let your servant
remain instead of the lad a slave to my lord,
and let the lad go up with his brothers.
34 "For how shall I go up to my father if the
lad is not with me—for fear that I see the evil
that would [1]overtake my father?"

Joseph Deals Kindly with His Brothers

45 Then Joseph could not control himself
before all those who stood by him, and
he cried, "Have everyone go out from me."
So there [1]was no man with him [a]when
Joseph made himself known to his brothers.
2 [a]He [1]wept so loudly that the Egyptians
heard *it,* and the household of Pharaoh
heard *of it.*
3 Then Joseph said to his brothers, "[a]I
am Joseph! [b]Is my father still alive?" But his
brothers could not answer him, for [c]they
were dismayed at his presence.
4 Then Joseph said to his brothers,
"Please come [1]closer to me." And they came
[1]closer. And he said, "I am your brother
Joseph, whom you [a]sold into Egypt.
5 "Now do not be grieved or angry [1]with
yourselves, because [a]you sold me here, for
[b]God sent me before you to preserve life.
6 "For the famine *has been* in the land

27 [a]Gen 46:19
28 [a]Gen 37:31-35
29 [1]Lit *my face* [2]Lit *evil* [a]Gen 42:38; 44:31
30 [1]Lit *his soul is bound with his soul* [a]1 Sam 18:1
31 [a]Gen 44:29
32 [1]Lit *and I shall have sinned for all the days before my father* [a]Gen 43:9
34 [1]Lit *find*
45:1 [1]Lit *stood* [a]Acts 7:13
2 [1]Lit *gave forth his voice in weeping* [a]Gen 45:14, 15; 46:29
3 [a]Acts 7:13 [b]Gen 43:27 [c]Gen 37:20-28; 42:21, 22
4 [1]Lit *near* [a]Gen 37:28
5 [1]Lit *in your eyes* [a]Gen 37:28 [b]Gen 45:7, 8; 50:20; Ps 105:17
6 [a]Gen 37:2; 41:46, 53
7 [1]Lit *escaped company* [a]Gen 45:5
8 [a]Judg 17:10
9 [a]Acts 7:14
10 [1]Lit *dwell* [a]Gen 46:28, 34; 47:1
11 [a]Gen 47:12
13 [a]Acts 7:14
14 [a]Gen 45:2
16 [1]Lit *voice* [2]Lit *saying, "Joseph's brothers have come"* [3]Lit *was good in the eyes of* [a]Acts 7:13
17 [1]Lit *come, go*
18 [1]Lit *good* [a]Gen 27:28
19 [1]Lit *take for yourselves* [a]Gen 45:21, 27; 46:5; Num 7:3-8

[a]these two years, and there are still five years
in which there will be neither plowing nor
harvesting.
7 "[a]God sent me before you to preserve
for you a remnant in the earth, and to keep
you alive by a great [1]deliverance.
8 "Now, therefore, it was not you who sent
me here, but God; and He has made me a
[a]father to Pharaoh and lord of all his household and ruler over all the land of Egypt.
9 "Hurry and go up to my father, and [a]say
to him, 'Thus says your son Joseph, "God
has made me lord of all Egypt; come down to
me, do not delay.
10 "You shall [1]live in the land of [a]Goshen,
and you shall be near me, you and your children and your children's children and your
flocks and your herds and all that you have.
11 "There I will also [a]provide for you, for
there are still five years of famine *to come,*
and you and your household and all that you
have would be impoverished." '
12 "Behold, your eyes see, and the eyes of
my brother Benjamin *see,* that it is my mouth
which is speaking to you.
13 "Now you must tell my father of all my
splendor in Egypt, and all that you have
seen; and you must hurry and [a]bring my
father down here."
14 Then he fell on his brother Benjamin's
neck and [a]wept, and Benjamin wept on his
neck.
15 He kissed all his brothers and wept on
them, and afterward his brothers talked with
him.
16 Now when [a]the [1]news was heard in
Pharaoh's house [2]that Joseph's brothers had
come, it [3]pleased Pharaoh and his servants.
17 Then Pharaoh said to Joseph, "Say to
your brothers, 'Do this: load your beasts and
[1]go to the land of Canaan,
18 and take your father and your households and come to me, and [a]I will give you
the [1]best of the land of Egypt and you will
eat the fat of the land.'
19 "Now you are ordered, 'Do this: [1]take
[a]wagons from the land of Egypt for your lit-

44:30 *his life is bound up in the lad's life.* The Hebrew underlying this clause is later used for "the soul of Jonathan" being "knit to the soul of David" (1 Sam 18:1).
44:33 *instead of the lad.* Judah's willingness to be a substitute for Benjamin helped make amends for his role in selling Joseph (see 37:26–27).
44:34 *for fear that I see the evil.* Judah remembers an earlier scene (37:34–35).
45:2 *wept.* See vv. 14–15; see also 43:30 and note.
45:3 *brothers . . . were dismayed.* Either because they thought they were seeing a ghost or because they were afraid of what Joseph would do to them.
45:4 *I am your brother Joseph.* See v. 3; Acts 7:13. This time Joseph emphasized his relationship to them. *you sold.* See note on 37:28.
45:5 *God sent me.* See vv. 7–9; Acts 7:9. God had a purpose to work through the brothers' thoughtless and cruel act (see Acts 2:23; 4:28).
45:6 Joseph was now 39 years old (see 41:46,53).
45:7 *a remnant.* Although none had been lost, they had escaped a great threat to them all; so Joseph called them a remnant in the confidence that they would live to produce a great people.
45:8 *father.* A title of honor given to viziers (see note on 41:43) and other high officials (in the Apocrypha see 1 Maccabees 11:32). All three titles of Joseph in this verse were originally Egyptian.
45:9 *Hurry . . . do not delay.* Joseph is anxious to see Jacob as soon as possible (see v. 13).
45:10 *Goshen.* A region in the eastern part of the Nile delta, it was very fertile (see v. 18) and remains so today.
45:12 *my mouth . . . is speaking.* Not through an interpreter as before (see 42:23).
45:14 *wept.* See 43:30 and note.
45:15 *his brothers talked with him.* In intimate fellowship and friendship, rather than hostility or fear, for the first time in over 20 years (see 37:2 and note on 45:6).
45:18 *you will eat the fat of the land.* An echo of Isaac's blessing on Jacob (see 27:28).

tle ones and for your wives, and bring your father and come.

20 ‘Do not [1]concern yourselves with your goods, for the [2]best of all the land of Egypt is yours.’ ”

21 Then the sons of Israel did so; and Joseph gave them [a]wagons according to the [1]command of Pharaoh, and gave them provisions for the journey.

22 To [1]each of them he gave [a]changes of garments, but to Benjamin he gave three hundred *pieces of* silver and [b]five changes of garments.

23 To his father he sent [1]as follows: ten donkeys loaded with the [2]best things of Egypt, and ten female donkeys loaded with grain and bread and sustenance for his father [3]on the journey.

24 So he sent his brothers away, and [1]as they departed, he said to them, “Do not [2]quarrel on the journey.”

25 Then they went up from Egypt, and came to the land of Canaan to their father Jacob.

26 They told him, saying, “Joseph is still alive, and indeed he is ruler over all the land of Egypt.” But [1]he was stunned, for [a]he did not believe them.

27 When they told him all the words of Joseph that he had spoken to them, and when he saw the [a]wagons that Joseph had sent to carry him, the spirit of their father Jacob revived.

28 Then Israel said, “It is enough; my son Joseph is still alive. I will go and see him before I die.”

Jacob Moves to Egypt

46 So Israel set out with all that he had, and came to [a]Beersheba, and offered sacrifices to the [b]God of his father Isaac.

2 [a]God spoke to Israel [1]in visions of the night and said, “[b]Jacob, Jacob.” And he said, “Here I am.”

3 He said, “[a]I am God, the God of your father; do not be afraid to go down to Egypt, for I will [b]make you a great nation there.

4 “[a]I will go down with you to Egypt, and [b]I will also surely bring you up again; and [c]Joseph will [1]close your eyes.”

5 Then Jacob arose from Beersheba; and the sons of Israel carried their father Jacob and their little ones and their wives in the [a]wagons which Pharaoh had sent to carry him.

6 They took their livestock and their property, which they had acquired in the land of Canaan, and [a]came to Egypt, Jacob and all his [1]descendants with him:

7 his sons and his grandsons with him, his daughters and his granddaughters, and all his [1]descendants he brought with him to Egypt.

Those Who Came to Egypt

8 Now these are the [a]names of the sons of Israel, Jacob and his sons, who went to Egypt: Reuben, Jacob’s firstborn.

9 The sons of Reuben: Hanoch and Pallu and Hezron and Carmi.

10 The [a]sons of Simeon: [1]Jemuel and Jamin and Ohad and [2]Jachin and [3]Zohar and Shaul the son of a Canaanite woman.

11 The sons of Levi: [1]Gershon, Kohath, and Merari.

12 The sons of Judah: Er and Onan and Shelah and Perez and Zerah (but Er and Onan died in the land of Canaan). And the [a]sons of Perez were Hezron and Hamul.

13 The sons of Issachar: Tola and [1]Puvvah and [2]Iob and Shimron.

14 The sons of Zebulun: Sered and Elon and Jahleel.

15 These are the sons of Leah, whom she bore to Jacob in Paddan-aram, with his daughter Dinah; [1]all his sons and his daughters *numbered* thirty-three.

16 The [a]sons of Gad: [1]Ziphion and Haggi, Shuni and [2]Ezbon, Eri and [3]Arodi and Areli.

17 The [a]sons of Asher: Imnah and Ishvah and Ishvi and Beriah and their sister Serah. And the [b]sons of Beriah: Heber and Malchiel.

18 These are the sons of Zilpah, whom Laban gave to his daughter Leah; and she bore to Jacob these sixteen persons.

19 The sons of Jacob’s wife Rachel: Joseph and Benjamin.

20 [1]Lit *let your eye look with regret upon your vessels* [2]Lit *good*
21 [1]Lit *mouth* [a]Gen 45:19
22 [1]Lit *all of them he gave each man* [a]2 Kin 5:5 [b]Gen 43:34
23 [1]Lit *like this* [2]Lit *good* [3]Lit *for*
24 [1]Lit *they departed; and he said* [2]Lit *be agitated*
26 [1]Lit *his heart grew numb* [a]Gen 37:31-35
27 [a]Gen 45:19
46:1 [a]Gen 21:31; 28:10 [b]Gen 26:24; 28:13; 31:42
2 [1]Lit *in the visions* [a]Gen 15:1; Num 12:6; Job 33:14, 15 [b]Gen 22:11; 31:11
3 [a]Gen 17:1; 28:13 [b]Gen 12:2; Ex 1:9; Deut 26:5
4 [1]Lit *put his hand on* [a]Gen 28:15; 48:21 [b]Gen 50:24; Ex 3:8 [c]Gen 50:1
5 [a]Gen 45:21
6 [1]Lit *seed* [a]Deut 26:5; Josh 24:4; Ps 105:23; Is 52:4; Acts 7:15
7 [1]Lit *seed*
8 [a]Ex 1:1-4; Num 26:4, 5; 1 Chr 2:1ff
10 [1]In Num 26:12 and 1 Chr 4:24, *Nemuel* [2]In 1 Chr 4:24, *Jarib* [3]In Num 26:13 and 1 Chr 4:24, *Zerah* [a]Ex 6:15
11 [1]In 1 Chr 6:16, *Gershom*
12 [a]1 Chr 2:5
13 [1]In Num 26:23, *Puvah;* in 1 Chr 7:1, *Puah* [2]In Num 26:24 and 1 Chr 7:1, *Jashub*
15 [1]Lit *all the souls of*
16 [1]In Num 26:15, *Zephon* [2]In Num 26:16, *Ozni* [3]In Num 26:17, *Arod* [a]Num 26:15-18
17 [a]1 Chr 7:30 [b]1 Chr 7:31

45:22 *to Benjamin he gave . . . five changes of garments.* See note on 43:34. *shekels.* See note on 20:16.

45:24 *Do not quarrel.* Joseph wanted nothing to delay their return (see note on v. 9), and he wanted them to avoid mutual accusation and recrimination concerning the past.

46:1 *set out.* Probably from the family estate at Hebron (see 35:27). *came to Beersheba, and offered sacrifices.* Abraham and Isaac had also worshiped the Lord there (see 21:33; 26:23–25).

46:2 *God spoke to Israel in visions of the night.* See 26:24. *Jacob, Jacob.* See note on 22:11. *Here I am.* See note on 22:1.

46:3–4 As Israel and his family were about to leave Canaan, God reaffirmed His covenant promises.

46:3 *I am . . . the God of your father; do not be afraid.* A verbatim repetition of God’s statement to Isaac in 26:24. *I will make you a great nation.* The Lord reaffirmed one aspect of His promise to Abraham (see 12:2). *there.* See Ex 1:7.

46:4 *I will go down with you to Egypt.* God would be with Jacob as he went south to Egypt just as He was with him when he went north to Haran, and would again bring him back as He had done before (see 28:15; see also 15:16; 48:21).

46:8 *these are the names of the sons of Israel . . . who went to Egypt.* The Hebrew here is repeated verbatim in Ex 1:1 (see note there), where it introduces the background for the story of the exodus (predicted here in v. 4).

46:15 *Paddan-aram.* See note on 25:20. *numbered thirty-three.* There are 34 names in vv. 8–15. To bring the number to 33 the name Ohad in v. 10 should probably be removed, since it does not appear in the parallel lists in Num 26:12–13; 1 Chr 4:24. The Hebrew form of “Ohad” looks very much like that of the nearby “Zohar” (see Ex 6:15), and a later scribe probably added Ohad to the text accidentally.

20 [a]Now to Joseph in the land of Egypt were born Manasseh and Ephraim, whom Asenath, the daughter of Potiphera, priest of On, bore to him.

21 The [a]sons of Benjamin: Bela and Becher and Ashbel, Gera and Naaman, [1]Ehi and Rosh, [2]Muppim and [3]Huppim and Ard.

22 These are the sons of Rachel, who were born to Jacob; *there were* fourteen persons in all.

23 The sons of Dan: [1]Hushim.

24 The sons of Naphtali: [1]Jahzeel and Guni and Jezer and [2]Shillem.

25 These are the [a]sons of Bilhah, whom [b]Laban gave to his daughter Rachel, and she bore these to Jacob; *there were* seven persons in all.

26 [a]All the persons belonging to Jacob, who came to Egypt, [1]his direct descendants, not including the wives of Jacob's sons, *were* sixty-six persons in all,

27 and the sons of Joseph, who were born to him in Egypt were [1]two; [a]all the persons of the house of Jacob, who came to Egypt, *were* seventy.

28 Now he sent Judah before him to Joseph, to point out *the way* before him to [a]Goshen; and they came into the land of Goshen.

29 Joseph [1]prepared his chariot and went up to Goshen to meet his father Israel; as soon as he appeared [2]before him, he fell on his neck and [a]wept on his neck a long time.

30 Then Israel said to Joseph, "Now let me die, since I have seen your face, that you are still alive."

31 Joseph said to his brothers and to his father's household, "[a]I will go up and tell Pharaoh, and will say to him, 'My brothers and my father's household, who *were* in the land of Canaan, have come to me;

32 and the men are shepherds, for they have been [1]keepers of livestock; and they have brought their flocks and their herds and all that they have.'

33 "When Pharaoh calls you and says, '[a]What is your occupation?'

34 you shall say, 'Your servants have been [1a]keepers of livestock from our youth even until now, both we and our fathers,' that you may [2]live in the land of [b]Goshen; for every shepherd is [3c]loathsome to the Egyptians."

Jacob's Family Settles in Goshen

47 Then [a]Joseph went in and told Pharaoh, and said, "My father and my brothers and their flocks and their herds and all that they have, have come out of the land of Canaan; and behold, they are in the land of [b]Goshen."

2 He took five men from among his brothers and [a]presented them to Pharaoh.

3 Then Pharaoh said to his brothers, "[a]What is your occupation?" So they said to Pharaoh, "Your servants are [b]shepherds, both we and our fathers."

4 They said to Pharaoh, "[a]We have come to sojourn in the land, for there is no pasture for your servants' flocks, for [b]the famine is severe in the land of Canaan. Now, therefore, please let your servants [1c]live in the land of Goshen."

5 Then Pharaoh said to [1]Joseph, "Your father and your brothers have come to you.

6 "The land of Egypt is [1]at your disposal; [2]settle your father and your brothers in [a]the best of the land, let them [3]live in the land of Goshen; and if you know any [b]capable men among them, then [4]put them in charge of my livestock."

7 Then Joseph brought his father Jacob and [1]presented him to Pharaoh; and Jacob [a]blessed Pharaoh.

8 Pharaoh said to Jacob, "How many [1]years have you lived?"

9 So Jacob said to Pharaoh, "The [1a]years of my sojourning are one hundred and [2]thirty; few and [3]unpleasant have been the [1]years of my life, nor have they [4]attained [b]the [1]years [5]that my fathers lived during the days of their sojourning."

10 And Jacob [a]blessed Pharaoh, and went out from [1]his presence.

11 So Joseph [1]settled his father and his brothers and gave them a possession in the land of Egypt, in [a]the best of the land, in the land of [b]Rameses, as Pharaoh had ordered.

12 Joseph [a]provided his father and his brothers and all his father's household with [1]food, according to their little ones.

13 Now there was no [1]food in all the land,

20 [a]Gen 41:50-52 **21** [1]In Num 26:38, *Ahiram* [2]In Num 26:39, *Shephupham;* in 1 Chr 7:12, *Shuppim* [3]In Num 26:39, *Hupham* [a]1 Chr 7:6 **23** [1]In Num 26:42, *Shuham* **24** [1]In 1 Chr 7:13, *Jahziel* [2]In 1 Chr 7:13, *Shallum* **25** [a]Gen 30:5, 7 [b]Gen 29:29 **26** [1]Lit *who came out of his loins* [a]Ex 1:5 **27** [1]Lit *two souls* [a]Ex 1:5; Deut 10:22; Acts 7:14 **28** [a]Gen 45:10 **29** [1]Lit *tied, harnessed* [2]Lit *to* [a]Gen 45:14, 15 **31** [a]Gen 47:1 **32** [1]Lit *men* **33** [a]Gen 47:2, 3 **34** [1]Lit *men* [2]Lit *dwell* [3]Lit *an abomination* [a]Gen 13:7, 8; 26:20; 37:2 [b]Gen 45:10, 18; 47:6, 11 [c]Gen 43:32; Ex 8:26

47:1 [a]Gen 46:31 [b]Gen 45:10; 46:28 **2** [a]Acts 7:13 **3** [a]Gen 46:33 [b]Gen 46:34 **4** [1]Lit *dwell* [a]Gen 15:13; Deut 26:5; Ps 105:23 [b]Gen 43:1; Acts 7:11 [c]Gen 46:34 **5** [1]Lit *Joseph, saying* **6** [1]Lit *before you* [2]Lit *cause them to dwell* [3]Lit *dwell* [4]Lit *appoint them rulers* [a]Gen 45:10, 18; 47:11 [b]Ex 18:21, 25; 1 Kin 11:28; Prov 22:29 **7** [1]Lit *set him before* [a]Gen 47:10; 2 Sam 14:22; 1 Kin 8:66 **8** [1]Lit *are the days of the years of your life* **9** [1]Lit *days of the years* [2]Lit *thirty years* [3]Lit *evil* [4]Lit *reached* [5]Lit *of the life of my fathers* [a]Heb 11:9, 13 [b]Gen 25:7; 35:28 **10** [1]Lit *Pharaoh's* [a]Gen 47:7 **11** [1]Lit *caused to dwell* [a]Gen 47:6, 27 [b]Ex 1:11; 12:37 **12** [1]Or *bread* [a]Gen 45:11 **13** [1]Or *bread*

46:20 See note on 41:45.

46:26 *All the persons belonging to Jacob, who came to Egypt . . . were sixty-six.* The total of 33 (see v. 15 and note), 16 (v. 18), 14 (v. 22) and 7 (see v. 25) is 70 (v. 27). To arrive at 66 we must subtract Er and Onan, who "died in the land of Canaan" (v. 12), and Manasseh and Ephraim (v. 20), who "were born . . . in Egypt" (v. 27).

46:27 *seventy.* See Deut 10:22. Seventy is the ideal and complete number (see Introduction: Literary Features; see also notes on 5:5; 10:2) of Jacob's descendants who would have been in Egypt if Er and Onan had not died earlier (see 38:7–10). For the number 75 in Acts 7:14 see note there.

46:28 *he sent Judah before him.* See note on 43:3.

46:29 *wept.* See 43:30 and note.

46:34 *every shepherd is loathsome to the Egyptians.* See note on 43:32.

47:9 *sojourning.* Jacob referred to the itinerant nature of patriarchal life in general and of his own in particular as he hopefully awaited the fulfillment of the promise of a land (see also Deut 26:5). *nor have they attained the years . . . my fathers lived.* Abraham lived to the age of 175 (25:7), Isaac to 180 (35:28).

47:11 *best of the land.* See note on 45:10. *land of Rameses.* The city of Rameses is mentioned in Ex 1:11; 12:37; Num 33:3,5. The name doubtless refers to the great Egyptian pharaoh Rameses II, who reigned centuries later (the designation here involves an editorial updating). In addition to being known as Goshen (see v. 27), the "land of Rameses" was called the "field of Zoan" in Ps 78:12,43

because the famine was very severe, so that
[a]the land of Egypt and the land of Canaan
languished because of the famine.
14 [a]Joseph gathered all the money that
was found in the land of Egypt and in the
land of Canaan for the grain which they
bought, and Joseph brought the money into
Pharaoh's house.
15 When the money was all spent in the
land of Egypt and in the land of Canaan, all
the Egyptians came to Joseph [1]and said,
"Give us [2]food, for [a]why should we die in
your presence? For *our* money [3]is gone."
16 Then Joseph said, "Give up your livestock, and I will give you *food* for your livestock, since *your* money [1]is gone."
17 So they brought their livestock to
Joseph, and Joseph gave them [1]food in
exchange for the horses and the [2]flocks and
the herds and the donkeys; and he [3]fed them
with [1]food in exchange for all their livestock
[4]that year.
18 When that year was ended, they came
to him the [1]next year and said to him, "We
will not hide from my lord that our money is
all spent, and the [2]cattle are my lord's. There
is nothing left [3]for my lord except our bodies
and our lands.
19 "Why should we die before your eyes,
both we and our land? Buy us and our land
for [1]food, and we and our land will be slaves
to Pharaoh. So give us seed, that we may live
and not die, and that the land may not be
desolate."

Result of the Famine

20 So Joseph bought all the land of Egypt
for Pharaoh, for [1]every Egyptian sold his
field, because the famine was severe upon
them. Thus the land became Pharaoh's.
21 As for the people, he removed them to
the cities from one end of Egypt's border to
the other.
22 Only the land of the priests he did not
buy, for the priests had an allotment from
Pharaoh, and they [1]lived off the allotment
which Pharaoh gave them. Therefore, they
did not sell their land.
23 Then Joseph said to the people,
"Behold, I have today bought you and your
land for Pharaoh; now, *here* is seed for you,
and you may sow the land.

13 [a]Gen 41:30; Acts 7:11
14 [a]Gen 41:56
15 [1]Lit *saying* [2]Or *bread* [3]Lit *ceases* [a]Gen 47:19
16 [1]Lit *ceases*
17 [1]Or *bread* [2]Lit *livestock of the flocks and livestock of the herds* [3]Lit *led them as a shepherd* [4]Lit *in that year*
18 [1]Lit *second* [2]Lit *livestock of the cattle* [3]Lit *in the presence of*
19 [1]Or *bread*
20 [1]Lit *Egypt, every man*
22 [1]Lit *ate their allotment*
24 [1]Lit *It shall come about...that you shall* [2]Lit *four parts* [a]Gen 41:34
26 [1]Lit *alone did* [a]Gen 47:22
27 [1]Lit *dwelt* [2]Lit *in the land of Goshen* [a]Gen 47:11 [b]Gen 17:6; 26:4; 35:11; Ex 1:7; Deut 26:5; Acts 7:17
28 [1]Lit *days of Jacob, the years of his life* [a]Gen 47:9
29 [1]Lit *the days of Israel to die drew near* [2]Lit *truth* [a]Deut 31:14; 1 Kin 2:1 [b]Gen 24:2 [c]Gen 24:49
30 [a]Gen 15:15; Deut 31:16 [b]Gen 23:17-20; 25:9, 10; 35:29; 49:29-32; 50:5, 13; Acts 7:15, 16
31 [a]Gen 21:23, 24; 24:3; 31:53; 50:25 [b]1 Kin 1:47
48:1 [1]Lit *one said to Joseph* [a]Gen 41:51, 52; Josh 14:4
2 [1]Lit *one told Jacob and said* [2]Lit *strengthened himself* [3]Lit *upon the bed*
3 [1]Heb *El Shaddai* [a]Gen 28:13f; 35:9-12 [b]Gen 28:19; 35:6
4 [1]Lit *seed* [a]Gen 17:8
5 [a]Gen 41:50-52; 46:20; 48:1; Josh 14:4 [b]1 Chr 5:1, 2

24 "[1]At the harvest you shall give a [a]fifth to
Pharaoh, and [2]four-fifths shall be your own
for seed of the field and for your food and for
those of your households and as food for
your little ones."
25 So they said, "You have saved our
lives! Let us find favor in the sight of my
lord, and we will be Pharaoh's slaves."
26 Joseph made it a statute concerning the
land of Egypt *valid* to this day, that Pharaoh
should have the fifth; [a]only the land of the
priests [1]did not become Pharaoh's.
27 Now Israel [1]lived in the land of Egypt, in
[2]Goshen, and they [a]acquired property in it and
[b]were fruitful and became very numerous.
28 Jacob lived in the land of Egypt [a]sev-
enteen years; so the [1]length of Jacob's life
was one hundred and forty-seven years.
29 When [1a]the time for Israel to die drew
near, he called his son Joseph and said to
him, "Please, if I have found favor in your
sight, [b]place now your hand under my thigh
and [c]deal with me in kindness and [2]faithful-
ness. Please do not bury me in Egypt,
30 but when I [a]lie down with my fathers,
you shall carry me out of Egypt and bury me
in [b]their burial place." And he said, "I will
do as you have said."
31 He said, "[a]Swear to me." So he swore
to him. Then [b]Israel bowed *in worship* at the
head of the bed.

Israel's Last Days

48 Now it came about after these things
that [1]Joseph was told, "Behold, your
father is sick." So he took his two sons
[a]Manasseh and Ephraim with him.
2 When [1]it was told to Jacob, "Behold,
your son Joseph has come to you," Israel
[2]collected his strength and sat [3]up in the bed.
3 Then Jacob said to Joseph, "[1a]God
Almighty appeared to me at [b]Luz in the land
of Canaan and blessed me,
4 and He said to me, 'Behold, I will make
you fruitful and numerous, and I will make
you a company of peoples, and will give this
land to your [1]descendants after you for [a]an
everlasting possession.'
5 "Now your two sons, who were born to
you in the land of Egypt before I came to you
in Egypt, are mine; [a]Ephraim and Manasseh
shall be mine, as [b]Reuben and Simeon are.

(see note on Gen 44:4).

47:13 *the famine was very severe.* After the people used up all their money to buy grain (see vv. 14–15), they traded their livestock (vv. 16–17), then their land (v. 20), then themselves (v. 21).

47:21 The Egyptians were to move temporarily into the cities until seed could be distributed to them for planting (see v. 23).

47:26 *Pharaoh should have the fifth.* The same was true "in the seven years of abundance" (41:34)—but now all the land on which the produce grew belonged to Pharaoh as well.

47:27 *Israel . . . were fruitful and became very numerous.* See 35:11–12; 46:3 and notes.

47:29 *place now your hand under my thigh.* See 24:2 and note. In both cases, ties of family kinship are being stressed.

47:30 *lie down with my fathers.* See note on 25:8. *bury me in their burial place.* In the cave of Machpelah (see 50:12–13).

47:31 *bowed in worship at the head of the bed.* Cf. 48:2.

48:3 *God Almighty.* See note on 17:1. *Luz.* The older name for Bethel (see 28:19).

48:5 *your two sons . . . are mine.* Jacob would adopt them as his own. *Ephraim and Manasseh.* See v. 1 for the expected order, since Manasseh was Joseph's firstborn (see 41:51). Jacob mentions Ephraim first because he intends to give him the primary blessing and thus "put Ephraim before Manasseh" (v. 20). *mine, as Reuben and Simeon are.* Joseph's first two sons would enjoy equal status

6 "But your offspring that [1]have been born after them shall be yours; they shall be called by the [2]names of their brothers in their inheritance.

7 "Now as for me, when I came from [a]Paddan, [b]Rachel died, [1]to my sorrow, in the land of Canaan on the journey, when there was still some distance to go to Ephrath; and I buried her there on the way to Ephrath (that is, Bethlehem)."

8 When Israel [a]saw Joseph's sons, he said, "Who are these?"

9 Joseph said to his father, "[a]They are my sons, whom God has given me here." So he said, "Bring them to me, please, that [b]I may bless them."

10 Now [a]the eyes of Israel were *so* dim from age *that* he could not see. Then [1]Joseph brought them close to him, and he [b]kissed them and embraced them.

11 Israel said to Joseph, "I never [1]expected to see your face, and behold, God has let me see your [2]children as well."

12 Then Joseph [1]took them from his knees, and [a]bowed with his face to the ground.

13 Joseph took them both, Ephraim with his right hand toward Israel's left, and Manasseh with his left hand toward Israel's right, and brought them close to him.

14 But Israel stretched out his right hand and laid it on the head of Ephraim, who was the younger, and his left hand on Manasseh's head, [1]crossing his hands, [2]although [a]Manasseh was the firstborn.

15 He blessed Joseph, and said,
"[a]The God before whom my fathers
Abraham and Isaac walked,
[b]The God who has been my shepherd
[1]all my life to this day,
16 [a]The angel who has redeemed me
from all evil,
[b]Bless the lads;
And may my name [1]live on in
them,
And the [2]names of my fathers
Abraham and Isaac;
And [c]may they grow into a multitude
in the midst of the earth."

17 When Joseph saw that his father [a]laid his right hand on Ephraim's head, it displeased him; and he grasped his father's hand to remove it from Ephraim's head to Manasseh's head.

18 Joseph said to his father, "Not so, my father, for this one is the firstborn. Place your right hand on his head."

19 But his father refused and said, "I know, my son, I know; he also will become a people and he also will be great. However, his younger brother shall be greater than he, and [a]his [1]descendants shall become a [2]multitude of nations."

20 [a]He blessed them that day, saying,
"By you Israel will pronounce blessing,
saying,
'May God make you like Ephraim and
Manasseh!'"
Thus he put Ephraim before Manasseh.

21 Then Israel said to Joseph, "Behold, I am about to die, but [a]God will be with you, and [b]bring you back to the land of your fathers.

22 "I give you one [1]portion more than your brothers, [a]which I took from the hand of the Amorite with my sword and my bow."

6 [1]Lit *you have begotten* [2]Lit *name*
7 [1]Lit *upon me* [a]Gen 33:18 [b]Gen 35:19, 20
8 [a]Gen 48:10
9 [a]Gen 33:5 [b]Gen 27:4
10 [1]Lit *he* [a]Gen 27:1 [b]Gen 27:27
11 [1]Lit *meditated, judged* [2]Lit *seed*
12 [1]Lit *made them come out* [a]Gen 42:6
14 [1]Or *consciously directing* [2]Lit *when* [a]Gen 41:51, 52
15 [a]Gen 17:1
15 [1]Lit *from the continuance of me* [b]Gen 49:24
16 [1]Lit *be called* [2]Lit *name* [a]Gen 22:11, 15-18; 28:13-15; 31:11 [b]Heb 11:21 [c]Gen 28:14; 46:3
17 [a]Gen 48:14
19 [1]Lit *seed* [2]Lit *fullness* [a]Gen 28:14; 46:3
20 [a]Heb 11:21
21 [a]Gen 26:3 [b]Gen 28:15; 46:4; 50:24
22 [1]Or *ridge;* lit *shoulder;* Heb *Shechem* [a]Josh 24:32; John 4:5

with Jacob's first two sons (35:23) and in fact would eventually supersede them. Because of an earlier sinful act (see 35:22 and note), Reuben would lose his birthright to Jacob's favorite son, Joseph (see 49:3–4; 1 Chr 5:2), and thus to Joseph's sons (see 1 Chr 5:1).

48:6 *offspring that have been born after them shall be yours.* They would take the place of Ephraim and Manasseh, whom Jacob had adopted. *they shall be called by the names of their brothers in their inheritance.* They would perpetuate the names of Ephraim and Manasseh for purposes of inheritance (for a similar provision see 38:8 and note; Deut 25:5–6). Joseph's territory would thus be divided between Ephraim and Manasseh, but Levi (Jacob's third son; see 35:23) would not receive a share of the land (Josh 14:4). The total number of tribal allotments would therefore remain the same.

48:7 *Paddan.* That is, Paddan-aram, meaning "plain of Aram," another name for Aram-naharaim (see note on 24:10). *Rachel died.* See 35:16–19. Adopted by Joseph's father, Ephraim and Manasseh in effect took the place of other sons whom Joseph's mother, Rachel, might have borne had she not died. *Ephrath.* See note on 35:16.

48:8 *Israel . . . said, "Who are these?"* Either because he had never met them or because, being old, he could not see them clearly.

48:10 *eyes . . . dim from age that he could not see.* See note on 27:1. *kissed them and embraced them.* While they were on Jacob's knees (see v. 12), probably symbolizing adoption (see note on 30:3).

48:13–20 See note on Acts 6:6.

48:13 *Manasseh . . . toward Israel's right.* Joseph wanted Jacob to bless Manasseh, Joseph's firstborn, by placing his right hand on Manasseh's head.

48:15 *blessed.* As his father Isaac had blessed him (27:27–29). *Joseph.* Used here collectively for Ephraim and Manasseh (the Hebrew for "you" and "yours in v. 21 is plural). *before whom . . . Abraham and Isaac walked.* See notes on 5:22; 17:1. *shepherd.* An intimate royal metaphor for God (see Ps 23:1), used in Genesis only here and in Jacob's later blessing of Joseph (49:24).

48:16 *angel.* See note on 16:7. The angel—God Himself—had earlier blessed Jacob (see 32:29; see also note on 32:24).

48:19 *his younger brother shall be greater than he.* See note on 25:23. During the divided monarchy (930–722 B.C.), Ephraim's descendants were the most powerful tribe in the north. "Ephraim" was often used to refer to the northern kingdom as a whole (see, e.g., Is 7:2,5,8–9; Hos 9:13; 12:1,8).

48:20 *he put Ephraim before Manasseh.* Jacob, the younger son who struggled with Esau for the birthright and blessing and who preferred the younger sister (Rachel) above the older (Leah), now advanced Joseph's younger son ahead of the older.

48:21 *Joseph.* See note on v. 15. *I am about to die.* Years later, Joseph spoke these words to his brothers (50:24).

48:22 *one portion more.* The Hebrew for this phrase is identical with the place-name Shechem, where Joseph was later buried in a plot of ground inherited by his descendants (see Josh 24:32; see also 33:19; John 4:5). *I took from . . . the Amorite.* Possibly referring to the event of 34:25–29.

Israel's Prophecy concerning His Sons

49 Then Jacob summoned his sons and
said, "Assemble yourselves that I may
tell you what will befall you [a]in the [1]days to
come.

2 "Gather together and hear, O sons of
Jacob;
And [a]listen to Israel your father.

3 "Reuben, you are my firstborn;
My might and [a]the beginning of my
strength,
[1]Preeminent in dignity and
[1]preeminent in power.
4 "[1]Uncontrolled as water, you shall not
have preeminence,
[a]Because you went up to your father's
bed;
Then you defiled *it*—he went up to
my couch.

5 "[a]Simeon and Levi are brothers;
Their swords are implements of
violence.
6 "[a]Let my soul not enter into their
council;
Let not my glory be united with their
assembly;
Because in their anger they slew
[1]men,
And in their self-will they lamed
[2]oxen.
7 "Cursed be their anger, for it is fierce;
And their wrath, for it is cruel.
[a]I will [1]disperse them in Jacob,
And scatter them in Israel.

8 "Judah, your brothers shall praise you;
Your hand shall be on the neck of
your enemies;
[a]Your father's sons shall bow down to
you.
9 "Judah is a [a]lion's whelp;
From the prey, my son, you have gone
up.
[b]He [1]couches, he lies down as a lion,
And as a [2]lion, who [3]dares rouse him
up?
10 "[a]The scepter shall not depart from
Judah,
Nor the ruler's staff from between his
feet,
[1]Until Shiloh comes,
And [b]to him *shall be* the obedience of
the peoples.
11 "[1][a]He ties *his* foal to the vine,
And his donkey's colt to the choice
vine;
[b]He washes his garments in wine,
And his robes in the blood of grapes.
12 "His eyes are [1]dull from wine,
And his teeth [2]white from milk.

13 "[a]Zebulun will dwell at the seashore;
And he *shall be* [1]a haven for ships,
And his flank *shall be* toward Sidon.

14 "Issachar is [1]a strong donkey,
[a]Lying down between the [2]sheepfolds.
15 "When he saw that a resting place was
good
And that the land was pleasant,
He bowed his shoulder to bear *burdens*,
And became a slave at forced labor.

16 "[a]Dan shall [b]judge his people,
As one of the tribes of Israel.
17 "Dan shall be a serpent in the way,
A horned snake in the path,
That bites the horse's heels,
So that his rider falls backward.

49:1 [1]Lit *end of the days* [a]Num 24:14
2 [a]Ps 34:11
3 [1]Lit *preeminence* [a]Deut 21:17; Ps 78:51; 105:36
4 [1]Or *Boiling over;* lit *Recklessness* [a]Gen 35:22; Deut 27:20; 1 Chr 5:1
5 [a]Gen 34:25-30
6 [1]Lit *a man* [2]Lit *an ox* [a]Ps 64:2
7 [1]Lit *divide* [a]Josh 19:1, 9; 21:1-42
8 [a]Gen 27:29; 1 Chr 5:2
9 [1]Lit *bows down* [2]Or *lioness* [3]Lit *shall* [a]Ezek 19:5-7; Mic 5:8 [b]Num 24:9
10 [1]Or *Until he comes to Shiloh;* or *Until he comes to whom it belongs* [a]Num 24:17; Ps 60:7; 108:8 [b]Ps 2:6-9; 72:8-11; Is 42:1, 4; 49:6
11 [1]Lit *Binding of* [a]Deut 8:7, 8; 2 Kin 18:32 [b]Is 63:2
12 [1]Or *darker than* [2]Or *whiter than*
13 [1]Lit *for a shore of ships* [a]Deut 33:18, 19
14 [1]Lit *a donkey of bone* [2]Or *saddlebags* [a]Judg 5:16; Ps 68:13
16 [a]Deut 33:22; Judg 18:26, 27 [b]Gen 30:6

49:2–27 Often called the "Blessing of Jacob," this is the longest poem in Genesis. Its various blessings were intended not only for Jacob's 12 sons but also for the tribes that descended from them (see v. 28). For other poetic blessings in Genesis see 9:26–27; 14:19–20; 27:27–29; 27:39–40; 48:15–16; 48:20.
49:4 *Uncontrolled.* Reuben's descendants were characterized by indecision (see Judg 5:15–16). *you shall not have preeminence, Because you went up to your father's bed.* See 35:22 and note; see also notes on 37:21; 48:5.
49:5 *Simeon and Levi are brothers.* They shared the traits of violence, anger and cruelty (see vv. 6–7).
49:7 *I will disperse them.* Fulfilled when Simeon's descendants were absorbed into the territory of Judah (see Josh 19:1,9) and when Levi's descendants were dispersed throughout the land, living in 48 towns and the surrounding pasturelands (see note on 48:6; see also Num 35:2,7; Josh 14:4; 21:41).
49:8 Cf. 27:29,40; 37:7,9. *Judah, your brothers . . . shall bow down to you.* See note on 43:3. As those who would become the leading tribes of southern and northern Israel respectively, Judah and Joseph were given the longest (vv. 8–12 and vv. 22–26) of Jacob's blessings. Judah was the fourth of Leah's sons and also the fourth son born to Jacob (29:35), but Reuben, Simeon and Levi had forfeited their right of leadership. So Jacob assigns leadership to Judah (a son of Leah) but a double portion to Joseph (a son of Rachel). See also 1 Chr 5:2.
49:9 *Judah is a lion's whelp.* A symbol of sovereignty, strength and courage. Judah (or Israel) is often pictured as a lion in later times (see Ezek 19:1–7; Mic 5:8; and especially Num 24:9). Judah's greatest descendant, Jesus Christ (see note on 43:3), is Himself called "the Lion that is from the tribe of Judah" (Rev 5:5).
49:10 Though difficult to translate, the verse has been traditionally understood as Messianic. It was initially fulfilled in David, and ultimately in Christ. *scepter.* See Num 24:17 and note. *Until Shiloh comes.* Or "Until he comes to whom it belongs," repeated almost verbatim in Ezek 21:27 in a section where Zedekiah, the last king of Judah, is told to "take off the crown" (Ezek 21:26) from his head because dominion over Jerusalem will ultimately be given to the one "whose right it is."
49:11 Judah's descendants would someday enjoy a settled and prosperous life.
49:13 Though landlocked by the tribes of Asher and Manasseh, the descendants of Zebulun were close enough to the Mediterranean (within ten miles) to "draw out the abundance of the seas" (Deut 33:19).
49:17 *Dan shall be a serpent.* The treachery of a group of Danites in later times is described in Judg 18:27. *That bites the horse's heels.* Samson, from the tribe of Dan, would single-handedly hold the Philistines at bay (Judg 14–16).

18 "[a]For Your salvation I wait, O LORD.

19 "[a]As for Gad, [1]raiders shall raid him,
But he will raid *at* their [2]heels.

20 "[1][a]As for [b]Asher, his [2]food shall be [3]rich,
And he will yield royal dainties.

21 "[a]Naphtali is a doe let loose,
He gives beautiful words.

22 "[a]Joseph is a fruitful [1]bough,
A fruitful [1]bough by a spring;
Its [2]branches run over a wall.
23 "The archers bitterly attacked him,
And shot *at him* and harassed him;
24 But his [a]bow remained [1]firm,
And [2][b]his arms were agile,
From the hands of the [c]Mighty One of Jacob
(From there is [d]the Shepherd, [e]the Stone of Israel),
25 From [a]the God of your father who helps you,
And [1][b]by the [2]Almighty who blesses you
With [c]blessings of heaven above,
Blessings of the deep that lies beneath,
Blessings of the breasts and of the womb.
26 "The blessings of your father
Have surpassed the blessings of my ancestors
Up to the [1]utmost bound of [a]the everlasting hills;

18 [a]Ex 15:2; Ps 25:5; 40:1-3; 119:166, 174; Is 25:9; Mic 7:7 **19** [1]Lit *a raiding band* [2]Lit *heel* [a]Deut 33:20 **20** [1]Lit *From* [2]Or *bread* [3]Lit *fat* [a]Deut 33:24, 25 [b]Gen 30:13 **21** [a]Deut 33:23 **22** [1]Lit *son* [2]Lit *daughters* [a]Deut 33:13-17 **24** [1]I.e. in an unyielding position [2]Lit *the arms of his hands* [a]Job 29:20 [b]Ps 18:34; 73:23; Is 41:10 [c]Ps 132:2, 5; Is 1:24; 49:26 [d]Ps 23:1; 80:1 [e]Ps 118:22; Is 28:16; 1 Pet 2:6-8

25 [1]Or *with* [2]Heb *Shaddai* [a]Gen 28:13; 32:9 [b]Gen 28:3; 48:3 [c]Gen 27:28 **26** [1]Lit *limit;* or *desire* [a]Deut 33:15, 16

49:18 Jacob pauses midway through his series of blessings to utter a brief prayer for God's help.
49:19 *Gad, raiders shall raid him.* Located east of the Jordan (see Josh 13:24–27), the descendants of Gad were vulnerable to raids by the Moabites to the south, as the Mesha (see 2 Kin 3:4) Stele (a Moabite inscription dating from the late ninth century B.C.) illustrates (see chart, p. xix).
49:20 *Asher, his food shall be rich.* Fertile farmlands near the Mediterranean (see Josh 19:24–30) would ensure the prosperity of Asher's descendants.
49:21 *Naphtali is a doe let loose.* Perhaps a reference to an independent spirit fostered in the descendants of Naphtali by their somewhat isolated location in the hill country north of the Sea of Galilee (see Josh 19:32–38).
49:22 *fruitful . . . fruitful.* A pun on the name Ephraim (see note on 41:52), who Jacob predicted would be greater than Joseph's firstborn son Manasseh (48:19–20). *branches run over a wall.* Ephraim's descendants tended to expand their territory (see Josh 17:14–18).
49:24 *his bow remained firm.* The warlike Ephraimites (see Judg 8:1; 12:1) would often prove victorious in battle (see Josh 17:18). *Mighty One of Jacob.* Stresses the activity of God in saving and redeeming His people (see Is 49:26). *Shepherd.* See note on 48:15. *Stone of Israel.* Israel's sure defense (see Deut 32:4,15,18, 30–31)—a figure often used also in Psalms and Isaiah.
49:25 *Almighty.* See note on 17:1. *blessings of heaven . . . of the deep.* The fertility of the soil watered by rains from above and springs and streams from below. *of the breasts and of the womb.* The fertility of man and animals. For the later prosperity of Ephraim's descendants see Hos 12:8.
49:26 *Joseph . . . the one distinguished among his brothers.* See note on v. 8. Ephraim would gain supremacy, especially over the northern tribes (see Josh 16:9; Is 7:1–2; Hos 13:1).
49:27 *Benjamin is a ravenous wolf.* See the exploits of Ehud (Judg

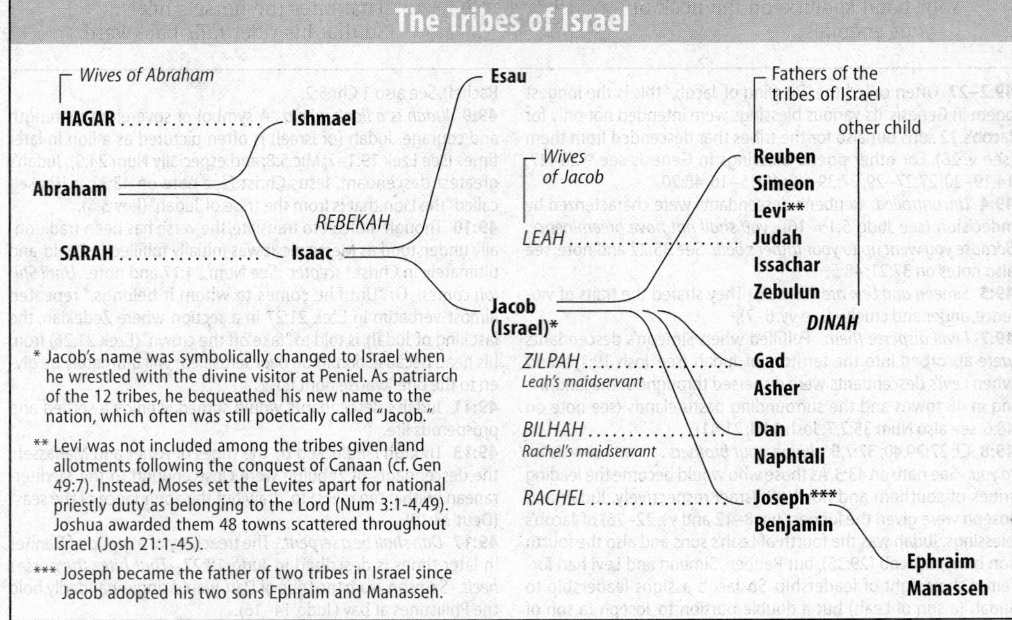
The Tribes of Israel
Wives of Abraham
HAGAR
Ishmael
Abraham
REBEKAH
SARAH
Isaac
Esau
Jacob (Israel)*
Wives of Jacob
LEAH
ZILPAH
Leah's maidservant
BILHAH
Rachel's maidservant
RACHEL
Fathers of the tribes of Israel
other child
Reuben
Simeon
Levi**
Judah
Issachar
Zebulun
DINAH
Gad
Asher
Dan
Naphtali
Joseph***
Benjamin
Ephraim
Manasseh
* Jacob's name was symbolically changed to Israel when he wrestled with the divine visitor at Peniel. As patriarch of the 12 tribes, he bequeathed his new name to the nation, which often was still poetically called "Jacob."
** Levi was not included among the tribes given land allotments following the conquest of Canaan (cf. Gen 49:7). Instead, Moses set the Levites apart for national priestly duty as belonging to the Lord (Num 3:1-4,49). Joshua awarded them 48 towns scattered throughout Israel (Josh 21:1-45).
*** Joseph became the father of two tribes in Israel since Jacob adopted his two sons Ephraim and Manasseh.

May they be on the head of Joseph,
And on the crown of the head of the
one distinguished among his
brothers.

27 "Benjamin is a [1]ravenous wolf;
In the morning he devours the prey,
And in the evening he divides the
spoil."

28 All these are the twelve tribes of Israel, and this is what their father said to them [1]when he blessed them. He blessed them, every one [2]with the blessing appropriate to him.

29 Then he charged them and said to them, "I am about to be [a]gathered to my people; [b]bury me with my fathers in the cave that is in [c]the field of Ephron the Hittite,

30 in the [a]cave that is in the field of Machpelah, which is before Mamre, in the land of Canaan, which Abraham bought along with the field from Ephron the Hittite for a [1]burial site.

31 "There they buried [a]Abraham and his wife [b]Sarah, there they buried [c]Isaac and his wife Rebekah, and there I buried Leah—

32 the field and the cave that is in it, purchased from the sons of Heth."

33 When Jacob finished charging his sons, he drew his feet into the bed and [a]breathed his last, and was [b]gathered to his people.

The Death of Israel

50 Then Joseph fell on his father's face, and wept over him and kissed him.

2 Joseph commanded his servants the physicians to embalm his father. So the physicians [a]embalmed Israel.

3 Now forty days were [1]required for [2]it, for [3]such is the period required for embalming. And the Egyptians [a]wept for him seventy days.

4 When the days of [1]mourning for him were past, Joseph spoke to the household of Pharaoh, saying, "If now I have found favor in your sight, please speak [2]to Pharaoh, saying,

5 '[a]My father made me swear, saying, "Behold, I am about to die; in my grave [b]which I dug for myself in the land of Canaan, there you shall bury me." Now therefore, please let me go up and bury my father; then I will return.' "

6 Pharaoh said, "Go up and bury your father, as he made you swear."

7 So Joseph went up to bury his father, and with him went up all the servants of Pharaoh, the elders of his household and all the elders of the land of Egypt,

8 and all the household of Joseph and his brothers and his father's household; they left only their little ones and their flocks and their herds in the land of Goshen.

9 There also went up with him both chariots and horsemen; and it was a very great company.

10 When they came to the [1]threshing floor of Atad, which is beyond the Jordan, they [a]lamented there with a very great and [2]sorrowful lamentation; and he [3]observed seven days mourning for his father.

11 Now when the inhabitants of the land, the Canaanites, saw the mourning at [1]the threshing floor of Atad, they said, "This is a [2]grievous [3]mourning for the Egyptians." Therefore it was named [4]Abel-mizraim, which is beyond the Jordan.

Burial at Machpelah

12 Thus his sons did for him as he had charged them;

13 for his sons carried him to the land of Canaan and buried him in [a]the cave of the field of Machpelah before Mamre, which Abraham had bought along with the field for a [1]burial site from Ephron the Hittite.

14 After he had buried his father, Joseph returned to Egypt, he and his brothers, and all who had gone up with him to bury his father.

15 When Joseph's brothers saw that their father was dead, they said, "[a]What if Joseph bears a grudge against us and pays us back in full for all the wrong which we did to him!"

16 So they [1]sent *a message* to Joseph, saying, "Your father charged before he died, saying,

17 'Thus you shall say to Joseph, "Please forgive, I beg you, the transgression of your brothers and their sin, for they did you wrong." ' And now, please forgive the trans-

27 [1]Lit *a wolf that tears*
28 [1]Lit *and* [2]Lit *according to his blessing*
29 [a]Gen 25:8 [b]Gen 47:30 [c]Gen 23:16-20; 50:13
30 [1]Lit *possession of a burial place* [a]Gen 23:3-20
31 [a]Gen 25:9 [b]Gen 23:19 [c]Gen 35:29
33 [a]Gen 25:8; Acts 7:15 [b]Gen 49:29
50:2 [a]Gen 50:26; 2 Chr 16:14; Matt 26:12; Mark 16:1; John 19:39, 40
3 [1]Lit *fulfilled* [2]Or *him* [3]Lit *so are fulfilled the days of embalming* [a]Gen 50:10; Num 20:29; Deut 34:8
4 [1]Lit *weeping* [2]Lit *In the ears of*
5 [a]Gen 47:29-31 [b]2 Chr 16:14; Is 22:16; Matt 27:60
10 [1]Heb *Goren ha-Atad* [2]Lit *heavy* [3]Lit *made a mourning for seven days* [a]Acts 8:2
11 [1]Heb *Goren ha-Atad* [2]Lit *heavy* [3]Heb *ebel* [4]I.e. the meadow (or mourning) of Egypt
13 [1]Lit *possession of a burial place* [a]Gen 23:16-20; Acts 7:16
15 [a]Gen 37:28; 42:21, 22
16 [1]Lit *commanded*

3:12–30) and Saul and Jonathan (1 Sam 11–15). See Judg 19–21 for examples of the savagery that characterized one group of Benjamin's descendants.

49:28 *twelve tribes of Israel.* See note on vv. 2–27.

49:29 *bury me with my fathers.* See note on 25:8. Jacob does not forget that the land of his fathers is his God-appointed homeland (see note on 23:19).

49:33 *was gathered to his people.* See note on 25:8.

50:1 *wept.* See note on 43:30.

50:2 *physicians embalmed Israel.* Professional embalmers could have been hired for the purpose, but Joseph perhaps wanted to avoid involvement with the pagan religious ceremonies accompanying their services.

50:3 *forty days . . . seventy days.* The two periods probably overlapped.

50:5 *My father made me swear.* See 47:29–31. *dug.* Or "bought," as the Hebrew for this verb is translated in Hos 3:2 (see also Deut 2:6). *go up.* To Hebron, which has a higher elevation than Goshen.

50:10 *threshing floor.* Grain was threshed on a flat circular area, either of rock or of pounded earth. Threshing floors were located on an elevated open place exposed to the wind, usually at the edge of town or near the main gate (see 1 Kin 22:10). See note on Ruth 1:22.

50:15 *bears a grudge . . . and pays us back.* Similarly, Esau had once planned to kill Jacob as soon as Isaac died (see 27:41).

gression of the servants of the God of your
father." And Joseph wept when they spoke
to him.
18 Then his brothers also came and [a]fell
down before him and said, "Behold, we are
your servants."
19 But Joseph said to them, "Do not be
afraid, for am I in God's place?
20 "As for you, [a]you meant evil against me,
but God meant it for good in order to bring
about [1]this present result, to preserve many
people alive.
21 "So therefore, do not be afraid; [a]I will
provide for you and your little ones." So he
comforted them and spoke [1]kindly to them.

Death of Joseph

22 Now Joseph stayed in Egypt, he and
his father's household, and Joseph lived one
hundred and ten years.
23 Joseph saw the third generation of
Ephraim's sons; also the sons of Machir, the
son of Manasseh, were [a]born on Joseph's
knees.
24 Joseph said to his brothers, "[a]I am
about to die, but God will surely [1]take care of
you and bring you up from this land to the
land which He [2]promised on oath to [b]Abraham, to [c]Isaac and to [d]Jacob."
25 Then Joseph made the sons of Israel
swear, saying, "God will surely [1]take care of
you, and [a]you shall carry my bones up from
here."
26 So Joseph died at the age of one hundred and ten years; and [1]he was [a]embalmed
and placed in a coffin in Egypt.

18 [a]Gen 37:8-10; 41:43 **20** [1]Lit *as it is this day* [a]Gen 37:26, 27; 45:5, 7 **21** [1]Lit *to their heart* [a]Gen 45:11; 47:12

23 [a]Gen 30:3 **24** [1]Or *visit* [2]Lit *swore* [a]Gen 48:21; Ex 3:16, 17; Heb 11:22 [b]Gen 13:15, 17; 15:7, 8, 18 [c]Gen 26:3 [d]Gen 28:13; 35:12 **25** [1]Or *visit* [a]Gen 47:29, 30; Ex 13:19; Josh 24:32; Heb 11:22 **26** [1]Lit *they embalmed him* [a]Gen 50:2

50:17 *Joseph wept.* See note on 43:30. Joseph may have been saddened by the thought that his brothers might be falsely implicating their father in their story. Or he may have regretted his failure to reassure them sooner that he had already forgiven them.
50:18 *fell down before him.* A final fulfillment of Joseph's earlier dreams (see note on 37:7; see also 37:9). *We are your servants.* They had earlier expressed a similar willingness, but under quite different circumstances (see 44:9,33).
50:19 *Am I in God's place?* See note on 30:2.
50:20 *God meant it for good.* Their act, out of personal animosity toward a brother, had been used by God to save life—the life of the Israelites, the Egyptians and all the nations that came to Egypt to buy food in the face of a famine that threatened the known world. At the same time, God showed by these events that his purpose for the nations is life and that this purpose would be effected through the descendants of Abraham.
50:23 *saw the third generation.* Cf. Job's experience (Job 42:16). *Machir.* Manasseh's firstborn son and the ancestor of the powerful Gileadites (Josh 17:1). The name of Machir later became almost interchangeable with that of Manasseh himself (see Judg 5:14). *were born on Joseph's knees.* Joseph probably adopted Machir's children (see note on 30:3).

50:24 *brothers.* Perhaps used here in a broader sense than siblings. *I am about to die.* See note on 48:21. *God will . . . bring you up from this land.* Joseph did not forget God's promises (cf. 15:16; 46:4; 48:21) concerning "the exodus" (Heb 11:22).

50:25 See 47:29–31 for a similar request by Jacob. *carry my bones up from here.* Centuries later Moses did so to fulfill his ancestor's oath (see Ex 13:19). Joseph's bones were eventually "buried . . . at Shechem, in the piece of ground which Jacob had bought from the sons of Hamor" (Josh 24:32; see Gen 33:19).

50:26 *Joseph died at the age of one hundred and ten years.* See v. 22. Ancient Egyptian records indicate that 110 years was considered to be the ideal life span; to the Egyptians this would have signified divine blessing upon Joseph.

Exodus

INTRODUCTION

Title

"Exodus" is a Latin word derived from Greek *Exodos,* the name given to the book by those who translated it into Greek. The word means "exit," "departure" (see Luke 9:31; Heb 11:22). The name was retained by the Latin Vulgate, by the Jewish author Philo (a contemporary of Christ) and by the Syriac version. In Hebrew the book is named after its first two words, *we'elleh shemoth* ("These are the names of"). The same phrase occurs in Gen 46:8, where it likewise introduces a list of the names of those Israelites "who came to Egypt" (1:1). Thus Exodus was not intended to exist separately, but was thought of as a continuation of a narrative that began in Genesis and was completed in Leviticus, Numbers and Deuteronomy. The first five books of the Bible are together known as the Pentateuch (see Introduction to Genesis: Author and Date of Writing).

Author and Date of Writing

Several statements in Exodus indicate that Moses wrote certain sections of the book (see 17:14; 24:4; 34:27). In addition, Josh 8:31 refers to the command of Ex 20:25 as having been "written in the book of the law of Moses." The NT also claims Mosaic authorship for various passages in Exodus (see, e.g., Mark 7:10; 12:26 and NASB marg.; see also Luke 2:22–23). Taken together, these references strongly suggest that Moses was largely responsible for writing the book of Exodus — a traditional view not convincingly challenged by the commonly held notion that the Pentateuch as a whole contains four underlying sources (see Introduction to Genesis: Author and Date of Writing).

Chronology

According to 1 Kin 6:1, the exodus took place 480 years before "the fourth year of Solomon's reign over Israel." Since that year was c. 966 B.C., it has been traditionally held that the exodus occurred c. 1446. The "three hundred years" of Judg 11:26 fits comfortably within this time span (see Introduction to Judges: Background). In addition, although Egyptian chronology relating to the 18th dynasty remains somewhat uncertain, recent research tends to support the traditional view that two of this dynasty's pharaohs, Thutmose III and his son Amunhotep II, were the pharaohs of the oppression and the exodus respectively (see notes on 2:15,23; 3:10).

On the other hand, the appearance of the name Raamses in 1:11 has led many to the conclusion that the 19th-dynasty pharaoh Seti I and his son Rameses II were the pharaohs of the oppression and the exodus respectively. Furthermore, archaeological evidence of the destruction of numerous Canaanite cities in the 13th century B.C. has been interpreted as proof that Joshua's troops invaded the promised land in that century. These and similar lines of argument lead to a date for the exodus of c. 1290 (see Introduction to Joshua: Historical Setting).

The identity of the cities' attackers, however, cannot be positively ascertained. The raids may have been initiated by later Israelite armies, or by Philistines or other outsiders. In addition, the archaeological evidence itself has become increasingly ambiguous, and recent evaluations have tended to redate some of it to the 18th dynasty. Also, the name Raamses in 1:11 could very well be the result of an editorial updating by someone who lived centuries after Moses — a procedure that probably accounts for the appearance of the same word in Gen 47:11 (see note there).

In short, there are no compelling reasons to modify in any substantial way the traditional 1446 B.C. date for the exodus of the Israelites from Egyptian bondage.

The Route of the Exodus

At least three routes of escape from Pithom and Raamses (1:11) have been proposed: (1) a northern route through the land of the Philistines (but see 13:17); (2) a middle route leading eastward across Sinai to Beersheba; and (3) a southern route along the west coast of Sinai to the southeastern extremities of the peninsula. The southern route seems most likely, since several of the sites in Israel's desert itinerary have been tentatively identified along it. See map No. 3 at the end of the study Bible. The exact place where Israel crossed the "Red Sea" is uncertain, however (see notes on 13:18; 14:2).

Themes and Theology

Exodus lays a foundational theology in which God reveals His name, His attributes, His redemption, His law and how He is to be worshiped. It also reports the appointment and work of the first covenant mediator (Moses), describes the beginnings of the priesthood, defines the role of the prophet and relates how the ancient covenant relationship between God and His people came under a new administration (the Sinai covenant).

Profound insights into the nature of God are found in chs. 3; 6; 33—34. The focus of these texts is on the fact and importance of His presence (as signified by His name Yahweh and by His glory). But emphasis is also placed on His attributes of justice, truthfulness, mercy, faithfulness and holiness. Thus to know God's "name" is to know Him and His character (see 3:13–15; 6:3).

God is also the Lord of history, for there is no one like Him: "majestic in holiness, Awesome in praises, working wonders" (15:11). Neither the affliction of Israel nor the plagues in Egypt were outside His control. Pharaoh, the Egyptians and all Israel saw the power of God.

It is reassuring to know that God remembers and is concerned about His people (see 2:24). What He had promised centuries earlier to Abraham, Isaac and Jacob He now begins to bring to fruition as Israel is freed from Egyptian bondage and sets out for the land of promise. The covenant at Sinai is but another step in God's fulfillment of His promise to the patriarchs (3:15–17; 6:2–8; 19:3–8).

The theology of salvation is likewise one of the strong emphases of the book. The verb "redeem" is used, e.g., in 6:6; 15:13. But the heart of redemption theology is best seen in the Passover narrative of ch. 12 and the sealing of the covenant in ch. 24. The apostle Paul viewed the death of the Passover lamb as fulfilled in Christ (1 Cor 5:7). Indeed, John the Baptist called Jesus the "Lamb of God who takes away the sin of the world" (John 1:29).

The foundation of Biblical ethics and morality is laid out first in the gracious character of God as revealed in the exodus itself and then in the Ten Commandments (20:1–17) and the ordinances of the book of the covenant (20:22—23:33), which taught Israel how to apply in a practical way the principles of the commandments.

The book concludes with an elaborate discussion of the theology of worship. Though costly in time, effort and monetary value, the tabernacle, in meaning and function, points to the chief end of man: "to glorify God and to enjoy him forever" (Westminster Shorter Catechism). By means of the tabernacle, the omnipotent, unchanging and transcendent God of the universe came to "dwell" or "tabernacle" with His people, thereby revealing His gracious nearness as well. God is not only mighty in Israel's behalf; He is also present in her midst.

However, these theological elements do not merely sit side by side in the Exodus narrative. They receive their fullest and richest significance from the fact that they are embedded in the account of God's raising up His servant Moses (1) to liberate His people from Egyptian bondage, (2) to inaugurate His earthly kingdom among them by bringing them into a special national covenant with Him, and (3) to erect within Israel God's royal tent. And this account of redemption from bondage leading to consecration in covenant and the pitching of God's royal tent in the earth, all through the ministry of a chosen mediator, discloses God's purpose in history—the purpose He would fulfill through Israel, and ultimately through Jesus Christ the supreme Mediator.

Outline

- I. Divine Redemption (chs. 1—18)
  - A. Fulfilled Multiplication (ch. 1)
    - 1. The promised increase (1:1 – 7)

   2. The first pogrom (1:8 – 14)
   3. The second pogrom (1:15 – 21)
   4. The third pogrom (1:22)
- B. Preparations for Deliverance (2:1—4:26)
   1. Preparing a leader (2:1 – 10)
   2. Extending the time of preparation (2:11 – 22)
   3. Preparing the people (2:23 – 25)
   4. Calling a deliverer (3:1 – 10)
   5. Answering inadequate objections (3:11 — 4:17)
   6. Preparing a leader's family (4:18 – 26)
- C. First Steps in Leadership (4:27—7:5)
   1. Reinforced by brothers (4:27 – 31)
   2. Rebuffed by the enemy (5:1 – 14)
   3. Rebuffed by the enslaved (5:15 – 21)
   4. Revisited by old objections (5:22 – 23)
   5. Reinforced by the name of God (6:1 – 8)
   6. Reminded of one's lowly origins (6:9 — 7:5)
- D. Judgment and Salvation through the Plagues (7:6—11:10)
   1. Presenting the signs of divine authority (7:6 – 13)
   2. First plague: water turned to blood (7:14 – 24)
   3. Second plague: frogs (7:25 — 8:15)
   4. Third plague: gnats (8:16 – 19)
   5. Fourth plague: insects (8:20 – 32)
   6. Fifth plague: against livestock (9:1 – 7)
   7. Sixth plague: boils (9:8 – 12)
   8. Seventh plague: hail (9:13 – 35)
   9. Eighth plague: locusts (10:1 – 20)
   10. Ninth plague: darkness (10:21 – 29)
   11. Tenth plague announced: death of the firstborn (ch. 11)
- E. The Passover (12:1 – 28)
   1. Preparations for the Passover (12:1 – 13)
   2. Preparations for Unleavened Bread (12:14 – 20)
   3. Celebration of the Passover (12:21 – 28)
- F. The Exodus from Egypt (12:29–51)
   1. Death at midnight (12:29 – 32)
   2. Expulsion from Egypt (12:33 – 42)
   3. Regulations for the Passover (12:43 – 51)
- G. The Consecration of the Firstborn (13:1 – 16)
- H. Crossing the "Red Sea" (13:17 — 15:21)
   1. Into the wilderness (13:17 – 22)
   2. At the "Red Sea" (14:1 – 14)
   3. Across the "Red Sea" (14:15 – 31)
   4. Song at the sea (15:1 – 21)
- I. Journey to Sinai (15:22—18:27)
   1. The waters of Marah (15:22 – 27)
   2. The manna and the quails (ch. 16)
   3. The waters of Meribah (17:1 – 7)
   4. The war with Amalek (17:8 – 16)
   5. The wisdom of Jethro (ch. 18)

II. Covenant at Sinai (chs. 19—24)
- A. The Covenant Proposed (ch. 19)

- B. The Decalogue (20:1 – 17)
- C. The Reaction of the People to God's Fiery Presence (20:18 – 21)
- D. The Book of the Covenant (20:22 — 23:33)
  1. Prologue (20:22 – 26)
  2. Laws on slaves (21:1 – 11)
  3. Laws on homicide (21:12 – 17)
  4. Laws on bodily injuries (21:18 – 32)
  5. Laws on property damage (21:33 — 22:15)
  6. Laws on society (22:16 – 31)
  7. Laws on justice and neighborliness (23:1 – 9)
  8. Laws on sacred seasons (23:10 – 19)
  9. Epilogue (23:20 – 33)
- E. Ratification of the Covenant (ch. 24)

III. Divine Worship (chs. 25 — 40)

- A. Instructions concerning the Tabernacle (chs. 25 — 31)
  1. Collection of the materials (25:1 – 9)
  2. Ark and mercy seat (25:10 – 22)
  3. Table of the bread of the Presence (25:23 – 30)
  4. Golden lampstand (25:31 – 40)
  5. Curtains and boards (ch. 26)
  6. Bronze altar (27:1 – 8)
  7. Court of the Tabernacle (27:9 – 19)
  8. Priesthood (27:20 — 28:5)
  9. Garments of the priests (28:6 – 43)
  10. Ordination of the priests (ch. 29)
  11. Altar of incense (30:1 – 10)
  12. Census tax (30:11 – 16)
  13. Laver of bronze (30:17 – 21)
  14. Anointing oil and incense (30:22 – 38)
  15. Appointment of craftsmen (31:1 – 11)
  16. Sabbath rest (31:12 – 18)
- B. False Worship (chs. 32 — 34)
  1. The golden calf (32:1 – 29)
  2. Moses' mediation (32:30 – 35)
  3. Threatened separation and Moses' prayer (ch. 33)
  4. Renewal of the covenant (ch. 34)
- C. The Building of the Tabernacle (chs. 35 — 40)
  1. Summons to build (35:1 – 19)
  2. Voluntary gifts (35:20 – 29)
  3. Bezalel and his craftsmen (35:30 — 36:7)
  4. Progress of the work (36:8 — 39:31)
  5. Moses' blessing (39:32 – 43)
  6. Erection of the tabernacle (40:1 – 33)
  7. Dedication of the tabernacle (40:34 – 38)

Israel Multiplies in Egypt

1 Now these are the [a]names of the sons of
Israel who came to Egypt with Jacob;
they came each one [1]with his household:
2 Reuben, Simeon, Levi and Judah;
3 Issachar, Zebulun and Benjamin;
4 Dan and Naphtali, Gad and Asher.
5 All the [1]persons who came from the
loins of Jacob were [a]seventy [2]in number, but
Joseph was *already* in Egypt.
6 [a]Joseph died, and all his brothers and
all that generation.
7 But the sons of Israel [a]were fruitful and
[1]increased greatly, and multiplied, and
became exceedingly [2]mighty, so that the land
was filled with them.
8 Now a new [a]king arose over Egypt,
who did not know Joseph.
9 [a]He said to his people, "Behold, the
people of the sons of Israel are [1]more and
mightier than we.
10 "Come, let us [a]deal wisely with them, or
else they will multiply and [1]in the event of
war, they will also join themselves to those
who hate us, and fight against us and
[2]depart from the land."
11 So they appointed [a]taskmasters over
them to afflict them with [1b]hard labor. And
they built for Pharaoh [c]storage cities, Pithom
and [d]Raamses.
12 But the more they afflicted them, [a]the
more they multiplied and the more they
[1]spread out, so that they were in dread of the
sons of Israel.
13 The Egyptians compelled the sons of
Israel [a]to labor rigorously;
14 and they made [a]their lives bitter with
hard labor in mortar and bricks and at all
kinds of labor in the field, all their labors
which they rigorously [1]imposed on them.
15 Then the king of Egypt spoke to the
Hebrew midwives, one of whom [1]was named
Shiphrah and the other [1]was named Puah;
16 and he said, "When you are helping
the Hebrew women to give birth and see
them upon the birthstool, [a]if it is a son, then
you shall put him to death; but if it is a
daughter, then she shall live."
17 But the midwives [1a]feared God, and
[b]did not do as the king of Egypt had [2]com-
manded them, but let the boys live.
18 So the king of Egypt called for the midwives and said to them, "Why have you
done this thing, and let the boys live?"
19 The midwives said to Pharaoh, "Because the Hebrew women are not as the
Egyptian women; for they are vigorous and
give birth before the midwife [1]can get to
them."
20 So [a]God was good to the midwives,
and [b]the people multiplied, and became very
[1]mighty.
21 Because the midwives [1a]feared God,
He [2b]established [3]households for them.
22 Then Pharaoh commanded all his people, saying, "[a]Every son who is born [1]you
are to cast into [b]the Nile, and every daughter
you are to keep alive."

The Birth of Moses

2 Now a man from [a]the house of Levi went
and [1]married a daughter of Levi.
2 The woman conceived and bore a son;

1:1 [1]Lit *and* [a]Gen 46:8-27 **5** [1]Lit *souls* [2]Lit *as to souls* [a]Gen 46:26, 27; Deut 10:22 **6** [a]Gen 50:26 **7** [1]Lit *swarmed* [2]Or *numerous* [a]Gen 12:2; 28:3; 35:11; 46:3; 47:27; 48:4; Deut 26:5; Ps 105:24; Acts 7:17 **8** [a]Acts 7:18, 19 **9** [1]Or *too many and too mighty for us* [a]Ps 105:24, 25 **10** [1]Lit *it came about when war befalls that* [2]Lit *go up from* [a]Acts 7:19 **11** [1]Lit *their burdens* [a]Gen 15:13; Ex 3:7; 5:6 [b]Ex 1:14; 2:11; 5:4-9; 6:6f [c]1 Kin 9:19; 2 Chr 8:4 [d]Gen 47:11 **12** [1]Lit *broke forth* [a]Ex 1:7 **13** [a]Gen 15:13; Deut 4:20 **14** [a]Ex 2:23; 6:9; Num 20:15; Acts 7:19

14 [1]Lit *worked through them* **15** [1]Lit *the name was* **16** [a]Acts 7:19 **17** [1]Or *revered* [2]Lit *spoken to* [a]Ex 1:21; Prov 16:6 [b]Acts 4:18-20; 5:29 **19** [1]Lit *comes to* **20** [1]Or *numerous* [a]Prov 11:18; Eccl 8:12; Heb 6:10 [b]Ex 1:12; Is 3:10

21 [1]Or *revered* [2]Lit *made* [3]Or *families* [a]Ex 1:17 [b]1 Sam 2:35; 2 Sam 7:11, 27; 1 Kin 2:24; 11:38 **22** [1]Some versions insert *to the Hebrews* [a]Acts 7:19 [b]Gen 41:1 **2:1** [1]Lit *took* [a]Ex 6:16, 18, 20

1:1–5 These verses clearly indicate that Exodus was written as a continuation of Genesis. The Israelites lived in Egypt 430 years (see 12:40).

1:1 *these are the names of.* The same expression appears in Gen 46:8 at the head of a list of Jacob's descendants. *Israel . . . Jacob.* Jacob had earlier been given the additional name Israel (see Gen 32:28; 35:10 and notes).

1:2–4 The sons of Leah (Reuben through Zebulun) and Rachel (Benjamin; Joseph is not mentioned because the list includes only those "who came to Egypt with Jacob," v. 1) are listed in the order of their seniority and before the sons of Rachel's and Leah's maidservants: Bilhah had Dan and Naphtali, Zilpah had Gad and Asher (see Gen 35:23–26).

1:5 *seventy.* See note on Gen 46:27.

1:6–7 From the death of Joseph to the rise of a new king (v. 8) was more than 200 years.

1:7 See Acts 7:17. God's promised blessing of fruitfulness and increase had been given to Adam (Gen 1:28), Noah (Gen 8:17; 9:1,7), Abraham (Gen 17:2,6; 22:17), Isaac (Gen 26:4) and Jacob (Gen 28:14; 35:11; 48:4). God continued to fulfill His promise during the 430-year sojourn in Egypt. *the land was filled with them.* The Hebrew used here echoes the blessing of Adam (Gen 1:28)—God's initial blessing of mankind was being fulfilled in Israel. The Israelites who left Egypt are said to number about 600,000 men, "aside from children" (12:37). *land.* Goshen (see note on Gen 45:10).

1:8 See Acts 7:18. *new king.* Probably Ahmose, the founder of the 18th dynasty, who expelled the Hyksos (foreign—predominantly Semitic—rulers of Egypt).

1:11 *taskmasters.* The same official Egyptian designation appears on a wall painting in the Theban tomb of Rekhmire during the reign of the 18th-dynasty pharaoh Thutmose III (see Introduction: Chronology). *Raamses.* See note on Gen 47:11. *Pharaoh.* The word, which is Egyptian in origin and means "great house," is a royal title rather than a personal name.

1:14 *made their lives bitter.* A fact commemorated in the Passover meal, which was eaten with "bitter herbs" (12:8). *all kinds of labor in the field.* Including pumping the waters of the Nile into the fields to irrigate them (see Deut 11:10).

1:15 *Hebrew.* See note on Gen 14:13. *Shiphrah and . . . Puah.* Semitic, not Egyptian, names. Since the Israelites were so numerous, there were probably other midwives under Shiphrah and Puah.

1:16 *birthstool.* The Hebrew term means lit. "two stones"; a woman sat on them while giving birth.

1:17 See Acts 5:29 for a parallel in the early church. *feared God.* See note on Gen 20:11.

2:1 *a man . . . a daughter of Levi.* Perhaps Amram and Jochebed (but see note on 6:20).

and when she saw [1]that he was [2][a]beautiful,
she hid him for three months.
3 But when she could hide him no
longer, she got him a [1][a]wicker [2]basket and
covered it over with tar and pitch. Then she
put the child into it and set *it* among the
[b]reeds by the bank of the Nile.
4 [a]His sister stood at a distance to [1]find
out what would [2]happen to him.
5 The daughter of Pharaoh came down
[a]to bathe at the Nile, with her maidens walking alongside the Nile; and she saw the [1]bas-
ket among the reeds and sent her maid, and
she brought it *to her.*
6 When she opened *it,* she [1]saw the
child, and behold, *the* [2]boy was crying. And
she had pity on him and said, "This is one of
the Hebrews' children."
7 Then his sister said to Pharaoh's
daughter, "Shall I go and call [1]a nurse for
you from the Hebrew women that she may
nurse the child for you?"
8 Pharaoh's daughter said to her, "Go
ahead." So the girl went and called the
child's mother.
9 Then Pharaoh's daughter said to her,
"Take this child away and nurse him for me
and I will give *you* your wages." So the
woman took the child and nursed him.
10 The child grew, and she brought him to
Pharaoh's daughter and [a]he became her son.
And she named him [1]Moses, and said,
"Because I [2]drew him out of the water."
11 Now it came about in those days,
[a]when Moses had grown up, that he went
out to his brethren and looked on their
[1][b]hard labors; and [c]he saw an Egyptian beating a Hebrew, one of his brethren.
12 So he [1]looked this way and that, and
when he saw there was no one *around,* he
[a]struck down the Egyptian and hid him in
the sand.
13 He went out [a]the next day, and behold,
two Hebrews were [1]fighting with each other;
and he said to the [2]offender, "Why are you
striking your companion?"
14 But he said, "[a]Who made you a [1]prince
or a judge over us? Are you [2]intending to kill
me as you killed the Egyptian?" Then Moses
was afraid and said, "Surely the matter has
become known."

Moses Escapes to Midian

15 When Pharaoh heard of this matter, he
tried to kill Moses. But [a]Moses fled from the
presence of Pharaoh and [1]settled in the land
of Midian, and he sat down [b]by a well.
16 Now [a]the priest of Midian had seven
daughters; and [b]they came to draw water and
filled the troughs to water their father's flock.
17 Then the shepherds came and drove
them away, but [a]Moses stood up and helped
them and watered their flock.
18 When they came to [a]Reuel their father,
he said, "Why have you come *back* so soon
today?"
19 So they said, "An Egyptian delivered us
from the hand of the shepherds, and what is
more, he even drew the water for us and
watered the flock."
20 He said to his daughters, "Where is he
then? Why is it that you have left the man
behind? Invite him [1]to have something to
eat."
21 [a]Moses was willing to dwell with the
man, and he gave his daughter [b]Zipporah to
Moses.
22 Then she gave birth to [a]a son, and he
named him [1]Gershom, for he said, "I have
been [b]a [2]sojourner in a foreign land."

2 [1]Lit *him that* [2]Lit *good* [a]Acts 7:20; Heb 11:23
3 [1]I.e. papyrus reeds [2]Or *chest* [a]Is 18:2 [b]Is 19:6
4 [1]Lit *know* [2]Lit *be done* [a]Ex 15:20; Num 26:59
5 [1]Or *chest* [a]Ex 7:15; 8:20
6 [1]Heb *saw it, the child* [2]Or *lad*
7 [1]Lit *a woman giving suck*
10 [1]Heb *Mosheh,* from *mashah* [2]Heb *mashah* [a]Acts 7:21
11 [1]Lit *burdens* [a]Acts 7:23; Heb 11:24-26 [b]Ex 1:11; 5:4, 5; 6:6, 7 [c]Acts 7:24
12 [1]Lit *turned* [a]Acts 7:24, 25
13 [1]Or *quarreling* [2]Or *the guilty one* [a]Acts 7:26-28
14 [1]Lit *man, a prince* [2]Lit *saying in your heart* [a]Gen 19:9; Acts 7:27, 28
15 [1]Lit *dwelt* [a]Acts 7:29; Heb 11:27 [b]Gen 24:11; 29:2
16 [a]Ex 3:1; 18:12 [b]Gen 24:11, 13, 19; 29:9, 10; 1 Sam 9:11
17 [a]Gen 29:3, 10
18 [a]Ex 3:1; Num 10:29
20 [1]Lit *that he may eat bread*
21 [a]Acts 7:29 [b]Ex 4:25; 18:2
22 [1]Cf Heb *ger sham, a stranger there* [2]Heb *ger* [a]Ex 4:20; 18:3, 4 [b]Gen 23:4; Lev 25:23; Acts 7:29; Heb 11:13, 14

2:2 *he was beautiful.* Moses was "lovely in the sight of God" (Acts 7:20; cf. Heb 11:23). The account of Moses' remarkable deliverance in infancy foreshadows the deliverance from Egypt that God would later effect through him.

2:3 *wicker basket.* Each of the two Hebrew words lying behind this phrase is of Egyptian origin. The word for "basket" is used only here and of Noah's ark (see note on Gen 6:14). Moses' basket was a miniature version of the large, seaworthy "papyrus vessels" mentioned in Is 18:2. *reeds.* A word of Egyptian derivation, reflected in the proper name "Red Sea" (Hebrew *Yam Suph,* "Sea of Reeds").

2:4 *His sister.* Miriam (see 15:20).

2:5 *the daughter of Pharaoh.* Perhaps the famous 18th-dynasty princess who later became Queen Hatshepsut. *maidens.* They stayed on the river bank to bathe the princess.

2:10 See Acts 7:21–22. *he became her son.* Throughout this early part of Exodus, all the pharaoh's efforts to suppress Israel were thwarted by women: the midwives (1:17), the Israelite mothers (1:19), Moses' mother and sister (vv. 3–4,7–9), the pharaoh's daughter (here). The pharaoh's impotence to destroy the people of God is thus ironically exposed. *Moses.* The name, of Egyptian origin, means "is born" and forms the second element in such pharaonic names as Ahmose (see note on 1:8), Thutmose and Raamses (see note on 1:11). *drew him out.* A Hebrew wordplay on the name Moses (which sounds like the Hebrew for "draw out"), emphasizing his providential rescue from the Nile. Thus Moses' name may also have served as a reminder of the great act of deliverance God worked through him at the "Red Sea" (see 13:17–14:31).

2:11–15 See Acts 7:23–29; Heb 11:24–27.

2:11 *Moses had grown up.* He was now 40 years old (see Acts 7:23).

2:14 *Who made you a prince or a judge . . . ?* Unwittingly, the speaker made a prediction that would be fulfilled 40 years later (see Acts 7:27,30,35). The Hebrew word for "judge" could also refer to a deliverer, as in the book of Judges (see Acts 7:35); it was often a synonym for "ruler" in the OT (see Gen 18:25 and note) as well as in ancient Canaanite usage. *Moses was afraid.* See note on Heb 11:27.

2:15 *Pharaoh.* Probably Thutmose III (see Introduction: Chronology). *Midian.* Named after one of Abraham's younger sons (see Gen 25:2; see also note on Gen 37:25). Midian was located in southeastern Sinai and west central Arabia, flanking the eastern arm of the Red Sea (Gulf of Aqaba) on both sides. Dry and desolate, it formed a stark contrast to Moses' former home in the royal court. He lived in Midian 40 years (see Acts 7:29–30).

2:16 *priest of Midian.* Reuel (see v. 18), which means "friend of God." His other name, Jethro (see 3:1), may be a title meaning "his excellency."

23 Now it came about in *the course of* those many days that the king of Egypt died. And the sons of Israel [a]sighed because of the bondage, and they cried out; and [b]their cry for help because of *their* bondage rose up to God.

24 So [a]God heard their groaning; and God remembered [b]His covenant with Abraham, Isaac, and Jacob.

25 [a]God saw the sons of Israel, and God [1]took notice *of them.*

The Burning Bush

3 Now Moses was pasturing the flock of [a]Jethro his father-in-law, the priest of Midian; and he led the flock to the [1]west side of the wilderness and came to [b]Horeb, the [c]mountain of God.

2 [a]The angel of the LORD appeared to him in a blazing fire from the midst of [1]a [b]bush; and he looked, and behold, the bush was burning with fire, yet the bush was not consumed.

3 So Moses said, "[1][a]I must turn aside now and see this [2]marvelous sight, why the bush is not burned up."

4 When the LORD saw that he turned aside to look, [a]God called to him from the midst of the bush and said, "Moses, Moses!" And he said, "Here I am."

5 Then He said, "Do not come near here; [a]remove your sandals from your feet, for the place on which you are standing is holy ground."

6 He said also, "[a]I am the God of your father, the God of Abraham, the God of Isaac, and the God of Jacob." [b]Then Moses hid his face, for he was [c]afraid to look at God.

7 The LORD said, "I have surely [a]seen the affliction of My people who are in Egypt, and have given heed to their cry because of their taskmasters, for I am aware of their sufferings.

8 "So I have come down [a]to deliver them from the [1]power of the Egyptians, and to bring them up from that land to a [b]good and spacious land, to a land flowing with milk and honey, to the place of [c]the Canaanite and the Hittite and the Amorite and the Perizzite and the Hivite and the Jebusite.

9 "Now, behold, [a]the cry of the sons of Israel has come to Me; furthermore, I have seen the oppression with which the Egyptians are oppressing them.

The Mission of Moses

10 "Therefore, come now, and I will send you to Pharaoh, [a]so that you may bring My people, the sons of Israel, out of Egypt."

11 But Moses said to God, "[a]Who am I, that I should go to Pharaoh, and that I should bring the sons of Israel out of Egypt?"

12 And He said, "Certainly [a]I will be with you, and this shall be the sign to you that it is I who have sent you: [b]when you have brought the people out of Egypt, [c]you shall [1]worship God at this mountain."

13 Then Moses said to God, "Behold, I am going to the sons of Israel, and I will say to them, 'The God of your fathers has sent me to you.' Now they may say to me, 'What is His name?' What shall I say to them?"

14 God said to Moses, "[1][a]I AM WHO [1]I AM"; and He said, "Thus you shall say to the sons of Israel, '[1]I AM has sent me to you.'"

23 [a]Ex 6:5, 9 [b]Ex 3:7, 9; Deut 26:7; James 5:4 **24** [a]Ex 6:5; Acts 7:34 [b]Gen 15:13f; 22:16-18; 26:2-5; 28:13-15; Ps 105:8, 42 **25** [1]Lit *knew them* [a]Ex 3:7; 4:31; Acts 7:34 **3:1** [1]Or *rear part* [a]Ex 2:18; 4:18; 18:12; Num 10:29 [b]Ex 3:12; 17:6; 33:6; 1 Kin 19:8 [c]Ex 4:27; 18:5; 24:13 **2** [1]Lit *the* [a]Gen 16:7-11; 21:17; 22:11, 15; Ex 3:4-11, 16; Judg 13:13-21; Acts 7:30 [b]Deut 33:16; Mark 12:26; Luke 20:37; Acts 7:30 **3** [1]Lit *Let me turn* [2]Lit *great* [a]Acts 7:31 **4** [a]Ex 4:5 **5** [a]Josh 5:15; Acts 7:33 **6** [a]Gen 28:13; Ex 3:16; 4:5; Matt 22:32; Mark 12:26; Luke 20:37 [b]Acts 7:32 [c]Judg 13:22; Rev 1:17 **7** [a]Ex 2:25; Neh 9:9; Ps 106:44; Is 63:9; Acts 7:34 **8** [1]Lit *hand* [a]Gen 15:13-16; 46:4; 50:24, 25; Ex 6:6-8; 12:51 [b]Ex 3:17; 13:5; Num 13:27; Deut 1:25; 8:7-9; Jer 11:5; Ezek 20:6 [c]Gen 15:19-21; Josh 24:11 **9** [a]Ex 2:23 **10** [a]Gen 15:13, 14; Ex 12:40, 41; Mic 6:4; Acts 7:6, 7

11 [a]Ex 4:10; 6:12; 1 Sam 18:18 **12** [1]Or *serve* [a]Gen 31:3; Ex 4:12, 15; 33:14-16; Deut 31:23; Josh 1:5; Is 43:2 [b]Ex 19:1 [c]Ex 19:2, 3; Acts 7:7 **14** [1]Related to the name of God, *YHWH*, rendered *LORD*, which is derived from the verb *HAYAH, to be* [a]Ex 6:3; John 8:24, 28, 58; Heb 13:8; Rev 1:8; 4:8

2:23 *in the course of those many days.* Thutmose III (see note on v. 15) enjoyed a long reign.
2:24 *covenant with Abraham.* See Gen 15:17–18; 17:7 and notes. *Isaac.* See Gen 17:19; 26:24. *Jacob.* See Gen 35:11–12.
3:1 Like David (2 Sam 7:8), Moses was called from tending the flock to be the shepherd of God's people. *Jethro.* See note on 2:16. *Horeb.* Means "desert," "desolation"; either (1) an alternate name for Mount Sinai or (2) another high mountain in the same vicinity in the southeast region of the Sinai peninsula. Tradition identifies Mount Horeb with Ras es-Safsaf ("willow peak"), 6,500 feet high, and Mount Sinai with Jebel Musa ("mountain of Moses"), 7,400 feet high, but both identifications are uncertain.
3:2 *angel of the LORD.* Used interchangeably with "the LORD" and "God" in v. 4 (see note on Gen 16:7). *appeared to him in a blazing fire.* God's revelation of Himself and His will was often accompanied by fire (see 13:21; 19:18; 1 Kin 18:24,38).
3:4 Every true prophet was called by God (see, e.g., 1 Sam 3:4; Is 6:8; Jer 1:4–5; Ezek 2:1–8; Hos 1:2; Amos 7:15; Jon 1:1–2; see also note on 7:1–2). *Moses, Moses! . . . Here I am.* See notes on Gen 22:1,11.
3:5 *remove your sandals.* A practice still followed by Muslims before entering a mosque. *holy.* The ground was not holy by nature but was made so by the divine presence (see, e.g., Gen 2:3). Holiness involves being consecrated to the Lord's service and thus being separated from the commonplace.
3:6 See 2:24 and note. *afraid to look at God.* See notes on Gen 16:13; 32:30. Later, as the Lord's servant, Moses would meet with God on Mount Sinai (19:3) and even ask to see God's glory (33:18).
3:8 *I have come down to deliver.* God may also come down to judge (see Gen 11:5–9; 18:21). *land flowing with milk and honey.* The traditional and proverbial description of the hill country of Canaan—in its original pastoral state (see note on Is 7:15). *Canaanite . . . Jebusite.* See notes on Gen 10:6,15–16; 13:7. The list of the Canaanite nations ranges from two names (see Gen 13:7) to five (see Num 13:29) to six (as here; see also Judg 3:5) to ten (see Gen 15:19–21) to twelve (see Gen 10:15–18). The classic description includes seven names (see, e.g., Deut 7:1), seven being the number of completeness (see note on Gen 4:17–18).
3:10 *Pharaoh.* Probably Amunhotep II (see Introduction: Chronology).
3:11 Moses' first expression of reluctance (see v. 13; 4:1,10,13).
3:12 *I will be with you.* See note on Gen 26:3. The Hebrew word translated "I will be" is the same as the one translated "I AM" in v. 14. *sign.* A visible proof or guarantee that what God had promised He would surely fulfill (see notes on 4:8; Gen 15:8).
3:13 Moses' second expression of reluctance. *What is His name?* God had not yet identified Himself to Moses by name (see v. 6; cf. Gen 17:1).
3:14 *I AM WHO I AM.* The name by which God wished to be

15 God, furthermore, said to Moses, "Thus you shall say to the sons of Israel, '[a]The LORD, the God of your fathers, the God of Abraham, the God of Isaac, and the God of Jacob, has sent me to you.' This is My name forever, and this is My [b]memorial-name [1]to all generations.

16 "Go and [a]gather the elders of Israel together and say to them, '[b]The LORD, the God of your fathers, the God of Abraham, Isaac and Jacob, has appeared to me, saying, "[1][c]I am indeed concerned about you and what has been done to you in Egypt.

17 "So [a]I said, I will bring you up out of the affliction of Egypt to the land of [b]the Canaanite and the Hittite and the Amorite and the Perizzite and the Hivite and the Jebusite, to a land [c]flowing with milk and honey." '

18 "[a]They will [1]pay heed to what you say; and [b]you with the elders of Israel will come to the king of Egypt and you will say to him, 'The LORD, the God of the Hebrews, has met with us. So now, please, let us go a [c]three days' journey into the wilderness, that we may sacrifice to the LORD our God.'

19 "But I know that the king of Egypt [a]will not permit you to go, [b]except [1]under compulsion.

20 "So I will stretch out [a]My hand and strike Egypt with all My [b]miracles which I shall do in the midst of it; and [c]after that he will let you go.

21 "I will grant this people [a]favor in the sight of the Egyptians; and it shall be that when you go, you will not go empty-handed.

22 "But every woman [a]shall ask of her neighbor and the woman who lives in her house, articles of silver and articles of gold, and clothing; and you will put them on your sons and daughters. Thus you will [b]plunder the Egyptians."

15 [1]Lit *to generation of generation* [a]Ex 3:6, 13 [b]Ps 30:4; 97:12; 102:12; 135:13; Hos 12:5
16 [1]Lit *Visiting I have visited* [a]Ex 4:29 [b]Gen 28:13; 48:15; Ex 3:2, 6; 4:5 [c]Ex 4:31; Ps 33:18f
17 [a]Gen 15:13-21; 46:4; 50:24, 25 [b]Josh 24:11 [c]Ex 3:8
18 [1]Lit *hear your voice* [a]Ex 4:31 [b]Ex 5:1 [c]Ex 5:3; 8:27
19 [1]Lit *by a strong hand* [a]Ex 5:2 [b]Ex 6:1
20 [a]Ex 6:1; 7:4, 5; 9:15; 13:3, 9, 14 [b]Ex 7:3; 15:11; Deut 6:22; Neh 9:10; Ps 105:27; 135:9; Jer 32:20; Acts 7:36 [c]Ex 11:1; 12:31-33
21 [a]Ex 11:3; 12:36; 1 Kin 8:50; Ps 105:37f; 106:46; Prov 16:7
22 [a]Gen 15:14; Ex 11:2; 12:35 [b]Ezek 39:10
4:1 [1]Lit *to my voice* [a]Ex 3:18; 6:30 [b]Ex 3:15, 16
2 [a]Ex 4:17, 20
3 [a]Ex 7:10-12
4 [1]Lit *palm*
5 [a]Ex 4:31; 19:9 [b]Gen 28:13; 48:15; Ex 3:6, 15
6 [a]Num 12:10; 2 Kin 5:27
7 [a]Num 12:13-15; Deut 32:39; 2 Kin 5:14; Matt 8:3; Luke 17:12-14
8 [1]Lit *listen to* [2]Lit *voice*
9 [a]Ex 7:19, 20
10 [1]Lit *a man of words* [2]Lit *yesterday* [3]Lit *heavy* [a]Ex 3:11; 4:1; 6:12; Jer 1:6

Moses Given Powers

4 Then Moses said, "What if they will not believe me or [a]listen [1]to what I say? For they may say, '[b]The LORD has not appeared to you.' "

2 The LORD said to him, "What is that in your hand?" And he said, "[a]A staff."

3 Then He said, "Throw it on the ground." So he threw it on the ground, and [a]it became a serpent; and Moses fled from it.

4 But the LORD said to Moses, "Stretch out your hand and grasp *it* by its tail"—so he stretched out his hand and caught it, and it became a staff in his [1]hand—

5 "that [a]they may believe that [b]the LORD, the God of their fathers, the God of Abraham, the God of Isaac, and the God of Jacob, has appeared to you."

6 The LORD furthermore said to him, "Now put your hand into your bosom." So he put his hand into his bosom, and when he took it out, behold, his hand was [a]leprous like snow.

7 Then He said, "Put your hand into your bosom again." So he put his hand into his bosom again, and when he took it out of his bosom, behold, [a]it was restored like *the rest of* his flesh.

8 "If they will not believe you or [1]heed the [2]witness of the first sign, they may believe the [2]witness of the last sign.

9 "But if they will not believe even these two signs or heed what you say, then you shall take some water from the Nile and pour it on the dry ground; and the water which you take from the Nile [a]will become blood on the dry ground."

10 Then Moses said to the LORD, "Please, Lord, [a]I have never been [1]eloquent, neither [2]recently nor in time past, nor since You have spoken to Your servant; for I am [3]slow of speech and [3]slow of tongue."

---

known and worshiped in Israel—the name that expressed His character as the dependable and faithful God who desires the full trust of His people (see v. 12, where "I will be" is completed by "with you"; see also 34:5–7). *I AM.* Jesus applied the phrase to Himself; in so doing He claimed to be God and risked being stoned for blasphemy (see John 8:58–59).

3:15 *The LORD.* The Hebrew for this name is *Yahweh* (often incorrectly spelled "Jehovah"; see note on Deut 28:58). It means "He is" or "He will be" and is the third-person form of the verb translated "I will be" in v. 12 and "I AM" in v. 14. When God speaks of Himself He says, "I AM," and when we speak of Him we say, "He is."

3:16 *elders.* The Hebrew for this word means lit. "bearded ones," perhaps reflecting the age, wisdom, experience and influence necessary for a man expected to function as an elder. As heads of local families and tribes, "elders" had a recognized position also among the Babylonians, Hittites, Egyptians (see Gen 50:7), Moabites and Midianites (see Num 22:7). Their duties included judicial arbitration and sentencing (see Deut 22:13–19) as well as military leadership (see Josh 8:10) and counsel (see 1 Sam 4:3).

3:18 *Hebrews.* See note on Gen 14:13. *three days' journey.* Probably a conventional expression for a short trip rather than a journey of exactly three days. *wilderness.* God had met with Moses there (see vv. 1–2) and would meet with him there again (see v. 12).

3:20 *miracles.* A prediction of the plagues that God would send against Egypt (see 7:14–12:30).

3:21–22 See 11:2–3; 12:35–36.

3:21 *when you go, you will not go empty-handed.* God had promised Abraham that after Israel had served for 400 years they would "come out with many possessions" (Gen 15:14; see Ps 105:37). Israel herself was to live by the same principle of providing gifts to a released slave (see Deut 15:12–15).

4:1 Moses' third expression of reluctance (in spite of God's assurance in 3:18).

4:2 *staff.* Probably a shepherd's crook.

4:3 *serpent.* See 7:9–10 and note. Throughout much of Egypt's history the pharaoh wore a cobra made of metal on the front of his headdress as a symbol of his sovereignty.

4:8 *sign.* A supernatural event or phenomenon designed to demonstrate authority, provide assurance (see Josh 2:12–13), bear testimony (see Is 19:19–20), give warning (see Num 17:10) or encourage faith. See note on 3:12.

4:10 Moses' fourth expression of reluctance. *I am slow of*

11 The LORD said to him, "Who has made man's mouth? Or [a]who makes *him* mute or deaf, or seeing or blind? Is it not I, the LORD?

12 "Now then go, and [a]I, even I, will be with your mouth, and [b]teach you what you are to say."

13 But he said, "Please, Lord, now [1]send *the message* by whomever You will."

Aaron to Be Moses' Mouthpiece

14 Then the anger of the LORD burned against Moses, and He said, "Is there not your brother Aaron the Levite? I know that [1]he speaks fluently. And moreover, behold, [a]he is coming out to meet you; when he sees you, he will be glad in his heart.

15 "You are to speak to him and [a]put the words in his mouth; and I, even I, will be with your mouth and his mouth, and I will teach you what you are to do.

16 "Moreover, [a]he shall speak for you to the people; and he will be as a mouth for you and you will be as God to him.

17 "You shall take in your hand [a]this staff, [b]with which you shall perform the signs."

18 Then Moses departed and returned to [1]Jethro [a]his father-in-law and said to him, "Please, let me go, that I may return to my brethren who are in Egypt, and see if they are still alive." And Jethro said to Moses, "Go in peace."

19 Now the LORD said to Moses in Midian, "Go [1]back to Egypt, for [a]all the men who were seeking your life are dead."

20 So Moses took his wife and his [a]sons and mounted them on a donkey, and returned to the land of Egypt. Moses also took the [b]staff of God in his hand.

21 The LORD said to Moses, "When you go [1]back to Egypt see that you perform before Pharaoh all [a]the wonders which I have put in your [2]power; but [b]I will harden his heart so that he will not let the people go.

22 "Then you shall say to Pharaoh, 'Thus says the LORD, "[a]Israel is My son, My firstborn.

23 "So I said to you, '[a]Let My son go that he may serve Me'; but you have refused to let him go. Behold, [b]I will kill your son, your firstborn." ' "

24 Now it came about at the lodging place on the way that the LORD met him and [a]sought to put him to death.

25 Then Zipporah took [a]a flint and cut off her son's foreskin and [1]threw it at Moses' feet, and she said, "You are indeed a bridegroom of blood to me."

26 So He let him alone. At that time she said, "*You are* a bridegroom of blood"—[1]because of the circumcision.

27 [a]Now the LORD said to Aaron, "Go to meet Moses in the wilderness." So he went and met him at the [b]mountain of God and kissed him.

28 [a]Moses told Aaron all the words of the LORD with which He had sent him, and [b]all the signs that He had commanded him *to do.*

29 Then Moses and Aaron went and [a]assembled all the elders of the sons of Israel;

30 and [a]Aaron spoke all the words which the LORD had spoken to Moses. He then performed the [b]signs in the sight of the people.

31 So [a]the people believed; and when they heard that the LORD [1][b]was concerned about the sons of Israel and that He had seen their affliction, then [c]they bowed low and worshiped.

11 [a]Ps 94:9; 146:8; Matt 11:5; Luke 1:20, 64
12 [a]Ex 4:15, 16; Deut 18:18; Is 50:4; Jer 1:9 [b]Matt 10:19, 20; Mark 13:11; Luke 12:11, 12; 21:14, 15
13 [1]Lit *send by the hand which You send*
14 [1]Lit *speaking he speaks* [a]Ex 4:27
15 [a]Ex 4:12, 30; 7:1f; Num 23:5, 12, 16; Deut 18:18; Is 51:16; 59:21; Jer 1:9
16 [a]Ex 7:1, 2
17 [a]Ex 4:2, 20; 17:9 [b]Ex 7:9-20; 14:16
18 [1]Heb *Jether* [a]Ex 2:21; 3:1
19 [1]Lit *return* [a]Ex 2:15, 23
20 [a]Ex 18:3, 4; Acts 7:29 [b]Ex 4:17; 17:9; Num 20:8, 9, 11
21 [1]Lit *to return* [2]Lit *hand* [a]Ex 3:20; 11:9, 10 [b]Ex 7:3, 13; 9:12, 35; 10:1, 20, 27; 14:4, 8; Deut 2:30; Josh 11:20; 1 Sam 6:6; Is 63:17; John 12:40; Rom 9:18
22 [a]Is 63:16; 64:8; Jer 31:9; Hos 11:1; Rom 9:4
23 [a]Ex 5:1; 6:11; 7:16 [b]Ex 11:5; 12:29; Ps 105:36; 135:8; 136:10
24 [a]Num 22:22
25 [1]Lit *made it touch at his feet* [a]Gen 17:14; Josh 5:2, 3
26 [1]Lit *with reference to*
27 [a]Ex 4:14 [b]Ex 3:1; 18:5; 24:13 **28** [a]Ex 4:15f [b]Ex 4:8f **29** [a]Ex 3:16 **30** [a]Ex 4:15, 16 [b]Ex 4:1-9 **31** [1]Lit *had visited* [a]Ex 3:18; 4:8f; 19:9 [b]Gen 50:24; Ex 3:16 [c]Gen 24:26; Ex 12:27; 1 Chr 29:20

speech and slow of tongue. Not in the sense of a speech impediment (see Acts 7:22). He complained, instead, of not being eloquent or quick-witted enough to respond to the pharaoh (see 6:12). Cf. the description of Paul in 2 Cor 10:10.

4:13 Moses' fifth and final expression of reluctance.

4:14 *the anger of the LORD burned against Moses.* Although the Lord is "slow to anger" (34:6), He does not withhold His anger or punishment from His disobedient children forever (see 34:7). *Levite.* Under Aaron's leadership Israel's priesthood would come from the tribe of Levi.

4:15–16 See note on 7:1–2.

4:19 *all the men . . . are dead.* Including Thutmose III (see 2:15,23; see also Introduction: Chronology).

4:20 *sons.* Gershom (see 2:22) and Eliezer. The latter, though unmentioned by name until 18:4, had already been born.

4:21 *wonders.* See note on 3:20. *I will harden his heart.* Nine times in Exodus the hardening of the pharaoh's heart is ascribed to God (here; 7:3; 9:12; 10:1,20,27; 11:10; 14:4,8; see Rom 9:17–18 and notes); another nine times the pharaoh is said to have hardened his own heart (7:13–14,22; 8:15,19,32; 9:7,34–35). The pharaoh alone was the agent of the hardening in each of the first five plagues. Not until the sixth plague did God confirm the pharaoh's willful action (see 9:12), as he had told Moses he would do (see similarly Rom 1:24–28).

4:22 *son.* Used collectively of the Israelites also in Hos 11:1. *My firstborn.* A figure of speech indicating Israel's special relationship with God (see Jer 31:9; Hos 11:1).

4:23 *kill . . . your firstborn.* Anticipates the tenth plague (see 11:5; 12:12).

4:24 *lodging place.* Perhaps near water, where travelers could spend the night. *The LORD . . . sought to put him to death.* Evidently because Moses had failed to circumcise his son (see Gen 17:9–14).

4:25 *Zipporah . . . cut off her son's foreskin.* Sensing that divine displeasure had threatened Moses' life, she quickly performed the circumcision on their young son. *flint.* Continued to be used for circumcision long after metal was introduced, probably because flint knives were sharper than the metal instruments available and thus more efficient for the surgical procedure (see Josh 5:2 and note). *feet.* Probably a euphemism for "genitals," as in Deut 28:57 ("between her legs," lit. "feet").

4:26 *bridegroom of blood.* Circumcision may have been repulsive to Zipporah—though it was practiced for various reasons among many peoples of the ancient Near East.

4:30 *Aaron spoke all the words which the LORD had spoken to Moses.* See note on 7:1–2.

Israel's Labor Increased

5 And afterward Moses and Aaron came and said to Pharaoh, "[a]Thus says the LORD, the God of Israel, '[b]Let My people go that they may celebrate a feast to Me in the wilderness.' "

2 But Pharaoh said, "[a]Who is the LORD that I should obey His voice to let Israel go? I do not know the LORD, and besides, [b]I will not let Israel go."

3 Then they said, "[a]The God of the Hebrews has met with us. Please, let us go a three days' journey into the wilderness that we may sacrifice to the LORD our God, otherwise He will fall upon us with pestilence or with the sword."

4 But the king of Egypt said to them, "Moses and Aaron, why do you [1]draw the people away from their [2]work? Get *back* to your [3a]labors!"

5 Again Pharaoh said, "Look, [a]the people of the land are now many, and you would have them cease from their labors!"

6 So the same day Pharaoh commanded [a]the taskmasters over the people and their [b]foremen, saying,

7 "You are no longer to give the people straw to make brick as previously; let them go and gather straw for themselves.

8 "But the quota of bricks which they were making previously, you shall impose on them; you are not to reduce any of it. Because they are [a]lazy, therefore they cry out, '[1]Let us go and sacrifice to our God.'

9 "Let the labor be heavier on the men, and let them work at it so that they will pay no attention to false words."

10 So [a]the taskmasters of the people and their foremen went out and spoke to the people, saying, "Thus says Pharaoh, 'I am not going to give you *any* straw.

11 'You go *and* get straw for yourselves wherever you can find *it,* but none of your labor will be reduced.' "

12 So the people scattered through all the land of Egypt to gather stubble for straw.

13 The taskmasters pressed them, saying, "Complete your [1]work quota, [2]*your* daily amount, just as when [3]you had straw."

14 Moreover, [a]the foremen of the sons of Israel, whom Pharaoh's taskmasters had set over them, [b]were beaten [1]and were asked, "Why have you not completed your required amount either yesterday or today in making brick as previously?"

15 Then the foremen of the sons of Israel came and cried out to Pharaoh, saying, "Why do you deal this way with your servants?

16 "There is no straw given to your servants, yet they keep saying to us, 'Make bricks!' And behold, your servants are being beaten; but it is the fault of your *own* people."

17 But he said, "You are [a]lazy, *very* lazy; therefore you say, 'Let us go *and* sacrifice to the LORD.'

18 "So go now *and* work; for you will be given no straw, yet you must deliver the quota of bricks."

19 The foremen of the sons of Israel saw that they were in trouble [1]because they were told, "You must not reduce [2]*your* daily amount of bricks."

20 When they left Pharaoh's presence, they met Moses and Aaron as they were [1]waiting for them.

21 [a]They said to them, "[b]May the LORD look upon you and judge *you,* for you have [c]made [1]us odious in Pharaoh's sight and in the sight of his servants, to put a sword in their hand to kill us."

22 Then Moses returned to the LORD and said, "[a]O Lord, why have You brought harm to this people? Why did You ever send me?

23 "Ever since I came to Pharaoh to speak in Your name, he has done harm to this people, [a]and You have not delivered Your people at all."

God Promises Action

6 Then the LORD said to Moses, "Now you shall see what I will do to Pharaoh; for [1a]under compulsion he will let them go, and [1]under compulsion he will drive them out of his land."

2 God spoke further to Moses and said to him, "I am [a]the LORD;

3 and I appeared to Abraham, Isaac, and Jacob, as [1a]God Almighty, but *by* [b]My name, [2]LORD, I did not make Myself known to them.

4 "I also established [a]My covenant with

5:1 [a]Ex 3:18 [b]Ex 4:23; 6:11; 7:16
2 [a]2 Kin 18:35; 2 Chr 32:14; Job 21:15 [b]Ex 3:19
3 [a]Ex 3:18
4 [1]Lit *loose* [2]Lit *works* [3]Lit *burdens* [a]Ex 1:11; 2:11; 6:5-7
5 [a]Ex 1:7, 9
6 [a]Ex 1:11; 3:7; 5:10, 13, 14 [b]Ex 5:10, 14, 15, 19
8 [1]Lit *saying, 'Let* [a]Ex 5:17
10 [a]Ex 1:11; 3:7; 5:6
13 [1]Lit *works* [2]Lit *the matter of a day in its day* [3]Lit *there was*
14 [a]Ex 5:6
14 [1]Lit *saying* [b]Is 10:24
17 [a]Ex 5:8
19 [1]Lit *saying* [2]Lit *from your bricks the matter of a day in its day*
20 [1]Lit *standing to meet*
21 [1]Lit *our savor to stink* [a]Ex 14:11; 15:24; 16:2 [b]Gen 16:5; 31:53 [c]Gen 34:30; 1 Sam 13:4; 27:12; 2 Sam 10:6; 1 Chr 19:6
22 [a]Num 11:11; Jer 4:10
23 [a]Ex 3:8
6:1 [1]Lit *by a strong hand* [a]Ex 3:19, 20; 7:4, 5; 11:1; 12:31, 33, 39; 13:3
2 [a]Ex 3:14, 15
3 [1]Heb *El Shaddai* [2]Heb *YHWH,* usually rendered *LORD* [a]Gen 17:1; 35:11; 48:3 [b]Ps 68:4; 83:18; Is 52:6; Jer 16:21; Ezek 37:6, 13
4 [a]Gen 12:7; 15:18; 17:4, 7; 26:3, 4; 28:4, 13

5:1 *Pharaoh.* See note on 3:10.
5:3 See 3:18 and note. The reason for sacrificing where the Egyptians could not see them is given in 8:26 (see note on Gen 43:32).
5:6 *taskmasters.* See note on 1:11. *foremen.* Israelite supervisors whose method of appointment and whose functions are indicated in vv. 14–16.
5:7 *straw.* Chopped and mixed with the clay as binder to make the bricks stronger.
5:9 *false words.* The pharaoh labels all hopes of a quick release for Israel as presumptuous and false.
5:21 *May the LORD look upon you and judge you.* See Gen 16:5; 31:49 and notes.
6:1 *Now.* Without further delay, God will act.
6:2 *I am the LORD.* Appears four times in this passage: (1) to introduce the message; (2) to confirm God's promise of redemption (v. 6) based on the evidence of vv. 2–5; (3) to underscore God's intention to adopt Israel (v. 7); (4) to confirm His promise of the land and to conclude the message (v. 8).
6:3 *God Almighty.* See note on Gen 17:1. *by My name, LORD, I did not make Myself known to them.* See notes on 3:14–15. This does not necessarily mean that the patriarchs were totally ignorant of the name Yahweh ("the LORD"), but it indicates that they did not understand its full implications as the name of the One who would redeem His people (see notes on v. 6; Gen 2:4). That fact could be comprehended only by the Israelites who were to experience the exodus, and by their descendants. *make Myself known.* This experiential sense of the verb "to know" is intend-

them, to give them the land of Canaan, the [1]land in which they sojourned.

5 "Furthermore I have [a]heard the groaning of the sons of Israel, because the Egyptians are holding them in bondage, and I have remembered My covenant.

6 "Say, therefore, to the sons of Israel, '[a]I am the LORD, and [b]I will bring you out from under the burdens of the Egyptians, and I will deliver you from their bondage. I will also [c]redeem you with [d]an outstretched arm and with great judgments.

7 'Then I will take you [1a]for My people, and [b]I will be [2]your God; and [c]you shall know that I am the LORD your God, who brought you out from under the burdens of the Egyptians.

8 'I will bring you to the land which [a]I [1]swore to give to Abraham, Isaac, and Jacob, and [b]I will give it to you *for* a possession; [c]I am the LORD.' "

9 So Moses spoke thus to the sons of Israel, but they did not listen to Moses on [a]account of *their* [1]despondency and cruel bondage.

10 Now the LORD spoke to Moses, saying,

11 "[a]Go, [1]tell Pharaoh king of Egypt [2]to let the sons of Israel go out of his land."

12 But Moses spoke before the LORD, saying, "Behold, the sons of Israel have not listened to me; [a]how then will Pharaoh listen to me, for I am [1b]unskilled in speech?"

13 Then the LORD spoke to Moses and to Aaron, and gave them a charge to the sons of Israel and to Pharaoh king of Egypt, to bring the sons of Israel out of the land of Egypt.

The Heads of Israel

14 These are the heads of their fathers' households. [a]The sons of Reuben, Israel's firstborn: Hanoch and Pallu, Hezron and Carmi; these are the families of Reuben.

15 The [a]sons of Simeon: Jemuel and Jamin and Ohad and Jachin and Zohar and Shaul the son of a Canaanite woman; these are the families of Simeon.

16 These are the names of [a]the sons of Levi according to their generations: Gershon and Kohath and Merari; and the [1]length of Levi's life was one hundred and thirty-seven years.

17 [a]The sons of Gershon: [1]Libni and Shimei, according to their families.

18 [a]The sons of Kohath: Amram and Izhar and Hebron and Uzziel; and the [1]length of Kohath's life was one hundred and thirty-three years.

19 [a]The sons of Merari: Mahli and Mushi. These are the families of the Levites according to their generations.

20 [a]Amram [1]married his father's sister Jochebed, and she bore him Aaron and Moses; and the [2]length of Amram's life was one hundred and thirty-seven years.

21 [a]The sons of Izhar: Korah and Nepheg and Zichri.

22 [a]The sons of Uzziel: Mishael and [1]Elzaphan and Sithri.

23 Aaron [1]married Elisheba, the daughter of [a]Amminadab, the sister of [b]Nahshon, and she bore him [c]Nadab and Abihu, Eleazar and Ithamar.

24 The [a]sons of Korah: Assir and Elkanah and [1]Abiasaph; these are the families of the Korahites.

25 Aaron's son [a]Eleazar [1]married one of the daughters of Putiel, and she bore him [b]Phinehas. These are the heads of the fathers' *households* of the Levites according to their families.

4 [1]Lit *land of their sojournings in which...*
5 [a]Ex 2:24
6 [a]Ex 13:3, 14; 20:2; Deut 6:12 [b]Ex 3:17; 7:4; 12:51; 16:6; 18:1; Deut 26:8; Ps 136:11 [c]Ex 15:13; Deut 7:8; 1 Chr 17:21; Neh 1:10 [d]Deut 4:34; 5:15; 26:8; Ps 136:11f
7 [1]Lit *to Me for a people* [2]Lit *to you for a God* [a]Ex 19:5; Deut 4:20; 7:6; 2 Sam 7:24 [b]Gen 17:7f; Ex 29:45f; Lev 11:45; 26:12, 13, 45; Deut 29:13 [c]Ex 16:12; Is 41:20; 49:23, 26; 60:16
8 [1]Lit *lifted up My hand* [a]Gen 15:18; 26:3; Num 14:30; Neh 9:15; Ezek 20:5, 6 [b]Josh 24:13; Ps 136:21, 22 [c]Ex 6:6
9 [1]Lit *shortness of spirit* [a]Ex 2:23
11 [1]Lit *speak to* [2]Lit *that he let* [a]Ex 4:22, 23
12 [1]Lit *uncircumcised of lips* [a]Ex 4:1, 10; 6:30 [b]Jer 1:6
14 [a]Gen 46:9; Num 26:5-11; 1 Chr 5:3
15 [a]Gen 46:10; 1 Chr 4:24
16 [1]Lit *years* [a]Gen 46:11; Num 3:17; 26:57f; 1 Chr 6:1, 16-19
17 [1]In 1 Chr 23:7, *Ladan* [a]Num 3:18-20; 1 Chr 6:17-19
18 [1]Lit *years* [a]Num 3:19; 1 Chr 6:2, 18
19 [a]Num 3:20; 1 Chr 6:19; 23:21

20 [1]Lit *took to him to wife* [2]Lit *years* [a]Ex 2:1, 2; Num 26:59 **21** [a]Num 16:1; 1 Chr 6:37, 38 **22** [1]In Num 3:30, *Elizaphan* [a]Lev 10:4; Num 3:30 **23** [1]Lit *took to him to wife* [a]Ruth 4:19, 20; 1 Chr 2:10 [b]Num 1:7; 2:3 [c]Lev 10:1; Num 3:2; 26:60; 1 Chr 6:3; 24:1 **24** [1]In 1 Chr 6:23 and 9:19, *Ebiasaph* [a]Num 26:11; 1 Chr 6:22, 23, 37 **25** [1]Lit *took to him to wife* [a]Josh 24:33 [b]Num 25:7-13; Josh 24:33; Ps 106:30

ed also in its repeated use throughout the account of the plagues (see v. 7; 7:17; 8:10,22; 9:14,29; 10:2; 11:7) and in connection with the exodus itself (see 14:4,18; 16:6,8,12; 18:11).

6:5 *remembered.* See note on Gen 8:1.

6:6 *I will bring you out . . . will deliver you . . . will also redeem you.* The verbs stress the true significance of the name Yahweh—"the LORD"—who is the Redeemer of His people (see note on v. 3). *great judgments.* See 7:4. The Lord's acts include redemption (for Israel) and judgment (against Egypt).

6:7–8 *brought you out from . . . will bring you to.* Redemption means not only release from slavery and suffering but also deliverance to freedom and joy.

6:7 *I will take you for My people, and I will be your God.* Words that anticipate the covenant at Mount Sinai (see 19:5–6; see also Jer 31:33).

6:8 See Gen 22:15–17. *swore.* See note on Gen 14:22.

6:12 *I am unskilled in speech.* See note on 4:10.

6:13 *to Moses and to Aaron.* The genealogy contained in vv. 14–25 gives details concerning the background of Moses and Aaron. Only the first three of Jacob's 12 sons (Reuben, Simeon and Levi) are listed since Moses and Aaron were from the third tribe.

6:16 *Merari.* The name is of Egyptian origin, as are those of Putiel and Phinehas (see v. 25) and of Moses himself (see note on 2:10). *the length of Levi's life was one hundred and thirty-seven years.* See vv. 18,20. In the OT, attention is usually called to a person's life span only when it exceeds 100 years.

6:20 *Amram . . . Aaron and Moses.* There is some reason to believe that Amram and Jochebed were not the immediate parents but the ancestors of Aaron and Moses. Kohath, Amram's father (see v. 18), was born before Jacob's (Israel's) descent into Egypt (see Gen 46:11), where the Israelites then stayed 430 years (see 12:40–41). Since Moses was 80 years old at the time of the exodus (see 7:7), he must have been born at least 350 years after Kohath, who consequently could not have been Moses' grandfather (see v. 18). Therefore Amram must not have been Moses' father, and the Hebrew verb for "bore" must have the same meaning it sometimes has in Gen 10 (see Gen 10:8, where it is translated "became the father of" and where "father" may mean "ancestor" or "predecessor" or "founder"; see also note on Gen 10:1). *Jochebed.* The name appears to mean "The LORD is glory." If so, it shows that the name Yahweh (here abbreviated as *Jo-*) was known before Moses was born (see note on v. 3). *Aaron and Moses.* Aaron, as the firstborn (see 7:7), is listed first in the official genealogy.

26 It was *the same* Aaron and Moses to whom the LORD said, "[a]Bring out the sons of Israel from the land of Egypt according to their [b]hosts."

27 They were the ones [a]who spoke to Pharaoh king of Egypt [1]about bringing out the sons of Israel from Egypt; it was *the same* Moses and Aaron.

28 Now it came about on the day when the LORD spoke to Moses in the land of Egypt,

29 that the LORD spoke to Moses, saying, "[a]I am the LORD; [b]speak to Pharaoh king of Egypt all that I speak to you."

30 But Moses said before the LORD, "Behold, I am [1][a]unskilled in speech; how then will Pharaoh listen to me?"

"I Will Stretch Out My Hand"

7 Then the LORD said to Moses, "[a]See, I make you *as* God to Pharaoh, and your brother Aaron shall be your prophet.

2 "You shall speak all that I command you, and your brother [a]Aaron shall speak to Pharaoh that he let the sons of Israel go out of his land.

3 "But [a]I will harden Pharaoh's heart that I may [b]multiply My signs and My wonders in the land of Egypt.

4 "When [a]Pharaoh does not listen to you, then I will lay My hand on Egypt and [b]bring out My hosts, My people the sons of Israel, from the land of Egypt by [c]great judgments.

5 "[a]The Egyptians shall know that I am the LORD, when I [b]stretch out My hand on Egypt and bring out the sons of Israel from their midst."

6 So Moses and Aaron did *it;* [a]as the LORD commanded them, thus they did.

7 Moses was [a]eighty years old and Aaron [1]eighty-three, when they spoke to Pharaoh.

Aaron's Rod Becomes a Serpent

8 Now the LORD spoke to Moses and Aaron, saying,

9 "When Pharaoh speaks to you, saying, '[1][a]Work a miracle,' then you shall say to Aaron, '[b]Take your staff and throw *it* down before Pharaoh, *that* it may become a serpent.' "

10 So Moses and Aaron came to Pharaoh, and thus they did just as the LORD had commanded; and Aaron threw his staff down before Pharaoh and [1]his servants, and it [a]became a serpent.

11 Then Pharaoh also [a]called for *the* wise men and *the* sorcerers, and they also, the [1][b]magicians of Egypt, did [2]the same with [c]their secret arts.

12 For each one threw down his staff and they turned into serpents. But Aaron's staff swallowed up their staffs.

13 Yet [a]Pharaoh's heart was [1]hardened, and he did not listen to them, as the LORD had said.

Water Is Turned to Blood

14 Then the LORD said to Moses, "Pharaoh's heart is [1]stubborn; he refuses to let the people go.

15 "Go to Pharaoh in the morning [1]as [a]he is going out to the water, and station yourself to meet him on the bank of the Nile; and you shall take in your hand [b]the staff that was turned into a serpent.

16 "[a]You shall say to him, 'The LORD, the God of the Hebrews, sent me to you, saying, "[b]Let My people go, that they may serve Me in the wilderness. But behold, you have not listened until now."

17 'Thus says the LORD, "[a]By this you shall know that I am the LORD: behold, I will strike [1]the water that is in the Nile with the staff that is in my hand, and [b]it will be turned to blood.

18 "[a]The fish that are in the Nile will die, and the Nile will [1]become foul, and the Egyptians will [2][b]find difficulty in drinking water from the Nile." ' "

19 Then the LORD said to Moses, "Say to Aaron, 'Take your staff and [a]stretch out your hand over the waters of Egypt, over their rivers, over their [1]streams, and over their

26 [a]Ex 3:10; 6:13 [b]Ex 7:4; 12:17, 51 **27** [1]Lit *to bring out* [a]Ex 5:1 **29** [a]Ex 6:2, 6, 8 [b]Ex 6:11; 7:2 **30** [1]Lit *uncircumcised of lips* [a]Ex 4:10; 6:12; Jer 1:6 **7:1** [a]Ex 4:16 **2** [a]Ex 4:15 **3** [a]Ex 4:21 [b]Ex 11:9; Acts 7:36 **4** [a]Ex 3:19, 20; 7:13, 16, 22; 8:15, 19; 9:12; 11:9 [b]Ex 12:51; 13:3, 9 [c]Ex 6:6 **5** [a]Ex 7:17; 8:19, 22; 10:7; 14:4, 18, 25 [b]Ex 3:20 **6** [a]Gen 6:22; 7:5; Ex 7:2 **7** [1]Lit *83 years old* [a]Deut 29:5; 31:2; 34:7; Acts 7:23, 30 **9** [1]Lit *Show a wonder for yourselves* [a]Is 7:11; John 2:18; 6:30 [b]Ex 4:2, 17 **10** [1]Lit *before his* [a]Ex 4:3; 7:9 **11** [1]Or *soothsayer priests* [2]Lit *thus* [a]Dan 2:2; 4:6; 5:7 [b]Gen 41:8; Ex 7:22; Dan 2:2; 2 Tim 3:8 [c]Ex 7:22; 8:7, 18; 2 Tim 3:9; Rev 13:13, 14 **13** [1]Lit *strong* [a]Ex 4:21; 7:3, 22; 8:15, 19, 32; 9:7, 12, 34, 35; 10:1, 20, 27 **14** [1]Or *hard;* lit *heavy* **15** [1]Lit *behold* [a]Ex 2:5; 8:20 [b]Ex 4:2, 3; 7:10 **16** [a]Ex 3:13, 18; 4:22; 5:1 [b]Ex 4:23; 5:1, 3 **17** [1]Lit *upon the waters* [a]Ex 5:2; 7:5; 10:2; Ps 9:16; Ezek 25:17 [b]Ex 4:9; 7:20; Rev 11:6; 16:4, 6 **18** [1]I.e. have a bad smell [2]Or *be weary of* [a]Ex 7:21 [b]Ex 7:24

19 [1]Or *canals* [a]Ex 8:5, 6, 16; 9:22; 10:12, 21; 14:21, 26

6:30 *unskilled in speech.* See v. 12 and note on 4:10.

7:1–2 As God transmits His word through His prophets to His people, so Moses will transmit God's message through Aaron to the pharaoh. The prophet's task was to speak God's word on God's behalf. He was God's "mouth" (4:15–16).

7:3 *harden.* See note on 4:21. *signs.* See notes on 3:12; 4:8.

7:4 *great judgments.* See note on 6:6.

7:7 *Moses was eighty years old.* See notes on 2:11,15.

7:9–10 *serpent.* The Hebrew for this word is different from that used in 4:3 (see Ps 74:13,"monster"). A related word (also translated "monster") is used in Ezek 29:3 as a designation for Egypt and her king.

7:11 *wise men and . . . magicians.* See note on Gen 41:8. According to tradition, two of the magicians who opposed Moses were named Jannes and Jambres (see 2 Tim 3:8; the first is also mentioned in the pre-Christian Dead Sea Scrolls). *the magicians of Egypt, did the same with their secret arts.* Either through sleight of hand or by means of demonic power.

7:12 *Aaron's staff swallowed up their staffs.* Demonstrating God's mastery over the pharaoh and the gods of Egypt.

7:13 *heart was hardened.* See note on 4:21.

7:14–10:29 The first nine plagues can be divided into three groups of three plagues each—7:14–8:19; 8:20–9:12; 9:13–10:29—with the first plague in each group (the first, the fourth and the seventh) introduced by a warning delivered to the pharaoh in the morning as he went out to the Nile (see v. 15; 8:20; 9:13).

7:17 *water . . . in the Nile . . . will be turned to blood.* See Ps 78:44; 105:29. The first nine plagues may have been a series of miraculous intensifications of natural events taking place in less than a year, and coming at God's bidding and timing. If so, the first plague resulted from the flooding of the Nile in late summer and early fall as large quantities of red sediment were washed down from Ethiopia, causing the water to become as red as blood (see the similar incident in 2 Kin 3:22). *my.* Moses'.

7:19 *your staff.* Aaron was acting on Moses' behalf (see v. 17).

pools, and over all their reservoirs of water, that they may become blood; and there will be blood throughout all the land of Egypt, both in *vessels of* wood and in *vessels of* stone.' "

20 So Moses and Aaron did even as the LORD had commanded. And he lifted up [1a]the staff and struck the water that *was* in the Nile, in the sight of Pharaoh and in the sight of his servants, and [b]all the water that *was* in the Nile was turned to blood.

21 The fish that *were* in the Nile died, and the Nile [1]became foul, so that the Egyptians could not drink water from the Nile. And the blood was through all the land of Egypt.

22 [a]But the [1]magicians of Egypt did [2]the same with their secret arts; and Pharaoh's heart was [3]hardened, and he did not listen to them, as the LORD had said.

23 Then Pharaoh turned and went into his house [1]with no concern even for this.

24 So all the Egyptians dug around the Nile for water to drink, for they could not drink of the water of the Nile.

25 Seven days [1]passed after the LORD had struck the Nile.

Frogs over the Land

8 [1]Then the LORD said to Moses, "Go to Pharaoh and say to him, 'Thus says the LORD, "[a]Let My people go, that they may serve Me.

2 "But if you refuse to let *them* go, behold, I will smite your whole territory with frogs.

3 "The Nile will [a]swarm with frogs, which will come up and go into your house and into your bedroom and on your bed, and into the houses of your servants and on your people, and into your ovens and into your kneading bowls.

4 "So the frogs will come up on you and your people and all your servants." ' "

5 [1]Then the LORD said to Moses, "Say to Aaron, '[a]Stretch out your hand with your staff over the rivers, over the [2]streams and over the pools, and make frogs come up on the land of Egypt.' "

6 So Aaron stretched out his hand over the waters of Egypt, and the [1a]frogs came up and covered the land of Egypt.

20 [1]Lit *with the staff* [a]Ex 17:5 [b]Ps 78:44; 105:29
21 [1]I.e. had a bad smell
22 [1]Or *soothsayer priests* [2]Lit *thus* [3]Lit *strong* [a]Ex 7:11; 8:7
23 [1]Lit *and he did not set his heart even to this*
25 [1]Lit *were fulfilled*
8:1 [1]Ch 7:26 in Heb [a]Ex 3:18; 4:23; 5:1, 3
3 [a]Ps 105:30
5 [1]Ch 8:1 in Heb [2]Or *canals* [a]Ex 7:19
6 [1]Lit *frog* [a]Ps 78:45; 105:30

7 [1]Or *soothsayer priests* [2]Lit *thus* [3]Lit *and made* [a]Ex 7:11, 22
8 [a]Ex 8:25; 9:27; 10:16 [b]Ex 8:28; 9:28; 10:17; Num 21:7; 1 Kin 13:6 [c]Ex 8:15, 29, 32
9 [1]Lit *Glory over me* [2]Lit *cut off*
10 [a]Ex 9:14; Deut 4:35, 39; 33:26; 2 Sam 7:22; 1 Chr 17:20; Ps 86:8; Is 46:9; Jer 10:6, 7
11 [a]Ex 8:13
12 [1]Lit *placed* [a]Ex 8:30; 9:33; 10:18
14 [1]I.e. had a bad smell
15 [1]Lit *made heavy* [a]Ex 7:4
16 [1]Or *lice*
17 [1]Or *lice* [a]Ps 105:31
18 [1]Or *soothsayer priests* [2]Or *lice* [a]Ex 7:11, 12; 8:7; 9:11
19 [1]Or *soothsayer priests* [2]Lit *strong* [a]Ex 7:5; 10:7; Ps 8:3; Luke 11:20

7 [a]The [1]magicians did [2]the same with their secret arts, [3]making frogs come up on the land of Egypt.

8 Then Pharaoh [a]called for Moses and Aaron and said, "[b]Entreat the LORD that He remove the frogs from me and from my people; and [c]I will let the people go, that they may sacrifice to the LORD."

9 Moses said to Pharaoh, "[1]The honor is yours to tell me: when shall I entreat for you and your servants and your people, that the frogs be [2]destroyed from you and your houses, *that* they may be left only in the Nile?"

10 Then he said, "Tomorrow." So he said, "*May it be* according to your word, that you may know that there is [a]no one like the LORD our God.

11 "The [a]frogs will depart from you and your houses and your servants and your people; they will be left only in the Nile."

12 Then Moses and Aaron went out from Pharaoh, and [a]Moses cried to the LORD concerning the frogs which He had [1]inflicted upon Pharaoh.

13 The LORD did according to the word of Moses, and the frogs died out of the houses, the courts, and the fields.

14 So they piled them in heaps, and the land [1]became foul.

15 But when Pharaoh saw that there was relief, he [1]hardened his heart and [a]did not listen to them, as the LORD had said.

The Plague of Insects

16 Then the LORD said to Moses, "Say to Aaron, 'Stretch out your staff and strike the dust of the earth, that it may become [1]gnats through all the land of Egypt.' "

17 They did so; and Aaron stretched out his hand with his staff, and struck the dust of the earth, and there were [1]gnats on man and beast. All the dust of the earth became [1a]gnats through all the land of Egypt.

18 The [1]magicians tried with their secret arts to bring forth [2]gnats, but [a]they could not; so there were [2]gnats on man and beast.

19 Then the [1]magicians said to Pharaoh, "[a]This is the finger of God." But Pharaoh's heart was [2]hardened, and he did not listen to them, as the LORD had said.

---

in vessels of wood and in vessels of stone. Lit. "in/on the wooden things and in/on the stone things." Some think that, since the Egyptians believed that their gods inhabited idols and images made of wood, clay and stone (see Deut 29:16–17), the plague may have been intended as a rebuke to their religion (see 12:12).

7:20 *Nile.* Egypt's dependence on the life-sustaining waters of the Nile led to its deification as the god Hapi, for whom hymns of adoration were composed. See note on v. 19.

7:24 *dug around the Nile for water to drink.* Filtered through sandy soil near the river bank, the polluted water would become safe for drinking.

7:25 *Seven days passed.* The plagues did not follow each other in rapid succession.

8:2 *I will smite your whole territory with frogs.* The frog (or toad) was deified in the goddess Heqt, who assisted women in childbirth.

8:3 *come up.* The frogs abandoned the Nile and swarmed over the land, perhaps because the unusually high concentration of bacteria-laden algae had by now proved fatal to most of the fish, thus polluting the river.

8:13 *the LORD did according to the word of Moses.* For similar occurrences see v. 31; 1 Sam 12:18; 1 Kin 18:42–45; Amos 7:1–6. *the frogs died.* Probably because they had been infected by the bacteria (*Bacillus anthracis*) in the Nile algae (see note on v. 3).

8:16 *dust . . . may become gnats.* The word "dust" is perhaps a reference to the enormous number (see, e.g., Gen 13:16) of the gnats, bred in the flooded fields of Egypt in late autumn.

8:19 *finger of God.* A concise and colorful figure of speech

20 Now the LORD said to Moses, "[a]Rise early in the morning and present yourself before Pharaoh, [1]as [b]he comes out to the water, and say to him, 'Thus says the LORD, "[c]Let My people go, that they may serve Me.

21 "For if you do not let My people go, behold, I will send swarms of insects on you and on your servants and on your people and into your houses; and the houses of the Egyptians will be full of swarms of insects, and also the ground on which they *dwell*.

22 "[a]But on that day I will set apart the land of Goshen, where My people are [1]living, so that no swarms of insects will be there, in order that you may know that [2][b]I, the LORD, am in the midst of the land.

23 "I will [1]put a division between My people and your people. Tomorrow this sign will occur." ' "

24 Then the LORD did so. And there came [1]great swarms of insects into the house of Pharaoh and the houses of his servants and the land was [a]laid waste because of the swarms of insects in all the land of Egypt.

25 Pharaoh [a]called for Moses and Aaron and said, "[b]Go, sacrifice to your God within the land."

26 But Moses said, "It is not right to do so, for we will sacrifice to the LORD our God [1]what is [a]an abomination to the Egyptians. If we sacrifice [1]what is an abomination to the Egyptians before their eyes, will they not then stone us?

27 "We must go a [a]three days' journey into the wilderness and sacrifice to the LORD our God as He [1]commands us."

28 Pharaoh said, "[a]I will let you go, that you may sacrifice to the LORD your God in the wilderness; only you shall not go very far away. [b]Make supplication for me."

29 Then Moses said, "Behold, I am going out from you, and I shall make supplication to the LORD that the swarms of insects may depart from Pharaoh, from his servants, and from his people tomorrow; only do not let Pharaoh [a]deal deceitfully again in not letting the people go to sacrifice to the LORD."

30 So [a]Moses went out from Pharaoh and made supplication to the LORD.

31 The LORD did [1]as Moses asked, and removed the swarms of insects from Pharaoh, from his servants and from his people; not one remained.

32 But Pharaoh [1]hardened his heart this time also, and [a]he did not let the people go.

Egyptian Cattle Die

9 Then the LORD said to Moses, "Go to Pharaoh and speak to him, 'Thus says the LORD, the God of the Hebrews, "[a]Let My people go, that they may serve Me.

2 "For [a]if you refuse to let *them* go and [1]continue to hold them,

3 behold, [a]the hand of the LORD [1]will come *with* a very severe pestilence on your livestock which are in the field, on the horses, on the donkeys, on the camels, on the herds, and on the flocks.

4 "[a]But the LORD will make a distinction between the livestock of Israel and the livestock of Egypt, so that [b]nothing will die of all that belongs to the sons of Israel." ' "

5 The LORD set a definite time, saying, "Tomorrow the LORD will do this thing in the land."

6 So the LORD did this thing on the next day, and [a]all the livestock of Egypt died; [b]but of the livestock of the sons of Israel, not one died.

7 Pharaoh sent, and behold, there was not even one of the livestock of Israel dead. But [a]the heart of Pharaoh was [1]hardened, and he did not let the people go.

The Plague of Boils

8 Then the LORD said to Moses and Aaron, "Take for yourselves handfuls of soot from a kiln, and let Moses throw it toward the sky in the sight of Pharaoh.

9 "It will become fine dust over all the

20 [1]Lit *behold* [a]Ex 7:15; 9:13 [b]Ex 2:5; 7:15 [c]Ex 3:18; 4:23; 5:1, 3; 8:1
22 [1]Lit *standing* [2]Or *I am the* LORD *in the midst of the earth* [a]Ex 9:4, 6, 24; 10:23; 11:7 [b]Ex 9:29; 19:5; 20:11
23 [1]Lit *set a ransom*
24 [1]Lit *heavy* [a]Ps 78:45; 105:31
25 [a]Ex 8:8; 9:27; 10:16 [b]Ex 9:28; 10:8, 24; 12:31
26 [1]Lit *the abomination of Egypt* [a]Gen 43:32; 46:34; Deut 7:25f
27 [1]Lit *says to us* [a]Ex 3:18; 5:3
28 [a]Ex 8:8, 15, 29, 32 [b]Ex 8:8; 9:28; 1 Kin 13:6
29 [a]Ex 8:8, 15
30 [a]Ex 8:12
31 [1]Lit *according to the word of Moses*
32 [1]Lit *made heavy* [a]Ex 4:21; 8:8, 15
9:1 [a]Ex 4:23; 8:1
2 [1]Lit *still hold* [a]Ex 8:2
3 [1]Lit *will be* [a]Ex 7:4; 1 Sam 5:6; Ps 39:10; Acts 13:11
4 [a]Ex 8:22 [b]Ex 9:6
6 [a]Ex 9:19, 20, 25; Ps 78:48 [b]Ex 9:4
7 [1]Lit *heavy* [a]Ex 7:14; 8:32

referring to God's miraculous power (see 31:18; Ps 8:3). Jesus drove out demons "by the finger of God" (Luke 11:20). Cf. the similar use of the phrase "hand of the LORD" in 9:3.

8:21 *I will send swarms of insects.* Probably *Stomoxys calcitrans,* which would have multiplied rapidly as the receding Nile left breeding places in its wake. Full-grown, such insects infest houses and stables and bite men and animals.

8:22 *I will set apart.* See 33:16. God makes a "division" (v. 23) between Moses' people and the pharaoh's people in this plague as well as in the fifth (see 9:4,6), the seventh (see 9:26), the ninth (see 10:23) and the tenth (see 11:7)—and probably also the sixth and eighth (see 9:11; 10:6)—demonstrating that the Lord can preserve His own people while judging Egypt. *Goshen.* See note on Gen 45:10.

8:26 *an abomination to the Egyptians.* See Gen 46:34; see also Gen 43:32 and note.

8:31 *The LORD did as Moses asked.* See note on v. 13.

9:3 *hand of the LORD.* See note on 8:19. *very severe pestilence on your livestock.* The flies of the fourth plague (see note on 8:21) probably carried the anthrax bacteria (see note on 8:13) that would now infect the animals, which had been brought into the fields again as the floodwaters subsided. The Egyptians worshiped many animals and animal-headed deities, including the bull-gods Apis and Mnevis, the cow-god Hathor and the ram-god Khnum. Thus Egyptian religion is again rebuked and ridiculed (see note on 7:19).

9:4 *distinction.* See note on 8:22.

9:5 *Tomorrow.* To give those Egyptians who feared God time to bring their livestock in from the fields and out of danger (see also v. 20).

9:6 *all the livestock of Egypt died.* That is, all that were left out in the fields. Protected livestock remained alive (see vv. 19–21).

9:8 *Take . . . soot . . . throw it toward the sky.* Perhaps symbolizing either the widespread extent of the plague of boils or their black coloration. *kiln.* Used for firing bricks, the symbol of Israel's bondage (see 1:14; 5:7–19). The same Hebrew word is translated "furnace" in Gen 19:28 and is used as a simile for the destruction of Sodom and Gomorrah.

land of Egypt, and will become [a]boils breaking out with sores on man and beast through
all the land of Egypt."
10 So they took soot from a kiln, and
stood before Pharaoh; and Moses threw it
toward the sky, and it became boils breaking
out with sores on man and beast.
11 [a]The [1]magicians could not stand before
Moses because of the boils, for the boils
were on the magicians [2]as well as on all the
Egyptians.
12 And [a]the LORD [1]hardened Pharaoh's
heart, and he did not listen to them, just as
the LORD had spoken to Moses.
13 Then the LORD said to Moses, "[a]Rise up
early in the morning and stand before Pharaoh and say to him, 'Thus says the LORD, the
God of the Hebrews, "[b]Let My people go,
that they may serve Me.
14 "For this time I will send all My plagues
[1]on you and your servants and your people,
so that [a]you may know that there is no one
like Me in all the earth.
15 "For *if by* now I had put forth My hand
and struck you and your people with pestilence, you would then have been cut off
from the earth.
16 "But, indeed, [a]for this reason I have
allowed you to [1]remain, in order to show you
My power and in order to proclaim My name
through all the earth.
17 "Still you exalt yourself against My people [1]by not letting them go.

The Plague of Hail

18 "Behold, about this time tomorrow, [a]I
will [1]send a very heavy hail, such as has not
been *seen* in Egypt from the day it was
founded [2]until now.
19 "Now therefore send, bring [a]your livestock and whatever you have in the field to
safety. [b]Every man and beast that is found in
the field and is not brought home, when the
hail comes down on them, will die." ' "
20 [a]The one among the servants of Pharaoh who [1]feared the word of the LORD made
his servants and his livestock flee into the
houses;
21 but he who [1]paid no regard to the word
of the LORD [2]left his servants and his livestock in the field.
22 Now the LORD said to Moses, "Stretch
out your hand toward the sky, that [1][a]hail
may fall on all the land of Egypt, on man and
on beast and on every plant of the field,
throughout the land of Egypt."
23 Moses stretched out his staff toward
the sky, and the LORD [1]sent [2]thunder and
[a]hail, and fire ran down to the earth. And the
LORD rained hail on the land of Egypt.
24 So there was hail, and fire [1]flashing
continually in the midst of the hail, very
severe, such as had not been in all the land
of Egypt since it became a nation.
25 [a]The hail struck all that was in the field
through all the land of Egypt, both man and
beast; the hail also struck every plant of the
field and shattered every tree of the field.
26 [a]Only in the land of Goshen, where the
sons of Israel *were,* there was no hail.
27 Then Pharaoh [1][a]sent for Moses and
Aaron, and said to them, "[b]I have sinned this
time; the LORD is the righteous one, and I and
my people are the wicked ones.
28 "[a]Make supplication to the LORD, for
there has been enough of God's [1]thunder
and hail; and [b]I will let you go, and you shall
stay no longer."
29 Moses said to him, "As soon as I go out
of the city, I will [a]spread out my [1]hands to
the LORD; the [2]thunder will cease and there
will be hail no longer, that you may know
that [b]the earth is the LORD's.
30 "[a]But as for you and your servants, I
know that [b]you do not yet [1]fear [2]the LORD
God."
31 (Now the flax and the [a]barley were
[1]ruined, for the barley was in the ear and the
flax was in bud.
32 But the wheat and the spelt were not
[1]ruined, for they *ripen* late.)
33 [a]So Moses went out of the city from
Pharaoh, and spread out his [1]hands to the
LORD; and the [2]thunder and the hail ceased,
and rain [3]no longer poured on the earth.

9 [a]Deut 28:27; Rev 16:2 **11** [1]Or *soothsayer priests* [2]Lit *and on all* [a]Ex 8:18 **12** [1]Lit *made strong* [a]Ex 4:21; 10:1, 20; 14:8; Josh 11:20; John 12:40 **13** [a]Ex 8:20 [b]Ex 4:23 **14** [1]Lit *to your heart* [a]Ex 8:10; Deut 3:24; 2 Sam 7:22; 1 Chr 17:20; Ps 86:8; Is 45:5-8; 46:9; Jer 10:6, 7 **16** [1]Lit *stand* [a]Prov 16:4; Rom 9:17 **17** [1]Lit *so as not to let* **18** [1]Lit *cause to rain* [2]Lit *and until now* [a]Ex 9:23, 24 **19** [a]Ex 9:6 [b]Ex 9:25 **20** [1]Or *revered* [a]Prov 13:13 **21** [1]Lit *did not set his heart to*

21 [2]Lit *then left* **22** [1]Lit *there may be hail* [a]Rev 16:21 **23** [1]Lit *gave* [2]Lit *sounds* [a]Gen 19:24; Josh 10:11; Ps 18:13; 78:47; 105:32; Is 30:30; Ezek 38:22; Rev 8:7 **24** [1]Lit *taking hold of itself* **25** [a]Ex 9:19; Ps 78:47, 48; 105:32, 33 **26** [a]Ex 8:22; 9:4, 6; 11:7 **27** [1]Lit *sent and called* [a]Ex 8:8 [b]Ex 10:16, 17; 2 Chr 12:6; Ps 129:4; 145:17; Lam 1:18 **28** [1]Lit *sounds* [a]Ex 8:8, 28; 10:17 [b]Ex 8:25; 10:8, 24 **29** [1]Lit *palms* [2]Lit *sounds* [a]1 Kin 8:22, 38; Ps 143:6; Is 1:15 [b]Ex 8:22; 19:5; 20:11; Ps 24:1; 1 Cor 10:26 **30** [1]Or *reverence* [2]Lit *before the LORD* [a]Ex 8:29 [b]Is 26:10 **31** [1]Lit *smitten* [a]Ruth 1:22; 2:23 **32** [1]Lit *smitten* **33** [1]Lit *palms* [2]Lit *sounds* [3]Lit *was not poured* [a]Ex 8:12; 9:29

9:9 *boils.* Probably skin anthrax (a variety of the plague that struck the livestock in vv. 1–7), a black, burning abscess that develops into a pustule. *man and beast.* The plague on the livestock now extended to other animals as well as to the people of Egypt.

9:11 *magicians could not stand.* The "boils of Egypt" (Deut 28:27) seriously affected the knees and legs (see Deut 28:35).

9:12 *the LORD hardened Pharaoh's heart.* See note on 4:21.

9:16 Paul quotes this verse as an outstanding illustration of the sovereignty of God (see Rom 9:17).

9:18 *I will send a very heavy hail.* The flooding of the Nile (the probable occasion of the first six plagues) came to an end late in the fall. The hailstorm is thus in the proper chronological position, taking place in January or February when the flax and barley were in flower but the wheat and spelt had not yet germinated (see vv. 31–32).

9:19–21 See note on v. 6.

9:27 *I have sinned this time.* For the first time the pharaoh acknowledges his sinfulness and perceives its devastating results.

9:29 *spread out my hands.* See 1 Kin 8:22,38,54; 2 Chr 6:12–13,29; Ezra 9:5; Ps 44:20; 88:9; 143:6; Is 1:15; 1 Tim 2:8. Statues of men praying with hands upraised have been found by archaeologists at several ancient sites in the Middle East.

9:30 *LORD God.* See note on Gen 2:4.

9:31–32 See note on v. 18.

9:32 *spelt.* Grains of spelt, a member of the grass family allied to wheat, have been found in ancient Egyptian tombs. Although inferior to wheat, it grows well in poorer and drier soil.

34 But when Pharaoh saw that the rain and the hail and the [1]thunder had ceased, he sinned again and [2]hardened his heart, he and his servants.

35 Pharaoh's heart was [1]hardened, and he did not let the sons of Israel go, just as the [a]LORD had spoken through Moses.

The Plague of Locusts

10 Then the LORD said to Moses, "Go to Pharaoh, for [a]I have [1]hardened his heart and the heart of his servants, that I may [2]perform these signs of Mine [3]among them,

2 and [a]that you may tell in the [1]hearing of your son, and of your grandson, how I made a mockery of the Egyptians and how I [2]performed My signs among them, [b]that you may know that I am the LORD."

3 Moses and Aaron went to Pharaoh and said to him, "Thus says the LORD, the God of the Hebrews, 'How long will you refuse to [a]humble yourself before Me? [b]Let My people go, that they may serve Me.

4 'For if you refuse to let My people go, behold, tomorrow I will bring locusts into your territory.

5 'They shall cover the surface of the land, so that no one will be able to see the land. [a]They will also eat the rest of what has escaped—what is left to you from the hail—and they will eat every tree which sprouts for you out of the field.

6 'Then [a]your houses shall be filled and the houses of all your servants and the houses of all the Egyptians, *something* which neither your fathers nor your grandfathers have seen, from the day that they [1]came upon the earth until this day.' " And he turned and went out from Pharaoh.

7 [a]Pharaoh's servants said to him, "How long will this man be [b]a snare to us? Let the men go, that they may serve the LORD their God. Do you not [1]realize that Egypt is destroyed?"

8 So Moses and Aaron [a]were brought back to Pharaoh, and he said to them, "[b]Go, serve the LORD your God! [1]Who are the ones that are going?"

9 Moses said, "[a]We shall go with our young and our old; with our sons and our daughters, [b]with our flocks and our herds we shall go, for we [1]must hold a feast to the LORD."

10 Then he said to them, "Thus may the LORD be with you, [1]if ever I let you and your little ones go! Take heed, for evil is [2]in your mind.

11 "Not so! Go now, the men *among you*, and serve the LORD, for [1]that is what you desire." So [a]they were driven out from Pharaoh's presence.

12 Then the LORD said to Moses, "[a]Stretch out your hand over the land of Egypt for the locusts, that they may come up on the land of Egypt and [b]eat every plant of the land, *even* all that the hail has left."

13 So Moses stretched out his staff over the land of Egypt, and the LORD directed an east wind on the land all that day and all that night; and when it was morning, the east wind [1]brought the [a]locusts.

14 [a]The locusts came up over all the land of Egypt and settled in all the territory of Egypt; *they were* very [1]numerous. There had never been so *many* [2]locusts, nor would there be so *many* [3]again.

15 For they covered the surface of the whole land, so that the land was darkened; and they [a]ate every plant of the land and all the fruit of the trees that the hail had left. Thus nothing green was left on tree or plant of the field through all the land of Egypt.

16 Then Pharaoh hurriedly [a]called for Moses and Aaron, and he said, "[b]I have sinned against the LORD your God and against you.

17 "Now therefore, please forgive my sin only this once, and [a]make supplication to the LORD your God, that He would only remove this death from me."

18 [a]He went out from Pharaoh and made supplication to the LORD.

19 So the LORD shifted *the wind* to a very strong west wind which took up the locusts and drove them into the [1]Red Sea; not one locust was left in all the territory of Egypt.

20 But [a]the LORD [1]hardened Pharaoh's heart, and he did not let the sons of Israel go.

Darkness over the Land

21 Then the LORD said to Moses, "[a]Stretch out your hand toward the sky, that there may be darkness over the land of Egypt, even a darkness [b]which may be felt."

22 So Moses stretched out his hand

---

34 [1]Lit *sounds* [2]Lit *made heavy*
35 [1]Lit *strong* [a]Ex 4:21
10:1 [1]Lit *made heavy* [2]Lit *put* [3]Lit *in his midst* [a]Ex 4:21; 7:13; Josh 11:20; John 12:40; Rom 9:18
2 [1]Lit *ears* [2]Lit *put* [a]Ex 12:26, 27; 13:8, 14, 15; Deut 4:9; Ps 44:1; 78:5; Joel 1:3 [b]Ex 7:5, 17
3 [a]1 Kin 21:29; 2 Chr 34:27; James 4:10; 1 Pet 5:6 [b]Ex 4:23
5 [a]Joel 1:4; 2:25
6 [1]Lit *were* [a]Ex 8:3, 21
7 [1]Lit *know* [a]Ex 7:5; 8:19; 12:33 [b]Ex 23:33; Josh 23:13; 1 Sam 18:21; Eccl 7:26
8 [1]Lit *Who and who are* [a]Ex 8:8 [b]Ex 8:25
9 [1]Lit *have a feast* [a]Ex 12:37, 38 [b]Ex 10:26
10 [1]Lit *when I* [2]Lit *before your face*
11 [1]Lit *you desire it* [a]Ex 10:28
12 [a]Ex 7:19 [b]Ex 10:5, 15
13 [1]Lit *carried* [a]Ps 78:46; 105:34
14 [1]Lit *heavy* [2]Lit *locusts like them before them* [3]Lit *after them* [a]Deut 28:38; Ps 78:46; 105:34; Joel 1:4, 7; 2:1-11; Rev 9:3
15 [a]Ex 10:5; Ps 105:34f
16 [a]Ex 8:8 [b]Ex 9:27
17 [a]Ex 8:8, 28; 9:28; 1 Kin 13:6
18 [a]Ex 8:30
19 [1]Lit *Sea of Reeds*
20 [1]Lit *made strong* [a]Ex 4:21; 11:10
21 [a]Ex 9:22 [b]Deut 28:29

10:2 *tell . . . your son.* The memory of God's redemptive acts is to be kept alive by reciting them to our descendants (see 12:26–27; 13:8,14–15; Deut 4:9; Ps 77:11–20; 78:4–6,43–53; 105:26–38; 106:7–12; 114:1–3; 135:8–9; 136:10–15).

10:4 *I will bring locusts.* In March or April the prevailing east winds (see v. 13) would bring in hordes of migratory locusts at their immature and most voracious stage. As also today, locust plagues were greatly feared in ancient times and became a powerful symbol of divine judgment (see Joel 1:4–7; 2:1–11; Amos 7:1–3).

10:7 *How long . . . ?* The pharaoh's officials ironically echo the phrase used by Moses in v. 3. *Egypt is destroyed.* Human rebellion and disobedience always bring death and destruction in their wake.

10:11 *Go now, the men.* From the pharaoh's standpoint, (1) the women and children should remain behind as hostages, and (2) it was typically only the men who participated fully in worship.

10:13 *east wind.* See note on v. 4.

10:19 *the LORD shifted the wind.* The forces of nature are compelled to obey His sovereign will (see 14:21; Matt 8:23–27). *Red Sea.* See note on 2:3.

10:21 *there may be darkness over . . . Egypt.* Like the third and

toward the sky, and there was [a]thick darkness in all the land of Egypt for three days.
23 They did not see one another, nor did
anyone rise from his place for three days,
[a]but all the sons of Israel had light in their
dwellings.
24 Then Pharaoh [a]called to Moses, and
said, "Go, serve the LORD; only let your
flocks and your herds be detained. Even
[b]your little ones may go with you."
25 But Moses said, "You must also [1]let us
have sacrifices and burnt offerings, that we
may [2]sacrifice *them* to the LORD our God.
26 "[a]Therefore, our livestock too shall go
with us; not a hoof shall be left behind, for
we shall take some of them to serve the LORD
our God. And until we arrive there, we ourselves do not know with what we shall serve
the LORD."
27 But [a]the LORD [1]hardened Pharaoh's
heart, and he was not willing to let them go.
28 Then Pharaoh said to him, "[a]Get away
from me! [1]Beware, do not see my face again,
for in the day you see my face you shall die!"
29 Moses said, "You are right; [a]I shall never see your face again!"

The Last Plague

11 Now the LORD said to Moses, "One
more plague I will bring on Pharaoh
and on Egypt; [a]after that he will let you go
from here. When he lets you go, he will surely drive you out from here completely.
2 "Speak now in the [1]hearing of the people that [a]each man ask from his neighbor
and each woman from her neighbor for articles of silver and articles of gold."
3 [a]The LORD gave the people favor in the
sight of the Egyptians. [b]Furthermore, the man
Moses *himself* was [1]greatly esteemed in the
land of Egypt, *both* in the sight of Pharaoh's
servants and in the sight of the people.
4 Moses said, "Thus says the LORD,
'About [a]midnight I am going out into the
midst of Egypt,
5 and [a]all the firstborn in the land of
Egypt shall die, from the firstborn of the
Pharaoh who sits on his throne, even to the
firstborn of the slave girl who is behind
the millstones; all the firstborn of the cattle
as well.
6 'Moreover, there shall be [a]a great cry in
all the land of Egypt, such as there has not
been *before* and such as shall never be again.
7 '[a]But against any of the sons of Israel a
dog will not *even* [1]bark, whether against
man or beast, that you may [2]understand
how the LORD makes a distinction between
Egypt and Israel.'
8 "[a]All these your servants will come down
to me and bow themselves [1]before me, saying, 'Go out, you and all the people who [2]fol-
low you,' and after that I will go out." [b]And he
went out from Pharaoh in hot anger.
9 Then the LORD said to Moses, "[a]Phar-
aoh will not listen to you, so [b]that My wonders will be multiplied in the land of Egypt."
10 [a]Moses and Aaron performed all these
wonders before Pharaoh; yet [b]the LORD
[1]hardened Pharaoh's heart, and he did not
let the sons of Israel go out of his land.

The Passover Lamb

12 Now the LORD said to Moses and Aaron
in the land of [1]Egypt,
2 "[a]This month shall be the beginning of
months for you; it is to be the first month of
the year to you.
3 "Speak to all the congregation of Israel,
saying, 'On the tenth of this month they are
each one to take a [1]lamb for themselves,
according to their fathers' households, a
[1]lamb for [2]each household.
4 'Now if the household is too small for a
[1]lamb, then he and his neighbor nearest to
his house are to take one according to the
[2]number of persons *in them;* according to
[3]what each man should eat, you are to
[4]divide the lamb.
5 'Your [1]lamb shall be [a]an unblemished
male a year old; you may take it from the
sheep or from the goats.

22 [a]Ps 105:28; Rev 16:10
23 [a]Ex 8:22
24 [a]Ex 8:8, 25 [b]Ex 10:10
25 [1]Lit *give into our hand* [2]Lit *make*
26 [a]Ex 10:9
27 [1]Lit *made strong* [a]Ex 4:21; 10:20; 14:4, 8
28 [1]Lit *Take heed to yourself* [a]Ex 10:11
29 [a]Ex 11:8; Heb 11:27
11:1 [a]Ex 12:31, 33, 39
2 [1]Lit *ears* [a]Ex 3:22; 12:35, 36
3 [1]Lit *very great* [a]Ex 3:21; 12:36; Ps 106:46 [b]Deut 34:10-12
4 [a]Ex 12:29
5 [a]Ex 12:12, 29; Ps 78:51; 105:36; 135:8; 136:10

6 [a]Ex 12:30
7 [1]Lit *sharpen his tongue* [2]Lit *know* [a]Ex 8:22; Josh 10:21
8 [1]Lit *to* [2]Lit *are at your feet* [a]Ex 12:31-33 [b]Heb 11:27
9 [a]Ex 7:4 [b]Ex 7:3
10 [1]Lit *made strong* [a]Ex 4:21 [b]Ex 7:3; 9:12; 10:20, 27; Josh 11:20; Is 63:17; John 12:40
12:1 [1]Lit *Egypt, saying*
2 [a]Ex 13:4; 23:15; 34:18; Deut 16:1
3 [1]Or *kid* [2]Lit *the*
4 [1]Or *kid* [2]Or *amount* [3]Lit *each man's eating* [4]Lit *compute for*
5 [1]Or *kid* [a]Lev 22:18-21; 23:12; Heb 9:14; 1 Pet 1:19

sixth plagues, this ninth plague was unannounced to Pharaoh. It was possibly caused by the arrival of an unusually severe khamsin, the blinding sandstorm that blows in from the desert each year in the early spring. The darkness was an insult to the sun-god Ra (or Re), one of the chief deities of Egypt.

10:28 Pharaoh declares that he will never again grant Moses an audience. *the day you see my face.* During a plague of darkness, these words are somewhat ironic.

11:1 *when he lets you go.* The Hebrew for this phrase can also be read "as one sends away [a bride]"—i.e., laden with gifts (see Gen 24:53).

11:2–3 See 12:35–36.

11:4 *Moses said.* Continuing the speech of 10:29.

11:5 *all the firstborn in . . . Egypt shall die.* See Ps 78:51; 105:36; 135:8; 136:10. This is the ultimate disaster, since all the plans and dreams of a father were bound up in his firstborn son, who received a double share of the family estate when the father died (see Deut 21:17 and note). Moreover, judgment on the firstborn represented judgment on the entire community. *slave girl who is behind the millstones.* The lowliest of occupations (see Is 47:2).

11:7 *distinction.* See note on 8:22.

12:2 *This month shall be the beginning of months.* The inauguration of the religious calendar in Israel (see chart, p. 92). In the ancient Near East, new year festivals normally coincided with the new season of life in nature. The designation of this month as Israel's religious New Year reminded Israel that her life as the people of God was grounded in God's redemptive act in the exodus. The Canaanite name for this month was Abib (see 13:4; 23:15; 34:18; Deut 16:1), which means "young head of grain." Later the Babylonian name Nisan was used (see Neh 2:1; Esth 3:7). Israel's agricultural calendar began in the fall (see note on 23:16), and during the monarchy it dominated the nation's civil calendar. Both calendars (civil and religious) existed side by side until after the exile. Judaism today uses only the calendar that begins in the fall.

12:3 *congregation of Israel.* The Israelites gathered in assembly.

12:5 *lamb . . . unblemished.* See Lev 22:18–25. Similarly, Jesus was like "a lamb unblemished and spotless" (1 Pet 1:19).

Hebrew Calendar and Selected Events

NUMBER OF MONTH		HEBREW NAME	MODERN EQUIVALENT	BIBLICAL REFERENCES	AGRICULTURE	FEASTS
1 Sacred sequence begins	7	**Abib; Nisan**	March–April	Ex 12:2; 13:4; 23:15; 34:18; Deut 16:1; Ne 2:1; Esth 3:7	Spring (later) rains; barley and flax harvest begins	Passover; Unleavened Bread; Firstfruits
2	8	**Ziv (Iyyar)***	April–May	1 Kin 6:1,37	Barley harvest; dry season begins	
3	9	**Sivan**	May–June	Esth 8:9	Wheat harvest	Pentecost (Weeks)
4	10	**(Tammuz)***	June–July		Tending vines	
5	11	**(Ab)***	July–August		Ripening of grapes, figs and olives	
6	12	**Elul**	August–September	Neh 6:15	Processing grapes, figs and olives	
7	1 Civil sequence	**Ethanim (Tishri)***	September–October	1 Kin 8:2	Autumn (early) rains begin; plowing	Trumpets; Atonement; Tabernacles (Booths)
8	2	**Bul (Marcheshvan)***	October–November	1 Kin 6:38	Sowing of wheat and barley	
9	3	**Kislev**	November–December	Neh 1:1; Zech 7:1	Winter rains begin (snow in some areas)	Hanukkah ("Dedication")
10	4	**Tebeth**	December–January	Esth 2:16		
11	5	**Shebat**	January–February	Zech 1:7		
12	6	**Adar**	February–March	Ezra 6:15; Esth 3:7,13; 8:12; 9:1,15,17,19,21	Almond trees bloom; citrus fruit harvest	Purim
		(Adar Sheni)* — Second Adar	This intercalary month was added about every three years so the lunar calendar would correspond to the solar year.			

*Names in parentheses are not in the Bible

6 '[1]You shall keep it until the [a]fourteenth day of the same month, then the whole assembly of the congregation of Israel is to kill it [2b]at twilight.

7 '[a]Moreover, they shall take some of the blood and put it on the two doorposts and on the lintel [1]of the houses in which they eat it.

8 'They shall eat the flesh [a]that *same* night, [b]roasted with fire, and they shall eat it with [c]unleavened bread [1d]and bitter herbs.

9 'Do not eat any of it raw or boiled at all with water, but rather [a]roasted with fire, *both* its head and its legs along with [b]its entrails.

10 '[a]And you shall not leave any of it over until morning, but whatever is left of it until morning, you shall burn with fire.

11 'Now you shall eat it in this manner: *with* your loins girded, your sandals on your feet, and your staff in your hand; and you shall eat it in haste—it is [a]the LORD's Passover.

12 'For [a]I will go through the land of Egypt on that night, and will strike down all the firstborn in the land of Egypt, both man and beast; and [b]against all the gods of Egypt I will execute judgments—[c]I am the LORD.

13 '[a]The blood shall be a sign for you on the houses where you [1]live; and when I see the blood I will pass over you, and no plague will befall you [2]to destroy *you* when I strike the land of Egypt.

Feast of Unleavened Bread

14 'Now [a]this day will be [b]a memorial to you, and you shall celebrate it *as* a feast to the LORD; throughout your generations you are to celebrate it *as* [1c]a permanent ordinance.

15 '[a]Seven days you shall eat unleavened bread, but on the first day you shall [1]remove leaven from your houses; for whoever eats anything leavened from the first day until the seventh day, [b]that [2]person shall be cut off from Israel.

16 '[a]On the first day you shall have a holy assembly, and *another* holy assembly on the seventh day; no work at all shall be done on them, except what must be eaten [1]by every person, that alone may be [2]prepared by you.

17 'You shall also observe [a]the *Feast of Unleavened Bread*, for on this [b]very day I brought your hosts out of the land of Egypt; therefore you shall observe this day throughout your generations as [c]a [1]permanent ordinance.

18 '[a]In the first *month*, on the fourteenth day of the month at evening, you shall eat unleavened bread, until the twenty-first day of the month at evening.

19 '[a]Seven days there shall be no leaven found in your houses; for whoever eats what is leavened, that [1b]person shall be cut off from the congregation of Israel, whether *he is* an alien or a native of the land.

20 'You shall not eat anything leavened; in all your dwellings you shall eat unleavened bread.' "

21 Then [a]Moses called for all the elders of Israel and said to them, "[1]Go and [b]take for yourselves [2]lambs according to your families, and slay [c]the Passover *lamb*.

22 "[a]You shall take a bunch of hyssop and dip it in the blood which is in the basin, and [1]apply some of the blood that is in the basin to the lintel and the two doorposts; and none of you shall go outside the door of his house until morning.

6 [1]Lit *It shall be to you for a guarding* [2]Lit *between the two evenings* [a]Ex 12:14, 17; Lev 23:5; Num 9:1-3, 11; 28:16 [b]Ex 16:12; Deut 16:4, 6
7 [1]Lit *upon* [a]Ex 12:22
8 [1]Lit *in addition to* [a]Ex 34:25; Num 9:12 [b]Deut 16:7 [c]Deut 16:3, 4; 1 Cor 5:8 [d]Num 9:11
9 [a]Ex 12:8 [b]Ex 29:13, 17, 22
10 [a]Ex 16:19; 23:18; 34:25
11 [a]Ex 12:13, 21, 27, 43
12 [a]Ex 11:4, 5 [b]Num 33:4; Ps 82:1 [c]Ex 6:2
13 [1]Lit *are* [2]Lit *for destruction* [a]Heb 11:28
14 [1]Or *an eternal* [a]Ex 12:6; Lev 23:4, 5; 2 Kin 23:21 [b]Ex 13:9 [c]Ex 12:17, 24; 13:10
15 [1]Lit *cause to cease* [2]Lit *soul* [a]Ex 13:6, 7; 23:15; 34:18; Lev 23:6; Num 28:17; Deut 16:3, 8 [b]Gen 17:14; Ex 12:19; Num 9:13
16 [1]Lit *pertaining to* [2]Lit *done* [a]Lev 23:7, 8; Num 28:18, 25
17 [1]Or *eternal* [a]Deut 16:3-8 [b]Ex 12:41 [c]Ex 12:14; 13:3, 10
18 [a]Ex 12:2; Lev 23:5-8; Num 28:16-25
19 [1]Lit *soul* [a]Ex 12:15; 23:15; 34:18 [b]Num 9:13

21 [1]Lit *Draw out* [2]Lit *sheep* [a]Num 9:4; Heb 11:28 [b]Ex 12:3 [c]Ex 12:11 **22** [1]Lit *cause to touch* [a]Ex 12:7

12:6 *at twilight.* Lit. "between the two evenings," an idiom meaning either (1) between the decline of the sun and sunset, or (2) between sunset and nightfall—which has given rise to disputes about when the Sabbath and other holy days begin.
12:7 *blood.* Symbolizes a sacrifice offered as a substitute, one life laid down for another (see Lev 17:11). Thus Israel escapes the judgment about to fall on Egypt only through the mediation of a sacrifice (see Heb 9:22; 1 John 1:7).
12:8 *unleavened bread.* Reflecting the haste with which the people left Egypt (see vv. 11,39; Deut 16:3). *bitter herbs.* Endive, chicory and other bitter-tasting plants are indigenous to Egypt. Eating them would recall the bitter years of servitude there (see 1:14).
12:9 *roasted . . . head . . . legs . . . entrails.* The method wandering shepherds used to cook meat.
12:11 *Passover.* Explained in vv. 13,23,27 to mean that the Lord would "pass over" and not destroy the occupants of houses that were under the sign of the blood.
12:12 *against all the gods of Egypt . . . judgments.* Some had already been judged (see notes on 7:19; 8:2; 9:3; 10:21), and now all would be: (1) They would be shown to be powerless to deliver from the impending slaughter, and (2) many animals sacred to the gods would be killed.
12:13 *sign.* Just as the plagues were miraculous signs of judgment on Pharaoh and his people (see 8:23), so the Lord's "passing over" the Israelites who placed themselves under the sign of blood was a pledge of God's mercy.
12:14 *celebrate it as a permanent ordinance.* Frequent references to Passover observance occur in the rest of Scripture (see Num 9:1–5; Josh 5:10; 2 Kin 23:21–23; 2 Chr 30:1–27; 35:1–19; Ezra 6:19–22; Luke 2:41–43; John 2:13,23; 6:4; 11:55—12:1). The ordinance is still kept by practicing Jews today.
12:15 *remove leaven from your houses.* Yeast later was often used as a symbol of sin, such as "hypocrisy" (Luke 12:1) or "malice and wickedness" (1 Cor 5:8). Before celebrating Passover, the observant Jew today conducts a systematic (often symbolic) search of his house to remove every crumb of leavened bread that might be there (see v. 19). *cut off from Israel.* Removed from the covenant people by execution (see, e.g., 31:14; Lev 20:2–3) or banishment. See also Gen 17:14 and note.
12:17 *Feast of Unleavened Bread.* Began with the Passover meal and continued for seven days (see vv. 18–19; see also Mark 14:12).
12:21 *Passover lamb.* Jesus is "our Passover" (1 Cor 5:7), sacrificed "once for all" (Heb 7:27) for us.
12:22 *hyssop.* Here probably refers to an aromatic plant (*Origanum maru*) of the mint family with a straight stalk (see John 19:29) and white flowers. The hairy surface of its leaves and branches held liquids well and made it suitable as a sprinkling

A Memorial of Redemption

23 "For [a]the LORD will pass through to
smite the Egyptians; and when He sees the
blood on the lintel and on the two doorposts,
the LORD will pass over the door and will
[b]not allow the [c]destroyer to come in to your
houses to smite *you*.
24 "And [a]you shall observe this event as
an ordinance for you and your children forever.
25 "When you enter the land which the
LORD will give you, as He has [1]promised, you
shall observe this [2]rite.
26 "[a]And when your children say to you,
'[1]What does this rite mean to you?'
27 you shall say, 'It is a Passover sacrifice
to [a]the LORD [1]who passed over the houses of
the sons of Israel in Egypt when He smote
the Egyptians, but [2]spared our homes.' "
[b]And the people bowed low and worshiped.
28 Then the sons of Israel went and did
so; just as the LORD had commanded Moses
and Aaron, so they did.
29 Now it came about at [a]midnight that
[b]the LORD struck all [c]the firstborn in the land
of Egypt, from the firstborn of Pharaoh who
sat on his throne to the firstborn of the captive who was in the dungeon, and all the
firstborn of [d]cattle.
30 Pharaoh arose in the night, he and all
his servants and all the Egyptians, and there
was [a]a great cry in Egypt, for there was no
home where there was not someone dead.
31 Then [a]he called for Moses and Aaron at
night and said, "Rise up, [b]get out from
among my people, both you and the sons of
Israel; and go, [1]worship the LORD, as you
have said.
32 "Take [a]both your flocks and your herds,
as you have said, and go, and bless me
also."

Exodus of Israel

33 [a]The Egyptians urged the people, to
send them out of the land in haste, for they
said, "We will all be dead."
34 So the people took [a]their dough before
it was leavened, *with* their kneading bowls
bound up in the clothes on their shoulders.
35 [a]Now the sons of Israel had done
according to the word of Moses, for they had
requested from the Egyptians articles of silver and articles of gold, and clothing;
36 and the LORD had given the people
favor in the sight of the Egyptians, so that
they let them have their request. Thus they
[a]plundered the Egyptians.
37 Now the [a]sons of Israel journeyed from
[b]Rameses to Succoth, about [c]six hundred
thousand men on foot, aside from children.
38 A [a]mixed multitude also went up with
them, [1]along with flocks and herds, a [b]very
large number of livestock.
39 They baked the dough which they had
brought out of Egypt into cakes of unleavened bread. For it had not become leavened,
since they were [a]driven out of Egypt and
could not delay, nor had they [1]prepared any
provisions for themselves.
40 Now the time [1]that the sons of Israel
lived in Egypt was [a]four hundred and thirty
years.
41 And at the end of four hundred and
thirty years, [1]to [a]the very day, [b]all the hosts
of the LORD went out from the land of Egypt.

Ordinance of the Passover

42 [a]It is a night [1]to be observed for the
LORD for having brought them out from the
land of Egypt; this night is for the LORD, [1]to
be observed [2]by all the sons of Israel
throughout their generations.
43 The LORD said to Moses and Aaron,
"This is the ordinance of [a]the Passover: no
[1b]foreigner is to eat of it;
44 but every man's [a]slave purchased with
money, after you have circumcised him, then
he may eat of it.
45 "[a]A sojourner or a hired servant shall
not eat of it.
46 "It is to be eaten in a single house; you
are not to bring forth any of the flesh outside

23 [a]Ex 11:4; 12:12, 13 [b]Rev 7:3; 9:4 [c]1 Cor 10:10; Heb 11:28
24 [a]Ex 12:14, 17; 13:5, 10
25 [1]Lit *spoken* [2]Lit *service*
26 [1]Lit *What is this service to you?* [a]Ex 10:2; 13:8, 14, 15; Deut 32:7; Josh 4:6; Ps 78:6
27 [1]Lit *because He* [2]Lit *delivered* [a]Ex 12:11 [b]Ex 4:31
29 [a]Ex 11:4, 5 [b]Num 8:17; 33:4; Ps 135:8; 136:10 [c]Ex 4:23; Ps 78:51; 105:36 [d]Ex 9:6
30 [a]Ex 11:6
31 [1]Or *serve* [a]Ex 8:8 [b]Ex 8:25
32 [a]Ex 10:9, 26
33 [a]Ex 10:7; 11:1; 12:39; Ps 105:38
34 [a]Ex 12:39
35 [a]Ex 3:21, 22; 11:2, 3; Ps 105:37
36 [a]Ex 3:22
37 [a]Num 33:3, 5 [b]Gen 47:11 [c]Ex 38:26; Num 1:46; 2:32; 11:21; 26:51
38 [1]Lit *and* [a]Num 11:4 [b]Ex 17:3; Num 20:19; 32:1; Deut 3:19
39 [1]Lit *made* [a]Ex 6:1; 11:1; 12:31-33
40 [1]Or *of the sons of Israel who dwelt* [a]Gen 15:13, 16; Acts 7:6; Gal 3:17
41 [1]Lit *that it happened on this very day* [a]Ex 12:17 [b]Ex 3:8, 10; 6:6
42 [1]Or *of vigil* [2]Lit *to the sons* [a]Ex 13:10; 34:18; Deut 16:1
43 [1]Lit *son of a stranger* [a]Ex 12:11; Num 9:14 [b]Ex 12:48
44 [a]Gen 17:12, 13; Lev 22:11
45 [a]Lev 22:10

device for use in purification rituals (see Lev 14:4,6,49,51–52; Num 19:6,18; Heb 9:19; see also Ps 51:7). *dip it in the blood.* Today at Passover meals a sprig of parsley or other plant is dipped in salt water to symbolize the lowly diet and tears of the Israelites during their time of slavery.

12:23 *pass over.* See note on v. 11. *the destroyer.* In Ps 78:49 the agent of God's wrath against the Egyptians is described as "a band of destroying angels." God often used angels to bring destructive plagues (see 2 Sam 24:15–16; 2 Kin 19:35; see also 1 Cor 10:10, a reference to Num 16:41–49).

12:26 *your children say to you, 'What does this rite mean to you?'* See 13:14. The Passover was to be observed as a memorial feast commemorating Israel's redemption and appropriating it anew. As observed today, it includes the asking of similar questions by the youngest child present.

12:27 *Passover sacrifice.* See note on v. 21. *passed over.* See note on v. 11.

12:29 *captive who was in the dungeon.* The lowliest of situations (see note on 11:5).

12:31 *he called for Moses.* Though he had sworn never again to grant Moses an audience (see 10:28 and note), Pharaoh now summons Moses (and Aaron) into his presence.

12:35–36 See 3:21–22; 11:2–3.

12:37 *journeyed from Rameses.* See 1:11; see also note on Gen 47:11. The Israelite departure took place "the next day after the Passover" (Num 33:3). *Succoth.* Probably modern Tell el-Maskhutah in the Wadi Tumeilat, west of the Bitter Lakes. *about six hundred thousand men.* A round number for 603,550 (see note on 38:26).

12:38 *a mixed multitude.* Possibly including such Egyptians as those mentioned in 9:20.

12:41 *four hundred and thirty years, to the very day.* See notes on Gen 15:13; Acts 7:6.

of the house, [a]nor are you to break any bone
of it.
47 "[a]All the congregation of Israel are to
[1]celebrate this.
48 "But [a]if a [1]stranger sojourns with you,
and [2]celebrates the Passover to the LORD, let
all his males be circumcised, and then let
him come near to [3]celebrate it; and he shall
be like a native of the land. But no uncircumcised person may eat of it.
49 "[1a]The same law shall [2]apply to the
native as to the [3]stranger who sojourns
among you."
50 Then all the sons of Israel did *so;* they
did just as the LORD had commanded Moses
and Aaron.
51 And on that same day [a]the LORD
brought the sons of Israel out of the land of
Egypt [1b]by their hosts.

Consecration of the Firstborn

13 Then the LORD spoke to Moses, saying,
2 "[a]Sanctify to Me every firstborn, the
first [1]offspring of every womb among the
sons of Israel, both of man and beast; it
belongs to Me."
3 Moses said to the people, "[a]Remember
this day in which you went out from Egypt,
from the house of [1]slavery; for [b]by [2]a powerful hand the LORD brought you out from this
place. [c]And nothing leavened shall be eaten.
4 "On this day in the [a]month of Abib, you
are about to go forth.
5 "It shall be when the LORD [a]brings you
to the land of the Canaanite, the Hittite, the
Amorite, the Hivite and the Jebusite, which
[b]He swore to your fathers to give you, a land
flowing with milk and honey, [c]that you shall
[1]observe this rite in this month.
6 "For [a]seven days you shall eat unleavened bread, and on the seventh day there
shall be a feast to the LORD.
7 "Unleavened bread shall be eaten
throughout the seven days; and [a]nothing
leavened shall be seen [1]among you, nor shall
any leaven be seen [1]among you in all your
borders.

46 [a]Num 9:12; Ps 34:20; John 19:33, 36
47 [1]Lit *do* [a]Ex 12:6; Num 9:13, 14
48 [1]Lit *sojourner* [2]Lit *does* [3]Lit *do* [a]Num 9:14
49 [1]Lit *One law* [2]Lit *be* [3]Lit *sojourner* [a]Lev 24:22; Num 15:15, 16, 29
51 [1]Lit *according to* [a]Ex 12:41 [b]Ex 6:26
13:2 [1]Lit *opening* [a]Ex 13:12, 13, 15; 22:29; Lev 27:26; Num 3:13; 8:16f; 18:15; Deut 15:19; Luke 2:23
3 [1]Lit *slaves* [2]Lit *strength of hand* [a]Ex 12:42; Deut 16:3 [b]Ex 3:20; 6:1 [c]Ex 12:19
4 [a]Ex 12:2; 23:15; 34:18; Deut 16:1
5 [1]Lit *serve this service* [a]Ex 3:8, 17; Josh 24:11 [b]Ex 6:8 [c]Ex 12:25
6 [a]Ex 12:15-20
7 [1]Lit *to* [a]Ex 12:19
8 [a]Ex 10:2; 12:26f; 13:14; Ps 44:1
9 [1]Lit *be for* [2]Lit *between your eyes* [a]Ex 12:14; 13:16; Num 15:39; Deut 6:8; 11:18 [b]Ex 13:3
10 [1]Lit *days to days* [a]Ex 12:24, 25; 13:5
11 [a]Ex 13:5 [b]Gen 15:18; 17:8; 28:15; Ps 105:42-45
12 [1]Lit *cause to pass over* [2]Lit *opening* [3]Lit *every issue the offspring of a beast* [a]Ex 13:1, 2; 22:29; 34:19; Lev 27:26; Num 18:15; Ezek 44:30; Luke 2:23
13 [1]Lit *opening* [a]Ex 34:20; Num 18:15 [b]Num 3:46 **14** [1]Lit *strength of hand* [2]Lit *slaves* [a]Ex 10:2; 12:26, 27; 13:8; Deut 6:20; Josh 4:6, 21 [b]Ex 13:3, 9
15 [1]Lit *opening* [a]Ex 12:29 **16** [1]Lit *be for* [2]Or *frontlet-bands* [3]Lit *between your eyes* [4]Lit *strength of hand* [a]Ex 13:9; Deut 6:8

8 "[a]You shall tell your son on that day,
saying, 'It is because of what the LORD did for
me when I came out of Egypt.'
9 "And [a]it shall [1]serve as a sign to you on
your hand, and as a reminder [2]on your forehead, that the law of the LORD may be in
your mouth; for with [b]a powerful hand the
LORD brought you out of Egypt.
10 "Therefore, you shall [a]keep this ordinance at its appointed time from [1]year to
year.
11 "Now when [a]the LORD brings you to the
land of the Canaanite, as [b]He swore to you
and to your fathers, and gives it to you,
12 [a]you shall [1]devote to the LORD the first
[2]offspring of every womb, and [3]the first offspring of every beast that you own; the
males belong to the LORD.
13 "But [a]every first [1]offspring of a donkey
you shall redeem with a lamb, but if you do
not redeem *it,* then you shall break its neck;
and [b]every firstborn of man among your
sons you shall redeem.
14 "[a]And it shall be when your son asks
you in time to come, saying, 'What is this?'
then you shall say to him, '[b]With a [1]power-
ful hand the LORD brought us out of Egypt,
from the house of [2]slavery.
15 'It came about, when Pharaoh was
stubborn about letting us go, that the [a]LORD
killed every firstborn in the land of Egypt,
both the firstborn of man and the firstborn of
beast. Therefore, I sacrifice to the LORD the
males, the first [1]offspring of every womb, but
every firstborn of my sons I redeem.'
16 "So [a]it shall [1]serve as a sign on your
hand and as [2]phylacteries [3]on your forehead,
for with a [4]powerful hand the LORD brought
us out of Egypt."

God Leads the People

17 Now when Pharaoh had let the people
go, God did not lead them by the way of the
land of the Philistines, even though it was

12:46 *nor . . . break any bone of it.* See Num 9:12; Ps 34:20; quoted in John 19:36 in reference to Jesus.
12:48 *no uncircumcised person may eat of it.* Only those consecrated to the Lord in covenant commitment could partake of Passover; only for them could it have its full meaning (see Gen 17:9–14). Concerning participants in the Lord's Supper see 1 Cor 11:28.
13:2 *Sanctify to Me every firstborn . . . among the sons.* God had adopted Israel as His firstborn (see 4:22) and had delivered every firstborn among the Israelites, whether man or animal, from the tenth plague (see 12:12–13). All the firstborn in Israel were therefore His. Jesus, Mary's firstborn son (see Luke 2:7), was presented to the Lord in accordance with this law (see Luke 2:22–23).
13:5 See note on 3:8.
13:9 *sign . . . on your hand, and as a reminder on your forehead.* A figure of speech (see v. 16; Deut 6:8; 11:18; see also Prov 3:3; 6:21; 7:3; Song 8:6). A literal reading of this verse has led to the practice of writing the texts of vv. 1–10, vv. 11–16, Deut 6:4–9 and Deut 11:13–21 on separate strips of parchment and placing them in two small leather boxes, which the observant Jew straps on his forehead and left arm before his morning prayers. The boxes are called "phylacteries" (Matt 23:5). This practice seems to have originated after the exile to Babylon.
13:13 *every first offspring of a donkey.* The economic importance of pack animals allowed for their redemption through sacrificing a lamb. *redeem.* See 6:6. The verb means "obtain release by means of payment." *every firstborn . . . among your sons.* Humans were to be consecrated to the Lord by their life, not by their death (see Gen 22:12; Num 3:39–51; cf. Rom 12:1).
13:14 See note on 12:26.
13:16 See note on v. 9.
13:17 *way of the land of the Philistines.* Although the most direct route from Goshen to Canaan, it was heavily guarded by a string of Egyptian fortresses.

near; for God said, "[a]The people might
change their minds when they see war, and
return to Egypt."
18 Hence God led the people around by
the way of the wilderness to the [1]Red Sea;
and the sons of Israel went up [a]in martial
array from the land of Egypt.
19 Moses took [a]the bones of Joseph with
him, for he had made the sons of Israel
solemnly swear, saying, "God will surely
[1]take care of you, and you shall carry my
bones from here with you."
20 Then they set out from [a]Succoth and
camped in Etham on the edge of the wilderness.
21 [a]The LORD was going before them in a
pillar of cloud by day to lead them on the
way, and in a pillar of fire by night to give
them light, that they might [1]travel by day
and by night.
22 [1]He [a]did not take away the pillar of
cloud by day, nor the pillar of fire by night,
from before the people.

Pharaoh in Pursuit

14 Now the LORD spoke to Moses, saying,
2 "Tell the sons of Israel to turn back
and camp before [a]Pi-hahiroth, between
[b]Migdol and the sea; you shall camp in front
of Baal-zephon, opposite it, by the sea.
3 "For Pharaoh will say of the sons of Israel, 'They are wandering aimlessly in the
land; the wilderness has shut them in.'
4 "Thus [a]I will [1]harden Pharaoh's heart,
and [b]he will chase after them; and I will be
honored through Pharaoh and all his army,
and [c]the Egyptians will know that I am the
LORD." And they did so.
5 When the king of Egypt was told that
the people had fled, [1]Pharaoh and his servants had a change of heart toward the people, and they said, "What is this we have
done, that we have let Israel go from serving
us?"
6 So he made his chariot ready and took
his people with him;
7 and he took six hundred select chariots, and all the *other* chariots of Egypt with
officers over all of them.
8 [a]The LORD [1]hardened the heart of Pharaoh, king of Egypt, and he chased after the
sons of Israel as the sons of Israel were going
out [2b]boldly.
9 Then [a]the Egyptians chased after them
with all the horses *and* chariots of Pharaoh,
his horsemen and his army, and they overtook them camping by the sea, [b]beside Pi-
hahiroth, in front of Baal-zephon.
10 As Pharaoh drew near, the sons of Israel [1]looked, and behold, the Egyptians were
marching after them, and they became very
frightened; [a]so the sons of Israel cried out to
the LORD.
11 Then [a]they said to Moses, "Is it
because there were no graves in Egypt that
you have taken us away to die in the wilderness? Why have you dealt with us in this
way, [1]bringing us out of Egypt?
12 "[a]Is this not the word that we spoke to
you in Egypt, saying, '[1]Leave us alone that
we may serve the Egyptians'? For it would
have been better for us to serve the Egyptians than to die in the wilderness."

The Sea Is Divided

13 But Moses said to the people, "[a]Do not
fear! [1]Stand by and see [b]the salvation of the
LORD which He will accomplish for you
today; for the Egyptians whom you have
seen today, you will never see them again
forever.
14 "[a]The LORD will fight for you while [b]you
keep silent."
15 Then the LORD said to Moses, "Why are
you crying out to Me? Tell the sons of Israel
to go forward.
16 "As for you, lift up [a]your staff and
stretch out your hand over the sea and divide
it, and the sons of Israel shall [1]go through
the midst of the sea on dry land.
17 "As for Me, behold, [a]I will [1]harden the
hearts of the Egyptians so that they will go in
after them; and I will be honored through

17 [a]Ex 14:11, 12; Num 14:1-4; Deut 17:16
18 [1]Lit *Sea of Reeds* [a]Josh 1:14; 4:12, 13
19 [1]Lit *visit* [a]Gen 50:24, 25; Josh 24:32; Acts 7:15, 16
20 [a]Ex 12:37; Num 33:6
21 [1]Lit *go* [a]Ex 14:19, 24; 33:9, 10; Num 9:15; 14:14; Deut 1:33; Neh 9:12; Ps 78:14; 99:7; 105:39; Is 4:5; 1 Cor 10:1
22 [1]Or *The pillar of cloud by day and the pillar of fire by night did not depart* [a]Neh 9:19
14:2 [a]Num 33:7 [b]Jer 44:1
4 [1]Lit *make strong* [a]Ex 4:21; 7:3; 14:17 [b]Ex 14:23 [c]Ex 7:5; 14:25
5 [1]Lit *the heart of Pharaoh...was changed*
8 [1]Lit *made strong* [2]Lit *with a high hand* [a]Ex 14:4 [b]Num 33:3; Acts 13:17
9 [a]Ex 15:9; Josh 24:6 [b]Ex 14:2
10 [1]Lit *lifted up their eyes* [a]Josh 24:7; Neh 9:9; Ps 34:17; 107:6
11 [1]Lit *so as to bring* [a]Ex 5:21; 15:24; 16:2; Ps 106:7, 8
12 [1]Lit *Cease from us* [a]Ex 6:9
13 [1]Or *Take your stand* [a]Gen 15:1; 46:3; Ex 20:20; 2 Chr 20:15, 17; Is 41:10, 13, 14 [b]Ex 14:30; 15:2
14 [a]Ex 14:25; 15:3; Deut 1:30; 3:22; Josh 23:3; 2 Chr 20:29; Neh 4:20 [b]Is 30:15
16 [1]Lit *enter the* [a]Ex 4:17, 20; 7:19; 14:21, 26; 17:5, 6, 9; Num 20:8, 9, 11; Is 10:26
17 [1]Lit *make strong* [a]Ex 14:4, 8

13:18 *way of the wilderness.* Leading south along the west coast of the Sinai peninsula. *Red Sea.* See note on 2:3. Various locations of the crossing have been proposed along the line of the modern Suez Canal and including the northern end of the Gulf of Suez (see map No. 3 at the end of the study Bible; but see also note on 14:2). *in martial array.* Probably armed only with spears, bows and slings.
13:19 See notes on Gen 50:24–25.
13:20 *Succoth.* See note on 12:37. *Etham.* Location unknown.
13:21 *pillar of cloud . . . pillar of fire.* The visible symbol of God's presence among His people (see 14:24; see also note on 3:2). The Lord often spoke to them from the pillar (see Num 12:5–6; Deut 31:15–16; Ps 99:6–7).
14:2 *turn back.* Northward, in the general direction from which they had come. *Pi-hahiroth.* "Faces Baal-zephon" (Num 33:7). *Migdol.* Location unknown. The name means "watchtower." *sea.* The sea that the NASB, in accordance with established tradition, calls the Red Sea—in Hebrew *Yam Suph*, i.e., Sea of Reeds (see notes on 2:3; 13:18). Reference can hardly be to the northern end of the Gulf of Suez since reeds do not grow in salt water. Moreover, an Egyptian papyrus locates Baal-zephon in the vicinity of Tahpanhes (see note on Jer 2:16), a site near Lake Menzaleh about 20 miles east of Rameses. The crossing of the "Red Sea" thus probably occurred at the southern end of Lake Menzaleh (see map, p. 97; but see note on 13:18). *Baal-zephon.* Means "Baal of the north" or "Baal of North (Mountain)"—also the name of a Canaanite god.
14:4 *know that I am the LORD.* See note on 6:3.
14:7 *officers.* The Hebrew for the singular of this word means "third man," perhaps referring to his place in a chariot crew.
14:14 *The LORD will fight for you.* A necessary reminder that although Israel was armed for battle ("in martial array," 13:18) and "going out boldly" (v. 8), the victory would be won by God alone.

The Exodus

The exodus and conquest narratives form the classic historical and spiritual drama of OT times. Subsequent ages looked back to this period as one of obedient and victorious living under divine guidance. Close examination of the environment and circumstances also reveals the strenuous exertions, human sin and bloody conflicts of the era.

Marah—Oasis
Rameses—City or settlement
Trade routes
Israelite route
Miles 0 20 40 60 80 100
Kms 0 50 100 150
Sea of Chinnereth
Jordan R.
CANAAN
AMMON
Rabbah
Jericho
Heshbon
Mt. Nebo
Ashdod
Lake Menzaleh
Way of the Land of the Philistines
Gaza
PHILISTIA
Lachish
Hebron
Salt Sea
Beersheba
Rameses
Migdol
WILDERNESS OF SHUR
AMALEKITES
WILDERNESS OF ZIN
GOSHEN
Way to Shur
Succoth
Pithom
Kadesh-barnea
Punon
EDOM
SHASU NOMADS
Brook of Egypt
On
Exact crossing place through the Biblical "Yam Suph" is unknown.
Trade route
Memphis
Way of the Land of the Red Sea
SINAI
WILDERNESS OF PARAN
EGYPT
Ezion Geber
Marah
Elim
MIDIAN
WILDERNESS OF SIN
Nile R.
Red Sea
Dophkah
Hazeroth
Rephidim
Mt. Sinai
WILDERNESS OF SINAI
Red Sea
Red Sea

The Israelite tribes fled past the Egyptian system of border posts, through the Red Sea and into the desert, where they avoided the main military and trade routes leading across northern Sinai. The less frequently traveled "Way of the Sea" led to the remote turquoise and copper mining region northwest of Mt. Sinai.

It was necessary for Moses to take refuge in Midian where the Egyptian authorities could not reach him. The decades spent on "the far west of the wilderness" were an important formative part of his life.

In historical terms, the exodus from Egypt was ignored by Egyptian scribes and recorders. No definitive monuments mention the event itself, but a stele of Pharaoh Merneptah (c. 1225 B.C.) claims that a people called Israel were encountered by Egyptian troops somewhere in northern Canaan.

Finding precise geographical and chronological details of the period is problematic, but new information has emerged from vast amounts of fragmentary archaeological and inscriptional evidence. Hittite cuneiform documents parallel the ancient covenant formula governing Israel's "national contract" with God at Mount Sinai.

The Late Bronze Age (c. 1550-1200 B.C.) was a time of major social migrations. Egyptian control over the Semites in the eastern Nile delta was harsh, with a system of brickmaking quotas imposed on the labor force, often the landless, low-class "Apiru." Numerous Canaanite towns were violently destroyed. New populations, including the "Sea Peoples," made their presence felt in Anatolia, Egypt, Canaan, Transjordan, and elsewhere in the eastern Mediterranean.

Correspondence from Canaanite town rulers to the Egyptian court in the time of Akhenaten (c. 1375 B.C.) reveals a weak structure of alliances, with an intermittent Egyptian military presence and an ominous fear of people called "Habiru" ("Apiru").

Pharaoh and all his army, through his chariots and his horsemen.

18 “[a]Then the Egyptians will know that I am the LORD, when I am honored through Pharaoh, through his chariots and his horsemen.”

19 [a]The angel of God, who had been going before the camp of Israel, moved and went behind them; and the pillar of cloud moved from before them and stood behind them.

20 So it came between the camp of Egypt and the camp of Israel; and there was the cloud [1]along with the darkness, yet it gave light at night. Thus the one did not come near the other all night.

21 [a]Then Moses stretched out his hand over the sea; and the LORD [1]swept the sea *back* by a strong east wind all night and turned the sea into [b]dry land, so [c]the waters were divided.

22 [a]The sons of Israel [1]went through the midst of the sea on the dry land, and [b]the waters *were like* a wall to them on their right hand and on their left.

23 Then [a]the Egyptians took up the pursuit, and all Pharaoh's horses, his chariots and his horsemen went in after them into the midst of the sea.

24 At the morning watch, [a]the LORD looked down on the [1]army of the Egyptians [2]through the pillar of fire and cloud and brought the [1]army of the Egyptians into confusion.

25 He [1]caused their chariot wheels to swerve, and He made them drive with difficulty; so the Egyptians said, “Let [2]us flee from Israel, [a]for the LORD is fighting for them against the Egyptians.”

26 Then the LORD said to Moses, “[a]Stretch out your hand over the sea so that the waters may come back over the Egyptians, over their chariots and their horsemen.”

27 So Moses stretched out his hand over the sea, and [a]the sea returned to its normal state at daybreak, while the Egyptians were fleeing [1]right into it; then the LORD [2][b]overthrew the Egyptians in the midst of the sea.

28 The waters returned and covered the chariots and the horsemen, [1]even Pharaoh's entire army that had gone into the sea after them; [a]not even one of them remained.

29 But the sons of Israel walked on [a]dry land through the midst of the sea, and the waters *were like* a wall to them on their right hand and on their left.

30 [a]Thus the LORD saved Israel that day from the hand of the Egyptians, and Israel [b]saw the Egyptians dead on the seashore.

31 When Israel saw the great [1]power which the LORD had [2]used against the Egyptians, the people [3]feared the LORD, and [a]they believed in the LORD and in His servant Moses.

18 [a]Ex 14:25
19 [a]Ex 13:21, 22
20 [1]Lit *and the darkness*
21 [1]Lit *caused to go* [a]Ex 7:19; 14:16 [b]Ps 66:6; 106:9; 136:13, 14 [c]Ex 15:8; Josh 3:16; 4:23; Neh 9:11; Ps 74:13; 78:13; 114:3, 5; Is 63:12, 13
22 [1]Lit *entered the* [a]Ex 15:19; Josh 3:17; 4:22; Neh 9:11; Ps 66:6; 78:13; Heb 11:29 [b]Ex 14:29; 15:8
23 [a]Ex 14:4, 17
24 [1]Lit *camp* [2]Or *in* [a]Ex 13:21
25 [1]Or *removed* [2]Lit *me* [a]Ex 14:4, 14, 18
26 [a]Ex 14:16
27 [1]Lit *to meet it* [2]Lit *shook off* [a]Josh 4:18 [b]Ex 15:1, 7; Deut 11:4; Neh 9:11; Ps 78:53; Heb 11:29
28 [1]Lit *in respect to* [a]Ps 78:53; 106:11
29 [a]Ex 14:22; Ps 66:6; Is 11:15
30 [a]Ex 14:13; Ps 106:8, 10; Is 63:8, 11 [b]Ps 58:10; 59:10
31 [1]Lit *hand* [2]Lit *done* [3]Or *revered* [a]Ex 4:31; 19:9; Ps 106:12; John 2:11; 11:45
15:1 [1]Lit *and said, saying* [2]Or *Let me sing* [3]Or *triumphed gloriously* [a]Ps 106:12; Rev 15:3 [b]Is 12:5; 42:10-12 [c]Jer 51:21
2 [1]Heb *YAH* [a]Ps 18:1, 2; Is 12:2; Hab 3:18f

The Song of Moses and Israel

15 [a]Then Moses and the sons of Israel sang this song to the LORD, [1]and said,

“[2][b]I will sing to the LORD, for He [3]is
highly exalted;
[c]The horse and its rider He has hurled
into the sea.
2 “[1][a]The LORD is my strength and song,
And He has become my salvation;
[b]This is my God, and I will praise
Him;
[c]My father's God, and I will [d]extol
Him.
3 “[a]The LORD is a warrior;
[1][b]The LORD is His name.

[b]Ps 48:14 [c]Ex 3:6, 15, 16 [d]2 Sam 22:47; Ps 99:5; Is 25:1
3 [1]Heb *YHWH*, usually rendered *LORD* [a]Ex 14:14; Rev 19:11 [b]Ex 3:15; 6:2, 3, 7, 8; Ps 24:8; 83:18

14:19 *angel of God.* See note on Gen 16:7; here associated with the cloud (see 13:21).
14:20 *came between the camp of Egypt and . . . Israel.* The pillar of cloud (signifying the Lord's presence) protected Israel (see Ps 105:39).
14:21 *strong east wind.* See 10:13. In 15:8 the poet praises the Lord and calls the wind the “blast of Your nostrils,” affirming (as here) that the miracle occurred in accordance with God's timing and under His direction (see 15:10).
14:22 *through . . . the sea on the dry ground.* In later times, psalmists and prophets reminded Israel of what God had done for them (see Ps 66:6; 106:9; 136:13–14; Is 51:10; 63:11–13). *waters were like a wall.* See v. 29. The waters were “piled up” (15:8) on both sides.
14:24 *morning watch.* Often the time for surprise attack (see Josh 10:9; 1 Sam 11:11). *the LORD looked down.* See note on 13:21.
14:25 *the LORD is fighting for them.* See note on v. 14.
14:27 *the LORD overthrew the Egyptians in the midst of the sea.* As He had done with the locusts of the eighth plague (see 10:19).
14:28 *not even one of them remained.* The Lord's victory over the pharaoh's army was complete.
14:31 *feared the LORD.* See note on Gen 20:11. *believed in the Lord and in His servant Moses.* Faith in God's mighty power and confidence in Moses' leadership. *His servant.* Here refers to one who has the status of a high official in the Lord's kingly administration (see Num 12:8; Deut 34:5). See also the same title applied to Joshua (Josh 24:29), Samuel (1 Sam 3:10), David (2 Sam 3:18) and Elijah (2 Kin 9:36).
15:1–18 A hymn celebrating God's spectacular victory over the pharaoh and his army. The focus of the song is God Himself (see v. 11); the divine name Yahweh (“the LORD”) appears ten times. Similes—“like a stone” (v. 5), “like a heap” (v. 8) and “like lead” (v. 10)—mark the conclusion of three of the five stanzas. The first four stanzas (vv. 1–5, 6–8, 9–10, 11–12) retell the story of the “salvation” (14:13) at the Red Sea, and the final stanza (vv. 13–18) anticipates the future approach to and conquest of Canaan (the promised land).
15:1 *Moses and the sons of Israel sang.* As though one person, the whole community praises God. *I will sing.* A common way to begin a hymn of praise (see Judg 5:3; Ps 89:1; 101:1; 108:1).
15:2 The first half of the verse is quoted verbatim in Ps 118:14 (see Is 12:2).
15:3 *The LORD is a warrior.* See note on 14:14. God is often pictured as a king leading His people into battle (see, e.g., Deut 1:30; Judg 4:14; 2 Sam 5:24; 2 Chr 20:17–18).

4 "[a]Pharaoh's chariots and his army He
has cast into the sea;
And the choicest of his officers are
[1]drowned in the [2]Red Sea.
5 "The deeps cover them;
[a]They went down into the depths like
a stone.
6 "[a]Your right hand, O LORD, is majestic
in power,
[b]Your right hand, O LORD, shatters the
enemy.
7 "And in the greatness of Your
[1]excellence You [a]overthrow those
who rise up against You;
[b]You send forth Your burning anger,
and it [c]consumes them as chaff.
8 "[a]At the blast of Your nostrils the
waters were piled up,
[b]The flowing waters stood up like a
heap;
The deeps were congealed in the heart
of the sea.
9 "[a]The enemy said, 'I will pursue, I will
overtake, I will [b]divide the spoil;
My [1]desire shall be [2]gratified against
them;
I will draw out my sword, my hand
will [3]destroy them.'
10 "[a]You blew with Your wind, the sea
covered them;
[b]They sank like lead in the [1]mighty
waters.
11 "[a]Who is like You among the gods,
O LORD?
Who is like You, [b]majestic in holiness,
[c]Awesome in praises, [d]working
wonders?
12 "[a]You stretched out Your right hand,
The earth swallowed them.
13 "In Your lovingkindness You have [a]led
the people whom You have
[b]redeemed;
In Your strength You have guided *them*
[c]to Your holy habitation.
14 "[a]The peoples have heard, they
tremble;
Anguish has gripped the inhabitants
of Philistia.
15 "Then the [a]chiefs of Edom were
dismayed;
[b]The leaders of Moab, trembling grips
them;
[c]All the inhabitants of Canaan have
melted away.
16 "[a]Terror and dread fall upon them;
[b]By the greatness of Your arm they are
motionless as stone;
Until Your people pass over,
O LORD,
Until the people pass over whom You
[c]have purchased.
17 "[a]You will bring them and [b]plant them
in [c]the mountain of Your
inheritance,
[d]The place, O LORD, which You have
made for Your dwelling,
[e]The sanctuary, O Lord, which Your
hands have established.
18 "[a]The LORD shall reign forever and
ever."
19 [a]For the horses of Pharaoh with his
chariots and his horsemen went into the
sea, and the LORD brought back the waters
of the sea on them, but the sons of Israel
walked on [b]dry land through the midst of
the sea.
20 [a]Miriam the prophetess, Aaron's sister,
took the [b]timbrel in her hand, and all the
women went out after her with timbrels and
with [1c]dancing.
21 Miriam answered them,
"[a]Sing to the LORD, for He [1]is highly
exalted;
The horse and his rider He has hurled
into the sea."

4 [1]Lit *sunk* [2]Lit *Sea of Reeds* [a]Ex 14:6, 7, 17, 28
5 [a]Ex 15:10; Neh 9:11
6 [a]Ex 3:20; 6:1 [b]Ps 118:15, 16
7 [1]Or *exaltation* [a]Ex 14:27 [b]Ps 78:49, 50 [c]Deut 4:24; Is 5:24; Heb 12:29
8 [a]Ex 14:22, 29; Job 4:9 [b]Ps 78:13
9 [1]Lit *soul* [2]Lit *be filled with them* [3]Or *dispossess, bring to ruin* [a]Ex 14:5, 8, 9 [b]Judg 5:30; Is 53:12; Luke 11:22
10 [1]Or *majestic* [a]Ex 14:27, 28 [b]Ex 15:5
11 [a]Ex 8:10; 9:14; Deut 3:24; 2 Sam 7:22; 1 Kin 8:23; Ps 71:19; 86:8; Mic 7:18 [b]Is 6:3; Rev 4:8 [c]Ps 22:23 [d]Ps 72:18; 136:4
12 [a]Ex 15:6
13 [a]Neh 9:12; Ps 77:20 [b]Ex 15:16; Ps 77:15 [c]Ex 15:17; Ps 78:54
14 [a]Deut 2:25; Hab 3:7
15 [a]Gen 36:15, 40 [b]Num 22:3, 4 [c]Josh 2:9, 11, 24; 5:1
16 [a]Ex 23:27; Deut 2:25; Josh 2:9 [b]Ex 15:5, 6 [c]Ex 15:13; Ps 74:2; Is 43:1; Jer 31:11; Titus 2:14; 2 Pet 2:1
17 [a]Ex 23:20; 32:34 [b]Ps 44:2; 80:8, 15 [c]Ps 2:6; 78:54, 68 [d]Ps 68:16; 76:2; 132:13, 14 [e]Ps 78:69
18 [a]Ps 10:16; 29:10; Is 57:15
19 [a]Ex 14:23, 28 [b]Ex 14:22, 29
20 [1]Lit *dances* [a]Ex 2:4; Num 26:59; 1 Chr 6:3; Mic 6:4 [b]Judg 11:34; 1 Sam 18:6; 1 Chr 15:16; Ps 68:25; 81:2; 149:3; Jer 31:4 [c]Judg 11:34; 21:21; 1 Sam 18:6; Ps 30:11; 150:4
21 [1]Or *has triumphed gloriously* [a]Ex 15:1

15:4 *officers.* See note on 14:7.

15:5 *went down . . . like a stone.* Babylon is similarly described in Jer 51:63–64.

15:8 See note on 14:22. *blast of Your nostrils.* See note on 14:21; see also Ps 18:15.

15:10 *You blew with Your wind.* See note on 14:21.

15:11 *Who is like You . . . ?* See Ps 35:10; 71:19; 89:6; 113:5; Mic 7:18. The Lord, who tolerates no rivals, has defeated all the gods of Egypt and their worshipers.

15:12 *earth.* Perhaps refers to Sheol or the grave (see Deut 32:22; Ps 63:9; 71:20), the realm of death below, since it was the sea that swallowed the Egyptians.

15:13 *people whom You have redeemed.* See note on 6:6. *Your holy habitation.* Perhaps a reference to the house of worship at Shiloh (see Jer 7:12), and ultimately the temple on Mount Zion (see Ps 76:2), the "place" God "chooses" (Deut 12:14,18,26; 14:25; 16:7,15–16; 17:8,10; 18:6; 31:11) to put "His name" (Deut 12:5,11,21; 14:23–24; 16:2,6,11; 26:2). But the phrase may refer to the promised land, which is called "Your dwelling" and "the sanctuary . . . Your hands have established" in v. 17.

15:14–15 *Philistia . . . Edom . . . Moab . . . Canaan.* The order is roughly that along the route Israel would follow from Mount Sinai to the promised land.

15:15 *chiefs.* The term used earlier of the Edomite rulers (see Gen 36:15–19,21,29–30,40,43).

15:16 *dread fall upon them.* See note on 1 Chr 14:17. *purchased.* Or "created" (the same alternative translation is possible in Deut 32:6). In Ps 74:2 the meaning "bought" or "purchased" is found in context with "redeemed" (see note on 13:13).

15:17 *inheritance.* The promised land (see 1 Sam 26:19; Ps 79:1).

15:20 *prophetess.* See Num 12:1–2 for a statement by Miriam concerning her prophetic gift (see note on 7:1–2). Other prophetesses in the Bible were Deborah (Judg 4:4), Isaiah's wife (Is 8:3, but see note there), Huldah (2 Kin 22:14), Noadiah (Neh 6:14), Anna (Luke 2:36) and Philip's daughters (Acts 21:9). *women went out after her with timbrels and with dancing.* Such celebration was common after victory in battle (see 1 Sam 18:6; 2 Sam 1:20).

15:21 Miriam repeats the first four lines of the victory hymn (see v. 1), changing only the form of the first verb.

The Lord Provides Water

22 [a]Then Moses [1]led Israel from the [2]Red
Sea, and they went out into [b]the wilderness
of [c]Shur; and they went three days in the
wilderness and found no water.
23 When they came to [a]Marah, they could
not drink the waters [1]of Marah, for they were
[2]bitter; therefore it was named [3]Marah.
24 So the people [a]grumbled at Moses, saying, "What shall we drink?"
25 Then he [a]cried out to the LORD, and the
LORD showed him [b]a tree; and he threw *it*
into the waters, and the waters became
sweet.
There He [c]made for them a statute and
regulation, and there He [d]tested them.
26 And He said, "[a]If you will give earnest
heed to the voice of the LORD your God, and
do what is right in His sight, and give ear [b]to
His commandments, and keep all His statutes, [c]I will put none of the diseases on you
which I have put on the Egyptians; for I, [d]the
LORD, am your healer."
27 Then they came to [a]Elim where there
were twelve springs of water and seventy
date palms, and they camped there beside
the waters.

The Lord Provides Manna

16 Then they set out from Elim, and all the
congregation of the sons of Israel came
to the wilderness of [a]Sin, which is between
Elim and Sinai, on [b]the fifteenth day of the
second month after their departure from the
land of Egypt.
2 The whole congregation of the sons of
Israel [a]grumbled against Moses and Aaron in
the wilderness.
3 The sons of Israel said to them,
"[a]Would that we had died by the LORD's
hand in the land of Egypt, [b]when we sat by
the pots of [1]meat, when we ate bread to the
full; for you have brought us out into this
wilderness to kill this whole assembly with
hunger."
4 Then the LORD said to Moses, "Behold,
[a]I will rain bread from heaven for you; and
the people shall go out and gather a day's
portion every day, that I may [b]test them,
whether or not they will walk in My [1]instruc-
tion.
5 "[a]On the sixth day, when they prepare
what they bring in, it will be twice as much
as they gather daily."
6 So Moses and Aaron said to all the sons
of Israel, "At evening [1][a]you will know that
the LORD has brought you out of the land of
Egypt;
7 and in the morning [1]you will see [a]the
glory of the LORD, for [b]He hears your grumblings against the LORD; and [c]what are we,
that you grumble against us?"

The Lord Provides Meat

8 Moses said, "*This will happen* when
the LORD gives you [1]meat to eat in the
evening, and bread to the full in the morning; for the LORD hears your grumblings
which you grumble against Him. And what
are we? Your grumblings are [a]not against us
but against the LORD."
9 Then Moses said to Aaron, "Say to all
the congregation of the sons of Israel,
'[a]Come near before the LORD, for He has
heard your grumblings.' "
10 It came about as Aaron spoke to the
whole congregation of the sons of Israel, that
they [1]looked toward the wilderness, and
behold, [a]the glory of the LORD appeared in
the cloud.
11 And the LORD spoke to Moses, saying,
12 "[a]I have heard the grumblings of the
sons of Israel; speak to them, saying, '[1]At

15:22 [1]Lit *caused Israel to journey* [2]Lit *Sea of Reeds* [a]Ps 77:20; 78:52, 53 [b]Num 33:8 [c]Gen 16:7; 20:1; 25:18
23 [1]Lit *from* [2]Heb *Marim* [3]I.e. bitterness [a]Num 33:8; Ruth 1:20
24 [a]Ex 14:11; 16:2; Ps 106:13
25 [a]Ex 14:10 [b]Ezek 47:7, 8 [c]Josh 24:25 [d]Ex 16:4; Deut 8:2, 16; Judg 2:22; 3:1, 4; Ps 66:10
26 [a]Ex 19:5, 6; Deut 7:12 [b]Ex 20:2-17 [c]Deut 7:15; 28:58, 60 [d]Ex 23:25; Deut 32:39; Ps 41:3, 4; 103:3; 147:3
27 [a]Num 33:9
16:1 [a]Num 33:10, 11; Ezek 30:15 [b]Ex 12:6, 51; 19:1
2 [a]Ex 14:11; 15:24; Ps 106:25; 1 Cor 10:10
3 [1]Or *flesh* [a]Ex 17:3; Num 14:2, 3; 20:3; Lam 4:9 [b]Num 11:4, 5
4 [1]Or *law* [a]Neh 9:15; Ps 78:23-25; 105:40; John 6:31; 1 Cor 10:3 [b]Ex 15:25; Deut 8:2, 16
5 [a]Ex 16:22
6 [1]Lit *and you* [a]Ex 6:7
7 [1]Lit *and you* [a]Ex 16:10, 12; Is 35:2; 40:5; John 11:4, 40 [b]Num 14:27; 17:5 [c]Num 16:11
8 [1]Or *flesh* [a]1 Sam 8:7; Luke 10:16; Rom 13:2; 1 Thess 4:8
9 [a]Num 16:16
10 [1]Lit *turned* [a]Ex 13:21; 16:7; Num 16:19; 1 Kin 8:10f
12 [1]Lit *Between the two evenings* [a]Ex 16:8; Num 14:27

15:22 *wilderness of Shur.* Located east of Egypt (see Gen 25:18; 1 Sam 15:7) in the northwestern part of the Sinai peninsula. In Num 33:8 it is called the "wilderness of Etham." Shur and Etham both mean "fortress wall" (Shur in Hebrew, Etham in Egyptian).
15:23 *Marah.* Probably modern Ain Hawarah, inland from the Gulf of Suez and 50 miles south of its northern end.
15:24 *grumbled.* During their wilderness wanderings, the Israelites grumbled against Moses and Aaron whenever they faced a crisis (see 16:2; 17:3; Num 14:2; 16:11,41). In reality, however, they were grumbling against the Lord (16:8). Paul warns us not to follow their example (see 1 Cor 10:10).
15:25 *he threw it into the waters, and the waters became sweet.* For a similar occurrence see 2 Kin 2:19–22. *a statute and regulation.* Technical terms presumably referring to what follows in v. 26. *tested.* See note on Gen 22:1. God tested Israel also in connection with His provision of manna (see 16:4; Deut 8:2–3) and the giving of the Ten Commandments (see 20:20).
15:27 *Elim.* Seven miles south of Ain Hawarah (see note on v. 23) in the well-watered valley of Gharandel. *date palms.* Elim means "large trees."
16:1 *from Elim . . . to the wilderness of Sin.* See Num 33:10–11. The wilderness of Sin was in southwestern Sinai ("Sin" is probably derived from "Sinai") in the region today called Debbet er-Ramleh. *fifteenth day of the second month.* Exactly one month had passed since Israel's exodus from Egypt (see 12:2,6,29,31).
16:2 *grumbled.* See note on 15:24.
16:3 *meat.* Num 11:5 lists additional items of food from Egypt that the Israelites craved.
16:4 *bread from heaven.* Jesus called Himself "the bread out of heaven" (John 6:32), "the bread of God" (John 6:33), "the bread of life" (John 6:35,48), "the living bread that came down out of heaven" (John 6:51)—all in the spiritual sense (John 6:63). For a similar application see Deut 8:3 and Jesus' quotation of it in Matt 4:4. *go out and gather a day's portion every day.* Probably the background for Jesus' model petition in Matt 6:11; Luke 11:3. *test.* See notes on 15:25; Gen 22:1.
16:5 *sixth day . . . twice as much as they gather daily.* To provide for "the seventh day, the sabbath" (v. 26), "a sabbath observance" (v. 23). See v. 29.
16:6 *know.* See note on 6:3.
16:8 *meat . . . in the evening, and bread . . . in the morning.* See vv. 13–14.
16:10 *glory of the LORD appeared in the cloud.* See 24:15–17; see also note on 13:21.

twilight you shall eat [2]meat, and in the
morning you shall be filled with bread; and
[b]you shall know that I am the LORD your
God.' "
13 So it came about at evening that [a]the
quails came up and covered the camp, and
in the morning [b]there was a layer of dew
around the camp.
14 [a]When the layer of dew [1]evaporated,
behold, on the [2]surface of the wilderness
[b]there was a fine flake-like thing, fine as the
frost on the ground.
15 When the sons of Israel saw *it,* they
said to one another, "[1]What is it?" For they
did not know what it was. And Moses said to
them, "[a]It is the bread which the LORD has
given you to eat.
16 "This is [1]what the LORD has commanded, 'Gather of it every man [2]as much as he
should eat; you shall take [3][a]an omer apiece
according to the number of persons each of
you has in his tent.' "
17 The sons of Israel did so, and *some*
gathered much and *some* little.
18 When they measured it with an omer,
[a]he who had gathered much had no excess,
and he who had gathered little had no lack;
every man gathered [1]as much as he should
eat.
19 Moses said to them, "[a]Let no man
leave any of it until morning."
20 But they did not listen to Moses, and
some left part of it until morning, and it bred
worms and became foul; and Moses was
angry with them.
21 They gathered it morning by morning,
every man [1]as much as he should eat; but
when the sun grew hot, it would melt.

The Sabbath Observed

22 [a]Now on the sixth day they gathered
twice as much bread, two omers for each
one. When all the [b]leaders of the congregation came and told Moses,
23 then he said to them, "This is what the
LORD [1]meant: [a]Tomorrow is a sabbath observance, a holy sabbath to the LORD. Bake what
you will bake and boil what you will boil,
and [b]all that is left over [2]put aside to be kept
until morning."
24 So they [1]put it aside until morning, as

12 [2]Or *flesh* [b]Ex 6:7; 16:7; 1 Kin 20:28; Joel 3:17
13 [a]Num 11:31; Ps 78:27-29; 105:40 [b]Num 11:9
14 [1]Lit *had gone up* [2]Lit *face of* [a]Num 11:7-9 [b]Ex 16:31; Neh 9:15; Ps 78:24; 105:40
15 [1]Heb *Man hu,* cf v 31 [a]Ex 16:4; Neh 9:15; Ps 78:24; John 6:31; 1 Cor 10:3
16 [1]Lit *the thing which* [2]Lit *according to his eating* [3]Lit *an omer for a head* [a]Ex 16:32, 36
18 [1]Lit *according to his eating* [a]2 Cor 8:15
19 [a]Ex 12:10; 16:23; 23:18
21 [1]Lit *according to his eating*
22 [a]Ex 16:5 [b]Ex 34:31
23 [1]Lit *spoke* [2]Lit *lay up for you* [a]Gen 2:3; Ex 20:8-11; 23:12; 31:15; 35:2; Lev 23:3; Neh 9:13, 14 [b]Ex 16:19
24 [1]Lit *laid it up*

24 [a]Ex 16:20
26 [1]Lit *none on it* [a]Ex 20:9, 10
28 [1]Or *laws* [a]2 Kin 17:14; Ps 78:10; 106:13
29 [1]Lit *for the* LORD
31 [1]Heb *man,* cf v 15 [a]Num 11:7-9; Deut 8:3, 16 [b]Ex 16:14
32 [1]Lit *the thing which*
33 [a]Heb 9:4; Rev 2:17
34 [a]Ex 25:16, 21; 27:21; 40:20; Num 17:10
35 [a]Deut 8:2f; Josh 5:12; Neh 9:20, 21
36 [1]I.e. Approx one bu [a]Ex 16:16
17:1 [1]Lit *their journeyings* [2]Lit *mouth* [a]Ex 16:1; Num 33:12 [b]Ex 19:2; Num 33:14

Moses had ordered, and [a]it did not become
foul nor was there any worm in it.
25 Moses said, "Eat it today, for today is a
sabbath to the LORD; today you will not find
it in the field.
26 "[a]Six days you shall gather it, but on the
seventh day, *the* sabbath, there will be
[1]none."
27 It came about on the seventh day that
some of the people went out to gather, but
they found none.
28 Then the LORD said to Moses, "[a]How
long do you refuse to keep My commandments and My [1]instructions?
29 "See, [1]the LORD has given you the sabbath; therefore He gives you bread for two
days on the sixth day. Remain every man in
his place; let no man go out of his place on
the seventh day."
30 So the people rested on the seventh
day.
31 The house of [a]Israel named it [1]manna,
and it was like [b]coriander seed, white, and
its taste was like wafers with honey.
32 Then Moses said, "This is [1]what the
LORD has commanded, 'Let an omerful of it
be kept throughout your generations, that
they may see the bread that I fed you in the
wilderness, when I brought you out of the
land of Egypt.' "
33 Moses said to Aaron, "[a]Take a jar and
put an omerful of manna in it, and place it
before the LORD to be kept throughout your
generations."
34 As the LORD commanded Moses, so
Aaron placed it before [a]the Testimony, to be
kept.
35 [a]The sons of Israel ate the manna forty
years, until they came to an inhabited land;
they ate the manna until they came to the
border of the land of Canaan.
36 (Now [a]an omer is a tenth of an
[1]ephah.)

Water in the Rock

17 Then all the congregation of the sons of
Israel journeyed by [1]stages from the
wilderness of [a]Sin, according to the [2]com-
mand of the LORD, and camped at [b]Rephi-
dim, and there was no water for the people
to drink.

16:12 *twilight.* See note on 12:6.
16:13 *quails came up.* For a similar incident see Num 11:31–33.
16:14 *fine flake-like thing.* See note on Num 11:7.
16:15 *What is it?* Manna (see v. 31) means "What is it?"
16:18 See 2 Cor 8:15, where Paul quotes the heart of the verse as an illustration of Christians who share with each other what they possess.
16:23 *sabbath.* The first occurrence of the word itself, though the principle of the seventh day as a day of rest and holiness is set forth in the account of creation (see note on Gen 2:3).
16:29 See note on v. 5.
16:31 *manna.* See note on Num 11:7.
16:33 *jar.* Said in Heb 9:4 to be made of gold.
16:34 *Testimony.* Anticipates the later description of the tablets containing the Ten Commandments as the "two tablets of the testimony" (31:18; 32:15; 34:29), which gave their name to the "ark of the testimony" (25:22; 26:33) in which they were placed (see 25:16,21) along with the jar of manna (see Heb 9:4; see also Rev 2:17 and note).
16:35 *ate the manna forty years . . . until they came to . . . Canaan.* The manna stopped at the time the Israelites celebrated their first Passover in Canaan (see Josh 5:10–12).
17:1 *journeyed by stages.* For the places to which they journeyed see Num 33:12–14. *Rephidim.* Probably either the Wadi Refayid or the Wadi Feiran, both near Jebel Musa (see note on 3:1) in southern Sinai.

2 Therefore the people [a]quarreled with Moses and said, "Give us water that we may drink." And Moses said to them, "[b]Why do you quarrel with me? [c]Why do you test the LORD?"

3 But the people thirsted there for water; and [1]they [a]grumbled against Moses and said, "Why, now, have you brought us up from Egypt, to kill [2]us and [3]our children and [3b]our livestock with thirst?"

4 So Moses cried out to the LORD, saying, "What shall I do to this people? A [a]little more and they will stone me."

5 Then the LORD said to Moses, "Pass before the people and take with you some of [a]the elders of Israel; and take in your hand your staff with which [b]you struck the Nile, and go.

6 "Behold, I will stand before you there on the rock at [a]Horeb; and [b]you shall strike the rock, and water will come out of it, that the people may drink." And Moses did so in the sight of the elders of Israel.

7 He named the place [1a]Massah and [2b]Meribah because of the quarrel of the sons of Israel, and because they [c]tested the LORD, saying, "Is the LORD among us, or not?"

Amalek Fought

8 Then [a]Amalek came and fought against Israel at [b]Rephidim.

9 So Moses said to [a]Joshua, "Choose men for us and go out, fight against Amalek. Tomorrow I will station myself on the top of the hill with [b]the staff of God in my hand."

10 Joshua did as Moses [1]told him, [2]and fought against Amalek; and Moses, Aaron, and [a]Hur went up to the top of the hill.

11 So it came about when Moses held his hand up, that Israel prevailed, and when he let his hand [1]down, Amalek prevailed.

12 But Moses' hands were heavy. Then they took a stone and put it under him, and he sat on it; and Aaron and Hur [a]supported his hands, one on one side and one on the other. Thus his hands were steady until the sun set.

13 So Joshua [1]overwhelmed Amalek and his people with the edge of the sword.

14 Then the LORD said to Moses, "[a]Write this in [1]a book as a memorial and [2]recite it to Joshua, [3]that [b]I will utterly blot out the memory of Amalek from under heaven."

15 Moses built an [a]altar and named it [b]The LORD is My Banner;

16 and he said, "[1a]The LORD has sworn; the LORD will have war against Amalek from generation to generation."

Jethro, Moses' Father-in-law

18 Now [a]Jethro, the priest of Midian, Moses' father-in-law, heard of all that God had done for Moses and for Israel His people, how the LORD had brought Israel out of Egypt.

2 Jethro, Moses' father-in-law, took Moses' wife [a]Zipporah, after he had sent her away,

3 and her [a]two sons, of whom [1]one was

2 [a]Ex 14:11; Num 20:2, 3, 13 [b]Ex 16:8 [c]Deut 6:16; Ps 78:18, 41; Matt 4:7; 1 Cor 10:9
3 [1]Lit *the people* [2]Lit *me* [3]Lit *my* [a]Ex 16:2, 3 [b]Ex 12:38
4 [a]Num 14:10; 1 Sam 30:6
5 [a]Ex 3:16, 18 [b]Ex 7:20
6 [a]Ex 3:1 [b]Num 20:10, 11; Deut 8:15; Neh 9:15; Ps 78:15; 105:41; 114:8; 1 Cor 10:4
7 [1]I.e. test [2]I.e. quarrel [a]Deut 6:16; 9:22; Ps 95:8 [b]Num 20:13, 24; 27:14; Ps 81:7 [c]Num 14:22; Deut 33:8
8 [a]Gen 36:12; Num 24:20; Deut 25:17-19; 1 Sam 15:2 [b]Ex 17:1
9 [a]Ex 24:13 [b]Ex 4:20
10 [1]Lit *said to* [2]Lit *to fight*
10 [a]Ex 24:14; 31:2
11 [1]Lit *rest*
12 [a]Is 35:3
13 [1]Lit *weakened*
14 [1]Lit *the book* [2]Lit *place it in the ears of* [3]Or *for* [a]Ex 24:4; 34:27; Num 33:2 [b]Deut 25:19; 1 Sam 15:3
15 [a]Ex 24:4 [b]Gen 22:14; Judg 6:24
16 [1]Or *Because a hand is against the throne of the LORD;* lit *Because a hand upon the throne of YAH* [a]Gen 22:16
18:1 [a]Ex 2:16, 18; 3:1 **2** [a]Ex 2:21; 4:25
3 [1]Lit *the name of the one was* [a]Ex 2:22; 4:20; Acts 7:29

17:2 *test the LORD.* Israel fails the Lord's testing of her (see 16:4) by putting the Lord to the test.
17:3 *grumbled.* See note on 15:24.
17:4 *this people.* The same note of distance and alienation ("this people" instead of "my people") in such situations (see also the interplay in 32:7, 9–11; 33:13) is found often in the prophets (see, e.g., Is 6:9; Hag 1:2).
17:6 *I will stand . . . there on the rock.* Paul may have had this incident in mind when he spoke of Christ as "a spiritual rock which followed" Israel (see 1 Cor 10:4; see also Heb 11:24–26). *Horeb.* See note on 3:1. *Strike the rock, and water will come out.* The event was later celebrated by Israel's hymn writers and prophets (see Ps 78:15–16,20; 105:41; 114:8; Is 48:21).
17:7 *Massah and Meribah.* Heb 3:7–8,15 (quoting Ps 95:7–8) gives the meaning "day of trial" for Massah and "provoked" for Meribah. Another Meribah, where a similar incident occurred near Kadesh-barnea (see note on Gen 14:7), is referred to in Num 20:13,24; 27:14; Deut 32:51; 33:8; Ps 81:7; 106:32; Ezek 47:19; 48:28.
17:8 *Amalek.* See note on Gen 14:7.
17:9 *Joshua.* The name given by Moses to Hoshea son of Nun (see Num 13:16). "Hoshea" means "salvation," while "Joshua" means "The LORD saves." The Greek form of the name Joshua is the same as that of the name Jesus. Joshua was from the tribe of Ephraim (Num 13:8), one of the most powerful of the 12 tribes (see notes on Gen 48:6,19). *fight against Amalek.* Joshua's military prowess uniquely suited him to be the conqueror of Canaan 40 years later, while his faith in God and loyalty to Moses suited him to be Moses' "servant" (24:13; 33:11) and successor (see Deut 1:38; 3:28; 31:14; 34:9; Josh 1:5).
17:10 *Hur.* Perhaps the same Hur who was the son of Caleb and the grandfather of Bezalel (see 1 Chr 2:19–20), one of the builders of the tabernacle (see 31:2–5).
17:11 *held his hand up.* A symbol of appeal to God for help and enablement (see note on 9:29; see also 9:22; 10:12; 14:16).
17:14 *Write.* See 24:4; 34:27–28; Num 33:2; Deut 28:58; 29:20,21,27; 30:10; 31:9,19,22,24; see also Introduction: Author and Date of Writing. *book.* Or "scroll," a long strip of leather or papyrus on which scribes wrote in columns (see Jer 36:23) with pen (see Is 8:1) and ink (see Jer 36:18), sometimes on both sides (see Ezek 2:10; Rev 5:1). After being rolled into a scroll, the "book" was often sealed (see Is 29:11; Dan 12:4; Rev 5:1–2,5,9) to protect its contents. Scrolls were of various sizes (see Is 8:1; Rev 10:2,9–10). Certain Egyptian examples reached lengths of over 100 feet; Biblical scrolls, however, rarely exceeded 30 feet in length, as in the case of a book like Isaiah (see Luke 4:17). Reading the contents of a scroll involved the awkward procedure of unrolling it with one hand while rolling it up with the other (see Is 34:4; Ezek 2:10; Luke 4:17,20; Rev 6:14). Shortly after the time of Christ the scroll gave way to the book form still used today.
17:15 *My Banner.* Recalling Moses' petition with upraised hands (see vv. 11–12,16) and testifying to the power of God displayed in defense of His people.
18:1 *Jethro, the priest of Midian.* See note on 2:16.
18:2 *sent her away.* Apparently Moses sent Zipporah to her father with the news that the Lord had blessed his mission (see v. 1) and that he was in the vicinity of Mount Sinai with Israel.

named Gershom, for Moses said, "I have been [b]a [2]sojourner in a foreign land."

4 [1]The other was named [2a]Eliezer, for *he said,* "[b]The God of my father was my help, and delivered me from the sword of Pharaoh."

5 Then Jethro, Moses' father-in-law, came with his sons and his wife to Moses [1]in the wilderness where he was camped, at [a]the mount of God.

6 He [1]sent word to Moses, "I, your father-in-law Jethro, am coming to you with your wife and her two sons with her."

7 Then Moses went out to meet his father-in-law, and [a]he bowed down and [b]kissed him; and they [c]asked each other of their welfare and went into the tent.

8 Moses told his father-in-law all that the LORD had done to Pharaoh and to the Egyptians [a]for Israel's sake, all the [b]hardship that had befallen them on the journey, and *how* [c]the LORD had delivered them.

9 Jethro rejoiced over all [a]the goodness which the LORD had done to Israel, [1]in delivering [2]them from the hand of the Egyptians.

10 So Jethro said, "[a]Blessed be the LORD who delivered you from the hand of the Egyptians and from the hand of Pharaoh, *and* who delivered the people from under the hand of the Egyptians.

11 "Now I know that [a]the LORD is greater than all the gods; [1]indeed, [b]it was proven when they dealt proudly against [2]the people."

12 [a]Then Jethro, Moses' father-in-law, took a burnt offering and sacrifices for God, and Aaron came with all the elders of Israel to eat [1]a meal with Moses' father-in-law before God.

13 It came about the next day that Moses sat to judge the people, and the people stood about Moses from the morning until the evening.

14 Now when Moses' father-in-law saw all that he was doing for the people, he said, "What is this thing that you are doing for the people? Why do you alone sit *as judge* and all the people stand about you from morning until evening?"

15 Moses said to his father-in-law, "Because the people come to me [a]to inquire of God.

16 "When they have a [1a]dispute, it comes to me, and I judge between a man and his neighbor and make known the statutes of God and His laws."

3 [2]Heb *ger* [b]Ex 2:22
4 [1]Lit *The name of the other was* [2]Heb *El-ezer;* i.e. my God is help [a]1 Chr 23:15, 17 [b]Gen 49:25
5 [1]Lit *unto* [a]Ex 3:1, 12; 4:27; 24:13
6 [1]Lit *said*
7 [a]Gen 43:26, 28 [b]Gen 29:13; Ex 4:27 [c]Gen 43:27; 2 Sam 11:7
8 [a]Ex 4:23; 7:4, 5 [b]Num 20:14; Neh 9:32 [c]Ex 15:6, 16
9 [1]Lit *in that He had delivered* [2]Lit *him* [a]Is 63:7-14
10 [a]Gen 14:20; 2 Sam 18:28; 1 Kin 8:56; Ps 68:19, 20
11 [1]Lit *indeed, in the thing in which they* [2]Lit *them* [a]Ex 12:12; 15:11; 2 Chr 2:5; Ps 95:3; 97:9; 135:5 [b]Luke 1:51
12 [1]Lit *bread* [a]Gen 31:54; Ex 24:5
15 [a]Num 9:6, 8; 27:5; Deut 17:8-13
16 [1]Lit *matter* [a]Ex 24:14
18 [1]Lit *this* [2]Lit *matter* [a]Num 11:14, 17; Deut 1:12 [b]Deut 1:9
19 [1]Lit *my voice* [2]Lit *You be for the people in front of God* [3]Lit *matters* [a]Num 27:5
20 [a]Deut 1:18; 4:1, 5; 5:1 [b]Ps 143:8
21 [1]Lit *see* [2]Lit *leaders of* [a]Ex 18:25; Deut 1:13, 15; 2 Chr 19:5-10; Ps 15:1-5; Acts 6:3 [b]Gen 42:18; 2 Sam 23:3 [c]Deut 16:19
22 [1]Lit *matter* [a]Deut 1:17, 18 [b]Num 11:17
23 [1]Lit *stand* [2]Lit *this* [3]Lit *his*
24 [1]Lit *to the voice of*
25 [1]Lit *leaders of* [a]Ex 18:21; Deut 1:15
26 [1]Lit *matter* [a]Ex 18:22
27 [1]Lit *sent off his father-in-law* [a]Num 10:29, 30

Jethro Counsels Moses

17 Moses' father-in-law said to him, "The thing that you are doing is not good.

18 "[a]You will surely wear out, both yourself and [1]these people who are with you, for the [2]task is too heavy for you; [b]you cannot do it alone.

19 "Now listen to [1]me: I will give you counsel, and God be with you. [2]You be the people's representative before God, and you [a]bring the [3]disputes to God,

20 [a]then teach them the statutes and the laws, and make known to them [b]the way in which they are to walk and the work they are to do.

21 "Furthermore, you shall [1]select out of all the people [a]able men [b]who fear God, men of truth, those who [c]hate dishonest gain; and you shall place *these* over them *as* leaders of thousands, [2]of hundreds, [2]of fifties and [2]of tens.

22 "Let them judge the people at all times; and let it be [a]that every major [1]dispute they will bring to you, but every minor [1]dispute they themselves will judge. So it will be easier for you, and [b]they will bear *the burden* with you.

23 "If you do this thing and God *so* commands you, then you will be able to [1]endure, and all [2]these people also will go to [3]their place in peace."

24 So Moses listened [1]to his father-in-law and did all that he had said.

25 Moses chose [a]able men out of all Israel and made them heads over the people, leaders of thousands, [1]of hundreds, [1]of fifties and [1]of tens.

26 They judged the people at all times; [a]the difficult [1]dispute they would bring to Moses, but every minor [1]dispute they themselves would judge.

27 Then Moses [1a]bade his father-in-law farewell, and he went his way into his own land.

Moses on Sinai

19 [a]In the third month after the sons of Israel had gone out of the land of Egypt, [1]on that very day they came into the wilderness of [b]Sinai.

2 When they set out from [a]Rephidim, they came to the wilderness of Sinai and camped in the wilderness; and there Israel camped in front of [b]the mountain.

19:1 [1]Lit *on this day* [a]Ex 12:6, 51; 16:1 [b]Deut 1:6; 4:10, 15; 5:2
2 [a]Ex 17:1; Num 33:15 [b]Ex 3:1, 12; 18:5

18:5 *mount of God.* See 3:1 and note.
18:11 *Now I know that the LORD is greater than all the gods.* See the similar confession of Naaman in 2 Kin 5:15.
18:12 *took.* The verb means "provided" an animal for sacrifice (see, e.g., 25:2; Lev 12:8), not "officiated at" a sacrifice. *eat a meal with.* A token of friendship (contrast the battle with the Amalekites, 17:8–16). Such a meal often climaxed the establishment of a treaty (see Gen 31:54; Ex 24:11).
18:15 *to inquire of God.* Usually by going to a place of worship (see Gen 25:22 and note; Num 27:21) or to a prophet (see 1 Sam 9:9; 1 Kin 22:8).
18:16 *statutes of God and His laws.* The process of compiling and systematizing the body of divine law that would govern the newly formed nation of Israel may have already begun (see 15:25–26 and note on Gen 26:5).
18:21 *men who fear God.* See note on Gen 20:11.
19:2 *wilderness of Sinai.* Located in the southeast region of the peninsula (see note on 3:1). The narrator locates there the

3 Moses went up to God, and [a]the LORD called to him from the mountain, saying, "Thus you shall say to the house of Jacob and tell the sons of Israel:

4 '[a]You yourselves have seen what I did to the Egyptians, and *how* I bore you on [b]eagles' wings, and brought you to Myself.

5 'Now then, [a]if you will indeed obey My voice and [b]keep My covenant, then you shall be [c]My [1]own possession among all the peoples, for [d]all the earth is Mine;

6 and you shall be to Me [a]a kingdom of priests and [b]a holy nation.' These are the words that you shall speak to the sons of Israel."

7 [a]So Moses came and called the elders of the people, and set before them all these words which the LORD had commanded him.

8 [a]All the people answered together and said, "All that the LORD has spoken we will do!" And Moses brought back the words of the people to the LORD.

9 The LORD said to Moses, "Behold, I will come to you in [a]a thick cloud, so that the [b]people may hear when I speak with you and may also believe in you forever." Then Moses told the words of the people to the LORD.

10 The LORD also said to Moses, "Go to the people and [a]consecrate them today and tomorrow, and let them [b]wash their garments;

11 and let them be ready for the third day, for on [a]the third day the LORD will come down on Mount Sinai in the sight of all the people.

12 "You shall set bounds for the people all around, saying, '[1]Beware that you do not go up on the mountain or touch the border of it; [a]whoever touches the mountain shall surely be put to death.

13 'No hand shall touch him, but [a]he shall surely be stoned or [1]shot through; whether beast or man, he shall not live.' When the ram's horn sounds a long blast, they shall come up to [b]the mountain."

14 So Moses went down from the mountain to the people and consecrated the people, and they washed their garments.

15 He said to the people, "Be ready for the third day; do not go near a woman."

16 [a]So it came about on the third day, when it was morning, that there were [1]thunder and lightning flashes and a thick cloud upon the mountain and a very loud trumpet sound, so that all the people who *were* in the camp trembled.

17 And Moses brought the people out of the camp to meet God, and they stood at the [1]foot of the mountain.

The LORD Visits Sinai

18 [a]Now Mount Sinai *was* all in smoke because the LORD descended upon it [b]in fire; and its smoke ascended like [c]the smoke of a furnace, and [d]the whole mountain [1]quaked violently.

19 When the sound of the trumpet grew louder and louder, Moses spoke and [a]God answered him with [1]thunder.

20 [a]The LORD came down on Mount Sinai, to the top of the mountain; and the LORD called Moses to the top of the mountain, and Moses went up.

21 Then the LORD spoke to Moses, "Go down, [1]warn the people, so that [a]they do not break through to the LORD to gaze, and many of them [2]perish.

22 "Also let the [a]priests who come near to the LORD consecrate themselves, or else the LORD will break out against them."

23 Moses said to the LORD, "The people cannot come up to Mount Sinai, for You

3 [a]Ex 3:4
4 [a]Deut 29:2 [b]Deut 32:11; Rev 12:14
5 [1]Or *special treasure* [a]Ex 15:26; Deut 5:2f [b]Ps 78:10 [c]Deut 4:20; 7:6; 14:2; 26:18; Ps 135:4; Titus 2:14; 1 Pet 2:9 [d]Ex 9:29; Deut 10:14; Job 41:11; Ps 50:12; 1 Cor 10:26
6 [a]1 Pet 2:5, 9; Rev 1:6; 5:10 [b]Deut 7:6; 14:21; 26:19; Is 62:12
7 [a]Ex 4:29, 30
8 [a]Ex 4:31; 24:3, 7; Deut 5:27; 26:17
9 [a]Ex 19:16; 24:15, 16; Deut 4:11; Ps 99:7 [b]Deut 4:12, 36
10 [a]Lev 11:44, 45 [b]Gen 35:2; Lev 15:5; Num 8:7, 21; 19:19; Rev 22:14
11 [a]Ex 19:16
12 [1]Lit *Take heed to yourselves* [a]Heb 12:20
13 [1]I.e. with arrows [a]Heb 12:20
13 [b]Ex 19:17
16 [1]Lit *sounds* [a]Heb 12:18, 19, 21
17 [1]Lit *lower part*
18 [1]Or *trembled* [a]Deut 4:11; Ps 104:32; 144:5 [b]Ex 3:2; 24:17; Deut 5:4; 2 Chr 7:1-3; Heb 12:18 [c]Gen 15:17; 19:28 [d]Judg 5:5; Ps 68:7, 8; Jer 4:24
19 [1]Or *a voice;* lit *a sound* [a]Ps 81:7
20 [a]Neh 9:13
21 [1]Lit *testify to* [2]Lit *fall* [a]Ex 3:5; 1 Sam 6:19 **22** [a]Ex 19:24; 24:5; Lev 10:3; 21:6-8

events recorded in the rest of Exodus, all of Leviticus, and Num 1:1–10:10.

19:3 *Jacob . . . Israel.* See note on 1:1.

19:4 *I bore you on eagles' wings.* The description best fits the female golden eagle.

19:5 *if . . . then.* The covenant between God and Israel at Mount Sinai is the outgrowth and extension of the Lord's covenant with Abraham and his descendants 600 years earlier (see chart, p. 16). Participation in the divine blessings is conditioned on obedience added to faith (see note on Gen 17:9). *My covenant.* See note on Gen 9:9. *My own possession among all the peoples.* The equivalent phrases used of Christians in 1 Pet 2:9 are "chosen race" and "people for God's own possession" (see Deut 7:6; 14:2; 26:18; Ps 135:4; Mal 3:17). *all the earth is Mine.* God is the Creator and Possessor of the earth and everything in it (see Gen 14:19,22; Ps 24:1–2).

19:6 *kingdom of priests.* Israel was to constitute the Lord's kingdom (the people who acknowledged Him as their King) and, like priests, was to be wholly consecrated to His service (see Is 61:6; cf. 1 Pet 2:5; Rev 1:6; 5:10; 20:6). *holy nation.* See 1 Pet 2:9. God's people, both individually and collectively, are to be set apart (see note on 3:5) to do His will (see Deut 7:6; 14:2,21; 26:19; Is 62:12).

19:8 *All that the LORD has spoken we will do.* The people promised to obey the terms of the covenant (see 24:3,7; Deut 5:27).

19:9 *thick cloud.* See 13:21 and note. *the people may hear when I speak.* See Deut 4:33. *may . . . believe in you forever.* See 14:31 and note.

19:10–11 Outward preparation to meet God symbolizes the inward consecration God requires of His people.

19:12–13 The whole mountain becomes holy because of God's presence (see 3:5 and note). Israel must keep herself from the mountain even as she is to keep herself from the tabernacle (see Num 3:10).

19:15 *do not go near a woman.* Not because sex is sinful but because it may leave the participants ceremonially unclean (see Lev 15:18; see also 1 Sam 21:4–5).

19:16 *thunder . . . lightning . . . loud trumpet sound.* God's appearance is often accompanied by an impressive display of meteorological sights and sounds (see, e.g., 1 Sam 7:10; 12:18; Job 38:1; 40:6; Ps 18:13–14). *thick cloud.* See 13:21 and note.

19:18 *fire . . . smoke of a furnace.* See Gen 15:17 and note.

19:22 *priests.* See also v. 24. Before the Aaronic priesthood was established (see 28:1), priestly functions were performed either by the elders (see note on 3:16; see also 3:18; 12:21; 18:12) or by designated younger men (see 24:5). But perhaps the verse

[1]warned us, saying, '[a]Set bounds about the
mountain and consecrate it.' "
24 Then the LORD said to him, "[1]Go down
and come up *again,* [a]you and Aaron with
you; but do not let the [b]priests and the people break through to come up to the LORD, or
He will break forth upon them."
25 So Moses went down to the people and
told them.

The Ten Commandments

20 Then God spoke all these words, saying,
2 "[a]I am the LORD your God, [b]who
brought you out of the land of Egypt, out of
the house of [1]slavery.
3 "[a]You shall have no other [b]gods [1]before
Me.
4 "[a]You shall not make for yourself [1]an
idol, or any likeness of what is in heaven
above or on the earth beneath or in the water
under the earth.
5 "[a]You shall not worship them or serve
them; for I, the LORD your God, am a [b]jealous
God, [c]visiting the iniquity of the fathers on
the children, on the third and the fourth generations of those who hate Me,
6 but showing lovingkindness to [a]thou-
sands, to those who love Me and keep My
commandments.
7 "[a]You shall not take the name of the LORD
your God in vain, for the LORD will not [1]leave
him unpunished who takes His name in vain.
8 "Remember [a]the sabbath day, to keep it
holy.
9 "[a]Six days you shall labor and do all
your work,
10 but the seventh day is a sabbath of the
LORD your God; *in it* [a]you shall not do any
work, you or your son or your daughter, your
male or your female servant or your cattle or
your sojourner who [1]stays with you.
11 "[a]For in six days the LORD made the
heavens and the earth, the sea and all that is
in them, and rested on the seventh day;
therefore the LORD blessed the sabbath day
and made it holy.

23 [1]Lit *testified to* [a]Ex 19:12 **24** [1]Lit *Go, descend* [a]Ex 24:1, 9, 12 [b]Ex 19:22 **20:2** [1]Lit *slaves* [a]Lev 26:1; Deut 5:6; Ps 81:10 [b]Ex 13:3; 15:13, 16; Deut 7:8 **3** [1]Or *besides Me* [a]Deut 6:14; 2 Kin 17:35; Jer 25:6; 35:15 [b]Ex 15:11; 20:23 **4** [1]Or *a graven image* [a]Lev 19:4; 26:1; Deut 4:15-19; 27:15 **5** [a]Ex 23:24; Josh 23:7; 2 Kin 17:35 [b]Ex 34:14; Deut 4:24; Josh 24:19; Nah 1:2 [c]Ex 34:6, 7; Num 14:18, 33; Deut 5:9, 10; 1 Kin 21:29; Jer 32:18 **6** [a]Deut 7:9 **7** [1]Or *hold him guiltless* [a]Lev 19:12; Deut 6:13; 10:20

8 [a]Ex 23:12; 31:13-16; Lev 26:2; Deut 5:12 **9** [a]Ex 34:21; 35:2, 3; Lev 23:3; Deut 5:13; Luke 13:14 **10** [1]Lit *is in your gates* [a]Neh 13:16-19 **11** [a]Gen 2:2, 3; Ex 31:17

anticipates the regulations for the Aaronic priests who will be appointed. *who come near to the LORD.* To officiate at sacrifices (see 40:32; Lev 21:23).

20:1–17 See Deut 5:6–21; see also Matt 5:21,27; 19:17–19; Mark 10:19; Luke 18:20; Rom 13:9; Eph 6:2–3.

20:1 *words.* A technical term for "(covenant) stipulations" in the ancient Near East (e.g., among the Hittites; see also 24:3,8; 34:28). The basic code in Israel's divine law is found in vv. 2–17, elsewhere called the "Ten Commandments" (34:28; Deut 4:13; 10:4), the Hebrew words for which mean lit. "Ten Words." "Decalogue," a term of Greek origin often used as a synonym for the Ten Commandments, also means lit. "Ten Words."

20:2 *I am the LORD your God, who brought you out.* The Decalogue reflects the structure of the contemporary royal treaties (see note on Gen 15:7). On the basis of (1) a preamble, in which the great king identified himself ("I am the LORD your God"), and (2) a historical prologue, in which he sketched his previous gracious acts toward the subject king or people ("who brought you out . . ."), the Lord then set forth (3) the treaty (covenant) stipulations (see Deut 5:1–3,7–21) to be obeyed (in this case, ten in number: vv. 3–17). Use of this ancient royal treaty pattern shows that the Lord is here formally acknowledged as Israel's King and that Israel is His subject people. As His subjects, His covenant people are to render complete submission, allegiance and obedience to Him out of gratitude for His mercies, reverence for His sovereignty, and trust in His continuing care. See chart, p. 16.

20:3 *before.* The Hebrew for this word is translated "in hostility toward" in Gen 16:12; 25:18. Something of that sense may be intended here. In any event, no deity, real or imagined, is to rival the one true God in Israel's heart and life.

20:4 *idol, or any likeness.* Because God has no visible form, any idol intended to resemble Him would be a sinful misrepresentation of Him (see Deut 4:12,15–18). Since other gods are not to be worshiped (see v. 5), making idols of them would be equally sinful (see Deut 4:19,23–28).

20:5 *jealous God.* God will not put up with rivalry or unfaithfulness. Usually His "jealousy" concerns Israel and assumes the covenant relationship (analogous to marriage) and the Lord's exclusive right to possess Israel and to claim her love and allegiance. Actually, jealousy is part of the vocabulary of love. The "jealousy" of God (1) demands exclusive devotion to Himself (see 34:14; Deut 4:24; 32:16,21; Josh 24:19; Ps 78:58; 1 Cor 10:22; James 4:5), (2) delivers to judgment all who oppose Him (see Deut 29:20; 1 Kin 14:22; Ps 79:5; Is 42:13; 59:17; Ezek 5:13; 16:38; 23:25; 36:5; Nah 1:2; Zeph 1:18; 3:8) and (3) vindicates His people (see 2 Kin 19:31; Is 9:7; 26:11; Ezek 39:25; Joel 2:18; Zech 1:14; 8:2). In some of these passages the meaning is closer to "zeal" (the same Hebrew word may be translated either way, depending on context). *on the third and fourth generations of those who hate Me.* Those Israelites who blatantly violate God's covenant and thus show that they reject the Lord as their King will bring down judgment on themselves and their households (see, e.g., Num 16:31–34; Josh 7:24 and note)—households were usually extended to "three or four" generations. See note on Ps 109:12. *hate.* In covenant contexts the terms "hate" and "love" (v. 6) were conventionally used to indicate rejection of or loyalty to the covenant Lord.

20:6 *to thousands, to those.* See 1 Chr 16:15; Ps 105:8. *love Me and keep My commandments.* See John 14:15; 1 John 5:3. In the treaty language of the ancient Near East the "love" owed to the great king was a conventional term for total allegiance and implicit trust expressing itself in obedient service.

20:7 *take the name of the LORD . . . in vain.* By profaning God's name—e.g., by swearing falsely by it (see Lev 19:12; see also Jer 7:9), as on the witness stand in court. Jesus elaborates on oath-taking in Matt 5:33–37.

20:8 See Gen 2:3. *sabbath.* See note on 16:23. *holy.* See note on 3:5.

20:9 *Six days.* The question of a shorter "work week" in a modern industrialized culture is not in view.

20:10 *in it you shall not do any work.* Two reasons (one here and one in Deuteronomy) are given: (1) Having completed His work of creation God "rested on the seventh day" (v. 11), and the Israelites are to observe the same pattern in their service of God in the creation; (2) the Israelites must cease all labor so that their servants can also participate in the Sabbath-rest—just as God had delivered His people from the burden of slavery in Egypt (see Deut 5:14–15). The Sabbath thus became a "sign" of the covenant between God and Israel at Mount Sinai (see 31:12–17; see also note on Gen 9:12).

12 "[a]Honor your father and your mother, that your [b]days may be prolonged in the land which the LORD your God gives you.

13 "[a]You shall not murder.

14 "[a]You shall not commit adultery.

15 "[a]You shall not steal.

16 "[a]You shall not bear false witness against your [b]neighbor.

17 "[a]You shall not covet your neighbor's house; [b]you shall not covet your neighbor's wife or his male servant or his female servant or his ox or his donkey or anything that belongs to your neighbor."

18 [a]All the people perceived the [1]thunder and the lightning flashes and the sound of the trumpet and the mountain smoking; and when the people saw *it,* they trembled and stood at a distance.

19 [a]Then they said to Moses, "Speak [1]to us yourself and we will listen; but let not God speak [1]to us, or we will die."

20 Moses said to the people, "[a]Do not be afraid; for God has come in order [b]to test you, and in order that [c]the fear of Him may [1]remain with you, so that you may not sin."

21 So the people stood at a distance, while Moses approached [a]the thick cloud where God *was.*

22 Then the LORD said to Moses, "Thus you shall say to the sons of Israel, 'You yourselves have seen that [a]I have spoken [1]to you from heaven.

23 '[a]You shall not make *other gods* besides Me; [b]gods of silver or gods of gold, you shall not make for yourselves.

24 'You shall make [a]an altar of earth for Me, and you shall sacrifice on it your [b]burnt offerings and your [c]peace offerings, [d]your sheep and your oxen; in every place [e]where I cause My name to be remembered, I will come to you and bless you.

25 'If you make an altar of stone for Me, [a]you shall not build it of cut stones, for if you wield your tool on it, you will profane it.

26 'And you shall not go up by steps to My altar, so that [a]your nakedness will not be exposed on it.'

Ordinances for the People

21 "Now these are the [a]ordinances which you are to set before them:

2 "If you buy [a]a Hebrew slave, he shall serve for six years; but on the seventh he shall go out as a free man without payment.

3 "If he comes [1]alone, he shall go out [1]alone; if he is the husband of a wife, then his wife shall go out with him.

4 "If his master gives him a wife, and she bears him sons or daughters, the wife and

12 [a]Lev 19:3; Deut 27:16; Matt 15:4; 19:19; Mark 7:10; 10:19; Luke 18:20; Eph 6:2 [b]Deut 5:16, 33; 6:2; 11:8, 9; Jer 35:7
13 [a]Gen 9:6; Ex 21:12; Lev 24:17; Matt 5:21; 19:18; Mark 10:19; Luke 18:20; Rom 13:9; James 2:11
14 [a]Lev 20:10; Deut 5:18; Matt 5:27; 19:18; Rom 13:9
15 [a]Ex 21:16; Lev 19:11, 13; Matt 19:18; Rom 13:9
16 [a]Ex 23:1, 7; Deut 5:20; Matt 19:18 [b]Lev 19:18
17 [a]Deut 5:21; Rom 7:7; 13:9; Eph 5:3, 5 [b]Prov 6:29; Matt 5:28
18 [1]Lit *sounds* [a]Ex 19:16, 18; Heb 12:18, 19
19 [1]Lit *with* [a]Deut 5:5, 23-27; Gal 3:19; Heb 12:19
20 [1]Lit *be before* [a]Ex 14:13; Is 41:10, 13 [b]Ex 15:25; Deut 13:3 [c]Deut 4:10; 6:24; Prov 3:7; 16:6; Is 8:13
21 [a]Ex 19:16; Deut 5:22

22 [1]Lit *with* [a]Deut 4:36; 5:24, 26; Neh 9:13 **23** [a]Ex 20:3 [b]Ex 32:1, 2, 4; Deut 29:17 **24** [a]Ex 20:25; 27:1-8 [b]Ex 10:25; 18:12 [c]Ex 24:5; Lev 1:2 [d]Deut 12:5; 16:6, 11; 26:2; 2 Chr 6:6 [e]Deut 12:5; 26:2 **25** [a]Deut 27:5, 6; Josh 8:31 **26** [a]Ex 28:42, 43
21:1 [a]Ex 24:3, 4; Deut 4:14; 6:1 **2** [a]Lev 25:39-43; Deut 15:12-18; Jer 34:14 **3** [1]Lit *by himself*

20:12 *Honor.* (1) Prize highly (see Prov 4:8), (2) care for (see Ps 91:15), (3) show respect for (see Lev 19:3; 20:9), and (4) obey (see Deut 21:18–21; cf. Eph 6:1). *that your days may be prolonged.* "The first commandment with a promise" (Eph 6:2). See also note on Deut 6:2.

20:13 See Matt 5:21–26. *murder.* The Hebrew for this verb usually refers to a premeditated and deliberate act.

20:14 See Matt 5:27–30. *adultery.* A sin "against God" (Gen 39:9) as well as against the marriage partner.

20:17 *covet.* Desire something with evil motivation (see Matt 15:19). To break God's commandments inwardly is equivalent to breaking them outwardly (see Matt 5:21–30).

20:18–21 Concludes the account of the giving of the Decalogue. The order of the narrative appears to be different from the order of events, since v. 18 is most likely a continuation of 19:25. On this reading, the proclamation of the Decalogue took place after Moses approached God (v. 21). Biblical writers often did not follow chronological sequence in their narratives for various literary reasons. The purpose of chronological displacement here may have been either (1) to keep the Decalogue distinct from the "book of the covenant" (24:7) that follows (20:22–23:19), or (2) to conclude the account with the formal institution of Moses' office as covenant mediator—or both.

20:19 See Heb 12:19–20. Israel requests a mediator to stand between them and God, a role fulfilled by Moses and subsequently by priests, prophets and kings—and ultimately by Jesus Christ (see 1 Tim 2:5).

20:20 *Do not be afraid.* Do not think that God's display of His majesty is intended simply to fill you with abject fear. He has come to enter into covenant with you as your heavenly King. *test.* See note on Gen 22:1. *fear of Him.* See note on Gen 20:11.

20:22–23:19 The stipulations of the "book of the covenant" (24:7), consisting largely of expansions on and expositions of the Ten Commandments. See chart, p. 255.

20:22–26 Initial stipulations governing Israel's basic relationship with God (cf. v. 3).

20:22 *heaven.* God's dwelling place. Even on "top of the mountain" (19:20) God spoke from heaven.

20:23 See vv. 3–4. The contrast between the one true God "in the heavens," who "does whatever He pleases" (Ps 115:3), and idols of silver or gold, who can do nothing at all (see Ps 115:4–7; see also Ps 135:5–6,15–17), is striking indeed.

20:24 *altar of earth.* Such an altar, with dimensions the same as those of the altar in the tabernacle (see 27:1), has been found in the excavated ruins of a small Iron Age (10th, or possibly 11th, century B.C.) Israelite temple at Arad in southern Israel. *burnt offerings.* See note on Lev 1:3. *peace offerings.* See note on Lev 3:1. *every place.* The numerous temporary places of worship (see, e.g., Josh 8:30–31; Judg 6:24; 21:4; 1 Sam 7:17; 14:35; 2 Sam 24:25; 1 Kin 18:30).

20:25 *you shall not build it of cut stones.* Many ancient altars of undressed stones (from various periods) have been found in Israel. *if you wield your tool on it, you will profane it.* For reasons not now clear, but perhaps related to pagan practices.

20:26 *steps.* The oldest stepped altar known in Israel is at Megiddo and dates between 3000 and 2500 B.C. *nakedness ... be exposed.* Men who ascended to such altars would expose their nakedness in the presence of God. Although Aaron and his descendants served at stepped altars (see Lev 9:22; Ezek 43:17), they were instructed to wear linen undergarments (see 28:42–43; Lev 6:10; 16:3–4; Ezek 44:17–18).

21:2–11 See Jer 34:8–22.

21:2 *Hebrew.* See note on Gen 14:13. *on the seventh he shall go out as a free man.* The Lord's servants are not to be anyone's perpetual slaves (see 20:10 and note).

her children shall belong to her master, and
he shall go out [1]alone.
5 "But [a]if the slave plainly says, 'I love my
master, my wife and my children; I will not
go out as a free man,'
6 then his master shall bring him to
[1]God, then he shall bring him to the door or
the doorpost. And his master shall pierce his
ear with an awl; and he shall serve him permanently.
7 "[a]If a man sells his daughter as a female
slave, she is not to [1]go free [b]as the male
slaves [1]do.
8 "If she is [1]displeasing in the eyes of her
master [2]who designated her for himself, then
he shall let her be redeemed. He does not
have authority to sell her to a foreign people
because of his [3]unfairness to her.
9 "If he designates her for his son, he shall
deal with her according to the custom of
daughters.
10 "If he takes to himself another woman,
he may not reduce her [1]food, her clothing, or
[a]her conjugal rights.
11 "If he will not do these three *things* for
her, then she shall go out for nothing, without *payment of* money.

Personal Injuries

12 "[a]He who strikes a man so that he dies
shall surely be put to death.
13 "[a]But [1]if he did not lie in wait *for him,*
but [b]God let *him* fall into his hand, then I will
appoint you a place to which he may flee.
14 "[a]If, however, a man acts presumptuously toward his neighbor, so as to kill him
craftily, you are to take him *even* from My
altar, that he may die.
15 "He who strikes his father or his mother
shall surely be put to death.
16 "[a]He who [1]kidnaps a man, whether he
sells him or he is found in his [2]possession,
shall surely be put to death.
17 "[a]He who curses his father or his mother shall surely be put to death.

4 [1]Lit *by himself*
5 [a]Deut 15:16, 17
6 [1]Or *the judges who acted in God's name*
7 [1]Lit *go out* [a]Neh 5:5 [b]Ex 21:2, 3
8 [1]Lit *bad* [2]Another reading is *so that he did not designate her* [3]Lit *dealing treacherously*
10 [1]Lit *flesh* [a]1 Cor 7:3, 5
12 [a]Gen 9:6; Lev 24:17; Num 35:30; Matt 26:52
13 [1]Lit *he who* [a]Num 35:10-34; Deut 19:1-13; Josh 20:1-9 [b]1 Sam 24:4, 10, 18
14 [a]Deut 19:11, 12; 1 Kin 2:28-34
16 [1]Lit *steals* [2]Lit *hand* [a]Deut 24:7
17 [a]Lev 20:9; Prov 20:20; Matt 15:4; Mark 7:10
18 [1]Lit *lies*
19 [1]Lit *his sitting* [2]Lit *healing, he shall cause to be healed*
20 [1]Lit *under* [2]Lit *suffer vengeance*
21 [1]Lit *stands* [2]Lit *money* [a]Lev 25:44-46
22 [1]Or *an untimely birth occurs;* lit *her children come out* [2]Lit *lays on him* [3]Lit *by arbitration* [a]Ex 21:30; Deut 22:18, 19
23 [a]Lev 24:19; Deut 19:21
24 [a]Lev 24:20; Deut 19:21; Matt 5:38
25 [1]Lit *welt*
27 [1]Lit *causes to fall*

18 "If men have a quarrel and one strikes
the other with a stone or with *his* fist, and he
does not die but [1]remains in bed,
19 if he gets up and walks around outside
on his staff, then he who struck him shall go
unpunished; he shall only pay for his [1]loss of
time, and [2]shall take care of him until he is
completely healed.
20 "If a man strikes his male or female
slave with a rod and he dies [1]at his hand, he
shall [2]be punished.
21 "If, however, he [1]survives a day or two,
no vengeance shall be taken; [a]for he is his
[2]property.
22 "If men struggle with each other and
strike a woman with child so that [1]she gives
birth prematurely, yet there is no injury, he
shall surely be fined as the woman's husband [2]may demand of him, and he shall
[a]pay [3]as the judges *decide.*
23 "But if there is *any further* injury, [a]then
you shall appoint *as a penalty* life for life,
24 [a]eye for eye, tooth for tooth, hand for
hand, foot for foot,
25 burn for burn, wound for wound,
[1]bruise for bruise.
26 "If a man strikes the eye of his male or
female slave, and destroys it, he shall let him
go free on account of his eye.
27 "And if he [1]knocks out a tooth of his
male or female slave, he shall let him go free
on account of his tooth.
28 "If an ox gores a man or a woman [1]to
death, [a]the ox shall surely be stoned and its
flesh shall not be eaten; but the owner of the
ox shall go unpunished.
29 "If, however, an ox was previously in
the habit of goring and its owner has been
warned, yet he does not confine it and it kills
a man or a woman, the ox shall be stoned
and its owner also shall be put to death.
30 "If a ransom is [1]demanded of him, then
he shall give for the redemption of his life
whatever is [1]demanded of him.

28 [1]Lit *so that he dies* [a]Gen 9:5; Ex 21:32 **30** [1]Lit *laid on him*

21:6 *God.* Or "the judges" (see 22:8–9,28). *pierce his ear with an awl.* See Deut 15:17. Submission to this rite symbolized willing service (see Ps 40:6–8 and note on Ps 40:6).

21:12–15 See 20:13 and note; see also Num 35:16–34; Deut 19:1–13; 21:1–9; 24:7; 27:24–25; Josh 20:1–9.

21:12 See Gen 9:6 and note.

21:13 *did not lie in wait for him.* Related terms and expressions are "unintentionally" (Num 35:11), "without enmity" (Num 35:22), "was not his enemy" (Num 35:23), "not seeking his injury" (Num 35:23) and "not hating him previously" (Deut 19:4). Premeditated murder is thus distinguished from accidental manslaughter. *God let him fall into his hand.* The event is beyond human control—in modern legal terminology, an "act of God." *place.* A city of refuge (see Num 35:6–32; Deut 19:1–13; Josh 20:1–9; 21:13,21,27,32,38).

21:14 *even from My altar.* The horns of the altar were a final refuge for those subject to judicial action (see 1 Kin 1:50–51; 2:28; Amos 3:14 and notes).

21:15 See 20:12.

21:16 See 20:15.

21:19 *walks around outside on his staff.* Is convalescing in a satisfactory way. *his loss of time.* Lit. "his sitting," i.e., his enforced idleness.

21:20–21 Benefit of doubt was granted to the slaveholder where no homicidal intentions could be proved.

21:23–25 See Deut 19:21. The so-called law of retaliation, as its contexts show, was meant to limit the punishment to fit the crime. By invoking the law of love, Jesus corrected the popular misunderstanding of the law of retaliation (see Matt 5:38–42). See note on Lev 24:20.

21:23 *any further injury.* Either to mother or to child.

21:26–27 Humane applications of the law of retaliation.

21:28–32 The law of the goring ox.

21:28 *the ox shall surely be stoned.* By killing someone, the ox becomes accountable for that person's life (see Gen 9:5).

21:30 *If a ransom is demanded.* If the victim's family is willing to accept a ransom payment instead of demanding the death penalty. *he shall give for the redemption of his life.* The ransom is not to compensate the victim's family but to save the negligent man's life.

31 "Whether it gores a son or [1]a daughter, it shall be done to him according to [2]the same rule.

32 "If the ox gores a male or female slave, [1]the owner shall give his *or her* master [a]thirty shekels of silver, and the ox shall be stoned.

33 "If a man opens a pit, or [1]digs a pit and does not cover it over, and an ox or a donkey falls into it,

34 the owner of the pit shall make restitution; he shall [1]give money to its owner, and the dead *animal* shall become his.

35 "If one man's ox hurts another's so that it dies, then they shall sell the live ox and divide its price equally; and also they shall divide the dead *ox*.

36 "Or *if* it is known that the ox was previously in the habit of goring, yet its owner has not confined it, he shall surely pay ox for ox, and the dead *animal* shall become his.

Property Rights

22 "[1]If a man steals an ox or a sheep and slaughters it or sells it, he shall pay five oxen for the ox and [a]four sheep for the sheep.

2 "[1]If the [a]thief is [2]caught while breaking in and is struck so that he dies, there will be no bloodguiltiness on his account.

3 "*But* if the sun has risen on him, there will be bloodguiltiness on his account. He shall surely make restitution; if he owns nothing, then he shall be [a]sold for his theft.

4 "If what he stole is actually found alive in his [1]possession, whether an ox or a donkey or a sheep, [a]he shall pay double.

5 "If a man lets a field or vineyard be grazed *bare* and lets his animal loose so that it grazes in another man's field, he shall make restitution from the best of his own field and the best of his own vineyard.

6 "If a fire breaks out and spreads to thorn bushes, so that stacked grain or the standing grain or the field *itself* is consumed, he who started the fire shall surely make restitution.

7 "[a]If a man gives his neighbor money or goods to keep *for him* and it is stolen from the man's house, if the thief is [1]caught, he shall pay double.

8 "If the thief is not [1]caught, then the owner of the house shall [2]appear before [3][a]the judges, *to* determine whether he [4]laid his hands on his neighbor's property.

9 "For every [1]breach of trust, *whether it is* for ox, for donkey, for sheep, for clothing, *or* for any lost thing about which one says, 'This is it,' the [2]case of both parties shall come before [3][a]the judges; he whom [3]the judges condemn shall pay double to his neighbor.

10 "If a man gives his neighbor a donkey, an ox, a sheep, or any animal to keep *for him*, and it dies or is hurt or is driven away while no one is looking,

11 an [a]oath before the LORD shall be made by the two of them [1]that he has not [2]laid hands on his neighbor's property; and its owner shall accept *it*, and he shall not make restitution.

12 "But if it is actually stolen from him, he shall make restitution to its owner.

13 "If it is all torn to pieces, let him bring it as evidence; he shall not make restitution for what has been torn to pieces.

14 "If a man [1]borrows *anything* from his neighbor, and it is injured or dies while its owner is not with it, he shall make full restitution.

15 "If its owner is with it, he shall not make restitution; if it is hired, it came for its hire.

Sundry Laws

16 "[a]If a man seduces a virgin who is not engaged, and lies with her, he must pay a dowry for her *to be* his wife.

17 "If her father absolutely refuses to give her to him, he shall [1]pay money equal to the [a]dowry for virgins.

18 "You shall not allow a [a]sorceress to live.

19 "[a]Whoever lies with an animal shall surely be put to death.

20 "[a]He who sacrifices to [1]any god, other than to the LORD alone, shall be [2]utterly destroyed.

21 "[a]You shall not wrong a stranger or oppress him, for you were strangers in the land of Egypt.

22 "[a]You shall not afflict any widow or orphan.

31 [1]Lit *gores a daughter* [2]Lit *this judgment*
32 [1]Lit *he* [a]Zech 11:12; Matt 26:15; 27:3, 9
33 [1]Lit *if a man digs*
34 [1]Lit *give back*
22:1 [1]Ch 21:37 in Heb [a]2 Sam 12:6; Luke 19:8
2 [1]Ch 22:1 in Heb [2]Lit *found* [a]Matt 6:19; 24:43; 1 Pet 4:15
3 [a]Matt 18:25
4 [1]Lit *hand* [a]Ex 22:7
7 [1]Lit *found* [a]Lev 6:1-7
8 [1]Lit *found* [2]Lit *approach to* [3]Or *God* [4]Lit *stretched his hand* [a]Ex 22:9; Deut 17:8, 9; 19:17
9 [1]Or *matter of transgression* [2]Lit *matter* [3]Or *God* [a]Ex 22:8, 28; Deut 25:1
11 [1]Lit *whether* [2]Lit *stretched his hand* [a]Heb 6:16
14 [1]Lit *asks*
16 [a]Deut 22:28, 29
17 [1]Lit *weigh out silver* [a]Gen 34:12; 1 Sam 18:25
18 [a]Lev 19:31; 20:6, 27; Deut 18:10, 11; 1 Sam 28:3; Jer 27:9, 10
19 [a]Lev 18:23; 20:15, 16; Deut 27:21
20 [1]Lit *the gods* [2]Lit *put under the ban* [a]Ex 32:8; 34:15; Lev 17:7; Num 25:2; Deut 17:2, 3, 5; 1 Kin 18:40; 2 Kin 10:25
21 [a]Ex 23:9; Lev 19:33, 34; 25:35; Deut 1:16; 10:19; 27:19; Zech 7:10
22 [a]Deut 24:17, 18; Prov 23:10, 11; Jer 7:6, 7

21:32 *thirty shekels of silver.* Apparently the standard price for a slave. It was also the amount Judas was willing to accept as his price for betraying Jesus (see Matt 26:14–15; see also Zech 11:12–13). *shekels.* See note on Gen 20:16.
21:33–36 Laws concerning injuries to animals.
22:1–15 Laws concerning property rights (see 20:15).
22:2 An act of self-defense in darkness does not produce bloodguilt.
22:3 Killing an intruder in broad daylight is not justifiable.
22:5 *from the best.* Restitution should always err on the side of quality and generosity.
22:6 *thorn bushes.* Often used as hedges (see Mic 7:4) bordering cultivated areas.
22:11 See 20:7 and note. *an oath before the LORD.* The judges were God's representatives in court cases (see 21:6; 22:8–9,28).
22:12–13 Similar laws apparently existed as early as the patriarchal period (see Gen 31:39).
22:16–31 General laws related to social obligations.
22:16 *dowry.* A gift, usually substantial, given by the prospective groom to the bride's family as payment for her (see Gen 24:53). The custom is still followed today in parts of the Middle East.
22:18 See Deut 18:10,14; 1 Sam 28:9; Is 47:12–14.
22:19 Ancient myths and epics describe acts of bestiality performed by pagan gods and demigods in Babylon and Canaan.
22:20 See 20:3–5. The total destruction (see NASB marg.) of the idolatrous Canaanites was later commanded by the Lord (see Num 21:2; Deut 2:34; 3:6; 7:2; 13:15; 20:17; Josh 2:10; 6:17,21; 8:25; 10:1,28,35,37,39–40; 11:11–12,20–21; Judg 1:17).
22:21–27 That the poor, the widow, the orphan, the alien—in

23 “If you afflict him at all, *and* [a]if he does
cry out to Me, [b]I will surely hear his cry;
24 and My anger will be kindled, and I
will kill you with the sword, [a]and your wives
shall become widows and your children
fatherless.
25 “[a]If you lend money to My people, to
the poor [1]among you, you are not to [2]act as
a creditor to him; you shall not [3]charge him
[b]interest.
26 “If you ever take your neighbor’s cloak
[a]as a pledge, you are to return it to him
before the sun sets,
27 for that is his only covering; it is his
cloak for his [1]body. What else shall he sleep
in? And it shall come about that [a]when he
cries out to Me, I will hear *him,* for [b]I am
gracious.
28 “You shall not [1a]curse God, [b]nor curse a
ruler of your people.
29 “[a]You shall not delay *the offering from*
[1]your harvest and your vintage. [b]The firstborn of your sons you shall give to Me.
30 “[a]You shall do the same with your oxen
and with your sheep. It shall be with its
mother seven days; [b]on the eighth day you
shall give it to Me.
31 “[a]You shall be holy men to Me, therefore
[b]you shall not eat *any* flesh torn to pieces in
the field; you shall throw it to the dogs.

Sundry Laws

23 “[a]You shall not bear a false report; do
not join your hand with a wicked man
to be a [b]malicious witness.
2 “You shall not follow [1]the masses in
doing evil, nor shall you [2]testify in a dispute
so as to turn aside after [1]a multitude in order
to [a]pervert *justice;*
3 [a]nor shall you [1]be partial to a poor man
in his dispute.
4 “[a]If you meet your enemy’s ox or his
donkey wandering away, you shall surely
return it to him.
5 “[a]If you see the donkey of one who
hates you lying *helpless* under its load, you
shall refrain from leaving it to him, you shall
surely release *it* with him.
6 “[a]You shall not pervert the justice *due* to
your needy *brother* in his dispute.
7 “[a]Keep far from a false charge, and [b]do
not kill the innocent or the righteous, for [c]I
will not acquit the guilty.
8 “[a]You shall not take a bribe, for a bribe
blinds the clear-sighted and [1]subverts the
cause of the just.
9 “[a]You shall not oppress a [1]stranger,
since you yourselves know the [2]feelings of a
[1]stranger, for you *also* were [1]strangers in the
land of Egypt.

The Sabbath and Land

10 “[a]You shall sow your land for six years
and gather in its yield,
11 but *on* the seventh year you shall let it
[1]rest and lie fallow, so that the needy of your
people may eat; and whatever they leave the
beast of the field may eat. You are to do the
same with your vineyard *and* your olive
grove.
12 “[a]Six days you are to do your work, but
on the seventh day you shall cease *from
labor* so that your ox and your donkey may
rest, and the son of your female slave, as
well as [1]your stranger, may refresh themselves.
13 “Now [a]concerning everything which I
have said to you, be on your guard; and [b]do
not mention the name of other gods, nor let
them be heard [1]from your mouth.

Three National Feasts

14 “[a]Three times a year you shall celebrate
a feast to Me.

23 [a]Deut 15:9; Job 35:9; Luke 18:7 [b]Deut 10:18; Job 34:28; Ps 10:14, 17, 18; 18:6; 68:5; James 5:4 **24** [a]Ps 109:2, 9 **25** [1]Lit *with* [2]Lit *be* [3]Lit *lay upon* [a]Lev 25:35-37; Deut 15:7-11 [b]Deut 23:19, 20; Neh 5:7; Ps 15:5; Ezek 18:8 **26** [a]Deut 24:6, 10-13; Job 24:3; Prov 20:16; Amos 2:8 **27** [1]Lit *skin* [a]Ex 22:23 [b]Ex 34:6 **28** [1]Or *revile* [a]Lev 24:15, 16 [b]Eccl 10:20; Acts 23:5 **29** [1]Lit *your fullness and your tears* [a]Ex 23:16, 19; Deut 26:2-11; Prov 3:9 [b]Ex 13:2, 12 **30** [a]Deut 15:19; Lev 22:27 [b]Gen 17:12; Lev 12:3 **31** [a]Ex 19:6; Lev 11:44; 19:2 [b]Lev 7:24; 17:15; Ezek 4:14 **23:1** [a]Ex 20:16; Lev 19:11f; Deut 5:20; Ps 101:5; Prov 10:18 [b]Deut 19:16-21; Ps 35:11; Prov 19:5; Acts 6:11 **2** [1]Lit *many men* [2]Or *answer* [a]Deut 16:19; 24:17 **3** [1]Lit *honor* [a]Ex 23:6; Lev 19:15; Deut 1:17; 16:19 **4** [a]Deut 22:1-4 **5** [a]Deut 22:4 **6** [a]Ex 23:2, 3; Lev 19:15 **7** [a]Ex 20:16; Ps 119:29; Eph 4:25 [b]Ex 20:13; Deut 27:25 [c]Ex 34:7; Deut 25:1; Rom 1:18 **8** [1]Or *distorts the words* [a]Deut 10:17; 16:19; Prov 15:27; 17:8, 23; Is 5:22, 23 **9** [1]Or *sojourner(s)* [2]Lit *soul* [a]Ex 22:21; Lev 19:33f; Deut 24:17f; 27:19 **10** [a]Lev 25:1-7 **11** [1]Lit *drop* **12** [1]Lit *the sojourner* [a]Ex 20:8-11; 31:15; 34:21; 35:2, 3; Lev 23:3; Deut 5:13f **13** [1]Lit *on* [a]Deut 4:9, 23; 1 Tim 4:16 [b]Josh 23:7; Ps 16:4; Hos 2:17 **14** [a]Ex 23:17; 34:22-24; Deut 16:16

fact, all defenseless people—are objects of God’s special concern and providential care is clear from the writings of Moses (see 21:26–27; 23:6–12; Lev 19:9–10; Deut 14:29; 16:11,14; 24:19–21; 26:12–13), the psalmists (see Ps 10:14,17–18; 68:5; 82:3; 146:9) and the prophets (see Is 1:23; 10:2; Jer 7:6; 22:3; Zech 7:10; Mal 3:5) as well as from the teachings of Jesus (see, e.g., Matt 25:34–45).

22:25–27 Laws dealing with interest on loans (see Lev 25:35–37; Deut 15:7–11; 23:19–20; see also Neh 5:7–12; Job 24:9; Prov 28:8; Ezek 18:13; 22:12). Interest for profit was not to be charged at the expense of the poor. Generosity in such matters was extended even further by Jesus (see Luke 6:34–35).

22:26–27 If all that a man had to offer as his pledge for a loan was his cloak, he was among the poorest of the poor (see Amos 2:8 and note).

22:28 *not curse God.* Or “not revile the judges.” *nor curse a ruler of your people.* A ruler was God’s representative; quoted by a penitent Paul after he had unwittingly insulted the high priest (see Acts 23:4–5).

22:29 *firstborn . . . give to Me.* See notes on 4:22; 13:2,13; see also 13:15.

22:30 *do the same with your oxen and with your sheep.* See notes on 13:2; 13:13; see also 13:12,15. *on the eighth day you shall give it to Me.* The same principle applied in a different way to firstborn sons as well (see note on Gen 17:12).

22:31 Since God’s people were “a kingdom of priests” (see 19:6 and note), they were to obey a law later specified for members of the Aaronic priesthood (see Lev 22:8) as well.

23:1–9 Most of the regulations in this section pertain to 20:16.

23:1 See Lev 19:16; Deut 22:13–19; 1 Kin 21:10–13.

23:4–5 Those hostile to you are to be shown the same consideration as others (see Deut 22:1–4; Prov 25:21). Jesus teaches that this means “love your enemies” (Matt 5:44).

23:7 1 Kin 21:10–13 is a vivid illustration of violation of this law.

23:8 See Deut 16:19. Samuel exemplifies faithful stewardship in this regard (see 1 Sam 12:3), while his sons do not (see 1 Sam 8:3).

23:10–13 Extensions of the principles taught in 20:8–11; Deut 5:12–15.

23:14–19 See 34:18–26; Lev 23:4–44; Num 28:16–29:40; Deut 16:1–17.

15 "You shall observe [a]the Feast of Unleavened Bread; for seven days you are to eat
unleavened bread, as I commanded you, at
the appointed time in the [b]month Abib, for
in it you came out of Egypt. And [1c]none shall
appear before Me empty-handed.
16 "Also *you shall observe* [a]the Feast of the
Harvest *of* the first fruits of your labors *from*
what you sow in the field; also the Feast of
the Ingathering at the end of the year [b]when
you gather in *the fruit of* your labors from the
field.
17 "[a]Three times a year all your males shall
appear before the Lord [1]GOD.
18 "[a]You shall not offer the blood of My sacrifice with leavened bread; [b]nor is the fat of
My [1]feast to remain overnight until morning.
19 "You shall bring [a]the choice first fruits of
your soil into the house of the LORD your
God.
"[b]You are not to boil a young goat in the
milk of its mother.

Conquest of the Land

20 "Behold, I am going to send [a]an angel
before you to guard you along the way and
[b]to bring you into the place which I have
prepared.
21 "Be on your guard before him and obey
his voice; [a]do not be rebellious toward him,
for he will not pardon your transgression,
since [b]My name is in him.
22 "But if you truly obey his voice and do
all that I say, then [a]I will be an enemy to
your enemies and an adversary to your
adversaries.
23 "[a]For My angel will go before you and
bring you in to *the land of* the Amorites, the
Hittites, the Perizzites, the Canaanites, the
Hivites and the Jebusites; and I will completely destroy them.
24 "[a]You shall not worship their gods, nor
serve them, nor do according to their deeds;
[b]but you shall utterly overthrow them and
break their [c]*sacred* pillars in pieces.
25 "[a]But you shall serve the LORD your God,
[1]and He will bless your bread and your water;
and [b]I will remove sickness from your midst.
26 "There shall be no one miscarrying or
[a]barren in your land; [b]I will fulfill the number of your days.
27 "I will [a]send My terror ahead of you,
and [b]throw into confusion all the people
among whom you come, and I will [c]make all
your enemies turn *their* backs to you.
28 "I will send [a]hornets ahead of you so
that they will [b]drive out the Hivites, the
Canaanites, and the Hittites before you.
29 "[a]I will not drive them out before you in
a single year, that the land may not become
desolate and the beasts of the field become
too numerous for you.
30 "I will drive them out before you [a]little
by little, until you become fruitful and take
possession of the land.
31 "[a]I will fix your boundary from the [1]Red
Sea to the sea of the Philistines, and from the
wilderness to the River *Euphrates;* [b]for I will
deliver the inhabitants of the land into your
hand, and you will [c]drive them out before
you.
32 "[a]You shall [1]make no covenant with
them [b]or with their gods.

15 [1]Lit *they...not* [a]Ex 12:14-20; Lev 23:6-8; Num 28:16-25 [b]Ex 12:2; 13:4 [c]Ex 22:29; 34:20 **16** [a]Ex 34:22; Lev 23:10; Num 28:26 [b]Lev 23:39 **17** [1]Heb *YHWH,* usually rendered *LORD* [a]Ex 23:14; 34:23; Deut 16:16 **18** [1]Or *festival* [a]Ex 34:25; Lev 2:11 [b]Ex 12:10; Lev 7:15; Deut 16:4 **19** [a]Ex 22:29; 34:26; Deut 26:2, 10; Neh 10:35; Prov 3:9 [b]Deut 14:21 **20** [a]Ex 3:2; 14:19; 23:23; 32:34; 33:2 [b]Ex 15:16, 17 **21** [a]Deut 9:7; Ps 78:40, 56 [b]Ex 3:14; 6:3; 34:5-7 **22** [a]Gen 12:3; Num 24:9; Deut 30:7 **23** [a]Ex 23:20; Josh 24:8, 11 **24** [a]Ex 20:5; 23:13, 33; Deut 12:30f [b]Num 33:52; Deut 7:5; 12:3; 2 Kin 18:4 [c]Ex 34:13; Lev 26:1; 2 Kin 3:2 **25** [1]Or *that He may bless* [a]Lev 26:3-13; Deut 6:13; 10:12; 28:1-14; Josh 22:5; 1 Sam 12:20; Matt 4:10 [b]Ex 15:26; Deut 7:15

26 [a]Deut 7:14 [b]Deut 4:40; Job 5:26 **27** [a]Gen 35:5; Ex 15:16; Deut 2:25; Josh 2:9 [b]Deut 7:23 [c]Ps 18:40; 21:12 **28** [a]Deut 7:20; Josh 24:12 [b]Ex 33:2; 34:11 **29** [a]Deut 7:22 **30** [a]Deut 7:22 **31** [1]Lit *Sea of Reeds* [a]Gen 15:18; Deut 1:7, 8; 11:24 [b]Deut 2:36; Josh 21:44 [c]Josh 24:12, 18 **32** [1]Lit *cut* [a]Ex 34:12; Deut 7:2 [b]Ex 23:13, 24

23:15 *Feast of Unleavened Bread.* Celebrated from the 15th through the 21st days of the first month (usually about mid-March to mid-April; see note on 12:2) at the beginning of the barley harvest; it commemorated the exodus.
23:16 *Feast of the Harvest.* Also called the "Feast of Weeks" (34:22) because it was held seven weeks after the Feast of Unleavened Bread. It was celebrated on the sixth day of the third month (usually about mid-May to mid-June) during the wheat harvest. In later Judaism it came to commemorate the giving of the law on Mount Sinai, though there is no evidence of this significance in the OT. In NT times it was called "(the day of) Pentecost" (Acts 2:1; 20:16; 1 Cor 16:8), which means "50" (see Lev 23:16). *Feast of the Ingathering.* Also called the "Feast of Booths" (Lev 23:34) because the Israelites lived in temporary shelters when God brought them out of Egypt (see Lev 23:43). It was celebrated from the 15th through the 22nd days of the seventh month (usually about mid-September to mid-October) when the produce of the orchards and vines had been harvested; it commemorated the wilderness wanderings after the exodus. *end of the year.* End of the agricultural year, which began in the fall (see note on 12:2).
23:17 *all your males.* Normally accompanied by their families (see, e.g., 1 Sam 1).
23:18 *not . . . with leavened bread.* See note on 12:15. *nor . . . remain overnight until morning.* See 12:9–10.
23:19 *first fruits.* Representative of the whole harvest. The offering of first fruits was an acknowledgment that the harvest was from the Lord and belonged wholly to Him. *You are not to boil a young goat in the milk of its mother.* Perhaps a protest against a Canaanite pagan ritual (see v. 33; 34:15).
23:20 *angel.* See 14:19; see also note on Gen 16:7. *place . . . I have prepared.* Canaan (cf. the similar statement of Jesus in John 14:2–3).
23:21 *name.* Representing God's presence.
23:22 *if.* See note on 19:5.
23:23 See 3:8 and note.
23:28 *hornets.* The meaning of the Hebrew for this word is uncertain. The Septuagint (the Greek translation of the OT) renders it "wasp," but the translators may have been guessing. In any event, the Lord promises to send some agent to disable or frighten the peoples of Canaan so that they will not be able to resist Israel's invasion. But probably the word involves concrete imagery and the focus of the statement is on the effects—therefore we are not to look for some historical agent to which the word metaphorically refers (cf. Is 7:18).
23:30 *little by little.* See Judg 1.
23:31 See Gen 15:18; 1 Kin 4:21. *Red Sea.* The (south)eastern border (here the modern Gulf of Aqaba; see note on 1 Kin 9:26). *sea of the Philistines.* The western border (the Mediterranean). *the wilderness.* The southern border (northeastern Sinai; see note on Gen 15:18). *the River.* The northern border (the Euphrates River).

33 "[a]They shall not live in your land,
because they will make you sin against Me;
for *if* you serve their gods, [b]it will surely be
a snare to you."

People Affirm Their Covenant with God

24 Then He said to Moses, "[a]Come up to
the LORD, you and Aaron, [b]Nadab and
Abihu and [c]seventy of the elders of Israel,
and you shall worship at a distance.
2 "Moses alone, however, shall come near
to the LORD, but they shall not come near,
nor shall the people come up with him."
3 Then Moses came and recounted to the
people all the words of the LORD and all the
[1]ordinances; and all the people answered
with one voice and said, "[a]All the words
which the LORD has spoken we will do!"
4 [a]Moses wrote down all the words of
the LORD. Then he arose early in the morning, and built an [b]altar [1]at the foot of the
mountain with twelve pillars for the twelve
tribes of Israel.
5 He sent young men of the sons of Israel, [a]and they offered burnt offerings and sacrificed young bulls as peace offerings to the
LORD.
6 [a]Moses took half of the blood and put
it in basins, and the *other* half of the blood
he sprinkled on the altar.
7 Then he took [a]the book of the covenant
and read *it* in the hearing of the people; and
they said, "[b]All that the LORD has spoken we
will do, and we will be obedient!"
8 So [a]Moses took the blood and sprinkled
it on the people, and said, "Behold [b]the blood
of the covenant, which the LORD has [1]made
with you [2]in accordance with all these
words."
9 Then Moses went up [1]with Aaron,
[a]Nadab and Abihu, and seventy of the elders
of Israel,
10 and [a]they saw the God of Israel; and
under His feet [1][b]there appeared to be a pavement of sapphire, [2]as clear as the sky itself.
11 Yet He did not stretch out His hand
against the nobles of the sons of Israel; and
[a]they saw God, and they ate and drank.
12 Now the LORD said to Moses, "Come up
to Me on the mountain and [1]remain there,
and [a]I will give you the stone tablets [2]with
the law and the commandment which I have
written for their instruction."
13 So Moses arose [1]with [a]Joshua his [2]ser-
vant, and Moses went up to [b]the mountain
of God.
14 But to the elders he said, "[a]Wait here
for us until we return to you. And behold,
[b]Aaron and Hur are with you; whoever [1]has
a legal matter, let him approach them."
15 Then Moses went up to the mountain,
and [a]the cloud covered the mountain.
16 [a]The glory of the LORD [1]rested on
Mount Sinai, and the cloud covered it for six
days; and on the seventh day He [b]called to
Moses from the midst of the cloud.
17 [a]And to the eyes of the sons of Israel
the appearance of the glory of the LORD was
like a [b]consuming fire on the mountain top.
18 Moses entered the midst of the cloud [1]as
he went up to the mountain; and Moses was
on the mountain [a]forty days and forty nights.

33 [a]Deut 7:1-5, 16 [b]Ex 34:12; Deut 12:30; Josh 23:13; Judg 2:3; Ps 106:36
24:1 [a]Ex 19:24 [b]Ex 6:23; 28:1; Lev 10:1, 2 [c]Num 11:16
3 [1]Or *judgments* [a]Ex 19:8; 24:7; Deut 5:27
4 [1]Lit *under* [a]Ex 17:14; 34:27; Deut 31:9 [b]Ex 17:15
5 [a]Ex 18:12
6 [a]Heb 9:18
7 [a]Ex 24:4; Heb 9:19 [b]Ex 24:3
8 [1]Lit *cut* [a]Heb 9:19, 20 [b]Zech 9:11; Matt 26:28; Mark 14:24; Luke 22:20; 1 Cor 11:25; Heb 13:20
8 [2]Lit *on all*
9 [1]Lit *and* [a]Ex 24:1
10 [1]Lit *like a pavement* [2]Lit *and as* [a]Ex 24:11; Num 12:8; Is 6:5; John 1:18; 6:46 [b]Ezek 1:26; 10:1; Rev 4:3
11 [a]Gen 16:13; 32:30; Ex 24:10
12 [1]Lit *be* [2]Lit *and* [a]Ex 31:18; 32:15; Deut 5:22
13 [1]Lit *and* [2]Or *minister* [a]Ex 17:9-14; 33:11 [b]Ex 3:1
14 [1]Lit *is a master of matters* [a]Gen 22:5 [b]Ex 17:10, 12
15 [a]Ex 19:9
16 [1]Lit *dwelt* [a]Ex 16:10; Num 14:10 [b]Ps 99:7
17 [a]Ex 3:2; Ezek 1:28 [b]Deut 4:24; 9:3; Heb 12:29
18 [1]Lit *and* [a]Ex 34:28; Deut 9:9; 10:10

23:33 *snare.* A symbol of destruction (see 10:7; Job 18:9; Ps 18:5; Prov 13:14; 21:6; Is 24:17–18).
24:1 *Come up.* The action, temporarily interrupted for the book of the covenant (20:22–23:33), is resumed from 20:21. Moses and his associates would ascend the mountain after the events of vv. 3–8. *Nadab and Abihu.* Aaron's two oldest sons. Nadab would have succeeded Aaron as high priest, but he and his brother died because they offered unauthorized fire before the Lord (see Lev 10:1–2; Num 3:4). *seventy . . . elders.* Cf. Num 11:16; perhaps representing Jacob's 70 descendants (see 1:5; Gen 46:27 and note). *elders.* See note on 3:16. *at a distance.* See 20:21.
24:2 *Moses alone.* The mediator between God and the people of Israel. Jesus, who is greater than Moses (see Heb 3:1–6), is the "mediator of a new covenant" (Heb 12:24).
24:3 *words.* Probably refers to the Ten Commandments (see 20:1 and note). *ordinances.* Probably refers to the stipulations of the book of the covenant (21:1–23:19). *we will do.* See v. 7; see also 19:8 and note.
24:4 *Moses wrote.* See note on 17:14; see also Introduction: Author and Date of Writing. *twelve pillars for.* See Josh 4:5,20; 1 Kin 18:31.
24:5 *young men . . . offered.* See note on 19:22.
24:6 *half of the blood . . . the other half.* The division of the blood points to the twofold aspect of the "blood of the covenant" (v. 8): The blood on the altar symbolizes God's forgiveness and His acceptance of the offering; the blood on the people points to an oath that binds them in obedience (see vv. 3,7).
24:7 *book of the covenant.* Strictly speaking, 20:22–23:19 (see note there)—but here implying also the stipulations of 20:2–17; 23:20–33. *we will do . . . we will be obedient.* See v. 3; see also 19:8 and note.
24:8 Only after the people agreed to obey the Lord could they participate in His covenant with them. *blood of the covenant.* See Mark 14:24 and note.
24:9 *went up.* See v. 1 and note.
24:10 *saw . . . God.* But not in the fullness of His glory (see 33:20; see also notes on 3:6; Gen 16:13; Num 12:8; Ezek 1:28). *sapphire.* Or "lapis lazuli." *sky.* Symbolized by the blue color of the "lapis lazuli" (see Ezek 1:26).
24:11 *stretch out His hand against.* See 9:15. *nobles.* Lit. "corners," "corner supports"; used in the sense of "nobles" only here. Cf. Gal 2:9. *ate and drank.* A covenant meal (cf. Gen 26:30; 31:54), celebrating the sealing of the covenant described in vv. 3–8. It foreshadows the Lord's Supper, which celebrates the new covenant sealed by Christ's death (see 1 Cor 11:25–26).
24:12 *Come up.* See note on v. 1. *stone tablets.* See note on 31:18. *their.* The people's. *instruction.* As instruction from the covenant Lord, the laws were divine directives.
24:13 *Joshua his servant.* See note on 17:9.
24:14 *Hur.* See note on 17:10.
24:17 *glory of the LORD.* See 16:10.
24:18 *was on the mountain.* Moses did not come down until he had received instructions concerning the tabernacle and its furnishings (see 32:15). *forty days and forty nights.* Jesus, the new Moses (see note on v. 2), fasted for the same length of time (see Matt 4:2).

Offerings for the Sanctuary

25 Then the LORD spoke to Moses, saying,
2 "[a]Tell the sons of Israel to [1]raise a
[2]contribution for Me; [b]from every man
whose heart moves him you shall [1]raise My
[2]contribution.
3 "This is the [1]contribution which you are
to [2]raise from them: gold, silver and bronze,
4 [1][a]blue, purple and scarlet *material,* fine
linen, goat *hair,*
5 rams' skins dyed red, porpoise skins,
acacia wood,
6 [a]oil for lighting, [b]spices for the anointing oil and for the fragrant incense,
7 onyx stones and setting stones for the
[a]ephod and for the [1][b]breastpiece.
8 "Let them [a]construct a sanctuary for
Me, [b]that I may dwell among them.
9 "[a]According to all that I am going to
show you, *as* the pattern of the tabernacle
and the pattern of all its furniture, just so you
shall construct *it.*

Ark of the Covenant

10 "[a]They shall construct an ark of acacia
wood two and a half [1]cubits [2]long, and one
and a half cubits [3]wide, and one and a half
cubits [4]high.
11 "You shall [a]overlay it with pure gold,
inside and out you shall overlay it, and you
shall make a gold molding [1]around it.
12 "You shall cast four gold rings for it and
[1]fasten them on its four feet, and two rings
shall be on one side of it and two rings on
the other side of it.
13 "You shall make poles of acacia wood
and overlay them with gold.
14 "You shall put the poles into the rings on
the sides of the ark, to carry the ark with them.
15 "The [a]poles shall [1]remain in the rings of
the ark; they shall not be removed from it.
16 "You shall [a]put into the ark the testimony which I shall give you.
17 "You shall [a]make a [1]mercy seat of pure
gold, two and a half [2]cubits [3]long and one
and a half cubits [4]wide.
18 "You shall make two cherubim of gold,
make them of hammered work [1]at the two
ends of the mercy seat.
19 "Make one cherub [1]at one end and one
cherub [1]at the other end; you shall make the
cherubim *of one piece* with the mercy seat at
its two ends.

25:2 [1]Lit *take* [2]Or *heave offering* [a]Ex 35:4-9 [b]Ex 35:21; 1 Chr 29:3, 5, 9; Ezra 2:68; 2 Cor 8:11, 12; 9:7 **3** [1]Or *heave offering* [2]Lit *take* **4** [1]Or *violet* [a]Ex 28:5, 6, 8 **6** [a]Ex 27:20 [b]Ex 30:23f **7** [1]Or *pouch* [a]Ex 28:4, 6-14 [b]Ex 28:4, 15-30 **8** [a]Ex 36:1-5 [b]Ex 29:45, 46; Num 5:3; Deut 12:11; 1 Kin 6:13; 2 Cor 6:16; Rev 21:3 **9** [a]Ex 25:40; 26:30; Acts 7:44; Heb 8:2, 5 **10** [1]I.e. One cubit equals approx 18 in. [2]Lit *its length* [3]Lit *its width* [4]Lit *its height* [a]Ex 37:1-9; Deut 10:3; Heb 9:4

11 [1]Lit *on it round about* [a]Heb 9:4 **12** [1]Or *put* **15** [1]Lit *be* [a]1 Kin 8:8 **16** [a]Ex 40:20; Deut 10:2; 31:26; 1 Kin 8:9; Heb 9:4 **17** [1]Lit *propitiatory*, and so through v 22 [2]I.e. One cubit equals approx 18 in. [3]Lit *its length* [4]Lit *its width* [a]Ex 37:6 **18** [1]Lit *from* **19** [1]Lit *from*

25:2 *contribution.* Here refers to a voluntary contribution.
25:4 *blue, purple and scarlet.* Royal colors. *blue, purple.* Dyes derived from various shellfish (primarily the *murex*) that swarm in the waters of the northeast Mediterranean. So important for the local economy was the dyeing industry that the promised land was known as Canaan (which means "land of purple"), later called Phoenicia (also meaning "land of purple") by the Greeks. *scarlet.* Derived from the eggs and carcasses of the worm *Coccus ilicis,* which attaches itself to the leaves of the holly plant. *fine linen.* A very high quality cloth (often used by Egyptian royalty) made from thread spun from the fibers of flax straw. The Hebrew for this term derives ultimately from Egyptian. Excellent examples of unusually white, tightly woven linen have been found in ancient Egyptian tombs. Some are so finely woven that they cannot be distinguished from silk without the use of a magnifying glass. *goat hair.* From long-haired goats. A coarse, black (cf. Song 1:5; 6:5) material, it was often used to weave cloth for tents.
25:5 *rams' skins dyed red.* After all the wool had been removed from the skins. The final product was similar to present-day morocco leather. *porpoise.* Native to the Red Sea. *acacia.* The wood is darker and harder than oak and is avoided by wood-eating insects. It is common in the Sinai peninsula.
25:6 *spices.* Those used in the anointing oil are identified in 30:23–24 as myrrh (balsam sap), cinnamon (bark of the cinnamon tree, a species of laurel), cane (pith from the root of a reed plant) and cassia (made from dried flowers of the cinnamon tree). Those used in the fragrant incense are identified in 30:34 as stacte (a powder taken from the middle of hardened drops of myrrh—rare and very valuable), onycha (made from mollusk shells) and galbanum (a rubbery resin taken from the roots of a flowering plant that thrives in Syria and Persia).
25:7 *setting stones.* See 28:17–20.
25:8 *sanctuary.* Lit. "holy place," "place set apart." See note on 3:5.
25:9 *tabernacle.* Lit. "dwelling place." The word is rarely used of human dwellings; it almost always signifies the place where God dwells among His people (see v. 8; 29:45–46; Lev 26:11; Ezek 37:27; cf. John 1:14; Rev 21:3). *pattern.* See note on v. 40.
25:10 *ark.* See v. 14. That is, "chest" (such was its form and function). The Hebrew for this word is translated by the more traditional term "ark" throughout the rest of Exodus (see note on Deut 10:1–3); it is different from that used to refer to Noah's ark and to the reed basket in which the infant Moses was placed (see note on 2:3). Of all the tabernacle furnishings, the ark is mentioned first probably because it symbolized the throne of the Lord (see 1 Sam 4:4; 2 Sam 6:2), the great King, who chose to dwell among His people (see note on v. 9).
25:11 *pure gold.* Uncontaminated by silver or other impurities.
25:12 *rings.* Lit. "houses," "housings," into which poles were inserted to carry the ark (see v. 14).
25:16 *testimony.* The two tablets on which were inscribed the Ten Commandments as the basic stipulations of the Sinai covenant (see 20:1–17; 31:18). The Hebrew word for "testimony" is related to a Babylonian word meaning "covenant stipulations." See also notes on v. 22; 16:34.
25:17 *mercy.* Or "atonement." It speaks of reconciliation, the divine act of grace whereby God draws to Himself and makes "at one" with Him those who were once alienated from Him. In the OT, the shed blood of sacrificial offerings effected atonement (see Lev 17:11 and note); in the NT, the blood of Jesus, shed once for all time, does the same (see Rom 3:25; 1 John 2:2). *mercy seat.* Or "atonement cover" (see note on Lev 16:2). That God's symbolic throne was capped with an atonement cover signified His great mercy toward His people—only such a God can be revered (see Ps 130:3–4).
25:18 *cherubim.* Probably similar to the carvings of winged sphinxes that adorned the armrests of royal thrones (see note on v. 10) in many parts of the ancient Near East (see also note on Gen 3:24). In the OT the cherubim were symbolic attendants that marked the place of the Lord's "enthronement" in His earthly kingdom (see 1 Sam 4:4; 2 Sam 6:2; 2 Kin 19:15; Ps 99:1). From the cover of the ark (God's symbolic throne) the Lord gave directions to Moses (see v. 22; Num 7:89). Later the ark's presence in

20 “[a]The cherubim shall have *their* wings spread upward, covering the mercy seat with their wings and [1]facing one another; the faces of the cherubim are to be *turned* toward the mercy seat.

21 “[a]You shall put the mercy seat [1]on top of the ark, and [b]in the ark you shall put the testimony which I will give to you.

22 “[a]There I will meet with you; and from above the mercy seat, from [b]between the two cherubim which are upon the ark of the testimony, I will speak to you about all that I will give you in commandment for the sons of Israel.

The Table of Showbread

23 “[a]You shall make a table of acacia wood, two cubits [1]long and one cubit [2]wide and one and a half cubits [3]high.

24 “You shall overlay it with pure gold and make a gold [a]border around it.

25 “You shall make for it a rim of a handbreadth around *it;* and you shall make a gold border for the rim around it.

26 “You shall make four gold rings for it and put rings on the four corners which are on its four feet.

27 “The rings shall be close to the rim as holders for the poles to carry the table.

28 “You shall make the poles of acacia wood and overlay them with gold, so that with them the table may be carried.

29 “You shall make its [1][a]dishes and its pans and its jars and its [2]bowls with which to pour drink offerings; you shall make them of pure gold.

30 “You shall set [a]the bread of the [1]Presence on the table before Me [2]at all times.

The Golden Lampstand

31 “[a]Then you shall make a lampstand of pure gold. The lampstand *and* its base and its shaft are to be made of hammered work; its cups, its [1]bulbs and its flowers shall be *of one piece* with it.

32 “[a]Six branches shall go out from its sides; three branches of the lampstand from its one side and three branches of the lampstand from its [1]other side.

33 “[a]Three cups *shall be* shaped like almond *blossoms* in the one branch, a [1]bulb and a flower, and three cups shaped like almond *blossoms* in the [2]other branch, a [1]bulb and a flower—so for six branches going out from the lampstand;

34 and [a]in the lampstand four cups shaped like almond *blossoms,* its [1]bulbs and its flowers.

35 “[a]A [1]bulb shall be under the *first* pair of branches *coming* out of it, and a [1]bulb under the *second* pair of branches *coming* out of it, and a [1]bulb under the *third* pair of branches *coming* out of it, for the six branches coming out of the lampstand.

36 “[a]Their [1]bulbs and their branches *shall be of one piece* with it; all of it shall be one piece of hammered work of pure gold.

37 “Then you shall make its lamps seven *in number;* and [a]they shall [1]mount its lamps so as to shed light on the space in front of it.

38 “Its snuffers and [1]their trays *shall be* of pure gold.

39 “It shall be made from a talent of pure gold, with all these utensils.

40 “[a]See that you make *them* [b]after the pattern for them, which was shown to you on the mountain.

Curtains of Linen

26 “[a]Moreover you shall make the tabernacle with ten curtains of fine twisted linen and [1]blue and purple and scarlet *material;* you shall make them with cherubim, the work of a skillful workman.

20 [1]Lit *their faces to* [a]1 Kin 8:7; 1 Chr 28:18; Heb 9:5
21 [1]Lit *above, upon* [a]Ex 26:34; 40:20 [b]Ex 25:16
22 [a]Ex 29:42, 43; 30:6, 36; Lev 16:2; Num 17:4 [b]Num 7:89; 1 Sam 4:4; 2 Sam 6:2; 2 Kin 19:15; Ps 80:1; Is 37:16
23 [1]Lit *its length* [2]Lit *its width* [3]Lit *its height* [a]Ex 37:10-16
24 [a]Ex 25:11
29 [1]Or *platters* [2]Lit *libation bowls* [a]Ex 37:16; Num 4:7
30 [1]Lit *Face* [2]Or *continually* [a]Ex 39:36; 40:23; Lev 24:5-9
31 [a]Ex 37:17-24; 1 Kin 7:49; Zech 4:2
31 [1]Or *calyx*
32 [1]Lit *second* [a]Ex 37:18
33 [1]Or *calyx* [2]Lit *one branch* [a]Ex 37:19
34 [1]Or *calyxes* [a]Ex 37:20
35 [1]Or *calyx* [a]Ex 37:21
36 [1]Or *calyxes* [a]Ex 37:22
37 [1]Lit *raise up* [a]Num 8:2
38 [1]Lit *its snuff dishes*
40 [a]Heb 8:5 [b]Ex 25:9; 26:30; Num 8:4; Acts 7:44
26:1 [1]Or *violet* [a]Ex 36:8-19

the temple at Jerusalem would designate it as God's earthly royal city (see Ps 9:11; 18:10 and notes).

25:22 *I will meet with you.* See note on 27:21. *ark of the testimony.* Called this because it contained the testimony (see note on v. 16). The phrase "ark of the testimony" is a synonym of the more familiar phrase "ark of the covenant" (see, e.g., Num 10:33).

25:23 *table.* The table taken from the second (Zerubbabel's) temple by Antiochus Epiphanes is depicted on the Arch of Titus among the items the Romans took back to Rome after conquering Jerusalem in A.D. 70.

25:26 *rings.* See note on v. 12.

25:30 *bread of the Presence.* Traditionally "showbread." In this phrase, "Presence" refers to the presence of God Himself (as in 33:14–15; Is 63:9). The bread (twelve loaves, one for each tribe) represented a perpetual bread offering to the Lord by which Israel declared that she consecrated to God the fruits of her labors, and by which she at the same time acknowledged that all such fruit had been hers only by God's blessing. See Lev 24:5–9.

25:31 *its cups, its bulbs and its flowers.* The design is patterned after an almond tree (see v. 33), the first of the trees in the Near East to blossom in spring. The cups of the lampstand resemble either the calyx (outer covering of the flower) or the almond nut.

25:37 *lamps.* The ancient lamp was a small clay saucer with part of its rim pinched together to form a spout from which protruded the top of a wick fed by oil contained in the saucer. (Examples of seven-spouted lamps come from the time of Moses.) The ruins of Beth Shan and Megiddo have yielded examples of a metal pedestal topped by a ledge designed to carry a lamp. The classic representation of the shape of the tabernacle lampstand comes from the time of Herod the Great and may be seen on the Arch of Titus in Rome. The lamps were to burn all night in the tabernacle, tended by the priests. Oil for the lamps was to be supplied by the people; the light from the lamps represented the glory of the Lord reflected in the consecrated lives of the Israelites—Israel's glory answering to God's glory in the tabernacle (29:43). See 27:20–21. *seven.* Signifying completeness.

25:40 Quoted in Heb 8:5 in order to contrast the "shadow" (the trappings of the old covenant) with the reality (the Christ of the new covenant). See also Heb 10:1.

26:1 *tabernacle.* See note on 25:9. Its basic structure was to be 15 feet wide by 45 feet long by 15 feet high. Over an inner lining of embroidered linen (vv. 1–6), it was to have a covering woven of goat hair (vv. 7–13) and two additional coverings of leather, one made from ram skins dyed red and one from the hides of porpoises (v. 14). Internally, the ceiling was probably

2 "The length of each curtain shall be twenty-eight [1]cubits, and the width of each curtain four [1]cubits; all the curtains shall have [2]the same measurements.

3 "Five curtains shall be [1]joined to one another, and *the other* five curtains *shall be* [1]joined to one another.

4 "You shall make loops of [1]blue on the edge of the [2]outermost curtain in the *first* set, and likewise you shall make *them* on the edge of the curtain that is outermost in the second [3]set.

5 "You shall make fifty loops in the one curtain, and you shall make fifty loops on the [1]edge of the curtain that is in the second [2]set; the loops shall be opposite each other.

6 "You shall make fifty clasps of gold, and [1]join the curtains to one another with the clasps so that the [2]tabernacle will be a unit.

Curtains of Goats' Hair

7 "Then [a]you shall make curtains of goats' *hair* for a tent over the tabernacle; you shall make eleven curtains in all.

8 "The length of each curtain *shall be* thirty [1]cubits, and the width of each curtain four cubits; the eleven curtains shall have [2]the same measurements.

9 "You shall [1]join five curtains by themselves and the *other* six curtains by themselves, and you shall double over the sixth curtain [2]at the front of the tent.

10 "You shall make fifty loops on the edge of the [1]curtain that is outermost in the *first* [2]set, and fifty loops on the edge of the curtain *that is outermost in* the second [2]set.

11 "You shall make fifty clasps of [1]bronze, and you shall put the clasps into the loops and [2]join the tent together so that it will be [3]a unit.

12 "The [1]overlapping part that is left over in the curtains of the tent, the half curtain that is left over, shall lap over the back of the tabernacle.

13 "The cubit on one side and the cubit on

2 [1]I.e. One cubit equals approx 18 in. [2]Lit *one measure*
3 [1]Or *coupled*
4 [1]Or *violet* [2]Lit *one curtain from the end in the coupling* [3]Lit *coupling*
5 [1]Lit *end* [2]Lit *coupling*
6 [1]Or *couple* [2]Or *dwelling place,* and so throughout the ch
7 [a]Ex 36:14
8 [1]I.e. One cubit equals approx 18 in. [2]Lit *one measure*
9 [1]Or *couple* [2]Lit *toward the front of the face of the tent*
10 [1]Lit *one curtain* [2]Lit *coupling*
11 [1]Or *copper* [2]Or *couple* [3]Lit *one*
12 [1]Lit *excess*

flat, but whether the leather coverings had a ridge line with sloping sides (like a tent) is not known. Symbolically the tabernacle represented God's royal tent. *fine twisted linen and blue and purple and scarlet material.* See note on 25:4. *cherubim.* Signifying a royal chamber (see 25:18 and note). **26:7** *goats' hair.* See note on 25:4.

The Tabernacle

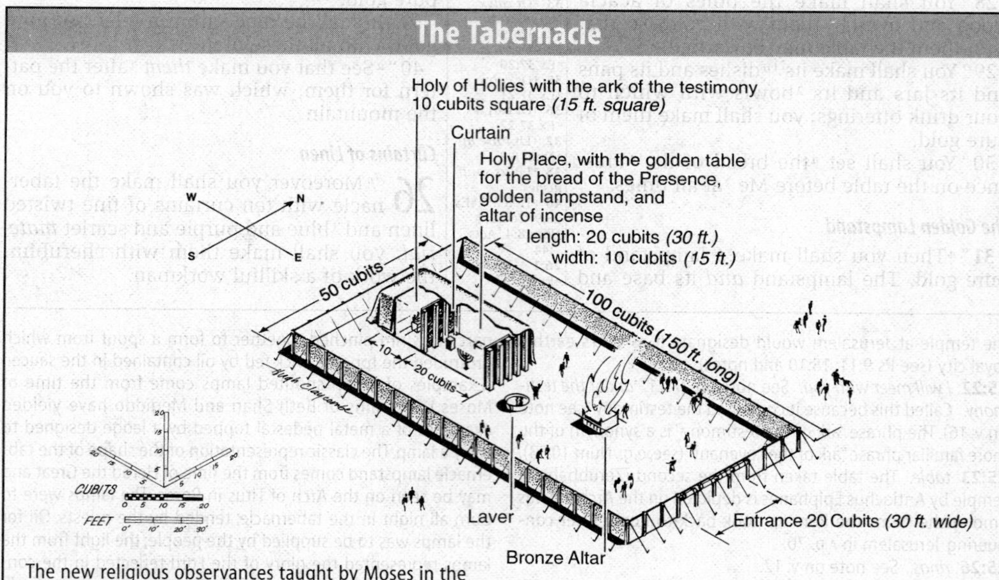
Holy of Holies with the ark of the testimony
10 cubits square (15 ft. square)
Curtain
Holy Place, with the golden table
for the bread of the Presence,
golden lampstand, and
altar of incense
length: 20 cubits (30 ft.)
width: 10 cubits (15 ft.)
W
N
S
E
50 cubits
100 cubits (150 ft. long)
10
20 cubits
Hugh Claycombe
CUBITS
0 5 10 15 20
FEET
0' 10' 20' 30'
Laver
Entrance 20 Cubits (30 ft. wide)
Bronze Altar

The new religious observances taught by Moses in the wilderness centered on rituals connected with the tabernacle, and amplified Israel's sense of separateness, purity and oneness under the Lordship of Yahweh.

A few wilderness shrines have been found in Sinai, notably at Serabit el-Khadem and at Timnah in the Negev, and show marked Egyptian influence.

Specific cultural antecedents to portable shrines carried on poles and covered with thin sheets of gold can be found in ancient Egypt as early as the Old Kingdom (2800-2250 B.C.), but were especially prominent in the 18th and 19th dynasties (1570-1180). The best examples come from the fabulous tomb of Tutankhamun, c. 1350.

Comparisons of construction details in the text of Ex 25-40 with the frames, shrines, poles, sheathing, draped fabric covers, gilt rosettes, and winged protective figures from the shrine of Tutankhamun are instructive. The period, the Late Bronze Age, is equivalent in all dating systems to the era of Moses and the exodus.

©1981 Hugh Claycombe

the other, of what is left over in the length of the curtains of the tent, shall lap over the sides of the tabernacle on one side and on the other, to cover it.

14 "[a]You shall make a covering for the tent of rams' skins [1]dyed red and a covering of porpoise skins above.

Boards and Sockets

15 "Then you shall make [a]the boards for the tabernacle of acacia wood, standing upright.

16 "Ten cubits *shall be* the length of [1]each board and one and a half cubits the width of each board.

17 "*There shall be* two tenons for each board, [1]fitted to one another; thus you shall do for all the boards of the tabernacle.

18 "You shall make the boards for the tabernacle: twenty boards [1]for the south side.

19 "You shall make forty [1a]sockets of silver under the twenty boards, two [1]sockets under one board for its two tenons and two [1]sockets under another board for its two tenons;

20 and for the second side of the tabernacle, on the north side, twenty boards,

21 and their forty [1]sockets of silver; two [1]sockets under one board and two [1]sockets under another board.

22 "For the [1]rear of the tabernacle, to the west, you shall make six boards.

23 "You shall make two boards for the corners of the tabernacle at the [1]rear.

24 "They shall be double beneath, and together they shall be complete [1]to its top [2]to the first ring; thus it shall be with both of them: they shall form the two corners.

25 "There shall be eight boards with their [1]sockets of silver, sixteen [1]sockets; two [1]sockets under one board and two [1]sockets under another board.

26 "Then you shall make [a]bars of acacia

14 [1]Or *tanned* [a]Ex 36:19
15 [a]Ex 36:20-34
16 [1]Lit *the*
17 [1]Lit *bound*
18 [1]Lit *toward the side of the Negev to the south*
19 [1]Or *bases* [a]Ex 38:27

19 [1]Or *bases*
21 [1]Or *bases*
22 [1]Lit *extreme parts*
23 [1]Lit *extreme parts*
24 [1]Or *at its head* [2]Or *with reference to*
25 [1]Or *bases*
26 [a]Ex 36:31

26:14 *rams' skins dyed red . . . porpoise.* See note on 25:5.
26:17 *tenons.* Lit. "hands"; probably the two at the bottom of each frame that were inserted into its two bases (see v. 19).
26:19 *forty sockets of silver.* These plus the 40 in v. 21, the 16 in v. 25 and the 4 in v. 32 make up a grand total of 100, the number of talents of silver obtained from the Israelite community to be used to cast the bases (see 38:27).
26:23 *corners.* Or "angles," perhaps referring to mitered joints at the corners.
26:26 *bars.* To strengthen the frames on the north, south and west sides.

Tabernacle Furnishings

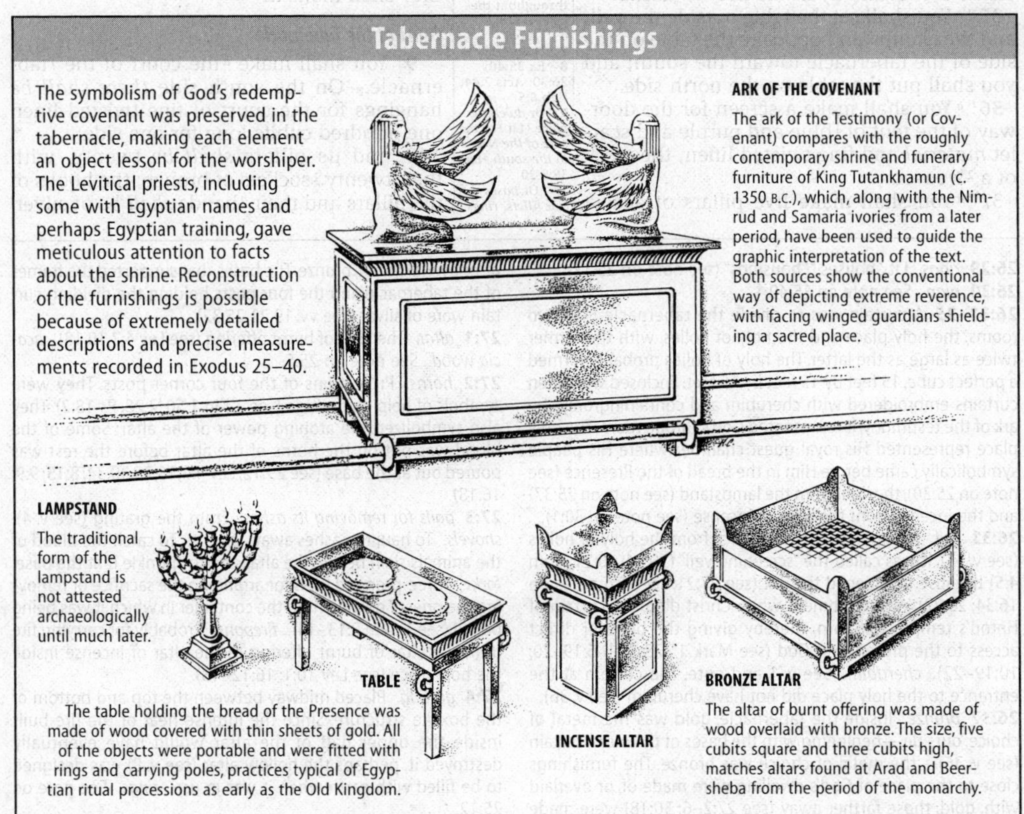

The symbolism of God's redemptive covenant was preserved in the tabernacle, making each element an object lesson for the worshiper. The Levitical priests, including some with Egyptian names and perhaps Egyptian training, gave meticulous attention to facts about the shrine. Reconstruction of the furnishings is possible because of extremely detailed descriptions and precise measurements recorded in Exodus 25–40.

ARK OF THE COVENANT
The ark of the Testimony (or Covenant) compares with the roughly contemporary shrine and funerary furniture of King Tutankhamun (c. 1350 B.C.), which, along with the Nimrud and Samaria ivories from a later period, have been used to guide the graphic interpretation of the text. Both sources show the conventional way of depicting extreme reverence, with facing winged guardians shielding a sacred place.

LAMPSTAND
The traditional form of the lampstand is not attested archaeologically until much later.

TABLE
The table holding the bread of the Presence was made of wood covered with thin sheets of gold. All of the objects were portable and were fitted with rings and carrying poles, practices typical of Egyptian ritual processions as early as the Old Kingdom.

INCENSE ALTAR

BRONZE ALTAR
The altar of burnt offering was made of wood overlaid with bronze. The size, five cubits square and three cubits high, matches altars found at Arad and Beersheba from the period of the monarchy.

wood, five for the boards of one side of the
tabernacle,
27 and five bars for the boards of the [1]oth-
er side of the tabernacle, and five bars for the
boards of the side of the tabernacle for the
[2]rear *side* to the west.
28 "The middle bar in the [1]center of the
boards shall pass through from end to end.
29 "You shall overlay the boards with gold
and make their rings of gold *as* holders for
the bars; and you shall overlay the bars with
gold.
30 "Then you shall erect the tabernacle
[a]according to its plan which you have been
shown in the mountain.

The Veil and Screen

31 "You shall make [a]a veil of [1]blue and purple and scarlet *material* and fine twisted
linen; it shall be made with cherubim, the
work of a skillful workman.
32 "You shall [1]hang it on four pillars of acacia overlaid with gold, their hooks *also being*
of gold, on four [2]sockets of silver.
33 "You shall [1]hang up the veil under the
clasps, and shall bring in [a]the ark of the testimony there within the veil; and the veil
shall [2]serve for you as a partition [b]between
the holy place and the holy of holies.
34 "[a]You shall put the mercy seat on the
ark of the testimony in the holy of holies.
35 "[a]You shall set the table outside the veil,
and the [b]lampstand opposite the table on the
side of the tabernacle toward the south; and
you shall put the table on the north side.
36 "[a]You shall make a screen for the doorway of the tent of [1]blue and purple and scarlet *material* and fine twisted linen, the work
of a [2]weaver.
37 "[a]You shall make five pillars of acacia
for the screen and overlay them with gold,
their hooks *also being of* gold; and you shall
cast five [1]sockets of [2]bronze for them.

27 [1]Lit *second* [2]Lit *extreme parts*
28 [1]Lit *midst*
30 [a]Ex 25:9, 40; Acts 7:44; Heb 8:5
31 [1]Or *violet* [a]Ex 36:35, 36; 2 Chr 3:14; Matt 27:51; Heb 9:3
32 [1]Lit *put* [2]Or *bases*
33 [1]Lit *put* [2]Lit *separate for you between* [a]Ex 25:16; 40:21 [b]Heb 9:2f
34 [a]Ex 25:21; 40:20; Lev 16:2
35 [a]Ex 40:22 [b]Ex 40:24
36 [1]Or *violet* [2]Lit *variegator;* i.e. a weaver in colors [a]Ex 36:37
37 [a]Ex 36:38
37 [1]Or *bases* [2]Or *copper*
27:1 [1]I.e. One cubit equals approx 18 in. [a]Ex 38:1-7
2 [1]Or *copper,* and so for *bronze* throughout the ch [a]Ps 118:27
4 [1]Lit *on*
7 [a]Num 4:15
8 [a]Ex 25:40; 26:30; Acts 7:44; Heb 8:5
9 [1]Or *dwelling place* [2]Lit *For the side of the Negev to the south* [a]Ex 38:9-20
10 [1]Or *bases* [2]Or *fillets, rings*

The Bronze Altar

27 "And you shall make [a]the altar of acacia wood, five [1]cubits long and five
cubits wide; the altar shall be square, and its
height shall be three cubits.
2 "You shall make [a]its horns on its four
corners; its horns shall be of one piece with
it, and you shall overlay it with [1]bronze.
3 "You shall make its pails for removing
its ashes, and its shovels and its basins and
its forks and its firepans; you shall make all
its utensils of bronze.
4 "You shall make for it a grating of network of bronze, and on the net you shall
make four bronze rings [1]at its four corners.
5 "You shall put it beneath, under the
ledge of the altar, so that the net will reach
halfway up the altar.
6 "You shall make poles for the altar, poles
of acacia wood, and overlay them with
bronze.
7 "Its poles shall be inserted into the
rings, so that the poles shall be on the two
sides of the altar [a]when it is carried.
8 "You shall make it hollow with planks;
[a]as it was shown to you in the mountain, so
they shall make *it*.

Court of the Tabernacle

9 "You shall make [a]the court of the [1]tab-
ernacle. [2]On the south side *there shall be*
hangings for the court of fine twisted linen
one hundred cubits long for one side;
10 and its pillars *shall be* twenty, with
their twenty [1]sockets of bronze; the hooks of
the pillars and their [2]bands *shall be* of silver.

26:29 *rings.* Lit. "houses," "housings" (see note on 25:12).
26:30 *plan.* See note on 25:40.
26:31–35 A curtain was to divide the tabernacle into two rooms, the holy place and the holy of holies, with the former twice as large as the latter. The holy of holies probably formed a perfect cube, 15 feet by 15 feet by 15 feet. Enclosed with linen curtains embroidered with cherubim and containing only the ark of the testimony, it represented God's throne room. The holy place represented His royal guest chamber where His people symbolically came before Him in the bread of the Presence (see note on 25:30), the light from the lampstand (see note on 25:37) and the incense from the altar of incense (see note on 30:1).
26:31 *veil.* To separate the holy place from the holy of holies (see v. 33). It was called the "screening veil" (39:34; 40:21; Num 4:5) because it screened the ark (see 27:21; see also notes on 16:34; 25:22). At the moment when Christ died, the curtain of Herod's temple was torn, thereby giving the believer direct access to the presence of God (see Mark 15:38; Heb 6:19–20; 10:19–22). *cherubim.* See v. 1 and note. The curtain at the entrance to the holy place did not have cherubim (see v. 36).
26:37 *bronze.* Inside the tabernacle, gold was the metal of choice; outside—beginning with the bases of the outer curtain (see v. 36)—the metal of choice was bronze. The furnishings close to the place of God's dwelling were made of, or overlaid with, gold; those farther away (see 27:2–6; 30:18) were made of, or overlaid with, bronze. The bases that supported the frames of the tabernacle and the four posts holding the dividing curtain were of silver (see vv. 19,21,25,32).
27:1 *altar.* The altar of burnt offering (see Lev 4:7,10,18). *acacia wood.* See note on 25:5.
27:2 *horns.* Projections of the four corner posts. They were symbols of help and refuge (see 1 Kin 1:50; 2:28; Ps 18:2). They also symbolized the atoning power of the altar: Some of the blood was put on the horns of the altar before the rest was poured out at the base (see 29:12; Lev 4:7,18,25,30,34; 8:15; 9:9; 16:18).
27:3 *pails for removing its ashes.* From the grating (see v. 4). *shovels.* To haul the ashes away. *basins.* To catch the blood of the animals slain beside the altar and to sprinkle it at the base. *forks.* Three-pronged forks for arranging the sacrifice or removing the priests' portion from the container in which it was being boiled (see 1 Sam 2:13–14). *firepans.* Probably for carrying fire from the altar of burnt offering to the altar of incense inside the holy place (see Lev 10:1; 16:12–13).
27:4 *grating.* Placed midway between the top and bottom of the boxlike structure. Since the intense heat of the fire built inside the upper half of the altar would have eventually destroyed it, perhaps the hollow altar (see v. 8) was designed to be filled with earth when it was in use. *rings.* See note on 25:12.

11 “Likewise for the north side in length
there shall be hangings one hundred *cubits*
long, and its twenty pillars with their twenty
[1]sockets of bronze; the hooks of the pillars
and their bands *shall be* of silver.
12 “*For* the width of the court on the west
side *shall be* hangings of fifty cubits *with*
their ten pillars and their ten [1]sockets.
13 “The width of the court on the [1]east side
shall be fifty cubits.
14 “The hangings for the *one* [1]side *of the*
gate shall be fifteen cubits *with* their three
pillars and their three [2]sockets.
15 “And for the [1]other [2]side *shall be* hangings of fifteen cubits *with* their three pillars
and their three [3]sockets.
16 “For the gate of the court *there shall be* a
screen of twenty cubits, of [1]blue and purple
and scarlet *material* and fine twisted linen,
the work of a [2]weaver, *with* their four pillars
and their four [3]sockets.
17 “All the pillars around the court shall be
furnished with silver bands *with* their hooks
of silver and their [1]sockets of bronze.
18 “The length of the court *shall be* one
hundred cubits, and the width fifty throughout, and the height five cubits of fine twisted
linen, and their [1]sockets of bronze.
19 “All the utensils of the tabernacle *used*
in all its service, and all its pegs, and all the
pegs of the court, *shall be* of bronze.
20 “You shall charge the sons of Israel, that
they bring you [a]clear oil of beaten olives for
the [1]light, to make a lamp [2]burn continually.
21 “In the [a]tent of meeting, outside [b]the
veil which is before the testimony, [c]Aaron
and his sons shall keep it in order from
evening to morning before the LORD; *it shall*
be a perpetual [d]statute throughout their generations [1]for the sons of Israel.

Garments of the Priests

28 “Then [a]bring near to yourself Aaron
your brother, and his sons with him,
from among the sons of Israel, to minister as
priest to Me—Aaron, [b]Nadab and Abihu,
Eleazar and Ithamar, Aaron’s sons.
2 “You shall make [a]holy garments for Aaron your brother, for glory and for beauty.
3 “You shall speak to all the [1a]skillful persons [b]whom I have endowed with [2]the spirit of wisdom, that they make Aaron’s garments to consecrate him, that he may
minister as priest to Me.
4 “These are the garments which they
shall make: a [1a]breastpiece and an ephod
and a robe and a tunic of checkered work, a
turban and a sash, and they shall make holy
garments for Aaron your brother and his
sons, that he may minister as priest to Me.
5 “They shall take [a]the gold and the [1]blue
and the purple and the scarlet *material* and
the fine linen.
6 “They shall also make [a]the ephod of
gold, of [1]blue and purple *and* scarlet *materi-*
al and fine twisted linen, the work of the
skillful workman.
7 “It shall have two shoulder pieces joined
to its two ends, that it may be joined.
8 “The skillfully woven band, which is on
it, shall be like its workmanship, [1]of the
same material: of gold, of [2]blue and purple
and scarlet *material* and fine twisted linen.
9 “You shall take two onyx stones and
engrave on them the names of the sons of
Israel,
10 six of their names on the one stone and
the names of the remaining six on the [1]other
stone, according to their birth.
11 “[1]As a jeweler engraves a signet, you
shall engrave the two stones according to the
names of the sons of Israel; you shall [2]set
them in filigree *settings* of gold.
12 “You shall put the two stones on the
shoulder pieces of the ephod, *as* stones of
memorial for the sons of Israel, and Aaron
shall [a]bear their names before the LORD on
his two shoulders [b]for a memorial.
13 “[a]You shall make filigree *settings* of
gold,

11 [1]Or *bases*
12 [1]Or *bases*
13 [1]Lit *east side eastward*
14 [1]Lit *shoulder* [2]Or *bases*
15 [1]Lit *second* [2]Lit *shoulder* [3]Or *bases*
16 [1]Or *violet* [2]Lit *variegator;* i.e. a weaver in colors [3]Or *bases*
17 [1]Or *bases*
18 [1]Or *bases*
20 [1]Or *luminary* [2]Lit *ascend* [a]Ex 35:8, 28; Lev 24:1-4
21 [1]Lit *from* [a]Ex 25:22; 29:42; 30:36 [b]Ex 26:31, 33 [c]Ex 30:8; 1 Sam 3:3; 2 Chr 13:11 [d]Ex 28:43; 29:9; Lev 3:17; 16:34; Num 18:23; 19:21; 1 Sam 30:25
28:1 [a]Num 18:7; Ps 99:6; Heb 5:1, 4
28:1 [b]Ex 24:1, 9
2 [a]Ex 29:5, 29; 31:10; 39:1-31; Lev 8:7-9, 30
3 [1]Lit *wise of heart* [2]I.e. artistic skill [a]Ex 31:6; 35:25, 31-35; 36:1 [b]Ex 31:3; Is 11:2; 1 Cor 12:7-11; Eph 1:17
4 [1]Or *pouch* [a]Ex 28:15-43
5 [1]Or *violet* [a]Ex 25:3
6 [1]Or *violet* [a]Ex 39:2-7; Lev 8:7
8 [1]Lit *from it* [2]Or *violet*
10 [1]Lit *second*
11 [1]Lit *A work of a lapidary, engravings of a seal* [2]Lit *make them to be surrounded*
12 [a]Ex 28:29; 39:6f [b]Ex 39:7; Lev 24:7; Num 31:54; Josh 4:7; 1 Cor 11:24f
13 [a]Ex 39:16-18

27:12–13 *west side . . . east side.* The courtyard is described as having two equal parts. The holy of holies probably occupied the central position in the western half, the altar of burnt offering the central position in the eastern half.

27:13–14 *east side . . . the gate.* The entry gate to the tabernacle courtyard faced east, as did that of Solomon’s temple (see Ezek 8:16) and of Herod’s temple.

27:18 *five cubits.* Five cubits equaled about seven and a half feet, high enough to block the view of people standing outside the courtyard, thus protecting the sanctity and privacy of the worship taking place inside.

27:20 *clear oil of beaten olives.* Unripe olives were crushed in a mortar. The pulpy mass was then placed in a cloth basket through the bottom of which the oil dripped, producing a clear fuel that burned with little or no smoke.

27:21 *tent of meeting.* The tabernacle; it was not a place where God’s people met for collective worship but one where God Himself met—by appointment, not by accident—with His people (see 29:42–43). *veil which is before the testimony.* See note on 26:31. *keep it in order from evening to morning.* The lamps were lit in the evening (see 30:8) and apparently extinguished in the morning (1 Sam 3:3).

28:1 *Nadab and Abihu.* See note on 24:1. *minister as priest to Me.* In order “to offer both gifts and sacrifices for sins” and to “deal gently with the ignorant and misguided” (Heb 5:1–2). Another important function of the priests was to read the law of Moses to the people and remind them of their covenant obligations (see Deut 31:9–13; Neh 8:2–3).

28:2 *for glory and for beauty.* The garments were to exalt the office and functions of lesser priests (see v. 40) as well as of the high priest.

28:6 *ephod.* A sleeveless vestment worn by the high priest. Sometimes the word refers to an otherwise unidentified object of worship (see, e.g., Judg 8:27; 18:17; Hos 3:4).

28:8 *band.* Apparently to hold the front and the back of the ephod to the priest’s body.

28:12 *Aaron shall bear their names . . . on his two shoulders.* To symbolize the fact that the high priest represents all Israel when he ministers in the tabernacle.

14 and two chains of pure gold; you shall make them of twisted cordage work, and you shall put the corded chains on the filigree *settings.*

15 “[a]You shall make a [1]breastpiece of judgment, the work of a skillful workman; like the work of the ephod you shall make it: of gold, of [2]blue and purple and scarlet *material* and fine twisted linen you shall make it.

16 “It shall be square *and* folded double, a span [1]in length and a span [1]in width.

17 “You shall [1]mount on it four rows of stones; the first row *shall be* a row of ruby, topaz and emerald;

18 and the second row a turquoise, a sapphire and a diamond;

19 and the third row a jacinth, an agate and an amethyst;

20 and the fourth row a beryl and an onyx and a jasper; they shall be [1]set in gold filigree.

21 “The stones shall be according to the names of the sons of Israel: twelve, according to their names; they shall be *like* the engravings of a seal, each [a]according to his name for the twelve tribes.

22 “You shall make on the [1]breastpiece chains of twisted cordage work in pure gold.

23 “You shall make on the breastpiece two rings of gold, and shall put the two rings on the two ends of the breastpiece.

24 “You shall put the two cords of gold on the two rings at the ends of the breastpiece.

25 “You shall put the *other* two ends of the two cords on the two filigree *settings,* and put them on the shoulder pieces of the ephod, at the front of it.

26 “You shall make two rings of gold and shall place them on the two ends of the breastpiece, on the edge of it, which is toward the inner side of the ephod.

27 “You shall make two rings of gold and put them on the bottom of the two shoulder pieces of the ephod, on the front of it close to the place where it is joined, above the skillfully woven band of the ephod.

28 “They shall bind the breastpiece by its rings to the rings of the ephod with a [1]blue cord, so that it will be on the skillfully woven band of the ephod, and that the breastpiece will not come loose from the ephod.

29 “Aaron shall carry the names of the sons of Israel in the breastpiece of judgment over his heart when he enters the holy place, for a memorial before the LORD continually.

30 “[a]You shall put in the breastpiece of judgment the [1b]Urim and the Thummim, and they shall be over Aaron’s heart when he goes in before the LORD; and Aaron shall carry the judgment of the sons of Israel over his heart before the LORD continually.

31 “[a]You shall make the robe of the ephod all of [1]blue.

32 “There shall be an opening [1]at its top in the middle of it; around its opening there shall be a binding of woven work, as like the opening of a coat of mail, so that it will not be torn.

33 “You shall make on its hem pomegranates of blue and purple and scarlet *material,* all around on its hem, and bells of gold between them all around:

34 a golden bell and a pomegranate, a golden bell and a pomegranate, all around on the hem of the robe.

35 “It shall be on Aaron [1]when he ministers; and [2]its tinkling shall be heard when he enters and [3]leaves the holy place before the LORD, so that he will not die.

36 “You shall also make [a]a plate of pure gold and shall engrave on it, like the engravings of a seal, ‘[b]Holy to the LORD.’

37 “You shall [1]fasten it on a [2]blue cord, and it shall be on the turban; it shall be at the front of the turban.

38 “It shall be on Aaron’s forehead, and Aaron shall [1a]take away the iniquity of the holy things which the sons of Israel consecrate, with regard to all their holy gifts; and it shall always be on his forehead, that [b]they may be accepted before the LORD.

39 “You shall weave [a]the tunic of checkered work of fine linen, and shall make a turban of fine linen, and you shall make a sash, the work of a [1]weaver.

40 “For Aaron’s sons you shall make [a]tunics; you shall also make sashes for them, and you shall make [1b]caps for them, for glory and for beauty.

41 “You shall put them on Aaron your brother and on his sons with him; and you shall [a]anoint them and [1]ordain them and consecrate them, that they may serve Me as priests.

15 [1]Or *pouch* [2]Or *violet* [a]Ex 39:8-21
16 [1]Lit *its*
17 [1]Lit *fill in a setting of stones, four rows of stones*
20 [1]Lit *interwoven with gold in their settings*
21 [a]Rev 7:4-8; 21:12
22 [1]Or *pouch,* and so through v 30
28 [1]Or *violet*
30 [1]I.e. lights and perfections [a]Lev 8:8 [b]Num 27:21; Deut 33:8; Ezra 2:63; Neh 7:65
31 [1]Or *violet* [a]Ex 39:22-26
32 [1]Or *for his head*
35 [1]Lit *for ministering* [2]Lit *its sound* [3]Lit *comes out* from
36 [a]Ex 39:30, 31; Lev 8:9 [b]Zech 14:20
37 [1]Lit *place* [2]Or *violet*
38 [1]Or *bear* [a]Lev 10:17; 22:16; Num 18:1 [b]Lev 1:4; 22:27; 23:11; Is 56:7
39 [1]Lit *variegator;* i.e. a weaver in colors [a]Ex 39:27-29
40 [1]Lit *headgear* [a]Ex 28:4; 39:27, 41 [b]Ex 29:9; 39:28; Lev 8:13; Ezek 44:18
41 [1]Lit *fill their hand* [a]Ex 29:7, 9; 30:30; 40:15; Lev 8:1-36; 10:7

28:15 *of judgment.* By means of the Urim and Thummim (see note on v. 30).

28:29 *Aaron shall carry the names . . . over his heart.* Thus the nation was doubly represented before the Lord (see v. 12 and note).

28:30 *the Urim and the Thummim.* The Hebrew for this phrase probably means “the lights [or possibly ‘curses’] and the perfections.” The Hebrew word *Urim* begins with the first letter of the Hebrew alphabet (*aleph*) and *Thummim* begins with the last letter (*taw*). They were sacred lots and were often used in times of crisis to determine the will of God (see Num 27:21). It has been suggested that if Urim (or “lights”) dominated when the lots were cast the answer was “no,” but if Thummim (or “perfections”) dominated it was “yes.” In any event, their “every decision” was “from the LORD” (Prov 16:33).

28:31 *robe.* Worn under the ephod.

28:35 According to Jewish tradition, one end of a length of rope was tied to the high priest’s ankle and the other end remained outside the tabernacle. If the bells on his robe stopped tinkling while he was in the holy place, the assumption that he had died could be tested by pulling gently on the rope.

28:38 *take away the iniquity.* Symbolically.

28:39 *tunic.* Worn under the robe.

28:40 *for glory and for beauty.* See note on v. 2.

42 "You shall make for them [a]linen breeches to cover *their* bare flesh; they shall [1]reach
from the loins even to the thighs.
43 "They shall be on Aaron and on his sons
when they enter the tent of meeting, or
[a]when they approach the altar to minister in
the holy place, so that they do not incur
[1]guilt and die. [b]It *shall be* a statute forever to
him and to his [2]descendants after him.

Consecration of the Priests

29 "[a]Now this is [1]what you shall do to
them to consecrate them to minister as
priests to Me: take one young bull and two
rams without blemish,
2 and [a]unleavened bread and unleavened cakes mixed with oil, and unleavened
wafers [1]spread with oil; you shall make them
of fine wheat flour.
3 "You shall put them in one basket, and
present them in the basket along with the
bull and the two rams.
4 "Then [a]you shall bring Aaron and his
sons to the doorway of the tent of meeting
and wash them with water.
5 "You shall take the garments, and put on
Aaron the [a]tunic and [b]the robe of the ephod
and [c]the ephod and [d]the [1]breastpiece, and
gird him with the skillfully [e]woven band of
the ephod;
6 and you shall set the [a]turban on his
head and put [b]the holy crown on the turban.
7 "Then you shall take [a]the anointing oil
and pour it on his head and anoint him.
8 "You shall bring his sons and put [a]tunics
on them.
9 "You shall gird them with [a]sashes, Aaron and his sons, and bind [1]caps on them,
and they shall have [b]the priesthood by a perpetual statute. So you shall [2c]ordain Aaron
and his sons.

The Sacrifices

10 "Then you shall bring the bull before the
tent of meeting, and Aaron and his sons shall
[a]lay their hands on the head of the bull.
11 "You shall slaughter the bull before the
LORD at the doorway of the tent of meeting.
12 "You shall [a]take some of the blood of
the bull and put *it* on [b]the horns of the altar
with your finger; and you shall pour out all
the blood at the base of the altar.

42 [1]Lit *be* [a]Ex 39:28; Lev 6:10; 16:4; Ezek 44:18
43 [1]Or *iniquity* [2]Lit *seed* [a]Ex 20:26 [b]Ex 27:21
29:1 [1]Lit *the thing which* [a]Lev 8:1-34
2 [1]Or *anointed* [a]Lev 2:4; 6:19-23
4 [a]Ex 40:12; Lev 8:6
5 [1]Or *pouch* [a]Ex 28:39; Lev 8:7 [b]Ex 28:31 [c]Ex 28:6 [d]Ex 28:15 [e]Ex 28:8
6 [a]Ex 28:4, 39 [b]Ex 28:36, 37; Lev 8:9
7 [a]Ex 30:25; Lev 8:12; 21:10; Num 35:25; Ps 133:2
8 [a]Ex 28:39, 40; Lev 8:13
9 [1]Lit *headgear* [2]Lit *fill the hand of* [a]Ex 28:40 [b]Ex 40:15; Num 3:10; 18:7; 25:13; Deut 18:5 [c]Ex 28:41; Lev 8:1-36
10 [a]Lev 1:4; 8:14
12 [a]Lev 8:15 [b]Ex 27:2; 30:2

13 "You shall [a]take all the fat that covers
the entrails and the [1]lobe of the liver, and the
two kidneys and the fat that is on them, and
offer them up in smoke on the altar.
14 "But [a]the flesh of the bull and its hide
and its refuse, you shall burn with fire outside the camp; it is a sin offering.
15 "[a]You shall also take the one ram, and
Aaron and his sons shall lay their hands on
the head of the ram;
16 and you shall slaughter the ram and
shall take its blood and sprinkle it around on
the altar.
17 "Then you shall cut the ram into its
pieces, and wash its entrails and its legs, and
put *them* [1]with its pieces and [2]its head.
18 "You shall offer up in smoke the whole
ram on the altar; it is a burnt offering to the
LORD: [a]it is a soothing aroma, an offering by
fire to the LORD.
19 "Then [a]you shall take the [1]other ram,
and Aaron and his sons shall lay their hands
on the head of the ram.
20 "You shall slaughter the ram, and take
some of its blood and put *it* on the lobe of
Aaron's right ear and on the lobes of his
sons' right ears and on the thumbs of their
right hands and on the big toes of their right
feet, and sprinkle the *rest of the* blood
around on the altar.
21 "Then you shall take some of the blood
that is on the altar and some of the [a]anoint-
ing oil, and sprinkle *it* on Aaron and on his
garments and on his sons and on his sons'
garments with him; so he and his garments
shall be consecrated, as well as his sons and
his sons' garments with him.
22 "You shall also take the fat from the ram
and the fat tail, and the fat that covers the
entrails and the [1]lobe of the liver, and the
two kidneys and the fat that is on them and
the right thigh (for it is a ram of [2]ordination),
23 and one cake of bread and [a]one cake of
bread *mixed with* oil and one wafer from the
basket of unleavened bread which is *set*
before the LORD;
24 and you shall put [1]all these [2]in the
[3]hands of Aaron and [2]in the [3]hands of his
sons, and shall wave them as a wave offering
before the LORD.
25 "[a]You shall take them from their hands,
and offer them up in smoke on the altar on

13 [1]Or *appendage on* [a]Lev 3:3, 4
14 [a]Lev 4:11, 12, 21; Heb 13:11
15 [a]Lev 8:18
17 [1]Lit *on* [2]Lit *on its*
18 [a]Gen 8:21; Ex 29:25
19 [1]Lit *second* [a]Lev 8:22f
21 [a]Ex 30:25, 31; Lev 8:30
22 [1]Or *appendage on* [2]Lit *filling*
23 [a]Lev 8:26
24 [1]Lit *the whole* [2]Lit *on* [3]Lit *palms*
25 [a]Lev 8:28

28:42–43 See note on 20:26.
28:43 *tent of meeting.* See note on 27:21.
29:1 *consecrate them.* See note on 19:10–11. *without blemish.* See note on 12:5.
29:4 *tent of meeting.* See note on 27:21. *wash them with water.* Symbolizing the removal of ceremonial uncleanness (cf. Heb 10:22) and thus signifying the purity that must characterize them.
29:7 *anoint him.* Symbolizing spiritual enduement for serving God (see Is 61:1).
29:10 *bring the bull.* As a sin offering (see v. 14) to atone for the past sins of Aaron and his sons (see Lev 4:3). *lay their hands on the head of the bull.* As a symbol of (1) the animal's becoming their substitute and (2) transferring their sins to the sin-bearer (see Lev 16:20–22 and note).
29:12 *horns of the altar.* See note on 27:2.
29:13 *fat.* The most select parts of the bull (see Lev 3:3–5,16) were burned on the altar as a sacrifice to the Lord.
29:14 *flesh . . . hide . . . refuse.* Thought of as bearing sin, and thus burned outside the camp (see Heb 13:11–13).
29:18 *offer . . . the whole ram.* Symbolizing total dedication.
29:20 *right ear.* Symbolizing sensitivity to God and His word. *right hands . . . right feet.* Symbolizing a life of service to others on God's behalf.
29:24 *wave offering.* See note on Lev 7:30–32.

the burnt offering for a soothing aroma before the LORD; it is an offering by fire to the LORD.

26 "Then you shall take [a]the breast of Aaron's ram of [1]ordination, and wave it as a wave offering before the LORD; and it shall be your portion.

27 "You shall consecrate the breast of the wave offering and the thigh of the heave offering which was waved and which was [1]offered from the ram of [2]ordination, from the one which was for Aaron and from the one which was for his sons.

28 "It shall be for Aaron and his sons as *their* portion forever from the sons of Israel, for it is a heave offering; and it shall be a heave offering from the sons of Israel from the sacrifices of their peace offerings, *even* their heave offering to the LORD.

29 "[a]The holy garments of Aaron shall be for his sons after him, [1]that in them they may be anointed and ordained.

30 "For seven days the one of his sons who is priest in his stead shall put them on when he enters the tent of meeting to minister in the holy place.

Food of the Priests

31 "You shall take the ram of [1]ordination and [a]boil its flesh in a holy place.

32 "Aaron and his sons shall eat the flesh of the ram and the bread that is in the basket, at the doorway of the tent of meeting.

33 "Thus [a]they shall eat [1]those things by which atonement was made [2]at their ordination *and* consecration; but a [3b]layman shall not eat *them*, because they are holy.

34 "[a]If any of the flesh of [1]ordination or any of the bread remains until morning, then you shall burn the remainder with fire; it shall not be eaten, because it is holy.

35 "Thus you shall do to Aaron and to his sons, according to all that I have commanded you; you shall [1]ordain them through [a]seven days.

36 "[a]Each day you shall offer a bull as a sin offering for atonement, and you shall [1]purify the altar when you make atonement [2]for it, and [b]you shall anoint it to consecrate it.

37 "For seven days you shall make atonement [1]for the altar and consecrate it; then [a]the altar shall be most holy, *and* whatever touches the altar shall be holy.

38 "Now [a]this is what you shall offer on the altar: two one year old lambs each day, continuously.

39 "The [a]one lamb you shall offer in the morning and the [1]other lamb you shall offer at [2]twilight;

40 and there *shall be* one-tenth *of an ephah* of fine flour mixed with one-fourth of a hin of beaten oil, and one-fourth of a hin of wine for a drink offering with one lamb.

41 "The [1]other lamb you shall offer at [2]twilight, and shall offer with it [3]the same grain offering and [4]the same drink offering as in the morning, for a soothing aroma, an offering by fire to the LORD.

42 "It shall be a continual burnt offering throughout your generations at the doorway of the tent of meeting before the LORD, [a]where I will meet with you, to speak to you there.

43 "I will meet there with the sons of Israel, and it shall be consecrated by My glory.

44 "I will consecrate the tent of meeting and the altar; I will also consecrate Aaron and his sons to minister as priests to Me.

45 "[a]I will dwell among the sons of Israel and will be their God.

46 "They shall know that [a]I am the LORD their God who brought them out of the land of Egypt, that I might dwell among them; I am the LORD their God.

The Altar of Incense

30 "Moreover, you shall make [a]an altar as a place for burning incense; you shall make it of acacia wood.

2 "Its length *shall be* a [1]cubit, and its width a cubit, it shall be square, and its height *shall be* two cubits; its horns *shall be* [2]of one piece with it.

3 "You shall overlay it with pure gold, its top and its [1]sides all around, and its horns; and you shall make a gold molding all around for it.

4 "You shall make two gold rings for it under its molding; you shall make *them* on its two side walls—on [1]opposite sides—and [2]they shall be holders for poles with which to carry it.

5 "You shall make the poles of acacia wood and overlay them with gold.

6 "You shall put [1]this altar in front of the veil that is [2]near the ark of the testimony, in front of the [3a]mercy seat that is over *the ark of* the testimony, where I will meet with you.

26 [1]Lit *filling* [a]Lev 7:31, 34; 8:29
27 [1]Lit *heaved; or lifted up* [2]Lit *filling*
29 [1]Lit *for anointing in them and filling their hand in them* [a]Num 20:26, 28
31 [1]Lit *filling* [a]Lev 8:31
33 [1]Lit *them* [2]Lit *to fill their hand to sanctify them* [3]Lit *stranger* [a]Lev 10:14 [b]Lev 22:10, 13
34 [1]Lit *filling* [a]Ex 12:10; 23:18; 34:25; Lev 8:32
35 [1]Lit *fill their hand* [a]Lev 8:33
36 [1]Or *offer a sin offering on the altar* [2]Lit *upon* [a]Heb 10:11 [b]Ex 40:10
37 [1]Lit *upon* [a]Ex 30:28f
38 [a]Num 28:3-31; 29:6-38
39 [1]Lit *second* [2]Lit *between the two evenings* [a]Ezek 46:13-15
41 [1]Lit *second* [2]Lit *between the two evenings* [3]Lit *according to the grain offering of the morning* [4]Lit *according to its*
42 [a]Ex 25:22; Num 17:4
45 [a]Ex 25:8; Lev 26:12; Num 5:3; Deut 12:11; Zech 2:10; 2 Cor 6:16; Rev 21:3
46 [a]Ex 20:2
30:1 [a]Ex 37:25-29
2 [1]I.e. One cubit equals approx 18 in. [2]Lit *from itself*
3 [1]Lit *walls*
4 [1]Lit *its two* [2]Lit *it*
6 [1]Lit *it* [2]Lit *upon or over* [3]Lit *propitiatory* [a]Ex 25:21f

29:28 *for Aaron and his sons . . . their portion forever.* Parts of certain sacrificial animals were set aside as food for the priests and their families (see Lev 10:14).
29:31 *a holy place.* Probably the tabernacle courtyard.
29:38–39 Institution of the daily morning and evening offerings—sometimes observed even during days of apostasy (see 2 Kin 16:15).
29:42–43 *I will meet.* See note on 27:21.
29:43 *My glory.* Symbolic of God's presence over the ark of the testimony (see note on 25:10; see also 40:34–35; 1 Kin 8:10–13).
29:45–46 *dwell among.* See note on 25:9.
29:45 *I will . . . be their God.* Commonly denotes the essence of the divine promise pledged in His covenant with His people (see note on 6:7).
29:46 *I am the LORD . . . who brought them out.* See note on 20:2.
30:1 *incense.* Its fragrant smoke symbolized the prayers of God's people (see Ps 141:2; Luke 1:10; Rev 5:8; 8:3–4).
30:3 *gold.* See note on 26:37.
30:4 *rings.* See note on 25:12.
30:6 *veil that is near the ark of the testimony.* See notes on 25:16,22; 26:31.

7 "Aaron shall burn fragrant incense on it; he shall burn it every morning when he trims the lamps.

8 "When Aaron [1]trims the lamps at [2]twilight, he shall burn incense. *There shall be* perpetual incense before the LORD throughout your generations.

9 "You shall not offer any strange incense on [1]this altar, or burnt offering or meal offering; and you shall not pour out a drink offering on it.

10 "Aaron shall [a]make atonement on its horns once a year; he shall make atonement on it with the blood of the sin offering of atonement once a year throughout your generations. It is most holy to the LORD."

11 The LORD also spoke to Moses, saying,

12 "When you take [a]a [1]census of the sons of Israel [2]to number them, then each one of them shall give [b]a ransom for [3]himself to the LORD, when you [4]number them, so that there will be no plague among them when you [4]number them.

13 "This is what everyone who [1]is numbered shall give: half a shekel according to the shekel of the sanctuary ([a]the shekel is twenty gerahs), half a shekel as a [2]contribution to the LORD.

14 "Everyone who [1]is numbered, from twenty years old and over, shall give the [2]contribution to the LORD.

15 "The rich shall not pay more and the poor shall not pay less than the half shekel, when you give the [1]contribution to the LORD to make atonement for [2]yourselves.

16 "You shall take the atonement money from the sons of Israel and shall give it for the service of the tent of meeting, that it may be a memorial for the sons of Israel before the LORD, to make atonement for [1]yourselves."

17 The LORD spoke to Moses, saying,

18 "You shall also make [a]a laver of [1]bronze, with its base of bronze, for washing; and you shall [b]put it between the tent of meeting and the altar, and you shall put water in it.

19 "Aaron and his sons shall [a]wash their hands and their feet from it;

20 when they enter the tent of meeting, they shall wash with water, so that they will not die; or when they approach the altar to minister, by offering up in smoke a fire *sacrifice* to the LORD.

21 "So they shall wash their hands and their feet, so that they will not die; and [a]it shall be a perpetual statute for them, for [1]Aaron and his [2]descendants throughout their generations."

8 [1]Lit *causes to ascend* [2]Lit *between the two evenings*
9 [1]Lit *it*
10 [a]Lev 16:18
12 [1]Lit *sum* [2]Lit *for their being mustered* [3]Lit *his soul* [4]Lit *muster* [a]Ex 38:25, 26; Num 1:2; 26:2 [b]Num 31:50
13 [1]Lit *passes over to those who are mustered* [2]Lit *heave offering* [a]Lev 27:25; Num 3:47; Ezek 45:12
14 [1]V 13, note 1 [2]Lit *heave offering of the* LORD
15 [1]Lit *heave offering of the* LORD [2]Lit *your souls*
16 [1]Lit *your souls*
18 [1]Or *copper* [a]Ex 38:8 [b]Ex 40:30
19 [a]Ex 40:31f; Is 52:11
21 [1]Lit *him* [2]Lit *seed*
25 [1]Lit *it* [a]Ex 37:29; 40:9; Lev 8:10
26 [a]Ex 40:9; Lev 8:10; Num 7:1
30 [a]Ex 29:7; Lev 8:12
32 [1]Lit *the flesh of man* [2]Lit *its proportion* [a]Ex 30:25, 37
33 [1]Lit *stranger* [2]Lit *even he shall* [a]Ex 30:38 [b]Gen 17:14; Ex 12:15; Lev 7:20f
36 [a]Ex 29:42
37 [1]Lit *its proportion* [a]Ex 30:32

The Anointing Oil

22 Moreover, the LORD spoke to Moses, saying,

23 "Take also for yourself the finest of spices: of flowing myrrh five hundred *shekels,* and of fragrant cinnamon half as much, two hundred and fifty, and of fragrant cane two hundred and fifty,

24 and of cassia five hundred, according to the shekel of the sanctuary, and of olive oil a hin.

25 "You shall make [1]of these a holy anointing oil, a perfume mixture, the work of a perfumer; it shall be [a]a holy anointing oil.

26 "With it [a]you shall anoint the tent of meeting and the ark of the testimony,

27 and the table and all its utensils, and the lampstand and its utensils, and the altar of incense,

28 and the altar of burnt offering and all its utensils, and the laver and its stand.

29 "You shall also consecrate them, that they may be most holy; whatever touches them shall be holy.

30 "[a]You shall anoint Aaron and his sons, and consecrate them, that they may minister as priests to Me.

31 "You shall speak to the sons of Israel, saying, 'This shall be a holy anointing oil to Me throughout your generations.

32 'It shall not be poured on [1]anyone's body, nor shall you make *any* like it in [2]the same proportions; [a]it is holy, *and* it shall be holy to you.

33 '[a]Whoever shall mix *any* like it or whoever puts any of it on a [1]layman [2][b]shall be cut off from his people.' "

The Incense

34 Then the LORD said to Moses, "Take for yourself spices, stacte and onycha and galbanum, spices with pure frankincense; there shall be an equal part of each.

35 "With it you shall make incense, a perfume, the work of a perfumer, salted, pure, *and* holy.

36 "You shall beat some of it very fine, and put part of it before the testimony in the tent of meeting [a]where I will meet with you; it shall be most holy to you.

37 "The incense which you shall make, [a]you shall not make in [1]the same proportions for yourselves; it shall be holy to you for the LORD.

30:10 *atonement . . . once a year.* See Lev 16:34.
30:12 *take a census.* Perhaps such censuses were taken on various occasions (and at stated intervals) to enter the Israelites into an official roll for public duties in the Lord's service (see Num 1:2; 26:2). *give a ransom for himself.* An extension of the principle stated in 13:13,15 (see note on 13:13).
30:14 *twenty years old and over.* Of military age (see Num 1:3).
30:16 *tent of meeting.* See note on 27:21.
30:18 *laver.* Made from bronze mirrors contributed by Israelite women (see 38:8). *washing.* See note on 29:4.
30:23–24 *myrrh . . . cinnamon . . . cane . . . cassia.* See note on 25:6.
30:33 *cut off from his people.* See note on 12:15.
30:34 *stacte and onycha and galbanum.* See note on 25:6. *frankincense.* A resin from the bark of *Boswellia carteri*, which grows in southern Arabia.

38 "[a]Whoever shall make *any* like it, to
[1]use as perfume, [2]shall be cut off from his
people."

The Skilled Craftsmen

31 [a]Now the LORD spoke to Moses, saying,
2 "See, I have called by name Bezalel,
the [a]son of Uri, the son of Hur, of the tribe of
Judah.
3 "I have [a]filled him with the Spirit of God
in wisdom, in understanding, in knowledge,
and in all *kinds of* [1]craftsmanship,
4 to [1]make artistic designs for work in
gold, in silver, and in [2]bronze,
5 and in the cutting of stones [1]for settings, and in the carving of wood, that he
may work in all *kinds of* [2]craftsmanship.
6 "And behold, I Myself have [1]appointed
with him [a]Oholiab, the son of Ahisamach, of
the tribe of Dan; and in the hearts of all who
are [2]skillful I have put [3]skill, that they may
make all that I have commanded you:
7 [a]the tent of meeting, and [b]the ark of
testimony, and [c]the [1]mercy seat upon it, and
all the furniture of the tent,
8 [a]the table also and its [1]utensils, and the
[b]pure *gold* lampstand with all its [1]utensils,
and [c]the altar of incense,
9 [a]the altar of burnt offering also with all
its [1]utensils, and [b]the laver and its stand,
10 the [1a]woven garments as well, and the
holy garments for Aaron the priest, and the
garments of his sons, *with which* to [2]carry on
their priesthood;
11 [a]the anointing oil also, and the [b]fra-
grant incense for the holy place, they are to
make *them* according to all that I have commanded you."

The Sign of the Sabbath

12 The LORD spoke to Moses, saying,
13 "But as for you, speak to the sons of
Israel, saying, '[a]You shall surely observe My
sabbaths; for *this* is [b]a sign between Me and
you throughout your generations, that you
may know that I am the LORD who sanctifies
you.
14 'Therefore you are to observe the sabbath, for it is holy to you. [a]Everyone who
profanes it shall surely be put to death; for
whoever does any work on it, that person
shall be cut off from among his people.
15 '[a]For six days work may be done, but
on the seventh day there is a [b]sabbath of
complete rest, holy to the LORD; [c]whoever
does any work on the sabbath day shall surely be put to death.
16 'So the sons of Israel shall observe the
sabbath, to [1]celebrate the sabbath throughout their generations as a perpetual covenant.'
17 "[a]It is a sign between Me and the sons of
Israel forever; [b]for in six days the LORD made
heaven and earth, but on the seventh day He
ceased *from labor,* and was refreshed."
18 When He had finished speaking with
him upon Mount Sinai, He gave Moses [a]the
two tablets of the testimony, tablets of stone,
[b]written by the finger of God.

The Golden Calf

32 Now when the people saw that Moses
[a]delayed to come down from the
mountain, the people assembled about Aaron and said to him, "Come, [b]make us [1]a god
who will go before us; as for [c]this Moses, the
man who brought us up from the land of
Egypt, we do not know what has become of
him."
2 Aaron said to them, "[a]Tear off the gold
rings which are in the ears of your wives,
your sons, and your daughters, and bring
them to me."
3 Then all the people tore off the gold
rings which were in their ears and brought
them to Aaron.
4 He took *this* from their hand, and fashioned it with a graving tool and made it into
a [a]molten calf; and they said, "[1]This is your

38 [1]Lit *smell of it* [2]Lit *even he shall* [a]Ex 30:33
31:1 [a]Ex 35:30-36:1
2 [a]1 Chr 2:20
3 [1]Or *workmanship* [a]Ex 35:31; 1 Kin 7:14; 1 Cor 12:4-8
4 [1]Lit *devise devices* [2]Or *copper*
5 [1]Lit *to fill in (for a setting)* [2]Or *workmanship*
6 [1]Lit *given* [2]Lit *wise of heart* [3]Lit *wisdom* [a]Ex 35:34
7 [1]Lit *propitiatory* [a]Ex 36:8-38 [b]Ex 37:1-5 [c]Ex 37:6-9
8 [1]Or *vessels* [a]Ex 37:10-16 [b]Ex 37:17-24; Lev 24:4 [c]Ex 37:25-29
9 [1]Or *vessels* [a]Ex 38:1-7 [b]Ex 38:8
10 [1]Or *service garments* [2]Lit *minister as priests* [a]Ex 39:1
11 [a]Ex 30:23-32 [b]Ex 30:34-38
13 [a]Ex 20:8 [b]Ex 31:17; Ezek 20:12, 20
14 [a]Ex 31:15; 35:2; Num 15:32, 35; John 7:23
15 [a]Ex 20:9-11; 23:12; 34:21; 35:2; Lev 23:3; Deut 5:12-14 [b]Gen 2:2f; Ex 16:23; 20:8; 35:2, 3 [c]Ex 31:14
16 [1]Lit *do*
17 [a]Ex 31:13; Ezek 20:12 [b]Gen 1:31; 2:2, 3; Ex 20:11
18 [a]Ex 24:12; 34:29; Deut 4:13; 5:22; 9:10f [b]Ex 32:15, 16; 34:1, 28; Deut 9:10

32:1 [1]Or *gods* [a]Ex 24:18; Deut 9:11, 12 [b]Acts 7:40 [c]Ex 14:11
2 [a]Ex 35:22 **4** [1]Or *These are your gods* [a]Deut 9:16; Neh 9:18; Ps 106:19; Acts 7:41

31:2 *Bezalel.* Means "in the shadow/protection of God." *Hur.* See note on 17:10.
31:3 *filled him with the Spirit of God.* Ability to work as a skilled craftsman was a spiritual gift, equipping a person for special service to God.
31:6 *Oholiab.* Means "The (divine) father is my tent/tabernacle." The names of Bezalel (see note on v. 2) and Oholiab were appropriate for the chief craftsmen working on the tabernacle.
31:7 *tent of meeting.* See note on 27:21.
31:13 *observe My Sabbaths.* Instructions for building the tabernacle and making the priestly garments are concluded by impressing on the Israelites the importance and necessity of keeping the Sabbath even while carrying out this special task.
31:14 *cut off from among his people.* See note on 12:15.
31:16–17 *covenant . . . sign.* In her rhythm of work and rest in the service of God, Israel is to emulate God's pattern in creation as an ever-renewed sign of her covenant with God (see note on Gen 9:12).
31:18 *two tablets.* In keeping with ancient Near Eastern practice, these were duplicates of the covenant document, not two sections of the Ten Commandments. One copy belonged to each party of the covenant. Since Israel's copy was to be laid up in the presence of her God (according to custom), both covenant tablets (God's and Israel's) were placed in the ark (see 25:21). *testimony.* See notes on 16:34; 25:16. *written by the finger of God.* Because it was God's covenant (see 19:5–6), and the stipulations of the covenant (20:1–17) were His.
32:1 *delayed.* Forty days and forty nights (see 24:18 and note). *the people.* Probably the tribe and clan leaders. *Moses . . . who brought us up from . . . Egypt.* A rebellious contrast to the gracious statement of Israel's covenant Lord (see 20:2 and note; 29:46).
32:2 *gold rings.* Probably part of the plunder brought from Egypt (see 3:21–22; 11:2–3; 12:35–36).
32:4 *made it into a molten calf.* Either gold plating over a carved wooden calf (it was later burned, v. 20) or crudely cast

god, O Israel, who brought you up from the land of Egypt."

5 Now when Aaron saw *this,* he built an altar before it; and Aaron made a proclamation and said, "Tomorrow *shall be* a feast to the LORD."

6 So the next day they rose early and [a]offered burnt offerings, and brought peace offerings; and [b]the people sat down to eat and to drink, and rose up [c]to play.

7 Then the LORD spoke to Moses, "Go [1]down at once, for your people, whom [a]you brought up from the land of Egypt, have [b]corrupted *themselves.*

8 "They have quickly turned aside from the way which I commanded them. [a]They have made for themselves a molten calf, and have worshiped it and [b]have sacrificed to it and said, '[1c]This is your god, O Israel, who brought you up from the land of Egypt!' "

9 [a]The LORD said to Moses, "I have seen this people, and behold, they are [1b]an obstinate people.

10 "Now then [a]let Me alone, that My anger may burn against them and that I may destroy them; and [b]I will make of you a great nation."

Moses' Entreaty

11 Then [a]Moses entreated the LORD his God, and said, "O LORD, why does Your anger burn against Your people whom You have brought out from the land of Egypt with great power and with a mighty hand?

12 "Why should [a]the Egyptians speak, saying, 'With evil *intent* He brought them out to kill them in the mountains and to destroy them from the face of the earth'? Turn from Your burning anger and change Your mind about *doing* harm to Your people.

13 "Remember Abraham, Isaac, and Israel, Your servants to whom You [a]swore by Yourself, and said to them, 'I will [b]multiply your [1]descendants as the stars of the heavens, and [c]all this land of which I have spoken I will give to your [1]descendants, and they shall inherit *it* forever.' "

14 [a]So the LORD changed His mind about the harm which He said He would do to His people.

15 [a]Then Moses turned and went down from the mountain with the two tablets of the testimony in his hand, [b]tablets which were written on both [1]sides; they were written on one *side* and the other.

16 The tablets were God's work, and the writing was God's writing engraved on the tablets.

17 Now when Joshua heard the sound of the people [1]as they shouted, he said to Moses, "There is a sound of war in the camp."

18 But he said,

"It is not the sound of the cry of
triumph,
Nor is it the sound of the cry of
defeat;
But the sound of singing I hear."

Moses' Anger

19 It came about, as soon as [1]Moses came near the camp, that [a]he saw the calf and *the* dancing; and Moses' anger burned, and [b]he threw the tablets from his hands and shattered them [2]at the foot of the mountain.

20 [a]He took the calf which they had made and burned *it* with fire, and ground it to powder, and scattered it over the surface of the water and made the sons of Israel drink *it.*

21 Then Moses said to Aaron, "What did this people do to you, that you have brought *such* great sin upon them?"

6 [a]Acts 7:41 [b]1 Cor 10:7 [c]Ex 32:17-19; Num 25:2
7 [1]Lit *go down* [a]Ex 32:4, 11; Deut 9:12 [b]Gen 6:11f
8 [1]Or *These are your gods* [a]Ex 20:3, 4, 23 [b]Ex 22:20; 34:15; Deut 32:17 [c]1 Kin 12:28
9 [1]Or *a stiff-necked* [a]Num 14:11-20 [b]Ex 33:3, 5; 34:9; Is 48:4; Acts 7:51
10 [a]Deut 9:14 [b]Num 14:12
11 [a]Deut 9:18, 26
12 [a]Num 14:13-19; Deut 9:28; Josh 7:9
13 [1]Lit *seed* [a]Gen 22:16-18; Heb 6:13 [b]Gen 15:5; 26:4 [c]Gen 12:7; 13:15; 15:18; 17:8; 35:12; Ex 13:5, 11; 33:1
14 [a]Ps 106:45
15 [1]Lit *their sides* [a]Deut 9:15 [b]Ex 31:18
17 [1]Lit *in its shouting*
19 [1]Lit *he* [2]Lit *beneath* [a]Ex 32:6; Deut 9:16 [b]Deut 9:17
20 [a]Deut 9:21

in solid gold and then further shaped with a tool, later to be melted down in the fire. The calf was probably similar to representations of the Egyptian bull-god Apis (see note on Jer 46:15). Its manufacture was a flagrant violation of the second commandment (20:4–5). *they.* The leaders among the people (see note on v. 1). *This is your god . . . up from the land of Egypt.* A parody of 20:2 (see note on v. 1). Centuries later, King Jeroboam would quote these words when he set up two golden calves in the northern kingdom of Israel (see 1 Kin 12:28–29).

32:5 *altar before it . . . feast to the LORD.* Apparently Aaron recognized the idolatrous consequences of his deed and acted quickly to keep the people from turning completely away from the Lord.

32:6 *the people sat down . . . rose up to play.* A pagan symbol evoked pagan religious practices. Paul quotes this sentence as a vivid example of Israel's tendency toward idolatry (see 1 Cor 10:7). The Hebrew verb translated "rose up to play" often has sexual connotations (see, e.g., "caressing," Gen 26:8). Immoral orgies frequently accompanied pagan worship in ancient times.

32:7,9 *your people . . . this people.* By not calling Israel "My people" (as, e.g., in 3:10), God indicates that He is disowning them for breaking His covenant with them.

32:7 *corrupted.* And, therefore, ripe for destruction (see v. 10; Gen 6:11–13).

32:9 *obstinate.* Like unresponsive oxen or horses (see Jer 27:11–12; see also note on Neh 3:5).

32:10 *I will make of you a great nation.* After Israel—Abraham's descendants—has been destroyed, God will transfer to Moses the pledge originally given to Abraham (see Gen 12:2).

32:11 *Your people.* Using God's own words (see v. 7 and note), Moses appeals to God's special relationship to Israel, then to God's need to vindicate His name in the eyes of the Egyptians (see v. 12), and finally to the great patriarchal promises (see v. 13).

32:13 *Israel.* Jacob (see 33:1; see also Gen 32:28).

32:14 *the LORD changed His mind.* See note on Jer 18:7–10; see also 2 Sam 24:16; Ps 106:45; Amos 7:1–6; James 5:16.

32:15 *went down from the mountain.* See note on 24:18. *two tablets.* See note on 31:18. *testimony.* See notes on 16:34; 25:16. *written on both sides.* Tablets were often thus inscribed in ancient times.

32:16 *God's work . . . God's writing.* See 31:18.

32:17 *Joshua.* Perhaps he had accompanied Moses part of the way up the mountain (see 24:13).

32:19 *shattered them.* Thus testifying against Israel that they had broken the covenant.

32:20 *burned it . . . ground it to powder.* King Jeroboam's altar (see note on v. 4) at Bethel received the same treatment (see 2 Kin 23:15).

22 Aaron said, "Do not let the anger of my lord burn; you know the people yourself, [a]that they are [1]prone to evil.

23 "For [a]they said to me, 'Make [1]a god for us who will go before us; for this Moses, the man who brought us up from the land of Egypt, we do not know what has become of him.'

24 "I said to them, 'Whoever has any gold, let them tear it off.' So they gave *it* to me, and [a]I threw it into the fire, and out came this calf."

25 Now when Moses saw that the people were [1]out of control—for Aaron had [a]let them [2]get out of control to be a derision among [3]their enemies—

26 then Moses stood in the gate of the camp, and said, "Whoever is for the LORD, *come* to me!" And all the sons of Levi gathered together to him.

27 He said to them, "Thus says the LORD, the God of Israel, 'Every man *of you* put his sword upon his thigh, and go back and forth from gate to gate in the camp, and kill every man his brother, and every man his friend, and every man his [1]neighbor.' "

28 So [a]the sons of Levi did [1]as Moses instructed, and about three thousand men of the people fell that day.

29 Then Moses said, "[1]Dedicate yourselves today to the LORD—for every man has been against his son and against his brother—in order that He may bestow a blessing upon you today."

30 On the next day Moses said to the people, "[a]You yourselves have [1]committed a great sin; and now I am going up to the LORD, perhaps I can [b]make atonement for your sin."

31 Then Moses returned to the LORD, and said, "Alas, this people has [1]committed a great sin, and they have made [2]a [a]god of gold for themselves.

32 "But now, if You will, forgive their sin—and if not, please blot me out from Your [a]book which You have written!"

33 The LORD said to Moses, "Whoever has sinned against Me, [a]I will blot him out of My book.

34 "But go now, lead the people [a]where I told you. Behold, [b]My angel shall go before you; nevertheless [c]in the day when I [1]punish, [d]I will [2]punish them for their sin."

35 [a]Then the LORD smote the people, because of [b]what they did with the calf which Aaron had made.

The Journey Resumed

33 Then the LORD spoke to Moses, "Depart, go up from here, you and the people whom you have brought up from the land of Egypt, to the land of which [a]I swore to Abraham, [b]Isaac, and [c]Jacob, saying, '[d]To your [1]descendants I will give it.'

2 "I will send [a]an angel before you and [b]I will drive out the Canaanite, the Amorite, the Hittite, the Perizzite, the Hivite and the Jebusite.

3 "*Go up* to a land [a]flowing with milk and honey; for I will not go up in your midst, because you are [1][b]an obstinate people, and [c]I might destroy you on the way."

4 When the people heard this [1]sad word, [a]they went into mourning, and none of them put on his ornaments.

5 For the LORD had said to Moses, "Say to the sons of Israel, 'You are [1][a]an obstinate people; should I go up in your midst for one moment, I would destroy you. Now therefore, put off your ornaments from you, that I may know what I shall do with you.' "

6 So the sons of Israel stripped them-

22 [1]Lit *in evil* [a]Deut 9:24
23 [1]Or *gods* [a]Ex 32:1-4
24 [a]Ex 32:4
25 [1]Lit *let loose* [2]Lit *go loose* [3]Lit *those who rise against them* [a]1 Kin 12:28-30; 14:16
27 [1]Or *kin*
28 [1]Lit *according to Moses' word* [a]Num 25:7-13; Deut 33:9
29 [1]Lit *Fill your hand*
30 [1]Lit *sinned* [a]1 Sam 12:20, 23 [b]Num 25:13
31 [1]Lit *sinned*
31 [2]Or *gods* [a]Ex 20:23
32 [a]Ps 69:28; Is 4:3; Dan 12:1; Mal 3:16, 17; Phil 4:3; Rev 3:5; 21:27
33 [a]Ex 17:14; Deut 29:20; Ps 9:5; Rev 3:5
34 [1]Lit *visit* [2]Lit *visit their sin upon them* [a]Ex 3:17 [b]Ex 23:20 [c]Deut 32:35; Rom 2:5, 6 [d]Ps 99:8
35 [a]Ex 32:28 [b]Ex 32:4, 24
33:1 [1]Lit *seed* [a]Ex 32:13 [b]Gen 26:1-3 [c]Gen 28:10 [d]Gen 12:7
2 [a]Ex 32:34 [b]Ex 23:27-31; Josh 24:11
3 [1]Lit *a stiff-necked* [a]Ex 3:8, 17 [b]Ex 32:9; 33:5 [c]Ex 32:10
4 [1]Lit *evil* [a]Num 14:1, 39
5 [1]Lit *a stiff-necked* [a]Ex 33:3

32:22–24 In his desperation, Aaron blamed the people (see notes on Gen 3:12–13).

32:24 *out came this calf.* Aaron could hardly have thought that Moses would believe such an incredible story.

32:25 *were out of control . . . get out of control.* The same Hebrew root underlies both phrases and is found also in Prov 29:18 ("unrestrained"). Anarchy reigns among people who refuse to obey and worship the Lord.

32:26 *Whoever is for the LORD, come to me.* See Josh 24:15; 1 Kin 18:21; Matt 6:24. *all.* A generalization since Deut 33:9 implies that some of the Levites were also slain. *sons of Levi.* The descendants of Levi (Gen 29:34) may have originally been regarded as priests (Deut 18:6–8). But at some stage they became subordinate to the priests who were descendants of Aaron, the brother of Moses (38:21; Num 3:9–10; 1 Chr 16:4–6,37–42).

32:27 *kill every man his brother . . . his friend . . . his neighbor.* See Matt 10:37; Luke 14:26.

32:28 *the sons of Levi did as Moses instructed.* Their zeal for the Lord is later matched by Aaron's grandson Phinehas, resulting in a perpetual covenant of the priesthood (see Num 25:7–13).

32:29 *Dedicate yourselves today to the LORD.* Because of their zeal for the Lord the Levites were set apart to be caretakers of the tabernacle and aides to the priests (see Num 1:47–53; 3:5–9, 12,41,45; 4:2–3).

32:30 *make atonement for your sin.* By making urgent intercession before God, as the mediator God had appointed between Himself and Israel. No sacrifice that Israel or Moses might bring could atone for this sin. But Moses so identified himself with Israel that he made his own death the condition for God's destruction of the nation (see v. 32). Jesus Christ, the great Mediator, offered Himself on the cross to make atonement for His people.

32:32 *book which You have written.* See notes on Ps 9:5; 51:1; 69:28.

32:33 *Whoever has sinned . . . I will blot him out.* Moses' gracious offer is refused, because the person who sins is responsible for his own sin (see Deut 24:16; Ezek 18:4 and note).

32:34 *Go now, lead the people.* Thus Moses received assurance that the Lord will continue His covenant with wayward Israel and fulfill His promise concerning the land. *where I told you.* Canaan (see 33:1).

33:2 *Canaanite . . . Jebusite.* See note on 3:8.

33:3 *land flowing with milk and honey.* See note on 3:8. *I will not go up in your midst.* The Lord's presence, earlier assured to His people (see 23:21 and note), is now temporarily withdrawn because of sin. *obstinate.* See note on 32:9.

33:6 *stripped themselves of their ornaments.* As a sign of mourning (see Ezek 26:16–17).

selves of their ornaments, from Mount Horeb *onward.*

7 Now Moses used to take [a]the tent and pitch it outside the camp, a good distance from the camp, and he called it the tent of meeting. And [b]everyone who sought the LORD would go out to the tent of meeting which was outside the camp.

8 And it came about, whenever Moses went out to the tent, that all the people would arise and stand, each at the entrance of his tent, and gaze after Moses until he entered the tent.

9 Whenever Moses entered the tent, [a]the pillar of cloud would descend and stand at the entrance of the tent; [b]and [1]the LORD would speak with Moses.

10 When all the people saw the pillar of cloud standing at the entrance of the tent, all the people would arise and worship, each at the entrance of his tent.

11 Thus [a]the LORD used to speak to Moses face to face, just as a man speaks to his friend. When [1]Moses returned to the camp, [b]his servant Joshua, the son of Nun, a young man, would not depart from the tent.

Moses Intercedes

12 Then Moses said to the LORD, "See, You say to me, '[a]Bring up this people!' But You Yourself have not let me know [b]whom You will send with me. [c]Moreover, You have said, 'I have known you by name, and you have also found favor in My sight.'

13 "Now therefore, I pray You, if I have found favor in Your sight, [a]let me know Your ways that I may know You, so that I may find favor in Your sight. [b]Consider too, that this nation is Your people."

14 And He said, "[a]My presence shall go *with you,* and [b]I will give you rest."

15 Then he said to Him, "[a]If Your presence does not go *with us,* do not lead us up from here.

16 "For how then can it be known that I have found favor in Your sight, I and Your people? Is it not by Your going with us, so that [a]we, I and Your people, may be distinguished from all the *other* people who are upon the face of the [1]earth?"

17 The LORD said to Moses, "I will also do this thing of which you have spoken; [a]for you have found favor in My sight and I have known you by name."

18 [a]Then [1]Moses said, "I pray You, show me Your glory!"

19 And He said, "[a]I Myself will make all My goodness pass before you, and will proclaim the name of the LORD before you; and [b]I will be gracious to whom I will be gracious, and will show compassion on whom I will show compassion."

20 But He said, "You cannot see My face, [a]for no man can see Me and live!"

21 Then the LORD said, "Behold, there is a place [1]by Me, and [a]you shall stand *there* on the rock;

22 and it will come about, while My glory is passing by, that I will put you in the cleft of the rock and [a]cover you with My hand until I have passed by.

23 "Then I will take My hand away and you shall see My back, but [a]My face shall not be seen."

The Two Tablets Replaced

34 Now the LORD said to Moses, "Cut out for yourself [a]two stone tablets like the former ones, and [b]I will write on the tablets the words that were on the former tablets which you shattered.

2 "So be ready by morning, and come up in the morning to [a]Mount Sinai, and [1]present yourself there to Me on the top of the mountain.

3 "[a]No man is to come up with you, nor let any man be seen [1]anywhere on the mountain; even the flocks and the herds may not graze in front of that mountain."

4 So he cut out [a]two stone tablets like the former ones, and Moses rose up early in the morning and went up to Mount Sinai, as the

7 [a]Ex 18:7, 12-16 [b]Ex 29:42f
9 [1]Lit *He* [a]Ex 13:21 [b]Ps 99:7
11 [1]Lit *he* [a]Num 12:8; Deut 34:10 [b]Ex 24:13
12 [a]Ex 3:10; 32:34 [b]Ex 33:2 [c]Ex 33:17
13 [a]Ps 25:4; 27:11; 51:13; 86:11; 119:33 [b]Ex 3:7, 10; 5:1; 32:12, 14; Deut 9:26, 29
14 [a]Deut 4:37; Is 63:9 [b]Deut 12:10; 25:19; Josh 21:44; 22:4
15 [a]Ps 80:3, 7, 19
16 [1]Lit *ground* [a]Lev 20:24, 26
17 [a]Ex 33:12
18 [1]Lit *he* [a]Ex 33:20-23
19 [a]Ex 34:6, 7 [b]Rom 9:15
20 [a]Is 6:5; 1 Tim 6:16
21 [1]Lit *with* [a]Ps 18:2, 46; 27:5; 61:2; 62:7
22 [a]Ps 91:1, 4; Is 49:2; 51:16
23 [a]Ex 33:20; John 1:18
34:1 [a]Ex 24:12; 31:18; 32:16, 19 [b]Deut 10:2, 4
2 [1]Or *place yourself before* [a]Ex 19:11, 18, 20
3 [1]Lit *on all* [a]Ex 19:12, 13
4 [a]Ex 34:1

33:7 *tent of meeting which was outside the camp.* Not the tabernacle (contrast 27:21), which occupied a central location within the Israelite camp, but a temporary structure where the people could inquire of the Lord until the more durable tabernacle was completed.

33:9 *pillar of cloud would descend.* Symbolizing God's communication with Moses "as a man speaks to his friend" (v. 11). Later, a similar descent crowned the completion of the tabernacle (see 40:33–34; see also note on 13:21).

33:11 *the LORD used to speak to Moses face to face.* As the OT mediator, Moses was unique among the prophets. *Joshua . . . would not depart from the tent.* Probably his task was to guard the tent against intrusion by others.

33:12 *You Yourself have not let me know whom You will send with me.* See note on v. 3. Moses objects that a mere angel is no substitute for God's own presence. *I have known you by name.* I have chosen you for my special purpose.

33:13 *let me know Your ways.* A prayer that is answered in 34:6–7.

33:14 *My presence shall go with you.* The Lord's gracious response to Moses' concern (see note on v. 12).

33:17 *for you have found favor in My sight.* How much more does God hear the prayers of His Son Jesus Christ (see Matt 17:5; Heb 3:1–6)!

33:18 See v. 22. In a sense, Moses' prayer was finally answered on the Mount of Transfiguration (Luke 9:30–32), where he shared a vision—however brief—of the Lord's glory with Elijah and three of Jesus' disciples.

33:19 *goodness.* God's nature and character. *name.* A further symbol of God's nature, character and person (see Ps 20:1; John 1:12; 17:6). Here His name implies His mercy (grace) and His compassion (as it does also in 34:6).

33:20 See note on Gen 16:13; see also John 1:18; 6:46; 1 Tim 1:17; 1 John 4:12.

33:21–23 God speaks of Himself in human language. See 34:5–7 for the fulfillment of His promise.

34:1 *two stone tablets . . . I will write on the tablets.* See note on 31:18. *words.* See note on 20:1.

LORD had commanded him, and he took two stone tablets in his hand.

5 [a]The LORD descended in the cloud and stood there with him as [1]he called upon the name of the LORD.

6 Then the LORD passed by in front of him and proclaimed, "The LORD, the LORD God, [a]compassionate and gracious, slow to anger, and abounding in lovingkindness and [1]truth;

7 who [a]keeps lovingkindness for thousands, who forgives iniquity, transgression and sin; yet He [b]will by no means leave *the guilty* unpunished, [c]visiting the iniquity of fathers on the children and on the grandchildren to the third and fourth generations."

8 Moses made haste [1a]to bow low toward the earth and worship.

9 He said, "[a]If now I have found favor in Your sight, O Lord, I pray, let the Lord go along in our midst, even though [1b]the people are so obstinate, and [c]pardon our iniquity and our sin, and [d]take us as Your own [2]possession."

The Covenant Renewed

10 Then [1]God said, "Behold, [a]I am going to make a covenant. Before all your people [b]I will perform miracles which have not been [2]produced in all the earth nor among any of the nations; and all the people [3]among whom you live will see the working of the LORD, for it is a fearful thing that I am going to perform with you.

11 "[1]Be sure to observe what I am commanding you this day: behold, [a]I am going to drive out the Amorite before you, and the Canaanite, the Hittite, the Perizzite, the Hivite and the Jebusite.

12 "[a]Watch yourself that you make no covenant with the inhabitants of the land into which you are going, or it will become a snare in your midst.

13 "[a]But *rather,* you are to tear down their altars and smash their *sacred* pillars and cut down their [1b]Asherim

14 —for [a]you shall not worship any other god, for the LORD, whose name is Jealous, is a jealous God—

15 otherwise you might make a covenant with the inhabitants of the land and they would play the harlot with their gods and [a]sacrifice to their gods, and someone [b]might invite you [1]to eat of his sacrifice,

16 and [a]you might take some of his daughters for your sons, and his daughters might play the harlot with their gods and cause your sons *also* to play the harlot with their gods.

17 "[a]You shall make for yourself no molten gods.

18 "You shall observe [a]the Feast of Unleavened Bread. For [b]seven days you are to eat unleavened bread, [1]as I commanded you, at the appointed time in the [c]month of Abib, for in the month of Abib you came out of Egypt.

19 "[a]The first offspring from every womb belongs to Me, and all your male livestock, the first offspring from [1]cattle and sheep.

20 "[a]You shall redeem with a lamb the [1]first offspring from a donkey; and if you do not redeem *it,* then you shall break its neck. You shall redeem [b]all the firstborn of your sons. [2c]None shall appear before Me empty-handed.

21 "You shall work [a]six days, but on the seventh day you shall rest; *even* during plowing time and harvest you shall rest.

22 "You shall celebrate [a]the Feast of Weeks, *that is,* the first fruits of the wheat harvest, and the Feast of Ingathering at the turn of the year.

23 "[a]Three times a year all your males are to appear before the Lord [1]GOD, the God of Israel.

24 "For I will [1a]drive out nations before you and enlarge your borders, and no man shall covet your land when you go up three times a year to appear before the LORD your God.

25 "[a]You shall not [1]offer the blood of My sacrifice with leavened bread, [b]nor is the sacrifice of the Feast of the Passover to [2]be left over until morning.

5 [1]Or *he called out with the name of the* LORD [a]Ex 19:9; 33:9
6 [1]Or *faithfulness* [a]Num 14:18; Deut 4:31; Neh 9:17; Ps 86:15; 103:8; 108:4; 145:8; Joel 2:13; Rom 2:4
7 [a]Ex 20:5, 6; Deut 5:10; 7:9; Ps 103:3; 130:3, 4; 1 John 1:9 [b]Ex 23:7; Deut 7:10; Job 10:14; Nah 1:3 [c]Deut 5:9
8 [1]Lit *and bowed...worshiped* [a]Ex 4:31
9 [1]Lit *it is a people stiff-necked* [2]Or *inheritance* [a]Ex 33:13 [b]Ex 32:9 [c]Ex 34:7 [d]Deut 4:20; 9:26, 29; 32:9; Ps 33:12
10 [1]Lit *He* [2]Lit *created* [3]Lit *in whose midst you are* [a]Ex 34:27, 28; Deut 5:2 [b]Deut 4:32; Ps 72:18; 136:4
11 [1]Lit *Observe for yourself* [a]Ex 33:2
12 [a]Ex 23:32, 33
13 [1]I.e. wooden symbols of a female deity [a]Ex 23:24; Deut 12:3 [b]Deut 16:21; Judg 6:25, 26; 2 Kin 18:4; 2 Chr 34:3f
14 [a]Ex 20:3, 5; Deut 4:24
15 [1]Lit *and you eat* [a]Ex 22:20; 32:8 [b]Num 25:1, 2; Deut 32:37, 38
16 [a]Deut 7:3; Josh 23:12, 13; 1 Kin 11:1-4
17 [a]Ex 20:4, 23; Lev 19:4; Deut 5:8
18 [1]Or *which* [a]Ex 12:17; Lev 23:6; Num 28:16f [b]Ex 12:15, 16 [c]Ex 12:2; 13:4
19 [1]Or *oxen* [a]Ex 13:2; 22:29f
20 [1]Lit *first opening of* [2]Lit *They shall not* [a]Ex 13:13 [b]Ex 13:15; Num 3:45 [c]Ex 22:29; 23:15; Deut 16:16 **21** [a]Ex 20:9f; 23:12; 31:15; 35:2; Lev 23:3; Deut 5:13f **22** [a]Ex 23:16; Num 28:26
23 [1]Heb *YHWH,* usually rendered LORD [a]Ex 23:14-17 **24** [1]Or *dispossess* [a]Ex 33:2; Ps 78:55 **25** [1]Lit *slaughter* [2]Lit *remain overnight* [a]Ex 23:18 [b]Ex 12:10

34:5 *name.* See note on 33:19.
34:6–7 See 33:19 and note. The Lord's proclamation of the meaning and implications of His name in these verses became a classic exposition that was frequently recalled elsewhere in the OT (see Num 14:18; Neh 9:17; Ps 86:15; 103:8; 145:8; Joel 2:13; Jon 4:2). See also notes on 3:14–15; 6:2–3.
34:7 *for thousands.* Or "to thousands" (see 20:6). *iniquity, transgression and sin.* See Is 59:12 and note.
34:10 *make a covenant.* Renewing the covenant he had earlier made (chs. 19–24). Verses 10–26, many of which are quoted almost verbatim from previous sections of Exodus (compare especially vv. 18–26 with 23:14–19), are sometimes referred to as the "Ritual Decalogue."
34:12 *make no covenant with the inhabitants of the land.* Israel is not to make a treaty of peace with any of the people of Canaan to let them live in the land.
34:13 *Asherim.* Symbols of Asherah, the name of the consort (wife) of El, the chief Canaanite god. Wooden poles, perhaps carved in her image, were often set up in her honor and placed near other pagan objects of worship (see, e.g., Judg 6:25).
34:14 *whose name is Jealous.* See note on 20:5.
34:15 *play the harlot.* See Judg 2:17 and note. *eat of his sacrifice.* Partaking of food sacrificed to a pagan deity invites compromise (cf. 1 Cor 8; 10:18–21).
34:17 *make . . . no molten gods.* As Aaron had done when he made the golden calf (see 32:4).
34:18–26 See notes on 23:14–19.
34:21 *even during plowing time and harvest you shall rest.* Just as they were also to rest while building the tabernacle (see notes on 31:13,16–17).

26 "You shall bring [a]the very first of the first fruits of your soil into the house of the LORD your God.

"You shall not boil a young goat in its mother's milk."

27 Then the LORD said to Moses, "[a]Write [1]down these words, for in accordance with these words I have made [b]a covenant with you and with Israel."

28 So he was there with the LORD [a]forty days and forty nights; he did not eat bread or drink water. And [b]he wrote on the tablets the words of the covenant, [c]the Ten [1]Commandments.

Moses' Face Shines

29 It came about when Moses was coming down from Mount Sinai (and the [a]two tablets of the testimony *were* in Moses' hand as he was coming down from the mountain), that Moses did not know that [b]the skin of his face shone because of his speaking with Him.

30 So when Aaron and all the sons of Israel saw Moses, behold, the skin of his face shone, and [a]they were afraid to come near him.

31 Then Moses called to them, and Aaron and all the rulers in the congregation returned to him; and Moses spoke to them.

32 Afterward all the sons of Israel came near, and he commanded them *to do* everything that the LORD had spoken [1]to him on Mount Sinai.

33 When Moses had finished speaking with them, [a]he put a veil over his face.

34 But whenever Moses went in before the LORD to speak with Him, [a]he would take off the veil until he came out; and whenever he came out and spoke to the sons of Israel what he had been commanded,

35 [a]the sons of Israel would see the face of Moses, that the skin of Moses' face shone. So Moses would replace the veil over his face until he went in to speak with Him.

The Sabbath Emphasized

35 Then Moses assembled all the congregation of the sons of Israel, and said to them, "[a]These are the things that the LORD has commanded *you* to [1]do:

2 "[a]For six days work may be done, but on the seventh day you shall have a holy *day,* [b]a sabbath of complete rest to the LORD; [c]whoever does any work on it shall be put to death.

3 "[a]You shall not kindle a fire in any of your dwellings on the sabbath day."

4 Moses spoke to all the congregation of the sons of Israel, saying, "This is the thing which the LORD has commanded, saying,

5 '[a]Take from among you a [1]contribution to the LORD; whoever is of a willing heart, let him bring it as the LORD's [1]contribution: gold, silver, and [2]bronze,

6 and [1]blue, purple and scarlet *material,* fine linen, goats' *hair,*

7 and rams' skins [1]dyed red, and porpoise skins, and acacia wood,

8 and oil for lighting, and spices for the anointing oil, and for the fragrant incense,

9 and onyx stones and setting stones for the ephod and for the [1]breastpiece.

Tabernacle Workmen

10 '[a]Let every skillful man among you come, and make all that the LORD has commanded:

11 the [1a]tabernacle, its tent and its covering, its hooks and its boards, its bars, its pillars, and its [2]sockets;

12 the [a]ark and its poles, the [1]mercy seat, and the curtain of the screen;

13 the [a]table and its poles, and all its [1]utensils, and the bread of the [2]Presence;

14 the [a]lampstand also for the light and its utensils and its lamps and the oil for the light;

15 and the [a]altar of incense and its poles, and the [b]anointing oil and the [c]fragrant incense, and the screen for the doorway at the [1]entrance of the tabernacle;

16 [a]the altar of burnt offering with its [1]bronze grating, its poles, and all its [2]utensils, the [3]basin and its stand;

17 [a]the hangings of the court, its pillars and its [1]sockets, and the screen for the gate of the court;

26 [a]Ex 23:19; Deut 26:2
27 [1]Lit *for yourself* [a]Ex 17:14; 24:4 [b]Ex 34:10
28 [1]Lit *Words* [a]Ex 24:18 [b]Ex 31:18; 34:1 [c]Deut 4:13; 10:4
29 [a]Ex 32:15 [b]Matt 17:2; 2 Cor 3:7
30 [a]2 Cor 3:7
32 [1]Lit *with*
33 [a]2 Cor 3:13
34 [a]2 Cor 3:16
35 [a]2 Cor 3:13

35:1 [1]Lit *do them* [a]Ex 34:32
2 [a]Ex 20:9, 10; 23:12; 31:15; 34:21; Lev 23:3; Deut 5:13f [b]Ex 16:23 [c]Num 15:32-36
3 [a]Ex 12:16; 16:23
5 [1]Or *heave offering* [2]Or *copper* [a]Ex 25:1-9
6 [1]Or *violet*
7 [1]Or *tanned*
9 [1]Or *pouch*
10 [a]Ex 31:6
11 [1]Lit *dwelling place* [2]Or *bases* [a]Ex 26:1-30
12 [1]Lit *propitiatory* [a]Ex 25:10-22
13 [1]Or *vessels* [2]Lit *Face* [a]Ex 25:23-30
14 [a]Ex 25:31ff
15 [1]Or *doorway* [a]Ex 30:1-6 [b]Ex 30:25 [c]Ex 30:34-38
16 [1]Or *copper* [2]Or *vessels* [3]Or *laver* [a]Ex 27:1-8
17 [1]Or *bases* [a]Ex 27:9-18

34:27 *Write down these words.* As he had earlier written down similar words (see 24:4).

34:28 *he wrote.* Here the Lord, rather than Moses, is probably the subject (see v. 1). *the words of the covenant, the Ten Commandments.* The two phrases are synonymous (see note on 20:1).

34:29 *testimony.* See notes on 16:34; 25:16. *shone.* He who had asked to see God's glory (33:18) now, quite unawares, reflects the divine glory. The Hebrew for "shone" is related to the Hebrew noun for "horn." The meaning of the phrase was therefore misunderstood by the Vulgate (the Latin translation), and thus European medieval art often showed horns sprouting from Moses' head.

34:33 *he put a veil over his face.* So that the Israelites would not see the fading away of the radiance but would continue to honor Moses as the one who represented God. For a NT reflection on Moses' action see 2 Cor 3:7–18 and notes.

35:1–3 Just as the Israelites had been reminded of the importance of Sabbath observance immediately after the instructions for building the tabernacle and making the priestly garments (see note on 31:13), so now—just before the fulfilling of those instructions—the people are given the same reminder.

35:4–39:43 For the most part repeated from chs. 25–28; 30:1–5; 31:1–11 (see notes on those passages), sometimes verbatim, but with the verbs primarily in the past rather than the future tense and with the topics arranged in a different order. Such repetition was a common feature of ancient Near Eastern literature and was intended to fix the details of a narrative in the reader's mind (see note on Gen 24:34–49).

35:5 *whoever is of a willing heart.* The voluntary motivation behind the offering of materials and services for the tabernacle is stressed (see vv. 21–22,26,29; 36:2–3).

18 the pegs of the tabernacle and the pegs of the court and their cords;

19 the [1][a]woven garments for ministering in the holy place, the holy garments for Aaron the priest and the garments of his sons, to minister as priests.' "

Gifts Received

20 Then all the congregation of the sons of Israel departed from Moses' presence.

21 [a]Everyone whose heart [1]stirred him and everyone whose spirit [2]moved him came *and* brought the LORD's [3]contribution for the work of the tent of meeting and for all its service and for the holy garments.

22 Then all [1]whose hearts moved them, both men and women, came *and* brought brooches and [2]earrings and signet rings and bracelets, all articles of gold; so *did* every man who [3]presented an offering of gold to the LORD.

23 Every man, [1]who had in his possession [2]blue and purple and scarlet *material* and fine linen and goats' *hair* and rams' skins [3]dyed red and porpoise skins, brought them.

24 Everyone who could make a [1]contribution of silver and [2]bronze brought the LORD's [1]contribution; and every man [3]who had in his possession acacia wood for any work of the service brought it.

25 All the [1]skilled women spun with their hands, and brought what they had spun, *in* [2]blue and purple *and* scarlet *material* and *in* fine linen.

26 All the women whose heart [1]stirred with a skill spun the goats' *hair.*

27 The rulers brought the onyx stones and the stones for setting for the ephod and for the [1]breastpiece;

28 and [a]the spice and the oil for the light and for the anointing oil and for the fragrant incense.

29 The [1]Israelites, all the men and women, whose heart [2]moved them to bring *material* for all the work, which the LORD had commanded through Moses to be done, brought a [a]freewill offering to the LORD.

30 [a]Then Moses said to the sons of Israel, "See, the LORD has called by name Bezalel the son of Uri, the son of Hur, of the tribe of Judah.

31 "And He has filled him with the Spirit of God, in wisdom, in understanding and in knowledge and in all [1]craftsmanship;

32 [1]to make designs for working in gold and in silver and in [2]bronze,

33 and in the cutting of stones for settings and in the carving of wood, so as to perform in every inventive work.

34 "He also has put in his heart to teach, both he and [a]Oholiab, the son of Ahisamach, of the tribe of Dan.

35 "[a]He has filled them with [1]skill to perform every work of an engraver and of a designer and of an embroiderer, in [2]blue and in purple *and* in scarlet *material,* and in fine linen, and of a weaver, as performers of every work and makers of designs.

The Tabernacle Underwritten

36 "Now Bezalel and Oholiab, and every [1]skillful person in whom the LORD has put [2]skill and understanding to know how to perform all the work [3]in the construction of the sanctuary, shall perform in accordance with all that the LORD has commanded."

2 Then Moses called Bezalel and Oholiab and every [1]skillful person in [2]whom the LORD had put [3]skill, [a]everyone whose heart stirred him, to come to the work to perform it.

3 They received from Moses all the [1]contributions which the sons of Israel had brought [2]to perform the work [3]in the construction of the sanctuary. And they still *continued* bringing to him freewill offerings every morning.

4 And all the [1]skillful men who were performing all the work of the sanctuary came, each from [2]the work which [3]he was performing,

5 and they said to [1]Moses, "[a]The people are bringing much more than enough for the [2]construction work which the LORD commanded *us* to [3]perform."

6 So Moses issued a command, and a [1]proclamation was circulated throughout the camp, saying, "Let no man or woman any longer perform work for the [2]contributions of the sanctuary." Thus the people were restrained from bringing *any more.*

7 [a]For the [1]material they had was sufficient and more than enough for all the work, to perform it.

Construction Proceeds

8 [a]All the [1]skillful men among those who were performing the work made the [2]tabernacle with ten curtains; of fine twisted linen and [3]blue and purple and scarlet *material,* with cherubim, the work of a skillful workman, [4]Bezalel made them.

9 The length of each curtain was twenty-eight [1]cubits and the width of each curtain four [1]cubits; all the curtains had [2]the same measurements.

10 He [1]joined five curtains to one another and *the other* five curtains he [1]joined to one another.

11 He made loops of [1]blue on the edge of the [2]outermost curtain in the first [3]set; he did likewise on the edge of the curtain that was [2]outermost in the second [3]set.

12 He made [a]fifty loops in the one curtain and he made fifty loops on the [1]edge of the curtain that was in the second [2]set; the loops were opposite each other.

19 [1]Or *service garments* [a]Ex 31:10; 39:1
21 [1]Lit *lifted up* [2]Or *made him willing* [3]Or *heave offering* [a]Ex 25:2; 35:5, 22, 26, 29; 36:2
22 [1]Or *who were willing-hearted* [2]Or *nose rings* [3]Lit *waved a wave offering*
23 [1]Lit *with whom was found* [2]Or *violet* [3]Or *tanned*
24 [1]Or *heave offering* [2]Or *copper* [3]Lit *with whom was found*
25 [1]Lit *women wise of heart* [2]Or *violet*
26 [1]Lit *lifted them up in wisdom*
27 [1]Or *pouch*
28 [a]Ex 30:23ff
29 [1]Lit *sons of Israel* [2]Lit *made them willing* [a]Ex 35:21; 1 Chr 29:9
30 [a]Ex 31:1-6
31 [1]Or *work*
32 [1]Lit *devise devices* [2]Or *copper*
34 [a]Ex 31:6
35 [1]Lit *wisdom of heart* [a]Ex 31:3, 6; 35:31; 1 Kin 7:14
35 [2]Or *violet*
36:1 [1]Lit *man wise of heart* [2]Lit *wisdom* [3]Or *connected with the service of;* lit *of the service of*
2 [1]Lit *man wise of heart* [2]Lit *whose heart* [3]Lit *wisdom* [a]Ex 35:21, 26
3 [1]Lit *lifted offering* [2]Lit *to perform it for the work* [3]Lit *of the service of*
4 [1]Lit *wise* [2]Lit *his* [3]Lit *they were*
5 [1]Lit *Moses, saying,* [2]Lit *service for the work* [3]Lit *perform it* [a]2 Chr 24:14; 31:6-10
6 [1]Lit *voice* [2]Lit *heave offering*
7 [1]Lit *work* [a]1 Kin 8:64
8 [1]Lit *wise of heart* [2]Lit *dwelling place* [3]Or *violet* [4]Lit *he* [a]Ex 26:1-14
9 [1]I.e. One cubit equals approx 18 in. [2]Lit *one measure*
10 [1]Or *coupled*
11 [1]Or *violet* [2]Lit *one curtain from the end in the coupling* [3]Lit *coupling*
12 [1]Lit *end* [2]Lit *coupling* [a]Ex 26:5

35:21 *tent of meeting.* See note on 27:21.

36:1–38 See note on 35:4–39:43.

13 He made [a]fifty clasps of gold and [1]joined the curtains to one another with the clasps, so the tabernacle was [2]a unit.

14 Then [a]he made curtains of goats' *hair* for a tent over the tabernacle; he made eleven curtains [1]in all.

15 The length of each curtain *was* thirty cubits and four cubits the width of each curtain; the eleven curtains had [1]the same measurements.

16 He [1]joined five curtains by themselves and *the other* six curtains by themselves.

17 Moreover, he made fifty loops on the edge of the curtain that was outermost in the *first* [1]set, and he made fifty loops on the edge of the curtain *that was outermost in* the second [1]set.

18 He made fifty clasps of [1]bronze to [2]join the tent together so that it would be [3]a unit.

19 He made a covering for the tent of rams' skins [1]dyed red, and a covering of porpoise skins above.

20 [a]Then he made the boards for the tabernacle of acacia wood, standing upright.

21 Ten cubits *was* the length of [1]each board and one and a half cubits the width of each board.

22 *There were* two tenons for each board, [1]fitted to one another; thus he did for all the boards of the tabernacle.

23 He made the boards for the tabernacle: twenty boards [1]for the south side;

24 and he made forty [1]sockets of silver under the twenty boards; two [1]sockets under one board for its two tenons and two [1]sockets under another board for its two tenons.

25 Then for the second side of the tabernacle, on the north side, he made twenty boards,

26 and their forty [1]sockets of silver; two [1]sockets under one board and two [1]sockets under another board.

27 For the [1]rear of the tabernacle, to the west, he made six boards.

28 He made two boards for the corners of the [1]tabernacle at the [2]rear.

29 They were double beneath, and together they were complete to its [1]top [2]to the first ring; thus he did with both of them for the two corners.

30 There were eight boards with their [1]sockets of silver, sixteen [1]sockets, [2]two under every board.

31 Then he made [a]bars of acacia wood, five for the boards of one side of the tabernacle,

32 and five bars for the boards of the [1]other side of the tabernacle, and five bars for the boards of the tabernacle for the [2]rear *side* to the west.

33 He made the middle bar to pass through in the [1]center of the boards from end to end.

34 He overlaid the boards with gold and made their rings of gold *as* holders for the bars, and overlaid the bars with gold.

35 [a]Moreover, he made the veil of [1]blue and purple and scarlet *material,* and fine twisted linen; he made it with cherubim, the work of a skillful workman.

36 He made four pillars of acacia for it, and overlaid them with gold, with their hooks of gold; and he cast four [1]sockets of silver for them.

37 He made a [a]screen for the doorway of the tent, of [1]blue and purple and scarlet *material,* and fine twisted linen, the work of a [2]weaver;

38 and *he made* its [a]five pillars with their hooks, and he overlaid their tops and their [1]bands with gold; but their five [2]sockets were of [3]bronze.

Construction Continues

37 [a]Now Bezalel made the ark of acacia wood; its length was two and a half [1]cubits, and its width one and a half cubits, and its height one and a half cubits;

2 and he overlaid it with pure gold inside and out, and made a gold molding for it all around.

3 He cast four rings of gold for it on its four feet; even two rings on one side of it, and two rings on the [1]other side of it.

4 He made poles of acacia wood and overlaid them with gold.

5 He put the poles into the rings on the sides of the ark, to carry [1]it.

6 He made a [1]mercy seat of pure gold, two and a half cubits [2]long and one and a half cubits [3]wide.

7 He made two cherubim of gold; he made them of hammered work [1]at the two ends of the mercy seat;

8 one cherub [1]at the one end and one cherub [1]at the other end; he made the cherubim *of one piece* with the mercy seat [1]at the two ends.

9 The cherubim had *their* wings spread upward, covering the [1]mercy seat with their wings, with their faces toward each other; the faces of the cherubim were toward the mercy seat.

10 [a]Then he made the table of acacia wood, two [1]cubits [2]long and a cubit [3]wide and one and a half cubits [4]high.

11 He overlaid it with pure gold, and made a gold molding for it all around.

12 He made a rim for it of a handbreadth all around, and made a gold molding for its rim all around.

13 He cast four gold rings for it and put the rings on the four corners that were on its four feet.

13 [1]Or *coupled* [2]Lit *one* [a]Ex 26:6
14 [1]Lit *in number* [a]Ex 26:7-14
15 [1]Lit *one measure*
16 [1]Or *coupled*
17 [1]Lit *coupling*
18 [1]Or *copper* [2]Or *couple* [3]Lit *one*
19 [1]Or *tanned*
20 [a]Ex 26:15-29
21 [1]Lit *the*
22 [1]Lit *bound*
23 [1]Lit *to the side of the Negev, to the south*
24 [1]Or *bases*
26 [1]Or *bases*
27 [1]Lit *extreme parts*
28 [1]Lit *dwelling place* [2]Lit *extreme parts*
29 [1]Or *head* [2]Or *with reference to*
30 [1]Or *bases* [2]Lit *two sockets*
31 [a]Ex 26:26-29
32 [1]Or *second* [2]Lit *extreme parts*
33 [1]Lit *midst*
35 [1]Or *violet* [a]Ex 26:31-37
36 [1]Or *bases*
37 [1]Or *violet* [2]Lit *variegator;* i.e. a weaver in colors [a]Ex 26:36
38 [1]Or *fillets, rings* [2]Or *bases* [3]Or *copper* [a]Ex 26:37
37:1 [1]I.e. One cubit equals approx 18 in. [a]Ex 25:10-20
3 [1]Lit *second*
5 [1]Lit *the ark*
6 [1]Lit *propitiatory* [2]Lit *its length* [3]Lit *its width*
7 [1]Lit *from*
8 [1]Lit *from*
9 [1]Lit *propitiatory*
10 [1]I.e. One cubit equals approx 18 in. [2]Lit *its length* [3]Lit *its width* [4]Lit *its height* [a]Ex 25:23-29

37:1–29 See note on 35:4–39:43.
37:1 *Bezalel made the ark.* The chief craftsman (see 31:2–3) was given the honor of making the most sacred object (see 25:10 and note) among the furnishings for the tabernacle.

14 Close by the rim were the rings, the holders for the poles to carry the table.

15 He made the poles of acacia wood and overlaid them with gold, to carry the table.

16 He made the utensils which were on the table, its [1]dishes and its pans and its [2]bowls and its jars, with which to pour out drink offerings, of pure gold.

17 [a]Then he made the lampstand of pure gold. He made the lampstand of hammered work, its base and its shaft; its cups, its [1]bulbs and its flowers were *of one piece* with it.

18 There were six branches going out of its sides; three branches of the lampstand from the one side of it and three branches of the lampstand from the [1]other side of it;

19 three cups shaped like almond *blossoms,* a [1]bulb and a flower in one branch, and three cups shaped like almond *blossoms,* a [1]bulb and a flower in the other branch—so for the six branches going out of the lampstand.

20 In the lampstand *there were* four cups shaped like almond *blossoms,* its [1]bulbs and its flowers;

21 and a [1]bulb was under the *first* pair of branches *coming* out of it, and a [1]bulb under the *second* pair of branches *coming* out of it, and a [1]bulb under the *third* pair of branches *coming* out of it, for the six branches coming out of the lampstand.

22 Their [1]bulbs and their branches were *of one piece* with it; the whole of it *was* a single hammered work of pure gold.

23 He made its seven lamps with its snuffers and its [1]trays of pure gold.

24 He made it and all its utensils from a talent of pure gold.

25 [a]Then he made the altar of incense of acacia wood: a cubit [1]long and a cubit [2]wide, square, and two cubits [3]high; its horns were *of one piece* with it.

26 He overlaid it with pure gold, its top and its [1]sides all around, and its horns; and he made a gold molding for it all around.

27 He made two golden rings for it under its molding, on its two sides—on opposite sides—as holders for poles with which to carry it.

28 He made the poles of acacia wood and overlaid them with gold.

29 [a]And he made the holy anointing oil and the pure, fragrant incense of spices, the work of a perfumer.

The Tabernacle Completed

38 [a]Then he made the altar of burnt offering of acacia wood, five [1]cubits [2]long, and five cubits [3]wide, square, and three cubits [4]high.

2 He made its horns on its four corners, its horns [1]being *of one piece* with it, and he overlaid it with [2]bronze.

3 He made all the utensils of the altar, the pails and the shovels and the basins, the flesh hooks and the firepans; he made all its utensils of bronze.

4 He made for the altar a grating of bronze network beneath, under its ledge, reaching halfway up.

5 He cast four rings on the four ends of the bronze grating *as* holders for the poles.

6 He made the poles of acacia wood and overlaid them with bronze.

7 He inserted the poles into the rings on the sides of the altar, with which to carry it. He made it hollow with planks.

8 [a]Moreover, he made the laver of bronze with its base of bronze, [1]from the mirrors of the serving women who served at the doorway of the tent of meeting.

9 [a]Then he made the court: [1]for the south side the hangings of the court were of fine twisted linen, one hundred cubits;

10 their twenty pillars, and their twenty [1]sockets, *made* of bronze; the hooks of the pillars and their [2]bands *were* of silver.

11 For the north side *there were* one hundred cubits; their twenty pillars and their twenty [1]sockets *were* of bronze, the hooks of the pillars and their [2]bands *were* of silver.

12 For the west side *there were* hangings of fifty cubits *with* their ten pillars and their ten [1]sockets; the hooks of the pillars and their [2]bands *were* of silver.

13 For the [1]east side fifty cubits.

14 The hangings for the *one* [1]side *of the gate were* fifteen cubits, *with* their three pillars and their three [2]sockets,

15 and so for the [1]other [2]side. [3]On both sides of the gate of the court *were* hangings of fifteen cubits, *with* their three pillars and their three [4]sockets.

16 All the hangings of the court all around *were* of fine twisted linen.

17 The [1]sockets for the pillars *were* of [2]bronze, the hooks of the pillars and their [3]bands, of silver; and the overlaying of their tops, of silver, and all the pillars of the court were furnished with silver [3]bands.

18 The screen of the gate of the court was the work of the [1]weaver, of [2]blue and purple and scarlet *material* and fine twisted linen. And the length *was* twenty cubits and the [3]height *was* five cubits, corresponding to the hangings of the court.

19 Their four pillars and their four [1]sockets *were* of bronze; their hooks *were* of silver, and the overlaying of their tops and their [2]bands *were* of silver.

20 All the pegs of the [1]tabernacle and of the court all around *were* of bronze.

The Cost of the Tabernacle

21 [1]This is the number of the things for

16 [1]Or *platters* [2]Lit *libation bowls* **17** [1]Or *calyxes* [a]Ex 25:31-39 **18** [1]Lit *second* **19** [1]Or *calyx* **20** [1]Or *calyxes* **21** [1]Or *calyx* **22** [1]Or *calyxes* **23** [1]Lit *snuff dishes* **25** [1]Lit *its length* [2]Lit *its width* [3]Lit *its height* [a]Ex 30:1-5 **26** [1]Lit *walls* **29** [a]Ex 30:23-25, 34, 35 **38:1** [1]I.e. One cubit equals approx 18 in. [2]Lit *its length* [3]Lit *its width* [4]Lit *its height* [a]Ex 27:1-8 **2** [1]Lit *were* [2]Or *copper,* and so for *bronze* throughout the ch

8 [1]Lit *with* [a]Ex 30:18 **9** [1]Lit *to the side of the Negev, to the south* [a]Ex 27:9-19 **10** [1]Or *bases* [2]Or *fillets, rings* **11** [1]Or *bases* [2]Or *fillets, rings* **12** [1]Or *bases* [2]Or *fillets, rings* **13** [1]Lit *east side, eastward* **14** [1]Lit *shoulder* [2]Or *bases* **15** [1]Lit *second* [2]Lit *shoulder* [3]Lit *On this side and on that side* [4]Or *bases* **17** [1]Or *bases* [2]Or *copper* [3]Or *fillets, rings* **18** [1]Lit *variegator;* i.e. a weaver in colors [2]Or *violet* [3]Lit *height in width* **19** [1]Or *bases* [2]Or *fillets, rings* **20** [1]Lit *dwelling place* **21** [1]Lit *These are the appointed things of the tabernacle*

38:1–31 See note on 35:4–39:43.

38:8 *bronze . . . mirrors.* Mirrored glass was unknown in ancient times, but highly polished bronze gave adequate reflection. *tent of meeting.* See note on 27:21.

the [2]tabernacle, the [2]tabernacle of the testimony, as they were [3]numbered according to the [4]command of Moses, for the service of the Levites, by the hand of Ithamar the son of Aaron the priest.

22 Now [a]Bezalel the son of Uri, the son of Hur, of the tribe of Judah, made all that the LORD had commanded Moses.

23 With him *was* [a]Oholiab the son of Ahisamach, of the tribe of Dan, an engraver and a skillful workman and a [1]weaver in [2]blue and in purple and in scarlet *material*, and fine linen.

24 All the gold that was used for the work, in all the work of the sanctuary, even the gold of the wave offering, was 29 talents and 730 shekels, according to [a]the shekel of the sanctuary.

25 [a]The silver of those of the congregation who were [1]numbered was 100 talents and 1,775 shekels, according to the shekel of the sanctuary;

26 [a]a beka a head (*that is*, half a shekel according to the shekel of the sanctuary), for each one who passed over to those who were [1]numbered, from twenty years old and upward, for [b]603,550 men.

27 The hundred talents of silver were for casting the [1]sockets of the sanctuary and the [1]sockets of the veil; one hundred [1]sockets for the hundred talents, a talent for a [1]socket.

28 Of the 1,775 *shekels*, he made hooks for the pillars and overlaid their tops and made [1]bands for them.

29 The bronze of the wave offering was 70 talents and 2,400 shekels.

30 With it he made the [1]sockets to the doorway of the tent of meeting, and the bronze altar and its bronze grating, and all the utensils of the altar,

31 and the [1]sockets of the court all around and the [1]sockets of the gate of the court, and all the pegs of the [2]tabernacle and all the pegs of the court all around.

The Priestly Garments

39 Moreover, from the [1a]blue and purple and scarlet *material*, they made finely [b]woven garments for ministering in the holy place [2]as well as the holy garments which were for Aaron, just as the LORD had commanded Moses.

2 [a]He made the ephod of gold, *and* of [1]blue and purple and scarlet *material*, and fine twisted linen.

3 Then they hammered out gold sheets and cut *them* into threads [1]to be woven in *with* the [2]blue and the purple and the scarlet *material*, and the fine linen, the work of a skillful workman.

4 They made attaching shoulder pieces for [1]the ephod; it was attached at its two *upper* ends.

5 The skillfully woven band which was on it was like its workmanship, [1]of the same material: of gold *and* of [2]blue and purple and scarlet *material*, and fine twisted linen, just as the LORD had commanded Moses.

6 [a]They made the onyx stones, set in gold filigree *settings;* they were engraved *like* the engravings of a signet, according to the names of the sons of Israel.

7 And [a]he placed them on the shoulder pieces of the ephod, *as* memorial stones for the sons of Israel, just as the LORD had commanded Moses.

8 [a]He made the breastpiece, the work of a skillful workman, like the workmanship of the ephod: of gold *and* of [1]blue and purple and scarlet *material* and fine twisted linen.

9 It was square; they made the breastpiece folded double, a span [1]long and a span [2]wide when folded double.

10 And they [1]mounted four rows of stones on it. The first row *was* a row of ruby, topaz, and emerald;

11 and the second row, a turquoise, a sapphire and a diamond;

12 and the third row, a jacinth, an agate, and an amethyst;

13 and the fourth row, a beryl, an onyx, and a jasper. They were set in gold filigree *settings* when they were [1]mounted.

14 The stones were corresponding to the names of the sons of Israel; they were twelve, corresponding to their names, *engraved with* the engravings of a signet, each with its name for the twelve tribes.

15 They made on the breastpiece chains like cords, of twisted cordage work in pure gold.

16 They made two gold filigree *settings* and two gold rings, and put the two rings on the two ends of the breastpiece.

17 Then they put the two gold cords in the two rings at the ends of the breastpiece.

18 They put the *other* two ends of the two cords on the two filigree *settings*, and put them on the shoulder pieces of the ephod at the front of it.

19 They made two gold rings and placed *them* on the two ends of the breastpiece, on its inner edge which was next to the ephod.

20 Furthermore, they made two gold rings and placed them on the bottom of the two shoulder pieces of the ephod, on the front of

21 [2]Lit *dwelling place* [3]Lit *appointed* [4]Lit *mouth*
22 [a]Ex 31:2
23 [1]Lit *variegator;* i.e. a weaver in colors [2]Or *violet* [a]Ex 31:6
24 [a]Ex 30:13; Lev 27:25; Num 3:47; 18:16
25 [1]Lit *mustered* [a]Ex 30:11-16
26 [1]Lit *mustered* [a]Ex 30:13, 15 [b]Ex 12:37; Num 1:46; 26:51
27 [1]Or *bases*
28 [1]Or *fillets, rings*
30 [1]Or *bases*
31 [1]Or *bases* [2]Lit *dwelling place*
39:1 [1]Or *violet* [2]Lit *and they made* [a]Ex 35:23 [b]Ex 31:10; 35:19
2 [1]Or *violet* [a]Ex 28:6-12
3 [1]Lit *to work* [2]Or *violet*
4 [1]Lit *it*
5 [1]Lit *from it* [2]Or *violet*
6 [a]Ex 28:9-11
7 [a]Ex 28:12
8 [1]Or *violet* [a]Ex 28:15-28
9 [1]Lit *its length* [2]Lit *its width*
10 [1]Lit *filled*
13 [1]Lit *filled*

38:25 *100 talents and 1,775 shekels.* Since there are 3,000 shekels in a talent, 100 talents equals 300,000 shekels, which, when added to the 1,775 shekels, gives a grand total of 301,775—half a shekel for each of the 603,550 men of military age (v. 26).

38:26 *603,550 men.* The number is doubtless to be understood literally, since the figures in the tribal census (see Num 1:21–43; 2:4–31) total 603,550 (see Num 1:46 and note). See Introduction to Numbers: Special Problem.

38:27 *a talent for a socket.* See note on 26:19.

39:1–43 See note on 35:4–39:43.

it, close to the place where it joined, above
the woven band of the ephod.
21 They bound the breastpiece by its rings
to the rings of the ephod with a [1]blue cord,
so that it would be on the woven band of the
ephod, and that the breastpiece would not
come loose from the ephod, just as the LORD
had commanded Moses.
22 [a]Then he made the robe of the ephod
of woven work, all of [1]blue;
23 [a]and the opening of the robe was *at the*
top in the center, as the opening of a coat of
mail, with a binding all around its opening,
so that it would not be torn.
24 They made pomegranates of [1]blue and
purple and scarlet *material and* twisted *linen*
on the hem of the robe.
25 They also made bells of pure gold, and
put the bells between the pomegranates all
around on the hem of the [1]robe,
26 [1]alternating a bell and a pomegranate
all around on the hem of the robe for the service, just as the LORD had commanded
Moses.
27 [a]They made the tunics of finely woven
linen for Aaron and his sons,
28 and the turban of fine linen, and the
decorated [1]caps of fine linen, and the linen
breeches of fine twisted linen,
29 and the sash of fine twisted linen, and
[1]blue and purple and scarlet *material,* the
work of the [2]weaver, just as the LORD had
commanded Moses.
30 [a]They made the plate of the holy crown
of pure gold, and [1]inscribed it like the
engravings of a signet, "Holy to the LORD."
31 They [1]fastened a [2]blue cord to it, to
[1]fasten it on the turban above, just as the
LORD had commanded Moses.
32 Thus all the work of the [1]tabernacle of
the tent of meeting was completed; and the
sons of Israel did according to all that the
LORD had commanded Moses; so they did.
33 They brought the tabernacle to Moses,
the tent and all its [1]furnishings: its clasps, its
boards, its bars, and its pillars and its [2]sock-
ets;
34 and the covering of rams' skins [1]dyed
red, and the covering of porpoise skins, and
the screening veil;
35 the ark of the testimony and its poles
and the [1]mercy seat;
36 the table, all its utensils, and the bread
of the [1]Presence;
37 the pure *gold* lampstand, [1]with its
arrangement of lamps and all its utensils,
and the oil for the light;
38 and the gold altar, and the anointing oil
and the fragrant incense, and the veil for the
doorway of the tent;
39 the [1]bronze altar and its [1]bronze grating, its poles and all its utensils, the laver
and its stand;
40 the hangings for the court, its pillars
and its [1]sockets, and the screen for the gate
of the court, its cords and its pegs and all the
[2]equipment for the service of the tabernacle,
for the tent of meeting;
41 the woven garments for ministering in
the holy place and the holy garments for
Aaron the priest and the garments of his
sons, to minister as priests.
42 So the sons of Israel did all the work
according to all that the LORD had commanded Moses.
43 And Moses [1]examined all the work and
behold, they had done it; just as the LORD
had commanded, this they had done. So
Moses [a]blessed them.

The Tabernacle Erected

40 Then the LORD spoke to Moses, saying,
2 "[a]On the first day of the first month
you shall set up the [1]tabernacle of the tent of
meeting.
3 "[a]You shall place the ark of the testimony there, and you shall screen the ark with
the veil.
4 "You shall [a]bring in the table and
[1b]arrange what belongs on it; and you shall
[c]bring in the lampstand and [2]mount its lamps.
5 "Moreover, you shall [a]set the gold altar
of incense before the ark of the testimony,
and set up the veil for the doorway to the
tabernacle.
6 "You shall set the altar of burnt offering
in front of the doorway of the tabernacle of
the tent of meeting.
7 "You shall [a]set the laver between the
tent of meeting and the altar and put water
[1]in it.
8 "You shall set up the court all around
and [1]hang up the veil for the gateway of the
court.
9 "Then you shall take the anointing oil
and [a]anoint the tabernacle and all that is in
it, and shall consecrate it and all its [1]furnish-
ings; and it shall be holy.
10 "You shall anoint the altar of burnt offering and all its utensils, and consecrate the
altar, and [a]the altar shall be most holy.
11 "You shall anoint the laver and its stand,
and consecrate it.
12 "Then you shall [a]bring Aaron and his
sons to the doorway of the tent of meeting
and wash them with water.

21 [1]Or *violet*
22 [1]Or *violet* [a]Ex 28:31, 34
23 [a]Ex 28:32
24 [1]Or *violet*
25 [1]Lit *robe, between the pomegranates*
26 [1]Lit *a bell and a pomegranate, a bell...*
27 [a]Ex 28:39, 40, 42
28 [1]Lit *headgear*
29 [1]Or *violet* [2]Lit *variegator;* i.e. a weaver in colors
30 [1]Lit *wrote on it a writing* [a]Ex 28:36, 37
31 [1]Lit *put* [2]Or *violet*
32 [1]Lit *dwelling place*
33 [1]Or *utensils* [2]Or *bases*
34 [1]Or *tanned*
35 [1]Lit *propitiatory*
36 [1]Lit *Face*
37 [1]Lit *its lamps, the lamps set in order*
39 [1]Or *copper*
40 [1]Or *bases* [2]Or *utensils*
43 [1]Lit *saw* [a]Lev 9:22, 23; Num 6:23-26
40:2 [1]Lit *dwelling place* [a]Ex 19:1; 40:17; Num 1:1
3 [a]Ex 26:33; 40:21; Num 4:5
4 [1]Lit *arrange its arrangement* [2]Or *light* [a]Ex 26:35; 40:22 [b]Ex 25:30; 40:23 [c]Ex 40:24f
5 [a]Ex 40:26
7 [1]Lit *there* [a]Ex 30:18; 40:30
8 [1]Lit *put the screen*
9 [1]Or *utensils* [a]Ex 30:26; Lev 8:10
10 [a]Ex 29:37
12 [a]Lev 8:1-6

39:30 *holy crown.* An official designation (not found in 28:36–37) for the plate of the turban.
39:32 *all the work on the tabernacle . . . was completed.* Reminiscent of the concluding words of the creation narrative (see Gen 2:1–3).
39:43 *Moses blessed them.* For the faithfulness with which the Israelites had donated their gifts, time and talents in building the tabernacle and all its furnishings—faithfulness in service brings divine benediction.
40:2 *first day of the first month.* The tabernacle was set up almost a year after the institution of the Passover (see v. 17; 12:2,6).

13 "[a]You shall put the holy garments on
Aaron and anoint him and consecrate him,
that he may minister as a priest to Me.
14 "You shall bring his sons and put tunics
on them;
15 and you shall anoint them even as you
have anointed their father, that they may
minister as priests to Me; and their anointing
will [1]qualify them for a [a]perpetual priesthood throughout their generations."
16 Thus Moses did; according to all that
the LORD had commanded him, so he did.
17 Now [a]in the first month [1]of the second
year, on the first *day* of the month, the [2]tab-
ernacle was erected.
18 Moses erected the tabernacle and [1]laid
its [2]sockets, and set up its boards, and
[1]inserted its bars and erected its pillars.
19 He spread the tent over the tabernacle
and put the covering of the tent [1]on top of it,
just as the LORD had commanded Moses.
20 Then he took [a]the testimony and put *it*
into the ark, and [1]attached the poles to the
ark, and put the [2]mercy seat [3]on top of the
ark.
21 He brought the ark into the tabernacle,
and [a]set up a veil for the screen, and
screened off the ark of the testimony, just as
the LORD had commanded Moses.
22 Then he [a]put the table in the tent of
meeting on the north side of the tabernacle,
outside the veil.
23 He set the arrangement of [a]bread in
order on it before the LORD, just as the LORD
had commanded Moses.
24 Then he placed the lampstand in the
tent of meeting, opposite the table, on the
south side of the tabernacle.
25 He [a]lighted the lamps before the LORD,
just as the LORD had commanded Moses.
26 Then he [a]placed the gold altar in the
tent of meeting in front of the veil;
27 and he [a]burned fragrant incense on it,
just as the LORD had commanded Moses.
28 Then he set up the [1]veil for the doorway of the tabernacle.
29 He [a]set the altar of burnt offering
before the doorway of the tabernacle of the
tent of meeting, and [b]offered on it the burnt
offering and the meal offering, just as the
LORD had commanded Moses.
30 He placed the laver between the tent of
meeting and the altar and put water in it for
washing.
31 [a]From it Moses and Aaron and his sons
washed their hands and their feet.
32 When they entered the tent of meeting,
and when they approached the altar, they
washed, just as the LORD had commanded
Moses.
33 He [a]erected the court all around the
[1]tabernacle and the altar, and [2]hung up the
veil for the gateway of the court. Thus Moses
finished the work.

The Glory of the LORD

34 [a]Then the cloud covered the tent of
meeting, and the [b]glory of the LORD filled the
tabernacle.
35 Moses [a]was not able to enter the tent of
meeting because the cloud had settled on it,
and the glory of the LORD filled the tabernacle.
36 Throughout all their journeys [a]when-
ever the cloud was taken up from over the
tabernacle, the sons of Israel would set out;
37 but [a]if the cloud was not taken up,
then they did not set out until the day when
it was taken up.
38 For throughout all their journeys, [a]the
cloud of the LORD was on the tabernacle by
day, and there was fire in it by night, in the
sight of all the house of Israel.

13 [a]Ex 28:41; Lev 8:13
15 [1]Lit *be for them* [a]Ex 29:9; Num 25:13
17 [1]Lit *in* [2]Lit *dwelling place* [a]Ex 40:2
18 [1]Lit *put* [2]Or *bases*
19 [1]Lit *over it above*
20 [1]Lit *set* [2]Lit *propitiatory* [3]Lit *over the ark above* [a]Ex 25:16; Deut 10:5; 1 Kin 8:9; 2 Chr 5:10; Heb 9:4
21 [a]Ex 26:33
22 [a]Ex 26:35
23 [a]Ex 25:30; Lev 24:5, 6
25 [a]Ex 25:37; 40:4
26 [a]Ex 30:6; 40:5
27 [a]Ex 30:7
28 [1]Or *screen*
29 [a]Ex 40:6 [b]Ex 29:38-42
31 [a]Ex 30:19, 20
33 [1]Or *dwelling place* [2]Lit *put the screen* [a]Ex 27:9-18; 40:8
34 [a]Num 9:15-23 [b]1 Kin 8:11; Ezek 43:4f; Rev 15:8
35 [a]1 Kin 8:11; 2 Chr 5:13, 14
36 [a]Num 9:17; Neh 9:19
37 [a]Num 9:19-22
38 [a]Ex 13:21; Num 9:12, 15; Ps 78:14; Is 4:5

40:16 *according to all that the LORD had commanded him, so he did.* Moses' obedience to God's command is a key theme of the final chapter of Exodus (see vv. 19,21,23,25,27,29,32). It was the people who provided all the resources and made all the components, but it was the Lord's servant Moses who was authorized to erect the tabernacle and prepare it for the Lord's entry.
40:33 *Moses finished the work.* See note on 39:32.
40:34 With the glory of the Lord entering the tabernacle, the great series of events that began with the birth of Moses and his rescue from the Nile, foreshadowing the deliverance of Israel from Egypt, comes to a grand climax. From now on, the Israelites march through the wilderness, and through history, with the Lord tenting among them and leading them to the land of fulfilled promises.
40:38 See note on 13:21. *house of Israel.* The nation, viewed as an extended family household.

Leviticus

INTRODUCTION

Author and Date

See note on 1:1 and Introduction to Genesis: Author and Date of Writing.

Title

Leviticus receives its name from the Septuagint (the Greek translation of the OT) and means "relating to the Levites." Its Hebrew title, *wayyiqra',* is the first word in the Hebrew text of the book and means "And He [i.e., the Lord] called." Although Leviticus does not deal only with the special duties of the Levites, it is so named because it concerns mainly the service of worship at the tabernacle, which was conducted by the priests who were the sons of Aaron, assisted by many from the rest of the tribe of Levi. Exodus gave the directions for building the tabernacle, and now Leviticus gives the laws and regulations for worship there, including instructions on ceremonial cleanness, moral laws, holy days, the sabbath year and the year of jubilee. These laws were given, at least for the most part, during the year that Israel camped at Mount Sinai, when God directed Moses in organizing Israel's worship, government and military forces. The book of Numbers continues the history with preparations for moving on from Sinai to Canaan.

Themes

The key thought of Leviticus is holiness (see note on 11:44)—the holiness of God and man (man must revere God in "holiness"). In Leviticus spiritual holiness is symbolized by physical perfection. Therefore the book demands perfect animals for its many sacrifices (chs. 1—7) and requires priests without deformity (chs. 8—10). A woman's hemorrhaging after giving birth (ch. 12); sores, burns or baldness (chs. 13—14); a man's bodily discharge (15:1–18); specific activities during a woman's monthly period (15:19–33)—all may be signs of blemish (a lack of perfection) and may symbolize man's spiritual defects, which break his spiritual wholeness. The person with visible skin disease must be banished from the camp, the place of God's special presence, just as Adam and Eve were banished from the Garden of Eden. Such a person can return to the camp (and therefore to God's presence) when he is pronounced whole again by the examining priests. Before he can reenter the camp, however, he has to offer the prescribed, perfect sacrifices (symbolizing the perfect, whole sacrifice of Christ).

After the covenant at Sinai, Israel was the earthly representation of God's kingdom (the theocracy), and, as her King, the Lord established His administration over all of Israel's life. Her religious, communal and personal life was so regulated as to establish her as God's holy people and to instruct her in holiness. Special attention was given to Israel's religious ritual. The sacrifices were to be offered at an approved sanctuary, which would symbolize both God's holiness and His compassion. They were to be controlled by the priests, who by care and instruction would preserve them in purity and carefully teach their meaning to the people. Each particular sacrifice was to have meaning for the people of Israel but would also have spiritual and symbolic import.

For more information on the meaning of sacrifice in general see the solemn ritual of the day of atonement (ch. 16). For the meaning of the blood of the offering see 17:11; Gen 9:4. For the emphasis on substitution see 16:21.

Some suppose that the OT sacrifices were remains of old agricultural offerings—a human desire to offer part of one's possessions as a love gift to the deity. But the OT sacrifices were specifically prescribed by God and received their meaning from the Lord's covenant relationship with Israel—whatever their superficial resemblances to pagan sacrifices. They indeed include the idea of a gift, but this is accompanied by such other values as dedication, communion, propitiation (appeasing God's judicial wrath against sin) and restitution.

The various offerings have differing functions, the primary ones being atonement (see note on Ex 25:17) and worship.

Outline

The subjects treated in Leviticus, as in any book of laws and regulations, cover several categories:

I. The Five Main Offerings (chs. 1 — 7)
   A. Their Content, Purpose and Manner of Offering (1:1 — 6:7)
   B. Additional Regulations (6:8 — 7:38)
II. The Ordination, Installation and Work of Aaron and His Sons (chs. 8 — 10)
III. Laws of Cleanness — Food, Childbirth, Diseases, etc. (chs. 11 — 15)
IV. The Day of Atonement and the Centrality of Worship at the Tabernacle (chs. 16 — 17)
V. Moral Laws Covering Incest, Honesty, Thievery, Idolatry, etc. (chs. 18 — 20)
VI. Regulations for the Priests, the Offerings and the Annual Feasts (21:1 — 24:9)
VII. Punishment for Blasphemy, Murder, etc. (24:10 – 23)
VIII. The Sabbath Year, Jubilee, Land Tenure and Reform of Slavery (ch. 25)
IX. Blessings and Curses for Covenant Obedience and Disobedience (ch. 26)
X. Regulations for Offerings Vowed to the Lord (ch. 27)

The Law of Burnt Offerings

1 Then [a]the LORD called to Moses and
spoke to him from the tent of meeting,
saying,
2 "Speak to the sons of Israel and say to
them, 'When any man of you brings an
[1a]offering to the LORD, you shall bring your
[1]offering of animals from [b]the herd or the
flock.
3 'If his offering is a [a]burnt offering from
the herd, he shall offer it, a male [b]without
defect; he shall offer it [c]at the doorway of the
tent of meeting, that he may be accepted
before the LORD.
4 '[a]He shall lay his hand on the head of
the burnt offering, that it may be accepted
for him to make [b]atonement on his behalf.
5 '[a]He shall slay the [1]young bull before
the LORD; and Aaron's sons the priests shall
offer up [b]the blood and [c]sprinkle the blood
around on the altar that is at the doorway of
the tent of meeting.
6 '[a]He shall then skin the burnt offering
and cut it into its pieces.
7 '[a]The sons of Aaron the priest shall put
fire on the altar and arrange wood on the
fire.
8 'Then Aaron's sons the priests shall
arrange the pieces, the head and the [a]suet
over the wood which is on the fire that is on
the altar.
9 'Its [a]entrails, however, and its legs he
shall wash with water. And [b]the priest shall
offer up in smoke all of it on the altar for a
burnt offering, an offering by fire of [c]a soothing aroma to the LORD.
10 'But if his offering is from the flock, of
the sheep or of the goats, for a burnt offering, he shall offer it a [a]male without defect.
11 '[a]He shall slay it on the side of the altar
northward before the LORD, and Aaron's sons
the priests shall sprinkle its blood around on
the altar.
12 'He shall then cut it into its pieces with
its head and its [a]suet, and the priest shall
arrange them on the wood which is on the
fire that is on the altar.
13 'The entrails, however, and the legs he
shall wash with water. And [a]the priest shall
offer all of it, and offer it up in smoke on the
altar; it is a burnt offering, an offering by fire
of a soothing aroma to the LORD.
14 'But if his offering to the LORD is a burnt
offering of birds, then he shall bring his
offering from the [a]turtledoves or from young
pigeons.
15 'The priest shall bring it to the altar, and
wring off its head and offer it up in smoke on
the altar; and its blood is to be drained out
[a]on the side of the altar.

1:1 [a]Ex 19:3; 25:22; Num 7:89 **2** [1]Heb *qorban* [a]Mark 7:11 [b]Lev 22:18f **3** [a]Lev 6:8-13 [b]Ex 12:5; Lev 22:20-24; Deut 15:21; 17:1 [c]Lev 17:8, 9; Deut 12:5, 6, 11 **4** [a]Ex 29:10, 15, 19; Lev 3:2, 8 [b]Ex 29:33; Lev 4:20, 26, 31; 2 Chr 29:23, 24 **5** [1]Or *one of the herd;* lit *son of the herd* [a]Ex 29:11, 16, 20 [b]Lev 17:11 [c]Lev 1:11; 3:2, 8, 13; Heb 12:24; 1 Pet 1:2 **6** [a]Lev 7:8 **7** [a]Lev 6:8-13 **8** [a]Lev 1:12; 3:3, 4; 8:20 **9** [a]Ex 12:9 [b]Num 15:8-10; 28:11-14 [c]Gen 8:21; Ex 29:18, 25; Lev 1:13; Num 15:3; Eph 5:2 **10** [a]Ex 12:5; Lev 1:3; Ezek 43:22; 1 Pet 1:19 **11** [a]Ex 24:6; Lev 1:5; 8:19; 9:12 **12** [a]Lev 3:3, 4 **13** [a]Num 15:4-7; 28:11-14 **14** [a]Gen 15:9; Lev 5:7, 11; 12:8; Luke 2:24 **15** [a]Lev 5:9

1:1 Emphasizes that the contents of Leviticus were given to Moses by God at Mount Sinai. Cf. also the concluding verse (27:34). In more than 50 places it is said that the Lord spoke to Moses. Modern criticism has attributed practically the whole book to priestly legislation written during or after the exile. But this is without objective evidence, is against the repeated claim of the book to be Mosaic, is against the traditional Jewish view, and runs counter to other OT and NT witness (Rom 10:5). Many items in Leviticus are now seen to be best explained in terms of a second-millennium B.C. date, which is also the most likely time for Moses to have written the Pentateuch (see Introduction to Genesis: Author and Date of Writing). There is no convincing reason not to take at face value the many references to Moses and his work. *tent of meeting.* The tabernacle, where God met with Israel (see note on Ex 27:21).

1:2 *brings an offering.* The Hebrew word for "offering" used here *(qorban)* comes from the word translated "brings." An "offering" is something that someone "brings" to God as a gift (most offerings were voluntary, such as the burnt offering). This word for "offering" is also used in Mark 7:11 ("Corban"), where Mark translates it as something "given" (see note there).

1:3 *burnt offering.* See further priestly regulations in 6:8–13 (see also chart, p. 139). A burnt offering was offered every morning and evening for all Israel (Ex 29:39–42). Double burnt offerings were brought on the Sabbath (Num 28:9–10) and extra ones on feast days (Num 28–29). In addition, anyone could offer special burnt offerings to express devotion to the Lord. *male.* The burnt offering had to be a male animal because of its greater value, and also perhaps because it was thought to better represent vigor and fertility. It was usually a young sheep or goat (for the average individual), but bulls (for the wealthy) and doves or pigeons (for the poor) were also specified. *without defect.* The animal had to be unblemished (cf. Mal 1:8). As in all offerings, the offerer was to lay his hand on the head of the animal to express identification between himself and the animal (16:21), whose death would then be accepted in "atonement" (v. 4). The blood was sprinkled on the sides of the great altar (located outside the tabernacle—later the temple—in the eastern half of the courtyard), where the fire of sacrifice was never to go out (6:13). The whole sacrifice was to be burned up (v. 9), including the head, legs, fat and inner organs. It is therefore sometimes called a holocaust offering (*holo* means "whole," and *caust* means "burnt"). When a bull was offered, however, the officiating priest could keep its hide (7:8). The burnt offering may have been the usual sacrifice offered by the patriarchs. It was the most comprehensive in its meaning. Its Hebrew name means "going up," perhaps symbolizing worship and prayer as its aroma ascended to the Lord (v. 17). The completeness of its burning also speaks of dedication on the part of the worshiper. *doorway of the tent of meeting.* Where the altar of burnt offering was (see Ex 40:29). *accepted before the LORD.* See Rom 12:1; Phil 4:18.

1:4 *lay his hand on.* See notes on v. 3; Ex 29:10. *atonement.* See notes on 16:20–22; 17:11.

1:5 Only after the offerer killed the animal (symbolizing substitution of a perfect animal sacrifice for a sinful human life) did the priestly work begin. *blood.* See notes on 17:11; Heb 9:18. *sprinkle . . . around the altar.* See Ex 24:6; Heb 9:19–21.

1:6 *skin.* The whole animal was burned except the hide, which was given to the priest (7:8).

1:9,13,17 *soothing aroma to the LORD.* The OT sacrifices foreshadowed Christ, who was an "offering . . . as a fragrant aroma" (Eph 5:2; cf. Phil 4:18).

1:11 *northward.* See diagram, p. 114.

1:14 *birds.* Three categories of sacrifices are mentioned: (1) herds (vv. 3–9), (2) flocks (vv. 10–13) and (3) birds (vv. 14–17). Sacrifices of birds were allowed for the poor (see 5:7; 12:8; Luke 2:24).

16 'He shall also take away its crop with its feathers and cast it beside the altar eastward, to the place of the [1a]ashes.

17 'Then he shall tear it by its wings, *but* [a]shall not sever *it*. And the priest shall offer it up in smoke on the altar on the wood which is on the fire; [b]it is a burnt offering, an offering by fire of a soothing aroma to the LORD.

The Law of Grain Offerings

2 'Now when anyone presents a [a]grain offering as an offering to the LORD, his offering shall be of fine flour, and he shall pour oil on it and put frankincense on it.

2 'He shall then bring it to Aaron's sons the priests; and shall take from it [a]his handful of its fine flour and of its oil with all of its frankincense. And the priest shall offer *it* up in smoke *as* its [b]memorial portion on the altar, an offering by fire of a soothing aroma to the LORD.

3 '[a]The remainder of the grain offering belongs to [b]Aaron and his sons: a thing most holy, of the offerings to the LORD by fire.

4 'Now when you bring an offering of a grain offering baked in an oven, *it shall be* [a]unleavened cakes of fine flour mixed with oil, or unleavened wafers [1]spread with oil.

5 'If your offering is a grain offering *made* [a]on the griddle, *it shall be* of fine flour, unleavened, mixed with oil;

6 you shall break it into bits and pour oil on it; it is a grain offering.

7 'Now if your offering is a grain offering *made* [a]in a [1]pan, it shall be made of fine flour with oil.

8 'When you bring in the grain offering which is made of these things to the LORD, it shall be presented to the priest and he shall bring it to the altar.

9 'The priest then shall take up from the grain offering [a]its memorial portion, and shall offer *it* up in smoke on the altar *as* an offering by fire of a soothing aroma to the LORD.

10 '[a]The remainder of the grain offering belongs to Aaron and his sons: a thing most holy of the offerings to the LORD by fire.

11 '[a]No grain offering, which you bring to the LORD, shall be made with leaven, for you shall not offer [1]up in smoke any leaven or any honey as an [b]offering by fire to the LORD.

12 '[a]As an offering of first fruits you shall bring them to the LORD, but they shall not ascend for a soothing aroma on the altar.

13 'Every grain offering of yours, moreover, you shall season with salt, so that [a]the salt of the covenant of your God shall not be lacking from your grain offering; with all your offerings you shall offer salt.

14 'Also if you bring a grain offering of early ripened things to the LORD, you shall bring [a]fresh heads of grain roasted in the fire, grits of new growth, for the grain offering of your early ripened things.

15 'You shall then put oil on it and lay incense on it; it is a grain offering.

16 'The priest shall offer up in smoke [a]its memorial portion, part of its grits and its oil with all its incense as an offering by fire to the LORD.

The Law of Peace Offerings

3 'Now if his offering is a [a]sacrifice of peace offerings, if he is going to offer out of the herd, whether male or female, he shall offer it [b]without defect before the LORD.

16 [1]Or *fat ashes* [a]Lev 6:10 **17** [a]Gen 15:10; Lev 5:8 [b]Lev 9:13 **2:1** [a]Lev 6:14-18; Num 15:4 **2** [a]Lev 5:12; 6:15 [b]Lev 2:9, 16; 5:12; 24:7; Acts 10:4 **3** [a]Lev 2:10; 6:16 [b]Lev 10:12, 13 **4** [1]Lit *anointed* [a]Ex 29:2 **5** [a]Lev 6:21; 7:9 **7** [1]Lit *lidded cooking pan* [a]Lev 7:9

9 [a]Lev 2:2, 16; 5:12 **10** [a]Lev 2:3; 6:16 **11** [1]Lit *up from it* [a]Ex 23:18; 34:25; Lev 6:16, 17 [b]Ex 29:25; Lev 1:13 **12** [a]Ex 34:22; Lev 7:13; 23:10, 17, 18 **13** [a]Num 18:19; 2 Chr 13:5; Ezek 43:24 **14** [a]Lev 23:14 **16** [a]Lev 2:2 **3:1** [a]Lev 7:11-34; 17:5 [b]Lev 1:3; 22:20-24

1:17 *not sever it.* See note on Gen 15:10.

2:1 *grain offering.* See further priestly regulations in 6:14–23; 7:9–10. It was made of grain or fine flour. If baked or cooked, it consisted of cakes or wafers made in a pan or oven or on a griddle. It was the only bloodless offering, but it was to accompany the burnt offering (see Num 28:3–6), sin offering (see Num 6:14–15) and peace offering (see 9:4; Num 6:17). The amounts of grain offering ingredients specified to accompany a bull, ram or lamb sacrificed as a burnt offering are given in Num 28:12–13. A representative handful of flour was to be burned on the altar with the accompanying offerings, and the balance was to be baked without yeast and eaten by the priests in their holy meals (6:14–17). The flour that was burned on the altar was mixed with olive oil for shortening, salted for taste and accompanied by incense, but it was to have no yeast or honey—neither of which was allowed on the altar (vv. 11–13). The cooked product was similar to pie crust. The worshiper was not to eat any of the grain offering, and the priests were not to eat any of their own grain offerings, which were to be totally burned (6:22–23). The Hebrew word for grain offering can mean "present" or "gift" and is often used in that way (see Gen 43:11). The sacred gifts expressed devotion to God (see v. 2). *fine flour.* Grain that was milled and sifted. *oil.* Olive oil is often mentioned in connection with grain and new wine as fresh products of the harvest (see Deut 7:13). Used extensively in cooking, it was a suitable part of the worshiper's gift. *frankincense.* The chief ingredient in incense (see Ex 30:34–35).

2:3 *thing most holy.* For this reason, the priests were to eat it in the sanctuary area proper and not feed their families with it (6:16–18).

2:4 *unleavened.* See notes on Ex 12:8,15.

2:5 *griddle.* A clay pan that rested on a stone heated by a fire. Later, iron pans were sometimes used.

2:11 *honey.* It was forbidden on the altar perhaps because of its use in brewing beer (as an aid to fermentation), though some suggest that it was because of its use in Canaanite cultic practice.

2:12 *first fruits.* See 23:10–11; Ex 23:16,19; Num 15:18–20; Deut 18:4–5; 26:1–11.

2:13 *salt of the covenant.* In ancient times salt was often costly and a valuable part of the diet. Perhaps this is why it was used as a covenant sign and was required for sacrifices.

3:1 *peace offerings.* See further priestly regulations in 7:11–21, 28–34. Two basic ideas are included in this offering: peace and fellowship. The traditional translation is "peace offering," a name that comes from the Hebrew word for the offering, which in turn is related to the Hebrew word *shalom,* meaning "peace" or "wholeness." Thus the offering perhaps symbolized peace between God and man as well as the inward peace that resulted. The peace offering was the only sacrifice of which the offerer might eat a part. Fellowship was involved because the offerer, on the basis of the sacrifice, had fellowship with God and

2 '[a]He shall lay his hand on the head of his offering and [b]slay it at the doorway of the tent of meeting, and Aaron's sons the priests shall sprinkle the blood around on the altar.

3 'From the sacrifice of the peace offerings he shall present an offering by fire to the LORD, the fat that covers the entrails and all the fat that is on the entrails,

4 and the two kidneys with the fat that is on them, which is on the loins, and the [1]lobe of the liver, which he shall remove with the kidneys.

5 'Then [a]Aaron's sons shall offer *it* up in smoke on the altar [b]on the burnt offering, which is on the wood that is on the fire; [c]it is an offering by fire of a soothing aroma to the LORD.

6 'But if his offering for a sacrifice of peace offerings to the LORD is from the flock, he shall offer it, male or female, [a]without defect.

7 'If he is going to offer [a]a lamb for his offering, then he shall offer it [b]before the LORD,

8 and [a]he shall lay his hand on the head of his offering and [b]slay it before the tent of meeting, and Aaron's sons shall [c]sprinkle its blood around on the altar.

9 'From the [a]sacrifice of peace offerings he shall bring as an offering by fire to the LORD, its fat, [1]the entire fat tail which he shall remove close to the backbone, and the fat that covers the entrails and all the fat that is on the entrails,

10 and the two kidneys with the fat that is on them, which is on the loins, and the [1]lobe of the liver, which he shall remove [a]with the kidneys.

11 'Then the priest shall offer *it* up in smoke [a]on the altar *as* [b]food, an offering by fire to the LORD.

12 'Moreover, if his offering is [a]a goat, then he shall offer it before the LORD,

13 and he shall lay his hand on its head and slay it before the tent of meeting, and the sons of Aaron shall sprinkle its blood around on the altar.

14 'From it he shall present his offering as an offering by fire to the LORD, the fat that covers the entrails and all the fat that is on the entrails,

15 and the two kidneys with the fat that is on them, which is on the loins, and the [1]lobe of the liver, which he shall remove [a]with the kidneys.

16 'The priest shall offer them up in smoke on the altar *as* food, an offering by fire for a soothing aroma; [a]all fat is the LORD's.

17 'It is a [a]perpetual statute throughout your generations in all your dwellings: you shall not eat any fat [b]or any blood.' "

The Law of Sin Offerings

4 Then the LORD spoke to Moses, saying,

2 "Speak to the sons of Israel, saying, 'If a person sins [a]unintentionally in any of the [1]things which the LORD has [b]commanded not to be done, and commits any of them,

3 [a]if the anointed priest sins so as to bring guilt on the people, then let him offer to the LORD a [1]bull without defect as a sin offering for the sin he has [2]committed.

4 'He shall bring the bull to the doorway of the tent of meeting before the LORD, and [a]he shall lay his hand on the head of the bull and slay the bull before the LORD.

5 'Then the [a]anointed priest is to take some of the blood of the bull and bring it to the tent of meeting,

2 [a]Lev 1:4 [b]Ex 29:11, 16, 20
4 [1]Or *appendage on*
5 [a]Lev 7:28-34 [b]Ex 29:38-42; Num 28:3-10 [c]Num 15:8-10; 28:12-14
6 [a]Lev 3:1; 22:20-24
7 [a]Num 15:4, 5; 28:4-8 [b]Lev 17:8, 9; 1 Kin 8:62
8 [a]Lev 1:4 [b]Lev 3:2 [c]Lev 1:5
9 [1]Lit *the fat tail, entire* [a]Lev 17:5; Num 7:88; 1 Sam 10:8; 2 Sam 6:17; 1 Kin 3:15; 8:63, 64; 1 Chr 16:1
10 [1]Or *appendage on* [a]Lev 3:4, 15
11 [a]Lev 3:5 [b]Lev 3:16; 21:6, 8, 17, 22
12 [a]Num 15:6-11
15 [1]Or *appendage on* [a]Lev 3:4; 7:4
16 [a]Lev 7:23-25
17 [a]Lev 6:18, 22; 7:34, 36; 10:9, 15; 16:29; 17:7; 23:14, 21; 24:3 [b]Lev 7:26; 17:10-16
4:2 [1]Lit *commands of the LORD which are not to be done* [a]Lev 4:22, 27; 5:15-18; 22:14 [b]Lev 4:13
3 [1]Or *bull of the herd* [2]Lit *sinned* [a]Lev 4:14, 23, 28
4 [a]Lev 1:4; 4:15; Num 8:12
5 [a]Lev 4:3, 17

with the priest, who also ate part of the offering (7:14–15, 31–34). This sacrifice—along with others—was offered by the thousands during the three annual festivals in Israel (see Ex 23:14–17; Num 29:39) because multitudes of people came to the temple to worship and share in a communal meal. During the monarchy, the animals offered by the people were usually supplemented by large numbers given by the king. At the dedication of the temple, Solomon offered 20,000 cattle and 120,000 sheep and goats as peace offerings over a period of 14 days (1 Kin 8:63–65).

3:2 *lay his hand on.* See notes on 1:3; Ex 29:10.

3:5 *on the burnt offering.* The burnt offerings for the nation as a whole were offered every morning and evening, and the peace offerings were offered on top of them.

3:9 *fat tail.* A breed of sheep still much used in the Middle East has a tail heavy with fat.

3:11,16 *on the altar as food.* Israelite sacrifices were not "food for the gods" (as in other ancient cultures; see Ezek 16:20; cf. Ps 50:9–13) but were sometimes called "food" metaphorically (21:6,8,17,21; 22:25) in the sense that they were gifts to God and that He received them with delight.

3:17 *not eat any fat or any blood.* See note on 17:11.

4:2 *unintentionally.* See 5:15; contrast Num 15:30–31. Four classes of people involved in committing unintentional sins are listed: (1) "the anointed priest" (vv. 3–12), (2) the "whole congregation of Israel" (vv. 13–21), (3) a "leader" (vv. 22–26) and (4) "anyone of the common people" (vv. 27–35). Heb 9:7 speaks of sins "committed in ignorance" in referring to the day of atonement.

4:3 *anointed priest.* The high priest (see 6:20,22). *sins.* All high priests sinned except the high priest Jesus Christ (Heb 5:1–3; 7:26–28). *on the people.* The relationship of the priests to the people was so intimate in Israel (as a nation consecrated to God) that the people became guilty when the priest sinned. *let him.* Although the burnt, grain and peace offerings (chs. 1–3) were voluntary, the sin offering was compulsory (see vv. 14,23,28). *without defect.* A defective sacrifice could not be a substitute for a defective people. The final perfect sacrifice for the sins of God's people was the crucified Christ, who was without any moral defect (Heb 9:13–14; 1 Pet 1:19). *sin offering.* See further priestly regulations in 6:24–30; Num 15:22–29. As soon as an "anointed priest" (or a person from one of the other classes of people) became aware of unintentional sin, he was to bring his sin offering to the Lord. On the other hand, should the priest (or others) remain unaware of unintentional sin, this lack was atoned for on the day of atonement.

4:4 Three principles of atonement are found in this verse: (1) substitution ("bring the bull"), (2) identification ("lay his hand on the head") and (3) the death of the substitute ("slay the bull").

4:5 *blood.* See note on 17:11. There were two types of sin offer-

Old Testament Sacrifices

SACRIFICE	OT REFERENCES	ELEMENTS	PURPOSE
Burnt Offering	Lev 1; 6:8-13; 8:18-21; 16:24	Bull, ram or male bird (dove or young pigeon for the poor); wholly consumed; no defect	Voluntary act of worship; atonement for unintentional sin in general; expression of devotion, commitment and complete surrender to God
Grain Offering	Lev 2; 6:14-23	Grain, fine flour, olive oil, incense, baked bread (cakes or wafers), salt; no yeast or honey; accompanied burnt offering and peace offering (along with drink offering)	Voluntary act of worship; recognition of God's goodness and provisions; devotion to God
Peace Offering	Lev 3; 7:11-34	Any animal without defect from herd or flock; variety of breads	Voluntary act of worship; thanksgiving and fellowship (it included a communal meal)
Sin Offering	Lev 4:1–5:13; 6:24-30; 8:14-17; 16:3-22	1. Young bull: for high priest and congregation 2. Male goat: for leader 3. Female goat or lamb: for common person 4. Turtledove or pigeon: for the poor 5. Tenth of an ephah of fine flour: for the very poor	Mandatory atonement for specific unintentional sin; confession of sin; forgiveness of sin; cleansing from defilement
Guilt Offering	Lev 5:14–6:7; 7:1-6	Ram or lamb	Mandatory atonement for unintentional sin requiring restitution; cleansing from defilement; make restitution; pay 20% fine

When more than one kind of offering was presented (as in Num 7:16,17), the procedure was usually as follows: (1) sin offering or guilt offering, (2) burnt offering, (3) peace offering and grain offering (along with a drink offering). This sequence furnishes part of the spiritual significance of the sacrificial system. First, sin had to be dealt with (sin offering or guilt offering). Second, the worshiper committed himself completely to God (burnt offering and grain offering). Third, fellowship or communion between the Lord, the priest and the worshiper (peace offering) was established. To state it another way, there were sacrifices of expiation (sin offerings and guilt offerings), consecration (burnt offerings and grain offerings) and communion (peace offerings—these included vow offerings, thank offerings and freewill offerings).

6 and the priest shall dip his finger in the blood and sprinkle some of the blood seven times before the LORD, in front of [a]the veil of the sanctuary.

7 'The priest shall also put some of the blood on the horns of [a]the altar of fragrant incense which is before the LORD in the tent of meeting; and all the blood of the bull he shall pour out at the base of the altar of burnt offering which is at the doorway of the tent of meeting.

8 '[a]He shall remove from it all the fat of the bull of the sin offering: the fat that covers the entrails, and all the fat which is on the entrails,

9 and the two kidneys with the fat that is on them, which is on the loins, and the [1]lobe of the liver, which he shall remove [a]with the kidneys

10 (just as it is removed from the ox of the sacrifice of peace offerings), and the priest is to offer them up in smoke on the altar of burnt offering.

11 'But [a]the hide of the bull and all its flesh with its head and its legs and its entrails and its refuse,

12 [1]that is, all *the rest of* the bull, he is to bring out to [a]a clean place outside the camp where the [2]ashes are poured out, and burn it on wood with fire; where the [2]ashes are poured out it shall be burned.

13 '[a]Now if the whole congregation of Israel commits error and the matter [1]escapes the notice of the assembly, and they commit any of the [2]things which the LORD has commanded not to be done, and they become guilty;

14 [a]when the sin [1]which they have [2]committed becomes known, then the assembly shall offer [b]a [3]bull of the herd for a sin offering and bring it before the tent of meeting.

15 'Then [a]the elders of the congregation shall lay their hands on the head of the bull before the LORD, and the bull shall be slain [b]before the LORD.

16 'Then the anointed priest is to bring some of the blood of the bull to the tent of meeting;

17 and [a]the priest shall dip his finger in the blood and sprinkle *it* seven times before the LORD, in front of the veil.

18 'He shall put some of the blood on the horns of [a]the altar which is before the LORD [1]in the tent of meeting; and all the blood he shall pour out at the base of the altar of burnt offering which is at the doorway of the tent of meeting.

19 '[a]He shall remove all its fat from it and offer it up in smoke on the altar.

20 'He shall also do with the bull just as he did with [a]the bull of the sin offering; thus he shall do with it. So [b]the priest shall make atonement for them, and they will be forgiven.

21 'Then he is to bring out the bull to *a place* outside the camp and burn it as he burned the first bull; it is [a]the sin offering for the assembly.

22 'When [a]a leader [b]sins and unintentionally does any one of all the [1]things which the LORD his God has commanded not to be done, and he becomes guilty,

23 [1][a]if his sin [2]which he has committed is made known to him, he shall bring for his offering a [3][b]goat, [c]a male without defect.

6 [a]Ex 40:21, 26
7 [a]Lev 4:18, 25, 30, 34; 8:15; 9:9; 16:18
8 [a]Lev 3:3, 4
9 [1]Or *appendage on* [a]Lev 3:4
11 [a]Lev 9:11; Num 19:5
12 [1]Lit *and* [2]Or *fat ashes are* [a]Lev 4:21; 6:10, 11; 16:27
13 [1]Lit *is hidden from the eyes of* [2]Lit *commands of the* LORD *which are not to be done* [a]Num 15:24-26
14 [1]Lit *concerning which* [2]Lit *sinned* [a]Lev 4:3
14 [3]Lit *son of the herd* [b]Lev 4:3, 23, 28
15 [a]Lev 8:14, 18, 22; Num 8:10, 12 [b]Lev 1:3
17 [a]Lev 4:6
18 [1]Lit *which is in* [a]Lev 4:7, 25, 30, 34
19 [a]Lev 4:8
20 [a]Lev 4:8, 21 [b]Num 15:25, 28
21 [a]Lev 4:13f; 16:15-17; Num 15:24-26
22 [1]Lit *commands of the* LORD *which are not to be done* [a]Num 31:13; 32:2 [b]Lev 4:2, 27
23 [1]Lit *or* [2]Lit *in which he has sinned* [3]Lit *buck of the goats* [a]Lev 4:3 [b]Lev 4:3, 14, 28 [c]Lev 4:28

ings. The first (vv. 3–21) and more important involved sprinkling the blood in the tabernacle in front of the inner curtain or, in the case of the solemn day of atonement (ch. 16), on and in front of the mercy seat itself. This type of sin offering was not eaten. The fat, kidneys and covering of the liver were burned on the great altar, but all the rest was burned outside the camp (v. 12). Heb 13:11–13 clearly draws the parallel to our sin offering, Jesus, who suffered outside the city gate. This type of sin offering was offered by and for a priest or by the elders for the whole community. In general, the animal to be sacrificed was a young bull, but on the day of atonement the sin offering was to be a goat (16:9).

The second type of sin offering (4:22–5:13) was for a leader of the nation or a private individual. Some of the blood was applied to the horns of the great altar, the rest poured out at its base. The fat, etc., was burned on the altar, but the rest of the offering was given to the priest and his male relatives as food to be eaten in a holy place (6:29–30; see 10:16–20). The sin offering brought by a private person was to be a female goat or lamb. If the person was poor, he could bring a turtledove or young pigeon (5:7–8; 12:6,8; cf. Luke 2:24), or even about two quarts of flour (5:11). The offering included confession (5:5) and the symbolic transfer of guilt by laying hands on the sacrifice (v. 29; 16:21). Then the priest who offered the sacrifice made atonement for the sin, and the Lord promised forgiveness (5:13). By bringing such a sin offering, a faithful Israelite under conviction of sin sought restoration of fellowship with God.

4:6 *finger.* The right forefinger (see 14:16). *seven.* The number was symbolic of perfection and completeness (see note on Gen 5:5). *veil.* The great curtain that separated the holy place from the holy of holies (Ex 26:33).

4:7 *horns.* The four horns of the altar (see Ex 30:1–3) were symbols of the atoning power of the sin offering (Ex 30:10).

4:8–10 See 3:3–5.

4:12 *outside the camp.* See note on 13:45–46. So also Jesus was crucified outside Jerusalem (Heb 13:11–13; see 9:11; 16:26–28; Num 19:3; Ezek 43:21). *clean.* The distinction between clean and unclean was a matter of ritual or religious purity, not a concern for physical cleanliness (see chs. 11–15 for examples; see also Mark 7:1–4). *burn.* Since the sins of the offerer were symbolically transferred to the sacrificial bull, the bull had to be entirely destroyed and not thrown on the ash pile of 1:16.

4:15 *elders.* See note on Ex 3:16.

4:18 *altar.* Of incense (see v. 7).

4:20 *sin offering.* The offering of the priest who had sinned (v. 3). *will be forgiven.* In 4:20–6:7 this is a key phrase, occurring nine times and referring to forgiveness by God.

4:23 *goat, a male.* Less valuable animals were sacrificed for those with lesser standing in the community or of lesser economic means. Thus a bull was required for the high priest (v. 3) and the whole community (v. 14), but a male goat for a civic leader (v. 23) and a female goat (v. 28) or lamb (v. 32) for an ordinary Israelite. If an offerer was too poor, then turtledoves and pigeons were sufficient (5:7) or even a handful of fine flour (5:11–12).

24 'He shall lay his hand on the head of the male goat and slay it in the place where [1]they slay the burnt offering before the LORD; it is a sin offering.

25 'Then the priest is to take some of the blood of the sin offering with his finger and put it on [a]the horns of the altar of burnt offering; and *the rest of* its blood he shall pour out at the base of the altar of burnt offering.

26 '[a]All its fat he shall offer up in smoke on the altar as *in the case of* the fat of the sacrifice of peace offerings. Thus [b]the priest shall make atonement for him in regard to his sin, and he will be forgiven.

27 'Now if [1]anyone of [2]the common people sins [a]unintentionally in doing any of the [3]things which the LORD has commanded not to be done, and becomes guilty,

28 [1][a]if his sin which he has [2]committed is made known to him, then he shall bring for his offering a [3][b]goat, a [c]female without defect, for his sin which he has [2]committed.

29 '[a]He shall lay his hand on the head of the sin offering and [b]slay the sin offering at the place of the burnt offering.

30 'The priest shall take some of its blood with his finger and put it on the horns of [a]the altar of burnt offering; and [b]all *the rest of* its blood he shall pour out at the base of the altar.

31 '[a]Then he shall remove all its fat, just as the fat was removed from the sacrifice of peace offerings; and the priest shall offer it up in smoke on the altar for [b]a soothing aroma to the LORD. Thus the priest shall make atonement for him, [1]and he will be forgiven.

32 'But if he brings [a]a lamb as his offering for a sin offering, he shall bring it, a female without defect.

33 '[a]He shall lay his hand on the head of the sin offering and slay it for a sin offering [b]in the place where [1]they slay the burnt offering.

34 'The priest is to take some of the blood of the sin offering with his finger and put it on the horns of [a]the altar of burnt offering, and [b]all *the rest of* its blood he shall pour out at the base of the altar.

35 'Then he shall remove [a]all its fat, just as the fat of the lamb is removed from the sacrifice of the peace offerings, and the priest shall offer them up in smoke on the altar, on the offerings by fire to the LORD. Thus [b]the priest shall make atonement for him in regard to his sin which he has [1]committed, and he will be forgiven.

24 [1]Lit *one slays*
25 [a]Lev 4:7, 18, 30, 34
26 [a]Lev 4:19 [b]Lev 4:20, 31; 5:10, 13, 16, 18; 6:7
27 [1]Lit *one soul* [2]Lit *the people of the land* [3]Lit *commands of the* LORD *which are not to be done* [a]Lev 4:2; Num 15:27
28 [1]Lit *or* [2]Lit *sinned* [3]Or *female goat* [a]Lev 4:3 [b]Lev 4:3, 14, 23, 32 [c]Lev 4:23
29 [a]Lev 1:4; 4:4, 24 [b]Lev 1:5, 11
30 [a]Lev 4:7, 18, 25, 34 [b]Lev 4:7
31 [1]Or *so that he may be* [a]Lev 4:8 [b]Gen 8:21; Ex 29:18; Lev 1:9, 13; 2:2, 9, 12
32 [a]Lev 4:28
33 [1]Lit *one slays* [a]Lev 1:4, 5 [b]Lev 4:29
34 [a]Lev 4:7, 18, 25, 30 [b]Lev 4:7
35 [1]Lit *sinned* [a]Lev 4:26, 31 [b]Lev 4:20

5:1 [1]Lit *voice of an oath* [2]Or *iniquity* [a]Prov 29:24; Jer 23:10
2 [a]Lev 11:8, 11, 24-40; Num 19:11-16; Deut 14:8
4 [a]Num 30:6, 8; Ps 106:33
5 [a]Lev 16:21; 26:40; Num 5:7; Prov 28:13
6 [1]Lit *sinned* [2]Lit *female goat* [a]Lev 4:28, 32
7 [1]Lit *his hand does not reach enough for* [a]Lev 12:6, 8; 14:22, 30, 31
8 [a]Lev 1:17
9 [a]Lev 1:15 [b]Lev 4:7, 18
10 [1]Lit *sinned* [a]Lev 1:14-17 [b]Lev 4:20, 26; 5:13, 16
11 [1]Lit *hand does not reach* [2]I.e. Approx one bu [a]Lev 14:21-32; 27:8 [b]Lev 2:1, 2

The Law of Guilt Offerings

5 'Now if a person sins after he hears a [1]public [a]adjuration *to testify* when he is a witness, whether he has seen or *otherwise* known, if he does not tell *it,* then he will bear his [2]guilt.

2 'Or if a person touches [a]any unclean thing, whether a carcass of an unclean beast or the carcass of unclean cattle or a carcass of unclean swarming things, though it is hidden from him and he is unclean, then he will be guilty.

3 'Or if he touches human uncleanness, of whatever *sort* his uncleanness *may* be with which he becomes unclean, and it is hidden from him, and then he comes to know *it,* he will be guilty.

4 'Or if a person [a]swears thoughtlessly with his lips to do evil or to do good, in whatever matter a man may speak thoughtlessly with an oath, and it is hidden from him, and then he comes to know *it,* he will be guilty in one of these.

5 'So it shall be when he becomes guilty in one of these, that he shall [a]confess that in which he has sinned.

6 'He shall also bring his guilt offering to the LORD for his sin which he has [1]committed, [a]a female from the flock, a lamb or a [2]goat as a sin offering. So the priest shall make atonement on his behalf for his sin.

7 'But if [1]he cannot afford a lamb, then he shall bring to the LORD his guilt offering for that in which he has sinned, two turtledoves or two young pigeons, [a]one for a sin offering and the other for a burnt offering.

8 'He shall bring them to the priest, who shall offer first that which is for the sin offering and shall nip its head at the front of its neck, but he [a]shall not sever *it.*

9 'He shall also sprinkle some of the blood of the sin offering [a]on the side of the altar, while the rest of the blood shall be drained out [b]at the base of the altar: it is a sin offering.

10 'The second he shall then prepare as a burnt offering [a]according to the ordinance. [b]So the priest shall make atonement on his behalf for his sin which he has [1]committed, and it will be forgiven him.

11 'But [a]if his [1]means are insufficient for two turtledoves or two young pigeons, then for his offering for that which he has sinned, he shall bring the tenth of an [2]ephah of fine flour for a sin offering; [b]he shall not put oil

---

4:25 *priest.* The priest who officiated for the civil authority or the lay person (see vv. 30,34).
4:28 *goat, a female.* See note on v. 23.
4:29 *lay his hand on.* See notes on 1:3; Ex 29:10.
4:30 *horns.* See note on v. 7.
4:32 *lamb . . . female.* See note on v. 23.
4:35 *fat . . . of the peace offering.* See 3:3–5.
5:1–4 Four examples of the unintentional sins (see 4:2–3,13, 22,27) the sin offering covers.
5:2 *unclean.* See note on 4:12.
5:3 *human uncleanness.* See chs. 11–15.
5:5 *confess.* The offerer had to acknowledge his sin to God in order to receive forgiveness.
5:7 *two turtledoves . . . pigeons.* See note on 4:23.
5:11 *fine flour.* See note on 4:23. Although no blood was used with a flour offering, it was offered "with the offerings of the LORD by fire" (v. 12). Heb 9:22 may refer to such a situation.

on it or place incense on it, for it is a sin
offering.
12 'He shall bring it to the priest, and the
priest shall take his handful of it as its
memorial portion and offer *it* up in smoke
on the altar, [1]with the offerings of the LORD
by fire: it is a sin offering.
13 'So the priest shall make atonement for
him concerning his sin which he has [1]com-
mitted from [a]one of these, and it will be forgiven him; then [b]*the rest* shall become the
priest's, like the grain offering.' "
14 Then the LORD spoke to Moses, saying,
15 "[a]If a person acts unfaithfully and sins
[b]unintentionally against the LORD's holy
things, then he shall bring his [c]guilt offering
to the LORD: [d]a ram without defect from the
flock, according to your valuation in silver
by shekels, in *terms of* the [e]shekel of the
sanctuary, for a guilt offering.
16 "[a]He shall make restitution for that
which he has sinned against the holy thing,
and shall add to it a fifth part of it and give it
to the priest. [b]The priest shall then make
atonement for him with the ram of the guilt
offering, and it will be forgiven him.
17 "Now if a person sins and does any of
the things [1]which the LORD has commanded
not to be done, [a]though he was unaware, still
he is guilty and shall bear his punishment.
18 "He is then to bring to the priest [a]a ram
without defect from the flock, according to
your valuation, for a guilt offering. So the
priest shall make atonement for him concerning his error in which he sinned [b]unin-
tentionally and did not know *it,* and it will
be forgiven him.
19 "It is a guilt offering; he was certainly
guilty before the LORD."

Guilt Offering

6 [1]Then the LORD spoke to Moses, saying,
2 "[a]When a person sins and acts unfaithfully against the LORD, and deceives his companion in regard to a deposit or a security
entrusted *to him,* or through robbery, or *if* he
has extorted from his companion,
3 or [a]has found what was lost and lied
about it and sworn falsely, so that he sins in
regard to any one of the things a man may do;
4 then it shall be, when he sins and
becomes guilty, that he shall [a]restore what
he took by robbery or what he got by extortion, or the deposit which was [1]entrusted to
him or the lost thing which he found,
5 or anything about which he swore
falsely; [a]he shall make restitution for it [1]in
full and add to it one-fifth more. [b]He shall
give it to the one to whom it belongs on the
day *he presents* his guilt offering.
6 "Then he shall bring to the priest his
guilt offering to the LORD, [a]a ram without
defect from the flock, according to your valuation, for a guilt offering,
7 and [a]the priest shall make atonement
for him before the LORD, and he will be forgiven for any one of the things which he may
have done to incur guilt."

The Priest's Part in the Offerings

8 [1]Then the LORD spoke to Moses, saying,
9 "Command Aaron and his sons, saying,
'This is [a]the law for the burnt offering: the
burnt offering itself *shall remain* on the
hearth on the altar all night until the morning, and [b]the fire on the altar is to be kept
burning on it.
10 'The priest is to put on [a]his linen robe,
and he shall put on undergarments next to
his flesh; and he shall take up the [1]ashes *to*
which the fire [2]reduces the burnt offering on
the altar and place them beside the altar.
11 'Then he shall take off his garments and
put on other garments, and carry the [1]ashes
outside the camp to a clean place.
12 'The fire on the altar shall be kept burning on it. It shall not go out, but the priest
shall burn wood on it every morning; and he
shall lay out the burnt offering on it, and
offer up in smoke the fat portions of the
peace offerings [a]on it.
13 'Fire shall be kept burning continually
on the altar; it is not to go out.
14 'Now this is the law of the grain offering: the sons of Aaron shall present it before
the LORD in front of the altar.
15 '[a]Then one *of them* shall lift up from it
a handful of the fine flour of the grain offering, [1]with its oil and all the incense that is on
the grain offering, and he shall offer *it* up in
smoke on the altar, a soothing aroma, as its
memorial offering to the LORD.
16 '[a]What is left of it Aaron and his sons
are to eat. It shall be eaten as unleavened
cakes in a holy place; they are to eat it in the
court of the tent of meeting.

12 [1]Lit *upon*
13 [1]Lit *sinned* [a]Lev 5:4, 5 [b]Lev 2:3
15 [a]Num 5:5-8 [b]Lev 4:2; 22:14 [c]Lev 7:1-10 [d]Lev 6:6 [e]Ex 30:13
16 [a]Lev 6:5; 22:14; Num 5:7, 8 [b]Lev 7:2-7
17 [1]Lit *the commands of the LORD which are* [a]Lev 4:2; 5:19
18 [a]Lev 5:15 [b]Lev 5:17
6:1 [1]Ch 5:20 in Heb
2 [a]Ex 22:7-15
3 [a]Ex 23:4; Deut 22:1-4
4 [a]Lev 24:18, 21

4 [1]Or *deposited with*
5 [1]Lit *in its sum* [a]Lev 5:16 [b]Num 5:8
6 [a]Lev 5:15
7 [a]Lev 7:2-5
8 [1]Ch 6:1 in Heb
9 [a]Ex 29:38-42; Num 28:3-10 [b]Lev 6:12, 13
10 [1]Or *fat ashes* [2]Lit *consumes* [a]Ex 28:39, 42; 39:27, 28
11 [1]Or *fat ashes*
12 [a]Lev 3:5
15 [1]Lit *and some of* [a]Lev 2:2, 9
16 [a]Lev 2:3; 10:12-14; Ezek 44:29

5:15 *guilt offering.* See further priestly regulations in 7:1–6 (see also Is 53:10). Traditionally called the "trespass offering," it was very similar to the sin offering (cf. 7:7), and the Hebrew words for the two were apparently sometimes interchanged. The major difference between the guilt and sin offerings was that the guilt offering was brought in cases where restitution for the sin was possible and therefore required (v. 16). Thus in cases of theft and cheating (6:2–5) the stolen property had to be returned along with 20 percent indemnity. By contrast, the sin offering was prescribed in cases of sin where no restitution was possible. The animal sacrificed as a guilt offering was always a ram.

6:3 *what was lost.* See Deut 22:1–3.

6:6 *to the priest . . . to the LORD.* Sacrifices were brought to the Lord, but priests were His authorized representatives.

6:8–7:36 Further regulations concerning the sacrifices, dealing mainly with the portions to be eaten by the priests or, in the case of the fellowship offering, by the one offering the sacrifice.

6:9 *burnt offering.* See ch. 1; Num 15:1–16 and notes.

6:13 The perpetual fire on the altar represented uninterrupted offering to and appeal to God on behalf of Israel.

6:14 *grain offering.* See ch. 2 and notes.

17 '[a]It shall not be baked with leaven. I
have given it as their share from My offerings
by fire; [b]it is most holy, like the sin offering
and [c]the guilt offering.
18 '[a]Every male among the sons of Aaron
may eat it; it is a permanent ordinance
throughout your generations, from the offerings by fire to the LORD. [b]Whoever touches
them will become consecrated.' "
19 Then the LORD spoke to Moses, saying,
20 "This is the offering which Aaron and his
sons are to present to the LORD on the day
when he is anointed; the tenth of an [a]ephah of
fine flour as [b]a [1]regular grain offering, half of
it in the morning and half of it in the evening.
21 "It shall be prepared with oil on a [a]grid-
dle. When it is *well* stirred, you shall bring it.
You shall present the grain offering in baked
pieces as a soothing aroma to the LORD.
22 "The anointed priest who will be in his
place [1]among his sons shall [2]offer it. By a
permanent ordinance it shall be entirely
offered up in smoke to the LORD.
23 "So every grain offering of the priest shall
be burned entirely. It shall not be eaten."
24 Then the LORD spoke to Moses, saying,
25 "Speak to Aaron and to his sons, saying,
'This is the law of the sin offering: [a]in the
place where the burnt offering is slain the sin
offering shall be slain before the LORD; it is
most holy.
26 '[a]The priest who offers it for sin shall
eat it. It shall be eaten in a holy place, in the
court of the tent of meeting.
27 '[a]Anyone who touches its flesh will
become consecrated; and when any of its
blood [1]splashes on a garment, in a holy
place you shall wash what was splashed on.
28 'Also [a]the earthenware vessel in which
it was boiled shall be broken; and if it was
boiled in a bronze vessel, then it shall be
scoured and rinsed in water.
29 '[a]Every male among the priests may eat
of it; [b]it is most holy.
30 'But no sin offering [a]of which any of the
blood is brought into the tent of meeting to
make atonement [b]in the holy place shall be
eaten; [c]it shall be burned with fire.

The Priest's Part in the Offerings

7 'Now this is the law of the [a]guilt offering;
it is most holy.
2 'In [a]the place where they slay the burnt
offering they are to slay the guilt offering,
and he shall sprinkle its blood around on the
altar.
3 'Then he shall offer from it all its fat:
the [a]fat tail and the fat that covers the
entrails,
4 and the two kidneys with the fat that is
on them, which is on the loins, and the lobe
on the liver he shall remove [a]with the kidneys.
5 'The priest shall offer them up in smoke
on the altar as an offering by fire to the LORD;
it is a guilt offering.
6 '[a]Every male among the priests may eat
of it. It shall be eaten in a holy place; it is
most holy.
7 'The guilt offering is like the [a]sin offering, there is one law for them; the [b]priest
who makes atonement with it [1]shall have it.
8 'Also the priest who presents any man's
burnt offering, [1]that priest shall have for
himself the skin of the burnt offering which
he has presented.
9 'Likewise, every grain offering that is
baked in the oven and everything prepared
in a [1]pan or on a [a]griddle [2]shall belong to
the priest who presents it.
10 'Every grain offering, mixed with oil or
dry, shall [1]belong to all the sons of Aaron,
[2]to all alike.
11 'Now this is the law of the [a]sacrifice of
peace offerings which shall be presented to
the LORD.
12 'If he offers it by way of [a]thanksgiving,
then along with the sacrifice of thanksgiving
he shall offer [b]unleavened cakes mixed with
oil, and unleavened wafers [1]spread with oil,
and cakes *of well* stirred fine flour mixed
with oil.
13 'With the sacrifice of his peace offerings
for thanksgiving, he shall present his offering
with cakes of [a]leavened bread.
14 'Of [1]this he shall present one of every
offering as a [2]contribution to the LORD; [a]it
shall [3]belong to the priest who sprinkles the
blood of the peace offerings.
15 '[a]Now *as for* the flesh of the sacrifice of
his thanksgiving peace offerings, it shall be
eaten on the day of his offering; he shall not
leave any of it over until morning.
16 'But if the sacrifice of his offering is a

17 [a]Lev 2:11 [b]Ex 40:10; Lev 6:25, 26, 29, 30; Num 18:9 [c]Lev 7:7; 10:16-18 **18** [a]Lev 6:29; 7:6; Num 18:10; 1 Cor 9:13 [b]Lev 6:27 **20** [1]Lit *grain offering continually* [a]Lev 5:11 [b]Num 4:16 **21** [a]Lev 2:5 **22** [1]Lit *from among* [2]Lit *do* **25** [a]Lev 1:11 **26** [a]Lev 6:29 **27** [1]Lit *one sprinkles* [a]Lev 7:19 **28** [a]Lev 11:33; 15:12 **29** [a]Lev 6:18 [b]Lev 6:17, 25 **30** [a]Lev 4:1-21 [b]Lev 4:7, 18 [c]Lev 4:11, 12, 21 **7:1** [a]Lev 5:14-6:7

2 [a]Lev 1:11 **3** [a]Lev 3:9 **4** [a]Lev 3:4 **6** [a]Lev 6:18, 29; Num 18:9 **7** [1]Lit *it shall be for him* [a]Lev 6:25, 26, 30 [b]1 Cor 9:13; 10:18 **8** [1]Lit *for the priest, it shall be for him* **9** [1]Lit *lidded cooking pan* [2]Lit *for the priest, it shall be for him* [a]Lev 2:5 **10** [1]Lit *be* [2]Lit *a man as his brother* **11** [a]Lev 3:1 **12** [1]Or *anointed* [a]Lev 7:15 [b]Lev 2:4; Num 6:15 **13** [a]Lev 2:12; 23:17, 18; Amos 4:5 **14** [1]Lit *it* [2]Or *heave offering* [3]Lit *be for* [a]Num 18:8, 11, 19 **15** [a]Lev 22:29, 30

6:25 *sin offering.* See 4:1–5:13 and notes.
6:28 *earthenware.* Ordinary kitchen utensils and domestic ware were made of clay, usually fired in a kiln and often painted or burnished.
7:2 *place.* On the north side of the altar of burnt offering in front of the tabernacle (1:11). *guilt offering.* See 5:14–6:7 and notes.
7:3 *fat tail.* See note on 3:9.
7:7–10 See Num 18:8–20; 1 Cor 9:13.
7:11–36 This section supplements ch. 3, adding regulations about (1) three types of peace offerings (thanksgiving, vv. 12–15; votive, v. 16; freewill, v. 16), (2) prohibition of eating fat and blood (vv. 22–27) and (3) the priests' share (vv. 28–36).
7:12–15 Thanksgiving offerings were given in gratitude for deliverance from sickness (Ps 116:17), trouble (Ps 107:22) or death (Ps 56:12), or for a blessing received.
7:13 *leavened.* This regulation was not against the prohibition of 2:11 or Ex 23:18 since the offering here was not burned on the altar.
7:15–18 See 19:5–8. All meat had to be eaten promptly (in the case of the thanksgiving offering on the same day, and in the case of the votive and freewill offerings within two days). One reason may have been that in Canaan meat spoiled quickly and thus became ceremonially impure (v. 18) because it was not

[a]votive or a freewill offering, it shall be eat-
en on the day that he offers his sacrifice, and
on the [1]next day what is left of it may be eat-
en;
17 [a]but what is left over from the flesh of
the sacrifice on the third day shall be burned
with fire.
18 'So if any of the flesh of the sacrifice of
his peace offerings should *ever* be eaten on
the third day, he who offers it will not be
accepted, *and* it will not be reckoned to his
benefit. It shall be an [a]offensive thing, and
the person who eats of it will bear his *own*
iniquity.
19 'Also the flesh that touches anything
unclean shall not be eaten; it shall be burned
with fire. [1]As for *other* flesh, anyone who is
clean may eat *such* flesh.
20 '[a]But the person who eats the flesh of
the sacrifice of peace offerings which belong
to the LORD, [1]in his uncleanness, that person
[b]shall be cut off from his people.
21 '[a]When anyone touches anything
unclean, whether human uncleanness, or an
unclean animal, or any unclean [1]detestable
thing, and eats of the flesh of the sacrifice of
peace offerings which belong to the LORD,
that person shall be cut off from his people.' "
22 Then the LORD spoke to Moses, saying,
23 "Speak to the sons of Israel, saying, 'You
shall not eat [a]any fat *from* an ox, a sheep or
a goat.
24 'Also the fat of *an animal* which dies
and the fat of an animal [a]torn *by beasts* may
be put to any other use, but you must certainly not eat it.
25 'For whoever eats the fat of the animal
from which [1]an offering by fire is offered to
the LORD, even the person who eats shall be
cut off from his people.
26 '[a]You are not to eat any blood, either of
bird or animal, in any of your dwellings.
27 'Any person who eats any blood, even
that person shall be cut off from his people.' "
28 Then the LORD spoke to Moses, saying,
29 "Speak to the sons of Israel, saying, 'He
who offers [a]the sacrifice of his peace offerings to the LORD shall bring his offering to
the LORD from the sacrifice of his peace offerings.
30 'His own hands are to bring offerings by
fire to the LORD. He shall bring the fat with
the breast, that the [a]breast may be [1]present-
ed as a wave offering before the LORD.
31 'The priest shall offer up the fat in
smoke on the altar, but [a]the breast shall
belong to Aaron and his sons.
32 'You shall give [a]the right thigh to the
priest as a [1]contribution from the sacrifices
of your peace offerings.
33 'The one among the sons of Aaron who
offers the blood of the peace offerings and
the fat, the right thigh shall be his as *his* portion.
34 'For I have taken [a]the breast of the wave
offering and the thigh of the [1]contribution
from the sons of Israel from the sacrifices of
their peace offerings, and have given them
to Aaron the priest and to his sons as *their*
due forever from the sons of Israel.
35 'This is [1]that which is consecrated to
Aaron and [1]that [a]which is consecrated to his
sons from the offerings by fire to the LORD, in
that day when he presented them to serve as
priests to the LORD.
36 '[1]These the LORD had commanded to be
given them from the sons of Israel in the day
that He [a]anointed them. It is *their* due forever throughout their generations.' "
37 This is the law of the burnt offering,
the grain offering and the sin offering and
the guilt offering and [a]the ordination offering
and the sacrifice of peace offerings,
38 [a]which the LORD commanded Moses at
Mount Sinai in the day that He commanded
the sons of Israel to [1]present their offerings
to the LORD in the wilderness of Sinai.

The Consecration of Aaron and His Sons

8 Then the LORD spoke to Moses, saying,
2 "[a]Take Aaron and his sons with him,
and the [b]garments and [c]the anointing oil and
the bull of the sin offering, and the two rams
and the basket of unleavened bread,

16 [1]Lit *morrow and what* [a]Lev 19:5-8
17 [a]Ex 12:10
18 [a]Lev 19:7; Prov 15:8
19 [1]Lit *And the flesh*
20 [1]Lit *and his uncleanness is on him* [a]Lev 22:3-7; Num 19:13 [b]Lev 7:25
21 [1]Some mss read *swarming thing* [a]Lev 5:2, 3
23 [a]Lev 3:17
24 [a]Ex 22:31; Lev 17:15; 22:8
25 [1]Lit *he offers an offering by fire*
26 [a]Gen 9:4; Lev 17:10-16; 19:26; Deut 12:23; 1 Sam 14:33; Acts 15:20
29 [a]Lev 3:1
30 [1]Lit *waved* [a]Ex 29:26, 27; Lev 8:29; Num 6:20
31 [a]Num 18:11; Deut 18:3
32 [1]Or *heave offering* [a]Ex 29:27; Lev 7:34; 9:21; Num 6:20
34 [1]Or *heave offering* [a]Ex 29:27; Lev 10:14, 15; Num 18:18
35 [1]Lit *the anointed portion of* [a]Num 18:8
36 [1]Lit *Which* [a]Ex 40:13-15; Lev 8:12, 30
37 [a]Ex 29:22-34; Lev 8:22, 23
38 [1]Or *offer* [a]Lev 1:1; 26:46; 27:34; Deut 4:5
8:2 [a]Ex 28:1 [b]Lev 6:10 [c]Ex 30:25

then perfect (1:3; see 21:16–23). The prohibition applied also to the Passover (Ex 12:10).

7:16 *votive.* See 22:18–23. A vow was a solemn promise to offer a gift to God in response to a divine deliverance or blessing. Such vows often accompanied prayers for deliverance or blessing (see note on Ps 7:17). *freewill offering.* See 22:18–23.

7:19 *unclean.* See note on 4:12.

7:20 *cut off from his people.* Removed from the covenant people through direct divine judgment (Gen 17:14), or (as here and in vv. 21,25,27; 17:4,9–10,14; 18:29; 19:8; 20:3,5–6,17–18; 23:29) through execution (see, e.g., 20:2–3; Ex 31:14), or possibly sometimes through banishment.

7:21 *detestable.* The penalty for doing things that were abominable in the Lord's eyes was severe (see note on v. 20; see also 18:29; 20:13).

7:22–27 See note on 17:11.

7:23 *fat.* The prohibition of fat for food was as strict as that of blood, but the reason was different. The fat of the peace offerings was the Lord's and was to be burned on the altar. There was no explicit prohibition of eating the fat of hunted animals like the gazelle or deer, but probably that was included (see 3:17; Deut 12:15–22).

7:26 *not to eat any blood.* See note on 17:11; see also 3:17; 19:26; Gen 9:4–6; Deut 12:16,23–25; 15:23; 1 Sam 14:32–34; Ezek 33:25.

7:28–36 See 10:12–15; Num 18:8–20; Deut 18:1–5.

7:30–32 *breast . . . right thigh.* The breast and right thigh given to the priest were first presented to the Lord with gestures described as waving the breast and presenting the thigh (v. 34). See 8:25–29; 9:21; 10:14–15; Ex 29:26–27; Num 6:20; 18:11,18.

7:37–38 A summary of chs. 1–7.

7:37 *ordination offering.* See 8:14–36; Ex 29:1–35.

8:2 *the garments.* See Ex 39:1–31; 40:12–16. The garments that the high priest was to wear when he ministered are detailed in

3 and assemble all the congregation at the doorway of the tent of meeting."

4 So Moses did just as the LORD commanded him. When the congregation was assembled at the doorway of the tent of meeting,

5 Moses said to the congregation, "This is the thing which the LORD has commanded to do."

6 Then [a]Moses had Aaron and his sons come near and [b]washed them with water.

7 He [a]put the tunic on him and girded him with the sash, and clothed him with the robe and put the ephod on him; and he girded him with the artistic band of the ephod, [1]with which he tied *it* to him.

8 He then placed the [1]breastpiece on him, and in the [1]breastpiece he put [2a]the Urim and the Thummim.

9 He also placed the turban on his head, and on the turban, at its front, he placed [a]the golden plate, the holy crown, just as the LORD had commanded Moses.

10 Moses then took [a]the anointing oil and anointed the [1]tabernacle and all that was in it, and consecrated them.

11 He sprinkled some of it on the altar seven times and anointed the altar and all its utensils, and the basin and its stand, to [a]consecrate them.

12 Then he poured some of the [a]anointing oil on Aaron's head and anointed him, to consecrate him.

13 [a]Next Moses had Aaron's sons come near and clothed them with tunics, and girded them with sashes and bound [1]caps on them, just as the LORD had commanded Moses.

14 Then he brought [a]the bull of the sin offering, and Aaron and his sons laid their hands on the head of the bull of the sin offering.

15 Next [1]Moses slaughtered *it* and took the blood and with his finger [a]put *some of it* around on the horns of the altar, and purified the altar. Then he poured out *the rest of* the blood at the base of the altar and consecrated it, to make atonement for it.

16 He also [a]took all the fat that was on the entrails and the [1]lobe of the liver, and the two kidneys and their fat; and Moses offered it up in smoke on the altar.

17 [a]But the bull and its hide and its flesh and its refuse he burned in the fire outside the camp, just as the LORD had commanded Moses.

18 Then he presented [a]the ram of the burnt offering, and Aaron and his sons laid their hands on the head of the ram.

19 [1]Moses slaughtered *it* and sprinkled the blood around on the altar.

20 When he had cut the ram into its pieces, Moses [a]offered up the head and the pieces and the suet in smoke.

21 After he had washed the entrails and the legs with water, Moses [a]offered up the whole ram in smoke on the altar. It was a burnt offering for a soothing aroma; it was an offering by fire to the LORD, just as the LORD had commanded Moses.

22 Then he presented the second ram, [a]the ram of [1]ordination, and Aaron and his sons laid their hands on the head of the ram.

23 [1]Moses slaughtered *it* and took some of its blood and [a]put it on the lobe of Aaron's right ear, and on the thumb of his right hand and on the big toe of his right foot.

24 He also had Aaron's sons come near; and Moses put some of the blood on the lobe of their right ear, and on the thumb of their right hand and on the big toe of their right foot. Moses then [a]sprinkled *the rest of* the blood around on the altar.

25 He took the fat, and the fat tail, and all the fat that was on the entrails, and the [1]lobe of the liver and the two kidneys and their fat and the right thigh.

26 [a]From the basket of unleavened bread that was before the LORD, he took one unleavened cake and one cake of bread *mixed with* oil and one wafer, and placed *them* on the portions of fat and on the right thigh.

27 He then [a]put all *these* on the hands of Aaron and on the hands of his sons and presented them as a wave offering before the LORD.

28 Then Moses [a]took them from their hands and offered them up in smoke on the altar with the burnt offering. They were an ordination offering for [b]a soothing aroma; it was an offering by fire to the LORD.

29 Moses also took [a]the breast and presented it for a wave offering before the LORD; it was [b]Moses' portion of the ram of ordination, just as the LORD had commanded Moses.

30 So Moses [a]took some of the anointing oil and some of the blood which was on the altar and sprinkled it on Aaron, on his gar-

6 [a]Ex 29:4-6 [b]Ex 30:19, 20; Ps 26:6; 1 Cor 6:11; Eph 5:26
7 [1]Lit *and with it* [a]Ex 28:4
8 [1]Lit *pouch* [2]I.e. the lights and perfections [a]Ex 28:30; Num 27:21; Deut 33:8; 1 Sam 28:6; Ezra 2:63; Neh 7:65
9 [a]Ex 28:36
10 [1]Or *dwelling place* [a]Ex 30:26-29; Lev 8:2
11 [a]Ex 29:36, 37; 30:29
12 [a]Ex 29:7; 30:30; Lev 21:10, 12; Ps 133:2
13 [1]Lit *headgear* [a]Ex 29:8, 9
14 [a]Ex 29:10; Lev 4:4; Ps 66:15; Ezek 43:19
15 [1]Lit *he slaughtered it and Moses took* [a]Ex 29:12; Lev 4:7; Ezek 43:20
16 [1]Or *appendage on* [a]Ex 29:13
17 [a]Ex 29:14; Lev 4:11, 12
18 [a]Ex 29:15; Lev 8:2
19 [1]Lit *He slaughtered it and Moses sprinkled*
20 [a]Lev 1:8
21 [a]Ex 29:18
22 [1]Lit *filling*, and so throughout the ch [a]Ex 29:31; Lev 8:2
23 [1]Lit *He slaughtered it and Moses took* [a]Ex 29:20, 21
24 [a]Heb 9:18-22
25 [1]Or *appendage on*
26 [a]Ex 29:23
27 [a]Ex 29:24
28 [a]Ex 29:25 [b]Gen 8:21
29 [a]Lev 7:31-34 [b]Ex 29:26; Ps 99:6
30 [a]Ex 29:21

Ex 28:4–43 (see notes there). *anointing oil.* See note on Ex 25:6. The oil was used to anoint the tabernacle, sacred objects and consecrated priests (vv. 10–12,30). It was later used to anoint leaders and kings (1 Sam 10:1; 16:13). See also note on Ex 29:7.
8:6 *washed them with water.* In the bronze basin (see v. 11) in the courtyard of the tabernacle (see Ex 30:17–21).
8:7 *ephod.* See note on Ex 28:6.
8:8 *Urim and Thummim.* See notes on Ex 28:30; 1 Sam 2:28.
8:9 *holy crown.* See note on Ex 39:30.
8:11 *seven times.* See note on 4:6.
8:12 *oil on Aaron's head.* See Ps 133.
8:14 *sin offering.* See 4:3–11 and notes. The consecration service included a sin offering for atonement, a burnt offering for worship (v. 18) and a "ram of ordination" (v. 22), whose blood was applied to the high priest on his right ear, thumb and toe (v. 23). After this was done, Aaron offered sacrifices for the people (9:15–21). Then he blessed the people in his capacity as priest, and the Lord accepted his ministry with the sign of miraculous fire (9:23–24). *laid their hands on.* See notes on 1:3; Ex 29:10.
8:28 *with the burnt offering.* See note on 3:5.

ments, on his sons, and on the garments of his sons with him; and he consecrated Aaron, his garments, and his sons, and the garments of his sons with him.

31 Then Moses said to Aaron and to his sons, "[a]Boil the flesh at the doorway of the tent of meeting, and eat it there together with the bread which is in the basket of the ordination offering, just as I commanded, [b]saying, 'Aaron and his sons shall eat it.'

32 "[a]The remainder of the flesh and of the bread you shall burn in the fire.

33 "[a]You shall not go outside the doorway of the tent of meeting for seven days, until the day that the period of your ordination is fulfilled; for he will [1]ordain you through seven days.

34 "The LORD has commanded to do as has been done this day, to make atonement on your behalf.

35 "At the doorway of the tent of meeting, moreover, you shall remain day and night for seven days and [a]keep the charge of the LORD, so that you will not die, for so I have been commanded."

36 Thus Aaron and his sons did all the things which the LORD had commanded through Moses.

Aaron Offers Sacrifices

9 Now it came about [a]on the eighth day that Moses called Aaron and his sons and the elders of Israel;

2 and he said to Aaron, "[a]Take for yourself a calf, a bull, for a sin offering and a ram for a burnt offering, *both* without defect, and offer *them* before the LORD.

3 "Then to the sons of Israel you shall speak, saying, 'Take a male goat for a sin offering, and a calf and a lamb, both one year old, without defect, for a burnt offering,

4 and an ox and a ram for peace offerings, to sacrifice before the LORD, and a grain offering mixed with oil; for today [a]the LORD will appear to you.' "

5 So they took what Moses had commanded to the front of the tent of meeting, and the whole congregation came near and stood before the LORD.

6 Moses said, "This is the thing which the LORD has commanded you to do, that [a]the glory of the LORD may appear to you."

7 Moses then said to Aaron, "Come near to the altar and [1][a]offer your sin offering and your burnt offering, that you may make atonement for yourself and for the people; then make the offering [2]for the people, that you may make atonement for them, just as the LORD has commanded."

8 [a]So Aaron came near to the altar and slaughtered the calf of the sin offering which was for himself.

9 [a]Aaron's sons presented the blood to him; and he dipped his finger in the blood and [b]put *some* on the horns of the altar, and poured out *the rest of* the blood at the base of the altar.

10 The fat and the kidneys and the [1]lobe of the liver of the sin offering, he then offered up in smoke on the altar just as the LORD had commanded Moses.

11 [a]The flesh and the skin, however, he burned with fire outside the camp.

12 Then he slaughtered the burnt offering; and Aaron's sons handed the blood to him and he sprinkled it around on the altar.

13 They handed the burnt offering to him in [1]pieces, with the head, and he offered *them* up in smoke on the altar.

14 He also washed the entrails and the legs, and offered *them* up in smoke with the burnt offering on the altar.

15 Then he presented the people's offering, and took the [a]goat of the sin offering which was for the people, and slaughtered it and offered it for sin, like the first.

16 He also presented the burnt offering, and [1]offered it according to [a]the ordinance.

17 Next he presented [a]the grain offering, and filled his [1]hand with some of it and offered *it* up in smoke on the altar, [b]besides the burnt offering of the morning.

18 Then [a]he slaughtered the ox and the ram, the sacrifice of peace offerings which was for the people; and Aaron's sons handed the blood to him and he sprinkled it around on the altar.

19 As for the portions of fat from the ox and from the ram, the fat tail, and the *fat* [a]covering, and the kidneys and the [1]lobe of the liver,

20 they now placed the portions of fat on the breasts; and he offered [1]them up in smoke on the altar.

21 But [a]the breasts and the right thigh Aaron [1]presented as a wave offering before the LORD, just as Moses had commanded.

22 Then Aaron lifted up his hands toward the people and [a]blessed them, and he stepped down after making the sin offering and the burnt offering and the peace offerings.

---

31 [a]Ex 29:31 [b]Ex 29:32
32 [a]Ex 29:34
33 [1]Lit *fill your hands* [a]Ex 29:35
35 [a]Num 3:7; 9:19; Deut 11:1; 1 Kin 2:3; Ezek 48:11
9:1 [a]Ezek 43:27
2 [a]Ezek 29:1; Lev 4:3
4 [a]Ex 29:43
6 [a]Ex 24:16; Lev 9:23
7 [1]Lit *make* [a]Heb 5:3; 7:27
7 [2]Lit *of*
8 [a]Lev 4:1-12
9 [a]Lev 9:12, 18 [b]Lev 4:7
10 [1]Or *appendage on*
11 [a]Lev 4:11, 12; 8:17
13 [1]Lit *its pieces*
15 [a]Lev 4:27-31
16 [1]Lit *made* [a]Lev 1:1-13
17 [1]Lit *palm* [a]Lev 2:1-3 [b]Lev 3:5
18 [a]Lev 3:1-11
19 [1]Or *appendage on* [a]Lev 3:9
20 [1]Lit *the portions of fat*
21 [1]Lit *waved* [a]Ex 29:26, 27; Lev 7:30-34
22 [a]Num 6:22-26; Deut 21:5; Luke 24:50

8:31 *saying, 'Aaron and his sons shall eat it.'* Quoted from Ex 29:32.
9:1 *eighth day.* After the seven days of ordination (8:33).
9:2 *sin offering.* See notes on 4:3,5. *burnt offering.* See note on 1:3.
9:4 *peace offering.* See note on 3:1. *grain offering.* See note on 2:1. *LORD will appear.* See vv. 6,23; see also note on Gen 12:7.
9:17 *burnt offering of the morning.* See Ex 29:38–42.
9:21 *wave offering.* See note on 7:30–32.
9:22 *blessed.* The Aaronic benediction, a threefold blessing, is given in Num 6:23–26. Cf. the threefold apostolic benediction in 2 Cor 13:14.
9:23 *glory of the LORD.* See v. 6; cf. the display of the Lord's glory at the erection of the tabernacle (Ex 40:34–35); cf. also God's acceptance of sacrifices at the dedication of Solomon's temple (2 Chr 7:1).

23 Moses and Aaron went into the tent of meeting. When they came out and blessed the people, [a]the glory of the LORD appeared to all the people.

24 [a]Then fire came out from before the LORD and consumed the burnt offering and the portions of fat on the altar; and when all the people saw *it,* they shouted and fell on their faces.

The Sin of Nadab and Abihu

10 Now [a]Nadab and Abihu, the sons of Aaron, took their respective [b]firepans, and after putting fire in them, placed incense on it and offered strange fire before the LORD, which He had not commanded them.

2 [a]And fire came out from the presence of the LORD and consumed them, and they died before the LORD.

3 Then Moses said to Aaron, "It is what the LORD spoke, saying,

'By those who [a]come near Me I [1][b]will
be treated as holy,
And before all the people I will [c]be
honored.' "

So Aaron, therefore, kept silent.

4 Moses called also to [a]Mishael and Elzaphan, the sons of Aaron's uncle Uzziel, and said to them, "Come forward, carry your [1]relatives away from the front of the sanctuary to the outside of the camp."

5 So they came forward and carried them still in their [a]tunics to the outside of the camp, as Moses had said.

6 Then Moses said to Aaron and to his sons Eleazar and Ithamar, "[a]Do not [1]uncover your heads nor tear your clothes, so that you will not die and that He will not [b]become wrathful against all the congregation. But your [2]kinsmen, the whole house of Israel, shall bewail the burning which the LORD has [3]brought about.

7 "You shall not even go out from the doorway of the tent of meeting, or you will die; for [a]the LORD's anointing oil is upon you." So they did according to the word of Moses.

8 The LORD then spoke to Aaron, saying,

9 "[a]Do not drink wine or strong drink, neither you nor your sons with you, when you come into the tent of meeting, so that you will not die—it is a perpetual statute throughout your generations—

10 and [a]so as to make a distinction between the holy and the profane, and between the unclean and the clean,

11 and [a]so as to teach the sons of Israel all the statutes which the LORD has spoken to them through Moses."

12 Then Moses spoke to Aaron, and to his surviving sons, [a]Eleazar and Ithamar, "[b]Take the grain offering that is left over from the LORD's offerings by fire and eat it unleavened beside the altar, for it is most holy.

13 "You shall eat it, moreover, in a holy place, because it is your due and your sons' due out of the LORD's offerings by fire; for thus I have been commanded.

14 "[a]The breast of the wave offering, however, and the thigh of the offering you may eat in a clean place, you and your sons and your daughters with you; for they have been given as your due and your sons' due out of the sacrifices of the peace offerings of the sons of Israel.

15 "[a]The thigh offered by lifting up and the breast offered by waving they shall bring along with the offerings by fire of the portions of fat, to present as a wave offering before the LORD; so it shall be a thing perpetually due you and your sons with you, just as the LORD has commanded."

16 But Moses searched carefully for the [a]goat of the sin offering, and behold, it had been burned up! So he was angry with Aaron's surviving sons Eleazar and Ithamar, saying,

17 "Why [a]did you not eat the sin offering at the holy place? For it is most holy, and [1]He gave it to you to bear away [b]the guilt of the congregation, to make atonement for them before the LORD.

18 "Behold, [a]since its blood had not been brought inside, into the sanctuary, you should certainly have [b]eaten it in the sanctuary, just as I commanded."

19 But Aaron spoke to Moses, "Behold, this very day they [a]presented their sin offering and their burnt offering before the LORD. When things like these happened to me, if I

23 [a]Lev 9:6; Num 16:19
24 [a]1 Kin 18:38, 39; 2 Chr 7:1
10:1 [a]Ex 24:1, 9; Num 3:2; 26:61 [b]Lev 16:12
2 [a]Num 3:4; 16:35; 26:61
3 [1]Or *will show Myself holy* [a]Ex 19:22; Lev 21:6 [b]Ex 30:30; Ezek 38:16 [c]Ex 14:4, 17; Is 49:3; Ezek 28:22
4 [1]Lit *brothers* [a]Ex 6:22
5 [a]Ex 29:5; Lev 8:13
6 [1]Lit *unbind* [2]Lit *brothers* [3]Lit *burned* [a]Lev 21:1-5, 10-12 [b]Num 1:53; 16:22, 46; 18:5; Josh 7:1; 22:18, 20; 2 Sam 24:1
7 [a]Ex 28:41; Lev 21:12
9 [a]Prov 20:1; 31:5; Is 28:7; Ezek 44:21; Hos 4:11; Luke 1:15; Eph 5:18; 1 Tim 3:3; Titus 1:7
10 [a]Lev 11:47; 20:25; Ezek 22:26
11 [a]Deut 17:10, 11; 33:10
12 [a]Ex 6:23; Num 3:2 [b]Lev 6:14-18
14 [a]Lev 7:30-34; Num 18:11
15 [a]Lev 7:34
16 [a]Lev 9:3, 15
17 [1]Or *was given* [a]Lev 6:24-30 [b]Ex 28:38; Lev 22:16; Num 18:1
18 [a]Lev 6:30 [b]Lev 6:26
19 [a]Lev 9:8, 12

9:24 *fire came out from before the LORD.* See 10:2; 1 Kin 18:38.
10:1 *firepans.* Ceremonial vessels containing hot coals and used for burning incense (see 16:12–13; 2 Chr 26:19; Rev 8:3–4).
10:2 *died before the LORD.* Aaron's older sons are mentioned also in Ex 6:23; 24:1,9; 28:1; Num 3:2–4; 26:60–61; 1 Chr 6:3; 24:1–2. They are regularly remembered as having died before the Lord and as having had no sons. Their death was tragic and at first seems harsh, but no more so than that of Ananias and Sapphira (Acts 5:1–11). In both cases a new era was being inaugurated (cf. also the judgment on Achan, Josh 7, and on Uzzah, 2 Sam 6:1–7). The new community had to be made aware that it existed for God, not vice versa.
10:6 *tear your clothes.* See 21:10; see also note on Gen 44:13.
10:7 *not . . . go out.* To join the mourners (see 21:11–12).
10:10 *between the holy and the profane.* The distinction between what was holy (sacred) and what was profane (common) was carefully maintained (see Ezek 22:26; 42:20; 44:23; 48:14–15).
10:12–15 See 7:28–36; Num 18:8–20; Deut 18:1–5.
10:18 *since its blood had not been brought inside . . . you should . . . have eaten.* There were two types of sin offerings: (1) those in which the blood was sprinkled within the tabernacle, and (2) those in which it was sprinkled only on the great altar. Portions of the second type normally should have been eaten (see note on 4:5). But Moses was satisfied when he learned that Aaron had acted sincerely and not in negligence or rebellion (vv. 19–20).
10:19 *things like these happened to me.* Perhaps referring to

had eaten a sin offering today, would it have been good in the sight of the LORD?"
20 When Moses heard *that,* it seemed good in his sight.

Laws about Animals for Food

11 The LORD spoke again to Moses and to Aaron, saying to them,
2 "Speak to the sons of Israel, saying, '[a]These are the creatures which you may eat from all the animals that are on the earth.
3 'Whatever divides a hoof, thus making split hoofs, *and* chews the cud, among the animals, that you may eat.
4 'Nevertheless, [a]you are not to eat of these, among those which chew the cud, or among those which divide the hoof: the camel, for though it chews cud, it does not divide the hoof, it is unclean to you.
5 'Likewise, the [1]shaphan, for though it chews cud, it does not divide the hoof, it is unclean to you;
6 the [1]rabbit also, for though it chews cud, it does not divide the hoof, it is unclean to you;
7 and the pig, for though it divides the hoof, thus making a split hoof, it does not chew cud, it is unclean to you.
8 'You shall not eat of their flesh nor touch their carcasses; they are unclean to you.
9 '[a]These you may eat, whatever is in the water: all that have fins and scales, those in the water, in the seas or in the rivers, you may eat.
10 '[a]But whatever is in the seas and in the rivers that does not have fins and scales among all the teeming life of the water, and among all the living creatures that are in the water, they are detestable things to you,
11 and they shall be [1]abhorrent to you; you may not eat of their flesh, and their carcasses you shall detest.
12 'Whatever in the water does not have fins and scales is [1]abhorrent to you.

Avoid the Unclean

13 'These, moreover, [a]you shall detest among the birds; they are [1]abhorrent, not to be eaten: the [2]eagle and the vulture and the [3]buzzard,
14 and the kite and the falcon in its kind,
15 every raven in its kind,
16 and the ostrich and the owl and the sea gull and the hawk in its kind,
17 and the little owl and the cormorant and the [1]great owl,
18 and the white owl and the [1]pelican and the carrion vulture,
19 and the stork, the heron in its kinds, and the hoopoe, and the bat.
20 'All the [1]winged insects that walk on *all* fours are detestable to you.
21 'Yet these you may eat among all the [1]winged insects which walk on *all* fours: those which have above their feet jointed legs with which to jump on the earth.
22 'These of them you may eat: the locust in its kinds, and the devastating locust in its kinds, and the cricket in its kinds, and the grasshopper in its kinds.
23 'But all other [1]winged insects which are four-footed are detestable to you.
24 'By these, moreover, you will be made unclean: whoever touches their carcasses becomes unclean until evening,
25 and [a]whoever picks up any of their carcasses shall wash his clothes and be unclean until evening.
26 'Concerning all the animals which divide the hoof but do not make a split *hoof,* or which do not chew cud, they are unclean to you: whoever touches them becomes unclean.
27 'Also whatever walks on its paws, among all the creatures that walk on *all* fours, are unclean to you; whoever touches their carcasses becomes unclean until evening,
28 and the one who picks up their carcasses shall wash his clothes and be unclean until evening; they are unclean to you.
29 'Now these are to you the unclean among the swarming things which swarm on the earth: the mole, and the mouse, and the [1]great lizard in its kinds,
30 and the gecko, and the [1]crocodile, and the lizard, and the [2]sand reptile, and the chameleon.
31 'These are to you the unclean among all the swarming things; whoever touches them when they are dead becomes unclean until evening.
32 'Also anything on which one of them may fall when they are dead becomes unclean, including any wooden article, or

11:2 [a]Deut 14:3-21
4 [a]Acts 10:14
5 [1]A small, shy, furry animal *(Hyrax syriacus)* found in the peninsula of the Sinai, northern Israel, and the region round the Dead Sea; KJV *coney,* orig NASB *rock badger*
6 [1]Or *hare*
9 [a]Deut 14:9
10 [a]Deut 14:10
11 [1]Lit *detestable things*
12 [1]Lit *detestable things*
13 [1]Lit *a detestable thing* [2]Or *vulture* [3]Or *black vulture* [a]Deut 14:12-19
17 [1]Specifically, *great horned owl*
18 [1]Or *owl* or *jackdaw*
20 [1]Lit *swarming things with wings*
21 [1]V 20, note 1
23 [1]V 20, note 1
25 [a]Lev 11:40
29 [1]Or *thorn-tailed lizard*
30 [1]Or *lizard* [2]Species as yet undefined

the death of his two oldest sons (v. 2), for which he mourned by fasting. Or possibly something had occurred that made him ceremonially unclean.

11:2 *These . . . you may eat.* Ch. 11 is closely paralleled in Deut 14:3–21 but is more extensive. The animals acceptable for human consumption were those that chewed the cud and had a split hoof (v. 3). Of marine life, only creatures with fins and scales were permissible (v. 9). Birds and insects are also covered in the instructions (vv. 13–23). The distinction between clean and unclean food was as old as the time of Noah (Gen 7:2). The main reason for the laws concerning clean and unclean food is the same as for other laws concerning the clean and unclean—to preserve the sanctity of Israel as God's holy people (see v. 44). Some hold that certain animal life was considered unclean for health considerations, but it is difficult to substantiate this idea. Uncleanness typified sin and defilement. For the uncleanness of disease and bodily discharges see chs. 13–15.

11:6 *rabbit.* Does not technically chew the cud with regurgitation. The apparent chewing movements of the rabbit caused it to be classified popularly with cud chewers.

11:20 *all fours.* Although insects have six legs, perhaps people in ancient times did not count as ordinary legs the two large hind legs used for jumping.

clothing, or a skin, or a sack—any article [1]of
which use is made—[a]it shall be put in the
water and be unclean until evening, then it
becomes clean.
33 'As for any [a]earthenware vessel into
which one of them may fall, whatever is in it
becomes unclean and you shall break [1]the
vessel.
34 'Any of the [1]food which may be eaten,
on which water comes, shall become
unclean, and any [1]liquid which may be
drunk in every vessel shall become unclean.
35 'Everything, moreover, on which part of
their carcass may fall becomes unclean; an
oven or a [1]stove shall be smashed; they are
unclean and shall continue as unclean to
you.
36 'Nevertheless a spring or a cistern [1]col-
lecting water shall be clean, though the one
who touches their carcass shall be unclean.
37 'If a part of their carcass falls on any
seed for sowing which is to be sown, it is
clean.
38 'Though if water is put on the seed and
a part of their carcass falls on it, it is unclean
to you.
39 'Also if one of the animals dies which
you have for food, the one who touches its
carcass becomes unclean until evening.
40 '[a]He too, who eats some of its carcass
shall wash his clothes and be unclean until
evening, and the one who picks up its carcass shall wash his clothes and be unclean
until evening.
41 '[a]Now every swarming thing that
swarms on the earth is detestable, not to be
eaten.
42 'Whatever crawls on its belly, and whatever walks on *all* fours, whatever has many
feet, in respect to every swarming thing that
swarms on the earth, you shall not eat them,
for they are detestable.
43 '[a]Do not render [1]yourselves detestable
through any of the swarming things that
swarm; and you shall not make yourselves
unclean with them so that you become
unclean.
44 'For [a]I am the LORD your God. Consecrate yourselves therefore, and [b]be holy, for I
am holy. And you shall not make yourselves
unclean with any of the swarming things
that swarm on the earth.
45 '[a]For I am the LORD who brought you up
from the land of Egypt to be your God; thus
[b]you shall be holy, for I am holy.' "
46 This is the law regarding the animal
and the bird, and every living thing that
moves in the waters and everything that
swarms on the earth,
47 [a]to make a distinction between the
unclean and the clean, and between the edible creature and the creature which is not to
be eaten.

Laws of Motherhood

12 Then the LORD spoke to Moses, saying,
2 "Speak to the sons of Israel, saying:
'When a woman [1]gives birth and bears a
male *child,* then she shall be unclean for sev-
en days, [a]as in the days of [2]her menstruation
she shall be unclean.
3 'On [a]the eighth day the flesh of his foreskin shall be circumcised.
4 'Then she shall remain in the blood of
her purification for thirty-three days; she
shall not touch any consecrated thing, nor
enter the sanctuary until the days of her
purification are completed.
5 'But if she bears a female *child,* then she
shall be unclean for two weeks, as in her
[1]menstruation; and she shall remain in the
blood of *her* purification for sixty-six days.
6 '[a]When the days of her purification are
completed, for a son or for a daughter, she
shall bring to the priest at the doorway of the
tent of meeting a one year old lamb for a
burnt offering and a young pigeon or a turtledove [b]for a sin offering.
7 'Then he shall offer it before the LORD
and make atonement for her, and she shall
be cleansed from the [1]flow of her blood. This
is the law for her who bears *a child, whether*
a male or a female.
8 'But if [1]she cannot afford a lamb, then
she shall take [a]two turtledoves or two young
pigeons, [b]the one for a burnt offering and the
other for a sin offering; and the [c]priest shall
make atonement for her, and she will be
clean.' "

32 [1]Lit *with which work is done* [a]Lev 15:12
33 [1]Lit *it* [a]Lev 6:28; 15:12
34 [1]I.e. if touched by a carcass; cf vv 29-32
35 [1]Lit *hearth for supporting (two) pots*
36 [1]Lit *of a gathering of*
40 [a]Lev 17:15; 22:8; Deut 14:21; Ezek 44:31
41 [a]Lev 11:29
43 [1]Lit *your souls* [a]Lev 20:25
44 [a]Ex 6:7; 16:12; 23:25; Is 43:3; 51:15 [b]Lev 19:2; 1 Pet 1:16
45 [a]Ex 6:7; 20:2; Lev 22:33; 25:38; 26:45 [b]Lev 19:2; 1 Pet 1:16
47 [a]Lev 10:10; Ezek 22:26; 44:23
12:2 [1]Lit *produces seed* [2]Lit *the impurity of her sickness* [a]Lev 15:19; 18:19
3 [a]Gen 17:12; Luke 1:59; 2:21
5 [1]Lit *impurity*
6 [a]Luke 2:22 [b]Lev 5:7
7 [1]Lit *fountain*
8 [1]Lit *her hand does not find a sufficiency of a lamb* [a]Luke 2:22-24 [b]Lev 5:7 [c]Lev 4:26

11:36 *cistern collecting water.* The use of waterproof plaster for lining cisterns dug in the ground was an important factor in helping the Israelites to settle the dry areas of Canaan after the conquest (cf. 2 Chr 26:10).

11:41 *earth.* Verses 29–30 identify the animals that move about (or swarm) on the ground.

11:44 *be holy, for I am holy.* Holiness is the key theme of Leviticus, ringing like a refrain in various forms throughout the book (e.g., v. 45; 19:2; 20:7,26; 21:8,15; 22:9,16,32). The word "holy" appears more often in Leviticus than in any other book of the Bible. Israel was to be totally consecrated to God. Her holiness was to be expressed in every aspect of her life, to the extent that all of life had a certain ceremonial quality. Because of who God is and what He has done (v. 45), His people must dedicate themselves fully to Him (cf. Matt 5:48). See Rom 12:1.

11:45 *brought . . . from the land of Egypt.* A refrain found 8 more times in Leviticus (19:36; 22:33; 23:43; 25:38,42,55; 26:13,45) and nearly 60 times in 18 other books of the OT.

11:46–47 A summary of ch. 11.

12:2 *unclean.* The uncleanness came from the bleeding (vv. 4–5,7), not from the birth. It is not clear why the period of uncleanness after the birth of a baby boy (40 days) was half the period for a girl (80 days). *menstruation.* See 15:19–24.

12:3 See notes on Gen 17:10,12.

12:6 *burnt offering.* See note on 1:3. *sin offering.* See notes on 4:3,5.

12:8 See 1:14–17 and note on 1:14; see also 5:7–10; 14:21–22; and especially Luke 2:24 (Mary's offering for Jesus).

The Test for Leprosy

13 Then the LORD spoke to Moses and to Aaron, saying,

2 "When a man has on the skin of his [1]body a swelling or a scab or a bright spot, and it becomes [2]an infection of leprosy on the skin of his [1]body, [a]then he shall be brought to Aaron the priest or to one of his sons the priests.

3 "The priest shall look at the mark on the skin of the [1]body, and if the hair in the infection has turned white and the infection appears to be deeper than the skin of his [1]body, it is an infection of leprosy; when the priest has looked at him, he shall pronounce him unclean.

4 "But if the bright spot is white on the skin of his [1]body, and [2]it does not appear to be deeper than the skin, and the hair on it has not turned white, then the priest shall [3]isolate *him who has* the infection for seven days.

5 "The priest shall look at him on the seventh day, and if in his eyes the infection [1]has not changed *and* the infection has not spread on the skin, then the priest shall [2]isolate him for seven more days.

6 "The priest shall look at him again on the seventh day, and if the infection has faded and the mark has not spread on the skin, then the priest shall pronounce him clean; it is *only* a scab. And he shall [a]wash his clothes and be clean.

7 "But if the scab spreads farther on the skin after he has shown himself to the priest for his cleansing, he shall appear again to the priest.

8 "The priest shall look, and if the scab has spread on the skin, then the priest shall pronounce him unclean; it is leprosy.

9 "When the infection of leprosy is on a man, then he shall be brought to the priest.

10 "The priest shall then look, and if there is a [a]white swelling in the skin, and it has turned the hair white, and there is quick raw flesh in the swelling,

11 it is [1]a chronic leprosy on the skin of his [2]body, and the priest shall pronounce him unclean; he shall not [3]isolate him, for he is unclean.

12 "If the leprosy breaks out farther on the skin, and the leprosy covers all the skin of *him who has* the infection from his head even to his feet, [1]as far as the priest can see,

13 then the priest shall look, and behold, *if* the leprosy has covered all his [1]body, he shall pronounce clean *him who has* the infection; it has all turned white *and* he is clean.

14 "But whenever raw flesh appears on him, he shall be unclean.

15 "The priest shall look at the raw flesh, and he shall pronounce him unclean; the raw flesh is unclean, it is leprosy.

16 "Or if the raw flesh turns again and is changed to white, then he shall [a]come to the priest,

17 and the priest shall look at him, and behold, *if* the infection has turned to white, then the priest shall pronounce clean *him who has* the infection; he is clean.

18 "When the [1]body has a boil on its skin and it is healed,

19 and in the place of the boil there is a white swelling or a reddish-white, bright spot, then it shall be shown to the priest;

20 and the priest shall look, and behold, *if* [1]it appears to be lower than the skin, and the hair on it has turned white, then the priest shall pronounce him unclean; it is the infection of leprosy, it has broken out in the boil.

21 "But if the priest looks at it, and behold, there are no white hairs in it and it is not lower than the skin and is faded, then the priest shall [1]isolate him for seven days;

22 and if it spreads farther on the skin, then the priest shall pronounce him unclean; it is an infection.

23 "But if the bright spot remains in its place and does not spread, it is *only* the scar of the boil; and the priest shall pronounce him clean.

24 "Or if the [1]body sustains in its skin a burn by fire, and the raw *flesh* of the burn becomes a bright spot, reddish-white, or white,

25 then the priest shall look at it. And if the hair in the bright spot has [a]turned white and it appears to be deeper than the skin, it is leprosy; it has broken out in the burn. Therefore, the priest shall pronounce him unclean; it is an infection of leprosy.

26 "But if the priest looks at it, and indeed, there is no white hair in the bright spot and it is no [1]deeper than the skin, but is dim, then the priest shall [2]isolate him for seven days;

27 and the priest shall look at him on the seventh day. If it spreads farther in the skin,

13:2 [1]Lit *flesh* [2]Lit *a mark, stroke,* and so throughout the ch [a]Deut 24:8
3 [1]Lit *flesh*
4 [1]Lit *flesh* [2]Lit *the appearance of it is not deeper* [3]Lit *shut up*
5 [1]Lit *has stood* [2]Lit *shut up*
6 [a]Lev 11:25; 14:8
10 [a]Num 12:10; 2 Kin 5:27; 2 Chr 26:19, 20
11 [1]Lit *an old* [2]Lit *flesh* [3]Lit *shut up*
12 [1]Lit *with regard to the whole sight of the priest's eyes*
13 [1]Lit *flesh*
16 [a]Luke 5:12-14
18 [1]Lit *flesh*
20 [1]Lit *the appearance of it is lower*
21 [1]Lit *shut up*
24 [1]Lit *flesh*
25 [a]Ex 4:6; Num 12:10; 2 Kin 5:27
26 [1]Lit *lower* [2]Lit *shut up*

13:1–46 This section deals with preliminary symptoms of skin diseases (vv. 1–8) and then with the symptoms of (1) raw flesh (vv. 9–17), (2) boils (vv. 18–23), (3) burns (vv. 24–28), (4) sores on the head or chin (vv. 29–37), (5) white spots (vv. 38–39) and (6) skin diseases on the head that cause baldness (vv. 40–44). **13:2** *infection . . . on the skin.* Occurs often in chs. 13–14; see also 22:4; Num 5:2. Since it is unlikely that ancient people would have understood the concept of infectiousness, this rendering is questionable; the Hebrew should perhaps be translated simply "skin disease." Such diseases show visible defects that could function aptly as a symbol for defilement—as could mildew (cf. vv. 47–59). *leprosy.* The Hebrew word was used for various diseases affecting the skin—not necessarily leprosy; see also 22:4–8; Num 5:2–4; Deut 24:8–9. The symptoms described, and the fact that they may rapidly change (vv. 6, 26–27, 32–37), show that the disease was not true leprosy (Hansen's disease). They apply also to a number of other diseases, as well as to rather harmless skin eruptions. The Hebrew word translated "infection of leprosy" can also mean "mildew" (v. 47; 14:34; and especially 14:57).

then the priest shall pronounce him unclean; it is an infection of leprosy.

28 "But if the bright spot remains in its place and has not spread in the skin, but is dim, it is the swelling from the burn; and the priest shall pronounce him clean, for it is *only* the scar of the burn.

29 "Now if a man or woman has an infection on the head or on the beard,

30 then the priest shall look at the infection, and if it appears to be deeper than the skin and there is thin yellowish hair in it, then the priest shall pronounce him unclean; it is a scale, it is leprosy of the head or of the beard.

31 "But if the priest looks at the infection of the scale, and indeed, it appears to be no deeper than the skin and there is no black hair in it, then the priest shall [1]isolate *the person* with the scaly infection for seven days.

32 "On the seventh day the priest shall look at the infection, and if the scale has not spread and no yellowish hair has [1]grown in it, and the appearance of the scale is no deeper than the skin,

33 then he shall shave himself, but he shall not shave the scale; and the priest shall [1]isolate *the person* with the scale seven more days.

34 "Then on the seventh day the priest shall look at the scale, and if the scale has not spread in the skin and it appears to be no deeper than the skin, the priest shall pronounce him clean; and he shall wash his clothes and be clean.

35 "But if the scale spreads farther in the skin after his cleansing,

36 then the priest shall look at him, and if the scale has spread in the skin, the priest need not seek for the yellowish hair; he is unclean.

37 "If in his sight the scale has remained, however, and black hair has grown in it, the scale has healed, he is clean; and the priest shall pronounce him clean.

38 "When a man or a woman has bright spots on the skin of the [1]body, *even* white bright spots,

39 then the priest shall look, and if the bright spots on the skin of their [1]bodies are a faint white, it is [2]eczema that has broken out on the skin; he is clean.

40 "Now if a [1]man loses the hair of his head, he is [a]bald; he is clean.

41 "If his head becomes bald at the [1]front and sides, he is bald on the forehead; he is clean.

42 "But if on the bald head or the bald forehead, there occurs a reddish-white infection, it is leprosy breaking out on his bald head or on his bald forehead.

43 "Then [a]the priest shall look at him; and if the swelling of the infection is reddish-white on his bald head or on his bald forehead, like the appearance of leprosy in the skin of the [1]body,

44 he is a leprous man, he is unclean. The priest shall surely pronounce him unclean; his infection is on his head.

45 "As for the leper who has the infection, his clothes shall be torn, and [a]the hair of his head shall be [1]uncovered, and he shall [b]cover his mustache and cry, '[c]Unclean! Unclean!'

46 "He shall remain unclean all the days during which he has the infection; he is unclean. He shall live alone; his dwelling shall be [a]outside the camp.

47 "When a garment has a [1]mark of leprosy in it, whether it is a wool garment or a linen garment,

48 whether in [1]warp or woof, of linen or of wool, whether in leather or in any article made of leather,

49 if the mark is greenish or reddish in the garment or in the leather, or in the [1]warp or in the woof, or in any article of leather, it is a leprous mark and shall be shown to the priest.

50 "Then [a]the priest shall look at the mark and shall [1]quarantine the article with the mark for seven days.

51 "He shall then look at the mark on the seventh day; if the mark has spread in the garment, whether in the warp or in the woof, or in the leather, whatever the purpose for which the leather is used, the mark is a [1]leprous malignancy, it is unclean.

52 "So he shall burn the garment, whether the warp or the woof, in wool or in linen, or any article of leather in which the mark occurs, for it is a [1]leprous malignancy; it shall be burned in the fire.

53 "But if the priest shall look, and indeed the mark has not spread in the garment, either in the warp or in the woof, or in any article of leather,

54 then the priest shall order them to wash the thing in which the mark occurs and he shall [1]quarantine it for seven more days.

55 "After the article with the mark has been washed, the priest shall again look, and if the mark has not changed its appearance, even though the mark has not spread, it is

31 [1]Lit *shut up*
32 [1]Lit *been*
33 [1]Lit *shut up*
38 [1]Lit *flesh*
39 [1]Lit *flesh* [2]Lit *tetter*
40 [1]Lit *man's head becomes bald* [a]2 Kin 2:23; Is 15:2; Amos 8:10
41 [1]Lit *border of his face*
43 [1]Lit *flesh* [a]Lev 10:10; Ezek 22:26
45 [1]Or *disheveled* [a]Lev 10:6 [b]Ezek 24:17, 22; Mic 3:7 [c]Lam 4:15
46 [a]Num 5:1-4; 12:14
47 [1]Lit *infection*, and so throughout the ch
48 [1]Or *weaving or texture*
49 [1]Or *weaving or texture*
50 [1]Lit *shut up* [a]Ezek 44:23
51 [1]Lit *malignant leprosy*
52 [1]Lit *malignant leprosy*
54 [1]Lit *shut up*

13:45–46 The ceremonially unclean were excluded from the camp (the area around the tabernacle and courtyard), where the Israelites lived in tents. Later, no unclean person was allowed in the temple area, where he could mingle with others. Not only was God present in the tabernacle in a special way, but also in the camp (Num 5:3; Deut 23:14). Therefore unclean people were not to be in the camp (see Num 5:1–4; 12:14–15, Miriam; 31:19–24; see also Lev 10:4–5; Num 15:35–36; 2 Kin 7:3–4; 2 Chr 26:21, Uzziah). As a result of their separation from God, the unclean were to exhibit their grief by tearing their clothes, by having unkempt hair and by partially covering their faces (v. 45).
13:47 *leprosy.* Or "mildew." During Israel's rainy season (October through March), mildew is a problem along the coast and by the Sea of Galilee, where it is very humid.
13:54 *wash.* See vv. 34,55–56,58. The treatment of disorders commonly included washing.

unclean; you shall burn it in the fire,
whether an eating away has produced bare-
ness on the top or on the front of it.
56 "Then if the priest looks, and if the mark
has faded after it has been washed, then he
shall tear it out of the garment or out of the
leather, whether from the warp or from the
woof;
57 and if it appears again in the garment,
whether in the warp or in the woof, or in any
article of leather, it is an outbreak; the article
with the mark shall be burned in the fire.
58 "The garment, whether the warp or the
woof, or any article of leather from which
the mark has departed when you washed it,
it shall then be washed a second time and
will be clean."
59 This is the law for the mark of leprosy
in a garment of wool or linen, whether in the
warp or in the woof, or in any article of
leather, for pronouncing it clean or unclean.

Law of Cleansing a Leper

14 Then the LORD spoke to Moses, saying,
2 "This shall be the law of the leper in
the day of his cleansing. [a]Now he shall be
brought to the priest,
3 and the priest shall go [a]out to the outside of the camp. Thus the priest shall look,
and if the [1]infection of leprosy has been
healed in the leper,
4 then the priest shall give orders to take
two live clean birds and [a]cedar wood and a
[1]scarlet string and hyssop for the one who is
to be cleansed.
5 "The priest shall also give orders to slay
the one bird in an earthenware vessel over
[1]running water.
6 "*As for* the live bird, he shall take it
together with [a]the cedar wood and the [1]scar-
let string and the [b]hyssop, and shall dip
them and the live bird in the blood of the
bird that was slain over the [2]running water.
7 "[a]He shall then sprinkle seven times the
one who is to be cleansed from the leprosy
and shall pronounce him clean, and shall let
the live bird go free over the open field.
8 "[a]The one to be cleansed shall then
wash his clothes and shave off all his hair
and bathe in water and [b]be clean. Now afterward, he may enter the camp, but he [c]shall
stay outside his tent for seven days.

9 "It will be on the seventh day that he
shall shave off all his hair: he shall shave his
head and his beard and his eyebrows, even
all his hair. He shall then wash his clothes
and bathe his [1]body in water and [a]be clean.
10 "Now on the eighth day he is to take
two male lambs without defect, and a yearling ewe lamb without defect, and three-
tenths *of an* [1]*ephah* of fine flour mixed with
oil for a grain offering, and one [2a]log of oil;
11 and the priest who pronounces him
clean shall present the man to be cleansed
and the [1]aforesaid before the LORD at the
doorway of the tent of meeting.
12 "Then the priest shall take the one male
lamb and bring it for a [a]guilt offering, with
the [1b]log of oil, and present them as a [c]wave
offering before the LORD.
13 "Next he shall slaughter the male lamb
in [a]the place where they slaughter the sin
offering and the burnt offering, at the place
of the sanctuary—for the guilt offering, [b]like
the sin offering, belongs to the priest; it is
most holy.
14 "The priest shall then take some of the
blood of the [a]guilt offering, and the priest
shall put *it* on [b]the lobe of the right ear of the
one to be cleansed, and on the thumb of his
right hand and on the big toe of his right
foot.
15 "The priest shall also take some of the
[1a]log of oil, and pour *it* into his left palm;
16 the priest shall then dip his right-hand
finger into the oil that is in his left palm, and
with his finger sprinkle some of the oil seven
times before the LORD.
17 "Of the remaining oil which is in his
palm, the priest shall put some on the right
ear lobe of the one to be cleansed, and on
the thumb of his right hand, and on the big
toe of his right foot, on the blood of the guilt
offering;
18 while the rest of the oil that is in the
priest's palm, he shall put on the head of the
one to be cleansed. So the priest shall make
[a]atonement on his behalf before the LORD.
19 "The priest shall next offer the [a]sin
offering and make atonement for the one to
be cleansed from his uncleanness. Then
afterward, he shall slaughter the burnt offering.
20 "The priest shall offer up the burnt offer-

14:2 [a]Matt 8:4; Mark 1:44; Luke 5:14; 17:14
3 [1]Lit *mark, stroke,* and so throughout the ch [a]Lev 13:46
4 [1]Lit *scarlet color and* [a]Lev 14:6, 49, 51, 52; Num 19:6
5 [1]Lit *living*
6 [1]Lit *scarlet color and* [2]Lit *living* [a]Lev 14:4 [b]Ps 51:7
7 [a]Ezek 36:25
8 [a]Lev 11:25; 13:6; Num 8:7 [b]Lev 14:9, 20 [c]Num 5:2, 3; 12:14, 15; 2 Chr 26:21

9 [1]Lit *flesh* [a]Lev 14:8, 20
10 [1]I.e. Approx one bu [2]I.e. Approx one pt [a]Lev 14:12, 15, 21, 24
11 [1]Lit *them*
12 [1]I.e. Approx one pt [a]Lev 5:6, 18; 6:6; 14:19 [b]Lev 14:10 [c]Ex 29:22-24, 26
13 [a]Ex 29:11; Lev 1:11; 4:24 [b]Lev 6:24-30; 7:7
14 [a]Lev 14:19 [b]Ex 29:20; Lev 8:23, 24
15 [1]I.e. Approx one pt [a]Lev 14:10
18 [a]Lev 4:26; Num 15:28; Heb 2:17
19 [a]Lev 14:12

13:59 A summary of ch. 13.

14:1–32 The ritual after the skin disease had been cured had three parts: (1) ritual for the first week (outside the camp, vv. 1–7), (2) ritual for the second week (inside the camp, vv. 8–20) and (3) special permission for the poor (vv. 21–32).

14:4 *hyssop.* A plant used in ceremonial cleansing (see note on Ex 12:22).

14:5 *slay.* Diseases and disorders were a symbol of sin and rendered a person or object ceremonially unclean. The prescribed cleansing included sacrifice as well as washing (see note on 13:54).

14:6 *cedar . . . string . . . hyssop.* Also used for cleansing in vv. 51–52; Num 19:6.

14:7,16,51 *seven times.* See note on 4:6.

14:7 *clean.* Perhaps the yarn and cedar stick were used as well as the hyssop plant to sprinkle the blood for cleansing (see Ps 51:7). Further sacrifices are specified in vv. 10–31. *let the live bird go free.* Cf. 16:22; see note on 16:5.

14:8 The Levites were similarly cleansed (see Num 8:7).

14:10 *grain offering.* See note on 2:1.

14:12 *guilt offering.* See 5:14–6:7 and note on 5:15. *wave offering.* See note on 7:30–32.

14:14 See note on 8:14.

14:19 *sin offering.* See 4:1–5:13 and notes on 4:3,5. *burnt offering.* See note on 1:3.

ing and the grain offering on the altar. Thus the priest shall make atonement for him, and [a]he will be clean.

21 "[a]But if he is poor and his [1]means are insufficient, then he is to take one male lamb for a [b]guilt offering as a wave offering to make atonement for him, and one-tenth *of an* [2]*ephah* of fine flour mixed with oil for a grain offering, and a [3c]log of oil,

22 and two turtledoves or two young pigeons which [1]are within his means, [a]the one shall be a [b]sin offering and the other a burnt offering.

23 "[a]Then the eighth day he shall bring them for his cleansing to the priest, at the doorway of the tent of meeting, before the LORD.

24 "The priest shall take the lamb of the guilt offering and [a]the [1]log of oil, and the priest shall offer them for a wave offering before the LORD.

25 "Next he shall slaughter the lamb of the guilt offering; and the priest is to take some of the blood of the guilt offering and put *it* on [a]the lobe of the right ear of the one to be cleansed and on the thumb of his right hand and on the big toe of his right foot.

26 "The priest shall also pour some of the oil into his left palm;

27 and with his right-hand finger the priest shall sprinkle some of the oil that is in his left palm seven times before the LORD.

28 "The priest shall then put some of the oil that is in his palm on the lobe of the right ear of the one to be cleansed, and on the thumb of his right hand and on the big toe of his right foot, on the place of the blood of the guilt offering.

29 "Moreover, the rest of the oil that is in the priest's palm he shall put on the head of the one to be cleansed, to make atonement on his behalf before the LORD.

30 "He shall then offer one of the turtledoves or young pigeons, [1]which are within his means.

31 "*He shall offer* what [1]he can afford, [a]the one for a sin offering and the other for a burnt offering, together with the grain offering. So the priest shall make atonement before the LORD on behalf of the one to be cleansed.

32 "This is the law *for him* in whom there is an infection of leprosy, whose [1]means are limited for his cleansing."

Cleansing a Leprous House

33 The LORD further spoke to Moses and to Aaron, saying:

34 "[a]When you enter the land of Canaan, which I give you for a possession, and I put a mark of leprosy on a house in the land of your possession,

35 then the one who owns the house shall come and tell the priest, saying, '*Something* like [a]a mark *of leprosy* has become visible to me in the house.'

36 "The priest shall then command that they empty the house before the priest goes in to look at the mark, so that everything in the house need not become unclean; and afterward the priest shall go in to look at the house.

37 "So he shall look at the mark, and if the mark on the walls of the house has greenish or reddish depressions and appears deeper than the [1]surface,

38 then the priest shall come out of the house, to the [1]doorway, and [2]quarantine the house for seven days.

39 "The priest shall return on the seventh day and [1]make an inspection. If the mark has indeed spread in the walls of the house,

40 then the priest shall order them to tear out the stones with the mark in them and throw them away [1]at an unclean place outside the city.

41 "He shall have the house scraped all around [1]inside, and they shall dump the plaster that they scrape off at an unclean place outside the city.

42 "Then they shall take other stones and replace *those* stones, and he shall take other plaster and replaster the house.

43 "If, however, the mark breaks out again in the house after he has torn out the stones and scraped the house, and after it has been replastered,

44 then the priest shall come in and [1]make an inspection. If he sees that the mark has indeed spread in the house, it is [a]a malignant mark in the house; it is unclean.

45 "He shall therefore tear down the house, its stones, and its timbers, and all the plaster of the house, and he shall take *them* outside the city to an [a]unclean place.

46 "Moreover, whoever goes into the house during the time that he has [1]quarantined it, becomes [a]unclean until evening.

47 "Likewise, whoever lies down in the house shall wash his clothes, and whoever eats in the house shall wash his clothes.

48 "If, on the other hand, the priest comes in and [1]makes an inspection and the mark has not indeed spread in the house after the house has been replastered, then the priest shall pronounce the house clean because the mark has [2]not reappeared.

49 "To cleanse the house then, he shall take [a]two birds and cedar wood and a [1]scarlet string and hyssop,

50 and he shall slaughter the one bird in an earthenware vessel over [1]running water.

51 "Then he shall take the cedar wood and

20 [a]Lev 14:8, 9 **21** [1]Lit *hand is not reaching* [2]I.e. Approx one bu [3]I.e. Approx one pt [a]Lev 5:11; 12:8; 27:8 [b]Lev 14:22 [c]Lev 14:10 **22** [1]Lit *his hand reaches* [a]Lev 5:7 [b]Lev 14:21, 24, 25 **23** [a]Lev 14:10, 11 **24** [1]I.e. Approx one pt [a]Lev 14:10 **25** [a]Lev 14:14 **30** [1]Lit *from those which his hand can reach* **31** [1]Lit *his hand can reach* [a]Lev 5:7 **32** [1]Lit *hand does not reach* **34** [a]Gen 17:8; Num 32:22; Deut 7:1; 32:49

35 [a]Ps 91:10 **37** [1]Lit *wall* **38** [1]Lit *doorway of the house* [2]Lit *shut up* **39** [1]Lit *look* **40** [1]Lit *to* **41** [1]Lit *from the house around* **44** [1]Lit *look* [a]Lev 13:51 **45** [a]Lev 14:41 **46** [1]Lit *shut up* [a]Num 19:7, 10, 21, 22 **48** [1]Lit *looks* [2]Lit *healed* **49** [1]Lit *scarlet color* [a]Lev 14:4 **50** [1]Lit *living*

14:20 *grain offering.* See note on 2:1.
14:33–53 There are many similarities between this section and the previous one, particularly in the manner of restoration.
14:45 *tear down.* A house desecrated by mildew (see note on 13:47), mold or fungus would be a defiled place to live in, so drastic measures had to be taken.

the [a]hyssop and the [1]scarlet string, with the
live bird, and dip them in the blood of the
slain bird as well as in the [2]running water,
and sprinkle the house seven times.
52 "He shall thus cleanse the house with
the blood of the bird and with the [1]running
water, along with the live bird and with the
cedar wood and with the hyssop and with
the [2]scarlet string.
53 "However, he shall let the live bird go
free outside the city into the open field. So he
shall make atonement for the house, and it
will be clean."
54 This is the law for any mark of leprosy—even for a [a]scale,
55 and for the [a]leprous garment or house,
56 and [a]for a swelling, and for a scab, and
for a bright spot—
57 to teach [1]when they are unclean and
[2]when they are clean. This is the law of leprosy.

Cleansing Unhealthiness

15 The LORD also spoke to Moses and to
Aaron, saying,
2 "Speak to the sons of Israel, and say to
them, '[a]When any man has a discharge from
his [1]body, [2]his discharge is unclean.
3 'This, moreover, shall be his uncleanness in his discharge: it is his uncleanness
whether his body allows its discharge to flow
or whether his body obstructs its discharge.
4 'Every bed on which the person with
the discharge lies becomes unclean, and
everything on which he sits becomes
unclean.
5 'Anyone, moreover, who touches his
bed shall wash his clothes and bathe in
water and be unclean until evening;
6 and whoever sits on the thing on which
the man with the discharge has been sitting,
shall wash his clothes and bathe in water
and be unclean until evening.
7 'Also whoever touches the [1]person with
the discharge shall wash his clothes and
bathe in water and be unclean until evening.
8 'Or if the man with the discharge spits
on one who is clean, he too shall wash his
clothes and bathe in water and be unclean
until evening.
9 'Every saddle on which the person with
the discharge rides becomes unclean.
10 'Whoever then touches any of the
things which were under him shall be
unclean until evening, and he who carries
them shall wash his clothes and bathe in
water and be unclean until evening.
11 'Likewise, whomever the one with the
discharge touches without having rinsed his
hands in water shall wash his clothes and
bathe in water and be unclean until evening.
12 'However, an [a]earthenware vessel
which the person with the discharge touches
shall be broken, and every wooden vessel
shall be rinsed in water.
13 'Now when the man with the discharge
becomes cleansed from his discharge, then
he [a]shall count off for himself seven days for
his cleansing; he shall then wash his clothes
and bathe his body in [1]running water and
will become clean.
14 'Then on the eighth day he shall take
for himself [a]two turtledoves or two young
pigeons, and come before the LORD to the
doorway of the tent of meeting and give
them to the priest;
15 and the priest shall offer them, [a]one for
a sin offering and the other for a burnt offering. So [b]the priest shall make atonement on
his behalf before the LORD because of his discharge.
16 '[a]Now if a [1]man has a seminal emission, he shall bathe all his body in water and
be unclean until evening.
17 'As for any garment or any leather on
which there is seminal emission, it shall be
washed with water and be unclean until
evening.
18 'If a man lies with a woman *so that*
there is a seminal emission, they shall both
bathe in water and be [a]unclean until
evening.
19 '[a]When a woman has a discharge, *if* her
discharge in her body is blood, she shall continue in her menstrual impurity for seven
days; and whoever touches her shall be
unclean until evening.
20 'Everything also on which she lies during her menstrual impurity shall be unclean,
and everything on which she sits shall be
unclean.
21 'Anyone who touches her bed shall
wash his clothes and bathe in water and be
unclean until evening.
22 'Whoever touches any thing on which
she sits shall wash his clothes and bathe in
water and be unclean until evening.
23 'Whether it be on the bed or on the
thing on which she is sitting, when he
touches it, he shall be unclean until evening.

51 [1]Lit *scarlet color* [2]Lit *living* [a]1 Kin 4:33; Ps 51:7
52 [1]Lit *living* [2]Lit *scarlet color*
54 [a]Lev 13:30
55 [a]Lev 13:47-52
56 [a]Lev 13:2
57 [1]Lit *in the day of uncleanness* [2]Lit *in the day of cleanness*
15:2 [1]Lit *flesh*, and so throughout the ch [2]Or *by his discharge, he is unclean* [a]Lev 22:4; Num 5:2; 2 Sam 3:29
7 [1]Lit *flesh*
12 [a]Lev 6:28; 11:33
13 [1]Lit *living* [a]Lev 8:33; 14:8
14 [a]Lev 14:22, 23
15 [a]Lev 5:7; 14:31 [b]Lev 14:19, 31
16 [1]Lit *man's...goes out from him* [a]Lev 22:4; Deut 23:10, 11
18 [a]1 Sam 21:4
19 [a]Lev 12:2

15:1–33 The chapter deals with (1) male uncleanness caused by bodily discharge (vv. 2–15) or emission of semen (vv. 16–18); (2) female uncleanness caused by her monthly period (vv. 19–24) or lengthy hemorrhaging (vv. 25–30); (3) summary (vv. 31–33).
15:2 *discharge from his body.* Probably either diarrhea or urethral discharge (various kinds of infections). The contamination of anything under the man (v. 10), whether he sat (vv. 4,6,9) or lay (v. 4) on it, indicates that the bodily discharge had to do with the buttocks or genitals.
15:4 *bed.* Something like a mat (cf. 2 Sam 11:13).
15:13 *cleansed.* God brought about the healing; the priest could only ascertain that a person was already healed.
15:16 *seminal.* Normal sexual activity and a woman's menstruation required no sacrifices but only washing and a minimal period of uncleanness.
15:19 *seven days.* See 12:2. This regulation is the background of 2 Sam 11:4 (Bathsheba).
15:20 See note on Gen 31:35.

24 '[a]If a man actually lies with her so that her menstrual impurity is on him, he shall be unclean seven days, and every bed on which he lies shall be unclean.

25 '[a]Now if a woman has a discharge of her blood many days, not at the period of her menstrual impurity, or if she has a discharge beyond [1]that period, all the days of her impure discharge she shall continue as though [2]in her menstrual impurity; she is unclean.

26 'Any bed on which she lies all the days of her discharge shall be to her like [1]her bed at menstruation; and every thing on which she sits shall be unclean, like [2]her uncleanness at that time.

27 'Likewise, whoever touches them shall be unclean and shall wash his clothes and bathe in water and be unclean until evening.

28 'When she becomes clean from her discharge, she shall count off for herself seven days; and afterward she will be clean.

29 'Then on the eighth day she shall take for herself two turtledoves or two young pigeons and bring them in to the priest, to the doorway of the tent of meeting.

30 'The priest shall offer the [a]one for a sin offering and the other for a burnt offering. So the priest shall make atonement on her behalf before the LORD because of her impure discharge.'

31 "Thus you shall keep the sons of Israel separated from their uncleanness, so that they will not die in their uncleanness by their [a]defiling My [1]tabernacle that is among them."

32 This is the law for the one with a discharge, and for the man [1]who has a seminal emission so that he is unclean by it,

33 and for the woman who is ill because of menstrual impurity, and for the one who has a discharge, whether a male or a female, or a man who lies with an unclean woman.

Law of Atonement

16 Now the LORD spoke to Moses after [a]the death of the two sons of Aaron, when they had approached the presence of the LORD and died.

2 The LORD said to Moses:

"Tell your brother Aaron that he shall not enter [a]at any time into the holy place inside the veil, before the [1]mercy seat which is on the ark, or he will die; for [b]I will appear in the cloud over the [1]mercy seat.

3 "Aaron shall enter the holy place with this: with a [1]bull for a [a]sin offering and a ram for a burnt offering.

4 "He shall put on the [a]holy linen tunic, and the linen undergarments shall be next to his [1]body, and he shall be girded with the linen sash and attired with the linen turban (these are holy garments). Then he shall [b]bathe his [1]body in water and put them on.

5 "He shall take from the congregation of the sons of Israel [a]two male goats for a sin offering and one ram for a burnt offering.

24 [a]Lev 18:19; 20:18
25 [1]Lit *her menstrual impurity* [2]Lit *in the days of* [a]Matt 9:20; Mark 5:25; Luke 8:43
26 [1]Lit *the bed of her menstrual impurity* [2]Lit *the uncleanness of her menstrual impurity*
30 [a]Lev 5:7
31 [1]Or *dwelling place* [a]Lev 20:3; Num 19:13, 20; Ezek 5:11; 36:17
32 [1]Lit *whose seminal emission goes out from him*
16:1 [a]Lev 10:1, 2
2 [1]Lit *propitiatory* [a]Ex 30:10; Heb 6:19; 9:7, 25 [b]Ex 25:21, 22; 40:34; 1 Kin 8:10-12
3 [1]Or *bull of the herd* [a]Lev 4:1-12; 16:6; Heb 9:7
4 [1]Lit *flesh* [a]Ex 28:39, 42 [b]Ex 30:20; Lev 16:24; Heb 10:22
5 [a]Lev 4:13-21; 2 Chr 29:21; Ezek 45:22

15:24 A case of the woman's period beginning during intercourse. This is different from 18:19 and 20:18. *menstrual impurity.* During her period a woman was protected from sexual activity. No offering was required for uncleanness contracted by a man in this way, but the uncleanness lasted seven days.

15:25 *discharge of her blood many days.* As, e.g., the woman in Matt 9:20. *beyond that period.* An unnatural discharge, possibly caused by disease, was treated like a sickness and required an offering upon recovery (vv. 28–30; see vv. 14–15).

15:31 Addressed to the priests, thus emphasizing the importance of the regulations. Since God dwelt in the tabernacle, any unholiness, symbolized by the discharges of ch. 15, could result in death if the people came into His presence. Sin separates all people from a holy God and results in their death, unless atonement is made (see the next chapter).

16:1–34 See 23:26–32; 25:9; Ex 30:10; Num 29:7–11; Heb 9:7. The order of ritual for the day of atonement was as follows: 1. The high priest went to the basin in the courtyard, removed his regular garments, washed himself (v. 4) and went into the holy place to put on the special garments for the day of atonement (v. 4). 2. He went out to sacrifice a bull at the altar of burnt offering as a sin offering for himself and the other priests (v. 11). 3. He went into the holy of holies with some of the bull's blood, with incense and with coals from the altar of burnt offering (vv. 12–13). The incense was placed on the burning coals, and the smoke of the incense hid the ark from view. 4. He sprinkled some of the bull's blood on and in front of the mercy seat (v. 14). 5. He went outside the tabernacle and cast lots for two goats to see which was to be sacrificed and which was to be the scapegoat (vv. 7–8). 6. At the altar of burnt offering the high priest killed the goat for the sin offering for the people, and for a second time he went into the holy of holies, this time to sprinkle the goat's blood in front of and on the mercy seat (vv. 5,9,15–16a). 7. He returned to the holy place (called "tent of meeting" in v. 16) and sprinkled the goat's blood there (v. 16b). 8. He went outside to the altar of burnt offering and sprinkled it (v. 18) with the blood of the bull (for himself, v. 11) and of the goat (for the people, v. 15). 9. While in the courtyard, he laid both hands on the second goat, thus symbolizing the transfer of Israel's sin, and sent it out into the wilderness (vv. 20–22). 10. The man who took the goat away, after he accomplished his task, washed himself and his clothes outside the camp (v. 26) before rejoining the people. 11. The high priest entered the holy place to remove his special garments (v. 23). 12. He went out to the basin to wash and put on his regular priestly clothes (v. 24). 13. As a final sacrifice he went out to the great altar and offered a ram (v. 3) as a burnt offering for himself, and another ram (v. 5) for the people (v. 24). 14. The conclusion of the entire day was the removal of the sacrifices for the sin offerings to a place outside the camp, where they were burned, and there the man who performed this ritual bathed and washed his clothes (vv. 27–28) before rejoining the people.

16:1 *death of the two sons of Aaron.* See 10:1–3.

16:2 *mercy seat.* See Ex 25:17 and note. Blood sprinkled on the lid of the ark made atonement for Israel on the day of atonement (vv. 15–17). In the Septuagint (the Greek translation of the OT) the word for "mercy seat" is the same one used of Christ and translated "propitiation" in Rom 3:25 (see note there).

16:3 *bull.* For Aaron's cleansing (vv. 6,11). Before Aaron could minister in the holy place for the nation, he himself had to be cleansed (Heb 5:1–3); not so Christ, who is our high priest and Aaron's antitype (Heb 7:26–28).

16:5 *two male goats for a sin offering.* One was the usual sin offering (see notes on 4:3,5) and the other a scapegoat. No sin-

6 "Then [a]Aaron shall offer the bull for the sin offering which is for himself, that he may make atonement for himself and for his household.

7 "He shall take the two goats and present them before the LORD at the doorway of the tent of meeting.

8 "Aaron shall cast lots for the two goats, one lot for the LORD and the other lot for the [1]scapegoat.

9 "Then Aaron shall offer the goat on which the lot for the LORD fell, and make it a sin offering.

10 "But the goat on which the lot for the [1]scapegoat fell shall be presented alive before the LORD, to make [a]atonement upon it, to send it into the wilderness as the [1]scapegoat.

11 "Then Aaron shall offer the bull of the sin offering [a]which is for himself and make atonement for himself and [b]for his household, and he shall slaughter the bull of the sin offering which is for himself.

12 "He shall take a [a]firepan full of coals of fire from upon the altar before the LORD and [1]two handfuls of finely ground [b]sweet incense, and bring *it* inside the veil.

13 "He shall put the incense on the fire before the LORD, that the cloud of incense may cover the [1a]mercy seat that is on *the ark of* the testimony, [b]otherwise he will die.

14 "Moreover, [a]he shall take some of the blood of the bull and sprinkle *it* [b]with his finger on the [1]mercy seat on the east *side;* also in front of the [1]mercy seat he shall sprinkle some of the blood with his finger seven times.

15 "Then he shall slaughter the goat of the sin offering [a]which is for the people, and bring its blood inside the veil and do with its blood as he did with the blood of the bull, and sprinkle it on the [1]mercy seat and in front of the [1]mercy seat.

16 "[a]He shall make atonement for the holy place, because of the impurities of the sons of Israel and because of their transgressions in regard to all their sins; and thus he shall do for the tent of meeting which abides with them in the midst of their impurities.

17 "When he goes in to make atonement in the holy place, no one shall be in the tent of meeting until he comes out, that he may make atonement for himself and for his household and for all the assembly of Israel.

6 [a]Heb 5:3
8 [1]Lit *goat of removal,* or else a name: *Azazel*
10 [1]Lit *goat of removal,* or else a name: *Azazel* [a]Is 53:4-10; Rom 3:25; 1 John 2:2
11 [a]Heb 7:27; 9:7 [b]Lev 16:33
12 [1]Lit *the filling of the hollow of his hands* [a]Lev 10:1; Num 16:18 [b]Ex 30:34-38
13 [1]Lit *propitiatory* [a]Ex 25:21 [b]Ex 28:43; Lev 22:9; Num 4:15, 20
14 [1]Lit *propitiatory* [a]Heb 9:25 [b]Lev 4:6, 17
15 [1]Lit *propitiatory* [a]Heb 7:27; 9:7, 12
16 [a]Ex 29:36, 37; 30:10; Heb 2:17
18 [a]Lev 4:25; Ezek 43:20, 22
19 [a]Lev 16:14; Ezek 43:20
21 [1]Lit *in addition to* [a]Lev 5:5
23 [a]Lev 16:4; Ezek 42:14; 44:19
24 [1]Lit *flesh* [a]Lev 16:4 [b]Ex 28:40, 41
26 [1]Lit *goat of removal,* or else a name: *Azazel* [2]Lit *flesh* [a]Lev 11:25, 40
27 [a]Lev 6:30; Heb 13:11
28 [a]Num 19:8
29 [a]Lev 23:27; Num 29:7

18 "Then he shall go out to the altar that is before the LORD and make atonement for it, and shall take some of the blood of the bull and of the blood of the goat and [a]put it on the horns of the altar on all sides.

19 "[a]With his finger he shall sprinkle some of the blood on it seven times and cleanse it, and from the impurities of the sons of Israel consecrate it.

20 "When he finishes atoning for the holy place and the tent of meeting and the altar, he shall offer the live goat.

21 "Then Aaron shall lay both of his hands on the head of the live goat, and [a]confess over it all the iniquities of the sons of Israel and all their transgressions [1]in regard to all their sins; and he shall lay them on the head of the goat and send *it* away into the wilderness by the hand of a man who *stands* in readiness.

22 "The goat shall bear on itself all their iniquities to a solitary land; and he shall release the goat in the wilderness.

23 "Then Aaron shall come into the tent of meeting and take off [a]the linen garments which he put on when he went into the holy place, and shall leave them there.

24 "[a]He shall bathe his [1]body with water in a holy place and put on [b]his clothes, and come forth and offer his burnt offering and the burnt offering of the people and make atonement for himself and for the people.

25 "Then he shall offer up in smoke the fat of the sin offering on the altar.

26 "The one who released the goat as the [1]scapegoat [a]shall wash his clothes and bathe his [2]body with water; then afterward he shall come into the camp.

27 "But the bull of the sin offering and the goat of the sin offering, [a]whose blood was brought in to make atonement in the holy place, shall be taken outside the camp, and they shall burn their hides, their flesh, and their refuse in the fire.

28 "Then the [a]one who burns them shall wash his clothes and bathe his body with water, then afterward he shall come into the camp.

An Annual Atonement

29 "*This* shall be a permanent statute for you: [a]in the seventh month, on the tenth day

---

gle offering could fully typify the atonement of Christ. The one goat was killed, its blood sprinkled in the holy place and its body burned outside the camp (vv. 15,27), symbolizing the payment of the price of Christ's atonement. The other goat, sent away alive and bearing the sins of the nation (v. 21), symbolized the removal of sin and its guilt. *ram.* For the sins of the people; the one in v. 3 was for the sins of the high priest. Both were sacrificed at the end of the ceremony (v. 24).

16:6–10 An outline of vv. 11–22.

16:11 *make atonement for himself.* See note on v. 3.

16:13 The smoke of the incense covered the ark so that the high priest would not see the glorious presence of God (v. 2) and thus die.

16:14 See Rom 3:25. *seven times.* See note on 4:6.

16:16 *tent of meeting.* Here and in vv. 17,20,33 the term means the holy place.

16:20–22 A summary description of substitutionary atonement. The sin of the worshipers was confessed and symbolically transferred to the sacrificial animal, on which hands were laid (see notes on 1:3; Ex 29:10; see also Lev 1:4; 3:8; 4:4).

16:24 *holy place.* Cf. 6:26. *burnt offering . . . burnt offering.* The two rams mentioned in vv. 3,5.

16:25 *fat of the sin offering.* See 4:8–10.

16:27 *outside the camp.* See note on 4:12.

of the month, you shall humble your souls and not [b]do any work, whether the native, or the alien who sojourns among you;

30 for it is on this day that [1]atonement shall be made for you to [a]cleanse you; you will be clean from all your sins before the LORD.

31 "It is to be a sabbath of solemn rest for you, that you may [a]humble your souls; it is a permanent statute.

32 "So the priest who is anointed and [1]ordained to serve as priest in his father's place shall make atonement: he shall thus put on [a]the linen garments, the holy garments,

33 and make atonement for the holy sanctuary, and he shall make atonement for the tent of meeting and for the altar. He shall also make atonement for [a]the priests and for all the people of the assembly.

34 "Now you shall have this as a [a]permanent statute, to [b]make atonement for the sons of Israel for all their sins once every year." And just as the LORD had commanded Moses, *so* he did.

Blood for Atonement

17 Then the LORD spoke to Moses, saying,

2 "Speak to Aaron and to his sons and to all the sons of Israel and say to them, 'This is what the LORD has commanded, saying,

3 "Any man from the house of Israel who slaughters an ox or a lamb or a goat in the camp, or who slaughters it outside the camp,

4 and [a]has not brought it to the doorway of the tent of meeting to present *it* as an offering to the LORD before the [1]tabernacle of the LORD, bloodguiltiness is to be reckoned to that man. He has shed blood and that man shall be cut off from among his people.

5 "[1]The reason is so that the sons of Israel may bring their sacrifices which they were sacrificing in the open field, that they may bring them in to the LORD, at the doorway of the tent of meeting to the priest, and sacrifice them as sacrifices of peace offerings to the LORD.

6 "The priest shall sprinkle the blood on the altar of the LORD at the doorway of the tent of meeting, and [a]offer up the fat in smoke as a soothing aroma to the LORD.

7 "[a]They shall no longer sacrifice their sacrifices to the [1]goat demons with which they play the harlot. This shall be a permanent statute to them throughout their generations." '

8 "Then you shall say to them, 'Any man from the house of Israel, or from the aliens who sojourn among them, who offers a burnt offering or sacrifice,

9 and [a]does not bring it to the doorway of the tent of meeting to [1]offer it to the LORD, that man also shall be cut off from his people.

10 '[a]And any man from the house of Israel, or from the aliens who sojourn among them, who eats any blood, [b]I will set My face against that person who eats blood and will cut him off from among his people.

11 'For [a]the [1]life of the flesh is in the blood, and I have given it to you on the altar to make atonement for your souls; for [b]it is the blood by reason of the [1]life that makes atonement.'

12 "Therefore I said to the sons of Israel, 'No person among you may eat blood, nor may any alien who sojourns among you eat blood.'

13 "So when any man from the sons of Israel, or from the aliens who sojourn among them, [1]in hunting catches a beast or a bird which may be eaten, [a]he shall pour out its blood and cover it with earth.

14 "[a]For *as for the* [1]life of all flesh, its blood is *identified* with its [1]life. Therefore I said to the sons of Israel, 'You are not to eat the blood of any flesh, for the [1]life of all flesh is its blood; whoever eats it shall be cut off.'

15 "[a]When any person eats *an animal* which dies or is torn *by beasts,* whether he is a native or an alien, he shall wash his clothes and bathe in water, and remain unclean until evening; then he will become clean.

16 "But if he does not wash *them* or bathe his body, then [a]he shall bear his [1]guilt."

29 [b]Ex 31:14, 15
30 [1]Lit *he shall make atonement* [a]Ps 51:2; Jer 33:8; Eph 5:26
31 [a]Lev 23:32; Ezra 8:21; Is 58:3, 5; Dan 10:12
32 [1]Lit *whose hand is filled* [a]Lev 16:4
33 [a]Lev 16:11
34 [a]Lev 23:31 [b]Heb 9:7
17:4 [1]Lit *dwelling place* [a]Deut 12:5-21
5 [1]Lit *In order that*
6 [a]Num 18:17
7 [1]Or *goat-idols* [a]Ex 22:20; 32:8; 34:15; Deut 32:17; 2 Chr 11:15; Ps 106:37f; 1 Cor 10:20
9 [1]Lit *do* [a]Ex 20:24; Lev 17:4
10 [a]Gen 9:4; Lev 3:17; 7:26, 27; Deut 12:16, 23-25; 1 Sam 14:33 [b]Lev 20:3, 6; Jer 44:11
11 [1]Lit *soul* [a]Gen 9:4; Lev 17:14 [b]Heb 9:22
13 [1]Lit *who in hunting* [a]Deut 12:16
14 [1]Lit *soul* [a]Gen 9:4; Lev 17:11
15 [a]Ex 22:31; Lev 7:24; 22:8; Deut 14:21
16 [1]Or *iniquity* [a]Num 19:20

16:29,31 *humble your souls.* The expression came to be used of fasting (Ps 35:13). The day of atonement was the only regular fast day stipulated in the OT (see 23:27,29,32, where humbling oneself probably implies fasting), though tradition later added other fast days to the Jewish calendar (see Zech 7:5; 8:19).
16:29 *seventh month.* Tishri, the seventh month, begins with the blowing of trumpets (see note on 23:24). The day of atonement follows on the 10th day, and on the 15th day the Feast of Booths begins (see 23:23–36).
16:30 *clean from all your sins.* On the day of atonement the repentant Israelite was assured of sins forgiven.
16:34 *once every year.* Heb 9:11–10:14 repeatedly points out this contrast with Christ's "once for all" sacrifice.
17:4 *tabernacle of the LORD.* The people, with few exceptions (e.g., Deut 12:15,20–21), were directed to sacrifice only at the central sanctuary (Deut 12:5–6). Sennacherib's representative referred to Hezekiah's requiring worship only in Jerusalem (2 Kin 18:22). One reason for such a regulation was to keep the Israelites from becoming corrupted by the Canaanites' pagan worship. *cut off from among his people.* See note on 7:20.
17:5 *to the priest . . . to the LORD.* See note on 6:6.
17:7 *play the harlot.* See 20:5–6; see also Judg 2:17 and note.
17:11 *the life of the flesh is in the blood.* See note on Gen 9:4. The blood shed in the sacrifices was sacred. It epitomized the life of the sacrificial victim. Since life was sacred, blood (a symbol of life) had to be treated with respect (Gen 9:5–6). Eating blood was therefore strictly forbidden (see 7:26–27; Deut 12:16,23–25; 15:23; 1 Sam 14:32–34). *blood . . . makes atonement.* Practically every sacrifice included the sprinkling or smearing of blood on the altar or within the tabernacle (v. 6; 1:5; 3:2; 4:6,25; 7:2), thus teaching that atonement involves the substitution of life for life. The blood of the OT sacrifice pointed forward to the blood of the Lamb of God, who obtained for His people "eternal redemption" (Heb 9:12). "Without shedding of blood there is no forgiveness" (Heb 9:22).
17:15 *dies or is torn.* Such animals would not have had the blood drained from them and therefore would be forbidden.

Laws on Immoral Relations

18 Then the LORD spoke to Moses, saying, 2 "Speak to the sons of Israel and say to them, '[a]I am the LORD your God.

3 'You shall not do [1]what is [a]done in the land of Egypt where you lived, nor are you to do [1]what is [b]done in the land of Canaan where I am bringing you; you shall not walk in their statutes.

4 'You are to perform My judgments and keep My statutes, [1]to live in accord with them; [a]I am the LORD your God.

5 'So you shall keep My statutes and My judgments, [a]by which a man may live if he does them; I am the LORD.

6 'None of you shall approach any blood relative [1]of his to uncover nakedness; I am the LORD.

7 '[a]You shall not uncover the nakedness of your father, that is, the nakedness of your mother. She is your mother; you are not to uncover her nakedness.

8 '[a]You shall not uncover the nakedness of your father's wife; it is your father's nakedness.

9 '[a]The nakedness of your sister, *either* your father's daughter or your mother's daughter, whether born at home or born outside, their nakedness you shall not uncover.

10 'The nakedness of your son's daughter or your daughter's daughter, their nakedness you shall not uncover; for [1]their nakedness is yours.

11 'The nakedness of your father's wife's daughter, [1]born to your father, she is your sister, you shall not uncover her nakedness.

12 '[a]You shall not uncover the nakedness of your father's sister; she is your father's blood relative.

13 'You shall not uncover the nakedness of your mother's sister, for she is your mother's blood relative.

14 '[a]You shall not uncover the nakedness of your father's brother; you shall not approach his wife, she is your aunt.

15 '[a]You shall not uncover the nakedness of your daughter-in-law; she is your son's wife, you shall not uncover her nakedness.

16 '[a]You shall not uncover the nakedness of your brother's wife; it is your brother's nakedness.

17 '[a]You shall not uncover the nakedness of a woman and of her daughter, nor shall you take her son's daughter or her daughter's daughter, to uncover her nakedness; they are blood relatives. It is [1]lewdness.

18 'You shall not [1]marry a woman in addition to [2]her sister [3]as a rival while she is alive, to uncover her nakedness.

19 '[a]Also you shall not approach a woman to uncover her nakedness during her [b]menstrual impurity.

20 '[a]You shall not have intercourse with your neighbor's wife, to be defiled with her.

21 'You shall not give any of your offspring [a]to [1]offer them to Molech, nor shall you [b]profane the name of your God; I am the LORD.

22 '[a]You shall not lie with a male as [1]one lies with a female; it is an abomination.

23 '[a]Also you shall not have intercourse with any animal to be defiled with it, nor shall any woman stand before an animal to [1]mate with it; it is a perversion.

24 'Do not defile yourselves by any of these things; for by all these [a]the nations

18:2 [a]Ex 6:7; Lev 11:44; Ezek 20:5
3 [1]Lit *according to the deed of* [a]Ezek 20:7, 8 [b]Lev 18:24-30; 20:23
4 [1]Lit *to walk in them* [a]Lev 18:2
5 [a]Neh 9:29; Ezek 18:9; 20:11; Luke 10:28; Rom 10:5; Gal 3:12
6 [1]Lit *of his flesh*
7 [a]Lev 20:11; Deut 27:20; Ezek 22:10
8 [a]Lev 20:11; Deut 22:30; 27:20; 1 Cor 5:1
9 [a]Lev 18:11; 20:17; Deut 27:22
10 [1]Lit *they are your nakedness*
11 [1]Lit *begotten of*
12 [a]Lev 20:19
14 [a]Lev 20:20
15 [a]Lev 20:12
16 [a]Lev 20:21
17 [1]Or *wickedness* [a]Lev 20:14
18 [1]Lit *take a wife* [2]Or *another* [3]Lit *to be*
19 [a]Lev 15:24; 20:18 [b]Lev 12:2
20 [a]Lev 20:10; Prov 6:29; Matt 5:27, 28; 1 Cor 6:9; Heb 13:4
21 [1]Lit *cause to pass over* [a]Lev 20:2-5; Deut 12:31 [b]Lev 19:12; 20:3; 21:6; Ezek 36:20; Mal 1:12
22 [1]Lit *those who lie* [a]Lev 20:13; Deut 23:18 mg; Rom 1:27
23 [1]Or *lie* [a]Ex 22:19; Lev 20:15, 16; Deut 27:21
24 [a]Lev 18:3; Deut 18:12

18:1–20:27 Here God's people are given instructions concerning interpersonal relations and a morality reflecting God's holiness. Israel was thereby prepared for a life different from the Canaanites, whose life-style was deplorably immoral. Ch. 18 contains prohibitions in the moral sphere, ch. 19 expands the Ten Commandments to detail correct morality, and ch. 20 assesses the penalties for violating God's standard of morality. See chart, p. 255.

18:2 In chs. 18–26 the phrase "I am the LORD" occurs 47 times. The Lord's name (i.e., His revealed character as Yahweh, "the LORD") is the authority that stands behind His instructions. See note on Ex 3:15.

18:3 Six times in this chapter Israel is warned not to follow the example of pagans (here, two times; see also vv. 24,26–27,30).

18:5 *live.* With God's full blessing. The law was the way of life for the redeemed (see Ezek 20:11,13,21), not a way of salvation for the lost (see Rom 10:5; Gal 3:12).

18:6 A summary of the laws against incest (vv. 7–18). Penalties for incestuous relations are given in ch. 20.

18:7 This prohibition applied also after the father's death. If the father was still living, the act was adulterous and therefore forbidden.

18:8 *your father's wife.* Other than your mother—assuming there is more than one wife.

18:11 *sister.* There would be many half-sisters in a polygamous society. Tamar claimed that an exception to this prohibition could be made (2 Sam 13:12–13; but see note there).

18:14 *your aunt.* See 20:20. If the father's brother was alive, the act would be adulterous. If he was dead, one could rationalize such a marriage because the aunt was not a blood relative—but it was forbidden.

18:15 Cf. the account of Judah and Tamar (Gen 38:18).

18:16 *your brother's wife.* The law also applied to a time after divorce or the brother's death. To marry one's brother's widow was not immoral but might damage the brother's inheritance. The levirate law of Deut 25:5–6 offered an exception that preserved the dead brother's inheritance and continued his line.

18:17 *daughter.* Stepdaughter (granddaughter-in-law is also covered in the verse). The law applied even after the mother's death.

18:18 Cf. the account of Jacob with Leah and Rachel (Gen 29:23–30).

18:19 See Ezek 18:6; 22:10.

18:21 *Molech.* The god of the Ammonites (see 20:2–5; 1 Kin 11:5 and note). The detestable practice of sacrificing children to Molech was common in Phoenicia and other surrounding countries. Cf. 2 Kin 3:26–27. King Manasseh evidently sacrificed his sons to Molech (2 Chr 33:6; see 2 Kin 23:10). Jer 32:35 protests the practice.

18:22 *lie with a male.* See 20:13, where the penalty for homosexual acts is death.

which I am casting out before you have
become defiled.
25 'For the land has become defiled, [a]there-
fore I have brought its [1]punishment upon it,
so the land [b]has spewed out its inhabitants.
26 'But as for you, you are to keep My statutes and My judgments and shall not do any
of these abominations, *neither* the native,
nor the alien who sojourns among you
27 (for the men of the land who have been
before you have done all these abominations, and the land has become defiled);
28 so that the land will not spew you out,
should you defile it, as it has spewed out the
nation which has been before you.
29 'For whoever does any of these abominations, [1]those persons who do *so* shall be
cut off from among their people.
30 'Thus you are to keep [a]My charge, that
you do not practice any of the abominable
customs which have been practiced before
you, so as not to defile yourselves with them;
[b]I am the LORD your God.' "

Idolatry Forbidden

19 Then the LORD spoke to Moses, saying:
2 "Speak to all the congregation of the
sons of Israel and say to them, '[a]You shall be
holy, for I the LORD your God am holy.
3 'Every one of you [a]shall reverence his
mother and his father, and you shall keep
[b]My sabbaths; [c]I am the LORD your God.
4 'Do not turn to [a]idols or make for yourselves molten [b]gods; I am the LORD your God.
5 'Now when you offer a sacrifice of
peace offerings to the LORD, you shall offer it
so that you may be accepted.
6 'It shall be eaten the same day you offer
it, and the next day; but what remains until
the third day shall be burned with fire.
7 'So if it is eaten at all on the third day, it
is an offense; it will not be accepted.
8 'Everyone who eats it will bear his iniquity, for he has profaned the holy thing of
the LORD; and that person shall be cut off
from his people.

Sundry Laws

9 '[a]Now when you reap the harvest of
your land, you shall not reap to the very corners of your field, nor shall you gather the
gleanings of your harvest.
10 'Nor shall you glean your vineyard, nor
shall you gather the fallen fruit of your vineyard; you shall leave them for the needy and
for the stranger. I am the LORD your God.
11 '[a]You shall not steal, nor deal falsely,
[b]nor lie to one another.
12 '[a]You shall not swear falsely by My
name, so as to [b]profane the name of your
God; I am the LORD.
13 '[a]You shall not oppress your neighbor,
nor rob *him*. [b]The wages of a hired man are
not to remain with you all night until morning.
14 'You shall not curse a deaf man, nor
[a]place a stumbling block before the blind,
but you shall revere your God; I am the LORD.
15 '[a]You shall do no injustice in judgment;
you shall not be partial to the poor nor defer
to the great, but you are to judge your neighbor fairly.
16 'You shall not go about as [a]a slanderer
among your people, and you are not to [1]act
against the [2b]life of your neighbor; I am the
LORD.
17 'You [a]shall not hate your [1]fellow countryman in your heart; you [b]may surely
reprove your neighbor, but shall not incur sin
because of him.
18 '[a]You shall not take vengeance, [b]nor
bear any grudge against the sons of your
people, but [c]you shall love your neighbor as
yourself; I am the LORD.
19 'You are to keep My statutes. You shall
not breed together two kinds of your cattle;
[a]you shall not sow your field with two kinds
of seed, nor wear a garment upon you of two
kinds of material mixed together.
20 '[a]Now if a man lies carnally with a
woman who is a slave acquired for *another*
man, but who has in no way been redeemed
nor given her freedom, there shall be punishment; they shall not, *however*, be put to
death, because she was not free.
21 'He shall bring his guilt offering to the
LORD to the doorway of the tent of meeting,
[a]a ram for a guilt offering.
22 'The priest shall also make atonement
for him with the ram of the guilt offering

25 [1]Lit *iniquity* [a]Lev 20:23; Deut 9:5; 18:12 [b]Lev 18:28; 20:22
29 [1]Or *and the*
30 [a]Lev 22:9; Deut 11:1 [b]Lev 18:2
19:2 [a]Ex 19:6; Lev 11:44; 20:7, 26; Eph 1:4; 1 Pet 1:16
3 [a]Ex 20:12; 31:13; Deut 5:16 [b]Ex 20:8 [c]Lev 11:44
4 [a]Lev 26:1; Ps 96:5; 115:4-7 [b]Ex 20:23; 34:17
9 [a]Lev 23:22; Deut 24:20-22
11 [a]Ex 20:15, 16 [b]Jer 9:3-5; Eph 4:25
12 [a]Ex 20:7; Deut 5:11; Matt 5:33 [b]Lev 18:21
13 [a]Ex 22:7-15, 21-27 [b]Deut 24:15; James 5:4
14 [a]Deut 27:18
15 [a]Ex 23:3, 6; Deut 1:17; 10:17; 16:19
16 [1]Lit *stand* [2]Lit *blood* [a]Ps 15:3; Jer 6:28; 9:4; Ezek 22:9 [b]Ex 23:7; Deut 27:25
17 [1]Lit *brother* [a]1 John 2:9, 11; 3:15 [b]Matt 18:15; Luke 17:3
18 [a]Deut 32:35; Rom 12:19; Heb 10:30 [b]Ps 103:9 [c]Matt 19:19; Mark 12:31; Luke 10:27; Rom 13:9; Gal 5:14; James 2:8
19 [a]Deut 22:9, 11
20 [a]Deut 22:23-27
21 [a]Lev 6:1-7

18:29 *abominations.* See note on 7:21. *cut off from among their people.* See note on 7:20.
19:1 See note on 18:1–20:27.
19:2 *be holy.* See note on 11:44.
19:3–4 See v. 30; Ex 20:4–6,8–11. See also chart, p. 255.
19:5 *peace offerings.* See note on 3:1.
19:6 *third day.* See note on 7:15–18.
19:8 *cut off from his people.* See note on 7:20.
19:9–10 See 23:22; see also Deut 24:19–21. Ruth 2 gives an example of the application of the law of gleaning.
19:11–12 See Ex 20:7,15–16.
19:13 *wages of a hired man.* See Deut 24:14–15; Matt 20:8.
19:17 *not hate your fellow countryman.* See 1 John 2:9,11; 3:15; 4:20.
19:18 *love your neighbor as yourself.* Quoted by Christ (Matt 22:39; Mark 12:31; Luke 10:27), Paul (Rom 13:9; Gal 5:14) and James (2:8). The stricter Pharisees (school of Shammai) added to this command what they thought it implied: "Hate your enemy" (Matt 5:43). Jesus' reaction, "Love your enemies," was in line with true OT teaching (see vv. 17,34) and was more in agreement with the middle-of-the-road Pharisees. Rabbi Nahmanides caught their sentiments: "One should place no limitations upon the love for the neighbor, but instead a person should love to do an abundance of good for his fellow being as he does for himself." "Neighbor" does not merely mean one who lives nearby, but anyone with whom one comes in contact.
19:21–22 *guilt offering.* See 5:14–6:7 and note on 5:15.

before the LORD for his sin which he has
committed, and the sin which he has committed will be forgiven him.
23 'When you enter the land and plant all
kinds of trees for food, then you shall count
their fruit as [1]forbidden. Three years it shall
be [1]forbidden to you; *it* shall not be eaten.
24 'But in the fourth year all its fruit shall
be holy, an offering of praise to the LORD.
25 'In the fifth year you are to eat of its
fruit, that its yield may increase for you; I am
the LORD your God.
26 'You shall not eat *anything* [a]with the
blood, nor practice [b]divination or soothsaying.
27 '[a]You shall not round off the side-
growth of your heads nor harm the edges of
your beard.
28 'You shall not make any cuts in your
[1]body for the [2]dead nor make any tattoo
marks on yourselves: I am the LORD.
29 '[a]Do not [1]profane your daughter by
making her a harlot, so that the land will not
fall to harlotry and the land become full of
lewdness.
30 'You shall [a]keep My sabbaths and
[b]revere My sanctuary; I am the LORD.
31 'Do not turn to [1a]mediums or spiritists;
do not seek them out to be defiled by them.
I am the LORD your God.
32 '[a]You shall rise up before the grayhead-
ed and honor the [1]aged, and you shall revere
your God; I am the LORD.
33 '[a]When a stranger resides with you in
your land, you shall not do him wrong.
34 'The stranger who resides with you
shall be to you as the native among you, and
[a]you shall love him as yourself, for you were
aliens in the land of Egypt; I am the LORD
your God.
35 '[a]You shall do no wrong in judgment, in
measurement of weight, or capacity.
36 'You shall have [a]just balances, just
weights, a just [1]ephah, and a just [2]hin; I am
the LORD your God, who brought you out
from the land of Egypt.
37 'You shall thus observe all My statutes
and all My ordinances and do them; I am the
LORD.' "

23 [1]Lit *uncircumcised*
26 [a]Gen 9:4; Lev 7:26f; 17:10; Deut 12:16, 23 [b]Deut 18:10; 2 Kin 17:17
27 [a]Lev 21:5; Deut 14:1
28 [1]Lit *flesh* [2]Lit *soul*
29 [1]Or *degrade* [a]Lev 21:9; Deut 22:21; 23:17, 18
30 [a]Lev 19:3 [b]Lev 26:2
31 [1]Or *ghosts or spirits* [a]Lev 20:6, 27; Deut 18:11; 1 Sam 28:3; Is 8:19
32 [1]Lit *face of the aged* [a]Prov 23:22; Lam 5:12; 1 Tim 5:1
33 [a]Ex 22:21; Deut 24:17, 18
34 [a]Lev 19:18
35 [a]Deut 25:13-16; Ezek 45:10
36 [1]I.e. Approx one bu [2]I.e. Approx one gal. [a]Deut 25:13-15; Prov 20:10

20:2 [1]Lit *seed* [a]Lev 18:21 [b]Lev 20:27; 24:14-23; Num 15:35, 36; Deut 21:21
3 [1]Lit *seed* [a]Lev 15:31 [b]Lev 18:21
4 [1]Lit *hiding they hide their eyes from* [2]Lit *seed*
6 [1]Or *ghosts and spirits* [a]Lev 19:31
7 [a]Eph 1:4; 1 Pet 1:16
8 [a]Ex 31:13
9 [a]Ex 21:17; Deut 27:16
10 [a]Ex 20:14; Lev 18:20; Deut 5:18
11 [a]Lev 18:7, 8; Deut 27:20
12 [1]Lit *confusion;* i.e. a violation of divine order [a]Lev 18:15

On Human Sacrifice and Immoralities

20 Then the LORD spoke to Moses, saying,
2 "You shall also say to the sons of Israel:
'Any man from the sons of Israel or from
the aliens sojourning in Israel [a]who gives
any of his [1]offspring to Molech, shall surely
be put to death; [b]the people of the land shall
stone him with stones.
3 'I will also set My face against that man
and will cut him off from among his people,
because he has given some of his [1]offspring
to Molech, [a]so as to defile My sanctuary and
[b]to profane My holy name.
4 'If the people of the land, however,
[1]should ever disregard that man when he
gives any of his [2]offspring to Molech, so as
not to put him to death,
5 then I Myself will set My face against
that man and against his family, and I will
cut off from among their people both him
and all those who play the harlot after him,
by playing the harlot after Molech.
6 'As for the person who turns to [1a]medi-
ums and to spiritists, to play the harlot after
them, I will also set My face against that person and will cut him off from among his
people.
7 'You shall consecrate yourselves therefore and [a]be holy, for I am the LORD your God.
8 '[a]You shall keep My statutes and practice them; I am the LORD who sanctifies you.
9 '[a]If *there is* anyone who curses his
father or his mother, he shall surely be put to
death; he has cursed his father or his mother, his bloodguiltiness is upon him.
10 '[a]If *there is* a man who commits adultery with another man's wife, one who commits adultery with his friend's wife, the adulterer and the adulteress shall surely be put to
death.
11 '[a]If *there is* a man who lies with his
father's wife, he has uncovered his father's
nakedness; both of them shall surely be put
to death, their bloodguiltiness is upon them.
12 '[a]If *there is* a man who lies with his
daughter-in-law, both of them shall surely be
put to death; they have committed [1]incest,
their bloodguiltiness is upon them.

19:26 *anything with the blood.* See note on 17:11. *soothsaying.* See v. 31; Ex 22:18; Deut 18:14; 1 Sam 28:9; Is 47:12–14.
19:27 *not round off the side-growth of your heads.* A prohibition still followed by orthodox Jews.
19:28 There was to be no disfiguring of the body, after the manner of the pagans (see note on 21:5).
19:34 *you were aliens in . . . Egypt.* See Deut 5:15.
19:35 *do no wrong in judgment.* In a culture with no bureau of weights and measures, cheating in business transactions by falsification of standards was common (see Deut 25:13–16; Prov 11:1; 16:11; 20:10,23). The prophets also condemned such sin (Amos 8:5; Mic 6:10–11).
20:1–27 In ch. 20 many of the same sins listed in ch. 18 are mentioned again, but this time usually with the death penalty specified. Israel's God is a jealous God and tolerates no rivals (see note on Ex 20:5). He requires exclusive allegiance (see Ex 20:3). See note on 18:1–20:27.
20:2–5 *Molech.* See note on 18:21.
20:3 *cut off from among his people.* See note on 7:20.
20:5 *play the harlot.* See v. 6; 17:7; see also note on Ex 34:15.
20:6 *to mediums and to spiritists.* Consulting a medium was no less a sin than being one (v. 27). See Deut 18:10–11. Only God was to be consulted—through either the priest or a prophet.
20:7 *be holy.* See note on 11:44.
20:8 *who sanctifies.* This phrase and the expression, "I am the LORD (your God)," are characteristic of chs. 18–26.
20:9 Cf. the penalty of a profligate son in Deut 21:20–21.
20:10 See 18:20.
20:12 See 18:15.

13 ‘[a]If *there is* a man who lies with a male as those who lie with a woman, both of them have committed a detestable act; they shall surely be put to death. Their bloodguiltiness is upon them.

14 ‘[a]If *there is* a man who [1]marries a woman and her mother, it is immorality; both he and they shall be burned with fire, so that there will be no immorality in your midst.

15 ‘[a]If *there is* a man who lies with an animal, he shall surely be put to death; you shall also kill the animal.

16 ‘If *there is* a woman who approaches any animal to [1]mate with it, you shall kill the woman and the animal; they shall surely be put to death. Their bloodguiltiness is upon them.

17 ‘[a]If *there is* a man who takes his sister, his father’s daughter or his mother’s daughter, so that he sees her nakedness and she sees his nakedness, it is a disgrace; and they shall be cut off in the sight of the sons of their people. He has uncovered his sister’s nakedness; he bears his guilt.

18 ‘[a]If *there is* a man who lies with a [1]menstruous woman and uncovers her nakedness, he has laid bare her flow, and she has [2]exposed the flow of her blood; thus both of them shall be cut off from among their people.

19 ‘[a]You shall also not uncover the nakedness of your mother’s sister or of your father’s sister, for such a one has made naked his [1]blood relative; they will bear their guilt.

20 ‘[a]If *there is* a man who lies with his uncle’s wife he has uncovered his uncle’s nakedness; they will bear their sin. They will die childless.

21 ‘[a]If *there is* a man who takes his brother’s wife, it is [1]abhorrent; he has uncovered his brother’s nakedness. They will be childless.

22 ‘You are therefore to keep all My statutes and all My ordinances and do them, so that the land to which I am bringing you to [1]live will not [a]spew you out.

23 ‘Moreover, you shall not [1]follow [a]the customs of the nation which I will drive out before you, for they did all these things, and [b]therefore I have abhorred them.

24 ‘Hence I have said to you, “[a]You are to possess their land, and I Myself will give it to you to possess it, a land flowing with milk and honey.” I am the LORD your God, who has [b]separated you from the peoples.

25 ‘[a]You are therefore to make a distinction between the clean animal and the unclean, and between the unclean bird and the clean; and you shall not make [1]yourselves detestable by animal or by bird or by anything [2]that creeps on the ground, which I have separated for you as unclean.

26 ‘Thus you are to be holy to Me, for I the LORD am holy; and I [a]have set you apart from the peoples to be Mine.

27 ‘Now a man or a woman [a]who is a medium or a [1]spiritist shall surely be put to death. They shall be stoned with stones, their bloodguiltiness is upon them.’ ”

Regulations concerning Priests

21 Then the LORD said to Moses, “Speak to the priests, the sons of Aaron, and say to them:

‘[a]**No** one shall defile himself for a *dead* person among his people,

2 [a]except for his relatives who are nearest to him, his mother and his father and his son and his daughter and his brother,

3 also for his virgin sister, who is near to him [1]because she has had no husband; for her he may defile himself.

4 ‘He shall not defile himself as a [1]relative by marriage among his people, and so profane himself.

5 ‘[a]They shall not make any baldness on their heads, [b]nor shave off the edges of their beards, [c]nor make any cuts in their flesh.

6 ‘They shall be holy to their God and [a]not profane the name of their God, for they present the offerings by fire [1]to the LORD, [b]the food of their God; so they shall be holy.

7 ‘[a]They shall not take a woman who is profaned by harlotry, nor shall they take a woman divorced from her husband; for he is holy to his God.

8 ‘You shall consecrate him, therefore, for he offers [a]the food of your God; he shall be holy to you; for I the LORD, who sanctifies you, am holy.

9 ‘[a]Also the daughter of any priest, if she profanes herself by harlotry, she profanes her father; she shall be burned with fire.

10 ‘The priest who is the highest among

13 [a]Lev 18:22
14 [1]Lit *takes* [a]Lev 18:17; Deut 27:23
15 [a]Lev 18:23; Deut 27:21
16 [1]Lit *lie*
17 [a]Lev 18:9; Deut 27:22
18 [1]Lit *sick* [2]Or *uncovered* [a]Lev 15:24; 18:19
19 [1]Lit *flesh* [a]Lev 18:12, 13
20 [a]Lev 18:14
21 [1]Or *an impure deed* [a]Lev 18:16
22 [1]Lit *dwell in it* [a]Lev 18:28
23 [1]Lit *walk in the statutes* [a]Lev 18:3 [b]Lev 18:25
24 [a]Ex 13:5; 33:1-3
24 [b]Ex 33:16; Lev 20:26
25 [1]Lit *your souls* [2]Lit *with which the ground creeps* [a]Lev 10:10; 11:1-47; Deut 14:3-21
26 [a]Lev 20:24
27 [1]Lit *spiritist among them* [a]Lev 19:31
21:1 [a]Lev 19:28; Ezek 44:25
2 [a]Lev 21:11
3 [1]Or *whom no man has had*
4 [1]Lit *husband among*
5 [a]Deut 14:1; Ezek 44:20 [b]Lev 19:27 [c]Deut 14:1
6 [1]Lit *of* [a]Lev 18:21 [b]Lev 3:11
7 [a]Lev 21:13, 14
8 [a]Lev 21:6
9 [a]Gen 38:24; Lev 19:29

20:13 *detestable.* See note on 7:21.
20:15–16 See 18:23.
20:18 See 18:19.
20:20 See 18:14.
20:21 See 18:16 and note.
20:24 *land flowing with milk and honey.* A common phrase in Exodus, Numbers and Deuteronomy (see Ex 3:8 and note; see also Josh 5:6; Jer 11:5; 32:22; Ezek 20:6,15).
20:25 See ch. 11 and notes.
20:27 See note on v. 6.
21:1–22:33 Directions for the priests’ conduct, especially about separation from ceremonial uncleanness.
21:1 *for a dead person.* Touching a corpse (Num 19:11) or entering the home of a person who had died (Num 19:14) made one unclean. A priest was only to contract such uncleanness at the death of a close relative (vv. 2–3), and the regulations for the high priest denied him even this (vv. 11–12).
21:5 *cuts in their flesh.* See 19:27–28. Such lacerations and disfigurement were common among pagans as signs of mourning and to secure the attention of their deity (see 1 Kin 18:28). Israelite faith had a much less grotesque view of death (see, e.g., vv. 1–4; Gen 5:24; 2 Sam 12:23; Heb 11:19).
21:8 *I . . . am holy.* See note on 11:44.
21:9 See Gen 38:24 and note.

his brothers, on whose head the anointing oil
has been poured and [1]who has been consecrated to wear the garments, [a]shall not
[2]uncover his head nor tear his clothes;
11 [a]nor shall he approach any dead person, nor defile himself *even* for his father or
his mother;
12 [a]nor shall he go out of the sanctuary
nor profane the sanctuary of his God, for
[b]the consecration of the anointing oil of his
God is on him; I am the LORD.
13 'He shall take a wife in her virginity.
14 '[a]A widow, or a divorced woman, or
one who is profaned by harlotry, these he
may not take; but rather he is to [1]marry a
virgin of his own people,
15 so that he will not profane his [1]off-
spring among his people; for I am the LORD
who sanctifies him.' "
16 Then the LORD spoke to Moses, saying,
17 "Speak to Aaron, saying, 'No man of
your [1]offspring throughout their generations
who has a defect shall approach to offer the
[a]food of his God.
18 '[a]For no one who has a defect shall
approach: a blind man, or a lame man, or he
who has a [1a]disfigured *face,* or any deformed
limb,
19 or a man who has a broken foot or broken hand,
20 or a hunchback or a dwarf, or *one who*
has a [1]defect in his eye or eczema or scabs or
[a]crushed testicles.
21 'No man among the [1]descendants of
Aaron the priest who has a defect is to come
near to offer the LORD's offerings by fire;
since he has a defect, he shall not come near
to offer [a]the food of his God.
22 'He may eat [a]the food of his God, *both*
of the most holy and of the holy,
23 only he shall not go in to the veil or
come near the altar because he has a defect,
so that he will not profane My sanctuaries.
For I am the LORD who sanctifies them.' "
24 So Moses spoke to Aaron and to his
sons and to all the sons of Israel.

Sundry Rules for Priests

22 Then the LORD spoke to Moses, saying,
2 "Tell Aaron and his sons to be careful
with the holy *gifts* of the sons of Israel,
which they dedicate to Me, so as not to profane My holy name; I am the LORD.
3 "Say to them, '[a]If any man among all
your [1]descendants throughout your generations approaches the holy *gifts* which the
sons of Israel dedicate to the LORD, while he
has an uncleanness, that person shall be cut
off from before Me; I am the LORD.
4 '[a]No man of the [1]descendants of Aaron,
who is a leper or who has a discharge, may
eat of the holy *gifts* until he is clean. [b]And if
one touches anything made unclean by a
corpse or if [c]a man has a seminal emission,
5 or [a]if a man touches any teeming
things by which he is made unclean, or any
man by whom he is made unclean, whatever his uncleanness;
6 a [1]person who touches any such shall
be unclean until evening, and shall not eat of
the holy *gifts* unless he has bathed his [2]body
in water.
7 'But when the sun sets, he will be clean,
and afterward he shall eat of the holy *gifts,*
for [a]it is his [1]food.
8 'He shall not eat [a]*an animal* which dies
or is torn *by beasts,* becoming unclean by it;
I am the LORD.
9 'They shall therefore keep [a]My charge,
so that [b]they will not bear sin because of it
and die thereby because they profane it; I am
the LORD who sanctifies them.
10 '[a]No [1]layman, however, is to eat the
holy *gift;* a sojourner with the priest or a
hired man shall not eat of the holy *gift.*
11 '[a]But if a priest buys a [1]slave as *his*
property with his money, [2]that one may eat
of it, and those who are born in his house
may eat of his [3]food.
12 'If a priest's daughter is married to a
[1]layman, she shall not eat of the [2]offering of
the *gifts.*
13 'But if a priest's daughter becomes a
widow or divorced, and has no child and
returns to her father's house as in her youth,
she shall eat of her father's [1]food; [a]but no
[2]layman shall eat of it.
14 '[a]But if a man eats a holy *gift* unintentionally, then he shall add to it a fifth of it
and shall give the holy *gift* to the priest.
15 '[a]They shall not profane the holy *gifts* of
the sons of Israel which they offer to the
LORD,
16 and *so* cause them [a]to bear [1]punish-
ment for guilt by eating their holy *gifts;* for I
am the LORD who sanctifies them.' "

Flawless Animals for Sacrifice

17 Then the LORD spoke to Moses, saying,
18 "Speak to Aaron and to his sons and to

10 [1]Lit *whose hand has been filled* [2]Lit *unbind* [a]Lev 10:6
11 [a]Lev 19:28; Num 19:14
12 [a]Lev 10:7 [b]Ex 29:6, 7
14 [1]Lit *take as wife* [a]Lev 21:7; Ezek 44:22
15 [1]Lit *seed*
17 [1]Lit *seed* [a]Lev 21:6
18 [1]Lit *slit* [a]Lev 22:19-25
20 [1]Lit *obscurity* [a]Deut 23:1; Is 56:3-5
21 [1]Lit *seed* [a]Lev 21:6
22 [a]1 Cor 9:13
22:3 [1]Lit *seed* [a]Lev 7:20, 21; Num 19:13
4 [1]Lit *seed* [a]Lev 14:1-32 [b]Lev 11:24-28, 39, 40 [c]Lev 15:16, 17
5 [a]Lev 11:23-28
6 [1]Lit *soul* [2]Lit *flesh*
7 [1]Lit *bread* [a]Num 18:11
8 [a]Lev 7:24; 11:39, 40; 17:15
9 [a]Lev 18:30 [b]Ex 28:43; Lev 22:16; Num 18:22
10 [1]Lit *stranger* [a]Ex 29:33; Lev 22:13; Num 3:10
11 [1]Lit *soul* [2]Lit *he may* [3]Lit *bread* [a]Gen 17:13; Ex 12:44
12 [1]Lit *stranger* [2]Lit *heave offering*
13 [1]Lit *bread* [2]Lit *stranger* [a]Lev 22:10
14 [a]Lev 5:15, 16
15 [a]Num 18:32
16 [1]Or *iniquity requiring a guilt offering* [a]Lev 10:17; 22:9

21:11–12 See note on v. 1.
21:17 *defect.* Like the sacrifices that had to be without defect, the priests were to typify Christ's perfection (Heb 9:13–14).
21:23 *veil.* Between the holy place and the holy of holies (see Ex 26:33).
22:3 *cut off from before Me.* Excluded from the worshiping community.
22:4 See 13:1–46 and note on 13:45–46; 15:1–18 and notes; 21:11.
22:5 See 11:29–31.
22:8 See 17:15 and note.
22:9 *die . . . because they profane it.* The laws of cleanness were the same for priests and people, but the penalties were far more severe for the priests, who had greater responsibility. Cf. Nadab and Abihu (10:1–3) and the faithless priests of Malachi's day (Mal 1:6–2:9). *sanctifies.* See note on 11:44.
22:14 *add to it a fifth . . . to the priest.* Cf. 5:16.
22:16 *holy.* See note on 11:44.

all the sons of Israel and say to them, '[a]Any
man of the house of Israel or of the aliens in
Israel who presents his offering, whether it is
any of their [1]votive or any of their freewill
offerings, which they present to the LORD for
a burnt offering—
19 [a]for you to be accepted—*it must be* a
male without defect from the cattle, the
sheep, or the goats.
20 '[a]Whatever has a defect, you shall not
offer, for it will not be accepted for you.
21 'When a man offers a sacrifice of peace
offerings to the LORD [a]to [1]fulfill a special vow
or for a freewill offering, of the herd or of the
flock, it must be perfect to be accepted; there
shall be no defect in it.
22 'Those *that are* blind or fractured or
maimed or having a running sore or eczema
or scabs, you shall not offer to the LORD, nor
make of them an offering by fire on the altar
to the LORD.
23 'In respect to an ox or a lamb which has
an [1]overgrown or stunted *member,* you may
present it for a freewill offering, but for a
vow it will not be accepted.
24 'Also [a]anything *with its testicles* bruised
or crushed or torn or cut, you shall not offer
to the LORD, or [1]sacrifice in your land,
25 nor shall you accept any such from the
hand of a foreigner for offering [a]as the [1]food
of your God; for their corruption is in them,
they have a defect, they shall not be accepted for you.' "
26 Then the LORD spoke to Moses, saying,
27 "When an ox or a sheep or a goat is
born, it shall [1]remain [a]seven days [2]with its
mother, and from the eighth day on it shall
be accepted as a sacrifice of an offering by
fire to the LORD.
28 "[a]But, *whether* it is an ox or a sheep,
you shall not kill *both* it and its young in one
day.
29 "When you sacrifice [a]a sacrifice of
thanksgiving to the LORD, you shall sacrifice
it so that you may be accepted.
30 "It shall be eaten on the same day, you
shall leave none of it until morning; I am the
LORD.

18 [1]Lit *vows* [a]Num 15:14
19 [a]Lev 21:18-21; Deut 15:21
20 [a]Deut 15:21; 17:1; Mal 1:8, 14; Heb 9:14; 1 Pet 1:19
21 [1]Or *make a special votive offering* [a]Num 15:3, 8
23 [1]Or *a deformed*
24 [1]Lit *do* [a]Lev 21:20
25 [1]Lit *bread* [a]Lev 21:22
27 [1]Lit *be* [2]Lit *under* [a]Ex 22:30
28 [a]Deut 22:6, 7
29 [a]Lev 7:12
31 [a]Lev 19:37; Num 15:40; Deut 4:40
33 [a]Lev 11:45
23:2 [a]Lev 23:4, 37, 44; Num 29:39 [b]Lev 23:21
3 [a]Ex 20:9, 10; 23:12; 31:13-17; 35:2, 3; Lev 19:3; Deut 5:13, 14
4 [a]Ex 23:14; Lev 23:2
5 [1]Lit *between the two evenings* [a]Ex 12:18, 19; Num 28:16-25; Deut 16:1; Josh 5:10
6 [a]Ex 12:14-20; 23:15; 34:18; Deut 16:3-8
7 [a]Lev 23:8, 21, 25, 35, 36
10 [a]Ex 23:19; 34:26

31 "[a]So you shall keep My commandments,
and do them; I am the LORD.
32 "You shall not profane My holy name,
but I will be sanctified among the sons of
Israel; I am the LORD who sanctifies you,
33 [a]who brought you out from the land of
Egypt, to be your God; I am the LORD."

Laws of Religious Festivals

23 The LORD spoke again to Moses, saying,
2 "Speak to the sons of Israel and say
to them, '[a]The LORD's appointed times which
you shall [b]proclaim as holy convocations—
My appointed times are these:
3 '[a]For six days work may be done, but
on the seventh day there is a sabbath of complete rest, a holy convocation. You shall not
do any work; it is a sabbath to the LORD in all
your dwellings.
4 'These are the [a]appointed times of the
LORD, holy convocations which you shall
proclaim at the times appointed for them.
5 '[a]In the first month, on the fourteenth
day of the month [1]at twilight is the LORD's
Passover.
6 'Then on the fifteenth day of the same
month there is the [a]Feast of Unleavened
Bread to the LORD; for seven days you shall
eat unleavened bread.
7 'On the first day you shall have a holy
convocation; you shall [a]not do any laborious
work.
8 'But for seven days you shall present an
offering by fire to the LORD. On the seventh
day is a holy convocation; you shall not do
any laborious work.' "
9 Then the LORD spoke to Moses, saying,
10 "Speak to the sons of Israel and say to
them, 'When you enter the land which I am
going to give to you and [a]reap its harvest,
then you shall bring in the sheaf of the first
fruits of your harvest to the priest.
11 'He shall wave the sheaf before the LORD
for you to be accepted; on the day after the
sabbath the priest shall wave it.
12 'Now on the day when you wave the
sheaf, you shall offer a male lamb one year old
without defect for a burnt offering to the LORD.

22:18 *burnt offering.* See note on 1:3.
22:20–22 See Mal 1:8.
22:21 *peace offerings.* See note on 3:1.
22:24 *bruised or crushed or torn or cut.* Castrated animals were not acceptable offerings.
22:28 Perhaps the prohibition was humanitarian (see v. 27), or possibly it was practical: The mother was to be saved to build up the flock (see Deut 22:6–7). Or it may have been a law to avoid an otherwise unknown pagan custom (see note on Ex 23:19).
22:30 *the same day.* The rule applied also to the Passover (Ex 34:25); however, the peace offering could be saved and eaten on the following day (7:16).
23:2 *appointed times.* See Ex 23:14–17 and notes; 34:18–25; Num 28–29; Deut 16:1–17. The parallel in Numbers (the fullest and closest to Leviticus) specifies in great detail the offerings to be made at each feast. See chart, pp. 164–165.
23:3 *sabbath.* See notes on Ex 16:23; 20:9–10. The sabbath is associated with the annual feasts also in Ex 23:12. Two additional lambs were to be sacrificed as a burnt offering every weekly sabbath (Num 28:9–10).
23:5 *first month.* See note on Ex 12:2. The Israelites had three systems of referring to months. In one, the months were simply numbered (as here and in v. 24). In another, the Canaanite names were used (Abib, Bul, etc.), of which only four are known. In the third system, the Babylonian names (Nisan, Adar, Tishri, Kislev, etc.) were used—in the exilic and postexilic books only—and are still used today. See chart, p. 92. *Passover.* See notes on Ex 12:11,14,21.
23:6 *Feast of Unleavened Bread.* See note on Ex 23:15. During the Feast the first sheaf of the barley harvest was brought (see vv. 10–11).

13 ‘Its [a]grain offering shall then be two-
tenths *of an ephah* of fine flour mixed with
oil, an offering by fire to the LORD *for* a soothing aroma, with its drink offering, a fourth of
a [1]hin of wine.
14 ‘Until this same day, until you have
brought in the offering of your God, [a]you
shall eat neither bread nor roasted grain nor
new growth. It is to be a perpetual statute
throughout your generations in all your
dwelling places.
15 ‘[a]You shall also count for yourselves
from the day after the sabbath, from the day
when you brought in the sheaf of the wave
offering; there shall be seven complete sabbaths.
16 ‘You shall count fifty days to the day
after the seventh sabbath; then you shall
present a [a]new grain offering to the LORD.
17 ‘You shall bring in from your dwelling
places two *loaves* of bread for a wave offering, made of two-tenths *of an* [1]*ephah;* they
shall be of a fine flour, baked [a]with leaven as
first fruits to the LORD.
18 ‘Along with the bread you shall present
seven one year old male lambs without
defect, and a bull of the herd and two rams;
they are to be a burnt offering to the LORD,
with their grain offering and their drink
offerings, an offering by fire of a soothing
aroma to the LORD.
19 ‘You shall also offer [a]one male goat for
a sin offering and two male lambs one year
old for a sacrifice of peace offerings.
20 ‘The priest shall then wave them with
the bread of the first fruits for a wave offering with two lambs before the LORD; they are
to be holy to the LORD for the priest.
21 ‘On this same day you shall [a]make a
proclamation as well; you are to have a holy
convocation. You shall do no laborious
[b]work. It is to be a perpetual statute in all

13 [1]I.e. Approx one gal. [a]Lev 6:20
14 [a]Ex 34:26; Num 15:20, 21
15 [a]Num 28:26-31; Deut 16:9-12
16 [a]Num 28:26
17 [1]I.e. Approx one bu [a]Lev 2:12; 7:13
19 [a]Lev 4:23; Num 28:30
21 [a]Lev 23:2, 4 [b]Lev 23:7

23:15 *seven complete sabbaths.* Or seven full weeks. See note on Ex 23:16.

23:16 *fifty days.* The NT name for the Feast of Weeks was Pentecost (see Acts 2:1; 20:16; 1 Cor 16:8), meaning “fifty.”

Old Testament Feasts and Other Sacred Days

NAME	OLD TESTAMENT REFERENCES	OT TIME	MODERN EQUIVALENT
Sabbath	Ex 20:8-11; 31:12-17; Lev 23:3; Deut 5:12-15	7th day	Same
Sabbath Year	Ex 23:10-11; Lev 25:1-7	7th year	Same
Year of Jubilee	Lev 25:8-55; 27:17-24; Num 36:4	50th year	Same
Passover	Ex 12:1-14; Lev 23:5; Num 9:1-14; 28:16; Deut 16:1-3a,4b-7	1st month (Abib) 14	Mar.–Apr.
Unleavened Bread	Ex 12:15-20; 13:3-10; 23:15; 34:18; Lev 23:6-8; Num 28:17-25; Deut 16:3b,4a,8	1st month (Abib) 15-21	Mar.–Apr.
First fruits	Lev 23:9-14	1st month (Abib) 16	Mar.–Apr.
Weeks (Pentecost)(Harvest)	Ex 23:16a; 34:22a; Lev 23:15-21; Num 28:26-31; Deut 16:9-12	3rd month (Sivan) 6	May–June
Trumpets (Later: Rosh Hashanah–New Year’s Day)	Lev 23:23-25; Num 29:1-6	7th month (Tishri) 1	Sept.–Oct.
Day of Atonement (Yom Kippur)	Lev 16; 23:26-32; Num 29:7-11	7th month (Tishri) 10	Sept.–Oct.
Booths (Tabernacles)(Ingathering)	Ex 23:16b; 34:22b; Lev 23:33-36a,39-43; Num 29:12-34; Deut 16:13-15; Zech 14:16-19	7th month (Tishri) 15-21	Sept.–Oct.
Holy Convocation	Lev 23:36b; Num 29:35-38	7th month (Tishri) 22	Sept.–Oct.
Purim	Esth 9:18-32	12th month (Adar) 14,15	Feb.–Mar.

On Kislev 25 (mid-December) Hanukkah, the feast of dedication or festival of lights, commemorated the purification of the temple and altar in the Maccabean period (165/4 B.C.). This feast is mentioned in John 10:22.

your dwelling places throughout your generations.
22 ‘[a]When you reap the harvest of your
land, moreover, you shall not reap to the
very corners of your field nor gather the
gleaning of your harvest; you are to leave
them for the needy and the alien. I am the
LORD your God.’ ”
23 Again the LORD spoke to Moses, saying,
24 “Speak to the sons of Israel, saying, ‘[a]In
the seventh month on the first of the month
you shall have a [1]rest, a [b]reminder by blowing *of trumpets*, a holy convocation.
25 ‘You shall [a]not do any laborious work,
but you shall present an offering by fire to
the LORD.’ ”

The Day of Atonement

26 The LORD spoke to Moses, saying,
27 “On exactly [a]the tenth day of this seventh month is [b]the day of atonement; it shall
be a holy convocation for you, and you shall
humble your souls and present an offering
by fire to the LORD.
28 “You shall not do any work on this same
day, for it is a [a]day of atonement, [b]to make
atonement on your behalf before the LORD
your God.

22 [a]Lev 19:9, 10; Deut 24:19; Ruth 2:15f
24 [1]Lit *sabbath rest* [a]Num 29:1 [b]Num 10:9, 10
25 [a]Lev 23:21
27 [a]Lev 16:29; 25:9; Num 29:7 [b]Ex 30:10; Lev 16:30; 23:28; Num 29:7-11
28 [a]Lev 23:27 [b]Lev 16:34

23:22 See note on 19:9–10.
23:24 *seventh month on the first of the month.* Today known as the Jewish New Year (*Rosh Hashanah*, "the beginning of the year"), but not so called in the Bible (the Hebrew expression is only used in Ezek 40:1 in a date formula). *blowing of trumpets.* Trumpets were blown on the first of every month (Ps 81:3). With no calendars available, the trumpets sounding across the land were an important signal of the beginning of the new season, the end of the agricultural year. See note on 16:29; see also chart, p. 92.
23:27 *day of atonement.* For details see notes on 16:1–34. Aaron was to enter the holy of holies only once a year (16:29–34) on the day called by modern Jews *Yom Kippur.* The Biblical name, however, is the plural *Yom Hakkippurim* (as in this verse), derived from the Hebrew words *yom* ("day") and *kipper* ("to atone"). The day was typological, foreshadowing the work of Christ, our high priest (see Heb 9:7; 13:11–12). *humble your souls.* See note on 16:29,31.

DESCRIPTION	PURPOSE	NEW TESTAMENT REFERENCES
Day of rest; no work	Rest for people and animals	Matt 12:1-14; 28:1; Luke 4:16; John 5:9; Acts 13:42; Col 2:16; Heb 4:1-11
Year of rest; fallow fields	Rest for land	
Canceled debts; liberation of slaves and indentured servants; land returned to original family owners	Help for poor; stabilize society	
Slaying and eating a lamb, together with bitter herbs and bread made without yeast, in every household	Remember Israel's deliverance from Egypt	Matt 26:17; Mark 14:12-26; John 2:13; 11:55; 1 Cor 5:7; Heb 11:28
Eating bread made without yeast; holding several assemblies; making designated offerings	Remember how the Lord brought the Israelites out of Egypt in haste	Mark 14:1; Acts 12:3; 1 Cor 5:6-8
Presenting a sheaf of the first of the barley harvest as a wave offering; making a burnt offering and a grain offering	Recognize the Lord's bounty in the land	Rom 8:23; 1 Cor 15:20-23
A festival of joy; mandatory and voluntary offerings, including the first fruits of the wheat harvest	Show joy and thankfulness for the Lord's blessing of harvest	Acts 2:1-4; 20:16; 1 Cor 16:8
An assembly on a day of rest commemorated with trumpet blasts and sacrifices	Present Israel before the Lord for his favor	
A day of rest, fasting and sacrifices of atonement for priests and people and atonement for the tabernacle and altar	Cleanse priests and people from their sins and purify the holy place	Rom 3:24-26; Heb 9:7; 10:3,19-22
A week of celebration for the harvest; living in booths and offering sacrifices	Memorialize the journey from Egypt to Canaan; give thanks for the productivity of Canaan	John 7:2,37
A day of convocation, rest and offering sacrifices	Commemorate the closing of the cycle of feasts	
A day of joy and feasting and giving presents	Remind the Israelites of their national deliverance in the time of Esther	

In addition, new moons were often special feast days (Num 10:10; 1 Chr 23:31; Ezra 3:5; Neh 10:33; Ps 81:3; Is 1:13-14; 66:23; Hosea 5:7; Amos 8:5; Col 2:16).

29 "If there is any [1]person who will not humble himself on this same day, [a]he shall be cut off from his people.

30 "As for any person who does any work on this same day, that person I will destroy from among his people.

31 "You shall do no work at all. It is to be a perpetual statute throughout your generations in all your dwelling places.

32 "It is to be a sabbath of complete rest to you, and you shall humble your souls; on the ninth of the month at evening, from evening until evening you shall keep your sabbath."

33 Again the LORD spoke to Moses, saying,

34 "Speak to the sons of Israel, saying, 'On [a]the fifteenth of this seventh month is the [b]Feast of Booths for seven days to the LORD.

35 'On the first day is a holy convocation; you shall do [a]no laborious work of any kind.

36 '[a]For seven days you shall present an offering by fire to the LORD. On [b]the eighth day you shall have a holy convocation and present an offering by fire to the LORD; it is an assembly. You shall do no laborious work.

37 'These are [a]the appointed times of the LORD which you shall proclaim as holy convocations, to present offerings by fire to the LORD—burnt offerings and grain offerings, sacrifices and drink offerings, [b]*each* day's matter on its own day—

38 besides *those of* the sabbaths of the LORD, and besides your gifts and besides all your [1]votive and freewill offerings, which you give to the LORD.

39 'On exactly the fifteenth day of the seventh month, [a]when you have gathered in the crops of the land, you shall celebrate the feast of the LORD for seven days, with a [1]rest on the first day and a [1]rest on the eighth day.

40 'Now on the first day you shall take for yourselves the [1]foliage of beautiful trees, palm branches and boughs of leafy trees and willows of the brook, and you shall rejoice before the LORD your God for seven days.

41 'You shall thus celebrate it *as* a feast to the LORD for seven days in the year. It *shall be* a perpetual statute throughout your generations; you shall celebrate it in the seventh month.

42 'You shall [1]live [a]in booths for seven days; all the native-born in Israel shall [1]live in booths,

43 so that [a]your generations may know that I had the sons of Israel live in booths when I brought them out from the land of Egypt. I am the LORD your God.' "

44 So Moses declared to the sons of Israel [a]the appointed times of the LORD.

The Lamp and the Bread of the Sanctuary

24 Then the LORD spoke to Moses, saying,
2 "Command the sons of Israel that
they bring to you [a]clear oil from beaten
olives for the [1]light, to make a lamp [2]burn
continually.

3 "Outside the veil of testimony in the tent of meeting, Aaron shall keep it in order from evening to morning before the LORD continually; *it shall be* a perpetual statute throughout your generations.

4 "He shall keep the lamps in order on the [a]pure *gold* lampstand before the LORD continually.

5 "[a]Then you shall take fine flour and bake twelve cakes with it; two-tenths *of an ephah* shall be *in* each cake.

6 "You shall set them *in* two rows, six *to* a row, on the [a]pure *gold* table before the LORD.

7 "You shall put pure frankincense on each row that it may be [a]a memorial portion for the bread, *even* an offering by fire to the LORD.

8 "[a]Every sabbath day he shall set it in order before the LORD [b]continually; it is an everlasting covenant [1]for the sons of Israel.

9 "[a]It shall be for Aaron and his sons, and they shall eat it in a holy place; for it is most holy to him from the LORD's offerings by fire, *his* portion forever."

10 Now the son of an Israelite woman, whose father was an Egyptian, went out among the sons of Israel; and the Israelite woman's son and a man of Israel struggled with each other in the camp.

11 The son of the Israelite woman blasphemed the [a]Name and cursed. So they brought him to Moses. (Now his mother's name was Shelomith, the daughter of Dibri, of the tribe of Dan.)

12 They put him in [1]custody [2]so that [a]the

29 [1]Lit *soul* [a]Gen 17:14; Lev 13:46; Num 5:2
34 [a]Num 29:12 [b]Lev 23:42, 43; Deut 16:13, 16; Ezra 3:4; Neh 8:14; Zech 14:16; John 7:2
35 [a]Lev 23:25
36 [a]Num 29:12-34 [b]Num 29:35-38
37 [a]Lev 23:2 [b]Num 28:1-29:38
38 [1]Lit *vows, and besides all your*
39 [1]Lit *sabbath rest* [a]Ex 23:16
40 [1]Lit *products, fruit*
42 [1]Lit *dwell* [a]Lev 23:34
42 [1]Lit *dwell*
43 [a]Deut 31:13; Ps 78:5f
44 [a]Lev 23:37
24:2 [1]Or *luminary* [2]Lit *ascend* [a]Ex 27:20, 21
4 [a]Ex 25:31; 31:8; 37:17
5 [a]Ex 25:30; 39:36; 40:23
6 [a]Ex 25:24; 1 Kin 7:48
7 [a]Lev 2:2, 9, 16
8 [1]Lit *from* [a]Matt 12:5 [b]Ex 25:30; Num 4:7; 2 Chr 2:4
9 [a]Matt 12:4; Mark 2:26; Luke 6:4
11 [a]Ex 3:15; 22:28; Job 2:5, 9; Is 8:21
12 [1]Or *prison* [2]Lit *to declare distinctly to them according to the mouth of the LORD* [a]Ex 18:15; Num 15:34

23:29 *cut off from his people.* See note on 7:20.
23:34 *Feast of Booths.* See notes on Ex 23:16; John 7:37–39. This was the last of the three annual pilgrimage festivals (Ex 23:14–17; Deut 16:16).
23:42 *booths.* The Hebrew for this word is *Sukkot* and can also be translated "tabernacles." Even today, orthodox Jews construct small booths (see Neh 8:13–17) to remind them of the booths they lived in when God brought them out of Egypt at the time of the exodus (v. 43).
24:2–4 See Ex 27:20–21.
24:3 *testimony.* See note on Ex 16:34. *keep it in order.* Keep the lamps burning (see vv. 2,4). *continually.* Every night without interruption, but not throughout the day. See 1 Sam 3:3 and note.
24:5 *two-tenths of an ephah.* About four quarts. Either the loaves were quite large or a smaller unit of measurement is intended (the Hebrew word *ephah* is not expressed).
24:7 *pure frankincense.* Not used as a condiment for the bread, but burned either in piles on the table or in small receptacles alongside the rows of bread.
24:8 *it.* Often called the "bread of the Presence" (see Ex 25:30 and note). It represented a gift from the 12 tribes and signified the fact that God sustained His people. It was eaten by the priests (24:9).
24:9 See 1 Sam 21:4–6.
24:10 *father was an Egyptian.* An alien. The laws, at least in the judicial sphere, applied equally to both the alien and the native-born Israelite (v. 22; see Ex 12:49).
24:11 *blasphemed.* See Ex 20:7 and note.

command of the LORD might be made clear
to them.
13 Then the LORD spoke to Moses, saying,
14 "Bring the one who has cursed outside
the camp, and let all who heard him [a]lay
their hands on his head; then [b]let all the congregation stone him.
15 "You shall speak to the sons of Israel,
saying, '[a]If anyone curses his God, then he
will bear his sin.
16 'Moreover, the one who [a]blasphemes the
name of the LORD shall surely be put to death;
all the congregation shall certainly stone him.
The alien as well as the native, when he blasphemes the Name, shall be put to death.

"An Eye for an Eye"

17 '[a]If a man [1]takes the life of any human
being, he shall surely be put to death.
18 '[a]The one who [1]takes the life of an animal shall make it good, life for life.
19 'If a man [1]injures his neighbor, just as
he has done, so it shall be done to him:
20 [a]fracture for fracture, [b]eye for eye,
tooth for tooth; just as he has [1]injured a
man, so it shall be [2]inflicted on him.
21 'Thus the one who [1]kills an animal shall
make it good, but [a]the one who [1]kills a man
shall be put to death.
22 'There shall be [a]one [1]standard for you;
it shall be for the stranger as well as the
native, for I am the LORD your God.' "
23 Then Moses spoke to the sons of Israel,
and they brought the one who had cursed
outside the camp and stoned him with
stones. Thus the sons of Israel did, just as
the LORD had commanded Moses.

The Sabbatic Year and Year of Jubilee

25 The LORD then spoke to Moses [1]at
Mount Sinai, saying,
2 "Speak to the sons of Israel and say to
them, 'When you come into the land which
I shall give you, then the land shall have a
sabbath to the LORD.
3 '[a]Six years you shall sow your field, and
six years you shall prune your vineyard and
gather in its crop,
4 but during [a]the seventh year the land
shall have a sabbath rest, a sabbath to the
LORD; you shall not sow your field nor prune
your vineyard.
5 'Your harvest's [1]aftergrowth you shall
not reap, and your grapes of untrimmed
vines you shall not gather; the land shall
have a sabbatical year.
6 '[a]All of you shall have the sabbath *products* of the land for food; yourself, and your
male and female slaves, and your hired man
and your foreign resident, those who live as
aliens with you.
7 'Even your cattle and the animals that
are in your land shall have all its crops to eat.
8 'You are also to count off seven sabbaths
of years for yourself, seven times seven years,
so that you have the time of the seven sabbaths of years, *namely,* forty-nine years.
9 'You shall then sound a ram's horn
abroad on [a]the tenth day of the seventh
month; on the day of atonement you shall
sound a horn all through your land.
10 'You shall thus consecrate the fiftieth
year and [a]proclaim [1]a release through the
land to all its inhabitants. It shall be a jubilee
for you, [2]and [b]each of you shall return to his
own property, [2]and each of you shall return
to his family.
11 'You shall have the fiftieth year as a
jubilee; you shall not sow, nor reap its after-
growth, nor gather in *from* its untrimmed
vines.
12 'For it is a jubilee; it shall be holy to
you. You shall eat its crops out of the field.
13 '[a]On this year of jubilee each of you
shall return to his own property.
14 'If you make a sale, moreover, to your
friend or buy from your friend's hand, [a]you
shall not wrong one another.
15 'Corresponding to the number of years
after the jubilee, you shall buy from your

14 [a]Deut 13:9; 17:7 [b]Lev 20:2, 27; Deut 21:21
15 [a]Ex 22:28
16 [a]1 Kin 21:10; Matt 12:31; Mark 3:28f
17 [1]Lit *smites* [a]Gen 9:6; Ex 21:12; Num 35:30, 31; Deut 27:24
18 [1]Lit *smites* [a]Lev 24:21
19 [1]Lit *gives a blemish*
20 [1]Lit *given a blemish* [2]Lit *given* [a]Ex 21:23; Deut 19:21 [b]Matt 5:38
21 [1]Lit *smites* [a]Lev 24:17
22 [1]Lit *judgment* [a]Ex 12:49; Num 9:14; 15:15, 16, 29
25:1 [1]Or *on*

3 [a]Ex 23:10, 11
4 [a]Lev 25:20
5 [1]Lit *growth from spilled kernels*
6 [a]Lev 25:20, 21
9 [a]Lev 23:27
10 [1]Or *liberty* [2]Or *when* [a]Jer 34:8, 15, 17 [b]Lev 25:13, 28, 54
13 [a]Lev 25:10; 27:24
14 [a]Lev 25:17

24:17,21 See Gen 9:6 and note.
24:20 *eye for eye, tooth for tooth.* See note on Ex 21:23–25. This represents a statement of principle: The penalty is to fit the crime, not exceed it. An actual eye or tooth was not to be required, nor is there evidence that such a penalty was ever exacted. A similar law of retaliation is found in the Code of Hammurapi, which also seems not to have been literally applied. Christ, like the middle-of-the-road Pharisees (school of Hillel), objected to an extremist use of this judicial principle to excuse private vengeance, such as by the strict Pharisees (school of Shammai); see Matt 5:38–42.
24:22 See note on v. 10.
25:4 *land shall have a sabbath.* See Ex 23:10–11. The Israelites did not practice crop rotation, but the fallow year (when the crops were not planted) served somewhat the same purpose. And just as the land was to have a sabbath year, so the servitude of a Hebrew slave was limited to six years, apparently whether or not the year he was freed was a sabbath year (see Ex 21:2 and note). Deut 15:1–11 specifies that debts were also to be canceled in the sabbath year. The care for the poor in the laws of Israel (see Ex 23:11) is noteworthy. See 23:7,35; Deut 31:10; Neh 10:31.

25:9 *day of atonement.* See notes on 16:1–34; see also 23:27.

25:10 *fiftieth year.* Possibly a fallow year in addition to the seventh sabbath year, or perhaps the same as the 49th year (counting the first and last years). Jewish sources from the period between the Testaments favor the latter interpretation. *proclaim a release . . . inhabitants.* See vv. 39–43,47–55. The Liberty Bell in Philadelphia is so named because this statement was written on it. Cf. Is 61:1–2; Luke 4:16–21. *jubilee.* The Hebrew for this word is the same as and may be related to one of the Hebrew words for "[ram's] horn," "trumpet" (see, e.g., Ex 19:13), though in v. 9 a different Hebrew word for "ram's horn" is used. Trumpets were blown at the close of the day of atonement to inaugurate the year of jubilee. Cf. 23:24.

25:13 *return to his own property.* See v. 10. The Lord prohibited the accumulation of property to the detriment of the poor. "The land is Mine," said the Lord (v. 23). God's people are only tenants (see 1 Chr 29:15; Heb 11:13).

[1]friend; he is to sell to you according to the
number of years of crops.
16 '[a]In proportion to the [1]extent of the
years you shall increase its price, and in proportion to the fewness of the years you shall
diminish its price, for *it is* a number of crops
he is selling to you.
17 'So [a]you shall not wrong one another,
but you shall [1]fear your God; for I am the
LORD your God.
18 'You shall thus observe My statutes and
keep My judgments, so as to carry them out,
that [a]you may live securely on the land.
19 'Then the land will yield its produce, so
that you can eat your fill and live securely
on it.
20 'But if you say, "[a]What are we going to
eat on the seventh year [1]if we do not sow or
gather in our crops?"
21 then [a]I will so order My blessing for
you in the sixth year that it will bring forth
the crop for three years.
22 'When you are sowing the eighth year,
you can still eat [a]old things from the crop,
eating *the old* until the ninth year when its
crop comes in.

The Law of Redemption

23 'The land, moreover, shall not be sold
permanently, for [a]the land is Mine; for [b]you
are *but* aliens and sojourners with Me.
24 'Thus for every [1]piece of your property,
you are to provide for the redemption of the
land.
25 '[a]If a [1]fellow countryman of yours
becomes so poor he has to sell part of his
property, then his nearest kinsman is to
come and buy back what his [1]relative has
sold.
26 'Or in case a man has no kinsman, but
so [1]recovers his means as to find sufficient
for its redemption,
27 [a]then he shall calculate the years since
its sale and refund the balance to the man to
whom he sold it, and so return to his property.
28 'But if [1]he has not found sufficient
means to get it back for himself, then what
he has sold shall remain in the hands of its
purchaser until the year of jubilee; but at the
jubilee it shall [2]revert, that [a]he may return to
his property.
29 'Likewise, if a man sells a dwelling
house in a walled city, then his redemption
right remains valid until a full year from its
sale; his right of redemption lasts a full year.
30 'But if it is not bought back for him
within the space of a full year, then the
house that is in the walled city passes permanently to its purchaser throughout his
generations; it does not [1]revert in the jubilee.
31 'The houses of the villages, however,
which have no surrounding wall shall be
considered [1]as open fields; they have
redemption rights and [2]revert in the jubilee.
32 'As for [a]cities of the Levites, the Levites
have a permanent right of redemption for the
houses of the cities which are their possession.
33 'What, therefore, [1]belongs to the Levites
may be redeemed and a house sale [2]in the
city of this possession [3]reverts in the jubilee,
for the houses of the cities of the Levites are
their possession among the sons of Israel.
34 '[a]But pasture fields of their cities shall
not be sold, for that is their perpetual possession.

Of Poor Countrymen

35 '[a]Now in case a [1]countryman of yours
becomes poor and his [2]means with regard to
you falter, then you are to sustain him, like a
stranger or a sojourner, that he may live with
you.
36 '[a]Do not take [1]usurious interest from
him, but revere your God, that your [2]coun-
tryman may live with you.
37 'You shall not give him your silver at
interest, nor your food for gain.
38 '[a]I am the LORD your God, who brought
you out of the land of Egypt to give you the
land of Canaan *and* [b]to be your God.
39 '[a]If a [1]countryman of yours becomes so
poor with regard to you that he sells himself
to you, you shall not subject him to a slave's
service.
40 'He shall be with you as a hired man, as
[a]if he were a sojourner; he shall serve with
you until the year of jubilee.
41 'He shall then go out from you, he and
his sons with him, and shall go back to his
family, that he may return to the property of
his forefathers.
42 'For they are My servants whom I
brought out from the land of Egypt; they are
not to be sold *in* a slave sale.
43 '[a]You shall not rule over him with
severity, but are to revere your God.
44 'As for your male and female slaves
whom you may have—you may acquire
male and female slaves from the pagan
nations that are around you.
45 'Then, too, *it is* out of the sons of the
sojourners who live as aliens among you that

15 [1]Lit *friend's hands*
16 [1]Lit *multitude* [a]Lev 25:27, 51, 52
17 [1]Or *reverence* [a]Lev 25:14; Prov 14:31; 22:22; Jer 7:5, 6; 1 Thess 4:6
18 [a]Lev 26:5; Deut 12:10; Jer 23:6
20 [1]Or *behold* [a]Lev 25:4
21 [a]Deut 28:8
22 [a]Lev 26:10
23 [a]Ex 19:5 [b]Gen 23:4; 1 Chr 29:15; Ps 39:12; Heb 11:13; 1 Pet 2:11
24 [1]Lit *land*
25 [1]Lit *brother* [a]Ruth 2:20; 4:4, 6
26 [1]Lit *his hand reaches*
27 [a]Lev 25:16
28 [1]Lit *his hand has not found sufficient to* [2]Lit *go out* [a]Lev 25:10, 13
30 [1]Lit *go out*
31 [1]Lit *according to* [2]Lit *go out*
32 [a]Num 35:1-8; Josh 21:2
33 [1]Lit *is from* [2]Lit *and* [3]Lit *goes out*
34 [a]Num 35:2-5
35 [1]Lit *brother* [2]Lit *hand* [a]Deut 15:7-11; 24:14, 15
36 [1]Lit *interest and usury* [2]Lit *brother* [a]Ex 22:25; Deut 23:19, 20
38 [a]Lev 11:45 [b]Gen 17:7
39 [1]Lit *brother* [a]Ex 21:2-6; Deut 15:12-18; 1 Kin 9:22
40 [a]Ex 21:2
43 [a]Ex 1:13, 14; Lev 25:46, 53; Ezek 34:4; Col 4:1

25:15 *number of years of crops.* The number of years left for harvesting. In a way, the sale of land in Israel was a lease until the year of jubilee (see 27:18,23).
25:24 *redemption of the land.* That is, the right to repurchase the land by (or for) the original family.
25:25 *nearest kinsman is to come and buy back.* See Jer 32:6–15. This is apparently what the nearest relative was to do for Naomi and Ruth (Ruth 4:1–4), but he was also obligated to marry the widow and support the family (see Deut 25:5–10). Only Boaz was willing to do both (Ruth 4:9–10).
25:33 *cities of the Levites.* See Num 35:1–8; Josh 21:1–42.
25:36 *usurious interest.* The main idea was not necessarily to forbid all interest, but to assist the poor. The law did not forbid lending so much as it encouraged giving.

you may gain acquisition, and out of their families who are with you, whom they will have [1]produced in your land; they also may become your possession.

46 'You may even bequeath them to your sons after you, to receive as a possession; you can use them as permanent slaves. [a]But in respect to your [1]countrymen, the sons of Israel, you shall not rule with severity over one another.

Of Redeeming a Poor Man

47 'Now if the [1]means of a stranger or of a sojourner with you becomes sufficient, and a [2]countryman of yours becomes so poor with regard to him as to sell himself to a stranger who is sojourning with you, or to the descendants of a stranger's family,

48 then he shall have redemption right after he has been sold. One of his brothers may redeem him,

49 or his uncle, or his uncle's son, may redeem him, or one of his blood relatives from his family may redeem him; or [1a]if he prospers, he may redeem himself.

50 'He then with his purchaser shall calculate from the year when he sold himself to him up to the year of jubilee; and the price of his sale shall correspond to the number of years. *It is* like the days of a hired man *that* he shall be with him.

51 'If there are still many years, [a]he shall refund part of his purchase price in proportion to them for his own redemption;

52 and if few years remain until the year of jubilee, he shall so calculate with him. In proportion to his years he is to refund *the amount for* his redemption.

53 'Like a man hired year by year he shall be with him; [a]he shall not rule over him with severity in your sight.

54 'Even if he is not redeemed by [1]these *means,* [a]he shall still go out in the year of jubilee, he and his sons with him.

55 'For the sons of Israel are My servants; they are My servants whom I brought out from the land of Egypt. I am the LORD your God.

Blessings of Obedience

26 'You shall not make for yourselves [1a]idols, nor shall you set up for yourselves [b]an image or [c]a *sacred* pillar, nor shall you place a [d]figured stone in your land to bow down [2]to it; for I am the LORD your God.

2 '[a]You shall keep My sabbaths and reverence My sanctuary; I am the LORD.

3 '[a]If you walk in My statutes and keep My commandments so as to carry them out,

4 then [a]I shall give you rains in their season, so that the land will yield its produce and the trees of the field will bear their fruit.

5 '[a]Indeed, your threshing will last for you until grape gathering, and grape gathering will last until sowing time. You will thus eat your [1]food to the full and [b]live securely in your land.

6 '[a]I shall also grant peace in the land, so that [b]you may lie down with no one making *you* tremble. [c]I shall also eliminate harmful beasts from the land, and [d]no sword will pass through your land.

7 'But you will chase your enemies and they will fall before you by the sword;

8 [a]five of you will chase a hundred, and a hundred of you will chase ten thousand, and your enemies will fall before you by the sword.

9 'So I will turn toward you and [a]make you fruitful and multiply you, and I will [b]confirm My covenant with you.

10 '[a]You will eat the old supply and clear out the old because of the new.

11 '[a]Moreover, I will make My [1]dwelling among you, and My soul will not [2]reject you.

12 '[a]I will also walk among you and be your God, and you shall be My people.

13 '[a]I am the LORD your God, who brought you out of the land of Egypt so that *you* would not be their slaves, and [b]I broke the bars of your yoke and made you walk erect.

Penalties of Disobedience

14 '[a]But if you do not obey Me and do not carry out all these commandments,

15 if, instead, you [a]reject My statutes, and if your soul abhors My ordinances so as not to carry out all My commandments, *and* so [b]break My covenant,

16 I, in turn, will do this to you: I will appoint over you a [a]sudden terror, consumption and fever that will waste away the eyes and cause the [b]soul to pine away; also, [c]you will sow your seed uselessly, for your enemies will eat it up.

17 'I will set My face against you so that you will be struck down before your enemies; and

45 [1]Lit *begotten*
46 [1]Lit *brothers* [a]Lev 25:43
47 [1]Lit *hand...reaches* [2]Lit *brother*
49 [1]Lit *if his hand has reached and* [a]Lev 25:26, 27
51 [a]Lev 25:16
53 [a]Lev 25:43
54 [1]Or *these years* [a]Lev 25:10, 13, 28
26:1 [1]Or *graven images* [a]Lev 19:4; Deut 5:8 [b]Ex 20:4; Deut 16:21f [c]Ex 23:24
26:1 [2]Lit *over* [d]Num 33:52
2 [a]Lev 19:30
3 [a]Deut 7:12-26; 11:13; 28:1-14
4 [a]Deut 11:14
5 [1]Lit *bread* [a]Deut 11:15; Joel 2:19, 26; Amos 9:13 [b]Lev 25:18, 19; Ezek 34:25
6 [a]Ps 29:11; 85:8; 147:14 [b]Zeph 3:13 [c]Lev 26:22 [d]Lev 26:25
8 [a]Deut 32:30
9 [a]Gen 17:6; 22:17; 48:4 [b]Gen 17:7
10 [a]Lev 25:22
11 [1]Or *tabernacle* [2]Lit *abhor* [a]Ex 25:8; 29:45, 46; Ezek 37:26
12 [a]Gen 3:8; Deut 23:14; 2 Cor 6:16
13 [a]Ex 20:2 [b]Ezek 34:27
14 [a]Deut 28:15-68; Josh 23:15
15 [a]Lev 26:11; 2 Kin 17:15 [b]Lev 26:9
16 [a]Deut 28:22; Ps 78:33 [b]1 Sam 2:33; Ezek 24:23; 33:10 [c]Judg 6:3-6; Job 31:8

25:55 *servants.* Covenant terminology, similar to "vassals." Slavery, however demeaning, is not brutal where the masters truly recognize themselves as God's servants. Cf. Paul's exhortation to both slaves and masters (Eph 6:5–9; Col 3:22–4:1).

26:1 *You shall not make . . . idols.* This verse probably does not forbid making statues, but it does forbid worshiping God in any material form (see Ex 20:4 and note). "God is spirit" (John 4:24; see Deut 4:15–19).

26:3 *keep My commandments.* Obedience is the key to blessing (see Gal 6:7–10; James 1:22–25). Compare the blessings promised in vv. 3–13 with those in Deut 28:1–14.

26:9 *fruitful and multiply.* See note on Gen 1:22; contrast Lev 26:22.

26:12 *your God . . . My people.* Covenantal terms later made famous by Hosea (1:9–10; 2:23). See Jer 31:33; Ezek 36:28; Heb 8:10.

26:14 *if you do not obey Me.* The list of curses for covenant disobedience (see vv. 14–39) is usually much longer than that of blessings for obedience (as in vv. 3–13; see Deut 28:15–29:28; cf. Deut 28:1–14).

26:17 See v. 36 and the allusion to this statement in Prov 28:1.

[a]those who hate you will rule over you, and [b]you will flee when no one is pursuing you.

18 'If also after these things you do not obey Me, then I will punish you [a]seven times more for your sins.

19 'I will also [a]break down your pride of power; I will also make your sky like iron and your earth like bronze.

20 '[a]Your strength will be spent uselessly, for your land will not yield its produce and the trees of the land will not yield their fruit.

21 'If then, you [1][a]act with hostility against Me and are unwilling to obey Me, I will increase the plague on you [b]seven times according to your sins.

22 '[a]I will let loose among you the beasts of the field, which will bereave you of your children and destroy your cattle and reduce your number so that [b]your roads lie deserted.

23 '[a]And if by these things you are not turned to Me, but act with hostility against Me,

24 then I will [a]act with hostility against you; and I, even I, will strike you [b]seven times for your sins.

25 'I will also bring upon you a sword which will execute [a]vengeance for the covenant; and when you gather together into your cities, I will send [b]pestilence among you, so that you shall be delivered into enemy hands.

26 '[a]When I break your staff of bread, ten women will bake your bread in one oven, and they will bring back your bread [1]in rationed amounts, so that you will [b]eat and not be satisfied.

27 'Yet if in spite of this you do not obey Me, but act with hostility against Me,

28 then [a]I will act with wrathful hostility against you, and I, even I, will punish you seven times for your sins.

29 'Further, [a]you will eat the flesh of your sons and the flesh of your daughters you will eat.

30 'I then [a]will destroy your high places, and cut down your [b]incense altars, and heap your [1]remains on the [1]remains of your idols, for My soul shall abhor you.

31 'I will [1]lay [a]waste your cities as well and will make your [b]sanctuaries desolate, and I will not [c]smell your soothing aromas.

32 'I will make [a]the land desolate [b]so that your enemies who settle in it will be appalled over it.

33 'You, however, I [a]will scatter among the nations and will draw out a sword after you, as your land becomes desolate and your cities become waste.

34 '[a]Then the land will [1]enjoy its sabbaths all the days of the desolation, while you are in your enemies' land; then the land will rest and [1]enjoy its sabbaths.

35 'All the days of *its* desolation it will observe the rest which it did not observe on your sabbaths, while you were living on it.

36 'As for those of you who may be left, I will also bring [a]weakness into their hearts in the lands of their enemies. And the sound of a driven leaf will chase them, and even when no one is pursuing they will flee [1]as though from the sword, and they will fall.

37 '[a]They will therefore stumble over each other as if *running* from the sword, although no one is pursuing; and you will have *no strength* [1]to stand up before your enemies.

38 'But [a]you will perish among the nations, and your enemies' land will consume you.

39 '[a]So those of you who may be left will rot away because of their iniquity in the lands of your enemies; and also because of the iniquities of their forefathers they will rot away with them.

40 '[a]If they confess their iniquity and the iniquity of their forefathers, in their unfaithfulness which they committed against Me, and also in their acting with hostility against Me—

41 I also was acting with hostility against them, to bring them into the land of their enemies—[a]or if their uncircumcised heart becomes humbled so that [b]they then make amends for their iniquity,

42 then I will remember [a]My covenant with Jacob, and I will remember also [b]My covenant with Isaac, and [c]My covenant with Abraham as well, and I will remember the land.

43 '[a]For the land will be abandoned by them, and will make up for its sabbaths while it is made desolate without them. They, meanwhile, will be making amends for their iniquity, [1]because they rejected My ordinances and their [b]soul abhorred My statutes.

44 'Yet in spite of this, when they are in the land of their enemies, I will not reject them, nor will I so [a]abhor them as [b]to destroy them, [c]breaking My covenant with them; for I am the LORD their God.

45 'But I will remember for them the [a]covenant with their ancestors, whom I brought out of the land of Egypt in the sight of the nations, that [b]I might be their God. I am the LORD.' "

46 [a]These are the statutes and ordinances and laws which the LORD established between Himself and the sons of Israel [1]through Moses at Mount Sinai.

Rules concerning Valuations

27 Again, the LORD spoke to Moses, saying,

2 "Speak to the sons of Israel and say to

17 [a]Ps 106:41 [b]Lev 26:36, 37; Ps 53:5; Prov 28:1
18 [a]Lev 26:21, 24, 28
19 [a]Is 28:1-3; Ezek 24:21
20 [a]Ps 127:1; Is 17:10, 11; 49:4; Jer 12:13
21 [1]Lit *walk,* and so throughout the ch [a]Lev 26:23, 27, 40 [b]Lev 26:18
22 [a]2 Kin 17:25 [b]Judg 5:6
23 [a]Lev 26:21; Jer 5:3
24 [a]Lev 26:28, 41 [b]Lev 26:21
25 [a]Jer 50:28; 51:11 [b]Num 14:12
26 [1]Lit *by weight* [a]Is 3:1; Ezek 4:16, 17; 5:16 [b]Mic 6:14
28 [a]Lev 26:24, 41; Is 59:18
29 [a]2 Kin 6:29
30 [1]Lit *corpses* [a]2 Kin 23:20; Ezek 6:3, 6; Amos 7:9 [b]2 Chr 34:4, 7; Is 27:9
31 [1]Lit *give desolation to* [a]Neh 2:3; Jer 44:2, 6, 22 [b]Is 63:18; Lam 2:7 [c]Amos 5:21
32 [a]Jer 9:11; 12:11; 25:11; 33:10 [b]Jer 18:16; 19:8
33 [a]Deut 4:27; 28:64; Ps 44:11; 106:27; Jer 31:10; Ezek 12:15; 20:23; Zech 7:14
34 [1]Lit *satisfy* [a]Lev 26:43; 2 Chr 36:21
36 [1]Lit *the flight of the sword* [a]Is 30:17; Lam 1:3, 6; 4:19; Ezek 21:7
37 [1]Lit *you will stand* [a]Jer 6:21; Nah 3:3
38 [a]Deut 4:26
39 [a]Ezek 4:17; 33:10
40 [a]Jer 3:12-15; 14:20; Hos 5:15
41 [a]Jer 4:4; 9:25, 26; Ezek 44:7, 9; Acts 7:51 [b]Ezek 20:43
42 [a]Gen 28:13-15; 35:11, 12 [b]Gen 26:2-5 [c]Gen 22:15-18
43 [1]Lit *because and by the cause* [a]Lev 26:34 [b]Lev 26:11
44 [a]Lev 26:11 [b]Deut 4:31; Jer 30:11 [c]Jer 33:20-26
45 [a]Ex 6:6-8 [b]Gen 17:7
46 [1]Lit *by the hand of* [a]Lev 7:38; 27:34; Deut 4:5; 29:1

26:41 *uncircumcised heart.* See note on Gen 17:10.
26:44 *not reject them.* See Jer 31:37; 33:25–26; Rom 11:1–29.
26:46 A summary statement concerning chs. 1–26.
27:1–34 This final chapter concerns things promised to the

them, '[a]When a man makes a difficult vow, he *shall be valued* according to your valuation of persons belonging to the LORD.

3 'If your valuation is of the male from twenty years even to sixty years old, then your valuation shall be fifty shekels of silver, after [a]the shekel of the sanctuary.

4 'Or if it is a female, then your valuation shall be thirty shekels.

5 'If it be from five years even to twenty years old then your valuation for the male shall be twenty shekels and for the female ten shekels.

6 'But if *they are* from a month even up to five years old, then your valuation shall be [a]five shekels of silver for the male, and for the female your valuation shall be three shekels of silver.

7 'If *they are* from sixty years old and upward, if it is a male, then your valuation shall be fifteen shekels, and for the female ten shekels.

8 'But if he is poorer than your valuation, then he shall be placed before the priest and the priest shall value him; [a]according to [1]the means of the one who vowed, the priest shall value him.

9 'Now if it is an animal of the kind which [1]men can present as an offering to the LORD, any such that one gives to the LORD shall be holy.

10 '[a]He shall not replace it or exchange it, a good for a bad, or a bad for a good; or if he does exchange animal for animal, then both it and its substitute shall become holy.

11 'If, however, it is any unclean animal of the kind which [1]men do not present as an offering to the LORD, then he shall place the animal before the priest.

12 'The priest shall value it [1]as either good or bad; as you, the priest, value it, so it shall be.

13 'But if he should ever *wish to* redeem it, then he shall add one-fifth of it to your valuation.

14 'Now if a man consecrates his house as holy to the LORD, then the priest shall value it [1]as either good or bad; as the priest values it, so it shall stand.

15 'Yet if the one who consecrates it should *wish to* redeem his house, then he shall add one-fifth of your valuation price to it, so that it may be his.

16 'Again, if a man consecrates to the LORD part of the fields of his own property, then your valuation shall be [1]proportionate to the seed needed for it: a homer of barley seed at fifty shekels of silver.

17 'If he consecrates his field as of the year of jubilee, according to your valuation it shall stand.

18 'If he consecrates his field after the jubilee, however, then the priest shall calculate the price for [1]him [2]proportionate to the years that are left until the year of jubilee; and it shall be deducted from your valuation.

19 'If the one who consecrates it should ever wish to redeem the field, then he shall add one-fifth of your valuation price to it, so that it may pass to him.

20 'Yet if he will not redeem the field, [1]but has sold the field to another man, it may no longer be redeemed;

21 and when it [1]reverts in the jubilee, the field shall be holy to the LORD, like a field [2]set apart; [a]it shall be for the priest as his [3]property.

22 'Or if he consecrates to the LORD a field which he has bought, which is not a part of the field of his own [1]property,

23 then the priest shall calculate for [1]him the amount of your valuation up to the year of jubilee; and he shall on that day give your valuation as holy to the LORD.

24 'In the year of jubilee the field shall return to the one from whom he bought it, to whom the possession of the land belongs.

25 'Every valuation of yours, moreover, shall be after [a]the shekel of the sanctuary. The shekel shall be twenty gerahs.

26 '[a]However, a firstborn among animals, which as a firstborn belongs to the LORD, no man may consecrate it; whether ox or sheep, it is the LORD'S.

27 'But if *it is* among the unclean animals, then he shall [1]redeem it according to your valuation and add to it one-fifth of it; and if it is not redeemed, then it shall be sold according to your valuation.

28 'Nevertheless, [a]anything which a man [1]sets apart to the LORD out of all that he has, of man or animal or of the fields of his own property, shall not be sold or redeemed. Anything [2]devoted to destruction is most holy to the LORD.

27:2 [a]Num 6:2; Deut 23:21-23
3 [a]Ex 30:13; Lev 27:25; Num 3:47; 18:16
6 [a]Num 18:16
8 [1]Lit *what the hand reaches* [a]Lev 5:11; 14:21-24
9 [1]Lit *they*
10 [a]Lev 27:33
11 [1]Lit *they*
12 [1]Lit *between*
14 [1]Lit *between good*
16 [1]Lit *according to its seed*
18 [1]Or *it* [2]Lit *according to the years*
20 [1]Or *if he*
21 [1]Lit *goes out* [2]Or *devoted, banned* [3]Lit *possession* [a]Num 18:14; Ezek 44:29
22 [1]Lit *possession*
23 [1]Or *it*
25 [a]Ex 30:13; Lev 27:3; Num 3:47; 18:16
26 [a]Ex 13:2
27 [1]Or *ransom*
28 [1]Lit *anything devoted;* or *banned* [2]Or *puts under the ban* [a]Num 18:14; Josh 6:17-19

Lord in kind—servants, animals, houses or lands. But provisions were made to give money instead of the item, in which case usually the adding of a fifth of its value was required. Such vows were expressions of special thanksgiving (cf. Hannah, 1 Sam 1:28) and were given over and above the expected sacrifices.

27:2 *a difficult vow.* Possibly to give slaves to the service of the temple, but more likely to offer oneself or a member of one's family. Since only Levites were acceptable for most work of this kind, other people gave the monetary equivalent—but see 1 Sam 1:11.

27:9 *shall be holy.* An animal given for a sacrifice could not be exchanged for another (v. 10). The people of Malachi's day chose the poorest animals after having vowed to offer good ones (Mal 1:13–14). If an unclean animal was given, it could be redeemed with the 20 percent penalty (vv. 11–13).

27:28 *sets apart to the LORD.* See NASB marg. Devoting something was far more serious than dedicating it to sacred use. The devoted thing became totally the Lord's. Achan's sin was the greater because he stole what had been devoted to the Lord (Josh 7:11). Persons devoted to destruction were usually the captives in the wars of Canaan (cf. 1 Sam 15:3,18).

29 'No [1]one who may have been [2]set apart
among men shall be ransomed; he shall
surely be put to death.
30 'Thus [a]all the tithe of the land, of the
seed of the land or of the fruit of the tree, is
the LORD's; it is holy to the LORD.
31 'If, therefore, a man wishes to redeem
part of his tithe, he shall add to it one-fifth of
it.
32 'For every tenth part of herd or flock,
whatever [a]passes under the rod, the tenth
one shall be holy to the LORD.
33 '[a]He is not to be concerned whether *it is*
good or bad, nor shall he exchange it; or if
he does exchange it, then both it and its substitute shall become holy. It shall not be
redeemed.' "
34 [a]These are the commandments which
the LORD commanded Moses for the sons of
Israel at Mount Sinai.

29 [1]Lit *one devoted;* or *banned* [2]Or *put under the ban* **30** [a]Gen 28:22; 2 Chr 31:5; Neh 13:12 **32** [a]Jer 33:13; Ezek 20:37 **33** [a]Lev 27:10 **34** [a]Lev 26:46; Deut 4:5

27:29 Saul sinned in this regard when he did not totally destroy the Amalekites (1Sa 15).
27:30 *tithe.* A tenth (see Num 18:21–29; Deut 12:6–18; 14:22–29; 26:12). From these passages it appears that Israel actually had three tithes: (1) the general tithe (here), paid to the Levites (Num 18:21), who in turn had to give a tenth of that to the priests (Num 18:26); (2) the tithe associated with the sacred meal involving offerer and Levite (Deut 14:22–27); (3) the tithe paid every three years to the poor (Deut 14:28–29).
27:34 *These are the commandments which the LORD commanded Moses.* See 1:1; 7:37–38; 25:1; 26:46. This is strong testimony for the Mosaic authorship and divine origin of the book.

Numbers

INTRODUCTION

Title

The English name of the book comes from the Septuagint (the Greek translation of the OT) and is based on the census lists found in chs. 1; 26. The Hebrew title of the book (*bemidbar,* "in the wilderness") is more descriptive of its contents. Numbers presents an account of the 38-year period of Israel's wandering in the wilderness following the establishment of the covenant of Sinai (compare 1:1 with Deut 1:1).

Author and Date

The book has traditionally been ascribed to Moses. This conclusion is based on (1) statements concerning Moses' writing activity (e.g., 33:1 – 2; Ex 17:14; 24:4; 34:27) and (2) the assumption that the first five books of the Bible, the Pentateuch, are a unit and come from one author. See Introduction to Genesis: Author and Date of Writing.

It is not necessary, however, to claim that Numbers came from Moses' hand complete and in final form. Portions of the book were probably added by scribes or editors from later periods of Israel's history. For example, the protestation of the humility of Moses (12:3) would hardly be convincing if it came from his own mouth. But it seems reasonable to assume that Moses wrote the essential content of the book.

Contents

Numbers relates the story of Israel's journey from Mount Sinai to the plains of Moab on the border of Canaan. Much of its legislation for people and priests is similar to that in Exodus, Leviticus and Deuteronomy. The book tells of the murmuring and rebellion of God's people and of their subsequent judgment. Those whom God had redeemed from slavery in Egypt and with whom He had made a covenant at Mount Sinai responded not with faith, gratitude and obedience but with unbelief, ingratitude and repeated acts of rebellion, which came to extreme expression in their refusal to undertake the conquest of Canaan (ch. 14). The community of the redeemed forfeited their part in the promised land. They were condemned to live out their lives in the wilderness; only their children would enjoy the fulfillment of the promise that had originally been theirs (cf. Heb 3:7 — 4:11).

Theological Teaching

In telling the story of Israel's wilderness wanderings, Numbers offers much that is theologically significant. During the first year after Israel's deliverance from Egypt, she entered into covenant with the Lord at Sinai to be the people of His kingdom, among whom He pitched His royal tent (the tabernacle) — this is the story of Exodus. As the account of Numbers begins, the Lord organizes Israel into a military camp. Leaving Sinai, she marches forth as His conquering army, with the Lord at her head, to establish His kingdom in the promised land in the midst of the nations. The book graphically portrays Israel's identity as the Lord's redeemed covenant people and her vocation as the servant people of God, charged with establishing His kingdom on earth. God's purpose in history is implicitly disclosed: to invade the arena of fallen humanity and effect the redemption of His creation — the mission in which His people are also to be totally engaged.

Numbers also presents the chastening wrath of God against His disobedient people. Because of her rebellion (and especially her refusal to undertake the conquest of Canaan), Israel was in breach of covenant. The fourth book of the Pentateuch presents a sobering reality: The God who had entered into covenant with Abraham (Gen 15; 17), who had delivered His people from bondage in the exodus (Ex 14 — 15), who had brought Israel into covenant with Himself as His "own possession" (Ex 19; see especially Ex 19:5 and NASB marg.) and

who had revealed His holiness and the gracious means of approaching Him (Lev 1—7) was also a God of wrath. His wrath extended to His errant children as well as to the enemy nations of Egypt and Canaan.

Even Moses, the great prophet and servant of the Lord, was not exempt from God's wrath when he disobeyed God. Ch. 20, which records his error, begins with the notice of Miriam's death (20:1) and concludes with the record of Aaron's death (20:22–29). Here is the passing of the old guard. Those whom God has used to establish the nation are dying before the nation has come into its own.

The questions arise: Is God finished with the nation as a whole (cf. Rom 11:1)? Are His promises a thing of the past? In one of the most remarkable sections of the Bible—the account of Balaam, the pagan diviner (chs. 22—24)—the reply is given. The Lord, working in a providential and direct way, proclaims His continued faithfulness to His purpose for His people despite their unfaithfulness to Him.

Balaam is Moab's answer to Moses, the man of God. He is an internationally known prophet who shares the pagan belief that the God of Israel is like any other deity who might be manipulated by acts of magic or sorcery. But from the early part of the narrative, when Balaam first encounters the one true God in visions, and in the narrative of the journey on the donkey (ch. 22), he begins to learn that dealing with the true God is fundamentally different from anything he has ever known. When he attempts to curse Israel at the instigation of Balak king of Moab, Balaam finds his mouth unable to express the curse he desires to pronounce. Instead, from his lips come blessings on Israel and curses on her enemies (chs. 23—24).

In his seven prophetic oracles, Balaam proclaims God's great blessing for His people (see 23:20). Though the immediate enjoyment of this blessing will always depend on the faithfulness of His people, the ultimate realization of God's blessing is sure—because of the character of God (see 23:19). Thus Numbers reaffirms the ongoing purposes of God. Despite His judgment on His rebellious people, God is still determined to bring Israel into the land of promise. His blessing to her rests in His sovereign will.

The teaching of the book has lasting significance for Israel and for the church (cf. Rom 15:4; 1 Cor 10:6,11). God does display His wrath even against His errant people, but His grace is renewed as surely as is the dawn and His redemptive purpose will not be thwarted.

Special Problem

The large numbers of men conscripted into Israel's army puzzle modern scholars (see, e.g., the figures in 1:46; 26:51). These numbers of men mustered for warfare demand a total population in excess of 2,000,000. Such numbers seem to be exceedingly large for the times, for the locale, for the wilderness wanderings, and in comparison with the inhabitants of Canaan. See note on 3:43.

Various possibilities have been suggested to solve this problem. Some have thought that the numbers may have been corrupted in transmission. The present text, however, does not betray textual difficulties with the numbers.

Others have felt that the Hebrew word for "thousand" might have a different meaning here from its usual numerical connotation. In some passages, for example, the word is a technical term for a company of men that may or may not equal 1,000 (e.g., Josh 22:14 and NASB marg.; 1 Sam 23:23). Further, some have postulated that this Hebrew word means "chief" (as in Gen 36:15). In this way the figure 53,400 (26:47) would mean "53 chiefs plus 400 men." Such a procedure would yield a greatly reduced total, but it would be at variance with the fact that the Hebrew text adds the "thousands" in the same way it adds the "hundreds" for a large total. Also, this would make the proportion of chiefs to fighting men top-heavy (59 chiefs for 300 men in Simeon).

Another option is to read the Hebrew word for "thousand" with a dual meaning of "chief" and "1,000," with the chiefs numbering one less than the stated figure. For example, the 46,500 of Reuben (1:21) is read as 45 chiefs and 1,500 fighting men, the 59,300 of Simeon (1:23) is read as 58 chiefs and 1,300 fighting men, etc. But in this case, as in the former, the totals of 1:46 and 2:32 must then be regarded as errors of understanding (perhaps by later scribes).

Still another approach is to regard the numbers as symbolic figures rather than as strictly mathematical. The numerical value of the Hebrew letters in the expression *bene yisra'el* ("all the congregation of the sons of Israel," 1:2) equals 603 (the number of the thousands of the fighting men, 1:46); the remaining 550 (plus 1 for Moses) might come from the numerical equivalent of the Hebrew letters in the expression "whoever is

able to go to war in Israel" (1:3). This symbolic use of numbers (called "gematria") is not unknown in the Bible (see Rev 13:18), but it is not likely in Numbers, where there are no literary clues pointing in that direction.

While the problem of the large numbers has not been satisfactorily solved, the Bible does point to a remarkable increase of Jacob's descendants during the four centuries of their sojourn in Egypt (see Ex 1:7 – 12). With all their difficulties, these numbers also point to the great role of providence and miracles in God's dealings with his people during their life in the wilderness (see note on 1:46).

Structure and Outline

The book has three major divisions, based on Israel's geographical locations. Each of the three divisions has two parts, as the following breakdown demonstrates: (1) Israel at Sinai, preparing to depart for the land of promise (1:1 — 10:10), followed by the journey from Sinai to Kadesh (10:11 — 12:16); (2) Israel at Kadesh, delayed as a result of rebellion (13:1 — 20:13), followed by the journey from Kadesh to the plains of Moab (20:14 — 22:1); (3) Israel on the plains of Moab, anticipating the conquest of the land of promise (22:2 — 32:42), followed by appendixes dealing with various matters (chs. 33 — 36).

- I. Israel at Sinai, Preparing to Depart for the Promised Land (1:1 — 10:10)
  - A. The Commands for the Census of the People (chs. 1 — 4)
    - 1. The numbers of men from each tribe mustered for war (ch. 1)
    - 2. The placement of the tribes around the tabernacle and their order for march (ch. 2)
    - 3. The placement of the Levites around the tabernacle, and the numbers of the Levites and the firstborn of Israel (ch. 3)
    - 4. The numbers of the Levites in their tabernacle service for the Lord (ch. 4)
  - B. The Commands for Purity of the People (5:1 — 10:10)
    - 1. The test for purity in the law of jealousy (ch. 5)
    - 2. The Nazirite vow and the Aaronic benediction (ch. 6)
    - 3. The offerings of the 12 leaders at the dedication of the tabernacle (ch. 7)
    - 4. The setting up of the lamps and the separation of the Levites (ch. 8)
    - 5. The observance of the Passover (9:1 – 14)
    - 6. The covering cloud and the silver trumpets (9:15 — 10:10)
- II. The Journey from Sinai to Kadesh (10:11 — 12:16)
  - A. The Beginning of the Journey (10:11 – 36)
  - B. The Beginning of the Sorrows: Fire and Quail (ch. 11)
  - C. The Opposition of Miriam and Aaron (ch. 12)
- III. Israel at Kadesh, the Delay Resulting from Rebellion (13:1 — 20:13)
  - A. The 12 Spies and Their Mixed Report of the Good Land (ch. 13)
  - B. The People's Rebellion against God's Commission, and Their Defeat (ch. 14)
  - C. A Collection of Laws on Offerings, the Sabbath and Tassels on Garments (ch. 15)
  - D. The Rebellion of Korah and His Allies (ch. 16)
  - E. The Budding of Aaron's Rod: A Sign for Rebels (ch. 17)
  - F. Concerning Priests, Their Duties and Their Support (ch. 18)
  - G. The Red Heifer and the Cleansing Water (ch. 19)
  - H. The Sin of Moses (20:1 – 13)
- IV. The Journey from Kadesh to the Plains of Moab (20:14 — 22:1)
  - A. The Resistance of Edom (20:14 – 21)
  - B. The Death of Aaron (20:22 – 29)
  - C. The Destruction of Arad (21:1 – 3)
  - D. The Bronze Serpent (21:4 – 9)
  - E. The Song of the Well and the Journey to Moab (21:10 – 20)
  - F. The Defeat of Sihon and Og (21:21 – 35)
  - G. Israel Returns to Moab (22:1)
- V. Israel on the Plains of Moab, in Anticipation of Taking the Promised Land (22:2 — 32:42)
  - A. Balak of Moab Hires Balaam to Curse Israel (22:2 – 41)

- B. Balaam Blesses Israel in Seven Oracles (chs. 23—24)
- C. The Baal of Peor and Israel's Apostasy (ch. 25)
- D. The Second Census (ch. 26)
- E. Instructions for the New Generation (chs. 27—30)
    1. The inheritance for women (27:1–11)
    2. The successor to Moses (27:12–23)
    3. Commands regarding offerings (28:1–15)
    4. Commands regarding festivals (28:16—29:40)
    5. Commands regarding vows (ch. 30)
- F. The War against Midian (ch. 31)
- G. The Settlement of the Transjordan Tribes (ch. 32)

VI. Appendixes Dealing with Various Matters (chs. 33—36)

- A. The Stages of the Journey (ch. 33)
- B. The Land of Inheritance (chs. 34—35)
- C. The Inheritance for Women (ch. 36)

The Census of Israel's Warriors

1 Then the LORD spoke to Moses in the wilderness of Sinai, in the tent of meeting, on [a]the first of the second month, in the second year after they had come out of the land of Egypt, saying,

2 "[a]Take a [1]census of all the congregation of the sons of Israel, by their families, by their fathers' households, according to the number of names, every male, head by head

3 from [a]twenty years old and upward, whoever *is able to* go out to war in Israel, you and Aaron shall [1]number them by their armies.

4 "With you, moreover, there shall be a man of each tribe, [a]each one head of his father's household.

5 "These then are the names of the men who shall stand with you: [a]of Reuben, Elizur the son of Shedeur;

6 of Simeon, Shelumiel the son of Zurishaddai;

7 of Judah, [a]Nahshon the son of Amminadab;

8 of Issachar, Nethanel the son of Zuar;

9 of Zebulun, Eliab the son of Helon;

10 of the sons of Joseph: of Ephraim, Elishama the son of Ammihud; of Manasseh, Gamaliel the son of Pedahzur;

11 of Benjamin, Abidan the son of Gideoni;

12 of Dan, Ahiezer the son of Ammishaddai;

13 of Asher, Pagiel the son of Ochran;

14 of Gad, Eliasaph the son of [a]Deuel;

15 of Naphtali, Ahira the son of Enan.

16 "These are they who were [a]called of the congregation, the leaders of their fathers' tribes; they were the [b]heads of [1]divisions of Israel."

17 So Moses and Aaron took these men who had been designated by name,

18 and they assembled all the congregation together on the [a]first of the second month. Then they registered by [b]ancestry in their families, by their fathers' households, according to the number of names, from twenty years old and upward, head by head,

19 just as [a]the LORD had commanded Moses. So he numbered them in the wilderness of Sinai.

20 [a]Now the sons of Reuben, Israel's firstborn, their genealogical registration by their families, by their fathers' households, according to the number of names, head by head, every male from twenty years old and upward, whoever *was able to* go out to war,

21 their numbered men of the tribe of Reuben *were* 46,500.

22 [a]Of the sons of Simeon, their genealogical registration by their families, by their fathers' households, their numbered men, according to the number of names, head by head, every male from twenty years old and upward, [b]whoever *was able to* go out to war,

23 their numbered men of the tribe of Simeon *were* 59,300.

24 [a]Of the sons of Gad, their genealogical registration by their families, by their fathers' households, according to the number of names, from twenty years old and upward, whoever *was able to* go out to war,

25 their numbered men of the tribe of Gad *were* 45,650.

26 [a]Of the sons of Judah, their genealogical registration by their families, by their fathers' households, according to the number of names, from twenty years old and upward, whoever *was able to* go out to war,

1:1 [a]Ex 40:2, 17 **2** [1]Lit *sum* [a]Ex 12:37; 38:25, 26; Num 26:2 **3** [1]Lit *muster,* and so throughout the ch [a]Ex 30:14; 38:26 **4** [a]Ex 18:21, 25; Num 1:16; Deut 1:15 **5** [a]Gen 29:32; Ex 1:2; Deut 33:6; Rev 7:5 **7** [a]Ruth 4:20; 1 Chr 2:10; Luke 3:32 **14** [a]Num 2:14 **16** [1]Lit *thousands;* or *clans* [a]Ex 18:21; Num 7:2; 16:2; 26:9 [b]Ex 18:25

18 [a]Num 1:1 [b]Ezra 2:59; Heb 7:3 **19** [a]2 Sam 24:1 **20** [a]Num 26:5-7 **22** [a]Num 26:12-14 [b]Ps 144:1 **24** [a]Gen 30:11; Num 26:15-18; Josh 4:12; Jer 49:1 **26** [a]Gen 29:35; Num 26:19-22; 2 Sam 24:9; Ps 78:68; Matt 1:2

1:1 *the* LORD *spoke to Moses.* One of the most pervasive emphases in Numbers is the fact that the Lord spoke to Moses and through Moses to Israel. From the opening words to the closing words (36:13), this is stated over 150 times and in more than 20 ways. The Lord's use of Moses as His prophet is described in 12:6–8. One of the Hebrew names for the book is *wayedabber* ("And He [the LORD] spoke"), from the first word in the Hebrew text. *tent of meeting.* The tabernacle. *wilderness of Sinai.* The more common Hebrew name for Numbers is *bemidbar* ("in the wilderness"), the fifth word in the Hebrew text. The events of Numbers cover a period of 38 years and nine or ten months, i.e., the period of Israel's wilderness wanderings. *first of the second month . . . second year.* Thirteen months after the exodus, Numbers begins. Israel had spent the previous year in the region of Mount Sinai receiving the law and erecting the tabernacle. Now she was to be mustered as a military force for an orderly march. Dating events from the exodus (for another example see 1 Kin 6:1) is similar to the Christian practice of dating years in reference to the incarnation of Christ (B.C. and A.D.). The exodus was God's great act of deliverance of His people from bondage.

1:2 *Take.* The Hebrew for this word is plural, indicating that Moses and Aaron were to complete this task together (see v. 3, "you and Aaron"), but the primary responsibility lay with Moses. *census.* Its main purpose was to form a military roster, not a social, political or taxing document.

1:3 *able to go out to war.* Refers to the principal military purpose of the census. The phrase occurs 14 times in ch. 1 and again in 26:2.

1:4 *a man of each tribe.* By having a representative from each tribe assist Moses and Aaron, the count would be regarded as legitimate by all.

1:5–16 The names of these men occur again in chs. 2; 7; 10. Most contain within them a reference to the name of God. Levi is not represented in the list (see vv. 47–53).

1:19 *So he numbered them in the wilderness of Sinai.* A summary statement; vv. 20–43 provide the details.

1:20–43 For each tribe there are two verses in repetitive formulaic structure, giving: (1) the name of the tribe, (2) the specifics of those numbered, (3) the name of the tribe again and (4) the total count for that tribe. The numbers for each tribe are rounded off to the hundred (but Gad to the 50, v. 25). The same numbers are given for each tribe in ch. 2, where there are four triads of tribes. A peculiarity in the numbers that leads some to believe that they are symbolic is that the hundreds are grouped between 200 and 700. Also, various speculations have arisen regarding the meaning of the Hebrew word for "thousand" (see Introduction: Special Problem). In this chapter, the word has been used to mean 1,000 in order for the totals to be achieved.

27 their numbered men of the tribe of Judah *were* 74,600.

28 [a]Of the sons of Issachar, their genealogical registration by their families, by their fathers' households, according to the number of names, from twenty years old and upward, whoever *was able to* go out to war,

29 their numbered men of the tribe of Issachar *were* 54,400.

30 [a]Of the sons of Zebulun, their genealogical registration by their families, by their fathers' households, according to the number of names, from twenty years old and upward, whoever *was able to* go out to war,

31 their numbered men of the tribe of Zebulun *were* 57,400.

32 [a]Of the sons of Joseph, *namely,* of the sons of Ephraim, their genealogical registration by their families, by their fathers' households, according to the number of names, from twenty years old and upward, whoever *was able to* go out to war,

33 their numbered men of the tribe of Ephraim *were* 40,500.

34 [a]Of the sons of Manasseh, their genealogical registration by their families, by their fathers' households, according to the number of names, from twenty years old and upward, whoever *was able to* go out to war,

35 their numbered men of the tribe of Manasseh *were* 32,200.

36 [a]Of the sons of Benjamin, their genealogical registration by their families, by their fathers' households, according to the number of names, from twenty years old and upward, whoever *was able to* go out to war,

37 their numbered men of the tribe of Benjamin *were* 35,400.

38 [a]Of the sons of Dan, their genealogical registration by their families, by their fathers' households, according to the number of names, from twenty years old and upward, whoever *was able to* go out to war,

39 their numbered men of the tribe of Dan *were* 62,700.

40 [a]Of the sons of Asher, their genealogical registration by their families, by their fathers' households, according to the number of names, from twenty years old and upward, whoever *was able to* go out to war,

41 their numbered men of the tribe of Asher *were* 41,500.

42 [a]Of the sons of Naphtali, their genealogical registration by their families, by their fathers' households, according to the number of names, from twenty years old and upward, whoever *was able to* go out to war,

43 their numbered men of the tribe of Naphtali *were* 53,400.

44 These are the ones who were numbered, whom Moses and Aaron numbered, with the leaders of Israel, twelve men, each of whom was of his father's household.

45 So all the numbered men of the sons of Israel by their fathers' households, from twenty years old and upward, whoever *was able to* go out to war in Israel,

46 even all the numbered men were [a]603,550.

Levites Exempted

47 [a]The Levites, however, were not numbered among them by their fathers' tribe.

48 For the LORD had spoken to Moses, saying,

49 "Only the tribe of Levi [a]you shall not number, nor shall you take their [1]census among the sons of Israel.

50 "But you shall [a]appoint the Levites over the [1]tabernacle of the testimony, and over all its furnishings and over all that belongs to it. They shall carry the tabernacle and all its furnishings, and they shall take care of it; they shall also camp around the [1]tabernacle.

51 "[a]So when the tabernacle is to set out, the Levites shall take it down; and when the tabernacle encamps, the Levites shall set it up. But [b]the [1]layman who comes near shall be put to death.

52 "[a]The sons of Israel shall camp, each man by his own camp, and each man by his own standard, according to their armies.

28 [a]Num 26:23-25
30 [a]Num 26:26, 27
32 [a]Num 26:35-37; Deut 33:13-17; Jer 7:15; Obad 19
34 [a]Num 26:28-34
36 [a]Gen 49:27; Num 26:38-41; 2 Chr 17:17; Rev 7:8
38 [a]Gen 30:6; 46:23; Num 2:25; 26:42, 43
40 [a]Num 26:44-47
42 [a]Num 26:48-50
46 [a]Ex 12:37; 38:26; Num 2:32; 26:51
47 [a]Num 2:33; 3:14-39; 4:49; 26:57-64
49 [1]Lit *sum* [a]Num 26:62
50 [1]Lit *dwelling place,* and so throughout the ch [a]Ex 38:21; Num 3:6-8, 25-37; 4:15, 25-27, 31, 32
51 [1]Lit *stranger* [a]Num 4:1-33 [b]Num 3:10, 38; 4:15, 19, 20
52 [a]Num 2:2, 34

1:32–35 Because the descendants of Levi were excluded from the census (see note on v. 47), the descendants of Joseph are listed according to the families of his two sons, Ephraim (vv. 32–33) and Manasseh (vv. 34–35). In this way the traditional tribal number of 12 is maintained, and Joseph is given the "double portion" of the ranking heir (cf. Gen 49:22–26; Deut 33:13–17; 2 Kin 2:9).

1:46 *603,550.* Except for Joshua and Caleb, all these died in the wilderness. The mathematics of these numbers is accurate and complex. It is complex in that the totals are reached in two ways: (1) a linear listing of 12 units (vv. 20–43), with the total given (v. 46); (2) four sets of triads, each with a subtotal, and then the grand total (2:3–32). These figures are also consistent with those in Ex 12:37; 38:26. This large number of men conscripted for the army suggests a population for the entire community in excess of 2,000,000 (see Introduction: Special Problem). Ex 1:7 describes the remarkable growth of the Hebrew people in Egypt during the 400-year sojourn. They had become so numerous that they were regarded as a grave threat to the security of Egypt (Ex 1:9–10,20). Israel's amazing growth from the 70 who entered Egypt (Ex 1:5) was an evidence of God's great blessing and His faithfulness to His covenant with Abraham (Gen 12:2; 15:5; 17:4–6; 22:17).

1:47 Because of their special tasks, the Levites were excluded from this military count. They too had to perform service to the Lord, but they were to be engaged in the ceremonies and maintenance of the tabernacle (see note on vv. 32–35).

1:50 *testimony.* The Ten Commandments written on stone tablets (see Ex 31:18; 32:15; 34:29), which were placed in the ark (Ex 25:16,21; 40:20), leading to the phrase the "ark of the testimony" (Ex 25:22; 26:33,34).

1:51 *layman.* The Hebrew for this phrase is often translated "stranger," "alien" or "foreigner" (e.g., Is 1:7; Hos 7:9). Thus a non-Levite Israelite was considered an alien to the religious duties of the tabernacle (see Ex 29:33; 30:33; Lev 22:12). *death.* See 3:10,38; 18:7; cf. 16:31–33; 1 Sam 6:19.

53 "[a]But the Levites shall camp around the tabernacle of the testimony, so that there will be [b]no wrath on the congregation of the sons of Israel. [c]So the Levites shall keep charge of the tabernacle of the testimony."
54 Thus the sons of Israel did; according to all which the LORD had commanded Moses, so they did.

Arrangement of the Camps

2 Now the LORD spoke to Moses and to Aaron, saying,
2 "[a]The sons of Israel shall camp, each by his own standard, with the [1]banners of their fathers' households; they shall camp around the tent of meeting [2]at a distance.
3 "Now those who camp on the east side toward the sunrise *shall be* of the standard of the camp of Judah, by their armies, and the leader of the sons of Judah: [a]Nahshon the son of Amminadab,
4 and his army, even their [1]numbered men, 74,600.
5 "Those who camp next to him *shall be* the tribe of Issachar, and the leader of the sons of Issachar: [a]Nethanel the son of Zuar,
6 and his army, even their numbered men, 54,400.
7 "*Then comes* the tribe of Zebulun, and the leader of the sons of Zebulun: [a]Eliab the son of Helon,
8 and his army, even his numbered men, 57,400.
9 "The total of the numbered men of the camp of Judah: 186,400, by their armies. [a]They shall set out first.

53 [a]Num 3:23, 29, 35, 38 [b]Lev 10:6; Num 16:46; 18:5 [c]Num 8:24; 18:2-4; 1 Chr 23:32
2:2 [1]Lit *signs* [2]Or *facing it* [a]Num 1:52; 24:2
3 [a]Num 1:7; 10:14; Ruth 4:20; 1 Chr 2:10; Luke 3:32, 33
4 [1]Lit *mustered*, and so throughout the ch
5 [a]Num 1:8; 7:18, 23
7 [a]Num 1:9
9 [a]Num 10:14

1:53 *camp around the tabernacle.* See 3:21–38. *wrath.* The Levites formed a protective hedge against trespassing by the non-Levites to keep them from experiencing divine wrath.
1:54 *the LORD had commanded Moses, so they did.* In view of Israel's great disobedience in the later chapters of Numbers, these words of initial compliance have a special poignancy.
2:1–34 This chapter is symmetrically structured:
Summary command (vv. 1–2)
  Details of execution (vv. 3–33)
    Eastern camp (vv. 3–9)
    Southern camp (vv. 10–16)
      Tent and Levites (v. 17)
    Western camp (vv. 18–24)
    Northern camp (vv. 25–31)
      Summary totals (vv. 32–33)
Summary conclusion (v. 34)
In ch. 1 the nation is mustered, and the genealogical relationships are clarified. In ch. 2 the nation is put in structural order, and the line of march and place of encampment are established. The numbers of ch. 1 are given in a new pattern, and the same leaders are named here again.
2:2 *each.* Each was to know his exact position within the camp. *standard . . . banners.* Each tribe had its banner, and each triad of tribes had its standard. Jewish tradition suggests that the tribal banners corresponded in color to the 12 stones in the breastpiece of the high priest (Ex 28:15–21). Tradition also holds that the standard of the triad led by Judah had the figure of a lion, that of Reuben the figure of a man, that of Ephraim the figure of an ox and that of Dan the figure of an eagle (see the four living creatures described by Ezek 1:10; cf. Rev 4:7). But these traditions are not otherwise substantiated. See diagram below. *at a distance.* See 1:52–53.
2:3–7 *Judah . . . Issachar . . . Zebulun.* The fourth, fifth and sixth sons of Jacob and Leah. It is somewhat surprising to have these three tribes first in the order of march, since Reuben is regularly noted as Jacob's firstborn son (1:20). However, because of the failure of the older brothers (Reuben, Simeon and Levi; see Gen 49:3–7), Judah is granted pride of place among his brothers (Gen 49:8). Judah produced the royal line from which the Messiah came (Gen 49:10; Ruth 4:18–21; Matt 1:1–16).

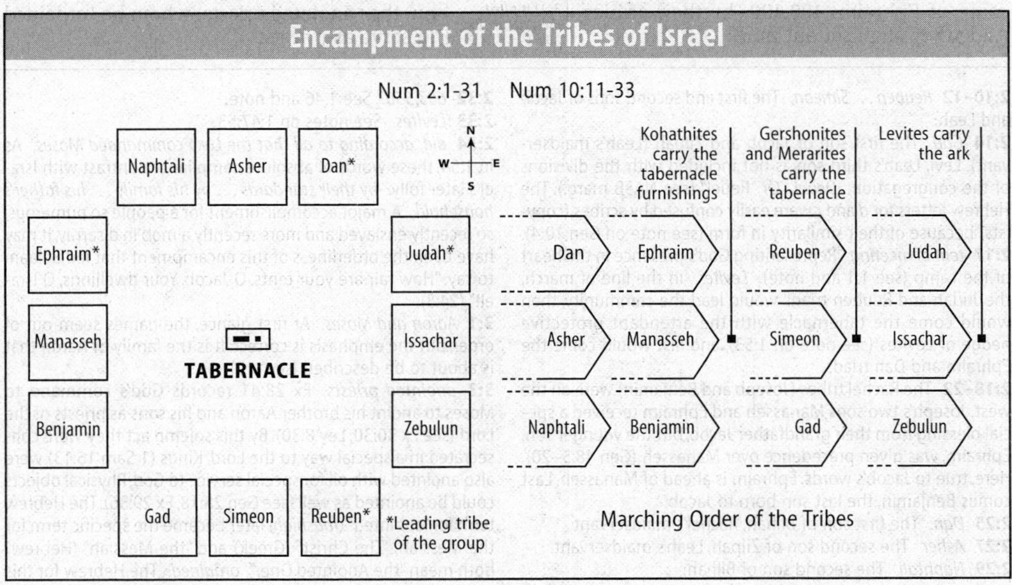
Encampment of the Tribes of Israel
Num 2:1-31
Num 10:11-33
Naphtali
Asher
Dan*
N
W
E
S
Ephraim*
Judah*
Manasseh
TABERNACLE
Issachar
Benjamin
Zebulun
Gad
Simeon
Reuben*
*Leading tribe of the group
Kohathites carry the tabernacle furnishings
Gershonites and Merarites carry the tabernacle
Levites carry the ark
Dan
Ephraim
Reuben
Judah
Asher
Manasseh
Simeon
Issachar
Naphtali
Benjamin
Gad
Zebulun
Marching Order of the Tribes

10"On the south side *shall be* the standard
of the camp of Reuben by their armies, and
the leader of the sons of Reuben: [a]Elizur the
son of Shedeur,
11 and his army, even their numbered
men, 46,500.
12"Those who camp next to him *shall be*
the tribe of Simeon, and the leader of the
sons of Simeon: [a]Shelumiel the son of Zurishaddai,
13 and his army, even their numbered
men, 59,300.
14"Then *comes* the tribe of Gad, and the
leader of the sons of Gad: [a]Eliasaph the son
of [1]Deuel,
15 and his army, even their numbered
men, 45,650.
16"The total of the numbered men of the
camp of Reuben: 151,450 by their armies.
And [a]they shall set out second.
17"[a]Then the tent of meeting shall set out
with the camp of the Levites in the midst of
the camps; just as they camp, so they shall set
out, every man in his place by their standards.
18"On the west side *shall be* the standard
of the camp of [a]Ephraim by their armies, and
the leader of the sons of Ephraim *shall be*
[b]Elishama the son of Ammihud,
19 and his army, even their numbered
men, 40,500.
20"Next to him *shall be* the tribe of Manasseh, and the leader of the sons of Manasseh:
[a]Gamaliel the son of Pedahzur,
21 and his army, even their numbered
men, 32,200.
22"Then *comes* the tribe of [a]Benjamin, and
the leader of the sons of Benjamin: [b]Abidan
the son of Gideoni,
23 and his army, even their numbered
men, 35,400.
24"The total of the numbered men of the
camp of Ephraim: 108,100, by their armies.
And [a]they shall set out third.

10 [a]Num 1:5 **12** [a]Num 1:6 **14** [1]Many mss read *Reuel* [a]Num 1:14; 7:42 **16** [a]Num 10:18 **17** [a]Num 1:53 **18** [a]Gen 48:14-20; Jer 31:9, 18-20 [b]Num 1:10 **20** [a]Num 1:10 **22** [a]Ps 68:27 [b]Num 1:11 **24** [a]Num 10:22

25"On the north side *shall be* the standard
of the camp of Dan by their armies, and the
leader of the sons of Dan: [a]Ahiezer the son
of Ammishaddai,
26 and his army, even their numbered
men, 62,700.
27"Those who camp next to him *shall be*
the tribe of Asher, and the leader of the sons
of Asher: [a]Pagiel the son of Ochran,
28 and his army, even their numbered
men, 41,500.
29"Then *comes* the tribe of [a]Naphtali, and
the leader of the sons of Naphtali: [b]Ahira the
son of Enan,
30 and his army, even their numbered
men, 53,400.
31"The total of the numbered men of the
camp of Dan *was* 157,600. [a]They shall set
out last by their standards."
32 These are the numbered men of the
sons of Israel by their fathers' households;
the total of the numbered men of the camps
by their armies, [a]603,550.
33 [a]The Levites, however, were not numbered among the sons of Israel, just as the
LORD had commanded Moses.
34 Thus the sons of Israel did; according
to all that the LORD commanded Moses, so
they camped by their standards, and so they
set out, every one by his family according to
his father's household.

Levites to Be Priesthood

3 [a]Now these are *the records of* the generations of Aaron and Moses at the time
when the LORD spoke with Moses on Mount
Sinai.
2 [a]These then are the names of the sons
of Aaron: Nadab the firstborn, and Abihu,
Eleazar and Ithamar.
3 These are the names of the sons of Aaron, the [a]anointed priests, whom he [1]ordained
to serve as priests.

25 [a]Num 1:12 **27** [a]Num 1:13 **29** [a]Gen 30:8 [b]Num 1:15 **31** [a]Num 10:25 **32** [a]Ex 38:26; Num 1:46 **33** [a]Num 1:47; 26:57-62 **3:1** [a]Ex 6:20-27 **2** [a]Ex 6:23; Num 26:60 **3** [1]Lit *filled their hand* [a]Ex 28:41

2:10–12 *Reuben . . . Simeon.* The first and second sons of Jacob and Leah.
2:14 *Gad.* The first son of Jacob and Zilpah (Leah's maidservant). Levi, Leah's third son, is not included with the divisions of the congregation. *Deuel.* Or "Reuel" (see NASB marg.). The Hebrew letters for *d* and *r* were easily confused by scribes (copyists) because of their similarity in form (see note on Gen 10:4).
2:17 *tent of meeting.* Representing God's presence in the heart of the camp (see 1:1 and note). *Levites.* In the line of march, the Judah and Reuben triads would lead the community, then would come the tabernacle with the attendant protective hedge of Levites (see note on 1:53), and last would come the Ephraim and Dan triads.
2:18–22 The Rachel tribes (Joseph and Benjamin) were on the west. Joseph's two sons Manasseh and Ephraim received a special blessing from their grandfather Jacob, but the younger son, Ephraim, was given precedence over Manasseh (Gen 48:5–20). Here, true to Jacob's words, Ephraim is ahead of Manasseh. Last comes Benjamin, the last son born to Jacob.
2:25 *Dan.* The first son of Bilhah, Rachel's maidservant.
2:27 *Asher.* The second son of Zilpah, Leah's maidservant.
2:29 *Naphtali.* The second son of Bilhah.
2:32 *603,550.* See 1:46 and note.
2:33 *Levites.* See notes on 1:47,53.
2:34 *did; according to all that the LORD commanded Moses.* As in 1:54, these words of absolute compliance contrast with Israel's later folly. *by their standards . . . by his family . . . his father's household.* A major accomplishment for a people so numerous, so recently enslaved and more recently a mob in disarray. It may have been the orderliness of this encampment that led Balaam to say: "How fair are your tents, O Jacob, Your dwellings, O Israel!" (24:5).
3:1 *Aaron and Moses.* At first glance, the names seem out of order, but the emphasis is correct: It is the family of Aaron that is about to be described (see v. 2).
3:3 *anointed priests.* Ex 28:41 records God's command to Moses to anoint his brother Aaron and his sons as priests of the Lord (see Ex 30:30; Lev 8:30). By this solemn act they were consecrated in a special way to the Lord. Kings (1 Sam 16:13) were also anointed with oil for special service to God. Physical objects could be anointed as well (see Gen 28:18; Ex 29:36). The Hebrew term for "anointed" (*mashiaḥ*) later became the specific term for the Messiah. "The Christ" (Greek) and "the Messiah" (Hebrew) both mean "the Anointed One." *ordained.* The Hebrew for this

4 [a]But Nadab and Abihu died before the LORD when they offered strange fire before the LORD in the wilderness of Sinai; and they had no children. So Eleazar and Ithamar served as priests [1]in the lifetime of their father Aaron.

5 Then the LORD spoke to Moses, saying,

6 "[a]Bring the tribe of Levi near and set them before Aaron the priest, that they may serve him.

7 "They shall perform the duties for [1]him and for the whole congregation before the tent of meeting, to do the [a]service of the tabernacle.

8 "They shall also keep all the furnishings of the tent of meeting, along with the duties of the sons of Israel, to do the service of the tabernacle.

9 "You shall thus [a]give the Levites to Aaron and to his sons; they are wholly given to him from among the sons of Israel.

10 "So you shall appoint Aaron and his sons that [a]they may keep their priesthood, but [b]the [1]layman who comes near shall be put to death."

11 Again the LORD spoke to Moses, saying,

12 "Now, behold, I [a]have taken the Levites from among the sons of Israel instead of every [b]firstborn, the first issue of the womb among the sons of Israel. So the Levites shall be Mine.

13 "For [a]all the firstborn are Mine; on the day that I struck down all the firstborn in the land of Egypt, I sanctified to Myself all the firstborn in Israel, from man to beast. They shall be Mine; I am the LORD."

14 Then the LORD spoke to Moses [a]in the wilderness of Sinai, saying,

15 "[1a]Number the sons of Levi by their fathers' households, by their families; every male from a month old and upward you shall number."

16 So Moses numbered them according to the [1]word of the LORD, just as he had been commanded.

17 [a]These then are the sons of Levi by their names: Gershon and Kohath and Merari.

18 These are the names of the [a]sons of Gershon by their families: Libni and Shimei;

19 and the sons of Kohath by their families: Amram and Izhar, Hebron and Uzziel;

20 and the sons of Merari by their families: Mahli and Mushi. These are the families of the Levites according to their fathers' households.

21 Of Gershon *was* the family of the Libnites and the family of the Shimeites; these *were* the families of the Gershonites.

22 Their numbered men, in the numbering of every male from a month old and upward, *even* their numbered men *were* 7,500.

23 The families of the Gershonites were to camp behind the [1]tabernacle westward,

24 and the leader of the fathers' households of the Gershonites *was* Eliasaph the son of Lael.

Duties of the Priests

25 Now [a]the duties of the sons of Gershon in the tent of meeting *involved* the tabernacle and [b]the tent, its covering, and [c]the screen for the doorway of the tent of meeting,

26 and [a]the hangings of the court, and [b]the screen for the doorway of the court which is around the tabernacle and the altar, and its cords, according to all the service [1]concerning them.

4 [1]Lit *before the face* [a]Lev 10:1, 2; Num 26:61
6 [a]Num 8:6-22; 18:1-7; Deut 10:8
7 [1]Lit *him and the duties of the whole congregation* [a]Num 1:50
9 [a]Num 18:6
10 [1]Lit *stranger* [a]Ex 29:9 [b]Num 1:51
12 [a]Num 3:45; 8:14 [b]Ex 13:2
13 [a]Ex 13:2; Lev 27:26; Neh 10:36
14 [a]Ex 19:1
15 [1]Lit *muster,* and so throughout the ch [a]Num 1:47
16 [1]Lit *mouth*
17 [a]Ex 6:16-22
18 [a]Ex 6:17
23 [1]Lit *dwelling place,* and so throughout the ch
25 [a]Num 4:24-26 [b]Ex 26:1, 7, 14 [c]Ex 26:36
26 [1]Lit *of it* [a]Ex 27:9, 12, 14, 15 [b]Ex 27:16

word means lit. "fill your hand" (see NASB marg. at Ex 32:29). By this act there was an investing of authority, a consecration and a setting apart.

3:4 *Nadab and Abihu.* See Lev 10:1–3 and notes. *strange fire.* This seems to be a deliberately obscure expression, as though the narrator finds the very concept distasteful. They were using fire that the Lord had not commanded (see Lev 10:1). Proximity to God's holiness requires righteousness and obedience from His priests. For all time, the deaths of Aaron's newly consecrated sons serve to warn God's ministers of the awesome seriousness of their tasks (cf. 1 Sam 2:12–17, 22–25,27–36; 3:11–14; 4:1–11). For similar divine judgments at the beginning of new stages in salvation history see Josh 7; 2 Sam 6:7; Acts 5:1–11.

3:5–10 These commands are not followed by a report of obedience as were the commands in chs. 1–2, but further details are given in ch. 8. Clear distinctions are made here between the priestly house (the sons of Aaron) and the Levites. The latter were to be aides to the priests, and they served not only Aaron but the whole nation in the process (see vv. 7–8).

3:9 *to him.* It appears that the issue here is service to Aaron (and through him to the Lord); in 8:16 the service is to the Lord.

3:10 *layman.* Lit. "stranger"—anyone lacking authorization. Service at the tabernacle may be performed only at the express appointment of the Lord. The words of v. 10 follow the paragraph telling of the death of Aaron's sons. They were authorized persons, but used unauthorized means. If the sons of Aaron were put to death at the commencement of their duties, how dare an unauthorized person even think to trespass? See v. 38; 18:7.

3:12–13 See note on Ex 13:2. *Mine.* Repeated for emphasis.

3:12 *instead of.* An example of the practice of substitution (see Gen 22:13 and note; Matt 20:28).

3:15 *a month old and upward.* The counting of the Levites corresponds to that of the other tribes in chs. 1–2, except that all males from the age of one month, rather than from 20 years, were to be counted. The Levites were not being mustered for war, but for special service in the sacred precincts of the Lord.

3:16 *as he had been commanded.* The obedience of Moses to the Lord's command is explicit and total.

3:21–38 The words of 1:53, "camp around the tabernacle of the testimony," are detailed by the four paragraphs in this section: (1) Gershon to the west (vv. 21–26); (2) Kohath to the south (vv. 27–32); (3) Merari to the north (vv. 33–37); (4) Moses and Aaron and sons to the east (v. 38). The other tribes began with the most favored: (1) Judah on the east (2:3); (2) Reuben on the south (2:10); (3) Ephraim on the west (2:18); (4) Dan on the north (2:25). The Levitical clans lead up to the most favored. The leaders of the Levitical houses correspond to the leaders of the other tribes (see note on 1:5–16). As the names of the other tribal leaders include a form of God's name, so do these names.

3:24 *Eliasaph.* Means "(My) God has added." *Lael.* Means "belonging to God."

3:25–26 There were three curtains or covering screens for the tabernacle: (1) at the gate of the courtyard (v. 26; 4:26); (2) at

27 Of Kohath *was* the family of the Amramites and the family of the Izharites and the family of the Hebronites and the family of the Uzzielites; these were the families of the Kohathites.

28 In the numbering of every male from a month old and upward, *there were* 8,600, performing the duties of the sanctuary.

29 The families of the sons of Kohath were to camp on the southward side of the tabernacle,

30 and the leader of the fathers' households of the Kohathite families was [1]Elizaphan the son of Uzziel.

31 Now [a]their duties *involved* [b]the ark, [c]the table, [d]the lampstand, [e]the altars, and the utensils of the sanctuary with which they minister, and the screen, and all the service [1]concerning them;

32 and Eleazar the son of Aaron the priest *was* the chief of the leaders of Levi, *and had* the oversight of those who perform the duties of the sanctuary.

33 Of Merari *was* the family of the Mahlites and the family of the Mushites; these *were* the families of Merari.

34 Their numbered men in the numbering of every male from a month old and upward, *were* 6,200.

35 The leader of the fathers' households of the families of Merari *was* Zuriel the son of Abihail. They *were* to [a]camp on the northward side of the tabernacle.

36 Now the appointed duties of the sons of Merari *involved* the frames of the tabernacle, its bars, its pillars, its sockets, all its equipment, and the service concerning them,

37 and the pillars around the court with their sockets and their pegs and their cords.

38 Now those who were to [a]camp before the tabernacle eastward, before the tent of meeting toward the sunrise, are Moses and Aaron and his sons, performing the duties of the sanctuary for the obligation of the sons of Israel; but [b]the [1]layman coming near was to be put to death.

39 All the numbered men of the Levites, whom Moses and Aaron numbered at the [1]command of the LORD by their families, every male from a month old and upward, *were* [a]22,000.

Firstborn Redeemed

40 Then the LORD said to Moses, "[a]Number every firstborn male of the sons of Israel from a month old and upward, and [1]make a list of their names.

41 "You [a]shall take the Levites for Me, I am the LORD, instead of all the firstborn among the sons of Israel, and the cattle of the Levites instead of all the firstborn among the cattle of the sons of Israel."

42 So Moses numbered all the firstborn among the sons of Israel, just as the LORD had commanded him;

43 and all the firstborn males by the number of names from a month old and upward, for their numbered men were [a]22,273.

44 Then the LORD spoke to Moses, saying,

45 "[a]Take the Levites instead of all the firstborn among the sons of Israel and the cattle of the Levites. And the Levites shall be Mine; I am the LORD.

46 "[a]For the ransom of the 273 of the firstborn of the sons of Israel who are in excess beyond the Levites,

47 you shall take [a]five shekels apiece, per head; you shall take *them* in [b]terms of the shekel of the sanctuary ([c]the shekel is twenty [1]gerahs),

48 and give the money, the ransom of those who are in excess among them, to Aaron and to his sons."

49 So Moses took the ransom money from those who were in excess, beyond those ransomed by the Levites;

50 from the firstborn of the sons of Israel he took the money in terms of the shekel of the sanctuary, 1,365.

51 Then Moses gave the ransom money to Aaron and to his sons, at the [1]command of the LORD, just as the LORD had commanded Moses.

30 [1]In Ex 6:22, *Elzaphan*
31 [1]Lit *of it* [a]Num 4:15 [b]Ex 25:10-22 [c]Ex 25:23-28 [d]Ex 25:31-40 [e]Ex 27:1, 2; 30:1-5
35 [a]Num 1:53; 2:25
38 [1]Lit *stranger* [a]Num 1:53; 2:3 [b]Num 1:51
39 [1]Lit *word* [a]Num 3:43; 4:48; 26:62
40 [1]Lit *take the number* [a]Num 3:15
41 [a]Num 3:12, 45
43 [a]Num 3:39
45 [a]Num 3:12
46 [a]Ex 13:13, 15; Num 18:15, 16
47 [1]I.e. A gerah equals approx one-fortieth oz [a]Lev 27:6; Num 18:16 [b]Ex 30:13 [c]Lev 27:25; Ezek 45:12
51 [1]Lit *mouth*

the entrance to the Tent (vv. 25,31; 4:25); (3) between the holy of holies and the holy place (4:5).

3:27 *Amramites.* Aaron was an Amramite (see Ex 6:20); thus he and Moses were from the family of Kohath. To the Kohathites was given the care of the most holy things (see 4:4–18).

3:28 *8,600.* The total number of Levites given in v. 39 is 22,000—300 less than the totals of 7,500 Gershonites (v. 22), 8,600 Kohathites (here) and 6,200 Merarites (v. 34). Many believe that a copyist may have made a mistake here, and that the correct number is 8,300.

3:30 *Elizaphan.* Means "(My) God has protected." *Uzziel.* Means "My strength is God."

3:35 *Zuriel.* Means "My Rock is God." *Abihail.* Means "My (divine) Father is power."

3:38 *toward the sunrise.* The most honored location, but Moses and Aaron were placed there for a representative ministry (on behalf of the Israelites). *the layman . . . was to be put to death.* Service in the tabernacle was an act of mercy, a means for the people to come before God. Yet it was marked by strict discipline—it had to be done in God's way. The sovereignty of God was evident in His limitations on the means to approach Him (see v. 10; 1:51; 18:7).

3:41 *I am the LORD.* What is being commanded conforms to God's character as Yahweh ("the LORD"; see note on Ex 3:14).

3:43 *22,273.* Seems too small for a population in excess of 2,000,000, and is used as an argument for attempting to find a means of reducing the total number of the people (calculations based on this number suggest a total population of about 250,000). Some suggest that the 22,273 firstborn of Israel were those born since the exodus, all the firstborn at the time of the exodus having already been set apart for the Lord at the first Passover (see Ex 12:22–23). This, however, creates a new problem since nowhere is that allegedly distinct group assigned any special service of the Lord. See Introduction: Special Problem.

Duties of the Kohathites

4 Then the LORD spoke to Moses and to Aaron, saying,

2 "Take [1]a census of the [2]descendants of Kohath from among the sons of Levi, by their families, by their fathers' households,

3 from [a]thirty years and upward, even to fifty years old, all who enter the service to do the work in the tent of meeting.

4 "This is the work of the [1]descendants of Kohath in the tent of meeting, *concerning* the most holy things.

5 "When the camp sets out, Aaron and his sons shall go in and they shall take down [a]the veil of the screen and cover the [b]ark of the testimony with it;

6 and they shall lay a [a]covering of porpoise skin on it, and shall spread over *it* a cloth of pure [1]blue, and shall insert its poles.

7 "Over the table of the bread of the Presence they shall also spread a cloth of [1]blue and put on it the dishes and the pans and the sacrificial bowls and the jars for the drink offering, and [a]the continual bread shall be on it.

8 "They shall spread over them a cloth of scarlet *material,* and cover the same with a covering of porpoise skin, and they shall insert its poles.

9 "Then they shall take a [1]blue cloth and cover the [a]lampstand for the light, [b]along with its lamps and its snuffers, and its [2]trays and all its oil vessels, by which they serve it;

10 and they shall put it and all its utensils in a covering of porpoise skin, and shall put it on the carrying bars.

11 "Over the golden altar they shall spread a [1]blue cloth and cover it with a covering of porpoise skin, and shall insert its poles;

12 and they shall take all the utensils of service, with which they serve in the sanctuary, and put them in a [1]blue cloth and cover them with a covering of porpoise skin, and put them on the carrying bars.

13 "Then they shall take away the [1]ashes from the [a]altar, and spread a purple cloth over it.

14 "They shall also put on it all its utensils by which they serve in connection with it: the firepans, the forks and shovels and the basins, all the utensils of the altar; and they shall spread a cover of porpoise skin over it and insert its poles.

15 "When Aaron and his sons have finished covering the holy *objects* and all the furnishings of the sanctuary, when the camp is to set out, after that the sons of Kohath shall come to carry *them,* so that they will not touch the holy *objects* [a]and die. These are the [1]things in the tent of meeting which the sons of Kohath are to carry.

16 "The responsibility of Eleazar the son of Aaron the priest is [a]the oil for the light and the [b]fragrant incense and [c]the continual grain offering and [d]the anointing oil—the responsibility of all the [1]tabernacle and of all that is in it, with the sanctuary and its furnishings."

17 Then the LORD spoke to Moses and to Aaron, saying,

18 "Do not let the tribe of the families of the Kohathites be cut off from among the Levites.

19 "But do this to them that they may live and [a]not die when they approach the most holy *objects:* Aaron and his sons shall go in and assign each of them to his work and to his load;

20 but [a]they shall not go in to see the holy *objects* even for a moment, or they will die."

Duties of the Gershonites

21 Then the LORD spoke to Moses, saying,

22 "Take [1]a census of the sons of Gershon [2]also, by their fathers' households, by their families;

23 from [a]thirty years and upward to fifty years old, you shall [1]number them; all who enter to perform the service to do the work in the tent of meeting.

24 "This is the service of the families of the Gershonites, in serving and in carrying:

25 they shall carry [a]the curtains of the tabernacle and the tent of meeting *with* its covering and [b]the covering of porpoise skin that is on top of it, and the screen for the doorway of the tent of meeting,

26 and [a]the hangings of the court, and the screen for the doorway of the gate of the court which is around the tabernacle and the altar, and their cords and all the equipment for their service; and all that is to be done, [1]they shall perform.

27 "All the service of the sons of the Gershonites, in all their loads and in all their work, shall be *performed* at the [1]command of Aaron and his sons; and you shall assign to them as a duty all their loads.

28 "This is the service of the families of the sons of the Gershonites in the tent of meeting, and their duties *shall be* [1]under the direction of Ithamar the son of Aaron the priest.

4:2 [1]Lit *the sum* [2]Lit *sons*
3 [a]Num 4:23, 30, 35; 8:24; 1 Chr 23:3, 24, 27; Ezra 3:8
4 [1]Lit *sons*
5 [a]Ex 40:5; Lev 16:2; 2 Chr 3:14; Matt 27:51; Heb 9:3 [b]Ex 25:10-16
6 [1]Or *violet* [a]Num 4:25
7 [1]Or *violet* [a]Ex 25:30; Lev 24:5-9
9 [1]Or *violet* [2]Lit *snuff dishes* [a]Ex 25:31 [b]Ex 25:37, 38
11 [1]Or *violet*
12 [1]Or *violet*
13 [1]Or *fat ashes;* i.e. soaked with fat [a]Ex 27:1-8
15 [1]Lit *burden...of the sons* [a]Num 1:51; 4:19, 20; 2 Sam 6:6, 7
16 [1]Lit *dwelling place,* and so throughout the ch [a]Lev 24:1-3 [b]Ex 30:34-38 [c]Lev 6:20 [d]Ex 30:22-33
19 [a]Num 4:15
20 [a]Ex 19:21; 1 Sam 6:19
22 [1]Lit *the sum* [2]Lit *also them*
23 [1]Lit *muster,* and so throughout the ch [a]Num 4:3; 1 Chr 23:3, 24, 27
25 [a]Ex 40:19 [b]Ex 26:14; Num 4:6
26 [1]Lit *so they shall serve* [a]Ex 38:9
27 [1]Lit *mouth*
28 [1]Lit *in the hand*

4:3 *thirty . . . to fifty years.* Ch. 3 listed all males over the age of one month (3:15). Ch. 4 lists those Levites who were of age to serve in the tabernacle. Of the 22,000 Levite males (3:39), 8,580 were of age for service (v. 48). From 8:24 we learn that the beginning age for service was 25; perhaps the first 5 years were something of an apprenticeship.

4:4 *most holy things.* Despite the fact that the primary care of these holy things was given to the Kohathites, they were forbidden to touch them (v. 15) or even to look at them (v. 20), on pain of death. All the work of the Kohathites was to be strictly supervised by Aaron and his sons, and only the priests were able to touch and look at the unveiled holy things.

4:16 *responsibility of Eleazar . . . the priest.* The high priest could draw near to the most holy things on behalf of the people. If he had not been able to do so, there could have been no worship by the community.

Duties of the Merarites

29 "*As for* the sons of Merari, you shall
number them by their families, by their
fathers' households;
30 from [a]thirty years and upward even to
fifty years old, you shall number them,
everyone who enters the service to do the
work of the tent of meeting.
31 "Now this is the duty of their loads, for
all their service in the tent of meeting: the
boards of the tabernacle and its bars and its
pillars and its [1]sockets,
32 and the pillars around the court and
their [1]sockets and their pegs and their cords,
with all their equipment and with all their
service; and you shall assign *each man* by
name the items [2]he is to carry.
33 "This is the service of the families of the
sons of Merari, according to all their service
in the tent of meeting, [1]under the direction
of Ithamar the son of Aaron the priest."
34 So Moses and Aaron and the leaders of
the congregation numbered the sons of the
Kohathites by their families and by their
fathers' households,
35 from [a]thirty years and upward even to
fifty years old, everyone who entered the service for work in the tent of meeting.
36 Their numbered men by their families
were 2,750.
37 These are the numbered men of the
Kohathite families, everyone who was serving in the tent of meeting, whom Moses and
Aaron numbered according to the [1]com-
mandment of the LORD [2]through Moses.
38 The numbered men of the sons of Gershon by their families and by their fathers'
households,
39 from thirty years and upward even to
fifty years old, everyone who entered the service for work in the tent of meeting.
40 Their numbered men by their families,
by their fathers' households, were 2,630.
41 These are the numbered men of the
families of the sons of Gershon, everyone
who was serving in the tent of meeting,
whom Moses and Aaron numbered according to the [1]commandment of the LORD.

30 [a]Num 4:3; 8:24-26
31 [1]Or *bases*
32 [1]Or *bases* [2]Lit *of the duty of their loads*
33 [1]Lit *in the hand*
35 [a]1 Chr 23:24
37 [1]Lit *mouth* [2]Lit *by the hand of*
41 [1]Lit *mouth*

42 The numbered men of the families of
the sons of Merari by their families, by their
fathers' households,
43 from [a]thirty years and upward even to
fifty years old, everyone who entered the service for work in the tent of meeting.
44 Their numbered men by their families
were 3,200.
45 These are the numbered men of the
families of the sons of Merari, whom Moses
and Aaron numbered according to the [1]com-
mandment of the LORD [2]through Moses.
46 All the numbered men of the Levites,
whom Moses and Aaron and the leaders of
Israel numbered, by their families and by
their fathers' households,
47 from thirty years and upward even to
fifty years old, everyone who could enter to
do the work of service and the work of carrying in the tent of meeting.
48 Their numbered men were [a]8,580.
49 According to the [1]commandment of the
LORD [2]through Moses, they [a]were numbered,
everyone by his serving or carrying; thus
these were his numbered men, just as the
LORD had commanded Moses.

On Defilement

5 Then the LORD spoke to Moses, saying,
2 "Command the sons of Israel that they
[a]send away from the camp every leper and
everyone having a [b]discharge and everyone
who is [c]unclean because of a *dead* person.
3 "You shall send away both male and
female; you shall send them outside the
camp so that they will not defile their camp
where I dwell [a]in their midst."
4 The sons of Israel did so and sent them
outside the camp; just as the LORD had spoken to Moses, thus the sons of Israel did.
5 Then the LORD spoke to Moses, saying,
6 "Speak to the sons of Israel, '[a]When a
man or woman commits any of the sins of
mankind, acting unfaithfully against the
LORD, and that person is guilty,
7 then [1]he shall [a]confess [2]his sins which
[3]he has committed, and he [b]shall make restitution in full for his wrong and add to it one-

43 [a]Num 8:24-26
45 [1]Lit *mouth* [2]Lit *by the hand of*
48 [a]Num 3:39
49 [1]Lit *mouth* [2]Lit *by the hand of* [a]Num 1:47
5:2 [a]Lev 13:8, 46; Num 12:10, 14, 15 [b]Lev 15:2 [c]Lev 21:1; Num 9:6-10; 19:11
3 [a]Lev 26:12; Num 35:34
6 [a]Lev 5:14-6:7
7 [1]Lit *they* [2]Lit *their* [3]Lit *they have* [a]Lev 5:5; 26:40, 41; Josh 7:19 [b]Lev 6:4, 5

5:2 *leper.* See note on Lev 13:2; cf. Luke 5:12–16; 17:11–19. *discharge.* See note on Lev 15:2. Such discharges were primarily from the sexual organs and were chronic in nature (cf. Luke 8:43–48). The people who suffered from them became living object lessons to the whole camp on the necessity for all people to be "clean" in their approach to God. *unclean.* Ceremonially unfit to be with the community, and a possible contaminant to the tabernacle and the pure worship of the Lord. Aspects of uncleanness were not left in the abstract or theoretical; the focus was on tangible issues, such as clearly evident skin diseases and discharges. *dead person.* The ultimate tangible sign of uncleanness. Processes of decay and disease in dead flesh were evident to all. Physical contact with a corpse was a sure mark of uncleanness; normal contacts with the living would have to be curtailed until proper cleansing had been made. See note on 6:6 for application to the Nazirite vow. Jesus reached out to the dead as well as to the living; His raising of Jairus's daughter began with holding her limp hand (Luke 8:54).

5:3 *male and female.* The concept of clean versus unclean cuts across sexual lines. The essential issue was the presence of the Lord in the camp; there can be no uncleanness where He dwells. In the new Jerusalem (Rev 21:2–3) the dwelling of God with man will be uncompromised by any form of uncleanness (Rev 21:27).

5:5–10 The connection of these verses (on personal wrongs) with the first paragraph (on ritual uncleanness) may be that of moving from the outward, visible defects to the inward, more secret faults that mar the purity of the community. Those with evident marks of uncleanness are to be expelled for the duration of their malady. But more insidious are those people who have overtly sinned against others in the community, and who think that they may continue to function as though they had done nothing wrong.

fifth of it, and give *it* to him whom he has wronged.

8 'But if the man has no [1]relative to whom restitution may be made for the wrong, the restitution which is made for the wrong *must go* to the LORD for the priest, besides the ram of atonement, by which atonement is made for him.

9 '[a]Also every [1]contribution pertaining to all the holy *gifts* of the sons of Israel, which they offer to the priest, shall be his.

10 'So every man's holy *gifts* shall be his; whatever any man gives to the priest, it [a]becomes his.' "

The Adultery Test

11 Then the LORD spoke to Moses, saying,

12 "Speak to the sons of Israel and say to them, 'If any man's wife [a]goes astray and is unfaithful to him,

13 and a man has [a]intercourse with her and it is hidden from the eyes of her husband and she is [1]undetected, although she has defiled herself, and there is no witness against her and she has not been caught in the act,

14 [1]if a spirit of [a]jealousy comes over him and he is jealous of his wife when she has defiled herself, or if a spirit of jealousy comes over him and he is jealous of his wife when she has not defiled herself,

15 the man shall then bring his wife to the priest, and shall bring *as* [1]an offering for her one-tenth of an [2]ephah of barley meal; he shall not pour oil on it nor put frankincense on it, for it is a grain offering of jealousy, a grain offering of memorial, [a]a reminder of iniquity.

16 'Then the priest shall bring her near and have her stand before the LORD,

17 and the priest shall take holy water in an earthenware vessel; and [1]he shall take some of the dust that is on the floor of the tabernacle and put *it* into the water.

18 'The priest shall then have the woman stand before the LORD and let *the hair of* the woman's head go loose, and place the grain offering of memorial [1]in her hands, which is the grain offering of jealousy, and in the hand of the priest is to be the water of bitterness that brings a curse.

19 'The priest shall have her take an oath and shall say to the woman, "If no man has lain with you and if you have not [a]gone astray into uncleanness, *being* under *the authority of* your husband, be [1]immune to this water of bitterness that brings a curse;

20 if you, however, have [a]gone astray, *being* under *the authority of* your husband, and if you have defiled yourself and a man other than your husband has had intercourse with you"

21 (then the priest shall have the woman [a]swear with the oath of the curse, and the priest shall say to the woman), "the LORD make you a curse and an oath among your people by the LORD's making your thigh [1]waste away and your abdomen swell;

22 and this water that brings a curse shall go into your [1]stomach, and make your abdomen swell and your thigh [2]waste away." And the woman [a]shall say, "Amen. Amen."

23 'The priest shall then write these curses on a scroll, and he shall [1]wash them off into the water of bitterness.

24 'Then he shall make the woman drink the water of bitterness that brings a curse, so that the water which brings a curse will go into her [1]and *cause* bitterness.

25 'The priest shall take the grain offering of jealousy from the woman's hand, and he shall wave the grain offering before the LORD and bring it to the altar;

8 [1]Lit *redeemer*
9 [1]Lit *heave offering* [a]Lev 7:32, 34; 10:14, 15
10 [a]Lev 10:13
12 [a]Num 5:19-21, 29
13 [1]Lit *concealed* [a]Lev 18:20; 20:10
14 [1]Lit *and* [a]Prov 6:34; Song 8:6
15 [1]Lit *her* [2]I.e. Approx one bu [a]1 Kin 17:18; Ezek 29:16
17 [1]Lit *the priest*
18 [1]Lit *on her palms*
19 [1]Lit *free from* [a]Num 5:12
20 [a]Num 5:12
21 [1]Lit *fall* [a]Josh 6:26; 1 Sam 14:24; Neh 10:29
22 [1]Or *inward parts* [2]Lit *fall* [a]Deut 27:15
23 [1]Lit *wipe*
24 [1]Lit *to*

5:11–31 Again, the connection with the preceding two paragraphs seems to be a movement from the more open, obvious sins to the more personal, hidden ones. Issues of purity begin with physical marks (vv. 1–4), are expanded to interpersonal relationships (vv. 5–10), and then intrude into the most intimate of relationships—the purity of a man and woman in their marriage bed. A test for marital fidelity is far more difficult to prove than a test for a skin disorder; hence, the larger part of the chapter is given to this most sensitive of issues.

5:14 *spirit of jealousy.* This may have been provoked on the basis of good cause, and the issue must be faced. The concern is not just for the bruised feelings of the husband but is ultimately based on the reality of God's dwelling among His people (v. 3). Yet the chapter is designed to prevent unfounded charges of unfaithfulness. This text was not to be used by a capricious, petty or malevolent husband to badger an innocent woman. *defiled.* The subject of the chapter is consistent; the purity of the camp where God dwells (v. 3) is the burden of the passage.

5:15–28 The actions presented here seem severe and harsh. But the consequences would have been worse for a woman charged with adultery by an angry husband if there was no provision for her guilt or innocence to be demonstrated. That she was taken to the priest (v. 15) is finally an act of mercy. The gravity of the ritual for a suspected unfaithful wife shows that the law regards marital infidelity most seriously. This was not just a concern of a jealous husband. The entire community was affected by this breach of faith; hence, the judgment was in the context of the community.

5:18 *let the hair . . . go loose.* A sign of openness; for the guilty, an expectation of judgment and mourning. *water of bitterness that brings a curse.* Or "curse-bringing water of bitterness." It is not just that the water was bitter tasting but that the water had the potential of bringing with it a bitter curse. The Lord's role in the proceedings (vv. 16,21,25) is emphasized repeatedly to show that this potion was neither simply a tool of magic nor merely a psychological device to determine stress. The verdict with respect to the woman was precipitated by her physiological and psychological responses to the bitter water, but the judgment was from the Lord.

5:21 *your thigh waste away and your abdomen swell.* The figurative language here (and in vv. 22,27) speaks of the loss of the capacity for childbearing (and, if pregnant, the miscarriage of the child). This is demonstrated by the determination of the fate of a woman wrongly charged (v. 28). For a woman in the ancient Near East to be denied the ability to bear children was a personal loss of inestimable proportions. Since it was in the bearing of children that a woman's worth was realized in the ancient world, this was a grievous punishment indeed.

26 and [a]the priest shall take a handful of
the grain offering as its memorial offering
and offer *it* up in smoke on the altar, and
afterward he shall make the woman drink
the water.
27 'When he has made her drink the water,
then it shall come about, if she has defiled
herself and has been unfaithful to her husband, that the water which brings a curse
will go into her [1]and *cause* bitterness, and
her abdomen will swell and her thigh will
[2]waste away, and the woman will become [a]a
curse among her people.
28 'But if the woman has not defiled herself and is clean, she will then be free and
conceive [1]children.
29 'This is the law of jealousy: when a
wife, *being* under *the authority of* her husband, [a]goes astray and defiles herself,
30 or when a spirit of jealousy comes over
a man and he is jealous of his wife, he shall
then make the woman stand before the LORD,
and the priest shall apply all this law to her.
31 'Moreover, the man will be free from
[1]guilt, but that woman shall [a]bear her
[1]guilt.' "

Law of the Nazirites

6 Again the LORD spoke to Moses, saying,
2 "Speak to the sons of Israel and say to
them, 'When a man or woman makes a [1]spe-
cial vow, the vow of [a]a [2]Nazirite, to [3]dedi-
cate himself to the LORD,
3 he shall [a]abstain from wine and strong
drink; he shall drink no vinegar, whether
made from wine or strong drink, nor shall he
drink any grape juice nor eat fresh or dried
grapes.
4 'All the days of his [1]separation he shall
not eat anything that is produced by the
grape vine, from *the* seeds even to *the* skin.
5 'All the days of his vow of separation
[a]no razor shall pass over his head. He shall
be holy until the days are fulfilled for which
he separated himself to the LORD; he shall let
the locks of hair on his head grow long.
6 '[a]All the days of his separation to the
LORD he shall not go near to a dead person.

26 [a]Lev 2:2, 9
27 [1]Lit *to* [2]Lit *fall* [a]Jer 29:18; 42:18; 44:12
28 [1]Lit *seed*
29 [a]Num 5:12
31 [1]Or *iniquity* [a]Lev 20:17
6:2 [1]Or *difficult* [2]I.e. one separated [3]Or *live as a Nazirite* [a]Judg 13:5; 16:17; Amos 2:11, 12
3 [a]Luke 1:15
4 [1]Or *living as a Nazirite,* and so through v 21
5 [a]1 Sam 1:11
6 [a]Lev 21:1-3; Num 19:11-22

7 'He [a]shall not make himself unclean for
his father or for his mother, for his brother or
for his sister, when they die, because his separation to God is on his head.
8 'All the days of his separation he is holy
to the LORD.
9 'But if a man dies very suddenly beside
him and he defiles his dedicated head *of
hair,* then [a]he shall shave his head on the
day when he becomes clean; [b]he shall shave
it on the seventh day.
10 'Then on the eighth day he shall bring
[a]two turtledoves or two young pigeons to the
priest, to the doorway of the tent of meeting.
11 'The priest shall offer [a]one for a sin
offering and *the* other for a burnt offering,
and make atonement for him [1]concerning
his sin because of the *dead* person. And that
same day he shall consecrate his head,
12 and shall dedicate to the LORD his days
[1]as a [2]Nazirite, and shall bring a male lamb
a year old for a guilt offering; but the former
days will be void because his separation was
defiled.
13 'Now this is the law of the Nazirite
[a]when the days of his separation are fulfilled, he shall bring [1]the offering to the doorway of the tent of meeting.
14 'He shall present his offering to the
LORD: one male lamb a year old without
defect for a burnt offering and one [a]ewe-lamb
a year old without defect for a sin offering
and one ram without defect for a peace offering,
15 and a basket of [a]unleavened cakes of
fine flour mixed with oil and unleavened
wafers spread with oil, along with [b]their
grain offering and their drink offering.
16 'Then the priest shall present *them*
before the LORD and shall offer his sin offering and his burnt offering.
17 'He shall also offer the ram for a sacrifice of peace offerings to the LORD, together
with the basket of unleavened cakes; the
priest shall likewise offer its grain offering
and its drink offering.
18 '[a]The Nazirite shall then shave his dedicated head *of hair* at the doorway of the tent

7 [a]Num 9:6
9 [a]Lev 14:8, 9 [b]Num 6:18
10 [a]Lev 5:7; 14:22
11 [1]Lit *because of that which he sinned* [a]Lev 5:7
12 [1]Or *of dedication* [2]I.e. one separated
13 [1]Lit *it* [a]Acts 21:26
14 [a]Lev 14:10; Num 15:27
15 [a]Ex 29:2; Lev 2:4 [b]Num 15:1-7
18 [a]Num 6:9; Acts 21:23, 24

6:2 *man or woman.* See ch. 30 for the differences between the vows of men and women. *vow . . . Nazirite.* Involved separation or consecration for a specific period of special devotion to God—on occasion even for life. Attention is usually given to the prohibitions for the Nazirite; more important to the Lord is the positive separation (see v. 8). This was not just a vow of personal self-discipline; it was an act of total devotion to the Lord.

6:4 *anything that is produced by the grape vine.* Not only was the fermented beverage forbidden, but even the seed and skin of the grape. During the period of a Nazirite's vow, three areas of his (or her) life were governed: (1) diet, (2) appearance and (3) associations. Every Israelite was regulated in these areas, but for the Nazirite each regulation was heightened. An analogy may be the practice of some Christians to forgo certain (good) foods during the period of Lent to enhance spiritual devotion to Christ in the special period of remembering His sufferings.

6:5 *no razor.* See Judg 13:5. The unusually long hair of a Nazirite would become a physical mark of his (or her) vow of special devotion to the Lord. Cf. Lev 21:5.

6:6 *dead person.* See note on 5:2. For the Nazirite, the prohibition of contact with dead bodies extended even to the deceased within his (or her) own family (v. 7; contrast Lev 21:1–3).

6:9–12 The provisions of the Nazirite vow concerned areas where he (or she) was able to make conscious decisions. This section deals with the unexpected and the unplanned events of daily living.

6:13–20 The offerings of the Nazirite at the completion of the period of the vow were extensive, expensive and expressive of the spirit of total commitment to the Lord during this time of special devotion. In addition to these several offerings the Nazirite burned his (or her) hair (the sign of the vow).

of meeting, and take the dedicated hair of his
head and put *it* on the fire which is under the
sacrifice of peace offerings.
19 '[a]The priest shall take the ram's shoulder *when it has been* boiled, and one unleavened cake out of the basket and one unleavened wafer, and shall put *them* on the
[1]hands of the Nazirite after he has shaved
his [2]dedicated *hair.*
20 'Then the priest shall wave them for a
wave offering before the LORD. It is holy for
the priest, together with the breast offered by
waving and the thigh offered by lifting up;
and [a]afterward the Nazirite may drink wine.'
21 "This is the law of the Nazirite who
vows his offering to the LORD according to
his separation, in addition to what *else* [1]he
can afford; according to his vow which he
takes, so he shall do according to the law of
his separation."

Aaron's Benediction

22 Then the LORD spoke to Moses, saying,
23 "Speak to Aaron and to his sons, saying,
'Thus [a]you shall bless the sons of Israel. You
shall say to them:
24 The LORD [a]bless you, and [b]keep you;
25 The LORD [a]make His face shine on you,
And [b]be gracious to you;
26 The LORD [a]lift up His countenance on
you,
And [b]give you peace.'
27 "So they shall [1][a]invoke My name on the
sons of Israel, and I *then* will bless them."

Offerings of the Leaders

7 Now on [a]the day that Moses had finished
setting up the tabernacle, he [b]anointed it
and consecrated it with all its furnishings
and the altar and all its utensils; he anointed
them and consecrated them also.
2 Then [a]the leaders of Israel, the heads
of their fathers' households, [b]made an offering (they were the leaders of the tribes; they
were the ones who [1]were over the [2]num-
bered men).
3 When they brought their offering
before the LORD, six [a]covered carts and
twelve oxen, a cart for *every* two of the leaders and an ox for each one, then they presented them before the tabernacle.
4 Then the LORD spoke to Moses, saying,
5 "Accept *these things* from them, that
they may be [1]used in the service of the tent
of meeting, and you shall give them to the
Levites, *to* each man according to his service."
6 So Moses took the carts and the oxen
and gave them to the Levites.
7 Two carts and four oxen he gave to the
sons of Gershon, according to [a]their service,
8 and four carts and eight oxen he gave
to the sons of Merari, according to [a]their service, under the [1]direction of Ithamar the son
of Aaron the priest.
9 But he did not give *any* to the sons of
Kohath because theirs *was* [a]the service of
the holy *objects, which* they carried on the
shoulder.
10 The leaders offered the dedication
offering [1]for the altar [2]when [a]it was anointed, so the leaders offered their offering
before the altar.
11 Then the LORD said to Moses, "Let
them present their offering, one leader each
day, for the dedication of the altar."
12 Now the one who presented his offering on the first day was Nahshon the son of
Amminadab, of the tribe of Judah;
13 and his offering *was* one silver [1][a]dish
whose weight *was* one hundred and thirty
shekels, one silver bowl of seventy shekels,
[b]according to [2]the shekel of the sanctuary,
both of them full of fine flour mixed with oil
for a grain offering;
14 one gold pan of ten *shekels,* full of
incense;
15 one [1]bull, one ram, one male lamb one
year old, for a burnt offering;
16 [a]one male goat for a sin offering;
17 and for the sacrifice of peace offerings,
two oxen, five rams, five male goats, five
male lambs one year old. This *was* the offering of [a]Nahshon the son of Amminadab.

19 [1]Lit *palms* [2]Or *separated* [a]Lev 7:28-34
20 [a]Eccl 9:7
21 [1]Lit *his hand can reach*
23 [a]1 Chr 23:13
24 [a]Deut 28:3-6; Ps 28:9 [b]1 Sam 2:9; Ps 17:8
25 [a]Ps 80:3, 7, 19 [b]Ps 86:16
26 [a]Ps 4:6; 44:3 [b]Ps 29:11; 37:37
27 [1]Lit *put* [a]2 Sam 7:23; 2 Chr 7:14
7:1 [a]Ex 40:17 [b]Ex 40:9-11; Num 7:10, 84, 88
2 [1]Lit *stood* [2]Lit *mustered* [a]Num 1:5-16 [b]2 Chr 35:8
3 [a]Is 66:20
5 [1]Lit *for serving*
7 [a]Num 4:24-26
8 [1]Lit *hand* [a]Num 4:31, 32
9 [a]Num 4:5-15
10 [1]Lit *of* [2]Lit *in the day that* [a]Num 7:1; 2 Chr 7:9
13 [1]Or *platter,* and so through v 85 [2]I.e. Approx one-half oz, and so through v 86 [a]Ex 25:29; 37:16 [b]Num 3:47
15 [1]Or *bull of the herd,* and so through v 81
16 [a]Lev 4:23
17 [a]Luke 3:32, 33

6:21 *This is the law of the Nazirite.* Summary statements such as this not only end a section, but also solemnize its contents.
6:24–26 The Aaronic benediction. The threefold repetition of the divine name Yahweh ("the LORD") is for emphasis and gives force to the expression in v. 27: "So they shall invoke my name on the sons of Israel." Each verse conveys two elements of benediction, and the verses are progressively longer (in the Hebrew text, the first verse has three words, the second has five and the third has seven).
6:25 *make His face shine on you.* In acceptance and favor.
6:26 *peace.* The Hebrew for this word is *shalom,* here seen in its most expressive fullness—not the absence of war, but a positive state of rightness and well-being. Such peace comes only from the Lord.
7:1–89 See Ex 40, which describes the setting up of the tabernacle and ends with the report of the cloud covering and the presence of the Lord filling the tabernacle. With much repetition of language, this chapter (the longest in the Pentateuch) records the magnificent (and identical) gifts to the Lord for tabernacle service from the leaders of the 12 tribes. The fact that the record of these gifts follows the text of the Aaronic benediction (6:24–26) seems fitting: In response to God's promise to bless His people, they bring gifts to Him in 12 sequential days of celebrative pageantry.
7:12–78 The leaders of the 12 tribes have already been named in 1:5–15; 2:3–32. The order of the presentation of their offerings to the Lord is the same as the order of march: first, the triad of tribes camped east of the tabernacle (Judah, Issachar and Zebulun: 2:3–9; 7:12,18,24); second, the triad camped to the south (Reuben, Simeon and Gad: 2:10–16; 7:30,36,42); third, the triad to the west (Ephraim, Manasseh and Benjamin: 2:18–24; 7:48,54,60); finally, those to the north (Dan, Asher and Naphtali: 2:25–31; 7:66,72,78). See diagram, p. 179.

18 On the second day Nethanel the son of Zuar, leader of Issachar, presented *an offering;*
19 he presented as his offering one silver dish whose weight *was* one hundred and thirty *shekels,* one silver bowl of seventy shekels, according to the shekel of the sanctuary, both of them full of fine flour mixed with oil for a grain offering;
20 one gold pan of ten *shekels,* full of incense;
21 one bull, one ram, one male lamb one year old, for a burnt offering;
22 one male goat for a sin offering;
23 and for the sacrifice of [a]peace offerings, two oxen, five rams, five male goats, five male lambs one year old. This *was* the offering of Nethanel the son of Zuar.
24 On the third day *it was* Eliab the son of Helon, leader of the sons of Zebulun;
25 his offering *was* one silver dish whose weight *was* one hundred and thirty *shekels,* one silver bowl of seventy shekels, according to the shekel of the sanctuary, both of them full of fine flour mixed with oil for a grain offering;
26 one gold pan of ten *shekels,* full of incense;
27 one young bull, one ram, one [a]male lamb one year old, for a burnt offering;
28 one male goat for a sin offering;
29 and for the sacrifice of peace offerings, two oxen, five rams, five male goats, five male lambs one year old. This *was* the offering of Eliab the son of Helon.
30 On the fourth day *it was* Elizur the son of Shedeur, leader of the sons of Reuben;
31 his offering *was* one silver dish whose weight *was* one hundred and thirty *shekels,* one silver bowl of seventy shekels, according to the shekel of the sanctuary, both of them full of fine flour mixed with oil for a grain offering;
32 one gold pan of ten *shekels,* full of incense;
33 one bull, one ram, one [a]male lamb one year old, for a burnt offering;
34 one male goat for a sin offering;
35 and for the sacrifice of peace offerings, two oxen, five rams, five male goats, five male lambs one year old. This *was* the offering of Elizur the son of Shedeur.
36 On the fifth day *it was* Shelumiel the son of Zurishaddai, leader of the children of Simeon;
37 his offering *was* one silver dish whose weight *was* one hundred and thirty *shekels,* one silver bowl of seventy shekels, according to the shekel of the sanctuary, both of them full of fine flour mixed with oil for a grain offering;
38 one gold pan of ten *shekels,* full of incense;
39 one bull, one ram, one male lamb one year old, for a burnt offering;
40 one male goat for a sin offering;
41 and for the sacrifice of peace offerings, two oxen, five rams, five male goats, five male lambs one year old. This *was* the offering of Shelumiel the son of Zurishaddai.
42 On the sixth day *it was* [a]Eliasaph the son of Deuel, leader of the sons of Gad;
43 his offering *was* one silver dish whose weight *was* one hundred and thirty *shekels,* one silver bowl of seventy shekels, according to the shekel of the sanctuary, both of them full of [a]fine flour mixed with oil for a grain offering;
44 one gold pan of ten *shekels,* full of incense;
45 [a]one bull, one ram, one male lamb one year old, for a burnt offering;
46 one male goat for a sin offering;
47 and for the sacrifice of peace offerings, two oxen, five rams, five male goats, five male lambs one year old. This *was* the offering of Eliasaph the son of Deuel.
48 On the seventh day *it was* [a]Elishama the son of Ammihud, leader of the sons of Ephraim;
49 his offering *was* one silver dish whose weight *was* one hundred and thirty *shekels,* one silver bowl of seventy shekels, according to the shekel of the sanctuary, both of them full of fine flour mixed with oil for a grain offering;
50 one gold pan of ten *shekels,* full of [a]incense;
51 [a]one bull, one ram, one male lamb one year old, for a burnt offering;
52 one male goat for a sin offering;
53 and for the sacrifice of peace offerings, two oxen, five rams, five male goats, five male lambs one year old. This *was* the offering of Elishama the son of Ammihud.
54 On the eighth day *it was* [a]Gamaliel the son of Pedahzur, leader of the sons of Manasseh;
55 his offering *was* one silver dish whose weight *was* one hundred and thirty *shekels,* one silver bowl of seventy shekels, according to the shekel of the sanctuary, both of them full of fine flour mixed with oil for a grain offering;
56 one gold pan of ten *shekels,* full of [a]incense;
57 one bull, one ram, one [a]male lamb one year old, for a burnt offering;
58 one male goat for a sin offering;
59 and for the [a]sacrifice of peace offerings, two oxen, five rams, five male goats, five male lambs one year old. This *was* the offering of Gamaliel the son of Pedahzur.
60 On the ninth day *it was* [a]Abidan the son of Gideoni, leader of the sons of Benjamin;
61 his offering *was* one silver dish whose weight *was* one hundred and thirty *shekels,* one silver bowl of seventy shekels, according to the shekel of the sanctuary, both of them full of fine flour mixed with oil for a grain offering;

23 [a]Lev 7:11-13
27 [a]Is 53:7; John 1:29; 1 Pet 1:19
33 [a]Heb 9:28
42 [a]Num 1:14; 10:20
43 [a]Lev 2:5; 14:10
45 [a]Ps 50:8-14; Is 1:11
48 [a]Num 1:10; 2:18; 1 Chr 7:26
50 [a]Deut 33:10; Ezek 8:11; Luke 1:10
51 [a]Mic 6:6-8
54 [a]Num 2:20
56 [a]Ex 30:7
57 [a]Ex 12:5; Acts 8:32; Rev 5:6
59 [a]Lev 3:1-17
60 [a]Num 1:11; 2:22

62 one gold pan of ten *shekels,* full of
[a]incense;
63 one bull, one ram, one male lamb one
year old, for a burnt offering;
64 one male goat for a [a]sin offering;
65 and for the sacrifice of [a]peace offerings, two oxen, five rams, five male goats,
five male lambs one year old. This *was* the
offering of Abidan the son of Gideoni.
66 On the tenth day *it was* [a]Ahiezer the
son of Ammishaddai, leader of the sons of
Dan;
67 his offering *was* one silver dish whose
weight *was* one hundred and thirty *shekels,*
one silver bowl of seventy shekels, according
to the [a]shekel of the sanctuary, both of them
full of fine flour mixed with oil for a grain
offering;
68 one gold pan of ten *shekels,* full of
[a]incense;
69 one bull, one ram, one male lamb one
year old, for a burnt offering;
70 one male goat for a sin offering;
71 and for the sacrifice of peace offerings,
two oxen, five rams, five male goats, five
male lambs one year old. This *was* the offering of Ahiezer the son of Ammishaddai.
72 On the eleventh day *it was* [a]Pagiel the
son of Ochran, leader of the sons of Asher;
73 his offering *was* one silver dish whose
weight *was* one hundred and thirty *shekels,*
one silver bowl of seventy shekels, according
to the shekel of the sanctuary, both of them
full of fine flour mixed with oil for a grain
offering;
74 one gold pan of ten *shekels,* full of
[a]incense;
75 one bull, one ram, one male lamb one
year old, for a burnt offering;
76 one male goat for a sin offering;
77 and for the sacrifice of peace offerings,
two oxen, five rams, five male goats, five
male lambs one year old. This *was* the offering of Pagiel the son of Ochran.
78 On the twelfth day *it was* [a]Ahira the
son of Enan, leader of the sons of Naphtali;
79 his offering *was* one [a]silver dish whose
weight *was* one hundred and thirty *shekels,*
one silver bowl of seventy shekels, according
to the shekel of the sanctuary, both of them
full of fine flour mixed with oil for a grain
offering;
80 one gold pan of ten *shekels,* full of
incense;
81 one bull, one ram, one male lamb one
year old, for a burnt offering;
82 one male goat for a sin offering;
83 and for the sacrifice of peace offerings,
two oxen, five rams, five male goats, five
male lambs one year old. This *was* the offering of Ahira the son of Enan.
84 This *was* [a]the dedication *offering* [1]for
the altar from the leaders of Israel [2]when [b]it
was anointed: twelve silver dishes, twelve
silver bowls, twelve gold pans,
85 each silver dish *weighing* one hundred
and thirty *shekels* and each bowl seventy; all
the silver of the utensils *was* 2,400 *shekels,*
according to the shekel of the sanctuary;
86 the twelve gold pans, full of incense,
weighing ten *shekels* apiece, according to the
[a]shekel of the sanctuary, all the gold of the
pans 120 *shekels;*
87 all the oxen for the burnt offering
twelve bulls, *all* the rams twelve, the male
lambs one year old with their grain offering
twelve, and the male goats for a sin offering
twelve;
88 and all the oxen for the sacrifice of
peace offerings 24 bulls, *all* the rams 60, the
male goats 60, the male lambs one year old
60. [a]This *was* the dedication *offering* for the
altar after it was anointed.
89 Now when [a]Moses went into the tent
of meeting to speak with Him, he heard the
voice speaking to him from above [b]the [1]mer-
cy seat that was on the ark of the testimony,
from [c]between the two cherubim, so He
spoke to him.

The Seven Lamps

8 Then the LORD spoke to Moses, saying,
2"Speak to Aaron and say to him, 'When
you [1]mount the lamps, the seven lamps will
[a]give light in the front of the lampstand.' "
3 Aaron therefore did so; he [1]mounted its
lamps at the front of the lampstand, just as
the LORD had commanded Moses.
4 [a]Now this was the workmanship of the
lampstand, hammered work of gold; from its
base to its flowers it was hammered work;
[b]according to the pattern which the LORD had
showed Moses, so he made the lampstand.

Cleansing the Levites

5 Again the LORD spoke to Moses, saying,
6"Take the Levites from among the sons
of Israel and [a]cleanse them.
7"Thus you shall do to them, for their
[1]cleansing: *sprinkle* [2]purifying [a]water on
them, and let them [3][b]use a razor over their

62 [a]Rev 5:8; 8:3, 4
64 [a]2 Cor 5:21
65 [a]Col 1:20
66 [a]Num 1:12; 2:25
67 [a]Ex 30:13; Lev 27:25
68 [a]Ps 141:2
72 [a]Num 1:13; 2:27
74 [a]Mal 1:11
78 [a]Num 1:15; 2:29
79 [a]Ezra 1:9, 10; Dan 5:2

84 [1]Lit *of* [2]Lit *in the day that* [a]Num 7:10 [b]Num 7:1
86 [a]Ex 30:13
88 [a]Num 7:1, 10
89 [1]Lit *propitiatory* [a]Ex 40:34, 35 [b]Ex 25:21, 22 [c]Ps 80:1; 99:1
8:2 [1]Lit *raise up* [a]Ex 25:37; Lev 24:2, 4
3 [1]Lit *raised up*
4 [a]Ex 25:31-40 [b]Ex 25:9, 31-40; 26:30; 37:17-24
6 [a]Is 52:11
7 [1]Lit *this their cleansing* [2]Lit *water of sin* [3]Lit *cause to pass* [a]Num 19:9, 13, 20 [b]Lev 14:8, 9

7:84–88 The totals of the 12 sets of gifts.
7:89 The climax: Communion is established between the Lord and His prophet. The people have an advocate with God.
8:2 *in the front of the lampstand.* The holy place in the tabernacle (see Ex 25:37; 26:33; 27:21).
8:5–26 Describes the cleansing of the Levites and may be compared with the account of the ordination of Aaron and his sons to the priesthood (Lev 8). The Levites are helpers to the priests, and the language describing their consecration is somewhat different from that of the priests. The priests were made holy, the Levites clean; the priests were anointed and washed, the Levites sprinkled; the priests were given new garments, the Levites washed theirs; blood was applied to the priests, it was waved over the Levites.
8:7 *use a razor over their whole body.* Symbolic of the completeness of their cleansing, as in the case of the ritual cleans-

whole [4]body and [c]wash their clothes, and they will be clean.

8 "Then let them take a [1]bull with [a]its grain offering, fine flour mixed with oil; and a second [1]bull you shall take for a sin offering.

9 "So [a]you shall present the Levites before the tent of meeting. [b]You shall also assemble the whole congregation of the sons of Israel,

10 and present the Levites before the LORD; and the sons of Israel [a]shall lay their hands on the Levites.

11 "Aaron then shall [1]present the Levites before the LORD as a [a]wave offering from the sons of Israel, that they may [2]qualify to perform the service of the LORD.

12 "Now [a]the Levites shall lay their hands on the heads of the bulls; then offer the one for a sin offering and the other for a burnt offering to the LORD, to make atonement for the Levites.

13 "You shall have the Levites stand before Aaron and before his sons so as to present them as a wave offering to the LORD.

14 "Thus you shall separate the Levites from among the sons of Israel, and [a]the Levites shall be Mine.

15 "Then after that the Levites may go in to serve the tent of meeting. But you shall cleanse them and [a]present them as a wave offering;

16 for they are [a]wholly given to Me from among the sons of Israel. I have taken them for Myself [b]instead of every first issue of the womb, the firstborn of all the sons of Israel.

17 "For [a]every firstborn among the sons of Israel is Mine, among the men and among the animals; on the day that I struck down all the firstborn in the land of Egypt I sanctified them for Myself.

18 "But I have taken the Levites instead of every firstborn among the sons of Israel.

19 "[a]I have given the Levites as [1]a gift to Aaron and to his sons from among the sons of Israel, to perform the service of the sons of Israel at the tent of meeting and to make atonement on behalf of the sons of Israel, so that there will be no [b]plague among the sons of Israel by [2]their coming near to the sanctuary."

20 Thus did Moses and Aaron and all the congregation of the sons of Israel to the Levites; according to all that the LORD had commanded Moses concerning the Levites, so the sons of Israel did to them.

21 [a]The Levites, too, purified themselves from sin and washed their clothes; and Aaron presented them as a wave offering before the LORD. Aaron also made atonement for them to cleanse them.

22 Then after that the Levites went in to perform their service in the tent of meeting before Aaron and before his sons; just as the LORD had commanded Moses concerning the Levites, so they did to them.

Retirement

23 Now the LORD spoke to Moses, saying,

24 "This is what *applies* to the Levites: from [a]twenty-five years old and upward [1]they shall enter to perform service in the work of the tent of meeting.

25 "But at the age of fifty years they shall [1]retire from service in the work and not work any more.

26 "They may, however, [1]assist their brothers in the tent of meeting, [a]to keep an obligation, but they *themselves* shall do no work. Thus you shall deal with the Levites concerning their obligations."

The Passover

9 Thus the LORD spoke to Moses in the wilderness of Sinai, in [a]the first month of the second year after they had come out of the land of Egypt, saying,

2 "Now, let the sons of Israel observe the Passover at [a]its appointed time.

3 "On the fourteenth day of this month,

7 [4]Lit *flesh* [c]Num 8:21
8 [1]Or *bull of the herd* [a]Lev 2:1; Num 15:8-10
8 [1]Or *bull of the herd*
9 [a]Ex 29:4; 40:12 [b]Lev 8:3
10 [a]Lev 1:4
11 [1]Lit *wave,* and so throughout the ch [2]Lit *be able* [a]Lev 7:30, 34
12 [a]Ex 29:10
14 [a]Num 3:12; 16:9
15 [a]Ex 29:24
16 [a]Num 3:9 [b]Ex 13:2; Num 3:12, 45
17 [a]Ex 13:2, 12, 13, 15; Luke 2:23
19 [1]Lit *given ones* [a]Num 3:9
19 [2]Lit *the sons of Israel's* [b]Num 1:53; 16:46
21 [a]Num 8:7
24 [1]Lit *he* [a]Num 4:3; 1 Chr 23:3, 24, 27
25 [1]Lit *return*
26 [1]Lit *serve* [a]Num 1:53
9:1 [a]Ex 40:2, 17; Num 1:1
2 [a]Ex 12:6; Lev 23:5; Deut 16:1, 2

ing of one cured of skin disease (Lev 14:8).

8:10 *sons of Israel shall lay their hands on the Levites.* The Levites were substitutes for the nation; by laying hands on them, the other people of the nation were acknowledging this substitutionary act (see vv. 16–18).

8:16 *to Me.* See note on 3:9.

8:19 *I have given the Levites as a gift to Aaron and to his sons.* The Levites were given to the Lord for His exclusive use (see v. 14). Now the Lord gives His Levites to the priests as their aides for the work of ministry in the tabernacle worship. *so that there will be no plague among the sons of Israel.* The Levites were a protective hedge for the community against trespassing in the sacred precincts of the tabernacle (see note on 1:53).

8:20 *according to all that the LORD had commanded Moses.* See vv. 4,22; 1:54; 2:34; 3:16,51; 4:49; 5:4; 9:5,23. The implicit obedience of Moses and the Israelites to God's commands in the areas of ritual and regimen stands in sharp contrast to the people's complaints against the Lord's loving character and to their breaches of faith that begin in ch. 11.

8:24 *twenty-five years old.* See note on 4:3. The age at which the Levites entered service was reduced to 20 by David (see 1 Chr 23:24,27), as the circumstances of their work had greatly changed by the time of the monarchy (see 1 Chr 23:26). It is difficult to imagine a change in circumstances between 4:3 and this verse, however. Therefore the rabbinical suggestion that these two verses indicate a five-year period of apprenticeship seems reasonable.

8:26 *They may . . . assist.* After a Levite had reached the mandatory retirement age of 50 (see v. 25), he was still free to assist his younger co-workers (perhaps at festivals), but he was no longer to do the difficult work he had done in his prime.

9:1–14 This unit is in four parts: (1) the command to keep the Passover (vv. 1–5); (2) the question concerning those ceremonially unclean (vv. 6–8); (3) the response of the Lord—giving permission for legitimate delay, but judgment for willful neglect (vv. 9–13); (4) the rights of the alien at Passover (v. 14). The first Passover was held in Egypt (see Ex 12). The second is here at Sinai a year later. Because of Israel's rebellion and God's judgment on her (ch. 14), Israel would not celebrate the Passover again until she entered the promised land (see Josh 5:10).

9:1 *first month of the second year.* The events of this chapter preceded the beginning of the census in ch. 1 (see 1:1).

[1]at twilight, you shall observe it at its appointed time; you shall observe it according to all its statutes and according to all its ordinances."

4 So Moses [1]told the sons of Israel to observe the Passover.

5 [a]They observed the Passover in the first *month,* on the fourteenth day of the month, at twilight, in the wilderness of Sinai; [b]according to all that the LORD had commanded Moses, so the sons of Israel did.

6 But there were *some* men who were [a]unclean because of *the* [1]dead person, so that they could not observe Passover on that day; so [b]they came before Moses and Aaron on that day.

7 Those men said to him, "*Though* we are unclean because of *the* [1]dead person, why are we restrained from presenting the offering of the LORD at its appointed time among the sons of Israel?"

8 Moses therefore said to them, "[1a]Wait, and I will listen to what the LORD will command concerning you."

9 Then the LORD spoke to Moses, saying,

10 "Speak to the sons of Israel, saying, 'If any one of you or of your generations becomes unclean because of a *dead* [1]person, or is on a distant journey, he may, however, observe the Passover to the LORD.

11 'In the second month on the [a]fourteenth day at twilight, they shall observe it; they [b]shall eat it with unleavened bread and bitter herbs.

12 'They [a]shall leave none of it until morning, [b]nor break a bone of it; according to all the statute of the Passover they shall observe it.

13 '[a]But the man who is clean and is not on a journey, and yet [1]neglects to observe the Passover, that [2]person shall then be cut off from his people, for he did not present the offering of the LORD at its appointed time. That man [b]will bear his sin.

14 '[a]If an alien sojourns among you and [1]observes the Passover to the LORD, according to the statute of the Passover and according to its ordinance, so he shall do; you shall have [b]one statute, both for the alien and for the native of the land.' "

3 [1]Lit *between the two evenings,* and so throughout the ch
4 [1]Lit *spoke to*
5 [a]Josh 5:10 [b]Ex 12:1-13
6 [1]Lit *soul of man* [a]Num 5:2; 19:11-22 [b]Ex 18:15; Num 27:2
7 [1]Lit *soul of man*
8 [1]Lit *Stand* [a]Ex 18:15; Ps 85:8
10 [1]Lit *soul*
11 [a]2 Chr 30:2, 15 [b]Ex 12:8
12 [a]Ex 12:10 [b]Ex 12:46; John 19:36
13 [1]Or *ceases* [2]Lit *soul* [a]Gen 17:14; Ex 12:15, 47 [b]Num 5:31
14 [1]Or *would observe* [a]Ex 12:48
14 [b]Ex 12:49; Lev 24:22; Num 15:15, 16, 29
15 [a]Ex 40:2, 17 [b]Ex 40:34 [c]Num 17:7 [d]Ex 13:21, 22
16 [a]Ex 40:34; Neh 9:12
17 [a]Ex 40:36-38; Num 10:11, 12
18 [1]Lit *mouth* [a]1 Cor 10:1
19 [1]Lit *and the*
20 [1]Lit *it was that* [2]Lit *mouth* [a]Ps 48:14; Prov 3:5, 6
21 [1]Lit *it was that* [2]Lit *was*
22 [a]Ex 40:36, 37
23 [1]Lit *mouth* [a]Ps 73:24; 107:7; Is 63:14

The Cloud on the Tabernacle

15 Now on [a]the day that the tabernacle was erected [b]the cloud covered the tabernacle, the [c]tent of the testimony, and [d]in the evening it was like the appearance of fire over the tabernacle, until morning.

16 So it was continuously; [a]the cloud would cover it *by day,* and the appearance of fire by night.

17 [a]Whenever the cloud was lifted from over the tent, afterward the sons of Israel would then set out; and in the place where the cloud settled down, there the sons of Israel would camp.

18 At the [1]command of the LORD the sons of Israel would set out, and at the [1]command of the LORD they would camp; [a]as long as the cloud settled over the tabernacle, they remained camped.

19 Even when the cloud lingered over the tabernacle for many days, [1]the sons of Israel would keep the LORD'S charge and not set out.

20 If [1]sometimes the cloud remained a few days over the tabernacle, [a]according to the [2]command of the LORD they remained camped. Then according to the [2]command of the LORD they set out.

21 If [1]sometimes the cloud [2]remained from evening until morning, when the cloud was lifted in the morning, they would move out; or *if it remained* in the daytime and at night, whenever the cloud was lifted, they would set out.

22 Whether it was two days or a month or a year that the cloud lingered over the tabernacle, staying above it, the sons of Israel remained camped and did not set out; but [a]when it was lifted, they did set out.

23 [a]At the [1]command of the LORD they camped, and at the [1]command of the LORD they set out; they kept the LORD'S charge, according to the [1]command of the LORD through Moses.

9:3 *twilight.* Traditional Jewish practice regards this period as the end of one day and the beginning of the next.

9:7 *why are we restrained from presenting the offering of the LORD. . . ?* Those with ceremonial uncleanness had a keen desire to worship the Lord "in spirit and truth" (John 4:24).

9:10 *he may . . . observe.* God's gracious provision for these people was an alternative day one month later (v. 11) so that they would not be excluded totally from the Passover celebration. The Lord thus demonstrates the reality of the distance that uncleanness brings between a believer and his (or her) participation in the worship of the community, but He also provides a merciful alternative.

9:12 *nor break a bone of it.* When Jesus ("our Passover," 1 Cor 5:7; cf. John 1:29) was crucified, it was reported that none of His bones was broken, in fulfillment of Scripture (John 19:36). See also Ex 12:46; Ps 34:20.

9:13 *neglects to observe . . . cut off.* The NT also issues grave warnings concerning the abuse or misuse of the celebration of the Lord's Supper (1 Cor 11:28–30). See note on Ex 12:15.

9:14 *alien.* Must first be circumcised before participating in the Passover celebration (Ex 12:48).

9:15 *cloud covered the tabernacle.* See notes on Ex 13:21; 40:34. The cloud was the visible symbol of the Lord's presence hovering above the tabernacle. That this was no ordinary cloud is attested not only by its spontaneous appearance at the completion of the setting up of the tabernacle, but also by the fact that at night it had the appearance of fire. The Lord also directed the movements of His people by means of the cloud (vv. 17–18).

9:18 *At the command of the LORD.* The lifting and settling of the cloud are identified with the Lord's command.

9:23 *kept the LORD'S charge.* The repetitious nature of vv. 15–23 enhances the expectation of continued complete obedience to the Lord's direction of Israel's movements through the wilderness. The role of Moses is mentioned for balance: Moses was

The Silver Trumpets

10 The LORD spoke further to Moses, saying,

2 "Make yourself two trumpets of silver, of hammered work you shall make them; and you shall use them for [a]summoning the congregation and for having the camps set out.

3 "[a]When both are blown, all the congregation shall gather themselves to you at the doorway of the tent of meeting.

4 "Yet if *only* one is blown, then the [a]leaders, the heads of the [1]divisions of Israel, shall assemble before you.

5 "But when you blow an alarm, the camps that are pitched [a]on the east side shall set out.

6 "When you blow an alarm the second time, the camps that are pitched on [a]the south side shall set out; an alarm is to be blown for them to set out.

7 "When convening the assembly, however, you shall blow without [a]sounding an alarm.

8 "[a]The priestly sons of Aaron, moreover, shall blow the trumpets; and [1]this shall be for you a perpetual statute throughout your generations.

9 "When you go to war in your land against the adversary who [a]attacks you, then you shall sound an alarm with the trumpets, that you may be [b]remembered before the LORD your God, and be saved from your enemies.

10 "Also in the day of your gladness and in your appointed [1]feasts, and on the first *days* of your months, [a]you shall blow the trumpets over your burnt offerings, and over the sacrifices of your peace offerings; and they shall be as a reminder of you before your God. I am the LORD your God."

The Tribes Leave Sinai

11 Now in [a]the second year, in the second month, on the twentieth of the month, the cloud was lifted from over the [1]tabernacle of the testimony;

12 and the sons of Israel set out on [a]their journeys from the wilderness of Sinai. Then the cloud settled down in the [b]wilderness of Paran.

13 [a]So they moved out for the first time according to the [1]commandment of the LORD through Moses.

14 The standard of the camp of the sons of Judah, according to their armies, [a]set out first, with Nahshon the son of Amminadab, over its army,

15 and Nethanel the son of Zuar, over the tribal army of the sons of Issachar;

16 and Eliab the son of Helon over the tribal army of the sons of Zebulun.

17 [a]Then the tabernacle was taken down; and the sons of Gershon and the sons of Merari, who were carrying the tabernacle, set out.

18 Next [a]the standard of the camp of Reuben, according to their armies, set out with Elizur the son of Shedeur, over its army,

19 and Shelumiel the son of Zurishaddai over the tribal army of the sons of Simeon,

20 and Eliasaph the son of Deuel was over the tribal army of the sons of Gad.

21 [a]Then the Kohathites set out, carrying the holy *objects;* and [b]the tabernacle was set up before their arrival.

22 [a]Next the standard of the camp of the sons of Ephraim, according to their armies, was set out, with Elishama the son of Ammihud over its army,

23 and Gamaliel the son of Pedahzur over the tribal army of the sons of Manasseh;

24 and Abidan the son of Gideoni over the tribal army of the sons of Benjamin.

25 [a]Then the standard of the camp of the sons of Dan, according to their armies, *which formed* the [b]rear guard for all the camps, set out, with Ahiezer the son of Ammishaddai over its army,

10:2 [a]Is 1:13
3 [a]Jer 4:5; Joel 2:15
4 [1]Lit *thousands;* or *clans* [a]Ex 18:21; Num 1:16; 7:2
5 [a]Num 10:14
6 [a]Num 10:18
7 [a]Joel 2:1
8 [1]Lit *it* [a]Num 31:6; Josh 6:4; 2 Chr 13:12
9 [a]Judg 2:18; 1 Sam 10:18; Ps 106:42 [b]Gen 8:1; Ps 106:4
10 [1]Or *times* [a]Ps 81:3-5
11 [a]Ex 40:17
11 [1]Lit *dwelling place,* and so throughout the ch
12 [a]Ex 40:36 [b]Gen 21:21; Num 12:16
13 [1]Lit *mouth* [a]Deut 1:6
14 [a]Num 2:3-9
17 [a]Num 4:21-32
18 [a]Num 2:10-16
21 [a]Num 4:4-20 [b]Num 10:17
22 [a]Num 2:18-24
25 [a]Num 2:25-31 [b]Josh 6:9, 13

the Lord's agent, who interpreted the movement of the cloud as signaling the movement of the people. The tragedy of their subsequent disobedience (ch. 11) is heightened by this paragraph on their obedience.

10:2 *trumpets.* Long, straight, slender metal tubes with flared ends. They were blown for order and discipline.

10:3 *blown.* Not only for assembling but also for marching (vv. 5–6), battle (v. 9) and festivals (v. 10). Since different signals were used (v. 7), a guild of priestly musicians was developed (v. 8). See Josh 6:4 for the use of seven trumpets of rams' horns (Hebrew *shophar*) in the battle of Jericho.

10:10 *in your appointed feasts . . . blow the trumpets.* As an introit to prepare the people for communion with God. Later, David expanded the instruments to include the full orchestra in the worship of the Lord (see, e.g., 1 Chr 25), but he maintained the playing of the silver trumpets regularly before the ark of the covenant (1 Chr 16:6).

10:11–28 The structure of this section is: (1) v. 11, time frame; (2) vv. 12–13, introductory summary of setting out; (3) vv. 14–17, setting out of the tribes led by Judah (see 2:3–9); (4) vv. 18–21, setting out of the tribes led by Reuben (see 2:10–16); (5) vv. 22–24, setting out of the tribes led by Ephraim (see 2:18–24); (6) vv. 25–27, setting out of the tribes led by Dan (see 2:25–31); (7) v. 28, concluding summary of the line of march.

10:11 *second month . . . twentieth of the month.* After 11 months in the region of Mount Sinai, the people set out for the promised land, led by the cloud. This verse begins the second great section of the book of Numbers (10:11–22:1). Israel leaves on a journey that in a few months should have led to the conquest of Canaan.

10:14–27 The names of the leaders of the 12 tribes are given for the fourth time in the book (see 1:5–15; 2:3–31; 7:12–83). The order of the line of march is essentially the same as that in ch. 2. The new details are that the Gershonites and Merarites, who carry the tabernacle, follow the triad of the Judah tribes (v. 17), and the Kohathites, who carry the holy things, follow the triad of the Reuben tribes (v. 21) (see diagram, p. 179).

10:14 *standard.* As in 2:3,10,18,25, each of the four triads of tribes had a standard or banner for rallying and organization.

26 and Pagiel the son of Ochran over the
tribal army of the sons of Asher;
27 and Ahira the son of Enan over the tribal army of the sons of Naphtali.
28 [1]This was the order of march of the
sons of Israel by their armies as they set out.
29 Then Moses said to [a]Hobab the son of
[b]Reuel the Midianite, Moses' father-in-law,
"We are setting out to the place of which the
LORD said, '[c]I will give it to you'; [d]come with
us and we will do you good, for the LORD
[e]has [1]promised good concerning Israel."
30 But he said to him, "[a]I will not come, but
rather will go to my *own* land and relatives."
31 Then he said, "Please do not leave us,
inasmuch as you know where we should
camp in the wilderness, and you [a]will be as
eyes for us.
32 "So it will be, if you go with us, that
[1][a]whatever good the LORD [2]does for us, [b]we
will [3]do for you."
33 [a]Thus they set out from the mount of
the LORD three days' journey, with [b]the ark of
the covenant of the LORD journeying in front
of them for the [1]three days, to seek out [c]a
resting place for them.
34 [a]The cloud of the LORD was over them
by day when they set out from the camp.
35 Then it came about when the ark set
out that Moses said,
"[a]Rise up, O LORD!
And let Your enemies be scattered,
And let those [b]who hate You flee
[1]before You."
36 When it came to rest, he said,
"[a]Return, O LORD,
To the myriad [b]thousands of Israel."

28 [1]Lit *These are the settings out of the sons*
29 [1]Lit *spoken* [a]Judg 4:11 [b]Ex 2:18; 3:1; 18:12 [c]Gen 12:7; Ex 6:4-8 [d]Ps 95:1-7; 100:1-5 [e]Deut 4:40; 30:5
30 [a]Judg 1:16; Matt 21:28, 29
31 [a]Job 29:15
32 [1]Lit *that good which* [2]Lit *does good* [3]Lit *do good* [a]Ps 22:27-31; 67:5-7 [b]Lev 19:34; Deut 10:18
33 [1]Lit *three days' journey* [a]Num 10:12 [b]Deut 1:33 [c]Is 11:10
34 [a]Num 9:15-23
35 [1]Or *from Your presence* [a]Ps 68:1, 2; Is 17:12-14 [b]Deut 7:10; 32:41
36 [a]Is 63:17 [b]Deut 1:10

11:1 [a]Num 14:2; 16:11; 17:5 [b]Num 11:18; 14:28
2 [1]Lit *sank down* [a]Num 12:11, 13; 21:7
3 [1]I.e. burning [a]Deut 9:22
4 [1]Lit *desired a desire* [2]Lit *flesh,* and so throughout the ch [a]Ex 12:38; 1 Cor 10:6 [b]Ps 78:20
5 [a]Ex 16:3
6 [1]Lit *soul is dried up* [2]Lit *for our eyes* [a]Num 21:5
7 [a]Ex 16:31 [b]Gen 2:12
8 [1]Lit *with* [2]Lit *juice of oil*
9 [1]Lit *on* [a]Ex 16:13, 14

The People Complain

11 Now the people became like [a]those
who complain of adversity [b]in the hearing of the LORD; and when the LORD heard *it,*
His anger was kindled, and the fire of the
LORD burned among them and consumed
some of the outskirts of the camp.
2 [a]The people therefore cried out to
Moses, and Moses prayed to the LORD and
the fire [1]died out.
3 So the name of that place was called
[1][a]Taberah, because the fire of the LORD
burned among them.
4 The [a]rabble who were among them
[1]had greedy desires; and also the sons of
Israel wept again and said, "[b]Who will give
us [2]meat to eat?
5 "[a]We remember the fish which we used
to eat free in Egypt, the cucumbers and the
melons and the leeks and the onions and the
garlic,
6 but now [a]our [1]appetite is gone. There is
nothing at all [2]to look at except this manna."
7 [a]Now the manna was like coriander
seed, and its appearance like that of [b]bdelli-
um.
8 The people would go about and gather
it and grind *it* [1]between two millstones or
beat *it* in the mortar, and boil *it* in the pot
and make cakes with it; and its taste was as
the taste of [2]cakes baked with oil.
9 [a]When the dew fell on the camp at
night, the manna would fall [1]with it.

10:29 *Hobab the son of Reuel.* Thus Hobab was Moses' brother-in-law. *Reuel.* Jethro (see Ex 2:18; 3:1).
10:31 *be as eyes.* Judg 1:16 indicates that Hobab acceded to Moses' request.
10:33 *three days' journey.* Because of the huge numbers of people in the tribes of Israel, and because this was their first organized march, it is not likely that this first journey covered much territory.
10:35–36 Reinforces the portrayal of Israel as the Lord's army on the march, with the Lord in the vanguard.
10:35 Later used in the opening words of a psalm celebrating God's triumphal march from Sinai to Jerusalem (see Ps 68:1).
11:1 *people . . . who complain.* The first ten chapters of Numbers repeatedly emphasize the complete obedience of Moses and the people to the dictates of the Lord. But only three days into their march, the people reverted to disloyal complaints. They had expressed the same complaints a year earlier only three days after their deliverance at the waters of the "Red Sea" (Ex 15:22–27) and subsequently had complained about manna (Ex 16) and a lack of water (Ex 17:1–7). *fire of the LORD.* By God's mercy, this purging fire was limited to the outskirts of the camp. The phrase sometimes refers to fire ignited by lightning (as probably in 1 Kin 18:38).
11:3 *Taberah.* Means "burning."
11:4 *rabble.* An apt term for the non-Israelite mixed group of people who followed the Israelites out of Egypt, pointing to a recurring source of complaints and trouble in the camp. Those who did not know the Lord and His mercies incited those who did know Him to rebel against Him. *Who will give us meat to eat?* As in Ex 16, the people began to complain about their diet, forgetting what God had done for them (see Ps 106:14). Certainly meat was not their common fare when they were slaves in Egypt. Now that they were in a new type of distress, the people romanticized the past and minimized its discomforts.
11:5 *fish . . . cucumbers . . . garlic.* Suggestive of the varieties of foods available in Egypt, in contrast to the diet of manna in the wilderness.
11:7 *manna.* Several naturalistic explanations for the manna have been given. For example, some equate it with the sticky and often granular honeydew that is excreted in Sinai in early June by various scale insects and that solidifies rapidly through evaporation. But no naturally occurring substance fits all the data of the text, and several factors suggest that manna was in fact the Lord's unique provision for His people in the wilderness: 1. The meaning of the Hebrew word for "manna" suggests that it was something unknown by the people at the time (see note on Ex 16:15). 2. The appearance and taste of the manna (see Ex 16:31) suggest that it is not something experienced by other peoples in other times. 3. The daily abundance of the manna and its regular periodic surge and slump (double amounts on the sixth day but none on the seventh day, Ex 16:22,27) hardly fit a natural phenomenon. 4. Its availability in ample supply for the entire wilderness experience, no matter where the people were (Ex 16:35), argues against a natural substance. 5. The keeping of a sample of the manna in the ark for future generations (Ex 16:33–34) suggests that it was a unique food.

The Complaint of Moses

10 Now Moses heard the people weeping
throughout their families, each man at the
doorway of his tent; and the anger of the
LORD was kindled greatly, and [1]Moses was
displeased.
11 [a]So Moses said to the LORD, "Why have
You [1]been so hard on Your servant? And why
have I not found favor in Your sight, that You
have laid the burden of all this people on me?
12 "Was it I who conceived all this people?
Was it I who brought them forth, that You
should say to me, 'Carry them in your bosom
as a [1a]nurse carries a nursing infant, to the
land which [b]You swore to their fathers'?
13 "Where am I to get meat to give to [a]all
this people? For they weep before me, saying, 'Give us meat that we may eat!'
14 "[a]I alone am not able to carry all this
people, because it is too [1]burdensome for
me.
15 "[a]So if You are going to deal thus with
me, please kill me at once, if I have found
favor in Your sight, and do not let me see my
wretchedness."

Seventy Elders to Assist

16 The LORD therefore said to Moses,
"Gather for Me [a]seventy men from the elders
of Israel, [b]whom you know to be the elders
of the people and their officers and bring
them to the tent of meeting, and let them
take their stand there with you.
17 "[a]Then I will come down and speak
with you there, and I will take of [b]the Spirit
who is upon you, and will put *Him* upon
them; and they shall bear the burden of the
people with you, so that you will not bear *it*
all alone.
18 "Say to the people, '[a]Consecrate yourselves for tomorrow, and you shall eat meat;
for you have wept [b]in the ears of the LORD,
saying, "Oh that someone would give us
meat to eat! For we were well-off in Egypt."
Therefore the LORD will give you meat and
you shall eat.
19 'You shall eat, not one day, nor two
days, nor five days, nor ten days, nor twenty
days,
20 [1]but a whole month, until it comes out
of your nostrils and becomes loathsome to
you; because [a]you have rejected the LORD
who is among you and have wept before
Him, saying, "Why did we ever leave
Egypt?" ' "
21 But Moses said, "The people, among
whom I am, are 600,000 on foot; yet You
have said, 'I will give them meat, so that
they may eat for a whole month.'
22 "Should flocks and herds be slaughtered
for them, to be sufficient for them? Or should
all the fish of the sea be gathered together
for them, to be sufficient for them?"
23 The LORD said to Moses, "Is [a]the LORD's
[1]power limited? Now you shall see whether
[b]My word will [2]come true for you or not."
24 So Moses went out and [a]told the people the words of the LORD. Also, he gathered
seventy men of the elders of the people, and
stationed them around the tent.
25 [a]Then the LORD came down in the
cloud and spoke to him; and He took of the
Spirit who was upon him and placed *Him*
upon the seventy elders. And when the Spirit rested upon them, they prophesied. But
they did not do *it* again.
26 But two men had remained in the camp;
the name of one was Eldad and the name of
the [1]other Medad. And [a]the Spirit rested upon

10 [1]Lit *it was evil in Moses' sight* **11** [1]Lit *dealt ill with* [a]Ex 5:22; Deut 1:12 **12** [1]Or *foster-father* [a]2 Kin 10:1, 5; Is 49:23 [b]Gen 24:7; Ex 13:5, 11; 33:1 **13** [a]Num 11:21, 22; John 6:5-9 **14** [1]Lit *heavy* [a]Ex 18:18; Deut 1:12 **15** [a]Ex 32:32 **16** [a]Ex 24:1, 9 [b]Ex 18:25 **17** [a]Num 11:25 [b]1 Sam 10:6; Joel 2:28

18 [a]Ex 19:10, 22 [b]Num 11:1 **20** [1]Lit *until* [a]Josh 24:27; 1 Sam 10:19 **23** [1]Lit *hand short* [2]Lit *befall you* [a]Is 50:2; 59:1 [b]Ezek 12:25; 24:14 **24** [a]Num 11:16 **25** [a]Num 11:17; 12:5 **26** [1]Lit *second* [a]Num 24:2; 1 Sam 10:6; 2 Chr 15:1; Neh 9:30

11:10 *the anger of the LORD was kindled greatly.* The rejection of His gracious gift of heavenly food (called "bread from heaven" in Ex 16:4) angered the Lord. God had said that the reception of the manna by the people would be a significant test of their obedience (Ex 16:4). In view of the good things He was to give them (10:32), the people were expected to receive each day's supply of manna as a gracious gift of a merciful God, and a promise of abundance to come. In spurning the manna, the people had spurned the Lord. They had failed the test of faith. *Moses was displeased.* The people's reaction to God's provision of manna was troubling to Moses as well. Instead of asking the Lord to understand the substance of their complaint, Moses asked Him why he was given such an ungrateful people to lead.
11:11–15 A prayer of distress and complaint, filled with urgency, irony and passion.
11:12 *Was it I who conceived all these people?* The implication is that the Lord conceived the people of Israel, that He was their nurse and that their promises were His. Moses asks that he be relieved of his mediatorial office, for "it is too burdensome for me" (v. 14; cf. Elijah, 1 Kin 19). Even death, Moses asserts (v. 15), would be preferable to facing the continuing complaints of the people.
11:16–34 The Lord's response to the great distress of His prophet was twofold—mercy and curse: 1. There was mercy to Moses in that his responsibility was now to be shared by 70 leaders (vv. 16–17). 2. There was a curse on the people that was analogous to their complaint: They asked for meat and would now become sick with meat (vv. 18–34).
11:18 *you shall eat meat.* Their distress at the lack of variety in the daily manna had led the people to challenge the Lord's goodness. They had wailed for meat. Now they were going to get their fill of meat, so much that it would make them physically ill (v. 20).
11:20 *you have rejected the LORD.* The principal issue was not meat at all, but a failure to demonstrate proper gratitude to the Lord, who was in their midst and who was their constant source of good.
11:21 *people . . . are 600,000 on foot.* The numbers are consistent: A marching force of this size suggests a total population of over 2,000,000 (see note on 1:46). Moses' distress at providing meat for this immense number of people (v. 22) is nearly comical—the task is impossible.
11:23 *Is the LORD's power limited?* The human impossibility is an occasion for demonstrating the Lord's power.
11:25 *they prophesied.* Probably means that they gave ecstatic expression to an intense religious experience (see 1 Sam 10:5–6; 18:10; 19:20–24; 1 Kin 18:29). *But they did not do it again.* It seems that the temporary gift of prophecy to the elders was primarily to establish their credentials as Spirit-empowered leaders.

them (now they were among those who had
been registered, but had not gone out to the
tent), and they prophesied in the camp.
27 So a young man ran and told Moses
and said, "Eldad and Medad are prophesying in the camp."
28 Then [a]Joshua the son of Nun, the
attendant of Moses from his youth, said,
"[b]Moses, my lord, restrain them."
29 But Moses said to him, "Are you jealous for my sake? [a]Would that all the LORD's
people were prophets, that the LORD would
put His Spirit upon them!"
30 Then Moses [1]returned to the camp,
both he and the elders of Israel.

The Quail and the Plague

31 [a]Now there went forth a wind from the
LORD and it brought quail from the sea, and
let *them* fall beside the camp, about a day's
journey on this side and a day's journey on
the other side, all around the camp and
[1]about two [2]cubits *deep* on the surface of the
ground.
32 The people [1]spent all day and all night
and all the next day, and gathered the quail
(he who gathered least gathered ten
[2a]homers) and they spread *them* out for
themselves all around the camp.
33 [a]While the meat was still between their
teeth, before it was chewed, the anger of the
LORD was kindled against the people, and the
LORD struck the people with a very severe
plague.
34 So the name of that place was called
[1a]Kibroth-hattaavah, because there they
buried the people who had been greedy.
35 From Kibroth-hattaavah [a]the people set
out for Hazeroth, and they [1]remained at
Hazeroth.

28 [a]Ex 33:11; Josh 1:1 [b]Mark 9:38-40
29 [a]1 Cor 14:5
30 [1]Lit *removed himself*
31 [1]Or from *about two cubits above* [2]I.e. One cubit equals approx 18 in. [a]Ex 16:13; Ps 78:26-28; 105:40
32 [1]Lit *rose* [2]I.e. One homer equals approx 11 bu [a]Ezek 45:11
33 [a]Ps 78:29-31; 106:15
34 [1]I.e. the graves of greediness [a]Deut 9:22
35 [1]Lit *were* [a]Num 33:17

The Murmuring of Miriam and Aaron

12 Then Miriam and Aaron spoke against
Moses because of the Cushite woman
whom he had married (for he had married a
[a]Cushite woman);
2 [a]and they said, "Has the LORD indeed
spoken only through Moses? Has He not spoken through us as well?" And the LORD heard
it.
3 (Now the man Moses was [a]very humble, more than any man who was on the face
of the earth.)
4 Suddenly the LORD said to Moses and
Aaron and to Miriam, "You three come out to
the tent of meeting." So the three of them
came out.
5 [a]Then the LORD came down in a pillar
of cloud and stood at the doorway of the
tent, and He called [1]Aaron and Miriam.
When they had both come forward,
6 He said,
"Hear now My words:
If there is a prophet among you,
I, the LORD, shall make Myself known
to him in a [a]vision.
I shall speak with him in a [b]dream.
7 "Not so, with [a]My servant Moses,
[b]He is faithful in all My household;
8 [a]With him I speak mouth to mouth,
Even openly, and not in dark sayings,
And he beholds [b]the form of the LORD.
Why then were you not afraid
To speak against My servant, against
Moses?"
9 So the anger of the LORD burned against
them and [a]He departed.
10 But when the cloud had withdrawn
from over the tent, behold, [a]Miriam *was*
leprous, as [b]*white as* snow. As Aaron

12:1 [a]Ex 2:21
2 [a]Num 16:3
3 [a]Matt 11:29
5 [1]Or *"Aaron and Miriam!"* [a]Ex 19:9; 34:5
6 [a]Gen 46:2; 1 Sam 3:15 [b]Gen 31:11; 1 Kin 3:5, 15
7 [a]Josh 1:1 [b]Heb 3:2, 5
8 [a]Deut 34:10; Hos 12:13 [b]Ex 20:4; 24:10, 11; Deut 5:8; Ps 17:15
9 [a]Gen 17:22; 18:33
10 [a]Deut 24:9 [b]Ex 4:6; 2 Kin 5:27

11:29 *Are you jealous for my sake?* Here the true spirit of Moses is demonstrated. Rather than being threatened by the public demonstration of the gifts of the Spirit by Eldad and Medad, Moses desired that all God's people might have the full gifts of the Spirit (cf. Phil 1:15–18). This verse is a fitting introduction to the inexcusable challenge to Moses' leadership in ch. 12.

11:31–32 Cf. the great provision of Jesus in the feeding of the 5,000 (John 6:5–13) and the 4,000 (Matt 15:29–39). In those cases the feeding was a demonstration of God's grace; in this instance it was of God's wrath.

11:34 *Kibroth-hattaavah.* Means "graves of greediness." These graves marked the death camp of those who had turned against the food of the Lord's mercy.

12:1 *Cushite woman . . . he had married.* Cush was the first son of Ham, the father of the southernmost peoples known to the Hebrews (Gen 10:6–7), living in the southern Nile valley. Moses' wife Zipporah may be referred to here (see Ex 2:15–22); if so, the term "Cushite" is used in contempt of her Midianite ancestry. It is more likely, however, that the reference is to a new wife taken by Moses, perhaps after the death of his first wife. The attack on the woman was a pretext; its focus was the prophetic gift of Moses and his special relationship with the Lord (v. 2).

12:2 *Has He not spoken through us as well?* Of course He had. Mic 6:4 speaks of Moses, Aaron and Miriam as God's gracious provision for Israel. The prophetic gifting of the 70 elders (11:24–30) seems to have been the immediate provocation for the attack of Miriam and Aaron on their brother.

12:3 Perhaps a later addition to the text, alerting the reader to the great unfairness of the charge of arrogance against Moses.

12:4 *Suddenly.* The abruptness of the Lord's response instilled terror (see Job 22:10; Is 47:11; Jer 4:20).

12:5 *came down.* Often used of divine manifestations. In 11:25 the Lord came down in grace; here and in Gen 11:5 He came down in judgment. In a sense every theophany (appearance of God) is a picture and promise of the grand theophany, the incarnation of Jesus, both in grace and in judgment.

12:6–8 The poetic cast of these words adds a sense of solemnity to them. The point of the poem is clear: All true prophetic vision is from the Lord, but in the case of Moses his position and faithfulness enhance his special relationship with the Lord.

12:7 *My servant.* See notes on Ex 14:31; Ps 18 title; Is 41:8–9; 42:1. *My household.* The household of God's people Israel.

12:8 *openly . . . not in dark sayings.* God's revelation does not come with equal clarity to His servants. There may be oracles of the Lord that a prophet might not fully understand at the time; to him they may be riddles and mysteries (cf. 1 Pet 1:10–11). But to Moses, God spoke with special clarity, as though face to face (see also Deut 34:10).

12:10 *leprous.* See note on Lev 13:2. Miriam, the principal offender against her brother Moses, has become an outcast, as

turned toward Miriam, behold, she *was*
leprous.
11 Then Aaron said to Moses, “Oh, my
lord, I beg you, [a]do not account *this* sin to
us, in which we have acted foolishly and in
which we have sinned.
12 “Oh, do not let her be like one dead,
whose flesh is half eaten away when he
comes from his mother’s womb!”
13 Moses cried out to the LORD, saying, “O
God, [a]heal her, I pray!”
14 But the LORD said to Moses, “If her
father had but [a]spit in her face, would she
not bear her shame for seven days? Let her
be shut up for seven days [b]outside the camp,
and afterward she may be received again.”
15 So [a]Miriam was shut up outside the
camp for seven days, and the people did not
move on until Miriam was received again.
16 Afterward, however, the people moved
out from Hazeroth and camped in the
wilderness of Paran.

Spies View the Land

13 Then [a]the LORD spoke to Moses saying,
2 “[a]Send out for yourself men so that
they may spy out the land of Canaan, which
I am going to give to the sons of Israel; you
shall send a man from each of their fathers’
tribes, every one a leader among them.”
3 So Moses sent them from the wilderness of Paran at the [1]command of the LORD,
all of them men who were heads of the sons
of Israel.
4 These then *were* their names: from the
tribe of Reuben, Shammua the son of Zaccur;
5 from the tribe of Simeon, Shaphat the
son of Hori;
6 from the tribe of Judah, [a]Caleb the son
of Jephunneh;
7 from the tribe of Issachar, Igal the son
of Joseph;
8 from the tribe of Ephraim, [a]Hoshea the
son of Nun;
9 from the tribe of Benjamin, Palti the
son of Raphu;
10 from the tribe of Zebulun, Gaddiel the
son of Sodi;
11 from the tribe of Joseph, from the tribe
of Manasseh, Gaddi the son of Susi;
12 from the tribe of Dan, Ammiel the son
of Gemalli;
13 from the tribe of Asher, Sethur the son
of Michael;
14 from the tribe of Naphtali, Nahbi the
son of Vophsi;
15 from the tribe of Gad, Geuel the son of
Machi.
16 These are the names of the men whom
Moses sent to spy out the land; but Moses
called [a]Hoshea the son of Nun, Joshua.
17 When Moses sent them to spy out the
land of Canaan, he said to them, “Go up
[1]there into [a]the [2]Negev; then go up into the
hill country.
18 “See what the land is like, and whether
the people who live in it are strong *or* weak,
whether they are few or many.
19 “How is the land in which they live, is it
good or bad? And how are the cities in which
they live, are *they* [1]like *open* camps or with
fortifications?
20 “[a]How is the land, is it fat or lean? Are
there trees in it or not? [1]Make an [b]effort then
to get some of the fruit of the land.” Now the
time was the time of the first ripe grapes.
21 So they went up and spied out the land
from [a]the wilderness of Zin as far as Rehob,
[1][b]at Lebo-hamath.
22 When they had gone up into [a]the Negev, [1]they came to Hebron where [b]Ahiman,
Sheshai and Talmai, the [2]descendants of
[c]Anak were. (Now Hebron was built seven
years before [d]Zoan in Egypt.)

11 [a]2 Sam 19:19; 24:10
13 [a]Ps 30:2; 41:4; Is 30:26; Jer 17:14
14 [a]Deut 25:9; Job 17:6; 30:10; Is 50:6 [b]Num 5:1-4
15 [a]Deut 24:9
13:1 [a]Deut 1:22, 23
2 [a]Deut 1:22; 9:23
3 [1]Lit *mouth*
6 [a]Num 14:6, 30; Josh 14:6
8 [a]Num 13:16; Deut 32:44
16 [a]Num 13:8; Deut 32:44
17 [1]Lit *here* [2]I.e. South country, and so throughout the ch [a]Gen 12:9; 13:1, 3
19 [1]Lit *in*
20 [1]Lit *Use your strength* [a]Deut 1:24, 25 [b]Deut 31:6, 23
21 [1]Or *to the entrance of Hamath* [a]Num 20:1; 27:14; 33:36 [b]Josh 13:5
22 [1]Lit Most mss read *one came* [2]Lit *children* [a]Num 13:17 [b]Josh 15:14 [c]Num 13:28, 33 [d]Ps 78:12, 43

---

she now suffers from a skin disease that would exclude her from the community of Israel (see 5:1–4).

12:11 *my lord, I beg you.* Aaron’s repentance for the sin of presumption is touching, both in its intensity and in his concern for his (and Moses’) sister.

12:14 *shame for seven days.* An act of public rebuke (see Deut 25:9) demands a period of public shame. A period of seven days was a standard time for uncleanness occasioned by being in contact with a dead body (see 19:11,14,16).

12:16 *wilderness of Paran.* The southernmost region of the promised land. The people’s opportunity to conquer the land was soon to come.

13:2 *spy out the land of Canaan.* The use of spies was a common practice in the ancient Near East (see note on Josh 2:1–24). From Deut 1:22–23 it appears that this directive of the Lord was in response to the people’s request. Thus the very sending of the spies was an expression of God’s grace.

13:4–15 The names listed here are different from those in chs. 1–2; 7; 10. Presumably the tribal leaders in the four earlier lists were older men. The task for the spies called for men who were younger and more robust, but no less respected by their peers.

13:16 *Moses called Hoshea the son of Nun, Joshua.* A parenthetical statement anticipating the later prominence of Joshua. The reader is alerted to the significance of this name in the list of the spies; here is a man of destiny. Hoshea means “salvation”; Joshua means “The LORD saves” (“Jesus” is the Greek form of Hebrew “Joshua”).

13:17–20 Moses’ instruction to the 12 spies was comprehensive; a thorough report of the land and its produce and the peoples and their towns was required in their reconnaissance mission.

13:21 *spied out the land.* The journey of the spies began in the southernmost extremity of the land (the wilderness of Zin) and took them to the northernmost point (Rehob, near Lebo Hamath; see 34:8). This journey of about 250 miles each way took them 40 days (v. 25), perhaps a round number.

13:22 *Hebron.* The first city the spies came to in Canaan. The parenthetical comment about the city’s being built seven years before Zoan in Egypt may have been prompted by their amazement at the size and fortifications of the city that was so closely associated with the lives of their ancestors four centuries before this time (see Gen 13:14–18; 14:13; 23:2; 25:9; 35:27–29; 50:13). In the stories of the ancestors of their people, Hebron had not been a great city, but a dwelling and trading place for shepherds and herdsmen. *descendants of Anak.* Three notable Anak descendants are mentioned as living at Hebron. The Ana-

23 Then they came to the [1]valley of [2][a]Esh-
col and from there cut down a branch with a
single cluster of grapes; and they carried it
on a pole between two *men*, with some of
the pomegranates and the figs.
24 That place was called the valley of
[1]Eshcol, because of the cluster which the
sons of Israel cut down from there.

The Spies' Reports

25 When they returned from spying out
the land, at the end of forty days,
26 they proceeded to come to Moses and
Aaron and to all the congregation of the sons
of Israel [1]in the wilderness of Paran, at
[a]Kadesh; and they brought back word to
them and to all the congregation and showed
them the fruit of the land.
27 Thus they told him, and said, "We
went in to the land where you sent us; and
[a]it certainly does flow with milk and honey,
and [b]this is its fruit.
28 "Nevertheless, [a]the people who live in
the land are strong, and the cities are fortified *and* very large; and moreover, we saw
[b]the [1]descendants of Anak there.
29 "Amalek is living in the land of [a]the
Negev and the Hittites and the Jebusites and
[b]the Amorites are living in the hill country,
and [c]the Canaanites are living by the sea and
by the side of the Jordan."
30 Then Caleb quieted the people [1]before
Moses and said, "We should by all means go
up and take possession of it, for we will surely overcome it."
31 But the men who had gone up with
him said, "[a]We are not able to go up against
the people, for they are too strong for us."
32 So they gave out to the sons of Israel [a]a
bad report of the land which they had spied
out, saying, "The land through which we
have gone, in spying it out, is [b]a land that
devours its [1]inhabitants; and [c]all the people
whom we saw in it are men of *great* size.
33 "There also we saw the [a]Nephilim (the
sons of Anak are part of the Nephilim); and
[b]we became like grasshoppers in our own
sight, and so we were in their sight."

The People Rebel

14 Then all the congregation [1]lifted up
their voices and cried, and the people
wept [2]that night.
2 All the sons of Israel [a]grumbled against
Moses and Aaron; and the whole congregation said to them, "[b]Would that we had died
in the land of Egypt! Or would that we had
died in this wilderness!
3 "Why is the LORD bringing us into this
land, [a]to fall by the sword? [b]Our wives and
our little ones will become plunder; would it
not be better for us to return to Egypt?"
4 So they said to one another, "[a]Let us
appoint a leader and return to Egypt."
5 [a]Then Moses and Aaron fell on their
faces in the presence of all the assembly of
the congregation of the sons of Israel.
6 Joshua the son of Nun and Caleb the
son of Jephunneh, of those who had spied
out the land, tore their clothes;
7 and they spoke to all the congregation
of the sons of Israel, saying, "[a]The land
which we passed through to spy out is an
exceedingly good land.
8 "[a]If the LORD is pleased with us, then He
will bring us into this land and give it to us—
[b]a land which flows with milk and honey.
9 "Only [a]do not rebel against the LORD;
and do not [b]fear the people of the land, for
they will be our [1]prey. Their [2]protection has
been removed from them, and the LORD is
with us; do not fear them."
10 [a]But all the congregation said to stone
them with stones. Then [b]the glory of the
LORD appeared in the tent of meeting to all
the sons of Israel.

Moses Pleads for the People

11 [a]The LORD said to Moses, "How long
will this people spurn Me? And how long
will [b]they not believe in Me, despite all the
signs which I have performed in their midst?

23 [1]Or *wadi* [2]I.e. cluster [a]Gen 14:13; Num 13:24; 32:9; Deut 1:24
24 [1]I.e. cluster
26 [1]Lit *to* [a]Num 20:1, 14; 32:8
27 [a]Ex 3:8, 17; 13:5 [b]Deut 1:25
28 [1]Lit *born ones* [a]Deut 1:28; 9:1, 2 [b]Num 13:33
29 [a]Num 13:17; 14:25, 45 [b]Josh 10:6 [c]Num 14:43, 45
30 [1]Lit *toward*
31 [a]Deut 1:28; 9:1-3
32 [1]Or *settlers* [a]Num 14:36, 37; Ps 106:24 [b]Ezek 36:13, 14 [c]Amos 2:9
33 [a]Gen 6:4
33 [b]Deut 1:28; 9:2; Josh 11:21
14:1 [1]Lit *lifted and gave their voice* [2]Lit *in that*
2 [a]Num 11:1 [b]Num 11:5; 16:13; 20:3, 4; 21:5
3 [a]Ex 5:21; 16:3 [b]Num 14:31; Deut 1:39
4 [a]Neh 9:17
5 [a]Num 16:4
7 [a]Num 13:27; Deut 1:25
8 [a]Deut 10:15 [b]Ex 3:8; Num 13:27
9 [1]Lit *food* [2]Lit *shadow* [a]Deut 1:26; 9:23, 24 [b]Deut 1:21, 29
10 [a]Ex 17:4 [b]Ex 16:10; Lev 9:23
11 [a]Ex 32:9-13 [b]Ps 106:24

kites were men of great stature; their physical size brought fear to the people (see vv. 32–33). In a later day of faith, Caleb was to drive them from their city (Josh 15:14; Judg 1:10).

13:23 *valley of Eshcol. Eschol* means "cluster." This valley is near Hebron; presumably the spies cut the cluster of grapes on their return journey. The size of the grape cluster should have indicated the goodness of the land God was giving them.

13:26–29 The first part of the spies' report was truthful, but the goodness of the land was offset in their fearful eyes by the powerful peoples who lived there.

13:30 *Caleb quieted the people.* Only Caleb and Hoshea (Joshua) gave a report prompted by faith in God.

13:32 *bad report of the land.* The promised land was a good land, a gracious gift from God. By speaking bad things about it, the faithless spies were speaking evil of the Lord (cf. 10:29).

13:33 Their words became exaggerations and distortions. The Anakites were now said to be Nephilim (see note on Gen 6:4). The reference to the Nephilim seems deliberately intended to evoke fear. The exaggeration of the faithless led to their final folly: "We became like grasshoppers."

14:1 *all . . . the people wept.* The frightening words of the faithless spies led to mourning by the entire community and to their great rebellion against the Lord. They forgot all the miracles the Lord had done for them, they despised His mercies, and they spurned His might. In their ingratitude they preferred death (v. 2).

14:3 *little ones.* The most reprehensible charge against God's grace was that concerning their children. Only their children would survive (see vv. 31–33).

14:9 *the LORD is with us.* There are no walls, no fortifications, no factors of size or bearing, and certainly no gods that can withstand the onslaught of God's people when the Lord is with them.

14:10 *the glory of the LORD appeared.* The theophany (manifestation of God) must have been staggering in its sudden and intense display of His majesty and wrath.

14:11 *spurn Me.* By refusing to believe in the Lord's power, especially in view of all the wonders they had experienced, the people of Israel were spurning Him.

12 "I will smite them with [1a]pestilence and
dispossess them, and I [b]will make you into a
nation greater and mightier than they."
13 [a]But Moses said to the LORD, "Then the
Egyptians will hear of it, for by Your strength
You brought up this people from their midst,
14 and they will tell *it* to the inhabitants of
this land. They have heard that You, O LORD,
are in the midst of this people, for [a]You, O
LORD, are seen eye to eye, while Your cloud
stands over them; and You go before them in
a pillar of cloud by day and in a pillar of fire
by night.
15 "Now if You slay this people as one
man, [a]then the nations who have heard of
Your fame will [1]say,
16 'Because the LORD [a]could not bring this
people into the land which He promised
them by oath, therefore He slaughtered them
in the wilderness.'
17 "But now, I pray, let the power of the
Lord be great, just as You have [1]declared,
18 '[a]The LORD is slow to anger and abundant in lovingkindness, forgiving iniquity
and transgression; but [b]He will by no means
clear *the guilty,* [c]visiting the iniquity of the
fathers on the children [1]to the third and the
fourth *generations.*'
19 "[a]Pardon, I pray, the iniquity of this people according to the greatness of Your lovingkindness, just as You also have forgiven
this people, from Egypt even until now."

The LORD Pardons and Rebukes

20 So the LORD said, "[a]I have pardoned
them according to your word;
21 but indeed, [a]as I live, [1b]all the earth
will be filled with the glory of the LORD.
22 "Surely [a]all the men who have seen My
glory and My signs which I performed in
Egypt and in the wilderness, yet [b]have put
Me to the test these ten times and have not
listened to My voice,
23 [a]shall by no means see the land which
I swore to their fathers, nor shall any of
those who spurned Me see it.
24 "But My servant Caleb, [a]because he has
had a different spirit and has followed Me
fully, [1b]I will bring into the land [2]which he
entered, and his [3]descendants shall take possession of it.
25 "[a]Now the Amalekites and the Canaanites live in the valleys; turn tomorrow and set
out to the wilderness by the way of the [1]Red
Sea."
26 The LORD spoke to Moses and Aaron,
saying,
27 "How long *shall I bear* with this evil
congregation who are [a]grumbling against
Me? I have heard the complaints of the sons
of Israel, which they are [1]making against Me.
28 "Say to them, '[a]As I live,' says the LORD,
'just as [b]you have spoken in My hearing, so
I will surely do to you;
29 [a]your corpses will fall in this wilderness, even all [b]your [1]numbered men, according to your complete number from twenty
years old and upward, who have grumbled
against Me.
30 'Surely you shall not come into the land
in which I [1]swore to settle you, [a]except
Caleb the son of Jephunneh and Joshua the
son of Nun.
31 '[a]Your children, however, whom you
said would become a prey—I will bring them
in, and they will know the land which you
have rejected.
32 '[a]But as for you, your corpses will fall in
this wilderness.
33 'Your sons shall be shepherds for [a]forty
years in the wilderness, and they will [1]suffer
for your [2]unfaithfulness, until your corpses
[3]lie in the wilderness.
34 'According to the [a]number of days
which you spied out the land, forty days, for
every day you shall bear your [1]guilt a year,
even forty years, and you will know My
opposition.
35 '[a]I, the LORD, have spoken, surely this I
will do to all this evil congregation who are
gathered together against Me. In this wilder-

12 [1]Lit *the pestilence* [a]Lev 26:25; Deut 28:21 [b]Ex 32:10
13 [a]Ex 32:11-14; Ps 106:23
14 [a]Ex 13:21; Deut 5:4
15 [1]Lit *speak, saying* [a]Ex 32:12
16 [a]Josh 7:7
17 [1]Lit *spoken, saying*
18 [1]Lit *on* [a]Ex 20:6; 34:6, 7; Deut 5:10; 7:9; Ps 103:8; 145:8; Jon 4:2 [b]Ex 20:5; Deut 5:9; 7:10 [c]Ex 34:7
19 [a]Ex 32:32; 34:9
20 [a]Mic 7:18-20
21 [1]Lit *and all* [a]Num 14:28; Deut 32:40; Is 49:18 [b]Is 6:3; Hab 2:14
22 [a]1 Cor 10:5 [b]Ex 5:21; 14:11; 15:24; 16:2; 17:2, 3; 32:1; Num 11:1, 4; 12:1; 14:2
23 [a]Num 26:65; 32:11; Heb 3:18
24 [1]Lit *him I* [2]Lit *where* [3]Lit *seed* [a]Num 14:6-9 [b]Num 26:65; 32:12; Deut 1:36; Josh 14:6-15
25 [1]Lit *Sea of Reeds* [a]Num 13:29
27 [1]Lit *complaining* [a]Num 11:1
28 [a]Num 14:21 [b]Num 14:2; Deut 2:14, 15; Heb 3:17
29 [1]Lit *mustered* [a]Heb 3:17 [b]Num 1:45, 46
30 [1]Lit *raised My hand* [a]Num 14:24
31 [a]Num 14:3
32 [a]Num 26:64, 65; 32:13; 1 Cor 10:5
33 [1]Lit *bear* [2]Lit *fornications* [3]Lit *are finished* [a]Deut 2:7; 8:2, 4; 29:5
34 [1]Or *iniquities* [a]Num 13:25 **35** [a]Num 23:19

14:12 *I will make you into a nation.* For the second time since the exodus, God speaks of starting over with Moses in creating a people faithful to Himself (see Ex 32:10).

14:13 *the Egyptians will hear of it.* Moses desires to protect the Lord's reputation. The enemies of God's people will charge the Lord with inability to complete His deliverance and will be contemptuous of His power.

14:17–19 Moses now moves from the Lord's reputation to His character, presenting a composite quotation of His own words of loyal love for and faithful discipline of His people (see Ex 20:6; 34:6–7).

14:22 *ten times.* Perhaps to be enumerated as follows: (1) Ex 14:10–12; (2) Ex 15:22–24; (3) Ex 16:1–3; (4) Ex 16:19–20; (5) Ex 16:27–30; (6) Ex 17:1–4; (7) Ex 32:1–35; (8) Num 11:1–3; (9) 11:4–34; (10) 14:3. But "ten times" may also be a way of saying "many times."

14:24 *My servant Caleb . . . has had a different spirit.* Caleb seems to be singled out; perhaps the words of vv. 7–9 were his, and he was joined in them by Joshua. Caleb's ultimate vindication came 45 years later (see note on 13:22; see also Josh 14:10).

14:28 *Just as you have spoken . . . I will surely do to you.* The people of Israel brought upon themselves their punishment. They had said that they would rather die in the wilderness (v. 2) than be led into Canaan to die by the sword. All those 20 years old or more, who were counted in the census, were to die in the wilderness (v. 29). The only exceptions would be Joshua and Caleb (v. 30). Only their children would survive (v. 31)—the children that the people said God would allow to die in the wilderness (v. 3).

14:34 The 40 days of the travels of the spies became the numerical pattern for their suffering: one year for one day—for 40 years they would recount their misjudgment, and for 40 years the people 20 years old or more would be dying, so that only the young generation might enter the land. Significantly, Israel's refusal to carry out the Lord's commission to conquer His land is the climactic act of rebellion for which God condemns Israel to die in the wilderness.

ness they shall be destroyed, and there they will die.' "

36 [a]As for the men whom Moses sent to spy out the land and who returned and made all the congregation grumble against him by bringing out a bad report concerning the land,

37 even [a]those men who brought out the very bad report of the land died by a [b]plague before the LORD.

38 But Joshua the son of Nun and Caleb the son of Jephunneh remained alive out of those men who went to spy out the land.

Israel Repulsed

39 When Moses spoke [a]these words to all the sons of Israel, [b]the people mourned greatly.

40 In the morning, however, they rose up early and went up to the [1]ridge of the hill country, saying, "[a]Here we are; [2]we have indeed sinned, but we will go up to the place which the LORD has promised."

41 But Moses said, "[a]Why then are you transgressing the [1]commandment of the LORD, when it will not succeed?

42 "[a]Do not go up, or you will be struck down before your enemies, for the LORD is not among you.

43 "For the Amalekites and the Canaanites will be there in front of you, and you will fall by the sword, inasmuch as you have turned back from following the LORD. And the LORD will not be with you."

44 But they went up heedlessly to the [1]ridge of the hill country; neither [a]the ark of the covenant of the LORD nor Moses left the camp.

45 Then the Amalekites and the Canaanites who lived in that hill country came down, and struck them and beat them down as far as [a]Hormah.

Laws for Canaan

15 Now the LORD spoke to Moses, saying,
2 "[a]Speak to the sons of Israel and say to them, 'When you enter the land [1]where you are to live, which I am giving you,

3 then make [a]an offering by fire to the LORD, a burnt offering or a sacrifice to [1][b]fulfill a special vow, or as a freewill offering or in your [c]appointed times, to make a [d]soothing aroma to the LORD, from the herd or from the flock.

4 '[a]The one who presents his offering shall present to the LORD a grain offering of one-tenth *of an ephah* of fine flour mixed with one-fourth of a [1]hin of oil,

5 and you shall prepare wine for the drink offering, one-fourth of a hin, with the burnt offering or for the sacrifice, for [a]each lamb.

6 'Or for a ram you shall prepare as a grain offering two-tenths *of an ephah* of fine flour mixed with one-third of a hin of oil;

7 and for the drink offering you shall offer one-third of a hin of wine as a soothing aroma to the LORD.

8 'When you prepare [a]a bull as a burnt offering or a sacrifice, to [1]fulfill a special vow, or for peace offerings to the LORD,

9 then you shall offer with the bull a grain offering of three-tenths *of an ephah* of fine flour mixed with one-half a hin of oil;

10 and you shall offer as the drink offering one-half a hin of wine as an offering by fire, as a soothing aroma to the LORD.

11 'Thus it shall be done for each ox, or for each ram, or for each of the male lambs, or of the goats.

12 'According to the number that you prepare, so you shall do for everyone according to their number.

13 'All who are native shall do these things in this manner, in presenting an offering by fire, as a soothing aroma to the LORD.

Law of the Sojourner

14 'If an alien sojourns with you, or one who may be among you throughout your generations, and he *wishes to* make an offering by fire, as a soothing aroma to the LORD, just as you do so he shall do.

15 '*As for* the assembly, there shall be [a]one statute for you and for the alien who sojourns *with you*, a perpetual statute

36 [a]Num 13:4-16, 32 **37** [a]1 Cor 10:10; Heb 3:17, 18 [b]Num 16:49 **39** [a]Num 14:28-35 [b]Ex 33:4 **40** [1]Or *top of the mountain* [2]Or *and we will go up...for we have sinned* [a]Deut 1:41-44 **41** [1]Lit *mouth* [a]2 Chr 24:20 **42** [a]Deut 1:42 **44** [1]Or *top of the mountain* [a]Num 31:6 **45** [a]Num 21:3 **15:2** [1]Lit *of your dwellings* [a]Lev 23:10

3 [1]Or *make a special votive offering* [a]Lev 1:2, 3 [b]Lev 22:21 [c]Lev 23:1-44 [d]Gen 8:21; 2 Cor 2:15, 16; Phil 4:18 **4** [1]I.e. Approx one gal., and so through v 10 [a]Num 28:1-29:40 **5** [a]Lev 1:10; 3:6; Num 15:11 **8** [1]Or *make a special votive offering* [a]Lev 1:3; 3:1 **15** [a]Num 9:14; 15:29

14:37 *those men who brought out the very bad report of the land died.* The judgment on the ten evil spies was immediate; the generation that they influenced would live out their lives in the wilderness.

14:40 *we will go up.* Now, too late, the people determine to go up to the land they had refused. Such a course of action was doomed to failure. Not only was the Lord not with them; He was against them (v. 41). Their subsequent defeat (v. 45) was another judgment the rebellious people brought down upon their own heads.

15:1–41 This chapter is divided into three units, each introduced by the phrase, "The LORD spoke to Moses" (vv. 1,17,37). The people were under terrible judgment because they had disobeyed the specific commands of the Lord and had despised His character.

15:2 *When you enter the land.* The juxtaposition of this clause with the sad ending of ch. 14 is dramatic. The sins of the people were manifold; they would be judged. The grace and mercy of the Lord are magnified as He points to the ultimate realization of His ancient promise to Abraham (Gen 12:7), as well as to His continuing promise to the nation that they would indeed enter the land.

15:3–12 Grain and wine offerings were to accompany the offerings by fire; the grain was to be mixed with oil. The offerings increased in amounts with the increase of size of the sacrificial animal (vv. 6–12). These passages are the first to indicate that wine offerings must accompany all burnt and fellowship offerings.

15:14 *alien.* As in the case of the celebration of the Passover (see note on 9:14), the alien had the same regulations as the native-born Israelite. The commonwealth of Israel would always be open to proselytes. Indeed, the charter of Israel's faith embraces all peoples of the earth (Gen 12:3).

throughout your generations; as you are, so shall the alien be before the LORD.

16 'There is to be [a]one law and one ordinance for you and for the alien who sojourns with you.' "

17 Then the LORD spoke to Moses, saying,

18 "Speak to the sons of Israel and say to them, 'When you enter the land where I bring you,

19 then it shall be, that when you eat of the [1a]food of the land, you shall lift up [2]an offering to the LORD.

20 '[a]Of the first of your [1]dough you shall lift up a cake as an [2]offering; as [b]the [2]offering of the threshing floor, so you shall lift it up.

21 'From the first of your [1]dough you shall give to the LORD an [2]offering throughout your generations.

22 'But when you [a]unwittingly fail and do not observe all these commandments, which the LORD has spoken to Moses,

23 *even* all that the LORD has commanded you [1]through Moses, from the day when the LORD gave commandment and onward throughout your generations,

24 then it shall be, if it is done [a]unintentionally, [1]without the knowledge of the congregation, that all the congregation shall offer one bull for a burnt offering, as a soothing aroma to the LORD, [b]with its grain offering and its drink offering, according to the ordinance, and one male goat for a sin offering.

25 'Then [a]the priest shall make atonement for all the congregation of the sons of Israel, and they will be forgiven; for it was an error, and they have brought their offering, an offering by fire to the LORD, and their sin offering before the LORD, for their error.

26 'So all the congregation of the sons of Israel will be forgiven, with the alien who sojourns among them, for *it happened* to all the people through [a]error.

27 'Also if one person sins [a]unintentionally, then he shall offer a one year old female goat for a sin offering.

28 '[a]The priest shall make atonement before the LORD for the person who goes astray when he sins unintentionally, making atonement for him [1]that he may be forgiven.

29 'You shall have one law for him who does *anything* unintentionally, for him who is native among the sons of Israel and for the alien who sojourns among them.

30 'But the person who does *anything* [a]defiantly, whether he is native or an alien, that one is blaspheming the LORD; and that person shall be cut off from among his people.

31 'Because he has [a]despised the word of the LORD and has broken His commandment, that person shall be completely cut off; [b]his [1]guilt *will be* on him.' "

Sabbath-breaking Punished

32 Now while the sons of Israel were in the wilderness, they found a man [a]gathering wood on the sabbath day.

33 Those who found him gathering wood brought him to Moses and Aaron and to all the congregation;

34 and they put him in [1]custody [a]because it had not been [2]declared what should be done to him.

35 Then the LORD said to Moses, "The man shall surely be put to death; [a]all the congregation shall stone him with stones outside the camp."

36 So all the congregation brought him outside the camp and stoned him [1]to death with stones, just as the LORD had commanded Moses.

37 The LORD also spoke to Moses, saying,

38 "Speak to the sons of Israel, and tell them that they shall make for themselves [a]tassels on the corners of their garments throughout their generations, and that they shall put on the tassel of each corner a cord of blue.

39 "It shall be a tassel for you [1]to look at and [a]remember all the commandments of the LORD, so as to do them and not [2]follow after your own heart and your own eyes, after which you played the harlot,

40 so that you may remember to do all My commandments and [a]be holy to your God.

41 "I am the LORD your God who brought

16 [a]Lev 24:22 **19** [1]Lit *bread* [2]Or *a heave offering* [a]Josh 5:11, 12 **20** [1]Or *coarse meal* [2]Or *heave offering* [a]Ex 34:26; Lev 23:14 [b]Deut 14:22, 23; 16:13 **21** [1]Or *coarse meal* [2]Or *offering lifted up* **22** [a]Lev 4:2 **23** [1]Lit *by the hand of* **24** [1]Lit *from the eyes of the congregation* [a]Lev 4:2, 22, 27; 5:15, 18 [b]Num 15:8-10 **25** [a]Lev 4:20; Heb 2:17 **26** [a]Num 15:24 **27** [a]Lev 4:27-31; Luke 12:48 **28** [a]Lev 4:35

28 [1]Or *and he shall* **30** [a]Num 14:40-44; Deut 1:43; 17:12, 13 **31** [1]Or *iniquity* [a]2 Sam 12:9; Prov 13:13 [b]Ezek 18:20 **32** [a]Ex 31:14, 15; 35:2, 3 **34** [1]Or *prison* [2]Lit *declared distinctly* [a]Num 9:8 **35** [a]Lev 20:2, 27; 24:14-23; Deut 21:21 **36** [1]Lit *with stones and he died* **38** [a]Deut 22:12; Matt 23:5 **39** [1]Lit *and you shall look at it* [2]Lit *seek* [a]Deut 4:23; 6:12; 8:11, 14, 19 **40** [a]Lev 11:44, 45

15:20 *Of the first of your dough.* This law also looks forward to the time when the Israelites would be in the land. The first of the threshed grain was to be made into a cake and presented to the Lord. This concept of the firstfruits is a symbol that all blessing is from the Lord and all produce belongs to Him.

15:22 *unwittingly fail.* Sins may be unintentional, but they still need to be dealt with (see note on Lev 4:2). Such unintentional sins may be committed by the people as a whole (vv. 22–26) or by an individual (vv. 27–29).

15:30 *defiantly.* Lit."with a high hand." Unlike unintentional sins, for which there are provisions of God's mercy, one who sets his hand defiantly to despise the word of God and to blaspheme His name must be punished. This was the experience of the nation in ch. 14, and it is described in the case of an individual here in vv. 32–36. *cut off from among his people.* See note on Ex 12:15.

15:32 *gathering wood on the sabbath day.* The penalty for breaking the sabbath was death (v. 36; Ex 31:15; 35:2). As in the case of the willful blasphemer (Lev 24:10–16), the sabbath-breaker was guilty of high-handed rebellion (see note on v. 30) and was judged with death. By the time of Christ, Sabbath-keeping had become distorted to the point that its regulations were regarded as more important than the needs of people. Jesus confronted the Pharisees on this issue on several occasions (see, e.g., Matt 12:1–14). From their point of view, these regulations (vv. 32–36) gave them reasons to seek His death (Matt 12:14).

15:38 *tassels on the corners of their garments.* As one would walk along, the tassels would swirl about at the edge of his garment (cf. v. 39), serving as excellent memory prods to obey God's commands (cf. Deut 6:4–9).

15:41 *I am the LORD your God who brought you out.* The demands that God made upon His people were grounded in His act of redemption (see Ex 20:2 and note).

you out from the land of Egypt to be your God; I am the LORD your God."

Korah's Rebellion

16 Now [a]Korah the son of Izhar, the son of Kohath, the son of Levi, with [b]Dathan and Abiram, the sons of Eliab, and On the son of Peleth, sons of Reuben, took *action*,

2 and they rose up before Moses, [1]together with some of the sons of Israel, two hundred and fifty leaders of the congregation, [2a]chosen in the assembly, men of renown.

3 They assembled together [a]against Moses and Aaron, and said to them, "[1b]You have gone far enough, for all the congregation are holy, every one of them, and [c]the LORD is in their midst; so why do you exalt yourselves above the assembly of the LORD?"

4 When Moses heard *this,* [a]he fell on his face;

5 and he spoke to Korah and all his company, saying, "Tomorrow morning the LORD will show who is His, and [a]who is holy, and will bring *him* near to Himself; even [b]the one whom He will choose, He will bring near to Himself.

6 "Do this: take censers for yourselves, Korah and all [1]your company,

7 and put fire in them, and lay incense upon them in the presence of the LORD tomorrow; and the man whom the LORD chooses *shall be* the one who is holy. [1a]You have gone far enough, you sons of Levi!"

8 Then Moses said to Korah, "Hear now, you sons of Levi,

9 [a]is it [1]not enough for you that the God of Israel has separated you from the *rest of* the congregation of Israel, [b]to bring you near to Himself, to do the service of the tabernacle of the LORD, and to stand before the congregation to minister to them;

10 and that He has brought you near, *Korah,* and all your brothers, sons of Levi, with you? And are you [a]seeking for the priesthood also?

11 "Therefore you and all your company are gathered together [a]against the LORD; but as for Aaron, [1]who is he that [b]you grumble against him?"

12 Then Moses sent [1]a summons to Dathan and Abiram, the sons of Eliab; but they said, "We will not come up.

13 "Is it [1]not enough that you have brought us up out of a [a]land flowing with milk and honey [b]to have us die in the wilderness, but you would also lord it over us?

14 "Indeed, you have not brought us [a]into a land flowing with milk and honey, nor have you given us an inheritance of [b]fields and vineyards. Would you [1c]put out the eyes of [2]these men? We will not come up!"

15 Then Moses became very angry and said to the LORD, "[a]Do not regard their offering! [b]I have not taken a single donkey from them, nor have I done harm to any of them."

16 Moses said to Korah, "You and all your company be present before the LORD tomorrow, both you and they along with Aaron.

17 "Each of you take his firepan and put incense on [1]it, and each of you bring his censer before the LORD, two hundred and fifty firepans; also you and Aaron *shall* each *bring* his firepan."

18 So they each took his *own* censer and put fire on [1]it, and laid incense on [1]it; and they stood at the doorway of the tent of meeting, with Moses and Aaron.

19 Thus Korah assembled all the congregation against them at the doorway of the tent of meeting. And [a]the glory of the LORD appeared to all the congregation.

20 Then the LORD spoke to Moses and Aaron, saying,

21 "[a]Separate yourselves from among this congregation, [b]that I may consume them instantly."

22 But they fell on their faces and said, "O God, [a]God of the spirits of all flesh, [b]when one man sins, will You be angry with the entire congregation?"

23 Then the LORD spoke to Moses, saying,

24 "Speak to the congregation, saying, '[a]Get back from around the dwellings of Korah, Dathan and Abiram.' "

16:1 [a]Ex 6:21; Jude 11 [b]Num 26:9; Deut 11:6
2 [1]Lit *and men from* [2]Lit *called ones of* [a]Num 1:16; 26:9
3 [1]Lit *It is much for you* [a]Num 12:2; Ps 106:16 [b]Num 16:7 [c]Num 5:3
4 [a]Num 14:5
5 [a]Lev 10:3; Ps 65:4 [b]Num 17:5, 8
6 [1]Lit *his*
7 [1]Lit *It is much for you* [a]Num 16:3
9 [1]Or *too little for you* [a]Is 7:13 [b]Num 3:6, 9; Deut 10:8
10 [a]Num 3:10; 18:1-7
11 [a]Ex 16:7
11 [1]Lit *what* [b]1 Cor 10:10
12 [1]Lit *to call*
13 [1]Lit *a little thing* [a]Ex 16:3; Num 11:4-6 [b]Num 14:2, 3
14 [1]Lit *bore out* [2]Lit *those* [a]Num 13:27; 14:8 [b]Ex 22:5; 23:10, 11; Num 20:5 [c]Judg 16:21; 1 Sam 11:2
15 [a]Gen 4:4, 5 [b]1 Sam 12:3
17 [1]Lit *them*
18 [1]Lit *them*
19 [a]Num 14:10; 16:42; 20:6
21 [a]Num 16:45 [b]Ex 32:10, 12
22 [a]Num 27:16 [b]Gen 18:23-32; Lev 4:3
24 [a]Num 16:45

16:1–7 Earlier, Miriam and Aaron had led a rebellion against the leadership of Moses (ch. 12). Now Korah and his allies attack the leadership of Moses and Aaron. Korah was descended from Levi through Kohath. As a Kohathite, he had high duties in the service of the Lord at the tabernacle (see 4:1–20), but he desired more. His passion was to assume the role of priest, and he used deception to advance his claim. Korah was joined by the Reubenites, Dathan, Abiram and On, and about 250 other leaders of Israel who had their own complaints. Their charge was that Moses had "gone far enough" (v. 3) in taking the role of spiritual leadership of the people; "all the congregation are holy" (v. 3). To this abusive charge Moses retorts, "You have gone far enough, you sons of Levi!" (v. 7), and sets up a trial by fire.
16:12 *Dathan and Abiram.* Their charge against Moses was that he had not led them into the land of promise. They claimed that Moses had in fact led the people "out of a land flowing with milk and honey" (v. 13). By this strange alchemy, in their minds the land of Egypt has been transformed from prison to paradise.
16:15 *nor have I done harm to any of them.* Moses' humanity is seen in his plea of innocence.
16:18–21 The trial was to be by fire: Which men would the Lord accept as His priests in the holy tabernacle? The 250 men allied with Korah came with arrogance to withstand Moses and Aaron at the entrance to the tent of meeting. The revelation of the Lord's glory was sure and sudden (v. 19), with words of impending doom for the rebellious people (v. 21). The punishment was fittingly ironic. Those 250 men who dared to present themselves as priests before the Lord with fire in their censers were themselves put to death by fire (perhaps lightning) from the Lord (see v. 35).
16:22 Here the magnanimity of Moses and Aaron is seen.
16:24 *Get back.* God's judgment was going to be severe, but He did not want to lash out against bystanders. It appears that Korah himself had left the 250 false priests and was standing with Dathan and Abiram to continue their opposition to Moses.

25 Then Moses arose and went to Dathan and Abiram, with the elders of Israel following him,

26 and he spoke to the congregation, saying, "[a]Depart now from the tents of these wicked men, and touch nothing that belongs to them, [b]or you will be swept away in all their sin."

27 So they got back from around the dwellings of Korah, Dathan and Abiram; and Dathan and Abiram came out *and* stood at the doorway of their tents, along with their wives and [a]their sons and their little ones.

28 Moses said, "By this you shall know that [a]the LORD has sent me to do all these deeds; for this is not [1]my doing.

29 "If these men die [1]the death of all men or [2]if they suffer the [a]fate of all men, *then* the LORD has not sent me.

30 "But [a]if the LORD [1]brings about an entirely new thing and the ground opens its mouth and swallows them up with all that is theirs, and they [b]descend alive into [2]Sheol, then you will understand that these men have spurned the LORD."

31 As he finished speaking all these words, the ground that was under them split open;

32 and [a]the earth opened its mouth and swallowed them up, and their households, and [b]all the men who belonged to Korah with *their* possessions.

33 So they and all that belonged to them went down alive to [1]Sheol; and the earth closed over them, and they perished from the midst of the assembly.

34 All Israel who *were* around them fled at their [1]outcry, for they said, "The earth may swallow us up!"

35 [a]Fire also came forth from the LORD and consumed the [b]two hundred and fifty men who were offering the incense.

36 [1]Then the LORD spoke to Moses, saying,

37 "Say to Eleazar, the son of Aaron the priest, that he shall take up the censers out of the midst of the [1]blaze, for they are holy; and you scatter the [2]burning coals abroad.

38 "As for the censers of these [1]men who have sinned at the cost of their lives, let them be made into hammered sheets for a plating of the altar, since they did present them before the LORD and they are holy; and [a]they shall be for a sign to the sons of Israel."

39 So Eleazar the priest took the bronze censers which the men who were burned had offered, and they hammered them out as a plating for the altar,

40 as a [1]reminder to the sons of Israel that [a]no [2]layman who is not of the [3]descendants of Aaron should come near [b]to burn incense before the LORD; so that he will not become like Korah and his company—just as the LORD had spoken to him [4]through Moses.

Murmuring and Plague

41 But on the next day all the congregation of the sons of Israel [a]grumbled against Moses and Aaron, saying, "You are the ones who have caused the death of the LORD's people."

42 It came about, however, when the congregation had assembled against Moses and Aaron, that they turned toward the tent of meeting, and behold, the cloud covered it and [a]the glory of the LORD appeared.

43 Then Moses and Aaron came to the front of the tent of meeting,

44 and the LORD spoke to Moses, saying,

45 "[1][a]Get away from among this congregation, that I may consume them instantly." Then they fell on their faces.

46 Moses said to Aaron, "Take your censer and put in it fire from the altar, and lay incense *on it;* then bring it quickly to the congregation and [a]make atonement for them, for [b]wrath has gone forth from the LORD, the plague has begun!"

47 Then Aaron took *it* as Moses had spoken, and ran into the midst of the assembly, for behold, the plague had begun among the people. [a]So he put *on* the incense and made atonement for the people.

48 He took his stand between the dead and the living, so that the plague was checked.

49 [a]But those who died by the plague were 14,700, besides those who [b]died on account of Korah.

50 Then Aaron returned to Moses at the doorway of the tent of meeting, for the plague had been checked.

Aaron's Rod Buds

17 [1]Then the LORD spoke to Moses, saying,
2 "Speak to the sons of Israel, and get from them a rod for each father's household:

26 [a]Is 52:11 [b]Gen 19:15, 17 **27** [a]Num 26:11 **28** [1]Lit *from my heart* [a]Ex 3:12-15; 4:12, 15 **29** [1]Lit *like the death* [2]Lit *the visitation of all men be visited upon them* [a]Eccl 3:19 **30** [1]Lit *creates a new creation* [2]I.e. the nether world [a]Job 31:2, 3 [b]Ps 55:15 **32** [a]Num 26:10; Deut 11:6; Ps 106:17 [b]Num 26:11 **33** [1]I.e. the nether world **34** [1]Or *voice* **35** [a]Num 11:1-3; 26:10 [b]Num 16:2 **36** [1]Ch 17:1 in Heb **37** [1]Or *place of burning* [2]Lit *the fire* **38** [1]Lit *sinners against their lives* [a]Ezek 14:8; 2 Pet 2:6

40 [1]Or *memorial* [2]Lit *stranger* [3]Lit *seed* [4]Lit *by the hand of* [a]Num 1:51 [b]Ex 30:7-10 **41** [a]Num 16:3 **42** [a]Num 16:19 **45** [1]Or *Arise* [a]Num 16:21, 24 **46** [a]Num 25:13; Is 6:6, 7 [b]Num 18:5; Deut 9:22 **47** [a]Num 25:6-8, 13 **49** [a]Num 25:9 [b]Num 16:32, 35 **17:1** [1]Ch 17:16 in Heb

---

16:30 *entirely new thing.* Moses wished to assure the people that the imminent judgment was the direct work of the Lord and not a chance event that might be interpreted differently. The opening of the earth to swallow the rebels was a sure sign of the wrath of God and the vindication of Moses and Aaron.

16:32 *swallowed them up, and their households.* The sons of Korah did not die (26:11); apparently they did not join their father in his rash plan. The households of the other rebels died with them.

16:37 *take up the censers.* The true priests took the censers of the 250 deceased impostors from their charred remains and hammered them into bronze sheets for the altar as a memorial of the folly of a self-proclaimed priest (v. 40).

16:41 *all the congregation . . . grumbled.* Again the community attacked Moses, unfairly charging him with the death of the Lord's people. Except for the intervention of Moses and Aaron (see vv. 4,22), the entire nation might have been destroyed because of their continued rebellion (see v. 45).

16:49 *those who died . . . were 14,700.* The number makes sense only if the community is as large as the census lists of ch. 2 suggest.

17:1–13 This story follows the account of the divine judgment of Korah (16:1–35) and the narrative of the symbolic use given to the censers of the rebels and its aftermath (16:36–50). Ch.

twelve rods, from all their leaders according to their fathers' households. You shall write each name on his rod,

3 and write Aaron's name on the rod of Levi; for there is one rod for the head *of each* of their fathers' households.

4 "You shall then deposit them in the tent of meeting in front of [a]the testimony, where I meet with you.

5 "It will come about that the rod of [a]the man whom I choose will sprout. Thus I will lessen from upon Myself the grumblings of the sons of Israel, who are grumbling against you."

6 Moses therefore spoke to the sons of Israel, and all their leaders gave him a rod apiece, for each leader according to their fathers' households, twelve rods, with the rod of Aaron among their rods.

7 So Moses deposited the rods before the LORD in [a]the tent of the testimony.

8 Now on the next day Moses went into the tent of the testimony; and behold, [a]the rod of Aaron for the house of Levi had sprouted and put forth buds and produced blossoms, and it bore ripe almonds.

9 Moses then brought out all the rods from the presence of the LORD to all the sons of Israel; and they looked, and each man took his rod.

10 But the LORD said to Moses, "Put back the rod of Aaron [a]before the testimony [1]to be kept as a sign against the [2b]rebels, that you may put an end to their grumblings against Me, so that they will not die."

11 Thus Moses did; just as the LORD had commanded him, so he did.

12 Then the sons of Israel spoke to Moses, saying, "[a]Behold, we perish, we are dying, we are all dying!

13 "[a]Everyone who comes near, who comes near to the tabernacle of the LORD, must die. Are we to perish completely?"

Duties of Levites

18 So the LORD said to Aaron, "You and your sons and your father's household with you shall [a]bear the guilt [1]in connection with the sanctuary, and you and your sons with you shall bear the guilt [2]in connection with your priesthood.

2 "But bring with you also your brothers, the tribe of Levi, the tribe of your father, that they may be [a]joined with you and serve you, while you and your sons with you are before the tent of the testimony.

3 "And they shall thus attend to your obligation and the obligation of all the tent, but [a]they shall not come near to the furnishings of the sanctuary and [b]the altar, or both they and you will die.

4 "They shall be joined with you and attend to the obligations of the tent of meeting, for all the service of the tent; but an [1]outsider may not come near you.

5 "So you shall attend to the [a]obligations of the sanctuary and the obligations of the altar, [b]so that there will no longer be wrath on the sons of Israel.

6 "Behold, I Myself [a]have taken your [1]fellow Levites from among the sons of Israel; they are [b]a gift to you, [2]dedicated to the LORD, to perform the service for the tent of meeting.

7 "But you and your sons with you shall [a]attend to your priesthood for everything concerning the altar and inside the veil, and you are to perform service. I am giving you the priesthood as [b]a [1]bestowed service, but [c]the [2]outsider who comes near shall be put to death."

The Priests' Portion

8 Then the LORD spoke to Aaron, "Now behold, I Myself have given you charge of My [1a]offerings, even all the holy gifts of the sons

4 [a]Ex 25:16, 21, 22; Num 17:7
5 [a]Num 16:5
7 [a]Num 1:50, 53; 9:15
8 [a]Ezek 17:24; Heb 9:4
10 [1]Lit *for preserving* [2]Lit *sons of rebellion* [a]Num 17:4 [b]Deut 9:7, 24
12 [a]Is 6:5
13 [a]Num 1:51

18:1 [1]Lit *of the sanctuary* [2]Lit *of your priesthood* [a]Ex 28:38; Lev 10:17; 22:16
2 [a]Num 3:5-10
3 [a]Num 4:15-20 [b]Num 1:51; 18:7
4 [1]Lit *a stranger*
5 [a]Ex 27:21; Lev 24:3 [b]Num 16:46
6 [1]Lit *brethren the* [2]Lit *given* [a]Num 3:12, 45 [b]Num 3:9
7 [1]Lit *service of gift* [2]Lit *stranger* [a]Ex 29:9 [b]Num 18:20; Deut 18:2; Matt 10:8; 1 Pet 5:2, 3 [c]Num 1:51
8 [1]Lit *heave offerings*, and so throughout the ch [a]Lev 6:16, 18; 7:28-34

---

17 is thus the third in a series of accounts vindicating the Aaronic priesthood against all opposition. The selection of 12 rods, one from each tribe, was a symbolic act whereby the divine choice of Aaron would be indicated again.

17:3 *write Aaron's name on the rod of Levi.* The test needed to be unequivocal because of the wide support given to Korah's rebellion. The 250 who had joined with Korah were from many, perhaps all, of the tribes.

17:4 *in front of the testimony.* In front of the ark, with the Ten Commandments, thus probably in the holy place, near the altar of incense.

17:8 *had sprouted and put forth buds . . . blossoms . . . ripe almonds.* God exceeded the demands of the test so that there might be no uncertainty as to who had acted or what He intended by His action.

17:10 *before the testimony.* Aaron's rod joined the stone tablets of the law of Moses (see note on Ex 25:16) and the jar of manna (Ex 16:33–34) within or near the ark of the covenant (see Heb 9:4). These holy symbols were ever before the Lord as memorials of His special deeds in behalf of His people. Moreover, should anyone of a later age dare to question the unique and holy place of the Aaronic priests in the Lord's service, this symbolic memorial of God's choice of Aaron would stand in opposition to his audacity. It is difficult to overestimate the importance of the role of Aaron and his sons in the worship of Israel (see note on 18:1–7).

17:12 *we perish . . .!* At last the people realized the sin of their arrogance in challenging Aaron's role. The appropriate ways of approaching the Lord are detailed in chs. 18–19.

18:1–7 Aaron and his family, chosen by the Lord to be the true priests of holy worship, faced a burdensome task. The lament of the people in 17:12–13 was real; grievous sins against the holy meeting place of the Lord and His people would be judged by death. The Lord's mercy in providing a legitimate priesthood was actually an aspect of His grace (cf. Ps 99:6–8), because it was the people's only hope for deliverance from judgment.

18:2 *bring . . . your brothers, the tribe of Levi.* The Aaronic priests were to be assisted by the others in the tribe of Levi, but the assistants were not to go beyond their serving role. If they did so, not only would they die, but so would the priests who were responsible (v. 3).

18:7 *giving you the priesthood as a bestowed service.* Of all men, the priests were privileged to approach the holy place and minister before the Lord. The priesthood was a gift of God's grace to both priests and people.

of Israel I have given them to you as a portion and to your sons as a perpetual allotment.

9 "This shall be yours from the most holy *gifts reserved* from the fire; every offering of theirs, even [a]every grain offering and every [b]sin offering and every guilt offering, which they shall render to Me, shall be most holy for you and for your sons.

10 "As the most holy *gifts* you shall eat it; every male shall eat it. It shall be holy to you.

11 "This also is yours, [a]the offering of their gift, even all the wave offerings of the sons of Israel; I have [b]given them to you and to your sons and daughters with you as a perpetual allotment. Everyone of your household who is clean may eat it.

12 "[a]All the [1]best of the fresh oil and all the [1]best of the fresh wine and of the grain, the first fruits of those which they give to the LORD, I give them to you.

13 "[a]The first ripe fruits of all that is in their land, which they bring to the LORD, shall be yours; everyone of your household who is clean may eat it.

14 "[a]Every devoted thing in Israel shall be yours.

15 "[1][a]Every first issue of the womb of all flesh, whether man or animal, which they offer to the LORD, shall be yours; nevertheless the firstborn of man you shall surely redeem, and the firstborn of unclean animals you shall redeem.

16 "As to their redemption price, from a month old you shall redeem them, by your valuation, five [1]shekels in silver, according to the [1]shekel of the sanctuary, which is twenty gerahs.

17 "But [a]the firstborn of an ox or the firstborn of a sheep or the firstborn of a goat, you shall not redeem; they are holy. [b]You shall sprinkle their blood on the altar and shall offer up their fat in smoke *as* an offering by fire, for a soothing aroma to the LORD.

18 "Their [1]meat shall be yours; it shall be yours like the [a]breast of a wave offering and like the right thigh.

19 "[a]All the offerings of the holy *gifts*, which the sons of Israel offer to the LORD, I have given to you and your sons and your daughters with you, as a perpetual allotment. It is [b]an everlasting covenant of salt before the LORD to you and your [1]descendants with you."

20 Then the LORD said to Aaron, "[a]You shall have no inheritance in their land nor own any portion among them; [b]I am your portion and your inheritance among the sons of Israel.

21 "To the sons of Levi, behold, I have given all the [a]tithe in Israel for an inheritance, in return for their service which they perform, the service of the tent of meeting.

22 "[a]The sons of Israel shall not come near the tent of meeting again, or they will bear sin and die.

23 "Only the Levites shall perform the service of the tent of meeting, and they shall [a]bear their iniquity; it shall be a perpetual statute throughout your generations, and among the sons of Israel [b]they shall have no inheritance.

24 "For the tithe of the sons of Israel, which they offer as an offering to the LORD, I have given to the Levites for an inheritance; therefore I have said concerning them, '[a]They shall have no inheritance among the sons of Israel.' "

25 Then the LORD spoke to Moses, saying,

26 "Moreover, you shall speak to the Levites and say to them, 'When you take from the sons of Israel [a]the tithe which I have given you from them for your inheritance, then you shall present an offering from it to the LORD, a [b]tithe of the tithe.

27 'Your offering shall be reckoned to you as the grain from the threshing floor or the full produce from the wine vat.

28 'So you shall also present an offering to the LORD from your tithes, which you receive from the sons of Israel; and from it you shall give the LORD'S offering to Aaron the priest.

29 'Out of all your gifts you shall present every offering due to the LORD, from all the [1]best of them, [2]the sacred part from them.'

9 [a]Lev 2:1-16 [b]Lev 6:30
11 [a]Num 18:1; Deut 18:3 [b]Lev 22:1-16
12 [1]Lit *fat* [a]Deut 18:4; 32:14; Ps 81:16; 147:14
13 [a]Ex 22:29; 23:19; 34:26
14 [a]Lev 27:1-33
15 [1]Lit *Everything that opens* [a]Ex 13:13, 15; Num 3:46
16 [1]I.e. A shekel equals approx one-half oz
17 [a]Deut 15:19 [b]Lev 3:2
18 [1]Lit *flesh* [a]Lev 7:31
19 [a]Num 18:11
19 [1]Lit *seed* [b]2 Chr 13:5
20 [a]Deut 10:9; 12:12; 14:27, 29 [b]Deut 18:2; Josh 13:33; Ezek 44:28
21 [a]Lev 27:30-33; Deut 14:22-29
22 [a]Num 1:51
23 [a]Num 18:1 [b]Num 18:20
24 [a]Deut 10:9
26 [a]Num 18:21 [b]Neh 10:38
29 [1]Lit *fat* [2]Lit *its*

18:8 *a portion and . . . a perpetual allotment.* The priests were to be supported in their work of ministry (see Lev 6:14–7:36). Since the Levites as a whole and the priests in particular had no part in the land that God was going to give them, it was necessary that the means for their provision be spelled out fully. They were not to have a part in the land; their share was the Lord Himself (v. 20).

18:11 *your sons and daughters.* Provision was made not only for the priests, but for their families as well. Only family members who were ceremonially unclean were forbidden to eat the gifts and offerings of the people (see v. 13). Provisions for cleansing were stated in Lev 22:4–8.

18:12 *best of the fresh oil . . . fresh wine . . . grain.* Since the best items of produce were to be given to the Lord, these became the special foods of the priests and their families. The NT writers similarly argue that those who minister the word of God in the present period should also be paid suitably for their work (see, e.g., 1 Cor 9:3–10 and notes).

18:19 *everlasting covenant of salt.* A permanent provision for the priests. The phrase "covenant of salt" (see 2 Chr 13:5) remains obscure. In Lev 2:13 the salt that must accompany grain offerings is called the "salt of the covenant." According to Ezek 43:24, salt is also to be sprinkled on burnt offerings, and Ex 30:35 specifies salt as one of the ingredients in the special incense compounded for the sanctuary. A "covenant of salt" is perhaps an allusion to the salt used in the sacrificial meal that commonly accompanied the making of a covenant (see Gen 31:54; Ex 24:5–11; Ps 50:5).

18:26–32 Although the Levites were the recipients of the tithe given to the Lord, they were not themselves exempt from worshiping God by tithing. They in turn were to give a tenth of their income to Aaron (v. 28) and were to be sure that the best part was given as the Lord's portion (v. 29). By obedient compliance the Levites would escape judicial death (v. 32).

30 "You shall say to them, 'When you have [1]offered from it the best of it, then *the rest* shall be reckoned to the Levites as the product of the threshing floor, and as the product of the wine vat.

31 'You may eat it anywhere, you and your households, for it is your compensation in return for your service in the tent of meeting.

32 'You will bear no sin by reason of it when you have [1]offered the [2]best of it. But you shall not [a]profane the sacred gifts of the sons of Israel, or you will die.'"

Ordinance of the Red Heifer

19 Then the LORD spoke to Moses and Aaron, saying,

2 "This is the statute of the law which the LORD has commanded, saying, 'Speak to the sons of Israel that they bring you an [a]unblemished red heifer in which is no defect *and* [b]on which a yoke has never [1]been placed.

3 'You shall give it to [a]Eleazar the priest, and it shall [b]be brought outside the camp and be slaughtered in his presence.

4 'Next Eleazar the priest shall take some of its blood with his finger and [a]sprinkle some of its blood toward the front of the tent of meeting seven times.

5 'Then the heifer shall be burned in his sight; [a]its hide and its flesh and its blood, with its refuse, shall be burned.

6 'The priest shall take [a]cedar wood and hyssop and scarlet *material* and cast it into the midst of the [1]burning heifer.

7 'The priest [a]shall then wash his clothes and bathe his [1]body in water, and afterward come into the camp, but the priest shall be unclean until evening.

8 'The one who burns it shall also wash his clothes in water and bathe his [1]body in water, and shall be unclean until evening.

9 'Now a man who is clean shall gather up the ashes of the heifer and deposit them outside the camp in a clean place, and [1]the congregation of the sons of Israel shall keep it as [a]water to remove impurity; it is [2]purification from sin.

10 'The one who gathers the ashes of the heifer [a]shall wash his clothes and be unclean until evening; and it shall be a perpetual statute to the sons of Israel and to the alien who sojourns among them.

11 '[a]The one who touches the corpse of any [1]person shall be unclean for seven days.

12 'That one shall [a]purify himself from uncleanness with [1]the water on the third day and on the seventh day, *and then* he will be clean; but if he does not purify himself on the third day and on the seventh day, he will not be clean.

13 '[a]Anyone who touches a corpse, the [1]body of a man who has died, and does not purify himself, [b]defiles the [2]tabernacle of the LORD; and that person shall be cut off from Israel. Because the water for impurity was not [3c]sprinkled on him, he shall be unclean; his uncleanness is still on him.

14 'This is the law when a man dies in a tent: everyone who comes into the tent and everyone who is in the tent shall be unclean for seven days.

15 'Every open vessel, which has no covering [1]tied down on it, shall be unclean.

16 '[a]Also, anyone who in the open field touches one who has been slain with a sword or who has died *naturally,* or a human bone or a grave, shall be unclean for seven days.

17 'Then for the unclean *person* they shall take some of the [1]ashes of the [2]burnt [3a]purification from sin and [4]flowing water shall be [5]added to them in a vessel.

18 'A clean person shall take hyssop and dip *it* in the water, and sprinkle *it* on the tent and on all the furnishings and on the persons who were there, and on the one who touched the bone or the one slain or the one dying *naturally* or the grave.

19 'Then the clean *person* [a]shall sprinkle on the unclean on the third day and on the seventh day; and on the seventh day he shall purify him from uncleanness, and he shall

30 [1]Lit *lifted*
32 [1]Lit *lifted* [2]Lit *fat* [a]Lev 22:15, 16
19:2 [1]Lit *come up* [a]Lev 22:20-25 [b]Deut 21:3
3 [a]Num 3:4 [b]Lev 4:11, 12, 21; Num 19:9
4 [a]Lev 4:6, 17; 16:14
5 [a]Ex 29:14; Lev 4:11, 12
6 [1]Lit *burning of the heifer* [a]Lev 14:4
7 [1]Lit *flesh* [a]Lev 16:26, 28; 22:6
8 [1]Lit *flesh*
9 [1]Lit *it shall be to the congregation... Israel, for a guarding as water of impurity*
9 [2]Or *a sin offering* [a]Num 8:7; 31:23
10 [a]Num 19:7
11 [1]Lit *soul of man* [a]Lev 21:1, 11; Num 5:2; 6:6; Acts 21:26, 27
12 [1]Lit *it* [a]Num 19:19; 31:19
13 [1]Lit *soul* [2]Lit *dwelling place* [3]Or *thrown* [a]Lev 7:21; 22:3-7 [b]Lev 15:31; 20:3; Num 19:20 [c]Num 19:19
15 [1]Lit *cord*
16 [a]Num 31:19
17 [1]Lit *dust* [2]Lit *burning of the* [3]Or *sin offering* [4]Lit *living* [5]Lit *put* [a]Num 19:9
19 [a]Ezek 36:25; Heb 10:22

19:2 *red heifer.* The qualifying words, "unblemished . . . no defect," are familiar in contexts of sacrificial worship in the OT. But this is not a sacrificial animal. It is a cow, not an ox; it is to be slaughtered, not sacrificed; and it is to be killed outside the camp, not at the holy altar. The ashes of the red heifer (v. 9) are the primary focus of this act, for they will be used in the ritual of the water of cleansing. The burning of the animal with its blood and offal (v. 5) is unprecedented in the OT. The normal pattern for the sacrifice of the burnt offering is given in Lev 1:3–9. In every respect the killing of the red heifer is distinct: A female animal was taken outside the camp to be killed; the priest had to be present, but he did not identify himself with it; and a bit of the heifer's blood was sprinkled from the priest's finger toward the tabernacle seven times, but the rest of the animal was to be burned in its entirety, without the draining of its blood or the cleansing of its offal.

19:6 *cedar wood and hyssop and scarlet material.* Associated with the cleansing properties of the ashes of the red heifer.

19:12 *purify himself . . . with the water.* The ashes from the red heifer were kept outside the camp and would be mixed as needed with water to provide a means of cleansing after contact with dead bodies.

19:13 *defiles the tabernacle of the LORD.* Willful neglect of the provision for cleansing brought not only judgment on the person, but also a pollution of the tabernacle itself. *cut off from Israel.* See note on Ex 12:15.

19:14 *everyone who is in the tent.* There would be many occasions in which a person would become unclean, not because of deliberate contact with a dead body, but just by being in the proximity of one who died.

19:18 *hyssop and dip it in the water, and sprinkle.* Here the method of the cleansing ritual is explained. A ceremonially clean person had to sprinkle the ceremonially unclean person or thing. The cleansing power of the blood of Christ is specifically contrasted ("much more"; Heb 9:13–14) with the cleansing effectiveness of the water of the ashes of the red heifer.

wash his clothes and bathe *himself* in water
and shall be clean by evening.
20 'But the man who is unclean and does
not purify himself from uncleanness, that
person shall be cut off from the midst of the
assembly, because he has [a]defiled the sanctuary of the LORD; the water for impurity has
not been sprinkled on him, he is unclean.
21 'So it shall be a perpetual statute for
them. And he [a]who sprinkles the water for
impurity shall wash his clothes, and he who
touches the water for impurity shall be
unclean until evening.
22 '[a]Furthermore, anything that the
unclean *person* touches shall be unclean;
and the person who touches *it* shall be
unclean until evening.' "

Death of Miriam

20 Then the sons of Israel, the whole congregation, came to the [a]wilderness of
Zin in the first month; and the people stayed
at Kadesh. Now Miriam died there and was
buried there.
2 [a]There was no water for the congregation, [b]and they assembled themselves
against Moses and Aaron.
3 [a]The people thus contended with Moses
and spoke, saying, "[b]If only we had perished
[c]when our brothers perished before the LORD!
4 "[a]Why then have you brought the
LORD's assembly into this wilderness, for us
and our beasts to die [1]here?
5 "Why have you made us come up from
Egypt, to bring us in to this wretched place?
[a]It is not a place of [1]grain or figs or vines or
pomegranates, nor is there water to drink."
6 Then Moses and Aaron came in from
the presence of the assembly to the doorway
of the tent of meeting and [a]fell on their faces.
Then the glory of the LORD appeared to them;
7 and the LORD spoke to Moses, saying,

The Water of Meribah

8 "Take [a]the rod; and you and your brother Aaron assemble the congregation and
speak to the rock before their eyes, that it
may yield its water. You shall thus bring
forth water for them out of the rock and let
the congregation and their beasts drink."
9 So Moses took the rod [a]from before the
LORD, just as He had commanded him;
10 and Moses and Aaron gathered the
assembly before the rock. And he said to
them, "[a]Listen now, you rebels; shall we
bring forth water for you out of this rock?"
11 Then Moses lifted up his hand and
struck the rock twice with his rod; and
[a]water came forth abundantly, and the congregation and their beasts drank.
12 But the LORD said to Moses and Aaron,
"[a]Because you have not believed Me, to treat
Me as holy in the sight of the sons of Israel,
therefore you shall not bring this assembly
into the land which I have given them."
13 Those *were* the waters of [1a]Meribah,
[2]because the sons of Israel contended with
the LORD, and He proved Himself holy
among them.
14 From Kadesh Moses then sent messengers to [a]the king of Edom: "Thus your brother Israel has said, 'You [b]know all the hardship that has befallen us;
15 that our fathers went down to Egypt,
and we stayed in Egypt a long time, and the
Egyptians treated us and our fathers badly.

20 [a]Num 19:13
21 [a]Num 19:7
22 [a]Lev 5:2, 3; 7:21; 22:5, 6
20:1 [a]Num 13:21; 27:14; 33:36
2 [a]Ex 17:1 [b]Num 16:19, 42
3 [a]Ex 17:2 [b]Num 14:2, 3 [c]Num 16:31-35
4 [1]Lit *there* [a]Ex 17:3
5 [1]Lit *seed* [a]Num 16:14
6 [a]Num 14:5
8 [a]Ex 4:17, 20; 17:5, 6
9 [a]Num 17:10
10 [a]Ps 106:33
11 [a]Ps 78:16; Is 48:21; 1 Cor 10:4
12 [a]Num 20:24; 27:14; Deut 1:37; 3:26, 27
13 [1]I.e. contention [2]Or *where* [a]Ex 17:7; Ps 95:8
14 [a]Gen 36:31-39; Deut 2:4 [b]Josh 2:9, 10; 9:9, 10, 24

20:1–29 This chapter begins with the death of Miriam (v. 1), concludes with the death of Aaron (v. 28), includes the record of the conflict with Edom (vv. 14–21) and centers on the tragic sin of Moses (vv. 11–12). Such was the sad beginning of Israel's last year in the wilderness.

20:1 *first month.* The year is not given, but a comparison of vv. 22–29 with 33:38 leads to the conclusion that this chapter begins in the 40th year after the exodus (see notes on 1:1; 9:1). Most of the people 20 years old or more at the time of the rebellion at Kadesh (chs. 13–14) would already have died. *at Kadesh.* The larger part of the wilderness wandering is left without record. The people may have gone through a cycle of roving travels, seeking the water sources and the sparse vegetation, supported primarily by manna. But their circuits would bring them back to the central camp at Kadesh, the scene of their great rebellion (chs. 13–14). They have now come full circle; the land of promise lies before them again.

20:2 *no water.* Forty years earlier, the Lord had instructed Moses to take the staff he had used to strike the Nile (Ex 7:17) and to strike the rock at Horeb to initiate a flow of water (Ex 17:1–7). Now, 40 years later, at the place of Israel's worst acts of rebellion, the scene was recurring. The children of the rebellious nation now desire to die with their parents; the complaints about the bread from heaven are repeated by the sons.

20:8 *speak to the rock.* Moses was told to take his rod, through which God had performed wonders in Egypt and in the wilderness all these years, but this time he was merely to speak to the rock and it would pour out its water for the people. Cf. Ps 114:8.

20:10 *Listen now, you rebels.* At once the accumulated anger, exasperation and frustration of 40 years came to expression (see Ps 106:33).

20:11 *struck the rock twice with his rod.* In his rage Moses disobeyed the Lord's instruction to speak to the rock (v. 8). Moses' rash action brought a stern rebuke from the Lord (v. 12). The nature of Moses' offense is not clearly stated in this text, but these factors appear to be involved: 1. Moses' action was a lack of trust in God (v. 12), as though he believed that a word alone would not suffice. 2. God's holiness was offended by Moses' rash action (v. 12), for he had not shown proper deference to God's presence.

20:12 *you shall not bring this assembly into the land.* The end result of Moses' action is sure: Neither Aaron nor Moses would enter the land of promise. Of their contemporaries only Joshua and Caleb would survive to enter the land. The inclusion of Aaron demonstrates his partnership with his brother in the breach against God's holiness.

20:13 *Meribah.* Means "contention." The same name was used 40 years earlier at the first occasion of bringing water from the rock (Ex 17:7, where it is also called Massah, "testing"). Ps 95:8 laments the rebellion at Meribah and Massah.

20:14–21 Moses' attempt to pass through the territory of Edom by peaceful negotiation and payment for services rendered is met by arrogant rebuff.

20:14 *your brother Israel.* The people of Edom were descended from Esau, the brother of Jacob (see Gen 36:1).

16 ‘But [a]when we cried out to the LORD, He
heard our voice and sent [b]an angel and
brought us out from Egypt; now behold, we
are at Kadesh, a town on the edge of your
territory.
17 ‘Please [a]let us pass through your land.
We will not pass through field or through
vineyard; we will not even drink water from
a well. We will go along the king’s highway,
not turning to the right or left, until we pass
through your territory.’ ”
18 [a]Edom, however, said to him, “You
shall not pass through [1]us, or I will come out
with the sword against you.”
19 Again, the sons of Israel said to him,
“We will go up by the highway, and if I and
[a]my livestock do drink any of your water,
[b]then I will [1]pay its price. Let me only pass
through on my feet, [2]nothing *else*.”
20 But he said, “[a]You shall not pass
through.” And Edom came out against him
with a heavy [1]force and with a strong hand.
21 [a]Thus Edom refused to allow Israel to
pass through his territory; [b]so Israel turned
away from him.
22 Now when they set out from [a]Kadesh,
the sons of Israel, the whole congregation,
came to Mount Hor.

Death of Aaron

23 Then the LORD spoke to Moses and Aaron at [a]Mount Hor by the border of the land
of Edom, saying,
24 “Aaron will be [a]gathered to his people;
for he shall not enter the land which I have
given to the sons of Israel, because [b]you
rebelled against My [1]command at the waters
of Meribah.
25 “Take Aaron and his son [a]Eleazar and
bring them up to Mount Hor;
26 and strip Aaron of his garments and
put them on his son Eleazar. So Aaron will
be [a]gathered *to his people,* and will die
there.”
27 So Moses did just as the LORD had commanded, and they went up to Mount Hor in
the sight of all the congregation.
28 After Moses had stripped Aaron of his
garments and [a]put them on his son Eleazar,
[b]Aaron died there on the mountain top.
Then Moses and Eleazar came down from
the mountain.
29 When all the congregation saw that
Aaron had died, all the house of Israel wept
for Aaron thirty [a]days.

Arad Conquered

21 When the Canaanite, the king of [a]Arad,
who lived in the [1]Negev, heard that
Israel was coming by the way of [2]Atharim,
then he fought against Israel and took some
of them captive.
2 So [a]Israel made a vow to the LORD and
said, “If You will indeed deliver this people
into my hand, then I will [1]utterly destroy
their cities.”
3 The LORD heard the voice of Israel and
delivered up the Canaanites; then they
[1]utterly destroyed them and their cities. Thus
the name of the place was called [2a]Hormah.
4 Then they set out from Mount Hor by
the way of the [1]Red Sea, to [a]go around the
land of Edom; and the [2]people became impatient because of the journey.
5 The people spoke against God and
Moses, “[a]Why have you brought us up out of
Egypt to die in the wilderness? For there is
no [1]food and no water, and [2b]we loathe this
miserable food.”

The Bronze Serpent

6 [a]The LORD sent fiery serpents among
the people and [b]they bit the people, so that
[c]many people of Israel died.

16 [a]Ex 2:23; 3:7 [b]Ex 14:19
17 [a]Num 21:22
18 [1]Lit *me* [a]Num 24:18
19 [1]Lit *give* [2]Or *no great thing* [a]Ex 12:38 [b]Deut 2:6, 28
20 [1]Lit *people* [a]Judg 11:17
21 [a]Judg 11:17 [b]Deut 2:8
22 [a]Num 20:1, 14
23 [a]Num 33:37
24 [1]Lit *mouth* [a]Gen 25:8 [b]Num 20:5, 10
25 [a]Num 3:4
26 [a]Num 20:24
28 [a]Ex 29:29 [b]Num 33:38; Deut 10:6; 32:50
29 [a]Gen 1:5; 50:3, 10; Deut 34:8
21:1 [1]I.e. South country [2]Or *the spies* [a]Num 33:40; Josh 12:14; Judg 1:16
2 [1]Lit *devote to destruction* [a]Gen 28:20; Judg 11:30
3 [1]Lit *devoted to destruction* [2]I.e. a devoted thing; or Destruction [a]Num 14:45
4 [1]Lit *Sea of Reeds* [2]Lit *soul of the people was short* [a]Deut 2:8
5 [1]Lit *bread* [2]Lit *our soul loathes* [a]Num 14:2, 3 [b]Num 11:6
6 [a]Deut 8:15 [b]Jer 8:17 [c]1 Cor 10:9

20:17 *king’s highway.* The major north-south trade route in Transjordan, extending from Arabia to Damascus.

20:20 *heavy force and . . . strong hand.* The show of force by Edom caused Israel to turn away so as not to risk conflict with this brother nation. Israel was forbidden by the Lord to take even a foothold in Edom (see Deut 2:4–6).

20:22 *Mount Hor.* Other than its proximity to the border of Edom (v. 23), nothing is known for certain about its location.

20:24 *gathered to his people.* A euphemism for death (see, e.g., Gen 25:8,17; 35:29). *you.* The Hebrew is plural. Aaron had joined Moses in rebellion against God (v. 12); his impending death was a precursor of Moses’ death as well (see Dt 34).

20:25 *Aaron and his son Eleazar.* There was no doubt about Aaron’s successor, just as there was no doubt about Moses’ successor (see Dt 34).

20:26–28 While Aaron was still alive, his garments were to be placed on his son; only then did he die.

20:29 *wept for Aaron.* His death (and that of Moses) marked the passing of a generation. The old generation was now nearly gone; in 40 years there had been almost a complete turnover of the people 20 years old or more.

21:1–3 The first battle of the new community against the Canaanites was provoked by the king of Arad, perhaps as he was raiding them. The result was a complete victory for the Israelites—a new day for them, since they had been defeated by the Amalekites and Canaanites a generation before (14:41–45).

21:2 *utterly destroy.* The Hebrew term refers to the irrevocable giving over of things or persons to the Lord, often by totally destroying them.

21:3 *Hormah.* Means “devoted to destruction”; the association with Israel’s earlier defeat is made certain by the use of this place-name (see 14:45).

21:4 With Moses’ determination not to engage Edom in battle (see note on 20:20), the people became impatient with him and with the direction the Lord was taking them. Flushed with victory, they were confident in themselves. They forgot that their victory over Arad was granted by the Lord in response to their solemn pledge (v. 2); now they were ready to rebel again.

21:5 *we loathe this miserable food.* The people’s impatience (v. 4) led them to blaspheme God, to reject His servant Moses and to despise the bread from heaven. This is the most bitter of their several attacks on the manna (see note on 11:7). Just as Moses’ attack on the rock was more than it appeared to be (see note on 20:11), so the people’s contempt for the heavenly bread was more serious than one might think. Rejecting the heavenly manna was tantamount to spurning God’s grace (cf. John 6:32–35,48–51,58).

7 [a]So the people came to Moses and
said, "We have sinned, because we have
spoken against the LORD and you; [b]intercede
with the LORD, that He may remove the serpents from us." And Moses interceded for
the people.
8 Then the LORD said to Moses, "[1]Make a
[a]fiery *serpent,* and set it on a standard; and it
shall come about, that everyone who is bitten, when he looks at it, he will live."
9 And Moses made a [a]bronze serpent
and set it on the standard; and it came
about, that if a serpent bit any man, when he
looked to the bronze serpent, he lived.
10 [a]Now the sons of Israel moved out and
camped in Oboth.
11 They journeyed from Oboth and
camped at Iyeabarim, in the wilderness
which is opposite Moab, to the [1]east.
12 [a]From there they set out and camped
in [1]Wadi Zered.
13 From there they journeyed and camped
on the other side of the Arnon, which is in
the wilderness that comes out of the border
of the Amorites, [a]for the Arnon is the border
of Moab, between Moab and the Amorites.
14 Therefore it is said in the Book of the
Wars of the LORD,
"Waheb in Suphah,
And the wadis of the Arnon,
15 And the slope of the wadis
That extends to the site of [a]Ar,
And leans to the border of Moab."
16 [a]From there *they continued* to [1]Beer,
that is the well where the LORD said to
Moses, "Assemble the people, that I may give
them water."
17 [a]Then Israel sang this song:
"Spring up, O well! Sing to it!
18 "The well, which the leaders sank,
Which the nobles of the people dug,
With the scepter *and* with their
staffs."
And from the wilderness *they continued* to
Mattanah,
19 and from Mattanah to Nahaliel, and
from Nahaliel to Bamoth,
20 and from Bamoth to the valley that is in
the land of Moab, at the top of Pisgah which
overlooks the [1]wasteland.

7 [a]Num 11:2; Ps 78:34; Is 26:16; Hos 5:15 [b]Ex 8:8; 1 Sam 12:19; Acts 8:24
8 [1]Lit *Make for yourself* [a]Is 14:29; 30:6; John 3:14
9 [a]2 Kin 18:4; John 3:14, 15
10 [a]Num 33:43, 44
11 [1]Lit *sunrise*
12 [1]I.e. a dry ravine except during rainy season [a]Num 33:45
13 [a]Num 22:36; Judg 11:18
15 [a]Num 21:28; Deut 2:9, 18, 29
16 [1]I.e. a well [a]Num 33:46-49
17 [a]Ex 15:1; Ps 105:2
20 [1]Or *Jeshimon*
21 [a]Deut 2:26-37; Judg 11:19
22 [a]Num 20:16, 17
23 [a]Num 20:21 [b]Deut 2:32
24 [1]Lit *smote,* so with Gr and Lat [2]M.T. reads *strong* [a]Amos 2:9 [b]Deut 2:37
25 [1]Lit *daughters* [a]Amos 2:10
28 [1]Lit *lords of the* [2]Or *Bamoth* [a]Jer 48:45 [b]Num 21:15 [c]Num 22:41; Is 15:2; 16:12
29 [a]Jer 48:46 [b]Judg 11:24; 1 Kin 11:33; 2 Kin 23:13 [c]Is 15:5 [d]Is 16:2
30 [a]Num 32:3, 34; Jer 48:18, 22
32 [a]Num 32:1, 3, 35; Jer 48:32
33 [a]Deut 3:1-7

Two Victories

21 [a]Then Israel sent messengers to Sihon,
king of the Amorites, saying,
22 "[a]Let me pass through your land. We
will not turn off into field or vineyard; we
will not drink water from wells. We will go
by the king's highway until we have passed
through your border."
23 [a]But Sihon would not permit Israel to
pass through his border. So Sihon gathered
all his people and went out against Israel in
the wilderness, and came to [b]Jahaz and
fought against Israel.
24 Then [a]Israel [1]struck him with the edge
of the sword, and took possession of his land
from the Arnon to the Jabbok, as far as the
sons of Ammon; for the [b]border of the sons
of Ammon *was* [2]Jazer.
25 Israel took all these cities and [a]Israel
lived in all the cities of the Amorites, in
Heshbon, and in all her [1]villages.
26 For Heshbon was the city of Sihon,
king of the Amorites, who had fought against
the former king of Moab and had taken all
his land out of his hand, as far as the Arnon.
27 Therefore those who use proverbs say,
"Come to Heshbon! Let it be built!
So let the city of Sihon be established.
28 "[a]For a fire went forth from Heshbon,
A flame from the town of Sihon;
It devoured [b]Ar of Moab,
The [1c]dominant [2]heights of the Arnon.
29 "[a]Woe to you, O Moab!
You are ruined, O people of
[b]Chemosh!
[c]He has given his sons as fugitives,
[d]And his daughters into captivity,
To an Amorite king, Sihon.
30 "But we have cast them down,
Heshbon is ruined as far as [a]Dibon,
Then we have laid waste even to
Nophah,
Which *reaches* to Medeba."
31 Thus Israel lived in the land of the
Amorites.
32 Moses sent to spy out [a]Jazer, and they
captured its villages and dispossessed the
Amorites who *were* there.
33 [a]Then they turned and went up by the
way of Bashan, and Og the king of Bashan

21:8–9 In response to the people's confession of sin (v. 7), God directed Moses to make an image of a serpent and put it on a pole, so that anyone who had been bitten could look at it and live. See the typological use of this incident in John 3:14–15.
21:10–13 The people skirt Edom and make their way to the Arnon, the wadi that serves as the border between Moab and the region of the Amorites and that flows west into the midpoint of the Dead Sea.
21:14 *Book of the Wars of the LORD.* Mentioned only here in the OT. This is not in existence today; it was presumably an ancient collection of songs of war in praise of God (see note on 10:3 for music in war). Cf. the "book of Jashar" (Josh 10:13; 2 Sam 1:18).
21:16 *I may give them water.* The quest for water had been a constant problem during the wilderness experience (see ch. 20; Ex 17).
21:17–18 The "song of the well" may also come from the Book of the Wars of the Lord (v. 14).
21:21–26 As with Edom (20:14–19), Israel requested freedom to pass through the land of the Amorites. When Sihon, their king, tried to meet Israel with a show of force, he suffered an overwhelming defeat. The land of the Amorites was in Transjordan, extending from the Arnon River (at the midpoint of the Dead Sea) to the Jabbok River (v. 24), which flows into the Jordan some 24 miles north of the Dead Sea.
21:27–30 This third ancient poem in ch. 21 was an Amorite taunt song about their earlier victory over Moab (v. 29). Perhaps the "song of Heshbon" was also preserved in the Book of the Wars of the Lord (v. 14).
21:33 *Bashan.* The region northeast of the Sea of Galilee.

went out [1]with all his people, for battle at
[b]Edrei.
34 But the LORD said to Moses, "[a]Do not
fear him, for I have given him into your
hand, and all his people and his land; and
you shall do to him as you did to Sihon, king
of the Amorites, who lived at Heshbon."
35 So [a]they [1]killed him and his sons and
all his people, until there was no remnant
left him; and they possessed his land.

Balak Sends for Balaam

22 [a]Then the sons of Israel journeyed, and
camped in the plains of Moab beyond
the Jordan *opposite* Jericho.
2 Now [a]Balak the son of Zippor saw all
that Israel had done to the Amorites.
3 [a]So Moab was in great fear because of
the people, for they were numerous; and
Moab was in dread of the sons of Israel.
4 Moab said to the elders of [a]Midian,
"Now this [1]horde will lick up all that is
around us, as the ox licks up the grass of the
field." And Balak the son of Zippor was king
of Moab at that time.
5 So he sent messengers to [a]Balaam the
son of Beor, at [b]Pethor, which is near the
[1]River, *in* the land of the sons of his people,
to call him, saying, "Behold, a people came
out of Egypt; behold, they cover the surface
of the land, and they are living opposite me.
6 "[a]Now, therefore, please come, [b]curse
this people for me since they are too [1]mighty
for me; perhaps I may be able to [2]defeat
them and drive them out of the land. For I
know that he whom you bless is blessed,
and he whom you curse is cursed."
7 So the elders of Moab and the elders of
Midian departed with the *fees for* [a]divination
in their hand; and they came to Balaam and
[1]repeated Balak's words to him.
8 He said to them, "Spend the night here,
and I will bring word back to you as the LORD

33 [1]Lit *he and* [b]Josh 13:12
34 [a]Deut 3:2
35 [1]Lit *smote* [a]Deut 3:3, 4
22:1 [a]Num 33:48, 49
2 [a]Judg 11:25
3 [a]Ex 15:15
4 [1]Lit *assembly* [a]Num 25:15-18; 31:1-3
5 [1]I.e. Euphrates [a]Josh 24:9; 2 Pet 2:15f; Jude 11 [b]Deut 23:4
6 [1]Or *numerous* [2]Lit *smite* [a]Num 22:17; 23:7, 8 [b]Num 22:12; 24:9
7 [1]Lit *spoke* [a]Num 23:23; 24:1; Josh 13:22
9 [a]Gen 20:3
12 [a]Num 23:8; 24:9 [b]Gen 12:2; 22:17
15 [1]Lit *these*
17 [a]Num 22:6
18 [1]Lit *mouth* [a]Num 22:38; 24:13; 1 Kin 22:14; 2 Chr 18:13
20 [a]Num 22:35; 23:5, 12, 16, 26; 24:13

may speak to me." And the leaders of Moab
stayed with Balaam.
9 Then [a]God came to Balaam and said,
"Who are these men with you?"
10 Balaam said to God, "Balak the son of
Zippor, king of Moab, has sent *word* to me,
11 'Behold, there is a people who came out
of Egypt and they cover the surface of the
land; now come, curse them for me; perhaps
I may be able to fight against them and drive
them out.'"
12 God said to Balaam, "Do not go with
them; [a]you shall not curse the people, for
they [b]are blessed."
13 So Balaam arose in the morning and
said to Balak's leaders, "Go back to your
land, for the LORD has refused to let me go
with you."
14 The leaders of Moab arose and went to
Balak and said, "Balaam refused to come
with us."
15 Then Balak again sent leaders, more
numerous and more distinguished than [1]the
former.
16 They came to Balaam and said to him,
"Thus says Balak the son of Zippor, 'Let
nothing, I beg you, hinder you from coming
to me;
17 for I will indeed honor you richly, and
I will do whatever you say to me. [a]Please
come then, curse this people for me.'"
18 Balaam replied to the servants of Balak,
"[a]Though Balak were to give me his house
full of silver and gold, I could not do anything, either small or great, contrary to the
[1]command of the LORD my God.
19 "Now please, you also stay here tonight,
and I will find out what else the LORD will
speak to me."
20 God came to Balaam at night and said
to him, "If the men have come to call you,
rise up *and* go with them; but [a]only the
word which I speak to you shall you do."

21:35 *killed him.* By defeating Og, Israel now controlled Transjordan from Moab to the heights of Bashan in the vicinity of Mount Hermon. The victory over Sihon and Og became a subject of song (Ps 135:11; 136:19–20), and is a regular part of the commemoration of the works of the Lord in the Passover celebration.
22:1 *plains of Moab.* Israel now marched back to their staging area east of the Jordan and just north of the Dead Sea. From this point they would launch their attack on Canaan, beginning with the ancient city of Jericho. Moab did not trust Israel's intentions, however. Moab's fear leads to a remarkable interval in the story of Israel: the account of Balak and Balaam (chs. 22–24).
22:3 *Moab was in great fear.* Balak king of Moab did not know that Israel had no plans against him.
22:4 *said to the elders of Midian.* Balak made an alliance with the Midianites to oppose Israel (see v. 7). *as the ox licks up the grass of the field.* A proverbial simile particularly fitting for a pastoral people.
22:5 *sent messengers to Balaam.* Since Balak believed that there was no military way to withstand Israel, he sought to oppose them through pagan divination (vv. 6–7), sending for a diviner with an international reputation. (One of Balaam's non-Biblical prophecies is preserved in an Aramaic text from Deir Alla in the Jordan Valley dating to c. 700 B.C.)
22:8 *bring word . . . as the LORD may speak.* The language here and in v. 18 ("the LORD my God") has led some to believe that Balaam was a believer in Yahweh ("the LORD"), God of Israel. Based on the subsequent narrative, however, it seems best to take Balaam's words as claiming to be the spokesman for any god. Balaam is universally condemned in Scripture for moral, ethical and religious faults (see 31:7–8,15–16; Deut 23:3–6; Josh 13:22; 24:9–10; Neh 13:1–3; Mic 6:5; 2 Pet 2:15–16; Jude 11; Rev 2:14).
22:9 *God came to Balaam.* The author shows his aversion to the pagan prophet Balaam by using "God" instead of "the LORD" (Yahweh), as Balaam does (e.g., in v. 8). By this subtle device, the narrator distances himself from Balaam's outrageous claims. That God spoke to Balaam is not to be denied, but Balaam did not yet realize that the God of Israel was unlike the supposed deities that he usually schemed against.
22:12 *they are blessed.* Israel was under the Lord's blessing promised to Abraham (see note on Gen 12:2–3).
22:20 *go with them.* There appears to be a contradiction between the permission God grants Balaam here and the prohibition He had given earlier (v. 12), and then the anger the Lord displayed against Balaam on his journey (v. 22). The diffi-

21 [a]So Balaam arose in the morning, and saddled his donkey and went with the leaders of Moab.

The Angel and Balaam

22 But God was angry because he was going, [a]and the angel of the LORD took his stand in the way as an adversary against him. Now he was riding on his donkey and his two servants were with him.

23 When the donkey saw the angel of the LORD standing in the way with his drawn sword in his hand, the donkey turned off from the way and went into the field; but Balaam struck the donkey to turn her back into the way.

24 Then the angel of the LORD stood in a narrow path of the vineyards, *with* a wall on this side and a wall on that side.

25 When the donkey saw the angel of the LORD, she pressed herself to the wall and pressed Balaam's foot against the wall, so he struck her again.

26 The angel of the LORD went further, and stood in a narrow place where there was no way to turn to the right hand or the left.

27 When the donkey saw the angel of the LORD, she lay down under Balaam; so [a]Balaam was angry and struck the donkey with his stick.

28 And [a]the LORD opened the mouth of the donkey, and she said to Balaam, "What have I done to you, that you have struck me these three times?"

29 Then Balaam said to the donkey, "Because you have made a mockery of me! If there had been a sword in my hand, [a]I would have killed you by now."

30 The donkey said to Balaam, "Am I not your donkey on which you have ridden all your life to this day? Have I ever been accustomed to do so to you?" And he said, "No."

31 Then the LORD opened the eyes of Balaam, and he saw [a]the angel of the LORD standing in the way with his drawn sword in his hand; and he bowed [1]all the way to the ground.

32 The angel of the LORD said to him, "Why have you struck your donkey these three times? Behold, I have come out as an adversary, because your way was [1a]contrary to me.

33 "But the donkey saw me and turned aside from me these three times. If she had not turned aside from me, I would surely have killed you just now, and let her live."

34 Balaam said to the angel of the LORD, "[a]I have sinned, for I did not know that you were standing in the way against me. Now then, if it is displeasing to you, I will turn back."

35 But the angel of the LORD said to Balaam, "Go with the men, but [a]you shall speak only the word which I [1]tell you." So Balaam went along with the leaders of Balak.

36 When Balak heard that Balaam was coming, he went out to meet him at the city of Moab, which is on the Arnon border, [1]at the extreme end of the border.

37 Then Balak said to Balaam, "Did I not urgently send to you to call you? Why did you not come to me? Am I really unable to honor you?"

38 So Balaam said to Balak, "Behold, I have come now to you! [a]Am I able to speak anything at all? The word that God puts in my mouth, that I shall speak."

39 And Balaam went with Balak, and they came to Kiriath-huzoth.

40 Balak sacrificed oxen and sheep, and sent *some* to Balaam and the leaders who were with him.

41 Then it came about in the morning that Balak took Balaam and brought him up to [1a]the high places of Baal, and he saw from there [2]a [b]portion of the people.

The Prophecies of Balaam

23 Then Balaam said to Balak, "Build seven altars for me here, and prepare seven bulls and seven rams for me here."

21 [a]2 Pet 2:15
22 [a]Ex 23:20
27 [a]James 1:19
28 [a]2 Pet 2:16
29 [a]Prov 12:10; Matt 15:19
31 [a]Josh 5:13-15

31 [1]Lit *and prostrated himself to his face*
32 [1]Lit *reckless* [a]2 Pet 2:15
34 [a]Num 14:40
35 [1]Or *speak to* [a]Num 22:20
36 [1]Lit *which is at*
38 [a]Num 22:18
41 [1]Or *Bamoth-baal* [2]Lit *the end of the camp* [a]Num 21:28 [b]Num 23:13

culty is best understood as lying in the contrary character of Balaam. God had forbidden him to go to curse Israel. He then allowed Balaam to go, but only if he would follow the Lord's direction. But Balaam's real intentions were known to the Lord, and so with severe displeasure He confronted the pagan prophet.

22:23 *the donkey saw the angel of the LORD.* The internationally known seer is blind to spiritual reality, but his proverbially dumb beast is able to see the angel of the Lord on the path. As a pagan prophet, Balaam was a specialist in animal divination, but his animal saw what he was blind to observe.

22:29 *If there had been a sword in my hand.* A ridiculous picture of the hapless Balaam. A sword was nearby (see vv. 23,31–33), but its victim was not going to be the donkey.

22:31 *Then the LORD opened the eyes of Balaam.* The language follows the same structure as the opening words of v. 28. In some ways, the opening of the eyes of the pagan prophet to see the reality of the angel was the greater miracle.

22:35 *speak only the word which I tell you.* The one great gain was that Balaam was now more aware of the seriousness of the task before him; he would not be able to change the word the Lord would give him (see 23:12,20,26).

22:37 *Did I not urgently send to you to call you?* The comic element of the story is seen not only in the hapless Balaam but also in the frustrated Balak (see 23:11,25; 24:10).

22:40 *Balak sacrificed oxen and sheep.* Not sacrifices to the Lord. The pieces given to Balaam would have included the livers, for, as a pagan diviner, Balaam was a specialist in liver divination. Balaam subsequently gave up his acts of sorcery as the power of the Lord's word came upon him (24:1).

23:1 *seven altars . . . seven bulls and seven rams.* These sacrifices were prepared as a part of Balaam's pagan actions. The number seven (signifying completeness) was held in high regard among Semitic peoples in general; the many animals would provide abundant liver and organ materials for the diviner from the east.

2 Balak did just as Balaam had spoken,
and Balak and Balaam offered up a bull and
a ram on each altar.
3 Then Balaam said to Balak, "Stand
beside your burnt offering, and I will go; perhaps the LORD will come to meet me, and
whatever He shows me I will tell you." So he
went to a bare hill.
4 Now God met Balaam, and he said to
Him, "I have set up the seven altars, and I
have offered up a bull and a ram on each
altar."
5 Then the LORD [a]put a word in Balaam's
mouth and said, "Return to Balak, and you
shall speak thus."
6 So he returned to him, and behold, he
was standing beside his burnt offering, he
and all the leaders of Moab.
7 He took up his [1]discourse and said,

"From [a]Aram Balak has brought me,
Moab's king from the mountains of
the East,
'[b]Come curse Jacob for me,
And come, denounce Israel!'
8 "[a]How shall I curse whom God has not
cursed?
And how can I denounce whom the
LORD has not denounced?
9 "As I see him from the top of the rocks,
And I look at him from the hills;
[a]Behold, a people *who* dwells apart,
And will not be reckoned among the
nations.
10 "[a]Who can count the dust of Jacob,
Or number the fourth part of Israel?
[b]Let [1]me die the death of the upright,
[c]And let my end be like his!"

11 Then Balak said to Balaam, "What
have you done to me? [a]I took you to curse
my enemies, but behold, you have actually
blessed them!"
12 He replied, "Must I not be careful to
speak [a]what the LORD puts in my mouth?"
13 Then Balak said to him, "Please come
with me to another place from where you
may see them, although you will only see the
extreme end of them and will not see all of
them; and curse them for me from there."
14 So he took him to the field of Zophim,
to the top of Pisgah, and built seven altars
and offered a bull and a ram on *each* altar.
15 And he said to Balak, "Stand here
beside your burnt offering while I myself
meet *the LORD* over there."
16 Then the LORD met Balaam and [a]put a
word in his mouth and said, "Return to
Balak, and thus you shall speak."
17 He came to him, and behold, he was
standing beside his burnt offering, and the
leaders of Moab with him. And Balak said to
him, "What has the LORD spoken?"
18 Then he took up his [1]discourse and
said,

"Arise, O Balak, and hear;
Give ear to me, O son of Zippor!
19 "[a]God is not a man, that He should lie,
Nor a son of man, that He should
repent;
[b]Has He said, and will He not do it?
Or has He spoken, and will He not
make it good?
20 "Behold, I have received *a command* to
bless;
[a]When He has blessed, then [b]I cannot
revoke it.
21 "[a]He has not observed [1]misfortune in
Jacob;
[b]Nor has He seen trouble in Israel;
[c]The LORD his God is with him,
[d]And the shout of a king is among
them.
22 "[a]God brings them out of Egypt,
He is for them like the [b]horns of the
wild ox.
23 "[a]For there is no omen against Jacob,
Nor is there any divination against
Israel;
At the proper time it shall be said to
Jacob
And to Israel, what God has done!

23:5 [a]Num 22:20; Deut 18:18; Jer 1:9
7 [1]Lit *parable* [a]Num 22:5; Deut 23:4 [b]Num 22:6
8 [a]Num 22:12
9 [a]Deut 32:8; 33:28
10 [1]Lit *my soul* [a]Gen 13:16; 28:14 [b]Is 57:1 [c]Ps 37:37
11 [a]Neh 13:2
12 [a]Num 22:20
16 [a]Num 22:20
18 [1]Lit *parable*
19 [a]1 Sam 15:29 [b]Is 40:8; 55:11
20 [a]Gen 12:2; 22:17; Num 22:12 [b]Is 43:13
21 [1]Or *iniquity* [a]Num 14:18, 19, 34; Ps 32:2, 5 [b]Deut 9:24; 32:5; Jer 50:20 [c]Ex 3:12; Deut 31:23 [d]Deut 33:5; Ps 89:15-18
22 [a]Num 24:8 [b]Deut 33:17
23 [a]Num 22:7; 24:1; Josh 13:22

23:2 *Balak did as Balaam had spoken.* Balaam is in charge; Balak is now his subordinate.

23:7–24:24 There are seven poetic oracles here: The first four are longer, have introductory narrative bridges and are written in exquisite poetry (23:7–10; 23:18–24; 24:3–9; 24:15–19). The last three are brief, are much more difficult to understand, and follow one another in a staccato pattern (24:20,21–22, 23–24).

23:7 *discourse.* Hebrew *mashal,* usually translated "proverb" or "oracle." By this word the distinctive nature of Balaam's prophecies is established; none of the prophecies of Israel's true prophets is described by this term.

23:8 *How shall I curse whom God has not cursed?* That which Balaam had been hired to do he was unable to do. God kept him from pronouncing a curse on His people, who were unlike the nations of the world (v. 9).

23:10 *Let me die the death of the upright.* A wish not granted (see 31:8,16). *let my end be like his!* He who had come to curse desired to share in Israel's blessing.

23:13 *will not see all of them.* Balak attempted to reduce Israel's power by selecting a point where their immense numbers would be obscured. Unfortunately for Balak, the oracle that followed (vv. 18–24) exceeded the first in its blessing on Israel.

23:19 *God is not a man, that He should lie.* These sublime words describe the immutability of the Lord and the integrity of His word. Balaam is a foil for God—constantly shifting, prevaricating, equivocating, changing—a prime example of the distinction between God and man.

23:21 *the shout of a king is among them.* That the first explicit declaration of the Lord's kingship in the Pentateuch was made by Balaam is a suitable improbability. Because God is King (Sovereign), He was able to use Balaam for his own ends—to bless his people in a new and wonderful manner.

23:22 *wild ox.* Or "aurochs" or "oryx," a traditional image of power in the ancient Near East (see also 24:8).

23:23 *no omen against Jacob.* Balaam speaks from his frightful experience. He had no means in his bag of tricks to withstand God's blessing of Israel.

24 “[a]Behold, a people rises like a lioness,
And as a lion it lifts itself;
It will not lie down until it devours the
prey,
And drinks the blood of the slain.”
25 Then Balak said to Balaam, “Do not
curse them at all nor bless them at all!”
26 But Balaam replied to Balak, “Did I not
tell you, ‘[1][a]Whatever the LORD speaks, that I
must do’?”
27 Then Balak said to Balaam, “Please
come, I will take you to another place; perhaps it will be [1]agreeable with God that you
curse them for me from there.”
28 So Balak took Balaam to the top of Peor
which overlooks the [1]wasteland.
29 Balaam said to Balak, “Build seven
altars for me here and prepare seven bulls
and seven rams for me here.”
30 Balak did just as Balaam had said, and
offered up a bull and a ram on *each* altar.

The Prophecy from Peor

24 When Balaam saw that it [1]pleased the
LORD to bless Israel, he did not go as at
other times to [2]seek [a]omens but he set his
face toward the [b]wilderness.
2 And Balaam lifted up his eyes and saw
Israel [1]camping tribe by tribe; and [a]the Spirit of God came upon him.
3 He took up his [1]discourse and said,
“[a]The oracle of Balaam the son of Beor,
And the oracle of the man whose eye
is opened;
4 The oracle of him who [a]hears the
[1]words of God,
Who sees the [b]vision of [2]the Almighty,
Falling down, yet having his eyes
uncovered,
5 How fair are your tents, O Jacob,
Your dwellings, O Israel!
6 “Like [1]valleys that stretch out,
Like gardens beside the river,
Like [a]aloes planted by the LORD,
Like [b]cedars beside the waters.
7 “Water will flow from his buckets,
And his seed *will be* by many waters,
And his king shall be higher than
[a]Agag,
[b]And his kingdom shall be exalted.
8 “[a]God brings him out of Egypt,
He is for him like the horns of the
wild ox.
[b]He will devour the nations *who are*
his adversaries,
And will crush their bones in pieces,
And shatter *them* with his [c]arrows.
9 “[a]He [1]couches, he lies down as a lion,
And as a [2]lion, who [3]dares rouse him?
[b]Blessed is everyone who blesses you,
And cursed is everyone who curses
you.”
10 Then Balak’s anger burned against
Balaam, and he struck his [1]hands together;
and Balak said to Balaam, “I called you to
curse my enemies, but behold, you have persisted in blessing them these three times!
11 “Therefore, [1]flee to your place now. I
said I would honor you greatly, but behold,
the LORD has held you back from honor.”
12 Balaam said to Balak, “[a]Did I not tell
your messengers whom you had sent to me,
saying,
13 ‘Though Balak were to give me his house
full of silver and gold, I could not do anything
contrary to the [1]command of the LORD, either
good or bad, [a]of my own [2]accord. [b]What the
LORD speaks, that I will speak’?
14 “And now, behold, [a]I am going to my
people; come, *and* I will advise you what
this people will do to your people in the
[1]days to come.”
15 He took up his discourse and said,
“[a]The oracle of Balaam the son of Beor,
And the oracle of the man whose eye
is opened,
16 The oracle of him who hears the
[1]words of God,

24 [a]Gen 49:9; Nah 2:11, 12
26 [1]Lit *saying, Whatever* [a]Num 22:18
27 [1]Lit *right in the sight of God*
28 [1]Or *Jeshimon*
24:1 [1]Lit *was good in the eyes of* [2]Lit *encounter* [a]Num 22:7; 23:23 [b]Num 23:28
2 [1]Lit *dwelling* [a]Num 11:26; 1 Sam 19:20; Rev 1:10
3 [1]Lit *parable,* and so throughout the ch [a]Num 24:15, 16
4 [1]Lit *sayings* [2]Heb *Shaddai* [a]Num 22:20 [b]Gen 15:1; Num 12:6
6 [1]Or possibly *palm trees* [a]Ps 45:8
6 [b]Ps 1:3
7 [a]Num 24:20; 1 Sam 15:8 [b]Ps 145:11-13
8 [a]Num 23:22 [b]Num 23:24; Ps 2:9 [c]Ps 45:5
9 [1]Lit *bows down* [2]Or *lioness* [3]Lit *shall* [a]Gen 49:9; Num 23:24 [b]Gen 12:3; 27:29
10 [1]Lit *palms*
11 [1]Lit *flee for yourself*
12 [a]Num 22:18
13 [1]Lit *mouth* [2]Lit *heart* [a]Num 16:28 [b]Num 22:20
14 [1]Lit *end of the days* [a]Num 31:8, 16; Josh 13:22
15 [a]Num 24:3, 4
16 [1]Lit *sayings*

23:24 *like a lioness.* Israel was about to arise and devour its foes, like a lioness on the hunt (see 24:9; Gen 49:9).
24:1 *go . . . to seek omens.* Balaam’s magic and sorcery are identified here (see notes on 22:40; 23:1).
24:2 *the Spirit of God came upon him.* Not to be confused with the filling of the Spirit (Acts 2:1–4), or with the anointing of the Spirit (Is 61:1). This unexpected language prepares the reader for the heightened revelation that is about to come from the unwitting messenger.
24:3–4 The extensive introduction of this oracle describes Balaam’s experience in the Lord’s presence. Now Balaam’s eyes were opened (see note on 22:31).
24:6–7 Balaam speaks here in general, but luxuriant, terms of the blessings that will come to the Israelites as they settle in their new land. The lushness of their blessing from the Lord is reminiscent of Eden.
24:7 *higher than Agag.* Possibly a specific future prophecy concerning the opponent of King Saul (1 Sam 15:32–33)—setting the stage for the even more remarkable words of the fourth oracle (vv. 15–19). But it may be that Agag was a common name among Amalekite kings and that the allusion here is to the Amalekites who attacked Israel when she came out of Egypt (see Ex 17:8–13) and again when she first approached Canaan (see 14:45).
24:8 *God brings him out of Egypt.* These central words about Israel’s salvation are recited by one who was a hostile outsider (see notes on 23:21; 25:1–18).
24:9 *Blessed is everyone who blesses you . . . curses you.* The theology of blessing and cursing in the promises made to Abraham (Gen 12:2–3) is now a part of this oracle of blessing. Perhaps here Balaam was reasserting his desire to be a part of Israel’s blessing (see note on 23:10).
24:11 *the LORD has held you back from honor.* In his disgust with Balaam’s failure to curse Israel, Balak now dismisses him without pay—the ultimate insult to his greed (see 2 Pet 2:15).
24:14 *in the days to come.* The distant (Messianic) future is usually indicated by this expression (see, e.g., Jer 48:47 and note).
24:15–16 As in the third oracle (see vv. 3–4), the introduction to the fourth oracle is lengthy, helping to prepare the reader for the startling words of the prophecy.

And knows the knowledge of the
[2]Most High,
Who sees the vision of [3]the Almighty,
Falling down, yet having his eyes
uncovered.
17 "I see him, but not now;
I behold him, but not near;
A star shall come forth from Jacob,
[a]A scepter shall rise from Israel,
[b]And shall crush through the
[1]forehead of Moab,
And [2]tear down all the sons of [3]Sheth.
18 "[a]Edom shall be a possession,
[b]Seir, its enemies, also will be a
possession,
While Israel performs valiantly.
19 "One from Jacob shall have dominion,
And will destroy the remnant from the
city."
20 And he looked at Amalek and took up
his discourse and said,
"Amalek was the first of the nations,
[a]But his end *shall be* [1]destruction."
21 And he looked at the [a]Kenite, and took
up his discourse and said,
"Your dwelling place is enduring,
And your nest is set in the cliff.
22 "Nevertheless Kain will be consumed;
How long will [a]Asshur [1]keep you
captive?"
23 Then he took up his discourse and
said,
"Alas, who can live except God has
ordained it?
24 "But ships *shall come* from the coast of
[a]Kittim,
And they shall afflict Asshur and will
afflict [b]Eber;
[c]So they also *will come* to destruction."
25 Then Balaam arose and departed and
returned to [a]his place, and Balak also went
his way.

16 [2]Heb *Elyon* [3]Heb *Shaddai* **17** [1]Lit *corners* [2]Another reading is *the crown of the head of* [3]I.e. tumult [a]Gen 49:10 [b]Num 21:29; Is 15:1-16:14 **18** [a]Gen 27:29; Amos 9:11, 12 [b]Gen 32:3 **20** [1]Lit *to destroying* [a]Num 24:24 **21** [a]Gen 15:19 **22** [1]Lit *take* [a]Gen 10:21, 22 **24** [a]Gen 10:4; Ezek 27:6 [b]Gen 10:21 [c]Num 24:20 **25** [a]Num 24:14

25:1 [a]Num 33:49; Josh 2:1 [b]Num 31:16; 1 Cor 10:8; Rev 2:14 **2** [a]Ex 34:15; Deut 32:38 **3** [1]Or *Baal-peor* [a]Ps 106:28, 29; Hos 9:10 **4** [1]Lit *in front of the sun* [a]Deut 13:17 **5** [1]Or *Baal-peor* [a]Ex 32:27 **6** [1]Lit *brothers* [a]Num 22:4 [b]Joel 2:17 **7** [a]Ps 106:30 **8** [1]Or *inner rooms* [2]Or *belly* [a]Num 16:46-48 **9** [a]Num 14:37; 16:48-50; 31:16 **11** [a]Ps 106:30

The Sin of Peor

25 While Israel remained at [a]Shittim, the
people began [b]to play the harlot with
the daughters of Moab.
2 For [a]they invited the people to the sacrifices of their gods, and the people ate and
bowed down to their gods.
3 So [a]Israel joined themselves to [1]Baal of
Peor, and the LORD was angry against Israel.
4 The LORD said to Moses, "Take all the
leaders of the people and execute them [1]in
broad daylight before the LORD, [a]so that the
fierce anger of the LORD may turn away from
Israel."
5 So Moses said to the judges of Israel,
"Each of you [a]slay his men who have joined
themselves to [1]Baal of Peor."
6 Then behold, one of the sons of Israel
came and brought to his [1]relatives a [a]Midi-
anite woman, in the sight of Moses and in
the sight of all the congregation of the sons
of Israel, [b]while they were weeping at the
doorway of the tent of meeting.
7 [a]When Phinehas the son of Eleazar, the
son of Aaron the priest, saw it, he arose from
the midst of the congregation and took a
spear in his hand,
8 and he went after the man of Israel into
the [1]tent and pierced both of them through,
the man of Israel and the woman, through
the [2]body. [a]So the plague on the sons of Israel was checked.
9 [a]Those who died by the plague were
24,000.

The Zeal of Phinehas

10 Then the LORD spoke to Moses, saying,
11 "[a]Phinehas the son of Eleazar, the son of
Aaron the priest, has turned away My wrath
from the sons of Israel in that he was jealous
with My jealousy among them, so that I did

24:17 *star . . . scepter.* Perhaps fulfilled initially in David, but ultimately in the coming Messianic ruler. Israel's future Deliverer will be like a star (cf. Rev 22:16) and scepter in his royalty and will bring victory over the enemies of his people (see v. 19). *Sheth.* Possibly the early inhabitants of Moab known as the Shutu people in ancient Egyptian documents.
24:20 *Amalek was the first.* The first to attack Israel and oppose the Lord's purpose with his people (see Ex 17:8–13).
24:21 *Kenite.* The name suggests a tribe of metal workers. In other passages the Kenites are allied with Israel (see, e.g., Judg 1:16; 4:11; 1 Sam 15:6). Since Moses' father-in-law was a Kenite but also associated with Midian (see Ex 2:16), it may be that Balaam's reference is to Midianites (see 22:4,7). *nest.* Hebrew *qen,* a wordplay on the word for Kenites (Hebrew *qeni*).
24:22 *Asshur.* Assyria.
24:24 *Kittim.* Probably ancient Kition in Cyprus. *they shall afflict Asshur and will afflict Eber; So . . . destruction.* One nation will rise and supplant another, only to face its own doom. By contrast, there is the implied ongoing blessing on Israel, and their sure promise of a future deliverer who will have the final victory (vv. 17–19).
25:1–18 It is not until 31:8,16 that we learn that the principal instigator of Israel's apostasy was Balaam (see notes on 22:5,8). Failing to destroy Israel by means of the mantic curse, Balaam seduced Israel by the Canaanite fertility rites of Baal.
25:1 *Shittim.* Another name for the region of Israel's staging for the conquest of Canaan; it was across the Jordan River opposite the ancient city of Jericho (see Josh 2:1). *play the harlot.* Israel's engagement in the fertility rites of Baal involved not only the evil of sexual immorality. It was also a breach of covenant with the Lord, a worship of the gods of the land (vv. 2–3) and a foretaste of the people's ruin in the unfolding of their history.
25:4 *execute them in broad daylight.* The special display of the corpses would warn survivors of the consequences of sin.
25:6 *brought to his relatives a Midianite woman.* The contempt for the holy things and the word of the Lord shown by Zimri (v. 14) and his lover Cozbi (v. 15) is unimaginable.
25:9 *24,000.* The number of those who died because of the flagrant actions of the people in their worship of Baal exceeded even those who died in the rebellion of Korah and his allies (14,700; see 16:49). Again, the large number of those who died fits well with the immense number of the people stated in the first census (1:46) and the second (26:51).
25:11 *he was jealous with My jealousy.* Cf. Ex 20:4–6. The zeal of Phinehas for the Lord's honor became the occasion for the

not destroy the sons of Israel [b]in My jealousy.

12 "Therefore say, '[a]Behold, I give him My [b]covenant of peace;

13 and it shall be for him and his [1]descendants after him, a covenant of a [a]perpetual priesthood, because he was jealous for his God and [b]made atonement for the sons of Israel.' "

14 Now the name of the [1]slain man of Israel who was [1]slain with the Midianite woman, was Zimri the son of Salu, a leader of a father's household among the Simeonites.

15 The name of the Midianite woman who was [1]slain was [a]Cozbi the daughter of [b]Zur, [2]who was head of the people of a father's household in Midian.

16 Then the LORD spoke to Moses, saying,

17 "[a]Be hostile to the Midianites and strike them;

18 for they have been hostile to you with their tricks, with which they have deceived you in the affair of Peor and in the affair of Cozbi, the daughter of the leader of Midian, their sister who was slain on the day of the plague because of Peor."

Census of a New Generation

26 [1]Then it came about after the [a]plague, [2]that the LORD spoke to Moses and to Eleazar the son of Aaron the priest, saying,

2 "[a]Take a [1]census of all the congregation of the sons of Israel from twenty years old and upward, by their fathers' households, whoever is able to go out to war in Israel."

3 So Moses and Eleazar the priest spoke with them [a]in the plains of Moab by the Jordan at Jericho, saying,

4 "*Take a census of the people* from twenty years old and upward, as the LORD has commanded Moses."

11 [b]Ex 20:5 **12** [a]Ps 106:30, 31 [b]Is 54:10; Ezek 34:25; 37:26 **13** [1]Lit *seed* [a]Ex 29:9 [b]Num 16:46 **14** [1]Lit *smitten* **15** [1]Lit *smitten* [2]Lit *he* [a]Num 25:18 [b]Num 31:8 **17** [a]Num 25:1; 22:4; 31:1-3 **26:1** [1]Ch 25:19 in Heb [2]Ch 26:1 in Heb [a]Num 25:9 **2** [1]Lit *sum* [a]Ex 30:11-16; 38:25, 26; Num 1:2 **3** [a]Num 22:1; 33:48; 35:1

7 [a]Num 1:21 **9** [a]Num 1:16; 16:2 **10** [1]Lit *sign* [a]Num 16:32 [b]Num 16:35, 38 **11** [a]Num 16:27, 33; Deut 24:16 **12** [1]In Gen 46:10 and Ex 6:15, *Jemuel* [2]In 1 Chr 4:24, *Jarib* **13** [1]In Gen 46:10, *Zohar* **14** [a]Num 1:23 **15** [1]In Gen 46:16, *Ziphion* **16** [1]In Gen 46:16, *Ezbon* **17** [1]In Gen 46:16, *Arodi*

Now the sons of Israel who came out of the land of Egypt *were:*

5 Reuben, Israel's firstborn, the sons of Reuben: *of* Hanoch, the family of the Hanochites; of Pallu, the family of the Palluites;

6 of Hezron, the family of the Hezronites; of Carmi, the family of the Carmites.

7 These are the families of the Reubenites, and those who were numbered of them were [a]43,730.

8 The son of Pallu: Eliab.

9 The sons of Eliab: Nemuel and Dathan and Abiram. These are the Dathan and Abiram who were [a]called by the congregation, who contended against Moses and against Aaron in the company of Korah, when they contended against the LORD,

10 and [a]the earth opened its mouth and swallowed them up along with Korah, when that company died, [b]when the fire devoured 250 men, so that they became a [1]warning.

11 [a]The sons of Korah, however, did not die.

12 The sons of Simeon according to their families: of [1]Nemuel, the family of the Nemuelites; of Jamin, the family of the Jaminites; of [2]Jachin, the family of the Jachinites;

13 of [1]Zerah, the family of the Zerahites; of Shaul, the family of the Shaulites.

14 These are the families of the Simeonites, [a]22,200.

15 The sons of Gad according to their families: of [1]Zephon, the family of the Zephonites; of Haggi, the family of the Haggites; of Shuni, the family of the Shunites;

16 of [1]Ozni, the family of the Oznites; of Eri, the family of the Erites;

17 of [1]Arod, the family of the Arodites; of Areli, the family of the Arelites.

18 These are the families of the sons of

Lord's covenanting with him and his descendants as God's true priests (see note on Gen 9:9). This son of Eleazar contrasts with the casual wickedness of his uncles, Nadab and Abihu (see Lev 10:1–3 and notes).

25:17 *Be hostile to the Midianites.* Because of their active participation in the seduction of the Israelites. Midianites had been in league with Balak from the beginning of the confrontation (see 22:4,7) and became the objects of a holy war (31:1–24).

26:1–51 The first census of those who were mustered for the war of conquest had been taken over 38 years earlier. That first generation of men 20 years old or more had nearly all died. It was now time for the new generation to be numbered and mustered for the campaign that awaited them. The aged Moses was joined in the task this time by his nephew Eleazar; Aaron was dead (see 20:28). In this second census the prominent clans of each tribe are listed. The numbers of most of the tribes increase. Reuben is one of the tribes that shows a decline. It is possible that the slight reduction of the families of Reuben was brought about by the judgment on their members during the rebellion of Korah and his Reubenite allies (see note on v. 9). In the intervening years the family of Reuben had nearly caught up with its former numbers (see note on v. 14). Note the comparison of the numbers of each tribe from the first census to the second:

Tribe	*First Census*	*Second Census*
Reuben	46,500	43,730
Simeon	59,300	22,200
Gad	45,650	40,500
Judah	74,600	76,500
Issachar	54,400	64,300
Zebulun	57,400	60,500
Ephraim	40,500	32,500
Manasseh	32,200	52,700
Benjamin	35,400	45,600
Dan	62,700	64,400
Asher	41,500	53,400
Naphtali	53,400	45,400
Total	603,550	601,730

26:9 *Dathan and Abiram.* The listing of Reuben's families becomes an occasion to remind the reader of the part that certain of their number had in Korah's rebellion (see 16:1; cf. Jude 11).

26:14 *22,200.* The greatest loss was in the tribe of Simeon (down from 59,300). Zimri was from the house of Simeon (25:14). Perhaps most of the 24,000 who died in the plague of that time were from Simeon. The judgment was so recent that the tribe had not had time to recover, as had the tribe of Reuben (see note on vv. 1–51).

Gad according to those who were numbered of them, [a]40,500.

19 The [a]sons of Judah *were* Er and Onan, but Er and Onan died in the land of Canaan.

20 The [a]sons of Judah according to their families were: of Shelah, the family of the Shelanites; of Perez, the family of the Perezites; of Zerah, the family of the Zerahites.

21 The sons of Perez were: of Hezron, the family of the Hezronites; of Hamul, the family of the Hamulites.

22 These are the families of Judah according to those who were numbered of them, [a]76,500.

23 The [a]sons of Issachar according to their families: *of* Tola, the family of the Tolaites; of [1]Puvah, the family of the Punites;

24 of [1]Jashub, the family of the Jashubites; of Shimron, the family of the Shimronites.

25 These are the families of Issachar according to those who were numbered of them, [a]64,300.

26 The [a]sons of Zebulun according to their families: of Sered, the family of the Seredites; of Elon, the family of the Elonites; of Jahleel, the family of the Jahleelites.

27 These are the families of the Zebulunites according to those who were numbered of them, [a]60,500.

28 The [a]sons of Joseph according to their families: Manasseh and Ephraim.

29 The sons of Manasseh: of Machir, the family of the Machirites; and [a]Machir [1]became the father of Gilead: of Gilead, the family of the Gileadites.

30 These are the sons of Gilead: *of* [1]Iezer, the family of the [a]Iezerites; of Helek, the family of the Helekites;

31 and *of* Asriel, the family of the Asrielites; and *of* Shechem, the family of the Shechemites;

32 and *of* Shemida, the family of the Shemidaites; and *of* Hepher, the family of the Hepherites.

33 Now Zelophehad the son of Hepher had no sons, but only daughters; and [a]the names of the daughters of Zelophehad were Mahlah, Noah, Hoglah, Milcah and Tirzah.

34 These are the families of Manasseh; and those who were numbered of them were [a]52,700.

35 These are the sons of Ephraim according to their families: of Shuthelah, the family of the Shuthelahites; of [1]Becher, the family of the Becherites; of Tahan, the family of the Tahanites.

36 These are the sons of Shuthelah: of Eran, the family of the Eranites.

37 These are the families of the sons of Ephraim according to those who were numbered of them, [a]32,500. These are the sons of Joseph according to their families.

38 The sons of Benjamin according to their families: of Bela, the family of the Belaites; of Ashbel, the family of the Ashbelites; of [1]Ahiram, the family of the Ahiramites;

39 of [1]Shephupham, the family of the Shuphamites; of [2]Hupham, the family of the Huphamites.

40 The sons of Bela were [1]Ard and Naaman: *of Ard,* the family of the Ardites; of Naaman, the family of the Naamites.

41 These are the sons of Benjamin according to their families; and those who were numbered of them were [a]45,600.

42 These are the sons of Dan according to their families: of [1]Shuham, the family of the Shuhamites. These are the families of Dan according to their families.

43 All the families of the Shuhamites, according to those who were numbered of them, were [a]64,400.

44 The [a]sons of Asher according to their families: of Imnah, the family of the Imnites; of Ishvi, the family of the Ishvites; of Beriah, the family of the Beriites.

45 Of the sons of Beriah: of Heber, the family of the Heberites; of Malchiel, the family of the Malchielites.

46 The name of the daughter of Asher *was* Serah.

47 These are the families of the sons of Asher according to those who were numbered of them, [a]53,400.

48 The [a]sons of Naphtali according to their families: of Jahzeel, the family of the Jahzeelites; of Guni, the family of the Gunites;

49 of Jezer, the family of the Jezerites; of [a]Shillem, the family of the Shillemites.

50 These are the families of Naphtali according to their families; and those who were numbered of them were [a]45,400.

51 These are those who were numbered of the sons of Israel, [a]601,730.

52 Then the LORD spoke to Moses, saying,

18 [a]Num 1:25 **19** [a]Gen 38:2; 46:12 **20** [a]Gen 49:8; 1 Chr 2:3; Rev 7:5 **22** [a]Num 1:27 **23** [1]In Gen 46:13, *Puvvah;* in 1 Chr 7:1, *Puah* [a]Gen 46:13; 1 Chr 7:1 **24** [1]In Gen 46:13, *Iob* **25** [a]Num 1:29 **26** [a]Gen 46:14 **27** [a]Num 1:31 **28** [a]Gen 46:20; Deut 33:16f **29** [1]Lit *begot* [a]Josh 17:1; 1 Chr 7:14f **30** [1]In Josh 17:2, *Abiezer* [a]Judg 6:11, 24, 34 **33** [a]Num 27:1 **34** [a]Num 1:35

35 [1]In 1 Chr 7:20, *Bered* **37** [a]Num 1:33 **38** [1]In Gen 46:21, *Ehi;* in 1 Chr 8:1, *Aharah* **39** [1]In Gen 46:21, *Muppim;* in 1 Chr 7:12, *Shuppim* [2]In Gen 46:21, *Muppim* and *Huppim* **40** [1]In 1 Chr 8:3, *Addar* **41** [a]Num 1:37 **42** [1]In Gen 46:23, *Hushim* **43** [a]Num 1:39 **44** [a]Gen 46:17; 1 Chr 7:30 **47** [a]Num 1:41 **48** [a]Gen 46:24; 1 Chr 7:13 **49** [a]1 Chr 7:13 **50** [a]Num 1:43 **51** [a]Ex 12:37; 38:26; Num 1:46; 11:21

26:19 *Er and Onan.* The names of the evil sons of Judah had not been forgotten, but they had no heritage (see Gen 38:1–10).
26:20 *Perez.* The line of David and Jesus would be traced through him (Ruth 4:18–22; Matt 1:1–3).
26:29,35 *Manasseh . . . Ephraim.* The order of the tribes is the same as in ch. 1, except for the inversion of Ephraim and Manasseh.
26:33 *Zelophehad . . . daughters.* See 27:1–11; 36.
26:34 *52,700.* The greatest gain was in the tribe of Manasseh (up from 32,200). The reason for this increase is not known.
26:46 *daughter . . . was Serah.* The listing of this solitary daughter is striking.
26:51 *601,730.* Despite all that the people had been through during the years of wilderness experience, their total number was nearly the same as that of those who were first numbered. This remarkable fact is to be regarded as the blessing of the Lord, in fulfillment of His many promises to give numerical strength to the people descended from Abraham through Jacob (see note on Gen 12:2–3). This grand total and its parts are in accord with the general pattern of the numbers in the book (see note on 1:46).

53 "[1]Among these the land shall be divided for an inheritance according to the number of names.

54 "[a]To the larger *group* you shall increase their inheritance, and to the smaller *group* you shall diminish their inheritance; each shall be given their inheritance according to those who were numbered of them.

55 "But the land shall be [a]divided by lot. They shall [1]receive their inheritance according to the names of the tribes of their fathers.

56 "According to the selection by lot, their inheritance shall be divided between the larger and the smaller *groups.*"

57 [a]These are those who were numbered of the Levites according to their families: of Gershon, the family of the Gershonites; of Kohath, the family of the Kohathites; of Merari, the family of the Merarites.

58 These are the families of Levi: the family of the Libnites, the family of the Hebronites, the family of the Mahlites, the family of the Mushites, the family of the Korahites. [a]Kohath [1]became the father of Amram.

59 The name of Amram's wife [a]was Jochebed, the daughter of Levi, who was born to Levi in Egypt; and she bore to Amram: Aaron and Moses and their sister Miriam.

60 [a]To Aaron were born Nadab and Abihu, Eleazar and Ithamar.

61 [a]But Nadab and Abihu died when they offered strange fire before the LORD.

62 Those who were numbered of them were [a]23,000, every male from a month old and upward, for [b]they were not numbered among the sons of Israel [c]since no inheritance was given to them among the sons of Israel.

63 These are those who were numbered by Moses and Eleazar the priest, who numbered the sons of Israel in the plains of Moab by the Jordan at Jericho.

64 [a]But among these there was not a man of those who were numbered by Moses and Aaron the priest, who numbered the sons of Israel in the wilderness of Sinai.

65 For the LORD had said [1]of them, "[a]They shall surely die in the wilderness." And not a man was left of them, [b]except Caleb the son of Jephunneh and Joshua the son of Nun.

53 [1]Lit *To*
54 [a]Num 33:54
55 [1]Lit *inherit according to* [a]Num 33:54; 34:13
57 [a]Gen 46:11; Ex 6:16; 1 Chr 6:1, 16
58 [1]Lit *begot* [a]Ex 6:20
59 [a]Ex 2:1, 2; 6:20
60 [a]Num 3:2
61 [a]Lev 10:1, 2; Num 3:4
62 [a]Num 3:39 [b]Num 1:47 [c]Num 18:23, 24
64 [a]Num 14:29-35; Deut 2:14-16; Heb 3:17
65 [1]Or *to* [a]Num 14:26-35; Ps 90:3-10; 1 Cor 10:5 [b]Deut 1:36; Josh 14:6-10

27:1 [a]Num 26:33; 36:1 [b]Num 26:33
3 [a]Num 26:64, 65 [b]Num 26:33
5 [a]Num 9:8; 27:21
7 [a]Num 36:2; Josh 17:4
11 [a]Num 35:29
12 [a]Deut 3:23-27; 32:48-52 [b]Num 33:47, 48
13 [1]Lit *was gathered* [a]Num 31:2 [b]Num 20:24, 28; Deut 10:6

A Law of Inheritance

27 Then [a]the daughters of Zelophehad, the son of Hepher, the son of Gilead, the son of Machir, the son of Manasseh, of the families of Manasseh the son of Joseph, came near; and these are [b]the names of his daughters: Mahlah, Noah and Hoglah and Milcah and Tirzah.

2 They stood before Moses and before Eleazar the priest and before the leaders and all the congregation, at the doorway of the tent of meeting, saying,

3 "Our father [a]died in the wilderness, yet he was not among the company of those who gathered themselves together against the LORD in the company of Korah; but he died in his own sin, and [b]he had no sons.

4 "Why should the name of our father be withdrawn from among his family because he had no son? Give us a possession among our father's brothers."

5 [a]So Moses brought their case before the LORD.

6 Then the LORD spoke to Moses, saying,

7 "[a]The daughters of Zelophehad are right in *their* statements. You shall surely give them a hereditary possession among their father's brothers, and you shall transfer the inheritance of their father to them.

8 "Further, you shall speak to the sons of Israel, saying, 'If a man dies and has no son, then you shall transfer his inheritance to his daughter.

9 'If he has no daughter, then you shall give his inheritance to his brothers.

10 'If he has no brothers, then you shall give his inheritance to his father's brothers.

11 'If his father has no brothers, then you shall give his inheritance to his nearest relative in his own family, and he shall possess it; and it shall be a [a]statutory ordinance to the sons of Israel, just as the LORD commanded Moses.' "

12 [a]Then the LORD said to Moses, "Go up to this [b]mountain of Abarim, and see the land which I have given to the sons of Israel.

13 "When you have seen it, you too [a]will be gathered to your people, [b]as Aaron your brother [1]was;

14 for in the wilderness of Zin, during the

26:53 *divided . . . according to the number.* Larger tribes would receive larger shares, but decisions of place would be made by lot (see 33:54).

26:57 *Levites.* As in the first census (ch. 3), the Levites were counted separately.

27:1–11 The daughters of a man who had no son (see 26:33) were concerned about their rights of inheritance and the preservation of their father's name in the land (v. 4). Their action in approaching Moses, Eleazar and the leaders of the nation was unprecedented, an act of courage and conviction.

27:3 *he died in his own sin.* A particular case from among those who died in the wilderness (see 26:64–65). These pious women had a sound understanding of the nature of the wilderness experience and a just claim for their family.

27:5 *Moses brought their case before the LORD.* This verse indicates how case law might have operated in Israel. The general laws would be proclaimed. Then legitimate exceptions or special considerations would come to the elders, and perhaps to Moses himself. He then would await a decision from the Lord. In this case, the Lord gave a favorable decision for these women. Ch. 36 provides an appendix to this account.

27:12–23 The juxtaposition of the story of Zelophehad's daughters' request for an inheritance in the land (vv. 1–11) and the Lord's words to Moses about his own exclusion from the land (vv. 12–14) is touching. Provisions are made for exceptions and irregularities in the inheritance laws, but there is no provision for Moses. His sin at the waters of Meribah at Kadesh (20:1–13) was always before him.

strife of the congregation, [a]you rebelled
against My [1]command [2]to treat Me as holy
before their eyes at the water." (These are
the waters of Meribah of Kadesh in the
wilderness of Zin.)

Joshua to Succeed Moses

15 Then Moses spoke to the LORD, saying,
16 "[a]May the LORD, the God of the spirits of
all flesh, appoint a man over the congregation,
17 who [a]will go out [1]and come in before
them, and who will lead them out and [2]bring
them in, so that the congregation of the LORD
will not be [b]like sheep which have no shepherd."
18 So the LORD said to Moses, "[1]Take Joshua the son of Nun, a man [a]in whom is the
Spirit, and [b]lay your hand on him;
19 and have him stand before Eleazar the
priest and before all the congregation, and
[a]commission him in their sight.
20 "You shall put some of your [1]authority
on him, in order that all the congregation of
the sons of Israel may obey *him.*
21 "Moreover, he shall stand before Eleazar
the priest, who shall inquire for him [a]by the
judgment of the Urim before the LORD. At his
[1]command they shall go out and at his [1]com-
mand they shall come in, *both* he and the
sons of Israel with him, even all the congregation."
22 Moses did just as the LORD commanded
him; and he took Joshua and set him before
Eleazar the priest and before all the congregation.
23 Then he laid his hands on him and
[a]commissioned him, just as the LORD had
spoken [1]through Moses.

Laws for Offerings

28 Then the LORD spoke to Moses, saying,
2 "Command the sons of Israel and say
to them, 'You shall [1]be careful to present My
offering, My [a]food for My offerings by fire, of
a soothing aroma to Me, at their appointed
time.'
3 "[a]You shall say to them, 'This is the
offering by fire which you shall offer to the
LORD: two male lambs one year old without
defect *as* a continual burnt offering every day.
4 'You shall offer the one lamb in the
morning and the other lamb you shall offer
[1]at twilight;
5 also [a]a tenth of an ephah of fine flour
for a [b]grain offering, mixed with a fourth of
a hin of beaten oil.
6 'It is a continual burnt offering which
was ordained in Mount Sinai as a soothing
aroma, an offering by fire to the LORD.
7 'Then the drink offering with it *shall be*
a fourth of a hin for each lamb, [a]in the holy
place you shall pour out a drink offering of
strong drink to the LORD.
8 'The other lamb you shall offer [1]at twilight; as the grain offering of the morning and
as its drink offering, you shall offer it, an
offering by fire, a soothing aroma to the LORD.
9 'Then on the sabbath day two male
lambs one year old without defect, and two-
tenths *of an* [1]*ephah* of fine flour mixed with
oil as a grain offering, and its drink offering:
10 '*This is* the burnt offering of every sabbath in addition to the [a]continual burnt
offering and its drink offering.
11 'Then [a]at the beginning of each of your
months you shall present a burnt offering to
the LORD: two [1]bulls and one ram, seven
male lambs one year old without defect;
12 [a]and three-tenths *of an* [1]*ephah* of fine
flour mixed with oil for a grain offering, for
each bull; and two-tenths of fine flour mixed
with oil for a grain offering, for the one ram;
13 and a tenth *of an* [1]*ephah* of fine flour
mixed with oil for a grain offering for each
lamb, for a burnt offering of a soothing aroma, an offering by fire to the LORD.
14 'Their drink offerings shall be half a hin
of wine for a bull and a third of a hin for the
ram and a fourth of a hin for a lamb; this is
the burnt offering of each month throughout
the months of the year.
15 'And one male goat for a sin offering to
the LORD; it shall be offered with its drink
offering in addition to the [a]continual burnt
offering.
16 '[a]Then on the fourteenth day of the first
month shall be the LORD's Passover.
17 '[a]On the fifteenth day of this month
shall be a [b]feast, unleavened bread *shall be*
eaten for seven days.

14 [1]Lit *mouth* [2]Lit *for My sanctity* [a]Num 20:12; Deut 32:51; Ps 106:32
16 [a]Num 16:22
17 [1]Lit *before them and who will* [2]Lit *who will bring* [a]Deut 31:2; 2 Chr 1:10 [b]1 Kin 22:17; Ezek 34:5; Matt 9:36; Mark 6:34
18 [1]Lit *Take for yourself* [a]Num 11:25-29; Deut 34:9 [b]Num 27:23
19 [a]Deut 3:28; 31:3, 7, 8, 23
20 [1]Lit *majesty*
21 [1]Lit *mouth* [a]Ex 28:30; 1 Sam 28:6
23 [1]Lit *by the hand of* [a]Deut 31:23
28:2 [1]Lit *watch* [a]Lev 3:11
3 [a]Ex 29:38-42

4 [1]Lit *between the two evenings*
5 [a]Ex 16:36; Num 15:4 [b]Lev 2:1
7 [a]Ex 29:42
8 [1]Lit *between the two evenings*
9 [1]I.e. Approx one bu
10 [a]Num 28:3
11 [1]Lit *bulls of the herd* [a]Num 10:10; Ezek 46:6, 7
12 [1]I.e. Approx one bu [a]Num 15:4-12
13 [1]I.e. Approx one bu
15 [a]Num 28:3
16 [a]Ex 12:1-20; Lev 23:5-8; Deut 16:1-8
17 [a]Lev 23:6 [b]Ex 23:15; 34:18; Deut 16:3-8

27:16 *appoint a man.* Moses' reaction to this reassertion of his restriction is a prayer for his successor.

27:18 *Take Joshua.* As Moses and Aaron needed to determine the true successor of Aaron before his death (20:22–29), so the true successor of Moses also needed to be established. Joshua and Caleb were the two heroes in the darkest hour of Israel's apostasy (chs. 13–14). It was fitting that the Lord selected one of them (cf. Ex 17:9–14; 24:13; 32:17; 33:11).

27:20 *put some of your authority on him.* The transition from Moses' leadership to that of any successor would be difficult. The change would be smoother by a gradual shift of power while Moses was still alive.

28:1–29:40 These chapters attest to the all-pervasiveness of sacrifice in the life of the people and to the enormity of the work of the priests. Perhaps the reason for these passages at this time is to give continuity to the impending transition from the leadership of Moses to that of Joshua (27:12–23).

28:1–8 See Ex 29:38–41; Lev 1–7 and notes.

28:9–10 The sabbath offerings were in addition to the daily offerings.

28:11–15 The sacrifices at the beginning of the month were of great significance. These were times for celebration and blowing of trumpets in worship (see 10:10).

28:16–25 The priests are instructed as to the proper preparation for the Passover in the first month of the year. Passover is also associated with the Feast of Unleavened Bread (see Ex 12:15; Lev 23:4–8). The number 7 (and 14, its multiple) reappears frequently in the paragraph.

18 ‘On the [a]first day *shall be* a holy convocation; you shall do no laborious work.

19 ‘You shall present an offering by fire, a burnt offering to the LORD: two [1]bulls and one ram and seven male lambs one year old, [a]having them without defect.

20 ‘For their grain offering, you shall offer fine flour mixed with oil: three-tenths *of an* [1]*ephah* for a bull and two-tenths for the ram.

21 ‘A tenth *of an* [1]*ephah* you shall offer for [2]each of the seven lambs;

22 and one male goat for a [a]sin offering to make atonement for you.

23 ‘You shall present these besides [a]the burnt offering of the morning, which is for a continual burnt offering.

24 ‘After this manner you shall present daily, for seven days, [a]the food of the offering by fire, of a soothing aroma to the LORD; it shall be presented with its drink offering in addition to the [b]continual burnt offering.

25 ‘On the seventh day you shall have a holy convocation; [a]you shall do no laborious work.

26 ‘Also on [a]the day of the first fruits, when you present a new grain offering to the LORD in your *Feast of* Weeks, you shall have a holy convocation; [b]you shall do no laborious work.

27 ‘You shall offer a burnt offering for a soothing aroma to the LORD: two young bulls, one ram, seven male lambs one year old;

28 and their grain offering, fine flour mixed with oil: three-tenths *of an* [1]*ephah* for each bull, two-tenths for the one ram,

29 a tenth for [1]each of the seven lambs;

30 *also* one male goat to make atonement for you.

31 ‘[a]Besides the continual burnt offering and its grain offering, you shall present *them* with their drink offerings. They shall be [1]without defect.

Offerings of the Seventh Month

29 ‘[a]Now in the seventh month, on the first day of the month, you shall also have a holy convocation; [b]you shall do no laborious work. It will be to you a day for blowing trumpets.

2 ‘You shall offer a burnt offering as a soothing aroma to the LORD: one [1]bull, one ram, *and* seven male lambs one year old without defect;

3 also their grain offering, fine flour mixed with oil: three-tenths *of an* [1]*ephah* for the bull, two-tenths for the ram,

4 and one-tenth for [1]each of the seven lambs.

5 ‘*Offer* one male goat for a sin offering, to make atonement for you,

6 [a]besides the burnt offering of the new moon and its grain offering, and the [b]continual burnt offering and its grain offering, and their drink offerings, according to their ordinance, for a soothing aroma, an offering by fire to the LORD.

7 ‘Then on [a]the tenth day of this seventh month you shall have a holy convocation, and you shall humble yourselves; you shall not do any work.

8 ‘You shall present a burnt offering to the LORD *as* a soothing aroma: one bull, one ram, seven male lambs one year old, [a]having them without defect;

9 and their grain offering, fine flour mixed with oil: three-tenths *of an* [1]*ephah* for the bull, two-tenths for the one ram,

10 a tenth for each of the seven lambs;

11 one male goat for a sin offering, besides [a]the sin offering of atonement and [b]the continual burnt offering and its grain offering, and their drink offerings.

12 ‘Then on [a]the fifteenth day of the seventh month you shall have a holy convocation; you [b]shall do no laborious work, and you shall observe a feast to the LORD for seven days.

13 ‘You shall present a burnt offering, an offering by fire as a soothing aroma to the LORD: thirteen bulls, two rams, fourteen male lambs one year old, which are without defect;

14 and their grain offering, fine flour mixed with oil: three-tenths *of an* [1]*ephah* for [2]each of the thirteen bulls, two-tenths for [3]each of the two rams,

15 and a tenth for each of the fourteen lambs;

16 and one male goat for a sin offering, [a]besides the continual burnt offering, its grain offering and its drink offering.

17 ‘Then on [a]the second day: twelve bulls, two rams, fourteen male lambs one year old without defect;

18 and their grain offering and their drink offerings for the bulls, for the rams and for the lambs, by their number [a]according to the ordinance;

19 and one male goat for a sin offering, [a]besides the continual burnt offering and its grain offering, and their drink offerings.

20 ‘Then on the third day: eleven bulls,

18 [a]Lev 23:7
19 [1]Or *bulls of the herd* [a]Deut 15:21
20 [1]I.e. Approx one bu
21 [1]I.e. Approx one bu [2]Lit *each lamb*
22 [a]Lev 16:18; Rom 8:3; Gal 4:4f
23 [a]Num 28:3
24 [a]Lev 3:11 [b]Num 28:3
25 [a]Num 28:18
26 [a]Ex 23:16; 34:22; Lev 23:15-21; Deut 16:9-12 [b]Num 28:18
28 [1]I.e. Approx one bu
29 [1]Lit *each lamb*
31 [1]Lit *without defect to you* [a]Num 28:3
29:1 [a]Ex 23:16; 34:22; Lev 23:23-25 [b]Num 28:26
2 [1]Or *bull of a herd,* and so throughout the ch
3 [1]I.e. Approx one bu
4 [1]Lit *each lamb,* and so throughout the ch
6 [a]Num 28:27 [b]Num 28:3
7 [a]Lev 16:29-34; 23:26-32
8 [a]Lev 22:20; Deut 15:21; 17:1
9 [1]I.e. Approx one bu
11 [a]Lev 16:3, 5 [b]Num 28:3
12 [a]Lev 23:33-35; Deut 16:13-15 [b]Num 29:1
14 [1]I.e. Approx one bu [2]Lit *each bull* [3]Lit *each ram*
16 [a]Num 28:3
17 [a]Lev 23:36
18 [a]Lev 2:1-16
19 [a]Num 28:8

28:26–31 The Feast of Weeks came 50 days after the Feast of Unleavened Bread (see Lev 23:9–22); from this number the term “Pentecost” (meaning “fifty”) was used in the NT (Ac 2:1).

29:1–6 The Feast of Trumpets came at the beginning of the seventh month, a busy month for the worship of the Lord in holy festivals (see Lev 23:23–25; see also chart, pp. 164–165). Later in Jewish tradition this feast commemorated the New Year, *Rosh Hashanah.* The trumpet used was the *shophar,* the ram’s horn.

29:7–11 The Feast of Trumpets leads into the day of atonement, a time of confession, contrition and celebration (see Lev 16; 23:26–32).

29:12–34 In the seventh month the Feast of Trumpets took place on the first day, the day of atonement occurred on the tenth day, and the Feast of Booths began on the 15th day and lasted for seven days (see Lev 23:33–44). Each day of the Feast of Booths had its own order for sacrifice.

two rams, fourteen male lambs one year old
without defect;
21 and their grain offering and their drink
offerings for the bulls, for the rams and for
the lambs, by their number according to the
ordinance;
22 and one male goat for a sin offering,
besides the continual burnt offering and its
grain offering and its drink offering.
23 'Then on the fourth day: ten bulls, two
rams, fourteen male lambs one year old
without defect;
24 their grain offering and their drink
offerings for the bulls, for the rams and for
the lambs, by their number according to the
ordinance;
25 and one male goat for a sin offering,
besides the continual burnt offering, its grain
offering and its drink offering.
26 'Then on the fifth day: nine bulls, two
rams, fourteen male lambs one year old
[a]without defect;
27 and their grain offering and their drink
offerings for the bulls, for the rams and for
the lambs, by their number according to the
ordinance;
28 and one male goat for a sin offering,
besides the continual burnt offering and its
grain offering and its drink offering.
29 'Then on the sixth day: eight bulls, two
rams, fourteen male lambs one year old
without defect;
30 and their grain offering and their drink
offerings for the bulls, for the rams and for
the lambs, by their number according to the
ordinance;
31 and one male goat for a sin offering,
besides the continual burnt offering, its grain
offering and its drink offerings.
32 'Then on the seventh day: seven bulls,
two rams, fourteen male lambs one year old
without defect;
33 and their grain offering and their drink
offerings for the bulls, for the rams and for
the lambs, by their number according to the
ordinance;
34 and one male goat for a sin offering,
besides the continual burnt offering, its grain
offering and its drink offering.
35 '[a]On the eighth day you shall have a
solemn assembly; you shall do no laborious
work.
36 'But you shall present a burnt offering,
an offering by fire, as a soothing aroma to
the LORD: one bull, one ram, seven male
lambs one year old without defect;
37 their grain offering and their drink
offerings for the bull, for the ram and for the
lambs, by their number according to the
ordinance;
38 and one male goat for a sin offering,
besides the continual burnt offering and its
grain offering and its drink offering.
39 'You shall present these to the LORD at
your [a]appointed times, besides your [1]votive
offerings and your freewill offerings, for your
burnt offerings and for your grain offerings
and for your drink offerings and for your
peace offerings.' "
40 [1]Moses spoke to the sons of Israel in
accordance with all that the LORD had commanded Moses.

The Law of Vows

30 Then Moses spoke to [a]the heads of the
tribes of the sons of Israel, saying,
"This is the word which the LORD has commanded.
2 "[a]If a man makes a vow to the LORD, or
takes an oath to bind himself with a binding
obligation, he shall not violate his word; he
shall do according to all that proceeds out of
his mouth.
3 "Also if a woman makes a vow to the
LORD, and binds herself by an obligation in
her father's house in her youth,
4 and her father hears her vow and her
obligation by which she has bound herself,
and her father [1]says nothing to her, then all
her vows shall stand and every obligation by
which she has bound herself shall stand.
5 "But if her father should forbid her on
the day he hears *of it,* none of her vows or
her obligations by which she has bound herself shall stand; and the LORD will forgive her
because her father had forbidden her.
6 "However, if she should [1]marry while
[2]under her vows or the rash statement of her
lips by which she has bound herself,
7 and her husband hears of it and says
nothing to her on the day he hears *it,* then
her vows shall stand and her obligations by
which she has bound herself shall stand.
8 "But if on the day her husband hears *of
it,* he forbids her, then he shall annul her
vow which [1]she is under and the rash statement of her lips by which she has bound
herself; and the LORD will forgive her.
9 "But the vow of a widow or of a
divorced woman, everything by which she
has bound herself, shall stand against her.
10 "However, if she vowed in her hus-

26 [a]Heb 7:26
35 [a]Lev 23:36
39 [1]Lit *vows* [a]Lev 23:2
40 [1]Ch 30:1 in Heb
30:1 [a]Num 1:4, 16; 7:2
2 [a]Deut 23:21-23; Matt 5:33
4 [1]Lit *is silent to her,* and so throughout the ch
6 [1]Lit *be to a husband* [2]Lit *her vows are on her*
8 [1]Lit *is on her*

29:40 *Moses spoke to the sons of Israel.* The recapitulation of these festivals was a necessary part of the transfer of power from Moses to Joshua.

30:1–16 The principal OT passage on vows (see Deut 23:21–23). A vow is not to be made rashly (cf. Eccl 5:1–7), and a vow to the Lord must be kept.

30:3–5 The vow of an unmarried woman still under her father's protection might be nullified by her father. This and the following law were probably designed for the protection of the woman, who in ancient Near Eastern society was subject to strong societal pressures, some of which would leave her without defense.

30:6–8 The vow of a married woman might be nullified by her husband.

30:9 *widow or . . . divorced woman.* She is her own agent in the taking of vows.

band's house, or bound herself by an obligation with an oath,
11 and her husband heard *it,* but said
nothing to her *and* did not forbid her, then
all her vows shall stand and every obligation
by which she bound herself shall stand.
12 "But if her husband indeed annuls them
on the day he hears *them,* then whatever
proceeds out of her lips concerning her vows
or concerning the obligation of herself shall
not stand; her husband has annulled them,
and the LORD will forgive her.
13 "Every vow and every binding oath to
humble herself, her husband may confirm it
or her husband may annul it.
14 "But if her husband indeed says nothing
to her from day to day, then he confirms all
her vows or all her obligations which are on
her; he has confirmed them, because he said
nothing to her on the day he heard them.
15 "But if he indeed annuls them after he
has heard them, then he shall bear her guilt."
16 These are the statutes which the LORD
commanded Moses, *as* between a man and
his wife, *and as* between a father and his
daughter, *while she is* in her youth in her
father's house.

The Slaughter of Midian

31 Then the LORD spoke to Moses, saying,
2 "[a]Take full vengeance for the sons of
Israel on the Midianites; afterward you will
be [b]gathered to your people."
3 Moses spoke to the people, saying,
"Arm men from among you for the war, that
they may [1]go against Midian to execute [a]the
LORD's vengeance on Midian.
4 "A thousand from each tribe of all the
tribes of Israel you shall send to the war."
5 So there were [1]furnished from the
thousands of Israel, a thousand from each
tribe, twelve thousand armed for war.
6 Moses sent them, a thousand from
each tribe, to the war, and Phinehas the son
of Eleazar the priest, to the war with them,
[a]and the holy vessels and [b]the trumpets for
the alarm in his hand.
7 So they made war against Midian, just
as the LORD had commanded Moses, and
[a]they killed every male.
8 They killed the kings of Midian along
with the *rest of* their slain: [a]Evi and Rekem
and [b]Zur and Hur and Reba, the five kings of
Midian; they also killed [c]Balaam the son of
Beor with the sword.
9 The sons of Israel captured the women
of Midian and their little ones; and all their
cattle and all their flocks and all their goods
they plundered.
10 Then they burned all their cities where
they lived and all their camps with fire.
11 [a]They took all the spoil and all the
prey, both of man and of beast.
12 They brought the captives and the prey
and the spoil to Moses, and to Eleazar the
priest and to the congregation of the sons of
Israel, to the camp at the plains of Moab,
which are by the Jordan *opposite* Jericho.
13 Moses and Eleazar the priest and all
the leaders of the congregation went out to
meet them outside the camp.
14 Moses was angry with the officers of
the army, the captains of thousands and the
captains of hundreds, who had come from
service in the war.
15 And Moses said to them, "Have you
[1]spared [a]all the women?
16 "[a]Behold, these [1]caused the sons of Israel, through the [2]counsel of [b]Balaam, to [3]tres-
pass against the LORD in the matter of Peor,
so the plague was among the congregation
of the LORD.
17 "[a]Now therefore, kill every male among
the little ones, and kill every woman who
has known man [1]intimately.
18 "But all the [1]girls who have not known
man [2]intimately, [3]spare for yourselves.
19 "[a]And you, camp outside the camp sev-
en days; whoever has killed any person and
whoever has touched any slain, purify your-

31:2 [a]Num 25:1, 16, 17 [b]Num 20:24, 26; 27:13
3 [1]Lit *be* [a]Lev 26:25
5 [1]Lit *delivered*
6 [a]Num 14:44 [b]Num 10:8, 9
7 [a]Deut 20:13; Judg 21:11; 1 Kin 11:15, 16
8 [a]Josh 13:21 [b]Num 25:15 [c]Num 31:16; Josh 13:22
11 [a]Deut 20:14
15 [1]Lit *let...live* [a]Deut 20:14
16 [1]Lit *were to* [2]Lit *word* [3]Possibly *defect from the Lord* [a]Num 25:1-9 [b]Num 31:8
17 [1]Lit *by lying with a man* [a]Deut 7:2; 20:16-18
18 [1]Lit *female children* [2]Lit *by lying with a man* [3]Lit *keep alive*
19 [a]Num 19:11-22

30:10–15 Further examples of the complications that come in the taking of vows within the husband-wife relationship. Such complications may have come up much as in the case of Zelophehad's daughters (27:1–11). One case after another presented itself, resulting in this final codification. Presumably, in the centuries leading up to the NT, the legal decisions on vows became even more complex. The words of Jesus that one is to avoid complications connected with oaths (Matt 5:33–37) are liberating.

31:1–24 The Lord declares a holy war (see essay, p. 271) against the Midianites as one of Moses' last actions before the end of his life. Moses was not motivated by petty jealousy; rather, the war was "the LORD's vengeance" (v. 3) for the Midianites' part in seducing the Israelites to engage in sexual immorality and to worship the Baal of Peor. (See 25:16–18, where the specific mention of Cozbi, a Midianite woman, heightens the anger expressed in ch. 31.)

31:2 *gathered to your people.* A euphemism for death (see, e.g., Gen 25:8,17; 35:29).

31:4 *A thousand from each tribe of . . . Israel.* The burden of the holy war had to be shared equally among the tribes.

31:6 *Phinehas.* His zeal for the Lord's honor led him to execute Zimri and Cozbi (25:8). Now he leads in the sacred aspects of the battle to demonstrate that this is a holy war. *trumpets.* See note on 10:3.

31:7 *as the LORD had commanded Moses.* The battle was the Lord's.

31:8 *they also killed Balaam.* Ch. 25 lacks the name of the principal instigator of the seduction of the Israelite men to the depraved worship of Baal. But here he is found among the dead. What Balaam had been unable to accomplish through acts of magic or sorcery (chs. 22–24) he was almost able to achieve by his advice to the Midianites (v. 16).

31:9–18 While the troops killed the men of Midian, they spared the women and children as plunder. Moses commanded that only the virgin women (who were thus innocent of the indecencies at Peor) could be spared; the guilty women and the boys (who might endanger the inheritance rights of Israelite men) were to be put to death (vv. 15–17).

31:19–24 Since this was holy war, both people (vv. 19–20) and things (vv. 21–24) had to be cleansed (cf. 19:11–13).

selves, you and your captives, on the third day and on the seventh day.

20 "You shall purify for yourselves every garment and every article of [1]leather and all the work of goats' *hair,* and all articles of wood."

21 Then Eleazar the priest said to the men of war who had gone to battle, "This is the statute of the law which the LORD has commanded Moses:

22 only the gold and the silver, the bronze, the iron, the tin and the lead,

23 everything that can stand the fire, you shall pass through the fire, and it shall be clean, but it shall be purified with [a]water for impurity. But whatever cannot stand the fire you shall pass through the water.

24 "And you shall wash your clothes on the seventh day and be clean, and afterward you may enter the camp."

Division of the Booty

25 Then the LORD spoke to Moses, saying,

26 "You and Eleazar the priest and the heads of the fathers' *households* of the congregation take a count of the booty [1]that was captured, both of man and of animal;

27 and [a]divide the booty between the warriors who went out to battle and all the congregation.

28 "[a]Levy a tax for the LORD from the men of war who went out to battle, one [1]in five hundred of the persons and of the cattle and of the donkeys and of the sheep;

29 take it from their half and give it to Eleazar the priest, as an [1]offering to the LORD.

30 "From the sons of Israel's half, you shall take one drawn out of every fifty of the persons, of the cattle, of the donkeys and of the sheep, from all the animals, and give them to the Levites who [a]keep charge of the tabernacle of the LORD."

31 Moses and Eleazar the priest did just as the LORD had commanded Moses.

32 Now the booty that remained from the spoil which the [1]men of war had plundered was 675,000 sheep,

33 and 72,000 cattle,

34 and 61,000 donkeys,

35 and of human beings, of the women who had not known man [1]intimately, all the persons were 32,000.

36 The half, the portion of those who went out to war, was *as follows:* the number of sheep was 337,500,

37 and the LORD's levy of the sheep was 675;

38 and the cattle were 36,000, from which the LORD's levy was 72;

39 and the donkeys were 30,500, from which the LORD's levy was 61;

40 and the human beings were 16,000, from whom the LORD's levy was 32 persons.

41 Moses gave the levy *which was* the LORD'S offering to Eleazar the priest, just [a]as the LORD had commanded Moses.

42 As for the sons of Israel's half, which Moses [1]separated from the men who had gone to war—

43 now the congregation's half was 337,500 sheep,

44 and 36,000 cattle,

45 and 30,500 donkeys,

46 and the human beings were 16,000—

47 and from the sons of Israel's half, Moses took one drawn out of every fifty, both of man and of animals, and gave them to the Levites, who kept charge of the tabernacle of the LORD, just as the LORD had commanded Moses.

48 Then the officers who were over the thousands of the army, the captains of thousands and the captains of hundreds, approached Moses,

49 and they said to Moses, "Your servants have taken a census of men of war who are in our charge, and no man of us is missing.

50 "So we have brought as an offering to the LORD what each man found, articles of gold, armlets and bracelets, signet rings, earrings and necklaces, [a]to make atonement for ourselves before the LORD."

51 Moses and Eleazar the priest took the gold from them, all kinds of wrought articles.

52 All the gold of the offering which they offered up to the LORD, from the captains of thousands and the captains of hundreds, was 16,750 shekels.

53 [a]The men of war had taken booty, every man for himself.

54 So Moses and Eleazar the priest took the gold from the captains of thousands and of hundreds, and brought it to the tent of meeting as [a]a memorial for the sons of Israel before the LORD.

Reuben and Gad Settle in Gilead

32 Now the sons of Reuben and the sons of Gad had an [a]exceedingly large number of livestock. So when they saw the land of [b]Jazer and the land of Gilead, that [1]it was indeed a place suitable for livestock,

2 the sons of Gad and the sons of Reuben came and spoke to Moses and to Eleazar the priest and to the leaders of the congregation, saying,

3 "[a]Ataroth, Dibon, Jazer, Nimrah, Heshbon, Elealeh, Sebam, Nebo and Beon,

20 [1]Or *skin* **23** [a]Num 19:9, 17 **26** [1]Lit *of captives* **27** [a]Josh 22:8 **28** [1]Lit *soul from* [a]Num 18:21-30 **29** [1]Lit *heave offering,* and so throughout the ch **30** [a]Num 3:7, 8, 25, 26, 31, 36, 37; 18:3, 4 **32** [1]Lit *people* **35** [1]Lit *by lying with a man*

41 [a]Num 5:9, 10; 18:19 **42** [1]Or *divided* **50** [a]Ex 30:12-16 **53** [a]Num 31:32; Deut 20:14 **54** [a]Ex 30:16 **32:1** [1]Lit *behold, the place, a place for* [a]Ex 12:38 [b]Num 21:32 **3** [a]Num 32:34-38

31:26–35 Another aspect of holy war was the fair distribution of the spoils of war, both among those who fought in the battle and among those who stayed with the community, with appropriate shares to be given to the Lord, whose battle it was (v. 28).

32:1 *sons of Reuben and the sons of Gad.* The abundance of fertile grazing land in Transjordan prompted the leaders of these two tribes to request that they be allowed to settle there and not cross the Jordan. This area too was a gift of God won by conquest.

4 the land [a]which the LORD [1]conquered before the congregation of Israel, is a land for livestock, and your servants have livestock."

5 They said, "If we have found favor in your sight, let this land be given to your servants as a possession; do not take us across the Jordan."

6 But Moses said to the sons of Gad and to the sons of Reuben, "Shall your brothers go to war while you yourselves sit here?

7 "[a]Now why are you [1]discouraging the sons of Israel from crossing over into the land which the LORD has given them?

8 "[1]This is what your fathers did when I sent them from [a]Kadesh-barnea to see the land.

9 "For when they went up to [a]the [1]valley of Eshcol and saw the land, they [2]discouraged the sons of Israel so that they did not go into the land which the LORD had given them.

10 "So [a]the LORD's anger burned in that day, and He swore, saying,

11 '[a]None of the men who came up from Egypt, from twenty years old and upward, shall see the land which I swore to Abraham, to Isaac and to Jacob; for they did not follow Me fully,

12 except Caleb the son of Jephunneh the Kenizzite and Joshua the son of Nun, [a]for they have followed the LORD fully.'

13 "[a]So the LORD's anger burned against Israel, and He made them wander in the wilderness forty years, until the entire generation of those who had done evil in the sight of the LORD was destroyed.

14 "Now behold, you have risen up in your fathers' place, a brood of sinful men, to add still more to the burning [a]anger of the LORD against Israel.

15 "For if you [a]turn away from following Him, He will once more abandon them in the wilderness, and you will destroy all these people."

16 Then they came near to him and said, "We will build here sheepfolds for our livestock and cities for our little ones;

17 [a]but we ourselves will be armed ready *to go* before the sons of Israel, until we have brought them to their place, while our little ones live in the fortified cities because of the inhabitants of the land.

18 "[a]We will not return to our homes until every one of the sons of Israel has possessed his inheritance.

19 "For we will not have an inheritance with them on the other side of the Jordan and beyond, because our inheritance has fallen to us [a]on this side of the Jordan toward the east."

20 [a]So Moses said to them, "If you will do [1]this, if you will arm yourselves before the LORD for the war,

21 and all of you armed men cross over the Jordan before the LORD until He has driven His enemies out from before Him,

22 [a]and the land is subdued before the LORD, then afterward you shall return and be free of obligation toward the LORD and toward Israel, and this land shall be yours for a possession before the LORD.

23 "But if you will not do so, behold, you have sinned against the LORD, and be sure [a]your sin will find you out.

24 "Build yourselves cities for your little ones, and sheepfolds for your sheep, and [a]do [1]what you have promised."

25 The sons of Gad and the sons of Reuben spoke to Moses, saying, "Your servants will do just as my lord commands.

26 "[a]Our little ones, our wives, our livestock and all our cattle shall [1]remain there in the cities of Gilead;

27 while your servants, everyone who is armed for war, will [a]cross over in the presence of the LORD to battle, just as my lord says."

28 So Moses gave command concerning them to Eleazar the priest, and to Joshua the son of Nun, and to the heads of the fathers' *households* of the tribes of the sons of Israel.

29 Moses said to them, "If the sons of Gad and the sons of Reuben, everyone who is armed for battle, will cross with you over the Jordan in the presence of the LORD, and the land is subdued before you, then you shall give them the land of Gilead for a possession;

30 but if they will not cross over with you armed, they shall have possessions among you in the land of Canaan."

31 The sons of Gad and the sons of Reuben answered, saying, "As the LORD has said to your servants, so we will do.

32 "We ourselves will cross over armed in the presence of the LORD into the land of Canaan, and the possession of our inheritance *shall remain* with us across the Jordan."

33 [a]So Moses gave to them, to the sons of Gad and to the sons of Reuben and to the half-tribe of Joseph's son Manasseh, the

4 [1]Lit *smote* [a]Num 21:34
7 [1]Lit *restraining the hearts of* [a]Num 13:27-14:4
8 [1]Lit *Thus your fathers* [a]Num 13:3, 26; Deut 1:19-25
9 [1]Or *wadi* [2]Lit *restrained the hearts of* [a]Num 13:24; Deut 1:24
10 [a]Num 14:11f; Deut 1:34
11 [a]Num 14:28-30
12 [a]Deut 1:36; Josh 14:8f
13 [a]Num 14:33-35
14 [a]Deut 1:34f
15 [a]Deut 30:17, 18; 2 Chr 7:19, 20
17 [a]Josh 4:12, 13
18 [a]Josh 22:1-4
19 [a]Josh 12:1; 13:8
20 [1]Lit *this thing* [a]Deut 3:18
22 [a]Deut 3:20
23 [a]Gen 4:7; 44:16; Is 59:12
24 [1]Lit *that which has come out of your mouth* [a]Num 30:2
26 [1]Lit *be* [a]Josh 1:14
27 [a]Josh 4:12
33 [a]Deut 3:8-17; Josh 12:1-6

32:8 *This is what your fathers did.* Moses' fear was that the failure of these two tribes to stay with the whole community in conquering Canaan would be the beginning of a general revolt against entering the land. It would be the failure of Kadesh (chs. 13–14) all over again. Moreover, the conquest of Canaan was a commission to all Israel.

32:17 *we ourselves will be armed.* The leaders of Reuben and Gad sought to assure Moses that they did not wish to shirk their duty in helping to conquer the land. They would join their brothers in battle but wished to leave their families and livestock behind in the territory of their choosing.

32:23 *be sure your sin will find you out.* The bargain was struck, but not without strong warnings if they failed to live up to their word.

32:33 *the half-tribe of . . . Manasseh.* It appears that after the requirements for Transjordan settlement were established with the tribes of Reuben and Gad, half the tribe of Manasseh joined with them.

kingdom of Sihon, king of the Amorites and
the kingdom of Og, the king of Bashan, the
land with its cities with *their* [1]territories, the
cities of the surrounding land.
34 The sons of Gad built Dibon and Ataroth and [a]Aroer,
35 and Atroth-shophan and Jazer and Jogbehah,
36 and [a]Beth-nimrah and Beth-haran as
fortified cities, and sheepfolds for sheep.
37 The sons of Reuben built Heshbon and
Elealeh and Kiriathaim,
38 and [a]Nebo and Baal-meon—*their* names
being changed—and Sibmah, and they gave
other names to the cities which they built.
39 The sons of [a]Machir the son of Manasseh went to Gilead and took it, and dispossessed the Amorites who were in it.
40 So Moses gave [a]Gilead to Machir the
son of Manasseh, and he lived in it.
41 Jair the son of Manasseh went and took
its [1]towns, and called them [2a]Havvoth-jair.
42 Nobah went and took Kenath and its
villages, and called it Nobah after [a]his own
name.

Review of the Journey from Egypt to Jordan

33 These are the journeys of the sons of
Israel, by which they came out from the
land of Egypt by their armies, under [a]the
[1]leadership of Moses and Aaron.
2 Moses recorded their starting places
according to their journeys by the [1]command
of the LORD, and these are their journeys
according to their starting places.
3 [a]They journeyed from Rameses in the
first month, on the fifteenth day of the first
month; on the [1]next day after the Passover
the sons of Israel [b]started out [2]boldly in the
sight of all the Egyptians,
4 while the Egyptians were burying all
their firstborn whom the LORD had struck
down among them. The LORD had also executed judgments [a]on their gods.
5 Then [a]the sons of Israel journeyed from
Rameses and camped in Succoth.
6 [a]They journeyed from Succoth and
camped in Etham, which is on the edge of
the wilderness.
7 [a]They journeyed from Etham and
turned back to Pi-hahiroth, which faces Baal-
zephon, and they camped before Migdol.
8 [a]They journeyed [1]from before Hahiroth
and passed through the midst of the sea into
the wilderness; and [b]they went three days'
journey in the wilderness of Etham and
camped at Marah.
9 [a]They journeyed from Marah and came
to Elim; and in Elim there were twelve
springs of water and seventy palm trees, and
they camped there.
10 They journeyed from Elim and camped
by the [1]Red Sea.
11 They journeyed from the [1]Red Sea and
camped in [a]the wilderness of Sin.
12 They journeyed from the wilderness of
Sin and camped at Dophkah.
13 They journeyed from Dophkah and
camped at Alush.
14 They journeyed from Alush and
camped [a]at Rephidim; now it was there that
the people had no water to drink.
15 They journeyed from Rephidim and
camped in [a]the wilderness of Sinai.
16 They journeyed from the wilderness of
Sinai and camped at [a]Kibroth-hattaavah.
17 They journeyed from Kibroth-hattaavah and camped at [a]Hazeroth.
18 They journeyed from Hazeroth and
camped at Rithmah.
19 They journeyed from Rithmah and
camped at Rimmon-perez.
20 They journeyed from Rimmon-perez
and camped at [a]Libnah.
21 They journeyed from Libnah and
camped at Rissah.
22 They journeyed from Rissah and
camped in Kehelathah.
23 They journeyed from Kehelathah and
camped at Mount Shepher.
24 They journeyed from Mount Shepher
and camped at Haradah.
25 They journeyed from Haradah and
camped at Makheloth.
26 They journeyed from Makheloth and
camped at Tahath.
27 They journeyed from Tahath and
camped at Terah.
28 They journeyed from Terah and
camped at Mithkah.
29 They journeyed from Mithkah and
camped at Hashmonah.
30 They journeyed from Hashmonah and
camped at [a]Moseroth.
31 They journeyed from Moseroth and
camped at Bene-jaakan.

33 [1]Lit *borders*
34 [a]Deut 2:36
36 [a]Num 32:3
38 [a]Is 46:1
39 [a]Gen 50:23
40 [a]Deut 3:12, 13, 15; Josh 17:1
41 [1]Lit *tent villages* [2]I.e. the towns of Jair [a]Deut 3:14; Judg 10:4
42 [a]2 Sam 18:18; Ps 49:11
33:1 [1]Lit *hand* [a]Ps 77:20; 105:26; Mic 6:4
2 [1]Lit *mouth*
3 [1]Lit *morrow* [2]Lit *with a high hand* [a]Ex 12:37 [b]Ex 14:8
4 [a]Ex 12:12
5 [a]Ex 12:37
6 [a]Ex 13:20
7 [a]Ex 14:1, 2
8 [1]Many mss read *from Pi-hahiroth* [a]Ex 14:22
8 [b]Ex 15:22, 23
9 [a]Ex 15:27
10 [1]Lit *Sea of Reeds*
11 [1]Lit *Sea of Reeds* [a]Ex 16:1
14 [a]Ex 17:1
15 [a]Ex 19:1
16 [a]Num 11:34
17 [a]Num 11:35
20 [a]Deut 1:1
30 [a]Deut 10:6

33:1–49 The numerous places (significantly 40 in number between Rameses and the plains of Moab) in Israel's wilderness experience are listed. Unfortunately, most of the sites were wilderness encampments, not cities with lasting archaeological records; so they are difficult to locate. Many of the places (e.g., in vv. 19–29) are not recorded elsewhere in Exodus and Numbers. Some of the places mentioned elsewhere (e.g., Taberah, 11:3; see 21:19) are missing here. The data warrant these conclusions: 1. Moses recorded the list at the Lord's command (v. 2). 2. The list should be taken seriously, as an accurate recapitulation of the stages of the journey, despite difficulty in locating many of the sites. 3. The numerical factor of 40 sites between Rameses and the plains of Moab suggests some styling of the list, which helps to account for the sites not included. 4. As in the case of genealogies in the Pentateuch, some factors of ancient significance may not be clear to us today. 5. Ultimately the record is a recital of the Lord's blessing on His people for the extended period of their wilderness experience. Although certainly not without geographical importance, the listing of the stages of Israel's experience in the wilderness is fundamentally a religious document, a litany of the Lord's deliverance of His people.

32 They journeyed from [a]Bene-jaakan and
camped at Hor-haggidgad.
33 They journeyed from Hor-haggidgad
and camped at [a]Jotbathah.
34 They journeyed from Jotbathah and
camped at Abronah.
35 They journeyed from Abronah and
camped at [a]Ezion-geber.
36 They journeyed from Ezion-geber and
camped in the wilderness of [a]Zin, that is,
Kadesh.
37 They journeyed from Kadesh and
camped at [a]Mount Hor, [b]at the edge of the
land of Edom.
38 [a]Then Aaron the priest went up to
Mount Hor at the [1]command of the LORD,
and died there in the fortieth year after the
sons of Israel had come from the land of
Egypt, on the first *day* in the fifth month.
39 Aaron was one hundred twenty-three
years old when he died on Mount Hor.
40 Now the Canaanite, the king of [a]Arad
[1]who lived in the [2]Negev in the land of
Canaan, heard of the coming of the sons of
Israel.
41 Then they journeyed from Mount Hor
and camped at Zalmonah.
42 They journeyed from Zalmonah and
camped at Punon.
43 They journeyed from Punon and
camped at [a]Oboth.
44 They journeyed from Oboth and
camped at Iye-abarim, at the border of Moab.
45 They journeyed from Iyim and camped
at Dibon-gad.
46 They journeyed from Dibon-gad and
camped at Almon-diblathaim.
47 They journeyed from Almon-diblathaim and camped in the mountains of [a]Aba-
rim, before Nebo.
48 They journeyed from the mountains of
Abarim and [a]camped in the plains of Moab
by the Jordan *opposite* Jericho.
49 They camped by the Jordan, from Beth-
jeshimoth as far as [a]Abel-shittim in the
plains of Moab.

Law of Possessing the Land

50 Then the LORD spoke to Moses in the
plains of Moab by the Jordan *opposite* Jericho, saying,
51 "Speak to the sons of Israel and say to
them, '[a]When you cross over the Jordan into
the land of Canaan,
52 then you shall drive out all the inhabitants of the land from before you, and
[a]destroy all their figured stones, and destroy
all their molten images and demolish all
their high places;
53 [a]and you shall take possession of the
land and live in it, for I have given the land
to you to possess it.
54 '[a]You shall inherit the land by lot
according to your families; to the larger you
shall give more inheritance, and to the smaller you shall give less inheritance. Wherever
the lot falls to anyone, that shall be his. You
shall inherit according to the tribes of your
fathers.
55 'But if you do not drive out the inhabitants of the land from before you, then it shall
come about that those whom you let remain
of them *will become* [a]as pricks in your eyes
and as thorns in your sides, and they will
trouble you in the land in which you live.
56 'And as I plan to do to them, so I will do
to you.' "

Instruction for Apportioning Canaan

34 Then the LORD spoke to Moses, saying,
2 "Command the sons of Israel and say
to them, 'When you enter [a]the land of
Canaan, this is the land that shall fall to you
as an inheritance, *even the* land of Canaan
according to its borders.
3 '[a]Your southern [1]sector shall [2]extend
from the wilderness of Zin along the side of
Edom, and your southern border shall
[2]extend from the end of the Salt Sea [b]east-
ward.
4 'Then your border shall turn *direction*
from the south to the ascent of Akrabbim
and [1]continue to Zin, and its [2]termination
shall be to the south of [a]Kadesh-barnea; and
it shall [3]reach Hazaraddar and [1]continue to
Azmon.
5 'The border shall turn *direction* from
Azmon to the brook of Egypt, and its termination shall be at [a]the sea.
6 'As for the western border, you shall
have the Great Sea, that is, *its* [1]coastline; this
shall be your west border.
7 '[a]And this shall be your north border:
you shall draw your *border* line from the
Great Sea to Mount Hor.
8 'You shall draw a line from Mount Hor
to [a]the [1]Lebo-hamath, and the termination
of the border shall be at Zedad;
9 and the border shall proceed to Ziph-
ron, and its termination shall be at Hazar-
enan. This shall be your north border.
10 'For your eastern border you shall also
draw a line from Hazar-enan to Shepham,
11 and the border shall go down from Shepham to [a]Riblah on the east side of Ain; and
the border shall go down and reach to the
[1]slope on the east side of the Sea of [b]Chin-
nereth.

32 [a]Gen 36:27; Deut 10:6; 1 Chr 1:42
33 [a]Deut 10:7
35 [a]Deut 2:8
36 [a]Num 20:1
37 [a]Num 20:22 [b]Num 20:16
38 [1]Lit *mouth* [a]Num 20:28; Deut 10:6
40 [1]Lit *and he* [2]I.e. South country [a]Num 21:1
43 [a]Num 21:10, 11
47 [a]Num 27:12
48 [a]Num 22:1
49 [a]Num 25:1
51 [a]Josh 3:17
52 [a]Ex 23:24; Lev 26:1; Deut 7:5; 12:3, 30; Ps 106:34-36
53 [a]Deut 11:31; 17:14; Josh 21:43
54 [a]Num 26:53-56
55 [a]Josh 23:13
34:2 [a]Gen 17:8; Ps 78:54, 55; 105:11
3 [1]Lit *side* [2]Lit *be* [a]Josh 15:1-3 [b]Josh 15:5
4 [1]Lit *pass along* [2]Lit *goings out,* and so throughout the ch [3]Lit *go forth to* [a]Num 32:8
5 [a]Josh 15:4
6 [1]Lit *border*
7 [a]Ezek 47:15-17
8 [1]Or *entrance of Hamath* [a]Josh 13:5
11 [1]Lit *shoulder* [a]2 Kin 23:33 [b]Deut 3:17; Josh 13:27

33:52 *drive out all the inhabitants of the land . . . destroy . . . all their molten images.* What Israel had accomplished in the war against the Midianites (ch. 31) was now to be extended to all the inhabitants of Canaan. Particularly important was the command to destroy all symbols of the pagan religious system of the Canaanites.

34:3–12 The listing of the four boundaries is not only for information, but also to display again the dimensions of God's great gift to His people.

12 'And the border shall go down to the Jordan and its termination shall be at the Salt Sea. This shall be your land according to its borders all around.' "

13 So Moses commanded the sons of Israel, saying, "[a]This is the land that you are to apportion by lot among you as a possession, which the LORD has commanded to give to the nine and a half tribes.

14 "[a]For the tribe of the sons of Reuben have received *theirs* according to their fathers' households, and the tribe of the sons of Gad according to their fathers' households, and the half-tribe of Manasseh have received their possession.

15 "The two and a half tribes have received their possession across the Jordan opposite Jericho, eastward toward the sunrising."

16 Then the LORD spoke to Moses, saying,

17 "[a]These are the names of the men who shall apportion the land to you for inheritance: Eleazar the priest and Joshua the son of Nun.

18 "You shall take one leader of every tribe to apportion the land for inheritance.

19 "These are the names of the men: of the tribe of [a]Judah, [b]Caleb the son of Jephunneh.

20 "Of the tribe of the sons of [a]Simeon, Samuel the son of Ammihud.

21 "Of the tribe of [a]Benjamin, Elidad the son of Chislon.

22 "Of the tribe of the sons of Dan a leader, Bukki the son of Jogli.

23 "Of the sons of Joseph: of the tribe of the sons of Manasseh a leader, Hanniel the son of Ephod.

24 "Of the tribe of the sons of Ephraim a leader, Kemuel the son of Shiphtan.

25 "Of the tribe of the sons of Zebulun a leader, Elizaphan the son of Parnach.

26 "Of the tribe of the sons of Issachar a leader, Paltiel the son of Azzan.

27 "Of the tribe of the sons of Asher a leader, Ahihud the son of Shelomi.

28 "Of the tribe of the sons of Naphtali a leader, Pedahel the son of Ammihud."

29 These are those whom the LORD commanded to apportion the inheritance to the sons of Israel in the land of Canaan.

Cities for the Levites

35 [a]Now the LORD spoke to Moses in the plains of Moab by the Jordan *opposite* Jericho, saying,

2 "Command the sons of Israel that they give to the Levites from the inheritance of their possession cities to live in; and you shall give to the Levites pasture lands around the cities.

3 "The cities shall be theirs to live in; and their pasture lands shall be for their cattle and for their herds and for all their beasts.

4 "The pasture lands of the cities which you shall give to the Levites *shall extend* from the wall of the city [1]outward a thousand cubits around.

5 "You shall also measure outside the city on the east side two thousand cubits, and on the south side two thousand cubits, and on the west side two thousand cubits, and on the north side two thousand cubits, with the city in the center. This shall become theirs as pasture lands for the cities.

Cities of Refuge

6 "The cities which you shall give to the Levites *shall be* the [a]six cities of refuge, which you shall give for the manslayer to flee to; and in addition to them you shall give forty-two cities.

7 "All the cities which you shall give to the Levites *shall be* [a]forty-eight cities, [1]together with their pasture lands.

8 "[a]As for the cities which you shall give from the possession of the sons of Israel, you shall take more from the larger and you shall take less from the smaller; each shall give some of his cities to the Levites in proportion to his possession which he inherits."

9 Then the LORD spoke to Moses, saying,

10 "[a]Speak to the sons of Israel and say to them, 'When you cross the Jordan into the land of Canaan,

11 [a]then you shall select for yourselves cities to be your [b]cities of refuge, that the manslayer who has [1]killed any person [c]unintentionally may flee there.

12 '[a]The cities shall be to you as a refuge from the avenger, so that the manslayer will not die until he stands before the congregation for [1]trial.

13 'The cities which you are to give shall be your six cities of refuge.

14 'You [a]shall give three cities across the Jordan and three cities [1]in the land of Canaan; they are to be cities of refuge.

15 'These six cities shall be for refuge for the sons of Israel, and for the alien and for the sojourner among them; that anyone who [1]kills a person [a]unintentionally may flee there.

13 [a]Gen 15:18; Num 26:52-56; Deut 11:24; Josh 14:1-5
14 [a]Num 32:33
17 [a]Josh 14:1, 2
19 [a]Gen 29:35; Deut 33:7; Ps 60:7 [b]Num 13:6, 30; 26:65; Deut 1:36
20 [a]Gen 29:33; 49:5; Ezek 48:24
21 [a]Gen 49:27; Deut 33:12; Ps 68:27
35:1 [a]Lev 25:32-34

4 [1]Lit *and outward*
6 [a]Josh 20:7-9
7 [1]Lit *them* [a]Josh 21:41
8 [a]Lev 25:32-34; Num 26:54; 33:54; Josh 21:1-42
10 [a]Josh 20:1-9
11 [1]Lit *smote* [a]Deut 19:1-13 [b]Josh 20:2f [c]Ex 21:13; Lev 4:2f, 22f; Num 35:22-25
12 [1]Lit *judgment* [a]Deut 19:4-6; Josh 20:2, 3
14 [1]Lit *you shall give in* [a]Deut 4:41
15 [1]Lit *smites* [a]Num 35:11

34:13–15 The new realities that the settlement of Reuben, Gad and the half-tribe of Manasseh in Transjordan brought about (see ch. 32).

34:16–29 The listing of the new tribal leaders recalls the listing of the leaders of the first generation (1:5–16). This time the promise will be realized; these new leaders will assist Eleazar and Joshua in actually allotting the land.

35:1–5 Since the Levites would not receive an allotment with the other tribes in the land (1:47–53), they would need towns in which to live and to raise their families and care for their livestock. The Levites were to be spread throughout the land, not in an isolated encampment. Josh 21 presents the fulfillment of this command.

35:6–15 Six Levitical cities were to be stationed strategically in the land—three in Transjordan and three in Canaan proper—as cities of refuge, where a person guilty of unintentional manslaughter might escape blood revenge. Josh 20 describes the sites that were chosen.

16 'ᵃBut if he struck him down with an iron object, so that he died, he is a murderer; the murderer shall surely be put to death.
17 'If he struck him down with a stone in the hand, by which he will die, and *as a result* he died, he is a murderer; the murderer ᵃshall surely be put to death.
18 'Or if he struck him with a wooden object in the hand, by which he might die, and *as a result* he died, he is a murderer; the murderer shall surely be put to death.
19 'The blood avenger himself shall put the murderer to death; he shall put him to death when he meets him.
20 'ᵃIf he pushed him of hatred, or threw something at him ᵇlying in wait and *as a result* he died,
21 or if he struck him down with his hand in enmity, and *as a result* he died, the one who struck him shall surely be put to death, he is a murderer; the blood avenger shall put the murderer to death when he meets him.
22 'ᵃBut if he pushed him suddenly without enmity, or threw something at him without lying in wait,
23 or with any [1]deadly object of stone, and without seeing it dropped on him so that he died, while he was not his enemy nor seeking his injury,

16 ᵃEx 21:12, 14; Lev 24:17 **17** ᵃNum 35:31 **20** ᵃGen 4:8; 2 Sam 3:27; 20:10 ᵇEx 21:14; Deut 19:11 **22** ᵃNum 35:11 **23** [1]Lit *by which he may die*

24 then ᵃthe congregation shall judge between the slayer and the blood avenger according to these ordinances.
25 'The congregation shall deliver the manslayer from the hand of the blood avenger, and the congregation shall restore him to his city of refuge to which he fled; and he shall live in it until the death of the high priest who was anointed with the holy oil.
26 'But if the manslayer at any time goes beyond the border of his city of refuge to which he may flee,
27 and the blood avenger finds him outside the border of his city of refuge, and the blood avenger kills the manslayer, he will not be guilty of blood
28 because he should have remained in his city of refuge until the death of the high priest. But after the death of the high priest the manslayer shall return to the land of his possession.
29 'These things shall be for a ᵃstatutory ordinance to you throughout your generations in all your dwellings.
30 'ᵃIf anyone kills a person, the murderer shall be put to death at the [1]evidence of witnesses, but ᵇno person shall be put to death on the testimony of one witness.

24 ᵃJosh 20:6 **29** ᵃNum 27:11 **30** [1]Lit *mouth* ᵃNum 35:16 ᵇDeut 17:6; 19:15; Matt 18:16; John 7:51; 8:17, 18

35:16–21 Various descriptions of the taking of life are presented that would indicate willful murder.
35:22 *without enmity.* The cities of refuge were to be established for the person who had committed an act of involuntary manslaughter.
35:24 *according to these ordinances.* Any gracious provision is subject to abuse. For this reason the case of the involuntary slayer had to be determined by the judges. Further, the accused man had to stay in the city of refuge until the death of the high priest (when there would be a general amnesty). If the accused left the city of refuge, he would become fair game again for the avenger of blood.
35:25–28 See note on Josh 20:6.
35:30 *witnesses.* To avoid the possibility of an innocent par-

Cities of Refuge

The idea of providing cities of refuge (Josh 20:1-9) for capital offenses is rooted in the tension between customary tribal law (retaliation or revenge, in which the blood relative is obligated to execute vengeance) and civil law (carried out less personally by an assembly according to a standard code of justice).

Blood feuds are usually associated with nomadic groups; legal procedures, with villages and towns. Israel, a society in the process of sedentarization, found it necessary to adopt an intermediate step regulating manslaughter, so that an innocent person would not be killed before standing trial. Absolution was possible only by being cleared by his hometown assembly, and by the eventual death of the high priest, which freed the offender from ritual pollution.

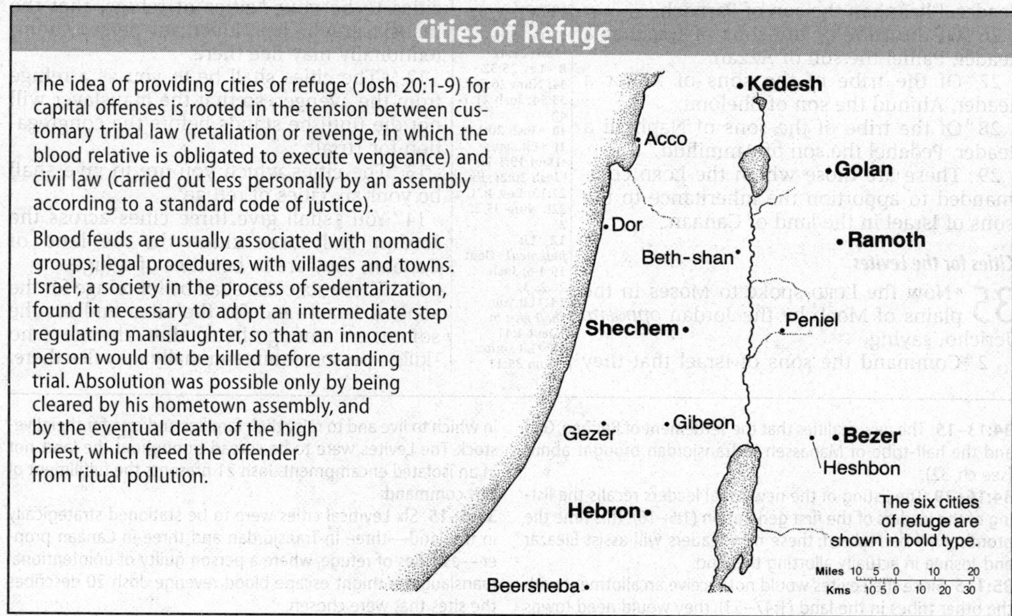
Kedesh
Acco
Golan
Dor
Ramoth
Beth-shan
Peniel
Shechem
Gibeon
Gezer
Bezer
Heshbon
Hebron
Beersheba
Miles 10 5 0 10 20
Kms 10 5 0 10 20 30
The six cities of refuge are shown in bold type.

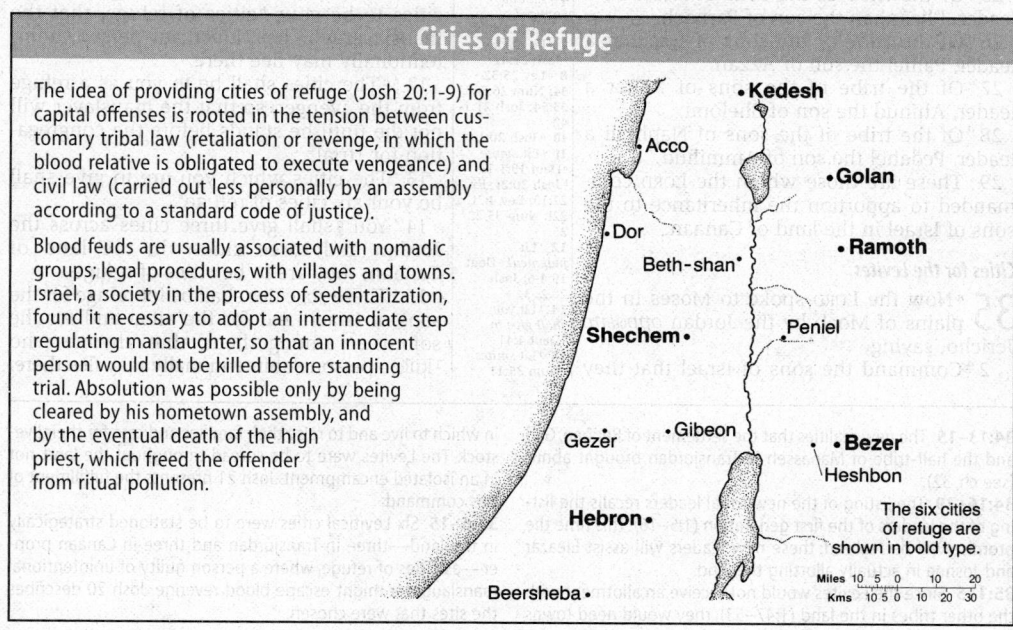

31 ‘Moreover, you shall not take ransom
for the life of a murderer who is guilty of
death, but he shall surely be put to death.
32 ‘You shall not take ransom for him who
has fled to his city of refuge, that he may
return to live in the land [1]before the death of
the priest.
33 ‘[a]So you shall not pollute the land in
which you are; for blood pollutes the land
and no expiation can be made for the land
for the blood that is shed on it, except [b]by
the blood of him who shed it.
34 ‘You shall not [a]defile the land in which
you live, in the midst of which [b]I dwell; for I
the LORD am dwelling in the midst of the
sons of Israel.’ ”

Inheritance by Marriage

36 [a]And the heads of the fathers’ *households* of the family of the sons of Gilead, the son of Machir, the son of Manasseh,
of the families of the sons of Joseph, came
near and spoke before Moses and before the
leaders, the heads of the fathers’ *households*
of the sons of Israel,
2 and they said, “The LORD commanded
my lord to give the land by lot to the sons of
Israel as an inheritance, and my lord [a]was
commanded by the LORD to give the inheritance of Zelophehad our brother to his
daughters.
3 “But if they [1]marry one of the sons of
the *other* tribes of the sons of Israel, their
inheritance will be withdrawn from the
inheritance of our fathers and will be added
to the inheritance of the tribe to which they
belong; thus it will be withdrawn from our
allotted inheritance.
4 “When the [a]jubilee of the sons of Israel
[1]comes, then their inheritance will be added
to the inheritance of the tribe to which they
belong; so their inheritance will be withdrawn from the inheritance of the tribe of
our fathers.”
5 Then Moses commanded the sons of
Israel according to the [1]word of the LORD,
saying, “The tribe of the sons of Joseph are
right in *their* statements.
6 “[a]This is [1]what the LORD has commanded concerning the daughters of Zelophehad,
saying, ‘Let them marry [2]whom they wish;
only they must marry within the family of
the tribe of their father.’
7 “Thus [a]no inheritance of the sons of
Israel shall [1]be transferred from tribe to tribe,
for the sons of Israel shall each [2]hold to the
inheritance of the tribe of his fathers.
8 “[a]Every daughter who comes into possession of an inheritance of any tribe of the
sons of Israel shall be wife to one of the family of the tribe of her father, so that the sons
of Israel each may possess the inheritance of
his fathers.
9 “Thus no inheritance shall [1]be transferred from one tribe to another tribe, for the
tribes of the sons of Israel shall each [2]hold to
his own inheritance.”
10 Just as the LORD had commanded
Moses, so the daughters of Zelophehad did:
11 [a]Mahlah, Tirzah, Hoglah, Milcah and
Noah, the daughters of Zelophehad married
their uncles’ sons.
12 They married *those* from the families of
the sons of Manasseh the son of Joseph, and
their inheritance [1]remained with the tribe of
the family of their father.
13 [a]These are the commandments and the
ordinances which the LORD commanded to
the sons of Israel through Moses in the plains
of Moab by the Jordan *opposite* Jericho.

32 [1]Or *until*
33 [a]Deut 21:7, 8; Ps 106:38 [b]Gen 9:6
34 [a]Lev 18:24, 25 [b]Num 5:3
36:1 [a]Num 27:1
2 [a]Num 27:5-7
3 [1]Lit *become wives to,* in this ch
4 [1]Lit *shall be* [a]Lev 25:10
5 [1]Lit *mouth*
6 [1]Lit *the thing which* [2]Lit *to the good one in their eyes* [a]Num 27:7
7 [1]Lit *turn about* [2]Lit *cleave* [a]1 Kin 21:3
8 [a]1 Chr 23:22
9 [1]Lit *turn about* [2]Lit *cleave*
11 [a]Num 26:33
12 [1]Lit *was*
13 [a]Lev 26:46; 27:34; Num 22:1

ty being accused and sentenced to death on insufficient evidence.

35:32 Not even an involuntary slayer could leave the city of refuge on the payment of a ransom.

35:33 *blood pollutes the land.* The crime of murder is not only an offense against the sanctity of life; it is in fact a pollutant to the Lord’s sacred land.

36:1–13 Presents an interesting further development of the account of Zelophehad’s daughters (see 27:1–11). Since the Lord had instructed Moses that the women might inherit their father’s land, new questions arose: What will happen to the family lands if these daughters marry among other tribes? Will not the original intention of the first provision be frustrated? Such questions led to the decision that marriage is to be kept within one’s own tribe, so that the family allotments will not pass “from one tribe to another tribe” (v. 9).

36:10 *Just as the LORD had commanded Moses, so the daughters of Zelophehad did.* The book of Numbers, which so often presents the rebellion of God’s people against His grace and in defiance of His will, ends on a happy note. These noble women, who were concerned for their father’s name and their own place in the land, obeyed the Lord.

Deuteronomy

INTRODUCTION

Title

The word "Deuteronomy" (meaning "repetition of the law"), the name of the last book of the Pentateuch, arose from a mistranslation in the Greek Septuagint and the Latin Vulgate of a phrase in Deut 17:18, which in Hebrew means "copy of this law." The error is not serious, however, since Deuteronomy is, in a certain sense, a "repetition of the law" (see Structure and Outline). The Hebrew name of the book is *'elleh haddebarim* ("These are the words") or, more simply, *debarim* ("words"; see 1:1).

Author

The book itself testifies that, for the most part, Moses wrote it (1:5; 31:9,22,24), and other OT books agree (1 Kin 2:3; 8:53; 2 Kin 14:6; 18:12) — though the preamble (1:1 – 5) may have been written by someone else, and the report of Moses' death (ch. 34) was almost certainly written by someone else. Jesus also bears testimony to Mosaic authorship (Matt 19:7 – 8; Mark 10:3 – 5; John 5:46 – 47), and so do other NT writers (Acts 3:22 – 23; 7:37 – 38; Rom 10:19). Moreover, Jesus quotes Deuteronomy as authoritative (Matt 4:4,7,10). In the NT there are almost 100 quotations of and allusions to Deuteronomy. Tradition uniformly testifies to the Mosaic authorship of the book (see, e.g., Mark 12:19). See Introduction to Genesis: Author and Date of Writing.

Date

The book is probably to be dated c. 1406 B.C. (see Introduction to Genesis: Author and Date of Writing).

Historical Setting

Deuteronomy locates Moses and the Israelites in the territory of Moab in the area where the Jordan flows into the Dead Sea (1:5). As his final act at this important time of transferring leadership to Joshua, Moses delivered his farewell addresses to prepare the people for their entrance into Canaan. These addresses were actually a covenant renewal (see Structure and Outline). In them, Moses emphasized the laws that were especially needed at such a time, and he presented them in a way appropriate to the situation. In contrast to the matter-of-fact narratives of Leviticus and Numbers, the book of Deuteronomy comes to us from Moses' heart in a warm, personal, sermonic form of expression.

Theological Teaching

The love relationship of the Lord to His people and that of the people to the Lord as their sovereign God pervade the whole book. Deuteronomy's spiritual emphasis and its call to total commitment to the Lord in worship and obedience inspired references to its message throughout the rest of Scripture.

Structure and Outline

Deuteronomy's literary structure supports its historical setting. By its interpretive, repetitious, reminiscent and somewhat irregular style it shows that it is a series of more or less extemporaneous addresses, sometimes describing events in nonchronological order (see, e.g., 10:3). But it also bears in its structure clear reflections of the suzerain-vassal treaties (see chart, p. 16) of the preceding and then-current Near Eastern states, a structure that lends itself to the Biblical emphasis on the covenant between the Lord and His people. In this sense Deuteronomy is a covenant renewal document, as the following outline shows:

- I. The Preamble (1:1–5)
- II. The Historical Prologue (1:6—4:43)
- III. The Stipulations of the Covenant (4:44—26:19)
  - A. The Great Commandment: The Demand for Absolute Allegiance (4:44—11:32)
  - B. Supplementary Requirements (chs. 12—26)
    - 1. Ceremonial consecration (12:1—16:17)
    - 2. Governmental leaders and a righteous nation (16:18—21:21)
    - 3. Sanctity of God's kingdom (21:22—25:19)
    - 4. Confession of God as Redeemer-King (ch. 26)
- IV. Ratification; Curses and Blessings (chs. 27—30)
- V. Leadership Succession under the Covenant (chs. 31—34)
  - A. Change of Leadership (31:1–29)
  - B. Song of Moses (31:30—32:47)
  - C. Moses' Testamental Blessing on the Tribes (32:48—33:29)
  - D. Death of Moses and Succession of Joshua (ch. 34)

The book is sometimes divided into three addresses:

- I. First Address (1:1—4:43)
- II. Second Address (4:44—28:68)
- III. Third Address (chs. 29—33)
- IV. Moses' Death (ch. 34)

Israel's History after the Exodus

1 These are the words which Moses spoke
to all Israel [a]across the Jordan in the
wilderness, in the [b]Arabah opposite [1]Suph,
between Paran and Tophel and Laban and
Hazeroth and Dizahab.
2 It is eleven days' *journey* from [a]Horeb
by the way of Mount [b]Seir to [c]Kadesh-barnea.
3 In the [a]fortieth year, on the first *day* of
the eleventh month, Moses spoke to the children of Israel, [b]according to all that the LORD
had commanded him *to give* to them,
4 after he had [1a]defeated Sihon the king
of the Amorites, who lived in Heshbon, and
[b]Og the king of Bashan, who lived in [c]Ashta-
roth [2]and Edrei.
5 Across the Jordan in the land of Moab,
Moses undertook to expound this law, saying,
6 "The LORD our God [a]spoke to us at
Horeb, saying, 'You have [1]stayed long
enough at this mountain.
7 'Turn and set your journey, and go to
[a]the hill country of the Amorites, and to all
their neighbors in the Arabah, in the hill
country and in the lowland and in [b]the
[1]Negev and by the seacoast, the land of the
Canaanites, and Lebanon, as far as the great
river, the river Euphrates.
8 'See, I have placed the land before you;
go in and possess the land which the LORD
[a]swore to give to your fathers, to Abraham,
to Isaac, and to Jacob, to them and their
[1]descendants after them.'
9 "I spoke to you at that time, saying, '[a]I
am not able to bear *the burden* of you alone.
10 'The LORD your God has [a]multiplied
you, and behold, you are this day like the
stars of heaven in number.
11 'May the LORD, the God of your fathers,
increase you a thousand-fold more than you
are and bless you, [a]just as He has [1]promised
you!
12 'How can I alone bear the load and burden of you and your strife?
13 '[1a]Choose wise and discerning and
experienced men from your tribes, and I will
appoint them as your heads.'
14 "You answered me and said, 'The thing
which you have said to do is good.'
15 "So I took the heads of your tribes, wise
and experienced men, and [1]appointed them
heads over you, leaders of thousands and [2]of
hundreds, [2]of fifties and [2]of tens, and officers for your tribes.
16 "Then I charged your judges at that
time, saying, 'Hear *the cases* between your
[1]fellow countrymen, and [a]judge righteously
between a man and his [2]fellow countryman,
or the alien who is with him.
17 '[a]You shall not show partiality in judgment; you shall hear the small and the great
alike. You shall [b]not fear [1]man, for the judgment is God's. [c]The case that is too hard for
you, you shall bring to me, and I will hear it.'
18 "[a]I commanded you at that time all the
things that you should do.
19 "Then we set out from [a]Horeb, and went
through all that [b]great and terrible wilderness which you saw on the way to the [c]hill
country of the Amorites, just as the LORD our
God had commanded us; and we came to
[a]Kadesh-barnea.
20 "I said to you, 'You have come to the hill
country of the Amorites which the LORD our
God is about to give us.
21 'See, the LORD your God has placed the
land before you; go up, take possession, as
the LORD, the God of your fathers, has spoken to you. [a]Do not fear or be dismayed.'

1:1 [1]Perhaps Red Sea [a]Deut 4:46 [b]Deut 2:8
2 [a]Ex 3:1; 17:6 [b]Gen 32:3 [c]Num 13:26; 32:8; Deut 9:23
3 [a]Num 33:38 [b]Deut 4:1, 2
4 [1]Lit *smitten* [2]So with ancient versions; M.T. omits *and* [a]Num 21:21-26; Deut 2:26-35; Josh 13:10; Neh 9:22 [b]Num 21:33-35; Josh 13:12 [c]Josh 12:4
6 [1]Lit *dwelt* [a]Num 10:11-13
7 [1]I.e. South country [a]Gen 15:18; Deut 11:24; Josh 10:40 [b]Gen 12:9
8 [1]Lit *seed* [a]Gen 12:7; 26:3; 28:13; Ex 33:1; Num 14:23; 32:11; Heb 6:13, 14
9 [a]Ex 18:18, 24; Num 11:14
10 [a]Gen 15:5; 22:17; Ex 32:13; Deut 7:7; 10:22; 26:5; 28:62
11 [1]Lit *spoken to* [a]Deut 1:8, 10
13 [1]Lit *Give for yourselves* [a]Ex 18:21
15 [1]Lit *gave* [2]Lit *leaders of*
16 [1]Lit *brothers* [2]Lit *brother* [a]Deut 16:18; John 7:24
17 [1]Lit *because of man* [a]Deut 10:17; 16:19; 24:17; 2 Chr 19:5, 6; Prov 24:23-26; Acts 10:34; James 2:1, 9 [b]Prov 29:25 [c]Ex 18:22, 26
18 [a]Ex 18:20
19 [a]Deut 1:2 [b]Deut 2:7; 8:15; 32:10; Jer 2:6 [c]Deut 1:7
21 [a]Josh 1:6, 9

1:1–5 The preamble gives the historical setting for the entire book.
1:1 *Moses spoke.* Almost all of Deuteronomy is made up of speeches by Moses during the final months of his life, just before the Israelites crossed the Jordan to enter Canaan. *Arabah.* Includes the valley of the Jordan (from the Sea of Galilee to the southern end of the Dead Sea) and the valley extending down to the Gulf of Aqaba. *Suph . . . Paran and Tophel and Laban and Hazeroth and Dizahab.* Places along the route from Sinai to the territory of Moab.
1:2 *Horeb.* The usual name for Mount Sinai in Deuteronomy (the only exception is in 33:2). *Kadesh-barnea.* See note on Gen 14:7. *Seir.* See note on Gen 36:8.
1:3 *fortieth year.* After leaving Egypt. The Lord had condemned Israel to 40 years of wandering in Sinai as punishment for not entering Canaan as He had commanded them to do at Kadesh (Num 14:33–34). The 40 years included the time spent at Sinai and on the journey to Kadesh as well as the next 38 years (see 2:14). See 8:2–5; 29:5–6; Num 14:29–35; 32:13; Heb 3:7–19. *eleventh month.* January-February.
1:5 *this law.* The Ten Commandments and other laws given at Mount Sinai and recorded in Ex 20–24, Leviticus and Numbers. In Deuteronomy the laws are summarized and interpreted, and adjusted to the new, specific situation Israel would face in Canaan. Thus Deuteronomy is, in essence, a covenant renewal (and updating) document.
1:7 See Josh 1:4. The land is described by its various geographical areas (see map No. 2 at the end of the study Bible). *Arabah.* See note on v. 1; here the Jordan Valley and the Dead Sea area. *hill country.* The midsection running north and south. *lowland.* Sloping toward the Mediterranean. *Negev.* See note on Gen 12:9. *seacoast.* The Mediterranean coastal strip. The "land of the Canaanites" and "Lebanon, as far as the . . . Euphrates" make up the northern sector. The "hill country of the Amorites" is, in general, the central and southern mountains. This description of the land agrees with that in the promise (see v. 8) to Abraham in Gen 15:18–21, a promise later limited to Isaac's descendants (Gen 26:2–4) and still later to the descendants of Jacob (Gen 35:11–12).
1:9–18 Cf. 16:18–20; Ex 18:13–26.
1:10 *The LORD your God.* This title occurs almost 300 times in Deuteronomy in addition to the many times that "LORD" is used alone or in other combinations. *like the stars of heaven.* See 10:22; 28:62; Gen 13:16 and note; 15:5 and note; 22:17; 26:4; Ex 32:13.
1:19–46 See Num 13–14.

22 "[a]Then all of you approached me and
said, 'Let us send men before us, that they
may search out the land for us, and bring
back to us word of the way by which we
should go up and the cities which we shall
enter.'
23 "The thing pleased me and I took twelve
of your men, one man for each tribe.
24 "[a]They turned and went up into the hill
country, and came to the valley of Eshcol
and spied it out.
25 "Then they took *some* of the fruit of the
land in their hands and brought it down to
us; and they brought us back a report and
said, 'It is a good land which the LORD our
God is about to give us.'
26 "[a]Yet you were not willing to go up, but
[b]rebelled against the [1]command of the LORD
your God;
27 and [a]you grumbled in your tents and
said, 'Because the LORD hates us, He has
brought us out of the land of Egypt to deliver us into the hand of the Amorites to
destroy us.
28 'Where can we go up? Our brethren have
made our hearts melt, saying, "The people are
bigger and taller than we; the cities are large
and fortified to heaven. And besides, we saw
[a]the sons of the Anakim there." '
29 "Then I said to you, 'Do not be shocked,
nor fear them.
30 'The LORD your God who goes before
you will [a]Himself fight on your behalf, [1]just
as He did for you in Egypt before your eyes,
31 and in the wilderness where you saw
how [a]the LORD your God carried you, just as
a man carries his son, in all the way which
you have walked until you came to this
place.'
32 "But [1a]for all this, you did not trust the
LORD your God,
33 [a]who goes before you on *your* way, [b]to
seek out a place for you to encamp, in fire by
night and cloud by day, to show you the way
in which you should go.

22 [a]Num 13:1-3 **24** [a]Num 13:21-25 **26** [1]Lit *mouth* [a]Num 14:1-4 [b]Deut 9:23 **27** [a]Deut 9:28; Ps 106:25 **28** [a]Num 13:28, 33; Deut 9:2 **30** [1]Lit *according to all that* [a]Ex 14:14; Deut 3:22; 20:4; Neh 4:20 **31** [a]Deut 32:10-12; Is 46:3, 4; 63:9; Hos 11:3; Acts 13:18 **32** [1]Lit *in this matter* [a]Num 14:11; Ps 106:24; Heb 3:19; 4:2; Jude 5 **33** [a]Ex 13:21; Num 9:15-23; Neh 9:12; Ps 78:14 [b]Num 10:33

34 [a]Num 14:28-30; Heb 3:18 **35** [a]Ps 95:11; 106:26; Ezek 20:15; 1 Cor 10:5; Heb 3:14-19 **36** [a]Num 14:24; Josh 14:9 **37** [a]Num 20:12; Deut 3:26; 4:21 [b]Num 27:13, 18 **38** [a]Num 14:30 [b]Num 34:17; Deut 3:28; 31:7; Josh 11:23 **39** [a]Num 14:3, 31 [b]Is 7:15, 16 **40** [1]Lit *Sea of Reeds* [a]Num 14:25 **41** [a]Num 14:40 **42** [1]Lit *smitten* [a]Num 14:41-43 **43** [1]Lit *mouth* [a]Num 14:40 **44** [1]Lit *dwelt* [a]Num 14:45 [b]Ps 118:12 **45** [a]Job 27:8, 9; Ps 66:18; John 9:31

34 "Then the LORD heard the sound of your
words, and He was angry and [a]took an oath,
saying,
35 '[a]Not one of these men, this evil generation, shall see the good land which I swore
to give your fathers,
36 except Caleb the son of Jephunneh; he
shall see it, and [a]to him and to his sons I will
give the land on which he has set foot,
because he has followed the LORD fully.'
37 "[a]The LORD was angry with me also on
your account, saying, '[b]Not even you shall
enter there.
38 'Joshua the son of Nun, who stands
before you, [a]he shall enter there; encourage
him, for [b]he will cause Israel to inherit it.
39 'Moreover, [a]your little ones who you
said would become a prey, and your sons,
who this day have [b]no knowledge of good or
evil, shall enter there, and I will give it to
them and they shall possess it.
40 'But as for you, [a]turn around and set
out for the wilderness by the way to the [1]Red
Sea.'
41 "[a]Then you said to me, 'We have sinned
against the LORD; we will indeed go up and
fight, just as the LORD our God commanded
us.' And every man of you girded on his
weapons of war, and regarded it as easy to
go up into the hill country.
42 "[a]And the LORD said to me, 'Say to them,
"Do not go up nor fight, for I am not among
you; otherwise you will be [1]defeated before
your enemies." '
43 "So I spoke to you, but you would not
listen. Instead [a]you rebelled against the
[1]command of the LORD, and acted presumptuously and went up into the hill country.
44 "[a]The Amorites who [1]lived in that hill
country came out against you and chased
you [b]as bees do, and crushed you from Seir
to Hormah.
45 "Then you returned and wept before the
LORD; but the [a]LORD did not listen to your
voice nor give ear to you.

1:21 *as the LORD . . . has spoken to you.* The promise of the land (see note on v. 7) was reaffirmed to Moses at the burning bush (v. 8; Ex 3:8,17). Now the Israelites are told to enter the land and conquer it. *Do not fear or be dismayed.* See 31:8; Josh 1:9; 8:1; 10:25.

1:23 *twelve.* They are named in Num 13:4–15.

1:24 *Eshcol.* See Num 13:23 and note.

1:26 *you . . . rebelled.* Although they themselves had not rebelled, the people were being addressed as a nation united with the earlier rebellious generation (see 5:2; cf. 29:1).

1:27 *grumbled.* See note on Ex 15:24. *the LORD hates us.* The people's statement is ironic indeed in the light of Deuteronomy's major theme (see Introduction: Theological Teaching).

1:28 *Anakim.* Earlier inhabitants of Canaan, described as giants (see 2:10,21; 9:2; Num 13:32).

1:30 *as He did for you in Egypt.* See Ex 14:1–15:19.

1:31 *God carried you.* See notes on Is 41:10,13; 43:1–2; cf. Is 40:11; Jer 31:10; Ezek 34:11–16.

1:33 *in fire by night and cloud by day.* The presence of the Lord was in the cloud over the tabernacle to guide the Israelites through their wilderness journeys (see Ex 13:21 and note; 40:34–38).

1:36 *Caleb.* See Num 13:30–14:38; Josh 14:6–15.

1:37 *on your account.* See 3:26; 4:21. God was angry with Moses when in a wrong spirit he struck the rock at Meribah to get water (Num 20:9–13; 27:12–14). And since it was the Israelites who had incited him to sin, God was angry with them too. This event (v. 37) occurred almost 40 years after that of the preceding verses (vv. 34–36), but Moses, interested in telling of the Israelites' sin and his own, brings the two events together.

1:39 *have no knowledge of good or evil.* See notes on Gen 2:9; Is 7:15.

1:41 *you.* See note on v. 26.

1:43 *you rebelled against the command of the LORD.* The same charge as in v. 26. First the people rebelled against the Lord's command to go into the land, then against His command not to enter the land. After their first rebellion the Lord would not go with them. His presence was essential, and Israel needed to learn that lesson.

1:44 *bees.* See note on Ex 23:28.

1:45 *before the LORD.* At the tabernacle.

46 "So you remained in [a]Kadesh many days, [1]the days that you spent *there.*

Wanderings in the Wilderness

2 "[a]Then we turned and set out for the wilderness by the way to the [1]Red Sea, as the LORD spoke to me, and circled [b]Mount Seir for many days.

2 "And the LORD spoke to me, saying,

3 'You have circled this mountain long enough. *Now* turn north,

4 [a]and command the people, saying, "You will pass through the [b]territory of your brothers the sons of Esau who live in Seir; and [c]they will be afraid of you. So be very careful;

5 do not [1]provoke them, for I will not give you any of their land, even *as little as* a [2]footstep [a]because I have given Mount Seir to Esau as a possession.

6 "You shall buy food from them with money so that you may eat, and you shall also purchase water from them with money so that you may drink.

7 "For the LORD your God has blessed you in all [1]that you have done; He has known your [2]wanderings through this [a]great wilderness. These [b]forty years the LORD your God has been with you; you have not lacked a thing." '

8 "So we passed beyond our brothers the sons of Esau, who live in Seir, away from the [a]Arabah road, away from Elath and [b]from Ezion-geber. And we turned and passed through by the way of the wilderness of Moab.

9 "Then the LORD said to me, 'Do not harass Moab, nor provoke them to war, for I will not give you any of [1]their land as a possession, because I have given [a]Ar to [b]the sons of Lot as a possession.

10 (The [a]Emim lived there formerly, a people as great, numerous, and tall as the Anakim.

11 Like the Anakim, they are also regarded as [a]Rephaim, but the Moabites call them Emim.

12 [a]The Horites formerly lived in Seir, but the sons of Esau dispossessed them and destroyed them from before them and settled in their place, [b]just as Israel did to the land of [1]their possession which the LORD gave to them.)

13 'Now arise and cross over the [1]brook Zered yourselves.' So we crossed over the [1]brook Zered.

14 "Now the [1]time that it took for us to come from Kadesh-barnea until we crossed over the [2]brook Zered was [a]thirty-eight years, until [b]all the generation of the men of war perished from within the camp, as [c]the LORD had sworn to them.

15 "[a]Moreover the hand of the LORD was against them, to destroy them from within the camp until they all perished.

16 "So it came about when [a]all the men of war had finally perished from among the people,

17 that the LORD spoke to me, saying,

18 'Today you shall cross over [a]Ar, the border of Moab.

19 'When you come opposite the [a]sons of Ammon, do not harass them nor provoke them, for I will not give you any of the land of the sons of Ammon as a possession, because I have given it to [b]the sons of Lot as a possession.'

20 (It is also regarded as the land of the [a]Rephaim, *for* Rephaim formerly lived in it, but the Ammonites call them Zamzummin,

21 a people as great, numerous, and tall as the Anakim, but the LORD destroyed them before them. And they dispossessed them and settled in their place,

22 just as He did for the sons of Esau, who [a]live in Seir, when He destroyed [b]the Horites from before them; they dispossessed them and settled in their place even to this day.

23 And the [a]Avvim, who lived in villages as far as Gaza, the [1b]Caphtorim who came from [2c]Caphtor, destroyed them and lived in their place.)

24 'Arise, set out, and pass through the [1a]valley of Arnon. Look! I have given Sihon the Amorite, king of Heshbon, and his land into your hand; begin to take possession and contend with him in battle.

46 [1]Lit *as the days* [a]Num 20:1, 22; Deut 2:7, 14; Judg 11:17
2:1 [1]Lit *Sea of Reeds* [a]Num 21:4 [b]Deut 1:2
4 [a]Num 20:14-21 [b]Gen 36:8 [c]Ex 15:15, 16
5 [1]Or *engage in strife with* [2]Lit *treading of a sole of a foot* [a]Gen 36:8; Josh 24:4
7 [1]Lit *the work of your hand* [2]Lit *goings* [a]Deut 1:19 [b]Num 14:33, 34; 32:13; Deut 2:14
8 [a]Deut 1:1 [b]Num 33:35; 1 Kin 9:26
9 [1]Lit *his* [a]Num 21:15, 28; Deut 2:18, 29 [b]Gen 19:36, 37
10 [a]Gen 14:5
11 [a]Gen 14:5; Deut 2:20
12 [a]Gen 36:20; Deut 2:22

12 [1]Lit *his* [b]Num 21:25, 35
13 [1]Or *wadi*
14 [1]Lit *days in which we went* [2]Or *wadi* [a]Deut 2:7 [b]Num 14:29-35; 26:64, 65; Ps 106:26; 1 Cor 10:5 [c]Deut 1:34, 35
15 [a]Jude 5
16 [a]Deut 2:14
18 [a]Deut 2:9
19 [a]Gen 19:38 [b]Deut 2:9
20 [a]Deut 2:11
22 [a]Gen 36:8; Deut 2:5 [b]Deut 2:12
23 [1]I.e. Philistines [2]I.e. Crete [a]Josh 13:3 [b]Gen 10:14; 1 Chr 1:12 [c]Jer 47:4; Amos 9:7
24 [1]Or *wadi* [a]Num 21:13, 14; Judg 11:18

2:1–3:11 See Num 20:14–21:35.
2:1 *Red Sea.* Here probably the Gulf of Aqaba (see note on 1 Kin 9:26). *Mount Seir.* The mountainous area south of the Dead Sea.
2:5 *I will not give you any of their land.* See vv. 9,19. The Lord told Moses to bypass Edom, Moab and Ammon because of their blood relationship to Israel. The Israelites were to take over only those lands east of the Jordan that were in the hands of the Amorites (see v. 24; 3:2). *I have given.* See vv. 9,19. The Lord had given the descendants of Esau (Edomites) and Lot (Moabites and Ammonites) their lands, just as He was giving the Israelites the territories of Transjordan and Canaan.
2:8 *Elath and . . . Ezion-geber.* At the head of the Gulf of Aqaba. The "Arabah road" ran from the head of the gulf northward and to the east of Moab.
2:9 *Ar.* Location unknown.
2:10 *Emim.* Possibly meaning "terrors." *Anakim.* See note on 1:28.
2:11 *Rephaim.* Ancient people of large stature.
2:12 *Horites.* See note on Gen 14:6. *the land . . . the LORD gave to them.* Either (1) the Transjordan regions (see 2:24–3:20), (2) Canaan itself or (3) Transjordan and Canaan. If either (2) or (3) is intended, editorial updating is involved (see note on Gen 14:14).
2:13 *Zered.* The main stream (intermittent) that flows into the southern end of the Dead Sea from the east (see map No. 4 at the end of the study Bible).
2:14 *thirty-eight years.* See note on 1:3.
2:20 *Zamzummin.* Possibly meaning "murmurers," and perhaps to be identified with the Zuzites of Gen 14:5.
2:23 *Avvim.* Pre-Philistine people otherwise unknown (Josh 13:3). *Captorim.* See note on Gen 10:14.
2:24 *Arnon.* See note on Num 21:10–13.

25 'This day I will begin to put [a]the dread
and fear of you [1]upon the peoples [2]every-
where under the heavens, who, when they
hear the report of you, [b]will tremble and be
in anguish because of you.'
26 "[a]So I sent messengers from the wilderness of Kedemoth to Sihon king of Heshbon
with words of peace, saying,
27 'Let me pass through your land, I will
[1]travel only on the highway; I will not turn
aside to the right or to the left.
28 'You will sell me food for money so that
I may eat, and give me water for money so
that I may drink, [a]only let me pass through
on [1]foot,
29 just as the sons of Esau who live in Seir
and the Moabites who live in [a]Ar did for me,
until I cross over the Jordan into the land
which the LORD our God is giving to us.'
30 "But [a]Sihon king of Heshbon was not
willing for us to pass [1]through his land; for
the [b]LORD your God hardened his spirit and
made his heart obstinate, in order to deliver
him into your hand, as *he is* today.
31 "The LORD said to me, 'See, I have begun
to deliver Sihon and his land [1]over to you.
Begin to [2]occupy, that you may possess his
land.'
32 "Then Sihon [1]with all his people came
out to meet us in battle at Jahaz.
33 "[a]The LORD our God delivered him [1]over
to us, and we [2b]defeated him with his sons
and all his people.
34 "So we captured all his cities at that time
and [1a]utterly destroyed [2]the men, women
and children of every city. We left no survivor.
35 "We took [a]only the animals as our booty
and the spoil of the cities which we had captured.
36 "From [a]Aroer which is on the edge of
the [1]valley of Arnon and *from* the city which
is in the [1]valley, even to Gilead, there was no
city that was too high for us; the LORD our
God delivered all [2]over to us.
37 "[a]Only you did not go near to the land
of the sons of Ammon, all along the [1]river
[b]Jabbok and the cities of the hill country,
and wherever the LORD our God had commanded us.

Conquests Recounted

3 "[a]Then we turned and went up the road
to Bashan, and Og, king of Bashan, [1]with
all his people came out to meet us in battle at
Edrei.
2 "But the LORD said to me, 'Do not fear
him, for I have delivered him and all his people and his land into your hand; and you
shall do to him just as you did to Sihon king
of the Amorites, who lived at Heshbon.'
3 "So the LORD our God delivered Og also,
king of Bashan, with all his people into our
hand, and we smote [1]them until no survivor
was [2]left.
4 "We captured all his cities at that time;
there was not a city which we did not take
from them: sixty cities, all the region of
[a]Argob, the kingdom of Og in Bashan.
5 "All these were cities fortified with high
walls, gates and bars, besides a great many
[1]unwalled towns.
6 "We [1]utterly destroyed them, as we did
to [a]Sihon king of Heshbon, [2b]utterly destroying [3]the men, women and children of every
city.
7 "[a]But all the animals and the spoil of the
cities we took as our booty.
8 "[a]Thus we took the land at that time
from the hand of the two kings of the Amorites who were beyond the Jordan, from the
[1]valley of Arnon to Mount Hermon
9 (Sidonians [a]call Hermon [b]Sirion, and
the Amorites call it [c]Senir):
10 all the cities of the plateau and all Gilead and [a]all Bashan, as far as Salecah and
Edrei, cities of the kingdom of Og in Bashan.
11 (For only Og king of Bashan was left of
the remnant of the [a]Rephaim. Behold, his
[1]bedstead was an iron [1]bedstead; it is in

25 [1]Lit *in front of* [2]Lit *under all the heavens* [a]Ex 23:27; Deut 11:25; Josh 2:9 [b]Ex 15:14-16
26 [a]Num 21:21-32; Deut 1:4; Judg 11:19-21
27 [1]Lit *go by the way*
28 [1]Lit *my feet* [a]Num 20:19
29 [a]Deut 2:9
30 [1]Lit *by him* [a]Num 21:23 [b]Ex 4:21; Josh 11:20
31 [1]Lit *before you* [2]Lit *possess*
32 [1]Lit *he and*
33 [1]Lit *before us* [2]Lit *smote* [a]Ex 23:31; Deut 7:2 [b]Deut 29:7
34 [1]Or *put under the ban* [2]Lit *every city of man...* [a]Deut 3:6; 7:2
35 [a]Deut 3:7
36 [1]Or *wadi* [2]Lit *before us* [a]Deut 3:12; 4:48; Josh 12:2; 13:9
37 [1]Or *wadi* [a]Deut 2:19 [b]Gen 32:22; Num 21:24; Deut 3:16
3:1 [1]Lit *he and* [a]Num 21:33-35
3 [1]Lit *him* [2]Lit *left to him*
4 [a]Deut 3:13, 14; 1 Kin 4:13
5 [1]Or *rural*
6 [1]Or *put them under the ban* [2]Or *putting under the ban* [3]Lit *every city of men...* [a]Deut 1:4 [b]Deut 2:34
7 [a]Deut 2:35
8 [1]Or *wadi* [a]Num 32:33; Josh 12:1-7; 13:8-12
9 [a]Deut 4:48; Josh 11:17; Ps 42:6; 133:3 [b]Ps 29:6 [c]1 Chr 5:23
10 [a]Josh 13:11
11 [1]Or *couch* [a]Gen 14:5; Deut 2:11, 20

2:26 *Kedemoth.* Means "eastern regions."
2:30 *hardened his spirit and made his heart obstinate.* In the OT, actions are often attributed to God without the mention of mediate or contributing situations or persons. Sihon by his own conscious will refused Israel passage, but it was God who would give Sihon's land to Israel (see note on Ex 4:21).
2:32 *Jahaz.* See note on Is 15:4.
2:34 *utterly destroyed.* The Hebrew for this expression usually denotes the destruction of everyone and everything that could be destroyed. Objects like gold, silver and bronze, not subject to destruction, were put in a secure place as God's possession. Destruction of people and things made them useless to the conquerors but put them in the hands of God. So the word is sometimes translated "destroyed" and sometimes "be under the ban" (see, e.g., Josh 6:17). The practice was sometimes limited, as when God assigned captured livestock and other plunder to His people as recompense for service in His army (see v. 35; 3:7; Jos 8:2).
2:36 *Aroer.* See note on Is 17:2. *Gilead.* See note on Gen 31:21.
2:37 *Jabbok.* See note on Gen 32:22.
3:3 *delivered Og . . . into our hand.* As in 2:26–37.
3:4 *sixty cities.* The cities were large and walled (1 Kin 4:13), implying a heavily populated territory (see v. 5). *region of Argob.* An otherwise unidentified area in Bashan (see vv. 13–14; 1 Kin 4:13).
3:6–7 See note on 2:34.
3:8 *Mount Hermon.* Snowcapped throughout the year and rising to a height of over 9,200 feet, it is one of the most prominent and beautiful mountains in Lebanon.
3:9 *Sirion.* This name for Mount Hermon is found also in a Canaanite document contemporary with Moses. *Senir.* This name for Mount Hermon is also found in Assyrian sources.
3:10 *Salecah.* A city marking the eastern boundary of Bashan (see Josh 13:11).
3:11 *iron bedstead.* Sarcophagi (stone coffins) of basalt have been found in Bashan, and the Hebrew for "bedstead" (which can be translated "sarcophagus") and "iron" may reflect this. If an actual bed, it was probably made of wood but with certain iron

[b]Rabbah of the sons of Ammon. Its length
was nine cubits and its width four cubits [2]by
ordinary cubit.)
12 "So we took possession of this land at
that time. From [a]Aroer, which is by the [1]val-
ley of Arnon, and half the hill country of
[b]Gilead and its cities I gave to the Reubenites
and to the Gadites.
13 "The rest of Gilead and all Bashan, the
kingdom of Og, I gave to the half-tribe of
Manasseh, all the region of Argob (concerning
all Bashan, it is called the land of Rephaim.
14 [a]Jair the son of Manasseh took all the
region of Argob as far as the border of the
Geshurites and the Maacathites, and called
[1]it, *that is,* Bashan, after his own name,
[2]Havvoth-jair, *as it is* to this day.)
15 "[a]To Machir I gave Gilead.
16 "To the Reubenites and to the Gadites I
gave from Gilead even as far as the [1]valley of
Arnon, the middle of the [1]valley [2]as a border
and as far as the [1]river [a]Jabbok, the border
of the sons of Ammon;
17 the Arabah also, with the Jordan [1]as *a*
border, from [2][a]Chinnereth [b]even as far as the
sea of the Arabah, [c]the Salt Sea, [3]at the foot
of the slopes of Pisgah on the east.
18 "Then I commanded you at that time,
saying, '[a]The LORD your God has given you
this land to possess it; [b]all you valiant men
shall cross over armed before your brothers,
the sons of Israel.
19 '[a]But your wives and your little ones
and your livestock (I know that you have
[b]much livestock) shall remain in your cities
which I have given you,
20 [a]until the LORD gives rest to your fellow
countrymen as to you, and they also possess
the land which the LORD your God will give
them beyond the Jordan. [b]Then you may
return every man to his possession which I
have given you.'
21 "I commanded Joshua at that time, saying, 'Your eyes have seen all that the LORD
your God has done to these two kings; so the
LORD shall do to all the kingdoms into which
you are about to cross.
22 'Do not fear them, for the LORD your
God [a]is the one fighting for you.'
23 "I also pleaded with the LORD at that
time, saying,
24 'O Lord [1]GOD, You have begun to show
Your servant [a]Your greatness and Your strong
hand; for what [b]god is there in heaven or on
earth who can do such works and mighty
acts as Yours?
25 'Let me, I pray, cross over and see the
[a]fair land that is beyond the Jordan, [1]that
good hill country and Lebanon.'
26 "But [a]the LORD was angry with me on
your account, and would not listen to me;
and the LORD said to me, '[1]Enough! Speak to
Me no more of this matter.
27 'Go up to the top of [a]Pisgah and lift up
your eyes to the west and north and south
and east, and see *it* with your eyes, [b]for you
shall not cross over this Jordan.
28 '[a]But charge Joshua and encourage him
and strengthen him, [b]for he shall go across
[1]at the head of this people, and he will give
them as an inheritance the land which you
will see.'
29 "So we remained in the valley opposite
[a]Beth-peor.

Israel Urged to Obey God's Law

4 "Now, O Israel, listen to the statutes and
the judgments which [a]I am teaching you
to perform, so that [b]you may live and go in
and take possession of the land which the
LORD, the God of your fathers, is giving you.
2 "[a]You shall not add to the word which [b]I
am commanding you, nor take away from it,
that you may keep the commandments of
the LORD your God which I command you.
3 "[a]Your eyes have seen what the LORD

11 [2]Lit *by a man's forearm* [b]2 Sam 11:1; 12:26; Jer 49:2
12 [1]Or *wadi* [a]Deut 2:36 [b]Num 32:32-38; Josh 13:8-13
14 [1]Lit *them* [2]I.e. the towns of Jair [a]Num 32:41; 1 Chr 2:22
15 [a]Num 32:39, 40
16 [1]Or *wadi* [2]Lit *and* [a]Num 21:24; Deut 2:37
17 [1]Lit *and* [2]I.e. the Sea of Galilee [3]Lit *under* [a]Num 34:11; Josh 13:27 [b]Josh 12:3 [c]Gen 14:3; Josh 3:16
18 [a]Josh 1:13 [b]Num 32:20; Josh 4:12, 13
19 [a]Josh 1:14 [b]Ex 12:38
20 [a]Josh 1:15 [b]Josh 22:4
22 [a]Ex 14:14; Deut 1:30; 20:4; Neh 4:20
24 [1]Heb *YHWH,* usually rendered *LORD* [a]Deut 11:2 [b]Ex 8:10; 15:11; 2 Sam 7:22; Ps 71:19; 86:8
25 [1]Lit *this* [a]Deut 4:22
26 [1]Lit *Enough for you* [a]Deut 1:37
27 [a]Num 23:14; 27:12 [b]Deut 1:37
28 [1]Lit *before this people* [a]Num 27:18; Deut 31:3, 7, 8, 23 [b]Deut 1:38
29 [a]Num 25:1-3; Deut 4:46; 34:6
4:1 [a]Deut 1:3 [b]Lev 18:5; Deut 5:33; 8:1; 16:20; 30:16, 19; Ezek 20:11; Rom 10:5
2 [a]Deut 12:32; Prov 30:6; Rev 22:18 [b]Deut 4:5, 14, 40
3 [a]Num 25:1-9

---

fixtures, as were the "iron chariots" (see note on Josh 17:16). *Rabbah of the sons of Ammon.* Called Philadelphia in NT times, Rabbah was the capital of ancient Ammon (Amos 1:13–14). Today its name is Amman, the capital of the kingdom of Jordan.

3:12–20 See Num 32; 34:13–15.

3:14 *Jair . . . Havvoth-jair.* See note on Judg 10:3. *the Geshurites and the Maacathites.* Two comparatively small kingdoms, Geshur was east of the Sea of Galilee and Maacah was east of the Waters of Merom (see note on Josh 11:5) and north of Geshur.

3:15 *Machir.* See note on Gen 50:23.

3:17 *Chinnereth.* See note on Mark 1:16. *Pisgah.* On the edge of the high plateau overlooking the Dead Sea from the east.

3:20 *rest.* A peaceful situation—free from external threat and oppression, and untroubled within by conflict, famine or plague (see 12:9–10; 25:19; see also notes on Josh 1:13; 1 Kin 5:4; Heb 4:1–11).

3:22 *God is the one.* The conquest narratives emphasize the truth that without the Lord's help Israel's victory would be impossible. The Lord's power, not Israel's unaided strength, achieved victory. Moses bolstered Israel's resolve and faith by this assurance (see 1:30; 2:21–22,31; 20:4).

3:23–25 Moses' final plea to be allowed to enter the land (see 1:37 and note; 31:2).

3:26 *on your account.* See note on 1:37.

3:27 *Go up to the top of Pisgah.* Moses did so after he had expounded the law to the Israelites to prepare them for life in the promised land (see 32:48–52; 34:1–6). *Pisgah.* See note on v. 17. *lift up your eyes to the west and north and south and east.* Like Abraham (see Gen 13:14), Moses would inherit the promised land only through his descendants (see 34:1–4).

3:28 *charge Joshua.* See 31:7–8.

3:29 *Beth-peor.* Means "house/sanctuary of Peor." Very likely, reference is to the cult place where the Baal of Peor was worshiped (see Num 23:28; 25:3,5).

4:1 *O Israel, listen.* God's call to His people to hear and obey is a frequent theme in Deuteronomy (see, e.g., 5:1; 6:3–4; 9:1; 20:3) and elsewhere in the OT. See also note on 6:4–9.

4:2 *You shall not add . . . nor take away.* The revelation the Lord gives is sufficient. All of it must be obeyed, and anything that adulterates or contradicts it cannot be tolerated (see 12:32; Prov 30:6; Gal 3:15; Rev 22:18–19).

has done in the case of Baal-peor, for all the men who followed Baal-peor, the LORD your God has destroyed [1]them from among you.

4 "But you who held fast to the LORD your God are alive today, every one of you.

5 "See, I have taught you statutes and judgments [a]just as the LORD my God commanded me, that you should do thus in the land where you are entering to possess it.

6 "So keep and do *them*, [a]for that is your wisdom and your understanding in the sight of the peoples who will hear all these statutes and say, 'Surely this great nation is a wise and understanding people.'

7 "For [a]what great nation is there that has a god [b]so near to it as is the LORD our God [c]whenever we call on Him?

8 "Or what great nation is there that has [a]statutes and judgments as righteous as this whole law which I am setting before you today?

9 "Only [a]give heed to yourself and keep your soul diligently, so that you do not forget the things which your eyes have seen and they do not depart from your heart [b]all the days of your life; but [c]make them known to your sons and your grandsons.

10 "*Remember* the day you stood before the LORD your God at Horeb, when the LORD said to me, 'Assemble the people to Me, that I may let them hear My words [a]so they may learn to [1]fear Me all the days they live on the earth, and that they may [b]teach their children.'

11 "You came near and stood at the foot of the mountain, [a]and the mountain burned with fire to the *very* heart of the heavens: darkness, cloud and thick gloom.

12 "Then the LORD spoke to you from the midst of the fire; you heard the sound of words, but you saw no form—only a voice.

13 "So He declared to you His covenant which He commanded you to perform, *that is,* [a]the Ten [1]Commandments; and [b]He wrote them on two tablets of stone.

14 "The LORD commanded me at that time to teach you statutes and judgments, that you might perform them in the land where you are going over to possess it.

3 [1]Lit *him*
5 [a]Lev 26:46; 27:34
6 [a]Deut 30:19, 20; 32:46, 47; Job 28:28; Ps 19:7; 111:10; Prov 1:7; 2 Tim 3:15
7 [a]Deut 4:32-34; 2 Sam 7:23 [b]Ps 34:17, 18; 145:18; 148:14; Is 55:6 [c]Ps 34:18; 85:9
8 [a]Ps 89:14; 97:2; 119:144, 160, 172
9 [a]Deut 4:23; 6:12; 8:11, 14, 19; Prov 4:23; 23:19 [b]Deut 6:2; 12:1; 16:3 [c]Gen 18:19; Deut 4:10; 6:7, 20-25; 11:19; 32:46; Ps 78:5, 6; Prov 22:6; Eph 6:4
10 [1]Or *reverence* [a]Deut 14:23; 17:19; 31:12, 13 [b]Deut 4:9
11 [a]Ex 19:18; Heb 12:18, 19
13 [1]Lit *Words* [a]Ex 34:28; Deut 10:4 [b]Ex 31:18; 34:1, 28
15 [a]Josh 23:11 [b]Is 40:18
16 [a]Deut 4:25; 9:12; 31:29 [b]Ex 20:4; Lev 26:1; Deut 5:8, 9; 27:15; Rom 1:23
17 [a]Rom 1:23
19 [a]Gen 2:1; Deut 17:3; 2 Kin 17:16; 21:3 [b]Deut 13:5, 10; Job 31:26-28
20 [a]1 Kin 8:51; Jer 11:4 [b]Ex 19:5; Deut 7:6; 14:2; 26:18; Titus 2:14; 1 Pet 2:9
21 [a]Num 20:12; Deut 1:37
22 [a]Num 27:13, 14 [b]Deut 3:25
23 [a]Deut 4:9 [b]Deut 4:16
24 [a]Ex 24:17; Deut 9:3; Is 30:27; 33:14; Heb 12:29 [b]Deut 5:9; 6:15
25 [1]Lit *beget*

15 "So [a]watch yourselves carefully, since you did not see any [b]form on the day the LORD spoke to you at Horeb from the midst of the fire,

16 so that you do not [a]act corruptly and [b]make a graven image for yourselves in the form of any figure, the likeness of male or female,

17 the likeness of any animal that is on the earth, the likeness of [a]any winged bird that flies in the sky,

18 the likeness of anything that creeps on the ground, the likeness of any fish that is in the water below the earth.

19 "And *beware* not to lift up your eyes to heaven and see the sun and the moon and the stars, [a]all the host of heaven, [b]and be drawn away and worship them and serve them, those which the LORD your God has allotted to all the peoples under the whole heaven.

20 "But the LORD has taken you and brought you out of [a]the iron furnace, from Egypt, to [b]be a people for His own possession, as today.

21 "[a]Now the LORD was angry with me on your account, and swore that I would not cross the Jordan, and that I would not enter the good land which the LORD your God is giving you as an inheritance.

22 "For [a]I will die in this land, I shall not cross the Jordan, but you shall cross and take possession of this [b]good land.

23 "So watch yourselves, [a]that you do not forget the covenant of the LORD your God which He made with you, and [b]make for yourselves a graven image in the form of anything *against* which the LORD your God has commanded you.

24 "For the LORD your God is a [a]consuming fire, a [b]jealous God.

25 "When you [1]become the father of children and children's children and have remained long in the land, and [a]act corruptly, and [b]make an [2]idol in the form of anything, and [c]do that which is evil in the sight of the LORD your God *so as* to provoke Him to anger,

[2]Or *a graven image* [a]Deut 4:16 [b]Deut 4:23 [c]2 Kin 17:17

4:4 *held fast.* See note on 10:20.

4:7 *near . . . whenever we call on Him.* The Israelites always had access to the Lord in prayer. His presence was symbolized by the tabernacle in the center of the camp, and by the pillar of cloud over the tabernacle (see Ex 40:34–38; Num 23:21).

4:9 *make them known to your sons.* See v. 10; 11:19; cf. Ex 12:26–27.

4:10–14 See Ex 19–24.

4:10 *Remember.* The divine call to Israel to remember the Lord's past redemptive acts—especially how He delivered them from slavery in Egypt—is a common theme in Deuteronomy (5:15; 7:18; 8:2,18; 9:7,27; 11:2; 15:15; 16:3,12; 24:9,18,22; 25:17) and is summarized in 32:7: "Remember the days of old."

4:12 *no form.* See v. 15; see also note on Ex 20:4. "God is spirit" (John 4:24; cf. Is 31:3).

4:13 *His covenant . . . the Ten Commandments.* See notes on Ex 20:1; 34:28. *two tablets of stone.* See note on Ex 31:18.

4:15–18 See note on Ex 20:4.

4:19 *not . . . be drawn away.* As kings of Judah would be later (2 Kin 23:5).

4:20 *iron furnace.* Suggests that the period in Egypt was a time of affliction, testing and refinement for the Israelites (see 1 Kin 8:51; Jer 11:4; see also Is 48:10).

4:21 *on your account.* See note on 1:37.

4:24 *consuming fire.* See 9:3; see also note on Ex 24:17. *jealous God.* See 5:9; 6:15; see also note on Ex 20:5.

4:25 *When you . . . have remained long in the land.* The pattern of Israel's rebellion, resulting in expulsion from the land, and then their repentance, leading to restoration to the land, is prominent in Deuteronomy (see, e.g., the blessing and curse formulas in chs. 27–28).

26 I [a]call heaven and earth to witness against you today, that you will [b]surely perish quickly from the land where you are going over the Jordan to possess it. You shall not [1]live long on it, but will be utterly destroyed.

27 "The LORD will [a]scatter you among the peoples, and you will be left few in number among the nations where the LORD drives you.

28 "[a]There you will serve gods, the work of man's hands, [b]wood and stone, [c]which neither see nor hear nor eat nor smell.

29 "[a]But from there you will seek the LORD your God, and you will find *Him* if you search for Him [b]with all your heart and all your soul.

30 "When you [a]are in distress and all these things have come upon you, [b]in the latter days [c]you will return to the LORD your God and listen to His voice.

31 "For the LORD your God is a [a]compassionate God; [b]He will not fail you nor [c]destroy you nor [d]forget the covenant with your fathers which He swore to them.

32 "Indeed, [a]ask now concerning the former days which were before you, since the [b]day that God created [1]man on the earth, and *inquire* [c]from one end of the heavens to the other. [d]Has *anything* been done like this great thing, or has *anything* been heard like it?

33 "[a]Has *any* people heard the voice of God speaking from the midst of the fire, as you have heard *it*, and survived?

34 "[a]Or has a god tried to go to take for himself a nation from within *another* nation [b]by trials, by signs and wonders and by war and [c]by a mighty hand and by an outstretched arm and by great terrors, [1]as the LORD your God did for you in Egypt before your eyes?

35 "To you it was shown that you might know that the LORD, He is God; [a]there is no other besides Him.

36 "[a]Out of the heavens He let you hear His voice [b]to discipline you; and on earth He let you see His great fire, and you heard His words from the midst of the fire.

37 "[1][a]Because He loved your fathers, therefore He chose [2]their descendants after them. And He [3][b]personally brought you from Egypt by His great power,

38 driving out from before you nations greater and mightier than you, to bring you in *and* [a]to give you their land for an inheritance, as it is today.

39 "Know therefore today, and take it to your heart, that [a]the LORD, He is God in heaven above and on the earth below; there is no other.

40 "[a]So you shall keep His statutes and His commandments which I am [1]giving you today, that [b]it may go well with you and with your children after you, and [c]that you may [2]live long on the land which the LORD your God is giving you for all time."

41 [a]Then Moses set apart three cities across the Jordan to the [1]east,

42 that a manslayer might flee there, who unintentionally slew his neighbor without having enmity toward him in time past; and by fleeing to one of these cities he might live:

43 [a]Bezer in the wilderness on the plateau for the Reubenites, and Ramoth in Gilead for the Gadites, and Golan in Bashan for the Manassites.

44 Now this is the law which Moses set before the sons of Israel;

45 these are the testimonies and the statutes and the ordinances which Moses spoke to the sons of Israel, when they came out from Egypt,

46 across the Jordan, in the valley [a]opposite Beth-peor, in the land of [b]Sihon king of the Amorites who lived at Heshbon, whom Moses and the sons of Israel [1]defeated when they came out from Egypt.

47 They took possession of his land and the land of [a]Og king of Bashan, the two kings of the Amorites, *who were* across the Jordan to the [1]east,

48 from [a]Aroer, which is on the edge of the [1]valley of Arnon, even as far as [b]Mount Sion (that is, Hermon),

49 with all the Arabah across the Jordan to the east, even as far as the sea of the Arabah, [1]at the foot of the slopes of Pisgah.

The Ten Commandments Repeated

5 Then Moses summoned all Israel and said to them:

26 [1]Lit *prolong your days* [a]Deut 30:19; 31:28; 32:1; Is 1:2; Mic 6:2 [b]Deut 7:4; 8:19, 20
27 [a]Lev 26:33; Deut 28:64; 29:28; Neh 1:8
28 [a]Deut 28:36, 64; Jer 16:13 [b]Deut 29:17 [c]Ps 115:4-8; 135:15-18; Is 44:12-20
29 [a]Deut 30:1-3, 10; 2 Chr 15:4; Is 55:6; Jer 29:13 [b]Deut 6:5; 10:12
30 [a]Ps 18:6; 59:16; 107:6, 13 [b]Deut 31:29; Jer 23:20; Hos 3:5; Heb 1:2 [c]Jer 4:1, 2
31 [a]Ex 34:6; 2 Chr 30:9; Neh 9:31; Ps 103:8; 111:4; 116:5; Jon 4:2 [b]Deut 31:6, 8; Josh 1:5; 1 Chr 28:20; Heb 13:5 [c]Jer 30:11 [d]Lev 26:45
32 [1]Or *Adam* [a]Deut 32:7; Job 8:8 [b]Gen 1:27; Is 45:12 [c]Deut 28:64; Matt 24:31 [d]Deut 4:7; 2 Sam 7:23
33 [a]Ex 20:22; Deut 5:24, 26
34 [1]Lit *according to all that* [a]Ex 14:30; Deut 33:29 [b]Deut 7:19 [c]Deut 5:15; 6:21; Ps 136:12
35 [a]Ex 8:10; 9:14; Deut 4:39; 32:12, 39; 1 Sam 2:2; Is 43:10-12; 44:6-8; 45:5-7; Mark 12:32
36 [a]Ex 19:9, 19; 20:18, 22; Deut 4:33; Neh 9:13; Heb 12:25 [b]Deut 8:5
37 [1]Lit *And instead, because* [2]Lit *his seed* [3]Lit *with His presence* [a]Deut 7:7, 8; 10:15; 33:3 [b]Ex 33:14; Is 63:9
38 [a]Num 32:4; 34:14, 15
39 [a]Deut 4:35; Josh 2:11
40 [1]Lit *commanding* [2]Lit *prolong your days* [a]Lev 22:31; Deut 4:2; Ps 105:45 [b]Deut 4:1; 5:16, 29, 33; 6:3, 18; 12:25, 28; 22:7 [c]Ex 23:26; Deut 32:47
41 [1]Lit *sunrise* [a]Num 35:6; Deut 19:2-13; Josh 20:7-9
43 [a]Josh 20:8
46 [1]Lit *smote* [a]Deut 3:29 [b]Num 21:21-25
47 [1]Lit *sunrise* [a]Deut 1:4; 3:3, 4
48 [1]Or *wadi* [a]Deut 2:36; 3:12 [b]Deut 3:9; Ps 133:3
49 [1]Lit *under*

4:26 *heaven and earth to witness.* See notes on 30:19; Ps 50:1; Isa 1:2.
4:27 *will scatter you.* See note on 28:64.
4:29 *with all your heart and . . . soul.* Indicates total involvement and commitment. The phrase is applied not only to how the Lord's people should seek Him, but also to how they should fear (revere) Him, live in obedience to Him, love and serve Him (6:5; 10:12; 11:13; 13:3; 30:6), and, after forsaking Him, renew their allegiance and commitment (26:16; 30:2,10).
4:31 *covenant . . . He swore to them.* See notes on Gen 21:23; 22:16; Heb 6:13,18. In ancient times, parties to a covenant were expected to confirm their intentions by means of a self-maledictory oath (see note on Gen 15:17).
4:35 *that you might know.* See v. 10. *there is no other besides Him.* See v. 39; 5:7; 6:4 and note; 32:39. Moses' belief in one God was total and uncompromising (see note on Ge 1:1).
4:37 *He loved.* The first reference in Deuteronomy to God's love for His people (see Introduction: Theological Teaching). See note on 7:8; see also 5:10; 7:9,13; 10:15; 23:5. The corollary truth is that His people should love Him (see note on 6:5).
4:39 See v. 35 and note.
4:41–43 See 19:1–13; Num 35:9–28; Jos 20.
4:43 *Bezer.* About 20 miles east of the northeast corner of the Dead Sea.

"**H**ear, O Israel, the statutes and the ordinances which I am speaking today in your [1]hearing, that you may learn them and observe [2]them carefully.

2 "The LORD our God made [a]a covenant with us at Horeb.

3 "[a]The LORD did not make this covenant with our fathers, but with us, *with* all those of [1]us alive here today.

4 "The LORD spoke to you [a]face to face at the mountain [b]from the midst of the fire,

5 *while* [a]I was standing between the LORD and you at that time, to declare to you the word of the LORD; [b]for you were afraid because of the fire and did not go up the mountain. [1]He said,

6 '[a]I am the LORD your God who brought you out of the land of Egypt, out of the house of [1]slavery.

7 '[a]You shall have no other gods [1]before Me.

8 '[a]You shall not make for yourself [1]an idol, *or* any likeness *of* what is in heaven above [2]or on the earth beneath [2]or in the water under the earth.

9 'You shall not worship them or serve them; for I, the LORD your God, am a jealous God, [a]visiting the iniquity of the fathers on the children, and on the third and the fourth *generations* of those who hate Me,

10 but [a]showing lovingkindness to thousands, to those who love Me and keep My commandments.

11 '[a]You shall not take the name of the LORD your God in vain, for the LORD will not [1]leave him unpunished who takes His name in vain.

12 '[a]Observe the sabbath day to keep it holy, as the LORD your God commanded you.

13 'Six days you shall labor and do all your work,

14 but [a]the seventh day is a sabbath of the LORD your God; *in it* you shall not do any work, you or your son or your daughter or your male servant or your female servant or your ox or your donkey or any of your cattle or your sojourner who [1]stays with you, so that your male servant and your female servant may rest as well as you.

15 '[a]You shall remember that you were a slave in the land of Egypt, and the LORD your God brought you out of there by a mighty hand and by an outstretched arm; therefore the LORD your God commanded you to observe the sabbath day.

16 '[a]Honor your father and your mother, as the LORD your God has commanded you, [b]that your days may be prolonged and that it may go well with you on the land which the LORD your God gives you.

17 '[a]You shall not murder.

18 '[a]You shall not commit adultery.

19 '[a]You shall not steal.

20 '[a]You shall not bear false witness against your neighbor.

21 '[a]You shall not covet your neighbor's wife, and you shall not desire your neighbor's house, his field or his male servant or his female servant, his ox or his donkey or anything that belongs to your neighbor.'

Moses Interceded

22 "These words the LORD spoke to all your assembly at the mountain from the midst of the fire, *of* the cloud and *of* the thick gloom, with a great voice, and He added no more. [a]He wrote them on two tablets of stone and gave them to me.

23 "And when you heard the voice from the midst of the darkness, while the mountain was burning with fire, you came near to me, all the heads of your tribes and your elders.

24 "You said, 'Behold, the LORD our God has shown us His glory and His greatness, and we have heard His voice from the midst of the fire; we have seen today that God speaks with man, yet he lives.

25 '[a]Now then why should we die? For this great fire will consume us; if we hear the voice of the LORD our God any longer, then we will die.

5:1 [1]Lit *ears* [2]Lit *to do them*
2 [a]Ex 19:5; Mal 4:4
3 [1]Lit *us ourselves* [a]Jer 31:32; Heb 8:9
4 [a]Num 14:14; Deut 34:10 [b]Deut 4:33
5 [1]Lit *saying* [a]Gal 3:19 [b]Ex 19:16, 21-24; 20:18; Heb 12:18-21
6 [1]Lit *slaves* [a]Ex 20:2-17; Lev 26:1; Deut 6:4; Ps 81:10
7 [1]Or *besides* [a]Ex 20:3
8 [1]Or *a graven image* [2]Lit *or what is* [a]Ex 20:4-6; Lev 26:1; Deut 4:15-18; 27:15; Ps 97:7
9 [a]Ex 34:7; Num 14:18; Deut 7:10
10 [a]Num 14:18; Deut 7:9; Jer 32:18
11 [1]Or *hold him guiltless* [a]Ex 20:7; Lev 19:12; Deut 6:13; 10:20; Matt 5:33
12 [a]Ex 16:23-30; 20:8-11; 31:13f; Mark 2:27f
14 [1]Lit *is in your gates* [a]Gen 2:2; Heb 4:4
15 [a]Ex 20:11
16 [a]Ex 20:12; Lev 19:3; Deut 27:16; Matt 15:4; 19:19; Mark 7:10; 10:19; Luke 18:20; Eph 6:2, 3; Col 3:20 [b]Deut 4:40
17 [a]Gen 9:6; Ex 20:13; Lev 24:17; Matt 5:21f; 19:18; Mark 10:19; Rom 13:9; James 2:11
18 [a]Ex 20:14; Lev 20:10; Matt 5:27f; 19:18; Mark 10:19; Luke 18:20; Rom 13:9; James 2:11
19 [a]Ex 20:15; Lev 19:11 **20** [a]Ex 20:16; 23:1; Matt 19:18
21 [a]Ex 20:17; Rom 7:7; 13:9 **22** [a]Ex 24:12; 31:18; Deut 4:13
25 [a]Ex 20:18, 19; Deut 18:16

5:1 *Hear, O Israel.* See note on 4:1.

5:2 *covenant with us at Horeb.* See note on Ex 19:5. God's covenant with Israel, given at Mount Horeb (Sinai) and now being confirmed, bound Israel to the Lord as their absolute Sovereign, and to His laws and regulations as their way of life. Adherence to the covenant would bring to Israel the blessings of the Lord, while breaking the covenant would bring against them the punishments described as "curses" (see, e.g., 28:15–20). Jer 31:31–34 predicted the establishing of a new covenant, which made the Sinaitic covenant obsolete (see Heb 7:22; see also Heb 8:6–13; 10:15–18 and notes). See chart, p. 16.

5:3 *not . . . with our fathers, but with us.* The covenant was made with those who were present at Sinai, but since they were representatives of the nation, it was made with all succeeding generations as well.

5:5 See vv. 23–26; Ex 20:18–21.

5:6–21 The Ten Commandments are both the basis and the heart of Israel's relationship with the Lord. It is almost impossible to exaggerate their effect on subsequent history. They constitute the basis of moral principles throughout the Western world, and they summarize what the one true God expects of His people in terms of faith, worship and conduct (see notes on Ex 20:3–17).

5:12 *as the* LORD *your God commanded you.* Missing from the parallel verse in Exodus (20:8), this clause reminds the people of the divine origin of the Ten Commandments 40 years earlier (see vv. 15–16).

5:14 *so that your male servant and your female servant may rest.* See note on Ex 20:10; see also v. 15.

5:15 *remember.* See note on 4:10.

5:16–21 The NT quotes often from this section of the Ten Commandments (see cross references).

5:20 See 19:18–19.

5:22 *words.* See note on Ex 20:1. *two tablets of stone.* See note on Ex 31:18.

5:25 *we will die.* See notes on Gen 16:13; 32:30.

26 ‘For [a]who is there of all flesh who has
heard the voice of the living God speaking
from the midst of the fire, as we *have,* and
lived?
27 ‘[1]Go near and hear all that the LORD our
God says; then speak to us all that the LORD
our God speaks to you, and we will hear and
do *it.*’
28 “The LORD heard the voice of your words
when you spoke to me, [a]and the LORD said to
me, ‘I have heard the voice of the words of
this people which they have spoken to you.
They have done well in all that they have
spoken.
29 ‘[a]Oh that they had such a heart in them,
that they would fear Me and [b]keep all My
commandments always, that [c]it may be well
with them and with their sons forever!
30 ‘Go, say to them, “Return to your tents.”
31 ‘[a]But as for you, stand here by Me, that
I may speak to you all the commandments
and the statutes and the judgments which
you shall teach them, that they may observe
them in the land which I give them to possess.’
32 “So you shall observe to do just as the
LORD your God has commanded you; [a]you
shall not turn aside to the right or to the left.
33 “[a]You shall walk in all the way which
the LORD your God has commanded you,
[b]that you may live and that it may be well
with you, and that you may prolong *your*
days in the land which you will possess.

Obey God and Prosper

6 “Now this is the commandment, the statutes and the judgments which the LORD
your God has commanded *me* to teach you,
that you might do *them* in the land where
you are going over to possess it,
2 so that you and your son and your
grandson might [a]fear the LORD your God, to
keep all His statutes and His commandments
which I command you, [b]all the days of your
life, and that your days may be prolonged.
3 “O Israel, you should listen and [1]be
careful to do *it,* that [a]it may be well with you
and that you may multiply greatly, just as the
LORD, the God of your fathers, has promised
you, *in* [b]a land flowing with milk and honey.
4 “[a]Hear, O Israel! The LORD is our God,
the [b]LORD is one!
5 “[a]You shall love the LORD your God
[b]with all your heart and with all your soul
and with all your might.
6 “[a]These words, which I am commanding you today, shall be on your heart.
7 [a]You shall teach them diligently to your
sons and shall talk of them when you sit in
your house and when you walk by the way
and when you lie down and when you rise
up.
8 “[a]You shall bind them as a sign on your
hand and they shall be as [1]frontals [2]on your
forehead.
9 “[a]You shall write them on the doorposts
of your house and on your gates.
10 “Then it shall come about when the
LORD your God brings you into the land
which He swore to your fathers, Abraham,
Isaac and Jacob, to give you, [a]great and
splendid cities which you did not build,
11 and houses full of all good things
which you did not fill, and hewn cisterns
which you did not dig, vineyards and olive
trees which you did not plant, and [a]you eat
and are satisfied,
12 then watch yourself, that [a]you do not
forget the LORD who brought you from the
land of Egypt, out of the house of [1]slavery.
13 “[a]You shall [1]fear *only* the LORD your
God; and you shall [2]worship Him and [b]swear
by His name.
14 “[a]You shall not follow other gods, any of
the gods of the peoples who surround you,
15 for the LORD your God in the midst of
you is a [a]jealous God; otherwise the anger of
the LORD your God will be kindled against
you, and He will [1]wipe you off the face of the
earth.

26 [a]Deut 4:33
27 [1]Lit *Go yourself*
28 [a]Deut 18:17
29 [a]Ps 81:13; Is 48:18 [b]Deut 11:1 [c]Deut 5:16, 33
31 [a]Ex 24:12
32 [a]Deut 17:20; 28:14; Josh 1:7; 23:6; Prov 4:27
33 [a]Deut 10:12; Jer 7:23; Luke 1:6 [b]Deut 4:1, 40; 12:25, 28; 22:7; Eph 6:3
6:2 [a]Ex 20:20; Deut 10:12; Ps 111:10; 128:1; Eccl 12:13 [b]Deut 4:9
3 [1]Lit *keep* [a]Deut 5:33 [b]Ex 3:8, 17
4 [a]Matt 22:37; Mark 12:29, 30; Luke 10:27 [b]Deut 4:35, 39; John 10:30; 1 Cor 8:4; Eph 4:6
5 [a]Matt 22:37; Mark 12:30; Luke 10:27 [b]Deut 4:29; 10:12
6 [a]Deut 11:18
7 [a]Deut 4:9; 11:19; Eph 6:4
8 [1]Or *frontlet bands* [2]Lit *between your eyes* [a]Ex 12:14; 13:9, 16; Deut 11:18; Prov 3:3; 6:21; 7:3
9 [a]Deut 11:20
10 [a]Deut 9:1; 19:1; Josh 24:13; Ps 105:44
11 [a]Deut 8:10; 11:15; 14:29
12 [1]Lit *slaves* [a]Deut 4:9
13 [1]Or *reverence* [2]Or *serve* [a]Deut 13:4; Matt 4:10; Luke 4:8 [b]Deut 5:11; 10:20; Ps 63:11; Matt 5:33
14 [a]Jer 25:6
15 [1]Lit *destroy* [a]Deut 4:24; 5:9

5:27 *we will hear and do it.* See note on Ex 19:8.
6:2 *fear the LORD.* See note on Gen 20:11. *days may be prolonged.* See 4:40; 5:16,33. By obeying the Lord and keeping His decrees, individual Israelites would enjoy long life in the land, and the people as a whole would enjoy a long national existence in the land.
6:3 *land flowing with milk and honey.* See note on Ex 3:8. The phrase is used 14 times from Exodus through Deuteronomy and 5 times elsewhere in the OT (see especially 32:13–14).
6:4–9 Known as the *Shema,* Hebrew for "Hear." It has become the Jewish confession of faith, recited daily by the pious (see Matt 22:37–38; Mark 12:29–30; Luke 10:27).
6:4 *Hear, O Israel.* See note on 4:1. *the LORD is one.* A divinely revealed insight, especially important in view of the multiplicity of Baals and other gods of Canaan and elsewhere (see, e.g., Judg 2:11–13).
6:5 *You shall love the LORD.* Love for God and neighbor (see Lev 19:18) is built on the love that the Lord has for His people (1 John 4:19–21) and on His identification with them. Such love is to be total, involving one's whole being (see notes on 4:29; Josh 22:5).
6:6 *words . . . shall be on your heart.* A feature that would especially characterize the "new covenant" (Jer 31:31; see Jer 31:33).
6:8–9 Many Jews take these verses literally and tie phylacteries (see note on Matt 23:5) to their foreheads and left arms. They also attach mezuzot (small wooden or metal containers in which passages of Scripture are placed) to the doorframes of their houses. But a figurative interpretation is supported by 11:18–20; Ex 13:9,16. See note on Ex 13:9.
6:10–12 Because the emphasis in Scripture is always on what God does and not on what His people achieve, they are never to forget what He has done for them.
6:13 Quoted in part by Jesus in response to Satan's temptation (Matt 4:10; Luke 4:8). Jesus quoted from Deuteronomy in response to the devil's other two temptations as well (see notes on v. 16; 8:3).
6:15 *jealous God.* See note on Ex 20:5.

16 "[a]You shall not put the LORD your God to the test, [b]as you tested *Him* at Massah.

17 "[a]You should diligently keep the commandments of the LORD your God, and His testimonies and His statutes which He has commanded you.

18 "You shall do what is right and good in the sight of the LORD, that [a]it may be well with you and that you may go in and possess the good land which the LORD swore to *give* your fathers,

19 by driving out all your enemies from before you, as the LORD has spoken.

20 "[a]When your son asks you in time to come, saying, 'What *do* the testimonies and the statutes and the judgments *mean* which the LORD our God commanded you?'

21 then you shall say to your son, 'We were slaves to Pharaoh in Egypt, and the LORD brought us from Egypt with a mighty hand.

22 'Moreover, the LORD showed great and distressing signs and wonders before our eyes against Egypt, Pharaoh and all his household;

23 He brought us out from there in order to bring us in, to give us the land which He had sworn to our fathers.'

24 "So the LORD commanded us to observe all these statutes, [a]to fear the LORD our God for our good always and [b]for our survival, as *it is* today.

25 "[a]It will be righteousness for us if we [1]are careful to observe all this commandment before the LORD our God, just as He commanded us.

Warnings

7 "[a]When the LORD your God brings you into the land where you are entering to possess it, and clears away many nations before you, the Hittites and the Girgashites and the Amorites and the Canaanites and the Perizzites and the Hivites and the Jebusites, [b]seven nations greater and stronger than you,

2 and when the LORD your God delivers them before you and you [1]defeat them, [a]then you shall [2]utterly destroy them. [b]You shall make no covenant with them [c]and show no favor to them.

3 "Furthermore, [a]you shall not intermarry with them; you shall not give your [1]daughters to [2]their sons, nor shall you take [3]their daughters for your [4]sons.

4 "For [1]they will turn your [2]sons away from [3]following Me to serve other gods; then the anger of the LORD will be kindled against you and [a]He will quickly destroy you.

5 "But thus you shall do to them: [a]you shall tear down their altars, and smash their *sacred* pillars, and hew down their [1]Asherim, and burn their graven images with fire.

6 "For you are [a]a holy people to the LORD your God; the LORD your God has chosen you to be [b]a people for His [1]own possession out of all the peoples who are on the face of the [2]earth.

7 "[a]The LORD did not set His love on you nor choose you because you were more in number than any of the peoples, for you were the fewest of all peoples,

8 but because the LORD loved you and kept the [a]oath which He swore to your forefathers, [b]the LORD brought you out by a mighty hand and redeemed you from the house of [1]slavery, from the hand of Pharaoh king of Egypt.

9 "Know therefore that the LORD your God, [a]He is God, [b]the faithful God, [c]who keeps [1]His covenant and [1]His lovingkindness to a thousandth generation with those who [d]love Him and keep His commandments;

10 but [a]repays those who hate Him to [1]their faces, to destroy [2]them; He will not delay [3]with him who hates Him, He will repay him to his face.

11 "Therefore, you shall keep the commandment and the statutes and the judgments which I am commanding you today, to do them.

Promises of God

12 "[a]Then it shall come about, because you listen to these judgments and keep and do them, that the LORD your God will keep with

16 [a]Matt 4:7; Luke 4:12 [b]Ex 17:7
17 [a]Deut 11:22; Ps 119:4
18 [a]Deut 4:40
20 [a]Ex 13:8, 14
24 [a]Deut 10:12; Jer 32:39 [b]Ps 41:2; Luke 10:28
25 [1]Lit *keep* [a]Deut 24:13; Rom 10:3
7:1 [a]Deut 20:16-18 [b]Acts 13:19
2 [1]Lit *smite* [2]Lit *surely devote to the ban* [a]Num 31:17; Josh 11:11 [b]Ex 23:32
2 [c]Deut 7:16; 13:8
3 [1]Lit *daughter* [2]Lit *his son* [3]Lit *his daughter* [4]Lit *son* [a]Ex 34:15, 16; Josh 23:12; Ezra 9:2
4 [1]Lit *he* [2]Lit *son* [3]Lit *after* [a]Deut 4:26
5 [1]I.e. wooden symbols of a female deity [a]Ex 23:24; 34:13; Deut 12:3
6 [1]Or *special treasure* [2]Lit *ground* [a]Ex 19:6; Deut 14:2, 21; Ps 50:5; Jer 2:3 [b]Ex 19:5; Deut 4:20; 14:2; 26:18; Ps 135:4; Titus 2:14; 1 Pet 2:9
7 [a]Deut 4:37
8 [1]Lit *slaves* [a]Ex 32:13 [b]Ex 13:3
9 [1]Lit *the* [a]Deut 4:35, 39 [b]Is 49:7; 1 Cor 1:9; 1 Thess 5:24; 2 Tim 2:13 [c]Ex 20:6; Dan 9:4 [d]Deut 5:10
10 [1]Lit *his face* [2]Lit *him* [3]Lit *to* [a]Is 59:18; Nah 1:2
12 [a]Lev 26:3-13; Deut 28:1-14

6:16 Quoted in part by Jesus in Matt 4:7; Luke 4:12 (see also note on v. 13). *as you tested Him at Massah.* See 9:22; 33:8; see also note on Ex 17:7.

6:20 See Ex 12:26 and note.

6:23 *brought us out . . . to bring us in.* See note on Ex 6:7–8.

6:25 *righteousness.* Probably here refers to a true, personal relationship with the covenant Lord that manifests itself in the daily lives of God's people (see 24:13).

7:1 *Hittites . . . Jebusites.* See 20:17; see also notes on Gen 10:6,15–18; 13:7. *seven nations.* See note on Ex 3:8.

7:2–5 *You shall make no covenant . . . not intermarry . . . tear down their altars.* Israel was to have no association—political, social or religious—with the idol worshipers of Canaan (see v. 16; see also note on 2:34).

7:2 *utterly destroy them.* See note on 2:34.

7:4 *turn your sons . . . to serve other gods.* The Lord's command against intermarriage with foreigners was not racially motivated but was intended to prevent spiritual contamination and apostasy (see, e.g., 1 Kin 11:1–11; Neh 13:25–27).

7:5 *altars . . . sacred pillars . . . Asherim.* Cult objects of Canaanite idolatrous worship (see 12:3; 16:21–22). Asherim were wooden symbols of the goddess Asherah (see Ex 34:13 and note.)

7:6 *holy.* Separated from all corrupting people or things and consecrated totally to the Lord (see note on Ex 3:5). *possession.* See note on Ex 19:5.

7:8 *because the LORD loved you.* "His covenant and His lovingkindness" (vv. 9,12) stem from God's love for His people, based on His character and embodied in His covenant; they do not stem from the numerical greatness of the people or any virtue of theirs. His love must be reciprocated by His people (see vv. 9–10; 9:4–6; see also note on 6:5).

7:9 *Know . . . that the LORD . . . is God.* See Ps 100:3. *thousandth generation with those who love Him.* See note on Ex 20:6.

7:12–15 The blessings are elaborated in 28:1–14; 30:1–10.

you [1]His covenant and [1]His lovingkindness which He swore to your forefathers.

13 "He will [a]love you and bless you and [b]multiply you; He will also bless the fruit of your womb and the fruit of your ground, your grain and your new wine and your oil, the increase of your herd and the young of your flock, [1]in the land which He swore to your forefathers to give you.

14 "You shall be blessed above all peoples; there will be no male or female [a]barren among you or among your cattle.

15 "[a]The LORD will remove from you all sickness; and He will not put on you any of the harmful diseases of Egypt which you have known, but He will lay them on all who hate you.

16 "You shall consume all the peoples whom the LORD your God will deliver to you; [a]your eye shall not pity them, nor shall you serve their gods, for that *would be* [b]a snare to you.

17 "If you should say in your heart, 'These nations are greater than I; how can I [a]dispossess them?'

18 you shall not be afraid of them; you shall well [a]remember what the LORD your God did to Pharaoh and to all Egypt:

19 [a]the great trials which your eyes saw and the signs and the wonders and the mighty hand and the outstretched arm by which the LORD your God brought you out. So shall the LORD your God do to all the peoples of whom you are afraid.

20 "Moreover, the LORD your God will send [a]the hornet against them, until those who are left and hide themselves from you perish.

21 "You shall not dread [1]them, for [a]the LORD your God is in your midst, [b]a great and awesome God.

22 "[a]The LORD your God will clear away these nations before you little by little; you will not be able to put an end to them quickly, for the [1]wild beasts would grow too numerous for you.

23 "[a]But the LORD your God will deliver them before you, and will [1]throw them into great confusion until they are destroyed.

24 "[a]He will deliver their kings into your hand so that you will make their name perish from under heaven; [b]no man will be able to stand before you until you have destroyed them.

25 "The graven images of their gods you are to [a]burn with fire; you shall [b]not covet the silver or the gold that is on them, nor take it for yourselves, or you will be [c]snared by it, for it is an [d]abomination to the LORD your God.

26 "You shall not bring an abomination into your house, and like it come under the [a]ban; you shall utterly detest it and you shall utterly abhor it, for it is something banned.

God's Gracious Dealings

8 "All the commandments that I am commanding you today you shall be careful to do, that you [a]may live and multiply, and go in and possess the land which the LORD swore *to give* to your forefathers.

2 "[a]You shall remember all the way which the LORD your God has [b]led you in the wilderness these forty years, that He might humble you, [c]testing you, to know what was in your heart, whether you would keep His commandments or not.

3 "He humbled you and let you be hungry, and fed you with manna which you did not know, nor did your fathers know, that He might make you [1]understand that [a]man does not live by bread alone, but man lives by everything that proceeds out of the mouth of the LORD.

4 "[a]Your clothing did not wear out on you, nor did your foot swell these forty years.

5 "[a]Thus you are to know in your heart that the LORD your God was disciplining you just as a man disciplines his son.

6 "Therefore, you shall keep the commandments of the LORD your God, to walk in His ways and to [1]fear Him.

7 "For [a]the LORD your God is bringing you into a good land, a land of brooks of water, of fountains and springs, flowing forth in valleys and hills;

8 a land of wheat and barley, of vines and fig trees and pomegranates, a land of olive oil and honey;

9 a land where you will eat food without scarcity, in which you will not lack anything; a land whose stones are iron, and out of whose hills you can dig copper.

12 [1]Lit *the*
13 [1]Lit *on the ground* [a]Ps 146:8; Prov 15:9; John 14:21 [b]Lev 26:9; Deut 13:17; 30:5
14 [a]Ex 23:26
15 [a]Ex 15:26
16 [a]Deut 7:2 [b]Ex 23:33; Judg 8:27; Ps 106:36
17 [a]Num 33:53
18 [a]Ps 105:5
19 [a]Deut 4:34
20 [a]Ex 23:28; Josh 24:12
21 [1]Lit *from before them* [a]Ex 29:45; Josh 3:10 [b]Deut 10:17; Neh 1:5; 9:32
22 [1]Lit *beasts of the field* [a]Ex 23:29, 30
23 [1]Lit *confuse them with* [a]Ex 23:27; Josh 10:10
24 [a]Josh 6:2; 10:23-25 [b]Deut 11:25; Josh 1:5; 10:8; 23:9
25 [a]Ex 32:20; Deut 12:3; 1 Chr 14:12 [b]Ex 20:17 [c]Deut 7:16; Judg 8:27 [d]Deut 17:1
26 [a]Lev 27:28f
8:1 [a]Deut 4:1
2 [a]Deut 8:16 [b]Ps 136:16; Amos 2:10 [c]Ex 15:25; 20:20; 2 Chr 32:31
3 [1]Lit *know* [a]Matt 4:4; Luke 4:4
4 [a]Deut 29:5; Neh 9:21
5 [a]Deut 4:36; 2 Sam 7:14; Prov 3:12; Heb 12:6; Rev 3:19
6 [1]Or *reverence*
7 [a]Deut 11:9-12; Jer 2:7

7:13 *grain . . . new wine . . . oil.* A common OT summary of the produce of field, vineyard and olive grove (see, e.g., 11:14; 14:23; 18:4; 28:51).

7:15 *not put on you . . . diseases.* See note on 28:60.

7:16 See essay, p. 271.

7:18 *remember.* See note on 4:10.

7:20 *hornet.* See note on Ex 23:28.

7:22 *God will clear away.* See note on 3:22.

7:25–26 Cf. the story of Achan (Josh 6:17–19; 7:1,20–25).

7:26 *come under the ban.* See note on 2:34.

8:2 *remember.* See note on 4:10. *testing.* See v. 16; see also note on Gen 22:1.

8:3 *manna.* See v. 16; see also note on Num 11:7. *man does not live by bread alone.* See note on 6:13; quoted by Jesus in response to the devil's temptation (see Matt 4:4; Luke 4:4). Bread sustains but does not guarantee life, which is God's gift to those who trust in and live by His word: His commands and promises (see vv. 1,18). God's "discipline" (v. 5) of His people by bringing them through the wilderness taught them this fundamental truth. There they were humbled (cf. v. 14) by being cast in total dependence on the Lord.

8:7–9 A concise description of the rich and fertile land of promise that the Israelites were about to enter and possess (see 11:8–12). See map No. 2 at the end of the study Bible.

8:9 *iron . . . copper.* The mountains of southern Lebanon and the regions east of the Sea of Galilee and south of the Dead Sea

10 "When [a]you have eaten and are satisfied, you shall bless the LORD your God for
the good land which He has given you.
11 "[1]Beware that you do not [a]forget the
LORD your God by not keeping His commandments and His ordinances and His statutes which I am commanding you today;
12 otherwise, [a]when you have eaten and
are satisfied, and have built good houses and
lived *in them,*
13 and when your herds and your flocks
multiply, and your silver and gold multiply,
and all that you have multiplies,
14 then your heart will become [1]proud
and you will [a]forget the LORD your God who
brought you out from the land of Egypt, out
of the house of [2]slavery.
15 "He led you through [a]the great and terrible wilderness, *with its* [b]fiery serpents and
scorpions and thirsty ground where there
was no water; He [c]brought water for you out
of the rock of flint.
16 "In the wilderness He fed you manna
[a]which your fathers did not know, that He
might humble you and that He might [b]test
you, to do good for you [1]in the end.
17 "Otherwise, [a]you may say in your heart,
'My power and the strength of my hand
made me this wealth.'
18 "But you shall remember the LORD your
God, for [a]it is He who is giving you power to
make wealth, that He may confirm His covenant which He swore to your fathers, as *it is*
this day.
19 "It shall come about if you ever forget
the LORD your God and go after other gods
and serve them and worship them, [a]I testify
against you today that you will surely perish.
20 "Like the nations that the LORD makes to
perish before you, so [a]you shall perish;
because you would not listen to the voice of
the LORD your God.

Israel Provoked God

9 "Hear, O Israel! You are crossing over the
Jordan today to go in to dispossess
[a]nations greater and mightier than you, great
cities [1b]fortified to heaven,
2 a people great and tall, the sons of the
Anakim, whom you know and of whom you
have heard *it said,* '[a]Who can stand before
the sons of Anak?'
3 "Know therefore today that [a]it is the
LORD your God who is crossing over before
you as [b]a consuming fire. He will destroy
them and He will subdue them before you,
so that [c]you may drive them out and destroy
them quickly, just as the LORD has spoken to
you.
4 "[a]Do not say in your heart when the
LORD your God has driven them out before
[1]you, 'Because of my righteousness the LORD
has brought me in to possess this land,' but *it*
is [b]because of the wickedness of these
nations *that* the LORD is dispossessing them
before you.
5 "It is [a]not for your righteousness or for
the uprightness of your heart that you are
going to possess their land, but *it is* because
of the wickedness of these nations *that* the
LORD your God is driving them out before
you, in order to confirm [b]the [1]oath which the
LORD swore to your fathers, to Abraham,
Isaac and Jacob.
6 "Know, then, *it is* not because of your
righteousness *that* the LORD your God is giving you this good land to possess, for you are
[a]a [1]stubborn people.
7 "Remember, do not forget how you provoked the LORD your God to wrath in the
wilderness; [a]from the day that you left the
land of Egypt until you arrived at this place,
you have been rebellious against the LORD.
8 "Even [a]at Horeb you provoked the LORD
to wrath, and the LORD was so angry with
you that He would have destroyed you.
9 "When I went up to the mountain to
receive the tablets of stone, the tablets of the
covenant which the LORD had made with
you, then I remained on the mountain forty
days and nights; [a]I neither ate bread nor
drank water.
10 "The LORD gave me the two tablets of
stone [a]written by the finger of God; and on
them *were* all the words which the LORD had
spoken with you at the mountain from the
midst of the fire on the day of the assembly.
11 "It came about [a]at the end of forty days
and nights that the LORD gave me the two
tablets of stone, the tablets of the covenant.

10 [a]Deut 6:11
11 [1]Lit *Take heed to yourself* [a]Deut 4:9
12 [a]Prov 30:9; Hos 13:6
14 [1]Lit *lifted up* [2]Lit *slaves* [a]Deut 8:11; Ps 106:21
15 [a]Deut 1:19; Jer 2:6 [b]Num 21:6 [c]Ex 17:6; Num 20:11; Deut 32:13; Ps 78:15; 114:8
16 [1]Lit *at your end* [a]Ex 16:15 [b]Deut 8:2
17 [a]Deut 9:4
18 [a]Prov 10:22; Hos 2:8
19 [a]Deut 4:26; 30:18
20 [a]Ezek 5:5-17
9:1 [1]Lit *and fortified* [a]Deut 4:38; 7:1; 11:23 [b]Deut 1:28
2 [a]Num 13:22, 28, 33; Josh 11:21, 22
3 [a]Deut 31:3; Josh 3:11 [b]Deut 4:24; Heb 12:29 [c]Ex 23:31; Deut 7:24
4 [1]Lit *you saying* [a]Deut 8:17; 9:7, 24; 31:27 [b]Lev 18:3, 24-30; Deut 12:31; 18:9-14
5 [1]Lit *word* [a]Titus 3:5 [b]Gen 12:7; 13:15; 15:7; 17:8; 26:4; 28:13
6 [1]Or *stiff-necked* [a]Deut 9:13; 10:16; 31:27
7 [a]Ex 14:10f; Num 14:22
8 [a]Ex 32:7-10; Ps 106:19
9 [a]Ex 24:18; 34:28; Deut 8:3; 9:18
10 [a]Deut 4:13
11 [a]Deut 9:9

---

contain iron. Both copper and iron were plentiful in the part of the Arabah south of the Dead Sea. Some of the copper mines date to the time of Solomon and earlier. Zarethan was a center for bronze works in Solomon's time (1 Kin 7:45–46). Some bronze objects from this site precede the Solomonic period, and today there are copper works at Timnah in the Negev.
8:11,14,19 *forget.* See note on 4:10.
8:15 *water . . . out of the rock.* See Ex 17:6 and note.
8:16 *test.* See v. 2; see also note on Gen 22:1.
8:17–18 See Zech 4:6 and note.
8:18 *remember.* See note on 4:10.
9:1 *Hear, O Israel!* See note on 4:1.
9:2 *Anakim.* See note on 1:28.
9:3 *consuming fire.* See 4:24; see also note on Ex 24:17. *He will subdue them before you . . . you may drive them out.* The Lord not only went ahead of the Israelites, but He also exerted His powder alongside them and through them to assure victory. The Lord's involvement, together with that of the Israelite armies, continues throughout Deuteronomy and the conquest narratives.
9:4 *Because of my righteousness.* See note on 7:8. *wickedness of these nations.* See note on Gen 15:16.
9:6,13 *stubborn.* See 10:16; 31:27; see also note on Ex 32:9.
9:7,27 *Remember.* See note on 4:10.
9:9 *tablets of stone . . . of the covenant.* See notes on Ex 20:1; 34:28.
9:10 *two tablets of stone.* See note on Ex 31:18. *finger of God.* See note on Ex 8:19.
9:11–21 See Ex 31:18–32:20.

12 “[a]Then the LORD said to me, ‘Arise, go down from here quickly, for your people whom you brought out of Egypt have acted corruptly. They have [b]quickly turned aside from the way which I commanded them; they have made a molten image for themselves.’

13 “The [a]LORD spoke further to me, saying, ‘I have seen this people, and indeed, it is a [1b]stubborn people.

14 ‘[a]Let Me alone, that I may destroy them and [b]blot out their name from under heaven; and I will make of you a nation mightier and greater than they.’

15 “[a]So I turned and came down from the mountain while the mountain was burning with fire, and the two tablets of the covenant were in my two hands.

16 “And I saw that you had indeed sinned against the LORD your God. You had made for yourselves a molten calf; you had turned aside quickly from the way which the LORD had commanded you.

17 “I took hold of the two tablets and threw them from my hands and smashed them before your eyes.

18 “[a]I fell down before the LORD, [b]as at the first, forty days and nights; [c]I neither ate bread nor drank water, [d]because of all your sin which you had committed in doing what was evil in the sight of the LORD to provoke Him to anger.

19 “For [a]I was afraid of the anger and hot displeasure with which the LORD was wrathful against you in order to destroy you, [b]but the LORD listened to me that time also.

20 “The LORD was angry enough with Aaron to destroy him; so I also prayed for Aaron at the same time.

21 “[a]I took your [1]sinful *thing*, the calf which you had made, and burned it with fire and crushed it, grinding it very small until it was as fine as dust; and I threw its dust into the brook that came down from the mountain.

22 “Again at [a]Taberah and at [b]Massah and at [c]Kibroth-hattaavah you provoked the LORD to wrath.

23 “When the LORD sent you from [a]Kadesh-barnea, saying, ‘[b]Go up and possess the land which I have given you,’ then you rebelled against the [1]command of the LORD your God; [c]you neither believed Him nor listened to His voice.

24 “[a]You have been rebellious against the LORD from the day I knew you.

12 [a]Ex 32:7, 8 [b]Judg 2:17
13 [1]Or *stiff-necked* [a]Ex 32:9 [b]Deut 10:16; 31:27; 2 Kin 17:14
14 [a]Ex 32:10 [b]Ps 9:5; 109:13
15 [a]Ex 32:15-19
18 [a]Ex 34:28 [b]Deut 10:10 [c]Deut 9:9 [d]Ex 34:9
19 [a]Ex 32:10f; Heb 12:21 [b]Ex 34:10; Deut 10:10
21 [1]Lit *sin* [a]Ex 32:20
22 [a]Num 11:3 [b]Ex 17:7 [c]Num 11:34
23 [1]Lit *mouth* [a]Deut 1:2 [b]Deut 1:21 [c]Deut 1:26; Ps 106:24
24 [a]Deut 9:7; 31:27

25 “[a]So I fell down before the LORD the forty days and nights, which I [1]did because the LORD had said He would destroy you.

26 “[a]I prayed to the LORD and said, ‘O Lord GOD, do not destroy Your people, even Your inheritance, whom You have redeemed through Your greatness, whom You have brought out of Egypt with a mighty hand.

27 ‘Remember Your servants, Abraham, Isaac, and Jacob; do not look at the stubbornness of this people or at their wickedness or their sin.

28 ‘Otherwise the land from which You brought us may say, “[a]Because the LORD was not able to bring them into the land which He had [1]promised them and because He hated them He has brought them out to slay them in the wilderness.”

29 ‘Yet they are Your people, even [a]Your inheritance, whom You have brought out by Your [b]great power and Your outstretched arm.’

The Tablets Rewritten

10 “At that time the LORD said to me, ‘[a]Cut out for yourself two tablets of stone like the former ones, and come up to Me on the mountain, and [b]make an ark of wood for yourself.

2 ‘[a]I will write on the tablets the words that were on the former tablets which you shattered, and [b]you shall put them in the ark.’

3 “So [a]I made an ark of acacia wood and [b]cut out two tablets of stone like the former ones, and went up on the mountain with the two tablets in my hand.

4 “He wrote on the tablets, like the former writing, [a]the Ten [1]Commandments [b]which the LORD had spoken to you on the mountain from the midst of the fire [c]on the day of the assembly; and the LORD gave them to me.

5 “Then I turned and [a]came down from the mountain and [b]put the tablets in the ark which I had made; [c]and there they are, as the LORD commanded me.”

6 (Now the sons of Israel set out from [1]Beeroth [a]Bene-jaakan to Moserah. [b]There Aaron died and there he was buried and Eleazar his son ministered as priest in his place.

7 [a]From there they set out to Gudgodah, and from Gudgodah to Jotbathah, a land of brooks of water.

8 [a]At that time the LORD set apart the tribe of Levi to carry the ark of the covenant of the LORD, to stand before the LORD [b]to serve Him and to bless in His name until this day.

25 [1]Lit *fell down* [a]Deut 9:18
26 [a]Ex 32:11-13; 1 Sam 7:9; Jer 15:1
28 [1]Lit *spoken to* [a]Ex 32:12; Num 14:16
29 [a]Deut 4:20; 1 Kin 8:51; Neh 1:10; Ps 106:40 [b]Deut 4:34
10:1 [a]Ex 34:1 [b]Ex 25:10
2 [a]Deut 4:13 [b]Ex 25:16
3 [a]Ex 25:5; 37:1-9 [b]Ex 34:4
4 [1]Lit *Words* [a]Ex 34:28; Deut 4:13 [b]Ex 20:1 [c]Deut 9:10; 18:16
5 [a]Ex 34:29 [b]Ex 40:20 [c]1 Kin 8:9
6 [1]Or *the wells of the sons of Jaakan* [a]Num 33:30, 31 [b]Num 20:25-28; 33:38
7 [a]Num 33:33, 34
8 [a]Num 3:6; 18:1-7; Deut 31:9 [b]Deut 17:12; 18:5; 21:5

9:19 *the LORD listened to me that time also.* Moses' intercessory prayer on this occasion (vv. 26–29) ranks among the great prayers for Israel's national survival (see 1 Sam 7:5,8–9; Jer 15:1).
9:22 *Taberah.* Means "burning"; see Num 11:3. *Massah.* See 6:16; 33:8; see also note on Ex 17:7. *Kibroth-hattaavah.* Means "graves of craving"; see Num 11:34.
9:23 *Kadesh-barnea.* See note on Gen 14:7.
9:27 *do not look at.* See note on Acts 17:30.
10:1–3 *ark.* See note on Ex 25:10.
10:1 *two tablets of stone.* See note on Ex 31:18.
10:2 *put them in the ark.* See notes on Ex 16:34; 25:16.
10:3 Ex 34–37 show that the order of events here is different from that in Exodus (see Introduction: Structure and Outline).
10:6–9 A historical parenthesis, apparently stemming from Moses' prayer for Aaron and the Israelites (9:26–29) and the reference to the ark (vv. 1–5).
10:8 *carry the ark.* See note on Num 1:50. *to serve.* See note on 21:5.

9 [a]Therefore, Levi does not have a portion or inheritance with his brothers; the LORD is his inheritance, just as the LORD your God spoke to him.)

10 "[a]I, moreover, stayed on the mountain forty days and forty nights like the first time, and the LORD listened to me that time also; the LORD was not willing to destroy you.

11 "Then the LORD said to me, 'Arise, proceed on your journey ahead of the people, that they may go in and possess the land which I swore to their fathers to give them.'

12 "[a]Now, Israel, what does the LORD your God require from you, but to [1]fear the LORD your God, to walk in all His ways and [b]love Him, and to serve the LORD your God with [c]all your heart and with all your soul,

13 *and* to keep the LORD's commandments and His statutes which I am commanding you today for your good?

14 "Behold, [a]to the LORD your God belong heaven and the [1]highest heavens, [b]the earth and all that is in it.

15 "[a]Yet on your fathers did the LORD set His affection to love them, and He chose their [1]descendants after them, *even* you above all peoples, as *it is* this day.

16 "[a]So circumcise [1]your heart, and [b]stiffen your neck no longer.

17 "[a]For the LORD your God is the God of gods and the [b]Lord of lords, the great, the mighty, and the awesome God [c]who does not show partiality nor [d]take a bribe.

18 "He executes justice for [a]the orphan and the widow, and shows His love for the alien by giving him food and clothing.

19 "[a]So show your love for the alien, for you were aliens in the land of Egypt.

20 "You shall fear the LORD your God; you shall serve Him and [a]cling to Him, and [b]you shall swear by His name.

21 "He is [a]your praise and He is your God, who has done these great and awesome things for you which your eyes have seen.

22 "[a]Your fathers went down to Egypt seventy persons *in all,* [b]and now the LORD your God has made you as numerous as the stars of heaven.

Rewards of Obedience

11 "You shall therefore [a]love the LORD your God, and always [b]keep His charge, His statutes, His ordinances, and His commandments.

2 "Know this day [a]that I *am* not *speaking* with your sons who have not known and who have not seen the [1]discipline of the LORD your God—His greatness, His mighty hand and His outstretched arm,

3 and [a]His signs and His works which He did in the midst of Egypt to Pharaoh the king of Egypt and to all his land;

4 and what He did to Egypt's army, to its horses and its chariots, [a]when He made the water of the [1]Red Sea to [2]engulf them while they were pursuing you, and the LORD [3]completely destroyed them;

5 and what He did to you in the wilderness until you came to this place;

6 and [a]what He did to Dathan and Abiram, the sons of Eliab, the son of Reuben, when the earth opened its mouth and swallowed them, their households, their tents, and [b]every living thing that [1]followed them, among all Israel—

7 but your own eyes have seen all the great work of the LORD which He did.

8 "You shall therefore keep every commandment which I am commanding you today, [a]so that you may be strong and go in and possess the land into which you are about to cross to possess it;

9 [a]so that you may prolong *your* days on the land which the LORD swore to your fathers to give to them and to their [1]descendants, [b]a land flowing with milk and honey.

10 "For the land, into which you are entering to possess it, is not like the land of Egypt from which you came, where you used to sow your seed and water it with your [1]foot like a vegetable garden.

11 "But [a]the land into which you are about to cross to possess it, a land of hills and valleys, drinks water from the rain of heaven,

12 a land for which the LORD your God cares; [a]the eyes of the LORD your God are always on it, from the [1]beginning even to the end of the year.

13 "It shall come about, [a]if you listen obediently to my commandments which I am commanding you today, [b]to love the LORD

9 [a]Num 18:20, 24; Deut 18:1, 2; Ezek 44:28
10 [a]Ex 34:28; Deut 9:18
12 [1]Or *reverence* [a]Mic 6:8 [b]Deut 6:5; Matt 22:37; 1 Tim 1:5 [c]Deut 4:29
14 [1]Lit *heaven of heavens* [a]1 Kin 8:27; Neh 9:6; Ps 68:33; 115:16 [b]Ps 24:1
15 [1]Lit *seed* [a]Deut 4:37
16 [1]Lit *the foreskin of your heart* [a]Lev 26:41; Jer 4:4 [b]Deut 9:6
17 [a]Josh 22:22; Ps 136:2; Dan 2:47; 1 Tim 6:15; Rev 19:16 [b]Rev 17:14 [c]Deut 1:17; Acts 10:34; Rom 2:11; Gal 2:6; Eph 6:9 [d]Deut 16:19
18 [a]Ex 22:22-24; Ps 68:5; 146:9
19 [a]Lev 19:34; Ezek 47:22, 23
20 [a]Deut 11:22; 13:4 [b]Deut 5:11; 6:13; Ps 63:11
21 [a]Ps 109:1; 148:14; Jer 17:14
22 [a]Gen 46:27 [b]Gen 15:5; 22:17; Deut 1:10
11:1 [a]Deut 6:5; 10:12 [b]Lev 18:30; 22:9

2 [1]Or *instruction* [a]Deut 4:34
3 [a]Ex 7:8-21
4 [1]Lit *Sea of Reeds* [2]Lit *flow over their faces* [3]Lit *to this day* [a]Ex 14:28; Deut 1:40; 2:1
6 [1]Lit *was at their feet* [a]Num 16:1-35; Ps 106:16-18 [b]Num 26:10, 11
8 [a]Deut 31:6, 7, 23; Josh 1:6, 7
9 [1]Lit *seed* [a]Deut 4:40; 5:16, 33; 6:2; Prov 10:27 [b]Ex 3:8
10 [1]I.e. probably a treadmill
11 [a]Deut 8:7
12 [1]Lit *beginning of the year* [a]1 Kin 9:3 **13** [a]Lev 26:3; Deut 7:12 [b]Deut 11:1

10:9 See Num 18:20,24.
10:12 *fear the LORD.* See note on Gen 20:11. *love Him.* See notes on 4:29,37; 6:5.
10:13 *for your good.* See 6:24; see also note on 6:2.
10:16 *circumcise your heart.* See note on Gen 17:10. *stiffen your neck.* See 9:6,13; 31:27; see also note on Ex 32:9.
10:20 *cling to.* As a man is "joined" to his wife (Gen 2:24), and as Ruth "clung" to Naomi (Ruth 1:14). See 4:4; 11:22; 13:4; 30:20.
10:22 *seventy.* See notes on Gen 46:26–27; see also Ex 1:5. *as the stars of heaven.* See note on 1:10.
11:2–7 Moses continually emphasizes the involvement of his listeners in the Lord's works of providence and deliverance. In 5:3 it was not the fathers but they themselves with whom the covenant was made. Here it is not their children but they themselves who saw God's great deeds.
11:2 *Know.* See note on 4:10.
11:8–12 See note on 8:7–9.
11:9 *prolong your days.* See note on 6:2.
11:10 *water it with your foot.* Irrigation channels dug by foot and/or fed by devices powered by foot brought the water of the Nile to the gardens in Egypt, in contrast to the rains that watered Canaan (v. 11).
11:13 See note on 4:29.

your God and to serve Him [c]with all your heart and all your soul,

14 that [1a]He will give the rain for your land in its season, the [2b]early and [3]late rain, that you may gather in your grain and your new wine and your oil.

15 "[1a]He will give grass in your fields for your cattle, and [b]you will eat and be satisfied.

16 "[1a]Beware that your hearts are not deceived, and that you do not turn away and serve other gods and worship them.

17 "Or [a]the anger of the LORD will be kindled against you, and He will [b]shut up the heavens [c]so that there will be no rain and the ground will not yield its fruit; and [d]you will perish quickly from the good land which the LORD is giving you.

18 "[a]You shall therefore [1]impress these words of mine on your heart and on your soul; and you shall bind them as a sign on your hand, and they shall be as [2]frontals [3]on your forehead.

19 "[a]You shall teach them to your sons, talking of them when you sit in your house and when you walk along the road and when you lie down and when you rise up.

20 "[a]You shall write them on the doorposts of your house and on your gates,

21 so that [a]your days and the days of your sons may be multiplied on the land which the LORD swore to your fathers to give them, as [1b]long as the heavens *remain* above the earth.

22 "For if you are [a]careful to keep all this commandment which I am commanding you to do, [b]to love the LORD your God, to walk in all His ways and [c]hold fast to Him,

23 then the LORD will [a]drive out all these nations from before you, and you will [b]dispossess nations greater and mightier than you.

24 "[a]Every place on which the sole of your foot treads shall be yours; [b]your border will be from the wilderness to Lebanon, *and* from the river, the river Euphrates, as far as [1]the western sea.

25 "[a]No man will be able to stand before you; the LORD your God will lay the dread of you and the fear of you on all the land on which you set foot, as He has spoken to you.

13 [c]Deut 4:29
14 [1]So some ancient versions; M.T. reads *I* [2]I.e. autumn [3]I.e. spring [a]Lev 26:4; Deut 28:12 [b]Joel 2:23; James 5:7
15 [1]So some ancient versions; M.T. reads *I* [a]Ps 104:14 [b]Deut 6:11
16 [1]Lit *Watch yourselves* [a]Job 31:27
17 [a]Deut 6:15; 9:19 [b]1 Kin 8:35; 2 Chr 6:26; 7:13 [c]Deut 28:24 [d]Deut 4:26
18 [1]Lit *put* [2]Lit *frontlet bands* [3]Lit *between your eyes* [a]Ex 13:9, 16; Deut 6:8
19 [a]Deut 4:9, 10; 6:7; Prov 22:6
20 [a]Deut 6:9
21 [1]Lit *the days of the heavens* [a]Prov 3:2; 4:10; 9:11 [b]Ps 72:5
22 [a]Deut 6:17 [b]Deut 11:1 [c]Deut 10:20
23 [a]Deut 4:38 [b]Deut 9:1
24 [1]I.e. the Mediterranean [a]Josh 1:3; 14:9 [b]Gen 15:18; Ex 23:31; Deut 1:7, 8
25 [a]Ex 23:27; Deut 7:24
26 [a]Deut 30:1, 19
27 [a]Deut 28:1-14
28 [1]Lit *to follow* [a]Deut 28:15-68
29 [a]Deut 27:12; Josh 8:33
30 [1]Lit *terebinths* [a]Josh 4:19 [b]Gen 12:6
31 [a]Deut 17:14; Josh 21:43
12:1 [1]Lit *all the days* [2]Lit *ground* [a]Deut 4:9, 10; 1 Kin 8:40
2 [a]2 Kin 16:4; 17:10, 11
3 [1]I.e. wooden symbols of a female deity [a]Num 33:52; Deut 7:5; Judg 2:2 [b]Ex 23:13; Ps 16:4; Zech 13:2

26 "[a]See, I am setting before you today a blessing and a curse:

27 the [a]blessing, if you listen to the commandments of the LORD your God, which I am commanding you today;

28 and the [a]curse, if you do not listen to the commandments of the LORD your God, but turn aside from the way which I am commanding you today, [1]by following other gods which you have not known.

29 "It shall come about, when the LORD your God brings you into the land where you are entering to possess it, [a]that you shall place the blessing on Mount Gerizim and the curse on Mount Ebal.

30 "Are they not across the Jordan, west of the way toward the sunset, in the land of the Canaanites who live in the Arabah, opposite [a]Gilgal, beside [b]the [1]oaks of Moreh?

31 "For you are about to cross the Jordan to go in to possess the land which the LORD your God is giving you, and [a]you shall possess it and live in it,

32 and you shall be careful to do all the statutes and the judgments which I am setting before you today.

Laws of the Sanctuary

12 "These are the statutes and the judgments which you shall carefully observe in the land which the LORD, the God of your fathers, has given you to possess [1a]as long as you live on the [2]earth.

2 "You shall utterly destroy all the places where the nations whom you shall dispossess serve their gods, on the [a]high mountains and on the hills and under every green tree.

3 "[a]You shall tear down their altars and smash their *sacred* pillars and burn their [1]Asherim with fire, and you shall cut down the engraved images of their gods and [b]obliterate their name from that place.

4 "You shall not act like this toward the LORD your God.

5 "[a]But you shall seek *the LORD* at the place which the LORD your God will choose from all your tribes, to establish His name there for His dwelling, and there you shall come.

5 [a]Ex 20:24; Deut 12:11, 13; 2 Chr 7:12; Ps 78:68

11:14 *early and late rain.* The rainy season in the Holy Land begins in October and ends in April.
11:17 *shut up the heavens.* The all-important seasonal rains (see v. 14) were controlled by the Lord—not by Baal, as the inhabitants of Canaan thought (cf. Hos 2:8,17).
11:18–20 See note on 6:8–9.
11:22 *hold fast.* See note on 10:20.
11:24 *Every place on which the sole of your foot treads.* See note on 1:7.
11:26–30 The blessings and curses proclaimed on Mount Gerizim and Mount Ebal are detailed in chs. 27–28.
11:28 *known.* Experienced or acknowledged (see 13:2,6,13; 28:64; 29:26; 32:17; see also note on Ex 6:3).
11:30 *way.* Probably the north-south road that ran parallel to the Jordan between the Sea of Galilee and the Dead Sea. *Arabah.* See note on 1:1. The Canaanites who lived there controlled the territory around Gerizim and Ebal. *oaks of Moreh.* See note on Gen 12:6.
12:3 *altars . . . sacred pillars . . . Asherim.* See note on 7:5.
12:4 *like this.* The rituals and accessories of idolatrous worship were not to be used to worship the Lord, the one true God (cf. vv. 29–31).
12:5 *the place which the LORD . . . will choose . . . to establish His name.* The tabernacle, the Lord's dwelling place during the wilderness journey, will be located in the city in Canaan where the Lord would choose to dwell. Moses stresses the importance of centralizing the place of worship as he prepares the people for settlement in the promised land, where the Canaanites had

6 "There you shall bring your burnt offerings, your sacrifices, [a]your tithes, the [1]con-
tribution of your hand, your votive offerings,
your freewill offerings, and the firstborn of
your herd and of your flock.
7 "There also you and your households
shall eat before the LORD your God, and
[a]rejoice in all [1]your undertakings in which
the LORD your God has blessed you.
8 "You shall not do at all what we are
doing here today, every man *doing* whatever
is right in his own eyes;
9 for you have not as yet come to [a]the
resting place and the [b]inheritance which the
LORD your God is giving you.
10 "When you cross the Jordan and live in
the land which the LORD your God is giving
you to inherit, and [a]He gives you rest from
all your enemies around *you* so that you live
in security,
11 [a]then it shall come about that the place
in which the LORD your God will choose for
His name to dwell, there you shall bring all
that I command you: your burnt offerings
and your sacrifices, your tithes and the [1]con-
tribution of your hand, and all your choice
votive offerings which you will vow to the
LORD.
12 "And you shall [a]rejoice before the LORD
your God, you and your sons and daughters,
your male and female servants, and the
[b]Levite who is within your gates, since [c]he
has no portion or inheritance with you.
13 "[a]Be careful that you do not offer your
burnt offerings in every *cultic* place you see,
14 but in the place which the LORD
chooses in one of your tribes, there you shall
offer your burnt offerings, and there you
shall do all that I command you.
15 "[a]However, you may slaughter and eat
meat within any of your gates, [1]whatever
you desire, according to the blessing of the
LORD your God which He has given you; the
unclean and the clean may eat of it, as of
[b]the gazelle and the deer.
16 "[a]Only you shall not eat the blood; [b]you
are to pour it out on the ground like water.
17 "[a]You are not allowed to eat within your
gates the tithe of your grain or new wine or
oil, or the firstborn of your herd or flock, or
any of your votive offerings which you vow,
or your freewill offerings, or the [1]contribu-
tion of your hand.
18 "But [a]you shall eat them before the LORD
your God in [b]the place which the LORD your
God will choose, you and your son and
daughter, and your male and female servants, and the [c]Levite who is within your
gates; and you shall [d]rejoice before the LORD
your God in all [1]your undertakings.
19 "[a]Be careful that you do not forsake the
Levite [1]as long as you live in your land.
20 "When the LORD your God extends your
border [a]as He has promised you, and you
say, 'I will eat meat,' because [1]you desire to
eat meat, *then* you may eat meat, [2]whatever
you desire.
21 "If the place which the LORD your God
chooses to put His name is too far from you,
then you may slaughter of your herd and
flock which the LORD has given you, as I
have commanded you; and you may eat
within your gates [1]whatever you desire.
22 "Just as a gazelle or a deer is eaten, so
you will eat it; the unclean and the clean
alike may eat of it.
23 "Only be sure [a]not to eat the blood, for
the blood is the [1]life, and you shall not eat
the [1]life with the flesh.
24 "You shall not eat it; you shall pour it
out on the ground like water.
25 "You shall not eat it, so that [a]it may be
well with you and your sons after you, for
[b]you will be doing what is right in the sight
of the LORD.
26 "[a]Only your holy things which you may
have and your votive offerings, you shall
take and go to the place which the LORD
chooses.
27 "And [a]you shall offer your burnt offerings, the flesh and the blood, on the altar of
the LORD your God; and the blood of your sacrifices shall be poured out on the altar of the
LORD your God, and [b]you shall eat the flesh.
28 "Be careful to listen to all these words
which I command you, so that [a]it may be
well with you and your sons after you forever, for you will be doing what is good and
right in the sight of the LORD your God.
29 "When [a]the LORD your God cuts off
before you the nations which you are going
in to dispossess, and you dispossess them
and dwell in their land,
30 beware that you are not ensnared [1]to
follow them, after they are destroyed before
you, and that you do not inquire after their
gods, saying, 'How do these nations serve
their gods, that I also may do likewise?'

6 [1]Or *heave offering* [a]Deut 14:22
7 [1]Lit *the putting forth of your hand* [a]Lev 23:40; Deut 12:12, 18; 14:26; 28:47; Eccl 3:12, 13; 5:18-20
9 [a]Deut 3:20; 25:19; Ps 95:11 [b]Deut 4:21
10 [a]Josh 11:23
11 [1]Or *heave offering* [a]Deut 12:5; 15:20; 16:2; 17:8; 18:6
12 [a]Deut 12:7 [b]Deut 12:18, 19; 26:11-13 [c]Deut 10:9; 14:29
13 [a]Deut 12:5, 11
15 [1]Lit *in every desire of your soul* [a]Deut 12:20-23 [b]Deut 12:22; 14:5; 15:22
16 [a]Gen 9:4; Lev 7:26; 17:10-12; 1 Sam 14:33f; Acts 15:20, 29 [b]Deut 15:23
17 [1]Lit *heave offering* [a]Deut 12:26
18 [a]Deut 14:23
18 [1]Lit *the putting forth of your hand* [b]Deut 12:5 [c]Deut 12:12 [d]Deut 12:7; Eccl 3:12f; 5:18-20
19 [1]Lit *all your days upon your land* [a]Deut 14:27
20 [1]Lit *your soul desires* [2]Lit *in every desire of your soul* [a]Gen 15:18; Deut 11:24; 19:8
21 [1]Lit *in every desire of your soul*
23 [1]Lit *soul* [a]Gen 9:4; Lev 17:10-14; Deut 12:16
25 [a]Deut 4:40; Is 3:10 [b]Ex 15:26; 1 Kin 11:38
26 [a]Num 5:9f; 18:19; Deut 12:17
27 [a]Lev 1:9, 13 [b]Lev 3:1-17
28 [a]Deut 4:40; Eccl 8:12
29 [a]Josh 23:4
30 [1]Lit *after them*

established many places of worship. See vv. 11,14,18,21,26; 14:23–24; 16:2,6,11; 26:2.

12:6 See v. 11 and chart, p. 139.

12:8 *what we are doing here today.* Israel was not able to follow all the procedures of the sacrificial system during the wilderness wandering and conquest periods. Moses was giving directives for their worship and way of life when settled in the land (vv. 10–14). *whatever is right in his own eyes.* See note on Judg 17:6.

12:9 *resting place.* See note on 3:20.

12:11 *for His name to dwell.* Equivalent to "a dwelling for Himself." See notes on Ex 3:13–15.

12:12 *rejoice before the LORD.* Joy, based on the Lord's blessings, was to be a major feature of Hebrew life and worship in the promised land (vv. 7,18). *Levite . . . has no . . . inheritance.* See 10:9; Num 18:20,24.

12:13 *not . . . in every cultic place you see.* Sacrifices and offerings to the Lord were to be brought only to the central sanctuary, not to the various Canaanite worship sites.

12:16 *you shall not eat the blood.* See v. 24; see also notes on Gen 9:4; Lev 17:11.

31 "[a]You shall not behave thus toward the LORD your God, for every abominable act which the LORD hates they have done for their gods; for [b]they even burn their sons and daughters in the fire to their gods.

32 "[1][a]Whatever I command you, you shall be careful to do; [b]you shall not add to nor take away from it.

Shun Idolatry

13 "[1][a]If a prophet or a dreamer of dreams arises among you and gives you a sign or a wonder,

2 and the sign or the wonder comes true, concerning which he spoke to you, saying, '[a]Let us go after other gods (whom you have not known) and let us serve them,'

3 you shall not listen to the words of that prophet or that dreamer of dreams; for the LORD your God is [a]testing you to find out if [b]you love the LORD your God with all your heart and with all your soul.

4 "[a]You shall follow the LORD your God and fear Him; and you shall keep His commandments, listen to His voice, serve Him, and [b]cling to Him.

5 "But that prophet or that dreamer of dreams shall be [a]put to death, because he has [1]counseled [2]rebellion against the LORD your God who brought you from the land of Egypt and redeemed you from the house of [3]slavery, [b]to seduce you from the way in which the LORD your God commanded you to walk. [c]So you shall purge the evil from among you.

6 "[a]If your brother, your mother's son, or your son or daughter, or the wife [1]you cherish, or your friend who is as your own soul, entice you secretly, saying, '[b]Let us go and serve other gods' (whom neither you nor your fathers have known,

7 of the gods of the peoples who are around you, near you or far from you, from one end of the earth to the other end),

8 [a]you shall not yield to him or listen to him; [b]and your eye shall not pity him, nor shall you spare or conceal him.

9 "[a]But you shall surely kill him; [b]your hand shall be first against him to put him to death, and afterwards the hand of all the people.

10 "So you shall stone him [1]to death because he has sought [a]to seduce you from the LORD your God who brought you out from the land of Egypt, out of the house of [2]slavery.

11 "Then [a]all Israel will hear and be afraid, and will never again do such a wicked thing among you.

12 "If you hear in one of your cities, which the LORD your God is giving you to live in, *anyone* saying *that*

13 some worthless men have gone out from among you and have seduced the inhabitants of their city, saying, '[a]Let us go and serve other gods' (whom you have not known),

14 then you shall investigate and search out and inquire thoroughly. If it is true *and* the matter established that this abomination has been done among you,

15 [a]you shall surely strike the inhabitants of that city with the edge of the sword, [1]utterly destroying it and all that is in it and its cattle with the edge of the sword.

16 "[a]Then you shall gather all its booty into the middle of its open square and burn the city and all its booty with fire as a whole burnt offering to the LORD your God; and it shall be a [1][b]ruin forever. It shall never be rebuilt.

17 "Nothing from that which is put under the ban shall cling to your hand, in order that the LORD may turn from [a]His burning anger and [b]show mercy to you, and have compassion on you and [c]make you increase, just [d]as He has sworn to your fathers,

18 [1]if you will listen to the voice of the LORD your God, [2]keeping all His commandments which I am commanding you today, [3]and doing what is right in the sight of the LORD your God.

Clean and Unclean Animals

14 "You are [a]the sons of the LORD your God; [b]you shall not cut yourselves nor [1]shave your forehead for the sake of the dead.

2 "For you are [a]a holy people to the LORD your God, and the LORD has chosen you to be

31 [a]Deut 9:5 [b]Lev 18:21; Deut 18:10; Ps 106:37; Jer 32:35
32 [1]Lit *Everything that* [a]Deut 4:2; Josh 1:7 [b]Prov 30:6; Rev 22:18
13:1 [1]Ch 13:2 in Heb [a]Matt 24:24; Mark 13:22; 2 Thess 2:9
2 [a]Deut 13:6, 13
3 [a]Ex 20:20; Deut 8:2, 16; 1 Cor 11:19 [b]Deut 6:5
4 [a]2 Kin 23:3; 2 Chr 34:31; 2 John 6 [b]Deut 10:20
5 [1]Lit *spoken* [2]Lit *turning aside* [3]Lit *slaves* [a]Deut 13:9, 15; 17:5; 1 Kin 18:40 [b]Deut 4:19; 13:10 [c]1 Cor 5:13
6 [1]Lit *of your bosom* [a]Deut 17:2-7; 29:18 [b]Deut 13:2
8 [a]Prov 1:10 [b]Deut 7:2
9 [a]Deut 13:5 [b]Lev 24:14; Deut 17:7
10 [1]Lit *with stones so that he dies* [2]Lit *slaves* [a]Deut 13:5
11 [a]Deut 19:20
13 [a]Deut 13:2
15 [1]Or *putting it under the ban* [a]Deut 13:5
16 [1]Lit *mound* [a]Deut 7:25, 26 [b]Josh 8:28; Is 17:1; 25:2; Jer 49:2
17 [a]Ex 32:12; Num 25:4 [b]Deut 30:3 [c]Deut 7:13 [d]Gen 22:17; 26:4, 24; 28:14
18 [1]Or *for* [2]Lit *to keep* [3]Lit *to do*
14:1 [1]Lit *make a baldness between your eyes* [a]Rom 8:16; 9:8, 26; Gal 3:26; 1 John 3:1 [b]Lev 19:28; 21:5; Jer 16:6; 41:5
2 [a]Lev 20:26; Deut 7:6; Rom 12:1

12:31 *burn . . . sons and daughters . . . in the fire.* See 18:10; see also note on Lev 18:21.
12:32 *shall not add to nor take away.* See note on 4:2.
13:1–5 Eventual fulfillment is one test of true prophecy (18:21–22), but the more stringent rule given here guards against intelligent foresight masquerading as prophecy and against coincidental fulfillment of the predictions of false prophets.
13:3 *testing.* See note on Gen 22:1. *all your heart.* See note on 4:29.
13:4 *cling.* See note on 10:20.
13:5 *prophet . . . shall be put to death.* See 18:20; Jer 28:15–17. *you shall purge the evil from among you.* Repeated in 17:7; 19:19; 21:21; 22:21,24; 24:7, and quoted in 1 Cor 5:13. The purpose was to eliminate the evildoers as well as the evil itself.
13:13 *worthless.* See 1 Sam 1:16; 2:12; 25:17. The same Hebrew word is also used, e.g., in 1 Sam 10:27; 30:22; 1 Kin 21:10,13; Prov 6:12. Later, this word (*Belial* in Hebrew) was used as a name for Satan (2 Cor 6:15), who is the personification of wickedness, lawlessness and worthlessness.
13:15 *utterly destroying it.* See note on 2:34.
14:1 *cut yourselves.* A pagan religious custom (see 1 Kin 18:28). *shave your forehead.* Shaving the forehead was a practice of mourners in Canaan.
14:2,21 *holy people to the LORD.* See note on Lev 11:44. The regulations regarding clean and unclean foods were intended to separate Israel from things the Lord had identified as detestable and ceremonially unclean.

a [b]people for His [1]own possession out of all
the peoples who are on the face of the earth.
3 "[a]You shall not eat any detestable thing.
4 "[a]These are the animals which you may
eat: the ox, the sheep, the goat,
5 [1]the deer, the gazelle, the roebuck, the
wild goat, the ibex, the antelope and the
mountain sheep.
6 "Any animal that divides the hoof and
has the hoof split in [1]two *and* [2]chews the
cud, among the animals, that you may eat.
7 "Nevertheless, you are not to eat of
these among those which [1]chew the cud, or
among those that divide the hoof in [2]two:
the camel and the [3]rabbit and the [4]shaphan,
for though they [1]chew the cud, they do not
divide the hoof; they are unclean for you.
8 "The pig, because it divides the hoof but
does not *chew* the cud, it is unclean for you.
You shall not eat any of their flesh nor touch
their carcasses.
9 "These you may eat of all that are in
water: anything that has fins and scales you
may eat,
10 but anything that does not have fins and
scales you shall not eat; it is unclean for you.
11 "You may eat any clean bird.
12 "But [a]these are the ones which you shall
not eat: the [1]eagle and the vulture and the
[2]buzzard,
13 and the red kite, the falcon, and the
kite in their kinds,
14 and every raven in its kind,
15 and the ostrich, the owl, the sea gull,
and the hawk in their kinds,
16 the little owl, the [1]great owl, the white
owl,
17 the pelican, the carrion vulture, the
cormorant,
18 the stork, and the heron in their kinds,
and the hoopoe and the bat.
19 "And all the [1]teeming life with wings are
unclean to you; they shall not be eaten.
20 "You may eat any clean bird.
21 "[a]You shall not eat anything which dies
of itself. You may give it to the alien who is
in your [1]town, so that he may eat it, or you
may sell it to a foreigner, for you are [b]a holy
people to the LORD your God. [c]You shall not
boil a young goat in its mother's milk.

2 [1]Or *special treasure* [b]Ex 19:5; Deut 4:20; 26:18; Titus 2:14; 1 Pet 2:9
3 [a]Ezek 4:14
4 [a]Lev 11:2-45; Acts 10:14
5 [1]Exact identification of these animals is uncertain
6 [1]Lit *two hoofs* [2]Lit *brings up*
7 [1]Lit *brings up* [2]Lit *a cleaving* [3]Or *hare* [4]A small, shy, furry animal *(Hyrax syriacus)* found in the peninsula of the Sinai, northern Israel, and the region round the Dead Sea; KJV *coney*, orig NASB *rock-badger*
12 [1]Or *vulture* [2]Or *black vulture* [a]Lev 11:13
16 [1]Or *great horned owl*
19 [1]I.e. flying insects
21 [1]Lit *gates* [a]Lev 17:15; 22:8; Ezek 4:14; 44:31 [b]Deut 14:2 [c]Ex 23:19; 34:26

22 "You [a]shall surely tithe all the produce
from [1]what you sow, which comes out of the
field every year.
23 "You shall eat in the presence of the LORD
your God, [a]at the place where He chooses to
establish His name, the tithe of your grain,
your new wine, your oil, and the firstborn of
your herd and your flock, so that you may
[b]learn to fear the LORD your God always.
24 "If the [1]distance is so great for you that
you are not able to [2]bring *the tithe,* since the
place where the LORD your God chooses [a]to
set His name is too far away from you when
the LORD your God blesses you,
25 then you shall [1]exchange *it* for money,
and bind the money in your hand and go to
the place which the LORD your God chooses.
26 "You may spend the money for whatever your [1]heart desires: for oxen, or sheep, or
wine, or strong drink, or whatever your
[1]heart [2]desires; and [a]there you shall eat in
the presence of the LORD your God and
rejoice, you and your household.
27 "Also you shall not neglect [a]the Levite
who is in your [1]town, [b]for he has no portion
or inheritance among you.
28 "[a]At the end of every third year you
shall bring out all the tithe of your produce
in that year, and shall deposit *it* in your
[1]town.
29 "The Levite, [a]because he has no portion
or inheritance among you, and [b]the alien,
the [1]orphan and the widow who are in your
[2]town, shall come and [c]eat and be satisfied,
in order that [d]the LORD your God may bless
you in all the work of your hand which you
do.

The Sabbatic Year

15 "[a]At the end of *every* seven years you
shall [1]grant a remission *of debts.*
2 "This is the manner of remission: every
creditor shall release what he has loaned to
his neighbor; he shall not exact it of his
neighbor and his brother, because the LORD's
remission has been proclaimed.
3 "[a]From a foreigner you may exact *it,* but
your hand shall release whatever of yours is
with your brother.

22 [1]Lit *your seed* [a]Lev 27:30; Deut 12:6, 17; Neh 10:37
23 [a]Deut 12:5 [b]Deut 4:10; Ps 2:11; 111:10; 147:11; Is 8:13; Jer 32:38-40
24 [1]Lit *way* [2]Lit *carry* it [a]Deut 12:5, 21
25 [1]Lit *give in money*
26 [1]Lit *soul* [2]Lit *asks of you* [a]Deut 12:7
27 [1]Lit *gates* [a]Deut 12:12 [b]Num 18:20; Deut 10:9; 18:12
28 [1]Lit *gates* [a]Deut 26:12
29 [1]Or *fatherless* [2]Lit *gates* [a]Deut 10:9 [b]Deut 16:11, 14; 24:19-21; 26:12; Ps 94:6; Is 1:17 [c]Deut 6:11 [d]Deut 15:10; Mal 3:10

15:1 [1]Lit *make a release* [a]Deut 31:10 **3** [a]Deut 23:20

14:2 *His own possession.* See note on Ex 19:5.
14:3–21 The subject of clean and unclean food is discussed in greater detail in Lev 11 (see notes there).
14:21 *shall not eat . . . dies of itself.* Because of the prohibition against eating blood, since the dead animal's blood would not be properly drained (see 12:16,24; see also notes on Gen 9:4; Lev 17:11). *shall not boil a young goat in its mother's milk.* See note on Ex 23:19.
14:22–29 See Num 18:21–29. Taken together, the two passages suggest the following: 1. Annually, a tenth of all Israelite produce was to be taken to the city of the central sanctuary for distribution to the Levites. 2. At that time, at an initial festival, all Israelites ate part of the tithe. 3. The rest, which would be by far the major part of it, belonged to the Levites. 4. Every third year the tithe was gathered in the towns and stored for distribution to the Levites and the less fortunate: aliens, fatherless and widows (see 26:12). 5. The Levites were to present to the Lord a tenth of their tithe. See note on Lev 27:30.
14:22 *tithe.* See notes on Gen 14:20; 28:22.
14:23 *establish His name.* See note on 12:5.
14:25 *money.* Pieces of silver of various weights were a common medium of exchange, but not in the form of coins (see note on Gen 20:16).
15:1 *every seven years.* See Ex 23:10–11; Lev 25:1–7.
15:3 *From a foreigner you may exact it.* Since he was not subject to the command to allow his fields to lie fallow during the seventh year, a foreigner would probably be financially able to pay his debts if asked to do so.

4 “However, there will be no poor among you, since [a]the LORD will surely bless you in the land which the LORD your God is giving you as an inheritance to possess,

5 if only you listen obediently to the voice of the LORD your God, to observe carefully all this commandment which I am commanding you today.

6 “[a]For the LORD your God will bless you as He has promised you, and you will lend to many nations, but you will not borrow; and you will rule over many nations, but they will not rule over you.

7 “If there is [a]a poor man with you, one of your brothers, in any of your [1]towns in your land which the LORD your God is giving you, [b]you shall not harden your heart, nor close your hand from your poor brother;

8 but [a]you shall freely open your hand to him, and shall generously lend him sufficient for his need *in* whatever he lacks.

9 “Beware that there is no base [1]thought in your heart, saying, ‘[a]The seventh year, the year of remission, is near,’ and [b]your eye is hostile toward your poor brother, and you give him nothing; then he [c]may cry to the LORD against you, and it will be a sin in you.

10 “You shall generously give to him, and your heart shall not be grieved when you give to him, because [a]for this thing the LORD your God will bless you in all your work and in all [1]your undertakings.

11 “[a]For the poor will never cease *to be* [1]in the land; therefore I command you, saying, ‘You shall freely open your hand to your brother, to your needy and poor in your land.’

12 “[a]If your [1]kinsman, a Hebrew man or woman, is sold to you, then he shall serve you six years, but in the seventh year you shall set him [2]free.

13 “When you set him [1]free, you shall not send him away empty-handed.

14 “You shall furnish him liberally from your flock and from your threshing floor and from your wine vat; you shall give to him as the LORD your God has blessed you.

15 “You shall remember that you were a slave in the land of Egypt, and the LORD your God redeemed you; therefore I command you [1]this today.

16 “It shall come about [a]if he says to you, ‘I will not go out from you,’ because he loves you and your household, since he fares well with you;

17 then you shall take an awl and pierce it through his ear into the door, and he shall be your servant forever. Also you shall do likewise to your maidservant.

18 “It shall not seem hard to you when you set him [1]free, for he has given you six years *with* [2]double the service of a hired man; so the LORD your God will bless you in whatever you do.

19 “[a]You shall consecrate to the LORD your God all the firstborn males that are born of your herd and of your flock; you shall not work with the firstborn of your herd, nor shear the firstborn of your flock.

20 “[a]You and your household shall eat it every year before the LORD your God in the place which the LORD chooses.

21 “[a]But if it has any [1]defect, *such as* lameness or blindness, *or* any serious [1]defect, you shall not sacrifice it to the LORD your God.

22 “You shall eat it within your gates; [a]the unclean and the clean alike *may eat it*, as [a]a gazelle or a deer.

23 “Only [a]you shall not eat its blood; you are to pour it out on the ground like water.

The Feasts of Passover, of Weeks, and of Booths

16 “Observe [a]the month of Abib and [1b]celebrate the Passover to the LORD your God, for in the month of Abib the LORD your God brought you out of Egypt by night.

2 “You shall sacrifice the Passover to the LORD your God from the flock and the herd, in the place where the LORD chooses to establish His name.

3 “[a]You shall not eat leavened bread with it; seven days you shall eat with it unleavened bread, the bread of affliction (for you came out of the land of Egypt in haste), so that you may remember [b]all the days of your

4 [a]Deut 28:8
6 [a]Deut 28:12, 13
7 [1]Lit *gates* [a]Lev 25:35; Deut 15:11 [b]1 John 3:17
8 [a]Matt 5:42; Luke 6:34; Gal 2:10
9 [1]Lit *word* [a]Deut 15:1 [b]Matt 20:15 [c]Ex 22:23; Deut 24:15; Job 34:28; Ps 12:5; James 5:4
10 [1]Lit *the putting forth of your hand* [a]Deut 14:29; Ps 41:1; Prov 22:9
11 [1]Lit *in the midst of* [a]Matt 26:11; Mark 14:7; John 12:8
12 [1]Lit *brother* [2]Lit *free from you* [a]Ex 21:2-6; Lev 25:39-43; Jer 34:14
13 [1]Lit *free from you*
15 [1]Lit *this thing*
16 [a]Ex 21:5, 6
18 [1]Lit *free from you* [2]Lit *double the amount*
19 [a]Ex 13:2, 12
20 [a]Lev 7:15-18; Deut 12:5; 14:23
21 [1]Lit *blemish* [a]Lev 22:19-25; Deut 17:1
22 [a]Deut 12:15, 16, 22
23 [a]Gen 9:4; Lev 7:26; 17:10; 19:26; Deut 12:16, 23
16:1 [1]Lit *perform* [a]Ex 12:2 [b]Num 28:16
3 [a]Ex 12:8, 15, 19, 39; 13:3; 34:18 [b]Deut 4:9

15:4 *there will be no poor among you.* Because of the Lord's reward for obedience (vv. 4–6), and because of the sabbath-year arrangement (vv. 7–11). This "year of remission" (v. 9) gave Israelites who had experienced economic reverses a way to gain release from indebtedness and so, in a measure, a way to equalize wealth. Cf. the provisions of the year of jubilee (Lev 25:8–38).
15:6 *you will lend.* If Israel failed to follow the Lord's commands, the reverse would be true (see 28:43–44).
15:11 *the poor will never cease . . . in the land.* See also Jesus' statement in Matt 26:11. Even in the best of societies under the most enlightened laws, the uncertainties of life and the variations among citizens result in some people becoming poor. In such cases the Lord commands that generosity and kindness be extended to them.
15:15 *remember.* See note on 4:10.
15:16 *because he loves you.* In Ex 21:5–6 an additional reason is given: The servant may want to stay with his family.
15:17 *take an awl and pierce it through his ear.* See note on Ex 21:6.
15:18 *double the service.* A Hebrew servant worked twice as many years as the Code of Hammurapi, e.g., required for release from debt (see chart, p. xix). Other ancient legal texts, however, support "equivalent to" as a possible translation of the phrase.
15:19 *consecrate . . . the firstborn males.* Because the Lord saved His people from the plague of death on the firstborn in Egypt (see Ex 12:12,29; 13:2 and note; 13:15).
15:21 *if it has any defect . . . you shall not sacrifice it.* See note on Lev 1:3.
15:23 See 12:16,24; see also notes on Gen 9:4; Lev 17:11.
16:1–17 See chart, pp. 164-165; see also Ex 23:14–19 and notes; 34:18–26; Lev 23:4–44 and notes; Num 28:16–29:40.
16:1–8 See Ex 12:1–28; 13:1–16 and notes.
16:1 *Abib.* See chart, p. 92.
16:3,12 *remember.* See note on 4:10.

life the day when you came out of the land of
Egypt.
4 "For seven days no leaven shall be seen
with you in all your territory, and [a]none of
the flesh which you sacrifice on the evening
of the first day shall remain overnight until
morning.
5 "You are not allowed to sacrifice the
Passover in any of your [1]towns which the
LORD your God is giving you;
6 but [a]at the place where the LORD your
God chooses to establish His name, you shall
sacrifice the Passover in the evening at sunset, at the time that you came out of Egypt.
7 "You shall [a]cook and eat *it* in the place
which the LORD your God chooses. In the
morning you are to return to your tents.
8 "Six days you shall eat unleavened
bread, and [a]on the seventh day there shall be
[b]a solemn assembly to the LORD your God;
you shall do no work *on it.*
9 "[a]You shall count seven weeks for yourself; you shall begin to count seven weeks
from the time you begin to put the sickle to
the standing grain.
10 "Then you shall [1]celebrate the Feast of
Weeks to the LORD your God with a tribute of
a freewill offering of your hand, which you
shall give just as the LORD your God blesses
you;
11 and you shall [a]rejoice before the LORD
your God, you and your son and your daughter and your male and female servants and
[b]the Levite who is in your [1]town, and [c]the
stranger and the [2]orphan and the widow
who are in your midst, in the place where
the LORD your God chooses to establish His
name.
12 "[a]You shall remember that you were a
slave in Egypt, and you shall be careful to
observe these statutes.
13 "[a]You shall [1]celebrate the Feast of
Booths seven days after you have gathered in
from your threshing floor and your wine vat;
14 and you shall [a]rejoice in your feast,
you and your son and your daughter and
your male and female servants and the
Levite and the stranger and the [1]orphan and
the widow who are in your [2]towns.
15 "Seven days you shall celebrate a feast
to the LORD your God in the place which the
LORD chooses, because the LORD your God
will bless you in all your produce and in all
the work of your hands, so that you will be
altogether joyful.
16 "[a]Three times in a year all your males
shall appear before the LORD your God in the
place which He chooses, at the Feast of
Unleavened Bread and at the Feast of Weeks
and at the Feast of Booths, and [b]they shall
not appear before the LORD empty-handed.
17 "Every man [1]shall give as he is able,
according to the blessing of the LORD your
God which He has given you.
18 "You shall appoint for yourself judges
and officers in all your [1]towns which the
LORD your God is giving you, according to
your tribes, and they shall judge the people
with righteous judgment.
19 "[a]You shall not distort justice; [b]you shall
not [1]be partial, and [c]you shall not take a
bribe, for a bribe blinds the eyes of the wise
and perverts the words of the righteous.
20 "Justice, *and only* justice, you shall pursue, that [a]you may live and possess the land
which the LORD your God is giving you.
21 "[a]You shall not plant for yourself an
[1]Asherah of any kind of tree beside the altar
of the LORD your God, which you shall make
for yourself.
22 "[a]You shall not set up for yourself a
sacred pillar which the LORD your God hates.

Administration of Justice

17 "[a]You shall not sacrifice to the LORD
your God an ox or a sheep which has a
blemish *or* any [1]defect, for that is a
detestable thing to the LORD your God.
2 "[a]If there is found in your midst, in any
of your [1]towns, which the LORD your God is
giving you, a man or a woman who does
what is evil in the sight of the LORD your
God, by transgressing His covenant,
3 and has gone and [a]served other gods
and worshiped them, [b]or the sun or the
moon or any of the heavenly host, [c]which I
have not commanded,
4 and if it is told you and you have
heard of it, then you shall inquire thoroughly. Behold, if it is true and the thing certain
that this detestable thing has been done in
Israel,
5 then you shall bring out that man or
that woman who has done this evil deed to
your gates, *that is,* the man or the woman,
and [a]you shall stone them to [1]death.

4 [a]Ex 12:8, 10; 34:25
5 [1]Lit *gates*
6 [a]Deut 12:5
7 [a]Ex 12:8; 2 Chr 35:13
8 [a]Num 28:25 [b]Ex 12:16; 13:6; Lev 23:8, 36
9 [a]Ex 23:16; 34:22; Lev 23:15; Num 28:26
10 [1]Lit *perform*
11 [1]Lit *gates* [2]Or *fatherless* [a]Deut 12:7 [b]Deut 12:12 [c]Deut 14:29
12 [a]Deut 15:15
13 [1]Lit *perform* [a]Lev 23:34-43
14 [1]Or *fatherless* [2]Lit *gates* [a]Deut 16:11
16 [a]Ex 23:14-17; 34:23, 24 [b]Ex 34:20
17 [1]Lit *according to the gift of his hand*
18 [1]Lit *gates*
19 [1]Lit *regard persons* [a]Ex 23:2; Lev 19:15; Deut 1:17; 10:17 [b]Prov 24:23 [c]Ex 23:8; Prov 17:23; Eccl 7:7
20 [a]Deut 4:1
21 [1]I.e. wooden symbol of a female deity [a]Deut 7:5; 2 Kin 17:16; 21:3; 2 Chr 33:3
22 [a]Lev 26:1
17:1 [1]Lit *evil thing* [a]Deut 15:21
2 [1]Lit *gates* [a]Deut 13:6-11
3 [a]Ex 22:20 [b]Job 31:26-28 [c]Jer 7:22
5 [1]Lit *death with stones* [a]Lev 24:14; Josh 7:25

16:6 *at the time that you came out of.* Or "on the anniversary of your departure from"; referring either to the time of day (as the NASB has translated), as the preceding phrases do, or to the anniversary of the day it first occurred.
16:7 *to your tents.* To wherever they were staying while at the festival, whether in permanent or temporary quarters.
16:8 *assembly.* Probably refers to closing assembly (cf. Lev 23:36).
16:9 *the time you begin to put the sickle to the standing grain.* Abib 16, the second day of the Passover Feast.
16:15 *you will be altogether joyful.* As a result of God's blessing (cf. John 3:29; 15:11; 16:24; Phil 2:2; 1 John 1:4; 2 John 12).
16:16 *Three times in a year.* The three annual pilgrimage festivals (see Ex 23:14,17; 34:23).
16:17 *give . . . according to the blessing of the LORD.* See v. 10; cf. 2 Cor 8:12.
16:18–20 Cf. 1:9–18; Ex 18:13–26.
16:19 See Ex 23:8 and note.
16:21–22 *Asherah. . . sacred pillar.* See note on 7:5.
17:1 *blemish or any defect.* See note on Lev 1:3.
17:3 *worshiped them, or the sun . . . moon . . . heavenly host.* See 2 Kin 17:16; 21:3,5; 23:4–5.

6 "[a]On the [1]evidence of two witnesses or three witnesses, he who is to die shall be put to death; he shall not be put to death on the [1]evidence of one witness.

7 "[a]The hand of the witnesses shall be first against him to put him to death, and afterward the hand of all the people. [b]So you shall purge the evil from your midst.

8 "[a]If any case is too difficult for you to decide, between [1]one kind of homicide or another, between [2]one kind of lawsuit or another, and between [3]one kind of assault or another, being cases of dispute in your [4]courts, then you shall arise and go up to [b]the place which the LORD your God chooses.

9 "So you shall come to [a]the Levitical priest or the judge who is *in office* in those days, and you shall inquire *of them* and they will declare to you the verdict in the case.

10 "You shall do according to the [1]terms of the verdict which they declare to you from that place which the LORD chooses; and you shall be careful to observe according to all that they teach you.

11 "[a]According to the [1]terms of the law which they teach you, and according to the verdict which they tell you, you shall do; you shall not turn aside from the word which they declare to you, to the right or the left.

12 "The man who acts [a]presumptuously by not listening to the priest who stands there to serve the LORD your God, nor to the judge, that man shall die; thus you shall purge the evil from Israel.

13 "Then all the people will hear and be afraid, and will not act [a]presumptuously again.

14 "When you enter the land which the LORD your God gives you, and you [a]possess it and live in it, and you say, '[b]I will set a king over me like all the nations who are around me,'

15 you shall surely set a king over you whom the LORD your God chooses, *one* [a]from among your [1]countrymen you shall set as king over yourselves; you may not put a foreigner over yourselves who is not your [1]countryman.

16 "[a]Moreover, he shall not multiply horses for himself, nor shall he [b]cause the people to return to Egypt to multiply horses, since [c]the LORD has said to you, 'You shall never again return that way.'

17 "[a]He shall not multiply wives for himself, [1]or else his heart will turn away; nor shall he greatly increase silver and gold for himself.

18 "Now it shall come about when he sits on the throne of his kingdom, he shall write for himself a copy of this law on a scroll [1][a]in the presence of the Levitical priests.

19 "It shall be with him and he shall read it [a]all the days of his life, that he may learn to fear the LORD his God, [1]by carefully observing all the words of this law and these statutes,

20 that his heart may not be lifted up above his [1]countrymen [a]and that he may not turn aside from the commandment, to the right or the left, so that he and his sons may continue long in his kingdom in the midst of Israel.

Portion of the Levites

18 "[a]The Levitical priests, the whole tribe of Levi, shall have no portion or inheritance with Israel; they shall eat the LORD's offerings by fire and His [1]portion.

2 "[a]They shall have no inheritance among their [1]countrymen; the LORD is their inheritance, as He [2]promised them.

3 "[a]Now this shall be the priests' due from the people, from those who offer a sacrifice, either an ox or a sheep, of which they shall give to the priest the shoulder and the two cheeks and the stomach.

4 "You shall give him the [a]first fruits of your grain, your new wine, and your oil, and the first shearing of your sheep.

5 "[a]For the LORD your God has chosen him and his sons from all your tribes, to [b]stand [1]and serve in the name of the LORD forever.

6 "Now if a Levite comes from any of your [1]towns throughout Israel where he [a]resides, and comes [2]whenever he desires to the place which the LORD chooses,

7 then he shall serve in the name of the

6 [1]Lit *mouth* [a]Num 35:30; Deut 19:15; Matt 18:16; John 8:17; 2 Cor 13:1; 1 Tim 5:19; Heb 10:28
7 [a]Lev 24:14; Deut 13:9 [b]1 Cor 5:13
8 [1]Lit *blood to blood* [2]Lit *judgment to judgment* [3]Lit *stroke to stroke* [4]Lit *gates* [a]2 Chr 19:10; Hag 2:11 [b]Deut 12:5; Ps 122:5
9 [a]Deut 19:17
10 [1]Lit *mouth*
11 [1]Lit *mouth* [a]Deut 25:1
12 [a]Num 15:30; Deut 1:43; 17:13; 18:20; Hos 4:4
13 [a]Deut 17:12
14 [a]Deut 11:31; Josh 21:43 [b]1 Sam 8:5, 19, 20; 10:19
15 [1]Lit *brother(s)* [a]Jer 30:21
16 [a]1 Kin 4:26; 10:26-29; Ps 20:7 [b]Is 31:1; Ezek 17:15 [c]Ex 13:17, 18; Hos 11:5
17 [1]Lit *nor* [a]2 Sam 5:13; 12:11; 1 Kin 11:3, 4
18 [1]Lit *from before* [a]Deut 31:24-26
19 [1]Lit *to keep to do them* [a]Deut 4:9, 10; Josh 1:8
20 [1]Lit *brothers* [a]Deut 5:32; 1 Kin 15:5
18:1 [1]Or *inheritance* [a]Deut 10:9; 1 Cor 9:13
2 [1]Lit *brothers* [2]Lit *spoke to* [a]Num 18:20
3 [a]Lev 7:32-34; Num 18:11, 12
4 [a]Num 18:12
5 [1]Lit *to* [a]Ex 29:9 [b]Deut 10:8
6 [1]Lit *gates* [2]Lit *with all the desire of his soul* [a]Num 35:2, 3

17:6 *two witnesses or three.* A further specification of the law set forth in Num 35:30. See 19:15; cf. Matt 18:16; 2 Cor 13:1; 1 Tim 5:19; Heb 10:28.

17:7 *you shall purge the evil from your midst.* See v. 12; see also note on 13:5.

17:14 *a king . . . like all the nations . . . around me.* Moses, Joshua and a succession of judges were chosen directly by the Lord to govern Israel on His behalf. As Gideon later said, "The LORD shall rule over you" (Judg 8:23; see note there). Moses here, however, anticipates a time when the people would ask for a king (see 1 Sam 8:4–9) contrary to the Lord's ideal for them (see notes on 7:2–5; 1 Sam 8:1–12:25; see also Lev 20:23). So Moses gives guidance concerning the eventual selection of a king.

17:16–17 The very things that later kings were guilty of, beginning especially with Solomon (1 Kin 4:26; 11:1–4)—except that they did not make Israel return to Egypt (but see Jer 42:13–43:7).

17:18 *write for himself a copy of this law.* As a sign of submission to the Lord as his King, and as a guide for his rule in obedience to his heavenly Suzerain. This was required procedure for vassal kings under the suzerainty treaties among the Hittites and others before and during this period (see note on 31:9). See chart, p. 16.

17:20 *his heart may not be lifted up.* The king was not above God's law, any more than were the humblest of his subjects.

18:1 *no portion or inheritance.* No private ownership of land. Towns and surrounding pasturelands were set aside for the use of the Levites (Josh 21:41–42), as were the tithes and parts of sacrifices (see 14:22–29 and note; Lev 27:30 and note; Num 18:21–29).

18:4 *first fruits.* See Ex 23:19 and note; 34:26; Lev 23:10–11; Num 15:18–20; 18:12–13.

18:5 See note on 21:5.

LORD his God, like all his fellow Levites who stand there before the LORD.

8 "[a]They shall eat [1]equal portions, except *what they receive* from the sale of their fathers' *estates*.

Spiritism Forbidden

9 "When you enter the land which the LORD your God gives you, you shall not learn to [1][a]imitate the detestable things of those nations.

10 "There shall not be found among you anyone [a]who makes his son or his daughter pass through the fire, one who uses divination, one [b]who practices witchcraft, or one who interprets omens, or a sorcerer,

11 or one who casts a spell, [a]or a medium, or a spiritist, or one who calls up the dead.

12 "For whoever does these things is detestable to the LORD; and [a]because of these detestable things the LORD your God will drive them out before you.

13 "[a]You shall be [1]blameless before the LORD your God.

14 "For those nations, which you shall dispossess, listen to those who [a]practice witchcraft and to diviners, but as for you, the LORD your God has not allowed you *to do* so.

15 "[a]The LORD your God will raise up for you a prophet like me from among you, from your [1]countrymen, you shall listen to him.

16 "This is [a]according to all that you asked of the LORD your God in Horeb on the day of the assembly, saying, 'Let me not hear again the voice of the LORD my God, let me not see this great fire anymore, or I will die.'

17 "[a]The LORD said to me, 'They have [1]spoken well.

18 'I will raise up a prophet from among their [1]countrymen like you, and [a]I will put My words in his mouth, and [b]he shall speak to them all that I command him.

19 '[a]It shall come about that whoever will not listen to My words which he shall speak in My name, I Myself will require *it* of him.

20 'But the prophet who speaks a word [a]presumptuously in My name which I have not commanded him to speak, or [b]which he speaks in the name of other gods, [1]that prophet shall die.'

21 "[1]You may say in your heart, 'How will we know the word which the LORD has not spoken?'

22 "[a]When a prophet speaks in the name of the LORD, if the thing does not come about or come true, that is the thing which the LORD has not spoken. The prophet has spoken it [b]presumptuously; you shall not be afraid of him.

Cities of Refuge

19 "[a]When the LORD your God cuts off the nations, whose land the LORD your God gives you, and you dispossess them and settle in their cities and in their houses,

2 [a]you shall set aside three cities for yourself in the midst of your land, which the LORD your God gives you to [1]possess.

3 "You shall prepare the [1]roads for yourself, and divide into three parts the territory of your land which the LORD your God will give you as a possession, [2]so that any manslayer may flee there.

4 "[a]Now this is the case of the manslayer who may flee there and live: when he [1]kills his friend [2]unintentionally, [3]not hating him previously—

5 as when *a man* goes into the forest with his friend to cut wood, and his hand [1]swings the axe to cut down the tree, and the iron *head* slips off the [2]handle and [3]strikes his friend so that he dies—he may flee to one of these cities and live;

6 otherwise the avenger of blood might pursue the manslayer [1]in the heat of his anger, and overtake him, because the way is long, and [2]take his life, though he was not deserving of death, since he had not hated him previously.

7 "Therefore, I command you, saying, 'You shall set aside three cities for yourself.'

8 "If the LORD your God [a]enlarges your territory, just as He has sworn to your fathers, and gives you all the land which He [1]promised to give your fathers—

9 if you [1]carefully observe all this commandment which I command you today, [a]to love the LORD your God, and to walk in His ways always—[b]then you shall add three more cities for yourself, besides these three.

8 [1]Lit *portion like portion* [a]Lev 27:30-33; Num 18:21-24; 2 Chr 31:4; Neh 12:44
9 [1]Lit *do according to* [a]Deut 9:5
10 [a]Deut 12:31 [b]Ex 22:18; Lev 19:26, 31; 20:6; Jer 27:9, 10; Mal 3:5
11 [a]Lev 19:31
12 [a]Lev 18:24
13 [1]Lit *complete, perfect;* or *having integrity* [a]Gen 6:9; 17:1; Matt 5:48
14 [a]2 Kin 21:6
15 [1]Lit *brothers* [a]Matt 21:11; Luke 2:25-34; 7:16; 24:19; John 1:21, 25; 4:19; Acts 3:22; 7:37
16 [a]Ex 20:18, 19; Deut 5:23-27
17 [1]Lit *done well what they have spoken* [a]Deut 5:28
18 [1]Lit *brothers* [a]Is 51:16; John 17:8 [b]John 4:25; 8:28; 12:49, 50
19 [a]Acts 3:23; Heb 12:25
20 [1]Lit *and that* [a]Deut 13:5; 17:12 [b]Deut 13:1, 2; Jer 14:14; Zech 13:3
21 [1]Lit *if you say*
22 [a]Jer 28:9 [b]Deut 18:20
19:1 [a]Deut 6:10, 11
2 [1]Lit *possess it* [a]Deut 4:41; Josh 20:2
3 [1]Lit *road* [2]Lit *and it shall be for every manslayer to flee there*
4 [1]Lit *smites* [2]Lit *without knowledge* [3]Lit *and he was not hating him previously* [a]Num 35:9-34
5 [1]Lit *is thrust with* [2]Lit *wood* [3]Lit *finds*
6 [1]Lit *while his heart is hot* [2]Lit *smite him in the soul*
8 [1]Lit *spoke* [a]Gen 15:18
9 [1]Lit *keep...to do it* [a]Deut 6:5 [b]Josh 20:7

18:9 *detestable things of those nations.* What follows is the most complete list of magical or spiritistic arts in the OT. All were practiced in Canaan, and all are condemned and prohibited. The people are not to resort to such sources for their information, guidance or revelation. Rather, they are to listen to the Lord's true prophets (see vv. 14–22; Is 8:19–20).
18:10 *makes his son or his daughter pass through the fire.* See 12:31; see also note on Lev 18:21.
18:15 *prophet like me.* Verse 16, as well as the general context (see especially vv. 20–22), indicates that a series of prophets is meant. At Mount Horeb the people requested that Moses take the message from God and deliver it to them (see Ex 20:19 and note). But now that Moses is to leave them, he says that another spokesman will take his place, and then another will be necessary for the next generation. This is therefore a collective reference to the prophets who will follow. As such, it is also the basis for Messianic expectation and receives a unique fulfillment in Jesus (see John 1:21,25,45; 5:46; 6:14; 7:40; Acts 3:22–26; 7:37).
18:16 See Ex 20:18–19; Heb 12:18–21.
18:18 *My words in his mouth.* See Ex 4:15–16; Jer 1:9; see also note on Ex 7:1–2.
18:20 *prophet who speaks . . . presumptuously.* See note on 13:1–5. *shall die.* See 13:5; Jer 28:15–17.
18:21–22 This negative form of statement is always true. But the positive statement, "If the prophecy comes true, it is from the Lord," may not always be true (see note on 13:1–5).
19:1–13 See 4:41–43; Num 35:9–28; Jos 20.

10 "So innocent blood will not be shed in the midst of your land which the LORD your God gives you as an inheritance, and [a]bloodguiltiness be on you.

11 "But [a]if there is a man who hates his neighbor and lies in wait for him and rises up against him and strikes [1]him so that he dies, and he flees to one of these cities,

12 then the elders of his city shall send and take him from there and deliver him into the hand of the avenger of blood, that he may die.

13 "[1][a]You shall not pity him, but [b]you shall purge the blood of the innocent from Israel, that it may go well with you.

Laws of Landmark and Testimony

14 "[a]You shall not move your neighbor's boundary mark, which the ancestors have set, in your inheritance which you will inherit in the land that the LORD your God gives you to [1]possess.

15 "[a]A single witness shall not rise up against a man on account of any iniquity or any sin [1]which he has committed; on the [2]evidence of two or three witnesses a matter shall be confirmed.

16 "[a]If a malicious witness rises up against a man to [1]accuse him of [2]wrongdoing,

17 then both the men who have the dispute shall stand [a]before the LORD, before the priests and the judges who will be *in office* in those days.

18 "The judges [a]shall investigate thoroughly, and if the witness is a false witness *and* he has [1]accused his brother falsely,

19 then [a]you shall do to him just as he had intended to do to his brother. Thus you shall purge the evil from among you.

20 "[a]The rest will hear and be afraid, and will never again do such an evil thing among you.

21 "Thus [1][a]you shall not show pity: [b]life for life, [c]eye for eye, tooth for tooth, hand for hand, foot for foot.

Laws of Warfare

20 "When you go out to battle against your enemies and see [a]horses and chariots *and* people more numerous than you, [b]do not be afraid of them; for the LORD your God, who brought you up from the land of Egypt, is with you.

2 "When you are approaching the battle, the priest shall come near and speak to the people.

3 "He shall say to them, 'Hear, O Israel, you are approaching the battle against your enemies today. Do not be fainthearted. [a]Do not be afraid, or panic, or tremble before them,

4 for the LORD your God [a]is the one who goes with you, to fight for you against your enemies, to save you.'

5 "The officers also shall speak to the people, saying, 'Who is the man that has built a new house and has not [a]dedicated it? Let him depart and return to his house, otherwise he might die in the battle and another man would dedicate it.

6 'Who is the man that has planted a vineyard and has not [1]begun to use its fruit? Let him depart and return to his house, otherwise he might die in the battle and another man [1]would begin to use its fruit.

7 '[a]And who is the man that is engaged to a woman and has not [1]married her? Let him depart and return to his house, otherwise he might die in the battle and another man [2]would marry her.'

8 "Then the officers shall speak further to the people and say, '[a]Who is the man that is afraid and fainthearted? Let him depart and return to his house, so that [1]he might not make his brothers' hearts melt like his heart.'

9 "When the officers have finished speaking to the people, they shall appoint commanders of armies at the head of the people.

10 "When you approach a city to fight against it, you shall [1]offer it terms of peace.

11 "If it [1]agrees to make peace with you and opens to you, then all the people who are found in it shall become your [a]forced labor and shall serve you.

12 "However, if it does not make peace with you, but makes war against you, then you shall besiege it.

13 "When the LORD your God gives it into your hand, [a]you shall strike all the [1]men in it with the edge of the sword.

14 "Only the women and the children and [a]the animals and all that is in the city, all its spoil, you shall take as booty for yourself; and you shall [1]use the spoil of your enemies which the LORD your God has given you.

15 "Thus you shall do to all the cities that

10 [a]Num 35:33; Deut 21:1-9
11 [1]Lit *him in the soul* [a]Ex 21:12; Num 35:16; 1 John 3:15
13 [1]Lit *Your eye* [a]Deut 7:2 [b]1 Kin 2:31
14 [1]Lit *possess it* [a]Deut 27:17; Job 24:2; Prov 22:28; Hos 5:10
15 [1]Lit *in any sin, which he sins* [2]Lit *mouth of two witnesses, or by the mouth of three* [a]Num 35:30; Deut 17:6; Matt 18:16; John 8:17; 2 Cor 13:1; 1 Tim 5:19; Heb 10:28
16 [1]Lit *testify against* [2]Lit *turning aside* [a]Ex 23:1; Ps 27:12
17 [a]Deut 17:9
18 [1]Lit *testified against* [a]Deut 25:1
19 [a]Prov 19:5
20 [a]Deut 17:13; 21:21
21 [1]Lit *your eye* [a]Deut 19:13 [b]Ex 21:23; Lev 24:20 [c]Matt 5:38
20:1 [a]Deut 3:22; 7:18; 31:6, 8; Ps 20:7; Is 31:1 [b]2 Chr 32:7, 8; Ps 23:4; Is 41:10

3 [a]Deut 20:1; Josh 23:10
4 [a]Deut 1:30; 3:22; Josh 23:10
5 [a]Neh 12:27
6 [1]Lit *treat(ed) it as common*
7 [1]Lit *taken* [2]Lit *take* [a]Deut 24:5
8 [1]So with Gr and other ancient versions [a]Judg 7:3
10 [1]Lit *call to it for peace*
11 [1]Lit *answers peace* [a]1 Kin 9:21
13 [1]Lit *males* [a]Num 31:7
14 [1]Lit *eat* [a]Josh 8:2

19:14 *boundary mark.* Such stones were set up to indicate the perimeters of fields and landed estates. Moving them illegally to increase one's own holdings was considered a serious crime.
19:15 See note on 17:6.
19:18 *false witness.* See 5:20; Lev 19:11–13; 1 Kin 21:10,13.
19:19 *you shall purge the evil from among you.* See note on 13:5.
19:21 *life for life.* See notes on Ex 21:23–25; Lev 24:20; see also Matt 5:38–42.
20:2 *priest shall . . . speak.* Not merely a recitation of ritual. Priests sometimes accompanied the army when it went into battle (see, e.g., Josh 6:4–21; 2 Chr 20:14–22).
20:3 *Hear, O Israel.* See note on 4:1.
20:4 See note on 3:22.
20:5–8 *Let him . . . return to his house.* See the curses in 28:30. Israel was not to trust in the size of its army but in the Lord. Exemptions from military duty were sometimes extensive (see, e.g., Judg 7:2–8).
20:10–15 Rules regarding warfare against nations outside the promised land.
20:11 *shall become your forced labor.* A fulfillment of Noah's curse on Canaan (see Gen 9:25 and note).

are very far from you, which are not of the cities of these nations [1]nearby.

16 "[a]Only in the cities of these peoples that the LORD your God is giving you as an inheritance, you shall not leave alive anything that breathes.

17 "But you shall [1]utterly destroy them, the Hittite and the Amorite, the Canaanite and the Perizzite, the Hivite and the Jebusite, as the LORD your God has commanded you,

18 so that they may not teach you to do [a]according to all their detestable things which they have done for their gods, so that you would [b]sin against the LORD your God.

19 "When you besiege a city a long time, to make war against it in order to capture it, you shall not destroy its trees by swinging an axe against them; for you may eat from them, and you shall not cut them down. [1]For is the tree of the field a man, that it should [2]be besieged by you?

20 "Only the trees which you know [1]are not fruit trees you shall destroy and cut down, that you may construct siegeworks against the city that is making war with you until it falls.

Expiation of a Crime

21 "If a slain person is found lying in the open country in the land which the LORD your God gives you to [1]possess, *and* it is not known who has struck him,

2 then your elders and your judges shall go out and measure *the distance* to the cities which are around the slain one.

3 "It shall be that the city which is nearest to the slain man, that is, the elders of that city, shall take a heifer of the herd, which has not been worked and which has not pulled in a yoke;

4 and the elders of that city shall bring the heifer down to a valley with running water, which has not been plowed or sown, and shall break the heifer's neck there in the valley.

5 "Then [a]the priests, the sons of Levi, shall come near, for the LORD your God has chosen them to serve Him and to bless in the name of the LORD; and every dispute and every [1]assault [2]shall be settled by them.

6 "All the elders of that city [1]which is nearest to the slain man shall [a]wash their hands over the heifer whose neck was broken in the valley;

7 and they shall answer and say, 'Our hands did not shed this blood, nor did our eyes see *it*.

8 '[1]Forgive Your people Israel whom You have redeemed, O LORD, and do not place the guilt of [a]innocent blood in the midst of Your people Israel.' And the bloodguiltiness shall be [2]forgiven them.

9 "[a]So you shall remove the guilt of innocent blood from your midst, when you do what is right in the eyes of the LORD.

Domestic Relations

10 "When you go out to battle against your enemies, and [a]the LORD your God delivers them into your hands and you take them away captive,

11 and see among the captives a beautiful woman, and have a desire for her and would take her as a wife for yourself,

12 then you shall bring her home to your house, and she shall [a]shave her head and [1]trim her nails.

13 "She shall also [1]remove the clothes of her captivity and shall remain in your house, and [a]mourn her father and mother a full month; and after that you may go in to her and be her husband and she shall be your wife.

14 "It shall be, if you are not pleased with her, then you shall let her go [1]wherever she wishes; but you shall certainly not sell her for money, you shall not [2]mistreat her, because you have [a]humbled her.

15 "If a man has two wives, the one loved and [a]the other [1]unloved, and *both* the loved and the [1]unloved have borne him sons, if the firstborn son belongs to the [1]unloved,

16 then it shall be in the day he [1]wills what he has to his sons, he cannot make the son of the loved the firstborn before the son of the [2]unloved, who is the firstborn.

17 "But he shall acknowledge the firstborn, the son of the [1]unloved, by giving him a double portion of all that [2]he has, for he is the

15 [1]Lit *here*
16 [a]Ex 23:31-33; Num 21:2, 3; Deut 7:1-5; Josh 11:14
17 [1]Or *put them under the ban*
18 [a]Ex 34:12-16; Deut 7:4; 9:5; 12:30, 31 [b]Ex 23:33; 2 Kin 21:3-15; Ps 106:34-41
19 [1]Read as interrogative with ancient versions [2]Lit *come before you in the siege*
20 [1]Lit *they are not trees for food*
21:1 [1]Lit *possess it*
5 [1]Lit *stroke* [2]Lit *shall be according to their mouth* [a]Deut 17:9-11; 19:17; 1 Chr 23:13
6 [1]Lit *who are* [a]Matt 27:24
8 [1]Lit *Cover over, atone for* [2]Lit *covered over, atoned for* [a]Num 35:33, 34; Jon 1:14
9 [a]Deut 19:13
10 [a]Josh 21:44
12 [1]Lit *do* [a]Lev 14:8, 9; Num 6:9
13 [1]Lit *remove from her* [a]Ps 45:10
14 [1]Lit *according to her soul* [2]Or *enslave* [a]Gen 34:2
15 [1]Lit *hated* [a]Gen 29:33
16 [1]Lit *makes to inherit* [2]Lit *hated*
17 [1]Lit *hated* [2]Lit *is found with him*

20:17 *Hittite . . . Jebusite.* See 7:1; see also notes on Gen 10:6,15–18; 13:7.
20:19 *you shall not destroy its trees.* The failure of later armies to follow this wise rule stripped bare much of the Holy Land (though the absence of woodlands there today is of relatively recent origin).
21:5 *to serve.* To officiate at the place of worship before the Lord on behalf of the people (see 10:8; 18:5). *to bless.* See Num 6:22–27.
21:6 *wash their hands.* Symbolic of a declaration of innocence (v. 7; see Matt 27:24).
21:10 *against your enemies.* The enemies here are those outside Canaan (see 20:14–15); so the woman (v. 11) could be taken captive and would not be subject to total destruction.
21:12 *shave her head.* Indicative of leaving her former life and beginning a new life, or perhaps symbolic of mourning (v. 13; see, e.g., Jer 47:5; Mic 1:16) or of humiliation (see note on Is 7:20). For cleansing rites see Lev 14:8; Num 8:7; cf. 2 Sam 19:24.
21:14 *humbled.* Twelve other times the Hebrew for this word is used of men forcing women to have sexual intercourse with them (22:24,29; Gen 34:2; Judg 19:24; 20:5; 2 Sam 13:12,14,22,32; Lam 5:11; Ezek 22:10–11).
21:15 *two wives.* See notes on Gen 4:19; 25:6.
21:16 *before.* The order of birth rather than parental favoritism governed succession, though the rule was sometimes set aside with divine approval (cf., e.g., Jacob or Solomon).
21:17 *double portion.* In Israel the oldest son enjoyed a double share of the inheritance. Parallels to this practice come from Nuzi, Larsa in the Old Babylonian period, and Assyria in the Mid-

[a]beginning of his strength; [b]to him belongs the right of the firstborn.

18 "If any man has a stubborn and rebellious son who will [a]not obey his father or his mother, and when they chastise him, he will not even listen to them,

19 then his father and mother shall seize him, and bring him out to the elders of his city [1]at the gateway of his hometown.

20 "They shall say to the elders of his city, 'This son of ours is stubborn and rebellious, he will not obey us, he is a glutton and a drunkard.'

21 "[a]Then all the men of his city shall stone him to death; so [b]you shall remove the evil from your midst, and [c]all Israel will hear *of it* and fear.

22 "If a man has committed a sin [a]worthy of death and he is put to death, and you hang him on a tree,

23 [a]his corpse shall not hang all night on the tree, but you shall surely bury him on the same day (for [b]he who is hanged is [1]accursed of God), so that you [c]do not defile your land which the LORD your God gives you as an inheritance.

Sundry Laws

22 "[a]You shall not see your [1]countryman's ox or his sheep straying away, and [2]pay no attention to them; you shall certainly bring them back to your countryman.

2 "If your countryman is not near you, or if you do not know him, then you shall bring it home to your house, and it shall remain with you until your countryman looks for it; then you shall restore it to him.

3 "Thus you shall do with his donkey, and you shall do the same with his garment, and you shall do likewise with anything lost by your countryman, which he has lost and you have found. You are not allowed to [1]neglect *them.*

4 "You shall not see your countryman's donkey or his ox fallen down on the way, and [1]pay no attention to them; you shall certainly help him to raise *them* up.

5 "A woman shall not wear man's clothing, nor shall a man put on a woman's clothing; for whoever does these things is an abomination to the LORD your God.

6 "If you happen to come upon a bird's nest along the way, in any tree or on the ground, with young ones or eggs, and the mother sitting on the young or on the eggs, [a]you shall not take the mother with the young;

7 you shall certainly let the mother go, but the young you may take for yourself, [a]in order that it may be well with you and that you may prolong your days.

8 "When you build a new house, you shall make a parapet for your roof, so that you will not bring bloodguilt on your house if anyone falls from it.

9 "[a]You shall not sow your vineyard with two kinds of seed, or [1]all the produce of the seed which you have sown and the increase of the vineyard will become defiled.

10 "[a]You shall not plow with an ox and a donkey together.

11 "[a]You shall not wear a material mixed of wool and linen together.

12 "[a]You shall make yourself tassels on the four corners of your garment with which you cover yourself.

Laws on Morality

13 "[a]If any man takes a wife and goes in to her and *then* [1]turns against her,

14 and charges her with shameful deeds and [1]publicly defames her, and says, 'I took this woman, *but* when I came near her, I did not find her a virgin,'

15 then the girl's father and her mother shall take and bring out the *evidence* of the girl's virginity to the elders of the city at the gate.

16 "The girl's father shall say to the elders, 'I gave my daughter to this man for a wife, but he [1]turned against her;

17 and behold, he has charged her with shameful deeds, saying, "I did not find your daughter a virgin." But [1]this is the evidence of my daughter's virginity.' And they shall spread the garment before the elders of the city.

18 "So [a]the elders of that city shall take the man and chastise him,

17 [a]Gen 49:3 [b]Gen 25:31 **18** [a]Ex 20:12; Lev 19:3; Prov 1:8; Eph 6:1-3 **19** [1]Lit *and to the gate of his place* **21** [a]Lev 20:2, 27; 24:14-23; Num 15:25, 36 [b]Deut 19:19 [c]Deut 13:11 **22** [a]Deut 22:26; Matt 26:66; Mark 14:64; Acts 23:29 **23** [1]Lit *the curse of God* [a]Josh 8:29; 10:26, 27; John 19:31 [b]Gal 3:13 [c]Lev 18:25; Num 35:34 **22:1** [1]Lit *brother,* and so through v 4 [2]Lit *hide yourself from them* [a]Ex 23:4, 5; Prov 27:10; Zech 7:9 **3** [1]Lit *hide yourself* **4** [1]Lit *hide yourself from them*

6 [a]Lev 22:28 **7** [a]Deut 4:40 **9** [1]Lit *the fullness* [a]Lev 19:19 **10** [a]2 Cor 6:14-16 **11** [a]Lev 19:19 **12** [a]Num 15:37-41; Matt 23:5 **13** [1]Lit *hates her* [a]Gen 29:21; Deut 24:1; Judg 15:1 **14** [1]Lit *causes an evil name to go out against her* **16** [1]Lit *hated her* **17** [1]Lit *these are* **18** [a]Ex 18:21; Deut 1:9-18

dle Assyrian period (see chart, p. xix). Receiving a double portion of an estate was also tantamount to succession. Thus Elisha succeeded Elijah (2 Kin 2:9). *beginning of his strength.* The first result of a man's procreative ability.

21:18 *stubborn and rebellious . . . will not obey.* In wicked defiance of the fifth commandment (see 5:16; Ex 20:12 and note).

21:21 *stone him to death.* See 5:16; 27:16; Ex 21:15,17. *you shall remove the evil from your midst.* See note on 13:5.

21:22 *put to death. . . on a tree.* The offender was first executed, then "hung on a tree" (see Gen 40:19), or, as the Hebrew for this phrase doubtless intends, "impaled on a pole" (see note on Esth 2:23).

21:23 *not hang all night on the tree.* Prolonged exposure gives undue attention to the crime and the criminal. *accursed of God.* God had condemned murder, and hanging on a tree symbolized divine judgment and rejection. Christ accepted the full punishment of our sins, thus becoming "a curse for us" (Gal 3:13).

22:1 *not see . . . and pay no attention.* See vv. 3–4. The Biblical legislation was intended not only to punish criminal behavior but also to express concern for people and their possessions. See chart, p. 255.

22:5 Probably intended to prohibit such perversions as transvestism and homosexuality, especially under religious auspices. The God-created differences between men and women are not to be disregarded (see Lev 18:22; 20:13).

22:14 *find her a virgin.* Find a blood-stained cloth or garment (see vv. 15,17,20).

22:15 *elders . . . at the gate.* See 25:7; see also notes on Gen 19:1; Ruth 4:1.

19 and they shall fine him a hundred *shekels* of silver and give it to the girl's father, because he [1]publicly defamed a virgin of Israel. And she shall remain his wife; he cannot [2]divorce her all his days.

20 "But if this [1][a]charge is true, that the girl was not found a virgin,

21 then they shall bring out the girl to the doorway of her father's house, and the men of her city shall stone her [1]to death because she has [a]committed an act of folly in Israel by playing the harlot in her father's house; thus [b]you shall purge the evil from among you.

22 "[a]If a man is found lying with a married woman, then both of them shall die, the man who lay with the woman, and the woman; thus you shall purge the evil from Israel.

23 "[a]If there is a girl who is a virgin engaged to a man, and *another* man finds her in the city and lies with her,

24 then you shall bring them both out to the gate of that city and you shall stone them [1]to death; the girl, because she did not cry out in the city, and the man, because he has violated his neighbor's wife. Thus you shall purge the evil from among you.

25 "But if in the field the man finds the girl who is engaged, and the man forces her and lies with her, then only the man who lies with her shall die.

26 "But you shall do nothing to the girl; there is no sin in the girl worthy of death, for just as a man rises against his neighbor and murders him, so is this case.

27 "When he found her in the field, the engaged girl cried out, but there was no one to save her.

28 "[a]If a man finds a girl who is a virgin, who is not engaged, and seizes her and lies with her and they are discovered,

29 then the man who lay with her shall give to the girl's father fifty *shekels* of silver,

19 [1]Lit *caused an evil name to go out against a virgin* [2]Lit *send her away*
20 [1]Lit *matter* [a]Deut 17:4
21 [1]Lit *with stones so that she dies* [a]Gen 34:7; Lev 19:29; 21:9; Deut 23:17, 18; Judg 20:5-10; 2 Sam 13:12, 13 [b]Deut 13:5; 17:7; 19:19
22 [a]Lev 20:10; Ezek 16:38; Matt 5:27, 28; John 8:5; 1 Cor 6:9; Heb 13:4
23 [a]Lev 19:20-22; Matt 1:18, 19
24 [1]Lit *with stones so that they die*
28 [a]Ex 22:16

22:19 *hundred shekels of silver.* A heavy fine—several times what Hosea paid to buy Gomer back (Hos 3:2) or what Jeremiah paid for the field at Anathoth (Jer 32:9). It may have been about twice the average bride-price (see note on v. 29). The high fine, in addition to the no-divorce rule, was intended to restrain not only a husband's charges against his wife but also easy divorce.
22:21,24 *you shall purge the evil from among you.* See v. 22; see also note on 13:5.
22:22 See Lev 20:10.
22:29 *fifty shekels of silver.* Probably equaled the average

Major Social Concerns in the Covenant

1. Personhood
Everyone's person is to be secure (Ex 20:13; Dt 5:17; Ex 21:16-21,26-31; Lev 19:14; Deut 24:7; 27:18).

2. False Accusation
Everyone is to be secure against slander and false accusation (Ex 20:16; Deut 5:20; Ex 23:1-3; Lev 19:16; Deut 19:15-21).

3. Woman
No woman is to be taken advantage of within her subordinate status in society (Ex 21:7-11,20,26-32; 22:16-17; Deut 21:10-14; 22:13-30; 24:1-5).

4. Punishment
Punishment for wrongdoing shall not be excessive so that the culprit is dehumanized (Deut 25:1-5).

5. Dignity
Every Israelite's dignity and right to be God's freedman and servant are to be honored and safeguarded (Ex 21:2,5-6; Lev 25; Deut 15:12-18).

6. Inheritance
Every Israelite's inheritance in the promised land is to be secure (Lev 25; Num 27:5-7; 36:1-9; Deut 25:5-10).

7. Property
Everyone's property is to be secure (Ex 20:15; Deut 5:19; Ex 21:33-36; 22:1-15; 23:4-5; Lev 19:35-36; Deut 22:1-4; 25:13-15).

8. Fruit of Labor
Everyone is to receive the fruit of his labors (Lev 19:13; Deut 24:14; 25:4).

9. Fruit of the Ground
Everyone is to share the fruit of the ground (Ex 23:10-11; Lev 19:9-10; 23:22; 25:3-55; Deut 14:28-29; 24:19-21).

10. Rest on Sabbath
Everyone, down to the humblest servant and the resident alien, is to share in the weekly rest of God's sabbath (Ex 20:8-11; Deut 5:12-15; Ex 23:12).

11. Marriage
The marriage relationship is to be kept inviolate (Ex 20:14; Deut 5:18; see also Lev 18:6-23; 20:10-21; Deut 22:13-30).

12. Exploitation
No one, however disabled, impoverished or powerless, is to be oppressed or exploited (Ex 22:21-27; Lev 19:14,33-34; 25:35-36; Deut 23:19; 24:6,12-15,17; 27:18).

13. Fair Trial
Everyone is to have free access to the courts and is to be afforded a fair trial (Ex 23:6,8; Lev 19:15; Deut 1:17; 10:17-18; 16:18-20; 17:8-13; 19:15-21).

14. Social Order
Every person's God-given place in the social order is to be honored (Ex 20:12; Deut 5:16; Ex 21:15,17; 22:28; Lev 19:3,32; 20:9; Deut 17:8-13; 21:15-21; 27:16).

15. Law
No one shall be above the law, not even the king (Deut 17:18-20).

16. Animals
Concern for the welfare of other creatures is to be extended to the animal world (Ex 23:5,11; Lev 25:7; Deut 22:4,6-7; 25:4).

and she shall become his wife because he
has violated her; he cannot divorce her all
his days.
30 "[1][a]A man shall not take his father's wife
so that he will not uncover his father's skirt.

Persons Excluded from the Assembly

23 "[a]No one who is [1]emasculated or has
his male organ cut off shall enter the
assembly of the LORD.
2 "No one of illegitimate birth shall enter
the assembly of the LORD; none of his *descendants,* even to the tenth generation, shall
enter the assembly of the LORD.
3 "[a]No Ammonite or Moabite shall enter
the assembly of the LORD; none of their
descendants, even to the tenth generation,
shall ever enter the assembly of the LORD,
4 [a]because they did not meet you with
[1]food and water on the way when you came
out of Egypt, and because they hired against
you [b]Balaam the son of Beor from Pethor of
[2]Mesopotamia, to curse you.
5 "Nevertheless, the LORD your God was
not willing to listen to Balaam, but the LORD
your God [a]turned the curse into a blessing for
you because the LORD your God [b]loves you.
6 "[a]You shall never seek their peace or
their prosperity all your days.
7 "You shall not detest an Edomite, for [a]he
is your brother; you shall not detest an Egyptian, [b]because you were an alien in his land.
8 "The sons of the third generation who
are born to them may enter the assembly of
the LORD.
9 "When you go out as [1]an army against
your enemies, you shall keep yourself from
every evil thing.
10 "[a]If there is among you any man who is
unclean because of a nocturnal emission,
then he must go outside the camp; he may
not [1]reenter the camp.
11 "But it shall be when evening approaches, he shall bathe himself with water, and at
sundown he may [1]reenter the camp.
12 "You shall also have a place outside the
camp and go out there,
13 and you shall have a [1]spade among
your tools, and it shall be when you sit down
outside, you shall dig with it and shall turn
[2]to cover up your excrement.
14 "Since [a]the LORD your God walks in the
midst of your camp to deliver you and to
[1]defeat your enemies before you, therefore
your camp must be [b]holy; and He must not
see [2]anything indecent among you [3]or He
will turn away from you.
15 "[a]You shall not hand over to his master
a slave who has [1]escaped from his master to
you.
16 "He shall live with you in your midst, in
the place which he shall choose in one of
your [1]towns where it pleases him; [a]you shall
not mistreat him.
17 "[a]None of the daughters of Israel shall
be a cult prostitute, [b]nor shall any of the
sons of Israel be a cult prostitute.
18 "You shall not bring the hire of a harlot
or the wages of a [1][a]dog into the house of the
LORD your God for any votive offering, for
both of these are an abomination to the LORD
your God.
19 "[a]You shall not charge interest to your
[1]countrymen: interest on money, food, *or*
anything that may be loaned at interest.
20 "[a]You may charge interest to a foreigner,
but to your [1]countrymen you shall not
charge interest, so that [b]the LORD your God
may bless you in all [2]that you undertake in
the land which you are about to enter to
[3]possess.
21 "[a]When you make a vow to the LORD
your God, you shall not delay to pay it, for it
would be sin in you, [1]and the LORD your God
will surely require it of you.
22 "However, if you refrain from vowing, it
would not be sin in you.
23 "You shall be careful to perform what
goes out from your lips, just as you have voluntarily vowed to the LORD your God, what
you have [1]promised.
24 "When you enter your neighbor's vineyard, then you may eat grapes [1]until you are
fully satisfied, but you shall not put any in
your [2]basket.

30 [1]Ch 23:1 in Heb [a]Lev 18:8; 20:11; Deut 27:20; 1 Cor 5:1
23:1 [1]Lit *wounded by crushing* of testicles [a]Lev 21:20; 22:24
3 [a]Neh 13:1, 2
4 [1]Lit *bread* [2]Heb *Aram-naharaim* [a]Neh 13:2 [b]Num 22:5; 23:7; Josh 24:9; 2 Pet 2:15; Jude 11
5 [a]Prov 26:2 [b]Deut 4:37
6 [a]Ezra 9:12
7 [a]Gen 25:24-26; Obad 10, 12 [b]Ex 22:21; 23:9; Lev 19:34; Deut 10:19
9 [1]Or *a camp*
10 [1]Lit *come to the midst of* [a]Lev 15:16
11 [1]Lit *come to the midst of*
13 [1]Lit *peg*
13 [2]Lit *and*
14 [1]Lit *give* [2]Lit *nakedness of anything* [3]Lit *and* [a]Lev 26:12 [b]Ex 3:5
15 [1]Lit *delivered himself* [a]1 Sam 30:15
16 [1]Lit *gates* [a]Ex 22:21; Prov 22:22
17 [a]Lev 19:29; Deut 22:21 [b]Gen 19:5; 2 Kin 23:7
18 [1]I.e. male prostitute, sodomite [a]Lev 18:22; 20:13
19 [1]Lit *brother* [a]Ex 22:25; Lev 25:35-37; Neh 5:2-7; Ps 15:5
20 [1]Lit *brother* [2]Lit *the putting forth of your hand* [3]Lit *possess it* [a]Deut 28:12 [b]Deut 15:10
21 [1]Lit *for* [a]Num 30:1, 2; Job 22:27; Ps 61:8; Eccl 5:4, 5; Matt 5:33
23 [1]Lit *spoken with your mouth*
24 [1]Lit *according to your satisfaction of your soul* [2]Or *vessel*

bride-price, which must have varied with the economic status of the participants (see note on Ex 22:16).
22:30 *his father's wife.* Refers to a wife other than his mother (see 27:20). *uncover his father's skirt.* Lit."uncover the corner of his father's garment" (see notes on Ruth 3:9; Ezek 16:8).
23:1 For blessings on eunuchs in later times see Is 56:4–5; Acts 8:26–39.
23:2–3 *even to the tenth generation.* Perhaps forever, since ten is symbolic of completeness or finality. In v. 6 the equivalent expression is "all your days" (lit. "all your days forever").
23:3 Ruth is an outstanding exception to Moabite exclusion from Israel (see Introduction to Ruth: Theme and Theology).
23:4 *Balaam the son of Beor.* See Num 22:4–24:25.
23:6 *never seek their peace or . . . prosperity.* See the prophets' denunciation of Moab, Ammon and Edom (Is 15–16; Jer 48:1–49:6; Ezek 25:1–11; Amos 1:13–2:3; Zeph 2:8–11).
23:7 *Edomite . . . your brother.* Edom (Esau) is often condemned for his hostility against his brother Jacob (Israel; see Amos 1:11; Obad 10; see also notes on Gen 25:22,26).
23:9–14 Sanitary rules for Israel's military camps. For similar rules for the people in general see Lev 15.
23:15 *a slave who has escaped . . . to you.* A foreign slave seeking freedom in Israel (see v. 16). Cf. 24:7.
23:17–18 See notes on Ex 34:15; Jdg 2:17.
23:18 *dog.* A word often associated with moral or spiritual impurity (cf. Matt 7:6; 15:26; Php 3:2). Here it probably refers to a male prostitute.
23:19 *interest.* See notes on Ex 22:25–27; Lev 25:36.
23:20 *charge . . . a foreigner.* A foreign businessman would come into Israel for financial advantage and so would be subject to paying interest.
23:21–23 See notes on Num 30; see also Eccl 5:4–6.

25 "[a]When you enter your neighbor's standing grain, then you may pluck the heads with your hand, but you shall not wield a sickle in your neighbor's standing grain.

Law of Divorce

24 "When a man takes a wife and marries her, and it happens [1]that she finds no favor in his eyes because he has found some [a]indecency in her, and [b]he writes her a certificate of divorce and puts *it* in her hand and sends her out from his house,

2 and she leaves his house and goes and becomes another man's *wife,*

3 and if the latter husband [1]turns against her and writes her a certificate of divorce and puts *it* in her hand and sends her out of his house, or if the latter husband dies who took her to be his wife,

4 *then* her [a]former husband who sent her away is not allowed to take her again to be his wife, since she has been defiled; for that is an abomination before the LORD, and you shall not bring sin on the land which the LORD your God gives you as an inheritance.

5 "[a]When a man takes a new wife, he shall not go out with the army nor be charged with any duty; he shall be free at home one year and shall [b]give happiness to his wife whom he has taken.

Sundry Laws

6 "No one shall take a handmill or an upper millstone in pledge, for he would be taking a life in pledge.

7 "[a]If a man is [1]caught kidnapping any of his [2]countrymen of the sons of Israel, and he deals with him violently or sells him, then that thief shall die; so you shall purge the evil from among you.

8 "[a]Be careful against [1]an infection of leprosy, that you diligently observe and do according to all that the Levitical priests teach you; as I have commanded them, so you shall be careful to do.

9 "Remember what the LORD your God did [a]to Miriam on the way as you came out of Egypt.

10 "[a]When you make your neighbor a loan of any sort, you shall not enter his house to take his pledge.

11 "You shall remain outside, and the man to whom you make the loan shall bring the pledge out to you.

25 [a]Matt 12:1; Mark 2:23; Luke 6:1
24:1 [1]Lit *if* [a]Num 5:12, 28; Deut 22:13-21 [b]Matt 5:31; 19:7-9; Mark 10:4, 5
3 [1]Lit *hates her*
4 [a]Jer 3:1
5 [a]Deut 20:7 [b]Prov 5:18
7 [1]Lit *found stealing* [2]Lit *brothers* [a]Ex 21:16
8 [1]Lit *a mark* or *stroke* [a]Lev 13:1-14, 57
9 [a]Num 12:10
10 [a]Ex 22:26, 27
13 [a]Ex 22:26 [b]Deut 6:25; Ps 106:31; Dan 4:27
14 [1]Lit *brothers* [2]Lit *gates* [a]Lev 19:13; 25:35-43; Deut 15:7-18; Prov 14:31; Amos 4:1; 1 Tim 5:18
15 [1]Lit *that the sun shall not go down on it* [2]Lit *soul* [a]Lev 19:13; Jer 22:13; James 5:4 [b]Ex 22:23; Deut 15:9; Job 35:9; James 5:4
16 [1]Or *with* [a]2 Kin 14:6; 2 Chr 25:4; Jer 31:29, 30; Ezek 18:20
17 [1]Lit *of* [2]Or *the fatherless* [a]Ex 23:9; Lev 19:33; Deut 1:17; 10:17; 16:19; 27:19 [b]Ex 22:22
19 [1]Or *fatherless* [a]Lev 19:9, 10; 23:22 [b]Deut 14:29 [c]Prov 19:17
20 [1]Lit *after yourself* [2]Or *fatherless* [a]Lev 19:10 [b]Deut 24:19
21 [1]Lit *glean it after yourself* [2]Or *fatherless*
25:1 [1]Lit *the judgment* [2]Lit *they judge them* [a]Deut 17:8-13; 19:17 [b]Deut 1:16, 17
2 [1]Lit *is a son of beating* [2]Or *wickedness* [a]Prov 19:29; Luke 12:48

12 "If he is a poor man, you shall not sleep with his pledge.

13 "[a]When the sun goes down you shall surely return the pledge to him, that he may sleep in his cloak and bless you; and [b]it will be righteousness for you before the LORD your God.

14 "[a]You shall not oppress a hired servant *who is* poor and needy, whether *he is* one of your [1]countrymen or one of your aliens who is in your land in your [2]towns.

15 "[a]You shall give him his wages on his day [1]before the sun sets, for he is poor and sets his [2]heart on it; so that [b]he will not cry against you to the LORD and it become sin in you.

16 "[a]Fathers shall not be put to death [1]for *their* sons, nor shall sons be put to death [1]for *their* fathers; everyone shall be put to death for his own sin.

17 "[a]You shall not pervert the justice [1]due an alien *or* [2]an orphan, nor [b]take a widow's garment in pledge.

18 "But you shall remember that you were a slave in Egypt, and that the LORD your God redeemed you from there; therefore I am commanding you to do this thing.

19 "[a]When you reap your harvest in your field and have forgotten a sheaf in the field, you shall not go back to get it; it shall be [b]for the alien, for the [1]orphan, and for the widow, in order that the LORD your God [c]may bless you in all the work of your hands.

20 "[a]When you beat your olive tree, you shall not go over the boughs [1]again; it shall be [b]for the alien, for the [2]orphan, and for the widow.

21 "When you gather the grapes of your vineyard, you shall not [1]go over it again; it shall be for the alien, for the [2]orphan, and for the widow.

22 "You shall remember that you were a slave in the land of Egypt; therefore I am commanding you to do this thing.

Sundry Laws

25 "[a]If there is a dispute between men and they go to [1]court, and [2]the judges decide their case, [b]and they justify the righteous and condemn the wicked,

2 then it shall be if the wicked man [1a]deserves to be beaten, the judge shall then make him lie down and be beaten in his presence with the number of stripes according to his [2]guilt.

24:1–4 In the books of Moses divorce was permitted and regulated (see Lev 21:7,14; 22:13; Num 30:9). Jesus conditioned the law of 24:1 in the Sermon on the Mount (Matt 5:31–32) and cited the higher law of creation (Matt 19:3–9).
24:5 *happiness.* Marital bliss was held in high regard.
24:6 *millstone.* Used for grinding grain for flour and daily food (see note on Judg 9:53).
24:7 *you shall purge the evil from among you.* See note on 13:5.
24:8 *leprosy.* See note on Lev 13:2.
24:9 *Remember.* See vv. 18, 22; see also note on 4:10.
24:10–13 See note on Ex 22:26–27.
24:16 *everyone shall be put to death for his own sin.* See Ezek 18:4 and note.
24:17–18 When the Israelites were in trouble, the Lord helped them. Therefore they were not to take advantage of others in difficulty.
24:19–21 See note on Lev 19:9–10.

3 “[a]He may beat him forty times *but* no more, so that he does not beat him with many more stripes than these and your brother is not [b]degraded in your eyes.

4 “[a]You shall not muzzle the ox while he is threshing.

5 “When brothers live together and one of them dies and has no son, the wife of the deceased shall not be *married* outside *the family* to a strange man. [a]Her husband’s brother shall go in to her and take her to himself as wife and perform the duty of a husband’s brother to her.

6 “It shall be that the firstborn whom she bears shall [1]assume the name of his dead brother, so that [a]his name will not be blotted out from Israel.

7 “[a]But if the man does not desire to take his brother’s wife, then his brother’s wife shall go up to the gate to the elders and say, ‘My husband’s brother refuses to establish a name for his brother in Israel; he is not willing to perform the duty of a husband’s brother to me.’

8 “Then the elders of his city shall summon him and speak to him. And *if* he persists and says, ‘I do not desire to take her,’

9 [a]then his brother’s wife shall come to him in the sight of the elders, and pull his sandal off his foot and [b]spit in his face; and she shall [1]declare, ‘Thus it is done to the man who does not build up his brother’s house.’

10 “In Israel his name shall be called, ‘The house of him whose sandal is removed.’

11 “If *two* men, a man and his [1]countryman, are struggling together, and the wife of one comes near to deliver her husband from the hand of the one who is striking him, and puts out her hand and seizes his genitals,

12 then you shall cut off her [1]hand; [2a]you shall not show pity.

13 “[a]You shall not have in your bag [1]differing weights, a large and a small.

14 “You shall not have in your house [1]differing measures, a large and a small.

15 “You shall have a full and just weight; you shall have a full and just [1]measure, [a]that your days may be prolonged in the [2]land which the LORD your God gives you.

3 [a]2 Cor 11:24 [b]Job 18:3
4 [a]Prov 12:10; 1 Cor 9:9; 1 Tim 5:18
5 [a]Matt 22:24; Mark 12:19; Luke 20:28
6 [1]Lit *stand on* [a]Ruth 4:5, 10
7 [a]Ruth 4:5, 6
9 [1]Lit *answer and say* [a]Ruth 4:7, 8 [b]Num 12:14
11 [1]Lit *brother*
12 [1]Lit *palm* [2]Lit *your eye* [a]Deut 7:2; 19:13
13 [1]Lit *a stone and a stone* [a]Lev 19:35-37; Prov 11:1; 20:23; Ezek 45:10; Mic 6:11
14 [1]Lit *an ephah and an ephah*
15 [1]Lit *ephah* [2]Lit *ground* [a]Ex 20:12
16 [a]Prov 11:1
17 [a]Ex 17:8-16
18 [1]Or *reverence* [a]Ps 36:1; Rom 3:18
19 [1]Lit *possess it* [a]Deut 12:9
26:2 [a]Ex 22:29; 23:16, 19; Num 18:13; Prov 3:9 [b]Deut 12:5
3 [1]So with Gr; Heb *your*
5 [1]Or *perishing* [2]Or *lived as an alien* [a]Gen 43:1-14 [b]Gen 46:27 [c]Deut 1:10; 10:22
6 [a]Ex 1:8-11
7 [a]Ex 2:23-25; 3:9

16 “For [a]everyone who does these things, everyone who acts unjustly is an abomination to the LORD your God.

17 “[a]Remember what Amalek did to you along the way when you came out from Egypt,

18 how he met you along the way and attacked among you all the stragglers at your rear when you were faint and weary; and he [a]did not [1]fear God.

19 “Therefore it shall come about when the LORD your God has given you [a]rest from all your surrounding enemies, in the land which the LORD your God gives you as an inheritance to [1]possess, you shall blot out the memory of Amalek from under heaven; you must not forget.

Offering First Fruits

26 “Then it shall be, when you enter the land which the LORD your God gives you as an inheritance, and you possess it and live in it,

2 that you shall take some of [a]the first of all the produce of the ground which you bring in from your land that the LORD your God gives you, and you shall put *it* in a basket and [b]go to the place where the LORD your God chooses to establish His name.

3 “You shall go to the priest who is in office at that time and say to him, ‘I declare this day to the LORD [1]my God that I have entered the land which the LORD swore to our fathers to give us.’

4 “Then the priest shall take the basket from your hand and set it down before the altar of the LORD your God.

5 “You shall answer and say before the LORD your God, ‘[a]My father was a [1]wandering Aramean, and he went down to Egypt and [2]sojourned there, [b]few in number; but there he became a [c]great, mighty and populous nation.

6 ‘And the [a]Egyptians treated us harshly and afflicted us, and imposed hard labor on us.

7 ‘Then [a]we cried to the LORD, the God of our fathers, and the LORD heard our voice and saw our affliction and our toil and our oppression;

25:3 *forty times but no more.* Beating could subject the culprit to abuse, so the law kept the punishment from becoming inhumane. Cf. Paul’s experience (2 Cor 11:24).

25:4 Applied to ministers of Christ in 1 Cor 9:9–10; 1 Tim 5:17–18. *threshing.* See notes on Gen 50:10; Ruth 1:22.

25:5–6 The continuity of each family and the decentralized control of land through family ownership were basic to the Mosaic economy (see note on Gen 38:8).

25:7 *if the man does not desire to take his brother’s wife.* See vv. 8–10; note the experiences, with some variations, described in Gen 38:8–10; Ruth 4:1–12. *to the gate to the elders.* See 22:15; see also notes on Gen 19:1; Ru 4:1.

25:11–12 Cf. Ex 21:22–25.

25:13–16 See note on Lev 19:35.

25:14 *measures.* Of quantity.

25:17 *Remember.* See note on 4:10. *Amalek.* See Ex 17:8–16; Num 14:45.

25:18 *fear God.* See note on Gen 20:11.

25:19 *rest.* See note on 3:20.

26:1 *inheritance.* See note on Ex 32:13.

26:2 *first of all the produce.* The offering described here occurred only once and must not be confused with the annual offerings of first fruits (see 18:4 and note). *the place where the LORD . . . chooses to establish His Name.* See note on 12:5.

26:5 *wandering Aramean.* A reference to Jacob, who had wandered from southern Canaan to Haran and back (Gen 27–35) and who later migrated to Egypt (see Gen 46:3–7). He also married two Aramean women (see Gen 28:5; 29:16,28). *few in number . . . became a great . . . nation.* See Ex 1:5; 1:7 and note.

8 [a]and the LORD brought us out of Egypt with a mighty hand and an outstretched arm and with great terror and with signs and wonders;
9 and He has brought us to this place and has given us this land, [a]a land flowing with milk and honey.
10 'Now behold, I have brought the first of the produce of the ground [a]which You, O LORD have given me.' And you shall set it down before the LORD your God, and worship before the LORD your God;
11 and you and [a]the Levite and the alien who is among you shall [b]rejoice in all the good which the LORD your God has given you and your household.
12 "[a]When you have finished [1]paying all the tithe of your increase in the third year, the year of tithing, then you shall give it to the Levite, to the stranger, to the [2]orphan and to the widow, that they may eat in your [3]towns and be satisfied.
13 "You shall say before the LORD your God, 'I have removed the sacred *portion* from *my* house, and also have given it to the Levite and the alien, the [1]orphan and the widow, according to all Your commandments which You have commanded me; [a]I have not transgressed or forgotten any of Your commandments.
14 'I have not eaten of it [1]while mourning, nor have I removed any of it while I was unclean, nor offered any of it to the dead. I have listened to the voice of the LORD my God; I have done according to all that You have commanded me.
15 '[a]Look down from Your holy habitation, from heaven, and bless Your people Israel, and the ground which You have given us, [b]a land flowing with milk and honey, as You swore to our fathers.'
16 "This day the LORD your God commands you to do these statutes and ordinances. You shall therefore be careful to do them [a]with all your heart and with all your soul.
17 "[a]You have today declared the LORD to be your God, and [1]that you would walk in His ways and keep His statutes, His commandments and His ordinances, and listen to His voice.
18 "The LORD has today declared you to be [a]His people, a treasured possession, as He promised you, and [1]that you should keep all His commandments;
19 and [1]that He will [a]set you high above all nations which He has made, for praise, fame, and honor; and that you shall be [b]a consecrated people to the LORD your God, as He has spoken."

The Curses of Mount Ebal

27 Then Moses and the elders of Israel charged the people, saying, "Keep all the commandments which I command you today.
2 "[a]So it shall be on the day when you cross the Jordan to the land which the LORD your God gives you, that you shall set up for yourself large stones and coat them with lime
3 and write on them all the words of this law, when you cross over, so that you may enter the land which the LORD your God gives you, [a]a land flowing with milk and honey, as the LORD, the God of your fathers, [1]promised you.
4 "So it shall be when you cross the Jordan, you shall set up [a]on Mount Ebal, these stones, [1]as I am commanding you today, and you shall coat them with lime.
5 "Moreover, you shall build there an altar to the LORD your God, an altar of stones; you [a]shall not [1]wield an iron *tool* on them.
6 "You shall build the altar of the LORD your God of [1]uncut stones, and you shall offer on it burnt offerings to the LORD your God;
7 and you shall sacrifice peace offerings and eat there, and [a]rejoice before the LORD your God.
8 "You shall write on the [1]stones all the words of this law very distinctly."
9 Then Moses and the Levitical priests spoke to all Israel, saying, "Be silent and listen, O Israel! This day you have become a people for the LORD your God.
10 "You shall therefore [1]obey the LORD your God, and do His commandments and His statutes which I command you today."
11 Moses also charged the people on that day, saying,
12 "When you cross the Jordan, these shall stand on [a]Mount Gerizim to bless the people: [b]Simeon, Levi, Judah, Issachar, Joseph, and Benjamin.

8 [a]Deut 4:34; 34:11, 12
9 [a]Ex 3:8, 17
10 [a]Deut 8:18; Prov 10:22
11 [a]Deut 12:12 [b]Deut 12:7; 16:11; Eccl 3:12, 13; 5:18-20
12 [1]Lit *tithing* [2]Or *fatherless* [3]Lit *gates* [a]Lev 27:30; Num 18:24; Deut 14:28, 29; Heb 7:5, 9, 10
13 [1]Or *fatherless* [a]Ps 119:141, 153, 176
14 [1]Lit *while in my*
15 [a]Ps 80:14; Is 63:15; Zech 2:13 [b]Deut 26:9
16 [a]Deut 4:29
17 [1]Lit *to walk in* [a]Ps 48:14
18 [a]Ex 6:7; 19:5; Deut 4:20; 7:6; 14:2; 28:9; 29:13; Titus 2:14; 1 Pet 2:9
18 [1]Lit *to keep all*
19 [1]Lit *to set you* [a]Deut 4:7, 8; 28:1, 13 [b]Ex 19:6; Deut 7:6; Is 62:12; Jer 2:3; 1 Pet 2:9
27:2 [a]Josh 8:30-32
3 [1]Lit *spoke to* [a]Deut 26:9
4 [1]Lit *which* [a]Deut 11:29; Josh 8:30
5 [1]Lit *lift up* [a]Ex 20:25; Josh 8:31
6 [1]Lit *whole*
7 [a]Deut 26:11
8 [1]I.e. stones coated with lime, cf v 4
10 [1]Lit *listen to the voice of*
12 [a]Deut 11:29 [b]Josh 8:33-35

26:11 *rejoice.* See note on 12:12.
26:12 See note on 14:22–29.
26:16 *with all your heart . . . soul.* See note on 4:29.
26:17 The terminology is that of a covenant or treaty, involving a renewal of Israel's vow that the Lord was God and that they would obey Him (see note on Ex 19:8).
26:18 *treasured possession.* See note on Ex 19:5.
27:2–8 Setting up stones inscribed with messages to be remembered was a common practice in the ancient Near East.
27:2,4 *coat them with lime.* So that the writing inscribed on them would stand out clearly (see v. 8).
27:3,8 *all the words of this law.* The stipulations (see note on Ex 20:1) of the covenant that Moses' reaffirmation contained.
27:5 *build . . . an altar of stones.* Different from the altars of the tabernacle, both in form and in use (see note on Ex 20:25).
27:9 *you have become a people for the LORD.* The language of covenant renewal.
27:12 *these shall stand on Mount Gerizim.* All six were descendants of Jacob by Leah and Rachel (see Gen 35:23–24). See 11:30 and note. *to bless.* No blessings appear in vv. 15–26, which consist entirely of 12 curses (see 28:15–68). Blessings, however, are listed and described in 28:1–14.

13 "For the curse, these shall stand on Mount Ebal: Reuben, Gad, Asher, Zebulun, Dan, and Naphtali.

14 "The Levites shall then answer and say to all the men of Israel with a loud voice,

15 'Cursed is the man who makes [1a]an idol or a molten image, an abomination to the LORD, the work of the hands of the craftsman, and sets *it* up in secret.' And [b]all the people shall answer and say, 'Amen.'

16 '[a]Cursed is he who dishonors his father or mother.' And all the people shall say, 'Amen.'

17 '[a]Cursed is he who moves his neighbor's boundary mark.' And all the people shall say, 'Amen.'

18 '[a]Cursed is he who misleads a blind *person* on the road.' And all the people shall say, 'Amen.'

19 '[a]Cursed is he who distorts the justice due an alien, [1]orphan, and widow.' And all the people shall say, 'Amen.'

20 '[a]Cursed is he who lies with his father's wife, because he has uncovered his father's skirt.' And all the people shall say, 'Amen.'

21 '[a]Cursed is he who lies with any animal.' And all the people shall say, 'Amen.'

22 '[a]Cursed is he who lies with his sister, the daughter of his father or of his mother.' And all the people shall say, 'Amen.'

23 '[a]Cursed is he who lies with his mother-in-law.' And all the people shall say, 'Amen.'

24 '[a]Cursed is he who strikes his neighbor in secret.' And all the people shall say, 'Amen.'

25 '[a]Cursed is he who accepts a bribe to strike down an innocent person.' And all the people shall say, 'Amen.'

26 '[a]Cursed is he who does not confirm the words of this law by doing them.' And all the people shall say, 'Amen.'

Blessings at Gerizim

28 "[a]Now it shall be, if you diligently [1]obey the LORD your God, being careful to do all His commandments which I command you today, the LORD your God [b]will set you high above all the nations of the earth.

2 "All these blessings will come upon you and [a]overtake you if you [1]obey the LORD your God:

3 "Blessed *shall* you *be* in the city, and blessed *shall* you *be* [a]in the [1]country.

4 "Blessed *shall be* the [1]offspring of your [2]body and the [1]produce of your ground and the [1]offspring of your beasts, the increase of your herd and the young of your flock.

5 "Blessed *shall be* your basket and your kneading bowl.

6 "Blessed *shall* you *be* [a]when you come in, and blessed *shall* you *be* when you go out.

7 "The LORD shall cause your enemies who rise up against you to be [1]defeated before you; they will come out against you one way and will flee before you seven ways.

8 "The LORD will command the blessing upon you in your barns and in [a]all that you put your hand to, and He will bless you in the land which the LORD your God gives you.

9 "[a]The LORD will establish you as a holy people to Himself, as He swore to you, if you keep the commandments of the LORD your God and walk in His ways.

10 "So all the peoples of the earth will see that [1a]you are called by the name of the LORD, and they will be afraid of you.

11 "[a]The LORD will make you abound in prosperity, in the [1]offspring of your [2]body and in the [1]offspring of your beast and in the [1]produce of your ground, in the land which the LORD swore to your fathers to give you.

12 "The LORD will open for you His good storehouse, the heavens, to give rain to your land in its season and to bless all the work of your hand; and [a]you shall lend to many nations, but you shall not borrow.

13 "[a]The LORD will make you the head and not the tail, and you only will be above, and you will not be underneath, if you listen to the commandments of the LORD your God, which I charge you today, to [1]observe *them* carefully,

14 and [a]do not turn aside from any of the words which I command you today, to the right or to the left, to go after other gods to serve them.

15 [1]Or *a graven image* [a]Ex 20:4, 23; 34:17; Lev 19:4; 26:1; Deut 4:16, 23; 5:8; Is 44:9 [b]1 Cor 14:16
16 [a]Ex 20:12; 21:17; Lev 19:3; 20:9; Deut 5:16; Ezek 22:7
17 [a]Deut 19:14; Prov 22:28
18 [a]Lev 19:14
19 [1]Or *fatherless* [a]Ex 22:21; 23:9; Lev 19:33; Deut 10:18; 24:17
20 [a]Lev 18:8; 20:11; Deut 22:30; 1 Cor 5:1
21 [a]Ex 22:19; Lev 18:23; 20:15
22 [a]Lev 18:9; 20:17
23 [a]Lev 20:14
24 [a]Ex 21:12; Lev 24:17; Num 35:30, 31
25 [a]Ex 23:7; Deut 10:17; Ps 15:5; Ezek 22:12
26 [a]Ps 119:21; Jer 11:3; Gal 3:10
28:1 [1]Lit *listen to the voice of* [a]Ex 15:26; 23:22-27; Lev 26:3-13; Deut 7:12-26; 11:13 [b]Deut 28:13; 26:19; 1 Chr 14:2
2 [1]Lit *listen to the voice of* [a]Zech 1:6
3 [1]Or *field* [a]Gen 39:5
4 [1]Lit *fruit* [2]Lit *womb*
6 [a]Ps 121:8
7 [1]Lit *smitten*
8 [a]Deut 15:10
9 [a]Ex 19:5
10 [1]Lit *the name of the LORD is called upon you* [a]2 Chr 7:14
11 [1]Lit *fruit* [2]Or *womb* [a]Deut 28:4; Prov 10:22
12 [a]Deut 23:20
13 [1]Lit *keep and do* [a]Deut 28:1, 44
14 [a]Deut 5:32; Josh 1:7

27:13 *these shall stand on Mount Ebal.* Reuben and Zebulun were descendants of Jacob by Leah; the rest were his descendants by the maidservants Zilpah and Bilhah (see Gen 35:23,25–26).

27:15 *makes an idol . . . molten image.* In violation of the first and second commandments of the Decalogue (see note on Ex 20:1). See 4:28; 5:6–10; 31:29; Is 40:19–20; 41:7; 44:9–20; 45:16; Jer 10:3–9; Hos 8:4–6; 13:2. *Amen.* Not simply approval but a solemn, formal assertion that the people accept and agree to the covenant and its curses and blessings (see vv. 16–26).

27:16 See 5:16; Ex 20:12 and note.

27:17 See note on 19:14.

27:19 See 24:17–18 and note.

27:20 Cf. 22:30; see Lev 18:8.

27:21 See Ex 22:19 and note; Lev 18:23; 20:15–16.

27:22 See Lev 18:9.

27:23 See Lev 18:8.

27:24–25 See 5:17; Ex 20:13; 21:12; Lev 24:17,21.

27:26 Quoted in Gal 3:10 to prove that mankind is under a curse because no one follows the law of God fully. *by doing them.* It is not enough to assert allegiance to the law; one must live according to its stipulations.

28:1–14 These blessings are the opposites of the curses in vv. 15–44 (compare especially vv. 3–6 with vv. 16–19).

28:5,17 *basket . . . kneading bowl.* Used at home for storage and for the preparation of foods, particularly bread.

28:7 For the reverse see v. 25.

28:12 *storehouse, the heavens.* For the heavens as the storehouse of rain, snow, hail and wind see Job 38:22; Ps 135:7; Jer 10:13; 51:16. *you shall lend.* For the opposite see v. 44; see also note on 15:6.

28:13 *the head and not the tail.* For the reverse see v. 44.

Consequences of Disobedience

15 "[a]But it shall come about, if you do not [1]obey the LORD your God, to observe to do all His commandments and His statutes with which I charge you today, that all these curses will come upon you and overtake you:

16 "[a]Cursed *shall* you *be* in the city, and cursed *shall* you *be* in the [1]country.

17 "[a]Cursed *shall be* your basket and your kneading bowl.

18 "[a]Cursed *shall be* the [1]offspring of your [2]body and the [1]produce of your ground, the increase of your herd and the young of your flock.

19 "[a]Cursed *shall* you *be* when you come in, and cursed *shall* you *be* when you go out.

20 "[a]The LORD will send upon you curses, confusion, and [b]rebuke, in all [1]you undertake to do, until you are destroyed and until [c]you perish quickly, on account of the evil of your deeds, because you have forsaken Me.

21 "[a]The LORD will make the pestilence cling to you until He has consumed you from the land where you are entering to possess it.

22 "[a]The LORD will smite you with consumption and with fever and with inflammation and with fiery heat and with [1]the sword and [b]with blight and with mildew, and they will pursue you until [c]you perish.

23 "[1]The heaven which is over your head shall be bronze, and the earth which is under you, iron.

24 "[a]The LORD will make the rain of your land powder and dust; from heaven it shall come down on you until you are destroyed.

25 "[a]The LORD shall cause you to be [1]defeated before your enemies; you will go out one way against them, but you will flee seven ways before them, and you will [b]be *an example of* terror to all the kingdoms of the earth.

26 "[a]Your carcasses will be food to all birds of the sky and to the beasts of the earth, and there will be no one to frighten *them* away.

27 "[a]The LORD will smite you with the boils of Egypt and with [b]tumors and with the scab and with the itch, from which you cannot be healed.

28 "The LORD will smite you with madness and with blindness and with bewilderment of heart;

29 and you will [1a]grope at noon, as the blind man gropes in darkness, and you will not prosper in your ways; but you shall only be oppressed and robbed continually, with none to save you.

30 "[a]You shall betroth a wife, but another man will violate her; [b]you shall build a house, but you will not live in it; you shall plant a vineyard, but you will not [1]use its fruit.

31 "Your ox shall be slaughtered before your eyes, but you will not eat of it; your donkey shall be torn away from you, and will not be restored to you; your sheep shall be given to your enemies, and you will have none to save you.

32 "[a]Your sons and your daughters shall be given to another people, while your eyes look on and yearn for them continually; but there will be nothing [1]you can do.

33 "[a]A people whom you do not know shall eat up the produce of your ground and all your labors, and you will never be anything but oppressed and crushed continually.

34 "You shall be driven mad by the sight of [1]what you see.

35 "[a]The LORD will strike you on the knees and legs with sore boils, from which you cannot be healed, from the sole of your foot to the crown of your head.

36 "[a]The LORD will bring you and your king, whom you set over you, to a nation which neither you nor your fathers have known, and there you shall serve other gods, [b]wood and stone.

37 "[a]You shall become a horror, a proverb, and a taunt among all the people where the LORD drives you.

38 "[a]You shall bring out much seed to the field but you will gather in little, for [b]the locust will consume it.

39 "[a]You shall plant and cultivate vineyards, but you will neither drink of the wine nor gather *the grapes,* for the worm will devour them.

40 "[a]You shall have olive trees throughout your territory but you will not anoint yourself with the oil, for your olives will drop off.

41 "[a]You shall [1]have sons and daughters but they will not be yours, for they will go into captivity.

42 "[a]The cricket shall possess all your trees and the produce of your ground.

43 "[a]The alien who is among you shall rise above you higher and higher, but you will go down lower and lower.

44 "[a]He shall lend to you, but you will not lend to him; [b]he shall be the head, and you will be the tail.

45 "So all these curses shall come on you and pursue you and overtake you [a]until you are destroyed, because you would not [1]obey the LORD your God by keeping His commandments and His statutes which He commanded you.

46 "They shall become [a]a sign and a wonder on you and your [1]descendants forever.

47 "[a]Because you did not serve the LORD your God with joy and a glad heart, for the abundance of all things;

15 [1]Lit *listen to the voice of* [a]Lev 26:14-43; Josh 23:15; Dan 9:11
16 [1]Or *field* [a]Deut 28:3
17 [a]Deut 28:5
18 [1]Lit *fruit* [2]Or *womb* [a]Deut 28:4
19 [a]Deut 28:6
20 [1]Lit *the putting forth of your hand which you do* [a]Deut 28:8; Mal 2:2 [b]Ps 80:16; Is 51:20; 66:15 [c]Deut 4:26
21 [a]Lev 26:25; Num 14:12; Jer 24:10; Amos 4:10
22 [1]Another reading is *drought* [a]Lev 26:16 [b]Amos 4:9 [c]Deut 4:26
23 [1]Lit *Your*
24 [a]Deut 11:17; 28:12
25 [1]Lit *smitten* [a]Deut 28:7; Is 30:17 [b]2 Chr 29:8; Jer 15:4; 24:9; Ezek 23:46
26 [a]Jer 7:33; 16:4; 19:7; 34:20
27 [a]Ex 9:9; Deut 7:15; 28:60, 61 [b]1 Sam 5:6
29 [1]Lit *be groping* [a]Ex 10:21
30 [1]Lit *begin it* [a]Job 31:10; Jer 8:10 [b]Amos 5:11
32 [1]Lit *in the power of your hand* [a]Deut 28:41
33 [a]Jer 5:15, 17
34 [1]Lit *your eyes which you*
35 [a]Deut 28:27
36 [a]2 Kin 17:4, 6; 24:12, 14; 25:7, 11; 2 Chr 36:1-21; Jer 39:1-9 [b]Deut 4:28; Jer 16:13
37 [a]1 Kin 9:7, 8; Jer 19:8; 24:9; 25:9; 29:18
38 [a]Is 5:10; Mic 6:15; Hag 1:6 [b]Ex 10:4; Joel 1:4
39 [a]Is 5:10; 17:10, 11
40 [a]Jer 11:16; Mic 6:15
41 [1]Lit *beget* [a]Deut 28:32
42 [a]Deut 28:38
43 [a]Deut 28:13
44 [a]Deut 28:12 [b]Deut 28:13
45 [1]Lit *listen to the voice of* [a]Deut 4:25, 26
46 [1]Lit *seed* [a]Num 26:10; Is 8:18; Ezek 5:15; 14:8
47 [a]Deut 12:7; Neh 9:35-37

28:23 *heaven . . . bronze . . . earth . . . iron.* No rain would pierce the sky or penetrate the ground (see v. 22).
28:25 For the reverse see v. 7.
28:27 *boils of Egypt.* See note on Ex 9:9.
28:30 See 20:5–7.
28:35 See note on Ex 9:11.
28:44 See notes on vv. 12–13.

48 therefore you shall serve your enemies
whom the LORD will send against you, [a]in
hunger, in thirst, in nakedness, and in the lack
of all things; and He [b]will put an iron yoke on
your neck until He has destroyed you.
49 "[a]The LORD will bring a nation against
you from afar, from the end of the earth, [b]as
the eagle swoops down, a nation whose language you shall not understand,
50 a nation of fierce countenance who will
[a]have no respect for the old, nor show favor
to the young.
51 "Moreover, it shall eat the [1]offspring of
your herd and the produce of your ground
until you are destroyed, who also leaves you
no grain, new wine, or oil, nor the increase
of your herd or the young of your flock until
they have caused you to perish.
52 "[a]It shall besiege you in all your [1]towns
until your high and fortified walls in which
you trusted come down throughout your
land, and it shall besiege you in all your
[1]towns throughout your land which the LORD
your God has given you.
53 "[a]Then you shall eat the [1]offspring of
your own body, the flesh of your sons and of
your daughters whom the LORD your God has
given you, during the siege and the distress
by which your enemy will [2]oppress you.
54 "The man who is [1]refined and very delicate among you [2]shall be hostile toward his
brother and toward the wife [3]he cherishes
and toward the rest of his children who
remain,
55 so that he will not give *even* one of
them any of the flesh of his children which
he will eat, since he has nothing *else* left,
during the siege and the distress by which
your enemy will [1]oppress you in all your
[2]towns.
56 "[a]The [1]refined and delicate woman
among you, who would not venture to set
the sole of her foot on the ground for deli-
cateness and [2]refinement, [3]shall be hostile
toward the husband [4]she cherishes and
toward her son and daughter,
57 and toward her afterbirth which issues
from between her [1]legs and toward her children whom she bears; for [a]she will eat them
secretly for lack of anything *else,* during the
siege and the distress by which your enemy
will [2]oppress you in your [3]towns.
58 "If you are not careful to observe all the
words of this law which are written in this
book, to [1a]fear this honored and awesome
[b]name, [2]the LORD your God,
59 then the LORD will bring extraordinary
plagues on you and [1]your descendants, even
[2]severe and lasting plagues, and miserable
and chronic sicknesses.
60 "[a]He will bring back on you all the diseases of Egypt of which you were afraid, and
they will cling to you.
61 "Also every sickness and every plague
which, not written in the book of this law,
the LORD will bring on you [a]until you are
destroyed.
62 "Then you shall be left few in number,
[a]whereas you were as numerous as the stars
of heaven, because you did not [1]obey the
LORD your God.
63 "It shall come about that as the LORD
[a]delighted over you to prosper you, and multiply you, so the LORD will [b]delight over you
to make you perish and destroy you; and you
will be [c]torn from the land where you are
entering to possess it.
64 "Moreover, the LORD will [a]scatter you
among all peoples, from one end of the earth
to the other end of the earth; and there you
shall [b]serve other gods, wood and stone,
which you or your fathers have not known.
65 "[a]Among those nations you shall find
no rest, and there will be no resting place for
the sole of your foot; but there [b]the LORD will
give you a trembling heart, failing of eyes,
and despair of soul.
66 "So your life shall [1]hang in doubt before
you; and you will be in dread night and day,
and shall have no assurance of your life.
67 "[a]In the morning you shall say, 'Would
that it were evening!' And at evening you
shall say, 'Would that it were morning!'
because of the dread of your heart which you
dread, and for the sight of your eyes which
you will see.

48 [a]Lam 4:4-6 [b]Jer 28:13, 14
49 [a]Is 5:26-30; 7:18-20; Jer 5:15; 6:22, 23 [b]Jer 48:40; 49:22; Lam 4:19; Hos 8:1
50 [a]Is 47:6
51 [1]Lit *fruit*
52 [1]Lit *gates* [a]Jer 10:17, 18; Zeph 1:15, 16
53 [1]Lit *fruit* [2]Or *distress* [a]Lev 26:29; 2 Kin 6:28, 29; Jer 19:9; Lam 2:20; 4:10
54 [1]Lit *tender* [2]Lit *his eye shall be evil toward* [3]Lit *of his bosom*
55 [1]Or *distress* [2]Lit *gates*
56 [1]Lit *tender* [2]Lit *tenderness* [3]Lit *her eye shall be evil toward* [4]Lit *of her bosom* [a]Lam 4:10
57 [1]Lit *feet*
57 [2]Or *distress* [3]Lit *gates* [a]2 Kin 6:28, 29; Lam 4:10
58 [1]Or *reverence* [2]Heb *YHWH* [a]Ps 99:3; Mal 1:14 [b]Is 42:8
59 [1]Lit *plague on your seed* [2]Lit *great*
60 [a]Deut 28:27
61 [a]Deut 4:25, 26
62 [1]Lit *listen to the voice of* [a]Deut 1:10; Neh 9:23
63 [a]Jer 32:41 [b]Prov 1:26 [c]Jer 12:14; 45:4
64 [a]Lev 26:33; Deut 4:27; Neh 1:8 [b]Deut 4:28; 29:26; 32:17
65 [a]Lam 1:3 [b]Lev 26:36
66 [1]Lit *be hung for you in front*
67 [a]Job 7:4

28:49 *end of the earth.* An indefinite figurative expression meaning "far away"—anywhere from the horizon to the perimeter of the then-known world. *eagle swoops down.* Symbolic of the speed and power of the Assyrians (see Hos 8:1) and Babylonians (see Jer 48:40; 49:22). *whose language you shall not understand.* Though related to Hebrew, the languages of Assyria and Babylonia were not understood by the average Israelite (see Is 28:11; 33:19 and note; 1 Cor 14:21).

28:53 *you shall eat . . . sons and . . . daughters.* For the actualizing of this curse see 2 Kin 6:24–29; Lam 2:20; 4:10. *the distress by which your enemy will oppress you.* See vv. 55, 57. The repetition of the clause emphasizes the distress that the Israelites would suffer if they refused to obey the Lord.

28:58 *words of this law.* See note on 31:24. *this honored and awesome name, the LORD.* See note on Ex 3:15. One of the oddities of history and revelation is the loss of the proper pronunciation of the Hebrew word *YHWH,* the most intimate and personal name of God in the OT (see note on Gen 2:4). "Jehovah" is a spelling that developed from combining the consonants of the name with the vowels of a word for "Lord" (*Adonai*). "Yahweh" is probably the original pronunciation. The name eventually ceased to be pronounced because later Jews thought it too holy to be uttered and feared violating Ex 20:7 and Lev 24:16. It is translated "LORD" in this version (see Preface to the NASB).

28:60 *diseases of Egypt.* Those brought on the Egyptians during the plagues (see 7:15; Ex 15:26).

28:61 *book of this law.* See note on 31:24.

28:62 *as the stars of heaven.* See 1:10; see also notes on Gen 13:16; 15:5.

28:64 *will scatter you.* Experienced by Israel in the Assyrian (722–721 B.C.) and Babylonian (586 B.C.) exiles (see 2 Kin 17:6; 25:21).

68 "The LORD will bring you back to Egypt
in ships, by the way about which I spoke to
you, 'You will never see it again!' And there
you will offer yourselves for sale to your enemies as male and female slaves, but there
will be no buyer."

The Covenant in Moab

29 [1a]These are the words of the covenant
which the LORD commanded Moses to
make with the sons of Israel in the land of
Moab, besides the [b]covenant which He had
made with them at Horeb.
2 [1]And Moses summoned all Israel and
said to them, "You have seen all that the
LORD did before your eyes in the land of
Egypt to Pharaoh and all his servants and all
his land;
3 [a]the great trials which your eyes have
seen, those great signs and wonders.
4 "Yet to this day [a]the LORD has not given
you a heart to know, nor eyes to see, nor ears
to hear.
5 "I have led you forty years in the wilderness; [a]your clothes have not worn out on
you, and your sandal has not worn out on
your foot.
6 "[a]You have not eaten bread, nor have
you drunk wine or strong drink, in order that
you might know that I am the LORD your God.
7 "[a]When you [1]reached this place, Sihon
the king of Heshbon and Og the king of
Bashan came out to meet us for battle, but
we [2]defeated them;
8 and we took their land and [a]gave it as
an inheritance to the Reubenites, the Gadites, and the half-tribe of the Manassites.
9 "[a]So keep the words of this covenant to
do them, [b]that you may prosper in all that
you do.
10 "You stand today, all of you, before the
LORD your God: your chiefs, your tribes, your
elders and your officers, *even* all the men of
Israel,
11 your little ones, your wives, and the
alien who is within your camps, from [a]the
one who chops your wood to the one who
draws your water,
12 that you may enter into the covenant
with the LORD your God, and into His oath
which the LORD your God is making with you
today,
13 in order that He may establish you
today as His people and that [a]He may be your
God, just as He spoke to you and as He swore
to your fathers, to Abraham, Isaac, and Jacob.
14 "Now not with you alone am I [a]making
this covenant and this oath,
15 [a]but both with those who stand here
with us today in the presence of the LORD our
God and with those who are not with us here
today
16 (for you know how we lived in the land
of Egypt, and how we came through the
midst of the nations through which you
passed;
17 moreover, you have seen their abominations and their idols *of* [a]wood, stone, silver, and gold, which *they had* with them);
18 [a]so that there will not be among you a
man or woman, or family or tribe, whose
heart turns away today from the LORD our
God, to go and serve the gods of those
nations; that there will not be among you [b]a
root bearing poisonous fruit and wormwood.
19 "It shall be when he hears the words of
this curse, that he will [1]boast, saying, 'I have
peace though I walk in the stubbornness of
my heart in order [2]to destroy the watered
land with the dry.'
20 "The LORD shall never be willing to forgive him, but rather the anger of the LORD
and [a]His jealousy will [1b]burn against that
man, and every curse which is written in this
book will [2]rest on him, and the LORD will
[c]blot out his name from under heaven.
21 "Then the LORD will single him out for
[1]adversity from all the tribes of Israel,
according to all the curses of the covenant
[a]which are written in this book of the law.
22 "Now the generation to come, your sons
who rise up after you and [a]the foreigner who
comes from a distant land, when they see
the plagues of the land and the diseases with
which the LORD has [1]afflicted it, will say,
23 'All its land is [a]brimstone and salt, [b]a
burning waste, [1]unsown and unproductive,
and no grass grows in it, like the overthrow
of [c]Sodom and Gomorrah, Admah and
Zeboiim, which the LORD overthrew in His
anger and in His wrath.'
24 "All the nations will say, '[a]Why has the
LORD done thus to this land? Why this great
[1]outburst of anger?'

29:1 [1]Ch 28:69 in Heb [a]Lev 26:46; 27:34 [b]Deut 5:2, 3
2 [1]Ch 29:1 in Heb
3 [a]Deut 4:34; 7:19
4 [a]Is 6:9, 10; Ezek 12:2; Matt 13:14; Acts 28:26, 27; Rom 11:8
5 [a]Deut 8:4
6 [a]Deut 8:3
7 [1]Lit *came to* [2]Lit *smote* [a]Num 21:21-24, 33, 35; Deut 2:26-3:17
8 [a]Num 32:32, 33; Deut 3:12, 13
9 [a]Deut 4:6; 1 Kin 2:3 [b]Josh 1:7
11 [a]Josh 9:21, 23, 27
13 [a]Gen 17:7; Ex 6:7
14 [a]Jer 31:31; Heb 8:7, 8
15 [a]Acts 2:39
17 [a]Ex 20:23; Deut 4:28; 28:36
18 [a]Deut 13:6 [b]Deut 32:32; Heb 12:15
19 [1]Lit *bless himself in his heart* [2]I.e. to destroy everything
20 [1]Lit *smoke* [2]Lit *lie down* [a]Ps 79:5; Ezek 23:25 [b]Ps 74:1; 80:4 [c]Ex 32:33; Deut 9:14; 2 Kin 14:27
21 [1]Lit *evil* [a]Deut 30:10
22 [1]Lit *made it sick* [a]Jer 19:8; 49:17; 50:13
23 [1]Lit *it is not sown and does not cause to sprout* [a]Gen 19:24; Is 34:9; Jer 17:6; Zeph 2:9 [b]Is 1:7; 64:11 [c]Jude 7
24 [1]Lit *heat* [a]1 Kin 9:8; Jer 22:8

28:68 *the way about which I spoke . . . 'You will never see it again!'* See 17:16; Ex 13:17; Num 14:3–4.

29:1 See notes on 5:2–3.

29:2 *You have seen.* Only those who were less than 20 years old (Num 14:29) when Israel followed the majority spy report at Kadesh-barnea and refused to enter Canaan would have actually experienced life in Egypt before the exodus. But Moses is speaking to the people as a nation and referring to the national experience (see note on 5:3).

29:4 Quoted in Rom 11:8 and applied to hardened Israel.

29:8 *gave it as an inheritance.* See 3:12–17.

29:9–15 A clear summary of the nature of covenant reaffirmation.

29:18 *root bearing poisonous fruit and wormwood.* The poison of idolatry, involving the rejection of the Lord.

29:20 *The LORD shall never be willing to forgive him.* Not to be taken as contradictory to 2 Pet 3:9 ("not wishing for any to perish"). Peter, too, says that those who deny the "Master" bring "swift destruction upon themselves" (2 Pet 2:1). *this book.* See note on 31:24. *blot out his name.* See 9:14; Ex 32:32–33; Rev 3:5.

29:21 *book of the law.* See note on 31:24.

29:23 *overthrow of Sodom.* See Gen 19:24–25; see also notes on Gen 10:19; 13:10.

25 "Then *men* will say, '[a]Because they forsook the covenant of the LORD, the God of
their fathers, which He made with them
when He brought them out of the land of
Egypt.
26 'They went and served other gods and
worshiped them, gods whom they have not
known and whom He had not [1]allotted to
them.
27 'Therefore, the anger of the LORD
burned against that land, [a]to bring upon it
every curse which is written in this book;
28 and [a]the LORD uprooted them from
their land in anger and in fury and in great
wrath, and cast them into another land, as *it*
is this day.'
29 "[a]The secret things belong to the LORD
our God, but [b]the things revealed belong to
us and to our sons forever, that we may
observe all the words of this law.

Restoration Promised

30 "So it shall be when all of these things
have come upon you, [a]the blessing and
the curse which I have set before you, and
you [1]call *them* to mind [b]in all nations where
the LORD your God has banished you,
2 and you [a]return to the LORD your God
and [1]obey Him [b]with all your heart and soul
according to all that I command you today,
you and your sons,
3 then the LORD your God will [a]restore
[1]you from captivity, and have compassion on
you, and [b]will gather you again from all the
peoples where the LORD your God has [c]scat-
tered you.
4 "If your outcasts are at the ends of the
[1]earth, [a]from there the LORD your God will
gather you, and from there He will [2]bring
you back.
5 "[a]The LORD your God will bring you into
the land which your fathers possessed, and
you shall possess it; and He will prosper you
and [b]multiply you more than your fathers.
6 "Moreover [a]the LORD your God will circumcise your heart and the heart of your
[1]descendants, [b]to love the LORD your God
with all your heart and with all your soul, so
that you may live.
7 "[a]The LORD your God will [1]inflict all
these curses on your enemies and on those
who hate you, who persecuted you.
8 "And you shall again [1]obey the LORD,
and observe all His commandments which I
command you today.
9 "[a]Then the LORD your God will [1]prosper
you abundantly in all the work of your hand,
in the [2]offspring of your [3]body and in the
[2]offspring of your cattle and in the [2]produce
of your ground, for [b]the LORD will again
rejoice over you for good, just as He rejoiced
over your fathers;
10 [1]if you [2]obey the LORD your God to
keep His commandments and His statutes
which [a]are written in this book of the law, [1]if
you turn to the LORD your God [b]with all your
heart and soul.
11 "For this commandment which I command you today is not too difficult for you,
nor is it [1]out of reach.
12 "It is not in heaven, [1]that you should
say, '[a]Who will go up to heaven for us to get
it for us and make us hear it, that we may
observe it?'
13 "Nor is it beyond the sea, [1]that you
should say, 'Who will cross the sea for us to
get it for us and make us hear it, that we may
observe it?'
14 "But the word is very near you, in your
mouth and in your heart, that you may
observe it.

Choose Life

15 "See, [a]I have set before you today life
and [1]prosperity, and death and [2]adversity;
16 in that I command you today [a]to love
the LORD your God, to walk in His ways and
to keep His commandments and His statutes
and His judgments, that you [b]may live and
multiply, and that the LORD your God may
bless you in the land where you are entering
to possess it.
17 "But if your heart turns away and you
will not obey, but are drawn away and worship other gods and serve them,
18 I declare to you today that [a]you shall
surely perish. You will not prolong *your* days
in the land where you are crossing the Jordan to enter [1]and possess it.
19 "[a]I call heaven and earth to witness
against you today, that I have set before you
life and death, [b]the blessing and the curse.
So choose life in order that you may live, you
and your [1]descendants,
20 [a]by loving the LORD your God, by obeying His voice, and [b]by holding fast to Him;

25 [a]2 Kin 17:9-23; 2 Chr 36:13-21
26 [1]Lit *portioned*
27 [a]Dan 9:11
28 [a]2 Chr 7:20; Ps 52:5; Prov 2:22; Ezek 19:12, 13
29 [a]Acts 1:7 [b]John 5:39; Acts 17:11; 2 Tim 3:16
30:1 [1]Lit *cause them to return to your heart* [a]Deut 11:26; 30:15, 19 [b]Lev 26:40-45; Deut 28:64; 29:28; 1 Kin 8:47
2 [1]Lit *listen to His voice* [a]Deut 4:29, 30; Neh 1:9 [b]Deut 4:29
3 [1]Lit *your captivity* [a]Gen 28:15; 48:21; Ps 126:1, 4; Jer 29:14 [b]Ps 147:2; Jer 32:37; Ezek 34:13 [c]Deut 4:27
4 [1]Lit *sky* [2]Lit *take you* [a]Neh 1:9; Is 43:6; 48:20; 62:11
5 [a]Jer 29:14; 30:3 [b]Deut 7:13; 13:17
6 [1]Lit *seed* [a]Deut 10:16 [b]Deut 6:5
7 [1]Lit *put* [a]Deut 7:15
8 [1]Lit *listen to the voice of*
9 [1]Lit *make you have excess for good* [2]Lit *fruit* [3]Lit *womb* [a]Jer 31:27, 28 [b]Jer 32:41
10 [1]Or *for you will* [2]Lit *listen to the voice of* [a]Deut 29:21 [b]Deut 4:29
11 [1]Lit *far off*
12 [1]Lit *to say* [a]Rom 10:6-8
13 [1]Lit *to say*
15 [1]Lit *good* [2]Lit *evil* [a]Deut 11:26
16 [a]Deut 6:5 [b]Deut 4:1; 30:19
18 [1]Lit *to* [a]Deut 4:26; 8:19
19 [1]Lit *seed* [a]Deut 4:26 [b]Deut 30:1
20 [a]Deut 6:5 [b]Deut 10:20

29:27 *this book.* See note on 31:24.
29:28 *as it is this day.* This would be said when Israel was in exile (see v. 25).
29:29 *secret things.* The hidden events of Israel's future relative to the blessings and curses; but the phrase can also have wider application. *things revealed.* Primarily the "words of this law."
30:2,6,10 *with all your heart . . . soul.* See note on 4:29.
30:6 *circumcise your heart.* See note on Gen 17:10.
30:7 *curses on your enemies.* Fulfilling Gen 12:3.
30:9 *your fathers.* The patriarchs (see v. 20).
30:10 *book of the law.* See note on 31:24.
30:12,14 *It is not in heaven . . . the word is very near you.* Moses declares that understanding, believing and obeying the covenant were not beyond them. Paul applies this passage to the availability of the "word of faith" (Rom 10:6–10).
30:19 *I call heaven and earth to witness.* The typical ancient covenant outside the OT contained a list of gods who served as "witnesses" to its provisions. The covenant in Deuteronomy was "witnessed" by heaven and earth (see 31:28; 32:1; see also notes on Ps 50:1; Isa 1:2).
30:20 *holding fast.* See note on 10:20. *this is your life.* When they chose the Lord, they chose life (v. 19). In 32:46–47 "all the

[c]for [1]this is your life and the length of your days, [2]that you may live in [d]the land which the LORD swore to your fathers, to Abraham, Isaac, and Jacob, to give them."

Moses' Last Counsel

31 So Moses went and spoke these words to all Israel.

2 And he said to them, "I am [a]a hundred and twenty years old today; [b]I am no longer able to come and go, and the LORD has said to me, '[c]You shall not cross this Jordan.'

3 "[a]It is the LORD your God who will cross ahead of you; He will destroy these nations before you, and you shall dispossess them. [b]Joshua is the one who will cross ahead of you, just as the LORD has spoken.

4 "The LORD will do to them just as He did to Sihon and Og, the kings of the Amorites, and to their land, when He destroyed them.

5 "[a]The LORD will deliver them up before you, and you shall do to them according to all the commandments which I have commanded you.

6 "[a]Be strong and courageous, [b]do not be afraid or tremble at them, for [c]the LORD your God is the one who goes with you. [d]He will not fail you or forsake you."

7 Then Moses called to Joshua and said to him in the sight of all Israel, "[a]Be strong and courageous, for you shall go with this people into the land which the LORD has sworn to their fathers to give them, and you shall give it to them as an inheritance.

8 "[a]The LORD is the one who goes ahead of you; He will be with you. [b]He will not fail you or forsake you. Do not fear or be dismayed."

9 So Moses wrote this law and gave it to the priests, the sons of Levi [a]who carried the ark of the covenant of the LORD, and to all the elders of Israel.

10 Then Moses commanded them, saying, "At the end of *every* seven years, at the time of [a]the year of remission of debts, at the [b]Feast of Booths,

11 when all Israel comes [a]to appear before the LORD your God at [b]the place which He will choose, [c]you shall read this law in front of all Israel in their hearing.

12 "Assemble the people, the men and the women and children and [1]the alien who is in your [2]town, so that they may hear and [a]learn and fear the LORD your God, and be careful to observe all the words of this law.

13 "Their children, who have not known, will hear and learn to fear the LORD your God, as long as you live on the land [1]which you are about to cross the Jordan to [2]possess."

Israel Will Fall Away

14 Then the LORD said to Moses, "Behold, [1][a]the time for you to die is near; call Joshua, and present yourselves at the tent of meeting, that I may commission him." [b]So Moses and Joshua went and presented themselves at the tent of meeting.

15 [a]The LORD appeared in the tent in a pillar of cloud, and the pillar of cloud stood at the doorway of the tent.

16 The LORD said to Moses, "Behold, [a]you are about to lie down with your fathers; and [b]this people will arise and play the harlot with the strange gods of the land, into the midst of which they are going, and [c]will forsake Me and break My covenant which I have made with them.

17 "[a]Then My anger will be kindled against them in that day, and [b]I will forsake them and [c]hide My face from them, and they will be consumed, and many evils and troubles will come upon them; so that they will say in that day, '[d]Is it not because our God is not among us that these evils have come upon us?'

18 "But I will surely hide My face in that day because of all the evil which they will do, for they will turn to other gods.

19 "Now therefore, [a]write this song for yourselves, and teach it to the sons of Israel; put it [1]on their lips, so that this song may be a witness for Me against the sons of Israel.

20 "[a]For when I bring them into the land flowing with milk and honey, which I swore to their fathers, and they have eaten and are satisfied and [b]become [1]prosperous, then they will turn to other gods and serve them, and spurn Me and break My covenant.

21 "Then it shall come about, [a]when many evils and troubles have come upon them, that this song will testify before them as a witness (for it shall not be forgotten from the

20 [1]Lit *that* [2]Lit *to dwell* [c]Deut 4:1; 32:47; Acts 17:25, 28 [d]Gen 12:7; 17:1-8
31:2 [a]Deut 34:7 [b]Num 27:17; 1 Kin 3:7 [c]Deut 1:37; 3:27
3 [a]Deut 9:3 [b]Num 27:18
5 [a]Deut 7:2
6 [a]Josh 10:25; 1 Chr 22:13 [b]Deut 1:29; 7:18; 20:1 [c]Deut 20:4 [d]Josh 1:5; Heb 13:5
7 [a]Deut 1:38; 3:28
8 [a]Ex 13:21; 33:14 [b]Deut 31:6; Josh 1:5; Heb 13:5
9 [a]Num 4:5, 6, 15; Deut 10:8; 31:25, 26; Josh 3:3
10 [a]Deut 15:1, 2 [b]Lev 23:34; Deut 16:13
11 [a]Deut 16:16 [b]Deut 12:5 [c]Josh 8:34; 2 Kin 23:2
12 [1]Lit *your alien* [2]Lit *gates* [a]Deut 4:10
13 [1]Lit *where* [2]Lit *possess it*
14 [1]Lit *your days to die are* [a]Num 27:12, 13; Deut 4:22; 32:50 [b]Ex 33:9-11
15 [a]Ex 33:9
16 [a]Gen 15:15 [b]Ex 34:15; Deut 4:25-28; Judg 2:11, 12, 17 [c]Judg 10:6; 1 Kin 18:18; 19:10; Jer 2:13
17 [a]Judg 2:14; 6:13 [b]2 Chr 15:2; 24:20 [c]Ps 104:29; Is 8:17 [d]Num 14:42
19 [1]Lit *in their mouths* [a]Deut 31:22
20 [1]Lit *fat* [a]Deut 6:10-12; 8:10, 19; 11:16, 17 [b]Deut 32:15-17
21 [a]Lev 26:41; Deut 4:30

words of this law" are said to be their life. The law, the Lord and life are bound together. "Life" in this context refers to all that makes life rich, full and productive—as God created it to be.

31:2 *no longer able to come and go.* Not a reference to physical disability (see 34:7). The Lord did not allow Moses to lead the people into Canaan because of his sin (see 1:37; 3:23–27; 4:21–22; 32:48–52; Num 20:2–13).

31:4 *just as He did to Sihon and Og.* See 2:26–3:11.

31:6 *Be strong and courageous.* The Lord's exhortation, often through His servants, to the people of Israel (Josh 10:25), to Joshua (vv. 7,23; Josh 1:6–7,9,18), to Solomon (1 Chr 22:13; 28:20) and to Hezekiah's military officers (2 Chr 32:7). By trusting in the Lord and obeying Him, His followers would be victorious in spite of great obstacles. *He will not fail you or forsake you.* See v. 8; Josh 1:5; 1 Kin 8:57; see also note on Gen 28:15.

31:9 *wrote this law and gave it to the priests.* Ancient treaties specified that a copy of the treaty was to be placed before the gods at the religious centers of the nations involved. For Israel, that meant to place it in or near the ark of the covenant (cf. notes on Ex 16:34; 31:18).

31:10 *every seven years.* See 15:4 and note; Ex 23:10–11; Lev 25:1–7; see also chart, pp. 164–165.

31:11 *place which He will choose.* See note on 12:5. *read this law in front of all Israel.* Reading the law to the Israelites (and teaching it to them) was one of the main duties of the priests (see 33:10; Mal 2:4–9).

31:14 *I may commission him.* See v. 23; cf. Num 27:18–23.

31:19 *write this song . . . and teach it.* See v. 22; 31:30–32:43.

[1]lips of their descendants); for [b]I know their intent which they are [2]developing today, before I have brought them into the land which I swore."

22 [a]So Moses wrote this song the same day, and taught it to the sons of Israel.

Joshua Is Commissioned

23 [a]Then He commissioned Joshua the son of Nun, and said, "[b]Be strong and courageous, for you shall bring the sons of Israel into the land which I swore to them, and [c]I will be with you."

24 It came about, when Moses finished writing the words of this law in a book until they were complete,

25 that Moses commanded the Levites [a]who carried the ark of the covenant of the LORD, saying,

26 "Take this book of the law and place it beside the ark of the covenant of the LORD your God, that it may [1]remain there as a witness against you.

27 "For I know [a]your rebellion and [b]your [1]stubbornness; behold, while I am still alive with you today, you have been rebellious against the LORD; how much more, then, after my death?

28 "Assemble to me all the elders of your tribes and your officers, that I may speak these words in their hearing and [a]call the heavens and the earth to witness against them.

29 "For I know that after my death you will [a]act corruptly and turn from the way which I have commanded you; and evil will befall you in the latter days, for you will do that which is evil in the sight of the LORD, provoking Him to anger with the work of your hands."

30 Then Moses spoke in the hearing of all the assembly of Israel the words of this song, until they were complete:

The Song of Moses

32 "[a]Give ear, O heavens, and let me
speak;
And let the earth hear the words of
my mouth.
2 "[a]Let my teaching drop as the rain,
My speech distill as the dew,
[b]As the droplets on the fresh grass
And as the showers on the herb.
3 "[a]For I proclaim the name of the LORD;
[b]Ascribe greatness to our God!
4 "[a]The Rock! His work is perfect,
[b]For all His ways are [1]just;
[c]A God of faithfulness and without
injustice,
Righteous and upright is He.
5 "[1a]They have acted corruptly toward
Him,
They are not His children, because of
their defect;
[b]*But are* a perverse and crooked
generation.
6 "Do you thus [a]repay the LORD,
[b]O foolish and unwise people?
[c]Is not He your Father who has bought
you?
[d]He has made you and established you.
7 "Remember the days of old,
Consider the years of all generations.
[a]Ask your father, and he will inform
you,
Your elders, and they will tell you.
8 "[a]When the Most High gave the
nations their inheritance,
When He separated the sons of [1]man,
He set the boundaries of the peoples
[b]According to the number of the sons
of Israel.
9 "[a]For the LORD's portion is His people;
Jacob is the allotment of His
inheritance.
10 "[a]He found him in a desert land,
And in the howling waste of a
wilderness;
He encircled him, He cared for him,
He guarded him as [b]the pupil of His
eye.
11 "[a]Like an eagle that stirs up its nest,
That hovers over its young,
[b]He spread His wings and caught them,
He carried them on His pinions.
12 "[a]The LORD alone guided him,
[b]And there was no foreign god with
him.
13 "[a]He made him ride on the high places
of the earth,

21 [1]Lit *mouth of its seed* [2]Lit *making* [b]1 Chr 28:9; John 2:24, 25
22 [a]Deut 31:19
23 [a]Num 27:23; Deut 31:7 [b]Josh 1:6 [c]Ex 3:12
25 [a]Deut 31:9
26 [1]Lit *be*
27 [1]Lit *stiff neck* [a]Deut 9:7, 24 [b]Ex 32:9; Deut 9:6, 13
28 [a]Deut 4:26; 30:19; 32:1
29 [a]Judg 2:19
32:1 [a]Deut 4:26; Ps 50:4; Is 1:2; Jer 6:19
2 [a]Is 55:10, 11
2 [b]Ps 72:6
3 [a]Ex 33:19; 34:5, 6 [b]Deut 3:24; 5:24
4 [1]Or *judgment* [a]Deut 32:15, 18, 30; 2 Sam 22:31 [b]Gen 18:25; Dan 4:37 [c]Deut 7:9
5 [1]Lit *It has* [a]Deut 4:25; 31:29 [b]Matt 17:17
6 [a]Ps 116:12 [b]Deut 32:28 [c]Deut 1:31; Ps 74:2; Is 63:16 [d]Deut 32:15
7 [a]Ex 12:26; Ps 78:5-8
8 [1]Or *Adam* [a]Acts 17:26 [b]Num 23:9; Deut 33:28
9 [a]1 Sam 10:1; 1 Kin 8:51, 53; Jer 10:16
10 [a]Deut 1:19 [b]Ps 17:8; Prov 7:2; Zech 2:8
11 [a]Ex 19:4; Deut 33:12 [b]Ps 18:10-18
12 [a]Deut 4:35, 39 [b]Deut 32:39; Is 43:12
13 [a]Is 58:14

31:23 *Be strong and courageous.* See note on v. 6.
31:24 *words of this law . . . complete.* The book of Deuteronomy up to this place (see note on v. 9).
31:26 *place it beside the ark.* See note on v. 9.
31:27 *stubbornness.* See 9:6,13; 10:16; see also note on Ex 32:9.
31:28 *heavens and the earth to witness.* See note on 30:19.
31:29 *the work of your hands.* A reference to idols (see 4:28; 27:15 and note).
31:30–32:43 The song of Moses (see notes on Ex 15:1–18; Rev 15:3).
32:1 *Give ear, O heavens.* For similar introductions see Is 1:2 and note; 34:1; Mic 1:2; 6:1–2.
32:4 *The Rock!* A major theme of the song of Moses (see vv. 15,18,30–31; see also note on Gen 49:24).
32:5 *perverse and crooked generation.* See Phil 2:15.
32:6 *Father.* See Is 63:16; 64:8.
32:7 *Remember the days of old.* See note on 4:10.
32:8 *Most High.* The only occurrence in Deuteronomy of this name for God (see note on Gen 14:19). It emphasizes the Lord's sovereignty over all creation. *gave the nations their inheritance.* See Gen 10. *According to the number of the sons of Israel.* Perhaps referring to the Lord's grant of Canaan to Israel as sufficient to sustain their expected population (see note on Gen 10:2).
32:10 *pupil of His eye.* Lit. "little man of his eye," referring to the pupil, a delicate part of the eye that is essential for vision and that therefore must be protected at all costs.
32:11 *hovers over.* See note on Ge 1:2.

And he ate the produce of the field;
[b]And He made him suck honey from
the rock,
And [c]oil from the flinty rock,
14 Curds of cows, and milk of the flock,
With fat of lambs,
And rams, the breed of Bashan, and
goats,
[a]With the finest of the wheat—
And of the [b]blood of grapes you drank
wine.

15 "[a]But [1]Jeshurun grew fat and kicked—
You are grown fat, thick, and sleek—
[b]Then he forsook God [c]who made him,
And scorned [d]the Rock of his salvation.
16 "[a]They made Him jealous with strange
gods;
[b]With abominations they provoked
Him to anger.
17 "[a]They sacrificed to demons who were
not God,
[b]To gods whom they have not known,
[c]New *gods* who came lately,
Whom your fathers did not dread.
18 "You neglected [a]the Rock who begot
you,
[b]And forgot the God who gave you
birth.

19 "[a]The LORD saw *this,* and spurned *them*
[b]Because of the provocation of His
sons and daughters.
20 "Then He said, 'I will hide My face
from them,
[a]I will see what their end *shall be;*
[b]For they are a perverse generation,
[c]Sons in whom is no faithfulness.
21 '[a]They have made Me jealous with
what is not God;
They have provoked Me to anger with
their [1][b]idols.
[c]So I will make them jealous with
those who are not a people;
I will provoke them to anger with a
foolish nation,
22 [a]For a fire is kindled in My anger,
And burns to the lowest part of [1]Sheol,
[b]And consumes the earth with its yield,
And sets on fire the foundations of the
mountains.

23 '[a]I will heap misfortunes on them;
[b]I will use My arrows on them.

13 [b]Deut 8:8; Ps 81:16 [c]Job 29:6
14 [a]Ps 81:16; 147:14 [b]Gen 49:11
15 [1]I.e. Israel [a]Deut 31:20 [b]Judg 10:6 [c]Deut 32:6 [d]Deut 32:4; Ps 89:26
16 [a]Ps 78:58 [b]Ps 106:29
17 [a]Lev 17:7; 1 Cor 10:20 [b]Deut 28:64 [c]Judg 5:8
18 [a]Deut 32:4 [b]Ps 106:21
19 [a]Lev 26:30; Ps 106:40 [b]Jer 44:21-23
20 [a]Deut 31:29 [b]Deut 32:5 [c]Deut 9:23
21 [1]Lit *vanities* [a]Deut 32:16; 1 Cor 10:22 [b]Deut 32:17; 1 Kin 16:13, 26 [c]Rom 10:19
22 [1]I.e. the nether world [a]Num 16:33-35; Ps 18:7, 8; Lam 4:11 [b]Lev 26:20
23 [a]Deut 29:21 [b]Ps 18:14; 45:5
24 [1]Lit *burning heat* [a]Deut 28:22, 48 [b]Ps 91:6 [c]Lev 26:22 [d]Amos 5:18, 19
25 [a]Lam 1:20; Ezek 7:15 [b]2 Chr 36:17; Lam 2:21
26 [a]Deut 4:27; 28:64 [b]Deut 9:14
27 [1]Lit *high* [a]Num 15:30
28 [1]Lit *perishing* [a]Deut 32:6
29 [1]Or *latter end* [a]Deut 5:29 [b]Deut 31:29
30 [a]Lev 26:7, 8 [b]Deut 32:4; Ps 44:12
31 [1]Lit *are judges* [a]Ex 14:25
32 [a]Deut 29:18
33 [1]Lit *dragons* [2]Lit *cruel*
34 [a]Job 14:17; Jer 44:21
35 [a]Ps 94:1; Rom 12:19; Heb 10:30 [b]Jer 23:12 [c]Ezek 7:5-10
36 [a]Ps 135:14; Heb 10:30

24 '[a]*They will be* wasted by famine, and
consumed by [1]plague
[b]And bitter destruction;
[c]And the teeth of beasts I will send
upon them,
[d]With the venom of crawling things of
the dust.
25 '[a]Outside the sword will bereave,
And inside terror—
[b]Both young man and virgin,
The nursling with the man of gray hair.
26 'I would have said, "[a]I will cut them to
pieces,
[b]I will remove the memory of them
from men,"
27 Had I not feared the provocation by
the enemy,
That their adversaries would misjudge,
That they would say, "[a]Our hand is
[1]triumphant,
And the LORD has not done all this." '

28 "[a]For they are a nation [1]lacking in
counsel,
And there is no understanding in
them.
29 "[a]Would that they were wise, that they
understood this,
[b]That they would discern their
[1]future!
30 "[a]How could one chase a thousand,
And two put ten thousand to flight,
Unless their [b]Rock had sold them,
And the LORD had given them up?
31 "Indeed their rock is not like our Rock,
[a]Even our enemies [1]themselves judge
this.
32 "For their vine is from the vine of
Sodom,
And from the fields of Gomorrah;
Their grapes are grapes of [a]poison,
Their clusters, bitter.
33 "Their wine is the venom of [1]serpents,
And the [2]deadly poison of cobras.

34 '[a]Is it not laid up in store with Me,
Sealed up in My treasuries?
35 '[a]Vengeance is Mine, and retribution,
[b]In due time their foot will slip;
[c]For the day of their calamity is near,
And the impending things are
hastening upon them.'
36 "[a]For the LORD will vindicate His
people,

32:13 *honey from the rock.* See Ps 81:16. In Canaan, bees sometimes built their hives in clefts of rocks (cf. Is 7:18–19). *oil from the flinty rock.* Olive trees often grew on rocky hillsides, as on the Mount of Olives east of Jerusalem.
32:14 *Bashan.* See note on Ezek 39:18. *blood of grapes.* Wine (see Gen 49:11).
32:15 *Jeshurun.* Means "the upright one," i.e., Israel; see also Is 44:2 and note. *Rock.* See v. 18 and note on v. 4.
32:21 Quoted in part in Rom 10:19 to illustrate Israel's failure to understand the good news about Christ.
32:22 *lowest part of Sheol.* See note on Gen 37:35.
32:30 *their Rock.* Israel's God.
32:31 *their rock.* The god of Israel's enemy.
32:34 *Sealed up in My treasuries.* The Lord's plans for the future are fixed and certain. Sin will be punished in due time.
32:35–36 Quoted in part in Heb 10:30 as a warning against rejecting the Son of God.
32:35 *Vengeance is Mine, and retribution.* Quoted in Rom 12:19 to affirm that avenging is God's prerogative.

[b]And will have compassion on His
servants,
When He sees that *their* [1]strength is
gone,
And there is none *remaining,* bond or
free.
37 " And He will say, '[a]Where are their
gods,
The rock in which they sought refuge?
38 '[a]Who ate the fat of their sacrifices,
And drank the wine of their drink
offering?
[b]Let them rise up and help you,
Let them be your hiding place!
39 '[a]See now that I, I am He,
[b]And there is no god besides Me;
[c]It is I who put to death and give life.
[d]I have wounded and it is I who heal,
[e]And there is no one who can deliver
from My hand.
40 'Indeed, [a]I lift up My hand to heaven,
And say, as I live forever,
41 [a]If I sharpen My [1]flashing sword,
And My hand takes hold on justice,
[b]I will render vengeance on My
adversaries,
And I will repay those who hate Me.
42 '[a]I will make My arrows drunk with
blood,
[b]And My sword will devour flesh,
With the blood of the slain and the
captives,
From the long-haired [1]leaders of the
enemy.'
43 " [a]Rejoice, O nations, *with* His people;
[b]For He will avenge the blood of His
servants,
[c]And will render vengeance on His
adversaries,
[d]And will atone for His land *and* His
people."

44 Then Moses came and spoke all the
words of this song in the hearing of the people, he, with [1][a]Joshua the son of Nun.
45 When Moses had finished speaking all
these words to all Israel,
46 he said to them, "[a]Take to your heart
all the words with which I am warning you
today, which you shall command [b]your sons
to observe [1]carefully, *even* all the words of
this law.
47 " For it is not an idle word for you;
indeed [a]it is your life. And [b]by this word you
will prolong your days in the land, [1]which
you are about to cross the Jordan to [2]pos-
sess."

48 [a]The LORD spoke to Moses that very
same day, saying,
49 " [a]Go up to this mountain of the Abarim,
Mount Nebo, which is in the land of Moab
[1]opposite Jericho, and look at the land of
Canaan, which I am giving to the sons of
Israel for a possession.
50 " Then die on the mountain where you
ascend, and be [a]gathered to your people, as
Aaron your brother died on Mount Hor and
was gathered to his people,
51 [a]because you broke faith with Me in
the midst of the sons of Israel at the waters
of Meribah-kadesh, in the [b]wilderness of
Zin, because you did not treat Me as holy in
the midst of the sons of Israel.
52 " [a]For you shall see the land at a distance, but [b]you shall not go there, into the
land which I am giving the sons of Israel."

The Blessing of Moses

33 Now this is the blessing with which
Moses [a]the man of God blessed the
sons of Israel before his death.
2 He said,
" [a]The LORD came from Sinai,
[b]And [1]dawned on them from Seir;
[c]He shone forth from Mount Paran,
And He came from [d]the [2]midst of ten
thousand holy ones;
[e]At His right hand there was [3]flashing
lightning for them.
3 " [a]Indeed, He loves [1]the people;
[b]All [2]Your holy ones are in Your hand,
[c]And they [3]followed in Your steps;
Everyone receives of Your words.
4 " [a]Moses charged us with a law,
[b]A possession for the assembly of
Jacob.
5 " [a]And He was king in Jeshurun,
When the heads of the people were
gathered,
The tribes of Israel together.
6 " [a]May Reuben live and not die,
Nor his men be few."
7 [a]And this regarding Judah; so he said,
" Hear, O LORD, the voice of Judah,
And bring him to his people.

36 [1]Lit *hand* [b]Lev 26:43-45; Deut 30:1-3
37 [a]Judg 10:14; Jer 2:28
38 [a]Num 25:1, 2 [b]Jer 11:12
39 [a]Is 41:4; 43:10 [b]Deut 32:12; Is 45:5 [c]1 Sam 2:6; Ps 68:20 [d]Ps 51:8 [e]Ps 50:22
40 [a]Ezek 20:5, 6; 21:4, 5
41 [1]Or *lightning* [a]Is 34:6-8 [b]Jer 50:28-32
42 [1]Lit *head* [a]Deut 32:23 [b]Jer 12:12; 46:10, 14
43 [a]Rom 15:10 [b]2 Kin 9:7; Rev 6:10; 19:2 [c]Is 1:24, 25 [d]Ps 65:3; 79:9; 85:1
44 [1]Lit *Hoshea* [a]Num 13:8, 16
46 [1]Lit *to do* [a]Ezek 40:4; 44:5 [b]Deut 4:9
47 [a]Deut 8:3; 30:20 [b]Deut 4:40; 33:25
47 [1]Lit *where* [2]Lit *possess it*
48 [a]Num 27:12
49 [1]Lit *which is opposite* [a]Num 27:12-14; Deut 3:27
50 [a]Gen 25:8
51 [a]Num 20:12 [b]Num 27:14
52 [a]Deut 34:1-3 [b]Deut 1:37; 3:27
33:1 [a]Josh 14:6
2 [1]Lit *rose to* [2]Lit *myriads of holiness* [3]Or *a fiery law* [a]Ex 19:18, 20; Ps 68:8, 17 [b]Judg 5:4 [c]Num 10:12; Hab 3:3 [d]Dan 7:10; Acts 7:53 [e]Ex 23:20-22
3 [1]Lit *peoples* [2]Lit *His* [3]Or *lie down at Your feet* [a]Deut 4:37; Mal 1:2 [b]Deut 7:6; 14:2 [c]Deut 6:1-9; Luke 10:39
4 [a]Deut 4:2; John 7:19 [b]Ps 119:111
5 [a]Num 23:21
6 [a]Gen 49:3, 4
7 [a]Gen 49:8-12

32:39 *no god besides Me.* See note on 4:35. *It is I who put to death and give life.* See Is 45:7 and note.
32:47 *it is your life.* See note on 30:20.
32:50 *gathered to your people.* See note on Gen 25:8. *Aaron . . . died on Mount Hor.* See 10:6; Num 20:22–29.
32:51 *you broke faith with Me.* See 1:37; 3:23–26; 4:21–22; 31:2; Num 20:12. *Meribah-kadesh, in the wilderness of Zin.* See 33:8; see also notes on Ex 17:7; Num 20:13.
33:1 *blessing.* See Gen 12:1–3; 22:15–18; 27:27–29; 28:10–15; 49:1–28. Moses' blessings on the tribes (vv. 6–25) should be compared particularly with Jacob's blessings on his sons in Gen 49. *man of God.* The first occurrence of this title. It appears next in Josh 14:6 (also of Moses; see Ps 90 title). Later it designates other messengers of God (see note on 1 Sam 2:27).
33:2 *Sinai . . . Seir . . . Paran.* Mountains associated with the giving of the law (see Gen 21:21 and note; Judg 5:4–5; Hab 3:3). *holy ones.* Angels.
33:3 *holy ones.* Israelites (see 7:6; 14:2; 26:19; 28:9).
33:5 *king.* The Lord, not an earthly monarch, was to be king over Israel (see Judg 8:23 and note). *Jeshurun.* Means "the upright one," i.e., Israel; also in v. 26 (see Is 44:2 and note).

With his hands he contended for
[1]them,
And may You be a help against his
adversaries."

8 Of Levi he said,
"*Let* Your [a]Thummim and Your Urim
belong to [1]Your [b]godly man,
[c]Whom You proved at Massah,
With whom You contended at the
waters of Meribah;
9 [a]Who said of his father and his
mother,
'I did not consider them';
And he did not acknowledge his
brothers,
Nor did he regard his own sons,
For [b]they observed Your word,
And kept Your covenant.
10 "[a]They shall teach Your ordinances to
Jacob,
And Your law to Israel.
[b]They shall put incense [1]before You,
And [c]whole burnt offerings on Your
altar.
11 "O LORD, bless his substance,
And accept the work of his hands;
Shatter the loins of those who rise up
against him,
And those who hate him, so that they
will not rise *again*."

12 Of Benjamin he said,
"[a]May the beloved of the LORD dwell in
security by Him,
[b]Who shields him all the day,
[c]And he dwells between His
shoulders."

13 Of Joseph he said,
"[a]Blessed of the LORD *be* his land,
With the choice things of heaven,
with the dew,
And from the deep lying beneath,
14 And with the choice yield of the
sun,
And with the choice produce of the
months.
15 "And with the [1]best things of [a]the
ancient mountains,
And with the choice things of the
everlasting hills,

7 [1]Lit *him*
8 [1]Lit *him* [a]Ex 28:30; Lev 8:8 [b]Ps 106:16 [c]Ex 17:7; Num 20:13, 24; Deut 6:16
9 [a]Ex 32:27-29 [b]Mal 2:5
10 [1]Lit *in Your nostrils* [a]Lev 10:11; Deut 31:9-13 [b]Lev 16:12, 13 [c]Ps 51:19
12 [a]Deut 4:37f; 12:10 [b]Deut 32:11 [c]Ex 28:12
13 [a]Gen 27:27, 28; 49:22-26
15 [1]Or *chief* [a]Hab 3:6
16 [a]Ex 2:2-6; 3:2, 4
17 [1]Or *together* [a]Num 23:22 [b]1 Kin 22:11; Ps 44:5
18 [a]Gen 49:13-15
19 [1]Lit *suck* [a]Ex 15:17; Ps 2:6; Is 2:3 [b]Ps 4:5; 51:19 [c]Is 60:5
20 [1]Or *lioness* [a]Gen 49:19 [b]Gen 49:9
21 [1]Lit *saw* [2]Or *covered up* [a]Num 32:1-5 [b]Num 34:14 [c]Josh 4:12 [d]Josh 22:1-3
22 [a]Gen 49:16 [b]Ezek 19:2, 3
23 [a]Gen 49:21

16 And with the choice things of the
earth and its fullness,
And the favor [a]of Him who dwelt in
the bush.
Let it come to the head of Joseph,
And to the crown of the head of the
one distinguished among his
brothers.
17 "As the firstborn of his ox, majesty is
his,
And his horns are the horns of [a]the
wild ox;
With them he will [b]push the peoples,
All [1]at once, *to* the ends of the earth.
And those are the ten thousands of
Ephraim,
And those are the thousands of
Manasseh."

18 [a]Of Zebulun he said,
"Rejoice, Zebulun, in your going forth,
And, Issachar, in your tents.
19 "[a]They will call peoples *to* the mountain;
There they will offer [b]righteous
sacrifices;
For they will [1]draw out [c]the
abundance of the seas,
And the hidden treasures of the sand."

20 [a]Of Gad he said,
"Blessed is the one who enlarges Gad;
He lies down [b]as a [1]lion,
And tears the arm, also the crown of
the head.
21 "[a]Then he [1]provided the first *part* for
himself,
[b]For there the ruler's portion was
[2]reserved;
[c]And he came *with* the leaders of the
people;
[d]He executed the justice of the LORD,
And His ordinances with Israel."

22 [a]Of Dan he said,
"Dan is [b]a lion's whelp,
That leaps forth from Bashan."

23 Of Naphtali he said,
"[a]O Naphtali, satisfied with favor,
And full of the blessing of the LORD,
Take possession of the sea and the
south."

33:8 *Thummim . . . Urim.* See note on Ex 28:30. *Massah.* See 6:16; 9:22; see also note on Ex 17:7. *Meribah.* See 32:51; see also note on Ex 17:7.
33:9 *they observed Your word.* The Levites had charge of the tabernacle with its ark, in which the book of the law was placed (see note on 31:9).
33:10 *teach Your ordinances to Jacob.* See note on 31:11.
33:13 *Of Joseph.* Moses included the blessing on the two tribes of Ephraim and Manasseh (v. 17), Joseph's sons, with that of Joseph himself. *the dew . . . the deep.* See note on Gen 49:25.
33:15–16 See Gen 49:26 and note.
33:16 *choice things of the earth.* Under the Lord's blessing, Joseph's land in the central part of Canaan was to be unusually fertile and productive. *who dwelt in the bush.* See Ex 3:1–6.
33:19 *abundance of the seas . . . hidden treasures of the sand.* References to maritime wealth (see note on Gen 49:13).
33:21 *he provided the first part.* For his livestock (see 3:12–20).
33:22 *leaps forth from Bashan.* The lion's cub, not Dan, is the subject. Another possible translation is "keeps away from the viper." Although someday he would be like a viper himself (see Gen 49:17), the early history of Dan pictured him as being somewhat more timid.
33:23 *sea.* The Sea of Galilee. Naphtali's area extended from north of the Waters of Merom to south of the Sea of Galilee.

24 [a]Of Asher he said,
"More blessed than sons is Asher;
May he be favored by his brothers,
[b]And may he dip his foot in oil.
25 "[a]Your locks will be iron and bronze,
[b]And according to your days, so will
your leisurely walk be.

26 "[a]There is none like the God of
[1]Jeshurun,
[b]Who rides the heavens [2]to your help,
And through the skies in His majesty.
27 "[a]The eternal God is a [1]dwelling place,
[b]And underneath are the everlasting
arms;
[c]And He drove out the enemy from
before you,
[d]And said, 'Destroy!'
28 "[a]So Israel dwells in security,
[b]The fountain of Jacob secluded,
[c]In a land of grain and new wine;
[d]His heavens also drop down dew.
29 "[a]Blessed are you, O Israel;
[b]Who is like you, a people saved by
the LORD,
[c]Who is the shield of your help
[d]And the sword of your majesty!
[e]So your enemies will cringe before
you,
[f]And you will tread upon their high
places."

The Death of Moses

34 [a]Now Moses went up from the plains
of Moab to Mount Nebo, to the top of
Pisgah, which is opposite Jericho. And the
LORD [b]showed him all the land, Gilead as far
as Dan,
2 and all Naphtali and the land of Ephraim and Manasseh, and all the land of Judah
as far as the [1a]western sea,
3 and the [1]Negev and the plain in the
valley of Jericho, [a]the city of palm trees, as
far as Zoar.
4 Then the LORD said to him, "This is the
land which [a]I swore to Abraham, Isaac, and
Jacob, saying, 'I will give it to your [1]descen-
dants'; I have let you see *it* with your eyes,
but you shall not go over there."
5 So Moses [a]the servant of the LORD
[b]died there in the land of Moab, according to
the [1]word of the LORD.
6 And He buried him in the valley in the
land of Moab, [a]opposite Beth-peor; but [b]no
man knows his burial place to this day.
7 Although Moses was [a]one hundred and
twenty years old when he died, [b]his eye was
not dim, nor his vigor abated.
8 So the sons of Israel wept for Moses in
the plains of Moab thirty days; then the days
of weeping *and* mourning for Moses came to
an end.
9 Now Joshua the son of Nun was [a]filled
with the spirit of wisdom, for Moses had laid
his hands on him; and the sons of Israel listened to him and did as the LORD had commanded Moses.
10 Since that time [a]no prophet has risen in
Israel like Moses, whom [b]the LORD knew face
to face,
11 for all the signs and wonders which the
LORD sent him to perform in the land of
Egypt against Pharaoh, all his servants, and
all his land,
12 and for all the mighty [1]power and for
all the great terror which Moses performed
in the sight of all Israel.

24 [a]Gen 49:20 [b]Job 29:6
25 [a]Ps 147:13 [b]Deut 4:40; 32:47
26 [1]I.e. Israel [2]Lit *in* [a]Ex 15:11; Deut 4:35; Ps 86:8; Jer 10:6 [b]Deut 10:14; Ps 68:33, 34; 104:3; Hab 3:8
27 [1]Or *refuge* [a]Ps 90:1, 2 [b]Gen 49:24 [c]Ex 34:11; Josh 24:18 [d]Deut 7:2
28 [a]Deut 33:12; Jer 23:6 [b]Num 23:9; Deut 32:8 [c]Gen 27:28, 37 [d]Deut 33:13
29 [a]Ps 1:1; 32:1, 2 [b]Deut 4:32; 2 Sam 7:23 [c]Gen 15:1; Ps 33:20; 115:9-11 [d]Ps 68:34 [e]Ps 66:3 [f]Num 33:52
34:1 [a]Deut 32:49 [b]Deut 32:52

2 [1]I.e. Mediterranean Sea [a]Deut 11:24
3 [1]I.e. South country [a]Judg 1:16; 3:13; 2 Chr 28:15
4 [1]Lit *seed* [a]Gen 12:7; 26:3; 28:13
5 [1]Lit *mouth* [a]Num 12:7; Josh 1:1, 2 [b]Deut 32:50
6 [a]Deut 3:29; 4:46 [b]Jude 9
7 [a]Deut 31:2 [b]Gen 27:1; 48:10
9 [a]Num 27:18, 23; Is 11:2
10 [a]Deut 18:15, 18 [b]Ex 33:11; Num 12:8; Deut 5:4
12 [1]Lit *hand*

33:26 *Jeshurun.* See note on 32:15. *rides . . . the skies.* See note on Ps 68:4.
33:29 *shield.* See note on Gen 15:1. *high places.* See note on 1Ki 3:2.
34:1 *Moses went up . . . to Mount Nebo.* In obedience to the Lord's command in 32:48–52.
34:4 *land which I swore.* See 1:8; Gen 12:1; 15:18 and note; Ex 33:1.
34:5 *servant of the LORD.* A special title used to refer to those whom the Lord, as the Great King, has taken into His service; they serve as members of God's royal administration. For example, it was used especially of Abraham (Gen 26:24), Moses (Ex 14:31), Joshua (Josh 24:29), David (2 Sam 7:5), the prophets (2 Kin 9:7), Israel collectively (Is 41:8), and even a foreign king the Lord used to carry out His purposes (Jer 25:9). See notes on Ex 14:31; Is 42:1–4.
34:6 *Beth-peor.* See note on 3:29.
34:7 *one hundred and twenty years old.* See 31:2; perhaps a round number, indicating three generations of about 40 years each.
34:8 *wept . . . thirty days.* See Gen 50:3 and note.
34:10 *no prophet has risen in Israel like Moses.* See note on 18:15. Until Jesus came, no one was superior to Moses. See Heb 3:1–6, where Moses the "servant" (Heb 3:5) is contrasted with Christ the "Son" (Heb 3:6). *face to face.* See Num 12:8 and note.

The Conquest and the Ethical Question of War

Many readers of Joshua (and other OT books) are deeply troubled by the role that warfare plays in this account of God's dealings with His people. Not a few relieve their ethical scruples by ascribing the author's perspective to a pre-Christian (and sub-Christian) stage of moral development that the Christian, in the light of Christ's teaching, must repudiate and transcend. Hence the main thread of the narrative line of Joshua is an offense to them.

It must be remembered, however, that the book of Joshua does not address itself to the abstract ethical question of war as a means for gaining human ends. It can only be understood in the context of the history of redemption unfolding in the Pentateuch, with its interplay of divine grace and judgment. Of that story it is the direct continuation.

Joshua is not an epic account of Israel's heroic generation or the story of Israel's conquest of Canaan with the aid of her national deity. It is rather the story of how God, to whom the whole world belongs, at one stage in the history of redemption reconquered a portion of the earth from the powers of this world that had claimed it for themselves, defending their claims by force of arms and reliance on their false gods. It tells how God commissioned His people, under His servant Joshua, to take Canaan in His name out of the hands of the idolatrous and dissolute Canaanites (whose measure of sin was now full; see Gen 15:16). It tells how He aided them in that enterprise and gave them conditional tenancy in His land in fulfillment of the ancient pledge.

Joshua is the story of the kingdom of God breaking into the world of nations at a time when national and political entities were viewed as the creation of the gods and living proofs of their power. Thus the Lord's triumph over the Canaanites testified to the world that the God of Israel is the one true and living God, whose claim on the world is absolute. It was also a warning to the nations that the irresistible advance of the kingdom of God would ultimately disinherit all those who opposed it, giving place in the earth only to those who acknowledge and serve the Lord. At once an act of redemption and of judgment, it gave notice of the outcome of history and anticipated the eschatological destiny of mankind and the creation.

The battles for Canaan were therefore the Lord's war, undertaken at a particular time in the program of redemption. God gave His people under Joshua no commission or license to conquer the world with the sword but a particular, limited mission. The conquered land itself would not become Israel's national possession by right of conquest, but it belonged to the Lord. So the land had to be cleansed of all remnants of paganism. Its people and their wealth were not for Israel to seize as the booty of war from which to enrich themselves (as Achan tried to do, ch. 7) but were placed under God's ban (were to be devoted to God to dispense with as He pleased). On that land Israel was to establish a commonwealth faithful to the righteous rule of God and thus be a witness (and a blessing) to the nations. If she herself became unfaithful and conformed to Canaanite culture and practice, she would in turn lose her place in the Lord's land—as she almost did in the days of the judges, and as she did eventually in the exile.

War is a terrible curse that the human race brings on itself as it seeks to possess the earth by its own unrighteous ways. But it pales before the curse that awaits all those who do not heed God's testimony to Himself or His warnings—those who oppose the rule of God and reject His offer of grace. The God of the second Joshua (Jesus) is the God of the first Joshua also. Although now for a time He reaches out to the whole world with the gospel (and commissions his people urgently to carry His offer of peace to all nations), the sword of His judgment waits in the wings—and His second Joshua will wield it (Rev 19:11–16).

Joshua

INTRODUCTION

Title and Theme

Joshua is a story of conquest and fulfillment for the people of God. After many years of slavery in Egypt and 40 years in the wilderness, the Israelites were finally allowed to enter the land promised to their fathers. Abraham, always a migrant, never possessed the country to which he was sent, but he left to his children the legacy of God's covenant that made them the eventual heirs of all of Canaan (see Gen 15:13,16,18; 17:8). Joshua was destined to turn that promise into reality.

Where Deuteronomy ends, the book of Joshua begins: The tribes of Israel are still camped on the east side of the Jordan River. The narrative opens with God's command to move forward and pass through the river on dry land. Then it relates the series of victories in central, southern and northern Canaan that gave the Israelites control of all the hill country and the Negev. It continues with a description of the tribal allotments and ends with Joshua's final addresses to the people. The theme of the book, therefore, is the establishment of Israel in the promised land.

Earlier in his life Joshua was called simply Hoshea (Num 13:8,16), meaning "salvation." But later Moses changed his name to Joshua, meaning "The LORD saves" (or "The LORD gives victory"). When this same name (the Greek form of which is Jesus) was given to Mary's firstborn son, it became the most loved of names.

In the Hebrew Bible the book of Joshua initiates a division called the Former Prophets, including also Judges, Samuel and Kings — all historical in content but written from a prophetic standpoint. They do more than merely record the nation's development from Moses to the fall of Judah in 586 B.C. They prophetically interpret God's covenant ways with Israel in history — how He fulfills and remains true to His promises (especially through His servants such as Joshua, the judges, Samuel and David) and how He deals with the waywardness of the Israelites. In Joshua it was the Lord who won the victories and "gave Israel all the land which He had sworn to give to their fathers" (21:43).

Author and Date

In the judgment of many scholars Joshua was not written until the end of the period of the kings, some 800 years after the actual events. But there are significant reasons to question this conclusion and to place the time of composition much earlier. The earliest Jewish traditions (Talmud) claim that Joshua wrote his own book except for the final section about his funeral, which is attributed to Eleazar son of Aaron (the last verse must have been added by a later editor).

On at least two occasions the text reports writing at Joshua's command or by Joshua himself. When the tribes received their territories, Joshua instructed his men, "Go and walk through the land and describe it" (18:8). Then in the last scene of the book, when Joshua led Israel in a renewal of the covenant with the Lord, he "made for them a statute and an ordinance" (24:25). On yet another occasion the one telling the story appears also to have been a participant in the event; he uses the pronoun "us" (5:6).

Moreover, the author's observations are accurate and precise. He is thoroughly at ease with the antiquated names of cities, such as "the Jebusite" city (15:8; 18:16,28) for Jerusalem, Kiriath-arba (14:15; 15:54; 20:7; 21:11) for Hebron, and Great Sidon (11:8; 19:28) for what later became simply Sidon. Tyre is mentioned (19:29), but in the days of Joshua it had not yet developed into a port of major importance.

But if some features suggest Joshua's own lifetime, others point to a time somewhat later. The account of the long day when the sun stood still at Aijalon is substantiated by a quotation from another source, the Book of Jashar (10:13). This would hardly be natural for an eyewitness of the miracle, writing shortly after it happened. Also, there are 12 instances where the phrase "until this day" is employed by the author.

It seems safe to conclude that the book, at least in its early form, dates from the beginning of the monarchy. Some think that Samuel may have had a hand in shaping or compiling the materials of the book, but in fact we are unsure who the final author or editor was.

The Life of Joshua

Joshua's remarkable life was filled with excitement, variety, success and honor. He was known for his deep trust in God and as "a man in whom is the Spirit" (Num 27:18). As a youth he lived through the bitter realities of slavery in Egypt, but he also witnessed the supernatural plagues and the miracle of Israel's escape from the army of the Egyptians when the waters of the sea opened before them. In the Sinai peninsula it was Joshua who led the troops of Israel to victory over the Amalekites (Ex 17:8–13). He alone was allowed to accompany Moses up the holy mountain where the tablets of the testimony were received (Ex 24:13–14). And it was he who stood watch at the temporary tent of meeting Moses set up before the tabernacle was erected (Ex 33:11).

Joshua was elected to represent his own tribe of Ephraim when the 12 spies were sent into Canaan to look over the land. Only Joshua and his friend Caleb were ready to follow God's will and take immediate possession of the land (see Num 14:26–34). The rest were condemned to die in the wilderness. Even Moses died short of the goal and was told to turn everything over to Joshua. God promised to guide and strengthen Joshua, just as he had Moses (Deut 31:23).

Joshua proved to be not only a military strategist in the battles that followed, but also a statesman in the way he governed the tribes. Above all, he was God's chosen servant (see 24:29 and note on Deut 34:5) to bring Moses' work to completion and establish Israel in the promised land. In that role he was a striking OT type (foreshadowing) of Christ (see notes on Heb 4:1,6–8).

Historical Setting

At the time of the Israelite migration into Canaan the superpowers of the ancient Near East were relatively weak. The Hittites had faded from the scene. Neither Babylon nor Egypt could maintain a military presence in Canaan, and the Assyrians would not send in their armies until centuries later.

As the tribes circled east of the Dead Sea, only the stronghold of Edom offered any resistance. Moab was forced to let Israel pass through her territory and camp in her plains. When Og and Sihon, two regional Amorite kings of Transjordan, tried to stop the Israelites, they were easily defeated and their lands occupied.

Biblical archaeologists call this period the Late Bronze Age (1550–1200 B.C.). Today thousands of artifacts give testimony to the richness of the Canaanite material culture, which was in many ways superior to that of the Israelites. When the ruins of the ancient kingdom of Ugarit were discovered at modern Ras Shamra on the northern coast of Syria (see chart on "Ancient Texts Relating to the OT," p. xix), a wealth of new information came to light concerning the domestic, commercial and religious life of the Canaanites. From a language close to Hebrew came stories of ancient kings and gods that revealed their immoral behavior and cruelty. In addition, pagan temples, altars, tombs and ritual vessels have been uncovered, throwing more light on the culture and customs of the peoples surrounding Israel.

Excavations at the ancient sites of Megiddo, Beth Shan and Gezer show how powerfully fortified these cities were and why they were not captured and occupied by Israel in Joshua's day. Many other fortified towns were taken, however, so that Israel became firmly established in the land as the dominant power. Apart from Jericho and Ai, Joshua is reported to have burned only Hazor (11:13), so attempts to date these events by destruction levels in the mounds of Canaan's ancient cities are questionable undertakings. It must also be remembered that other groups were involved in campaigns in the region about this time, among whom were Egyptian rulers and the Sea Peoples (including the Philistines). There had also been much intercity warfare among the Canaanites, and afterward the period of the judges was marked by general turbulence.

Much of the data from archaeology appears to support a date for Joshua's invasion c. 1250 B.C. This fits well with an exodus that would then have taken place 40 years earlier under the famous Rameses II, who ruled from the Nile delta at a city with the same name (Ex 1:11). It also places Joseph in Egypt in a favorable situation. Four hundred years before Rameses II the pharaohs were the Semitic Hyksos, who also ruled from the delta near the land of Goshen.

On the other hand, a good case can be made for the traditional viewpoint that the invasion occurred c. 1406 B.C. The oppression would have taken place under Amunhotep II after the death of his father Thutmose III, who is known to have used slave labor in his building projects. The earlier date also fits better with the two numbers found in Judg 11:26 and 1 Kin 6:1, since it allows for an additional 150 years between Moses and the monarchy. See also the Introductions to Genesis: Author and Date of Writing; Exodus: Chronology; and Judges: Background.

Outline

- I. The Entrance into the Land (1:1—5:12)
  - A. The Exhortations to Conquer (ch. 1)
  - B. The Reconnaissance of Jericho (ch. 2)
  - C. The Crossing of the Jordan (chs. 3—4)
  - D. The Consecration at Gilgal (5:1–12)
- II. The Conquest of the Land (5:13—12:24)
  - A. The Initial Battles (5:13—8:35)
    - 1. The victory at Jericho (5:13—6:27)
    - 2. The failure at Ai because of Achan's sin (ch. 7)
    - 3. The victory at Ai (8:1–29)
    - 4. The covenant renewed at Shechem (8:30–35)
  - B. The Campaign in the South (chs. 9—10)
    - 1. The treaty with the Gibeonites (ch. 9)
    - 2. The long day of Joshua (10:1–15)
    - 3. The southern cities conquered (10:16–43)
  - C. The Campaign in the North (ch. 11)
  - D. The Defeated Kings of Canaan (ch. 12)
- III. The Distribution of the Land (chs. 13—21)
  - A. Areas Yet to Be Conquered (13:1–7)
  - B. The Land East of the Jordan for Reuben, Gad and Half of Manasseh (13:8–33)
  - C. The Lands Given to Judah and "Joseph" at Gilgal (chs. 14—17)
  - D. The Lands Given to the Remaining Tribes at Shiloh (chs. 18—19)
    - 1. The tabernacle at Shiloh (18:1–10)
    - 2. The allotments for Benjamin, Simeon, Zebulun, Issachar, Asher, Naphtali and Dan (18:11—19:48)
    - 3. The town given to Joshua (19:49–51)
  - E. The Cities Assigned to the Levites (chs. 20—21)
    - 1. The 6 cities of refuge (ch. 20)
    - 2. The 48 cities of the priests (ch. 21)
- IV. Epilogue: Tribal Unity and Loyalty to the Lord (chs. 22—24)
  - A. The Altar of Witness by the Jordan (ch. 22)
  - B. Joshua's Farewell Exhortation (ch. 23)
  - C. The Renewal of the Covenant at Shechem (24:1–28)
  - D. The Death and Burial of Joshua and Eleazar (24:29–33)

God's Charge to Joshua

1 Now it came about after the death of
Moses the servant of the LORD, that the
LORD spoke to Joshua the son of Nun, Moses'
[1]servant, saying,
2 "Moses [a]My servant is dead; now therefore arise, [b]cross this Jordan, you and all this
people, to the land which I am giving to
them, to the sons of Israel.
3 "[a]Every place on which the sole of your
foot treads, I have given it to you, just as I
spoke to Moses.
4 "[a]From the wilderness and this Lebanon, even as far as the great river, the river
Euphrates, all the land of the Hittites, and as
far as the Great Sea toward the setting of the
sun will be your territory.
5 "[a]No man will *be able to* stand before
you all the days of your life. Just as I have
been with Moses, I will be with you; [b]I will
not fail you or forsake you.
6 "[a]Be strong and courageous, for you
shall give this people possession of the land
which I swore to their fathers to give them.
7 "Only be strong and very courageous;
[1a]be careful to do according to all the law
which Moses My servant commanded you; do
not turn from it to the right or to the left, so
that you may [2]have success wherever you go.
8 "[a]This book of the law shall not depart
from your mouth, but you shall meditate on
it day and night, so that you may [1]be careful
to do according to all that is written in it; [b]for
then you will make your way prosperous,
and then you will [2]have success.
9 "Have I not commanded you? [a]Be strong
and courageous! [b]Do not tremble or be dismayed, for the LORD your God is with you
wherever you go."

Joshua Assumes Command

10 Then Joshua commanded the officers
of the people, saying,
11 "Pass through the midst of the camp and
command the people, saying, 'Prepare provisions for yourselves, for within [a]three days
you are to cross this Jordan, to go in to possess the land which the LORD your God is giving you, to possess it.'"
12 [a]To the Reubenites and to the Gadites
and to the half-tribe of Manasseh, Joshua
[1]said,
13 "Remember the word which Moses the
servant of the LORD commanded you, saying,
'[a]The LORD your God gives you rest and will
give you this land.'
14 "Your wives, your little ones, and your
cattle shall remain in the land which Moses
gave you beyond the Jordan, but you shall
cross before your brothers in battle array, all
your valiant warriors, and shall help them,
15 until the LORD gives your brothers rest,
as *He gives* you, and they also possess the
land which the LORD your God is giving

1:1 [1]Or *minister*
2 [a]Num 12:7; Deut 34:5 [b]Josh 1:11
3 [a]Deut 11:24
4 [a]Gen 15:18; Num 34:3
5 [a]Deut 7:24 [b]Deut 31:6, 7; Heb 13:5
6 [a]Deut 31:6, 7, 23
7 [1]Lit *observe* [2]Or *act wisely* [a]Deut 5:32
8 [1]Lit *observe*
8 [2]Or *act wisely* [a]Deut 31:24; Josh 8:34 [b]Deut 29:9; Ps 1:1-3
9 [a]Josh 1:7 [b]Deut 31:8
11 [a]Josh 3:2
12 [1]Lit *said, saying* [a]Num 32:20-22
13 [a]Deut 3:18-20

1:1–18 The Lord initiates the action by charging Joshua, His chosen replacement for Moses (see Deut 31:1–8), to lead Israel across the Jordan and take possession of the promised land. He urges courage and promises success—but only if Israel obeys the law of God that Moses has given them. The chapter consists of speeches significant in their content and order: The Lord commands Joshua as His appointed leader over His people (vv. 1–9); Joshua, as the Lord's representative, addresses Israel (vv. 10–15); Israel responds to Joshua as the Lord's representative and successor to Moses (vv. 16–18). Thus the events of the book are set in motion and the roles of the main actors indicated.

1:1 *after the death of Moses.* Immediately the time and occasion of the action are set forth, showing that the story will continue where Deuteronomy ended, with the death of Moses. Cf. "after the death of Joshua" (Judg 1:1). *servant of the LORD.* See notes on Ex 14:31; Deut 34:5; Ps 18 title; Is 41:8–9; 42:1. *Moses' servant.* The title by which Joshua served for many years as second in command (see Num 11:28; see also Ex 24:13; 33:11; Deut 1:38).

1:2 *Jordan.* The flow of the Jordan near Jericho was not large during most of the year (only 80–100 feet wide), but at flood stage in the spring it filled its wider bed, which at places was a mile wide and far more treacherous to cross. *land which I am giving to them.* A central theme of the Pentateuch (see Gen 12:1; 50:24; Ex 3:8; 23:31; Deut 1:8). Joshua records the fulfillment of this promise of God.

1:3–5 See Deut 11:24–25.

1:4 The dimensions of the land promised to Israel vary (compare this text and Gen 15:18 with Deut 34:1–4), but these are the farthest limits—conquered and held only by David and Solomon. Canaan was still called "Hatti-land" centuries after the Hittites had withdrawn to the north. But Joshua was to take all he set out to conquer; wherever he set his foot was his. His victories gave to the 12 tribes most of the central hill country and much of the Negev.

1:5 *I will be with you.* To direct, sustain and assure success.

1:6 *land which I swore to their fathers.* The long-awaited inheritance pledged to the descendants of Abraham (Gen 15:7,8–21) and of Jacob (Gen 28:13).

1:7 *be careful to do.* Success was not guaranteed unconditionally (see Deut 8:1; 11:8,22–25).

1:8 *book of the law.* A documentary form of the laws from Sinai was already extant. *mouth.* See Deut 4:9–10; 6:6–7; 11:19. The law was usually read orally (cf. Deut 30:9–14; Acts 8:30). *meditate.* See Ps 1:2.

1:9 *Have I not commanded you?* A rhetorical question that emphasizes the authority of the speaker.

1:10 *Joshua commanded.* At this point Joshua assumes full command. *officers.* May refer to those whom Moses had appointed over the divisions within the tribes (Ex 18:21; Deut 1:15).

1:11 *provisions.* Foodstuffs needed for the next several days of march.

1:12–15 The threat from the two kings of Transjordan was overcome by military victory and the occupation of the lands north of Moab and east of the Jordan River. The two and a half tribes who asked to remain had been charged by Moses to send their fighting men across with the rest to conquer Canaan (Num 21:21–35; 32:1–27). The conquest of the promised land must be an undertaking by all Israel.

1:13 *rest.* An important OT concept (see notes on Deut 3:20; 2 Sam 7:1,11), implying secure borders, peace with neighboring countries and absence of threat to life and well-being within the land (see note on 1 Kin 5:4).

1:14 *in battle array, all your valiant warriors.* Those over 20 (see, e.g., Ex 38:26), known for their valor and able to equip themselves with the weapons of war.

them. [a]Then you shall return to [1]your own
land, and possess [2]that which Moses [b]the
servant of the LORD gave you beyond the Jordan toward the sunrise."
16 They answered Joshua, saying, "All
that you have commanded us we will do,
and wherever you send us we will go.
17 "Just as we obeyed Moses in all things,
so we will obey you; only [a]may the LORD
your God be with you as He was with Moses.
18 "Anyone who rebels against your [1]com-
mand and does not obey your words in all
that you command him, shall be put to
death; only be strong and courageous."

Rahab Shelters Spies

2 Then Joshua the son of Nun sent two
men as spies secretly from [a]Shittim, saying, "Go, view the land, especially Jericho."
So they went and came into the house of [b]a
harlot whose name was Rahab, and [1]lodged
there.
2 It was told the king of Jericho, saying,
"Behold, men from the sons of Israel have
come here tonight to search out the land."
3 And the king of Jericho sent *word* to
Rahab, saying, "Bring out the men who have
come to you, who have entered your house,
for they have come to search out all the land."
4 But the [a]woman had taken the two
men and hidden them, and she said, "Yes,
the men came to me, but I did not know
where they were from.
5 "It came about when *it was time* to shut
the gate at dark, that the men went out; I do
not know where the men went. Pursue them
quickly, for you will overtake them."
6 But [a]she had brought them up to the
roof and hidden them in the stalks of flax
which she had laid in order on the roof.
7 So the men pursued them on the road
to the Jordan to the fords; and as soon as
those who were pursuing them had gone
out, they shut the gate.
8 Now before they lay down, [1]she came
up to them on the roof,
9 and said to the men, "[a]I know that the
LORD has given you the land, and that the
[b]terror of you has fallen on us, and that all
the inhabitants of the land have [1]melted
away before you.
10 "[a]For we have heard how the LORD dried
up the water of the [1]Red Sea before you
when you came out of Egypt, and [b]what you
did to the two kings of the Amorites who
were beyond the Jordan, to Sihon and Og,
whom you [2]utterly destroyed.
11 "When we heard *it*, [a]our hearts melted
and no [1]courage remained in any man any
longer because of you; for the [b]LORD your
God, He is God in heaven above and on
earth beneath.
12 "Now therefore, please swear to me by
the LORD, since I have dealt kindly with you,
that you also will deal kindly with my
father's household, and give me a [a]pledge of
[1]truth,
13 and [1]spare my father and my mother
and my brothers and my sisters, with all who
belong to them, and deliver our [2]lives from
death."
14 So the men said to her, "Our [1]life [2]for
yours if you do not tell this business of ours;
and it shall come about when the LORD gives

15 [1]Lit *the land of your possession* [2]Lit *it* [a]Josh 22:4 [b]Josh 1:1
17 [a]Josh 1:5, 9
18 [1]Lit *mouth*
2:1 [1]Lit *lay down* [a]Num 25:1; Josh 3:1 [b]Heb 11:31; James 2:25
4 [a]2 Sam 17:19
6 [a]James 2:25
8 [1]Lit *then she*
9 [1]Or *become demoralized* [a]Num 20:24; Josh 9:24 [b]Ex 23:27; Deut 2:25; Josh 9:9, 10
10 [1]Lit *Sea of Reeds* [2]Or *put under the ban* [a]Ex 14:21; Num 23:22; 24:8 [b]Num 21:21-35
11 [1]Lit *spirit arose* [a]Josh 5:1; 7:5; Ps 22:14; Is 13:7; 19:1 [b]Deut 4:39
12 [1]Or *faithfulness* [a]Josh 2:18, 19
13 [1]Lit *let live* [2]Lit *souls*
14 [1]Lit *soul* [2]Lit *instead of you to die*

1:18 *Anyone who rebels.* Having just taken the oath of allegiance to Joshua, they now agree to the death penalty for any act of treason (e.g., the sin of Achan, 7:15). *be strong and courageous.* The people's words of encouragement to Joshua echo and reinforce those from the Lord (vv. 6–7,9).

2:1–24 The mission of the two spies and the account of Rahab. The practice of reconnaissance and espionage is as old as war itself (cf. Judg 7:10–11; 1 Sam 26:6–12). Rahab became a convert to the God of Israel and a famous woman among the Hebrews. She is honored in the NT for her faith (Heb 11:31) and for her good works (James 2:25).

2:1 *sent . . . from Shittim.* The invasion point was in the plains of Moab facing toward the Jordan and Jericho (Num 33:48–49). The Hebrew word *Shittim* means "acacia trees," which grow in the semi-arid conditions of the wilderness. *especially Jericho.* The primary focus of the spies. It was a fortified city, was well supplied by strong springs, which helped to make it an oasis, and was located just five miles west of the Jordan. Its name probably means "moon city," and archaeological excavations there reveal continuous occupation back to at least 7000 B.C. *harlot.* Josephus and other early sources refer to Rahab as an "innkeeper", but see Heb 11:31; James 2:25.

2:2 *king of Jericho.* The major cities of Canaan were in reality small kingdoms, each ruled by a local king (attested also in the Amarna letters of the 14th century B.C.; see chart, p. xix).

2:6 *hidden . . . in the stalks of flax.* Rooftops in the Near East are still used for drying grain or stalks. Rahab's cunning saved the lives of the two Israelites but put her own life in jeopardy.

2:7 *Jordan . . . fords.* Shallow crossings of the Jordan, where the depth of normal flow averages only three feet.

2:8–11 Rahab's confession has a significant concentric structure:

a. "I know";

b. "terror. . . has fallen on us . . . the inhabitants of the land";

c. "we have heard";

bb. "our hearts melted and no courage remained in any man";

aa. "the LORD your God, He is God."

Rahab's personal confession forms the outer frame (a.–aa.); the inner frame (b.–bb.) offers the military intelligence that the spies report back to Joshua; the center (c., v. 10) sums up the news about the Lord that occasioned both the Canaanite fear and Rahab's abandonment of Canaan and its gods for the Lord and Israel. Her confession of faith in the Lord and her accurate information about the Lord's triumphs over powerful enemies are astounding. That the hearts of the Canaanites were "melted away" (v. 9) was vital information to the spies.

2:10 *utterly destroyed.* See note on Num 21:2.

2:12 *deal kindly with my father's household.* The Hebrew for "kindness" or "kindly" is frequently translated "love" or "unfailing love" and often summarizes God's covenant favor toward His people or the love that people are to show to others. Rahab had acted toward the spies as though she was an Israelite, and now she asks that Israel treat her similarly. *pledge of truth.* Their oath to spare the whole family (v. 14).

2:14 *kindly and faithfully.* The terms of the pledge made by

us the land that we will [a]deal kindly and [3]faithfully with you."

The Promise to Rahab

15 Then she let them down by a rope through the window, for her house was on the city wall, so that she was living on the wall.

16 She said to them, "[a]Go to the hill country, so that the pursuers will not happen upon you, and hide yourselves there for three days until the pursuers return. Then afterward you may go on your way."

17 The men said to her, "[a]We *shall be* free from this oath [1]to you which you have made us swear,

18 [1]unless, when we come into the land, you tie this cord of scarlet thread in the window through which you let us down, and [a]gather to yourself into the house your father and your mother and your brothers and all your father's household.

19 "It shall come about that anyone who goes out of the doors of your house into the street, his blood *shall be* on his own head, and we *shall be* free; but anyone who is with you in the house, [a]his blood *shall be* on our head if a hand is *laid* on him.

20 "But if you tell this business of ours, then we shall be free from the oath which you have made us swear."

21 She said, "According to your words, so be it." So she sent them away, and they departed; and she tied the scarlet cord in the window.

22 They departed and came to the hill country, and remained there for three days until the pursuers returned. Now the pursuers had sought *them* [1]all along the road, but had not found *them*.

23 Then the two men returned and came down from the hill country and crossed over and came to Joshua the son of Nun, and they related to him all that had happened to them.

24 They said to Joshua, "Surely the LORD has given all the land into our hands; moreover, [a]all the inhabitants of the land have [1]melted away before us."

Israel Crosses the Jordan

3 Then Joshua rose early in the morning; and he and all the sons of Israel set out from [a]Shittim and came to the Jordan, and they lodged there before they crossed.

2 [a]At the end of three days the officers went through the midst of the camp;

3 and they commanded the people, saying, "When you see the [a]ark of the covenant of the LORD your God with the Levitical priests carrying it, then you shall set out from your place and go after it.

4 "However, there shall be between you and it a distance of about 2,000 [1]cubits by measure. Do not come near it, that you may know the way by which you shall go, for you have not passed this way before."

5 Then Joshua said to the people, "[a]Consecrate yourselves, for tomorrow the LORD will do wonders among you."

6 And Joshua spoke to the priests, saying, "Take up the ark of the covenant and cross over ahead of the people." So they took up the ark of the covenant and went ahead of the people.

7 Now the LORD said to Joshua, "This day I will begin to [a]exalt you in the sight of all

14 [3]Or *truly* [a]Gen 24:49
16 [a]James 2:25
17 [1]Lit *of yours* [a]Gen 24:8
18 [1]Lit *behold* [a]Josh 2:12
19 [a]Matt 27:25
22 [1]Lit *through all the road*
24 [1]Or *become demoralized* [a]Josh 2:9
3:1 [a]Josh 2:1
2 [a]Josh 1:11
3 [a]Deut 31:9
4 [1]I.e. One cubit equals approx 18 in.
5 [a]Ex 19:10, 11; Josh 7:13
7 [a]Josh 4:14

the spies echo Rahab's request (v. 12). *when the LORD gives us the land.* All were convinced of the inevitable victory of the Israelites over the city of Jericho.

2:15 *her house was on the city wall.* There is archaeological evidence that the people of Jericho would occasionally build their houses onto the city wall. Although this evidence predates the time of Joshua, it may still serve to illumine this verse. Alternatively, the Late Bronze fortifications at Jericho may have included a casemate wall (a hollow wall with partitions), and Rahab may have occupied one or more rooms inside it.

2:18 *cord of scarlet thread in the window.* The function of the red marker was similar to that of the blood of the Passover lamb when the Lord struck down the firstborn of Egypt (see Ex 12:13,22–23). The early church viewed the blood-colored cord as a type (symbol) of Christ's atonement.

2:19 *his blood shall be on our head.* A vow that accepted responsibility for the death of another, with its related guilt and the retribution meted out by either relatives or the state.

2:22 *the hill country.* Directly west of ancient Jericho were the high, rugged hills of the central mountain ridge in Canaan. They are honeycombed with caves, making the concealment and escape of the two spies relatively easy.

3:1–4:24 Details of the river crossing and the memorial of 12 stones set up in the camp at Gilgal. The great significance of this account can hardly be overemphasized, since it marks the crossing of the boundary into the promised land and parallels the miracle of the "Red Sea" crossing in the exodus (Ex 14–15). The Israelites' faith in the God of their fathers was renewed and strengthened when it was about to be most severely challenged, while at the same time the Canaanites' fear was greatly increased (5:1). In this account the author uses an "overlay" technique in which, having narrated the crossing to its conclusion (ch. 3), he returns to various points in the event to enlarge on several details: the stones for a memorial (4:1–9); the successful crossing by all Israel (4:10–14); the renewed flow of the river after the crossing was completed (4:15–18). The final paragraph of ch. 4 (vv. 19–24) picks up the story again from 3:17 and completes the account by noting Israel's encampment at Gilgal and the erecting of the stone memorial.

3:3 *ark of the covenant.* The most sacred of the tabernacle furnishings (see Ex 25:10–22). Since it signified the Lord's throne, the Lord Himself went into the Jordan ahead of His people as He led them into the land of rest (see Num 10:33–36).

3:4 *distance of about 2,000 cubits.* There was evidently a line of march, with the priests and ark leading the way. Respect for the sacred symbol of the Lord's holy presence accounts for this gap of about 1,000 yards between the people and the priests bearing the ark.

3:5 *Consecrate yourselves.* Before their meeting with God at Sinai this had involved washing all their garments as well as their bodies, and also abstinence from sexual intercourse (see Ex 19:10,14–15).

3:7 *I will begin to exalt you.* A prime objective for the divine intervention at the Jordan was to validate the leadership of

Israel, that they may know that just as I have
been with Moses, I will be with you.
8 "You shall, moreover, command the
priests who are carrying the ark of the covenant, saying, 'When you come to the edge
of the waters of the Jordan, you shall stand
still in the Jordan.' "
9 Then Joshua said to the sons of Israel,
"Come here, and hear the words of the LORD
your God."
10 Joshua said, "By this you shall know
that [a]the living God is among you, and that
He will assuredly [b]dispossess from before
you the Canaanite, the Hittite, the Hivite, the
Perizzite, the Girgashite, the Amorite, and
the Jebusite.
11 "Behold, the ark of the covenant of [a]the
Lord of all the earth is crossing over ahead of
you into the Jordan.
12 "Now then, [a]take for yourselves twelve
men from the tribes of Israel, one man for
each tribe.
13 "It shall come about when the soles of
the feet of the priests who carry the ark of
the LORD, the Lord of all the earth, rest in the
waters of the Jordan, the waters of the Jordan will be cut off, *and* the waters which are
[1]flowing down from above [2]will [a]stand in
one heap."
14 So when the people set out from their
tents to cross the Jordan with the priests carrying [a]the ark of the covenant before the
people,
15 and when those who carried the ark
came into the Jordan, and the feet of the
priests carrying the ark were dipped in the
edge of the water (for the [a]Jordan overflows
all its banks all the days of harvest),
16 [a]the waters which were [1]flowing down
from above stood *and* rose up in [b]one heap,
a great distance away at Adam, the city that
is beside Zarethan; and those which were
[1]flowing down toward the sea of the [c]Ara-
bah, the Salt Sea, were completely cut off. So
the people crossed opposite Jericho.
17 And the priests who carried the ark of
the covenant of the LORD stood firm [a]on dry
ground in the middle of the Jordan while all
Israel crossed on dry ground, until all the
nation had finished crossing the Jordan.

Memorial Stones from Jordan

4 Now when all the nation had finished
crossing the [a]Jordan, the LORD spoke to
Joshua, saying,
2 "[a]Take for yourselves twelve men from
the people, one man from each tribe,
3 and command them, saying, 'Take up
for yourselves twelve stones from here out of
the middle of the Jordan, from the place
where the priests' feet are standing firm, and
carry them over with you and lay them down
in [a]the lodging place where you will lodge
tonight.' "
4 So Joshua called the twelve men whom
he had appointed from the sons of Israel, one
man from each tribe;
5 and Joshua said to them, "[1]Cross again
to the ark of the LORD your God into the middle of the Jordan, and each of you take up a
stone on his shoulder, according to the number of the tribes of the sons of Israel.

10 [a]Deut 5:26; 1 Thess 1:9 [b]Ex 33:2; Deut 7:1
11 [a]Job 41:11; Ps 24:1; Zech 6:5
12 [a]Josh 4:2
13 [1]Lit *going* [2]Lit *and they will* [a]Ex 15:8
14 [a]Ps 132:8; Acts 7:44f
15 [a]1 Chr 12:15; Jer 12:5; 49:19
16 [1]Lit *going* [a]Ps 66:6; 74:15; 114:3, 5 [b]Josh 3:13 [c]Deut 1:1
17 [a]Ex 14:21, 22, 29
4:1 [a]Deut 27:2; Josh 3:17
2 [a]Josh 3:12
3 [a]Josh 4:20
5 [1]Lit *Cross before the ark*

Joshua. With a miraculous event so much like that of the "Red Sea" crossing, Joshua's position as the Lord's servant would be shown to be comparable to that of Moses.

3:10 *By this you shall know.* The manner by which God is about to bring Israel across the Jordan River, the watery boundary of the promised land, will bring assurance that the one true God is with them and that He will surely dislodge the present inhabitants of Canaan. Two fundamental issues are at stake: 1. Who is the true and mighty God—the God of Israel or the god on whom the Canaanites depend (Baal, who was believed to reign as king among the gods because he had triumphed over the sea-god)? By opening the way through the flooded Jordan the Lord would show both Israel and the Canaanites that He is Lord over the waters (as He was at the "Red Sea," at the flood and at creation) and that He is able to establish His own order in the world. See 1 Kin 20:23; 2 Kin 18:32–35. 2. Who has the rightful claim to the land—the Lord or the Canaanites? (For the juridical aspect of such wars see Judg 11:27.) By passing safely through the Jordan at the head of His army the Lord showed the rightness of His claim on the land. In the ancient Near East a common way for obtaining the judicial verdict of the gods was by compelling the accused to submit to trial by water ordeal. Usually this involved casting him into a river (if the accused drowned, the gods had found him guilty; if not, the gods had declared him innocent). In Israel, however, another form of water ordeal was practiced (see Num 5:16–28). Significantly, the Lord would enter the Jordan first and then remain there until His whole army had crossed safely over. Thus His claim to the land was vindicated before the eyes of all who heard about it. And it was His claim, not Israel's; she came through the Jordan only with Him and as His army, "baptized" to His service. *Canaanite . . . Jebusite.* See notes on Gen 9:25; 10:6,15–16; 13:7; 15:16; 23:3; Ex 3:8; Judg 3:3; 6:10.

3:12 *take . . . twelve men.* Joshua seems to anticipate the Lord's instructions concerning a stone monument of the event (see 4:2–3).

3:13 *cut off.* Blocked, stopped in its flow. *stand in one heap.* The Hebrew for "heap" is found here, in v. 16 and also in the poetic accounts of the "Red Sea" crossing (Ex 15:8; Ps 78:13). It is possible that God used a physical means (such as a landslide) to dam up the Jordan at the place called Adam (v. 16), near the entrance of the Jabbok. (As recently as 1927 a blockage of the water in this area was recorded that lasted over 20 hours.) But if so, the miraculous element is not diminished (see Ex 14:21).

3:15 *when.* The stoppage nearly 20 miles upstream (v. 16) would have happened several hours earlier to make the events coincide. *overflows all its banks.* Because of the spring rains and the melting of snow on Mount Hermon. *harvest.* Grain harvest took place in April and May.

3:17 *the priests who carried the ark . . . stood firm on dry ground in the middle of the Jordan.* Signifying that the Lord Himself remained in the place of danger until all Israel had crossed the Jordan.

4:3 *in the lodging place where you will lodge tonight.* Indicating that the entire nation made the crossing in one day.

6 "[1]Let this be a sign among you, so that
[a]when your children ask [2]later, saying,
'What do these stones mean to you?'
7 then you shall say to them, 'Because
the [a]waters of the Jordan were cut off before
the ark of the covenant of the LORD; when it
crossed the Jordan, the waters of the Jordan
were cut off.' So these stones shall become a
[b]memorial to the sons of Israel forever."
8 Thus the sons of Israel did as Joshua
commanded, and took up twelve stones from
the middle of the Jordan, just as the LORD
spoke to Joshua, according to the number of
the tribes of the sons of Israel; and they carried them over with them to [a]the lodging
place and put them down there.
9 Then Joshua set up twelve [a]stones in
the middle of the Jordan at the place where
the feet of the priests who carried the ark of
the covenant were standing, and they are
there to this day.
10 For the priests who carried the ark were
standing in the middle of the Jordan until
everything was completed that the LORD had
commanded Joshua to speak to the people,
according to all that Moses had commanded
Joshua. And the people hurried and crossed;
11 and when all the people had finished
crossing, the ark of the LORD and the priests
crossed before the people.
12 [a]The sons of Reuben and the sons of
Gad and the half-tribe of Manasseh crossed
over in battle array before the sons of Israel,
just as Moses had spoken to them;
13 about 40,000 equipped for war, crossed
for battle before the LORD to the desert plains
of Jericho.
14 [a]On that day the LORD exalted Joshua
in the sight of all Israel; so that they [1]revered
him, just as they had [1]revered Moses all the
days of his life.
15 Now the LORD said to [1]Joshua,
16 "Command the priests who carry [a]the
ark of the testimony that they come up from
the Jordan."

6 [1]Lit *That this may be* [2]Lit *tomorrow* [a]Ex 12:26; 13:14; Josh 4:21
7 [a]Josh 3:13 [b]Ex 12:14; Num 16:40
8 [a]Josh 4:20
9 [a]Gen 28:18; Josh 24:26f; 1 Sam 7:12
12 [a]Num 32:17
14 [1]Or *feared* [a]Josh 3:7
15 [1]Lit *Joshua, saying*
16 [a]Ex 25:16
18 [1]Lit *drawn out*
19 [a]Deut 1:3
20 [1]Lit *these* [a]Josh 4:8 [b]Josh 4:3, 8
21 [1]Lit *Israel, saying,*
22 [a]Josh 3:17
23 [1]Lit *Sea of Reeds* [a]Ex 14:21
24 [1]Or *reverence* [2]Lit *all the days* [a]1 Kin 8:42; 2 Kin 19:19; Ps 106:8 [b]Ex 15:16; 1 Chr 29:12; Ps 89:13 [c]Ex 14:31; Ps 76:7f; Jer 10:7
5:1 [1]Other mss read *we* [a]Num 13:29 [b]Josh 2:10, 11
2 [a]Ex 4:25

17 So Joshua commanded the priests, saying, "Come up from the Jordan."
18 It came about when the priests who
carried the ark of the covenant of the LORD
had come up from the middle of the Jordan,
and the soles of the priests' feet were [1]lifted
up to the dry ground, that the waters of the
Jordan returned to their place, and went over
all its banks as before.
19 Now the people came up from the Jordan on the [a]tenth of the first month and
camped at Gilgal on the eastern edge of Jericho.
20 [1][a]Those twelve stones which they had
taken from the Jordan, Joshua set up [b]at Gilgal.
21 He said to the sons of [1]Israel, "When
your children ask their fathers in time to
come, saying, 'What are these stones?'
22 then you shall inform your children,
saying, 'Israel crossed this Jordan on [a]dry
ground.'
23 "For the LORD your God dried up the
waters of the Jordan before you until you
had crossed, just as the LORD your God had
done to the [1]Red Sea, [a]which He dried up
before us until we had crossed;
24 that [a]all the peoples of the earth may
know that the [b]hand of the LORD is mighty,
so that you may [1][c]fear the LORD your God
[2]forever."

Israel Is Circumcised

5 Now it came about when all the kings of
the Amorites who *were* beyond the Jordan to the west, and all the kings of the
[a]Canaanites who *were* by the sea, [b]heard
how the LORD had dried up the waters of the
Jordan before the sons of Israel until [1]they
had crossed, that their hearts melted, and
there was no spirit in them any longer
because of the sons of Israel.
2 At that time the LORD said to Joshua,
"Make for yourself [a]flint knives and circumcise again the sons of Israel the second time."

4:6 *What do these stones mean . . . ?* A stone monument was commonly used as a memorial to remind future generations of what had happened at that place (24:26; 1 Sam 7:12).
4:9 *Joshua set up twelve stones in.* Suggesting that Joshua set up a second pile in the middle of the river. An alternative translation ("Joshua set up the twelve stones that had been in") suggests that each tribe brought a stone for the monument from the riverbed to the new campsite at Gilgal, and Joshua constructed the monument there (see v. 20).
4:13 *about 40,000.* Seems too few for the number of men listed in Num 26 for Reuben, Gad and half of Manasseh; the contingents were very likely representative since it would have been imprudent to leave the people undefended who settled in Transjordan (cf. 22:8, "brothers"; Num 32:17).
4:19 *tenth of the first month.* The day the Passover lamb was to be selected (Ex 12:3). *Gilgal.* Usually identified with the ruins at Khirbet el-Mafjer, two miles northeast of Jericho.
4:23 *God dried up the . . . Jordan.* Still another descriptive phrase for the miracle, along with "the waters . . . cut off," "rose up in one heap" and "waters . . . stood" (3:16).
4:24 *that all . . . may know.* The Lord's revelation of His power to the Israelites was a public event that all the Canaanites heard about (see 5:1), just as they had heard of the crossing of the "Red Sea" and defeat of Sihon and Og (2:10). *you.* The Hebrew can also be read as "they." *fear the LORD.* Worship and serve Him according to His commandments.
5:1–12 Two covenantal ceremonies were resumed at Gilgal in accordance with the laws from Sinai: the rite of circumcision and the Feast of the Passover. Both were significant preparations for the conquest of the promised land.
5:1 *Amorites . . . Canaanites.* Usually interchangeable, these general names included the many smaller nations in the land. Amorite meant "westerner," and Canaanite referred to the people living along the Mediterranean coast. This verse perhaps concludes the account of the crossing since it notes the effect of that event on the peoples of Canaan (see note on 3:10).
5:2 *flint knives.* Metal knives were available, but flint made a more efficient surgical tool, as modern demonstrations have

3 So Joshua made himself flint knives and circumcised the sons of Israel at [1]Gibeath-haaraloth.

4 This is the reason why Joshua circumcised them: [a]all the people who came out of Egypt who were males, all the men of war, died in the wilderness along the way after they came out of Egypt.

5 For all the people who came out were circumcised, but all the people who were born in the wilderness along the way as they came out of Egypt had not been circumcised.

6 For the sons of Israel walked [a]forty years in the wilderness, until all the nation, *that is*, the men of war who came out of Egypt, [1]perished because they did not listen to the voice of the LORD, [b]to whom the LORD had sworn that He would not let them see the land which the LORD had sworn to their fathers to give us, a land flowing with milk and honey.

7 Their children whom He raised up in their place, Joshua [1]circumcised; for they were uncircumcised, because they had not circumcised them along the way.

8 Now when they had finished circumcising all the nation, they remained in their places in the camp until they were [1]healed.

9 Then the LORD said to Joshua, "Today I have rolled away [a]the reproach of Egypt from you." So the name of that place is called [1]Gilgal to this day.

3 [1]I.e. the hill of the foreskins
4 [a]Deut 2:14
6 [1]Lit *were finished* [a]Deut 2:7, 14 [b]Num 14:29-35; 26:63-65
7 [1]Lit *circumcised them*
8 [1]Lit *revived*
9 [1]I.e. rolling [a]Zeph 2:8

10 While the sons of Israel camped at Gilgal [a]they observed the Passover on the evening of the [b]fourteenth day of the month on the desert plains of Jericho.

11 On the [1]day after the Passover, on [2]that very day, they ate some of the produce of the land, unleavened cakes and parched *grain*.

12 [a]The manna ceased on the [1]day after they had eaten some of the produce of the land, so that the sons of Israel no longer had manna, but they ate some of the yield of the land of Canaan during that year.

13 Now it came about when Joshua was by Jericho, that he lifted up his eyes and looked, and behold, [a]a man was standing opposite him with his sword drawn in his hand, and Joshua went to him and said to him, "Are you for us or for our adversaries?"

14 He said, "No; rather I indeed come now *as* captain of the host of the LORD." And Joshua [a]fell on his face to the earth, and bowed down, and said to him, "What has my lord to say to his servant?"

15 The captain of the LORD's host said to Joshua, "[a]Remove your sandals from your feet, for the place where you are standing is holy." And Joshua did so.

The Conquest of Jericho

6 Now Jericho was tightly shut because of the sons of Israel; no one went out and no one came in.

10 [a]Ex 12:18 [b]Josh 4:19
11 [1]Lit *morrow* [2]Lit *this*
12 [1]Lit *morrow* [a]Ex 16:35
13 [a]Gen 18:1, 2; 32:24, 30; Num 22:31
14 [a]Gen 17:3
15 [a]Ex 3:5

shown. Israel had to be consecrated to the Lord's service before she could undertake the Lord's warfare and take possession of the land (cf. Ex 4:24–26). *circumcise.* Circumcision marked every male as a son of Abraham (Gen 17:10–11) bound to the service of the Lord, and it was a prerequisite for the Passover (Ex 12:48).

5:3 *Gibeath-haaraloth.* See NASB marg.

5:6 *forty years.* The time between their departure from Egypt and the crossing of the Jordan. Only 38 years had passed since they turned back at Kadesh-barnea (Num 14:20–22; Deut 2:14).

5:9 *reproach of Egypt.* Although the reference may be to Egypt's enslavement of Israel, it is much more likely that the author had in mind the reproach the Egyptians would have cast upon her and her God if Israel had perished in the wilderness (see Ex 32:12; Num 14:13; Deut 9:28). Now that the wilderness journey is over and Israel is safely in the promised land as His special people consecrated to Him by circumcision, the reproach of Egypt is rolled away.

5:10 *Passover.* The ceremonies took place in the month of Abib, the first month of the year (Ex 12:2). At twilight on the 14th day of the month the Passover lamb was to be slaughtered, then roasted and eaten that same night (Ex 12:5–8). Israel had not celebrated Passover since Sinai, one year after her release from Egypt (Num 9:1–5). Before the next season she had rebelled at the border of Canaan, and the generation of the exodus had been condemned to die in the wilderness (Num 14:21–23, 29–35). For that generation the celebration of Passover (deliverance from judgment) could have had little meaning.

5:11 *unleavened cakes.* Bread baked without yeast. It was to be eaten during the seven feast days that followed (Ex 12:15; Lev 23:6).

5:12 *manna ceased.* This transition from eating manna to eating the "produce of the land" (v. 11) ended 40 years of dependence on God's special provision. Manna was God's gift for the wilderness journey; from now on He provided Israel with food from the promised land.

5:13–6:5 The narration of the conquest is introduced by the sudden appearance of a heavenly figure who calls himself the "captain of the host of the LORD" (5:14).

5:13 *Joshua was by Jericho.* The leader of God's army went to scout the nearest Canaanite stronghold, but another warrior was already on the scene. *a man was standing.* The experience is taken by many to be an encounter with God in human form (theophany), or with Christ (Christophany). But angels also were sent on missions of this kind (Judg 6:11; 13:3), and some were identified as captains over the heavenly armies (Dan 10:5,20; 12:1).

5:14 *No; rather.* Joshua and Israel must know their place—it is not that God is on their side; rather, they must fight God's battles. *captain of the host of the LORD.* God has sent the commander of His heavenly armies to take charge of the battle on earth. Joshua must take orders from him (6:2–5), and he can also know that the armies of heaven are committed to this war—as later events confirm. *my lord.* A term of respect for a superior.

5:15 Joshua is commissioned to undertake the Lord's battles for Canaan, just as Moses had been commissioned to confront Pharaoh (Ex 3:5).

6:1 *Jericho.* Modern Tell es-Sultan, site of more than two dozen ancient cities, built and destroyed, one above the other. Many had powerful, double walls, but none of the levels has been positively identified as the one that fell under Joshua. The tell (mound) is roughly 400 by 200 yards in size. Since Jericho may have been a center for the worship of the moon-god (Jericho probably means "moon city"), God was destroying not only Canaanite cities, but also Canaanite religion. See map No. 3 at the end of the study Bible.

2 The LORD said to Joshua, "See, I have given Jericho into your hand, with [a]its king *and* the valiant warriors.

3 "You shall march around the city, all the men of war circling the city once. You shall do so for six days.

4 "Also seven priests shall carry seven [a]trumpets of rams' horns before the ark; then on the seventh day you shall march around the city seven times, and the priests shall blow the trumpets.

5 "It shall be that when they make a long blast with the ram's horn, and when you hear the sound of the trumpet, all the people shall shout with a great shout; and the wall of the city will fall down [1]flat, and the people will go up every man [2]straight ahead."

6 So Joshua the son of Nun called the priests and said to them, "Take up the ark of the covenant, and let seven priests carry seven trumpets of rams' horns before the ark of the LORD."

7 Then [1]he said to the people, "Go forward, and march around the city, and let the armed men go on before the ark of the LORD."

8 And it was *so,* that when Joshua had spoken to the people, the seven priests carrying the seven trumpets of rams' horns before the LORD went forward and blew the trumpets; and the ark of the covenant of the LORD followed them.

9 The armed men went before the priests who blew the trumpets, and [a]the rear guard came after the ark, while they continued to blow the trumpets.

10 But Joshua commanded the people, saying, "You shall not shout nor let your voice be heard nor let a word proceed out of your mouth, until the day I tell you, 'Shout!' Then you shall shout!"

11 So he had the ark of the LORD [1]taken around the city, circling *it* once; then they came into the camp and spent the night in the camp.

12 Now Joshua rose early in the morning, and the priests took up the ark of the LORD.

13 [a]The seven priests carrying the seven trumpets of rams' horns before the ark of the LORD went on continually, and blew the trumpets; and the armed men went before them and [b]the rear guard came after the ark of the LORD, while they continued to blow the trumpets.

14 Thus the second day they marched around the city once and returned to the camp; they did so for six days.

15 Then on the seventh day they rose early at the dawning of the day and marched around the city in the same manner seven times; only on that day they marched around the city seven times.

16 At the seventh time, when the priests blew the trumpets, Joshua said to the people, "[a]Shout! For the LORD has given you the city.

17 "The city shall be [a]under the ban, it and all that is in it belongs to the LORD; only Rahab the harlot [1]and all who are with her in the house shall live, because she hid the messengers whom we sent.

18 "But as for you, only keep yourselves from the things under the ban, so that you do not [1]covet *them* and [a]take some of the things under the ban, and make the camp of Israel accursed and bring trouble on it.

6:2 [a]Deut 7:24
4 [a]Lev 25:9
5 [1]Lit *in its place* [2]Lit *before himself*
7 [1]Or *they*
9 [a]Josh 6:13; Is 52:12
11 [1]Lit *to go around*
13 [a]Josh 6:4 [b]Josh 6:9
16 [a]2 Chr 13:14f
17 [1]Lit *she and all* [a]Lev 27:28; Deut 20:17
18 [1]Lit *devote* [a]Josh 7:1

6:2 *The LORD.* The Lord's command no doubt comes to Joshua through the "captain of the host of the LORD" (5:14), who orders the first conquest of a Canaanite city.

6:3 *march around the city.* A ritual act, signifying a siege of the city, that was to be repeated for six days.

6:4 *trumpets of rams' horns.* Instruments not of music but of signaling, in both religious and military contexts (which appear to come together here). The trumpets were to be sounded (v. 8), as on the seventh day, announcing the presence of the Lord (see 2 Sam 6:15; 1 Chr 15:28; Zech 9:14). *ark.* Signified that the Lord was laying siege to the city. *seventh day.* No note is taken of the sabbath during this seven-day siege, but perhaps that was the day the Lord gave the city to Israel as the first pledge of the land of rest. To arrive at the goal of a long march on the seventh day is a motif found also in other ancient Near Eastern literature. In any event, the remarkable constellation of sevens (seven priests with trumpets, seven days, seven encirclements on the seventh day) underscores the sacred significance of the event (see Introduction to Revelation: Distinctive Feature) and is, perhaps, a deliberate evoking of the seven days of creation to signal the beginning of God's new order in the world.

6:5 *long blast . . . great shout.* Signaling the onset of the attack—psychological warfare, intended to create panic and confusion (see Judg 7). In the Dead Sea Scroll of "The War of the Sons of Light against the Sons of Darkness," the Levites are instructed to blow in unison a great battle fanfare to melt the heart of the enemy (see essay, p. 1356.) *every man straight ahead.* Not a breach here and there but a general collapse of the walls, giving access to the city from all sides.

6:7 *armed men.* The Hebrew for this term differs from that in v. 3 but may be synonymous with it. It is to be expected that the ark led the procession. If so, the present reference may be to a kind of royal guard (but see v. 9 and note).

6:8–14 Throughout these verses the ark of the Lord is made the center of focus, highlighting the fact that it was the Lord Himself who besieged the city.

6:9 *rear guard.* If the rear guard was made up of the final contingents of the army (see Num 10:25), the armed guard of vv. 7,9 constituted the main body of troops.

6:12–14 Literary repetition reflects repetition in action, a common feature in ancient Near Eastern literature.

6:17 *under the ban.* See vv. 18, 21; 2:10; see also note on Num 21:2. The ban placed all of Jericho's inhabitants under the curse of death and all of the city's treasures that could not be destroyed under consignment to the Lord's house (v. 19). According to the law of Moses this ban could be applied to animals for sacrifice, to property given to God, or to any person found worthy of death (Lev 27:28–29). It was Moses himself who ruled that all the inhabitants of Canaan be "devoted" by execution for their idolatry and all its accompanying moral corruption (Deut 20:16–18). See note on Deut 2:34. *Rahab . . . and all who are with her in the house shall live.* Honoring the pledge made by the two spies (2:14).

6:18 *make the camp of Israel accursed.* See note on v. 17. If Israel took for herself anything that was under God's ban, she herself would fall under the ban.

19 "[a]But all the silver and gold and articles of bronze and iron are holy to the LORD; they shall go into the treasury of the LORD."

20 So the people shouted, and [1]*priests* blew the trumpets; and when the people heard the sound of the trumpet, the people shouted with a great shout and the [a]wall fell down [2]flat, so that the people went up into the city, every man straight [3]ahead, and they took the city.

21 [a]They [1]utterly destroyed everything in the city, both man and woman, young and old, and ox and sheep and donkey, with the edge of the sword.

22 Joshua said to the two men who had spied out the land, "[a]Go into the harlot's house and bring the woman and all she has out of there, as you have sworn to her."

23 So the young men who were spies went in and [a]brought out Rahab and her father and her mother and her brothers and all she had; they also brought out all her relatives and placed them outside the camp of Israel.

24 [a]They burned the city with fire, and all that was in it. Only the silver and gold, and articles of bronze and iron, they put into the treasury of the [1]house of the LORD.

25 However, [a]Rahab the harlot and her father's household and all she had, Joshua [1]spared; and she has lived in the midst of Israel to this day, for [b]she hid the messengers whom Joshua sent to spy out Jericho.

26 Then Joshua made them take an oath at that time, saying, "[a]Cursed before the LORD is the man who rises up and builds this city Jericho; with *the loss of* his firstborn he shall lay its foundation, and with *the loss of* his youngest son he shall set up its gates."

27 So [a]the LORD was with Joshua, and his [b]fame was in all the land.

19 [a]Num 31:11, 12, 21-23
20 [1]Or *they* [2]Lit *in its place* [3]Lit *before himself* [a]Heb 11:30
21 [1]Or *put under the ban* [a]Deut 20:16
22 [a]Josh 2:12-19
23 [a]Heb 11:31
24 [1]I.e. tabernacle [a]Deut 20:16-18
25 [1]Lit *let live* [a]Heb 11:31 [b]Josh 2:6
26 [a]1 Kin 16:34
27 [a]Gen 39:2; Judg 1:19 [b]Josh 9:1, 3

Israel Is Defeated at Ai

7 [a]But the sons of Israel acted unfaithfully in regard to the things under the ban, for Achan, the son of Carmi, the son of Zabdi, the son of Zerah, from the tribe of Judah, took some of the things under the ban, therefore the anger of the LORD burned against the sons of Israel.

2 Now Joshua sent men from Jericho to Ai, which is near [a]Beth-aven, east of Bethel, and said to them, "[1]Go up and spy out the land." So the men went up and spied out Ai.

3 They returned to Joshua and said to him, "Do not let all the people go up; *only* about two or three thousand men need go up [1]to Ai; do not make all the people toil up there, for they are few."

4 So about three thousand men from the people went up there, but [a]they fled [1]from the men of Ai.

5 The men of Ai struck down about thirty-six of their men, and pursued them [1]from the gate as far as Shebarim and struck them down on the descent, so the [a]hearts of the people melted and became as water.

6 Then Joshua [a]tore his clothes and fell to the earth on his face before the ark of the LORD until the evening, *both* he and the elders of Israel; and [b]they put dust on their heads.

7 Joshua said, "Alas, O Lord [1]GOD, why did You ever bring this people over the Jordan, *only* to deliver us into the hand of the Amorites, to destroy us? If only we had been willing [2]to dwell beyond the Jordan!

8 "O Lord, what can I say since Israel has turned *their* [1]back before their enemies?

9 "[a]For the Canaanites and all the inhabitants of the land will hear of it, and they will surround us and cut off our name from the earth. And what will You do for Your great name?"

7:1 [a]Josh 6:17-19
2 [1]Lit *saying, Go* [a]Josh 18:12; 1 Sam 13:5; 14:23
3 [1]Lit *and smite*
4 [1]Lit *before* [a]Lev 26:17; Deut 28:25
5 [1]Or *before* [a]Lev 26:36; Josh 2:11; Ezek 21:7; Nah 2:10
6 [a]Job 2:12 [b]Job 42:6; Lam 2:10; Rev 18:19
7 [1]Heb *YHWH*, usually rendered *LORD* [2]Lit *and had dwelt*
8 [1]Lit *neck*
9 [a]Ex 32:12; Deut 9:28

6:25 *she has lived in . . . Israel.* The faith of Rahab is noted twice in the NT (Heb 11:31; James 2:25).

6:26 *Cursed . . . is the man.* Jericho itself was to be devoted to the Lord as a perpetual sign of God's judgment on the wicked Canaanites and as a first fruits offering of the land. This was a way of signifying that the conquered land belonged to the Lord. The curse was fulfilled in the rebellious days of King Ahab (1 Kin 16:34).

7:1–26 The tragic story of Achan, which stands in sharp contrast to the story of Rahab. In the earlier event a Canaanite prostitute, because of her courageous allegiance to Israel and her acknowledgment of the Lord, was spared and received into Israel. She abandoned Canaan and its gods on account of the Lord and Israel, and so received Canaan back. In the present event an Israelite (of the tribe of Judah, no less), because of his disloyalty to the Lord and Israel, is executed as the Canaanites were. He stole the riches of Canaan from the Lord, and so lost his inheritance in the promised land. This is also a story of how one man's sin adversely affected the entire nation. Throughout this account (as often in the OT) Israel is considered a corporate unity in covenant with and in the service of the Lord. Thus even in the acts of one (Achan) or a few (the 3,000 defeated at Ai) all Israel is involved (see vv. 1,11; 22:20).

7:2 *from Jericho to Ai.* An uphill march of some 15 miles through a ravine to the top of the central Palestinian ridge. Strategically, an advance from Gilgal to Ai would bring Israel beyond the Jordan Valley and provide them a foothold in the central highlands. Ai in Hebrew means "the ruin." It is usually identified with et-Tell (meaning "the ruin" in Arabic), just two miles east of Bethel, but some dispute this precise identification. *Beth-aven.* Means "house of wickedness," a derogatory designation of either Bethel itself or a pagan shrine nearby (see 1 Sam 13:5; Hos 4:15; Amos 5:5). *spy out the land.* See note on 2:1–24.

7:5 *Shebarim.* Means "breaks," a fitting term for the rocky bluffs overlooking the Jordan Valley.

7:6 *Joshua tore his clothes.* A sign of great distress (see Gen 37:29,34; 44:13; Judg 11:35). Joshua's dismay (and that of the people), as indicated by his prayer, arose from his recognition that the Lord had not been with Israel's troops in the battle. And without the Lord the whole venture for which Israel had crossed the Jordan would be impossible. Moreover, the Canaanites would now judge that neither Israel nor her God was invincible. They would pour out of their fortified cities, combine forces and descend on Israel in the Jordan Valley, from which Israel could not escape across the flooding Jordan.

7:9 *Your great name.* Joshua pleads, as Moses had (Num

10 So the LORD said to Joshua, "Rise up! Why is it that you have fallen on your face?

11 "Israel has sinned, and [a]they have also transgressed My covenant which I commanded them. And they have even taken some of the things under the ban and have both stolen and deceived. Moreover, they have also put *them* among their own things.

12 "Therefore the [a]sons of Israel cannot stand before their enemies; they turn *their* [1]backs before their enemies, for they have become accursed. I will not be with you anymore unless you destroy the things under the ban from your midst.

13 "Rise up! [a]Consecrate the people and say, 'Consecrate yourselves for tomorrow, for thus the LORD, the God of Israel, has said, "[b]There are things under the ban in your midst, O Israel. You cannot stand before your enemies until you have removed the things under the ban from your midst."

14 'In the morning then you shall come near by your tribes. And it shall be that the tribe which [a]the LORD takes *by lot* shall come near by families, and the family which the LORD takes shall come near by households, and the household which the LORD takes shall come near man by man.

15 '[a]It shall be that the one who is taken with the things under the ban shall be burned with fire, he and all that belongs to him, because he has transgressed the covenant of the LORD, and because he [b]has committed a disgraceful thing in Israel.' "

The Sin of Achan

16 So Joshua arose early in the morning and brought Israel near by [1]tribes, and the tribe of Judah was taken.

17 He brought the family of Judah near, and he took the family of the Zerahites; and he brought the family of the Zerahites near man by man, and Zabdi was taken.

11 [a]Josh 6:18, 19
12 [1]Lit *necks* [a]Num 14:39, 45; Judg 2:14
13 [a]Josh 3:5 [b]Josh 6:18
14 [a]Prov 16:33
15 [a]1 Sam 14:38f [b]Gen 34:7; Judg 20:6
16 [1]Lit *its tribes*

18 He brought his household near man by man; and [a]Achan, son of Carmi, son of Zabdi, son of Zerah, from the tribe of Judah, was taken.

19 Then Joshua said to Achan, "My son, I implore you, [a]give glory to the LORD, the God of Israel, and give praise to Him; and tell me now what you have done. Do not hide it from me."

20 So Achan answered Joshua and said, "Truly, I have sinned against the LORD, the God of Israel, and [1]this is what I did:

21 when I saw among the spoil a beautiful mantle from Shinar and two hundred shekels of silver and a bar of gold fifty shekels in weight, then I [a]coveted them and took them; and behold, they are concealed in the earth inside my tent with the silver underneath it."

22 So Joshua sent messengers, and they ran to the tent; and behold, it was concealed in his tent with the silver underneath it.

23 They took them from inside the tent and brought them to Joshua and to all the sons of Israel, and they poured them out before the LORD.

24 Then Joshua and all Israel with him, took Achan the son of Zerah, the silver, the mantle, the bar of gold, his sons, his daughters, his [1]oxen, his donkeys, his sheep, his tent and all that belonged to him; and they brought them up to [a]the valley of [2]Achor.

25 Joshua said, "Why have you [a]troubled us? The LORD will trouble you this day." And all Israel stoned [1]them with stones; and they burned them with fire [2]after they had stoned them with stones.

26 They raised over him a great heap of stones that stands to this day, and the LORD turned from the fierceness of His anger. Therefore the name of that place has been called [a]the valley of [1]Achor to this day.

18 [a]Num 32:23; Acts 5:1-10
19 [a]1 Sam 6:5; 2 Chr 30:22; Jer 13:16; John 9:24
20 [1]Lit *thus and thus I did*
21 [a]Eph 5:5; 1 Tim 6:10
24 [1]Or *cattle* [2]I.e. trouble [a]Josh 15:7
25 [1]Lit *him* [2]Lit *and they stoned* [a]Josh 6:18
26 [1]I.e. trouble [a]Is 65:10; Hos 2:15

14:13–16; Deut 9:28–29), that God's honor in the eyes of all the world was at stake in the fortunes of His people.

7:11 *Israel has sinned.* One soldier's theft of the devoted goods brought collective guilt on the entire nation (see 22:20). *transgressed My covenant.* See v. 15. This is the main indictment; what follows is further specification.

7:12 *become accursed.* See note on 6:18.

7:13 *Consecrate yourselves.* A series of purifications to be undertaken by every Israelite in preparation for meeting with God, as before a solemn religious feast or a special assembly called by the Lord (see note on 3:5). Here God summons His people before Him for His judgment.

7:14 *tribe which the LORD takes.* When the lots are cast, one of the tribes is taken by the LORD so that the search is narrowed until the Lord exposes the guilty persons. The lots may have been the Urim and Thummim from the ephod of the high priest (see notes on Ex 28:30; 1 Sam 2:28; see also 1 Sam 14:41).

7:15 *disgraceful thing in Israel.* An act that within Israel, as the covenant people of the Lord, is an outrage of utter folly (see Deut 22:21; Judg 19:23–24; 20:6,10; 2 Sam 13:12).

7:19 *My son.* Joshua took a fatherly attitude toward Achan. *give glory to the LORD.* A solemn charge to tell the truth. *give praise to Him.* Or "confess to Him."

7:21 *mantle from Shinar.* A valuable import. *two hundred shekels . . . fifty shekels.* The silver would have weighed about five pounds, the gold about one and one-fourth pounds.

7:23 *before the LORD.* Who is here the Judge.

7:24 *Joshua . . . all Israel.* Joshua and all Israel were God's agents for executing His judgment on both the Canaanites and this violator of the covenant. *all that belonged to him.* As the head of (and example for) his family, Achan involved his whole household in his guilt and punishment. This is in accordance with the principle of corporate solidarity—the whole community is represented in one member (especially the head of that community).

7:25 *stoned them.* Because Achan had been found guilty of violating the covenant of the holy Lord (see Ex 19:13; Lev 24:23; Num 15:36). Afterward the bodies were burned to purge the land of the evil.

7:26 *great heap of stones.* A second monument in the land to the events of the conquest—alongside the memorial at Gilgal (4:20). *Achor.* Means "trouble." Achor was also another form of Achan's name (see 1 Chr 2:7, where Achan is called "Achar").

The Conquest of Ai

8 Now the LORD said to Joshua, "[a]Do not fear or be dismayed. Take all the people of war with you and arise, go up to Ai; see, [b]I have given into your hand the king of Ai, his people, his city, and his land.

2 "You shall do to Ai and its king just as you did to Jericho and its king; you shall [a]take only its spoil and its cattle as plunder for yourselves. [1]Set an ambush for the city behind it."

3 So Joshua rose with all the people of war to go up to Ai; and Joshua chose 30,000 men, valiant warriors, and sent them out at night.

4 He commanded them, saying, "See, you are [a]going to ambush the city from behind [1]it. Do not go very far from the city, but all of you be ready.

5 "Then I and all the people who are with me will approach the city. And when they come out to meet us as at the first, [a]we will flee before them.

6 "They will come out after us until we have drawn them away from the city, for they will say, '*They* are fleeing before us as at the first.' So we will flee before them.

7 "And you shall rise from *your* ambush and take possession of the city, for the LORD your God will deliver it into your hand.

8 "Then it will be when you have seized the city, that you shall set the city on fire. You shall do *it* [a]according to the word of the LORD. See, I have commanded you."

9 So Joshua sent them away, and they went to the place of ambush and remained between Bethel and Ai, on the west side of Ai; but Joshua spent that night among the people.

10 Now Joshua [a]rose early in the morning and mustered the people, and he went up with the elders of Israel before the people to Ai.

11 Then all the people of war who *were* with him went up and drew near and arrived in front of the city, and camped on the north side of Ai. Now *there was* a valley between him and Ai.

12 And he took about 5,000 men and set them in ambush between [a]Bethel and Ai, on the west side of the [1]city.

13 So they stationed the people, all the army that was on the north side of the city, and its rear guard on the west side of the city, and Joshua spent that night in the midst of the valley.

8:1 [a]Josh 1:9; 10:8 [b]Josh 6:2
2 [1]Lit *Set for yourself* [a]Deut 20:14; Josh 8:27
4 [1]Lit *the city* [a]Judg 20:29
5 [a]Judg 20:32
8 [a]Deut 20:16-18; Josh 8:2
10 [a]Gen 22:3
12 [1]I.e. Ai [a]Gen 12:8; 28:19; Judg 1:22
15 [a]Josh 15:61; 16:1; 18:12
16 [a]Judg 20:31
17 [1]Lit *open*
18 [a]Ex 14:16; 17:9-13; Josh 8:26
20 [1]Lit *behind them*
21 [1]Lit *smote*
22 [1]Lit *These came* [2]Lit *these...those* [3]Lit *smote* [4]Lit *for it* [a]Josh 8:8
25 [1]Lit *men* [a]Deut 20:16-18
26 [a]Ex 17:11, 12

14 It came about when the king of Ai saw *it,* that the men of the city hurried and rose up early and went out to meet Israel in battle, he and all his people at the appointed place before the desert plain. But he did not know that *there was* an ambush against him behind the city.

15 Joshua and all Israel pretended to be beaten before them, and fled [a]by the way of the wilderness.

16 And all the people who were in the city were called together to pursue them, and they pursued Joshua and [a]were drawn away from the city.

17 So not a man was left in Ai or Bethel who had not gone out after Israel, and they left the city [1]unguarded and pursued Israel.

18 Then the LORD said to Joshua, "[a]Stretch out the javelin that is in your hand toward Ai, for I will give it into your hand." So Joshua stretched out the javelin that was in his hand toward the city.

19 The *men in* ambush rose quickly from their place, and when he had stretched out his hand, they ran and entered the city and captured it, and they quickly set the city on fire.

20 When the men of Ai turned [1]back and looked, behold, the smoke of the city ascended to the sky, and they had no place to flee this way or that, for the people who had been fleeing to the wilderness turned against the pursuers.

21 When Joshua and all Israel saw that the *men in* ambush had captured the city and that the smoke of the city ascended, they turned back and [1]slew the men of Ai.

22 [1]The others came out from the city to encounter them, so that they were *trapped* in the midst of Israel, [2]some on this side and some on that side; and they [3]slew them until [a]no one was left [4]of those who survived or escaped.

23 But they took alive the king of Ai and brought him to Joshua.

24 Now when Israel had finished killing all the inhabitants of Ai in the field in the wilderness where they pursued them, and all of them were fallen by the edge of the sword until they were destroyed, then all Israel returned to Ai and struck it with the edge of the sword.

25 [a]All who fell that day, both men and women, were 12,000—all the [1]people of Ai.

26 For Joshua [a]did not withdraw his hand with which he stretched out the javelin until

---

8:1–29 Renewal of the conquest and the taking of Ai.
8:1 *Do not fear.* Now that Israel is purged, the Lord reassures Joshua once more (see 1:3–5; 3:11–13; 6:2–5).
8:2 *you shall take . . . as plunder.* The Lord now assigns the wealth of Canaan to His troops who fight His battles. *Set an ambush.* Still in command, the Lord directs the attack.
8:12 *5,000.* Verse 3 speaks of a contingent of 30,000 assigned to the ambush. Perhaps Joshua assigned two different units to the task to assure success. Or from the original 30,000 a unit of 5,000 may have been designated to attack Ai itself while the remaining 25,000 served as a covering force to block the threat from Bethel (see v. 17).
8:13 *army . . . on the north side.* In full visibility Joshua's main force moved north of the city, then pretended to flee to the east, drawing out the entire army of defenders.
8:17 *Ai or Bethel.* Their joint action indicates that the two cities were closely allied, though each is said to have had a king (12:9,16).

he had [1]utterly destroyed all the inhabitants of Ai.

27 [a]Israel took only the cattle and the spoil of that city as plunder for themselves, according to the word of the LORD which He had commanded Joshua.

28 So Joshua burned Ai and made it [a]a heap forever, a desolation until this day.

29 [a]He hanged the king of Ai on a tree until evening; and at sunset Joshua gave command and they took his body down from the tree and threw it at the entrance of the city gate, and raised over it a great heap of stones *that stands* to this day.

30 Then Joshua built an altar to the LORD, the God of Israel, in [a]Mount Ebal,

31 just as Moses the servant of the LORD had commanded the sons of Israel, as it is written in the book of the law of Moses, [a]an altar of uncut stones on which no man had wielded an iron *tool;* and they offered burnt offerings on it to the LORD, and sacrificed peace offerings.

32 He [a]wrote there on the stones a copy of the law of Moses, which [1]he had written, in the presence of the sons of Israel.

33 [a]All Israel with their elders and officers and their judges were standing on both sides of the ark before the Levitical priests who carried the ark of the covenant of the LORD, the stranger as well as the native. Half of them *stood* in front of [b]Mount Gerizim and half of them in front of Mount Ebal, just as Moses the servant of the LORD had given command at first to bless the people of Israel.

34 Then afterward he read all the words of the law, the blessing and the curse, according to all that is written in [a]the book of the law.

35 There was not a word of all that Moses had commanded which Joshua did not read before all the assembly of Israel [a]with the women and the little ones and the strangers who were [1]living among them.

Guile of the Gibeonites

9 Now it came about when [a]all the kings who were beyond the Jordan, in the hill country and in the lowland and on all the [b]coast of the Great Sea toward Lebanon, [c]the Hittite and the Amorite, the Canaanite, the Perizzite, the Hivite and the Jebusite, heard of it,

2 that they gathered themselves together with [1a]one accord to fight with Joshua and with Israel.

3 When the inhabitants of [a]Gibeon heard what Joshua had done to Jericho and to Ai,

4 they also acted craftily and [1]set out as

26 [1]Or *put under the ban*
27 [a]Josh 8:2
28 [a]Deut 13:16
29 [a]Deut 21:22, 23
30 [a]Deut 27:2-8
31 [a]Ex 20:25
32 [1]I.e. Moses [a]Deut 27:2, 3, 8
33 [a]Deut 27:11-14
33 [b]Deut 11:29
34 [a]Josh 1:8
35 [1]Lit *walking* [a]Ex 12:38; Deut 31:12; Zech 8:23
9:1 [a]Num 13:29; Josh 3:10 [b]Num 34:6 [c]Ex 3:17; 23:23
2 [1]Lit *one mouth* [a]Ps 83:3, 5
3 [a]Josh 9:17, 22; 10:2; 21:17
4 [1]Lit *went and traveled as envoys*

8:26 *he had utterly destroyed.* For the second time Joshua ordered the holy ban on the inhabitants of a Canaanite city (see notes on Num 21:2; Deut 2:34).
8:28 *burned Ai.* As he had Jericho (6:24) and would later do to Hazor (11:11). *a desolation until this day.* If the ruins of Ai have been correctly identified (see note on 7:2), the site shows signs of later occupation only from c. 1200 to 1100 B.C.
8:29 *hanged the king of Ai on a tree.* The Israelites did not execute by hanging. "Tree" may refer to a pole on which the king's body was impaled after execution (see note on Deut 21:22). *until evening.* According to Mosaic instructions (see Deut 21:22–23). *great heap of stones.* A third monument in the land (see note on 7:26).
8:30–35 The renewal of the covenant with the Lord as Moses had ordered (Deut 11:26–30; 27:1–8) concludes the account of the initial battles (see Introduction: Outline). The conquest of Canaan has already been put into rich theological perspective. This final event (see also Joshua's final official act, ch. 24) underscores Israel's servant relationship to the Lord. In conquest and occupation she must faithfully acknowledge her one identity as the people of the kingdom of God, subject to His commission and rule (see note on 5:14).

How Israel could assemble peacefully between Mount Ebal and Mount Gerizim without further conquest is a worrisome question—and has led to some radical reconstructions of Israel's history. It must be noted, however, that Biblical narrators at times followed a thematic rather than a strictly chronological order of events. That may be the case here, since it is clear that the story of the Gibeonite deception and submission (ch. 9) is included in the thematic development of how Israel came into possession of the rest of Canaan (see the author's introduction in 9:1–2). The Shechemites (Shechem was a major city lying between the two mountains mentioned) were Hivites (or were under Hivite domination; see Gen 34:2) and thus were related to the people of the Gibeonite cities (9:7; 11:19). Also, there was no important town between Gibeon and Shechem (Bethel and Ai had been subdued). Perhaps the treaty of submission established between Israel and the Gibeonites (ch. 9) applied also to the Hivites of Shechem, and the covenant renewal ceremony that concludes ch. 8 (and the previous narrative section) actually took place chronologically after the events narrated in ch. 9. If this suggestion is correct, the Gibeonites or their representatives would have been among the "aliens" who participated with Israel in the covenant event (vv. 33,35).
8:30 *Mount Ebal.* At the foot of this peak was the fortress city of Shechem, where Abraham had built an altar (Gen 12:6–7).
8:31 *burnt offerings.* See Lev 1:1–17. *peace offerings.* See Lev 3:1–17; 7:11–18.
8:32 *wrote . . . on the stones.* Moses had ordered the people first to plaster the stones, then to inscribe on them the words of the law (Deut 27:2–4). These stones are the fourth monument in the land (see note on v. 29).
8:33 *stranger as well as the native.* Israel now included those who were part of the "mixed multitude" (Ex 12:38) who had come out of Egypt, plus others who had associated with them during the wilderness wanderings (see note on vv. 30–35).
8:34 *the blessing and the curse.* See Deut 27–28 and notes.
9:1–27 The account of how the Gibeonites deceived the leaders of the tribes and obtained a treaty of submission to Israel. It is the first of three sections telling how Israel came into possession of the bulk of the land. Verses 1–2 introduce the three units.
9:1 *kings who were beyond the Jordan.* Small, independent city-kingdoms were scattered over Canaan, inhabited by a variety of peoples who had come earlier from outside the land (compare vv. 1–2 with Gen 15:19).
9:3 *Gibeon.* A site just north of Jerusalem called el-Jib, showing the remains of a Late Bronze Age city with an excellent water supply. The Gibeonites were in league with a number of neighboring towns (v. 17) but seem to have been dominant in the confederation.
9:4 *they also acted craftily.* Motivated by their fear of Israel's

envoys, and took worn-out sacks on their donkeys, and wineskins worn-out and torn and [2]mended,

5 and worn-out and patched sandals on their feet, and worn-out clothes on themselves; and all the bread of their provision was dry *and* had become crumbled.

6 They went to Joshua to the [a]camp at Gilgal and said to him and to the men of Israel, "We have come from a far country; now therefore, make a covenant with us."

7 The men of Israel said to the [a]Hivites, "Perhaps you are living [1]within our land; [b]how then shall we make a covenant with you?"

8 But they said to Joshua, "[a]We are your servants." Then Joshua said to them, "Who are you and where do you come from?"

9 They said to him, "Your servants have come from [a]a very far country because of the [1]fame of the LORD your God; for [b]we have heard the report of Him and all that He did in Egypt,

10 and all that He did to the two kings of the Amorites who were beyond the Jordan, to Sihon king of Heshbon and to Og king of Bashan who was at Ashtaroth.

11 "So our elders and all the inhabitants of our country spoke to us, saying, 'Take provisions in your hand for the journey, and go to meet them and say to them, "[a]We are your servants; now then, make a covenant with us." '

12 "This our bread *was* warm *when* we took it for our provisions out of our houses on the day that we left to come to you; but now behold, it is dry and has become crumbled.

13 "These wineskins which we filled were new, and behold, they are torn; and these our clothes and our sandals are worn out because of the very long journey."

14 So the men *of Israel* took some of their provisions, and [a]did not ask for the [1]counsel of the LORD.

15 [a]Joshua made peace with them and made a covenant with them, to let them live; and the leaders of the congregation swore *an oath* to them.

16 It came about at the end of three days after they had made a covenant with them, that they heard that they were neighbors and that they were living [1]within their land.

17 Then the sons of Israel set out and came to their cities on the third day. Now their cities *were* [a]Gibeon and Chephirah and Beeroth and Kiriath-jearim.

18 The sons of Israel did not strike them because the leaders of the congregation had sworn to them by the LORD the God of Israel. And the whole congregation grumbled against the leaders.

19 But all the leaders said to the whole congregation, "We have sworn to them by the LORD, the God of Israel, and now we cannot touch them.

20 "This we will do to them, even let them live, so that wrath will not be upon us for the oath which we swore to them."

21 The leaders said to them, "Let them live." So they became [a]hewers of wood and drawers of water for the whole congregation, just as the leaders had spoken to them.

22 Then Joshua called for them and spoke to them, saying, "Why have you deceived us, saying, 'We are very far from you,' [a]when you are living [1]within our land?

23 "Now therefore, you are [a]cursed, and [1]you shall never cease being slaves, both hewers of wood and drawers of water for the house of my God."

24 So they answered Joshua and said, "[a]Because it was certainly told your servants that the LORD your God had commanded His servant Moses to give you all the land, and to destroy all the inhabitants of the land before you; therefore we feared greatly for our lives because of you, and have done this thing.

25 "Now behold, [a]we are in your hands; do as it seems good and right in your sight to do to us."

26 Thus he did to them, and delivered

4 [2]Lit *tied up*
6 [a]Josh 5:10
7 [1]Lit *among us* [a]Josh 9:1; 11:19 [b]Ex 23:32; Deut 7:2
8 [a]Deut 20:11; 2 Kin 10:5
9 [1]Or *name* [a]Josh 9:16, 17 [b]Josh 2:9; 9:24
11 [a]Josh 9:8
14 [1]Lit *mouth* [a]Num 27:21
15 [a]Ex 23:32

16 [1]Lit *among them*
17 [a]Josh 18:25
21 [a]Deut 29:11
22 [1]Lit *among us* [a]Josh 9:16
23 [1]Lit *a servant shall not be cut off from you* [a]Gen 9:25
24 [a]Josh 9:9
25 [a]Gen 16:6

God, the Gibeonites used pretense to trick Joshua into a treaty that would allow them to live.

9:6 *make a covenant with us.* In this request they were offering to submit themselves by treaty to be subjects of the Israelites (see v. 11, where they call themselves "your servants"—unmistakable language in the international diplomacy of that day). They chose submission rather than certain death (v. 24).

9:7 *Hivites.* Possibly Horites, an ethnic group living in Canaan related to the Hurrians of northern Mesopotamia (11:19; Gen 10:17; Ex 23:23; Jdg 3:3).

9:9 *heard the report of Him.* The same reports that had been heard in Jericho (see 2:10).

9:14 *did not ask . . . the LORD.* Did not consult their King, whose mission they were on.

9:15 *made peace . . . a covenant.* A covenant to let them live was sworn by the heads of the tribes—i.e., an oath was taken in the holy name of God. All such oaths were binding in Israel (see Ex 20:7; Lev 19:12; 1 Sam 14:24).

9:18 *the whole congregation grumbled.* Perhaps the people feared the consequences of not following through on the earlier divine order to destroy all the Canaanites, but more likely they grumbled because they could not take over the Gibeonite cities and possessions.

9:21 *hewers of wood and drawers of water.* A conventional phrase for household servants.

9:23 *cursed.* Noah's prediction that Canaan would someday "be the servant of Shem" (Gen 9:25–26) has part of its fulfillment in this event. *for the house of my God.* Probably specifies how the Gibeonites were to serve "the whole congregation" (v. 21). Worship at the tabernacle (and later at the temple) required much wood and water (for sacrifices and washing) and consequently a great deal of menial labor. From now on, that labor was to be supplied by the Gibeonites, perhaps on a rotating basis. In this way they entered the Lord's service. When Solomon became king, the tabernacle and altar were at Gibeon (2 Chr 1:3,5).

them from the hands of the sons of Israel,
and they did not kill them.
27 But Joshua made them that day hewers
of wood and drawers of water for the congregation and for the altar of the LORD, to this
day, [a]in the place which He would choose.

Five Kings Attack Gibeon

10 Now it came about when Adoni-zedek
king of Jerusalem heard that Joshua
had captured Ai, and had [1]utterly destroyed
it (just [a]as he had done to Jericho and its
king, so he had done to Ai and its king), and
that the inhabitants of Gibeon had [b]made
peace with Israel and were [2]within their
land,
2 that [1]he [a]feared greatly, because Gibeon *was* a great city, like one of the royal cities, and because it was greater than Ai, and
all its men *were* mighty.
3 Therefore Adoni-zedek king of Jerusalem sent *word* [a]to Hoham king of Hebron
and to Piram king of Jarmuth and to Japhia
king of Lachish and to Debir king of Eglon,
saying,
4 "Come up to me and help me, and let us
[1]attack Gibeon, for it has [a]made peace with
Joshua and with the sons of Israel."
5 So the five kings of [a]the Amorites, the
king of Jerusalem, the king of Hebron, the
king of Jarmuth, the king of Lachish, *and* the
king of Eglon, gathered together and went
up, they with all their armies, and camped
by Gibeon and fought against it.
6 Then the men of Gibeon sent *word* to
Joshua to the camp at Gilgal, saying, "Do not
[1]abandon your servants; come up to us
quickly and save us and help us, for all the
kings of the Amorites that live in the hill
country have assembled against us."

27 [a]Deut 12:5
10:1 [1]Or *put under the ban* [2]Lit *among them* [a]Josh 8:21f [b]Josh 9:15
2 [1]Lit *they* [a]Ex 15:14-16
3 [a]Josh 10:23
4 [1]Lit *smite* [a]Josh 9:15
5 [a]Num 13:29
6 [1]Lit *slacken your hands from*

7 So Joshua went up from Gilgal, he and
[a]all the people of war with him and all the
valiant warriors.
8 The LORD said to Joshua, "[a]Do not fear
them, for I have given them into your hands;
not [1]one of them shall stand before you."
9 So Joshua came upon them suddenly
[1]by marching all night from Gilgal.
10 [a]And the LORD confounded them
before Israel, and He [1]slew them with a
great slaughter at Gibeon, and pursued them
by the way of the ascent of Beth-horon and
struck them as far as Azekah and Makkedah.
11 As they fled from before Israel, *while*
they were at the descent of Beth-horon, [a]the
LORD threw large stones from heaven on
them as far as Azekah, and they died; *there*
were more who died [1]from the hailstones
than those whom the sons of Israel killed
with the sword.
12 Then Joshua spoke to the LORD in the
day when the LORD delivered up the Amorites before the sons of Israel, and he said in
the sight of Israel,
"O [a]sun, stand still at Gibeon,
And O moon in the valley of Aijalon."
13 [a]So the sun stood still, and the moon
stopped,
Until the nation avenged themselves
of their enemies.
Is it not written in [b]the book of Jashar? And
[c]the sun stopped in the middle of the sky
and did not hasten to go *down* for about a
whole day.
14 There was no day like that before it or
after it, when the LORD listened to the voice
of a man; for [a]the LORD fought for Israel.
15 Then Joshua and all Israel with him
returned to the camp to Gilgal.

7 [a]Josh 8:1
8 [1]Lit *a man* [a]Josh 1:5, 9
9 [1]Lit *he went up*
10 [1]Lit *struck* [a]Deut 7:23
11 [1]Lit *with* [a]Ps 18:12f; Is 28:2
12 [a]Hab 3:11
13 [a]Hab 3:11 [b]2 Sam 1:18 [c]Is 38:8
14 [a]Ex 14:14; Deut 1:30; Josh 10:42

9:27 *the place which He would choose.* Joshua moved the tabernacle (and its altar) to Shiloh, and there it would reside at least until the days of Samuel (1 Sam 4:3). Later, the Lord chose Jerusalem (1 Kin 9:3).

10:1–43 The army under Joshua comes to the defense of Gibeon and defeats the coalition of southern kings at Aijalon, then subdues all the southern cities of Judah and the Negev.

10:1 *Adoni-zedek.* Means "lord of righteousness" or "My (divine) lord is righteous." An earlier king of Jerusalem had a similar name (Melchizedek; see Gen 14:18 and note). *Jerusalem.* City of the Jebusites.

10:2 *great city.* Gibeon was not only larger in size than Bethel or Ai, but also closer to Jerusalem. With Bethel and Ai conquered and the Gibeonite league in submission, the Israelites were well established in the central highlands, virtually cutting the land in two. Naturally the king of Jerusalem felt threatened, and he wanted to reunite all the Canaanites against Israel. Perhaps he also held (or claimed) some political dominion over the Gibeonite cities and viewed their submission to Israel as rebellion. *mighty.* Men famous for their courage in battle, yet wise enough to have made peace with the Israelites.

10:5 *five kings of the Amorites.* Rulers over five of the major cities in the southern mountains. The Amorites of the hills are here distinguished from the Canaanites along the coast.

10:6 *come . . . and save us.* An urgent appeal for deliverance to a man whose name means "The LORD saves." A treaty such as Joshua had made with the Gibeonites usually obliged the ruling nation to come to the aid of the subject peoples if they were attacked.

10:9 *marching all night.* Gilgal was about 20 miles east of Gibeon, a steep uphill climb for Joshua's men. *suddenly.* Joshua attacked early in the morning, perhaps while the moon was still up (v. 12).

10:10 *confounded.* The Hebrew for this word implies terror or panic.

10:11 *descent of Beth-horon.* A long descent to the plain of Aijalon below, following the main east-west crossroad just north of Jerusalem. *large stones from heaven.* For the Lord's use of the elements of nature as His armaments see Judg 5:20; 1 Sam 7:10; Job 38:22.

10:13 *book of Jashar.* An early account of Israel's wars (perhaps all in poetic form; see 2 Sam 1:18; see also note on Judg 5:1–31), but never a part of canonical Scripture. *did not . . . go down.* Some believe that God extended the hours of daylight for the Israelites to defeat their enemies. Others suggest that the sun remained cool (perhaps as the result of an overcast sky) for an entire day, allowing the fighting to continue through the afternoon. The fact is we do not know what happened, except that it involved divine intervention.

Victory at Makkedah

16 Now these [a]five kings had fled and hidden themselves in the cave at Makkedah.

17 It was told Joshua, saying, "The five kings have been found hidden in the cave at Makkedah."

18 Joshua said, "Roll large stones against the mouth of the cave, and assign men by it to guard them,

19 but do not stay *there* yourselves; pursue your enemies and [1]attack them in the rear. Do not allow them to enter their cities, for the LORD your God has delivered them into your hand."

20 It came about when Joshua and the sons of Israel had finished [1]slaying them with a very great slaughter, [a]until they were destroyed, and the survivors *who* remained of them [2]had entered the fortified cities,

21 that all the people returned to the camp to Joshua at Makkedah in peace. No one [1]uttered a word against any of the sons of Israel.

22 Then Joshua said, "Open the mouth of the cave and bring these five kings out to me from the cave."

23 They did so, and [a]brought these five kings out to him from the cave: the king of Jerusalem, the king of Hebron, the king of Jarmuth, the king of Lachish, *and* the king of Eglon.

24 When they brought these kings out to Joshua, Joshua called for all the men of Israel, and said to the chiefs of the men of war who had gone with him, "Come near, [a]put your feet on the necks of these kings." So they came near and put their feet on their necks.

25 Joshua then said to them, "[a]Do not fear or be dismayed! Be strong and courageous, for thus the LORD will do to all your enemies with whom you fight."

26 So afterward Joshua struck them and put them to death, and he [a]hanged them on five trees; and they hung on the trees until evening.

27 It came about at [1]sunset that Joshua gave a command, and [a]they took them down from the trees and threw them into the cave where they had hidden themselves, and put large stones over the mouth of the cave, to this very day.

28 Now Joshua captured Makkedah on that day, and struck it and its king with the edge of the sword; [a]he [1]utterly destroyed [2]it and every [3]person who was in it. He left no survivor. Thus he did to the king of Makkedah [b]just as he had done to the king of Jericho.

Joshua's Conquest of Southern Palestine

29 Then Joshua and all Israel with him passed on from Makkedah to [a]Libnah, and fought against Libnah.

30 The LORD gave it also with its king into the hands of Israel, and he struck it and every person who *was* in it with the edge of the sword. He left no survivor in it. Thus he did to its king just as he had done to the king of Jericho.

31 And Joshua and all Israel with him passed on from Libnah to Lachish, and they camped by it and fought against it.

32 The LORD gave Lachish into the hands of Israel; and he captured it on the second day, and struck it and every person who *was* in it with the edge of the sword, according to all that he had done to Libnah.

33 Then Horam king of [a]Gezer came up to help Lachish, and Joshua [1]defeated him and his people until he had left him no survivor.

34 And Joshua and all Israel with him passed on from Lachish to Eglon, and they camped by it and fought against it.

35 They captured it on that day and struck it with the edge of the sword; and he [1]utterly destroyed that day every person who *was* in it, according to all that he had done to Lachish.

36 Then Joshua and all Israel with him went up from Eglon to [a]Hebron, and they fought against it.

37 They captured it and struck it and its king and all its cities and all the persons who *were* in it with the edge of the sword. He left no survivor, according to all that he had done to Eglon. And he [1]utterly destroyed it and every person who *was* in it.

38 Then Joshua and all Israel with him returned to [a]Debir, and they fought against it.

39 He captured it and its king and all its cities, and they struck them with the edge of the sword, and [1]utterly destroyed every person *who was* in it. He left no survivor. Just as

16 [a]Josh 10:5
19 [1]Lit *smite their tail*
20 [1]Lit *striking* [2]Lit *and had* [a]Deut 20:16
21 [1]Lit *sharpened his tongue*
23 [a]Deut 7:24
24 [a]Mal 4:3
25 [a]Josh 10:8
26 [a]Josh 8:29
27 [1]Lit *the time of the going of the sun* [a]Deut 21:22, 23
28 [1]Or *put under the ban* [2]Some mss read *them* [3]Lit *soul,* and so throughout the ch [a]Deut 20:16 [b]Josh 6:21
29 [a]Josh 15:42; 21:13
33 [1]Lit *smote* [a]Josh 16:3, 10; Judg 1:29; 1 Kin 9:16f
35 [1]Or *put under the ban*
36 [a]Num 13:22; Judg 1:10, 20; 2 Sam 5:1, 3, 5, 13; 2 Chr 11:10
37 [1]Or *put it under the ban*
38 [a]Josh 15:15; Judg 1:11; 1 Chr 6:58
39 [1]Or *put it under the ban*

10:16 *Makkedah.* A town near Azekah (v. 10) in the western foothills where Joshua's troops made their camp.

10:19 *pursue your enemies.* Most of the fighting men defending the southern cities were caught and killed before they could reach the safety of their fortresses.

10:21 *No one uttered a word.* The thought here appears to be that no one dared even to raise his voice against the Israelites anymore.

10:24 *put your feet on the necks.* Public humiliation of defeated enemy chieftains was the usual climax of warfare in the ancient Near East.

10:26 *hanged them on five trees.* See note on Deut 21:22.

10:27 *put large stones.* A fifth monument in the land to the events of the conquest (see note on 8:32).

10:28 *destroyed . . . every person.* The holy ban was placed on the people of Makkedah, meaning they were "devoted to death" for their wicked deeds (see notes on Num 21:2; Deut 2:34). The same fate came to the other major cities of the south (vv. 29–42).

10:33 *Horam king of Gezer.* An important detail: the defeat of the king of the most powerful city in the area. Gezer was eventually taken over by the Egyptians and given to King Solomon as a wedding gift (see 1 Kin 9:16).

10:38 *Debir.* In the past, Debir (also known as Kiriath-sepher, 15:15) was identified with Tell Beit Mirsim. More recently, however, it has been equated with Khirbet Rabud, about five miles southwest of Hebron.

he had done to Hebron, so he did to Debir
and its king, as he had also done to Libnah
and its king.
40 Thus Joshua struck all the land, [a]the
hill country and the [1]Negev and the lowland
and the slopes and [b]all their kings. He left
no survivor, but [c]he [2]utterly destroyed all
who breathed, just as the LORD, the God of
Israel, had commanded.
41 Joshua struck them from Kadesh-barnea even as far as Gaza, and all the country
of [a]Goshen even as far as Gibeon.
42 Joshua captured all these kings and
their lands at one time, because [a]the LORD,
the God of Israel, fought for Israel.
43 So Joshua and all Israel with him
returned to the camp at Gilgal.

Northern Palestine Taken

11 Then it came about, when Jabin king of
[a]Hazor heard *of it,* that he sent to
Jobab king of Madon and to the king of
Shimron and to the king of Achshaph,
2 and to the kings who were of the north
in the hill country, and in the [a]Arabah—
south of [1]Chinneroth and in the lowland and
on the [2]heights of Dor on the west—
3 to the Canaanite on the east and on the
west, and the Amorite and the Hittite and the
Perizzite and the Jebusite in the hill country,
and [a]the Hivite [1]at the foot of [b]Hermon in
the land of [c]Mizpeh.
4 They came out, they and all their
armies with them, [a]*as* many people as the
sand that is on the seashore, with very many
horses and chariots.
5 So all of these kings having agreed to
meet, came and encamped together at the
waters of Merom, to fight against Israel.
6 Then the LORD said to Joshua, "[a]Do not
be afraid because of them, for tomorrow at
this time I will deliver all of them slain before
Israel; you shall [b]hamstring their horses and
burn their chariots with fire."
7 So Joshua and all the people of war
with him came upon them suddenly by the
waters of Merom, and attacked them.
8 The LORD delivered them into the hand
of Israel, so that they [1]defeated them, and
pursued them as far as Great Sidon and
[a]Misrephoth-maim and the valley of
[b]Mizpeh to the east; and they struck them
until no survivor was left to them.
9 Joshua did to them as the LORD had
told him; he [a]hamstrung their horses and
burned their chariots with fire.
10 Then Joshua turned back at that time,
and captured [a]Hazor and struck its king with
the sword; for Hazor formerly was the head
of all these kingdoms.
11 [a]They struck every person who was in
it with the edge of the sword, [1]utterly
destroying *them;* there was no one left who
breathed. And he burned Hazor with fire.
12 Joshua captured all the cities of these
kings, and all their kings, and he struck them
with the edge of the sword, *and* utterly
destroyed them; just [a]as Moses the servant
of the LORD had commanded.
13 However, Israel did not burn any cities
that stood on their mounds, except Hazor
alone, *which* Joshua burned.
14 [a]All the spoil of these cities and the cattle, the sons of Israel took as their plunder;
but they struck every man with the edge of
the sword, until they had destroyed them.
They left no one who breathed.
15 Just as the LORD had commanded
Moses his servant, so Moses commanded
Joshua, and so Joshua did; he left nothing
undone of all that the LORD had commanded
Moses.

40 [1]I.e. South country [2]Or *put it under the ban* [a]Deut 1:7 [b]Deut 7:24 [c]Deut 20:16
41 [a]Josh 11:16; 15:51
42 [a]Josh 10:14
11:1 [a]Josh 11:10
2 [1]I.e. Sea of Galilee [2]Or *Naphoth-dor* [a]Josh 12:3; 13:27
3 [1]Lit *under* [a]Deut 7:1; Judg 3:3, 5; 1 Kin 9:20 [b]Josh 11:17; 13:5, 11 [c]Josh 15:38; 18:26
4 [a]Judg 7:12
6 [a]Josh 10:8
6 [b]2 Sam 8:4
8 [1]Lit *smote* [a]Josh 13:6 [b]Josh 11:3
9 [a]Josh 11:6
10 [a]Josh 11:1
11 [1]Or *putting them under the ban,* and so throughout the ch [a]Deut 20:16
12 [a]Num 33:50-52; Deut 7:2; 20:16f
14 [a]Num 31:11, 12

10:41 *Kadesh-barnea . . . Gaza.* The south-to-north limits in the western part of the region. *Goshen.* A seldom-used name for the eastern Negev, not to be confused with the Goshen in the delta of Egypt; it is also the name of a town (15:51). Goshen and Gibeon mark the south-to-north limits in the eastern part of the region.

11:1–23 Only the northern cities remained to be conquered. The major battle for the hills of Galilee is fought and won against Hazor and the coalition of other northern city-states. A summary follows of all Joshua's victories in the southern and central regions as well.

11:1 *Jabin king of Hazor.* Jabin is perhaps a dynastic name, used again in the days of Deborah (Judg 4:2). The archaeological excavation of Hazor shows that it was the largest and best fortified of all the Canaanite cities. Its lower city measured 175 acres.

11:2 *Chinneroth.* Means "harp"; the Sea of Galilee.

11:4 *as many . . . as the sand . . . on the seashore.* A widely used figure of speech for indicating large numbers (see note on Gen 22:17).

11:5 *all of these kings.* Jabin's muster extended as far as the Arabah (v. 2) in the Jordan Valley and as far as Dor on the Mediterranean, south of Mount Carmel. *Merom.* Probably modern Meirun, just northwest of Safed near the source of the Wadi Ammud (Marun)—some eight miles northwest of the Sea of Galilee.

11:6 *hamstring their horses.* Done by cutting the tendon above the hock or ankle, crippling the horse so that it cannot walk again. *burn their chariots.* These advanced implements of war were not used by the armies of Israel until the time of Solomon (see 1 Kin 9:22; 10:26–29).

11:10 *Joshua . . . captured Hazor.* Perhaps his greatest victory. Hazor's armed forces, however, had been defeated earlier at Merom. The archaeological site reveals extensive damage and the burning of the Canaanite city c. 1400 B.C., c. 1300 and again c. 1230. Since the destruction level at c. 1300 probably indicates the burning of the city by Pharaoh Seti I, this leaves the destruction levels at c. 1400 and c. 1230 for Joshua's conquest. Those who hold to the late date of the conquest opt for the 1230 level; those who hold to the early date opt for 1400 (see Introduction: Historical Setting). Once again the ban of total destruction was applied (v. 11).

11:13 *mounds.* The Hebrew word is *tel* (Arabic *tell*), a hill formed by the accumulated debris of many ancient settlements one above the other (see note on 7:2).

11:15 *he left nothing undone.* Joshua's success should be measured in the light of the specific orders given by God, which he carried out fully, rather than by the total area that

16 Thus Joshua took all that land: [a]the hill
country and all the [1]Negev, all that land of
Goshen, the lowland, [b]the Arabah, the hill
country of Israel and its lowland
17 from [a]Mount Halak, that rises toward
Seir, even as far as Baal-gad in the valley of
Lebanon [1]at the foot of Mount Hermon. And
he captured [b]all their kings and struck them
down and put them to death.
18 Joshua waged war a long time with all
these kings.
19 There was not a city which made peace
with the sons of Israel except [a]the Hivites
living in Gibeon; they took them all in battle.
20 [a]For it was of the LORD to [1]harden their
hearts, to meet Israel in battle in order that
he might [b]utterly destroy them, that they
might [2]receive no mercy, but that he might
destroy them, just as the LORD had commanded Moses.
21 Then Joshua came at that time and cut
off [a]the Anakim from the hill country, from
Hebron, from Debir, from Anab and from all
the hill country of Judah and from all the hill
country of Israel. Joshua utterly destroyed
them with their cities.
22 There were no Anakim left in the land
of the sons of Israel; only in Gaza, in [a]Gath,
and in [b]Ashdod some remained.
23 So Joshua took the whole land, according to all that the LORD had spoken to Moses,
and [a]Joshua gave it for an inheritance to
Israel according to their divisions by their
tribes. [b]Thus the land had rest from war.

Kings Defeated by Israel

12 Now these are the [a]kings of the land
whom the sons of Israel [1]defeated, and
whose land they possessed beyond the Jordan toward the sunrise, from the valley of
the Arnon as far as Mount Hermon, and all
the Arabah to the east:
2 Sihon king of the Amorites, who lived
in Heshbon, *and* ruled [a]from Aroer, which is
on the edge of the valley of the Arnon, both
the middle of the valley and half of Gilead,
even as far as the brook Jabbok, the border
of the sons of Ammon;
3 and the [a]Arabah as far as the Sea of
[1]Chinneroth toward the east, and as far as
the sea of the Arabah, *even* the Salt Sea, eastward [2]toward [b]Beth-jeshimoth, and on the
south, [3]at the foot of the slopes of Pisgah;
4 and the territory of Og king of Bashan,
one of [a]the remnant of Rephaim, who lived
at [b]Ashtaroth and at Edrei,
5 and ruled over Mount Hermon and
[a]Salecah and all Bashan, as far as [b]the border of the Geshurites and the Maacathites,
and half of Gilead, *as far as* the border of
Sihon king of Heshbon.
6 Moses the servant of the LORD and the
sons of Israel [1]defeated them; and [a]Moses
the servant of the LORD gave it to the Reubenites and the Gadites and the half-tribe of
Manasseh as a possession.
7 Now these are the kings of the land
whom Joshua and the sons of Israel [1]defeat-
ed beyond the Jordan toward the west, from
Baal-gad in the valley of Lebanon even as far
as [a]Mount Halak, which rises toward Seir;
and Joshua gave it to the tribes of Israel as a
possession according to their divisions,
8 in [a]the hill country, in the lowland, in
the Arabah, on the slopes, and in the wilderness, and in the [1]Negev; the Hittite, the
Amorite and the Canaanite, the Perizzite, the
Hivite and the Jebusite:
9 the [a]king of Jericho, one; the [b]king of
Ai, which is beside Bethel, one;
10 the [a]king of Jerusalem, one; the king of
Hebron, one;
11 the king of Jarmuth, one; the king of
Lachish, one;
12 the king of Eglon, one; the king of
Gezer, one;
13 the king of Debir, one; the king of
Geder, one;
14 the king of Hormah, one; the king of
[a]Arad, one;
15 the king of Libnah, one; the king of
Adullam, one;

16 [1]I.e. South country [a]Josh 10:40, 41 [b]Josh 11:2
17 [1]Lit *under* [a]Josh 12:7 [b]Deut 7:24
19 [a]Josh 9:3, 7
20 [1]Lit *make strong* [2]Lit *have* [a]Ex 14:17 [b]Deut 7:16
21 [a]Num 13:33; Deut 9:2
22 [a]1 Sam 17:4; 1 Kin 2:39; 1 Chr 8:13 [b]Josh 15:46f; 1 Sam 5:1; Is 20:1
23 [a]Deut 1:38 [b]Deut 12:9, 10; 25:19; Heb 4:8
12:1 [1]Lit *smote* [a]Num 32:33; Deut 3:8-17
2 [a]Deut 2:36

3 [1]I.e. Galilee [2]Lit *the way of* [3]Lit *under* [a]Josh 11:2 [b]Josh 13:20
4 [a]Deut 3:11 [b]Deut 1:4
5 [a]Deut 3:10; Josh 13:11; 1 Chr 5:11 [b]Deut 3:14; 1 Sam 27:8
6 [1]Lit *smote* [a]Num 32:33; Deut 3:12
7 [1]Lit *smote* [a]Josh 11:17
8 [1]I.e. South country [a]Josh 11:16
9 [a]Josh 6:2 [b]Josh 8:29
10 [a]Josh 10:23
14 [a]Num 21:1

eventually would have to be occupied by Israel.

11:16 *all that land.* A lesson in the geography of Canaan follows. See map No. 2 at the end of the study Bible.

11:17 *Mount Halak.* A wilderness peak to the east of Kadesh-barnea marking Israel's southern extremity. *Baal-gad.* The first valley west of Mount Hermon.

11:18 *a long time.* An estimation of the duration of Joshua's conquests can be made from the life-span of Caleb: Seven years had elapsed from the beginning of the conquest (age 78; compare 14:7 with Deut 2:14) until he took Hebron (age 85; see 14:10).

11:20 *the LORD . . . their hearts.* God has sovereign control of history, yet His will never denies our personal and moral freedom (cf. the case of Pharaoh, Ex 8:32; 9:12).

11:21 *Anakim.* Had been reported by the 12 spies to be a people "of great size" (Num 13:32), whom the Israelites had feared so much that they had refused to undertake the conquest. They were related to the Nephilim (see note on Gen 6:4) and were named after their forefather, Anak. Joshua shared with Caleb his victory over the Anakites (14:12–15).

12:1–24 A conclusion to the first section of Joshua, and a summary of the victories of the Israelites and the cities whose kings had been defeated (see map No. 3 at the end of the study Bible).

12:1 *land . . . beyond the Jordan.* The unity of the nation is reaffirmed by the inclusion of these lands in Transjordan. *Arnon Gorge.* Marked the border with Moab to the south. *Mount Hermon.* The upper limits of Israel's land to the north.

12:4 *Og king of Bashan.* Og and Sihon (v. 2) met defeat under the command of Moses, a long-remembered tribute to God's mighty power (see Neh 9:22; Ps 135:11).

12:7 *the land . . . toward the west.* Canaan proper (9:1; 11:16–17; 24:11; Gen 15:18–19).

12:12 *king of Gezer.* Had been defeated in the siege of Lachish (10:33), but the city itself was not captured by Joshua, nor were the cities of Aphek, Taanach, Megiddo or Dor (vv. 18–23; see Judg 1:27–31).

16 the king of Makkedah, one; the king of
Bethel, one;
17 the king of Tappuah, one; the [a]king of
Hepher, one;
18 the king of [a]Aphek, one; the king of
Lasharon, one;
19 the king of Madon, one; the king of
Hazor, one;
20 the king of Shimron-meron, one; the
king of Achshaph, one;
21 the king of Taanach, one; the king of
Megiddo, one;
22 the king of [a]Kedesh, one; the king of
Jokneam in Carmel, one;
23 the king of Dor in the [1]heights of Dor,
one; the king of [a]Goiim in Gilgal, one;
24 the king of Tirzah, one: [a]in all, thirty-
one kings.

Canaan Divided among the Tribes

13 Now [a]Joshua was old *and* advanced in
years when the LORD said to him, "You
are old *and* advanced in years, and very
much of the land remains to be possessed.
2 "This is the land that remains: all the
regions *of* the Philistines and all *those of* the
[a]Geshurites;
3 from the Shihor which is [1]east of
Egypt, even as far as the border of Ekron to
the north (it is counted as Canaanite); the
[a]five lords of the Philistines: the Gazite,
the Ashdodite, the Ashkelonite, the Gittite,
the Ekronite; and the Avvite
4 [1]to the south, all the land of the
Canaanite, and Mearah that belongs to the
Sidonians, as far as [a]Aphek, to the border of
the [b]Amorite;
5 and the land of the [a]Gebalite, and all of
Lebanon, toward the [1]east, [b]from Baal-gad
below Mount Hermon as far as [2]Lebo-
hamath.
6 "All the inhabitants of the hill country
from Lebanon as far as [a]Misrephoth-maim,
all the Sidonians, I will [1]drive them out from
before the sons of Israel; [b]only allot it to Israel for an inheritance as I have commanded
you.
7 "Now therefore, apportion this land for
an inheritance to the nine tribes and the half-
tribe of Manasseh."
8 With [1]the other half-tribe, the Reubenites and the Gadites received their inheritance which Moses gave them [a]beyond the
Jordan to the east, just as Moses the servant
of the LORD gave to them;
9 from Aroer, which is on the edge of the
valley of the Arnon, with the city which is in
the middle of the valley, and all the plain of
Medeba, as far as Dibon;
10 and all the cities of Sihon king of the
Amorites, who reigned in Heshbon, as far as
the border of the sons of Ammon;
11 and [a]Gilead, and the [1]territory of the
Geshurites and Maacathites, and all Mount
Hermon, and all Bashan as far as Salecah;
12 all the kingdom of [a]Og in Bashan, who
reigned in Ashtaroth and in Edrei (he alone
was left of the remnant of the Rephaim); for
Moses [b]struck them and dispossessed them.
13 But the sons of Israel did not dispossess the Geshurites or the Maacathites; for
Geshur and Maacath live among Israel until
this day.
14 [a]Only to the tribe of Levi he did not
give an inheritance; the offerings by fire to
the LORD, the God of Israel, are [1]their inheritance, as He spoke to him.
15 So Moses gave *an inheritance* to the
tribe of the sons of Reuben according to their
families.
16 Their [1]territory was [a]from Aroer, which
is on the edge of the valley of the Arnon,
with the city which is in the middle of the
valley and all the plain by Medeba;
17 Heshbon, and all its cities which are on
the plain: Dibon and Bamoth-baal and Beth-
baal-meon,
18 and [a]Jahaz and Kedemoth and Mephaath,
19 and [a]Kiriathaim and Sibmah and
Zereth-shahar on the hill of the valley,
20 and Beth-peor and the slopes of Pisgah
and Beth-jeshimoth,
21 even all the cities of the plain and all
the kingdom of Sihon king of the Amorites
who reigned in Heshbon, whom Moses
struck with the chiefs of Midian, [a]Evi and
Rekem and Zur and Hur and Reba, the
princes of Sihon, who lived in the land.
22 The sons of Israel also killed [a]Balaam

17 [a]1 Kin 4:10
18 [a]Josh 13:4; 2 Kin 13:17
22 [a]Josh 19:37; 20:7; 21:32
23 [1]Or *Naphath-dor* [a]Gen 14:1
24 [a]Deut 7:24
13:1 [a]Josh 14:10
2 [a]Josh 13:11; 1 Sam 27:8
3 [1]Lit *on the face of* [a]1 Sam 6:4, 16
4 [1]Or *from the Teman* [a]Josh 12:18; 19:30; 1 Sam 4:1; 1 Kin 20:26, 30 [b]Ezek 16:3; Amos 2:10
5 [1]Lit *sunrise* [2]Or *the entrance of Hamath* [a]1 Kin 5:18 [b]Josh 12:7
6 [1]Or *dispossess* [a]Josh 11:8 [b]Num 33:54
8 [1]Lit *it, the* [a]Josh 12:1-6
11 [1]Or *border* [a]Gen 37:25; Num 32:29; Josh 13:25; 17:5f
12 [a]Deut 3:11 [b]Num 21:24
14 [1]Lit *his* [a]Deut 18:1, 2
16 [1]Or *border* [a]Josh 13:9
18 [a]Num 21:23; Judg 11:20; Is 15:4; Jer 48:34
19 [a]Num 32:37; Jer 48:1, 23; Ezek 25:9
21 [a]Num 31:8
22 [a]Num 31:8

13:1–32 The heavenly King, who has conquered the land, begins the administration of His realm by assigning specific territories to the several tribes. Much of chs. 13–21 reads like administrative documents. The account begins by noting the land still to be subdued (but to be allotted) and by recalling the assignments already made by Moses to the two and a half tribes east of the Jordan (see map No. 4 at the end of the study Bible).
13:1 *Joshua was old.* Between 90 and 100 years of age; Caleb was 85 (14:10).
13:3 *Shihor.* Another name for the Wadi el-Arish below Gaza at the eastern entrance to the Sinai. *lords.* The Hebrew for this word is probably derived from a Greek term for "tyrant," indicating the Aegean background of the Philistines. See map, p. 312.
13:5 *Gebalite.* Inhabitants of the ancient city of Byblos just north of modern Beirut. The Phoenicians and the Philistines held most of the territory still to be occupied by Israel.
13:9 *Aroer.* This town on the Arnon River marked the southern boundary of Israel. From here the land extended through Gilead and Bashan to the slopes of Mount Hermon in the north, the territory once dominated by the two kings of the Amorites, Sihon and Og.
13:14 *the offerings . . . are their inheritance.* See Deut 18:1–8 and note on Deut 18:1.
13:15 *Moses gave . . . to . . . Reuben.* The land east of the Jordan between the Arnon River (boundary of Moab) and Heshbon (the old royal city of Sihon).
13:22 *Balaam the son of Beor.* The one who supposedly had influence with the gods (Num 22–24) was slain when the Lord

the son of Beor, the diviner, with the sword among *the rest of* their slain.

23 The border of the sons of Reuben was the [1]Jordan. This was the inheritance of the sons of Reuben according to their families, the cities and their villages.

24 Moses also gave *an inheritance* to the tribe of Gad, to the sons of Gad, according to their families.

25 Their territory was [a]Jazer, and all the cities of Gilead, and half the land of the sons of Ammon, as far as Aroer which is before Rabbah;

26 and from Heshbon as far as Ramath-mizpeh and Betonim, and from Mahanaim as far as the border of [1]Debir;

27 and in the valley, Beth-haram and Beth-nimrah and Succoth and Zaphon, the rest of the kingdom of Sihon king of Heshbon, with the Jordan [1]as a border, as far as the *lower* end of the Sea of [2a]Chinnereth beyond the Jordan to the east.

28 This is the inheritance of the sons of Gad according to their families, the cities and their villages.

29 Moses also gave *an inheritance* to the half-tribe of Manasseh; and it was for the half-tribe of the sons of Manasseh according to their families.

30 Their territory was from Mahanaim, all Bashan, all the kingdom of Og king of Bashan, and all [a]the [1]towns of Jair, which are in Bashan, sixty cities;

31 also half of Gilead, with [a]Ashtaroth and Edrei, the cities of the kingdom of Og in Bashan, *were* for the sons of Machir the son of Manasseh, for half of the sons of Machir according to their families.

23 [1]Lit *Jordan and border*
25 [a]Num 21:32; Josh 21:39; 2 Sam 24:5; 1 Chr 6:81; 26:31; Is 16:8f; Jer 48:32
26 [1]Or *Lidebir*
27 [1]Lit *and border* [2]I.e. Galilee [a]Num 34:11; Deut 3:17
30 [1]Lit *tent villages* [a]Num 32:41
31 [a]Josh 9:10; 12:4; 13:12; Judg 10:6; 1 Sam 7:3f; 12:10; 1 Chr 6:71

punished the Midianites for trying to seduce Israel into idolatry and sexual immorality (see Num 25; 31:8).

13:24 *Moses . . . to the tribe of Gad.* The central area, beginning near Heshbon on the south and reaching, along the Jordan, to the southern end of the Sea of Galilee. It included most of Gilead, but the exact boundary between Gad and the half-tribe of Manasseh remains somewhat uncertain since not all the places named can now be located.

13:29 *Moses . . . to the half-tribe of Manasseh.* The lands east and north of the Sea of Galilee, but also including the upper part of Gilead. Makir led in the occupation of these lands (see Num 32:32,39–42).

Conquest of Canaan

Damascus
Great Sea
Mt. Hermon
NORTHERN CAMPAIGN
BASHAN
Hazor
Acco
Chinnereth
Sea of Chinnereth
Edrei
Dor
Megiddo
Beth-shan
Taanach
Ibleam
Dothan
Jordan R.
Mt. Ebal
Mt. Gerizim
CENTRAL CAMPAIGN
See right-hand page
Bethel
Gibeon
Jericho
Heshbon
Mt. Nebo
Gath
Salt Sea
Jahaz
Hebron
Dibon
SOUTHERN CAMPAIGN
See right-hand page
Beersheba
Miles 10 5 0 10 20
Kms 10 5 0 10 20 30

4. THE NORTHERN CAMPAIGN

Late Bronze Age Hazor was burned by Joshua (Jos 11:13). Excavations have revealed three clearly datable destruction layers, one of which may provide the strongest evidence yet for a historically verifiable date for the conquest.

The excavator thought Joshua burned the latest level (c. 1230 B.C.), but others argue that it must actually have been the earliest of the three levels, c. 1400 B.C.

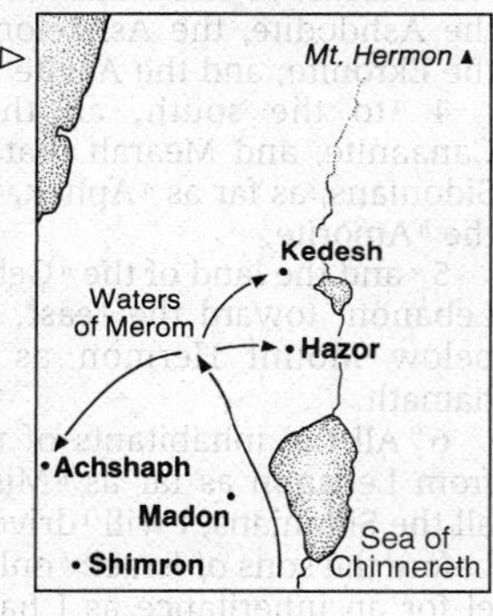

Mt. Hermon
Kedesh
Waters of Merom
Hazor
Achshaph
Madon
Shimron
Sea of Chinnereth

1. ENTRY INTO CANAAN

When the Israelite tribes approached Canaan after four decades of desert existence, they had to overcome the two Amorite kingdoms on the plain of Medeba and in Bashan. Under Moses' leadership, they also subdued the Midianites in order to consolidate their control over the Transjordanian region.

The conquest of Canaan followed a course that in retrospect appears as though it had been planned by a brilliant strategist. Taking Jericho gave Israel control of its strategic plains, fords and roads as a base of operations. When Israel next gained control of the Bethel, Gibeon and Upper Beth-horon region, she dominated the center of the north-south Palestinian ridge. Subsequently, she was able to break the power of the allied urban centers in separate campaigns south and north.

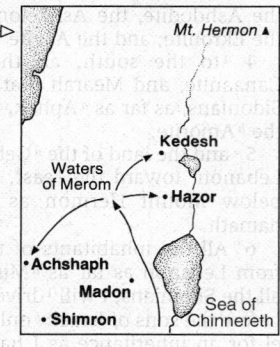

32 These are *the territories* which Moses
apportioned for an inheritance in the plains
of Moab, beyond the Jordan at Jericho to the
east.
33 But [a]to the tribe of Levi, Moses did not
give an inheritance; the LORD, the God of
Israel, is their inheritance, as He had [1]prom-
ised to them.

Caleb's Request

14 Now these are *the territories* which the
sons of Israel inherited in the land of
Canaan, which [a]Eleazar the priest, and Joshua the son of Nun, and the heads of the
[1]households of the tribes of the sons of Israel apportioned to them for an inheritance,
2 by the [a]lot of their inheritance, as the
LORD commanded [1]through Moses, for the
nine tribes and the half-tribe.
3 For [a]Moses had given the inheritance
of the two tribes and the half-tribe beyond
the Jordan; but [b]he did not give an inheritance to the Levites among them.
4 For the sons of Joseph were two tribes,
[a]Manasseh and Ephraim, and they did not
give a portion to the Levites in the land,
except cities to live in, with their pasture
lands for their livestock and for their property.
5 Thus the sons of Israel did just [a]as the
LORD had commanded Moses, and they
divided the land.
6 Then the sons of Judah drew near to
Joshua in Gilgal, and [a]Caleb the son of
Jephunneh the Kenizzite said to him, "You
know the word which the LORD spoke to

33 [1]Lit *spoken to* [a]Deut 18:1f; Josh 13:14
14:1 [1]Lit *fathers'* [a]Num 34:16-29
2 [a]Num 26:55; 33:54; 34:13
2 [1]Lit *by the hand of*
3 [a]Num 32:33 [b]Josh 13:14
4 [a]Gen 41:51f; 46:20; 48:1, 5; Num 26:28; 2 Chr 30:1
5 [a]Num 35:1f; Josh 21:2
6 [a]Num 13:6, 30; 14:6, 24, 30

13:33 *the LORD . . . is their inheritance.* See v.14; see also Deut 18:1–8 and note on Deut 18:1.

14:1–15 A short introductory chapter for the following section (chs. 15–19), with a special note on the Lord's faithfulness to Caleb.

14:1 *Eleazar the priest.* Son of Aaron, Eleazar as high priest was the highest official over the casting of the lots. The Urim and Thummim (see notes on Ex 28:30; 1 Sam 2:28) may have been used.

14:4 *Manasseh and Ephraim.* Sons of Joseph. Since Jacob had adopted them as his own sons (Gen 48:5), they constituted two separate tribes. This made possible the 12-part nation, with the Levites serving as a nonpolitical tribe.

14:6 *the word . . . the LORD spoke.* Caleb now recalls the prom-

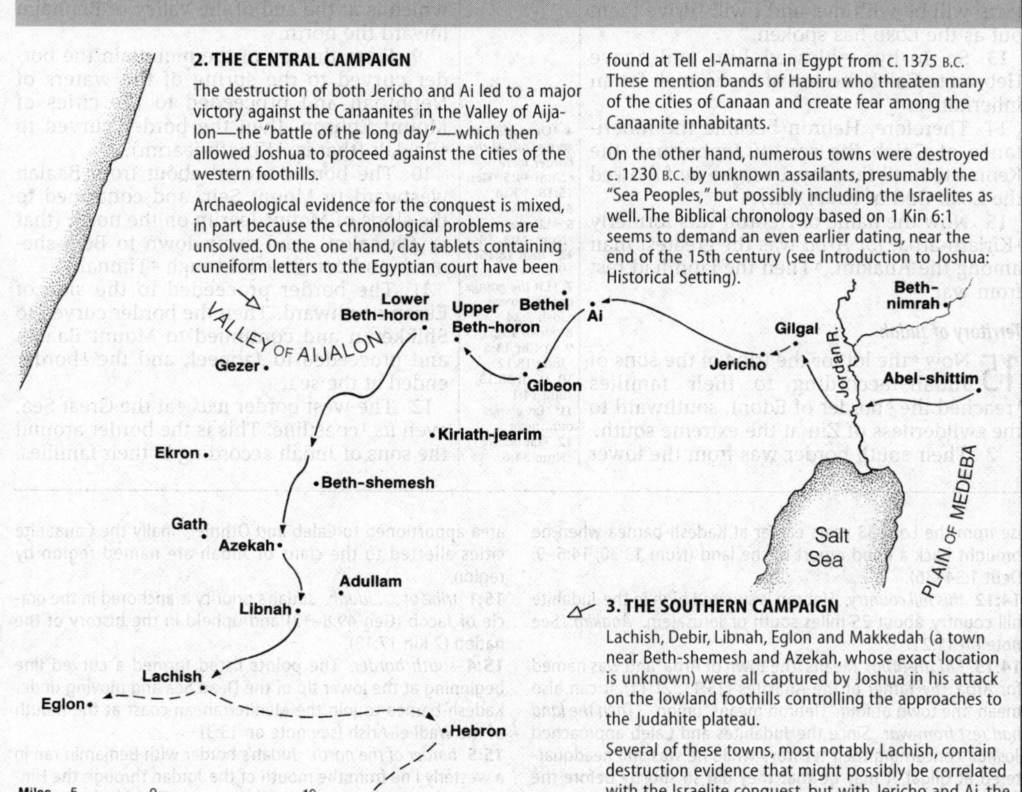

Lower Beth-horon
Upper Beth-horon
Bethel
Ai
Beth-nimrah
Gilgal
Jordan R.
Jericho
Abel-shittim
VALLEY OF AIJALON
Gezer
Gibeon
Kiriath-jearim
Ekron
Beth-shemesh
Gath
Azekah
Adullam
Libnah
Salt Sea
PLAIN OF MEDEBA
Lachish
Eglon
Hebron
Debir
Miles 5 0 10
Kms 5 0 10

2. THE CENTRAL CAMPAIGN

The destruction of both Jericho and Ai led to a major victory against the Canaanites in the Valley of Aijalon—the "battle of the long day"—which then allowed Joshua to proceed against the cities of the western foothills.

Archaeological evidence for the conquest is mixed, in part because the chronological problems are unsolved. On the one hand, clay tablets containing cuneiform letters to the Egyptian court have been found at Tell el-Amarna in Egypt from c. 1375 B.C. These mention bands of Habiru who threaten many of the cities of Canaan and create fear among the Canaanite inhabitants.

On the other hand, numerous towns were destroyed c. 1230 B.C. by unknown assailants, presumably the "Sea Peoples," but possibly including the Israelites as well. The Biblical chronology based on 1 Kin 6:1 seems to demand an even earlier dating, near the end of the 15th century (see Introduction to Joshua: Historical Setting).

3. THE SOUTHERN CAMPAIGN

Lachish, Debir, Libnah, Eglon and Makkedah (a town near Beth-shemesh and Azekah, whose exact location is unknown) were all captured by Joshua in his attack on the lowland foothills controlling the approaches to the Judahite plateau.

Several of these towns, most notably Lachish, contain destruction evidence that might possibly be correlated with the Israelite conquest, but with Jericho and Ai, the historical implications are not clear.

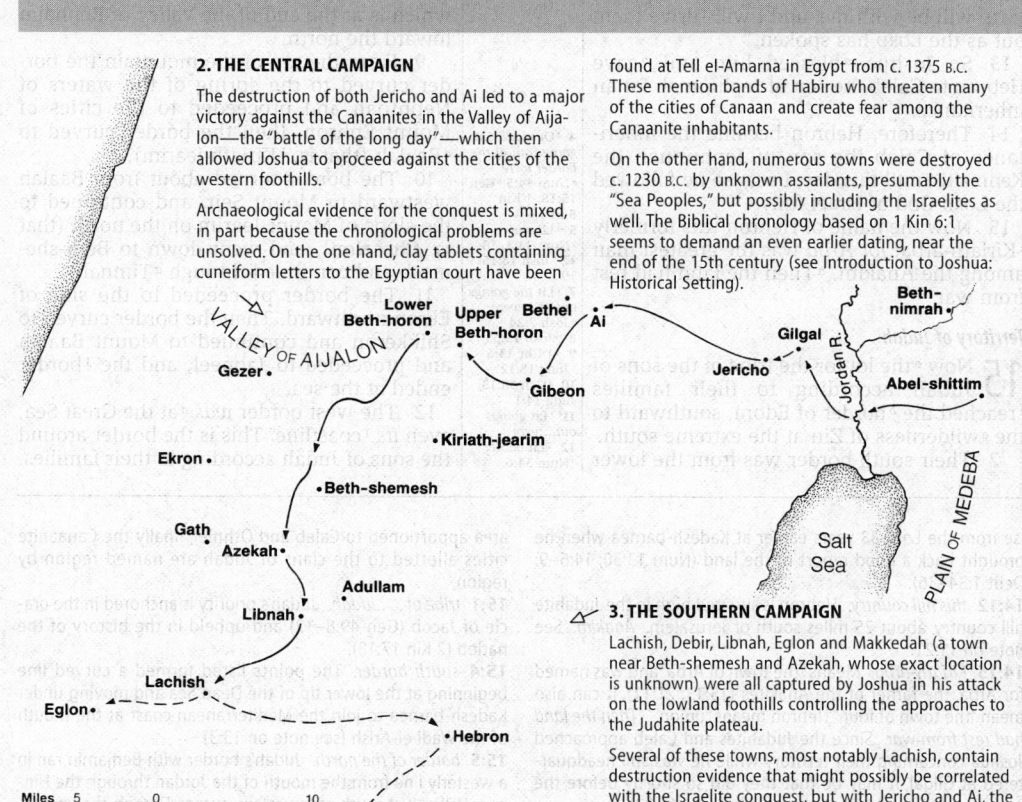

Moses the man of God concerning [1]you and me in Kadesh-barnea.

7 "I was forty years old when [a]Moses the servant of the LORD sent me from Kadesh-barnea to spy out the land, and I brought word back to him as *it was* in my heart.

8 "Nevertheless my brethren who went up with me made the heart of the people [1]melt with fear; but [a]I followed the LORD my God fully.

9 "So Moses swore on that day, saying, 'Surely [a]the land on which your foot has trodden will be an inheritance to you and to your children forever, because you have followed the LORD my God fully.'

10 "Now behold, the LORD has let me live, just as He spoke, these forty-five years, from the time that the LORD spoke this word to Moses, when Israel walked in the wilderness; and now behold, I am eighty-five years old today.

11 "[a]I am still as strong today as I was in the day Moses sent me; as my strength was then, so my strength is now, for war and for [b]going out and coming in.

12 "Now then, give me this hill country about which the LORD spoke on that day, for you heard on that day that [a]Anakim *were* there, with great fortified cities; perhaps the LORD will be with me, and I will [1]drive them out as the LORD has spoken."

13 So Joshua [a]blessed him and [b]gave Hebron to Caleb the son of Jephunneh for an inheritance.

14 Therefore, Hebron became the inheritance of Caleb the son of Jephunneh the Kenizzite until this day, because he followed the LORD God of Israel fully.

15 Now the name of Hebron was formerly [1]Kiriath-arba; *for Arba* was the greatest man among the Anakim. [a]Then the land had rest from war.

Territory of Judah

15 Now [a]the lot for the tribe of the sons of Judah according to their families [1]reached the [b]border of Edom, southward to the [c]wilderness of Zin at the extreme south.

2 Their south border was from the lower end of the Salt Sea, from the bay that turns to the south.

3 Then it proceeded southward to the ascent of Akrabbim and continued to Zin, then went up by the south of Kadesh-barnea and continued to Hezron, and went up to Addar and turned about to Karka.

4 It [a]continued to Azmon and proceeded to the [1b]brook of Egypt, and the [2]border ended at the sea. This shall be your south border.

5 The [a]east border *was* the Salt Sea, as far as the [1]mouth of the Jordan. And the [b]border of the north side was from the bay of the sea at the [1]mouth of the Jordan.

6 Then the border went up to Beth-hoglah, and continued on the north of Beth-arabah, and the border went up to the stone of Bohan the son of Reuben.

7 The border went up to Debir from [a]the valley of Achor, and turned northward toward Gilgal which is opposite the ascent of Adummim, which is on the south of the valley; and the border continued to the waters of En-shemesh and [1]it ended at En-rogel.

8 Then the border went up the valley of Ben-hinnom to the slope of the [a]Jebusite on the south (that is, Jerusalem); and the border went up to the top of the mountain which is before the valley of Hinnom to the west, which is at the end of the valley of Rephaim toward the north.

9 From the top of the mountain the border curved to the spring of the waters of Nephtoah and proceeded to the cities of Mount Ephron, then the border curved to [a]Baalah (that is, [b]Kiriath-jearim).

10 The border turned about from Baalah westward to Mount Seir, and continued to the slope of Mount Jearim on the north (that is, Chesalon), and went down to Beth-shemesh and continued through [a]Timnah.

11 The border proceeded to the side of Ekron northward. Then the border curved to Shikkeron and continued to Mount Baalah and proceeded to Jabneel, and the [1]border ended at the sea.

12 The west border *was* [a]at the Great Sea, even *its* [1]coastline. This is the border around the sons of Judah according to their families.

6 [1]Lit *me and concerning you* **7** [a]Num 13:1-31 **8** [1]Lit *become demoralized* [a]Num 14:24; Deut 1:36 **9** [a]Deut 1:36 **11** [a]Deut 34:7 [b]Deut 31:2 **12** [1]Or *dispossess* [a]Num 13:33 **13** [a]Josh 22:6 [b]Judg 1:20; 1 Chr 6:55f **15** [1]I.e. the city of Arba [a]Josh 11:23 **15:1** [1]Lit *was to* [a]Num 34:3, 4 [b]Num 20:16 [c]Deut 32:51

4 [1]Or *wadi* [2]Lit *goings out of the border were* [a]Num 34:5 [b]Gen 15:18; 1 Kin 8:65 **5** [1]Lit *end* [a]Num 34:3, 10-12 [b]Josh 18:15-19 **7** [1]Lit *the goings out of it were* [a]Josh 7:24 **8** [a]Josh 15:63 **9** [a]1 Chr 13:6 [b]Judg 18:12 **10** [a]Gen 38:13; Judg 14:1 **11** [1]Lit *goings out...were* **12** [1]Lit *border* [a]Num 34:6

ise from the Lord 38 years earlier at Kadesh-barnea when he brought back a good report of the land (Num 13:30; 14:6–9; Deut 1:34–36).

14:12 *this hill country.* Hebron is situated high in the Judahite hill country, about 25 miles south of Jerusalem. *Anakim.* See note on 11:21.

14:15 *Kiriath-arba.* Means "the town of Arba" and was named for Arba, the father of the Anakites (15:13; 21:11). It can also mean "the town of four." Hebron means "union." *Then the land had rest from war.* Since the Judahites and Caleb approached Joshua concerning their territory while he was still headquartered at Gilgal, it may be that they did so shortly before the wars fought under Joshua were ended (see 11:23).

15:1–63 Judah is the first of the west bank tribes to have its territory delineated. First the outer limits are listed, then the area apportioned to Caleb and Othniel; finally the Canaanite cities allotted to the clans of Judah are named region by region.

15:1 *tribe of . . . Judah.* Judah's priority is anchored in the oracle of Jacob (Gen 49:8–12) and upheld in the history of the nation (2 Kin 17:18).

15:4 *south border.* The points listed formed a curved line beginning at the lower tip of the Dead Sea and moving under Kadesh-barnea to join the Mediterranean coast at the mouth of the Wadi el-Arish (see note on 13:3).

15:5 *border of the north.* Judah's border with Benjamin ran in a westerly line from the mouth of the Jordan through the Hinnom Valley, just south of Jerusalem, over to Timnah, then northwest to the coastal city of Jabneel (later called Jamnia), about ten miles south of Joppa.

13 Now [a]he gave to Caleb the son of Jephunneh a portion [b]among the sons of Judah, according to the [1]command of the LORD to Joshua, *namely,* [2]Kiriath-arba, *Arba being* the father of Anak (that is, Hebron).

14 [a]Caleb [1]drove out from there the three [b]sons of Anak: Sheshai and Ahiman and Talmai, the children of Anak.

15 Then [a]he went up from there against the inhabitants of Debir; now the name of Debir formerly was Kiriath-sepher.

16 And Caleb said, "The one who [1]attacks Kiriath-sepher and captures it, [2]I will give him Achsah my daughter as a wife."

17 [a]Othniel the son of Kenaz, the brother of Caleb, captured it; so he gave him Achsah his daughter as a wife.

18 [a]It came about that when she came *to him,* she persuaded him to ask her father for a field. So she alighted from the donkey, and Caleb said to her, "What do you want?"

19 Then she said, "Give me a blessing; since you have given me the land of the [1]Negev, give me also springs of water." So he gave her the upper springs and the lower springs.

20 This is the inheritance of the tribe of the sons of Judah according to their families.

21 Now the cities at the extremity of the tribe of the sons of Judah toward the border of Edom in the south were Kabzeel and [a]Eder and Jagur,

22 and Kinah and Dimonah and Adadah,

23 and Kedesh and Hazor and Ithnan,

24 Ziph and Telem and Bealoth,

25 and Hazor-hadattah and Kerioth-hezron (that is, Hazor),

26 Amam and Shema and Moladah,

27 and Hazar-gaddah and Heshmon and Beth-pelet,

28 and Hazar-shual and [a]Beersheba and Biziothiah,

29 Baalah and Iim and Ezem,

30 and Eltolad and Chesil and Hormah,

31 and [a]Ziklag and Madmannah and Sansannah,

32 and Lebaoth and Shilhim and Ain and Rimmon; in all, twenty-nine cities with their villages.

33 In the lowland: [a]Eshtaol and Zorah and Ashnah,

34 and Zanoah and En-gannim, Tappuah and Enam,

35 Jarmuth and [a]Adullam, Socoh and Azekah,

36 and Shaaraim and Adithaim and Gederah and Gederothaim; fourteen cities with their villages.

37 Zenan and Hadashah and Migdal-gad,

38 and Dilean and Mizpeh and Joktheel,

39 [a]Lachish and Bozkath and Eglon,

40 and Cabbon and Lahmas and Chitlish,

41 and Gederoth, Beth-dagon and Naamah and Makkedah; sixteen cities with their villages.

42 Libnah and Ether and Ashan,

43 and Iphtah and Ashnah and Nezib,

44 and Keilah and Achzib and Mareshah; nine cities with their villages.

45 Ekron, with its towns and its villages;

46 from Ekron even to the sea, all that were by the [1]side of Ashdod, with their villages.

47 Ashdod, its towns and its villages; Gaza, its towns and its villages; as far as [a]the [1]brook of Egypt and the Great Sea, even *its* [2]coastline.

48 In the hill country: Shamir and Jattir and Socoh,

49 and Dannah and Kiriath-sannah (that is, Debir),

50 and Anab and Eshtemoh and Anim,

51 and Goshen and Holon and Giloh; eleven cities with their villages.

52 Arab and Dumah and Eshan,

53 and Janum and Beth-tappuah and Aphekah,

54 and Humtah and Kiriath-arba (that is, Hebron), and Zior; nine cities with their villages.

55 Maon, Carmel and Ziph and Juttah,

56 and Jezreel and Jokdeam and Zanoah,

57 Kain, Gibeah and Timnah; ten cities with their villages.

58 Halhul, Beth-zur and Gedor,

59 and Maarath and Beth-anoth and Eltekon; six cities with their villages.

60 Kiriath-baal (that is, Kiriath-jearim), and Rabbah; two cities with their villages.

61 In the wilderness: Beth-arabah, Middin and Secacah,

62 and Nibshan and the City of Salt and Engedi; six cities with their villages.

63 Now as for the [a]Jebusites, the inhabitants of Jerusalem, the sons of Judah could not [1]drive them out; so the Jebusites live

13 [1]Lit *mouth* [2]I.e. the city of Arba [a]Josh 14:13-15 [b]Num 13:6
14 [1]Or *dispossessed* [a]Josh 11:21, 22 [b]Num 13:33; Deut 9:2
15 [a]Josh 10:38
16 [1]Lit *smites* [2]Lit *and I*
17 [a]Judg 1:13; 3:9
18 [a]Judg 1:14
19 [1]I.e. South country
21 [a]Gen 35:21
28 [a]Gen 21:31
31 [a]1 Sam 27:6; 30:1
33 [a]Judg 13:25; 16:31
35 [a]1 Sam 22:1
39 [a]Josh 10:3; 2 Kin 14:19
46 [1]Lit *hand*
47 [1]Or *wadi* [2]Lit *border* [a]Josh 15:4
63 [1]Or *dispossess them* [a]Judg 1:21; 2 Sam 5:6; 1 Chr 11:4

15:15 *he went up . . . against . . . Debir.* See note on 10:38.

15:17 *Othniel.* See Judg 3:7–11 for his service as judge in Israel.

15:19 *upper . . . lower springs.* They still water the local farms in Hebron.

15:21 *cities at the extremity . . . of Judah . . . in the south.* Most of the first 29 villages were assigned to the tribe of Simeon (cf. 19:1–9).

15:33 *lowland.* The Hebrew for this term is *Shephelah.* This area between the highlands of central Judah and the Philistine coast was for the most part not occupied by Israel until the victories of King David. Some of the places on this list were reassigned to the tribe of Dan (cf. 19:41–43).

15:48 *hill country.* The high region south of Jerusalem. The Septuagint adds 11 names, including Tekoa and Bethlehem, to this list.

15:61 *wilderness.* The chalky, dry region east and south of Jerusalem that borders the Dead Sea.

15:62 Only Engedi can be positively located, though the "City of Salt" is believed by many to be Qumran, where, centuries later, the scribes who produced the Dead Sea Scrolls lived.

15:63 *Jebusites.* A victory over the city of the Jebusites by the men of Judah is recorded in Judg 1:8, but evidently this did not result in its permanent occupation. Both Benjamin and Judah

with the sons of Judah at Jerusalem until this day.

Territory of Ephraim

16 Then the lot for the sons of Joseph went from the Jordan at Jericho to the waters of Jericho on the east into [a]the wilderness, going up from Jericho through the hill country to Bethel.

2 It went from Bethel to Luz, and [a]continued to the border of the Archites at Ataroth.

3 It went down westward to the territory of the Japhletites, as far as the territory of lower [a]Beth-horon even to [b]Gezer, and [1]it ended at the sea.

4 The [a]sons of Joseph, Manasseh and Ephraim, received their inheritance.

5 Now *this* was the territory of the sons of Ephraim according to their families: the border of their inheritance eastward was [a]Ataroth-addar, as far as upper Beth-horon.

6 Then the border went westward at [a]Michmethath on the north, and the border turned about eastward to Taanath-shiloh and continued *beyond* it to the east of Janoah.

7 It went down from Janoah to Ataroth and to [a]Naarah, then reached Jericho and came out at the Jordan.

8 From [a]Tappuah the border continued westward to the [1]brook of Kanah, and [2]it ended at the sea. This is the inheritance of the tribe of the sons of Ephraim according to their families,

9 *together* with the cities which were set apart for the sons of Ephraim in the midst of the inheritance of the sons of Manasseh, all the cities with their villages.

10 [a]But they did not [1]drive out the Canaanites who lived in Gezer, so [b]the Canaanites live in the midst of Ephraim to this day, and they became forced laborers.

Territory of Manasseh

17 Now *this* was the lot for the tribe of [a]Manasseh, for he was the firstborn of Joseph. To Machir the firstborn of Manasseh, the father of Gilead, [1]were allotted Gilead and Bashan, because he was a man of war.

2 So *the lot* was *made* for the rest of the sons of Manasseh according to their families: for the sons of Abiezer and for the sons of Helek and for the sons of Asriel and for the sons of Shechem and for the sons of Hepher and for the sons of Shemida; these *were* the male [1]descendants of Manasseh the son of Joseph according to their families.

3 However, [a]Zelophehad, the son of Hepher, the son of Gilead, the son of Machir, the son of Manasseh, had no sons, only daughters; and these are the names of his daughters: Mahlah and Noah, Hoglah, Milcah and Tirzah.

4 They came near before Eleazar the priest and before Joshua the son of Nun and before the leaders, saying, "The LORD commanded Moses to give us an inheritance among our brothers." So [a]according to the [1]command of the LORD he gave them an inheritance among their father's brothers.

5 Thus there fell ten portions to Manasseh, besides the land of Gilead and Bashan, which is beyond the Jordan,

6 because the daughters of Manasseh received an inheritance among his sons. And the [a]land of Gilead belonged to the rest of the sons of Manasseh.

7 The border of Manasseh [1]ran from Asher to Michmethath which was east of Shechem; then the border went [2]southward to the inhabitants of En-tappuah.

8 The land of Tappuah belonged to Manasseh, but [a]Tappuah on the border of Manasseh *belonged* to the sons of Ephraim.

9 The [a]border went down to the [1]brook of Kanah, southward of the [1]brook (these cities *belonged* to Ephraim among the cities of Manasseh), and the border of Manasseh *was* on the north side of the [1]brook and [2]it ended at the sea.

10 The south side *belonged* to Ephraim and the north side to Manasseh, and the sea was [1]their border; and they reached to Asher on the north and to Issachar on the east.

11 In Issachar and in Asher, [a]Manasseh had Beth-shean and its towns and Ibleam and its towns, and the inhabitants of Dor and its towns, and the inhabitants of En-dor and its towns, and the inhabitants of Taanach and

16:1 [a]Josh 8:15; 18:12
2 [a]Josh 18:13
3 [1]Lit *the goings out of it were* [a]Josh 18:13; 1 Kin 9:17 [b]Josh 10:33
4 [a]Josh 17:14
5 [a]Josh 18:13
6 [a]Josh 17:7
7 [a]1 Chr 7:28
8 [1]Or *wadi* [2]Lit *the goings out of it were* [a]Josh 17:8
10 [1]Or *dispossess* [a]Judg 1:29; 1 Kin 9:16 [b]Josh 17:12, 13
17:1 [1]Lit *and there was to him* [a]Gen 41:51; 46:20; 48:17f
2 [1]Lit *sons*
3 [a]Num 26:33; 27:1-7
4 [1]Lit *mouth* [a]Num 27:5-7
6 [a]Josh 13:30, 31
7 [1]Lit *was* [2]Lit *to the right hand*
8 [a]Josh 16:8
9 [1]Or *wadi* [2]Lit *goings out of it were* [a]Josh 16:8f
10 [1]Lit *its*
11 [a]1 Chr 7:29

failed to take the Jebusite fortress of Jerusalem (Judg 1:21).

16:1–17:18 Two chapters are devoted to the lands given to the "house of Joseph" (Ephraim and the half-tribe of Manasseh that settled west of the Jordan). Following Judah, the Joseph tribes were given priority.

16:1 *lot for . . . Joseph.* Ephraim's southern border moved west from Jericho past Bethel and down to Gezer and the Mediterranean coast.

16:5 *border.* Ephraim's northern border began down by the Jordan and ran west near Shiloh, but south of Shechem, then followed the Wadi Kanah down to the Mediterranean Sea.

16:10 *Gezer.* See note on 10:33. *became forced laborers.* Since Gezer does not appear to have come under Israelite control until the days of Solomon (1 Kin 9:15–16), this may be a note added after that event (but see 2 Sam 5:25).

17:1 *Manasseh . . . the firstborn of Joseph.* A reminder to the proud Ephraimites that Manasseh had been the firstborn, though Jacob gave priority to Ephraim when he adopted Joseph's two sons (Gen 48:14,19).

17:3 *Zelophehad . . . had . . . only daughters.* Before Moses died, he promised the daughters an allotment along with their relatives (see Num 26:33; 27:1–7).

17:5 *ten portions.* Manasseh's territory was second only to Judah's in size. The ten portions went to the five brothers (minus Hepher) and to the five granddaughters of Hepher. For the law protecting the inheritance rights of a daughter without brothers see Num 27:8–11.

17:11 *Beth-shean . . . Megiddo.* These powerfully fortified cities, and others along Manasseh's common border with Issachar and Asher, were not conquered until later. When King Saul died

its towns, and the inhabitants of Megiddo and its towns, the third is [b]Napheth.

12 [a]But the sons of Manasseh could not take possession of these cities, because the Canaanites persisted in living in that land.

13 It came about when the sons of Israel became strong, [a]they put the Canaanites to forced labor, but they did not [1]drive them out completely.

14 Then the [a]sons of Joseph spoke to Joshua, saying, "Why have you given me only one lot and one portion for an inheritance, since I am a numerous people whom the LORD has thus far blessed?"

15 Joshua said to them, "If you are a numerous people, go [1]up to the forest and [2]clear a place for yourself there in the land of the Perizzites and of the Rephaim, since the hill country of Ephraim is too narrow for you."

16 The sons of Joseph said, "The hill country is not enough for us, and all the Canaanites who live in the valley land have [a]chariots of iron, both those who are in Beth-shean and its towns and those who are in the valley of Jezreel."

17 Joshua spoke to the house of Joseph, to Ephraim and Manasseh, saying, "You are a numerous people and have great power; you shall not have one lot *only,*

18 but the hill country shall be yours. For though it is a forest, you shall [1]clear it, and to its [2]farthest borders it shall be yours; for you shall [3]drive out the Canaanites, even though they have [a]chariots of iron *and* though they are strong."

Rest of the Land Divided

18 Then the whole congregation of the sons of Israel assembled themselves at [a]Shiloh, and set up the tent of meeting there; and the land was subdued before them.

2 There remained among the sons of Israel seven tribes who had not divided their inheritance.

3 So Joshua said to the sons of Israel, "[a]How long will you put off entering to take possession of the land which the LORD, the God of your fathers, has given you?

4 "Provide for yourselves three men from [1]each tribe that I may send them, and that they may arise and walk through the land and write a description of it according to their inheritance; then they shall [2]return to me.

5 "They shall divide it into seven portions; [a]Judah shall stay in its territory on the south, and the house of Joseph shall stay in their territory on the north.

6 "You shall describe the land in seven divisions, and bring *the description* here to me. [a]I will cast lots for you here before the LORD our God.

7 "For [a]the Levites have no portion among you, because the priesthood of the LORD is [1]their inheritance. Gad and Reuben and the half-tribe of Manasseh also have received their inheritance eastward beyond the Jordan, which Moses the servant of the LORD gave them."

8 Then the men arose and went, and Joshua commanded those who went to describe the land, saying, "Go and walk through the land and describe it, and return to me; then I will cast lots for you here before the LORD in [a]Shiloh."

9 So the men went and passed through the land, and described it by cities in seven divisions in a book; and they came to Joshua to the camp at Shiloh.

10 And [a]Joshua cast lots for them in Shiloh before the LORD, and there Joshua divided the land to the sons of Israel according to their divisions.

11 [b]Josh 11:2; 12:23 **12** [a]Judg 1:27 **13** [1]Or *dispossess* [a]Josh 16:10 **14** [a]Num 13:7 **15** [1]Lit *up for yourself* [2]Lit *cut down* **16** [a]Josh 17:18; Judg 1:19; 4:3, 13 **18** [1]Lit *cut it down* [2]Lit *goings out* [3]Or *dispossess* [a]Josh 17:16 **18:1** [a]Judg 21:19; Jer 7:12; 26:6, 9

3 [a]Judg 18:9 **4** [1]Lit *the* [2]Lit *come* **5** [a]Josh 15:1 **6** [a]Josh 14:2 **7** [1]Lit *his* [a]Num 18:7, 20; Josh 13:33 **8** [a]Josh 18:1 **10** [a]Num 34:16-29; Josh 19:51

in battle, the victorious Philistines fastened his body to the wall of Beth-shean (see 1 Sam 31:10), which suggests that that city was in league with the Philistines.

17:13 *when the sons of Israel became strong.* Possibly referring to the days of David and Solomon (see note on 16:10).

17:14 *sons of Joseph . . . numerous.* The reference is to both Ephraim and Manasseh (see v. 17). The allotment to the Joseph tribes is here handled as one (see 16:1,4)—though the two subdivisions are then described separately (16:5–17:11).

17:15 *clear a place for yourself.* This region of Canaan was still heavily forested. It seems that the Israelites viewed their assigned territories primarily in terms of the number of cities that had their land cleared for farming and pasturage, not in terms of the size of the region in which these cities were located. The region assigned to the Joseph tribes was at the time not as heavily populated as others. *Perizzites and . . . Rephaim.* Here listed as neighboring peoples, though elsewhere the Perizzites are said to have lived on the west bank in Canaan (3:10; 12:8) and the Rephaites in the Transjordan kingdom of Og (12:4; 13:12). See notes on Gen 13:7; Deut 2:11. *hill country of Ephraim.* The territory of the Joseph tribes—under the name of the legal firstborn (see note on v. 1).

17:16 *in the valley land.* Only in the plains were chariots effective. *chariots of iron.* Chariots with certain parts made of iron (see note on 2 Sam 8:7), perhaps the axles—the use of iron was a new development (see note on 11:6).

18:1–19:51 Seven tribes remained to be assigned land: Benjamin, Simeon, Zebulun, Issachar, Asher, Naphtali and Dan. Their lots were cast at Shiloh, after which a special portion was awarded to Joshua.

18:1 *Shiloh.* About ten miles northeast of Bethel, a little east of the main road from Bethel to Shechem. *tent of meeting.* The tabernacle (see note on Ex 27:21) with its sacred ark of the covenant. It would remain at Shiloh until the time of Samuel (1 Sam 4:3).

18:3 *take possession.* Conquest had to be followed by settlement, which required a survey, then a fair distribution, and then a full occupation of the land. A distinction must therefore be made between the national wars of conquest (Joshua) and the tribal wars of occupation (Judg 1–2).

18:5 *north.* Relative to the territory of Judah.

18:6 *I will cast lots for you.* See note on 14:1.

18:7 *priesthood of the LORD is their inheritance.* See 13:14; see also Deut 18:1-8 and note on Deut 18:1.

18:9 *book.* The actual form of the document was probably that of a scroll.

The Territory of Benjamin

11 Now the lot of the tribe of the sons of Benjamin came up according to their families, and the territory of their lot [1]lay between the sons of Judah and the sons of Joseph.

12 [a]Their border on the north side was from the Jordan, then the border went up to the side of Jericho on the north, and went up through the hill country westward, and [1]it ended at the wilderness of Beth-aven.

13 From there the border continued to [a]Luz, to the side of Luz (that is, Bethel) southward; and the border went down to Ataroth-addar, near the hill which *lies* on the south of [b]lower Beth-horon.

14 The border extended *from there* and turned round on the west side southward, from the hill which *lies* before Beth-horon southward; and [1]it ended at Kiriath-baal (that is, Kiriath-jearim), a city of the sons of Judah. This *was* the west side.

15 Then the [a]south side *was* from the edge of Kiriath-jearim, and the border went westward and went to the fountain of the waters of Nephtoah.

16 The border went down to the edge of the hill which is in the [a]valley of Ben-hinnom, which is in the valley of Rephaim northward; and it went down to the valley of Hinnom, to the slope of the Jebusite southward, and went down to En-rogel.

17 It extended northward and went to En-shemesh and went to Geliloth, which is opposite the ascent of Adummim, and it went down to the [a]stone of Bohan the son of Reuben.

18 It continued to the side in front of the Arabah northward and went down to the Arabah.

19 The border continued to the side of Beth-hoglah northward; and the [1]border ended at the north bay of the Salt Sea, at the south end of the Jordan. This *was* the south border.

20 Moreover, the Jordan was its border on the east side. This *was* the inheritance of the sons of Benjamin, according to their families *and* according to its borders all around.

21 Now the cities of the tribe of the sons of Benjamin according to their families were Jericho and Beth-hoglah and Emek-keziz,

22 and Beth-arabah and Zemaraim and Bethel,

23 and Avvim and Parah and Ophrah,

24 and Chephar-ammoni and Ophni and [a]Geba; twelve cities with their villages.

25 Gibeon and Ramah and Beeroth,

26 and Mizpeh and Chephirah and Mozah,

27 and Rekem and Irpeel and Taralah,

28 and [a]Zelah, Haeleph and the Jebusite (that is, Jerusalem), Gibeah, Kiriath; fourteen cities with their villages. This is the inheritance of the [b]sons of Benjamin according to their families.

Territory of Simeon

19 Then the second lot [1]fell to Simeon, to the tribe of the sons of Simeon according to their families, and their inheritance was in the midst of the inheritance of the sons of Judah.

2 So they had as their inheritance Beer-sheba or [1]Sheba and Moladah,

3 and Hazar-shual and Balah and Ezem,

4 and Eltolad and Bethul and Hormah,

5 and Ziklag and Beth-marcaboth and Hazar-susah,

6 and Beth-lebaoth and Sharuhen; thirteen cities with their villages;

7 Ain, Rimmon and Ether and Ashan; four cities with their villages;

8 and all the villages which *were* around these cities as far as Baalath-beer, Ramah of the [1]Negev. This *was* the inheritance of the tribe of the sons of Simeon according to their families.

9 The inheritance of the sons of Simeon *was taken* from the portion of the sons of Judah, for the share of the sons of Judah was too large for them; so the sons of Simeon received *an* inheritance in the midst of [1]Judah's inheritance.

Territory of Zebulun

10 Now the third lot came up for the sons of Zebulun according to their families. And the territory of their inheritance was as far as Sarid.

11 Then their border went up to the west and to Maralah, it then [1]touched Dabbesheth and reached to the [2]brook that is before Jokneam.

12 Then it turned from Sarid to the east toward the sunrise as far as the border of Chisloth-tabor, and it proceeded to Daberath and [1]up to Japhia.

13 From there it continued eastward toward the sunrise to Gath-hepher, to Eth-kazin, and it proceeded to Rimmon [1]which stretches to Neah.

14 The border circled around it on the north to Hannathon, and [1]it ended at the valley of Iphtahel.

15 *Included* also *were* Kattah and Nahalal and Shimron and Idalah and Bethlehem; twelve cities with their villages.

11 [1]Lit *went out* **12** [1]Lit *the goings out of it were* [a]Josh 16:1 **13** [a]Gen 28:19; Judg 1:23 [b]Josh 16:3 **14** [1]Lit *the goings out of it were* **15** [a]Josh 15:5-9 **16** [a]2 Kin 23:10 **17** [a]Josh 15:6 **19** [1]Lit *goings out of the border were* **24** [a]Ezra 2:26; Is 10:29

28 [a]2 Sam 21:14 [b]Num 26:38 **19:1** [1]Lit *came out* **2** [1]In Josh 15:26, *Shema* **8** [1]I.e. South country **9** [1]Lit *their* **11** [1]Or *reached to* [2]Or *wadi* **12** [1]Lit *went up* **13** [1]Or *and is marked off* **14** [1]Lit *the goings out of it were*

18:11 *lot . . . Benjamin.* A buffer zone between Judah and Ephraim, the two dominant tribes. Its northern line was the same as Ephraim's southern border (see note on 16:1), and its southern line the same as Judah's northernmost boundary (see note on 15:5).

18:23 *Avvim.* The people of Ai.

19:1 *second lot . . . Simeon.* Cities within the borders of Judah (15:21) in the Negev along Judah's southern border (1 Chr 4:24–42).

19:10 *third lot came up for the sons of Zebulun.* To this tribe went a portion of lower Galilee west of the Sea of Galilee and in the vicinity of NT Nazareth.

16 This *was* the inheritance of the sons of Zebulun according to their families, these cities with their villages.

Territory of Issachar

17 The fourth lot [1]fell to Issachar, to the sons of Issachar according to their families.

18 Their territory was to Jezreel and *included* Chesulloth and [a]Shunem,

19 and Hapharaim and Shion and Anaharath,

20 and Rabbith and Kishion and Ebez,

21 and Remeth and En-gannim and En-haddah and Beth-pazzez.

22 The border reached to [a]Tabor and Shahazumah and Beth-shemesh, and [1]their border ended at the Jordan; sixteen cities with their villages.

23 This *was* the inheritance of the tribe of the sons of Issachar according to their families, the cities with their villages.

Territory of Asher

24 Now the fifth lot [1]fell to the tribe of the sons of Asher according to their families.

25 Their territory was Helkath and Hali and Beten and Achshaph,

26 and Allammelech and Amad and Mishal; and it reached to Carmel on the west and to Shihor-libnath.

27 It turned toward the [1]east to Beth-dagon and reached to Zebulun, and to the valley of Iphtahel northward to Beth-emek and Neiel; then it proceeded on [2]north to [a]Cabul,

28 and Ebron and Rehob and Hammon and Kanah, as far as Great [a]Sidon.

29 The border turned to Ramah and to the fortified city of Tyre; then the border turned to Hosah, and [1]it ended at the sea by the region of [a]Achzib.

30 *Included* also *were* Ummah, and Aphek and Rehob; twenty-two cities with their villages.

31 This *was* the inheritance of the tribe of the sons of Asher according to their families, these cities with their villages.

Territory of Naphtali

32 The sixth lot [1]fell to the sons of Naphtali; to the sons of Naphtali according to their families.

33 Their border was from Heleph, from the oak in Zaanannim and Adami-nekeb and Jabneel, as far as Lakkum, and [1]it ended at the Jordan.

34 Then the border turned westward to Aznoth-tabor and proceeded from there to Hukkok; and it reached to Zebulun on the south and [1]touched Asher on the west, and to Judah at the Jordan toward the [2]east.

35 The fortified cities *were* Ziddim, Zer and [a]Hammath, Rakkath and [b]Chinnereth,

36 and Adamah and Ramah and Hazor,

37 and Kedesh and Edrei and En-hazor,

38 and Yiron and Migdal-el, Horem and Beth-anath and Beth-shemesh; nineteen cities with their villages.

39 This *was* the inheritance of the tribe of the sons of Naphtali according to their families, the cities with their villages.

Territory of Dan

40 The seventh lot [1]fell to the tribe of the sons of Dan according to their families.

41 The territory of their inheritance was Zorah and Eshtaol and Ir-shemesh,

42 and Shaalabbin and Aijalon and Ithlah,

43 and Elon and Timnah and Ekron,

44 and Eltekeh and Gibbethon and Baalath,

45 and Jehud and Bene-berak and Gath-rimmon,

46 and Me-jarkon and Rakkon, with the territory over against [1]Joppa.

47 The territory of the [a]sons of Dan proceeded [1]beyond them; for the sons of Dan went up and fought with Leshem and captured it. Then they struck it with the edge of the sword and possessed it and [2]settled in it; and they called [3b]Leshem Dan after the name of Dan their father.

48 This *was* the inheritance of the tribe of the sons of Dan according to their families, these cities with their villages.

49 When they finished apportioning the land for inheritance by its borders, the sons of Israel gave an inheritance in their midst to Joshua the son of Nun.

17 [1]Lit *came out* **18** [a]1 Sam 28:4; 2 Kin 4:8 **22** [1]Lit *the goings out of their border were* [a]Judg 4:6; Ps 89:12 **24** [1]Lit *came out* **27** [1]Lit *sunrise* [2]Lit *from the left hand* [a]1 Kin 9:13 **28** [a]Gen 10:19; Judg 1:31; Acts 27:3 **29** [1]Lit *the goings out of it were* [a]Judg 1:31 **32** [1]Lit *came out*

33 [1]Lit *the goings out of it were* **34** [1]Or *reached to* [2]Lit *sunrise* **35** [a]Gen 10:18; 1 Kin 8:65 [b]Deut 3:17 **40** [1]Lit *came out* **46** [1]Heb *Japho* **47** [1]Lit *from* [2]Lit *dwelt* [3]I.e. Laish [a]Judg 18:1 [b]Judg 18:29

19:17 *fourth lot . . . to Issachar.* Southwest of the Sea of Galilee reaching down to Beth-shan and west to the Jezreel Valley. Mount Tabor marked its northern border.

19:24 *fifth lot . . . to . . . Asher.* Asher was given the coastal area as far north as Sidon in Phoenicia and as far south as Mount Carmel.

19:32 *sixth lot . . . to . . . Naphtali.* An area mostly to the north of the Sea of Galilee, taking in the modern Huleh Valley and the mountains bordering on Asher to the west. Its southernmost point was at the lower edge of the Sea of Galilee.

19:40 *seventh lot . . . to . . . Dan.* An elbow of land squeezed between Ephraim and Judah and west of Benjamin. The port of Joppa marked the northwestern corner of Dan.

19:47 *territory of . . . Dan proceeded beyond them.* Lit. "went out from them," probably indicating they were not able to maintain control over it. The Amorites of this area "forced the sons of Dan to the hill country" (Judg 1:34), so most of the tribe migrated to the upper Jordan Valley, where they seized the town of Leshem (or Laish, Judg 18:2–10,27–29) and renamed it Dan.

19:49 *gave an inheritance. . . to Joshua.* In the account of the distribution of the promised land (the territory west of the Jordan), the assignment to Caleb is treated first (14:6–15), the assignment to Joshua last. Thus the allotting of inheritance to these two dauntless servants of the Lord from the wilderness generation (see Num 13:30; 14:6,24,30) frames the whole account—and both received the territory they asked for. Appropriately, Joshua's allotment came last; he was not a king or a warlord but the servant of God commissioned to bring the Lord's people into the promised land.

50 In accordance with the [1]command of
the LORD they gave him the city for which he
asked, [a]Timnath-serah in the hill country of
Ephraim. So he built the city and [2]settled in it.
51 [a]These are the inheritances which Eleazar the priest, and Joshua the son of Nun,
and the heads of the [1]households of the
tribes of the sons of Israel distributed by lot
in Shiloh before the LORD at the doorway of
the tent of meeting. So they finished dividing
the land.

Six Cities of Refuge

20 Then the LORD spoke to Joshua, saying,
2 "Speak to the sons of Israel, saying,
'[1]Designate [a]the cities of refuge, of which I
spoke to you [2]through Moses,
3 that the manslayer who [1]kills any person unintentionally, without premeditation,
may flee there, and they shall become your
refuge from the avenger of blood.
4 'He shall flee to one of these cities, and
shall stand at the entrance of the [a]gate of the
city and state his case in the hearing of the
elders of that city; and they shall [1]take him
into the city to them and give him a place, so
that he may dwell among them.
5 'Now [a]if the avenger of blood pursues
him, then they shall not deliver the manslayer into his hand, because he struck his
neighbor without premeditation and did not
hate him beforehand.
6 'He shall dwell in that city [a]until he
stands before the congregation for judgment,
until the death of the one who is high priest
in those days. Then the manslayer shall
[1]return to his own city and to his own house,
to the city from which he fled.' "
7 So they [1]set apart [a]Kedesh in [2]Galilee
in the hill country of Naphtali and Shechem
in the hill country of Ephraim, and Kiriath-
arba (that is, Hebron) in [b]the hill country of
Judah.
8 Beyond the Jordan east of Jericho, they
[1]designated Bezer in the wilderness on the
plain from the tribe of Reuben, and Ramoth
in Gilead from the tribe of Gad, and Golan in
Bashan from the tribe of Manasseh.
9 [a]These were the appointed cities for all
the sons of Israel and for the stranger who
sojourns among them, that whoever [1]kills
any person unintentionally may flee there,
and not die by the hand of the avenger of
blood until he stands before the congregation.

Forty-eight Cities of the Levites

21 Then the heads of [1]households of [a]the
Levites approached Eleazar the priest,
and Joshua the son of Nun, and the heads
of [1]households of the tribes of the sons of
Israel.
2 They spoke to them at Shiloh in the land
of Canaan, saying, "[a]The LORD commanded
[1]through Moses to give us cities to live in,
with their pasture lands for our cattle."
3 So the sons of Israel gave the Levites
from their inheritance these cities with their
pasture lands, according to the [1]command of
the LORD.
4 Then the lot came out for the families
of the Kohathites. And the sons of Aaron the
priest, who were of the Levites, [1]received
thirteen cities by lot from the tribe of Judah
and from the tribe of the Simeonites and
from the tribe of Benjamin.
5 The rest of the sons of Kohath
[1]received ten cities by lot from the families of
the tribe of Ephraim and from the tribe of
Dan and from the half-tribe of Manasseh.
6 The sons of Gershon [1]received thirteen
cities by lot from the families of the tribe of

50 [1]Lit *mouth* [2]Lit *dwelt* [a]Num 13:8; Josh 24:30
51 [1]Lit *fathers* [a]Josh 18:10
20:2 [1]Lit *Set for yourselves* [2]Lit *by the hand of* [a]Num 35:6-34; Deut 4:41-43; 19:2ff
3 [1]Lit *smites*
4 [1]Lit *gather* [a]Ruth 4:1; Job 5:4; Jer 38:7
5 [a]Num 35:12
6 [1]Lit *return and come* [a]Num 35:12
7 [1]Lit *sanctified* [2]Heb *Galil* [a]Josh 21:32; 1 Chr 6:76
7 [b]Josh 21:11; Luke 1:39
8 [1]Lit *set*
9 [1]Lit *smites* [a]Num 35:13ff
21:1 [1]Lit *fathers* [a]Num 35:1-8
2 [1]Lit *by the hand of* [a]Num 35:2
3 [1]Lit *mouth*
4 [1]Lit *had*
5 [1]Lit *had*
6 [1]Lit *had*

19:50 *Timnath-serah.* Located in the southwestern corner of Ephraim, facing out to the sea. Here Joshua was also buried (24:30).

20:1–9 Having distributed the land to the tribes, the Lord's next administrative regulation (see note on 13:1–32) provided an elementary system of government, specifically a system of regional courts to deal with capital offenses having to do with manslaughter. Thus this most inflammatory of cases was removed from local jurisdiction, and a safeguard was created against the easy miscarriage of justice (with its potential for endless blood feuds) when retribution for manslaughter was left in the hands of family members. The cities chosen were among those also assigned to the Levites, where ideally the law of Moses would especially be known and honored.

20:2 *of which I spoke to you through Moses.* See Num 35:6–34.

20:3 *avenger of blood.* Also translated "close relative" (Ruth 3:9), or "Redeemer" (Ps 19:14). The avenger was a near relative with the obligation of exacting retribution (see Lev 24:17; Num 35:16–28).

20:4 *gate of the city.* Traditional place for trials, where the elders sat to hold court (see Ruth 4:1 and note; see also Job 29:7).

20:6 *congregation.* Made up of the adult males of the city. Their function in the trial before the elders (v. 4) is not clear, but perhaps they witnessed the trial to see that it was fair (closed courts are notoriously corruptible). *death of the . . . high priest.* See Num 35:25–28. Either an atoning effect or a kind of amnesty was achieved by the high priest's death.

20:7 *they set apart Kedesh.* A wordplay in the Hebrew: "they consecrated (the town of) consecration." The other two cities west of the Jordan already had sacred associations: For Shechem see 8:30–35 and note; Gen 12:6–7; for Hebron see Gen 23:2; 49:29–32. The geographical distribution of the cities was important: one in the north, one in the midlands and one in the south. (See v. 8, where the order of the three cities of refuge that served in Transjordan is reversed: Bezer in the south, Ramoth in the midlands and Golan in the north.) See map, p. 226.

20:9 *the stranger.* Evidence of the equal protection granted to the foreigners living in Israel (cf. Lev 19:33–34; Deut 10:18–19).

21:1–45 Finally the Levites are allotted their towns and adjoining pasturelands—with the priestly families being given precedence (see v. 10).

21:4 *Kohathites.* The three sons of Levi were Kohath, Gershon and Merari (Ex 6:16; Num 3:17). *Judah . . . Simeonites . . . Benjamin.* Tribal areas close to Jerusalem, which would later be the site of the temple. The remaining Kohathites received cities in adjoining tribes.

Issachar and from the tribe of Asher and
from the tribe of Naphtali and from the half-
tribe of Manasseh in Bashan.
7 The sons of Merari according to their
families [1]received twelve cities from the tribe
of Reuben and from the tribe of Gad and
from the tribe of Zebulun.
8 Now the [a]sons of Israel gave by lot to
the Levites these cities with their pasture
lands, as the LORD had commanded [1]through
Moses.
9 They gave these cities which are *here*
mentioned by name from the tribe of the
sons of Judah and from the tribe of the sons
of Simeon;
10 and they were for the sons of Aaron,
one of the families of the Kohathites, of the
sons of Levi, for the lot was theirs first.
11 Thus [a]they gave them Kiriath-arba,
Arba being the [b]father of Anak (that is,
Hebron), in the hill country of Judah, with
its surrounding pasture lands.
12 But the fields of the city and its villages
they gave to Caleb the son of Jephunneh as
his possession.
13 So [a]to the sons of Aaron the priest they
gave [b]Hebron, the city of refuge for the
manslayer, with its pasture lands, and [c]Lib-
nah with its pasture lands,
14 and [a]Jattir with its pasture lands and
[b]Eshtemoa with its pasture lands,
15 and [1]Holon with its pasture lands and
[a]Debir with its pasture lands,
16 and [1]Ain with its pasture lands and
[a]Juttah with its pasture lands *and* [b]Beth-she-
mesh with its pasture lands; nine cities from
these two tribes.
17 From the tribe of Benjamin, [a]Gibeon
with its pasture lands, [b]Geba with its pasture
lands,
18 Anathoth with its pasture lands and
[1]Almon with its pasture lands; four cities.
19 All the cities of the sons of Aaron, the
priests, were thirteen cities with their pasture
lands.
20 Then the cities from the tribe of Ephraim were allotted to the [a]families of the sons
of Kohath, the Levites, *even to* the rest of the
sons of Kohath.
21 They gave them [a]Shechem, the city of
refuge for the manslayer, with its pasture
lands, in the hill country of Ephraim, and
Gezer with its pasture lands,
22 and Kibzaim with its pasture lands and
Beth-horon with its pasture lands; four cities.
23 From the tribe of Dan, Elteke with its
pasture lands, Gibbethon with its pasture
lands,
24 Aijalon with its pasture lands, Gath-
rimmon with its pasture lands; four cities.

7 [1]Lit *had*
8 [1]Lit *by the hand of* [a]Gen 49:5ff
11 [a]1 Chr 6:55 [b]Josh 14:15; 15:13
13 [a]1 Chr 6:57 [b]Josh 15:54 [c]Josh 15:42
14 [a]Josh 15:48 [b]Josh 15:50
15 [1]In 1 Chr 6:58, *Hilen* [a]Josh 15:49
16 [1]In 1 Chr 6:59, *Ashan* [a]Josh 15:55 [b]Josh 15:10
17 [a]Josh 18:25 [b]Josh 18:24
18 [1]In 1 Chr 6:60, *Allemeth*
20 [a]1 Chr 6:66
21 [a]Josh 20:7
27 [a]1 Chr 6:71
32 [a]Josh 20:7
34 [a]1 Chr 6:77
36 [a]Deut 4:43; Josh 20:8
38 [a]Deut 4:43; 1 Kin 4:13 [b]Gen 32:2; 2 Sam 2:8
41 [a]Num 35:7
43 [a]Deut 34:4

25 From the half-tribe of Manasseh, *they
allotted* Taanach with its pasture lands and
Gath-rimmon with its pasture lands; two cities.
26 All the cities with their pasture lands
for the families of the rest of the sons of
Kohath were ten.
27 [a]To the sons of Gershon, one of the
families of the Levites, from the half-tribe of
Manasseh, *they gave* Golan in Bashan, the
city of refuge for the manslayer, with its pasture lands, and Be-eshterah with its pasture
lands; two cities.
28 From the tribe of Issachar, *they gave*
Kishion with its pasture lands, Daberath
with its pasture lands,
29 Jarmuth with its pasture lands, En-gannim with its pasture lands; four cities.
30 From the tribe of Asher, *they gave*
Mishal with its pasture lands, Abdon with its
pasture lands,
31 Helkath with its pasture lands and
Rehob with its pasture lands; four cities.
32 From the tribe of Naphtali, *they gave*
[a]Kedesh in Galilee, the city of refuge for the
manslayer, with its pasture lands and Ham-
moth-dor with its pasture lands and Kartan
with its pasture lands; three cities.
33 All the cities of the Gershonites according to their families were thirteen cities with
their pasture lands.
34 To the families of [a]the sons of Merari,
the rest of the Levites, *they gave* from the
tribe of Zebulun, Jokneam with its pasture
lands and Kartah with its pasture lands.
35 Dimnah with its pasture lands, Nahalal
with its pasture lands; four cities.
36 From the tribe of Reuben, *they gave*
[a]Bezer with its pasture lands and Jahaz with
its pasture lands,
37 Kedemoth with its pasture lands and
Mephaath with its pasture lands; four cities.
38 From the tribe of Gad, *they gave*
[a]Ramoth in Gilead, the city of refuge for the
manslayer, with its pasture lands and [b]Maha-
naim with its pasture lands,
39 Heshbon with its pasture lands, Jazer
with its pasture lands; four cities in all.
40 All *these were* the cities of the sons of
Merari according to their families, the rest of
the families of the Levites; and their lot was
twelve cities.
41 [a]All the cities of the Levites in the
midst of the possession of the sons of Israel
were forty-eight cities with their pasture
lands.
42 These cities each had its surrounding
pasture lands; thus *it was* with all these cities.
43 [a]So the LORD gave Israel all the land

21:11 *Hebron.* Caleb's city (14:13–15). The priests and Levites were to be given space in their assigned cities along with the other inhabitants.
21:27 *sons of Gershon.* Received cities in the northern tribes of Asher, Naphtali and Issachar.
21:34 *families of the sons of Merari.* Their 12 cities were scattered over Reuben, Gad and Zebulun.
21:43–45 A concluding summary statement of how the Lord

which He had sworn to give to their fathers, and [b]they possessed it and lived in it.

44 And the LORD [a]gave them rest on every side, according to all that He had sworn to their fathers, and [b]no one of all their enemies stood before them; [c]the LORD gave all their enemies into their hand.

45 [a]Not [1]one of the good promises which the LORD had [2]made to the house of Israel failed; all came to pass.

Tribes beyond Jordan Return

22 [a]Then Joshua summoned the Reubenites and the Gadites and the half-tribe of Manasseh,

2 and said to them, "You have kept all that Moses the servant of the LORD commanded you, [a]and have listened to my voice in all that I commanded you.

3 "You have not forsaken your brothers these many days to this day, but have kept the charge of the commandment of the LORD your God.

4 "And now [a]the LORD your God has given rest to your brothers, as He spoke to them; therefore turn now and go to your tents, to the land of your possession, which Moses the servant of the LORD gave you beyond the Jordan.

5 "Only be very careful to observe the commandment and the law which Moses the servant of the LORD commanded you, to [a]love the LORD your God and walk in all His ways and keep His commandments and hold fast to Him and serve Him [b]with all your heart and with all your soul."

6 So Joshua [a]blessed them and sent them away, and they went to their tents.

7 Now [a]to the one half-tribe of Manasseh Moses had given *a possession* in Bashan, but [b]to the other half Joshua gave *a possession* among their brothers westward beyond the Jordan. So when Joshua sent them away to their tents, he blessed them,

8 and said to [1]them, "Return to your tents with great riches and with very much livestock, with silver, gold, bronze, iron, and with very many clothes; [a]divide the spoil of your enemies with your brothers."

9 The sons of Reuben and the sons of Gad and the half-tribe of Manasseh returned *home* and departed from the sons of Israel at Shiloh which is in the land of Canaan, to go to the [a]land of Gilead, to the land of their possession which they had possessed, according to the [1]command of the LORD [2]through Moses.

The Offensive Altar

10 When they came to the region of the Jordan which is in the land of Canaan, the sons of Reuben and the sons of Gad and the half-tribe of Manasseh built an altar there by the Jordan, a large altar in appearance.

11 And the sons of Israel heard *it* [1]said, "Behold, the sons of Reuben and the sons of Gad and the half-tribe of Manasseh have [a]built an altar at the [2]frontier of the land of Canaan, in the region of the Jordan, on the side *belonging to* the sons of Israel."

12 When the sons of Israel heard *of it,* the whole congregation of the sons of Israel gathered themselves at [a]Shiloh to go up against them in war.

13 Then the sons of Israel sent to the sons of Reuben and to the sons of Gad and to the half-tribe of Manasseh, into the land of Gilead, [a]Phinehas the son of Eleazar the priest,

14 and with him ten chiefs, one chief for each father's household from each of the tribes of Israel; and [a]each one of them *was* the head of his father's household among the [1]thousands of Israel.

15 They came to the sons of Reuben and to the sons of Gad and to the half-tribe of Manasseh, to the land of Gilead, and they spoke with them saying,

16 "Thus says the whole congregation of the LORD, 'What is this unfaithful act which you have committed against the God of Israel, turning away from following the LORD this day, by [a]building yourselves an altar, to rebel against the LORD this day?

43 [b]Num 33:53; Deut 11:31; 17:14
44 [a]Josh 1:13; 23:1 [b]Deut 7:24 [c]Ex 23:31
45 [1]Lit *a word from every good word* [2]Lit *spoken* [a]Josh 23:14; 1 Kin 8:56
22:1 [a]Num 32:20-22
2 [a]Josh 1:12-18
4 [a]Num 32:18; Deut 3:20
5 [a]Deut 5:10 [b]Deut 4:29
6 [a]Gen 47:7; Josh 14:13; 2 Sam 6:18; Luke 24:50
7 [a]Num 32:33 [b]Josh 17:1-13
8 [1]Lit *them, saying, "Return*
8 [a]Num 31:27; 1 Sam 30:16
9 [1]Lit *mouth* [2]Lit *by the hand of* [a]Num 32:1, 26, 29
11 [1]Lit *saying* [2]Lit *front* [a]Deut 12:5; Josh 22:19
12 [a]Josh 18:1
13 [a]Num 25:7, 11; 31:6
14 [1]Or *families* [a]Num 1:4
16 [a]Josh 22:11

had fulfilled His sworn promise to give Israel this land (see Gen 15:18–21). The occupation of the land was not yet complete (see 23:4–5; Judg 1–2), but the national campaign was over and Israel was finally established in the promised land. No power was left in Canaan that could threaten to dislodge her.

21:44 *rest on every side.* See note on 1:13.

22:1–34 The two and a half tribes from east of the Jordan, faithful in battle, are now commended by Joshua and sent to their homes. But their "altar of witness" (see vv. 26–27,34) was misunderstood, and disciplinary action against them was narrowly averted.

22:2 *all that Moses . . . commanded.* Moses had ordered them to join the other tribes in the conquest of Canaan (Num 32:16–27; Deut 3:18).

22:5 *love the LORD . . . serve Him with all your heart.* Both Moses and Joshua saw that obedience to the laws of God would require love and service from the heart. In the ancient Near East, "love" was also a political term, indicating truehearted loyalty to one's king.

22:8 *divide . . . with your brothers.* Moses also had seen the need for a fair sharing of the spoils of war (Num 31:25–27).

22:10 *region of the Jordan.* Understood in the Septuagint to be Gilgal, next to Jericho; more likely it was a site east of Shiloh along the Jordan River (18:17).

22:11 *and the sons of Israel heard.* Anxiety about apostasy led to hasty conclusions. They thought the altar had been set up as a rival to the true altar at Shiloh.

22:12 *gathered . . . at Shiloh.* In the presence of God at the tabernacle. *to go up against them in war.* To take disciplinary action (cf. Deut 13:12–18; Judg 20).

22:13–14 A prestigious delegation is sent to try to turn the Transjordan tribes from their (supposed) act of rebellion against the Lord.

22:16 *What is this unfaithful act . . . ?* The accusations were very grave: You have committed apostasy and rebellion.

17 'Is not [a]the iniquity of Peor [1]enough for us, from which we have not cleansed ourselves to this day, although a plague came on the congregation of the LORD,

18 that you must turn away this day from following the LORD? If you rebel against the LORD today, [a]He will be angry with the whole congregation of Israel tomorrow.

19 'If, however, the land of your possession is unclean, then [1]cross into the land of the possession of the LORD, where the LORD's tabernacle [2]stands, and take possession among us. Only do not rebel against the LORD, or rebel against us by [a]building an altar for yourselves, besides the altar of the LORD our God.

20 'Did not [a]Achan the son of Zerah act unfaithfully in the things under the ban, and wrath fall on all the congregation of Israel? And that man did not perish alone in his iniquity.' "

21 Then the sons of Reuben and the sons of Gad and the half-tribe of Manasseh answered and spoke to the heads of the [1]families of Israel.

22 "The [a]Mighty One, God, the LORD, the Mighty One, God, the LORD! [b]He knows, and may Israel itself know. If *it was* in rebellion, or if in an unfaithful act against the LORD do not save us this day!

23 "If we have built us an altar to turn away from following the LORD, or if to [a]offer a burnt offering or grain offering on it, or if to offer sacrifices of peace offerings on it, may the LORD Himself require it.

24 "But truly we have done this out of concern, [1]for a reason, saying, 'In time to come your sons may say to our [2]sons, "What have you to do with the LORD, the God of Israel?

25 "For the LORD has made the Jordan a border between us and you, *you* sons of Reuben and sons of Gad; you have no portion in the LORD." So your sons may make our sons stop fearing the LORD.'

26 "Therefore we said, 'Let us [1]build an altar, not for burnt offering or for sacrifice;

27 rather it shall be [a]a witness between us and you and between our generations after us, that we are to [b]perform the service of the LORD before Him with our burnt offerings, and with our sacrifices and with our peace offerings, so that your sons will not say to our sons in time to come, "You have no portion in the LORD." '

28 "Therefore we said, 'It shall also come about if they say *this* to us or to our generations in time to come, then we shall say, "See the copy of the altar of the LORD which our fathers made, not for burnt offering or for sacrifice; rather it is a witness between us and you." '

29 "Far be it from us that we should rebel against the LORD and turn away from following the LORD this day, by [a]building an altar for burnt offering, for grain offering or for sacrifice, besides the altar of the LORD our God which is before His [1]tabernacle."

30 So when Phinehas the priest and the leaders of the congregation, even the heads of the [1]families of Israel who *were* with him, heard the words which the sons of Reuben and the sons of Gad and the sons of Manasseh spoke, it pleased them.

31 And Phinehas the son of Eleazar the priest said to the sons of Reuben and to the sons of Gad and to the sons of Manasseh, "Today we know that the [a]LORD is in our midst, because you have not committed this unfaithful act against the LORD; now you have delivered the sons of Israel from the hand of the LORD."

32 Then Phinehas the son of Eleazar the priest and the leaders returned from the sons of Reuben and from the sons of Gad, from the land of Gilead to the land of Canaan, to the sons of Israel, and brought back word to them.

33 The word pleased the sons of Israel, and the sons of Israel [a]blessed God; and they did not speak of going up against them in war to destroy the land in which the sons of Reuben and the sons of Gad were living.

34 The sons of Reuben and the sons of Gad [a]called the altar *Witness;* "For," *they said,* "it is a witness between us that the LORD is God."

Joshua's Farewell Address

23 Now it came about after many days, when the LORD had given [a]rest to Israel

17 [1]Lit *little for us* [a]Num 25:1-9 **18** [a]Num 16:22 **19** [1]Lit *cross for yourselves* [2]Lit *abides* [a]Josh 22:11 **20** [a]Josh 7:1-26 **21** [1]Lit *thousands* **22** [a]Deut 10:17 [b]1 Kin 8:39; Job 10:7; Ps 44:21 **23** [a]Deut 12:11 **24** [1]Lit *from* [2]Lit *sons, saying* **26** [1]Lit *prepare to build for ourselves* **27** [a]Gen 31:48; Josh 24:27 [b]Deut 12:6, 11, 26f **29** [1]Lit *dwelling place* [a]Deut 12:13f **30** [1]Lit *thousands* **31** [a]Ex 25:8; Lev 26:11f; 2 Chr 15:2 **33** [a]1 Chr 29:20; Dan 2:19; Luke 2:28 **34** [a]Gen 31:47-49 **23:1** [a]Josh 21:44

22:17 *Peor.* Where some of the Israelites became involved in the Moabite worship of Baal of Peor (Num 25:1–5).

22:19 *is unclean.* By pagan worship, corrupting its inhabitants. *the land of the . . . LORD.* The promised land proper had never included Transjordan territory. Canaan was the land the Lord especially claimed as His own and promised to the descendants of Abraham, Isaac and Jacob.

22:20 *Achan . . . all the congregation of Israel?* See note on 7:1–26.

22:22 *The Mighty One, God, the LORD.* See note on Ps 50:1. The repetition of the sacred names gives an oath-like quality to this strong denial of any wrongdoing.

22:27 *witness.* The altar, presumably of uncut stone (see 8:31; Ex 20:25), was to serve as a testimony to the commitment of the Transjordan tribes to remain loyal to the Lord, and to their continued right to worship the Lord at the tabernacle—even though they lived outside the land of promise. It constitutes the sixth memorial monument in the land noted by the author of Joshua (see note on 10:27).

22:31 *you have delivered the sons of Israel.* Their words prevented a terrible punishment that the other tribes were about to inflict as a divine act of judgment (consider the implications of v. 20).

23:1–16 Joshua, the Lord's servant, delivers a farewell address recalling the victories the Lord has given, but also reminding the people of areas yet to be possessed and of the need to be loyal to God's covenant laws. Their mission remains—to be the people of God's kingdom in the world.

23:1 *rest.* See note on 1:13. *advanced in years.* Joshua was approaching the age of 110 (24:29).

from all their enemies [1]on every side, and Joshua was old, advanced in years,

2 that [a]Joshua called for all Israel, for their elders and their heads and their judges and their officers, and said to them, "I am old, advanced in years.

3 "And you have seen all that the LORD your God has done to all these nations because of you, for [a]the LORD your God is He who has been fighting for you.

4 "See, [a]I have apportioned to you these nations which remain as an inheritance for your tribes, with all the nations which I have cut off, from the Jordan even to the Great Sea toward the setting of the sun.

5 "The LORD your God, He will thrust them out from before you and [1a]drive them from before you; and [b]you will possess their land, just as the LORD your God [2]promised you.

6 "[a]Be very firm, then, to keep and do all that is written in the book of the law of Moses, so that you may not turn aside from it to the right hand or to the left,

7 so that you will not [1]associate with these nations, these which remain among you, or [a]mention the name of their gods, or [b]make *anyone* swear *by them,* or [c]serve them, or bow down to them.

8 "But you are to cling to the LORD your God, as you have done to this day.

9 "[a]For the LORD has [1]driven out great and strong nations from before you; and as for you, [b]no man has stood before you to this day.

10 "[a]One of your men puts to flight a thousand, for the LORD your God is [b]He who fights for you, just as He [1]promised you.

11 "So take diligent heed to yourselves to love the LORD your God.

12 "For if you ever go back and [a]cling to the rest of these nations, these which remain among you, and [b]intermarry with them, so that you [1]associate with them and they with you,

13 know with certainty that the LORD your God will not continue to [1]drive these nations out from before you; but they will be a [a]snare and a trap to you, and a whip on your sides and thorns in your eyes, until you perish from off this good land which the LORD your God has given you.

14 "Now behold, today [a]I am going the way of all the earth, and you know in all your hearts and in all your souls that [b]not one word of all the good words which the LORD your God spoke concerning you has failed; all have [1]been fulfilled for you, not [2]one of them has failed.

15 "It shall come about that just as all the good words which the LORD your God spoke to you have come upon you, so [a]the LORD will bring upon you all the threats, until He has destroyed you from off this good land which the LORD your God has given you.

16 "[a]When you transgress the covenant of the LORD your God, which He commanded you, and go and serve other gods and bow down to them, then the anger of the LORD will burn against you, and you will perish quickly from off the good land which He has given you."

Joshua Reviews Israel's History

24 Then [a]Joshua gathered all the tribes of Israel to Shechem, and called for the elders of Israel and for their heads and their judges and their officers; and they presented themselves before God.

2 Joshua said to all the people, "Thus says the LORD, the God of Israel, 'From ancient times your fathers lived beyond the [1]River, *namely,* [a]Terah, the father of Abraham and the father of Nahor, and they served other gods.

3 'Then [a]I took your father Abraham from beyond the [1]River, and led him through all the land of Canaan, and [b]multiplied his [2]descendants and gave him [c]Isaac.

4 'To Isaac I gave [a]Jacob and Esau, and [b]to Esau I gave Mount Seir to possess it; but [c]Jacob and his sons went down to Egypt.

5 'Then [a]I sent Moses and Aaron, and I plagued Egypt [1]by what I did in its midst; and afterward I brought you out.

6 'I brought your fathers out of Egypt, and [a]you came to the sea; and Egypt pursued

23:1 [1]Lit *from round about*
2 [a]Josh 24:1
3 [a]Deut 1:30
4 [a]Ex 23:30
5 [1]Or *dispossess* [2]Lit *spoke to* [a]Ex 23:20 [b]Num 33:53
6 [a]Deut 5:32; Josh 1:7
7 [1]Lit *go among* [a]Ex 23:13; Ps 16:4 [b]Deut 6:13; 10:20 [c]Ex 20:5
9 [1]Or *dispossessed* [a]Ex 23:23, 30 [b]Deut 7:24
10 [1]Lit *spoke to* [a]Lev 26:8; Deut 28:7; 32:20 [b]Deut 3:22; Josh 23:3
12 [1]Lit *go among* [a]Ex 34:15, 16; Ps 106:34, 35 [b]Deut 7:3, 4; Ezra 9:2; Neh 13:25
13 [1]Or *dispossess* [a]Ex 23:33; 34:12; Deut 7:16
14 [1]Lit *come* [2]Lit *one word* [a]1 Kin 2:2 [b]Josh 21:45
15 [a]Lev 26:14-33; Deut 28:15
16 [a]Deut 4:25, 26
24:1 [a]Josh 23:2
2 [1]I.e. Euphrates [a]Gen 11:27-32
3 [1]I.e. Euphrates [2]Lit *seed* [a]Gen 12:1; 24:7 [b]Gen 15:5 [c]Gen 21:3
4 [a]Gen 25:25, 26 [b]Gen 36:8; Deut 2:5 [c]Gen 46:6, 7
5 [1]Lit *according to* [a]Ex 4:14-17
6 [a]Ex 14:2-31

23:6 *Be very firm, then, to . . . do.* Echoing the Lord's instructions at the beginning (1:7–8; see 22:5). *book of the law.* A reference to canonical written materials from the time of Moses (cf. Deut 30:10,19; 31:9,24,26).
23:11 *love the LORD your God.* A concluding summation (see note on 22:5).
23:12 *if you ever go back.* Remaining in the promised land was conditioned on faithfulness to the Lord and separation from the idolaters still around them. Failure to meet these conditions would bring Israel's banishment from the land (cf. vv. 13,15–16; 2 Kin 17:7–8; 2 Chr 7:14–20). *cling to . . . intermarry.* The Lord prohibited alliances, either national or domestic, with the peoples of Canaan because such alliances would tend to compromise Israel's loyalty to the Lord (see Ex 34:15–16; Deut 7:2–4).
23:13 *a snare and a trap.* Joshua's warning echoes Ex 23:33; 34:12; Deut 7:16.
24:1–33 Once more Joshua assembled the tribes at Shechem to call Israel to a renewal of the covenant (see 8:30–35). It was his final official act as the Lord's servant, mediator of the Lord's rule over His people. In this he followed the example of Moses, whose final official act was also a call to covenant renewal—of which Deuteronomy is the preserved document.
24:2 *Thus says the LORD.* Only a divinely appointed mediator would dare to speak for God with direct discourse, as in vv. 2–13. *From ancient times.* In accordance with the common ancient Near Eastern practice of making treaties (covenants), a brief recital of the past history of the relationship precedes the making of covenant commitments. Joshua here focuses on the separation of Abraham from his polytheistic family, the deliverance of Israel from Egypt and the Lord's establishment of His people in Canaan. *the River.* See NASB marg.
24:6 *Red Sea.* See NASB marg.

your fathers with chariots and horsemen to the [1]Red Sea.

7 'But when they cried out to the LORD, He put darkness between you and the Egyptians, and brought the sea upon them and covered them; and your own eyes saw what I did in Egypt. And [a]you lived in the wilderness for a long time.

8 'Then [a]I brought you into the land of the Amorites who lived beyond the Jordan, and they fought with you; and I gave them into your hand, and you took possession of their land when I destroyed them before you.

9 'Then [a]Balak the son of Zippor, king of Moab, arose and fought against Israel, and he sent and summoned Balaam the son of Beor to curse you.

10 'But I [a]was not willing to listen to Balaam. So he had to bless you, and I delivered you from his hand.

11 '[a]You crossed the Jordan and came to Jericho; and the citizens of Jericho fought against you, *and* [b]the Amorite and the Perizzite and the Canaanite and the Hittite and the Girgashite, the Hivite and the Jebusite. Thus [c]I gave them into your hand.

12 'Then I [a]sent the hornet before you and it [1]drove out the two kings of the Amorites from before you, *but* [b]not by your sword or your bow.

13 '[a]I gave you a land on which you had not labored, and cities which you had not built, and you have lived in them; you are eating of vineyards and olive groves which you did not plant.'

"We Will Serve the LORD"

14 "Now, therefore, [1][a]fear the LORD and serve Him in sincerity and [2]truth; and put away the gods which your fathers served beyond the [3]River and in Egypt, and serve the LORD.

15 "If it is disagreeable in your sight to serve the LORD, choose for yourselves today whom you will serve: whether the gods which your fathers served which were beyond the River, or [a]the gods of the Amorites in whose land you are living; but as for me and my house, we will serve the LORD."

16 The people answered and said, "Far be it from us that we should forsake the LORD to serve other gods;

17 for the LORD our God is He who brought us and our fathers up out of the land of Egypt, from the house of [1]bondage, and who did these great signs in our sight and preserved us through all the way in which we went and among all the peoples through whose midst we passed.

18 "The LORD drove out from before us all the peoples, even the Amorites who lived in the land. We also will serve the LORD, for He is our God."

19 Then Joshua said to the people, "You will not be able to serve the LORD, [a]for He is a holy God. He is [b]a jealous God; [c]He will not forgive your transgression or your sins.

20 "[a]If you forsake the LORD and serve foreign gods, then He will turn and do you harm and consume you after He has done good to you."

21 The people said to Joshua, "No, but we will serve the LORD."

22 Joshua said to the people, "You are witnesses against yourselves that [a]you have chosen for yourselves the LORD, to serve Him." And they said, "We are witnesses."

23 "Now therefore, put away the foreign gods which are in your midst, and [a]incline your hearts to the LORD, the God of Israel."

24 [a]The people said to Joshua, "We will serve the LORD our God and we will [1]obey His voice."

25 [a]So Joshua made a covenant with the people that day, and made for them a statute and an ordinance in Shechem.

26 And Joshua [a]wrote these words in the book of the law of God; and he took a large stone and set it up there under the oak that was by the sanctuary of the LORD.

6 [1]Lit *Sea of Reeds*
7 [a]Deut 1:46; 2:14
8 [a]Num 21:21-32
9 [a]Num 22:2-6
10 [a]Deut 23:5
11 [a]Josh 3:14-17 [b]Ex 23:23, 28; Deut 7:1 [c]Ex 23:31
12 [1]Lit *drove them out* [a]Ex 23:28; Deut 7:20 [b]Ps 44:3
13 [a]Deut 6:10, 11
14 [1]Or *reverence* [2]Or *faithfulness* [3]I.e. Euphrates [a]Deut 10:12; 18:13; 1 Sam 12:24
15 [a]Judg 6:10
17 [1]Lit *bondmen*
19 [a]Lev 19:2; 20:7, 26 [b]Ex 20:5; 34:14 [c]Ex 23:21
20 [a]Deut 4:25, 26
22 [a]Ps 119:173
23 [a]1 Kin 8:57, 58; Ps 119:36; 141:4
24 [1]Lit *listen to* [a]Ex 19:8; 24:3, 7; Deut 5:27
25 [a]Ex 24:8
26 [a]Deut 31:24

24:10 *I was not willing to listen to Balaam.* Not only did the Lord reject Balaam's prayers; He also turned his curse into a blessing (see Num 23–24).

24:12 *the hornet.* Lower (northern) Egypt had long used the hornet as a national symbol, so Egypt's military campaigns in Canaan may have been in mind. But "the hornet" may also refer to the reports about Israel that spread panic among the Canaanites (2:11; 5:1; 9:24). See note on Ex 23:28.

24:14 *fear the LORD.* Trust, serve and worship Him. *gods which your fathers served beyond the River and in Egypt.* See v. 2. Joshua appealed to the Israelites to put away the gods their forefathers had worshiped in Mesopotamia and Egypt. In Ur and Haran, Terah's family would have been exposed to the worship of the moon-god, Nanna(r) or Sin. The golden calf of Ex 32:4 may be an example of their worship of the gods of Egypt. It was probably patterned after Apis, the sacred bull of Egypt; see note on Ex 32:4. (Jeroboam's golden calves at Bethel and Dan, on the other hand, probably represented mounts or pedestals for a riding or standing deity; see 1 Kin 12:28–29.)

24:15 *as for me.* Joshua publicly makes his commitment, hoping to elicit the same from Israel.

24:17–18 A creedal statement based on the miraculous events of the exodus and ending with "He is our God."

24:19 *You will not be able.* Strong words to emphasize the danger of overconfidence.

24:22 *witnesses.* See v. 27; a normal part of treaty/covenant-making (see Deut 30:19).

24:23 *foreign gods.* The other gods were represented by idols of wood and metal, which could be thrown away and destroyed.

24:25 *covenant with the people.* Consisting of the pledges they had agreed to and the decrees and laws from God.

24:26 *large stone.* Set up as a witness to the covenant renewal that closed Joshua's ministry, this is the seventh memorial in the land reminding Israel of what the Lord had done for them through His servant (see note on 22:27). To these memorials were added the perpetual ruins of Jericho (6:26). Thus the promised land itself bore full testimony to Israel (seven being the

27 Joshua said to all the people, "Behold,
[a]this stone shall be for a witness against us,
for it has heard all the words of the LORD
which He spoke [1]to us; thus it shall be for a
witness against you, so that you do not deny
your God."
28 Then Joshua dismissed the people,
each to his inheritance.

Joshua's Death and Burial

29 It came about after these things that
Joshua the son of Nun, the servant of the
LORD, died, being one hundred and ten years
old.
30 And they buried him in the territory of
his inheritance in [a]Timnath-serah, which is
in the hill country of Ephraim, on the north
of Mount Gaash.
31 [a]Israel served the LORD all the days of
Joshua and all the days of the elders who [1]sur-
vived Joshua, and had known all the deeds of
the LORD which He had done for Israel.
32 Now [a]they buried the bones of Joseph,
which the sons of Israel brought up from
Egypt, at Shechem, in the piece of ground
[b]which Jacob had bought from the sons of
Hamor the father of Shechem for one hundred [1]pieces of money; and they became the
inheritance of Joseph's sons.
33 And Eleazar the son of Aaron died; and
they buried him [1]at Gibeah of [a]Phinehas his
son, which was given him in the hill country
of Ephraim.

27 [1]Lit *with* [a]Josh 22:27, 34
30 [a]Josh 19:50
31 [1]Lit *prolonged days after* [a]Judg 2:6f
32 [1]Heb *qesitah* [a]Gen 50:24, 25; Ex 13:19 [b]Gen 33:19; John 4:5; Acts 7:15f
33 [1]Or *on the hill* [a]Josh 22:13

number of completeness)—how she had come into possession of the land and how she would remain in the land only by fulfilling the covenant conditions. The land shouted its own story. *oak.* See note on Gen 12:6.

24:29–33 Three burials. Since it was a deep desire of the ancients to be buried in their homeland, these notices not only mark the conclusion of the story and the close of an era but also underscore the fact that Israel had indeed been established in the promised homeland—the Lord had kept His covenant.

24:29 *one hundred and ten.* For the significance of this number see note on Gen 50:26.

24:30 *buried him . . . in Timnath-serah.* See 19:50 and note.

24:31 The story told in Joshua is a testimony to Israel's faithfulness in that generation. The author anticipates the quite different story that would follow.

24:32 *bones of Joseph.* Returning his bones to Shechem was significant not only because of the ancient plot of land Jacob bought from Hamor (Gen 33:19), but also because Shechem was to be the center of the tribes of Ephraim and Manasseh, the two sons of Joseph. Also, the return fulfilled an oath sworn to Joseph on his deathbed (Gen 50:25; Ex 13:19).

24:33 *Eleazar.* The high priest who served Joshua, as Aaron had served Moses. *Gibeah.* Not the Benjamite city, but a place in Ephraim near Shiloh.

Judges

INTRODUCTION

Title

The title describes the leaders Israel had from the time of the elders who outlived Joshua until the time of the monarchy. Their principal purpose is best expressed in 2:16: "Then the LORD raised up judges, who delivered them from the hands of . . . those who plundered them." Since it was God who permitted the oppressions and raised up deliverers, He Himself was Israel's ultimate Judge and Deliverer (11:27; see 8:23, where Gideon, a judge, insists that the Lord is Israel's true ruler).

Author and Date

Although, according to tradition, Samuel wrote the book, authorship is actually uncertain. It is possible that Samuel assembled some of the accounts from the period of the judges and that such prophets as Nathan and Gad, both of whom were associated with David's court, had a hand in shaping and editing the material (see 1 Chr 29:29).

The date of composition is also unknown, but it was undoubtedly during the monarchy. The frequent expression "In those days there was no king in Israel" (17:6; 18:1; 19:1; 21:25) suggests a date after the establishment of the monarchy. The observation that the Jebusites still controlled Jerusalem (1:21) has been taken to indicate a time before David's capture of the city c. 1000 B.C. (see 2 Sam 5:6 – 10). But the new conditions in Israel alluded to in chs. 17 — 21 suggest a time after the Davidic dynasty had been effectively established (tenth century B.C.).

Theme and Theology

The book of Judges describes the life of Israel in the promised land from the death of Joshua to the rise of the monarchy. On the one hand, it is an account of frequent apostasy, provoking divine chastening. On the other hand, it tells of urgent appeals to God in times of crisis, moving the Lord to raise up leaders (judges) through whom He throws off foreign oppressors and restores the land to peace.

After Israel was established in the promised land through the ministry of Joshua, her pilgrimage ended. Many of the covenant promises God had given to the patriarchs in Canaan and to the fathers in the wilderness had now been fulfilled. The Lord's land, where Israel was to enter into rest, lay under her feet; it remained only for her to occupy it, to displace the Canaanites and to cleanse it of paganism. The time had come for Israel to be the kingdom of God in the form of an established commonwealth on earth.

But in Canaan Israel quickly forgot the acts of God that had given her birth and had established her in the land. Consequently she lost sight of her unique identity as God's people, chosen and called to be His army and the loyal citizens of His emerging kingdom. She settled down and attached herself to Canaan's peoples, morals, gods, and religious beliefs and practices as readily as to Canaan's agriculture and social life.

Throughout Judges the fundamental issue is the lordship of God in Israel — i.e., Israel's acknowledgment of and loyalty to His rule. His kingship over Israel had been uniquely established by the covenant at Sinai (Ex 19 — 24), which was later renewed by Moses on the plains of Moab (Deut 29) and by Joshua at Shechem (Josh 24). The author accuses Israel of having rejected the kingship of the Lord again and again. She stopped fighting the Lord's battles, turned to the gods of Canaan to secure the blessings of family, flocks and fields, and abandoned God's laws for daily living. In the very center of the cycle of the judges (see Outline), Gideon had to remind Israel that the Lord was her King (see note on 8:23). The recurring lament, and indictment, of chs. 17 — 21 (see Outline) is: "In those days there was no king in Israel; every man did what was right in his own eyes" (see note on 17:6). The primary reference here is doubtless to the earthly mediators of the Lord's

rule (i.e., human kings), but the implicit charge is that Israel did not truly acknowledge or obey her heavenly King either.

Only by the Lord's sovereign use of foreign oppression to chasten His people — thereby implementing the covenant curses (see Lev 26:14–45; Deut 28:15–68) — and by His raising up deliverers when His people cried out to Him did He maintain His kingship in Israel and preserve the embryonic kingdom from extinction. Israel's flawed condition was graphically exposed; she continued to need new saving acts by God in order to enter into the promised rest (see note on Josh 1:13).

Out of the recurring cycles of disobedience, foreign oppression, cries of distress, and deliverance (see 2:11–19; Neh 9:26–31) emerges another important theme — the covenant faithfulness of the Lord. The amazing patience and long-suffering of God are no better demonstrated than during this unsettled period.

Remarkably, this age of Israel's failure, following directly on the redemptive events that came through Moses and Joshua, is in a special way the OT age of the Spirit. God's Spirit enabled men to accomplish feats of victory in the Lord's holy war against the powers that threatened His kingdom (see 3:10; 6:34; 11:29; 13:25; 14:6,19; 15:14; see also 1 Sam 10:6,10; 11:6; 16:13). This same Spirit, poured out on the church following the redemptive work of the second Joshua (Jesus), empowered the people of the Lord to begin the task of preaching the gospel to all nations and of advancing the kingdom of God (see notes on Acts 1:2,8).

Background

Fixing precise dates for the judges is difficult and complex. The dating system followed here is based primarily on 1 Kin 6:1, which speaks of an interval of 480 years between the exodus and the fourth year of Solomon's reign. This would place the exodus c. 1446 B.C. and the period of the judges between c. 1380 and the rise of Saul, c. 1050. Jephthah's statement that Israel had occupied Heshbon for 300 years (11:26) generally agrees with these dates.

Some maintain, however, that the number 480 in 1 Kin 6:1 is somewhat artificial, arrived at by multiplying 12 (perhaps in reference to the 12 judges) by 40 (a conventional number of years for a generation). They point out the frequent use of the round numbers 10, 20, 40 and 80 in the book of Judges itself. A later date for the exodus would of course require a much shorter period of time for the judges (see Introduction to Exodus: Chronology).

Literary Features

Even a quick reading of Judges discloses its basic threefold division: (1) a prologue (1:1—3:6), (2) a main body (3:7—16:31) and (3) an epilogue (chs. 17—21). Closer study brings to light a more complex structure, with interwoven themes that bind the whole into an intricately designed portrayal of the character of an age.

The prologue (1:1—3:6) has two parts, and each serves a different purpose. They are not chronologically related, nor does either offer a strict chronological scheme of the time as a whole. The first part (1:1—2:5) sets the stage historically for the narratives that follow. It describes Israel's occupation of the promised land — from her initial success to her large-scale failure and divine rebuke.

The second part (2:6—3:6) indicates a basic perspective on the period from the time of Joshua to the rise of the monarchy, a time characterized by recurring cycles of apostasy, oppression, cries of distress and gracious divine deliverance. The author summarizes and explains the Lord's dealings with his rebellious people and introduces some of the basic vocabulary and formulas he will use in the later narratives: "did evil in the sight of the LORD," 2:11 (see 3:7,12; 4:1; 6:1; 10:6); "gave them into the hands of," 2:14 (see 6:1; 13:1); and "sold them," 2:14 (see 3:8; 4:2; 10:7).

The main body of the book (3:7—16:31), which gives the actual accounts of the recurring cycles (apostasy, oppression, distress, deliverance), has its own unique design. Each cycle has a similar beginning ("The sons of Israel did what was evil in the sight of the LORD"; see note on 3:7) and a recognizable conclusion ("the land had rest . . . years" or "judged Israel . . . years"; see note on 3:11). The first of these cycles (Othniel; see 3:7–11 and note) provides the "report form" used for each successive story of oppression and deliverance. The remaining five cycles form the following narrative units, built around the rest of the major judges:

1. Ehud (3:12–30), a lone hero from the tribe of Benjamin who delivers Israel from oppression from the east.

2. Deborah (chs. 4—5), a woman from one of the Joseph tribes (Ephraim, west of the Jordan) who judges at a time when Israel is being overrun by a coalition of Canaanites under Sisera.

3. Gideon and his son Abimelech (chs. 6—9), who form the central account. In many ways Gideon is the ideal judge, evoking memory of Moses, while his son is the very antithesis of a responsible and faithful judge.

4. Jephthah (10:6—12:7), a social outcast from the other Joseph tribe (Manasseh, east of the Jordan) who judges at a time when Israel is being threatened by a coalition of powers under the king of Ammon.

5. Samson (chs. 13—16), a lone hero from the tribe of Dan who delivers Israel from oppression from the west.

The arrangement of these narrative units is significant. The central accounts of Gideon (the Lord's ideal judge) and Abimelech (the anti-judge) are bracketed by the parallel narratives of the woman Deborah and the social outcast Jephthah—which in turn are framed by the stories of the lone heroes Ehud and Samson. In this way even the structure focuses attention on the crucial issue of the period of the judges: Israel's attraction to the Baals of Canaan (shown by Abimelech; see note on 9:1–57) versus the Lord's kingship over His people (encouraged by Gideon; see note on 8:23).

The epilogue (chs. 17—21) characterizes the era in yet another way, depicting religious and moral corruption on the part of individuals, cities and tribes. Like the introduction, it has two divisions that are neither chronologically related nor expressly dated to the careers of specific judges. The events must have taken place, however, rather early in the period of the judges (see notes on 18:30; 20:1,28).

By dating the events of the epilogue only in relationship to the monarchy (see the recurring refrain in 17:6; 18:1; 19:1; 21:25), the author contrasts the age of the judges with the better time that the monarchy inaugurated, undoubtedly having in view the rule of David and his dynasty (see note on 17:1—21:25). The book mentions two instances of the Lord's assigning leadership to the tribe of Judah: (1) in driving out the Canaanites (1:1–2), and (2) in disciplining a tribe in Israel (20:18). The author views the ruler from the tribe of Judah as the savior of the nation.

The first division of the epilogue (chs. 17—18) relates the story of Micah's development of a paganized place of worship and tells of the tribe of Dan abandoning their allotted territory while adopting Micah's corrupted religion. The second division (chs. 19—21) tells the story of a Levite's sad experience at Gibeah in Benjamin and records the disciplinary removal of the tribe of Benjamin because it had defended the degenerate town of Gibeah.

The two divisions have several interesting parallels:

1. Both involve a Levite's passing between Bethlehem (in Judah) and Ephraim across the Benjamin-Dan corridor.

2. Both mention 600 warriors—those who led the tribe of Dan and those who survived from the tribe of Benjamin.

3. Both conclude with the emptying of a tribal area in that corridor (Dan and Benjamin).

Not only are these Benjamin-Dan parallels significant within the epilogue, but they also form a notable link to the main body of the book. The tribe of Benjamin, which in the epilogue undertook to defend gross immorality, setting ties of blood above loyalty to the Lord, was the tribe from which the Lord raised up the deliverer Ehud (3:15). The tribe of Dan, which in the epilogue retreated from its assigned inheritance and adopted pagan religious practices, was the tribe from which the Lord raised up the deliverer Samson (13:2,5). Thus the tribes that in the epilogue depict the religious and moral corruption of Israel are the very tribes from which the deliverers were chosen whose stories frame the central account of the book (Gideon-Abimelech).

The whole design of the book from prologue to epilogue, the unique manner in which each section deals with the age as a whole, and the way the three major divisions are interrelated clearly portray an age gone awry—an age when "there was no king in Israel" and "every man did what was right in his own eyes" (see note on 17:6). Of no small significance is the fact that the story is in episodes and cycles. It is given as the story of all Israel, though usually only certain areas are directly involved. The book portrays the centuries after Joshua as a time of Israelite unfaithfulness to the Lord and of her surrender to the allurements of Canaan. Only by the mercies of God was Israel not overwhelmed and absorbed by the pagan nations around her. Meanwhile, however, the history of redemption virtually stood still—awaiting the forward thrust of the Lord's servant David and the establishment of his dynasty.

Outline

- I. Prologue: Incomplete Conquest and Apostasy (1:1—3:6)
  - A. First Episode: Israel's Failure to Purge the Land (1:1—2:5)
  - B. Second Episode: God's Dealings with Israel's Rebellion (2:6—3:6)
- II. Oppression and Deliverance (3:7—16:31)

Major Judges	*Minor Judges*
A. Othniel Defeats Mesopotamia (3:7–11)	
B. Ehud Defeats Moab (3:12–30)	
	1. Shamgar (3:31)
C. Deborah Defeats Canaan (chs. 4—5)	
D. Gideon Defeats Midian (chs. 6—8)	
(Abimelech, the anti-judge, ch. 9)	
	2. Tola (10:1–2)
	3. Jair (10:3–5)
E. Jephthah Defeats Ammon (10:6—12:7)	
	4. Ibzan (12:8–10)
	5. Elon (12:11–12)
	6. Abdon (12:13–15)
F. Samson Checks Philistia (chs. 13—16)	

- III. Epilogue: Religious and Moral Disorder (chs. 17—21)
  - A. First Episode (chs. 17—18; see 17:6; 18:1)
    1. Micah's corruption of religion (ch. 17)
    2. The Danites' departure from their tribal territory (ch. 18)
  - B. Second Episode (chs. 19—21; see 19:1; 21:25)
    1. Gibeah's corruption of morals (ch. 19)
    2. The Benjamites' removal from their tribal territory (chs. 20—21)

Jerusalem Is Captured

1 Now it came about after the death of Joshua that the sons of Israel [a]inquired of the LORD, saying, "Who shall go up first for us [b]against the Canaanites, to fight against them?"

2 The LORD said, "[a]Judah shall go up; behold, I have given the land into his hand."

3 Then Judah said to Simeon his brother, "Come up with me into [1]the territory allotted me, that we may fight against the Canaanites; and [2]I in turn will go with you into [3]the territory allotted you." So Simeon went with him.

4 Judah went up, and [a]the LORD gave the Canaanites and the Perizzites into their hands, and they [1]defeated ten thousand men at Bezek.

5 They found Adoni-bezek in Bezek and fought against him, and they [1]defeated the Canaanites and the Perizzites.

6 But Adoni-bezek fled; and they pursued him and caught him and cut off his [1]thumbs and big toes.

7 Adoni-bezek said, "Seventy kings with their thumbs and their big toes cut off used to gather up *scraps* under my table; [a]as I have done, so God has repaid me." So they brought him to Jerusalem and he died there.

8 Then the sons of Judah fought against [a]Jerusalem and captured it and struck it with the edge of the sword and set the city on fire.

9 Afterward the sons of Judah went down to fight against the Canaanites living in the hill country and in the [1]Negev and in the lowland.

10 [a]So Judah went against the Canaanites who lived in Hebron (now the name of Hebron formerly *was* Kiriath-arba); and they struck Sheshai and Ahiman and Talmai.

Capture of Other Cities

11 Then [a]from there he went against the inhabitants of Debir (now the name of Debir formerly *was* Kiriath-sepher).

12 And Caleb said, "The one who attacks Kiriath-sepher and captures it, I will even give him my daughter Achsah for a wife."

13 [a]Othniel the son of Kenaz, Caleb's younger brother, captured it; so he gave him his daughter Achsah for a wife.

14 Then [a]it came about when she came *to him*, that she persuaded him to ask her father for a field. Then she alighted from [1]her donkey, and Caleb said to her, "What [2]do you want?"

15 She said to him, "Give me a blessing, since you have given me the land of the [1]Negev, give me also springs of water." So Caleb gave her the upper springs and the lower springs.

16 The [1]descendants of [a]the Kenite, Moses' father-in-law, went up from the [b]city of palms with the sons of Judah, to the wilderness of Judah which is in the south of [c]Arad; and they went and lived with the people.

17 Then Judah went with Simeon his brother, and they struck the Canaanites liv-

1:1 [a]Num 27:21 [b]Judg 1:27; 2:21-23; 3:1-6
2 [a]Gen 49:8
3 [1]Lit *my lot* [2]Lit *I, even I* [3]Lit *your lot*
4 [1]Lit *smote them* [a]Ps 44:2; 78:55
5 [1]Lit *smote*
6 [1]Lit *thumbs of his hands and his feet*
7 [a]Lev 24:19
8 [a]Josh 15:63; Judg 1:21
9 [1]I.e. South country
10 [a]Josh 15:13-19
11 [a]Josh 15:15
13 [a]Judg 3:9
14 [1]Lit *the* [2]Lit *for yourself* [a]Josh 15:18
15 [1]I.e. South country
16 [1]Lit *sons* [a]Num 10:29-32; Judg 4:11 [b]Deut 34:3; Judg 3:13 [c]Num 21:1

1:1–3:6 An introduction in two parts: (1) an account of Israel's failure to lay claim completely to the promised land as the Lord had directed (1:1–36) and of His rebuke for their disloyalty (2:1–5); (2) an overview of the main body of the book (3:7–16:31), portraying Israel's rebellious ways in the centuries after Joshua's death and showing how the Lord dealt with her in that period (2:6–3:6). See Introduction: Literary Features.

1:1–36 Judah is assigned leadership in occupying the land (v. 2; see 20:18). Her vigorous efforts (together with those of Simeon) highlight by contrast the sad story of failure that follows. Only Ephraim's success at Bethel (vv. 22–26) breaks the monotony of that story.

1:1 *after the death of Joshua.* The book of Judges, like that of Joshua, tells of an era following the death of a leading figure in the history of redemption (see Josh 1:1). Joshua probably died c. 1390 B.C. The battles under his leadership broke the power of the Canaanites to drive the Israelites out of the land. The task that now confronted Israel was the actual occupation of Canaanite territory (see notes on Josh 18:3; 21:43–45). *inquired of the LORD.* Probably by the priestly use of Urim and Thummim (see notes on Ex 28:30; 1 Sam 2:28). *go up.* The main Israelite encampment was at Gilgal, near Jericho in the Jordan Valley (about 800 feet below sea level), while the Canaanite cities were mainly located in the central hill country (about 2,500–3,500 feet above sea level).

1:2 *Judah shall go up.* See 20:18. Judah was also the first to be assigned territory west of the Jordan (Josh 15). The leadership role of the tribe of Judah had been anticipated in the blessing of Jacob (Gen 49:8–12).

1:3 *Simeon.* Joshua assigned to Simeon cities within the territory of Judah (Josh 19:1,9; see Gen 49:5–7).

1:4 *Canaanites.* See note on Gen 10:6. *Perizzites.* See note on Gen 13:7. *Bezek.* Location unknown. Saul marshaled his army there before going to Jabesh-gilead (1 Sam 11:8).

1:5 *Adoni-bezek.* Means "lord of Bezek."

1:6 *cut off his thumbs and big toes.* Physically mutilating prisoners of war was a common practice in the ancient Near East (see note on 16:21). It rendered them unfit for military service.

1:7 *Seventy kings.* Canaan was made up of many small city-states, each of which was ruled by a king. "Seventy" may be a round number, or it may be symbolic of a large number. *under my table.* Humiliating treatment, like that given to a dog (see Matt 15:27; Luke 16:21). *God has repaid me.* See note on Ex 21:23–25.

1:8 *fought against Jerusalem.* Although the city was defeated, it was not occupied by the Israelites at this time (see v. 21). Israel did not permanently control the city until David captured it c. 1000 B.C. (2 Sam 5:6–10).

1:10 *Kiriath-arba.* See note on Josh 14:15.

1:11 *Debir.* See note on Josh 10:38.

1:12 *Caleb.* He and Joshua had brought back an optimistic report about the prospects of conquering Canaan (Num 14:6–9). *daughter . . . for a wife.* Victory in battle was one way to pay the bride-price for a girl (see 1 Sam 18:25).

1:13 *Othniel.* First major judge (see 3:7–11).

1:15 *upper . . . lower springs.* They still water the local farms in Hebron.

1:16 *Moses' father-in-law.* See note on Ex 2:16.

1:17 *Judah . . . Simeon.* Judah was fulfilling her commitment (v. 3).

ing in Zephath, and utterly destroyed it. So
the name of the city was called [a]Hormah.
18 And Judah took [a]Gaza with its territory and Ashkelon with its territory and Ekron
with its territory.
19 Now the LORD was with Judah, and
they took possession of the hill country; but
they could not [1]drive out the inhabitants of
the valley because they had [a]iron chariots.
20 Then they gave Hebron to Caleb, [a]as
Moses had [1]promised; and he drove out from
there [b]the three sons of Anak.
21 [a]But the sons of Benjamin did not drive
out the [b]Jebusites who lived in Jerusalem; so
the Jebusites have lived with the sons of
Benjamin in Jerusalem to this day.
22 Likewise the house of Joseph went up
against Bethel, and the LORD was with them.
23 The house of Joseph spied out Bethel
([a]now the name of the city was formerly Luz).
24 The spies saw a man coming out of the
city and they said to him, "Please show us
the entrance to the city and [a]we will treat
you kindly."
25 So he showed them the entrance to the
city, and they struck the city with the edge of

17 [a]Num 21:3
18 [a]Josh 11:22
19 [1]Or *dispossess* [a]Josh 17:16; Judg 4:3, 13
20 [1]Lit *spoken* [a]Josh 14:9 [b]Josh 15:14; Judg 1:10
21 [a]Josh 15:63; Judg 1:8
21 [b]1 Chr 11:4
23 [a]Gen 28:19
24 [a]Josh 2:12

1:18 *Gaza . . . Ashkelon . . . Ekron.* Three of the five main cities inhabited by the Philistines (see map below).
1:19 *could not drive out the inhabitants.* Israel failed to comply with God's commands (Deut 7:1–5; 20:16–18) to drive the Canaanites out of the land. Five factors were involved in that failure: (1) The Canaanites possessed superior weapons (v. 19); (2) Israel disobeyed God by making treaties with the Canaanites (2:1–3); (3) Israel violated the covenant the Lord had made with their forefathers (2:20–21); (4) God was testing Israel's faithfulness to obey His commands (2:22–23; 3:4); (5) God was giving Israel, as His army, the opportunity to develop her skills in warfare (3:1–2). *iron chariots.* Wooden vehicles with certain iron fittings, perhaps axles.
1:20 *as Moses had promised.* See Num 14:24; Deut 1:36; Josh 14:9–14. *Anak.* See note on Num 13:22.
1:21 *sons of Benjamin did not drive out.* See note on v. 8. Jerusalem lay on the border between Benjamin and Judah but was allotted to Benjamin (Josh 18:28). *Jebusites.* See note on Gen 10:16.
1:22 *house of Joseph.* Ephraim and West Manasseh. *Bethel.* See note on Gen 12:8. There is archaeological evidence of a destruction in the 13th century B.C. that may reflect the battle mentioned in this verse.
1:23 *spied out.* See note on Num 13:2.

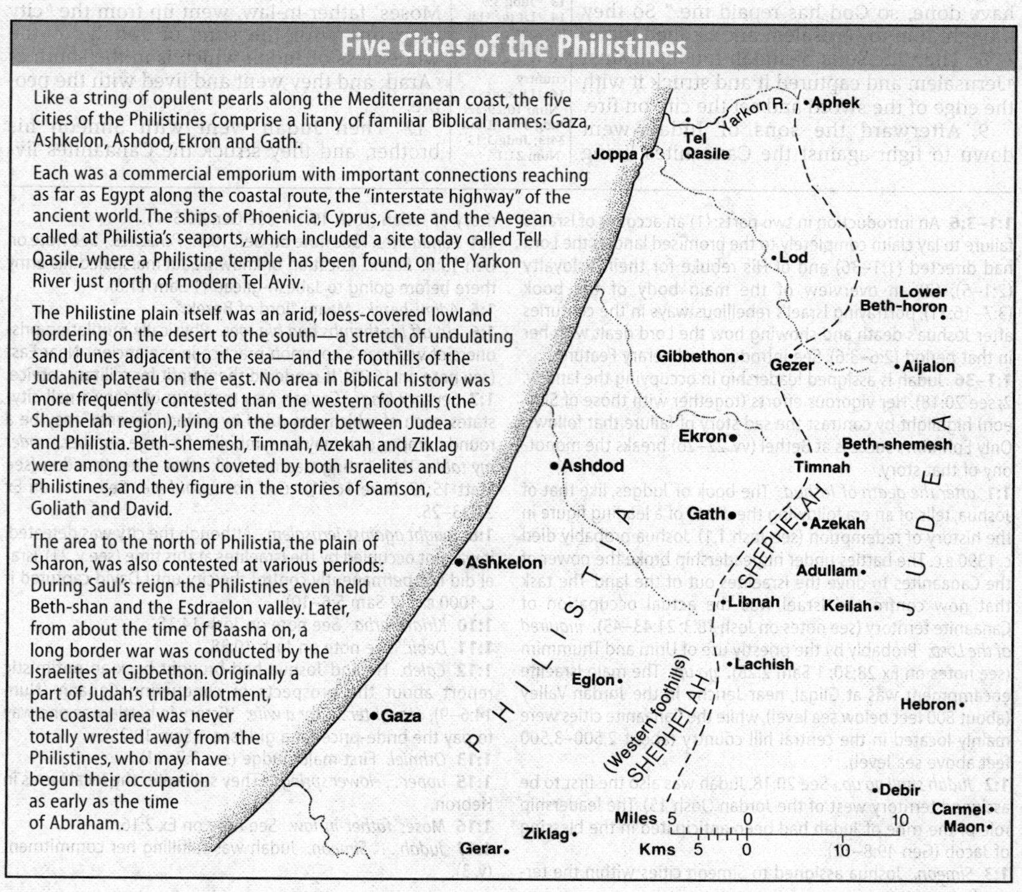

Five Cities of the Philistines

Like a string of opulent pearls along the Mediterranean coast, the five cities of the Philistines comprise a litany of familiar Biblical names: Gaza, Ashkelon, Ashdod, Ekron and Gath.

Each was a commercial emporium with important connections reaching as far as Egypt along the coastal route, the "interstate highway" of the ancient world. The ships of Phoenicia, Cyprus, Crete and the Aegean called at Philistia's seaports, which included a site today called Tell Qasile, where a Philistine temple has been found, on the Yarkon River just north of modern Tel Aviv.

The Philistine plain itself was an arid, loess-covered lowland bordering on the desert to the south—a stretch of undulating sand dunes adjacent to the sea—and the foothills of the Judahite plateau on the east. No area in Biblical history was more frequently contested than the western foothills (the Shephelah region), lying on the border between Judea and Philistia. Beth-shemesh, Timnah, Azekah and Ziklag were among the towns coveted by both Israelites and Philistines, and they figure in the stories of Samson, Goliath and David.

The area to the north of Philistia, the plain of Sharon, was also contested at various periods: During Saul's reign the Philistines even held Beth-shan and the Esdraelon valley. Later, from about the time of Baasha on, a long border war was conducted by the Israelites at Gibbethon. Originally a part of Judah's tribal allotment, the coastal area was never totally wrested away from the Philistines, who may have begun their occupation as early as the time of Abraham.

the sword, [a]but they let the man and all his family go free.

26 The man went into the land of the Hittites and built a city and named it Luz [1]which is its name to this day.

Places Not Conquered

27 [a]But Manasseh did not take possession of Beth-shean and its villages, or Taanach and its villages, or the inhabitants of Dor and its villages, or the inhabitants of Ibleam and its villages, or the inhabitants of Megiddo and its villages; so [b]the Canaanites persisted in living in that land.

28 It came about when Israel became strong, that they put the Canaanites to forced labor, but they did not drive them out completely.

29 [a]Ephraim did not drive out the Canaanites who were living in Gezer; so the Canaanites lived in Gezer among them.

30 Zebulun did not drive out the inhabitants of Kitron, or the inhabitants of [1]Nahalol; so the Canaanites lived among them and became subject to forced labor.

31 Asher did not drive out the inhabitants of Acco, or the inhabitants of Sidon, or of Ahlab, or of Achzib, or of Helbah, or of Aphik, or of Rehob.

32 So the Asherites lived among the Canaanites, the inhabitants of the land; for they did not drive them out.

33 Naphtali did not drive out the inhabitants of Beth-shemesh, or the inhabitants of Beth-anath, but lived among the Canaanites, the inhabitants of the land; and the inhabitants of Beth-shemesh and Beth-anath became forced labor for them.

34 Then the Amorites [1]forced the sons of Dan into the hill country, for they did not allow them to come down to the valley;

35 yet the Amorites persisted in [1]living in Mount Heres, in Aijalon and in Shaalbim; but when the [2]power of the house of Joseph [3]grew strong, they became forced labor.

36 The border of the Amorites ran from the [a]ascent of Akrabbim, from Sela and upward.

Israel Rebuked

2 Now [a]the angel of the LORD came up from Gilgal to [b]Bochim. And he said, "[c]I brought you up out of Egypt and led you into the land which I have sworn to your fathers; and I said, '[d]I will never break My covenant with you,

2 and as for you, [a]you shall make no covenant with the inhabitants of this land; [b]you shall tear down their altars.' But you have not [1]obeyed Me; what is this you have done?

3 "Therefore I also said, '[a]I will not drive them out before you; but they will [1]become [b]*as thorns* in your sides and their gods will be a snare to you.' "

4 When the angel of the LORD spoke these words to all the sons of Israel, the people lifted up their voices and wept.

5 So they named that place [1]Bochim; and there they sacrificed to the LORD.

Joshua Dies

6 [a]When Joshua had dismissed the people, the sons of Israel went each to his inheritance to possess the land.

7 The people served the LORD all the days of Joshua, and all the days of the elders who [1]survived Joshua, who had seen all the great work of the LORD which He had done for Israel.

8 Then Joshua the son of Nun, the servant of the LORD, died at the age of one hundred and ten.

25 [a]Josh 6:25
26 [1]Lit *it*
27 [a]Josh 17:12 [b]Judg 1:1
29 [a]Josh 16:10
30 [1]Perhaps same as *Nahalal*
34 [1]Lit *pressed*
35 [1]Lit *dwelling* [2]Lit *hand* [3]Lit *was heavy*
36 [a]Josh 15:3
2:1 [a]Judg 6:11; 13:2-21 [b]Judg 2:5 [c]Ex 20:2 [d]Gen 17:7, 8; Lev 26:42, 44; Deut 7:9
2 [1]Lit *listened to My voice* [a]Ex 23:32; Deut 7:2-5 [b]Ex 34:12, 13
3 [1]Some ancient mss read *be adversaries, and* [a]Josh 23:13 [b]Num 33:55
5 [1]I.e. weepers
6 [a]Josh 24:28-31
7 [1]Lit *prolonged days after*

1:25 *let the man . . . go free.* Cf. the treatment of Rahab (Josh 6:25).
1:26 *land of the Hittites.* A name for Aram (Syria) at the time of the conquest (see note on Gen 10:15).
1:27–29 See Josh 17:16–18.
1:28 *forced labor.* See note on 1 Kin 5:13.
1:33 *Beth-shemesh.* Location unknown. The name means "house of the sun(-god)." There was also a Beth-shemesh in Judah (see note on v. 35). *Beth-anath.* Means "house of (the goddess) Anath" (see note on 3:31).
1:34 *Amorites.* See note on Gen 10:16. *forced the sons of Dan.* Joshua had defeated the Amorites earlier (Josh 10:5–11), but they were still strong enough to withstand the Danites. For this reason a large number of Danites migrated northward a short time later (see ch. 18).
1:35 *Mount Heres.* Means "mountain of the sun(-god)"; probably the Beth-shemesh in Judah, which is also called Ir-shemesh, "city of the sun(-god)" (Josh 19:41).
1:36 *border of the Amorites.* Their southern boundary (see Josh 15:2–3).
2:1–5 Because Israel had not zealously laid claim to the land as the Lord had directed (see 1:27–36), He withdrew His helping hand. On this note the first half of the introduction ends. Although the actual time of the Lord's rebuke is not indicated, it was probably early in the period of the judges and may even have been connected with the event in Josh 9 (or possibly Josh 18:1–3).
2:1 *angel of the LORD.* See note on Gen 16:7. The role of the angel of the Lord in this passage parallels that of the unnamed prophet in 6:8–10 and the word of the Lord in 10:11–14, calling His people to account. *Gilgal.* The place where Israel first became established in the land under Joshua (see Josh 4:19–5:12). *out of Egypt.* The theme of Exodus, frequently referred to as the supreme evidence of God's redemptive love for His people (see Ex 20:2). *sworn.* See Gen 15:18; see also note on Heb 6:13.
2:2 *make no covenant.* To have done so would have broken their covenant with the Lord (see Ex 23:32).
2:6–3:6 The second half of the introduction continues the narrative of Josh 24:28–31. It is a preliminary survey of the accounts narrated in Judg 3:7–16:31, showing that Israel's first centuries in the promised land are a recurring cycle of apostasy, oppression, cries of distress and gracious deliverance (see Introduction: Literary Features). The author reminds Israel that she will enjoy God's promised rest in the promised land only when she is loyal to Him and to His covenant.
2:6 *possess the land.* See note on 1:1.
2:8 *servant of the LORD.* Joshua is identified as the Lord's official representative (see notes on Ex 14:31; Ps 18 title; Is 41:8–9;

9 And they buried him in the territory of
[a]his inheritance in Timnath-heres, in the hill
country of Ephraim, north of Mount Gaash.
10 All that generation also were gathered
to their fathers; and there arose another generation after them who [a]did not know the
LORD, nor yet the work which He had done
for Israel.

Israel Serves Baals

11 Then the sons of Israel did [a]evil in the
sight of the LORD and [1]served the [b]Baals,
12 and [a]they forsook the LORD, the God of
their fathers, who had brought them out of
the land of Egypt, and followed other gods
from *among* the gods of the peoples who
were around them, and bowed themselves
down to them; thus they provoked the LORD
to anger.
13 So they forsook the LORD and [a]served
Baal and the Ashtaroth.
14 [a]The anger of the LORD burned against
Israel, and He gave them into the hands of
plunderers who plundered them; and [b]He
sold them into the hands of their enemies
around *them,* so that they could no longer
stand before their enemies.
15 Wherever they went, the hand of the
LORD was against them for evil, as the LORD
had spoken and [a]as the LORD had sworn to
them, so that they were severely distressed.
16 [a]Then the LORD raised up judges [1]who
delivered them from the hands of those who
plundered them.
17 Yet they did not listen to their judges,
for they played the harlot after other gods
and bowed themselves down to them. They
turned aside quickly from the way [a]in which
their fathers had walked in obeying the commandments of the LORD; they did not do as
their fathers.
18 When the LORD raised up judges for
them, [a]the LORD was with the judge and
delivered them from the hand of their enemies all the days of the judge; for the LORD
was [b]moved to pity by their groaning
because of those who oppressed and afflicted them.
19 But it came about when the judge died,
that they would turn back and act more corruptly than their fathers, in following other
gods to serve them and bow down to them;
they did not abandon their practices or their
stubborn ways.
20 [a]So the anger of the LORD burned
against Israel, and He said, "Because this
nation has transgressed My covenant which
I commanded their fathers and has not listened to My voice,
21 [a]I also will no longer drive out before
them any of the nations which Joshua left
when he died,
22 in order to [a]test Israel by them,
whether they will keep the way of the LORD
to walk in it as their fathers [1]did, or not."
23 So the LORD allowed those nations to
remain, not driving them out quickly; and
He did not give them into the hand of Joshua.

Idolatry Leads to Servitude

3 [a]Now these are the nations which the
LORD left, to test Israel by them (*that is,* all
who had not [1]experienced any of the wars of
Canaan;
2 only in order that the generations of the

9 [a]Josh 19:49f **10** [a]Ex 5:2; 1 Sam 2:12 **11** [1]Or *worshiped* [a]Judg 3:7, 12; 4:1; 6:1 [b]Judg 6:25; 8:33; 10:6 **12** [a]Deut 31:16 **13** [a]Judg 10:6 **14** [a]Deut 31:17; Ps 106:40-42 [b]Deut 28:25; 32:30 **15** [a]Lev 26:14-39; Deut 28:15-68 **16** [1]Lit *and they* [a]Ps 106:43-45 **17** [a]Judg 2:7 **18** [a]Josh 1:5 [b]Deut 32:36; Ps 106:44 **20** [a]Judg 2:14 **21** [a]Josh 23:4, 5, 13 **22** [1]Lit *kept* [a]Deut 8:2; 13:3 **3:1** [1]Lit *known* [a]Judg 1:1; 2:21, 22

42:1). *one hundred and ten.* For the significance of this number see note on Gen 50:26.

2:10–15 The Lord withdraws His help because of Israel's apostasy. He "sells" the people He had "bought" (Ex 15:16) and redeemed (Ex 15:13; cf. Ps 74:2).

2:10 *gathered to their fathers.* See Gen 15:15; see also note on Gen 25:8. *who did not know the LORD . . . Israel.* They had no direct experience of the Lord's acts (see Ex 1:8).

2:11 *did evil in the sight of the LORD.* The same expression is used in 3:7,12; 4:1; 6:1; 10:6. *Baals.* The many local forms of this Canaanite deity (see note on v. 13).

2:12 *provoked the LORD to anger.* See Deut 4:25; see also note on Zec 1:2.

2:13 *Baal.* Means "lord." Baal, the god worshiped by the Canaanites and Phoenicians, was variously known to them as the son of Dagon and the son of El. In Aram (Syria) he was called Hadad and in Babylonia Adad. Believed to give fertility to the womb and life-giving rain to the soil, he is pictured as standing on a bull, a popular symbol of fertility and strength (see 1 Kin 12:28). The storm cloud was his chariot, thunder his voice, and lightning his spear and arrows. The worship of Baal involved sacred prostitution and sometimes even child sacrifice (see Jer 19:5). The stories of Elijah and Elisha (1 Kin 17–2 Kin 13), as well as many other OT passages, directly or indirectly protest Baalism (e.g., Ps 29:3–9; 68:1–4,32–34; 93:1–5; 97:1–5; Jer 10:12–16; 14:22; Hos 2:8,16–17; Amos 5:8). *Ashtaroth.* Female deities such as Ashtoreth (consort of Baal) and Asherah (consort of El, the chief god of the Canaanite pantheon). Ashtoreth was associated with the evening star and was the beautiful goddess of war and fertility. She was worshiped as Ishtar in Babylonia and as Athtart in Aram. To the Greeks she was Astarte or Aphrodite, and to the Romans, Venus. Worship of the Ashtoreths involved extremely lascivious practices (1 Kin 14:24; 2 Kin 23:7).

2:14 *gave them into the hands of.* The same expression is used in 6:1; 13:1. *sold them.* The same expression is used in 3:8; 4:2; 10:7.

2:16–19 The Lord was merciful to His people in times of distress, sending deliverers to save them from oppression. But Israel continually forgot these saving acts, just as she had those He had performed through Moses and Joshua.

2:16 *judges.* See Introduction: Title. There were six major judges (Othniel, Ehud, Deborah, Gideon, Jephthah and Samson) and six minor ones (Shamgar, Tola, Jair, Ibzan, Elon and Abdon).

2:17 *played the harlot.* Since the Hebrew for Baal (meaning "lord") was also used by women to refer to their husbands, it is understandable that the metaphor of adultery was commonly used in connection with Israelite worship of Baal (see Hos 2:2–3,16–17).

2:18 *groaning . . . oppressed.* The language of the Egyptian bondage (see Ex 2:24; 3:9; 6:5).

2:20–23 The Lord decided to leave the remaining nations to test Israel's loyalty.

3:1–6 The list of nations the Lord left roughly describes an arc along the western and northern boundaries of the area actu-

sons of Israel might [1]be taught war, [2]those who had not [3]experienced it formerly).

3 *These nations are:* the five lords of the Philistines and all the Canaanites and the Sidonians and [a]the Hivites who lived in Mount Lebanon, from Mount Baal-hermon as far as [1]Lebo-hamath.

4 They were for [1][a]testing Israel, to find out if they would [2]obey the commandments of the LORD, which He had commanded their fathers [3]through Moses.

5 [a]The sons of Israel lived among the Canaanites, the Hittites, the Amorites, the Perizzites, the Hivites, and the Jebusites;

6 and [a]they took their daughters for themselves as wives, and gave their own daughters to their sons, and served their gods.

7 The sons of Israel did [a]what was evil in the sight of the LORD, and [b]forgot the LORD their God and [c]served the Baals and the [1]Asheroth.

8 Then the anger of the LORD was kindled against Israel, so that He sold them into the hands of Cushan-rishathaim king of [1]Mesopotamia; and the sons of Israel served Cushan-rishathaim eight years.

The First Judge Delivers Israel

9 When the sons of Israel cried to the LORD, the LORD raised up a deliverer for the sons of Israel to deliver them, [a]Othniel the son of Kenaz, Caleb's younger brother.

10 [a]The Spirit of the LORD came upon him, and he judged Israel. When he went out to war, the LORD gave Cushan-rishathaim king of [1]Mesopotamia into his hand, so that [2]he prevailed over Cushan-rishathaim.

11 Then the land had rest forty years. And Othniel the son of Kenaz died.

12 Now the sons of Israel again [a]did evil in the sight of the LORD. So [b]the LORD strengthened Eglon the king of Moab against Israel, because they had done evil in the sight of the LORD.

13 And he gathered to himself the sons of Ammon and Amalek; and he went and [1]defeated Israel, and they possessed [a]the city of the palm trees.

14 The sons of Israel served Eglon the king of Moab eighteen years.

Ehud Delivers from Moab

15 But when the sons of Israel [a]cried to the LORD, the LORD raised up a deliverer for them, Ehud the son of Gera, the Benjamite, a left-handed man. And the sons of Israel sent tribute by [1]him to Eglon the king of Moab.

16 Ehud made himself a sword which had two edges, a cubit in length, and he bound it on his right thigh under his cloak.

2 [1]Lit *know, to teach them* [2]Lit *only* [3]Lit *known*
3 [1]Or *the entrance of Hamath* [a]Josh 9:7; 11:19
4 [1]Lit *testing by them* [2]Lit *hear* [3]Lit *by the hand of* [a]Deut 8:2
5 [a]Ps 106:35
6 [a]Ex 34:15, 16; Deut 7:3, 4; Josh 23:12
7 [1]I.e. wooden symbol of a female deity [a]Judg 2:11 [b]Deut 4:9 [c]Judg 2:13
8 [1]Heb *Aram-naharaim*
9 [a]Judg 1:13
10 [1]Heb *Aram* [2]Lit *his hand was strong* [a]Num 11:25-29; 24:2
12 [a]Judg 2:11 [b]Judg 2:14
13 [1]Lit *smote* [a]Deut 34:3; Judg 1:16
15 [1]Lit *his hand* [a]Ps 78:34

---

ally occupied by Israel at the death of Joshua (vv. 1–4). Within Israelite-occupied territory there were large groups of native peoples (v. 5; see 1:27–36) with whom the Israelites intermingled, often adopting their religions (v. 6).

3:2 *might be taught war.* As His covenant servant, Israel was the Lord's army for fighting against the powers of the world that were settled in His land. In view of the incomplete conquest, succeeding generations in Israel needed to become capable warriors. "Only" probably here means "especially."

3:3 *five lords.* The Hebrew for "lords" is related to the word "tyrant" (see note on Josh 13:3) and is used only of Philistine rulers. These rulers had control of a five-city confederacy. At one point Judah defeated three of these cities (1:18) but was unable to hold them. *Sidonians.* Here used collectively of the Phoenicians. *Hivites.* Here identified with a region in northern Canaan reaching all the way to Hamath (see also Josh 11:3). *Mount Baal-hermon.* Probably Mount Hermon (see 1 Chr 5:23).

3:6 *took their daughters . . . and served their gods.* See note on Josh 23:12. The degenerating effect of such intermarriage is well illustrated in Solomon's experience (1 Kin 11:1–8).

3:7–11 In the account of Othniel's judgeship the author provides the basic literary form he uses in his accounts of the major judges (i.e., beginning statement; cycle of apostasy, oppression, distress, deliverance; recognizable conclusion), adding only the brief details necessary to complete the report (see Introduction: Literary Features).

3:7 *did . . . evil in the sight of the LORD.* A recurring expression (see v. 12; 4:1; 6:1; 10:6; 13:1) used to introduce the cycles of the judges (see Introduction: Literary Features). *Baals.* See note on 2:13. *Asheroth.* See notes on 2:13; Ex 34:13.

3:8 *Cushan-rishathaim.* Probably means "doubly wicked Cushan," perhaps a caricature of his actual name (see note on 10:6 regarding Baal-zebub). *Mesopotamia.* See note on Gen 24:10.

3:9 *Israel cried to the LORD.* The Israelites' cries of distress occurred in each recurring cycle of the judges (see Introduction: Literary Features). *Othniel.* See 1:13.

3:10 *Spirit of the LORD came upon him.* The Spirit empowered Othniel to deliver His people, as He did Gideon (6:34), Jephthah (11:29), Samson (14:6,19) and also David (1 Sam 16:13). Cf. Num 11:25–29.

3:11 *the land had rest . . . years.* A recognizable conclusion to the cycle of a judge (noted only here and in v. 30; 5:31; 8:28). After the judgeship of Gideon this formula is replaced by "judged Israel . . . years" (12:7; 15:20; 16:31). See Introduction: Literary Features. *forty years.* A conventional number of years for a generation (see Introduction: Background).

3:12–30 Ehud's triumph over Eglon king of Moab. The left-handed Benjamite was an authentic hero. All alone, and purely by his wits, he cut down the king of Moab, who had established himself in Canaan near Jericho. This account balances that of Samson in the five narrative units central to the book of Judges (see Introduction: Literary Features).

3:12 *Moab.* See note on Gen 19:36–38.

3:13 *sons of Ammon.* See note on Gen 19:33. *sons of . . . Amalek.* These descendants of Esau (Gen 36:12,16) lived in the Negev (Num 13:29). See note on Gen 14:7.

3:14 *sons of Israel.* Here mainly Benjamin and Ephraim.

3:15 *left-handed man.* Left-handedness was noteworthy among Benjamites (see 20:15–16)—which is ironic since Benjamin means "son of (my) right hand." Being left-handed, Ehud could conceal his dagger on the side where it was not expected (see v. 21). *tribute.* An annual payment, perhaps of agricultural products (cf. 2Ki 3:4).

3:16 *a sword which had two edges.* During the period of the judges, Israelite weapons were often fashioned or improvised for the occasion: Shamgar's oxgoad (v. 31), Jael's tent peg (4:22), Gideon's jars and torches (7:20), the woman's millstone (9:53) and Samson's donkey jawbone (15:15). See 1 Sam 13:19.

17 He presented the tribute to Eglon king
of Moab. Now Eglon was a very fat man.
18 It came about when he had finished
presenting the tribute, that he sent away the
people who had carried the tribute.
19 But he himself turned back from the
idols which were at Gilgal, and said, "I have
a secret message for you, O king." And he
said, "Keep silence." And all who attended
him left him.
20 Ehud came to him while he was sitting
alone in his cool roof chamber. And Ehud
said, "I have a message from God for you."
And he arose from his seat.
21 Ehud stretched out his left hand, took
the sword from his right thigh and thrust it
into his belly.
22 The handle also went in after the blade,
and the fat closed over the blade, for he did
not draw the sword out of his belly; and the
refuse came out.
23 Then Ehud went out into the vestibule
and shut the doors of the roof chamber
behind him, and locked *them.*
24 When he had gone out, his servants
came and looked, and behold, the doors of
the roof chamber were locked; and they said,
"[a]He is only [1]relieving himself in the cool
room."
25 They waited until they [1]became anxious; but behold, he did not open the doors
of the roof chamber. Therefore they took the
key and opened them, and behold, their
master had fallen to the [2]floor dead.
26 Now Ehud escaped while they were
delaying, and he passed by the idols and
escaped to Seirah.
27 It came about when he had arrived,
that [a]he blew the trumpet in the hill country
of Ephraim; and the sons of Israel went
down with him from the hill country, and he
was in front of them.
28 He said to them, "Pursue *them,* for the
LORD has given your enemies the Moabites
into your hands." So they went down after
him and seized [a]the fords of the Jordan opposite Moab, and did not allow anyone to cross.
29 They struck down at that time about
ten thousand Moabites, all robust and
valiant men; and no one escaped.
30 So Moab was subdued that day under
the hand of Israel. And the land was undisturbed for eighty years.

Shamgar Delivers from Philistines

31 After him came [a]Shamgar the son of
Anath, who struck down six hundred Philistines with an oxgoad; and he also saved Israel.

Deborah and Barak Deliver from Canaanites

4 Then [a]the sons of Israel again did evil in
the sight of the LORD, after Ehud died.
2 And the LORD sold them into the hand
of [a]Jabin king of Canaan, who reigned in
Hazor; and the commander of his army was
Sisera, who lived in [b]Harosheth-hagoyim.
3 The sons of Israel cried to the LORD; for
he had nine hundred [a]iron chariots, and he
oppressed the sons of Israel severely for
twenty years.
4 Now Deborah, a [1]prophetess, the wife
of Lappidoth, was judging Israel at that time.
5 She used to [1]sit under the [a]palm tree of

24 [1]Lit *covering his feet* [a]1 Sam 24:3
25 [1]Lit *were ashamed* [2]Lit *earth*

27 [a]Judg 6:34; 1 Sam 13:3
28 [a]Judg 7:24; 12:5
31 [a]Judg 5:6
4:1 [a]Judg 2:19
2 [a]Josh 11:1, 10 [b]Judg 4:13, 16
3 [a]Judg 1:19
4 [1]Lit *woman prophetess*
5 [1]Or *live* [a]Gen 35:8

3:19 *idols.* Lit."carved (stone) things," a frequent Hebrew word for stone idols. But here the reference may be to carved stone statues of Eglon, marking the boundary of the territory he now claims as part of his expanded realm—a common practice in the ancient Near East.

3:20 *roof chamber.* Rooms were built on the flat roofs of houses (2 Kin 4:10–11) and palaces (Jer 22:13–14), and had latticed windows (2 Kin 1:2) that provided comfort in the heat of summer.

3:28 *seized the fords.* This move prevented the Moabites from sending reinforcements and also enabled the Israelites to cut off the Moabites fleeing Jericho.

3:30 *eighty years.* Round numbers are frequently used in Judges (see Introduction: Background).

3:31 *Shamgar.* The first of six minor judges and a contemporary of Deborah (see 5:6–7). His name is foreign, so he was probably not an Israelite. *son of Anath.* Indicates either that Shamgar came from the town of Beth-anath (see 1:33) or that his family worshiped the goddess Anath. Since Anath, Baal's sister, was a goddess of war who fought for Baal, the expression "son of Anath" may have been a military title, meaning "a warrior." *oxgoad.* A long, wooden rod, sometimes having a metal tip, used for driving draft animals (see 1 Sam 13:21).

4:1–5:31 Deborah's triumph over Sisera (commander of a Canaanite army)—first narrated in prose (ch. 4), then celebrated in song (ch. 5). At the time of the Canaanite threat from the north, Israel remained incapable of united action until a woman (Deborah) summoned them to the Lord's battle. Because the warriors of Israel lacked the courage to rise up and face the enemy, the glory of victory went to a woman (Jael)—and she may not have been an Israelite.

4:1–2 Except for the Canaanites, Israel's enemies came from outside the territory she occupied. Nations like Mespotamia, Moab, Midian and Ammon were mainly interested in plunder, but the Canaanite uprising of chs. 4–5 was an attempt to restore Canaanite power in the north. The Philistines engaged in continual struggle with Israel for permanent control of the land in the southern and central regions.

4:2 *Jabin.* See Ps 83:9–10. The name was possibly royal rather than personal. Joshua is credited with having earlier slain a king by the same name (Josh 11:1,10). *Hazor.* The original royal city of the Jabin dynasty; it may still have been in ruins (see note on Josh 11:10). Sisera sought to recover the territory once ruled by the kings of Hazor. *Sisera.* His name suggests he was not a Canaanite.

4:3 *nine hundred.* The number probably represents a coalition rather than the chariot force of one city. In the 15th century B.C., Pharaoh Thutmose III boasted of having captured 924 chariots at the battle of Megiddo. *sons of Israel.* Mainly Zebulun and Naphtali, but West Manasseh, Issachar and Asher were also affected.

4:4 *Deborah.* Means "bee"; cf. Deut 1:44. She is the only judge said to have been a prophet(ess). Other women spoken of as prophetesses are Miriam (Ex 15:20), Huldah (2 Kin 22:14), Noadiah (Neh 6:14) and Anna (Luke 2:36), but see also Acts 21:9.

Deborah between Ramah and Bethel in the
hill country of Ephraim; and the sons of Israel came up to her for judgment.
6 Now she sent and summoned [a]Barak
the son of Abinoam from Kedesh-naphtali,
and said to him, "[1]Behold, the LORD, the God
of Israel, has commanded, 'Go and march to
Mount Tabor, and take with you ten thousand men from the sons of Naphtali and
from the sons of Zebulun.
7 'I will draw out to you Sisera, the commander of Jabin's army, with his chariots
and his [1]many *troops* to the river Kishon,
and [a]I will give him into your hand.' "
8 Then Barak said to her, "If you will go
with me, then I will go; but if you will not go
with me, I will not go."
9 She said, "I will surely go with you;
nevertheless, the honor shall not be yours on
the journey that you are about to take, [a]for
the LORD will sell Sisera into the hands of a
woman." Then Deborah arose and went with
Barak to Kedesh.
10 Barak called [a]Zebulun and Naphtali
together to Kedesh, and ten thousand men
went up [1b]with him; Deborah also went up
with him.
11 Now Heber [a]the Kenite had separated
himself from the Kenites, from the sons of
Hobab the father-in-law of Moses, and had
pitched his tent as far away as the [1]oak in
[b]Zaanannim, which is near Kedesh.
12 Then they told Sisera that Barak the
son of Abinoam had gone up to Mount
Tabor.
13 Sisera called together all his chariots,
[a]nine hundred iron chariots, and all the people who *were* with him, from [b]Harosheth-
hagoyim to the river Kishon.
14 Deborah said to Barak, "Arise! For this
is the day in which the LORD has given Sisera
into your hands; [1]behold, [a]the LORD has
gone out before you." So Barak went down
from Mount Tabor with ten thousand men
following him.
15 [a]The LORD [1]routed Sisera and all *his*
chariots and all *his* army with the edge of the
sword before Barak; and Sisera alighted from
his chariot and fled away on foot.
16 But Barak pursued the chariots and the
army as far as Harosheth-hagoyim, and all
the army of Sisera fell by the edge of the
sword; [a]not even one was left.
17 Now Sisera fled away on foot to the
tent of Jael the wife of Heber the Kenite, for
there was peace between Jabin the king of
Hazor and the house of Heber the Kenite.
18 Jael went out to meet Sisera, and said
to him, "Turn aside, my master, turn aside to
me! Do not be afraid." And he turned aside
to her into the tent, and she covered him
with a [1]rug.
19 [a]He said to her, "Please give me a little
water to drink, for I am thirsty." So she
opened a [1]bottle of milk and gave him a
drink; then she covered him.
20 He said to her, "Stand in the doorway
of the tent, and it shall be if anyone comes
and inquires of you, and says, 'Is there anyone here?' that you shall say, 'No.' "
21 But Jael, Heber's wife, [a]took a tent peg
and [1]seized a hammer in her hand, and went
secretly to him and drove the peg into his
temple, and it went through into the ground;

6 [1]Or *Has not... commanded...?* [a]Heb 11:32
7 [1]Lit *multitude* [a]Ps 83:9
9 [a]Judg 4:21
10 [1]Lit *at his feet* [a]Judg 5:18 [b]Judg 4:14; 5:15
11 [1]Or *terebinth* [a]Judg 1:16 [b]Josh 19:33
13 [a]Judg 4:3
13 [b]Judg 4:2
14 [1]Or *has not the LORD gone...?* [a]Deut 9:3; 2 Sam 5:24; Ps 68:7
15 [1]Lit *confused* [a]Deut 7:23; Josh 10:10
16 [a]Ex 14:28; Ps 83:9
18 [1]Or *blanket*
19 [1]I.e. skin container [a]Judg 5:24-27
21 [1]Lit *placed* [a]Judg 5:26

4:6 *Barak.* Means "thunderbolt"—which suggests that he is summoned to be the Lord's "flashing sword" (Deut 32:41). He is named among the heroes of faith in Heb 11:32. *Kedesh-naphtali.* A town affected by the Canaanite oppression. *Mount Tabor.* A mountain about 1,300 feet high, northeast of the battle site. *Naphtali and . . . Zebulun.* Issachar, a near neighbor of these tribes, is not mentioned here but is included in the poetic description of the battle in 5:15. In all, six tribes are mentioned as having participated in the battle.
4:7 With the Israelites encamped on the slopes of Mount Tabor, safe from chariot attack, the Lord's strategy was to draw Sisera into a trap. For the battle site, Sisera cleverly chose the Valley of Jezreel along the Kishon River, where his chariot forces would have ample maneuvering space to range the battlefield and attack in numbers from any quarter. But that was his undoing, for he did not know the power of the Lord, who would fight from heaven for Israel with storm and flood (see 5:20–21), as He had done in the days of Joshua (Josh 10:11–14). Even in modern times storms have rendered the plain along the Kishon virtually impassable. In April of 1799 the flooded Kishon River aided Napoleon's victory over a Turkish army.
4:9 *a woman.* Barak's timidity (and that of Israel's other warriors, whom he exemplified) was due to lack of trust in the Lord and was thus rebuked (see note on 9:54).
4:11 *Heber the Kenite.* Since one meaning of Heber's name is "ally," and since "Kenite" identifies him as belonging to a clan of metalworkers, the author hints at the truth that this member of a people allied with Israel since the days of Moses has moved from south to north to ally himself (see v. 17) with the Canaanite king who is assembling a large force of "iron chariots." It is no doubt he who informs Sisera of Barak's military preparations. *the Kenites.* Settled in the south not far from Kadesh Barnea in the Negev (see 1:16). *Hobab.* See Num 10:29.
4:14 *gone out before you.* As a king at the head of his army (see 1 Sam 8:20). See also Ex 15:3 ("The LORD is a warrior"); Josh 10:10–11; 2 Sam 5:24; 2 Chr 20:15–17,22–24. *Barak went down from Mount Tabor.* The Lord's "thunderbolt" (see note on v. 6) descends the mountain to attack the Canaanite army.
4:15 *routed.* See note on v. 7. The Hebrew for this word is also used of the panic that overcame the Egyptians at the "Red Sea" (Ex 14:24) and the Philistines at Mizpah (1 Sam 7:10).
4:18 *he turned aside to her . . . tent.* Since ancient Near Eastern custom prohibited any man other than a woman's husband or father from entering her tent, Jael seemed to offer Sisera an ideal hiding place.
4:19 *bottle.* Containers for liquids were normally made from the skins of goats or lambs. *milk.* See note on 5:25. Jael, whose name means "mountain goat," gave him milk to drink—and it was most likely goat's milk (see Ex 23:19; Prov 27:27).
4:21 *drove the peg into his temple.* The laws of hospitality normally meant that one tried to protect a guest from any harm (see 19:23; Gen 19:8). Jael remained true to her family's previous alliance with Israel (she may not have been an Israelite) and so undid her husband's deliberate breach of faith. Armed only with domestic implements, this dauntless woman destroyed the great warrior whom Barak had earlier feared.

for he was sound asleep and exhausted. So
he died.
22 And behold, as Barak pursued Sisera,
Jael came out to meet him and said to him,
"Come, and I will show you the man whom
you are seeking." And he entered [1]with her,
and behold Sisera was lying dead with the
tent peg in his temple.
23 So [a]God subdued on that day Jabin the
king of Canaan before the sons of Israel.
24 The hand of the sons of Israel pressed
heavier and heavier upon Jabin the king of
Canaan, until they had [1]destroyed Jabin the
king of Canaan.

The Song of Deborah and Barak

5 [a]Then Deborah and Barak the son of
Abinoam sang on that day, saying,
2 "[a]That [1]the leaders led in Israel,
That [b]the people volunteered,
Bless the LORD!
3 "Hear, O kings; give ear, O rulers!
[a]I—to the LORD, I will sing,
I will sing praise to the LORD, the God
of Israel.
4 "[a]LORD, when You went out from Seir,
When You marched from the field of
Edom,
[b]The earth quaked, the heavens also
dripped,
Even the clouds dripped water.
5 "[a]The mountains [1]quaked at the
presence of the LORD,
[b]This Sinai, at the presence of the
LORD, the God of Israel.

6 "In the days of [a]Shamgar the son of
Anath,
In the days of [b]Jael, the highways
[1]were deserted,
And travelers [2]went by [3]roundabout
ways.
7 "The peasantry ceased, they ceased in
Israel,
Until I, Deborah, arose,
Until I arose, a mother in Israel.
8 "[a]New gods were chosen;
Then war *was* in the gates.
Not a shield or a spear was seen
Among forty thousand in Israel.
9 "My heart *goes out* to [a]the commanders
of Israel,
The volunteers among the people;
Bless the LORD!
10 "[a]You who ride on [1]white donkeys,
You who sit on *rich* carpets,
And you who travel on the road—[2]sing!
11 "At the sound of those who divide
flocks among [a]the watering places,
There they shall recount [b]the
righteous deeds of the LORD,
The righteous deeds for His
[1]peasantry in Israel.
Then the people of the LORD went
down [c]to the gates.
12 "[a]Awake, awake, Deborah;
Awake, awake, [1]sing a song!
Arise, Barak, and [b]take away your
captives, O son of Abinoam.
13 "Then survivors came down to the
nobles;
The people of the LORD came down to
me as warriors.
14 "From Ephraim those whose root is [a]in
Amalek *came down*,

22 [1]Lit *to*
23 [a]Neh 9:24; Ps 18:47
24 [1]Lit *cut off*
5:1 [a]Ex 15:1
2 [1]Or *locks hung loose in* [a]Judg 5:9 [b]Ps 110:3
3 [a]Ps 27:6
4 [a]Deut 33:2; Ps 68:7 [b]Ps 68:8, 9
5 [1]Lit *flowed* [a]Ex 19:18 [b]Ps 68:8
6 [a]Judg 3:31
6 [1]Lit *had ceased* [2]Lit *walked* [3]Lit *twisted* [b]Judg 4:17
8 [a]Deut 32:17
9 [a]Judg 5:2
10 [1]Or *tawny* [2]Or *declare it* [a]Judg 10:4; 12:14
11 [1]Or *rural dwellers* [a]Gen 24:11; 29:2, 3 [b]1 Sam 12:7; Mic 6:5 [c]Judg 5:8
12 [1]Or *utter* [a]Ps 57:8 [b]Ps 68:18; Eph 4:8
14 [a]Judg 12:15

4:22 *Sisera was lying dead.* With Sisera dead the kingdom of Jabin was no longer a threat. The land "flowing with milk and honey" had been saved by the courage and faithfulness of "Bee" (see note on v. 4) and "Mountain Goat" (see note on v. 19).

5:1–31 To commemorate a national victory with songs was a common practice (see Ex 15:1–18; Num 21:27–30; Deut 32:1–43; 1 Sam 18:7). The "Book of the Wars of the LORD" (see note on Num 21:14) and the "book of Jashar" (see note on Josh 10:13) were probably collections of such songs.

The song was probably written by Deborah (see v. 7) and is thus one of the oldest poems in the Bible. It highlights some of the central themes of the narrative (cf. Ex 15:1–18; 1 Sam 2:1–10; 2 Sam 22; 23:1–7; Luke 1:46–55,68–79). In particular, it celebrates before the nations (v. 3) the righteous acts of the Lord and of His warriors (v. 11). The song may be divided into the following sections: (1) the purpose of the song (praise) and the occasion for the deeds it celebrates (vv. 2–9); (2) the exhortation to Israel to act in accordance with her heroic past (vv. 10–11a); (3) the people's appeal to Deborah (vv. 11b–12); (4) the gathering of warriors (vv. 13–18); (5) the battle (vv. 19–23); (6) the crafty triumph of Jael over Sisera (vv. 24–27); (7) the anxious waiting of Sisera's mother (vv. 28–30); and (8) the conclusion (v. 31).

5:4–5 Poetic recalling of the Lord's terrifying appearance in a storm cloud many years before, when he had brought Israel through the wilderness into Canaan (see Deut 33:2; Ps 68:7–8; Mic 1:3–4; see also Ps 18:7–15).

5:4 *Seir.* Mt. Seir, in Edom. For a similar association of Seir (and Mount Paran) with Sinai see Deut 33:2. *the heavens also dripped.* See Ps 68:7–10.

5:5 *This Sinai.* See Ps 68:8. An earthquake and thunderstorm occurred when God appeared at Mount Sinai (Ex 19:16–18).

5:6 *Shamgar.* See note on 3:31. *highways were deserted.* Because of enemy garrisons and marauding bands (see note on 4:1–2) the roads were unsafe.

5:7 *peasantry ceased.* The inhabitants of villages fled to walled towns for protection.

5:8 *Not a shield or spear was seen.* Either because Israel had made peace with the native Canaanites (see 3:5–6) or because she had been disarmed (see 1 Sam 13:19–22).

5:10 *who ride on white donkeys.* An allusion to the nobles and the wealthy (see 10:4; 12:14).

5:11 *sound of those who divide flocks.* The leaders are encouraged by the songs ("sound"; cf. "sing" in v. 10) of the minstrels at the watering places—songs that rehearse the past heroic achievements of the Lord and His warriors.

5:12 *Awake.* A plea to take action (see Ps 44:23; Is 51:9). *take away your captives.* The same action is applied to God in Ps 68:18 and to Christ in Eph 4:8.

5:13–18 The warriors of the Lord who gathered for the battle. The tribes who came were Ephraim, Benjamin, Manasseh ("Machir" is possibly both East and West Manasseh; see Deut 3:15; Josh 13:29–31; 17:1), Zebulun (vv. 14,18), Issachar (v. 15) and Naphtali (v. 18). Especially involved were Zebulun and Naphtali (v. 18; see 4:10), the tribes most immediately affected

Following you, Benjamin, with your
peoples;
From Machir commanders came
down,
And from Zebulun those who wield
the staff of [1]office.
15 "And the [1]princes of Issachar *were* with
Deborah;
As *was* Issachar, so *was* Barak;
Into the valley they rushed [a]at his
[2]heels;
Among the divisions of Reuben
There were great resolves of heart.
16 "Why did you sit among [a]the
[1]sheepfolds,
To hear the piping for the flocks?
Among the divisions of Reuben
There were great searchings of heart.
17 "[a]Gilead [1]remained across the Jordan;
And why did Dan stay in ships?
Asher sat at the seashore,
And [1]remained by its landings.
18 "[a]Zebulun *was* a people who despised
their lives *even* to death,
And Naphtali also, on the high places
of the field.

19 "[a]The kings came *and* fought;
Then fought the kings of Canaan
[b]At Taanach near the waters of
Megiddo;
[c]They took no plunder in silver.
20 "[a]The stars fought from heaven,
From their courses they fought against
Sisera.
21 "The torrent of Kishon swept them
away,
The ancient torrent, the torrent
Kishon.
[a]O my soul, march on with strength.
22 "[a]Then the horses' hoofs beat
From the dashing, the dashing of his
[1]valiant steeds.
23 'Curse Meroz,' said the angel of the
LORD,
'Utterly curse its inhabitants;
[a]Because they did not come to the
help of the LORD,
To the help of the LORD against the
warriors.'

24 "[a]Most blessed of women is Jael,
The wife of Heber the Kenite;
Most blessed is she of women in the
tent.
25 "He asked for water *and* she gave him
milk;
In a magnificent bowl she brought
him curds.
26 "She reached out her hand for the tent
peg,
And her right hand for the workmen's
hammer.
Then she struck Sisera, she smashed
his head;
And she shattered and pierced his
temple.
27 "Between her feet he bowed, he fell, he
lay;
Between her feet he bowed, he fell;
Where he bowed, there he fell [1]dead.

28 "Out of the window she looked and
lamented,
The mother of Sisera through the
[1]lattice,
'Why does his chariot delay in coming?
Why do the [2]hoofbeats of his chariots
tarry?'
29 "Her wise princesses would answer her,
Indeed she repeats her words to
herself,

14 [1]Lit *the scribe* [a]Judg 12:15
15 [1]So with ancient versions; Heb *My princes* [2]Lit *feet* [a]Judg 4:10
16 [1]Or *saddlebags* [a]Num 32:1, 2, 24, 36
17 [1]Or *dwelt* [a]Josh 22:9
18 [a]Judg 4:6, 10
19 [a]Josh 11:1-5; Judg 4:13 [b]Judg 1:27 [c]Judg 5:30
20 [a]Josh 10:12-14
21 [a]Ex 15:2; Ps 44:5
22 [a]Job 39:19-25

22 [1]Lit *mighty ones*
23 [a]Judg 5:13
24 [a]Judg 4:19-21
27 [1]Lit *devastated*
28 [1]Or *window* [2]Lit *steps*

by Sisera's tyranny. Reuben (vv. 15–16) and Gad (here referred to as Gilead, v. 17), from east of the Jordan, and Dan and Asher, from along the coast (v. 17), are rebuked for not responding. Judah and Simeon are not even mentioned, perhaps because they were already engaged with the Philistines. Levi is not mentioned because it did not have military responsibilities in the theocracy (kingdom of God).

5:14 *root is in Amalek.* Some Amalekites apparently once lived in the hill country of Ephraim (see 12:15). *Machir.* The firstborn son of Manasseh (Josh 17:1). Although the descendants of Machir settled on both sides of the Jordan (see Deut 3:15; Josh 13:29–31; 17:1; 1 Chr 7:14–19), reference here is to those west of the Jordan (see v. 17; Josh 17:5).

5:18 *on the high places of the field.* Perhaps connected to Gen 49:21, where Naphtali is described as a "doe let loose."

5:19 *Megiddo.* Megiddo and Taanach dominated the main pass that runs northeast through the hill country from the plain of Sharon to the Valley of Jezreel. Because of its strategic location, the "plain of Megiddo" (2 Chr 35:22) has been a frequent battleground from the earliest times. There Pharaoh Thutmose III defeated a Canaanite coalition in 1468 B.C., and there in A.D. 1917 the British under General Allenby ended the rule of the Turks in Palestine by vanquishing them in the Valley of Jezreel opposite Megiddo. In Biblical history the forces of Israel under Deborah and Barak crushed the Canaanites "near the waters of Megiddo" (v. 19), and there Judah's good king Josiah died in battle against Pharaoh Neco II in 609 B.C. (2 Kin 23:29). See also the reference in Rev 16:16 to "the place which in Hebrew is called Har-Magedon" (i.e., "Mount Megiddo") as the site of the "war of the great day of God, the Almighty" (Rev 16:14).

5:20 *stars fought.* A poetic way of saying that the powers of heaven fought in Israel's behalf (see note on 4:7).

5:21 *swept them away.* See note on 4:7.

5:23 *Meroz.* Because of its refusal to help the army of the Lord, this Israelite town in Naphtali was cursed. Other cities were also punished severely for refusing to participate in the wars of the Lord (see 8:15–17; 21:5–10).

5:25 *curds.* Artificially soured milk made by shaking milk in a skin-bottle and then allowing it to ferment (due to bacteria that remained in the skin from previous use).

5:28 This graphic picture of the anxious waiting of Sisera's mother heightens the triumph of Jael over the powerful Canaanite general and presents a contrast between this mother in Canaan and the triumphant Deborah, "a mother in Israel" (v. 7).

30 ‘[a]Are they not finding, are they not
dividing the spoil?
A maiden, two maidens for every
warrior;
To Sisera a spoil of dyed work,
A spoil of dyed work embroidered,
Dyed work of double embroidery on
the [1]neck of the spoiler?’
31 “[a]Thus let all Your enemies perish,
O LORD;
[b]But let those who love Him be like
the rising of the sun in its might.”
And the land was undisturbed for forty
years.

Israel Oppressed by Midian

6 Then the sons of Israel [a]did what was evil
in the sight of the LORD; and the LORD
gave them into the hands of [b]Midian seven
years.
2 The [1]power of Midian prevailed against
Israel. Because of Midian the sons of Israel
made for themselves [a]the dens which were in
the mountains and the caves and the strongholds.
3 For it was when Israel had sown, that
the Midianites would come up with the
Amalekites and the sons of the east and [1]go
against them.
4 So they would camp against them and
[a]destroy the produce of the earth [1]as far as
Gaza, and [b]leave no sustenance in Israel as
well as no sheep, ox, or donkey.
5 For they would come up with their livestock and their tents, they would come in
[a]like locusts for number, both they and their
camels were innumerable; and they came
into the land to devastate it.
6 So Israel was brought [a]very low
because of Midian, and the sons of Israel
cried to the LORD.
7 Now it came about when the sons of
Israel cried to the LORD on account of Midian,
8 that the LORD sent a prophet to the sons
of Israel, and [a]he said to them, “Thus says
the LORD, the God of Israel, ‘It was I who
brought you up from Egypt and brought you
out from the house of [1]slavery.
9 ‘I delivered you from the hands of the
Egyptians and from the hands of all your
oppressors, and dispossessed them before
you and gave you their land,
10 and I said to you, “I am the LORD your
God; you [a]shall not fear the gods of the
Amorites in whose land you live. But you
have not [1]obeyed Me.” ’ ”

Gideon Is Visited

11 Then [a]the angel of the LORD came and
sat under the [1]oak that was in Ophrah, which
belonged to Joash the [b]Abiezrite as his son
[c]Gideon was beating out wheat in the wine
press in order to save *it* from the Midianites.
12 The angel of the LORD appeared to him
and said to him, “The LORD is with you, O
valiant warrior.”
13 Then Gideon said to him, “O my lord, if
the LORD is with us, why then has all this
happened to us? And where are all His miracles which our fathers told us about, saying,
‘Did not the LORD bring us up from Egypt?’
But [a]now the LORD has abandoned us and
given us into the hand of Midian.”
14 The LORD [1]looked at him and said, “[a]Go
in this your strength and deliver Israel from
the hand of Midian. Have I not sent you?”

30 [1]Lit *necks of the spoil* [a]Ex 15:9
31 [a]Ps 68:2; 92:9 [b]Ps 19:4-6; 89:36, 37
6:1 [a]Judg 2:11 [b]Num 22:4; 25:15-18; 31:1-3
2 [1]Lit *hand* [a]1 Sam 13:6; Heb 11:38
3 [1]Lit *go up*
4 [1]Lit *until your coming to* [a]Lev 26:16 [b]Deut 28:31
5 [a]Judg 7:12; 8:10
6 [a]Deut 28:43
8 [1]Lit *slaves* [a]Judg 2:1, 2
10 [1]Lit *listened to My voice* [a]2 Kin 17:35; Jer 10:2
11 [1]Or *terebinth* [a]Judg 2:1; 6:14; 13:3 [b]Josh 17:2; Judg 6:15 [c]Heb 11:32
13 [a]Judg 6:1; Ps 44:9
14 [1]Or *turned toward* [a]Heb 11:32-34

5:31 The song ends with a prayer that the present victory would be the pattern for all future battles against the Lord's enemies (see Num 10:35; Ps 68:1–2). *Your enemies . . . those who love Him.* The two basic attitudes of people toward the Lord. As Lord of the covenant and royal Head of His people Israel, He demanded their love (see Ex 20:6), just as kings in the ancient Near East demanded the love of their subjects. *forty years.* A conventional number of years for a generation (see Introduction: Background).

6:1–9:57 The Gideon and Abimelech narratives are a literary unit and constitute the center account of the judges. They are bracketed by the stories of Deborah (from Ephraim, a son of Joseph; west of the Jordan) and Jephthah (from Manasseh, the other son of Joseph; east of the Jordan)—which in turn are bracketed by the stories of the heroes Ehud (from Benjamin) and Samson (from Dan). In this center narrative, the crucial issues of the period of the judges are emphasized: the worship of Baal, and the Lord's kingship over His covenant people Israel (see note on 8:23).

6:1 *Midian.* See notes on Gen 37:25; Ex 2:15. Since they were apparently not numerous enough to wage war against the Israelites alone, they often formed coalitions with surrounding peoples—as with the Moabites (Num 22:4–6; 25:6–18), the Amalekites and other tribes from the east (v. 3). Their defeat was an event long remembered in Hebrew history (see Ps 83:9; Is 9:4; 10:26; Hab 3:7).

6:3 *Amalekites.* See note on Gen 14:7. Normally they were a people of the Negev, but they are in coalition here with the Midianites and other eastern peoples, who were nomads from the desert east of Moab and Ammon.

6:5 *like locusts for number.* A vivid picture of the marauders who swarmed across the land, leaving it stripped bare (see 7:12; Ex 10:13–15; Joel 1:4). *camels.* The earliest OT reference to the use of mounted camels in warfare.

6:7 *cried to the LORD.* The Israelites' cries of distress occurred in each recurring cycle of the judges (see Introduction: Literary Features).

6:8 *prophet.* See notes on 2:1; 10:11. The unnamed prophet rebuked Israel for forgetting that the Lord had saved them from Egyptian bondage and had given them the land (vv. 9–10).

6:10 *Amorites.* Probably here includes all the inhabitants of Canaan (see note on Gen 10:16).

6:11 *angel of the LORD.* See note on Gen 16:7. *Ophrah.* To be distinguished from the Benjamite Ophrah (Josh 18:23). *Abiezrite.* The Abiezrites (v. 24) were from the tribe of Manasseh (Josh 17:2). *beating out wheat in the wine press.* Rather than in the usual, exposed area (see note on Ruth 1:22). Gideon felt more secure threshing in this better protected but very confined space.

6:12 *valiant warrior.* Apparently Gideon belonged to the upper class, perhaps a kind of aristocracy (see v. 27), in spite of his disclaimer in v. 15.

6:14 *LORD looked.* See vv. 22–23. Apparently this appearance of the "angel of the LORD" (v. 11) was a theophany (a manifes-

15 [a]He said to Him, "O Lord, [1]how shall I deliver Israel? Behold, my family is the least in [b]Manasseh, and I am the youngest in my father's house."

16 [a]But the LORD said to him, "Surely I will be with you, and you shall [1]defeat Midian as one man."

17 So [1]Gideon said to Him, "If now I have found favor in Your sight, then show me [a]a sign that it is You who speak with me.

18 "Please do not depart from here, until I come *back* to You, and bring out my offering and lay it before You." And He said, "I will remain until you return."

19 Then Gideon went in and [a]prepared a young goat and unleavened bread from an [1]ephah of flour; he put the meat in a basket [2]and the broth in a pot, and brought *them* out to him under the [3]oak and presented *them.*

20 The angel of God said to him, "Take the meat and the unleavened bread and lay them on this rock, and pour out the broth." And he did so.

21 Then the angel of the LORD put out the end of the staff that was in his hand and touched the meat and the unleavened bread; and [a]fire sprang up from the rock and consumed the meat and the unleavened bread. Then the angel of the LORD [1]vanished from his sight.

22 [a]When Gideon saw that he was the angel of the LORD, [1]he said, "Alas, O Lord [2]GOD! For now I have seen the angel of the LORD face to face."

23 The LORD said to him, "Peace to you, do not fear; you shall not die."

24 Then Gideon built an altar there to the LORD and named it [1]The LORD is Peace. To this day it is still [a]in Ophrah of the Abiezrites.

25 Now on the same night the LORD said to him, "Take your father's bull [1]and a second bull seven years old, and pull down the altar of Baal which belongs to your father, and cut down the [2a]Asherah that is beside it;

26 and build an altar to the LORD your God on the top of this stronghold in an orderly manner, and take a second bull and offer a burnt offering with the wood of the Asherah which you shall cut down."

27 Then Gideon took ten men of his servants and did as the LORD had spoken to him; and because he was too afraid of his father's household and the men of the city to do it by day, he did it by night.

The Altar of Baal Destroyed

28 When the men of the city arose early in the morning, behold, the altar of Baal was torn down, and the Asherah which was beside it was cut down, and the second bull was offered on the altar which had been built.

29 They said to one another, "Who did this thing?" And when they searched about and inquired, they said, "Gideon the son of Joash did this thing."

30 Then the men of the city said to Joash, "Bring out your son, that he may die, for he has torn down the altar of Baal, and indeed, he has cut down the Asherah which was beside it."

31 But Joash said to all who stood against him, "Will you contend for Baal, or will you deliver him? Whoever will [1]plead for him shall be put to death by morning. If he is a god, let him contend for himself, because someone has torn down his altar."

32 Therefore on that day he named him [a]Jerubbaal, that is to say, "Let Baal contend against him," because he had torn down his altar.

33 Then all the Midianites and the Amalekites and the sons of the east assembled themselves; and they crossed over and camped in [a]the valley of Jezreel.

34 So [a]the Spirit of the LORD [1]came upon Gideon; and he [b]blew a trumpet, and the Abiezrites were called together to follow him.

35 He sent messengers throughout Manasseh, and they also were called together to follow him; and he sent messengers to Asher, [a]Zebulun, and Naphtali, and [b]they came up to meet them.

15 [1]Lit *with what* [a]Ex 3:11 [b]Judg 6:11
16 [1]Lit *smite* [a]Ex 3:12; Josh 1:5
17 [1]Lit *he* [a]Judg 6:37; Is 38:7, 8
19 [1]I.e. Approx one bu [2]Lit *and he put* [3]Or *terebinth* [a]Gen 18:6-8
21 [1]Or *departed* [a]Lev 9:24
22 [1]Lit *Gideon* [2]Heb *YHWH,* usually rendered *LORD* [a]Gen 32:30; Ex 33:20; Judg 13:21, 22
24 [1]Heb *Yahweh-shalom* [a]Judg 8:32
25 [1]Or *even* [2]I.e. wooden symbol of a female deity, also vv 26, 28, 30 [a]Ex 34:13
31 [1]Or *contend*
32 [a]Judg 7:1
33 [a]Josh 17:16
34 [1]Lit *clothed* [a]Judg 3:10 [b]Judg 3:27
35 [a]Judg 4:6, 10; 5:18 [b]Judg 7:3

tation of God). *Go... Have I not sent you?* Gideon was commissioned to deliver Israel as Moses had been (see Ex 3:7–10).
6:15 *how shall I . . . ?* The Lord usually calls the lowly rather than the mighty to act for Him (see notes on Gen 25:23; 1 Sam 9:21).
6:17 *show me a sign.* See vv. 36–40; cf. the signs the Lord gave Moses as assurance that He would be with him in his undertaking (see Ex 3:12; 4:1–17).
6:21 *consumed the meat.* Indicating that Gideon's offering was accepted (see Lev 9:24).
6:23 *shall not die.* See 13:22 and notes on Gen 16:13; 32:30.
6:25 *pull down the altar.* Gideon's first task as the Lord's warrior was to tear down an altar to Baal, as Israel had been commanded to do (see 2:2; Ex 34:13; Deut 7:5). *Baal.* See note on 2:13. *Asherah.* See NASB marg.; see also notes on 2:13; Ex 34:13.
6:26 *altar . . . in an orderly manner.* See Ex 20:25.
6:30 *he may die.* The Israelites were so apostate that they were willing to kill one of their own people for the cause of Baal (contrast Deut 13:6–10, where God told Moses that idolaters must be stoned).
6:32 *Jerubbaal.* Means "let Baal contend." This name later occurs as Jerubbesheth (2 Sam 11:21) by substituting a degrading term (Hebrew *bosheth,* "shameful thing") for the name of Baal, as in the change of the names Eshbaal and Merib-baal (1 Chr 8:33–34) to Ish-bosheth and Mephibosheth (see notes on 2 Sam 2:8; 4:4). *Let Baal contend against him.* Let Baal defend himself against Gideon.
6:33 *valley of Jezreel.* See note on 5:19.
6:34 *Spirit . . . came upon.* Lit. "Spirit . . . clothed Himself with." This vivid figure, used only three times (here; 1 Chr 12:18; 2 Chr 24:20), emphasizes that the Spirit of the Lord empowered the human agent and acted through him (see note on 3:10).
6:35 *Manasseh.* West Manasseh. *Asher.* This tribe earlier had failed to answer the call to arms (5:17).

Sign of the Fleece

36 Then Gideon said to God, "[a]If You will
deliver Israel [1]through me, as You have spoken,
37 behold, I will put a fleece of wool on
the threshing floor. If there is dew on the
fleece only, and it is dry on all the ground,
then I will know that You will deliver Israel
[1]through me, as You have spoken."
38 And it was so. When he arose early the
next morning and squeezed the fleece, he
drained the dew from the fleece, a bowl full
of water.
39 Then Gideon said to God, "[a]Do not let
Your anger burn against me that I may speak
once more; please let me make a test once
more with the fleece, let it now be dry only
on the fleece, and let there be dew on all the
ground."
40 God did so that night; for it was dry
only on the fleece, and dew was on all the
ground.

Gideon's 300 Chosen Men

7 Then [a]Jerubbaal (that is, Gideon) and all
the people who were with him, rose early
and camped beside [1]the spring of Harod; and
the camp of Midian was on the north side of
[2]them by the hill of [b]Moreh in the valley.
2 The LORD said to Gideon, "The people
who are with you are too many for Me to
give Midian into their hands, [a]for Israel
[1]would become boastful, saying, 'My own
[2]power has delivered me.'
3 "Now therefore [1]come, proclaim in the
hearing of the people, saying, '[a]Whoever is
afraid and trembling, let him return and
depart from Mount Gilead.' " So 22,000 people returned, but 10,000 remained.
4 [a]Then the LORD said to Gideon, "The
people are still too many; bring them down
to the water and I will test them for you
there. Therefore it shall be that he of whom I
say to you, 'This one shall go with you,' he
shall go with you; but everyone of whom I
say to you, 'This one shall not go with you,'
he shall not go."
5 So he brought the people down to the
water. And the LORD said to Gideon, "You
shall separate everyone who laps the water
with his tongue as a dog laps, as well as
everyone who kneels to drink."
6 Now the number of those who lapped,
putting their hand to their mouth, was 300
men; but all the rest of the people kneeled to
drink water.
7 The LORD said to Gideon, "I will deliver
you [a]with the 300 men who lapped and will
give the Midianites into your hands; so let all
the *other* people go, each man to his [1]home."
8 So [1]the 300 men took the people's provisions and their trumpets into their hands.
And [2]Gideon sent all the *other* men of Israel,
each to his tent, but retained the 300 men;
and the camp of Midian was below him in
the valley.
9 Now the same night it came about that
the LORD said to him, "Arise, go down against
the camp, [a]for I have given it into your
hands.
10 "But if you are afraid to go down, go
with Purah your servant down to the camp,
11 and you will hear what they say; and
[a]afterward your hands will be strengthened
that you may go down against the camp." So
he went with Purah his servant down to the
[1]outposts of the army that was in the camp.
12 Now the Midianites and the Amalekites
and all the sons of the east were lying in the
valley [a]as numerous as locusts; and their
camels were without number, [b]as numerous
as the sand on the seashore.
13 When Gideon came, behold, a man
was relating a dream to his friend. And he
said, "Behold, I [1]had a dream; [2]a loaf of barley bread was tumbling into the camp of
Midian, and it came to the tent and struck it
so that it fell, and turned it [3]upside down so
that the tent lay flat."
14 His friend replied, "This is nothing less
than the sword of Gideon the son of Joash, a
man of Israel; God has given Midian and all
the camp [a]into his hand."
15 When Gideon heard the account of the
dream and its interpretation, he bowed in
worship. He returned to the camp of Israel
and said, "Arise, for the LORD has given the
camp of Midian into your hands."
16 He divided the 300 men into three
[1]companies, and he put trumpets and empty

36 [1]Lit *by my hand* [a]Judg 6:14, 16, 17
37 [1]Lit *by my hand*
39 [a]Gen 18:32
7:1 [1]Or *En-Harod* [2]Lit *him* [a]Judg 6:32 [b]Gen 12:6; Deut 11:30
2 [1]Lit *glorify itself against me* [2]Lit *hand* [a]Deut 8:17, 18
3 [1]Or *please* [a]Deut 20:8
4 [a]1 Sam 14:6
7 [1]Lit *place* [a]1 Sam 14:6
8 [1]Lit *they* [2]Lit *he*
9 [a]Josh 2:24; 10:8; 11:6
11 [1]Lit *extremity of the battle array* [a]Judg 7:15; 1 Sam 14:9, 10
12 [a]Judg 6:5; 8:10 [b]Josh 11:4
13 [1]Lit *dreamed* [2]Lit *and behold, a loaf* [3]Lit *upwards*
14 [a]Josh 2:9
16 [1]Lit *heads*

6:39 *speak once more.* Cf. Abraham's words in Gen 18:32.

7:1–8 As supreme commander of Israel, the Lord reduced the army so that Israel would know that the victory was by His power, not theirs.

7:1 *Harod.* Means "trembling" and may refer to either the timidity of the Israelites (v. 3) or the great panic of the Midianites when Gideon attacked (v. 21). The Hebrew verb form is translated "routed" in 8:12. *hill of Moreh.* Located across the Valley of Jezreel, approximately four miles from the Israelite army.

7:3 *let him return.* Those who were afraid to fight the Lord's battle were not to go out with His army so that they would not demoralize the others (Deut 20:8). *Mount Gilead.* Perhaps used here as another name for Mount Gilboa.

7:6 *lapped.* The 300 remained on their feet, prepared for any emergency.

7:8–14 The Lord provided Gideon with encouraging intelligence information for the battle.

7:13–14 Although revelations by dreams are frequently mentioned in the OT, here both dreamer and interpreter are non-Israelite. Contrast Joseph, who interpreted dreams in Egypt (Gen 40:1–22; 41:1–32), and Daniel, who interpreted dreams in Babylon (Dan 2:1–45; 4:4–27).

7:13 *loaf of barley bread.* Since barley was considered an inferior grain and only one-half the value of wheat (see 2 Kin 7:1), it is a fitting symbol for Israel, which was inferior in numbers.

7:16 *three companies.* A strategy adopted by Israel on several occasions (9:43; 1 Sam 11:11; 2 Sam 18:2). *trumpets.* Rams' horns (see Ex 19:13).

pitchers into the hands of all of them, with
torches inside the pitchers.
17 He said to them, "Look at me and do
likewise. And behold, when I come to the
outskirts of the camp, [1]do as I do.
18 "When I and all who are with me blow
the trumpet, then you also blow the trumpets all around the camp and say, 'For the
LORD and for Gideon.' "

Confusion of the Enemy

19 So Gideon and the hundred men who
were with him came to the outskirts of the
camp at the beginning of the middle watch,
when they had just posted the watch; and
they blew the trumpets and smashed the
pitchers that were in their hands.
20 When the three [1]companies blew the
trumpets and broke the pitchers, they held
the torches in their left hands and the trumpets in their right hands for blowing, and
cried, "A sword for the LORD and for Gideon!"
21 Each stood in his place around the
camp; and [a]all the [1]army ran, crying out as
they fled.
22 When they blew 300 trumpets, the
[a]LORD set the sword of one against another
even throughout the whole [1]army; and the
[1]army fled as far as Beth-shittah toward Zererah, as far as the edge of [b]Abel-meholah, by
Tabbath.
23 The men of Israel were summoned
from [a]Naphtali and Asher and all Manasseh,
and they pursued Midian.
24 Gideon sent messengers throughout all
the hill country of Ephraim, saying, "Come
down [1]against Midian and [a]take the waters
before them, as far as Beth-barah and the

17 [1]Lit *it shall come about that just as I do, so you shall do*
20 [1]Lit *heads*
21 [1]Or *camp* [a]2 Kin 7:7
22 [1]Or *camp* [a]1 Sam 14:20 [b]1 Kin 4:12; 19:16
23 [a]Judg 6:35
24 [1]Lit *to meet* [a]Judg 3:28

7:19 *middle watch.* The Hebrews divided the night into three watches (see note on Matt 14:25). The "beginning of the middle watch" would be after the enemy had gone to sleep.
7:22 *300 trumpets.* Normally only a comparatively small number of men in an army carried trumpets. *one against another.* A similar panic occurred among the Ammonites, Moabites and Edomites (2 Chr 20:23) and, on a somewhat smaller scale, among the Philistines at Gibeah (1 Sam 14:20). See Ezek 38:21; Zech 14:13; see also note on Judg 4:15. *toward Zererah.* Toward the southeast.
7:23 *were summoned.* Encouraged by the turn of events, many of those who had departed now joined the battle.
7:24 *hill country of Ephraim.* Gideon needed the aid of the Ephraimites to cut off the retreat of the Midianites into the Jor-

Gideon's Battles

The story of Gideon begins with a graphic portrayal of one of the most striking facts of life in the Fertile Crescent: the periodic migration of nomadic people from the Aramean desert into the settled areas of Canaan. Each spring the tents of the bedouin herdsmen appeared overnight almost as if by magic, scattered on the hills and fields of the farming districts. Conflict between these two ways of life (herdsmen and farmers) was inevitable.

In the Biblical period, the vast numbers and warlike practice of the herdsmen reduced the village people to near vassalage. Gideon's answer was twofold: (1) religious reform, starting with his own family; and (2) military action, based on a coalition of northern Israelite tribes. The location of Gideon's hometown, "Ophrah of the Abiezrites," is not known with certainty, but probably was ancient Aper (modern Afula) in the Valley of Jezreel.

The battle at the spring of Harod is justly celebrated for its strategic brilliance. Denied the use of the only local water source, the Midianites camped in the valley and fell victim to the small band of Israelites, who attacked them from the heights of the hill of Moreh.

The main battle took place north of the hill near the village of En-dor at the foot of Mount Tabor. Fleeing by way of the Jordan Valley, the Midianites were trapped when the Ephraimites seized the fords of the Jordan from below Beth-shan to Beth-barah near Adam.

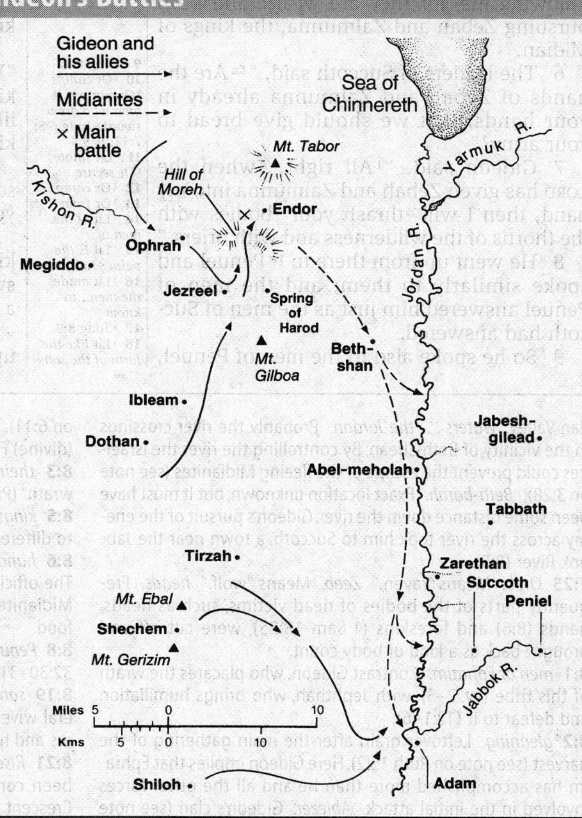

Jordan." So all the men of Ephraim were summoned and they took the waters as far as Beth-barah and the Jordan.

25 They captured the two leaders of Midian, [a]Oreb and Zeeb, and they killed Oreb at the rock of Oreb, and they killed Zeeb at the wine press of Zeeb, while they pursued Midian; and they brought the heads of Oreb and Zeeb to Gideon [b]from across the Jordan.

Zebah and Zalmunna Routed

8 Then the men of Ephraim said to him, "[a]What is this thing you have done to us, not calling us when you went to fight against Midian?" And they contended with him vigorously.

2 But he said to them, "What have I done now in comparison with you? Is not the gleaning *of the grapes* of Ephraim better than the vintage of Abiezer?

3 "God has given the leaders of Midian, Oreb and Zeeb into your hands; and what was I able to do in comparison with you?" Then their [1]anger toward him subsided when he said [2]that.

4 Then Gideon and the 300 men who were with him came [a]to the Jordan *and* crossed over, weary yet pursuing.

5 He said to the men of [a]Succoth, "Please give loaves of bread to the people who are following me, for they are weary, and I am pursuing Zebah and Zalmunna, the kings of Midian."

6 The leaders of Succoth said, "[1a]Are the hands of Zebah and Zalmunna already in your hands, that we should give bread to your army?"

7 Gideon said, "[1]All right, [a]when the LORD has given Zebah and Zalmunna into my hand, then I will [2]thrash your [3]bodies with the thorns of the wilderness and with briers."

8 He went up from there to [1a]Penuel and spoke similarly to them; and the men of Penuel answered him just as the men of Succoth had answered.

9 So he spoke also to the men of Penuel, saying, "When I return safely, [a]I will tear down this tower."

10 Now Zebah and Zalmunna were in Karkor, and their [1]armies with them, about 15,000 men, all who were left of the entire [2]army of the sons of the east; [a]for the fallen were 120,000 [3]swordsmen.

11 Gideon went up by the way of those who lived in tents on the east of Nobah and Jogbehah, and [1]attacked the camp when the camp was [2]unsuspecting.

12 When Zebah and Zalmunna fled, he pursued them and captured the two kings of Midian, Zebah and Zalmunna, and routed the whole [1]army.

13 Then Gideon the son of Joash returned from the battle [1]by the ascent of Heres.

14 And he captured a youth [1]from Succoth and questioned him. Then *the youth* wrote down for him the princes of Succoth and its elders, seventy-seven men.

15 He came to the men of Succoth and said, "Behold Zebah and Zalmunna, concerning whom you taunted me, saying, '[1a]Are the hands of Zebah and Zalmunna already in your hand, that we should give bread to your men who are weary?' "

16 He took the elders of the city, and thorns of the wilderness and briers, and he [1]disciplined the men of Succoth with them.

17 [a]He tore down the tower of Penuel and killed the men of the city.

18 Then he said to Zebah and Zalmunna, "What kind of men *were* they whom you killed at Tabor?" And they said, "They were like you, each one [1]resembling the son of a king."

19 He said, "They *were* my brothers, the sons of my mother. *As* the LORD lives, if only you had let them live, I would not kill you."

20 So he said to Jether his firstborn, "Rise, kill them." But the youth did not draw his sword, for he was afraid, because he was still a youth.

21 Then Zebah and Zalmunna said, "Rise up yourself, and fall on us; for as the man, so

25 [a]Ps 83:11; Is 10:26 [b]Judg 8:4
8:1 [a]Judg 12:1
3 [1]Lit *spirit* [2]Lit *this thing*
4 [a]Judg 7:25
5 [a]Gen 33:17
6 [1]Lit *Is the palm* [a]Judg 8:15
7 [1]Lit *For thus* [2]Or *trample* [3]Lit *flesh* [a]Judg 7:15
8 [1]In Gen 32:30, *Peniel* [a]Gen 32:31
9 [a]Judg 8:17
10 [1]Or *camps* [2]Or *camp* [3]Lit *men who drew sword* [a]Judg 6:5; 7:12; Is 9:4
11 [1]Lit *smote* [2]Or *secure*
12 [1]Or *camp*
13 [1]Or *from*
14 [1]Lit *of the men of*
15 [1]Lit *Is the palm* [a]Judg 8:6
16 [1]Lit *made the men...to know*
17 [a]Judg 8:9
18 [1]Lit *like the form of the sons*

dan Valley. *waters . . . the Jordan.* Probably the river crossings in the vicinity of Beth-shean. By controlling the river the Israelites could prevent the escape of the fleeing Midianites (see note on 3:28). *Beth-barah.* Exact location unknown, but it must have been some distance down the river. Gideon's pursuit of the enemy across the river took him to Succoth, a town near the Jabbok River (8:5).

7:25 *Oreb.* Means "raven." *Zeeb.* Means "wolf." *heads.* Frequently parts of the bodies of dead victims, such as heads, hands (8:6) and foreskins (1 Sam 18:25), were cut off and brought back as a kind of body count.

8:1 *men of Ephraim.* Contrast Gideon, who placates the wrath of this tribe (vv. 2–3), with Jephthah, who brings humiliation and defeat to it (12:1–6).

8:2 *gleaning.* Leftover grain after the main gathering of the harvest (see note on Ruth 1:22). Here Gideon implies that Ephraim has accomplished more than he and all the other forces involved in the initial attack. *Abiezer.* Gideon's clan (see note on 6:11). The name means "My (divine) Father is helper" or "My (divine) Father is strong."

8:3 *their anger . . . subsided.* "A gentle answer turns away wrath" (Prov 15:1).

8:5 *kings of Midian.* Zebah and Zalmunna may have belonged to different Midianite tribes (see Num 31:8).

8:6 *hands.* See note on 7:25. *that we should give bread . . . ?* The officials of Succoth doubted Gideon's ability to defeat the Midianite coalition and feared reprisal if they gave his army food.

8:8 *Penuel.* The place where Jacob had wrestled with God (Gen 32:30–31).

8:19 *sons of my mother.* In an age when men often had several wives it was necessary to distinguish between full brothers and half brothers.

8:21 *Rise up yourself.* Dying at the hands of a boy may have been considered a disgrace (see 1 Sam 17:42). *ornaments.* Crescent necklaces, as in Is 3:18.

is his strength." [a]So Gideon arose and killed
Zebah and Zalmunna, and [b]took the crescent
ornaments which were on their camels'
necks.
22 Then the men of Israel said to Gideon,
"Rule over us, both you and your son, also
your son's son, for you have delivered us
from the hand of Midian."
23 But Gideon said to them, "I will not
rule over you, nor shall my son rule over
you; [a]the LORD shall rule over you."
24 Yet Gideon said to them, "I would
[1]request of you, that each of you give me [2]an
earring from his spoil." (For they had gold
earrings, because they were [a]Ishmaelites.)
25 They said, "We will surely give *them*."
So they spread out a garment, and every one
of them threw an earring there from his
spoil.
26 The weight of the gold earrings that he
requested was 1,700 *shekels* of gold, besides
the crescent ornaments and the pendants
and the purple robes which *were* on the
kings of Midian, and besides the neck bands
that *were* on their camels' necks.
27 Gideon made it into [a]an ephod, and
placed it in his city, Ophrah, and all Israel
played the harlot with it there, so that it
became a snare to Gideon and his household.

Forty Years of Peace

28 So Midian was subdued before the sons
of Israel, and they did not lift up their heads
anymore. And the land was undisturbed for
forty years in the days of Gideon.
29 Then [a]Jerubbaal the son of Joash went
and lived in his own house.
30 Now Gideon had [a]seventy sons who
[1]were his direct descendants, for he had
many wives.
31 His concubine who was in Shechem
also bore him a son, and he [1]named him
Abimelech.
32 And Gideon the son of Joash died at a
ripe old age and was buried in the tomb of
his father Joash, in Ophrah of the Abiezrites.
33 Then it came about, as soon as Gideon
was dead, [a]that the sons of Israel again
played the harlot with the Baals, and made
[b]Baal-berith their god.
34 Thus the sons of Israel [a]did not remember the LORD their God, who had delivered
them from the hands of all their enemies on
every side;
35 [a]nor did they show kindness to the
household of Jerubbaal (*that is,* Gideon) in
accord with all the good that he had done to
Israel.

Abimelech's Conspiracy

9 And [a]Abimelech the son of Jerubbaal
went to Shechem to his mother's [1]relatives, and spoke to them and to the whole
clan of the household of his mother's father,
saying,
2 "Speak, now, in the hearing of all the
leaders of Shechem, 'Which is better for you,
that [a]seventy men, all the sons of Jerubbaal,
rule over you, or that one man rule over
you?' Also, remember that I am [b]your bone
and your flesh."
3 And his mother's [1]relatives spoke all
these words on his behalf in the hearing of
all the leaders of Shechem; and [2]they were

21 [a]Ps 83:11 [b]Judg 8:26
23 [a]1 Sam 8:7; 10:19; 12:12; Ps 10:16
24 [1]Lit *request a request* [2]Or *a nose ring* [a]Gen 25:13-16
27 [a]Ex 28:6-35; Judg 17:5; 18:14-20
29 [a]Judg 7:1
30 [1]Lit *came from his loins* [a]Judg 9:2, 5
31 [1]Lit *appointed his name*
33 [a]Judg 2:11, 12 [b]Judg 9:4, 27, 46
34 [a]Deut 4:9; Judg 3:7
35 [a]Judg 9:16-18
9:1 [1]Lit *brothers* [a]Judg 8:31, 35
2 [a]Judg 8:30; 9:5, 18 [b]Gen 29:14
3 [1]Lit *brothers* [2]Lit *their hearts inclined after*

8:23 *I will not rule . . . the LORD shall rule.* Gideon, like Samuel (1 Sam 8:4–20), rejected the establishment of a monarchy because he regarded it as a replacement of the Lord's rule. God's rule over Israel (theocracy) is a central issue in Judges.
8:24 *earring.* Or possibly "nose ring" (see Gen 24:47; Ezek 16:12). *Ishmaelites.* Related to the Midianites (Gen 25:1–2) and sometimes identified with them (vv. 22,24; Gen 37:25–28; 39:1). See note on Gen 37:25.
8:27 *ephod.* Sometimes a holy garment associated with the priesthood (Ex 28:6–30; 39:2–26; Lev 8:7), at other times a pagan object associated with idols (17:5; 18:14,17).
8:28 *forty years.* A conventional number of years for a generation (see Introduction: Background).
8:29 *Jerubbaal.* See note on 6:32.
8:30 *seventy sons.* A sign of power and prosperity (see 12:14; 2 Kin 10:1).
8:31 *concubine.* She was originally a slave in his household (9:18; see note on Gen 16:2). *Abimelech.* Appears elsewhere as a royal title (Gen 20:2; 26:1; Ps 34 title) and means "My (divine) Father is King." Gideon, in naming his son, acknowledges that the Lord (here called "Father") is King.
8:32 *at a ripe old age.* A phrase used elsewhere only of Abraham (Gen 15:15; 25:8) and David (1 Chr 29:28).
8:33 *Baals.* See notes on 2:11,13. *Baal-berith.* Means "lord of the covenant"; the same deity is called El-berith ("god of the covenant") in 9:46. There was a temple dedicated to him (see 9:4) in Shechem. The word "covenant" in his name probably refers to a solemn treaty that bound together a league of Canaanite cities whose people worshiped him as their god. Ironically, Shechem (v. 31), near Mount Ebal, was the site at which Joshua had twice renewed the Lord's covenant with Israel after they had entered Canaan (Josh 8:30–35; 24:25–27). See also note on 2:11.
9:1–57 The stories of Gideon and Abimelech form the literary center of Judges (see Introduction: Literary Features). Abimelech, who tried to set himself up like a Canaanite city king with the help of Baal (v. 4), stands in sharp contrast to his father Gideon (Jerubbaal), who had attacked Baal worship and insisted that the Lord ruled over Israel. Abimelech attempted this Canaanite revival in the very place where Joshua had earlier reaffirmed Israel's allegiance to the Lord (Josh 24:14–27). In every respect Abimelech was the antithesis of the Lord's appointed judges.
9:1 *Shechem.* See note on Gen 33:18. Ruins dating from the Canaanite era give evidence of a sacred area, probably to be associated with the temple of Baal-berith or El-berith (vv. 4,46). Archaeological evidence, which is compatible with the destruction of Shechem by Abimelech, indicates that its sacred area was never rebuilt after this time.
9:2 *leaders.* The singular form of the Hebrew for this word is *ba'al.* It means "lord" or "owner" and probably refers here to the aristocracy or landowners of the city. *your bone and your flesh.* Being half-Canaanite, Abimelech intimated that it was in their best interest to make him king rather than be under the rule of Gideon's 70 sons. The following he gathered was based on this relationship and became a threat to the people of Israel.

inclined to follow Abimelech, for they said,
"He is [a]our [3]relative."
4 They gave him seventy *pieces* of silver
from the house of [a]Baal-berith with which
Abimelech hired worthless and reckless fellows, and they followed him.
5 Then he went to his father's house at
Ophrah and [a]killed his brothers the sons of
Jerubbaal, [b]seventy men, on one stone. But
Jotham the youngest son of Jerubbaal was
left, for he hid himself.
6 All the men of Shechem and all [1]Beth-
millo assembled together, and they went and
made Abimelech king, by the [2]oak of the pillar which was in Shechem.
7 Now when they told Jotham, he went
and stood on the top of [a]Mount Gerizim, and
lifted his voice and called out. Thus he said
to them, "Listen to me, O men of Shechem,
that God may listen to you.
8 "Once the trees went forth to anoint a
king over them, and they said to the olive
tree, 'Reign over us!'
9 "But the olive tree said to them, 'Shall I
leave my fatness with [1]which God and men
are honored, and go to wave over the trees?'
10 "Then the trees said to the fig tree, 'You
come, reign over us!'
11 "But the fig tree said to them, 'Shall I
leave my sweetness and my good [1]fruit, and
go to wave over the trees?'
12 "Then the trees said to the vine, 'You
come, reign over us!'
13 "But the vine said to them, 'Shall I leave
my new wine, which cheers God and men,
and go to wave over the trees?'
14 "Finally all the trees said to the bramble,
'You come, reign over us!'
15 "The bramble said to the trees, 'If in
[1]truth you are anointing me as king over
you, come and take refuge in my shade; but
if not, may fire come out from the bramble
and consume the cedars of Lebanon.'
16 "Now therefore, if you have dealt in
[1]truth and integrity in making Abimelech
king, and if you have dealt well with [a]Jerub-
baal and his house, and [2]have dealt with him
[3]as he deserved—
17 for my father fought for you and
[1]risked his life and delivered you from the
hand of Midian;
18 but you have risen against my father's
house today and have killed [a]his sons, seventy men, on one stone, and have made
Abimelech, [b]the son of his maidservant, king
over the men of Shechem, because he is your
[1]relative—
19 if then you have dealt in [1]truth and
integrity with Jerubbaal and his house this
day, rejoice in Abimelech, and let him also
rejoice in you.
20 "But if not, let fire come out from Abimelech and consume the men of Shechem and
[1]Beth-millo; and let fire come out from the
men of Shechem and from [1]Beth-millo, and
consume Abimelech."
21 Then Jotham escaped and fled, and
went to Beer and remained there because of
Abimelech his brother.

Shechem and Abimelech Fall

22 Now Abimelech ruled over Israel three
years.
23 [a]Then God sent an evil spirit between
Abimelech and the men of Shechem; and the
men of Shechem [b]dealt treacherously with
Abimelech,
24 [a]so that the violence [1]done to the seventy sons of Jerubbaal might come, and
[b]their blood might be laid on Abimelech

3 [3]Lit *brother* [a]Gen 29:15
4 [a]Judg 8:33
5 [a]2 Kin 11:1, 2 [b]Judg 8:30; 9:2, 18
6 [1]Or *the house of Millo* [2]Or *terebinth*
7 [a]Deut 11:29, 30
9 [1]Lit *which by me*
11 [1]Or *produce*
15 [1]Or *sincerity*
16 [1]Or *sincerity* [2]Lit *if you have* [3]Lit *according to the dealing of his hands* [a]Judg 8:35
17 [1]Lit *cast his soul in front*
18 [1]Lit *brother* [a]Judg 8:30; 9:2, 5 [b]Judg 8:31
19 [1]Or *sincerity*
20 [1]Or *the house of Millo*
23 [a]1 Sam 16:14; Is 19:2, 14 [b]Is 33:1
24 [1]Lit *of the seventy* [a]Deut 27:25; Judg 9:56, 57 [b]Num 35:33

9:4 *from the house.* Ancient temples served as depositories for personal and civic funds. The payments of vows and penalties, as well as gifts, were also part of the temple treasury. The temple of Baal-berith is probably to be identified with a large building found at Shechem by archaeologists. *worthless and reckless fellows.* Use of mercenaries to accomplish political or military goals was common in ancient times. Others who used them are Jephthah (11:3), David (1 Sam 22:1–2), Absalom (2 Sam 15:1), Adonijah (1 Kin 1:5), Rezon (1 Kin 11:23–24) and Jeroboam (2 Chr 13:6–7).

9:5 *on one stone.* Abimelech's 70 brothers were slaughtered like sacrificial animals (see 13:19–20; 1 Sam 14:33–34). In effect he inaugurated his kingship by using his Israelite half brothers as his coronation sacrifices (see 2 Sam 15:10,12; 1 Kin 1:5,9; 3:4).

9:6 *Beth-millo.* "Millo" is derived from a Hebrew verb meaning "to fill" and probably refers to the earthen fill used to erect a platform on which walls and other large structures were built. Beth-millo may be identical to the "inner chamber" of v. 46. *oak.* See Josh 24:25–26; see also note on Gen 12:6.

9:7 *top.* Probably a ledge that overlooked the city.

9:8 *trees went forth.* Fables of this type, in which inanimate objects speak and act, were popular among Eastern peoples of that time (see 2 Kin 14:9).

9:9–13 The olive tree, the fig tree and the vine were all plants that produced fruit of great importance to the people of the Near East.

9:13 *cheers God.* Cf. Ex 29:40.

9:14 *bramble.* Probably the well-known buckthorn, a scraggly bush common in the hills of Canaan and a constant menace to farming. It produced nothing of value and was an apt figure for Abimelech.

9:15 *shade.* Ironically, in offering shade to the trees, the thornbush symbolized the traditional role of kings as protectors of their subjects (see Is 30:2–3; 32:1–2; Lam 4:20; Dan 4:12). *cedars of Lebanon.* The most valuable of Near Eastern trees, here symbolic of the leading men of Shechem (see v. 20).

9:20 *fire come out . . . and consume.* A grim prediction that Abimelech and the people of Shechem would destroy each other. Fire spreads rapidly through bramble bushes and brings about swift destruction (see Ex 22:6; Is 9:18).

9:21 *Beer.* A very common name, meaning "a well."

9:22 *Israel.* Those Israelites who recognized Abimelech's authority, mainly in the vicinity of Shechem.

9:23 *evil spirit.* Perhaps a spirit of distrust and bitterness. The Hebrew for "spirit" is often used to describe an attitude or disposition. *dealt treacherously.* The one who founded his kingdom by treachery is himself undone by treachery.

their brother, who killed them, and on the
men of Shechem, who strengthened his
hands to kill his brothers.
25 The men of Shechem set [1]men in
ambush against him on the tops of the
mountains, and they robbed all who might
pass by them along the road; and it was told
to Abimelech.
26 Now Gaal the son of Ebed came with
his [1]relatives, and crossed over into Shechem; and the men of Shechem put their
trust in him.
27 They went out into the field and gathered *the grapes of* their vineyards and trod
them, and held a [1]festival; and they went
into the house of [a]their god, and ate and
drank and cursed Abimelech.
28 Then Gaal the son of Ebed said, "Who
is Abimelech, and who is Shechem, that we
should serve him? Is he not the son of Jerubbaal, and *is* Zebul *not* his [1]lieutenant? Serve
the men of [a]Hamor the father of Shechem;
but why should we serve him?
29 "[1][a]Would, therefore, that this people
were under my authority! Then I would
remove Abimelech." And he said to Abimelech, "Increase your army and come out."
30 When Zebul the ruler of the city heard
the words of Gaal the son of Ebed, his anger
burned.
31 He sent messengers to Abimelech
[1]deceitfully, saying, "Behold, Gaal the son of
Ebed and his [2]relatives have come to Shechem; and behold, they are [3]stirring up the
city against you.
32 "Now therefore, arise by night, you and
the people who are with you, and lie in wait
in the field.
33 "In the morning, as soon as the sun is
up, you shall rise early and rush upon the
city; and behold, when he and the people
who are with him come out against you, you
shall [a]do to them [1]whatever you can."
34 So Abimelech and all the people who
were with him arose by night and lay in wait
against Shechem in four [1]companies.
35 Now Gaal the son of Ebed went out
and stood in the entrance of the city gate;
and Abimelech and the people who *were*
with him arose from the ambush.
36 When Gaal saw the people, he said to
Zebul, "[1]Look, people are coming down
from the tops of the mountains." But Zebul
said to him, "You are seeing the shadow of
the mountains as *if they were* men."
37 Gaal spoke again and said, "Behold,
people are coming down from [a]the [1]highest
part of the land, and one [2]company comes
by the way of [3]the diviners' [4]oak."
38 Then Zebul said to him, "Where is
your [1]boasting now with which you said,
'Who is Abimelech that we should serve
him?' Is this not the people whom you
despised? Go out now and fight with them!"
39 So Gaal went out before the leaders of
Shechem and fought with Abimelech.
40 Abimelech chased him, and he fled
before him; and many fell wounded up to
the entrance of the gate.
41 Then Abimelech remained at Arumah,
but Zebul drove out Gaal and his [1]relatives
so that they could not remain in Shechem.
42 Now it came about the next day, that
the people went out to the field, and it was
told to Abimelech.
43 So he took [1]his people and divided
them into three [2]companies, and lay in wait
in the field; when he looked and [3]saw the
people coming out from the city, he arose
against them and [4]slew them.
44 Then Abimelech and the [1]company
who was with him dashed forward and
stood in the entrance of the city gate; the
other two [2]companies then dashed against
all who *were* in the field and [3]slew them.
45 Abimelech fought against the city all
that day, and he captured the city and killed
the people who *were* in it; then he [a]razed the
city and sowed it with salt.
46 When all the leaders of the tower of
Shechem heard of *it,* they entered the inner
chamber of the [1]temple of [a]El-berith.
47 It was told Abimelech that all the leaders of the tower of Shechem were gathered
together.
48 So Abimelech went up to Mount [a]Zal-
mon, he and all the people who *were* with
him; and Abimelech took [1]an axe in his hand
and cut down a branch from the trees, and
lifted it and laid *it* on his shoulder. Then he
said to the people who *were* with him,
"What you have seen me do, hurry *and* do
[2]likewise."
49 All the people also cut down each one
his branch and followed Abimelech, and put
them on the inner chamber and set the inner

25 [1]Lit *liers-in-wait for*
26 [1]Lit *brothers*
27 [1]Lit *rejoicing* [a]Judg 8:33; 9:46
28 [1]Lit *overseer* [a]Gen 34:2
29 [1]Lit *And who will give this people into my hand* [a]2 Sam 15:4
31 [1]Or *in Tormah* [2]Lit *brothers* [3]Lit *besieging*
33 [1]Lit *as your hand can find* [a]1 Sam 10:7
34 [1]Lit *heads*
36 [1]Lit *Behold*
37 [1]Or *center* [2]Lit *head* [3]Heb *Elommeonenim* [4]Or *terebinth* [a]Ezek 38:12
38 [1]Lit *mouth*
41 [1]Lit *brothers*
43 [1]Lit *the* [2]Lit *heads* [3]Lit *behold* [4]Lit *smote*
44 [1]Singular with Gr; Heb plural, *heads* [2]Lit *heads* [3]Lit *smote*
45 [a]2 Kin 3:25
46 [1]Lit *house* [a]Judg 8:33
48 [1]Lit *the axes* [2]Lit *like me* [a]Ps 68:14

9:26 *put their trust in him.* Just as the fickle population had followed Abimelech, so they are now swayed by the deceptive proposals of Gaal.
9:27 *held a festival.* The vintage harvest was one of the most joyous times of the year (see Is 16:9–10; Jer 25:30), but festivals and celebrations held at pagan temples often degenerated into debauched drinking affairs.
9:28 *Hamor.* The Hivite ruler who had founded the city of Shechem (Gen 33:19; 34:2; Josh 24:32).
9:32 *lie in wait.* Ambush succeeded against Gibeah in Benjamin (20:37) and against Ai (Jos 8:2).
9:34 *four companies.* Smaller segments meant less chance of detection. Also, attack from several directions was good strategy.
9:37 *highest part of the land.* See note on Ezek 38:12. *diviner's oak.* Probably a sacred tree in some way related to the temple of Baal-berith (see note on Gen 12:6).
9:43 *three companies.* See note on 7:16.
9:45 *sowed it with salt.* To condemn it to perpetual barrenness and desolation (see Deut 29:23; Ps 107:33–34; Jer 17:6; Zep 2:9).
9:46 *inner chamber.* Probably the Beth-millo of v. 6. *El-berith.* Baal-berith (v. 4).

chamber on fire over those *inside,* so that all
the men of the tower of Shechem also died,
about a thousand men and women.
50 Then Abimelech went to Thebez, and
he camped against Thebez and captured it.
51 But there was a strong tower in the
center of the city, and all the men and
women with all the leaders of the city fled
there and shut themselves in; and they went
up on the roof of the tower.
52 So Abimelech came to the tower and
fought against it, and approached the
entrance of the tower to burn it with fire.
53 But [a]a certain woman threw an upper
millstone on Abimelech's head, crushing his
skull.
54 Then [a]he called quickly to the young
man, his armor bearer, and said to him, "Draw
your sword and kill me, so that it will not be
said of me, 'A woman slew him.' " So [1]the
young man pierced him through, and he died.
55 When the men of Israel saw that Abimelech was dead, each departed to his [1]home.
56 Thus [a]God repaid the wickedness of
Abimelech, which he had done to his father
in killing his seventy brothers.
57 Also God returned all the wickedness
of the men of Shechem on their heads, and
the curse of Jotham the son of Jerubbaal
came [1]upon them.

Oppression of Philistines and Ammonites

10 Now after Abimelech died, Tola the son
of Puah, the son of Dodo, a man of
Issachar, [a]arose to save Israel; and he lived
in Shamir in the hill country of Ephraim.
2 He judged Israel twenty-three years.
Then he died and was buried in Shamir.
3 After him, Jair the Gileadite arose and
judged Israel twenty-two years.
4 He had thirty sons who rode on thirty
donkeys, and they had thirty cities [1]in the
land of Gilead [a]that are called [2]Havvoth-jair
to this day.
5 And Jair died and was buried in
Kamon.
6 Then the sons of Israel again did evil in
the sight of the LORD, [a]served the Baals and
the Ashtaroth, the gods of Aram, the gods of
Sidon, the gods of Moab, [b]the gods of the
sons of Ammon, and the gods of the Philistines; thus [c]they forsook the LORD and did
not serve Him.
7 The anger of the LORD burned against
Israel, and He [a]sold them into the hands of
the Philistines and into the hands of the sons
of Ammon.
8 They [1]afflicted and crushed the sons of
Israel [2]that year; for eighteen years they
afflicted all the sons of Israel who were
beyond the Jordan [3]in Gilead in the land of
the Amorites.
9 The sons of Ammon crossed the Jordan
to fight also against Judah, Benjamin, and
the house of Ephraim, so that Israel was
greatly distressed.
10 Then the [a]sons of Israel cried out to the
LORD, saying, "We have sinned against You,
for indeed, we have forsaken our God and
served the Baals."
11 The LORD said to the sons of Israel,
"*Did I* not *deliver you* [a]from the Egyptians,

53 [a]2 Sam 11:21
54 [1]Lit *his* [a]1 Sam 31:4
55 [1]Lit *place*
56 [a]Gen 9:5, 6; Ps 94:23
57 [1]Lit *to*
10:1 [a]Judg 2:16
4 [1]Lit *which are in* [2]I.e. the towns of Jair [a]Num 32:41
6 [a]Judg 2:13 [b]Judg 11:24 [c]Deut 31:16, 17; 32:15
7 [a]1 Sam 12:9
8 [1]Lit *shattered* [2]Lit *in that* [3]Lit *which is in*
10 [a]1 Sam 12:10
11 [a]Judg 2:12

9:49 *set the inner chamber on fire.* In fulfillment of Jotham's curse (v. 20).

9:53 *woman.* While the men used bows, arrows and spears, women helped to defend the tower by dropping heavy stones on those who came near it. *upper millstone.* See note on 3:16. The upper, revolving stone of a mill was circular, with a hole in the center. Grinding grain was women's work (see Ex 11:5), usually considered too lowly for men to perform (see 16:21). Abimelech was killed by a woman using a domestic implement (see also 4:21).

9:54 *armor bearer.* A military leader usually had a young man carry his shield and spear (see 1 Sam 14:6; 31:4). *A woman slew him.* It was considered a disgrace for a soldier to die at the hands of a woman. Abimelech's shameful death was long remembered (2 Sam 11:21).

9:56 *God repaid.* God was in control of the events. As Israel's true King, He brought Abimelech's wickedness to a quick and shameful end.

9:57 *curse of Jotham.* See v. 20.

10:1 *Tola the son of Puah . . . a man of Issachar.* Tola and Puah bear names of two of the sons of Issachar (Gen 46:13; Num 26:23; 1Ch 7:1).

10:3 *Jair.* Since Jair came from Gilead (the territory assigned to Manasseh) and since a descendant of Manasseh bore the same name (Num 32:41; Deut 3:14; 1 Kin 4:13), it appears that Jair was a Manassite.

10:4 *thirty sons . . . thirty donkeys . . . thirty cities.* Evidence of wealth and position. *Havvoth-jair.* See NASB marg.

10:6–12:7 Israel now turned to Jephthah, a social outcast whom they had driven from the land and caused to become an outlaw without an inheritance in Israel. The author notes this to Israel's shame. The account of Jephthah's judgeship balances that of Deborah in the story of the judges (see note on 4:1–5:31; see also Introduction: Literary Features).

10:6 *gods of Aram.* The chief gods were Hadad (Baal), Mot, Anath and Rimmon. *gods of Sidon.* The Sidonians worshiped essentially the same gods as the Canaanites (see notes on 2:11,13). *gods of Moab.* The chief deity of Moab was Chemosh. *gods of the sons of Ammon.* Molech was the chief Ammonite deity (see 1 Kin 11:7) and was sometimes worshiped by the offering of human sacrifice (Lev 18:21; 20:2–5; 2 Kin 23:10). This god is also called Milcom (see 1 Kin 11:5; 2 Kin 23:13; see also note on Lev 18:21). Both Molech and Milcom are forms of a Semitic word for "king." *gods of the Philistines.* While the Philistines worshiped most of the Canaanite gods, their most popular deities appear to have been Dagon and Baal-zebub. The name Dagon is the same as a Hebrew word for "grain," suggesting that he was a vegetation deity. He was worshiped in Babylonia as early as the second millennium B.C. Baal-zebub was worshiped in Ekron (2 Kin 1:2–3,6,16). The name means "lord of the flies," a deliberate change by followers of the Lord (Yahweh) to ridicule and protest the worship of Baal-zebul ("Baal the prince"), a name known from ancient Canaanite texts (see Matt 10:25; 12:24 and notes).

10:7 *Philistines.* The account of Philistine oppression is resumed in 13:1.

10:11 *The LORD said.* See note on 2:1. The Lord rebuked Israel for forgetting that He had delivered them from their oppres-

[b]the Amorites, [c]the sons of Ammon, and the
Philistines?
12 "Also when the Sidonians, the Amalekites and the Maonites [a]oppressed you, you
cried out to Me, and I delivered you from
their hands.
13 "Yet [a]you have forsaken Me and served
other gods; therefore I will no longer deliver
you.
14 "[a]Go and cry out to the gods which you
have chosen; let them deliver you in the time
of your distress."
15 The sons of Israel said to the LORD, "We
have sinned, [a]do to us whatever seems good
to You; only please deliver us this day."
16 [a]So they put away the foreign gods from
among them and served the LORD; and [1b]He
could bear the misery of Israel no longer.
17 Then the sons of Ammon were summoned and they camped in Gilead. And the
sons of Israel gathered together and camped
in [a]Mizpah.
18 The people, the leaders of Gilead, said
to one another, "Who is the man who will
begin to fight against the sons of Ammon?
He shall become head over all the inhabitants of Gilead."

Jephthah the Ninth Judge

11 Now [a]Jephthah the Gileadite was a
[1]valiant warrior, but he was the son of
a harlot. And Gilead [2]was the father of Jephthah.
2 Gilead's wife bore him sons; and when
his wife's sons grew up, they drove Jephthah
out and said to him, "You shall not have an
inheritance in our father's house, for you are
the son of another woman."
3 So Jephthah fled from his brothers and
lived in the land of [a]Tob; and worthless fellows gathered themselves [1]about Jephthah,
and they went out with him.
4 It came about after a while that [a]the
sons of Ammon fought against Israel.
5 When the sons of Ammon fought
against Israel, the elders of Gilead went to
get Jephthah from the land of Tob;
6 and they said to Jephthah, "Come and
be our chief that we may fight against the
sons of Ammon."
7 Then Jephthah said to the elders of Gilead, "[a]Did you not hate me and drive me
from my father's house? So why have you
come to me now when you are in trouble?"
8 The elders of Gilead said to Jephthah,
"For this reason we have now returned to
you, that you may go with us and fight with
the sons of Ammon and [a]become head over
all the inhabitants of Gilead."
9 So Jephthah said to the elders of Gilead, "If you take me back to fight against the
sons of Ammon and the LORD gives them up
[1]to me, will I become your head?"
10 The elders of Gilead said to Jephthah,
"[a]The LORD is [1]witness between us; surely
we will do [2]as you have said."
11 Then Jephthah went with the elders of
Gilead, and the people made him head and
chief over them; and Jephthah spoke all his
words before the LORD at [a]Mizpah.
12 Now Jephthah sent messengers to the
king of the sons of Ammon, saying, "What is
between you and me, that you have come to
me to fight against my land?"
13 The king of the sons of Ammon said to
the messengers of Jephthah, "Because Israel
[a]took away my land when they came up
from Egypt, from the Arnon as far as the
[b]Jabbok and the Jordan; therefore, return
them peaceably now."
14 But Jephthah sent messengers again to
the king of the sons of Ammon,
15 and they said to him, "Thus says Jephthah, 'Israel did not take away the land of
Moab nor the land of the sons of Ammon.
16 'For when they came up from Egypt,
and Israel [a]went through the wilderness to
the [1]Red Sea and [b]came to Kadesh,
17 then Israel [a]sent messengers to the
king of Edom, saying, "Please let us pass

11 [b]Num 21:21-25 [c]Judg 3:13
12 [a]Ps 106:42
13 [a]Jer 2:13
14 [a]Deut 32:37
15 [a]1 Sam 3:18
16 [1]Lit *His soul was short with the misery* [a]Josh 24:23 [b]Deut 32:36
17 [a]Judg 11:29
11:1 [1]Or *mighty man of valor* [2]Lit *begat* [a]Heb 11:32
3 [1]Lit *to* [a]2 Sam 10:6, 8
4 [a]Judg 10:9, 17
7 [a]Gen 26:27
8 [a]Judg 10:18
9 [1]Lit *before*
10 [1]Lit *hearer* [2]Lit *according to your word* [a]Gen 31:50; Jer 29:23; 42:5; Mic 1:2
11 [a]Judg 10:17; 11:29; 20:1; 1 Sam 10:17
13 [a]Num 21:24 [b]Gen 32:22
16 [1]Lit *Sea of Reeds* [a]Num 14:25; Deut 1:40 [b]Num 20:1, 4-21
17 [a]Num 20:14-21

sors in Canaan (see notes on 2:16–19; 6:8).

10:12 *Maonites.* Perhaps the same as the Meunites, who along with the Philistines and Arabs opposed Israel (2 Chr 26:7).

10:17 *Mizpah.* Means "watchtower." Several places bore this name. Jephthah's headquarters was a town or fortress in Gilead (11:11) called "Mizpah of Gilead" (11:29). It may have been the same as Ramath-mizpeh (Josh 13:26), located about 30 miles east of Beth-shean.

10:18 The Gileadites wanted to resist the Ammonite incursion but lacked the courageous military leadership to press their cause. *people.* Fighting men.

11:1 *the son of a harlot.* Therefore Jephthah was a social outcast.

11:3 *Tob.* The men of Tob were later allied with the Ammonites against David (2 Sam 10:6–8). *worthless fellows.* See note on 9:4.

11:8 *become head.* In addition to their initial offer of military command during the war with Ammon (v. 6), the Gileadites now also offer to make Jephthah regional head after the fighting is over.

11:11 The proposal of the elders was ratified by the people, a process followed in the election of Saul (1 Sam 11:15), Rehoboam (1 Kin 12:1) and Jeroboam (1 Kin 12:20).

11:13 *my land.* When the Israelites had first approached Canaan, this area was ruled by the Amorite king Sihon, who had taken it from the Moabites (Num 21:29). The Ammonites had since become dominant over Moab and now claimed all previous Moabite territory.

11:14–27 Jephthah responded in accordance with international policies of the time; his letter is a classic example of contemporary international correspondence. It also reflects—and appeals to—the common recognition that the god(s) of a people established and protected their political boundaries and decided all boundary disputes. Jephthah's defense of Israel's claim to the land is threefold: (1) Israel took it from Sihon king of the Amorites, not from the Ammonites (vv. 15–22); (2) the Lord gave the land to Israel (vv. 23–25); (3) Israel had long possessed it (vv. 26–27).

11:16 *Kadesh.* Kadesh-barnea; see note on Num 20:1.

through your land," but the king of Edom would not listen. [b]And they also sent to the king of Moab, but he would not consent. So Israel remained at Kadesh.

18 'Then they went through the wilderness and [a]around the land of Edom and the land of Moab, and came to the east side of the land of Moab, and they camped beyond the Arnon; but they [b]did not enter the territory of Moab, for the Arnon *was* the border of Moab.

19 'And Israel sent [a]messengers to Sihon king of the Amorites, the king of Heshbon, and Israel said to him, "Please let us pass through your land to our place."

20 'But Sihon did not trust Israel to pass through his territory; so Sihon gathered all his people and camped in Jahaz and fought with Israel.

21 'The LORD, the God of Israel, gave Sihon and all his people into the hand of Israel, and they [1a]defeated them; so Israel possessed all the land of the Amorites, the inhabitants of that country.

22 '[a]So they possessed all the territory of the Amorites, from the Arnon as far as the Jabbok, and from the wilderness as far as the Jordan.

23 'Since now the LORD, the God of Israel, drove out the Amorites from before His people Israel, are you then to possess it?

24 'Do you not possess what [a]Chemosh your god gives you to possess? So whatever the LORD our God has driven out before us, we will possess it.

25 'Now are you any better than [a]Balak the son of Zippor, king of Moab? Did he ever strive with Israel, or did he ever fight against them?

26 '[a]While Israel lived in Heshbon and its villages, and in Aroer and its villages, and in all the cities that are on the banks of the Arnon, three hundred years, why did you not recover them within that time?

27 'I therefore have not sinned against you, but you are doing me wrong by making war against me; [a]may the LORD, the Judge, judge today between the sons of Israel and the sons of Ammon.'"

28 But the king of the sons of Ammon [1]disregarded the message which Jephthah sent him.

Jephthah's Tragic Vow

29 Now [a]the Spirit of the LORD came upon Jephthah, so that he passed through Gilead and Manasseh; then he passed through Mizpah of Gilead, and from Mizpah of Gilead he went on to the sons of Ammon.

30 Jephthah made a vow to the LORD and said, "If You will indeed give the sons of Ammon into my hand,

31 then it shall be that whatever comes out of the doors of my house to meet me when I return in peace from the sons of Ammon, it shall be the LORD's, and I will offer it up as a burnt offering."

32 So Jephthah crossed over to the sons of Ammon to fight against them; and the LORD gave them into his hand.

33 He struck them with a very great slaughter from Aroer [1]to the entrance of [a]Minnith, twenty cities, and as far as Abel-keramim. So the sons of Ammon were subdued before the sons of Israel.

34 When Jephthah came to his house at [a]Mizpah, behold, his daughter was coming out to meet him [b]with tambourines and with dancing. Now she was his one *and* only child; besides her he had no son or daughter.

35 When he saw her, he tore his clothes and said, "Alas, my daughter! You have brought me very low, and you are among those who trouble me; for I have [1]given my word to the LORD, and [a]I cannot take *it* back."

36 So she said to him, "My father, you have [1]given your word to the LORD; [a]do to me [2]as you have said, since the LORD has avenged you of your enemies, the sons of Ammon."

37 She said to her father, "Let this thing be done for me; let me alone two months, that I may [1]go to the mountains and weep because of [a]my virginity, I and my companions."

38 Then he said, "Go." So he sent her away for two months; and she left with her

17 [b]Josh 24:9
18 [a]Num 21:4; Deut 2:8 [b]Deut 2:9, 18, 19
19 [a]Num 21:21-32; Deut 2:26-36
21 [1]Lit *smote* [a]Num 21:24; Deut 2:32-34
22 [a]Deut 2:36, 37
24 [a]Num 21:29; 1 Kin 11:7
25 [a]Num 22:2; Josh 24:9; Mic 6:5
26 [a]Num 21:25, 26; Deut 2:36
27 [a]Gen 16:5; 18:25; 31:53; 1 Sam 24:12, 15
28 [1]Lit *did not listen to the words*
29 [a]Judg 3:10
33 [1]Lit *even until you are coming to* [a]Ezek 27:17
34 [a]Judg 10:17; 11:11 [b]Ex 15:20; 1 Sam 18:6; Jer 31:4
35 [1]Lit *opened my mouth* [a]Num 30:2; Eccl 5:4, 5
36 [1]Lit *opened your mouth* [2]Lit *according to what has proceeded from your mouth* [a]Num 30:2
37 [1]Lit *go and go down on* [a]Gen 30:23; Luke 1:25

11:21 *LORD, the God of Israel.* War was viewed not only in military terms but also as a contest between deities (see v. 24; Ex 12:12; Num 33:4).

11:24 *Chemosh.* The chief deity of the Moabites. At this time either the king of Ammon also ruled Moab or there was a military confederacy of the two peoples.

11:25 *Balak.* See Num 22–24.

11:26 *three hundred years.* For the relevance of this phrase in establishing the time span for Judges see Introduction: Background.

11:27 *Judge.* See 1 Sam 24:15. As the divine Judge, the Lord is the final court of appeal. It is significant that in the book of Judges the singular noun "judge" is found only here, where it is used of the Lord, Israel's true Judge.

11:29 *Spirit of the LORD.* See note on 3:10. In the OT the unique empowering of the Spirit was given to an individual primarily to enable him to carry out the special responsibilities God had given him.

11:30 *made a vow.* A common practice among the Israelites (see Gen 28:20; 1 Sam 1:11; 2 Sam 15:8). The precise nature of this vow has been the subject of wide speculation, but v. 31 indicates the promise of a burnt offering and leads to the conclusion that Jephthah probably offered his daughter as a human sacrifice (v. 39). A vow was not to be broken (see Num 30:2; Deut 23:21–23; see also Eccl 5:4–5).

11:34 *dancing.* It was customary for women to greet armies returning victoriously from battle in this way (see Ex 15:20; 1 Sam 18:6).

11:35 *tore his clothes.* A common practice for expressing extreme grief (see Gen 37:34 and note).

11:37 *my virginity.* To be kept from marrying and rearing children was a bitter prospect for an Israelite girl.

companions, and wept on the mountains
because of her virginity.
39 At the end of two months she returned
to her father, who did to her according to the
vow which he had made; and she [1]had no
relations with a man. Thus it became a custom in Israel,
40 that the daughters of Israel went yearly
to [1]commemorate the daughter of Jephthah
the Gileadite four days in the year.

Jephthah and His Successors

12 Then the men of Ephraim were summoned, and they crossed [1]to Zaphon
and [a]said to Jephthah, "Why did you cross
over to fight against the sons of Ammon
without calling us to go with you? We will
burn your house down on you."
2 Jephthah said to them, "I and my people were at great strife with the sons of
Ammon; when I called you, you did not
deliver me from their hand.
3 "When I saw that you would not deliver
me, I [1a]took my life in my hands and crossed
over against the sons of Ammon, and the
LORD gave them into my hand. Why then
have you come up to me this day to fight
against me?"
4 Then Jephthah gathered all the men of
Gilead and fought Ephraim; and the men of
Gilead [1]defeated Ephraim, because they said,
"You are fugitives of Ephraim, O Gileadites,
in the midst of Ephraim *and* in the midst of
Manasseh."
5 The Gileadites [a]captured the fords of
the Jordan opposite Ephraim. And it happened when *any of* the fugitives of Ephraim
said, "Let me cross over," the men of Gilead
would say to him, "Are you an Ephraimite?"
If he said, "No,"
6 then they would say to him, "Say now,
'Shibboleth.' " But he said, "Sibboleth," for
he could not [1]pronounce it correctly. Then
they seized him and slew him at the fords of
the Jordan. Thus there fell at that time
42,000 of Ephraim.
7 Jephthah judged Israel six years. Then
Jephthah the Gileadite died and was buried
in *one of* the cities of Gilead.
8 Now Ibzan of Bethlehem judged Israel
after him.
9 He had thirty sons, and thirty daughters *whom* he [1]gave in marriage outside *the*
family, and he brought in thirty daughters
from outside for his sons. And he judged
Israel seven years.
10 Then Ibzan died and was buried in
Bethlehem.
11 Now Elon the Zebulunite judged Israel
after him; and he judged Israel ten years.
12 Then Elon the Zebulunite died and was
buried at Aijalon in the land of Zebulun.
13 Now Abdon the son of Hillel the Pirathonite judged Israel after him.
14 He had forty sons and thirty grandsons
who rode on seventy donkeys; and he judged
Israel eight years.
15 Then Abdon the son of Hillel the Pirathonite died and was buried at Pirathon in
the land of Ephraim, in the hill country of
the Amalekites.

Philistines Oppress Again

13 Now the sons of Israel [a]again did evil
in the sight of the LORD, so that the
LORD gave them into the hands of the Philistines forty years.
2 There was a certain man of [a]Zorah, of
the family of the Danites, whose name was
Manoah; and his wife was barren and had
borne no *children*.
3 [a]Then the angel of the LORD appeared
to the woman and said to her, "Behold now,
you are barren and have borne no *children*,

39 [1]Lit *knew no man*
40 [1]Lit *recount;* ancient versions, *lament*
12:1 [1]Or *northward* [a]Judg 8:1
3 [1]Lit *put my soul in my palm* [a]1 Sam 19:5; 28:21; Job 13:14
4 [1]Lit *smote*
5 [a]Judg 3:28
6 [1]Lit *speak so*
9 [1]Lit *sent outside*
13:1 [a]Judg 2:11
2 [a]Josh 19:41
3 [a]Judg 6:11, 14; 13:6, 8, 10, 11; Luke 1:11-13

11:39 *custom in Israel.* Probably a local custom, since no other mention of it is found in the OT.

12:1 *burn your house down.* The Philistines issued a similar threat to Samson's wife (14:15). See also 20:48.

12:2 *said.* Again Jephthah tried diplomacy first (see 11:12,14; see also note on 8:1). *I called.* New information on the sequence of events.

12:6 *Shibboleth.* Ironically, the word meant "floods" (see, e.g., Ps 69:2,15). Apparently the Israelites east of the Jordan pronounced its initial letter with a strong "sh" sound, while those in Canaan gave it a softer "s" sound. (Peter was similarly betrayed by his accent; see Matt 26:73.)

12:7 *judged Israel . . . years.* A new formula for closing out the account of a judge (see note on 3:11; see also Introduction: Literary Features).

12:8 *Bethlehem.* Probably the Bethlehem in western Zebulun.

12:9 *thirty sons, and thirty daughters.* See note on 10:4.

12:11 *Elon.* Also the name of a clan in the tribe of Zebulun (Gen 46:14; Num 26:26).

12:14 *forty sons and thirty grandsons.* A total of 70 (see notes on 8:30; 10:4).

12:15 *hill country of the Amalekites.* See note on 5:14. The background of this reference is unknown; the Amalekites are otherwise associated with the Negev (Num 13:29).

13:1–16:31 Samson (from the tribe of Dan), like Ehud (from the tribe of Benjamin), was a loner, whose heroic exploits involved single-handed triumphs over powerful enemies. His story therefore balances that of Ehud (3:12–30). He typifies the nation of Israel—born by special divine provision, consecrated to the Lord from birth and endowed with unique power among his fellowmen. The likeness is even more remarkable in light of his foolish chasing of foreign women, some of ill repute, until he was cleverly subdued by one of them. In this he exemplified Israel, who during the period of the judges constantly prostituted herself to Canaanite gods to her own destruction.

13:1 *did evil in the sight of the LORD.* See note on 3:7.

13:2 *Zorah.* A town first assigned to Judah (Josh 15:33), but later given to Dan (Josh 19:41). It became the point of departure for the Danite migration northward (18:2,8,11). *Danites.* See 1:34 and note. *barren . . . no children.* The same condition, before divine intervention, as that of Sarah, the mother of Isaac (Gen 11:30; 16:1); Rebekah, the mother of Jacob (Gen 25:21); Hannah, the mother of Samuel (1 Sam 1:2); and Elizabeth, the mother of John the Baptist (Lk 1:7).

13:3 *angel of the LORD.* See note on Gen 16:7. *you shall. . . give*

but you shall conceive and give birth to a son.

4 "Now therefore, be careful [a]not to drink wine or strong drink, nor eat any unclean thing.

5 "[a]For behold, you shall conceive and give birth to a son, and no razor shall come upon his head, for the boy shall be a [b]Nazirite to God from the womb; and he shall begin to deliver Israel from the hands of the Philistines."

6 Then the woman came and told her husband, saying, "[a]A man of God came to me and his appearance was like the appearance of the angel of God, very awesome. And I did not ask him where he *came* from, nor did he tell me his name.

7 "But he said to me, 'Behold, you shall conceive and give birth to a son, and now you shall not drink wine or strong drink nor eat any unclean thing, for the boy shall be a Nazirite to God from the womb to the day of his death.' "

8 Then Manoah entreated the LORD and said, "O Lord, please let [a]the man of God whom You have sent come to us again that he may teach us what to do for the boy who is to be born."

9 God listened to the voice of Manoah; and [a]the angel of God came again to the woman as she was sitting in the field, but Manoah her husband was not with her.

10 So the woman ran quickly and told her [1]husband, "Behold, [a]the man who [2]came the *other* day has appeared to me."

11 Then Manoah arose and followed his wife, and when he came to the man he said to him, "Are you [a]the man who spoke to the woman?" And he said, "I am."

12 Manoah said, "Now when your words come *to pass,* what shall be the boy's mode of life and his vocation?"

13 So [a]the angel of the LORD said to Manoah, "[b]Let the woman pay attention [1]to all that I said.

4 [a]Num 6:2, 3; Luke 1:15
5 [a]Luke 1:15 [b]Num 6:2-5
6 [a]Judg 6:11; 13:8, 10, 11
8 [a]Judg 13:3, 7
9 [a]Judg 13:8
10 [1]Lit *husband, and said to him* [2]Lit *came to me* [a]Judg 13:9
11 [a]Judg 13:8
13 [1]Lit *from* [a]Judg 13:11 [b]Judg 13:4

14 [a]Num 6:4
15 [a]Judg 13:3
16 [1]Lit *bread* [a]Judg 6:20
17 [a]Gen 32:29
18 [1]I.e. incomprehensible [a]Is 9:6
19 [a]Judg 6:20, 21
20 [a]Lev 9:24; 1 Chr 21:16; Ezek 1:28; Matt 17:6
21 [a]Judg 13:16
22 [a]Gen 32:30; Deut 5:26; Judg 6:22
23 [a]Ps 25:14
24 [a]1 Sam 3:19; Luke 1:80
25 [1]I.e. the camp of Dan [a]Judg 3:10 [b]Judg 18:11, 12

14 "She should not eat anything that comes from the [a]vine nor drink wine or strong drink, nor eat any unclean thing; let her observe all that I commanded."

15 Then Manoah said to [a]the angel of the LORD, "Please let us detain you so that we may prepare a young goat for you."

16 The angel of the LORD said to Manoah, "Though you detain me, [a]I will not eat your [1]food, but if you prepare a burnt offering, *then* offer it to the LORD." For Manoah did not know that he was the angel of the LORD.

17 Manoah said to the angel of the LORD, "[a]What is your name, so that when your words come *to pass,* we may honor you?"

18 But the angel of the LORD said to him, "Why do you ask my name, seeing it is [1a]wonderful?"

19 So [a]Manoah took the young goat with the grain offering and offered it on the rock to the LORD, and He performed wonders while Manoah and his wife looked on.

20 For it came about when the flame went up from the altar toward heaven, that the angel of the LORD ascended in the flame of the altar. When Manoah and his wife saw *this,* they [a]fell on their faces to the ground.

21 Now the angel of the LORD did not appear to Manoah or his wife again. [a]Then Manoah knew that he was the angel of the LORD.

22 So Manoah said to his wife, "[a]We will surely die, for we have seen God."

23 But his wife said to him, "If the LORD had desired to kill us, He would not have accepted a burnt offering and a grain offering from our hands, nor would He have [a]shown us all these things, nor would He have let us hear *things* like this at this time."

24 Then the woman gave birth to a son and named him Samson; and the [a]child grew up and the LORD blessed him.

25 And [a]the Spirit of the LORD began to stir him in [1b]Mahaneh-dan, between Zorah and Eshtaol.

---

birth to a son. Cf. the announcements of the births of Ishmael (Gen 16:11), Isaac (Gen 18:10), Immanuel (Is 7:14), John the Baptist (Luke 1:13) and Jesus (Luke 1:31).

13:5 *Nazirite.* From the Hebrew word meaning "separated" or "dedicated." For the stipulations of this vow see Num 6:1–21 and notes. Samson's vow was not voluntary, and it applied to his whole lifetime (v. 7). The same was true of Samuel (1 Sam 1:11) and John the Baptist (Luke 1:15). *begin to deliver Israel from the . . . Philistines.* The deliverance was continued in the time of Samuel (1 Sam 7:10–14) and completed under David (2 Sam 5:17–25; 8:1).

13:6 *man of God.* An expression often used of prophets (see Deut 33:1; 1 Sam 2:27; 9:6–10; 1 Kin. 12:22), though it is clear from vv. 3,21 that this messenger was not a prophet but the angel of the Lord.

13:8 *teach us.* Not the usual parental concern, but a special concern based on the boy's special calling.

13:12 *when your words come to pass.* A declaration of faith. To Manoah it was not a matter of whether these events would occur, but of when (v. 17).

13:15 *detain you . . . prepare a young goat.* Such food was considered a special delicacy. Hospitality of this kind was common in the ancient Near East (see 6:18–19; Gen 18:1–8).

13:17 *What is your name . . . ?* A messenger's identity was considered very important. *when your words come to pass.* Fulfilled prophecy was a sign of the authenticity of a prophet (Deut 18:21–22; 1Sa 9:6).

13:18 *wonderful.* In Is 9:6 the Hebrew for this phrase (translated "Wonderful") applies to One who would come as "Mighty God."

13:22 *surely die.* See 6:23 and notes on Gen 16:13; 32:30.

13:24 *Samson.* The name is derived from a Hebrew word meaning "sun" or "brightness," and is used here either as an expression of joy over the birth of the child or as a reference to the nearby town of Beth-shemesh, "house of the sun(-god)." *the child grew up and the LORD blessed him.* Cf. 1 Sam 2:26 (Samuel) and Luke 2:52 (Jesus).

13:25 *began to stir him.* See notes on 3:10; 11:29. *Mahaneh-dan.* Means "Dan's camp" (see NASB marg.; see also 18:12).

Samson's Marriage

14 Then Samson went down to Timnah
and saw a woman in Timnah, *one* of
the daughters of the Philistines.
2 So he came [1]back and told his father
and [2]mother, "I saw a woman in Timnah,
one of the daughters of the Philistines; now
therefore, get her for me as a wife."
3 Then his father and his mother said to
him, "Is there no woman among the daughters of your [1a]relatives, or among all [2]our
people, that you go to [b]take a wife from the
uncircumcised Philistines?" But Samson said
to his father, "Get her for me, for she [3]looks
good to me."
4 However, his father and mother did not
know that [a]it was of the LORD, for He was
seeking an occasion against the Philistines.
Now at that time the Philistines were ruling
over Israel.
5 Then Samson went down to Timnah
with his father and mother, and came as far
as the vineyards of Timnah; and behold, a
young lion *came* roaring toward him.
6 [a]The Spirit of the LORD [1]came upon
him mightily, so that [b]he tore him as one
tears a young goat though he had nothing in
his hand; but he did not tell his father or
mother what he had done.
7 So he went down and talked to the
woman; and she [1]looked good to Samson.
8 When he returned later to take her, he
turned aside to look at the carcass of the
lion; and behold, a swarm of bees and honey were in the body of the lion.
9 So he scraped [1]the honey into his
[2]hands and went on, eating as he went.
When he came to his father and mother, he
gave *some* to them and they ate *it;* but he did
not tell them that he had scraped the honey
out of the body of the lion.
10 Then his father went down to the
woman; and Samson made a feast there, for
the young men customarily did this.
11 When they saw him, they brought thirty companions to be with him.

Samson's Riddle

12 Then Samson said to them, "Let me
now [a]propound a riddle to you; if you will
indeed tell it to me within the seven days of
the feast, and find it out, then I will give you
thirty linen wraps and thirty [b]changes of
clothes.
13 "But if you are unable to tell me, then
you shall give me thirty linen wraps and thirty changes of clothes." And they said to him,
"Propound your riddle, that we may hear it."
14 So he said to them,
"Out of the eater came something to
eat,
And out of the strong came something
sweet."
But they could not tell the riddle in three
days.
15 Then it came about on the [1]fourth day
that they said to Samson's wife, "[a]Entice
your husband, so that he will tell us the riddle, [b]or we will burn you and your father's
house with fire. Have you invited us to
impoverish us? Is this not *so?*"
16 Samson's wife wept before him and
said, "[a]You only hate me, and you do not
love me; you have propounded a riddle to
the sons of my people, and have not told *it* to
me." And he said to her, "Behold, I have not
told *it* to my father or mother; so should I
tell you?"
17 However she wept before him seven
days while their feast lasted. And on the seventh day he told her because she pressed
him so hard. She then told the riddle to the
sons of her people.
18 So the men of the city said to him on
the seventh day before the sun went down,
"What is sweeter than honey?
And what is stronger than a lion?"
And he said to them,

14:2 [1]Lit *up* [2]Lit *mother, saying,* **3** [1]Lit *brothers* [2]Lit *my* [3]Lit *is right in my eyes* [a]Gen 24:3, 4 [b]Ex 34:16; Deut 7:3 **4** [a]Josh 11:20 **6** [1]Lit *rushed upon* [a]Judg 3:10 [b]1 Sam 17:34-36 **7** [1]Lit *was right in Samson's eyes* **9** [1]Lit *it* [2]Lit *palms*

12 [a]Ezek 17:2 [b]Gen 45:22; 2 Kin 5:22 **15** [1]So with some ancient versions; Heb *seventh* [a]Judg 16:5 [b]Judg 15:6 **16** [a]Judg 16:15

14:1 *Timnah.* Identified as Tell Batash in the Sorek Valley, west of Beth-shemesh. Archaeologists have uncovered the Philistine layer of the town. *one of the daughters of the Philistines.* The disappointment of Samson's parents (v. 3; cf. Esau, Gen 26:35; 27:46; 28:1) is understandable in light of the prohibition against marriage with the peoples of Canaan (Ex 34:11,16; Deut 7:1,3; see also Judg 3:5–6).

14:2 *get her for me.* See Gen 34:4. As the head of the family, the father exercised authority in all matters, often including the choice of wives for his sons (see 12:9; Gen 24:3–9; Neh 10:30).

14:3 *uncircumcised.* A term of scorn, referring to those not bound by covenant to the Lord, used especially of the Philistines (see note on 1 Sam 14:6). *she looks good to me.* The Hebrew for this expression is similar to that translated "did what was right in his own eyes" in 17:6; 21:25. The author anticipates this theme, which recurs in chs. 17–21.

14:4 *it was of the LORD.* See Josh 11:20; 1 Kin 12:15. The Lord uses even the sinful weaknesses of men to accomplish His purposes and bring praise to His name (see Gen 45:8; 50:20; 2 Chr 25:20; Acts 2:23; 4:28; Rom 8:28–29).

14:5 *vineyards of Timnah.* The Sorek Valley (in which Timnah was located) and its surrounding areas were noted for their luxurious vineyards. *young lion.* Lions were once common in southern Canaan (see 1 Sam 17:34; 2 Sam 23:20; 1 Kin 13:24; 20:36).

14:6 *Spirit . . . came upon him.* See 13:25; 14:19; 15:14; see also notes on 3:10; 11:29. *tore him.* David (1 Sam 17:34–37) and Benaiah (2 Sam 23:20) later performed similar feats.

14:10 *feast.* Such a special feast was common in the ancient Near East (see Gen 29:22) and here lasted seven days (v. 12; see Gen 29:27). Since it would have included drinking wine, Samson may have violated his Nazirite vow (see 13:4,7).

14:11 *companions.* These are the "attendants of the bridegroom" (cf. Matt 9:15). They were probably charged with protecting the wedding party against marauders.

14:12 *riddle.* The use of riddles at feasts and special occasions was popular in the ancient world. *changes of clothes.* Mentioned, together with silver, as gifts of great value in Gen 45:22; 2 Kin 5:22 (see also Zech 14:14).

14:16 *do not love me.* Delilah used the same tactics (16:15).

"If you had not plowed with my heifer,
You would not have found out my
riddle."

19 Then [a]the Spirit of the LORD [1]came upon him mightily, and he went down to Ashkelon and killed thirty of them and took their spoil and gave the changes *of clothes* to those who told the riddle. And his anger burned, and he went up to his father's house.

20 But Samson's wife was [a]*given* to his companion who had been his [1]friend.

Samson Burns Philistine Crops

15 But after a while, in the time of wheat harvest, Samson visited his wife [a]with a young goat, and said, "I will go in to my wife in *her* room." But her father did not let him enter.

2 Her father said, "I really thought that you hated her intensely; so I [a]gave her to your companion. Is not her younger sister [1]more beautiful than she? Please let her be yours [2]instead."

3 Samson then said to them, "This time I shall be blameless in regard to the Philistines when I do them harm."

4 Samson went and caught three hundred foxes, and took torches, and turned *the foxes* tail to tail and put one torch in the middle between two tails.

5 When he had set fire to the torches, he released [1]the foxes into the standing grain of the Philistines, thus burning up both the shocks and the standing grain, along with the vineyards *and* groves.

6 Then the Philistines said, "Who did this?" And they said, "Samson, the son-in-law of the Timnite, because [1]he took his wife and gave her to his companion." So the Philistines came up and [a]burned her and her father with fire.

7 Samson said to them, "Since you act like this, I will surely take revenge on you, but after that I will quit."

8 He struck them [1]ruthlessly with a great slaughter; and he went down and lived in the cleft of the rock of Etam.

9 Then the Philistines went up and camped in Judah, and spread out in Lehi.

10 The men of Judah said, "Why have you come up against us?" And they said, "We have come up to bind Samson in order to do to him as he did to us."

11 Then 3,000 men of Judah went down to the cleft of the rock of Etam and said to Samson, "Do you not know [a]that the Philistines are rulers over us? What then is this that you have done to us?" And he said to them, "As they did to me, so I have done to them."

12 They said to him, "We have come down to bind you so that we may give you into the hands of the Philistines." And Samson said to them, "Swear to me that you will not [1]kill me."

13 So they said to [1]him, "No, but we will bind you fast and give you into their hands; yet surely we will not kill you." Then they bound him with two new ropes and brought him up from the rock.

14 When he came to Lehi, the Philistines shouted as they met him. And [a]the Spirit of the LORD [1]came upon him mightily so that the ropes that were on his arms were as flax that is burned with fire, and his bonds [2]dropped from his hands.

15 He found a fresh jawbone of a donkey, so he [1]reached out and took it and [2]killed [a]a thousand men with it.

16 Then Samson said,

"With the jawbone of a donkey,
[1]Heaps upon heaps,
With the jawbone of a donkey
I have [2]killed a thousand men."

17 When he had finished speaking, he

19 [1]Lit *rushed upon* [a]Judg 3:10; 13:25 **20** [1]Or *best man* [a]Judg 15:2 **15:1** [a]Gen 38:17 **2** [1]Lit *better* [2]Lit *instead of her* [a]Judg 14:20 **5** [1]Lit *them* **6** [1]I.e. the Timnite [a]Judg 14:15

8 [1]Lit *leg on thigh* **11** [a]Lev 26:25; Deut 28:43f; Judg 13:1; 14:4; Ps 106:40-42 **12** [1]Lit *fall upon me yourselves* **13** [1]Lit *him, saying* **14** [1]Lit *rushed upon* [2]Lit *were melted* [a]Judg 14:19; 1 Sam 11:6 **15** [1]Lit *stretched out his hand* [2]Lit *smote* [a]Lev 26:8; Josh 23:10 **16** [1]Lit *Heap, two heaps;* Heb is same root as donkey [2]Lit *smitten*

14:18 *my heifer.* Samson's wife (see v. 15). Since heifers were not used for plowing, Samson is accusing them of unfairness.
14:19 *Spirit . . . came upon him.* God's purposes for Samson included humbling the Philistines. *Ashkelon.* One of the five principal cities of the Philistines (see map, p. 312).
14:20 *companion.* See 15:2; probably the young man who had attended Samson (cf. John 3:29), in all likelihood one of his 30 companions (v. 11).
15:1 *time of wheat harvest.* Near the end of May or the beginning of June (see note on Ruth 1:22). *young goat.* Such a gift was customary, as with Judah and Tamar (Gen 38:17).
15:2 *younger sister.* Samson's father-in-law felt he had to make a counterproposal because he had received the bride-price from Samson. Similar marital transactions were made by Laban and Jacob (Gen 29:16–28) and Saul and David (1 Sam 18:19–21).
15:4 *foxes.* The Hebrew word may refer to foxes or jackals, both of which are still found in modern Israel.
15:5 *burning up.* The wheat harvest (v. 1) comes at the end of a long dry season, thus making the fields extremely vulnerable to fire.
15:7 *revenge.* A common feature of life in the ancient Near East. Six cities of refuge were designated by the Lord to prevent endless killings (Josh 20:1–9).
15:9 *Lehi.* Means "jawbone." This locality probably did not receive the name until after the events described here; the author uses the name in anticipation of those events—a common device in Hebrew narrative. The exact site of Lehi is not known.
15:11 *3,000 men of Judah.* The only time a force from Judah is explicitly mentioned in connection with any of the judges (but see note on 1:2). The men of Judah were well aware of Samson's capabilities, and even with a large force they did not attempt to tie him up without his consent (vv. 12–13). *Philistines are rulers over us.* Much of Judah was under Philistine rule, and the tribe was apparently content to accept it. They mustered a force, not to support Samson, but to capture him for the Philistines.
15:14 *shouted.* A battle cry (see 1 Sam 17:52). They came shouting against Samson as the lion had come roaring against him (14:5). *Spirit of the LORD.* See notes on 3:10; 11:29; 14:19.
15:15 *killed a thousand men with it.* Cf. the exploits of Shamgar, who struck down 600 Philistines with an oxgoad (3:31).

threw the jawbone from his hand; and he
named that place [1]Ramath-lehi.
18 Then he became very thirsty, and he
[a]called to the LORD and said, "You have giv-
en this great deliverance by the hand of Your
servant, and now [1]shall I die of thirst [2]and
fall into the hands of the uncircumcised?"
19 But God split the hollow place that is in
Lehi so that water came out of it. When he
drank, [a]his [1]strength returned and he
revived. Therefore he named it [2]En-hakkore,
which is in Lehi to this day.
20 So [a]he judged Israel twenty years in
[b]the days of the Philistines.

Samson's Weakness

16 Now Samson went to [a]Gaza and saw a
harlot there, and went in to her.
2 *When it was told* to the Gazites, saying,
"Samson has come here," they [a]surrounded
the place and lay in wait for him all night at
the gate of the city. And they kept silent all
night, saying, "*Let us wait* until the morning
light, then we will kill him."
3 Now Samson lay until midnight, and at
midnight he arose and took hold of the doors
of the city gate and the two posts and pulled
them up along with the bars; then he put
them on his shoulders and carried them up
to the top of the mountain which is opposite
Hebron.
4 After this it came about that he loved a
woman in the valley of Sorek, whose name
was Delilah.
5 The [a]lords of the Philistines came up to
her and said to her, "[b]Entice him, and see
where his great strength *lies* and [1]how we
may overpower him that we may bind him to
afflict him. Then we will each give you
eleven hundred *pieces* of silver."
6 So Delilah said to Samson, "Please tell
me where your great strength is and [1]how
you may be bound to afflict you."
7 Samson said to her, "If they bind me
with seven fresh cords that have not been
dried, then I will become weak and be like
any *other* man."
8 Then the lords of the Philistines
brought up to her seven fresh cords that had
not been dried, and she bound him with
them.
9 Now she had *men* lying in wait in an
inner room. And she said to him, "The Philistines are upon you, Samson!" But he
snapped the cords as a string of tow snaps
when it [1]touches fire. So his strength was not
discovered.
10 Then Delilah said to Samson, "Behold,
you have deceived me and told me lies; now
please tell me [1]how you may be bound."
11 He said to her, "If they bind me tightly
with new ropes [1]which have not been used,
then I will become weak and be like any *other* man."
12 So Delilah took new ropes and bound
him with them and said to him, "The Philistines are upon you, Samson!" For the *men*
were lying in wait in the inner room. But he
snapped [1]the ropes from his arms like a
thread.
13 Then Delilah said to Samson, "Up to
now you have deceived me and told me lies;
tell me [1]how you may be bound." And he
said to her, "If you weave the seven locks of
my [2]hair with the web [3][and fasten it with a
pin, then I will become weak and be like any
other man."
14 So while he slept, Delilah took the sev-
en locks of his [1]hair and wove them into the
web]. And she fastened *it* with the pin and
said to him, "The Philistines are upon you,
Samson!" But he awoke from his sleep and
pulled out the pin of the loom and the web.

Delilah Extracts His Secret

15 Then she said to him, "[a]How can you
say, 'I love you,' when your heart is not with
me? You have deceived me these three times

17 [1]I.e. the high place of the jawbone
18 [1]Or *I shall... uncircumcised* [2]Or *or* [a]Judg 16:28
19 [1]Lit *spirit* [2]I.e. the spring of him who called [a]Is 40:29
20 [a]Judg 16:31; Heb 11:32 [b]Judg 13:1
16:1 [a]Josh 15:47
2 [a]1 Sam 23:26; Ps 118:10-12
5 [1]Lit *by what* [a]Josh 13:3 [b]Judg 14:15
6 [1]Lit *by what*

9 [1]Lit *smells*
10 [1]Lit *by what*
11 [1]Lit *with which work has not been done*
12 [1]Lit *them*
13 [1]Lit *by what* [2]Lit *head* [3]The passage in brackets is found in Gr but not in any Heb mss
14 [1]Lit *head*
15 [a]Judg 14:16

15:18 *shall I die of thirst . . . ?* Mighty Samson was, after all, only a mortal man.
15:19 *water came out of it.* God provided for Samson as He had for Israel in the wilderness. See Ex 17:1–7 (Massah and Meribah); Num 20:2–13 (Meribah).
15:20 *judged Israel . . . years.* See note on 12:7. *twenty years.* Round numbers are frequently used in Judges (see Introduction: Background).
16:1 *Gaza.* An important Philistine seaport on the Mediterranean coast of the southwest portion of Canaan. *harlot.* While Samson certainly possessed physical strength, he lacked moral strength, which ultimately led to his ruin.
16:2 *morning light.* By that time they expected Samson to be exhausted and sleeping soundly.
16:3 *bars.* Probably made of bronze (1 Kin 4:13) or iron (Ps 107:16; Is 45:2). *opposite Hebron.* That is, in the direction of Hebron, which was 38 miles away in the hill country. Since Hebron was the chief city of Judah, this must be seen as Samson's response to what the men of Judah had done to him (see 15:11–13).
16:5 *lords of the Philistines.* See note on 3:3. *overpower him.* The Philistines were not interested in killing him quickly; they sought revenge by a prolonged period of torture. *eleven hundred pieces of silver.* An extraordinarily generous payment in light of 17:10 (see note there). (The total amount paid by the five Philistines would have been equivalent to the price of 275 slaves, at the rate offered for Joseph centuries earlier; see Gen 37:28.) Micah stole a similar amount of silver from his mother (17:2).
16:7 *seven fresh cords.* The number seven had special significance to the ancients, symbolizing completeness or fullness. Note that Samson's hair was divided into seven braids (v. 13).
16:11 *new ropes.* The Philistines apparently did not know that this method had already been tried and had failed (15:13–14).
16:13 Out of disdain, Samson arrogantly played with his Philistine adversaries. *fasten it with a pin.* Probably from a weaver's shuttle. The details of the account suggest that the loom in question was the vertical type with a crossbeam from which warp threads were suspended. Samson's long hair was woven into the warp and beaten up into the web with the pin, thus forming a tight fabric.

and have not told me where your great
strength is."
16 It came about when she pressed him
daily with her words and urged him, that his
soul was [1]annoyed to death.
17 So he told her all *that was* in his heart
and said to her, "A razor has never come on
my head, for I have been a [a]Nazirite to God
from my mother's womb. If I am shaved,
then my strength will leave me and I will
become weak and be like any *other* man."
18 When Delilah saw that he had told her
all *that was* in his heart, she sent and called
the lords of the Philistines, saying, "Come up
once more, for he has told me all *that is* in
his heart." Then the lords of the Philistines
came up to her and brought the money in
their hands.
19 She made him sleep on her knees, and
called for a man and had him shave off the
seven locks of his [1]hair. Then she began to
afflict him, and his strength left him.
20 She said, "The Philistines are upon
you, Samson!" And he awoke from his sleep
and said, "I will go out as at other times and
shake myself free." But he did not know that
[a]the LORD had departed from him.
21 Then the Philistines seized him and
gouged out his eyes; and they brought him
down to Gaza and bound him with bronze
chains, and he was a grinder in the prison.
22 However, the hair of his head began to
grow again after it was shaved off.
23 Now the lords of the Philistines assembled to offer a great sacrifice to [a]Dagon their
god, and to rejoice, for they said,

"Our god has given Samson our enemy
into our hands."

24 When the people saw him, [a]they
praised their god, for they said,

"Our god has given our enemy into our
hands,
Even the destroyer of our country,
Who has slain many of us."

25 It so happened when [1]they were in high
spirits, that they said, "Call for Samson, that
he may amuse us." So they called for Samson
from the prison, and he [2]entertained them.
And they made him stand between the pillars.
26 Then Samson said to the boy who was
holding his hand, "Let me feel the pillars on
which the house rests, that I may lean
against them."
27 Now the house was full of men and
women, and all the lords of the Philistines
were there. And about 3,000 men and
women were on the roof looking on while
Samson was amusing *them*.

Samson Is Avenged

28 [a]Then Samson called to the LORD and
said, "O Lord [1]GOD, please remember me
and please strengthen me just this time, O
God, that I may at once [b]be avenged of the
Philistines for my two eyes."
29 Samson grasped the two middle pillars
on which the house rested, and braced himself against them, the one with his right
hand and the other with his left.
30 And Samson said, "Let me die with the
Philistines!" And he bent with [1]all his might
so that the house fell on the lords and all the
people who were in it. So the dead whom he
killed at his death were more than those
whom he killed in his life.
31 Then his brothers and all his father's
household came down, took him, brought
him up and buried him between Zorah and
Eshtaol in the tomb of Manoah his father.
[a]Thus he had judged Israel twenty years.

Micah's Idolatry

17 Now there was a man of the hill country of Ephraim whose name was Micah.

16 [1]Lit *impatient to the point of* **17** [a]Num 6:2, 5; Judg 13:5 **19** [1]Lit *head* **20** [a]Num 14:42, 43; Josh 7:12; 1 Sam 16:14 **23** [a]1 Sam 5:2 **24** [a]1 Sam 31:9; 1 Chr 10:9; Ps 97:7

25 [1]Lit *their heart was pleasant* [2]Lit *made sport before them* **28** [1]Heb *YHWH*, usually rendered *LORD* [a]Judg 15:18 [b]Jer 15:15 **30** [1]Lit *strength* **31** [a]Judg 15:20

16:19–20 *his strength left him . . . the LORD had departed from him.* The source of Samson's strength was ultimately God Himself.
16:20 *he did not know.* One of the most tragic statements in the OT. Samson was unaware that he had betrayed his calling. He had permitted a Philistine woman to rob him of the sign of his special consecration to the Lord. The Lord's champion lay asleep and helpless in the arms of his paramour.
16:21 *gouged out his eyes.* Brutal treatment of prisoners of war to humiliate and incapacitate them was common (see 1 Sam 11:2; 2 Kin 25:7; see also note on Judg 1:6). *to Gaza.* In shame and weakness, Samson was led to Gaza, the place where he had displayed great strength (vv. 1–3). *he was a grinder.* See note on 9:53.
16:23 *Dagon.* See note on 10:6. *Our god has given.* It was common to attribute a victory to the national deities.
16:27 *on the roof.* The temple complex probably surrounded an open court and had a flat roof where a large number of people had gathered to get a glimpse of the fallen champion.
16:30 *bent.* Samson pushed the wooden pillars from their stone bases. Archaeologists have discovered a Philistine temple with a pair of closely spaced pillar bases. *killed . . . were more.* Samson previously had slain well over 1,000 people (see 15:15; see also 14:19; 15:8).
16:31 *came down, took him.* The freedom of his family to secure his body and give it a burial indicates that the Philistines had no intention of further dishonoring him (contrast Saul's death, 1 Sam 31:9–10). *judged Israel . . . years.* See note on 12:7. *twenty years.* Round numbers are frequently used in Judges (see Introduction: Background).
17:1–21:25 Two episodes forming an epilogue to the story of the judges (see Introduction: Literary Features). The events narrated evidently took place fairly early in the period of the judges (see notes on 18:30; 20:1,28). They illustrate the religious and moral degeneracy that characterized the age—when "there was no king in Israel" and "every man did what was right in his own eyes" (17:6; 21:25). Writing at a time when the monarchy under the Davidic dynasty had brought cohesion and order to the land and had reestablished a center for the worship of the Lord, the author portrays this earlier era of the judges as a dismal period of national decay, from which it was to be rescued by the house of David.
17:1–18:31 The first episode illustrates corruption in Israelite worship by telling of Micah's establishment of a local place of

2 He said to his mother, "The eleven hundred *pieces* of silver which were taken from you, about which you uttered a curse [1]in my hearing, behold, the silver is with me; I took it." And his mother said, "Blessed be my son by the LORD."

3 He then returned the eleven hundred *pieces* of silver to his mother, and his mother said, "I wholly dedicate the silver from my hand to the LORD for my son [a]to make a graven image and a molten image; now therefore, I will return [1]them to you."

4 So when he returned the silver to his mother, his mother took two hundred *pieces* of silver and gave them to the silversmith who made [1]them into a graven image and a molten image, and [2]they were in the house of Micah.

5 And the man Micah had a [1a]shrine and he made an [b]ephod and [2c]household idols and [3]consecrated one of his sons, [d]that he might become his priest.

6 In those days [a]there was no king in Israel; [b]every man did what was right in his own eyes.

7 Now there was a young man from [a]Bethlehem in Judah, of the family of Judah, who was a Levite; and he was [1]staying there.

8 Then the man departed from the city, from Bethlehem in Judah, to [1]stay wherever he might find *a place;* and as he made his journey, he came to the [a]hill country of Ephraim to the house of Micah.

9 Micah said to him, "Where do you come from?" And he said to him, "I am a Levite from Bethlehem in Judah, and I am going to [1]stay wherever I may find *a place.*"

10 Micah then said to him, "Dwell with me and be [a]a father and a priest to me, and I will give you ten *pieces* of silver a year, a suit of clothes, and your maintenance." So the Levite went *in.*

11 The Levite agreed to live with the man, and the young man became to him like one of his sons.

12 So Micah [1]consecrated the Levite, and the young man [a]became his priest and [2]lived in the house of Micah.

13 Then Micah said, "Now I know that the LORD will prosper me, seeing I have a Levite as priest."

Danites Seek Territory

18 [a]In those days there was no king of Israel; and [b]in those days the tribe of the Danites was seeking an inheritance for themselves to live in, for until that day [1]an inheritance had not [2]been allotted to them as a possession among the tribes of Israel.

2 So the sons of Dan sent from their family five men out of their whole number, [1]valiant men from [a]Zorah and Eshtaol, to spy out the land and to search it; and they said to them, "Go, search the land." And they came to [b]the hill country of Ephraim, to the house of Micah, and lodged there.

3 When they were near the house of Micah, they recognized the voice of the young man, the Levite; and they turned aside there and said to him, "Who brought you here? And what are you doing in this *place?* And what do you have here?"

4 He said to them, "Thus and so has Micah done to me, and he has hired me and [a]I have become his priest."

5 They said to him, "Inquire of God, please, that we may know whether our way on which we are going will be prosperous."

17:2 [1]Lit *and also spoke it in my ears* **3** [1]Lit *it* [a]Ex 20:4, 23; 34:17 **4** [1]Lit *it* [2]Lit *it was* **5** [1]Lit *house of gods* [2]Heb *teraphim* [3]Lit *filled the hand of* [a]Judg 18:24 [b]Judg 8:27; 18:14 [c]Gen 31:19 [d]Num 3:10 **6** [a]Judg 18:1; 19:1 [b]Deut 12:8; Judg 21:25 **7** [1]Or *sojourning* [a]Judg 19:1; Ruth 1:1, 2; Mic 5:2; Matt 2:1 **8** [1]Or *sojourn* [a]Josh 24:33 **9** [1]Or *sojourn* **10** [a]Judg 18:19

12 [1]Lit *filled the hand of* [2]Lit *was* [a]Num 16:10; 18:1-7 **18:1** [1]Lit *it* [2]Lit *fallen* [a]Judg 17:6; 19:1 [b]Josh 19:40-48 **2** [1]Lit *men, sons of valor* [a]Judg 13:25 [b]Judg 17:1 **4** [a]Judg 17:12

worship in Ephraim, aided by a Levite claiming descent from Moses. This paganized worship of the Lord is taken over by the tribe of Dan when that tribe abandons its appointed inheritance and migrates to Israel's northern frontier.

17:2 *eleven hundred pieces of silver.* See note on 16:5. *about which you uttered a curse.* Fear of the curse seems to have motivated his returning the stolen money. *Blessed be my son.* A blessing to counteract the curse.

17:3 *mother . . . son.* With their paganized view of the God of Israel, both were idolaters in disobedience to the law (Ex 20:4,23; Deut 4:16). *a graven image and a molten image.* The first was probably made of wood overlaid with silver; the second was made of solid silver or of cheaper metal overlaid with silver.

17:4 *silversmith.* A maker of idols, as in Acts 19:24 (cf. Is 40:19 and Jer 10:9, where the Hebrew for this word is translated "goldsmith").

17:5 *ephod.* See 8:27 and note on Ex 28:6. *idols.* Household gods, used in this case for divining (cf. Ezek 21:21; Zech 10:2). Some of them were in human form (1 Sam 19:13).

17:6 *was no king.* See 18:1; 19:1; 21:25; suggests that Judges was written after the establishment of the monarchy (see Introduction: Author and Date). *did what was right in his own eyes.* The expression implies that Israel had departed from the covenant standards of conduct found in the law (see Deut 12:8).

17:7 *Bethlehem in Judah.* Not among the 48 designated Levitical cities (Jos 21).

17:8 *departed from the city.* The failure of the Israelites to obey the law probably resulted in a lack of support for the Levites, which explains the man's wandering in search of his fortune.

17:10 *father.* A term of respect used also for Elijah (2 Kin 2:12) and Elisha (2 Kin 6:21; 13:14). See Gen 45:8; Matt 23:9. *ten pieces.* About four ounces. In the light of this remuneration for a year's service, the stated amounts in 16:5 and 17:2 take on special significance. The offer of wages, clothing and food was more than this Levite could resist (v. 11). Clearly material concerns were at the root of his decision, because later he accepts an even more attractive offer (18:19–20).

17:12 *consecrated the Levite.* An attempt to make his shrine legitimate and give it prestige. Micah probably removed his son (see v. 5).

18:1 *seeking an inheritance.* The Danite allotment was at the west end of the strip of land between Judah and Ephraim (Josh 19:41–46), but, due to the opposition of the Amorites (Judg 1:34) and the Philistines, the Danites were unable to occupy that territory (see note on 13:2).

18:2 *spy out.* See 1:23 and note on Num 13:2.

18:3 *recognized the voice.* Perhaps they recognized him by his dialect or accent.

18:5 *Inquire of God.* The request is for an oracle, probably by using the ephod and household gods (see note on 17:5). God had already revealed His will by the allotments given to the var-

6 The priest said to them, "Go in peace;
your way in which you are going [1]has the
LORD's approval."
7 Then the five men departed and came
to [a]Laish and saw the people who were in it
living in security, after the manner of the
Sidonians, quiet and secure; for there was no
[1]ruler humiliating *them* for anything in the
land, and they were far from the Sidonians
and had no dealings with anyone.
8 When they came back to their brothers
at Zorah and Eshtaol, their brothers said to
them, "What *do* you *report?*"
9 They said, "Arise, and let us go up
against them; for we have seen the land, and
behold, it is very good. And will you [1]sit
still? Do not delay to go, to enter, to possess
the land.
10 "When you enter, you will come to a
secure people with a spacious land; for God
has given it into your hand, [a]a place where
there is no lack of anything that is on the
earth."
11 Then from the family of the Danites,
from Zorah and from Eshtaol, six hundred
men armed with weapons of war set out.
12 They went up and camped at Kiriath-
jearim in Judah. Therefore they called that
place [1][a]Mahaneh-dan to this day; behold, it
is [2]west of Kiriath-jearim.
13 They passed from there to the hill
country of Ephraim and came to the house of
Micah.

Danites Take Micah's Idols

14 Then the five men who went to spy out
the country of Laish said to their kinsmen,
"Do you know that there are in these houses
[a]an ephod and [1]household idols and a
graven image and a molten image? Now
therefore, consider what you should do."
15 They turned aside there and came to
the house of the young man, the Levite, to
the house of Micah, and asked him of his
welfare.
16 The six hundred men armed with their
weapons of war, who were of the sons of
Dan, stood by the entrance of the gate.
17 Now the five men who went to spy out
the land went up *and* entered there, *and*
took [a]the graven image and the ephod and
[1]household idols and the molten image,
while the priest stood by the entrance of the
gate with the six hundred men armed with
weapons of war.
18 When these went into Micah's house
and took the graven image, the ephod and
[1]household idols and the molten image, the
priest said to them, "What are you doing?"
19 They said to him, "Be silent, [a]put your
hand over your mouth and come with us, and
be to us [b]a father and a priest. Is it better for
you to be a priest to the house of one man, or
to be priest to a tribe and a family in Israel?"
20 The priest's heart was glad, and he
took the ephod and [1]household idols and the
graven image and went among the people.
21 Then they turned and departed, and
put the little ones and the livestock and the
valuables in front of them.
22 When they had gone some distance
from the house of Micah, the men who *were*
in the houses near Micah's house assembled
and overtook the sons of Dan.
23 They cried to the sons of Dan, who
turned [1]around and said to Micah, "What is
the matter with you, that you have assembled together?"
24 He said, "You have taken away my
gods which I made, and the priest, and have
gone away, and what do I have besides? So
how can you say to me, 'What is *the matter*
with you?' "
25 The sons of Dan said to him, "Do not let
your voice be heard among us, or else [1]fierce
men will fall upon you and you will [2]lose
your life, with the lives of your household."
26 So the sons of Dan went on their way;
and when Micah saw that they were too
strong for him, he turned and went back to
his house.
27 Then they took what Micah had made
and the priest who had belonged to him, and

6 [1]Lit *is before the LORD*
7 [1]Lit *possessor of restraint* [a]Josh 19:47; Judg 18:29
9 [1]Lit *be*
10 [a]Deut 8:9
12 [1]I.e. the camp of Dan [2]Lit *behind* [a]Judg 13:25
14 [1]Heb *teraphim* [a]Judg 17:5
17 [1]Heb *teraphim* [a]Gen 31:19, 30; Is 41:29; Mic 5:13
18 [1]Heb *teraphim*
19 [a]Job 21:5; 29:9; 40:4 [b]Judg 17:10
20 [1]Heb *teraphim*
23 [1]Lit *their faces*
25 [1]Lit *bitter of soul* [2]Lit *gather*

---

ious tribes (Josh 14–20). They were searching for an oracle that would guarantee the success of their journey.

18:6 *Go in peace.* The Levite gave them the message they wanted to hear. He was even careful to use the name of the Lord to give the message credibility and authority.

18:7 *Laish.* The journey northward was about 100 miles from Zorah and Eshtaol (v. 2). This town is called Leshem in Josh 19:47. After its capture by the Danites, Laish was renamed Dan (v. 29), and it was Israel's northernmost settlement (see 20:1; 1 Sam 3:20; 2 Sam 3:10). Excavations there have disclosed that the earliest Israelite occupation of Dan was in the 12th century B.C. and that the first Israelite inhabitants apparently lived in tents or temporary huts. Occupation of the site continued into the Assyrian period, but the town was destroyed and rebuilt many times. A large high place attached to the city was often extensively rebuilt and refurbished and was in use into the Hellenistic period. *Sidonians.* A peaceful Phoenician people who engaged in commerce throughout the Mediterranean world. *had no dealings.* They did not feel threatened by other powers and therefore sought no treaties for mutual defense.

18:11 *six hundred men.* As leaders of the tribe of Dan, they represented the entire tribe's migration to its new location in the north. Cf. the 600 men who constituted the remnant of the tribe of Benjamin (20:47).

18:19 *father.* See note on 17:10. *a tribe and family.* Only one clan from the tribe of Dan is ever mentioned—Shuham (Num 26:42; called Hushim in Gen 46:23). The Danites appealed to the Levite's vanity and materialism.

18:21 *in front of them.* For protection in case of attack; see Gen 33:2–3 (Jacob and Esau).

18:24 *You have taken away my gods.* Micah was concerned about the loss of gods that could not even protect themselves. *what do I have besides?* The agonizing cry of one whose faith is centered in helpless gods.

came to [a]Laish, to a people quiet and secure, and struck them with the edge of the sword; and they burned the city with fire.

28 And there was no one to deliver *them,* because it was far from Sidon and they had no dealings with anyone, and it was in the valley which is near [a]Beth-rehob. And they rebuilt the city and lived in it.

29 [a]They called the name of the city Dan, after the name of Dan their father who was born in Israel; however, the name of the city formerly was Laish.

30 The sons of Dan set up for themselves [a]the graven image; and Jonathan, the son of [b]Gershom, the son of [1]Manasseh, [a]he and his sons were priests to the tribe of the Danites until the day of the captivity of the land.

31 So they set up for themselves Micah's graven image which he had made, all the time that the [a]house of God was at Shiloh.

A Levite's Concubine Degraded

19 Now it came about in those days, when [a]there was no king in Israel, that there was a certain Levite [1]staying in the remote part of the hill country of Ephraim, who took a concubine for himself from Bethlehem in Judah.

2 But his concubine played the harlot against him, and she went away from him to her father's house in Bethlehem in Judah, and was there for a period of four months.

3 Then her husband arose and went after her to [a]speak [1]tenderly to her in order to bring her back, [2]taking with him his servant and a pair of donkeys. So she brought him into her father's house, and when the girl's father saw him, he was glad to meet him.

4 His father-in-law, the girl's father, detained him; and he remained with him three days. So they ate and drank and lodged there.

5 Now on the fourth day they got up early in the morning, and he [1]prepared to go; and the girl's father said to his son-in-law, "[a]Sustain [2]yourself with a piece of bread, and afterward you may go."

6 So both of them sat down and ate and drank together; and the girl's father said to the man, "Please be willing to spend the night, and [a]let your heart be merry."

7 Then the man arose to go, but his father-in-law urged him so that he spent the night there again.

8 On the fifth day he arose to go early in the morning, and the girl's father said, "Please sustain [1]yourself, and wait until [2]afternoon"; so both of them ate.

9 When the man arose to go along with his concubine and servant, his father-in-law, the girl's father, said to him, "Behold now, the day has drawn [1]to a close; please spend the night. Lo, the day is [2]coming to an end; spend the night here that your heart may be merry. Then tomorrow you may arise early for your journey so that you may go [3]home."

10 But the man was not willing to spend the night, so he arose and departed and came to *a place* opposite [a]Jebus (that is, Jerusalem). And there were with him a pair of saddled donkeys; his concubine also was with him.

11 When they *were* near Jebus, the day was almost gone; and [a]the servant said to his master, "Please come, and let us turn aside into this city of the Jebusites and spend the night in it."

12 However, his master said to him, "We will not turn aside into the city of foreigners who are not of the sons of Israel; but we will go on as far as Gibeah."

13 He said to his servant, "Come and let us approach one of these places; and we will spend the night in Gibeah or Ramah."

14 So they passed along and went their way, and the sun set on them near Gibeah which belongs to Benjamin.

27 [a]Josh 19:47; Judg 18:7
28 [a]2 Sam 10:6
29 [a]Josh 19:47
30 [1]Some ancient versions read *Moses* [a]Judg 17:3, 5 [b]Ex 2:22; 18:3
31 [a]Josh 18:1
19:1 [1]Or *sojourning* [a]Judg 18:1
3 [1]Lit *to her heart* [2]Lit *and* [a]Gen 34:3; 50:21
5 [1]Lit *arose*

5 [2]Lit *your heart* [a]Gen 18:5; Judg 19:8
6 [a]Judg 16:25; 19:9, 22; Ruth 3:7; 1 Kin 21:7; Esth 1:10
8 [1]Lit *your heart* [2]Lit *the day declines*
9 [1]Lit *toward evening* [2]Lit *declining* [3]Lit *to your tent*
10 [a]1 Chr 11:4, 5
11 [a]Judg 19:19

18:28 *Beth-rehob.* Probably the same as Rehob in Num 13:21.
18:30 *Manasseh.* The original reading appears to have been "Moses" (supported by an ancient Hebrew scribal tradition, some Greek Septuagint manuscripts and the Latin Vulgate). The Levite Jonathan would then be identified as the son of Gershom, the son of Moses (Ex 2:22; 18:3; 1 Chr 23:14–15). In an effort to prevent desecration of the name of Moses, later scribes modified the name slightly, making it read "Manasseh." If Jonathan was the grandson of Moses, the events in this chapter must have occurred early in the period of the judges (see notes on 20:1,28). *captivity of the land.* The date of this captivity has not been determined (see note on v. 7 regarding Laish).
18:31 *all the time that the house of God was at Shiloh.* See Josh 18:1. For Shiloh's destruction see Ps 78:60; Jer 7:12,14; 26:6. Archaeological work at Shiloh indicates that the site was destroyed c. 1050 B.C. and was left uninhabited for many centuries.
19:1–21:25 The second episode of the epilogue (see note on 17:1–18:31). It illustrates Israel's moral corruption by telling of the degenerate act of the men of Gibeah—an act remembered centuries later (Hos 9:9; 10:9). Although that town showed itself to be as wicked as any Canaanite town, it was defended by the rest of the tribe of Benjamin against the Lord's discipline through the Israelites, until nearly the whole tribe was destroyed.
19:1–30 An account of an Israelite town that revived the ways of Sodom (see Ge 19).
19:1 *Levite.* Unlike the Levite of chs. 17–18, this man is not named. *concubine.* See note on Gen 25:6.
19:3 *glad to meet him.* The separation of the concubine from the Levite was probably a matter of family disgrace, and so his father-in-law was glad for the prospect of the two being reunited.
19:10 *Jebus.* See 1:21; see also note on Gen 10:16.
19:12 *city of foreigners.* With the city under the control of the Jebusites, the Levite was afraid that he would receive no hospitality and might be in mortal danger.
19:14 *Gibeah . . . Benjamin.* Distinguished from the Gibeah in Judah (Josh 15:20,57) and the Gibeah in the hill country of Ephraim (Josh 24:33). As the political capital of Saul's kingdom, it is called Gibeah of Saul in 1 Sam 11:4; see also 1 Sam 13:15.

15 They turned aside there in order to enter *and* lodge in Gibeah. When [1]they entered, [1]they sat down in the open square of the city, for no one took them into *his* house to spend the night.

16 Then behold, an old man was coming out of the field from his work at evening. Now the man was from [a]the hill country of Ephraim, and he was [1]staying in Gibeah, but the men of the place [b]were Benjamites.

17 And he lifted up his eyes and saw the traveler in the open square of the city; and the old man said, "Where are you going, and where do you come from?"

18 He said to him, "We are passing from Bethlehem in Judah to the remote part of the hill country of Ephraim, *for* I am from there, and I went to Bethlehem in Judah. But I am *now* going to [1]my house, and no man will take me into his house.

19 "Yet there is both straw and fodder for our donkeys, and also bread and wine for me, [1]your maidservant, and [a]the young man who is with your servants; there is no lack of anything."

20 The old man said, "[a]Peace to you. Only let me *take care of* all your needs; however, do not spend the night in the open square."

21 [a]So he took him into his house and gave the donkeys fodder, and they washed their feet and ate and drank.

22 While they were [1]celebrating, behold, [a]the men of the city, certain [2][b]worthless fellows, surrounded the house, pounding the door; and they spoke to the owner of the house, the old man, saying, "Bring out the man who came into your house that we may have [3]relations with him."

23 Then the man, the owner of the house, went out to them and said to them, "No, my fellows, please do not act so wickedly; since this man has come into my house, [a]do not commit this act of folly.

24 "[a]Here is my virgin daughter and his concubine. Please let me bring them out that you may ravish them and do to them [1]whatever you wish. But do not commit such an act of folly against this man."

25 But the men would not listen to him. So the man seized his concubine and brought *her* out to them; and they raped her and abused her all night until morning, then let her go at the approach of dawn.

26 [1]As the day began to dawn, the woman came and fell down at the doorway of the man's house where her master was, until *full* daylight.

27 When her master arose in the morning and opened the doors of the house and went out to go on his way, then behold, his concubine was lying at the doorway of the house with her hands on the threshold.

28 He said to her, "Get up and let us go," [a]but there was no answer. Then he placed her on the donkey; and the man arose and went to his [1]home.

29 When he entered his house, he took a knife and laid hold of his concubine and [a]cut her in twelve pieces, limb by limb, and sent her throughout the territory of Israel.

30 All who saw *it* said, "Nothing like this has *ever* happened or been seen from the day when the sons of Israel came up from the land of Egypt to this day. Consider it, [a]take counsel and speak up!"

Resolve to Punish the Guilty

20 Then all the sons of Israel from Dan to Beersheba, including the land of Gilead, came out, and the congregation assembled as one man to the LORD at [a]Mizpah.

2 The [1]chiefs of all the people, *even* of all

15 [1]So with Gr; M.T. *he*
16 [1]Or *sojourning* [a]Judg 19:1 [b]Judg 19:14
18 [1]Heb *the house of the LORD*, cf v 29
19 [1]I.e. my concubine [a]Judg 19:11
20 [a]Gen 43:23; Judg 6:23
21 [a]Gen 24:32, 33
22 [1]Lit *making their hearts merry* [2]Lit *sons of Belial* [3]Lit *intercourse* [a]Gen 19:4, 5; Ezek 16:46-48 [b]Deut 13:13; 1 Sam 2:12; 1 Kin 21:10; 2 Cor 6:15
23 [a]Gen 34:7; Deut 22:21; Judg 20:6; 2 Sam 13:12
24 [1]Lit *the good in your eyes* [a]Gen 19:8
26 [1]Lit *At the turning of the morning*
28 [1]Lit *place* [a]Judg 20:5
29 [a]1 Sam 11:7
30 [a]Judg 20:7; Prov 13:10
20:1 [a]1 Sam 7:5
2 [1]Lit *cornerstones*

19:15 *took them into his house.* See notes on 13:15; Gen 18:2.

19:18 *my house.* Apparently the Levite was planning to go to Shiloh (see 18:31; Josh 18:1) to present a thank offering to the Lord or a sin offering for himself and his concubine.

19:21 *washed their feet.* An evidence of hospitality in the ancient Near East, where travelers commonly wore sandals as they walked the dusty roads (see Gen 18:4; 24:32; 43:24; Luke 7:44; John 13:5–14).

19:22 *worthless fellows.* The Hebrew for this expression refers to the morally depraved (see note on Deut 13:13). Elsewhere the expression is associated with idolatry (Deut 13:13), drunkenness (1 Sam 1:16) and rebellion (1 Sam 2:12). Here the reference is to homosexuality. *Bring out the man.* The sexual perversion of these wicked men is yet another example of the decadence of an age when "every man did what was right in his own eyes" (17:6; 21:25). A similar request was made by the men of Sodom (Gen 19:5). Homosexuality was common among the Canaanites.

19:23 *do not act so wickedly.* An expression of outrage at the willful perversion of what is right and natural (see Gen 19:7; 2 Sam 13:12; see also Rom 1:27).

19:24 *my virgin daughter and his concubine.* The tragedy of this story lies not only in the decadence of Gibeah, but also in the callous selfishness of men who would betray defenseless women to be brutally violated for a whole night. Cf. Gen 19:8, where Lot offered his two daughters to the men of Sodom.

19:29 *cut her in twelve pieces.* Dismembering the concubine's body and sending parts to each of the 12 tribes was intended to awaken Israel from its moral lethargy and to marshal the tribes to face up to their responsibility. It is ironic that the one who issued such a call was himself so selfish and insensitive. See also Saul's similar action in 1 Sam 11:7.

20:1–48 All Israel (except Jabesh-gilead; see 21:8–9) assembled before the Lord to deal with the moral outrage committed by the men of Gibeah. Having first inquired of God for divine direction, they marched against Gibeah and the Benjamites as the disciplinary arm of the Lord (see Josh 22:11–34), following Him as their King.

20:1 *Dan to Beersheba.* A conventional way of speaking of all Israel from north (Dan) to south (Beersheba); see 1 Sam 3:20; 2 Sam 3:10; 24:2; 1 Chr 21:2; 2 Chr 30:5. The use of this expression, however, does not mean that the events of this chapter occurred after Dan's move to the north (18:27–29); rather, it indicates the author's perspective at the time of writing

the tribes of Israel, took their stand in the
assembly of the people of God, 400,000 foot
[2]soldiers [a]who drew the sword.
3 (Now the sons of Benjamin heard that
the sons of Israel had gone up to Mizpah.)
And the sons of Israel said, "Tell *us,* how did
this wickedness take place?"
4 So the Levite, the husband of the woman who was murdered, answered and said,
"I came with my concubine to spend the
night at Gibeah which belongs to Benjamin.
5 "But the [a]men of Gibeah rose up against
me and surrounded the house at night
because of me. They intended to kill me;
instead, they [b]ravished my concubine so that
she died.
6 "And I [a]took hold of my concubine and
cut her in pieces and sent her throughout
the land of Israel's inheritance; for [b]they
have committed a lewd and disgraceful act
in Israel.
7 "Behold, all you sons of Israel, [a]give
your advice and counsel here."
8 Then all the people arose as one man,
saying, "Not one of us will go to his tent, nor
will any of us return to his house.
9 "But now this is the thing which we will
do to Gibeah; *we will go up* against it by lot.
10 "And we will take 10 men out of 100
throughout the tribes of Israel, and 100 out of
1,000, and 1,000 out of 10,000 to [1]supply
food for the people, that when they come to
[2]Gibeah of Benjamin, they may [3]punish
them for all the disgraceful acts that they
have committed in Israel."
11 Thus all the men of Israel were gathered against the city, united as one man.
12 Then the tribes of Israel sent men
through the entire [1]tribe of Benjamin, saying, "What is this wickedness that has taken
place among you?
13 "Now then, deliver up the men, the
[1a]worthless fellows in Gibeah, that we may
put them to death and [b]remove *this* wickedness from Israel." But the sons of Benjamin
would not listen to the voice of their brothers, the sons of Israel.

2 [2]Lit *men* [a]Judg 8:10
5 [a]Judg 19:22 [b]Judg 19:25f
6 [a]Judg 19:29 [b]Gen 34:7; Josh 7:15
7 [a]Judg 19:30
10 [1]Lit *take* [2]Heb *Geba* [3]Lit *do*
12 [1]Lit *tribes*
13 [1]Lit *sons of Belial* [a]2 Cor 6:15 [b]Deut 13:5; 17:12; 1 Cor 5:13

14 The sons of Benjamin gathered from
the cities to Gibeah, to go out to battle
against the sons of Israel.
15 From the cities on that day the [a]sons of
Benjamin were [1]numbered, 26,000 men who
draw the sword, besides the inhabitants of
Gibeah who were [1]numbered, 700 choice
men.
16 Out of all these people 700 [a]choice men
were left-handed; each one could sling a
stone at a hair and not miss.
17 Then the men of Israel besides Benjamin were [1]numbered, 400,000 men who
draw the sword; all these were men of war.

Civil War, Benjamin Defeated

18 Now the sons of Israel arose, went up
to Bethel, and [a]inquired of God and said,
"Who shall go up first for us to battle against
the sons of Benjamin?" Then the LORD said,
"Judah *shall go up* first."
19 So the sons of Israel arose in the morning and camped against Gibeah.
20 The men of Israel went out to battle
against Benjamin, and the men of Israel
arrayed for battle against them at Gibeah.
21 Then the sons of Benjamin came out of
Gibeah and [1a]felled to the ground on that
day 22,000 men of Israel.
22 But the people, the men of Israel,
encouraged themselves and arrayed for battle again in the place where they had arrayed
themselves the first day.
23 [a]The sons of Israel went up and wept
before the LORD until evening, and [b]inquired
of the LORD, saying, "Shall we again draw
near for battle against the sons of my brother Benjamin?" And the LORD said, "Go up
against him."
24 Then the sons of Israel [1]came against
the sons of Benjamin the second day.
25 Benjamin went out [1]against them from
Gibeah the second day and [2]felled to the
ground again 18,000 men of the sons of Israel; all these drew the sword.
26 Then [a]all the sons of Israel and all the
people went up and came to Bethel and

15 [1]Or *mustered* [a]Num 1:36, 37; 2:23; 26:41
16 [a]Judg 3:15; 1 Chr 12:2
17 [1]Or *mustered*
18 [a]Num 27:21; Judg 20:23, 27
21 [1]Lit *destroyed* [a]Judg 20:25
23 [a]Josh 7:6, 7 [b]Judg 20:18
24 [1]Lit *approached*
25 [1]Lit *to meet* [2]Lit *destroyed*
26 [a]Judg 20:23; 21:2

(Judges was probably written after the Davidic dynasty was fully established; see Introduction: Author and Date). Here the expression refers to the disciplinary action of all Israel (except Jabesh-gilead; see 21:8–9) against Gibeah and the rest of the Benjamites. Such a united response must have occurred early in the time of the judges, before the period of foreign domination of various parts of the land. *assembled . . . at Mizpah.* A gathering place of the tribes during the days of Saul (1 Sam 7:5–17; 10:17). *as one man.* Cf. vv. 8,11; 1 Sam 11:7.

20:9 *lot.* Casting lots was a common method of determining the will of God (see notes on Ex 28:30; Jon 1:7; Acts 1:26).

20:10 *10 men.* Support for the large army had to be well organized and efficient. One man was responsible for providing food for nine men fighting at the front.

20:13 *deliver up . . . the worthless fellows.* The demand of Israel was not unreasonable. They wanted to punish only those directly involved in the crime. *worthless fellows.* See note on Deut 13:13. *put them to death.* The sin of the men of Gibeah called for the death penalty, and Israel had to punish the sin if she was to avoid guilt herself (see Deut 13:5; 17:7; 19:19–20).

20:16 *left-handed.* The Benjamite Ehud was also left-handed (3:15). *sling a stone.* Cf. Zech 9:15. The sling was a very effective weapon, as David later demonstrated in his encounter with Goliath (1 Sam 17:49). A slingstone, weighing one pound or more, could be hurled at 90–100 miles an hour. *miss.* In other contexts the Hebrew for this verb is translated "to sin."

20:18 *Bethel.* At this time the ark of the covenant and the high priest Phinehas were at Bethel (see vv. 26–28). *inquired of God.* Probably by priestly use of Urim and Thummim (see notes on Ex 28:30; 1 Sam 2:28). *Who shall go up first . . . ?* See 1:1–36. *Judah.* See note on 1:2.

20:21 *22,000 men of Israel.* A rousing victory for the Benjamites, who numbered 25,700 and therefore had slain nearly one man apiece.

wept; thus they remained there before the
LORD and fasted that day until evening. And
they offered burnt offerings and peace offerings before the LORD.
27 The sons of Israel [a]inquired of the LORD
(for the ark of the covenant of God *was* there
in those days,
28 and Phinehas the son of Eleazar, Aaron's son, stood before it to *minister* in those
days), saying, "Shall I yet again go out to
battle against the sons of my brother Benjamin, or shall I cease?" And the LORD said,
"Go up, [a]for tomorrow I will deliver them
into your hand."
29 [a]So Israel set men in ambush around
Gibeah.
30 The sons of Israel went up against the
sons of Benjamin on the third day and arrayed
themselves against Gibeah as at other times.
31 [a]The sons of Benjamin went out
[1]against the people and were drawn away
from the city, and they began to strike [2]and
kill some of the people as at other times, on
the highways, one of which goes up to Bethel and the other to Gibeah, *and* in the field,
about thirty men of Israel.
32 The sons of Benjamin said, "They are
struck down before us, as at the first." But
the sons of Israel said, "Let us flee that we
may draw them away from the city to the
highways."
33 Then all the men of Israel arose from
their place and arrayed themselves at Baal-
tamar; [a]and the men of Israel in ambush
broke out of their place, even out of Maareh-
geba.
34 When ten thousand choice men from
all Israel came against Gibeah, the battle
became [1]fierce; [a]but [2]Benjamin did not
know that [3]disaster was [4]close to them.
35 And the LORD struck Benjamin before
Israel, so that the sons of Israel destroyed
25,100 men of Benjamin that day, all [1]who
draw the sword.
36 So the sons of Benjamin saw that they
were [1]defeated. [a]When the men of Israel
gave [2]ground to Benjamin because they
relied on the men in ambush whom they had
set against Gibeah,
37 [a]the men in ambush hurried and
rushed against Gibeah; the men in ambush
also deployed and struck all the city with the
edge of the sword.
38 Now the appointed sign between the
men of Israel and the men in ambush was
[a]that they would make a great cloud of
smoke rise from the city.
39 Then the men of Israel turned in the
battle, and Benjamin began to strike [1]and kill
about thirty men of Israel, [a]for they said,
"Surely they are [2]defeated before us, as in
the first battle."
40 But when the cloud began to rise from
the city in a column of smoke, Benjamin
looked [a]behind them; and behold, the whole
city was going up *in smoke* to heaven.
41 Then the men of Israel turned, and the
men of Benjamin were terrified; for they saw
that [1a]disaster was [2]close to them.
42 Therefore, they turned their backs
before the men of Israel [a]toward the direction of the wilderness, but the battle overtook them while those who came out of the
cities destroyed them in the midst of them.
43 [a]They surrounded Benjamin, pursued
them without rest *and* trod them down
opposite Gibeah toward the [1]east.
44 Thus 18,000 men of Benjamin fell; all
these were valiant warriors.
45 [1]The rest turned and fled toward the
wilderness to the rock of [a]Rimmon, but they
[2]caught 5,000 of them on the highways and
overtook them [3]at Gidom and [4]killed 2,000
of them.
46 So all of Benjamin who fell that day
were 25,000 men who draw the sword; all
these were valiant warriors.
47 But 600 men turned and fled toward the
wilderness to the rock of Rimmon, and they
remained at the rock of Rimmon four months.
48 The men of Israel then turned back
against the sons of Benjamin and struck
them with the edge of the sword, both the
entire city with the cattle and all that they
found; they also set on fire all the cities
which they found.

Mourning Lost Tribe

21 Now the men of Israel [a]had sworn in
Mizpah, saying, "None of us shall give
his daughter to Benjamin [1]in marriage."
2 [a]So the people came to Bethel and sat

27 [a]Judg 20:18 **28** [a]Judg 7:9 **29** [a]Josh 8:4 **31** [1]Lit *to meet* [2]Lit *slain ones* [a]Josh 8:16 **33** [a]Josh 8:19 **34** [1]Lit *heavy* [2]Lit *they* [3]Lit *evil* [4]Lit *touching* [a]Josh 8:14; Job 21:13 **35** [1]Lit *these* **36** [1]Lit *smitten* [2]Lit *place* [a]Josh 8:15 **37** [a]Josh 8:19

38 [a]Josh 8:20 **39** [1]Lit *slain ones* [2]Lit *smitten* [a]Judg 20:32 **40** [a]Josh 8:20 **41** [1]Lit *evil* [2]Lit *touching* [a]Prov 5:22; 11:5, 6; 29:6 **42** [a]Josh 8:15, 24 **43** [1]Lit *sunrise* [a]Hos 9:9; 10:9 **45** [1]So with Gr; Heb *And they* [2]Lit *gleaned* [3]Lit *as far as* [4]Lit *smote* [a]Judg 21:13 **21:1** [1]Lit *for a wife* [a]Judg 21:7, 18 **2** [a]Judg 20:26

20:27 *ark.* The only mention of the ark in Judges.
20:28 *Phinehas.* Phinehas was the priest in the tabernacle in the days of Joshua (Josh 22:13), and the fact that he was still serving is further evidence that these events took place early in the days of the judges (see notes on v. 1; 18:30).
20:29 *set men in ambush.* See 9:32; Jos 8:2.
20:33 *Baal-tamar.* Location unknown.
20:36b–45 Details of the account in vv. 29–36a.
20:46 *25,000.* A round number for 25,100 (v. 35).
20:47 *600 men.* If these had not escaped, the tribe of Benjamin would have been annihilated. The same number of Danites went to Laish (18:11).
21:1–25 Second thoughts about the slaughter of their Benjamite brothers caused the Israelites to grieve over the loss. Only 600 Benjamites were left alive, and the men of Israel decided to provide wives for them in order to keep the tribe from disappearing. After slaughtering most of the people of Jabesh Gilead, the Israelites took 400 girls from the survivors and gave them to 400 Benjamites. Shortly afterward, each of the remaining Benjamites seized a wife from the girls of Shiloh, and Benjamin began to be restored.
21:1 *sworn.* This vow, probably taken in the name of the Lord, was not an ordinary vow but invoked a curse on oneself if the vow was broken (v. 18; see also Acts 23:12–15).
21:2 *Bethel.* See 20:18,26–27. *wept bitterly.* Earlier the Israelites wept because they were defeated by the Benjamites

there before God until evening, and lifted up their voices and wept [1]bitterly.

3 They said, “Why, O LORD, God of Israel, has this come about in Israel, so that one tribe should be *missing* today in Israel?”

4 It came about the next day that the people arose early and built [a]an altar there and offered burnt offerings and peace offerings.

5 Then the sons of Israel said, “Who is there among all the tribes of Israel who did not come up in the assembly to the LORD?” For [1]they had taken a great oath concerning him [a]who did not come up to the LORD at Mizpah, saying, “He shall surely be put to death.”

6 And the sons of Israel were sorry for their brother Benjamin and said, “One tribe is cut off from Israel today.

7 “What shall we do for wives for those who are left, since we have [a]sworn by the LORD not to give them any of our daughters in marriage?”

Provision for Their Survival

8 And they said, “What one is there of the tribes of Israel who did not come up to the LORD at Mizpah?” And behold, no one had come to the camp from Jabesh-gilead to the assembly.

9 For when the people were [1]numbered, behold, not one of the inhabitants of Jabesh-gilead was there.

10 And the congregation sent 12,000 of the valiant warriors there, and commanded them, saying, “Go and [a]strike the inhabitants of Jabesh-gilead with the edge of the sword, with the women and the little ones.

11 “This is the thing that you shall do: you [a]shall utterly destroy every man and every woman who has [1]lain with a man.”

12 And they found among the inhabitants of Jabesh-gilead 400 young virgins who had not known a man by lying with [1]him; and they brought them to the camp at Shiloh, which is in the land of Canaan.

2 [1]Lit *with great weeping*
4 [a]Deut 12:5; 2 Sam 24:25
5 [1]Lit *there was a great oath* [a]Judg 5:23
7 [a]Judg 21:1
9 [1]Or *mustered*
10 [a]Num 31:17; Judg 5:23; 1 Sam 11:7
11 [1]Lit *known lying with* [a]Num 31:17
12 [1]Lit *a male*
13 [a]Judg 20:47 [b]Deut 20:10
14 [1]Lit *did not find it so*
18 [a]Judg 21:1
19 [a]Josh 18:1; Judg 18:31; 1 Sam 1:3
21 [1]Lit *dance* [a]Ex 15:20; Judg 11:34
22 [1]Lit *his* [2]Lit *because* [a]Judg 21:1, 18

13 Then the whole congregation sent *word* and spoke to the sons of Benjamin who were [a]at the rock of Rimmon, and [b]proclaimed peace to them.

14 Benjamin returned at that time, and they gave them the women whom they had kept alive from the women of Jabesh-gilead; yet they [1]were not enough for them.

15 And the people were sorry for Benjamin because the LORD had made a breach in the tribes of Israel.

16 Then the elders of the congregation said, “What shall we do for wives for those who are left, since the women are destroyed out of Benjamin?”

17 They said, “*There must be* an inheritance for the survivors of Benjamin, so that a tribe will not be blotted out from Israel.

18 “But we cannot give them wives of our daughters.” For the sons of Israel [a]had sworn, saying, “Cursed is he who gives a wife to Benjamin.”

19 So they said, “Behold, there is a feast of the LORD from year to year in [a]Shiloh, which is on the north side of Bethel, on the east side of the highway that goes up from Bethel to Shechem, and on the south side of Lebonah.”

20 And they commanded the sons of Benjamin, saying, “Go and lie in wait in the vineyards,

21 and watch; and behold, if the daughters of Shiloh come out to [1a]take part in the dances, then you shall come out of the vineyards and each of you shall catch his wife from the daughters of Shiloh, and go to the land of Benjamin.

22 “It shall come about, when their fathers or their brothers come to complain to us, that we shall say to them, ‘Give them to us voluntarily, because we did not take for each man *of Benjamin* [1]a wife in battle, [2a]nor did you give *them* to them, *else* you would now be guilty.’ ”

23 The sons of Benjamin did so, and took wives according to their number from those

---

(20:23,26). Now they weep because the disciplinary action against the Benjamites has nearly annihilated one of the tribes (see v. 3).

21:5 *not come . . . in the assembly.* The tribes had a mutual responsibility in times of military action (see note on 5:13–18). Those who failed to participate were often singled out and sometimes punished (5:15–17,23). *great oath.* Complicating the situation for Israel was the fact that they had taken a second oath, calling for the death of those who did not participate in the battle.

21:10 *12,000.* A thousand from each tribe (see Num 31:6), with 1,000 supplied to represent the tribe of Benjamin.

21:11 *destroy every man.* The punishment of Jabesh Gilead seems brutal, but the covenant bond between the tribes was extremely important. Even though delinquency on some occasions was not punished (5:15–17), the nature of the crime in this case, coupled with Benjamin's refusal to turn over the criminals, caused Israel to take this oath (v. 5).

21:12 *Canaan.* Emphasizes the fact that the women were brought across the Jordan from the east.

21:19 *feast of the LORD.* In light of the mention of vineyards (v. 20), it is likely that this reference is to the Feast of Booths (see note on 1 Sam 1:3), though it may have been a local festival. *north side of Bethel . . . south side of Lebonah.* This detailed description of Shiloh's location may indicate that this material was written at a time when Shiloh was in ruins, perhaps after its destruction during the battle of Aphek (1 Sam 4:1–11).

21:21 *catch his wife.* With the Benjamites securing wives in this manner, the other tribes were not actually “giving” their daughters to them (see note on v. 22).

21:22 *when their fathers or their brothers . . . complain.* It was customary for the brothers of a girl who had been abducted to demand satisfaction (see Gen 34:7–31; 2 Sam 13:20–38). It was therefore important that the elders anticipate this response and be prepared to get cooperation from the girls' families.

who danced, whom they carried away. And
they went and returned to their inheritance
and [a]rebuilt the cities and lived in them.
24 The sons of Israel departed from there
at that time, every man to his tribe and family, and each one of them went out from
there to his inheritance.
25 [a]In those days there was no king in
Israel; everyone did what was right in his
own eyes.

23 [a]Judg 20:48
25 [a]Judg 17:6; 18:1; 19:1

21:24 *went out from there.* These soldiers had probably been away from home at least five months (see 20:47).

21:25 *there was no king in Israel.* See note on 17:6.

Ruth

INTRODUCTION

Title

The book is named after one of its main characters, a young woman of Moab, the great-grandmother of David and an ancestress of Jesus (Matt 1:1,5). The only other Biblical book bearing the name of a woman is Esther.

Background

The story is set in the time of the judges, a time characterized in the book of Judges as a period of religious and moral degeneracy, national disunity and general foreign oppression. The book of Ruth reflects a temporary time of peace between Israel and Moab (contrast Judg 3:12 – 30). Like 1 Sam 1 — 2, it gives a series of intimate glimpses into the private lives of the members of an Israelite family. It also presents a delightful account of the remnant of true faith and piety in the period of the judges, relieving an otherwise wholly dark picture of that era.

Author and Date of Writing

The author is unknown. Jewish tradition points to Samuel, but it is unlikely that he is the author because the mention of David (4:17,22) implies a later date. Further, the literary style of Hebrew used in Ruth suggests that it was written during the period of the monarchy.

Theme and Theology

The author focuses on Ruth's unswerving and selfless devotion to desolate Naomi (1:16 – 17; 2:11 – 12; 3:10; 4:15) and on Boaz's kindness to these two widows (chs. 2 — 4). He presents striking examples of lives that embody in their daily affairs the self-giving love that fulfills God's law (Lev 19:18; cf. Rom 13:10). Such love also reflects God's love, in a marvelous joining of man's actions with God's (compare 2:12 with 3:9). In God's benevolence such lives are blessed and are made a blessing.

It may seem surprising that one who reflects God's love so clearly is a Moabitess (see map, p. 347). Yet her complete loyalty to the Israelite family into which she has been received by marriage and her total devotion to her desolate mother-in-law mark her as a true daughter of Israel and a worthy ancestress of David. She strikingly exemplifies the truth that participation in the coming kingdom of God is decided, not by blood and birth, but by the conformity of one's life to the will of God through the "obedience of faith" (Rom 1:5). Her place in the ancestry of David signifies that all nations will be represented in the kingdom of David's greater Son.

As an episode in the ancestry of David, the book of Ruth sheds light on his role in the history of redemption. Redemption is a key concept throughout the account; the Hebrew word in its various forms occurs 23 times. The book is primarily a story of Naomi's transformation from despair to happiness through the selfless, God-blessed acts of Ruth and Boaz. She moves from emptiness to fullness (1:21; 3:17; see notes on 1:1,3,5 – 6,12,21 – 22; 3:17; 4:15), from destitution (1:1 – 5) to security and hope (4:13 – 17). Similarly, Israel was transformed from national desperation at the death of Eli (1 Sam 4:18) to peace and prosperity in the early days of Solomon (1 Kin 4:20 – 34; 5:4) through the selfless devotion of David, a true descendant of Ruth and Boaz. The author thus reminded Israel that the reign of the house of David, as the means of God's benevolent rule in Israel, held the prospect of God's promised peace and rest. But this rest would continue only so long as those who participated in the kingdom — prince and people alike — reflected in their daily lives the selfless love exemplified by Ruth and Boaz. In Jesus, the great "son of David" (Matt 1:1), and His redemptive work, the promised blessings of the kingdom of God find their fulfillment.

Literary Features

The book of Ruth is a Hebrew short story, told with consummate skill. Among historical narratives in Scripture it is unexcelled in its compactness, vividness, warmth, beauty and dramatic effectiveness — an exquisitely wrought jewel of Hebrew narrative art.

Marvelously symmetrical throughout (see Outline), the action moves from a briefly sketched account of distress (1:1 – 5; 71 words in Hebrew) through four episodes to a concluding account of relief and hope that is drawn with equal brevity (4:13 – 17; 71 words in Hebrew). The crucial turning point occurs exactly midway (see note on 2:20). The opening line of each of the four episodes signals its main development (1:6, the return; 2:1, the meeting with Boaz; 3:1, finding a home for Ruth; 4:1, the decisive event at the gate), while the closing line of each episode facilitates transition to what follows (see notes on 1:22; 2:23; 3:18; 4:12). Contrast is also used to good effect: pleasant (the meaning of "Naomi") and bitter (1:20), full and empty (1:21), and the living and the dead (2:20). Most striking is the contrast between two of the main characters, Ruth and Boaz: The one is a young, alien, destitute widow, while the other is a middle-aged, well-to-do Israelite securely established in his home community. For each there is a corresponding character whose actions highlight, by contrast, his or her selfless acts: Ruth — Orpah, Boaz — the unnamed kinsman.

When movements in space, time and circumstance all correspond in some way, a harmony results that both satisfies the reader's artistic sense and helps open doors to understanding. The author of Ruth keeps his readers from being distracted from the central story — Naomi's passage from emptiness to fullness through the selfless acts of Ruth and Boaz (see Theme and Theology). That passage, or restoration, first takes place in connection with her return from Moab to the promised land and to Bethlehem ("house of food"; see note on 1:1). It then progresses with the harvest season, when the fullness of the land is gathered in. All aspects of the story keep the reader's attention focused on the central issue. Consideration of these and other literary devices (mentioned throughout the notes) will aid understanding of the book of Ruth.

Outline

- I. Introduction: Naomi Emptied (1:1 – 5)
- II. Naomi Returns from Moab (1:6 – 22)
  - A. Ruth Clings to Naomi (1:6 – 18)
  - B. Ruth and Naomi Return to Bethlehem (1:19 – 22)
- III. Ruth and Boaz Meet in the Harvest Fields (ch. 2)
  - A. Ruth Begins Work (2:1 – 7)
  - B. Boaz Shows Kindness to Ruth (2:8 – 16)
  - C. Ruth Returns to Naomi (2:17 – 23)
- IV. Ruth Goes to Boaz at the Threshing Floor (ch. 3)
  - A. Naomi Instructs Ruth (3:1 – 5)
  - B. Boaz Pledges to Secure Redemption (3:6 – 15)
  - C. Ruth Returns to Naomi (3:16 – 18)
- V. Boaz Arranges to Marry Ruth (4:1 – 12)
  - A. Boaz Confronts the Unnamed Kinsman (4:1 – 8)
  - B. Boaz Buys Naomi's Property and Announces His Marriage to Ruth (4:9 – 12)
- VI. Conclusion: Naomi Filled (4:13 – 17)
- VII. Epilogue: Genealogy of David (4:18 – 22)

Naomi Widowed

1 Now it came about in the days [a]when the
judges [1]governed, that there was [b]a
famine in the land. And a certain man [c]of
Bethlehem in Judah went to sojourn in the
land of Moab [2]with his wife and his two
sons.
2 The name of the man *was* Elimelech,
and the name of his wife, Naomi; and the
names of his two sons *were* Mahlon and
Chilion, Ephrathites of Bethlehem in Judah.
Now they [a]entered the land of Moab and
remained there.
3 Then Elimelech, Naomi's husband,
died; and she was left with her two sons.
4 They took for themselves Moabite
women *as* wives; the name of the one was
Orpah and the name of the other Ruth. And
they lived there about ten years.
5 Then [1]both Mahlon and Chilion also
died, and the woman was bereft of her two
children and her husband.
6 Then she arose with her daughters-in-
law that she might return from the land of
Moab, for she had heard in the land of Moab
that the LORD had [a]visited His people in [b]giv-
ing them food.
7 So she departed from the place where
she was, and her two daughters-in-law with
her; and they went on the way to return to
the land of Judah.
8 And Naomi said to her two daughters-
in-law, "Go, return each of you to her mother's house. [a]May the LORD deal kindly with
you as you have dealt with the dead and
with me.
9 "May the LORD grant that you may find
rest, each in the house of her husband."

1:1 [1]Or *judged* [2]Lit *he, and* [a]Judg 2:16-18 [b]Gen 12:10; 26:1; 2 Kin 8:1 [c]Judg 17:8; Mic 5:2
2 [a]Judg 3:30
5 [1]Lit *both of them*
6 [a]Ex 4:31; Jer 29:10; Zeph 2:7 [b]Ps 132:15; Matt 6:11
8 [a]2 Tim 1:16

1:1 *when the judges governed.* Probably from c. 1380 to c. 1050 B.C. (see Introduction to Judges: Background). By mentioning the judges, the author calls to mind that period of Israel's apostasy, moral degradation and oppression. *famine.* Not mentioned in Judges. *Bethlehem in Judah.* David's hometown (1 Sam 16:18). Bethlehem (the name suggests "house of food") is empty.
1:2 *Elimelech.* Means "(My) God is King" (see note on Judg 8:23). *Naomi.* Means "pleasant." *Ephrathites.* Ephrathah was a name for the area around Bethlehem (see 4:11; Gen 35:19; 1 Sam 17:12; Mic 5:2).
1:3 *Elimelech, Naomi's husband, died.* Naomi's emptying begins (see v. 21).
1:4 *They took . . . Moabite women.* Prospect of continuing the family line remained. *Moabite women.* See Gen 19:36–37. Marriage with Moabite women was not forbidden, though no Moabite—or his sons to the tenth generation—was allowed to "enter the assembly of the LORD" (Deut 23:3). *Ruth.* The name sounds like the Hebrew for "friendship." Ruth is one of four women in Matthew's genealogy of Jesus. The others are Tamar, Rahab and Bathsheba (Matt 1:3,5–6).
1:5 *Mahlon.* Ruth's husband (4:10), whose name probably means "weakling." *the woman was bereft of her . . . husband.* Naomi's emptiness is complete: She has neither husband nor sons. She has only two young daughters-in-law, both of them foreigners and childless.
1:6 *arose . . . that she might return.* Empty Naomi returns to the newly filled land of promise. *the LORD had visited His people.* At several points in the account, God's sovereign control of events is acknowledged (here; vv. 13,21; 2:20; 4:12–15). *food.* Bethlehem ("house of food") again has food.
1:8 *Go, return.* Desolate Naomi repeatedly urges her daughters-in-law to return to their original homes in Moab (here; vv. 11–12,15); she has nothing to offer them. *deal kindly.* See 2:20; 3:10.

The Book of Ruth

Set in the dark and bloody days of the judges, the story of Ruth is silent about the underlying hostility and suspicion the two peoples—Judahites and Moabites—felt for each other. The original onslaught of the invading Israelite tribes against towns that were once Moabite had never been forgotten or forgiven, while the Hebrew prophets denounced Moab's pride and arrogance for trying to bewitch, seduce and oppress Israel from the time of Balaam on. The Mesha stele (c. 830 B.C.) boasts of the massacre of entire Israelite towns.

Moab encompassed the expansive, grain-filled plateau between the Dead Sea and the eastern desert on both sides of the enormous rift of the Arnon River gorge. Much of eastern Maob was steppeland—semi-arid wastes not profitable for cultivation, but excellent for grazing flocks of sheep and goats. The tribute Moab paid to Israel in the days of Ahab was 100,000 lambs and the wool of 100,000 rams (see 2 Kin 3:4 and note).

to Jericho
Jordan R.
Heshbon
ISRAEL
Mt. Nebo
Bethlehem
Dead Sea
Dibon
Aroer
Arnon R.
King's Highway
MOAB
Kir-hareseth
Miles 10 5 0 10 20
Kms 10 5 0 10 20 30

The main route through Moab was the King's Highway, a track connecting the cities of Heshbon, Dibon and Kir-hareseth with points north and south.

Then she kissed them, and they lifted up their voices and wept.

10 And they said to her, "*No,* but we will surely return with you to your people."

11 But Naomi said, "Return, my daughters. Why should you go with me? Have I yet sons in my womb, that [a]they may be your husbands?

12 "Return, my daughters! Go, for I am too old to have a husband. If I said I have hope, if I should even have a husband tonight and also bear sons,

13 would you therefore wait until they were grown? Would you therefore refrain from marrying? No, my daughters; for it is [1]harder for me than for you, for [a]the hand of the LORD has gone forth against me."

Ruth's Loyalty

14 And they lifted up their voices and wept again; and Orpah kissed her mother-in-law, but Ruth clung to her.

15 Then she said, "Behold, your sister-in-law has gone back to her people and her [a]gods; return after your sister-in-law."

16 But Ruth said, "Do not urge me to leave you *or* turn back from following you; for where you go, I will go, and where you lodge, I will lodge. Your people *shall be* my people, and your God, my God.

17 "Where you die, I will die, and there I will be buried. Thus may [a]the LORD do to me, and worse, if *anything but* death parts you and me."

18 When [a]she saw that she was determined to go with her, she [1]said no more to her.

19 So they both went until they came to Bethlehem. And when they had come to Bethlehem, [a]all the city was stirred because of them, and [1]the women said, "Is this Naomi?"

20 She said to them, "Do not call me [1]Naomi; call me [2]Mara, for [3][a]the Almighty has dealt very bitterly with me.

21 "I went out full, but [a]the LORD has brought me back empty. Why do you call me Naomi, since the LORD has witnessed against me and [1]the Almighty has afflicted me?"

22 So Naomi returned, and with her Ruth the Moabitess, her daughter-in-law, who returned from the land of Moab. And they came to Bethlehem at [a]the beginning of barley harvest.

Ruth Gleans in Boaz' Field

2 Now Naomi had [1]a kinsman of her husband, a [2]man of great wealth, of the family of [a]Elimelech, whose name was Boaz.

2 And Ruth the Moabitess said to Naomi, "Please let me go to the field and [a]glean among the ears of grain after one in whose sight I may find favor." And she said to her, "Go, my daughter."

3 So she departed and went and gleaned in the field after the reapers; and [1]she hap-

11 [a]Gen 38:11; Deut 25:5
13 [1]Lit *more bitter* [a]Judg 2:15; Job 19:21; Ps 32:4
15 [a]Josh 24:15; Judg 11:24
17 [a]1 Sam 3:17; 2 Kin 6:31
18 [1]Lit *ceased to speak* [a]Acts 21:14
19 [1]Lit *they* [a]Matt 21:10
20 [1]I.e. pleasant [2]I.e. bitter [3]Heb *Shaddai* [a]Ex 6:3; Job 6:4
21 [1]Heb *Shaddai* [a]Job 1:21
22 [a]Ex 9:31; Lev 23:10, 11
2:1 [1]Or *an acquaintance* [2]Or *mighty, valiant man* [a]Ruth 1:2
2 [a]Lev 19:9, 10; 23:22; Deut 24:19; Ruth 2:7
3 [1]Lit *her chance chanced upon*

1:11 *sons . . . may be your husbands.* Naomi alludes to the Israelite law (Deut 25:5–6) regarding levirate marriage (see notes on Gen 38:8; Deut 25:5–10; see also Mark 12:18–23), which was given to protect the widow and guarantee continuance of the family line.
1:12 *I am too old.* Naomi can have no more sons; even her womb is empty.
1:13 *the hand of the LORD . . . against me.* See notes on vv. 5–6; see also vv. 20–21.
1:14 Orpah's departure highlights the loyalty and selfless devotion of Ruth to her desolate mother-in-law.
1:15 *her gods.* The chief god of the Moabites was Chemosh.
1:16 This classic expression of loyalty and love discloses the true character of Ruth. Her commitment to Naomi is complete, even though it holds no prospect for her but to share in Naomi's desolation. For a similar declaration of devotion see 2 Sam 15:21.
1:17 *may the LORD do to me, and worse.* See note on 1 Sam 3:17. Ruth, a Gentile, swears her commitment to Naomi in the name of Israel's God, thus acknowledging Him as her God (see v. 16).
1:20 *Naomi . . . Mara.* See NASB marg. In the ancient Near East a person's name was often descriptive. *Almighty.* See note on Gen 17:1.
1:21 *full . . . empty.* These words highlight the central theme of the story—how the empty Naomi becomes full again.
1:22 *Ruth the Moabitess.* Several times the author reminds the reader that Ruth is a foreigner from a despised people (2:2,6,21; 4:5,10; see 2:10). *beginning.* Naomi and Ruth arrive in Bethlehem just as the renewed fullness of the land is beginning to be harvested—an early hint that Naomi will be full again. Reference to the barley harvest also prepares the reader for the next major scene in the harvest fields (see Introduction: Literary Features). *harvest.* Harvesting grain in ancient Canaan took place in April and May (barley first, wheat a few weeks later; see 2:23). It involved the following steps: (1) cutting the ripened standing grain with hand sickles (Deut 16:9; 23:25; Jer 50:16; Joel 3:13)—usually done by men; (2) binding the grain into sheaves—usually done by women; (3) gleaning, i.e., gathering stalks of grain left behind (2:7); (4) transporting the sheaves to the threshing floor—often by donkey, sometimes by cart (Amos 2:13); (5) threshing, i.e., loosening the grain from the straw—usually done by the treading of cattle (Deut 25:4; Hos 10:11), but sometimes by toothed threshing sledges (Is 41:15; Amos 1:3) or the wheels of carts (Is 28:28); (6) winnowing—done by tossing the grain into the air with winnowing forks (Jer 15:7) so that the wind, which usually came up for a few hours in the afternoon, blew away the straw and chaff (Ps 1:4), leaving the grain at the winnower's feet; (7) sifting the grain (Amos 9:9) to remove any residual foreign matter; (8) bagging for transportation and storage (Gen 42–44). Threshing floors, where both threshing and winnowing occurred, were hard, smooth, open places, prepared on either rock or clay and carefully chosen for favorable exposure to the prevailing winds. They were usually on the east side—i.e., downwind—of the village.
2:1 *kinsman.* A sign of hope (see note on v. 20). *Boaz.* Probably means "In him is strength." Boaz is included in both genealogies of Jesus (Matt 1:5; Luke 3:32).
2:2 *let me go.* Although Ruth is an alien and, as a young woman alone, obviously quite vulnerable in the harvest fields, she undertakes to provide for her mother-in-law. In 3:1 Naomi undertakes to provide for Ruth. *glean among the . . . grain.* The law of Moses instructed landowners to leave what the harvesters missed so that the poor, the alien, the widow and the fatherless could glean for their needs (Lev 19:9; 23:22; Deut 24:19).
2:3 *she happened to come.* Divine providence is at work (vv. 19–20).

pened to come to the portion of the field belonging to Boaz, who was of the family of Elimelech.

4 Now behold, Boaz came from Bethlehem and said to the reapers, "[a]May the LORD be with you." And they said to him, "May the LORD bless you."

5 Then Boaz said to his servant who was [1]in charge of the reapers, "Whose young woman is this?"

6 The servant [1]in charge of the reapers replied, "She is the young Moabite woman who returned with Naomi from the land of Moab.

7 "And she said, 'Please let me glean and gather after the reapers among the sheaves.' Thus she came and has remained from the morning until now; she has been sitting in the house for a little while."

8 Then Boaz said to Ruth, "[1]Listen carefully, my daughter. Do not go to glean in another field; furthermore, do not go on from this one, but stay here with my maids.

9 "Let your eyes be on the field which they reap, and go after them. Indeed, I have commanded the servants not to touch you. When you are thirsty, go to the [1]water jars and drink from what the servants draw."

10 Then she [a]fell on her face, bowing to the ground and said to him, "Why have I found favor in your sight that you should take notice of me, since I am a foreigner?"

11 Boaz replied to her, "All that you have done for your mother-in-law after the death of your husband has been fully reported to me, and how you left your father and your mother and the land of your birth, and came to a people that you did not previously know.

12 "[a]May the LORD reward your work, and your wages be full from the LORD, the God of Israel, [b]under whose wings you have come to seek refuge."

13 Then she said, "I have found favor in your sight, my lord, for you have comforted me and indeed have spoken [1]kindly to your maidservant, though I am not like one of your maidservants."

14 At mealtime Boaz said to her, "[1]Come here, that you may eat of the bread and dip your piece of bread in the vinegar." So she sat beside the reapers; and he [2]served her roasted grain, and she ate and was satisfied [a]and had some left.

15 When she rose to glean, Boaz commanded his servants, saying, "Let her glean even among the sheaves, and do not insult her.

16 "Also you shall purposely pull out for her *some grain* from the bundles and leave *it* that she may glean, and do not rebuke her."

17 So she gleaned in the field until evening. Then she beat out what she had gleaned, and it was about an ephah of barley.

18 She took *it* up and went into the city, and her mother-in-law saw what she had gleaned. She also took *it* out and [a]gave [1]Naomi what she had left after [2]she was satisfied.

19 Her mother-in-law then said to her, "Where did you glean today and where did you work? May he who [a]took notice of you be blessed." So she told her mother-in-law with whom she had worked and said, "The name of the man with whom I worked today is Boaz."

20 Naomi said to her daughter-in-law, "[a]May he be blessed of the LORD who has not withdrawn his kindness to the living and to the dead." Again Naomi said to her, "The man is [1]our relative, he is one of our [2]closest relatives."

21 Then Ruth the Moabitess said, "[1]Furthermore, he said to me, 'You should stay close to my servants until they have finished all my harvest.' "

22 Naomi said to Ruth her daughter-in-law, "It is good, my daughter, that you go out with his maids, so that *others* do not fall upon you in another field."

23 So she stayed close by the maids of Boaz in order to glean until [a]the end of the

4 [a]Judg 6:12; Ps 129:8; Luke 1:28; 2 Thess 3:16
5 [1]Lit *appointed over*
6 [1]Lit *who was appointed over*
8 [1]Lit *Have you not heard*
9 [1]Lit *vessels*
10 [a]1 Sam 25:23
12 [a]1 Sam 24:19 [b]Ruth 1:16; Ps 17:8; 36:7; 57:1; 61:4; 63:7; 91:4
13 [1]Lit *to the heart of your*
14 [1]Lit *Draw near* [2]Lit *held out to* [a]Ruth 2:18
18 [1]Lit *her* [2]Lit *her satiety* [a]Ruth 2:14
19 [a]Ps 41:1
20 [1]Lit *near to us* [2]Lit *redeemers* [a]2 Sam 2:5
21 [1]Lit *Also that*
23 [a]Deut 16:9

2:4 The exchange of greetings between Boaz and his laborers characterizes Boaz as a godly man with a kind spirit.
2:9 *go after them.* It was customary for the men to cut the grain and for the servant girls to go behind them to bind the grain into sheaves. Then Ruth could glean what they had left behind (see note on 1:22).
2:11 Ruth's commitment to care for her desolate mother-in-law remains the center of attention throughout the book.
2:12 *under whose wings.* A figure of a bird protecting her young under her wings (see Matt 23:37; see also note on 3:9).
2:13 *your maidservant.* A polite reference to herself.
2:15 *commanded his servants.* Boaz goes beyond the requirement of the law in making sure that Ruth's labors are abundantly productive (see 3:15).
2:17 *beat out.* See note on 1:22. In Ruth's case, as in that of Gideon (Judg 6:11), the amount was small and could be threshed by hand simply by beating it with a club or stick. *ephah.* An ephah was probably about three-fifths of a bushel—an unusually large amount for one day's gleaning.
2:20 *the LORD who has not withdrawn his kindness.* See 1:8. In 3:10 Boaz credits Ruth with demonstrating this same virtue. *closest relatives.* Redemption is a key concept in Ruth (see Introduction: Theme and Theology). The "closest relative," also known as a kinsman-redeemer, was responsible for protecting the interests of needy members of the extended family—e.g., to provide an heir for a brother who had died (Deut 25:5–10), to redeem land that a poor relative had sold outside the family (Lev 25:25–28), to redeem a relative who had been sold into slavery (Lev 25:47–49) and to avenge the killing of a relative (Num 35:19–21; "avenger" and "kinsman-redeemer" are translations of the same Hebrew word). Naomi is encouraged when she hears that the Lord has led Ruth to the fields of a relative who might serve as their kinsman-redeemer. This moment of Naomi's awakened hope is the crucial turning point of the story.
2:23 *until the end of the . . . harvest.* This phrase rounds out the harvest episode and prepares for the next major scene on the threshing floor (see Introduction: Literary Features).

barley harvest and the wheat harvest. And
she lived with her mother-in-law.

Boaz Will Redeem Ruth

3 Then Naomi her mother-in-law said to
her, "My daughter, shall I not seek [1]secu-
rity for you, that it may be well with you?
2 "Now is not Boaz [a]our [1]kinsman, with
whose maids you were? Behold, he winnows
barley at the threshing floor tonight.
3 "Wash yourself therefore, and anoint
yourself and put on your *best* clothes, and go
down to the threshing floor; *but* do not make
yourself known to the man until he has finished eating and drinking.
4 "It shall be when he lies down, that you
shall [1]notice the place where he lies, and you
shall go and uncover his feet and lie down;
then he will tell you what you shall do."
5 She said to her, "[a]All that you say I will
do."
6 So she went down to the threshing
floor and did according to all that her mother-in-law had commanded her.
7 When Boaz had eaten and drunk and
[a]his heart was merry, he went to lie down at
the end of the heap of grain; and she came
secretly, and uncovered his feet and lay
down.
8 It happened in the middle of the night
that the man was startled and [1]bent forward;
and behold, a woman was lying at his feet.
9 He said, "Who are you?" And she
answered, "I am Ruth your maid. So spread
your covering over your maid, for you are a
[1]close relative."
10 Then he said, "[a]May you be blessed of
the LORD, my daughter. You have shown your
last kindness to be better than the first by not
going after young men, whether poor or rich.
11 "Now, my daughter, do not fear. I will
do for you whatever you [1]ask, for all my people in the [2]city know that you are [a]a woman
of excellence.
12 "Now it is true I am a [1]close relative;
however, there is a [1]relative closer than I.
13 "Remain this night, and when morning
comes, [a]if he will [1]redeem you, good; let him
redeem you. But if he does not wish to
[1]redeem you, then I will redeem you, [b]as the
LORD lives. Lie down until morning."
14 So she lay at his feet until morning and
rose before one could recognize another; and
he said, "[a]Let it not be known that the
woman came to the threshing floor."
15 Again he said, "Give me the cloak that
is on you and hold it." So she held it, and he
measured six *measures* of barley and laid *it*
on her. Then [1]she went into the city.
16 When she came to her mother-in-law,
she said, "[1]How did it go, my daughter?"
And she told her all that the man had done
for her.
17 She said, "These six *measures* of barley
he gave to me, for he said, 'Do not go to your
mother-in-law empty-handed.'"
18 Then she said, "Wait, my daughter,
until you know how the matter [1]turns out;
for the man will not rest until he has [2]settled
it today."

The Marriage of Ruth

4 Now Boaz went up to the gate and sat
down there, and behold, [a]the [1]close relative of whom Boaz spoke was passing by, so
he said, "Turn aside, [2]friend, sit down here."
And he turned aside and sat down.
2 He took ten men of the [a]elders of the
city and said, "Sit down here." So they sat
down.

3:1 [1]Lit *rest*
2 [1]Or *acquaintance* [a]Deut 25:5-10
4 [1]Lit *know*
5 [a]Eph 6:1; Col 3:20
7 [a]Judg 19:6, 9; 2 Sam 13:28; 1 Kin 21:7; Esth 1:10
8 [1]Lit *twisted himself*
9 [1]Or *redeemer*
10 [a]Ruth 2:20
11 [1]Lit *say* [2]Lit *gate* [a]Prov 12:4; 31:10
12 [1]Or *redeemer*
13 [1]Or *act as close relative to* [a]Deut 25:5; Matt 22:24 [b]Judg 8:19; Jer 4:2; 12:16
14 [a]Rom 14:16; 2 Cor 8:21
15 [1]So with many mss; M.T. *he*
16 [1]Lit *Who are you?*
18 [1]Lit *falls* [2]Lit *a finished the matter*
4:1 [1]Or *redeemer* [2]Lit *a certain one* [a]Ruth 3:12
2 [a]1 Kin 21:8; Prov 31:23

3:1 Naomi's awakened hope (cf. 1:8–13) now moves her to undertake provision for Ruth's future (see note on 2:2).
3:2 *he winnows . . . tonight.* See note on 1:22. In the threshing season it was customary for the landowner to spend the night near the threshing floor to protect his grain from theft.
3:3 Ruth is instructed to prepare herself like a bride (see Ezek 16:9–12). *go down to the threshing floor.* Women were not normally present at the evening revelries of the threshers (v. 14). *eating and drinking.* Harvest was a time of festivity (Is 9:3; 16:9–10; Jer 48:33).
3:4 *uncover his feet and lie down.* Although Naomi's instructions may appear forward, the moral integrity of Naomi and Ruth is never in doubt (see v. 11). Naomi's advice to Ruth is clearly for the purpose of appealing to Boaz's kinsman obligation. Ruth's actions were a request for marriage. Tamar, the mother of Perez (4:12), had also laid claim to the provision of the levirate (or kinsman-redeemer) law (Gen 38:13–30).
3:9 *spread your covering over your maid.* A request for marriage (see Ezek 16:8); a similar custom is still practiced in some parts of the Middle East today. There is a play on the words "wings" of the Lord (2:12) and "covering" (lit. "wings") of the garment (here), both signifying protection. Boaz is vividly reminded that he must serve as the Lord's protective wing to watch over Ruth.
3:10 *last kindness . . . better than the first.* See 2:11–12.
3:11 *woman of excellence.* See Prov 31:10. The Hebrew for this expression is similar to that used of Boaz in 2:1; thus the author maintains a balance between his descriptions of Ruth and Boaz.
3:12 *a relative closer than I.* How Boaz was related to Ruth's former husband (Mahlon) is unknown, but the closest male relative had the primary responsibility to marry a widow. Naomi instructed Ruth to approach Boaz because he had already shown himself willing to be Ruth's protector. Boaz, however, would not bypass the directives of the law, which clearly gave priority to the nearest relative.
3:13 *as the LORD lives.* Boaz commits himself by oath (cf. 1:17) to redeem the family property and to arrange Ruth's honorable marriage.
3:15 Boaz goes beyond the requirement of the law in supplying Ruth with grain from the threshing floor (see 2:15).
3:17 *empty-handed.* Again the empty-full motif (see note on 1:21).
3:18 *Wait.* The Hebrew underlying this word is translated "sat" in 4:1. Thus the author prepares the reader for the next major scene, in which Boaz sits at the town gate to see the matter through.
4:1 *gate.* The "town hall" of ancient Israel, the normal place for business and legal transactions, where witnesses were readily available (vv. 9–12; see note on Gen 19:1). *friend.* The other kinsman remains unnamed.
4:2 *ten men of the elders.* A full court for legal proceedings.

3 Then he said to the [1]closest relative, "Naomi, who has come back from the land of Moab, has to sell the piece of land [a]which belonged to our brother Elimelech.

4 "So I thought to [1]inform you, saying, '[a]Buy *it* before those who are sitting *here,* and before the elders of my people. If you will redeem *it,* redeem *it;* but if [2]not, tell me that I may know; for [b]there is no one but you to redeem *it,* and I am after you.' " And he said, "I will redeem *it.*"

5 Then Boaz said, "On the day you buy the field from the hand of Naomi, you must also acquire Ruth the Moabitess, the widow of the deceased, in order [a]to raise up the name of the deceased on his inheritance."

6 [a]The [1]closest relative said, "I cannot redeem *it* for myself, because I would [2]jeopardize my own inheritance. Redeem *it* for yourself; you *may have* my right of redemption, for I cannot redeem *it.*"

7 Now this was [a]*the custom* in former times in Israel concerning the redemption and the exchange *of land* to confirm any matter: a man removed his sandal and gave it to another; and this was the *manner of* attestation in Israel.

8 So the [1]closest relative said to Boaz, "Buy *it* for yourself." And he removed his sandal.

9 Then Boaz said to the elders and all the people, "You are witnesses today that I have bought from the hand of Naomi all that belonged to Elimelech and all that belonged to Chilion and Mahlon.

10 "Moreover, I have acquired Ruth the Moabitess, the widow of Mahlon, to be my wife in order to raise up the name of the deceased on his inheritance, so [a]that the name of the deceased will not be cut off from his brothers or from the [1]court of his *birth* place; you are witnesses today."

11 All the people who were in the [1]court, and the elders, said, "*We are* witnesses. May the LORD make the woman who is coming into your home [a]like Rachel and Leah, both of whom built the house of Israel; and may you achieve [2]wealth in Ephrathah and [3]become famous in Bethlehem.

12 "Moreover, may your house be like the house of [a]Perez whom Tamar bore to Judah, through the [1]offspring which the LORD will give you by this young woman."

13 So Boaz took Ruth, and she became his wife, and he went in to her. And [a]the LORD [1]enabled her to conceive, and she gave birth to a son.

14 Then the [a]women said to Naomi, "Blessed is the LORD who has not left you without a [1]redeemer today, and may his name [2]become famous in Israel.

15 "May he also be to you a restorer of life and a sustainer of your old age; for your daughter-in-law, who loves you [1][a]and is better to you than seven sons, has given birth to him."

3 [1]Lit *redeemer* [a]Lev 25:25
4 [1]Lit *uncover your ear* [2]Lit *no one will redeem* [a]Jer 32:7f [b]Lev 25:25
5 [a]Gen 38:8; Deut 25:5f; Matt 22:24
6 [1]Lit *redeemer* [2]Lit *ruin* [a]Lev 25:25
7 [a]Deut 25:8-10
8 [1]Lit *redeemer*
10 [1]Lit *gate* [a]Deut 25:6
11 [1]Lit *gate* [2]Or *power* [3]Lit *call the name in* [a]Gen 29:25-30
12 [1]Lit *seed* [a]Gen 38:29; 46:12; Ruth 4:18
13 [1]Lit *gave her conception* [a]Gen 29:31; 33:5
14 [1]Or *closest relative* [2]Lit *be called in* [a]Luke 1:58
15 [1]Lit *who* [a]Ruth 1:16, 17; 2:11, 12

4:3 *sell the piece of land.* See note on 2:20. Two interpretations are possible: 1. Naomi owns the land but is so destitute that she is forced to sell. It was the duty of the kinsman-redeemer to buy any land in danger of being sold outside the family. 2. Naomi does not own the land—it had been sold by Elimelech before the family left for Moab—but by law she retains the right of redemption to buy the land back. Lacking funds to do so herself, she is dependent on a kinsman-redeemer to do it for her. It is the right of redemption that Naomi is "selling." *brother.* Used in the broader sense of "relative."

4:5 *also acquire . . . the widow of the deceased.* Now Boaz reveals the other half of the obligation—the acquisition of Ruth. Levirate law (Deut 25:5–6) provided that Ruth's firstborn son would keep Mahlon's name alive and would possess the right of ownership of the family inheritance.

4:6 *I cannot redeem it.* Possibly he fears that, if he has a son by her and if that son is his only surviving heir, his own property will transfer to the family of Elimelech (see note on Gen 38:9). In that case his risk was no greater than that assumed by Boaz. This kinsman's refusal to assume the kinsman-redeemer's role highlights the kindness and generosity of Boaz toward the two widows—just as Orpah's return to her family highlights Ruth's selfless devotion and loyalty to Naomi.

4:7 *a man removed his sandal.* The process of renouncing one's property rights and passing them to another was publicly attested by taking off a sandal and transferring it to the new owner (cf. Amos 2:6; 8:6). The Nuzi documents (see chart, p. xix) refer to a similar custom.

4:9 *witnesses.* The role of public witnesses was to attest to all legal transactions and other binding agreements.

4:10 *name of the deceased.* See Deut 25:6.

4:11 *Rachel and Leah . . . built the house of Israel.* Cf. Deut 25:9. The Israelite readers of Ruth would have associated the house of Jacob (Israel), built up by Rachel and Leah, with the house of Israel, rebuilt by David, the descendant of Ruth and Boaz, after it had been threatened with extinction (1 Sam 4). They also knew that the Lord had covenanted to "build" the house of David as an enduring dynasty, through which Israel's blessed destiny would be assured (see 2 Sam 7:27–29). *Ephrathah.* See note on 1:2.

4:12 *Perez whom Tamar bore to Judah.* Perez was Boaz's ancestor (vv. 18–21; Matt 1:3; Luke 3:33). His birth to Judah was from a union based on the levirate practice (Gen 38:27–30; see note on 1:11). Perez was therefore an appropriate model within Boaz's ancestry for the blessing the elders gave to Boaz. Moreover, the descendants of Perez had raised the tribe of Judah to a prominent place in Israel. So the blessing of the elders—that, through the offspring Ruth would bear to Boaz, his family would be like that of Perez—was fully realized in David and his dynasty. Thus also v. 12 prepares the reader for the events briefly narrated in the conclusion.

4:13–17 The conclusion of the story balances the introduction (1:1–5): (1) In the Hebrew both have the same number of words; (2) both compress much into a short space; (3) both focus on Naomi; (4) the introduction emphasizes Naomi's emptiness, and the conclusion portrays her fullness.

4:13 *the LORD enabled her to conceive.* See note on 1:6.

4:14 *redeemer.* The child Obed, as vv. 15–17 make clear. *may his name become famous.* This same wish is expressed concerning Boaz in v. 11.

4:15 *better to you than seven sons.* See 1 Sam 1:8. Since seven was considered a number of completeness, to have seven sons was the epitome of all family blessings in Israel (see 1 Sam 2:5; Job 1:2; 42:13). Ruth's selfless devotion to Naomi receives its climactic acknowledgment.

The Line of David Began Here

16 Then Naomi took the child [1]and laid
him in her lap, and became his nurse.
17 The neighbor women gave him a
name, saying, "A son has been born to Naomi!" So they named him Obed. He is the
father of Jesse, the father of David.
18 Now these are the generations of Perez:
[a]to Perez [1]was born Hezron,
19 and to Hezron was born Ram, and to
Ram, Amminadab,
20 and to Amminadab was born Nahshon,
and to Nahshon, Salmon,
21 and to Salmon was born Boaz, and to
Boaz, Obed,
22 and to Obed was born Jesse, and to Jesse, David.

16 [1]I.e. as her own **18** [1]Lit *begot,* and so through v 22 [a]Matt 1:3-6

4:16 *laid him in her lap.* Possibly symbolizing adoption (see note on Gen 30:3).

4:17 *A son has been born to Naomi!* Through Ruth, aged Naomi, who can no longer bear children, obtains an heir in place of Mahlon. *Obed.* The name means "servant," in its full form possibly "servant of the Lord."

4:18–22 See 1 Chr 2:5–15; Matt 1:3–6; Luke 3:31–33. Like the genealogies of Gen 5:3–32; 11:10–26, this genealogy has ten names (see note on Gen 5:5). It brings to mind the reign of David, during which, in contrast to the turbulent period of the judges recalled in 1:1, Israel finally entered into rest in the promised land (see 1 Kin 5:4). It signifies that, just as Naomi was brought from emptiness to fullness through the selfless love of Ruth and Boaz, so the Lord brought Israel from unrest to rest through their descendant David, who selflessly gave himself to fight Israel's battles on the Lord's behalf. The ultimate end of this genealogy is Jesus Christ, the great "son of David" (Matt 1:1), who fulfills prophecy and will bring the Lord's people into final rest.

1 Samuel

INTRODUCTION

Title

1 and 2 Samuel are named after the person God used to establish kingship in Israel. Samuel not only anointed both Saul and David, Israel's first two kings, but he also gave definition to the new order of God's rule over Israel that began with the incorporation of kingship into its structure. Samuel's importance as God's representative in this period of Israel's history is close to that of Moses (see Ps 99:6; Jer 15:1) since he, more than any other person, provided for covenant continuity in the transition from the rule of the judges to that of the monarchy.

1 and 2 Samuel were originally one book. It was divided into two parts by the translators of the Septuagint (the Greek translation of the OT) — a division subsequently followed by Jerome (the Latin Vulgate) and by modern versions. The title of the book has varied from time to time, having been designated "The First and Second Books of Kingdoms" (Septuagint), "First and Second Kings" (Vulgate) and "First and Second Samuel" (Hebrew tradition and most modern versions).

Literary Features, Authorship and Date

Many questions have arisen pertaining to the literary character, authorship and date of 1,2 Samuel. Certain literary characteristics of the book suggest that it was compiled with the use of a number of originally independent sources, which the author may have incorporated into his own composition as much as possible in their original, unedited form.

Who the author was cannot be known with certainty since the book itself gives no indication of his identity. Some have suggested Zabud, son of Nathan the prophet, who is referred to in 1 Kin 4:5 as King Solomon's "friend." He would have had access to information about David's reign from his father Nathan, as well as from court records. Whoever the author was, he must have lived shortly after Solomon's death (930 B.C.) and the division of the kingdom (see references to "Israel and Judah" in 11:8; 17:52; 18:16; 2 Sam 5:5; 24:1 – 9 and the expression "kings of Judah" in 1 Sam 27:6). Also, he doubtless had access to records of the life and times of Samuel, Saul and David. Explicit reference in the book itself is made to only one such source (the book of Jashar, 2 Sam 1:18), but the writer of Chronicles refers to four others that pertain to this period (the account of the chronicles of King David, 1 Chr 27:24; the chronicles of Samuel the seer; the chronicles of Nathan the prophet; the chronicles of Gad the seer, 1 Chr 29:29).

Contents and Theme: Kingship and Covenant

1 Samuel portrays the establishment of kingship in Israel. Before the author describes this momentous change in the structure of the theocracy (God's rule), he effectively depicts the complexity of its context. The following events provide both historical and theological context for the birth of the monarchy:

1. *The birth, youth and calling of Samuel (chs. 1 — 3).* In a book dealing for the most part with the reigns of Israel's first two kings, Saul and David, it is significant that the author chose not to include a birth narrative of either of these men, but to describe the birth of their forerunner and anointer, the prophet Samuel. This in itself accentuates the importance the author attached to Samuel's role in the events that follow. He seems to be saying in a subtle way that flesh and blood are to be subordinated to word and Spirit in the process of the establishment of kingship. For this reason chs. 1 — 3 should be viewed as integrally related to what follows, not as a more likely component of the book of Judges or as a loosely attached prefix to the rest of 1,2 Samuel. Kingship is given its birth and then nurtured by the prophetic word and work of the prophet Samuel. Moreover, the events of Samuel's nativity thematically anticipate the story of God's working that is narrated in the rest of the book.

2. *The "ark narratives" (chs. 4—6).* This section describes how the ark of God was captured by the Philistines and then, after God wreaked havoc on several Philistine cities, how it was returned to Israel. These narratives reveal the folly of Israel's notion that possession of the ark automatically guaranteed victory over her enemies. They also display the awesome power of the Lord (Yahweh, the God of Israel) and His superiority over the Philistine god Dagon. The Philistines were forced to confess openly their helplessness against God's power by their return of the ark to Israel. The entire ark episode performs a vital function in placing Israel's subsequent sinful desire for a human king in proper perspective.

3. *Samuel as a judge and deliverer (ch. 7).* When Samuel called Israel to repentance and renewed dedication to the Lord, the Lord intervened mightily in Israel's behalf and gave victory over the Philistines. This narrative reaffirms the authority of Samuel as a divinely ordained leader; at the same time it provides evidence of divine protection and blessing for God's people when they place their confidence in the Lord and live in obedience to their covenant obligations.

All the material in chs. 1—7 serves as a necessary preface for the narratives of chs. 8—12, which describe the rise and establishment of kingship in Israel. The author has masterfully arranged the stories in chs. 8—12 in order to accentuate the serious theological conflict surrounding the historical events. In the study of these chapters, scholars have often noted the presence of a tension or ambivalence in the attitude toward the monarchy: On the one hand, Samuel is commanded by the Lord to give the people a king (8:7,9,22; 9:16–17; 10:24; 12:13); on the other hand, their request for a king is considered a sinful rejection of the Lord (8:7; 10:19; 12:12,17,19–20). These seemingly conflicting attitudes toward the monarchy must be understood in the context of Israel's covenant relationship with the Lord.

Moses had anticipated Israel's desire for a human king (Deut 17:18–20), but Israelite kingship was to be compatible with the continued rule of the Lord over His people as their Great King. Instead, when the elders asked Samuel to give them a king (8:5,19–20), they rejected the Lord's kingship over them (8:7; 10:19; 12:17,19). Their desire was for a king such as the nations around them had—to lead them in battle and give them a sense of national security and unity. The request for a king constituted a denial of their covenant relationship to the Lord, who was their King. Moreover, the Lord not only had promised to be their protector but had also repeatedly demonstrated His power in their behalf, most recently in the ark narratives (chs. 4—6), as well as in the great victory won over the Philistines under the leadership of Samuel (ch. 7).

Nevertheless the Lord instructed Samuel to give the people a king (8:7,9,22). By divine appointment Saul was brought into contact with Samuel, and Samuel was directed to anoint him privately as king (9:1—10:16). Subsequently, Samuel gathered the people at Mizpah, where, after again admonishing them concerning their sin in desiring a king (10:18–19), he presided over the selection of a king by lot. The lot fell on Saul and publicly designated him as the one whom God had chosen (10:24). Saul did not immediately assume his royal office, but returned home to work his fields (11:5,7). When the inhabitants of Jabesh-gilead were threatened by Nahash the Ammonite, Saul rose to the challenge, gathered an army and led Israel to victory in battle. His success placed a final seal of divine approval on Saul's selection to be king (cf. 10:24; 11:12–13) and occasioned the inauguration of his reign at Gilgal (11:14—12:25).

The question that still needed resolution, then, was not so much whether Israel should have a king (it was clearly the Lord's will to give them a king), but rather how they could maintain their covenant with God (i.e., preserve the theocracy) now that they had a human king. The problem was resolved when Samuel called the people to repentance and renewal of their allegiance to the Lord on the very occasion of the inauguration of Saul as king (11:14—12:25; see note on 10:25). By establishing kingship in the context of covenant renewal, Samuel placed the monarchy in Israel on a radically different footing from that in surrounding nations. The king in Israel was not to be autonomous in his authority and power; rather, he was to be subject to the law of the Lord and the word of the prophet (10:25; 12:23). This was to be true not only for Saul but also for all the kings who would occupy the throne in Israel in the future. The king was to be an instrument of the Lord's rule over His people, and the people as well as the king were to continue to recognize the Lord as their ultimate Sovereign (12:14–15).

Saul very quickly demonstrated that he was unwilling to submit to the requirements of his theocratic office (chs. 13—15). When he disobeyed the instructions of the prophet Samuel in preparation for battle against the Philistines (13:13), and when he refused to totally destroy the Amalekites as he had been com-

manded to do by the word of the Lord through Samuel (ch. 15), he ceased to be an instrument of the Lord's rule over His people. These abrogations of the requirements of his theocratic office led to his rejection as king (15:23).

The remainder of 1 Samuel (chs. 16—31) depicts the Lord's choice of David to be Saul's successor, and then describes the long road by which David is prepared for accession to the throne. Although Saul's rule became increasingly anti-theocratic in nature, David refused to usurp the throne by forceful means but left his accession to office in the Lord's hands. Eventually Saul was wounded in a battle with the Philistines and, fearing capture, took his own life. Three of Saul's sons, including David's loyal friend Jonathan, were killed in the same battle (ch. 31).

Chronology

Even though the narratives of 1,2 Samuel contain some statements of chronological import (see, e.g., 1 Sam 6:1; 7:2; 8:1,5; 13:1; 25:1; 2 Sam 2:10–11; 5:4–5; 14:28; 15:7), the data are insufficient to establish a precise chronology for the major events of this period of Israel's history. Except for the dates of David's birth and the duration of his reign, which are quite firm (see 2 Sam 5:4–5), most other dates can only be approximated. The textual problem with the chronological data on the age of Saul when he became king and the length of his reign (see 1 Sam 13:1, NASB marg.) contributes to uncertainty concerning the precise time of his birth and the beginning of his reign. No information is given concerning the time of Samuel's birth (1 Sam 1:1) or death (25:1). His lifetime must have spanned, at least in part, that of Samson and that of Obed, son of Ruth and Boaz and grandfather of David. It is indicated that he was well along in years when the elders of Israel asked him to give them a king (see 8:1,5). One other factor contributing to chronological uncertainty is that the author has not always arranged his material in strict chronological sequence. It seems clear, for example, that 2 Sam 7 is to be placed chronologically after David's conquests described in 2 Sam 8:1–14 (see notes on 2 Sam 7:1; 8:1). The story of the famine sent by God on Israel during the reign of David because of Saul's violation of a treaty with the Gibeonites is found in 2 Sam 21:1–4, though chronologically it occurred prior to the time of Absalom's rebellion recorded in 2 Sam 15—18 (see further the notes on 2 Sam 21:1–2). The following dates, however, provide an approximate chronological framework for the times of Samuel, Saul and David.

1105 B.C.	Birth of Samuel (1 Sam 1:20)
1080	Birth of Saul
1050	Saul anointed to be king (1 Sam 10:1)
1040	Birth of David
1025	David anointed to be Saul's successor (1 Sam 16:1–13)
1010	Death of Saul and beginning of David's reign over Judah in Hebron (2 Sam 1:1; 2:1,4,11)
1003	Beginning of David's reign over all Israel and capture of Jerusalem (2 Sam 5)
997–992	David's wars (2 Sam 8:1–14)
991	Birth of Solomon (2 Sam 12:24; 1 Kin 3:7; 11:42)
980	David's census (2 Sam 24:1)
970	End of David's reign (2 Sam 5:4–5; 1 Kin 2:10–11)

Outline

I. Historical Setting for the Establishment of Kingship in Israel (1 Sam 1—7)
  A. Samuel's Birth, Youth and Calling to Be a Prophet; Judgment on the House of Eli (1 Sam 1—3)
  B. Israel Defeated by the Philistines, the Ark of God Taken and the Ark Restored; Samuel's Role as Judge and Deliverer (1 Sam 4—7)

II. The Establishment of Kingship in Israel under the Guidance of Samuel the Prophet (1 Sam 8—12)
  A. The People's Sinful Request for a King and God's Intent to Give Them a King (1 Sam 8)
  B. Samuel Anoints Saul Privately to Be King (1 Sam 9:1—10:16)
  C. Saul Chosen to Be King Publicly by Lot at Mizpah (1 Sam 10:17–27)
  D. The Choice of Saul as King Confirmed by Victory over the Ammonites (1 Sam 11:1–13)

- E. Saul's Reign Inaugurated at a Covenant Renewal Ceremony Convened by Samuel at Gilgal (1 Sam 11:14 — 12:25)

III. Saul's Kingship a Failure (1 Sam 13 — 15)

IV. David's Rise to the Throne; Progressive Deterioration and End of Saul's Reign (1 Sam 16:1 — 2 Sam 5:5)

- A. David Is Anointed Privately, Enters the Service of King Saul and Flees for His Life (1 Sam 16 — 26)
- B. David Seeks Refuge in Philistia, and Saul and His Sons Are Killed in Battle (1 Sam 27 — 31)
- C. David Becomes King over Judah (2 Sam 1 — 4)
- D. David Becomes King over All Israel (2 Sam 5:1 – 5)

V. David's Kingship in Its Accomplishments and Glory (2 Sam 5:6 — 9:12)

- A. David Conquers Jerusalem and Defeats the Philistines (2 Sam 5:6 – 25)
- B. David Brings the Ark to Jerusalem (2 Sam 6)
- C. God Promises David an Everlasting Dynasty (2 Sam 7)
- D. The Extension of David's Kingdom Externally and the Justice of His Rule Internally (2 Sam 8)
- E. David's Faithfulness to His Covenant with Jonathan (2 Sam 9)

VI. David's Kingship in Its Weaknesses and Failures (2 Sam 10 — 20)

- A. David Commits Adultery and Murder (2 Sam 10 — 12)
- B. David Loses His Sons Amnon and Absalom (2 Sam 13 — 20)

VII. Final Reflections on David's Reign (2 Sam 21 — 24)

Elkanah and His Wives

1 Now there was a certain man from [a]Ramathaim-zophim from the [b]hill country of Ephraim, and his name was [c]Elkanah the son of Jeroham, the son of Elihu, the son of Tohu, the son of Zuph, an Ephraimite.

2 He had [a]two wives: the name of one was [b]Hannah and the name of the other Peninnah; and Peninnah had children, but Hannah had no children.

3 Now this man would go up from his city [a]yearly [b]to worship and to sacrifice to the LORD of hosts in [c]Shiloh. And the two sons of Eli, Hophni and Phinehas, were priests to the LORD there.

4 When the day came that Elkanah sacrificed, he [a]would give portions to Peninnah his wife and to all her sons and her daughters;

5 but to Hannah he would give a double portion, for he loved Hannah, [a]but the LORD had closed her womb.

6 Her rival, however, [a]would provoke her bitterly to irritate her, because the LORD had closed her womb.

7 It happened year after year, as often as she went up to the house of the LORD, she would provoke her; so she wept and would not eat.

8 Then Elkanah her husband said to her, "Hannah, why do you weep and why do you not eat and why is your heart sad? [a]Am I not better to you than ten sons?"

9 Then Hannah rose after eating and drinking in Shiloh. Now Eli the priest was sitting on the seat by the doorpost of [a]the temple of the LORD.

10 She, [1]greatly distressed, prayed to the LORD and wept bitterly.

11 She [a]made a vow and said, "O LORD of hosts, if You will indeed [b]look on the affliction of Your maidservant and remember me, and not forget Your maidservant, but will give Your maidservant a [1]son, then I will give him to the LORD all the days of his life, and [c]a razor shall never come on his head."

12 Now it came about, as she [1]continued praying before the LORD, that Eli was watching her mouth.

13 As for Hannah, [a]she was speaking in her heart, only her lips were moving, but her voice was not heard. So Eli thought she was drunk.

14 Then Eli said to her, "[a]How long will you make yourself drunk? Put away your wine from you."

15 But Hannah replied, "No, my lord, I am a woman [1]oppressed in spirit; I have drunk

1:1 [a]1 Sam 1:19 [b]Josh 17:17, 18; 24:33 [c]1 Chr 6:22-28, 33-38
2 [a]Deut 21:15-17 [b]Luke 2:36
3 [a]Ex 34:23; 1 Sam 1:21; Luke 2:41 [b]Ex 23:14; Deut 12:5-7; 16:16 [c]Josh 18:1
4 [a]Deut 12:17, 18
5 [a]Gen 16:1; 30:1
6 [a]Job 24:21
8 [a]Ruth 4:15
9 [a]1 Sam 3:3
10 [1]Lit *bitter of soul*
11 [1]Lit *seed of men* [a]Num 30:6-11 [b]Gen 29:32 [c]Num 6:5; Judg 13:5
12 [1]Lit *multiplied*
13 [a]Gen 24:42-45
14 [a]Acts 2:4, 13
15 [1]Lit *severe*

1:1 *Ramathaim-zophim.* The name occurs only here in the OT and appears to be another name for Ramah (see 1:19; 2:11; 7:17; 19:18; 25:1). It is perhaps to be identified with the Ramah of Benjamin (see Josh 18:25) located in the hill country about five miles north of Jerusalem near the border of Ephraim and Benjamin. *-zophim.* Or "a Zuphite." It is not entirely clear whether this word refers to the man or the place. If it refers to the man, it indicates his descent from Zuph (see 1 Chr 6:34–35). If it refers to the place, it designates the general area in which Ramathaim is located (see 9:5). *Ephraimite.* Although Elkanah is here called an Ephraimite, he was probably a Levite whose family belonged to the Kohathite clans that had been allotted towns in Ephraim (see Josh 21:20–21; 1 Chr 6:22–26).

1:2 *two wives.* See notes on Gen 4:19; 16:2; 25:6.

1:3 *this man would go up . . . yearly.* Three times a year every Israelite male was required to appear before the Lord at the central sanctuary (Ex 23:14–19; 34:23; Deut 16:16–17). The festival referred to here was probably the Feast of Booths, which not only commemorated God's care for His people during the wilderness journey to Canaan (see Lev 23:43) but more especially celebrated, with joy and feasting, God's blessing on the year's crops (see Deut 16:13–15). On such festive occasions Hannah's deep sorrow because of her own barrenness was the more poignant. *the LORD of hosts.* This is the first time in the Bible that God is designated by this title. The Hebrew for "host(s)" can refer to (1) human armies (Ex 7:4; Ps 44:9); (2) the celestial bodies such as the sun, moon and stars (Gen 2:1; Deut 4:19; Is 40:26); or (3) the heavenly creatures such as angels (Josh 5:14; 1 Kin 22:19; Ps 148:2). The title, "the LORD of hosts," is perhaps best understood as a general reference to the sovereignty of God over all powers in the universe. In the account of the establishment of kingship in Israel it became particularly appropriate as a reference to God as the God of armies—both of the heavenly army (Deut 33:2; Josh 5:14; Ps 68:17; Hab 3:8) and of the army of Israel (1 Sam 17:45). *Shiloh.* The town in Ephraim between Bethel and Shechem where the central sanctuary and the ark of the covenant were located (see Josh 18:1; Judg 21:19).

1:4 *sacrificed.* Here refers to a sacrifice that was combined with a festive meal signifying fellowship and communion with the Lord and grateful acknowledgment of His mercies (see Lev 7:11–18; Deut 12:7,17–18).

1:5 *the LORD had closed her womb.* The Lord gives and withholds children (see Gen 18:10; 29:31; 30:2,22).

1:6 *Her rival.* See note on Gen 16:4.

1:9 *temple.* Here and in 3:3 the central sanctuary, the tabernacle (the temple in Jerusalem had not yet been built), is referred to as "the temple of the LORD." It is also called "the house of the LORD" (v. 7; 3:15), "the tent of meeting" (2:22) and "My dwelling" (2:32). The references to the tabernacle as a "house" and a "temple," as well as references to sleeping quarters and doors (3:2,15), give the impression that at this time the tabernacle was part of a larger, more permanent building complex to which the term "temple" could legitimately be applied (cf. Jer 7:12,14; 26:6).

1:11 *vow.* See Gen 28:20–22; Num 21:2; Ps 50:14; 76:11; 116:14,18; 132:2–5; Prov 20:25; 31:2. Regulations for the making of vows by women are found in Num 30. *remember.* To remember is more than simply to recall that Hannah existed. It is to go into action in her behalf (see v. 19; see also note on Gen 8:1). *all the days of his life.* In contrast to the normal period of service for Levites, which was from age 25 to 50 (see Num 8:23–26). *razor shall never.* Hannah voluntarily vows for her son that which God had required of Samson (Judg 13:5). Long hair was a symbol of dedication to the service of the Lord and was one of the characteristics of the Nazirite vow (see Num 6:1–21). The vow was normally taken for a limited time rather than for life.

1:13 *drunk.* Eli's mistake suggests that in those days it was not uncommon for drunken people to enter the sanctuary. Further evidence of the religious and moral deterioration of the time is found in the stories of Judg 17–21.

neither wine nor strong drink, but I [a]have poured out my soul before the LORD.

16 "Do not [1]consider your maidservant as a worthless woman, for I have spoken until now out of my great concern and [2]provocation."

17 Then Eli answered and said, "[a]Go in peace; and may the God of Israel [b]grant your petition that you have asked of Him."

18 She said, "[a]Let your maidservant find favor in your sight." So the woman went her way and ate, and [b]her face was no longer *sad*.

Samuel Is Born to Hannah

19 Then they arose early in the morning and worshiped before the LORD, and returned again to their house in [a]Ramah. And Elkanah [1]had relations with Hannah his wife, and [b]the LORD remembered her.

20 It came about [1]in due time, after Hannah had conceived, that she gave birth to a son; and she named him Samuel, *saying*, "[a]Because I have asked him of the LORD."

21 Then the man Elkanah [a]went up with all his household to offer to the LORD the yearly sacrifice and *pay* his vow.

22 But Hannah did not go up, for she said to her husband, "*I will not go up* until the child is weaned; then I will [a]bring him, that he may appear before the LORD and [b]stay there forever."

23 [a]Elkanah her husband said to her, "Do what seems best [1]to you. Remain until you have weaned him; only [b]may the LORD confirm His word." So the woman remained and nursed her son until she weaned him.

24 Now when she had weaned him, [a]she took him up with her, with a three-year-old bull and one ephah of flour and a jug of wine, and brought him to [b]the house of the LORD in Shiloh, although the child was young.

25 Then [a]they slaughtered the bull, and [b]brought the boy to Eli.

26 She said, "Oh, my lord! [a]As your soul lives, my lord, I am the woman who stood here beside you, praying to the LORD.

27 "[a]For this boy I prayed, and the LORD has given me my petition which I asked of Him.

28 "[a]So I have also [1]dedicated him to the LORD; as long as he lives he is [1]dedicated to the LORD." And [b]he worshiped the LORD there.

Hannah's Song of Thanksgiving

2 Then Hannah [a]prayed and said,
"My heart exults in the LORD;
[b]My [1]horn is exalted in the LORD,
My mouth [2]speaks boldly against my enemies,
Because [c]I rejoice in Your salvation.
2 "[a]There is no one holy like the LORD,
Indeed, [b]there is no one besides You,
[c]Nor is there any rock like our God.
3 "[1]Boast no more so very proudly,
[a]Do not let arrogance come out of your mouth;
[b]For the LORD is a God of knowledge,
[c]And with Him actions are weighed.
4 "[a]The bows of the mighty are shattered,
[b]But the feeble gird on strength.
5 "Those who were full hire themselves out for bread,
But those who were hungry cease *to hunger*.

15 [a]Job 30:16; Ps 42:4; 62:8; Lam 2:19 **16** [1]Lit *give* [2]Lit *my provocation* **17** [a]Judg 18:6; 1 Sam 25:35; 2 Kin 5:19; Mark 5:34; Luke 7:50 [b]Ps 20:3-5 **18** [a]Gen 33:15; Ruth 2:13 [b]Rom 15:13 **19** [1]Lit *knew* [a]1 Sam 1:1; 2:11 [b]Gen 21:1; 30:22 **20** [1]Lit *at the circuit of the days* [a]Gen 41:51, 52; Ex 2:10, 22; Matt 1:21 **21** [a]Deut 12:11; 1 Sam 1:3 **22** [a]Luke 2:22 [b]1 Sam 1:11, 28 **23** [1]Lit *in your eyes* [a]Num 30:7, 10, 11 [b]1 Sam 1:17 **24** [a]Num 15:9, 10; Deut 12:5, 6

24 [b]Josh 18:1; 1 Sam 4:3, 4 **25** [a]Lev 1:5 [b]Luke 2:22 **26** [a]2 Kin 2:2, 4, 6; 4:30 **27** [a]1 Sam 1:11-13; Ps 6:9; 66:19, 20 **28** [1]Lit *lent* [a]1 Sam 1:11, 22 [b]Gen 24:26, 52 **2:1** [1]I.e. strength [2]Lit *is enlarged* [a]1 Sam 2:1-10; Luke 1:46-55 [b]Deut 33:17; Job 16:15; Ps 75:10; 89:17, 24; 92:10; 112:9 [c]Ps 9:14; 13:5; 35:9; Is 12:2, 3 **2** [a]Ex 15:11; Lev 19:2; Ps 86:8 [b]2 Sam 22:32 [c]Deut 32:30, 31 **3** [1]Lit *Talk much* [a]Prov 8:13 [b]1 Sam 16:7; 1 Kin 8:39 [c]Prov 16:2; 24:12 **4** [a]Ps 37:15; 46:9 [b]Ps 18:39; Heb 11:32-34

1:16 *worthless.* See note on Deut 13:13.
1:20 *Samuel.* "Samuel" sounds like the Hebrew for "heard of God."
1:21 *yearly sacrifice.* See notes on vv. 3–4. *his vow.* Making vows to God was a common feature of OT piety, usually involving thank offerings and praise (see Lev 7:16; Ps 50:14; 56:12; 66:13–15; 116:17–18; Is 19:21). Elkanah no doubt annually made vows to the Lord as he prayed for God's blessing on his crops and flocks, and fulfilled those vows at the Feast of Booths (see note on v. 3).
1:22 *weaned.* It was customary in the East to nurse children for three years or longer (in the Apocrypha see 2 Maccabees 7:27) since there was no way to keep milk sweet.
1:23 *His word.* No previous word from God is mentioned, unless this refers to the pronouncement of Eli in v. 17. The Dead Sea Scrolls, Septuagint (the Greek translation of the OT) and Syriac version resolve this problem by reading "your word."
1:26 *As your soul lives.* A customary way of emphasizing the truthfulness of one's words.
2:1 *prayed.* Hannah's prayer is a song of praise and thanksgiving to God (see Ps 72:20, where the psalms of David are designated "prayers"). This song has sometimes been termed the "Magnificat of the OT" because it is so similar to the Magnificat of the NT (Mary's song, Luke 1:46–55). It also has certain resemblances to the "Benedictus" (the song of Zechariah, Luke 1:67–79). Hannah's song of praise finds many echoes in David's song near the end of the book (2 Sam 22). These two songs frame the main narrative, and their themes highlight the ways of God that the narrative relates—they contain the theology of the book in the form of praise. Hannah speaks prophetically at a time when Israel is about to enter an important new period of her history with the establishment of kingship through her son, Samuel. *exults in the LORD.* The supreme source of Hannah's joy is not in the child, but in the God who has answered her prayer. *My horn is exalted in the LORD.* See NASB marg.; cf. Deut 33:17; Ps 75:5,10; 92:10; 112:9; Luke 1:69. To have one's horn lifted up by God is to be delivered from disgrace to a position of honor and strength.
2:2 *no one besides You.* See 2 Sam 7:22; Deut 4:39; Is 45:6. *rock.* A metaphor to depict the strength and stability of the God of Israel as the unfailing source of security for His people (see 2 Sam 22:32; Deut 32:4,31; Ps 18:31; Is 30:29; 44:8).
2:3 *so very proudly . . . arrogance.* After the manner of Peninnah (and others in the narratives of 1,2 Samuel—Eli's sons, the Philistines, Saul, Nabal, Goliath, Absalom, Shimei and Sheba). *the LORD is a God of knowledge.* See 16:7; 1 Kin 8:39; Ps 139:1–6.
2:4–5 In a series of examples derived from everyday life Hannah shows that God often works contrary to natural expectations and brings about surprising reversals—seen frequently in the stories that follow.

[a]Even the barren gives birth to seven,
But [b]she who has many children
languishes.
6 "[a]The LORD kills and makes alive;
[b]He brings down to [1]Sheol and raises
up.
7 "[a]The LORD makes poor and rich;
[b]He brings low, He also exalts.
8 "[a]He raises the poor from the dust,
[b]He lifts the needy from the ash heap
[c]To make them sit with nobles,
And inherit a seat of honor;
[d]For the pillars of the earth are the
LORD's,
And He set the world on them.
9 "[a]He keeps the feet of His godly ones,
[b]But the wicked ones are silenced in
darkness;
[c]For not by might shall a man prevail.
10 "[a]Those who contend with the LORD
will be shattered;
[b]Against them He will thunder in the
heavens,
[c]The LORD will judge the ends of the
earth;
[d]And He will give strength to His
king,
[e]And will exalt the [1]horn of His
anointed."

11 Then Elkanah went to his home at [a]Ramah. [b]But the boy ministered to the LORD before Eli the priest.

The Sin of Eli's Sons

12 Now the sons of Eli were [1][a]worthless men; they did not know the LORD

13 [a]and the custom of the priests with the people. When any man was offering a sacrifice, the priest's servant would come while the meat was boiling, with a three-pronged fork in his hand.

14 Then he would thrust it into the pan, or kettle, or caldron, or pot; all that the fork brought up the priest would take for himself. Thus they did in Shiloh to all the Israelites who came there.

15 Also, before [a]they burned the fat, the priest's servant would come and say to the man who was sacrificing, "Give the priest meat for roasting, as he will not take boiled meat from you, only raw."

16 If the man said to him, "They must surely [1]burn the fat [2]first, and then take as much as [3]you desire," then he would say, "No, but you shall give *it to me* now; and if not, I will take it by force."

17 Thus the sin of the young men was very great before the LORD, for the men [a]despised the offering of the LORD.

5 [a]Ruth 4:15; Ps 113:9 [b]Jer 15:9
6 [1]I.e. the nether world [a]Deut 32:39; 2 Kin 5:7; Rev 1:18 [b]Is 26:19
7 [a]Deut 8:17, 18 [b]Job 5:11; Ps 75:7; James 4:10
8 [a]Job 42:10-12; Ps 75:7; 113:7 [b]2 Sam 7:8; Dan 2:48; James 2:5 [c]Job 36:7; Ps 113:8 [d]Job 38:4-6; Ps 75:3; 104:5
9 [a]Ps 91:11, 12; 121:3; Prov 3:26; 1 Pet 1:5 [b]Matt 8:12 [c]Ps 33:16, 17
10 [1]I.e. strength [a]Ex 15:6; Ps 2:9 [b]1 Sam 7:10; 2 Sam 22:14; Ps 18:13, 14 [c]Ps 96:13; 98:9; Matt 25:31, 32 [d]Ps 21:1, 7 [e]Ps 89:24
11 [a]1 Sam 1:1, 19 [b]1 Sam 1:28; 2:18; 3:1
12 [1]Lit *sons of Belial* [a]Jer 2:8; 9:3, 6; 2 Cor 6:15
13 [a]Lev 7:29-34
15 [a]Lev 3:3-5, 16
16 [1]Lit *offer up in smoke* [2]Lit *like the day* [3]Lit *your soul*
17 [a]Mal 2:7-9

2:5 *birth to seven.* See note on Ruth 4:15.

2:6–8 Hannah declares that life and death, prosperity and adversity, are determined by the sovereign power of God—another theme richly illustrated in the following narrative (see Deut 32:39; 1 Kin 17:20–24; 2 Kin 4:32–35; John 5:21; 11:41–44).

2:6 *Sheol.* See NASB marg.; see also note on Gen 37:35.

2:8 *pillars of the earth.* A common figure in the OT for the solid base on which the earth (the dry land on which man lives, not planet earth; Gen 1:10) is founded. The phrase does not teach a particular theory of the structure of the universe (see Job 9:6; 38:6; Ps 75:3; 104:5; Zech 12:1).

2:9 *keeps the feet.* Travel in ancient Israel was for the most part by foot over trails that were often rocky and dangerous (see Ps 91:11–12; 121:3). *godly ones.* People who are faithful to the Lord. The Hebrew root underlying this word is used of both God and His people in 2 Sam 22:26 (see also Ps 18:25) to characterize the nature of their mutual relationship. The word is also found in Ps 12:1; 32:6; Prov 2:8.

2:10 *judge.* Impose His righteous rule upon (see Ps 96:13; 98:9). *ends of the earth.* All nations and peoples (see Deut 33:17; Is 45:22). *His king.* Hannah's prayer is here prophetic, anticipating the establishment of kingship in Israel and the initial realization of the Messianic ideal in David (Luke 1:69). Ultimately her expectation finds fulfillment in Christ and His complete triumph over the enemies of God. *horn.* See note on v. 1. *anointed.* The first reference in the Bible to the Lord's anointed—i.e., His anointed king. (Priests were also anointed for God's service; see Ex 28:41; Lev 4:3.) The word is often synonymous with "king" (as here) and provides part of the vocabulary basis for the Messianic idea in the Bible. "Anointed" and "Messiah" are the translation and transliteration respectively of the same Hebrew word. The Greek translation of this Hebrew term is *Christos,* from which comes the English word "Christ" (see note on Matt 1:17). A king (coming from the tribe of Judah) is first prophesied by Jacob (Gen 49:10); kingship is further anticipated in the oracles of Balaam in Num 24:7,17. Also Deut 17:14–20 looks forward to the time when the Lord will place a king of His choice over His people after they enter the promised land. 1,2 Samuel shows how this expectation of the theocratic king is realized in the person of David. Hannah's prophetic anticipation of a king at the time of the dedication of her son Samuel, who was to be God's agent for establishing kingship in Israel, is entirely appropriate.

2:11 *ministered.* Performed such services as a boy might render while assisting the high priest. *to the LORD.* At the "house of the LORD" (1:24).

2:12 *worthless.* See note on Deut 13:13. *did not know.* In OT usage, to "know" the Lord is not just intellectual or theoretical recognition. To know the Lord is to enter into fellowship with Him and acknowledge His claims on one's life. The term often has a covenantal connotation (see Jer 31:34; Hos 13:4).

2:13–16 Apparently vv. 13–14 describe the practice that had come to be accepted for determining the priests' portion of the peace offerings (Lev 7:31–36; 10:14–15; Deut 18:1–5)—a tradition presumably based on the assumption that a random thrust of the fork would providentially determine a fair portion. Verses 15–16 then describe how Eli's sons arrogantly violated that custom and the law.

2:15 *before they burned the fat.* On the altar as the Lord's portion, which He was to receive first (see Lev 3:16; 4:10,26,31,35; 7:28,30–31; 17:6). *roasting.* Boiling is the only form of cooking specified in the law for the priests' portion (Num 6:19–20). Roasting this portion is nowhere expressly forbidden in the law, but it is specified only for the Passover lamb (Ex 12:8–9; Deut 16:7). The present passage seems to imply that for the priests to roast their portion of the sacrifices was unlawful.

2:16 *by force.* Presenting the priests' portion was to be a voluntary act on the part of the worshipers (see Lev 7:28–36; Deut 18:3).

Samuel before the Lord as a Boy

18 Now [a]Samuel was ministering before
the LORD, *as* a boy [1b]wearing a linen ephod.
19 And his mother would make him a little [a]robe and bring it to him from year to
year when she would come up with her husband to offer [b]the yearly sacrifice.
20 Then Eli would [a]bless Elkanah and his
wife and say, "May the LORD give you [1]chil-
dren from this woman in place of [2]the one
she [b]dedicated to the LORD." And they went
to their own [3]home.
21 [a]The LORD visited Hannah; and she
conceived and gave birth to three sons and
two daughters. And [b]the boy Samuel grew
before the LORD.

Eli Rebukes His Sons

22 Now Eli was very old; and he heard [a]all
that his sons were doing to all Israel, and
how they lay with [b]the women who served
at the doorway of the tent of meeting.
23 He said to them, "Why do you do such
things, the evil things that I hear from all
these people?
24 "No, my sons; for the report is not good
[a]which I hear [1]the LORD's people circulating.
25 "If one man sins against another, [a]God
will mediate for him; but [b]if a man sins
against the LORD, who can intercede for
him?" But they would not listen to the voice
of their father, for the [c]LORD desired to put
them to death.
26 Now the boy [a]Samuel [1]was growing in
stature and in favor both with the LORD and
with men.
27 Then [a]a man of God came to Eli and
said to him, "Thus says the LORD, '[b]Did I *not*
indeed reveal Myself to the house of your
father when they were in Egypt *in bondage*
to Pharaoh's house?
28 '[a]Did I *not* choose them from all the
tribes of Israel to be My priests, to go up to
My altar, to burn incense, to carry an ephod
before Me; and did I *not* [b]give to the house of
your father all the fire *offerings* of the sons of
Israel?
29 'Why do you [a]kick at My sacrifice and at
My offering [b]which I have commanded *in My*
[c]*dwelling*, and [d]honor your sons above Me,
by making yourselves fat with the [1]choicest
of every offering of My people Israel?'
30 "Therefore the LORD God of Israel
declares, '[a]I did indeed say that your house
and the house of your father should walk
before Me forever'; but now the LORD
declares, 'Far be it from Me—for [b]those who
honor Me I will honor, and those [c]who
despise Me will be lightly esteemed.
31 'Behold, [a]the days are coming when I
will break your [1]strength and the [1]strength of
your father's house so that there will not be
an old man in your house.
32 'You will see [a]the distress of *My* dwell-

31 [1]Or *arm* [a]1 Sam 4:11-18; 22:17-20 **32** [a]1 Kin 2:26, 27

18 [1]Lit *girded with* [a]1 Sam 2:11; 3:1 [b]1 Sam 2:28; 22:18; 2 Sam 6:14; 1 Chr 15:27
19 [a]Ex 28:31 [b]1 Sam 1:3, 21
20 [1]Lit *seed* [2]Lit *the one asked for which was lent* [3]Lit *place* [a]Luke 2:34 [b]1 Sam 1:11, 27, 28
21 [a]Gen 21:1 [b]Judg 13:24; 1 Sam 2:26; 3:19-21; Luke 1:80; 2:40
22 [a]1 Sam 2:13-17 [b]Ex 38:8
24 [1]Or *making the LORD's people transgress* [a]1 Kin 15:26
25 [a]Deut 1:17 [b]Num 15:30; 1 Sam 3:14; Heb 10:26, 27 [c]Josh 11:20
26 [1]Lit *was going on both great and good* [a]1 Sam 2:21; Luke 2:52
27 [a]Deut 33:1; Judg 13:6 [b]Ex 4:14-16; 12:1, 43
28 [a]Ex 28:1-4; 30:7, 8; Lev 8:7, 8 [b]Lev 7:35, 36
29 [1]Or *first* [a]1 Sam 2:13-17 [b]Deut 12:5-9 [c]Ps 26:8 [d]Matt 10:37
30 [a]Ex 29:9; Num 25:13 [b]Ps 50:23 [c]Mal 2:9

2:18 *Now Samuel.* Between 2:11 and 4:1 the author presents a series of sharp contrasts between Samuel and Eli's sons. *linen ephod.* A priestly garment worn by those who served before the Lord at His sanctuary (see 22:18; 2 Sam 6:14). It was a close-fitting, sleeveless pullover, usually of hip length, and is to be distinguished from the special ephod worn by the high priest (see note on v. 28; cf. Ex 39:1–26).

2:19 *little robe.* A sleeveless garment reaching to the knees, worn over the undergarment and under the ephod (see 15:27; 18:4). *yearly sacrifice.* See note on 1:3.

2:22 *lay with the women who served.* See Ex 38:8. There is no further reference to such women in the OT. Perhaps these women performed various menial tasks, but certainly their service is not to be confused with that of the Levites, which is prescribed in the Pentateuch (Num 1:50; 3:6–8; 8:15; 16:9; 18:2–3). The immoral acts of Eli's sons are reminiscent of the religious prostitution (fertility rites) at the Canaanite sanctuaries (see 1 Kin 14:24; 15:12; 22:46)—acts that were an abomination to the Lord and a desecration of His house (Deut 23:17–18).

2:23 *He said to them.* Eli rebuked his sons but did not remove them from office. God would do that.

2:25 *God.* Eli's argument is that when someone commits an offense against another man, there is recourse to a third party to decide the issue (whether this be understood as God or as God's representatives, the judges; see Ex 22:8–9 and note on Ex 22:11); but when the offense is against the Lord, there is no recourse, for God is both the one wronged and the judge. *the LORD desired to put them to death.* This comment by the author of the narrative is not intended to excuse Eli's sons, but to indicate that Eli's warning was much too late. Eli's sons had persisted in their evil ways for so long that God's judgment on them was determined (v. 34; see Josh 11:20).

2:26 *growing in stature and in favor both with the LORD and with men.* Cf. Luke's description of Jesus (Luke 2:52).

2:27 *man of God.* Often a designation for a prophet (see 9:6,10; Deut 33:1; Josh 14:6; 1 Kin 13:1,6–8; 17:18,24; 2 Kin 4:7). *house of your father.* The descendants of Aaron.

2:28 *to be My priests.* Three tasks of the priests are mentioned: 1. *to go up to My altar.* To perform the sacrificial rites at the altar of burnt offering in the courtyard of the tabernacle. 2. *to burn incense.* At the altar of incense in the holy place (Ex 30:1–10). 3. *to carry an ephod.* See note on v. 18. It would appear that the reference here is to the special ephod of the high priest (see Ex 28:4–13). The breastplate containing the Urim and Thummim was attached to the ephod of the high priest. The Urim and Thummim were a divinely ordained means of communication with God, placed in the custody of the high priest (see Ex 28:30 and note; see also 1 Sam 23:9–12; 30:7–8).

2:30 *I did indeed say.* See Ex 29:9; Lev 8–9; Num 16–17; 25:13. *Far be it from Me.* This is not to say that the promise of the priesthood to Aaron's house has been annulled, but that Eli and his house are to be excluded from participation in this privilege because of their sin. *those who honor Me I will honor.* See v. 29. Spiritual privileges bring responsibilities and obligations; they are not to be treated as irrevocable rights (see 2 Sam 22:26–27).

2:31 *strength . . . strength.* Lit. "arm . . . arm," symbolic of strength. Eli's "arm" and that of his priestly family will be cut off (contrast David, 2 Sam 22:35). *not be an old man in your house.* A prediction of the decimation of Eli's priestly family in the death of his sons (4:11), in the massacre of his descendants by Saul at Nob (22:18–19) and in the removal of Abiathar from his priestly office (1 Kin 2:26–27).

2:32 *distress of My dwelling.* Including the capture of the ark by the Philistines (4:1–10), the destruction of Shiloh (Jer 7:14) and

ing, in *spite of* all the good that [1]I do for Israel; and an [b]old man will not be in your house
forever.
33 'Yet I will not cut off every man of yours
from My altar [1]so that your eyes will fail
from weeping and your soul grieve, and all
the increase of your house will die [2]in the
prime of life.
34 'This will be [a]the sign to you which will
come concerning your two sons, Hophni and
Phinehas: [b]on the same day both of them will
die.
35 'But [a]I will raise up for Myself a faithful
priest who will do according to what is in My
heart and in My soul; and [b]I will build him
an enduring house, and he will walk before
[c]My anointed always.
36 'Everyone who is left in your house will
come and bow down to him for a [1]piece of
silver or a loaf of bread and say, "Please
[2]assign me to one of the priest's offices so
that I may eat a piece of bread." ' "

The Prophetic Call to Samuel

3 Now [a]the boy Samuel was ministering to
the LORD before Eli. And [b]word from the
LORD was rare in those days, [1]visions were
infrequent.
2 It happened at that time as Eli was
lying down in his place (now [a]his eyesight
had begun to grow dim *and* he could not see
well),
3 and [a]the lamp of God had not yet gone
out, and Samuel was lying down in the temple of the LORD where the ark of God *was*,
4 that the LORD called Samuel; and he
said, "[a]Here I am."
5 Then he ran to Eli and said, "Here I
am, for you called me." But he said, "I did
not call, lie down again." So he went and lay
down.
6 The LORD called yet again, "Samuel!" So
Samuel arose and went to Eli and said, "Here
I am, for you called me." But he [1]answered,
"I did not call, my son, lie down again."
7 [a]Now Samuel did not yet know the
LORD, nor had the word of the LORD yet been
revealed to him.
8 So the LORD called Samuel again for the
third time. And he arose and went to Eli and
said, "Here I am, for you called me." Then
Eli discerned that the LORD was calling the
boy.
9 And Eli said to Samuel, "Go lie down,
and it shall be if He calls you, that you shall
say, 'Speak, LORD, for Your servant is listening.' " So Samuel went and lay down in his
place.
10 Then the LORD came and stood and
called as at other times, "Samuel! Samuel!"
And Samuel said, "Speak, for Your servant is
listening."
11 The LORD said to Samuel, "Behold, [a]I
am about to do a thing in Israel at which both
ears of everyone who hears it will tingle.
12 "In that day [a]I will carry out against Eli
all that I have spoken concerning his house,
from beginning to end.
13 "For [a]I have told him that I am about to
judge his house forever for [b]the iniquity
which he knew, because [c]his sons brought a
curse on themselves and [d]he did not rebuke
them.
14 "Therefore I have sworn to the house of
Eli that [a]the iniquity of Eli's house shall not
be atoned for by sacrifice or offering forever."
15 So Samuel lay down until morning.
Then he [a]opened the doors of the house of

32 [1]Lit *He does* [b]Zech 8:4
33 [1]Lit *to waste away your eyes and to grieve your soul* [2]Lit *as men*
34 [a]1 Sam 10:7-9; 1 Kin 13:3 [b]1 Sam 4:11, 17
35 [a]1 Sam 3:1; 7:9; 9:12, 13 [b]1 Sam 8:3-5; 25:28; 2 Sam 7:11, 27; 1 Kin 11:38 [c]1 Sam 10:9, 10; 12:3; 16:13
36 [1]Or *payment* [2]Lit *attach*
3:1 [1]Lit *no vision spread abroad* [a]1 Sam 2:11, 18 [b]Ps 74:9; Ezek 7:26; Amos 8:11, 12
2 [a]Gen 27:1; 48:10; 1 Sam 4:15
3 [a]Ex 25:31-37; Lev 24:2, 3
4 [a]Is 6:8
6 [1]Lit *said*
7 [a]Acts 19:2; 1 Cor 13:11
11 [a]2 Kin 21:12; Jer 19:3
12 [a]1 Sam 2:27-36
13 [a]1 Sam 2:29-31 [b]1 Sam 2:22 [c]1 Sam 2:12, 17, 22 [d]Deut 17:12; 21:18
14 [a]Lev 15:31; Is 22:14
15 [a]1 Chr 15:23

the relocation of the tabernacle to Nob (21:1–6; see note on 21:1).

2:33 A reference apparently to Abiathar, who was expelled from office by Solomon (see 1 Kin 2:26–27) after an unsuccessful attempt to make Adonijah king as the successor to David.

2:34 *the sign to you.* The death of Hophni and Phinehas (4:11) will confirm the longer-term predictions. Such confirmation of a prophetic word was not uncommon (see 10:7–9; 1 Kin 13:3; Jer 28:15–17; Luke 1:18–20).

2:35 *I will raise up for Myself a faithful priest.* Initially fulfilled in the person of Zadok, who served as a priest during the time of David (see 2 Sam 8:17; 15:24,35; 20:25) and who eventually replaced Abiathar as high priest in the time of Solomon (see 1 Kin 2:35; 1 Chr 29:22). *build him an enduring house.* Lit. "build for him a faithful house"; the faithful priest will be given a "faithful" (i.e., enduring) priestly family. See the similar word spoken concerning David (25:28, "enduring house"; see also 2 Sam 7:16; 1 Kin 11:38). The line of Zadok was continued by his son Azariah (see 1 Kin 4:1) and was still on the scene at the time of the return from the exile (see 1 Chr 6:14–15; Ezra 3:2). It continued in intertestamental times until Antiochus IV Epiphanes (175–164 B.C.) sold the priesthood to Menelaus (in the Apocrypha see 2 Maccabees 4:23–50), who was not of the priestly line. *My anointed.* David and his successors (see note on v. 10).

3:1 *boy Samuel.* See 2:11,18. Samuel is now no longer a little child (see 2:21,26). The Jewish historian Josephus places his age at 12 years; he may have been older. *word from the LORD was rare.* See Prov 29:18; Amos 8:11. During the entire period of the judges, apart from the prophet of 2:27–36, we are told of only two prophets (Judg 4:4; 6:8) and of five revelations (Judg 2:1–3; 6:11–23; 7:2–11; 10:11–14; 13:3–21). Possibly 2 Chr 15:3 also refers to this period. *visions.* Cf. Gen 15:1.

3:3 *the lamp of God had not yet gone out.* The reference is to the golden lampstand, which stood opposite the table of the bread of the Presence (Ex 25:31–40) in the holy place. It was still night, but the early morning hours were approaching when the flame grew dim or went out (see Ex 27:20–21; 30:7–8; Lev 24:3–4; 2 Chr 13:11; Prov 31:18). For the lamp to be permitted to go out before morning was a violation of the Pentateuchal regulations. *temple.* See note on 1:9.

3:5 *he said.* Eli's failure to recognize at once that the Lord had called Samuel may be indicative of his own unfamiliarity with the Lord.

3:7 *did not yet know the LORD.* In the sense of having a direct experience of Him (see Ex 1:8), such as receiving a revelation from God (see the last half of the verse).

3:11–14 The Lord's first revelation to Samuel repeats the message Eli had already received from the "man of God" (2:27–36), thus confirming the fact that the youth had indeed received a revelation from God.

3:15 *doors of the house of the LORD.* See note on 1:9. The tabernacle itself did not have doors. This may refer to an enclosure in which it stood. *vision.* See note on vv. 11–14.

the LORD. But Samuel was afraid to tell [b]the vision to Eli.

16 Then Eli called Samuel and said, "Samuel, my son." And he said, "Here I am."

17 He said, "What is the word that He spoke to you? Please do not hide it from me. [a]May God do so to you, and more also, if you hide anything from me of all the words that He spoke to you."

18 So Samuel told him everything and hid nothing from him. And he said, "[a]It is the LORD; let Him do what seems good to Him."

19 Thus [a]Samuel grew and [b]the LORD was with him and [c]let none of his words [1]fail.

20 All Israel [a]from Dan even to Beersheba knew that Samuel was confirmed as a prophet of the LORD.

21 And [a]the LORD appeared again at Shiloh, [b]because the LORD revealed Himself to Samuel at Shiloh by the word of the LORD.

Philistines Take the Ark in Victory

4 Thus the word of Samuel came to all Israel. Now Israel went out to meet the Philistines in battle and camped beside [a]Ebenezer while the Philistines camped in [b]Aphek.

2 The Philistines drew up in battle array to meet Israel. When the battle spread, Israel was [1]defeated before the Philistines who killed about four thousand men on the battlefield.

3 When the people came into the camp, the elders of Israel said, "[a]Why has the LORD defeated us today before the Philistines? [b]Let us take to ourselves from Shiloh the ark of the covenant of the LORD, that [1]it may come among us and deliver us from the power of our enemies."

4 So the people sent to Shiloh, and from there they carried the ark of the covenant of the LORD of hosts [a]who sits *above* the cherubim; and the two sons of Eli, Hophni and Phinehas, *were* there with the ark of the covenant of God.

5 As the ark of the covenant of the LORD came into the camp, [a]all Israel shouted with a great shout, so that the earth resounded.

6 When the Philistines heard the noise of the shout, they said, "What *does* the noise of this great shout in the camp of the Hebrews *mean?*" Then they understood that the ark of the LORD had come into the camp.

7 The Philistines were afraid, for they said, "God has come into the camp." And they said, "[a]Woe to us! For nothing like this has happened before.

8 "Woe to us! Who shall deliver us from the hand of these mighty gods? These are the gods who smote the Egyptians with all *kinds of* plagues in the wilderness.

9 "[a]Take courage and be men, O Philistines, or you will become slaves to the Hebrews, [b]as they have been slaves to you; therefore, be men and fight."

10 So the Philistines fought and [a]Israel was [1]defeated, and [b]every man fled to his tent; and the slaughter was very great, for there fell of Israel thirty thousand foot soldiers.

11 And the ark of God was taken; and [a]the two sons of Eli, Hophni and Phinehas, died.

15 [b]1 Sam 3:10 **17** [a]2 Sam 3:35 **18** [a]Ex 34:5-7; Lev 10:3; Job 2:10; Is 39:8 **19** [1]Lit *fall to the ground* [a]1 Sam 2:21 [b]Gen 21:22; 28:15; 39:2 [c]1 Sam 9:6 **20** [a]Judg 20:1 **21** [a]Gen 12:7 [b]1 Sam 3:10 **4:1** [a]1 Sam 7:12 [b]Josh 12:18; 1 Sam 29:1 **2** [1]Lit *smitten* **3** [a]Josh 7:7, 8 [b]Num 10:35; Josh 6:6

3 [1]Or *he* **4** [a]Ex 25:22; 2 Sam 6:2; Ps 80:1 **5** [a]Josh 6:5, 20 **7** [a]Ex 15:14 **9** [a]1 Cor 16:13 [b]Judg 13:1; 1 Sam 14:21 **10** [1]Lit *smitten* [a]Deut 28:15, 25; 1 Sam 4:2 [b]2 Sam 18:17; 19:8; 2 Kin 14:12; 2 Chr 25:22 **11** [a]1 Sam 2:34; Ps 78:56-64

3:17 *May God do so to you, and more.* A curse formula (see 14:44; 20:13; 25:22; 2 Sam 3:9,35; 19:13; Ruth 1:17; 1 Kin 2:23; 2 Kin 6:31), usually directed against the speaker but here used by Eli against Samuel if he conceals anything the Lord said (see also note on 14:24).

3:18 *let Him do what seems good to Him.* Eli bows before God, accepting the judgment as righteous (see Ex 34:5–7).

3:19 *let none of his words fail.* Because none of Samuel's words proved unreliable, he was recognized as a prophet who spoke the word of the Lord (see vv. 20–21).

3:20 *Dan even to Beersheba.* A conventional expression often used in Samuel, Kings and Chronicles to denote the entire land (Dan was located in the far north and Beersheba in the far south).

3:21 *at Shiloh.* But not after the events narrated in chs. 4–6 (see Jer 7:12–14; 26:6).

4:1 *the word of Samuel came to all Israel.* Contrast 3:1. *Ebenezer.* Means "stone of help." The precise location is unknown, but it was probably a short distance (see v. 6) to the east of Aphek—not to be confused with the location of the stone named Ebenezer that was later erected by Samuel between Mizpah and Shen (see 7:12) to commemorate a victory over the Philistines. *Aphek.* A town about 12 miles northeast of the coastal city of Joppa. Philistine presence this far north suggests an attempt to spread their control over the Israelite tribes of central Canaan (see v. 9; Judg 15:11).

4:3 *Why has the LORD defeated us . . . ?* The elders understood that their defeat was more an indication of God's displeasure than it was of Philistine military might. Israel's pagan neighbors also believed that the outcome of battle was decided by the gods. *that it may come among us and deliver us.* See NASB marg. In an attempt to secure the Lord's presence with them in the struggle against the Philistines, the elders sent for the ark of the covenant. They were correct in thinking there was a connection between God's presence with His people and the ark (cf. v. 4), and no doubt they remembered the presence of the ark at notable victories in Israel's past history (see Num 10:33–36; Josh 3:3,11,14–17; 6:6,12–20). But they incorrectly believed that the Lord's presence with the ark was guaranteed, rather than being subject to His free decision. They reflect the pagan notion that the deity is identified with the symbol of His presence, and that God's favor could automatically be gained by manipulating the symbol.

4:4 *sits above the cherubim.* On each end of the atonement cover of the ark of the covenant were golden cherubim with their wings spread upward over the ark (see Ex 25:17–22). In the space between these cherubim God's presence with His people was localized in a special way, so that the atonement cover of the ark came to be viewed as the throne of Israel's divine King (see 2 Sam 6:2; Ps 80:1; 99:1). *Hophni and Phinehas.* These wicked priests (see 2:12) did not restrain the army from its improper use of the ark but actually accompanied the ark to the battlefield.

4:6 *Hebrews.* See note on Gen 14:13.

4:7 *God has come into the camp.* The Philistines also identified the God of Israel with the symbol of His presence (see note on v. 3).

4:8 *mighty gods.* The Philistines could think only in polytheistic terms. *Egyptians . . . plagues.* See note on 6:6.

4:11 *the ark of God was taken.* This phrase or a variation of it occurs five times in the chapter (here, vv. 17,19,21–22) and is

12 Now a man of Benjamin ran from the battle line and came to Shiloh the same day with [a]his clothes torn and [1]dust on his head.

13 When he came, behold, [a]Eli was sitting on *his* seat [1]by the road eagerly watching, because his heart was trembling for the ark of God. So the man came to tell *it* in the city, and all the city cried out.

14 When Eli heard the noise of the outcry, he said, "What *does* the noise of this commotion *mean?*" Then the man came hurriedly and told Eli.

15 Now Eli was ninety-eight years old, and [a]his eyes were set so that he could not see.

16 The man said to Eli, "I am the one who came from the battle line. Indeed, I escaped from the battle line today." And he said, "[a]How did things go, my son?"

17 Then the one who brought the news replied, "Israel has fled before the Philistines and there has also been a great slaughter among the people, and your two sons also, Hophni and Phinehas, are dead, and the ark of God has been taken."

18 When he mentioned the ark of God, [1][a]Eli fell off the seat backward beside the gate, and his neck was broken and he died, for [2]he was old and heavy. Thus he judged Israel forty years.

19 Now his daughter-in-law, Phinehas's wife, was pregnant and about to give birth; and when she heard the news that the ark of God was taken and that her father-in-law and her husband had died, she kneeled down and gave birth, for her pains came upon her.

20 And about the time of her death the women who stood by her said to her, "[a]Do not be afraid, for you have given birth to a son." But she did not answer or pay attention.

21 And she called the boy [1]Ichabod, saying, "[a]The glory has departed from Israel," because [b]the ark of God was taken and because of her father-in-law and her husband.

22 She said, "The glory has departed from Israel, for the ark of God was taken."

Capture of the Ark Provokes God

5 Now the Philistines took the ark of God and [a]brought it from Ebenezer to [b]Ashdod.

2 Then the Philistines took the ark of God and brought it to [a]the house of Dagon and set it by Dagon.

3 When the Ashdodites arose early the next morning, behold, [a]Dagon had fallen on his face to the ground before the ark of the LORD. So they took Dagon and [b]set him in his place again.

4 But when they arose early the next morning, behold, [a]Dagon had fallen on his face to the ground before the ark of the LORD. And the head of Dagon and both the palms of his hands *were* cut off on the threshold; [1]only the trunk of Dagon was left to him.

5 Therefore neither the priests of Dagon nor all who enter Dagon's house [a]tread on the threshold of Dagon in Ashdod to this day.

12 [1]Lit *ground* [a]Josh 7:6; 2 Sam 1:2; 15:32; Neh 9:1; Job 2:12
13 [1]Gr version reads *beside the gate watching the road* [a]1 Sam 1:9; 4:18
15 [a]1 Sam 3:2; 1 Kin 14:4
16 [a]2 Sam 1:4
18 [1]Lit *he* [2]Lit *the man* [a]1 Sam 4:13
20 [a]Gen 35:16-19
21 [1]I.e. No glory [a]Ps 26:8; Jer 2:11 [b]1 Sam 4:11
5:1 [a]1 Sam 4:1; 7:12 [b]Josh 13:3
2 [a]Judg 16:23-30; 1 Chr 10:8-10
3 [a]Is 19:1; 46:1, 2 [b]Is 46:7
4 [1]So with ancient versions; Heb *only Dagon* [a]Ezek 6:4, 6; Mic 1:7
5 [a]Zeph 1:9

the focal point of the narrative. In this disastrous event, God's word in 3:11 finds a swift fulfillment. *Hophni and Phinehas, died.* The fulfillment of 2:34; 3:12.

4:12 *his clothes torn and dust on his head.* A sign of grief and sorrow, here marking the messenger as a bearer of bad news (see 2 Sam 1:2; 13:19; 15:32).

4:13 *his heart was trembling for the ark of God.* Eli had sufficient spiritual sensitivity to be aware of the danger inherent in the sinful and presumptuous act of taking the ark of God into the battle. And he seems to have been even more concerned for the ark than for his sons (see v. 18).

4:18 *he died.* The death of Eli marked the end of an era that had begun with the death of Joshua and the elders who served with him (see Josh 24:29,31). Incapable of restraining Israel or his sons from their wicked ways, and weakened and blinded by age, the old priest is an apt symbol of the flawed age now coming to its tragic close. He is also a striking contrast to the reign of David, which is the main focus of this narrative. *heavy.* A bit of information that not only helps explain why Eli's fall was fatal but also links his death with the judgment announced earlier: "Why do you . . . honor your sons above Me, by making yourselves fat . . .?" (2:29). *he judged Israel forty years.* Eli is here included among the judges (see 2 Sam 7:11; Judg 2:16–19; Ruth 1:1), who served as leaders of Israel in the period between the deaths of Joshua and of the elders who outlived him and the establishment of kingship. It is likely that Eli's leadership of 40 years overlapped that of Jephthah, Ibzan, Elon and Abdon (Judg 12:7–14), as well as that of Samson (Judg 13–16).

4:21 *The glory has departed.* The glory of Israel was Israel's God, not the ark, and loss of the ark did not mean that God had abandoned His people—God was not inseparably bound to the ark (see Jer 3:16–17). Yet the removal of the ark from Israel did signal estrangement in the relationship between God and His people, and it demonstrated the gravity of their error in thinking that in spite of their wickedness they had the power to coerce God into doing their will simply because they possessed the ark.

5:1 *Ashdod.* One of the five major cities of the Philistines (Josh 13:3), it was located near the Mediterranean coast about 35 miles west of Jerusalem. See map, p.312.

5:2 *Dagon.* In Canaanite mythology the son (or brother) of El and the father of Baal. He was the principal god of the Philistines and was worshiped in temples at Gaza (Judg 16:21,23,26), Ashdod (here) and Beth-shan (31:10–12; 1 Chr 10:10). Veneration of this deity was widespread in the ancient world, extending from Mesopotamia to the Aramean and Canaanite area and attested in non-Biblical sources dating from the late third millennium B.C. until Maccabean times (second century B.C.; in the Apocrypha see 1 Maccabees 10:83–85). The precise nature of the worship of Dagon is obscure. Some have considered Dagon to be a fish god, but more recent evidence suggests either a storm or grain god. His name is related to a Hebrew word for "grain."

5:3 *Dagon had fallen on his face.* The ark was placed next to the image of Dagon by the Philistines in order to demonstrate Dagon's superiority over the God of Israel, but the symbolism was reversed when Dagon was toppled to a position of homage before the ark of the Lord.

5:5 *tread on the threshold.* Apparently the threshold was considered to possess supernatural power because of its contact with parts of the fallen image of Dagon. Zeph 1:9 appears to be a reference to a more general and rather widespread pagan

6 Now [a]the hand of the LORD was heavy on the Ashdodites, and [b]He ravaged them and smote them with [c]tumors, both Ashdod and its territories.

7 When the men of Ashdod saw that it was so, they said, "The ark of the God of Israel must not remain with us, for His hand is severe on us and on Dagon our god."

8 So they sent and [a]gathered all the lords of the Philistines to them and said, "What shall we do with the ark of the God of Israel?" And they said, "Let the ark of the God of Israel be brought around to Gath." And they brought the ark of the God of Israel *around*.

9 After they had brought it around, [a]the hand of the LORD was against the city with very great confusion; and He smote the men of the city, both young and old, so that [b]tumors broke out on them.

10 So they sent the ark of God to Ekron. And as the ark of God came to Ekron the Ekronites cried out, saying, "They have brought the ark of the God of Israel around to [1]us, to kill [1]us and [2]our people."

11 They [a]sent therefore and gathered all the lords of the Philistines and said, "Send away the ark of the God of Israel, and let it return to its own place, so that it will not kill [1]us and [2]our people." For there was a deadly confusion throughout the city; [b]the hand of God was very heavy there.

12 And the men who did not die were smitten with tumors and [a]the cry of the city went up to heaven.

The Ark Returned to Israel

6 Now the ark of the LORD had been in the [1]country of the Philistines seven months.

2 And [a]the Philistines called for the priests and the diviners, saying, "What shall we do with the ark of the LORD? Tell us [1]how we shall send it to its place."

3 They said, "If you send away the ark of the God of Israel, [a]do not send it empty; but you shall surely [b]return to Him a guilt offering. Then you will be healed and it will be known to you why His hand is not removed from you."

4 Then they said, "What shall be the guilt offering which we shall return to Him?" And they said, "Five golden [a]tumors and five golden mice [b]*according to* the number of the lords of the Philistines, for one plague was on all of [1]you and on your lords.

5 "So you shall make likenesses of your tumors and likenesses of your mice that ravage the land, and [a]you shall give glory to the God of Israel; perhaps [b]He will ease His hand from you, [c]your gods, and your land.

6 "Why then do you harden your hearts [a]as the Egyptians and Pharaoh hardened their hearts? When He had severely dealt with them, [b]did they not allow [1]the people to go, and they departed?

7 "Now therefore, take and [a]prepare a new cart and two milch cows on which there [b]has never been a yoke; and hitch the cows to the cart and take their calves home, away from them.

8 "Take the ark of the LORD and place it on the cart; and put [a]the articles of gold which you return to Him as [b]a guilt offering in a box by its side. Then send it away that it may go.

9 "Watch, if it goes up by the way of its own territory to [a]Beth-shemesh, then He has done us this great evil. But if not, then [b]we will know that it was not His hand that struck us; it happened to us by chance."

6 [a]Ex 9:3; 1 Sam 5:7, 11; Ps 32:4; 145:20; 147:6; Acts 13:11 [b]1 Sam 6:5 [c]Deut 28:27; Ps 78:66
8 [a]1 Sam 5:11; 29:6-11
9 [a]Deut 2:15; 1 Sam 5:11; 7:13; 12:15 [b]1 Sam 5:6
10 [1]Lit *me* [2]Lit *my*
11 [1]Lit *me* [2]Lit *my* [a]1 Sam 5:8 [b]1 Sam 5:6, 9
12 [a]Ex 12:30; Is 15:3
6:1 [1]Lit *field*
2 [a]Gen 41:8; Ex 7:11; Is 2:6
2 [1]Or *with what*
3 [a]Ex 23:15; Deut 16:16 [b]Lev 5:15, 16
4 [1]Lit *them* [a]1 Sam 5:6, 9, 12; 6:17 [b]Josh 13:3; Judg 3:3; 1 Sam 6:17, 18
5 [a]Josh 7:19; 1 Chr 16:28, 29; Is 42:12; Jer 13:16; John 9:24; Rev 14:7 [b]1 Sam 5:6, 11 [c]1 Sam 5:3, 4, 7
6 [1]Lit *them* [a]Ex 7:13; 8:15, 32; 9:34; 14:17 [b]Ex 12:31
7 [a]2 Sam 6:3 [b]Num 19:2; Deut 21:3, 4
8 [a]1 Sam 6:4, 5 [b]1 Sam 6:3
9 [a]Josh 15:10; 21:16 [b]1 Sam 6:3

idea that the threshold was the dwelling place of spirits. *this day.* The time of the writing of 1,2 Samuel (see Introduction: Literary Features, Authorship and Date).

5:6 *the hand of the LORD was heavy.* Dagon's broken hand lay on the ground (v. 4), but the Lord shows the reality and strength of His own hand by bringing a plague (see note on 6:4) on the people of Ashdod and the surrounding area (see vv. 9,11). God would not be manipulated by His own people (see note on 4:3), nor would He permit the Philistines to think that their victory over the Israelites and the capture of the ark demonstrated the superiority of their god over the God of Israel.

5:8 *lords.* Of the five major cities of the Philistines (see 6:16; Josh 13:3; Judg 3:3). *Let the ark of the God of Israel be brought ... to Gath.* Evidently the leaders of the Philistines did not share the opinion of the Ashdodites that there was a direct connection between what had happened in Ashdod and the presence of the ark; they seem to have suspected that the sequence of events was merely coincidental (see 6:9). The removal of the ark to Gath put the matter to a test.

5:10 *Ekron.* The northernmost of the five major Philistine cities, located 11 miles northeast of Ashdod and close to Israelite territory (see map, p. 312).

5:11 *Send away the ark of the God of Israel.* After three successive towns had been struck by disease upon the arrival of the ark, there was little doubt in the people's minds that the power of the God of Israel was the cause of their distress.

6:2 *priests and ... diviners.* The experts on religious matters (priests) and the discerners of hidden knowledge by interpretation of omens (diviners) were consulted (see Deut 18:10; Is 2:6; Ezek 21:21).

6:3 *guilt offering.* The priests and diviners suggest returning the ark with a gift, signifying recognition of guilt in taking the ark from Israel and compensation for this violation of the Lord's honor (see v. 5). For the guilt offering in Israel see Lev 5:14–6:7.

6:4 *Five golden tumors.* Corresponding to the symptoms of the plague (see 5:6). *five golden mice.* The disease was accompanied by a plague of mice (v. 5). The Greek translation of the OT (the Septuagint) includes this information earlier in the narrative (at the end of 5:6). It is likely that the mice were carriers of the disease, which may have been a form of the plague.

6:5 *make likenesses ... and you shall give glory to the God of Israel.* The golden models were an acknowledgment that the disease and the mice were a judgment from the hand of the God of Israel (see note on v. 3).

6:6 *the Egyptians and Pharaoh.* The plagues that God inflicted on the Egyptians at the time of the exodus made a lasting impression on the surrounding nations (see 4:8; Josh 2:10).

6:7 *has never been a yoke.* Have not been trained to pull a cart. *take their calves home.* Normally cows do not willingly leave their suckling calves.

6:9 *Beth-shemesh.* A town near the Philistine border, belong-

10 Then the men did so, and took two
milch cows and hitched them to the cart, and
shut up their calves at home.
11 They put the ark of the LORD on the
cart, and the box with the golden mice and
the likenesses of their tumors.
12 And the cows took the straight way in
the [1]direction of [a]Beth-shemesh; they went
along [b]the highway, lowing as they went,
and did not turn aside to the right or to the
left. And the lords of the Philistines followed
them to the border of Beth-shemesh.
13 Now *the people of* Beth-shemesh were
reaping their wheat harvest in the valley, and
they raised their eyes and saw the ark and
were glad to see *it*.
14 The cart came into the field of Joshua
the Beth-shemite and stood there where
there *was* a large stone; and they split the
wood of the cart and [a]offered the cows as a
burnt offering to the LORD.
15 [a]The Levites took down the ark of the
LORD and the box that was with it, in which
were the articles of gold, and put them on
the large stone; and the men of Beth-shemesh offered burnt offerings and sacrificed
sacrifices that day to the LORD.
16 When the [a]five lords of the Philistines
saw it, they returned to Ekron that day.
17 [a]These are the golden tumors which
the Philistines returned for a guilt offering to
the LORD: one for Ashdod, one for Gaza, one
for Ashkelon, one for Gath, one for Ekron;
18 and the golden mice, *according* to the
number of all the cities of the Philistines
belonging to the five lords, [a]both of fortified
cities and of country villages. [b]The large
[1]stone on which they set the ark of the LORD
is a witness to this day in the field of Joshua
the Beth-shemite.
19 [a]He struck down some of the men of
Beth-shemesh because they had looked into
the ark of the LORD. He struck down of all
the people, 50,070 men, and the people
mourned because the LORD had struck the
people with a great slaughter.
20 The men of Beth-shemesh said, "[a]Who
is able to stand before the LORD, this holy
God? And to whom shall He go up from us?"
21 So they sent messengers to the inhabitants of [a]Kiriath-jearim, saying, "The Philistines have brought back the ark of the LORD;
come down and take it up to you."

Deliverance from the Philistines

7 And the men of Kiriath-jearim came and
took the ark of the LORD and [a]brought it
into the house of Abinadab on the hill, and
consecrated Eleazar his son to keep the ark
of the LORD.
2 From the day that the ark remained at
Kiriath-jearim, the time was long, for it was
twenty years; and all the house of Israel
lamented after the LORD.
3 Then Samuel spoke to all the house of
Israel, saying, "[a]If you return to the LORD
with all your heart, [b]remove the foreign gods
and the [c]Ashtaroth from among you and
[d]direct your hearts to the LORD and [e]serve
Him alone; and He will deliver you from the
hand of the Philistines."
4 So the sons of Israel removed the Baals
and the Ashtaroth and served the LORD alone.
5 Then Samuel said, "Gather all Israel to
[a]Mizpah and [b]I will pray to the LORD for
you."

12 [1]Lit *way* [a]1 Sam 6:9 [b]Num 20:19 **14** [a]2 Sam 24:22; 1 Kin 19:21 **15** [a]Josh 3:3 **16** [a]Josh 13:3; Judg 3:3 **17** [a]1 Sam 6:4 **18** [1]So some mss and versions; Heb *Abel* [a]Deut 3:5 [b]1 Sam 6:14, 15 **19** [a]Ex 19:21; Num 4:5, 15, 20; 2 Sam 6:7 **20** [a]Lev 11:44, 45; 2 Sam 6:9; Mal 3:2; Rev 6:17 **21** [a]Josh 9:17; 15:9, 60; 1 Chr 13:5, 6 **7:1** [a]2 Sam 6:3, 4 **3** [a]1 Kin 8:48; Is 55:7; Hos 6:1; Joel 2:12-14 [b]Gen 35:2; Josh 24:14, 23; Judg 10:16 [c]Judg 2:13; 1 Sam 31:10 [d]Deut 13:4; 2 Chr 19:3 [e]Deut 6:13; 10:20; 13:4; Josh 24:14; Matt 4:10; Luke 4:8 **5** [a]Judg 10:17; 20:1 [b]1 Sam 8:6; 12:17-19

ing to Judah (see Josh 15:10). Its name means "house (or sanctuary) of the sun(-god)."

6:13 *reaping their wheat harvest.* The time of wheat harvest is from mid-April until mid-June.

6:14–15 The termination of the trip at Beth-shemesh is just as much a revelation of the hand of God as the journey itself, because it was one of the towns of Judah assigned to the priests at the time of the conquest (see Josh 21:13–16).

6:17 *guilt offering.* See note on v. 3.

6:18 *witness.* A kind of monument to the event. *this day.* The time of the writing of 1,2 Samuel (see Introduction: Literary Features, Authorship and Date).

6:19 *looked into the ark.* The men of Beth-shemesh (Levites and priests among them) were judged by God for their irreverent curiosity. Because God had so closely linked the manifestation of His own presence among His people with the ark, it was to be treated with great honor and respect (see 2 Sam 6:7; Num 4:17–20). This attitude of respect, however, is quite different from the superstitious attitude that led the elders to take the ark into battle against the Philistines, thus treating it as an object with magical power (see note on 4:3). *50,070.* A few Hebrew manuscripts read "70." The additional 50,000 in most Hebrew manuscripts is apparently a copyist's mistake because it is added in an ungrammatical way (no conjunction). Furthermore, this small town could not have contained that many inhabitants.

6:20 *to whom shall He go up from us?* The inhabitants of Beth-shemesh respond to God's judgment in much the same way as the inhabitants of Ashdod, Gath and Ekron (see 5:8–10).

7:1 *house of Abinadab.* The ark remained in relative obscurity at Abinadab's house until David brought it to Jerusalem (2 Sam 6:2–3). Somehow the tent of meeting (and the altar of burnt offering) escaped the destruction of Shiloh (Jer 7:12,14; 26:6). It apparently was first moved to Nob (21:1–9). In David's and Solomon's days it was located at Gibeon (1 Chr 16:39; 21:29; 2 Chr 1:3,13), the city whose people had been condemned to be menial laborers at the Lord's sanctuary (Josh 9:23,27). Later, we are told, Solomon brought the "tent of meeting" to the completed temple (see notes on 1 Kin 3:4; 8:4).

7:2 *twenty years.* Probably the 20-year interval between the return of the ark to Israel and the assembly called by Samuel at Mizpah (see v. 5).

7:3 *Ashtaroth.* The Hebrew plural of Ashtoreth, who was a goddess of love, fertility and war, worshiped in various forms by many peoples of the ancient Near East, including the Canaanites (see note on Judg 2:13). The worship of Ashtoreth is frequently combined with the worship of Baal (see v. 4; 12:10; Judg 2:13; 3:7; 10:6), in accordance with the common practice in fertility cults to associate male and female deities.

7:5 *Mizpah.* A town in the territory of Benjamin (Josh 18:26), located about seven and a half miles north of Jerusalem. It was here that the Israelites had previously gathered to undertake disciplinary action against Benjamin (Judg 20:1; 21:1) after the abuse and murder of the concubine of a traveling Levite in Gibeah of Benjamin. Several other places bore the same name (see

6 They gathered to Mizpah, and drew
water and [a]poured it out before the LORD,
and [b]fasted on that day and said there, "[c]We
have sinned against the LORD." And Samuel
judged the sons of Israel at Mizpah.
7 Now when the Philistines heard that
the sons of Israel had gathered to Mizpah,
the lords of the Philistines went up against
Israel. And when the sons of Israel heard it,
[a]they were afraid of the Philistines.
8 Then the sons of Israel said to Samuel,
"[a]Do not cease to cry to the LORD our God for
us, that He may save us from the hand of the
Philistines."
9 Samuel took [a]a suckling lamb and
offered it for a whole burnt offering to the
LORD; and Samuel cried to the LORD for Israel and [b]the LORD answered him.
10 Now Samuel was offering up the burnt
offering, and the Philistines drew near to battle against Israel. But [a]the LORD thundered
with a great [1]thunder on that day against the
Philistines and [b]confused them, so that they
were [2]routed before Israel.
11 The men of Israel went out of Mizpah
and pursued the Philistines, and struck them
down as far as below Beth-car.
12 Then Samuel [a]took a stone and set it
between Mizpah and Shen, and named it
[1]Ebenezer, saying, "Thus far the LORD has
helped us."
13 [a]So the Philistines were subdued and
[b]they did not come anymore within the border of Israel. And the hand of the LORD was
against the Philistines all the days of Samuel.
14 The cities which the Philistines had
taken from Israel were restored to Israel,
from Ekron even to Gath; and Israel delivered their territory from the hand of the Philistines. So there was peace between Israel
and [a]the Amorites.

Samuel's Ministry

15 Now Samuel [a]judged Israel all the days
of his life.
16 He used to go annually on circuit to
[a]Bethel and [b]Gilgal and [c]Mizpah, and he
judged Israel in all these places.
17 Then his return *was* to [a]Ramah, for his
house *was* there, and there he judged Israel;
and he [b]built there an altar to the LORD.

Israel Demands a King

8 And it came about when Samuel was old
that [a]he appointed his sons judges over
Israel.
2 Now the name of his firstborn was
Joel, and the name of his second, Abijah;
they were judging in [a]Beersheba.
3 His sons, however, did not walk in his
ways, but turned aside after dishonest gain
and [a]took bribes and perverted justice.
4 Then all the elders of Israel gathered
together and came to Samuel at [a]Ramah;
5 and they said to him, "Behold, you
have grown old, and your sons do not walk
in your ways. Now [a]appoint a king for us to
judge us like all the nations."
6 But the thing was [1a]displeasing in the
sight of Samuel when they said, "Give us a
king to judge us." And [b]Samuel prayed to the
LORD.
7 The LORD said to Samuel, "Listen to the
voice of the people in regard to all that they
say to you, for [a]they have not rejected you,
but they have rejected Me from being king
over them.
8 "Like all the deeds which they have

6 [a]1 Sam 1:15; Ps 62:8; Lam 2:19 [b]Lev 16:29; Neh 9:1 [c]Judg 10:10; 1 Kin 8:47; Ps 106:6
7 [a]1 Sam 13:6; 17:11
8 [a]1 Sam 12:19-24; Is 37:4
9 [a]Lev 22:27 [b]Ps 99:6; Jer 15:1
10 [1]Lit *voice* [2]Lit *smitten* [a]1 Sam 2:10; 2 Sam 22:14, 15; Ps 29:3, 4 [b]Josh 10:10; Ps 18:14
12 [1]I.e. The stone of help [a]Gen 35:14; Josh 4:9; 24:26
13 [a]Judg 13:1-15 [b]1 Sam 13:5
14 [a]Num 13:29; Josh 10:5-10
15 [a]1 Sam 7:6
16 [a]Gen 28:19; 35:6 [b]Josh 5:9, 10 [c]1 Sam 7:5
17 [a]1 Sam 1:1, 19; 2:11 [b]Judg 21:4
8:1 [a]Deut 16:18, 19
2 [a]Gen 22:19; 1 Kin 19:3; Amos 5:5
3 [a]Ex 23:6, 8; Deut 16:19
4 [a]1 Sam 7:17
5 [a]Deut 17:14, 15
6 [1]Or *evil* [a]1 Sam 12:17 [b]1 Sam 15:11
7 [a]Ex 16:8; 1 Sam 10:19

22:3; Gen 31:49; Josh 11:3,8; 15:38). *I will pray.* See 7:8–9; 8:6; 12:17–19, 23; 15:11. Samuel, like Moses, was later remembered as a great intercessor (see Ps 99:6; Jer 15:1). Both were appointed by God to mediate His rule over His people, representing God to Israel and speaking on Israel's behalf to God.

7:6 *drew water and poured it out before the LORD.* There is no other reference to this type of ceremony in the OT. It appears to symbolize the pouring out of one's heart in repentance and humility before the Lord. For related expressions see 1:15; Ps 62:8; Lam 2:19. *Samuel judged.* See v. 15; see also note on 4:18.

7:10 *the LORD thundered with a great thunder.* The Lord had promised to be the protector of His people when they were obedient to their covenant obligations (see Ex 23:22; Deut 20:1–4; see also 2 Sam 5:19–25; Josh 10:11–14; Judg 5:20–21; 2 Kin 7:6; 19:35; 2 Chr 20:17,22).

7:12 *Ebenezer.* See NASB marg.; see also note on 4:1.

7:13 *did not come anymore within the border of Israel.* Some interpreters see a contradiction between this statement and subsequent references to the Philistines in 9:16; 10:5; 13:3,5; 17:1; 23:27. This statement, however, only indicates that the Philistines did not immediately counterattack. See 2 Kin 6:23–24 for a similar situation.

7:15 A summary statement marking the end of the author's account of Samuel's ministry as Israel's leader (see v. 6).

7:16 *judged Israel.* See note on 4:18.

7:17 *Ramah.* See note on 1:1.

8:1–12:25 See Introduction: Contents and Theme.

8:1 *when Samuel was old.* Probably about 20 years after the victory at Mizpah, when Samuel was approximately 65 years old (see Introduction: Chronology).

8:3 *took bribes.* Perversion of justice through bribery was explicitly forbidden in Pentateuchal law (see Ex 23:8; Deut 16:19).

8:5 *appoint a king . . . to judge us.* The elders cite Samuel's age and the misconduct of his sons as justifications for their request for a king. It soon becomes apparent, however, that the more basic reason for their request was a desire to be like the surrounding nations—to have a human king as a symbol of national power and unity who would lead them in battle and guarantee their security (see v. 20; 10:19; 12:12; see also Introduction: Contents and Theme).

8:7 *Listen to the voice of the people . . . that they say to you.* Anticipations of kingship in Israel are present already in the Pentateuch (Gen 49:10; Num 24:7,17; Deut 17:14–20); Samuel is therefore instructed to listen to the people's request (see vv. 9,22). *they have not rejected you, but . . . Me from being king over them.* Cf. Judg 8:23. The sin of Israel in requesting a king (see 10:19; 12:12,17,19–20) did not rest in any evil inherent in kingship itself, but in the kind of kingship the people envisioned and their reasons for requesting it (see Introduction: Contents and Theme). Their desire was for a form of kingship that denied their covenant relationship with the Lord, who Himself was pledged to be their savior and deliverer. In requesting a king

done since the day that I brought them up from Egypt even to this day—in that they have forsaken Me and served other gods—so they are doing to you also.

9 "Now then, listen to their voice; [a]however, you shall solemnly [1]warn them and tell them of [b]the [2]procedure of the king who will reign over them."

Warning concerning a King

10 So Samuel spoke all the words of the LORD to [a]the people who had asked of him a king.

11 He said, "[a]This will be the [1]procedure of the king who will reign over you: [b]he will take your sons and place *them* for himself in his chariots and among his horsemen and [c]they will run before his chariots.

12 "[a]He will appoint for himself commanders of thousands and of fifties, and *some* to [1]do his plowing and to reap his harvest and to make his weapons of war and equipment for his chariots.

13 "He will also take your daughters for perfumers and cooks and bakers.

14 "[a]He will take the best of your fields and your vineyards and your olive groves and give *them* to his servants.

15 "He will take a tenth of your seed and of your vineyards and give to his officers and to his servants.

16 "He will also take your male servants and your female servants and your best young men and your donkeys and [1]use *them* for his work.

17 "He will take a tenth of your flocks, and you yourselves will become his servants.

18 "Then [a]you will cry out in that day because of your king whom you have chosen for yourselves, but [b]the LORD will not answer you in that day."

19 Nevertheless, the people [a]refused to listen to the voice of Samuel, and they said, "No, but there shall be a king over us,

20 [a]that we also may be like all the nations, that our king may judge us and go out before us and fight our battles."

9 [1]Lit *testify to* [2]Lit *custom* [a]Ezek 3:18 [b]1 Sam 8:11-18; 10:25
10 [a]1 Sam 8:4
11 [1]Lit *custom* [a]Deut 17:14-20; 1 Sam 10:25 [b]1 Sam 14:52 [c]2 Sam 15:1
12 [1]Lit *plow his plowing* [a]Num 31:14; 1 Sam 22:7
14 [a]1 Kin 21:7; Ezek 46:18
16 [1]Lit *make*
18 [a]Is 8:21 [b]Prov 1:25-28; Is 1:15; Mic 3:4
19 [a]Is 66:4; Jer 44:16
20 [a]1 Sam 8:5
21 [a]Judg 11:11
22 [1]Lit *cause a king to reign for them* [a]1 Sam 8:7
9:1 [1]Or *wealth or influence* [a]1 Sam 14:51; 1 Chr 8:33; 9:36-39
2 [a]1 Sam 10:24 [b]1 Sam 10:23
4 [a]Josh 24:33 [b]2 Kin 4:42 [c]Josh 19:42
5 [a]1 Sam 1:1 [b]1 Sam 10:2
6 [a]Deut 33:1; 1 Kin 13:1; 2 Kin 5:8 [b]1 Sam 3:19 [c]Gen 24:42
7 [a]1 Kin 14:3; 2 Kin 5:15; 8:8, 9; Ezek 13:19

21 Now after Samuel had heard all the words of the people, [a]he repeated them in the LORD's hearing.

22 The LORD said to Samuel, "[a]Listen to their voice and [1]appoint them a king." So Samuel said to the men of Israel, "Go every man to his city."

Saul's Search

9 Now there was a man of Benjamin whose name was [a]Kish the son of Abiel, the son of Zeror, the son of Becorath, the son of Aphiah, the son of a Benjamite, a mighty man of [1]valor.

2 He had a son whose name was Saul, a [a]choice and handsome *man*, and there was not a more handsome person than he among the sons of Israel; [b]from his shoulders and up he was taller than any of the people.

3 Now the donkeys of Kish, Saul's father, were lost. So Kish said to his son Saul, "Take now with you one of the servants, and arise, go search for the donkeys."

4 He passed through [a]the hill country of Ephraim and passed through the land of [b]Shalishah, but they did not find *them*. Then they passed through the land of [c]Shaalim, but *they were* not *there*. Then he passed through the land of the Benjamites, but they did not find *them*.

5 When they came to the land of [a]Zuph, Saul said to his servant who was with him, "Come, and let us return, [b]or else my father will cease *to be concerned* about the donkeys and will become anxious for us."

6 He said to him, "Behold now, there is [a]a man of God in this city, and the man is held in honor; [b]all that he says surely comes true. Now let us go there, [c]perhaps he can tell us about our journey on which we have set out."

7 Then Saul said to his servant, "But behold, if we go, what shall we bring the man? For the bread is gone from our sack and there is [a]no present to bring to the man of God. What do we have?"

8 The servant answered Saul again and

"like all the nations" (v. 20) they broke the covenant, rejected the Lord who was their King (12:12; Num 23:21; Deut 33:5) and forgot His constant provision for their protection in the past (10:18; 12:8–11).

8:11 *the procedure of the king.* Using a description of the policies of contemporary Canaanite kings (vv. 11–17), Samuel warns the people of the burdens associated with the type of kingship they long for.

8:15 *tenth.* This king's portion would be over and above the tenth Israel was to devote to the Lord (Lev 27:30–32; Num 18:26; Deut 14:22,28; 26:12). In fact, the demands of the king would parallel all that Israel was to consecrate to the Lord as her Great King (persons, lands, crops, livestock)—even the whole population (v. 17).

8:18 *cry out . . . because of your king.* See 1 Kin 12:4; Jer 22:13–17.

8:20 *like all the nations.* See notes on vv. 5,7.

9:2 *taller than any of the people.* Physically of kingly stature (see 10:23).

9:3 *donkeys . . . were lost.* Saul is introduced as a donkey wrangler sent in search of donkeys that had strayed from home—perhaps symbolizing Saul and the rebellious people who had asked for a king (cf. Is 1:3). David would be introduced as a shepherd caring for his father's flock and later pictured as the shepherd over the Lord's flock (2 Sam 5:2; 7:7–8; Ps 78:71–72).

9:6 *He said to him.* Saul's ignorance of Samuel is indicative of his character. *man of God.* See note on 2:27; here a reference to Samuel. *this city.* Probably Ramah (see 7:17), the hometown of Samuel, to which he had just returned from a journey (see v. 12; 7:16). *all that he says . . .* See 3:19 and note.

9:7 *what shall we bring the man?* Other examples of gifts offered to prophets are found in 1 Kin 14:3; 2 Kin 4:42; 5:15–16; 8:8–9. Whether Samuel accepted the gift and whether he was dependent on such gifts for a livelihood are not clear. Elisha

said, "Behold, I have in my hand a fourth of
a shekel of silver; I will give *it* to the man of
God and he will [a]tell us our way."
9 (Formerly in Israel, when a man went
to inquire of God, he used to say, "Come,
and let us go to the seer"; for *he who is called*
a prophet now was formerly called [a]a seer.)
10 Then Saul said to his servant, "Well
said; come, let us go." So they went to the
city where the man of God was.
11 As they went up the slope to the city,
[a]they found young women going out to draw
water and said to them, "Is the seer here?"
12 They answered them and said, "He is;
[1]see, *he is* ahead of you. Hurry now, for he
has come into the city today, for [a]the people
have a sacrifice on [b]the high place today.
13 "As soon as you enter the city you will
find him before he goes up to the high place
to eat, for the people will not eat until he
comes, because [a]he must bless the sacrifice;
afterward those who are invited will eat.
Now therefore, go up for you will find him at
once."
14 So they went up to the city. As they
came into the city, behold, Samuel was coming out toward them to go up to the high
place.

God's Choice for King

15 Now a day before Saul's coming, [a]the
LORD had [1]revealed *this* to Samuel saying,
16 "About this time tomorrow I will send
you a man from the land of Benjamin, and
[a]you shall anoint him to be prince over My
people Israel; and he will deliver My people
from the hand of the Philistines. For [b]I have

8 [a]1 Sam 9:6
9 [a]2 Sam 24:11; 2 Kin 17:13; 1 Chr 9:22; 26:28; 29:29; Is 30:10; Amos 7:12
11 [a]Gen 24:11, 15; 29:8, 9; Ex 2:16
12 [1]Or *behold* [a]Gen 31:54; Num 28:11-15; 1 Kin 3:2 [b]1 Sam 7:17; 10:5
13 [a]Luke 9:16; John 6:11
15 [1]Lit *uncovered the ear* [a]1 Sam 15:1; Acts 13:21
16 [a]1 Sam 10:1 [b]Ex 3:7, 9
17 [1]Lit *answered* [a]1 Sam 16:12
20 [a]1 Sam 9:3 [b]1 Sam 8:5; 12:13
21 [1]So some ancient versions; Heb *tribes* [a]1 Sam 15:17 [b]Judg 20:46-48
23 [1]Lit *Give* [2]Lit *with you*
24 [1]Lit *saying* [a]Ex 29:22, 27; Lev 7:32, 33; Num 18:18

regarded My people, because their cry has
come to Me."
17 When Samuel saw Saul, the LORD [1]said
to him, "[a]Behold, the man of whom I spoke
to you! This one shall rule over My people."
18 Then Saul approached Samuel in the
gate and said, "Please tell me where the
seer's house is."
19 Samuel answered Saul and said, "I am
the seer. Go up before me to the high place,
for you shall eat with me today; and in the
morning I will let you go, and will tell you all
that is on your mind.
20 "[a]As for your donkeys which were lost
three days ago, do not set your mind on
them, for they have been found. And [b]for
whom is all that is desirable in Israel? Is it not
for you and for all your father's household?"
21 Saul replied, "[a]Am I not a Benjamite, of
[b]the smallest of the tribes of Israel, and my
family the least of all the families of the
[1]tribe of Benjamin? Why then do you speak
to me in this way?"
22 Then Samuel took Saul and his servant
and brought them into the hall and gave
them a place at the head of those who were
invited, who were about thirty men.
23 Samuel said to the cook, "[1]Bring the
portion that I gave you, concerning which I
said to you, 'Set it [2]aside.' "
24 Then the cook [a]took up the leg with
what was on it and set *it* before Saul. And
Samuel said, "Here is what has been
reserved! Set *it* before you *and* eat, because
it has been kept for you until the appointed
time, [1]since I said I have invited the people."
So Saul ate with Samuel that day.

---

refused the gift of Naaman (2 Kin 5:16). In later times false prophets adjusted their message to the desires of those who supported them (1 Kin 22:6,8,18; Mic 3:5,11).

9:8 *a fourth of a shekel.* That is, about one-tenth of an ounce. Before the use of coins, gold or silver was weighed out for each monetary transaction (see 13:21; Job 28:15). The value of that amount of silver in Saul's time is not known.

9:9 *he who is called a prophet . . . formerly called a seer.* There was no essential difference between a seer and a prophet. The person popularly designated as a prophet at the time of the writing of 1,2 Samuel was termed a seer in the time of Saul. This need not mean that the term "prophet" was unknown in the time of Saul or that the term "seer" was unknown in later times (see Is 30:10). The reference is to popular usage.

9:12 *high place.* See Lev 26:30. After entrance into the promised land, the Israelites often followed the custom of the Canaanites in building local altars on hills. (At this time the central sanctuary was not functioning because the ark of God was separated from the tabernacle; Shiloh had been destroyed, and the priestly family, after the death of Eli's sons, was apparently still inactive.) In later times, worship at these "high places" provided a means for the entrance of pagan practices into Israel's religious observances and, for this reason, it was condemned (see note on 1Ki 3:2).

9:13 *he must bless the sacrifice.* Samuel presided over the sacrificial meal (see 1:4; 2:13–16), at which he gave a prayer, probably similar to those referred to in the NT (see Matt 26:26–27; John 6:11, 23; 1 Tim 4:3–5).

9:16 *anoint him.* Priests were also anointed (see Ex 29:7; 40:12–15; Lev 4:3; 8:12), but from this point in the OT it is usually the king who is referred to as "the anointed of the LORD" (see note on 2:10; cf. 12:3; 24:6; 26:9,11,16; 2 Sam 1:14,16; 19:21; 22:51; 23:1; Ps 2:2,6; but see also Zech 4:14). Anointing signifies separation to the Lord for a particular task and divine equipping for the task (see 10:1,6; 16:13; Is 61:1). *prince.* The Hebrew for this word indicates one designated (here by the Lord) to be the chief in rank. It served as a useful term to ease the transition between the time of the judges and that of the kings. *Philistines.* See note on 7:13.

9:20 *all that is desirable in Israel.* A reference to Israel's desire for a king.

9:21 *smallest of the tribes . . . least of all the families.* Saul's origins were among the humblest in Israel (Benjamin was the last of Jacob's sons, and the tribe had been greatly reduced in the time of the judges; see Judg 20:46–48). His elevation to king shows that God "raises the poor" (2:8), which is one of the central themes running throughout Samuel. God's use of the powerless to promote His kingdom in the world is a common feature in the Biblical testimony and underscores the truth that His kingdom is not of this world.

9:24 *leg.* The Hebrew for this word specifies the thigh, which was normally reserved for the Lord's consecrated priest (see Ex 29:22,27; Lev 7:32–33,35; Num 6:20; 18:18). The presentation of this choice piece of the sacrificial animal to Saul was a distinct honor and anticipated his being designated the Lord's anointed.

25 When they came down from the high
place into the city, *Samuel* spoke with Saul
[a]on the [1]roof.
26 And they arose early; and at daybreak
Samuel called to Saul on the roof, saying,
"Get up, that I may send you away." So Saul
arose, and both he and Samuel went out into
the street.
27 As they were going down to the edge of
the city, Samuel said to Saul, "Say to the servant that he might go ahead of us and pass
on, but you remain standing now, that I may
proclaim the word of God to you."

Saul among Prophets

10 Then [a]Samuel took the flask of oil,
poured it on his head, [b]kissed him and
said, "Has not [c]the LORD anointed you a ruler
over [d]His inheritance?
2 "When you go from me today, then you
will find two men close to [a]Rachel's tomb in
the territory of Benjamin at Zelzah; and they
will say to you, '[b]The donkeys which you
went to look for have been found. Now
behold, your father has [1]ceased to be concerned about the donkeys and is anxious for
you, saying, "What shall I do about my
son?"'
3 "Then you will go on further from
there, and you will come as far as the [1a]oak
of Tabor, and there three men going up [b]to
God at Bethel will meet you, one carrying
three young goats, another carrying three
loaves of bread, and another carrying a jug
of wine;
4 and they will greet you and give you
two *loaves* of bread, which you will accept
from their hand.
5 "Afterward you will come to [1a]the hill of
God where the Philistine garrison is; and it
shall be as soon as you have come there to
the city, that you will meet [b]a group of
prophets coming down from the high place
with harp, tambourine, flute, and a lyre
before them, and [c]they will be prophesying.
6 "Then [a]the Spirit of the LORD will come
upon you mightily, and [b]you shall prophesy
with them and be changed into another man.
7 "It shall be when these signs come to
you, [a]do for yourself what [1]the occasion
requires, for [b]God is with you.
8 "And [a]you shall go down before me to
Gilgal; and behold, I will come down to you
to offer burnt offerings and [b]sacrifice peace
offerings. [c]You shall wait seven days until I
come to you and show you what you should
do."
9 Then it happened when he turned his
back to leave Samuel, God [a]changed [1]his
heart; and all those signs came about on that
day.
10 [a]When they came to [1]the hill there,
behold, a group of prophets met him; and
the Spirit of God came upon him mightily, so
that he prophesied among them.
11 It came about, when all who knew him
previously saw that he prophesied now with
the prophets, that the people said to one
another, "What has happened to the son of
Kish? [a]Is Saul also among the prophets?"
12 A man there said, "Now, who is their
father?" Therefore it became a proverb: "[a]Is
Saul also among the prophets?"
13 When he had finished prophesying, he
came to the high place.
14 Now [a]Saul's uncle said to him and his
servant, "Where did you go?" And he said,
"[b]To look for the donkeys. When we saw
that they could not be found, we went to
Samuel."
15 Saul's uncle said, "Please tell me what
Samuel said to you."
16 So Saul said to his uncle, "[a]He told us
plainly that the donkeys had been found."
But he did not tell him about the matter of
the kingdom which Samuel had mentioned.

25 [1]Gr adds *and they spread a bed for Saul on the roof and he slept* [a]Deut 22:8; Luke 5:19; Acts 10:9
10:1 [a]Ex 30:23-33; 1 Sam 16:13; 2 Kin 9:3, 6 [b]Ps 2:12 [c]1 Sam 16:13; 26:9; 2 Sam 1:14 [d]Deut 32:9; Ps 78:71
2 [1]Lit *abandoned the matter of* [a]Gen 35:16-20; 48:7 [b]1 Sam 9:3-5
3 [1]Or *terebinth* [a]Gen 35:8 [b]Gen 28:19; 35:1, 3, 7
5 [1]Or *Gibeath-haelohim* [a]1 Sam 13:2, 3 [b]1 Sam 19:20; 2 Kin 2:3, 5, 15
5 [c]2 Kin 3:15; 1 Chr 25:1-6; 1 Cor 14:1
6 [a]Num 11:25, 29; Judg 14:6 [b]1 Sam 10:10; 19:23, 24
7 [1]Lit *your hand finds* [a]Eccl 9:10 [b]Josh 1:5; Judg 6:12; Heb 13:5
8 [a]1 Sam 11:14; 13:8 [b]1 Sam 11:15 [c]1 Sam 13:8
9 [1]Lit *for him another heart* [a]1 Sam 10:6
10 [1]Or *Gibeah* [a]1 Sam 10:5, 6; 19:20
11 [a]1 Sam 19:24; Amos 7:14, 15; Matt 13:54-57; John 7:15
12 [a]1 Sam 19:23, 24
14 [a]1 Sam 14:50 [b]1 Sam 9:3-6
16 [a]1 Sam 9:20

10:1 *oil.* Perhaps spiced olive oil (see Ex 30:22–33). *Has not the LORD anointed you . . . ?* See note on 9:16. *ruler.* See 9:16 and note on "prince" (same word in Hebrew). *His inheritance.* "My people Israel" (9:16). The Lord's inheritance includes both the people (see Ex 34:9) and the land (see Ex 15:17). After departing from Samuel, Saul is to receive three signs (see vv. 2–7) to authenticate Samuel's words and to assure him that the Lord has indeed chosen him to be king.

10:5 *the hill of God.* Or "Gibeah of God" (see NASB marg.). Gibeah was Saul's hometown (see v. 26; 11:4), located in the tribal area of Benjamin (Josh 18:28; Judg 19:12–14). It was usually called "Gibeah" or "Gibeah of Benjamin" (as in 13:2,15), but twice "Gibeah of Saul" (15:34; 2 Sam 21:6). The present designation (used only here) may have been Samuel's way of reminding Saul that the land of Canaan belonged to God and not to the Philistines (see Deut 32:43; Is 14:2; Hos 9:3). *prophets.* The bands of prophets with which Samuel was associated (as also the "sons of the prophets" with whom Elijah and Elisha were associated; see note on 1 Kin 20:35) appear to have been small communities of men who banded together in spiritually decadent times for mutual cultivation of their religious zeal. *prophesying.* Here (and in vv. 6,10–11,13) appears to designate an enthusiastic praising of God inspired by the Holy Spirit (see Num 11:24–30 for similar use of the term).

10:7 *do . . . what the occasion requires.* Saul is to take whatever action is appropriate when the situation presents itself to manifest publicly his royal leadership (see 11:4–11).

10:8 *go down before me to Gilgal.* At some unspecified future time, perhaps previously discussed (see 9:25), Saul is to go to Gilgal and wait seven days for Samuel's arrival (see 13:7–14).

10:11 *Is Saul also among the prophets?* An expression of surprise at Saul's behavior (see note on v. 5) by those who had known him previously—another subtle indication of his character (see notes on 9:3,6).

10:12 *who is their father?* Some understand the question as an expression of contempt for prophets generally, others as implying the recognition that prophetic inspiration comes from God and therefore could be imparted to whomever God chose. However, since leading prophets were sometimes called "father" (2 Kin 2:12; 6:21; 13:14), the speaker may have intended a disdainful reference to Samuel or an ironical gibe at Saul.

Saul Publicly Chosen King

17 Thereafter Samuel called the [a]people together to the LORD at Mizpah;

18 and he said to the sons of Israel, "[a]Thus says the LORD, the God of Israel, 'I brought Israel up from Egypt, and I delivered you from the hand of the Egyptians and from the [1]power of all the kingdoms that were oppressing you.'

19 "But you [a]have today rejected your God, who delivers you from all your calamities and your distresses; yet you have [1]said, 'No, but set a king over us!' Now therefore, [b]present yourselves before the LORD by your tribes and by your clans."

20 Thus Samuel brought all the tribes of Israel near, and the tribe of Benjamin was taken by lot.

21 Then he brought the tribe of Benjamin near by its families, and the Matrite family was taken. And Saul the son of Kish was taken; but when they looked for him, he could not be found.

22 Therefore [a]they inquired further of the LORD, "Has the man come here yet?" So the LORD said, "Behold, he is hiding himself by the baggage."

23 So they ran and took him from there, and when he stood among the people, [a]he was taller than any of the people from his shoulders upward.

24 Samuel said to all the people, "Do you see him [a]whom the LORD has chosen? Surely there is no one like him among all the people." So all the people shouted and said, "[1b]*Long* live the king!"

17 [a]Judg 20:1; 1 Sam 7:5 **18** [1]Lit *hand* [a]Judg 6:8, 9 **19** [1]So with several mss and versions; M.T. *said to Him* [a]1 Sam 8:6, 7; 12:12 [b]Josh 7:14-18; 24:1; Prov 16:33 **22** [a]1 Sam 23:2, 4 **23** [a]1 Sam 9:2 **24** [1]Lit *May the king live* [a]Deut 17:15; 2 Sam 21:6 [b]1 Kin 1:25, 34, 39

25 [a]Deut 17:14-20; 1 Sam 8:11-18 [b]Deut 31:26 **26** [a]1 Sam 11:4; 15:34 **27** [1]Lit *sons of Belial*, cf 2 Cor 6:15 [a]Deut 13:13; 1 Sam 25:17 [b]1 Kin 10:25; 2 Chr 17:5 **11:1** [1]Lit *camped against* [a]1 Sam 12:12 [b]Judg 21:8; 1 Sam 31:11 [c]Gen 26:28; 1 Kin 20:34; Job 41:4; Ezek 17:13 **2** [a]Num 16:14 [b]1 Sam 17:26; Ps 44:13 **3** [a]1 Sam 8:4 **4** [a]1 Sam 10:26; 15:34 [b]Gen 27:38; Judg 2:4; 20:23, 26; 21:2; 1 Sam 30:4 **5** [1]Lit *Saul* [a]1 Kin 19:19

25 Then Samuel told the people [a]the ordinances of the kingdom, and wrote *them* in the book and [b]placed *it* before the LORD. And Samuel sent all the people away, each one to his house.

26 Saul also went [a]to his house at Gibeah; and the valiant *men* whose hearts God had touched went with him.

27 But certain [1a]worthless men said, "How can this one deliver us?" And they despised him and [b]did not bring him any present. But he kept silent.

Saul Defeats the Ammonites

11 Now [a]Nahash the Ammonite came up and [1]besieged [b]Jabesh-gilead; and all the men of Jabesh said to Nahash, "Make [c]a covenant with us and we will serve you."

2 But Nahash the Ammonite said to them, "I will make *it* with you on this condition, [a]that I will gouge out the right eye of every one of you, thus I will make it [b]a reproach on all Israel."

3 [a]The elders of Jabesh said to him, "Let us alone for seven days, that we may send messengers throughout the territory of Israel. Then, if there is no one to deliver us, we will come out to you."

4 Then the messengers came [a]to Gibeah of Saul and spoke these words in the hearing of the people, and all the people [b]lifted up their voices and wept.

5 Now behold, Saul was coming from the field [a]behind the oxen, and [1]he said, "What is *the matter* with the people that they

---

10:17 *Samuel called the people.* After the private designation and anointing of Saul to be king (9:1–10:16), an assembly is called by Samuel to make the Lord's choice known to the people (v. 21) and to define the king's task (v. 25). *Mizpah.* See note on 7:5.
10:18 *I delivered you.* Speaking through Samuel, the Lord emphasizes to the people that He has been their deliverer throughout their history. He brought them out of Egypt and delivered them from all their enemies during the time of the judges. Although the judges themselves are sometimes referred to as Israel's deliverers (see Judg 3:9,15,31; 6:14; 10:1; 13:5), this was true only in a secondary sense, for they were instruments of the Lord's deliverance (see Judg 2:18). It was the Lord who sent them (see 12:11; Judg 6:14).
10:19 *rejected your God.* See note on 8:7.
10:20 *tribe of Benjamin was taken.* Probably by casting lots (see 14:41–42; Josh 7:15–18). The Urim and Thummim were used for this purpose (see notes on 2:28; Ex 28:30).
10:24 *Long live the king!* See 2 Sam 16:16.
10:25 *ordinances of the kingdom.* Samuel here takes the first step toward resolving the tension that existed between Israel's misdirected desire for a king (and their misconceived notion of what the king's role and function should be) and the Lord's intent to give them one (see Introduction: Contents and Theme). This description of the duties and prerogatives of the Israelite king was given for the benefit of both the people and the king-designate. It was intended to clearly distinguish Israelite kingship from that of the surrounding nations and to ensure that the king's role in Israel was compatible with the continued rule of the Lord over Israel as her Great King (see Deut 17:14–20). *placed it before the LORD.* The written constitutional-legal document defining the role of the king in governing God's covenant people was preserved at the sanctuary (the tabernacle, later the temple). Other written documents defining Israel's covenant relationship with the Lord are referred to in Ex 24:7; Deut 31:26; Josh 24:26.
10:27 *worthless men.* See note on Deut 13:13. *How can this one deliver us?* Reflects the people's continued apostate idea that national security was to be sought in the person of the human king (see note on v. 18; cf. 8:20).
11:1 *Ammonite.* The Ammonites were descended from Lot (see Gen 19:38; Deut 2:19) and lived east of the tribal territory of Gad near the upper regions of the Jabbok River (see Deut 2:37; Josh 12:2). Previous attempts by the Ammonites to occupy Israelite territory are referred to in Judg 3:13; 11:4–32. The Philistine threat to Israel in the west presented the Ammonites with an opportunity to move against Israel from the east with supposed impunity. *Jabesh-gilead.* A town east of the Jordan in the tribal area of Manasseh.
11:2 *gouge out the right eye.* Besides causing humiliation (see note on Judg 16:21), the loss of the right eye would destroy the military capability of the archers.
11:4 *Gibeah of Saul.* See 10:26 and note on 10:5. Close family ties undoubtedly prompted the inhabitants of Jabesh to seek help from the tribe of Benjamin (see Judg 21:12–14).
11:5 *Saul was coming from the field.* After Saul's public selection as the king-designate at Mizpah (10:17–27), he returned home (10:26) to resume his normal private activities and to wait for the Lord's leading for the next step in his elevation to the throne (see notes on v. 15; 10:7).

weep?" So they related to him the words of the men of Jabesh.

6 Then [a]the Spirit of God came upon Saul mightily when he heard these words, and [1]he became very angry.

7 He took a yoke of oxen and [a]cut them in pieces, and sent *them* throughout the territory of Israel by the hand of messengers, saying, "[b]Whoever does not come out after Saul and after Samuel, so shall it be done to his oxen." Then the dread of the LORD fell on the people, and they came out [c]as one man.

8 He [1]numbered them in [a]Bezek; and the [b]sons of Israel were 300,000, and the men of Judah 30,000.

9 They said to the messengers who had come, "Thus you shall say to the men of Jabesh-gilead, 'Tomorrow, by the time the sun is hot, you will have deliverance.' " So the messengers went and told the men of Jabesh; and they were glad.

10 Then the men of Jabesh said, "[a]Tomorrow we will come out to you, and you may do to us whatever seems good [1]to you."

11 The next morning Saul put the people [a]in three companies; and they came into the midst of the camp at the morning watch and struck down the Ammonites until the heat of the day. Those who survived were scattered, so that no two of them were left together.

12 Then the people said to Samuel, "[a]Who is he that said, 'Shall Saul reign over us?' [1][b]Bring the men, that we may put them to death."

13 But Saul said, "[a]Not a man shall be put to death this day, for today [b]the LORD has accomplished deliverance in Israel."

14 Then Samuel said to the people, "Come and let us go to [a]Gilgal and [b]renew the kingdom there."

15 So all the people went to Gilgal, and there they made Saul king [a]before the LORD in Gilgal. There they also [b]offered sacrifices of peace offerings before the LORD; and there Saul and all the men of Israel rejoiced greatly.

Samuel Addresses Israel

12 Then Samuel said to all Israel, "Behold, [a]I have listened to your voice in all that you said to me and I [b]have [1]appointed a king over you.

2 "Now, [a]here is the king walking before you, but [b]I am old and gray, and behold [c]my sons are with you. And [d]I have walked before you from my youth even to this day.

3 "Here I am; bear witness against me before the LORD and [a]His anointed. [b]Whose ox have I taken, or whose donkey have I taken, or whom have I defrauded? Whom have I oppressed, or [c]from whose hand have I taken a bribe to blind my eyes with it? I will restore *it* to you."

4 They said, "You have not defrauded us or oppressed us or taken anything from any man's hand."

5 He said to them, "The LORD is witness against you, and His anointed is witness this day that [a]you have found nothing [b]in my hand." And they said, "*He is* witness."

6 Then Samuel said to the people, "It is

6 [1]Lit *his anger burned exceedingly* [a]Judg 3:10; 6:34; 11:29; 13:25; 14:6; 1 Sam 10:10; 16:13
7 [a]Judg 19:29 [b]Judg 21:5, 8 [c]Judg 20:1
8 [1]Lit *mustered* [a]Judg 1:5 [b]Judg 20:2
10 [1]Lit *in your sight* [a]1 Sam 11:3
11 [a]Judg 7:16, 20
12 [1]Lit *Give* [a]1 Sam 10:27 [b]Luke 19:27
13 [a]1 Sam 10:27; 2 Sam 19:22
13 [b]Ex 14:13, 30; 1 Sam 19:5
14 [a]1 Sam 7:16; 10:8 [b]1 Sam 10:25
15 [a]1 Sam 10:17 [b]1 Sam 10:8
12:1 [1]Lit *made* [a]1 Sam 8:7, 9, 22 [b]1 Sam 10:24; 11:14, 15
2 [a]1 Sam 8:20 [b]1 Sam 8:1, 5 [c]1 Sam 8:3, 5 [d]1 Sam 3:10, 19, 20
3 [a]1 Sam 10:1; 24:6; 2 Sam 1:14 [b]Ex 20:17; Num 16:15; Acts 20:33 [c]Ex 23:8; Deut 16:19
5 [a]Acts 23:9; 24:20 [b]Ex 22:4

11:6 *the Spirit of God came upon Saul mightily.* For similar endowment of Israel's deliverers with extraordinary vigor by God's Spirit see 10:6,10; Judg 14:6,19; 15:14.

11:7 *sent them throughout . . . Israel.* For a similar case see Judg 19:29.

11:8 *Bezek.* Located north of Shechem, west of the Jordan River but within striking distance of Jabesh-gilead.

11:11 *the morning watch.* The third watch, from about 2:00 A.M. until about 6:00 A.M. (see note on Matt 14:25).

11:13 *the LORD has accomplished deliverance in Israel.* Saul recognizes Israel's true deliverer (see note on 10:18). The victory, in combination with Saul's confession, places yet another seal of divine approval on Saul as the man the Lord has chosen to be king.

11:14 *let us go to Gilgal and renew the kingdom.* Samuel perceives that it is now the appropriate time for the people to renew their allegiance to the Lord. The kingship of which he speaks is the Lord's, not Saul's. Samuel calls for an assembly to restore the covenant relationship between the Lord and His people. He wants to inaugurate Saul's rule in a manner demonstrating that the continued rule of the Lord as Israel's Great King is in no way diminished or violated in the new era of the monarchy (see Introduction: Contents and Theme). Verses 14–15 are a brief synopsis of the Gilgal assembly and are prefaced to the more detailed account of the same assembly in ch. 12. *Gilgal.* Located east of Jericho near the Jordan River. It was a particularly appropriate place for Israel to renew her allegiance to the Lord (see Josh 4:19–5:11; 10:8–15).

11:15 *made Saul king before the LORD.* Saul had previously been anointed in private by Samuel at Ramah (10:1) and publicly selected as the king-designate at Mizpah (10:17–27). In the subsequent Ammonite crisis (vv. 1–13) his leadership did not rest on public recognition of his royal authority, but on the military victory. Now at Gilgal Saul is inaugurated as God's chosen king and formally assumes the privileges and responsibilities of this office. *peace offerings.* This type of offering was an important element in the original ceremony of covenant ratification at Sinai (Ex 24:5,11). It represented the communion or peace between the Lord and His people when the people lived in conformity with their covenant obligations (see Lev 7:11–17; 22:21–23). *rejoiced greatly.* Rejoicing is the expression of people who have renewed their commitment to the Lord, confessed their sin (see 12:19) and been given a king.

12:3 *bear witness against me.* When Samuel presents the newly inaugurated king to the people, he seeks to establish publicly his own past faithfulness to the covenant as leader of the nation. His purpose is to exonerate himself and provide an example for Saul in his new responsibilities. *Whose ox have I taken, or whose donkey have I taken . . . ?* See Ex 20:17; 22:1,4,9. Samuel has not used his position for personal gain (see Num 16:15). *whom have I defrauded? Whom have I oppressed . . . ?* See Lev 19:13; Deut 24:14. *from whose hand have I taken a bribe . . . ?* See Ex 23:8; Deut 16:19.

12:6 *Samuel said to the people.* Samuel turns from consideration of his previous leadership to the matter of the people's request for a king, which he views as a covenant-breaking act and a serious apostasy. *It is the LORD.* Samuel emphasizes that in the past the Lord had provided the necessary leadership for the nation.

the LORD who [1a]appointed Moses and Aaron and who brought your fathers up from the land of Egypt.

7 "So now, take your stand, [a]that I may plead with you before the LORD concerning all the righteous acts of the LORD which He did for you and your fathers.

8 "[a]When Jacob went into Egypt and [b]your fathers cried out to the LORD, then [c]the LORD sent Moses and Aaron [1d]who brought your fathers out of Egypt and settled them in this place.

9 "But [a]they forgot the LORD their God, so [b]He sold them into the hand of Sisera, captain of the army of Hazor, and [c]into the hand of the Philistines and [d]into the hand of the king of Moab, and they fought against them.

10 "[a]They cried out to the LORD and said, 'We have sinned because we have forsaken the LORD and have served [b]the Baals and the Ashtaroth; but [c]now deliver us from the hands of our enemies, and we will serve You.'

11 "Then the LORD sent [a]Jerubbaal and [1b]Bedan and [c]Jephthah and [d]Samuel, and delivered you from the hands of your enemies all around, so that you lived in security.

The King Confirmed

12 "When you saw [a]that Nahash the king of the sons of Ammon came against you, you said to me, '[b]No, but a king shall reign over us,' [c]although the LORD your God *was* your king.

13 "Now therefore, [a]here is the king whom you have chosen, [b]whom you have asked for, and behold, the LORD has set a king over you.

14 "[a]If you will fear the LORD and serve Him, and listen to His voice and not rebel against the [1]command of the LORD, then both you and also the king who reigns over you will follow the LORD your God.

15 "[a]If you will not listen to the voice of the LORD, but rebel against the [1]command of the LORD, then [b]the hand of the LORD will be against you, [c]*as it was* against your fathers.

16 "Even now, [a]take your stand and see this great thing which the LORD will do before your eyes.

17 "[a]Is it not the wheat harvest today? [b]I will call to the LORD, that He may send [1]thunder and rain. Then you will know and see that [c]your wickedness is great which you have done in the sight of the LORD by asking for yourselves a king."

18 So Samuel called to the LORD, and the LORD sent [1]thunder and rain that day; and [a]all the people greatly feared the LORD and Samuel.

19 Then all the people said to Samuel, "[a]Pray for your servants to the LORD your God, so that we may not die, for we have added to all our sins [b]*this* evil by asking for ourselves a king."

20 Samuel said to the people, "Do not fear. You have committed all this evil, yet [a]do not turn aside from following the LORD, but serve the LORD with all your heart.

21 "You must not turn aside, for *then you would go* after [a]futile things which can not profit or deliver, because they are futile.

22 "For [a]the LORD will not abandon His

6 [1]Lit *made* [a]Ex 6:26; Mic 6:4
7 [a]Ezek 20:35; Mic 6:1-5
8 [1]Lit *and they brought* [a]Gen 46:5, 6 [b]Ex 2:23-25 [c]Ex 3:10; 4:14-16 [d]1 Sam 10:18
9 [a]Deut 32:18; Judg 3:7 [b]Judg 4:2 [c]Judg 3:31; 10:7; 13:1 [d]Judg 3:12-30
10 [a]Judg 10:10 [b]Judg 2:13; 3:7 [c]Judg 10:15, 16
11 [1]Gr and Syr read *Barak* [a]Judg 6:31, 32; 7:1 [b]Judg 4:6; 11:1 [c]Judg 11:29 [d]1 Sam 3:20
12 [a]1 Sam 11:1, 2 [b]1 Sam 8:6, 19 [c]Judg 8:23; 1 Sam 8:7
13 [a]1 Sam 10:24 [b]1 Sam 8:5; 12:17, 19; Hos 13:11
14 [1]Lit *mouth* [a]Josh 24:14
15 [1]Lit *mouth* [a]Lev 26:14, 15; Josh 24:20; Is 1:20 [b]1 Sam 5:9 [c]1 Sam 12:9
16 [a]Ex 14:13, 31
17 [1]Lit *sounds* [a]Prov 26:1 [b]1 Sam 7:9, 10; James 5:16ff [c]1 Sam 8:7
18 [1]Lit *sounds* [a]Ex 14:31
19 [a]Ex 9:28; 1 Sam 12:23; Jer 15:1; 1 John 5:16 [b]1 Sam 12:17, 20
20 [a]Deut 11:16
21 [a]Deut 11:16; Is 41:29; Hab 2:18
22 [a]Deut 31:6; 1 Kin 6:13

12:7 *plead with you.* The terminology is that of a legal proceeding, as in vv. 2–5, but now the relationship of the parties is reversed. This time Samuel is the accuser, the people are the defendants, and the Lord is the Judge. *righteous acts of the LORD.* These righteous acts (see vv. 8–11) demonstrate the constancy of the Lord's covenant faithfulness toward His people in the past and, by way of contrast, serve as an indictment of their present apostasy.

12:11 *LORD . . . delivered you.* The Lord repeatedly delivered Israel from her enemies right up to Samuel's own lifetime (see 7:3,8,10,12), demonstrating again the people's apostasy in desiring a king.

12:12 *When you saw that Nahash . . . came against you.* In the face of the combined threat from the Philistines in the west (9:16) and the Ammonites in the east (11:1–13), the Israelites sought to find security in the person of a human king. *the LORD your God was your king.* The Israelite desire for and trust in a human leader constituted a rejection of the kingship of the Lord and betrayed a loss of confidence in His care, in spite of His faithfulness during the time of the exodus, conquest and judges (see note on 8:7).

12:13 *the LORD has set a king over you.* In spite of the sinfulness of the people's request, the Lord had chosen to incorporate kingship into the structure of the theocracy (His kingdom). Kingship was given by the Lord to His people and was to function as an instrument of His rule over them (see Introduction: Contents and Theme).

12:14 *If you will fear the LORD.* Samuel relates the old covenant condition (see Ex 19:5–6; Deut 8:19; 11:13–15,22–28; 28; 30:17–18; Josh 24:20) to the new era Israel is entering with the establishment of the monarchy. *you and also the king . . . will follow the LORD your God.* Israel and her king are to demonstrate that although human kingship has been established, they will continue to recognize the Lord as their true King. In this new era where potential for divided loyalty between the Lord and the human king arises, Israel's loyalty to the Lord must remain inviolate. For similar use of the expression "to follow" see 2 Sam 2:10; 15:13; 1 Kin 12:20; 16:21.

12:15 *If you will not listen.* Samuel confronts Israel with the same alternatives Moses had expressed centuries earlier (see Deut 28; 30:15–20). The introduction of kingship into Israel's socio-political structure has not changed the fundamental nature of Israel's relationship to the Lord.

12:16 *see this great thing.* Samuel calls the people to observe as the Lord Himself demonstrates His existence and power and authenticates the truthfulness and seriousness of Samuel's words.

12:17 *wheat harvest.* See note on 6:13.

12:19 *Pray . . . to the LORD your God.* Samuel's indictment (vv. 6–15) combined with the awesome sign of thunder and rain in the dry season (vv. 16–18) prompted the people to confess their sin and request Samuel's intercession for them.

12:20 *yet do not turn aside from following the LORD.* Samuel again brings into focus the central issue in the controversy surrounding the establishment of kingship in Israel.

12:21 *futile things.* No rivals to the Lord can deliver or guarantee security.

people [b]on account of His great name, because the LORD [c]has been pleased to make you a people for Himself.

23 "Moreover, as for me, [a]far be it from me that I should sin against the LORD by ceasing to pray for you; but [b]I will instruct you in the good and right way.

24 "[a]Only [1]fear the LORD and serve Him in truth with all your heart; for consider [b]what great things He has done for you.

25 "[a]But if you still do wickedly, [b]both you and your king [c]will be swept away."

War with the Philistines

13 Saul was [1]*thirty* years old when he began to reign, and he reigned [2]*forty* two years over Israel.

2 Now Saul chose for himself 3,000 men of Israel, of which 2,000 were with Saul in [a]Michmash and in the hill country of Bethel, while 1,000 were with Jonathan at [b]Gibeah of Benjamin. But he sent away the rest of the people, each to his tent.

3 Jonathan smote [a]the garrison of the Philistines that was in [b]Geba, and the Philistines heard of *it.* Then Saul [c]blew the trumpet throughout the land, saying, "Let the Hebrews hear."

4 All Israel heard [1]the news that Saul had smitten the garrison of the Philistines, and also that Israel [a]had become odious to the Philistines. The people were then summoned [2]to Saul at Gilgal.

5 Now the Philistines assembled to fight with Israel, 30,000 chariots and 6,000 horsemen, and [a]people like the sand which is on the seashore in abundance; and they came up and camped in Michmash, east of [b]Beth-aven.

6 When the men of Israel saw that they were in a strait (for the people were hard-pressed), then [a]the people hid themselves in caves, in thickets, in cliffs, in cellars, and in pits.

7 Also *some of* the Hebrews crossed the Jordan into the land of [a]Gad and Gilead. But as for Saul, he *was* still in Gilgal, and all the people followed him trembling.

8 Now [a]he waited seven days, according to the appointed time set by Samuel, but Samuel did not come to Gilgal; and the people were scattering from him.

9 So Saul said, "Bring to me the burnt offering and the peace offerings." And [a]he offered the burnt offering.

10 As soon as he finished offering the burnt offering, behold, Samuel came; and [a]Saul went out to meet him *and* to [1]greet him.

11 But Samuel said, "What have you done?" And Saul said, "Because I saw that the people were scattering from me, and that you did not come within the appointed days, and that [a]the Philistines were assembling at Michmash,

12 therefore I said, 'Now the Philistines will come down against me at Gilgal, and I have not asked the favor of the LORD.' So I forced myself and offered the burnt offering."

13 Samuel said to Saul, "[a]You have acted foolishly; [b]you have not kept the commandment of the LORD your God, which He commanded you, for now the LORD would have established your kingdom [1]over Israel [c]forever.

14 "But [a]now your kingdom shall not endure. [b]The LORD has sought out for Himself a man after His own heart, and the LORD has appointed him as ruler over His people, because you have not kept what the LORD commanded you."

22 [b]Ex 32:12; Num 14:13; Josh 7:9; Ps 106:8; Jer 14:21 [c]Deut 7:6-11; 1 Pet 2:9
23 [a]Rom 1:9; 1 Cor 9:16; Col 1:9; 1 Thess 3:10; 2 Tim 1:3 [b]1 Kin 8:36; Ps 34:11; Prov 4:11
24 [1]Or *reverence* [a]Eccl 12:13 [b]Deut 10:21; Is 5:12
25 [a]Is 1:20; 3:11 [b]Josh 24:20 [c]1 Sam 31:1-5; Hos 10:3
13:1 [1]As in some mss of the LXX; Heb omits *thirty* [2]See Acts 13:21; Heb omits *forty*
2 [a]1 Sam 13:5; 14:31 [b]1 Sam 10:26
3 [a]1 Sam 10:5 [b]1 Sam 13:16; 14:5 [c]Judg 3:27; 6:34
4 [1]Lit *saying* [2]Lit *after* [a]Gen 34:30; Ex 5:21; 2 Sam 10:6
5 [a]Josh 11:4 [b]Josh 18:12; 1 Sam 14:23
6 [a]Judg 6:2
7 [a]Num 32:33
8 [a]1 Sam 10:8
9 [a]Deut 12:5-14; 2 Sam 24:25; 1 Kin 3:4
10 [1]Lit *bless* [a]1 Sam 15:13
11 [a]1 Sam 13:2, 5, 16, 23
13 [1]Lit *to* [a]2 Chr 16:9 [b]1 Sam 15:11, 22, 28 [c]1 Sam 1:22
14 [a]1 Sam 15:28 [b]Acts 7:46; 13:22

12:23 *I will instruct you in the good and right way.* Samuel is not retiring from his prophetic role when he presents the people with their king. He will continue to intercede for the people (see v. 19; 7:8–9) and will instruct them in their covenant obligations (see Deut 6:18; 12:28). Saul and all future kings are to be subject to instruction and correction by the Lord's prophets.

12:24 *fear the LORD.* Samuel summarizes Israel's obligation of loyalty to the Lord as an expression of gratitude for the great things He has done for them.

12:25 *you and your king will be swept away.* Should the nation persist in covenant-breaking conduct, it will bring upon itself its own destruction.

13:1 *thirty years old . . . forty two years.* The wording of the verse follows the regularly used formula that introduces the reigns of later kings (see, e.g., 2 Sam 2:10; 5:4; 1 Kin 14:21; 2 Kin 8:26).

13:2 *Michmash.* Located southeast of Bethel and northeast of Gibeah near a pass (see v. 23). *Jonathan.* Saul's oldest son (see 14:49), mentioned here for the first time.

13:3 *Geba.* Located across a ravine and south of Michmash.

13:4 *odious.* A metaphor depicting an object of strong hostility, as in 2 Sam 10:6; 16:21; Gen 34:30; Ex 5:21. *Gilgal.* See note on 11:14. By prearrangement Saul had been instructed to wait for Samuel there (see notes on v. 8; 10:8).

13:5 *30,000 chariots.* The Canaanites under Sisera (see Judg 4:13) had 900 chariots. The Israelites did not acquire chariots until the time of Solomon (see 1 Kin 4:26).

13:8 *time set by Samuel.* See note on 10:8. Saul is fully aware that Samuel's previous instructions had reference to this gathering at Gilgal. *the people were scattering.* The seven-day delay heightened the fear of the Israelite soldiers.

13:9 *Saul . . . offered the burnt offering.* Samuel had promised to make these offerings himself (see 10:8) before Israel went to battle (see 7:9), and he had directed Saul to await his arrival and instructions.

13:13 *You have acted foolishly.* The foolish and sinful aspect (see 26:21; 2 Sam 24:10; 1 Chr 21:8; 2 Chr 16:9) of Saul's act was that he thought he could strengthen Israel's chances against the Philistines while disregarding the instruction of the Lord's prophet Samuel. *you have not kept the commandment of the LORD your God.* Saul was to recognize the word of the prophet Samuel as the word of the Lord (see 3:20; 15:1; Ex 20:18–19; see also note on Ex 7:1–2). In disobeying Samuel's instructions, Saul violated a fundamental requirement of his theocratic office. His kingship was not to function independently of the law and the prophets (see notes on 12:14,23; 15:11).

13:14 *your kingdom shall not endure.* Saul will not be followed by his sons; there will be no dynasty bearing his name (contrast the Lord's word to David, 2 Sam 7:11–16). There is a striking parallel in the word of the Lord to Eli (see 2:30,35). *The LORD has*

15 Then Samuel arose and went up from Gilgal to [a]Gibeah of Benjamin. And Saul [1]numbered the people who were present with him, [b]about six hundred men.

16 Now Saul and his son Jonathan and the people who were present with them were staying in [a]Geba of Benjamin while the Philistines camped at Michmash.

17 And [a]the [1]raiders came from the camp of the Philistines in three [2]companies: one [3]company turned [4]toward [b]Ophrah, to the land of Shual,

18 and another [1]company turned [2]toward [a]Beth-horon, and another [1]company turned [2]toward the border which overlooks the valley of [b]Zeboim toward the wilderness.

19 Now [a]no blacksmith could be found in all the land of Israel, for the Philistines said, "Otherwise the Hebrews will make [1b]swords or spears."

20 So all Israel went down to the Philistines, each to sharpen his plowshare, his mattock, his axe, and his hoe.

21 The charge was [1]two-thirds of a shekel for the plowshares, the mattocks, the forks, and the axes, and to fix the hoes.

22 So it came about on the day of battle that [a]neither sword nor spear was found in the hands of any of the people who *were* with Saul and Jonathan, but they were found with Saul and his son Jonathan.

23 And [a]the garrison of the Philistines went out to [b]the pass of Michmash.

Jonathan's Victory

14 Now the day came that Jonathan, the son of Saul, said to the young man who was carrying his armor, "Come and let us cross over to the Philistines' garrison that is on the other side." But he did not tell his father.

2 Saul was staying in the outskirts of [a]Gibeah under the pomegranate tree which is in [b]Migron. And the people who *were* with him *were* [c]about six hundred men,

3 and Ahijah, the [a]son of Ahitub, [b]Ichabod's brother, the son of Phinehas, the son of Eli, the priest of the LORD at [c]Shiloh, [d]was [1]wearing an ephod. And the people did not know that Jonathan had gone.

4 [a]Between the passes by which Jonathan sought to cross over to the Philistines' garrison, there was a sharp crag on the one side and a sharp crag on the other side, and the name of the one was Bozez, and the name of the other Seneh.

5 The one crag rose on the north opposite Michmash, and the other on the south opposite Geba.

6 Then Jonathan said to the young man who was carrying his armor, "Come and let us cross over to the garrison of [a]these uncircumcised; perhaps the LORD will work for us, for [b]the LORD is not restrained to save by many or by few."

7 His armor bearer said to him, "Do all that is in your heart; turn yourself, *and* here I am with you according to your [1]desire."

8 Then Jonathan said, "[a]Behold, we will cross over to the men and reveal ourselves to them.

9 "If they [1]say to us, 'Wait until we come to you'; then we will stand in our place and not go up to them.

10 "But if they [1]say, 'Come up to us,' then we will go up, for the LORD has given them into our hands; and [a]this shall be the sign to us."

11 When both of them revealed themselves to the garrison of the Philistines, the Philistines said, "Behold, [a]Hebrews are coming out of the holes where they have hidden themselves."

12 So the men of the garrison [1]hailed Jonathan and his armor bearer and said, "Come up to us and [a]we will tell you something." And Jonathan said to his armor bearer, "Come up after me, for [b]the LORD has given them into the hands of Israel."

13 Then Jonathan climbed up on his hands and feet, with his armor bearer behind him; and they fell before Jonathan, and his armor bearer put some to death after him.

15 [1]Lit *mustered* [a]1 Sam 13:2 [b]1 Sam 13:2, 6, 7; 14:2
16 [a]1 Sam 13:2, 3
17 [1]Lit *destroyers* [2]Lit *heads* [3]Lit *head* [4]Lit *toward the direction of* [a]1 Sam 14:15 [b]Josh 18:23
18 [1]Lit *head* [2]Lit *the direction of* [a]Josh 16:3; 18:13, 14 [b]Neh 11:34
19 [1]Lit *sword or spear* [a]Judg 5:8; 2 Kin 24:14; Jer 24:1; 29:2 [b]Judg 5:8
21 [1]Heb *pim*
22 [a]Judg 5:8
23 [a]1 Sam 14:1; 2 Sam 23:14 [b]1 Sam 14:4, 5; Is 10:28
14:2 [a]1 Sam 13:15, 16 [b]Is 10:28 [c]1 Sam 13:15
3 [a]1 Sam 22:9-12, 20 [b]1 Sam 4:21
3 [1]Lit *carrying* [c]1 Sam 1:3 [d]1 Sam 2:28
4 [a]1 Sam 13:23
6 [a]1 Sam 17:26, 36; Jer 9:25, 26 [b]Judg 7:4, 7; 1 Sam 17:46, 47; Ps 115:3; 135:6; Zech 4:6; Matt 19:26
7 [1]Lit *heart*
8 [a]Judg 7:9-14
9 [1]Lit *say thus*
10 [1]Lit *say thus* [a]Gen 24:14; Judg 6:36
11 [a]1 Sam 13:6; 14:22
12 [1]Lit *answered* [a]1 Sam 17:43, 44 [b]2 Sam 5:24

---

sought out . . . a man after His own heart, and . . . appointed him. Paul quotes from this passage at Antioch (Acts 13:22). *ruler.* See 10:16 and note on "prince" in 9:16 (same word in Hebrew).

13:15 *six hundred.* The seven-day delay had greatly depleted Saul's forces (see vv. 2,4,6–8).

13:17 *raiders.* The purpose of these Philistine contingents was not to engage the Israelites in battle, but to plunder the land and demoralize its inhabitants.

13:18 *valley of Zeboim.* Located to the east toward the Jordan Valley.

13:19 *no blacksmith.* A Philistine monopoly on the technology of iron production placed the Israelites at a great disadvantage in the fashioning and maintenance of agricultural implements and military weapons.

13:22 *neither sword nor spear.* The Israelites fought with bow and arrow and slingshot.

14:1 *on the other side.* The Philistines were encamped to the north of the pass and the Israelites to the south.

14:2 *Gibeah.* Saul had retreated farther south from Geba (13:3) to Gibeah. *under the pomegranate tree.* It appears to have been customary for leaders in early Israel to hold court under well-known trees (see 22:6; Jdg 4:5).

14:3 *Ahijah.* Either the brother and predecessor of Ahimelech son of Ahitub (referred to in 21:1; 22:9,11) or an alternate name for Ahimelech. *Ichabod's brother.* See 4:21. *wearing an ephod.* See note on 2:28.

14:6 *uncircumcised.* A term of contempt (see 17:26,36; 31:4; 2 Sam 1:20; Judg 14:3; 15:18; 1 Chr 10:4), which draws attention to Israel's covenant relationship to the Lord (see note on Gen 17:10) and, by implication, to the illegitimacy of the Philistine presence in the land. *by many or by few.* See note on 17:47. Jonathan's bold plan is undertaken as an act of faith (cf. Heb 11:33–34) founded on God's promise (9:16).

14:10 *sign to us.* See Judg 6:36–40; Is 7:11.

14:11 *Hebrews.* See 4:6; 13:3,7 and note on Gen 14:13.

14 That first slaughter which Jonathan and his armor bearer made was about twenty men within about half a furrow in an acre of land.

15 And there was a trembling in the camp, in the field, and among all the people. Even the garrison and [a]the raiders trembled, and [b]the earth quaked so [c]that it became a [1]great trembling.

16 Now Saul's watchmen in Gibeah of Benjamin looked, and behold, the multitude melted away; and they went here and *there.*

17 Saul said to the people who *were* with him, "[1]Number now and see who has gone from us." And when they had [1]numbered, behold, Jonathan and his armor bearer were not *there.*

18 Then Saul said to Ahijah, "[a]Bring the ark of God here." For the ark of God was at that time with the sons of Israel.

19 [a]While Saul talked to the priest, the commotion in the camp of the Philistines continued and increased; so Saul said to the priest, "Withdraw your hand."

20 Then Saul and all the people who *were* with him rallied and came to the battle; and behold, [a]every man's sword was against his fellow, *and there was* very great confusion.

21 Now the Hebrews *who* were with the Philistines previously, who went up with them all around in the camp, even [a]they also *turned* to be with the Israelites who *were* with Saul and Jonathan.

22 When all the [a]men of Israel who had hidden themselves in the hill country of Ephraim heard that the Philistines had fled, even they also pursued them closely in the battle.

15 [1]Lit *trembling of God* [a]1 Sam 13:17, 18 [b]1 Sam 7:10 [c]Gen 35:5; 2 Kin 7:6
17 [1]Lit *muster(ed)*
18 [a]1 Sam 23:9; 30:7
19 [a]Num 27:21
20 [a]Judg 7:22; 2 Chr 20:23
21 [a]1 Sam 29:4
22 [a]1 Sam 13:6
23 [1]Lit *passed over* [a]Ex 14:30; 1 Sam 10:19; 14:23; 1 Chr 11:14; 2 Chr 32:22; Ps 44:7 [b]1 Sam 13:5
24 [1]Lit *until* [a]Josh 6:26
26 [a]Matt 3:4
27 [a]1 Sam 14:43 [b]1 Sam 30:12
29 [a]Josh 7:25; 1 Kin 18:18
31 [a]1 Sam 14:5 [b]Josh 10:12

23 So [a]the LORD delivered Israel that day, and the battle [1]spread beyond [b]Beth-aven.

Saul's Foolish Order

24 Now the men of Israel were hard-pressed on that day, for Saul had [a]put the people under oath, saying, "Cursed be the man who eats food [1]before evening, and until I have avenged myself on my enemies." So none of the people tasted food.

25 All *the people of* the land entered the forest, and there was honey on the ground.

26 When the people entered the forest, behold, [a]*there was* a flow of honey; but no man put his hand to his mouth, for the people feared the oath.

27 But Jonathan had not heard when his father put the people under oath; therefore, [a]he put out the end of the staff that *was* in his hand and dipped it in the honeycomb, and put his hand to his mouth, and [b]his eyes brightened.

28 Then one of the people said, "Your father strictly put the people under oath, saying, 'Cursed be the man who eats food today.' " And the people were weary.

29 Then Jonathan said, "[a]My father has troubled the land. See now, how my eyes have brightened because I tasted a little of this honey.

30 "How much more, if only the people had eaten freely today of the spoil of their enemies which they found! For now the slaughter among the Philistines has not been great."

31 They struck among the Philistines that day from [a]Michmash to [b]Aijalon. And the people were very weary.

14:15 *earth quaked.* See 7:10; Josh 10:11–14; Ps 77:18 for other instances of divine intervention in nature to bring deliverance to Israel.

14:18 *Bring the ark of God.* Saul decides to seek God's will before entering into battle with the Philistines (see Num 27:21; Deut 20:2). Here the Septuagint (the Greek translation of the OT) may preserve the original text ("'Bring the ephod.' At that time he wore the ephod before the Israelites") for the following reasons: 1. In 7:1 the ark was located at Kiriath-jearim, where it remained until David brought it to Jerusalem (2 Sam 6), but the ephod was present in Saul's camp at Gibeah (see v. 3). 2. Nowhere else in the OT is the ark used to determine God's will, but the ephod (with the Urim and Thummim) was given for this purpose (see 23:9; 30:7 and notes on 2:18,28). 3. The command to the priest to withdraw his hand (v. 19) is more appropriate with the ephod than with the ark.

14:19 *Withdraw your hand.* Due to the urgency of the moment, Saul decides that to wait for the word of the Lord might jeopardize his military advantage. As in 13:8–12, his decision rests on his own insight rather than on dependence upon the Lord and a commitment to obey Him.

14:23 *So the LORD delivered Israel that day.* The writer attributes the victory to the Lord, not to either Saul or Jonathan (see vv. 6,10,15; 11:13).

14:24–46 Following the account of the great victory the Lord had given, the author relates Saul's actions that strikingly illustrated his lack of fitness to be king. This foolish curse before the battle (see note on v. 24) made the army "hard-pressed" and, as Jonathan tellingly observed, "troubled the land" (v. 29) rather than contributing to the victory. And later, when hindered from taking advantage of the battle's outcome by the Lord's refusal to answer (v. 37), Saul was ready to execute Jonathan as the cause, though Jonathan had contributed most to the victory, as everyone else recognized (v. 45). Saul's growing egocentrism was turning into an all-consuming passion that threatened the very welfare of the nation. Rather than serving the cause of the Lord and His people, he was in fact becoming a king "like all the nations" (8:5).

14:24 *hard-pressed.* Saul's rash action in requiring his troops to fast placed them at an unnecessary disadvantage in the battle (see vv. 29–30). *Cursed.* Thus Saul as king "put the people under oath" (v. 28), a most serious matter because an oath directly invoked God's involvement, whether it concerned giving testimony (Ex 20:7; Lev 19:12), making commitments (Gen 21:23–24; 24:3–4) or prohibiting action (here; Josh 6:24). It appealed to God as the supreme enforcement power and the all-knowing Judge of human actions. *I have avenged myself on my enemies.* Saul perceives the conflict with the Philistines more as a personal vendetta (see note on 15:12) than as a battle for the honor of the Lord and the security of the Lord's people (note the contrast between his attitude and that of Jonathan in vv. 6,10,12).

14:31 *Aijalon.* Located to the west near the Philistines' own territory (see Josh 10:12).

32 [a]The people [1]rushed greedily upon the spoil, and took sheep and oxen and calves, and slew *them* on the ground; and the people ate *them* [b]with the blood.

33 Then they told Saul, saying, "Behold, the people are [a]sinning against the LORD by eating with the blood." And he said, "You have acted treacherously; roll a great stone to me today."

34 Saul said, "Disperse yourselves among the people and say to them, 'Each one of you bring me his ox or his sheep, and slaughter *it* here and eat; and do not sin against the LORD by eating with the blood.' " So all the people that night brought each one his ox [1]with him and slaughtered *it* there.

35 And [a]Saul built an altar to the LORD; it was the first altar that he built to the LORD.

36 Then Saul said, "Let us go down after the Philistines by night and take spoil among them until the morning light, and let us not leave a man of them." And they said, "Do whatever seems good [1]to you." So [a]the priest said, "Let us draw near to God here."

37 Saul [a]inquired of God, "Shall I go down after the Philistines? Will You give them into the hand of Israel?" But [b]He did not answer him on that day.

38 Saul said, "[a]Draw near here, all you [1]chiefs of the people, and investigate and see how this sin has happened today.

39 "For [a]as the LORD lives, who delivers Israel, though it is in Jonathan my son, he shall surely die." But not one of all the people answered him.

40 Then he said to all Israel, "You shall be on one side and I and Jonathan my son will be on the other side." And the people said to Saul, "Do what seems good [1]to you."

41 Therefore, Saul said to the LORD, the God of Israel, "[a]Give a perfect *lot.*" And Jonathan and Saul were taken, but the people escaped.

42 Saul said, "Cast *lots* between me and Jonathan my son." And Jonathan was taken.

43 Then Saul said to Jonathan, "[a]Tell me what you have done." So Jonathan told him and said, "[b]I indeed tasted a little honey with the end of the staff that was in my hand. Here I am, I must die!"

44 Saul said, "[a]May God do [1]this *to me* and more also, for [b]you shall surely die, Jonathan."

45 But the people said to Saul, "Must Jonathan die, who has [1]brought about this great deliverance in Israel? Far from it! As the LORD lives, [a]not one hair of his head shall fall to the ground, for [b]he has worked with God this day." So the people [2]rescued Jonathan and he did not die.

46 Then Saul went up from [1]pursuing the Philistines, and the Philistines went to their own place.

Constant Warfare

47 Now when Saul had taken the kingdom over Israel, he fought against all his enemies on every side, against Moab, [a]the sons of Ammon, Edom, [b]the kings of Zobah, and [c]the Philistines; and wherever he turned, he [1]inflicted punishment.

48 He acted valiantly and [1a]defeated the Amalekites, and delivered Israel from the hands of [2]those who plundered them.

49 Now [a]the sons of Saul were Jonathan and Ishvi and Malchi-shua; and the names of his two daughters *were these:* the name of the firstborn [b]Merab and the name of the younger [c]Michal.

50 The name of Saul's wife was Ahinoam the daughter of Ahimaaz. And [a]the name of the captain of his army was Abner the son of Ner, Saul's uncle.

51 [a]Kish *was* the father of Saul, and Ner the father of Abner *was* the son of Abiel.

52 Now the war against the Philistines was severe all the days of Saul; and when Saul saw any mighty man or any valiant man, he [1a]attached him to [2]his staff.

Saul's Disobedience

15 Then Samuel said to Saul, "[a]The LORD sent me to anoint you as king over His people, over Israel; now therefore, listen to the [1]words of the LORD.

32 [1]Lit *did with regard to the spoil* [a]1 Sam 15:19 [b]Gen 9:4; Lev 3:17; 17:10-14; 19:26; Deut 12:16, 23; Acts 15:20
33 [a]Lev 7:26, 27; 19:26; Deut 12:16, 23-25; 15:23
34 [1]Lit *in his hand*
35 [a]1 Sam 7:12, 17; 2 Sam 24:25; James 4:8
36 [1]Lit *in your eyes* [a]1 Sam 14:3, 18, 19
37 [a]1 Sam 10:22 [b]1 Sam 28:6
38 [1]Lit *corners* [a]Josh 7:11, 12; 1 Sam 10:19, 20
39 [a]1 Sam 14:24, 44; 2 Sam 12:5
40 [1]Lit *in your eyes*
41 [a]Acts 1:24
43 [a]Josh 7:19 [b]1 Sam 14:27
44 [1]Lit *thus* [a]Ruth 1:17; 1 Sam 25:22 [b]1 Sam 14:39
45 [1]Lit *worked* [2]Lit *ransomed* [a]2 Sam 14:11; 1 Kin 1:52; Luke 21:18; Acts 27:34 [b]2 Cor 6:1
46 [1]Lit *after*
47 [1]Or *condemned* [a]1 Sam 11:1-13 [b]2 Sam 8:3-10 [c]1 Sam 14:52
48 [1]Lit *smote* [2]Lit *its plunderers* [a]1 Sam 15:3, 7
49 [a]1 Sam 31:2; 1 Chr 8:33; 10:2 [b]1 Sam 18:17-19 [c]1 Sam 18:20, 27; 19:12; 2 Sam 6:20-23
50 [a]2 Sam 2:8
51 [a]1 Sam 9:1, 21
52 [1]Lit *gathered* [2]Lit *himself* [a]1 Sam 8:11
15:1 [1]Lit *sound of the words* [a]1 Sam 9:16; 10:1

14:33 *eating with the blood.* The Israelites were not permitted to eat blood (see Gen 9:4; Lev 17:11; 19:26; Deut 12:16; Ezek 33:25; Acts 15:20 and notes). *acted treacherously.* The same Hebrew term is translated "faithless" in Jer 3:8–11.

14:35 *first altar that he built.* Another indication of Saul's personal lack of interest in religious matters (see notes on 9:6; 10:11).

14:36 *priest.* Ahijah (see v. 3).

14:37 *Saul inquired of God.* The means of ascertaining God's will appears to have been the ephod with its Urim and Thummim (see v. 3 and note on v. 18). *He did not answer.* Because an oath had been broken in the battle, God refused to answer Saul's inquiry concerning further military action.

14:39 *as the LORD lives.* An oath formula (see note on v. 24; see also 19:6; Jer 4:2; Hos 4:15).

14:41 *taken.* See 10:20–21; Josh 7:14–18; Prov 16:33.

14:44 A curse formula (see note on v. 24; see also 3:17 and note).

14:45 *he has worked with God this day.* The men of Saul's army recognize the inappropriateness of taking the life of the one through whom God has delivered His people.

14:47–48 A summary of Saul's military victories to the east (Moab and the Ammonites), south (Edom), west (Philistines) and north (Zobah).

14:47 *sons of Ammon.* See Deut 2:19–21,37.

14:48 *Amalekites.* See note on 15:2.

14:49 *sons of Saul.* See 2 Sam 2:8,10; 1 Chr 9:39; 10:2. *Merab . . . Michal.* See 18:17,20,27; 19:11–17; 25:44; 2 Sam 6:16–23.

14:50 *Ahinoam.* The only reference to a wife of Saul. His concubine Rizpah is mentioned in 2 Sam 3:7; 21:8–11.

14:52 *all the days of Saul.* Closes the main account of Saul's reign. *he attached him to his staff.* Saul developed a special cadre of professional soldiers bound to himself, much as David was to do later (see 22:2; 23:13; 25:13; 27:2–3; 29:2; 30:1,9; 2 Sam 2:3; 5:6; 8:18; 15:18; 23:8–39).

15:1–35 The event that occasioned Saul's rejection. Although

2 "Thus says the LORD of hosts, 'I will [1]punish Amalek [a]*for* what he did to Israel, how he set himself against him on the way while he was coming up from Egypt.

3 'Now go and strike Amalek and [a]utterly destroy all that he has, and do not spare him; but [b]put to death both man and woman, child and infant, ox and sheep, camel and donkey.' "

4 Then Saul summoned the people and [1]numbered them in [a]Telaim, 200,000 foot soldiers and 10,000 men of Judah.

5 Saul came to the city of Amalek and set an ambush in the valley.

6 Saul said to [a]the Kenites, "Go, depart, go down from among the Amalekites, so that I do not destroy you with them; for [b]you showed kindness to all the sons of Israel when they came up from Egypt." So the Kenites departed from among the Amalekites.

7 So [a]Saul [1]defeated the Amalekites, from [b]Havilah as you go to [c]Shur, which is [2]east of Egypt.

8 He captured [a]Agag the king of the Amalekites alive, and [b]utterly destroyed all the people with the edge of the sword.

9 But Saul and the people [a]spared Agag and the best of the sheep, the oxen, the fatlings, the lambs, and all that was good, and were not willing to destroy them utterly; but everything despised and worthless, that they utterly destroyed.

Samuel Rebukes Saul

10 Then the word of the LORD came to Samuel, saying,

11 "[a]I regret that I have made Saul king, for [b]he has turned back from [1]following Me and has not carried out My commands." And Samuel was distressed and [c]cried out to the LORD all night.

12 Samuel rose early in the morning to meet Saul; and it was told Samuel, saying, "Saul came to [a]Carmel, and behold, he set up a monument for himself, then turned and proceeded on [1]down to [b]Gilgal."

13 Samuel came to Saul, and Saul said to him, "[a]Blessed are you of the LORD! I have carried out the command of the LORD."

14 But Samuel said, "[a]What then is this [1]bleating of the sheep in my ears, and the [1]lowing of the oxen which I hear?"

15 Saul said, "They have brought them from the Amalekites, for [a]the people spared the best of the sheep and oxen, to sacrifice to the LORD your God; but the rest we have utterly destroyed."

16 Then Samuel said to Saul, "Wait, and let me tell you what the LORD said to me last night." And he said to him, "Speak!"

17 Samuel said, "Is it not true, [a]though you were little in your own eyes, you were *made* the head of the tribes of Israel? And the LORD anointed you king over Israel,

18 and the LORD sent you on a [1]mission, and said, '[a]Go and utterly destroy the sinners, the Amalekites, and fight against them until they are exterminated.'

19 "Why then did you not obey the voice of the LORD, [a]but rushed upon the spoil and did what was evil in the sight of the LORD?"

2 [1]Or *visit* [a]Ex 17:8-16; Num 24:20; Deut 25:17-19
3 [a]Num 24:20; Deut 20:16-18; Josh 6:17-21 [b]1 Sam 22:19
4 [1]Lit *mustered* [a]Josh 15:24
6 [a]Num 24:21; Judg 1:16; 4:11 [b]Ex 18:9, 10; Num 10:29-32
7 [1]Lit *smote* [2]Lit *before* [a]1 Sam 14:48 [b]Gen 25:18 [c]Gen 16:7; Ex 15:22; 1 Sam 27:8
8 [a]Num 24:7; 1 Sam 15:20; Esth 3:1 [b]1 Sam 27:8, 9; 30:1; 2 Sam 8:12
9 [a]1 Sam 15:3, 15, 19
11 [a]Gen 6:6, 7; Ex 32:14; 1 Sam 15:35; 2 Sam 24:16
11 [1]Lit *after* [b]Josh 22:16; 1 Sam 13:13; 1 Kin 9:6, 7 [c]Ex 32:11-13; Luke 6:12
12 [1]Lit *and went down* [a]Josh 15:55; 1 Sam 25:2 [b]1 Sam 13:12, 15
13 [a]Gen 14:19; Judg 17:2; Ruth 3:10; 2 Sam 2:5
14 [1]Lit *sound* [a]Ex 32:21-24
15 [a]Gen 3:12, 13; Ex 32:22, 23; 1 Sam 15:9, 21
17 [a]1 Sam 9:21; 10:22
18 [1]Lit *way* [a]1 Sam 15:3 **19** [a]1 Sam 14:32

no time designation is given, it evidently occurred after the conflicts of 14:47, in a time of relative peace and security. It is likely that David was anointed (16:1–13) shortly after the rejection of Saul (vv. 22,26,28), thus c. 1025 B.C.

15:2 *Amalek.* A Bedouin people descended from Esau (see Gen 36:12,16) usually located in the Negev and Sinai regions (see 27:8; 30:1; Gen 14:7; Ex 17:8; Num 13:29). *what he did to Israel.* See Ex 17:8–13; Num 14:43, 45; Deut 25:17–19; cf. Judg 3:13; 6:3–5,33; 7:12; 10:12.

15:3 *utterly destroy.* See notes on Lev 27:28–29; Deut 2:34; Josh 6:17–18; see also Deut 13:12–18. Saul is given an opportunity as king to demonstrate his allegiance to the Lord by obedience in this assigned task.

15:4 *Telaim.* Probably the same as Telem in Josh 15:24, located in the southern part of Judah.

15:5 *city of Amalek.* A settlement of Amalekites, most likely located between Telaim and Kadesh-barnea, possibly the residence of their king.

15:6 *Kenites.* A Bedouin people of the Sinai, closely related to the Midianites. Moses had married a Kenite woman (see Ex 2:16,21–22; Num 10:29; Judg 1:16; 4:11), and some of the Kenites had accompanied the Israelites when they settled in the land of Canaan (see 27:10; Judg 1:16; 4:17–23; 5:24; 1 Chr 2:55).

15:7 *Havilah . . . to Shur.* The location of Havilah is uncertain. Shur was on the eastern frontier of Egypt (see 27:8; Gen 16:7; 20:1). Ishmael's descendants occupied this area (see Gen 25:18).

15:8 *all the people.* All the Amalekites they encountered. Some Amalekites survived (see 27:8; 30:1,18; 2 Sam 8:12; 1 Chr 4:43).

15:9 When Israel refused to obey the Lord's command (v. 3), their holy war against the Amalekites degenerated into personal aggrandizement, much like that of Achan at the time of the conquest of Canaan (see Josh 7:1). Giving to the Lord by destruction only what was despised and weak was a contemptible act (see Mal 1:7–12), not to be excused (see v. 19) by the protestation that the best had been preserved for sacrifice to the Lord (vv. 15,21).

15:11 *regret.* See note on v. 29. *he has turned back from following Me.* A violation of the fundamental requirement of his office as king (see notes on 12:14–15).

15:12 *Carmel.* Located about seven miles south of Hebron (see 25:2; Josh 15:55). *monument for himself.* Saul's self-glorification here contrasts sharply with his self-abasement after the victory over the Ammonites (see note on 11:13; cf. v. 17; 2 Sam 18:18). *Gilgal.* Saul returns to the place where he was inaugurated and instructed in the responsibilities of his office (see 11:14–12:25). This was also the place where he had been told that he would not have a continuing dynasty because of his disobedience (see 13:13–14).

15:13 *I have carried out the command of the LORD.* Here and in v. 20 Saul is clearly less than honest in his statements to Samuel.

15:15 *the people spared the best . . . to sacrifice.* Saul attempts to shift responsibility from himself to the people and to excuse their action by claiming pious intentions. *the LORD your God.* Saul's use of the pronoun "your" instead of "my" here and in vv. 21,30 indicates an awareness of his own alienation from the Lord (see 12:19 for a similar case), even though he speaks of obedience and the intent to honor God by sacrifice.

15:17 *you were little in your own eyes.* See 9:21; 10:22.

20 Then Saul said to Samuel, "[a]I did obey
the voice of the LORD, and went on the [1]mis-
sion on which the LORD sent me, and have
brought back Agag the king of Amalek, and
have utterly destroyed the Amalekites.
21 "But [a]the people took *some* of the spoil,
sheep and oxen, the choicest of the things
devoted to destruction, to sacrifice to the
LORD your God at Gilgal."
22 Samuel said,

"[a]Has the LORD as much delight in
burnt offerings and sacrifices
As in obeying the voice of the LORD?
Behold, [b]to obey is better than
sacrifice,
And to heed than the fat of rams.
23 "For rebellion is as the sin of
[a]divination,
And insubordination is as [b]iniquity
and idolatry.
Because you have rejected the word of
the LORD,
[c]He has also rejected you from *being*
king."

24 Then Saul said to Samuel, "[a]I have
sinned; [b]I have indeed transgressed the [1]com-
mand of the LORD and your words, because I
feared the people and listened to their voice.
25 "Now therefore, [a]please pardon my sin
and return with me, that I may worship the
LORD."
26 But Samuel said to Saul, "I will not
return with you; for [a]you have rejected the
word of the LORD, and the LORD has rejected
you from being king over Israel."
27 As Samuel turned to go, [a]*Saul* seized
the edge of his robe, and it tore.
28 So Samuel said to him, "[a]The LORD has
torn the kingdom of Israel from you today
and has given it to your neighbor, who is better than you.
29 "Also the [1a]Glory of Israel [b]will not lie
or change His mind; for He is not a man that
He should change His mind."
30 Then he said, "I have sinned; [a]*but*
please honor me now before the elders of my
people and before Israel, and go back with
me, [b]that I may worship the LORD your God."
31 So Samuel went back following Saul,
and Saul worshiped the LORD.
32 Then Samuel said, "Bring me Agag, the
king of the Amalekites." And Agag came to
him [1]cheerfully. And Agag said, "Surely the
bitterness of death is past."
33 But Samuel said, "[a]As your sword has
made women childless, so shall your mother be childless among women." And Samuel
hewed Agag to pieces before the LORD at Gilgal.
34 Then Samuel went to [a]Ramah, but Saul
went up to his house at [b]Gibeah of Saul.
35 [a]Samuel did not see Saul again until
the day of his death; for Samuel [b]grieved
over Saul. And the LORD regretted that He
had made Saul king over Israel.

Samuel Goes to Bethlehem

16 Now the LORD said to Samuel, "[a]How
long will you grieve over Saul, since [b]I
have rejected him from being king over Israel? [c]Fill your horn with oil and go; I will send
you to [d]Jesse the Bethlehemite, for I have
[e]selected a king for Myself among his sons."
2 But Samuel said, "How can I go? When

20 [1]Lit *way* [a]1 Sam 15:13 **21** [a]Ex 32:22, 23; 1 Sam 15:15 **22** [a]Ps 40:6-8; 51:16, 17; Is 1:11-15; Mic 6:6-8; Heb 10:6-9 [b]Jer 7:22, 23; Hos 6:6; Matt 12:7; Mark 12:33 **23** [a]Deut 18:10 [b]Gen 31:19, 34 [c]1 Sam 13:14 **24** [1]Lit *mouth* [a]Num 22:34; 2 Sam 12:13; Ps 51:4 [b]Prov 29:25; Is 51:12, 13 **25** [a]Ex 10:17 **26** [a]1 Sam 13:14; 16:1 **27** [a]1 Kin 11:30, 31 **28** [a]1 Sam 28:17, 18; 1 Kin 11:31 **29** [1]Or *Eminence* [a]1 Chr 29:11 [b]Num 23:19; Ezek 24:14; Titus 1:2 **30** [a]John 5:44; 12:43 [b]Is 29:13 **32** [1]Or *in bonds* **33** [a]Gen 9:6; Judg 1:7; Matt 7:2 **34** [a]1 Sam 7:17 [b]1 Sam 11:4 **35** [a]1 Sam 19:24 [b]1 Sam 16:1 **16:1** [a]1 Sam 15:35 [b]1 Sam 13:13, 14; 15:23 [c]1 Sam 9:16; 10:1; 2 Kin 9:1 [d]Ruth 4:17-22 [e]Ps 78:70, 71; Acts 13:22

15:22 Samuel does not suggest that sacrifice is unimportant but that it is acceptable only when brought with an attitude of obedience and devotion to the Lord (see Ps 15; Is 1:11–17; Hos 6:6; Amos 5:21–27; Mic 6:6–8). *fat of rams.* The fat of sacrificed animals belonged to the Lord (see 2:15; Ex 23:18; Lev 3:14–16; 7:30).

15:23 *rebellion.* Samuel charges Saul with violating the central requirement of the covenant condition given to him when he became king (see 12:14–15). *sin of divination.* A serious offense against the Lord (see Lev 19:26; Deut 18:9–12), which Saul himself condemned (28:3,9). *you have rejected the word of the LORD.* A king who sets his own will above the command of the Lord ceases to be an instrument of the Lord's rule over His people, violating the very nature of his theocratic office. *He has also rejected you from being king.* The judgment here goes beyond the one given earlier (see note on 13:14). Now Saul himself is to be set aside as king. Although this did not happen immediately, as chs. 16–31 show, the process began that led to his death. It included in its relentless course the removal of God's Spirit and favor from him (16:14), the defection of his son Jonathan and daughter Michal to David, and the insubordination of his own officials (22:17).

15:24 Saul's confession retains an element of self-justification and a shift of blame (contrast David's confession, 2 Sam 12:13; Ps 51). Previously (vv. 15,21) he had attempted to justify the actions of those under him.

15:25 *return with me.* Saul's greatest concern was not to worship God but to avoid an open break with the prophet Samuel, a break that would undermine his authority as king (see v. 30).

15:28 *your neighbor.* David (see note on 13:14).

15:29 *Glory of Israel.* A title of God used elsewhere only in Mic 1:15 (but see note there), though in Ps 106:20 "glory" should probably be capitalized as referring to God (see note on 4:21). Cf. 2 Sam 1:19; Ps 89:17; Is 13:19. *will not lie or change His mind.* See Num 23:19; Ps 110:4; Jer 4:28; Mal 3:6 and notes. There is no conflict between this statement and vv. 11,35, where the Lord is said to "regret" that he had made Saul king. God has real emotions (one of the marks of personality).

15:31 *So Samuel went back following Saul.* Samuel's purpose in agreeing to Saul's request is not to honor Saul, but to carry out the divine sentence on Agag and in so doing to reemphasize Saul's neglect of duty.

15:34 *Ramah.* Samuel's home (see 7:17). *Gibeah of Saul.* See note on 10:5.

15:35 *Samuel grieved.* Samuel regarded Saul as if dead (see the use of "mourned" in 6:19). Even though his love for him remained (see v. 11; 16:1), he sought no further contact with him because God had rejected him as king. Saul did come to Samuel on one other occasion (see 19:24).

16:1 *the LORD said to Samuel.* Probably c. 1025 B.C. (see note on 15:1–35). *Jesse.* For Jesse's genealogy see Ruth 4:18–22; Matt 1:3–6. *Bethlehemite.* Bethlehem was a town five miles south of Jerusalem, formerly known as Ephrath (Gen 48:7). It was later to become renowned as the "city of David" (Luke 2:4) and the birthplace of Christ (Mic 5:2; Matt 2:1; Luke 2:4–7). *I have selected a king . . . among his sons.* See notes on 13:14; 15:28.

Saul hears *of it,* he will kill me." And the
LORD said, "[a]Take a heifer with you and say,
'I have come to sacrifice to the LORD.'
3 "You shall invite Jesse to the sacrifice,
and [a]I will show you what you shall do; and
[b]you shall anoint for Me the one whom I
[1]designate to you."
4 So Samuel did what the LORD said, and
came to [a]Bethlehem. And the elders of the
city came trembling to meet him and said,
"[b]Do you come in peace?"
5 He said, "In peace; I have come to sacrifice to the LORD. [a]Consecrate yourselves
and come with me to the sacrifice." He also
consecrated Jesse and his sons and invited
them to the sacrifice.
6 When they entered, he looked at [a]Eliab
and thought, "Surely the LORD's anointed is
before Him."
7 But the LORD said to Samuel, "Do not
look at his appearance or at the height of his
stature, because I have rejected him; for
[1]God *sees* not as man sees, for man looks at
the outward appearance, [a]but the LORD looks
at the heart."
8 Then Jesse called [a]Abinadab and made
him pass before Samuel. And he said, "The
LORD has not chosen this one either."

2 [a]1 Sam 20:29
3 [1]Lit *say to you* [a]Ex 4:15; Acts 9:6 [b]Deut 17:14, 15; 1 Sam 9:16
4 [a]Gen 48:7; Luke 2:4 [b]1 Kin 2:13; 2 Kin 9:22; 1 Chr 12:17, 18
5 [a]Gen 35:2; Ex 19:10
6 [a]1 Sam 17:13
7 [1]So with Gr; Heb He does *not* see *what man sees* [a]1 Sam 2:3; 1 Kin 8:39; 1 Chr 28:9; Luke 16:15
8 [a]1 Sam 17:13

16:2 *Saul . . . will kill me.* The road from Ramah (where Samuel was, 15:34) to Bethlehem passed through Gibeah of Saul. Saul already knew that the Lord had chosen someone to replace him as king (see 15:28). Samuel fears that jealousy will incite Saul to violence. Later incidents (18:10–11; 19:10; 20:33) demonstrate that Samuel's fears were well-founded. *say, 'I have come to sacrifice to the LORD.'* This response is true but incomplete, and it was intended to deceive Saul.

16:3 *anoint.* See note on 9:16.

16:5 *Consecrate yourselves.* Involves preparing oneself spiritually as well as making oneself ceremonially clean by washing and putting on clean clothes (see Ex 19:10,14; Lev 15; Num 19:11–22).

16:6 *Eliab.* Jesse's oldest son (17:13).

16:7 *his appearance or at the height.* Samuel is not to focus on these outward features, which had characterized Saul (see 9:2; 10:23–24). *heart.* The Lord is concerned with man's inner disposition and character (see 1 Kin 8:39; 1 Chr 28:9; Luke 16:15; John 2:25; Acts 1:24).

16:8 *Abinadab.* Jesse's second son.

David's Family Tree

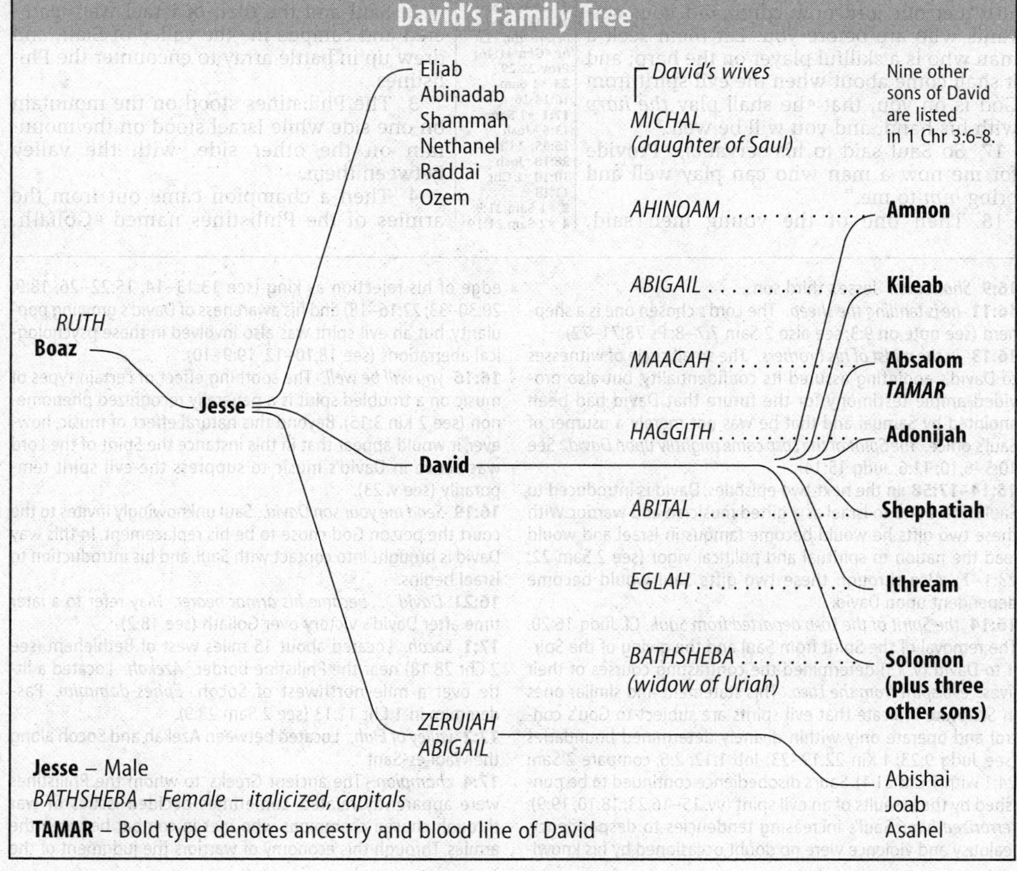

RUTH
Boaz
Jesse
Eliab
Abinadab
Shammah
Nethanel
Raddai
Ozem
David
ZERUIAH
ABIGAIL
David's wives
MICHAL (daughter of Saul)
AHINOAM
ABIGAIL
MAACAH
HAGGITH
ABITAL
EGLAH
BATHSHEBA (widow of Uriah)
Amnon
Kileab
Absalom
TAMAR
Adonijah
Shephatiah
Ithream
Solomon (plus three other sons)
Nine other sons of David are listed in 1 Chr 3:6-8.
Abishai
Joab
Asahel
Jesse – Male
BATHSHEBA – Female – italicized, capitals
TAMAR – Bold type denotes ancestry and blood line of David

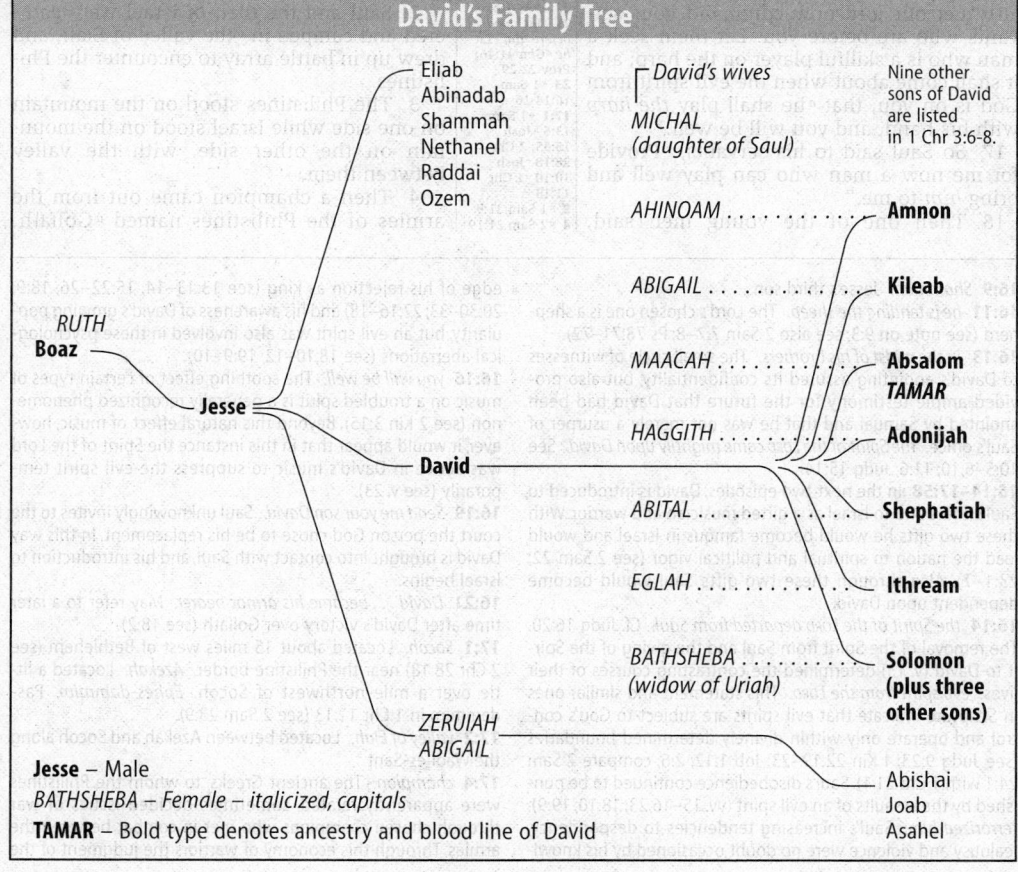

9 Next Jesse made [1a]Shammah pass by. And he said, "The LORD has not chosen this one either."

10 Thus Jesse made seven of his sons pass before Samuel. But Samuel said to Jesse, "The LORD has not chosen these."

11 And Samuel said to Jesse, "Are these all the children?" And he said, "[a]There remains yet the youngest, and behold, he is tending the sheep." Then Samuel said to Jesse, "Send and [1]bring him; for we will not sit down until he comes here."

David Anointed

12 So he sent and brought him in. Now he was ruddy, with [a]beautiful eyes and a handsome appearance. And the LORD said, "[b]Arise, anoint him; for this is he."

13 Then Samuel took the horn of oil and [a]anointed him in the midst of his brothers; and [b]the Spirit of the LORD came mightily upon David from that day forward. And Samuel arose and went to Ramah.

14 [a]Now the Spirit of the LORD departed from Saul, and [b]an evil spirit from the LORD terrorized him.

15 Saul's servants then said to him, "Behold now, an evil spirit from God is terrorizing you.

16 "Let our lord now command your servants who are before you. Let them seek a man who is a skillful player on the harp; and it shall come about when the evil spirit from God is on you, that [a]he shall play *the harp* with his hand, and you will be well."

17 So Saul said to his servants, "Provide for me now a man who can play well and bring *him* to me."

18 Then one of the young men said, "Behold, I have seen a son of Jesse the Bethlehemite who is a skillful musician, [a]a mighty man of valor, a warrior, one prudent in speech, and a handsome man; and [b]the LORD is with him."

19 So Saul sent messengers to Jesse and said, "Send me your son David who is with the flock."

20 Jesse [a]took a donkey *loaded with* bread and a jug of wine and a young goat, and sent *them* to Saul by David his son.

21 Then David came to Saul and [1a]attended him; and [2]Saul loved him greatly, and he became his armor bearer.

22 Saul sent to Jesse, saying, "Let David now stand before me, for he has found favor in my sight."

23 So it came about whenever [a]the *evil* spirit from God came to Saul, David would take the harp and play *it* with his hand; and Saul would be refreshed and be well, and the evil spirit would depart from him.

Goliath's Challenge

17 Now [a]the Philistines gathered their armies for battle; and they were gathered at Socoh which belongs to Judah, and they camped between [b]Socoh and [c]Azekah, in [d]Ephes-dammim.

2 Saul and the men of Israel were gathered and camped in [a]the valley of Elah, and drew up in battle array to encounter the Philistines.

3 The Philistines stood on the mountain on one side while Israel stood on the mountain on the other side, with the valley between them.

4 Then a champion came out from the armies of the Philistines named [a]Goliath,

9 [1]In 2 Sam 13:3, *Shimeah;* in 1 Chr 2:13, *Shimea* [a]1 Sam 17:13
11 [1]Lit *take* [a]1 Sam 17:12; 2 Sam 13:3
12 [a]Gen 39:6; Ex 2:2; Acts 7:20 [b]1 Sam 9:17
13 [a]1 Sam 10:1 [b]Num 27:18; 1 Sam 10:6, 9, 10
14 [a]Judg 16:20; 1 Sam 11:6; 18:12; 28:15 [b]Judg 9:23; 1 Sam 16:15, 16; 18:10; 19:9; 1 Kin 22:19-22
16 [a]1 Sam 18:10; 19:9; 2 Kin 3:15
18 [a]1 Sam 17:32-36 [b]1 Sam 3:19
20 [a]1 Sam 10:4, 27; Prov 18:16
21 [1]Lit *stood before him* [2]Lit *he* [a]Gen 41:46; Prov 22:29
23 [a]1 Sam 16:14-16
17:1 [a]1 Sam 13:5 [b]Josh 15:35; 2 Chr 28:18 [c]Josh 10:10 [d]1 Chr 11:13
2 [a]1 Sam 21:9
4 [a]2 Sam 21:19

16:9 *Shammah.* Jesse's third son.
16:11 *he is tending the sheep.* The Lord's chosen one is a shepherd (see note on 9:3; see also 2 Sam 7:7–8; Ps 78:71–72).
16:13 *in the midst of his brothers.* The small circle of witnesses to David's anointing assured its confidentiality, but also provided ample testimony for the future that David had been anointed by Samuel and that he was not merely a usurper of Saul's office. *the Spirit of the LORD came mightily upon David.* See 10:5–6,10; 11:6; Judg 15:14.
16:14–17:58 In the next two episodes, David is introduced to Saul's court and to Israel as a gifted musician and warrior. With these two gifts he would become famous in Israel and would lead the nation to spiritual and political vigor (see 2 Sam 22; 23:1–7). Also through these two gifts Saul would become dependent upon David.
16:14 *the Spirit of the LORD departed from Saul.* Cf. Judg 16:20. The removal of the Spirit from Saul and the giving of the Spirit to David (v. 13) determined the contrasting courses of their lives. *evil spirit from the LORD.* This statement and similar ones in Scripture indicate that evil spirits are subject to God's control and operate only within divinely determined boundaries (see Judg 9:23; 1 Kin 22:19–23; Job 1:12; 2:6; compare 2 Sam 24:1 with 1 Chr 21:1). Saul's disobedience continued to be punished by the assaults of an evil spirit (vv. 15–16,23; 18:10; 19:9). *terrorized him.* Saul's increasing tendencies to despondency, jealousy and violence were no doubt occasioned by his knowledge of his rejection as king (see 13:13–14; 15:22–26; 18:9; 20:30–33; 22:16–18) and his awareness of David's growing popularity, but an evil spirit was also involved in these psychological aberrations (see 18:10–12; 19:9–10).
16:16 *you will be well.* The soothing effect of certain types of music on a troubled spirit is a generally recognized phenomenon (see 2 Kin 3:15). Beyond this natural effect of music, however, it would appear that in this instance the Spirit of the Lord was active in David's music to suppress the evil spirit temporarily (see v. 23).
16:19 *Send me your son David.* Saul unknowingly invites to the court the person God chose to be his replacement. In this way David is brought into contact with Saul, and his introduction to Israel begins.
16:21 *David . . . became his armor bearer.* May refer to a later time after David's victory over Goliath (see 18:2).
17:1 *Socoh.* Located about 15 miles west of Bethlehem (see 2 Chr 28:18) near the Philistine border. *Azekah.* Located a little over a mile northwest of Socoh. *Ephes-dammim.* Pasdammim in 1 Chr 11:13 (see 2 Sam 23:9).
17:2 *valley of Elah.* Located between Azekah and Socoh along the Wadi es-Sant.
17:4 *champion.* The ancient Greeks, to whom the Philistines were apparently related, sometimes decided issues of war through chosen champions who met in combat between the armies. Through this economy of warriors the judgment of the

from [b]Gath, whose height was six [1]cubits and a span.

5 *He had* a bronze helmet on his head, and he was clothed with scale-armor [1]which weighed five thousand shekels of bronze.

6 *He* also *had* bronze [1]greaves on his legs and a [a]bronze javelin *slung* between his shoulders.

7 [a]The shaft of his spear was like a weaver's beam, and the head of his spear *weighed* six hundred shekels of iron; [b]his shield-carrier also walked before him.

8 He stood and shouted to the ranks of Israel and said to them, "Why do you come out to draw up in battle array? Am I not the Philistine and you [a]servants of Saul? Choose a man for yourselves and let him come down to me.

9 "[a]If he is able to fight with me and [1]kill me, then we will become your servants; but if I prevail against him and [1]kill him, then you shall become our servants and serve us."

10 Again the Philistine said, "[a]I defy the ranks of Israel this day; give me a man that we may fight together."

11 When Saul and all Israel heard these words of the Philistine, they were dismayed and greatly afraid.

12 Now David was [a]the son of [1]the [b]Ephrathite of Bethlehem in Judah, whose name was Jesse, and [c]he had eight sons. And [2]Jesse was old in the days of Saul, advanced *in years* among men.

13 The three older sons of Jesse had [1]gone after Saul to the battle. And [a]the names of his three sons who went to the battle were Eliab the firstborn, and the second to him Abinadab, and the third Shammah.

14 [a]David was the youngest. Now the three oldest followed Saul,

15 [a]but David went back and forth from Saul [b]to tend his father's flock at Bethlehem.

16 The Philistine came [1]forward morning and evening for forty days and took his stand.

17 Then Jesse said to David his son, "[a]Take now for your brothers an ephah of this roasted grain and these ten loaves and run to the camp to your brothers.

18 "[a]Bring also these ten cuts of cheese to the commander of *their* thousand, [b]and look into the welfare of your brothers, and bring back [1]news of them.

19 "For Saul and they and all the men of Israel are in the valley of Elah, fighting with the Philistines."

David Accepts the Challenge

20 So David arose early in the morning and left the flock with a keeper and took *the supplies* and went as Jesse had commanded him. And he came to the [a]circle of the camp while the army was going out in battle array shouting the war cry.

21 Israel and the Philistines drew up in battle array, army against army.

22 Then David left his [a]baggage in the [1]care of the baggage keeper, and ran to the battle line and entered in order to greet his brothers.

23 As he was talking with them, behold, the champion, the Philistine from Gath named Goliath, was coming up from the army of the Philistines, and he spoke [a]these same words; and David heard *them*.

24 When all the men of Israel saw the man, they fled from him and were greatly afraid.

25 The men of Israel said, "Have you seen this man who is coming up? Surely he is coming up to defy Israel. And it will be that the king will enrich the man who kills him with great riches and [a]will give him his daughter and make his father's house [1]free in Israel."

26 Then David spoke to the men who were standing by him, saying, "What will be done for the man who kills this Philistine and takes away [a]the reproach from Israel? For who is this [b]uncircumcised Philistine, that he should [c]taunt the armies of [d]the living God?"

27 The people [1]answered him in accord with this word, saying, "[a]Thus it will be done for the man who kills him."

28 Now Eliab his oldest brother heard when he spoke to the men; and [a]Eliab's anger burned against David and he said, "Why have you come down? And with whom have you left those few sheep in the wilderness? I know your insolence and the

4 [1]I.e. One cubit equals approx 18 in. [b]Josh 11:22
5 [1]Lit *and the weight of the armor* was
6 [1]Or *shin guards* [a]1 Sam 17:45
7 [a]2 Sam 21:19; 1 Chr 11:23 [b]1 Sam 17:41
8 [a]1 Sam 8:17
9 [1]Lit *smite* [a]2 Sam 2:12-16
10 [a]1 Sam 17:26, 36, 45; 2 Sam 21:21
12 [1]Lit *this* [2]Lit *the man* [a]Ruth 4:22; 1 Sam 16:18 [b]Gen 35:19 [c]1 Sam 16:10, 11; 1 Chr 2:13-15
13 [1]Lit *gone; they went* [a]1 Sam 16:6, 8, 9
14 [a]1 Sam 16:11
15 [a]1 Sam 16:21-23 [b]1 Sam 16:11, 19
16 [1]Lit *near*
17 [a]1 Sam 25:18
18 [a]1 Sam 16:20 [b]Gen 37:13, 14
18 [1]Lit *their pledge*
20 [a]1 Sam 26:5, 7
22 [1]Lit *hand* [a]Judg 18:21; Is 10:28
23 [a]1 Sam 17:8-10
25 [1]I.e. free from taxes and public service [a]Josh 15:16
26 [a]1 Sam 11:2 [b]1 Sam 14:6; 17:36; Jer 9:25, 26 [c]1 Sam 17:10 [d]Deut 5:26; 2 Kin 19:4; Jer 10:10
27 [1]Lit *said to* [a]1 Sam 17:25
28 [a]Gen 37:4, 8-36; Prov 18:19; Matt 10:36

gods on the matter at stake was determined (trial by battle ordeal). Israel too may have known this practice (see 2 Sam 2:14–16).

17:11 *Saul and all Israel . . . were . . . greatly afraid.* Israel's giant warrior (see 9:2; 10:23) quails before the Philistine champion. The fear of Saul and the Israelite army (see vv. 24,32) betrays a loss of faith in the covenant promises of the Lord (see Ex 23:22; Deut 3:22; 20:1–4). Their fear also demonstrates that the Israelite search for security in a human king (apart from trust in the Lord; see notes on 8:5,7) had failed. On the basis of God's covenant promises, Israel was never to fear her enemies but to trust in the Lord (see 2 Sam 10:12; Ex 14:13–14; Num 14:9; Josh 10:8; 2 Chr 20:17).

17:12 *Ephrathite.* See note on Ru 1:2.

17:15 *David went back and forth from Saul.* David's position at the court (see 16:21–23) was not permanent, but was performed on an intermittent basis. For the relationship between chs. 16 and 17 see note on v. 55.

17:24 *greatly afraid.* See note on v. 11.

17:25 *the king will enrich . . . great riches.* See 8:14; 22:7. *give him his daughter.* See 18:17–26; cf. Josh 15:16.

17:26 *who is this . . . ?* David sees the issues clearly—which sets him apart from Saul and all the other Israelites on that battlefield.

17:28 *Eliab's anger burned.* Eliab's anger may arise from jealousy toward his brother and a sense of guilt for the defeatist attitude of the Israelites. He recognizes, but does not comprehend, David's indomitable spirit (see 16:13).

wickedness of your heart; for you have come down in order to see the battle."

29 But David said, "What have I done now? Was it not just a [1]question?"

30 Then he turned [1]away from him to another and [a]said the same thing; and the people answered the same thing as [2]before.

David Kills Goliath

31 When the words which David spoke were heard, they told *them* [1]to Saul, and he sent for him.

32 David said to Saul, "[a]Let no man's heart fail on account of him; [b]your servant will go and fight with this Philistine."

33 Then Saul said to David, "[a]You are not able to go against this Philistine to fight with him; for you are *but* a youth while he has been a warrior from his youth."

34 But David said to Saul, "Your servant was tending his father's sheep. When a lion or a bear came and took a lamb from the flock,

35 I went out after him and [1]attacked him, and [a]rescued *it* from his mouth; and when he rose up against me, I seized *him* by his beard and [1]struck him and killed him.

36 "Your servant has [1]killed both the lion and the bear; and this uncircumcised Philistine will be like one of them, since he has taunted the armies of the living God."

37 And David said, "[a]The LORD who delivered me from the paw of the lion and from the paw of the bear, He will deliver me from the hand of this Philistine." And Saul said to David, "[b]Go, and may the LORD be with you."

38 Then Saul clothed David with his garments and put a bronze helmet on his head, and he clothed him with armor.

39 David girded his sword over his armor and tried to walk, for he had not tested *them.* So David said to Saul, "I cannot go with these, for I have not tested *them.*" And David took them [1]off.

40 He took his stick in his hand and chose for himself five smooth stones from the brook, and put them in the shepherd's bag which he had, even in *his* pouch, and [a]his sling was in his hand; and he approached the Philistine.

41 Then the Philistine came on and approached David, with the shield-bearer in front of him.

42 When the Philistine looked and saw David, [a]he disdained him; for he was *but* a youth, and [b]ruddy, with a handsome appearance.

43 The Philistine said to David, "[a]Am I a dog, that you come to me with sticks?" And [b]the Philistine cursed David by his gods.

44 The Philistine also said to David, "Come to me, and I will give your flesh [a]to the birds of the sky and the beasts of the field."

45 Then David said to the Philistine, "You come to me with a sword, a spear, and a javelin, [a]but I come to you in the name of the LORD of hosts, the God of the armies of Israel, whom you have taunted.

46 "This day the LORD will deliver you up into my hands, and I will strike you down and remove your head from you. And I will give the [a]dead bodies of the army of the Philistines this day to the birds of the sky and the wild beasts of the earth, [b]that all the earth may know that there is a God in Israel,

47 and that all this assembly may know that [a]the LORD does not deliver by sword or by spear; [b]for the battle is the LORD's and He will give you into our hands."

48 Then it happened when the Philistine rose and came and drew near to meet David, that [a]David ran quickly toward the battle line to meet the Philistine.

49 And David put his hand into his bag and took from it a stone and slung *it,* and struck the Philistine on his forehead. And the stone sank into his forehead, so that he fell on his face to the ground.

50 Thus David prevailed over the Philistine with a sling and a stone, and he struck the Philistine and killed him; but there was no sword in David's hand.

29 [1]Lit *word*
30 [1]Lit *from beside him* [2]Lit *the former word* [a]1 Sam 17:26, 27
31 [1]Lit *before*
32 [a]Deut 20:1-4 [b]1 Sam 16:18
33 [a]Num 13:31
35 [1]Lit *smote* [a]Amos 3:12
36 [1]Lit *smitten*
37 [a]2 Cor 1:10; 2 Tim 4:17, 18 [b]1 Sam 20:13; 1 Chr 22:11, 16
39 [1]Lit *off from himself*
40 [a]Judg 20:16
42 [a]Ps 123:4; Prov 16:18 [b]1 Sam 16:12
43 [a]1 Sam 24:14; 2 Sam 3:8; 2 Kin 8:13 [b]1 Kin 20:10
44 [a]1 Sam 17:46
45 [a]2 Sam 22:35; 2 Chr 32:8; Ps 124:8; Heb 11:32-34
46 [a]Deut 28:26 [b]Josh 4:24; 1 Kin 8:43; 18:36; 2 Kin 19:19; Is 37:20
47 [a]1 Sam 14:6; 2 Chr 14:11; 20:15; Ps 44:6; Hos 1:7; Zech 4:6 [b]2 Chr 20:15
48 [a]Ps 27:3

17:32 *Let no man's heart fail on account of him.* David's confidence does not rest in his own prowess (see vv. 37,47) but in the power of the living God, whose honor has been violated by the Philistines and whose covenant promises have been scorned by the Israelites.
17:33 *You are not able.* Saul does not take into account the power of God (see vv. 37,47).
17:34 *lion.* For the presence of lions in Canaan at that time see 2 Sam 23:20; Judg 14:5–18; 1 Kin 13:24–26; Amos 3:12. *bear.* See 2 Sam 17:8; 2 Kin 2:24; Amos 5:19.
17:36 *this uncircumcised Philistine.* See note on 14:6.
17:37 *The LORD . . . will deliver me.* Reliance on the Lord was essential for the true theocratic king (see notes on 10:18; 11:13). Here David's faith contrasts sharply with Saul's loss of faith (see 11:6–7 for Saul's earlier fearlessness). *Saul said to David, "Go."* Saul is now dependent on David not only for his sanity (see note on 16:16) but also for the security of his realm.
17:40 *his stick.* God's newly appointed shepherd of His people (see 2 Sam 5:2; 7:7; Ps 78:72) goes to defend the Lord's threatened and frightened flock. *stones.* Usually the stones chosen were round and smooth and somewhat larger than a baseball. When hurled by a master slinger, they probably traveled at close to 100 miles per hour. *his sling.* For the Benjamites' skill with a sling see Judg 20:16.
17:43 *Am I a dog . . . ?* See note on 2 Sam 9:8.
17:45 *in the name of the LORD of hosts.* David's strength was his reliance on the Lord (see Ps 9:10; Prov 18:10). For the expression "name of the LORD" see notes on Ex 3:13–14; Deut 12:11.
17:46 *all the earth may know.* The victory that David anticipates will demonstrate to all the world the existence and power of Israel's God (see Ex 7:17; 9:14,16,29; Deut 4:34–35; Josh 2:10–11; 4:23–24; 1 Kin 8:59–60; 18:36–39; 2 Kin 5:15; 19:19).
17:47 *the battle is the LORD's.* Both the Israelite and the Philistine armies will be shown the error of placing trust in human devices for personal or national security (see 2:10; 14:6; 2 Chr 14:11; 20:15; Ps 33:16–17; 44:6–7; Eccl 9:11; Hos 1:7; Zec 4:6).

51 Then David ran and stood over the Philistine and [a]took his sword and drew it out of its sheath and killed him, and cut off his head with it. [b]When the Philistines saw that their champion was dead, they fled.

52 The men of Israel and Judah arose and shouted and pursued the Philistines [1]as far as the valley, and to the gates of [a]Ekron. And the slain Philistines [2]lay along the way to [b]Shaaraim, even to Gath and Ekron.

53 The sons of Israel returned from chasing the Philistines and plundered their camps.

54 Then David took the Philistine's head and brought it to Jerusalem, but he put his weapons in his tent.

55 Now when Saul saw David going out against the Philistine, he said to Abner the commander of the army, "Abner, whose son is [a]this young man?" And Abner said, "By your life, O king, I do not know."

56 The king said, "You inquire whose son the youth is."

57 So when David returned from killing the Philistine, Abner took him and [a]brought him before Saul with the Philistine's head in his hand.

58 Saul said to him, "Whose son are you, young man?" And David answered, "[a]*I am* the son of your servant Jesse the Bethlehemite."

Jonathan and David

18 Now it came about when he had finished speaking to Saul, that [a]the soul of Jonathan was knit to the soul of David, and [b]Jonathan loved him as himself.

2 Saul took him that day and [a]did not let him return to his father's house.

3 Then [a]Jonathan made a covenant with David because he loved him as himself.

4 [a]Jonathan stripped himself of the robe that was on him and gave it to David, with his armor, including his sword and his bow and his belt.

5 So David went out wherever Saul sent him, *and* [1]prospered; and Saul set him over the men of war. And it was pleasing in the sight of all the people and also in the sight of Saul's servants.

6 It happened as they were coming, when David returned from killing the Philistine, that [a]the women came out of all the cities of Israel, singing and dancing, to meet King Saul, with tambourines, with joy and with [1]musical instruments.

7 The women [a]sang as they [1]played, and said,

"[b]Saul has slain his thousands,
[c]And David his ten thousands."

8 Then Saul became very angry, for this saying [1]displeased him; and he said, "They have ascribed to David ten thousands, but to me they have ascribed thousands. Now [a]what more can he have but the kingdom?"

9 Saul looked at David with suspicion from that day on.

Saul Turns against David

10 Now it came about on the next day that [a]an evil spirit from God came mightily upon Saul, and [b]he raved in the midst of the house, while David was playing *the harp* with his hand, [1c]as usual; and [2d]a spear *was* in Saul's hand.

11 [a]Saul hurled the spear for he thought,

51 [a]1 Sam 21:9; 2 Sam 23:21 [b]Heb 11:34
52 [1]Lit *until your coming to* [2]Lit *fell* [a]Josh 15:11 [b]Josh 15:36
55 [a]1 Sam 16:12, 21, 22
57 [a]1 Sam 17:54
58 [a]1 Sam 17:12
18:1 [a]Gen 44:30 [b]Deut 13:6; 1 Sam 20:17; 2 Sam 1:26
2 [a]1 Sam 17:15
3 [a]1 Sam 20:8-17
4 [a]Gen 41:42; 1 Sam 17:38; Esth 6:8
5 [1]Or *acted wisely*
6 [1]I.e. triangles; or three-stringed instruments [a]Ex 15:20, 21; Judg 11:34; Ps 68:25; 149:3
7 [1]Or *danced* [a]Ex 15:21; 1 Sam 21:11; 29:5 [b]1 Sam 21:11 [c]2 Sam 18:3
8 [1]Lit *was evil in his eyes* [a]1 Sam 15:28
10 [1]Lit *day by day* [2]Lit *the* [a]1 Sam 16:14 [b]1 Sam 19:23, 24 [c]1 Sam 16:23 [d]1 Sam 19:9
11 [a]1 Sam 19:10; 20:33

17:51 *they fled.* Most likely the Philistines saw the fall of their champion as the judgment of the gods, but they did not honor Goliath's original proposal (see v. 9).
17:54 *brought it to Jerusalem.* Jerusalem had not at this time been conquered by the Israelites. David may have kept Goliath's head as a trophy of victory and brought the skull with him to Jerusalem when he took that city and made it his capital (see 2 Sam 5:1–9). Or, having grown up almost under the shadow of the Jebusite city, he may have displayed Goliath's head to its defiant inhabitants as a warning of what the God of Israel was able to do and eventually would do. *put his weapons in his tent.* As his personal spoils of the battle. Since Goliath's sword is later in the custody of the priest at Nob (see 21:9), he must have dedicated it to the Lord, the true victor in the fight (cf. 31:10).
17:55 *whose son is this young man?* The seeming contradiction between vv. 55–58 and 16:14–23 may be resolved by noting that prior to this time David was not a permanent resident at Saul's court (see v. 15; 18:2; see also note on 16:21), so that Saul's knowledge of David and his family may have been minimal. Further, Saul may have been so incredulous at David's courage that he was wondering if his family background and social standing might explain his extraordinary conduct.
18:1 It appears that David spoke with Saul at length, and he may have explained his actions as an expression of his faith in the Lord, thus attracting the love and loyalty of Jonathan (see v. 3; 14:6; 19:5). Their friendship endured even when it became clear that David was to replace him as the successor to his father's throne.
18:2 *Saul . . . did not let him return.* See note on 17:15.
18:3 *Jonathan made a covenant with David.* The initiative comes from Jonathan. The terms of the agreement are not here specified (see further 19:1; 20:8,13–16,41–42; 23:18) but would appear to involve a pledge of mutual loyalty and friendship. At the very least, Jonathan accepts David as his equal.
18:4 *stripped himself of the robe . . . and gave it to David.* Jonathan ratifies the covenant in an act that symbolizes giving himself to David. His act may even signify his recognition that David was to assume his place as successor to Saul (see 20:14–15,31; 23:17)—a possibility that seems the more likely in that he also gave David "his sword and his bow and his belt" (cf. 13:22).
18:5 *wherever Saul sent him.* During the rest of the campaign.
18:7 *David his ten thousands.* In accordance with the normal conventions of Hebrew poetry, this was the women's way of saying "Saul and David have slain thousands" (10,000 was normally used as the parallel of 1,000—see Deut 32:30; Ps 91:7; Mic 6:7; also in Canaanite poetry found at Ugarit). It is a measure of Saul's insecurity and jealousy that he read their intentions incorrectly and took offense. His resentment may have been initially triggered by the mention of David's name alongside his own. See note on 21:11 for how the Philistines interpreted the song.
18:10 *evil spirit from God.* See note on 16:14. *raved.* The Hebrew for this word is sometimes used to indicate uncontrolled ecstatic behavior (see note on 1 Kin 18:29) and is best understood in that sense in this context (see also note on 10:5). *as usual.* See 16:14,23.

"I will [1]pin David to the wall." But David [2]escaped from his presence twice.

12 Now [a]Saul was afraid of David, [b]for the LORD was with him but [c]had departed from Saul.

13 Therefore Saul removed him from [1]his presence and appointed him as his commander of a thousand; and [a]he went out and came in before the people.

14 David was [1]prospering in all his ways for [a]the LORD *was* with him.

15 When Saul saw that he was [1]prospering greatly, he dreaded him.

16 But [a]all Israel and Judah loved David, and he went out and came in before them.

17 Then Saul said to David, "[a]Here is my older daughter Merab; I will give her to you as a wife, only be a valiant man for me and fight [b]the LORD's battles." For Saul thought, "My hand shall not be against him, but [c]let the hand of the Philistines be against him."

18 But David said to Saul, "[a]Who am I, and what is my life *or* my father's family in Israel, that I should be the king's son-in-law?"

19 So it came about at the time when Merab, Saul's daughter, should have been given to David, that she was given to [a]Adriel [b]the Meholathite for a wife.

David Marries Saul's Daughter

20 Now [a]Michal, Saul's daughter, loved David. When they told Saul, the thing was agreeable [1]to him.

21 Saul thought, "I will give her to him that she may become a snare to him, and [a]that the hand of the Philistines may be against him." Therefore Saul said to David, "[b]For a second time you may be my son-in-law today."

22 Then Saul commanded his servants, "Speak to David secretly, saying, 'Behold, the king delights in you, and all his servants love you; now therefore, become the king's son-in-law.' "

23 So Saul's servants spoke these words [1]to David. But David said, "Is it trivial in your sight to become the king's son-in-law, [a]since I am a poor man and lightly esteemed?"

24 The servants of Saul reported to him [1]according to these words *which* David spoke.

25 Saul then said, "Thus you shall say to David, 'The king does not desire any [a]dowry except a hundred foreskins of the Philistines, [b]to take vengeance on the king's enemies.' " Now [c]Saul planned to make David fall by the hand of the Philistines.

26 When his servants told David these words, [1]it pleased David to become the king's son-in-law. [2][a]Before the days had expired

27 David rose up and went, [a]he and his men, and struck down two hundred men among the Philistines. Then [b]David brought their foreskins, and they gave them in full number to the king, that he might become the king's son-in-law. So Saul gave him Michal his daughter for a wife.

28 When Saul saw and knew that the LORD was with David, and *that* Michal, Saul's daughter, loved him,

29 then Saul was even more afraid of David. Thus Saul was David's enemy continually.

30 Then the commanders of the Philistines [a]went out *to battle,* and it happened as often as they went out, that David [b]behaved himself more wisely than all the servants of Saul. So his name was highly esteemed.

David Protected from Saul

19 Now Saul told Jonathan his son and all his servants [a]to put David to death. But [b]Jonathan, Saul's son, greatly delighted in David.

2 So Jonathan told David saying, "Saul my father is seeking to put you to death. Now therefore, please be on guard in the morning, and stay in a secret place and hide yourself.

3 "I will go out and stand beside my father in the field where you are, and I will speak with my father about you; [a]if I [1]find out anything, then I will tell you."

4 Then Jonathan [a]spoke well of David to Saul his father and said to him, "[b]Do not let the king sin against his servant David, since

11 [1]Lit *strike David and the wall* [2]Lit *turned about* **12** [a]1 Sam 18:15, 29 [b]1 Sam 16:13, 18 [c]1 Sam 16:14; 28:15 **13** [1]Lit *with him* [a]Num 27:17; 1 Sam 18:16; 2 Sam 5:2 **14** [1]Or *acting wisely* [a]Gen 39:2, 3, 23; Josh 6:27; 1 Sam 16:18 **15** [1]Or *acting very wisely* **16** [a]1 Sam 18:5 **17** [a]1 Sam 17:25 [b]Num 21:14; 1 Sam 17:36, 47; 25:28 [c]1 Sam 18:21, 25 **18** [a]1 Sam 9:21; 18:23; 2 Sam 7:18 **19** [a]2 Sam 21:8 [b]Judg 7:22; 1 Kin 19:16 **20** [1]Lit *in his sight* [a]1 Sam 18:28 **21** [a]1 Sam 18:17 [b]1 Sam 18:26 **23** [1]Lit *in the ears of* [a]Gen 29:20; 34:12

24 [1]Lit *by saying according* **25** [a]Gen 34:12; Ex 22:17 [b]1 Sam 14:24 [c]1 Sam 18:17 **26** [1]Lit *it was agreeable in the sight of* [2]Lit *And the days had not expired* [a]1 Sam 18:21 **27** [a]1 Sam 18:17 [b]2 Sam 3:14 **30** [a]2 Sam 11:1 [b]1 Sam 18:5 **19:1** [a]1 Sam 18:8, 9 [b]1 Sam 18:1-3 **3** [1]Lit *see* [a]1 Sam 20:9, 13 **4** [a]1 Sam 20:32; Prov 31:8, 9 [b]Gen 42:22; Prov 17:13; Jer 18:20

18:12 *the LORD was with him but had departed from Saul.* See 16:14 and note.

18:13 *Saul removed him from his presence.* His apparent motive was the hope that David would be killed in battle (see vv. 17, 21, 25; 19:1), but the result was greater acclaim for David (see vv. 14,16,30).

18:17 *Here is my older daughter.* David was entitled to have Saul's daughter as his wife because of his victory over Goliath (see 17:25). This promise had not been kept and is now made conditional on further military service, in which Saul hoped David would be killed. *the LORD's battles.* See 25:28.

18:25 *any dowry except.* Normally a bride-price was paid by the bridegroom to the father of the bride (see Gen 34:12; Ex 22:16) as compensation for the loss of his daughter and insurance for her support if widowed. Saul requires David instead to pass a test appropriate for a great warrior, hoping that he will "fall" (see vv. 17,21).

18:28 *Michal . . . loved him.* God's favor on David is revealed not only in his military accomplishments, but also in Michal's love for him—now added to that of Jonathan. Everything Saul seeks to use against David turns to David's advantage.

18:29 *Saul was even more afraid of David.* Saul's perception that God's hand was on David did not lead him to repentance and acceptance of his own lot (see 15:26) but into greater fear and jealousy toward David.

19:1 *Saul told Jonathan . . . to put David to death.* Saul now abandons his indirect attempts on David's life (see 18:13,17,25) and adopts a more direct approach, leading to David's departure from the court and from service to Saul (see vv. 12,18; 20:42).

19:4 *Jonathan spoke well of David.* Jonathan does not let his own personal ambition distort his perception of David's true theocratic spirit (see v. 5 and notes on 14:6; 17:11; 18:1).

he has not sinned against you, and since his
deeds *have been* very [1]beneficial to you.
5 "For [a]he took his life in his hand and
struck the Philistine, and [b]the LORD brought
about a great deliverance for all Israel; you
saw *it* and rejoiced. [c]Why then will you sin
against innocent blood by putting David to
death without a cause?"
6 Saul listened to the voice of Jonathan,
and Saul vowed, "As the LORD lives, he shall
not be put to death."
7 Then Jonathan called David, and Jonathan told him all these words. And Jonathan
brought David to Saul, and he was in his
presence as [a]formerly.
8 When there was war again, David went
out and fought with the Philistines and
[1]defeated them with great slaughter, so that
they fled before him.
9 Now there was [a]an evil spirit from the
LORD on Saul as he was sitting in his house
[b]with his spear in his hand, [c]and David was
playing *the harp* with *his* hand.
10 [a]Saul tried to [1]pin David to the wall
with the spear, but he slipped away out of
Saul's presence, so that he [2]stuck the spear
into the wall. And David fled and escaped
that night.
11 Then [a]Saul sent messengers to David's
house to watch him, in order to put him to
death in the morning. But Michal, David's
wife, told him, saying, "If you do not save
your life tonight, tomorrow you will be put
to death."
12 [a]So Michal let David down through a
window, and he went out and fled and
escaped.
13 Michal took [a]the [1]household idol and
laid *it* on the bed, and put a quilt of goats'
hair at its head, and covered *it* with clothes.
14 When Saul sent messengers to take
David, she said, "[a]He is sick."
15 Then Saul sent messengers to see
David, saying, "Bring him up to me on [1]his
bed, that I may put him to death."
16 When the messengers entered, behold,
the [1]household idol *was* on the bed with the
quilt of goats' *hair* at its head.
17 So Saul said to Michal, "Why have you
deceived me like this and let my enemy go,
so that he has escaped?" And Michal said to
Saul, "He said to me, 'Let me go! [a]Why
should I put you to death?' "
18 Now David fled and escaped and came
[a]to Samuel at Ramah, and told him all that
Saul had done to him. And he and Samuel
went and stayed in [b]Naioth.
19 It was told Saul, saying, "Behold, David
is at Naioth in Ramah."
20 Then [a]Saul sent messengers to take
David, but when they saw [b]the company of
the prophets prophesying, with Samuel
standing *and* presiding over them, the Spirit
of God came upon the messengers of Saul;
and [c]they also prophesied.
21 When it was told Saul, he sent other
messengers, and they also prophesied. So
Saul sent messengers again the third time,
and they also prophesied.
22 Then he himself went to Ramah and
came as far as the large well that is in Secu;
and he asked and said, "Where are Samuel
and David?" And *someone* said, "Behold,
they are at Naioth in Ramah."
23 He [1]proceeded there to Naioth in
Ramah; and [a]the Spirit of God came upon
him also, so that he went along prophesying
continually until he came to Naioth in Ramah.
24 He also stripped off his clothes, and he
too prophesied before Samuel and [1]lay down
[2a]naked all that day and all that night.
Therefore they say, "[b]Is Saul also among the
prophets?"

David and Jonathan Covenant

20 Then David fled from Naioth in Ramah,
and came and [a]said [1]to Jonathan,
"What have I done? What is my iniquity?
And what is my sin before your father, that
he is seeking my life?"
2 He said to him, "Far from it, you shall
not die. Behold, my father does nothing
either great or small [1]without disclosing it to
me. So why should my father hide this thing
from me? It is not so!"
3 Yet David [a]vowed again, [1]saying, "Your
father knows well that I have found favor in
your sight, and he has said, 'Do not let Jonathan know this, or he will be grieved.' But
truly [b]as the LORD lives and as your soul
lives, there is [2]hardly a step between me and
death."

4 [1]Lit *good*
5 [a]Judg 9:17; 1 Sam 17:49, 50; 28:21; Ps 119:109 [b]1 Sam 11:13; 1 Chr 11:14 [c]Deut 19:10-13; 1 Sam 20:32; Ps 94:21; Matt 27:4
7 [a]1 Sam 16:21; 18:2, 10, 13
8 [1]Lit *smote*
9 [a]1 Sam 16:14; 18:10, 11 [b]1 Sam 18:10 [c]1 Sam 16:16
10 [1]Lit *strike David and the wall* [2]Lit *struck* [a]1 Sam 18:11; 20:33; Prov 1:16
11 [a]Judg 16:2; Ps 59: title
12 [a]Josh 2:15; Acts 9:25; 2 Cor 11:33
13 [1]Heb *teraphim* [a]Gen 31:19; Judg 18:14, 17
14 [a]Josh 2:5
15 [1]Lit *the*
16 [1]Heb *teraphim*
17 [a]2 Sam 2:22
18 [a]1 Sam 7:17 [b]1 Sam 19:22, 23
20 [a]1 Sam 19:11, 14; John 7:32 [b]1 Sam 10:5, 6, 10 [c]Num 11:25; Joel 2:28
23 [1]Lit *went* [a]1 Sam 10:10
24 [1]Lit *fell* [2]I.e. without outward garments [a]2 Sam 6:20; Is 20:2; Mic 1:8 [b]1 Sam 10:10-12
20:1 [1]Lit *before* [a]1 Sam 24:9
2 [1]Lit *and he does not uncover my ear*
3 [1]Lit *and said* [2]Lit *about* [a]Deut 6:13 [b]1 Sam 25:26; 2 Kin 2:6

19:6 *Saul listened . . . Saul vowed.* See 14:24,44 for previous oaths that Saul did not keep (see note on 14:39).
19:9 *evil spirit from the LORD.* See note on 16:14; cf. 18:10–11.
19:10 *with the spear.* See 18:10–11; 20:33.
19:12 *through a window.* For similar escapes see Josh 2:15; Acts 9:25.
19:13 *household idol.* See NASB marg. and note on Gen 31:19.
19:18 *Ramah.* Samuel's home (see 7:17 and note on 1:1). *Naioth.* Means "habitations" or "dwellings." The term appears to designate a complex of houses in a certain section of Ramah where a company of prophets resided (see vv. 19–20,22–23).
19:20 *company of the prophets.* See 10:5 and note. *prophesying.* See notes on 10:5; 18:10.
19:24 *he . . . lay down naked all that day and . . . night.* Saul was so overwhelmed by the power of the Spirit of God that he was prevented from carrying out his intention to take David's life. His frustrated attempts to kill David—his own inability to harm David and the thwarting of his plans by Jonathan's loyalty, by Michal's deception and by David's own cleverness—all reach their climax here. *Is Saul also among the prophets?* This second occasion reinforced the first (see 10:11 and note). Its repetition underscores how alien Saul's spirit was from that of these zealous servants of the Lord.
20:1 *Naioth in Ramah.* See note on 19:18.
20:3 *truly as the LORD lives.* See note on 14:39.

4 Then Jonathan said to David, "Whatever [1]you say, I will do for you."
5 So David said to Jonathan, "Behold,
tomorrow is [a]the new moon, and I ought [b]to
sit down to eat with the king. But let me go,
[c]that I may hide myself in the field until the
third evening.
6 "If your father misses me at all, then
say, 'David earnestly asked *leave* of me to
run to [a]Bethlehem his city, because it is [b]the
yearly sacrifice there for the whole family.'
7 "If he [1]says, 'It is good,' your servant
will be safe; but if he is very angry, [a]know
that he has decided on evil.
8 "Therefore deal kindly with your servant, for [a]you have brought your servant
into a covenant of the LORD with you. But [b]if
there is iniquity in me, put me to death yourself; for why then should you bring me to
your father?"
9 Jonathan said, "Far be it from you! For
if I should indeed learn that evil has been
decided by my father to come upon you,
then would I not tell you about it?"
10 Then David said to Jonathan, "Who
will tell me [1]if your father answers you
harshly?"
11 Jonathan said to David, "Come, and let
us go out into the field." So both of them
went out to the field.
12 Then Jonathan said to David, "The
LORD, the God of Israel, *be witness!* When I
have sounded out my father about this time
tomorrow, *or* the third day, behold, if there is
good *feeling* toward David, shall I not then
send to you and [1]make it known to you?
13 "If it please my father *to do* you harm,
[a]may the LORD do so to Jonathan and more
also, if I do not [1]make it known to you and
send you away, that you may go in safety.
And [b]may the LORD be with you as He has
been with my father.
14 "If I am still alive, will you not show me
the lovingkindness of the LORD, that I may
not die?
15 "[a]You shall not cut off your lovingkindness from my house forever, not even when
the LORD cuts off every one of the enemies of
David from the face of the earth."
16 So Jonathan made a *covenant* with the

4 [1]Lit *your soul says*
5 [a]Num 10:10; 28:11-15; Amos 8:5 [b]1 Sam 20:24, 27 [c]1 Sam 19:2
6 [a]1 Sam 17:58 [b]Deut 12:5; 1 Sam 9:12
7 [1]Lit *says thus* [a]1 Sam 25:17
8 [a]1 Sam 18:3; 23:18 [b]2 Sam 14:32
10 [1]Lit *or what*
12 [1]Lit *uncover your ear*
13 [1]Lit *uncover your ear* [a]Ruth 1:17; 1 Sam 3:17 [b]Josh 1:5; 1 Sam 17:37; 18:12; 1 Chr 22:11, 16
15 [a]2 Sam 9:1, 3

20:5 *new moon.* Each month of the year was consecrated to the Lord by the bringing of special sacrifices (Num 28:11–15) and the blowing of trumpets (Num 10:10; Ps 81:3). This observance also involved cessation from normal work, especially at the beginning of the seventh month (Lev 23:24–25; Num 29:1–6; 2 Kin 4:23; Is 1:13; Am 8:5).
20:6 *yearly sacrifice.* David's statement indicates that it was customary for families to observe the new moon festival together once in the year. There is no other reference in the OT to this practice.
20:8 *covenant.* See note on 18:3.
20:13 *may the LORD do so to Jonathan and more.* A common curse formula (see note on 3:17). *may the LORD be with you as He has been with my father.* A clear indication that Jonathan expects David to become king.
20:14 *that I may not die.* It was quite common in the ancient world for the first ruler of a new dynasty to secure his position by murdering all potential claimants to the throne from the preceding dynasty (see 1 Kin 15:29; 16:11; 2 Kin 10:7; 11:1).
20:15 *your lovingkindness from my house.* This request was based on the covenant previously concluded between Jonathan and David (see note on 18:3) and was subsequently honored in David's dealings with Jonathan's son Mephibosheth (see 2 Sam 9:3,7; 21:7).

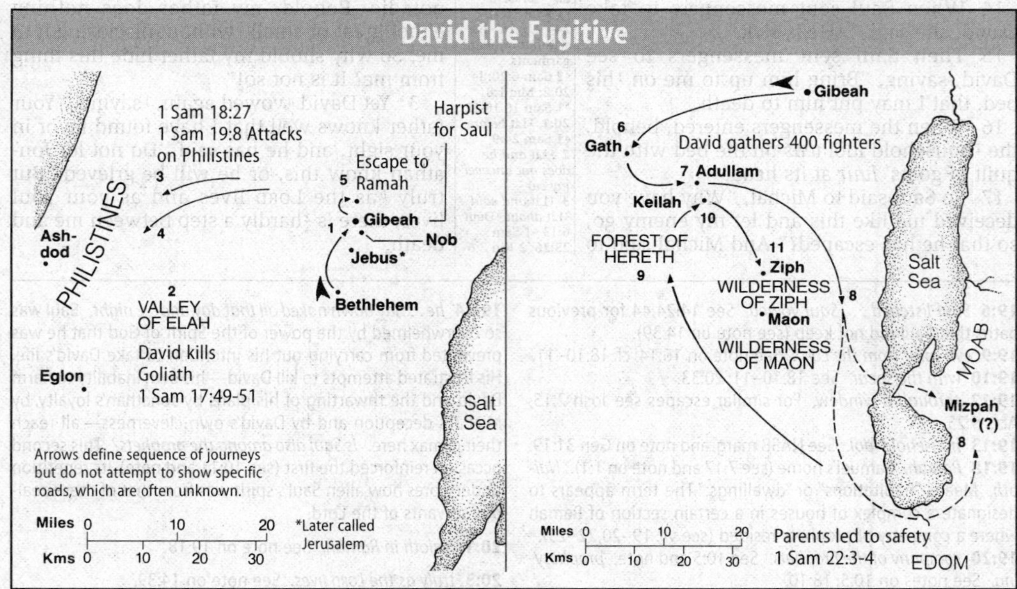
David the Fugitive
1 Sam 18:27
1 Sam 19:8 Attacks on Philistines
Harpist for Saul
Escape to Ramah
3
5
4
1
Gibeah
Nob
Jebus*
Ash-dod
PHILISTINES
Bethlehem
2
VALLEY OF ELAH
David kills Goliath
1 Sam 17:49-51
Eglon
Salt Sea
Arrows define sequence of journeys but do not attempt to show specific roads, which are often unknown.
Miles 0 10 20
Kms 0 10 20 30
*Later called Jerusalem
Gibeah
6
Gath
David gathers 400 fighters
7 Adullam
Keilah
10
FOREST OF HERETH
9
11
Ziph
WILDERNESS OF ZIPH
8
Maon
WILDERNESS OF MAON
Salt Sea
MOAB
Mizpah (?)
8
Miles 0 10 20
Kms 0 10 20 30
Parents led to safety
1 Sam 22:3-4
EDOM

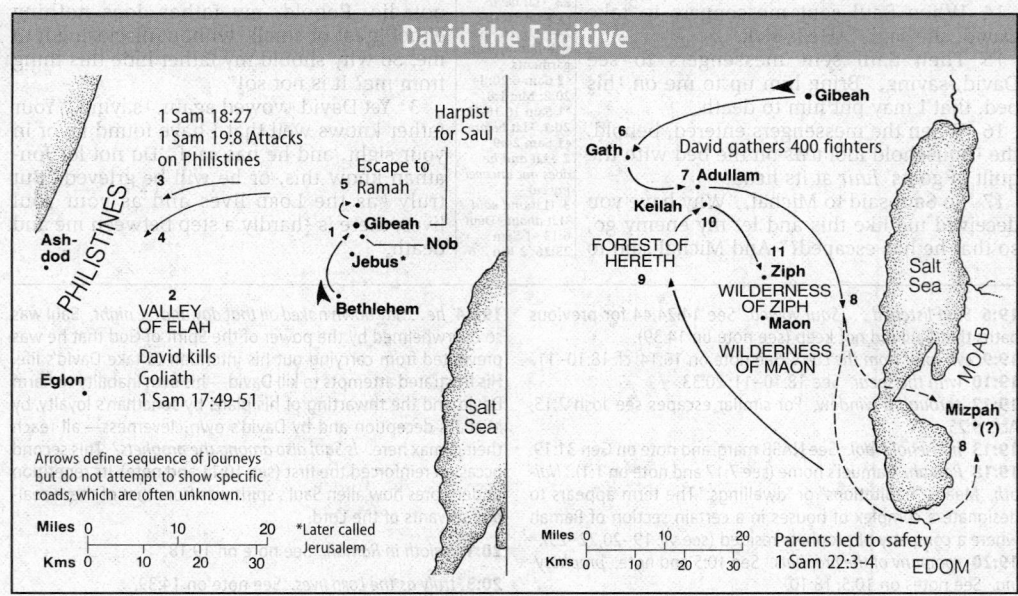

house of David, *saying,* "[a]May the LORD require *it* at the hands of David's enemies."

17 Jonathan made David vow again because of his love for him, because [a]he loved him as he loved his own life.

18 Then Jonathan said to him, "[a]Tomorrow is the new moon, and you will be missed because your seat will be empty.

19 "When you have stayed for three days, you shall go down quickly and come to the place where you hid yourself on that eventful day, and you shall remain by the stone Ezel.

20 "I will shoot three arrows to the side, as though I shot at a target.

21 "And behold, I will send the lad, *saying,* 'Go, find the arrows.' If I specifically say to the lad, 'Behold, the arrows are on this side of you, get them,' then come; for there is safety for you and [1]no harm, as the LORD lives.

22 "But if I [1]say to the youth, '[a]Behold, the arrows are beyond you,' go, for the LORD has sent you away.

23 "[a]As for the [1]agreement of which you and I have spoken, behold, [b]the LORD is between you and me forever."

24 So David hid in the field; and when the new moon came, the king sat down to eat food.

25 The king sat on his seat as usual, the seat by the wall; then Jonathan rose up and Abner sat down by Saul's side, but [a]David's place was empty.

26 Nevertheless Saul did not speak anything that day, for he thought, "It is an accident, [a]he is not clean, surely *he is* not clean."

27 It came about the next day, the second *day* of the new moon, that David's place was empty; so Saul said to Jonathan his son, "Why has the son of Jesse not come to the meal, either yesterday or today?"

28 Jonathan then answered Saul, "[a]David earnestly asked leave of me *to go* to Bethlehem,

29 for he said, 'Please [1]let me go, since our family has a sacrifice in the city, and my brother has commanded me to attend. And now, if I have found favor in your sight, please let me get away that I may see my brothers.' For this reason he has not come to the king's table."

16 [a]Deut 23:21; 1 Sam 25:22
17 [a]1 Sam 18:1
18 [a]1 Sam 20:5, 25
21 [1]Lit *there is nothing*
22 [1]Lit *say thus* [a]1 Sam 20:37
23 [1]Lit *word* [a]1 Sam 20:14, 15 [b]Gen 31:49, 53; 1 Sam 20:42
25 [a]1 Sam 20:18
26 [a]Lev 7:20, 21; 15:5; 1 Sam 16:5
28 [a]1 Sam 20:6
29 [1]Lit *send me away*
31 [1]Lit *all the days which* [2]Lit *is a son of death* [a]2 Sam 12:5
32 [a]Gen 31:36; 1 Sam 19:5; Prov 31:9; Matt 27:23
33 [a]1 Sam 18:11; 19:10 [b]1 Sam 20:7
36 [1]Lit *the* [a]1 Sam 20:20, 21
37 [a]1 Sam 20:22
41 [a]Gen 42:6 [b]1 Sam 18:3
42 [a]1 Sam 20:22

Saul Is Angry with Jonathan

30 Then Saul's anger burned against Jonathan and he said to him, "You son of a perverse, rebellious woman! Do I not know that you are choosing the son of Jesse to your own shame and to the shame of your mother's nakedness?

31 "For [1]as long as the son of Jesse lives on the earth, neither you nor your kingdom will be established. Therefore now, send and bring him to me, for [a]he [2]must surely die."

32 But Jonathan answered Saul his father and said to him, "[a]Why should he be put to death? What has he done?"

33 Then [a]Saul hurled his spear at him to strike him down; [b]so Jonathan knew that his father had decided to put David to death.

34 Then Jonathan arose from the table in fierce anger, and did not eat food on the second day of the new moon, for he was grieved over David because his father had dishonored him.

35 Now it came about in the morning that Jonathan went out into the field for the appointment with David, and a little lad *was* with him.

36 He said to his lad, "[a]Run, find now the arrows which I am about to shoot." As the lad was running, he shot [1]an arrow past him.

37 When the lad reached the place of the arrow which Jonathan had shot, Jonathan called after the lad and said, "[a]Is not the arrow beyond you?"

38 And Jonathan called after the lad, "Hurry, be quick, do not stay!" And Jonathan's lad picked up the arrow and came to his master.

39 But the lad was not aware of anything; only Jonathan and David knew about the matter.

40 Then Jonathan gave his weapons to his lad and said to him, "Go, bring *them* to the city."

41 When the lad was gone, David rose from the south side and fell on his face to the ground, and [a]bowed three times. And they kissed each other and wept together, but [b]David *wept* the more.

42 Jonathan said to David, "[a]Go in safety, inasmuch as we have sworn to each other in

20:16 *May the LORD require it at the hands of David's enemies.* Jonathan aligns himself completely with David, calling for destruction of his enemies, even if that should include his father, Saul.
20:17 *vow again.* See vv. 14–15, 42; 18:3. *he loved him as he loved his own life.* See 18:3; 2 Sam 1:26.
20:18 *new moon.* See note on v. 5.
20:19 *the place where you hid.* Perhaps the place referred to in 19:2.
20:23 *the agreement of which you and I have spoken.* See vv. 15–17. *the LORD is between.* The invoking of God to act as witness and judge between them ensures that their agreement will be kept.
20:25 *Abner.* Saul's cousin and the commander of his army (see 14:50).
20:26 *not clean.* See note on 16:5; cf. Lev 7:19–21; 15:16; Deut 23:10.
20:30 *son of a perverse, rebellious woman.* The Hebrew idiom intends to characterize Jonathan, not his mother.
20:31 *neither you nor your kingdom will be established.* Saul is now convinced that David will succeed him if David is not killed (see notes on 18:13,17,29; 19:1), and he is incapable of understanding Jonathan's lack of concern for his own succession to the throne.
20:33 *hurled his spear.* See 18:11; 19:10.
20:41 *bowed three times.* A sign of submission and respect (see Gen 33:3; 42:6).
20:42 *sworn to each other.* See vv. 14–15,23; 18:3. *the city.* Gibeah (see 10:26).

the name of the LORD, saying, '[b]The LORD
will be between me and you, and between
my [1]descendants and your [1]descendants forever.' " [2]Then he rose and departed, while
Jonathan went into the city.

David Takes Consecrated Bread

21 Then David came to [a]Nob to Ahimelech the priest; and Ahimelech [b]came
trembling to meet David and said to him,
"Why are you alone and no one with you?"
2 David said to Ahimelech the priest,
"The king has commissioned me with a matter and has said to me, '[a]Let no one know
anything about the matter on which I am
sending you and with which I have commissioned you; and I have directed the young
men to a certain place.'
3 "Now therefore, what [1]do you have on
hand? Give [2]me five loaves of bread, or
whatever can be found."
4 The priest answered David and said,
"There is no ordinary bread [1]on hand, but
there is [a]consecrated bread; if only the young
men have [b]kept themselves from women."
5 David answered the priest and said to
him, "[a]Surely women have been kept from
us as previously when I set out and the [b]ves-
sels of the young men were holy, though it
was an ordinary journey; how much more
then today will [1]their vessels *be holy?"*
6 So [a]the priest gave him consecrated
bread; for there was no bread there but the
[b]bread of the Presence which was removed
from before the LORD, in order to put hot
bread *in its place* when it was taken away.
7 Now one of the servants of Saul was
there that day, detained before the LORD; and
his name was [a]Doeg the Edomite, the [b]chief
of Saul's shepherds.
8 David said to Ahimelech, "Now is there
not a spear or a sword [1]on hand? For I
brought neither my sword nor my weapons
[2]with me, because the king's matter was
urgent."
9 Then the priest said, "[a]The sword of
Goliath the Philistine, whom you [1]killed [b]in
the valley of Elah, behold, it is wrapped in a
cloth behind the ephod; if you would take it
for yourself, take *it.* For there is no other
except it here." And David said, "There is
none like it; give it to me."
10 Then David arose and fled that day
from Saul, and went to [a]Achish king of Gath.
11 But the [a]servants of Achish said to him,
"Is this not David the king of the land? [b]Did
they not sing of this one as they danced, saying,

'Saul has slain his thousands,
And David his ten thousands'?"

12 David [a]took these words [1]to heart and
greatly feared Achish king of Gath.
13 So he [a]disguised his sanity before
them, and acted insanely in their hands, and
scribbled on the doors of the gate, and let his
saliva run down into his beard.
14 Then Achish said to his servants,
"Behold, you see the man behaving as a
madman. Why do you bring him to me?
15 "Do I lack madmen, that you have
brought this one to act the madman in my
presence? Shall this one come into my
house?"

The Priests Slain at Nob

22 So David departed from there and
[a]escaped to [b]the cave of Adullam; and
when his brothers and all his father's household heard *of it,* they went down there to him.
2 Everyone who was in distress, and
everyone who [1]was in debt, and everyone
who was [2]discontented gathered to him; and
he became captain over them. Now there
were [a]about four hundred men with him.
3 And David went from there to Mizpah
of Moab; and he said to the king of Moab,

42 [1]Lit *seed* [2]Ch 21:1 in Heb [b]1 Sam 20:15, 16, 23
21:1 [a]1 Sam 22:19; Neh 11:32; Is 10:32 [b]1 Sam 16:4
2 [a]Ps 141:3
3 [1]Lit *is under your hand?* [2]Lit *in my hand*
4 [1]Lit *under my hand* [a]Ex 25:30; Lev 24:5-9; Matt 12:4 [b]Ex 19:15
5 [1]Lit *it* be holy *in the vessel* [a]Ex 19:14, 15 [b]1 Thess 4:4
6 [a]Matt 12:3, 4; Luke 6:3, 4 [b]Lev 24:5-9
7 [a]1 Sam 14:47; 22:9; Ps 52: title [b]1 Chr 27:29, 31
8 [1]Lit *under your hand*
8 [2]Lit *in my hand*
9 [1]Lit *smote* [a]1 Sam 17:51, 54 [b]1 Sam 17:2
10 [a]Ps 34: title
11 [a]Ps 56: title [b]1 Sam 18:7; 29:5
12 [1]Lit *in his* [a]Luke 2:19
13 [a]Ps 34: title
22:1 [a]Ps 57: title [b]Josh 12:15; 15:35; 2 Sam 23:13; Ps 142: title
2 [1]Lit *had a creditor* [2]Lit *bitter of soul* [a]1 Sam 23:13; 25:13

21:1 *Nob.* A town northeast of Jerusalem and south of Gibeah where the tabernacle was relocated after the destruction of Shiloh (4:2–3; Jer 7:12). Although it appears that no attempt was made to bring the ark to this sanctuary (see note on 7:1), Ahimelech the high priest, 85 other priests (22:17–18), the ephod (v. 9) and the table of consecrated bread (v. 6) are mentioned in connection with it. *Ahimelech the priest.* See note on 14:3. It appears from 22:10,15 that David's purpose in coming to Nob was to seek the Lord's guidance by means of the Urim and Thummim (see notes on 2:28; Ex 28:30).

21:2 It is not clear why David resorts to deception in his response to Ahimelech. Perhaps it was an attempt to protect Ahimelech from the charge of involvement in David's escape from Saul. If so, his strategy was not successful (see 22:13–18).

21:4 *consecrated bread.* The "bread of the Presence" (see v. 6; Ex 25:30), which was placed in the holy place in the tabernacle and later in the temple as a thank offering to the Lord, symbolizing His provision of daily bread. *if only the young men have kept themselves from women.* Although the bread was to be eaten only by the priests (see Lev 24:9), Ahimelech agreed to give it to David and his men on the condition that they were ceremonially clean (see Ex 19:15; Lev 15:18). Jesus uses this incident to illustrate the principle that the ceremonial law was not to be viewed in a legalistic manner (see Matt 12:3–4). He also teaches that it is always lawful to do good and to save life (see Luke 6:9). Such compassionate acts are within the true spirit of the law.

21:9 *sword of Goliath.* See note on 17:54. *ephod.* See note on 2:28.

21:10 *Achish.* See note on Ps 34 title. *Gath.* One of the five major towns of the Philistines (Josh 13:3).

21:11 *king of the land.* The designation of David as "king" by the Philistines may be understood as a popular exaggeration expressing an awareness of the enormous success and popularity of David among the Israelite people.

22:1 *cave of Adullam.* See 2 Sam 23:13; Gen 38:1; Josh 12:15; 15:35; 1 Chr 11:15 and note on Ps 142 title.

22:2 *four hundred men with him.* David, officially an outlaw, was joined by others in similar circumstances, so that he began to develop the power base that would sustain him throughout his later years as king.

22:3 *Mizpah of Moab.* Precise location unknown. *let my father and my mother come and stay with you.* The king of Moab was

"Please let my father and my mother come
and stay with you until I know what God
will do for me."
4 Then he left them with the king of
Moab; and they stayed with him all the time
that David was in the stronghold.
5 [a]The prophet Gad said to David, "Do
not stay in the stronghold; depart, and go
into the land of Judah." So David departed
and went into the forest of Hereth.
6 Then Saul heard that David and the
men who were with him had been discovered. Now [a]Saul was sitting in Gibeah, under
the tamarisk tree on the height with his
spear in his hand, and all his servants were
standing around him.
7 Saul said to his servants who stood
around him, "Hear now, O Benjamites! Will
the son of Jesse also give to all of you fields
and vineyards? [a]Will he make you all commanders of thousands and commanders of
hundreds?
8 "For all of you have conspired against
me so that there is no one who [1]discloses to
me [a]when my son makes *a covenant* with
the son of Jesse, and there is none of you
[b]who is sorry for me or [1]discloses to me that
my son has stirred up my servant against me
to lie in ambush, as *it is* this day."
9 Then [a]Doeg the Edomite, who was
[1]standing by the servants of Saul, said, "[b]I
saw the son of Jesse coming to Nob, to
[c]Ahimelech the son of Ahitub.
10 "[a]He inquired of the LORD for him, [b]gave
him provisions, and [c]gave him the sword of
Goliath the Philistine."
11 Then the king sent someone to summon Ahimelech the priest, the son of Ahitub,
and all his father's household, the priests
who were in Nob; and all of them came to
the king.
12 Saul said, "Listen now, son of Ahitub."
And he [1]answered, "Here I am, my lord."
13 Saul then said to him, "Why have you
and the son of Jesse conspired against me, in
that you have given him bread and a sword
and have inquired of God for him, so that he
would rise up against me [a]by lying in
ambush as *it is* this day?"
14 [a]Then Ahimelech answered the king
and said, "And who among all your servants
is as faithful as David, even the king's son-
in-law, who [1]is captain over your guard, and
is honored in your house?
15 "Did I *just* begin [a]to inquire of God for
him today? Far be it from me! [b]Do not let the
king impute anything to his servant *or* to any
of the household of my father, for your servant knows nothing [1]at all of this whole
affair."
16 But the king said, "You shall surely die,
Ahimelech, you and all your father's household!"
17 And [a]the king said to the [1]guards who
were attending him, "Turn around and put
the priests of the LORD to death, because
their hand also is with David and because
they knew that he was fleeing and did not
[2]reveal it to me." But the [b]servants of the
king were not willing to put forth their hands
to [3]attack the priests of the LORD.
18 Then the king said to Doeg, "You turn
around and [1]attack the priests." And Doeg
the Edomite turned around and [2]attacked the
priests, and [a]he killed that day eighty-five
men [b]who wore the linen ephod.
19 And [a]he struck Nob the city of the
priests with the edge of the sword, both men
and women, children and infants; also oxen,
donkeys, and sheep *he struck* with the edge
of the sword.
20 But [a]one son of Ahimelech the son of
Ahitub, named Abiathar, [b]escaped and fled
after David.
21 Abiathar told David that Saul had killed
the priests of the LORD.
22 Then David said to Abiathar, "I knew
on that day, when [a]Doeg the Edomite was

5 [a]2 Sam 24:11; 1 Chr 21:9; 29:29; 2 Chr 29:25
6 [a]Judg 4:5; 1 Sam 14:2
7 [a]1 Sam 8:12; 1 Chr 12:16-18
8 [1]Lit *uncovers my ear* [a]1 Sam 18:3; 20:16 [b]1 Sam 23:21
9 [1]Or *set over* [a]Ps 52: title [b]1 Sam 21:1 [c]1 Sam 14:3; 21:1
10 [a]Num 27:21; 1 Sam 10:22 [b]1 Sam 21:6 [c]1 Sam 21:9
12 [1]Lit *said*
13 [a]1 Sam 22:8
14 [1]So with Gr; Heb *turns aside to* [a]1 Sam 19:4, 5; 20:32
15 [1]Lit *small or great* [a]2 Sam 5:19, 23 [b]2 Sam 19:18, 19
17 [1]Lit *runners* [2]Lit *uncover my ear* [3]Lit *fall upon* [a]2 Kin 10:25 [b]Ex 1:17
18 [1]Lit *smite* [2]Lit *smote* [a]1 Sam 2:31 [b]1 Sam 2:18
19 [a]1 Sam 15:3
20 [a]1 Sam 23:6, 9; 30:7; 1 Kin 2:26, 27 [b]1 Sam 23:6
22 [a]1 Sam 21:7

a natural ally for David because Saul had warred against him (see 14:47) and David's own great-grandmother was a Moabitess (see Ruth 4:13,22).

22:4 *stronghold.* Perhaps a specific fortress, but more likely a reference to a geographical area in which it was easy to hide (see 23:14; 2 Sam 5:17; 23:14).

22:5 *prophet Gad.* The king-designate is now served also by a prophet. Later a priest would come to him (v. 20) and complete the basic elements of a royal entourage—and they were all refugees from Saul's administration. This is the first appearance of the prophet who later assisted David in musical arrangements for the temple services (see 2 Chr 29:25), wrote a history of David's reign (see 1 Chr 29:29) and confronted David with the Lord's rebuke for his sin of numbering the Israelites (see 2 Sam 24:11–25). *forest of Hereth.* Located in the tribal area of Judah.

22:6 *Gibeah.* See note on 10:5. *tamarisk tree.* See note on 14:2.

22:7 *Benjamites.* Saul, a Benjamite (9:1–2; 10:21), seeks to strengthen his position with his own officials by emphasizing tribal loyalty. David was from the tribe of Judah (see note on 16:1; 2 Sam 2:4). *give to all of you fields and vineyards?* Saul does exactly what Samuel had warned him that he would do—become like the kings of other nations (see 8:14). His actions are contrary to the covenantal ideal for kingship (see notes on 8:7; 10:25). *commanders of thousands and commanders of hundreds.* See 8:12.

22:10 *He inquired of the LORD for him.* See note on 21:1.

22:17 *they knew that he was fleeing.* How much the priests really knew is not clear. David himself had not told them (see 21:2–3,8).

22:18 *linen ephod.* See note on 2:18.

22:19 *struck Nob . . . with the edge of the sword.* Thus the prophecy of judgment against the house of Eli is fulfilled (see 2:31).

22:20 *Abiathar, escaped and fled after David.* See note on v. 5. Abiathar brought the high priestly ephod with him (see 23:6) and subsequently "inquired of the LORD" for David (see 23:2 and note; see also 23:4,9; 30:7–8; 2 Sam 2:1; 5:19,23). He served as high priest until removed from office by Solomon for participating in the rebellion of Adonijah (see 1 Kin 2:26–27).

there, that he would surely tell Saul. I have
brought about *the death* of every person in
your father's household.
23 "Stay with me; do not be afraid, for [a]he
who seeks my life seeks your life, for you are
[1]safe with me."

David Delivers Keilah

23 Then they told David, saying, "Behold,
the Philistines are fighting against [a]Kei-
lah and are plundering the threshing floors."
2 So David [a]inquired of the LORD, saying,
"Shall I go and [1]attack these Philistines?"
And the LORD said to David, "Go and [1]attack
the Philistines and deliver Keilah."
3 But David's men said to him, "Behold,
we are afraid here in Judah. How much more
then if we go to Keilah against the ranks of
the Philistines?"
4 Then David inquired of the LORD once
more. And the LORD answered him and said,
"Arise, go down to Keilah, for [a]I will give the
Philistines into your hand."
5 So David and his men went to Keilah
and fought with the Philistines; and he led
away their livestock and struck them with a
great slaughter. Thus David delivered the
inhabitants of Keilah.
6 Now it came about, when Abiathar the
son of Ahimelech [a]fled to David at Keilah,
that he came down *with* an ephod in his
hand.
7 When it was told Saul that David had
come to Keilah, Saul said, "God has [1]deliv-
ered him into my hand, for he shut himself
in by entering a city with double gates and
bars."
8 So Saul summoned all the people for
war, to go down to Keilah to besiege David
and his men.
9 Now David knew that Saul was plotting
evil against him; so he said to [a]Abiathar the
priest, "[b]Bring the ephod here."
10 Then David said, "O LORD God of Israel, Your servant has heard for certain that
Saul is seeking to come to Keilah to destroy
the city on my account.
11 "Will the men of Keilah surrender me
into his hand? Will Saul come down just as
Your servant has heard? O LORD God of Israel, I pray, tell Your servant." And the LORD
said, "He will come down."
12 Then David said, "Will the men of Keilah surrender me and my men into the hand
of Saul?" And the LORD said, "[a]They will surrender you."
13 Then David and his men, [a]about six
hundred, arose and departed from Keilah,
and they went [b]wherever they could go.
When it was told Saul that David had
escaped from Keilah, he [1]gave up the pursuit.
14 David stayed in the wilderness in the
strongholds, and remained in the hill country
in the wilderness of [a]Ziph. And Saul sought
him every day, but [b]God did not deliver him
into his hand.

Saul Pursues David

15 Now David [1]became aware that Saul
had come out to seek his life while David
was in the wilderness of Ziph at Horesh.
16 And Jonathan, Saul's son, arose and
went to David at Horesh, and [1a]encouraged
him in God.
17 Thus he said to him, "[a]Do not be
afraid, because the hand of Saul my father
will not find you, and you will be king over
Israel and I will be next to you; and [b]Saul my
father knows that also."
18 So [a]the two of them made a covenant
before the LORD; and David stayed at Horesh
while Jonathan went to his house.
19 Then [a]Ziphites came up to Saul at Gibeah, saying, "Is David not hiding with us in
the strongholds at Horesh, on [b]the hill of
Hachilah, which is on the [1]south of [2]Jeshi-
mon?
20 "Now then, O king, come down according to all the desire of your soul to [1]do so;
and [a]our part *shall be* to surrender him into
the king's hand."
21 Saul said, "May you be blessed of the
LORD, [a]for you have had compassion on me.
22 "Go now, make more sure, and investigate and see his place where his [1]haunt is,
and who has seen him there; for I am told
that he is very cunning.
23 "So look, and learn about all the hiding
places where he hides himself and return to
me with certainty, and I will go with you;
and if he is in the land, I will search him out
among all the thousands of Judah."
24 Then they arose and went to Ziph
before Saul. Now David and his men were in
the wilderness of [a]Maon, in the Arabah to
the [1]south of [2]Jeshimon.
25 When Saul and his men went to seek
him, they told David, and he came down to

23 [1]Lit *a charge* [a]1 Kin 2:26
23:1 [a]Josh 15:44; Neh 3:17, 18
2 [1]Lit *smite* [a]1 Sam 23:4, 6, 9-12; 2 Sam 5:19, 23
4 [a]Josh 8:7; Judg 7:7
6 [a]1 Sam 22:20
7 [1]Lit *alienated*
9 [a]1 Sam 22:20 [b]1 Sam 23:6; 30:7
12 [a]Judg 15:10-13; 1 Sam 23:20
13 [1]Lit *ceased going out* [a]1 Sam 22:2; 25:13 [b]2 Sam 15:20
14 [a]Josh 15:55; 2 Chr 11:8 [b]Ps 32:7
15 [1]Lit *saw*
16 [1]Lit *strengthened his hand* [a]1 Sam 30:6; Neh 2:18
17 [a]Ps 27:1, 3; 118:6; Is 54:17; Heb 13:6 [b]1 Sam 20:31; 24:20
18 [a]1 Sam 18:3; 20:12-17, 42; 2 Sam 9:1; 21:7
19 [1]Lit *right side* [2]Or *the desert* [a]1 Sam 26:1; Ps 54: title [b]1 Sam 26:3
20 [1]Lit *come down* [a]1 Sam 23:12
21 [a]1 Sam 22:8
22 [1]Lit *foot*
24 [1]Lit *right side* [2]Or *the desert* [a]Josh 15:55; 1 Sam 25:2

23:2 *David inquired of the LORD.* By means of the Urim and Thummim through the high priest Abiathar (see vv. 6,9 and note on 2:28).

23:9 *Bring the ephod.* See note on v. 2.

23:13 *about six hundred.* The number of David's men has grown significantly (cf. 22:2).

23:14 *wilderness . . . strongholds.* Inaccessible places (see note on 22:4). *wilderness of Ziph.* Located south of Hebron. *God did not deliver him into his hand.* The reality of God's protection over David portrayed here contrasts sharply with the wishful thinking of Saul in v. 7.

23:17 *you will be king over Israel.* See notes on 18:4; 20:13, 16,31. *I will be next to you.* Jonathan's love and respect for David enable him to accept a role subordinate to David without any sign of resentment or jealousy (see notes on 18:3; 19:4). This is the last recorded meeting between Jonathan and David. *Saul . . . knows that.* See 18:8 and note on 20:31.

23:18 *covenant.* See notes on 18:3; 20:14–15.

23:19 *strongholds.* Inaccessible places (see note on 22:4).

the rock and stayed in the wilderness of
Maon. And when Saul heard *it,* he pursued
David in the wilderness of Maon.
26 Saul went on one side of the mountain,
and David and his men on the other side of
the mountain; and David was hurrying to get
away from Saul, for Saul and his men [a]were
surrounding David and his men to seize them.
27 But a messenger came to Saul, saying,
"Hurry and come, for the Philistines have
made a raid on the land."
28 So Saul returned from pursuing David
and went to meet the Philistines; therefore
they called that place [1]the Rock of Escape.
29 [1]David went up from there and stayed
in the strongholds of [a]Engedi.

David Spares Saul's Life

24 Now [a]when Saul returned from pursuing the Philistines, [b]he was told, saying, "Behold, David is in the wilderness of
Engedi."
2 Then [a]Saul took three thousand chosen
men from all Israel and went to seek David
and his men in front of the Rocks of the Wild
Goats.
3 He came to the sheepfolds on the way,
where there *was* a cave; and Saul [a]went in to
[1]relieve himself. Now [b]David and his men
were sitting in the inner recesses of the cave.
4 The men of David said to him, "Behold,
[a]*this is* the day of which the LORD said to you,
'Behold; [b]I am about to give your enemy into
your hand, and you shall do to him as it
seems good [1]to you.' " Then David arose and
cut off the edge of Saul's robe secretly.
5 It came about afterward that [a]David's
[1]conscience bothered him because he had
cut off the edge of Saul's *robe.*
6 So he said to his men, "[a]Far be it from
me because of the LORD that I should do this
thing to my lord, the LORD's anointed, to
stretch out my hand against him, since he is
the LORD's anointed."
7 David [1]persuaded his men with *these*
words and did not allow them to rise up
against Saul. And Saul arose, [2]left the cave,
and went on *his* way.
8 Now afterward David arose and went
out of the cave and called after Saul, saying,
"My lord the king!" And when Saul looked
behind him, [a]David bowed with his face to
the ground and prostrated himself.
9 David said to Saul, "Why do you listen
to the words of men, saying, 'Behold, David
seeks [1]to harm you'?
10 "[a]Behold, this day your eyes have seen
that the LORD had given you today into my
hand in the cave, and [b]some said to kill you,
but *my eye* had pity on you; and I said, 'I will
not stretch out my hand against my lord, for
he is the LORD's anointed.'
11 "Now, [a]my father, see! Indeed, see the
edge of your robe in my hand! For in that I
cut off the edge of your robe and did not kill
you, know and perceive that there is no evil
or [1]rebellion in my hands, and I have not
sinned against you, though you [b]are lying in
wait for my life to take it.
12 "[a]May the LORD judge between [1]you and
me, and may the LORD avenge me on you;
but my hand shall not be against you.
13 "As the proverb of the ancients says,
'[a]Out of the wicked comes forth wickedness'; but my hand shall not be against you.
14 "After whom has the king of Israel come
out? Whom are you pursuing? [a]A dead dog,
[b]a single flea?
15 "[a]The LORD therefore be judge and
decide between [1]you and me; and may He
see and [b]plead my cause and [2]deliver me
from your hand."
16 When David had finished speaking
these words to Saul, Saul said, "[a]Is this your
voice, my son David?" Then Saul lifted up
his voice and wept.
17 [a]He said to David, "You are more righteous than I; for [b]you have dealt well with
me, while I have dealt wickedly with you.
18 "You have declared today that you have
done good to me, that [a]the LORD delivered me
into your hand and *yet* you did not kill me.
19 "For if a man [a]finds his enemy, will he
let him go away [1]safely? May the LORD therefore reward you with good in return for what
you have done to me this day.
20 "Now, behold, [a]I know that you will
surely be king, and that [b]the kingdom of
Israel will be established in your hand.
21 "So now [a]swear to me by the LORD that
you will not cut off my [1]descendants after
me and that you will not destroy my name
from my father's household."
22 David swore to Saul. And Saul went to
his home, but David and his men went up to
[a]the stronghold.

26 [a]Ps 17:9
28 [1]Heb *Sela-hammahlekoth*
29 [1]Ch 24:1 in Heb [a]Josh 15:62; 2 Chr 20:2
24:1 [a]1 Sam 23:28, 29 [b]1 Sam 23:19
2 [a]1 Sam 26:2
3 [1]Lit *cover his feet* [a]Judg 3:24 [b]Ps 57: title; 142: title
4 [1]Lit *in your sight* [a]1 Sam 23:17; 25:28-30 [b]1 Sam 26:8, 11
5 [1]Lit *heart struck* [a]2 Sam 24:10
6 [a]1 Sam 26:11
7 [1]Lit *tore apart* [2]Lit *from*
8 [a]1 Sam 25:23, 24; 1 Kin 1:31
9 [1]Lit *your hurt*
10 [a]Ps 7:3, 4 [b]1 Sam 24:4
11 [1]Lit *transgression* [a]2 Kin 5:13 [b]1 Sam 23:14, 23; 26:20
12 [1]Lit *me and you* [a]Gen 16:5; 31:53; Judg 11:27; 1 Sam 26:10, 23
13 [a]Matt 7:16-20
14 [a]2 Sam 9:8 [b]1 Sam 26:20
15 [1]Lit *me and you* [2]Lit *vindicate* [a]1 Sam 24:12 [b]Ps 35:1; 43:1; 119:154; Mic 7:9
16 [a]1 Sam 26:17
17 [a]1 Sam 26:21 [b]Matt 5:44
18 [a]1 Sam 26:23
19 [1]Lit *on a good road* [a]1 Sam 23:17
20 [a]1 Sam 23:17 [b]1 Sam 13:14
21 [1]Lit *seed* [a]Gen 21:23; 1 Sam 20:14-17; 2 Sam 21:6-8
22 [a]1 Sam 23:29

24:4 *this is the day of which the LORD said.* There is no previous record of the divine revelation here alluded to by David's men. Perhaps this was their own interpretation of the anointing of David to replace Saul (see 16:13–14), or of assurances given to David that he would survive Saul's vendetta against him and ultimately become king (see 20:14–15; 23:17). This clause may also be rendered "today the LORD is saying." Then the reference would not be to a verbal communication from the Lord but to the providential nature of the incident itself, which David's men understood as a revelation from God that David should not ignore.
24:6 *he is the LORD's anointed.* Because Saul's royal office carried divine sanction by virtue of his anointing (see note on 9:16), David is determined not to wrest the kingship from Saul but to leave its disposition to the Lord who gave it (see vv. 12,15; 26:10).
24:11 *my father.* Saul was David's father-in-law (see 18:27).
24:16 *lifted up his voice and wept.* Saul experiences temporary remorse (see 26:21) for his actions against David but quickly reverts to his former determination to kill him (see 26:2).
24:21 *not cut off my descendants.* See notes on 20:14–15.
24:22 *stronghold.* An inaccessible place (see note on 22:4). From previous experience David did not place any confidence in Saul's words of repentance.

Samuel's Death

25 [a]Then Samuel died; and all Israel gathered together and [b]mourned for him, and [c]buried him at his house in Ramah. And David arose and went down to the [d]wilderness of Paran.

Nabal and Abigail

2 Now *there was* a man in [a]Maon whose business was in [b]Carmel; and the man was very [1]rich, and he had three thousand sheep and a thousand goats. And it came about while [c]he was shearing his sheep in Carmel

3 (now the man's name was Nabal, and his [a]wife's name was Abigail. And the woman was [1]intelligent and beautiful in appearance, but the man was harsh and evil in *his* dealings, and he was [b]a Calebite),

4 that David heard in the wilderness that Nabal was shearing his sheep.

5 So David sent ten young men; and David said to the young men, "Go up to Carmel, [1]visit Nabal and greet him in my name;

6 and thus you shall say, '[1]Have a long life, [a]peace be to you, and peace be to your house, and peace be to all that you have.

7 'Now I have heard [a]that you have shearers; now your shepherds have been with us and we have not insulted them, [b]nor have they missed anything all the days they were in Carmel.

8 'Ask your young men and they will tell you. Therefore let *my* young men find favor in your eyes, for we have come on [a]a [1]festive day. Please give whatever you find at hand to your servants and to your son David.' "

9 When David's young men came, they spoke to Nabal according to all these words in David's name; then they waited.

10 But Nabal answered David's servants and said, "[a]Who is David? And who is the son of Jesse? There are many servants today who are each breaking away from his master.

11 "Shall I then [a]take my bread and my water and my meat that I have slaughtered for my shearers, and give it to men [1]whose origin I do not know?"

12 So David's young men retraced their way and went back; and they came and told him according to all these words.

13 David said to his men, "Each *of you* gird on his sword." So each man girded on his sword. And David also girded on his sword, and about [a]four hundred men went up behind David while two hundred [b]stayed with the baggage.

14 But one of the young men told Abigail, Nabal's wife, saying, "Behold, David sent messengers from the wilderness to [1a]greet our master, and he scorned them.

15 "Yet the men were very good to us, and we were not [a]insulted, nor did we miss anything [1]as long as we went about with them, while we were in the fields.

16 "[a]They were a wall to us both by night and by day, all the time we were with them tending the sheep.

17 "Now therefore, know and [1]consider what you should do, for evil is plotted against our master and against all his household; and he is such a [2]worthless man that no one can speak to him."

Abigail Intercedes

18 Then Abigail hurried and [a]took two hundred *loaves* of bread and two jugs of wine and five sheep already prepared and five measures of roasted grain and a hundred clusters of raisins and two hundred cakes of figs, and loaded *them* on donkeys.

25:1 [a]1 Sam 28:3 [b]Num 20:29; Deut 34:8 [c]2 Kin 21:18; 2 Chr 33:20 [d]Gen 21:21; Num 10:12; 13:3
2 [1]Lit *great* [a]1 Sam 23:24 [b]Josh 15:55 [c]Gen 38:13; 2 Sam 13:23
3 [1]Lit *of good understanding* [a]Prov 31:10 [b]Josh 15:13; 1 Sam 30:14
5 [1]Lit *go into*
6 [1]Lit *To life* [a]1 Chr 12:18; Ps 122:7; Luke 10:5
7 [a]2 Sam 13:23, 24 [b]1 Sam 25:15, 21
8 [1]Lit *good* [a]Neh 8:10-12; Esth 9:19, 22
10 [a]Judg 9:28
11 [1]Lit *from where they are* [a]Judg 8:6, 15
13 [a]1 Sam 23:13 [b]1 Sam 30:24
14 [1]Lit *bless* [a]1 Sam 13:10; 15:13
15 [1]Lit *all the days* [a]1 Sam 25:7, 21
16 [a]Ex 14:22; Job 1:10
17 [1]Lit *see* [2]Lit *son of Belial*
18 [a]2 Sam 16:1; 1 Chr 12:40

25:1 *all Israel . . . mourned for him.* Samuel was recognized as a leader of national prominence who played a key role in the restructuring of the theocracy with the establishment of the monarchy (see chs. 8–12). The loss of his leadership was mourned much like that of other prominent figures in Israel's past history, including Jacob (Gen 50:10), Aaron (Num 20:29) and Moses (Deut 34:8). *Ramah.* See 7:17 and note on 1:1.

25:2–44 Nabal, the "fool" (see v. 25 and note), lived near Carmel, where Saul had erected a monument in his own honor (see 15:12) and had committed the act that led to his rejection (see 15:26). The account of Nabal effectively serves the author's purpose in a number of ways: 1. Nabal's general character, his disdainful attitude toward David though David had guarded his flocks, and his sudden death at the Lord's hand all parallel Saul (whose "flock" David had also protected). This allows the author indirectly to characterize Saul as a fool (see 13:13; 26:21) and to foreshadow his end. 2. David's vengeful attitude toward Nabal displays his natural tendency and highlights his restraint toward Saul, the Lord's anointed (this event is sandwiched between the two instances in which David spared Saul in spite of the urging of his men). 3. Abigail's prudent action prevents David from using his power as leader for personal vengeance (the very thing Saul was doing). In this way the Lord (who avenged His servant) keeps David's sword clean, teaching him a lesson he does not forget. 4. Abigail's confident acknowledgment of David's future accession to the throne foreshadows that event and even anticipates the Lord's commitment to establish David's house as an "enduring house" (v. 28; cf. 2 Sam 7:11–16). 5. Abigail's marriage to David provides him with a wise and worthy wife, while Saul gives away David's wife Michal to another, illustrating how the Lord counters every move Saul makes against David.

25:3 *Calebite.* A descendant of Caleb (see Num 14:24), who settled at Hebron (see Josh 14:13) after the conquest of Canaan. Since Caleb's name can mean "dog," Nabal is subtly depicted as a dog as well as a fool. He would soon be a dead dog (see note on 2 Sam 9:8), when the Lord would avenge his acts of contempt toward David. The hint is strong that, when the Lord avenges Saul's sins against David (see 24:12,15), the king will no longer pursue a dead dog (see 24:14) but will himself become one—a case of biting irony.

25:4 *shearing his sheep.* A festive occasion (see v. 8; 2 Sam 13:23–24).

25:8 *whatever you find at hand.* David and his men ask for some remuneration for their protection of Nabal's shepherds and flocks against pillage (see vv. 15–16,21).

25:17 *worthless man.* See note on Deut 13:13. *no one can speak to him.* In this way, too, Nabal is like Saul (cf., e.g., 20:27–33).

19 She said to her young men, "[a]Go on before me; behold, I am coming after you." But she did not tell her husband Nabal.

20 It came about as she was riding on her donkey and coming down by the hidden part of the mountain, that behold, David and his men were coming down toward her; so she met them.

21 Now David had said, "Surely in vain I have guarded all that this *man* has in the wilderness, so that nothing was missed of all that belonged to him; and he has [a]returned me evil for good.

22 "[a]May God do so to the enemies of David, and more also, [b]if by morning I leave *as much as* one [1]male of any who belong to him."

23 When Abigail saw David, she hurried and dismounted from her donkey, and fell on her face before David [a]and bowed herself to the ground.

24 She fell at his feet and said, "On me [1]alone, my lord, be the blame. And please let your maidservant speak [2]to you, and listen to the words of your maidservant.

25 "Please do not let my lord [1]pay attention to this [2]worthless man, Nabal, for as his name is, so is he. [3]Nabal is his name and folly is with him; but I your maidservant did not see the young men of my lord whom you sent.

26 "Now therefore, my lord, as the LORD lives, and as your soul lives, since the LORD has restrained you from [1]shedding blood, and [a]from [2]avenging yourself by your own hand, now then [b]let your enemies and those who seek evil against my lord, be as Nabal.

27 "Now let [a]this [1]gift which your maidservant has brought to my lord be given to the young men who [2]accompany my lord.

28 "Please forgive [a]the transgression of your maidservant; for [b]the LORD will certainly make for my lord an enduring house, because my lord is [c]fighting the battles of the LORD, and [d]evil will not be found in you all your days.

29 "Should anyone rise up to pursue you and to seek your [1]life, then the [1]life of my lord shall be bound in the bundle of the living with the LORD your God; but the [1]lives of your enemies [a]He will sling out [2]as from the hollow of a sling.

30 "And when the LORD does for my lord according to all the good that He has spoken concerning you, and [a]appoints you ruler over Israel,

31 this will not [1]cause grief or a troubled heart to my lord, both by having shed blood without cause and by my lord having [2]avenged himself. [a]When the LORD deals well with my lord, then remember your maidservant."

32 Then David said to Abigail, "[a]Blessed be the LORD God of Israel, who sent you this day to meet me,

33 and blessed be your discernment, and blessed be you, [a]who have kept me this day from [1]bloodshed and from [2]avenging myself by my own hand.

34 "Nevertheless, as the LORD God of Israel lives, [a]who has restrained me from harming you, unless you had come quickly to meet me, surely there would not have been left to Nabal until the morning light *as much as* one [1]male."

35 So David received from her hand what she had brought him and said to her, "[a]Go up to your house in peace. See, I have listened to [1]you and [2b]granted your request."

36 Then Abigail came to Nabal, and behold, he was holding [a]a feast in his house, like the feast of a king. And Nabal's heart was merry within him, [b]for he was very drunk; so [c]she did not tell him anything [1]at all until the morning light.

37 But in the morning, when the wine had gone out of Nabal, his wife told him these things, and his heart died within him so that he became *as* a stone.

38 About ten days later, [a]the LORD struck Nabal and he died.

19 [a]Gen 32:16, 20 **21** [a]Ps 109:5; Prov 17:13 **22** [1]Lit *who urinates against the wall* [a]1 Sam 3:17; 20:13 [b]1 Kin 14:10 **23** [a]1 Sam 20:41 **24** [1]Lit *even me* [2]Lit *in your ears* **25** [1]Lit *set his heart to* [2]Lit *man of Belial* [3]I.e. Fool **26** [1]Lit *coming in with blood* [2]Lit *saving* [a]Heb 10:30 [b]2 Sam 18:32 **27** [1]Lit *blessing* [2]Lit *walk at the feet of* [a]Gen 33:11; 1 Sam 30:26 **28** [a]1 Sam 25:24 [b]1 Sam 22:14; 2 Sam 7:11, 16 [c]1 Sam 18:17 [d]1 Sam 24:11; Ps 7:3

29 [1]Lit *soul* [2]Lit *in the midst* [a]Jer 10:18 **30** [a]1 Sam 13:14 **31** [1]Lit *become staggering to you or a stumbling of the heart* [2]Lit *saved* [a]Gen 40:14; 1 Sam 25:30 **32** [a]Ex 18:10; 1 Kin 1:48; Ps 41:13; 72:18; 106:48; Luke 1:68 **33** [1]Lit *coming in with blood* [2]Lit *saving* [a]1 Sam 25:26 **34** [1]Lit *who urinates against the wall* [a]1 Sam 25:26 **35** [1]Lit *your voice* [2]Lit *lifted up your face* [a]1 Sam 20:42; 2 Kin 5:19 [b]Gen 19:21 **36** [1]Lit *small or large* [a]2 Sam 13:28 [b]Prov 20:1; Is 5:11; Hos 4:11 [c]1 Sam 25:19 **38** [a]1 Sam 26:10; 2 Sam 6:7; Ps 104:29

25:19 *did not tell her husband.* Cf. Michal's treatment of Saul (19:11–14).
25:22 *May God do so to the enemies of David, and more also.* See note on 3:17. The sense may be: "As surely as God will punish my (David's) enemies, so surely will I kill every male in Nabal's household."
25:25 *worthless man.* See note on Deut 13:13. *as his name is, so is he.* In ancient times a person's name was believed to reflect his nature and character. *Nabal is his name.* In Hebrew the name Nabal means "fool."
25:26 *as the LORD lives.* See note on 14:39.
25:28 *the LORD will certainly make . . . an enduring house.* While the idea that David was destined to become king in place of Saul may have spread among the general populace, Abigail's assessment of David contrasts sharply with that of her husband (see v. 10). *fighting the battles of the LORD.* Abigail is familiar with David's victories over the Philistines, in which he sought to glorify the Lord rather than advance his own honor (see 17:26,45–47; 18:16–17). *evil will not be found in you.* Abigail shows concern for the preservation of David's integrity in view of the office he was later to assume (see vv. 30–31,39).
25:29 *bound in the bundle of the living.* Using the figure of placing a valuable possession in a carefully wrapped package for safekeeping, Abigail assures David that the Lord will preserve his life in the midst of danger.
25:30 *ruler.* See note on "prince" in 9:16 (same word in Hebrew).
25:31 *shed blood without cause.* See note on v. 28.
25:32 *who sent you.* David recognizes the providential leading of the Lord in his encounter with Abigail (see v. 39).
25:36 *holding a feast.* See Prov 30:21–22. *like the feast of a king.* Another clue that the author is using Nabal as a subtle portrayal of Saul.
25:37 *became as a stone.* Perhaps he suffered a stroke—he who was without moral sensitivity (was a *nabal;* see v. 25 and note) became as senseless as a stone.

David Marries Abigail

39 When David heard that Nabal was
dead, he said, "Blessed be the LORD, who has
[a]pleaded the cause of my reproach from the
hand of Nabal and [b]has kept back His servant from evil. The LORD has also returned
the evildoing of Nabal on his own head."
Then David sent [1c]a proposal to Abigail, to
take her as his wife.
40 When the servants of David came to
Abigail at Carmel, they spoke to her, saying,
"David has sent us to you to take you as his
wife."
41 She arose [a]and bowed with her face to
the ground and said, "Behold, your maidservant is a maid [b]to wash the feet of my lord's
servants."
42 Then [a]Abigail quickly arose, and rode
on a donkey, with her five maidens who
[1]attended her; and she followed the messengers of David and became his wife.
43 David had also taken Ahinoam of [a]Jez-
reel, and [b]they both became his wives.
44 Now Saul had given [a]Michal his
daughter, David's wife, to Palti the son of
Laish, who was from [b]Gallim.

David Again Spares Saul

26 Then the Ziphites came to Saul at Gibeah, saying, "[a]Is not David hiding on the
hill of Hachilah, *which is* before [1]Jeshimon?"
2 So Saul arose and went down to the
wilderness of Ziph, having with him [a]three
thousand chosen men of Israel, to search for
David in the wilderness of Ziph.
3 Saul camped in the hill of Hachilah,
which is before [1]Jeshimon, [a]beside the road,
and David was staying in the wilderness.
When [b]he saw that Saul came after him into
the wilderness,
4 David sent out spies, and he knew that
Saul was definitely coming.
5 David then arose and came to the place
where Saul had camped. And David saw the
place where Saul lay, and [a]Abner the son of
Ner, the commander of his army; and Saul
was lying in the circle of the camp, and the
people were camped around him.
6 Then David said to Ahimelech [a]the Hittite and to [b]Abishai the son of Zeruiah,
Joab's brother, saying, "Who [c]will go down
with me to Saul in the camp?" And Abishai
said, "I will go down with you."
7 So David and Abishai came to the people by night, and behold, Saul lay sleeping
inside the circle of the camp with his spear
stuck in the ground at his head; and Abner
and the people were lying around him.
8 Then Abishai said to David, "Today
God has delivered your enemy into your
hand; now therefore, please let me strike him
with the spear [1]to the ground with one
stroke, and I will not [2]strike him the second
time."
9 But David said to Abishai, "Do not
destroy him, for [a]who can stretch out his
hand against the LORD's anointed and be
without guilt?"
10 David also said, "As the LORD lives,
[a]surely the LORD will strike him, or [b]his day
will come that he dies, or [c]he will go down
into battle and perish.
11 "[a]The LORD forbid that I should stretch
out my hand against the LORD's anointed; but
now please take the spear that is at his head
and the jug of water, and let us go."
12 So David took the spear and the jug of
water from *beside* Saul's head, and they
went away, but no one saw or knew *it*, nor
did any awake, for they were all asleep,
because [a]a sound sleep from the LORD had
fallen on them.
13 Then David crossed over to the other
side and stood on top of the mountain at a
distance *with* a large area between them.
14 David called to the people and to Abner
the son of Ner, saying, "Will you not answer,
Abner?" Then Abner replied, "Who are you
who calls to the king?"
15 So David said to Abner, "Are you not a
man? And who is like you in Israel? Why
then have you not guarded your lord the
king? For one of the people came to destroy
the king your lord.
16 "This thing that you have done is not
good. As the LORD lives, *all* of you [1a]must
surely die, because you did not guard your
lord, the LORD's anointed. And now, see
where the king's spear is and the jug of
water that was at his head."
17 Then Saul recognized David's voice
and said, "[a]Is this your voice, my son

39 [1]Lit *and spoke* [a]1 Sam 24:15; Prov 22:23 [b]1 Sam 25:26, 34 [c]Song 8:8
41 [a]1 Sam 25:23 [b]Mark 1:7
42 [1]Lit *walked at her feet* [a]Gen 24:61-67
43 [a]Josh 15:56 [b]1 Sam 27:3; 30:5
44 [a]1 Sam 18:27; 2 Sam 3:14 [b]Is 10:30
26:1 [1]Or *the desert* [a]1 Sam 23:19; Ps 54: title
2 [a]1 Sam 13:2; 24:2
3 [1]Or *the desert* [a]1 Sam 24:3 [b]1 Sam 23:15
5 [a]1 Sam 14:50, 51; 17:55
6 [a]Gen 23:3; 26:34; Josh 3:10; 1 Kin 10:29; 2 Kin 7:6 [b]1 Chr 2:16 [c]Judg 7:10, 11
8 [1]Lit *even into* [2]Lit *repeat with respect to him*
9 [a]1 Sam 24:6, 7; 2 Sam 1:14, 16
10 [a]Deut 32:35; 1 Sam 25:26, 38; Rom 12:19; Heb 10:30 [b]Gen 47:29; Deut 31:14; Ps 37:13 [c]1 Sam 31:6
11 [a]1 Sam 24:6, 12; Rom 12:17, 19; 1 Pet 3:9
12 [a]Gen 2:21; 15:12; Is 29:10
16 [1]Lit *are surely sons of death* [a]1 Sam 20:31
17 [a]1 Sam 24:16

25:43 *Ahinoam.* David's first wife (see 27:3; 30:5; 2 Sam 2:2) and mother of his first son, Amnon (see 2 Sam 3:2). *Jezreel.* Located near Carmel (see v. 2; Josh 15:55) and not to be confused with the northern town of the same name, where Israel camped against the Philistines (see 29:1,11) and where Ahab resided in later times (see 1 Kin 18:45–46).
25:44 *Michal . . . David's wife.* See 18:27.
26:1 *Ziphites.* See 23:19; see also note on 23:14. *Gibeah.* Saul's residence (see 10:26).
26:2 *three thousand.* Apparently Saul's standing army (see 24:2).
26:5 *lay.* David arrived at Saul's camp during the night when the men were sleeping. *Abner.* Saul's cousin (see 14:50).
26:6 *Ahimelech the Hittite.* Not referred to elsewhere. Hittites had long resided in Canaan (see note on Gen 10:15; see also Gen 15:20; 23:3–20; Deut 7:1; 20:17). Another Hittite in David's service was Uriah (see 2 Sam 11:3; 23:39). *Abishai the son of Zeruiah, Joab's brother.* Zeruiah was an older sister of David (1 Chr 2:16), so Abishai and Joab (and their brother Asahel, 2 Sam 2:18) were David's nephews as well as trusted military leaders. Joab would long serve as the commander of his army.
26:9 See note on 24:6.
26:10 *As the LORD lives.* See note on 14:39.
26:12 *David took the spear and the jug of water.* In this way he sought to prove again to Saul that he did not seek his life.

David?" And David said, "It is my voice, my
lord the king."
18 He also said, "[a]Why then is my lord
pursuing his servant? For what have I done?
Or what evil is in my hand?
19 "Now therefore, please let my lord the
king listen to the words of his servant. If [a]the
LORD has stirred you up against me, [b]let Him
[1]accept an offering; but [c]if it is [2]men, cursed
are they before the LORD, for [d]they have driv-
en me out today so that I would have no
attachment with the inheritance of the LORD,
saying, 'Go, serve other gods.'
20 "Now then, do not let my blood fall to
the ground away from the presence of the
LORD; for the king of Israel has come out to
search for [a]a single flea, just as one hunts a
partridge in the mountains."
21 Then Saul said, "[a]I have sinned.
Return, my son David, for I will not harm
you again because my life was precious in
your sight this day. Behold, I have played the
fool and have committed a serious error."

18 [a]1 Sam 24:9, 11-14
19 [1]Lit *smell* [2]Lit *sons of men* [a]2 Sam 16:11 [b]Gen 8:21 [c]1 Sam 24:9 [d]Josh 22:25-27
20 [a]1 Sam 24:14
21 [a]Ex 9:27; 1 Sam 15:24, 30; 24:17
23 [a]1 Sam 24:19; Ps 7:8; 18:20; 62:12 [b]1 Sam 24:12
24 [a]1 Sam 18:30 [b]Ps 54:7
25 [a]1 Sam 24:19 [b]1 Sam 24:22
27:1 [1]Lit *in his heart* [2]Lit *that I should surely escape* [a]1 Sam 26:19

22 David replied, "Behold the spear of the
king! Now let one of the young men come
over and take it.
23 "[a]The LORD will repay each man *for* his
righteousness and his faithfulness; for the
LORD delivered you into *my* hand today, but
[b]I refused to stretch out my hand against the
LORD's anointed.
24 "Now behold, as your life was [a]highly
valued in my sight this day, so may my life
be highly valued in the sight of the LORD, and
may He [b]deliver me from all distress."
25 Then Saul said to David, "[a]Blessed are
you, my son David; you will both accomplish much and surely prevail." So [b]David
went on his way, and Saul returned to his
place.

David Flees to the Philistines

27 Then David said [1]to himself, "Now I
will perish one day by the hand of Saul.
[a]There is nothing better for me than [2]to
escape into the land of the Philistines. Saul

26:19 *let Him accept an offering.* David knows no reason why God should be angry with him; but if for some reason God is behind Saul's determined effort to kill him, David appeals for God to accept an offering of appeasement (cf. 16:5)—in any event, to let the matter be settled between David and God, without Saul's involvement. *cursed are they before the LORD.* David commits any such men to the judgment of God. *the inheritance of the LORD.* See note on 10:1. David appeals to Saul's conscience by describing his present exclusion from the fellowship of God's people and from living at peace in the Lord's land. *Go, serve other gods.* In their view, to be expelled from the Lord's land was to be separated from the Lord's sanctuary (an OT form of excommunication) and left to serve the gods of whatever land one may settle in (see Josh 22:24–27).

26:20 *search for a . . . flea.* See 24:14. David suggests that Saul is making a fool of himself in his fanatical pursuit of an innocent and undesigning man.

26:21 *I have sinned.* See 24:17. *I have played the fool.* Saul confesses that his behavior has been not only unwise but also ungodly (see notes on 13:13; 25:2–44).

26:23 *I refused to stretch out my hand against the LORD's anointed.* See v. 9 and note on 24:6.

26:25 *you will . . . prevail.* Saul makes a veiled reference to his own conviction that David will replace him as king (see 24:20).

27:1 *I will perish . . . by the hand of Saul.* David falters in his faith (see 23:14; 25:29) and under pressure of Saul's superior forces feels compelled to seek security outside Israel's borders. *land of the Philistines.* For the second time David seeks refuge

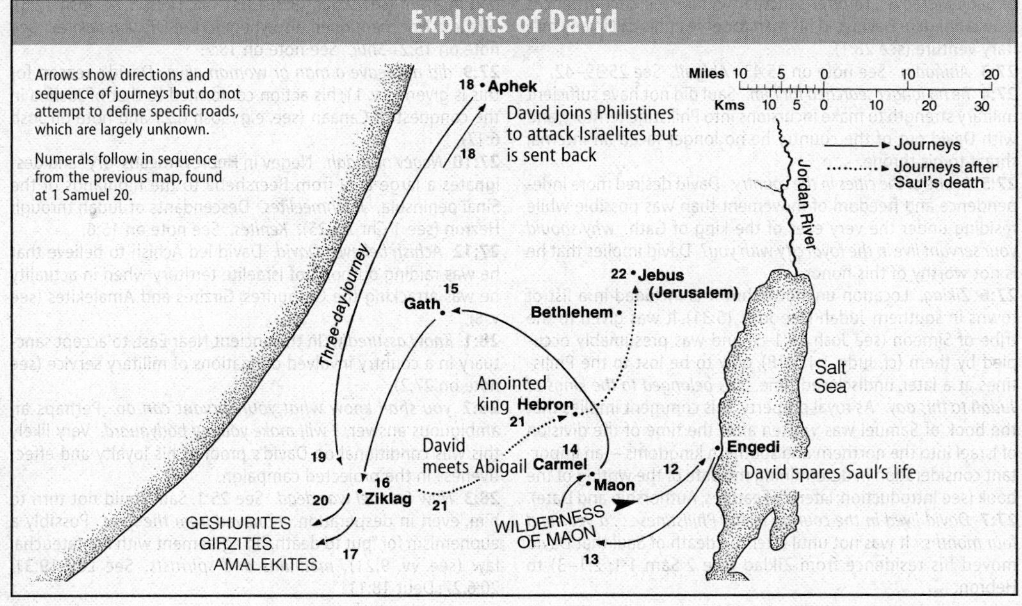
Exploits of David
Arrows show directions and sequence of journeys but do not attempt to define specific roads, which are largely unknown.
Numerals follow in sequence from the previous map, found at 1 Samuel 20.
18 • Aphek
David joins Philistines to attack Israelites but is sent back
18
Miles 10 5 0 10 20
Kms 10 5 0 10 20 30
Journeys
Journeys after Saul's death
Jordan River
Three-day-journey
22 • Jebus (Jerusalem)
15
Gath
Bethlehem
Salt Sea
Anointed king Hebron
21
David meets Abigail
Carmel
14
Maon
19
16
Ziklag
20
21
12
Engedi
David spares Saul's life
GESHURITES
GIRZITES
AMALEKITES
17
WILDERNESS OF MAON
13

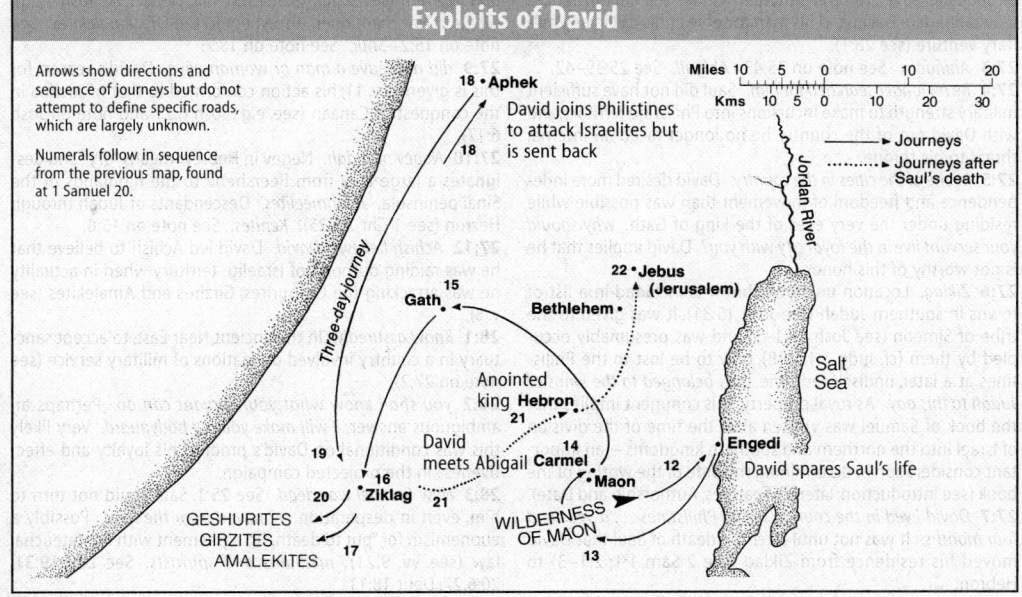

then will despair of searching for me anymore in all the territory of Israel, and I will
escape from his hand."
2 So David arose and crossed over, he and
[a]the six hundred men who were with him, to
[b]Achish the son of Maoch, king of Gath.
3 And David lived with Achish at Gath,
he and his men, [a]each with his household,
even David with [b]his two wives, Ahinoam
the Jezreelitess, and Abigail the Carmelitess,
Nabal's [1]widow.
4 Now it was told Saul that David had
fled to Gath, so he no longer searched for
him.
5 Then David said to Achish, "If now I
have found favor in your sight, let them give
me a place in one of the cities in the country,
that I may live there; for why should your
servant live in the royal city with you?"
6 So Achish gave him Ziklag that day;
therefore [a]Ziklag has belonged to the kings
of Judah to this day.
7 The number of days that David lived in
the country of the Philistines was [a]a year
and four months.
8 Now David and his men went up and
raided [a]the Geshurites and the Girzites and
[b]the Amalekites; for they were the inhabitants of the land from ancient times, as you
come to [c]Shur even as far as the land of
Egypt.
9 David [1]attacked the land and did not
leave a man or a woman alive, and he [a]took
away the sheep, the cattle, the donkeys, the

2 [a]1 Sam 25:13 [b]1 Sam 21:10; 1 Kin 2:39
3 [1]Lit *wife* [a]1 Sam 30:3; 2 Sam 2:3 [b]1 Sam 25:42, 43
6 [a]Josh 15:31; 19:5; Neh 11:28
7 [a]1 Sam 29:3
8 [a]Josh 13:2, 13 [b]Ex 17:8; 1 Sam 15:7, 8 [c]Ex 15:22
9 [1]Lit *smote* [a]1 Sam 15:3; Job 1:3
10 [1]I.e. South country [a]1 Sam 23:27 [b]1 Sam 30:29; 1 Chr 2:9, 25 [c]Judg 1:16; 4:11
28:1 [a]1 Sam 29:1
2 [1]Lit *keeper of my head* [a]1 Sam 1:22, 28
3 [a]1 Sam 25:1 [b]1 Sam 7:17 [c]Lev 19:31; 20:27; Deut 18:10; 1 Sam 15:23

camels, and the clothing. Then he returned
and came to Achish.
10 Now Achish said, "Where have you
[a]made a raid today?" And David said,
"Against the [1]Negev of Judah and against the
[1]Negev of [b]the Jerahmeelites and against the
[1]Negev of [c]the Kenites."
11 David did not leave a man or a woman
alive to bring to Gath, saying, "Otherwise
they will tell about us, saying, 'So has David
done and so *has been* his practice all the
time he has lived in the country of the Philistines.' "
12 So Achish believed David, saying, "He
has surely made himself odious among his
people Israel; therefore he will become my
servant forever."

Saul and the Spirit Medium

28 Now it came about in those days that
[a]the Philistines gathered their armed
camps for war, to fight against Israel. And
Achish said to David, "Know assuredly that
you will go out with me in the camp, you
and your men."
2 David said to Achish, "Very well, you
shall know what your servant can do." So
Achish said to David, "Very well, I will make
you [1]my bodyguard [a]for life."
3 Now [a]Samuel was dead, and all Israel
had lamented him and buried him [b]in
Ramah, his own city. And Saul had removed
from the land those who [c]were mediums and
spiritists.

in the land of the Philistines (see 21:10–15).

27:2 *Achish . . . king of Gath.* See 21:10. In contrast to David's previous excursion into Philistia, Achish is now ready to receive him because he has become known as a formidable adversary of Saul. Moreover, to offer sanctuary under the circumstances would obligate David and his men to serve at his call in any military venture (see 28:1).

27:3 *Ahinoam.* See note on 25:43. *Abigail.* See 25:39–42.

27:4 *he no longer searched for him.* Saul did not have sufficient military strength to make incursions into Philistine territory, and with David out of the country he no longer faced an internal threat to his throne.

27:5 *in one of the cities in the country.* David desired more independence and freedom of movement than was possible while residing under the very eyes of the king of Gath. *why should your servant live in the royal city with you?* David implies that he is not worthy of this honor.

27:6 *Ziklag.* Location unknown, but it is included in a list of towns in southern Judah (see Josh 15:31). It was given to the tribe of Simeon (see Josh 19:1–5) and was presumably occupied by them (cf. Judg 1:17–18), only to be lost to the Philistines at a later, undisclosed time. *has belonged to the kings of Judah to this day.* As royal property. This comment implies that the book of Samuel was written after the time of the division of Israel into the northern and southern kingdoms—an important consideration in determining the date of the writing of the book (see Introduction: Literary Features, Authorship and Date).

27:7 *David lived in the country of the Philistines . . . a year and four months.* It was not until after the death of Saul that David moved his residence from Ziklag (see 2 Sam 1:1; 2:1–3) to Hebron.

27:8 *Geshurites.* A people residing in the area south of Philistia who were not defeated by the Israelites at the time of the conquest (see Josh 13:1–3) and who are to be distinguished from the Geshurites residing in the north near the upper Jordan in Aram (see 2 Sam 3:3; 13:37–38; Deut 3:14; Josh 12:5). *Girzites.* Not mentioned elsewhere in the OT. *Amalekites.* See note on 15:2. *Shur.* See note on 15:7.

27:9 *did not leave a man or woman alive.* David's reason for this is given in v. 11; his action conformed to that of Joshua in the conquest of Canaan (see, e.g., Josh 6:21 and note on Josh 6:17).

27:10 *Negev of Judah.* Negev in Hebrew means "dry" and designates a large area from Beersheba to the highlands of the Sinai peninsula. *Jerahmeelites.* Descendants of Judah through Hezron (see 1 Chr 2:9,25). *Kenites.* See note on 15:6.

27:12 *Achish believed David.* David led Achish to believe that he was raiding outposts of Israelite territory when in actuality he was attacking the Geshurites, Girzites and Amalekites (see v. 8).

28:1 *Know assuredly.* In the ancient Near East, to accept sanctuary in a country involved obligations of military service (see note on 27:2).

28:2 *you shall know what your servant can do.* Perhaps an ambiguous answer. *I will make you my bodyguard.* Very likely this was conditional on David's proof of his loyalty and effectiveness in the projected campaign.

28:3 *Now Samuel was dead.* See 25:1. Saul could not turn to him, even in desperation. *removed from the land.* Possibly a euphemism for "put to death," in agreement with Pentateuchal law (see vv. 9,21). *mediums and spiritists.* See Lev 19:31; 20:6,27; Deut 18:11.

4 So the Philistines gathered together and came and camped [a]in Shunem; and Saul gathered all Israel together and they camped in [b]Gilboa.

5 When Saul saw the camp of the Philistines, he was afraid and his heart trembled greatly.

6 [a]When Saul inquired of the LORD, [b]the LORD did not answer him, either by [c]dreams or by [d]Urim or by prophets.

7 Then Saul said to his servants, "Seek for me a woman who is a medium, that I may go to her and inquire of her." And his servants said to him, "Behold, [a]there is a woman who is a medium at [b]En-dor."

8 Then Saul [a]disguised himself by putting on other clothes, and went, he and two men with him, and they came to the woman by night; and he said, "[b]Conjure up for me, please, and [c]bring up for me whom I shall [1]name to you."

9 But the woman said to him, "Behold, you know [a]what Saul has done, how he has cut off those who are mediums and spiritists from the land. Why are you then laying a snare for my life to bring about my death?"

10 Saul vowed to her by the LORD, saying, "As the LORD lives, no punishment shall come upon you for this thing."

11 Then the woman said, "Whom shall I bring up for you?" And he said, "Bring up Samuel for me."

12 When the woman saw Samuel, she cried out with a loud voice; and the woman spoke to Saul, saying, "Why have you deceived me? For you are Saul."

13 The king said to her, "Do not be afraid; but what do you see?" And the woman said to Saul, "I see a [1]divine being coming up out of the earth."

14 He said to her, "What is his form?" And she said, "An old man is coming up, and [a]he is wrapped with a robe." And Saul knew that it was Samuel, and [b]he bowed with his face to the ground and did homage.

15 Then Samuel said to Saul, "Why have you disturbed me by bringing me up?" And Saul answered, "I am greatly distressed; for the Philistines are waging war against me, and [a]God has departed from me and [b]no longer answers me, either through prophets or by dreams; therefore I have called you, that you may make known to me what I should do."

16 Samuel said, "Why then do you ask me, since the LORD has departed from you and has become your adversary?

17 "The LORD has done [1]accordingly [a]as He spoke through me; for the LORD has torn the kingdom out of your hand and given it to your neighbor, to David.

18 "As [a]you did not [1]obey the LORD and did not execute His fierce wrath on Amalek, so the LORD has done this thing to you this day.

19 "Moreover the LORD will also give over Israel along with you into the hands of the Philistines, therefore tomorrow [a]you and your sons will be with me. Indeed the LORD will give over the army of Israel into the hands of the Philistines!"

20 Then Saul immediately fell full length upon the ground and was very afraid because of the words of Samuel; also there was no strength in him, for he had eaten no [1]food all day and all night.

21 The woman came to Saul and saw that he was terrified, and said to him, "Behold, your maidservant has [1]obeyed you, and [a]I have [2]taken my life in my hand and have listened to your words which you spoke to me.

4 [a]Josh 19:18; 1 Sam 28:4; 1 Kin 1:3; 2 Kin 4:8 [b]1 Sam 31:1
6 [a]1 Chr 10:13, 14 [b]1 Sam 14:37; Prov 1:24-31 [c]Num 12:6; Joel 2:28 [d]Ex 28:30; Num 27:21
7 [a]Acts 16:16 [b]Josh 17:11; Ps 83:10
8 [1]Lit *say* [a]2 Chr 18:29; 35:22 [b]1 Chr 10:13; Is 8:19 [c]Deut 18:10, 11
9 [a]1 Sam 28:3
13 [1]Or *god*
14 [a]1 Sam 15:27 [b]1 Sam 24:8
15 [a]1 Sam 16:14; 18:12 [b]1 Sam 28:6
17 [1]Lit *for himself* [a]1 Sam 15:28
18 [1]Lit *listen to the voice of* [a]1 Sam 15:20, 26; 1 Kin 20:42
19 [a]1 Sam 31:2; Job 3:17-19
20 [1]Lit *bread*
21 [1]Lit *listened to your voice* [2]Lit *put* [a]Judg 12:3; 1 Sam 19:5; Job 13:14

28:4 *Shunem.* The Philistines assembled their forces far to the north, along the plain of Jezreel in the territory of Issachar (see Josh 19:18). *Gilboa.* A range of mountains east of the plain of Jezreel.

28:5 *his heart trembled greatly.* Because he is estranged from the Lord and is not performing his role as the true theocratic king (see note on 17:11).

28:6 *Saul inquired of the LORD.* Presumably through the agency of a priest. Saul seems to sense disaster in the approaching battle and seeks divine revelation concerning its outcome. *dreams.* Direct personal revelation (see Num 12:6 and note). *Urim.* Revelation through the priest (see note on 2:28). Since the authentic ephod and its Urim were with Abiathar, who was aligned with David (see 23:2,6,9), either Saul had fabricated another ephod for his use or the author used a conventional statement including the three visual forms of revelation to underscore his point. *prophets.* David had a prophet (Gad, 22:5), but after Samuel's alienation from Saul (15:35) no prophet served Saul.

28:7 *Seek for me a woman who is a medium.* In his desperation Saul turns to a pagan practice that he himself had previously outlawed (v. 3) in accordance with the Mosaic law (see Lev 19:26,31). *En-dor.* Located about six miles northwest of Shunem (see v. 4; Josh 17:11).

28:9 *Why are you then laying a snare for my life . . .?* The woman is very cautious about practicing her trade with strangers lest she be betrayed to Saul (see note on v. 3).

28:10 *As the LORD lives.* See note on 14:39.

28:12 *When the woman saw Samuel.* The episode has been understood in many different ways, among them the following: 1. God permitted the spirit of Samuel to appear to the woman. 2. The woman had contact with an evil or devilish spirit in the form of Samuel by whom she was deceived and controlled. 3. By using parapsychological powers such as telepathy or clairvoyance, the woman was able to discern Saul's thoughts and picture Samuel in her own mind. Whatever the explanation of this mysterious affair, the medium was used in some way to convey to Saul that the impending battle would bring death, would dash his hopes for a dynasty and would conclude his reign with a devastating defeat of Israel that would leave the nation at the mercy of the Philistines, the very people against whom he had struggled all his years as king. And this would come, as Samuel had previously announced (15:26,28), because of his unfaithfulness to the Lord. *she cried out . . . you are Saul.* By whatever means, the medium suddenly becomes aware that she is dealing with Saul.

28:14 *An old man . . . wrapped with a robe.* Saul remembers Samuel as customarily dressed in this apparel (see 15:27).

28:21 *The woman came to Saul.* This statement suggests that the woman removed herself from the direct view of Saul while she gave her oracles.

22 "So now also, please listen to the voice of your maidservant, and let me set a piece of bread before you that *you may* eat and have strength when you go on *your* way."

23 But he refused and said, "[a]I will not eat." [b]However, his servants together with the woman urged him, and he listened to [1]them. So he arose from the ground and sat on [c]the bed.

24 The woman had a [a]fattened calf in the house, and she quickly slaughtered it; and she [b]took flour, kneaded it and baked unleavened bread from it.

25 She brought *it* before Saul and his servants, and they ate. Then they arose and went away that night.

The Philistines Mistrust David

29 Now [a]the Philistines gathered together all their armies to [b]Aphek, while the Israelites were camping by the spring which is in [c]Jezreel.

2 And the lords of the Philistines were proceeding on by hundreds and by thousands, and [a]David and his men were proceeding on in the rear with Achish.

3 Then the commanders of the Philistines said, "What *are* these Hebrews *doing here?*" And Achish said to the commanders of the Philistines, "Is this not David, the servant of Saul the king of Israel, [a]who has been with me these days, or *rather* these years, and [b]I have found no fault in him from the day he [1]deserted *to me* to this day?"

4 But the commanders of the Philistines were angry with him, and the commanders of the Philistines said to him, "Make the man go back, that he may return [a]to his place where you have assigned him, and do not let him go down to battle with us, [b]or in the battle he may become an adversary to us. For with what could this *man* make himself acceptable to his lord? *Would it* not *be* with the heads of [1]these men?

5 "Is this not David, [a]of whom they sing in the dances, saying,

'Saul has slain his thousands,
And David his ten thousands'?"

6 Then Achish called David and said to him, "*As* the LORD lives, you *have been* upright, and [a]your going out and your coming in with me in the army are pleasing in my sight; [b]for I have not found evil in you from the day of your coming to me to this day. Nevertheless, you are not pleasing in the sight of the lords.

7 "Now therefore return and go in peace, that you may not displease the lords of the Philistines."

8 David said to Achish, "[a]But what have I done? And what have you found in your servant from the day when I came before you to this day, that I may not go and fight against the enemies of my lord the king?"

9 But Achish replied to David, "I know that you are pleasing in my sight, [a]like an angel of God; nevertheless [b]the commanders of the Philistines have said, 'He must not go up with us to the battle.'

10 "Now then arise early in the morning [a]with the servants of your lord who have come with you, and as soon as you have arisen early in the morning and have light, depart."

11 So David arose early, he and his men, to depart in the morning to return to the land of the Philistines. And the Philistines went up to Jezreel.

David's Victory over the Amalekites

30 Then it happened when David and his men came to [a]Ziklag on the third day, that [b]the Amalekites had made a raid on the [1]Negev and on [c]Ziklag, and had [2]overthrown Ziklag and burned it with fire;

2 and they took captive the women *and all* who were in it, both small and great, [1][a]without killing anyone, and carried *them* off and went their way.

3 When David and his men came to the city, behold, it was burned with fire, and their wives and their sons and their daughters had been taken captive.

4 Then David and the people who were with him [a]lifted their voices and wept until there was no strength in them to weep.

5 Now [a]David's two wives had been tak-

23 [1]Lit *their voices* [a]1 Kin 21:4 [b]2 Kin 5:13 [c]Esth 1:6; Ezek 23:41
24 [a]Gen 18:7; Luke 15:23, 27, 30 [b]Gen 18:6
29:1 [a]1 Sam 28:1 [b]Josh 12:18; 19:30; 1 Sam 4:1; 1 Kin 20:30 [c]1 Kin 21:1; 2 Kin 9:30
2 [a]1 Sam 28:1, 2
3 [1]Lit *fell* [a]1 Sam 27:7 [b]1 Sam 27:1-6; 1 Chr 12:19, 20; Dan 6:5
4 [1]Lit *those* [a]1 Sam 27:6 [b]1 Sam 14:21
5 [a]1 Sam 18:7; 21:11
6 [a]2 Sam 3:25; 2 Kin 19:27; Is 37:28 [b]1 Sam 27:8-12; 29:3
8 [a]1 Sam 27:10-12
9 [a]2 Sam 14:17, 20; 19:27 [b]1 Sam 29:4
10 [a]1 Chr 12:19, 22
30:1 [1]I.e. South country [2]Lit *smote* [a]1 Sam 29:4, 11 [b]1 Sam 15:7; 27:8-10 [c]1 Sam 27:6, 8
2 [1]Lit *they did not kill* [a]1 Sam 27:11
4 [a]Num 14:1
5 [a]1 Sam 25:42, 43; 2 Sam 2:2

29:1 *the Philistines gathered . . . all their armies.* The narrative flow broken at 28:2 is resumed. *Aphek.* A place in the vicinity of Shunem (28:4), to be distinguished from another place of the same name referred to in 4:1 (see 1 Kin 20:26,30; 2 Kin 13:17).
29:2 *lords of the Philistines.* See note on 5:8.
29:3 *I have found no fault in him.* David's tactics described in 27:10–12 were highly successful.
29:4 *place where you have assigned him.* See 27:6. *in the battle he may become an adversary to us.* The Philistines had experienced just such a reversal on a previous occasion (see 14:21).
29:6 *As the LORD lives.* See note on 14:39. Achish swears by the God of Israel apparently as a means of proving his sincerity to David.
29:8 *But what have I done?* David pretends disappointment in order to keep intact his strategy of deception. In reality this turn of events rescued David from a serious dilemma. *what have you found . . . that I may not go and fight against the enemies of my lord the king?* David again uses an ambiguous statement (see 28:2). To whom was he referring as "my lord the king"—Achish or Saul or the Lord?
29:9 *like an angel of God.* A common simile.
29:11 *Jezreel.* The place of Israel's camp (see v. 1).
30:1–31:13 While Saul goes to his death at the hands of the Philistines, David is drawn into and pursues the Lord's continuing war with the Amalekites (see 15:2–3 and notes).
30:1 *Ziklag.* See note on 27:6. *Amalekites.* See 27:8 and note on 15:2. The absence of David and his warriors gave the Amalekites opportunity for revenge. *Negev.* See note on 27:10.

en captive, Ahinoam the Jezreelitess and
Abigail the [1]widow of Nabal the Carmelite.
6 Moreover David was greatly distressed
because [a]the people spoke of stoning him,
for all the people were [1]embittered, each one
because of his sons and his daughters. But
[b]David strengthened himself in the LORD his
God.
7 Then [a]David said to [b]Abiathar the
priest, the son of Ahimelech, "Please bring
me the ephod." So Abiathar brought the
ephod to David.
8 [a]David inquired of the LORD, saying,
"[b]Shall I pursue this band? Shall I overtake
them?" And He said to him, "Pursue, for you
will surely overtake them, [c]and you will
surely rescue *all*."
9 So David went, [a]he and the six hundred men who were with him, and came to
the brook Besor, *where* those left behind
remained.
10 But David pursued, he and four hundred men, for [a]two hundred who were too
exhausted to cross the brook Besor remained
behind.
11 Now they found an Egyptian in the
field and brought him to David, and gave
him bread and he ate, and they provided him
water to drink.
12 They gave him a piece of fig cake and
two clusters of raisins, and he ate; [a]then his
spirit [1]revived. For he had not eaten bread or
drunk water for three days and three nights.
13 David said to him, "To whom do you
belong? And where are you from?" And he
said, "I am a young man of Egypt, a servant
of an Amalekite; and my master left me
behind when I fell sick three days ago.
14 "We made a raid on [a]the [1]Negev of the
Cherethites, and on that which belongs to
Judah, and on [b]the [1]Negev of Caleb, and [c]we
burned Ziklag with fire."
15 Then David said to him, "Will you
bring me down to this band?" And he said,
"Swear to me by God that you will not kill
me or deliver me into the hands of my master, and I will bring you down to this band."
16 When he had brought him down,
behold, they were [1]spread over all the land,
[a]eating and drinking and [2]dancing because
of [b]all the great spoil that they had taken
from the land of the Philistines and from the
land of Judah.
17 David [1]slaughtered them [a]from the twilight [2]until the evening of [3]the next day; and
not a man of them escaped, except four hundred young men who rode on [b]camels and
fled.
18 So David [a]recovered all that the Amalekites had taken, and [1]rescued his two wives.
19 But nothing of theirs was missing,
whether small or great, sons or daughters,
spoil or anything that they had taken for
themselves; [a]David brought *it* all back.
20 So David had [1]captured all the sheep
and the cattle *which the people* drove ahead
of [2]the *other* livestock, and they said, "[a]This
is David's spoil."

The Spoils Are Divided

21 When [a]David came to the two hundred
men who were too exhausted to follow David,
who had also been left at the brook Besor, and
they went out to meet David and to meet the
people who were with him, then David
approached the people and greeted them.
22 Then all the wicked and worthless men
among those who went with David said,
"Because they did not go with [1]us, we will
not give them any of the spoil that we have
recovered, except to every man his wife and
his children, that they may lead *them* away
and depart."
23 Then David said, "You must not do so,
my brothers, with what the LORD has given
us, who has kept us and delivered into our
hand the band that came against us.
24 "And who will listen to you in this matter? For [a]as his share is who goes down to
the battle, so shall his share be who stays by
the baggage; they shall share alike."
25 So it has been from that day forward,
that he made it a statute and an ordinance
for Israel to this day.
26 Now when David came to Ziklag, he
sent *some* of the spoil to the elders of Judah,
to his friends, saying, "Behold, [a]a [1]gift for you
from the spoil of [b]the enemies of the LORD:
27 to those who were in [a]Bethel, and to
those who were in [b]Ramoth of the [1]Negev,
and to those who were in [c]Jattir,
28 and to those who were in [a]Aroer, and
to those who were in Siphmoth, and to those
who were in [b]Eshtemoa,
29 and to those who were in Racal, and to
those who were in the cities of [a]the Jerahmeelites, and to those who were in the cities
of [b]the Kenites,

5 [1]Lit *wife*
6 [1]Lit *bitter in soul* [a]Ex 17:4; John 8:59 [b]1 Sam 23:16; Ps 18:2; 27:14; 31:24; 71:4, 5; Rom 4:20
7 [a]1 Sam 23:6, 9 [b]1 Sam 22:20-23
8 [a]1 Sam 23:2, 4; Ps 50:15; 91:15 [b]Ex 15:9 [c]1 Sam 30:18
9 [a]1 Sam 27:2
10 [a]1 Sam 30:9, 21
12 [1]Lit *returned to him* [a]Judg 15:19
14 [1]I.e. South country [a]1 Sam 30:1, 16; 2 Sam 8:18; 1 Kin 1:38, 44; Ezek 25:16; Zeph 2:5 [b]Josh 14:13; 15:13; 21:12 [c]1 Sam 30:1
16 [1]Lit *left* [2]Lit *keeping a pilgrim-feast* [a]Luke 12:19; 17:27f [b]1 Sam 30:14
17 [1]Lit *smote* [a]1 Sam 11:11
17 [2]Lit *even until* [3]Lit *their* [b]Judg 7:12; 1 Sam 15:3
18 [1]Lit *David rescued* [a]Gen 14:16
19 [a]1 Sam 30:8
20 [1]Lit *taken* [2]Lit *those livestock* [a]1 Sam 30:26-31
21 [a]1 Sam 30:10
22 [1]Lit *me*
24 [a]Num 31:27; Josh 22:8
26 [1]Lit *blessing* [a]1 Sam 25:27 [b]1 Sam 18:17; 25:28
27 [1]I.e. South country [a]Gen 12:8; Josh 7:2; 8:9; 16:1 [b]Josh 19:8 [c]Josh 15:48; 21:14
28 [a]Josh 13:16; 1 Chr 11:44 [b]Josh 15:50
29 [a]1 Sam 27:10 [b]Judg 1:16; 1 Sam 15:6

30:5 *Ahinoam.* See note on 25:43. *Abigail.* See 25:42.
30:7 *Abiathar the priest.* See note on 22:20. *ephod.* See note on 2:28.
30:14 *Negev.* See note on 27:10. *Cherethites.* Along with the Pelethites, they later contributed contingents of professional warriors to David's private army (see 2 Sam 15:18; 20:7; 1 Kin 1:38). The name may indicate that they originally came from the island of Crete (see note on "Caphtor" in Jer 47:4). *Negev of Caleb.* The area south of Hebron (see Josh 14:13).
30:22 *worthless men.* See note on Deut 13:13.
30:23 *what the LORD has given us.* David gently but firmly rejects the idea that their victory is to be attributed to their own prowess. Because the Lord gave the victory, no segment of David's men could claim any greater right to the spoils than any other.
30:26 *elders of Judah . . . his friends.* David sent the plunder as an expression of gratitude to those who had assisted him during his flight from Saul (see v. 31), thus preparing the way for his later elevation to kingship in Judah (see 2 Sam 2:1–4).
30:29 *Jerahmeelites.* See note on 27:10. *Kenites.* See note on 15:6.

30 and to those who were in [a]Hormah,
and to those who were in [b]Bor-ashan, and to
those who were in Athach,
31 and to those who were in [a]Hebron, and
to all the places where David himself and his
men were accustomed to [b]go."

Saul and His Sons Slain

31 [a]Now the Philistines were fighting
against Israel, and the men of Israel
fled from before the Philistines and fell slain
[b]on Mount Gilboa.
2 The Philistines overtook Saul and his
sons; and the Philistines [1]killed [a]Jonathan
and Abinadab and Malchi-shua the sons of
Saul.
3 [a]The battle went heavily against Saul,
and the archers [1]hit him; and he was badly
wounded by the archers.
4 [a]Then Saul said to his armor bearer,
"Draw your sword and pierce me through
with it, otherwise [b]these uncircumcised will
come and pierce me through and make sport
of me." But his armor bearer would not, for
he was greatly afraid. [c]So Saul took his
sword and fell on it.
5 When his armor bearer saw that Saul
was dead, he also fell on his sword and died
with him.
6 Thus Saul died with his three sons, his
armor bearer, and all his men on that day
together.
7 When the men of Israel who were on the
other side of the valley, with those who were
beyond the Jordan, saw that the men of Israel
had fled and that Saul and his sons were dead,
they abandoned the cities and fled; then the
Philistines came and lived in them.
8 It came about on the [1]next day when
the Philistines came to strip the slain, that
they found Saul and his three sons fallen on
Mount Gilboa.
9 They cut off his head and stripped off his
weapons, and sent *them* [1]throughout the land
of the Philistines, [a]to carry the good news [b]to
the house of their idols and to the people.
10 They put his weapons in the [1]temple of
[a]Ashtaroth, and [b]they fastened his body to
the wall of [c]Beth-shan.
11 Now when [a]the inhabitants of Jabesh-
gilead heard [1]what the Philistines had done
to Saul,
12 [a]all the valiant men rose and walked all
night, and took the body of Saul and the
bodies of his sons from the wall of Beth-
shan, and they came to Jabesh and [b]burned
them there.
13 They took their bones and [a]buried
them under [b]the tamarisk tree at Jabesh, and
[c]fasted seven days.

30 [a]Num 14:45; 21:3; Josh 12:14; 15:30; 19:4; Judg 1:17 [b]Josh 15:42; 19:7
31 [a]Num 13:22; Josh 14:13-15; 21:11-13; 2 Sam 2:1 [b]1 Sam 23:22
31:1 [a]1 Chr 10:1-12 [b]1 Sam 28:4
2 [1]Lit *smote* [a]1 Chr 8:33f
3 [1]Lit *found* [a]2 Sam 1:6
4 [a]Judg 9:54; 1 Chr 10:4 [b]Judg 14:3; 1 Sam 14:6; 17:26, 36 [c]2 Sam 1:6, 10
8 [1]Lit *morrow*
9 [1]Lit *into...around* [a]2 Sam 1:20 [b]Judg 16:23, 24
10 [1]Lit *house* [a]Judg 2:13; 1 Sam 7:3 [b]1 Sam 31:12; 2 Sam 21:12 [c]Josh 17:11
11 [1]Lit *about him what* [a]1 Sam 11:1-13
12 [a]2 Sam 2:4-7 [b]2 Chr 16:14
13 [a]2 Sam 21:12-14 [b]1 Sam 22:6 [c]2 Sam 1:12

30:31 *Hebron.* The most important city in the southern part of Judah. The other locations mentioned are to the southwest and southeast of Hebron.
31:2 *Jonathan and Abinadab and Malki-shua.* See note on 14:49. The surviving son, Ish-bosheth or Eshbaal (1 Chr 8:33; 9:39), was afterward promoted by Abner, who somehow survived the battle, to succeed his father as king (2 Sam 2:8–9).
31:4 *uncircumcised.* See 14:6 and note. *make sport of me.* A practice that was not uncommon; previously the Philistines had mutilated and humiliated Samson after his capture (see Judg 16:23–25). *took his sword and fell on it.* The culmination of a long process of self-destruction.
31:6 *all his men.* Those who had served around him in his administration (but see note on v. 2).
31:9 *They cut off his head.* David had done the same to Goliath (see 17:51). *sent them throughout the land.* Saul's head and armor served as proof and trophies of their victory.
31:10 *They put his weapons in the temple.* Symbolic of ascribing the victory to the Philistine gods.
31:11 *Jabesh-gilead.* See note on 11:1.
31:12 *took the body of Saul and . . . his sons.* The men of Jabesh-gilead had not forgotten how Saul had come to their defense when they were threatened by the Ammonites (see ch. 11). *burned them.* Cremation was not customary in ancient Israel and here appears to have been done to prevent any further abuse of the bodies of Saul and his sons by the Philistines.
31:13 *took their bones and buried them.* David later had their remains removed from Jabesh and placed in the family burial grounds of Zela in Benjamin (see 2 Sam 21:12–14). *fasted seven days.* As an indication of their mourning for Saul (cf. 2 Sam 1:12; 3:35; 12:16,21–23).

2 Samuel

INTRODUCTION

Title

1 and 2 Samuel were originally one book (see Introduction to 1 Samuel: Title).

Literary Features, Authorship and Date

See Introduction to 1 Samuel: Literary Features, Authorship and Date.

Contents and Theme: Kingship and Covenant

2 Samuel depicts David as a true (though imperfect) representative of the ideal theocratic king. David was initially acclaimed king at Hebron by the tribe of Judah (chs. 1—4), and subsequently was accepted by the remaining tribes after the murder of Ish-bosheth, one of Saul's surviving sons (5:1–5). David's leadership was decisive and effective. He captured Jerusalem from the Jebusites and made it his royal city and residence (5:6–14). Shortly afterward he brought the ark of the Lord from the house of Abinadab to Jerusalem, publicly acknowledging the Lord's kingship and rule over himself and the nation (ch. 6; Ps 132:3–5).

Under David's rule the Lord caused the nation to prosper, to defeat its enemies and, in fulfillment of His promise (see Gen 15:18), to extend its borders from Egypt to the Euphrates (ch. 8). David wanted to build a temple for the Lord—as His royal house, as a place for His throne (the ark) and as a place for Israel to worship Him. But the prophet Nathan told David that he was not to build the Lord a house (temple); rather, the Lord would build David a house (dynasty). Ch. 7 announces the Lord's promise that this Davidic dynasty would endure forever. This climactic chapter also describes the establishment of the Davidic covenant (see Ps 89:34–37), a covenant that promises ultimate victory over the evil one through the offspring of Eve (see Gen 3:15 and note). This promise—which had come to be focused on Shem and his descendants (see Gen 9:26–27 and notes), then on Abraham and his descendants (see Gen 12:2–3; 13:16; 15:5 and notes) and then on Judah and his (royal) descendants (see Gen 49:8–11 and notes)—is now focused specifically on the royal family of David. Later the prophets make clear that a descendant of David who sits on David's throne will perfectly fulfill the role of the theocratic king. He will complete the redemption of God's people (see Is 9:6–7; 11:1–16; Jer 23:5–6; 30:8–9; 33:14–16; Ezek 34:23–24; 37:24–25), thus enabling them to achieve the promised victory with Him (Rom 16:20).

After the description of David's rule in its glory and success, chs. 10—20 depict the darker side of his reign and describe David's weaknesses and failures. Even though David remained a king after God's own heart because he was willing to acknowledge his sin and repent (12:13), he nevertheless fell far short of the theocratic ideal and suffered the disciplinary results of his disobedience (12:10–12). His sin with Bathsheba (chs. 11—12) and his leniency both with the wickedness of his sons (13:21; 14:1,33; 19:4–6) and with the insubordination of Joab (3:29,39; 20:10,23) led to intrigue, violence and bloodshed within his own family and the nation. It eventually drove him from Jerusalem at the time of Absalom's rebellion. Nonetheless the Lord was gracious to David, and his reign became a standard by which the reigns of later kings were measured (see 2 Kin 18:3; 22:2).

The book ends with David's own words of praise to God, who had delivered him from all his enemies (22:31–51), and with words of expectation for the fulfillment of God's promise that a king will come from the house of David and rule "over men righteously" (23:3–5). These songs echo many of the themes of Hannah's song (1 Sam 2:1–10), and together they frame (and interpret) the basic narrative.

Chronology

See Introduction to 1 Samuel: Chronology.

Outline

Below is an abbreviated outline for 2 Samuel. For the complete outline see Introduction to 1 Samuel: Outline.

- IV. David's Rise to the Throne; Progressive Deterioration and End of Saul's Reign (1 Sam 16:1—2 Sam 5:5)
  - A. David Is Anointed Privately, Enters the Service of King Saul and Flees for His Life (1 Sam 16—26)
  - B. David Seeks Refuge in Philistia, and Saul and His Sons Are Killed in Battle (1 Sam 27—31)
  - C. David Becomes King over Judah (2 Sam 1—4)
  - D. David Becomes King over All Israel (2 Sam 5:1–5)
- V. David's Kingship in Its Accomplishments and Glory (2 Sam 5:6—9:12)
  - A. David Conquers Jerusalem and Defeats the Philistines (2 Sam 5:6–25)
  - B. David Brings the Ark to Jerusalem (2 Sam 6)
  - C. God Promises David an Everlasting Dynasty (2 Sam 7)
  - D. The Extension of David's Kingdom Externally and the Justice of His Rule Internally (2 Sam 8)
  - E. David's Faithfulness to His Covenant with Jonathan (2 Sam 9)
- VI. David's Kingship in Its Weaknesses and Failures (2 Sam 10—20)
  - A. David Commits Adultery and Murder (2 Sam 10—12)
  - B. David Loses His Sons Amnon and Absalom (2 Sam 13—20)
- VII. Final Reflections on David's Reign (2 Sam 21—24)

David Learns of Saul's Death

1 Now it came about after [a]the death of
Saul, when David had returned from [b]the
slaughter of the Amalekites, that David
remained two days in Ziklag.
2 On the third day, behold, [a]a man came
out of the camp from Saul, [b]with his clothes
torn and [1]dust on his head. And it came
about when he came to David that [c]he fell to
the ground and prostrated himself.
3 Then David said to him, "From where
do you come?" And he said to him, "I have
escaped from the camp of Israel."
4 David said to him, "[a]How did things
go? Please tell me." And he said, "The people have fled from the battle, and also many
of the people have fallen and are dead; and
Saul and Jonathan his son are dead also."
5 So David said to the young man who
told him, "How do you know that Saul and
his son Jonathan are dead?"
6 The young man who told him said, "By
chance I happened to be on [a]Mount Gilboa,
and behold, [b]Saul was leaning on his spear.
And behold, the chariots and the horsemen
pursued him closely.
7 "When he looked behind him, he saw
me and called to me. And I said, 'Here I am.'
8 "He said to me, 'Who are you?' And I
[1]answered him, '[a]I am an Amalekite.'
9 "Then he said to me, 'Please stand
beside me and kill me, for agony has seized
me because my [1]life still lingers in me.'
10 "So I stood beside him [a]and killed him,
because I knew that he could not live after
he had fallen. And [b]I took the crown which
was on his head and the bracelet which *was*
on his arm, and I have brought them here to
my lord."
11 Then [a]David took hold of his clothes
and tore them, and *so* also *did* all the men
who *were* with him.
12 They mourned and wept and [a]fasted
until evening for Saul and his son Jonathan
and for the people of the LORD and the house
of Israel, because they had fallen by the
sword.
13 David said to the young man who told
him, "Where are you from?" And he [1]an-
swered, "[a]I am the son of an alien, an Amalekite."
14 Then David said to him, "How is it you
were not afraid [a]to stretch out your hand to
destroy the LORD's anointed?"
15 And David called one of the young men
and said, "Go, [1]cut him down." [a]So he
struck him and he died.
16 David said to him, "[a]Your blood is on
your head, for [b]your mouth has testified
against you, saying, 'I have killed the LORD's
anointed.'"

David's Dirge for Saul and Jonathan

17 Then David [a]chanted with this lament
over Saul and Jonathan his son,
18 and he told *them* to teach the sons of
Judah *the song of* the bow; behold, it is written in [a]the book of Jashar.
19 "[1]Your beauty, O Israel, is slain on your
high places!
[a]How have the mighty fallen!
20 "[a]Tell *it* not in Gath,

1:1 [a]1 Sam 31:6 [b]1 Sam 30:1, 17, 26
2 [1]Lit *ground* [a]2 Sam 4:10 [b]1 Sam 4:12 [c]1 Sam 25:23
4 [a]1 Sam 4:16
6 [a]1 Sam 28:4; 31:1-6; 1 Chr 10:4-10 [b]1 Sam 31:2-4
8 [1]Lit *said to* [a]1 Sam 15:3; 30:1, 13, 17
9 [1]Lit *whole life is still in me*
10 [a]Judg 9:54 [b]2 Kin 11:12
11 [a]Gen 37:29, 34; Josh 7:6; 2 Chr 34:27; Ezra 9:3
12 [a]2 Sam 3:35
13 [1]Lit *said* [a]2 Sam 1:8
14 [a]1 Sam 24:6; 26:9, 11, 16
15 [1]Lit *fall upon him* [a]2 Sam 4:10, 12
16 [a]1 Sam 26:9; 2 Sam 3:28, 29; 1 Kin 2:32 [b]2 Sam 1:10; Luke 19:22
17 [a]2 Chr 35:25
18 [a]Josh 10:13
19 [1]Lit *The* [a]2 Sam 1:25, 27
20 [a]1 Sam 31:8-13; Mic 1:10

1:1 *after the death of.* See Josh 1:1; Judg 1:1. The narrative thread of 1 Samuel is continued. 1 and 2 Samuel were originally one book (see Introduction to 1 Samuel: Title). *David had returned from the slaughter of the Amalekites.* See 1 Sam 30:26. *Ziklag.* See note on 1 Sam 27:6.
1:2 *his clothes torn and dust on his head.* See note on 1 Sam 4:12; see also Josh 7:6; Acts 14:14.
1:8 *Amalekite.* It is not necessary to conclude from v. 3 that this Amalekite was a member of Saul's army. His statement that he "happened to be on Mount Gilboa" (v. 6) is probably not as innocent as it appears. He may have been there as a scavenger to rob the fallen soldiers of their valuables and weapons. It is ironic that Saul's death is reported by an Amalekite (see 1 Sam 15).
1:10 *I stood beside him and killed him.* The Amalekite's story conflicts with 1 Sam 31:3–6, where Saul is depicted as taking his own life. It appears that the Amalekite fabricated this version of Saul's death, expecting David to reward him (see 4:10). His miscalculation of David's response cost him his life (see v. 15). *I took the crown.* Apparently he got to Saul before the Philistines did (see 1 Sam 31:8–9).
1:11 *took hold of his clothes and tore them.* See note on 1 Sam 4:12.
1:12 *mourned and wept.* David and his men expressed their grief in typical Near Eastern fashion (see Gen 23:2; 1 Kin 13:30; Jer 22:18). *fasted.* See 3:35; 1 Sam 31:13.
1:13 *Amalekite.* The man was probably unaware of David's recent hostile encounters with the Amalekites (see v. 1; 1 Sam 30; see also note on 1 Sam 15:2).
1:14 The Amalekite understood nothing of the deep significance that David attached to the sanctity of the royal office in Israel (see note on 1 Sam 24:6). *the LORD's anointed.* See note on 1 Sam 9:16.
1:15 *cut him down* David displays no personal satisfaction over Saul's death and condemns to death the one he believes to be his murderer (see note on v. 10; see also 4:10).
1:16 *Your blood is on your head.* The Amalekite's own testimony brought about his execution (see Josh 2:19; 1 Kin 2:37).
1:17 *lament.* It was a common practice in the ancient Near East to compose laments for fallen leaders and/or heroes.
1:18 *song of the bow.* Perhaps David taught his men to sing this lament while they practiced the bow (Israel's most common weapon; see, e.g., 22:35) as a motivation to master the weapon thoroughly so they would not experience a similar defeat (see note on Ezek 21:9). *book of Jashar.* See note on Josh 10:13.
1:19 *Your beauty.* A reference to Saul and Jonathan as divinely designated leaders of God's covenant people, who had achieved many significant victories over Israel's enemies (see 1 Sam 14:47–48 and note). *high places.* Of Gilboa (see vv. 21,25; 1 Sam 31:1). *How have the mighty fallen!* The theme of David's lament (see v. 27). David's words contain no suggestion of bitterness toward Saul but rather recall the good qualities and accomplishments of Saul and Jonathan.
1:20 *Tell it not in Gath . . . Ashkelon.* As the major Philistine cities located the closest and farthest from Israel's borders, Gath and Ashkelon represent the entire Philistine nation. David does not want the enemies of God's covenant people to take pleasure in Israel's defeat (as he knew they would; see 1 Sam

Proclaim it not in the streets of
Ashkelon,
Or [b]the daughters of the Philistines
will rejoice,
The daughters of [c]the uncircumcised
will exult.
21 "[a]O mountains of Gilboa,
[b]Let not dew or rain be on you, nor
fields of offerings;
For there the shield of the mighty was
defiled,
The shield of Saul, not [c]anointed with
oil.
22 "[a]From the blood of the slain, from the
fat of the mighty,
[b]The bow of Jonathan did not turn
back,
And the sword of Saul did not return
empty.
23 "Saul and Jonathan, beloved and
pleasant in their life,
And in their death they were not
parted;
[a]They were swifter than eagles,
[b]They were stronger than lions.
24 "O daughters of Israel, weep over Saul,
Who clothed you luxuriously in
scarlet,
Who put ornaments of gold on your
apparel.
25 "[a]How have the mighty fallen in the
midst of the battle!
Jonathan is slain on your high places.
26 "I am distressed for you, my brother
Jonathan;
You have been very pleasant to me.
[a]Your love to me was more wonderful
Than the love of women.

20 [b]Ex 15:20, 21; 1 Sam 18:6 [c]1 Sam 14:6
21 [a]1 Sam 31:1 [b]Ezek 31:15 [c]Is 21:5
22 [a]Deut 32:42; Is 34:6 [b]1 Sam 18:4
23 [a]Jer 4:13 [b]Judg 14:18
25 [a]2 Sam 1:19, 27
26 [a]1 Sam 18:1-4
27 [a]2 Sam 1:19, 25 [b]Is 13:5
2:1 [a]1 Sam 23:2, 4, 9-12 [b]Josh 14:13; 1 Sam 30:31
2 [1]Lit *wife* [a]1 Sam 25:42, 43
3 [a]1 Sam 30:9; 1 Chr 12:1
4 [a]1 Sam 16:13; 2 Sam 5:3, 5 [b]1 Sam 31:11-13
5 [1]Lit *done* [a]1 Sam 23:21; Ps 115:15
6 [1]Lit *do* [a]Ex 34:6; 2 Tim 1:16
7 [1]Lit *sons of valor*
8 [1]I.e. man of shame; cf 1 Chr 8:33, *Eshbaal* [a]1 Sam 14:50 [b]Gen 32:2; 2 Sam 17:24

27 "[a]How have the mighty fallen,
And [b]the weapons of war perished!"

David Made King over Judah

2 Then it came about afterwards that [a]David
inquired of the LORD, saying, "Shall I go up
to one of the cities of Judah?" And the LORD
said to him, "Go up." So David said, "Where
shall I go up?" And He said, "[b]To Hebron."
2 So David went up there, and [a]his two
wives also, Ahinoam the Jezreelitess and
Abigail the [1]widow of Nabal the Carmelite.
3 And [a]David brought up his men who
were with him, each with his household; and
they lived in the cities of Hebron.
4 Then the men of Judah came and there
[a]anointed David king over the house of
Judah.
And they told David, saying, "It was [b]the
men of Jabesh-gilead who buried Saul."
5 David sent messengers to the men of
Jabesh-gilead, and said to them, "[a]May you
be blessed of the LORD because you have
[1]shown this kindness to Saul your lord, and
have buried him.
6 "Now [a]may the LORD [1]show lovingkindness and truth to you; and I also will [1]show
this goodness to you, because you have done
this thing.
7 "Now therefore, let your hands be strong
and be [1]valiant; for Saul your lord is dead,
and also the house of Judah has anointed me
king over them."

Ish-bosheth Made King over Israel

8 But [a]Abner the son of Ner, commander
of Saul's army, had taken [1]Ish-bosheth the son
of Saul and brought him over to [b]Mahanaim.

31:9–10) and thus bring reproach on the name of the Lord (see Ex 32:12; Num 14:13–19; Deut 9:28; Josh 7:9; Mic 1:10). *uncircumcised.* See note on 1 Sam 14:6.

1:21 *O mountains of Gilboa.* As an expression of profound grief, David rhetorically pronounces a curse on the place where Israel was defeated and Saul and Jonathan were killed (for other such rhetorical curses see Job 3:3–26; Jer 20:14–18). *not anointed with oil.* Leather shields were rubbed with oil to preserve them (see Is 21:5).

1:23 *in their death they were not parted.* Even though Jonathan opposed his father's treatment of David, he gave his life beside his father in Israel's defense.

1:26 *more wonderful Than the love of women.* David is not suggesting that marital love is inferior to that of friendship, nor do his remarks have any sexual implications. He is simply calling attention to Jonathan's nearly inexplicable self-denying commitment to David, whom he had long recognized as the Lord's choice to succeed his father rather than himself (see notes on 1 Sam 20:13–16).

1:27 *weapons of war.* Probably a metaphor for Saul and Jonathan.

2:1 *David inquired of the LORD.* By means of the ephod through the priest Abiathar (see notes on Ex 28:30; 1 Sam 2:28; 23:2). *one of the cities of Judah.* Even though Saul was dead and David had many friends and contacts among the people of his own tribe (see 1 Sam 30:26–31), David did not presume to return from Philistine territory to assume the kingship promised to him without first seeking the Lord's guidance. *Hebron.* An old and important city (see Gen 13:18; 23:2; Josh 15:13–15; see also note on 1 Sam 30:31) centrally located in the tribe of Judah.

2:2 *Ahinoam the Jezreelitess.* See note on 1 Sam 25:43. *Abigail.* See 1Sa 25.

2:3 *men who were with him.* See 1 Sam 22:2; 23:13; 30:3,9.

2:4 *anointed David king.* See notes on 1 Sam 2:10; 9:16. David had previously been anointed privately by Samuel in the presence of his own family (see note on 1 Sam 16:13). Here the anointing ceremony is repeated as a public recognition by his own tribe of his divine calling to be king. *over the house of Judah.* Very likely the tribe of Simeon was also involved (see Josh 19:1; Judg 1:3), but the Judahites in every way dominated the area. *men of Jabesh-gilead.* See notes on 1 Sam 11:1; 31:12. *buried Saul.* See note on 1 Sam 31:13.

2:7 *your lord is dead . . . the house of Judah has anointed me king over them.* David's concluding statement to the men of Jabesh-gilead is a veiled invitation to them to recognize him as their king just as the tribe of Judah had done. This appeal for their support, however, was ignored (see 1 Sam 2:8–9).

2:8 *Saul's army.* His small standing army of professionals loyal to him and his family (see 1 Sam 13:2,15; 14:2,52). *Ish-bosheth.* The name was originally Eshbaal (1 Chr 8:33) but was changed by the author of Samuel to Ish-bosheth, meaning "man of shame" (see note on 4:4). Evidently Baal (meaning "lord" or "master") was at this time still used to refer to the Lord. Later this was discontinued because of confusion with the Canaan-

9 He made him king over [a]Gilead, over the [b]Ashurites, over [c]Jezreel, over Ephraim, and over Benjamin, even over all Israel.

10 Ish-bosheth, Saul's son, was forty years old when he became king over Israel, and he was king for two years. The house of Judah, however, followed David.

11 [a]The [1]time that David was king in Hebron over the house of Judah was seven years and six months.

Civil War

12 Now Abner the son of Ner, went out from Mahanaim to [a]Gibeon with the servants of Ish-bosheth the son of Saul.

13 And [a]Joab the son of Zeruiah and the servants of David went out and met [1]them by the pool of Gibeon; and they sat down, [2]one on the one side of the pool and [2]the other on the other side of the pool.

14 Then Abner said to Joab, "Now let the young men arise and [1][a]hold a contest before us." And Joab said, "Let them arise."

15 So they arose and went over by count, twelve for Benjamin and Ish-bosheth the son of Saul, and twelve of the servants of David.

16 Each one of them seized his [1]opponent by the head and *thrust* his sword in his [2]opponent's side; so they fell down together. Therefore that place was called [3]Helkath-hazzurim, which is in Gibeon.

17 That day the battle was very severe, and [a]Abner and the men of Israel were beaten before the servants of David.

18 Now [a]the three sons of Zeruiah were there, Joab and Abishai and Asahel; and Asahel *was* [b]*as* [1]swift-footed as one of the gazelles which is in the field.

19 Asahel pursued Abner and did not [1]turn to the right or to the left from following Abner.

20 Then Abner looked behind him and said, "Is that you, Asahel?" And he answered, "It is I."

21 So Abner said to him, "[1]Turn to your right or to your left, and take hold of one of the young men for yourself, and take for yourself his spoil." But Asahel was not willing to turn aside from following him.

22 Abner repeated again to Asahel, "Turn [1]aside from following me. Why should I strike you to the ground? [a]How then could I lift up my face to your brother Joab?"

23 However, he refused to turn aside; therefore Abner struck him in the belly with the butt end of the spear, so that the spear came out at his back. And he fell there and died on the spot. And it came about that all who came to the place where [a]Asahel had fallen and died, stood still.

24 But Joab and Abishai pursued Abner, and when the sun was going down, they came to the hill of Ammah, which is in front of Giah by the way of the wilderness of Gibeon.

25 The sons of Benjamin gathered together behind Abner and became one band, and they stood on the top of a certain hill.

26 Then Abner called to Joab and said, "Shall the sword devour forever? Do you not know that it will be bitter in the end? How long will you [1]refrain from telling the people to turn back from following their brothers?"

27 Joab said, "As God lives, if you had not

9 [a]Josh 22:9 [b]Judg 1:32 [c]1 Sam 29:1
11 [1]Lit *number of days* [a]2 Sam 5:5
12 [a]Josh 10:12; 18:25
13 [1]Lit *them together* [2]Lit *these* [a]2 Sam 8:16; 1 Chr 2:16; 11:6
14 [1]Lit *make sport* [a]2 Sam 2:16, 17
16 [1]Lit *fellow* [2]Lit *fellow's* [3]I.e. the field of sword-edges
17 [a]2 Sam 3:1
18 [a]1 Chr 2:16
18 [1]Lit *light in his feet* [b]1 Chr 12:8; Hab 3:19
19 [1]Lit *turn to go to*
21 [1]Lit *Turn for yourself*
22 [1]Lit *aside for yourself* [a]2 Sam 3:27
23 [a]2 Sam 20:12
26 [1]Lit *not tell the people*

ite god Baal, and the author of Samuel reflects the later sensitivity. *son of Saul.* See notes on 1 Sam 14:49; 31:2. *brought him.* Abner takes the initiative in the power vacuum created by Saul's death, using the unassertive Ish-bosheth as a pawn for his own ambitions (see 3:11; see also note on 4:1). There is no evidence that Ish-bosheth had strong support among the Israelites generally. *Mahanaim.* A Gileadite town in Transjordan and thus beyond the sphere of Philistine domination—a kind of refugee capital.

2:9 *He made him king.* As a relative of Saul (see 1 Sam 14:50), Abner had both a family and a career interest in ensuring dynastic succession for Saul's house. *Gilead . . . all Israel.* This delineation of Ish-bosheth's realm suggests that his actual rule, while involving territory both east and west of the Jordan, was quite limited and that the last entry ("all Israel") was more claim than reality. David ruled over Judah and Simeon, and the Philistines controlled large sections of the northern tribal regions.

2:11 *seven years and six months.* Cf. Ish-bosheth's two-year reign in Mahanaim (v. 10). Because it appears that David was made king over all Israel shortly after Ish-bosheth's death (5:1–5) and moved his capital to Jerusalem not long afterward (5:6–12), reconciling the lengths of David's and Ish-bosheth's reigns is difficult. The difficulty is best resolved by assuming that it took Ish-bosheth a number of years to be recognized as his father's successor, and that the two years of his reign roughly correspond to the last two or three years of David's reign in Hebron.

2:12 Abner initiates an action to prevent David's sphere of influence from spreading northward out of Judah. Gibeon was located in the tribal area of Benjamin, to which Saul and his family belonged, and which the Philistines had not occupied.

2:13 *Joab the son of Zeruiah.* See note on 1 Sam 26:6. Joab became a figure of major importance during David's reign as a competent but ruthless military leader (see 10:7–14; 11:1; 12:26; 1 Kin 11:15–16). At times David was unable to control him (3:39; 18:5,14; 1 Kin 2:5–6), and he was eventually executed for his wanton assassinations and his part in the conspiracy to place Adonijah rather than Solomon on David's throne (1 Kin 2:28–34). *servants of David.* Some, at least, of David's small force of professionals that had gathered around him (see 1 Sam 22:1–2; 23:13; 27:2; 30:9).

2:15 *Benjamin.* At this time Ish-bosheth seems to have been supported mainly by his own tribesmen.

2:17 *That day the battle was very severe.* Because the representative combat (see note on 1 Sam 17:4) by 12 men from each side was indecisive, a full-scale battle ensued in which David's forces were victorious. The attempt to use representative combat to avoid the decimation of civil war failed (see 3:1).

2:21 *Turn.* Abner tried unsuccessfully to avoid the necessity of killing Asahel.

2:22 *How then could I lift up my face to your brother Joab?* Abner did not want the hostility between himself and Joab to be intensified by the practice of blood revenge (see note on 3:27).

2:26 *Shall the sword devour forever?* Abner proposes an armistice as a means of avoiding the awful consequences of civil war.

2:27 *As God lives.* An oath formula (see note on 1 Sam 14:39).

spoken, surely then the people would have gone away in the morning, each from following his brother."

28 So Joab blew the trumpet; and all the people halted and pursued Israel no longer, [a]nor did they continue to fight anymore.

29 Abner and his men then went through the Arabah all that night; so they crossed the Jordan, walked all morning, and came to [a]Mahanaim.

30 Then Joab returned from following Abner; when he had gathered all the people together, [1]nineteen of David's servants besides Asahel were missing.

31 But the servants of David had struck down many of Benjamin and Abner's men, *so that* three hundred and sixty men died.

32 And they took up Asahel and buried him [a]in his father's tomb which was in Bethlehem. Then Joab and his men went all night until the day [1]dawned at Hebron.

The House of David Strengthened

3 Now [a]there was a long war between the house of Saul and the house of David; and David grew steadily stronger, but the house of Saul grew weaker continually.

2 [a]Sons were born to David at Hebron: his firstborn was Amnon, by [b]Ahinoam the Jezreelitess;

3 and his second, Chileab, by Abigail the [1]widow of Nabal the Carmelite; and the third, Absalom the son of [a]Maacah, the daughter of Talmai, king of [b]Geshur;

4 and the fourth, [a]Adonijah the son of Haggith; and the fifth, Shephatiah the son of Abital;

5 and the sixth, Ithream, by David's wife Eglah. These were born to David at Hebron.

28 [a]2 Sam 3:1
29 [a]2 Sam 2:8
30 [1]Lit *nineteen men*
32 [1]Lit *lighted on them* [a]Gen 47:29, 30; Judg 8:32
3:1 [a]1 Kin 14:30; Ps 46:9
2 [a]1 Chr 3:1-3 [b]1 Sam 25:42, 43
3 [1]Lit *wife* [a]1 Sam 27:8; 1 Chr 3:2 [b]2 Sam 14:32; 15:8
4 [a]1 Kin 1:5
6 [a]2 Sam 2:8, 9
7 [1]So some ancient mss and versions; M.T. *he* [a]2 Sam 21:8-11
8 [a]1 Sam 24:14; 2 Sam 9:8
9 [a]1 Kin 19:2 [b]1 Sam 15:28
10 [a]1 Sam 15:28 [b]1 Sam 3:20
13 [1]Lit *saying* [2]Lit *my face* [a]Gen 43:3 [b]1 Sam 18:20; 19:11

Abner Joins David

6 It came about while there was war between the house of Saul and the house of David that [a]Abner was making himself strong in the house of Saul.

7 Now Saul had a concubine whose name was [a]Rizpah, the daughter of Aiah; and [1]Ish-bosheth said to Abner, "Why have you gone in to my father's concubine?"

8 Then Abner was very angry over the words of Ish-bosheth and said, "[a]Am I a dog's head that belongs to Judah? Today I show kindness to the house of Saul your father, to his brothers and to his friends, and have not delivered you into the hands of David; and yet today you charge me with a guilt concerning the woman.

9 "[a]May God do so to Abner, and more also, if [b]as the LORD has sworn to David, I do not accomplish this for him,

10 [a]to transfer the kingdom from the house of Saul and to establish the throne of David over Israel and over Judah, [b]from Dan even to Beersheba."

11 And he could no longer answer Abner a word, because he was afraid of him.

12 Then Abner sent messengers to David in his place, saying, "Whose is the land? Make your covenant with me, and behold, my hand shall be with you to bring all Israel over to you."

13 He said, "Good! I will make a covenant with you, but I demand one thing of you, [1]namely, [a]you shall not see my face unless you [b]first bring Michal, Saul's daughter, when you come to see [2]me."

14 So David sent messengers to Ish-bosheth, Saul's son, saying, "Give me my

2:28 *nor did they continue to fight anymore.* For the present the open conflict ceased, but the hostility remained (see 3:1).
2:29 *Arabah.* See note on Dt 1:1.
3:2–5 The list of six sons born to David in Hebron is given as an evidence of the strengthening of David's house in contrast to that of Saul (v. 1). That these six sons were each born of a different mother indirectly informs us that David married four additional wives (see 2:2) during his time in Hebron. The writer does not offer any direct criticism of this polygamous practice (see 5:13), which conflicts with Deut 17:17, but he lets the disastrous results in David's family life speak for themselves (see chs. 13–19; 1 Kin 1–2). *Amnon.* Later raped his sister Tamar and was killed by his brother Absalom (see ch. 13). *Ahinoam the Jezreelitess.* See note on 1 Sam 25:43.
3:3 *Chileab.* Called Daniel in 1 Chr 3:1. *Abigail.* See 1 Sam 25. *Absalom.* Later avenged the rape of Tamar by killing Amnon, and conspired against his father David in an attempt to make himself king (see chs. 13–18). *Maacah, the daughter of Talmai.* David's marriage to Maacah undoubtedly had political implications. With Talmai as an ally on Ish-bosheth's northern border, David flanked the northern kingdom both south and north. *Geshur.* A small Aramean city kingdom (see 15:8) located northeast of the Sea of Galilee (see Josh 12:5; 13:11–13).
3:4 *Adonijah.* Was put to death for attempting to take over the throne before Solomon could be crowned (see 1 Kin 1–2).
3:7 *Rizpah.* See 21:8–11. *Why have you gone in to my father's concubine?* Ish-bosheth suspects that Abner's act was part of a conspiracy to seize the kingship (cf. v. 6). Great significance was attached to taking the concubine of a former king (see note on 12:8; see also 16:21; 1 Kin 2:22).
3:9 *May God do so to Abner, and more also.* A curse formula (see note on 1 Sam 3:17). *as the LORD has sworn to David.* The knowledge of David's divine designation as successor to Saul had spread widely (see notes on 2:4; 1 Sam 16:13; 25:28).
3:10 *transfer the kingdom.* Abner was the real power behind the throne. *Dan even to Beersheba.* See note on 1 Sam 3:20.
3:12 *Whose is the land?* Possibly a rhetorical question that presumed that the land belonged either to Abner or to David. The former seems more likely from the following sentence. *Make your covenant with me.* Abner wants assurance that he will face no reprisals for his past loyalty to the house of Saul.
3:13 *Michal, Saul's daughter.* Although Saul had given Michal to David (1 Sam 18:27), he later gave her to another man after David fled from his court (1 Sam 25:44). In the minds of the northern elders, the reunion of David and Michal would strengthen David's claim to the throne as a legitimate son-in-law of Saul.
3:14 *David sent messengers to Ish-bosheth.* David wanted Michal returned as an open and official act of Ish-bosheth himself, rather than as part of a subterfuge planned by Abner. David knew that Ish-bosheth would not dare to defy Abner's wishes (see v. 11). *a hundred foreskins of the Philistines.* See 1 Sam

wife Michal, to whom I was betrothed [a]for a hundred foreskins of the Philistines."

15 Ish-bosheth sent and took her from *her* husband, from [1]Paltiel the son of Laish.

16 But her husband went with her, weeping as he went, and followed her as far as [a]Bahurim. Then Abner said to him, "Go, return." So he returned.

17 Now Abner had [1]consultation with [a]the elders of Israel, saying, "In times past you were seeking for David to be king over you.

18 "Now then, do *it!* For the LORD has spoken of David, saying, '[a]By the hand of My servant David [1]I will save My people Israel from the hand of the Philistines and from the hand of all their enemies.' "

19 Abner also spoke in the hearing of Benjamin; and in addition Abner went to speak in the hearing of David in Hebron all that seemed good to Israel and to [a]the whole house of Benjamin.

20 Then Abner and twenty men with him came to David at Hebron. And David made a feast for Abner and the men who were with him.

21 Abner said to David, "Let me arise and go and [a]gather all Israel to my lord the king, that they may make a covenant with you, and that [b]you may be king over all that your soul desires." So David sent Abner away, and he went in peace.

22 And behold, [a]the servants of David and Joab came from a raid and brought much spoil with them; but Abner was not with David in Hebron, for he had sent him away, and he had gone in peace.

23 When Joab and all the army that was with him arrived, they told Joab, saying, "Abner the son of Ner came to the king, and he has sent him away, and he has gone in peace."

24 Then Joab came to the king and said, "What have you done? Behold, Abner came to you; why then have you sent him away and he is already gone?

25 "You know Abner the son of Ner, that he came to deceive you and to learn of [a]your going out and coming in and to find out all that you are doing."

Joab Murders Abner

26 When Joab came out from David, he sent messengers after Abner, and they brought him back from the well of Sirah; but David did not know *it.*

27 So when Abner returned to Hebron, Joab took him aside into the middle of the gate to speak with him privately, and there [a]he struck him in the belly so that he died on account of the blood of Asahel his brother.

28 Afterward when David heard it, he said, "I and my kingdom are innocent before the LORD forever of the blood of Abner the son of Ner.

29 "[a]May it [1]fall on the head of Joab and on all his father's house; and may there not fail from the house of Joab [b]one who has a discharge, or who is a leper, or who takes hold of a distaff, or who falls by the sword, or who lacks bread."

30 So Joab and Abishai his brother killed Abner [a]because he had put their brother Asahel to death in the battle at Gibeon.

David Mourns Abner

31 Then David said to Joab and to all the people who were with him, "[a]Tear your clothes and gird on sackcloth and lament before Abner." And King David walked behind the bier.

32 Thus they buried Abner in Hebron; and the king lifted up his voice and wept at [a]the grave of Abner, and all the people wept.

14 [a]1 Sam 18:25, 27
15 [1]In 1 Sam 25:44, *Palti*
16 [a]2 Sam 16:5; 19:16
17 [1]Lit *a word* [a]1 Sam 8:4
18 [1]So many ancient mss and versions; M.T. *he* [a]1 Sam 9:16; 15:28
19 [a]1 Sam 10:20, 21; 1 Chr 12:29
21 [a]2 Sam 3:10, 12 [b]1 Kin 11:37
22 [a]1 Sam 27:8
25 [a]Deut 28:6; 1 Sam 29:6; Is 37:28
27 [a]2 Sam 2:23; 20:9, 10; 1 Kin 2:5
29 [1]Lit *whirl* [a]Deut 21:6-9; 1 Kin 2:31-33 [b]Lev 13:46
30 [a]2 Sam 2:23
31 [a]Gen 37:34; Judg 11:35
32 [a]Job 31:28, 29; Prov 24:17

18:25. Saul had required 100 Philistine foreskins; David presented him with 200 (1 Sam 18:27).

3:16 *Bahurim.* The last Benjamite city on the way to Hebron (see 16:5; 17:18).

3:17 *elders of Israel.* The collective leadership of the various tribes comprised an informal national ruling body (see notes on Ex 3:16; Joel 1:2; Matt 15:2; Acts 24:1; see also 1 Sam 8:4; 2 Sam 5:3; 1 Kin 8:1,3; 20:7; 2 Kin 10:1; 23:1). *you were seeking for David to be king.* Apparently Ish-bosheth's support came mainly from the tribe of Benjamin (see 2:15 and note) and from Gilead in Transjordan (see 2:8; 1 Sam 11:9–11; 31:11–13).

3:18 *the LORD has spoken of David.* By this time Samuel's anointing of David must have become common knowledge (see 5:2). Abner probably interpreted the anointing as a promise from the Lord, since Samuel was the Lord's much-revered prophet.

3:19 *Abner also spoke in the hearing of Benjamin.* Because Saul and his family were from the tribe of Benjamin, Abner was careful to consult the Benjamites concerning the transfer of kingship to the tribe of Judah. Apparently they consented, but Abner was not above representing matters in a way that was favorable to his purpose.

3:21 *make a covenant with you.* See 5:3 and note.

3:25 *he came to deceive you.* Joab despised Abner for killing his brother (2:18,23; 3:27) and sought to discredit him in David's eyes as a mere opportunist. Perhaps he also sensed that his own position of leadership would be threatened if Abner joined forces with David, since Abner was obviously a power among the northern tribes.

3:27 *Joab . . . struck him in the belly so that he died.* Joab's murder of Abner is not to be excused either as an act of war or as justifiable blood revenge (cf. Num 35:12; Deut 19:11–13). Asahel had been killed by Abner in the course of battle (see 2:23; see also note on 2:21).

3:29 *May it fall on the head of Joab and on all his father's house.* After disclaiming any personal or official involvement in the plot to assassinate Abner (v. 28), David cursed Joab and thereby called on God to judge his wicked act. In this crucial hour when David's relationship to the northern tribes hung in the balance, he appears not to have felt sufficiently secure in his own position to bring Joab publicly to justice (see v. 39). The crime went unpunished until early in the reign of Solomon (1 Kin 2:5–6,29–35).

3:31 *Joab.* He too was compelled to join the mourners. It may be that Joab's involvement was not widely known and that David hoped to keep the matter secret for the time being.

3:32 *Hebron.* David's royal city at the time. *the king lifted up his*

33 [a]The king chanted a *lament* for Abner
and said,
“Should Abner die as a fool dies?
34 “Your hands were not bound, nor your
feet put in fetters;
As one falls before the [1]wicked, you
have fallen.”
And all the people wept again over him.
35 Then all the people came [a]to [1]persuade
David to eat bread while it was still day; but
David vowed, saying, “[b]May God do so to
me, and more also, if I taste bread or anything else [c]before the sun goes down.”
36 Now all the people took note *of it,* and
it [1]pleased them, just as everything the king
did [2]pleased all the people.
37 So all the people and all Israel understood that day that it had not been *the will* of
the king to put Abner the son of Ner to death.
38 Then the king said to his servants, “Do
you not know that a prince and a great man
has fallen this day in Israel?
39 “I am [a]weak today, though anointed
king; and these men [b]the sons of Zeruiah are
too difficult for me. [c]May the LORD repay the
evildoer according to his evil.”

Ish-bosheth Murdered

4 Now when [1]Ish-bosheth, Saul's son, heard
that [a]Abner had died in Hebron, [2b]he lost
courage, and all Israel was disturbed.
2 Saul's son *had* two men who were
commanders of bands: the name of the one
was Baanah and the name of the other
Rechab, sons of Rimmon the Beerothite, of
the sons of Benjamin (for [a]Beeroth is also
considered [b]*part* of Benjamin,
3 and the Beerothites fled to [a]Gittaim
and have been aliens there until this day).
4 Now [a]Jonathan, Saul's son, had a son
crippled in his feet. He was five years old
when the [b]report of Saul and Jonathan came
from Jezreel, and his nurse took him up and
fled. And it happened that in her hurry to
flee, he fell and became lame. And his name
was [1c]Mephibosheth.

33 [a]2 Sam 1:17; 2 Chr 35:25 **34** [1]Lit *sons of wickedness* **35** [1]Lit *cause* [a]2 Sam 12:17 [b]1 Sam 3:17 [c]2 Sam 1:12 **36** [1]Lit *was good in their eyes* [2]Lit *was good in the eyes of all* **39** [a]1 Chr 29:1; 2 Chr 13:7 [b]2 Sam 19:5-7 [c]1 Kin 2:32-34 **4:1** [1]So some ancient mss; M.T. *he* [2]Lit *his hands dropped* [a]2 Sam 3:27 [b]Ezra 4:4 **2** [a]Josh 9:17 [b]Josh 18:25 **3** [a]Neh 11:33 **4** [1]I.e. Merib-baal [a]2 Sam 9:3, 6 [b]1 Sam 31:1-4 [c]1 Chr 8:34; 9:40

5 [a]2 Sam 2:8 **6** [1]Lit *And here* [2]Lit *takers of wheat* [a]2 Sam 2:23 **7** [1]Lit *went* [a]2 Sam 2:29 **8** [1]Lit *seed* [a]1 Sam 24:4; 25:29 **9** [a]Gen 48:16; 1 Kin 1:29; Ps 31:7 **10** [1]Lit *he was as a bearer of good news in his own eyes* [a]2 Sam 1:2, 4, 15 **11** [1]Lit *burn* [a]Gen 9:5; Ps 9:12 **12** [a]2 Sam 1:15 [b]2 Sam 3:32 **5:1** [1]Lit *said, saying* [a]1 Chr 11:1-3 [b]2 Sam 19:13

5 So the sons of Rimmon the Beerothite,
Rechab and Baanah, departed and came to
the house of [a]Ish-bosheth in the heat of the
day while he was taking his midday rest.
6 [1]They came to the middle of the house
as [2]if to get wheat, and [a]they struck him in
the belly; and Rechab and Baanah his brother escaped.
7 Now when they came into the house,
as he was lying on his bed in his bedroom,
they struck him and killed him and beheaded him. And they took his head and [1a]trav-
eled by way of the Arabah all night.
8 Then they brought the head of Ish-
bosheth to David at Hebron and said to the
king, “Behold, the head of Ish-bosheth [a]the
son of Saul, your enemy, who sought your
life; thus the LORD has given my lord the king
vengeance this day on Saul and his [1]descen-
dants.”
9 David answered Rechab and Baanah
his brother, sons of Rimmon the Beerothite,
and said to them, “As the LORD lives, [a]who
has redeemed my life from all distress,
10 [a]when one told me, saying, ‘Behold,
Saul is dead,’ and [1]thought he was bringing
good news, I seized him and killed him in
Ziklag, which was the reward I gave him for
his news.
11 “How much more, when wicked men
have killed a righteous man in his own
house on his bed, shall I not now [a]require
his blood from your hand and [1]destroy you
from the earth?”
12 Then [a]David commanded the young
men, and they killed them and cut off their
hands and feet and hung them up beside the
pool in Hebron. But they took the head of
Ish-bosheth [b]and buried it in the grave of
Abner in Hebron.

David King over All Israel

5 [a]Then all the tribes of Israel came to
David at Hebron and [1]said, “Behold, we
are [b]your bone and your flesh.
2 “Previously, when Saul was king over

---

voice and wept at the grave of Abner. Because Abner's murder had the potential of destroying the union of the nation under David's rule, David did everything possible to demonstrate his innocence to the people. In this he was successful (see vv. 36–37).
3:35 *May God do so to me, and more also.* A curse formula (see note on 1 Sam 3:17).
3:39 *May the LORD repay the evildoer.* See note on v. 29.
4:1 *he lost courage.* Ish-bosheth was very much aware of his dependence on Abner (see note on 2:8). *all Israel was disturbed.* Civil strife threatened, and the northern tribes were now without a strong leader.
4:2 *Beeroth.* One of the Gibeonite cities (Josh 9:17) assigned to Benjamin (Josh 18:25).
4:3 *Gittaim.* Its location is not known (but see Neh 11:33).
4:4 *Jonathan, Saul's son, had a son crippled in his feet.* The writer emphasizes that with the death of Ish-bosheth (see v. 6) there was no other viable claimant to the throne from the house of Saul. *report of Saul and Jonathan.* See 1:4; 1 Sam 31:2–4. *Mephibosheth.* See 9:1–13; 16:1–4; 19:24–30; 21:7–8. The name was originally Merib-baal (apparently meaning “opponent of Baal”; see 1 Chr 8:34), perhaps to be spelled “Meri-baal” (meaning “loved by Baal”), but was changed by the author of Samuel to Mephibosheth (meaning “from the mouth of the shameful thing”). See note on 2:8.
4:7 *Arabah.* See note on Deut 1:1.
4:8 *the LORD has given my lord the king vengeance . . . on Saul.* Recab and Baanah depict their assassination of Ish-bosheth in pious terms, expecting David to commend them for their act—a serious miscalculation.
4:9 *As the LORD lives.* An oath formula (see note on 1 Sam 14:39).
4:11 *require his blood from your hand.* An expression for the death penalty (see Gen 9:5–6). David here does what he was unable to do with Joab (see note on 3:29).
4:12 *their hands and feet.* The hands that had assassinated Ish-bosheth and the feet that had run with the news.
5:1–24:25 Beginning with ch. 5 there are sections of 2 Sam-

us, [a]you were the one who led Israel out and
in. And the LORD said to you, '[b]You will shepherd My people Israel, and you will be [c]a
ruler over Israel.' "
3 So all the elders of Israel came to the
king at Hebron, and King David [a]made a covenant with them before the LORD at Hebron;
then [b]they anointed David king over Israel.
4 David was [a]thirty years old when he
became king, *and* [b]he reigned forty years.
5 At Hebron [a]he reigned over Judah sev-
en years and six months, and in Jerusalem
he reigned thirty-three years over all Israel
and Judah.
6 [a]Now the king and his men went to
[b]Jerusalem against the Jebusites, the inhabitants of the land, and they said to [1]David,
"You shall not come in here, but the blind
and lame will turn you away"; [2]thinking,
"David cannot enter here."

2 [a]1 Sam 18:5, 13, 16 [b]Gen 49:24; 2 Sam 7:7 [c]1 Sam 25:30
3 [a]2 Sam 3:21 [b]1 Sam 16:13; 2 Sam 2:4
4 [a]Gen 41:46; Num 4:3; Luke 3:23 [b]1 Kin 2:11; 1 Chr 26:31
5 [a]2 Sam 2:11; 1 Chr 3:4; 29:27

6 [1]Lit *David, saying* [2]Lit *saying* [a]1 Chr 11:4-9 [b]Josh 15:63; 18:28; Judg 1:21

uel that have parallel passages in 1 Chronicles. In some instances these parallel accounts are nearly identical; in others there are variations.

5:1 *all the tribes of Israel.* Representatives of each tribe, including elders and armed soldiers (see 1 Chr 12:23–40). *your bone and your flesh.* The representatives of the various tribes cite three reasons for recognizing David as their king. The first of these is the acknowledgment that David is an Israelite. Even though national unity had been destroyed in the civil strife following Saul's death (2:8–3:1), this blood relationship had not been forgotten.

5:2 *the one who led Israel out and in.* The second reason (see note on v. 1) for recognizing David as king (see 1 Sam 18:5, 13–14,16,30). *the LORD said to you.* The third and most important reason (see 1 Sam 13:13–14; 16:1,13; 23:17; 25:26–31).

5:3 *King David made a covenant with them before the LORD.* David and Israel entered into a covenant in which both the king and the people obligated themselves before the Lord to carry out their mutual responsibilities (see 2 Kin 11:17 and note). Thus, while David was king over Judah as the one elevated to that position by his tribe and later became king over Jerusalem by conquest (vv. 6–10), his rule over the northern tribes was by virtue of a treaty (covenant) of submission. That treaty was not renewed with David's grandson Rehoboam because he refused to negotiate its terms at the time of his accession to the throne (1 Kin 12:1–16). *they anointed David king over Israel.* The third time David was anointed (see note on 2:4).

5:5 *At Hebron he reigned . . . seven years and six months.* See 2:11. *Israel and Judah.* The specific relationship of David to these two segments of his realm appears to have remained distinct (see note on v. 3).

5:6 *Jerusalem.* One of the most significant accomplishments of David's reign was the establishment of Jerusalem as his royal city and the nation's capital (see Introduction: Contents and Theme). The site was first occupied in the third millennium B.C. and was a royal city in the time of Abraham (see note on Gen 14:18). It was located on the border between Judah and Benjamin but was controlled by neither tribe. At the time of the conquest both Judah and Benjamin had attacked the city (see notes on Judg 1:8,21), but it was quickly lost again to the Jebusites (Josh 15:63) and was sometimes referred to by the name Jebus (see Judg 19:10; 1 Chr 11:4). The city David conquered covered somewhat less than 11 acres and could have housed not many more than 3,500 inhabitants. By locating his royal city in a newly conquered town on the border between the two segments of his realm, David united the kingdom under his rule without seeming to subordinate one part to the other. *Jebusites.* A Canaanite people (Gen 10:15–16) inhabiting the

The City of the Jebusites/David's Jerusalem

Substantial historical evidence, both Biblical and extra-Biblical, places the temple of Herod (and before it the temples of Zerubbabel and of Solomon) on the holy spot where King David built an altar to the Lord. David had purchased the land from Araunah the Jebusite, who was using the exposed bedrock as a threshing floor (2 Sam 24:18-25). Tradition claims a much older sanctity for the site, associating it with the altar of Abraham on Mount Moriah (Gen 22:1-19). The writer of Genesis equates Moriah with "the mount of the LORD," and other OT shrines originated in altars erected by Abraham.

c. 1000 B.C.

Barely 12 acres in size, Jebus, a Canaanite city, could well defend itself against attack, with walls atop steep canyons and shafts reaching an underground water source. David captured the stronghold c. 1000 B.C. and made it his capital.

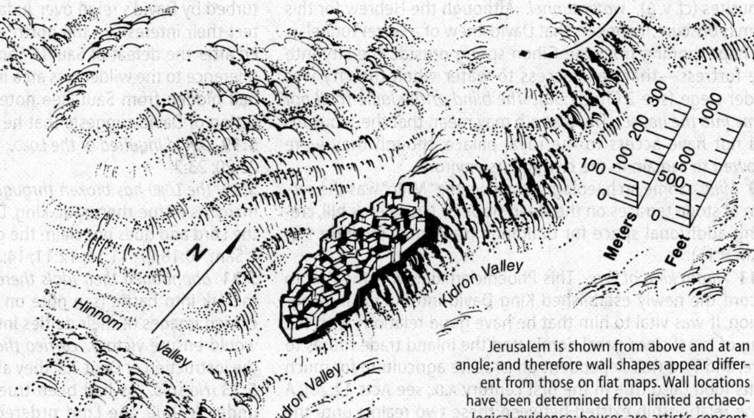

Jerusalem is shown from above and at an angle; and therefore wall shapes appear different from those on flat maps. Wall locations have been determined from limited archaeological evidence; houses are artist's concept.

© Hugh Claycombe 1982

7 Nevertheless, David captured the stronghold of Zion, that is [a]the city of David.

8 David said on that day, "Whoever would strike the Jebusites, let him reach the lame and the blind, who are hated by David's soul, through the water tunnel." Therefore they say, "The blind or the lame shall not come into the house."

9 So David lived in the stronghold and called it [a]the city of David. And David built all around from the [1b]Millo and inward.

10 [a]David became greater and greater, for the LORD God of hosts was with him.

11 [a]Then Hiram king of Tyre sent messengers to David with cedar trees and carpenters and stonemasons; and [b]they built a house for David.

12 And David realized that the LORD had established him as king over Israel, and that He had exalted his kingdom for the sake of His people Israel.

13 Meanwhile [a]David took more concubines and wives from Jerusalem, after he came from Hebron; and more sons and daughters were born to David.

14 Now [a]these are the names of those who were born to him in Jerusalem: Shammua, Shobab, Nathan, Solomon,

15 Ibhar, Elishua, Nepheg, Japhia,

16 Elishama, Eliada and Eliphelet.

War with the Philistines

17 When the Philistines heard that they had anointed David king over Israel, [a]all the Philistines went up to seek out David; and when David heard *of it,* he went down to the [b]stronghold.

18 Now the Philistines came and spread themselves out in [a]the valley of Rephaim.

19 Then [a]David inquired of the LORD, saying, "Shall I go up against the Philistines? Will You give them into my hand?" And [b]the LORD said to David, "Go up, for I will certainly give the Philistines into your hand."

20 So David came to [a]Baal-perazim and [1]defeated them there; and he said, "The LORD has broken through my enemies before me like the breakthrough of waters." Therefore he named that place [2]Baal-perazim.

21 They abandoned their idols there, so [a]David and his men carried them away.

22 Now [a]the Philistines came up once again and spread themselves out in the valley of Rephaim.

23 When [a]David inquired of the LORD, He said, "You shall not go *directly* up; circle

7 [a]2 Sam 6:12, 16; 1 Kin 2:10; 9:24
9 [1]I.e. citadel [a]2 Sam 5:7 [b]1 Kin 9:15, 24
10 [a]2 Sam 3:1
11 [a]1 Kin 5:1, 10, 18; 1 Chr 14:1 [b]Ps 30: title
13 [a]Deut 17:17; 1 Chr 3:9
14 [a]1 Chr 3:5-8
17 [a]1 Sam 29:1 [b]2 Sam 23:14; 1 Chr 11:16
18 [a]Gen 14:5; Josh 15:8; 17:15; 18:16
19 [a]1 Sam 23:2 [b]2 Sam 2:1
20 [1]Lit *David smote* [2]I.e. the master of breakthrough [a]1 Chr 14:11; Is 28:21
21 [a]1 Chr 14:12
22 [a]2 Sam 5:18
23 [a]2 Sam 5:19

area in (Josh 15:8; 18:16) and around (Num 13:29; Josh 11:3) Jerusalem. *the blind and lame will turn you away.* Jerusalem was a natural fortress because of its location on a rise surrounded on three sides by deep valleys; so the Jebusites were confident that their walls could easily be defended.

5:7 *stronghold.* Probably the fortified city itself. *Zion.* The first occurrence of the name in the OT (its meaning is unknown). Originally the name appears to have been given to the southernmost hill of the city on which the Jebusite fortress was located. As the city expanded (from the days of Solomon onward), the name continued to be applied to the entire city (see Is 1:8; 2:3).

5:8 *David said on that day.* 1 Chr 11:6 may be combined with this verse for a more complete account. Joab's part in the conquest of the city demonstrated again his military prowess and reconfirmed him in the position of commander of David's armies. *the lame and the blind.* An ironic reference to the Jebusites (cf. v. 6). *water tunnel.* Although the Hebrew for this term is obscure, it appears that David knew of a secret tunnel—perhaps running from the Gihon spring outside the city into the fortress—that gave access to water when the city was under siege (see 2 Chr 32:30). *The blind or the lame shall not come into the house.* The proverb may mean that the Jebusites did not have access to the royal palace, though they were allowed to remain in the city and its environs.

5:9 *Millo.* Some archaeologists believe the "Millo" was the system of stone terraces on the steep slope of Jerusalem's hill, creating additional space for buildings (see notes on Judg 9:6; 1 Kin 9:15).

5:11 *Hiram king of Tyre.* This Phoenician king was the first to accord the newly established King David international recognition. It was vital to him that he have good relations with the king of Israel since Israel dominated the inland trade routes to Tyre, and Tyre was dependent on Israelite agriculture for much of its food (also true in the first century A.D.; see Acts 12:20). A close relationship existed between these two realms until the Babylonian invasions. *Tyre.* An important Phoenician seaport on the Mediterranean coast north of Israel (see Ezek 26–27).

5:12 *David realized that the LORD had established him as king.* In the ideology of the ancient Near East the king's possession of a palace was the chief symbolic indication of his status. *for the sake of His people Israel.* David acknowledged that his elevation to kingship over all Israel was the Lord's doing and that it was an integral part of His continuing redemptive program for Israel—just as the ministries of Moses, Joshua, the judges and Samuel had been.

5:13 *David took more concubines and wives.* See note on 3:2–5.

5:14 *Shammua, Shobab, Nathan, Solomon.* 1 Chr 3:5 designates Bathsheba as their mother.

5:17 *When the Philistines heard that they had anointed David king.* Chronologically it is likely that the Philistine attack followed immediately after the events of v. 3 and before the capture of Jerusalem (vv. 6–14). (The author arranged his narrative by topics; see note on 7:1.) The Philistines had not been disturbed by David's reign over Judah, but now they acted to protect their interests in the north, much of which they dominated after the defeat of Saul (1 Sam 31). *stronghold.* Probably a reference to the wilderness area in southern Judah where David had hidden from Saul (see notes on 1 Sam 22:4; 23:14). This action of David suggests that he had not yet taken Jerusalem.

5:19 *David inquired of the LORD.* See notes on 2:1; 1 Sam 2:28; 22:20; 23:2.

5:20 *the LORD has broken through . . . Baal-perazim.* See NASB marg. As a true theocratic king, David attributes the victory to the Lord and does not claim the glory for himself (see notes on 1 Sam 10:18,27; 11:13; 12:11; 14:23; 17:11,45–47).

5:21 *abandoned their idols there.* As the Israelites had taken the ark into battle (see note on 1 Sam 4:3), so the Philistines carried images of their deities into battle in the hope that this would ensure victory. *carried them away.* In compliance with the instruction of Deut 7:5, they also burned them (1 Chr 14:12).

5:23 *He said.* As had been true in the case of the conquest under Joshua, the Lord ordered the battle and He Himself marched against the enemy with His heavenly host (see Josh

around behind them and come at them in
front of the [1]balsam trees.
24 "It shall be, when [a]you hear the sound
of marching in the tops of the [1]balsam trees,
then you shall act promptly, for then [b]the
LORD will have gone out before you to strike
the army of the Philistines."
25 Then David did so, just as the LORD had
commanded him, and struck down the Philistines from [1a]Geba [2]as far as [b]Gezer.

Peril in Moving the Ark

6 [a]Now David again gathered all the chosen men of Israel, thirty thousand.
2 And David arose and went with all the
people who were with him to [1a]Baale-judah,
to bring up from there the ark of God which
is called by the [b]Name, the very name of the
LORD of hosts who [c]is [2]enthroned *above* the
cherubim.
3 They [1]placed the ark of God on [a]a new
cart that they might bring it from the house
of Abinadab which was on the hill; and
Uzzah and Ahio, the sons of Abinadab, were
leading the new cart.
4 So [a]they brought it with the ark of God
from the house of Abinadab, which was on
the hill; and Ahio was walking ahead of the
ark.
5 Meanwhile, David and all the house of
Israel [a]were celebrating before the LORD
[b]with all kinds of *instruments made of* [1]fir
wood, and with lyres, harps, tambourines,
castanets and cymbals.
6 But when they came to the [a]threshing
floor of Nacon, Uzzah [b]reached out toward
the ark of God and took hold of it, for the
oxen nearly upset *it*.

23 [1]Or *baka-shrubs*
24 [1]Or *baka-shrubs* [a]2 Kin 7:6 [b]Judg 4:14
25 [1]In 1 Chr 14:16, *Gibeon* [2]Lit *until you are coming to* [a]Is 28:21 [b]Josh 12:12; 21:21
6:1 [a]1 Chr 13:5-14
2 [1]I.e. Kiriath-jearim [2]Lit *sitting* [a]Josh 15:9, 10; 1 Sam 7:1 [b]Lev 24:16 [c]Ex 25:22
3 [1]Lit *caused to ride* [a]Num 7:4-9; 1 Sam 6:7
4 [a]1 Sam 7:1; 1 Chr 13:7
5 [1]Or *cypress* [a]1 Sam 18:6, 7 [b]1 Chr 13:8
6 [a]1 Chr 13:9 [b]Num 4:15, 19, 20
7 [1]Lit *the* [a]1 Sam 6:19
8 [1]Lit *the* LORD *broke through a breakthrough* [2]I.e. the breakthrough of Uzzah
9 [a]Ps 119:120; Luke 5:8
10 [a]1 Chr 26:4-8
11 [a]Gen 30:27; 39:5
12 [a]1 Chr 15:25-16:3 [b]1 Kin 8:1
13 [a]Num 4:15; Josh 3:3; 1 Chr 15:2, 15 [b]1 Kin 8:5
14 [1]Lit *girded with* [a]Ex 15:20, 21; Judg 11:34 [b]Ex 19:6; 1 Sam 2:18, 28
16 [a]2 Sam 3:14

7 And the anger of the LORD burned
against Uzzah, and [a]God struck him down
there for [1]his irreverence; and he died there
by the ark of God.
8 David became angry because [1]of the
LORD'S outburst against Uzzah, and that
place is called [2]Perez-uzzah to this day.
9 So [a]David was afraid of the LORD that
day; and he said, "How can the ark of the
LORD come to me?"
10 And David was unwilling to move the
ark of the LORD into the city of David with
him; but David took it aside to the house of
[a]Obed-edom the Gittite.
11 Thus the ark of the LORD remained in
the house of Obed-edom the Gittite three
months, and the LORD [a]blessed Obed-edom
and all his household.

The Ark Is Brought to Jerusalem

12 Now it was told King David, saying,
"The LORD has blessed the house of Obed-
edom and all that belongs to him, on account
of the ark of God." [a]David went and brought
up the ark of God from the house of Obed-
edom into [b]the city of David with gladness.
13 And so it was, that when the [a]bearers
of the ark of the LORD had gone six paces, he
sacrificed an [b]ox and a fatling.
14 And [a]David was dancing before the
LORD with all *his* might, and David was
[1b]wearing a linen ephod.
15 So David and all the house of Israel
were bringing up the ark of the LORD with
shouting and the sound of the trumpet.
16 Then it happened *as* the ark of the
LORD came into the city of David that
[a]Michal the daughter of Saul looked out of

6:2–5; 8:1–2; 10:8,14; 11:6). David's wars were a continuation and completion of the wars fought by Joshua.

5:24 *sound of marching.* The heavenly host of the Lord going into battle.

6:2 *Baale-judah.* That is, Kiriath-jearim (see Josh 15:60; 18:14; 1 Sam 6:21; 7:1; se also note on 1 Ch 13:6). *ark of God.* See Ex 25:10–22; see also notes on 1 Sam 4:3–4,21. The ark had remained at Kiriath-jearim during the reign of Saul. *called by the Name.* Used elsewhere to designate ownership (see 12:28; Deut 28:10; Is 4:1; 63:19). *LORD of hosts.* See note on 1 Sam 1:3. *enthroned above the cherubim.* See note on 1 Sam 4:4; see also 1 Chr 28:2 ("footstool of our God"). David recognized the great significance of the ark as the earthly throne of Israel's God. As a true theocratic king, he wished to acknowledge the Lord's kingship and rule over both himself and the people by restoring the ark to a place of prominence in the nation.

6:3 *new cart.* David follows the example of the Philistines (see 1 Sam 6:7) rather than the instructions of Ex 25:12–14; Num 4:5–6,15, which require that the ark be carried on the shoulders of the Levites (see 1 Chr 15:13–15). *from the house of Abinadab.* See 1 Sam 7:1. *Uzzah and Ahio, the sons of Abinadab.* 1 Sam 7:1 speaks of Eleazar as the son of Abinadab. The Hebrew word for "son" can have the broader meaning of "descendant."

6:7 *his irreverence.* Although Uzzah's intent may have been good, he violated the clear instructions the Lord had given for handling the ark (see note on v. 3; cf. Ex 25:15; Num 4:5–6,15; 1 Chr 15:13–15; see also note on 1 Sam 6:19). At this important new beginning in Israel's life with the Lord, the Lord gives a shocking and vivid reminder to David and Israel that those who claim to serve Him must acknowledge His rule with absolute seriousness (see Lev 10:1–3; Josh 7:24–25; 24:19–20; Acts 5:1–11).

6:8 *David became angry.* David's initial reaction was resentment that his attempt to honor the Lord had resulted in a display of God's wrath. *Perez-uzzah.* See NASB marg. The place-name memorialized a divine warning that was not soon forgotten (see Josh 7:26 and note). *to this day.* Until the time of the writing of 2 Samuel.

6:9 *David was afraid of the LORD.* David's anger was accompanied by fear—not the wholesome fear of proper honor and respect for the Lord (1 Sam 12:24; Josh 24:14) but an anxiety arising from an acute sense of his own guilt (Gen 3:10; Dt 5:5).

6:10 *Obed-edom.* Perhaps means "servant of man." *Gittite.* He appears to have been a Levite (see note on 1 Chr 13:13; cf. 1 Chr 15:18,24; 16:5; 26:4–8,15; 2 Chr 25:24), though many think the term "Gittite" fixes his place of birth at the Philistine city of Gath (see 15:18). However, Gittite may be a reference to the Levitical city Gath-rimmon in Dan or Manasseh (Josh 21:20–25).

6:12 *David . . . brought up the ark.* God's blessing on the household of Obed-edom showed David that God's anger had been appeased.

6:13 *bearers of the ark.* David had become aware of his previous error (1 Chr 15:13–15). *six paces.* Sufficient to show that now God's blessing was on the Levites (see 1 Chr 15:26).

6:14 *linen ephod.* See note on 1 Sam 2:18.

the window and saw King David leaping and dancing before the LORD; and she despised him in her heart.

17 So they brought in the ark of the LORD and set it [a]in its place inside the tent which David had pitched for it; and [b]David offered burnt offerings and peace offerings before the LORD.

18 When David had finished offering the burnt offering and the peace offering, [a]he blessed the people in the name of the LORD of hosts.

19 Further, he distributed to all the people, to all the multitude of Israel, both to men and women, a cake of bread and one of dates and one of raisins to each one. Then all the people departed each to his house.

20 But when David returned to bless his household, Michal the daughter of Saul came out to meet David and said, "How the king of Israel distinguished himself today! [a]He uncovered himself today in the eyes of his servants' maids as one of the [b]foolish ones shamelessly uncovers himself!"

21 So David said to Michal, "[a]*It was* before the LORD, who chose me above your father and above all his house, to appoint me ruler over the people of the LORD, over Israel; therefore I will celebrate before the LORD.

22 "I will be more lightly esteemed than this and will be humble in my own eyes, but with the maids of whom you have spoken, with them I will be distinguished."

23 Michal the daughter of Saul had no child to the day of her death.

David Plans to Build a Temple

7 [a]Now it came about when the king lived in his house, and the LORD had given him rest on every side from all his enemies,

2 that the king said to [a]Nathan the prophet, "See now, I dwell in [b]a house of cedar, but the ark of God [c]dwells within tent curtains."

3 Nathan said to the king, "[a]Go, do all that is in your mind, for the LORD is with you."

4 But in the same night the word of the LORD came to Nathan, saying,

5 "Go and say to My servant David, 'Thus says the LORD, "[a]Are you the one who should build Me a house to dwell in?

6 "For [a]I have not dwelt in a house since the day I brought up the sons of Israel from Egypt, even to this day; but I have been moving about [b]in a tent, even in a [1]tabernacle.

7 "[a]Wherever I have gone with all the sons of Israel, did I speak a word with one of the tribes of Israel, [b]which I commanded to shepherd My people Israel, saying, 'Why have you not built Me a house of cedar?' " '

God's Covenant with David

8 "Now therefore, thus you shall say to My servant David, 'Thus says the LORD of hosts, "[a]I took you from the pasture, from following the sheep, [b]to be ruler over My people Israel.

9 "[a]I have been with you wherever you have gone and [b]have cut off all your enemies from before you; and I will make you a great name, like the names of the great men who are on the earth.

10 "I will also appoint a place for My people Israel and [a]will plant them, that they may live in their own place and not be disturbed again, [b]nor will the [1]wicked afflict them any more as formerly,

11 even [a]from the day that I commanded judges to be over My people Israel; and [b]I

17 [a]1 Chr 15:1; 2 Chr 1:4 [b]1 Kin 8:62-65
18 [a]1 Kin 8:14, 15
20 [a]2 Sam 6:14, 16; Eccl 7:17 [b]Judg 9:4
21 [a]1 Sam 13:14; 15:28
7:1 [a]1 Chr 17:1-27
2 [a]2 Sam 7:17; 12:1; 1 Kin 1:22; 1 Chr 29:29; 2 Chr 9:29 [b]2 Sam 5:11 [c]Ex 26:1
3 [a]1 Kin 8:17, 18; 1 Chr 22:7
5 [a]1 Kin 5:3, 4; 8:19
6 [1]Lit *dwelling place* [a]Josh 18:1; 1 Kin 8:16 [b]Ex 40:18, 34
7 [a]Lev 26:11, 12 [b]2 Sam 5:2
8 [a]1 Sam 16:11, 12; Ps 78:70, 71 [b]2 Sam 6:21
9 [a]1 Sam 5:10 [b]Ps 18:37-42
10 [1]Lit *sons of wickedness* [a]Ex 15:17; Is 5:2, 7 [b]Ps 89:22, 23; Is 60:18
11 [a]Judg 2:14-16; 1 Sam 12:9-11 [b]2 Sam 7:1

6:16 *she despised him.* Michal had no appreciation for the significance of the event and deeply resented David's public display as unworthy of the dignity of a king (see vv. 20–23).
6:17 *burnt offerings.* See Lev 1. *peace offerings.* See note on 1 Sam 11:15.
6:18 *he blessed the people.* As Solomon would later do at the dedication of the temple (1 Kin 8:55–61).
6:20 *uncovered himself.* An allusion to David's having worn only a linen ephod (v. 14) rather than his royal robe.
6:23 *Michal . . . had no child.* Probably a punishment for her pride and at the same time another manifestation of God's judgment on the house of Saul.
7:1–29 God's great promise to David (see Introduction: Contents and Theme). Although it is not expressly called a covenant here, it is elsewhere (23:5; Ps 89:3,28,34,39; cf. Ps 132:11), and David responds with language suggesting his recognition that a covenant had been made (see notes on vv. 20,28).
7:1 *when the king lived in his house.* See 5:11; see also note on 5:12. *and the LORD had given him rest . . . from all his enemies.* Chronologically the victories noted in 8:1–14 probably preceded the events of this chapter. The arrangement of material is topical (see also note on 5:17)—ch. 6 records the bringing of the ark to Jerusalem; ch. 7 tells of David's desire to build a temple in Jerusalem in which to house the ark.
7:2 *Nathan.* The first reference to this prophet (see 12:1–14; 1 Kin 1). *tent.* See v. 6; 6:17. Now that he himself had a royal palace (symbolic of his established kingship), a tent did not seem to David to be an appropriate place for the throne of Israel's divine King (see note on 6:2; see also Ps 132:2–5; Acts 7:46). He wanted to build Israel's heavenly King a royal house in the capital city of his kingdom.
7:3 *Nathan said.* In consulting a prophet, David sought God's will, but Nathan boldly voiced approval of David's plans in the Lord's name before he had received a revelation from the Lord.
7:5 *Are you the one . . . ?* David's desire was commendable (1 Kin 8:18–19), but his gift and mission were to fight the Lord's battles until Israel was securely at rest in the promised land (see v. 10; 1 Kin 5:3).
7:7 *did I speak . . . saying, "Why have you not built Me a house . . . ?"* David misunderstood the Lord's priorities. He reflected the pagan notion that the gods were interested in human beings only as builders and maintainers of their temples and as practitioners of their cult. Instead, the Lord had raised up rulers in Israel only to shepherd His people (that is also why he had brought David "from the pasture," v. 8).
7:9 *I . . . have cut off all your enemies.* See note on v. 1.
7:10 *I will also appoint a place for My people Israel.* It is for this purpose that the Lord has made David king, and through David He will do it. *as formerly.* In Egypt.
7:11 *judges.* Leaders during the period of the judges (see

will give you rest from all your enemies. The
LORD also declares to you that [c]the LORD will
make a house for you.
12 "[a]When your days are complete and you
[b]lie down with your fathers, [c]I will raise up
your [1]descendant after you, who will come
forth from [2]you, and I will establish his kingdom.
13 "[a]He shall build a house for My name,
and [b]I will establish the throne of his kingdom forever.
14 "[a]I will be a father to him and he will be
a son to Me; [b]when he commits iniquity, I
will correct him with the rod of men and the
strokes of the sons of men,
15 but My lovingkindness shall not depart
from him, [a]as I took *it* away from Saul,
whom I removed from before you.
16 "[a]Your house and your kingdom shall
endure before [1]Me forever; your throne shall
be established forever." ' "
17 In accordance with all these words and
all this vision, so Nathan spoke to David.

David's Prayer

18 Then David the king went in and sat
before the LORD, and he said, "[a]Who am I, O
Lord [1]GOD, and what is my house, that You
have brought me this far?
19 "And yet this was insignificant in Your
eyes, O Lord GOD, [a]for You have spoken also
of the house of Your servant concerning the
distant future. And [b]this is the [1]custom of
man, O Lord GOD.
20 "Again what more can David say to You?
For [a]You know Your servant, O Lord GOD!
21 "[a]For the sake of Your word, and according to Your own heart, You have done all this
greatness to let Your servant know.
22 "For this reason [a]You are great, O Lord
GOD; for [b]there is none like You, and there is
no God besides You, [c]according to all that we
have heard with our ears.
23 "And [a]what one nation on the earth is
like Your people Israel, whom God went to
redeem for Himself as a people and to make
a name for Himself, and [b]to do a great thing
for You and awesome things for Your land,
before [c]Your people whom [d]You have
redeemed for Yourself from Egypt, *from*
nations and their gods?
24 "For [a]You have established for Yourself
Your people Israel as Your own people forever, and [b]You, O LORD, have become their
God.

11 [c]1 Sam 25:28; 2 Sam 7:27
12 [1]Lit *seed* [2]Lit *your bowels* [a]1 Kin 2:1 [b]Deut 31:16; Acts 13:36 [c]1 Kin 8:20; Ps 132:11
13 [a]1 Kin 6:12; 8:19 [b]Is 9:7; 49:8
14 [a]Ps 89:26, 27; 2 Cor 6:18; Heb 1:5 [b]1 Kin 11:34; Ps 89:30-33
15 [a]1 Sam 15:23; 16:14
16 [1]So with Gr and some ancient mss; M.T. *you* [a]2 Sam 7:13; Ps 89:36, 37
18 [1]Heb *YHWH,* usually rendered *LORD,* and so throughout the ch [a]Ex 3:11; 1 Sam 18:18
19 [1]Or *law* [a]2 Sam 7:11-16; 1 Chr 17:17 [b]Is 55:8, 9
20 [a]1 Sam 16:7; John 21:17
21 [a]1 Chr 17:19; Eph 4:32
22 [a]Deut 3:24; Ps 48:1; 86:10 [b]Ex 15:11; 1 Sam 2:2 [c]Ex 10:2; Ps 44:1
23 [a]Deut 4:32-38 [b]Deut 10:21 [c]Deut 15:15 [d]Deut 9:26
24 [a]Deut 32:6 [b]Gen 17:7, 8; Ex 6:7

Introduction to Judges: Title). *I will give you rest from all your enemies.* See vv. 1,9. David's victories over threatening powers will be complete, so that the rest already enjoyed will be assured for the future. *the LORD will make a house for you.* Compare this statement with the rhetorical question of v. 5. In a beautiful play on words God says that David is not to build Him a house (temple); rather, God will build David a house (royal dynasty) that will last forever (v. 16). God has been building Israel ever since the days of Abraham, and now He commits Himself to build David's royal house so that the promise to Israel may be fulfilled—rest in the promised land. It is God's building that effects His kingdom. This covenant with David is unconditional, like those with Noah, Abram and Phinehas (see note on Gen 9:9; see also chart, p. 16), grounded only in God's firm and gracious purpose. It finds its ultimate fulfillment in the kingship of Christ, who was born of the tribe of Judah and the house of David (see Ps 89:30–38; Is 9:1–7; Matt 1:1; Luke 1:32–33,69; Acts 2:30; 13:23; Rom 1:2–3; 2 Tim 2:8; Rev 3:7; 22:16).

7:12 *raise up your descendant after you.* The royal line of David, in contrast to that of Saul, would continue after David's death by dynastic succession.

7:13 *He shall build a house for My name.* God's priorities are that His own royal house, where His throne (the ark) can finally come to rest (1 Chr 6:31; 28:2), will wait until Israel is at rest and David's dynasty (in the person of his son) is secure. "Name" is equivalent to "Me" in v. 5 (see note on 1 Sam 25:25).

7:14 *father to him... son to Me.* This familial language expresses the special relationship God promises to maintain with the descendant(s) of David whom He will establish on David's throne. It marks him as the one God has chosen and enthroned to rule in His name as the official representative of God's rule over His people (see notes on Ps 2:7; 45:6; 89:27). In Jesus Christ this promise comes to ultimate fulfillment (see Matt 1:1; Mark 1:11; Heb 1:5).

7:15 *My lovingkindness.* God's special and unfailing favor (see note on Ps 6:4).

7:16 *your throne shall be established forever.* See note on v. 11; see also Introduction: Contents and Theme. The promise of an everlasting kingdom for the house of David became the focal point for many later prophecies and powerfully influenced the development of the Messianic hope in Israel.

7:18–29 David's prayer expresses wonder that God would make such commitments to him and his descendants. But he also acknowledges that what God had pledged to him is for Israel's sake, that its purpose is the fulfillment of God's covenanted promises to His people—and that its ultimate effect will be the honor and praise of God throughout the world.

7:18 *went in.* Presumably into the tent (6:17) in which the ark was kept. *sat before the LORD.* The ark was the symbol of God's presence with His people (see Ex 25:22; see also notes on 1 Sam 4:3–4,21).

7:19 *And this is the custom of man, O Lord GOD.* The meaning of this clause is uncertain (cf. 1 Chr 17:17). It has also been taken as an exclamation ("This is Your law for man, O Sovereign LORD!") and understood as a summation of the divine decree concerning David and his house.

7:20 *know.* Or "especially acknowledge" or "choose" (see Gen 18:19, "chosen"; Amos 3:2, "chosen"). David recognizes God's promise as a covenant (23:5).

7:21 *Your word.* Probably God's covenant word of promise to His people.

7:22 *no God besides You.* See 22:32; 1 Sam 2:2.

7:23 *one nation . . . God went to redeem for Himself as a people.* Israel's uniqueness did not consist in her national achievements but in God's choice of her to be His own people (see Deut 7:6–8; 33:26–29). *to make a name for Himself.* The basis for God's electing love, revealed in His dealings with Israel, did not lie in any meritorious characteristic of the Israelite people but in His own sovereign purposes (see Deut 7:6–8; 9:4–5; 1 Sam 12:22; Neh 9:10; Is 63:12; Jer 32:20–21; Ezek 36:22–38).

7:24 *You, O LORD, have become their God.* What God has pledged to David, He has pledged as the God of Israel.

25 "Now therefore, O LORD God, the word that You have spoken concerning Your servant and his house, confirm *it* forever, and do as You have spoken,

26 [a]that Your name may be magnified forever, by saying, 'The LORD of hosts is God over Israel'; and may the house of Your servant David be established before You.

27 "For You, O LORD of hosts, the God of Israel, have [1]made a revelation to Your servant, saying, '[a]I will build you a house'; therefore Your servant has found [2]courage to pray this prayer to You.

28 "Now, O Lord GOD, You are God, and [a]Your words are truth, and You have [1]promised this good thing to Your servant.

29 "Now therefore, may it please You to bless the house of Your servant, that it may continue forever before You. For You, O Lord GOD, have spoken; and [a]with Your blessing may the house of Your servant be blessed forever."

David's Triumphs

8 [a]Now after this it came about that David [1]defeated the Philistines and subdued them; and David took [2]control of the chief city from the hand of the Philistines.

2 [a]He [1]defeated [b]Moab, and measured them with the line, making them lie down on the ground; and he measured two lines to put to death and one full line to keep alive. And [c]the Moabites became servants to David, [d]bringing tribute.

3 Then David [1]defeated [a]Hadadezer, the son of Rehob king of Zobah, as [b]he went to restore his [2]rule at the [3]River.

4 David captured from him 1,700 horsemen and 20,000 foot soldiers; and David [a]hamstrung the chariot horses, but reserved *enough* of them for 100 chariots.

5 When [a]the Arameans of Damascus came to help Hadadezer, king of Zobah, David [1]killed 22,000 Arameans.

6 Then David put garrisons among the Arameans of Damascus, and [a]the Arameans became servants to David, bringing tribute. And [b]the LORD helped David wherever he went.

7 David took the shields of gold which were [1]carried by the servants of Hadadezer and brought them to Jerusalem.

8 From [1]Betah and from [a]Berothai, cities of Hadadezer, King David took a very large amount of bronze.

9 Now when Toi king of [a]Hamath heard that David had [1]defeated all the army of Hadadezer,

10 Toi sent [1]Joram his son to King David to [2]greet him and bless him, because he had fought against Hadadezer and [3]defeated him; for Hadadezer [4]had been at war with Toi. And [5]*Joram* brought with him articles of silver, of gold and of bronze.

11 King David also [a]dedicated these to the LORD, with the silver and gold that he had dedicated from all the nations which he had subdued:

12 from [1]Aram and [a]Moab and [b]the sons of Ammon and [c]the Philistines and [d]Amalek, and from the spoil of Hadadezer, son of Rehob, king of Zobah.

13 So [a]David made a name *for himself* when he returned from [1]killing 18,000 [2]Arameans in [b]the Valley of Salt.

14 He put garrisons in Edom. In all Edom he put garrisons, and [a]all the Edomites became servants to David. And [b]the LORD helped David wherever he went.

15 So David reigned over all Israel; and David [1]administered justice and righteousness for all his people.

26 [a]Ps 72:18, 19; Matt 6:9 **27** [1]Lit *uncovered the ear of* [2]Lit *his heart* [a]2 Sam 7:13 **28** [1]Or *spoken* [a]Ex 34:6; John 17:17 **29** [a]Num 6:24-26 **8:1** [1]Lit *smote* [2]Lit *the bridle of the mother city* [a]1 Chr 18 **2** [1]Lit *smote* [a]Num 24:17 [b]1 Sam 22:3, 4 [c]2 Sam 8:6; 1 Kin 4:21 [d]2 Kin 3:4; 17:3 **3** [1]Lit *smote* [2]Lit *hand* [3]I.e. Euphrates [a]1 Sam 14:47; 2 Sam 10:16, 19 [b]2 Sam 10:15-19 **4** [a]Josh 11:6, 9 **5** [a]1 Kin 11:23-25

5 [1]Lit *smote* **6** [a]2 Sam 8:2 [b]2 Sam 3:18 **7** [1]Lit *on* **8** [1]In 1 Chr 18:8, *Tibhath* [a]Ezek 47:16 **9** [1]Lit *smitten* [a]1 Kin 8:65; 2 Chr 8:4 **10** [1]In 1 Chr 18:10, *Hadoram* [2]Lit *ask him of his welfare* [3]Lit *smitten* [4]Lit *was a man of wars* [5]Lit *there were in his hand* **11** [a]1 Kin 7:51 **12** [1]Some mss read *Edom* [a]2 Sam 8:2 [b]2 Sam 10:14 [c]2 Sam 5:17-25 [d]1 Sam 27:8; 30:17-20 **13** [1]Lit *smiting* [2]Some mss read *Edom* [a]2 Sam 7:9 [b]2 Kin 14:7

14 [a]Gen 27:37-40; Num 24:17, 18 [b]2 Sam 8:6 **15** [1]Lit *was doing*

7:27 *Your servant has found courage to pray this prayer to You.* David's prayer lays claim on God's promise.

7:28 *good thing.* A common summary expression for covenant benefits from God (see, e.g., 1 Sam 2:32, "good"; Num 10:29,32; Deut 26:11; Josh 21:45; 23:14, "good words"; Is 63:7; Jer 29:32; 32:40–41, "good"; 33:9).

8:1 *after this it came about.* Chronologically the events of this chapter, or many of them, are probably to be placed between chs. 5 and 6 (see 7:1 and note). *the chief city.* An unknown site, perhaps near Gath (see 1 Chr 18:1).

8:2 *Moab.* Descendants of Lot (Gen 19:37), occupying territory east of the Dead Sea. Saul fought with the Moabites (1 Sam 14:47), and David sought refuge in Moab for his parents during his exile from Israel (1 Sam 22:3–4). See note on Ruth 1:22.

8:3 *Hadadezer.* Means "Hadad is (my) help." Hadad was an Aramean deity equivalent to the Canaanite Baal. *Zobah.* Saul had previously fought against the kings of Zobah (1 Sam 14:47), whose territory was apparently located in the Beqaa Valley between the Lebanon and Anti-Lebanon mountains, thus on Israel's northern border. *restore.* Saul's earlier victories over the kings of Zobah had extended Israelite control, if only briefly, as far as the fringes of the Euphrates Valley. *the River.* The land promised to Abraham had included borders from Egypt to the Euphrates River (Gen 15:18–21; Deut 1:7; 11:24; Josh 1:4). Here is at least another provisional fulfillment of this promise (see 1 Kin 4:21–24; see also Gen 17:8; Josh 21:43–45). See map No. 5 at the end of the study Bible.

8:4 *hamstrung the chariot horses.* See Josh 11:6 and note. David may not have understood the value of the chariot as a military weapon.

8:5 *came to help Hadadezer.* They feared Israelite expansion to the north.

8:7 *shields of gold.* Shields adorned with gold—the phrase is similar to "chariots of iron" (see Josh 17:16 and note).

8:8 *bronze.* Later used by Solomon in the construction of the temple (1 Chr 18:8).

8:9 *Hamath.* A kingdom centered on the Orontes River, north of Zobah (see v. 3 and note).

8:13 *Valley of Salt.* See 2 Kin 14:7; see also Ps 60 title.

8:15 *justice and righteousness.* As a true theocratic king, David's reign was characterized by adherence to God's standards of right rule (see notes on 1 Sam 8:3; 12:3), as no doubt laid down in Samuel's "ordinances of the kingdom" (see 1 Sam 10:25 and note; 1 Kin 2:3–4).

16 [a]Joab the son of Zeruiah *was* over the army, and [b]Jehoshaphat the son of Ahilud *was* [c]recorder.

17 [a]Zadok the son of Ahitub and Ahimelech the son of Abiathar *were* [b]priests, and Seraiah *was* [c]secretary.

18 [a]Benaiah the son of Jehoiada [1]was over the [b]Cherethites and the Pelethites; and David's sons were [2c]chief ministers.

David's Kindness to Mephibosheth

9 Then David said, "Is there yet [1]anyone left of the house of Saul, [a]that I may show him kindness for Jonathan's sake?"

2 Now there was a servant of the house of Saul whose name was Ziba, and they called him to David; and the king said to him, "Are you [a]Ziba?" And he said, "*I am* your servant."

3 The king said, "Is there not yet anyone of the house of Saul to whom I may show the [a]kindness of God?" And Ziba said to the king, "[b]There is still a son of Jonathan who is crippled in both feet."

4 So the king said to him, "Where is he?" And Ziba said to the king, "Behold, he is [a]in the house of Machir the son of Ammiel in Lo-debar."

5 Then King David sent and brought him from the house of Machir the son of Ammiel, from Lo-debar.

6 [a]Mephibosheth, the son of Jonathan the son of Saul, came to David and [b]fell on his face and prostrated himself. And David said, "Mephibosheth." And he said, "Here is your servant!"

7 David said to him, "Do not fear, for [a]I will surely show kindness to you for the sake of your father Jonathan, and [b]will restore to you all the [1]land of your [2]grandfather Saul; and [c]you shall [3]eat at my table regularly."

8 Again he prostrated himself and said, "What is your servant, that you should regard [a]a dead dog like me?"

9 Then the king called Saul's servant Ziba and said to him, "[a]All that belonged to Saul and to all his house I have given to your master's [1]grandson.

16 [a]1 Chr 11:6 [b]1 Kin 4:3 [c]2 Kin 18:18, 37
17 [a]1 Chr 6:4-8 [b]1 Chr 16:39, 40 [c]2 Kin 18:18
18 [1]Lit *and the Cherethites* [2]Lit *priests* [a]1 Kin 4:4 [b]1 Sam 30:14; 2 Sam 15:18; 20:7, 23; 1 Kin 1:38, 44 [c]1 Chr 18:17
9:1 [1]Lit *he who is* [a]1 Sam 20:14-17, 42
2 [a]2 Sam 16:1-4; 19:17, 29
3 [a]1 Sam 20:14 [b]2 Sam 4:4
4 [a]2 Sam 17:27-29
6 [a]2 Sam 16:4; 19:24-30 [b]1 Sam 25:23
7 [1]Lit *field* [2]Lit *father* [3]Lit *eat bread* [a]2 Sam 9:1, 3 [b]2 Sam 12:8 [c]2 Sam 19:28; 1 Kin 2:7; 2 Kin 25:29
8 [a]2 Sam 16:9; 24:14
9 [1]Lit *son* [a]2 Sam 16:4; 19:29

8:16 *Joab the son of Zeruiah was over the army.* See notes on 2:13;5:8. *recorder.* The precise duties of this official are not indicated, though the position was an important one in the court and was maintained throughout the period of the monarchy (see 2 Kin 18:18,37; 2 Chr 34:8; Is 36:3,11,22). He may have been a kind of chancellor or chief administrator of royal affairs, responsible among other things for the royal chronicles and annals.

8:17 *Zadok the son of Ahitub.* First mentioned here, Zadok was a descendant of Eleazar son of Aaron (see 1 Chr 6:4–8,50–52; 24:1–3). His father, Ahitub, is not to be identified with Ichabod's brother of the same name (1 Sam 14:3). Zadok remained loyal to David throughout his reign (15:24–29; 17:15–16; 19:11) and eventually anointed Solomon as David's successor (1 Kin 1:8,45; 2:35; 4:4). *Ahimelech the son of Abiathar.* It appears that a copyist's error may have occurred here (repeated in 1 Chr 24:3,6,31) in which these two names have been transposed. Abiathar is referred to as son of Ahimelech in 1 Sam 22:20. While it is true that the Abiathar of 1 Sam 22:20 could have had a son named Ahimelech (after his grandfather), such a person does not appear elsewhere in the narratives of Samuel and Kings as a colleague of Zadok, but Abiathar consistently does (15:29,35; 17:15; 19:11; 20:25; 1 Kin 1:7–8,19; 2:27,35; 4:4). Abiathar was a descendant of Aaron through Ithamar (1 Chr 24:3) in the line of Eli (see notes on 1 Sam 2:31,33). *Seraiah.* Also called Sheva (20:25), Shisha (1 Kin 4:3) and Shavsha (1 Chr 18:16). *secretary.* His duties presumably included domestic and foreign correspondence, perhaps keeping records of important political events, and various administrative functions (2 Kin 12:10–12).

8:18 *Cherethites and the Pelethites.* See note on 1 Sam 30:14. Under the leadership of Benaiah, they formed a sort of special royal guard for David (23:22–23). "Pelethite" is probably an alternate form of "Philistine." *chief ministers.* The Hebrew has the common word for "priests" (see NASB marg.; see also 20:26), but the usage is obscure since that sense appears unlikely. Chronicles has "chiefs at the king's side" (see 1 Chr 18:17 and note), which supports the meaning "chief ministers."

9:1–20:26 These chapters, together with 1 Kin 1:1–2:46, are often referred to as the "Court History of David" and hailed as one of the finest examples of historical narrative to have been produced in the ancient world. Their intimate and precise detail marks them as the work of an eyewitness.

9:1–13 The events of this chapter cannot be dated precisely, but they occurred a number of years after David's capture of Jerusalem. Mephibosheth was five years old at the time of his father's death (4:4); now he has a son of his own (v. 12).

9:1 *I may show him kindness for Jonathan's sake.* David has not forgotten his promise to Jonathan (see 1 Sam 20:15,42).

9:2 *Ziba.* The chief steward of Saul's estate, which had been inherited by Mephibosheth son of Jonathan, Saul's firstborn (see 16:1–4; 19:17).

9:3 *There is still a son of Jonathan.* Saul had other descendants (see 21:8), but Ziba mentions only the one in whom David would be chiefly interested.

9:4 *Machir.* Apparently a wealthy benefactor of Mephibosheth who later also came to David's aid (17:27). *Lo-debar.* A town deep in Gileadite territory in Transjordan (Josh 13:26, "Debir"), far from the family estate and from David's court (see note on 2:8).

9:7 *restore to you.* The property Saul had acquired as king had either been taken over by David, or Ziba as steward had virtually taken possession of it and was profiting from its income (see 16:1–4; 19:26–30). *you shall eat at my table regularly.* More a matter of high honor than economic assistance. Mephibosheth's general financial needs were to be cared for by the produce of Saul's estate (v. 10).

9:8 *dead dog like me.* An expression of deep self-abasement. The author has used the "dead dog" motif with great effect. First Goliath, scornfully disdaining the young warrior David, asks, "Am I a dog . . . ?" (1 Sam 17:43)—and unwittingly foreshadows his own end. Then David, in a self-deprecating manner, describes himself as a "dead dog" (1 Sam 24:14) to suggest to Saul that the king of Israel should not consider him worth so much attention. In the Nabal episode, that "dog" (a Calebite) and his sudden death characterize Saul and foreshadow his unhappy end (see note on 1 Sam 25:3). Here a grandson of Saul and in 16:9 a relative of the dead king who curses David are similarly described. For the author, "dead dog" fittingly characterizes those who foolishly scorn or oppose the Lord's anointed, while David's own self-deprecation (see 1 Sam 18:18; 2 Sam 7:18) is conducive to his exaltation.

10 "You and your sons and your servants shall cultivate the land for him, and you shall bring in *the produce* so that your master's grandson may have food; nevertheless [a]Mephibosheth your master's grandson [b]shall [1]eat at my table regularly." Now Ziba had fifteen sons and twenty servants.

11 Then Ziba said to the king, "According [a]to all that my lord the king commands his servant so your servant will do." So Mephibosheth ate at [1]David's table as one of the king's sons.

12 Mephibosheth had a young son whose name was Mica. And all who lived in the house of Ziba were servants to Mephibosheth.

13 So Mephibosheth lived in Jerusalem, for [a]he ate at the king's table regularly. Now [b]he was lame in both feet.

Ammon and Aram Defeated

10 [a]Now it happened afterwards that [b]the king of the Ammonites died, and Hanun his son became king in his place.

2 Then David said, "I will show kindness to Hanun the son of [a]Nahash, just as his father showed kindness to me." So David sent [1]some of his servants to console him concerning his father. But when David's servants came to the land of the Ammonites,

3 the princes of the Ammonites said to Hanun their lord, "[1]Do you think that David is honoring your father because he has sent consolers to you? [a]Has David not sent his servants to you in order to search the city, to spy it out and overthrow it?"

4 So Hanun took David's servants and [a]shaved off half of their beards, and [b]cut off their garments in the middle as far as their hips, and sent them away.

5 When they told *it* to David, he sent to meet them, for the men were greatly humiliated. And the king said, "[1]Stay at Jericho until your beards grow, and *then* return."

6 Now when the sons of Ammon saw that [a]they had become odious to David, the sons of Ammon sent and [b]hired the Arameans of [c]Beth-rehob and the [d]Arameans of Zobah, 20,000 foot soldiers, and the king of [e]Maacah with 1,000 men, and the men of Tob with 12,000 men.

7 When David heard *of it,* he sent Joab and all the army, the mighty men.

8 The sons of Ammon came out and drew up in battle array [a]at the entrance of the [1]city, while the Arameans of Zobah and of Rehob and the men of [b]Tob and Maacah *were* by themselves in the field.

9 Now when Joab saw that [1]the battle was set against him in front and in the rear, he selected from all the choice men of Israel, and arrayed *them* against the Arameans.

10 But the remainder of the people he placed in the hand of Abishai his brother, and he arrayed *them* against the sons of Ammon.

11 He said, "If the Arameans are too strong for me, then you shall help me, but if the sons of Ammon are too strong for you, then I will come to help you.

12 "[a]Be strong, and let us show ourselves courageous for the sake of our people and for the cities of our God; and [b]may the LORD do what is good in His sight."

13 So Joab and the people who were with him drew near to the battle against the Arameans, and [a]they fled before him.

14 When the sons of Ammon saw that the Arameans fled, they *also* fled before Abishai and entered the city. [a]Then Joab returned from *fighting* against the sons of Ammon and came to Jerusalem.

15 When the Arameans saw that they had been [1]defeated by Israel, they gathered themselves together.

16 [a]And Hadadezer sent and brought out the Arameans who were beyond the [1]River, and they came to Helam; and [b]Shobach the commander of the army of Hadadezer [2]led them.

17 Now when it was told David, he gathered all Israel together and crossed the Jordan, and came to Helam. And the Arameans arrayed themselves to meet David and fought against him.

18 But the Arameans fled before Israel, and David killed [a]700 charioteers of the Arameans and 40,000 horsemen and struck down Shobach the commander of their army, and he died there.

19 When all the kings, servants of Hadadezer, saw that they were [1]defeated by Israel, [a]they made peace with Israel and

10 [1]Lit *eat bread* [a]2 Sam 9:7, 11, 13 [b]2 Sam 19:28; 1 Kin 2:7
11 [1]Lit *my* [a]2 Sam 16:1-4; 19:24-30
13 [a]2 Sam 9:7, 11 [b]2 Sam 9:3
10:1 [a]1 Chr 19:1-19 [b]1 Sam 11:1
2 [1]Lit *by the hand of* [a]1 Sam 11:1
3 [1]Lit *In your eyes is David honoring* [a]Gen 42:9, 16
4 [a]Is 15:2; Jer 41:5 [b]Is 20:4
5 [1]Lit *Return to*
6 [a]Gen 34:30; 1 Sam 27:12 [b]2 Sam 8:3, 5; 2 Kin 7:6 [c]Judg 18:28 [d]2 Sam 8:3 [e]Deut 3:14
8 [1]Lit *gate* [a]1 Chr 19:9 [b]Judg 11:3, 5
9 [1]Lit *the faces of the battle were against*
12 [a]Deut 31:6; Josh 1:6; 1 Cor 16:13 [b]1 Sam 3:18
13 [a]1 Kin 20:13-21
14 [a]2 Sam 11:1
15 [1]Lit *smitten before*
16 [1]I.e. Euphrates [2]Lit *before* [a]2 Sam 8:3-8 [b]1 Chr 19:16
18 [a]1 Chr 19:18
19 [1]Lit *smitten before* [a]2 Sam 8:6

9:12 *Mica.* See 1 Chr 8:35–39 for his descendants.
10:1 *king.* Nahash (see v. 2; 1 Sam 11). *Ammonites.* See note on 1 Sam 11:1.
10:2 *show kindness.* The Hebrew for this expression suggests that a formal treaty existed between the Israelites and the Ammonites. Perhaps this explains why there is no account of a war against the Ammonites in ch. 8, and why the Ammonites did not come to the assistance of the Moabites (8:2).
10:3 *city.* Rabbah, the capital (11:1; 12:26).
10:4 *shaved off half of their beards.* In the Eastern world of that time this was considered an insult of the most serious kind. A beard was shaved only as a sign of deep mourning (see Is 15:2; Jer 41:5; Ezek 5:1). *cut off their garments . . . as far as their hips.* A customary way of degrading prisoners of war (see Is 20:4).
10:5 *Jericho.* See notes on Josh 6:1,26; 1 Kin 16:34. Jericho remained unrestored during the centuries between Joshua's conquest and the time of Ahab.
10:6 *Beth-rehob.* See Num 13:21; Judg 18:28. *Zobah.* See note on 8:3. *Maacah.* See Deut 3:14; Josh 12:5; 13:13. *Tob.* See Judg 11:3,5.
10:10 *Abishai.* See note on 1 Sam 26:6.
10:16 *Hadadezer.* See note on 8:3. *Helam.* A town close to the northern border of Gilead.
10:18 *700.* Evidently a copyist's mistake; in 1 Chr 19:18 the figure is 7,000.
10:19 *they made peace with Israel.* There is no indication that

served them. So the Arameans feared to help
the sons of Ammon anymore.

Bathsheba, David's Great Sin

11 [a]Then it happened [1][b]in the spring, at
the time when kings go out *to battle,*
that David sent Joab and his servants with
him and all Israel, and they destroyed the
sons of Ammon and [c]besieged Rabbah. But
David stayed at Jerusalem.
2 Now when evening came David arose
from his bed and walked around on [a]the roof
of the king's house, and from the roof he saw
a woman bathing; and the woman was very
beautiful in appearance.
3 So David sent and inquired about the
woman. And one said, "Is this not [a]Bathshe-
ba, the daughter of Eliam, the wife of [b]Uriah
the Hittite?"
4 David sent messengers and took her,
and when she came to him, [a]he lay with her;
[b]and when she had purified herself from her
uncleanness, she returned to her house.
5 The woman conceived; and she sent
and told David, and said, "[a]I am pregnant."
6 Then David sent to Joab, *saying,* "Send
me Uriah the Hittite." So Joab sent Uriah to
David.
7 When Uriah came to him, [a]David
asked concerning the welfare of Joab and
[1]the people and the state of the war.
8 Then David said to Uriah, "Go down to
your house, and [a]wash your feet." And Uriah went out of the king's house, and a present from the king [1]was sent out after him.
9 But Uriah slept [a]at the door of the
king's house with all the servants of his lord,
and did not go down to his house.

11:1 [1]Lit *at the return of the year* [a]1 Chr 20:1 [b]2 Sam 10:14; 1 Kin 20:22, 26 [c]2 Sam 12:26-29; Jer 49:2, 3; Amos 1:14
2 [a]Deut 22:8; 1 Sam 9:25; Matt 24:17; Acts 10:9
3 [a]1 Chr 3:5 [b]2 Sam 23:39
4 [a]Ps 51: title; James 1:14, 15 [b]Lev 12:2-5; 15:18-28; 18:19
5 [a]Lev 20:10; Deut 22:22
7 [1]Lit *welfare of* [a]Gen 37:14; 1 Sam 17:22
8 [1]Lit *went out* [a]Gen 43:24; Luke 7:44
9 [a]1 Kin 14:27, 28
11 [1]Or *booths* [a]2 Sam 7:2, 6 [b]2 Sam 20:6
12 [1]Lit *morrow* [a]Job 20:12-14
13 [a]Prov 20:1; 23:29-35 [b]2 Sam 11:9
14 [a]1 Kin 21:8-10
15 [1]Lit *Give* [2]Lit *strong* [a]Eccl 8:11; Jer 17:9 [b]2 Sam 12:9
17 [a]2 Sam 11:21

10 Now when they told David, saying,
"Uriah did not go down to his house," David
said to Uriah, "Have you not come from a
journey? Why did you not go down to your
house?"
11 Uriah said to David, "[a]The ark and
Israel and Judah are staying in [1]temporary
shelters, and my lord Joab and [b]the servants
of my lord are camping in the open field.
Shall I then go to my house to eat and to
drink and to lie with my wife? By your life
and the life of your soul, I will not do this
thing."
12 Then David said to Uriah, "[a]Stay here
today also, and tomorrow I will let you go."
So Uriah remained in Jerusalem that day and
the [1]next.
13 Now David called him, and he ate and
drank before him, and he [a]made him drunk;
and in the evening he went out to lie on his
bed [b]with his lord's servants, but he did not
go down to his house.
14 Now in the morning David [a]wrote a letter to Joab and sent *it* by the hand of Uriah.
15 [a]He had written in the letter, saying,
"[1]Place Uriah in the front line of the [2]fiercest
battle and withdraw from him, [b]so that he
may be struck down and die."
16 So it was as Joab kept watch on the
city, that he put Uriah at the place where he
knew there *were* valiant men.
17 The men of the city went out and
fought against Joab, and some of the people
among David's servants fell; and [a]Uriah the
Hittite also died.
18 Then Joab sent and reported to David
all the events of the war.
19 He charged the messenger, saying,

Hadadezer himself made peace with Israel as his vassals did in the aftermath of this defeat. These events represent David's last major campaign against combined foreign powers.

11:1 *the spring.* Of the year following the events reported in ch. 10. The time must have been about ten years after David became established in Jerusalem. *the time when kings go out to battle.* Directly after the grain harvest in April and May. *Rabbah.* See note on 10:3. Though now alone (see 10:19), the Ammonites had not yet been subjugated.

11:2 *walked around on the roof.* The roofs were flat (see 1 Sam 9:25). David had probably gone there to enjoy the cool evening air.

11:3 *Eliam.* Perhaps the same Eliam who was a member of David's personal bodyguard (23:34) and a son of his counselor Ahithophel. *Uriah.* Also listed among those comprising David's royal guard (23:39). His name suggests that even though he was a Hittite, he had adopted the Israelite faith (Uriah means "My light is the LORD"). *Hittite.* See note on 1 Sam 26:6.

11:4 *David sent messengers and took her.* Through this action David eventually becomes guilty of breaking the sixth, seventh, ninth and tenth commandments (Ex 20:13–17). *when she came to him, he lay with her.* Bathsheba appears to have been an unprotesting partner in this adulterous relationship with David. *when she had purified herself from her uncleanness.* Lev 15:18 required purification after sexual relations.

11:5 *I am pregnant.* Bathsheba leaves the next step up to David. The law prescribed the death penalty for both David and Bathsheba (Lev 20:10; Deut 22:22), as they well knew.

11:6 *Send me Uriah.* Under the pretense of seeking information about the course of the war, David brings Uriah back to Jerusalem.

11:8 *Go down to your house, and wash your feet.* In essence, David tells Uriah to go home and relax. What he does not say specifically is what is most important, and well understood by Uriah (v. 11). *a present from the king was sent out after him.* The Hebrew word for "present" has the meaning of "food" in Gen 43:34 ("portions" from the king's table). David wanted Uriah and Bathsheba to enjoy their evening together.

11:11 *ark.* Uriah's statement suggests that the ark was in the field camp with the army rather than in the tent that David had set up for it in Jerusalem (6:17). If so, it was probably there for purposes of worship and to seek guidance for the war. But then the circumstances are even more damning for David—the Lord is in the field with His army while David stays at home in leisure. *Shall I then go to my house . . . ?* Uriah's devotion to duty exposes by sharp contrast David's dalliance at home while his men are in the field. *By your life and the life of your soul.* See note on 1 Sam 1:26.

11:13 *he made him drunk.* In the hope that in this condition he would relent and go to Bathsheba.

11:15 *so that he may be struck down and die.* Unsuccessful in making it appear that Uriah was the father of Bathsheba's child, David plotted Uriah's death so he could marry Bathsheba himself as quickly as possible.

"When you have finished telling all the events of the war to the king,

20 and if it happens that the king's wrath rises and he says to you, 'Why did you go so near to the city to fight? Did you not know that they would shoot from the wall?

21 'Who [a]struck down Abimelech the son of Jerubbesheth? Did not a woman throw an upper millstone on him from the wall so that he died at Thebez? Why did you go so near the wall?'—then you shall say, 'Your servant Uriah the Hittite is dead also.' "

22 So the messenger departed and came and reported to David all that Joab had sent him *to tell.*

23 The messenger said to David, "The men prevailed against us and came out against us in the field, but we [1]pressed them as far as the entrance of the gate.

24 "Moreover, the archers shot at your servants from the wall; so some of the king's servants are dead, and your servant Uriah the Hittite is also dead."

25 Then David said to the messenger, "Thus you shall say to Joab, 'Do not let this thing [1]displease you, for the sword devours one as well as another; make your battle against the city stronger and overthrow it'; and *so* encourage him."

26 Now when the wife of Uriah heard that Uriah her husband was dead, [a]she mourned for her husband.

27 When the *time of* mourning was over, David sent and [1]brought her to his house and [a]she became his wife; then she bore him a son. But [b]the thing that David had done was evil in the sight of the LORD.

Nathan Rebukes David

12 Then the LORD sent [a]Nathan to David. And [b]he came to him and [1]said,
"There were two men in one city, the
one rich and the other poor.
2 "The rich man had a great many flocks
and herds.
3 "But the poor man had nothing except
[a]one little ewe lamb
Which he bought and nourished;
And it grew up together with him and
his children.
It would eat of his [1]bread and drink of
his cup and lie in his bosom,
And was like a daughter to him.
4 "Now a traveler came to the rich man,
And he [1]was unwilling to take from
his own flock or his own herd,
To prepare for the wayfarer who had
come to him;
Rather he took the poor man's ewe
lamb and prepared it for the man
who had come to him."

5 Then David's anger burned greatly against the man, and he said to Nathan, "As the LORD lives, surely the man who has done this [1a]deserves to die.

6 "He must make restitution for the lamb [a]fourfold, because he did this thing and had no compassion."

7 Nathan then said to David, "[a]You are the man! Thus says the LORD God of Israel, '[b]It is I who anointed you king over Israel and it is I who delivered you from the hand of Saul.

8 'I also gave you [a]your master's house and your master's wives into your [1]care, and I gave you the house of Israel and Judah; and if *that had been* too little, I would have added to you many more things like these!

9 'Why [a]have you despised the word of the LORD by doing evil in His sight? [b]You have struck down Uriah the Hittite with the sword, [c]have taken his wife to be your wife, and have killed him with the sword of the sons of Ammon.

10 'Now therefore, [a]the sword shall never depart from your house, because you have despised Me and have taken the wife of Uriah the Hittite to be your wife.'

11 "Thus says the LORD, 'Behold, I will raise up evil against you from your own house-

21 [a]Judg 9:50-54
23 [1]Lit *were upon*
25 [1]Lit *be evil in your sight*
26 [a]Gen 50:10; Deut 34:8; 1 Sam 31:13
27 [1]Lit *gathered* [a]2 Sam 12:9 [b]Ps 51:4, 5
12:1 [1]Lit *said to him* [a]2 Sam 7:2, 4, 17 [b]Ps 51: title
3 [1]Lit *morsel* [a]2 Sam 11:3
4 [1]Lit *spared*
5 [1]Lit *is a son of death* [a]1 Sam 26:16
6 [a]Ex 22:1; Luke 19:8
7 [a]1 Kin 20:42 [b]1 Sam 16:13
8 [1]Lit *bosom* [a]2 Sam 9:7
9 [a]1 Sam 15:23, 26 [b]2 Sam 11:14-17 [c]2 Sam 11:27
10 [a]2 Sam 13:28; 18:14; 1 Kin 2:25

11:21 *Jerubbesheth.* That is, Gideon. Another possible spelling is "Jerubbosheth." In Judges he is called Jerubbaal (see note on Judg 6:32). For similar name changes by the author of Samuel see notes on 2:8; 4:4. *millstone.* See Judg 9:52–53. *Uriah . . . is dead.* Joab knows that this news is of great importance to David, and he uses it to squelch any criticism David might otherwise have had of the battle tactics.
11:25 *David said to the messenger.* David hid his satisfaction over the news with a hypocritical statement that war is war and the death of Uriah should not be a discouragement.
11:27 *time of mourning was over.* Presumably a period of seven days (Gen 50:10; 1 Sam 31:13). *she became his wife.* See notes on 3:2–5; 5:14. *the thing that David had done was evil in the sight of the LORD.* Not only had David brazenly violated God's laws (see note on v. 4) but, even worse, he had shamelessly abused his royal power, which the Lord had entrusted to him to shepherd the Lord's people (5:2; 7:7–8).
12:1 *The LORD sent.* Prophets were messengers from the Lord. Here the Great King sends His emissary to rebuke and announce judgment on the king He had enthroned over His people. *Nathan.* See note on 7:2. *There were two men.* Nathan begins one of the most striking parables in the OT.
12:5 *As the LORD lives.* See note on 1 Sam 14:39.
12:6 *fourfold.* In agreement with the requirements of Ex 22:1.
12:8 *your master's wives.* Earlier narratives refer to only one wife of Saul (Ahinoam, 1 Sam 14:50) and one concubine (Rizpah, 2 Sam 3:7; 21:8). This statement suggests that there were others. But since it was customary for new kings to assume the harem of their predecessors (see note on 3:7), it may be that Nathan merely uses conventional language to emphasize that the Lord had placed David on Saul's throne. *I gave you the house of Israel and Judah.* See 2:4; 5:2–3.
12:9 *despised the word of the LORD.* See notes on 11:4,27. *You . . . killed him.* David is held directly responsible for Uriah's death even though he fell in battle (see 11:15).
12:10 *the sword shall never depart from your house.* Three of David's sons came to violent deaths: Amnon (13:28–29), Absalom (18:14) and Adonijah (1 Kin 2:25).

hold; [a]I will even take your wives before your eyes and give *them* to your companion, and he will lie with your wives in [1]broad daylight.

12 'Indeed [a]you did it secretly, but [b]I will do this thing before all Israel, and [1]under the sun.' "

13 Then David said to Nathan, "[a]I have sinned against the LORD." And Nathan said to David, "The LORD also has [1b]taken away your sin; you shall not die.

14 "However, because by this deed you have [a]given occasion to the enemies of the LORD to blaspheme, the child also that is born to you shall surely die."

15 So Nathan went to his house.

Loss of a Child

Then the LORD struck the child that Uriah's [1]widow bore to David, so that he was *very* sick.

16 David therefore inquired of God for the child; and David [a]fasted and went and [b]lay all night on the ground.

17 [a]The elders of his household stood beside him in order to raise him up from the ground, but he was unwilling and would not eat food with them.

18 Then it happened on the seventh day that the child died. And the servants of David were afraid to tell him that the child was dead, for they said, "Behold, while the child was *still* alive, we spoke to him and he did not listen to our voice. How then can we tell him that the child is dead, since he might do *himself* harm!"

19 But when David saw that his servants were whispering together, David perceived that the child was dead; so David said to his servants, "Is the child dead?" And they said, "He is dead."

20 So David arose from the ground, [a]washed, anointed *himself,* and changed his clothes; and he came into the house of the LORD and [b]worshiped. Then he came to his own house, and when he requested, they set food before him and he ate.

21 Then his servants said to him, "What is this thing that you have done? [1]While the child was alive, you fasted and wept; but when the child died, you arose and ate food."

22 He said, "While the child was *still* alive, [a]I fasted and wept; for I said, '[b]Who knows, the LORD may be gracious to me, that the child may live.'

23 "But now he has died; why should I fast? Can I bring him back again? [a]I will go to him, but [b]he will not return to me."

Solomon Born

24 Then David comforted his wife Bathsheba, and went in to her and lay with her; and she gave birth to a son, and [1a]he named him Solomon. Now the LORD loved him

25 and sent *word* through Nathan the prophet, and he named him [1]Jedidiah for the LORD's sake.

War Again

26 [a]Now Joab fought against [b]Rabbah of the sons of Ammon and captured the royal city.

27 Joab sent messengers to David and said, "I have fought against Rabbah, I have even captured the city of waters.

28 "Now therefore, gather the rest of the people together and camp against the city and capture it, or I will capture the city myself and it will be named after me."

29 So David gathered all the people and went to Rabbah, fought against it and captured it.

30 Then [a]he took the crown of [1]their king from his head; and its weight *was* a talent of gold, and *in it* [2]*was* a precious stone; and it was *placed* on David's head. And he brought out the spoil of the city in great amounts.

31 He also brought out the people who

11 [1]Lit *the sight of this sun* [a]Deut 28:30; 2 Sam 16:21, 22
12 [1]Lit *before* [a]2 Sam 11:4-15 [b]2 Sam 16:22
13 [1]Lit *caused your sin to pass away* [a]1 Sam 15:24, 30; 2 Sam 24:10; Luke 18:13 [b]Lev 20:10; 24:17; Prov 28:13; Mic 7:18
14 [a]Is 52:5; Rom 2:24
15 [1]Lit *wife*
16 [a]Neh 1:4 [b]2 Sam 13:31
17 [a]Gen 24:2
20 [a]Ruth 3:3; Matt 6:17 [b]Ps 95:6-8; 103:1, 8-17; Prov 3:7
21 [1]Lit *On account of*
22 [a]Is 38:1-3 [b]Jon 3:9
23 [a]Gen 37:35 [b]Job 7:8-10
24 [1]Some mss read *she* [a]1 Chr 22:9; Matt 1:6
25 [1]I.e. beloved of the LORD
26 [a]1 Chr 20:1-3 [b]Deut 3:11
30 [1]Or *Malcam;* cf Zeph 1:5 [2]Or were *precious stones* [a]1 Chr 20:2

12:11 *I will raise up evil against you from your own household.* David was driven from Jerusalem by Absalom's conspiracy to seize the kingship from his own father (15:1–15). *he will lie with your wives in broad daylight.* Fulfilled at the time of Absalom's rebellion (see note on 16:22).

12:13 *I have sinned against the LORD.* David recognizes his guilt and confesses his sin in response to Nathan's rebuke (see Ps 51). There is a clear contrast between David's confession and Saul's (see note on 1 Sam 15:24). *The LORD also has taken away your sin.* David experienced the joy of knowing his sin was forgiven (see Ps 32:1,5; cf. Ps 51:8,12). *you shall not die.* The Lord, in his grace, released David from the customary death penalty for adultery and murder (Lev 20:10; 24:17).

12:14 *you have given occasion to the enemies of the LORD to blaspheme.* David is required to suffer the disciplinary results of his sin in a manner open to public view.

12:20 *he came into the house of the LORD and worshiped.* In this way David clearly demonstrated his humble acceptance of the disciplinary results of his sin. Again (see note on v. 13) there is a contrast between David's attitude and Saul's (see note on 1 Sam 15:25).

12:23 *I will go to him.* Like the child, David will die and join him in the grave (see note on Gen 37:35).

12:24 *Solomon.* See 1 Chr 22:9 and note.

12:25 *Jedidiah.* Means "beloved of the LORD." The giving of this name suggests that the Lord's special favor rested on Solomon from his birth. And since the name also contained an echo of David's name, it provided assurance to David that the Lord also loved him and would continue his dynasty.

12:26 *Joab fought against Rabbah.* The writer now returns to the outcome of the attack against the Ammonites (11:1,25), which provided the background for the story of David and Bathsheba. Even while the Lord was displeased with David, He gave the Israelites victory over a people who had abused them.

12:30 *the crown . . . was placed on David's head.* A crown of such weight (about 75 pounds) would have been worn only briefly and on very special occasions. Perhaps it was worn only once in a symbolic act of transferring to David sovereignty over Ammon.

David's Conquests

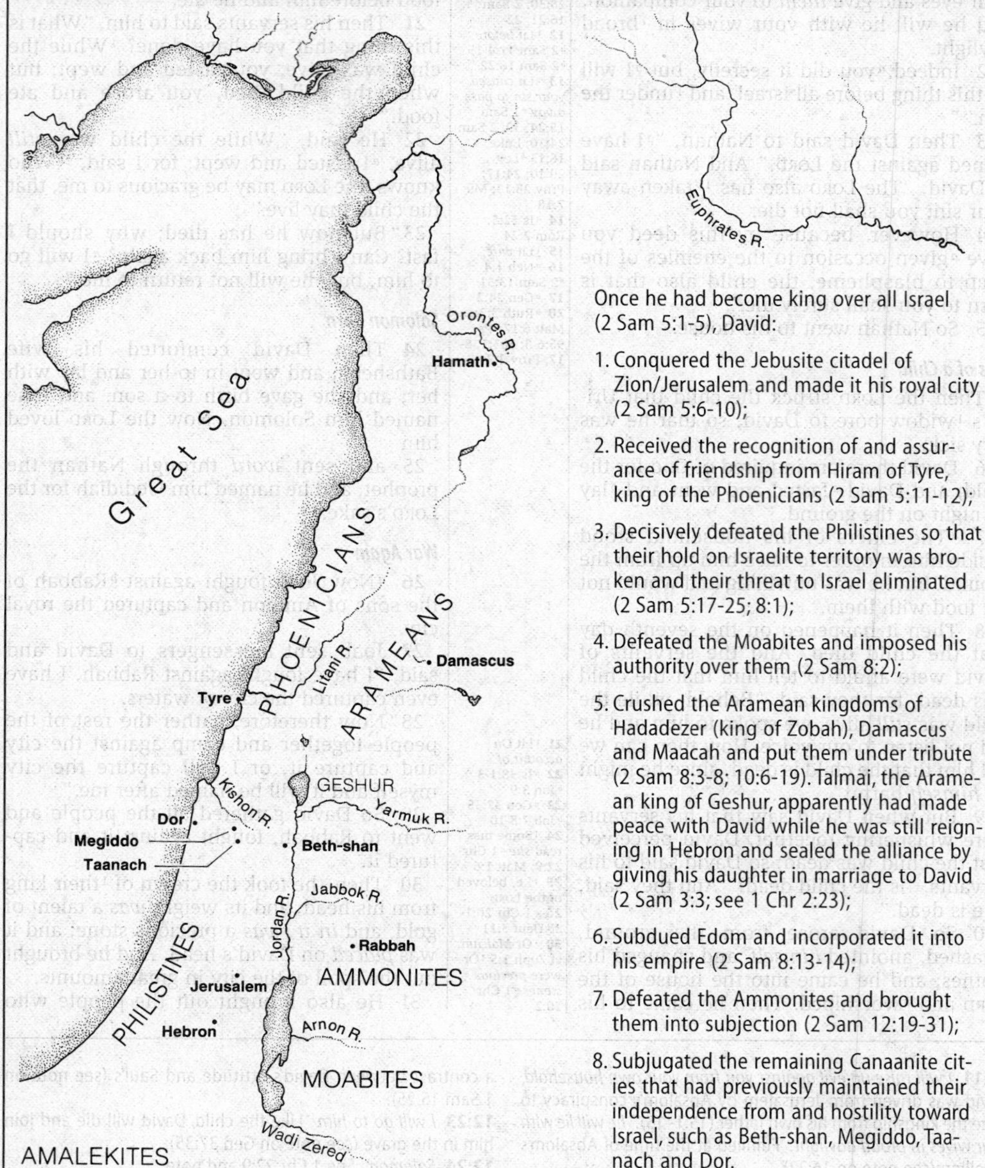

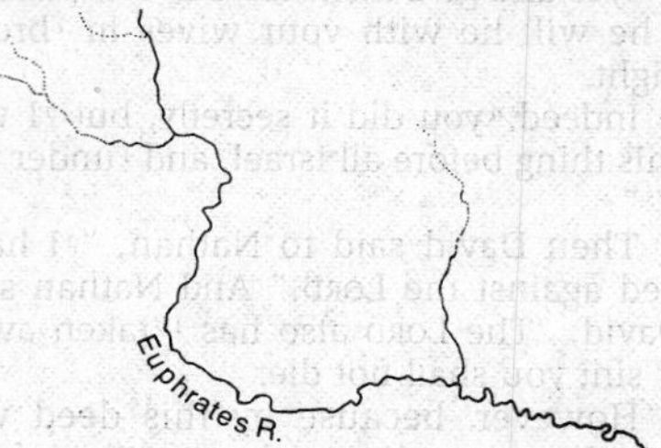

Euphrates R.
Great Sea
Orontes R.
Hamath
PHOENICIANS
ARAMEANS
Litani R.
Damascus
Tyre
GESHUR
Kishon R.
Yarmuk R.
Dor
Megiddo
Taanach
Beth-shan
Jabbok R.
Jordan R.
Rabbah
AMMONITES
PHILISTINES
Jerusalem
Hebron
Arnon R.
MOABITES
Wadi Zered
AMALEKITES
EDOMITES
Eastern arm of the
Red Sea
Miles 0 20 40 60 80 100
Kms 0 20 40 60 80 100 120 140

Once he had become king over all Israel (2 Sam 5:1-5), David:

1. Conquered the Jebusite citadel of Zion/Jerusalem and made it his royal city (2 Sam 5:6-10);
2. Received the recognition of and assurance of friendship from Hiram of Tyre, king of the Phoenicians (2 Sam 5:11-12);
3. Decisively defeated the Philistines so that their hold on Israelite territory was broken and their threat to Israel eliminated (2 Sam 5:17-25; 8:1);
4. Defeated the Moabites and imposed his authority over them (2 Sam 8:2);
5. Crushed the Aramean kingdoms of Hadadezer (king of Zobah), Damascus and Maacah and put them under tribute (2 Sam 8:3-8; 10:6-19). Talmai, the Aramean king of Geshur, apparently had made peace with David while he was still reigning in Hebron and sealed the alliance by giving his daughter in marriage to David (2 Sam 3:3; see 1 Chr 2:23);
6. Subdued Edom and incorporated it into his empire (2 Sam 8:13-14);
7. Defeated the Ammonites and brought them into subjection (2 Sam 12:19-31);
8. Subjugated the remaining Canaanite cities that had previously maintained their independence from and hostility toward Israel, such as Beth-shan, Megiddo, Taanach and Dor.

Since David had earlier crushed the Amalekites (1 Sam 30:17), his wars thus completed the conquest begun by Joshua and secured all the borders of Israel. His empire (united Israel plus the subjugated kingdoms) reached from Ezion-geber on the eastern arm of the Red Sea to the Euphrates River.

were in it, and [a]set *them* under saws, sharp
iron instruments, and iron axes, and made
them pass through the brickkiln. And thus
he did to all the cities of the sons of Ammon.
Then David and all the people returned *to*
Jerusalem.

Amnon and Tamar

13 Now it was after this that [a]Absalom the
son of David had a beautiful sister
whose name was [b]Tamar, and [c]Amnon the
son of David loved her.
2 Amnon was so frustrated because of
his sister Tamar that he made himself ill, for
she was a virgin, and it seemed [1]hard to
Amnon to do anything to her.
3 But Amnon had a friend whose name
was Jonadab, the son of [1a]Shimeah, David's
brother; and Jonadab was a very shrewd man.
4 He said to him, "O son of the king, why
are you so depressed morning after morning?
Will you not tell me?" Then Amnon said to
him, "I am in love with Tamar, the sister of
my brother Absalom."
5 Jonadab then said to him, "Lie down on
your bed and pretend to be ill; when your
father comes to see you, say to him, 'Please let
my sister Tamar come and give me *some* food
to eat, and let her prepare the food in my sight,
that I may see *it* and eat from her hand.' "
6 So Amnon lay down and pretended to
be ill; when the king came to see him,
Amnon said to the king, "Please let my sister
Tamar come and [a]make me a couple of cakes
in my sight, that I may eat from her hand."
7 Then David sent to the house for
Tamar, saying, "Go now to your brother
Amnon's house, and prepare food for him."
8 So Tamar went to her brother Amnon's
house, and he was lying down. And she took
dough, kneaded *it*, made cakes in his sight,
and baked the cakes.
9 She took the pan and [1]dished *them* out
before him, but he refused to eat. And
Amnon said, "[a]Have everyone go out from
me." So everyone went out from him.
10 Then Amnon said to Tamar, "Bring the
food into the [1]bedroom, that I may eat from
your hand." So Tamar took the cakes which
she had made and brought them into the
bedroom to her brother Amnon.
11 When she brought *them* to him to eat,
he [a]took hold of her and said to her, "Come,
lie with me, my sister."
12 But she answered him, "No, my brother, do not violate me, for [a]such a thing is not
done in Israel; do not do this [b]disgraceful
thing!
13 "As for me, where could I [1]get rid of my
reproach? And as for you, you will be like
one of the [2]fools in Israel. Now therefore,
please speak to the king, for [a]he will not
withhold me from you."
14 However, he would not listen to [1]her;
since he was stronger than she, he [a]violated
her and lay with her.
15 Then Amnon hated her with a very
great hatred; for the hatred with which he
hated her was greater than the love with
which he had loved her. And Amnon said to
her, "Get up, go away!"
16 But she said to him, "No, because this
wrong in sending me away is greater than
the other that you have done to me!" Yet he
would not listen to her.
17 Then he called his young man who
attended him and said, "Now throw this
woman out of my *presence*, and lock the
door behind her."
18 Now she had on [a]a [1]long-sleeved garment; for in this manner the virgin daughters of the king dressed themselves in robes.
Then his attendant took her out and locked
the door behind her.
19 [a]Tamar put [1]ashes on her head and
[b]tore her [2]long-sleeved garment which *was*
on her; and [c]she put her hand on her head
and went away, crying aloud as she went.
20 Then Absalom her brother said to her,
"Has Amnon your brother been with you?
But now keep silent, my sister, he is your
brother; do not take this matter to heart." So
Tamar remained and was desolate in her
brother Absalom's house.
21 Now when King David heard of all
these matters, he was very angry.

31 [a]1 Chr 20:3; Heb 11:37
13:1 [a]2 Sam 3:2, 3; 1 Chr 3:2 [b]1 Chr 3:9 [c]2 Sam 3:2
2 [1]Lit *hard in Amnon's eyes*
3 [1]In 1 Sam 16:9, *Shammah;* in 1 Chr 2:13, *Shimea* [a]1 Sam 16:9
6 [a]Gen 18:6
9 [1]Lit *poured* [a]Gen 45:1
10 [1]Or *inner room*
11 [a]Gen 39:12
12 [a]Lev 20:17 [b]Judg 19:23; 20:6
13 [1]Lit *cause to go* [2]Or *disgraceful ones* [a]Gen 20:12
14 [1]Lit *her voice* [a]Lev 18:9; Deut 22:25; 27:22; 2 Sam 12:11
18 [1]Lit *a varicolored tunic* [a]Gen 37:3, 23
19 [1]Or *dust* [2]Lit *varicolored tunic* [a]1 Sam 4:12; Esth 4:1 [b]Gen 37:29; 2 Sam 1:11 [c]Jer 2:37

12:31 *set them under saws . . . brickkiln.* Had them tortured and/or killed in keeping with their own cruel practices (see 1 Sam 11:2; Amos 1:13).
13:1–39 The trouble within David's family begins (see note on 12:10).
13:1 *Tamar.* David's daughter by Maacah of Geshur (3:3), and Absalom's full sister. *Amnon.* David's oldest son (3:2).
13:3 *Shimeah.* Called Shammah in 1 Sam 16:9.
13:13 *as for you.* This act would jeopardize Amnon's position as crown prince and heir to the throne. *he will not withhold me from you.* Possibly a futile attempt by Tamar to escape Amnon's immediate designs rather than a serious proposal, since such a marriage was prohibited in Israel (see Lev 18:9; 20:17; Deut 27:22).
13:15 *Amnon hated her.* The reversal in Amnon's feelings toward Tamar demonstrates that his former "love" (v. 1) was nothing but sensual desire.
13:16 *this wrong in sending me away is greater.* No longer a virgin, she could not be offered by her father to any other potential husband (see v. 21 and note).
13:18 *long-sleeved garment.* See NASB marg. See also Gen 37:3 and note.
13:19 *put ashes on her head.* A sign of great mourning. *tore her long-sleeved garment.* Thus expressing her anguish and announcing that her virginity had been violated. *put her hand on her head.* Also a sign of grief (see Jer 2:37).
13:20 *now keep silent, my sister . . . do not take this matter to heart.* Absalom urges his sister not to make the matter a public scandal, and attempts to quiet her by minimizing its significance. Meanwhile, he formulates his own secret plans for revenge (see vv. 22,28,32).
13:21 *he was very angry.* Although David was incensed by Amnon's rape of Tamar, there is no record that he took any puni-

22 But Absalom did not speak to Amnon [a]either good or bad; for [b]Absalom hated Amnon because he had violated his sister Tamar.

23 Now it came about after two full years that Absalom [a]had sheepshearers in Baal-hazor, which is near Ephraim, and Absalom invited all the king's sons.

Absalom Avenges Tamar

24 Absalom came to the king and said, "Behold now, your servant has sheepshearers; please let the king and his servants go with your servant."

25 But the king said to Absalom, "No, my son, we should not all go, for we will be burdensome to you." Although he [1]urged him, he would not go, but blessed him.

26 Then [a]Absalom said, "If not, please let my brother Amnon go with us." And the king said to him, "Why should he go with you?"

27 But when Absalom [1]urged him, he let Amnon and all the king's sons go with him.

28 Absalom commanded his servants, saying, "See now, [a]when Amnon's heart is merry with wine, and when I say to you, 'Strike Amnon,' then put him to death. Do not fear; have not I myself commanded you? Be courageous and be [1]valiant."

29 The servants of Absalom did to Amnon just as Absalom had commanded. Then all the king's sons arose and each mounted [a]his mule and fled.

30 Now it was while they were on the way that the report came to David, saying, "Absalom has struck down all the king's sons, and not one of them is left."

31 Then the king arose, [a]tore his clothes and [b]lay on the ground; and all his servants were standing by with clothes torn.

22 [a]Gen 31:24 [b]Lev 19:17; 1 John 2:9, 11; 3:10, 12, 15 **23** [a]1 Sam 25:7 **25** [1]Lit *broke through* **26** [a]2 Sam 3:27; 11:13-15 **27** [1]Lit *broke through* **28** [1]Lit *sons of valor* [a]Judg 19:6, 9, 22; 1 Sam 25:36-38 **29** [a]2 Sam 18:9; 1 Kin 1:33, 38 **31** [a]2 Sam 1:11 [b]2 Sam 12:16

32 [1]Lit *answered and said* [2]Lit *say* [3]Lit *mouth* [a]2 Sam 13:3-5 **33** [1]Lit *his heart* [a]2 Sam 19:19 **34** [a]2 Sam 13:37, 38 [b]2 Sam 18:24 **36** [1]Lit *with a very great weeping* **37** [a]2 Sam 13:34 [b]2 Sam 3:3 [c]2 Sam 14:23, 32 **38** [a]2 Sam 13:34 **39** [a]2 Sam 12:19-23 **14:1** [a]2 Sam 13:39 **2** [1]Lit *took* [a]2 Sam 23:26; 2 Chr 11:6; Amos 1:1 [b]2 Sam 12:20

32 [a]Jonadab, the son of Shimeah, David's brother, [1]responded, "Do not let my lord [2]suppose they have put to death all the young men, the king's sons, for Amnon alone is dead; because by the [3]intent of Absalom this has been determined since the day that he violated his sister Tamar.

33 "Now therefore, do not let my lord the king [a]take the report to [1]heart, namely, 'all the king's sons are dead,' for only Amnon is dead."

34 Now [a]Absalom had fled. And [b]the young man who was the watchman raised his eyes and looked, and behold, many people were coming from the road behind him by the side of the mountain.

35 Jonadab said to the king, "Behold, the king's sons have come; according to your servant's word, so it happened."

36 As soon as he had finished speaking, behold, the king's sons came and lifted their voices and wept; and also the king and all his servants wept [1]very bitterly.

37 Now [a]Absalom fled and went to [b]Talmai the son of Ammihud, the king of [c]Geshur. And *David* mourned for his son every day.

38 [a]So Absalom had fled and gone to Geshur, and was there three years.

39 *The heart of* King David longed to go out to Absalom; for [a]he was comforted concerning Amnon, since he was dead.

The Woman of Tekoa

14 Now Joab the son of Zeruiah perceived that [a]the king's heart *was inclined* toward Absalom.

2 So Joab sent to [a]Tekoa and [1]brought a wise woman from there and said to her, "Please pretend to be a mourner, and put on mourning garments now, and do not [b]anoint

tive action against him. Perhaps the memory of his own sin with Bathsheba adversely affected his judicious handling of the matter. Whatever the reason, David abdicated his responsibility both as king and as father. This disciplinary leniency toward his sons (see notes on 14:33; 1 Kin 1:6) eventually led to the death of Amnon and the revolts of Absalom and Adonijah.

13:22 *Absalom did not speak to Amnon . . . Absalom hated Amnon.* He quietly bided his time.

13:23 *Absalom invited all the king's sons.* The time of sheep-shearing was a festive occasion (see 1 Sam 25:4,8).

13:26 *let my brother Amnon go with us.* Upon David's refusal of the invitation, Absalom diplomatically requested that Amnon, the crown prince and oldest son, be his representative. *Why should he go with you?* David's question suggests some misgivings because of the strained relationship between the two half brothers (see v. 22).

13:28 *put him to death.* Absalom arranged for the murder of his half brother in violation of Eastern hospitality. In the wicked acts of Amnon and Absalom, David's oldest sons became guilty of sexual immorality and murder, as their father had before them. With the murder of Amnon, Absalom not only avenged the rape of his sister but also secured for himself the position of successor to the throne (see 3:3; 15:1–6). Kileab, David's second son (3:3), may have died in his youth since there is no reference to him beyond the announcement of his birth.

13:29 *mule.* Apparently the normal mount for royalty in David's kingdom (see 18:9; 1 Kin 1:33,38,44; see also note on 1 Kin 1:33).

13:31 *tore his clothes and lay on the ground.* Common ways of expressing grief (see Josh 7:6; 1 Kin 21:27; Esth 4:1,3; Job 1:20; 2:8).

13:37 *Talmai the son of Ammihud, the king of Geshur.* Absalom's grandfather (see 3:3).

13:39 *longed to go out to Absalom.* With Absalom a refugee, David had lost both of his oldest living sons.

14:1 *Joab the son of Zeruiah.* See note on 2:13. *the king's heart was inclined toward Absalom.* Torn between anger and love (and perhaps remorse), David again leaves the initiative to others.

14:2 *So Joab sent.* Joab appears to have been motivated by a concern for the political implications of the unresolved dispute between David and the son in line for the throne. He attempts to move David to action by means of a story designed to elicit a response clearly applicable, by analogy, to David's own predicament. A similar technique was used by Nathan the prophet (12:1–7; see 1 Kin 20:38–43). *Tekoa.* A town a few miles south of Bethlehem, from which the prophet Amos also came (Amos 1:1).

yourself with oil, but be like a woman who
has been mourning for the dead many days;
3 then go to the king and speak to him in
this manner." So Joab put [a]the words in her
mouth.
4 Now when the woman of Tekoa [1]spoke
to the king, she fell on her face to the ground
and [a]prostrated herself and said, "[b]Help, O
king."
5 The king said to her, "What is your
trouble?" And she [1]answered, "Truly I am a
widow, for my husband is dead.
6 "Your maidservant had two sons, but
the two of them struggled together in the
field, and there was no [1]one to separate
them, so one struck the other and killed him.
7 "Now behold, [a]the whole family has
risen against your maidservant, and they say,
'Hand over the one who struck his brother,
that we may put him to death for the life of
his brother whom he killed, [b]and destroy the
heir also.' Thus they will extinguish my coal
which is left, so as to [1]leave my husband neither name nor remnant on the face of the
earth."
8 Then the king said to the woman, "Go
to your house, and I will give orders concerning you."
9 The woman of Tekoa said to the king,
"O my lord, the king, [a]the iniquity is on me
and my father's house, but [b]the king and his
throne are guiltless."
10 So the king said, "Whoever speaks to
you, bring him to me, and he will not touch
you anymore."
11 Then she said, "Please let the king
remember the LORD your God, [a]*so that* the
avenger of blood will not continue to
destroy, otherwise they will destroy my son."
And he said, "[b]As the LORD lives, not one
hair of your son shall fall to the ground."
12 Then the woman said, "Please let your
maidservant speak a word to my lord the
king." And he said, "Speak."
13 The woman said, "[a]Why then have you
planned such a thing against the people of
God? For in speaking this word the king is as
one who is guilty, *in that* the king does not
bring back [b]his banished one.
14 "For [a]we will surely die and are [b]like
water spilled on the ground which cannot be
gathered up again. Yet God does not take
away life, but plans [1]ways so that [c]the banished one will not be cast out from him.
15 "Now [1]the reason I have come to speak
this word to my lord the king is that the people have made me afraid; so your maidservant said, 'Let me now speak to the king,
perhaps the king will perform the [2]request of
his maidservant.
16 'For the king will hear [1]and deliver his
maidservant from the [2]hand of the man who
would destroy [3]both me and my son from
[a]the inheritance of God.'
17 "Then your maidservant said, 'Please let
the word of my lord the king be [1]comforting,
for as [a]the angel of God, so is my lord the
king to discern good and evil. And may the
LORD your God be with you.' "
18 Then the king answered and said to the
woman, "Please do not hide anything from
me that I am about to ask you." And the
woman said, "Let my lord the king please
speak."
19 So the king said, "Is the hand of Joab
with you in all this?" And the woman replied,
"As your soul lives, my lord the king, no one
can turn to the right or to the left from anything that my lord the king has spoken.
Indeed, it was [a]your servant Joab who commanded me, and it was he who put all these
words in the mouth of your maidservant;

3 [a]2 Sam 14:19
4 [1]Many mss and ancient versions read *came* [a]1 Sam 25:23 [b]2 Kin 6:26-28
5 [1]Lit *said*
6 [1]Lit *deliverer between*
7 [1]Lit *set* [a]Num 35:19; Deut 19:12, 13 [b]Matt 21:38
9 [a]Gen 43:9; 1 Sam 25:24 [b]1 Kin 2:33
11 [a]Num 35:19, 21; Deut 19:4-10 [b]1 Sam 14:45; 1 Kin 1:52; Matt 10:30
13 [a]2 Sam 12:7; 1 Kin 20:40-42 [b]2 Sam 13:37, 38
14 [1]Lit *devices* [a]Job 30:23; 34:15; Heb 9:27 [b]Ps 58:7 [c]Num 35:15, 25, 28
15 [1]Lit *that* [2]Lit *word*
16 [1]Lit *to* [2]Lit *palm* [3]Lit *together* [a]Deut 32:9; 1 Sam 26:19
17 [1]Lit *for rest* [a]1 Sam 29:9; 2 Sam 14:20; 19:27
19 [a]2 Sam 14:3

14:7 *the whole family has risen against your maidservant.* It was customary in Israel for a murder victim's next of kin to avenge the blood of his relative by putting the murderer to death (see note on 3:27; see also Num 35:12; Deut 19:11–13). In the case presented, however, blood revenge would wipe out the family line, which was something Israelite law and custom tried to avoid if at all possible (see notes on Deut 25:5–6; Ruth 2:20). *destroy the heir as well.* The woman suggests that the motivation for blood revenge was more a selfish desire to acquire the family inheritance than a desire for justice (see Num 27:11). *leave my husband neither name nor remnant.* The implication is that it would be a more serious offense to terminate the woman's family line than to permit a murder to go unpunished by blood revenge. Apparently Joab hoped subtly to suggest to David that if he did not restore Absalom, a struggle for the throne would eventually ensue.
14:8 *I will give orders concerning you.* David's judicial action may have rested on the legal ground that the murder was not premeditated (see Deut 19:4–6).
14:9 *iniquity.* For the unpunished crime.
14:11 *let the king remember the LORD your God.* The woman wants David to confirm his promise by an oath in the Lord's name. *As the LORD lives.* An oath formula (see notes on Gen 42:15; 1 Sam 14:39) that solemnly binds David to his commitment.
14:13 *against the people of God.* The woman's suggestion is that David has done the same thing to Israel that her family members have done to her. The people of Israel want their crown prince returned safely to them. *the king is as one who is guilty.* The argument is that when David exempted the fictitious murderer from blood revenge, he in effect rendered himself guilty for not doing the same in the case of Absalom. The analogy places David in the position of the blood avenger.
14:14 *like water spilled on the ground.* Blood revenge will not return the victim of murder to life, just as water spilled on the ground cannot be recovered. *God does not take away life.* In the suggestion that the avenging of blood is contrary to God's ways of dealing with people, the woman apparently distorts Biblical teaching of God's justice (see note on Gen 9:6). But she dwells on the mercy of God, who would rather preserve life than take it (see Ezek 18:23,32; 33:11). David's own guilt and subsequent experience of God's mercy appear to give added weight to the woman's argument (see notes on 12:13; 13:21).
14:15 *the people have made me afraid.* The woman reverts to her own fabricated story. "The people" are evidently those of her own family who are seeking blood revenge.
14:17 *as the angel of God . . . discern good and evil.* Possessing superhuman powers of discernment—as a king ideally should (see v. 20; 19:27).

20 in order to change the appearance of things your servant Joab has done this thing. But my lord is wise, [a]like the wisdom of the angel of God, to know all that is in the earth."

Absalom Is Recalled

21 Then the king said to Joab, "Behold now, [a]I will surely do this thing; go therefore, bring back the young man Absalom."

22 Joab fell on his face to the ground, prostrated himself and blessed the king; then Joab said, "Today your servant knows that I have found favor in your sight, O my lord, the king, in that the king has performed the [1]request of his servant."

23 So Joab arose and went to [a]Geshur and brought Absalom to Jerusalem.

24 However the king said, "Let him turn to [a]his own house, and let him not see my face." So Absalom turned to his own house and did not see the king's face.

25 Now in all Israel was no one as handsome as Absalom, so highly praised; [a]from the sole of his foot to the crown of his head there was no defect in him.

26 When he [a]cut the hair of his head (and it was at the end of every year that he cut *it,* for it was heavy on him so he cut it), he weighed the hair of his head at 200 shekels by the king's weight.

27 [a]To Absalom there were born three sons, and one daughter whose name was [b]Tamar; she was a woman of beautiful appearance.

28 Now Absalom lived two full years in Jerusalem, [a]and did not see the king's face.

29 Then Absalom sent for Joab, to send him to the king, but he would not come to him. So he sent again a second time, but he would not come.

30 Therefore he said to his servants, "See, [a]Joab's [1]field is next to mine, and he has barley there; go and set it on fire." So Absalom's servants set the [1]field on fire.

20 [a]2 Sam 14:17; 19:27
21 [a]2 Sam 14:11
22 [1]Lit *word*
23 [a]Deut 3:14; 2 Sam 13:37, 38
24 [a]2 Sam 13:20
25 [a]Deut 28:35; Job 2:7; Is 1:6
26 [a]Ezek 44:20
27 [a]2 Sam 18:18 [b]2 Sam 13:1
28 [a]2 Sam 14:24
30 [1]Lit *portion* [a]Judg 15:3-5

31 Then Joab arose, came to Absalom at his house and said to him, "Why have your servants set my [1]field on fire?"

32 Absalom [1]answered Joab, "Behold, I sent for you, saying, 'Come here, that I may send you to the king, to say, "Why have I come from Geshur? It would be better for me still to be there." ' Now therefore, let me see the king's face, [a]and if there is iniquity in me, let him put me to death."

33 So when Joab came to the king and told him, he called for Absalom. Thus he came to the king and prostrated himself on his face to the ground before the king, and [a]the king kissed Absalom.

Absalom's Conspiracy

15 Now it came about after this that [a]Absalom provided for himself a chariot and horses and fifty men as runners before him.

2 Absalom used to rise early and [a]stand beside the way to the gate; and when any man had a suit to come to the king for judgment, Absalom would call to him and say, "From what city are you?" And he would say, "Your servant is from one of the tribes of Israel."

3 Then Absalom would say to him, "See, [a]your [1]claims are good and right, but no man listens to you on the part of the king."

4 Moreover, Absalom would say, "[a]Oh that one would appoint me judge in the land, then every man who has any suit or cause could come to me and I would give him justice."

5 And when a man came near to prostrate himself before him, he would put out his hand and take hold of him and [a]kiss him.

6 In this manner Absalom dealt with all Israel who came to the king for judgment; [a]so Absalom stole away the hearts of the men of Israel.

7 Now it came about at the end of [1]forty

31 [1]Lit *portion*
32 [1]Lit *said to* [a]1 Sam 20:8; Prov 28:13
33 [a]Gen 33:4; Luke 15:20
15:1 [a]1 Kin 1:5
2 [a]Ruth 4:1; 2 Sam 19:8
3 [1]Lit *words* [a]Prov 12:2
4 [a]Judg 9:29
5 [a]2 Sam 14:33; 20:9
6 [a]Rom 16:18
7 [1]Some ancient versions render *four*

14:21 *Joab.* He appears to have been present the whole time.

14:23 *Joab . . . went to Geshur.* See 13:37.

14:24 *let him not see my face.* David still vacillates (see note on v. 1); he does not offer forgiveness and restoration.

14:25 *no one . . . so highly praised.* Absalom's handsomeness brought him attention and popular favor—which he was soon to cultivate.

14:26 *hair of his head.* For the people of that time, hair was apparently a sign of vigor. Kings and heroic figures were usually portrayed with abundant locks, while baldness was a disgrace (see 2 Kin 2:23). In this, too, Absalom seemed destined for the throne. *king's weight.* The royal shekel was perhaps heavier than the sanctuary shekel (see Ex 30:13; Lev 5:15; Num 3:47).

14:27 *three sons.* Their names are unknown; 18:18 suggests that they died in their youth. *Tamar.* Absalom named his daughter after his sister (13:1). Maacah (1 Kin 15:2) was probably a daughter of Tamar, and Absalom's granddaughter (see note on 2 Chr 11:20).

14:32 *if there is iniquity in me, let him put me to death.* Absalom demands either full pardon and restoration or death, but he still gives no sign of repentance.

14:33 *the king kissed Absalom.* Signifying his forgiveness and Absalom's reconciliation with the royal family. David sidesteps repentance and justice, and in this way he probably contributes to the fulfillment of the prophecy of Nathan (12:10–12).

15:1 *chariot and horses.* As far as is known, Absalom was the first Israelite leader to acquire a chariot and horses (cf. Deut 17:16). *fifty men.* They probably functioned as bodyguards and provided a display of royal pomp that appealed to the masses. Adonijah later followed Absalom's example (1 Kin 1:5).

15:3 *your claims are good.* Absalom seeks to ingratiate himself with the people by endorsing their grievances apart from any investigation into their legitimacy.

15:4 *Oh that one would appoint me judge in the land.* Absalom presents himself as the solution to the people's legal grievances. In the case of Amnon, he had taken matters into his own hands because of his father's laxity. He has found, he believes, the weakness in his father's reign, and he capitalizes on it with political astuteness.

15:7 *forty years.* Some ancient manuscripts read "four years,"

years that Absalom said to the king, "Please
let me go and pay my vow which I have
vowed to the LORD, in [a]Hebron.
8 "For your servant [a]vowed a vow while I
was living at Geshur in Aram, saying, '[b]If the
LORD shall indeed bring me back to
Jerusalem, then I will serve the LORD.' "
9 The king said to him, "Go in peace." So
he arose and went to Hebron.
10 But Absalom sent spies throughout all
the tribes of Israel, saying, "As soon as you
hear the sound of the trumpet, then you
shall say, '[a]Absalom is king in Hebron.' "
11 Then two hundred men went with
Absalom from Jerusalem, [a]who were invited
and [b]went [1]innocently, and they did not
know anything.
12 And Absalom sent for [a]Ahithophel the
Gilonite, David's counselor, from his city
[b]Giloh, while he was offering the sacrifices.
And the conspiracy was strong, for [c]the people increased continually with Absalom.

David Flees Jerusalem

13 Then a messenger came to David, saying, "[a]The hearts of the men of Israel are
[1]with Absalom."
14 David said to all his servants who were
with him at Jerusalem, "[a]Arise and let us
flee, for *otherwise* none of us will escape from
Absalom. Go in haste, or he will overtake us
quickly and bring down calamity on us and
strike the city with the edge of the sword."
15 Then the king's servants said to the
king, "Behold, your servants *are ready to do*
whatever my lord the king chooses."
16 So the king went out and all his household [1]with him. But [a]the king left ten concubines to keep the house.
17 The king went out and all the people
[1]with him, and they stopped at the last
house.
18 Now all his servants passed on beside
him, [a]all the Cherethites, all the Pelethites
and all the Gittites, [b]six hundred men who
had come [1]with him from Gath, passed on
before the king.
19 Then the king said to [a]Ittai the Gittite,
"Why will you also go with us? Return and
remain with the king, for you are a foreigner
and also an exile; *return* to your own place.
20 "You came *only* yesterday, and shall I
today make you wander with us, while [a]I go
where I will? Return and take back your
brothers; [b]mercy and [1]truth be with you."
21 But Ittai answered the king and said,
"As the LORD lives, and as my lord the king
lives, surely [a]wherever my lord the king may
be, whether for death or for life, there also
your servant will be."
22 Therefore David said to Ittai, "Go and
pass over." So Ittai the Gittite passed over
with all his men and all the little ones who
were with him.
23 While all the country was weeping
with a loud voice, all the people passed over.
The king also passed over [a]the brook Kidron,
and all the people passed over toward [b]the
way of the wilderness.
24 Now behold, [a]Zadok also *came,* and all
the Levites with him [b]carrying the ark of the
covenant of God. And they set down the ark
of God, and [c]Abiathar came up until all the
people had finished passing from the city.
25 The king said to Zadok, "Return the ark
of God to the city. If I find favor in the sight of
the LORD, then [a]He will bring me back again
and show me both it and [b]His habitation.
26 "But if He should say thus, '[a]I have no
delight in you,' behold, here I am, [b]let Him
do to me as seems good [1]to Him."
27 The king said also to Zadok the priest,
"Are you *not* [a]a seer? Return to the city in

7 [a]2 Sam 3:2, 3 **8** [a]2 Sam 13:37, 38 [b]Gen 28:20, 21 **10** [a]1 Kin 1:34; 2 Kin 9:13 **11** [1]Lit *in their integrity* [a]1 Sam 9:13 [b]1 Sam 22:15 **12** [a]2 Sam 15:31 [b]Josh 15:51 [c]Ps 3:1 **13** [1]Lit *after* [a]Judg 9:3; 2 Sam 15:6 **14** [a]2 Sam 12:11; Ps 3: title **16** [1]Lit *at his feet* [a]2 Sam 16:21, 22 **17** [1]Lit *at his feet*

18 [1]Lit *at his feet* [a]2 Sam 8:18 [b]1 Sam 23:13; 25:13; 30:1, 9 **19** [a]2 Sam 18:2 **20** [1]Or *faithfulness* [a]1 Sam 23:13 [b]2 Sam 2:6 **21** [a]Ruth 1:16, 17; Prov 17:17 **23** [a]1 Kin 15:13; 2 Chr 29:16 [b]2 Sam 15:28; 16:2 **24** [a]2 Sam 8:17; 20:25 [b]Num 4:15; 1 Sam 4:4, 5 [c]1 Sam 22:20 **25** [a]Ps 43:3 [b]Ex 15:13; Jer 25:30 **26** [1]Lit *in His sight* [a]2 Sam 11:27; 1 Chr 21:7 [b]1 Sam 3:18 **27** [a]1 Sam 9:6-9

i.e. four years after Absolom's return to the court (14:33). By this time he must have been about 30 years old, so his revolt must be dated early in the last decade of David's reign. *Hebron.* Where David was first proclaimed king (see notes on 2:1,4; 5:3,5) and where Absalom was born (3:2–3). Absalom may have had reason to believe that he could count on some local resentment over David's transfer of the capital to Jerusalem. Hebron was also the site of an important sanctuary.

15:8 *Geshur.* See 13:37.

15:12 *Ahithophel.* Bathsheba's grandfather (see 11:3; 23:34) and a wise and respected counselor (16:23). He appears to have secretly aligned himself with Absalom's rebellion in its planning stage, perhaps in retaliation against David for his treatment of Bathsheba and Uriah. This unsuspected betrayal by a trusted friend may have prompted David's statements in Ps 41:9; 55:12–14. *Gilonite.* Giloh was near Hebron (see Josh 15:51).

15:14 *none of us will escape from Absalom.* Uncertain of the extent of Absalom's support (see v. 13), David fears being trapped in Jerusalem, and he wants to spare the city a bloodbath.

15:16 *the king left ten concubines to keep the house.* See 5:13; see also note on 3:2. David unknowingly arranges for the fulfillment of one of Nathan's prophecies (see note on 12:11; see also 20:3).

15:18 *Cherethites . . . Pelethites.* See note on 8:18. *Gittites, six hundred men.* Philistine soldiers from Gath under the command of Ittai who for some unknown reason had joined David's personal military force (see 18:2).

15:19 *Return and remain with the king.* David releases the Philistine contingent from further obligations to him.

15:21 *As the LORD lives.* An oath of loyalty and devotion taken in the name of Israel's God (see note on 1 Sam 14:39). For a similar oath see Ruth 1:16–17.

15:24 *Zadok.* See note on 8:17. *Abiathar.* See note on 8:17; see also 1 Sam 22:20–23.

15:25 *Return the ark of God to the city.* David reveals a true understanding of the connection between the ark and God's presence with His people. He knows that possession of the ark does not guarantee God's blessing (see notes on 1 Sam 4:3,21). He also recognizes that the ark belongs in the capital city as a symbol of the Lord's rule over the nation (see note on 6:2), no matter who the king might be.

15:26 *let Him do to me as seems good to Him.* David confesses that he has no exclusive claim to the throne and that Israel's divine King is free to confer the kingship on whomever He chooses.

15:27 *Are you not a seer?* Perhaps an allusion to the high

peace and your [b]two sons with you, your son
Ahimaaz and Jonathan the son of Abiathar.
28 "See, I am going to wait [a]at the fords of
the wilderness until word comes from you to
inform me."
29 Therefore Zadok and Abiathar returned
the ark of God to Jerusalem and remained
there.
30 And David went up the ascent of the
Mount of Olives, and wept as he went, and
[a]his head was covered and he walked [b]bare-
foot. Then all the people who were with him
each covered his head and went up weeping
as they went.
31 Now someone told David, saying,
"[a]Ahithophel is among the conspirators with
Absalom." And David said, "O LORD, I pray,
[b]make the counsel of Ahithophel foolishness."
32 It happened as David was coming to
the summit, where God was worshiped, that
behold, Hushai the [a]Archite met him with
his [1]coat torn and [2]dust on his head.
33 David said to him, "If you pass over
with me, then you will be [a]a burden to me.
34 "But if you return to the city, and [a]say to
Absalom, 'I will be your servant, O king; as I
have been your father's servant in time past,
so I will now be your servant,' then you can
thwart the counsel of Ahithophel for me.
35 "Are not Zadok and Abiathar the priests
with you there? So it shall be that [a]whatever
you hear from the king's house, you shall
report to Zadok and Abiathar the priests.
36 "Behold [a]their two sons are with them
there, Ahimaaz, Zadok's son and Jonathan,
Abiathar's son; and [b]by them you shall send
me everything that you hear."
37 So Hushai, [a]David's friend, came into
the city, and [b]Absalom came into Jerusalem.

Ziba, a False Servant

16 Now when David had passed [a]a little
beyond the summit, behold, [b]Ziba the
servant of Mephibosheth met him [c]with a
couple of saddled donkeys, and on them
were two hundred loaves of bread, a hundred
clusters of raisins, a hundred summer fruits,
and a jug of wine.
2 The king said to Ziba, "Why do you
have these?" And Ziba said, "[a]The donkeys
are for the king's household to ride, and the
bread and summer fruit for the young men to
eat, and the wine, [b]for whoever is faint in
the wilderness to drink."
3 Then the king said, "And where is
[a]your master's son?" And [b]Ziba said to the
king, "Behold, he is staying in Jerusalem, for
he said, 'Today the house of Israel will
restore the kingdom of my father to me.' "
4 So the king said to Ziba, "Behold, all
that belongs to Mephibosheth is yours." And
Ziba said, "I prostrate myself; let me find
favor in your sight, O my lord, the king!"

David Is Cursed

5 When King David came to [a]Bahurim,
behold, there came out from there a man of
the family of the house of Saul [b]whose name
was Shimei, the son of Gera; he came out
[c]cursing continually as he came.
6 He threw stones at David and at all the
servants of King David; and all the people
and all the mighty men were at his right
hand and at his left.
7 Thus Shimei said when he cursed, "Get
out, get out, [a]you man of bloodshed, and
worthless fellow!
8 "[a]The LORD has returned upon you all
[b]the bloodshed of the house of Saul, in
whose place you have reigned; and the LORD
has given the kingdom into the hand of your
son Absalom. And behold, you are *taken* in
your own evil, for you are a man of bloodshed!"
9 Then [a]Abishai the son of Zeruiah said
to the king, "Why should [b]this dead dog
[c]curse my lord the king? Let me go over now
and [1]cut off his head."
10 But the king said, "[a]What have I to do

27 [b]2 Sam 17:17
28 [a]Josh 5:10; 2 Sam 17:16
30 [a]Esth 6:12; Ezek 24:17, 23 [b]Is 20:2-4
31 [a]2 Sam 15:12 [b]2 Sam 16:23; 17:14, 23
32 [1]Or *tunic* [2]Lit *ground* [a]Josh 16:2
33 [a]2 Sam 19:35
34 [a]2 Sam 16:19
35 [a]2 Sam 17:15, 16
36 [a]2 Sam 15:27 [b]2 Sam 17:17
37 [a]2 Sam 16:16; 1 Chr 27:33 [b]2 Sam 16:15
16:1 [a]2 Sam 15:32 [b]2 Sam 9:2-13 [c]1 Sam 25:18
2 [a]Judg 10:4 [b]2 Sam 17:29
3 [a]2 Sam 9:9, 10 [b]2 Sam 19:26, 27
5 [a]2 Sam 3:16; 17:18 [b]2 Sam 19:16-23; 1 Kin 2:8, 9, 44 [c]Ex 22:28; 1 Sam 17:43
7 [a]2 Sam 12:9
8 [a]2 Sam 21:1-9 [b]2 Sam 1:16; 3:28, 29; 4:11, 12
9 [1]Lit *take off* [a]1 Sam 26:8; 2 Sam 19:21; Luke 9:54 [b]2 Sam 9:8 [c]Ex 22:28
10 [a]2 Sam 3:39; 19:22

priest's custody of the Urim and Thummim as a means of divine revelation (see notes on Ex 28:30; 1 Sam 2:28). See also note on 1Sa 9:9.

15:28 *fords of the wilderness.* Fords across the Jordan in the vicinity of Gilgal.

15:30 *his head was covered.* A sign of sorrow (see Esth 6:12; Jer 14:3–4). *he walked barefoot.* Another sign of sorrow (see Is 20:2,4; Ezek 24:17; Mic 1:8).

15:31 *Ahithophel.* See note on v. 12.

15:32 *Hushai the Archite.* The Archites were a clan (some think non-Israelite) that inhabited an area southwest of Bethel (Josh 16:2). Since Hushai was a trusted member of David's court (see note on v. 37), his appearance was the beginning of an answer to David's prayer (v. 31).

15:37 *Hushai, David's friend.* 1 Chr 27:33 calls him the "king's friend," which seems to be an official title for the king's most trusted adviser (see 1 Kin 4:5).

16:1 *Ziba.* See ch. 9. *Mephibosheth.* See note on 4:4.

16:2 *Ziba said.* Since David assumed control of Saul's estate (9:7–10), Ziba, always the opportunist, seeks to profit from the political crisis.

16:3 *your master's son.* "Son" here means "grandson," i.e. Mephibosheth (see 9:2–3,9).

16:4 *all that belongs to Mephibosheth is yours.* Because the revolt was so widespread and loyalties so uncertain, David was quick to assume the worst.

16:5 *Bahurim.* On the eastern slope of the Mount of Olives (see note on 3:16). *of the family of the house of Saul.* The clan of Matri (see 1 Sam 10:21). *Gera.* His exact relation to Saul is unknown (see note on 1Ki 2:8).

16:6 *people and . . . mighty men.* The Cherethites, Pelethites and 600 Gittites (see 15:18).

16:7 *worthless fellow.* See note on Deut 13:13.

16:8 *bloodshed of the house of Saul.* Shimei may be referring to the executions reported in 21:1–14, but the time of that event is uncertain (see note on 21:1).

16:9 *Abishai.* See note on Sam 26:6. *this dead dog.* An expression of absolute contempt (see note on 9:8).

with you, O sons of Zeruiah? [b]If he curses,
and if the LORD has told him, 'Curse David,'
[c]then who shall say, 'Why have you done
so?' "
11 Then David said to Abishai and to all
his servants, "Behold, [a]my son who came
out from [1]me seeks my life; how much more
now this Benjamite? Let him alone and let
him curse, [b]for the LORD has told him.
12 "Perhaps the LORD will look on my affliction and [1][a]return good to me instead of his
cursing this day."
13 So David and his men went on the
way; and Shimei went along on the hillside
parallel with him and as he went he cursed
and cast stones and threw dust at him.
14 The king and all the people who were
with him arrived weary and he refreshed
himself there.

Absalom Enters Jerusalem

15 [a]Then Absalom and all the people, the
men of Israel, entered Jerusalem, and
Ahithophel with him.
16 Now it came about when [a]Hushai the
Archite, David's friend, came to Absalom,
that [b]Hushai said to Absalom, "[c]*Long* live
the king! *Long* live the king!"
17 Absalom said to Hushai, "Is this your
[1]loyalty to your friend? [a]Why did you not go
with your friend?"
18 Then Hushai said to Absalom, "No! For
whom the LORD, this people, and all the men
of Israel have chosen, his I will be, and with
him I will remain.
19 "Besides, [a]whom should I serve? *Should*
I not *serve* in the presence of his son? As I
have served in your father's presence, so I
will be in your presence."
20 Then Absalom said to Ahithophel,
"Give your advice. What shall we do?"
21 Ahithophel said to Absalom, "[a]Go in to
your father's concubines, whom he has left
to keep the house; then all Israel will hear
that you have made yourself odious to your
father. The hands of all who are with you
will also be strengthened."
22 So they pitched a tent for Absalom on
the roof, [a]and Absalom went in to his
father's concubines [b]in the sight of all Israel.
23 [a]The advice of Ahithophel, which he
[1]gave in those days, *was* as if one inquired of
the word of God; [b]so was all the advice of
Ahithophel *regarded* by both David and
Absalom.

Hushai's Counsel

17 Furthermore, Ahithophel said to Absalom, "Please let me choose 12,000 men
that I may arise and pursue David tonight.
2 "[a]I will come upon him while he is
weary and [1]exhausted and terrify him, so
that all the people who are with him will
flee. Then [b]I will strike down the king alone,
3 and I will bring back all the people to
you. [1]The return of everyone depends on the
man you seek; *then* all the people will be at
[a]peace."
4 So the [1]plan pleased Absalom and all
the elders of Israel.
5 Then Absalom said, "Now call [a]Hushai
the Archite also, and let us hear what [1]he
has to say."
6 When Hushai had come to Absalom,
Absalom said to [1]him, "Ahithophel has spoken [2]thus. Shall we [3]carry out his plan? If
not, you speak."
7 So Hushai said to Absalom, "[a]This time
the advice that Ahithophel has [1]given is not
good."
8 Moreover, Hushai said, "You know
your father and his men, that they are
mighty men and they are [1]fierce, [a]like a bear
robbed of her cubs in the field. And your
father is an [2]expert in warfare, and will not
spend the night with the people.
9 "Behold, he has now hidden himself in
one of the [1]caves or in another place; and it
will be [2]when he falls on them at the first
attack, that whoever hears *it* will say, 'There
has been a slaughter among the people who
follow Absalom.'
10 "And even the one who is valiant,
whose heart is like the heart of a lion, [a]will
completely [1]lose heart; for all Israel knows
that your father is a mighty man and those
who are with him are valiant men.
11 "But I counsel that all Israel be surely
gathered to you, [a]from Dan even to Beersheba, [b]as the sand that is by the sea in abundance, and that [1]you personally go into battle.
12 "So we shall come to him in one of the
places where he can be found, and we will
[1]fall on him [a]as the dew falls on the ground;

10 [b]John 18:11 [c]Rom 9:20
11 [1]Lit *my body* [a]2 Sam 12:11 [b]Gen 45:5; 1 Sam 26:19
12 [1]Lit *the* LORD *will return* [a]Deut 23:5; Rom 8:28
15 [a]2 Sam 15:12, 37
16 [a]2 Sam 15:37 [b]2 Sam 15:34 [c]1 Sam 10:24; 2 Kin 11:12
17 [1]Or *kindness* [a]2 Sam 19:25
19 [a]2 Sam 15:34
21 [a]2 Sam 15:16; 20:3
22 [a]2 Sam 15:16; 20:3 [b]2 Sam 12:11, 12
23 [1]Lit *advised* [a]2 Sam 17:14, 23
23 [b]2 Sam 15:12
17:2 [1]Lit *slack of hands* [a]2 Sam 16:14 [b]1 Kin 22:31
3 [1]Lit *Like the return of the whole is the man whom you seek* [a]Jer 6:14
4 [1]Lit *word was pleasing in the sight of*
5 [1]Lit *is in his mouth—even he* [a]2 Sam 15:32-34
6 [1]Lit *him, saying* [2]Lit *according to this word* [3]Lit *do his word*
7 [1]Lit *advised* [a]2 Sam 16:21
8 [1]Lit *bitter of soul* [2]Lit *man of war* [a]Hos 13:8
9 [1]Lit *pits* [2]Lit *according to a falling among them*
10 [1]Lit *melt* [a]Josh 2:9-11
11 [1]Lit *your face go* [a]1 Sam 3:20 [b]Gen 22:17; 1 Sam 13:5
12 [1]Lit *settle down* [a]Ps 110:3; Mic 5:7

16:10 *If . . . the LORD has told him, 'Curse David.'* David leaves open the possibility that God has seen fit to terminate his rule—the verdict is not yet in (see 15:26). For David's later actions regarding Shimei see 19:18–23; 1 Kin 2:8–9.

16:15 *Ahithophel.* See note on 15:12.

16:16 *Hushai the Archite, David's friend.* See notes on 15:32,37.

16:21 *Go in to your father's concubines.* This would signify Absalom's assumption of royal power; it would also be a definitive and irreversible declaration of the break between father and son (see notes on 3:7; 12:8; 1 Kin 2:22).

16:22 *Absalom went in to his father's concubines.* A fulfillment of Nathan's prophecy (12:11–12). For additional significance see note on v. 21.

17:1–3 Ahithophel's advice to Absalom envisioned a cheap and easy victory that would not leave the nation weakened.

17:4 *all the elders of Israel.* See note on 3:17. Absalom's rebellion appears to have gained extensive backing from prominent tribal leaders.

17:5 *Hushai the Archite.* See 16:16–19; see also notes on 15:32,37.

17:7–13 Hushai's advice subtly capitalizes on Absalom's uncertainty, his fear and his egotism.

17:12 *we . . . we.* Hushai carefully links himself with the revolt.

and of him and of all the men who are with
him, not even one will be left.
13 "If he withdraws into a city, then all
Israel shall bring ropes to that city, and we
will [a]drag it into the [1]valley until not even a
small stone is found there."
14 Then Absalom and all the men of Israel said, "The counsel of Hushai the Archite is
better than the counsel of Ahithophel." For
[a]the LORD had ordained to thwart the good
counsel of Ahithophel, so that the LORD
might bring calamity on Absalom.

Hushai's Warning Saves David

15 Then [a]Hushai said to Zadok and to
Abiathar the priests, "[1]This is what Ahithophel counseled Absalom and the elders of
Israel, and [1]this is what I have counseled.
16 "Now therefore, send quickly and tell
David, saying, '[a]Do not spend the night at
the fords of the wilderness, but by all means
cross over, or else the king and all the people
who are with him will be [1]destroyed.'"
17 [a]Now Jonathan and Ahimaaz were
staying at [b]En-rogel, and a maidservant
would go and tell them, and they would go
and tell King David, for they could not be
seen entering the city.
18 But a lad did see them and told Absalom; so the two of them departed quickly
and came to the house of a man [a]in Bahurim, who had a well in his courtyard, and
they went down [1]into it.
19 And [a]the woman [1]took a covering and
spread it over the well's mouth and scattered
grain on it, so that nothing was known.
20 Then Absalom's servants came to the
woman at the house and said, "Where are
Ahimaaz and Jonathan?" And [a]the woman
said to them, "They have crossed the brook
of water." And when they searched and could
not find *them,* they returned to Jerusalem.
21 It came about after they had departed
that they came up out of the well and went
and told King David; and they said to David,
"[a]Arise and cross over the water quickly for
thus Ahithophel has counseled against you."
22 Then David and all the people who
were with him arose and crossed the Jordan;
and by [1]dawn not even one remained who
had not crossed the Jordan.
23 Now when Ahithophel saw that his
counsel was not [1]followed, he [2]saddled *his*
donkey and arose and went to his home, to
[a]his city, and [3b]set his house in order, and
[c]strangled himself; thus he died and was
buried in the grave of his father.
24 Then David came to [a]Mahanaim. And
Absalom crossed the Jordan, he and all the
men of Israel with him.
25 Absalom set [a]Amasa over the army in
place of Joab. Now Amasa was the son of a
man whose name was [1]Ithra the Israelite,
who went in to Abigail the daughter of
[b]Nahash, sister of Zeruiah, Joab's mother.
26 And Israel and Absalom camped in the
land of Gilead.
27 Now when David had come to Mahanaim, Shobi [a]the son of Nahash from [b]Rab-
bah of the sons of Ammon, [c]Machir the son
of Ammiel from Lo-debar, and [d]Barzillai the
Gileadite from Rogelim,
28 brought [a]beds, basins, pottery, wheat,
barley, flour, parched *grain,* beans, lentils,
parched *seeds,*
29 honey, curds, sheep, and cheese of the
herd, for David and for the people who *were*
with him, [a]to eat; for they said, "The people
are hungry and weary and thirsty in the
wilderness."

Absalom Slain

18 Then David [1]numbered the people who
were with him and [a]set over them commanders of thousands and commanders of
hundreds.
2 David sent the people out, [a]one third
under the [1]command of Joab, one third
under the [1]command of Abishai the son of
Zeruiah, Joab's brother, and one third under
the [1]command of [b]Ittai the Gittite. And the
king said to the people, "I myself will surely
go out with you also."
3 But the people said, "[a]You should not

13 [1]Or *wadi* [a]Mic 1:6
14 [a]2 Sam 15:31, 34; Ps 9:15, 16
15 [1]Lit *Thus and thus* [a]2 Sam 15:35, 36
16 [1]Lit *swallowed up* [a]2 Sam 15:28
17 [a]2 Sam 15:27, 36 [b]Josh 15:7; 18:16
18 [1]Lit *there* [a]2 Sam 3:16; 16:5
19 [1]Lit *took and spread the covering* [a]Josh 2:4-6
20 [a]Lev 19:11; Josh 2:3-5; 1 Sam 19:12-17
21 [a]2 Sam 17:15, 16
22 [1]Lit *the light of the morning*
23 [1]Lit *done* [2]Lit *bound* [3]Lit *gave charge to* [a]2 Sam 15:12 [b]2 Kin 20:1 [c]Matt 27:5
24 [a]Gen 32:2, 10; 2 Sam 2:8
25 [1]In 1 Chr 2:17, *Jether the Ishmaelite* [a]2 Sam 19:13; 20:9-12; 1 Kin 2:5, 32 [b]1 Chr 2:16
27 [a]1 Sam 11:1; 2 Sam 10:1, 2 [b]2 Sam 12:26, 29 [c]2 Sam 9:4 [d]2 Sam 19:31-39; 1 Kin 2:7
28 [a]Prov 11:25; Matt 5:7
29 [a]2 Sam 16:2, 14; Prov 21:26; Eccl 11:1; Rom 12:13
18:1 [1]Lit *mustered* [a]Ex 18:25; Num 31:14; 1 Sam 22:7
2 [1]Lit *hand* [a]Judg 7:16; 1 Sam 11:11 [b]2 Sam 15:19-22
3 [a]2 Sam 21:17

17:14 *the LORD had ordained to thwart the good counsel of Ahithophel.* An answer to David's prayer (see 15:31; cf. Ps 33:10; Prov 21:30).

17:15 *Zadok and to Abiathar.* See 15:24–29,35–36.

17:16 *fords of the wilderness.* See 15:28 and note. *cross over.* Hushai advises David to cross the Jordan River, knowing that Absalom might change his mind and immediately set out after him.

17:17 *Jonathan and Ahimaaz.* See 15:36. *En-rogel.* A spring in the Kidron Valley just outside the walls of Jerusalem. *a maidservant.* A servant girl going to the spring for water would attract no attention.

17:18 *Bahurim.* See note on 16:5.

17:23 *his city.* Giloh (see note on 15:12). *strangled himself.* Ahithophel was convinced that the rebellion would fail and that he would be found guilty of treason as a co-conspirator.

17:24 *Mahanaim.* Ironically the same place where Ish-bosheth had sought refuge after Saul's death (2:8).

17:25 *Amasa.* Nephew of David and cousin of both Absalom and Joab son of Zeruiah. *Abigail the daughter of Nahash, sister of Zeruiah.* Zeruiah was David's sister (1 Chr 2:16). Since the father of Abigail and Zeruiah is Nahash rather than Jesse, it would appear that their unnamed mother married Jesse after the death of Nahash.

17:27 *Shobi the son of Nahash.* Apparently the brother of Hanun (see 10:2–4), whom David had defeated earlier in his reign (12:26–31). *Rabbah of the sons of Ammon.* See note on 10:3. *Machir.* See note on 9:4. *Barzillai.* A wealthy benefactor of David during his flight to Mahanaim (see 19:32; 1 Kin 2:7). After the Babylonian exile, there were claimants to the priesthood among his descendants (Ezra 2:61–63; Neh 7:63).

18:2 *Ittai the Gittite.* See 15:18–22.

18:3 *You should not go out.* In addition to the reason given, David was growing old and was no longer the warrior he had

go out; for if we indeed flee, they will not care about us; even if half of us die, they will not care about us. But [1]you are worth ten thousand of us; therefore now it is better that you *be ready* to help us from the city."

4 Then the king said to them, "Whatever seems best to you I will do." So [a]the king stood beside the gate, and all the people went out by hundreds and thousands.

5 The king charged Joab and Abishai and Ittai, saying, "*Deal* gently for my sake with the young man Absalom." And [a]all the people heard when the king charged all the commanders concerning Absalom.

6 Then the people went out into the field against Israel, and the battle took place in [a]the forest of Ephraim.

7 The people of Israel were [1]defeated there before the servants of David, and the slaughter there that day was great, 20,000 men.

8 For the battle there was spread over the whole countryside, and the forest devoured more people that day than the sword devoured.

9 Now Absalom happened to meet the servants of David. For Absalom was riding on *his* mule, and the mule went under the thick branches of a great oak. And [a]his head caught fast in the oak, so he was [1]left hanging between heaven and earth, while the mule that was under him kept going.

10 When a certain man saw *it*, he told Joab and said, "Behold, I saw Absalom hanging in an oak."

11 Then Joab said to the man who had told him, "Now behold, you saw *him!* Why then did you not strike him there to the ground? And I would have given you ten *pieces* of silver and a belt."

12 The man said to Joab, "Even if I should receive a thousand *pieces of* silver in my hand, I would not put out my hand against the king's son; for [a]in our hearing the king charged you and Abishai and Ittai, saying, '[1]Protect for me the young man Absalom!'

13 "Otherwise, if I had dealt treacherously against his life (and [a]there is nothing hidden from the king), then you yourself would have stood aloof."

14 Then Joab said, "I will not [1]waste time here with you." [a]So he took three spears in his hand and thrust them through the heart of Absalom while he was yet alive in the [2]midst of the oak.

15 And ten young men who carried Joab's armor gathered around and struck Absalom and killed him.

16 Then [a]Joab blew the trumpet, and the people returned from pursuing Israel, for Joab restrained the people.

17 They took Absalom and cast him into [1]a deep pit in the forest and [a]erected over him a very great heap of stones. And [b]all Israel fled, each to his tent.

18 Now Absalom in his lifetime had taken and [a]set up for himself a pillar which is in [b]the King's Valley, for he said, "[c]I have no son [1]to preserve my name." So he named the pillar after his own name, and it is called Absalom's Monument to this day.

David Is Grief-stricken

19 Then [a]Ahimaaz the son of Zadok said, "Please let me run and bring the king news [b]that the LORD has [1]freed him from the hand of his enemies."

20 But Joab said to him, "You are not the man to carry news this day, but you shall carry news another day; however, you shall carry no news today because the king's son is dead."

21 Then Joab said to the Cushite, "Go, tell the king what you have seen." So the Cushite bowed to Joab and ran.

22 Now Ahimaaz the son of Zadok said once more to Joab, "But whatever happens, please let me also run after the Cushite." And Joab said, "Why would you run, my son, since [a]you will have no reward for going?"

23 "But whatever happens," *he said,* "I will

3 [1]So with some ancient versions; M.T. *for now there are ten thousand like us*
4 [a]2 Sam 18:24
5 [a]2 Sam 18:12
6 [a]Josh 17:15, 18; 2 Sam 17:26
7 [1]Lit *smitten*
9 [1]Lit *placed* [a]2 Sam 14:26
12 [1]So with some mss and the ancient versions; M.T. *Take care whoever* you are *of* [a]2 Sam 18:5
13 [a]2 Sam 14:19, 20
14 [1]Lit *tarry thus* [2]Lit *heart* [a]2 Sam 14:30
16 [a]2 Sam 2:28; 20:22
17 [1]Lit *the great* [a]Deut 21:20, 21; Josh 7:26; 8:29 [b]2 Sam 19:8; 20:1, 22
18 [1]Lit *for the sake of remembering* [a]1 Sam 15:12 [b]Gen 14:17 [c]2 Sam 14:27
19 [1]Lit *vindicated* [a]2 Sam 15:36 [b]2 Sam 18:31
22 [a]2 Sam 18:29

been (see note on 15:7). This is essentially the same idea that Ahithophel had expressed to Absalom (see 17:2).

18:5 *Deal gently for my sake with . . . Absalom.* David's love for his (now) oldest son was undying—and almost his undoing (see 19:5–7).

18:6 *Israel.* Absalom's army (see 15:13; 16:15; 17:4,11,24–26). *forest of Ephraim.* The battle was apparently fought in Gilead, east of the Jordan (see 17:24,26). Why this area is termed the "forest of Ephraim" is not clear (perhaps it comes from an Ephraimite claim on the area; see Judg 12:1–4).

18:8 *the battle there was spread.* The armies apparently became dispersed, and many of the men got lost in the forest.

18:9 *his mule.* See note on 13:29. *his head caught fast in the oak.* Whether by the entanglement of his abundant hair (14:26) or by some other means is not stated, but his handsome head (see 14:25) was in the end—ironically—his undoing.

18:11 *I would have given you.* Joab must be referring to an announced intent on his part to reward anyone killing Absalom. His actions and interests did not always coincide with David's wishes (see note on 2:13).

18:15 *killed him.* The easiest and most certain way of ending the rebellion—but the brutal overkill is indicative of the deep animosity felt by David's men against Absalom.

18:17 *great heap of stones.* A mound of rocks that mocked the monument Absalom himself had erected (v. 18). *all Israel.* See note on v. 6.

18:18 *set up for himself a pillar.* As Saul had done (1 Sam 15:12). *King's Valley.* Thought to be located near Jerusalem (see Gen 14:17; Josephus, *Antiquities,* 7.10.3). *I have no son.* See 14:27 and note. *Absalom's Monument.* Not to be confused with the much later monument of the same name that is still visible today in the valley east of Jerusalem.

18:19 *Ahimaaz the son of Zadok.* See 15:27; 17:17–21.

18:20 *not the man to carry news.* The choice of a messenger depended on the content of the message (see v. 27 and note).

18:21 *Cushite.* An alien (see notes on Gen 10:6–8; Amos 9:7).

run." So he said to him, "Run." Then Ahimaaz ran by way of the plain and passed up
the Cushite.
24 Now [a]David was sitting between the
two gates; and [b]the watchman went up to
the roof of the gate by the wall, and raised
his eyes and looked, and behold, a man running by himself.
25 The watchman called and told the
king. And the king said, "If he is by himself
there is good news in his mouth." And he
came nearer and nearer.
26 Then the watchman saw another man
running; and the watchman called to the
gatekeeper and said, "Behold, *another* man
running by himself." And the king said,
"This one also is bringing good news."
27 The watchman said, "I [1]think the running of the first one [a]is like the running of
Ahimaaz the son of Zadok." And the king
said, "[b]This is a good man and comes with
good news."
28 Ahimaaz called and said to the king,
"[1]All is well." And [a]he prostrated himself
before the king with his face to the ground.
And he said, "[b]Blessed is the LORD your God,
who has delivered up the men who lifted
their hands against my lord the king."
29 The king said, "[a]Is it well with the
young man Absalom?" And Ahimaaz
answered, "When Joab sent the king's servant, and your servant, I saw a great tumult,
but [b]I did not know what *it was*."
30 Then the king said, "Turn aside and
stand here." So he turned aside and stood
still.
31 Behold, the Cushite arrived, and the
Cushite said, "Let my lord the king receive
good news, for [a]the LORD has [1]freed you this
day from the hand of all those who rose up
against you."
32 Then the king said to the Cushite, "[a]Is
it well with the young man Absalom?" And
the Cushite answered, "[b]Let the enemies of
my lord the king, and all who rise up against
you for evil, be as that young man!"
33 [1]The king was deeply moved and went
up to the chamber over the gate and wept.
And thus he said as he walked, "[a]O my son
Absalom, my son, my son Absalom! [b]Would
I had died instead of you, O Absalom, my
son, my son!"

Joab Reproves David's Lament

19 Then it was told Joab, "Behold, [a]the
king is weeping and mourns for Absalom."
2 The [1]victory that day was turned to
mourning for all the people, for the people
heard *it* said that day, "The king is grieved
for his son."
3 So the people went by stealth into the
city that day, as people who are humiliated
steal away when they flee in battle.
4 The king [a]covered his face and [1]cried
out with a loud voice, "[b]O my son Absalom,
O Absalom, my son, my son!"
5 Then Joab came into the house to the
king and said, "Today you have covered with
shame the faces of all your servants, who
today have saved your life and the lives of
your sons and daughters, the lives of your
wives, and the lives of your concubines,
6 by loving those who hate you, and by
hating those who love you. For you have
shown today that [1]princes and servants are
nothing to you; for I know this day that if
Absalom were alive and all of us were dead
today, then [2]you would be pleased.
7 "Now therefore arise, go out and speak
[1]kindly to your servants, for I swear by the
LORD, if you do not go out, surely [a]not a man
will pass the night with you, and this will be
worse for you than all the evil that has come
upon you from your youth until now."

David Restored as King

8 So the king arose and sat in the gate.
When they told all the people, saying,
"Behold, the king is [a]sitting in the gate,"
then all the people came before the king.
Now [b]Israel had fled, each to his tent.
9 All the people were quarreling throughout all the tribes of Israel, saying, "[a]The king
delivered us from the [1]hand of our enemies
and [b]saved us from the [1]hand of the Philistines, but now [c]he has fled out of the land
from Absalom.
10 "However, Absalom, whom we anointed over us, has died in battle. Now then,
why are you silent about bringing the king
back?"
11 Then King David sent to [a]Zadok and
Abiathar the priests, saying, "Speak to the
elders of Judah, saying, 'Why are you the

24 [a]2 Sam 19:8 [b]2 Sam 13:34; 2 Kin 9:17
27 [1]Lit *see* [a]2 Kin 9:20 [b]1 Kin 1:42
28 [1]Lit *Peace* [a]1 Sam 25:23; 2 Sam 14:4 [b]1 Sam 17:46
29 [a]2 Sam 20:9; 2 Kin 4:26 [b]2 Sam 18:22
31 [1]Lit *vindicated* [a]Judg 5:31; 2 Sam 18:19
32 [a]2 Sam 18:29 [b]1 Sam 25:26
33 [1]Ch 19:1 in Heb [a]2 Sam 19:4 [b]Ex 32:32; Rom 9:3

19:1 [a]2 Sam 18:5, 14
2 [1]Lit *salvation*
4 [1]Lit *the king cried* [a]2 Sam 15:30 [b]2 Sam 18:33
6 [1]Or *commanders* [2]Lit *it would be right in your eyes*
7 [1]Lit *to the heart* [a]Prov 14:28
8 [a]2 Sam 15:2; 18:24 [b]2 Sam 18:17
9 [1]Lit *palm* [a]2 Sam 8:1-14 [b]2 Sam 5:20; 8:1 [c]2 Sam 15:14
11 [a]2 Sam 15:29

18:27 *comes with good news.* David presumed that Joab would not have sent someone like Ahimaaz to carry bad news (see v. 20 and note).
18:29 *I saw a great tumult.* Ahimaaz avoids a direct answer to David's question, though he knew Absalom was dead.
18:33 *O my son Absalom . . . !* One of the most moving expressions in all literature of a father's love for a son—in spite of all that Absalom had done.
19:5 *Joab came . . . to the king.* Apparently confident that the king was unaware of his part in Absalom's death. David never indicates that he learned of it (see 1 Kin 2:5). *you have covered with shame the faces of all your servants.* Joab boldly rebukes David for allowing his personal grief to keep him from expressing his appreciation for the loyalty of those who risked their lives to preserve his throne. Joab warns David that his love for Absalom can still undo him.
19:9 *The king delivered us.* With Absalom dead, the northern tribes remember what David had done for them (see 3:17–18; 5:2).
19:11 *Speak to the elders of Judah.* Even though the rebellion had begun in Hebron in Judah (see 15:9–12), David appeals to the elders of his own tribe to take the initiative in restoring him to the throne in Jerusalem (see 2:4; 1 Sam 30:26). This appeal produced the desired result, but it also led to the arousal of tribal jealousies (see vv. 41–42).

last to bring the king back to his house, since
the word of all Israel has come to the king,
even to his house?
12 'You are my brothers; [a]you are my bone
and my flesh. Why then should you be the
last to bring back the king?'
13 "Say to [a]Amasa, 'Are you not my bone
and my flesh? [b]May God do so to me, and
more also, if you will not be [c]commander of
the army before me continually [d]in place of
Joab.' "
14 Thus he turned the hearts of all the
men of Judah [a]as one man, so that they sent
word to the king, *saying*, "Return, you and
all your servants."
15 The king then returned and came as far
as the Jordan. And Judah came to [a]Gilgal in
order to go to meet the king, to bring the
king across the Jordan.
16 Then [a]Shimei the son of Gera, the Benjamite who was from Bahurim, hurried and
came down with the men of Judah to meet
King David.
17 There were a thousand men of Benjamin with him, with [a]Ziba the servant of the
house of Saul, and his fifteen sons and his
twenty servants with him; and they rushed
to the Jordan before the king.
18 Then they kept crossing the ford to
bring over the king's household, and to do
what was good in his sight. And Shimei the
son of Gera fell down before the king as he
was about to cross the Jordan.
19 So he said to the king, "[a]Let not my
lord consider me guilty, nor remember what
your servant did wrong on the day when my
lord the king came out from Jerusalem, so
that the king would [1]take *it* to heart.
20 "For your servant knows that I have
sinned; therefore behold, I have come today,
[a]the first of all the house of Joseph to go
down to meet my lord the king."
21 But Abishai the son of Zeruiah said,
"[a]Should not Shimei be put to death for this,
[b]because he cursed the LORD's anointed?"
22 David then said, "[a]What have I to do
with you, O sons of Zeruiah, that you should
this day be an adversary to me? [b]Should any
man be put to death in Israel today? For do I
not know that I am king over Israel today?"
23 The king said to Shimei, "[a]You shall
not die." Thus the king swore to him.
24 Then [a]Mephibosheth the [1]son of Saul
came down to meet the king; and [b]he had
neither [2]cared for his feet, nor [2]trimmed his
mustache, nor [c]washed his clothes, from the
day the king departed until the day he came
home in peace.
25 It was when he came from Jerusalem
to meet the king, that the king said to him,
"[a]Why did you not go with me, Mephibosheth?"
26 So he answered, "O my lord, the king,
my servant deceived me; for your servant
said, 'I will saddle a donkey for myself that I
may ride on it and go with the king,'
[a]because your servant is lame.
27 "Moreover, [a]he has slandered your servant to my lord the king; but my lord the
king is [b]like the angel of God, therefore do
what is good in your sight.
28 "For [a]all my father's household was
nothing but dead men before my lord the
king; [b]yet you set your servant among those
who ate at your own table. What right do I
have yet that I should [1]complain anymore to
the king?"
29 So the king said to him, "Why do you
still speak of your affairs? I have [1]decided,
'You and Ziba shall divide the land.' "
30 Mephibosheth said to the king, "Let
him even take it all, since my lord the king
has come safely to his own house."
31 Now [a]Barzillai the Gileadite had come
down from Rogelim; and he went on to the
Jordan with the king to [1]escort him over the
Jordan.
32 Now Barzillai was very old, being
eighty years old; and he had [1a]sustained the
king while he stayed at Mahanaim, for he
was a very great man.
33 The king said to Barzillai, "You cross

12 [a]2 Sam 5:1
13 [a]2 Sam 17:25 [b]1 Kin 19:2 [c]2 Sam 8:16 [d]2 Sam 3:27-39; 19:5-7
14 [a]Judg 20:1
15 [a]Josh 5:9; 1 Sam 11:14, 15
16 [a]2 Sam 16:5-13; 1 Kin 2:8
17 [a]2 Sam 16:1-4; 19:26, 27
19 [1]Lit *set* [a]1 Sam 22:15; 2 Sam 16:6-8
20 [a]2 Sam 16:5
21 [a]2 Sam 16:7, 8 [b]Ex 22:28
22 [a]2 Sam 3:39; 16:9, 10
22 [b]1 Sam 11:13
23 [a]1 Kin 2:8
24 [1]I.e. grandson [2]Lit *done* [a]2 Sam 9:6-10 [b]2 Sam 12:20 [c]Ex 19:10
25 [a]2 Sam 16:17
26 [a]2 Sam 9:3
27 [a]2 Sam 16:3, 4 [b]2 Sam 14:17, 20
28 [1]Lit *cry out* [a]2 Sam 21:6-9 [b]2 Sam 9:7, 10, 13
29 [1]Lit *said*
31 [1]Lit *send* [a]2 Sam 17:27-29; 1 Kin 2:7
32 [1]Or *provided food for* [a]2 Sam 17:27-29

19:13 *Amasa.* See 17:25 and note. Although Amasa deserved death for treason, David appointed him commander of his army in place of Joab, hoping to secure the allegiance of those who had followed Amasa, especially the Judahites (see 20:5). *May God do so to me, and more also.* A curse formula (see note on 1 Sam 3:17).
19:15 *Gilgal.* See note on Josh 4:19.
19:17 *a thousand men of Benjamin.* No doubt fearing they would be suspected by the king of being implicated in Shimei's deed.
19:20 *your servant knows that I have sinned.* Shimei's guilt was common knowledge; he could only seize the most appropriate time to plead for mercy. *house of Joseph.* A common way of referring to the northern tribes (see 1 Kin 11:28; Ezek 37:19; Amos 5:6; Zech 10:6)—of which Ephraim and Manasseh (sons of Joseph) were the most prominent (see Num 26:28; Josh 18:5; Judg 1:22).
19:21 *Abishai.* See 16:9; see also note on 1 Sam 26:6. *the LORD's anointed.* See note on 1 Sam 9:16; see also 1 Sam 24:6; 26:9–11; Ex 22:28; 1 Kin 21:10.
19:22 *Should any man be put to death in Israel today?* It was a day for general amnesty (see 1 Sam 11:13).
19:23 *You shall not die.* David kept his pledge; he would not himself avenge the wrong committed against him (see note on 1 Sam 25:2–44). But on his deathbed he instructed Solomon to take Shimei's case in hand (see 1 Kin 2:8–9,36–46).
19:24 *Mephibosheth.* See 9:6–13.
19:25 *Why did you not go with me . . . ?* David remembers Ziba's previous allegations (see 16:3).
19:26 *lame.* See 4:4; 9:3.
19:27 *he has slandered your servant.* See 16:3. *like the angel of God.* See 14:17 and note. *do what is good in your sight.* Mephibosheth discreetly requests David to reconsider the grant of his property to Ziba (see 16:4).
19:29 *divide the land.* Faced with conflicting testimony that could not be corroborated, David withholds judgment and orders the division of Saul's estate.
19:31 *Barzillai.* See note on 17:27.

over with me and I will [1]sustain you in Jerusalem with me."

34 But Barzillai said to the king, "[a]How long [1]have I yet to live, that I should go up with the king to Jerusalem?

35 "I am [1]now [a]eighty years old. Can I distinguish between good and bad? Or can your servant taste what I eat or what I drink? Or can I hear anymore [b]the voice of singing men and women? [c]Why then should your servant be an added burden to my lord the king?

36 "Your servant would merely cross over the Jordan with the king. Why should the king compensate me *with* this reward?

37 "Please let your servant return, that I may die in my own city near the grave of my father and my mother. However, here is your servant [a]Chimham, let him cross over with my lord the king, and do for him what is good in your sight."

38 The king answered, "Chimham shall cross over with me, and I will do for him what is good in your sight; and whatever you [1]require of me, I will do for you."

39 All the people crossed over the Jordan and the king crossed too. The king then [a]kissed Barzillai and blessed him, and he returned to his place.

40 Now the king went on to Gilgal, and Chimham went on with him; and all the people of Judah and also [a]half the people of Israel [1]accompanied the king.

41 And behold, all the men of Israel came to the king and said to the king, "[a]Why had our brothers [b]the men of Judah stolen you away, and brought the king and his household and all David's men with him over the Jordan?"

42 Then all the men of Judah answered the men of Israel, "Because [a]the king is a close relative to [1]us. Why then [2]are you angry about this matter? Have we eaten at all at the king's *expense*, or has [3]anything been taken for us?"

43 But the men of Israel answered the men of Judah and said, "[1][a]We have ten parts in the king, therefore [1]we also have more *claim* on David than you. Why then did you treat us with contempt? Was it not [1]our advice first to bring back [1]our king?" Yet the words of the men of Judah were harsher than the words of the men of Israel.

Sheba's Revolt

20 Now [a]a worthless fellow happened to be there whose name was Sheba, the son of [b]Bichri, a Benjamite; and he blew the trumpet and said,

"[c]We have no portion in David,
Nor do we have inheritance in [d]the son of Jesse;
[e]Every man to his tents, O Israel!"

2 So all the men of Israel [1]withdrew from following David *and* followed Sheba the son of Bichri; but the men of Judah [2]remained steadfast to their king, from the Jordan even to Jerusalem.

3 Then David came to his house at Jerusalem, and [a]the king took the ten women, the concubines whom he had left to keep the house, and placed them under guard and provided them with sustenance, but did not go in to them. So they were shut up until the day of their death, living as widows.

4 Then the king said to [a]Amasa, "Call out the men of Judah for me within three days, and be present here yourself."

5 So Amasa went to call out *the men of* Judah, but he [a]delayed longer than the set time which he had appointed him.

6 And David said to [a]Abishai, "Now Sheba the son of Bichri will do us more harm than Absalom; [b]take your lord's servants and pursue him, so that he does not find for himself fortified cities and escape from our sight."

7 So Joab's men went out after him, [a]along with the Cherethites and the Pelethites and all the mighty men; and they went out from Jerusalem to pursue Sheba the son of Bichri.

33 [1]Or *provide food for*
34 [1]Lit *are the days of the years of my life* [a]Gen 47:8
35 [1]Lit *today* [a]Ps 90:10 [b]Eccl 2:8; Is 5:11, 12 [c]2 Sam 15:33
37 [a]2 Sam 19:40; 1 Kin 2:7; Jer 41:17
38 [1]Lit *choose*
39 [a]Gen 31:55; Ruth 1:14; 2 Sam 14:33
40 [1]Lit *crossed over with* [a]2 Sam 19:9, 10
41 [a]Judg 8:1; 12:1 [b]2 Sam 19:11, 12
42 [1]Lit *me* [2]Lit *is it hot to you* [3]Or *a gift* [a]2 Sam 19:12
43 [1]Singular in Heb [a]2 Sam 5:1; 1 Kin 11:30, 31
20:1 [a]2 Sam 16:7 [b]Gen 46:21 [c]2 Sam 19:43; 1 Kin 12:16 [d]1 Sam 22:7-9 [e]1 Sam 13:2; 2 Sam 18:17; 2 Chr 10:16
2 [1]Lit *went up* [2]Lit *clung to*
3 [a]2 Sam 15:16; 16:21, 22
4 [a]2 Sam 17:25; 19:13
5 [a]1 Sam 13:8
6 [a]2 Sam 21:17 [b]2 Sam 11:11; 1 Kin 1:33
7 [a]2 Sam 8:18; 1 Kin 1:38

19:35 *distinguish between good and bad.* At his age, he would be indifferent to all the pleasures of the court.
19:37 *Chimham.* Likely a son of Barzillai (see 1Ki 2:7).
19:41 *Why had . . . the men of Judah stolen you away, and brought the king . . . over the Jordan?* It seems that the Jordan was a kind of psychological border to the land of Israel (see Josh 22:19,25; Judg 12:4)—which may also explain why Ish-bosheth (2:8), Mephibosheth (9:4) and even David himself (17:22) had sought refuge in Transjordan. That being the case, the protest of the Israelites may be that the Judahites had not waited for all Israel to assemble before bringing David across the Jordan, thus leaving the Israelites in a bad light—as though they were reluctant to receive the king back (see v. 43).
19:43 *ten parts.* The ten tribes, excluding Judah and Simeon (see note on 2:4). *we also have more claim on David.* The grounds for this assertion may be that the Lord had chosen David to reign in the place of Saul (see 3:17–18; 5:2).
20:1 *worthless fellow.* See note on Deut 13:13. *there.* In Gilgal (19:40–43). *Bichri.* Benjamin's second son (Beker, Gen 46:21; 1 Chr 7:6–9). *Benjamite.* Tribal jealousy still simmered over the transfer of the royal house from Benjamin (Saul's tribe) to Judah. *We have no portion in David.* Sheba appeals to the Israelite suspicion that David favored his own tribe Judah over the other tribes (see 1 Kin 12:16).
20:2 *all the men of Israel.* Those referred to in 19:41–43.
20:3 *ten . . . concubines.* See notes on 15:16; 16:22.
20:4 *Amasa.* See notes on 17:25; 19:13. David bypasses Joab.
20:6 *Abishai.* David bypasses Joab a second time (see v. 7). *your lord's servants.* "Joab's men" (v. 7).
20:7 *Joab's men.* See 18:2. It becomes clear that Joab also accompanied the soldiers and, though not in command (by the king's order), he was obviously the leader recognized by the soldiers (see vv. 7,11,15). *Cherethites and the Pelethites.* See note on 8:18. *mighty men.* See 23:8–39. Once more in a time of crisis David depended mainly on the small force of professionals (many of them non-Israelite) who made up his private army.

8 When they were at the large stone
which is in [a]Gibeon, Amasa came [1]to meet
them. Now Joab was [2]dressed in his military
attire, and over it was a belt with a sword in
its sheath fastened at his waist; and as he
went forward, it fell out.
9 Joab said to Amasa, "Is it well with
you, my brother?" And [a]Joab took Amasa by
the beard with his right hand to kiss him.

Amasa Murdered

10 But Amasa was not on guard against
the sword which was in Joab's hand so [a]he
struck him in the belly with it and poured
out his inward parts on the ground, and did
not *strike* him again, and he died. Then Joab
and Abishai his brother pursued Sheba the
son of Bichri.
11 Now there stood by him one of Joab's
young men, and said, "Whoever favors Joab
and whoever is for David, [a]*let him* follow
Joab."
12 But Amasa lay wallowing in *his* blood
in the middle of the highway. And when the
man saw that all the people stood still, he
[1]removed Amasa from the highway into the
field and threw a garment over him when he
saw that everyone who came by him stood
still.

Revolt Put Down

13 As soon as he was removed from the
highway, all the men passed on after Joab to
pursue Sheba the son of Bichri.
14 Now he went through all the tribes of
Israel to Abel, even Beth-maacah, and all the
Berites; and they were gathered together and
also went after him.
15 They came and besieged him in [a]Abel
Beth-maacah, and [b]they [1]cast up a siege
ramp against the city, and it stood by the
rampart; and all the people who were with

8 [1]Lit *before* [2]Lit *girded with military garment as clothing* [a]2 Sam 2:13; 3:30
9 [a]Matt 26:49
10 [a]2 Sam 2:23; 3:27; 1 Kin 2:5
11 [a]2 Sam 20:13
12 [1]Lit *caused to turn*
15 [1]Lit *poured out* [a]1 Kin 15:20; 2 Kin 15:29 [b]2 Kin 19:32; Ezek 4:2

16 [a]2 Sam 14:2
19 [a]Deut 20:10 [b]1 Sam 26:19; 2 Sam 14:16; 21:3
21 [a]Josh 24:33 [b]2 Sam 20:2
22 [a]2 Sam 20:16; Eccl 9:13-16 [b]2 Sam 20:1
23 [a]2 Sam 8:16-18; 1 Kin 4:3-6
24 [a]1 Kin 4:3
25 [a]1 Kin 4:4

Joab were wreaking destruction in order to
topple the wall.
16 Then [a]a wise woman called from the
city, "Hear, hear! Please tell Joab, 'Come
here that I may speak with you.' "
17 So he approached her, and the woman
said, "Are you Joab?" And he answered, "I
am." Then she said to him, "Listen to the
words of your maidservant." And he answered,
"I am listening."
18 Then she spoke, saying, "Formerly they
used to say, 'They will surely ask *advice* at
Abel,' and thus they ended *the dispute.*
19 "I am of those who are peaceable *and*
faithful in Israel. [a]You are seeking to destroy a
city, even a mother in Israel. Why would you
swallow up [b]the inheritance of the LORD?"
20 Joab replied, "Far be it, far be it from
me that I should swallow up or destroy!
21 "Such is not the case. But a man from
[a]the hill country of Ephraim, [b]Sheba the son
of Bichri by name, has lifted up his hand
against King David. Only hand him over, and
I will depart from the city." And the woman
said to Joab, "Behold, his head will be
thrown to you over the wall."
22 Then the woman [a]wisely came to all
the people. And they cut off the head of Sheba
the son of Bichri and threw it to Joab. So
[b]he blew the trumpet, and they were dispersed
from the city, each to his tent. Joab
also returned to the king at Jerusalem.
23 [a]Now Joab was over the whole army of
Israel, and Benaiah the son of Jehoiada was
over the Cherethites and the Pelethites;
24 and Adoram was over the forced labor,
and [a]Jehoshaphat the son of Ahilud was the
recorder;
25 and Sheva was scribe, and Zadok and
[a]Abiathar were priests;
26 and Ira the Jairite was also a priest to
David.

20:8 *Gibeon.* See note on 2:12. *Amasa came.* Apparently with some troops (see v. 11 and note).
20:10 *in the belly.* See 2:23; 3:27. For the second time Joab commits murder to secure his position as commander of David's army (see 1 Kin 2:5–6). *Joab and Abishai his brother.* In defiance of David's order, Joab reassumes command on his own initiative (see v. 23).
20:11 *Whoever favors Joab and whoever is for David.* To dispel any idea that Joab was aligned with Sheba's conspiracy, an appeal is made to Amasa's troops to support Joab if they are truly loyal to David.
20:14 *Abel . . . Beth-maacah.* Located to the north of Dan (see 1 Kin 15:20; 2 Chr 16:4). Sheba's strategy was to gather as many volunteers for his revolt as possible, but he was obviously afraid to assemble his ragtag army anywhere within close reach of David's men. *Berites.* Otherwise unknown.
20:18 *ask advice at Abel.* The city was famous for the wisdom of its inhabitants.
20:19 *a mother in Israel.* A town that produced faithful Israelites—cities were commonly personified as women (see Jer 50:12; Gal 4:26). *the inheritance of the LORD.* See note on 1 Sam 10:1.
20:21 *hill country of Ephraim.* Either Sheba, a Benjamite (see v. 1), lived in the tribal territory of Ephraim or this was the designation of a geographical, rather than a strictly tribal, region.
20:22 *Joab also returned to the king at Jerusalem.* See notes on vv. 7,10.
20:23–26 These royal officials apparently served David during most of his reign (see 8:15–18).
20:23 *Joab was over the whole army of Israel.* Though in some disfavor, he held this position until he participated in Adonijah's conspiracy (1 Kin 1:7; 2:28–35). *Cherethites and the Pelethites.* See note on 8:18.
20:24 *Adoram was over the forced labor.* A position not established in the early years of David's reign (see 8:15–16). Adoram (a variant of Adoniram) must have been a late appointee of David since he continued to serve under Solomon (1 Kin 4:6; 5:14) and was eventually killed in the early days of the reign of Rehoboam (1 Kin 12:18; 2 Chr 10:18). *forced labor.* Labor performed for the most part by prisoners of war from defeated nations (see Josh 9:21; 1 Kin 9:15,20–21). *recorder.* See note on 8:16.
20:25 *Sheva.* See note on 8:17 ("Seraiah"). *scribe.* See note on 8:17. *Zadok and Abiathar.* See note on 8:17.
20:26 *Jairite.* A reference either to Jair of the tribe of Manas-

Gibeonite Revenge

21 Now there was [a]a famine in the days of
David for three years, year after year;
and [b]David sought the presence of the LORD.
And the LORD said, "It is for Saul and his
bloody house, because he put the Gibeonites
to death."
2 So the king called the Gibeonites and
spoke to them (now the Gibeonites were not
of the sons of Israel but of the remnant of the
Amorites, and [a]the sons of Israel [1]made a
covenant with them, but Saul had sought to
[2]kill them in his zeal for the sons of Israel
and Judah).
3 Thus David said to the Gibeonites,
"What should I do for you? And how can I
make atonement that you may bless [a]the
inheritance of the LORD?"
4 Then the Gibeonites said to him, "[a]We
have no *concern* of silver or gold with Saul or
his house, nor is it for us to put any man to
death in Israel." And he said, "I will do for
you whatever you say."
5 So they said to the king, "[a]The man
who consumed us and who planned [1]to
exterminate us from remaining within any
border of Israel,
6 let seven men from his sons be given to
us, and we will [1]hang them [a]before the LORD
in Gibeah of Saul, [b]the chosen of the LORD."
And the king said, "I will give *them.*"
7 But the king spared [a]Mephibosheth,
the son of Jonathan the son of Saul,
[b]because of the oath of the LORD which was
between them, between David and Saul's
son Jonathan.
8 So the king took the two sons of [a]Riz-
pah the daughter of Aiah, Armoni and
Mephibosheth whom she had borne to Saul,
and the five sons of [1b]Merab the daughter of
Saul, whom she had borne to Adriel the son
of Barzillai the [c]Meholathite.
9 Then he gave them into the hands of
the Gibeonites, and they [1]hanged them in
the mountain before the LORD, so that the
seven of them fell together; and they were
put to death in the first days of harvest at
[a]the beginning of barley harvest.
10 [a]And Rizpah the daughter of Aiah took
sackcloth and spread it for herself on the
rock, from the beginning of harvest until [1]it
rained on them from the sky; and [b]she
[2]allowed neither the birds of the sky to rest
on them by day nor the beasts of the field by
night.
11 When it was told David what Rizpah
the daughter of Aiah, the concubine of Saul,
had done,
12 then David went and took [a]the bones
of Saul and the bones of Jonathan his son
from the men of Jabesh-gilead, who had
stolen them from the open square of [b]Beth-

21:1 [a]Gen 12:10; 26:1; 42:5 [b]Num 27:21
2 [1]Lit *had sworn to* [2]Lit *smite* [a]Josh 9:3, 15-20
3 [a]1 Sam 26:19; 2 Sam 20:19
4 [a]Num 35:31, 32
5 [1]Lit *against us that we should be exterminated* [a]2 Sam 21:1
6 [1]Lit *expose them* [a]Num 25:4 [b]1 Sam 10:24
7 [a]2 Sam 4:4; 9:10 [b]1 Sam 18:3; 20:12-17; 23:18; 2 Sam 9:1-7
8 [1]So Gr and Heb mss [a]2 Sam 3:7 [b]1 Sam 18:19 [c]1 Kin 19:16
9 [1]Lit *exposed them* [a]Ex 9:31, 32
10 [1]Lit *water was poured* [2]Lit *gave* [a]Deut 21:23 [b]1 Sam 17:44, 46
12 [a]1 Sam 31:11-13 [b]Josh 17:11

seh (Num 32:41) or to a judge from Gilead (Judg 10:3,5). *priest.* See note on 8:18.

21:1–24:25 This concluding section forms an appendix to 1,2 Samuel and contains additional materials (without concern for chronology) relating to David's reign. While its topical arrangement is striking, it also employs a literary pattern, *a-b-c/c-b-a,* frequently found elsewhere in OT literature. The first and last units (21:1–14; 24:1–25) are narratives of two events in which David had to deal with God's wrath against Israel (the first occasioned by an act of Saul, the second by his own). The second and fifth units (21:15–22; 23:8–39) are accounts of David's warriors (the second much longer than the first). At the center (22:1–23:7) are two songs of David (the first much longer than the second), one of which celebrates David's victories as warrior-king while the other recalls his role as psalmist (see note on 1 Sam 16:14–17:58). It is unknown if motivation for this arrangement went beyond aesthetic considerations. The triumph song of ch. 22 and the song of Hannah in 1 Sam 2:1–10 clearly form a literary frame enclosing the main composition (see note on 1 Sam 2:1).

21:1–14 This event appears to have occurred after David's kindness was extended to Mephibosheth (ch. 9) and before Absalom's rebellion (16:7–8; 18:28; see note on 16:8).

21:1 *he put the Gibeonites to death.* Saul's action against the Gibeonites is not related elsewhere but appears to have been instituted early in his reign, motivated by an excessive nationalism (if not tribalism—the Gibeonites occupied territory partly assigned to Benjamin, and Saul's great-grandfather was known as the "father of Gibeon," 1 Chr 8:29; 9:35).

21:2 *Amorites.* A comprehensive name sometimes used to designate all the pre-Israelite inhabitants of Canaan (Gen 15:16; Josh 24:18; Judg 6:10; Amos 2:10). More precisely, the Gibeonites were called Hivites (Josh 9:7; 11:19). *the sons of Israel made a covenant with them.* A pledge sworn in the name of the Lord (Josh 9:15,18–26). *sought to kill them.* The reason Saul was unsuccessful is not known.

21:3 *bless.* Since the oath sworn to them had been violated, they could rightly call down God's curse on the land. *the inheritance of the LORD.* See note on 1 Sam 10:1.

21:4 *nor is it for us to put any man to death in Israel.* Bloodguilt could only be redressed by the shedding of blood, but as subject aliens the Gibeonites had no right to legal redress against an Israelite. This restriction must have been Saul's since it is contrary to the Mosaic law (see Ex 22:21; Lev 19:34; 24:22; Deut 1:16–17; 24:17; 27:19).

21:5 *The man.* Saul. *exterminate us from . . . Israel.* Those who escaped Saul's attack had been driven from their towns and lands (see 4:2–3 and notes).

21:6 *seven.* Because it would represent a full number (seven symbolized completeness)—though many more Gibeonites had been slain. *Gibeah.* The place of Saul's residence (see 1 Sam 10:26).

21:7 *oath of the LORD . . . between David and . . . Jonathan.* See 4:4; 9:1–13; 1 Sam 18:3; 20:15.

21:8 *Rizpah.* See 3:7. *Merab.* See 1 Sam 18:19. *Barzillai the Meholathite.* Not to be confused with Barzillai the Gileadite (17:27; 19:31).

21:9 *the seven of them fell together.* This nearly extinguished the house of Saul, which God had rejected (see 1 Sam 13:13–14; 15:23–26). In 1 Chr 8:29–39; 9:35–44 no descendants of Saul are listed other than from the line of Jonathan. *the beginning of barley harvest.* About the middle of April (see note on Ruth 1:22).

21:10 *sackcloth.* See note on Gen 37:34. *rained.* An indication that the famine was caused by drought and evidence that the judgment on Israel for breaking the oath sworn to the Gibeonites (see v. 1) was now over.

21:12 *bones of Saul and . . . Jonathan his son.* See 1 Sam 31:11–13. David's final act toward Saul and Jonathan was a deed

shan, [c]where the Philistines had hanged them on the day [d]the Philistines struck down Saul in Gilboa.

13 He brought up the bones of Saul and the bones of Jonathan his son from there, and they gathered the bones of those who had been [1]hanged.

14 They buried the bones of Saul and Jonathan his son in the country of Benjamin in [a]Zela, in the grave of Kish his father; thus they did all that the king commanded, and after that [b]God was moved by prayer for the land.

15 Now when [a]the Philistines were at war again with Israel, David went down and his servants with him; and as they fought against the Philistines, David became weary.

16 Then Ishbi-benob, who was [a]among the descendants of the [1]giant, the weight of whose spear was three hundred *shekels* of bronze in weight, [2]was girded with a new *sword,* and he [3]intended to kill David.

17 But [a]Abishai the son of Zeruiah helped him, and struck the Philistine and killed him. Then the men of David swore to him, saying, "[b]You shall not go out again with us to battle, so that you do not extinguish [c]the lamp of Israel."

18 [a]Now it came about after this that there was war again with the Philistines at Gob; then [b]Sibbecai the Hushathite struck down Saph, who was among the descendants of the [1]giant.

19 There was war with the Philistines again at Gob, and Elhanan the son of Jaare-oregim the Bethlehemite [1]killed [2]Goliath the Gittite, [a]the shaft of whose spear was like a weaver's beam.

12 [c]1 Sam 31:10 [d]1 Sam 31:3, 4
13 [1]Lit *exposed*
14 [a]Josh 18:28 [b]Josh 7:26; 2 Sam 24:25
15 [a]2 Sam 5:17-25
16 [1]Heb *Raphah* [2]Lit *and he was* [3]Lit *said* [a]Num 13:22, 28; Josh 15:14; 2 Sam 21:18-22
17 [a]2 Sam 20:6-10 [b]2 Sam 18:3 [c]2 Sam 22:29 1 Kin 11:36
18 [1]Heb *Raphah* [a]1 Chr 20:4-8 [b]1 Chr 11:29; 27:11
19 [1]Lit *smote* [2]In 1 Chr 20:5, *Lahmi, the brother of Goliath* [a]1 Sam 17:7
20 [1]Heb *Raphah* [a]2 Sam 21:16, 18
22 [1]Heb *Raphah* [a]1 Chr 20:8
22:1 [1]Lit *palm* [a]Ps 18:2-50 [b]Ex 15:1; Deut 31:30
2 [1]Lit *crag* [a]1 Sam 23:25; 24:2; Ps 31:3; 71:3
3 [1]Lit *God of my rock* [a]Deut 32:4, 37; 1 Sam 2:2 [b]Gen 15:1; Deut 33:29 [c]Luke 1:69 [d]Ps 9:9
4 [a]Ps 48:1; 96:4
5 [1]Heb *Belial* [2]Or *terrified* [a]Ps 93:4; Jon 2:3 [b]Ps 69:14, 15
6 [1]I.e. the nether world [a]Ps 116:3
7 [1]Or *called* [a]Ps 116:4; 120:1

20 There was war at Gath again, where there was a man of *great* stature who had six fingers on each hand and six toes on each foot, twenty-four in number; and he also had been born [a]to the [1]giant.

21 When he defied Israel, Jonathan the son of Shimei, David's brother, struck him down.

22 [a]These four were born to the [1]giant in Gath, and they fell by the hand of David and by the hand of his servants.

David's Psalm of Deliverance

22 [a]And David spoke [b]the words of this song to the LORD in the day that the LORD delivered him from the [1]hand of all his enemies and from the [1]hand of Saul.

2 He said,
"[a]The LORD is my [1]rock and my fortress
and my deliverer;
3 [1][a]My God, my rock, in whom I take
refuge,
My [b]shield and [c]the horn of my
salvation, my stronghold and [d]my
refuge;
My savior, You save me from violence.
4 "I call upon the LORD, [a]who is worthy
to be praised,
And I am saved from my enemies.
5 "For [a]the waves of death encompassed
me;
[b]The torrents of [1]destruction
[2]overwhelmed me;
6 [a]The cords of [1]Sheol surrounded me;
The snares of death confronted me.
7 "[a]In my distress I called upon the
LORD,
Yes, I [1]cried to my God;

---

of deep respect for the king he had honored and the friend he had loved.

21:15–22 These four Philistine episodes (vv. 15–17, 18, 19, 20–21) cannot be chronologically located with any certainty (see note on 21:1–24:25). Each involves a heroic accomplishment by one of David's mighty men, resulting in the death of a "descendant of the giant" (see vv. 16,18,20,22).

21:16 *giant.* In saying the four formidable enemy warriors referred to in this series were "born to the giant in Gath" (v. 22), the writer may be linking them to Deut 2:10–11,20–21. In that case, they may have been related to the Anakites (see Josh 11:21–22). Cf. Gen 15:19–20, which in its list of ten peoples of Canaan mentions Rephaites but not Anakites, though the Anakites (but not Rephaites) figure significantly in the accounts of the conquest (Num 13:22,28,33; Deut 1:28; 9:2; Josh 14:12,15; Judg 1:20).

21:17 *Abishai.* See note on 1 Sam 26:6. *so that you do not extinguish the lamp of Israel.* A striking metaphor depicting Israel's dependence on David for its security and continuing existence as a nation—its national hope (see 22:29; 23:3–4; 1 Kin 11:36).

21:18 *Gob.* Probably in the near vicinity of Gezer, where 1 Chr 20:4 locates this same battle. *Saph.* Called Sippai in 1 Chr 20:4.

21:19 *Elhanan . . . killed Goliath.* Since it is clear from 1 Sam 17 that David killed Goliath, it is possible that an early copyist misread the Hebrew for "Lahmi the brother of" (see 1 Chr 20:5) as "the Bethlehemite" (in Hebrew the word for "killed" stands first in the clause).

21:21 *defied Israel.* As Goliath had done (see 1 Sam 17:10,25). *Shimei.* Also called Shammah (1 Sam 16:9; 17:13).

22:1 *this song.* Preserved also as Ps 18 (see notes on that psalm). Besides an introduction (vv. 2–4) and conclusion (vv. 47–51), the song consists of three major sections: The first describes David's deliverance from mortal danger at the hands of his enemies (vv. 5–20); the second sets forth the moral grounds for God's saving help (vv. 21–30); the third recounts the help that the Lord gave him (vv. 31–46). The song was probably composed shortly after David's victories over foreign enemies (8:1–14) and before his sin with Bathsheba (compare vv. 21–25 with 1 Kin 15:5). *from . . . all his enemies.* See 8:1–14. *from . . . Saul.* See 1 Sam 18–31.

22:2 *my rock.* A figure particularly appropriate to David's experience (see vv. 32,47; 23:3; Deut 32:4,15,18,31; Ps 28:1; 31:2; 61:2; 78:35; 89:26; 94:22; 95:1). He had often taken refuge among the rocks of the wilderness (1 Sam 23:25; 24:2), but he realized that true security was found only in the Lord. *fortress.* The Hebrew for this word occurs in 5:17; 23:14; 1 Sam 22:4–5; 24:22, referring to places where David sought refuge.

22:3 *My shield.* See vv. 31,36; Gen 15:1; Deut 33:29. *horn.* Here symbolizes strength (see Deut 33:17; Jer 48:25; see also note on Luke 1:69).

22:5 *waves of death.* In vv. 5–6 David depicts his experiences in poetic figures of mortal danger.

22:6 *Sheol.* See note on Jnh 2:2.

And from His temple He heard my voice,
And my cry for help *came* into His ears.
8 "Then [a]the earth shook and quaked,
[b]The foundations of heaven were trembling
And were shaken, because He was angry.
9 "Smoke went up [1]out of His nostrils,
[a]Fire from His mouth devoured;
[b]Coals were kindled by it.
10 "He bowed the heavens also, and came down
With [a]thick darkness under His feet.
11 "[a]And He rode on a cherub and flew;
And He [1]appeared on [b]the wings of the wind.
12 "[a]And He made darkness [1]canopies around Him,
A mass of waters, thick clouds of the sky.
13 "From the brightness before Him
[a]Coals of fire were kindled.
14 "[a]The LORD thundered from heaven,
And the Most High uttered His voice.
15 "[a]And He sent out arrows, and scattered them,
Lightning, and [1]routed them.
16 "Then the channels of the sea appeared,
The foundations of the world were [1]laid bare
By the rebuke of the LORD,
[a]At the blast of the breath of His nostrils.
17 "[a]He sent from on high, He took me;
[b]He drew me out of many waters.
18 "He delivered me from my strong enemy,
From those who hated me, for they were too strong for me.
19 "They confronted me in the day of my calamity,
[a]But the LORD was my support.
20 "[a]He also brought me forth into a broad place;
He rescued me, [b]because He delighted in me.
21 "[a]The LORD has rewarded me according to my righteousness;
[b]According to the cleanness of my hands He has recompensed me.
22 "[a]For I have kept the ways of the LORD,
And have not acted wickedly against my God.
23 "[a]For all His ordinances *were* before me,
And *as for* His statutes, I did not depart from [1]them.
24 "[a]I was also [1]blameless toward Him,
And I kept myself from my iniquity.
25 "[a]Therefore the LORD has recompensed me according to my righteousness,
According to my cleanness before His eyes.
26 "[a]With the [1]kind You show Yourself [1]kind,
With the [2]blameless You show Yourself [2]blameless;
27 [a]With the pure You show Yourself pure,
[b]And with the perverted You show Yourself [1]astute.
28 "[a]And You save an afflicted people;
[b]But Your eyes are on the haughty *whom* You abase.
29 "[a]For You are my lamp, O LORD;
And the LORD illumines my darkness.
30 "[a]For by You I can [1]run upon a troop;
By my God I can leap over a wall.
31 "[a]As for God, His way is [1]blameless;
[b]The word of the LORD is tested;
[c]He is a shield to all who take refuge in Him.
32 "[a]For who is God, besides the LORD?
[b]And who is a rock, besides our God?

8 [a]Judg 5:4; Ps 97:4 [b]Job 26:11
9 [1]Or *in His wrath* [a]Ps 97:3; Heb 12:29 [b]2 Sam 22:13
10 [a]Ex 19:16; 1 Kin 8:12; Ps 97:2; Nah 1:3
11 [1]Many mss read *sped* [a]2 Sam 6:2 [b]Ps 104:3
12 [1]Or *pavilions* [a]Job 36:29
13 [a]2 Sam 22:9
14 [a]Job 37:2-5; Ps 29:3
15 [1]Lit *confused* [a]Deut 32:23; Josh 10:10; 1 Sam 7:10
16 [1]Or *uncovered* [a]Ex 15:8; Nah 1:4
17 [a]Ps 144:7 [b]Ex 2:10
19 [a]Ps 23:4
20 [a]Ps 31:8; 118:5 [b]2 Sam 15:26
21 [a]1 Sam 26:23; 1 Kin 8:32 [b]Ps 24:4
22 [a]Gen 18:19; Ps 128:1; Prov 8:32
23 [1]Lit *it* [a]Deut 6:6-9; Ps 119:30, 102
24 [1]Lit *complete;* or *having integrity* [a]Gen 6:9; 7:1; Eph 1:4; Col 1:21, 22
25 [a]2 Sam 22:21
26 [1]Or *loyal* [2]Lit *complete;* or *having integrity* [a]Matt 5:7
27 [1]Lit *twisted* [a]Matt 5:8; 1 John 3:3 [b]Lev 26:23, 24; Rom 1:28
28 [a]Ex 3:7, 8; Ps 72:12, 13 [b]Is 2:11, 12, 17; 5:15
29 [a]2 Sam 21:17; 1 Kin 11:36; Ps 27:1
30 [1]Or *crush a troop* [a]2 Sam 5:6-8
31 [1]Lit *complete;* or *having integrity* [a]Deut 32:4; Matt 5:48 [b]Ps 12:6; 119:140; Prov 30:5 [c]2 Sam 22:3; Ps 84:9
32 [a]1 Sam 2:2 [b]2 Sam 22:2

22:7 *His temple.* Heaven, where the Lord is enthroned as King (see Ps 11:4; Is 6:1; Jnh 2:7).
22:8–16 See note on Ps 18:7–15.
22:9 *Smoke went up out of His nostrils.* God's power is portrayed in terms similar to those applied to the awesome beast, the Leviathan (Job 41:19–21).
22:11 *cherub.* See Ezek 1 and 10, where cherubim are said to be the bearers of the throne of God; see also notes on Gen 3:24; 1 Sam 4:4; Ezek 1:5.
22:14 *The LORD thundered.* The reference to thunder as the voice of God is common in the OT (see Ps 29; Job 37:2–5). Thunder is particularly suited to expressing God's power and majesty.
22:17 *He sent from on high.* In vv. 17–20 David describes his deliverance, initially in figurative terms (v. 17; cf. v. 5) and subsequently in more literal language (vv. 18–20).
22:20 *delighted in.* The Hebrew underlying this expression is used in 15:26; Ps 22:8 (cf. Matt 3:17, "well-pleased") and expresses the idea of the sovereign good pleasure and favor of God toward His anointed one (v. 51).
22:21 *according to my righteousness.* In vv. 21–25 David refers to the Lord's deliverances as a reward for his own righteousness. While these statements may give the impression of self-righteous boasting and a meritorious basis for divine favor, they should be understood in their context as: (1) David's desire to please the Lord in his service as the Lord's anointed (see note on v. 51); (2) his recognition that the Lord rewards those who faithfully seek to serve Him.
22:26–30 Because God responds to man in kind (see Job 34:11; Prov 3:34), David has experienced the Lord's favor.
22:28 *the haughty whom You abase.* The words of this verse fit well with David's experience in his conflict with Saul (see Hannah's song, 1 Sam 2:3–8).
22:29 *You are my lamp.* The Lord causes David's life and undertakings to flourish (see Job 18:5–6; 21:17; see also note on Ps 27:1).
22:31 *His way is blameless.* The remainder of the song (vv. 31–51) accentuates David's praise to God for His deliverances.
22:32 *rock.* See note on v. 2.

33 "[a]God is my strong fortress;
And He [1]sets the [2]blameless in [3]His way.
34 "[a]He makes [1]my feet like hinds' *feet,*
[b]And sets me on my high places.
35 "[a]He trains my hands for battle,
[b]So that my arms can bend a bow of bronze.
36 "You have also given me [a]the shield of Your salvation,
And Your [1]help makes me great.
37 "[a]You enlarge my steps under me,
And my [1]feet have not slipped.
38 "I pursued my enemies and [a]destroyed them,
And I did not turn back until they were consumed.
39 "And I have devoured them and shattered them, so that they did not rise;
And [a]they fell under my feet.
40 "For You have girded me with strength for battle;
You have [1]subdued under me [a]those who rose up against me.
41 "You have also [a]made my enemies turn *their* backs to me,
And I [1]destroyed those who hated me.
42 "[a]They looked, but there was none to save;
[b]*Even* to the LORD, but He did not answer them.
43 "[a]Then I pulverized them as the dust of the earth;
[b]I crushed *and* stamped them as the mire of the streets.
44 "[a]You have also delivered me from the contentions of my people;
[b]You have kept me as head of the nations;
[c]A people whom I have not known serve me.
45 "[a]Foreigners pretend obedience to me;
As soon as they hear, they obey me.
46 "Foreigners [1]lose heart,
[a]And [2]come trembling out of their [3]fortresses.
47 "The LORD lives, and blessed be my rock;
And exalted be [1][a]God, the rock of my salvation,
48 [a]The God who executes vengeance for me,
[b]And brings down peoples under me,
49 Who also brings me out from my enemies;
You even lift me above [a]those who rise up against me;
[b]You rescue me from the violent man.
50 "[a]Therefore I will give thanks to You, O LORD, among the nations,
And I will sing praises to Your name.
51 "[a]*He* is a tower of [1]deliverance to His king,
And [b]shows lovingkindness to His anointed,
[c]To David and his [2]descendants forever."

David's Last Song

23 Now these are the last words of David.
David the son of Jesse declares,
[a]The man who was raised on high declares,
[b]The anointed of the God of Jacob,
And the sweet psalmist of Israel,
2 "[a]The Spirit of the LORD spoke by me,
And His word was on my tongue.
3 "The God of Israel said,
[a]The Rock of Israel spoke to me,
'[b]He who rules over men righteously,
[c]Who rules in the fear of God,
4 [a]Is as the light of the morning *when* the sun rises,
A morning without clouds,
When the tender grass *springs* out of the earth,
Through sunshine after rain.'
5 "Truly is not my house so with God?
For [a]He has made an everlasting covenant with me,
Ordered in all things, and secured;
For all my salvation and all *my* desire,
Will He not indeed make *it* grow?

33 [1]Or *sets free* [2]Lit *complete;* or *having integrity* [3]Another reading is *my* [a]2 Sam 22:2; Ps 31:3, 4
34 [1]Another reading is *His* [a]2 Sam 2:18; Hab 3:19 [b]Deut 32:13
35 [a]Ps 144:1 [b]Job 20:24
36 [1]Lit *answering* [a]Eph 6:16, 17
37 [1]Lit *ankles* [a]2 Sam 22:20; Prov 4:12
38 [a]Ex 15:9
39 [a]Mal 4:3
40 [1]Lit *caused to bow down* [a]Ps 44:5
41 [1]Or *silenced* [a]Ex 23:27; Josh 10:24
42 [a]Is 17:7, 8 [b]1 Sam 28:6; Is 1:15
43 [a]2 Kin 13:7 [b]Is 10:6; Mic 7:10
44 [a]2 Sam 3:1; 19:9, 14 [b]2 Sam 8:1-14 [c]Is 55:5
45 [a]Ps 66:3; 81:15
46 [1]Lit *languish* [2]Lit *gird themselves* [3]Lit *fastnesses* [a]1 Sam 14:11; Mic 7:17
47 [1]Lit *the God of the rock* [a]2 Sam 22:3; Ps 89:26
48 [a]1 Sam 24:12; 25:39; 2 Sam 4:8; Ps 94:1 [b]Ps 144:2
49 [a]Ps 44:5 [b]Ps 140:1, 4, 11
50 [a]Rom 15:9
51 [1]I.e. victories; lit *salvation* [2]Lit *seed* [a]Ps 144:10 [b]Ps 89:24 [c]2 Sam 7:12-16
23:1 [a]2 Sam 7:8, 9; Ps 78:70, 71 [b]1 Sam 16:12, 13; Ps 89:20
2 [a]Matt 22:43; 2 Pet 1:21
3 [a]2 Sam 22:2, 3, 32 [b]Ps 72:1-3; Is 11:1-5 [c]2 Chr 19:7, 9
4 [a]Judg 5:31; Ps 72:6
5 [a]2 Sam 7:12-16; Ps 89:29; Is 55:3

22:47 *The LORD lives.* God's interventions and blessings in David's behalf have shown Him to be the living God (see Deut 5:26).
22:50 *I will give thanks to You, O LORD, among the nations.* For Paul's reference to this vow see Rom 15:9.
22:51 *His king . . . His anointed.* See notes on 1 Sam 10:25; 12:14–15. David refers to himself in the third person in a way that acknowledges the covenantal character of his kingship. It is in the context of David's official capacity as the LORD's anointed that the entire song is to be read and understood (see note on v. 21). *his descendants forever.* David speaks of God's promise through Nathan (see 7:12–16).
23:1 *last words of David.* Probably to be understood as David's last poetic testimony (in the manner of his psalms), perhaps composed at the time of his final instructions and warnings to his son Solomon (see 1 Kin 2:1–10).
23:2 *The Spirit of the LORD spoke by me.* David was conscious of God's Spirit at work in him enabling him to speak under the Spirit's guidance (see notes on 2 Tim 3:16; 2 Pet 1:21).
23:3 *Rock.* See note on 22:2; see also 1 Sam 2:2; Deut 32:4,15,18,30–31. *He who rules over men righteously.* In brief and vivid strokes David portrays the ideal theocratic king—to be fully realized only in the rule of David's greater son, Jesus Christ. This prophetic utterance complements that of 7:12–16 and anticipates those of Is 9:7; 11:1–5; Jer 23:5–6; 33:15–16; Zec 9:9.
23:4 *as the light of the morning.* See notes on Ps 27:1; 36:9.
23:5 *is not my house so with God?* A rhetorical question recalling God's covenant with him and his dynasty (see 7:12–16). *everlasting covenant.* David expressly calls God's promise to him a covenant that will not be abrogated (see notes on 7:20,28; Is 55:3; see also Ps 89:3,28,34,39; 132:11). *make it grow.* Through David's promised descendants.

6 "[a]But the worthless, every one of them
will be thrust away like thorns,
Because they cannot be taken in hand;
7 But the man who touches them
Must be [1]armed with iron and the
shaft of a spear,
And [a]they will be completely burned
with fire in *their* [2]place."

His Mighty Men

8 [a]These are the names of the mighty men whom David had: Josheb-basshebeth a Tahchemonite, chief of the [1]captains, he was *called* Adino the Eznite, because of eight hundred slain *by him* at one time;

9 and after him was Eleazar the son of [a]Dodo the [b]Ahohite, one of the three mighty men with David when they [1]defied the Philistines who were gathered there to battle and the men of Israel had [2]withdrawn.

10 [a]He arose and struck the Philistines until his hand was weary and [1]clung to the sword, and [b]the LORD brought about a great [2]victory that day; and the people returned after him only to strip *the slain*.

11 Now after him was Shammah the son of Agee a [a]Hararite. And the Philistines were gathered [1]into a troop where there was a plot of ground full of lentils, and the people fled from the Philistines.

12 But he took his stand in the midst of the plot, defended it and struck the Philistines; and [a]the LORD brought about a great [1]victory.

13 Then three of the thirty chief men went down and came to David in the harvest time to the [a]cave of Adullam, while the troop of the Philistines was camping in [b]the valley of Rephaim.

14 David was then [a]in the stronghold, while the garrison of the Philistines was then in Bethlehem.

15 [a]David had a craving and said, "Oh that someone would give me water to drink from the well of Bethlehem which is by the gate!"

6 [a]Matt 13:41
7 [1]Lit *filled* [2]Lit *sitting* [a]Matt 3:10; 13:30; Heb 6:8
8 [1]Or *three* [a]1 Chr 11:11-47
9 [1]Lit *reproached* [2]Lit *gone up* [a]1 Chr 27:4 [b]1 Chr 8:4
10 [1]Lit *his hand clung* [2]Lit *salvation* [a]1 Chr 11:13 [b]1 Sam 11:13; 19:5
11 [1]Possibly at Lehi [a]2 Sam 23:33
12 [1]Lit *salvation* [a]2 Sam 23:10
13 [a]1 Sam 22:1 [b]2 Sam 5:18
14 [a]1 Sam 22:4, 5
15 [a]1 Chr 11:17
16 [a]1 Chr 11:18 [b]Gen 35:14
17 [a]Lev 17:10
18 [1]So two Heb mss and Syriac; M.T. *three* [2]Lit *slain ones* [a]2 Sam 10:10, 14; 18:2 [b]1 Chr 11:20, 21
20 [1]Lit *smote* [2]Or *two lion-like heroes* [a]2 Sam 8:18; 20:23 [b]Josh 15:21
21 [1]Lit *smote* [2]Lit *a man of appearance*
22 [a]2 Sam 23:20
24 [a]2 Sam 2:18; 1 Chr 27:7
25 [a]1 Chr 11:27 [b]Judg 7:1
26 [a]2 Sam 14:2
27 [a]Josh 21:18
28 [a]2 Kin 25:23

16 [a]So the three mighty men broke through the camp of the Philistines, and drew water from the well of Bethlehem which was by the gate, and took *it* and brought *it* to David. Nevertheless he would not drink it, but [b]poured it out to the LORD;

17 and he said, "Be it far from me, O LORD, that I should do this. [a]*Shall I drink* the blood of the men who went in *jeopardy* of their lives?" Therefore he would not drink it. These things the three mighty men did.

18 [a]Abishai, the brother of Joab, the son of Zeruiah, was [b]chief of the [1]thirty. And he swung his spear against three hundred [2]and killed *them*, and had a name as well as the three.

19 He was most honored of the thirty, therefore he became their commander; however, he did not attain to the three.

20 Then [a]Benaiah the son of Jehoiada, the son of a valiant man of [b]Kabzeel, who had done mighty deeds, [1]killed the [2]two *sons of* Ariel of Moab. He also went down and killed a lion in the middle of a pit on a snowy day.

21 He [1]killed an Egyptian, [2]an impressive man. Now the Egyptian *had* a spear in his hand, but he went down to him with a club and snatched the spear from the Egyptian's hand and killed him with his own spear.

22 These *things* [a]Benaiah the son of Jehoiada did, and had a name as well as the three mighty men.

23 He was honored among the thirty, but he did not attain to the three. And David appointed him over his guard.

24 [a]Asahel the brother of Joab was among the thirty; Elhanan the son of Dodo of Bethlehem,

25 [a]Shammah the [b]Harodite, Elika the Harodite,

26 Helez the Paltite, Ira the son of Ikkesh the [a]Tekoite,

27 Abiezer the [a]Anathothite, Mebunnai the Hushathite,

28 Zalmon the Ahohite, Maharai the [a]Netophathite,

23:6 *worthless ... thrust away.* Godless people who have no interest in the righteous king will be destroyed (see Ps 2:9; 110:5–6).

23:8–39 See note on 21:1–24:25. This list of 37 (see v. 39) of David's most valiant warriors and the description of some of their exploits are paralleled in 1 Chr 11:11–41. There the list is expanded by 16 names (1 Chr 11:41–47).

23:8 *Tahchemonite.* 1 Chr 11:11 reads "Hachmonite," derived from an unknown place-name. *captains.* Two groups of three warriors (vv. 8–12 and 13–23) and one group of 30 warriors (vv. 23–39) are mentioned (see note on v. 39 for the total number of warriors).

23:9 *Ahohite.* A descendant of Ahoah from the tribe of Benjamin (1Ch 8:4).

23:13 *three.* Not the same as the three mighty men of v. 9. *thirty chief men.* See vv. 23–24,39. *harvest time.* See 11:1 and note. The circumstances of this event suggest that it happened shortly after David had fled from Saul, when men first began to gather to his cause (see 1 Sam 22:1–4), or shortly after his conquest of Jerusalem (see 2 Sam 5:17–18). *cave of Adullam.* See 1 Sam 22:1. *Rephaim.* See 5:18.

23:14 *stronghold.* See note on 1 Sam 22:4.

23:15–16 See note on 1 Chr 11:15–19.

23:18 *Abishai.* See 10:10,14; 18:2; see also note on 1 Sam 26:6. *three.* Presumably those referred to in vv. 13–17.

23:20 *Benaiah the son of Jehoiada.* Commander of the Cherethites and Pelethites (8:18; 20:23; see v. 23 below) and of the division of troops for the third month of the year (1 Chr 27:5). He supported Solomon's succession to the throne (1 Kin 1–2) and eventually replaced Joab as commander of the army (1 Kin 2:35).

23:24 *Asahel.* See 2:18–23. *thirty.* Twenty-nine names are listed in vv. 24–39. Since the three of vv. 13–17 are also included in the thirty (see v. 13), the total number of warriors mentioned is 32. 1 Chr 11:26–47 lists 16 additional names for this group, so it appears that the list includes the names of replacements for vacancies when a warrior either dropped out or died.

29 [a]Heleb the son of Baanah the Netophathite, Ittai the son of Ribai of [b]Gibeah of the sons of Benjamin,

30 Benaiah a [a]Pirathonite, Hiddai of the brooks of [b]Gaash,

31 Abi-albon the Arbathite, Azmaveth the [a]Barhumite,

32 Eliahba the [a]Shaalbonite, the sons of Jashen, Jonathan,

33 [a]Shammah the Hararite, Ahiam the son of Sharar the Ararite,

34 Eliphelet the son of Ahasbai, the son of [a]the Maacathite, [b]Eliam the son of [c]Ahithophel the Gilonite,

35 [a]Hezro the [b]Carmelite, Paarai the Arbite,

36 Igal the son of Nathan of [a]Zobah, Bani the Gadite,

37 Zelek the Ammonite, Naharai the [a]Beerothite, armor bearers of Joab the son of Zeruiah,

38 Ira the [a]Ithrite, Gareb the Ithrite,

39 [a]Uriah the Hittite; thirty-seven in all.

The Census Taken

24 [a]Now [b]again the anger of the LORD burned against Israel, and it incited David against them to say, "[c]Go, number Israel and Judah."

2 The king said to Joab the commander of the army who was with him, "Go about now through all the tribes of Israel, [a]from Dan to Beersheba, and [1]register the people, that I may know the number of the people."

3 But Joab said to the king, "[a]Now may the LORD your God add to the people a hundred times as many as they are, while the eyes of my lord the king *still* see; but why does my lord the king delight in this thing?"

4 Nevertheless, the king's word prevailed against Joab and against the commanders of the army. So Joab and the commanders of the army went out from the presence of the king to [1]register the people of Israel.

5 They crossed the Jordan and camped in [a]Aroer, on the right side of the city that is in the middle of the valley of Gad and toward [b]Jazer.

6 Then they came to Gilead and to [1]the land of Tahtim-hodshi, and they came to Dan-jaan and around to [a]Sidon,

7 and came to the [a]fortress of Tyre and to all the cities of the [b]Hivites and of the Canaanites, and they went out to the south of Judah, *to* [c]Beersheba.

8 So when they had gone about through the whole land, they came to Jerusalem at the end of nine months and twenty days.

9 And Joab gave [a]the number of the [1]registration of the people to the king; and there were in Israel [b]eight hundred thousand valiant men who drew the sword, and the men of Judah were five hundred thousand men.

10 Now [a]David's heart [1]troubled him after he had numbered the people. So David said to the LORD, "[b]I have sinned greatly in what I have done. But now, O LORD, please [2]take away the iniquity of Your servant, for [c]I have acted very foolishly."

11 When David arose in the morning, the word of the LORD came to [a]the prophet Gad, David's [b]seer, saying,

12 "Go and speak to David, 'Thus the LORD says, "I am offering you three things; choose for yourself one of them, which I will do to you." ' "

13 So Gad came to David and told him,

29 [a]1 Chr 11:30 [b]Josh 18:28 **30** [a]Judg 12:13, 15 [b]Josh 24:30 **31** [a]2 Sam 3:16 **32** [a]Josh 19:42 **33** [a]2 Sam 23:11 **34** [a]2 Sam 10:6, 8; 20:14 [b]2 Sam 11:3 [c]2 Sam 15:12 **35** [a]1 Chr 11:37 [b]Josh 15:55 **36** [a]2 Sam 8:3 **37** [a]2 Sam 4:2 **38** [a]1 Chr 2:53 **39** [a]2 Sam 11:3, 6
24:1 [a]1 Chr 21:1 [b]2 Sam 21:1, 2 [c]1 Chr 27:23, 24 **2** [1]Lit *muster* [a]Judg 20:1; 2 Sam 3:10 **3** [a]Deut 1:11
4 [1]Lit *muster* **5** [a]Deut 2:36; Josh 13:9, 16 [b]Num 21:32; 32:35 **6** [1]Or *Kadesh in the land of the Hittite* [a]Josh 19:28; Judg 1:31 **7** [a]Josh 19:29 [b]Josh 11:3; Judg 3:3 [c]Gen 21:22-33 **9** [1]Lit *muster* [a]Num 1:44-46 [b]1 Chr 21:5 **10** [1]Lit *smote* [2]Lit *cause to pass away* [a]1 Sam 24:5 [b]2 Sam 12:13 [c]1 Sam 13:13; 2 Chr 16:9 **11** [a]1 Sam 22:5; 1 Chr 29:29 [b]1 Sam 9:9

23:34 *Eliam.* Father of Bathsheba (see 11:3) and son of David's counselor Ahithophel, who joined in Absalom's conspiracy (see 15:12,31,34; 16:20–23; 17:1–23).
23:39 *Uriah.* Husband of Bathsheba (see 11:3–27). *thirty-seven.* The total number of warriors referred to in vv. 8–39, including the three of vv. 8–12, the three of vv. 13–17, Abishai (vv. 18–19), Benaiah (vv. 20–23) and the 29 whose names are recorded in vv. 24–39 (see note on v. 24).
24:1 *again.* The previous occasion may have been the famine of 21:1. *the anger of the LORD burned against Israel.* The specific reason for the Lord's displeasure is not stated. Because the anger is said to be directed against Israel rather than David, some have concluded that it was occasioned by the widespread support among the people for the rebellions of Absalom and Sheba against David (see 15:12; 17:11,24–26; 18:7; 20:1–2), the divinely chosen and anointed theocratic king. This would mean that the events of this chapter are to be placed chronologically shortly after those of chs. 15–20 and so after 980 B.C. (see note on 15:7). *the LORD . . . incited David against them.* 1 Chr 21:1 says that Satan inspired David to take the census. Although Scripture is clear that God does not cause anyone to sin (James 1:13–15), it is also clear that man's—and Satan's—evil acts are under God's sovereign control (see Ex 4:21; 7:3; 9:12; 10:1,20,27; 11:10; 14:4; Josh 11:20; 1 Kin 22:22–23; Job 1:12; 2:10; Ezek 3:20; 14:9; Acts 4:28). *number Israel and Judah.* David's military census (see vv. 2–3) does not appear to have been prompted by any immediate external threat. Since he wanted to "know the number of the people" (v. 2), it is evident that his action was motivated either by pride in the size of the empire he had acquired or by reliance for his security on the size of the reserve of manpower he could muster in an emergency or, more likely, both. The mere taking of a census was hardly sinful (see Num 1:2–3; 26:2–4), but in this instance it represented an unwarranted glorying in and dependence on human power rather than the Lord (not much different from Israel's initial desire to have a king for their security; see 1 Sam 8–12). The act was uncharacteristic of David (see 1 Sam 17:26,37,45–47; 2 Sam 22:2–4,47–51).
24:2 *Dan to Beersheba.* See note on 1 Sam 3:20.
24:3 *but why . . . ?* David's directive does not go unchallenged. The fact that he does not answer suggests that he knew his reasons were highly questionable. In any event, Joab's challenge renders David the more guilty.
24:5–8 The military census was begun in southern Transjordan and moved northward, then back across the Jordan, moving from north to south.
24:9 *eight hundred thousand . . . five hundred thousand.* These figures differ from those of 1 Chr 21:5 (see notes on 1 Chr 21:5–6).
24:10 *I have sinned greatly.* See note on v. 1.
24:11 *the prophet Gad, David's seer.* See notes on 1 Sam 9:9; 22:5.
24:12 *Go and speak to David.* See 12:1 and note. *three things.*

and said to him, “Shall [a]seven years of
famine come to you in your land? Or will you
flee three months before your foes while they
pursue you? Or shall there be three days’
pestilence in your land? Now consider and
see what answer I shall return to Him who
sent me.”
14 Then David said to Gad, “I am in great
distress. Let us now fall into the hand of the
LORD [a]for His mercies are great, but do not
let me fall into the hand of man.”

Pestilence Sent

15 So [a]the LORD [1]sent a pestilence upon
Israel from the morning until the appointed
time, and seventy thousand men of the people [b]from Dan to Beersheba died.
16 [a]When the angel stretched out his
hand toward Jerusalem to destroy it, [b]the
LORD relented from the calamity and said to
the angel who destroyed the people, “It is
enough! Now relax your hand!” And the
angel of the LORD was by the threshing floor
of Araunah the Jebusite.
17 Then David spoke to the LORD when he
saw the angel who was striking down the
people, and said, “Behold, [a]it is I who have
sinned, and it is I who have done wrong; but
[b]these sheep, what have they done? Please
let Your hand be against me and against my
father’s house.”

David Builds an Altar

18 So Gad came to David that day and
said to him, “[a]Go up, erect an altar to the
LORD on the threshing floor of [1]Araunah the
Jebusite.”
19 David went up according to the word of
Gad, just as the LORD had commanded.
20 Araunah looked down and saw the
king and his servants crossing over toward
him; and Araunah went out and bowed his
face to the ground before the king.
21 Then Araunah said, “Why has my lord
the king come to his servant?” And David
said, “To buy the threshing floor from you,
in order to build an altar to the LORD, [a]that
the plague may be held back from the people.”
22 Araunah said to David, “Let my lord
the king take and offer up what is good in his
sight. Look, [a]the oxen for the burnt offering,
the threshing sledges and the yokes of the
oxen for the wood.
23 “Everything, O king, Araunah gives to
the king.” And Araunah said to the king,
“May the LORD your God [a]accept you.”
24 However, the king said to Araunah,
“No, but I will surely buy *it* from you for a
price, for [a]I will not offer burnt offerings to
the LORD my God [1]which cost me nothing.”
So [b]David bought the threshing floor and the
oxen for fifty shekels of silver.
25 David built there an altar to the LORD
and offered burnt offerings and peace offerings. [a]Thus the LORD was moved by prayer
for the land, and the plague was held back
from Israel.

13 [a]1 Chr 21:12; Ezek 14:21
14 [a]Ps 51:1; 130:4, 7
15 [1]Lit *gave* [a]1 Chr 21:14; 27:24 [b]2 Sam 24:2
16 [a]Ex 12:23; 2 Kin 19:35; Acts 12:23 [b]Ex 32:14; 1 Sam 15:11
17 [a]2 Sam 24:10 [b]2 Sam 7:8; Ps 74:1
18 [1]In 2 Chr 3:1, *Ornan* [a]1 Chr 21:18
21 [a]Num 16:44-50
22 [a]1 Sam 6:14; 1 Kin 19:21
23 [a]Ezek 20:40, 41
24 [1]Lit *gratuitously* [a]Mal 1:13, 14 [b]1 Chr 21:24, 25
25 [a]2 Sam 21:14

The three alternative judgments were all included in the curses that Moses said would come on God’s people when they failed to adhere to their covenant obligations (see Deut 28:15–25).

24:14 *not . . . into the hand of man.* David, who knew both God and war, knew that even in His anger God is more merciful than man let loose in the rampages of war (see Ps 30:5).

24:15 *Dan to Beersheba.* See note on 1 Sam 3:20.

24:16 *angel.* Angels appear elsewhere in Scripture as instruments of God’s judgment (see Ex 33:2; 2 Kin 19:35; Ps 35:5–6; 78:49; Matt 13:41; Acts 12:23). *the LORD relented.* See note on 1 Sam 15:29. *threshing floor of Araunah.* Located on Mount Moriah, immediately north of David’s city and overlooking it. Later it would become the site of the temple (see 1 Chr 22:1; 2 Chr 3:1). *Jebusite.* See note on 5:6.

24:17 *let Your hand be against me and against my father’s house.* Although the people of Israel were not without guilt (see v. 1), David assumes full blame for his own act and acknowledges his responsibility as king for the well-being of the Lord’s people (see 5:2; 7:7–8).

24:19 *as the LORD had commanded.* The Lord Himself appointed the atoning sacrifice in answer to David’s prayer.

24:21 *To buy the threshing floor from you.* David does not simply expropriate the property for his royal purposes (see 1 Sam 8:14).

24:24 *burnt offerings.* See Lev 1:1–17. *David bought the threshing floor.* Thus the later site of the temple (see note on v. 16) became the royal property of the house of David. *and the oxen.* David’s haste could not wait for oxen to be brought some distance from his own herds. *fifty shekels.* See note on 1 Chr 21:25.

24:25 *peace offerings.* See note on 1 Sam 11:15. Reconciliation and restoration of covenant fellowship were obtained by the king’s repentance, intercessory prayer and the offering of sacrifices.

1 Kings

INTRODUCTION

Title

1 and 2 Kings (like 1 and 2 Samuel and 1 and 2 Chronicles) are actually one literary work, called in Hebrew tradition simply "Kings." The division of this work into two books was introduced by the translators of the Septuagint (the Greek translation of the OT) and subsequently followed in the Latin Vulgate and most modern versions. In 1448 the division into two sections also appeared in a Hebrew manuscript and was perpetuated in later printed editions of the Hebrew text. Both the Septuagint and the Latin Vulgate further designated Samuel and Kings in a way that emphasized the relationship of these two works (Septuagint: First, Second, Third and Fourth Book of Kingdoms; Latin Vulgate: First, Second, Third and Fourth Kings). Together Samuel and Kings relate the whole history of the monarchy, from its rise under the ministry of Samuel to its fall at the hands of the Babylonians.

The division between 1 and 2 Kings has been made at an appropriate but somewhat arbitrary place, shortly after the deaths of Ahab of the northern kingdom (22:37) and Jehoshaphat of the southern kingdom (22:50). Placing the division at this point causes the account of the reign of Ahaziah of Israel to overlap the end of 1 Kings (22:51 – 53) and the beginning of 2 Kings (ch. 1). The same is true of the narration of the ministry of Elijah, which for the most part appears in 1 Kings (chs. 17 — 19). However, his final act of judgment and the passing of his cloak to Elisha at the moment of his ascension to heaven in a whirlwind are contained in 2 Kings (1:1 — 2:17).

Author, Sources and Date

There is little conclusive evidence as to the identity of the author of 1,2 Kings. Although Jewish tradition credits Jeremiah, few today accept this as likely. Whoever the author was, it is clear that he was familiar with the book of Deuteronomy — as were many of Israel's prophets. It is also clear that he used a variety of sources in compiling his history of the monarchy. Three such sources are named: "the book of the acts of Solomon" (11:41), "the Book of the Chronicles of the Kings of Israel" (14:19), "the Book of the Chronicles of the Kings of Judah" (14:29). It is likely that other written sources were also employed (such as those mentioned in Chronicles; see below).

Although some scholars have concluded that the three sources specifically cited in 1,2 Kings are to be viewed as official court annals from the royal archives in Jerusalem and Samaria, this is by no means certain. It seems at least questionable whether official court annals would have included details of conspiracies such as those referred to in 16:20; 2 Kin 15:15. It is also questionable whether official court annals would have been readily accessible for public scrutiny, as the author clearly implies in his references to them. Such considerations have led some scholars to conclude that these sources were probably records of the reigns of the kings of Israel and Judah compiled by the succession of Israel's prophets spanning the kingdom period. 1,2 Chronicles makes reference to a number of such writings: "in the chronicles of Samuel the seer, in the chronicles of Nathan the prophet and in the chronicles of Gad the seer" (1 Chr 29:29), "the prophecy of Ahijah the Shilonite" and "the visions of Iddo the seer" (2 Chr 9:29), "the records of Shemaiah the prophet" (2 Chr 12:15), "the annals of Jehu son of Hanani" (2 Chr 20:34), "the treatise of the Book of the Kings" (2 Chr 24:27), the "acts of Uzziah . . . the prophet Isaiah, the son of Amoz has written" (2 Chr 26:22; see also 2 Chr 32:32) — and there may have been others. It is most likely, for example, that for the ministries of Elijah and Elisha the author depended on a prophetic source (perhaps from the eighth century) that had drawn up an account of those two prophets in which they were already compared with Moses and Joshua.

Some scholars place the date of composition of 1,2 Kings in the time subsequent to Jehoiachin's release from prison (562 B.C.; 2 Kin 25:27 – 30) and prior to the end of the Babylonian exile in 538. This position is

challenged by others on the basis of statements in 1,2 Kings that speak of certain things in the preexilic period that are said to have continued in existence "to this day" (see, e.g., 8:8, the poles used to carry the ark; 9:20–21, conscripted labor; 12:19, Israel in rebellion against the house of David; 2 Kin 8:22, Edom in rebellion against the kingdom of Judah). From such statements it is argued that the writer must have been a person living in Judah in the preexilic period rather than in Babylon in postexilic times. If this argument is accepted, one must conclude that the original book was composed about the time of the death of Josiah and that the material pertaining to the time subsequent to his reign was added during the exile c. 550. While this "two-edition" viewpoint is possible, it rests largely on the "to this day" statements.

An alternative is to understand these statements as those of the original source used by the author rather than statements of the author himself. A comparison of 2 Chr 5:9 with 1 Kin 8:8 suggests that this is a legitimate conclusion. Chronicles is clearly a postexilic writing, yet the wording of the statement concerning the poles used to carry the ark ("they are there to this day") is the same in Chronicles as it is in Kings. Probably the Chronicler was simply quoting his source, namely, 1 Kin 8:8. There is no reason that the author of 1,2 Kings could not have done the same thing in quoting from his earlier sources. This explanation allows for positing a single author living in exile and using the source materials at his disposal.

Theme: Kingship and Covenant

1,2 Kings contains no explicit statement of purpose or theme. Reflection on its content, however, reveals that the author has selected and arranged his material in a manner that provides a sequel to the history found in 1,2 Samuel — a history of kingship regulated by covenant. In general, 1,2 Kings describes the history of the kings of Israel and Judah in the light of God's covenants. The guiding thesis of the book is that the welfare of Israel and her kings depended on their obedience to their obligations as defined in the Mosaic covenant.

It is clearly not the author's intention to present a socio-politico-economic history of Israel's monarchy in accordance with the principles of modern historiography. The author repeatedly refers the reader to other sources for more detailed information about the reigns of the various kings (see, e.g., 11:41; 14:19,29; 15:7,31; 16:5,14,20,27), and he gives a covenantal rather than a social or political or economic assessment of their reigns. From the standpoint of a political historian, Omri would be considered one of the more important rulers in the northern kingdom. He established a powerful dynasty and made Samaria the capital city. According to the Moabite Stone (see chart, p. xix), Omri was the ruler who subjugated the Moabites to the northern kingdom. Long after Omri's death, Assyrian rulers referred to Jehu as the "son of Omri" (either mistakenly or merely in accordance with their literary conventions when speaking of a later king of a realm). Yet in spite of Omri's political importance, his reign is dismissed in six verses (16:23–28) with the statement that he "did evil in the sight of the LORD, and acted more wickedly than all who were before him" (16:25). Similarly, the reign of Jeroboam II, who presided over the northern kingdom during the time of its greatest political and economic power, is treated only briefly (2 Kin 14:23–29).

Another example of the writer's covenantal rather than merely political or economic interest can be seen in the description of the reign of Josiah of Judah. Nothing is said about the early years of his reign, but a detailed description is given of the reformation and renewal of the covenant that he promoted in his 18th year as king (2 Kin 22:3 — 23:28). Nor is anything said of the motives leading Josiah to oppose Pharaoh Neco of Egypt at Megiddo, or of the major shift in geopolitical power from Assyria to Babylon that was connected with this incident (see notes on 2 Kin 23:29–30).

It becomes apparent, then, that the kings who receive the most attention in 1,2 Kings are those during whose reigns there was either notable deviation from or affirmation of the covenant (or significant interaction between a king and God's prophet; see below). Ahab son of Omri is an example of the former (17:1 — 22:39). His reign is given extensive treatment, not so much because of its extraordinary political importance, but because of the serious threat to covenant fidelity and continuity that arose in the northern kingdom during his reign. Ultimately the pagan influence of Ahab's wife Jezebel through Ahab's daughter Athaliah (whether she was Jezebel's daughter is unknown) nearly led to the extermination of the house of David in Judah (see 2 Kin 11:1–3).

Manasseh (2 Kin 21:1–18) is an example of a similar sort. Here again it is deviation from the covenant that is emphasized in the account of his reign rather than political features, such as involvement in the Assyrian-Egyptian conflict (mentioned in Assyrian records but not in 2 Kings). The extreme apostasy characterizing Manasseh's reign made exile for Judah inevitable (2 Kin 21:10–15; 23:26–27).

On the positive side, Hezekiah (2 Kin 18:1—20:21) and Josiah (2 Kin 22:1—23:29) are given extensive treatment because of their involvement in covenant renewal. These are the only two kings given unqualified approval by the writer for their loyalty to the Lord (2 Kin 18:3; 22:2). It is noteworthy that all the kings of the northern kingdom are said to have done evil in the eyes of the Lord and walked in the ways of Jeroboam, who caused Israel to sin (see, e.g., 16:26,31; 22:52; 2 Kin 3:3; 10:29). It was Jeroboam who established the golden calf worship at Bethel and Dan shortly after the division of the kingdom (see 12:26–33; 13:1–6).

While the writer depicts Israel's obedience or disobedience to the Sinai covenant as decisive for her historical destiny, he also recognizes the far-reaching historical significance of the Davidic covenant, which promised that David's dynasty would endure forever. This is particularly noticeable in references to the "lamp" that the Lord had promised David (see 11:36; 15:4; 2 Kin 8:19; see also note on 2 Sam 21:17). It also appears in more general references to the promise to David (8:20,25) and its consequences for specific historical developments in Judah's later history (11:12–13,32; 2 Kin 19:34; 20:6). In addition, the writer uses the life and reign of David as a standard by which the lives of later kings are measured (see, e.g., 9:4; 11:4,6,33,38; 14:8; 15:3,5,11; 2 Kin 16:2; 18:3; 22:2).

Another prominent feature of the narratives of 1,2 Kings is the emphasis on the relationship between prophecy and fulfillment in the historical developments of the monarchy. On at least 11 occasions a prophecy is recorded that is later said to have been fulfilled (see, e.g., 2 Sam 7:13 and 1 Kin 8:20; 1 Kin 11:29–39 and 1 Kin 12:15; 1 Kin 13 and 2 Kin 23:16–18). The result of this emphasis is that the history of the kingdom is not presented as a chain of chance occurrences or the mere interplay of human actions but as the unfolding of Israel's historical destiny under the guidance of an omniscient and omnipotent God—Israel's covenant Lord, who rules all history in accordance with His sovereign purposes (see 8:56; 2 Kin 10:10).

The author also stresses the importance of the prophets themselves in their role as official emissaries from the court of Israel's covenant Lord, the Great King to whom Israel and her king were bound in service through the covenant. The Lord sent a long succession of such prophets to call king and people back to covenant loyalty (2 Kin 17:13). For the most part their warnings and exhortations fell on deaf ears. Many of these prophets and prophetesses are mentioned in the narratives of 1,2 Kings (see, e.g., Ahijah, 11:29–40; 14:5–18; Shemaiah, 12:22–24; Micaiah, 22:8–28; Jonah, 2 Kin 14:25; Isaiah, 2 Kin 19:1–7,20–34; Huldah, 2 Kin 22:14–20), but particular attention is given to the ministries of Elijah and Elisha (1 Kin 17—19; 2 Kin 1—13).

Reflection on these features of 1,2 Kings suggests that it was written to explain to a people in exile that the reason for their condition of humiliation was their stubborn persistence in breaking the covenant. In bringing the exile upon His people, God, after much patience, imposed the curses of the covenant, which had stood as a warning to them from the beginning (see Lev 26:27–45; Deut 28:64–68). This is made explicit with respect to the captivity of the northern kingdom in 2 Kin 17:7–23; 18:10–12, and with respect to the southern kingdom in 2 Kin 21. The reformation under Josiah in the southern kingdom is viewed as too little, too late (see 2 Kin 23:26–27; 24:3).

The book, then, provides a retrospective analysis of Israel's history. It explains the reasons both for the destruction of Samaria and Jerusalem and their respective kingdoms and for the bitter experience of being forced into exile. This does not mean, however, that there is no hope for the future. The writer consistently keeps the promise to David in view as a basis on which Israel in exile may look to the future with hope rather than with despair. In this connection the final four verses of the book, reporting Jehoiachin's release from prison in Babylon and his elevation to a place of honor in the court there (2 Kin 25:27–30), take on added significance. The future remains open for a new work of the Lord in faithfulness to His promise to the house of David.

It is important to note that, although the author was undoubtedly a Judahite exile, and although the northern kingdom had been dispersed for well over a century and a half at the time of his writing, the scope of his concern was all Israel—the whole covenant people. Neither he nor the prophets viewed the division

of the kingdom as an excommunication of the ten tribes, nor did they see the earlier exile of the northern kingdom as a final exclusion of the northern tribes from Israel's future.

Chronology

1,2 Kings presents the reader with abundant chronological data. Not only is the length of the reign of each king given, but during the period of the divided kingdom the beginning of the reign of each king is synchronized with the regnal year of the ruling king in the opposite kingdom. Often additional data, such as the age of the ruler at the time of his accession, are also provided.

By integrating Biblical data with those derived from Assyrian chronological records, the year 853 B.C. can be fixed as the year of Ahab's death, and the year 841 as the year Jehu began to reign. The years in which Ahab and Jehu had contacts with Shalmaneser III of Assyria can also be given definite dates (by means of astronomical calculations based on an Assyrian reference to a solar eclipse). With these fixed points, it is then possible to work both forward and backward in the lines of the kings of Israel and Judah to give dates for each king. By the same means it can be determined that the division of the kingdom occurred in 930, that Samaria fell to the Assyrians in 722–721 and that Jerusalem fell to the Babylonians in 586.

The synchronistic data correlating the reigns of the kings of Israel and Judah present some knotty problems, which have long been considered nearly insoluble. In more recent times, most of these problems have been resolved in a satisfactory way through recognizing such possibilities as overlapping reigns, co-regencies of sons with their fathers, differences in the time of the year in which the reign of a king officially began, and differences in the way a king's first year was reckoned (e.g., see notes on 15:33; 2 Kin 8:25; see also chart, pp. 478–479).

Content

1,2 Kings describes the history of Israel's monarchy from the closing days of the rule of David until the time of the Babylonian exile. After an extensive account of Solomon's reign, the narrative records the division of the kingdom and then, by means of its synchronistic accounts, presents an interrelated picture of developments within the two kingdoms.

Kingship in the northern kingdom was plagued with instability and violence. Twenty rulers represented nine different dynasties during the approximately 210 years from the division of the kingdom in 930 B.C. until the fall of Samaria in 722–721. In the southern kingdom there were also 20 rulers, but these were all descendants of David (except Athaliah, whose usurping of the throne interrupted the sequence for a few years) and spanned a period of about 345 years from the division of the kingdom until the fall of Jerusalem in 586.

Outline

1,2 Kings can be broadly outlined by relating its contents to the major historical periods it describes and to the ministries of Elijah and Elisha.

- I. The Solomonic Era (1:1—12:24)
  - A. Solomon's Succession to the Throne (1:1—2:12)
  - B. Solomon's Throne Consolidated (2:13–46)
  - C. Solomon's Wisdom (ch. 3)
  - D. Solomon's Reign Characterized (ch. 4)
  - E. Solomon's Building Projects (5:1—9:9)
    - 1. Preparation for building the temple (ch. 5)
    - 2. Building the temple (ch. 6)
    - 3. Building the palace (7:1–12)
    - 4. The temple furnishings (7:13–51)
    - 5. Dedication of the temple (ch. 8)
    - 6. The Lord's response and warning (9:1–9)
  - F. Solomon's Reign Characterized (9:10—10:29)
  - G. Solomon's Folly (11:1–13)
  - H. Solomon's Throne Threatened (11:14–43)

- I. Rehoboam's Succession to the Throne (12:1–24)

II. Israel and Judah from Jeroboam I/Rehoboam to Ahab/Asa (12:25—16:34)
- A. Jeroboam I of Israel (12:25—14:20)
- B. Rehoboam of Judah (14:21–31)
- C. Abijam of Judah (15:1–8)
- D. Asa of Judah (15:9–24)
- E. Nadab of Israel (15:25–32)
- F. Baasha of Israel (15:33—16:7)
- G. Elah of Israel (16:8–14)
- H. Zimri of Israel (16:15–20)
- I. Omri of Israel (16:21–28)
- J. Ahab of Israel (16:29–34)

III. The Ministries of Elijah and Elisha and Other Prophets from Ahab/Asa to Joram/Jehoshaphat (17:1—2 Kin 8:15)
- A. Elijah (and Other Prophets) in the Reign of Ahab (17:1—22:40)
  1. Elijah and the drought (ch. 17)
  2. Elijah on Mount Carmel (ch. 18)
  3. Elijah's flight to Horeb (ch. 19)
  4. A prophet condemns Ahab for sparing Ben-hadad (ch. 20)
  5. Elijah condemns Ahab for seizing Naboth's vineyard (ch. 21)
  6. Micaiah prophesies Ahab's death; its fulfillment (22:1–40)
- B. Jehoshaphat of Judah (22:41–50)
- C. Ahaziah of Israel; Elijah's Last Prophecy (22:51—2 Kin 1:18)
- D. Elijah's Translation; Elisha's Inauguration (2 Kin 2:1–18)
- E. Elisha in the Reign of Jehoram (2:19—8:15)
  1. Elisha's initial miraculous signs (2:19–25)
  2. Elisha during the campaign against Moab (ch. 3)
  3. Elisha's ministry to needy ones in Israel (ch. 4)
  4. Elisha heals Naaman (ch. 5)
  5. Elisha's deliverance of one of the prophets (6:1–7)
  6. Elisha's deliverance of Joram from Aramean raiders (6:8–23)
  7. Aramean siege of Samaria lifted, as Elisha prophesied (6:24—7:20)
  8. The Shunammite's land restored (8:1–6)
  9. Elisha prophesies Hazael's oppression of Israel (8:7–15)

IV. Israel and Judah from Joram/Jehoram to the Exile of Israel (2 Kin 8:16—17:41)
- A. Jehoram of Judah (8:16–24)
- B. Ahaziah of Judah (8:25–29)
- C. Jehu's Revolt and Reign (chs. 9—10)
  1. Elisha orders Jehu's anointing (9:1–13)
  2. Jehu's assassination of Joram and Ahaziah (9:14–29)
  3. Jehu's execution of Jezebel (9:30–37)
  4. Jehu's slaughter of Ahab's family (10:1–17)
  5. Jehu's eradication of Baal worship (10:18–36)
- D. Athaliah and Joash of Judah; Repair of the Temple (chs. 11—12)
- E. Jehoahaz of Israel (13:1–9)
- F. Jehoash of Israel; Elisha's Last Prophecy (13:10–25)
- G. Amaziah of Judah (14:1–22)
- H. Jeroboam II of Israel (14:23–29)
- I. Azariah of Judah (15:1–7)
- J. Zechariah of Israel (15:8–12)
- K. Shallum of Israel (15:13–16)

- L. Menahem of Israel (15:17–22)
- M. Pekahiah of Israel (15:23–26)
- N. Pekah of Israel (15:27–31)
- O. Jotham of Judah (15:32–38)
- P. Ahaz of Judah (ch. 16)
- Q. Hoshea of Israel (17:1–6)
- R. Exile of Israel; Resettlement of the Land (17:7–41)

V. Judah from Hezekiah to the Babylonian Exile (2 Kin 18—25)
- A. Hezekiah (chs. 18—20)
  1. Hezekiah's good reign (18:1–8)
  2. The Assyrian threat and deliverance (18:9—19:37)
  3. Hezekiah's illness and alliance with Babylon (ch. 20)
- B. Manasseh (21:1–18)
- C. Amon (21:19–26)
- D. Josiah (22:1—23:30)
  1. Repair of the temple; discovery of the book of the law (ch. 22)
  2. Renewal of the covenant; end of Josiah's reign (23:1–30)
- E. Jehoahaz Exiled to Egypt (23:31–35)
- F. Jehoiakim: First Babylonian Invasion (23:36—24:7)
- G. Jehoiachin: Second Babylonian Invasion (24:8–17)
- H. Zedekiah (24:18–20)
- I. Babylonian Exile of Judah (25:1–21)
- J. Removal of the Remnant to Egypt (25:22–26)
- K. Elevation of Jehoiachin in Babylon (25:27–30)

David in Old Age

1 Now King David was old, advanced in age; and they covered him with clothes, but he could not keep warm.

2 So his servants said to him, "Let them seek a young virgin for my lord the king, and let her [1]attend the king and become his nurse; and let her lie in your bosom, that my lord the king may keep warm."

3 So they searched for a beautiful girl throughout all the territory of Israel, and found Abishag the [a]Shunammite, and brought her to the king.

4 The girl was very beautiful; and she became the king's nurse and served him, but the king did not [1]cohabit with her.

5 Now [a]Adonijah the son of Haggith exalted himself, saying, "I will be king." So [b]he prepared for himself chariots and horsemen with fifty men to run before him.

6 His father had never [1]crossed him at any time by asking, "Why have you done so?" And he was also a very handsome man, and [2a]he was born after Absalom.

7 [1]He had conferred with [a]Joab the son of Zeruiah and with [b]Abiathar the priest; and following [c]Adonijah they helped him.

8 But [a]Zadok the priest, [b]Benaiah the son of Jehoiada, [c]Nathan the prophet, [d]Shimei, Rei, and [e]the mighty men who belonged to David, were not with Adonijah.

9 Adonijah sacrificed sheep and oxen and fatlings by the [1]stone of Zoheleth, which is beside [a]En-rogel; and he invited all his brothers, the king's sons, and all the men of Judah, the king's servants.

10 But he did not invite Nathan the prophet, Benaiah, the mighty men, and [a]Solomon his brother.

Nathan and Bathsheba

11 Then Nathan spoke to [a]Bathsheba the mother of Solomon, saying, "Have you not heard that Adonijah the son of Haggith has become king, and David our lord does not know *it?*

12 "So now come, please let me [a]give you counsel and save your life and the life of your son Solomon.

13 "Go [1]at once to King David and say to him, 'Have you not, my lord, O king, sworn to your maidservant, saying, "[a]Surely Solomon your son shall be king after me, and he shall sit on my throne"? Why then has Adonijah become king?'

14 "Behold, while you are still there speaking with the king, I will come in after you and confirm your words."

15 So Bathsheba went in to the king in the bedroom. Now [a]the king was very old, and Abishag the Shunammite was ministering to the king.

16 Then Bathsheba bowed and prostrated herself [1]before the king. And the king said, "What [2]do you wish?"

1:2 [1]Lit *stand before*
3 [a]Josh 19:18; 1 Sam 28:4
4 [1]Lit *know her*
5 [a]2 Sam 3:4 [b]2 Sam 15:1
6 [1]Lit *pained him* [2]Lit *she gave him birth* [a]2 Sam 3:3, 4
7 [1]Lit *his words were* [a]1 Chr 11:6 [b]1 Sam 22:20, 23; 2 Sam 20:25 [c]1 Kin 2:22
8 [a]2 Sam 20:25; 1 Chr 16:39 [b]2 Sam 8:18 [c]2 Sam 12:1 [d]1 Kin 4:18 [e]2 Sam 23:8-39
9 [1]Or *Gliding* or *Serpent Stone* [a]Josh 15:7; 18:16; 2 Sam 17:17
10 [a]2 Sam 12:24
11 [a]2 Sam 12:24
12 [a]Prov 15:22
13 [1]Lit *and enter* [a]1 Kin 1:30; 1 Chr 22:9-13
15 [a]1 Kin 1:1
16 [1]Lit *to* [2]Lit *to you*

1:1–12:24 The narrative of the Solomonic era is an exquisite example of literary inversion, in this case consisting of nine sections. The first and last are parallel, as well as the second and eighth, etc.—and the fifth section, which occupies the central position in the structure, is the longest of the nine and describes Solomon's building projects (see Introduction: Outline).

1:1 *advanced in age.* 2 Sam 5:4 indicates that David died at about 70 years of age (cf. 1 Kin 2:11).

1:3 *Shunammite.* Abishag came from Shunem (2 Kin 4:8; Josh 19:18; 1 Sam 28:4), located near the plain of Jezreel in the tribal territory of Issachar.

1:4 *did not cohabit with her.* Significant in connection with Adonijah's request to be given Abishag as his wife after the death of David (see notes on 2:17,22).

1:5 *Adonijah.* The fourth son of David (see 2 Sam 3:4), who was at this time approximately 35 years of age. It is likely that he was the oldest surviving son of David (see note on 2 Sam 13:28; see also 2 Sam 18:14). *exalted himself.* A unilateral attempt to usurp the throne, bypassing King David's right to designate his own successor (Adonijah must at least have known that his father favored Solomon; see v. 10). If successful, it would have thwarted God's and David's choice of Solomon (see vv. 13,17,30; 1 Chr 22:9–10; see also note on 2 Sam 12:25). *fifty men to run before him.* Adonijah here follows the example of Absalom before him (see note on 2 Sam 15:1).

1:6 *never crossed him.* David appears to have been consistently negligent in disciplining his sons (see notes on 2 Sam 13:21; 14:33). *very handsome.* Attractive physical appearance was an important asset to an aspirant to the throne (see 1 Sam 9:2; 16:12; 2 Sam 14:25).

1:7 *Joab the son of Zeruiah.* See notes on 1 Sam 26:6; 2 Sam 2:13; 19:13; 20:10,23. Joab's alignment with Adonijah may have been motivated by a struggle for power with Benaiah (see v. 8; 2 Sam 8:18; 20:23; 23:20–23). Joab held his position more by his standing with the army than by the favor and confidence of David (see 2:5–6). *Abiathar the priest.* See note on 2 Sam 8:17.

1:8 *Zadok the priest.* See note on 2 Sam 8:17. *Benaiah the son of Jehoiada.* See note on 2 Sam 23:20. *Nathan the prophet.* See 2 Sam 12:1–25. *Shimei.* Not the Shimei of 2:8,46; 2 Sam 16:5–8; perhaps the same as Shimei son of Ela (4:18). *Rei.* Or "and his friends," i.e., friends of Shimei. If Rei is a proper name, this is its only occurrence in the OT. *mighty men who belonged to David.* See 2 Sam 23:8–39.

1:9 *Adonijah sacrificed.* Here also (see note on v. 5) Adonijah followed the example of Absalom (see 2 Sam 15:7–12). *En-rogel.* Means "the spring of Rogel"; located just south of Jerusalem in the Kidron Valley. Apparently the site of a spring had some kind of symbolic significance for the business at hand (see v. 33 and note).

1:11 *Bathsheba the mother of Solomon.* The queen mother held an important and influential position in the royal court (see 2:19; 15:13; 2 Kin 10:13; 2 Chr 15:16). *has become king.* Although the preceding narrative does not relate the actual proclamation of Adonijah's kingship, it can be assumed (see v. 25; 2:15; cf. 2 Sam 15:10).

1:12 *save your life and the life of your son Solomon.* It was common in the ancient Near East for a usurper to liquidate all potential claimants to the throne in an attempt to secure his own position (see 15:29; 2 Kin 10:11; 11:1).

1:13 *Have you not . . . sworn to your maidservant . . . ?* Although 2 Samuel does not record David's oath concerning the succession of Solomon, it does suggest that Solomon was the son through whom the Lord's promise to David for an eternal dynasty would be carried forward (see note on v. 5).

17 She said to him, "My lord, you swore to your maidservant by the LORD your God, *saying*, '[a]Surely your son Solomon shall be king after me and he shall sit on my throne.'

18 "Now, behold, Adonijah is king; and now, my lord the king, you do not know *it*.

19 "[a]He has sacrificed oxen and fatlings and sheep in abundance, and has invited all the sons of the king and Abiathar the priest and Joab the commander of the army, but he has not invited Solomon your servant.

20 "As for you now, my lord the king, the eyes of all Israel are on you, to tell them who shall sit on the throne of my lord the king after him.

21 "Otherwise it will come about, [a]as soon as my lord the king sleeps with his fathers, that I and my son Solomon will be considered [1]offenders."

22 Behold, while she was still speaking with the king, Nathan the prophet came in.

23 They told the king, saying, "Here is Nathan the prophet." And when he came in before the king, he prostrated himself [1]before the king with his face to the ground.

24 Then Nathan said, "My lord the king, have you said, 'Adonijah shall be king after me, and he shall sit on my throne'?

25 "[a]For he has gone down today and has sacrificed oxen and fatlings and sheep in abundance, and has invited all the king's sons and the commanders of the army and Abiathar the priest, and behold, they are eating and drinking before him; and they say, '[b]*Long* live King Adonijah!'

26 "[a]But me, *even* me your servant, and Zadok the priest and Benaiah the son of Jehoiada and your servant Solomon, he has not invited.

27 "Has this thing been done by my lord the king, and you have not shown to your [1]servants who should sit on the throne of my lord the king after him?"

28 Then King David said, "Call Bathsheba to me." And she came into the king's presence and stood before the king.

29 The king vowed and said, "[a]As the LORD lives, who has redeemed my life from all distress,

30 surely as [a]I vowed to you by the LORD the God of Israel, saying, 'Your son Solomon shall be king after me, and he shall sit on my throne in my place'; I will indeed do so this day."

31 Then Bathsheba bowed with her face to the ground, and prostrated herself [1]before the king and said, "[a]May my lord King David live forever."

32 Then King David said, "Call to me [a]Zadok the priest, Nathan the prophet, and Benaiah the son of Jehoiada." And they came into the king's presence.

33 The king said to them, "Take with you [a]the servants of your lord, and have my son Solomon ride on my own mule, and bring him down to [b]Gihon.

34 "Let Zadok the priest and Nathan the prophet [a]anoint him there as king over Israel, and [b]blow the trumpet and say, '[c]*Long* live King Solomon!'

35 "Then you shall come up after him, and he shall come and sit on my throne and be king in my place; for I have appointed him to be ruler over Israel and Judah."

36 Benaiah the son of Jehoiada answered the king and said, "Amen! Thus may the LORD, the God of my lord the king, say.

37 "[a]As the LORD has been with my lord the king, so may He be with Solomon, and [b]make his throne greater than the throne of my lord King David!"

Solomon Anointed King

38 So [a]Zadok the priest, Nathan the prophet, Benaiah the son of Jehoiada, [b]the Cherethites, and the Pelethites went down and had Solomon ride on King David's mule, and brought him to [c]Gihon.

39 Zadok the priest then [a]took the horn of

17 [a]1 Kin 1:13
19 [a]1 Kin 1:9
21 [1]Lit *sinners* [a]Deut 31:16; 2 Sam 7:12; 1 Kin 2:10
23 [1]Lit *to*
25 [a]1 Kin 1:9 [b]1 Sam 10:24
26 [a]1 Kin 1:8, 10
27 [1]Some mss read *servant*
29 [a]2 Sam 4:9
30 [a]1 Kin 1:13, 17
31 [1]Lit *to* [a]Dan 2:4; 3:9
32 [a]1 Kin 1:8
33 [a]2 Sam 20:6, 7 [b]2 Chr 32:30; 33:14
34 [a]1 Sam 10:1; 16:3, 12; 2 Sam 5:3; 1 Kin 19:16; 2 Kin 9:3 [b]2 Sam 15:10 [c]1 Kin 1:25
37 [a]Josh 1:5, 17; 1 Sam 20:13 [b]1 Kin 1:47
38 [a]1 Kin 1:8 [b]2 Sam 8:18 [c]1 Kin 1:33
39 [a]Ex 30:23-32; Ps 89:20

1:17 *you swore to your maidservant by the LORD your God.* An oath taken in the Lord's name was inviolable (see Ex 20:7; Lev 19:12; Josh 9:15,18,20; Judg 11:30,35; Eccl 5:4–7).

1:21 *sleeps with his fathers.* A conventional expression for death (see Gen 47:30; Deut 31:16).

1:24 Nathan approached David diplomatically by raising a question that revealed the dilemma. Either David had secretly encouraged Adonijah to claim the throne and thereby had broken his oath to Bathsheba and Solomon (see v. 27), or he had been betrayed by Adonijah.

1:25 *Long live King Adonijah!* An expression of recognition and acclamation of the new king (see 1 Sam 10:24; 2 Sam 16:16; 2 Kin 11:12).

1:31 *May my lord King David live forever.* An expression of Bathsheba's thanks in the stereotyped hyperbolic language of the court (see Neh 2:3; Dan 2:4; 3:9; 5:10; 6:21).

1:33 *the servants of your lord.* Presumably including the Cherethites and Pelethites (see v. 38). *my own mule.* Although crossbreeding was forbidden in the Mosaic law (Lev 19:19); mules (perhaps imported; see Ezek 27:14) were used in the time of David, at least as mounts for royalty (see 2 Sam 13:29; 18:9). To ride on David's own mule was a public proclamation that Solomon's succession to the throne was sanctioned by David (see Gen 41:43; Esth 6:7–8). *Gihon.* The site of a spring on the eastern slope of Mount Zion (see notes on v. 9; 2Sa 5:8).

1:34 *anoint him.* See notes on 1 Sam 2:10; 9:16. *blow the trumpet.* See 2 Kin 9:13; 2 Sam 15:10; 20:1. *Long live King Solomon!* See note on v. 25.

1:35 *Israel and Judah.* The distinction between Israel and Judah was rooted in the separate arrangements by which David became king over these two tribal units (see 2 Sam 2:4; 5:3).

1:36 *Amen! Thus may the LORD . . . say.* See Jer 28:6.

1:37 *greater.* Not a deprecation of David's accomplishments, but an expression of total loyalty to David and Solomon. Benaiah shared David's own desire for his chosen successor (see vv. 47–48).

1:38 *the Cherethites, and the Pelethites.* See note on 2 Sam 8:18.

1:39 *Zadok . . . anointed Solomon.* Kings chosen by God to rule over His people who were not in a line of dynastic succession

oil from the tent and [b]anointed Solomon.
Then they [c]blew the trumpet, and all the
people said, "[d]*Long* live King Solomon!"
40 All the people went up after him, and
the people [1]were playing on flutes and rejoicing with great joy, so that the earth [2]shook at
their noise.
41 Now Adonijah and all the guests who
were with him heard *it* as they finished eating. When Joab heard the sound of the trumpet, he said, "Why [1]is the city making such
an uproar?"
42 While he was still speaking, behold,
[a]Jonathan the son of Abiathar the priest
came. Then Adonijah said, "Come in, for
[b]you are a valiant man and bring good
news."
43 But Jonathan replied to Adonijah, "No!
Our lord King David has made Solomon king.
44 "The king has also sent with him Zadok
the priest, Nathan the prophet, Benaiah the
son of Jehoiada, the Cherethites, and the
Pelethites; and they have made him ride on
the king's mule.
45 "Zadok the priest and Nathan the prophet have anointed him king in Gihon, and
they have come up from there rejoicing, [a]so
that the city is in an uproar. This is the noise
which you have heard.
46 "Besides, [a]Solomon has even taken his
seat on the throne of the kingdom.
47 "Moreover, the king's servants came to
bless our lord King David, saying, 'May
[a]your God make the name of Solomon better
than your name and his throne greater than
your throne!' And [b]the king bowed himself
on the bed.
48 "The king has also said thus, 'Blessed be
the LORD, the God of Israel, who [a]has granted one to sit on my throne today while my
own eyes see *it.*' "
49 Then all the guests of Adonijah were
terrified; and they arose and each went on
his way.
50 And Adonijah was afraid of Solomon,
and he arose, went and [a]took hold of the
horns of the altar.
51 Now it was told Solomon, saying,
"Behold, Adonijah is afraid of King Solomon,
for behold, he has taken hold of the horns of
the altar, saying, 'Let King Solomon swear to
me today that he will not put his servant to
death with the sword.' "
52 Solomon said, "If he is a worthy man,
[a]not one of his hairs will fall to the ground;
but if wickedness is found in him, he will
die."
53 So King Solomon sent, and they
brought him down from the altar. And he
came and prostrated himself [1]before King
Solomon, and Solomon said to him, "Go to
your house."

David's Charge to Solomon

2 As David's [1][a]time to die drew near, he
charged Solomon his son, saying,
2 "[a]I am going the way of all the earth. [b]Be
strong, therefore, and [1]show yourself a man.
3 "Keep the charge of the LORD your God,
to walk in His ways, to keep His statutes, His
commandments, His ordinances, and His
testimonies, [a]according to what is written in
the Law of Moses, that [b]you may succeed in
all that you do and wherever you turn,
4 so that [a]the LORD may carry out His
promise which He spoke concerning me, saying, '[b]If your sons are careful of their way, [c]to
walk before Me in [1]truth with all their heart

39 [b]1 Chr 29:22 [c]1 Kin 1:34 [d]1 Sam 10:24
40 [1]Lit *fluting* [2]Lit *was split*
41 [1]Lit *is the sound of the city an uproar*
42 [a]2 Sam 15:27, 36; 17:17 [b]2 Sam 18:27
45 [a]1 Kin 1:40
46 [a]1 Chr 29:23
47 [a]1 Kin 1:37 [b]Gen 47:31
48 [a]2 Sam 7:12; 1 Kin 3:6
50 [a]Ex 27:2; 30:10; 1 Kin 2:28
52 [a]1 Sam 14:45; 2 Sam 14:11; Acts 27:34
53 [1]Lit *to*
2:1 [1]Lit *days* [a]Gen 47:29; Deut 31:14
2 [1]Lit *become a man* [a]Josh 23:14 [b]Deut 31:7, 23; Josh 1:6, 7
3 [a]Deut 17:18-20 [b]1 Chr 22:12, 13
4 [1]Or *faithfulness* [a]2 Sam 7:25 [b]Ps 132:12 [c]2 Kin 20:3

---

were anointed by prophets (Saul, 1 Sam 9:16; David, 1 Sam 16:12; Jehu, 2 Kin 9). Kings who assumed office in the line of dynastic succession were anointed by priests (Solomon, here; Joash, 2 Kin 11:12). The distinction seems to be that the priest worked within the established order while the prophets introduced new divine initiatives. *horn of oil.* Perhaps containing the anointing oil described in Ex 30:22–33. *tent.* The tent David had erected in Jerusalem to house the ark (see 2 Sam 6:17) rather than the tabernacle at Gibeon (see 3:4 and note; 2 Chr 1:3).

1:41 *heard it.* Although Gihon may not have been visible from En-rogel, the distance was not great and the sound would carry down the Kidron Valley.

1:42 *Jonathan the son of Abiathar.* See 2 Sam 17:17–21.

1:47 *better.* See note on v. 37.

1:48 *one to sit on my throne.* In Solomon's succession to the throne David sees a fulfillment of the promise in 2 Sam 7:12,16.

1:49 *went on his way.* No one wanted to be identified with Adonijah's abortive coup now that it appeared certain to fail.

1:50 *took hold of the horns of the altar.* The horns of the altar were vertical projections at each corner. The idea of seeking asylum at the altar was rooted in the Pentateuch (see Ex 21:13–14). The priest smeared the blood of the sacrifice on the horns of the altar (see Ex 29:12; Lev 4:7,18,25,30,34) during the sacrificial ritual. Adonijah thus seeks to place his own destiny under the protection of God.

1:52 *worthy man.* Who recognizes and submits to Solomon's office and authority. *if wickedness is found in him.* If he shows evidence of continuing opposition to Solomon's succession to the throne.

2:1 *he charged.* Moses (Deut 31:1–8), Joshua (Josh 23:1–16) and Samuel (1 Sam 12:1–25), as representatives of the Lord's rule, had all given final instructions and admonitions shortly before their deaths.

2:2 *the way of all the earth.* To the grave (see Josh 23:14). *Be strong.* See Deut 31:7,23; Josh 1:6–7,9,18.

2:3 *Keep the charge of the LORD your God.* See Gen 26:5; Lev 18:30; Deut 11:1. *walk in His ways.* A characteristic expression of Deuteronomy for obedience to covenant obligations (Deut 5:33; 8:6; 10:12; 11:22; 19:9; 26:17; 28:9; 30:16). *His statutes, His commandments, His ordinances, and His testimonies.* Four generally synonymous terms for covenant obligations (see 6:12; 8:58; 2 Kin 17:37; Deut 8:11; 11:1; 26:17; 28:15,45; 30:10,16). *that you may succeed.* See Deut 29:9.

2:4 *that the LORD may carry out His promise . . . concerning me.* David here alludes to the covenanted promise of an everlasting dynasty given to him by God through Nathan the prophet (see notes on 2 Sam 7:11–16). Although the covenant promise to David was unconditional, individual participation in its blessing on the part of David's royal descendants was conditioned on obedience to the obligations of the Mosaic covenant (see 2 Chr 7:17–22). *with all their heart and . . . soul.* See Deut 4:29; 6:5; 10:12; 30:6. *you shall not lack a man on the throne of*

and with all their soul, [2][d]you shall not lack a
man on the throne of Israel.'
5 "Now you also know what Joab the
[a]son of Zeruiah did to me, what he did to the
two commanders of the armies of Israel, to
[b]Abner the son of Ner, and to [c]Amasa the
son of Jether, whom he killed; he also [1]shed
the blood of war in peace. And he put the
blood of war on his belt [2]about his waist,
and on his sandals [3]on his feet.
6 "[a]So act according to your wisdom, and
do not let his gray hair go down to [1]Sheol in
peace.
7 "But [a]show kindness to the sons of
Barzillai the Gileadite, and [b]let them be
among those who eat at your table; [c]for they
[1]assisted me when I fled from Absalom your
brother.
8 "Behold, [a]there is with you Shimei the
son of Gera the Benjamite, of Bahurim; now
it was he who cursed me with a [1]violent
curse on the day I went to Mahanaim. But
when [b]he came down to me at the Jordan, I
swore to him by the LORD, saying, 'I will not
put you to death with the sword.'
9 "Now therefore, do not let him go
unpunished, [a]for you are a wise man; and
you will know what you ought to do to him,
and you will bring his gray hair down to
[1]Sheol with blood."

Death of David

10 Then [a]David slept with his fathers and
was buried in [b]the city of David.
11 [a]The days that David reigned over Israel *were* forty years: [b]seven years he reigned
in Hebron and thirty-three years he reigned
in Jerusalem.
12 And [a]Solomon sat on the throne of

4 [2]Lit *there shall not be cast off to you a man from before Me* [d]2 Sam 7:12, 13; 1 Kin 8:25; 9:5
5 [1]Lit *made* [2]Lit *that was about* [3]Lit *that were on* [a]2 Sam 2:13, 18 [b]2 Sam 3:27; 1 Kin 2:32 [c]2 Sam 20:10
6 [1]I.e. the nether world [a]1 Kin 2:9
7 [1]Lit *came near to* [a]2 Sam 19:31-38 [b]2 Sam 9:7, 10 [c]2 Sam 17:27-29
8 [1]Or *grievous* [a]2 Sam 16:5-8
8 [b]2 Sam 19:18-23
9 [1]I.e. the nether world [a]1 Kin 2:6
10 [a]Acts 2:29; 13:36 [b]2 Sam 5:7; 1 Kin 3:1 **11** [a]2 Sam 5:4, 5; 1 Chr 3:4; 29:26, 27 [b]2 Sam 5:5 **12** [a]1 Chr 29:23; 2 Chr 1:1

Israel. Both Solomon and his descendants fell short of their covenant obligations. This led to the division of the kingdom and eventually to the exile of both the northern and southern kingdoms. It was only in the coming of Christ that the fallen tent of David would be restored (see notes on Amos 9:11–15; Acts 15:16) and the promise of David's eternal dynasty ultimately fulfilled. When the nation and its king turned away from the requirements of the Sinai covenant, they experienced the covenant curses rather than blessings; but in all this God remained faithful to His covenant promises to Abraham and to David (see Lev 26:42–45; Is 9:6–7; 11:1–16; 16:5; 55:3; Jer 23:5–6; 30:9; 33:17,20–22,25–26; Ezek 34:23–24; 37:24–28).

2:5 *Joab the son of Zeruiah.* See note on 1:7. *Abner the son of Ner.* See notes on 2 Sam 3:25–32. *Amasa the son of Jether.* See 2 Sam 20:10. *shed the blood of war in peace.* Joab's actions were unlawful assassinations (see Deut 19:1–13; 21:1–9) and only served his own self-interest.

2:7 *sons of Barzillai.* See note on 2 Sam 17:27. *eat at your table.* A position of honor that brought with it other benefits (see 18:19; 2 Kin 25:29; 2 Sam 9:7; 19:28; Neh 5:17).

2:8 See 2 Sam 16:5–13. *Shimei the son of Gera the Benjamite.* Gera was probably the ancestor of Shimei's particular line of descent rather than his immediate father (see Gen 46:21; Judg 3:15). The Hebrew for "son" may mean "descendant," "successor," or "nation."

2:9 *do not let him go unpunished.* The Mosaic law prohibited cursing a ruler (21:10; Ex 22:28).

2:10 *slept with his fathers.* See note on 1:21. *city of David.* See 2 Sam 5:7 and note. Peter implies that David's tomb is still known in his day (Acts 2:29).

2:11 *forty years.* See 2 Sam 5:4–5. David ruled c. 1010–970 B.C. (see Introduction to 1 Samuel: Chronology).

Solomon's Jerusalem

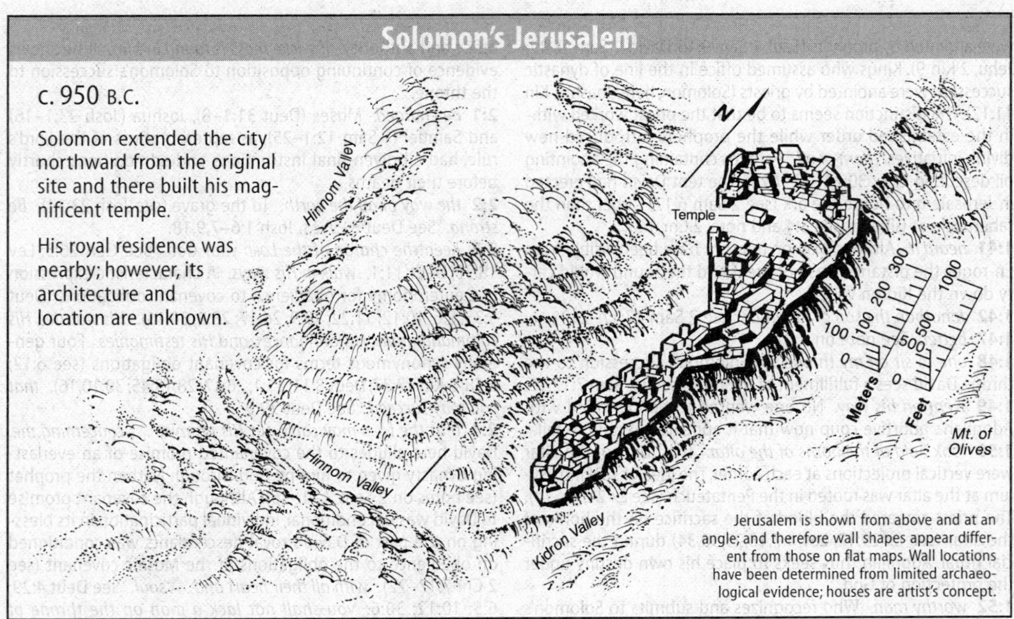

c. 950 B.C.
Solomon extended the city northward from the original site and there built his magnificent temple.
His royal residence was nearby; however, its architecture and location are unknown.
N
Hinnom Valley
Temple
Hinnom Valley
Kidron Valley
Mt. of Olives
0 100 200 300
Meters
0 500 1000
Feet

Jerusalem is shown from above and at an angle; and therefore wall shapes appear different from those on flat maps. Wall locations have been determined from limited archaeological evidence; houses are artist's concept.

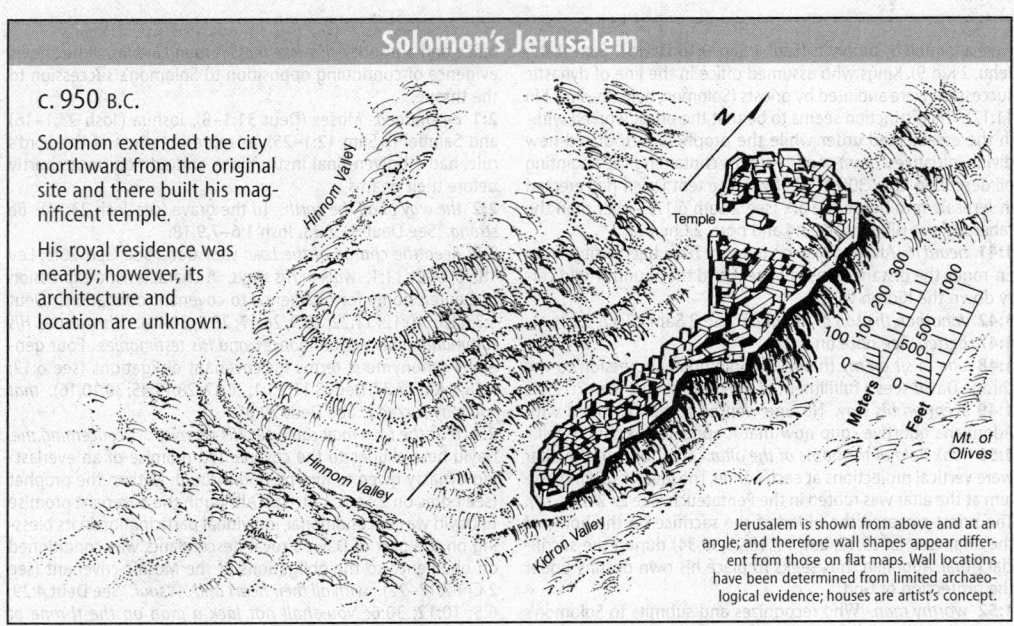

David his father, and his kingdom was firmly established.
13 Now Adonijah the son of Haggith came
to Bathsheba the mother of Solomon. And
she said, "[a]Do you come peacefully?" And
he said, "Peacefully."
14 Then he said, "I have something *to say*
to you." And she said, "Speak."
15 So he said, "You know that [a]the kingdom was mine and [b]that all Israel [1]expected
me to be king; [c]however, the kingdom has
turned about and become my brother's, [d]for
it was his from the LORD.
16 "Now I am making one request of you;
do not [1]refuse me." And she said to him,
"Speak."
17 Then he said, "Please speak to Solomon
the king, for he will not [1]refuse you, that he
may give me [a]Abishag the Shunammite as a
wife."
18 Bathsheba said, "Very well; I will speak
to the king for you."

Adonijah Executed

19 So Bathsheba went to King Solomon to
speak to him for Adonijah. And the king
arose to meet her, bowed before her, and sat
on his throne; then he [a]had a throne set for
the king's mother, and [b]she sat on his right.
20 Then she said, "I am making one small
request of you; [a]do not [1]refuse me." And the
king said to her, "Ask, my mother, for I will
not [2]refuse you."
21 So she said, "[a]Let Abishag the Shunammite be given to Adonijah your brother
as a wife."
22 King Solomon answered and said to his
mother, "And why are you asking Abishag
the Shunammite for Adonijah? [a]Ask for him
also the kingdom—[b]for he is my older brother—even for him, for [c]Abiathar the priest,
and for Joab the son of Zeruiah!"
23 Then King Solomon swore by the LORD,
saying, "May God do so to me and more
also, if Adonijah has [a]not spoken this word
against his own [1]life.
24 "Now therefore, as the LORD lives, who
has established me and set me on the throne
of David my father and [a]who has made me a
house as He promised, surely Adonijah shall
be put to death today."
25 So King Solomon [a]sent Benaiah the son
of Jehoiada; and he fell upon him so that he
died.
26 Then to Abiathar the priest the king
said, "[a]Go to Anathoth to your own field,
[b]for you [1]deserve to die; but I will not put
you to death at this time, because [c]you carried the ark of the Lord [2]GOD before my
father David, and because [d]you were afflicted in everything with which my father was
afflicted."
27 So Solomon dismissed Abiathar from
being priest to the LORD, in order to fulfill
[a]the word of the LORD, which He had spoken
concerning the house of Eli in Shiloh.

Joab Executed

28 Now the news came to Joab, [a]for Joab
had followed Adonijah, [b]although he had not
followed Absalom. And Joab fled to the tent
of the LORD and [c]took hold of the horns of
the altar.
29 It was told King Solomon that Joab had
fled to the tent of the LORD, and behold, he is
beside the altar. Then Solomon [a]sent Benaiah the son of Jehoiada, saying, "[b]Go, fall
upon him."
30 So Benaiah came to the tent of the LORD
and said to him, "Thus the king has said,

13 [a]1 Sam 16:4 **15** [1]Lit *set their faces on me* [a]2 Sam 3:3, 4; 1 Kin 2:22 [b]1 Kin 1:5-25 [c]1 Kin 1:38-50 [d]1 Chr 22:9, 10; 28:5-7 **16** [1]Lit *turn away my face* **17** [1]Lit *turn away your face* [a]1 Kin 1:3, 4 **19** [a]1 Kin 15:13 [b]Ps 45:9 **20** [1]Lit *turn away my face* [2]Lit *turn away your face* [a]1 Kin 2:16 **21** [a]1 Kin 1:3, 4 **22** [a]2 Sam 12:8 [b]1 Kin 1:6; 2:15; 1 Chr 3:2, 5

22 [c]1 Kin 1:7 **23** [1]Lit *soul* [a]Ruth 1:17 **24** [a]2 Sam 7:11, 13; 1 Chr 22:10 **25** [a]2 Sam 8:18 **26** [1]Lit *are a man of death* [2]Heb *YHWH,* usually rendered LORD [a]Josh 21:18; Jer 1:1 [b]1 Sam 26:16 [c]1 Sam 23:6; 2 Sam 15:24-29 [d]1 Sam 22:20-23; 23:8, 9 **27** [a]1 Sam 2:27-36 **28** [a]1 Kin 1:7 [b]2 Sam 17:25; 18:2 [c]1 Kin 1:50 **29** [a]1 Kin 2:25 [b]Ex 21:14

2:13 *Adonijah the son of Haggith.* See note on 1:5. *Do you come peacefully?* The question (see 1 Sam 16:4; 2 Kin 9:22) reveals Bathsheba's apprehension concerning Adonijah's intention (see 1:5).
2:15 *the kingdom was mine.* See 1:11. *All Israel expected me to be king.* A gross exaggeration (see 1:7–8). *it was his from the LORD.* Adonijah professes to view Solomon's kingship as God's will and to have no further intentions of seeking the position for himself.
2:17 *give me Abishag the Shunammite as a wife.* Adonijah's request has the appearance of being innocent (but see note on v. 22) since Abishag had remained a virgin throughout the period of her care for David (see 1:1–4; Deut 22:30).
2:19 *right.* The position of honor (see Ps 110:1; Matt 20:21).
2:20 *one small request.* Bathsheba does not seem to have attached any great significance to Adonijah's request.
2:22 *Ask for him also the kingdom.* Solomon immediately understood Adonijah's request as another attempt to gain the throne. Possession of the royal harem was widely regarded as signifying the right of succession to the throne (see notes on 2 Sam 3:7; 12:8; 16:21). Although Abishag was a virgin, she would be regarded by the people as belonging to David's harem; so marriage to Abishag would greatly strengthen Adonijah's claim to the throne. *for Abiathar the priest, and for Joab son of Zeruiah.* See note on 1:7. Solomon assumes that Abiathar and Joab continue to be involved in Adonijah's treacherous schemes.
2:23 *May God do so to me and more also.* A curse formula (see note on 1 Sam 3:17).
2:24 *has made me a house.* Solomon's son and successor, Rehoboam, was born shortly before Solomon became king (cf. 11:42; 14:21). *as He promised.* See 1 Chr 22:9–10.
2:25 *Benaiah the son of Jehoiada.* See notes on 1:7; 2 Sam 23:20.
2:26 *you carried the ark.* See 2 Sam 15:24–25,29; 1 Chr 15:11–12. *were afflicted in everything with which my father was afflicted.* See 1 Sam 22:20–23; 23:6–9; 30:7; 2 Sam 17:15; 19:11.
2:27 *to fulfill the word of the LORD, which He had spoken concerning the house of Eli in Shiloh.* See notes on 1 Sam 2:30–35.
2:28 *news.* Of Adonijah's death and Abiathar's banishment. *followed Adonijah.* See 1:7. *tent of the LORD.* See note on 1:39. *took hold of the horns of the altar.* See note on 1:50.
2:29 *fall upon him.* The right of asylum was extended only to those who accidentally caused someone's death (see Ex 21:14). Solomon was completely justified in denying this right to Joab, not only for his complicity in Adonijah's conspiracy, but also for his murder of Abner and Amasa (see vv. 31–33). In this incident Solomon finds a suitable occasion for carrying out his father's instruction (see vv. 5–6).

'Come out.' " But he said, "No, for I will die here." And Benaiah brought the king word again, saying, "Thus spoke Joab, and thus he answered me."

31 The king said to him, "[a]Do as he has spoken and fall upon him and bury him, [b]that you may remove from me and from my father's house the blood which Joab shed without cause.

32 "[a]The LORD will return his blood on his own head, [b]because he fell upon two men more righteous and better than he and killed them with the sword, while my father David did not know *it:* [c]Abner the son of Ner, commander of the army of Israel, and [d]Amasa the son of Jether, commander of the army of Judah.

33 "[a]So shall their blood return on the head of Joab and on the head of his [1]descendants forever; but to David and his [1]descendants and his house and his throne, may there be peace from the LORD forever."

34 Then [a]Benaiah the son of Jehoiada went up and fell upon him and put him to death, and he was buried at his own house [b]in the wilderness.

35 [a]The king appointed Benaiah the son of Jehoiada over the army in his place, and the king appointed [b]Zadok the priest [c]in the place of Abiathar.

Shimei Executed

36 Now the king sent and called for [a]Shimei and said to him, "Build for yourself a house in Jerusalem and live there, and do not go out from there to any place.

37 "For on the day you go out and [a]cross over the [1]brook Kidron, you will know for certain that you shall surely die; [b]your blood shall be on your own head."

38 Shimei then said to the king, "The word is good. As my lord the king has said, so your servant will do." So Shimei lived in Jerusalem many days.

39 But it came about at the end of three years, that two of the servants of Shimei ran away [a]to Achish son of Maacah, king of Gath. And they told Shimei, saying, "Behold, your servants are in Gath."

40 Then Shimei arose and saddled his donkey, and went to Gath to Achish to look for his servants. And Shimei went and brought his servants from Gath.

41 It was told Solomon that Shimei had gone from Jerusalem to Gath, and had returned.

42 So the king sent and called for Shimei and said to him, "Did I not make you swear by the LORD and solemnly warn you, saying, 'You will know for certain that on the day you depart and go anywhere, you shall surely die'? And you said to me, 'The word which I have heard is good.'

43 "Why then have you not kept the oath of the LORD, and the command which I [1]have laid on you?"

44 The king also said to Shimei, "[a]You know all the evil which [1]you acknowledge in your heart, which you did to my father David; therefore [b]the LORD shall return your evil on your own head.

45 "But King Solomon shall be blessed, and [a]the throne of David shall be established before the LORD forever."

46 [a]So the king commanded Benaiah the son of Jehoiada, and he went out and fell upon him so that he died.

[b]Thus the kingdom was established in the hands of Solomon.

Solomon's Rule Consolidated

3 Then [a]Solomon [1]formed a marriage alliance with Pharaoh king of Egypt, and took Pharaoh's daughter [b]and brought her to

31 [a]Ex 21:14 [b]Num 35:33; Deut 19:13; 21:8, 9
32 [a]Gen 9:6; Judg 9:24, 57; Ps 7:16 [b]2 Chr 21:13, 14 [c]2 Sam 3:27 [d]2 Sam 20:9, 10
33 [1]Lit *seed* [a]2 Sam 3:29
34 [a]1 Kin 2:25 [b]Josh 15:61; Matt 3:1
35 [a]1 Kin 4:4 [b]1 Chr 6:53; 24:3; 29:22 [c]1 Kin 2:27
36 [a]2 Sam 16:5; 1 Kin 2:8
37 [1]Or *wadi* [a]2 Sam 15:23; 2 Kin 23:6; John 18:1 [b]Josh 2:19; 2 Sam 1:16; Ezek 18:13
39 [a]1 Sam 27:2
43 [1]Lit *commanded*
44 [1]Lit *your heart acknowledges* [a]2 Sam 16:5-13 [b]1 Sam 25:39; 2 Kin 11:1, 12-16; Ps 7:16
45 [a]2 Sam 7:13; Prov 25:5
46 [a]1 Kin 2:25, 34 [b]1 Kin 2:12; 2 Chr 1:1
3:1 [1]Lit *made himself a son-in-law of Pharaoh* [a]1 Kin 7:8; 9:16, 24; 2 Chr 8:11 [b]1 Kin 9:24

2:32 *fell upon two men . . . and killed them.* See 2 Sam 3:27; 20:9–10. *army of Israel.* See 2 Sam 2:8–9. *army of Judah.* See 2 Sam 20:4.

2:34 *at his own house.* The tomb of Joab's father was located near Bethlehem (see 2 Sam 2:32). *wilderness.* Of Judah, east of Bethlehem.

2:35 *Benaiah the son of Jehoiada.* See note on 2 Sam 23:20. *Zadok the priest.* See notes on 1 Sam 2:35; 2 Sam 8:17.

2:36 *do not go out from there to any place.* Confinement to Jerusalem would greatly reduce the possibility of Shimei's (see v. 8) conspiring with any remaining followers of Saul against Solomon's rule.

2:39 *Achish son of Maacah, king of Gath.* Gath was a major Philistine city (see Josh 13:3; 1 Sam 6:16–17). It is likely that Gath was ruled successively by Maoch, Achish the elder (1 Sam 27:2), Maacah and Achish the younger (here).

2:46 *fell upon him so that he died.* The third execution carried out by Benaiah (see vv. 25,34). It brought to completion the tasks assigned to Solomon by David just before his death (vv. 6,9).

3:1 *formed a marriage alliance with Pharaoh.* It appears likely that Solomon established his marriage alliance with either Siamun or Psusennes II, the last kings of the 21st Egyptian dynasty (the first Egyptian pharaoh mentioned by name in the OT is Shishak—11:40; 14:25–26—who established the 22nd Egyptian dynasty c. 945 B.C.). Such an alliance attests Egyptian recognition of the growing importance and strength of the Israelite state. 1 Kin 9:16 indicates that the pharaoh gave his daughter the Canaanite town of Gezer as a dowry at the time of her marriage to Solomon. Gezer was located near the crossing of two important trade routes. One, to the west of Gezer, went from Egypt to the north and was very important for Egypt's commercial interests. The other, to the north of Gezer, went from Jerusalem to the Mediterranean Sea and the port of Joppa and was important to Solomon as a supply line for his building projects. The marriage alliance enabled both Solomon and the pharaoh to accomplish important economic and political objectives. No precise date is given for the conclusion of the marriage alliance, though it appears to have occurred in the third or fourth year of Solomon's reign (see 2:39). Solomon began construction of the temple in his fourth year (6:1), and control of the Gezer area was important to him for the beginning of this project. *city of David.* The Egyptian princess was given a temporary residence in the old fortress (see 2 Sam 5:7 and note)

the city of David [c]until he had finished building his own house and the house of the LORD
and [d]the wall around Jerusalem.
2 [a]The people were still sacrificing on the
high places, because there was no house
built for the name of the LORD until those
days.
3 Now [a]Solomon loved the LORD, [b]walk-
ing in the statutes of his father David, except
he sacrificed and burned incense on the high
places.
4 [a]The king went to [b]Gibeon to sacrifice
there, [c]for that was the great high place;
Solomon offered a thousand burnt offerings
on that altar.
5 [a]In Gibeon the LORD appeared to
Solomon [b]in a dream at night; and God said,
"[c]Ask what *you wish* me to give you."

Solomon's Prayer

6 Then Solomon said, "[a]You have shown
great lovingkindness to Your servant David
my father, [b]according as he walked before
You in [1]truth and righteousness and uprightness of heart toward You; and [c]You have
[2]reserved for him this great lovingkindness,
that You have given him a son to sit on his
throne, as *it is* this day.
7 "Now, O LORD my God, [a]You have made
Your servant king in place of my father
David, yet [b]I am but a little child; [c]I do not
know how to go out or come in.
8 "[a]Your servant is in the midst of Your
people which You have chosen, [b]a great people who are too many to be numbered or
counted.
9 "So [a]give Your servant [1]an understanding heart to judge Your people [b]to discern
between good and evil. For who is able to
judge this [2]great people of Yours?"

God's Answer

10 [1]It was pleasing in the sight of the Lord
that Solomon had asked this thing.
11 God said to him, "Because you have
asked this thing and have [a]not asked for
yourself [1]long life, nor have asked riches for
yourself, nor have you asked for the life of
your enemies, but have asked for yourself
[2]discernment to understand justice,
12 behold, [a]I have done according to your
words. Behold, [b]I have given you a wise and
discerning heart, so that there has been no
one like you before you, nor shall one like
you arise after you.
13 "[a]I have also given you what you have
not asked, both [b]riches and honor, so that
there will not be any among the kings like
you all your days.
14 "[a]If you walk in My ways, keeping My
statutes and commandments, as your father
David walked, then I will [b]prolong your
days."
15 Then [a]Solomon awoke, and behold, it
was a dream. And he came to Jerusalem and
stood before the ark of the covenant of the

3:1 [c]1 Kin 7:1; 9:10 [d]1 Kin 9:15 **2** [a]Lev 17:3-5; Deut 12:2, 13, 14; 1 Kin 22:43 **3** [a]Deut 6:5; 10:12, 13; 11:13; 30:16; Ps 31:23; 145:20; 1 Cor 8:3 [b]1 Kin 2:3; 9:4; 11:4, 6, 38 **4** [a]2 Chr 1:3 [b]Josh 18:21-25 [c]1 Chr 16:39; 21:29 **5** [a]1 Kin 9:2; 11:9 [b]Num 12:6; Matt 1:20; 2:13 [c]John 15:7 **6** [1]Or *faithfulness* [2]Lit *kept* [a]2 Sam 7:8-17; 2 Chr 1:8 [b]1 Kin 9:4 [c]1 Kin 1:48 **7** [a]1 Chr 22:9-13 [b]1 Chr 29:1; Jer 1:6, 7 [c]Num 27:17 **8** [a]Ex 19:6; Deut 7:6 [b]Gen 15:5; 22:17

9 [1]Lit *a hearing* [2]Lit *heavy* [a]2 Chr 1:10; Ps 72:1, 2; Prov 2:3-9; James 1:5 [b]2 Sam 14:17; Heb 5:14 **10** [1]Lit *the thing* **11** [1]Lit *many days* [2]Lit *hearing* [a]James 4:3 **12** [a]1 John 5:14, 15 [b]1 Kin 4:29-31; 5:12; 10:23, 24; Eccl 1:16

13 [a]1 Kin 4:21-24; 10:23, 27; Matt 6:33; Eph 3:20 [b]Prov 3:16 **14** [a]1 Kin 3:6 [b]Ps 91:16; Prov 3:2 **15** [a]Gen 41:7

until a separate palace of her own could be constructed some 20 years later (7:8; 9:10; 2 Chr 8:11).

3:2 *high places.* Upon entering Canaan, the Israelites often followed the Canaanite custom of locating their altars on high hills, probably on the old Baal sites. The question of the legitimacy of Israelite worship at these high places has long been a matter of debate. It is clear that the Israelites were forbidden to take over pagan altars and high places and use them for the worship of the Lord (Num 33:52; Deut 7:5; 12:3). It is also clear that altars were to be built only at divinely sanctioned sites (see Ex 20:24; Deut 12:5,8,13–14). It is not so clear whether multiplicity of altars was totally forbidden provided the above conditions were met (see 19:10,14; Lev 26:30–31; Deut 12; 1 Sam 9:12). It seems, however, that these conditions were not followed even in the time of Solomon, and pagan high places were being used for the worship of the Lord. This would eventually lead to religious apostasy and syncretism and was strongly condemned (2 Kin 17:7–18; 21:2–9; 23:4–25). *because there was no house built.* Worship at a variety of places was apparently considered normal prior to the building of the temple (see Judg 6:24; 13:19; 1 Sam 7:17; 9:12–13).

3:3 *except.* Solomon's one major fault early in his reign was inconsistency in meeting the Mosaic requirements concerning places of legitimate worship.

3:4 *Gibeon.* The Gibeonites tricked Joshua and Israel into a peace treaty at the time of the conquest of Canaan (see Josh 9:3–27). The city was subsequently given to the tribe of Benjamin and set apart for the Levites (Josh 18:25; 21:17). David avenged Saul's violation of the Gibeonite treaty by the execution of seven of Saul's descendants (see 2 Sam 21:1–9). *great high place.* The reason for Gibeon's importance was the presence there of the tabernacle and the ancient bronze altar (see 1 Chr 21:29; 2 Chr 1:2–6). These must have been salvaged after the destruction of Shiloh by the Philistines (see note on 1 Sam 7:1).

3:5 *dream.* Revelation through dreams is found elsewhere in the OT (see Gen 28:12; 31:11; 46:2; Num 12:6; Judg 7:13; Dan 2:4; 7:1), as well as in the NT (see, e.g., Matt 1:20; 2:12,22).

3:6 *lovingkindness.* The Hebrew for this word refers to God's covenant favors (see note on 2 Sam 7:15). Solomon is praising the Lord for faithfulness to His promises to David (2 Sam 7:8–16). *according as.* See note on 2 Sam 22:21.

3:7 *I am but a little child.* The birth of Solomon is generally placed in approximately the middle of David's 40-year reign, meaning that Solomon was about 20 years old at the beginning of his own reign (see 2:11–12) and lacked experience in assuming the responsibilities of his office (cf. Jer 1:6).

3:8 *great people who are too many to be . . . counted.* From the small beginnings of a single family living in Egypt (see Gen 46:26–27; Deut 7:7), the Israelites had increased to an extent approaching that anticipated in the promise given to Abraham (Gen 13:16; 22:17–18) and Jacob (Gen 32:12). See 4:20.

3:11 *long life . . . riches . . . life of your enemies.* Typical desires of ancient Near Eastern monarchs.

3:12 *no one like you.* See 4:29–34; 10:1–13.

3:13 *I have also given you what you have not asked.* Cf. Jesus' promise in Luke 12:31.

3:14 *if you walk in My ways . . . I will prolong your days.* Echoes Deut 6:2; 17:20; 22:7. Unfortunately Solomon did not remain obedient to the covenant as his father David had (11:6), and he did not live to be much more than 60 years of age (see note on v. 7; cf. 11:42).

3:15 *ark of the covenant of the Lord.* See notes on 6:19; 2 Sam

Lord, and offered burnt offerings and made
peace offerings, and [b]made a feast for all his
servants.

Solomon Wisely Judges

16 Then two women who were harlots
came to the king and stood before him.
17 The one woman said, "Oh, my lord,
[1]this woman and I live in the same house;
and I gave birth to a child while she *was* in
the house.
18 "It happened on the third day after I
gave birth, that this woman also gave birth
to a child, and we were together. There was
no stranger with us in the house, only the
two of us in the house.
19 "This woman's son died in the night,
because she lay on it.
20 "So she arose in the middle of the night
and took my son from beside me while your
maidservant slept, and laid him in her bosom, and laid her dead son in my bosom.
21 "When I rose in the morning to nurse my
son, behold, he was dead; but when I looked
at him carefully in the morning, behold, he
was not my son, whom I had borne."
22 Then the other woman said, "No! For
the living one is my son, and the dead one is
your son." But [1]the first woman said, "No!
For the dead one is your son, and the living
one is my son." Thus they spoke before the
king.
23 Then the king said, "[1]The one says,
'This is my son who is living, and your son is
the dead one'; and [1]the other says, 'No! For
your son is the dead one, and my son is the
living one.' "
24 The king said, "Get me a sword." So
they brought a sword before the king.
25 The king said, "Divide the living child
in two, and give half to the one and half to
the other."
26 Then the woman whose child *was* the
living one spoke to the king, for [1a]she was
deeply stirred over her son and said, "Oh,
my lord, give her the living child, and by no
means kill him." But the other said, "He
shall be neither mine nor yours; divide *him!*"
27 Then the king said, "Give [1]the first
woman the living child, and by no means kill
him. She is his mother."
28 When all Israel heard of the judgment
which the king had [1]handed down, they
feared the king, for [a]they saw that the wisdom of God was in him to [2]administer justice.

Solomon's Officials

4 Now King Solomon was king over all Israel.
2 These were his officials: Azariah the
son of Zadok *was* [a]the priest;
3 Elihoreph and Ahijah, the sons of Shisha *were* secretaries; [a]Jehoshaphat the son
of Ahilud *was* the recorder;
4 and [a]Benaiah the son of Jehoiada *was*
over the army; and Zadok and [b]Abiathar
were priests;
5 and Azariah the son of Nathan *was*
over [a]the deputies; and Zabud the son of
Nathan, a priest, *was* the king's friend;
6 and Ahishar was over the household;
and Adoniram the son of Abda *was* over the
men subject to forced labor.
7 Solomon had twelve deputies over all
Israel, who [1]provided for the king and his
household; each man had to [2]provide for a
month in the year.
8 These are their names: Ben-hur, in the
[a]hill country of Ephraim;
9 Ben-deker in Makaz and [a]Shaalbim
and [b]Beth-shemesh and Elonbeth-hanan;
10 Ben-hesed, in Arubboth ([a]Socoh *was*
his and all the land of [b]Hepher);
11 Ben-abinadab, *in* all [1]the [a]height of Dor
(Taphath the daughter of Solomon was his
wife);

15 [b]1 Kin 8:65
17 [1]Lit *I and this woman*
22 [1]Lit *this one was saying*
23 [1]Lit *this one*
26 [1]Lit *her compassion grew warm* [a]Gen 43:30; Is 49:15; Jer 31:20; Hos 11:8
27 [1]Lit *her the living child*
28 [1]Lit *judged* [2]Lit *do* [a]1 Kin 3:9, 11, 12; Dan 1:17; Col 2:2, 3
4:2 [a]1 Chr 6:10
3 [a]2 Sam 8:16
4 [a]1 Kin 2:35 [b]1 Kin 2:27
5 [a]1 Kin 4:7
7 [1]Lit *nourished* [2]Lit *nourish*
8 [a]Josh 24:33
9 [a]Judg 1:35 [b]Josh 21:16
10 [a]Josh 15:35 [b]Josh 12:17
11 [1]Or *Naphoth-dor* [a]Josh 11:1, 2

6:2. *peace offerings.* See note on 1 Sam 11:15.

3:16 *two . . . harlots.* It is not known if these two were Israelites or Jebusites— possibly the latter. *came to the king.* It was possible for Israelites (and others within the realm) to bypass lower judicial officials (Deut 16:18) and appeal directly to the king (see 2 Kin 8:3; 2 Sam 15:2).

3:17 *live in the same house.* Brothels were common in ancient Near Eastern cities.

3:28 *they saw that the wisdom of God was in him.* This episode strikingly demonstrated that the Lord had answered Solomon's prayer for a discerning heart (vv. 9,12).

4:1 *king over all Israel.* Solomon ruled over an undivided kingdom, as his father had before him (see 2 Sam 8:15).

4:2 *son.* According to 2 Sam 15:27,36 and 1 Chr 6:8–9, Azariah was the son of Ahimaaz and the grandson of Zadok (see note on 2:8). Apparently Zadok's son Ahimaaz had died, so that Zadok was succeeded by his grandson Azariah. *Zadok.* See 2:27,35.

4:3 *Shisha.* See note on 2 Sam 8:17. *secretaries.* See note on 2 Sam 8:17. *Jehoshaphat the son of Ahilud.* The same person who served in David's court (see 2 Sam 8:16). *recorder.* See note on 2 Sam 8:16.

4:4 *Benaiah.* Replaced Joab as commander of the army (see 2:35; 2 Sam 8:18). *Zadok and Abiathar.* Abiathar was banished at the beginning of Solomon's reign (2:27,35), and Zadok was succeeded by his grandson Azariah (v. 2).

4:5 *Nathan.* Either the prophet (1:11) or the son of David (2 Sam 5:14). *deputies.* See vv. 7–19. *priest.* See note on 2 Sam 8:18 ("chief ministers"). *the king's friend.* See note on 2 Sam 15:37.

4:6 *over the household.* The first OT reference to an office mentioned frequently in 1,2 Kings (1 Kin 16:9; 18:3; 2 Kin 18:18,37; 19:2). It is likely that this official was administrator of the palace and steward of the king's properties. *Adoniram.* Served not only under Solomon, but also under David before him (2 Sam 20:24) and Rehoboam after him (1 Kin 12:18). *forced labor.* See notes on 9:15; 2 Sam 20:24.

4:7 *Solomon had twelve deputies.* The 12 districts were not identical to tribal territories, possibly because the tribes varied greatly in agricultural productivity. But Solomon's administrative decision violated traditional tribal boundaries and probably stirred up ancient tribal loyalties, eventually contributing to the disruption of the united kingdom.

4:8 *Ben-hur.* The Hebrew *Ben* means "son of."

4:11 *Ben-abinadab.* Most likely the "son of" David's brother

12 Baana the son of Ahilud, *in* [a]Taanach
and Megiddo, and all [b]Beth-shean which is
beside [c]Zarethan below Jezreel, from Beth-
shean to [d]Abel-meholah as far as the other
side of [e]Jokmeam;
13 Ben-geber, in [a]Ramoth-gilead ([b]the
towns of Jair, the son of Manasseh, which
are in Gilead were his: [c]the region of Argob,
which is in Bashan, sixty great cities with
walls and bronze bars *were* his);
14 Ahinadab the son of Iddo, *in* [a]Mahana-
im;
15 [a]Ahimaaz, in Naphtali (he also married
Basemath the daughter of Solomon);
16 Baana the son of [a]Hushai, in Asher and
[1]Bealoth;
17 Jehoshaphat the son of Paruah, in Issachar;
18 [a]Shimei the son of Ela, in Benjamin;
19 Geber the son of Uri, in the land of Gilead, [a]the country of Sihon king of the Amorites and of Og king of Bashan; and *he was*
the only deputy who *was* in the land.

Solomon's Power, Wealth and Wisdom

20 [a]Judah and Israel *were* as numerous as
the sand that is on the [1]seashore in abundance; *they* were eating and drinking and
rejoicing.
21 [1][a]Now Solomon ruled over all the kingdoms [b]from the [2]River *to* the land of the Philistines and to the border of Egypt; [c]*they*
brought tribute and served Solomon all the
days of his life.
22 Solomon's [1]provision for one day was
thirty [2]kors of fine flour and sixty [2]kors of
meal,
23 ten fat oxen, twenty [1]pasture-fed oxen,
a hundred sheep besides deer, gazelles, roe-
bucks, and fattened fowl.

12 [a]Judg 5:19 [b]Josh 17:11 [c]Josh 3:16 [d]1 Kin 19:16 [e]1 Chr 6:68
13 [a]1 Kin 22:3-15 [b]Num 32:41 [c]Deut 3:4
14 [a]Josh 13:26
15 [a]2 Sam 15:27
16 [1]Or *in Aloth* [a]2 Sam 15:32
18 [a]1 Kin 1:8
19 [a]Deut 3:8-10
20 [1]Lit *sea* [a]Gen 22:17; 32:12; 1 Kin 3:8
21 [1]Ch 5:1 in Heb [2]I.e. Euphrates [a]2 Chr 9:26 [b]Gen 15:18; Josh 1:4 [c]2 Sam 8:2, 6
22 [1]Lit *bread* [2]I.e. One kor equals approx 10 bu
23 [1]Lit *oxen of the pasture*
24 [1]Lit *beyond* [2]I.e. Euphrates [a]Judg 1:18 [b]Ps 72:11 [c]1 Chr 22:9
25 [a]Jer 23:6; Mic 4:4; Zech 3:10 [b]1 Sam 3:20
26 [1]One ms reads *4000*, cf 2 Chr 9:25 [a]1 Kin 10:26; 2 Chr 1:14
27 [1]Or *nourished*
28 [a]Esth 8:10, 14; Mic 1:13
29 [1]Lit *heart* [a]1 Kin 3:12 [b]1 Kin 4:20
30 [a]Gen 29:1; Judg 6:33 [b]Is 19:11; Acts 7:22
31 [1]In 1 Chr 2:6, *Dara* [2]Lit *name* [a]1 Kin 3:12 [b]1 Chr 15:19; Ps 89: title [c]1 Chr 2:6
32 [a]Prov 1:1; 10:1; 25:1; Eccl 12:9; Song 1:1
34 [1]Lit *they* [a]1 Kin 10:1; 2 Chr 9:23

24 For he had dominion over everything
[1]west of the [2]River, from Tiphsah even to
[a]Gaza, [b]over all the kings [1]west of the [2]Riv-
er; and [c]he had peace on all sides around
about him.
25 [a]So Judah and Israel lived in safety,
every man under his vine and his fig tree,
[b]from Dan even to Beersheba, all the days of
Solomon.
26 [a]Solomon had [1]40,000 stalls of horses
for his chariots, and 12,000 horsemen.
27 Those deputies [1]provided for King
Solomon and all who came to King
Solomon's table, each in his month; they left
nothing lacking.
28 They also brought barley and straw for
the horses and [a]swift steeds to the place where
it should be, each according to his charge.
29 Now [a]God gave Solomon wisdom and
very great discernment and breadth of
[1]mind, [b]like the sand that is on the seashore.
30 Solomon's wisdom surpassed the wisdom of all [a]the sons of the east and [b]all the
wisdom of Egypt.
31 For [a]he was wiser than all men, than
[b]Ethan the Ezrahite, Heman, [c]Calcol and
[1]Darda, the sons of Mahol; and his [2]fame
was *known* in all the surrounding nations.
32 [a]He also spoke 3,000 proverbs, and his
songs were 1,005.
33 He spoke of trees, from the cedar that is
in Lebanon even to the hyssop that grows on
the wall; he spoke also of animals and birds
and creeping things and fish.
34 [1]Men [a]came from all peoples to hear
the wisdom of Solomon, from all the kings of
the earth who had heard of his wisdom.

Abinadab (see 1 Sam 16:8; 17:13), making him Solomon's first cousin (he was also his son-in-law).

4:12 *Baana the son of Ahilud.* Probably a brother of Jehoshaphat the recorder (v. 3).

4:16 *Baana the son of Hushai.* Perhaps the son of David's trusted adviser (see notes on 2 Sam 15:32,37).

4:18 *Shimei the son of Ela.* Perhaps the same Shimei mentioned in 1:8.

4:20 *as numerous as the sand that is on the seashore.* See 3:8 and note; see also v. 29; Gen 22:17; 2 Sam 17:11; Is 10:22; Jer 33:22; Hos 1:10; cf. Gen 41:49; Josh 11:4; Judg 7:12; Ps 78:27. *they were eating and drinking and rejoicing.* Judah and Israel prospered (see 5:4).

4:21 *from the River to the land of the Philistines and to the border of Egypt.* The borders of Solomon's empire extended to the limits originally promised to Abraham (see note on 2 Sam 8:3). However, rebellion was brewing in Edom (11:14–21) and Damascus (11:23–25).

4:22 *Solomon's provision for one day.* For all his household, his palace servants and his court officials and their families.

4:24 *Tiphsah.* A city on the west bank of the Euphrates River. *Gaza.* The southernmost city of the Philistines on the Mediterranean coast.

4:26 *40,000.* See NASB marg. 1 Kin 10:26 and 2 Chr 1:14 indicate that Solomon had 1,400 chariots, meaning he maintained stalls for two horses for each chariot, with places for about 1,200 reserve horses. By way of comparison, an Assyrian account of the battle of Qarqar in 853 B.C. (about a century after Solomon) speaks of 1,200 chariots from Damascus, 700 chariots from Hamath and 2,000 chariots from Israel (the northern kingdom).

4:29 *like the sand . . . on the seashore.* See note on v. 20.

4:30 *sons of the east.* The phrase is general and appears to refer to the peoples of Mesopotamia (see Gen 29:1) and Arabia (see Jer 49:28; Ezek 25:4,10)—those associated with Israel's northeastern and eastern horizons, just as Egypt was the main region on her southwestern horizon. Many examples of Mesopotamian wisdom literature have been recovered. *wisdom of Egypt.* See Gen 41:8; Ex 7:11; Acts 7:22. Examples of Egyptian wisdom literature are to be found in the proverbs of Ptahhotep (c. 2450 B.C.) and Amenemope (see Introduction to Proverbs: Date).

4:31 *he was wiser than all men.* Until Jesus came (see Luke 11:31). *Ethan the Ezrahite.* See Ps 89 title. *Heman, Calcol and Darda.* See note on 1 Chr 2:6.

4:32 *3,000 proverbs.* Only some of these are preserved in the book of Proverbs.

4:33 *animals and birds and creeping things and fish.* Examples of Solomon's knowledge of these creatures are found in Prov 6:6–8; 26:2–3,11; 27:8; 28:1,15.

4:34 *all peoples . . . all the kings of the earth.* A general statement referring to the Near Eastern world (cf. Gen 41:57).

Alliance with King Hiram

5 [1][a]Now Hiram king of Tyre sent his servants to Solomon, when he heard that
they had anointed him king in place of his
father, for [b]Hiram had [2]always been a friend
of David.
2 Then [a]Solomon sent *word* to Hiram,
saying,
3 "You know that [a]David my father was
unable to build a house for the name of the
LORD his God because of the wars which surrounded him, until the LORD put them under
the soles of his feet.
4 "But now [a]the LORD my God has given
me rest on every side; there is neither adversary nor [1]misfortune.
5 "Behold, [a]I [1]intend to build a house for
the name of the LORD my God, as the LORD
spoke to David my father, saying, 'Your son,
whom I will set on your throne in your place,
he will build the house for My name.'
6 "Now therefore, command that they cut
for me [a]cedars from Lebanon, and my servants will be with your servants; and I will
give you wages for your servants according
to all that you say, for you know that there is
no one among us who knows how to cut
timber like the Sidonians."
7 When Hiram heard the words of
Solomon, he rejoiced greatly and said,
"Blessed be the LORD today, who has given to
David a wise son over this great people."
8 So Hiram sent *word* to Solomon, saying, "I have heard *the message* which you
have sent me; I will do [1]what you desire concerning the cedar and cypress timber.
9 "My servants will bring *them* down from
Lebanon to the sea; and I will make them
into rafts *to go* by sea [a]to the place where
you [1]direct me, and I will have them broken
up there, and you shall carry *them* away.
Then [b]you shall accomplish my desire by
giving food to my household."
10 So [1]Hiram [2]gave Solomon [3]as much as
he desired of the cedar and cypress timber.
11 [a]Solomon then gave Hiram 20,000
[1]kors of wheat as food for his household,
and twenty [1]kors of beaten oil; thus Solomon
would give Hiram year by year.
12 [a]The LORD gave wisdom to Solomon,
just as He [1]promised him; and there was
peace between Hiram and Solomon, and the
two of them made a covenant.

Conscription of Laborers

13 Now [a]King Solomon [1]levied forced
laborers from all Israel; and the forced laborers [2]numbered 30,000 men.
14 He sent them to Lebanon, 10,000 a
month in relays; they were in Lebanon a
month *and* two months at home. And [a]Ado-
niram *was* over the forced laborers.
15 Now [a]Solomon had 70,000 [1]trans-
porters, and 80,000 hewers *of stone* in the
mountains,
16 [a]besides Solomon's 3,300 chief deputies
who *were* over the [1]project *and* who ruled
over the people who were doing the work.
17 Then [a]the king commanded, and they
quarried great stones, costly stones, to lay
the foundation of the house with cut stones.
18 So Solomon's builders and [1]Hiram's

5:1 [1]Ch 5:15 in Heb [2]Lit *all the day* [a]2 Chr 2:3 [b]2 Sam 5:11; 1 Chr 14:1
2 [a]2 Chr 2:3
3 [a]2 Sam 7:5; 1 Chr 28:2, 3
4 [1]Lit *evil occurrence* [a]1 Kin 4:24; 1 Chr 22:9
5 [1]Lit *say* [a]2 Sam 7:12, 13; 1 Chr 17:12; 22:10; 28:6; 2 Chr 2:4
6 [a]2 Chr 2:8
8 [1]Lit *all your pleasure*
9 [1]Lit *send* [a]2 Chr 2:16 [b]Ezra 3:7; Ezek 27:17
10 [1]Heb *Hirom* [2]Lit *was giving* [3]Lit *all his desire*
11 [1]I.e. One kor equals approx 10 bu [a]2 Chr 2:10
12 [1]Lit *spoke to* [a]1 Kin 3:12
13 [1]Lit *raised up* [2]Lit *was* [a]1 Kin 4:6; 9:15
14 [a]1 Kin 4:6; 12:18
15 [1]Or *burden bearers* [a]1 Kin 9:20-22; 2 Chr 2:17, 18
16 [1]Lit *work* [a]1 Kin 9:23
17 [a]1 Kin 6:7; 1 Chr 22:2
18 [1]Heb *Hirom's*

5:1 *Hiram king of Tyre.* Hiram ruled over Tyre c. 978–944 B.C. He may have also served as co-regent with his father Abibaal as early as 993. Before Solomon was born, Hiram provided timber and workmen for the building of David's palace (see 2 Sam 5:11).
5:3 *unable to build a house.* Although David was denied the privilege of building the temple, he did make plans and provisions for its construction (see 1 Chr 22:2–5; 28:2; cf. also Ps 30 title).
5:4 *rest.* Described here as "neither adversary nor misfortune." God's promises to His people (see Ex 33:14; Deut 25:19; Josh 1:13,15) and to David (2 Sam 7:11) have now been fulfilled (see 8:56), so that the Israelites are free to concentrate their strength and resources on building their Great King's royal house (see note on 2 Sam 7:11).
5:5 *name.* Signifies God's revealed character or self-revelation as a person (see, e.g., 8:16; Ex 20:24; Deut 12:5; 2 Sam 6:2; 7:13). *as the LORD spoke to David my father.* See 2 Sam 7:12–13; 1 Chr 22:8–10.
5:6 *command.* A more detailed account of Solomon's request is found in 2 Chr 2:3–10. *cedars from Lebanon.* Widely used in the ancient Near East in the construction of royal houses and temples.
5:7 *Blessed be the LORD.* In polytheistic cultures it was common practice for the people of one nation to recognize the deities of another nation (see 10:9; 11:5) and even to ascribe certain powers to them (see 2 Kin 18:25; see also 2 Chr 2:12).
5:9 *place where you direct me.* Joppa (2 Chr 2:16; see note on 1 Kin 3:1). *giving food to my household.* Provision of food for Hiram's court personnel appears to cover only the cost of the wood itself. In addition, Solomon would have to provide for the wages of the Phoenician laborers (v. 6). Comparison of v. 11 with 2 Chr 2:10 indicates that besides wheat and olive oil for Hiram's court, Solomon also sent barley and wine for labor costs. Hiram may have sold some of these provisions in order to pay the laborers.
5:11 *20,000 kors of wheat.* About 125,000 bushels. By way of comparison, Solomon's court received 10,950 kors of flour and 21,900 kors of meal on an annual basis (see 4:22). Solomon's whole grain payment to Hiram of 20,000 kors of wheat and 20,000 kors of barley (2 Chr 2:10) would probably yield about 26,666 kors of refined flour and meal, or about 20 percent less than the requirements of Solomon's own court.
5:13 *forced laborers.* See notes on 9:15; 2 Sam 20:24. Resentment among the people toward this sort of forced labor eventually led to a civil uprising and the division of Solomon's kingdom immediately after his death (12:1–18).
5:15 *70,000 transporters . . . 80,000 hewers.* Conscripted from the non-Israelite population that David had subdued and incorporated into his kingdom (see 2 Chr 2:17–18). *mountains.* The limestone hills of the Holy Land where the stone was quarried.
5:16 *3,300 chief deputies..* 1 Kin 9:23 refers to 550 chief officers. If these are two different categories of supervisory personnel, the total is 3,850 men. 2 Chr 2:2 refers to 3,600 supervisors, and 2 Chr 8:10 speaks of 250 chief officers, which again yields a total of 3,850 men in a supervisory capacity.
5:17 *great stones, costly stones.* For the size of these stones see 7:10. Transportation of such stones to Jerusalem would require enormous manpower.

builders and [a]the Gebalites [2]cut them, and prepared the timbers and the stones to build the house.

The Building of the Temple

6 [a]Now it came about in the four hundred and eightieth year after the sons of Israel came out of the land of Egypt, in the fourth year of Solomon's reign over Israel, in the month of Ziv which is the second month, that he [1]began to build the house of the LORD.

2 As for the house which King Solomon built for the LORD, its length *was* sixty [1]cubits and its width twenty *cubits* and its height thirty cubits.

3 The porch in front of the nave of the house *was* twenty cubits [1]in length, [2]corresponding to the width of the house, *and* its [3]depth along the front of the house *was* ten cubits.

4 Also for the house [a]he made windows with *artistic* frames.

5 [a]Against the wall of the house he built stories encompassing the walls of the house around both the nave and the [b]inner sanctuary; thus he made [c]side chambers all around.

6 The lowest story *was* five cubits wide, and the middle *was* six cubits wide, and the third *was* seven cubits wide; for on the outside he [1]made offsets *in the wall* of the house all around in order that *the beams* would not [2]be inserted in the walls of the house.

7 [a]The house, while it was being built, was built of stone [1]prepared at the quarry, and there was neither hammer nor axe nor any iron tool heard in the house while it was being built.

8 The doorway for the [1]lowest side chamber *was* on the right side of the house; and they would go up by winding stairs to the middle *story,* and from the middle to the third.

9 So [a]he built the house and finished it; and he covered the house with beams and [1]planks of cedar.

10 He also built the stories against the whole house, each five [1]cubits high; and they [2]were fastened to the house with timbers of cedar.

11 Now the word of the LORD came to Solomon saying,

12 "*Concerning* this house which you are building, [a]if you will walk in My statutes and execute My ordinances and keep all My commandments by walking in them, then I will carry out My word with you which I spoke to David your father.

13 "[a]I will dwell among the sons of Israel, and [b]will not forsake My people Israel."

14 [a]So Solomon built the house and finished it.

15 Then he [a]built the walls of the house on the inside with boards of cedar; from the floor of the house to the [1]ceiling he overlaid *the walls* on the inside with wood, and he overlaid the floor of the house with boards of cypress.

16 [a]He built twenty cubits on the rear part of the house with boards of cedar from the floor to the [1]ceiling; he built *them* for it on the inside as an inner sanctuary, *even* as [b]the most holy place.

17 The house, that is, the nave in front of *the inner sanctuary,* was forty [1]cubits *long.*

18 There was cedar on the house within, carved *in the shape* of [a]gourds and open flowers; all was cedar, there was no stone seen.

19 Then he prepared an inner sanctuary within the house in order to place there the ark of the covenant of the LORD.

18 [2]Or *chiseled* [a]Josh 13:5; Ezek 27:9
6:1 [1]Lit *built* [a]2 Chr 3:1, 2
2 [1]I.e. One cubit equals approx 18 in.
3 [1]Lit *in its length* [2]Lit *on the face of* [3]Lit *width*
4 [a]Ezek 40:16; 41:16
5 [a]Ezek 41:6 [b]1 Kin 6:16, 19, 20 [c]Ezek 41:5
6 [1]Lit *gave* [2]Lit *take hold*
7 [1]Lit *finished* [a]Ex 20:25; Deut 27:5, 6
8 [1]So with Gr and versions; M.T. *middle*
9 [1]Lit *rows* [a]1 Kin 6:14, 38
10 [1]I.e. One cubit equals approx 18 in. [2]Lit *took hold*
12 [a]2 Sam 7:5-16; 1 Kin 9:4
13 [a]Ex 25:8; 29:45; Lev 26:11 [b]Deut 31:6; Josh 1:5; Heb 13:5
14 [a]1 Kin 6:9, 38
15 [1]Lit *walls of ceiling* [a]1 Kin 7:7
16 [1]Lit *walls* [a]2 Chr 3:8 [b]Ex 26:33, 34; Lev 16:2; 1 Kin 8:6; Heb 9:3
17 [1]I.e. One cubit equals approx 18 in.
18 [a]1 Kin 7:24

5:18 *Gebalites.* Gebal is also known as Byblos (see note on Ezek 27:9).

6:1–38 See drawing, p. 458.

6:1 *four hundred and eightieth year . . . fourth year.* Synchronizations between certain events in the reigns of later Israelite kings and Assyrian chronological records fix the fourth year of Solomon's reign at c. 966 B.C. (see Introduction: Chronology). If Israel's exodus is placed 480 years prior to 966, it would have occurred c. 1446 (the chronology followed in this study Bible) during the rule of the 18th-dynasty Egyptian pharaoh, Amunhotep II. On the basis of Ex 1:11 and certain other historical considerations, however, some have concluded that the exodus could not have occurred prior to the rule of the 19th-dynasty pharaoh, Rameses II—thus not until c. 1290 (see note on Gen 47:11). This would mean that the 480 years of this verse would be understood as either a schematic (perhaps representative of 12 generations multiplied by the conventional, but not always actual, 40-year length of a generation) or aggregate figure (the combined total of a number of subsidiary time periods, which in reality were partly concurrent, examples of which are to be found in Egyptian and Mesopotamian records).

6:2 *house which King Solomon built.* The temple was patterned after the tabernacle (and, in general, other temples of the time) and was divided into three major areas: the most holy place, the holy place and the outer courtyard. The most holy place in the temple was cubical, as it probably was in the tabernacle. The dimensions of the temple in most instances seem to be double those of the tabernacle (see Ex 26:15–30; 36:20–34).

6:6 *offsets.* To avoid making holes in the temple wall, it was built with a series of ledges on which the beams for the three floors of side chambers rested. This accounts for the different widths of the rooms on each floor.

6:11 *the word of the LORD came to Solomon.* As the temple neared completion the Lord spoke to Solomon, perhaps through an unnamed prophet (but see 3:5,11–14; 9:2–9).

6:12 *if you will walk in My statutes . . . I will carry out My word with you.* In words similar to those spoken by David (see notes on 2:1–4), the Lord assures Solomon of a continuing dynasty (see 2 Sam 7:12–16) if he is faithful to the covenant.

6:13 *I will dwell among the sons of Israel.* In the temple being built (see 9:3). To avoid any apprehension among the Israelites concerning His presence with them (cf. Ps 78:60; Jer 26:6,9; see note on 1 Sam 7:1), the Lord gives assurance that He will dwell in their midst (see 8:10–13; Lev 26:11).

6:16 *most holy place.* Similar terminology ("holy of holies") was used for the inner sanctuary housing the ark in the tabernacle (see Ex 26:33–34; Lev 16:2,16–17, 20, 23).

6:19 *ark of the covenant of the LORD.* The Ten Commandments are called the "words of the covenant" in Ex 34:28. The stone tablets on which the Ten Commandments were inscribed are

20 [1]The inner sanctuary *was* twenty cubits in length, twenty cubits in width, and twenty cubits in height, and he overlaid it with pure gold. He also overlaid the altar with cedar.
21 So Solomon overlaid the inside of the house with pure gold. And he drew chains of gold across the front of the inner sanctuary, and he overlaid it with gold.
22 He overlaid the whole house with gold, until all the house was finished. Also [a]the whole altar which was by the inner sanctuary he overlaid with gold.
23 [a]Also in the inner sanctuary he made two cherubim of olive wood, each ten cubits high.
24 Five cubits *was* the one wing of the cherub and five cubits the other wing of the cherub; from the end of one wing to the end of the other wing *were* ten cubits.
25 The other cherub *was* ten cubits; both the cherubim were of the same measure and the same form.
26 The height of the one cherub *was* ten cubits, and so *was* the other cherub.
27 He placed the cherubim in the midst of the inner house, and [a]the wings of the cherubim were spread out, so that the wing of

20 [1]Lit *before*
22 [a]Ex 30:1, 3, 6
23 [a]Ex 37:7-9; 2 Chr 3:10-12
27 [a]Ex 25:20; 37:9; 1 Kin 8:7

called the "tablets of the covenant" in Deut 9:9. The ark in which the tablets were kept (see Ex 25:16,21; 40:20; Deut 10:1–5) is thus sometimes called the "ark of the covenant of the LORD" (see Deut 10:8; 31:9,25; Josh 3:11). Elsewhere the ark is variously designated as the "ark of the LORD" (Josh 3:13; 4:11), the "ark of the testimony" (Ex 30:6; 31:7) and the "ark of God" (1 Sam 3:3; 4:11,17,21; 5:1–2).

6:20 *pure gold.* The extensive use of gleaming gold probably symbolized the glory of God and His heavenly temple (cf. Rev 21:10–11,18,21).

6:21 *chains of gold.* The curtain covering the entrance to the most holy place was probably hung on these chains (see 2 Chr 3:14; Matt 27:51; Heb 6:19).

6:22 *altar which was by the inner sanctuary.* The incense altar (see 7:48; Ex 30:1,6; 37:25–28; Heb 9:3–4).

6:23 *cherubim.* See note on Ex 25:18. They were to stand as sentries on either side of the ark (8:6–7; 2 Chr 3:10–13). Two additional cherubim stood on the ark—one on each end of its atonement cover (Ex 25:17–22). *ten cubits high.* The most holy place, where the cherubim stood, was 20 cubits high (v. 16).

Solomon's Temple

960–586 B.C.

Temple source materials are subject to academic interpretation, and subsequent art reconstructions vary.

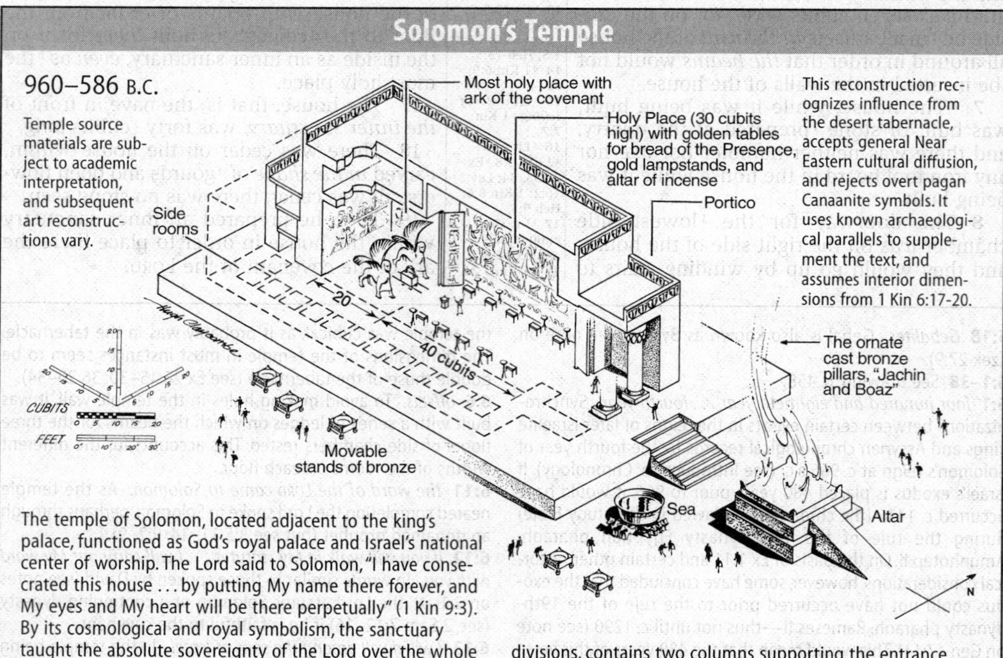

Most holy place with ark of the covenant
Holy Place (30 cubits high) with golden tables for bread of the Presence, gold lampstands, and altar of incense
Portico
Side rooms
20
40 cubits
The ornate cast bronze pillars, "Jachin and Boaz"
Movable stands of bronze
Sea
Altar
CUBITS
FEET
N

This reconstruction recognizes influence from the desert tabernacle, accepts general Near Eastern cultural diffusion, and rejects overt pagan Canaanite symbols. It uses known archaeological parallels to supplement the text, and assumes interior dimensions from 1 Kin 6:17-20.

The temple of Solomon, located adjacent to the king's palace, functioned as God's royal palace and Israel's national center of worship. The Lord said to Solomon, "I have consecrated this house . . . by putting My name there forever, and My eyes and My heart will be there perpetually" (1 Kin 9:3). By its cosmological and royal symbolism, the sanctuary taught the absolute sovereignty of the Lord over the whole creation and His special headship over Israel.

The floor plan is a type that has a long history in Semitic religion, particularly among the West Semites. An early example of the tripartite division into *'ulam*, *hekal*, and *debir* (portico, main hall, and inner sanctuary) has been found at Syrian Ebla (c. 2300 B.C.) and, much later but more contemporaneous with Solomon, at Tell Tainat in the Orontes basin (c. 900 B.C.). Like Solomon's, the later temple has three divisions, contains two columns supporting the entrance, and is located adjacent to the royal palace.

Many archaeological parallels can be drawn to the methods of construction used in the temple, e.g., the "stone and cedar beam" technique described in 1 Kin 6:36. Interestingly, evidence for the largest bronze-casting industry ever found in Palestine comes from the same locale and period as that indicated in Scripture: Zarethan in the Jordan Valley c. 1000 B.C.

©1986 Hugh Claycombe

the one was touching the *one* wall, and the wing of the other cherub was touching the other wall. So their wings were touching each other in the center of the house.

28 He also overlaid the cherubim with gold.

29 Then he carved all the walls of the house round about with carved engravings of cherubim, palm trees, and open flowers, inner and outer *sanctuaries.*

30 He overlaid the floor of the house with gold, inner and outer *sanctuaries.*

31 For the entrance of the inner sanctuary he made doors of olive wood, the lintel *and* five-sided doorposts.

32 So *he made* two doors of olive wood, and he carved on them carvings of cherubim, palm trees, and open flowers, and overlaid them with gold; and he spread the gold on the cherubim and on the palm trees.

33 So also he made for the entrance of the nave four-sided doorposts of olive wood

34 and [a]two doors of cypress wood; the two leaves of the one door turned on pivots, and the two [1]leaves of the other door turned on pivots.

35 He carved *on it* cherubim, palm trees, and open flowers; and he overlaid *them* with gold evenly applied on the engraved work.

36 [a]He built the inner court with three rows of cut stone and a row of cedar beams.

37 [a]In the fourth year the foundation of the house of the LORD was laid, in the month of Ziv.

38 In the eleventh year, in the month of Bul, which is the eighth month, the house was finished throughout all its parts and according to all its plans. So he was seven years in building it.

Solomon's Palace

7 Now [a]Solomon was building his own house thirteen years, and he finished all his house.

2 [a]He built the house of the forest of Lebanon; its length was 100 [1]cubits and its width 50 cubits and its height 30 cubits, on four rows of cedar pillars with cedar beams on the pillars.

3 It was paneled with cedar above the side chambers which were on the 45 pillars, 15 in each row.

4 *There were artistic window* frames in three rows, and window was opposite window in three ranks.

5 All the doorways and doorposts *had* squared *artistic* frames, and window was opposite window in three ranks.

6 Then he made [a]the hall of pillars; its length was 50 cubits and its width 30 cubits, and a porch *was* in front of them and pillars and a [b]threshold in front of them.

7 He made the hall of the [a]throne where he was to judge, the hall of judgment, and [b]it was paneled with cedar from floor to floor.

8 His house where he was to live, the other court inward from the hall, was of the same workmanship. [a]He also made a house like this hall for Pharaoh's daughter, [b]whom Solomon had married.

9 All these were of costly stones, of stone cut according to measure, sawed with saws, inside and outside; even from the foundation to the coping, and so on the outside to the great court.

10 The foundation was of costly stones, *even* large stones, stones of ten cubits and stones of eight cubits.

11 And above were costly stones, stone cut according to measure, and cedar.

12 So [a]the great court all around *had* three rows of cut stone and a row of cedar beams even as the inner court of the house of the LORD, and [b]the porch of the house.

Hiram's Work in the Temple

13 Now [a]King Solomon sent and brought Hiram from Tyre.

34 [1]So with Gr; M.T. *curtains* [a]Ezek 41:23-25
36 [a]1 Kin 7:12; Jer 36:10
37 [a]1 Kin 6:1
7:1 [a]1 Kin 3:1; 9:10; 2 Chr 8:1

2 [1]I.e. One cubit equals approx 18 in. [a]1 Kin 10:17, 21; 2 Chr 9:16
6 [a]1 Kin 7:12 [b]Ezek 41:25, 26
7 [a]Ps 122:5; Prov 20:8 [b]1 Kin 6:15, 16
8 [a]1 Kin 9:24; 2 Chr 8:11 [b]1 Kin 3:1
12 [a]1 Kin 6:36 [b]1 Kin 7:6
13 [a]2 Chr 2:13, 14; 4:11

6:29 *he carved . . . cherubim.* Not a violation of the second commandment, which prohibited making anything to serve as a representation of God and worshiping it (see note on Ex 20:4). *palm trees, and open flowers.* Early Jewish synagogues were adorned with similar motifs. The depiction of cherubim and beautiful trees and flowers is reminiscent of the Garden of Eden, from which man had been driven as a result of sin (Gen 3:24). In a symbolic sense, readmission to the paradise of God is now to be found only by means of atonement for sin at the sanctuary.
6:36 *inner court.* Suggests that there was an outer courtyard (see 8:64). 2 Chr 4:9 refers to the "court of the priests" (inner) and the "great court" (outer). The inner court is also called the upper court (Jer 36:10) because of its higher position on the temple mount.
6:37 *fourth year.* Of Solomon's reign (see v. 1 and note).
6:38 *eleventh year.* Of Solomon's reign (959 B.C.).
7:1 *thirteen years.* Solomon spent almost twice as long building his own house as he did the Lord's house (see 6:38; see also Hag 1:2–4).
7:2 *house of the forest of Lebanon.* Four rows of cedar pillars in the palace created the impression of a great forest. *length was 100 cubits and its width 50 cubits and its height 30 cubits.* About 150 feet long, 75 feet wide and 45 feet high. Compare these measurements with those of the temple in 6:2.
7:3 *45 pillars, 15 in each row.* Suggests that there were three floors in the building above the main hall on the ground level. The building included storage area for weaponry (see 10:16–17).
7:6 *hall.* Apparently an entrance hall to the palace of the forest of Lebanon. Its length (50 cubits) corresponds to the width of the palace.
7:7 *hall of the throne.* It is not clear whether the throne hall, the hall of judgment, Solomon's own living quarters (v. 8) and the palace for Pharaoh's daughter (v. 8) were separate buildings or locations within the palace of the forest of Lebanon.
7:9 *sawed with saws.* The pinkish white limestone of the Holy Land is easily cut when originally quarried, but gradually hardens with exposure.
7:12 *great court.* Constructed in the same way as the inner court of the temple (6:36).
7:13 *King Solomon sent.* Prior to the completion of the temple and the construction of Solomon's palace (see 2 Chr 2:7, 13–14). *Hiram.* His full name is Huram-abi (Huram is a variant of Hiram; 2 Chr 2:13).

14 [a]He was a widow's son from the tribe
of Naphtali, and his father was a man of
Tyre, a worker in bronze; and [b]he was filled
with wisdom and understanding and skill for
doing any work in bronze. So he came to
King Solomon and [c]performed all his work.
15 He fashioned [a]the two pillars of
bronze; [b]eighteen cubits was the height of
one pillar, and a line of twelve cubits [1]meas-
ured the circumference of both.
16 He also made two capitals of molten
bronze to set on the tops of the pillars; the
height of the one capital was five [1]cubits and
the height of the other capital was five cubits.
17 *There were* nets of network and twisted
threads of chainwork for the capitals which
were on the top of the pillars; seven for the
one capital and seven for the other capital.
18 So he made the pillars, and two rows
around on the one network to cover the capitals which were on the top of the pomegranates; and so he did for the other capital.
19 The capitals which *were* on the top of
the pillars in the porch were of lily design,
four cubits.
20 *There were* capitals on the two pillars,
even above *and* close to the [1]rounded projection which was beside the network; and
[a]the pomegranates *numbered* two hundred
in rows around [2]both capitals.
21 [a]Thus he set up the pillars at the
[b]porch of the nave; and he set up the right
pillar and named it [1]Jachin, and he set up
the left pillar and named it [2]Boaz.
22 On the top of the pillars was lily design.
So the work of the pillars was finished.
23 [a]Now he made the sea of [b]cast *metal*
ten cubits from brim to brim, circular in
form, and its height was five cubits, and
[1]thirty cubits in circumference.

14 [a]2 Chr 2:14 [b]Ex 28:3; 31:3-5; 35:31; 36:1 [c]2 Chr 4:11-16
15 [1]Lit *went around the other pillar* [a]2 Kin 25:17; 2 Chr 3:15; 4:12; Jer 52:21 [b]1 Kin 7:41
16 [1]I.e. One cubit equals approx 18 in.
20 [1]Lit *belly* [2]Lit *on the other capital* [a]1 Kin 7:42; 2 Chr 3:16; 4:13; Jer 52:23
21 [1]I.e. he shall establish [2]I.e. in it is strength [a]2 Chr 3:17 [b]1 Kin 6:3
23 [1]Lit *a line of 30 cubits went around it* [a]2 Chr 4:2 [b]2 Kin 16:17; 25:13

7:14 *widow's son from the tribe of Naphtali.* 2 Chr 2:14 indicates that Huram-abi's mother was from Dan. Apparently she was born in the city of Dan in northern Israel close to the tribe of Naphtali, from which came her first husband. After he died, she married a man from Tyre. *any work in bronze.* Huram-abi had a much wider range of skills as well (see 2 Chr 2:7,14).
7:15 *two pillars of bronze.* One was placed on each side of the main entrance to the temple (v. 21). Surely decorative, they may also have embodied a symbolism not known to us. It has been suggested that they were not freestanding but supported a roof (forming a portico to the temple) and an architrave.
7:21 *the right pillar.* The temple, like the tabernacle before it, faced east (see Ezek 8:16).
7:23 *sea of cast metal.* This enormous reservoir of water corresponded to the bronze basin made for the tabernacle (see Ex 30:17–21; 38:8). Its water was used by the priests for ritual cleansing (2 Chr 4:6). *thirty cubits.* Technically speaking, this should be 31.416 cubits because of the ten-cubit diameter of

Temple Furnishings

Glimpses of the rich ornamentation of Solomon's temple can be gained through recent discoveries that illumine the text of 1 Kin 6-7.

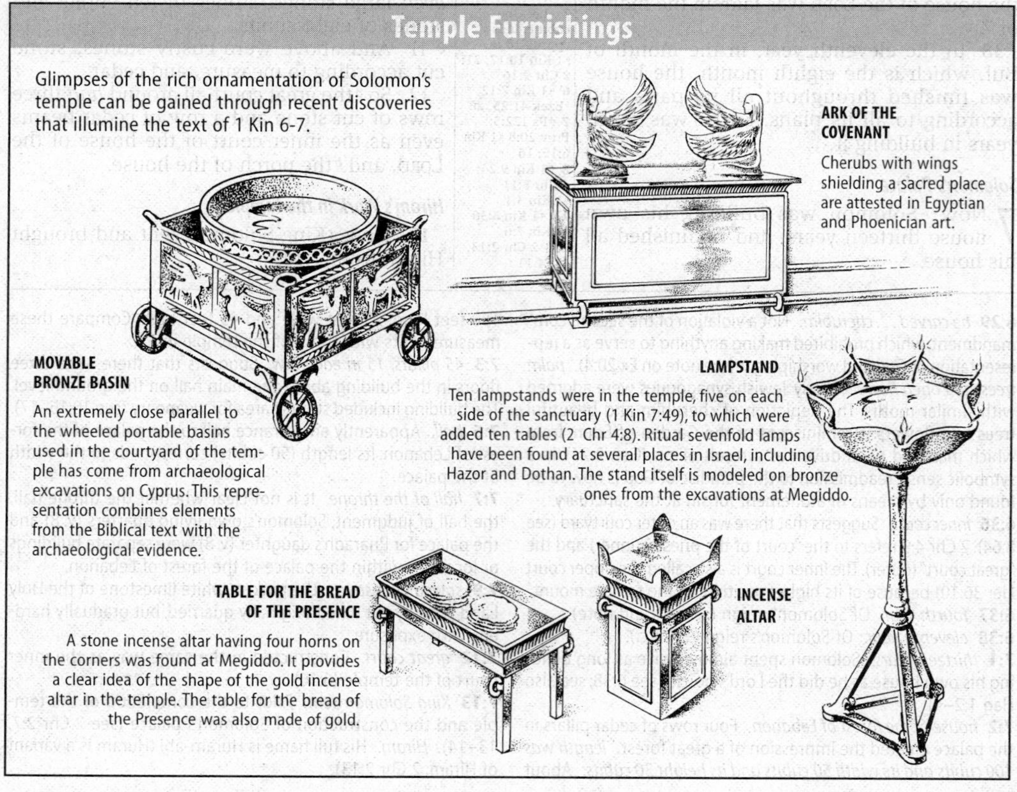

ARK OF THE COVENANT Cherubs with wings shielding a sacred place are attested in Egyptian and Phoenician art.

MOVABLE BRONZE BASIN An extremely close parallel to the wheeled portable basins used in the courtyard of the temple has come from archaeological excavations on Cyprus. This representation combines elements from the Biblical text with the archaeological evidence.

LAMPSTAND Ten lampstands were in the temple, five on each side of the sanctuary (1 Kin 7:49), to which were added ten tables (2 Chr 4:8). Ritual sevenfold lamps have been found at several places in Israel, including Hazor and Dothan. The stand itself is modeled on bronze ones from the excavations at Megiddo.

TABLE FOR THE BREAD OF THE PRESENCE / INCENSE ALTAR A stone incense altar having four horns on the corners was found at Megiddo. It provides a clear idea of the shape of the gold incense altar in the temple. The table for the bread of the Presence was also made of gold.

24 Under its brim [a]gourds went around
encircling it ten to a cubit, [b]completely surrounding the sea; the gourds were in two
rows, cast [1]with the rest.
25 [a]It stood on twelve oxen, three facing
north, three facing west, three facing south,
and three facing east; and the sea *was set* on
top of them, and all their rear parts *turned*
inward.
26 It was a handbreadth thick, and its brim
was made like the brim of a cup, *as* a lily
blossom; it could hold two thousand baths.
27 Then [a]he made the ten stands of
bronze; the length of each stand was four
cubits and its width four cubits and its
height three cubits.
28 This was the design of the stands: they
had borders, even borders between the
[1]frames,
29 and on the borders which were
between the [1]frames *were* lions, oxen and
cherubim; and on the [1]frames there *was* a
pedestal above, and beneath the lions and
oxen *were* wreaths of hanging work.
30 Now each stand had four bronze
wheels with bronze axles, and its four feet
had supports; beneath the basin *were* cast
supports with wreaths at each side.
31 Its opening inside the crown at the top
was a cubit, and its opening *was* round like
the design of a pedestal, a cubit and a half;
and also on its opening *there were* engravings,
and their borders were square, not round.
32 The four wheels *were* underneath the
borders, and the axles of the wheels *were* on
the stand. And the height of a wheel *was* a
cubit and a half.
33 The workmanship of the wheels *was*
like the workmanship of a chariot wheel.
Their axles, their rims, their spokes, and
their hubs *were* all cast.
34 Now *there were* four supports at the
four corners of each stand; its supports *were*
part of the stand itself.
35 On the top of the stand *there was* a circular form half a [1]cubit high, and on the top
of the stand its [2]stays and its borders *were*
part of it.
36 He engraved on the plates of its stays
and on its borders, cherubim, lions and palm
trees, according to the clear space on each,
with wreaths *all* around.
37 [a]He made the ten stands like this: all of
them had one casting, one measure and one
form.
38 [a]He made ten basins of bronze, one
basin held forty baths; each basin *was* four
cubits, *and* on each of the ten stands *was*
one basin.
39 Then he set the stands, five on the right
side of the house and five on the left side of
the house; and he set the sea *of cast metal* on
the right side of the house eastward toward
the south.
40 Now Hiram made the basins and the
shovels and the bowls. So Hiram finished
doing all the work which he performed for
King Solomon *in* the house of the LORD:
41 the two pillars and the *two* bowls of the
capitals which *were* on the top of the [a]two
pillars, and the two networks to cover the
two bowls of the capitals which *were* on the
top of the pillars;
42 and the [a]four hundred pomegranates
for the two networks, two rows of pomegranates for each network to cover the two
bowls of the capitals which *were* on the tops
of the pillars;
43 and the ten stands with the ten basins
on the stands;
44 and [a]the one sea and the twelve oxen
under the sea;
45 and [a]the pails and the shovels and the
bowls; even all these utensils which Hiram
made for King Solomon *in* the house of the
LORD *were* of polished bronze.
46 [a]In the plain of the Jordan the king cast
them, in the clay ground between [b]Succoth
and [c]Zarethan.
47 Solomon left all the utensils *unweighed*,
because *they were* too many; [a]the weight of
the bronze could not be ascertained.
48 Solomon made all the furniture which
was in the house of the LORD: [a]the golden
altar and the golden table on which *was* the
[b]bread of the Presence;

24 [1]Lit *in its casting* [a]1 Kin 6:18 [b]2 Chr 4:3
25 [a]2 Chr 4:4, 5; Jer 52:20
27 [a]1 Kin 7:38; 2 Kin 25:13; 2 Chr 4:14
28 [1]Or *crossbars*
29 [1]Or *crossbars*
35 [1]I.e. One cubit equals approx 18 in. [2]Lit *hands*
37 [a]2 Chr 4:14
38 [a]Ex 30:18; 2 Chr 4:6
41 [a]1 Kin 7:17, 18
42 [a]1 Kin 7:20
44 [a]1 Kin 7:23, 25
45 [a]Ex 27:3; 2 Chr 4:16
46 [a]2 Chr 4:17 [b]Gen 33:17; Josh 13:27 [c]Josh 3:16
47 [a]1 Chr 22:3, 14
48 [a]Ex 30:1-3; 37:10-29; 2 Chr 4:8 [b]Ex 25:30

the circular top. Thirty may be a round number here, or perhaps the measurement was taken a bit below the rim or on the inside circumference (see v. 26).

7:24 *ten to a cubit.* With ten gourds to a cubit it took 300 gourds to span the entire reservoir, or 600 gourds counting both rows.

7:27 *ten stands.* These movable bronze stands were designed to hold water basins (see v. 38) of much smaller dimensions than the bronze sea. The water from the basins was used to wash certain prescribed parts of the animals that were slaughtered for burnt offerings (see Lev 1:9,13; 2Ch 4:6).

7:36 *He engraved . . . cherubim, lions and palm trees.* See note on 6:29.

7:40 *basins.* Perhaps used for cooking meat to be eaten in connection with the peace offerings (see Lev 7:11–17; 22:21–23). *shovels.* Used for removing ashes from the altar. *bowls.* For use by the priests in various rites involving the sprinkling of blood or water (see Ex 27:3).

7:41 *two networks.* See v. 17.

7:42 *four hundred pomegranates.* See vv. 18,20.

7:43 *ten stands with the ten basins.* See vv. 27–37.

7:44 *the one sea and the twelve oxen.* See vv. 23–26.

7:45 *pails and the shovels and the bowls.* See v. 40.

7:46 *Succoth.* Located on the east side of the Jordan (Gen 33:17; Josh 13:27; Judg 8:4–5) just north of the Jabbok River. Excavations in this area have confirmed that Succoth was a center of metallurgy during the period of the monarchy. *Zarethan.* Located near Adam (see Josh 3:16) and Abel-meholah (4:12).

7:48 *golden altar.* See 6:22. *golden table.* The bread of the Presence was placed on this table (see Ex 25:23–30; 1 Chr 9:32; 2 Chr 13:11; 29:18). Ten such golden tables are mentioned in 1 Chr 28:16 and 2 Chr 4:8,19, five on the right side and five on the left of the temple.

49 and the lampstands, five on the right side and five on the left, in front of the inner sanctuary, of pure gold; and [a]the flowers and the lamps and the tongs, of gold;

50 and the cups and the snuffers and the bowls and the spoons and the [a]firepans, of pure gold; and the hinges both for the doors of the inner house, the most holy place, *and* for the doors of the house, *that is,* of the nave, of gold.

51 [a]Thus all the work that King Solomon performed *in* the house of the LORD was finished. And [b]Solomon brought in the things dedicated by his father David, the silver and the gold and the utensils, *and* he put them in the treasuries of the house of the LORD.

The Ark Brought into the Temple

8 [a]Then Solomon assembled the elders of Israel and all [b]the heads of the tribes, the leaders of the fathers' *households* of the sons of Israel, to King Solomon in Jerusalem, [c]to bring up the ark of the covenant of the LORD from [d]the city of David, which is Zion.

2 All the men of Israel assembled themselves to King Solomon at [a]the feast, in the month Ethanim, which is the seventh month.

3 Then all the elders of Israel came, and [a]the priests took up the ark.

4 They brought up the ark of the LORD and [a]the tent of meeting and all the holy utensils, which were in the tent, and the priests and the Levites brought them up.

5 And King Solomon and all the congregation of Israel, who were assembled to him, [a]were with him before the ark, sacrificing [1]so many sheep and oxen they could not be counted or numbered.

6 Then [a]the priests brought the ark of the covenant of the LORD [b]to its place, into the inner sanctuary of the house, to the most holy place, [c]under the wings of the cherubim.

7 For the cherubim spread *their* wings over the place of the ark, and the cherubim made a covering over the ark and its poles from above.

8 But [a]the poles were so long that the ends of the poles could be seen from the holy place before the inner sanctuary, but they could not be seen outside; they are there to this day.

9 [a]There was nothing in the ark except the two tablets of stone which Moses put there at Horeb, where [b]the LORD made a covenant with the sons of Israel, when they came out of the land of Egypt.

10 It happened that when the priests came from the holy place, [a]the cloud filled the house of the LORD,

11 so that the priests could not stand to minister because of the cloud, for the glory of the LORD filled the house of the LORD.

Solomon Addresses the People

12 [a]Then Solomon said,

"The LORD has said that [b]He would
dwell in the thick cloud.

13 "[a]I have surely built You a lofty house,
[b]A place for Your dwelling forever."

14 Then the king [1]faced about and [a]blessed all the assembly of Israel, while all the assembly of Israel was standing.

15 He said, "[a]Blessed be the LORD, the God of Israel, [b]who spoke with His mouth to my father David and has fulfilled *it* with His hand, saying,

16 '[a]Since the day that I brought My people Israel from Egypt, I did not choose a city out of all the tribes of Israel *in which* to build a house that [b]My name might be there, but [c]I chose David to be over My people Israel.'

17 "[a]Now it was [1]in the heart of my father David to build a house for the name of the LORD, the God of Israel.

18 "But the LORD said to my father David, 'Because it was [1]in your heart to build a

49 [a]Ex 25:31-38 **50** [a]Ex 27:3; 2 Kin 25:15 **51** [a]2 Chr 5:1 [b]2 Sam 8:11; 1 Chr 18:11; 2 Chr 5:1 **8:1** [a]2 Chr 5:2-10 [b]Num 1:4; 7:2 [c]2 Sam 6:12-17; 1 Chr 15:25-29 [d]2 Sam 5:7 **2** [a]Lev 23:34; 1 Kin 8:65; 2 Chr 7:8-10 **3** [a]Num 7:9; Deut 31:9; Josh 3:3, 6 **4** [a]1 Kin 3:4; 2 Chr 1:3 **5** [1]Lit *sheep and oxen...numbered for multitude* [a]2 Sam 6:13; 2 Chr 1:6 **6** [a]1 Kin 8:3 [b]1 Kin 6:19 [c]1 Kin 6:27

8 [a]Ex 25:13-15; 37:4, 5 **9** [a]Ex 25:16, 21; Deut 10:2-5; Heb 9:4 [b]Ex 24:7, 8; 40:20; Deut 4:13 **10** [a]Ex 40:34, 35; 2 Chr 7:1, 2 **12** [a]2 Chr 6:1 [b]Lev 16:2; Ps 18:11; 97:2 **13** [a]2 Sam 7:13 [b]Ex 15:17; Ps 132:14 **14** [1]Lit *turned his face about* [a]2 Sam 6:18; 1 Kin 8:55 **15** [a]1 Chr 29:10, 20; Neh 9:5; Luke 1:68 [b]2 Sam 7:12, 13; 1 Chr 22:10 **16** [a]2 Sam 7:4, 5; 1 Chr 17:3-10; 2 Chr 6:5 [b]Deut 12:5, 11 [c]1 Sam 16:1; 2 Sam 7:8 **17** [1]Lit *with* [a]2 Sam 7:2, 3; 1 Chr 17:1, 2

7:49 *lampstands . . . of pure gold.* Only one lampstand with seven arms had stood in the tabernacle, opposite the table for the bread of the Presence (Ex 25:31–40; 26:35). The ten lampstands in the temple, five on the right side and five on the left, created a lane of light in the holy place. *flowers of . . . gold.* See Ex 25:33. *lamps.* See Ex 25:37. *tongs.* See 2 Chr 4:21; Isa 6:6.
7:50 *firepans.* See 2 Kin 25:15; 2 Chr 4:22; Jer 52:18–19.
7:51 *things dedicated by his father David.* Valuable objects of silver and gold, either taken as booty in war or received as tribute from kings seeking David's favor (see 2 Sam 8:9–12; 1 Chr 18:7–11; 2 Chr 5:1). *treasuries of the house of the LORD.* See 15:18; 2 Kin 12:18; 1 Chr 9:26; 26:20–26; 28:12.
8:1 *bring up the ark of the covenant.* David had previously brought the ark from the house of Obed-edom to Jerusalem (see 2Sam 6). *the city of David, which is Zion.* See note on 2Sam 5:7.
8:2 *feast.* It is probable that Solomon waited 11 months (see 6:38) to dedicate the temple during the Feast of Booths, which was observed in the seventh month of the year (Lev 23:34; Deut 16:13–15). *seventh month.* Presumably in the 12th year of Solomon's reign.
8:4 *tent of meeting.* The tabernacle, which had been preserved at Gibeon (see notes on 3:4; 1 Sam 7:1; see also 2 Chr 5:4–5).
8:6 *under the wings of the cherubim.* See 6:23–28.
8:8 *the ends . . . could be seen.* The carrying poles were always to remain in the gold rings of the ark (Ex 25:15). *they are there to this day.* These words must be those of the original author of this description of the dedication of the temple rather than those of the final compiler of the books of Kings (see Introduction: Author, Sources and Date; see also 2 Chr 5:9).
8:9 *two tablets of stone.* See Ex 25:16; 40:20. *the LORD made a covenant.* See Ex 24.
8:10 *the cloud filled the house of the LORD.* Just as a visible manifestation of the presence of the Lord had descended on the tabernacle at Sinai, so now the Lord came to take up His abode in the temple (see Ex 40:33–35; Ezek 10:3–5,18–19; 43:4–5).
8:12 *He would dwell in the thick cloud.* See Ex 19:9; 24:15,18; 33:9–10; 34:5; Lev 16:2; Deut 4:11; 5:22; Ps 18:10–11.
8:15 *fulfilled it.* See 2 Sam 7:5–16.
8:16 *My name.* Equivalent to the Lord Himself (see note on 5:5).

house for My name, you did well that it was
[1]in your heart.
19 '[a]Nevertheless you shall not build the
house, but your son who [1]will be born to
you, he will build the house for My name.'
20 "Now the LORD has fulfilled His word
which He spoke; for [a]I have risen in place of
my father David and sit on the throne of Israel, as the LORD [1]promised, and have built the
house for the name of the LORD, the God of
Israel.
21 "There I have set a place for the ark, [a]in
which is the covenant of the LORD, which He
made with our fathers when He brought
them from the land of Egypt."

The Prayer of Dedication

22 Then [a]Solomon stood before the altar
of the LORD in the presence of all the assembly of Israel and [b]spread out his hands
toward heaven.
23 He said, "O LORD, the God of Israel,
[a]there is no God like You in heaven above or
on earth beneath, [b]keeping covenant and
showing lovingkindness to Your servants
who walk before You with all their heart,
24 who have kept with Your servant, my
father David, that which You have [1]promised
him; indeed, You have spoken with Your
mouth and have fulfilled it with Your hand
as it is this day.
25 "Now therefore, O LORD, the God of Israel, keep with Your servant David my father
that which You have [1]promised him, saying,
'[2][a]You shall not lack a man to sit on the
throne of Israel, if only your sons take heed
to their way to walk before Me as you have
walked.'
26 "Now therefore, O God of Israel, let Your
word, I pray, be confirmed [a]which You have
spoken to Your servant, my father David.
27 "But will God indeed dwell on the earth?
Behold, [a]heaven and the [1]highest heaven
cannot contain You, how much less this
house which I have built!
28 "Yet have regard to the [a]prayer of Your
servant and to his supplication, O LORD my
God, to listen to the cry and to the prayer
which Your servant prays before You today;
29 [a]that Your eyes may be open toward
this house night and day, toward [b]the place
of which You have said, 'My name shall be
there,' to listen to the prayer which Your servant shall pray toward this place.
30 "[a]Listen to the supplication of Your servant and of Your people Israel, [b]when they
pray toward this place; hear in heaven Your
dwelling place; hear and [c]forgive.
31 "[a]If a man sins against his neighbor and
is made to take an oath, and he comes *and*
takes an oath before Your altar in this house,
32 then hear in heaven and act and judge
Your servants, [a]condemning the wicked by
bringing his way on his own head and justifying the righteous by giving him according
to his righteousness.
33 "[a]When Your people Israel are [1]defeated
before an enemy, because they have sinned
against You, [b]if they turn to You again and
confess Your name and pray and make supplication to You in this house,
34 then hear in heaven, and forgive the
sin of Your people Israel, and bring them
back to the land which You gave to their
fathers.
35 "[a]When the heavens are shut up and
there is no rain, because they have sinned
against You, and they pray toward this place
and confess Your name and turn from their
sin when You afflict them,
36 then hear in heaven and forgive the sin
of Your servants and of Your people Israel,
[a]indeed, teach them the good way in which
they should walk. And [b]send rain on Your

18 [1]Lit *with*
19 [1]Lit *will come forth from your loins* [a]2 Sam 7:5, 12, 13; 1 Kin 5:3, 5; 1 Chr 17:11, 12; 22:8-10
20 [1]Lit *spoke* [a]1 Chr 28:5, 6
21 [a]Deut 31:26; 1 Kin 8:9
22 [a]1 Kin 8:54; 2 Chr 6:12 [b]Ex 9:33; Ezra 9:5
23 [a]1 Sam 2:2; 2 Sam 7:22 [b]Deut 7:9; Neh 1:5; 9:32; Dan 9:4
24 [1]Lit *spoken to*
25 [1]Lit *spoken to* [2]Lit *There shall not be cut off to you a man from before Me* [a]1 Kin 2:4
26 [a]2 Sam 7:25
27 [1]Lit *heaven of heavens* [a]2 Chr 2:6; Ps 139:7-16; Is 66:1; Jer 23:24; Acts 7:49
28 [a]Phil 4:6
29 [a]2 Chr 7:15; Neh 1:6 [b]Deut 12:11
30 [a]Neh 1:6 [b]Dan 6:10 [c]Ex 34:6, 7; Ps 85:2; Dan 9:9; 1 John 1:9
31 [a]Ex 22:8-11
32 [a]Deut 25:1
33 [1]Lit *smitten* [a]Lev 26:17, 25; Deut 28:25, 48 [b]Lev 26:40-42
35 [a]Lev 26:19; Deut 11:16, 17; 2 Sam 24:10-13
36 [a]1 Sam 12:23; Ps 5:8; 25:4, 5; 27:11; 86:11; 119:133; Jer 6:16 [b]1 Kin 18:1, 41-45; Jer 14:22

8:23 *no God like You.* No other god has acted in history as has the God of Israel, performing great miracles and directing the course of events so that His long-range covenant promises are fulfilled (see Ex 15:11; Deut 4:39; 7:9; Ps 86:8–10).
8:24 *that which You have promised.* See v. 15; 2 Sam 7:5–16.
8:25 *if only your sons . . . walk before Me.* See 9:4–9; 2 Chr 7:17–22; see also note on 1 Kin 2:4.
8:27 *how much less this house which I have built!* With the construction of the temple and the appearance of a visible manifestation of the presence of God within its courts, the erroneous notion that God was irreversibly and exclusively bound to the temple in a way that guaranteed His assistance to Israel no matter how the people lived could very easily arise (see Jer 7:4–14; Mic 3:11). Solomon confessed that even though God had chosen to dwell among His people in a special and localized way, He far transcended containment by anything in all creation.
8:29 *My name.* I the Lord (see note on 5:5).
8:30 *pray toward this place.* When an Israelite was unable to pray in the temple itself, he was to direct his prayers toward the place where God had pledged to be present among His people (see Dan 6:10). *heaven Your dwelling place.* See note on v. 27.
8:31 *made to take an oath.* In cases such as default in pledges (Ex 22:10–12) or alleged adultery (Num 5:11–31), when there was insufficient evidence to establish the legitimacy of the charge, the supposed offender was required to take an oath of innocence at the sanctuary. Such an oath, with its attendant blessings and curses, was considered a divinely given means of determining innocence or guilt since the consequences of the oath became apparent in the life of the individual either by his experiencing the blessing or the curse or by direct divine revelation through the Urim and Thummim (see Ex 28:29–30; Lev 8:8; Num 27:21).
8:32 *hear in heaven.* It is clear that Solomon viewed the oath as an appeal to God to act and not as an automatic power that worked in a magical way.
8:33 *defeated before an enemy, because they have sinned against You.* Defeat by enemies was listed in Deut 28:25 as one of the curses that would come on Israel if she disobeyed the covenant. Solomon's prayer reflects an awareness of the covenant obligations the Lord had placed on His people and a knowledge of the consequences that disobedience would entail.
8:34 *bring them back to the land.* A reference to prisoners taken in battle.
8:35 *no rain.* Drought was another of the covenant curses listed in Deut 28:22–24.
8:36 *good way . . . they should walk.* In accordance with covenant obligations (see Deut 6:18; 12:25; 13:18; 1 Sam 12:23).

land, which You have given Your people for
an inheritance.

37 "[a]If there is famine in the land, if there
is pestilence, if there is blight *or* mildew,
locust *or* grasshopper, if their enemy
besieges them in the land of their [1]cities,
whatever plague, whatever sickness *there is,*

38 whatever prayer or supplication is
made by any man *or* by all Your people Israel, [1]each knowing the [2]affliction of his own
heart, and spreading his [3]hands toward this
house;

39 then hear in heaven Your dwelling
place, and forgive and act and render to each
according to all his ways, [a]whose heart You
know, for [b]You alone know the hearts of all
the sons of men,

40 that they may [1]fear You all the days
that they live [2]in the land which You have
given to our fathers.

41 "Also concerning the foreigner who is
not of Your people Israel, when he comes
from a far country for Your name's sake

42 (for they will hear of Your great name
[a]and Your mighty hand, and of Your outstretched arm); when he comes and prays
toward this house,

43 hear in heaven Your dwelling place,
and do according to all for which the foreigner calls to You, in order [a]that all the peoples of the earth may know Your name, to
[1]fear You, as *do* Your people Israel, and that
they may know that [2]this house which I have
built is called by Your name.

44 "When Your people go out to battle
against [1]their enemy, by whatever way You
shall send them, and [a]they pray to the LORD
[2]toward the city which You have chosen and
the house which I have built for Your name,

45 then hear in heaven their prayer and
their supplication, and maintain their [1]cause.

46 "When they sin against You (for [a]there
is no man who does not sin) and You are
angry with them and deliver them to an enemy, so that [1]they take them away captive [b]to
the land of the enemy, far off or near;

47 [a]if they [1]take thought in the land where
they have been taken captive, and repent
and make supplication to You in the land of
those who have taken them captive, saying,
'[b]We have sinned and have committed iniquity, we have acted wickedly';

48 [a]if they return to You with all their
heart and with all their soul in the land of
their enemies who have taken them captive,
and [b]pray to You toward their land which
You have given to their fathers, the city
which You have chosen, and the house
which I have built for Your name;

49 then hear their prayer and their supplication in heaven Your dwelling place, and
maintain their [1]cause,

50 and forgive Your people who have
sinned against You and all their transgressions which they have transgressed against
You, and [a]make them *objects of* compassion
before those who have taken them captive,
that they may have compassion on them

51 ([a]for they are Your people and Your
inheritance which You have brought forth
from Egypt, [b]from the midst of the iron furnace),

52 [a]that Your eyes may be open to the
supplication of Your servant and to the supplication of Your people Israel, to listen to
them whenever they call to You.

53 "For You have separated them from all
the peoples of the earth as Your inheritance,
[a]as You spoke through Moses Your servant,
when You brought our fathers forth from
Egypt, O Lord [1]GOD."

Solomon's Benediction

54 [a]When Solomon had finished praying
this entire prayer and supplication to the
LORD, [b]he arose from before the altar of the

37 [1]Lit *gates* [a]Lev 26:16, 25, 26; Deut 28:21-23, 38-42
38 [1]Lit *who shall know each* [2]Lit *plague* [3]Lit *palms*
39 [a]1 Sam 2:3; 16:7 [b]1 Chr 28:9; Ps 11:4; Jer 17:10; John 2:24, 25; Acts 1:24
40 [1]Or *revere* [2]Lit *on the face of the land*
42 [a]Ex 13:3; Deut 3:24
43 [1]Or *reverence* [2]Lit *Your name is called upon this house which I have built* [a]Josh 4:23, 24; 1 Sam 17:46; Ps 67:2
44 [1]Lit *his* [2]Lit in *the way of* [a]2 Chr 14:11
45 [1]Lit *right* or *justice*
46 [a]Ps 130:3, 4; 143:2; Prov 20:9; Eccl 7:20; Rom 3:23; 1 John 1:8-10
46 [1]Lit *their captors take them captive* [b]Lev 26:34-39; 2 Kin 17:6, 18; 25:21
47 [1]Lit *return to their heart* [a]Lev 26:40-42; Neh 9:2 [b]Ezra 9:6, 7; Neh 1:6; Ps 106:6; Dan 9:5
48 [a]Deut 4:29; 1 Sam 7:3, 4; Neh 1:9 [b]Dan 6:10; Jon 2:4
49 [1]Lit *judgment*
50 [a]2 Chr 30:9; Ps 106:46; Acts 7:10
51 [a]Ex 32:11, 12; Deut 9:26-29 [b]Deut 4:20; Jer 11:4
52 [a]1 Kin 8:29
53 [1]Heb *YHWH,* usually rendered *LORD* [a]Ex 19:5, 6; Deut 9:26-29
54 [a]2 Chr 7:1 [b]2 Chr 6:13

8:37 *famine.* See Deut 32:24. *pestilence.* See Deut 28:21–22; 32:24. *locust or grasshopper.* See Deut 28:38,42. *their enemy besieges them in the land of their cities.* See Deut 28:52. *plague.* See Deut 28:61; 31:29; 32:23–25. *sickness.* See Deut 28:22.

8:38 *knowing the affliction of his own heart.* Conscious of one's guilt before God, with an attitude of repentance and the desire for God's forgiveness and grace (see 2 Chr 6:29; Ps 38:17–18; Jer 17:9).

8:39 *render to each according to all his ways.* Not to be viewed as a request for retribution for the wrong committed (forgiveness and retribution are mutually exclusive), but as a desire for whatever discipline God in His wisdom may use to correct His people and to instruct them in the way of the covenant (see v. 40; Prov 3:11; Heb 12:5–15).

8:40 *fear You.* Honor and obediently serve You (see Deut 5:29; 6:1–2; 8:6; 31:13; 2 Chr 6:31; Ps 130:4).

8:41 *foreigner who is not of Your people Israel.* One who comes from a foreign land to pray to Israel's God at the temple, as distinguished from a resident alien.

8:42 *they will hear.* See 9:9 (foreign nations generally); 10:1 (queen of Sheba); Josh 2:9–11 (Rahab); 1 Sam 4:6–8 (Philistines). *Your great name and Your mighty hand, and of Your outstretched arm.* God's great power, demonstrated by His interventions in the history of His people (see Deut 4:34; 5:15; 7:19; 11:2; 26:8).

8:44 *go out to battle . . . whatever way You shall send them.* Military initiatives undertaken with divine sanction (see, e.g., Lev 26:7; Deut 20; 21:10; 1 Sam 15:3; 23:2,4; 30:8; 2 Sam 5:19,24). *toward the city which You have chosen.* See note on v. 30.

8:46 *an enemy, so that they take them away captive.* On the basis of Lev 26:33–45; Deut 28:64–68; 30:1–5 Solomon knew that stubborn disobedience would lead to exile from the promised land.

8:51 *iron furnace.* See Deut 4:20 and note.

8:53 *You have separated them . . . as Your inheritance.* Solomon began his prayer with an appeal to the Davidic covenant (vv. 23–30), and he closes with an appeal to the Sinaitic covenant (see Ex 19:5; Lev 20:24,26; Deut 7:6; 32:9).

8:54 *kneeling on his knees.* Cf. v. 22; 2 Sam 7:18; 2 Chr 6:13; Luke 22:41; Eph 3:14.

LORD, from kneeling on his knees with his
[1]hands spread toward heaven.
55 And he stood and [a]blessed all the
assembly of Israel with a loud voice, saying:
56 "Blessed be the LORD, who has given
rest to His people Israel, [a]according to all
that He [1]promised; [b]not one word has [2]failed
of all His good [3]promise, which He [1]prom-
ised through Moses His servant.
57 "May the LORD our God be with us, as
He was with our fathers; [a]may He not leave
us or forsake us,
58 that [a]He may incline our hearts to Himself, to walk in all His ways and to keep His
commandments and His statutes and His ordinances, which He commanded our fathers.
59 "And may these words of mine, with
which I have made supplication before the
LORD, be near to the LORD our God day and
night, that He may maintain the [1]cause of
His servant and the [1]cause of His people Israel, [2]as each day requires,
60 so [a]that all the peoples of the earth
may know that [b]the LORD is God; there is no
one else.
61 "[a]Let your heart therefore be [1]wholly
devoted to the LORD our God, to walk in His
statutes and to keep His commandments, as
at this day."

Dedicatory Sacrifices

62 [a]Now the king and all Israel with him
[b]offered sacrifice before the LORD.
63 Solomon offered for the sacrifice of
peace offerings, which he offered to the
LORD, 22,000 oxen and 120,000 sheep. [a]So
the king and all the sons of Israel dedicated
the house of the LORD.
64 On the same day the king consecrated
the middle of the court that *was* before the
house of the LORD, because there he [1]offered
the burnt offering and the grain offering and

54 [1]Lit *palms* **55** [a]Num 6:23-26; 2 Sam 6:18; 1 Kin 8:14 **56** [1]Lit *spoke* [2]Lit *fallen* [3]Lit *word* [a]Deut 12:10 [b]Josh 21:45; 23:14, 15 **57** [a]Deut 31:6, 17; Josh 1:5; 1 Sam 12:22; Rom 8:31; Heb 13:5 **58** [a]Ps 119:36; Jer 31:33 **59** [1]Lit *judgment* [2]Lit *the thing of a day in its day* **60** [a]Josh 4:24; 1 Sam 17:46; 1 Kin 8:43; 2 Kin 19:19 [b]Deut 4:35; 1 Kin 18:39; Jer 10:10-12 **61** [1]Lit *complete with* [a]Deut 18:13; 1 Kin 11:4; 2 Kin 20:3 **62** [a]2 Chr 7:4-10 [b]2 Sam 6:17-19; Ezra 6:16, 17 **63** [a]Ezra 6:15-18; Neh 12:27 **64** [1]Lit *made*

64 [a]2 Chr 4:1 **65** [a]Lev 23:34-42; 1 Kin 8:2 [b]Num 34:8; Josh 13:5; Judg 3:3; 2 Kin 14:25 [c]Gen 15:18; Ex 23:31; Num 34:5; Josh 13:3 **66** [1]Lit *done* **9:1** [1]Lit *Solomon's desire which he was pleased to do* [a]2 Chr 7:11 [b]1 Kin 7:1, 2 [c]2 Chr 8:6 **2** [a]1 Kin 3:5; 11:9; 2 Chr 1:7 **3** [a]2 Kin 20:5; Ps 10:17; 34:17 [b]1 Kin 8:29 [c]Deut 11:12; 2 Chr 6:40

the fat of the peace offerings; for [a]the bronze
altar that *was* before the LORD *was* too small
to hold the burnt offering and the grain offering and the fat of the peace offerings.
65 So [a]Solomon observed the feast at that
time, and all Israel with him, a great assembly [b]from the entrance of Hamath [c]to the
brook of Egypt, before the LORD our God, for
seven days and seven *more* days, *even* fourteen days.
66 On the eighth day he sent the people
away and they blessed the king. Then they
went to their tents joyful and glad of heart for
all the goodness that the LORD had [1]shown to
David His servant and to Israel His people.

God's Promise and Warning

9 [a]Now it came about when Solomon had
finished building the house of the LORD,
and [b]the king's house, and [c]all [1]that Solomon desired to do,
2 that [a]the LORD appeared to Solomon a
second time, as He had appeared to him at
Gibeon.
3 The LORD said to him, "[a]I have heard
your prayer and your supplication, which
you have made before Me; I have consecrated this house which you have built [b]by putting My name there forever, and [c]My eyes
and My heart will be there perpetually.
4 "As for you, [a]if you will walk before Me
as your father David walked, in integrity of
heart and uprightness, doing according to all
that I have commanded you *and* will keep
My statutes and My ordinances,
5 then [a]I will establish the throne of your
kingdom over Israel forever, just as I [1]prom-
ised to your father David, saying, '[2]You shall
not lack a man on the throne of Israel.'

4 [a]1 Kin 3:6, 14; 11:4, 6, 8; 2 Kin 20:3; Ps 128:1 **5** [1]Lit *spoke* [2]Lit *There shall not be cut off to you a man* [a]2 Sam 7:12, 16; 1 Kin 2:4; 6:12; 1 Chr 22:10

8:56 *Blessed be the LORD.* Solomon understood this historic day to be a testimony to God's covenant faithfulness. *rest to His people.* After the conquest of Canaan under the leadership of Joshua, the Lord gave the Israelites a period of rest from their enemies (Josh 11:23; 21:44; 22:4), even though there remained much land to be possessed (Josh 13:1; Judg 1). It was only with David's victories that the rest was made durable and complete (see 2 Sam 7:1; see also note on 1 Kin 5:4).

8:58 *incline our hearts to Himself.* Solomon asks for a divine work of grace within his people that will enable them to be faithful to the covenant (see Deut 30:6; Ps 51:10; Phil 2:13).

8:59 *His servant.* The king, who, as the Lord's anointed, serves as the earthly representative of God's rule over His people (see notes on Ps 2:2,7).

8:60 *so that all . . . may know.* See note on Ps 46:10.

8:63 *peace offerings.* Involved a communion meal (see note on 1 Sam 11:15). *22,000 oxen and 120,000 sheep.* Although these numbers may seem large, there were vast numbers of people who participated in the dedication ceremony, which lasted 14 days (see vv. 1–2; see also v. 65).

8:65 *entrance of Hamath.* See note on Ezek 47:15. *brook of Egypt.* Probably Wadi el-Arish (see note on Gen 15:18). People came to Jerusalem for the dedication of the temple from nearly the entire area of Solomon's dominion (see note on 4:21). *seven days and seven more days, even fourteen days.* It appears that the seven-day celebration for the dedication of the temple was followed by the seven-day Feast of Booths (see note on v. 2), which was observed from the 15th to the 21st of the seventh month. According to Chronicles, this was followed by a final assembly on the next day, in accordance with Lev 23:33–36; then on the 23rd of the month the people were sent to their homes (see 2 Chr 7:8–10).

9:1 *when Solomon had finished.* At the earliest this would be in the 24th year (4 + 7 + 13 = 24) of Solomon's reign—946 B.C. (see 6:1,37–38; 7:1; 9:10).

9:2 *He had appeared to him at Gibeon.* See 3:4–15.

9:3 *putting My name there forever.* See 8:10–13. *My eyes and My heart will be there perpetually.* See 8:29.

9:4–5 *if you will walk before Me . . . in integrity of heart . . . I will establish the throne of your kingdom over Israel forever.* See 8:25 and note on 2:4. The Lord reemphasizes to Solomon the importance of obedience to the covenant in order to experience its blessings rather than its curses. This was particularly necessary as Solomon's kingdom grew in influence and wealth, with all the potential for covenant-breaking that prosperity brought (see Deut 8:12–14,17; 31:20; 32:15).

6 "[a]But if you or your sons indeed turn
away from following Me, and do not keep
My commandments and My statutes which I
have set before you, and go and serve other
gods and worship them,
7 [a]then I will cut off Israel from the land
which I have given them, and [b]the house
which I have consecrated for My name, I will
[1]cast out of My sight. So [c]Israel will become
a proverb and a byword among all peoples.
8 "And this house will become [1a]a heap of
ruins; everyone who passes by will be astonished and hiss and say, '[b]Why has the LORD
done thus to this land and to this house?'
9 "And they will say, '[a]Because they forsook the LORD their God, who brought their
fathers out of the land of Egypt, and adopted
other gods and worshiped them and served
them, therefore the LORD has brought all this
adversity on them.' "

Cities Given to Hiram

10 [a]It came about [b]at the end of twenty
years in which Solomon had built the two
houses, the house of the LORD and the king's
house
11 (Hiram king of Tyre had supplied
Solomon with cedar and cypress timber and
gold according to all his desire), then King
Solomon gave Hiram twenty cities in the
land of Galilee.
12 So Hiram came out from Tyre to see the
cities which Solomon had given him, and
they [1]did not please him.
13 He said, "What are these cities which
you have given me, my brother?" So [1]they
were called the land of [2a]Cabul to this day.
14 [a]And Hiram sent to the king 120 talents
of gold.

15 Now this is the account of the forced
labor which King Solomon [a]levied to build
the house of the LORD, his own house, the
[1b]Millo, the wall of Jerusalem, [c]Hazor,
[d]Megiddo, and [e]Gezer.
16 *For* Pharaoh king of Egypt had gone up
and captured Gezer and burned it with fire,
and killed the [a]Canaanites who lived in the
city, and had [b]given it *as* a dowry to his
daughter, Solomon's wife.
17 So Solomon rebuilt Gezer and the lower [a]Beth-horon
18 and [a]Baalath and Tamar in the wilderness, in the land *of Judah*,
19 and all the storage cities which Solomon
had, even [a]the cities for [1]his chariots and the
cities for [1b]his horsemen, and [2c]all that it
pleased Solomon to build in Jerusalem, in
Lebanon, and in all the land [3]under his rule.
20 *As for* all the people who were left of
the Amorites, the Hittites, the Perizzites, the
Hivites and the Jebusites, who were not of
the sons of Israel,
21 [a]their descendants who were left after
them in the land [b]whom the sons of Israel
were unable to destroy utterly, [c]from them
Solomon levied [d]forced laborers, even to this
day.
22 But Solomon [a]did not make slaves of
the sons of Israel; for they were men of war,
his servants, his princes, his captains, his
chariot commanders, and his horsemen.
23 These *were* the [1a]chief officers who *were*
over Solomon's work, five hundred and fifty,
[b]who ruled over the people doing the work.
24 As soon as [a]Pharaoh's daughter came
up from the city of David to her house which

23 [1]Or *officers of the deputies* [a]2 Chr 8:10 [b]1 Kin 5:16
24 [a]1 Kin 3:1; 7:8

6 [a]2 Sam 7:14-16; 1 Chr 28:9; Ps 89:30ff
7 [1]Lit *send* [a]Lev 18:24-29; Deut 4:26; 2 Kin 17:23 [b]Jer 7:4-14 [c]Deut 28:37; Ps 44:14; Jer 24:9
8 [1]Heb *high* [a]2 Kin 25:9; 2 Chr 36:19 [b]Deut 29:24-26; 2 Chr 7:21; Jer 22:8, 9, 28
9 [a]Deut 29:25-28; Jer 2:10-13
10 [a]2 Chr 8:1 [b]1 Kin 6:37, 38; 7:1; 9:1
12 [1]Lit *were not right in his sight*
13 [1]Lit *he called them* [2]I.e. as good as nothing [a]Josh 19:27
14 [a]1 Kin 9:11
15 [1]I.e. citadel [a]1 Kin 5:13 [b]2 Sam 5:9; 1 Kin 9:24 [c]Josh 11:1; 19:36 [d]Josh 17:11 [e]Judg 1:29
16 [a]Josh 16:10 [b]1 Kin 3:1; 7:8
17 [a]Josh 10:10; 16:3; 21:22; 2 Chr 8:5
18 [a]Josh 19:44
19 [1]Lit *the* [2]Lit *the desire of Solomon which he desired to build in Jerusalem* [3]Lit *of* [a]1 Kin 10:26; 2 Chr 1:14 [b]1 Kin 4:26 [c]1 Kin 9:1
21 [a]Judg 1:21-29; 3:1 [b]Josh 15:63; 17:12, 13 [c]Judg 1:28, 35 [d]Gen 9:25, 26; Ezra 2:55, 58
22 [a]Lev 25:39

9:6 *serve other gods and worship them.* See 11:4–8.
9:7 *a proverb and a byword among all peoples.* See the covenant curse in Deut 28:37.
9:9 *therefore the LORD has brought all this adversity on them.* See Deut 29:22–28; Jer 22:8–30.
9:10–28 See map No. 5 at the end of the study Bible.
9:11 *Solomon gave Hiram twenty cities in the land of Galilee.* Comparison of vv. 10–14 with 5:1–12 suggests that during Solomon's 20 years of building activity he became more indebted to Hiram than anticipated in their original agreement (see note on 5:9), which had provided for payment for labor (5:6) and wood (5:10–11). From vv. 11,14 it is evident that in addition to wood and labor Solomon had also acquired great quantities of gold from Hiram. It appears that Solomon gave Hiram the 20 towns in the Phoenician-Galilee border area as a surety for repayment of the gold. 2 Chr 8:1–2 indicates that at some later date when Solomon's gold reserves were increased, perhaps after the return of the expedition to Ophir (1 Kin 9:26–28; 10:11) or the visit of the queen of Sheba (10:1–13), he settled his debt with Hiram and recovered the 20 towns held as collateral.
9:15 *forced labor.* Non-Israelite slave labor of a permanent nature (in contrast to the temporary conscription of Israelite workmen described in 5:13–16). *the Millo.* Probably for Solomon's expansion of Jerusalem on the ridge north from David's city (see note on 2 Sam 5:9). *Hazor.* Solomon's building activity at Hazor, Megiddo and Gezer was intended to strengthen the fortifications of these ancient, strategically located towns (Solomonic gates, probably built by the same masons, have been found at all three sites). Hazor was the most important fortress in the northern Galilee area, controlling the trade route running from the Euphrates River to Egypt. *Megiddo.* Another fortress along the great north-south trade route; it commanded the pass through the Carmel range from the plain of Jezreel to the coastal plain of Sharon. *Gezer.* See note on 3:1.
9:16 *killed the Canaanites . . . in the city.* Although Joshua had killed the king of Gezer at the time of the conquest (Josh 10:33; 12:12), the tribe of Ephraim had been unable to drive out its inhabitants (Josh 16:10; Judg 1:29).
9:17 *lower Beth-horon.* Located about eight miles northwest of Jerusalem at a pass giving entrance to the Judahite highlands and Jerusalem from the coastal plain.
9:18 *Baalath.* To be identified with either the Bealoth of Josh 15:24 located to the south of Hebron in the tribe of Judah or the Baalath southwest of Beth-horon in the tribe of Dan (Josh 19:44). *Tamar.* Perhaps Tadmor (see 2 Chr 8:4).
9:20 *Amorites . . . Jebusites.* See Deut 7:1; 20:17; see also notes on Gen 10:15–18; 13:7; 15:16; 23:9; Josh 5:1; Judg 3:3; 6:10; 2 Sam 21:2.
9:22 *Solomon did not make slaves of the sons of Israel.* See note on v. 15.
9:23 *five hundred and fifty, who ruled.* See note on 5:16.

Solomon had built for her, [b]then he built the
Millo.
25 Now [a]three times in a year Solomon
offered burnt offerings and peace offerings
on the altar which he built to the LORD, burning incense with them *on the altar* which
was before the LORD. So he finished the
house.
26 King Solomon also built a [a]fleet of
ships in [b]Ezion-geber, which is near Eloth on
the shore of the [1]Red Sea, in the land of
Edom.
27 [a]And Hiram sent his servants with the
fleet, sailors who knew the sea, along with
the servants of Solomon.
28 They went to [a]Ophir and took four
hundred and twenty talents of gold from
there, and brought *it* to King Solomon.

The Queen of Sheba

10 [a]Now when the [a]queen of [b]Sheba
heard about the fame of Solomon concerning the name of the LORD, she came [c]to
test him with difficult questions.
2 So she came to Jerusalem with a very
large retinue, with camels [a]carrying spices
and very much gold and precious stones.
When she came to Solomon, she spoke with
him about all that was in her heart.
3 Solomon [1]answered all her questions;
nothing was hidden from the king which he
did not [2]explain to her.
4 When the queen of Sheba perceived all
the wisdom of Solomon, the house that he
had built,
5 the food of his table, the seating of his
servants, the attendance of his waiters and
their attire, his cupbearers, and [1]his stairway
by which he went up to the house of the
LORD, there was no more spirit in her.
6 Then she said to the king, "It was a
true report which I heard in my own land
about your words and your wisdom.
7 "Nevertheless I did not believe the
[1]reports, until I came and my eyes had seen
it. And behold, the half was not told me. You
exceed *in* wisdom and prosperity the report
which I heard.
8 "How [a]blessed are your men, how
blessed are these your servants who stand
before you continually *and* hear your wisdom.
9 "[a]Blessed be the LORD your God who
delighted in you to set you on the throne of
Israel; [b]because the LORD loved Israel forever,
therefore He made you king, [c]to do justice
and righteousness."
10 [a]She gave the king a hundred and
twenty talents of gold, and a very great
amount of spices and precious stones. Never
again did such abundance of spices come in
as that which the queen of Sheba gave King
Solomon.
11 [a]Also the ships of Hiram, which
brought gold from Ophir, brought in from
Ophir a very great *number of* almug trees
and precious stones.
12 [a]The king made of the almug trees supports for the house of the LORD and for the
king's house, also lyres and harps for the
singers; such almug trees have not come in
again nor have they been seen to this day.
13 King Solomon gave to the queen of
Sheba all her desire which she requested,
besides what he gave her according to [1]his
royal bounty. Then she turned and went to
her own land [2]together with her servants.

24 [b]2 Sam 5:9; 1 Kin 9:15; 11:27; 2 Chr 32:5
25 [a]Ex 23:14-17; Deut 16:16
26 [1]Lit *Sea of Reeds* [a]1 Kin 22:48 [b]Num 33:35; Deut 2:8; 1 Kin 22:48
27 [a]1 Kin 5:6, 9; 10:11
28 [a]1 Chr 29:4; 2 Chr 8:18
10:1 [a]2 Chr 9:1; Matt 12:42; Luke 11:31 [b]Gen 10:7, 28; Ps 72:10, 15 [c]Judg 14:12-14; Ps 49:4
2 [a]1 Kin 10:10
3 [1]Lit *told her all her words* [2]Lit *tell her*
5 [1]Or *his burnt offering which he offered*
7 [1]Lit *words*
8 [a]Prov 8:34
9 [a]1 Kin 5:7 [b]1 Chr 17:22; 2 Chr 2:11 [c]2 Sam 8:15; 23:3; Ps 72:2
10 [a]1 Kin 10:2
11 [a]1 Kin 9:27, 28; Job 22:24
12 [a]2 Chr 9:11
13 [1]Lit *the hand of King Solomon* [2]Lit *she and*

9:25 *three times in a year.* On the occasion of the three important annual festivals: the Feast of Unleavened Bread, the Feast of Weeks, and the Feast of Booths (see Ex 23:14–17; 2 Chr 8:13).
9:26 *ships.* Used in a large trading business that brought great wealth to Solomon's court (see v. 28; 10:11). *Ezion-geber.* Located at the northern tip of the Gulf of Aqaba (see 22:48; Num 33:35; Deut 2:8). *Red Sea.* The Hebrew for this term, normally read as *Yam Suph* ("sea of reeds"), refers to the body of water through which the Israelites passed at the time of the exodus (see notes on Ex 13:18; 14:2). It can also be read, however, as *Yam Soph* ("sea of ⌊land's⌋ end"), a more likely reading when referring to the Red Sea, and especially (as here) to its eastern arm (the Gulf of Aqaba).
9:28 *Ophir.* A source for gold (2 Chr 8:18; Job 28:16; Ps 45:9; Is 13:12), almug trees and precious stones (10:11), and silver, ivory, apes and baboons (10:22). Its location is disputed: Southeastern Arabia, southwestern Arabia, the northeastern African coast (in the area of Somalia), India and Zimbabwe have all been suggested. If Ophir was located in Arabia, it was probably a trading center for goods from farther east as well as from east Africa. But the three-year voyages of Solomon's merchant vessels (10:22) suggest a more distant location than the Arabian coast.
10:1 *Sheba.* Archaeological evidence suggests that Sheba is to be identified with a mercantile kingdom that flourished in southwest Arabia (see notes on Gen 10:28; Joel 3:8) c. 900–450 B.C. It profited from the sea trade of India and east Africa by transporting luxury commodities north to Damascus and Gaza on caravan routes through the Arabian Desert. It is possible that Solomon's fleet of ships threatened Sheba's continued dominance of this trading business. *concerning the name of the LORD.* The queen of Sheba recognized a connection between the wisdom of Solomon and the God he served. Jesus used her example to condemn the people of His own day who had not recognized that "something greater than Solomon" was in their midst (Matt 12:42; Luke 11:31).
10:9 *Blessed be the LORD your God.* The queen of Sheba's confession is beautifully worded and reflects a profound understanding of Israel's covenant relationship with the Lord. However, it does not necessarily imply anything more than her recognition of the Lord as Israel's national God in conformity with the ideas of polytheistic paganism (see note on 5:7; see also 2 Chr 2:12; Dan 3:28–29). There is no confession that Solomon's God has become her God to the exclusion of all others.
10:10 *a hundred and twenty talents of gold.* See notes on 9:11,28.
10:11 *ships of Hiram.* See 9:26–28. Hiram had supplied the wood, the sailors and the expertise in construction that Israel lacked. *almug trees.* Perhaps a variant of "algum trees" (2 Chr 9:10–11). Its identity is unknown, though some suggest it is juniper. It was apparently available from Lebanon as well as Ophir (2 Chr 2:8).
10:13 *all her desire which she requested.* The exchange of gifts between Solomon and the queen may have signified the effecting of a trade agreement (see note on v. 1). There is no basis for

Wealth, Splendor and Wisdom

14 [a]Now the weight of gold which came in to Solomon in one year was 666 talents of gold,

15 besides *that* from the traders and the [1]wares of the merchants and all the kings of the [a]Arabs and the governors of the country.

16 [a]King Solomon made 200 large shields of beaten gold, [1]using 600 *shekels of* gold on each large shield.

17 *He made* [a]300 shields of beaten gold, [1]using three minas of gold on each shield, and [b]the king put them in the house of the forest of Lebanon.

18 Moreover, the king made a great throne of [a]ivory and overlaid it with refined gold.

19 *There were* six steps to the throne and a round top to the throne at its rear, and [1]arms [2]on each side of the seat, and two lions standing beside the [1]arms.

20 Twelve lions were standing there on the six steps on the one side and on the other; nothing like *it* was made for any other kingdom.

21 All King Solomon's drinking vessels *were* of gold, and all the vessels of the house of the forest of Lebanon *were* of pure gold. None was of silver; it was not considered [1]valuable in the days of Solomon.

22 For [a]the king had at sea the ships of Tarshish with the ships of Hiram; once every three years the ships of Tarshish came bringing gold and silver, ivory and apes and peacocks.

23 [a]So King Solomon became greater than all the kings of the earth in riches and in wisdom.

24 All the earth was seeking the presence of Solomon, [a]to hear his wisdom which God had put in his heart.

25 [a]They brought every man his gift, articles of silver and gold, garments, weapons, spices, horses, and mules, so much year by year.

26 [a]Now Solomon gathered chariots and horsemen; and he had 1,400 chariots and 12,000 horsemen, and he [1]stationed them in the [b]chariot cities and with the king in Jerusalem.

27 [a]The king made silver *as common* as stones in Jerusalem, and he made cedars as plentiful as sycamore trees that are in the [1]lowland.

28 [a]Also Solomon's import of horses was from Egypt and Kue, *and* the king's merchants procured *them* from Kue for a price.

29 A chariot [1]was imported from Egypt for 600 *shekels* of silver, and a horse for 150; and [2]by the same means they exported them [a]to all the kings of the Hittites and to the kings of the Arameans.

Solomon Turns from God

11 Now [a]King Solomon loved many foreign women along with the daughter of Pharaoh: Moabite, Ammonite, Edomite, Sidonian, and Hittite women,

2 from the nations concerning which the LORD had said to the sons of Israel, "[a]You shall not [1]associate with them, nor shall they [1]associate with you, *for* they will surely turn your heart away after their gods." Solomon held fast to these in love.

3 [a]He had seven hundred wives, princesses, and three hundred concubines, and his wives turned his heart away.

4 For when Solomon was old, his wives turned his heart away after other gods; and [a]his heart was not [1]wholly devoted to the LORD his God, as the heart of David his father *had been*.

5 For Solomon went after [a]Ashtoreth the

14 [a]2 Chr 9:13-28
15 [1]Or *traffic* [a]2 Chr 9:14
16 [1]Lit *he brought up* [a]1 Kin 14:26-28; 2 Chr 12:9, 10
17 [1]Lit *he brought up* [a]1 Kin 14:26 [b]1 Kin 7:2
18 [a]1 Kin 10:22; 2 Chr 9:17; Ps 45:8
19 [1]Lit *hands* [2]Lit *on this side and on this at the place of the seat*
21 [1]Lit *anything*
22 [a]1 Kin 9:26-28; 22:48; 2 Chr 20:36
23 [a]1 Kin 3:12, 13; 4:30
24 [a]1 Kin 3:9, 12, 28
25 [a]Ps 68:29
26 [1]So with ancient versions; Heb *led* [a]1 Kin 4:26; 2 Chr 1:14-17; 9:25 [b]1 Kin 9:19
27 [1]Heb *Shephelah* [a]Deut 17:17; 2 Chr 1:15
28 [a]Deut 17:16; 2 Chr 1:16; 9:28
29 [1]Lit *came up and went out from* [2]Lit *in like manner by their hand* [a]2 Kin 7:6, 7
11:1 [a]Deut 17:17; Neh 13:23-27
2 [1]Lit *go among* [a]Ex 23:31-33; 34:12-16; Deut 7:3
3 [a]2 Sam 5:13-16
4 [1]Lit *complete with* [a]1 Kin 9:4
5 [a]Judg 2:13; 10:6; 1 Sam 7:3, 4

---

the idea sometimes suggested that she desired offspring fathered by Solomon and left Jerusalem carrying his child.

10:15 *that from . . . the kings of the Arabs.* Tribute from Bedouin sheiks for passage of their caravans into Israelite territory. *governors of the country.* See 4:7–19.

10:16 *large shields.* Rectangular shields that afforded maximum protection (in distinction from the smaller round shields). These gold shields were probably not intended for battle but for ceremonial use, symbolizing Israel's wealth and glory. They were probably made of wood overlaid with gold. Shishak of Egypt carried them off as plunder in the fifth regnal year of Solomon's son Rehoboam (see 14:25–26).

10:22 *ships of Tarshish.* See 2 Chr 9:21. The same fleet is referred to in v. 11; 9:26–28. "Ships of Tarshish" are not necessarily ships that sail to Tarshish (see note on Jon 1:3) but can designate large trading vessels.

10:26 *chariots and horsemen.* See note on 4:26. Accumulation of chariots and horses by the king was forbidden in the Mosaic law (Deut 17:16).

10:29 *exported them.* Through his agents Solomon was the middleman in a lucrative trading business. *Hittites.* See note on Gen 10:15. *Arameans.* A people who occupied a large area north and east of the Sea of Galilee (cf. note on Aram in Gen 10:22).

11:1 *loved many foreign women.* Many of Solomon's marriages were no doubt for the purpose of sealing international relationships with various kingdoms, large and small—a common practice in the ancient Near East. But this violated not only Deut 17:17 with respect to the multiplicity of wives, but also the prohibition against taking wives from the pagan peoples among whom Israel settled (see Ex 34:16; Deut 7:1–3; Josh 23:12–13; Ezra 9:2; 10:2–3; Neh 13:23–27). *Moabite.* See note on Gen 19:36–38. *Ammonite.* See note on Gen 19:36–38; see also 14:21; Deut 23:3. *Edomite.* See notes on Gen 25:26; 36:1; Amos 1:11; 9:12; see also Deut 23:7–8. *Sidonian.* See 16:31.

11:2 *they will surely turn your heart away after their gods.* An example in Israel's earlier history is found in Num 25:1–15.

11:3 *seven hundred . . . three hundred.* Cf. Song 6:8, but see note there.

11:4 *his heart was not wholly devoted to the LORD his God.* See 8:61. The atmosphere of paganism and idolatry introduced into Solomon's court by his foreign wives gradually led Solomon into syncretistic religious practices.

11:5 *Ashtoreth.* See v. 33; 14:15; 2 Kin 23:13; see also note on Judg 2:13. *Milcom.* See 2 Kin 23:10,13. Molech and Milcom are alternate names for the same pagan deity. Worship of this god not only severely jeopardized the continued recognition of the

goddess of the Sidonians and after [1][b]Milcom
the detestable idol of the Ammonites.
6 Solomon did what was evil in the sight
of the LORD, and did not follow the LORD fully, as David his father *had done.*
7 Then Solomon built a high place for
[a]Chemosh the detestable idol of Moab, on
the mountain which is [1]east of Jerusalem,
and for [b]Molech the detestable idol of the
sons of Ammon.
8 Thus also he did for all his foreign
wives, who burned incense and sacrificed to
their gods.
9 Now [a]the LORD was angry with Solomon [b]because his heart was turned away
from the LORD, the God of Israel, [c]who had
appeared to him twice,
10 and [a]had commanded him concerning
this thing, that he should not go after other
gods; but he did not observe what the LORD
had commanded.
11 So the LORD said to Solomon, "Because
[1]you have done this, and you have not kept
My covenant and My statutes, which I have
commanded you, [a]I will surely tear the kingdom from you, and will give it to your servant.
12 "Nevertheless I will not do it in your
days for the sake of your father David, *but* I
will tear it out of the hand of your son.
13 "However, [a]I will not tear away all the
kingdom, *but* [b]I will give one tribe to your
son for the sake of My servant David and [c]for
the sake of Jerusalem which I have chosen."

God Raises Adversaries

14 Then the LORD raised up an adversary
to Solomon, Hadad the Edomite; he was of
the [1]royal line in Edom.

5 [1]In Jer 49:1, 3, *Malcam* [b]1 Kin 11:7
7 [1]Lit *before* [a]Num 21:29; Judg 11:24; 2 Kin 23:13 [b]Lev 20:2-5; 2 Kin 23:10; Acts 7:43
9 [a]Ps 90:7 [b]1 Kin 11:2, 4 [c]1 Kin 3:5; 9:2
10 [a]1 Kin 6:12; 9:6, 7
11 [1]Lit *this is with you* [a]1 Sam 2:30; 1 Kin 11:29-31; 12:15, 16, 20; 2 Kin 17:15, 21
13 [a]2 Sam 7:15; 1 Chr 17:13; Ps 89:33 [b]1 Kin 11:32, 36; 12:20 [c]1 Kin 8:29
14 [1]Lit *king's seed*
15 [a]2 Sam 8:14; 1 Chr 18:12, 13 [b]Deut 20:13
17 [1]Lit *to go into*
18 [a]Num 10:12; Deut 1:1
19 [1]Lit *in the sight of*
21 [a]1 Kin 2:10
22 [1]Lit *send me away*
23 [a]1 Kin 11:14 [b]2 Sam 8:3; 10:16
24 [a]2 Sam 10:8, 18

15 For it came about, [a]when David was in
Edom, and Joab the commander of the army
had gone up to bury the slain, and had
[b]struck down every male in Edom
16 (for Joab and all Israel stayed there six
months, until he had cut off every male in
Edom),
17 that Hadad fled [1]to Egypt, he and certain Edomites of his father's servants with
him, while Hadad *was* a young boy.
18 They arose from Midian and came to
[a]Paran; and they took men with them from
Paran and came to Egypt, to Pharaoh king of
Egypt, who gave him a house and assigned
him food and gave him land.
19 Now Hadad found great favor [1]before
Pharaoh, so that he gave him in marriage the
sister of his own wife, the sister of Tahpenes
the queen.
20 The sister of Tahpenes bore his son
Genubath, whom Tahpenes weaned in Pharaoh's house; and Genubath was in Pharaoh's
house among the sons of Pharaoh.
21 But [a]when Hadad heard in Egypt that
David slept with his fathers and that Joab the
commander of the army was dead, Hadad
said to Pharaoh, "Send me away, that I may
go to my own country."
22 Then Pharaoh said to him, "But what
have you lacked with me, that behold, you
are seeking to go to your own country?" And
he answered, "Nothing; nevertheless you
must surely [1]let me go."
23 [a]God also raised up *another* adversary
to him, Rezon the son of Eliada, who had
fled from his lord [b]Hadadezer king of Zobah.
24 He gathered men to himself and
became leader of a marauding band, [a]after
David slew them of *Zobah;* and they went to

absolute kingship of the Lord over His people, but also involved (on rare occasions) the abomination of child sacrifice (see 2 Kin 16:3; 17:17; 21:6; Lev 18:21; 20:2–5; see also note on Judg 10:6).

11:6 *as David his father had done.* Although David committed grievous sins, he was repentant, and he was never involved in idolatrous worship.

11:7 *high place.* See note on 3:2. *Chemosh.* See note on 2 Kin 3:27.

11:9 *appeared to him twice.* See 3:4–5; 9:1–9.

11:11 *not kept My covenant.* Solomon had broken the most basic demands of the covenant (see Ex 20:2–5) and thereby severely undermined the entire covenant relationship between God and His people.

11:12 *for the sake of your father David.* Because of David's unwavering loyalty to the Lord and God's covenant with him (see 2 Sam 7:11–16).

11:13 *one tribe.* Judah (see note on vv. 31–32; see also 12:20). *for the sake of Jerusalem which I have chosen.* Now that Jerusalem contained the temple built by David's son in accordance with 2 Sam 7:13, the destiny of Jerusalem and the Davidic dynasty were closely linked (see 2 Kin 19:34; 21:7–8; Ps 132). The temple represented God's royal palace, where His earthly throne (the ark) was situated and where He had pledged to be present as Israel's Great King (9:3).

11:14 *Hadad.* A familiar name among Edomite kings (see Gen 36:35,39).

11:15 *David was in Edom.* See 2 Sam 8:13–14.

11:16 *all Israel . . . every male in Edom.* All those, on both sides, who took part in the campaign.

11:17 *a young boy.* Probably in his early teens.

11:18 *Midian.* At this time Midianites inhabited a region on the eastern borders of Moab and Edom. *Paran.* A wilderness area southeast of Kadesh in the central area of the Sinai peninsula (see Num 10:12; 12:16; 13:3). *Pharaoh king of Egypt.* See note on 3:1. *gave him a house and . . . food and . . . land.* In a time of Israel's growing strength it was in Egypt's interest to befriend those who would harass Israel and keep her power in check.

11:21 *Send me away.* It appears that Hadad returned to Edom during the early days of Solomon's reign.

11:22 *what have you lacked with me . . . ?* Because Egypt had by this time established relatively good relations with Israel (see note on 3:1), the pharaoh was reluctant to see Hadad return to Edom and provoke trouble with Solomon.

11:24 *leader of a marauding band.* As David had been (1 Sam 22:1–2), and Jephthah before him (Judg 11:3). *they went to Damascus and stayed there, and reigned.* Presumably this took place in the early part of Solomon's reign (see 2 Sam 8:6 for the situation in Damascus during the time of David). It is likely that Solomon's expedition (2 Chr 8:3) against Hamath-zobah (the kingdom formerly ruled by Hadadezer, 2 Sam 8:3–6) was provoked by opposition led by Rezon. Even though Solomon was able to retain control of the territory north of Damascus to the

Damascus and stayed [1]there, and reigned in
Damascus.
25 So he was an adversary to Israel all the
days of Solomon, along with the evil that
Hadad *did;* and he abhorred Israel and
reigned over Aram.
26 Then [a]Jeroboam the son of Nebat, an
Ephraimite of Zeredah, Solomon's servant,
whose mother's name was Zeruah, a widow,
[b]also [1]rebelled against the king.
27 Now this was the reason why he
[1]rebelled against the king: [a]Solomon built
the [2]Millo, *and* closed up the breach of the
city of his father David.
28 Now the man Jeroboam was a valiant
warrior, and when [a]Solomon saw that the
young man was [1]industrious, he appointed
him over all the [2]forced labor of the house of
Joseph.
29 It came about at that time, when Jeroboam went out of Jerusalem, that [a]the
prophet Ahijah the Shilonite found him on
the road. Now [1]Ahijah had clothed himself
with a new cloak; and both of them were
alone in the field.
30 Then [a]Ahijah took hold of the new
cloak which was on him and tore it into
twelve pieces.
31 He said to Jeroboam, "Take for yourself
ten pieces; for thus says the LORD, the God of
Israel, 'Behold, [a]I will tear the kingdom out
of the hand of Solomon and give you ten
tribes
32 ([a]but he will have one tribe, for the
sake of My servant David and for the sake of
Jerusalem, [b]the city which I have chosen
from all the tribes of Israel),
33 because they have forsaken Me, and
[a]have worshiped Ashtoreth the goddess of the
Sidonians, [b]Chemosh the god of Moab, and
Milcom the god of the sons of Ammon; and
they have not walked in My ways, doing what
is right in My sight and *observing* My statutes
and My ordinances, as his father David *did.*
34 'Nevertheless I will not take the whole
kingdom out of his hand, but I will make
him [1]ruler all the days of his life, for the sake
of My servant David whom I chose, who
observed My commandments and My statutes;
35 but [a]I will take the kingdom from his
son's hand and give it to you, *even* ten tribes.
36 'But [a]to his son I will give one tribe,
[b]that My servant David may have a lamp
always before Me in Jerusalem, [a]the city
where I have chosen for Myself to put My
name.
37 'I will take you, and you shall reign over
whatever [1]you desire, and you shall be king
over Israel.
38 'Then it will be, that if you listen to all
that I command you and walk in My ways,
and do what is right in My sight by observing My statutes and My commandments, as
My servant David did, then [a]I will be with
you and [b]build you an enduring house as I
built for David, and I will give Israel to you.
39 'Thus I will afflict the [1]descendants of
David for this, but not always.' "
40 Solomon sought therefore to put Jero-

24 [1]Lit *in it*
26 [1]Lit *lifted up a hand* [a]1 Kin 11:11, 28; 12:2, 20; 2 Chr 13:6 [b]2 Sam 20:21
27 [1]Lit *lifted up a hand* [2]I.e. citadel [a]1 Kin 9:15, 24
28 [1]Lit *a doer of work* [2]Lit *burden* [a]Prov 22:29
29 [1]Lit *he* [a]1 Kin 12:15; 14:2; 2 Chr 9:29
30 [a]1 Sam 15:27, 28
31 [a]1 Kin 11:11, 12
32 [a]1 Kin 11:13; 12:21
32 [b]1 Kin 11:13; 14:21
33 [a]1 Sam 7:3; 1 Kin 11:5-8 [b]Num 21:29; Jer 48:7, 13
34 [1]Or *prince*
35 [a]1 Kin 11:12; 12:16, 17
36 [a]1 Kin 11:13 [b]1 Kin 15:4; 2 Kin 8:19; Ps 132:17
37 [1]Lit *your soul desires*
38 [a]Deut 31:8; Josh 1:5 [b]2 Sam 7:11, 27
39 [1]Lit *seed*

Euphrates (4:21,24), he was not able to drive Rezon from Damascus itself.

11:26 *rebelled against the king.* See note on v. 40.

11:27 *the Millo.* See 9:15 and note.

11:28 *all the forced labor of the house of Joseph.* See 5:13–18. Jeroboam's supervision of the conscripted laborers from the tribes of Ephraim and Manasseh made him aware of the smoldering discontent among the people over Solomon's policies (see 12:4).

11:31–32 *ten tribes . . . one tribe.* The tradition of considering the ten northern tribes as a unit distinct from the southern tribes (Judah and Simeon—Levi received no territorial inheritance; see Josh 21) goes back to the period of the judges (see Judg 5:14–16). The reason, no doubt, was the continuing presence of a non-Israelite corridor (Jerusalem, Gibeonite league, Gezer) that separated the two Israelite regions (see map No. 4 at the end of the study Bible). Political division along the same line during the early years of David's reign and the different arrangements that brought the southern and northern segments under David's rule (see 2 Sam 2:4; 5:3) reinforced this sense of division. With the conquest of Jerusalem by David (2 Sam 5:6–7) and the pharaoh's gift of Gezer to Solomon's wife (9:16–17), all Israel was for the first time territorially united. (Now that Jerusalem and Gezer were under Israelite control, the Gibeonite league, which had submitted already to Joshua—see Josh 9—could be effectively absorbed politically.) In the division here announced, the "one tribe" refers to the area dominated by Judah (but including Simeon; see Josh 19:1–9), and the "ten tribes" refers to the region that came under David's rule at the later date (Ephraim and Manasseh, Joseph's sons, being counted as two tribes; see Gen 48:5; see also note on Josh 14:4). For further refinement of the new boundaries that came about see note on 12:21.

11:33 *forsaken Me.* See vv. 5–7. *have not walked in My ways.* See vv. 1–2; 3:14.

11:34 *I will make him ruler all the days of his life.* See vv. 12–13.

11:35 *from his son's hand.* From Rehoboam (see 12:1–24).

11:36 *a lamp always before Me in Jerusalem.* Symbolizes the continuance of the Davidic dynasty in the city where God had chosen to cause His name to dwell (see v. 13 and note). In a number of passages, the burning or snuffing out of one's lamp signifies the flourishing or ceasing of one's life (Job 18:6; 21:17; Prov 13:9; 20:20; 24:20). Here (and in 15:4; 2 Kin 8:19; 2 Chr 21:7; Ps 132:17) the same figure is applied to David's dynasty (see especially Ps 132:17, where "prepared a lamp for Mine anointed" is parallel to "cause the horn of David to spring forth"). In David's royal sons his "lamp" continues to burn before the Lord in Jerusalem.

11:37 *Israel.* The northern ten tribes.

11:38 *If you listen to all that I command you . . . I will be with you.* Jeroboam was placed under the same covenant obligations as David and Solomon before him (see 2:3–4; 3:14; 6:12–13).

11:39 *afflict the descendants of David.* The division of the kingdom considerably reduced the status and power of the house of David. *not always.* Anticipates a restoration (announced also in the Messianic prophecies of Jer 30:9; Ezek 34:23; 37:15–28; Hos 3:5; Amos 9:11–12) in which the nation is reunited under the rule of the house of David.

11:40 *Solomon sought therefore to put Jeroboam to death.* Jeroboam, perhaps indifferent to the timing announced by Ahijah

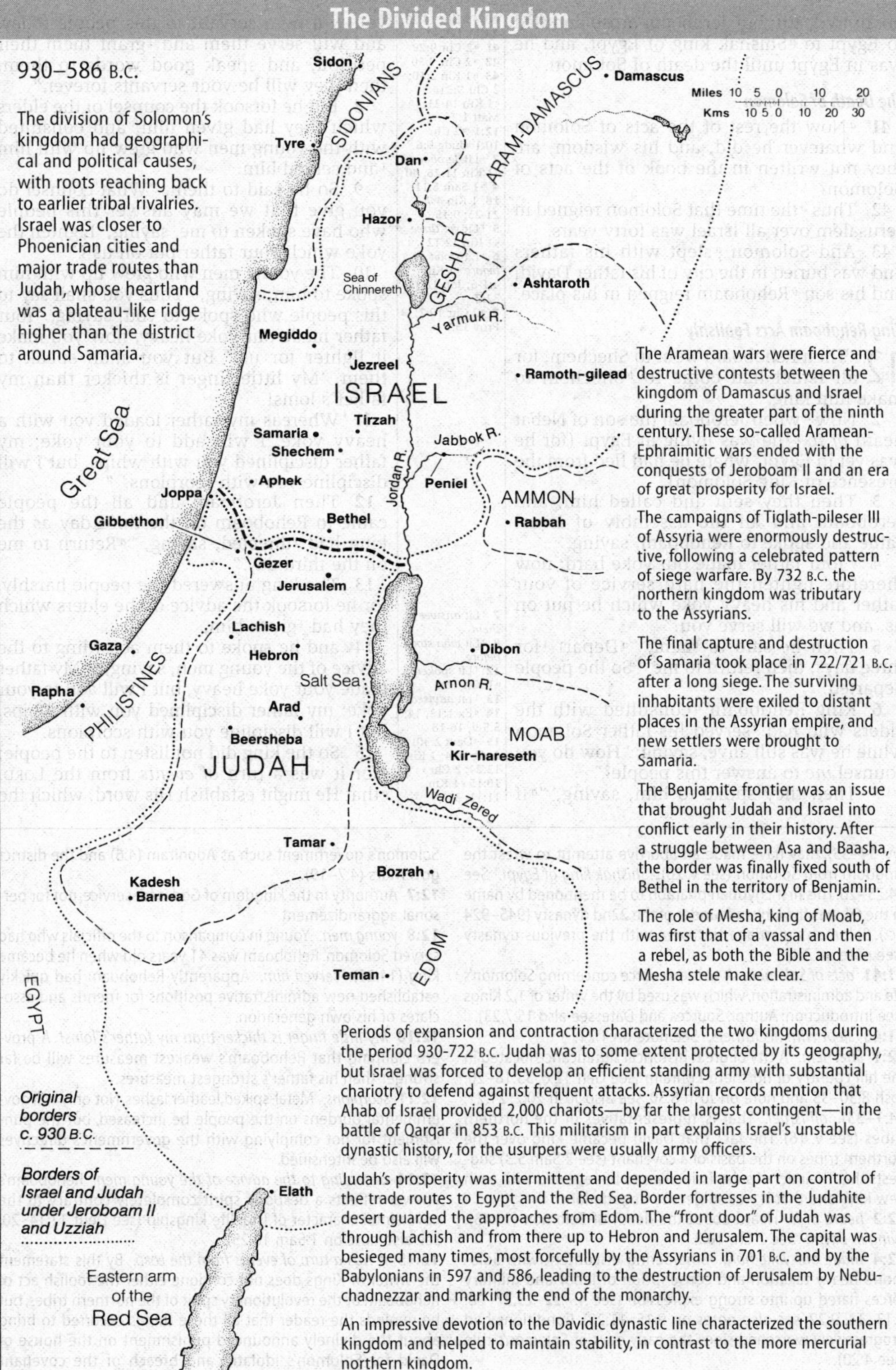
The Divided Kingdom
930–586 B.C.
The division of Solomon's kingdom had geographical and political causes, with roots reaching back to earlier tribal rivalries. Israel was closer to Phoenician cities and major trade routes than Judah, whose heartland was a plateau-like ridge higher than the district around Samaria.
Sidon
SIDONIANS
Tyre
Dan
ARAM-DAMASCUS
Damascus
Miles 10 5 0 10 20
Kms 10 5 0 10 20 30
Hazor
GESHUR
Sea of Chinnereth
Ashtaroth
Yarmuk R.
Megiddo
Jezreel
Ramoth-gilead
ISRAEL
Great Sea
Tirzah
Samaria
Shechem
Jabbok R.
Aphek
Jordan R.
Peniel
Joppa
AMMON
Gibbethon
Bethel
Rabbah
Gezer
Jerusalem
Lachish
Gaza
Hebron
Dibon
PHILISTINES
Salt Sea
Arnon R.
Rapha
Arad
Beersheba
MOAB
JUDAH
Kir-hareseth
Wadi Zered
Tamar
Bozrah
Kadesh Barnea
EDOM
Teman
EGYPT
Elath
Eastern arm of the Red Sea
Original borders c. 930 B.C.
Borders of Israel and Judah under Jeroboam II and Uzziah
The Aramean wars were fierce and destructive contests between the kingdom of Damascus and Israel during the greater part of the ninth century. These so-called Aramean-Ephraimitic wars ended with the conquests of Jeroboam II and an era of great prosperity for Israel.
The campaigns of Tiglath-pileser III of Assyria were enormously destructive, following a celebrated pattern of siege warfare. By 732 B.C. the northern kingdom was tributary to the Assyrians.
The final capture and destruction of Samaria took place in 722/721 B.C. after a long siege. The surviving inhabitants were exiled to distant places in the Assyrian empire, and new settlers were brought to Samaria.
The Benjamite frontier was an issue that brought Judah and Israel into conflict early in their history. After a struggle between Asa and Baasha, the border was finally fixed south of Bethel in the territory of Benjamin.
The role of Mesha, king of Moab, was first that of a vassal and then a rebel, as both the Bible and the Mesha stele make clear.
Periods of expansion and contraction characterized the two kingdoms during the period 930-722 B.C. Judah was to some extent protected by its geography, but Israel was forced to develop an efficient standing army with substantial chariotry to defend against frequent attacks. Assyrian records mention that Ahab of Israel provided 2,000 chariots—by far the largest contingent—in the battle of Qarqar in 853 B.C. This militarism in part explains Israel's unstable dynastic history, for the usurpers were usually army officers.
Judah's prosperity was intermittent and depended in large part on control of the trade routes to Egypt and the Red Sea. Border fortresses in the Judahite desert guarded the approaches from Edom. The "front door" of Judah was through Lachish and from there up to Hebron and Jerusalem. The capital was besieged many times, most forcefully by the Assyrians in 701 B.C. and by the Babylonians in 597 and 586, leading to the destruction of Jerusalem by Nebuchadnezzar and marking the end of the monarchy.
An impressive devotion to the Davidic dynastic line characterized the southern kingdom and helped to maintain stability, in contrast to the more mercurial northern kingdom.

boam to death; but Jeroboam arose and fled
to Egypt to [a]Shishak king of Egypt, and he
was in Egypt until the death of Solomon.

The Death of Solomon

41 [a]Now the rest of the acts of Solomon
and whatever he did, and his wisdom, are
they not written in the book of the acts of
Solomon?
42 Thus [a]the time that Solomon reigned in
Jerusalem over all Israel was forty years.
43 And Solomon [a]slept with his fathers
and was buried in the city of his father David,
and his son [b]Rehoboam reigned in his place.

King Rehoboam Acts Foolishly

12 [a]Then Rehoboam went to Shechem, for
all Israel had come to [b]Shechem to
make him king.
2 Now [a]when Jeroboam the son of Nebat
heard *of it,* [1]he was living in Egypt (for he
was yet in Egypt, where he had fled from the
presence of King Solomon).
3 Then they sent and called him, and
Jeroboam and all the assembly of Israel
came and spoke to Rehoboam, saying,
4 "[a]Your father made our yoke hard; now
therefore lighten the hard service of your
father and his heavy yoke which he put on
us, and we will serve you."
5 Then he said to them, "[a]Depart [1]for
three days, then return to me." So the people
departed.
6 King Rehoboam [a]consulted with the
elders who had [1]served his father Solomon
while he was still alive, saying, "How do you
counsel *me* to answer this people?"
7 Then they spoke to him, saying, "[a]If
you will be a servant to this people today,
and will serve them and [1]grant them their
petition, and speak good words to them,
then they will be your servants forever."
8 But he forsook the counsel of the elders
which they had given him, and consulted
with the young men who grew up with him
[1]and served him.
9 So he said to them, "What counsel do
you give that we may answer this people
who have spoken to me, saying, 'Lighten the
yoke which your father put on us'?"
10 The young men who grew up with him
spoke to him, saying, "Thus you shall say to
this people who spoke to you, saying, 'Your
father made our yoke heavy, now you make
it lighter for us!' But you shall speak to
them, 'My little finger is thicker than my
father's loins!
11 'Whereas my father loaded you with a
heavy yoke, I will add to your yoke; my
father disciplined you with whips, but I will
discipline you with scorpions.' "
12 Then Jeroboam and all the people
came to Rehoboam on the third day as the
king had [1]directed, saying, "[a]Return to me
on the third day."
13 The king answered the people harshly,
for he forsook the advice of the elders which
they had [1]given him,
14 and he spoke to them according to the
advice of the young men, saying, "[a]My father
made your yoke heavy, but I will add to your
yoke; my father disciplined you with whips,
but I will discipline you with scorpions."
15 So the king did not listen to the people;
[a]for it was a turn *of events* from the LORD,
[b]that He might establish His word, which the

40 [a]1 Kin 14:25; 2 Chr 12:2-9
41 [a]2 Chr 9:29
42 [a]2 Chr 9:30
43 [a]1 Kin 2:10; 2 Chr 9:31 [b]1 Kin 14:21; Matt 1:7
12:1 [a]2 Chr 10:1 [b]Judg 9:6
2 [1]Lit *Jeroboam* [a]1 Kin 11:26, 40
4 [a]1 Sam 8:11-18; 1 Kin 4:7, 21-25; 9:15
5 [1]Lit *yet three* [a]1 Kin 12:12
6 [1]Lit *stood before* [a]1 Kin 4:1-6; Job 12:12; 32:7
7 [a]2 Chr 10:7; Prov 15:1
7 [1]Lit *answer them*
8 [1]Lit *who stood before*
12 [1]Lit *spoken* [a]1 Kin 12:5
13 [1]Lit *advised*
14 [a]Ex 1:13, 14; 5:5-9, 16-18
15 [a]Deut 2:30; Judg 14:4; 1 Kin 12:24; 2 Chr 10:15 [b]1 Kin 11:11, 31

(vv. 34–35), may have made an abortive attempt to wrest the kingdom from Solomon (see v. 26). *Shishak king of Egypt.* See 14:25–26. This first Egyptian pharaoh to be mentioned by name in the OT was the Libyan founder of the 22nd dynasty (945–924 B.C.). Solomon's marriage ties were with the previous dynasty (see note on 3:1).

11:41 *acts of Solomon.* A written source concerning Solomon's life and administration, which was used by the writer of 1,2 Kings (see Introduction: Author, Sources and Date; see also 15:7,23).

11:43 *slept with his fathers.* See note on 1:21.

12:1 *Shechem.* A city of great historical significance located in the hill country of northern Ephraim (see Gen 12:6; 33:18–20; Josh 8:30–35 and note on Josh 8:30; see also Josh 20:7; 21:21; 24:1–33). *all Israel.* That is, representatives of the northern tribes (see v. 16). The fact that David became king over the northern tribes on the basis of a covenant (see 2 Sam 5:3) suggests that their act of submission was to be renewed with each new king and that it was subject to negotiation.

12:2 *heard of it.* Heard about the death of Solomon (11:43). *living in Egypt.* See 2 Chr 10:2.

12:4 *made our yoke hard.* Smoldering discontent with Solomon's heavy taxation and conscription of labor and military forces flared up into strong expression (see 4:7,22–23,27–28; 5:13–14; 9:22; see also notes on 9:15; 11:28). Conditions had progressively worsened since the early days of Solomon's rule (see 4:20).

12:6 *elders who had served his father Solomon.* Officials of Solomon's government such as Adoniram (4:6) and the district governors (4:7–19).

12:7 Authority in the kingdom of God is for service, not for personal aggrandizement.

12:8 *young men.* Young in comparison to the officials who had served Solomon. Rehoboam was 41 years old when he became king (14:21). *served him.* Apparently Rehoboam had quickly established new administrative positions for friends and associates of his own generation.

12:10 *My little finger is thicker than my father's loins!* A proverb claiming that Rehoboam's weakest measures will be far stronger than his father's strongest measures.

12:11 *scorpions.* Metal-spiked leather lashes. Not only will governmental burdens on the people be increased, but the punishment for not complying with the government's directives will also be intensified.

12:14 *according to the advice of the young men.* Rehoboam's answer reflects a despotic spirit completely contrary to the covenantal character of Israelite kingship (see Deut 17:14–20; see also note on 1 Sam 10:25).

12:15 *it was a turn of events from the LORD.* By this statement the writer of Kings does not condone either the foolish act of Rehoboam or the revolutionary spirit of the northern tribes, but he reminds the reader that all these things occurred to bring about the divinely announced punishment on the house of David for Solomon's idolatry and breach of the covenant (11:9–13). For the relationship between divine sovereignty over

LORD spoke through Ahijah the Shilonite to Jeroboam the son of Nebat.

The Kingdom Divided

16 When all Israel *saw* that the king did not listen to them, the people answered the king, saying,

"What portion do we have in David?
We have no inheritance in the son of
Jesse;
[a]To your tents, O Israel!
Now look after your own house,
David!"

So Israel departed to their tents.

17 But [a]as for the sons of Israel who lived in the cities of Judah, Rehoboam reigned over them.

18 Then King Rehoboam sent [a]Adoram, who was over the forced labor, and all Israel stoned him [1]to death. And King Rehoboam made haste to mount his chariot to flee to Jerusalem.

19 [a]So Israel has been in rebellion against the house of David to this day.

20 It came about when all Israel heard that Jeroboam had returned, that they sent and called him to the assembly and made him king over all Israel. [a]None but the tribe of Judah followed the house of David.

21 [a]Now when Rehoboam had come to Jerusalem, he assembled all the house of Judah and the tribe of Benjamin, 180,000 chosen men who were warriors, to fight against the house of Israel to restore the kingdom to Rehoboam the son of Solomon.

22 But the word of God came to [a]Shemaiah the man of God, saying,

23 "Speak to Rehoboam the son of Solomon, king of Judah, and to all the house of Judah and Benjamin and to the [a]rest of the people, saying,

24 'Thus says the LORD, "You must not go up and fight against your [1]relatives the sons of Israel; return every man to his house, [a]for this thing has come from Me." ' " So they listened to the word of the LORD, and returned and went *their way* according to the word of the LORD.

Jeroboam's Idolatry

25 Then [a]Jeroboam built Shechem in the hill country of Ephraim, and lived [1]there. And he went out from there and built [b]Penuel.

26 Jeroboam said in his heart, "Now the kingdom will return to the house of David.

27 "[a]If this people go up to offer sacrifices in the house of the LORD at Jerusalem, then the heart of this people will return to their lord, *even* to Rehoboam king of Judah; and they will kill me and return to Rehoboam king of Judah."

28 So the king [1]consulted, and [a]made two golden [b]calves, and he said to them, "It is too much for you to go up to Jerusalem; [c]behold your gods, O Israel, that brought you up from the land of Egypt."

29 He set [a]one in [b]Bethel, and the other he put in [c]Dan.

30 Now [a]this thing became a sin, for the

16 [a]2 Sam 20:1
17 [a]1 Kin 11:13, 36
18 [1]Lit *with stones that he died* [a]2 Sam 20:24; 1 Kin 4:6; 5:14
19 [a]2 Kin 17:21
20 [a]1 Kin 11:13, 32, 36
21 [a]2 Chr 11:1
22 [a]2 Chr 11:2; 12:5-7
23 [a]1 Kin 12:17
24 [1]Lit *brothers* [a]1 Kin 12:15
25 [1]Lit *in it* [a]Gen 12:6; Judg 9:45-49 [b]Gen 32:30, 31; Judg 8:8, 17
27 [a]Deut 12:5-7, 14
28 [1]Lit *took counsel* [a]2 Kin 10:29; 17:16; Hos 8:4-7 [b]Hos 10:5 [c]Ex 32:4, 8
29 [a]Hos 10:5 [b]Gen 28:19 [c]Judg 18:26-31
30 [a]1 Kin 13:34; 2 Kin 17:21

all things and human responsibility for evil acts see note on 2 Sam 24:1. *His word, which the LORD spoke through Ahijah . . . to Jeroboam.* See 11:29–39.

12:16 *all Israel.* The northern tribes (see note on v. 1). *David.* The Davidic dynasty (see 2 Sam 20:1 for an earlier expression of the same sentiment).

12:17 *sons of Israel who lived in the cities of Judah.* People originally from the northern tribes who had settled in Judah. They were later to be joined by others from the north who desired to serve the Lord and worship at the temple (see 2 Chr 11:16–17).

12:18 *Adoram, who was over the forced labor.* Adoram (a variant of Adoniram) had served in the same capacity under both David (2 Sam 20:24) and Solomon (1 Kin 4:6; 5:14).

12:19 *this day.* The time of the writing of the source from which the author of 1 Kings derived this account (see Introduction: Author, Sources and Date).

12:21 *tribe of Benjamin.* Although the bulk of Benjamin was aligned with the northern tribes (see note on 11:31–32), the area around Jerusalem remained under Rehoboam's control (as did the Gibeonite cities and Gezer). The northern boundary of Judah must have reached almost to Bethel (12 miles north of Jerusalem)—which Abijah, Rehoboam's son, even held for a short while (see 2 Chr 13:19). *180,000 . . . warriors.* Probably includes all support personnel together with those who would actually be committed to battle.

12:22 *Shemaiah.* Wrote a history of Rehoboam's reign (2 Chr 12:15). Another of his prophecies is recorded in 2 Chr 12:5–8. *man of God.* A common way of referring to a prophet (see, e.g., 13:1; Deut 18:18; 33:1; 1 Sam 2:27; 9:9–10).

12:23 *rest of the people.* See note on v. 17.

12:24 *went their way.* Although full-scale civil war was averted, intermittent skirmishes and battles between Israel and Judah continued throughout the reigns of Rehoboam, Abijah and Asa, until political instability in Israel after the death of Baasha finally brought the conflict to a halt. Asa's son Jehoshaphat entered into an alliance with Ahab and sealed the relationship by the marriage of his son Jehoram to Ahab's daughter Athaliah (see 14:30; 15:6,16; 22:2,44; 2 Kin 8:18).

12:25 *Penuel.* A town in Transjordan (see Gen 32:31; Judg 8:9,17) of strategic importance for defense against the Arameans of Damascus (see 11:23–25) and the Ammonites.

12:26 *return to the house of David.* Jeroboam did not have confidence in the divine promise given to him through Ahijah (see 11:38) and thus took action that forfeited the theocratic basis for his kingship.

12:28 *two golden calves.* Pagan gods of the Arameans and Canaanites were often represented as standing on calves or bulls as symbols of their strength and fertility (see note on Judg 2:13). *behold your gods, O Israel, that brought you up from the land of Egypt.* Like Aaron (Ex 32:4–5), Jeroboam attempted to combine the pagan calf symbol with the worship of the Lord, though he attempted no physical representation of the Lord—no "god" stood on the backs of his bulls.

12:29 *Bethel.* Located about 12 miles north of Jerusalem close to the border of Ephraim but within the territory of Benjamin (Josh 18:11–13,22). Bethel held a prominent place in the history of Israel's worship of the Lord (see Gen 12:8; 28:11–19; 35:6–7; Judg 20:26–28; 1 Sam 7:16). *Dan.* Located in the far north of the land near Mount Hermon. A similarly paganized worship was practiced here during the period of the judges (Judg 18:30–31).

people went *to worship* before the one as far
as Dan.
31 And [a]he made houses on high places,
and [b]made priests from among [1]all the people who were not of the sons of Levi.
32 Jeroboam [1]instituted a feast in the
eighth month on the fifteenth day of the
month, [a]like the feast which is in Judah, and
he [2]went up to the altar; thus he did in Bethel, sacrificing to the calves which he had
made. And he stationed in Bethel [b]the priests
of the high places which he had made.
33 Then he [1]went up to the altar which he
had made in Bethel on the fifteenth day in
the eighth month, even in the month which
he had [2a]devised [3]in his own heart; and he
[2]instituted a feast for the sons of Israel and
[1]went up to the altar [b]to burn [4]incense.

Jeroboam Warned, Stricken

13 Now behold, there came [a]a man of God
from Judah to Bethel by the word of the
LORD, while Jeroboam was standing by the
altar [b]to burn incense.
2 [a]He cried against the altar by the word
of the LORD, and said, "O altar, altar, thus
says the LORD, 'Behold, a son shall be born to
the house of David, [b]Josiah by name; and on
you he shall sacrifice the priests of the high
places who burn incense on you, and human
bones shall be burned on you.' "
3 Then he gave a [1]sign the same day, saying, "[a]This is the [1]sign which the LORD has
spoken, 'Behold, the altar shall be split apart
and the [2]ashes which are on it shall be
poured out.' "
4 Now when the king heard the saying of
the man of God, which he cried against the
altar in Bethel, Jeroboam stretched out his
hand from the altar, saying, "Seize him." But
his hand which he stretched out against him
dried up, so that he could not draw it back to
himself.
5 The altar also was split apart and the
[1]ashes were poured out from the altar,
according to the [2]sign which the man of God
had given by the word of the LORD.
6 The king said to the man of God,
"Please [1a]entreat the LORD your God, and
pray for me, that my hand may be restored to
me." So [b]the man of God [2]entreated the
LORD, and the king's hand was restored to
him, and it became as it was before.
7 Then the king said to the man of God,
"Come home with me and refresh yourself,
and [a]I will give you a reward."
8 But the man of God said to the king,
"[a]If you were to give me half your house I
would not go with you, nor would I eat
bread or drink water in this place.
9 "For so [1]it was commanded me by the
word of the LORD, saying, 'You shall eat no
bread, nor drink water, nor return by the
way which you came.' "
10 So he went another way and did not
return by the way which he came to Bethel.

The Disobedient Prophet

11 Now [a]an old prophet was living in
Bethel; and his [1]sons came and told him all
the deeds which the man of God had done
that day in Bethel; the words which he had
spoken to the king, these also they related to
their father.
12 Their father said to them, "[1]Which way
did he go?" Now his sons [2]had seen the way
which the man of God who came from Judah
had gone.

31 [1]Or *extremities of* [a]1 Kin 13:32 [b]1 Kin 13:33; 2 Kin 17:32; 2 Chr 11:15; 13:9
32 [1]Lit *made* [2]Or *offered upon* [a]Lev 23:33, 34; Num 29:12; 1 Kin 8:2, 5 [b]Amos 7:10-13
33 [1]Or *offered upon* [2]Lit *made* [3]Lit *from* [4]Or *sacrifices* [a]Num 15:39 [b]1 Kin 13:1
13:1 [a]1 Kin 12:22; 2 Kin 23:17 [b]1 Kin 12:33
2 [a]1 Kin 13:32 [b]2 Kin 23:15, 16
3 [1]Lit *wonder* [2]Lit *ashes of fat* [a]Ex 4:1-5; Judg 6:17; Is 38:7; John 2:18; 1 Cor 1:22
5 [1]Lit *ashes of fat* [2]Lit *wonder*
6 [1]Lit *soften the face of* [2]Lit *softened the face of* [a]Ex 8:8, 28; 9:28; 10:17; Acts 8:24; James 5:16 [b]Luke 6:27, 28
7 [a]1 Sam 9:7, 8; 2 Kin 5:15
8 [a]Num 22:18; 24:13; 1 Kin 13:16, 17
9 [1]Lit *he commanded me*
11 [1]Lit *son* [a]1 Kin 13:25; 2 Kin 23:18
12 [1]Lit *Where is the way he went* [2]Some ancient versions read *showed him*

12:30 *this thing became a sin.* Jeroboam's royal policy promoted violation of the second commandment (Ex 20:4–6). It inevitably led to Israel's violation of the first commandment also (Ex 20:3) and opened the door for the entrance of fully pagan practices into Israel's religious rites (especially in the time of Ahab). Jeroboam foolishly abandoned religious principle for political expediency and in so doing forfeited the promise given him by the prophet Ahijah (see 11:38).

12:31 *he made houses on high places.* See note on 3:2. *not of the sons of Levi.* Many of the priests and Levites of the northern kingdom migrated to Judah because Jeroboam bypassed them when appointing cult personnel in the north (see 2 Chr 11:13–14).

12:32 *feast which is in Judah.* Apparently the Feast of Booths, observed in Judah on the 15th to the 21st of the seventh month (see 8:2; Lev 23:34). *went up to the altar.* Jeroboam overstepped the limits of his prerogatives as king and assumed the role of a priest (see 2 Chr 26:16–21).

13:1 *man of God.* See note on 12:22. *from Judah to Bethel.* God sent a prophet from the southern kingdom to Bethel in the northern kingdom. Possibly He did this to emphasize that the divinely appointed political division (11:11,29–39; 12:15,24) was not intended to establish rival religious systems in the two kingdoms. Two centuries later the prophet Amos from Tekoa in Judah also went to Bethel in the northern kingdom to pronounce God's judgment on Jeroboam II (Amos 7:10–17).

13:2 *Josiah.* A prophetic announcement of the rule of King Josiah, who came to the throne in Judah nearly 300 years after the division of the kingdom. *shall sacrifice the priests of the high places.* Fulfilled in 2 Kin 23:15–20.

13:3 *sign.* The immediate fulfillment of a short-term prediction would serve to authenticate the reliability of the longer-term prediction (see Deut 18:21–22).

13:5 *ashes were poured out.* Visibly demonstrating God's power to fulfill the words of the prophet (see note on v. 3) and providing a clear sign that Jeroboam's offering was unacceptable to the Lord (see Lev 6:10–11).

13:6 *your God.* Should not be taken as implying that Jeroboam no longer considered the Lord as his own God (cf. 2:3; Gen 27:20), but as suggesting that he recognized the prophet as his superior in the theocratic order. *king's hand was restored.* The Lord's gracious response to Jeroboam's request is to be seen as an additional sign (see v. 3) given to confirm the word of the prophet and to move Jeroboam to repentance.

13:7 *Come home with me.* Jeroboam attempted to renew his prestige in the eyes of the people by creating the impression that there was no fundamental break between himself and the prophetic order (see 1 Sam 15:30 for a similar situation).

13:9 *You shall eat no bread.* The prophet's refusal of Jeroboam's invitation rested on a previously given divine command. It underscored God's extreme displeasure with the apostate worship at Bethel.

13 Then he said to his sons, "Saddle the
donkey for me." So they saddled the donkey
for him and he rode away on it.
14 So he went after the man of God and
found him sitting under [1]an oak; and he said
to him, "Are you the man of God who came
from Judah?" And he said, "I am."
15 Then he said to him, "Come home with
me and eat bread."
16 He said, "[a]I cannot return with you,
nor go with you, nor will I eat bread or drink
water with you in this place.
17 "For a command *came* to me [a]by the
word of the LORD, 'You shall eat no bread,
nor drink water there; do not return by going
the way which you came.' "
18 He said to him, "[a]I also am a prophet
like you, and [b]an angel spoke to me by the
word of the LORD, saying, 'Bring him back
with you to your house, that he may eat
bread and drink water.' " *But* [c]he lied to him.
19 So he went back with him, and ate
bread in his house and drank water.
20 Now it came about, as they were sitting
down at the table, that the word of the LORD
came to the prophet who had brought him
back;
21 and he cried to the man of God who
came from Judah, saying, "Thus says the
LORD, 'Because you have [1]disobeyed the
[2]command of the LORD, and have not
observed the commandment which the LORD
your God commanded you,
22 but have returned and eaten bread and
drunk water in the place of which He said to
you, "Eat no bread and drink no water";
your body shall not come to the grave of
your fathers.' "
23 It came about after he had eaten bread
and after he had drunk, that he saddled the
donkey for him, for the prophet whom he
had brought back.
24 Now when he had gone, [a]a lion met
him on the way and killed him, and his body
was thrown on the road, with the donkey
standing beside it; the lion also was standing
beside the body.
25 And behold, men passed by and saw the
body thrown on the road, and the lion standing beside the body; so they came and told *it*
in the city where [a]the old prophet lived.
26 Now when the prophet who brought
him back from the way heard *it,* he said, "It
is the man of God, who [1]disobeyed the
[2]command of the LORD; therefore the LORD
has given him to the lion, which has torn
him and killed him, according to the word of
the LORD which He spoke to him."
27 Then he spoke to his sons, saying, "Saddle the donkey for me." And they saddled *it.*
28 He went and found his body thrown on
the road with the donkey and the lion standing beside the body; the lion had not eaten
the body nor torn the donkey.
29 So the prophet took up the body of the
man of God and laid it on the donkey and
brought it back, and he came to the city of
the old prophet to mourn and to bury him.
30 He laid his body in his own grave, and
they mourned over him, *saying,* "[a]Alas, my
brother!"
31 After he had buried him, he spoke to
his sons, saying, "When I die, bury me in the
grave in which the man of God is buried;
[a]lay my bones beside his bones.
32 "[a]For the thing shall surely come to pass
which he cried by the word of the LORD
against the altar in Bethel and [b]against all
the houses of the high places which are in
the cities of [c]Samaria."
33 After this event Jeroboam did not
return from his evil way, but [a]again he made
priests of the high places from among [1]all
the people; [b]any who would, he ordained, to
be priests of the high places.
34 [1a]This event became sin to the house
of Jeroboam, [b]even to blot *it* out and destroy
it from off the face of the earth.

14 [1]Or a *terebinth*
16 [a]1 Kin 13:8, 9
17 [a]1 Kin 20:35
18 [a]Matt 7:15; 1 John 4:1 [b]Gal 1:8 [c]Prov 12:19, 22; 19:5; Jer 29:31, 32; Ezek 13:8, 9; 1 Tim 4:1, 2
21 [1]Lit *rebelled against* [2]Lit *mouth*
24 [a]1 Kin 20:36
25 [a]1 Kin 13:11
26 [1]Lit *rebelled against* [2]Lit *mouth*
30 [a]Jer 22:18
31 [a]Ruth 1:17; 2 Kin 23:17, 18
32 [a]1 Kin 13:2 [b]Lev 26:30; 1 Kin 12:31 [c]1 Kin 16:24; John 4:5; Acts 8:14
33 [1]Or *extremities of* [a]1 Kin 12:31, 32 [b]Judg 17:5
34 [1]Lit *by this thing he became* [a]1 Kin 12:30; 2 Kin 17:21 [b]1 Kin 14:10; 15:29, 30

13:18 *I also am a prophet like you.* A half-truth. It is likely that the old prophet in Bethel had faithfully proclaimed the word of the Lord in former days, but those days had long since passed.
13:19 *he went back with him.* Neither the old prophet's lie nor his own need justified disobedience to the direct and explicit command of the Lord. His public action in this matter undermined respect for the divine authority of all he had said at Bethel.
13:20 *the word of the* LORD *came to the prophet.* The fundamental distinction between a true and a false prophecy here becomes apparent. The false prophecy arises from one's own imagination (Jer 23:16; Ezek 13:2,7) while the true prophecy is from God (Ex 4:16; Deut 18:18; Jer 1:9; 2 Pet 1:21).
13:22 *your body shall not come to the grave of your fathers.* The man of God from Judah will die far from his own home and family burial plot.
13:24 *killed him.* A stern warning to Jeroboam that God takes His word very seriously. *the donkey standing beside it; the lion also.* The remarkable fact that the donkey did not run and the lion did not attack the donkey or disturb the man's body (v. 28) clearly stamped the incident as a divine judgment. This additional miracle was reported in Bethel (v. 25) and provided yet another sign authenticating the message that the man of God from Judah had delivered at Jeroboam's altar. But Jeroboam was still not moved to repentance (v. 33).
13:30 *laid his body in his own grave.* See v. 22. The old prophet did the only thing left for him to do in order to make amends for his deliberate and fatal deception.
13:31 *grave in which the man of God is buried.* The old prophet chose in this way to identify himself with the message that the man of God from Judah had given at Bethel.
13:32 *Samaria.* As the capital of the northern kingdom, Samaria is used to designate the entire territory of the northern ten tribes (see note on 16:24). However, Samaria was not established until about 50 years after this (16:23–24). The use of the name here reflects the perspective of the author of Kings (see note on Gen 14:14 for a similar instance of the use of a place-name—Dan—of later origin than the historical incident with which it is connected).
13:33 *made priests . . . from among all the people.* See 12:31 and note.
13:34 *sin.* The sin in 12:30 was the establishment of a

Ahijah Prophesies against the King

14 At that time Abijah the son of Jeroboam became sick.
2 Jeroboam said to his wife, "Arise now,
and [a]disguise yourself so that they will not
know that you are the wife of Jeroboam, and
go to [b]Shiloh; behold, Ahijah the prophet is
there, who [c]spoke concerning me *that I*
would be king over this people.
3 "[a]Take ten loaves with you, *some* cakes
and a jar of honey, and go to him. He will tell
you what will happen to the boy."
4 Jeroboam's wife did so, and arose and
went to [a]Shiloh, and came to the house of
[b]Ahijah. Now Ahijah could not see, [c]for his
eyes were [1]dim because of his age.
5 Now the LORD had said to Ahijah,
"Behold, the wife of Jeroboam is coming to
[1]inquire of you concerning her son, for he is
sick. You shall say thus and thus to her, for it
will be when she arrives that [a]she will pretend to be another woman."
6 When Ahijah heard the sound of her
feet coming in the doorway, he said, "Come
in, wife of Jeroboam, why do you pretend to
be another woman? For I am sent to you *with*
a harsh *message.*
7 "Go, say to Jeroboam, 'Thus says the
LORD God of Israel, "[a]Because I exalted you
from among the people and made you leader
over My people Israel,
8 and [a]tore the kingdom away from the
house of David and gave it to you—[b]yet you
have not been like My servant David, who
kept My commandments and who followed
Me with all his heart, [c]to do only that which
was right in My sight;
9 you also have done more evil than all
who were before you, and [a]have gone and
made for yourself other gods and [b]molten
images to provoke Me to anger, and have
[c]cast Me behind your back—
10 therefore behold, I am bringing calamity on the house of Jeroboam, and [a]will cut
off from Jeroboam [1]every male person, [b]both
bond and free in Israel, and I [c]will make a
clean sweep of the house of Jeroboam, as
one sweeps away dung until it is all gone.
11 "[a]Anyone belonging to Jeroboam who
dies in the city the dogs will eat. And he who
dies in the field the birds of the heavens will
eat; for the LORD has spoken *it.*" '
12 "Now you, arise, go to your house.
[a]When your feet enter the city the child will
die.
13 "All Israel shall mourn for him and bury
him, for [1]he alone of Jeroboam's *family* will
come to the grave, because in him [a]some-
thing good was found toward the LORD God
of Israel in the house of Jeroboam.
14 "Moreover, [a]the LORD will raise up for
Himself a king over Israel who will cut off
the house of Jeroboam this day [1]and from
now on.
15 "For the LORD will strike Israel, as a reed is
shaken in the water; and [a]He will uproot Israel from [b]this good land which He gave to their
fathers, and [c]will scatter them beyond the
Euphrates River, [d]because they have made
their [1]Asherim, provoking the LORD to anger.

14:2 [a]1 Sam 28:8; 2 Sam 14:2; 2 Chr 18:29 [b]Josh 18:1 [c]1 Kin 11:29-31
3 [a]1 Sam 9:7, 8; 1 Kin 13:7; 2 Kin 4:42
4 [1]Lit *set* [a]1 Kin 14:2 [b]1 Kin 11:29 [c]1 Sam 3:2; 4:15
5 [1]Lit *seek a word from* [a]2 Sam 14:2
7 [a]2 Sam 12:7; 1 Kin 11:28-31; 16:2
8 [a]1 Kin 11:31 [b]1 Kin 11:33, 38
8 [c]1 Kin 15:5
9 [a]1 Kin 12:28; 2 Chr 11:15 [b]Ex 34:17 [c]Neh 9:26; Ps 50:17; Ezek 23:35
10 [1]Lit *him who urinates against the wall* [a]1 Kin 21:21; 2 Kin 9:8 [b]Deut 32:36; 2 Kin 14:26 [c]1 Kin 15:29
11 [a]1 Kin 16:4; 21:24
12 [a]1 Kin 14:17
13 [1]Lit *the one* [a]2 Chr 19:3
14 [1]Lit *and what even now?* [a]1 Kin 15:27-29
15 [1]I.e. wooden symbols of a female deity [a]Deut 29:28; 2 Kin 17:6; Ps 52:5 [b]Josh 23:15, 16 [c]2 Kin 15:29 [d]Ex 34:13, 14; Deut 12:3, 4

paganized worship; here it is persistence in this worship with all its attendant evils.

14:1 *At that time.* Probably indicating a time not far removed from the event narrated in ch. 13. *Abijah.* Means "My (divine) Father is the LORD," suggesting that Jeroboam, at least to some degree, desired to be regarded as a worshiper of the Lord.

14:2 *disguise yourself.* Jeroboam's attempt to mislead the prophet Ahijah into giving a favorable prophecy concerning the sick boy indicates (1) his consciousness of his own guilt, (2) his superstition that prophecy worked in a magical way and (3) his confused but real respect for the power of the Lord's prophet. *who spoke concerning me that I would be king over this people.* See 11:29–39.

14:3 *ten loaves.* The gift of an ordinary farmer (like Saul in 1 Sam 9:7–8) rather than that of a king (see 2 Kin 8:7–9).

14:5 *the LORD had said to Ahijah.* See 1 Sam 9:15–17; 2 Kin 6:32 for other examples of divine revelation concerning an imminent visit.

14:6 *Come in, wife of Jeroboam.* Ahijah's recognition of the woman and his knowledge of the purpose of her visit served to authenticate his message as truly being the word of the Lord.

14:7–8 *exalted you . . . made you leader . . . tore the kingdom away.* Jeroboam is first reminded of the gracious acts of the Lord in his behalf (see 11:26,30–38).

14:8 *you have not been like My servant David.* Jeroboam had not responded to God's gracious acts and had ignored the requirements given when Ahijah told him he would become king (see 11:38).

14:9 *all who were before you.* Jeroboam's wickedness surpassed that of Saul, David and Solomon in that he implemented a paganized system of worship for the entire populace of the northern kingdom. *other gods.* See notes on 12:28,30.

14:10 *bond and free.* Without exception (see 21:21; 2 Kin 9:8; 14:26).

14:11 *he who dies in the field the birds of the heavens will eat.* See note on 16:4. The covenant curse of Deut 28:26 is applied to Jeroboam's male descendants, none of whom will receive an honorable burial.

14:12 *child.* The Hebrew for this word allows for wide latitude in age (the same term is used for the young advisers of Rehoboam; see 12:8 and note). *will die.* Although the death of Abijah was a severe disappointment to Jeroboam and his wife, it was an act of God's mercy to the prince, sparing him the disgrace and suffering that were to come on his father's house (see Is 57:1–2).

14:13 *All Israel shall mourn for him and bury him.* Perhaps an indication that Abijah was the crown prince, and was well known and loved by the people. *grave.* He alone of Jeroboam's descendants would receive an honorable burial.

14:14 *a king . . . who will cut off the house of Jeroboam.* Ahijah looked beyond the brief reign of Nadab, Jeroboam's son (15:25–26), to the revolt of Baasha (15:27–16:7).

14:15 *as a reed is shaken in the water.* Descriptive of the instability of the royal house in the northern kingdom, which was to be characterized by assassinations and revolts (see 15:27–28; 16:16; 2 Kin 9:24; 15:10,14,25,30). *He will uproot Israel.* The list of curses for covenant breaking found in Deuteronomy climaxes in forced exile for God's people from the land of promise (Deut 28:63–64; 29:25–28). *Asherim.* Ahijah perceived that Jeroboam's use of golden bulls in worship would inevitably lead to the adoption of other elements of Canaanite nature religion.

16 "He will give up Israel [a]on account of
the sins of Jeroboam, which he [1]committed
and with which he made Israel to sin."
17 Then Jeroboam's wife arose and departed and came to [a]Tirzah. [b]As she was
entering the threshold of the house, the child
died.
18 [a]All Israel buried him and mourned for
him, according to the word of the LORD
which He spoke through His servant Ahijah
the prophet.
19 Now the rest of the acts of Jeroboam,
[a]how he made war and how he reigned,
behold, they are written in the Book of the
Chronicles of the Kings of Israel.
20 The time that Jeroboam reigned *was*
twenty-two years; and he slept with his
fathers, and Nadab his son reigned in his
place.

Rehoboam Misleads Judah

21 [a]Now Rehoboam the son of Solomon
reigned in Judah. Rehoboam was forty-one
years old when he became king, and he
reigned seventeen years in Jerusalem, [b]the
city which the LORD had chosen from all the
tribes of Israel to put His name there. And his
mother's name was Naamah the Ammonitess.
22 [a]Judah did evil in the sight of the LORD,
and they [b]provoked Him to jealousy more
than all that their fathers had done, with [1]the
sins which they [2]committed.
23 For they also built for themselves [a]high
places and *sacred* [b]pillars and [1c]Asherim on
every high hill and [d]beneath every luxuriant
tree.
24 There were also [a]male cult prostitutes
in the land. They did according to all the
abominations of the nations which the LORD
dispossessed before the sons of Israel.
25 [a]Now it happened in the fifth year of
King Rehoboam, that Shishak the king of
Egypt came up against Jerusalem.
26 He took away the treasures of the
house of the LORD and the treasures of the
king's house, and [a]he took everything,
[1b]even taking all the shields of gold which
Solomon had made.
27 So King Rehoboam made shields of
bronze in their place, and [a]committed them
to the [1]care of the commanders of the [2]guard
who guarded the doorway of the king's
house.
28 Then it happened as often as the king
entered the house of the LORD, that the
[1]guards would carry them and would bring
them back into the [1]guards' room.
29 [a]Now the rest of the acts of Rehoboam
and all that he did, are they not written in the
Book of the Chronicles of the Kings of Judah?
30 [a]There was war between Rehoboam
and Jeroboam continually.
31 And Rehoboam slept with his fathers
and was buried with his fathers in the city of
David; and [a]his mother's name was Naamah
the Ammonitess. And Abijam his son
became king in his place.

16 [1]Lit *sinned* [a]1 Kin 12:30; 13:34; 15:30, 34; 16:2
17 [a]1 Kin 15:21, 33; 16:6-9, 15, 23; Song 6:4 [b]1 Kin 14:12
18 [a]1 Kin 14:13
19 [a]1 Kin 14:30; 2 Chr 13:2-20
21 [a]2 Chr 12:13 [b]1 Kin 11:32, 36
22 [1]Lit *their* [2]Lit *sinned* [a]2 Chr 12:1, 14 [b]Deut 32:21; Ps 78:58; 1 Cor 10:22
23 [a]Deut 12:2; Ezek 16:24
23 [1]I.e. wooden symbols of a female deity [b]Deut 16:22 [c]1 Kin 14:15 [d]2 Kin 17:10; Is 57:5; Jer 2:20
24 [a]Gen 19:5; Deut 23:17; 1 Kin 15:12; 22:46; 2 Kin 23:7
25 [a]1 Kin 11:40; 2 Chr 12:2, 9
26 [1]Lit *and he took away* [a]1 Kin 15:18; 2 Chr 12:9 [b]1 Kin 10:17; 2 Chr 9:15, 16
27 [1]Lit *hand* [2]Lit *runner* [a]1 Sam 8:11; 22:17
28 [1]Lit *runners*
29 [a]2 Chr 12:15, 16
30 [a]1 Kin 12:21; 15:6
31 [a]1 Kin 14:21

The goddess Asherah was the consort of El (see notes on Ex 34:13; Judg 2:13), and the Asherim were probably wooden representations of the goddess (see note on Ex 34:13).

14:16 *sins of Jeroboam.* See 12:26–33; 13:33–34. *which he made Israel to sin.* A phrase repeated often in 1,2 Kings (e.g., 15:26; 16:2,13,19,26).

14:17 *Tirzah.* Used by the kings of Israel as the royal city until Omri purchased and built up Samaria to serve that purpose (16:24). It is probably modern Tell el-Far'ah, about seven miles north of Shechem (see note on SS 6:4).

14:19 *war.* See v. 30; 15:6; 2 Chr 13:2–20. *Chronicles of the Kings of Israel.* A record of the reigns of the kings of the northern kingdom used by the author of 1,2 Kings and apparently accessible to those interested in further details of the history of the reigns of Israelite kings. It is not to be confused with the canonical book of 1,2 Chronicles, which was written later than 1,2 Kings and contains the history of the reigns of the kings of Judah only (see Introduction: Author, Sources and Date).

14:20 *twenty-two years.* 930–909 B.C. *slept with his fathers.* See note on 1:21. *Nadab.* See 15:25–32.

14:21 *forty-one years old.* Rehoboam was born shortly before David's death (see 11:42; see also note on 2:24). *seventeen years.* 930–913 B.C. *city which the LORD had chosen . . . to put His name.* See 9:3; Ps 132:13.

14:22 *Judah did evil in the sight of the LORD.* The reign of Rehoboam is described in greater detail in 2 Chr 11–12. The priests and Levites who immigrated to Judah from the north led the country to follow the way of David and Solomon for the first three years of Rehoboam's reign (see 12:24; 2 Chr 11:17). In later years Rehoboam and the people of Judah turned away from the Lord (2 Chr 12:1).

14:23 *high places.* See note on 3:2. *sacred pillars.* Stone pillars, bearing a religious significance, that were placed next to the altars. The use of such pillars was common among the Canaanites and was explicitly forbidden to the Israelites in the Mosaic law (Ex 23:24; Lev 26:1; Deut 16:21–22). It is likely that the pillars were intended to be representations of the deity (2 Kin 3:2). For legitimate uses of stone pillars see Gen 28:18; 31:45; Ex 24:4. *Asherim.* See note on v. 15.

14:24 *male cult prostitutes.* Ritual prostitution was an important feature of Canaanite fertility religion. The Israelites had been warned by Moses not to engage in this abominable practice (see Deut 23:17–18; see also 1 Kin 15:12; 2 Kin 23:7; Hos 4:14).

14:25 *fifth year of King Rehoboam.* 926 B.C. *Shishak.* See notes on 3:1; 11:40. *came up against Jerusalem.* Shishak's invasion is described in more detail in 2 Chr 12:2–4 and is also attested in a victory inscription found on the walls of the temple of Amun in Thebes, where numerous cities that Shishak plundered in both Judah and the northern kingdom are listed. 2 Chr 12:5–8 indicates that fear of the impending invasion led to a temporary reformation in Judah.

14:26 *shields of gold which Solomon had made.* See 10:16–17.

14:27 *shields of bronze.* The reduced realm could not match the great wealth Solomon had accumulated in Jerusalem (see 10:21,23,27).

14:29 *Chronicles of the Kings of Judah.* A record of the reigns of the kings of Judah similar to the one for the kings of the northern kingdom (see note on v. 19; see also Introduction: Author, Sources and Date).

14:30 *war . . . continually.* See notes on v. 19; 12:24.

14:31 *slept with his fathers.* See note on 1:21.

Rulers of the Divided Kingdom of Israel and Judah

DATA AND DATES IN ORDER OF SEQUENCE

	SCRIPTURE	KINGS	SYNCHRONISM OR CORRELATION	LENGTH OF REIGN	HISTORICAL DATA	DATES
1.	*1 Kin 12:1-24* *1 Kin 14:21-31*	***Rehoboam** (Judah)*		*17 years*		*930-913*
2.	1 Kin 12:25–14:20	**Jeroboam I** (Israel)		22 years		930-909
3.	*1 Kin 15:1-8*	***Abijah (Abijam)** (Judah)*	*18th of Jeroboam*	*3 years*		*913-910*
4.	*1 Kin 15:9-24*	***Asa** (Judah)*	*20th of Jeroboam*	*41 years*		*910-869*
5.	1 Kin 15:25-31	**Nadab** (Israel)	2nd of Asa	2 years		909-908
6.	1 Kin 15:32–16:7	**Baasha** (Israel)	3rd of Asa	24 years		908-886
7.	1 Kin 16:8-14	**Elah** (Israel)	26th of Asa	2 years		886-885
8.	1 Kin 16:15-20	**Zimri** (Israel)	27th of Asa	7days		885
9.	1 Kin 16:21-22	**Tibni** (Israel)			Overlap with Omri	885-880
10.	1 Kin 16:23-28	**Omri** (Israel)	27th of Asa		Made king by the people	885
					Overlap with Tibni	885-880
				12 years	Official reign = 11 actual years	885-874
			31st of Asa		Beginning of sole reign	880
11.	1 Kin 16:29–22:40	**Ahab** (Israel)	38th of Asa	22 years	Official reign = 21 actual years	874-853
12.	*1 Kin 22:41-50*	***Jehoshaphat** (Judah)*			*Co-regency with Asa*	*872-869*
				25 years	*Official reign*	*872-848*
			4th of Ahab		*Beginning of sole reign*	*869*
					Has Jehoram as regent	*853-848*
13.	1 Kin 22:51– 2 Kin 1:18	**Ahaziah** (Israel)	17th of Jehoshaphat	2 years	Official reign = 1 yr. actual reign	853-852
14.	2 Kin 1:17	**Joram (Jehoram)**	2nd of Jehoram			852
	2 Kin 3:1–8:15	(Israel)	18th of Jehoshaphat	12 years	Official reign = 11 actual years	852-841
15.	*2 Kin 8:16-24*	***Jehoram** (Judah)*	*5th of Joram*		*Beginning of sole reign*	*848*
				8 years	*Official reign = 7 actual years*	*848-841*
16.	*2 Kin 8:25-29*	***Ahaziah** (Judah)*	*12th of Joram*	*1 year*	*Nonaccession-year reckoning*	*841*
	2 Kin 9:29		*11th of Joram*		*Accession-year reckoning*	*841*
17.	2 Kin 9:30–10:36	**Jehu** (Israel)		28 years		841-814
18.	*2 Kin 11*	***Athaliah** (Judah)*		*7 years*		*841-835*
19.	*2 Kin 12*	***Joash (Jehoash)** (Judah)*	*7th of Jehu*	*40 years*		*835-796*
20.	2 Kin 13:1-9	**Jehoahaz** (Israel)	23rd of Joash	17 years		814-798
21.	2 Kin 13:10-25	**Jehoash (Joash)** (Israel)	37th of Joash	16 years		798-782

Adapted from: A Chronology of the Hebrew Kings by Edwin R. Thiele. ©1977 by The Zondervan Corporation. Used by permission.

SCRIPTURE	KINGS	SYNCHRONISM OR CORRELATION	LENGTH OF REIGN	HISTORICAL DATA	DATES
22. *2 Kin 14:1-22*	***Amaziah*** *(Judah)*	*2nd of Jehoash*	*29 years*		*796-767*
				Overlap with Azariah	*792-767*
23. *2 Kin 14:23-29*	***Jeroboam II*** *(Israel)*			*Co-regency with Jehoash*	*793-782*
			41 years	*Total reign*	*793-753*
		15th of Amaziah		*Beginning of sole reign*	*782*
24. *2 Kin 15:1-7*	***Azariah (Uzziah)***			*Overlap with Amaziah*	*792-767*
	(Judah)		*52 years*	*Total reign*	*792-740*
		27th of Jeroboam		*Beginning of sole reign*	*767*
25. 2 Kin 15:8-12	**Zechariah** (Israel)	38th of Azariah	6 months		753
26. 2 Kin 15:13-15	**Shallum** (Israel)	39th of Azariah	1 month		752
27. 2 Kin 15:16-22	**Menahem** (Israel)	39th of Azariah	10 years	Ruled in Samaria	752-742
28. 2 Kin 15:23-26	**Pekahiah** (Israel)	50th of Azariah	2 years		742-740
29. 2 Kin 15:27-31	**Pekah** (Israel)			In Gilead; overlapping years	752-740
			20 years	Total reign	752-732
		52nd of Azariah		Beginning of sole reign	740
30. *2 Kin 15:32-38*	***Jotham*** *(Judah)*			*Co-regency with Azariah*	*750-740*
2 Kin 15:30			*16 years*	*Official reign*	*750-735*
				Reign to his 20th year	*750-732*
		2nd of Pekah		*Beginning of co-regency*	*750*
31. *2 Kin 16*	***Ahaz*** *(Judah)*			*Total reign*	*735-715*
		17th of Pekah			*735*
			16 years	*From 20th of Jotham*	*732-715*
32. 2 Kin 15:30	**Hoshea** (Israel)			20th of Jotham	732
2 Kin 17		12th of Ahaz*	9 years		732-722
33. *2 Kin 18:1–20:21*	***Hezekiah*** *(Judah)*	*3rd of Hoshea**	*29 years*		*715-686*
34. *2 Kin 21:1-18*	***Manasseh*** *(Judah)*			*Co-regency with Hezekiah*	*697-686*
			55 years	*Total reign*	*697-642*
35. *2 Kin 21:19-26*	***Amon*** *(Judah)*		*2 years*		*642-640*
36. *2 Kin 22:1–23:30*	***Josiah*** *(Judah)*		*31 years*		*640-609*
37. *2 Kin 23:31-33*	***Jehoahaz*** *(Judah)*		*3 months*		*609*
38. *2 Kin 23:34–24:7*	***Jehoiakim*** *(Judah)*		*11 years*		*609-598*
39. *2 Kin 24:8-17*	***Jehoiachin*** *(Judah)*		*3 months*		*598-597*
40. *2 Kin 24:18–25:26*	***Zedekiah*** *(Judah)*		*11 years*		*597-586*

*These data arise when the reign of Hoshea is thrown 12 years in advance of its historical position.

*Italics denote kings of **Judah**.*
Non-italic type denotes kings of **Israel**.

Abijam Reigns over Judah

15 [a]Now in the eighteenth year of King
Jeroboam, the son of Nebat, Abijam
became king over Judah.
2 He reigned three years in Jerusalem;
and his mother's name was [1a]Maacah the
daughter of [2b]Abishalom.
3 He walked in all the sins of his father
which he had committed before him; and [a]his
heart was not [1]wholly devoted to the LORD his
God, like the heart of his father David.
4 But for David's sake the LORD his God
gave him a [a]lamp in Jerusalem, to raise up
his son after him and to establish Jerusalem;
5 [a]because David did what was right in
the sight of the LORD, and had not turned
aside from anything that He commanded
him all the days of his life, [b]except in the
case of Uriah the Hittite.
6 [a]There was war between Rehoboam
and Jeroboam all the days of his life.
7 Now [a]the rest of the acts of Abijam and
all that he did, are they not written in the
Book of the Chronicles of the Kings of
Judah? [b]And there was war between Abijam
and Jeroboam.

Asa Succeeds Abijam

8 [a]And Abijam slept with his fathers and
they buried him in the city of David; and Asa
his son became king in his place.
9 So in the twentieth year of Jeroboam
the king of Israel, Asa began to reign as king
of Judah.
10 He reigned forty-one years in Jerusalem; and [a]his mother's name was Maacah
the daughter of Abishalom.
11 [a]Asa did what was right in the sight of
the LORD, like David his father.
12 [a]He also put away the male cult prostitutes from the land and [b]removed all the
idols which his fathers had made.
13 [1a]He also removed Maacah his mother
from *being* queen mother, because she had
made a horrid image [2]as an Asherah; and
Asa cut down her horrid image and [b]burned
it at the brook Kidron.
14 [a]But the high places were not taken
away; nevertheless [b]the heart of Asa was
[1]wholly devoted to the LORD all his days.
15 [a]He brought into the house of the LORD
the dedicated things of his father and his own
dedicated things: silver and gold and utensils.
16 [a]Now there was war between Asa and
Baasha king of Israel all their days.
17 [a]Baasha king of Israel went up against
Judah and [1b]fortified Ramah [c]in order to prevent *anyone* from going out or coming in to
Asa king of Judah.
18 Then [a]Asa took all the silver and the

15:1 [a]2 Chr 13:1 **2** [1]In 2 Chr 13:2, *Micaiah, the daughter of Uriel* [2]In 2 Chr 11:20, *Absalom* [a]2 Chr 13:2 [b]2 Chr 11:21 **3** [1]Lit *complete with* [a]1 Kin 11:4; Ps 119:80 **4** [a]2 Sam 21:17; 1 Kin 11:36; 2 Chr 21:7 **5** [a]1 Kin 9:4; 14:8; Luke 1:6 [b]2 Sam 11:3f, 15-17; 12:9, 10 **6** [a]1 Kin 14:30; 2 Chr 12:15-13:20 **7** [a]2 Chr 13:2, 21, 22 [b]2 Chr 13:3-20 **8** [a]2 Chr 14:1 **10** [a]1 Kin 15:2 **11** [a]2 Chr 14:2 **12** [a]Deut 23:17; 1 Kin 14:24; 22:46 [b]1 Kin 11:7, 8; 14:23; 2 Chr 14:2-5 **13** [1]Lit *also Maacah his mother and he removed her* [2]Or *for Asherah* [a]2 Chr 15:16-18 [b]Ex 32:20 **14** [1]Lit *complete with* [a]1 Kin 22:43; 2 Kin 12:3 [b]1 Kin 8:61; 15:3 **15** [a]1 Kin 7:51

16 [a]1 Kin 15:32 **17** [1]Lit *built* [a]2 Chr 16:1-6 [b]Josh 18:25; 1 Kin 15:21, 22 [c]1 Kin 12:26-29 **18** [a]1 Kin 14:26; 15:15

15:1 *eighteenth year of King Jeroboam.* The first of numerous synchronisms in 1,2 Kings between the reigns of the kings in the north and those in Judah (see, e.g., vv. 9,25,33; 16:8,15,29; see also Introduction: Chronology). *Abijam.* A variant of Abijah; see note on 14:1. Both Rehoboam and Jeroboam had sons by this name.

15:2 *three years.* 913–910 B.C. *Maacah the daughter of Abishalom.* See NASB marg. Abijah's mother is said to be a daughter of Uriel of Gibeah in 2 Chr 13:2. It is likely that Maacah was the granddaughter of Absalom and the daughter of a marriage between Tamar (Absalom's daughter; see 2 Sam 14:27) and Uriel. Absalom's mother was also named Maacah (2 Sam 3:3).

15:3 *sins of his father.* See 14:22–24. *not wholly devoted to the LORD his God, like . . . his father David.* Although David fell into grievous sin, his heart was never divided between serving the Lord and serving the nature deities of the Canaanites.

15:4 *lamp in Jerusalem.* See note on 11:36.

15:5 *Uriah the Hittite.* See 2 Sam 11.

15:6 *Rehoboam.* See note on 12:24.

15:7 *rest of the acts of Abijam.* See 2 Chr 13. *Chronicles of the Kings of Judah.* See note on 14:29. *war between Abijam and Jeroboam.* Cf. v. 6; 14:30. From 2 Chr 13 it is clear that the chronic hostile relations of preceding years flared into serious combat in which Abijam defeated Jeroboam and took several towns from him, including Bethel (2 Chr 13:19).

15:8 *slept with his fathers.* See note on 1:21.

15:9 *twentieth year of Jeroboam.* 910 B.C. (see note on 14:20).

15:10 *forty-one years.* 910–869 B.C. *Maacah the daughter of Abishalom.* See note on v. 2.

15:12 *male cult prostitutes.* See note on 14:24. *removed all the idols which his fathers had made.* See 14:23.

15:13 *removed Maacah his mother.* 2 Chr 14:1–15:16 indicates a progression in Asa's reform over a period of years. Although Asa had destroyed pagan idols and altars early in his reign (2 Chr 14:2–3), it was not until after a victory over Zerah the Cushite (2 Chr 14:8–15) that Asa responded to the message of the prophet Azariah son of Oded by calling for a covenant renewal assembly in Jerusalem in the 15th year of his reign (2 Chr 15:10). After this assembly Asa deposed his grandmother (the Hebrew for "mother" here means "grandmother," a common usage) Maacah because of her idolatry (2 Chr 15:16). *made a horrid image as an Asherah.* See note on 14:15. It appears that Maacah's action was a deliberate attempt to counter Asa's reform.

15:14 *the high places were not taken away.* The reference here and in 2 Chr 15:17 is to those high places where the Lord was worshiped (for the question of legitimacy of worship of the Lord at high places see note on 3:2). When 2 Chr 14:3 indicates that Asa removed the high places, it is to be taken as a reference to the high places that were centers of pagan Canaanite worship (see 2 Chr 17:6; 20:33 for the same distinction). This same statement of qualified approval that is made of Asa is made of five other kings of Judah prior to the time of Hezekiah (Jehoshaphat, 22:43; Joash, 2 Kin 12:3; Amaziah, 2 Kin 14:4; Azariah, 2 Kin 15:4; Jotham, 2 Kin 15:35). *wholly devoted to the LORD.* See note on v. 3.

15:15 *dedicated things: silver and gold.* Most likely consisting of war booty that Abijam had taken from Jeroboam (2 Chr 13) and that Asa acquired from Zerah the Cushite (2 Chr 14:8–15).

15:16 *war between Asa and Baasha . . . all their days.* A reference to the chronic hostile relations that had existed ever since the division of the kingdom, rather than to full-scale combat (see notes on v. 7; 12:24; see also 2 Chr 15:19).

15:17 *fortified Ramah.* Baasha had recaptured the territory previously taken from Jeroboam by Abijam (see note on v. 7; see also 2 Chr 13:19) since Ramah was located south of Bethel and only about five miles north of Jerusalem. *prevent anyone from going out or coming in to Asa.* See 2 Chr 15:9–10.

15:18 *silver and the gold which were left.* That which remained

gold which were left in the treasuries of the house of the LORD and the treasuries of the king's house, and delivered them into the hand of his servants. And [b]King Asa sent them to Ben-hadad the son of Tabrimmon, the son of Hezion, king of Aram, who lived in [c]Damascus, saying,

19 "*Let there be* a [a]treaty between [1]you and me, *as* between my father and your father. Behold, I have sent you a present of silver and gold; go, break your treaty with Baasha king of Israel so that he will withdraw from me."

20 So Ben-hadad listened to King Asa and sent the commanders of his armies against the cities of Israel, and [1]conquered [a]Ijon, [b]Dan, [c]Abel-beth-maacah and all [d]Chinneroth, besides all the land of Naphtali.

21 When Baasha heard *of it,* [a]he ceased [1]fortifying Ramah and remained in [b]Tirzah.

22 Then King Asa made a proclamation to all Judah—none was exempt—and they carried away the stones of Ramah and its timber with which Baasha had built. And King Asa built with them [a]Geba of Benjamin and Mizpah.

Jehoshaphat Succeeds Asa

23 [a]Now the rest of all the acts of Asa and all his might and all that he did and the cities which he built, are they not written in the Book of the Chronicles of the Kings of Judah? But in the time of his old age he was diseased in his feet.

24 And Asa slept with his fathers and was buried with his fathers in the city of David his father; and [a]Jehoshaphat his son reigned in his place.

Nadab, then Baasha, Rules over Israel

25 Now [a]Nadab the son of Jeroboam became king over Israel in the second year of Asa king of Judah, and he reigned over Israel two years.

26 He did evil in the sight of the LORD, and [a]walked in the way of his father and [b]in his sin which he made Israel sin.

27 Then [a]Baasha the son of Ahijah of the house of Issachar conspired against him, and Baasha struck him down at [b]Gibbethon, which belonged to the Philistines, while Nadab and all Israel were laying siege to Gibbethon.

28 So Baasha killed him in the third year of Asa king of Judah and reigned in his place.

29 It came about as soon as he was king, he struck down all the household of Jeroboam. He did not leave to Jeroboam [1]any persons alive, until he had destroyed them, [a]according to the word of the LORD, which He spoke by His servant Ahijah the Shilonite,

30 *and* because of the sins of Jeroboam which he sinned, and [a]which he made Israel sin, because of his provocation with which he provoked the LORD God of Israel to anger.

31 [a]Now the rest of the acts of Nadab and all that he did, are they not written in the Book of the Chronicles of the Kings of Israel?

War with Judah

32 [a]There was war between Asa and Baasha king of Israel all their days.

18 [b]2 Kin 12:17, 18; 2 Chr 16:2 [c]Gen 14:15; 1 Kin 11:23, 24
19 [1]Lit *me and you* [a]2 Chr 16:7
20 [1]Lit *smote* [a]2 Kin 15:29 [b]Judg 18:29; 1 Kin 12:29 [c]2 Sam 20:15; 2 Kin 15:29 [d]Josh 11:2; 12:3
21 [1]Lit *building* [a]1 Kin 15:17 [b]1 Kin 14:17; 16:15-18
22 [a]Josh 18:24; 21:17
23 [a]2 Chr 16:11-14
24 [a]1 Kin 22:41-44; 2 Chr 17:1; Matt 1:8
25 [a]1 Kin 14:20
26 [a]1 Kin 12:28-33; 13:33, 34 [b]1 Kin 14:16; 15:30, 34
27 [a]1 Kin 14:14 [b]Josh 19:44; 21:23; 1 Kin 16:15
29 [1]Lit *any breath* [a]1 Kin 14:9-16
30 [a]1 Kin 15:26
31 [a]1 Kin 14:19
32 [a]1 Kin 15:16

after the plundering of Jerusalem by Shishak of Egypt (see 14:25). *Hezion.* It is not clear whether Hezion is to be identified with Rezon of Damascus (see 11:23–25) or regarded as the founder of a new dynasty.

15:19 *treaty . . . between my father and your father.* A reference to a previously unmentioned treaty between Abijam and Tabrimmon of Aram. When Tabrimmon died, Baasha succeeded in establishing a treaty with his successor Ben-hadad. Asa saw no hope for success against Baasha without the assistance provided by a renewal of the old treaty with Aram. Although his plan seemed to be successful, it was condemned by Hanani the prophet as a foolish act and a denial of reliance on the Lord (see 2 Chr 16:7–10). The true theocratic king was never to fear his enemies but to trust in the God of the covenant for security and protection (see note on 1 Sam 17:11). Ahaz was later to follow Asa's bad example and seek Assyria's help when he was attacked by Israel and Aram (see 2 Kin 16:5–9; Is 7).

15:20 *Naphtali.* The cities that Ben-hadad conquered in Naphtali were of particular importance because the major trade routes from Damascus going west to Tyre and southwest through the plain of Jezreel to the coastal plain and Egypt transversed this area. This same territory was later seized by the Assyrian ruler Tiglath-pileser III (2 Kin 15:29).

15:21 *Tirzah.* See note on 14:17.

15:22 *proclamation to all Judah.* Asa's action is reminiscent of the labor force conscripted by Solomon (5:13–14; 11:28). *Geba . . . Mizpah.* Asa established two border fortresses to check Baasha's desire to expand his territory southward. Geba was east of Ramah, and Mizpah was southwest of Ramah.

15:23 *rest of all the acts of Asa.* See 2 Chr 14:2–16:14. *Chronicles of the Kings of Judah.* See note on 14:29. *diseased in his feet.* See 2 Chr 16:12.

15:24 *slept with his fathers.* See note on 1:21. *Jehoshaphat his son reigned in his place.* For the reign of Jehoshaphat see 22:41–50; 2 Chr 17:1–21:1.

15:25 *second year of Asa.* See note on v. 1. The second year of Asa of Judah corresponded to the 22nd and last year of Jeroboam of Israel (see v. 9; 14:20). *two years.* 909–908 B.C.

15:26 *his sin which he made Israel sin.* Jeroboam's sin (see note on 14:16). Although Abijam of Judah occupied Bethel during the reign of Jeroboam (see note on v. 7), it is probable that the paganized worship Jeroboam initiated was continued elsewhere until control of Bethel was regained by Baasha.

15:27 *Gibbethon.* A town located between Jerusalem and Joppa (probably a few miles west of Gezer) in the territory originally assigned to Dan (Josh 19:43–45). This Levitical city (Josh 21:23) probably fell into Philistine hands at the time of the Philistine expansion in the period of the judges.

15:28 *third year of Asa.* 908 B.C. (see note on v. 10). It is likely that Baasha was a commander in Nadab's army and was able to secure the support of the military for his revolt.

15:29 *the word . . . He spoke by . . . Ahijah.* See 14:10–11.

15:30 *sins of Jeroboam which he sinned, and which he made Israel sin.* See note on 14:16.

15:31 *Chronicles of the Kings of Israel.* See note on 14:19.

15:32 *war . . . all their days.* See note on v. 16. The demise of Jeroboam's dynasty did not improve relations between the two kingdoms.

33 In the third year of Asa king of Judah, Baasha the son of Ahijah became king over all Israel at Tirzah, *and reigned* twenty-four years.

34 He did evil in the sight of the LORD, and [a]walked in the way of Jeroboam and in his sin which he made Israel sin.

Prophecy against Baasha

16 Now the word of the LORD came to [a]Jehu the son of [b]Hanani against Baasha, saying,

2 "Inasmuch as I [a]exalted you from the dust and made you leader over My people Israel, and [b]you have walked in the way of Jeroboam and have made My people Israel sin, provoking Me to anger with their sins,

3 behold, [a]I will consume [b]Baasha and his house, and [c]I will make your house like the house of Jeroboam the son of Nebat.

4 "[a]Anyone of Baasha who dies in the city the dogs will eat, and anyone of his who dies in the field the birds of the heavens will eat."

5 [a]Now the rest of the acts of Baasha and what he did and his might, are they not written in the Book of the Chronicles of the Kings of Israel?

The Israelite Kings

6 And Baasha slept with his fathers and was buried in [a]Tirzah, and Elah his son became king in his place.

7 Moreover, the word of the LORD through [a]the prophet Jehu the son of Hanani also came against Baasha and his household, both because of all the evil which he did in the sight of the LORD, provoking Him to anger with [b]the work of his hands, in being like the house of Jeroboam, and because [c]he struck [1]it.

8 In the twenty-sixth year of Asa king of Judah, Elah the son of Baasha became king over Israel at Tirzah, *and reigned* two years.

9 His servant [a]Zimri, commander of half his chariots, conspired against him. Now he *was* at Tirzah drinking himself drunk in the house of Arza, [b]who *was* over the household at Tirzah.

10 Then Zimri went in and struck him and put him to death in the twenty-seventh year of Asa king of Judah, and became king in his place.

11 It came about when he became king, as soon as he sat on his throne, that [a]he [1]killed all the household of Baasha; he did not leave [2]a single male, neither of his [3]relatives nor of his friends.

12 Thus Zimri destroyed all the household of Baasha, [a]according to the word of the LORD, which He spoke against Baasha through [b]Jehu the prophet,

13 for all the sins of Baasha and the sins of Elah his son, which they sinned and which they made Israel sin, [a]provoking the LORD God of Israel to anger with their [1]idols.

14 [a]Now the rest of the acts of Elah and all that he did, are they not written in the Book of the Chronicles of the Kings of Israel?

15 In the twenty-seventh year of Asa king of Judah, Zimri reigned seven days at Tirzah. Now the people were camped against [a]Gibbethon, which belonged to the Philistines.

16 The people who were camped heard [1]it said, "Zimri has conspired and has also struck down the king." Therefore all Israel

34 [a]1 Kin 15:26
16:1 [a]1 Kin 16:7; 2 Chr 19:2; 20:34 [b]2 Chr 16:7-10
2 [a]1 Sam 2:8; 1 Kin 14:7 [b]1 Kin 15:34
3 [a]1 Kin 14:10; 21:21 [b]1 Kin 16:11 [c]1 Kin 15:29
4 [a]1 Kin 14:11; 21:24
5 [a]1 Kin 14:19; 15:31
6 [a]1 Kin 14:17; 15:21
7 [a]1 Kin 16:1 [b]Ps 115:4; Is 2:8
7 [1]Or *him* [c]1 Kin 14:14; 15:27, 29
9 [a]2 Kin 9:30-33 [b]Gen 24:2; 39:4; 1 Kin 18:3
11 [1]Lit *smote* [2]Lit *him who urinates against the wall* [3]Lit *redeemers* [a]1 Kin 15:29; 16:3
12 [a]1 Kin 16:3 [b]2 Chr 19:2; 20:34
13 [1]Lit *vanities* [a]Deut 32:21; 1 Kin 15:30
14 [a]1 Kin 16:5
15 [a]1 Kin 15:27
16 [1]Lit *saying*

15:33 *third year of Asa.* 908 B.C. (see note on v. 10). *Tirzah.* See note on 14:17. *twenty-four years.* 908–886 B.C. His official years were counted as 24, though his actual years were 23 (see 16:8; see also Introduction: Chronology).

15:34 *his sin which he made Israel sin.* See note on 14:16. The assessment of Baasha's reign indicates no improvement over the reign of Nadab, whom he replaced (see v. 26).

16:1 *Jehu.* Like his father before him (see 2 Chr 16:7–10), Jehu brought God's word of condemnation to a king. Much as the man of God from Judah (see note on 13:1) and later the prophet Amos, he was sent from the south to a northern king. His ministry continued for about 50 years until the reign of Jehoshaphat of Judah (2 Chr 19:2; 20:34).

16:2 *I exalted you from the dust.* Cf. 14:7. *walked in the way of Jeroboam.* See note on 14:16.

16:3 *consume Baasha and his house.* Cf. 14:10 (the house of Jeroboam); 21:21 (the house of Omri and Ahab).

16:4 Identical to the prophecy against Jeroboam's dynasty in 14:11.

16:5 *his might.* For the purposes of the writer of Kings (see Introduction: Theme), it was not necessary to list any of Baasha's achievements. He may have been a very successful ruler from a military-political point of view. *Chronicles of the Kings of Israel.* See note on 14:19.

16:6 *slept with his fathers.* See note on 1:21.

16:7 *evil which he did . . . like the house of Jeroboam.* See v. 2; 15:34. *he struck it.* Although Baasha fulfilled God's purpose (14:10,14) in destroying the house of Jeroboam, he remained responsible for this violent and unlawful act (cf. Gen 50:20; Is 10:5–7,12).

16:8 *twenty-sixth year of Asa.* 886 B.C. (see note on 15:10; see also Introduction: Chronology). *two years.* 886–885 B.C.

16:9 *drinking himself drunk.* The fact that Elah was carousing at Tirzah while the army was laying siege to Gibbethon (v. 15) indicates he had little perception of his responsibilities as king.

16:10 *twenty-seventh year of Asa.* 885 B.C.

16:11 *killed all the household of Baasha.* See 15:29; 2 Kin 10:1–7; 11:1. *friends.* Probably including the chief adviser to the king (see note on 2 Sam 15:37).

16:12 *word of the LORD . . . through Jehu the prophet.* See vv. 1–4. Zimri did not consciously decide to fulfill Jehu's prophecy, but unwittingly he became the instrument by which Jehu's prediction was fulfilled (see note on v. 7) when he conspired against Elah and destroyed the dynasty of Baasha.

16:13 *sins of Baasha and . . . Elah his son, which they sinned.* See 15:34. *idols.* A reference to all the paganism in Israel's religious observances, including the use of the golden calves in worship (see 12:28; 14:9).

16:14 *Chronicles of the Kings of Israel.* See note on 14:19.

16:15 *twenty-seventh year of Asa.* 885 B.C. (see notes on 15:1,10). *Gibbethon.* See notes on v. 9; 15:27.

16:16 *conspired and . . . struck down the king.* See vv. 9–12. *Omri, the commander of the army.* He held a higher rank than Zimri did under Elah (v. 9).

made Omri, the commander of the army,
king over Israel that day in the camp.
17 Then Omri and all Israel with him went
up from Gibbethon and besieged Tirzah.
18 When Zimri saw that the city was tak-
en, he went into the citadel of the king's
house and burned the king's house over him
with fire, and [a]died,
19 because of his sins which he sinned,
doing evil in the sight of the LORD, [a]walking
in the way of Jeroboam, and in his sin which
he did, making Israel sin.
20 [a]Now the rest of the acts of Zimri and
his conspiracy which he [1]carried out, are
they not written in the Book of the Chronicles of the Kings of Israel?
21 Then the people of Israel were divided
into two parts: half of the people followed
Tibni the son of Ginath, to make him king;
the *other* half followed Omri.
22 But the people who followed Omri prevailed over the people who followed Tibni
the son of Ginath. And Tibni died and Omri
became king.
23 In the thirty-first year of Asa king of
Judah, Omri became king over Israel *and
reigned* twelve years; he reigned six years at
[a]Tirzah.
24 He bought the hill [1]Samaria from Shemer for two talents of silver; and he built on
the hill, and named the city which he built
[1][a]Samaria, after the name of Shemer, the
owner of the hill.
25 [a]Omri did evil in the sight of the LORD,
and [b]acted more wickedly than all who *were*
before him.
26 For he [a]walked in all the way of Jeroboam the son of Nebat and in his sins which
he made Israel sin, provoking the LORD God
of Israel with their [1]idols.
27 Now the rest of the acts of Omri which
he did and his might which he [1]showed, are
they not written in the Book of the Chronicles of the Kings of Israel?
28 So Omri slept with his fathers and was
buried in Samaria; and Ahab his son became
king in his place.
29 Now Ahab the son of Omri became king
over Israel in the thirty-eighth year of Asa king
of Judah, and Ahab the son of Omri reigned
over Israel in Samaria twenty-two years.
30 Ahab the son of Omri did evil in the
sight of the LORD [a]more than all who were
before him.
31 It came about, as though it had been a
trivial thing for him to walk in the sins of Jeroboam the son of Nebat, that [a]he married
Jezebel the daughter of Ethbaal king of the
[b]Sidonians, and went to serve Baal and worshiped him.

18 [a]1 Sam 31:4, 5; 2 Sam 17:23
19 [a]1 Kin 12:28; 14:16; 15:26
20 [1]Lit *conspired* [a]1 Kin 16:5, 14, 27
23 [a]1 Kin 15:21
24 [1]Heb *Shomeron*

24 [1]Heb *Shomeron* [a]1 Kin 16:28, 29, 32
25 [a]Mic 6:16 [b]1 Kin 14:9; 16:30-33
26 [1]Lit *vanities* [a]1 Kin 16:19
27 [1]Lit *did*
30 [a]1 Kin 14:9; 16:25
31 [a]Deut 7:1-5 [b]Judg 18:7; 1 Kin 11:1-5; 2 Kin 10:18; 17:16

16:17 *Tirzah.* The royal residence (see vv. 8–10; see also note on 14:17).
16:19 *way of Jeroboam.* See note on 14:16.
16:20 *Chronicles of the Kings of Israel.* See note on 14:19.
16:22 *Tibni died.* It is not clear whether Tibni's death was due to natural causes or the result of the military struggle for control of the land.
16:23 *thirty-first year of Asa.* 880 B.C. (see note on 15:10; see also Introduction: Chronology). *became king.* Became sole king. The struggle for control of the northern kingdom between Omri and Tibni lasted four years (compare this verse with v. 15). *twelve years.* 885–874. The 12 years of Omri's reign include the four years of struggle between Omri and Tibni (cf. vv. 15,29). *Tirzah.* See note on 14:17. Omri had been able to capture Tirzah in a matter of days (vv. 15–19).
16:24 *Samaria.* Seven miles northwest of Shechem, Samaria rose about 300 feet above the surrounding fertile valleys (referred to as a "crown" in Is 28:1). The original owner may have been persuaded to sell his property (see 21:3) on the condition that the city be named after him (cf. Ruth 4:5). The site provided an ideal location for a nearly impregnable capital city for the northern kingdom (see 20:1–21; 2 Kin 6:25; 18:9–10). With the establishment of this royal city, the kings of the north came to possess a royal citadel-city like that of the Davidic dynasty (see 2 Sam 5:6–12). Archaeologists have discovered that Omri and Ahab also adorned it with magnificent structures to rival those Solomon had erected in Jerusalem. From this time on, the northern kingdom could be designated by the name of the royal city, just as the southern kingdom could be designated by its capital, Jerusalem (see, e.g., 21:1; Is 10:10; Amos 6:1).
16:25 *acted more wickedly than all.* Omri's alliance with Ethbaal of Tyre and Sidon (Omri's son Ahab married Ethbaal's daughter Jezebel to seal the alliance) led to widespread Baal worship in the northern kingdom (vv. 31–33) and eventually to the near extinction of the Davidic line in the southern kingdom (see 2 Kin 11; see also note on 2 Kin 8:18). This marriage alliance must have been established in the early years of Omri's reign (see note on v. 23), perhaps to strengthen his hand against Tibni (see vv. 21–22).
16:26 *sins which he made Israel sin.* See 12:26–33; see also note on 14:16. *idols.* See note on v. 13.
16:27 *his might which he showed.* Omri's military and political accomplishments were not of importance for the purposes of the writer of Kings (see Introduction: Theme). Apart from establishing Samaria as the capital of the northern kingdom, about all that is known of him is that he organized a governmental structure in the northern kingdom that was in place during the rule of his son, Ahab (see 20:14–15). Omri's dynasty, however, endured for over 40 years. A century and a half later (732 B.C.) Tiglath-pileser III of Assyria referred to Israel as the "house of Omri" in his annals. *Chronicles of the Kings of Israel.* See note on 14:19.
16:28 *slept with his fathers.* See note on 1:21.
16:29 *thirty-eighth year of Asa.* 874 B.C. (see notes on 15:9–10). *twenty-two years.* 874–853 B.C.
16:30 *did evil . . . more than all.* Omri sinned more than those before him (see v. 25), and Ahab sinned more than his father had. Evil became progressively worse in the royal house of the northern kingdom. Nearly a third of the narrative material in 1,2 Kings concerns the 34-year period of the reigns of Ahab and his two sons, Ahaziah and Joram. In this period the struggle between the kingdom of God (championed especially by Elijah and Elisha) and the kingdom of Satan was especially intense.
16:31 *married Jezebel the daughter of Ethbaal.* The Jewish historian Josephus refers to Ethbaal as a king-priest who ruled over Tyre and Sidon for 32 years. Ahab had already married Jezebel during the reign of his father (see note on v. 25). *Baal.* Perhaps Melqart, the local manifestation of Baal in Tyre, whose worship was brought to Israel by Jezebel. It is probable that Ahab participated in the worship of this deity at the time of his marriage.

32 So he erected an altar for Baal in [a]the
house of Baal which he built in Samaria.
33 Ahab also made [a]the [1]Asherah. Thus
[b]Ahab did more to provoke the LORD God of
Israel than all the kings of Israel who were
before him.
34 [a]In his days Hiel the Bethelite built Jericho; he laid its foundations with the *loss of*
Abiram his firstborn, and set up its gates
with the *loss of* his youngest son Segub,
according to the word of the LORD, which He
spoke by Joshua the son of Nun.

Elijah Predicts Drought

17 Now Elijah the Tishbite, who was of
[1a]the settlers of Gilead, said to Ahab,
"[b]As the LORD, the God of Israel lives, before
whom I stand, surely [c]there shall be neither
dew nor rain these years, except by my word."
2 The word of the LORD came to him, saying,
3 "Go away from here and turn eastward,
and hide yourself by the brook Cherith,
which is [1]east of the Jordan.
4 "It shall be that you will drink of the
brook, and [a]I have commanded the ravens
to provide for you there."
5 So he went and did according to the
word of the LORD, for he went and lived by
the brook Cherith, which is [1]east of the Jordan.
6 The ravens brought him bread and
meat in the morning and bread and meat in
the evening, and he would drink from the
brook.
7 It happened after a while that the
brook dried up, because there was no rain in
the land.
8 Then the word of the LORD came to
him, saying,
9 "Arise, go to [a]Zarephath, which belongs
to Sidon, and stay there; behold, [b]I have commanded a widow there to provide for you."
10 So he arose and went to Zarephath,
and when he came to the gate of the city,
behold, a widow was there gathering sticks;
and [a]he called to her and said, "Please get
me a little water in a [1]jar, that I may drink."
11 As she was going to get *it,* he called to
her and said, "Please bring me a piece of
bread in your hand."
12 But she said, "[a]As the LORD your God
lives, [b]I have no [1]bread, only a handful of
flour in the [2]bowl and a little oil in the jar;

32 [a]2 Kin 10:21, 26, 27
33 [1]I.e. wooden symbol of a female deity [a]2 Kin 13:6 [b]1 Kin 14:9; 16:29, 30; 21:25
34 [a]Josh 6:26
17:1 [1]Or *Tishbe in Gilead* [a]Judg 12:4 [b]1 Kin 18:10; 22:14; 2 Kin 3:14; 5:20 [c]1 Kin 18:1; Luke 4:25; James 5:17
3 [1]Lit *before*
4 [a]1 Kin 17:9
5 [1]Lit *before*
9 [a]Obad 20; Luke 4:26 [b]1 Kin 17:4
10 [1]Or *vessel* [a]Gen 24:17; John 4:7
12 [1]Lit *cake* [2]Lit *pitcher* [a]1 Kin 17:1 [b]2 Kin 4:2-7

The names of Ahab's sons (Ahaziah, "The LORD grasps"; Joram, "The LORD is exalted") suggest that Ahab did not intend to replace the worship of the Lord with the worship of Baal but to worship both deities in a syncretistic way.
16:32 *house of Baal which he built in Samaria.* Ahab imported the Phoenician Baal worship of his wife Jezebel into the northern kingdom by constructing a temple of Baal in Samaria, just as Solomon had erected the temple of the Lord in Jerusalem. This pagan temple and its sacred stone (see note on 14:23) were later destroyed by Jehu (2 Kin 10:21–27).
16:33 *Asherah.* See note on 14:15. *than all the kings of Israel.* See note on v. 30. Ahab elevated the worship of Baal to an official status in the northern kingdom at the beginning of his reign.
16:34 *built Jericho.* Does not mean that Jericho had remained uninhabited since its destruction by Joshua (see Josh 18:21; Judg 1:16; 3:13; 2 Sam 10:5), but that it had remained an unwalled town or village. During the rule of Ahab, Hiel fortified the city by reconstructing its walls and gates (see 9:17 for a similar use of "rebuilt"). This violated God's intention that the ruins of Jericho (Josh 6:26) be a perpetual reminder that Israel had received the land of Canaan from God's hand as a gift of grace. Accordingly, Hiel suffered the curse Joshua had pronounced.
17:1 *Elijah.* Elijah's name (meaning "The LORD is my God") was the essence of his message (18:21,39). He was sent to oppose vigorously, by word and action, both Baal worship and those who engaged in it. *of the settlers of Gilead.* See NASB marg. Gilead was in the northern Transjordan area. The precise location of Tishbe is unknown. *before whom I stand.* A technical expression indicating one who stands in the service of a king. Kings and priests in Israel were supposed to be anointed to serve as official representatives of the Lord, Israel's Great King, leading Israel in the way of faithfulness to the Lord and channeling His covenantal care and blessings to them. Since the days of Jeroboam the northern kingdom had not had such a priest (12:31), and its kings had all been unfaithful. Now, in the great crisis brought on by Ahab's promotion of Baal worship, the Lord sent Elijah (and after him Elisha) to serve as His representative (instead of king and priest), much as Moses had done long ago. The author of Kings highlights many parallels between the ministries of Elijah and Moses. *neither dew nor rain.* The drought was not only a divine judgment on a nation that had turned to idolatry, but also a demonstration that even though Baal was considered the god of fertility and lord of the rain clouds, he was powerless to give rain (cf. Lev 26:3–4; Hos 2:5,8).
17:3 *Go away from here.* With this command God withdrew His prophet from His land and people to leave them isolated from His word and blessings. The absence of the prophet confirmed and intensified the judgment. *brook Cherith . . . east of the Jordan.* The location of Cherith is uncertain. Perhaps it was a gorge formed by one of the northern tributaries to the Yarmuk River.
17:4 *ravens to provide for you there.* The Lord's faithful servant Elijah was miraculously sustained beyond the Jordan (like Israel in the wilderness in the time of Moses) while Israel in the promised land was going hungry—a clear testimony against Israel's reliance on Baal. The fact that Elijah was sustained in a miraculous way apart from living among his own people demonstrated that the word of God was not dependent on the people, but the people were dependent on the word of God.
17:9 *Zarephath, which belongs to Sidon.* A coastal town located between Tyre and Sidon in the territory ruled by Jezebel's father Ethbaal (16:31). Elijah is commanded to go and reside in the heart of the very land from which the Baal worship now being promoted in Israel had come. *I have commanded a widow there to provide for you.* Elijah, as the bearer of God's word, was now to be sustained by human hands, but they were the hands of a poor widow facing starvation (v. 12). She was, moreover, from outside the circle of God's own people (cf. Luke 4:25–26)—in fact, she was from the pagan nation that at that time (much like Egypt earlier and Babylon later) represented the forces arrayed against God's kingdom.
17:10 *So he arose and went.* Elijah's reliance on the Lord demonstrated the faith in the Lord that Israel should have been living by.
17:12 *As the LORD your God lives.* Her oath in the name of the Lord was either an accommodation to Elijah, whom she recognized as an Israelite (see notes on 5:7; 10:9), or a genuine expres-

and behold, I am gathering [3]a few sticks that I may go in and prepare for me and my son, that we may eat it and [c]die."

13 Then Elijah said to her, "Do not fear; go, do as you have said, but make me a little bread cake from [1]it first and bring *it* out to me, and afterward you may make *one* for yourself and for your son.

14 "For thus says the LORD God of Israel, 'The [1]bowl of flour shall not be exhausted, nor shall the jar of oil [2]be empty, until the day that the LORD sends rain on the face of the earth.' "

15 So she went and did according to the word of Elijah, and she and he and her household ate for *many* days.

16 The [1]bowl of flour was not exhausted nor did the jar of oil [2]become empty, according to the word of the LORD which He spoke through Elijah.

Elijah Raises the Widow's Son

17 Now it came about after these things that the son of the woman, the mistress of the house, became sick; and his sickness was so severe that there was no breath left in him.

18 So she said to Elijah, "[a]What do I have to do with you, O [b]man of God? [1]You have come to me to bring my iniquity to remembrance and to put my son to death!"

19 He said to her, "Give me your son." Then he took him from her bosom and carried him up to the upper room where he was living, and laid him on his own bed.

20 He called to the LORD and said, "O LORD my God, have You also brought calamity to the widow with whom I am [1]staying, by causing her son to die?"

21 [a]Then he stretched himself upon the child three times, and called to the LORD and said, "O LORD my God, I pray You, let this child's life return [1]to him."

22 The LORD heard the voice of Elijah, [a]and the life of the child returned [1]to him and he revived.

23 Elijah took the child and brought him down from the upper room into the house and gave him to his mother; and Elijah said, "See, your son is alive."

24 Then the woman said to Elijah, "[a]Now I know that you are a man of God and that the word of the LORD in your mouth is truth."

Obadiah Meets Elijah

18 Now it happened [a]*after* many days that the word of the LORD came to Elijah in the third year, saying, "Go, show yourself to Ahab, and [b]I will send rain on the face of the earth."

2 So Elijah went to show himself to Ahab. Now the famine *was* severe in Samaria.

3 Ahab called Obadiah [a]who *was* over the household. (Now Obadiah [1b]feared the LORD greatly;

4 for [a]when Jezebel [1]destroyed the prophets of the LORD, Obadiah took a hundred prophets and hid them by fifties in a cave, and [b]provided them with bread and water.)

12 [3]Lit *two* [c]Gen 21:15, 16
13 [1]Lit *there*
14 [1]Lit *pitcher* [2]Lit *lack*
16 [1]Lit *pitcher* [2]Lit *lack*
18 [1]Or *Have you come... death?* [a]2 Sam 16:10; 2 Kin 3:13; Luke 4:34; John 2:4 [b]1 Kin 12:22
20 [1]Lit *sojourning*
21 [1]Lit *upon his inward part* [a]2 Kin 4:34, 35; Acts 20:10
22 [1]Lit *upon his inward part* [a]Luke 7:14; Heb 11:35
24 [a]John 2:11; 3:2; 16:30
18:1 [a]1 Kin 17:1; Luke 4:25; James 5:17 [b]Deut 28:12
3 [1]Or *revered* [a]1 Kin 16:9 [b]Neh 7:2; Job 28:28
4 [1]Lit *cut off* [a]1 Kin 18:13 [b]Matt 10:40-42

---

sion of previous knowledge of and commitment to the God of Israel.

17:13 *make me a little bread cake from it first and . . . afterward you may make one for yourself and for your son.* As a prophet, Elijah's words are the command of the Lord. The widow is asked to give all she has to sustain the bearer of the word of God. The demand to give her all is in essence the demand of the covenant that Israel had broken.

17:14 *thus says the LORD God of Israel.* Elijah can tell the widow "Do not fear" (v. 13) because the demand of the covenant is not given without the promise of the covenant. The Lord does not ask more than He promises to give.

17:15 *did according to the word of Elijah.* By an act of faith the woman received the promised blessing. Israel had forsaken the covenant and followed Baal and Asherah in search of prosperity. Now in the midst of a pagan kingdom a widow realized that trustful obedience to the word of God is the way that leads to life.

17:16 *bowl of flour was not exhausted.* God miraculously provided for this non-Israelite who, in an act of faith in the Lord's word, had laid her life on the line. He gave her "manna" from heaven even while He was withholding food from His unfaithful people in the promised land. The warning of Deut 32:21 was being fulfilled (cf. Rom 10:19; 11:11,14).

17:18 *You have come . . . to bring my iniquity to remembrance and to put my son to death!* The widow concluded that Elijah's presence in her house had called God's attention to her sin, and that the death of her son was a divine punishment for this sin. Although her sense of guilt seems to have been influenced by pagan ideas, both she and Elijah are confronted with the question: Why did the God who promised life bring death instead?

17:21 *stretched himself upon the child three times.* The apparent intent of this physical contact was to transfer the bodily warmth and stimulation of the prophet to the child. Elijah's prayer, however, makes it clear that he expected the life of the child to return as an answer to prayer, not as a result of bodily contact. *let this child's life return to him.* Moved by a faith like that of Abraham (Rom 4:17; Heb 11:19), Elijah prayed for the child's return to life so that the veracity and trustworthiness of God's word might be demonstrated.

17:22 *the life of the child returned to him.* The first instance of raising the dead recorded in Scripture. This non-Israelite widow was granted the supreme covenant blessing, the gift of life rescued from the power of death. This blessing came in the person of her son, the only hope for a widow in ancient society (see 2 Kin 4:14; Ruth 1:11–12; 4:15–17; Luke 7:12).

17:24 *you are a man of God.* The widow had addressed Elijah as a man of God previously (v. 18), but now she knew in a much more experiential way that he truly was a prophet of the Lord (see note on 12:22). *the word of the LORD in your mouth is truth.* God used this experience to convince the Phoenician widow that His word was completely reliable. Her confession was one that the Lord's own people in Israel had failed to make.

18:1 *third year.* Apparently of the drought. Later Jewish tradition indicates that the drought lasted three and a half years (cf. Luke 4:25; James 5:17), but that probably represents a symbolic number for a drought cut short (half of seven years; see Gen 41:27; 2 Kin 8:1). *show yourself to Ahab, and I will send rain on the face of the earth.* Elijah's return is not occasioned by repentance in Israel but by the command of the Lord, who in His sovereign grace determined to reveal Himself anew to His people.

18:3 *Obadiah.* A common OT name, meaning "servant of the LORD." *over the household.* See note on 4:6.

5 Then Ahab said to Obadiah, "Go through the land to all the springs of water and to all the valleys; perhaps we will find grass and keep the horses and mules alive, and not [1]have to kill some of the cattle."

6 So they divided the land between them to [1]survey it; Ahab went one way by himself and Obadiah went another way by himself.

7 Now as Obadiah was on the way, behold, Elijah [1]met him, [a]and he recognized him and fell on his face and said, "Is this you, Elijah my master?"

8 He said to him, "It is I. Go, say to your master, 'Behold, Elijah *is here.*'"

9 He said, "What [1]sin have I committed, that you are giving your servant into the hand of Ahab to put me to death?

10 "[a]As the LORD your God lives, there is no nation or kingdom where my master has not sent to search for you; and when they said, 'He is not *here,*' he made the kingdom or nation swear that they could not find you.

11 "And now you are saying, 'Go, say to your master, "Behold, Elijah *is here.*"'

12 "It will come about when I leave you [a]that the Spirit of the LORD will carry you where I do not know; so when I come and tell Ahab and he cannot find you, he will kill me, although *I* your servant have [1]feared the LORD from my youth.

13 "[a]Has it not been told to my master what I did when Jezebel killed the prophets of the LORD, that I hid [1]a hundred prophets of the LORD by fifties in a cave, and provided them with bread and water?

14 "And now you are saying, 'Go, say to your master, "Behold, Elijah *is here*"'; he will then kill me."

15 Elijah said, "[a]As the LORD of hosts lives, before whom I stand, I will surely show myself to him today."

16 So Obadiah went to meet Ahab and told him; and Ahab went to meet Elijah.

17 When Ahab saw Elijah, [a]Ahab said to him, "Is this you, you troubler of Israel?"

18 He said, "I have not troubled Israel, but you and your father's house *have,* because [a]you have forsaken the commandments of the LORD and [b]you have followed the Baals.

19 "Now then send *and* gather to me all Israel at [a]Mount Carmel, [b]*together* with 450 prophets of Baal and 400 prophets of [c]the Asherah, who eat at Jezebel's table."

God or Baal on Mount Carmel

20 So Ahab sent *a message* among all the sons of Israel and brought the prophets together at Mount Carmel.

21 Elijah came near to all the people and said, "[a]How long *will* you [1]hesitate between two opinions? [b]If the LORD is God, follow Him; but if Baal, follow him." But the people did not answer him a word.

22 Then Elijah said to the people, "I [a]alone am left a prophet of the LORD, but Baal's prophets are [b]450 men.

23 "Now let them give us two oxen; and let them choose one ox for themselves and cut it up, and place it on the wood, but put no fire *under it;* and I will prepare the other ox and lay it on the wood, and I will not put a fire *under it.*

24 "Then you call on the name of your god, and I will call on the name of the LORD, and [a]the God who answers by fire, He is God." And all the people said, "[1]That is a good idea."

25 So Elijah said to the prophets of Baal, "Choose one ox for yourselves and prepare it first for you are many, and call on the name of your god, but put no fire *under it.*"

26 Then they took the ox which [1]was giv-

5 [1]Lit *cut off*
6 [1]Lit *pass through*
7 [1]Lit *to meet* [a]2 Kin 1:6-8
9 [1]Lit *have I sinned*
10 [a]1 Kin 17:1
12 [1]Or *revered* [a]2 Kin 2:16; Ezek 3:12, 14; Acts 8:39
13 [1]Lit *a hundred men of the prophets* [a]1 Kin 18:4
15 [a]1 Kin 17:1
17 [a]Josh 7:25; 1 Kin 21:20
18 [a]1 Kin 9:9; 2 Chr 15:2 [b]1 Kin 16:31; 21:25, 26
19 [a]Josh 19:26; 2 Kin 2:25 [b]1 Kin 18:22 [c]1 Kin 16:33
21 [1]Lit *limp on the two divided opinions* [a]2 Kin 17:41; Matt 6:24 [b]Josh 24:15
22 [a]1 Kin 19:10, 14 [b]1 Kin 18:19
24 [1]Lit *The matter is good* [a]1 Kin 18:38
26 [1]Lit *he gave*

18:5 The famine did not move Ahab to repentance (contrast Ahab's response to the famine with that of David years earlier, 2 Sam 21:1). But when his military strength seemed to be jeopardized, he scoured the land for food and water (see 10:26; according to the annals of the Assyrian ruler Shalmaneser III, Ahab had a force of at least 2,000 chariots).

18:8 *say to your master, 'Behold, Elijah is here.'* This action would publicly identify Obadiah with Elijah in contrast to his previous clandestine support of the prophets sought by Jezebel (see vv. 4,13).

18:12 *the Spirit of the LORD will carry you where I do not know.* Elijah's disappearance earlier and now his sudden reappearance suggested to Obadiah that God's Spirit was miraculously transporting the prophet about (see 2 Kin 2:16).

18:13 *Jezebel killed the prophets.* Possibly in an attempt to please Baal so he would send rain. *prophets of the LORD.* Probably members of the communities of "prophets" that had sprung up in Israel during this time of apostasy (see note on 20:35).

18:17 *you troubler of Israel.* Ahab holds Elijah to account for the drought and charges him with a crime against the state worthy of death (he calls him a trouble bringer; see Josh 7:25).

18:18 *You have forsaken the commandments of the LORD and . . . followed the Baals.* The source of Israel's trouble was not Elijah or even the drought, but the breach of covenantal loyalty.

18:19 *Mount Carmel.* A high ridge next to the Mediterranean Sea, where the effects of the drought would be least apparent (see Amos 1:2) and the power of Baal to nurture life would seem to be strongest. *prophets of Baal . . . prophets of the Asherah.* See v. 29 and note. *Asherah.* See note on 14:15. *eat at Jezebel's table.* See note on 2:7.

18:21 *hesitate.* The Hebrew for this word is the same as that used for "leaped" in v. 26 (see note there). Elijah speaks with biting irony: In her religious ambivalence Israel is but engaging in a wild and futile religious "dance." *If the LORD is God, follow Him; but if Baal, follow him.* Elijah placed a clear choice before the people. He drew a sharp contrast between the worship of the Lord and that of Baal, to eliminate the apostate idea that both deities could be worshiped in a syncretistic way.

18:22 *I alone am left.* At least the only one to stand boldly and publicly against the king and the prophets of Baal (but see v. 4; 19:10,14; 20:13,28,35; 22:6,8; see also 19:18 and note).

18:24 *The God who answers by fire, He is God.* Both the Lord and Baal were said to ride the thunderstorm as their divine chariot (see Ps 104:3 and note); thunder was their voice (see Ps 29:3–9 and note) and lightning ("fire") their weapon (see Ps 18:14 and note). Elijah's challenge is direct. Cf. Lev 9:24.

en them and they prepared it and called on
the name of Baal from morning until noon
saying, "O Baal, answer us." But there was
[a]no voice and no one answered. And they
[2]leaped about the altar which [3]they made.
27 It came about at noon, that Elijah
mocked them and said, "Call out with a loud
voice, for he is a god; either he is occupied or
gone aside, or is on a journey, or perhaps he
is asleep and needs to be awakened."
28 So they cried with a loud voice and
[a]cut themselves according to their custom
with swords and lances until the blood
gushed out on them.
29 When midday was past, they [1]raved
[a]until the time of the offering of the *evening*
sacrifice; but there was no voice, no one
answered, and no [2]one paid attention.
30 Then Elijah said to all the people,
"Come near to me." So all the people came
near to him. And [a]he repaired the altar of the
LORD which had been torn down.
31 Elijah took twelve stones according to
the number of the tribes of the sons of Jacob,
to whom the word of the LORD had come,
saying, "[a]Israel shall be your name."
32 So with the stones he built an altar in
[a]the name of the LORD, and he made a trench
around the altar, large enough to hold two
[1]measures of seed.
33 [a]Then he arranged the wood and cut
the ox in pieces and laid *it* on the wood.
34 And he said, "Fill four pitchers with
water and pour *it* on the burnt offering and
on the wood." And he said, "Do it a second
time," and they did it a second time. And he
said, "Do it a third time," and they did it a
third time.
35 The water flowed around the altar and
he also filled the trench with water.

Elijah's Prayer

36 [a]At the time of the offering of the
evening sacrifice, Elijah the prophet came
near and said, "[b]O LORD, the God of Abraham, Isaac and Israel, today let it be known
that [c]You are God in Israel and that I am Your
servant and [d]I have done all these things at
Your word.
37 "Answer me, O LORD, answer me, that
this people may know that You, O LORD, are
God, and *that* You have turned their heart
back again."
38 Then the [a]fire of the LORD fell and consumed the burnt offering and the wood and
the stones and the dust, and licked up the
water that was in the trench.
39 When all the people saw it, they fell on
their faces; and they said, "[a]The LORD, He is
God; the LORD, He is God."
40 Then Elijah said to them, "Seize the
prophets of Baal; do not let one of them
escape." So they seized them; and Elijah
brought them down to [a]the brook Kishon,
[b]and slew them there.
41 Now Elijah said to Ahab, "Go up, eat
and drink; for there is the sound of the roar
of a *heavy* shower."
42 So Ahab went up to eat and drink. But
Elijah went up to the top of [a]Carmel; and he
[b]crouched down on the earth and put his
face between his knees.
43 He said to his servant, "Go up now,
look toward the sea." So he went up and
looked and said, "There is nothing." And he
said, "Go back" seven times.
44 It came about at the seventh *time*, that
he said, "Behold, [a]a cloud as small as a
man's hand is coming up from the sea." And
he said, "Go up, say to Ahab, '[1]Prepare *your*

26 [2]Lit *limped;* i.e. a type of ceremonial dance [3]So some mss and the ancient versions; M.T. *he* [a]Ps 115:4, 5; Jer 10:5
28 [a]Lev 19:28; Deut 14:1
29 [1]Lit *prophesied* [2]Lit *attentiveness* [a]Ex 29:39, 41
30 [a]1 Kin 19:10, 14; 2 Chr 33:16
31 [a]Gen 32:28; 35:10; 2 Kin 17:34
32 [1]Heb *seahs;* i.e. one seah equals approx 11 qts [a]Col 3:17
33 [a]Gen 22:9; Lev 1:7, 8
36 [a]1 Kin 18:29 [b]Gen 28:13; Ex 3:6; 4:5; Matt 22:32 [c]1 Kin 8:43 [d]Num 16:28-32
38 [a]Gen 15:17; Lev 9:24; 10:1, 2; Judg 6:21; 2 Kin 1:12; 1 Chr 21:26; 2 Chr 7:1; Job 1:16
39 [a]1 Kin 18:21, 24
40 [a]Judg 4:7; 5:21 [b]Deut 13:5; 18:20; 2 Kin 10:24, 25
42 [a]1 Kin 18:19, 20 [b]James 5:18
44 [1]Lit *Tie, harness* [a]Luke 12:54

18:26 *leaped about the altar.* The ecstatic cultic dance was part of the pagan ritual intended to arouse the deity to perform some desired action.
18:27 *occupied . . . asleep.* Elijah ridicules, but as he does he shows knowledge of the Baal myths.
18:28 *until the blood gushed out.* Self-inflicted wounds (causing blood to flow) were symbolic of self-sacrifice as an extreme method of arousing the deity to action. Such mutilation of the body was strictly forbidden in the Mosaic law (Lev 19:28; Deut 14:1).
18:29 *raved.* Indicative of ecstatic raving, in which the ritual reached its climax (see notes on 1 Sam 10:5; 18:10). *time of the . . . evening sacrifice.* See Ex 29:38–41; Num 28:3–8. *no voice.* Dramatic demonstration of Baal's impotence (see Ps 115:5–8; 135:15–18; Jer 10:5).
18:30 *altar of the LORD which had been torn down.* It is possible that the altar had been built by people of the northern ten tribes after the division of the kingdom (see note on 3:2) and that it had been destroyed by the agents of Jezebel (vv. 4,13; 19:10,14).
18:31 *twelve stones according to the number of the tribes.* In this way Elijah called attention to the covenant unity of Israel as the people of God in spite of her political division. What was about to happen concerned the entire nation, not just the northern ten tribes.
18:34 *water.* By drenching the whole installation Elijah showed to all that he was using no tricks.
18:36 *said.* Elijah's simple but earnest prayer stands in sharp contrast to the frantic shouts and "dancing" and self-mutilation of the Baal prophets. *God of Abraham, Isaac and Israel.* An appeal to the Lord to remember His ancient covenant with the patriarchs, and to Israel to remember all that the Lord has done for her since the days of her forefathers.
18:38 *fire of the LORD fell.* See note on v. 24.
18:40 *slew them there.* Elijah, acting on the authority of the Lord, who sent him, carried out the sentence pronounced in the Mosaic law for prophets of pagan deities (Deut 13:13–18; 17:2–5).
18:41 *sound of . . . a heavy shower.* Now that Baal worship has been struck a devastating blow, there is the promise of rain (see 17:1). Significantly, Ahab takes no action—either to carry out the Mosaic sentence or to halt Elijah.
18:42 *Elijah . . . crouched down on the earth and put his face between his knees.* Now that the people had confessed that the Lord alone was God, Elijah prayed for the covenant curse to be lifted (see note on 17:1) by the coming of rain (see 8:35; 2 Chr 7:13–14).
18:43 *Seven times.* The number symbolic of completeness.
18:44 *coming up from the sea.* Appearing on the western horizon.

chariot and go down, so that the *heavy* shower does not stop you.' "

45 In a little while the sky grew black with clouds and wind, and there was a heavy shower. And Ahab rode and went to [a]Jezreel.

46 Then [a]the hand of the LORD was on Elijah, and [b]he girded up his loins and [1]outran Ahab [2]to Jezreel.

Elijah Flees from Jezebel

19 Now Ahab told Jezebel all that Elijah had done, and [1][a]how he had killed all the prophets with the sword.

2 Then Jezebel sent a messenger to Elijah, saying, "[a]So may the gods do to me and even more, if I do not make your [1]life as the [1]life of one of them by tomorrow about this time."

3 And he [1]was afraid and arose and ran for his [2]life and came to [a]Beersheba, which belongs to Judah, and left his servant there.

4 But he himself went a day's journey into the wilderness, and came and sat down under a [1]juniper tree; and [a]he requested for himself that he might die, and said, "It is enough; now, O LORD, take my [2]life, for I am not better than my fathers."

5 He lay down and slept under a [1]juniper tree; and behold, there was [a]an angel touching him, and he said to him, "Arise, eat."

6 Then he looked and behold, there was at his head a bread cake *baked on* hot stones, and a jar of water. So he ate and drank and lay down again.

7 The angel of the LORD came again a second time and touched him and said, "Arise, eat, because the journey is too great for you."

8 So he arose and ate and drank, and went in the strength of that food [a]forty days and forty nights to [b]Horeb, the mountain of God.

Elijah at Horeb

9 Then he came there to a cave and lodged there; and behold, [a]the word of the LORD *came* to him, and He said to him, "What are you doing here, Elijah?"

10 He said, "[a]I have been very zealous for the LORD, the God of hosts; for the sons of Israel have forsaken Your covenant, [b]torn down Your altars and killed Your prophets with the sword. And [c]I alone am left; and they seek my life, to take it away."

11 So He said, "[a]Go forth and stand on the mountain before the LORD." And behold, the LORD was passing by! And [b]a great and strong wind was rending the mountains and breaking in pieces the rocks before the LORD; *but* the LORD *was* not in the wind. And after the wind an earthquake, *but* the LORD *was* not in the earthquake.

12 After the earthquake a fire, *but* the LORD *was* not in the fire; and after the fire [a]a sound of a gentle blowing.

13 When Elijah heard *it*, [a]he wrapped his face in his mantle and went out and stood in the entrance of the cave. And behold, [b]a voice *came* to him and said, "What are you doing here, Elijah?"

45 [a]Josh 17:16; Judg 6:33
46 [1]Lit *ran before* [2]Lit *until you are coming to* [a]2 Kin 3:15; Is 8:11; Ezek 3:14 [b]2 Kin 4:29; Jer 1:17; 1 Pet 1:13
19:1 [1]Lit *all about how* [a]1 Kin 18:40
2 [1]Lit *soul* [a]Ruth 1:17; 1 Kin 20:10; 2 Kin 6:31
3 [1]Reading of many mss; Heb text may read *saw* [2]Lit *soul* [a]Gen 21:31
4 [1]Or *broom-tree* [2]Lit *soul* [a]Num 11:15; Jer 20:14-18; Jon 4:3, 8
5 [1]Or *broom-tree* [a]Gen 28:12
8 [a]Ex 24:18; 34:28; Deut 9:9-11, 18; Matt 4:2 [b]Ex 3:1; 4:27
9 [a]Ex 33:21, 22
10 [a]Ex 20:5; 34:14 [b]Rom 11:3, 4 [c]1 Kin 18:22
11 [a]Ex 19:20; 24:12, 18 [b]Ezek 1:4
12 [a]Job 4:16; Zech 4:6
13 [a]Ex 3:6 [b]1 Kin 19:9

18:46 *outran Ahab to Jezreel.* Divinely energized by extraordinary strength, Elijah ran before Ahab's chariot to Jezreel. This dramatic scene, with the Lord's prophet running before the king and the Lord Himself racing behind him riding His mighty thundercloud chariot (see note on v. 24), served as a powerful appeal to Ahab to break once for all with Baal and henceforth to rule as the servant of the Lord.

19:2 *May the gods do to me and even more.* A curse formula (see note on 1 Sam 3:17). *one of them.* The dead prophets of Baal (v. 1).

19:3 *he was afraid and arose and ran for his life.* In spite of Elijah's great triumph in the trial on Mount Carmel and the dramatic demonstration that Elijah's God is the Lord of heaven and earth and the source of Israel's blessings, Jezebel is undaunted. Hers is no empty threat, and Ahab has shown that he is either unwilling or unable to restrain her. So Elijah knows that one of the main sources of Israel's present apostasy is still spewing out its poison and that his own life is in danger. *Beersheba.* The southernmost city in Judah (see notes on Gen 21:31; Amos 5:5; see also Judg 20:1).

19:4 *juniper tree.* A wilderness shrub, sometimes large enough to offer some shade. *requested for himself that he might die.* Cf. Jon 4:3,8. Elijah concluded that his work was fruitless and consequently that life was not worth living. He had lost his confidence in the triumph of the kingdom of God and was withdrawing from the arena of conflict.

19:7 *angel of the LORD.* See note on Gen 16:7. God in His mercy provided sustenance and rest for His discouraged servant. *the journey is too great for you.* Evidently Elijah had already determined to go to Mount Horeb, where God had established His covenant with His people. There is no indication that the Lord had instructed him to do this as He had previously directed him to go to Cherith (17:2–3) and to Zarephath (17:8–9) and to meet Ahab (18:1).

19:8 *forty days and forty nights.* Sustained by the Lord as Moses had been for the same length of time on Mount Sinai (Ex 24:18; 34:28) and as Jesus would be in the wilderness (Matt 4:2,11). *Horeb, the mountain of God.* Probably an alternate name for Mount Sinai (see Ex 3:1; 19:1–3), located in the wilderness apparently about 250 miles south of Beersheba.

19:9 *What are you doing here, Elijah?* The question implies that Elijah had come to Sinai for his own misguided reasons and not because the Lord had sent him.

19:10 Elijah did not give a direct answer to the Lord's question but implied that the work the Lord had begun centuries earlier with the establishment of the Sinai covenant had now come to nothing. Whereas Moses had interceded for Israel when they sinned with the golden calf (Ex 32:11–13), Elijah condemned the Israelites for breaking the covenant, and bitterly complained over the fruitlessness of his own work. *I alone am left.* See note on 18:22.

19:12 *gentle blowing.* In the symbolism of these occurrences (vv. 11–12) the Lord appears to be telling Elijah that although His servant's indictment of Israel was a call for God to judge His people with windstorm, earthquake and fire, it was not God's will to do so now. Elijah must return to continue God's mission to His people, and Elisha is to carry it on for another generation (v. 16).

19:13 *What are you doing here, Elijah?* After demonstrating His presence in the gentle whisper rather than in the wind, earthquake or fire, the Lord gave Elijah an opportunity to revise the answer he had previously given to the same question (vv. 9–10).

14 Then he said, "[a]I have been very zealous for the LORD, the God of hosts; for the
sons of Israel have forsaken Your covenant,
torn down Your altars and killed Your prophets with the sword. And I alone am left; and
they seek my life, to take it away."
15 The LORD said to him, "Go, return on
your way to the wilderness of Damascus,
and when you have arrived, [a]you shall
anoint Hazael king over Aram;
16 and [a]Jehu the son of Nimshi you shall
anoint king over Israel; and [b]Elisha the son
of Shaphat of Abel-meholah you shall anoint
as prophet in your place.

14 [a]1 Kin 19:10
15 [a]2 Kin 8:8-15
16 [a]2 Kin 9:1-10 [b]1 Kin 19:19-21; 2 Kin 2:9, 15

19:14 Elijah's unrevised answer demonstrated that he did not understand the significance of the divine revelation he had just witnessed.
19:15 *The LORD said to him.* Giving instructions to Elijah that revealed His sovereign power over people and nations. Even though Israel would experience divine judgment through Hazael, Jehu and Elisha, God would continue to preserve a remnant faithful to Himself among the people. *return . . . to the wilderness of Damascus.* Apparently Elijah is to go back by way of the road east of the Dead Sea and the Jordan. As it turns out, all three anointings take place east of the Jordan, though it is Elisha who effects the anointing of the two kings. *anoint.* Appears to mean here no more than "designate as divinely appointed." This anointing was actually done by Elijah's successor Elisha (see 2 Kin 8:7–15). *Hazael.* Subsequently became a serious threat to Israel during the reigns of Joram, Jehu and Jehoahaz (see 2 Kin 8:28–29; 10:32–33; 12:17–18; 13:3,22).

19:16 *Jehu . . . you shall anoint.* Jehu was a military commander under Ahab and Joram, Ahab's son (2 Kin 9:5–6). He was anointed king over Israel by "one of the sons of the prophets" at the instruction of Elisha (2 Kin 9:1–16), with the mandate to destroy the house of Ahab. *Elisha.* As with Elijah (see note on 17:1), Elisha's name (meaning "God is salvation" or "God saves") was the essence of his ministry. His name evokes memory of Joshua ("The LORD saves"). Elijah is given someone to finish his work just as Moses was, and Elisha channels the covenant blessings to the faithful in Israel just as Joshua brought Israel into the promised land (see the account of Elisha's ministry in 2 Kin 2:19–8:15; 9:1–3; 13:14–20). In the NT John the Baptist ("Elijah," Matt 11:14; 17:12) was followed by Jesus ("Joshua"; see note on Matt 1:21) to complete God's saving work. *son of Shaphat.* Shaphat means "He judges," which is also in accordance with Elisha's ministry. *of Abel-meholah.* See map below.

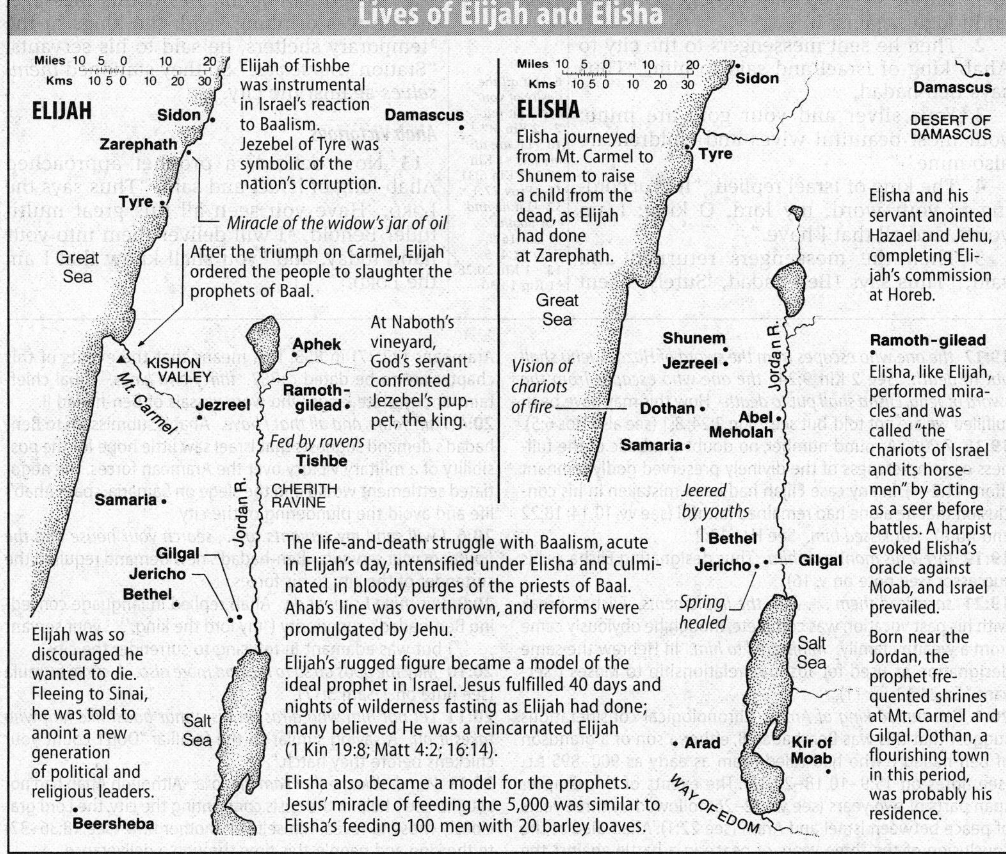

Lives of Elijah and Elisha
Miles 10 5 0 10 20
Kms 10 5 0 10 20 30
ELIJAH
Sidon
Zarephath
Tyre
Damascus
Elijah of Tishbe was instrumental in Israel's reaction to Baalism. Jezebel of Tyre was symbolic of the nation's corruption.
Miracle of the widow's jar of oil
Great Sea
After the triumph on Carmel, Elijah ordered the people to slaughter the prophets of Baal.
KISHON VALLEY
Mt. Carmel
Aphek
At Naboth's vineyard, God's servant confronted Jezebel's puppet, the king.
Jezreel
Ramoth-gilead
Fed by ravens
Tishbe
CHERITH RAVINE
Samaria
Jordan R.
Gilgal
Jericho
Bethel
Elijah was so discouraged he wanted to die. Fleeing to Sinai, he was told to anoint a new generation of political and religious leaders.
Salt Sea
Beersheba
The life-and-death struggle with Baalism, acute in Elijah's day, intensified under Elisha and culminated in bloody purges of the priests of Baal. Ahab's line was overthrown, and reforms were promulgated by Jehu.
Elijah's rugged figure became a model of the ideal prophet in Israel. Jesus fulfilled 40 days and nights of wilderness fasting as Elijah had done; many believed He was a reincarnated Elijah (1 Kin 19:8; Matt 4:2; 16:14).
Elisha also became a model for the prophets. Jesus' miracle of feeding the 5,000 was similar to Elisha's feeding 100 men with 20 barley loaves.
Miles 10 5 0 10 20
Kms 10 5 0 10 20 30
ELISHA
Sidon
Damascus
DESERT OF DAMASCUS
Elisha journeyed from Mt. Carmel to Shunem to raise a child from the dead, as Elijah had done at Zarephath.
Tyre
Elisha and his servant anointed Hazael and Jehu, completing Elijah's commission at Horeb.
Great Sea
Shunem
Jezreel
Vision of chariots of fire
Dothan
Abel Meholah
Samaria
Jordan R.
Ramoth-gilead
Elisha, like Elijah, performed miracles and was called "the chariots of Israel and its horsemen" by acting as a seer before battles. A harpist evoked Elisha's oracle against Moab, and Israel prevailed.
Jeered by youths
Bethel
Jericho
Gilgal
Spring healed
Salt Sea
Born near the Jordan, the prophet frequented shrines at Mt. Carmel and Gilgal. Dothan, a flourishing town in this period, was probably his residence.
Arad
Kir of Moab
WAY OF EDOM

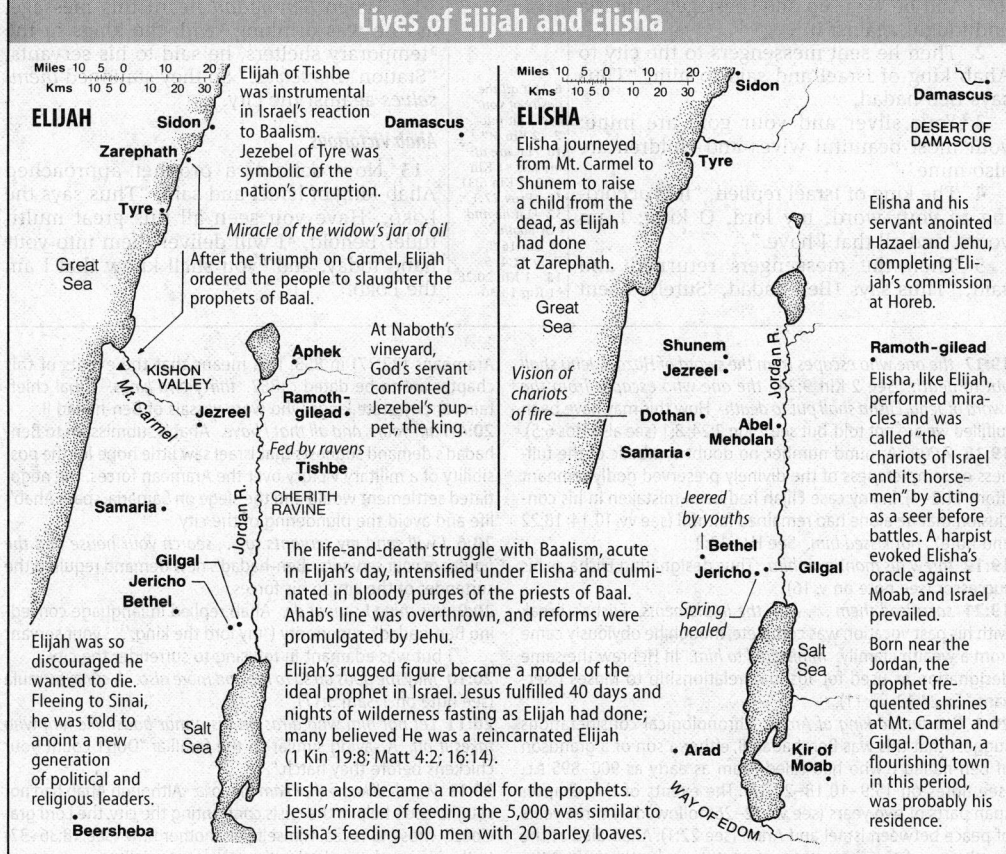

17 "It shall come about, the [a]one who escapes from the sword of Hazael, Jehu [b]shall put to death, and the one who escapes from the sword of Jehu, Elisha shall put to death.

18 "[a]Yet I will leave 7,000 in Israel, all the knees that have not bowed to Baal and every mouth that has not [b]kissed him."

19 So he departed from there and found Elisha the son of Shaphat, while he was plowing with twelve pairs *of oxen* before him, and he with the twelfth. And Elijah passed over to him and threw [a]his mantle on him.

20 He left the oxen and ran after Elijah and said, "Please [a]let me kiss my father and my mother, then I will follow you." And he said to him, "Go back again, for what have I done to you?"

21 So he returned from following him, and took the pair of oxen and sacrificed them and [a]boiled their flesh with the implements of the oxen, and gave *it* to the people and they ate. Then he arose and followed Elijah and ministered to him.

War with Aram

20 Now [a]Ben-hadad king of Aram gathered all his army, [b]and there *were* thirty-two kings with him, and horses and chariots. And he went up and [c]besieged Samaria and fought against it.

2 Then he sent messengers to the city to Ahab king of Israel and said to him, "Thus says Ben-hadad,

3 'Your silver and your gold are mine; your most beautiful wives and children are also mine.' "

4 The king of Israel replied, "It is according to your word, my lord, O king; I am yours, and all that I have."

5 Then the messengers returned and said, "Thus says [1]Ben-hadad, 'Surely, I sent to you saying, "You shall give me your silver and your gold and your wives and your children,"

6 but about this time tomorrow I will send my servants to you, and they will search your house and the houses of your servants; and [1]whatever is desirable in your eyes, they will [2]take in their hand and carry away.' "

7 Then the king of Israel called all the elders of the land and said, "Please observe and [a]see how this man is looking for trouble; for he sent to me for my wives and my children and my silver and my gold, and I did not refuse him."

8 All the elders and all the people said to him, "Do not listen or consent."

9 So he said to the messengers of Ben-hadad, "Tell my lord the king, 'All that you sent for to your servant at the first I will do, but this thing I cannot do.' " And the messengers departed and brought him word again.

10 Ben-hadad sent to him and said, "May [a]the gods do so to me and more also, if the dust of Samaria will suffice for handfuls for all the people who [1]follow me."

11 Then the king of Israel replied, "Tell *him*, '[a]Let not him who girds on *his armor* boast like him who takes *it* off.' "

12 When *Ben-hadad* heard this message, as [a]he was drinking [1]with the kings in the [2]temporary shelters, he said to his servants, "Station *yourselves*." So they stationed *themselves* against the city.

Ahab Victorious

13 Now behold, a prophet approached Ahab king of Israel and said, "Thus says the LORD, 'Have you seen all this great multitude? Behold, [a]I will deliver them into your hand today, and [b]you shall know that I am the LORD.' "

17 [a]2 Kin 8:12; 13:3, 22 [b]2 Kin 9:14-10:25
18 [a]Rom 11:4 [b]Hos 13:2
19 [a]1 Sam 28:14; 2 Kin 2:8, 13, 14
20 [a]Matt 8:21, 22; Luke 9:61, 62; Acts 20:37
21 [a]2 Sam 24:22
20:1 [a]1 Kin 15:18, 20; 2 Kin 6:24 [b]1 Kin 22:31 [c]1 Kin 16:24; 2 Kin 6:24
5 [1]Lit *Ben-hadad, saying*
6 [1]Lit *all the desire of your eyes* [2]Lit *put*
7 [a]2 Kin 5:7
10 [1]Lit *are at my feet* [a]1 Kin 19:2; 2 Kin 6:31
11 [a]Prov 27:1
12 [1]Lit *he and* [2]Or *booths* [a]1 Kin 16:9; Prov 31:4, 5
13 [a]1 Kin 20:28 [b]1 Kin 18:36

19:17 *the one who escapes from the sword of Hazael, Jehu shall put to death.* See 2 Kin 9:24. *the one who escapes from the sword of Jehu, Elisha shall put to death.* How this may have been fulfilled we are not told, but see 2 Kin 2:24; 8:1 (see also Hos 6:5).
19:18 *7,000.* A round number, no doubt symbolic of the fullness or completeness of the divinely preserved godly remnant (Rom 11:2–4). In any case Elijah had been mistaken in his conclusion that he alone had remained faithful (see vv. 10,14; 18:22 and note). *not kissed him.* See Hos 13:2.
19:19 *threw his mantle on him.* Thus designating Elisha as his successor (see note on v. 16).
19:21 *sacrificed them . . . with the implements.* Elisha's break with his past vocation was complete, though he obviously came from a wealthy family. *ministered to him.* In Hebrew the same designation as used for Joshua's relationship to Moses ("servant," Ex 24:13; 33:11).
20:1 *Ben-hadad king of Aram.* Chronological considerations suggest that this was Ben-hadad II, either a son or a grandson of Ben-hadad I, who had ruled Aram as early as 900–895 B.C. (see notes on 15:9–10,18–20,33). The events of this chapter span parts of two years (see vv. 22–26) followed by three years of peace between Israel and Aram (see 22:1). Ahab died at the conclusion of the three years of peace in a battle against the Arameans (22:37) in 853. This means that the events of this chapter are to be dated c. 857. *thirty-two kings.* Tribal chieftains or city-state kings who were vassals of Ben-hadad II.
20:4 *I am yours, and all that I have.* Ahab's submission to Ben-hadad's demand suggests that Israel saw little hope for the possibility of a military victory over the Aramean forces. The negotiated settlement would end the siege on Samaria, spare Ahab's life and avoid the plundering of the city.
20:6 *I will send my servants to . . . search your house and the houses of your servants.* Ben-hadad's new demand required the surrender of the city to his forces.
20:9 *this thing I cannot do.* Ahab replied in language conceding Ben-hadad's superiority ("my lord the king,'. . . your servant . . . ' ") but was adamant in refusing to surrender the city.
20:10 *May the gods do so to me and more also.* A curse formula (see note on 1 Sam 3:17).
20:11 *Let not him who girds on his armor boast like him who takes it off.* A saying similar to the familiar "Don't count your chickens before they hatch."
20:13 *you shall know that I am the LORD.* Although Ahab had not sought God's help in the crisis confronting the city, the Lord graciously chose to reveal Himself yet another time (see 18:36–37) to the king and people, this time through a deliverance.

14 Ahab said, "By whom?" So he said, "Thus says the LORD, 'By the young men of the rulers of the provinces.'" Then he said, "Who shall [1]begin the battle?" And he [2]answered, "You."

15 Then he mustered the young men of the rulers of the provinces, and there were 232; and after them he mustered all the people, *even* all the sons of Israel, 7,000.

16 They went out at noon, while [a]Ben-hadad was drinking himself drunk in the [1]temporary shelters [2]with the thirty-two kings who helped him.

17 The young men of the rulers of the provinces went out first; and Ben-hadad sent out and they told him, saying, "Men have come out from Samaria."

18 [a]Then he said, "If they have come out for peace, take them alive; or if they have come out for war, take them alive."

19 So these went out from the city, the young men of the rulers of the provinces, and the army which followed them.

20 They [1]killed each his man; and the Arameans fled and Israel pursued them, and Ben-hadad king of Aram escaped on a horse with horsemen.

21 The king of Israel went out and [1]struck the horses and chariots, and [1]killed the Arameans with a great slaughter.

22 Then [a]the prophet came near to the king of Israel and said to him, "Go, strengthen yourself and observe and see what you have to do; for [b]at the turn of the year the king of Aram will come up against you."

23 Now the servants of the king of Aram said to him, "[a]Their gods are gods of the mountains, therefore they were stronger than we; but rather let us fight against them in the plain, *and* surely we will be stronger than they.

24 "Do this thing: remove the kings, each from his place, and put captains in their place,

25 and [1]muster an army like the army that you have lost, horse for horse, and chariot for chariot. Then we will fight against them in the plain, and surely we will be stronger than they." And he listened to their voice and did so.

Another Aramean War

26 [a]At the turn of the year, Ben-hadad mustered the Arameans and went up to [b]Aphek to fight against Israel.

27 The sons of Israel were mustered and were provisioned and went to meet them; and the sons of Israel camped before them like two little flocks of goats, [a]but the Arameans filled the country.

28 Then [a]a man of God came near and spoke to the king of Israel and said, "Thus says the LORD, 'Because the Arameans have said, "[b]The LORD is a god of *the* mountains, but He is not a god of *the* valleys," therefore [c]I will give all this great multitude into your hand, and you shall know that I am the LORD.'"

29 So they camped one over against the other seven days. And on the seventh day the battle was joined, and the sons of Israel [1]killed *of* the Arameans 100,000 foot soldiers in one day.

30 But the rest fled to [a]Aphek into the city, and the wall fell on 27,000 men who were left. And Ben-hadad fled and came into the city [b]into an inner chamber.

31 [a]His servants said to him, "Behold now, we have heard that the kings of the house of Israel are merciful kings, please let us [b]put sackcloth on our loins and ropes on our heads, and go out to the king of Israel; perhaps he will save your [1]life."

14 [1]Lit *bind* [2]Lit *said*
16 [1]Or *booths* [2]Lit *he and the 32 kings* [a]1 Kin 16:9; 20:12; Prov 20:1
18 [a]2 Kin 14:8-12
20 [1]Lit *smote*
21 [1]Lit *smote*
22 [a]1 Kin 20:13 [b]2 Sam 11:1; 1 Kin 20:26
23 [a]1 Kin 14:23; Jer 16:19-21; Rom 1:21-23
25 [1]Lit *number*
26 [a]1 Kin 20:22 [b]2 Kin 13:17
27 [a]Judg 6:3-5; 1 Sam 13:5-8
28 [a]1 Kin 17:18 [b]1 Kin 20:23 [c]1 Kin 20:13
29 [1]Lit *smote*
30 [a]1 Kin 20:26 [b]1 Kin 22:25; 2 Chr 18:24
31 [1]Lit *soul* [a]1 Kin 20:23-26 [b]Gen 37:34; 2 Sam 3:31

20:14 *young men of the rulers of the provinces.* See note on 16:27. Organizational details of the provincial government of the northern kingdom are unknown.

20:15 *the young men . . . were 232 . . . all the sons of Israel, 7,000.* Not a large military force (though a significant number for a city under siege) but one of fitting size for demonstrating that the imminent victory was from the Lord rather than from Israel's own military superiority (cf. Jdg 7:2).

20:20 *They killed each his man.* Apparently they were met by a small advance force like their own (see 2 Sam 2:15–16). *escaped on a horse with horsemen.* Since fighting on horseback did not come until later, reference must be to chariot horses and charioteers. After their defeat, the Arameans seem to have withdrawn to Damascus.

20:22 *the king of Aram will come up against you.* The anonymous prophet (see v. 13) warned Ahab against undue self-confidence. The prophet's announcement of an impending renewed attack by Ben-hadad should have driven Ahab to more complete reliance on the God who had revealed Himself on Mount Carmel and in the recent military victory.

20:23 *gods of the mountains.* An expression of the pagan idea that a deity's power extended only over the limited area of his particular jurisdiction. *therefore they were stronger than we.* The Arameans believed that the outcome of military conflicts depended on the relative strength of the gods of the opposing forces rather than on the inherent strength of the two armies. For this reason, their strategy was to fight the next battle in a way that advantageously maximized the supposed strengths and weaknesses of the deities involved.

20:26 *Aphek.* Presumably the Aphek located a few miles east of the Sea of Galilee. The battle apparently took place in the Jordan Valley near the juncture of the Yarmuk and Jordan rivers.

20:28 *man of God.* Apparently the same prophet mentioned in vv. 13,22. *you shall know that I am the LORD.* See note on v. 13. God will again demonstrate that He is the sovereign ruler over all nature and history and that the pagan nature deities are powerless before Him.

20:29 *killed . . . 100,000 foot soldiers.* Probably includes all those who were driven from the field and the Aramean encampment, including support personnel.

20:30 *wall fell.* The God of Israel not only gave Israel's army a victory in battle but also caused an additional disaster to fall on the Aramean army. *27,000.* Aphek was certainly not so large a city that its wall could literally have collapsed on so many. Perhaps this is the number of troops that had taken refuge in Aphek and were left defenseless when the city walls gave way.

20:31 *kings of the house of Israel are merciful.* The Arameans recognized that Israel's kings were different from, e.g., the ruth-

32 So [a]they girded sackcloth on their loins and *put* ropes on their heads, and came to the king of Israel and said, "[b]Your servant Ben-hadad says, 'Please let me live.' " And he said, "Is he still alive? He is my brother."

33 Now the men [1]took this as an omen, and quickly [2]catching his word said, "Your brother Ben-hadad." Then he said, "Go, bring him." Then Ben-hadad came out to him, and he [3]took him up into the chariot.

34 *Ben-hadad* said to him, "[a]The cities which my father took from your father I will restore, and you shall make streets for yourself in Damascus, as my father made in Samaria." *Ahab said,* "And I will let you go with this covenant." So he made a covenant with him and let him go.

35 Now a certain man of [a]the sons of the prophets said to [1]another [b]by the word of the LORD, "Please strike me." But the man refused to strike him.

36 Then he said to him, "Because you have not listened to the voice of the LORD, behold, as soon as you have departed from me, [a]a lion will [1]kill you." And as soon as he had departed from him a lion found him and [2]killed him.

37 Then he found another man and said, "Please [1]strike me." And the man [2]struck him, [3]wounding him.

38 So the prophet departed and waited for the king by the way, and [a]disguised himself with a bandage over his eyes.

39 As the king passed by, he cried to the king and said, "Your servant went out into the midst of the battle; and behold, a man turned aside and brought a man to me and said, 'Guard this man; if for any reason he is missing, [a]then your life shall be for his life, or else you shall pay a talent of silver.'

40 "While your servant was busy here and there, he was gone." And the king of Israel said to him, "So shall your judgment be; you yourself have decided *it.*"

41 Then he hastily took the bandage away from his eyes, and the king of Israel recognized him that he was of the prophets.

42 He said to him, "Thus says the LORD, 'Because you have let go out of *your* hand the man whom I had devoted to destruction, therefore [a]your [1]life shall go for his [1]life, and your people for his people.' "

43 So [a]the king of Israel went to his house sullen and vexed, and came to Samaria.

Ahab Covets Naboth's Vineyard

21 Now it came about after these things that Naboth the Jezreelite had a vineyard which *was* in [a]Jezreel beside the palace of Ahab king of Samaria.

2 Ahab spoke to Naboth, saying, "[a]Give me your vineyard, that I may have it for a

32 [a]1 Kin 20:31 [b]1 Kin 20:3-6
33 [1]Lit *divined* [2]Lit *caught from him* [3]Lit *caused him to come up*
34 [a]1 Kin 15:20
35 [1]Lit *his neighbor* [a]2 Kin 2:3-7 [b]1 Kin 13:17, 18
36 [1]Lit *smite* [2]Lit *smote* [a]1 Kin 13:24
37 [1]Lit *smite* [2]Lit *smote* [3]Lit *striking and wounding*
38 [a]1 Kin 14:2
39 [a]2 Kin 10:24
42 [1]Lit *soul* [a]1 Kin 20:39
43 [a]1 Kin 21:4
21:1 [a]Judg 6:33; 1 Kin 18:45, 46
2 [a]1 Sam 8:14

less Assyrian kings. *sackcloth . . . ropes.* Perhaps here symbolic of humility and submission.

20:32 *Your servant.* In the diplomatic language of the time, Ben-hadad acknowledged his inferiority and subordination to Ahab by designating himself Ahab's servant (see note on v. 9). *my brother.* Ahab disregarded Ben-hadad's concession and responded in terminology used by rulers who considered themselves equals (see 9:13). In doing this, Ahab gave much more than Ben-hadad had asked or expected.

20:33 *took him up into the chariot.* Not the treatment normally accorded a defeated military opponent.

20:34 *cities which my father took from your father.* Perhaps Ramoth-gilead (see 22:3) along with some of the cities Ben-hadad I had taken from Baasha (15:20) at an even earlier time. *make streets for yourself.* Outlets for engaging in the lucrative international trade—a distinct economic advantage; usually such privileges were a jealously guarded local monopoly. *made a covenant with him and let him go.* A parity treaty (a peace treaty between equals) that included among its provisions the political and trade agreements proposed by Ben-hadad.

20:35 *sons of the prophets.* An expression designating members of prophetic companies (see 2 Kin 2:3,5,7,15; 4:1,38; 5:22; 6:1; 9:1). "Son" is not to be understood here as "male child" or "descendant" but as the member of a group. These companies of prophets were apparently religious communities that sprang up in the face of general indifference and apostasy for the purpose of mutual edification and the cultivation of the experience of God. It seems likely that they were known as prophets because their religious practices (sometimes ecstatic) were called prophesying (see 18:29; Num 11:25–27; 1 Sam 10:5–6,10–11; 18:10; 19:20–24)—to be distinguished from "prophet" in the sense of one bringing ("prophesying") a word from the Lord. The relationship of the Lord's great prophets (such as Samuel, Elijah and Elisha) to these communities was understandably a close one, the Lord's prophets probably being viewed as their spiritual mentors.

20:36 *as soon as you have departed from me, a lion will kill you.* A penalty reminiscent of what happened to the man of God from Judah (13:23–24).

20:39 *talent.* About 75 pounds. Because few soldiers could have paid such a large sum, it would appear to Ahab that the man's life was at stake.

20:40 *So shall your judgment be.* Ahab refused to grant clemency. Little did he know that he was pronouncing his own death sentence (cf. the similar technique used by Nathan the prophet, 2 Sam 12:1–12).

20:42 *the man whom I had devoted to destruction.* The Hebrew refers to the irrevocable giving over of things or persons to the Lord, often by totally destroying them (see notes on Lev 27:28; Josh 6:17). It is not clear whether Ahab violated a previous revelation or erred by simply neglecting to inquire of the Lord before releasing Ben-hadad. In any case, the Lord had given Ben-hadad into Ahab's hand (see v. 28), and Ahab was responsible to the Lord for his custody. *your life shall go for his life, and your people for his people.* Because Ahab sinned in his official capacity as king, the sentence fell not only on Ahab personally but also on the people of the northern kingdom. Ahab died in battle against the Arameans (22:29–39), and Israel was severely humiliated by them during the reigns of Jehu and Jehoahaz (2 Kin 10:32; 13:3).

21:1 *beside the palace of Ahab.* Ahab maintained a residence in Jezreel in addition to his official palace in Samaria (see 18:45; 2 Kin 9:30). *Samaria.* The entire northern kingdom is here represented by its capital city (see note on 16:24).

21:2 *Give me your vineyard.* Because royal power in Israel was limited by covenantal law (see Deut 17:14–20; 1 Sam 10:25), Ahab was unable simply to confiscate privately held land, as was customary with Canaanite kings (see note on v. 7; see also 1 Sam 8:9–17).

vegetable garden because it is close beside
my house, and I will give you a better vineyard than it in its place; if [1]you like, I will
give you the price of [2]it in money."
3 But Naboth said to Ahab, "The LORD
forbid me [a]that I should give you the inheritance of my fathers."
4 [a]So Ahab came into his house sullen
and vexed because of the word which
Naboth the Jezreelite had spoken to him; for
he said, "I will not give you the inheritance
of my fathers." And he lay down on his bed
and turned away his face and ate no [1]food.
5 But Jezebel his wife came to him and
said to him, "How is it that your spirit is so
sullen that you are not eating [1]food?"
6 So he said to her, "Because I spoke to
Naboth the Jezreelite and said to him, 'Give
me your vineyard for money; or else, if it
pleases you, I will give you a vineyard in its
place.' But he said, 'I will not give you my
vineyard.' "
7 Jezebel his wife said to him, "[a]Do you
now [1]reign over Israel? Arise, eat bread, and
let your heart be joyful; I will give you the
vineyard of Naboth the Jezreelite."
8 [a]So she wrote letters in Ahab's name
and sealed them with his seal, and sent letters to [b]the elders and to the nobles who
were living with Naboth in his city.
9 Now she wrote in the letters, saying,
"Proclaim a fast and seat Naboth at the head
of the people;
10 and seat two [a]worthless men before
him, and let them testify against him, saying, '[b]You cursed God and the king.' Then
take him out and [c]stone him [1]to death."

Jezebel's Plot

11 So the men of his city, the elders and
the nobles who lived in his city, did as Jezebel had sent *word* to them, just as it was
written in the letters which she had sent
them.
12 They [a]proclaimed a fast and seated
Naboth at the head of the people.
13 Then the two worthless men came in
and sat before him; and the worthless men
testified against him, even against Naboth,
before the people, saying, "Naboth cursed
God and the king." [a]So they took him outside
the city and stoned him [1]to death with stones.
14 Then they sent *word* to Jezebel, saying,
"Naboth has been stoned and is dead."
15 When Jezebel heard that Naboth had
been stoned and was dead, Jezebel said to
Ahab, "Arise, take possession of the vineyard
of Naboth, the Jezreelite, which he refused
to give you for money; for Naboth is not
alive, but dead."
16 When Ahab heard that Naboth was
dead, Ahab arose to go down to the vineyard
of Naboth the Jezreelite, to take possession
of it.
17 Then the word of the LORD came to Elijah the Tishbite, saying,
18 "Arise, go down to meet Ahab king of
Israel, [a]who is in Samaria; behold, he is in
the vineyard of Naboth where he has gone
down to take possession of it.
19 "You shall speak to him, saying, 'Thus
says the LORD, "[a]Have you murdered and
also taken possession?" ' And you shall
speak to him, saying, 'Thus says the LORD,
"[b]In the place where the dogs licked up the
blood of Naboth the dogs will lick up your
blood, even yours." ' "
20 Ahab said to Elijah, "[a]Have you found
me, O my enemy?" And he [1]answered, "I
have found *you,* [b]because you have sold
yourself to do evil in the sight of the LORD.
21 "Behold, I will bring evil upon you, and
[a]will utterly sweep you away, and will cut
off from Ahab every male, both bond and
free in Israel;
22 and [a]I will make your house [b]like the
house of Jeroboam the son of Nebat, and like
the house of Baasha the son of Ahijah,

2 [1]Lit *it is good in your eyes* [2]Lit *this*
3 [a]Lev 25:23; Num 36:7; Ezek 46:18
4 [1]Lit *bread* [a]1 Kin 20:43
5 [1]Lit *bread*
7 [1]Lit *exercise kingship* [a]1 Sam 8:14
8 [a]Esth 3:12; 8:8, 10 [b]1 Kin 20:7
10 [1]Lit *so that he dies* [a]1 Sam 2:12; 2 Sam 20:1 [b]Ex 22:28; Lev 24:15, 16; Acts 6:11 [c]Lev 24:14
12 [a]Is 58:4
13 [1]Lit *with stones so that he died* [a]2 Kin 9:26; 2 Chr 24:21; Acts 7:58, 59; Heb 11:37
18 [a]1 Kin 16:29
19 [a]2 Sam 12:9 [b]1 Kin 22:38; 2 Kin 9:26
20 [1]Lit *said* [a]1 Kin 18:17 [b]1 Kin 21:25; 2 Kin 17:17; Rom 7:14
21 [a]1 Kin 14:10; 2 Kin 9:8
22 [a]1 Kin 15:29 [b]1 Kin 16:3, 11

21:3 Naboth's refusal to dispose of his land was based on the conviction that the land was the Lord's, that He had granted a perpetual lease to each Israelite family and that this lease was to be jealously preserved as the family's permanent inheritance in the promised land.

21:7 *Do you now reign over Israel?* A sarcastic remark of incredulity spoken by one accustomed to the despotic practices of the Phoenician and Canaanite kings, who would not hesitate a moment to use their power to satisfy personal interests (contrast the attitude and practice of Samuel in the exercise of his civil power, 1 Sam 12:3–4).

21:9 *Proclaim a fast.* Jezebel attempted to create the impression that a disaster threatened the people that could be averted only if they would humble themselves before the Lord and remove any person whose sin had brought God's judgment on them (cf. Judg 20:26; 1 Sam 7:5–6; 2 Chr 20:2–4).

21:10 *two.* Mosaic law required two witnesses for capital offenses (Num 35:30; Deut 17:6; 19:15). *worthless men.* See note on Deut 13:13. *let them testify.* The entire scenario was designed to give an appearance of legitimate judicial procedure (see Ex 20:16; 23:7; Lev 19:16). *You cursed God and the king.* For this the Mosaic law prescribed death by stoning (Lev 24:15–16).

21:13 *outside the city.* In accordance with Mosaic law (Lev 24:14; Num 15:35–36). Naboth was stoned on his own field (compare v. 19 with 2 Kin 9:21,26), and his sons were stoned with him (see 2 Kin 9:26; cf. the case of Achan, Josh 7: 24–25), thus also eliminating his heirs.

21:19 *Have you murdered and also taken possession?* Ahab's willing compliance with Jezebel's scheme made him guilty of murder and theft. *In the place where the dogs licked up the blood of Naboth the dogs will lick up your blood.* Ahab's subsequent repentance (v. 29) occasioned the postponement of certain aspects of this prophecy until the time of his son Joram, whose body was thrown on the field of Naboth (2 Kin 9:25–26). Ahab himself was killed in battle at Ramoth-gilead (22:29–37) and his body brought to Samaria, where the dogs licked the blood being washed from his chariot (22:38).

21:21 *bond and free.* See note on 14:10.

21:22 *like the house of Jeroboam.* See 14:10; 15:28–30. *the house of Baasha.* See 16:3–4,11–13.

because of the provocation with which you
have provoked *Me* to anger, and *because* you
[c]have made Israel sin.
23 "Of Jezebel also has the LORD spoken,
saying, '[a]The dogs will eat Jezebel in the
[1]district of Jezreel.'
24 "[a]The one belonging to Ahab, who dies
in the city, the dogs will eat, and the one who
dies in the field the birds of heaven will eat."
25 [a]Surely there was no one like Ahab
who sold himself to do evil in the sight of the
LORD, [1]because Jezebel his wife incited him.
26 [a]He acted very abominably in following idols, [b]according to all that the Amorites
had done, whom the LORD cast out before the
sons of Israel.
27 It came about when Ahab heard these
words, that [a]he tore his clothes and put [1]on
sackcloth and fasted, and he lay in sackcloth
and went about [2]despondently.
28 Then the word of the LORD came to Elijah the Tishbite, saying,
29 "Do you see how Ahab has humbled
himself before Me? Because he has humbled
himself before Me, I will not bring the evil in
his days, *but* I will bring the evil upon his
house [a]in his son's days."

Ahab's Third Campaign against Aram

22 Three [1]years passed without war
between Aram and Israel.
2 [a]In the third year [b]Jehoshaphat the king
of Judah came down to the king of Israel.
3 Now the king of Israel said to his servants, "Do you know that [a]Ramoth-gilead
belongs to us, and we [1]are still doing nothing
to take it out of the hand of the king of Aram?"
4 And he said to Jehoshaphat, "Will you
go with me to battle at Ramoth-gilead?" And
Jehoshaphat said to the king of Israel, "[a]I am
as you are, my people as your people, my
horses as your horses."
5 Moreover, Jehoshaphat said to the king
of Israel, "Please inquire [1]first for the word
of the LORD."
6 Then [a]the king of Israel gathered the
prophets together, about four hundred men,
and said to them, "Shall I go against Ramoth-
gilead to battle or shall I refrain?" And they
said, "Go up, for the Lord will give *it* into the
hand of the king."
7 But [a]Jehoshaphat said, "Is there not yet
a prophet of the LORD here that we may
inquire of him?"
8 The king of Israel said to Jehoshaphat,
"There is yet one man by whom we may
inquire of the LORD, but I hate him, because
he does not prophesy good concerning me,
but evil. *He is* Micaiah son of Imlah." But
Jehoshaphat said, "Let not the king say so."
9 Then the king of Israel called an officer
and said, "[1]Bring quickly Micaiah son of
Imlah."
10 Now the king of Israel and Jehoshaphat
king of Judah were sitting each on his
throne, arrayed in *their* robes, at the threshing floor at the entrance of the gate of
Samaria; and [a]all the prophets were prophesying before them.
11 Then Zedekiah the son of Chenaanah
made [a]horns of iron for himself and said,
"Thus says the LORD, '[b]With these you will
gore the Arameans until they are consumed.' "
12 All the prophets were prophesying
thus, saying, "Go up to Ramoth-gilead and
prosper, for the LORD will give *it* into the
hand of the king."

22 [c]1 Kin 12:30; 13:34; 14:16
23 [1]Lit *portion; some mss read rampart* [a]2 Kin 9:10, 30-37
24 [a]1 Kin 14:11; 16:4
25 [1]Or *whom Jezebel his wife incited* [a]1 Kin 16:30-33; 21:20
26 [a]1 Kin 15:12; 2 Kin 17:12 [b]Gen 15:16; Lev 18:25-30; 2 Kin 21:11
27 [1]Lit *sackcloth on his flesh* [2]Or *softly* [a]Gen 37:34; 2 Sam 3:31; 2 Kin 6:30
29 [a]2 Kin 9:25-37
22:1 [1]Lit *they sat for three years*
2 [a]2 Chr 18:2 [b]1 Kin 15:24
3 [1]Lit *are silent so as not* [a]Deut 4:43; Josh 21:38; 1 Kin 4:13
4 [a]2 Kin 3:7
5 [1]Lit *as the day*
6 [a]1 Kin 18:19
7 [a]2 Kin 3:11
9 [1]Lit *Hasten Micaiah*
10 [a]1 Kin 22:6
11 [a]Zech 1:18-21 [b]Deut 33:17

21:24 See notes on 14:11; 16:4.
21:25 *Jezebel his wife incited him.* See 16:31; 18:4; 19:1–2; 21:7.
21:26 *Amorites.* Here a designation for the entire pre-Israelite population of Canaan (see Gen 15:16; Dt 1:7).
21:27 *sackcloth.* See note on Gen 37:34.
21:29 *in his son's days.* The judgment was postponed but not rescinded (see note on v. 19).
22:1 *Three years.* See note on 20:1. *without war between Aram and Israel.* The annals of the Assyrian ruler Shalmaneser III (859–824 B.C.) record the participation of both "Ahab the Israelite" and Hadadezer (Ben-hadad) of Damascus in a coalition of 12 rulers that fought against Assyrian forces at Qarqar on the Orontes River in 853. According to the Assyrian records, Ahab contributed 2,000 chariots and 10,000 foot soldiers to the allied forces. Assyrian claims of victory appear exaggerated since they withdrew and did not venture westward again for four or five years.
22:2 *Jehoshaphat the king of Judah came down to the king of Israel.* Perhaps to congratulate him on the success of the western alliance against the Assyrian threat (see notes on v. 1; 2 Chr 18:2).
22:3 *Ramoth-gilead.* Located near the Yarmuk River in Transjordan; an Israelite city since the days of Moses (see 4:13; Deut 4:43; Josh 20:8). *belongs to us.* Israel could lay claim to Ramoth-gilead also by virtue of the treaty concluded with Ben-hadad a few years earlier (see 20:34), the provisions of which he had apparently failed to honor.
22:4 *Will you go with me . . . ?* Even though Ahab had just been allied with the Arameans against the Assyrians, now that the Assyrian threat was over he did not hesitate to seize an opportunity to free Ramoth-gilead from Aramean control. *I am as you are, my people as your people, my horses as your horses.* Jehoshaphat was later to be condemned by the prophet Jehu (2 Chr 19:2) for violating the Lord's will by joining forces with Ahab. In this alliance, Jehoshaphat completely reversed the policy of his father Asa, who had entered into an alliance with the Arameans against Baasha of the northern kingdom (see 15:17–23).
22:5 *inquire first for the word of the LORD.* Jehoshaphat hesitated to proceed with the planned action without the assurance of the Lord's favor (see 1 Sam 23:1–4; 2Sa 2:1).
22:6 *prophets.* No doubt associated with the paganized worship at Bethel (see notes on 12:28–29), they exercised their "office" by proclaiming messages designed to please the king (see Amos 7:10–13).
22:7 *Is there not yet a prophet of the LORD here . . . ?* Jehoshaphat recognized that the 400 prophets were not to be relied on (see Ezek 13:2–3) and asked for consultation with a true prophet of the Lord.
22:8 *does not prophesy good.* Ahab's assessment of a prophet depended on whether his message was favorable to him (see 18:17; 21:20).
22:11 *Zedekiah.* Evidently the spokesman for the 400 prophets. *horns of iron.* A symbol of power (see Deut 33:17).

Micaiah Predicts Defeat

13 Then the messenger who went to summon Micaiah spoke to him saying, "Behold now, the words of the prophets are uniformly favorable to the king. Please let your word be like the word of one of them, and speak favorably."

14 But Micaiah said, "[a]As the LORD lives, what [b]the LORD says to me, that I shall speak."

15 When he came to the king, the king said to him, "Micaiah, shall we go to Ramoth-gilead to battle, or shall we refrain?" And he [1]answered him, "[a]Go up and succeed, and the LORD will give *it* into the hand of the king."

16 Then the king said to him, "How many times must I adjure you to speak to me nothing but the truth in the name of the LORD?"

17 So he said,

"I saw all Israel
 Scattered on the mountains,
 [a]Like sheep which have no shepherd.
 And the LORD said, 'These have no master.
 Let each of them return to his house in peace.' "

18 Then the king of Israel said to Jehoshaphat, "[a]Did I not tell you that he would not prophesy good concerning me, but evil?"

19 [1]Micaiah said, "Therefore, hear the word of the LORD. [a]I saw the LORD sitting on His throne, and [b]all the host of heaven standing by Him on His right and on His left.

20 "The LORD said, 'Who will entice Ahab to go up and fall at Ramoth-gilead?' And one said this while another said that.

21 "Then a spirit came forward and stood before the LORD and said, 'I will entice him.'

22 "The LORD said to him, 'How?' And he said, 'I will go out and [a]be a deceiving spirit in the mouth of all his prophets.' Then He said, 'You are to entice *him* and also prevail. Go and do so.'

23 "Now therefore, behold, [a]the LORD has put a deceiving spirit in the mouth of all these your prophets; and the LORD has proclaimed disaster against you."

24 Then [a]Zedekiah the son of Chenaanah came near and struck Micaiah on the cheek and said, "[b]How did the Spirit of the LORD pass from me to speak to you?"

25 Micaiah said, "Behold, you shall see on that day when you [a]enter an inner room to hide yourself."

26 Then the king of Israel said, "Take Micaiah and return him to Amon the governor of the city and to Joash the king's son;

27 and say, 'Thus says the king, "[a]Put this man in prison and feed him [1]sparingly with bread and water until I return safely." ' "

28 Micaiah said, "[a]If you indeed return safely the LORD has not spoken by me." And he said, "[b]Listen, all you people."

Defeat and Death of Ahab

29 So [a]the king of Israel and Jehoshaphat king of Judah went up against Ramoth-gilead.

30 The king of Israel said to Jehoshaphat, "[a]I will disguise myself and go into the battle, but you put on your robes." So the king of Israel disguised himself and went into the battle.

31 Now [a]the king of Aram had commanded the thirty-two captains of his chariots, saying, "Do not fight with small or great, but with the king of Israel alone."

32 So when the captains of the chariots saw Jehoshaphat, they said, "Surely it is the king of Israel," and they turned aside to fight against him, and Jehoshaphat cried out.

33 When the captains of the chariots saw that it was not the king of Israel, they turned back from pursuing him.

34 Now a certain man drew his bow at random and struck the king of Israel [1]in a joint of the armor. So he said to the driver of

14 [a]1 Kin 18:10, 15 [b]Num 22:18; 24:13
15 [1]Lit *said to* [a]1 Kin 22:12
17 [a]Num 27:17; 1 Kin 22:34-36; 2 Chr 18:16; Matt 9:36; Mark 6:34
18 [a]1 Kin 22:8
19 [1]Lit *he* [a]Is 6:1; Ezek 1:26-28; Dan 7:9, 10 [b]Job 1:6; 2:1; Ps 103:20, 21; Dan 7:10; Matt 18:10; Heb 1:7, 14
22 [a]Judg 9:23; 1 Sam 16:14; 18:10; 19:9; Ezek 14:9; 2 Thess 2:11
23 [a]Ezek 14:9
24 [a]1 Kin 22:11; Matt 5:39; Acts 23:2, 3 [b]2 Chr 18:23
25 [a]1 Kin 20:30
27 [1]Lit *with bread of affliction and water of affliction* [a]2 Chr 16:10; 18:25-27
28 [a]Deut 18:22 [b]Mic 1:2
29 [a]1 Kin 22:3, 4
30 [a]2 Chr 35:22
31 [a]1 Kin 20:1, 16, 24; 2 Chr 18:30
34 [1]Lit *between the scale-armor and the breastplate*

22:13 *let your word be like the word of one of them.* A bit of advice reflecting the view that all prophets were merely self-serving.

22:15 *we.* A subtle shift (see v. 6) that seeks a favorable response by including Jehoshaphat as a co-sponsor of the enterprise. *Go up . . . the LORD will give it into the hand of the king.* Micaiah sarcastically mimics the 400 false prophets (see v. 12).

22:16 *speak to me nothing but the truth.* Micaiah apparently betrayed his lack of seriousness, and Ahab immediately recognizes this.

22:17 *Like sheep which have no shepherd . . . These have no master.* Using the imagery of shepherd and sheep (see Num 27:16–17; Zech 13:7; Matt 9:36; 26:31), Micaiah depicts Ahab's death in the upcoming battle.

22:19 *I saw the LORD sitting on His throne.* A true prophet was one who had, as it were, been made privy to what had transpired in God's heavenly throne room and so could truthfully declare what God intended to do (see Is 6:1; Jer 23:16–22).

22:23 *the LORD has put a deceiving spirit in the mouth of all these your prophets.* Some view the lying spirit as Satan or one of his agents. Others have suggested a spirit of God who undertakes the task of a lying spirit (but see 1 Sam 15:29). Still others understand the lying spirit as a symbolic picture of the power of the lie. The Lord had given the 400 prophets over to the power of the lie because they did not love the truth and had chosen to speak out of their own hearts (see Jer 14:14; 23:16,26; Ezek 13:2–3,17; see also note on 2 Sam 24:1; cf. 2 Thess 2:9–12).

22:24 *How did the Spirit of the LORD pass from me to speak to you?* By this sarcastic question Zedekiah suggests that one prophet can be a liar just as well as another.

22:25 *enter an inner room to hide.* Where Zedekiah will seek refuge (cf. 20:30). This will vindicate Micaiah's prophetic authority.

22:30 *disguise.* By this strategy he thought he could direct attention away from himself and so minimize any chance for fulfillment of Micaiah's prediction.

22:31 *with the king of Israel alone.* If the leader was killed or captured, ancient armies usually fell apart (cf. vv. 35–36).

22:34 *driver of his chariot.* A war chariot normally carried two men—a fighter and a driver. Sometimes, it appears, there were three men, but the third seems to have been an officer who commanded a chariot unit (see 9:22; 2 Kin 9:25; Ex 14:7; 15:4).

his chariot, "Turn [2]around and take me out of the [3]fight; [a]for I am severely wounded."
35 The battle [1]raged that day, and the king was propped up in his chariot in front of the Arameans, and died at evening, and the blood from the wound ran into the bottom of the chariot.
36 [a]Then a cry passed throughout the army close to sunset, saying, "Every man to his city and every man to his [1]country."
37 So the king died and was brought to Samaria, and they buried the king in Samaria.
38 They washed the chariot by the pool of Samaria, and the dogs licked up his blood (now the harlots bathed themselves *there*), [a]according to the word of the LORD which He spoke.
39 Now the rest of the acts of Ahab and all that he did and [a]the ivory house which he built and all the cities which he built, are they not written in the Book of the Chronicles of the Kings of Israel?
40 So Ahab slept with his fathers, and Ahaziah his son became king in his place.

The New Rulers

41 [a]Now Jehoshaphat the son of Asa became king over Judah in the fourth year of Ahab king of Israel.
42 Jehoshaphat was thirty-five years old when he became king, and he reigned twenty-five years in Jerusalem. And his mother's name was Azubah the daughter of Shilhi.
43 [a]He walked in all the way of Asa his father; he did not turn aside from it, doing right in the sight of the LORD. [b]However, the high places were not taken away; the people still sacrificed and burnt incense on the high places.
44 [a]Jehoshaphat also made peace with the king of Israel.
45 Now the rest of the acts of Jehoshaphat, and his might which he showed and how he warred, are they not written [a]in the Book of the Chronicles of the Kings of Judah?
46 The remnant of [a]the sodomites who remained in the days of his father Asa, he [1]expelled from the land.
47 Now [a]there was no king in Edom; a deputy was king.
48 Jehoshaphat made [a]ships of Tarshish to go to [b]Ophir for gold, but [c]they did not go for the ships were broken at [d]Ezion-geber.
49 Then Ahaziah the son of Ahab said to Jehoshaphat, "Let my servants go with your servants in the ships." But Jehoshaphat was not willing.
50 [a]And Jehoshaphat slept with his fathers and was buried with his fathers in the city of his father David, and Jehoram his son became king in his place.
51 Ahaziah the son of Ahab [a]became king over Israel in Samaria in the seventeenth year of Jehoshaphat king of Judah, and he reigned two years over Israel.
52 He did evil in the sight of the LORD and [a]walked in the way of his father and in the way of his mother and in the way of Jeroboam the son of Nebat, who caused Israel to sin.
53 [a]So he served Baal and worshiped him and provoked the LORD God of Israel to anger, according to all that his father had done.

34 [2]Lit *your hand* [3]Lit *camp* [a]2 Chr 35:23
35 [1]Lit *went up*
36 [1]Lit *land* [a]2 Kin 14:12
38 [a]1 Kin 21:19
39 [a]Amos 3:15
41 [a]2 Chr 20:31
43 [a]2 Chr 17:3 [b]1 Kin 15:14; 2 Kin 12:3
44 [a]1 Kin 22:2; 2 Kin 8:16, 18; 2 Chr 19:2
45 [a]2 Chr 20:34
46 [1]Lit *consumed* [a]Gen 19:5; Deut 23:17; 1 Kin 14:24; 15:12; Jude 7
47 [a]2 Sam 8:14; 2 Kin 3:9
48 [a]1 Kin 10:22; 2 Chr 20:36 [b]1 Kin 9:28 [c]2 Chr 20:37 [d]1 Kin 9:26
50 [a]2 Chr 21:1
51 [a]1 Kin 22:40
52 [a]1 Kin 15:26; 21:25
53 [a]Judg 2:11; 1 Kin 16:30-32

22:35 *died at evening.* Fulfilling Micaiah's prophecy (vv. 17,28).
22:38 *according to the word of the LORD.* A partial fulfillment of Elijah's prophecy concerning Ahab's death (see note on 21:19).
22:39 *ivory house which he built.* Excavators of Samaria have found ivory inlays in some of the buildings dating from this period of Israel's history. Ahab's use of ivory in this way is indicative of the realm's economic prosperity during his reign. *cities which he built.* Excavators have found evidence that Ahab strengthened the fortifications of Megiddo and Hazor. *Chronicles of the Kings of Israel.* See note on 14:19.
22:40 *slept with his fathers.* See note on 1:21. *Ahaziah his son became king in his place.* For the reign of Ahaziah see vv. 51–53; 2Ki 1.
22:41 *Jehoshaphat . . . became king over Judah in the fourth year of Ahab.* Appears to refer to the beginning of Jehoshaphat's reign as sole king in 869 B.C. (see notes on v. 42; 16:29; see also Introduction: Chronology).
22:42 *twenty-five years.* 872–848 B.C. The full span of Jehoshaphat's reign dates from the 39th year of King Asa, when he became co-regent with his father (see note on 15:10; see also 2 Chr 16:12).
22:43 *the high places were not taken away.* See notes on 3:2; 15:14.
22:44 *king.* Probably to be understood in the collective sense and as including Ahab, Ahaziah and Joram, all of whom ruled in the north during the reign of Jehoshaphat in the south (see note on v. 4).
22:45 *how he warred.* See 2 Kin 3; 2 Chr 17:11; 20. *Chronicles of the Kings of Judah.* See note on 14:29.
22:46 *sodomites.* See note on 14:24.
22:47 *no king in Edom.* Suggests that Edom was subject to Judah (see 2 Sam 8:14; 2 Kin 8:20).
22:48 *Ophir.* See note on 9:28. *broken at Ezion-geber.* The destruction of the trading ships was a judgment of God on Jehoshaphat for entering into an alliance with Ahaziah of the northern kingdom (see 2 Chr 20:35–37).
22:50 *slept with his fathers.* See note on 1:21. *Jehoram his son became king in his place.* For the reign of Jehoram see 2 Kin 8:16–24; 2 Chr 21.
22:51 *seventeenth year of Jehoshaphat.* 853 B.C. (see notes on vv. 41–42). *two years.* 853–852 (see note on 2 Kin 1:17).
22:52 *way of his father and . . . mother.* See 16:30–33. *way of Jeroboam.* See 12:28–33.

2 Kings

INTRODUCTION

See Introduction to 1 Kings.

Outline

Below is an abbreviated outline for 2 Kings. For the complete outline see Introduction to 1 Kings: Outline.

III. The Ministries of Elijah and Elisha and Other Prophets from Ahab/Asa to Joram/Jehoshaphat (1 Kin 17:1 — 2 Kin 8:15)
   A. Elijah (and Other Prophets) in the Reign of Ahab (1 Kin 17:1 — 22:40)
   B. Jehoshaphat of Judah (1 Kin 22:41 – 50)
   C. Ahaziah of Israel; Elijah's Last Prophecy (22:51 — 2 Kin 1:18)
   D. Elijah's Translation; Elisha's Inauguration (2 Kin 2:1 – 18)
   E. Elisha in the Reign of Jehoram (2:19 — 8:15)

IV. Israel and Judah from Joram/Jehoram to the Exile of Israel (2 Kin 8:16 — 17:41)
   A. Jehoram of Judah (8:16 – 24)
   B. Ahaziah of Judah (8:25 – 29)
   C. Jehu's Revolt and Reign (chs. 9 — 10)
   D. Athaliah and Joash of Judah; Repair of the Temple (chs. 11 — 12)
   E. Jehoahaz of Israel (13:1 – 9)
   F. Jehoash of Israel; Elisha's Last Prophecy (13:10 – 25)
   G. Amaziah of Judah (14:1 – 22)
   H. Jeroboam II of Israel (14:23 – 29)
   I. Azariah of Judah (15:1 – 7)
   J. Zechariah of Israel (15:8 – 12)
   K. Shallum of Israel (15:13 – 16)
   L. Menahem of Israel (15:17 – 22)
   M. Pekahiah of Israel (15:23 – 26)
   N. Pekah of Israel (15:27 – 31)
   O. Jotham of Judah (15:32 – 38)
   P. Ahaz of Judah (ch. 16)
   Q. Hoshea of Israel (17:1 – 6)
   R. Exile of Israel; Resettlement of the Land (17:7 – 41)

V. Judah from Hezekiah to the Babylonian Exile (2 Kin 18 — 25)
   A. Hezekiah (chs. 18 — 20)
   B. Manasseh (21:1 – 18)
   C. Amon (21:19 – 26)
   D. Josiah (22:1 — 23:30)
   E. Jehoahaz Exiled to Egypt (23:31 – 35)
   F. Jehoiakim: First Babylonian Invasion (23:36 — 24:7)
   G. Jehoiachin: Second Babylonian Invasion (24:8 – 17)
   H. Zedekiah (24:18 – 20)
   I. Babylonian Exile of Judah (25:1 – 21)
   J. Removal of the Remnant to Egypt (25:22 – 26)
   K. Elevation of Jehoiachin in Babylon (25:27 – 30)

Ahaziah's Messengers Meet Elijah

1 Now [a]Moab rebelled against Israel after
the death of Ahab.
2 And Ahaziah fell through the lattice in
his upper chamber which *was* in Samaria,
and became ill. So he sent messengers and
said to them, "Go, [a]inquire of Baal-zebub,
the god of Ekron, [b]whether I will recover
from this sickness."
3 But the angel of the LORD said to [a]Elijah
the Tishbite, "Arise, go up to meet the messengers of the king of Samaria and say to
them, 'Is it because there is no God in Israel
that you are going to inquire of [b]Baal-zebub,
the god of Ekron?'
4 "Now therefore thus says the LORD,
'[1][a]You shall not come down from the bed
where you have gone up, but you shall surely die.' " Then Elijah departed.
5 When the messengers returned to him
he said to them, "[1]Why have you returned?"
6 They said to him, "A man came up to
meet us and said to us, 'Go, return to the
king who sent you and say to him, "Thus
says the LORD, 'Is it because there is no God
in Israel *that* you are sending [a]to inquire of
Baal-zebub, the god of Ekron? Therefore
[1]you shall not come down from the bed
where you have gone up, but shall surely
die.' " ' "

1:1 [a]2 Sam 8:2; 2 Kin 3:5
2 [a]2 Kin 1:3, 6, 16; Matt 10:25; Mark 3:22 [b]2 Kin 8:7-10
3 [a]1 Kin 17:1; 21:17 [b]2 Kin 1:2
4 [1]Lit *The bed where you went up, you shall not come down from it* [a]2 Kin 1:6, 16
5 [1]Lit *What is this that you have returned?*
6 [1]V 4, note 1 [a]2 Kin 1:2
8 [1]Lit *said* [2]Or *girt* [a]Zech 13:4; Matt 3:4; Mark 1:6
9 [a]2 Kin 6:13, 14
10 [a]1 Kin 18:36-38; Luke 9:54 [b]Job 1:16
13 [a]Is 1:5; Jer 5:3

7 He said to them, "What kind of man
was he who came up to meet you and spoke
these words to you?"
8 They [1]answered him, "[a]*He was* a hairy
man with a leather girdle [2]bound about his
loins." And he said, "It is Elijah the Tishbite."
9 Then *the king* [a]sent to him a captain of
fifty with his fifty. And he went up to him,
and behold, he was sitting on the top of the
hill. And he said to him, "O man of God, the
king says, 'Come down.' "
10 Elijah replied to the captain of fifty, "If
I am a man of God, [a]let fire come down from
heaven and consume you and your fifty."
[b]Then fire came down from heaven and consumed him and his fifty.
11 So he again sent to him another captain of fifty with his fifty. And he said to him,
"O man of God, thus says the king, 'Come
down quickly.' "
12 Elijah replied to them, "If I am a man
of God, let fire come down from heaven and
consume you and your fifty." Then the fire of
God came down from heaven and consumed
him and his fifty.
13 So he [a]again sent the captain of a third
fifty with his fifty. When the third captain of
fifty went up, he came and bowed down on
his knees before Elijah, and begged him and
said to him, "O man of God, please let my

1:1 *Moab rebelled.* Moab had been brought into subjection by David (see 2 Sam 8:2), but when the northern and Transjordan tribes rebelled and made Jeroboam their king, political domination of Moab probably also shifted to the northern kingdom. An inscription of Mesha king of Moab (see chart, p. xix) indicates that during the reign of Omri's "son" (probably a reference to his grandson Joram, not to Ahab) the Moabites were able to free the area of Medeba from Israelite control (see map No. 5 at the end of the study Bible). *after the death of Ahab.* See 1 Kin 22:37.

1:2 *Baal-zebub.* See note on Judg 10:6. *Ekron.* The northernmost of the five major Philistine cities (see Josh 13:3; 1 Sam 5:10 and notes). *whether I will recover.* Ahaziah appears to have feared that his injury would be fatal. He turned to the pagan deity for a revelatory oracle, not for healing.

1:3 *angel of the LORD.* See 1 Kin 19:7; see also note on Gen 16:7. The Lord usually spoke directly to the consciousness of the prophet (1 Kin 17:2,8; 18:1; 19:9; 21:17). Perhaps the means of revelation was changed in this instance to heighten the contrast between the messengers of Ahaziah (vv. 2–3,5) and the angel (which means "messenger") of the Lord. *Elijah the Tishbite.* See note on 1 Kin 17:1. *king of Samaria.* See note on 1 Kin 21:1.

1:4 *you shall surely die.* Ahaziah will receive the oracle he sought, but it will come from the Lord through Elijah, not from Baal-zebub.

1:5 *Why have you returned?* Ahaziah realized the messengers could not have traveled so quickly to Ekron and back.

1:8 *hairy man.* See 1 Kin 19:19. That is, he wore a garment (probably his cloak) made of sheepskin or camel's hair, tied with a simple leather thong (cf. Matt 3:4). His dress contrasted sharply with the fine linen clothing (see Jer 13:1) of his wealthy contemporaries and constituted a protest against the materialistic attitudes of the king and the upper classes (cf. Matt 11:7–8; Luke 7:24–25). *It is Elijah the Tishbite.* Ahaziah was familiar with Elijah's appearance because of the prophet's many encounters with Ahab, his father.

1:9 *the king sent to him a captain of fifty with his fifty.* The pagan people of that time thought that the magical power of curses could be nullified either by forcing the pronouncer of the curse to retract his statement or by killing him so that his curse would go with him to the netherworld. It appears that Ahaziah shared this view and desired to take Elijah prisoner in order to counteract the pronouncement of his death. *O man of God, the king says, 'Come down.'* Ahaziah attempted to place the prophet under the authority of the king. This constituted a violation of the covenant nature of Israelite kingship, in which the king's actions were always to be placed under the scrutiny and authority of the word of the Lord spoken by His prophets (see notes on 1 Sam 10:25; 12:23).

1:10 *fire came down from heaven and consumed him and his fifty.* See 1 Kin 18:38. Another link between the ministries of Elijah and Moses (see Lev 10:2; Num 16:35). At stake in this incident was the question of who was sovereign in Israel. Would Ahaziah recognize that the king in Israel was only a vice-regent under the authority and kingship of the Lord, or would he exercise despotic power, like pagan kings (see notes on 1 Sam 12:14–15)? At Mount Carmel the Lord had revealed Himself and authenticated His prophet by fire from heaven (see 1 Kin 18:38–39). Now this previous revelation is confirmed to Ahaziah. Jesus' rebuke of His disciples for suggesting that fire be called down from heaven to destroy the Samaritans (Luke 9:51–56) is not to be understood as a disapproval of Elijah's action, but as an indication that the disciples failed to discern the difference between the issue at stake in Elijah's day and the unbelief of the Samaritans in their own day.

1:11 *he again sent to him another captain of fifty with his fifty.* Ahaziah refused to submit to the word of the Lord in spite of the dramatic revelation of God's power.

1:13 *bowed down on his knees before Elijah.* The third captain, recognizing that Elijah was the bearer of the word of the Lord, feared for his life and bowed before him with a humble request.

life and the lives of these fifty servants of yours be precious in your sight."

14 "Behold fire came down from heaven and consumed the first two captains of fifty with their fifties; but now let my [1]life be precious in your sight."

15 [a]The angel of the LORD said to Elijah, "Go down with him; [b]do not be afraid of him." So he arose and went down with him to the king.

16 Then he said to him, "Thus says the LORD, 'Because you have sent messengers [a]to inquire of Baal-zebub, the god of Ekron—is it because there is no God in Israel to inquire of His word?—therefore [1]you shall not come down from the bed where you have gone up, but shall surely die.'"

Jehoram Reigns over Israel

17 So Ahaziah died according to the word of the LORD which Elijah had spoken. And because he had no son, Jehoram became king in his place [a]in the second year of Jehoram the son of Jehoshaphat, king of Judah.

18 Now the rest of the acts of Ahaziah which he did, are they not written in the Book of the Chronicles of the Kings of Israel?

Elijah Taken to Heaven

2 And it came about when the LORD was about to [a]take up Elijah by a [1]whirlwind to heaven, that Elijah went with [b]Elisha from [c]Gilgal.

2 Elijah said to Elisha, "[a]Stay here please, for the LORD has sent me as far as [b]Bethel." But Elisha said, "[c]As the LORD lives and as you yourself live, I will not leave you." So they went down to Bethel.

3 Then [a]the sons of the prophets who *were at* Bethel came out to Elisha and said to him, "Do you know that the LORD will take away your master from over [1]you today?" And he said, "Yes, I know; be still."

4 Elijah said to him, "Elisha, please [a]stay here, for the LORD has sent me to [b]Jericho." But he said, "[a]As the LORD lives, and as you yourself live, I will not leave you." So they came to Jericho.

5 [a]The sons of the prophets who *were* at Jericho approached Elisha and said to him, "[b]Do you know that the LORD will take away your master from over [1]you today?" And he [2]answered, "Yes, I know; be still."

6 Then Elijah said to him, "Please [a]stay here, for the LORD has sent me to [b]the Jordan." And he said, "As the LORD lives, and as you yourself live, I will not leave you." So the two of them went on.

7 Now [a]fifty men of the sons of the prophets went and stood opposite *them* at a distance, while the two of them stood by the Jordan.

8 Elijah [a]took his mantle and folded it together and [b]struck the waters, and they were divided here and there, so that the two of them crossed over on dry ground.

9 When they had crossed over, Elijah said to Elisha, "Ask what I shall do for you before I am taken from you." And Elisha said, "Please, let a [a]double portion of your spirit be upon me."

10 He said, "You have asked a hard thing. *Nevertheless,* if you [a]see me when I am taken from you, it shall be so for you; but if not, it shall not be *so.*"

11 As they were going along and talking, behold, *there appeared* [a]a chariot of fire and horses of fire which separated the two of them. And Elijah went up by a [1]whirlwind to heaven.

12 Elisha saw *it* and cried out, "[a]My father, my father, the [1]chariots of Israel and

14 [1]Lit *soul* **15** [a]2 Kin 1:3 [b]Is 51:12; Jer 1:17; Ezek 2:6 **16** [1]V 4, note 1 [a]2 Kin 1:3 **17** [a]2 Kin 3:1; 8:16 **2:1** [1]Or *windstorm* [a]Gen 5:24; Heb 11:5 [b]1 Kin 19:16-21 [c]Josh 4:19 **2** [a]Ruth 1:15 [b]1 Kin 12:28, 29 [c]1 Sam 1:26; 2 Kin 2:4, 6 **3** [a]2 Kin 4:1, 38; 5:22

3 [1]Lit *your head* **4** [a]2 Kin 2:2 [b]Josh 6:26 **5** [1]Lit *your head* [2]Lit *said* [a]2 Kin 2:3 [b]2 Kin 2:3 **6** [a]2 Kin 2:2 [b]Josh 3:8, 15-17 **7** [a]2 Kin 2:15, 16 **8** [a]1 Kin 19:13, 19 [b]Ex 14:21, 22; 2 Kin 2:14 **9** [a]Num 11:17-25; Deut 21:17 **10** [a]Acts 1:10 **11** [1]Or *windstorm* [a]2 Kin 6:17 **12** [1]Lit *chariot* [a]2 Kin 13:14

1:15 *The angel of the LORD said to Elijah.* See note on v. 3.
1:17 *died according to the word of the LORD.* In the end Ahaziah was punished for turning away from the God of Israel to a pagan deity, and the word of the Lord was shown to be both reliable and beyond the power of the king to annul. *Jehoram.* Ahaziah's younger brother (see 3:1; 1 Kin 22:51). *second year of Jehoram the son of Jehoshaphat.* Jehoram's reign overlapped that of his father Jehoshaphat from 853 to 848 B.C. (see note on 8:16). The reference here is to the second year of that co-regency. The 18th year of Jehoshaphat (3:1) is therefore the same as the second year of Jehoram's co-regency (852).
1:18 *Chronicles of the Kings of Israel.* See note on 1 Kin 14:19.
2:2 *I will not leave you.* Elisha was aware that Elijah's ministry was almost finished and that his departure was near (v. 5). He was determined to accompany him until the moment the Lord took him. His commitment to Elijah and to Elijah's ministry was unfailing (see v. 9; 1 Kin 19:21).
2:3 *sons of.* See note on 1 Kin 20:35. During the days of Elijah and Elisha, companies of prophets were located at Bethel (here), Jericho (v. 5) and Gilgal (4:38). It appears that Elijah journeyed by divine instruction to Gilgal (v. 1), Bethel (v. 2) and Jericho (v. 4) for a last meeting with each of these companies.
2:7 *Fifty men.* These men were to witness the miracle by which Elijah and Elisha crossed the river.
2:8 *Elijah took his mantle . . . and struck the waters.* Elijah used his cloak much as Moses had used his staff at the time of Israel's passage through the "Red Sea" (see Ex 14:16,21,26).
2:9 *let a double portion . . . be upon me.* Elisha was not expressing a desire for a ministry twice as great as Elijah's, but he was using terms derived from inheritance law to express his desire to carry on Elijah's ministry. Inheritance law assigned a double portion of a father's possessions to the firstborn son (see Deut 21:17 and note).
2:10 *hard thing.* Although Elijah had previously been told to anoint Elisha as his successor (1 Kin 19:16,19–21), Elijah's response clearly showed that the issue rested solely with the Lord's sovereign good pleasure. *if you see me . . . it shall be so . . . but if not, it shall not be so.* Elijah left the answer to Elisha's request in the Lord's hands.
2:11 *chariot of fire and horses of fire.* The Lord's heavenly host has accompanied and supported Elijah's ministry (as it had that of Moses; see Ex 15:1–10), and now at his departure Elisha is allowed to see it (cf. 6:17). *Elijah went up by a whirlwind to heaven.* Elijah, like Enoch before him (Gen 5:24), was taken up to heaven bodily without experiencing death; like Moses (Deut 34:4–6), he was taken away outside the promised land.
2:12 *chariots of Israel and its horsemen!* Elisha depicted Elijah as embodying the true strength of the nation. He, rather than

its horsemen!" And he saw [2]Elijah no more. Then [b]he took hold of his own clothes and tore them in two pieces.

13 He also took up the mantle of Elijah that fell from him and returned and stood by the bank of the Jordan.

14 He took the mantle of Elijah that fell from him and struck the waters and said, "Where is the LORD, the God of Elijah?" And when he also had [a]struck the waters, they were divided here and there; and Elisha crossed over.

Elisha Succeeds Elijah

15 Now when [a]the sons of the prophets who *were* at Jericho opposite *him* saw him, they said, "The spirit of Elijah rests on Elisha." And they came to meet him and bowed themselves to the ground before him.

16 They said to him, "Behold now, there are with your servants fifty strong men, please let them go and search for your master; perhaps [a]the Spirit of the LORD has taken him up and cast him on some mountain or into some valley." And he said, "You shall not send."

17 But when [a]they urged him until he was ashamed, he said, "Send." They sent therefore fifty men; and they searched three days but did not find him.

18 They returned to him while he was staying at Jericho; and he said to them, "Did I not say to you, 'Do not go'?"

19 Then the men of the city said to Elisha, "Behold now, the situation of this city is pleasant, as my lord sees; but the water is bad and the land [1]is unfruitful."

20 He said, "Bring me a new jar, and put salt [1]in it." So they brought *it* to him.

21 He went out to the spring of water and [a]threw salt [1]in it and said, "Thus says the LORD, 'I have [2]purified these waters; there shall not be from there death or [3]unfruitfulness any longer.' "

22 So the waters have been [1]purified to this day, according to the word of Elisha which he spoke.

23 Then he went up from there to Bethel; and as he was going up by the way, young lads came out from the city and [a]mocked him and said to him, "Go up, you baldhead; go up, you baldhead!"

24 When he looked behind him and saw them, he [a]cursed them in the name of the LORD. Then two female bears came out of the woods and tore up forty-two lads of [1]their number.

25 He went from there to [a]Mount Carmel, and from there he returned to Samaria.

Jehoram Meets Moab Rebellion

3 Now Jehoram the son of Ahab became king over Israel at Samaria [a]in the eighteenth year of Jehoshaphat king of Judah, and reigned twelve years.

2 He did evil in the sight of the LORD,

12 [2]Lit *him* [b]Gen 37:34; Job 1:20
14 [a]2 Kin 2:8
15 [a]2 Kin 2:7
16 [a]1 Kin 18:12; Acts 8:39
17 [a]2 Kin 8:11
19 [1]Lit *causes barrenness*
20 [1]Lit *there*
21 [1]Lit *there* [2]Lit *healed* [3]Lit *barrenness* [a]Ex 15:25, 26; 2 Kin 4:41; 6:6
22 [1]Lit *healed*
23 [a]2 Chr 36:16; Ps 31:17, 18
24 [1]Lit *them* [a]Neh 13:25-27
25 [a]1 Kin 18:19, 20; 2 Kin 4:25
3:1 [a]2 Kin 1:17

the apostate king, is the Lord's representative. The same description was later used of Elisha (13:14).

2:13 *He also took up the mantle.* See note on v. 8. Possession of Elijah's cloak symbolized Elisha's succession to Elijah's ministry (see 1 Kin 19:19).

2:14 *when he . . . struck the waters, they were divided.* See v. 8. The Lord authenticated Elisha's succession to Elijah's ministry and demonstrated that the same divine power that had accompanied Elijah's ministry was now operative in the ministry of Elisha. In crossing the Jordan as Joshua had before him, Elisha is shown to be Elijah's "Joshua" (Elisha and Joshua are very similar names, Elisha meaning "God saves" and Joshua "The LORD saves").

2:15 *bowed themselves to the ground before him.* Indicated their recognition of Elisha's succession to Elijah's position. Elisha was now the Lord's official representative in this time of royal apostasy.

2:16 *Perhaps the Spirit of the LORD has taken him up and cast him on.* Obadiah expressed the same idea years earlier (see 1 Kin 18:12). *You shall not send.* Elisha knew their search would be fruitless.

2:17 *Send.* When the company of prophets refused to be satisfied with Elisha's answer, he permitted them to go so that the authority and truth of his words would be confirmed to them.

2:19 *city.* Evidently Jericho (see v. 18). *the water is bad and the land is unfruitful.* The inhabitants of Jericho were experiencing the effects of the covenant curse (contrast Deut 28:15–18 with Ex 23:25–26; Lev 26:9; Deut 28:1–4). See 1 Kin 16:34; Josh 6:26.

2:20 *new jar.* That which was to be used in the service of the Lord was to be undefiled by profane use (see Lev 1:3,10; Num 19:2; Deut 21:3; 1 Sam 6:7). *put salt in it.* Elisha may have used salt because of its known preservative qualities, but it is more likely that he used it to symbolize the covenant faithfulness of the Lord (see note on Num 18:19; see also 2 Chr 13:5).

2:21 *I have purified these waters.* Any idea of a magical effect of the salt in the purification of the water is excluded by the explicit statement that the Lord Himself healed the water. In this symbolic way Elisha was able, as the first act of his ministry, to proclaim to the people that in spite of their disobedience the Lord was merciful and was still reaching out to them in His grace (see 13:23).

2:23 *Go up.* Since Bethel was the royal cult center of the northern kings (1 Kin 12:29; Amos 7:13) and Elijah and Elisha were known to frequent Samaria (perhaps even as their main residence; see note on 5:3), the youths from Bethel no doubt assumed that Elisha was going up to Samaria to continue Elijah's struggle against royal apostasy. (Some believe that the youths, in their mocking, were telling Elisha to ascend to heaven as Elijah had done.) *you baldhead!* Baldness was uncommon among the ancient Jews, and luxuriant hair seems to have been viewed as a sign of strength and vigor (see note on 2 Sam 14:26). By calling Elisha "baldhead," the youths from Bethel expressed that city's utter disdain for the Lord's representative, who, they felt, had no power.

2:24 *cursed them in the name of the LORD.* Elisha pronounced a curse similar to the covenant curse of Lev 26:21–22. The result gave warning of the judgment that would come on the entire nation should it persist in disobedience and apostasy (see 2 Chr 36:16). Thus Elisha's first acts were indicative of his ministry that would follow: God's covenant blessings would come to those who looked to Him (vv. 19–22), but God's covenant curses would fall on those who turned away from Him.

3:1 *Jehoram the son of Ahab became king . . . in the eighteenth year of Jehoshaphat.* See note on 1:17. *twelve years.* 852–841 B.C.

though not like his father and his mother; for
[a]he put away the *sacred* pillar of Baal [b]which
his father had made.
3 Nevertheless, [a]he clung to the sins of
Jeroboam the son of Nebat, [b]which he made
Israel sin; he did not depart from them.
4 Now Mesha king of Moab was a sheep
breeder, and [a]used to pay the king of Israel
100,000 lambs and the wool of 100,000 rams.
5 But [a]when Ahab died, the king of
Moab rebelled against the king of Israel.
6 And King Jehoram went out of Samaria
[1]at that time and mustered all Israel.
7 Then he went and sent *word* to Jehoshaphat the king of Judah, saying, "The king of
Moab has rebelled against me. Will you go
with me to fight against Moab?" And he said,
"I will go up; [a]I am as you are, my people as
your people, my horses as your horses."
8 He said, "Which way shall we go up?"
And he [1]answered, "The way of the wilderness of Edom."
9 So [a]the king of Israel went with [b]the
king of Judah and [c]the king of Edom; and
they made a circuit of seven days' journey,
and there was no water for the army or for
the cattle that followed them.
10 Then the king of Israel said, "Alas! For
the LORD has called these three kings to give
them into the hand of Moab."
11 But Jehoshaphat said, "[a]Is there not a
prophet of the LORD here, that we may
inquire of the LORD by him?" And one of the
king of Israel's servants answered and said,
"[b]Elisha the son of Shaphat is here, [c]who
used to pour water on the hands of Elijah."
12 Jehoshaphat said, "The word of the
LORD is with him." So the king of Israel and
Jehoshaphat and the king of Edom went
down to him.
13 Now Elisha said to the king of Israel,
"What do I have to do with you? [a]Go to the
prophets of your father and to the prophets
of your mother." And the king of Israel said
to him, "No, for the LORD has called these
three kings *together* to give them into the
hand of Moab."
14 Elisha said, "[a]As the LORD of hosts lives,
before whom I stand, were it not that I regard
the presence of Jehoshaphat the king of
Judah, I would not look at you nor see you.
15 "But now [a]bring me a minstrel." And it
came about, when the minstrel played, that
[b]the hand of the LORD came upon him.
16 He said, "Thus says the LORD, 'Make
this valley full of trenches.'
17 "For thus says the LORD, 'You shall not
see wind nor shall you see rain; yet that valley [a]shall be filled with water, so that you
shall drink, both you and your cattle and
your beasts.
18 'This is but a [a]slight thing in the sight of
the LORD; He will also give the Moabites into
your hand.
19 '[a]Then you shall strike every fortified
city and every choice city, and fell every
good tree and stop all springs of water, and
mar every good piece of land with stones.' "

2 [a]Ex 23:24; 2 Kin 10:18, 26-28 [b]1 Kin 16:31, 32
3 [a]1 Kin 12:28-32 [b]1 Kin 14:9, 16
4 [a]2 Sam 8:2; Is 16:1, 2
5 [a]2 Kin 1:1
6 [1]Lit *in that day*
7 [a]1 Kin 22:4
8 [1]Lit *said*
9 [a]2 Kin 3:1 [b]2 Kin 3:7 [c]1 Kin 22:47
11 [a]1 Kin 22:7
11 [b]2 Kin 2:25 [c]1 Kin 19:21; John 13:4, 5, 13, 14
13 [a]1 Kin 18:19; 22:6-11, 22-25
14 [a]1 Kin 17:1; 2 Kin 5:16
15 [a]1 Sam 16:23; 1 Chr 25:1 [b]1 Kin 18:46; Ezek 1:3
17 [a]Ps 107:35
18 [a]Jer 32:17, 27; Mark 10:27; Luke 1:37
19 [a]2 Kin 3:25

3:2 *not like his father and his mother.* Not as Ahab (see notes on 1 Kin 16:30–34) and Jezebel (see 1 Kin 18:4; 19:1–2; 21:7–15). *sacred pillar of Baal which his father had made.* Apparently a reference to the stone representation of the male deity (see note on 1 Kin 14:23) that Ahab placed in the temple he had constructed for Jezebel in Samaria (see 1 Kin 16:32–33). From 10:27 it appears that this stone was later reinstated, perhaps by Jezebel.

3:3 *sins of Jeroboam . . . which he made Israel sin.* See note on 1 Kin 14:16.

3:4 *Mesha king of Moab.* See note on 1:1. *100,000 lambs and the wool of 100,000 rams.* The heavy annual tribute (see Is 16:1) that Israel required from the Moabites as a vassal state.

3:5 *king of Moab rebelled.* See note on 1:1.

3:7 *Will you go with me to fight against Moab?* Jehoram wished to attack Moab from the rear (v. 8), but to do that his army had to pass through Judah. *I am as you are, my people as your people, my horses as your horses.* See 1 Kin 22:4. Jehoshaphat had already been condemned by prophets of the Lord for his alliance with the northern kings Ahab (see 2 Chr 18:1; 19:1–2) and Ahaziah (2 Chr 20:35–37), yet he agreed to join with Jehoram against Moab. Perhaps he was disturbed by the potential danger to Judah posed by the growing strength of Moab (see 2 Chr 20), and he may have considered Jehoram less evil than his predecessors (see v. 2).

3:8 *the way of the wilderness of Edom.* This route of attack took the armies of Israel and Judah south of the Dead Sea, enabling them to circumvent the fortifications of Moab's northern frontier and to avoid the possibility of a rearguard action against them by the Arameans of Damascus. The Edomites, who were subject to Judah, were in no position to resist the movement of Israel's army through their territory.

3:9 *king of Edom.* Although here designated a king, he was in reality a governor appointed by Jehoshaphat (see 8:20; 1 Kin 22:47).

3:11 *Is there not a prophet of the LORD here . . . ?* See 1 Kin 22:7. Only after the apparent failure of their own strategies did the three rulers seek the word of the Lord (v. 12). *Elisha the son of Shaphat is here.* Since Elijah is reported to have sent a letter to Jehoshaphat's son Jehoram after his father's death (2 Chr 21:12–15), it seems that Elisha accompanied the armies on this campaign as the representative of the aged Elijah. The event is narrated here after the account of Elisha's initiation as Elijah's successor and the two events that foreshadowed the character of his ministry. Following this introduction to Elisha's ministry, the present episode is topically associated with the series of Elisha's acts that now occupies the narrative.

3:13 *Go to the prophets of your father and . . . mother.* See 1 Kin 22:6.

3:14 *were it not that I regard . . . Jehoshaphat . . . I would not look at you.* Jehoram will share in the blessing of the word of God only because of his association with Jehoshaphat.

3:15 *bring me a minstrel.* To create a disposition conducive to receiving the word of the Lord.

3:16 *this valley.* The Israelite armies were encamped in the broad valley (the Arabah) between the highlands of Moab on the east and those of Judah on the west, just south of the Dead Sea.

3:17 *shall be filled with water.* The word of the Lord contained a promise and a directive. The Lord will graciously provide for His people, but they must respond to His word in faith and obedience (v. 16).

3:19 The two armies will devastate the rebellious country.

20 It happened in the morning [a]about the
time of offering the sacrifice, that behold,
water came by the way of Edom, and the
country was filled with water.
21 Now all the Moabites heard that the
kings had come up to fight against them. And
all who were able to [1]put on armor and older
were summoned and stood on the border.
22 They rose early in the morning, and the
sun shone on the water, and the Moabites
saw the water opposite *them* as red as blood.
23 Then they said, "This is blood; the
kings have surely fought together, and they
have slain one another. Now therefore,
Moab, to the spoil!"
24 But when they came to the camp of
Israel, the Israelites arose and struck the
Moabites, so that they fled before them; and
they went forward [1]into the land, [2]slaughter-
ing the Moabites.
25 [a]Thus they destroyed the cities; and
each one threw a stone on every piece of
good land and filled it. So they stopped all
the springs of water and felled all the good
trees, until in [b]Kir-hareseth *only* they left its
stones; however, the slingers went about *it*
and struck it.
26 When the king of Moab saw that the
battle was too fierce for him, he took with
him 700 men who drew swords, to break
through to the king of Edom; but they could
not.
27 Then he took his oldest son who was to
reign in his place, and [a]offered him as a
burnt offering on the wall. And there came
great wrath against Israel, and they departed
from him and returned to their own land.

The Widow's Oil

4 Now a certain woman of the wives of
[a]the sons of the prophets cried out to [1]Eli-
sha, "Your servant my husband is dead, and
you know that your servant feared the LORD;
and [b]the creditor has come to take my two
children to be his slaves."
2 Elisha said to her, "What shall I do for
you? Tell me, what do you have in the
house?" And she said, "Your maidservant
has nothing in the house except [a]a jar of oil."
3 Then he said, "Go, borrow vessels at
large for yourself from all your neighbors,
even empty vessels; do not get a few.
4 "And you shall go in and shut the door
behind you and your sons, and pour out into
all these vessels, and you shall set aside
what is full."
5 So she went from him and shut the
door behind her and her sons; they were
bringing *the vessels* to her and she poured.
6 When [a]the vessels were full, she said
to her son, "Bring me another vessel." And
he said to her, "There is not one vessel
more." And the oil stopped.
7 Then she came and told [a]the man of
God. And he said, "Go, sell the oil and pay
your debt, and you *and* your sons can live on
the rest."

The Shunammite Woman

8 Now there came a day when Elisha
passed over to [a]Shunem, where there was a
[1]prominent woman, and she persuaded him
to eat [2]food. And so it was, as often as he
passed by, he turned in there to eat [2]food.
9 She said to her husband, "Behold now,
I perceive that this is a holy [a]man of God
passing by us continually.
10 "Please, let us [a]make a little walled
upper chamber and let us set a bed for him
there, and a table and a chair and a lampstand; and it shall be, when he comes to us,
that he can turn in there."

20 [a]Ex 29:39, 40
21 [1]Lit *gird themselves with a belt*
24 [1]Lit *into it* [2]Lit *smiting*
25 [a]2 Kin 3:19 [b]Is 16:7; Jer 48:31, 36
27 [a]Amos 2:1; Mic 6:7
4:1 [1]Lit *Elisha, saying* [a]2 Kin 2:3
4:1 [b]Lev 25:39-41, 48; 1 Sam 22:2; Neh 5:2-5
2 [a]1 Kin 17:12
6 [a]Matt 14:20
7 [a]1 Kin 12:22
8 [1]Lit *great* [2]Lit *bread* [a]Josh 19:18
9 [a]2 Kin 4:7
10 [a]Matt 10:41, 42; 25:40; Rom 12:13

3:20 *time of offering.* See Ex 29:38–39; Num 28:3–4. *water came by the way of Edom.* Flash floods in the distant mountains of Edom caused water to flow north through the broad, usually dry, valley that sloped toward the Dead Sea (see note on v. 16).
3:23 *the kings have surely . . . slain one another.* The Moabites would have good reason to suspect that an internal conflict had arisen between the parties of an alliance whose members had previously been mutually hostile.
3:25 *Kir-hareseth.* The capital city of Moab (see Is 16:7,11; Jer 48:31,36), usually identified with present-day Kerak, located about 11 miles east of the Dead Sea and 15 miles south of the Arnon River.
3:26 *break through to the king of Edom.* A desperate attempt by the king of Moab to induce Edom to turn against Israel and Judah.
3:27 *offered him as a burnt offering on the wall.* King Mesha offered his oldest son, the crown prince, as a burnt offering (see 16:3; Jer 7:31) to the Moabite god Chemosh (see 1 Kin 11:7; Num 21:29; Jer 48:46) in an attempt to induce the deity to come to his aid. *there came great wrath against Israel.* The Hebrew underlying this clause would normally refer to a visitation of God's wrath. It may be that just when total victory appeared to be in Israel's grasp, God's displeasure with the Ahab dynasty showed itself in some way that caused the Israelite kings to give up the campaign. Comparing Aramaic and later Hebrew usage, a few scholars suggest that the Hebrew here can be translated, "There was great dismay upon/in Israel."
4:1 *sons of the prophets.* See notes on 2:3; 1 Kin 20:35. *to take my two children to be his slaves.* Servitude as a means of debt payment by labor was permitted in the Mosaic law (Ex 21:1–2; Lev 25:39–41; Deut 15:1–11). It appears that the practice was much abused (see Neh 5:5,8; Amos 2:6; 8:6), even though the law limited the term of such bondage and required that those so held be treated as hired workers.
4:4 *shut the door behind you and your sons.* The impending miracle was not intended to be a public sensation but to demonstrate privately God's mercy and grace to this widow (cf. Ps 68:5). She did not hesitate to respond to the instructions of the Lord's prophet in faith and obedience.
4:8 *Shunem.* See note on 1 Kin 1:3.
4:9 *holy man of God.* The woman recognized that Elisha was a person set apart to the Lord's work in a very special sense. Nowhere else in the OT is the term "holy" applied to a prophet.
4:10 *when he comes to us . . . he can turn in there.* By her hospitality the woman was able to assist in sustaining the proclamation of God's word through Elisha.

11 [1]One day he came there and turned in
to the upper chamber and [2]rested.
12 Then he said to [a]Gehazi his servant,
"Call this Shunammite." And when he had
called her, she stood before him.
13 He said to him, "Say now to her,
'Behold, you have been [1]careful for us with
all this [2]care; what can I do for you? Would
you be spoken for to the king or to the captain of the army?' " And she [3]answered, "I
live among my own people."
14 So he said, "What then is to be done
for her?" And Gehazi [1]answered, "Truly she
has no son and her husband is old."
15 He said, "Call her." When he had
called her, she stood in the doorway.
16 Then he said, "[a]At this season [1]next
year you will embrace a son." And she said,
"No, my lord, O man of God, [b]do not lie to
your maidservant."
17 The woman conceived and bore a son
at that season [1]the next year, as Elisha had
said to her.

The Shunammite's Son

18 When the child was grown, the day
came that he went out to his father to the
reapers.
19 He said to his father, "My head, my
head." And he said to his servant, "Carry
him to his mother."
20 When he had taken him and brought
him to his mother, he sat on her [1]lap until
noon, and *then* died.
21 She went up and [a]laid him on the bed
of [b]the man of God, and shut *the door*
behind him and went out.
22 Then she called to her husband and
said, "Please send me one of the servants
and one of the donkeys, that I may run to the
man of God and return."
23 He said, "Why will you go to him
today? It is neither [a]new moon nor sabbath."
And she said, "*It will be* well."
24 Then she saddled a donkey and said to
her servant, "Drive and go forward; do not
slow down [1]the pace for me unless I tell
you."
25 So she went and came to the man of
God to [a]Mount Carmel.
When the man of God saw her at a distance, he said to Gehazi his servant,
"Behold, [1]there is the Shunammite.
26 "Please run now to meet her and say to
her, 'Is it well with you? Is it well with your
husband? Is it well with the child?' " And she
[1]answered, "It is well."
27 When she came to the man of God [a]to
the hill, she caught hold of his feet. And
Gehazi came near to push her away; but the
man of God said, "Let her alone, for her soul
is [1]troubled within her; and the LORD has
hidden it from me and has not told me."
28 Then she said, "Did I ask for a son
from my lord? Did I not say, '[a]Do not deceive
me'?"
29 Then he said to Gehazi, "[a]Gird up your
loins and [b]take my staff in your hand, and go
your way; if you meet any man, do not
[c]salute him, and if anyone salutes you, do
not answer him; and [d]lay my staff on the
lad's face."
30 The mother of the lad said, "[a]As the
LORD lives and as you yourself live, I will not
leave you." And he arose and followed her.
31 Then Gehazi passed on before them
and laid the staff on the lad's face, but there
was no sound or [1]response. So he returned

11 [1]Lit *Now a day came that* [2]Lit *lay there*
12 [a]2 Kin 4:29-31; 5:20-27; 8:4, 5
13 [1]Lit *fearful* [2]Lit *fear* [3]Lit *said*
14 [1]Lit *said*
16 [1]Lit *when the time revives* [a]Gen 18:14 [b]2 Kin 4:28
17 [1]Lit *when the time revived*
20 [1]Lit *knees*
21 [a]2 Kin 4:32 [b]2 Kin 4:7
23 [a]Num 10:10; 28:11; 1 Chr 23:31
24 [1]Lit *riding*
25 [1]Lit *this Shunammite* [a]2 Kin 2:25
26 [1]Lit *said*
27 [1]Lit *bitter* [a]2 Kin 4:25
28 [a]2 Kin 4:16
29 [a]1 Kin 18:46; 2 Kin 9:1 [b]Ex 4:17; 2 Kin 2:14 [c]Luke 10:4 [d]Ex 7:19, 20; 14:16
30 [a]2 Kin 2:2, 4
31 [1]Lit *attentiveness*

4:12 *Gehazi.* Referred to here for the first time; he appears to have served Elisha in some of the same ways as Elisha had served Elijah, though the two men were of drastically different character (see 5:19–27; 6:15).

4:13 *I live among my own people.* The Shunammite woman felt secure and content in the community of her own family and tribe, and she had no need or desire for favors from high government officials.

4:14 *she has no son and her husband is old.* A great disappointment because it meant that the family's name would cease and its land and possessions would pass on to others. It was also a great threat to this young wife's future in that she faced the likelihood of many years as a widow with no provider or protector—children were a widow's only social security in old age (see 8:1–6; see also note on 1 Kin 17:22).

4:16 *At this season next year.* See Gen 17:21; 18:14. *O man of God, do not lie to your maidservant.* The woman's response revealed the depths of her desire for a son and her fear of disappointment more than it showed a lack of confidence in the word of Elisha.

4:17 *as Elisha had said to her.* The trustworthiness of Elisha's word was confirmed, and the birth of the son was shown to be the result of God's gracious intervention in her behalf.

4:20 *he . . . died.* The child, given as an evidence of God's grace and the reliability of His word, was suddenly taken from the woman in a severe test of her faith. Her subsequent actions demonstrate the strength of her faith in the face of great calamity.

4:21 *laid him on the bed of the man of God.* In this way the woman concealed the child's death from the rest of the household while she went to seek the prophet at whose word the child had been born.

4:23 *Why will you go to him today?* The question suggests that it was not uncommon for the woman to go to Elisha, but that on this occasion the timing of her visit was unusual. *It is neither new moon nor sabbath.* The sabbath and new moon were observed by cessation from work (see notes on Gen 2:3; Ex 16:23; 20:9–10; 1 Sam 20:5; see also Lev 23:3).

4:26 *It is well.* The woman was determined to share her distress with no one but the prophet from whom she had received the promise of the birth of her son.

4:28 *Did I not say, 'Do not deceive me'?* The woman struggled with the question of why the Lord would take from her that which she had been given as a special demonstration of His grace and the trustworthiness of His word.

4:29 *lay my staff on the lad's face.* It appears that Elisha expected the Lord to restore the boy's life when the staff was placed on him. This does not suggest that Elisha attributed magical power to the staff, but that he viewed it as a representation of his own presence and a symbol of divine power (see note on 2:8; cf. Ex 14:16; Acts 19:12).

4:30 *I will not leave you.* The woman was not convinced that

to meet him and told [2]him, "The lad [a]has not
awakened."
32 When Elisha came into the house,
behold the lad was dead and laid on his bed.
33 So he entered and [a]shut the door
behind them both and prayed to the LORD.
34 And [a]he went up and lay on the child,
and put his mouth on his mouth and his eyes
on his eyes and his hands on his hands, and
he stretched himself on him; and the flesh of
the child became warm.
35 Then he returned and walked in the
house once back and forth, and went up and
[a]stretched himself on him; and the lad
sneezed seven times and the lad opened his
eyes.
36 He called Gehazi and said, "Call this
Shunammite." So he called her. And when
she came in to him, he said, "Take up your
son."
37 Then she went in and fell at his feet
and bowed herself to the ground, and [a]she
took up her son and went out.

The Poisonous Stew

38 When Elisha returned to [a]Gilgal, *there*
was [b]a famine in the land. [1]As [c]the sons of
the prophets [d]were sitting before him, he
said to his servant, "[e]Put on the large pot
and boil stew for the sons of the prophets."
39 Then one went out into the field to
gather herbs, and found a wild vine and
gathered from it his lap full of wild gourds,
and came and sliced them into the pot of
stew, for they did not know *what they were.*
40 So they poured *it* out for the men to
eat. And as they were eating of the stew, they
cried out and said, "O man of God, there is
[a]death in the pot." And they were unable to
eat.
41 But he said, "Now bring meal." [a]He
threw it into the pot and said, "Pour *it* out for
the people that they may eat." Then there
was no harm in the pot.
42 Now a man came from Baal-shalishah,
and brought the man of God bread of the
first fruits, twenty loaves of barley and fresh
ears of grain in his sack. And he said, "[a]Give
them to the people that they may eat."
43 His attendant said, "What, [a]will I set
this before a hundred men?" But he said,
"Give *them* to the people that they may eat,
for thus says the LORD, 'They shall eat and
have *some* left over.' "
44 So he set *it* before them, and they ate
and [a]had *some* left over, according to the
word of the LORD.

Naaman Is Healed

5 Now [a]Naaman, captain of the army of the
king of Aram, was a great man [1]with his
master, and highly respected, because by him
the LORD had given victory to Aram. The man
was also a valiant warrior, *but he was* a leper.
2 Now the Arameans had gone out [a]in
bands and had taken captive a little girl from
the land of Israel; and she [1]waited on Naaman's wife.
3 She said to her mistress, "I wish that
my master were [1]with the prophet who is in
Samaria! Then he would cure him of his leprosy."

31 [2]Lit *him, saying* [a]John 11:11
33 [a]2 Kin 4:4; Matt 6:6; Luke 8:51
34 [a]1 Kin 17:21-23
35 [a]1 Kin 17:21
37 [a]Heb 11:35
38 [1]Lit *And* [a]2 Kin 2:1 [b]2 Kin 8:1 [c]2 Kin 2:3 [d]Luke 10:39; Acts 22:3 [e]Ezek 11:3, 7, 11; 24:3
40 [a]Ex 10:17
41 [a]Ex 15:25; 2 Kin 2:21
42 [a]Matt 14:16-21; 15:32-38
43 [a]Luke 9:13; John 6:9
44 [a]Matt 14:20; 15:37; John 6:13
5:1 [1]Lit *before* [a]Luke 4:27
2 [1]Lit *was before* [a]2 Kin 6:23; 13:20
3 [1]Lit *before*

Gehazi's mission would be successful and insisted that Elisha himself accompany her to Shunem.

4:33 *shut the door behind them both and prayed.* Just as Elijah had done in a similar situation years before (see 1 Kin 17:20–22), Elisha first turned to the Lord in earnest prayer for restoration of life to the dead child. His prayer is clear evidence that his subsequent actions were not intended as a magical means of restoring life.

4:34 *lay on the child.* See note on 1 Kin 17:21. Perhaps Elisha was familiar with the earlier similar action of Elijah.

4:37 *fell at his feet and bowed herself to the ground.* The woman gratefully acknowledged the special favor granted to her by the Lord through Elisha, and silently reaffirmed the verbal confession of the widow of Zarephath (see 1 Kin 17:24).

4:38 *famine in the land.* Perhaps the same famine mentioned in 8:1. Famine was a covenant curse (see Lev 26:19–20,26; Deut 28:18,23–24; 1 Kin 8:36–37) and evidence of God's anger with His people's disobedience to their covenant obligations. *sons of the prophets.* See note on 2:3.

4:39 *wild vine . . . gourds.* The precise type of plant is not specified.

4:41 *meal.* The flour itself did not make the stew edible (see 2:21 and note). It was simply a means by which the Lord provided for those who were faithful to the covenant, at a time when others suffered under the covenant curse.

4:42 *first fruits.* Instead of bringing the first fruits of the new harvest (see Lev 2:14; 23:15–17; Deut 18:3–5) to the apostate priests at Bethel and Dan (see 1 Kin 12:28–31), godly people in the northern kingdom may have contributed their offerings for the sustenance of Elisha and those associated with him (see note on v. 23). Thus they looked upon Elisha rather than the apostate king and priests as the true representative of their covenant Lord.

4:43 *says the LORD.* The bread was multiplied at the word of the Lord through Elisha apart from any intermediate means (contrast v. 41; 2:20; cf. Mark 6:35–43).

5:1 *king of Aram.* Probably Ben-hadad II (see notes on 8:7; 13:3; 1 Kin 20:1). *the LORD had given victory to Aram.* Probably a reference to an otherwise undocumented Aramean victory over the Assyrians in the aftermath of the battle of Qarqar in 853 B.C. (see note on 1 Kin 22:1). In the narrator's theological perspective, this victory is attributable to the sovereignty of the God of Israel, who is seen as the ruler and controller of the destinies of all nations, not just that of Israel (see Ezek 30:24; Amos 2:1–3; 9:7). *leper.* The Hebrew word was used for various diseases affecting the skin—not necessarily leprosy.

5:2 *gone out in bands.* Although Israel had concluded a peace treaty with the Arameans during the reign of Ahab (see 1 Kin 20:34), minor border skirmishes continued between the two states in the aftermath of the battle for control of Ramoth-gilead, in which Ahab had been killed (see note on 1 Kin 22:4; see also 1 Kin 22:35). *little girl from the land of Israel.* In sharp contrast to the Israelite king in Samaria, this young girl held captive in Damascus was very much aware of God's saving presence with His people through His servant Elisha, and she selflessly shared that knowledge with her Aramean captors.

5:3 *prophet who is in Samaria.* Elisha, who maintained a residence in Samaria (see v. 9; 2:25; 6:19).

4 [1]Naaman went in and told his master,
saying, "Thus and thus spoke the girl who is
from the land of Israel."
5 Then the king of Aram said, "Go [1]now,
and I will send a letter to the king of Israel."
He departed and [a]took with him ten talents
of silver and six thousand *shekels* of gold and
ten [b]changes of clothes.
6 He brought the letter to the king of Israel, saying, "And now as this letter comes to
you, behold, I have sent Naaman my servant
to you, that you may cure him of his leprosy."
7 When the king of Israel read the letter,
[a]he tore his clothes and said, "[b]Am I God, to
kill and to make alive, that this man is sending *word* to me to cure a man of his leprosy?
But [c]consider now, and see how he is seeking [1]a quarrel against me."
8 It happened when Elisha [a]the man of
God heard that the king of Israel had torn his
clothes, that he sent *word* to the king, saying,
"Why have you torn your clothes? Now let
him come to me, and he shall know that
there is a prophet in Israel."
9 So Naaman came with his horses and
his chariots and stood at the doorway of the
house of Elisha.
10 Elisha sent a messenger to him, saying,
"[a]Go and wash in the Jordan seven times,
and your flesh will be restored to you and
you will be clean."
11 But Naaman was furious and went
away and said, "Behold, I [1]thought, 'He will
surely come out to me and stand and call on
the name of the LORD his God, and wave his
hand over the place and cure the leper.'
12 "Are not [1]Abanah and Pharpar, the
rivers of Damascus, better than all the waters
of Israel? Could I not wash in them and be
clean?" So he turned and [a]went away in a
rage.
13 [a]Then his servants came near and
spoke to him and said, "[b]My father, had the
prophet told you *to do some* great thing,
would you not have done *it?* How much
more *then,* when he says to you, 'Wash, and
be clean'?"
14 So he went down and dipped *himself*
seven times in the Jordan, according to the
word of the man of God; and [a]his flesh was
restored like the flesh of a little child and [b]he
was clean.

Gehazi's Greed

15 When he returned to the man of God
[1]with all his company, and came and stood
before him, he said, "Behold now, [a]I know
that there is no God in all the earth, but in
Israel; so please [b]take a [2]present from your
servant now."
16 But he said, "[a]As the LORD lives, before
whom I stand, [b]I will take nothing." And he
urged him to take *it,* but he refused.
17 Naaman said, "If not, please let your
servant at least be given two mules' load of
[a]earth; for your servant will no longer offer

4 [1]Lit *He*
5 [1]Lit *enter* [a]1 Sam 9:7; 2 Kin 4:42 [b]Judg 14:12; 2 Kin 5:22, 23
7 [1]Lit *an occasion* [a]Gen 37:29 [b]Gen 30:2; 1 Sam 2:6 [c]1 Kin 20:7; Luke 11:54
8 [a]1 Kin 12:22
10 [a]John 9:7
11 [1]Lit *said*
12 [1]Another reading is *Amanah* [a]Prov 14:17; 16:32; 19:11
13 [a]1 Sam 28:23 [b]2 Kin 2:12; 6:21; 8:9
14 [a]2 Kin 5:10; Job 33:25 [b]Luke 4:27; 5:13
15 [1]Lit *he and* [2]Lit *blessing* [a]Josh 2:11; 1 Sam 17:46, 47; 2 Kin 5:8 [b]1 Sam 25:27
16 [a]2 Kin 3:14 [b]Gen 14:22, 23; 2 Kin 5:20, 26
17 [a]Ex 20:24

5:5 *I will send a letter to the king of Israel.* The border skirmishes had not nullified the official peace between the two nations as established by treaty. The king of Israel was Jehoram (see 1:17; 3:1; 9:24). *ten talents of silver.* About 750 pounds of silver. An idea of the relative value of this amount of silver can be seen by comparing it with the price Omri paid for the hill of Samaria (see 1 Kin 16:24).

5:6 *that you may cure him of his leprosy.* Ben-hadad assumed that the prophet described by the Israelite slave girl was subject to the authority of the king and that his services could be bought with a sufficiently large gift. He thought he could buy with worldly wealth one of the chief blessings of God's saving presence among His people.

5:7 *he is seeking a quarrel against me.* Jehoram concluded that the entire incident was an attempt by Ben-hadad to create a pretext for a declaration of war. So blind was the king to God's saving presence through Elisha that he could think only of international intrigue.

5:8 *Why have you torn your clothes?* Elisha chided Jehoram for his fear (see note on 1 Sam 17:11) and for his failure to consult the Lord's prophet (see 3:13–14 for evidence of the tension that existed between Jehoram and Elisha).

5:9 *with his horses and his chariots.* This proud pagan would command the healing by his lordly presence.

5:10 *wash in the Jordan seven times.* The instruction is designed to demonstrate to Naaman that healing would come by the power of the God of Israel, but only if he obeyed the word of the Lord's prophet. The prophet himself was not a healer. Ritual washings were practiced among Eastern religions as a purification rite, and the number seven was generally known as a symbol of completeness. Naaman was to wash in the muddy waters of the Jordan River, demonstrating that there was no natural connection between the washing and the desired healing. Perhaps it also suggested that one needed to pass through the Jordan, as Israel had done (Josh 3–4), in order to obtain healing from the God of Israel.

5:11 *wave his hand over the place and cure the leper.* Naaman expected to be healed by the magical technique of the prophet rather than by the power of God operative in connection with his own obedient response to God's word.

5:12 *Abanah and Pharpar.* The Abanah was termed the Golden River by the Greeks. It is usually identified with the Barada River of today, rising in the Anti-Lebanon mountains and flowing through the city of Damascus. The Pharpar River flows east from Mount Hermon just to the south of Damascus.

5:14 *his flesh was restored like the flesh of a little child and he was clean.* Physically he was reborn (see also v. 15 and note). As he obeyed God's word, Naaman received the gift of God's grace. Naaman is here a sign to disobedient Israel that God's blessing is found only in the path of trustful obedience. When His own people turn away from covenant faithfulness, God will raise up those who will follow His word from outside the covenant nation (see notes on 1 Kin 17:9–24; see also Matt 8:10–12; Luke 4:27).

5:15 *no God in all the earth, but in Israel.* Naaman's confession put to shame the Israelites who continued to waver in their opinion on whether Baal and the Lord (Yahweh) were both gods, or whether Yahweh alone was God (see note on 1 Kin 18:21).

5:16 *I will take nothing.* Elisha did not seek monetary gain for proclaiming the word of the Lord (see Matt 10:8). Naaman was healed solely by divine grace, not by the power of Elisha.

5:17 *let your servant at least be given two mules' load of earth.* In the ancient world it was commonly thought that a deity could be worshiped only on the soil of the nation to which he

burnt offering nor will he sacrifice to other
gods, but to the LORD.
18 "In this matter may the LORD pardon
your servant: when my master goes into the
house of Rimmon to worship there, and [a]he
leans on my hand and I bow myself in the
house of Rimmon, when I bow myself in the
house of Rimmon, the LORD pardon your servant in this matter."
19 He said to him, "[a]Go in peace." So he
departed from him some distance.
20 But [a]Gehazi, the servant of Elisha the
man of God, [1]thought, "Behold, my master
has spared this Naaman the Aramean, [2]by
not receiving from his hands what he
brought. [b]As the LORD lives, I will run after
him and take something from him."
21 So Gehazi pursued Naaman. When
Naaman saw one running after him, he came
down from the chariot to meet him and said,
"Is all well?"
22 He said, "[a]All is well. My master has
sent me, saying, 'Behold, just now two
young men of the sons of the prophets have
come to me from [b]the hill country of Ephraim. Please give them a talent of silver and
[c]two changes of clothes.' "
23 Naaman said, "[a]Be pleased to take two
talents." And he urged him, and bound two
talents of silver in two bags with two
changes of clothes and gave them to two of
his servants; and they carried *them* before
him.
24 When he came to the [1]hill, he took
them from their hand and [a]deposited them
in the house, and he sent the men away, and
they departed.
25 But he went in and stood before his
master. And Elisha said to him, "Where have
you been, Gehazi?" And he said, "[a]Your servant went nowhere."
26 Then he said to him, "Did not my heart
go *with you,* when the man turned from his
chariot to meet you? [a]Is it a time to receive
money and to receive clothes and olive
groves and vineyards and sheep and oxen
and male and female servants?
27 "Therefore, the leprosy of Naaman shall
cling to you and to your [1]descendants forever." So he went out from his presence [a]a leper *as white* as snow.

The Axe Head Recovered

6 Now [a]the sons of the prophets said to Elisha, "Behold now, the place before you
where we are living is too limited for us.
2 "Please let us go to the Jordan and each
of us take from there a beam, and let us
make a place there for ourselves where we
may live." So he said, "Go."
3 Then one said, "Please be willing to go
with your servants." And he [1]answered, "I
shall go."
4 So he went with them; and when they
came to the Jordan, they cut down trees.
5 But as one was felling a beam, [1]the axe
head fell into the water; and he cried out and
said, "Alas, my master! For it was borrowed."
6 Then the man of God said, "Where did
it fall?" And when he showed him the place,
[a]he cut off a stick and threw *it* in there, and
made the iron float.
7 He said, "Take it up for yourself." So he
put out his hand and took it.

The Arameans Plot to Capture Elisha

8 Now the king of Aram was warring
against Israel; and he [1]counseled with his

18 [a]2 Kin 7:2, 17
19 [a]Ex 4:18; 1 Sam 1:17; Mark 5:34
20 [1]Lit *said* [2]Lit *from* [a]2 Kin 4:12, 31, 36 [b]Ex 20:7; 2 Kin 6:31
22 [a]2 Kin 4:26 [b]Josh 24:33 [c]2 Kin 5:5
23 [a]2 Kin 6:3
24 [1]Lit *Ophel* [a]Josh 7:1, 11, 12, 21; 1 Kin 21:16
25 [a]2 Kin 5:22
26 [a]2 Kin 5:16
27 [1]Lit *seed* [a]Ex 4:6; Num 12:10
6:1 [a]2 Kin 2:3
3 [1]Lit *said*
5 [1]Lit *as for the iron, it fell*
6 [a]Ex 15:25; 2 Kin 2:21; 4:41
8 [1]Lit *took counsel*

was bound (see v. 15). For this reason Naaman wanted to take Israelite soil with him in order to have a place in Damascus for the worship of the Lord.

5:18 *my master.* Ben-hadad, king of Aram. *Rimmon.* Also known as Hadad (and in Canaan and Phoenicia as Baal), this Aramean deity was the god of storm ("Rimmon" means "thunderer") and war. The two names were sometimes combined (see note on Zech 12:11).

5:19 *Go in peace.* Elisha did not directly address Naaman's problem of conscience (v. 18), but commended him to the leading and grace of God as he returned to his pagan environment and official responsibilities.

5:20 *As the LORD lives.* An oath formula (see note on 1 Sam 14:39).

5:22 *sons of the prophets.* See note on 2:3. *Please give them a talent of silver and two changes of clothes.* Gehazi deceived Naaman in order to satisfy his desire for material gain. The evil of his lie was compounded in that it obscured the gracious character of the Lord's work in Naaman's healing and blurred the distinction between Elisha's function as a true prophet of the Lord and the self-serving actions of false prophets and pagan soothsayers.

5:24 *house.* Of Elisha (see v. 9).

5:26 *Is it a time to receive money . . . ?* Gehazi sought to use the grace of God granted to another individual for his own material advantage. This was equivalent to making merchandise of God's grace (see note on 2 Cor 2:17). "Money" here and elsewhere in 2 Kings refers to gold or silver in various weights, not to coins, which were a later invention. *clothes . . . female servants.* Evidently what Gehazi secretly hoped to acquire with the two talents of silver (see note on v. 5).

5:27 *leprosy.* See note on v. 1. *to you and to your descendants forever.* For the extension of punishment to the children of an offender of God's law see Ex 20:5 and note; see also note on Josh 7:24. *white as snow.* See Ex 4:6.

6:1 *sons of the prophets.* See note on 2:3.

6:2 *a place there for ourselves where we may live.* Some have suggested that the company of prophets lived in a communal housing structure. The Hebrew for this phrase, however, could be translated "a place there for us to sit," referring to some type of assembly hall. It is implied in 4:1–7 that there were separate dwellings for the members of the prophetic companies (see note on 1 Sam 19:18).

6:5 *it was borrowed.* At that time an iron axe head was a costly tool, too expensive for the members of the prophetic company to purchase. Having lost it, the borrower faced the prospect of having to work off the value as a bondservant.

6:6 *he cut off a stick and threw it in there, and made the iron float.* The Lord demonstrated here His concern for the welfare of His faithful ones.

6:8 *king of Aram.* Probably Ben-hadad II (see note on 5:1). *warring against Israel.* A reference to border clashes rather than full-

servants saying, "In such and such a place
shall be my camp."
9 [a]The man of God sent *word* to the king
of Israel saying, "Beware that you do not
pass this place, for the Arameans are coming
down there."
10 The king of Israel sent to the place
about which the man of God had told him;
thus he warned him, so that he guarded himself there, [1]more than once or twice.
11 Now the heart of the king of Aram was
enraged over this thing; and he called his
servants and said to them, "Will you tell me
which of us is for the king of Israel?"
12 One of his servants said, "No, my lord,
O king; but Elisha, the prophet who is in
Israel, tells the king of Israel the words that
you speak in your bedroom."
13 So he said, "Go and see where he is,
that I may send and take him." And it was
told him, saying, "Behold, he is in [a]Dothan."
14 He sent horses and chariots and a great
army there, and they came by night and surrounded the city.
15 Now when the attendant of the man of
God had risen early and gone out, behold,
an army with horses and chariots was circling the city. And his servant said to him,
"Alas, my master! [1]What shall we do?"
16 So he [1]answered, "[a]Do not fear, for
[b]those who are with us are more than those
who are with them."
17 Then Elisha prayed and said, "[a]O LORD,
I pray, open his eyes that he may see." And
the LORD opened the servant's eyes and he
saw; and behold, the mountain was full of
[b]horses and chariots of fire all around Elisha.
18 When they came down to him, Elisha
prayed to the LORD and said, "Strike this
[1]people with blindness, I pray." So He
[a]struck them with blindness according to the
word of Elisha.
19 Then Elisha said to them, "This is not
the way, nor is this the city; follow me and I
will bring you to the man whom you seek."
And he brought them to Samaria.
20 When they had come into Samaria, Elisha said, "O [a]LORD, open the eyes of these
men, that they may see." So the LORD opened
their eyes and they saw; and behold, they
were in the midst of Samaria.
21 Then the king of Israel when he saw
them, said to Elisha, "[a]My father, shall I [1]kill
them? Shall I [1]kill them?"
22 He [1]answered, "You shall not [2]kill
them. Would you [2][a]kill those you have taken
captive with your sword and with your bow?
[b]Set bread and water before them, that they
may eat and drink and go to their master."
23 So he prepared a great feast for them;
and when they had eaten and drunk he sent
them away, and they went to their master.
And [a]the marauding bands of Arameans did
not come again into the land of Israel.

The Siege of Samaria—Cannibalism

24 Now it came about after this, that
[a]Ben-hadad king of Aram gathered all his
army and went up and besieged Samaria.
25 There was a great [a]famine in Samaria;
and behold, they besieged it, until a donkey's head was sold for eighty *shekels* of silver, and a fourth of a [1]kab of dove's dung for
five *shekels* of silver.

9 [a]2 Kin 4:1, 7; 6:12
10 [1]Lit *not once or twice*
13 [a]Gen 37:17
15 [1]Lit *How*
16 [1]Lit *said* [a]Ex 14:13 [b]2 Chr 32:7, 8; Rom 8:31
17 [a]2 Kin 6:20 [b]2 Kin 2:11; Ps 68:17; Zech 6:1-7
18 [1]Lit *nation* [a]Gen 19:11
20 [a]2 Kin 6:17
21 [1]Lit *smite* [a]2 Kin 2:12; 5:13; 8:9
22 [1]Lit *said* [2]Lit *smite* [a]Deut 20:11-16; 2 Chr 28:8-15 [b]Rom 12:20
23 [a]2 Kin 5:2; 24:2
24 [a]1 Kin 20:1
25 [1]I.e. One kab equals approx 2 qts [a]Lev 26:26

scale hostility (see v. 23; see also note on 5:2). Some indication of Israelite weakness and Aramean strength is seen in the ability of the Arameans to send forces to Dothan (only about 11 miles north of Samaria) without apparent difficulty (see vv. 13–14).

6:9 *man of God.* Elisha (see v. 10). *king of Israel.* Probably Jehoram (see 1:17; 3:1; 9:24).

6:11 *which of us is for the king of Israel?* Repeated evidence that Israel possessed advance knowledge of Aramean military plans led the king of Aram to suspect that there was a traitor among his top officials.

6:12 *king of Israel.* Jehoram (see 3:1).

6:13 *take him.* The king of Aram thought he could eliminate Elisha's influence by denying him contact with Israel's king. *Dothan.* Located on a hill about halfway between Jezreel and Samaria, where the main royal residences were (see 1:2; 3:1; 8:29; 9:15; 10:1; 1 Kin 21:1).

6:16 *those who are with us are more than those who are with them.* Elisha knew that there was greater strength in the unseen reality of the hosts of heaven than in the visible reality of the Aramean forces (see 2 Chr 32:7–8; Ps 34:7; 1 John 4:4).

6:17 *he saw . . . the mountain was full of horses and chariots.* In response to Elisha's prayer, his servant was able to see the protecting might of the heavenly hosts gathered about Elisha (see Gen 32:1–2; Ps 34:7; 91:11–12; Matt 18:10; 26:53; see also note on 2 Kin 2:11).

6:18 *Strike this people with blindness.* Elisha had prayed for the eyes of his servant to be opened to the unseen reality of the heavenly hosts; now he prays for the eyes of the Aramean soldiers to be closed to earthly reality (see Gen 19:11).

6:19 *This is not the way, nor is this the city.* Elisha's statement led the Aramean soldiers to believe that they were being directed to the city where Elisha could be found. Technically this statement was not an untruth, since Elisha accompanied them to Samaria, but it was a means of deceiving the Aramean soldiers into a trap inside Samaria, the fortress-like capital city of the northern kingdom (see Ex 1:19–20; Josh 2:6; 1 Sam 16:1–2 for other instances of deception recorded in the OT).

6:20 *they were in the midst of Samaria.* The power of the Lord operative through Elisha turned the intended captors into captives.

6:21 *king of Israel.* Jehoram (see note on v. 9).

6:22 *You shall not kill them.* In reality the Aramean soldiers had been taken captive by the power of the Lord, not by Jehoram's military prowess. The Lord's purpose was to demonstrate to them and their king and to the Israelites and their king that Israel's national security ultimately was grounded in the Lord, not in military forces or strategies.

6:23 *bands of Arameans did not come again into the land of Israel.* See notes on v. 8; 5:2. Temporarily the Arameans recognized the futility of opposition to the power of the God of Israel.

6:24 *Ben-hadad.* The same Ben-hadad who had besieged Samaria on a previous occasion (see notes on 13:3; 1 Kin 20:1). This siege is probably to be dated c. 850 B.C.

6:25 *donkey's head.* According to Pentateuchal law the donkey was unclean and not to be eaten (see Lev 11:2–7; Deut 14:4–8). The severity of the famine caused the inhabitants of Samaria

26 As the king of Israel was passing by on the wall a woman cried out to him, saying, "Help, my lord, O king!"

27 He said, "[1]If the LORD does not help you, from where shall I help you? From the threshing floor, or from the wine press?"

28 And the king said to her, "[a]What [1]is the matter with you?" And she [2]answered, "This woman said to me, 'Give your son that we may eat him today, and we will eat my son tomorrow.'

29 "[a]So we boiled my son and ate him; and I said to her on the next day, 'Give your son, that we may eat him'; but she has hidden her son."

30 When the king heard the words of the woman, [a]he tore his clothes—now he was passing by on the wall—and the people looked, and behold, he had sackcloth [1]beneath on his [2]body.

31 Then he said, "May [a]God do so to me and more also, if the head of Elisha the son of Shaphat [1]remains on him today."

32 Now Elisha was sitting in his house, and [a]the elders were sitting with him. And *the king* sent a man from his presence; but before the messenger came to him, he said to the elders, "Do you [b]see how this son of a murderer has sent to take away my head? Look, when the messenger comes, shut the door and [1]hold the door shut against him. Is not the sound of his master's feet behind him?"

33 While he was still talking with them, behold, the messenger came down to him and he said, "[a]Behold, this evil is from the LORD; why should I wait for the LORD any longer?"

Elisha Promises Food

7 Then Elisha said, "Listen to the word of the LORD; thus says the LORD, '[a]Tomorrow about this time a [1]measure of fine flour will be *sold* for a shekel, and two measures of barley for a shekel, in the gate of Samaria.' "

2 [a]The royal officer on whose hand the king was leaning answered the man of God and said, "Behold, [b]if the LORD should make windows in heaven, could this thing be?" Then he said, "Behold, you will see it with your own eyes, but you will not eat [1]of it."

Four Lepers Relate Arameans' Flight

3 Now there were four [a]leprous men at the entrance of the gate; and they said to one another, "Why do we sit here until we die?

4 "If we say, 'We will enter the city,' then the famine is in the city and we will die there; and if we sit here, we die also. Now therefore come, and let us [1]go over to [a]the camp of the Arameans. If they spare us, we will live; and if they kill us, we will but die."

5 They arose at twilight to go to the camp of the Arameans; when they came to the outskirts of the camp of the Arameans, behold, there was no one there.

6 For [a]the Lord had caused the army of the Arameans to hear a sound of chariots and a sound of horses, *even* the sound of a great army, so that they said to one another, "Behold, the king of Israel has hired against us [b]the kings of the Hittites and [c]the kings of the Egyptians, to come upon us."

7 Therefore they [a]arose and fled in the twilight, and left their tents and their horses and their donkeys, *even* the camp just as it was, and fled for their life.

8 When these lepers came to the outskirts of the camp, they entered one tent and ate and drank, and [a]carried from there silver and gold and clothes, and went and hid *them;* and they returned and entered another tent and carried from there *also,* and went and hid *them.*

9 Then they said to one another, "We are not doing right. This day is a day of good

27 [1]Lit *No, let the LORD help you*
28 [1]Lit *to you* [2]Lit *said* [a]Judg 18:23
29 [a]Lev 26:27-29; Deut 28:52, 53, 57; Lam 4:10
30 [1]Lit *within* [2]Lit *flesh* [a]1 Kin 21:27
31 [1]Lit *stands* [a]Ruth 1:17; 1 Kin 19:2
32 [1]Lit *press him with the door* [a]Ezek 8:1; 14:1; 20:1 [b]1 Kin 18:4, 13, 14; 21:10, 13
33 [a]Is 8:21
7:1 [1]Heb *seah* [a]2 Kin 7:18
2 [1]Lit *from there* [a]2 Kin 5:18; 7:17, 19 [b]Gen 7:11; Mal 3:10
3 [a]Lev 13:45, 46; Num 5:2-4; 12:10-14
4 [1]Lit *fall* [a]2 Kin 6:24
6 [a]2 Sam 5:24 [b]1 Kin 10:29 [c]2 Chr 12:2, 3; Is 31:1; 36:9
7 [a]Ps 48:4-6; Prov 28:1
8 [a]Josh 7:21

not only to disregard the laws of uncleanness, but also to place a high value on the least edible part of the donkey. *eighty shekels of silver.* About two pounds of silver; see also note on 5:5.

6:27 *If the LORD does not help you, from where shall I help you?* Jehoram correctly recognized his own inability to assist the woman if the Lord Himself did not act in Israel's behalf, but he wrongly implied that the Lord was to be blamed for a situation brought on by Israel's own disobedience and idolatry.

6:28 *we will eat my son tomorrow.* The sins of the king and people were so great that the covenant curses of Lev 26:29 and Deut 28:53,57 were being inflicted (cf. Lam 4:10).

6:30 *tore his clothes.* More an expression of anger toward Elisha and the Lord (see v. 31) than one of repentance and sorrow for the sins that had provoked the covenant curse. *sackcloth.* A coarse cloth usually worn as a sign of mourning (see note on Gen 37:34). It is not clear why Jehoram wore sackcloth hidden under his royal robe. Perhaps it was a testing of the Lord, a private ritual to attempt to gain divine favor.

6:31 *May God do so to me and more also.* A curse formula (see note on 1 Sam 3:17). *if the head of Elisha . . . remains on him today.* Joram considered Elisha in some way responsible for the conditions in the city. Cf. Ahab's attitude toward Elijah (1 Kin 18:10,16; 21:20).

6:32 *elders.* Leaders of the city (see notes on Ex 3:16; 2 Sam 3:17). They sit with Elisha rather than with the king.

6:33 *why should I wait for the LORD any longer?* Jehoram felt himself deceived by Elisha and abandoned by the Lord, whom he blamed for the disastrous conditions in the city.

7:1 *a measure of fine flour will be sold for a shekel.* See NASB marg. A seah was about seven quarts, and a shekel was about two-fifths of an ounce. This was about double the normal cost of flour, but a phenomenal improvement over the highly inflated prices the famine had caused.

7:2 *windows in heaven.* See v. 19; Gen 8:2; Is 24:18.

7:3 *entrance of the gate.* Pentateuchal law excluded persons with skin diseases from residence in the community (Lev 13:46; Num 5:2–3).

7:6 *the LORD had caused the . . . Arameans to hear a sound.* See 2 Sam 5:24 and note. *kings of the Hittites and . . . Egyptians.* Kings of small city-states ruled by dynasties of Hittite origin, which had arisen in northern Aram after the fall of the Hittite empire c. 1200 B.C.

news, but we are keeping silent; if we wait until morning light, punishment will [1]overtake us. Now therefore come, let us go and tell the king's household."

10 So they came and called to the gatekeepers of the city, and they told them, saying, "We came to the camp of the Arameans, and behold, there was no one there, nor the voice of man, only the horses tied and the donkeys tied, and the tents just as they were."

11 The gatekeepers called and told *it* within the king's household.

12 Then the king arose in the night and said to his servants, "I will now tell you what the Arameans have done to us. They know that [a]we are hungry; therefore they have gone from the camp [b]to hide themselves in the field, saying, 'When they come out of the city, we will capture them alive and get into the city.' "

13 One of his servants said, "Please, let some *men* take five of the horses which remain, which are left [1]in the city. Behold, they *will be in any case* like all the multitude of Israel who are left in it; behold, they *will be in any case* like all the multitude of Israel who have already perished, so let us send and see."

14 They took therefore two chariots with horses, and the king sent after the army of the Arameans, saying, "Go and see."

The Promise Fulfilled

15 They went after them to the Jordan, and behold, all the way was full of clothes and equipment which the Arameans had thrown away in their haste. Then the messengers returned and told the king.

16 So the people went out and plundered the camp of the Arameans. Then a [1]measure of fine flour *was sold* for a shekel and two [1]measures of barley for a shekel, [a]according to the word of the LORD.

17 Now the king appointed [a]the royal officer on whose hand he leaned [1]to have charge of the gate; but the people trampled on him at the gate, and he died just as the man of God had said, [b]who spoke when the king came down to him.

18 It happened just as the man of God had spoken to the king, saying, "[a]Two [1]measures of barley for a shekel and a [1]measure of fine flour for a shekel, will be *sold* tomorrow about this time at the gate of Samaria."

19 Then the royal officer answered the man of God and said, "Now behold, [a]if the LORD should make windows in heaven, could such a thing be?" And he said, "Behold, you will see it with your own eyes, but you will not eat [1]of it."

20 And so it happened to him, for the people trampled on him at the gate and he died.

Jehoram Restores the Shunammite's Land

8 Now [a]Elisha spoke to the woman whose son he had restored to life, saying, "Arise and go [1]with your household, and sojourn wherever you can sojourn; for the [b]LORD has called for a famine, and [c]it will even come on the land for seven years."

2 So the woman arose and did according to the word of the man of God, and she went with her household and sojourned in the land of the Philistines seven years.

3 At the end of seven years, the woman returned from the land of the Philistines; and she went out to [1]appeal to the king for her house and for her field.

4 Now the king was talking with [a]Gehazi, the servant of the man of God, saying, "Please relate to me all the great things that Elisha has done."

5 As he was relating to the king [a]how he had restored to life the one who was dead, behold, the woman whose son he had restored to life [1]appealed to the king for her house and for her field. And Gehazi said, "My lord, O king, this is the woman and this is her son, whom Elisha restored to life."

6 When the king asked the woman, she related *it* to him. So the king appointed for her a certain officer, saying, "Restore all that was hers and all the produce of the field from the day that she left the land even until now."

9 [1]Lit *find*
12 [a]2 Kin 6:25-29 [b]Josh 8:4-12
13 [1]Lit *in it*
16 [1]Heb *seah;* i.e. one seah equals approx 11 qts [a]2 Kin 7:1
17 [1]Lit *over the gate* [a]2 Kin 7:2
17 [b]2 Kin 6:32
18 [1]Heb *seah;* i.e. one seah equals approx 11 qts [a]2 Kin 7:1
19 [1]Lit *from there* [a]2 Kin 7:2
8:1 [1]Lit *you and your* [a]2 Kin 4:18, 31-35 [b]Ps 105:16; Hag 1:11 [c]Gen 41:27, 54
3 [1]Lit *cry out*
4 [a]2 Kin 4:12; 5:20-27
5 [1]Lit *cried out* [a]2 Kin 4:35

7:12 *what the Arameans have done to us.* Jehoram's unbelief caused him to conclude that the report of the four leprous men was part of an Aramean war strategy rather than an evidence of the fulfillment of Elisha's prophecy (see v. 1).

7:16–20 *according to the word of the LORD . . . as the man of God had said . . . as the man of God had spoken . . . so it happened to him.* Emphasizing the trustworthiness of the prophetic word spoken by Elisha. In the fulfillment of Elisha's prophecy Israel was reminded that deliverance from her enemies was a gift of God's grace and that rejection of God's word provoked the wrath of divine judgment.

8:1 *the LORD has called for a famine.* The famine should have been perceived by the people of the northern kingdom as a covenant curse sent on them because of their sin (see note on 4:38). *seven years.* It is not clear whether this famine began before or after the Aramean siege of Samaria (see 4:38; 6:24–7:20).

8:2 *she went with her household.* Elisha's instruction enabled the woman and her family to escape the privations of the famine.

8:3 *went . . . to the king.* See note on 1 Kin 3:16. *appeal . . . for her house and for her field.* Either someone had illegally occupied the woman's property during her absence, or it had fallen to the domain of the king by virtue of its abandonment.

8:4 *Gehazi.* See 5:27. *relate to me all the great things that Elisha has done.* The king's lack of familiarity with Elisha's ministry is perhaps an indication that this incident occurred in the early days of the reign of Jehu rather than in the time of Jehoram, who had had numerous contacts with Elisha (see 3:13–14; 5:7–10; 6:10–23; 6:24–7:20). But see note on 5:7.

8:5 *As he was relating to the king.* The woman's approach to the king providentially coincided with Gehazi's story of her son's miraculous restoration to life through the ministry of Elisha.

8:6 *Restore all that was hers.* The widow and her son were living examples of the Lord's provision and blessing for those who were obedient to the word of the Lord through His prophets.

Elisha Predicts Evil from Hazael

7 Then Elisha came to [a]Damascus. Now
[b]Ben-hadad king of Aram was sick, and it
was told him, saying, "[c]The man of God has
come here."
8 The king said to [a]Hazael, "[b]Take a gift
in your hand and go to meet the man of God,
and [c]inquire of the LORD by him, saying,
'Will I recover from this sickness?' "
9 So Hazael went to meet him and took a
gift in his hand, even every kind of good
thing of Damascus, forty camels' loads; and
he came and stood before him and said,
"[a]Your son Ben-hadad king of Aram has sent
me to you, saying, 'Will I recover from this
sickness?' "
10 Then Elisha said to him, "[a]Go, say to
him, 'You will surely recover,' but the [b]LORD
has shown me that he will certainly die."
11 He [1]fixed his gaze steadily *on him* [a]until
he was ashamed, and [b]the man of God wept.
12 Hazael said, "Why does my lord weep?"
Then he [1]answered, "Because [a]I know the
evil that you will do to the sons of Israel: their
strongholds you will set on fire, and their
young men you will kill with the sword, and
their little ones you [b]will dash in pieces, and
their women with child you will rip up."
13 Then Hazael said, "But what is your
servant, [a]*who is but* a dog, that he should do
this great thing?" And Elisha [1]answered,
"[b]The LORD has shown me that you will be
king over Aram."
14 So he departed from Elisha and returned to his master, who said to him, "What
did Elisha say to you?" And he [1]answered,
"He told me that [a]you would surely recover."
15 On the following day, he took the cover and dipped it in water and spread it on his
face, [a]so that he died. And Hazael became
king in his place.

Another Jehoram Reigns in Judah

16 Now in the fifth year of [a]Joram the son
of Ahab king of Israel, Jehoshaphat being
then the king of Judah, Jehoram the son of
Jehoshaphat king of Judah became king.
17 He was [a]thirty-two years old when he
became king, and he reigned eight years in
Jerusalem.
18 He walked in the way of the kings of
Israel, just as the house of Ahab had done,
for [a]the daughter of Ahab became his wife;
and he did evil in the sight of the LORD.
19 However, the LORD was not willing to
destroy Judah, for the sake of David His servant, [a]since He had [1]promised him to give a
[2]lamp to him through his sons always.
20 In his days [a]Edom revolted from under
the hand of Judah, and made a king over
themselves.
21 Then Joram crossed over to Zair, and
all his chariots with him. And he arose by
night and struck the Edomites who had surrounded him and the captains of the chariots; [a]but *his* [1]army fled to their tents.

7 [a]1 Kin 11:24 [b]2 Kin 6:24 [c]2 Kin 5:20
8 [a]1 Kin 19:15, 17 [b]1 Kin 14:3 [c]2 Kin 1:2
9 [a]2 Kin 5:13
10 [a]2 Kin 8:14 [b]2 Kin 8:15
11 [1]Lit *made his face stand fast and he set* [a]2 Kin 2:17 [b]Luke 19:41
12 [1]Lit *said* [a]2 Kin 10:32, 33; 12:17; 13:3, 7 [b]2 Kin 15:16; Nah 3:10
13 [1]Lit *said* [a]1 Sam 17:43; 2 Sam 9:8 [b]1 Kin 19:15
14 [1]Lit *said* [a]2 Kin 8:10
15 [a]2 Kin 8:10
16 [a]2 Kin 1:17; 3:1
17 [a]2 Chr 21:5-10
18 [a]2 Kin 8:27
19 [1]Lit *said* [2]I.e. descendant on the throne [a]2 Sam 7:12-15; 1 Kin 11:36
20 [a]1 Kin 22:47; 2 Kin 3:9, 26, 27; 8:22
21 [1]Lit *the people* [a]2 Sam 18:17; 19:8

8:7 *Elisha came to Damascus.* The time had come for Elisha to carry out one of the three tasks originally given to Elijah at Mount Horeb (see notes on 1 Kin 19:15–16). The annals of the Assyrian ruler Shalmaneser III record Assyrian victories over Ben-hadad (Hadadezer) of Damascus in 846 B.C. and Hazael of Damascus in 842. Elisha's visit to Damascus is to be dated c. 843.
8:8 *inquire of the LORD by him.* In a reversal of the situation described in 1:1–4, a pagan king seeks an oracle from Israel's God. *Will I recover . . . ?* The question is the same as that of Ahaziah in 1:2.
8:9 *every kind of good thing of Damascus, forty camels' loads.* Damascus was the center for trade between Egypt, Asia Minor and Mesopotamia. Ben-hadad evidently thought a generous gift would favorably influence Elisha's oracle. *Your son Ben-hadad.* Use of father-son terminology is a tacit acknowledgment by Ben-hadad of Elisha's superiority (see 6:21; 1 Sam 25:8).
8:10 *You will surely recover.* An assertion that Ben-hadad's illness was not terminal (see v. 14).
8:12 *evil that you will do to the sons of Israel.* The Lord gave Elisha a clear picture of the severity of the judgment He was about to send on Israel by the hand of Hazael (see 9:14–16; 10:32; 12:17–18; 13:3,22). *set on fire . . . their women with child you will rip up.* These actions were characteristic of victorious armies at that time (see 15:16; Hos 10:14; 13:16; Amos 1:13). Elisha's words do not sanction such acts but simply describe Hazael's future attacks on Israel.
8:13 *what is your servant, who is but a dog, that he should do this great thing?* Hazael did not show repulsion at these violent acts but saw no possibility to gain the power necessary to accomplish them (for this metaphorical use of "dog" see note on 2 Sam 9:8). *you will be king over Aram.* Elisha's prophecy suggests that Hazael was not a legitimate successor to Ben-hadad. In an Assyrian inscription Hazael is designated "the son of a nobody" (i.e., a commoner) who usurped the throne.
8:15 *died.* Elisha's prophecy of Hazael's kingship did not legitimize the assassination. Hazael's murder of Ben-hadad as well as his future acts of violence against Israel were wicked acts arising out of his own sinful heart (see Is 10:5–19). His reign extended from c. 842 B.C. to c. 806 or 796, and he was followed by a son he named Ben-hadad (13:24).
8:16 *fifth year of Joram.* 848 B.C. Jehoram had been co-regent with his father since 853 (see note on 1:17), but he now began his reign as sole king.
8:17 *reigned eight years in Jerusalem.* Jehoram's sole reign is to be dated 848–841 B.C.
8:18 *as the house of Ahab had done.* Jehoram introduced Baal worship in Judah, as Ahab had done in the northern kingdom (see 11:18). Baal worship now spread to the southern kingdom at the same time it was being restricted in the northern kingdom by Ahab's son Joram (see 3:1–2). *the daughter of Ahab became his wife.* Jehoram's wife was Athaliah, a daughter of Ahab but probably not of Jezebel (see v. 26; 2 Chr 18:1). Athaliah's influence on Jehoram paralleled that of Jezebel on Ahab (see 1 Kin 16:31; 18:4; 19:1–2; 2 Chr 21:6).
8:19 *lamp to him.* See note on 1 Kin 11:36; see also Ps 132:17. The Lord spared Judah and its royal house the judgment He brought on the house of Ahab because of the covenant He had made with David (see 2 Sam 7:16,29; 2 Chr 21:7).
8:20 *made a king over themselves.* Previously Edom had been subject to Judah and had been ruled by a deputy (see note on 3:9; see also 1 Kin 22:47).
8:21 *his army fled.* Although Jehoram and his army were able

22 [a]So Edom revolted [1]against Judah to this
day. Then [b]Libnah revolted at the same time.
23 The rest of the acts of Joram and all
that he did, are they not written in the Book
of the Chronicles of the Kings of Judah?

Ahaziah Succeeds Jehoram in Judah

24 So Joram slept with his fathers and
[a]was buried with his fathers in the city of
David; and [b]Ahaziah his son became king in
his place.
25 [a]In the twelfth year of Joram the son of
Ahab king of Israel, Ahaziah the son of Jehoram king of Judah began to reign.
26 [a]Ahaziah *was* twenty-two years old
when he became king, and he reigned one
year in Jerusalem. And his mother's name
was Athaliah the granddaughter of Omri king
of Israel.
27 [a]He walked in the way of the house of
Ahab and did evil in the sight of the LORD,
like the house of Ahab *had done,* because he
was a son-in-law of the house of Ahab.
28 Then he went with Joram the son of
Ahab to war against [a]Hazael king of Aram at
[b]Ramoth-gilead, and the Arameans [1]wound-
ed Joram.
29 So [a]King Joram returned to be healed
in Jezreel of the wounds which the Arameans had [1]inflicted on him at [b]Ramah when
he fought against Hazael king of Aram. Then
[c]Ahaziah the son of Jehoram king of Judah
went down to see Joram the son of Ahab in
Jezreel because he was sick.

Jehu Reigns over Israel

9 Now Elisha the prophet called one of [a]the
sons of the prophets and said to him,
"[b]Gird up your loins, and [c]take this flask of
oil in your hand and go to [d]Ramoth-gilead.

22 [1]Lit *from under the hand of* [a]Gen 27:40 [b]Josh 21:13; 2 Kin 19:8
24 [a]2 Chr 21:20 [b]2 Chr 21:1, 7
25 [a]2 Chr 22:1-6
26 [a]2 Chr 22:2
27 [a]2 Chr 22:3
28 [1]Lit *smote* [a]2 Kin 8:15 [b]1 Kin 22:3, 29
29 [1]Lit *struck* [a]2 Kin 9:15 [b]2 Kin 8:28; 2 Chr 22:5, 6 [c]2 Kin 9:16
9:1 [a]2 Kin 2:3 [b]2 Kin 4:29 [c]1 Sam 10:1; 16:1; 1 Kin 1:39 [d]2 Kin 8:28, 29
2 [1]Lit *and look there for* [2]Lit *cause him to* [a]1 Kin 19:16, 17; 2 Kin 9:14, 20 [b]2 Kin 9:5, 11
3 [a]2 Chr 22:7
4 [a]2 Kin 9:1
5 [1]Lit *To whom of us all?*
6 [a]1 Sam 2:7, 8; 1 Kin 19:16; 2 Kin 9:3; 2 Chr 22:7
7 [a]Deut 32:35, 43 [b]1 Kin 18:4; 21:15, 21, 25 [c]2 Kin 9:32-37
8 [a]1 Kin 21:21; 2 Kin 10:17 [b]1 Sam 25:22 [c]Deut 32:36; 2 Kin 14:26
9 [a]1 Kin 14:10, 11; 15:29 [b]1 Kin 16:3-5, 11, 12
10 [a]1 Kin 21:23; 2 Kin 9:35, 36
11 [a]2 Kin 9:17, 19, 22 [b]Jer 29:26; Hos 9:7; Mark 3:21

2 "When you arrive there, [1]search out
[a]Jehu the son of Jehoshaphat the son of
Nimshi, and go in and [2][b]bid him arise from
among his brothers, and bring him to an
inner room.
3 "Then take the flask of oil and pour it on
his head and say, 'Thus says the LORD, "[a]I
have anointed you king over Israel." ' Then
open the door and flee and do not wait."
4 So [a]the young man, the servant of the
prophet, went to Ramoth-gilead.
5 When he came, behold, the captains of
the army were sitting, and he said, "I have a
word for you, O captain." And Jehu said,
"[1]For which *one* of us?" And he said, "For
you, O captain."
6 He arose and went into the house, and
he poured the oil on his head and said to
him, "Thus says the LORD, the God of Israel,
'[a]I have anointed you king over the people of
the LORD, *even* over Israel.
7 'You shall strike the house of Ahab your
master, [a]that I may avenge [b]the blood of My
servants the prophets, and the blood of all
the servants of the LORD, [c]at the hand of Jezebel.
8 'For the whole house of Ahab shall perish, and [a]I will cut off from Ahab [b]every
male person [c]both bond and free in Israel.
9 '[a]I will make the house of Ahab like the
house of Jeroboam the son of Nebat, and
[b]like the house of Baasha the son of Ahijah.
10 '[a]The dogs shall eat Jezebel in the territory of Jezreel, and none shall bury *her.*' "
Then he opened the door and fled.
11 Now Jehu came out to the servants of
his master, and one said to him, "[a]Is all well?
Why did this [b]mad fellow come to you?"
And he said to them, "You know *very well*
the man and his talk."

---

to break through an encirclement by Edomite forces, they were soundly defeated and forced to retreat to their own territory.
8:22 *to this day.* Until the time of the writing of the account of Jehoram's reign used by the author of 1,2 Kings (see Introduction to 1 Kings: Author, Sources and Date; see also note on 1 Kin 8:8). Later, Amaziah of Judah was able to inflict a serious defeat on Edom (14:7), and his successor Azariah regained control of the trade route to Elath through Edomite territory (14:22; 2 Chr 26:2). *Libnah revolted at the same time.* Libnah appears to have been located close to the Philistine border near Lachish (see 19:8). It is likely that the revolt of Libnah was connected with that of the Philistines and Arabs described in 2 Chr 21:16–17.
8:23 *the acts of Joram* [Jehoram]. See 2 Chr 21:4–20. *Chronicles of the Kings of Judah.* See note on 1 Kin 14:29.
8:24 *slept with his fathers.* See notes on 1 Kin 1:21; 2 Chr 21:20.
8:25 *twelfth year of Joram.* 841 B.C. In 9:29 the first year of Joram's reign was counted as his accession year and his second year as the first year of his reign, whereas here his accession year was counted as the first year of his reign (see Introduction to 1 Kings: Chronology).
8:26 *twenty-two years old when he became king.* See note on 2 Chr 22:2. *Athaliah.* See note on v. 18.
8:27 *way of the house of Ahab.* See 2 Chr 22:3–5.
8:28 *he went with Joram . . . to war against Hazael . . . at Ramoth-gilead.* As Jehoshaphat had joined Ahab in battle against the Arameans at Ramoth-gilead (1 Kin 22), so now Ahaziah joined his uncle Joram in a similar venture. On the previous occasion Ahab met his death (1 Kin 22:37). On this occasion Joram was wounded and, while recuperating in Jezreel (see note on 1 Kin 21:1), both he and his nephew Ahaziah were assassinated by Jehu (see 9:14–28).
9:1 *sons of the prophets.* See note on 2:3.
9:3 *I have anointed you king.* See notes on 1 Sam 2:10; 9:16; 1 Kin 19:16.
9:7 *strike the house of Ahab.* Jehu learned that he was the divinely appointed agent to inflict the judgment Elijah had pronounced many years earlier in his own hearing against the house of Ahab (see vv. 25–26; 1 Kin 21:21–24). *blood of all the servants of the LORD, at the hand of Jezebel.* A reference to people such as Naboth and his family (1 Kin 21:13), who were unjustly put to death through Jezebel's influence.
9:8 *bond and free.* See note on 1 Kin 14:10.
9:9 *like the house of Jeroboam.* See 1 Kin 14:7–11; 15:27–30. *like the house of Baasha.* See 1 Kin 16:1–4,8–12. Elijah had spoken the same words to Ahab years before (see 1 Kin 21:21–24).
9:11 *this mad fellow.* The epithet betrays a scornful attitude on the part of the military officers of the northern kingdom toward members of the prophetic companies.

12 They said, "It is a lie, tell us now." And he said, "Thus and thus he said to me, 'Thus says the LORD, "I have anointed you king over Israel." ' "

13 Then [a]they hurried and each man took his garment and placed it under him on the bare steps, and [b]blew the trumpet, saying, "Jehu is king!"

Jehoram (Joram) Is Assassinated

14 So Jehu the son of Jehoshaphat the son of Nimshi conspired against Joram. [a]Now Joram [1]with all Israel was [2]defending Ramoth-gilead against Hazael king of Aram,

15 but [a]King [1]Joram had returned to Jezreel to be healed of the wounds which the Arameans had [2]inflicted on him when he fought with Hazael king of Aram. So Jehu said, "If this is your mind, *then* let no one escape *or* [3]leave the city to go tell *it* in Jezreel."

16 Then Jehu rode in a chariot and went to Jezreel, for Joram was lying there. [a]Ahaziah king of Judah had come down to see Joram.

17 Now the watchman was standing on the tower in Jezreel and he saw the [1]company of Jehu as he came, and said, "I see a [1]company." And Joram said, "Take a horseman and send him to meet them and let him say, 'Is it peace?' "

18 So a horseman went to meet him and said, "Thus says the king, 'Is it peace?' " And Jehu said, "[a]What have you to do with peace? Turn behind me." And the watchman [1]reported, "The messenger came to them, but he did not return."

19 Then he sent out a second horseman, who came to them and said, "Thus says the king, 'Is it peace?' " And Jehu [1]answered, "What have you to do with peace? Turn behind me."

20 The watchman [1]reported, "He came even to them, and he did not return; and [a]the driving is like the driving of [b]Jehu the son of Nimshi, for he drives furiously."

21 Then [1]Joram said, "[2]Get ready." And they made his chariot ready. [1][a]Joram king of Israel and Ahaziah king of Judah went out, each in his chariot, and they went out to meet Jehu and found him in the [3][b]property of Naboth the Jezreelite.

22 When [1]Joram saw Jehu, he said, "Is it peace, Jehu?" And he [2]answered, "What peace, [a]so long as the harlotries of your mother Jezebel and her witchcrafts are so many?"

23 So [1]Joram [2]reined about and fled and said to Ahaziah, "[a]*There is* treachery, O Ahaziah!"

24 And [a]Jehu [1]drew his bow with his full strength and [2]shot [3]Joram between his arms; and the arrow went [4]through his heart and he sank in his chariot.

25 Then *Jehu* said to Bidkar his officer, "Take *him* up and [a]cast him into the [1]property of the field of Naboth the Jezreelite, for I remember when [2]you and I were riding together after Ahab his father, that the [b]LORD laid this [c]oracle against him:

26 'Surely [a]I have seen yesterday the blood of Naboth and the blood of his sons,' says the LORD, 'and [b]I will repay you in this [1]property,' says the LORD. Now then, take and cast him into the [1]property, according to the word of the LORD."

Jehu Assassinates Ahaziah

27 [a]When Ahaziah the king of Judah saw *this,* he fled by the way of the garden house. And Jehu pursued him and said, "[1]Shoot him too, in the chariot." *So they shot him* at the ascent of Gur, which is at [b]Ibleam. But he fled to Megiddo and died there.

28 [a]Then his servants carried him in a chariot to Jerusalem and buried him in his grave with his fathers in the city of David.

29 Now in [a]the eleventh year of Joram, the son of Ahab, Ahaziah became king over Judah.

30 When Jehu came to Jezreel, Jezebel heard *of it,* and [a]she painted her eyes and adorned her head and looked out the window.

31 As Jehu entered the gate, she said, "[a]Is it [1]well, Zimri, [2]your master's murderer?"

32 Then he lifted up his face to the window and said, "Who is on my side? Who?" And two or three officials looked down at him.

Jezebel Is Slain

33 He said, "Throw her down." So they threw her down, and some of her blood was sprinkled on the wall and on the horses, and he trampled her under foot.

13 [a]Matt 21:7, 8; Mark 11:7, 8 [b]2 Sam 15:10; 1 Kin 1:34, 39
14 [1]Lit *he and* [2]Lit *keeping* [a]1 Kin 22:3; 2 Kin 8:28
15 [1]Heb *Jehoram* [2]Lit *struck* [3]Lit *go out from* [a]2 Kin 8:29
16 [a]2 Kin 8:29
17 [1]Lit *multitude*
18 [1]Lit *told, saying* [a]2 Kin 9:19, 22
19 [1]Lit *said*
20 [1]Lit *told, saying* [a]2 Sam 18:27 [b]1 Kin 19:17
21 [1]Heb *Jehoram* [2]Lit *Yoke the chariot* [3]Lit *portion* [a]2 Chr 22:7 [b]1 Kin 21:1-7, 15-19; 2 Kin 9:26
22 [1]Heb *Jehoram*
22 [2]Lit *said* [a]1 Kin 16:30-33; 18:19; 2 Chr 21:13
23 [1]Heb *Jehoram* [2]Lit *turned his hands* [a]2 Kin 11:14
24 [1]Lit *filled his hand with the bow* [2]Lit *smote* [3]Heb *Jehoram* [4]Lit *out at* [a]1 Kin 22:34
25 [1]Lit *portion* [2]Lit *I and you* [a]1 Kin 21:1 [b]1 Kin 21:19, 24-29 [c]Is 13:1
26 [1]Lit *portion* [a]1 Kin 21:13, 19 [b]2 Kin 9:21, 25
27 [1]Lit *smite* [a]2 Chr 22:7, 9 [b]Josh 17:11; Judg 1:27
28 [a]2 Kin 23:30
29 [a]2 Kin 8:25
30 [a]Jer 4:30; Ezek 23:40
31 [1]Lit *peace* [2]Lit *his* [a]1 Kin 16:9-20; 2 Kin 9:18-22

9:15 *let no one escape . . . to go tell it in Jezreel.* For the success of Jehu's revolt and to avoid a civil conflict it was important to take Joram totally by surprise.
9:16 *Jezreel.* About 45 miles from Ramoth-gilead. *Ahaziah . . . had come down to see Joram.* See 8:29.
9:21 *property of Naboth.* See notes on 1 Kin 21:2–3,13,19.
9:22 *harlotries . . . and her witchcrafts.* Both punishable by death (see Deut 13; 18:10–12). As long as these evils were promoted in the northern kingdom, there could be no peace.
9:26 *according to the word of the LORD.* Jehu saw himself providentially placed in the position of fulfilling the prophecy of Elijah given years before (see 1 Kin 21:18–24). Even though Ahab's own blood was not shed on Naboth's field (see 1 Kin 21:29 and note), Jehu saw in Joram's death the fulfillment of Elijah's prophecy (see note on 1 Kin 21:19).
9:27 *fled to Megiddo and died there.* It may be questioned whether Jehu was justified in extending the purge of Ahab's house (see Hos 1:4) to the descendants of the house of David through Ahab's daughter Athaliah (see 8:18,26).
9:31 *Zimri, your master's murderer.* In bitter sarcasm Jezebel called Jehu by the name Zimri. About 45 years earlier Zimri had seized the throne from Elah by assassination and then had destroyed the whole house of Baasha. He ruled, however, for only seven days before Omri seized power (see 1 Kin 16:8–20).

34 When he came in, he ate and drank;
and he said, "See now to [a]this cursed woman
and bury her, for [b]she is a king's daughter."
35 They went to bury her, but they found
nothing more of her than the skull and the
feet and the palms of her hands.
36 Therefore they returned and told him.
And he said, "This is the word of the LORD,
which He spoke by His servant Elijah the
Tishbite, saying, '[a]In the [1]property of Jezreel
the dogs shall eat the flesh of Jezebel;
37 and [a]the corpse of Jezebel will be as
dung on the face of the field in the [1]property
of Jezreel, so they cannot say, "This is Jezebel." ' "

Judgment upon Ahab's House

10 Now Ahab had seventy sons in
[a]Samaria. And Jehu wrote letters and
sent *them* to Samaria, to the rulers of Jezreel, the elders, and to the guardians of *the
children of* Ahab, saying,
2 "Now, [a]when this letter comes to you,
since your master's sons are with you, [1]as
well as the chariots and horses and a fortified city and the weapons,
3 select the best and [1]fittest of your master's sons, and set *him* on his father's throne,
and fight for your master's house."
4 But they feared greatly and said,
"Behold, [a]the two kings did not stand before
him; how then can we stand?"
5 And the one who *was* over the household, and he who *was* over the city, the elders, and the guardians of *the children*, sent
word to Jehu, saying, "[a]We are your ser-

34 [a]1 Kin 21:25 [b]1 Kin 16:31
36 [1]Lit *portion* [a]1 Kin 21:23
37 [1]Lit *portion* [a]Jer 8:1-3
10:1 [a]1 Kin 16:24-29
2 [1]Lit *and with you the* [a]2 Kin 5:6
3 [1]Lit *most upright*
4 [a]2 Kin 9:24, 27
5 [a]Josh 9:8, 11; 1 Kin 20:4, 32; 2 Kin 18:14
7 [a]Judg 9:5; 2 Kin 11:1
9 [1]Lit *just* [2]Lit *smote* [a]2 Kin 9:14-24 [b]2 Kin 10:6
10 [1]Lit *by the hand of* [a]2 Kin 9:7-10 [b]1 Kin 21:19-29
11 [1]Lit *smote* [a]Hos 1:4
12 [1]I.e. house of binding

vants, all that you say to us we will do, we
will not make any man king; do what is good
in your sight."
6 Then he wrote a letter to them a second
time saying, "If you are on my side, and you
will listen to my voice, take the heads of the
men, your master's sons, and come to me at
Jezreel tomorrow about this time." Now the
king's sons, seventy persons, *were* with the
great men of the city, *who* were rearing them.
7 When the letter came to them, they
took the king's sons and [a]slaughtered *them*,
seventy persons, and put their heads in baskets, and sent *them* to him at Jezreel.
8 When the messenger came and told
him, saying, "They have brought the heads
of the king's sons," he said, "Put them in
two heaps at the entrance of the gate until
morning."
9 Now in the morning he went out and
stood and said to all the people, "You are
[1]innocent; behold, [a]I conspired against my
master and killed him, but [b]who [2]killed all
these?
10 "Know then that [a]there shall fall to the
earth nothing of the word of the LORD, which
the LORD spoke concerning the house of
Ahab, for the LORD has done [b]what He spoke
[1]through His servant Elijah."
11 So Jehu [1]killed all who remained of the
house of Ahab in [a]Jezreel, and all his great
men and his acquaintances and his priests,
until he left him without a survivor.
12 Then he arose and departed and went
to Samaria. On the way while he was at
[1]Beth-eked of the shepherds,

9:36 *the word of the LORD, which He spoke by His servant Elijah.* In the manner of Jezebel's death the word of the Lord was confirmed—the word she had defied during her life (see 1 Kin 21:23).

10:1 *Ahab had seventy sons.* The number of Ahab's wives is unknown (see 1 Kin 20:5). The 70 presumably included both sons and grandsons. *Samaria.* In order to consolidate his coup and establish control of the northern kingdom, Jehu still faced the formidable problems of taking the nearly impregnable fortress of Samaria (see note on 1 Kin 16:24) and then of completing the destruction of Ahab's house. *rulers.* Officers appointed by the king (see 1 Kin 4:1–6). *elders.* Local leaders by virtue of their position in the tribal and family structure (see notes on Ex 3:16; 2 Sam 3:17). *guardians of the children of Ahab.* Those entrusted with the care and upbringing of the princes in the royal family.

10:3 *fight for your master's house.* Jehu's strategy was to induce the leaders of Samaria into submission to his rule by bluffing a military confrontation.

10:4 *feared greatly.* The leaders of Samaria were completely intimidated by Jehu's challenge.

10:5 *the one . . . over the household.* See note on 1 Kin 4:6. *he who was over the city.* Probably an official appointed by the king who served as commander of the militia of the capital city. *the elders, and the guardians.* See note on v. 1.

10:6 *take the heads of . . . your master's sons, and come to me.* The wording of Jehu's command contains what appears to be a deliberate ambiguity. The "heads of the men, your master's sons" could be understood as a reference to the leading figures among the 70 descendants of Ahab, such as the crown prince and several other sons of special ability and standing. On the other hand, the expression could be taken as a reference to the literal heads of all 70 princes.

10:7 *slaughtered them, seventy persons.* The leaders of the city understood the communiqué in the literal sense, as Jehu most certainly had hoped they would. *put their heads in baskets, and sent them to him.* The leaders of Samaria did not carry the heads of the princes to Jezreel themselves as they had been ordered to do by Jehu (see v. 6). It is likely that they feared for their lives.

10:8 *Put them in two heaps at the entrance of the gate.* This gruesome procedure imitated the barbaric practice of the Assyrian rulers Ashurnasirpal and Shalmaneser III, whose reigns were characterized by acts of terror.

10:9 *I conspired . . . and killed him.* Jehu openly confessed his own part in the overthrow of the government of Joram. *who killed all these?* Because of the ambiguous communiqué Jehu sent to the leaders of Samaria (see note on v. 6), he can now deny any personal responsibility for the slaughter of the 70 sons of Ahab and can lay the blame for it on the leaders of Samaria.

10:10 *what He spoke through His servant Elijah.* See 1 Kin 21:20–24,29. Jehu implies a divine sanction not only for what had already been done but also for his intent to continue the purge of Ahab's house and associates.

10:11 *all his great men and his acquaintances and his priests.* Jehu went beyond the responsibility given to him (see 9:7; Hos 1:4) and acted solely on grounds of political self-interest. Jehu himself had been in the service of Ahab (see 9:25).

13 [a]Jehu [1]met the [2]relatives of Ahaziah
king of Judah and said, "Who are you?" And
they [3]answered, "We are the [2]relatives of
Ahaziah; and we have come down [4]to greet
the sons of the king and the sons of the
queen mother."
14 He said, "Take them alive." So they took
them alive and killed them at the pit of Beth-
eked, forty-two men; and he left none of them.
15 Now when he had departed from there,
he [1]met [a]Jehonadab the son of [b]Rechab *coming* to meet him; and he [2]greeted him and
said to him, "Is your heart right, as my heart
is with your heart?" And Jehonadab [3]an-
swered, "It is." *Jehu said,* "If it is, [c]give *me*
your hand." And he gave him his hand, and
he took him up to him into the chariot.
16 He said, "Come with me and [a]see my
zeal for the LORD." So [1]he made him ride in
his chariot.
17 When he came to Samaria, [a]he [1]killed
all who remained to Ahab in Samaria, until
he had destroyed him, [b]according to the
word of the LORD which He spoke to Elijah.

Jehu Destroys Baal Worshipers

18 Then Jehu gathered all the people and
said to them, "[a]Ahab served Baal a little;
Jehu will serve him much.
19 "Now, [a]summon all the prophets of
Baal, all his worshipers and all his priests;
let no one be missing, for I have a great sacrifice for Baal; whoever is missing shall not
live." But Jehu did it in [1]cunning, so that he
might destroy the worshipers of Baal.
20 And Jehu said, "[a]Sanctify a solemn
assembly for Baal." And [b]they proclaimed *it*.
21 Then Jehu sent [1]throughout Israel and
all the worshipers of Baal came, so that there
was not a man left who did not come. And
when they went into [a]the house of Baal, the
house of Baal was filled from one end to the
other.
22 He said to the one who *was* [1]in charge
of the wardrobe, "Bring out garments for all
the worshipers of Baal." So he brought out
garments for them.
23 Jehu went into the house of Baal with
Jehonadab the son of Rechab; and he said to
the worshipers of Baal, "Search and see that
there is here with you none of the servants of
the LORD, but only the worshipers of Baal."
24 Then they went in to offer sacrifices
and burnt offerings.
Now Jehu had stationed for himself eighty
men outside, and he had said, "[a]The one
who permits any of the men whom I bring
into your hands to escape [1]shall give up his
life in exchange."
25 Then it came about, as soon as he had
finished offering the burnt offering, that Jehu
said to the [1a]guard and to the royal officers,
"[b]Go in, [2]kill them; let none come out." And
they [3]killed them with the edge of the sword;
and the [1]guard and the royal officers threw
them out, and went to the [4]inner room of the
house of Baal.
26 They brought out the *sacred* [a]pillars of
the house of Baal and burned them.
27 They also broke down the *sacred* pillar
of Baal and broke down the house of Baal,
and [a]made it a latrine to this day.
28 Thus Jehu eradicated Baal out of Israel.
29 However, [a]*as for* the sins of Jeroboam
the son of Nebat, which he made Israel sin,
from these Jehu did not depart, *even* the
[b]golden calves that *were* at Bethel and that
were at Dan.
30 The LORD said to Jehu, "Because you
have done well in executing what is right in
My eyes, *and* have done to the house of
Ahab according to all that *was* in My heart,
[a]your sons of the fourth generation shall sit
on the throne of Israel."
31 But Jehu [1a]was not careful to walk in
the law of the LORD, the God of Israel, with
all his heart; [b]he did not depart from the sins
of Jeroboam, which he made Israel sin.

13 [1]Lit *found* [2]Lit *brothers* [3]Lit *said* [4]Lit *about the welfare of* [a]2 Kin 8:24, 29; 2 Chr 21:17; 22:8
15 [1]Lit *found* [2]Lit *blessed* [3]Lit *said* [a]Jer 35:6-19 [b]1 Chr 2:55 [c]Ezra 10:19; Ezek 17:18
16 [1]Lit *they* [a]1 Kin 19:10
17 [1]Lit *smote* [a]2 Kin 9:8 [b]2 Kin 10:10
18 [a]1 Kin 16:31, 32
19 [1]Lit *insidiousness* [a]1 Kin 18:19; 22:6
20 [a]Joel 1:14 [b]Ex 32:4-6
21 [1]Lit *in all* [a]1 Kin 16:32; 2 Kin 11:18
22 [1]Lit *over the*
24 [1]Lit *his soul for his soul* [a]1 Kin 20:30-42
25 [1]Lit *runners* [2]Lit *smite* [3]Lit *smote* [4]Lit *city* [a]1 Sam 22:17 [b]1 Kin 18:40
26 [a]1 Kin 14:23; 2 Kin 3:2
27 [a]Ezra 6:11; Dan 2:5; 3:29
29 [a]1 Kin 12:28-30; 13:33, 34 [b]1 Kin 12:29
30 [a]2 Kin 15:12
31 [1]Lit *did not watch* [a]Prov 4:23 [b]2 Kin 10:29

10:13 *relatives of Ahaziah.* See 2 Chr 21:17. *sons of the king and . . . the queen mother.* Members of the royal family from Judah who had not yet heard of the deaths of Joram and Jezebel.
10:15 *Jehonadab the son of Rechab.* Jehonadab was the leader of a conservative movement among the Israelites that was characterized by strong opposition to Baalism as well as to various practices of a settled agricultural society, including the building of houses, the sowing of crops and the use of wine. His followers still adhered to these principles over 200 years later and were known as Rechabites (see Jer 35:6–10).
10:16 *made him ride in his chariot.* Public association with Jehonadab gave Jehu added credentials among the rural populace as a follower of the Lord.
10:18 *Ahab served Baal a little; Jehu will serve him much.* After settling in Samaria, Jehu gave the appearance of having previously appealed to the word of the Lord as a mere political maneuver.
10:19 *shall not live.* Jehu's reputation made this no idle threat.
10:26 *burned them.* May refer to the Asherim (see note on 1 Kin 14:15) that usually accompanied a sacred pillar (see 1 Kin 16:32–33).
10:27 *sacred pillar of Baal.* See note on 1 Kin 14:23. *to this day.* See note on 8:22.
10:29 *sins of Jeroboam . . . he made Israel sin.* See 1 Kin 12:26–32; 13:33–34; 14:16.
10:30 *Because you have done . . . to the house of Ahab according to all that was in My heart.* Jehu was the Lord's instrument to bring judgment on the house of Ahab, for which he was commended. But he was later condemned by the prophet Hosea for the killing of all Ahab's associates, as well as Ahaziah of Judah and the 42 Judahite princes—the "bloodshed of Jezreel" (Hos 1:4). *fourth generation.* The restriction of this blessing to four generations is reflective of the qualified approval given to Jehu's reign. Nevertheless, his dynasty survived longer than any other dynasty of the northern kingdom, lasting nearly 100 years. It included the reigns of Jehoahaz, Jehoash, Jeroboam II and Zechariah (see note on 15:12).
10:31 *was not careful to walk in the law of the LORD . . . with all his heart.* Jehu seems to have been driven more by a political desire to secure his own position on the throne of the northern kingdom than by a desire to serve the Lord. In this he was

32 In those days the [a]LORD began to cut off *portions* [1]from Israel; and [b]Hazael [2]defeated them throughout the territory of Israel:

33 from the Jordan eastward, all the land of Gilead, the Gadites and the Reubenites and the Manassites, from [a]Aroer, which is by the valley of the Arnon, even [b]Gilead and Bashan.

Jehoahaz Succeeds Jehu

34 Now the rest of the acts of Jehu and all that he did and all his might, are they not written in the Book of the Chronicles of the Kings of Israel?

35 And Jehu slept with his fathers, and they buried him in Samaria. And Jehoahaz his son became king in his place.

36 Now the [1]time which Jehu reigned over Israel in Samaria *was* twenty-eight years.

Athaliah Queen of Judah

11 [a]When Athaliah the mother of Ahaziah saw that her son was dead, she rose and destroyed all the royal [1]offspring.

2 But Jehosheba, the daughter of King Joram, sister of Ahaziah, [a]took Joash the son of Ahaziah and stole him from among the king's sons who were being put to death, and placed him and his nurse in the bedroom. So they hid him from Athaliah, and he was not put to death.

3 So he was hidden with her in the house of the LORD six years, while Athaliah was reigning over the land.

4 [a]Now in the seventh year Jehoiada sent and brought the captains of hundreds of [b]the Carites and of the [1]guard, and brought them to him in the house of the LORD. Then he made a covenant with them and put them under oath in the house of the LORD, and showed them the king's son.

5 He commanded them, saying, "This is the thing that you shall do: [a]one third of you, who come in on the sabbath and keep watch over the king's house

6 (one third also *shall be* at the gate Sur, and one third at the gate behind the [1]guards), [2]shall keep watch over the house for defense.

7 "Two parts of you, *even* all who go out on the sabbath, shall also keep watch over the house of the LORD for the king.

8 "Then you shall surround the king, each with his weapons in his hand; and whoever comes within the ranks shall be put to death. And [a]be with the king when he goes out and when he comes in."

9 So the captains of hundreds [a]did according to all that Jehoiada the priest commanded. And each one of them took his men who were to come in on the sabbath, with those who were to go out on the sabbath, and came to Jehoiada the priest.

10 [a]The priest gave to the captains of hundreds the spears and shields that *had been* King David's, which *were* in the house of the LORD.

11 The [1]guards stood each with his weapons in his hand, from the right [2]side of the house to the left [2]side of the house, by the altar and by the house, around the king.

12 Then he brought the king's son out and [a]put the crown on him and *gave him* [b]the testimony; and they made him king and

32 [1]Lit *in* [2]Lit *smote* [a]2 Kin 13:25; 14:25 [b]1 Kin 19:17; 2 Kin 8:12; 13:22
33 [a]Deut 2:36 [b]Amos 1:3-5
36 [1]Lit *days*
11:1 [1]Lit *seed* [a]2 Chr 22:10-12
2 [a]2 Kin 11:21; 12:1
4 [1]Lit *runners* [a]2 Chr 23:1-21 [b]2 Sam 20:23; 2 Kin 11:19
5 [a]1 Chr 9:25
6 [1]Lit *runners* [2]Lit *and shall*
8 [a]Num 27:16, 17
9 [a]2 Chr 23:8
10 [a]2 Sam 8:7; 1 Chr 18:7
11 [1]Lit *runners* [2]Lit *shoulder*
12 [a]2 Sam 1:10 [b]Ex 25:16; 31:18

guilty of using God's judgment on the house of Ahab to satisfy his self-interest.

10:32 *the LORD began to cut off portions from Israel.* The climax of the covenant curses enumerated in Lev 26 and Deut 28 was Israel's expulsion from Canaan. During the rule of Jehu the northern kingdom experienced the beginnings of this curse (see 17:7–18 for its full realization).

10:33 All of Transjordan was lost to Hazael and the Arameans of Damascus.

10:34 *rest of the acts of Jehu.* The Black Obelisk of the Assyrian ruler Shalmaneser III informs us that Jehu paid tribute to the Assyrians shortly after coming to the throne of the northern kingdom in 841 B.C. In the Assyrian inscription Jehu is incorrectly called the "son of Omri," but this may simply be Shalmaneser's way of identifying Jehu with Samaria (or Israel). There is no reference to this payment of tribute in the Biblical narratives of Jehu's reign. *Chronicles of the Kings of Israel.* See note on 1 Kin 14:19.

10:35 *slept with his fathers.* See note on 1 Kin 1:21. *Jehoahaz his son became king in his place.* For the reign of Jehoahaz see 13:1–9.

10:36 *twenty-eight years.* 841–814 B.C.

11:1 *Athaliah.* See note on 8:18. *her son was dead.* See 9:27. *destroyed all the royal offspring.* To secure the throne in Judah for herself. By this time the royal family in Judah had already been reduced to a mere remnant. Joram, the late husband of Athaliah and the father of Ahaziah, had killed all his brothers when he succeeded his father Jehoshaphat on the throne (see 2 Chr 21:4). Jehu had slain another 42 members of the royal house of Judah, perhaps including many of the sons of Joram's brothers (10:12–14; 2 Chr 22:8–9), and the brothers of Ahaziah had been killed by marauding Arabs (2 Chr 22:1). It is likely that Athaliah's purge focused primarily on the children of Ahaziah, i.e., her own grandchildren. Ahaziah had died at the young age of 22 (see 8:26). This attempt to completely destroy the house of David was an attack on God's redemptive plan—a plan that centered in the Messiah, which the Davidic covenant promised (see notes on 2 Sam 7:11,16; 1 Kin 8:25).

11:2 *daughter of King Joram, sister of Ahaziah.* It is likely that Jehosheba was the daughter of Joram by a wife other than Athaliah, and thus she was a half sister of Ahaziah. She was married to the high priest Jehoiada (see 2 Chr 22:11). *him and his nurse.* The child was not more than a year old and had not yet been weaned (see vv. 3,21).

11:4 *seventh year.* Of Athaliah's rule. *captains of hundreds.* 2 Chr 23:1 lists the names of five commanders, all native Israelites. *Carites.* Mercenary soldiers from Caria in southwest Asia Minor who served as royal bodyguards. *brought them to him in the house of the LORD.* 2 Chr 23:2 includes the Levites and family leaders of Judah in the conspiracy.

11:10 *spears and shields that had been King David's, which were in the house of LORD.* David had probably taken the spears and gold shields as plunder in his battle with Hadadezer and then dedicated them to the Lord (see 2 Sam 8:7–11).

11:12 *testimony.* Either (1) the Ten Commandments, (2) the entire Mosaic covenant or (3) a document dealing more specifically with the covenant responsibilities of the king (see Deut 17:14–20; see also note on 1 Sam 10:25). The third option is

anointed him, and they clapped their hands and said, "[c]*Long* live the king!"

13 [a]When Athaliah heard the noise of the guard *and of* the people, she came to the people in the house of the LORD.

14 She looked and behold, the king was standing [a]by the pillar, according to the custom, with the captains and the [1]trumpeters beside the king; and [b]all the people of the land rejoiced and blew trumpets. Then Athaliah [c]tore her clothes and cried, "[d]Treason! Treason!"

15 And Jehoiada the priest commanded the captains of hundreds who were appointed over the army and said to them, "Bring her out [1]between the ranks, and whoever follows her put to death with the sword." For the priest said, "Let her not be put to death in the house of the LORD."

16 So they [1]seized her, and when she arrived at the horses' entrance of the king's house, she was [a]put to death there.

17 Then [a]Jehoiada made a covenant between the LORD and the king and the people, that they would be the LORD's people, also [b]between the king and the people.

18 All the people of the land went to [a]the house of Baal, and tore it down; [b]his altars and his images they broke in pieces thoroughly, and [c]killed Mattan the priest of Baal before the altars. And the priest appointed [1]officers over the house of the LORD.

19 He took the captains of hundreds and the [a]Carites and the [1]guards and all the people of the land; and they brought the king down from the house of the LORD, and came by the way of [b]the gate of the [1]guards to the king's house. And he sat on the throne of the kings.

20 So [a]all the people of the land rejoiced and the city was quiet. For they had put Athaliah to death with the sword at the king's house.

21 [1][a]Jehoash was seven years old when he became king.

12 [c]1 Sam 10:24 13 [a]2 Chr 23:12 14 [1]Lit *trumpets* [a]2 Kin 23:3; 2 Chr 34:31 [b]1 Kin 1:39, 40 [c]Gen 37:29; 44:13 [d]2 Kin 9:23 15 [1]Lit *from within* 16 [1]Lit *placed hands to her* [a]Gen 9:6; Lev 24:17 17 [a]Josh 24:25; 2 Chr 15:12-14; 34:31 [b]1 Sam 10:25; 2 Sam 5:3 18 [1]Lit *offices* [a]2 Kin 10:26, 27 [b]Deut 12:2, 3 [c]1 Kin 18:40 19 [1]Lit *runners* [a]2 Kin 11:4 [b]2 Kin 11:6

20 [a]Prov 11:10 21 [1]Ch 12:1 in Heb [a]2 Chr 24:1-14 12:1 [a]2 Chr 24:1 3 [a]2 Kin 14:4; 15:35 4 [1]Lit *which it comes into...to bring* [a]2 Kin 22:4 [b]Ex 30:13-16; 35:5, 22, 29; 1 Chr 29:3-9 5 [1]Lit *breaches, and so through v 12* 6 [a]2 Chr 24:5

Joash (Jehoash) Reigns over Judah

12 In the seventh year of Jehu, [a]Jehoash became king, and he reigned forty years in Jerusalem; and his mother's name was Zibiah of Beersheba.

2 Jehoash did right in the sight of the LORD all his days in which Jehoiada the priest instructed him.

3 Only [a]the high places were not taken away; the people still sacrificed and burned incense on the high places.

The Temple to Be Repaired

4 Then Jehoash said to the priests, "All the money of the sacred things [a]which is brought into the house of the LORD, in current money, *both* [b]the money of each man's assessment *and* all the money [1]which any man's heart prompts him to bring into the house of the LORD,

5 let the priests take it for themselves, each from his acquaintance; and they shall repair the [1]damages of the house wherever any damage may be found."

6 But it came about that in the twenty-third year of King Jehoash [a]the priests had not repaired the damages of the house.

7 Then King Jehoash called for Jehoiada

most likely. *anointed him.* See notes on 1 Sam 2:10; 9:16; 1 Kin 1:39. *Long live the king!* See 1 Sam 10:24; 1 Kin 1:34,39.

11:14 *pillar.* Apparently one of the two bronze pillars of the portico of the temple, named Jachin and Boaz (see 23:3; 1 Kin 7:15–22; 2 Chr 23:13). *all the people of the land.* It is likely that Jehoiada had chosen to stage his coup on a sabbath during one of the major religious festivals, when many from the realm who were loyal to the Lord would be in Jerusalem.

11:17 *covenant between the LORD and the king and people, that they would be the LORD's people.* A renewal of the Mosaic covenant, by which Israel had been constituted as the Lord's people (see Ex 19:5–6; Deut 4:20). The years of apostasy, involving both the royal house and the people of Judah, necessitated a renewal of allegiance to the Lord at the time of an important new beginning for the southern kingdom (see notes on 1 Sam 11:14–15; 12:14–15,24–25). *also between the king and the people.* Defined responsibilities and mutual obligations of king and people that were compatible with Israel's covenant relationship with the Lord (see notes on 1 Sam 10:25; 2 Sam 5:3).

11:18 *images.* Stone pillars (see note on 1 Kin 14:23) and Asherim (see note on 1 Kin 14:15).

11:19 *captains of hundreds and the Carites and the guards.* See note on v. 4.

11:21 See v. 3. The Lord had preserved a lamp for David in Jerusalem (see 1 Kin 11:36).

12:1 *seventh year of Jehu.* 835 B.C. (see note on 10:36). *forty years.* 835–796.

12:2 *all his days in which Jehoiada the priest instructed him.* After Jehoiada died, Jehoash turned away from the Lord (see 2 Chr 24:17–27).

12:3 *high places were not taken away.* These were high places where the Lord was worshiped rather than pagan deities (see note on 1 Kin 15:14). They were nevertheless potential sources for the entrance of pagan practices into Israel's worship (see note on 1Ki 3:2).

12:4 *money of the sacred things . . . brought into the house of the LORD.* The money was derived from three different sources: 1. *money collected in the census.* At the age of 20, Israelite youths were required to register for military service and to make an offering of half a shekel (see note on 5:26) for use in the service of the central sanctuary (see Ex 30:11–16; 38:25–26; Num 2:32). 2. *money received from personal vows.* Various types of vows and their equivalence in monetary assessments are described in Lev 27:1–25. 3. *money brought voluntarily to the temple.* For voluntary offerings see Lev 22:18–23; Deut 16:10.

12:5 *acquaintance.* Or, more likely, "treasurer," a temple functionary who handled financial matters for the priests relative to the people's sacrifices and offerings. *wherever any damage may be found.* Construction of the temple had been completed 124 years before the beginning of the reign of Jehoash (see notes on v. 1; 1 Kin 6:38). In addition to deterioration due to age, it had fallen into disrepair and abuse during the rule of Athaliah (see 2 Chr 24:7).

12:6 *twenty-third year of King Jehoash.* Jehoash may have instituted his plan for restoration of the temple a few years before

the priest, and for the *other* priests and said to them, "Why do you not repair the damages of the house? Now therefore take no *more* money from your acquaintances, but pay it for the damages of the house."

8 So the priests agreed that they would take no *more* money from the people, nor repair the damages of the house.

9 But [a]Jehoiada the priest took a chest and bored a hole in its lid and put it beside the altar, on the right side as one comes into the house of the LORD; and the priests who guarded the threshold put in it all the money which was brought into the house of the LORD.

10 When they saw that there was much money in the chest, [a]the king's scribe and the high priest came up and tied *it* in bags and counted the money which was found in the house of the LORD.

11 They gave the money which was weighed out into the hands of those who did the work, who had the oversight of the house of the LORD; and they [1]paid it out to the carpenters and the builders who worked on the house of the LORD;

12 and [a]to the masons and the stonecutters, and for buying timber and hewn stone to repair the damages to the house of the LORD, and for all that was [1]laid out for the house to repair it.

13 But [a]there were not made for the house of the LORD [b]silver cups, snuffers, bowls, trumpets, any vessels of gold, or vessels of silver from the money which was brought into the house of the LORD;

14 for they gave that to those who did the work, and with it they repaired the house of the LORD.

15 Moreover, [a]they did not require an accounting from the men into whose hand they gave the money to pay to those who did the work, for they dealt faithfully.

16 The [a]money from the guilt offerings and [b]the money from the sin offerings was not brought into the house of the LORD; [c]it was for the priests.

17 Then [a]Hazael king of Aram went up and fought against Gath and captured it, and [b]Hazael set his face to go up to Jerusalem.

18 [a]Jehoash king of Judah took all the sacred things that Jehoshaphat and Jehoram and Ahaziah, his fathers, kings of Judah, had dedicated, and [b]his own sacred things and all the gold that was found among the treasuries of the house of the LORD and of the king's house, and sent *them* to Hazael king of Aram. Then he went away from Jerusalem.

Joash (Jehoash) Succeeded by Amaziah in Judah

19 Now the rest of the acts of Joash and all that he did, are they not written in the Book of the Chronicles of the Kings of Judah?

20 [a]His servants arose and made a conspiracy and [b]struck down Joash at [c]the house of Millo *as he was* going down to Silla.

9 [a]Mark 12:41; Luke 21:1 **10** [a]2 Sam 8:17; 2 Kin 19:2; 22:3, 4, 12 **11** [1]Lit *brought* **12** [1]Lit *went out* [a]2 Kin 22:5, 6 **13** [a]2 Chr 24:14 [b]1 Kin 7:48, 50

15 [a]2 Kin 22:7; 1 Cor 4:2; 2 Cor 8:20 **16** [a]Lev 5:15-18 [b]Lev 4:24, 29 [c]Lev 7:7; Num 18:19 **17** [a]1 Kin 19:17; 2 Kin 8:12; 10:32, 33 [b]2 Chr 24:23, 24 **18** [a]1 Kin 14:26; 15:18; 2 Kin 16:8; 18:15, 16 [b]2 Kin 12:4 **20** [a]2 Chr 24:25-27 [b]2 Kin 14:5 [c]Judg 9:6; 2 Sam 5:9; 1 Kin 11:27

the 23rd year of his reign. Now at age 30 he asserts his royal authority and takes charge of the temple repairs.

12:7 *Take no more money from your acquaintances.* The proceeds from the sources of revenue mentioned in v. 4 were no longer to be given to the priests.

12:8 *priests agreed.* Apparently a compromise was reached: The priests would no longer take the money received from the people, but neither would they pay for the temple repairs from the money they had already received.

12:9 *priests who guarded the threshold.* Three high-ranking priests charged with protecting the temple from unlawful (profane) entry (see 25:18; Jer 52:24). *put in it all the money.* When the people were assured that all their offerings would be used for the temple restoration, they responded with greater generosity. See 22:3–7 for continuation (or renewal) of this practice in the reign of Josiah.

12:10 *king's scribe.* See note on 2 Sam 8:17. Jehoash arranges for direct royal supervision of the temple's monetary affairs.

12:11 *those . . . who had the oversight.* The whole matter is taken out of the hands of the priests.

12:13 *there were not made for the house of the LORD . . . vessels of gold, or . . . silver.* All the money was initially designated for the restoration of the temple. When the restoration was completed, additional funds were used for the acquisition of silver and gold articles for use in the temple service (see 2 Chr 24:14).

12:16 *money from the guilt offerings and . . . sin offerings.* See Lev 5:16; 6:5; Num 5:7–10 for references to priestly income in connection with the bringing of a guilt offering. There is no Pentateuchal reference to priestly income in connection with the bringing of a sin offering (but see Lev 7:7).

12:17 *Then.* These events must have taken place toward the end of Jehoash's reign. From 2 Chr 24:17–24 it is clear that the Aramean attack was occasioned by Jehoash's turning away from the Lord after Jehoiada's death. Jehoash's apostasy reached its climax in the stoning of Jehoiada's son Zechariah (2 Chr 24:22). Probably because of Jehoash's earlier zeal for the temple, the author of Kings did not choose to relate these matters. *Hazael.* See 8:7–15; 10:32–33; 13:3,22. *Gath.* One of the major Philistine cities (see Josh 13:3) that David had conquered (1 Chr 18:1) and that continued to be subject to Judah during the reign of Rehoboam (2 Chr 11:8). In the latter years of the reign of Jehoash of Judah (835–796 B.C.) and during the reign of Jehoahaz of Israel (814–798; see 13:3,7), the Arameans had virtually overrun the northern kingdom, enabling them to advance against the Philistines and the kingdom of Judah with little resistance. *Hazael set his face to go up to Jerusalem.* See 2 Chr 24:23–24.

12:18 *sacred things . . . gold . . . sent them to Hazael.* Years earlier, Asa had sought to secure assistance from the Arameans with a similar gift (see 1 Kin 15:18).

12:19 *Chronicles of the Kings of Judah.* See note on 1 Kin 14:29. A fuller account of the reign of Joash (Jehoash) is also found in 2 Chr 22:10–24:27.

12:20 *made a conspiracy.* The conspiracy was aroused in response to Joash's murder of Zechariah son of Jehoiada (see 2 Chr 24:25). *house of Millo.* For the meaning of Millo see note on Judg 9:6. Here the reference may be to a building (perhaps a kind of barracks) built on the "Millo" in the old City of David (see 2 Sam 5:9 and note; 1 Kin 11:27). Perhaps the king was staying there temporarily with his troops at the time of his assassination; Chronicles says he was killed "on his bed" (2 Chr 24:25). *Silla.* Perhaps refers to a steep descent from the City of David down into the Kidron Valley.

21 For Jozacar the son of Shimeath and Jehozabad the son of [a]Shomer, his servants, struck *him* and he died; and they buried him with his fathers in the city of David, and [b]Amaziah his son became king in his place.

Kings of Israel: Jehoahaz and Jehoash

13 In the twenty-third year of Joash the son of Ahaziah, king of Judah, Jehoahaz the son of Jehu became king over Israel at Samaria, *and he reigned* seventeen years.

2 He did evil in the sight of the LORD, and followed the sins of Jeroboam the son of Nebat, [a]with which he made Israel sin; he did not turn from them.

3 [a]So the anger of the LORD was kindled against Israel, and He gave them continually into the hand of [b]Hazael king of Aram, and into the hand of [c]Ben-hadad the son of Hazael.

4 Then [a]Jehoahaz entreated the favor of the LORD, and the LORD listened to him; for [b]He saw the oppression of Israel, how the king of Aram oppressed them.

5 The LORD gave Israel a [1][a]deliverer, so that they [2]escaped from under the hand of the Arameans; and the sons of Israel lived in their tents as formerly.

6 Nevertheless they did not turn away from the sins of the house of Jeroboam, [a]with which he made Israel sin, but walked in [1]them; and [b]the Asherah also remained standing in Samaria.

7 For he left to Jehoahaz of the [1]army not more than fifty horsemen and ten chariots and 10,000 footmen, for the king of Aram had destroyed them and [a]made them like the dust at threshing.

8 Now the rest of the acts of Jehoahaz, and all that he did and his might, are they not written in the Book of the Chronicles of the Kings of Israel?

9 And Jehoahaz slept with his fathers, and they buried him in Samaria; and Joash his son became king in his place.

10 In the thirty-seventh year of Joash king of Judah, Jehoash the son of Jehoahaz became king over Israel in Samaria, *and reigned* sixteen years.

11 He did evil in the sight of the LORD; he did not turn away from all the sins of Jeroboam the son of Nebat, with which he made Israel sin, but he walked in [1]them.

12 [a]Now the rest of the acts of Joash and all that he did and his might with which he fought against Amaziah king of Judah, are they not written in the Book of the Chronicles of the Kings of Israel?

13 So Joash slept with his fathers, and Jeroboam sat on his throne; and Joash was buried in Samaria with the kings of Israel.

Death of Elisha

14 When Elisha [1]became sick with the illness of which he was to die, Joash the king of Israel came down to him and wept over [2]him and said, "[a]My father, my father, the chariots of Israel and its horsemen!"

15 Elisha said to him, "Take a bow and arrows." So he [1]took a bow and arrows.

16 Then he said to the king of Israel, "Put your hand on the bow." And he put his hand

21 [a]2 Chr 24:26 [b]2 Kin 14:1
13:2 [a]1 Kin 12:26-33
3 [a]Judg 2:14 [b]2 Kin 12:17 [c]2 Kin 13:24, 25
4 [a]Num 21:7-9 [b]Ex 3:7, 9; 2 Kin 14:26
5 [1]Or *savior* [2]Lit *went out* [a]2 Kin 13:25; 14:25, 27; Neh 9:27
6 [1]Lit *it* [a]2 Kin 13:2 [b]1 Kin 16:33
7 [1]Lit *people*
7 [a]Amos 1:3
11 [1]Lit *it*
12 [a]2 Kin 13:14-19; 14:8-15
14 [1]Lit *was sick with his sickness* [2]Lit *his face* [a]2 Kin 2:12
15 [1]Lit *took to himself*

12:21 *servants.* Sons of Ammonite and Moabite mothers (2 Chr 24:26), suggesting that they may have been mercenary military officers whose services could have been bought by others. *buried him with his fathers.* But see 2 Chr 24:25. *Amaziah his son became king in his place.* For the reign of Amaziah see 14:1–22.
13:1 *twenty-third year of Joash.* 814 B.C. (see note on 12:1; see also Introduction to 1 Kings: Chronology). *seventeen years.* 814–798.
13:2 *sins of Jeroboam.* See 1 Kin 12:26–32; 13:33–34; 14:16.
13:3 *Hazael.* See notes on 8:12,13,15; 10:33. *Ben-hadad.* See v. 24. His reign began in either 806 or 796 B.C.
13:4 *the LORD listened to him.* Although deliverance did not come during the lifetime of Jehoahaz (see v. 22), the Lord was merciful to His people in spite of their sin, because of His covenant with Abraham, Isaac and Jacob (v. 23).
13:5 *Israel a deliverer.* Probably either (1) the Assyrian ruler Adadnirari III (810–783 B.C.), whose attacks on the Arameans of Damascus in 806 and 804 enabled the Israelites to break Aramean control over Israelite territory (see v. 25; 14:25), or (2) Jehoash son of Jehoahaz (vv. 17,19,25), or (3) Jeroboam II, who was able to extend Israel's boundaries far to the north (see 14:25,27) after the Assyrians had broken the military power of the Arameans.
13:6 *Asherah also remained standing.* This idol had been set up by Ahab (see 1 Kin 16:33) and had either escaped destruction by Jehu when he purged Baal worship from Samaria (see 10:27–28) or had been reintroduced during the reign of Jehoahaz.
13:7 *ten chariots.* In effect, a small police force. According to the Assyrian annals of Shalmaneser III, Ahab had contributed 2,000 chariots to the coalition of forces that opposed the Assyrians at the battle of Qarqar in 853 B.C. (see note on 1 Kin 22:1). *10,000 footmen.* At the battle of Qarqar Ahab had supplied 10,000 foot soldiers to the coalition of forces opposing the Assyrians. At that time this would have represented only a contingent of Israel's army, while now it represented the entire Israelite infantry. In 857 Ahab had inflicted 100,000 casualties on the Aramean foot soldiers in one day (see 1 Kin 20:29).
13:8 *Chronicles of the Kings of Israel.* See note on 1 Kin 14:19.
13:9 *slept with his fathers.* See note on 1 Kin 1:21.
13:10 *thirty-seventh year of Joash.* 798 B.C. (see note on 12:1). *sixteen years.* 798–782.
13:11 *sins of Jeroboam.* See 1 Kin 12:26–32; 13:33–34; 14:16.
13:12 *fought against Amaziah.* See 14:8–14; 2 Chr 25:17–24. *Chronicles of the Kings of Israel.* See note on 1 Kin 14:19.
13:13 *slept with his fathers.* See note on 1 Kin 1:21. *Jeroboam sat on his throne.* For the reign of Jeroboam II see 14:23–29.
13:14 *Elisha became sick.* Ch. 9 contains the last previous reference to Elisha. Since Jehu had been anointed in 841 B.C. (see note on 10:36) and Joash began to reign in 798 (see note on v. 10), there is at least a 43-year period in which we are told nothing of Elisha's activities. Based on Elisha's relationship with Elijah, he must have been born prior to 880 and he must have lived to be more than 80 years of age. *the chariots of Israel and its horsemen!* An expression of recognition by Joash that Elisha was of greater significance for Israel's military success than Israel's military forces were (see notes on 2:12; 6:13,16–23).
13:16 *laid his hands on the king's hands.* By this symbolic act

on it, then Elisha laid his hands on the king's
hands.
17 He said, "Open the window toward the
east," and he opened *it*. Then Elisha said,
"Shoot!" And he shot. And he said, "The
LORD's arrow of victory, even the arrow of victory over Aram; for you will [1]defeat the Arameans at [a]Aphek until you have [2]destroyed
them."
18 Then he said, "Take the arrows," and
he took them. And he said to the king of
Israel, "Strike the ground," and he struck *it*
three times and [1]stopped.
19 So [a]the man of God was angry with him
and said, "You should have struck five or six
times, then you would have struck Aram
until you would have [1]destroyed *it*. But now
you shall strike Aram [b]*only* three times."
20 Elisha died, and they buried him. Now
[a]the bands of the Moabites would invade the
land in the spring of the year.
21 As they were burying a man, behold,
they saw a marauding band; and they cast
the man into the grave of Elisha. And when
the man [1]touched the bones of Elisha he
[a]revived and stood up on his feet.
22 Now [a]Hazael king of Aram had
oppressed Israel all the days of Jehoahaz.
23 But the [a]LORD was gracious to them and
[b]had compassion on them and turned to them
because of [c]His covenant with Abraham,
Isaac, and Jacob, and would not destroy them
or cast them from His presence until now.
24 When Hazael king of Aram died, Ben-
hadad his son became king in his place.
25 Then [a]Jehoash the son of Jehoahaz
took again from the hand of Ben-hadad the
son of Hazael the cities which he had taken
in war from the hand of Jehoahaz his father.
[b]Three times Joash [1]defeated him and recovered the cities of Israel.

Amaziah Reigns over Judah

14 [a]In the second year of Joash son of
Joahaz king of Israel, [b]Amaziah the son
of Joash king of Judah became king.
2 He was twenty-five years old when he
became king, and he reigned twenty-nine
years in Jerusalem. And his mother's name
was Jehoaddin of Jerusalem.
3 He did right in the sight of the LORD,
yet not like David his father; he did according to all that Joash his father had done.
4 Only [a]the high places were not taken
away; [b]the people still sacrificed and burned
incense on the high places.
5 Now it came about, as soon as the
kingdom was firmly in his hand, that he
[1a]killed his servants who had slain the king
his father.
6 But the sons of the [1]slayers he did not
put to death, according to what is written in
the book of the Law of Moses, as the LORD
commanded, saying, "[a]The fathers shall not
be put to death for the sons, nor the sons be
put to death for the fathers; but [b]each shall
be put to death for his own sin."
7 He [1]killed *of* Edom in [a]the Valley of Salt
10,000 and took [b]Sela by war, and named it
[c]Joktheel to this day.

17 [1]Lit *smite* [2]Lit *made an end of* [a]1 Kin 20:26
18 [1]Lit *stood*
19 [1]Lit *made an end of* [a]2 Kin 5:20 [b]2 Kin 13:25
20 [a]2 Kin 3:7; 24:2
21 [1]Lit *went and touched* [a]Matt 27:52
22 [a]2 Kin 8:12, 13
23 [a]2 Kin 14:27 [b]1 Kin 8:28 [c]Gen 13:16, 17; 17:2-5
25 [1]Lit *smote* [a]2 Kin 10:32, 33; 14:25 [b]2 Kin 13:18, 19
14:1 [a]2 Chr 25:1 [b]2 Kin 13:10
4 [a]2 Kin 12:3 [b]2 Kin 16:4
5 [1]Lit *smote* [a]2 Kin 12:20
6 [1]Lit *smiters* [a]Deut 24:16 [b]Jer 31:30; Ezek 18:4, 20
7 [1]Lit *smote* [a]2 Sam 8:13; 1 Chr 18:12; 2 Chr 25:11 [b]Is 16:1 [c]Josh 15:38

Elisha indicated that Joash was to engage the Arameans in battle with the Lord's blessing on him.

13:17 *window toward the east.* Faced Transjordan, which was controlled by the Arameans (see 10:32–33). *Aphek.* About 60 years earlier Ahab had won a decisive victory at Aphek over the Arameans and Ben-hadad II (see 1 Kin 20:26–30 and note on 1 Kin 20:26).

13:18 *struck it three times and stopped.* The moderately enthusiastic response to Elisha's directive reflected insufficient zeal for accomplishing the announced task.

13:19 *strike Aram only three times.* Joash's moderate enthusiasm in striking the ground with arrows symbolized the moderate success he would have against the Arameans. It would be left for Jeroboam II son of Joash to gain complete victory over them (see 14:25,28).

13:21 *when the man touched the bones of Elisha he revived and stood up on his feet.* The life-giving power of the God Elisha represented is demonstrated once again in this last OT reference to Elisha (for previous demonstrations of this power see 4:32–37 and 1 Kin 17:17–24; for Elijah's translation to heaven without dying see 2:11–12).

13:23 *until now.* Until the time of the writing of the source from which the author derived this account (see note on 1 Kin 8:8; see also Introduction to 1 Kings: Author, Sources and Date). *would not destroy them or cast them from His presence.* In His mercy and grace the Lord was long-suffering toward His people and refrained from full implementation of the covenant curse of exile from Canaan (see note on 10:32). This postponement of judgment provided Israel with the opportunity to repent and return to covenant faithfulness.

13:24 *Ben-hadad.* See note on v. 3.

13:25 *cities which he had taken . . . from . . . Jehoahaz.* Probably towns west of the Jordan, since the area east of the Jordan had been lost already in the time of Jehu (see 10:32–33). It was not until the time of Jeroboam II that the area east of the Jordan was fully recovered for Israel (see 14:25). *Three times.* In fulfillment of Elisha's prophecy (v. 19).

14:1 *second year of Joash.* 796 B.C. (see note on 13:10).

14:2 *twenty-nine years.* 796–767. Amaziah's 29-year reign included a 24-year co-regency with his son Azariah (see notes on v. 21; 15:1–2).

14:3 *not like David his father.* Amaziah did not remain completely free from involvement with the worship of pagan deities (see 2 Chr 25:14–16). His loyalty to the Lord fell short of that of Asa and Jehoshaphat before him (see 1 Kin 15:11,14; 22:43; see also 1 Kin 9:4; 11:4).

14:4 *high places were not taken away.* See note on 1 Kin 15:14.

14:7 *killed of Edom . . . 10,000.* Amaziah was able to regain temporarily (see 2 Chr 28:17) some of Judah's control over the Edomites, which had been lost during the reign of Jehoram (see 8:20–22). *Valley of Salt.* The same battlefield on which David had defeated the Edomites (see 2 Sam 8:13; 1 Chr 18:12; Ps 60 title), generally identified with the Arabah directly south of the Dead Sea. *Sela.* Means "rock"; often regarded as the Edomite stronghold presently known as Petra (a Greek word meaning "rock"; see Judg 1:36; Is 16:1; 42:11; Obad 3). *to this day.* Until the time of the writing of the account of Amaziah's reign used by the author (see note on 1 Kin 8:8; see also Introduction to 1 Kings: Author, Sources and Date).

8 [a]Then Amaziah sent messengers to
Jehoash, the son of Jehoahaz son of Jehu,
king of Israel, saying, "[b]Come, let us face
each other."
9 Jehoash king of Israel sent to Amaziah
king of Judah, saying, "[a]The thorn bush
which was in Lebanon sent to the cedar
which was in Lebanon, saying, 'Give your
daughter to my son in marriage.' But there
passed by a wild beast that was in Lebanon,
and trampled the thorn bush.
10 "[a]You have indeed [1]defeated Edom, and
[b]your heart has [2]become proud. Enjoy your
glory and stay at home; for why should you
provoke trouble so that you, even you,
would fall, and Judah with you?"
11 But Amaziah would not listen. So Jehoash king of Israel went up; and he and Amaziah king of Judah faced each other at [a]Beth-
shemesh, which belongs to Judah.
12 Judah was defeated [1]by Israel, and
[a]they fled each to his tent.
13 Then Jehoash king of Israel captured
Amaziah king of Judah, the son of Jehoash
the son of Ahaziah, at Beth-shemesh, and
came to Jerusalem and tore down the wall of
Jerusalem from [a]the Gate of Ephraim to [b]the
Corner Gate, 400 [1]cubits.
14 [a]He took all the gold and silver and all
the utensils which were found in the house
of the LORD, and in the treasuries of the
king's house, the hostages also, and returned
to Samaria.

Jeroboam II Succeeds Jehoash in Israel

15 [a]Now the rest of the acts of Jehoash
which he did, and his might and how he
fought with Amaziah king of Judah, are they
not written in the Book of the Chronicles of
the Kings of Israel?
16 So Jehoash slept with his fathers and
was buried in Samaria with the kings of Israel; and Jeroboam his son became king in his
place.

Azariah (Uzziah) Succeeds Amaziah in Judah

17 [a]Amaziah the son of Joash king of
Judah lived fifteen years after the death of
Jehoash son of Jehoahaz king of Israel.
18 Now the rest of the acts of Amaziah,
are they not written in the Book of the
Chronicles of the Kings of Judah?
19 They conspired against him in
Jerusalem, and he fled to [a]Lachish; but they
sent after him to Lachish and killed him
there.
20 Then they brought him on horses and
he was buried at Jerusalem with his fathers
in the city of David.
21 All the people of Judah took [1]Azariah,
who *was* sixteen years old, and made him
king in the place of his father Amaziah.
22 [a]He built Elath and restored it to Judah
after the king slept with his fathers.
23 In the fifteenth year of Amaziah the
son of Joash king of Judah, Jeroboam the
son of Joash king of Israel became king in
Samaria, *and reigned* forty-one years.
24 He did evil in the sight of the LORD; he
did not depart from all the sins of Jeroboam
the son of Nebat, which he made Israel sin.
25 [a]He restored the border of Israel from

8 [a]2 Chr 25:17-24 [b]2 Sam 2:14-17
9 [a]Judg 9:8-15
10 [1]Lit *smitten* [2]Lit *lifted you up* [a]2 Kin 14:7 [b]Deut 8:14; 2 Chr 26:16
11 [a]Josh 19:38
12 [1]Lit *before* [a]2 Sam 18:17
13 [1]I.e. One cubit equals approx 18 in. [a]Neh 8:16; 12:39 [b]2 Chr 25:23
14 [a]1 Kin 14:26; 2 Kin 12:18
15 [a]2 Kin 13:12, 13
17 [a]2 Chr 25:25-28
19 [a]Josh 10:31; 2 Kin 18:14, 17
21 [1]In 2 Chr 26:1, *Uzziah*
22 [a]1 Kin 9:26; 2 Kin 16:6; 2 Chr 8:17
25 [a]2 Kin 10:32; 13:25

14:8 *let us face each other.* A challenge amounting to a declaration of war. Perhaps it was provoked by the hostile actions of mercenary troops from the northern kingdom after their dismissal from the Judahite army (see 2 Chr 25:10,13) and by the refusal of Jehoash to establish a marriage alliance with Amaziah (see v. 9).
14:9 *Jehoash . . . sent . . . saying.* For his reply Jehoash used a fable (see Judg 9:8–15) in which he represented himself as a strong cedar and Amaziah as an insignificant thistle that could easily be trampled underfoot.
14:11 *would not listen.* See 2 Chr 25:20. *Beth-shemesh.* A town about 15 miles west of Jerusalem near the border between Judah and Dan (see Josh 15:10; 1Sa 6:9).
14:13 *Jehoash . . . captured Amaziah.* It is likely that Amaziah was taken back to the northern kingdom as a prisoner, where he remained until being released to return to Judah after the death of Jehoash (see vv. 15–16; see also note on v. 21). *Gate of Ephraim to the Corner Gate.* The Corner Gate (see Jer 31:38; Zech 14:10) was at the northwest corner of the wall around Jerusalem. The Ephraim Gate was on the north side of Jerusalem (see Neh 12:39), 600 feet east of the Corner Gate. This northwestern section of the wall of Jerusalem was the point at which the city was most vulnerable to attack.
14:14 *gold and silver and all the utensils . . . found in the house of the LORD, and . . . the king's house.* The value of the plundered articles was probably not great, because Joash had previously stripped the temple and palace to pay tribute to Hazael of Damascus (see 12:17–18). *hostages also.* The hostages were probably intended to secure additional payments of tribute in view of the meager war booty.
14:15 *Chronicles of the Kings of Israel.* See note on 1 Kin 14:19.
14:16 *slept with his fathers.* See 13:12–13; see also note on 1 Kin 1:21.
14:17 *lived fifteen years after the death of Jehoash.* Jehoash died in 782 B.C. and Amaziah in 767.
14:18 *Chronicles of the Kings of Judah.* See note on 1 Kin 14:29.
14:19 *conspired against him.* 2 Chr 25:27 connects the conspiracy against Amaziah with his turning away from the Lord, but it did not serve the purpose of the author of Kings to note this. *Lachish.* A fortress city in southern Judah 15 miles west of Hebron, presently known as Tell ed-Duweir (see 18:14; 2 Chr 11:9).
14:21 *All the people of Judah took Azariah, who was.* Or "Now all the people of Judah had taken Azariah, when he was." Azariah is also called Uzziah (see 15:13). *made him king in place of his father Amaziah.* It is likely that this occurred after Amaziah had been taken prisoner by Jehoash (see v. 13). Thus Azariah's reign substantially overlapped that of his father Amaziah (see notes on v. 2; 15:2).
14:22 *built Elath and restored it to Judah.* Azariah extended the subjection of the Edomites begun by his father (see v. 7) and reestablished Israelite control over the important port city on the Gulf of Aqaba (see 1 Kin 9:26).
14:23 *fifteenth year of Amaziah.* 782 B.C. (see note on v. 2). This was the beginning of Jeroboam's sole reign. He had previously served as co-regent with his father Joash. *forty-one years.* 793–753 (including the co-regency with his father).
14:24 *sins of Jeroboam.* See 1 Kin 12:26–32; 13:33–34; 14:16; Amos 3:13–14; 4:4–5; 5:4–6; 7:10–17.

[b]the entrance of Hamath as far as [c]the Sea of
the Arabah, according to the word of the
LORD, the God of Israel, which He spoke
[1]through His servant [d]Jonah the son of Amittai, the prophet, who was of [e]Gath-hepher.
26 For the [a]LORD saw the affliction of Israel, *which was* very bitter; for [b]there was neither bond nor free, nor was there any helper
for Israel.
27 The [a]LORD did not say that He would
blot out the name of Israel from under heav-
en, but He saved them by the hand of Jeroboam the son of Joash.

Zechariah Reigns over Israel

28 Now the rest of the acts of Jeroboam
and all that he did and his might, how he
fought and how he recovered for Israel,
[a]Damascus and [b]Hamath, *which had
belonged* to Judah, are they not written in
the Book of the Chronicles of the Kings of
Israel?
29 And Jeroboam slept with his fathers,
even with the kings of Israel, and Zechariah
his son became king in his place.

Series of Kings: Azariah (Uzziah) over Judah

15 [a]In the twenty-seventh year of Jeroboam king of Israel, Azariah son of Amaziah king of Judah became king.
2 He was [a]sixteen years old when he
became king, and he reigned fifty-two years
in Jerusalem; and his mother's name was
[1]Jecoliah of Jerusalem.
3 He did right in the sight of the LORD,
according to all that his father Amaziah had
done.
4 Only [a]the high places were not taken
away; the people still sacrificed and burned
incense on the high places.
5 [a]The LORD struck the king, so that he
was a leper to the day of his death. And he
[b]lived in a separate house, [1]while Jotham the
king's son was over the household, judging
the people of the land.
6 Now the rest of the acts of Azariah and
all that he did, are they not written in the
Book of the Chronicles of the Kings of
Judah?
7 And Azariah slept with his fathers, and
they buried him with his fathers in the city of
David, and Jotham his son became king in
his place.

Zechariah over Israel

8 [a]In the thirty-eighth year of Azariah
king of Judah, Zechariah the son of Jeroboam became king over Israel in Samaria *for*
six months.
9 He did evil in the sight of the LORD, as
his fathers had done; he did not depart from
the sins of Jeroboam the son of Nebat, which
he made Israel sin.
10 Then Shallum the son of Jabesh con-

25 [1]Lit *by* [b]1 Kin 8:65 [c]Deut 3:17 [d]Jon 1:1; Matt 12:39, 40 [e]Josh 19:13
26 [a]2 Kin 13:4 [b]Deut 32:36
27 [a]2 Kin 13:23
28 [a]1 Kin 11:24 [b]2 Chr 8:3
15:1 [a]2 Kin 14:17
2 [a]2 Chr 26:3, 4

2 [1]In 2 Chr 26:3, *Jechiliah*
4 [a]2 Kin 12:3
5 [1]Lit *and* [a]2 Chr 26:21-23 [b]Lev 13:46; Num 12:14
8 [a]2 Kin 15:1

14:25 *entrance of Hamath.* Jeroboam II was able to free the northern kingdom from the oppression it had suffered at the hands of Hazael and Ben-hadad (see 10:32; 12:17; 13:3,22,25). He also extended Israelite political control over the Arameans of Damascus, an undertaking that had been begun by his father Joash (see 13:25). Assyrian pressure on the Arameans, including attacks on Damascus by Shalmaneser IV in 773 B.C. and Ashur-dan III in 772, had weakened the Arameans enough to enable Jeroboam II to gain the upper hand over them. Meanwhile, Assyria also became too weak to suppress Jeroboam's expansion. *Sea of the Arabah.* The Dead Sea. According to Amos 6:14 the southern limit of Jeroboam's kingdom in Transjordan was the "brook of the Arabah"—probably to be connected with the Valley of Salt (see note on v. 7). If so, Jeroboam had also subdued Moab and the Ammonites. *Jonah . . . the prophet . . . of Gath-hepher.* See Jon 1:1. Gath-hepher was located in the tribe of Zebulun, northeast of Nazareth (see Josh 19:13). This reference to Jonah is of help in dating the ministry of the prophet.
14:26 *affliction.* At the hands of the Arameans (see 10:32–33; 13:3–7), the Moabites (13:20) and the Ammonites (Amos 1:13). *bond nor free.* See note on 1 Kin 14:10.
14:27 *did not say.* The sin of the Israelites had not yet reached its full measure, and the Lord mercifully extended to the nation an additional period of grace in which there was opportunity to repent (see note on 13:23). Persistence in apostasy, however, would bring certain judgment (see Amos 4:2–3; 6:14). *saved them by the hand of Jeroboam.* See note on 13:5.
14:28 *all that he did.* During Jeroboam's reign the northern kingdom enjoyed greater material prosperity than at any time since the rule of David and Solomon. Unfortunately, it was also a time of religious formalism and apostasy as well as social injustice (see the books of Amos and Hosea, who prophesied during Jeroboam's reign). *Damascus and Hamath.* See note on v. 25. *Judah.* Damascus and Hamath were once included in territory ruled by David and Solomon (see 2 Sam 8:6; 2 Chr 8:3). *Chronicles of the Kings of Israel.* See note on 1 Kin 14:19.
14:29 *slept with his fathers.* See note on 1 Kin 1:21. *Zechariah his son became king in his place.* For the reign of Zechariah see 15:8–12.
15:1 *twenty-seventh year of Jeroboam.* 767 B.C., based on dating the beginning of Jeroboam's co-regency with Joash in 793 (see note on 14:23). *Azariah . . . became king.* He began his sole reign, after a 24-year co-regency with his father Amaziah (see notes on v. 2; 14:2,21). (His actual years were one less than his official years.)
15:2 *fifty-two years.* 792–740 B.C. (but he was co-regent with his father Amaziah 792–767). See note on v. 1.
15:3 *according to all that his father Amaziah had done.* See note on 14:3.
15:4 *high places were not taken away.* See 14:4; see also note on 1 Kin 15:14.
15:5 *struck the king, so that he was a leper.* A punishment for usurping the priestly function of burning incense on the altar in the temple (see 2 Chr 26:16–21; cf. Lev 13:46). *was over the household, judging the people of the land.* Jotham ruled for his father for the remainder of Azariah's life (750–740 B.C.; see note on v. 33).
15:6 *all that he did.* A more detailed account of Azariah's accomplishments is found in 2 Chr 26:1–15. *Chronicles of the Kings of Judah.* See note on 1 Kin 14:29.
15:7 *slept with his fathers.* See note on 1 Kin 1:21. *Jotham his son became king in his place.* For the reign of Jotham see vv. 32–38.
15:8 *thirty-eighth year of Azariah.* 753 B.C. (see note on v. 2).
15:9 *sins of Jeroboam.* See 1 Kin 12:26–32; 13:33–34; 14:16.

Assyrian Campaigns against Israel and Judah

The Assyrian invasions of the eighth century B.C. were the most traumatic political events in the entire history of Israel.

The brutal Assyrian style of warfare relied on massive armies, superbly equipped with the world's first great siege machines manipulated by an efficient corps of engineers.

Psychological terror, however, was Assyria's most effective weapon. It was ruthlessly applied, with corpses impaled on stakes, severed heads stacked in heaps, and captives skinned alive.

The shock of bloody military sieges on both Israel and Judah was profound. The prophets did not fail to scream out against their horror, while at the same time pleading with the people to see God's hand in history, to recognize spiritual causes in the present punishment.

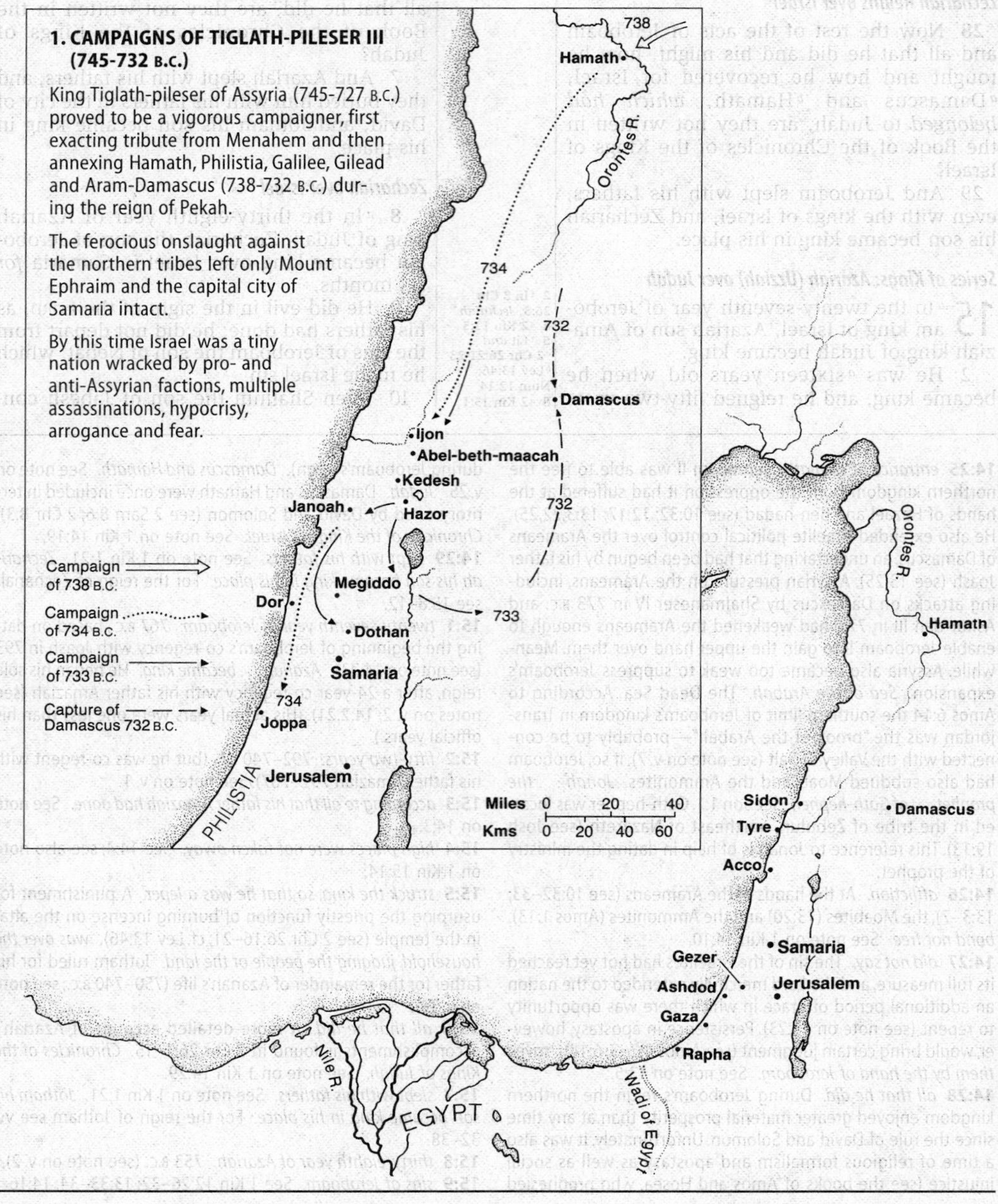

1. CAMPAIGNS OF TIGLATH-PILESER III (745-732 B.C.)

King Tiglath-pileser of Assyria (745-727 B.C.) proved to be a vigorous campaigner, first exacting tribute from Menahem and then annexing Hamath, Philistia, Galilee, Gilead and Aram-Damascus (738-732 B.C.) during the reign of Pekah.

The ferocious onslaught against the northern tribes left only Mount Ephraim and the capital city of Samaria intact.

By this time Israel was a tiny nation wracked by pro- and anti-Assyrian factions, multiple assassinations, hypocrisy, arrogance and fear.

Campaign of 738 B.C.
Campaign of 734 B.C.
Campaign of 733 B.C.
Capture of Damascus 732 B.C.
738
Hamath
Orontes R.
734
732
Damascus
Ijon
Abel-beth-maacah
Kedesh
Janoah
Hazor
732
Megiddo
Dor
733
Dothan
Samaria
734
Joppa
Jerusalem
PHILISTIA
Miles 0 20 40
Kms 0 20 40 60
Orontes R.
Hamath
Sidon
Damascus
Tyre
Acco
Gezer
Samaria
Ashdod
Jerusalem
Gaza
Rapha
Wadi of Egypt
Nile R.
EGYPT

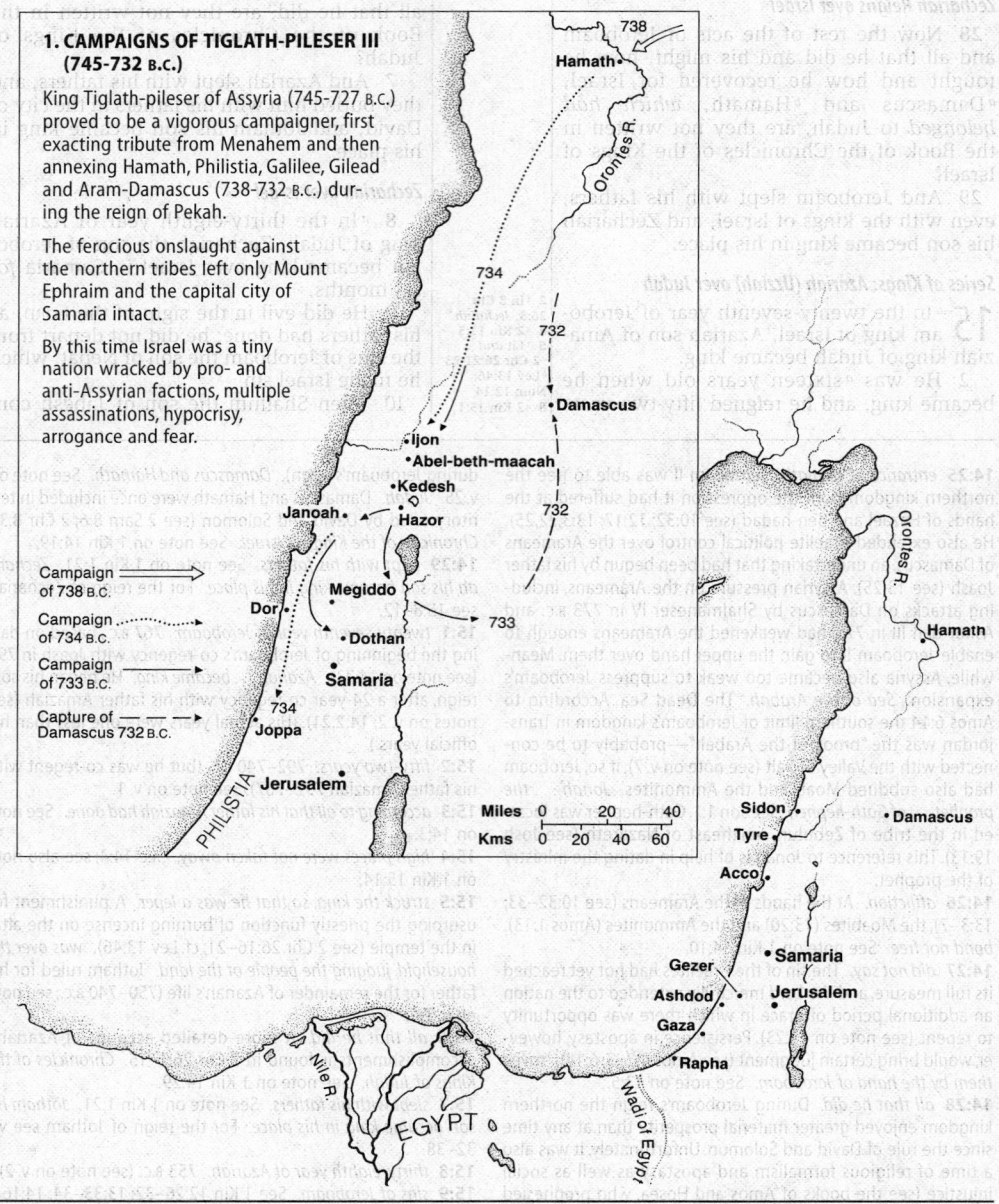

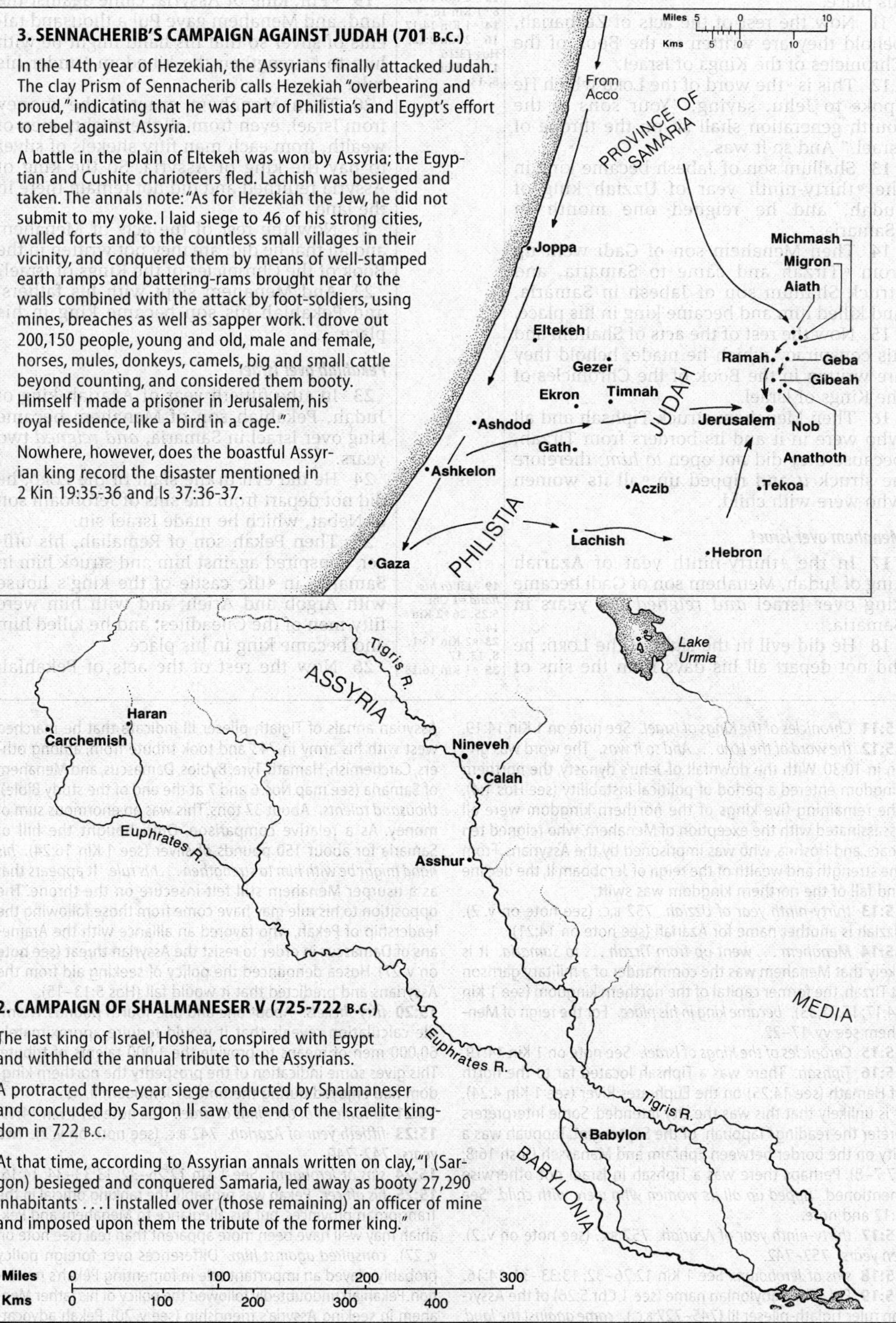
3. SENNACHERIB'S CAMPAIGN AGAINST JUDAH (701 B.C.)
In the 14th year of Hezekiah, the Assyrians finally attacked Judah. The clay Prism of Sennacherib calls Hezekiah "overbearing and proud," indicating that he was part of Philistia's and Egypt's effort to rebel against Assyria.
A battle in the plain of Eltekeh was won by Assyria; the Egyptian and Cushite charioteers fled. Lachish was besieged and taken. The annals note: "As for Hezekiah the Jew, he did not submit to my yoke. I laid siege to 46 of his strong cities, walled forts and to the countless small villages in their vicinity, and conquered them by means of well-stamped earth ramps and battering-rams brought near to the walls combined with the attack by foot-soldiers, using mines, breaches as well as sapper work. I drove out 200,150 people, young and old, male and female, horses, mules, donkeys, camels, big and small cattle beyond counting, and considered them booty. Himself I made a prisoner in Jerusalem, his royal residence, like a bird in a cage."
Nowhere, however, does the boastful Assyrian king record the disaster mentioned in 2 Kin 19:35-36 and Is 37:36-37.
Miles 0 5 10
Kms 0 5 10
From Acco
PROVINCE OF SAMARIA
Joppa
Michmash
Migron
Aiath
Eltekeh
Gezer
Ramah
Geba
Gibeah
Ekron
Timnah
JUDAH
Jerusalem
Nob
Ashdod
Gath
Anathoth
Ashkelon
Aczib
Tekoa
PHILISTIA
Lachish
Hebron
Gaza
Lake Urmia
Tigris R.
ASSYRIA
Haran
Carchemish
Nineveh
Calah
Euphrates R.
Asshur
MEDIA
2. CAMPAIGN OF SHALMANESER V (725-722 B.C.)
The last king of Israel, Hoshea, conspired with Egypt and withheld the annual tribute to the Assyrians. A protracted three-year siege conducted by Shalmaneser and concluded by Sargon II saw the end of the Israelite kingdom in 722 B.C.
At that time, according to Assyrian annals written on clay, "I (Sargon) besieged and conquered Samaria, led away as booty 27,290 inhabitants . . . I installed over (those remaining) an officer of mine and imposed upon them the tribute of the former king."
Euphrates R.
Tigris R.
Babylon
BABYLONIA
Miles 0 100 200 300
Kms 0 100 200 300 400

spired against him and [a]struck him before
the people and [1]killed him, and reigned in
his place.
11 Now the rest of the acts of Zechariah,
behold they are written in the Book of the
Chronicles of the Kings of Israel.
12 This is [a]the word of the LORD which He
spoke to Jehu, saying, "Your sons to the
fourth generation shall sit on the throne of
Israel." And so it was.
13 Shallum son of Jabesh became king in
the [a]thirty-ninth year of Uzziah king of
Judah, and he reigned one month in
[b]Samaria.
14 Then Menahem son of Gadi went up
from [a]Tirzah and came to Samaria, and
struck Shallum son of Jabesh in Samaria,
and killed him and became king in his place.
15 Now the rest of the acts of Shallum and
his conspiracy which he made, behold they
are written in the Book of the Chronicles of
the Kings of Israel.
16 Then Menahem struck Tiphsah and all
who were in it and its borders from Tirzah,
because they did not open *to him;* therefore
he struck *it* and ripped up [a]all its women
who were with child.

Menahem over Israel

17 In the [a]thirty-ninth year of Azariah
king of Judah, Menahem son of Gadi became
king over Israel *and reigned* ten years in
Samaria.
18 He did evil in the sight of the LORD; he
did not depart all his days from the sins of
Jeroboam the son of Nebat, which he made
Israel sin.
19 [a]Pul, king of Assyria, came against the
land, and Menahem gave Pul a thousand talents of silver so that his hand might be with
him to [b]strengthen the kingdom [1]under his
rule.
20 Then Menahem exacted the money
from Israel, even from all the mighty men of
wealth, from each man fifty shekels of silver
to pay the king of Assyria. So the king of
Assyria returned and did not remain there in
the land.
21 Now the rest of the acts of Menahem
and all that he did, are they not written in the
Book of the Chronicles of the Kings of Israel?
22 And Menahem slept with his fathers,
and Pekahiah his son became king in his
place.

Pekahiah over Israel

23 In [a]the fiftieth year of Azariah king of
Judah, Pekahiah son of Menahem became
king over Israel in Samaria, *and reigned* two
years.
24 He did evil in the sight of the LORD; he
did not depart from the sins of Jeroboam son
of Nebat, which he made Israel sin.
25 Then Pekah son of Remaliah, his officer, conspired against him and struck him in
Samaria, in [a]the castle of the king's house
with Argob and Arieh; and with him were
fifty men of the Gileadites; and he killed him
and became king in his place.
26 Now the rest of the acts of Pekahiah

10 [1]Lit *smote* [a]Amos 7:9
12 [a]2 Kin 10:30
13 [a]2 Kin 15:1, 8 [b]1 Kin 16:24
14 [a]1 Kin 14:17
16 [a]2 Kin 8:12; Hos 13:16
17 [a]2 Kin 15:1, 8, 13
19 [1]Lit *in his hand* [a]1 Chr 5:25, 26 [b]2 Kin 14:5
23 [a]2 Kin 15:1, 8, 13, 17
25 [a]1 Kin 16:18

15:11 *Chronicles of the Kings of Israel.* See note on 1 Kin 14:19.
15:12 *the word of the LORD . . . And so it was.* The word was given in 10:30. With the downfall of Jehu's dynasty, the northern kingdom entered a period of political instability (see Hos 1:4). The remaining five kings of the northern kingdom were all assassinated with the exception of Menahem, who reigned ten years, and Hoshea, who was imprisoned by the Assyrians. From the strength and wealth of the reign of Jeroboam II, the decline and fall of the northern kingdom was swift.
15:13 *thirty-ninth year of Uzziah.* 752 B.C. (see note on v. 2). Uzziah is another name for Azariah (see note on 14:21).
15:14 *Menahem . . . went up from Tirzah . . . to Samaria.* It is likely that Menahem was the commander of a military garrison at Tirzah, the former capital of the northern kingdom (see 1 Kin 14:17; 15:21,33). *became king in his place.* For the reign of Menahem see vv. 17–22.
15:15 *Chronicles of the Kings of Israel.* See note on 1 Kin 14:19.
15:16 *Tiphsah.* There was a Tiphsah located far to the north of Hamath (see 14:25) on the Euphrates River (see 1 Kin 4:24). It is unlikely that this was the city intended. Some interpreters prefer the reading "Tappuah" of the Septuagint. Tappuah was a city on the border between Ephraim and Manasseh (Josh 16:8; 17:7–8). Perhaps there was a Tiphsah in Israel not otherwise mentioned. *ripped up all its women who were with child.* See 8:12 and note.
15:17 *thirty-ninth year of Azariah.* 752 B.C. (see note on v. 2). *ten years.* 752–742.
15:18 *sins of Jeroboam.* See 1 Kin 12:26–32; 13:33–34; 14:16.
15:19 *Pul.* The Babylonian name (see 1 Chr 5:26) of the Assyrian ruler Tiglath-pileser III (745–727 B.C.). *came against the land.* Assyrian annals of Tiglath-pileser III indicate that he marched west with his army in 743 and took tribute from, among others, Carchemish, Hamath, Tyre, Byblos, Damascus, and Menahem of Samaria (see map Nos. 6 and 7 at the end of the study Bible). *thousand talents.* About 37 tons. This was an enormous sum of money. As a relative comparison, Omri bought the hill of Samaria for about 150 pounds of silver (see 1 Kin 16:24). *his hand might be with him to strengthen . . . his rule.* It appears that as a usurper Menahem still felt insecure on the throne. The opposition to his rule may have come from those following the leadership of Pekah, who favored an alliance with the Arameans of Damascus in order to resist the Assyrian threat (see note on v. 27). Hosea denounced the policy of seeking aid from the Assyrians and predicted that it would fail (Hos 5:13–15).
15:20 *fifty shekels.* About one and one-fourth pounds. A simple calculation reveals that it would require approximately 60,000 men of means to provide the 1,000 talents of tribute. This gives some indication of the prosperity the northern kingdom had enjoyed during the time of Jeroboam II.
15:21 *Chronicles of the Kings of Israel.* See note on 1 Kin 14:19.
15:23 *fiftieth year of Azariah.* 742 B.C. (see note on v. 2). *two years.* 742–740.
15:24 *sins of Jeroboam.* See 1 Kin 12:26–32; 13:33–34; 14:16.
15:25 *his officer.* Pekah was probably the ranking official in the Transjordan provinces, but his allegiance to Menahem and Pekahiah may well have been more apparent than real (see note on v. 27). *conspired against him.* Differences over foreign policy probably played an important role in fomenting Pekah's revolution. Pekahiah undoubtedly followed the policy of his father Menahem in seeking Assyria's friendship (see v. 20). Pekah advocat-

and all that he did, behold they are written
in the Book of the Chronicles of the Kings of
Israel.

Pekah over Israel

27 In [a]the fifty-second year of Azariah
king of Judah, [b]Pekah son of Remaliah
became king over Israel in Samaria, *and
reigned* twenty years.
28 He did evil in the sight of the LORD; he
did not depart from the sins of Jeroboam son
of Nebat, which he made Israel sin.
29 In the days of Pekah king of Israel,
[1a]Tiglath-pileser king of Assyria came and
[2]captured Ijon and Abel-beth-maacah and
Janoah and Kedesh and Hazor and Gilead
and Galilee, all the land of Naphtali; and [b]he
carried them captive to Assyria.
30 And Hoshea the son of Elah made a
conspiracy against Pekah the son of Remaliah, and struck him and put him to death and
became king in his place, in the twentieth
year of Jotham the son of Uzziah.
31 Now the rest of the acts of Pekah and all
that he did, behold, they are written in the
Book of the Chronicles of the Kings of Israel.

Jotham over Judah

32 In the second year of Pekah the son of
Remaliah king of Israel, Jotham the son of
[1]Uzziah king of Judah became king.

27 [a]2 Kin 15:23 [b]2 Chr 28:6; Is 7:1
29 [1]In 1 Chr 5:6, 26, *Tilgath-pilneser* [2]Lit *took* [a]2 Kin 15:19 [b]2 Kin 17:6
32 [1]I.e. Azariah
33 [a]2 Chr 27:1
34 [a]2 Kin 15:3, 4; 2 Chr 26:4, 5
35 [a]2 Kin 12:3 [b]2 Chr 23:20; 27:3
37 [a]2 Kin 16:5; Is 7:1
16:1 [a]2 Chr 28:1
2 [a]2 Chr 28:1-4

33 [a]He was twenty-five years old when he
became king, and he reigned sixteen years in
Jerusalem; and his mother's name *was* Jeru-
sha the daughter of Zadok.
34 [a]He did what was right in the sight of
the LORD; he did according to all that his
father Uzziah had done.
35 Only [a]the high places were not taken
away; the people still sacrificed and burned
incense on the high places. [b]He built the
upper gate of the house of the LORD.
36 Now the rest of the acts of Jotham and
all that he did, are they not written in the
Book of the Chronicles of the Kings of Judah?
37 In those days [a]the LORD began to send
Rezin king of Aram and Pekah the son of
Remaliah against Judah.
38 And Jotham slept with his fathers, and
he was buried with his fathers in the city of
David his father; and Ahaz his son became
king in his place.

Ahaz Reigns over Judah

16 In the seventeenth year of Pekah the
son of Remaliah, [a]Ahaz the son of
Jotham, king of Judah, became king.
2 [a]Ahaz *was* twenty years old when he
became king, and he reigned sixteen years in
Jerusalem; and he did not do what was right
in the sight of the LORD his God, as his father
David *had done.*

ed friendly relations with the Arameans of Damascus in order to counter potential Assyrian aggression (see 16:1–9; Is 7:1–2,4–6).
15:26 *Chronicles of the Kings of Israel.* See note on 1 Kin 14:19.
15:27 *fifty-second year of Azariah.* 740 B.C. (see note on v. 2). *twenty years.* 752–732, based on the assumptions (which the data seem to require) that Pekah had established in Transjordan virtually a rival government to that of Menahem when Menahem assassinated Shallum (see notes on vv. 17,19,25), and that the number of regnal years given here includes this period of rival rule.
15:28 *sins of Jeroboam.* See 1 Kin 12:26–32; 13:33–34; 14:16.
15:29 *Tiglath-pileser king of Assyria came.* See note on v. 19. The historical background for this attack is found in 16:5–9; 2 Chr 28:16–21; Is 7:1–17. *Ijon . . . Naphtali.* Over 150 years earlier Ben-hadad I of Damascus had taken this same territory from the northern kingdom in response to an appeal by a king of Judah (see notes on 1 Kin 15:19–20). *carried them captive to Assyria.* See 1 Chr 5:26. The forced exile of Israelites from their homeland was a fulfillment of the covenant curse (see note on 10:32).
15:30 *Hoshea . . . made a conspiracy against Pekah.* Hoshea probably represented the faction in the northern kingdom that favored cooperation with Assyria rather than resistance. In one of his annals Tiglath-pileser III claims to have placed Hoshea on the throne of the northern kingdom and to have taken ten talents of gold and 1,000 talents of silver as tribute from him. *twentieth year of Jotham.* 732 B.C. (see notes on vv. 32–33). Reference is to his 20th official year, which was his 19th actual year.
15:31 *Chronicles of the Kings of Israel.* See note on 1 Kin 14:19.
15:32 *second year of Pekah.* 750 B.C. (see note on v. 27).
15:33 *sixteen years.* 750–735 B.C. Jotham was co-regent with his father 750–740 (see note on v. 5). Jotham's reign was in some sense terminated in 735, and his son Ahaz took over. However, Jotham continued to live until at least 732 (see notes on vv. 30,37).
15:34 *that his father Uzziah had done.* See note on v. 3; see also 2 Chr 27:2.
15:35 *high places were not taken away.* See v. 4; see also note on 1 Kin 15:14. *upper gate of the house of the LORD.* See 2 Chr 23:20; Jer 20:2; Ezek 8:3; 9:2. Additional information on Jotham's building activities is given in 2 Chr 27:3–4.
15:36 *the rest of the acts of Jotham.* See 2 Chr 27:1–6. *Chronicles of the Kings of Judah.* See note on 1 Kin 14:29.
15:37 This parenthetical statement concerning Jotham's reign supports the idea of an overlap between the reigns of Jotham and Ahaz (see note on v. 33), since 16:5–12; 2 Chr 28:5–21; Is 7:1–17 all place the major effort of Rezin and Pekah in the time of Ahaz.
15:38 *slept with his fathers.* See note on 1 Kin 1:21.
16:1 *seventeenth year of Pekah.* 735 B.C. (see note on 15:27). The reign of Ahaz apparently overlapped that of Jotham, with Ahaz serving as a senior partner beginning in 735 (see notes on 15:33,37; see also notes on v. 2; 17:1).
16:2 *twenty years old when he became king.* Perhaps the age at which Ahaz became a senior co-regent with his father Jotham in 735 B.C. (see note on v. 1). Otherwise, according to the ages and dates provided, Ahaz would have been 11 or 12 instead of 14 or 15 years old when his son Hezekiah was born (cf. 18:1–2). *sixteen years.* The synchronizations of the reigns of Ahaz and Hezekiah of Judah with those of Pekah and Hoshea of the northern kingdom present some apparent chronological difficulties (see notes on v. 1; 17:1; 18:1,9–10). It seems best to take the 16 years specified here as the number of years Ahaz reigned after the death of Jotham, thus 732–715 (see notes on 15:30,33). The beginning of his reign appears to be dated in a variety of ways in the Biblical text: (1) in 744/743, which presupposes a co-regency with his grandfather Azariah at the tender age of 11 or 12 (see 17:1); (2) in 735, when he became senior co-regent with Jotham (see v. 1); and (3) in 732, when he

3 But he walked in the way of the kings
of Israel, [a]and even made his son pass
through the fire, [b]according to the abominations of the nations whom the LORD had
[1]driven out from before the sons of Israel.
4 He [a]sacrificed and burned incense on
the high places and on the hills and under
every green tree.
5 Then [a]Rezin king of Aram and Pekah
son of Remaliah, king of Israel, came up to
Jerusalem to *wage* war; and they besieged
Ahaz, [b]but could not [1]overcome him.
6 At that time Rezin king of Aram recovered [a]Elath for Aram, and cleared the Judeans
out of [1]Elath entirely; and the [2]Arameans
came to Elath and have lived there to this day.

Ahaz Seeks Help of Aram

7 [a]So Ahaz sent messengers to [b]Tiglath-
pileser king of Assyria, saying, "I am your
servant and your son; come up and deliver
me from the [1]hand of the king of Aram and
from the [1]hand of the king of Israel, who are
rising up against me."
8 [a]Ahaz took the silver and gold that was
found in the house of the LORD and in the
treasuries of the king's house, and sent a
present to the king of Assyria.
9 [a]So the king of Assyria listened to him;
and the king of Assyria went up against
Damascus and [b]captured it, and carried *the
people of* it away into exile to [c]Kir, and put
Rezin to death.

Damascus Falls

10 Now King Ahaz went to Damascus to
meet [a]Tiglath-pileser king of Assyria, and
saw the altar which *was* at Damascus; and
King Ahaz sent to [b]Urijah the priest the [1]pat-
tern of the altar and its model, according to
all its workmanship.
11 So Urijah the priest built an altar;
according to all that King Ahaz had sent
from Damascus, thus Urijah the priest made
it, [1]before the coming of King Ahaz from
Damascus.
12 When the king came from Damascus,
the king saw the altar; then [a]the king
approached the altar and [1]went up to it,
13 and [1]burned his burnt offering and his
meal offering, and poured his drink offering
and sprinkled the blood of his peace offerings on the altar.
14 [a]The bronze altar, which *was* before
the LORD, [1]he brought from the front of the
house, from between [b]*his* altar and the
house of the LORD, and he put it on the north
side of *his* altar.
15 Then King Ahaz [1]commanded Urijah
the priest, saying, "Upon the great altar [2]burn

3 [1]Or *dispossessed* [a]Lev 18:21; 2 Kin 17:17; 21:6 [b]Deut 12:31; 2 Kin 21:2, 11
4 [a]Deut 12:2; 2 Kin 14:4
5 [1]Lit *fight* [a]2 Kin 15:37; Is 7:1 [b]2 Chr 28:5, 6
6 [1]Heb *Eloth* [2]So with some ancient versions; Heb *Edomites* [a]2 Kin 14:22; 2 Chr 26:2
7 [1]Lit *palm* [a]2 Chr 28:16 [b]2 Kin 15:29
8 [a]2 Kin 12:17, 18; 18:15
9 [a]2 Chr 28:21
9 [b]Amos 1:3-5 [c]Is 22:6; Amos 9:7
10 [1]Lit *likeness* [a]2 Kin 15:29 [b]Is 8:2
11 [1]Lit *until*
12 [1]Or *offered on it* [a]2 Chr 26:16, 19
13 [1]Lit *offered in smoke*
14 [1]Lit *he also* [a]Ex 27:1, 2; 40:6, 29; 2 Chr 4:1 [b]2 Kin 16:11
15 [1]Lit *commanded him, Urijah* [2]Lit *offer in smoke*

began his sole reign after the death of Jotham. *did not do . . . as his father David had done.* Ahaz does not even receive the qualified approval given to Amaziah (14:3), Azariah (15:3) and Jotham (15:34).

16:3 *way of the kings of Israel.* It is unlikely that Ahaz adhered to the calf worship introduced by Jeroboam I at Bethel and Dan (see 1 Kin 12:26–32; 13:33–34; 14:16). The reference here is probably to Baal worship in the spirit of Ahab (see notes on 1 Kin 16:31–33; see also 2 Chr 28:2). *made his son pass through the fire.* Israel had been warned by Moses not to engage in this pagan rite (see Lev 18:21; Deut 18:10). In Israel the firstborn son in each household was to be consecrated to the Lord and redeemed by a payment of five shekels to the priests (see Ex 13:1,11–13; Num 18:16). See also 3:27; 17:17; 21:6; 23:10; 2 Chr 28:3; Jer 7:31; 32:35.

16:4 *high places.* See 15:4,35; see also note on 1 Kin 15:14. These high places appear to be those assimilated from pagan Baal worship and used for the worship of the Lord in a syncretistic fashion. *under every green tree.* Large trees were viewed as symbols of fertility by the pre-Israelite inhabitants of Canaan. Immoral pagan rites were performed at shrines located under such trees. Contrary to the explicit prohibition of the Mosaic covenant, the Israelites adopted this pagan custom (see 17:10; 1 Kin 14:23; Deut 12:2; Jer 2:20; 3:6; 17:2; Ezek 6:13; 20:28; Hos 4:13–14).

16:5 *Rezin . . . and Pekah . . . came up to Jerusalem to wage war.* See notes on 15:25,37. *could not overcome.* See Is 7:1–17; 2 Chr 28:5–21. Rezin and Pekah desired to replace Ahaz on the throne of the southern kingdom with the son of Tabeel in order to gain another ally in their anti-Assyrian political policy (see notes on 15:19,25). The Lord delivered Judah and Ahaz from this threat in spite of their wickedness because of the promises of the Davidic covenant (see 1 Kin 11:36; 2 Sam 7:13; Is 7:3–7,14).

16:6 *Rezin king of Aram recovered Elath.* See note on 14:22. *Arameans came to Elath.* The Hebrew for "Arameans" can also be read as "Edomites" (see 2 Chr 28:17). The Philistines also took this opportunity to avenge previous defeats (compare 2 Chr 26:5–7 with 2 Chr 28:18). *to this day.* See note on 1 Kin 8:8.

16:7 *Tiglath-pileser.* See notes on 15:19, 29. *your servant and your son.* Ahaz preferred to seek security for Judah by means of a treaty with Assyria rather than by obedience to the Lord and trust in His promises (see Ex 23:22; Is 7:10–16).

16:8 *silver and gold . . . in the house of the LORD.* The temple treasure must have been restored to some degree by Jotham (see 12:18; 14:14). The name "Jehoahaz of Judah" (Ahaz) appears on a list of rulers (including those of the Philistines, Ammonites, Moabites and Edomites) who brought tribute to Tiglath-pileser in 734 B.C.

16:9 *went up against Damascus and captured it.* In 732 B.C. Tiglath-pileser III moved against Damascus and destroyed it (see the prophecies of Is 7:16; Amos 1:3–5). *carried the people of it away . . . to Kir.* The Arameans were sent back to the place from which they had come (Amos 9:7) in fulfillment of the prophecy of Amos (Amos 1:5). The location of Kir is unknown, though it is mentioned in connection with Elam in Is 22:6.

16:10 *Ahaz went to Damascus to meet Tiglath-pileser.* As a vassal king to express his gratitude and loyalty to the victorious Assyrian ruler. *altar . . . at Damascus.* Perhaps that of the god Rimmon (see 5:18; 2 Chr 28:23), but more likely a royal altar of Tiglath-pileser. Ahaz's reproduction of such an altar would have been a further sign of submission to the Assyrians.

16:13 *burnt offering . . . meal offering . . . drink offering . . . peace offerings.* With the exception of the drink offering, these same sacrifices were offered at the dedication of the temple (1 Kin 8:64).

16:14 *north side of his altar.* Ahaz removed the bronze altar from its prominent place in front of the temple and gave it a place alongside the new stone altar.

16:15 *great altar.* Even though fire from heaven had inaugurated and sanctioned the use of the bronze altar for the worship of the Lord (see 2 Chr 7:1), Ahaz now replaced it with an altar

[a]the morning burnt offering and the evening meal offering and the king's burnt offering and his meal offering, with the burnt offering of all the people of the land and their meal offering and their drink offerings; and sprinkle on it all the blood of the burnt offering and all the blood of the sacrifice. But [b]the bronze altar shall be for me to inquire *by*."

16 So Urijah the priest did according to all that King Ahaz commanded.

17 Then King Ahaz [a]cut off the borders of the stands, and removed the laver from them; he also [b]took down the sea from the bronze oxen which were under it and put it on a pavement of stone.

18 The covered way for the sabbath which they had built in the house, and the outer entry of the king, he removed from the house of the LORD because of the king of Assyria.

Hezekiah Reigns over Judah

19 Now the rest of the acts of Ahaz which he did, are they not written [a]in the Book of the Chronicles of the Kings of Judah?

20 So [a]Ahaz slept with his fathers, and [b]was buried with his fathers in the city of David; and his son Hezekiah reigned in his place.

Hoshea Reigns over Israel

17 In the twelfth year of Ahaz king of Judah, [a]Hoshea the son of Elah became king over Israel in Samaria, *and reigned* nine years.

2 He did evil in the sight of the LORD, only not as the kings of Israel who were before him.

3 [a]Shalmaneser king of Assyria came up [b]against him, and Hoshea became his servant and paid him tribute.

4 But the king of Assyria found conspiracy in Hoshea, who had sent messengers to So king of Egypt and had offered no tribute to the king of Assyria, as *he had done* year by year; so the king of Assyria shut him up and bound him in prison.

5 Then the king of Assyria invaded the whole land and went up to [a]Samaria and besieged it three years.

Israel Captive

6 In the ninth year of Hoshea, [a]the king of Assyria captured Samaria and [b]carried Israel away into exile to Assyria, and [c]settled them in Halah and Habor, *on* the river of [d]Gozan, and [e]in the cities of the Medes.

Why Israel Fell

7 Now [a]*this* came about because the sons of Israel had sinned against the LORD their God, [b]who had brought them up from the land of Egypt from under the hand of Pharaoh, king of Egypt, [c]and they had [1]feared other gods

15 [a]Ex 29:39-41 [b]2 Kin 16:14
17 [a]1 Kin 7:27, 28, 38 [b]1 Kin 7:23, 25
19 [a]2 Chr 28:26
20 [a]Is 14:28 [b]2 Chr 28:27
17:1 [a]2 Kin 15:30
3 [a]Hos 10:14 [b]2 Kin 18:9-12
5 [a]Hos 13:16
6 [a]Hos 13:16 [b]Deut 28:64; 29:27, 28 [c]2 Kin 18:11; 1 Chr 5:26 [d]Is 37:12 [e]Is 13:17; 21:2
7 [1]Lit *revered,* and so throughout the ch [a]Josh 23:16 [b]Ex 14:15-30 [c]Judg 6:10

built on the pattern of the pagan altar from Damascus. Although the bronze altar was quite large (see 2 Chr 4:1), the new altar was larger. *morning burnt offering.* See 3:20; Ex 29:38–39; Num 28:3–4. *evening meal offering.* See note on 1 Kin 18:29. *king's burnt offering and his meal offering.* There is no other reference to these special offerings of the king in the OT, with the possible exception of Ezekiel's depiction of the offerings of a future prince (Ezek 46:12). *the bronze altar shall be for me to inquire by.* Seeking omens by the examination of the entrails of sacrificed animals is well attested in ancient Near Eastern texts. Here Ahaz states his intention to follow an Assyrian divination technique in an attempt to secure the Lord's guidance.

16:17 *borders of the stands, and removed the laver.* See 1 Kin 7:27–39. *took down the sea from the bronze oxen.* See 1 Kin 7:23–26. Perhaps the bronze was needed for tribute required by Tiglath-pileser III.

16:18 *because of the king of Assyria.* As a vassal of Tiglath-pileser, Ahaz was forced to relinquish some of the symbols of his own royal power.

16:19 *rest of the acts of Ahaz.* See 2 Chr 28, where, among other things, it is said that Ahaz even "closed the doors of the house of the LORD" (2 Chr 28:24). *Chronicles of the Kings of Judah.* See note on 1 Kin 14:29.

16:20 *slept with his fathers.* See note on 1 Kin 1:21; see also 2 Chr 28:27. *his son Hezekiah reigned in his place.* For the reign of Hezekiah see 18:1–20:21.

17:1 *twelfth year of Ahaz.* 732 B.C. (see note on 15:30), on the assumption that Ahaz began a co-regency with Azariah in 744/743 (see notes on 16:1–2). Some interpreters prefer to place the beginning of the reign of Ahaz in 735 on the assumption that the "twelfth" year of his reign in this text is a copyist's error for the "fourth" year of his reign (i.e., 732). *nine years.* 732–722 (see Introduction to 1 Kings: Chronology).

17:3 *Shalmaneser.* Hoshea had become a vassal to Assyria under the rule of Tiglath-pileser III (see note on 15:30). The latter was succeeded on the Assyrian throne by Shalmaneser V, who ruled 727–722 B.C.

17:5 *three years.* 725–722 B.C. Samaria was a strongly fortified city and extremely difficult to subdue (see note on 1 Kin 16:24).

17:6 *ninth year of Hoshea.* 722 B.C. (see note on v. 1). *king of Assyria captured Samaria.* In the winter (December) of 722–721 Shalmaneser V died (possibly by assassination), and the Assyrian throne was seized by Sargon II (722–705). In his annals Sargon II lays claim to the capture of Samaria at the beginning of his reign, but it was hardly more than a mopping-up operation. *carried Israel away into exile.* Because the northern kingdom refused to be obedient to their covenant obligations, the Lord brought on them the judgment pronounced already by Ahijah during the reign of the northern kingdom's first king, Jeroboam I (see note on 1 Kin 14:15). In his annals Sargon II claims to have deported 27,290 Israelites. He then settled other captured people in the vacated towns of the northern kingdom (see v. 24). *Halah.* Location uncertain. *Habor, on the river of Gozan.* Or, more likely, "Gozan, on the river of Habor." Gozan was an Assyrian provincial capital located on a tributary of the Euphrates River. *cities of the Medes.* Towns located in the area south of the Caspian Sea and northeast of the Tigris River.

17:7–23 A theological explanation for the downfall of the northern kingdom. Israel had repeatedly spurned the Lord's gracious acts, had refused to heed the prophets' warnings of impending judgment (vv. 13–14,23) and had failed to keep her covenant obligations (v. 15). The result was the implementation of the covenant curse precisely as it had been presented to the Israelites by Moses before they entered into Canaan (Deut 28:49–68; 32:1–47).

17:7 *brought them up from the land of Egypt.* The deliverance

8 and [a]walked in the [1]customs of the
nations whom the LORD had driven out before
the sons of Israel, and *in the customs* [b]of the
kings of Israel which they had [2]introduced.
9 The sons of Israel [1]did things secretly
which were not right against the LORD their
God. Moreover, they built for themselves
high places in all their towns, from [a]watch-
tower to fortified city.
10 [a]They set for themselves *sacred* pillars
and [1][b]Asherim on every high hill and under
every green tree,
11 and there they burned incense on all
the high places as the nations *did* which the
LORD had carried away to exile before them;
and they did evil things provoking the LORD.
12 They served idols, [a]concerning which
the LORD had said to them, "You shall not do
this thing."
13 Yet the [a]LORD warned Israel and Judah
[b]through all His prophets *and* [c]every seer,
saying, "[d]Turn from your evil ways and keep
My commandments, My statutes according
to all the law which I commanded your
fathers, and which I sent to you through My
servants the prophets."
14 However, they did not listen, but [a]stiff-
ened their neck [1]like their fathers, who did
not believe in the LORD their God.
15 [a]They rejected His statutes and [b]His
covenant which He made with their fathers
and His warnings with which He warned
them. And [c]they followed vanity and
[d]became vain, and *went* after the nations
which surrounded them, concerning which
the [e]LORD had commanded them not to do
like them.
16 They forsook all the commandments of
the LORD their God and made for themselves
molten images, *even* [a]two calves, and [b]made
an [1]Asherah and [c]worshiped all the host of
heaven and [d]served Baal.
17 Then [a]they made their sons and their
daughters pass through the fire, and [b]prac-
ticed divination and enchantments, and
[c]sold themselves to do evil in the sight of the
LORD, provoking Him.
18 So the LORD was very angry with Israel
and [a]removed them from His [1]sight; [b]none
was left except the tribe of Judah.
19 Also [a]Judah did not keep the commandments of the LORD their God, but [b]walked in
the [1]customs [2]which Israel had [3]introduced.
20 The LORD rejected all the [1]descendants
of Israel and afflicted them and [a]gave them
into the hand of plunderers, until He had
cast them [2]out of His sight.
21 When [a]He had torn Israel from the
house of David, [b]they made Jeroboam the
son of Nebat king. Then [c]Jeroboam drove
Israel away from following the LORD and
made them [1]commit a great sin.
22 The sons of Israel walked in all the sins
of Jeroboam which he did; they did not
depart from them
23 [a]until the LORD removed Israel from His
sight, [b]as He spoke through all His servants

8 [1]Lit *statutes* [2]Lit *made* [a]Lev 18:3; Deut 18:9 [b]2 Kin 16:3; 17:19
9 [1]Or *uttered words which* [a]2 Kin 18:8
10 [1]I.e. wooden symbols of a female deity [a]Ex 34:12-14 [b]1 Kin 14:23; Mic 5:14
12 [a]Ex 20:4
13 [a]Neh 9:29, 30 [b]2 Kin 17:23 [c]1 Sam 9:9 [d]Jer 7:3-7; 18:11; Ezek 18:31
14 [1]Lit *like the neck of* [a]Ex 32:9; 33:3; Acts 7:51
15 [a]Jer 8:9 [b]Ex 24:6-8; Deut 29:25 [c]Deut 32:21 [d]Jer 2:5; Rom 1:21-23
15 [e]Deut 12:30, 31
16 [1]I.e. a wooden symbol of a female deity [a]1 Kin 12:28 [b]1 Kin 14:15, 23 [c]Deut 4:19; 2 Kin 21:3 [d]1 Kin 16:31
17 [a]2 Kin 16:3 [b]Lev 19:26; Deut 18:10-12 [c]1 Kin 21:20
18 [1]Lit *face* [a]2 Kin 17:6 [b]1 Kin 11:13, 32, 36
19 [1]Lit *statutes* [2]Lit *of Israel which they* [3]Lit *made* [a]1 Kin 14:22, 23 [b]2 Kin 16:3
20 [1]Lit *seed* [2]Lit *from His face* [a]2 Kin 15:29 **21** [1]Lit *sin* [a]1 Kin 11:11, 31 [b]1 Kin 12:20 [c]1 Kin 12:28-33 **23** [a]2 Kin 17:6 [b]2 Kin 17:13

from Egypt was the fundamental redemptive event in Israel's history. She owed her very existence as a nation to this gracious and mighty act of the Lord (see Ex 20:2; Deut 5:15; 26:8; Josh 24:5–7,17; Judg 10:11; 1 Sam 12:6; Neh 9:9–13; Mic 6:4). *feared other gods.* A violation of the most basic obligation of Israel's covenant with the Lord (see v. 35; Deut 5:7; 6:14; Josh 24:14–16,20; Jer 1:16; 2:5–6; 25:6; 35:15).

17:8 *customs of the nations.* See Deut 18:9; Judg 2:12–13. *customs of the kings of Israel which they had introduced.* See, e.g., 10:31 (Jehu); 14:24 (Jeroboam II); 1 Kin 12:28–33 (Jeroboam I); 16:25–26 (Omri); 16:30–34 (Ahab).

17:9 *high places in all their towns.* See 14:4; 15:4,35; see also notes on 16:4; 1 Kin 3:2; 15:14.

17:10 *sacred pillars.* See note on 1 Kin 14:23. *Asherim.* See note on 1 Kin 14:15. *on every high hill and under every green tree.* See 16:4; 1 Kin 14:23; Jer 2:20; 3:6,13; 17:2.

17:11 *evil things.* Perhaps a reference to ritual prostitution (see note on 1 Kin 14:24; see also Hos 4:13–14).

17:12 *You shall not do this thing.* See Ex 20:4–5; see also Ex 23:13; Lev 26:1; Deut 5:6–10.

17:13 *warned Israel and Judah through all His prophets.* Israel not only violated the requirements of the Sinai covenant, but she also spurned the words of prophets the Lord had graciously sent to call His people back to the covenant (see, e.g., 1 Kin 13:1–3; 14:6–16; Judg 6:8–10; 1 Sam 3:19–21 as well as the ministries of Elijah, Elisha, Amos and Hosea). *seer.* See note on 1 Sam 9:9.

17:14 *stiffened their neck.* A figure derived from the obstinate resistance of an ox to being placed under a yoke (see Deut 10:16; Jer 2:20; 7:26; 17:23; 19:15; Hos 4:16).

17:15 *followed vanity.* See Deut 32:21; Jer 2:5; 8:19; 10:8; 14:22; 51:18.

17:16 *molten images, even two calves.* The golden calves of Bethel and Dan (see 1 Kin 12:28–30). *Asherah.* See note on 1 Kin 14:15. *all the host of heaven.* Israel had been commanded not to follow the astral cults of her pagan neighbors (see Deut 4:19; 17:3). Although this form of idolatry is not mentioned previously in 1,2 Kings, the prophet Amos apparently alludes to its practice in the northern kingdom during the reign of Jeroboam II (see note on Amos 5:26). It was later introduced in the southern kingdom during the reign of Manasseh (see 21:3,5) and abolished during the reformation of Josiah (see 23:4–5,12; see also Ezek 8:16).

17:17 *made their sons and their daughters pass through the fire.* See note on 16:3. *divination and enchantments.* Such practices were forbidden in the Mosaic covenant (see note on 16:15; see also Lev 19:26; Deut 18:10).

17:18 *removed them from His sight.* The exile of the northern kingdom (see v. 6; 23:27). *none was left except the tribe of Judah.* The southern kingdom included elements of the tribes of Simeon and Benjamin, but Judah was the only tribe in the south to retain its complete integrity (see notes on 1 Kin 11:31–32; see also note on 2 Kin 19:4).

17:20 *afflicted them and gave them into the hand of plunderers.* See 10:32–33; 13:3,20; 24:2; 2 Chr 21:16; 28:18; Amos 1:13.

17:21 *torn Israel from the house of David.* See 1 Kin 11:11,31; 12:24. The division of the kingdom was of the Lord, but it came to the nation as a punishment for their sins. *Jeroboam . . . made them commit a great sin.* See 1 Kin 12:26–32; 13:33–34.

17:23 *spoke through all His servants the prophets.* See 1 Kin 14:15–16; Hos 10:1–7; 11:5; Amos 5:27.

Exile of the Northern Kingdom

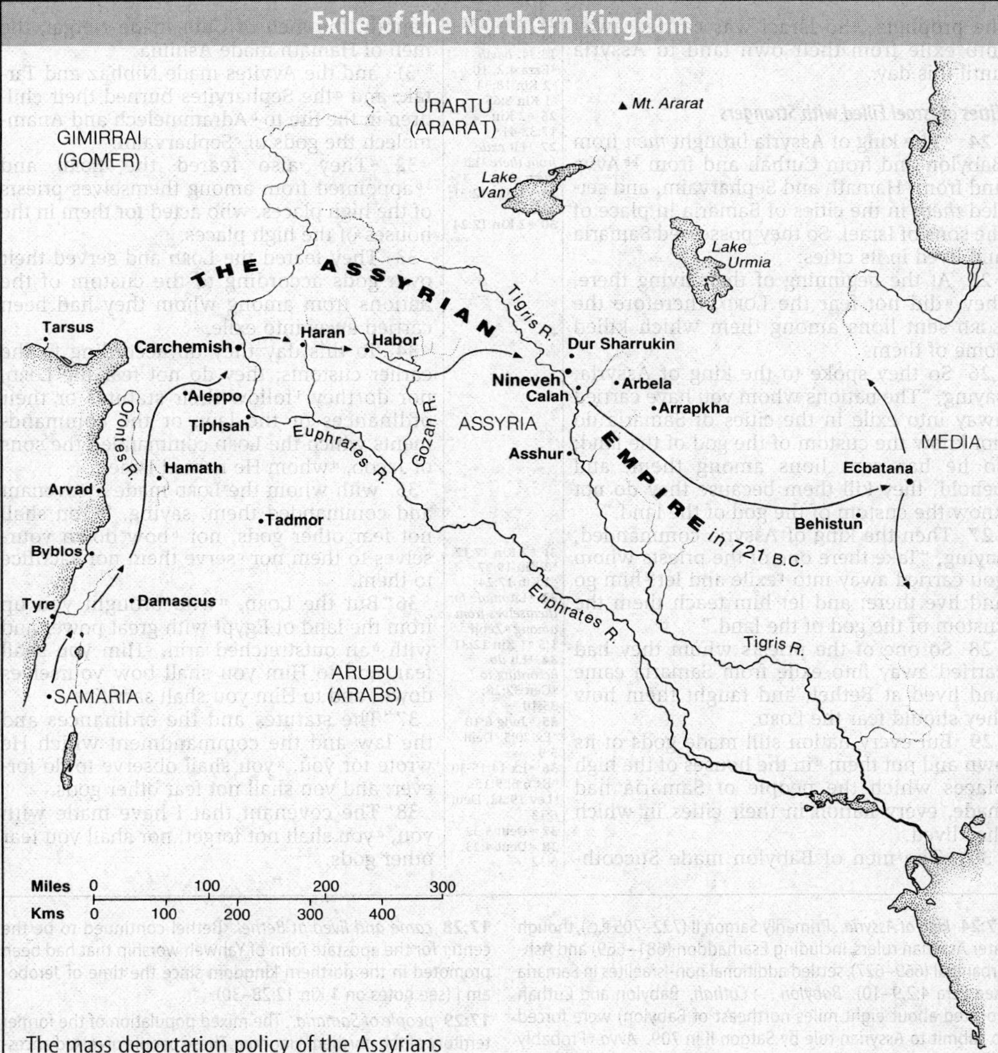

Mt. Ararat
URARTU
(ARARAT)
GIMIRRAI
(GOMER)
Lake Van
Lake Urmia
THE ASSYRIAN EMPIRE in 721 B.C.
Tigris R.
Tarsus
Carchemish
Haran
Habor
Dur Sharrukin
Nineveh
Calah
Arbela
Arrapkha
Aleppo
Orontes R.
Tiphsah
Euphrates R.
Gozan R.
ASSYRIA
MEDIA
Asshur
Ecbatana
Hamath
Arvad
Tadmor
Behistun
Byblos
Euphrates R.
Tyre
Damascus
Tigris R.
ARUBU
(ARABS)
SAMARIA
Miles 0 100 200 300
Kms 0 100 200 300 400

The mass deportation policy of the Assyrians was a companion piece to the brutal and calculated terror initiated by Ashurnasirpal and followed by all his successors. It was intended to forestall revolts but, like all Draconian measures, it merely spread misery and engendered hatred. In the end, it hastened the disintegration of the Assyrian empire.

There is some evidence that Israel experienced its first deportations under Tiglath-pileser III (745-727 B.C.), a cruelty repeated by Sargon II (722-705 B.C.) at the time of the fall of Samaria. The latter king's inscriptions boast of carrying away 27,290 inhabitants of the city "as booty." According to 2 Kin 17:6, they were sent to Assyria, to Halah (Calah?), to Habor on the Gozan River, and apparently to the eastern frontiers of the empire (to the towns of the Medes, most probably somewhere in the vicinity of Ecbatana, the modern Hamadan).

The sequel is provided by the inscriptions of Sargon: "The Arabs who live far away in the desert, who know neither overseers nor officials, and who had not yet brought their tribute to any king, I deported . . . and settled them in Samaria."

Much mythology has developed around the theme of the so-called ten lost tribes of Israel. A close examination of Assyrian records reveals that the deportations approximated only a limited percentage of the population, usually consisting of noble families. Agricultural workers, no doubt the majority, were deliberately left to care for the crops (cf. the Babylonian practice, 2Ki 24:14; 25:12).

the prophets. [a]So Israel was carried away
into exile from their own land to Assyria
until this day.

Cities of Israel Filled with Strangers

24 [a]The king of Assyria brought *men* from
Babylon and from Cuthah and from [1b]Avva
and from [c]Hamath and Sepharvaim, and settled *them* in the cities of Samaria in place of
the sons of Israel. So they possessed Samaria
and lived in its cities.
25 At the beginning of their living there,
they [a]did not fear the LORD; therefore the
LORD sent lions among them which killed
some of them.
26 So they spoke to the king of Assyria,
saying, "The nations whom you have carried
away into exile in the cities of Samaria do
not know the custom of the god of the land;
so he has sent lions among them, and
behold, they kill them because they do not
know the custom of the god of the land."
27 Then the king of Assyria commanded,
saying, "Take there one of the priests whom
you carried away into [1]exile and let [2]him go
and live there; and let him teach them the
custom of the god of the land."
28 So one of the priests whom they had
carried away into exile from Samaria came
and lived at Bethel, and taught them how
they should fear the LORD.
29 But every nation still made gods of its
own and put them [a]in the houses of the high
places which the people of Samaria had
made, every nation in their cities in which
they lived.
30 [a]The men of Babylon made Succoth-
benoth, the men of Cuth made Nergal, the
men of Hamath made Ashima,
31 and the Avvites made Nibhaz and Tar-
tak; and [a]the Sepharvites burned their children in the fire to [b]Adrammelech and Anammelech the gods of [c]Sepharvaim.
32 [a]They also feared the LORD and
[1b]appointed from among themselves priests
of the high places, who acted for them in the
houses of the high places.
33 They feared the LORD and served their
own gods according to the custom of the
nations from among whom they had been
carried away into exile.
34 To this day they do according to the
earlier customs: they do not fear the LORD,
nor do they [1]follow their statutes or their
ordinances or the law, or the commandments which the LORD commanded the sons
of Jacob, [a]whom He named Israel;
35 with whom the LORD made a covenant
and commanded them, saying, "[a]You shall
not fear other gods, nor [b]bow down yourselves to them nor [c]serve them nor sacrifice
to them.
36 "But the LORD, [a]who brought you up
from the land of Egypt with great power and
with [b]an outstretched arm, [c]Him you shall
fear, and to Him you shall bow yourselves
down, and to Him you shall sacrifice.
37 "The statutes and the ordinances and
the law and the commandment which He
wrote for you, [a]you shall observe to do forever; and you shall not fear other gods.
38 "The covenant that I have made with
you, [a]you shall not forget, nor shall you fear
other gods.

23 [a]2 Kin 17:6
24 [1]In 2 Kin 18:34, *Ivvah* [a]Ezra 4:2, 10 [b]2 Kin 18:34 [c]1 Kin 8:65
25 [a]2 Kin 17:32-41
27 [1]Lit *exile from there* [2]Lit *them*
29 [a]1 Kin 12:31; 13:32
30 [a]2 Kin 17:24
31 [a]2 Kin 17:17 [b]2 Kin 19:37 [c]2 Kin 17:24
32 [1]Lit *made for themselves from among* [a]Zeph 1:5 [b]1 Kin 12:31
34 [1]Lit *do according to* [a]Gen 32:28; 35:10
35 [a]Judg 6:10 [b]Ex 20:5 [c]Deut 5:9
36 [a]Ex 14:15-30 [b]Ex 6:6; 9:15 [c]Lev 19:32; Deut 6:13
37 [a]Deut 5:32
38 [a]Deut 4:23; 6:12

17:24 *king of Assyria.* Primarily Sargon II (722–705 B.C.), though later Assyrian rulers, including Esarhaddon (681–669) and Ashurbanipal (669–627), settled additional non-Israelites in Samaria (see Ezra 4:2,9–10). *Babylon . . . Cuthah.* Babylon and Cuthah (located about eight miles northeast of Babylon) were forced to submit to Assyrian rule by Sargon II in 709. *Avva.* Probably the same as Ivvah (see 18:34; 19:13). Its association with Hamath, Arpad and Sepharvaim suggests a location somewhere in Aram (Syria). *Hamath.* Located on the Orontes River (see 14:25; 18:34; see also note on Ezek 47:15). In 720 Sargon II made the kingdom of Hamath into an Assyrian province. *Sepharvaim.* Perhaps located in Aramean territory, possibly between Damascus and Hamath. *Samaria.* Here a designation for the entire northern kingdom (see note on 1 Kin 13:32).

17:25 *did not fear the LORD.* They worshiped their own national deities. *sent lions among them.* Lions had always been present in Canaan (see 1 Kin 13:24; 20:36; Judg 14:5; 1 Sam 17:34; Amos 3:12). In the aftermath of the disruption and depopulation caused by the conflict with the Assyrians, the lions greatly increased in number (see Ex 23:29). This was viewed by the inhabitants of the land and the writer of Kings as a punishment from the Lord (see Lev 26:21–22).

17:26 *king of Assyria.* Sargon II. *the custom of the god of the land.* According to the religious ideas of that time, each regional deity required special ritual observances, which, if ignored or violated, would bring disaster on the land.

17:27 *one of the priests.* Of the golden calf cult established in the northern kingdom by Jeroboam I (see 1 Kin 12:31 and note).

17:28 *came and lived at Bethel.* Bethel continued to be the center for the apostate form of Yahweh worship that had been promoted in the northern kingdom since the time of Jeroboam I (see notes on 1 Kin 12:28–30).

17:29 *people of Samaria.* The mixed population of the former territory of the northern kingdom. These people of mixed ancestry eventually came to be known as Samaritans. In later times the Samaritans rejected the idolatry of their polytheistic origins and followed the teachings of Moses, including monotheism. In NT times Jesus testified to a Samaritan woman (John 4:4–26), and many Samaritans were converted under the ministry of Philip (Acts 8:4–25).

17:32 *acted for them in the houses of the high places.* See note on 1 Kin 12:31.

17:33 *They feared the LORD and served their own gods.* A classic statement of syncretistic religion.

17:34 *To this day.* Until the time of the writing of 1,2 Kings. *fear the LORD.* Here used in the sense of faithful worship. In vv. 32–33 "fear the LORD" refers to a paganized worship.

17:35 *You shall not fear other gods.* The Mosaic covenant demanded exclusive worship of the Lord (Ex 20:5; Deut 5:9). This was the first and great commandment, and it was to distinguish Israel from all other peoples.

17:36 *the LORD, who brought you up from the land of Egypt . . . you shall fear.* Here, as in v. 7, the deliverance from Egypt is cited as the gracious act of the Lord par excellence that entitled Him to exclusive claim on Israel's loyalty.

39 "But the LORD your God you shall fear; and He will deliver you from the hand of all your enemies."
40 However, they did not listen, but they did according to their earlier custom.
41 [a]So while these nations feared the LORD, they also served their [1]idols; their children likewise and their grandchildren, as their fathers did, so they do to this day.

Hezekiah Reigns over Judah

18 Now it came about [a]in the third year of Hoshea, the son of Elah king of Israel, that [b]Hezekiah the son of Ahaz king of Judah became king.
2 He was [a]twenty-five years old when he became king, and he reigned twenty-nine years in Jerusalem; and his mother's name was Abi the daughter of Zechariah.
3 [a]He did right in the sight of the LORD, according to all that his father David had done.
4 [a]He removed the high places and broke down the *sacred* pillars and cut down the [1]Asherah. He also broke in pieces [b]the bronze serpent that Moses had made, for until those days the sons of Israel burned incense to it; and it was called [2]Nehushtan.
5 [a]He trusted in the LORD, the God of Israel; [b]so that after him there was none like him among all the kings of Judah, nor *among those* who were before him.
6 For he [a]clung to the LORD; he did not depart from following Him, but kept His commandments, which the LORD had commanded Moses.

Hezekiah Victorious

7 [a]And the LORD was with him; wherever he went he prospered. And [b]he rebelled against the king of Assyria and did not serve him.
8 [a]He [1]defeated the Philistines as far as Gaza and its territory, from [b]watchtower to fortified city.
9 Now in the fourth year of King Hezekiah, which was the seventh year of Hoshea son of Elah king of Israel, [a]Shalmaneser king of Assyria came up against Samaria and besieged it.
10 At the end of three years they captured it; in the sixth year of Hezekiah, which was [a]the ninth year of Hoshea king of Israel, Samaria was captured.
11 Then the king of Assyria carried Israel away into exile to Assyria, and put them in [a]Halah and on the Habor, the river of Gozan, and in the cities of the Medes,
12 because they [a]did not obey the voice of the LORD their God, but transgressed His covenant, *even* all that Moses the servant of the LORD commanded; they would neither listen nor do *it*.

Invasion of Judah

13 [a]Now in the fourteenth year of King Hezekiah, Sennacherib king of Assyria came

41 [1]Or *graven images* [a]Zeph 1:5; Matt 6:24
18:1 [a]2 Kin 16:2; 17:1 [b]2 Chr 28:27
2 [a]2 Chr 29:1, 2
3 [a]2 Kin 20:3; 2 Chr 31:20
4 [1]I.e. a wooden symbol of a female deity [2]I.e. a piece of bronze [a]2 Kin 18:22; 2 Chr 31:1 [b]Num 21:8, 9
5 [a]2 Kin 19:10 [b]2 Kin 23:25
6 [a]Deut 10:20; Josh 23:8
7 [a]Gen 39:2, 3; 1 Sam 18:14 [b]2 Kin 16:7
8 [1]Lit *smote* [a]2 Chr 28:18; Is 14:29 [b]2 Kin 17:9
9 [a]2 Kin 17:3-7
10 [a]2 Kin 17:6
11 [a]1 Chr 5:26
12 [a]1 Kin 9:6; Dan 9:6, 10
13 [a]2 Chr 32:1; Is 36:1-39:8

17:39 *will deliver you from . . . all your enemies.* See Ex 23:22; Deut 20:1–4; 23:14.
17:41 *to this day.* See note on v. 34.
18:1 *third year of Hoshea . . . Hezekiah . . . became king.* 729 B.C. (see 17:1). Hezekiah was co-regent with his father Ahaz from 729 to 715 (see note on 16:2 and Is 36:1).
18:2 *became king.* Became sole king of Judah. *twenty-nine years.* 715–686 B.C. See also 2 Chr 29–32 and Is 36–39 for a description of the events of his reign, including a more detailed account of the reformation he led (2 Chr 29–31). One of his first acts was to reopen the temple, which had been closed by his father Ahaz (see note on 16:19; see also 2 Chr 29:3).
18:3 *right . . . according to all that his father David had done.* Hezekiah is one of the few kings who is compared favorably with David. The others are Asa (1 Kin 15:11), Jehoshaphat (1 Kin 22:43) and Josiah (2 Kin 22:2). A qualification is introduced, however, with both Asa and Jehoshaphat: They did not remove the high places (see 1 Kin 15:14; 22:43).
18:4 *removed the high places.* Hezekiah was not the first king to destroy high places (see notes on 1 Kin 3:2; 15:14), but he was the first to destroy high places dedicated to the worship of the Lord (see 12:3; 14:4; 15:4,35; 17:9; 1 Kin 22:43). This became known even to the Assyrian king, Sennacherib (see v. 22). *sacred pillars.* See 3:2; 10:26–27; 17:10; see also note on 1 Kin 14:23. *Asherah.* See 13:6; 17:10,16; 1 Kin 16:23; see also note on 1 Kin 14:15. *sons of Israel burned incense to it.* It is unlikely that the bronze snake had been an object of worship all through the centuries of Israel's existence as a nation. Just when an idolatrous significance was attached to it is not known, but perhaps it occurred during the reign of Hezekiah's father Ahaz (see ch. 16). Snake worship of various types was common among ancient Near Eastern peoples.
18:5 *after him there was none like him . . . nor among those . . . before him.* A difference of emphasis is to be seen in this statement when compared to that of 23:25. Hezekiah's uniqueness is to be found in his trust in the Lord, while Josiah's uniqueness is to be found in his scrupulous observance of the Mosaic law.
18:7 *rebelled against the king of Assyria.* Judah had become a vassal to Assyria under Ahaz (see 16:7)—which required at least formal recognition of Assyrian deities. Hezekiah reversed the policy of his father Ahaz and sought independence from Assyrian dominance. It is likely that sometime shortly after 705 B.C., when Sennacherib replaced Sargon II on the Assyrian throne, Hezekiah refused to pay the annual tribute due the Assyrians.
18:8 *defeated the Philistines.* In a reversal of the conditions existing during the time of Ahaz, in which the Philistines captured Judahite cities in the hill country and Negev (see 2 Chr 28:18), Hezekiah was able once again to subdue the Philistines. Probably Hezekiah tried to coerce the Philistines into joining his anti-Assyrian policy. In one of his annals Sennacherib tells of forcing Hezekiah to release Padi, king of the Philistine city of Ekron, whom Hezekiah held prisoner in Jerusalem. This occurred in connection with Sennacherib's military campaign in 701 B.C.
18:9 *fourth year of King Hezekiah.* 725 B.C., the fourth year of Hezekiah's co-regency with Ahaz (see notes on v. 1; 17:1).
18:10 *three years.* See note on 17:5. *ninth year of Hoshea.* See note on 17:6.
18:11 *king of Assyria carried Israel away.* See note on 17:6.
18:12 *transgressed His covenant.* See 17:7–23.
18:13 *fourteenth year.* Of Hezekiah's sole reign: 701 B.C. (see note on v. 2). *Sennacherib . . . came up against.* Verses 13–16 correspond very closely with Sennacherib's own account of his 701 campaign against Phoenicia, Judah and Egypt. *seized them.* In his annals, Sennacherib claims to have captured 46 of Heze-

up against all the fortified cities of Judah and
seized them.
14 Then Hezekiah king of Judah sent to
the king of Assyria at Lachish, saying, "[a]I
have done wrong. [1]Withdraw from me;
whatever you [2]impose on me I will bear." So
the king of Assyria [3]required of Hezekiah
king of Judah three hundred talents of silver
and thirty talents of gold.
15 [a]Hezekiah gave *him* all the silver
which was found in the house of the LORD,
and in the treasuries of the king's house.
16 At that time Hezekiah cut off *the gold*
from the doors of the temple of the LORD, and
from the doorposts which Hezekiah king of
Judah had overlaid, and gave it to the king of
Assyria.
17 Then the king of Assyria sent [a]Tartan
and Rab-saris and Rabshakeh from Lachish
to King Hezekiah with a large army to Jerusalem. So they went up and came to Jerusalem. And when they went up, they came and
stood by the [b]conduit of the upper pool,
which is on the highway of the [1]fuller's field.
18 When they called to the king, [a]Eliakim
the son of Hilkiah, who was over the household, and [b]Shebnah the scribe and Joah the
son of Asaph the recorder, came out to them.
19 Then Rabshakeh said to them, "Say
now to Hezekiah, 'Thus says the great king,
the king of Assyria, "[a]What is this confidence that you [1]have?
20 "You say (but *they are* [1]only empty
words), '*I have* counsel and strength for the
war.' Now on whom do you rely, [a]that you
have rebelled against me?

14 [1]Lit *Return* [2]Lit *give* [3]Lit *put on* [a]2 Kin 18:7
15 [a]1 Kin 15:18, 19; 2 Kin 12:18; 16:8
17 [1]I.e. launderer's [a]Is 20:1 [b]2 Kin 20:20; Is 7:3
18 [a]2 Kin 19:2; Is 22:20 [b]Is 22:15
19 [1]Lit *trust* [a]2 Chr 32:10
20 [1]Lit *a word of the lips* [a]2 Kin 18:7

21 "Now behold, you [1a]rely on the staff of
this crushed reed, *even* on Egypt; on which if
a man leans, it will go into his [2]hand and
pierce it. So is Pharaoh king of Egypt to all
who rely on him.
22 "But if you say to me, 'We trust in the
LORD our God,' is it not He whose high places
and [a]whose altars Hezekiah has taken away,
and has said to Judah and to Jerusalem, 'You
shall worship before this altar in Jerusalem'?
23 "Now therefore, [1]come, make a bargain
with my master the king of Assyria, and I
will give you two thousand horses, if you are
able on your part to set riders on them.
24 "How then can you [1]repulse one [2]official
of the least of my master's servants, and [3]rely
on Egypt for chariots and for horsemen?
25 "Have I now come up [1]without the
LORD'S approval against this place to destroy
it? The LORD said to me, 'Go up against this
land and destroy it.'" '"
26 Then Eliakim the son of Hilkiah, and
Shebnah and Joah, said to Rabshakeh,
"Speak now to your servants in Aramaic, for
we [1]understand *it;* and do not speak with us
in [2a]Judean in the hearing of the people who
are on the wall."
27 But Rabshakeh said to them, "Has my
master sent me only to your master and to
you to speak these words, *and* not to the
men who sit on the wall, *doomed* to eat their
own dung and drink their own urine with
you?"
28 Then Rabshakeh stood and cried with a
loud voice in Judean, [1]saying, "Hear the
word of the great king, the king of Assyria.

21 [1]Lit *rely for yourself* [2]Lit *palm* [a]Is 30:2, 3, 7; Ezek 29:6, 7
22 [a]2 Kin 18:4; 2 Chr 31:1
23 [1]Lit *please exchange pledges*
24 [1]Lit *turn away the face of* [2]Or *governor* [3]Lit *rely for yourself*
25 [1]Lit *without the LORD*
26 [1]Lit *hear* [2]I.e. Hebrew [a]Ezra 4:7; Dan 2:4
28 [1]Lit *and spoke, saying,*

kiah's fortified cities, as well as numerous open villages, and to have taken 200,150 of the people captive. He says he made Hezekiah "a prisoner in Jerusalem his royal residence, like a bird in a cage," but he does not say he took Jerusalem.

18:14 *three hundred talents of silver and thirty talents of gold.* About eleven tons of silver and one ton of gold. The Assyrian and Biblical reports of the amount of tribute paid by Hezekiah to Sennacherib agree with respect to the 30 talents of gold, but Sennacherib claims to have received 800 talents of silver rather than the 300 specified in the Biblical text. This discrepancy may be the result of differences in the weight of Assyrian and Israelite silver talents, or it may simply be due to the Assyrian propensity for exaggeration. For the relative value of this amount of silver and gold see note on 15:19.

18:15 *silver . . . in the house of the LORD, and in the treasuries of the king's house.* See 12:10,18; 14:14; 16:8; 1 Kin 7:51; 14:26; 15:18.

18:17–19:37 See Is 36–37; cf. 2Ch 32.

18:17 *Lachish.* See note on Is 36:2. *conduit . . . field.* See note on Is 7:3. It is ironic that the Assyrian officials demand Judah's surrender on the very spot where Isaiah had warned Ahaz to trust in the Lord rather than in an alliance with Assyria for deliverance from the threat against him from Aram and the northern kingdom of Israel (see 16:5–10; Is 7:1–17).

18:18 *over the household.* See note on 1 Kin 4:6. *scribe.* See note on 2 Sam 8:17. *recorder.* See note on 2 Sam 8:16.

18:19 *great king.* A frequently used title of the Assyrian rulers—and occasionally of the Lord (Ps 47:2; 48:2; 95:3; Mal 1:14; Matt 5:35). *says.* The following address is a masterpiece of calculated intimidation and psychological warfare designed to break the resistance of the inhabitants of Jerusalem (see vv. 26–27).

18:21 *rely on . . . Egypt.* See 19:9; Is 30:1–5; 31:1–3.

18:22 *is it not He whose high places and whose altars Hezekiah has taken away . . . ?* The Assyrians cleverly attempted to drive a wedge between Hezekiah and the people. They attempted to exploit any resentment that may have existed among those who opposed Hezekiah's reformation and his destruction of the high places (see note on v. 4).

18:23 *if you are able . . . to set riders on them.* With this sarcastic taunt, the Assyrians undoubtedly accurately suggest that the Judahites were so weak in military personnel that they could not even take advantage of such a generous offer. In contrast with the Assyrians, the army of Judah at the time consisted largely of foot soldiers. The city under siege would have contained few chariots, and it is not known whether the Israelites ever employed mounted men in combat.

18:25 *The LORD said to me.* Possibly Assyrian spies had informed Sennacherib of the prophecies of Isaiah and Micah.

18:26 *Aramaic.* Had become the international language of the Near East, known and used by those experienced in diplomacy and commerce. It is surprising that the Assyrian officials were able to speak the Hebrew dialect of the common people of Judah (see 2 Chr 32:18).

18:27 *men who sit on the wall.* The Assyrian strategy was to negotiate in the hearing of the people in order to demoralize them and turn them against Hezekiah. *eat their own dung and drink their own urine.* A vivid portrayal of the potential hardship of a prolonged siege.

29 "Thus says the king, '[a]Do not let Hezekiah deceive you, for he will not be able to
deliver you from [1]my hand;
30 nor let Hezekiah make you trust in the
LORD, saying, "The LORD will surely deliver
us, and this city will not be given into the
hand of the king of Assyria."
31 'Do not listen to Hezekiah, for thus says
the king of Assyria, "[1]Make your peace with
me and come out to me, and eat [a]each of his
vine and each of his fig tree and drink each
of the waters of his own cistern,
32 until I come and take you away [a]to a
land like your own land, a land of grain and
new wine, a land of bread and vineyards, a
land of olive trees and honey, that you may
live and not die." But do not listen to Hezekiah when he misleads you, saying, "The
LORD will deliver us."
33 '[a]Has any one of the gods of the nations
delivered his land from the hand of the king
of Assyria?
34 '[a]Where are the gods of Hamath and
[b]Arpad? Where are the gods of Sepharvaim,
Hena and [1c]Ivvah? Have they delivered
Samaria from my hand?
35 'Who among all the gods of the lands
[1]have delivered their land from my hand,
[a]that the LORD should deliver Jerusalem from
my hand?' "
36 But the people were silent and answered him not a word, for the king's commandment was, "Do not answer him."
37 Then [a]Eliakim the son of Hilkiah, who
was over the household, and Shebna the
scribe and Joah the son of Asaph, the recorder, came to Hezekiah [b]with their clothes
torn and told him the words of Rabshakeh.

Isaiah Encourages Hezekiah

19 [a]And when King Hezekiah heard *it*, he
[b]tore his clothes, [c]covered himself with
sackcloth and entered the house of the LORD.
2 Then he sent Eliakim who was over the
household with Shebna the scribe and the
elders of the priests, [a]covered with sackcloth,
to [b]Isaiah the prophet the son of Amoz.
3 They said to him, "Thus says Hezekiah, 'This day is a day of distress, rebuke, and
rejection; for children have come to birth and
there is no strength to *deliver.*
4 '[a]Perhaps the LORD your God will hear
all the words of Rabshakeh, whom his master
the king of Assyria has sent [b]to reproach the
living God, and will rebuke the words which
the LORD your God has heard. Therefore, offer
a prayer for [c]the remnant that is left.' "
5 So the servants of King Hezekiah came
to Isaiah.
6 Isaiah said to them, "Thus you shall
say to your master, 'Thus says the LORD, "Do
not be afraid because of the words that you
have heard, with which the [a]servants of the
king of Assyria [b]have blasphemed Me.
7 "Behold, I will put a spirit in him so that
[a]he will hear a rumor and return to his own
land. And [b]I will make him fall by the sword
in his own land." ' "

29 [1]Heb *his* [a]2 Chr 32:15
31 [1]Lit *Make with me a blessing* [a]1 Kin 4:20, 25
32 [a]Deut 8:7-9; 11:12
33 [a]2 Kin 19:12; Is 10:10, 11
34 [1]In 2 Kin 17:24, *Avva* [a]2 Kin 19:13 [b]Is 10:9 [c]2 Kin 17:24
35 [1]Lit *who have* [a]Ps 2:1-3; 59:7
37 [a]2 Kin 18:26
37 [b]2 Kin 6:30
19:1 [a]2 Chr 32:20-22; Is 37:1 [b]2 Kin 18:37 [c]1 Kin 21:27
2 [a]2 Sam 3:31 [b]Is 1:1; 2:1
4 [a]Josh 14:12; 2 Sam 16:12 [b]2 Kin 18:35 [c]Is 1:9
6 [a]2 Kin 18:17 [b]2 Kin 18:22-25, 30, 35
7 [a]2 Kin 7:6 [b]2 Kin 19:37

18:29 *Thus says the king.* The Assyrian officials now address their remarks directly to the populace rather than to the officials of Hezekiah, as in vv. 19–27. *Do not let Hezekiah deceive you.* Here and in vv. 30–31 the people are urged three times to turn against Hezekiah.
18:30 *this city will not be given into the hand of the king of Assyria.* Hezekiah could say this on the basis of God's promise to him (see 20:6; see also note on Is 38:6).
18:31 *eat each of his vine and each of his fig tree and drink . . . of his own cistern.* Depicting peaceful and prosperous times (see 1 Kin 4:25; Mic 4:4; Zech 3:10).
18:32 *until I come and take you away to a land like your own.* Ultimately surrender meant deportation, but Sennacherib pictured it as something desirable. *that you may live and not die.* The alternatives depicted for the people are: (1) Trust in the Lord and Hezekiah and die, or (2) trust in the Assyrians and enjoy prosperity and peace. These words directly contradict the alternatives placed before Israel by Moses in Deut 30:15–20.
18:33–35 *Has any one of the gods of the nations delivered his land from the hand of the king of Assyria? . . . that the LORD should deliver Jerusalem from my hand?* The flaw in the Assyrian reasoning was to equate the one true and living God with the no-gods (Deut 32:21) of the pagan peoples the Assyrians had defeated (see 19:4,6; 2 Chr 32:13–19; Is 10:9–11).
18:34 *Hamath.* See notes on 14:25; 17:24. *Arpad.* A city located near Hamath and taken by the Assyrians in 740 B.C. (see 19:13; Is 10:9; Jer 49:23). *Sepharvaim.* See note on 17:24. *Hena.* Probably located in the vicinity of the other cities mentioned. *Ivvah.* See note on 17:24.
18:36 *for the king's commandment was, "Do not answer him."* The Assyrian attempt to stir up a popular revolt against the leadership and authority of Hezekiah had failed.
18:37 *clothes torn.* An expression of great emotion (see 6:30; 1 Kin 21:27). Perhaps in this instance it was motivated by the Assyrian blasphemy against the true God (see 19:4,6; Matt 26:65; Mark 14:63–64).
19:1 *sackcloth.* See note on 6:30.
19:2 *over the household.* See note on 1 Kin 4:6. *scribe.* See note on 2 Sam 8:17. *elders of the priests.* Probably the oldest members of various priestly families (see Jer 19:1). The crisis involved not only the city of Jerusalem, but also the temple. *Isaiah the prophet.* The first reference to Isaiah in the book of Kings, though he had been active in the reigns of Uzziah, Jotham and Ahaz (see Isa 1:1).
19:3 *for children have come to birth and there is no strength to deliver.* Depicts the critical nature of the threat facing the city.
19:4 *living God.* In contrast to the no-gods of 18:33–35. See 1 Sam 17:26,36,45 for another example of ridiculing the living and true God. *offer a prayer.* Intercessory prayer was an important aspect of the ministry of the prophets (see, e.g., the intercession of Moses and Samuel: Ex 32:31–32; 33:12–17; Num 14:13–19; 1 Sam 7:8–9; 12:19, 23; Ps 99:6; Jer 15:1). *remnant.* Those left in Judah after Sennacherib's capture of many towns and numerous people (see note on 18:13; cf. Is 10:28–32). Archaeological evidence reveals that many Israelites fled the northern kingdom during the Assyrian assaults and settled in Judah, so that the nation of Judah became the remnant of all Israel.
19:7 *spirit.* Of insecurity and fear. *rumor.* Some interpreters link this "rumor" with the challenge to Sennacherib from Tirhakah of Egypt (v. 9). Others regard it as disturbing information from Sennacherib's homeland. *fall by the sword.* See v. 37. Here

Sennacherib Defies God

8 Then Rabshakeh returned and found
the king of Assyria fighting against [a]Libnah,
for he had heard that [1]the king had left
[b]Lachish.
9 When he heard *them* say concerning
Tirhakah king of [1]Cush, "Behold, he has
come out to fight against you," he sent messengers again to Hezekiah saying,
10 "Thus you shall say to Hezekiah king of
[1]Judah, 'Do not [a]let your God in whom you
trust deceive you saying, "[b]Jerusalem will
not be given into the hand of the king of
Assyria."
11 'Behold, you have heard what the kings
of Assyria have done to all the lands, destroying them completely. So will you be [1]spared?
12 '[a]Did the gods of [1]those nations which
my fathers destroyed deliver them, *even*
[b]Gozan and [c]Haran and Rezeph and [d]the
sons of Eden who *were* in Telassar?
13 '[a]Where is the king of Hamath, the king
of Arpad, the king of the city of Sepharvaim,
and *of* Hena and Ivvah?' "

Hezekiah's Prayer

14 Then [a]Hezekiah took the [1]letter from
the hand of the messengers and read it, and
he went up to the house of the LORD and
[2]spread it out before the LORD.
15 Hezekiah prayed before the LORD and
said, "O LORD, the God of Israel, [a]who are
[1]enthroned *above* the cherubim, [b]You are the
God, You alone, of all the kingdoms of the
earth. You have made heaven and earth.
16 "[a]Incline Your ear, O LORD, and hear;
[b]open Your eyes, O LORD, and see; and listen
to the words of Sennacherib, which he has
sent [c]to reproach the living God.
17 "Truly, O LORD, the kings of Assyria have
devastated the nations and their lands
18 and have cast their gods into the fire,
[a]for they were not gods but the work of
men's hands, wood and stone. So they have
destroyed them.

8 [1]Lit *he* [a]Josh 10:29 [b]2 Kin 18:14
9 [1]Or *Ethiopia*
10 [1]Lit *Judah, saying,* [a]2 Kin 18:5 [b]2 Kin 18:30
11 [1]Lit *delivered*
12 [1]Lit *the* [a]2 Kin 18:33 [b]2 Kin 17:6 [c]Gen 11:31 [d]Is 37:12
13 [a]2 Kin 18:34
14 [1]Lit *letters...read them* [2]Lit *Hezekiah spread* [a]Is 37:14
15 [1]Lit *seated* [a]Ex 25:22; Is 37:14 [b]2 Kin 5:15
16 [a]Ps 31:2; Is 37:17 [b]1 Kin 8:29; 2 Chr 6:40 [c]2 Kin 19:4
18 [a]Is 44:9-20; Acts 17:29
19 [a]1 Kin 8:42, 43 [b]2 Kin 19:15
20 [a]2 Kin 20:5
21 [a]Jer 14:17; Lam 2:13 [b]Ps 109:25; Matt 27:39
22 [1]Lit *on high* [a]2 Kin 19:4 [b]2 Kin 19:6 [c]Is 5:24; 30:11-15
23 [1]So with some ancient versions; M.T. *will cut...will enter* [a]2 Kin 18:17 [b]2 Chr 26:10; Is 10:18
24 [1]So with some ancient versions; M.T. *will dry up* [2]Lit *the besieged place* [a]Is 19:6
25 [a]Is 45:7 [b]Is 10:5

19 "Now, O LORD our God, I pray, deliver
us from his hand [a]that all the kingdoms of
the earth may know that You alone, O [b]LORD,
are God."

God's Answer through Isaiah

20 Then Isaiah the son of Amoz sent to
Hezekiah saying, "Thus says the LORD, the
God of Israel, 'Because you have prayed to
Me about Sennacherib king of Assyria, [a]I
have heard *you.*'
21 "This is the word that the LORD has spoken against him:

'She has despised you and mocked you,
[a]The virgin daughter of Zion;
She [b]has shaken *her* head behind you,
The daughter of Jerusalem!
22 'Whom have you [a]reproached and
[b]blasphemed?
And against whom have you raised
your voice,
And [1]haughtily lifted up your eyes?
Against the [c]Holy One of Israel!
23 '[a]Through your messengers you have
reproached the Lord,
And you have said, "With my many
chariots
I came up to the heights of the
mountains,
To the remotest parts of Lebanon;
And I [1]cut down its tall cedars *and* its
choice cypresses.
And I [1]entered its farthest lodging
place, its [b]thickest forest.
24 "I dug *wells* and drank foreign waters,
And with the sole of my feet I [1][a]dried
up
All the rivers of [2]Egypt."

25 '[a]Have you not heard?
Long ago I did it;
From ancient times I planned it.
[b]Now I have brought it to pass,
That you should turn fortified cities
into ruinous heaps.

---

the eventual murder of Sennacherib is connected with his blasphemy against the living God.

19:8 *Libnah.* See note on 8:22. *Lachish.* See 18:17 (see also note on Is 36:2).

19:9 *Tirhakah.* See note on Is 37:9. *Cush.* The upper Nile region.

19:12 *Gozan.* See note on 17:6. *Haran.* See note on Gen 11:31. It is not known just when Haran was taken by the Assyrians. *Rezeph.* Located south of the Euphrates River and northeast of Hamath. *Eden.* See Ezek 27:23; Amos 1:5; a district along the Euphrates River south of Haran. It was incorporated into the Assyrian empire by Shalmaneser III in 855 B.C. *Telassar.* Location unknown.

19:13 *Hamath . . . Ivvah.* See note on 18:34.

19:14 *letter.* See 2 Chr 32:17.

19:15 *enthroned above the cherubim.* See notes on Ex 25:18; 1 Sam 4:4. *You are the God, You alone.* See notes on 18:33–35; Dt 6:4.

19:18 *work of men's hands.* For the foolishness and futility of idolatry see Ps 115:3–8; 135:15–18; Is 2:20; 40:19–20; 41:7; 44:9–20.

19:20 *I have heard you.* On this occasion Isaiah's message to Hezekiah was unsolicited by the king (contrast v. 2).

19:21–28 The arrogance of the Assyrians and their ridicule of the Israelites and their God are countered with a derisive pronouncement of judgment (cf. Ps 2) on the misconceived Assyrian pride (see Is 10:5–34).

19:21 *virgin daughter of Zion.* A personification of Jerusalem and its inhabitants.

19:22 *Holy One of Israel.* A designation of the God of Israel characteristic of Isaiah (see note on Isa 1:4).

19:24 *dried up All the rivers of Egypt.* A presumptuous boast for one who had not even conquered Egypt.

19:25 *I planned it. Now I have brought it to pass.* The God of Israel is the ruler of all nations and history. The Assyrians attributed their victories to their own military superiority. However, Isaiah said that God alone ordained these victories (see Is 10:5–19; cf. Ezek 30:24–26).

26 'Therefore their inhabitants were short
of strength,
They were dismayed and put to shame;
They were [a]as the vegetation of the
field and as the green herb,
As grass on the housetops is scorched
before it is grown up.
27 'But [a]I know your sitting down,
And your going out and your coming
in,
And your raging against Me.
28 'Because of your raging against Me,
And because your [1]arrogance has
come up to My ears,
Therefore I [a]will put My hook in your
nose,
And My bridle in your lips,
And [b]I will turn you back by the way
which you came.
29 'Then this shall be [a]the sign for you:
[1]you will eat this year what grows of itself, in
the second year what springs from the same,
and in the third year sow, reap, plant vineyards, and eat their fruit.
30 '[a]The surviving remnant of the house of
Judah will again take root downward and
bear fruit upward.
31 'For out of Jerusalem will go forth a
remnant, and [a]out of Mount Zion [1]survivors.
[b]The zeal of [2]the LORD will perform this.
32 'Therefore thus says the LORD concerning the king of Assyria, "[a]He will not come
to this city or shoot an arrow there; and he
will not come before it with a shield or throw
up a siege ramp against it.
33 "[a]By the way that he came, by the same
he will return, and he shall not come to this
city," ' declares the LORD.
34 '[a]For I will defend this city to save it for
My own sake and [b]for My servant David's
sake.' "
35 [a]Then it happened that night that the
angel of the LORD went out and struck
185,000 in the camp of the Assyrians; and
when [1]men rose early in the morning,
behold, all of them were [2]dead.
36 So [a]Sennacherib king of Assyria
departed and returned *home,* and lived at
[b]Nineveh.
37 It came about as he was worshiping in
the house of Nisroch his god, that [1][a]Adram-
melech and Sharezer killed him with the
sword; and they escaped into [b]the land of
Ararat. And [c]Esarhaddon his son became
king in his place.

26 [a]Ps 129:6
27 [a]Ps 139:1
28 [1]Lit *complacency* [a]Ezek 19:9; 29:4 [b]2 Kin 19:33, 36
29 [1]Lit *eating* [a]Ex 3:12; 2 Kin 20:8, 9
30 [a]2 Kin 19:4; 2 Chr 32:22, 23
31 [1]Lit *those who escape* [2]Some ancient mss read *the LORD of hosts* [a]Is 10:20 [b]Is 9:7
32 [a]Is 8:7-10
33 [a]2 Kin 19:28
34 [a]2 Kin 20:6; Is 31:5 [b]1 Kin 11:12, 13
35 [1]Lit *they* [2]Lit *dead bodies* [a]2 Sam 24:16; 2 Chr 32:21
36 [a]2 Kin 19:7, 28, 33 [b]Jon 1:2
37 [1]Some ancient mss read *Adrammelech and Sharezer his sons smote him* [a]2 Kin 19:17, 31 [b]Gen 8:4; Jer 51:27 [c]Ezra 4:2
20:1 [1]Lit *sick to the point of death* [a]2 Chr 32:24; Is 38:1-22 [b]2 Sam 17:23
3 [1]Lit *great weeping* [a]Neh 5:19; 13:14, 22, 31 [b]2 Kin 18:3-6 [c]2 Sam 12:21, 22

Hezekiah's Illness and Recovery

20 [a]In those days Hezekiah became [1]mor-
tally ill. And Isaiah the prophet the son
of Amoz came to him and said to him, "Thus
says the LORD, '[b]Set your house in order, for
you shall die and not live.' "
2 Then he turned his face to the wall and
prayed to the LORD, saying,
3 "[a]Remember now, O LORD, I beseech
You, [b]how I have walked before You in truth
and with a whole heart and have done what
is good in Your sight." And [c]Hezekiah wept
[1]bitterly.
4 Before Isaiah had gone out of the mid-

19:27 *I know.* See Ps 121:8.

19:28 *hook in your nose.* At the top of an Assyrian obelisk an Assyrian king (probably Esarhaddon, 681–669 B.C.) is pictured holding ropes attached to rings in the noses of four of his enemies. Here Isaiah portrays the same thing happening to Sennacherib (see note on Is 37:29; cf. Ezek 38:4; Amos 4:2).

19:29 *you will eat this year what grows of itself.* Sennacherib had apparently either destroyed or confiscated the entire harvest that had been sown the previous fall. The people would only have use of the later, second growth that came from seeds dropped from the previous year's harvest (see Lev 25:5). This suggests that Sennacherib came to Judah in March or April about the time of harvest. *the second year what springs from the same.* Sennacherib's departure would be too late in the fall (October) for new crops to be planted for the coming year. In the Holy Land crops are normally sown in September and October. *in the third year sow, reap.* The routine times for sowing and harvesting could be observed in the following year. The third year is likely a reference to the third year of harvests detrimentally affected by the Assyrian presence.

19:30–31 *remnant.* See note on v. 4. For use of the term "remnant" as a designation for those who will participate in the future unfolding of God's redemptive program see Is 11:11,16; 28:5; Mic 4:7; Rom 11:5.

19:32 *not come to this city.* Sennacherib, who was presently at Libnah (see v. 8; see also note on 8:22), would not be able to carry out his threats against Jerusalem (see note on 18:13).

19:34 *for My servant David's sake.* See note on 1 Kin 11:13.

19:35 *angel of the LORD.* See note on Gen 16:7. *185,000.* See Is 37:36.

19:36 *Nineveh.* The capital of the Assyrian empire.

19:37 *Nisroch.* The name of this deity does not appear in preserved Assyrian records. *his sons Adrammelech and Sharezer.* Ancient records refer to the murder of Sennacherib by an unnamed son on the 20th of the month of Tebet in the 23rd year of Sennacherib's reign. *Ararat.* See note on Gen 8:4. *Esarhaddon his son became king in his place.* And reigned 681–669 B.C. Assyrian inscriptions speak of a struggle among Sennacherib's sons for the right of succession to the Assyrian throne. Sennacherib's designation of Esarhaddon as heir apparent, even though he was younger than several of his brothers, may have sparked the abortive attempt at a coup by Adrammelech and Sharezer.

20:1 *In those days.* Hezekiah's illness (vv. 1–11) as well as his reception of envoys from Babylon (vv. 12–19) must have preceded the Assyrian campaign in 701 B.C. (see v. 6; see also notes on vv. 12–13). Babylonian records indicate that Merodach-baladan (v. 12) died in Elam after being expelled from Babylon in 703. *Set your house in order.* Arrangements of a testamentary nature needed to be made, especially with respect to throne succession. *you shall die.* Assuming that Hezekiah was 25 years old in 715 when he began his sole reign (see 18:2) and that his illness occurred a little more than 15 years prior to his death (see note on v. 6), he would have been about 37 or 38 years old at this time.

20:3 *walked before You in truth . . . and have done what is good.* Hezekiah's prayer is not an appeal for divine favor that is based on good works, but it expresses the realization that the Lord graciously favors those who earnestly serve Him (see note on 2 Sam 22:21).

dle court, the word of the LORD came to him,
saying,
5 "Return and say to [a]Hezekiah the leader
of My people, 'Thus says the LORD, the God
of your father David, "[b]I have heard your
prayer, [c]I have seen your tears; behold, I will
heal you. On the third day you shall go up to
the house of the LORD.
6 "I will add fifteen years to your [1]life, and
I will deliver you and this city from the hand
of the king of Assyria; and [a]I will defend this
city for My own sake and for My servant
David's sake." ' "
7 Then Isaiah said, "Take a cake of figs."
And they took and laid *it* on the boil, and he
recovered.
8 Now Hezekiah said to Isaiah, "What
will be the sign that the LORD will heal me,
and that I shall go up to the house of the
LORD the third day?"
9 Isaiah said, "[a]This shall be the sign
to you from the LORD, that the LORD will do
the thing that He has spoken: shall the
shadow go forward ten steps or go back ten
steps?"
10 So Hezekiah [1]answered, "It is easy for
the shadow to decline ten steps; no, but let
the shadow turn backward ten steps."
11 Isaiah the prophet cried to the LORD,
and [a]He brought the shadow on the [1]stair-
way back ten steps by which it had gone
down on the [1]stairway of Ahaz.

Hezekiah Shows Babylon His Treasures

12 [a]At that time [1]Berodach-baladan a son
of Baladan, king of Babylon, sent letters and
a present to Hezekiah, for he heard that Hezekiah had been sick.
13 Hezekiah listened to them, and showed
them [a]all his treasure house, the silver and
the gold and the spices and the precious oil
and the house of his armor and all that was
found in his treasuries. There was nothing in
his house nor in all his dominion that Hezekiah did not show them.
14 Then Isaiah the prophet came to King
Hezekiah and said to him, "What did these
men say, and from where have they come to
you?" And Hezekiah said, "They have come
from a far country, from Babylon."
15 He said, "What have they seen in your
house?" So Hezekiah [1]answered, "They have
seen all that is in my house; there is nothing
among my treasures that I have not shown
them."
16 Then Isaiah said to Hezekiah, "Hear
the word of the LORD.
17 'Behold, the days are coming when [a]all
that is in your house, and all that your
fathers have laid up in store to this day will
be carried to Babylon; nothing shall be left,'
says the LORD.
18 'Some [a]of your sons who shall issue
from you, whom you will beget, will be tak-
en away; and they will become [b]officials in
the palace of the king of Babylon.' "
19 Then Hezekiah said to Isaiah, "The
word of the LORD which you have spoken is
[a]good." For he [1]thought, "Is it not so, if there
will be peace and truth in my days?"
20 [a]Now the rest of the acts of Hezekiah
and all his might, and how he [b]made the

5 [a]1 Sam 9:16; 10:1 [b]2 Kin 19:20 [c]Ps 39:12
6 [1]Lit *days* [a]2 Kin 19:34
9 [a]Is 38:7
10 [1]Lit *said*
11 [1]Lit *steps* [a]Josh 10:12-14; Is 38:8
12 [1]Many mss and ancient versions read *Merodach-baladan;* cf Is 39:1 [a]2 Chr 32:31; Is 39:1-8
13 [a]2 Chr 32:27
15 [1]Lit *said*
17 [a]2 Kin 24:13; 25:13-15; 2 Chr 36:10; Jer 52:17-19
18 [a]2 Kin 24:12; 2 Chr 33:11 [b]Dan 1:3-7
19 [1]Lit *said* [a]1 Sam 3:18
20 [a]2 Chr 32:32 [b]Neh 3:16

20:5 *I will heal you.* God is the one who sovereignly ordains all that comes to pass (Ps 139:16; Eph 1:11). Hezekiah's petition and God's response demonstrate that (1) divine sovereignty does not make prayer inappropriate but, on the contrary, it establishes it, and (2) both prayer and the divine response to prayer are to be included in one's conception of God's sovereign plan (see 1 Kin 21:29; Ezek 33:13–16).
20:6 *add fifteen years to your life.* Hezekiah died in 686 B.C. The beginning of the extension of his life is thus to be placed no later than 702. *for My own sake and for My servant David's sake.* See 19:34; see also note on 1 Kin 11:13.
20:7 *cake.* The Lord healed Hezekiah (see v. 5), but divine healing does not necessarily exclude the use of known remedies.
20:9 *steps.* See v. 11 (see also note on Is 38:8).
20:12 *Berodach-baladan.* Or, as in NASB marg., "Merodach-baladan." The name means "(The god) Marduk has given me a son." He ruled in Babylon 721–710 B.C. before being forced to submit to Assyrian domination by Sargon II of Assyria. Sometime after Sargon's death in 705, Berodach-baladan briefly reestablished Babylonian independence and ruled in Babylon until Sennacherib forced him to flee in 703 (see note on v. 1). *sent letters and a present to Hezekiah.* See 2 Chr 32:31; Is 39. It is likely that Berodach-baladan was attempting to draw Hezekiah into an alliance against Assyria. Although Hezekiah rejected the pro-Assyrian policies of his father Ahaz (see 16:7) and rebelled against Assyria (see 18:7), he erred in seeking to strengthen Israel's security by friendship with Babylon and Egypt (see 2 Chr 32:31; Is 30–31; see also notes on 1 Sam 17:11; 1 Kin 15:19).
20:13 *listened to them, and showed them all.* Hezekiah's reception of the delegation from Babylon was overly hospitable. Perhaps it was an attempt to bolster Judah's security by impressing the Babylonians with the wealth and power of his kingdom as a basis for mutual cooperation against the Assyrians. In principle this was a denial of the covenantal nature of the royal office in Israel (see note on 2 Sam 24:1). *silver . . . oil.* The presence of these treasures in Jerusalem is evidence that this incident occurred before the payment of tribute to Sennacherib in 701 B.C. (see 18:15–16).
20:14 *What did these men say . . . ?* Hezekiah gave no response to Isaiah's question concerning the diplomatic purpose of the Babylonian envoys.
20:17 *carried to Babylon.* Hezekiah's reception of the Babylonians would bring the exact opposite of what he desired and expected. Isaiah's prediction of Babylonian exile at least 115 years before it happened is all the more remarkable because, when he spoke, it appeared that Assyria rather than Babylon was the world power from whom Judah had the most to fear.
20:18 *Some of your sons . . . will be taken away.* Hezekiah's own son Manasseh was taken by the Assyrians and held prisoner for a while in Babylon (see 2 Chr 33:11); later, many more from the house of David were to follow (see 24:15; 25:7; Dan 1:3).
20:19 *word . . . is good.* Although it is possible to understand Hezekiah's statement as a selfish expression of relief that he himself would not experience the announced adversity, it seems better to take it as a humble acceptance of the Lord's judgment (see 2 Chr 32:26) and as gratefulness for the intervening time of peace that the Lord in His mercy was granting to His people.

pool and the conduit and brought water into
the city, are they not written in the Book of
the Chronicles of the Kings of Judah?
21 [a]So Hezekiah slept with his fathers,
and Manasseh his son became king in his
place.

Manasseh Succeeds Hezekiah

21 [a]Manasseh was twelve years old when
he became king, and he reigned fifty-
five years in Jerusalem; and his mother's
name was Hephzibah.
2 [a]He did evil in the sight of the LORD,
[b]according to the abominations of the
nations whom the LORD dispossessed before
the sons of Israel.
3 For [a]he rebuilt the high places which
Hezekiah his father had destroyed; and [b]he
erected altars for Baal and made an [1]Ashe-
rah, as Ahab king of Israel had done, and
[c]worshiped all the host of heaven and served
them.
4 [a]He built altars in the house of the
LORD, of which the LORD had said, "[b]In
Jerusalem I will put My name."
5 For he built altars for [a]all the host of
heaven in [b]the two courts of the house of the
LORD.
6 [a]He made his son pass through the fire,
[b]practiced witchcraft and used divination,
and dealt with mediums and spiritists. He
did much evil in the sight of the LORD provoking *Him to anger.*
7 Then [a]he set the carved image of Asherah that he had made, in the house of which
the LORD said to David and to his son
Solomon, "[b]In this house and in Jerusalem,
which I have chosen from all the tribes of
Israel, I will put My name forever.
8 "And I [a]will not make the feet of Israel
wander anymore from the land which I gave
their fathers, if only they will observe to do
according to all that I have commanded
them, and according to all the law that My
servant Moses commanded them."
9 But they did not listen, and Manasseh
[a]seduced them to do evil more than the
nations whom the LORD destroyed before the
sons of Israel.

The King's Idolatries Rebuked

10 Now the LORD spoke through His servants the prophets, saying,
11 "[a]Because Manasseh king of Judah has
done these abominations, [b]having done
wickedly more than all the Amorites did who
were before him, and [c]has also made Judah
sin [d]with his idols;
12 therefore thus says the LORD, the God of
Israel, 'Behold, I am bringing *such* calamity
on Jerusalem and Judah, that whoever hears
of it, [a]both his ears will tingle.
13 '[a]I will stretch over Jerusalem the line
of Samaria and the plummet of the house of
Ahab, and I will wipe Jerusalem as one
wipes a dish, wiping it and turning it upside
down.
14 'I will abandon the remnant of My
inheritance and deliver them into the hand
of their enemies, and they will become as
plunder and spoil to all their enemies;
15 because they have done evil in My
sight, and have been provoking Me to anger
since the day their fathers came from Egypt,
even to this day.' "
16 [a]Moreover, Manasseh shed very much
innocent blood until he had filled Jerusalem
from one end to another; besides his sin

21 [a]2 Chr 32:33 **21:1** [a]2 Chr 33:1-9 **2** [a]Jer 15:4 [b]2 Kin 16:3 **3** [1]I.e. a wooden symbol of a female deity [a]2 Kin 18:4 [b]1 Kin 16:31-33 [c]Deut 17:2-5; 2 Kin 17:16; 23:5 **4** [a]2 Kin 16:10-16 [b]2 Sam 7:13; 1 Kin 8:29 **5** [a]2 Kin 23:4, 5 [b]1 Kin 7:12; 2 Kin 23:12 **6** [a]Lev 18:21; 2 Kin 16:3; 17:17 [b]Lev 19:26, 31; Deut 18:10-14 **7** [a]Deut 16:21; 2 Kin 23:6 [b]1 Kin 8:29; 9:3; 2 Chr 7:12, 16

8 [a]2 Sam 7:10; 2 Kin 18:11, 12 **9** [a]Prov 29:12 **11** [a]2 Kin 21:2; 24:3, 4 [b]Gen 15:16; 1 Kin 21:26 [c]2 Kin 21:16 [d]2 Kin 21:21 **12** [a]1 Sam 3:11; Jer 19:3 **13** [a]Is 34:11; Amos 7:7, 8 **16** [a]2 Kin 24:4

20:20 *the pool and the conduit.* Hezekiah built a tunnel from the Gihon spring (see 1 Kin 1:33,38) to a cistern (2 Chr 32:30) inside the city's walls (see diagram No. 8 at the end of the study Bible). This greatly reduced Jerusalem's vulnerability to siege by guaranteeing a continuing water supply. In 1880 an inscription (the Siloam inscription; see chart, p. xix) was found in the rock wall at the entrance to this tunnel, describing the method of its construction. The tunnel, cut through solid rock, is over 1,700 feet long; its height varies from 3 2/3 feet to 11 1/2 feet and it averages 2 feet in width. *Chronicles of the Kings of Judah.* See note on 1 Kin 14:29.

20:21 *slept with his fathers.* See note on 1 Kin 1:21.

21:1 *twelve years old.* Manasseh was born after Hezekiah's serious illness (see 20:6). *fifty-five years.* 697–642 B.C., including a ten-year co-regency (697–686) with his father Hezekiah. This was the longest reign of any king in either Israel or Judah.

21:2 *abominations.* Manasseh reversed the religious policies of his father Hezekiah (see 18:3–5) and reverted to those of Ahaz (see 16:3).

21:3 *high places . . . Hezekiah . . . had destroyed.* See note on 18:4; see also 2 Chr 31:1. *Asherah.* See 1 Kin 14:15,23; 15:13; 16:33. *as Ahab.* Manasseh was the Ahab of Judah (see 1 Kin 16:30–33). *worshiped all the host of heaven.* See note on 17:16.

21:4 *In Jerusalem I will put My name.* See 1 Kin 8:20,29; 9:3.

21:6 *made his son pass through the fire.* See note on 16:3; see also 17:17. *practiced witchcraft and used divination.* See notes on 16:15; 17:17. *dealt with mediums and spiritists.* See Lev 19:31; Deut 18:11; 1 Sam 28:3,7–9 and notes.

21:7 *carved image of Asherah.* See note on 1 Kin 14:15. *David.* See 2 Sam 7:13. *Solomon.* See 1 Kin 9:3. *chosen from all the tribes.* See 1 Kin 11:13,32,36.

21:9 *nations whom the LORD destroyed.* See 1 Kin 14:24; Deut 12:29–31; 31:3.

21:10 *His servants the prophets.* See 2 Chr 33:10,18.

21:11 *done wickedly more than all the Amorites.* See note on 1 Kin 21:26.

21:12 *whoever hears of it, both his ears will tingle.* See Jer 19:3.

21:13 *line . . . plummet.* Instruments normally associated with construction are used here as symbols of destruction (see Is 34:11; Amos 7:7–9,17).

21:14 *I will abandon.* In the sense of giving over to judgment (see Jer 12:7), not in the sense of abrogation of the covenant (see 1 Sam 12:22; Is 43:1–7). *remnant of My inheritance.* Upon the destruction of the northern kingdom, Judah had become the remnant of the Lord's inheritance (see 1 Kin 8:51; Deut 4:20; 1 Sam 10:1; Ps 28:9; see also note on 2 Kin 19:4).

21:15 The history of Israel was a history of covenant breaking. With the reign of Manasseh the cup of God's wrath overflowed, and the judgment of exile from the land of promise (see note on 17:7–23) became inevitable (see 24:1–4).

21:16 *innocent blood.* A reference to godly people and perhaps even prophets who were martyred for opposition to

[b]with which he made Judah sin, in doing evil in the sight of the LORD.

17 [a]Now the rest of the acts of Manasseh and all that he did and his sin which he [1]committed, are they not written in the Book of the Chronicles of the Kings of Judah?

18 [a]And Manasseh slept with his fathers and was buried in the garden of his own house, [b]in the garden of Uzza, and Amon his son became king in his place.

Amon Succeeds Manasseh

19 [a]Amon was twenty-two years old when he became king, and he reigned two years in Jerusalem; and his mother's name *was* Meshullemeth the daughter of Haruz of Jotbah.

20 He did evil in the sight of the LORD, [a]as Manasseh his father had done.

21 For he walked in all the way that his father had walked, and served the idols that his father had served and worshiped them.

22 So [a]he forsook the LORD, the God of his fathers, and did not walk in the way of the LORD.

23 [a]The servants of Amon conspired against him and killed the king in his own house.

24 Then [a]the people of the land [1]killed all those who had conspired against King Amon, and the people of the land made Josiah his son king in his place.

25 Now the rest of the acts of Amon which he did, are they not written in the Book of the Chronicles of the Kings of Judah?

26 He was buried in his grave [a]in the garden of Uzza, and Josiah his son became king in his place.

16 [b]2 Kin 21:11
17 [1]Lit *sinned* [a]2 Chr 33:11-19
18 [a]2 Chr 33:20 [b]2 Kin 21:26
19 [a]2 Chr 33:21-23
20 [a]2 Kin 21:2-6, 11, 16
22 [a]2 Kin 22:17; 1 Chr 28:9
23 [a]2 Kin 12:20; 14:19
24 [1]Lit *smote* [a]2 Kin 14:5
26 [a]2 Kin 21:18

22:1 [a]2 Chr 34:1 [b]Josh 15:39
2 [a]Deut 5:32; Josh 1:7
3 [a]2 Chr 34:8
4 [1]Or *total* [a]2 Kin 12:4, 9, 10
5 [1]Lit *breach* [a]2 Kin 12:11-14
7 [a]2 Kin 12:15; 1 Cor 4:2
8 [a]Deut 31:24-26; 2 Chr 34:14, 15

Josiah Succeeds Amon

22 [a]Josiah was eight years old when he became king, and he reigned thirty-one years in Jerusalem; and his mother's name *was* Jedidah the daughter of Adaiah of [b]Bozkath.

2 He did right in the sight of the LORD and walked in all the way of his father David, nor did he [a]turn aside to the right or to the left.

3 Now [a]in the eighteenth year of King Josiah, the king sent Shaphan, the son of Azaliah the son of Meshullam the scribe, to the house of the LORD saying,

4 "[a]Go up to Hilkiah the high priest that he may [1]count the money brought in to the house of the LORD which the doorkeepers have gathered from the people.

5 "[a]Let them deliver it into the hand of the workmen who have the oversight of the house of the LORD, and let them give it to the workmen who are in the house of the LORD to repair the [1]damages of the house,

6 to the carpenters and the builders and the masons and for buying timber and hewn stone to repair the house.

7 "Only [a]no accounting shall be made with them for the money delivered into their hands, for they deal faithfully."

The Lost Book

8 Then Hilkiah the high priest said to Shaphan the scribe, "[a]I have found the book of the law in the house of the LORD." And Hilkiah gave the book to Shaphan who read it.

9 Shaphan the scribe came to the king and brought back word to the king and said, "Your servants have emptied out the money

---

Manasseh's evil practices (see vv. 10–11). According to a Jewish tradition (not otherwise substantiated) Isaiah was sawed in two during Manasseh's reign (cf. Heb 11:37).

21:17 *rest of the acts of Manasseh.* See 2 Chr 33:12–19. *Chronicles of the Kings of Judah.* See note on 1 Kin 14:29.

21:18 *slept with his fathers.* See note on 1 Kin 1:21. *Uzza.* Probably a shortened form of Uzziah (see 14:21–22 and 15:1–7, Azariah; 2 Chr 26, Uzziah).

21:19 *two years.* 642–640 B.C. *Jotbah.* Some identify it with the Jotbathah of Num 33:33–34 and Deut 10:7, near Eziongeber. Others, including the church father Jerome, have located it in Judah.

21:20 *did evil.* Amon did not share in the change of heart that characterized his father Manasseh in the last days of his life (see 2 Chr 33:12–19). He must have restored the idolatrous practices that Manasseh abolished because these were again in existence in the time of Josiah (see 23:5–7,12).

21:23 *conspired against him.* Whether this palace revolt was motivated by religious or political considerations is not known.

21:24 *people of the land.* The citizenry in general (see 11:14,18; 14:21; 23:30). *killed all those who had conspired against King Amon.* It is not clear whether this counterinsurgency was motivated simply by loyalty to the house of David or by other factors.

21:25 *Chronicles of the Kings of Judah.* See note on 1 Kin 14:29.

21:26 *Uzza.* See note on v. 18.

22:1 *thirty-one years.* 640–609 B.C. (see note on 21:19). *Bozkath.* Located in Judah in the vicinity of Lachish (see Josh 15:39).

22:2 *way of his father David.* See note on 18:3. Josiah was the last godly king of the Davidic line prior to the exile. Jeremiah, who prophesied during the time of Josiah (see Jer 1:2), spoke highly of him (Jer 22:15–16). Zephaniah also prophesied in the early days of his reign (Zeph 1:1).

22:3 *eighteenth year.* 622 B.C. Josiah was then 26 years old (see v. 1). He had begun to serve the Lord faithfully at the age of 16 (the 8th year of his reign, 2 Chr 34:3). When he was 20 years old (the 12th year of his reign, 2 Chr 34:3), he had already begun to purge the land of its idolatrous practices. *the scribe.* Probably refers back to Shaphan (see v. 12). For the duties of such a scribe see note on 2 Sam 8:17. Two additional individuals are mentioned as accompanying Shaphan in 2 Chr 34:8.

22:4 *Hilkiah.* Father of Azariah and grandfather of Seraiah, the high priest executed at the time of the destruction of Jerusalem by the Babylonians (see 25:18–20). It is unlikely that this Hilkiah was also the father of Jeremiah (see Jer 1:1). *money . . . the doorkeepers have gathered.* Josiah used the method devised by Joash for collecting funds for the restoration of the temple (see 12:1–16; 2 Chr 34:9).

22:5 *workmen who have the oversight.* See 2 Chr 34:12–13.

22:8 *book of the law.* Some interpreters hold that this refers to a copy of the entire Pentateuch, while others understand it as a reference to a copy of part or all of Deuteronomy alone (see Deut 31:24,26; 2 Chr 34:14).

that was found in the house, and have delivered it into the hand of the workmen who have the oversight of the house of the LORD."

10 Moreover, Shaphan the scribe told the king saying, "Hilkiah the priest has given me a book." And Shaphan read it in the presence of the king.

11 When the king heard the words of the book of the law, [a]he tore his clothes.

12 Then the king commanded Hilkiah the priest, [a]Ahikam the son of Shaphan, [1][b]Achbor the son of Micaiah, Shaphan the scribe, and Asaiah the king's servant saying,

13 "Go, inquire of the LORD for me and the people and all Judah concerning the words of this book that has been found, for [a]great is the wrath of the LORD that burns against us, because our fathers have not listened to the words of this book, to do according to all that is written concerning us."

Huldah Predicts

14 So Hilkiah the priest, Ahikam, Achbor, Shaphan, and Asaiah went to Huldah the prophetess, the wife of Shallum the son of [1][a]Tikvah, the son of Harhas, keeper of the wardrobe (now she lived in Jerusalem in the [b]Second Quarter); and they spoke to her.

15 She said to them, "Thus says the LORD God of Israel, 'Tell the man who sent you to me,

16 thus says the LORD, "Behold, I [a]bring evil on this place and on its inhabitants, *even* all the words of the book which the king of Judah has read.

17 "[a]Because they have forsaken Me and have burned incense to other gods that they might provoke Me to anger with all the work of their hands, therefore My wrath burns against this place, and it shall not be quenched." '

18 "But to [a]the king of Judah who sent you to inquire of the LORD thus shall you say to him, 'Thus says the LORD God of Israel, "*Regarding* the words which you have heard,

19 [a]because your heart was tender and [b]you humbled yourself before the LORD when you heard what I spoke against this place and against its inhabitants that they should become [c]a desolation and a [d]curse, and you have [e]torn your clothes and wept before Me, I truly have heard you," declares the LORD.

20 "Therefore, behold, I will gather you to your fathers, and [a]you will be gathered to your grave in peace, and your eyes will not see all the evil which I will bring on this place." ' " So they brought back word to the king.

Josiah's Covenant

23 [a]Then the king sent, and they gathered to him all the elders of Judah and of Jerusalem.

2 The king went up to the house of the LORD and all the men of Judah and all the inhabitants of Jerusalem with him, and the priests and the prophets and all the people, both small and great; and [a]he read in their hearing all the words of the book of the covenant [b]which was found in the house of the LORD.

3 [a]The king stood by the pillar and made a covenant before the LORD, [b]to walk after the LORD, and to keep His commandments and His testimonies and His statutes with all *his* heart and all *his* soul, to carry out the words of this covenant that were written in this book. And all the people [1]entered into the covenant.

Reforms under Josiah

4 Then the king commanded Hilkiah the high priest and [a]the priests of the second order and the [1]doorkeepers, [b]to bring out of

11 [a]Gen 37:34; Josh 7:6
12 [1]In 2 Chr 34:20, *Abdon, son of Micah* [a]2 Kin 25:22; Jer 26:24 [b]2 Chr 34:20
13 [a]Deut 29:23-28; 31:17, 18
14 [1]In 2 Chr 34:22, *Tokhath, son of Hasrah* [a]2 Chr 34:22 [b]Zeph 1:10
16 [a]Deut 29:27; Dan 9:11-14
17 [a]Deut 29:25, 26; 2 Kin 21:22
18 [a]2 Chr 34:26
19 [a]1 Sam 24:5; Ps 51:17 [b]Ex 10:3; 1 Kin 21:29 [c]Lev 26:31 [d]Jer 26:6 [e]2 Kin 22:11
20 [a]2 Kin 23:30
23:1 [a]2 Chr 34:29-32
2 [a]Deut 31:10-13 [b]2 Kin 22:8
3 [1]Lit *took a stand in* [a]2 Kin 11:14, 17 [b]Deut 13:4
4 [1]Lit *keepers of the threshold* [a]2 Kin 25:18; Jer 52:24 [b]2 Kin 21:3, 7; 2 Chr 33:3

22:11 *tore his clothes.* See note on 18:37; contrast Josiah's reaction with that of Jehoiakim to the words of the scroll written by Jeremiah (see Jer 36:24). Perhaps the covenant curses of Lev 26 and/or Deut 28, climaxing with the threat of exile, were the statements that especially disturbed Josiah.

22:12 *Ahikam.* Father of Gedaliah, who was later to be appointed governor of Judah by Nebuchadnezzar (see 25:22; Jer 39:14). He was also the protector of Jeremiah when his life was threatened during the reign of Jehoiakim (see Jer 26:24). *Achbor.* His son Elnathan is mentioned in 24:8; Jer 26:22; 36:12. *Shaphan the scribe.* See note on v. 3.

22:14 *Huldah the prophetess.* Why the delegation sought out Huldah rather than Jeremiah or Zephaniah is not known. Perhaps it was merely a matter of her accessibility in Jerusalem. *Shallum . . . keeper of the wardrobe.* Perhaps the same Shallum who was the uncle of Jeremiah (see Jer 32:7). *Second Quarter.* A section of the city probably located in a newly developed area between the first and second walls in the northwest part of Jerusalem (see 2 Chr 33:14; Zeph 1:10).

22:16 *this place.* Jerusalem.

22:19 *your heart was tender.* See v. 11.

22:20 *gather you to your fathers.* See note on 1 Kin 1:21. *you will be gathered to your grave in peace.* This prediction refers to Josiah's death before God's judgment on Jerusalem through Nebuchadnezzar and so is not contradicted by his death in battle with Pharaoh Neco of Egypt (see 23:29–30). Josiah was assured that the final judgment on Judah and Jerusalem would not come in his own days.

23:1 *elders.* See note on 10:1.

23:2 *book of the covenant.* Although this designation is used in Ex 24:7 with reference to the contents of Ex 20–23, it is here applied to either all or part of the book of Deuteronomy or the entire Mosaic law. Whatever else the scroll contained, it clearly included the covenant curses of Lev 26 and/or Deut 28 (see notes on v. 21; 22:8,11).

23:3 *pillar.* See note on 11:14. *made a covenant.* Josiah carries out the function of covenant mediator; cf. Moses (Ex 24:3–8; Deut 1–34), Joshua (Josh 24), Samuel (1 Sam 11:14–12:25) and Jehoiada (2 Kin 11:17). *walk after the LORD.* See notes on 1 Sam 12:14,20. *entered into the covenant.* It is likely that some sort of ratification rite was performed, in which the people participated and pledged by oath to be loyal to their covenant obligations. Whether this was done symbolically (see Jer 34:18) or verbally (see Deut 27:11–26) is not clear.

23:4 *doorkeepers.* See 12:9. *Baal, for Asherah.* See note on 1 Kin 14:15. *host of heaven.* See note on 17:16. *carried their*

the temple of the LORD all the vessels that
were made for Baal, for [2]Asherah, and for all
the host of heaven; and [c]he burned them
outside Jerusalem in the fields of the Kidron,
and carried their ashes to Bethel.
5 He did away with the idolatrous priests
whom the kings of Judah had appointed to
burn incense in the high places in the cities
of Judah and in the surrounding area of
Jerusalem, also those who burned incense to
Baal, to the sun and to the moon and to the
constellations and to all the [a]host of heaven.
6 He brought out the Asherah from the
house of the LORD outside Jerusalem to the
brook Kidron, and burned it at the brook Kidron, and [a]ground *it* to dust, and [b]threw its
dust on the graves of the [1]common people.
7 He also broke down the houses of the
[a]*male* cult prostitutes which *were* in the
house of the LORD, where [b]the women were
weaving [1]hangings for the Asherah.
8 Then he brought all the priests from
the cities of Judah, and defiled the high
places where the priests had burned incense,
from [a]Geba to Beersheba; and he broke
down the high places of the gates which
were at the entrance of the gate of Joshua the
governor of the city, which *were* on one's left
at the city gate.
9 Nevertheless [a]the priests of the high
places did not go up to the altar of the LORD
in Jerusalem, but they ate unleavened bread
among their brothers.
10 [a]He also defiled [1]Topheth, which is in
the valley of the son of Hinnom, [b]that no
man might make his son or his daughter
pass through the fire for [c]Molech.

4 [2]I.e. a wooden symbol of a female deity, and so throughout the ch [c]2 Kin 23:15
5 [a]2 Kin 21:3
6 [1]Lit *sons of the people* [a]2 Kin 23:15 [b]2 Chr 34:4
7 [1]Or *tents;* lit *houses* [a]1 Kin 14:24; 15:12 [b]Ex 35:25, 26; Ezek 16:16
8 [a]Josh 21:17; 1 Kin 15:22
9 [a]Ezek 44:10-14
10 [1]I.e. place of burning [a]Is 30:33; Jer 7:31, 32; 19:4-6 [b]Lev 18:21 [c]1 Kin 11:7
11 [a]Deut 4:19; Job 31:26; Ezek 8:16
12 [1]Or *ran from there* [a]Jer 19:13; Zeph 1:5 [b]2 Kin 21:5; 2 Chr 33:5 [c]2 Kin 23:4, 6
13 [a]1 Kin 11:7 [b]1 Kin 11:5 [c]Num 21:29
14 [a]Deut 7:5, 25 [b]2 Kin 23:16
15 [1]So the Gr; Heb *burned the high place* [a]1 Kin 13:1 [b]1 Kin 12:28-33 [c]2 Kin 23:6
16 [a]1 Kin 13:2

11 He did away with the horses which the
kings of Judah had given to the [a]sun, at the
entrance of the house of the LORD, by the
chamber of Nathan-melech the official,
which *was* in the precincts; and he burned
the chariots of the sun with fire.
12 [a]The altars which *were* on the roof, the
upper chamber of Ahaz, which the kings of
Judah had made, and [b]the altars which
Manasseh had made in the two courts of the
house of the LORD, the king broke down; and
he [1]smashed them there and [c]threw their
dust into the brook Kidron.
13 The high places which *were* before
Jerusalem, which *were* on the right of [a]the
mount of destruction which Solomon the
king of Israel had built for [b]Ashtoreth the
abomination of the Sidonians, and for [c]Che-
mosh the abomination of Moab, and for Milcom the abomination of the sons of Ammon,
the king defiled.
14 [a]He broke in pieces the *sacred* pillars
and cut down the Asherim and [b]filled their
places with human bones.
15 Furthermore, [a]the altar that *was* at Bethel *and* the [b]high place which Jeroboam the
son of Nebat, who made Israel sin, had made,
even that altar and the high place he broke
down. Then he [1c]demolished its stones,
ground them to dust, and burned the Asherah.
16 Now when Josiah turned, he saw the
graves that *were* there on the mountain, and
he sent and took the bones from the graves
and burned *them* on the altar and defiled it
[a]according to the word of the LORD which the
man of God proclaimed, who proclaimed
these things.

ashes to Bethel. See vv. 15–16. Bethel was located just over the border between Judah and the former northern kingdom in territory nominally under Assyrian control. With a decline in Assyrian power, Josiah was able to exert his own influence in the north. He apparently deposited the ashes at Bethel in order to desecrate (see note on v. 14) the very place where golden calf worship had originally polluted the land (see notes on 1 Kin 12:28–30).

23:5 *idolatrous priests.* See Hos 10:5; Zeph 1:4. *kings of Judah.* A reference to Manasseh and Amon, and perhaps to Ahaz before them. *high places.* See note on 18:4.

23:6 *Asherah.* See note on 1 Kin 14:15. The Asherah destroyed by Hezekiah (18:4) was reintroduced by Manasseh (21:7). When Manasseh turned to the Lord, it is likely that he too got rid of the Asherah (see 2 Chr 33:15) and that it was then again reintroduced by Amon (2 Kin 21:21; 2 Chr 33:22). *threw its dust on the graves of the common people.* Intended as a defilement of the goddess, not as a desecration of the graves of the poor (see Jer 26:23).

23:7 *male cult prostitutes.* See note on 1 Kin 14:24.

23:8 *defiled the high places.* See note on 18:4. *Geba to Beersheba.* Geba was on the northern border of the southern kingdom (see 1 Kin 15:22), and Beersheba was on its southern border (see note on 1 Sam 3:20).

23:9 *ate unleavened bread among their brothers.* Although not permitted to serve at the temple altar, these priests were to be sustained by a share of the priestly provisions (see Lev 2:10; 6:16–18). They occupied a status similar to that of priests with physical defects (see Lev 21:16–23).

23:10 *Topheth.* The name of an area in the Valley of Hinnom where altars used for child sacrifice were located (see Is 30:33; Jer 7:31; 19:5–6). *make his son or his daughter pass through the fire.* See 17:17; 21:6; see also note on 16:3. *Molech.* See note on 1 Kin 11:5.

23:11 *horses . . . given to the sun.* If live, the horses may have been used to pull chariots bearing images of a sun-god in religious processions. Small images of horses have recently been found in a cult place just outside one of the ancient walls of Jerusalem. *Nathan-melech.* Perhaps the official in charge of the chariots.

23:12 *altars . . . on the roof.* Altars dedicated to the worship of all the starry hosts (see Jer 19:13; Zeph 1:5)—erected by Ahaz (2 Kin 16:3–4,10–16), Manasseh (21:3) and Amon (21:21–22).

23:13 *high places . . . Solomon . . . had built.* See note on 1 Kin 11:5.

23:14 *filled their places with human bones.* The bones would defile these sites and make them unsuitable for cultic use in the future (see Num 19:16).

23:15 *altar that was at Bethel.* See 1 Kin 12:32–33. Nothing is said of the golden calf, which undoubtedly had been sent to Assyria as tribute at the time of the captivity of the northern kingdom (see Hos 10:5–6).

23:16 *graves.* Of the priests of the Bethel sanctuary (see 1 Kin 13:2). *burned them on the altar and defiled it.* See notes on vv. 6,14. *the man of God . . . who proclaimed these things.* See 1 Kin 13:1–2,32.

17 Then he said, "What is this monument
that I see?" And the men of the city told him,
"[a]It is the grave of the man of God who came
from Judah and proclaimed these things
which you have done against the altar of
Bethel."
18 He said, "Let him alone; let no one disturb his bones." So they [1]left his bones
undisturbed [a]with the bones of the prophet
who came from Samaria.
19 Josiah also removed all the houses of
the high places which *were* [a]in the cities of
Samaria, which the kings of Israel had made
provoking [1]the LORD; and he did to them
[2]just as he had done in Bethel.
20 All the priests of the high places who
were there [a]he slaughtered on the altars and
burned human bones on them; then he
returned to Jerusalem.

Passover Reinstituted

21 Then the king commanded all the people saying, "[a]Celebrate the Passover to the
LORD your God [b]as it is written in this book
of the covenant."
22 [a]Surely such a Passover had not been
celebrated from the days of the judges who
judged Israel, nor in all the days of the kings
of Israel and of the kings of Judah.
23 But in the eighteenth year of King Josiah, this Passover was observed to the LORD in
Jerusalem.
24 Moreover, Josiah [1]removed [a]the mediums and the spiritists and the [b]teraphim and
[c]the idols and all the abominations that were

17 [a]1 Kin 13:1, 30, 31 **18** [1]Lit *let his bones escape with* [a]1 Kin 13:11, 31 **19** [1]So with ancient versions [2]Lit *according to all the acts* [a]2 Chr 34:6, 7 **20** [a]2 Kin 10:25; 11:18 **21** [a]2 Chr 35:1-17 [b]Num 9:2-4; Deut 16:2-8 **22** [a]2 Chr 35:18, 19 **24** [1]Lit *consumed* [a]Lev 19:31; 2 Kin 21:6 [b]Gen 31:19 mg [c]2 Kin 21:11, 21

seen in the land of Judah and in Jerusalem,
[d]that he might [2]confirm the words of the law
which were written [e]in the book that Hilkiah
the priest found in the house of the LORD.
25 Before him there was no king [a]like him
who turned to the LORD with all his heart and
with all his soul and with all his might,
according to all the law of Moses; nor did
any like him arise after him.
26 However, the LORD did not turn from
the fierceness of His great wrath with which
His anger burned against Judah, [a]because of
all the provocations with which Manasseh
had provoked Him.
27 The LORD said, "I will remove Judah
also from My sight, [a]as I have removed Israel. And [b]I will cast off Jerusalem, this city
which I have chosen, and the [1]temple of
which I said, 'My name shall be there.' "

Jehoahaz Succeeds Josiah

28 Now the rest of the acts of Josiah and
all that he did, are they not written in the
Book of the Chronicles of the Kings of
Judah?
29 [a]In his days [b]Pharaoh Neco king of
Egypt went up to the king of Assyria to the
river Euphrates. And King Josiah went to
meet him, and when *Pharaoh Neco* saw him
he killed him at [c]Megiddo.
30 [a]His servants drove [1]his body in a chariot from Megiddo, and brought him to
Jerusalem and buried him in his own tomb.
[b]Then the people of the land took Jehoahaz
the son of Josiah and anointed him and

24 [2]Or *perform* [d]Deut 18:10-22 [e]2 Kin 22:8 **25** [a]2 Kin 18:5 **26** [a]2 Kin 21:11-13; Jer 15:4 **27** [1]Lit *house* [a]2 Kin 18:11 [b]2 Kin 21:13, 14 **29** [a]2 Chr 35:20-24 [b]Jer 46:2 [c]Judg 5:19 **30** [1]Lit *him, dead* [a]2 Kin 9:28 [b]2 Chr 36:1-4

23:18 *prophet who came from Samaria.* See 1 Kin 13:31–32. Samaria is here not to be understood as the city by that name since the prophet came from Bethel (see 1 Kin 13:11), and the city Samaria did not yet exist (see 1 Kin 16:24). Rather, it is to be taken as a designation for the entire area of the former northern kingdom (see notes on 17:24,29; 1 Kin 13:32).

23:20 *All the priests of the high places . . . he slaughtered.* These were non-Levitical priests of the apostate worship practiced in the area of the former northern kingdom (see notes on 17:27–28,33–34). They were treated like the pagan priests of Judah (see v. 5) in contrast to Josiah's treatment of the priests at the high places in Judah (see vv. 8–9). Josiah's actions in this matter conformed to the requirements of Deut 13; 17:2–7.

23:21 *Celebrate the Passover.* A more complete description of this observance is found in 2 Chr 35:1–19. *as it is written in this book of the covenant.* See note on v. 2. This appears to refer to Deut 16:1–8, where the Passover is described in a communal setting at a sanctuary (see Ex 23:15–17; 34:23–24; Lev 23:4–14) rather than in the family setting of Ex 12:1–14,43–49.

23:22 The uniqueness of Josiah's Passover celebration seems to be in the fact that all the Passover lambs were slaughtered exclusively by the Levites (see 2 Chr 35:1–19; cf. 2 Chr 30:2–3,17–20 for the Passover observed in the time of Hezekiah).

23:23 *eighteenth year.* See note on 22:3.

23:24 *teraphim.* See note on Gen 31:19. *words of the law.* See notes on v. 2; 22:8.

23:25 *no king like him.* See note on 18:5. *with all his heart . . . soul and . . . might.* See Dt 6:5.

23:26 *However, the LORD did not turn from the fierceness of His great wrath.* The judgment against Judah and Jerusalem was postponed but not rescinded because of Josiah's reformation (see notes on 21:15; 22:20).

23:27 *as I have removed Israel.* See 17:18–23. *Jerusalem, this city which I have chosen.* See 21:4,7,13. *the temple of which I said, 'My name shall be there.'* See note on 1 Kin 8:16.

23:28 *Chronicles of the Kings of Judah.* See note on 1 Kin 14:29.

23:29 *Pharaoh Neco king of Egypt.* Ruled 610–595 B.C. *went up to the king of Assyria.* Pharaoh Neco intended to help Ashur-uballit II, the last Assyrian king, in his struggle against the rising power of Babylon under Nabopolassar. The Assyrian capital, Nineveh, had already fallen to the Babylonians and Medes in 612 (see the book of Nahum). The remaining Assyrian forces had regrouped at Haran, but in 609 they were forced west of the Euphrates. It appears to be at this time that the Egyptians under Neco were coming to the Assyrians' aid. *King Josiah went to meet him.* Perhaps Josiah opposed the passage of Neco's army through the pass at Megiddo (see 2 Chr 35:20–24) because he feared that the growth of either Egyptian or Assyrian power would have adverse results for the continued independence of Judah.

23:30 *buried him in his own tomb.* See 2 Chr 35:24–25. *people of the land.* See note on 21:24. *Jehoahaz the son of Josiah.* Jehoahaz's name was originally Shallum (see 1 Chr 3:15; Jer 22:11), which was probably changed to Jehoahaz at the time of his accession to the throne. Perhaps Jehoahaz was chosen by the people over Jehoiakim because it was known that Jehoiakim favored a pro-Egyptian policy instead of the anti-Egyptian policy of Josiah and Jehoahaz. *anointed him.* See note on 1 Sam 9:16.

made him king in place of his father.
31 [a]Jehoahaz was twenty-three years old
when he became king, and he reigned three
months in Jerusalem; and his mother's name
was [b]Hamutal the daughter of Jeremiah of
Libnah.
32 He did evil in the sight of the LORD,
[a]according to all that his fathers had done.
33 [a]Pharaoh Neco imprisoned him at
[b]Riblah in the land of [c]Hamath, that he
might not reign in Jerusalem; and he
imposed on the land a fine of one hundred
talents of silver and a talent of gold.

Jehoiakim Made King by Pharaoh

34 Pharaoh Neco made [a]Eliakim the son
of Josiah king in the place of Josiah his
father, and [b]changed his name to Jehoiakim.
But he took Jehoahaz away and [1c]brought
him to Egypt, and he died there.
35 So Jehoiakim [a]gave the silver and gold
to Pharaoh, but he taxed the land in order to
give the money at the [1]command of Pharaoh.
He exacted the silver and gold from the
people of the land, each according to his valuation,
to give it to Pharaoh Neco.
36 [a]Jehoiakim was twenty-five years old
when he became king, and he reigned eleven
years in Jerusalem; and his mother's name
was Zebidah the daughter of Pedaiah of
Rumah.

31 [a]1 Chr 3:15; Jer 22:11 [b]2 Kin 24:18
32 [a]2 Kin 21:2-7
33 [a]2 Kin 23:29 [b]2 Kin 25:6 [c]1 Kin 8:65
34 [1]So with Gr; Heb *he came* [a]1 Chr 3:15 [b]2 Kin 24:17; 2 Chr 36:4 [c]Jer 22:11, 12; Ezek 19:3, 4
35 [1]Lit *mouth* [a]2 Kin 23:33
36 [a]2 Chr 36:5; Jer 22:18, 19; 26:1
37 [a]2 Kin 23:32
24:1 [a]2 Chr 36:6; Jer 25:1; Dan 1:1, 2
2 [a]Jer 35:11f [b]2 Kin 6:23 [c]2 Kin 13:20 [d]2 Kin 23:27
3 [1]Lit *mouth* [a]2 Kin 18:25 [b]2 Kin 23:26
4 [a]2 Kin 21:16
6 [a]Jer 22:18, 19

37 He did evil in the sight of the LORD,
[a]according to all that his fathers had done.

Babylon Controls Jehoiakim

24 [a]In his days Nebuchadnezzar king of
Babylon came up, and Jehoiakim
became his servant *for* three years; then he
turned and rebelled against him.
2 The LORD sent against him [a]bands of
Chaldeans, [b]bands of Arameans, [c]bands of
Moabites, and bands of Ammonites. So He
sent them against Judah to destroy it,
[d]according to the word of the LORD which He
had spoken through His servants the prophets.
3 [a]Surely at the [1]command of the LORD it
came upon Judah, to remove *them* from His
sight [b]because of the sins of Manasseh,
according to all that he had done,
4 and [a]also for the innocent blood which
he shed, for he filled Jerusalem with innocent
blood; and the LORD would not forgive.
5 Now the rest of the acts of Jehoiakim
and all that he did, are they not written in
the Book of the Chronicles of the Kings of
Judah?

Jehoiachin Reigns

6 So [a]Jehoiakim slept with his fathers,
and Jehoiachin his son became king in his
place.

23:31 *three months.* In 609 B.C. *Jeremiah.* Not the prophet (see Jer 1:1). *Libnah.* See note on 8:22.

23:32 *evil . . . according to . . . his fathers.* See 16:3; 21:2,21; Ezek 19:3.

23:33 *imprisoned him at Riblah.* By either deception or overt force the Egyptians were able to take Jehoahaz captive and impose tribute on Judah (see 2 Chr 36:3). Jehoahaz was imprisoned at Neco's military headquarters established at Riblah on the Orontes River. Nebuchadnezzar was later to make his headquarters at the same place (see 25:6,20).

23:34 *Eliakim the son of Josiah.* Eliakim was an older brother of Jehoahaz (see 1 Chr 3:15). Perhaps he had been bypassed earlier as a successor to Josiah because of a pro-Egyptian political stance. *changed his name to Jehoiakim.* The meaning of these two names is similar (Eliakim, "God has established"; Jehoiakim, "Yahweh has established"). Perhaps Neco wanted to use the name change to imply that his actions were sanctioned by Yahweh, the God of Judah (see 18:25; 2 Chr 35:21). In any case, the change in name indicated that Jehoiakim was subject to Neco's authority. *took Jehoahaz . . . to Egypt, and he died there.* See 2 Chr 36:4; Jer 22:10–12.

23:35 *from the people of the land.* The tribute for Neco was raised by a graduated tax placed on the very people who had supported the kingship of Jehoahaz (see v. 30). Menahem of the northern kingdom had used a similar method of raising funds for tribute (see 15:20).

23:36 *eleven years.* 609–598 B.C.

23:37 *did evil in the sight of the LORD.* Jehoiakim was responsible for the murder of the prophet Uriah from Kiriath-jearim (Jer 26:20–24), and his rule was characterized by dishonesty, oppression and injustice (see Jer 22:13–19). He reintroduced idolatrous worship in the temple (see Ezek 8:5–17) and refused to accept the word of the Lord through Jeremiah (see Jer 36). *his fathers.* Manasseh (21:1–18) and Amon (21:19–26).

24:1 *Nebuchadnezzar.* Means "O (god) Nabu, protect my son!" He was the son of Nabopolassar (see note on 23:29) and the most powerful king of the Neo-Babylonian empire (612–539 B.C.), reigning 605–562 (see Dan 1–4). *came up.* In 605 Nebuchadnezzar, the crown prince and commander of the Babylonian army, defeated Pharaoh Neco and the Egyptians at the battle of Carchemish and again at Hamath (see 23:29; Jer 46:2). These victories had far-reaching implications in the geopolitical power structure of the eastern Mediterranean world. Nebuchadnezzar went on to conquer all of the "Hatti-country," which, according to Babylonian records, included the "city of Judah." Daniel was among the Judahite hostages taken at this time (see Dan 1:1). Perhaps as early as Sept. 6, 605, Nebuchadnezzar acceded to the Babylonian throne upon the death of his father. *three years.* Probably 604–602. In 604 Nebuchadnezzar returned to the west and took tribute from "all the kings of Hatti-land." It is likely that Jehoiakim was included among these kings. *turned and rebelled.* In 601 Nebuchadnezzar again marched west against Egypt and was repulsed by strong Egyptian resistance. This may have encouraged Jehoiakim's rebellion, even though Jeremiah had warned against it (see Jer 27:9–11).

24:2 *The LORD sent against him . . . Chaldeans . . . Arameans . . . Moabites . . . Ammonites.* Reaction to Jehoiakim's rebellion was swift. Babylonian (Chaldean) troops, perhaps garrisoned in Aram, along with troops of other loyal vassals, were sent to put down the Judahite rebellion.

24:3 *sins of Manasseh.* See 21:11–12; 23:26–27; Jer 15:3–4.

24:4 *innocent blood.* See note on 21:16. *would not forgive.* See 22:17.

24:5 *Chronicles of the Kings of Judah.* See note on 1 Kin 14:29.

24:6 *slept with his fathers.* See note on 1 Kin 1:21. Jehoiakim died shortly before Jerusalem fell to the Babylonian siege (see vv. 8–12). Whether his death was due to natural causes or political intrigue is not indicated.

7 [a]The king of Egypt did not come out of his land again, [b]for the king of Babylon had taken all that belonged to the king of Egypt from [c]the brook of Egypt to the river Euphrates.

8 [a]Jehoiachin was [b]eighteen years old when he became king, and he reigned three months in Jerusalem; and his mother's name *was* Nehushta the daughter of Elnathan of Jerusalem.

9 He did evil in the sight of the LORD, [a]according to all that his father had done.

Deportation to Babylon

10 At that time the servants of Nebuchadnezzar king of Babylon went up to Jerusalem, and the city came under siege.

11 And Nebuchadnezzar the king of Babylon came to the city, while his servants were besieging it.

12 [a]Jehoiachin the king of Judah went out to the king of Babylon, he and his mother and his servants and his captains and his officials. So [b]the king of Babylon took him captive in the eighth year of his reign.

13 [a]He carried out from there all the treasures of the house of the LORD, and the treasures of the king's house, and [b]cut in pieces all the vessels of gold [c]which Solomon king of Israel had made in the temple of the LORD, just as the LORD had said.

14 Then [a]he led away into exile all Jerusalem and all the captains and all the mighty men of valor, [b]ten thousand captives, and [c]all the craftsmen and the smiths. None remained [d]except the poorest people of the land.

7 [a]Jer 37:5-7 [b]Jer 46:2 [c]Gen 15:18
8 [a]1 Chr 3:16 [b]2 Chr 36:9
9 [a]2 Kin 21:2-7
12 [a]Jer 22:24-30; 24:1; 29:1, 2 [b]2 Chr 36:10
13 [a]2 Kin 20:17; Is 39:6 [b]2 Kin 25:13-15 [c]1 Kin 7:48-50
14 [a]Jer 24:1 [b]2 Kin 24:16; Jer 52:28 [c]Jer 24:1; 29:2 [d]2 Kin 25:12
15 [a]2 Chr 36:10; Jer 22:24-28; Ezek 17:12
16 [a]2 Kin 24:14
17 [1]I.e. Jehoiachin's uncle [a]2 Chr 36:10-13; Jer 37:1
18 [a]Jer 27:1; 28:1; 52:1 [b]2 Kin 23:31
19 [a]2 Kin 23:37
20 [a]Deut 4:24; 29:27; 2 Kin 23:26 [b]2 Chr 36:13; Ezek 17:15
25:1 [1]Lit *against it* [a]2 Chr 36:17-20; Jer 39:1-7 [b]Jer 21:2; 34:1, 2; Ezek 24:2 [c]Ezek 21:22

15 So [a]he led Jehoiachin away into exile to Babylon; also the king's mother and the king's wives and his officials and the leading men of the land, he led away into exile from Jerusalem to Babylon.

16 All the men of valor, [a]seven thousand, and the craftsmen and the smiths, one thousand, all strong and fit for war, and these the king of Babylon brought into exile to Babylon.

Zedekiah Made King

17 [a]Then the king of Babylon made [1]his uncle Mattaniah king in his place, and changed his name to Zedekiah.

18 [a]Zedekiah was twenty-one years old when he became king, and he reigned eleven years in Jerusalem; and his mother's name was [b]Hamutal the daughter of Jeremiah of Libnah.

19 He did evil in the sight of the LORD, [a]according to all that Jehoiakim had done.

20 For [a]through the anger of the LORD *this* came about in Jerusalem and Judah until He cast them out from His presence. And [b]Zedekiah rebelled against the king of Babylon.

Nebuchadnezzar Besieges Jerusalem

25 [a]Now in the ninth year of his reign, on the tenth day of the tenth month, [b]Nebuchadnezzar king of Babylon came, he and all his army, against Jerusalem, camped against it and [c]built a siege wall all around [1]it.

2 So the city was under siege until the eleventh year of King Zedekiah.

24:7 *The king of Egypt did not come out of his land again.* This was due to the Egyptian defeat at Carchemish (see Jer 46:2) in 605 B.C., and it explains why Jehoiakim received no help from Egypt in his rebellion against the Babylonians. *brook of Egypt.* See note on 1 Kin 8:65.

24:8 *three months.* In 598–597 B.C. Babylonian records place the fall of Jerusalem to Nebuchadnezzar on Mar. 16, 597. This means that the three-month and ten-day reign (see 2 Chr 36:9–10) of Jehoiachin began in December, 598.

24:9 *according to all that his father had done.* See 23:37; Jer 22:20–30.

24:11 *Nebuchadnezzar the king . . . came to the city.* Babylonian records say that Nebuchadnezzar "encamped against the city of Judah, and on the second day of the month of Addaru [i.e., Mar. 16, 597 B.C.] he seized the city and captured the king."

24:12 *eighth year.* April, 597 B.C. (see 2 Chr 36:10; see also note on Jer 52:28, where a different system of dating is reflected).

24:13 *As the LORD had said.* See 20:13,17.

24:14 *ten thousand.* This figure may include the 7,000 fighting men and 1,000 craftsmen mentioned in v. 16 (see note on Jer 52:28, where a different number of captives is mentioned).

24:15 *Jehoiachin away into exile to Babylon.* Fulfilling Jeremiah's prophecy (Jer 22:24–27; see 2 Kin 25:27–30).

24:17 *his uncle Mattaniah.* Mattaniah was a son of Josiah (see 1 Chr 3:15; Jer 1:3) and brother of Jehoiachin's father, Jehoiakim. *changed his name to Zedekiah.* Mattaniah's name (meaning "gift of Yahweh") was changed to Zedekiah ("righteousness of Yahweh"). Perhaps Nebuchadnezzar wanted to imply that his actions against Jerusalem and Jehoiachin were just. In any case, the name change signified subjection to Nebuchadnezzar (see note on 23:34).

24:18 *eleven years.* 597–586 B.C. *Jeremiah.* See note on 23:31. *Libnah.* See note on 8:22.

24:19 *did evil . . . according to all that Jehoiakim had done.* See note on 23:37. During Zedekiah's reign idolatrous practices continued to increase in Jerusalem (see 2 Chr 36:14; Ezek 8–11). He was a weak and indecisive ruler (see Jer 38:5,19), who refused to heed the word of the Lord given through Jeremiah (2 Chr 36:12).

24:20 *Zedekiah rebelled.* Most interpreters link Zedekiah's revolt with the succession to the Egyptian throne in 589 B.C. of the ambitious pharaoh Apries (Hophra). Zedekiah had sworn allegiance to Nebuchadnezzar (Ezek 17:13), he had sent envoys to Babylon (see Jer 29:3), and he had made a personal visit (see Jer 51:59). However, he seems to have capitulated to the seductive propaganda of the anti-Babylonian and pro-Egyptian faction in Jerusalem (see Jer 37:5; Ezek 17:15–16) in a tragically miscalculated effort to gain independence from Babylon.

25:1 *ninth year . . . tenth day . . . tenth month.* Jan. 15, 588 B.C. (see Jer 39:1; 52:4; Ezek 24:1–2). *Nebuchadnezzar . . . came . . . against Jerusalem.* Earlier, Nebuchadnezzar had subdued all the fortified cities in Judah except Lachish and Azekah (see Jer 34:7). A number of Hebrew inscriptions on potsherds were found at Lachish in 1935 and 1938. These Lachish ostraca (or letters; see chart, p. xix) describe conditions at Lachish and Azekah during the Babylonian siege.

25:2–3 *eleventh year . . . ninth day . . . fourth month.* July 18, 586 B.C. (see Jer 39:2; 52:5–7). Some scholars follow a different dat-

Nebuchadnezzar's Campaigns against Judah

605–586 B.C.

Events in Judah moved swiftly following the death of Josiah. Pharaoh Neco pressed his advantage by deporting the new ruler and appointing a second son of Josiah, Jehoiakim, as king.

The Persian conquest of Lydia in 546 B.C. brought the Greeks into conflict with Persia, a series of events chronicled in great detail by Herodotus.

The prophet Jeremiah was taken to Egypt by Judahite refugees fleeing from Babylonian-controlled territory. They brought him to Tahpanhes, where he continued his prophecies.

LYDIA
Great Sea
Haran
Tiphsah
Hamath
Riblah
Sidon
Tyre
Tahpanhes
Migdol
AMMON
Jerusalem
JUDAH
KEDAR
EDOM
On
Memphis
Brook of Egypt
EGYPT

CONQUEST OF JERUSALEM 597 B.C.

- Route of main Babylonian army
- Captives deported
- Raids by Babylonian allies 602 B.C.

Sea of Galilee
Megiddo
Samaria
Shechem
Shiloh
Great Sea
Mizpah
Gibeon
Ramah
Jerusalem
Azekah
Lachish
Hebron
Dead Sea
Miles 10 5 0 10 20
Kms 10 5 0 10 20 30

Soon a stronger power appeared in the north in the person of Nebuchadnezzar, king of the Chaldeans (Neo-Babylonians), who determined to follow the fierce policies of his Assyrian predecessors.

The tribute of Jehoiakim was paid at a distance when he heard of Nebuchadnezzar's approach. After three years as a Babylonian vassal, he rebelled, bringing a rapid response in the form of small-scale raids from Babylonians, Arameans, Moabites and Ammonites (c. 602 B.C.). Finally, Nebuchadnezzar's forces controlled all of the coastal territory north of the brook of Egypt.

When 18-year-old Jehoiachin had ruled just three months (597 B.C.), the main Babylonian army struck, capturing Jerusalem and exiling the king as a captive in Babylon. Ten thousand persons were deported.

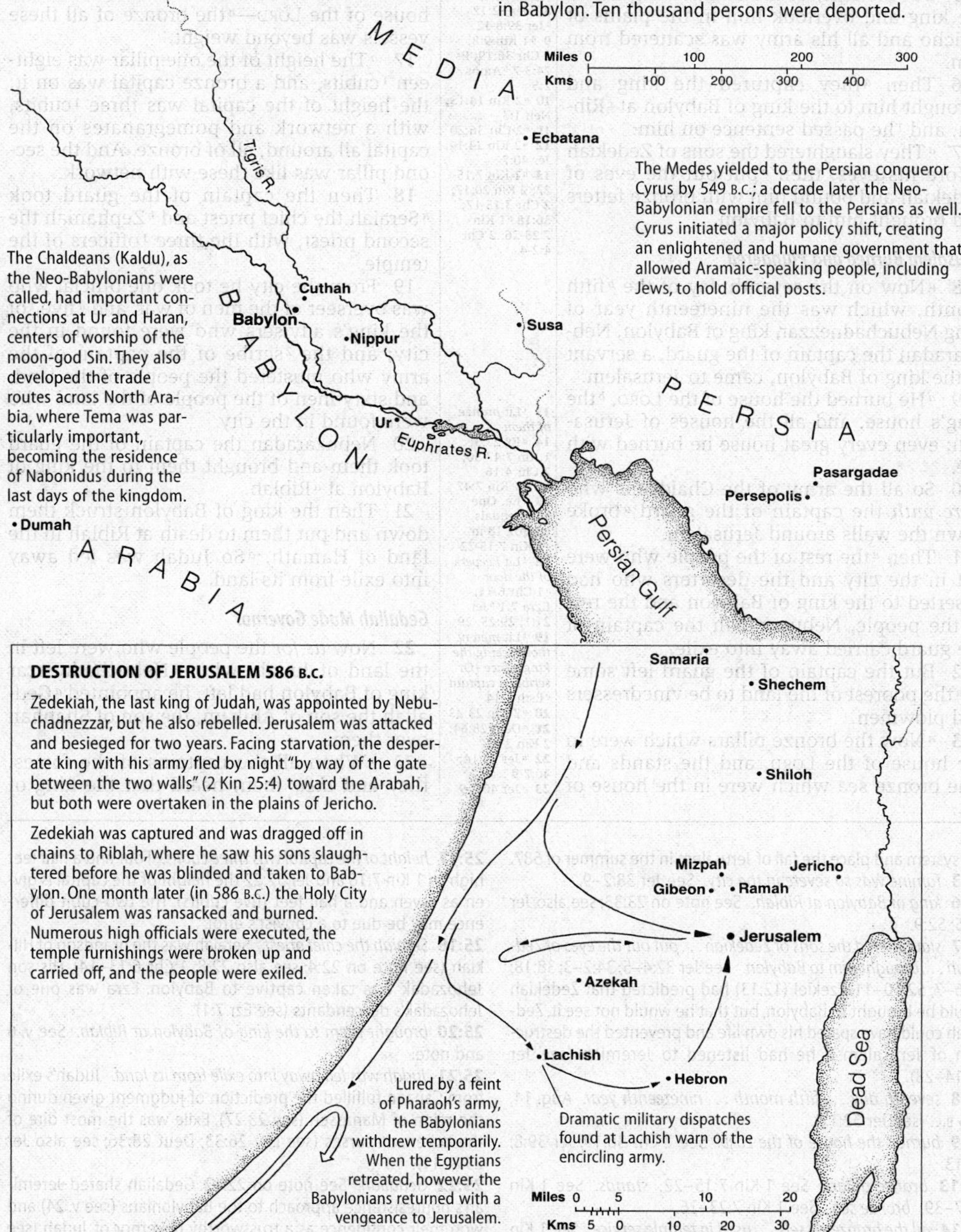
Miles 0 100 200 300
Kms 0 100 200 300 400
MEDIA
Ecbatana
The Medes yielded to the Persian conqueror Cyrus by 549 B.C.; a decade later the Neo-Babylonian empire fell to the Persians as well. Cyrus initiated a major policy shift, creating an enlightened and humane government that allowed Aramaic-speaking people, including Jews, to hold official posts.
Tigris R.
The Chaldeans (Kaldu), as the Neo-Babylonians were called, had important connections at Ur and Haran, centers of worship of the moon-god Sin. They also developed the trade routes across North Arabia, where Tema was particularly important, becoming the residence of Nabonidus during the last days of the kingdom.
Cuthah
Babylon
Nippur
BABYLON
Susa
Ur
Euphrates R.
PERSIA
Pasargadae
Persepolis
Persian Gulf
Dumah
ARABIA
DESTRUCTION OF JERUSALEM 586 B.C.
Zedekiah, the last king of Judah, was appointed by Nebuchadnezzar, but he also rebelled. Jerusalem was attacked and besieged for two years. Facing starvation, the desperate king with his army fled by night "by way of the gate between the two walls" (2 Kin 25:4) toward the Arabah, but both were overtaken in the plains of Jericho.
Zedekiah was captured and was dragged off in chains to Riblah, where he saw his sons slaughtered before he was blinded and taken to Babylon. One month later (in 586 B.C.) the Holy City of Jerusalem was ransacked and burned. Numerous high officials were executed, the temple furnishings were broken up and carried off, and the people were exiled.
Samaria
Shechem
Shiloh
Mizpah
Jericho
Gibeon
Ramah
Jerusalem
Azekah
Lachish
Hebron
Dead Sea
Lured by a feint of Pharaoh's army, the Babylonians withdrew temporarily. When the Egyptians retreated, however, the Babylonians returned with a vengeance to Jerusalem.
Dramatic military dispatches found at Lachish warn of the encircling army.
Miles 0 5 10 20
Kms 5 0 10 20 30

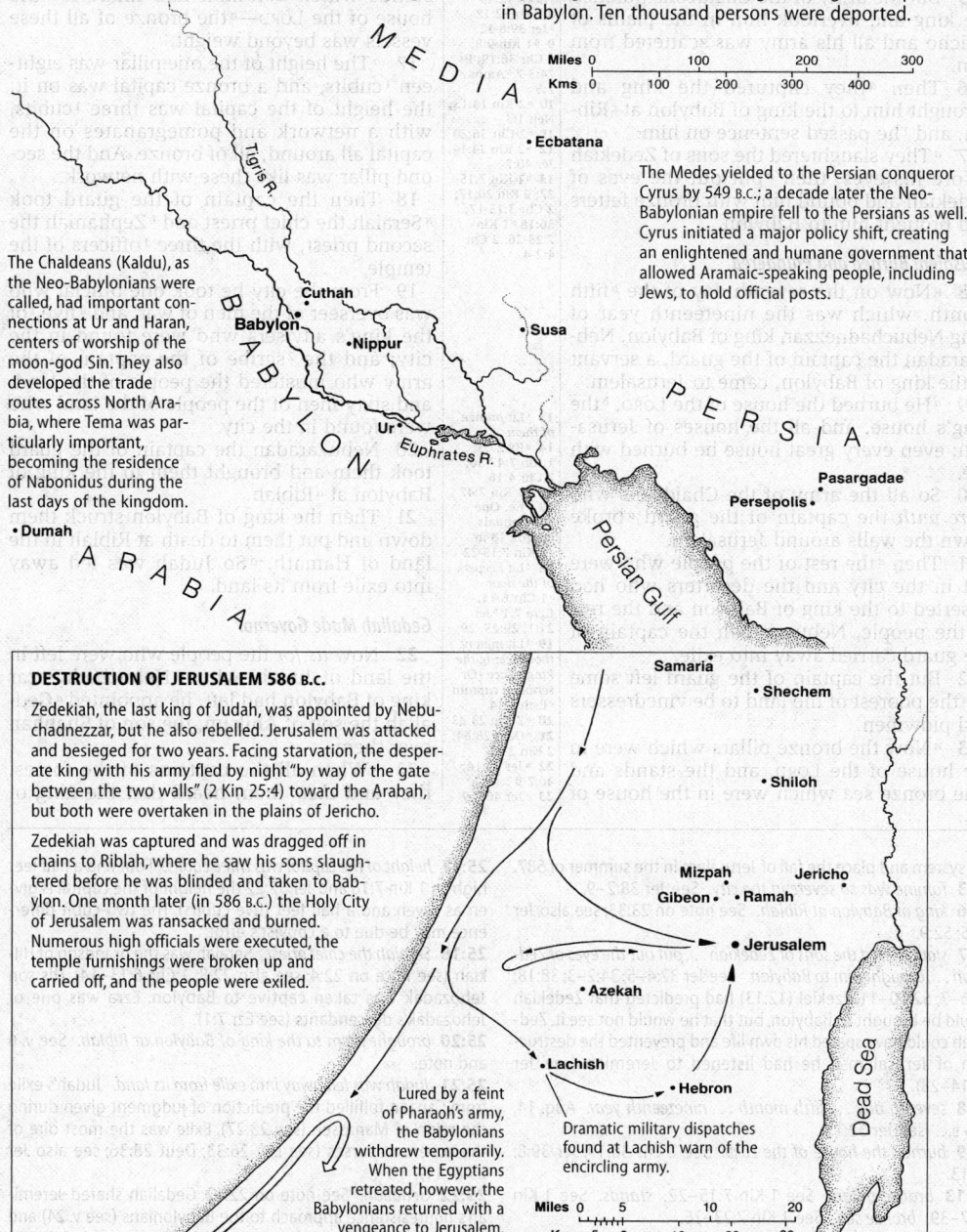

3 On the ninth day of the *fourth* month [a]the famine was so severe in the city that there was no food for the people of the land.

4 [a]Then the city was broken into, and all the men of war *fled* by night by way of the gate between the two walls beside [b]the king's garden, though the Chaldeans were all around the city. And [1]they went by way of the Arabah.

5 But the army of the Chaldeans pursued the king and overtook him in the plains of Jericho and all his army was scattered from him.

6 Then [a]they captured the king and [b]brought him to the king of Babylon at [c]Riblah, and [1]he passed sentence on him.

7 [a]They slaughtered the sons of Zedekiah before his eyes, then [b]put out the eyes of Zedekiah and bound him with bronze fetters and brought him to Babylon.

Jerusalem Burned and Plundered

8 [a]Now on the seventh day of the [b]fifth month, which was the nineteenth year of King Nebuchadnezzar, king of Babylon, Nebuzaradan the captain of the guard, a servant of the king of Babylon, came to Jerusalem.

9 [a]He burned the house of the LORD, [b]the king's house, and all the houses of Jerusalem; even every great house he burned with fire.

10 So all the army of the Chaldeans who *were with* the captain of the guard [a]broke down the walls around Jerusalem.

11 Then [a]the rest of the people who were left in the city and the deserters who had deserted to the king of Babylon and the rest of the people, Nebuzaradan the captain of the guard carried away into exile.

12 But the captain of the guard left some of [a]the poorest of the land to be vinedressers and plowmen.

13 [a]Now the bronze pillars which were in the house of the LORD, and the stands and [b]the bronze sea which were in the house of the LORD, the Chaldeans broke in pieces and carried the [1]bronze to Babylon.

14 [a]They took away the pots, the shovels, the snuffers, the spoons, and all the bronze vessels which were used in *temple* service.

15 The captain of the guard also took away the firepans and the basins, what was fine gold and what was fine silver.

16 The two pillars, the one sea, and the stands which Solomon had made for the house of the LORD—[a]the bronze of all these vessels was beyond weight.

17 [a]The height of the one pillar was eighteen [1]cubits, and a bronze capital was on it; the height of the capital was three [1]cubits, with a network and pomegranates on the capital all around, all of bronze. And the second pillar was like these with network.

18 Then the captain of the guard took [a]Seraiah the chief priest and [b]Zephaniah the second priest, with the three [1]officers of the temple.

19 From the city he took one official who was overseer of the men of war, and [a]five [1]of the king's advisers who were found in the city; and the [2]scribe of the captain of the army who mustered the people of the land; and sixty men of the people of the land who were found in the city.

20 Nebuzaradan the captain of the guard took them and brought them to the king of Babylon at [a]Riblah.

21 Then the king of Babylon struck them down and put them to death at Riblah in the land of Hamath. [a]So Judah was led away into exile from its land.

Gedaliah Made Governor

22 Now *as for* the people who were left in the land of Judah, whom Nebuchadnezzar king of Babylon had left, he appointed [a]Gedaliah the son of Ahikam, the son of Shaphan over them.

23 [a]When all the captains of the forces, they and *their* men, heard that the king of

3 [a]2 Kin 6:24, 25; Lam 4:9, 10
4 [1]So some ancient mss and versions; M.T. *he* [a]Ezek 33:21 [b]Neh 3:15
6 [1]Lit *they spoke judgment with him* [a]Jer 34:21, 22 [b]Jer 32:4 [c]2 Kin 23:33
7 [a]Jer 39:6, 7 [b]Ezek 12:13
8 [a]Jer 52:12 [b]Jer 39:8-12
9 [a]1 Kin 9:8; 2 Chr 36:19; Ps 74:3-7 [b]Amos 2:5
10 [a]2 Kin 14:13; Neh 1:3
11 [a]2 Chr 36:20
12 [a]2 Kin 24:14; Jer 40:7
13 [a]1 Kin 7:15-22; 2 Kin 20:17; 2 Chr 3:15-17; 36:18 [b]1 Kin 7:23-26; 2 Chr 4:2-4
13 [1]Lit *bronze of them*
14 [a]Ex 27:3; 1 Kin 7:47-50; 2 Chr 4:16
16 [a]1 Kin 7:47
17 [1]I.e. One cubit equals approx 18 in. [a]1 Kin 7:15-22
18 [1]Lit *keepers of the door* [a]1 Chr 6:14; Ezra 7:1 [b]Jer 21:1; 29:25, 29
19 [1]Lit *men of those seeing the king's face* [2]Or *scribe, a captain* [a]Esth 1:14
20 [a]2 Kin 23:33
21 [a]Deut 28:64; 2 Kin 23:27
22 [a]Jer 39:14; 40:7-9
23 [a]Jer 40:7-9

---

ing system and place the fall of Jerusalem in the summer of 587.
25:3 *famine was so severe in the city.* See Jer 38:2–9.
25:6 *king of Babylon at Riblah.* See note on 23:33; see also Jer 39:5; 52:9.
25:7 *slaughtered the sons of Zedekiah . . . put out the eyes of Zedekiah . . . brought him to Babylon.* See Jer 32:4–5; 34:2–3; 38:18; 39:6–7; 52:10–11. Ezekiel (12:13) had predicted that Zedekiah would be brought to Babylon, but that he would not see it. Zedekiah could have spared his own life and prevented the destruction of Jerusalem if he had listened to Jeremiah (see Jer 38:14–28).
25:8 *seventh day . . . fifth month . . . nineteenth year.* Aug. 14, 586 B.C. (see Jer 52:12).
25:9 *burned the house of the LORD.* See 2 Chr 36:19; Jer 39:8; 52:13.
25:13 *bronze pillars.* See 1 Kin 7:15–22. *stands.* See 1 Kin 7:27–39. *bronze sea.* See 1 Kin 7:23–26.
25:14 *all the bronze vessels . . . used in temple service.* See 1 Kin 7:40,45.
25:17 *height of the capital was three cubits.* Four and a half feet high. In 1 Kin 7:16 and Jer 52:22 the height of the capital is given as seven and a half feet (five cubits). The two-cubit difference may be due to a copyist's error.
25:18 *Seraiah the chief priest.* Seraiah was the grandson of Hilkiah (see note on 22:4; see also 22:8; 1 Chr 6:13–14). His son Jehozadak was taken captive to Babylon. Ezra was one of Jehozadak's descendants (see Ezr 7:1).
25:20 *brought them to the king of Babylon at Riblah.* See v. 6 and note.
25:21 *Judah was led away into exile from its land.* Judah's exile from Canaan fulfilled the prediction of judgment given during the reign of Manasseh (see 23:27). Exile was the most dire of the covenant curses (see Lev 26:33; Deut 28:36; see also Jer 25:8–11).
25:22 *Gedaliah.* See note on 22:12. Gedaliah shared Jeremiah's nonresistance approach to the Babylonians (see v. 24) and won their confidence as a trustworthy governor of Judah (see Jer 41:10).

Babylon had appointed Gedaliah *governor,*
they came to Gedaliah to [b]Mizpah, namely,
Ishmael the son of Nethaniah, and Johanan
the son of Kareah, and Seraiah the son of
Tanhumeth the Netophathite, and Jaazaniah
the son of the Maacathite, they and their
men.
24 Gedaliah swore to them and their men
and said to them, "Do not be afraid of the
servants of the Chaldeans; live in the land
and serve the king of Babylon, and it will be
well with you."
25 [a]But it came about in the seventh
month, that Ishmael the son of Nethaniah,
the son of Elishama, of the royal [1]family,
came [2]with ten men and struck Gedaliah
down so that he died along with the Jews and
the Chaldeans who were with him at Mizpah.
26 [a]Then all the people, both small and
great, and the captains of the forces arose
and went to Egypt; for they were afraid of
the Chaldeans.
27 [a]Now it came about in the thirty-
seventh year of [b]the exile of Jehoiachin king

23 [b]Josh 18:26
25 [1]Lit *seed* [2]Lit *and ten men with him* [a]Jer 41:1, 2
26 [a]Jer 43:4-7
27 [a]Jer 52:31-34 [b]2 Kin 24:12, 15

25:23 *Mizpah.* Had been a town of important political significance in the time just before the establishment of the monarchy (see note on 1 Sam 7:5). Jeremiah found Gedaliah there (see Jer 40:1–6). *Ishmael the son of Nethaniah.* Verse 25 gives a fuller genealogy. Elishama, Ishmael's grandfather, was the royal secretary under Jehoiakim (Jer 36:12). *Jaazaniah the son of the Maacathite.* In 1932 an agate seal was found at Tell en-Nasbeh (Mizpah) bearing the name of Jaazaniah (perhaps the man mentioned here) with the inscription: "Belonging to Jaazaniah the servant of the king."
25:24 Gedaliah urged submission to the Babylonians as the judgment of God. He advocated the restoration of the normal pursuits of a peacetime society (see Jer 27). A similar message had been given by Jeremiah to the captives taken to Babylon in 597 B.C. (see Jer 29:4–7).
25:25 *seventh month.* October, 586 B.C. *struck Gedaliah down.* A more complete account of the assassination of Gedaliah is given in Jer 40:13–41:15. Ishmael appears to have had personal designs on the throne, to have resented Gedaliah's ready submission to the Babylonians, and to have been manipulated by the Ammonites, who also chafed under Babylonian domination (see Jer 40:14; 41:10,15).
25:26 *went to Egypt.* Pharaoh Apries (Hophra) was then ruler in Egypt (see note on 24:20).
25:27 *thirty-seventh year . . . twelfth month . . . twenty-seventh day.* Mar. 22, 561 B.C. *in the year that he became king.* 561

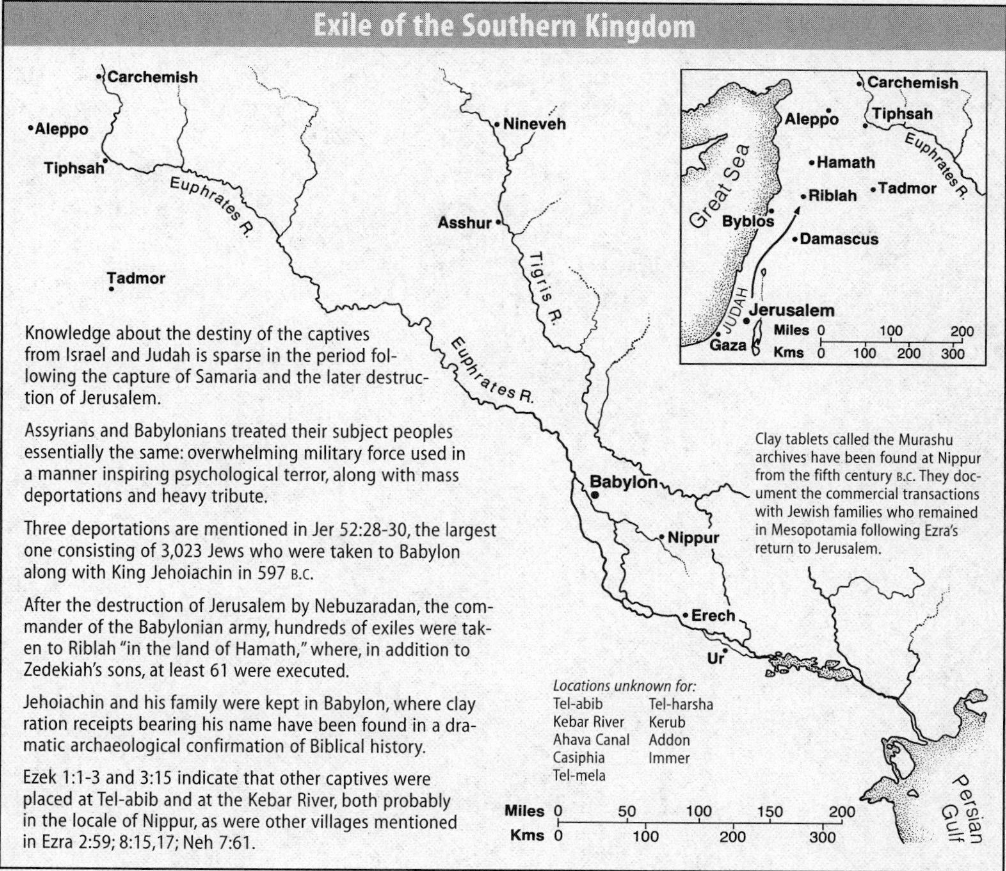
Exile of the Southern Kingdom
Carchemish
Aleppo
Tiphsah
Euphrates R.
Nineveh
Asshur
Tigris R.
Tadmor
Babylon
Nippur
Erech
Ur
Persian Gulf
Great Sea
Hamath
Riblah
Tadmor
Byblos
Damascus
Jerusalem
JUDAH
Gaza
Miles 0 100 200
Kms 0 100 200 300
Knowledge about the destiny of the captives from Israel and Judah is sparse in the period following the capture of Samaria and the later destruction of Jerusalem.
Assyrians and Babylonians treated their subject peoples essentially the same: overwhelming military force used in a manner inspiring psychological terror, along with mass deportations and heavy tribute.
Three deportations are mentioned in Jer 52:28-30, the largest one consisting of 3,023 Jews who were taken to Babylon along with King Jehoiachin in 597 B.C.
After the destruction of Jerusalem by Nebuzaradan, the commander of the Babylonian army, hundreds of exiles were taken to Riblah "in the land of Hamath," where, in addition to Zedekiah's sons, at least 61 were executed.
Jehoiachin and his family were kept in Babylon, where clay ration receipts bearing his name have been found in a dramatic archaeological confirmation of Biblical history.
Ezek 1:1-3 and 3:15 indicate that other captives were placed at Tel-abib and at the Kebar River, both probably in the locale of Nippur, as were other villages mentioned in Ezra 2:59; 8:15,17; Neh 7:61.
Clay tablets called the Murashu archives have been found at Nippur from the fifth century B.C. They document the commercial transactions with Jewish families who remained in Mesopotamia following Ezra's return to Jerusalem.
Locations unknown for:
Tel-abib
Kebar River
Ahava Canal
Casiphia
Tel-mela
Tel-harsha
Kerub
Addon
Immer
Miles 0 50 100 150 200
Kms 0 100 200 300

of Judah, in the twelfth month, on the twenty-seventh *day* of the month, that Evil-merodach king of Babylon, in the year that he
became king, [1c]released Jehoiachin king of
Judah from prison;
28 and he [a]spoke kindly to him and set his
throne above the throne of the kings who
were with him in Babylon.

29 [1]Jehoiachin changed his prison clothes
and [2a]had his meals in [3]the king's presence
regularly all the days of his life;
30 and for his [a]allowance, a regular
allowance was given him by the king, a portion for each day, all the days of his life.

27 [1]Lit *lifted up the head of* [c]Gen 40:13, 20
28 [a]Dan 2:37; 5:18, 19
29 [1]Lit *he* [2]Lit *ate bread* [3]Lit *his presence* [a]2 Sam 9:7
30 [a]Neh 11:23; 12:47

(some scholars place Evil-merodach's succession to the throne in October, 562; see note on 24:1). His name means "man of (the god) Marduk." *released Jehoiachin . . . from prison.* Babylonian administrative tablets (see chart, p. xix), recording the payment of rations in oil and barley to prisoners held in Babylon, mention Yaukin (Jehoiachin) king of Iahudu (Judah) and five of his sons (cf. 24:15). No reason is given for Jehoiachin's release. Perhaps it was part of a general amnesty proclaimed at the beginning of Evil-merodach's reign.

25:28 *spoke kindly to him and set his throne above the throne of the kings.* The book of Kings ends on a hopeful note. The judgment of exile will not destroy the people of Israel or the line of David. God's promise concerning David's house remains (see 2 Sam 7:14–16).

1 Chronicles

INTRODUCTION

Title

The Hebrew title (*dibre hayyamim*) can be translated "the events (or annals) of the days (or years)." The same phrase occurs in references to sources used by the author or compiler of Kings (translated "chronicles" in, e.g., 1 Kin 14:19,29; 15:7,23,31; 16:5,14,20,27; 22:45). The Septuagint translators (who translated the OT into Greek) called the book "the things omitted," indicating that they regarded it as a supplement to Samuel and Kings. Jerome (A.D. 347 – 420), translator of the Latin Vulgate, suggested that a more appropriate title would be "chronicle of the whole sacred history." Luther took over this suggestion in his German version, and others have followed him. Chronicles was first divided into two books by the Septuagint translators.

Author, Date and Sources

According to ancient Jewish tradition, Ezra wrote Chronicles, Ezra and Nehemiah (see Introduction to Ezra: Literary Form and Authorship), but this cannot be established with certainty. A growing consensus dates Chronicles in the latter half of the fifth century B.C., thus possibly within Ezra's lifetime. And it must be acknowledged that the author, if not Ezra himself, at least shared many basic concerns with that reforming priest — though Chronicles is not so narrowly "priestly" in its perspective as was long affirmed.

Some believe the text contains evidence here and there of later expansions after the basic work had been composed. While editorial revisions are not unlikely, all specific proposals regarding them remain tentative.

In his recounting of history long past, the Chronicler relied on many written sources. About half his work was taken from Samuel and Kings; he also drew on the Pentateuch, Judges, Ruth, Psalms, Isaiah, Jeremiah, Lamentations and Zechariah (though he used texts of these books that varied somewhat from those that have been preserved in the later standardized Hebrew texts). And there are frequent references to still other sources: "the Book of the Kings of Israel" (9:1; 2 Chr 20:34; cf. 2 Chr 33:18), "the account of the chronicles of King David" (27:24), "the Book of the Kings of Judah and Israel" or ". . . of Israel and Judah" (2 Chr 16:11; 25:26; 27:7; 28:26; 32:32; 35:27; 36:8), "the treatise of the Book of the Kings" (2 Chr 24:27). It is unclear whether these all refer to the same source or to different sources, and what their relationship is to Samuel and Kings or to the royal annals referred to in Kings. In addition, the author cites a number of prophetic writings: those of "Samuel the seer" (29:29), "Nathan the prophet" (29:29; 2 Chr 9:29), "Gad the seer" (29:29), "Ahijah the Shilonite" (2 Chr 9:29), "Iddo the seer" (2 Chr 9:29; 12:15; 13:22), "Shemaiah the prophet" (2 Chr 12:15), "the prophet Isaiah" (2 Chr 26:22), "the Hozai" (2 Chr 33:19). All these he used, often with only minor changes, to tell his own story of the past. He did not invent, but he did select, arrange and integrate his sources to compose a narrative "sermon" for postexilic Israel as she struggled to reorient herself as the people of God in a new situation.

Purpose and Themes

Just as the author of Kings had organized and interpreted the data of Israel's history to address the needs of the exiled community, so the Chronicler wrote for the restored community. The burning issue was the question of continuity with the past: Is God still interested in us? Are His covenants still in force? Now that we have no Davidic king and are subject to Persia, do God's promises to David still have meaning for us? After the great judgment (the dethroning of the house of David, the destruction of the nation, of Jerusalem and of the temple, and the exile to Babylon), what is our relationship to Israel of old? Several elements go into the Chronicler's answer:

1. Continuity with the past is signified by the temple in Jerusalem, rebuilt by the Lord's sovereign influence over a Persian imperial edict (2 Chr 36:22 – 23). For a generation that had no independent political status and no Davidic king the author takes great pains to show that the temple of the Lord and its service

(including its book of prayer and praise, an early edition of the Psalms) are supreme gifts of God given to Israel through the Davidic dynasty. For that reason his account of the reigns of David and Solomon is largely devoted to David's preparation for and Solomon's building of the temple and David's instructions for the temple service (with the counsel of Gad the seer and Nathan the prophet, 2 Chr 29:25, and also of the Levites Asaph, Heman and Jeduthun, 2 Chr 35:15). See also the Chronicler's accounts of the reigns of Asa, Jehoshaphat, Joash, Hezekiah and Josiah. The temple of the Lord in the ancient holy city and its service (including the Psalms) were the chief legacy left to the restored community by the house of David.

2. The value of this legacy is highlighted by the author's emphasis on God's furtherance of His gracious purposes toward Israel through His sovereign acts of election: (1) of the tribe of Levi to serve before the ark of the covenant (15:2; see 23:24–32), (2) of David to be king over Israel (28:4; 2 Chr 6:6), (3) of Solomon his son to be king and to build the temple (28:5–6,10; 29:1), (4) of Jerusalem (2 Chr 6:6,34,38; 12:13; 33:7) and (5) of the temple (2 Chr 7:12,16; 33:7) to be the place where God's Name would be present among His people. These divine acts give assurance to postexilic Israel that her rebuilt temple in Jerusalem and its continuing service mark her as God's people whose election has not been annulled.

3. In addition to the temple, Israel has the law and the prophets as a major focus of her covenant life under the leadership of the house of David. Neither the Davidic kings nor the temple had in themselves assured Israel's security and blessing. All had been conditional on Israel's and the king's faithfulness to the law (28:7; 2 Chr 6:16; 7:17; 12:1; 33:8). In the Chronicler's account, a primary feature of the reign of every faithful Davidic king was his attempt to bring about compliance with the law: David (6:49; 15:13,15; 16:40; 22:12–13; 29:19), Asa (2 Chr 14:4; 15:12–14), Jehoshaphat (2 Chr 17:3–9; 19:8–10), Joash (2 Chr 24:6,9), Hezekiah (2 Chr 29:10,31; 30:15–16; 31:3–4,21), Josiah (2 Chr 34:19–21, 29–33; 35:6,12,26). And to heed God's prophetic word was no less crucial. The faithful kings, such as David, Asa, Jehoshaphat, Hezekiah and Josiah—and even Rehoboam (2 Chr 11:4; 12:6) and Amaziah (2 Chr 25:7–10)—honored it; the unfaithful kings disregarded it to their destruction (Jehoram, 2 Chr 21:12–19; Joash, 2 Chr 24:19–25; Amaziah, 2 Chr 25:15–16,20; Manasseh, 2 Chr 33:10–11; see 36:15–16). Chronicles, in fact, notes the ministries of more prophets than do Samuel and Kings. Jehoshaphat's word to Israel expresses the Chronicler's view succinctly: "Put your trust in the LORD your God and you will be established. Put your trust in his prophets and succeed" (2 Chr 20:20). In the Chronicler's account of Israel's years under the kings, her response to the law and the prophets was more decisive for her destiny than the reigns of kings.

Thus the law and the prophets, like the temple, are more crucial to Israel's continuing relationship with the Lord than the presence or absence of a king, the reigns of the Davidic kings themselves being testimony.

4. The Chronicler further underscores the importance of obedience to the law and the prophets by emphasizing the theme of immediate retribution. See the express statements of David (28:9), of the Lord (2 Chr 7:14) and of the prophets (2 Chr 12:5; 15:2,7; 16:7,9; 19:2–3; 21:14–15; 24:20; 25:15–16; 28:9; 34:24–28). In writing his accounts of individual reigns, he never tires of demonstrating how sin always brings judgment in the form of disaster (usually either illness or defeat in war), whereas repentance, obedience and trust yield peace, victory and prosperity.

5. Clearly the author of Chronicles wished to sustain Israel's hope for the promised Messiah, son of David, in accordance with the Davidic covenant (2 Sam 7) and the assurances of the prophets, including those near to him (Haggai, Zechariah and Malachi). He was careful to recall the Lord's pledge to David (1 Chr 17) and to follow this with many references back to it (see especially his account of Solomon's reign and also 2 Chr 13:5; 21:7; 23:3). But perhaps even more indicative are his idealized depictions of David, Solomon, Asa, Jehoshaphat, Hezekiah and Josiah. While not portrayed as flawless, these kings are presented as prime examples of the Messianic ideal, i.e., as royal servants of the Lord whose reigns promoted godliness and covenant faithfulness in Israel. They were crowned with God's favor toward His people in the concrete forms of victories, deliverances and prosperity. They sat, moreover, on the "throne of the LORD" (29:23; see 28:5; 2 Chr 9:8) and ruled over the Lord's kingdom (17:14; 2 Chr 13:8). Thus they served as types, foreshadowing the David to come of whom the prophets had spoken, and their remembrance nurtured hope in the face of much discouragement (see the book of Malachi). See further the next section on "Portrait of David and Solomon."

6. Yet another major theme of the Chronicler's history is his concern with "all Israel" (see, e.g., 9:1; 11:1–4; 12:38–40; 16:1–3; 18:14; 21:1–5; 28:1–8; 29:21–26; 2 Chr 1:1–3; 7:8–10; 9:30; 10:1–3,16; 12:1; 18:16; 28:23;

29:24; 30:1–13,23–27; 34:6–9,33). As a matter of fact, he viewed the restored community as the remnant of all Israel, both north and south (9:2–3). This was more than a theological conceit. His narrative makes frequent note of movements of godly people from Israel to Judah for specifically religious reasons. The first were Levites in the time of Rehoboam (2 Chr 11:14). In the reign of Asa others followed from Ephraim and Manasseh (2 Chr 15:9). Shortly after the Assyrian destruction of the northern kingdom, many from that devastated land resettled in Judah at Hezekiah's invitation (2 Chr 30). Presumably not all who came for Hezekiah's great Passover remained, but archaeology has shown a sudden large increase in population in the region around Jerusalem at this time, and the Chronicler specifically mentions "sons of Israel . . . who lived in the cities of Judah" (2 Chr 31:6). He also speaks of the people of "Manasseh and Ephraim and from all the remnant of Israel" who joined with the people of "Judah and Benjamin and the inhabitants of Jerusalem" in restoring the temple in the days of Josiah (2 Chr 34:9). These were also present at Josiah's Passover (2 Chr 35:17–18). So the kingdom of "Judah" had absorbed many from the northern kingdom through the years, and the Chronicler viewed it as the remnant of all Israel from the time of Samaria's fall.

7. The genealogies also demonstrate continuity with the past. To the question "Is God still interested in us?" the Chronicler answers, "He has always been." God's grace and love for the restored community did not begin with David or the conquest or the exodus — but with creation (1:1). For the genealogies see below.

8. The Chronicler often introduces speeches not found in Samuel and Kings, using them to convey some of his main emphases. Of the 165 speeches in Chronicles of varying lengths, only 95 are found in the parallel texts of Samuel and Kings. Cf., e.g., the speeches of Abijah (2 Chr 13:4–12), Asa (2 Chr 14:11) and Jehoshaphat (2 Chr 20:5–12).

Portrait of David and Solomon

The bulk of the Chronicler's history is devoted to the reigns of David (chs. 11—29) and Solomon (2 Chr 1—9). His portraits of these two kings are quite distinctive and provide a key to his concerns:

1. The Chronicler has idealized David and Solomon. Anything in his source material (mainly Samuel and Kings) that might tarnish his picture of them is omitted. He makes no reference to the seven-year reign in Hebron before the uniting of the kingdom, the wars between Saul's house and David, the negotiations with Abner, the difficulties over David's wife Michal, or the murders of Abner and Ish-bosheth (2 Sam 1—4). The Chronicler presents David as being immediately anointed king over all Israel after the death of Saul (ch. 11) and enjoying the total support of the people (11:10—12:40; see note on 3:1–9). Subsequent difficulties for David are also not recounted. No mention is made of David's sin with Bathsheba, the crime and death of Amnon, the fratricide by Absalom and his plot against his father, the flight of David from Jerusalem, the rebellions of Sheba and Shimei, and other incidents that might diminish the glory of David's reign (2 Sam 11—20). David is presented without blemish, apart from the incident of the census (the Chronicler had a special purpose for including it; see ch. 21 and notes).

The Chronicler handles Solomon similarly. Solomon is specifically named in a divine oracle as David's successor (22:7–10; 28:6). His accession to the throne is announced publicly by David and is greeted with the unanimous support of all Israel (chs. 28—29). No mention is made of the bedridden David, who must overturn the attempted coup by Adonijah at the last moment to secure the throne for Solomon. Nor is there mention that the military commander Joab and the high priest Abiathar supported Adonijah's attempt (1 Kin 1). Solomon's execution of those who had wronged David (1 Kin 2) is also omitted. The accession of Solomon is without competition or detracting incident. The account of his reign is devoted almost wholly to the building of the temple (2 Chr 2—8), and no reference to his failures is included. No mention is made of his idolatry, his foreign wives or the rebellions against his rule (1 Kin 11). Even the blame for the schism is removed from Solomon (1 Kin 11:26–40; 12:1–4) and placed on the scheming of Jeroboam. Solomon's image in Chronicles is such that he can be paired with David in the most favorable light (2 Chr 11:17).

The David and Solomon of the Chronicler, then, must be seen not only as the David and Solomon of history, but also as typifying the Messianic king of the Chronicler's expectation.

2. Not only is there idealization of David and Solomon, but the author also appears to consciously adopt the account of the succession of Moses and Joshua as a model for the succession of David and Solomon:

a. Both David and Moses fail to attain their goals — one to build the temple and the other to enter the promised land. In both cases the divine prohibition is related to the appointment of a successor (22:5 – 13; 28:2 – 8; Deut 1:37 – 38; 31:2 – 8).

b. Both Solomon and Joshua bring the people of God into rest (22:8 – 9; Josh 11:23; 21:44).

c. There are a number of verbal parallels in the appointments of Solomon and Joshua (compare 22:11 – 13,16; 28:7 – 10,20; 2 Chr 1:1 with Deut 31:5 – 8,23; Josh 1:5,7 – 9).

d. There are both private and public announcements of the appointment of the successors: private (22:6; Deut 31:23); public (28:8; Deut 31:7 — both "in the sight of all Israel").

e. Both enjoy the immediate and wholehearted support of the people (29:23 – 24; Deut 34:9; Josh 1:16 – 18).

f. It is twice reported that God "highly exalted" or "exalted . . . greatly" Solomon and Joshua (29:25; 2 Chr 1:1; Josh 3:7; 4:14).

The Chronicler also uses other models from Pentateuchal history in his portrayal of David and Solomon. Like Moses, David received the plans for the temple from God (28:11 – 19; Ex 25:9) and called on the people to bring voluntary offerings for its construction (29:1 – 9; Ex 25:1 – 7). Solomon's relationship to Huram-abi, the craftsman from Tyre (2 Chr 2:13 – 14), echoes the role of Bezalel and Oholiab in the building of the tabernacle (Ex 35:30 — 36:7). See note on 2 Chr 1:5.

Genealogies

Analysis of genealogies, both inside and outside the Bible, has disclosed that they serve a variety of functions (with different principles governing the lists), that they vary in form (some being segmented, others linear) and depth (number of generations listed), and that they are often fluid (subject to change).

There are three general areas in which genealogies function: the familial or domestic, the legal-political, and the religious. In the domestic area an individual's social status, privileges and obligations may be reflected in his placement in the lineage (see 7:14 – 19); the rights of the firstborn son and the secondary status of the children of concubines are examples from the Bible. In the political sphere genealogies substantiate claims to hereditary office or settle competing claims when the office is contested. Land organization and territorial groupings of social units may also be determined by genealogical reckoning — e.g., the division of the land among the 12 tribes. In Israel military levies also proceeded along genealogical lines; several of the genealogies in Chronicles reflect military conscription (5:1 – 26; 7:1 – 12,30 – 40; 8:1 – 40). Genealogies function in the religious sphere primarily by establishing membership among the priests and Levites (6:1 – 30; 9:10 – 34; Neh 7:61 – 65).

As to form, some genealogical lists trace several lines of descent (segmented genealogies) while others are devoted to a single line (linear genealogies).

Comparison of genealogical lists of the same tribal or family line often brings to light surprising differences. This fluidity of the lists may reflect variation in function. But sometimes changes in the status or relations of social structures are reflected in genealogies by changes in the relationships of names in the genealogy (see notes on 1:35 – 42; 6:22,27) or by the addition of names or segments to a lineage (see notes on 5:11 – 22; 6:27; 7:6 – 12). The most common type of fluidity in Biblical materials is telescoping, the omission of names from the list. Unimportant names are left out in order to relate an individual to a prominent ancestor, or possibly to achieve the desired number of names in the genealogy. Some Biblical genealogies, for example, omit names to achieve multiples of 7: For the period from David to the exile Matthew gives 14 generations (2 times 7), while Luke gives 21 (3 times 7), and the same authors give similar multiples of 7 for the period from the exile to Jesus (Matt 1:1 – 17; Luke 3:23 – 38).

The genealogies of Chronicles show variation in all these properties; the arrangements often reflect the purpose for which the genealogies were composed prior to their being adopted by the Chronicler as part of his record.

Outline

I. Genealogies: Creation to Restoration (1 Chr 1 — 9)
   A. The Patriarchs (ch. 1)
   B. The 12 Sons of Jacob/Israel (2:1 – 2)

   - C. The Family of Judah (2:3—4:23)
   - D. The Sons of Simeon (4:24–43)
   - E. Reuben, Gad and the Half-Tribe of Manasseh (ch. 5)
   - F. Levi and Families (ch. 6)
   - G. Issachar, Benjamin, Naphtali, Manasseh, Ephraim and Asher (chs. 7—9)
- II. The Reign of David (1 Chr 10—29)
   - A. Death of Saul (ch. 10)
   - B. Capture of Jerusalem; David's Power Base (chs. 11—12)
   - C. Return of the Ark; Establishment of David's Kingdom (chs. 13—16)
   - D. Dynastic Promise (ch. 17)
   - E. David's Conquests (chs. 18—20)
   - F. The Census (ch. 21)
   - G. Preparations for the Temple (ch. 22)
   - H. Organization of the Temple Service (chs. 23—26)
   - I. Administrative Structures of the Kingdom (ch. 27)
   - J. David's Final Preparations for Succession and the Temple (28:1—29:20)
   - K. Succession of Solomon; Death of David (29:21–30)
- III. The Reign of Solomon (2 Chr 1—9)
   - A. The Gift of Wisdom (ch. 1)
   - B. Building the Temple (2:1—5:1)
   - C. Dedication of the Temple (5:2—7:22)
   - D. Solomon's Other Activities (ch. 8)
   - E. Solomon's Wisdom, Splendor and Death (ch. 9)
- IV. The Schism, and the History of the Kings of Judah (2 Chr 10—36)
   - A. Rehoboam (chs. 10—12)
   - B. Abijah (13:1—14:1)
   - C. Asa (14:2—16:14)
   - D. Jehoshaphat (17:1—21:3)
   - E. Jehoram and Ahaziah (21:4—22:9)
   - F. Joash (22:10—24:27)
   - G. Amaziah (ch. 25)
   - H. Uzziah (ch. 26)
   - I. Jotham (ch. 27)
   - J. Ahaz (ch. 28)
   - K. Hezekiah (chs. 29—32)
   - L. Manasseh (33:1–20)
   - M. Amon (33:21–25)
   - N. Josiah (34:1—36:1)
   - O. Josiah's Successors (36:2–14)
   - P. Exile and Restoration (36:15–23)

Genealogy from Adam

1 [a]Adam, Seth, Enosh,
2 Kenan, Mahalalel, Jared,
3 Enoch, Methuselah, Lamech,
4 Noah, Shem, Ham and Japheth.
5 [a]The sons of Japheth *were* Gomer,
Magog, Madai, Javan, Tubal, Meshech and
Tiras.
6 The sons of Gomer *were* Ashkenaz,
[1]Diphath, and Togarmah.
7 The sons of Javan *were* Elishah, Tarshish, Kittim and [1]Rodanim.
8 The sons of Ham *were* Cush, Mizraim,
Put, and Canaan.
9 The sons of Cush *were* Seba, Havilah,
Sabta, Raama and Sabteca; and the sons of
Raamah *were* Sheba and Dedan.
10 Cush [1]became the father of Nimrod; he
began to be a mighty one in the earth.
11 [a]Mizraim became the father of the people of Lud, Anam, Lehab, Naphtuh,
12 Pathrus, Casluh, from which the [1]Phi-
listines came, and Caphtor.
13 Canaan became the father of Sidon, his
firstborn, Heth,
14 and the Jebusites, the Amorites, the
Girgashites,
15 the Hivites, the Arkites, the Sinites,
16 the Arvadites, the Zemarites and the
Hamathites.
17 [a]The sons of Shem *were* Elam, Asshur,
Arpachshad, Lud, Aram, Uz, Hul, Gether
and [1]Meshech.
18 Arpachshad became the father of Shelah and Shelah became the father of Eber.
19 Two sons were born to Eber, the name
of the one was Peleg, for in his days the earth
was divided, and his brother's name was
Joktan.
20 Joktan became the father of Almodad,
Sheleph, Hazarmaveth, Jerah,
21 Hadoram, Uzal, Diklah,
22 [1]Ebal, Abimael, Sheba,
23 Ophir, Havilah and Jobab; all these
were the sons of Joktan.
24 [a]Shem, Arpachshad, Shelah,
25 Eber, Peleg, Reu,
26 Serug, Nahor, Terah,
27 Abram, that is Abraham.

Descendants of Abraham

28 The sons of Abraham *were* Isaac and
Ishmael.
29 [a]These are their genealogies: the firstborn of Ishmael *was* Nebaioth, then Kedar,
Adbeel, Mibsam,
30 Mishma, Dumah, Massa, Hadad, Tema,
31 Jetur, Naphish and Kedemah; these
were the sons of Ishmael.
32 [a]The sons of Keturah, Abraham's concubine, *whom* she bore, *were* Zimran, Jokshan, Medan, Midian, Ishbak and Shuah. And
the sons of Jokshan *were* Sheba and Dedan.
33 The sons of Midian were Ephah, Epher,
Hanoch, Abida and Eldaah. All these were
the sons of Keturah.
34 [a]Abraham became the father of Isaac.
The sons of Isaac *were* [b]Esau and Israel.
35 [a]The sons of Esau *were* Eliphaz, Reuel,
Jeush, Jalam and Korah.
36 The sons of Eliphaz *were* Teman, Omar,
[1]Zephi, Gatam, Kenaz, Timna and Amalek.

1:1 [a]Gen 4:25-5:32
5 [a]Gen 10:2-4
6 [1]In Gen 10:3, *Riphath*
7 [1]In Gen 10:4, *Dodanim*
10 [1]Lit *begot,* and so throughout the ch
11 [a]Gen 10:13-18
12 [1]Or *people of Pelisht*
17 [1]In Gen 10:23, *Mash*
[a]Gen 10:22-29
22 [1]In Gen 10:28, *Obal*
24 [a]Gen 11:10-26; Luke 3:34-36
29 [a]Gen 25:13-16
32 [a]Gen 25:1-4
34 [a]1 Chr 1:28
[b]Gen 25:25, 26; 32:28
35 [a]Gen 36:4-10
36 [1]In Gen 36:11, *Zepho*

1:1–9:44 The genealogies succinctly show the restored community's continuity with the past. The great deeds of God on Israel's behalf prior to the rise of David are passed over in silence, but the genealogies serve as a skeleton of history to show that the Israel of the restoration stands at the center of the divine purpose from the beginning (from Adam, v. 1). And the genealogies also serve the very practical purpose of legitimizing the present. They provide the framework by which the ethnic and religious purity of the people can be maintained. They also establish the continuing line of royal succession and the legitimacy of the priests for the postexilic temple service. (See Introduction: Genealogies.)

1:1–2:1 The Chronicler here covers the period from Adam to Jacob, and the materials are drawn almost entirely from Genesis. The subsidiary lines of descent are presented first: Japheth and Ham (vv. 5–16) are given before Shem (vv. 17–27), the sons of Shem other than those in Abraham's ancestry (vv. 17–23) before that line (vv. 24–27), the sons of Abraham's concubines (vv. 28–33) before Isaac's line (v. 34), the descendants of Esau and the Edomite ruling houses (vv. 35–54) before the sons of Israel (2:1). In each case the elect lineage is given last.

Several features of this genealogy are striking when compared with non-Biblical materials. The genealogy begins without an introduction. Two sections of the genealogy have no kinship terms and are only lists of names: the first 13 names (vv. 1–4; see note on v. 4) and vv. 24–27. In vv. 5–16 (and following v. 27) kinship terms are used. Both segmented (those tracing several lines of descent) and linear (those tracing a single line) genealogies are included. This identical structure is found in a copy of the Assyrian King List: There is no introduction, and the scribe has drawn lines across the tablet dividing it into four sections, two of which are lists of names without kinship terms, alternating with two lists in which relations are specified; both segmented and linear genealogies are used. This suggests that the Chronicler was following a known literary pattern for his composition.

1:1–4 From creation to the flood. This list is taken from Gen 5:1–32 (see notes there). The omission of Cain and Abel demonstrates the Chronicler's interest in the chosen line (see Gen 4:17–25).

1:4 *Noah.* Shem, Ham, and Japheth were the sons of Noah. The Chronicler's readers would have known this and would not have needed a kinship notice in the text; the Septuagint (the Greek translation of the OT) and some modern translations read "the sons of Noah" to clarify the relationship of the four names.

1:5–23 This genealogy is drawn from the table of nations in Gen 10:2–29 (see notes there). The arrangement is primarily geographical and cultural rather than biological. Omitting the Philistines (v. 12) as a parenthesis, a total of 70 nations is achieved: Japheth, 14; Ham, 30; Shem, 26 (see note on Gen 10:2)—an example of a genealogy telescoped to attain multiples of 7 (see Introduction: Genealogies).

1:24–27 See notes on 1:1–2:1; Gen 11:10–26.

1:28–34 See notes on Gen 25:1–18.

1:35–42 See Gen 36:10–28 and notes.

1:36 *sons of Eliphaz.* These correspond to Gen 36:11–12, but with one difficulty: Listing Timna and Amalek as sons of Eliphaz is in apparent conflict with Gen 36:12, where Timna is the con-

37 The sons of Reuel *were* Nahath, Zerah,
Shammah and Mizzah.
38 [a]The sons of Seir *were* Lotan, Shobal,
Zibeon, Anah, Dishon, Ezer and Dishan.
39 The sons of Lotan *were* Hori and
[1]Homam; and Lotan's sister *was* Timna.
40 The sons of Shobal *were* [1]Alian, Manahath, Ebal, [2]Shephi and Onam. And the sons
of Zibeon *were* Aiah and Anah.
41 The [1]son of Anah *was* Dishon. And the
sons of Dishon *were* [2]Hamran, Eshban, Ithran and Cheran.
42 The sons of Ezer *were* Bilhan, Zaavan
and [1]Jaakan. The sons of Dishan *were* Uz
and Aran.
43 [a]Now these are the kings who reigned
in the land of Edom before any king of the
sons of Israel reigned. Bela was the son of
Beor, and the name of his city was Dinhabah.
44 When Bela died, Jobab the son of
Zerah of [a]Bozrah became king in his place.
45 When Jobab died, Husham of the land
of [a]the Temanites became king in his place.
46 When Husham died, Hadad the son of
Bedad, who [1]defeated Midian in the field of
Moab, became king in his place; and the
name of his city *was* Avith.
47 When Hadad died, Samlah of Masrekah became king in his place.
48 When Samlah died, Shaul of Rehoboth
by the River became king in his place.
49 When Shaul died, Baal-hanan the son
of Achbor became king in his place.
50 When Baal-hanan died, [1]Hadad
became king in his place; and the name of
his city was [2]Pai, and his wife's name was
Mehetabel, the daughter of Matred, the
daughter of Mezahab.
51 Then Hadad died.
Now the chiefs of Edom were: chief Timna, chief [1]Aliah, chief Jetheth,
52 chief Oholibamah, chief Elah, chief
Pinon,
53 chief Kenaz, chief Teman, chief Mibzar,
54 chief Magdiel, chief Iram. These *were*
the chiefs of Edom.

Genealogy: Twelve Sons of Jacob (Israel)

2 [a]These are the sons of Israel: Reuben,
Simeon, Levi, Judah, Issachar, Zebulun,
2 Dan, Joseph, Benjamin, Naphtali, Gad
and Asher.
3 [a]The sons of Judah *were* Er, Onan and
Shelah; *these* three were born to him by
Bath-shua the Canaanitess. And Er, Judah's
firstborn, was wicked in the sight of the
LORD, so He put him to death.
4 [a]Tamar his daughter-in-law bore him
Perez and Zerah. Judah had five sons in all.
5 The sons of Perez *were* Hezron and
Hamul.
6 The sons of Zerah *were* [1]Zimri, Ethan,
Heman, Calcol and [2]Dara; five of them in all.
7 The [1]son of Carmi *was* [2a]Achar, the
troubler of Israel, who violated the ban.
8 The [1]son of Ethan *was* Azariah.

Genealogy of David

9 Now the sons of Hezron, who were
born to him *were* Jerahmeel, Ram and
Chelubai.
10 Ram [1]became the father of Ammin-

38 [a]Gen 36:20-28
39 [1]In Gen 36:22, *Hemam*
40 [1]In Gen 36:23, *Alvan* [2]In Gen 36:23, *Shepho*
41 [1]Lit *sons* [2]In Gen 36:26, *Hemdan*
42 [1]Or *Akan*, as in Gen 36:27
43 [a]Gen 36:31-43
44 [a]Is 34:6
45 [a]Job 2:11
46 [1]Lit *smote*
50 [1]In Gen 36:39, *Hadar* [2]In Gen 36:39, *Pau*
51 [1]In Gen 36:40, *Alvah*
2:1 [a]Gen 35:22-26; 46:8-25
3 [a]Gen 38:2-10
4 [a]Gen 38:13-30
6 [1]In Josh 7:1, *Zabdi* [2]In 1 Kin 4:31, *Darda*
7 [1]Lit *sons* [2]In Josh 7:18, *Achan* [a]Josh 7:1
8 [1]Lit *sons*
10 [1]Lit *begot*, and so throughout the ch

cubine of Eliphaz and mother of Amalek. The Septuagint (the Greek translation of the OT) assumes a mistake in the Hebrew text and lists Amalek as Eliphaz's son by Timna. Perhaps the Chronicler has once again omitted kinship terminology (see notes on 1:1–2:1; v. 4). Alternatively, some regard this as an example of genealogical fluidity (see Introduction: Genealogies): Since the name Timna also became the name of a chiefdom in Edom (v. 51; Gen 36:40), during the course of time Timna was "promoted" in the Edomite genealogies to the position of a son of Eliphaz and brother of Amalek.

1:43–54 See Gen 36:31–43. The Chronicler continues with extensive coverage of Edom. This is striking in contrast to his omission of the line of Cain and the brief treatment of the line of Ishmael. It probably reflects the fact that the Edomites were important in the Chronicler's own day (see 18:11–13; 2 Chr 8:17; 21:8; 25:20; 28:17).

2:1–2 Although there are numerous lists of the 12 tribes in the OT, only four are given in genealogical form: (1) Gen 29:31–30:24; 35:16–20; (2) Gen 35:22–26; (3) Gen 46:8–27; (4) here. Other lists of the tribes are found in 12:24–37; 27:16–22; Ex 1:2–5; Deut 27:12–13; 33; Ezek 48:31–34. In other lists the tribe of Levi is omitted, and the number 12 is achieved by dividing Joseph into the tribes of Ephraim and Manasseh (Num 1:5–15; 1:20–43; 2:3–31; 7:12–83; 10:14–28; 13:4–15; 26:5–51). In this passage the Chronicler appears to follow Gen 35:22–26 except for the position of the tribe of Dan, which is found in seventh instead of ninth place. The list here does not set the order in which the Chronicler will take up the tribes; rather, he moves immediately to his major concern with the house of David and the tribe of Judah (2:3–4:23), even though Judah is fourth in the genealogy. In the lists of these chapters the Chronicler maintains the number 12, but with the following names: Judah, Simeon, Reuben, Gad, half of Manasseh, Levi, Issachar, Benjamin, Naphtali, Ephraim, Manasseh and Asher. Zebulun and Dan are omitted.

2:3–9 The lineage of Judah is traced to Hezron's sons (v. 9), whose descendants are given in 2:10–3:24. Of Judah's five sons, the first two (Er and Onan) died as the result of sin recorded in Gen 38. The lineage of the third son, Shelah, is taken up in 4:21; this section focuses on the remaining two (see Gen 46:12; Num 26:19–22).

2:6 *Ethan, Heman, Calcol and Dara.* Not immediate descendants of Zerah; rather, they are from the later period of the reign of Solomon (1 Kin 4:31). A Heman and an Ethan were David's musicians (see 15:19; Ps 88–89 titles), but whether these are the same individuals is uncertain. If they are the same, the fact that in 6:33–42 and 15:19 Heman and Ethan are assigned to the tribe of Levi may be another example of genealogical fluidity, where these men's musical skills brought them into the Levitical lineage. Or the reverse may have occurred: As Levites associated with Judah, they were brought into that lineage.

2:7 *Achar.* Achar (meaning "trouble") is called Achan in Josh 7; 22:20. The change from Achan to Achar is probably a play on words reflecting the trouble Achan brought to Israel.

2:10–3:24 That the Chronicler's primary concern in the genealogy of Judah is with the line of David is seen in his arrangement of this section's material as an inversion:

adab, and Amminadab became the father of Nahshon, leader of the sons of Judah;

11 Nahshon became the father of Salma, Salma became the father of Boaz,

12 Boaz became the father of Obed, and Obed became the father of Jesse;

13 and Jesse became the father of Eliab his firstborn, then Abinadab the second, [1]Shimea the third,

14 Nethanel the fourth, Raddai the fifth,

15 Ozem the sixth, David the seventh;

16 and their sisters *were* Zeruiah and Abigail. And the three sons of Zeruiah *were* [1]Abshai, Joab and Asahel.

17 Abigail bore Amasa, and the father of Amasa was [1]Jether the Ishmaelite.

18 Now Caleb the son of Hezron had sons by Azubah *his* wife, and by Jerioth; and these were her sons: Jesher, Shobab, and Ardon.

19 When Azubah died, Caleb married Ephrath, who bore him Hur.

20 Hur became the father of Uri, and Uri became the father of Bezalel.

21 Afterward Hezron went in to the daughter of Machir the father of Gilead, whom he married when he was sixty years old; and she bore him Segub.

22 Segub became the father of Jair, who had twenty-three cities in the land of Gilead.

23 But Geshur and Aram took [1]the towns of Jair from them, with Kenath and its villages, *even* sixty cities. All these were the sons of Machir, the father of Gilead.

24 After the death of Hezron in Calebephrathah, Abijah, Hezron's wife, bore him Ashhur the father of Tekoa.

25 Now the sons of Jerahmeel the firstborn of Hezron *were* Ram the firstborn, then Bunah, Oren, Ozem *and* Ahijah.

26 Jerahmeel had another wife, whose name was Atarah; she was the mother of Onam.

27 The sons of Ram, the firstborn of Jerahmeel, were Maaz, Jamin and Eker.

28 The sons of Onam were Shammai and Jada. And the sons of Shammai *were* Nadab and Abishur.

29 The name of Abishur's wife *was* Abihail, and she bore him Ahban and Molid.

30 The sons of Nadab *were* Seled and Appaim, and Seled died without sons.

31 The [1]son of Appaim *was* Ishi. And the [1]son of Ishi *was* Sheshan. And the [1]son of Sheshan *was* Ahlai.

32 The sons of Jada the brother of Shammai *were* Jether and Jonathan, and Jether died without sons.

33 The sons of Jonathan *were* Peleth and Zaza. These were the sons of Jerahmeel.

34 Now Sheshan had no sons, only daughters. And Sheshan had an Egyptian servant whose name was Jarha.

35 Sheshan gave his daughter to Jarha his servant in marriage, and she bore him Attai.

36 Attai became the father of Nathan, and Nathan became the father of Zabad,

37 and Zabad became the father of Ephlal, and Ephlal became the father of Obed,

38 and Obed became the father of Jehu, and Jehu became the father of Azariah,

39 and Azariah became the father of Helez, and Helez became the father of Eleasah,

40 and Eleasah became the father of Sismai, and Sismai became the father of Shallum,

41 and Shallum became the father of Jekamiah, and Jekamiah became the father of Elishama.

42 Now the sons of Caleb, the brother of Jerahmeel, *were* Mesha his firstborn, who

13 [1]In 1 Sam 16:9, *Shammah;* in 2 Sam 13:3, *Shimeah*
16 [1]In 2 Sam 2:18, *Abishai*
17 [1]In 2 Sam 17:25, *Ithra the Israelite*
23 [1]Or *Havvoth-jair*
31 [1]Lit *sons*

Descendants of Ram (David's ancestry), 2:10–17
Descendants of Caleb, 2:18–24
Descendants of Jerahmeel, 2:25–33
Supplementary material on Jerahmeel, 2:34–41
Supplementary material on Caleb, 2:42–55
Supplementary material on Ram (David's descendants), ch. 3

The Chronicler has structured this central portion of the Judah genealogy to highlight the Davidic ancestry and descent, which frame this section and emphasize the position of David—in line with the Chronicler's interests in the historical portions that follow (see note on 4:1–23).

2:10–17 Verses 10–12 are a linear genealogy from Ram to Jesse; then Jesse's lineage is segmented, reminiscent of 1 Sam 16:1–13. The source for most of the material is Ruth 4:19–22. In 1 Sam 16:10–13 David was the eighth of Jesse's sons to appear before Samuel; in this passage only seven are named, enabling David to occupy the favored place of the seventh son (v. 15; see Introduction: Genealogies). David was the half-uncle of his famous warriors Abishai, Joab, Asahel and Amasa (11:6,20,26; 2 Sam 2:13,18; 17:25; 19:13).

2:18–24 For the Chronicler the important name in this genealogy of the Calebites is Bezalel (v. 20), the wise master craftsman who supervised the building of the tabernacle (Ex 31:1–5). He is mentioned in the Bible only in Exodus and Chronicles. The Chronicler uses Bezalel and Oholiab (Ex 31:6) as a model for his portrait of Solomon and Huram-abi in the building of the temple (see note on 2 Chr 1:5). By inserting a reference to the builder of the tabernacle next to the genealogy of David in vv. 10–17, the Chronicler characteristically juxtaposes the themes of king and temple—so important to his historical narrative.

2:25–33 This section is identified as a separate entity from the supplementary material by its opening and closing formulas: "the sons of Jerahmeel" (v. 25) and "These were the sons of Jerahmeel" (v. 33). Verses 25–41 are the only genealogical materials on the Jerahmeelites in the Bible. 1 Sam 27:10 and 30:27–29 place their settlements in the Negev.

2:34–41 Supplementary material on the line of Sheshan (v. 31); it is a linear genealogy to a depth of 13 generations. The generation of Elishama (v. 41) would be the 23rd since Judah, if there has been no telescoping in this lineage. If no names are omitted, Elishama would likely be contemporary with David, though we know nothing of him.

2:42–55 The same opening and closing formulas noted in vv. 25,33 occur in vv. 42,50a: "Now the sons of Caleb . . . These were the sons of Caleb." The list in this section is a mixture of personal and place-names; the phrase "father of" can be under-

was the father of Ziph; and [1]his son was Mareshah, the father of Hebron.

43 The sons of Hebron *were* Korah and Tappuah and Rekem and Shema.

44 Shema became the father of Raham, the father of Jorkeam; and Rekem became the father of Shammai.

45 The son of Shammai was Maon, and Maon *was* the father of Bethzur.

46 Ephah, Caleb's concubine, bore Haran, Moza and Gazez; and Haran became the father of Gazez.

47 The sons of Jahdai *were* Regem, Jotham, Geshan, Pelet, Ephah and Shaaph.

48 Maacah, Caleb's concubine, bore Sheber and Tirhanah.

49 She also bore Shaaph the father of Madmannah, Sheva the father of Machbena and the father of Gibea; and the daughter of Caleb *was* Achsah.

50 These were the sons of Caleb.

The [1]sons of Hur, the firstborn of Ephrathah, *were* Shobal the father of Kiriath-jearim,

51 Salma the father of Bethlehem *and* Hareph the father of Beth-gader.

52 Shobal the father of Kiriath-jearim had sons: Haroeh, half of the Manahathites,

53 and the families of Kiriath-jearim: the Ithrites, the Puthites, the Shumathites and the Mishraites; from these came the Zorathites and the Eshtaolites.

54 The sons of Salma *were* Bethlehem and the Netophathites, Atroth-beth-joab and half of the Manahathites, the Zorites.

55 The families of scribes who lived at Jabez *were* the Tirathites, the Shimeathites *and* the Sucathites. Those are the Kenites who came from Hammath, the father of the house of Rechab.

Family of David

3 [a]Now these were the sons of David who were born to him in Hebron: the firstborn *was* Amnon, by Ahinoam the Jezreelitess; the second *was* Daniel, by Abigail the Carmelitess;

2 the third *was* Absalom the son of Maacah, the daughter of Talmai king of Geshur; the fourth *was* Adonijah the son of Haggith;

3 the fifth *was* Shephatiah, by Abital; the sixth *was* Ithream, by his wife Eglah.

4 Six were born to him in Hebron, and [a]there he reigned seven years and six months. And in Jerusalem he reigned thirty-three years.

5 [a]These were born to him in Jerusalem: Shimea, Shobab, Nathan and [b]Solomon, four, by [c]Bath-shua the daughter of Ammiel;

6 and Ibhar, Elishama, Eliphelet,

7 Nogah, Nepheg and Japhia,

8 Elishama, Eliada and Eliphelet, nine.

9 All *these were* the sons of David, besides the sons of the concubines; and [a]Tamar *was* their sister.

10 Now Solomon's son *was* Rehoboam, Abijah *was* his son, Asa his son, Jehoshaphat his son,

11 Joram his son, Ahaziah his son, Joash his son,

12 Amaziah his son, Azariah his son, Jotham his son,

13 Ahaz his son, Hezekiah his son, Manasseh his son,

14 Amon his son, Josiah his son.

15 The sons of Josiah *were* Johanan the firstborn, and the second *was* Jehoiakim, the third Zedekiah, the fourth Shallum.

16 The sons of Jehoiakim *were* Jeconiah his son, Zedekiah his son.

17 The sons of Jeconiah, the prisoner, *were* Shealtiel his son,

42 [1]Lit *the sons of*
50 [1]Lit *son*

3:1 [a]2 Sam 3:2-5
4 [a]2 Sam 2:11; 5:4, 5; 1 Kin 2:11; 1 Chr 29:27
5 [a]2 Sam 5:14-16; 1 Chr 14:4-7 [b]2 Sam 12:24, 25 [c]2 Sam 11:3
9 [a]2 Sam 13:1

stood not only as ancestor or predecessor, but also (as likely here) as "founder of" or "leader of" a city.

2:50b–55 Resumes the genealogy of Hur (v. 20). The same formulas for identifying the genealogical sections in vv. 25,33 and in vv. 42,50a are used in v. 50b and 4:4: "The sons of Hur . . . These were the sons of Hur." The presence of these formulas suggests that this section and 4:1–4 were once a unit; the Chronicler has inserted his record of the Davidic descent (ch. 3) into the middle of this other genealogy, apparently to balance the sections of his material (see notes on 2:10–3:24; 4:1–23). Otherwise the disruption of the genealogy of Hur may have already occurred in the Chronicler's sources.

2:55 *Tirathites, the Shimeathites and the Sucathites.* May refer to three families, as translated here, or possibly to three different classes of scribes, perhaps those who (1) read, (2) copied and (3) checked the work. *Kenites.* Originally a foreign people, many of the Kenites were incorporated into Judah (see Num 10:29–32; Judg 1:16; 4:11).

3:1–24 See note on 2:10–3:24.

3:1–9 This list of David's children is largely drawn from 2 Sam 3:2–5; 5:13–16; 13:1 (see notes there). The sons born in Jerusalem are repeated in 1 Chr 14:3–7. The name Eliphelet occurs twice (vv. 6,8); in 14:5,7 two spellings of the name are given (only one son having this name is mentioned in 2 Sam 5:14–16). The reference to David's seven-year rule in Hebron (v. 4) is repeated in 29:27, though the Chronicler does not deal with this period in his narrative. The references to Absalom, Tamar, Adonijah, Amnon and Bathsheba all recall unhappy incidents in the life of David, incidents the Chronicler has omitted from his later narrative (see 2 Sam 11–15; 17–18; 1 Kin 1).

3:10 *Rehoboam.* See 2 Chr 10–12. *Abijah.* See 2 Chr 13:1–14:1. *Asa.* See 2 Chr 14–16. *Jehoshaphat.* See 1 Kin 22.

3:11 *Joram.* See 2 Chr 21.

3:13 *Ahaz.* See 2 Chr 28. *Hezekiah.* See 2 Chr 29–32. *Manasseh.* See 2 Chr 33:1–20.

3:14 *Amon.* See 2 Chr 33:21–25. *Josiah.* See 2 Kin 22:1–23:30; 2 Chr 34:1–36:1.

3:15–16 "Johanan the firstborn" is not mentioned elsewhere and may have died before Josiah. The genealogy is segmented at this point, instead of linear as in vv. 10–14. Since Josiah's other three sons would all occupy the throne, the succession was not uniformly father to son. Shallum/Jehoahaz (2 Chr 36:2–4; 2 Kin 23:30–35) was replaced by Jehoiakim (2 Chr 36:5–8; 2 Kin 23:34–24:6); Jehoiakim was succeeded by his son Jehoiachin (2 Chr 36:9–10; 2 Kin 24:8–16). After Jehoiachin was taken captive to Babylon by Nebuchadnezzar, Josiah's son Zedekiah (2 Kin 24:17–25:7; 2 Chr 36:11–14) became the last king of Judah.

3:17–20 Seven sons are attributed to Jeconiah (Jehoiachin), but

18 and Malchiram, Pedaiah, Shenazzar, Jekamiah, Hoshama and Nedabiah.

19 The sons of Pedaiah *were* Zerubbabel and Shimei. And the [1]sons of Zerubbabel *were* Meshullam and Hananiah, and Shelomith *was* their sister;

20 and Hashubah, Ohel, Berechiah, Hasadiah and Jushab-hesed, five.

21 The [1]sons of Hananiah *were* Pelatiah and Jeshaiah, the sons of Rephaiah, the sons of Arnan, the sons of Obadiah, the sons of Shecaniah.

22 The [1]descendants of Shecaniah *were* Shemaiah, and the sons of Shemaiah: Hattush, Igal, Bariah, Neariah and Shaphat, six.

23 The [1]sons of Neariah *were* Elioenai, Hizkiah and Azrikam, three.

24 The sons of Elioenai *were* Hodaviah, Eliashib, Pelaiah, Akkub, Johanan, Delaiah and Anani, seven.

Line of Hur, Asher

4 [a]The sons of Judah *were* Perez, Hezron, Carmi, Hur and Shobal.

2 Reaiah the son of Shobal [1]became the father of Jahath, and Jahath became the father of Ahumai and Lahad. These *were* the families of the Zorathites.

3 These *were* the [1]sons of Etam: Jezreel, Ishma and Idbash; and the name of their sister *was* Hazzelelponi.

4 Penuel *was* the father of Gedor, and Ezer the father of Hushah. These *were* the sons of Hur, the firstborn of Ephrathah, the father of Bethlehem.

5 Ashhur, the father of Tekoa, had two wives, Helah and Naarah.

6 Naarah bore him Ahuzzam, Hepher, Temeni and Haahashtari. These were the sons of Naarah.

7 The sons of Helah *were* Zereth, [1]Izhar and Ethnan.

8 Koz became the father of Anub and Zobebah, and the families of Aharhel the son of Harum.

9 Jabez was more honorable than his brothers, and his mother named him Jabez saying, "Because I bore *him* with pain."

10 Now Jabez called on the God of Israel, saying, "Oh that You would bless me indeed and enlarge my border, and that Your hand might be with me, and that You would keep *me* from harm that *it* may not pain me!" And God granted him what he requested.

11 Chelub the brother of Shuhah became the father of Mehir, who was the father of Eshton.

12 Eshton became the father of Beth-rapha and Paseah, and Tehinnah the father of [1]Ir-nahash. These are the men of Recah.

13 Now the sons of Kenaz *were* Othniel and Seraiah. And the [1]sons of Othniel *were* Hathath and Meonothai.

14 Meonothai became the father of Oph-

19 [1]Lit *son*
21 [1]Lit *son*
22 [1]Lit *sons*
23 [1]Lit *son*
4:1 [a]1 Chr 2:3
2 [1]Lit *begot,* and so throughout the ch
3 [1]So with some ancient versions; Heb *father*
7 [1]Another reading is *Zohar*
12 [1]Or *the city of Nahash*

not one succeeded him (see notes on vv. 15–16; Jer 22:30). Tablets found in Babylon dating from the 10th to the 35th year of Nebuchadnezzar (595–570 B.C.) and listing deliveries of rations mention Jeconiah and five sons as well as other Judahites held in Babylon. Jeconiah received similar largess from Nebuchadnezzar's successor Evil-merodach (562–560 B.C.; see 2 Kin 25:27–30).

3:18 *Shenazzar.* May be another spelling of the name Sheshbazzar. If so, the treasures of the temple were consigned to his care for return to Judah (Ezra 1:11). He also served for a short time as the first governor of the returnees and made an initial attempt at rebuilding the temple (Ezra 5:14–16). Little is known of him; he soon disappeared from the scene and was overshadowed by his nephew Zerubbabel, who assumes such importance in Ezra, Haggai and Zechariah. But see note on Ezra 1:8.

3:19 *Pedaiah.* Other texts name Shealtiel (v. 17) as Zerubbabel's father (Ezra 3:2,8; Neh 12:1; Hag 1:12,14; 2:2,23). Suggestions offered to resolve this difficulty are: 1. Shealtiel may have died early, and Pedaiah became the head of the family. 2. Pedaiah may have married the childless widow of Shealtiel; Zerubbabel would then be regarded as the son of Shealtiel according to the law of levirate marriage (Deut 25:5–6). In Luke 3:27 Neri instead of Jehoiachin (v. 17) is identified as the father of Shealtiel. Similar suggestions to those above could be made in this instance as well. It is also interesting to note that the genealogies of Jesus in Matt 1 and Luke 3 both trace his descent to Zerubbabel, but that none of the names subsequent to Zerubbabel (v. 19–24) is found in the NT genealogies.

3:20 *five.* May have been sons of Zerubbabel, but no kinship terms are provided. Since the sons of Hananiah (v. 19) are specified in v. 21, they could also be the sons of Meshullam (v. 19).

3:21 *sons of Rephaiah . . . Shecaniah.* Probably other Davidic families at the time of Zerubbabel (v. 19) or Pelatiah and Jeshaiah. If they are understood as contemporary with Zerubbabel, his genealogy was carried only two generations (his sons and grandsons) and a date for Chronicles as early as 450 B.C. is possible (see Introduction: Author, Date and Sources).

3:22 *six.* Perhaps a copyist accidentally omitted one name.

4:1–23 None of the genealogies of Judah in this section appears elsewhere in Scripture. Although the section may have the appearance of miscellaneous notes, the careful shaping of the Chronicler is evident in light of the overall inverted structure of the genealogies of Judah:

2:3	Shelah
2:4–8	Perez
2:9—3:24	Hezron
4:1–20	Perez
4:21–23	Shelah

This balancing of the material in inverse order shows the centrality of the section of the lineage of Hezron and the house of David; the same balancing in inverse order is observed within the Hezron section (see note on 2:10–3:24). The record of Judah's oldest surviving son, Shelah, frames the entire genealogy of Judah. There are 15 fragmentary genealogies in this section, with two to six generations in each.

4:1–2 The descendants of Judah here are not brothers; rather, the genealogy is linear.

4:1 *Carmi.* Either a scribal confusion or an alternative name for Chelubai (2:9); the confusion may have been induced by 2:7.

4:2 *Reaiah.* A variant of Haroeh (2:52).

4:5–8 Supplementary to 2:24.

4:9–10 The practice of inserting short historical notes into genealogical records is amply attested in non-Biblical genealogical texts from the ancient Near East as well as in other Biblical genealogies (Gen 4:19–24; 10:8–12).

4:13 *Othniel.* The first of Israel's judges (Josh 15:17; Judg 1:13; 3:9–11).

rah, and Seraiah became the father of Joab
the father of [1]Ge-harashim, for they were
craftsmen.
15 The sons of Caleb the son of Jephunneh *were* Iru, Elah and Naam; and the [1]son
of Elah *was* [2]Kenaz.
16 The sons of Jehallelel *were* Ziph and
Ziphah, Tiria and Asarel.
17 The [1]sons of Ezrah *were* Jether, Mered,
Epher and Jalon. ([2]And these are the sons of
Bithia the daughter of Pharaoh, whom Mered
took) and she conceived *and bore* Miriam,
Shammai and Ishbah the father of Eshtemoa.
18 His Jewish wife bore Jered the father of
Gedor, and Heber the father of Soco, and
Jekuthiel the father of Zanoah.
19 The sons of the wife of Hodiah, the sister of Naham, *were* the [1]fathers of Keilah the
Garmite and Eshtemoa the Maacathite.
20 The sons of Shimon *were* Amnon and
Rinnah, Benhanan and Tilon. And the sons
of Ishi *were* Zoheth and Ben-zoheth.
21 The sons of Shelah the son of Judah
were Er the father of Lecah and Laadah the
father of Mareshah, and the families of the
house of the linen workers at Beth-ashbea;
22 and Jokim, the men of Cozeba, Joash,
Saraph, who ruled in Moab, and Jashubi-
lehem. And the [1]records are ancient.
23 These were the potters and the inhabitants of Netaim and Gederah; they lived
there with the king for his work.

Descendants of Simeon

24 The sons of Simeon *were* [1]Nemuel and
Jamin, [2]Jarib, [3]Zerah, Shaul;
25 Shallum his son, Mibsam his son,
Mishma his son.
26 The sons of Mishma *were* Hammuel his
son, Zaccur his son, Shimei his son.
27 Now Shimei had sixteen sons and six
daughters; but his brothers did not have
many sons, nor did all their family multiply
like the sons of Judah.
28 They lived at Beersheba, Moladah and
Hazar-shual,
29 at Bilhah, Ezem, Tolad,
30 Bethuel, Hormah, Ziklag,
31 Beth-marcaboth, Hazar-susim, Beth-
biri and Shaaraim. These *were* their cities
until the reign of David.
32 Their villages *were* Etam, Ain, Rimmon, Tochen and Ashan, five cities;
33 and all their villages that *were* around
the same cities as far as [1]Baal. These *were*
their settlements, and they have their genealogy.
34 Meshobab and Jamlech and Joshah the
son of Amaziah,
35 and Joel and Jehu the son of Joshibiah,
the son of Seraiah, the son of Asiel,
36 and Elioenai, Jaakobah, Jeshohaiah,
Asaiah, Adiel, Jesimiel, Benaiah,
37 Ziza the son of Shiphi, the son of Allon,
the son of Jedaiah, the son of Shimri, the son
of Shemaiah;
38 these mentioned by name *were* leaders
in their families; and their fathers' houses
increased greatly.
39 They went to the entrance of Gedor,
even to the east side of the valley, to seek
pasture for their flocks.
40 They found rich and good pasture, and
[a]the land was broad and quiet and peaceful;
for those who lived there formerly *were*
Hamites.
41 [a]These, recorded by name, came in the
days of Hezekiah king of Judah, and
[1]attacked their tents and the Meunites who
were found there, and destroyed them utterly to this day, and lived in their place,
because there was pasture there for their
flocks.
42 From them, from the sons of Simeon,
five hundred men went to [a]Mount Seir, with
Pelatiah, Neariah, Rephaiah and Uzziel, the
sons of Ishi, as their leaders.
43 [a]They [1]destroyed the remnant of the
Amalekites who escaped, and have lived
there to this day.

Genealogy from Reuben

5 Now the sons of Reuben the firstborn of
Israel (for [a]he was the firstborn, but

14 [1]Or *valley of craftsmen*
15 [1]Lit *sons* [2]Lit *and Kenaz*
17 [1]Lit *son* [2]In the Heb the words in ( ) are at the end of v 18
19 [1]Lit *father*
22 [1]Lit *words*
24 [1]In Gen 46:10 and Ex 6:15, *Jemuel* [2]In Num 26:12, *Jachin* [3]In Gen 46:10 and Ex 6:15, *Zohar*
33 [1]In Josh 19:8, *Baalath*
40 [a]Judg 18:7-10
41 [1]Lit *smote* [a]1 Chr 4:33-38
42 [a]Gen 36:8, 9
43 [1]Lit *smote* [a]1 Sam 15:7, 8; 30:17
5:1 [a]Gen 29:32; 1 Chr 2:1

4:16–20 This portion of the genealogy is from preexilic times; several of the places named were not included in the province of Judah in the restoration period (e.g., Ziph and Eshtemoa).

4:17 *Bithia the daughter of Pharaoh, whom Mered took.* Mered is otherwise unknown; the fact that he married a daughter of Pharaoh suggests his prominence. The event may be associated with the fortunes of Israel in Egypt under Joseph.

4:21,23 This section accurately reflects a feature of ancient Near Eastern society. Clans were often associated not only with particular localities but also with special trades or guilds, such as linen workers (v. 21), potters (v. 23), royal patronage (v. 23) and scribes (2:55).

4:24–43 The genealogy of Simeon is also found in Gen 46:10; Ex 6:15; Num 26:12–13. Simeon settled in part of the territory of Judah; the list of occupied towns should be compared with Josh 15:26–32,42; 19:2–7. Since Simeon occupied areas allotted to Judah, this tribe was politically incorporated into Judah and appears to have lost much of its own identity in history (see Gen 34:24–31; 49:5–7; see also notes on Gen 34:25; 49:7). Geographical and historical notes are inserted in the genealogy (see note on vv. 9–10). Apparently two genealogies are included here: vv. 24–33—ending with the formula, "they have their genealogy"—and vv. 34–43. Overpopulation (v. 38) caused them to expand toward Gedor and east toward Edom at the time of Hezekiah (vv. 39–43). The long hostility between Israel and Amalek surfaced once again (v. 43; cf. Ex 17:8–16; Deut 25:17–19; 1 Sam 15; see Introduction to Esther: Purpose, Themes and Literary Features).

5:1–26 The genealogical records of the Transjordan tribes: Reuben, Gad and half of Manasseh (see Num 32:33–42). The Chronicler's concern with "all Israel" includes incorporating the genealogical records of these tribes that were no longer significant entities in Israel's life in the restoration period, having been swept away in the Assyrian conquests.

5:1–10 The necessity to explain why the birthright of the firstborn did not remain with Reuben (see Gen 35:22; 49:4 for Reu-

because [b]he defiled his father's bed, [c]his
birthright was given to the sons of Joseph
the son of Israel; so that he is not enrolled in
the genealogy according to the birthright.
2 [a]Though Judah prevailed over his
brothers, and [b]from him *came* the leader, yet
the birthright belonged to Joseph),
3 [a]the sons of Reuben the firstborn of Israel *were* Hanoch and Pallu, Hezron and Carmi.
4 The sons of Joel *were* Shemaiah his
son, Gog his son, [a]Shimei his son,
5 Micah his son, Reaiah his son, Baal his
son,
6 Beerah his son, whom [1]Tilgath-pilneser
king of Assyria carried away into exile; he
was leader of the Reubenites.
7 His [1]kinsmen by their families, [a]in the
genealogy of their generations, *were* Jeiel the
chief, then Zechariah
8 and Bela the son of Azaz, the son of
Shema, the son of Joel, who lived in [a]Aroer,
even to Nebo and Baal-meon.
9 To the east he settled as far as the
entrance of the wilderness from the river
Euphrates, [a]because their cattle had increased in the land of Gilead.
10 In the days of Saul [a]they made war
with the Hagrites, who fell by their hand, so
that they [1]occupied their tents throughout
[2]all the land east of Gilead.
11 Now the sons of Gad lived opposite
them in the land of [a]Bashan as far as [b]Sale-
cah.
12 Joel *was* the chief and Shapham the
second, then Janai and Shaphat in Bashan.
13 Their [1]kinsmen of their fathers' households *were* Michael, Meshullam, Sheba,
Jorai, Jacan, Zia and Eber, seven.
14 These *were* the sons of Abihail, the son
of Huri, the son of Jaroah, the son of Gilead,
the son of Michael, the son of Jeshishai, the
son of Jahdo, the son of Buz;
15 Ahi the son of Abdiel, the son of Guni,
was head of their fathers' households.
16 They lived in Gilead, in Bashan and in
its towns, and in all the pasture lands of
[a]Sharon, as far as their [1]borders.
17 All of these were enrolled in the
genealogies in the days of [a]Jotham king of
Judah and in the days of [b]Jeroboam king of
Israel.
18 The sons of Reuben and the Gadites
and the half-tribe of Manasseh, *consisting* of
valiant men, men who bore shield and
sword and shot with bow and *were* skillful in
battle, *were* 44,760, who [a]went to war.
19 They made war against [a]the Hagrites,
[b]Jetur, Naphish and Nodab.
20 They were helped against them, and
the Hagrites and all who *were* with them
were given into their hand; for [a]they cried
out to God in the battle, and He answered
their prayers because [b]they trusted in Him.
21 They took away their cattle: their
50,000 camels, 250,000 sheep, 2,000 donkeys; and 100,000 [1]men.
22 For many fell slain, because [a]the war
was of God. And [b]they settled in their place
until the [c]exile.
23 Now the sons of the half-tribe of
Manasseh lived in the land; from Bashan to
Baal-hermon and [a]Senir and Mount Hermon
they were numerous.
24 These were the heads of their fathers'
households, even Epher, Ishi, Eliel, Azriel,
Jeremiah, Hodaviah and Jahdiel, mighty
men of valor, famous men, heads of their
fathers' households.
25 But they [a]acted treacherously against
the God of their fathers and [b]played the har-

5:1 [b]Gen 35:22; 49:4 [c]Gen 48:15-22 **2** [a]Gen 49:8-10; Ps 60:7; 108:8 [b]Mic 5:2; Matt 2:6 **3** [a]Gen 46:9; Ex 6:14; Num 26:5-9 **4** [a]1 Chr 5:8 **6** [1]In 2 Kin 15:29, *Tiglath-pileser* **7** [1]Lit *brothers* [a]1 Chr 5:17 **8** [a]Num 32:34; Josh 12:2 **9** [a]Josh 22:8, 9 **10** [1]Lit *dwelt in* [2]Lit *all the face of the east* [a]1 Chr 5:18-21 **11** [a]Josh 13:11 [b]Deut 3:10 **13** [1]Lit *brother*

16 [1]Lit *goings out* [a]1 Chr 27:29; Song 2:1; Is 35:2; 65:10 **17** [a]2 Kin 15:5, 32 [b]2 Kin 14:16, 28 **18** [a]Num 1:3 **19** [a]1 Chr 5:10 [b]Gen 25:15; 1 Chr 1:31 **20** [a]2 Chr 14:11-13 [b]Ps 9:10; 20:7, 8; 22:4, 5 **21** [1]Lit *souls of men* **22** [a]Josh 23:10; 2 Chr 32:8; Rom 8:31 [b]1 Chr 4:41 [c]2 Kin 15:29; 17:6 **23** [a]Deut 3:9 **25** [a]Deut 32:15-18 [b]Ex 34:15

ben's sin) interrupts the initial statement (v. 1), which is then repeated after the explanation (v. 3). The parenthetical material (vv. 1–2) shows the writer's partiality for Judah, even though Joseph received the double portion (Ephraim and Manasseh) of the firstborn. The Hebrew term translated "leader" (v. 2) is used of David in 11:2; 17:7; 2 Sam 5:2; 6:21; 7:8; cf. 1 Chr 28:4. The use of military titles (vv. 6–7) and a battle account (v. 10) suggest that this genealogy may have functioned in military organization (see Introduction: Genealogies). The source for some of this material on Reuben is Num 26:5–11. The Chronicler has omitted reference to Eliab and his three sons who perished in the rebellion of Korah (see Num 26:8–10) and so were not relevant to his purpose.

5:6 *Tilgath-pilneser.* Tiglath-pileser. This Assyrian king (745–727 B.C.) attacked Israel (v. 26; 2 Kin 15:29) and also imposed tribute on Ahaz of Judah (2 Chr 28:19–20; 2 Kin 16:7–10).

5:10 *Hagrites.* See vv. 19–22. Named among the enemies of Israel (Ps 83:6), this tribe is apparently associated with Hagar, the mother of Ishmael (Gen 16), but see note on Ps 83:6.

5:11–22 The materials in this list for the tribe of Gad have no parallels in the Bible. The other genealogies of Gad are organized around his seven sons (Gen 46:16; Num 26:15–18); here four names are given, none found in the other lists. The Chronicler states (v. 17) that these records came from the period of Jotham of Judah (750–732 B.C.) and Jeroboam of Israel (793–753). The presence of military titles and narratives (vv. 12,18–22) suggests that this genealogy originated as part of a military census. The territory of Gad is delineated in Deut 3:12.

5:18–22 The first example of the Chronicler's theme of immediate retribution (see Introduction: Purpose and Themes). Success in warfare is attributed to their crying out to God (v. 20; cf. 2 Chr 6:24–25,34–39; 12:7–12; 13:13–16; 14:9–15; 18:31; 20:1–30; 32:1–23).

5:23–26 Manasseh is treated further in 7:14–19; the half-tribe that settled in Transjordan is dealt with here since it shared the same fate as Reuben and Gad, and possibly also so that the Chronicler could keep the total of 12 for his tribal genealogies (see note on 2:1–2). Again immediate retribution is apparent: Just as trust in God can bring victory (vv. 18–22), so also defeat comes to the unfaithful (vv. 25–26). The use of the retributive theme in these two accounts argues for the unity of the genealogies with the historical portions of Chronicles. The list of names given here is not properly a genealogy but a list of clans. Since they are described as brave warriors in connection with a battle report (vv. 24–26), this section too is likely derived from records of military conscription (see note on vv. 1–10; see also 2 Kin 15:19,29; 17:6; 18:11).

lot [c]after the gods of the peoples of the land,
whom God had destroyed before them.
26 So the God of Israel stirred up the spirit of [a]Pul, king of Assyria, even the spirit of
[1]Tilgath-pilneser king of Assyria, and he
[b]carried them away into exile, namely the
Reubenites, the Gadites and the half-tribe of
Manasseh, and brought them to Halah,
Habor, Hara and to the river of Gozan, to this
day.

Genealogy: The Priestly Line

6 [1a]The sons of Levi *were* [2]Gershon, Kohath
and Merari.
2 The sons of Kohath *were* Amram, Izhar,
Hebron and Uzziel.
3 The children of Amram *were* Aaron,
Moses and Miriam. And the sons of Aaron
were Nadab, Abihu, Eleazar and Ithamar.
4 Eleazar [1]became the father of Phinehas, *and* Phinehas became the father of
Abishua,
5 and Abishua became the father of Bukki, and Bukki became the father of Uzzi,
6 and Uzzi became the father of Zerahiah, and Zerahiah became the father of Meraioth,
7 Meraioth became the father of Amariah, and Amariah became the father of Ahitub,
8 and [a]Ahitub became the father of
Zadok, and Zadok [b]became the father of
Ahimaaz,
9 and Ahimaaz became the father of Azariah, and Azariah became the father of Johanan,
10 and Johanan became the father of Azariah ([a]it was he who served as the priest in
the house [b]which Solomon built in Jerusalem),
11 and [a]Azariah became the father of
Amariah, and Amariah became the father of
Ahitub,
12 and Ahitub became the father of Zadok,
and Zadok became the father of [1]Shallum,
13 and Shallum became the father of Hilkiah, and Hilkiah became the father of Azariah,
14 and Azariah became the father of
[a]Seraiah, and Seraiah became the father of
Jehozadak;
15 and Jehozadak went *along* when the
LORD carried Judah and Jerusalem away into
exile [1]by Nebuchadnezzar.
16 [1a]The sons of Levi *were* [2]Gershom,
Kohath and Merari.
17 These are the names of the sons of Gershom: Libni and Shimei.
18 The sons of Kohath *were* Amram, Izhar,
Hebron and Uzziel.
19 The sons of [a]Merari *were* Mahli and
Mushi. And these are the families of the
Levites according to their fathers' *households*.
20 Of Gershom: Libni his son, Jahath his
son, Zimmah his son,
21 Joah his son, Iddo his son, Zerah his
son, Jeatherai his son.
22 The sons of Kohath *were* Amminadab
his son, Korah his son, Assir his son,
23 Elkanah his son, Ebiasaph his son and
Assir his son,

25 [c]2 Kin 17:7
26 [1]In 2 Kin 15:29, *Tiglath-pileser* [a]2 Kin 15:19, 29; 2 Chr 28:20 [b]2 Kin 17:6
6:1 [1]Ch 5:27 in Heb [2]In v 16, *Gershom* [a]Gen 46:11; Ex 6:16-25
4 [1]Lit *begot*, and so throughout the ch
8 [a]2 Sam 8:17 [b]2 Sam 15:27
10 [a]2 Chr 26:17 [b]1 Kin 6:1; 2 Chr 3:1
11 [a]Ezra 7:3
12 [1]In ch 9:11, *Meshullam*
14 [a]Neh 11:11
15 [1]Lit *by the hand of*
16 [1]Ch 6:1 in Heb [2]In v 1, *Gershon* [a]Gen 46:11; Ex 6:16
19 [a]Num 3:33; 1 Chr 23:21

5:26 *Pul.* Probably Tilgath-pilneser's (Tiglath-pileser's) throne name in Babylon (the Babylonians called him Pulu).
6:1–81 This chapter is devoted to a series of lists, all pertaining to the tribe of Levi. The first section (vv. 1–15) records the line of the high priests down to the exile; the clans of Levi follow (vv. 16–30). David's appointees as temple musicians came from the three clans of Levi: Gershon, Kohath and Merari (vv. 31–47). The generations between Aaron and Ahimaaz are given a separate listing (vv. 49–53), reinforcing the separate duties of priests and Levites (see note on Ex 32:26). The listing of the Levitical possessions among the tribes concludes the chapter (vv. 54–81).
6:1–3 A short segmented genealogy narrows the descendants of Levi to the lineage of Eleazar, in whose line the high priests are presented in linear form (vv. 4–15). The sons of Levi (v. 1) always appear in this order, based on age (v. 16; Gen 46:11; Ex 6:16; Num 3:17; 26:57). Of Aaron's four sons (v. 3), the first two died as a result of sacrilege (Lev 10:2; Num 26:61); succeeding generations of priests would trace their lineage to either Eleazar or Ithamar.
6:4–15 This list of high priests from the time of Eleazar to the exile has been sharply telescoped. The following high priests known from the OT are not mentioned: Jehoiada (2 Kin 12:2), Urijah (2 Kin 16:10–16), possibly two other Azariahs (2 Chr 26:17,20; 31:10–13), Eli (1 Sam 1:9; 14:3) and Abiathar (2 Sam 8:17). The list is repeated with some variation in Ezra 7:1–5 (see notes there).
6:8 *Ahitub became the father of Zadok.* This Zadok was one of David's two priests (18:16; 2 Sam 8:17). When David's other priest, Abiathar (see note on vv. 4–15), supported the rebellion of Adonijah, Zadok supported Solomon (1 Kin 1). After the expulsion of Abiathar (1 Kin 2:26–27), Zadok alone held the office (1 Chr 29:22), which continued in his line (1 Kin 4:2). The Ahitub mentioned here should not be confused with the priest who was the grandson of Eli (1 Sam 14:3) and grandfather of Abiathar (1 Sam 22:20); the line of Zadok replaced the line of Eli (1 Sam 2:27–36; 1 Kin 2:26–27). For the importance of the line of Zadok see Ezek 40:46; 43:19; 44:15; 48:11. Ezra was concerned to trace his own priestly lineage to this house (Ezra 7:1–5).
6:13 *Hilkiah.* Discovered the Book of the Law in the temple at the time of Josiah (2 Kin 22; 2 Chr 34).
6:14 *Seraiah.* Executed by the Babylonians after the conquest of Jerusalem in 586 B.C. (2 Kin 25:18–21). *Jehozadak.* Father of Jeshua, the high priest in the first generation of the restoration. His name is spelled "Jozadak" in Ezra 3:2,8; 5:2; 10:18; Neh 12:26 and "Jehozadak" elsewhere (see Hag 1:1; 2:2; Zech 6:11).
6:16–19a Repeated from Ex 6:16–19; Num 3:17–20; 26:57–61.
6:22–23 *Assir . . . Elkanah . . . Ebiasaph.* Ex 6:24 names these men as sons of Korah, but here they are presented in the form ordinarily used for a linear genealogy of successive generations (see vv. 20–21,25–26,29–30). Either this is another example of genealogical fluidity, or one must understand "his son" as referring to Kohath and not to the immediately preceding name.
6:22 *Amminadab.* The almost parallel genealogy later in this chapter lists Izhar in the place of Amminadab—who is nowhere else listed as a son of Kohath, while every other list includes Izhar (vv. 2,37–38; Ex 6:18,21). Either Amminadab is an otherwise unattested alternative name of Izhar, or he is an otherwise unknown son. Or this may be another example of genealogical

24 Tahath his son, Uriel his son, Uzziah his son and Shaul his son.

25 The sons of Elkanah *were* Amasai and Ahimoth.

26 *As for* Elkanah, the sons of Elkanah *were* Zophai his son and Nahath his son,

27 Eliab his son, Jeroham his son, Elkanah his son.

28 The sons of Samuel *were* [a]Joel the firstborn, and Abijah the second.

29 The sons of Merari *were* Mahli, Libni his son, Shimei his son, Uzzah his son,

30 Shimea his son, Haggiah his son, Asaiah his son.

31 [a]Now these are those whom David appointed over the service of song in the house of the LORD, [b]after the ark rested *there.*

32 They ministered with song before the tabernacle of the tent of meeting, until Solomon had built the house of the LORD in Jerusalem; and they [1]served in their office according to their order.

33 These are those who [1]served with their sons: From the sons of the Kohathites *were* Heman the singer, the son of Joel, the son of Samuel,

34 the son of Elkanah, the son of Jeroham, the son of Eliel, the son of Toah,

35 the son of Zuph, the son of Elkanah, the son of Mahath, the son of Amasai,

36 the son of Elkanah, the son of Joel, the son of Azariah, the son of Zephaniah,

37 the son of Tahath, the son of Assir, the son of Ebiasaph, the son of Korah,

38 the son of Izhar, the son of Kohath, the son of Levi, the son of Israel.

39 *Heman's* brother Asaph stood at his right hand, even Asaph the son of Berechiah, the son of Shimea,

40 the son of Michael, the son of Baaseiah, the son of Malchijah,

41 the son of Ethni, the son of Zerah, the son of Adaiah,

42 the son of Ethan, the son of Zimmah, the son of Shimei,

43 the son of Jahath, the son of Gershom, the son of Levi.

28 [a]1 Sam 8:2; 1 Chr 6:33
31 [a]1 Chr 15:16-22, 27; 16:4-6 [b]2 Sam 6:17; 1 Kin 8:4; 1 Chr 15:25-16:1
32 [1]Lit *stood over*
33 [1]Lit *stood*
44 [1]Lit *brothers*
48 [1]Lit *brothers* [2]Lit *given*
49 [1]Lit *offered up in smoke* [a]Ex 27:1-8 [b]Ex 30:1-7 [c]Ex 30:10-16
50 [a]1 Chr 6:4-8; Ezra 7:5
54 [a]Josh 21:4, 10
55 [a]Josh 14:13; 21:11f
56 [a]Josh 15:13
57 [a]Josh 21:13, 19
58 [1]In Josh 21:15, *Holon*
59 [1]In Josh 21:16, *Ain*
60 [1]In Josh 21:18, *Almon*

44 On the left hand *were* their [1]kinsmen the sons of Merari: Ethan the son of Kishi, the son of Abdi, the son of Malluch,

45 the son of Hashabiah, the son of Amaziah, the son of Hilkiah,

46 the son of Amzi, the son of Bani, the son of Shemer,

47 the son of Mahli, the son of Mushi, the son of Merari, the son of Levi.

48 Their [1]kinsmen the Levites were [2]appointed for all the service of the tabernacle of the house of God.

49 But Aaron and his sons [1a]offered on the altar of burnt offering and [b]on the altar of incense, for all the work of the most holy place, and [c]to make atonement for Israel, according to all that Moses the servant of God had commanded.

50 [a]These are the sons of Aaron: Eleazar his son, Phinehas his son, Abishua his son,

51 Bukki his son, Uzzi his son, Zerahiah his son,

52 Meraioth his son, Amariah his son, Ahitub his son,

53 Zadok his son, Ahimaaz his son.

54 Now these are their settlements according to their camps within their borders. To the sons of Aaron of the families of the Kohathites (for theirs was the [a]*first* lot),

55 to them they gave [a]Hebron in the land of Judah and its pasture lands around it;

56 [a]but the fields of the city and its villages, they gave to Caleb the son of Jephunneh.

57 [a]To the sons of Aaron they gave the *following* cities of refuge: Hebron, Libnah also with its pasture lands, Jattir, Eshtemoa with its pasture lands,

58 [1]Hilen with its pasture lands, Debir with its pasture lands,

59 [1]Ashan with its pasture lands and Beth-shemesh with its pasture lands;

60 and from the tribe of Benjamin: Geba with its pasture lands, [1]Allemeth with its pasture lands, and Anathoth with its pasture lands. All their cities throughout their families were thirteen cities.

---

fluidity in which the Levites are linked with the tribe of Judah and the lineage of David (see Ruth 4:18–22; see also Matt 1:4; Luke 3:33) in view of Aaron's marriage to the daughter of Amminadab of Judah (Ex 6:23; see 1 Chr 2:10).

6:24 *Uriel.* Possibly the one who led the Kohathites in David's day (15:5).

6:26–27 *Zophai . . . Nahath . . . Eliab.* Apparently variant names for Zuph, Toah and Eliel (vv. 34–35).

6:28 *Samuel.* His lineage is also given in 1 Sam 1:1, where his family is identified as Ephraimite (see note there). Either this is an example of genealogical fluidity, in which Samuel's involvement in the tabernacle (1 Sam 3) and performance of priestly duties (9:22; 1 Sam 2:18; 3:1) resulted in his incorporation into the Levites, or the term "Ephraimite" is to be understood as a place of residence, not as a statement of lineage.

6:31–48 Each of the three Levitical clans contributed musicians for the temple: Heman from the family of Kohath, Asaph from Gershon, and Ethan from Merari. The Chronicler makes frequent reference to the appointment of the musical guilds by David (15:16,27; 25:1–31; 2 Chr 29:25–26; see Neh 12:45–47). The frequent mention of the role of the Levites has led many to assume that the author was a member of the musicians. Non-Biblical literature also attests to guilds of singers and musicians in Canaanite temples. This genealogy appears to function as a means of legitimizing the Levites of the restoration period (Ezra 2:40–41; Neh 7:43–44; 10:9–13, 28–29; 11:15–18; 12:24–47).

6:49–53 Repeats vv. 4–8 but presumably serves a different function: to legitimize the line of Zadok, which is traced down to Solomon's time, as the only Levitical division authorized to offer sacrifices.

6:54–81 This list of Levitical possessions is taken from Josh 21 with only minor differences (see notes there). The Levites, who were given no block of territory of their own, were distributed throughout Israel.

61 [a]Then to the rest of the sons of Kohath *were given* by lot, from the family of the tribe, from the half-tribe, the half of Manasseh, ten cities.

62 To the sons of Gershom, according to their families, *were given* from the tribe of Issachar and from the tribe of Asher, the tribe of Naphtali, and the tribe of Manasseh, thirteen cities in Bashan.

63 [a]To the sons of Merari *were given* by lot, according to their families, from the tribe of Reuben, the tribe of Gad and the tribe of Zebulun, twelve cities.

64 [a]So the sons of Israel gave to the Levites the cities with their pasture lands.

65 They gave by lot from the tribe of the sons of Judah, the tribe of the sons of Simeon and the tribe of the sons of Benjamin, [a]these cities which are mentioned by name.

66 [a]Now some of the families of the sons of Kohath had cities of their territory from the tribe of Ephraim.

67 They gave to them the *following* cities of refuge: Shechem in the hill country of Ephraim with its pasture lands, Gezer also with its pasture lands,

68 Jokmeam with its pasture lands, Beth-horon with its pasture lands,

69 Aijalon with its pasture lands and Gath-rimmon with its pasture lands;

70 and from the half-tribe of Manasseh: Aner with its pasture lands and Bileam with its pasture lands, for the rest of the family of the sons of Kohath.

71 To the sons of Gershom *were given,* from the family of the half-tribe of Manasseh: Golan in Bashan with its pasture lands and Ashtaroth with its pasture lands;

72 and from the tribe of Issachar: Kedesh with its pasture lands, Daberath with its pasture lands

73 and Ramoth with its pasture lands, Anem with its pasture lands;

74 and from the tribe of Asher: Mashal with its pasture lands, Abdon with its pasture lands,

75 Hukok with its pasture lands and Rehob with its pasture lands;

76 and from the tribe of Naphtali: Kedesh in Galilee with its pasture lands, Hammon with its pasture lands and Kiriathaim with its pasture lands.

77 To the rest of *the Levites,* the sons of Merari, *were given,* from the tribe of Zebulun: Rimmono with its pasture lands, Tabor with its pasture lands;

78 and beyond the Jordan at Jericho, on the east side of the Jordan, *were given them,* from the tribe of Reuben: Bezer in the wilderness with its pasture lands, Jahzah with its pasture lands,

79 Kedemoth with its pasture lands and Mephaath with its pasture lands;

80 and from the tribe of Gad: Ramoth in Gilead with its pasture lands, Mahanaim with its pasture lands,

81 Heshbon with its pasture lands and Jazer with its pasture lands.

Genealogy from Issachar

7 Now the sons of Issachar *were* four: Tola, [1]Puah, [2]Jashub and Shimron.

2 The sons of Tola *were* Uzzi, Rephaiah, Jeriel, Jahmai, Ibsam and Samuel, heads of their fathers' households. *The sons* of Tola *were* mighty men of valor in their generations; [a]their number in the days of David was 22,600.

3 The [1]son of Uzzi *was* Izrahiah. And the sons of Izrahiah *were* Michael, Obadiah, Joel, Isshiah; all five of them *were* [a]chief men.

4 With them by their generations according to their fathers' households were 36,000 [1]troops of the army for war, for they had many wives and sons.

5 Their [1]relatives among all the families of Issachar *were* mighty men of valor, enrolled by genealogy, in all 87,000.

Descendants of Benjamin

6 [a]*The sons of* Benjamin *were* three: Bela and Becher and Jediael.

7 The sons of Bela were five: Ezbon, Uzzi, Uzziel, Jerimoth and Iri. They *were* heads of fathers' households, mighty men of valor, and were 22,034 enrolled by genealogy.

8 The sons of Becher *were* Zemirah, Joash, Eliezer, Elioenai, Omri, Jeremoth, Abijah, Anathoth and Alemeth. All these *were* the sons of Becher.

9 They were enrolled by genealogy, according to their generations, heads of their fathers' households, 20,200 mighty men of valor.

10 The [1]son of Jediael *was* Bilhan. And the sons of Bilhan *were* Jeush, Benjamin, Ehud, Chenaanah, Zethan, Tarshish and Ahishahar.

11 All these *were* sons of Jediael, according to the heads of their fathers' households, 17,200 mighty men of valor, who were [1]ready to go out with the army to war.

12 [1]Shuppim and [2]Huppim *were* the sons of [3]Ir; Hushim *was* the [4]son of [5]Aher.

61 [a]Josh 21:5; 1 Chr 6:66-70
63 [a]Josh 21:7, 34-40
64 [a]Num 35:1-8; Josh 21:3, 41, 42
65 [a]1 Chr 6:57-60
66 [a]Josh 21:20-26

7:1 [1]In Gen 46:13, *Puvvah;* in Num 26:23, *Puvah* [2]In Gen 46:13, *Iob*
2 [a]2 Sam 24:1-9
3 [1]Lit *sons* [a]1 Chr 5:24
4 [1]Or *bands*
5 [1]Lit *brothers,* and so throughout the ch
6 [a]1 Chr 8:1-40
10 [1]Lit *sons*
11 [1]Lit *going out*
12 [1]In Num 26:39, *Shephupham* [2]In Num 26:39, *Hupham* [3]In v 7, *Iri* [4]Lit *sons* [5]In Num 26:38, *Ahiram*

7:1–5 Parts of the genealogy of Issachar are taken from Gen 46:13; Num 1:28; 26:23–25, though many of the names are otherwise unattested. This list of the clans appears to come from a military muster (vv. 2,4–5) from the time of David (v. 2), perhaps reflecting the census of ch. 21 and 2 Sam 24.

7:6–12 There is considerable fluidity among the Biblical sources listing the sons of Benjamin. This list gives three sons; Gen 46:21 records ten; Num 26:38–39 and 1 Chr 8:1–2 both list five (the only name appearing in all these sources is Bela, the firstborn). The variations reflect different origins and functions for these genealogies. The list here appears to function in the military sphere (vv. 7,9,11).

Sons of Naphtali

13 The sons of Naphtali *were* [1]Jahziel, Guni, Jezer, and [2]Shallum, the sons of Bilhah.

Descendants of Manasseh

14 The sons of Manasseh *were* Asriel, whom his Aramean concubine bore; she bore Machir the father of Gilead.

15 Machir took a wife for Huppim and Shuppim, [1]whose sister's name was Maacah. And the name of the second was Zelophehad, and Zelophehad had daughters.

16 Maacah the wife of Machir bore a son, and she named him Peresh; and the name of his brother *was* Sheresh, and his sons *were* Ulam and Rakem.

17 The [1]son of Ulam *was* Bedan. These *were* the sons of Gilead the son of Machir, the son of Manasseh.

18 His sister Hammolecheth bore Ishhod and [1]Abiezer and Mahlah.

19 The sons of Shemida were Ahian and Shechem and Likhi and Aniam.

Descendants of Ephraim

20 [a]The sons of Ephraim *were* Shuthelah and [1]Bered his son, Tahath his son, Eleadah his son, Tahath his son,

21 Zabad his son, Shuthelah his son, and Ezer and Elead whom the men of Gath who were born in the land killed, because they came down to take their livestock.

22 Their father Ephraim [a]mourned many days, and his relatives [b]came to comfort him.

23 Then he went in to his wife, and she conceived and bore a son, and he named him [1]Beriah, because misfortune had come upon his house.

24 His daughter was Sheerah, [a]who built lower and upper Beth-horon, also Uzzen-sheerah.

25 Rephah was his son *along* with Resheph, Telah his son, Tahan his son,

26 Ladan his son, Ammihud his son, Elishama his son,

27 [1]Non his son and [a]Joshua his son.

28 [a]Their possessions and settlements *were* Bethel with its towns, and to the east [1]Naaran, and to the west Gezer with its towns, and Shechem with its towns as far as [2]Ayyah with its towns,

29 and along the borders of the sons of Manasseh, Beth-shean with its towns, Taanach with its towns, Megiddo with its towns, Dor with its towns. In these lived the [a]sons of Joseph the son of Israel.

Descendants of Asher

30 [a]The sons of Asher *were* Imnah, Ishvah, Ishvi and Beriah, and Serah their sister.

31 The sons of Beriah *were* Heber and Malchiel, who was the father of Birzaith.

32 Heber [1]became the father of Japhlet, [2]Shomer and Hotham, and Shua their sister.

33 The sons of Japhlet *were* Pasach, Bimhal and Ashvath. These were the sons of Japhlet.

34 The sons of [1]Shemer *were* Ahi and Rohgah, Jehubbah and Aram.

35 The [1]sons of his brother Helem *were* Zophah, Imna, Shelesh and Amal.

36 The sons of Zophah *were* Suah, Harnepher, Shual, Beri and Imrah,

37 Bezer, Hod, Shamma, Shilshah, Ithran and Beera.

38 The sons of Jether *were* Jephunneh, Pispa and Ara.

39 The sons of Ulla *were* Arah, Hanniel and Rizia.

40 All these *were* the sons of Asher, heads of the fathers' houses, choice and mighty men of valor, heads of the princes. And the number of them enrolled by genealogy for service in war was 26,000 men.

Genealogy from Benjamin

8 And [a]Benjamin [1]became the father of Bela his firstborn, Ashbel the second, [b]Aharah the third,

2 Nohah the fourth and Rapha the fifth.

3 Bela had sons: [1]Addar, Gera, Abihud,

13 [1]In Gen 46:24, *Jahzeel* [2]In Gen 46:24 and Num 26:49, *Shillem*
15 [1]Lit *and his*
17 [1]Lit *sons*
18 [1]In Num 26:30, *Iezer*
20 [1]In Num 26:35, *Becher* [a]Num 26:35, 36
22 [a]Gen 37:34 [b]Job 2:11; John 11:19
23 [1]I.e. on misfortune
24 [a]Josh 16:3, 5; 2 Chr 8:5
27 [1]In Ex 33:11, *Nun* [a]Ex 17:9-14; 24:13
28 [1]In Josh 16:7, *Naarah* [2]Many mss read *Azzah* [a]Josh 16:2
29 [a]Judg 1:22-29
30 [a]Gen 46:17; Num 26:44-46
32 [1]Lit *begot* [2]In v 34, *Shemer*
34 [1]In v 32, *Shomer*
35 [1]Lit *son*
8:1 [1]Lit *begot,* and so throughout the ch [a]Gen 46:21; 1 Chr 7:6-12 [b]1 Chr 7:12
3 [1]In Gen 46:21 and Num 26:40, *Ard*

7:13 Repeats Gen 46:24; Num 26:48–50. *sons of Bilhah.* Dan and Naphtali were the actual "sons" of Jacob's concubine Bilhah (Gen 30:3–8), so Naphtali's sons are Bilhah's "descendants."

7:14–19 See note on 5:23–26. The sources for this genealogy are Num 26:29–34; Josh 17:1–18. The daughters of Zelophehad (v. 15) prompted the rulings on the inheritance rights of women (Num 26:29–34; 27:1–11; 36:1–12; Josh 17:3–4). Of the 13 different clans of the tribe of Manasseh known from these genealogies, seven are mentioned in the Samaria ostraca (about 65 inscribed potsherds containing records of deliveries of wine, oil, barley and other commodities in the eighth century B.C.). The prominence of women in this genealogy is unusual; this suggests that it may have functioned in the domestic sphere, perhaps as a statement of the social status of the various clans of Manasseh (see Introduction: Genealogies).

7:20–29 The source for part of the genealogy of Ephraim is Num 26:35. If Rephah (v. 25) is the grandson of Ephraim, ten generations are recorded from Ephraim to Joshua, a number that fits very well the 400-year interval when Israel was in Egypt. Joshua's Ephraimite ancestry is also mentioned in Num 13:8 (where he is called "Hoshea"; see Num 13:16). The raid against Gath (vv. 21–22) must have taken place well before the conquest of Canaan and must have originated in Egypt. The list of settlements (vv. 28–29) summarizes Josh 16–17.

7:30–40 The genealogy of Asher follows Gen 46:17 for the first three generations; it is also parallel to Num 26:44–46, except that the name Ishvah (v. 30) is missing there. This genealogy too reflects a military function (v. 40).

8:1–40 The inclusion of a second and even more extensive genealogy of Benjamin (see note on 7:6–12) reflects both the importance of this tribe and the Chronicler's interest in Saul. Judah, Simeon and part of Benjamin had composed the southern kingdom (1 Kin 12:1–21), and their territory largely comprised the restoration province of Judah in the Chronicler's own time. The genealogy of Benjamin is more extensive than that of all the other tribes except Judah and Levi. The Chronicler is also concerned with the genealogy of Saul (vv. 29–38) in order to set the stage for the historical narrative that begins with the

4 Abishua, Naaman, Ahoah,

5 Gera, Shephuphan and Huram.

6 These are the sons of Ehud: these are the heads of fathers' *households* of the inhabitants of Geba, and they carried them into exile to Manahath,

7 namely, Naaman, Ahijah and Gera—he carried them into exile; and he became the father of Uzza and Ahihud.

8 Shaharaim became the father of children in the [1]country of Moab after he had [2]sent away Hushim and Baara his wives.

9 By Hodesh his wife he became the father of Jobab, Zibia, Mesha, Malcam,

10 Jeuz, Sachia, Mirmah. These were his sons, heads of fathers' *households.*

11 By Hushim he became the father of Abitub and Elpaal.

12 The sons of Elpaal *were* Eber, Misham, and Shemed, who built Ono and Lod, with its towns;

13 and Beriah and Shema, who were heads of fathers' *households* of the inhabitants of Aijalon, who put to flight the inhabitants of Gath;

14 and [1]Ahio, Shashak and Jeremoth.

15 Zebadiah, Arad, Eder,

16 Michael, Ishpah and Joha *were* the sons of Beriah.

17 Zebadiah, Meshullam, Hizki, Heber,

18 Ishmerai, Izliah and Jobab *were* the sons of Elpaal.

19 Jakim, Zichri, Zabdi,

20 Elienai, Zillethai, Eliel,

21 Adaiah, Beraiah and Shimrath *were* the sons of [1]Shimei.

22 Ishpan, Eber, Eliel,

23 Abdon, Zichri, Hanan,

24 Hananiah, Elam, Anthothijah,

25 Iphdeiah and Penuel *were* the sons of Shashak.

26 Shamsherai, Shehariah, Athaliah,

27 Jaareshiah, Elijah and Zichri *were* the sons of Jeroham.

28 These were heads of the fathers' *households* according to their generations, chief men [1]who lived in Jerusalem.

29 [a]Now in Gibeon, *Jeiel,* the father of Gibeon lived, and his wife's name was Maacah;

30 and his firstborn son *was* Abdon, then Zur, Kish, Baal, Nadab,

31 Gedor, Ahio and [1]Zecher.

32 Mikloth became the father of [1]Shimeah. And they also lived with their [2]relatives in Jerusalem opposite their *other* [2]relatives.

Genealogy from King Saul

33 [a]Ner became the father of Kish, and Kish became the father of Saul, and Saul became the father of Jonathan, Malchi-shua, [1]Abinadab and [2]Eshbaal.

34 The son of Jonathan *was* [1]Merib-baal, and Merib-baal became the father of Micah.

35 The sons of Micah *were* Pithon, Melech, [1]Tarea and Ahaz.

36 Ahaz became the father of [1]Jehoaddah, and Jehoaddah became the father of Alemeth, Azmaveth and Zimri; and Zimri became the father of Moza.

37 Moza became the father of Binea; [1]Raphah *was* his son, Eleasah his son, Azel his son.

38 Azel had six sons, and these *were* their names: Azrikam, Bocheru, Ishmael, Sheariah, Obadiah and Hanan. All these *were* the sons of Azel.

39 The sons of Eshek his brother *were* Ulam his firstborn, Jeush the second and Eliphelet the third.

40 The sons of Ulam were mighty men of valor, archers, and had many sons and grandsons, 150 *of them.* All these *were* of the sons of Benjamin.

People of Jerusalem

9 So all Israel was enrolled by genealogies; and behold, they are written in the Book of the Kings of Israel. And [a]Judah was carried away into exile to Babylon for their unfaithfulness.

2 [a]Now the first who lived in their possessions in their cities *were* Israel, the priests, the Levites and [b]the [1]temple servants.

3 Some of the sons of Judah, of the sons of Benjamin and of the sons of Ephraim and Manasseh lived in [a]Jerusalem:

4 Uthai the son of Ammihud, the son of

8 [1]Lit *field* [2]Lit *sent them away*
14 [1]Or *his brothers*
21 [1]In v 13, *Shema*
28 [1]Lit *these*
29 [a]1 Chr 9:35-38
31 [1]In ch 9:37, *Zechariah*
32 [1]In ch 9:38, *Shimeam* [2]Lit *brothers*
33 [1]1 Sam 14:49, *Ishvi* [2]In 2 Sam 2:8, *Ish-bosheth* [a]1 Chr 9:39-44
34 [1]In 2 Sam 4:4, *Mephibosheth*
35 [1]In 9:41, *Tahrea*
36 [1]In 9:42, *Jarah*
37 [1]In 9:43, *Rephaiah*
9:1 [a]1 Chr 5:25, 26
2 [1]Heb *Nethinim* [a]Ezra 2:70; Neh 7:73; 11:3-22 [b]Ezra 2:43, 58; 8:20
3 [a]Neh 11:1

end of his reign (ch. 10); Saul's genealogy is repeated in 9:35–44. Several references suggest that this genealogy also originated in the military sphere (vv. 6,10,13,28,40).

8:1–5 Cf. the lists in 7:6–12; Gen 46:21–22; Num 26:38–41.

8:6–27 Unique to Chronicles.

8:29–38 Essentially the same as the list in 9:35–44.

8:33 For the sons of Saul see 1 Sam 14:49; 31:2. *Jonathan.* The firstborn and the best known of the sons of Saul, both for his military prowess and for his friendship with David (1 Sam 13–14; 18:1–4; 19:1–7; 20:1–42; 23:16–18; 2 Sam 21:13–14). *Eshbaal.* See NASB marg.; see also note on 2 Sam 2:8.

8:34 *Merib-baal.* See NASB marg.; see also note on 2 Sam 4:4.

9:1 *All Israel.* The Chronicler's concern with "all Israel" is one key to why he included the genealogies (see Introduction: Purpose and Themes).

9:2–34 This list of the members of the restored community reflects the Chronicler's concern with the institutions of his own day, especially the legitimacy of officeholders. He lists laity ("Israel," v. 2) in vv. 3–9, priests in vv. 10–13 and Levites in vv. 14–34. He mentions a fourth class of returnees—the temple servants (v. 2)—but does not give them separate listing in the material that follows. They may have been originally foreigners who were incorporated into the Levites (Josh 9:23; Ezra 8:20) and so are not listed apart from that tribe. A similar office is known in the temple at ancient Ugarit. The list here is related to the one in Neh 11, but less than half the names are the same in the two lists.

9:3 *Ephraim and Manasseh.* Again reflecting his concern with "all Israel," the Chronicler shows that the returnees were not only from Judah and Benjamin but also from the northern tribes.

Omri, the son of Imri, the son of Bani, from
the sons of Perez the [a]son of Judah.
5 From the Shilonites *were* Asaiah the
firstborn and his sons.
6 From the sons of Zerah *were* Jeuel and
their [1]relatives, 690 *of them.*
7 From the sons of Benjamin *were* Sallu
the son of Meshullam, the son of Hodaviah,
the son of Hassenuah,
8 and Ibneiah the son of Jeroham, and
Elah the son of Uzzi, the son of Michri, and
Meshullam the son of Shephatiah, the son of
Reuel, the son of Ibnijah;
9 and their relatives according to their generations, [a]956. All these *were* heads of fathers'
households according to their fathers' houses.
10 [a]From the priests *were* Jedaiah,
Jehoiarib, Jachin,
11 and [1]Azariah the son of Hilkiah, the
son of Meshullam, the son of Zadok, the son
of Meraioth, the son of Ahitub, [a]the chief
officer of the house of God;
12 and Adaiah the son of Jeroham, the son
of Pashhur, the son of Malchijah, and Maasai
the son of Adiel, the son of Jahzerah, the son
of Meshullam, the son of Meshillemith, the
son of Immer;
13 and their relatives, heads of their
fathers' households, 1,760 very able men for
the work of the service of the house of God.
14 [a]Of the Levites *were* Shemaiah the son
of Hasshub, the son of Azrikam, the son of
Hashabiah, of the sons of Merari;
15 and Bakbakkar, Heresh and Galal and
Mattaniah the son of Mica, the son of
[1]Zichri, the son of Asaph,
16 and [1]Obadiah the son of [2]Shemaiah, the
son of Galal, the son of Jeduthun, and
Berechiah the son of Asa, the son of Elkanah,
who lived in the villages of the Netophathites.
17 Now the gatekeepers *were* [1]Shallum
and Akkub and Talmon and Ahiman and
their relatives (Shallum the chief
18 *being stationed* until now at [a]the king's
gate to the east). These *were* the gatekeepers
for the camp of the sons of Levi.
19 Shallum the son of Kore, the son of
[1]Ebiasaph, the son of Korah, and his relatives of his father's house, the Korahites,
were over the work of the service, keepers of
the thresholds of the tent; and their fathers
had been over the camp of the LORD, keepers
of the entrance.
20 [a]Phinehas the son of Eleazar was ruler
over them previously, *and* the LORD was with
him.
21 [a]Zechariah the son of Meshelemiah
was gatekeeper of the entrance of the tent of
meeting.
22 All these who were chosen to be gatekeepers at the thresholds were 212. These
were enrolled by genealogy in their villages,
[a]whom David and Samuel the seer appointed [b]in their office of trust.
23 So they and their sons [1]had charge of
the gates of the house of the LORD, *even* the
house of the tent, as guards.
24 The gatekeepers were [1]on the four
sides, to the east, west, north and south.
25 Their relatives in their villages [a]*were* to
come in every seven days from time to time
to be with [1]them;
26 for the four chief gatekeepers who *were*
Levites, were in an office of trust, and were
over the chambers and over the treasuries in
the house of God.
27 They spent the night around the house
of God, [a]because the watch was [1]committed
to them; and they *were* [2]in charge of opening
it morning by morning.
28 Now some of them [1]had charge of the
utensils of service, for [2]they counted them
when they brought them in and when they
took them out.
29 Some of them also were appointed over
the furniture and over all the utensils of the
sanctuary and [a]over the fine flour and the
wine and the oil and the frankincense and
the spices.
30 Some of [a]the sons of the priests prepared the mixing of the spices.
31 Mattithiah, one of the Levites, who was
the firstborn of Shallum the Korahite, had
[a]the [1]responsibility over the things which
were baked in pans.
32 Some of their relatives of the sons of
the Kohathites [a]*were* over the showbread to
prepare it every sabbath.

4 [a]Gen 46:12; Num 26:20
6 [1]Lit *brothers,* and so throughout the ch
9 [a]Neh 11:8
10 [a]Neh 11:10-14
11 [1]In Neh 11:11, *Seraiah* [a]Jer 20:1
14 [a]Neh 11:15-19
15 [1]In Neh 11:17, *Zabdi*
16 [1]In Neh 11:17, *Abda* [2]In Neh 11:17, *Shammua*
17 [1]In v 21, *Meshelemiah;* in 26:14, *Shelemiah;* in Neh 12:25, *Meshullam*
18 [a]Ezek 44:1; 46:1, 2
19 [1]In Ex 6:24, *Abiasaph*
20 [a]Num 25:7-13
21 [a]1 Chr 26:2, 14
22 [a]1 Chr 26:1 [b]2 Chr 31:15, 18
23 [1]Lit *were over the gates*
24 [1]Lit *to the four winds*
25 [1]Lit *these* [a]2 Kin 11:5, 7; 2 Chr 23:8
27 [1]Lit *on them* [2]Lit *over the opening* [a]1 Chr 23:30-32
28 [1]Lit *were over the* [2]Lit *by count they brought them in and by count they took them out*
29 [a]1 Chr 23:29
30 [a]Ex 30:23-25
31 [1]Lit *office of trust* [a]1 Chr 9:22
32 [a]Lev 24:5-8

9:4–6 See 2:3–6; 4:21. The returnees of Judah are traced to Judah's sons Perez, Zerah and Shelah—if the word "Shilonites" (v. 5) is read as "Shelanites" (Num 26:20). If the reading "Shilonites" is retained, the reference is to Shiloh, the important sanctuary city (Judg 18:31; Jer 7:12–14; 26:9).

9:10–13 The list of priests is essentially the same as that in Neh 11:10–14. Since it is tied to the list of priests earlier in the genealogies (6:1–15,50–53), contemporary Israel's continuity with her past is shown.

9:15–16 *Asaph . . . Jeduthun.* Leaders of musical groups (6:39; 16:41). Later the Chronicler also lists the musicians (ch. 25) before the gatekeepers (ch. 26).

9:16 *Netophathites.* See note on Neh 12:28.

9:17–21 The Chronicler gives the names of four gatekeepers, while Neh 11:19 mentions only two. The chief of the gatekeepers had the honor of responsibility for the gate used by the king (Ezek 46:1–2). The gatekeepers are also listed in ch. 26; Ezra 2:42. These officers traced their origin to Phinehas (v. 20; 6:4; Num 3:32; 25:6–13).

9:22–27 Twenty-four guard stations were manned in three shifts around the clock; 72 men would be needed for each week. With a total of 212 men, each would have a tour of duty approximately every three weeks (26:12–18).

9:28–34 The Levites not only were responsible for the temple precincts and for opening the gates in the morning, but they also had charge of the chambers and supply rooms (23:28; 26:20–29) as well as the implements, supplies and furnishings (28:13–18; Ezra 1:9–11). In addition they were responsible for the preparation of baked goods (Ex 25:30; Lev 2:5–7; 7:9). The priests alone prepared the perfumed anointing oil and spices (Ex 30:23–33).

33 Now these are [a]the singers, heads of
fathers' *households* of the Levites, *who lived*
in the chambers *of the temple* free *from other*
service; for they were [1]engaged [b]in their
work day and night.
34 These were heads of fathers' *house-*
holds of the Levites according to their generations, chief men, [1]who lived in Jerusalem.

Ancestry and Descendants of Saul

35 [a]In Gibeon Jeiel the father of Gibeon
lived, and his wife's name was Maacah,
36 and his firstborn son *was* Abdon, then
Zur, Kish, Baal, Ner, Nadab,
37 Gedor, Ahio, Zechariah and Mikloth.
38 Mikloth became the father of Shimeam.
And they also lived with their relatives in
Jerusalem opposite their *other* relatives.
39 [a]Ner became the father of Kish, and
Kish became the father of Saul, and Saul
became the father of Jonathan, Malchi-shua,
Abinadab and Eshbaal.
40 The son of Jonathan *was* Merib-baal;
and Merib-baal became the father of Micah.
41 The sons of Micah *were* Pithon,
Melech, Tahrea [a]*and Ahaz.*
42 Ahaz became the father of Jarah, and
Jarah became the father of Alemeth, Azmaveth and Zimri; and Zimri became the father
of Moza,
43 and Moza became the father of Binea
and Rephaiah his son, Eleasah his son, Azel
his son.
44 Azel had six sons whose names are
these: Azrikam, Bocheru and Ishmael and
Sheariah and Obadiah and Hanan. These
were the sons of Azel.

Defeat and Death of Saul and His Sons

10 [a]Now the Philistines fought against
Israel; and the men of Israel fled before
the Philistines and fell slain on Mount Gilboa.
2 The Philistines closely pursued Saul
and his sons, and the Philistines struck down
Jonathan, [1a]Abinadab and Malchi-shua, the
sons of Saul.
3 The battle became heavy against Saul,
and the archers [1]overtook him; and he was
wounded by the archers.
4 Then Saul said to his armor bearer,
"Draw your sword and thrust me through
with it, otherwise these uncircumcised will
come and abuse me." But his armor bearer
would not, for he was greatly afraid. [a]There-
fore Saul took his sword and fell on it.
5 When his armor bearer saw that Saul
was dead, he likewise fell on his sword and
died.
6 [a]Thus Saul died with his three sons,
and all *those* of his house died together.
7 When all the men of Israel who were in
the valley saw that they had fled, and that
Saul and his sons were dead, they forsook
their cities and fled; and the Philistines came
and lived in them.
8 It came about the next day, when the
Philistines came to strip the slain, that they
found Saul and his sons fallen on Mount Gilboa.
9 [a]So they stripped him and took his
head and his armor and sent *messengers*
around the land of the Philistines to carry the
good news to their idols and to the people.
10 They put his armor in the house of
their gods and fastened his head in the house
of Dagon.

Jabesh-gilead's Tribute to Saul

11 When all Jabesh-gilead heard all that
the Philistines had done to Saul,
12 [a]all the valiant men arose and took
away the body of Saul and the bodies of his
sons and brought them to Jabesh, and they
buried their bones under the oak in Jabesh,
and fasted seven days.
13 [a]So Saul died for his trespass which he
committed against the LORD, because of the
word of the LORD which he did not keep; and
also [b]because he asked counsel of a medium, making inquiry *of it,*
14 and did not inquire of the LORD. Therefore He killed him and [a]turned the kingdom
to David the son of Jesse.

David Made King over All Israel

11 [a]Then all Israel gathered to David at
Hebron [1]and said, "Behold, we are
your bone and your flesh.
2 "In times past, even when Saul was
king, you *were* the one who led out and
brought in Israel; and the LORD your God said
to you, '[a]You shall shepherd My people Isra-

33 [1]Lit *over them in the work* [a]1 Chr 6:31-47; 25:1 [b]Ps 134:1 **34** [1]Lit *these* **35** [a]1 Chr 8:29-32 **39** [a]1 Chr 8:33-38 **41** [a]1 Chr 8:35-37 **10:1** [a]1 Sam 31:1-13 **2** [1]In 1 Sam 14:49, *Ishvi* [a]1 Sam 31:2 **3** [1]Lit *found him*

4 [a]1 Sam 31:4 **6** [a]1 Sam 31:6 **9** [a]1 Sam 31:9 **12** [a]1 Sam 31:12f **13** [a]1 Sam 13:13, 14; 15:23 [b]Lev 19:31; 20:6; 1 Sam 28:7 **14** [a]1 Sam 15:28; 1 Chr 12:23 **11:1** [1]Lit *saying* [a]2 Sam 5:1, 3, 6-10 **2** [a]2 Sam 5:2; 7:7

9:35–44 The genealogy of Saul is duplicated here (see 8:29–38) as a transition to the short account of his reign that begins the Chronicler's narration (ch. 10).
10:2 For the strategy of pursuing the king in battle see note on 1 Kin 22:31.
10:6 *his three sons.* See v. 2 (Ish-bosheth survived; see note on 1 Sam 31:2). *all those of his house.* His three sons and his chief officials (his official "house"), not all his descendants (see 8:33–34 and notes; 1 Sam 31:6).
10:13–14 These verses are not paralleled in the Samuel account; they were put here by the Chronicler in line with his concern with immediate retribution (see Introduction: Purpose and Themes). Seeking mediums was forbidden (Deut 18:9–14) and brought death to Saul. The Chronicler is obviously writing to an audience already familiar with Samuel and Kings, and he frequently assumes that knowledge. Here the consultation with the medium at Endor is alluded to (see 1 Sam 28), but the Chronicler does not recount the incident.
11:1–2 Chr 9:31 See Introduction: Portrait of David and Solomon.
11:1–3 The material here parallels that in 2 Sam 5:1–3, but is recast by the Chronicler in accordance with his emphasis on the popular support given David by "all Israel" (v. 1). While the Chronicler twice mentions the seven-year reign at Hebron before the death of Ish-bosheth and the covenant with the northern tribes (3:4; 29:27), these incidents are bypassed in the

el, and you shall be prince over My people Israel.' "

3 So all the elders of Israel came to the king at Hebron, and David made a covenant with them in Hebron before the LORD; and [a]they anointed David king over Israel, [b]according to the word of the LORD through Samuel.

Jerusalem, Capital City

4 Then David and all Israel went to Jerusalem ([a]that is, Jebus); and the Jebusites, the inhabitants of the land, *were* there.

5 The inhabitants of Jebus said to David, "You shall not enter here." Nevertheless David captured the stronghold of Zion (that is, the city of David).

6 Now David had said, "Whoever strikes down a Jebusite first shall be chief and commander." [a]Joab the son of Zeruiah went up first, so he became chief.

7 Then David dwelt in the stronghold; therefore it was called the city of David.

8 He [1]built the city all around, from the [2]Millo even to the surrounding area; and Joab [3]repaired the rest of the city.

9 [a]David became greater and greater, for the LORD of hosts *was* with him.

David's Mighty Men

10 [a]Now these are the heads of the mighty men whom David had, who gave him strong support in his kingdom, together with all Israel, to make him king, [b]according to the word of the LORD concerning Israel.

11 These *constitute* the list of the mighty men whom David had: [a]Jashobeam, the son of a Hachmonite, [b]the chief of the thirty; he lifted up his spear against three hundred [1]whom he killed at one time.

12 After him was Eleazar the son of [a]Dodo, the Ahohite, who *was* [1]one of the three mighty men.

13 He was with David at [1]Pasdammim [a]when the Philistines were gathered together there to battle, and there was a plot of ground full of barley; and the people fled before the Philistines.

14 They took their stand in the midst of the plot and defended it, and struck down the Philistines; and the LORD saved them by a great [1]victory.

15 Now three of the thirty chief men went down to the rock to David, into the cave of Adullam, while [a]the army of the Philistines was camping in the valley of Rephaim.

16 David was then in the stronghold, while [a]the garrison of the Philistines *was* then in Bethlehem.

17 David had a craving and said, "Oh that someone would give me water to drink from the well of Bethlehem, which is by the gate!"

18 So the three broke through the camp of the Philistines and drew water from the well of Bethlehem which *was* by the gate, and took *it* and brought *it* to David; nevertheless David would not drink it, but poured it out to the LORD;

19 and he said, "Be it far from me before my God that I should do this. Shall I drink the blood of these men *who went* [1]at the risk of their lives? For at the risk of their lives they brought it." Therefore he would not drink it. These things the three mighty men did.

20 As for [1]Abshai the brother of Joab, he was chief of the [2]thirty, and he swung his spear against three hundred [3]and killed them; and he had a name as well as the [2]thirty.

21 Of the three in the second *rank* he was the most honored and became their commander; however, he did not attain to the *first* three.

22 [a]Benaiah the son of Jehoiada, the son of a valiant man of Kabzeel, mighty in deeds, struck down the [1]two *sons of* Ariel of Moab. He also went down and [2]killed a lion inside a pit on a snowy day.

23 He [1]killed an Egyptian, a man of *great* stature five [2]cubits tall. Now in the Egyptian's hand *was* [a]a spear like a weaver's beam, but he went down to him with a club and snatched the spear from the Egyptian's hand and [1]killed him with his own spear.

24 These *things* Benaiah the son of Jehoiada did, and had a name as well as the three mighty men.

25 Behold, he was honored among the thirty, but he did not attain to the three; and David appointed him over his guard.

26 Now the mighty men of the armies *were* Asahel the brother of Joab, Elhanan the son of Dodo of Bethlehem,

27 [1]Shammoth the Harorite, Helez the [2]Pelonite,

28 Ira the son of Ikkesh the Tekoite, Abiezer the Anathothite,

3 [a]2 Sam 2:4; 5:3, 5 [b]1 Sam 16:1, 3, 12, 13
4 [a]Josh 15:8, 63; Judg 1:21
6 [a]2 Sam 8:16
8 [1]Or *fortified* [2]I.e. citadel [3]Lit *revived*
9 [a]2 Sam 3:1
10 [a]2 Sam 23:8-39 [b]1 Chr 11:3
11 [1]Lit *slain ones* [a]2 Sam 23:8 [b]1 Chr 12:18
12 [1]Lit *among* [a]1 Chr 27:4
13 [1]In 1 Sam 17:1, *Ephesdammim* [a]2 Sam 23:11, 12
14 [1]Or *salvation*
15 [a]1 Chr 14:9
16 [a]1 Sam 10:5
19 [1]Lit *with their souls*
20 [1]In 2 Sam 23:18, *Abishai* [2]So Syriac; M.T. *three* [3]Lit *slain ones*
22 [1]Or *two lion-like heroes of* [2]Lit *smote* [a]2 Sam 8:18
23 [1]Lit *smote* [2]I.e. One cubit equals approx 18 in. [a]1 Sam 17:7
27 [1]In 2 Sam 23:25, *Shammah the Harodite* [2]In 2 Sam 23:26, *Paltite*

narrative portion of the book. Most striking is the elimination at this point of the information in 2 Sam 5:4–5. Rather, the Chronicler paints a picture of immediate accession over "all Israel," followed by the immediate conquest of Jerusalem (see Introduction: Portrait of David and Solomon). The author once again assumes the reader's knowledge of the parallel account.

11:4–9 See 2 Sam 5:6–10 and notes. The "all Israel" theme appears in v. 4 as a substitute for "the king and his men" (2 Sam 5:6).

11:10–41a See 2 Sam 23:8–39 and notes. In the Samuel account this list of David's mighty men is given near the end of his reign. The Chronicler has moved the list to the beginning of his reign and has greatly expanded it (11:41b–12:40), again as part of his emphasis on the broad support of "all Israel" for the kingship of David (v. 10).

11:11 *three hundred.* Actually 800 (see 2 Sam 23:8), 300 here apparently being a copyist's mistake, perhaps influenced by the same number in v. 20.

11:12–14 See 2 Sam 23:9b–11a.

11:15–19 David recognizes that he is not worthy of such devotion and makes the water a drink offering to the Lord (see Gen 35:14; 2 Kin 16:13; Jer 7:18; Hos 9:4).

29 [1]Sibbecai the Hushathite, [2]Ilai the Ahohite,
30 Maharai the Netophathite, [1]Heled the son of Baanah the Netophathite,
31 Ithai the son of Ribai of Gibeah of the sons of Benjamin, Benaiah the Pirathonite,
32 [1]Hurai of the brooks of Gaash, [2]Abiel the Arbathite,
33 Azmaveth the Baharumite, Eliahba the Shaalbonite,
34 the sons of [1]Hashem the Gizonite, Jonathan the son of Shagee the Hararite,
35 Ahiam the son of [1]Sacar the Hararite, [2]Eliphal the son of Ur,
36 Hepher the Mecherathite, Ahijah the Pelonite,
37 Hezro the Carmelite, [1]Naarai the son of Ezbai,
38 Joel the brother of Nathan, Mibhar the son of Hagri,
39 Zelek the Ammonite, Naharai the Berothite, the armor bearer of Joab the son of Zeruiah,
40 Ira the Ithrite, Gareb the Ithrite,
41 Uriah the Hittite, Zabad the son of Ahlai,
42 Adina the son of Shiza the Reubenite, a chief of the Reubenites, and thirty with him,
43 Hanan the son of Maacah and Joshaphat the Mithnite,
44 Uzzia the Ashterathite, Shama and Jeiel the sons of Hotham the Aroerite,
45 Jediael the son of Shimri and Joha his brother, the Tizite,
46 Eliel the Mahavite and Jeribai and Joshaviah, the sons of Elnaam, and Ithmah the Moabite,
47 Eliel and Obed and Jaasiel the Mezobaite.

29 [1]In 2 Sam 23:27, *Mebunnai* [2]In 2 Sam 23:28, *Zalmon*
30 [1]In 2 Sam 23:29, *Heleb*
32 [1]In 2 Sam 23:30, *Hiddai* [2]In 2 Sam 23:31, *Abi-albon*
34 [1]In 2 Sam 23:32, *Jashen*
35 [1]In 2 Sam 23:33, *Sharar* [2]In 2 Sam 23:34, *Eliphelet the son of Ahasbai*
37 [1]In 2 Sam 23:35, *Paarai the Arbite*
12:1 [a]1 Sam 27:2-6
2 [a]Judg 3:15; 20:16 [b]1 Chr 12:29
4 [1]In Heb the beginning of v 5, making 41 vv in ch

David's Supporters in Ziklag

12 [a]Now these are the ones who came to David at Ziklag, while he was still restricted because of Saul the son of Kish; and they were among the mighty men who helped *him* in war.
2 They were equipped with bows, [a]using both the right hand and the left *to sling* stones and *to shoot* arrows from the bow; [b]*they were* Saul's kinsmen from Benjamin.
3 The chief was Ahiezer, then Joash, the sons of Shemaah the Gibeathite; and Jeziel and Pelet, the sons of Azmaveth, and Beracah and Jehu the Anathothite,
4 and Ishmaiah the Gibeonite, a mighty man among the thirty, and over the thirty. [1]Then Jeremiah, Jahaziel, Johanan, Jozabad the Gederathite,
5 [1]Eluzai, Jerimoth, Bealiah, Shemariah, Shephatiah the Haruphite,
6 Elkanah, Isshiah, Azarel, Joezer, Jashobeam, the Korahites,
7 and Joelah and Zebadiah, the sons of Jeroham of Gedor.
8 From the Gadites there [1]came over to David in the stronghold in the wilderness, mighty men of valor, men trained for war, who could handle shield and spear, and whose faces were like the faces of lions, and [a]*they were* as swift as the gazelles on the mountains.
9 Ezer *was* the first, Obadiah the second, Eliab the third,
10 Mishmannah the fourth, Jeremiah the fifth,
11 Attai the sixth, Eliel the seventh,
12 Johanan the eighth, Elzabad the ninth,
13 Jeremiah the tenth, Machbannai the eleventh.
14 These of the sons of Gad were [1]captains of the army; [a]he who was least was equal to a hundred and the greatest to a thousand.
15 [a]These are the ones who crossed the Jordan in the first month when it was overflowing all its banks and they put to flight all those in the valleys, both to the east and to the west.
16 Then some of the sons of Benjamin and Judah came to the stronghold to David.
17 David went out to meet them, and said to them, "If you come peacefully to me to help me, my heart shall be united with you; but if to betray me to my adversaries, since there is no [1]wrong in my hands, may the God of our fathers look on *it* and decide."
18 Then [a]the Spirit [1]came upon [b]Amasai, who was the chief of the thirty, *and he said,*

"*We* are yours, O David,
And with you, O son of Jesse!
[c]Peace, peace to you,
And peace to him who helps you;
Indeed, your God helps you!"

Then David received them and made them [2]captains of the band.
19 [a]From Manasseh also some defected to David when he was about to go to battle with the Philistines against Saul. But they did not help them, for the lords of the Philistines after consultation sent him away, saying, "At *the cost of* our heads he may defect to his master Saul."
20 As he went to Ziklag there defected to him from Manasseh: Adnah, Jozabad, Jediael, Michael, Jozabad, Elihu and Zillethai,

5 [1]V 6 in Heb
8 [1]Lit *separated themselves* [a]2 Sam 2:18
14 [1]Or *chiefs* [a]Deut 32:30
15 [a]Josh 3:15; 4:18
17 [1]Lit *violence*
18 [1]Lit *clothed* [2]Or *chiefs* [a]Judg 3:10; 6:34 [b]1 Chr 2:17 [c]1 Sam 25:5, 6
19 [a]1 Sam 29:2-9

11:41b–12:40 See note on vv. 10–41a. The list in 2 Sam 23 ends with Uriah the Hittite (2 Sam 11); the source for the additional names is not known. The emphasis continues to be on the support of "all Israel"—even Saul's own kinsmen recognized the legitimacy of David's kingship before Saul's death (12:1–7,16–18,23,29).
12:1 The Chronicler assumes the reader's knowledge of the events at Ziklag (1 Sam 27); see vv. 19–20.
12:8–15 The men of Gad were from Transjordan. Melting snows to the north would have brought the Jordan to flood stage in the first month (March-April) at the time of their crossing (v. 15). The most appropriate time for this incident would have been in the period of David's wandering in the region of the Dead Sea (1 Sam 23:14; 24:1; 25:1; 26:1).

[1]captains of thousands who belonged to Manasseh.

21 They helped David against [a]the band of raiders, for they were all mighty men of valor, and were captains in the army.

22 For day by day *men* came to David to help him, until there was a great army [a]like the army of God.

Supporters Gathered at Hebron

23 Now these are the numbers of the [1]divisions equipped for war, [a]who came to David at Hebron, [b]to turn the kingdom of Saul to him, [c]according to the [2]word of the LORD.

24 The sons of Judah who bore shield and spear *were* 6,800, equipped for war.

25 Of the sons of Simeon, mighty men of valor for war, 7,100.

26 Of the sons of Levi 4,600.

27 Now Jehoiada was the leader of *the house of* Aaron, and with him were 3,700,

28 also [a]Zadok, a young man mighty of valor, and of his father's house twenty-two captains.

29 Of the sons of Benjamin, [a]Saul's kinsmen, 3,000; for until now [b]the greatest part of them had kept their allegiance to the house of Saul.

30 Of the sons of Ephraim 20,800, mighty men of valor, famous men in their fathers' households.

31 Of the half-tribe of Manasseh 18,000, who were designated by name to come and make David king.

32 Of the sons of Issachar, [a]men who understood the times, with knowledge of what Israel should do, their chiefs *were* two hundred; and all their kinsmen *were* at their command.

20 [1]Or *chiefs*
21 [a]1 Sam 30:1
22 [a]Gen 32:2; Josh 5:13-15
23 [1]Lit *heads* [2]Lit *mouth* [a]2 Sam 2:3, 4 [b]1 Chr 10:14 [c]1 Chr 11:10
28 [a]2 Sam 8:17; 1 Chr 6:8, 53
29 [a]1 Chr 12:2 [b]2 Sam 2:8, 9
32 [a]Esth 1:13

33 Of Zebulun, there were 50,000 who went out in the army, who could draw up in battle formation with all kinds of weapons of war and helped *David* [1]with [a]an undivided heart.

34 Of Naphtali *there were* 1,000 captains, and with them 37,000 with shield and spear.

35 Of the Danites who could draw up in battle formation, *there were* 28,600.

36 Of Asher *there were* 40,000 who went out in the army to draw up in battle formation.

37 From the other side of the Jordan, of the Reubenites and the Gadites and of the half-tribe of Manasseh, *there were* 120,000 with all *kinds* of weapons of war for the battle.

38 All these, being men of war who could draw up in battle formation, came to Hebron with [a]a perfect heart to make David king over all Israel; and all the rest also of Israel were of one mind to make David king.

39 They were there with David three days, eating and drinking, for their kinsmen had prepared for them.

40 Moreover those who were near to them, *even* as far as Issachar and Zebulun and Naphtali, [a]brought food on donkeys, camels, mules and on oxen, great quantities of flour cakes, fig cakes and bunches of raisins, wine, oil, oxen and sheep. There was joy indeed in Israel.

Peril in Transporting the Ark

13 Then David consulted with the captains of the thousands and the hundreds, even with every leader.

2 David said to all the assembly of Israel, "If it seems good to you, and if it is from the LORD our God, let us send everywhere to our

33 [1]Lit *not of double heart* [a]Ps 12:2
38 [a]2 Sam 5:1-3; 1 Chr 12:33
40 [a]1 Sam 25:18

12:23–37 The emphasis remains on "all Israel" (v. 38). Though 13 tribes are named, they are grouped in order to maintain the traditional number of 12 (see note on 2:1–2). The northernmost and the Transjordan tribes send the largest number of men (vv. 33–37), reinforcing the degree of support that David enjoyed not only in Judah and Benjamin but throughout the other tribes as well. The numbers in this section seem quite high. Essentially two approaches are followed on this question: 1. It is possible to explain the numbers so that a lower figure is actually attained. The Hebrew word for "thousand" may represent a unit of a tribe, each having its own commander (13:1; see Num 31:14,48,52,54). In this case the numbers would be read not as a total figure, but as representative commanders. For example, the 6,800 from Judah (v. 24) would be read either as six commanders of 1,000 and eight commanders of 100 (see 13:1), or possibly as six commanders of thousands and 800 men. Reducing the numbers in this fashion fits well with 13:1 and with the list of commanders alone found for Zadok's family (v. 28) and the tribe of Issachar (v. 32). Taking the numbers as straight totals would require the presence of 340,800 persons in Hebron for a feast at the same time. 2. Another approach is to allow the numbers to stand and to view them as hyperbole on the part of the Chronicler to achieve a number "like the army of God" (v. 22). This approach would fit well with the Chronicler's glorification of David and with the banquet scene that follows.

12:38–40 The Chronicler's portrait of David is influenced by his Messianic expectations (see Introduction: Purpose and Themes). In the presence of a third of a million people (see note on vv. 23–37) David's coronation banquet typifies the future Messianic feast (Is 25:6–8). The imagery of the Messianic banquet became prominent in the intertestamental literature (*Apocalypse of Baruch* 29:4–8; *Enoch* 62:14) and in the NT (see Matt 8:11–12 and Luke 13:28–30; Matt 22:1–10 and Luke 14:16–24; see also Matt 25:1–13; Luke 22:28–30; Rev 19:7–9). The Lord's Supper anticipates that coming banquet (Matt 26:29; Mark 14:25; Luke 22:15–18; 1 Cor 11:23–26).

13:1–14 See 2 Sam 6:1–11 and notes. The author abandons the chronological order as given in 2 Sam 5–6 and puts the transfer of the ark first, delaying his account of the palace building and the Philistine campaign until later (ch. 14). This is in accordance with his portrayal of David; David's concern with the ark was expressed immediately upon his accession—his consultation with the leaders appears to be set in the context of the coronation banquet (12:38–40).

13:1–4 These verses are not found in Samuel and reflect the Chronicler's own concerns with "all Israel." The semi-military expedition to retrieve the ark in 2 Sam 6:1 is here broadened by consultation with and support from the whole assembly of Israel, "all the land" (v. 2), including the priests and Levites—an important point for the Chronicler since only they are allowed to move the ark (15:2,13; 23:25–27; Deut 10:8).

kinsmen who remain in all the land of Israel,
also to the priests and Levites who are with
them in their cities with pasture lands, that
they may meet with us;
3 and let us bring back the ark of our
God to us, [a]for we did not seek it in the days
of Saul."
4 Then all the assembly said that they
would do so, for the thing was right in the
eyes of all the people.
5 [a]So David assembled all Israel together,
from the Shihor of Egypt even to the
entrance of Hamath, [b]to bring the ark of God
from Kiriath-jearim.
6 [a]David and all Israel went up to [b]Baal-
ah, *that is,* to Kiriath-jearim, which belongs
to Judah, to bring up from there the ark of
God, the LORD [c]who is enthroned *above* the
cherubim, where His name is called.
7 They [1]carried the ark of God on a new
cart from [a]the house of Abinadab, and Uzza
and Ahio drove the cart.
8 David and all Israel were celebrating
before God with all *their* might, [a]even with
songs and with lyres, harps, tambourines,
cymbals and with trumpets.
9 When they came to [a]the threshing floor
of Chidon, Uzza put out his hand to hold the
ark, because the oxen nearly upset *it.*
10 The anger of the LORD burned against
Uzza, so He struck him down [a]because he
put out his hand to the ark; [b]and he died
there before God.
11 Then David became angry because [1]of
the LORD's outburst against Uzza; and he
called that place [2]Perez-uzza to this day.
12 David was afraid of God that day, saying, "How can I bring the ark of God *home* to
me?"
13 So David did not take the ark with him

13:3 [a]1 Sam 7:1, 2
5 [a]2 Sam 6:1; 1 Kin 8:65; 1 Chr 15:3 [b]1 Sam 6:21; 7:1
6 [a]2 Sam 6:2-11 [b]Josh 15:9 [c]Ex 25:22; 2 Kin 19:15
7 [1]Lit *caused to ride* [a]1 Sam 7:1
8 [a]1 Chr 15:16
9 [a]2 Sam 6:6
10 [a]1 Chr 15:13, 15 [b]Lev 10:2
11 [1]Lit *the LORD had broken through a breakthrough* [2]I.e. the breakthrough of Uzza
13 [a]1 Chr 15:25
14 [a]1 Chr 26:4, 5
14:1 [a]2 Sam 5:11
3 [1]Lit *begot*
4 [1]Lit *were to* [a]1 Chr 3:5-8
9 [a]1 Chr 11:15; 14:13
11 [1]Lit *smote*

to the city of David, but took it aside [a]to the
house of Obed-edom the Gittite.
14 Thus the ark of God remained with the
family of Obed-edom in his house three
months; and [a]the LORD blessed the family of
Obed-edom with all that he had.

David's Family Enlarged

14 [a]Now Hiram king of Tyre sent messengers to David with cedar trees, masons
and carpenters, to build a house for him.
2 And David realized that the LORD had
established him as king over Israel, *and* that
his kingdom was highly exalted, for the sake
of His people Israel.
3 Then David took more wives at
Jerusalem, and David [1]became the father of
more sons and daughters.
4 [a]These are the names of the children
[1]born *to him* in Jerusalem: Shammua, Shobab, Nathan, Solomon,
5 Ibhar, Elishua, Elpelet,
6 Nogah, Nepheg, Japhia,
7 Elishama, Beeliada and Eliphelet.

Philistines Defeated

8 When the Philistines heard that David
had been anointed king over all Israel, all the
Philistines went up in search of David; and
David heard of it and went out against them.
9 Now the Philistines had come and
[a]made a raid in the valley of Rephaim.
10 David inquired of God, saying, "Shall I
go up against the Philistines? And will You
give them into my hand?" Then the LORD
said to him, "Go up, for I will give them into
your hand."
11 So they came up to Baal-perazim, and
David [1]defeated them there; and David said,
"God has broken through my enemies by my

13:3 *we did not seek it in the days of Saul.* 1 Sam 14:18 may be an exception (but see note there).
13:5–6 The emphasis remains on the united action of "all Israel." Israelites came to participate in this venture all the way from Lebo Hamath in the north and from the Shihor River in the south.
13:5 *Shihor.* An Egyptian term meaning "the pool of Horus." It appears to be a part of the Nile or one of the major canals of the Nile (see Josh 13:3; Is 23:3; Jer 2:18 and notes).
13:6 *Baalah.* The Canaanite name for Kiriath-jearim, also known as Kiriath-baal (Josh 18:14). The Chronicler assumes that his readers are familiar with the account of how the ark came to be at Kiriath-jearim (1 Sam 6:1–7:1).
13:7 *Uzza and Ahio.* Sons or descendants of Abinadab (2 Sam 6:3).
13:10 *because he put out his hand to the ark.* The ark was to be moved only by Levites, who carried it with poles inserted through rings in the sides of the ark (Ex 25:12–15). None of the holy things was to be touched, on penalty of death (Num 4:15). These strictures were observed in the second and successful attempt to move the ark to Jerusalem (15:1–15). It cannot be known whether Uzza and Ahio were Levites—the Samuel account does not mention the presence of Levites, but the Chronicler's careful inclusion of Levites in this expedition suggests that they were present (see note on vv. 1–4). In any case, the ark should not have been moved on a cart (as done by the Philistines, 1 Sam 6) or touched.
13:13 *Obed-edom.* Perhaps the same man mentioned in 15:18,21,24. In 26:4 God's blessing on Obed-edom included numerous sons. This reference also establishes that Obed-edom was a Levite and that the ark was properly left in his care.
14:1–17 The Chronicler backtracks to pick up material from 2 Sam 5 deferred to this point (see note on 13:1–14). The three-month period that the ark remained with Obed-edom (13:14) was filled with incidents showing God's blessing on David: the building of his royal house (vv. 1–2), his large family (vv. 3–7) and his success in warfare (vv. 8–16)—all because of the Lord's blessing (vv. 2,17).
14:1–2 See 2 Sam 5:11–12 and notes.
14:1 *Hiram.* Later provided materials and labor for building the temple (2 Chr 2). His mention here implies international recognition of David as king over Israel and a treaty between David and Hiram.
14:3–7 See 3:5–9; 2 Sam 5:13–16. David's children born in Hebron are omitted (3:1–4; 2 Sam 3:2–5; see note on 11:1–3).
14:7 *Beeliada.* Eliada in 3:8; 2 Sam 5:16.
14:8–12 See 2 Sam 5:17–21 and notes.
14:11 *broken through . . . Baal-perazim.* The Hebrew underlying the name of this place where the Lord broke out against the Philistines is the same as that underlying the word used in

hand, like the breakthrough of waters." Therefore they named that place [2]Baal-perazim.

12 They abandoned their gods there; so David gave the order and they were burned with fire.

13 The Philistines made [a]yet another raid in the valley.

14 David inquired again of God, and God said to him, "You shall not go up after them; circle around [1]behind them and come at them in front of the [2]balsam trees.

15 "It shall be when you hear the sound of marching in the tops of the balsam trees, then you shall go out to battle, for God will have gone out before you to strike the army of the Philistines."

16 David did just as God had commanded him, and they struck down the army of the Philistines from [1]Gibeon even as far as Gezer.

17 Then the fame of David went out into all the lands; and [a]the LORD brought the fear of him on all the nations.

Plans to Move the Ark to Jerusalem

15 Now *David* built houses for himself in the city of David; and he prepared a place for the ark of God and [a]pitched a tent for it.

2 Then David said, "[a]No one is to carry the ark of God but the Levites; for the LORD chose them to carry the ark of God and to minister to Him forever."

3 And [a]David assembled all Israel at Jerusalem to bring up the ark of the LORD [b]to its place which he had prepared for it.

4 David gathered together the sons of Aaron and [a]the Levites:

5 of the sons of Kohath, Uriel the chief, and 120 of his [1]relatives;

6 of the sons of Merari, Asaiah the chief, and 220 of his relatives;

7 of the sons of Gershom, Joel the chief, and 130 of his relatives;

8 of the sons of Elizaphan, Shemaiah the chief, and 200 of his relatives;

9 of the sons of Hebron, Eliel the chief, and 80 of his relatives;

10 of the sons of Uzziel, Amminadab the chief, and 112 of his relatives.

11 Then David called for [a]Zadok and [b]Abiathar the priests, and for the Levites, for Uriel, Asaiah, Joel, Shemaiah, Eliel and Amminadab,

12 and said to them, "You are the heads of the fathers' *households* of the Levites; [a]consecrate yourselves both you and your relatives, that you may bring up the ark of the LORD God of Israel [b]to *the place* that I have prepared for it.

13 "[a]Because you did not *carry it* at the first, the LORD our God made an outburst on us, for we did not seek Him according to the ordinance."

14 [a]So the priests and the Levites consecrated themselves to bring up the ark of the LORD God of Israel.

15 The sons of [a]the Levites carried the ark of God on their shoulders with the poles thereon, as Moses had commanded according to the word of the LORD.

16 Then David spoke to the chiefs of the Levites [a]to appoint their relatives the singers, with instruments of music, harps, lyres, loud-sounding cymbals, to raise sounds of joy.

17 So [a]the Levites appointed Heman the son of Joel, and from his relatives, Asaph the son of Berechiah; and from the sons of Merari their relatives, Ethan the son of Kushaiah,

18 and with them their relatives of the second rank, Zechariah, [1]Ben, Jaaziel, Shemiramoth, Jehiel, Unni, Eliab, Benaiah, Maaseiah, Mattithiah, Eliphelehu, Mikneiah, Obed-edom and Jeiel, the gatekeepers.

19 So the singers, Heman, Asaph and Ethan *were appointed* to sound aloud cymbals of bronze;

11 [2]I.e. the master of breakthrough
13 [a]1 Chr 14:9
14 [1]Lit *from upon* [2]Or *baka shrubs*
16 [1]In 2 Sam 5:25, *Geba*
17 [a]Ex 15:14-16; Deut 2:25
15:1 [a]1 Chr 15:3; 16:1; 17:1-5
2 [a]Num 4:15; Deut 10:8
3 [a]1 Kin 8:1; 1 Chr 13:5 [b]Ex 40:20f; 2 Sam 6:12, 17; 1 Chr 15:1, 12
4 [a]1 Chr 6:16-30; 12:26
5 [1]Lit *brothers;* i.e. fellow tribesmen, and so throughout the ch
11 [a]1 Chr 12:28 [b]1 Sam 22:20-23; 1 Kin 2:26, 35
12 [a]Ex 19:14, 15; 2 Chr 35:6 [b]1 Chr 15:1, 3
13 [a]2 Sam 6:3; 1 Chr 13:7
14 [a]1 Chr 15:12
15 [a]Ex 25:14; Num 4:5f
16 [a]1 Chr 13:8; 25:1
17 [a]1 Chr 25:1
18 [1]Omitted in Gr and many mss

13:11 when the Lord broke out against Uzza (see note there; see also NASB marg. here). Perez-uzza means "breakthrough of Uzza."

14:12 *gave the order and they were burned.* 2 Sam 5:21 does not mention burning but says that David and his men carried the idols away. Many have seen here an intentional change on the part of the Chronicler in order to bring David's actions into strict conformity with the law, which required that pagan idols be burned (Deut 7:5,25). However, some Septuagint (the Greek translation of the OT) manuscripts of Samuel agree with Chronicles that David burned the idols. This would indicate that the Chronicler was not innovating for theological reasons but was carefully reproducing the text he had before him, which differed from the Masoretic (traditional Hebrew) text of Samuel.

14:13–16 See 2 Sam 5:22–25 and notes.

14:17 *the LORD brought the fear of him on all the nations.* Here and elsewhere the Chronicler uses an expression that refers to an incapacitating terror brought on by the sense that the awful power of God is present in behalf of His people (see Ex 15:16). Thus David is seen by the nations as the very representative of God (similarly Asa, 2 Chr 14:14; Jehoshaphat, 2 Chr 17:10; 20:29).

15:1–16:3 This account of the successful attempt to move the ark to Jerusalem is greatly expanded over the material in 2 Samuel. Only 15:25–16:3 has a parallel (2 Sam 6:12–19); the rest of the material is unique to the Chronicler and reflects his own interests, especially in the Levites and cultic musicians (vv. 3–24; see Introduction: Purpose and Themes). Ps 132 should also be read in connection with this account.

15:1 *built houses for himself.* See 14:1–2 and note on 13:1–14.

15:2–3 See note on 13:10.

15:4–10 The three clans of Levi are represented (Kohath, Merari and Gershon), as well as three distinct subgroups within Kohath (Elizaphan, Hebron and Uzziel)—862 in all.

15:12 *consecrate yourselves.* Through ritual washings and avoidance of ceremonial defilement (Ex 29:1–37; 30:19–21; 40:31–32; Lev 8:5–35).

15:13–15 The Chronicler provides the explanation for the failure in the first attempt to move the ark, an explanation not found in the Samuel account (see note on 13:10).

15:18,21,24 *Obed-edom.* See note on 13:13.

20 and Zechariah, Aziel, Shemiramoth, Jehiel, Unni, Eliab, Maaseiah and Benaiah, with [1]harps *tuned* to [a]alamoth;

21 and Mattithiah, Eliphelehu, Mikneiah, Obed-edom, Jeiel and Azaziah, to lead with [1]lyres tuned to [a]the sheminith.

22 Chenaniah, chief of the Levites, was *in charge of* the singing; he gave instruction in singing because he was skillful.

23 Berechiah and Elkanah were gatekeepers for the ark.

24 Shebaniah, Joshaphat, Nethanel, Amasai, Zechariah, Benaiah and Eliezer, the priests, [a]blew the trumpets before the ark of God. Obed-edom and Jehiah also *were* gatekeepers for the ark.

25 [a]So *it was* David, with the elders of Israel and the captains over thousands, who went to bring up the ark of the covenant of the LORD from [b]the house of Obed-edom with joy.

26 Because God was helping the Levites who were carrying the ark of the covenant of the LORD, they sacrificed [a]seven bulls and seven rams.

27 Now David was clothed with a robe of fine linen with all the Levites who were carrying the ark, and the singers and Chenaniah the leader of the singing *with* the singers. [a]David also wore an ephod of linen.

28 Thus all Israel brought up the ark of the covenant of the LORD with shouting, and with sound of the horn, with trumpets, with loud-sounding cymbals, with harps and lyres.

29 It happened when the ark of the covenant of the LORD came to the city of David, that [a]Michal the daughter of Saul looked out of the window and saw King David leaping and celebrating; and she despised him in her heart.

A Tent for the Ark

16 And they brought in the ark of God and [a]placed it inside the tent which David had pitched for it, and they offered burnt offerings and peace offerings before God.

2 When David had finished offering the burnt offering and the peace offerings, he blessed the people in the name of the LORD.

3 He distributed to everyone of Israel, both man and woman, to everyone a loaf of bread and a portion *of meat* and a raisin cake.

4 He appointed some of the Levites *as* ministers before the ark of the LORD, even to celebrate and to thank and praise the LORD God of Israel:

5 Asaph the chief, and second to him Zechariah, *then* [1]Jeiel, Shemiramoth, Jehiel, Mattithiah, Eliab, Benaiah, Obed-edom and Jeiel, with musical instruments, harps, lyres; also Asaph *played* loud-sounding cymbals,

6 and Benaiah and Jahaziel the priests *blew* trumpets continually before the ark of the covenant of God.

7 Then on that day David [a]first assigned [1]Asaph and his [2]relatives to give thanks to the LORD.

Psalm of Thanksgiving

8 [a]Oh give thanks to the LORD, call upon
His name;
[b]Make known His deeds among the
peoples.
9 Sing to Him, sing praises to Him;
[1]Speak of all His [2]wonders.
10 [1]Glory in His holy name;
Let the heart of those who seek the
LORD be glad.
11 [a]Seek the LORD and His strength;
Seek His face continually.
12 [a]Remember His wonderful deeds
which He has done,
[b]His marvels and the judgments from
His mouth,
13 O seed of Israel His servant,
Sons of Jacob, His chosen ones!
14 He is the LORD our God;
[a]His judgments are in all the earth.
15 Remember His covenant forever,
The word which He commanded to a
thousand generations,
16 [a]*The covenant* which He made with
Abraham,
And His oath to Isaac.
17 [a]He also confirmed it to Jacob for a
statute,
To Israel as an everlasting covenant,

20 [1]Or *harps of maiden-like tone* [a]Ps 46: title
21 [1]Or *octave harps* [a]Ps 6: title
24 [a]1 Chr 15:28; 16:6
25 [a]2 Sam 6:12, 15 [b]1 Chr 13:13
26 [a]Num 23:1-4, 29
27 [a]2 Sam 6:14
29 [a]2 Sam 3:13f; 6:16
16:1 [a]1 Chr 15:1

5 [1]In 1 Chr 15:18, *Jaaziel*
7 [1]Lit *by the hand of Asaph* [2]Lit *brothers* [a]2 Sam 22:1; 23:1
8 [a]1 Chr 16:8-36; Ps 105:1-15 [b]1 Kin 8:43; 2 Kin 19:19
9 [1]Or *Meditate on* [2]I.e. wonderful acts
10 [1]Or *Boast*
11 [a]Ps 24:6
12 [a]Ps 103:2 [b]Ps 78:43-68
14 [a]Ps 48:10
16 [a]Gen 12:7; 17:2; 22:16-18; 26:3
17 [a]Gen 35:11, 12

15:24 *priests, blew the trumpets.* See 16:6; Num 10:1–10.
15:27 Both 2 Sam 6:14 and the Chronicler mention David's wearing a linen ephod, a garment worn by priests (1 Sam 2:18; 22:18). The Chronicler adds, however, that David (as well as the rest of the Levites in the procession) was wearing a robe of fine linen, further associating him with the dress of the cultic functionaries. Apparently the Chronicler viewed David as a priest-king, a kind of Messianic figure (see Ps 110; Zech 6:9–15).
15:29 Parallel to 2 Sam 6:16, but the Chronicler omits the remainder of this incident recorded there (2 Sam 6:20–23). Some interpreters regard this omission as part of the Chronicler's positive view of David, so that a possibly unseemly account is omitted. On the other hand, it is equally plausible that the Chronicler here simply assumes the reader's knowledge of the other account (see notes on 10:13–14; 11:1–3; 12:1; 13:6).
16:1–3 David is further associated with the priests in his supervision of the sacrifices and his exercising the priestly prerogative of blessing the people (Num 6:22–27; see note on 15:27). The baked goods provided by David were for the sacrificial meal following the peace offerings (Lev 3:1–17; 7:11–21,28–36).
16:8–36 Similar to various parts of the book of Psalms (for vv. 8–22 see Ps 105:1–15; for vv. 23–33, Ps 96; for vv. 34–36, Ps 106:1,47–48). This psalm is not found in the Samuel account. The use of the lengthy historical portion from Ps 105 emphasizing the promises to Abraham would be particularly relevant to the Chronicler's postexilic audience, for whom the faithfulness of God was a fresh reality in their return to the land. The citation from Ps 106 would also be of immediate relevance to the Chronicler's audience as those who had been gathered and delivered from the nations (v. 35).

18 Saying, "[a]To you I will give the land of
Canaan,
As the portion of your inheritance."
19 [a]When they were only a few in
number,
Very few, and strangers in it,
20 And they wandered about from nation
to nation,
And from *one* kingdom to another
people,
21 He permitted no man to oppress them,
And [a]He reproved kings for their
sakes, *saying,*
22 "Do not touch My anointed ones,
And [a]do My prophets no harm."
23 [a]Sing to the LORD, all the earth;
Proclaim good tidings of His salvation
from day to day.
24 Tell of His glory among the nations,
His wonderful deeds among all the
peoples.
25 For [a]great is the LORD, and greatly to
be praised;
He also is [b]to be feared above all gods.
26 For all the gods of the peoples are
[1a]idols,
[b]But the LORD made the heavens.
27 Splendor and majesty are before Him,
Strength and joy are in His place.
28 Ascribe to the LORD, O families of the
peoples,
Ascribe to the LORD glory and strength.
29 Ascribe to the LORD the glory due His
name;
Bring an [1]offering, and come before
Him;
[a]Worship the LORD in [2]holy array.
30 Tremble before Him, all the earth;
Indeed, the world is firmly
established, it will not be moved.
31 [a]Let the heavens be glad, and let the
earth rejoice;
And let them say among the nations,
"[b]The LORD reigns."
32 [a]Let the sea [1]roar, and [2]all it contains;
Let the field exult, and all that is in it.
33 Then the trees of the forest will sing
for joy before the LORD;
For He is coming to judge the earth.
34 [a]O give thanks to the LORD, for *He is*
good;
For His lovingkindness is everlasting.
35 [a]Then say, "Save us, O God of our
salvation,
And gather us and deliver us from the
nations,
To give thanks to Your holy name,
And [1]glory in Your praise."
36 [a]Blessed be the LORD, the God of
Israel,
From everlasting even to everlasting.
Then all the people [b]said, "Amen," and praised the LORD.

Worship before the Ark

37 So he left Asaph and his [1]relatives there [a]before the ark of the covenant of the LORD to minister before the ark continually, [b]as every day's work required;
38 and [a]Obed-edom with [1]his 68 relatives; Obed-edom, also the son of Jeduthun, and [b]Hosah as gatekeepers.
39 *He left* [a]Zadok the priest and his [1]relatives the priests [b]before the [2]tabernacle of the LORD in the high place which *was* at Gibeon,
40 to offer burnt offerings to the LORD on the altar of burnt offering continually morning and evening, [a]even according to all that is written in the law of the LORD, which He commanded Israel.
41 With them *were* [a]Heman and Jeduthun, and [b]the rest who were chosen, who were designated by name, to [c]give thanks to the LORD, because His lovingkindness is everlasting.
42 And with them *were* Heman and Jeduthun *with* trumpets and cymbals for those who should sound aloud, and *with* instruments *for* [a]the songs of God, and the sons of Jeduthun for the gate.
43 [a]Then all the people departed each to his house, and David returned to bless his household.

God's Covenant with David

17 [a]And it came about, when David dwelt in his house, that David said to Nathan the prophet, "Behold, I am dwelling in a house of cedar, but the ark of the covenant of the LORD is under curtains."
2 Then Nathan said to David, "Do all that is in your heart, for God is with you."
3 It came about the same night that the word of God came to Nathan, saying,

18 [a]Gen 13:15 **19** [a]Gen 34:30; Deut 7:7 **21** [a]Gen 12:17; 20:3; Ex 7:15-18 **22** [a]Gen 20:7 **23** [a]Ps 96:1-13 **25** [a]Ps 144:3-6 [b]Ps 89:7 **26** [1]Or *non-existent things* [a]Lev 19:4 [b]Ps 102:25 **29** [1]Or *a grain offering* [2]Or *the splendor of holiness* [a]Ps 29:2 **31** [a]Is 44:23; 49:13 [b]Ps 93:1; 96:10 **32** [1]Or *thunder* [2]Lit *its fullness* [a]Ps 98:7 **34** [a]2 Chr 5:13; 7:3; Ezra 3:11; Ps 106:1; 136:1; Jer 33:11

35 [1]Lit *boast* [a]Ps 106:47, 48 **36** [a]1 Kin 8:15, 56; Ps 72:18 [b]Deut 27:15; Neh 8:6 **37** [1]Lit *brothers* [a]1 Chr 16:4, 5 [b]2 Chr 8:14; Ezra 3:4 **38** [1]Lit *their brothers, 68* [a]1 Chr 13:14 [b]1 Chr 26:10 **39** [1]Lit *brothers* [2]Lit *dwelling place* [a]1 Chr 15:11 [b]1 Kin 3:4 **40** [a]Ex 29:38-42; Num 28:3, 4 **41** [a]1 Chr 6:33 [b]1 Chr 25:1-6 [c]2 Chr 5:13 **42** [a]1 Chr 25:7; 2 Chr 7:6; 29:27 **43** [a]2 Sam 6:19 **17:1** [a]2 Sam 7:1-29

16:29 *holy array.* See note on Ps 29:2.
16:39 *tabernacle . . . at Gibeon.* The tabernacle remained at Gibeon until Solomon's construction of the temple in Jerusalem (2 Chr 1:13; 5:5), when it was stored within the temple. The existence of these two shrines—the tabernacle and the temporary structure for the ark in Jerusalem (v. 1)—accounts for the two high priests: Zadok serving in Gibeon and Abiathar in Jerusalem (18:16; 27:34; see note on 6:8).
16:42 *trumpets . . . sound aloud.* See Num 10:1–10.
17:1–27 See 2 Sam 7 and notes.
17:1,10 In these verses the Chronicler omits the statement that David had rest from his enemies (2 Sam 7:1,11). Several factors may be at work in this omission: 1. The account of David's major wars is yet to come (chs. 18–20). Chronologically, this passage should follow the account of the wars (v. 8), but the author has placed it here to continue his concern with the ark and the building of the temple (vv. 4–6,12). 2. The Chronicler also views David as a man of war through most of his life (22:6–8), in contrast to Solomon, who is the man of "rest" (22:9) and who will build the temple (22:10). For the Chronicler, David has rest from enemies only late in his life (22:18). 3. As part of his concern to parallel David and Solomon to Moses and Joshua, Solomon (like Joshua) brings the people to rest from enemies (see Introduction: Portrait of David and Solomon).

4 "Go and tell David My servant, 'Thus says the LORD, "[a]You shall not build a house for Me to dwell in;

5 for I have not dwelt in a house since the day that I brought up Israel to this day, [a]but I have [1]gone from tent to tent and from *one* dwelling place *to another.*

6 "In all places where I have walked with all Israel, have I spoken a word [a]with any of the judges of Israel, whom I commanded to shepherd My people, saying, 'Why have you not built for Me a house of cedar?' " '

7 "Now, therefore, thus shall you say to My servant David, 'Thus says the LORD of hosts, "I took you from the pasture, from following the sheep, to be leader over My people Israel.

8 "I have been with you wherever you have gone, and have cut off all your enemies from before you; and I will make you a name like the name of the great ones who are in the earth.

9 "I will appoint a place for My people Israel, and will plant them, so that they may dwell in their own place and not be moved again; and the [1]wicked will not waste them anymore as formerly,

10 even from the day that I commanded judges *to be* over My people Israel. And I will subdue all your enemies.

Moreover, I tell you that the LORD will build a house for you.

11 "When your days are fulfilled that you must go *to be* with your fathers, that I will set up *one of* your [1]descendants after you, who will be of your sons; and I will establish his kingdom.

12 "He shall build for Me a house, and I will establish his throne forever.

13 "[a]I will be his father and he shall be My son; and I will not take My lovingkindness away from him, [b]as I took it from him who was before you.

14 "But I will settle him in My house and in My kingdom forever, and his throne shall be established forever." ' "

15 According to all these words and according to all this vision, so Nathan spoke to David.

David's Prayer in Response

16 Then David the king went in and sat before the LORD and said, "[a]Who am I, O LORD God, and what is my house that You have brought me this far?

17 "This was a small thing in Your eyes, O God; but You have spoken of Your servant's house for a great while to come, and have regarded me according to the standard of a man of high degree, O LORD God.

18 "What more can David still *say* to You concerning the honor *bestowed* on Your servant? For You know Your servant.

19 "O LORD, [a]for Your servant's sake, and according to Your own heart, You have wrought all this greatness, to make known all these great things.

20 "O LORD, there is none like You, nor is there any God besides You, according to all that we have heard with our ears.

21 "And what one nation in the earth is like Your people Israel, whom God went to redeem for Himself *as* a people, to make You a name by great and terrible things, [1]in driving out nations from before Your people, whom You redeemed out of Egypt?

22 "[a]For Your people Israel You made Your own people forever, and You, O LORD, became their God.

23 "Now, O LORD, let the word that You have spoken concerning Your servant and concerning his house be established forever, and do as You have spoken.

24 "Let Your name be established and magnified forever, saying, 'The LORD of hosts is the God of Israel, *even* a God to Israel; and the house of David Your servant is established before You.'

25 "For You, O my God, have revealed to Your servant that You will build for him a house; therefore Your servant has found *courage* to pray before You.

26 "Now, O LORD, You are God, and have [1]promised this good thing to Your servant.

27 "And now it has pleased You to bless the house of Your servant, that it may [1]continue forever before You; for You, O LORD, have blessed, and it is blessed forever."

David's Kingdom Strengthened

18 Now after this [a]it came about that David [1]defeated the Philistines and subdued them and took Gath and its towns from the hand of the Philistines.

4 [a]1 Chr 28:2, 3
5 [1]Lit *been* [a]Ex 40:2, 3; 2 Sam 7:6
6 [a]2 Sam 7:7
9 [1]Lit *sons of wickedness*
11 [1]Lit *seed*
13 [a]2 Cor 6:18; Heb 1:5 [b]1 Chr 10:14
16 [a]2 Sam 7:18
19 [a]2 Sam 7:21; Is 37:35
22 [a]Ex 19:5, 6
26 [1]Lit *said*
27 [1]Lit *be*
18:1 [1]Lit *smote,* and so in vv 1-3 [a]2 Sam 8:1-18

17:12–14 Though in this context these words refer to Solomon, the NT applies them to Jesus (Mark 1:11; Luke 1:32–33; Heb 1:5).

17:13 The Chronicler omits from his source (2 Sam 7:14) any reference to "punishment with the rod" or "flogging" as discipline for Solomon. This omission reflects his idealization of Solomon as a Messianic figure, for whom such punishment would not be appropriate (see Introduction: Portrait of David and Solomon).

17:14 The Chronicler introduces his own concerns by the changes in the pronouns found in his source (2 Sam 7:16); instead of "Your house and your kingdom," the Chronicler reads "My house and My kingdom." This same emphasis on theocracy (God's rule) is found in several other passages unique to Chronicles (28:5–6; 29:23; 2 Chr 1:11; 9:8; 13:4–8).

17:16 *sat.* Aside from its parallel in 2 Sam 7:18, the only other reference in the OT to sitting as a posture for prayer is 1 Kin 19:4.

17:21–22 The references to the exodus from Egypt would remind the Chronicler's audience of the second great exodus, the release of the restoration community from the period of Babylonian captivity.

18:1–20:8 The accounts of David's wars serve to show the blessing of God on his reign; God keeps His promise to subdue

2 He defeated Moab, and the Moabites
became servants to David, bringing tribute.
3 David also defeated Hadadezer king of
Zobah *as far as* Hamath, as he went to establish his [1]rule to the Euphrates River.
4 David took from him 1,000 chariots and
7,000 horsemen and 20,000 foot soldiers, and
David hamstrung all the chariot horses, but
reserved *enough* of them for 100 chariots.
5 When the Arameans of [1]Damascus
came to help Hadadezer king [a]of Zobah,
David [2]killed 22,000 men of the Arameans.
6 Then David put *garrisons* among the
Arameans of [1]Damascus; and the Arameans
became servants to David, bringing tribute.
And the LORD helped David wherever he
went.
7 David took the shields of gold which
were [1]carried by the servants of Hadadezer
and brought them to Jerusalem.
8 Also from [1]Tibhath and from Cun, cities of Hadadezer, David took a very large
amount of bronze, with which [a]Solomon
made the bronze sea and the pillars and the
bronze utensils.
9 Now when [1]Tou king of Hamath heard
that David had [2]defeated all the army of
Hadadezer king of Zobah,
10 he sent [1]Hadoram his son to King
David to [2]greet him and to bless him,
because he had fought against Hadadezer
and had [3]defeated him; for Hadadezer had
been at war with Tou. And *Hadoram brought*
all kinds of articles of gold and silver and
bronze.
11 King David also dedicated these to the
LORD with the silver and the gold which he
had carried away from all the nations: from
Edom, Moab, the sons of Ammon, the Philistines, and from Amalek.
12 Moreover Abishai the son of Zeruiah
[1]defeated 18,000 Edomites in the Valley of
Salt.
13 Then he put garrisons in Edom, and all
the Edomites became servants to David. And
the LORD helped David wherever he went.
14 So David reigned over all Israel; and he
[1]administered justice and righteousness for
all his people.
15 [a]Joab the son of Zeruiah *was* over the
army, and Jehoshaphat the son of Ahilud
was recorder;
16 and Zadok the son of Ahitub and
Abimelech the son of Abiathar *were* priests,
and Shavsha *was* secretary;
17 and Benaiah the son of Jehoiada *was*
over the Cherethites and the Pelethites, and
the sons of David *were* chiefs at the king's
side.

3 [1]Lit *hand* **5** [1]Heb *Darmeseq* [2]Lit *smote* [a]1 Chr 19:6 **6** [1]Heb *Darmeseq* **7** [1]Lit *on* **8** [1]In 2 Sam 8:8, *Betah* [a]1 Kin 7:40-47; 2 Chr 4:11-18 **9** [1]In 2 Sam 8:9, *Toi* [2]Lit *smitten* **10** [1]In 2 Sam 8:10, *Joram* [2]Lit *ask him of his welfare* [3]Lit *smitten*

12 [1]Lit *smote* **14** [1]Lit *was doing* **15** [a]1 Chr 11:6 **19:1** [a]2 Sam 10:1-19

David's Messengers Abused

19 [a]Now it came about after this, that
Nahash the king of the sons of Ammon
died, and his son became king in his place.

David's enemies (17:10). These accounts are also particularly relevant to a theme developed in the postexilic prophets: that the silver and gold of the nations would flow to Jerusalem; the tribute of enemy peoples builds the temple of God (18:7–8,11; 22:2–5,14–15; cf. Hag 2:1–9,20–23; Zech 2:7–13; 6:9–15; 14:12–14). While this passage of Chronicles portrays God's blessing on David, it simultaneously explains the Chronicler's report later (22:6–8; 28:3) that David could not build the temple because he was a man of war. The material in these chapters essentially follows the Chronicler's source in 2 Samuel. The major differences are not changes the Chronicler introduces into the text, but items he chooses not to deal with—in particular 2 Sam 9; 11:2–12:25, where accounts not compatible with his portrait of David occur.

18:1–13 See 2 Sam 8:1–14 and notes.

18:2 The Chronicler omits the harsh treatment of the Moabites recorded in 2 Sam 8:2, perhaps so that no unnecessary cruelty or brutality would tarnish his portrait of David.

18:5 *Arameans.* Mentioned also among the enemies of Saul (1 Sam 14:47, "Zobah"). By the time of David they were united north (Zobah) and south (Beth-rehob, 2 Sam 10:6) under Hadadezer. They persisted as a foe of Israel for two centuries until they fell to Assyria shortly before the northern kingdom likewise fell (2 Kin 16:7–9).

18:8 *Tibhath and from Cun.* Located in the valley between the Lebanon and Anti-Lebanon mountain ranges. *with which Solomon made the bronze . . . utensils.* See 2 Chr 4:2–5,18.

18:12 *Abishai.* 2 Sam 8:13 speaks only of David (see 1 Kin 11:15–16; Ps 60 title).

18:15–17 The titles and duties of these officers at David's court appear to be modeled on the organization of Egyptian functionaries serving Pharaoh.

18:15 For the account of how Joab attained his position over the army see 11:4–6; 2 Sam 5:6–8.

18:16 *Zadok . . . Abimelech the son of Abiathar.* See notes on 6:8; 16:39; 2 Sam 8:17.

18:17 *Cherethites and the Pelethites.* Apparently a group of foreign mercenaries who constituted part of the royal bodyguard (2 Sam 8:18; 20:23; see note on 1 Sam 30:14). They remained loyal to David at the time of the rebellions of Absalom (2 Sam 15:18) and Sheba (2 Sam 20:7) and supported the succession of Solomon against his rival Adonijah (1 Kin 1:38,44). *chiefs.* The earlier narrative at this point uses the Hebrew term ordinarily translated "priests" (see note on 2 Sam 8:18). The Chronicler has used a term for civil service instead of sacral service. Two approaches to this passage are ordinarily followed: 1. Some scholars see here an attempt by the Chronicler to keep the priesthood restricted to the Levitical line as part of his larger concern with legitimacy of cultic institutions in his own day. 2. Others argue that the Hebrew term used in 2 Sam 8:18 could earlier have had a broader meaning than "priest" and could be used of some other types of officials (cf. 2 Sam 20:26; 1 Kin 4:5). The Chronicler used an equivalent term, since by his day the Hebrew term for "priest" was restricted to cultic functionaries. The Septuagint, Targum, Old Latin and Josephus all translate the term in Samuel by some word other than "priest."

19:1–20:3 The Chronicler follows 2 Sam 10–12 closely (see notes there), apart from his omission of the account of David's sin with Bathsheba (11:2–12:25). The Ammonites were a traditional enemy of Israel (2 Chr 20:1–2,23; 27:5; Judg 3:13; 10:7–9; 10:17–11:33; 1 Sam 11:1–13; 14:47; 2 Kin 10:32–33; Jer 49:1–6; Zeph 2:8–11). Even during the postexilic period Tobiah the Ammonite troubled Jerusalem (Neh 2:19; 4:3,7; 6:1,12,14; 13:4–9).

19:1 *Nahash.* Possibly the same as Saul's foe (1 Sam 11:1), or perhaps his descendant.

2 Then David said, "I will show kindness to Hanun the son of Nahash, because his father showed kindness to me." So David sent messengers to console him concerning his father. And David's servants came into the land of the sons of Ammon to Hanun to console him.

3 But the princes of the sons of Ammon said to Hanun, "[1]Do you think that David is honoring your father, in that he has sent comforters to you? Have not his servants come to you to search and to overthrow and to spy out the land?"

4 So Hanun took David's servants and shaved them and cut off their garments in the middle as far as their hips, and sent them away.

5 Then *certain persons* went and told David about the men. And he sent to meet them, for the men were greatly humiliated. And the king said, "[1]Stay at Jericho until your beards grow, and *then* return."

6 When the sons of Ammon saw that they had made themselves odious to David, Hanun and the sons of Ammon sent 1,000 talents of silver to hire for themselves chariots and horsemen from Mesopotamia, from Aram-maacah and [a]from Zobah.

7 So they hired for themselves 32,000 chariots, and the king of Maacah and his people, who came and camped before [a]Medeba. And the sons of Ammon gathered together from their cities and came to battle.

8 When David heard *of it,* he sent Joab and all the army, the mighty men.

9 The sons of Ammon came out and drew up in battle array at the entrance of the city, and the kings who had come were by themselves in the field.

Ammon and Aram Defeated

10 Now when Joab saw that the [1]battle was set against him in front and in the rear, he selected from all the choice men of Israel and they arrayed themselves against the Arameans.

11 But the remainder of the people he placed in the hand of [1]Abshai his brother; and they arrayed themselves against the sons of Ammon.

12 He said, "If the Arameans are too strong for me, then you shall help me; but if the sons of Ammon are too strong for you, then I will help you.

13 "Be strong, and let us show ourselves courageous for the sake of our people and for the cities of our God; and may the LORD do what is good in His sight."

14 So Joab and the people who were with him drew near to the battle against the Arameans, and they fled before him.

15 When the sons of Ammon saw that the Arameans fled, they also fled before Abshai his brother and entered the city. Then Joab came to Jerusalem.

16 When the Arameans saw that they had been [1]defeated by Israel, they sent messengers and brought out the Arameans who were beyond the [2]River, with Shophach the commander of the army of Hadadezer [3]leading them.

17 When it was told David, he gathered all Israel together and crossed the Jordan, and came upon them and drew up in formation against them. And when David drew up in battle array against the Arameans, they fought against him.

18 The Arameans fled before Israel, and David killed of the Arameans 7,000 charioteers and 40,000 foot soldiers, and put to death Shophach the commander of the army.

19 So when the servants of Hadadezer saw that they were [1]defeated by Israel, they made peace with David and served him. Thus the Arameans were not willing to help the sons of Ammon anymore.

War with Philistine Giants

20 [a]Then it happened [1]in the spring, at the time when kings go out *to battle,* that Joab led out the army and ravaged the land of the sons of Ammon, and came and besieged Rabbah. But David stayed at Jerusalem. And [b]Joab struck Rabbah and overthrew it.

2 [a]David took the crown of [1]their king from his head, and he found it to weigh a talent of gold, and there was a precious stone in it; and it was placed on David's head. And he brought out the spoil of the city, a very great amount.

3 He brought out the people who *were* in it, [a]and cut *them* with saws and with sharp instruments and with axes. And thus David did to all the cities of the sons of Ammon. Then David and all the people returned *to* Jerusalem.

4 [a]Now it came about after this, that war [1]broke out at [2]Gezer with the Philistines;

3 [1]Lit *In your eyes is David honoring your father because*
5 [1]Lit *Return to*
6 [a]1 Chr 18:5, 9
7 [a]Num 21:30; Josh 13:9, 16
10 [1]Lit *the face of the battle*
11 [1]In 2 Sam 10:10, *Abishai*
16 [1]Lit *smitten before* [2]I.e. Euphrates [3]Lit *before*
19 [1]Lit *smitten before*
20:1 [1]Lit *at the return of the year* [a]2 Sam 11:1 [b]2 Sam 12:26
2 [1]In Zeph 1:5, *Malcam* [a]2 Sam 12:30, 31
3 [a]2 Sam 12:31
4 [1]Lit *stood up* [2]In 2 Sam 21:18, *Gob* [a]2 Sam 21:18-22

19:6 *Mesopotamia, from Aram-maacah and from Zobah.* 2 Sam 10:6 also mentions Beth-rehob and Tob. All these states were north and northeast of Israel and formed a solid block from the region of Lake Huleh through the Anti-Lebanons to beyond the Euphrates.

19:7 *Medeba.* A town in Moab apparently in the hands of Ammon.

19:9 *the city.* The capital city, Rabbah, to which Joab would lay siege the following year (20:1–3).

19:18 *7,000.* 2 Sam 10:18 has 700, which is evidently a copyist's mistake.

20:1 *when kings go out to battle.* Immediately following the spring harvest when there was some relaxation of agricultural labors and armies on the move could live off the land. *Rabbah.* See note on 19:9. Rabbah is the site of modern Amman, Jordan.

20:2–3 The Chronicler assumes that the reader is familiar with 2 Sam 12:26–29; he does not offer an explanation of how David, who had remained in Jerusalem (v. 1), came to be at Rabbah.

then Sibbecai the Hushathite [3]killed Sippai,
one of the descendants of the [4]giants, and
they were subdued.
5 And there was war with the Philistines
again, and Elhanan the son of [a]Jair [1]killed
Lahmi the brother of Goliath the Gittite, the
[b]shaft of whose spear *was* like a weaver's
beam.
6 Again there was war at Gath, where
there was a man of *great* stature who had
twenty-four fingers and toes, six *fingers on*
each hand and six *toes on each foot;* and he
also was descended from the giants.
7 When he taunted Israel, Jonathan the
son of Shimea, David's brother, [1]killed him.
8 These were descended from the giants
in Gath, and they fell by the hand of David
and by the hand of his servants.

Census Brings Pestilence

21 [a]Then Satan stood up against Israel
and moved David to number Israel.
2 So David said to Joab and to the
princes of the people, "[a]Go, number Israel
from Beersheba even to Dan, and bring me
word that I may know their number."
3 Joab said, "[a]May the LORD add to His
people a hundred times as many as they are!
But, my lord the king, are they not all my
lord's servants? Why does my lord seek this
thing? Why should he be a cause of guilt to
Israel?"
4 Nevertheless, the king's word prevailed
against Joab. Therefore, Joab departed and
went throughout all Israel, and came to Jerusalem.
5 Joab gave the number of the [1]census of
all the people to David. And [a]all Israel were
1,100,000 men who drew the sword; and
Judah *was* 470,000 men who drew the sword.
6 [a]But he did not [1]number Levi and Benjamin among them, for the king's [2]command
was abhorrent to Joab.
7 [1]God was displeased with this thing, so
He struck Israel.
8 David said to God, "I have sinned
greatly, in that I have done this thing. [a]But
now, please take away the iniquity of Your
servant, for I have done very foolishly."
9 The LORD spoke to [a]Gad, David's [b]seer,
saying,
10 "Go and speak to David, saying, 'Thus
says the LORD, "I [1]offer you three things;
choose for yourself one of them, which I will
do to you." ' "
11 So Gad came to David and said to him,
"Thus says the LORD, 'Take for yourself
12 [a]either three years of famine, or three
months to be swept away before your foes,
while the sword of your enemies overtakes
you, or else three days of the sword of the
LORD, even pestilence in the land, and the
angel of the LORD destroying throughout all
the territory of Israel.' Now, therefore, consider what answer I shall return to Him who
sent me."
13 David said to Gad, "I am in great distress; please let me fall into the hand of the
LORD, [a]for His mercies are very great. But do
not let me fall into the hand of man."
14 [a]So the LORD [1]sent a pestilence on Israel; 70,000 men of Israel fell.
15 And God sent an angel to Jerusalem to
destroy it; but as he was about to destroy *it,*
the LORD saw and [a]was sorry over the
calamity, and said to the destroying angel, "It
is enough; now relax your hand." And the
angel of the LORD was standing by the threshing floor of [1]Ornan the Jebusite.
16 Then David lifted up his eyes and saw
the angel of the LORD standing between earth
and heaven, with his drawn sword in his

4 [3]Lit *smote* [4]Heb *Raphah,* and so in vv 6, 8
5 [1]Lit *smote* [a]2 Sam 21:19 [b]1 Sam 17:7; 1 Chr 11:23
7 [1]Lit *smote*
21:1 [a]2 Sam 24:1-25
2 [a]1 Chr 27:23, 24
3 [a]Deut 1:11
5 [1]Lit *muster* [a]2 Sam 24:9
6 [1]Lit *muster* [a]1 Chr 27:24
6 [2]Lit *word*
7 [1]Lit *it was evil in the sight of God*
8 [a]2 Sam 12:13
9 [a]2 Sam 24:11; 1 Chr 29:29 [b]1 Sam 9:9
10 [1]Lit *stretch out to*
12 [a]2 Sam 24:13
13 [a]Ps 51:1; 130:4, 7
14 [1]Lit *gave* [a]1 Chr 27:24
15 [1]In 2 Sam 24:16, *Araunah* [a]Ex 32:14; 1 Sam 15:11; Jon 3:10

20:4 *Sibbecai.* See 11:29; 27:11. *giants.* See Gen 14:5; Deut 2:10–11; see also note on 2 Sam 21:16.
20:5 See note on 2 Sam 21:19. *weaver's beam.* See 11:23; 1 Sam 17:7.
20:6 *the giants.* See note on 2 Sam 21:16.
21:1–22:1 See 2 Sam 24 and notes. Although the story of David's census is quite similar in both narratives, the two accounts function differently. In Samuel the account belongs to the appendix (2 Sam 21–24), which begins and ends with accounts of the Lord's anger against Israel during the reign of David because of actions by her kings (in ch. 21, an act of Saul; in ch. 24, an act of David). See note on 2 Sam 21:1–24:25. The Chronicler appears to include it in order to account for the purchase of the ground on which the temple would be built. The additional material in Chronicles that is not found in Samuel (21:28–22:1) makes this interest clear. The census is the preface to David's preparations for the temple (chs. 22–29).
21:1 See note on 2 Sam 24:1. *Satan.* Satan means "accuser" (see Job 1:6; Zech 3:1 and notes).
21:4 The Chronicler abridges the more extensive account of Joab's itinerary found in 2 Sam 24:4–8; he does not mention that the census required nine months and 20 days (2 Sam 24:8).
21:5 *all Israel were 1,100,000 men . . . Judah was 470,000.* 2 Sam 24:9 has 800,000 in Israel and 500,000 (which could be a round number for 470,000) in Judah. The reason for the difference is unclear. Perhaps it is to be related to the unofficial and incomplete nature of the census (see 27:23–24), with the differing figures representing the inclusion or exclusion of certain unspecified groupings among the people (see v. 6). Or perhaps it is simply due to a copyist's mistake.
21:6 The Chronicler adds the note that Joab exempted Levi and Benjamin from the counting. This additional note reflects the Chronicler's concern with the Levites and with the worship of Israel. The tabernacle in Gibeon and the ark in Jerusalem both fell within the borders of Benjamin.
21:9 *Gad.* A longtime friend of David, having been with him when he was a fugitive from Saul (1 Sam 22:3–5; cf. 1 Chr 29:29; 2 Chr 29:25).
21:12 *three years of famine.* 2 Sam 24:13 reads "seven years of famine," but the Septuagint reads "three years" there.
21:16 The verse has no parallel in the traditional Hebrew text of 2 Sam 24, so some scholars regard it as an addition by the Chronicler reflecting the more developed doctrine of angels in the postexilic period. However, a fragmentary Hebrew text of Samuel from the third century B.C., discovered at Qumran, contains the verse. It now appears that the Chronicler was carefully copying the Samuel text at his disposal, which differed in some respects from the Masoretic (traditional Hebrew) text.

hand stretched out over Jerusalem. Then David and the elders, [a]covered with sackcloth, fell on their faces.

17 David said to God, "Is it not I who [1]commanded to count the people? Indeed, I am the one who has sinned and done very wickedly, [a]but these sheep, what have they done? O LORD my God, please let Your hand be against me and my father's household, but not against Your people that they should be plagued."

David's Altar

18 [a]Then the angel of the LORD [1]commanded Gad to say to David, that David should go up and build an altar to the LORD on the threshing floor of Ornan the Jebusite.

19 So David went up at the word of Gad, which he spoke in the name of the LORD.

20 Now Ornan turned back and saw the angel, and his four sons *who were* with him hid themselves. And Ornan was threshing wheat.

21 As David came to Ornan, Ornan looked and saw David, and went out from the threshing floor and prostrated himself [1]before David with his face to the ground.

22 Then David said to Ornan, "Give me the [1]site of *this* threshing floor, that I may build on it an altar to the LORD; for the full price you shall give it to me, that the plague may be restrained from the people."

23 Ornan said to David, "Take *it* for yourself; and let my lord the king do what is good in his sight. See, I will give the oxen for burnt offerings and the threshing sledges for wood and the wheat for the grain offering; I will give *it* all."

24 But King David said to Ornan, "No, but I will surely buy *it* for the full price; for I will not take what is yours for the LORD, or offer a burnt offering [1]which costs me nothing."

25 So [a]David gave Ornan 600 shekels of gold by weight for the [1]site.

26 Then David built an altar to the LORD there and offered burnt offerings and peace offerings. And he called to the LORD and [a]He answered him with fire from heaven on the altar of burnt offering.

27 The LORD commanded the angel, and he put his sword back in its sheath.

28 At that time, when David saw that the LORD had answered him on the threshing floor of Ornan the Jebusite, he offered sacrifice there.

29 [a]For the tabernacle of the LORD, which Moses had made in the wilderness, and the altar of burnt offering *were* in the high place at Gibeon at that time.

30 But David could not go before it to inquire of God, for he was terrified by the sword of the angel of the LORD.

David Prepares for Temple Building

22 Then David said, "[a]This is the house of the LORD God, and this is the altar of burnt offering for Israel."

2 So David [1]gave orders to gather [a]the foreigners who were in the land of Israel, and [b]he set stonecutters to hew out stones to build the house of God.

3 David [a]prepared large quantities of iron [1]to make the nails for the doors of the gates and for the clamps, and more [b]bronze than could be weighed;

4 and timbers of cedar logs beyond number, for [a]the Sidonians and Tyrians brought large quantities of cedar timber to David.

5 David said, "My son [a]Solomon is young and inexperienced, and the house that is to

16 [a]1 Kin 21:27 **17** [1]Lit *said* [a]2 Sam 7:8; Ps 74:1 **18** [1]Lit *said to* [a]2 Chr 3:1 **21** [1]Lit *to* **22** [1]Lit *place*

24 [1]Lit *gratuitously* **25** [1]Lit *place* [a]2 Sam 24:24 **26** [a]Lev 9:24; Judg 6:21 **29** [a]1 Kin 3:4; 1 Chr 16:39 **22:1** [a]1 Chr 21:18-28; 2 Chr 3:1 **2** [1]Lit *said to* [a]1 Kin 9:20, 21; 2 Chr 2:17 [b]1 Kin 5:17, 18 **3** [1]Lit *for* [a]1 Chr 29:2, 7 [b]1 Chr 22:14 **4** [a]1 Kin 5:6-10 **5** [a]1 Kin 3:7; 1 Chr 29:1

Josephus, who appears to be following the text of Samuel, also reported this information. Presumably, he too used a text of Samuel similar to that followed by the Chronicler.

21:20–21 The Chronicler reports that Ornan (a variant of Araunah; see 2 Sam 24:16) was threshing wheat as the king approached—information not found in 2 Sam 24:20. However, Josephus and the fragmentary text of Samuel from Qumran both mention this information (see note on v. 16).

21:25 *600 shekels of gold.* 2 Sam 24:24 says 50 shekels of silver were paid for the threshing floor and oxen. The difference has been explained by some as the Chronicler's attempt to glorify David and the temple by inflating the price. However, the difference is more likely explained by the Chronicler's statement that this was the price for the "site," i.e., for a much larger area than the threshing floor alone.

21:26 *fire from heaven.* Underscores the divine approval and the sanctity of the site (see 2 Chr 7:1; Lev 9:24; 1 Kin 18:37–38).

21:28–22:1 This material is not found in 2 Sam 24. It reflects the Chronicler's main concern in reporting this narrative (see note on 21:1–22:1).

21:30 *it.* The tabernacle.

22:1–29:30 This material is unique to Chronicles and displays some of the Chronicler's most characteristic interests: the preparations for the building of the temple, the legitimacy of the priests and Levites, and the royal succession. The chapters portray a theocratic "Messianic" kingdom as it existed under David and Solomon.

22:1 David dedicates this property (21:18–30) as the site for the temple (see vv. 2–6). See note on Ps 30 title.

22:2–19 Solomon's appointment to succeed David was twofold: (1) a private audience, with David and some leaders in attendance (vv. 17–19), and (2) a public announcement to the people (ch. 28), similar to when Joshua succeeded Moses (see Introduction: Portrait of David and Solomon).

22:2 *foreigners . . . stonecutters.* 2 Sam 20:24 confirms the use of forced labor by David, but does not specify that these laborers were aliens, not Israelites. Solomon used Israelites in conscripted labor (1 Kin 5:13–18; 9:15–23; 11:28), but the Chronicler mentions only his use of aliens (2 Chr 8:7–10). Though they were personally free, aliens were without political rights and could be easily exploited. The OT frequently warns that they were not to be oppressed (Ex 22:21; 23:9; Lev 19:33; Deut 24:14; Jer 7:6; Zech 7:10). Isaiah prophesies the participation of foreigners in the building of Jerusalem's walls in the future (Is 60:10–12).

22:3 *bronze.* See note on 18:8.

22:5 *young.* Solomon's age at the time of his accession is not known with certainty. He came to the throne in 970 B.C. and was likely born c. 991.

be built for the LORD shall be exceedingly
magnificent, famous and glorious throughout
all lands. *Therefore* now I will make preparation for it." So David made ample preparations before his death.

Solomon Charged with the Task

6 Then [a]he called for his son Solomon,
and charged him to build a house for the
LORD God of Israel.
7 David said to Solomon, "[a]My son, [1]I
had intended to build a house to the name of
the LORD my God.
8 "But the word of the LORD came to me,
saying, '[a]You have shed much blood and
have [1]waged great wars; you shall not build
a house to My name, because you have shed
so much blood on the earth before Me.
9 'Behold, a son will be born to you, who
shall be a man of rest; and [a]I will give him
rest from all his enemies on every side; for
[b]his name shall be [1]Solomon, and I will give
peace and quiet to Israel in his days.
10 '[a]He shall build a house for My name,
and he shall be My son and I will be his
father; and I will establish the throne of his
kingdom over Israel forever.'
11 "Now, my son, [a]the LORD be with you
that you may be successful, and build the
house of the LORD your God just as He has
spoken concerning you.
12 "[a]Only the LORD give you discretion and
understanding, and give you charge over
Israel, so that you may [b]keep the law of the
LORD your God.
13 "[a]Then you will prosper, if you are careful to observe the statutes and the ordinances which the LORD commanded Moses
concerning Israel. [b]Be strong and courageous, do not fear nor be dismayed.
14 "Now behold, [1]with great pains I have
prepared for the house of the LORD [a]100,000
talents of gold and 1,000,000 talents of silver,
and [b]bronze and iron beyond weight, for
[2]they are in great quantity; also timber and

6 [a]1 Kin 2:1
7 [1]Lit *as for me, it was in my heart* [a]2 Sam 7:2, 3; 1 Chr 17:1
8 [1]Lit *made* [a]1 Chr 28:3
9 [1]I.e. peaceful [a]1 Kin 4:20, 25 [b]2 Sam 12:24, 25
10 [a]2 Sam 7:13, 14; 1 Chr 17:12
11 [a]1 Chr 22:16
12 [a]1 Kin 3:9-12; 2 Chr 1:10 [b]1 Kin 2:3
13 [a]1 Chr 28:7 [b]Josh 1:6-9
14 [1]Lit *in my affliction* [2]Lit *it is* [a]1 Chr 29:4 [b]1 Chr 22:3

stone I have prepared, and you may add to
them.
15 "Moreover, there are many workmen
with you, stonecutters and masons of stone
and carpenters, and all men who are skillful
in every kind of work.
16 "Of the gold, the silver and the bronze
and the iron there is no limit. Arise and
work, and may [a]the LORD be with you."
17 [a]David also commanded all the leaders
of Israel to help his son Solomon, *saying,*
18 "Is not the LORD your God with you?
And [a]has He not given you rest on every
side? For He has given the inhabitants of the
land into my hand, and the land is subdued
before the LORD and before His people.
19 "Now [a]set your heart and your soul to
seek the LORD your God; arise, therefore, and
build the sanctuary of the LORD God, [b]so that
you may bring the ark of the covenant of the
LORD and the holy vessels of God into the
house that is to be built [c]for the name of the
LORD."

Solomon Reigns

23 [a]Now when David [1]reached old age,
[b]he made his son Solomon king over
Israel.
2 And he gathered together all the leaders of Israel with the priests and the Levites.

Offices of the Levites

3 [a]The Levites were numbered from thirty years old and upward, and [b]their number
by [1]census of men was 38,000.
4 Of these, 24,000 were [a]to oversee the
work of the house of the LORD; and 6,000
were [b]officers and judges,
5 and 4,000 *were* gatekeepers, and [a]4,000
were praising the LORD with the instruments
which [1]David made for giving praise.
6 David divided them into divisions
[a]according to the sons of Levi: Gershon,
Kohath, and Merari.

16 [a]1 Chr 22:11
17 [a]1 Chr 28:1-6
18 [a]1 Chr 22:9; 23:25
19 [a]1 Chr 28:9 [b]1 Kin 8:6, 21; 2 Chr 5:7 [c]1 Chr 22:7
23:1 [1]Lit *became old and sated with days* [a]1 Chr 29:28 [b]1 Kin 1:1-40; 2:12; 1 Chr 28:5; 29:22
3 [1]Lit *their heads* [a]Num 4:3-49 [b]Num 4:48; 1 Chr 23:24
4 [a]Ezra 3:8, 9 [b]1 Chr 26:29
5 [1]Lit *I made* [a]1 Chr 15:16
6 [a]1 Chr 6:1

22:8–9 See note on 17:1. In 1 Kin 5:3 Solomon explains that David could not build the temple because he was too busy with wars. The Chronicler's nuance is slightly different—not just that wars took so much of his time, but that David was in some sense defiled by them because of the bloodshed. A pun on Solomon's name is woven into the divine oracle ("Solomon" sounds like and may be derived from the Hebrew word for "peace").

22:10 See note on 17:12–14.

22:12–13 See Introduction: Portrait of David and Solomon.

22:19 See 2 Chr 5:1–7.

23:1–27:34 David's preparations for the temple were not restricted to amassing materials for the building; he also arranged for its administration and worship. Unique to Chronicles (see note on 22:1–29:30), these details of the organization of the theocracy (God's kingdom) were of vital concern in the Chronicler's own day. Characteristically for the Chronicler, details about religious and cultic matters (chs. 23–26) take precedence over those that are civil and secular (ch. 27). David's arrangements provided the basis and authority for the practices of the restored community.

23:1 *made his son Solomon king.* The account of Solomon's succession is resumed in chs. 28–29. The Chronicler omits the accounts of disputed succession and bloody consolidation recorded in 1 Kin 1–2 (see note on 28:1–29:30) since these would not be in accord with his overall portrait of David and Solomon (see Introduction: Portrait of David and Solomon).

23:2–5 The Levites were not counted in the census that had provoked the wrath of God (21:6–7).

23:3 *Levites . . . from thirty years old and upward.* The census of Levites was made first in accordance with the Mosaic prescription (Num 4:1–3). Apparently soon after this count, David instructed that the age be lowered to 20 years (vv. 24,27); a similar adjustment to age 25 had been made under Moses (Num 8:23–24, but see note on Num 8:24).

23:6 *Gershon, Kohath, and Merari.* The Levites were organized by their three clans (ch. 6; Ex 6:16–19; Num 3). This list parallels those in 6:16–30; 24:20–30.

Gershonites

7 Of the Gershonites *were* [1]Ladan and Shimei.

8 The sons of Ladan *were* Jehiel the first and Zetham and Joel, three.

9 The sons of Shimei *were* Shelomoth and Haziel and Haran, three. These were the heads of the fathers' *households* of Ladan.

10 The sons of Shimei *were* Jahath, [1]Zina, Jeush and Beriah. These four *were* the sons of Shimei.

11 Jahath was the first and Zizah the second; but Jeush and Beriah did not have many sons, so they became a father's household, one [1]class.

Kohathites

12 The sons of Kohath were four: Amram, Izhar, Hebron and Uzziel.

13 [a]The sons of Amram were Aaron and Moses. And [b]Aaron was set apart to sanctify him as most holy, he and his sons forever, [c]to burn incense before the LORD, to minister to Him and to bless in His name forever.

14 But *as for* [a]Moses the man of God, his sons were named among the tribe of Levi.

15 The sons of Moses *were* Gershom and Eliezer.

16 The [1]son of Gershom *was* [2]Shebuel the chief.

17 The [1]son of Eliezer was Rehabiah the chief; and Eliezer had no other sons, but the sons of Rehabiah were very many.

18 The [1]son of Izhar was [2]Shelomith the chief.

19 The sons of Hebron *were* Jeriah the first, Amariah the second, Jahaziel the third and Jekameam the fourth.

20 The sons of Uzziel *were* Micah the first and Isshiah the second.

Merarites

21 The sons of Merari were Mahli and Mushi. The sons of Mahli *were* Eleazar and Kish.

22 Eleazar died and had no sons, but daughters only, so their brothers, the sons of Kish, took them *as wives.*

23 The sons of Mushi *were* three: Mahli, Eder and Jeremoth.

Duties Revised

24 [a]These were the sons of Levi according to their fathers' households, *even* the heads of the fathers' *households* of those of them who were [1]counted, in the number of names by their [2]census, doing the work for the service of the house of the LORD, [b]from twenty years old and upward.

25 For David said, "The LORD God of Israel [a]has given rest to His people, and He dwells in Jerusalem forever.

26 "Also, [a]the Levites will no longer need to carry the tabernacle and all its utensils for its service."

27 For by the last words of David the sons of Levi *were* numbered from twenty years old and upward.

28 For their office is [1]to assist the sons of Aaron with the service of the house of the LORD, in the courts and in the chambers and in the purifying of all holy things, even the work of the service of the house of God,

29 [a]and with the showbread, and [b]the fine flour for a grain offering, and unleavened wafers, or [c]*what is baked in* the pan or [d]what is well-mixed, and [e]all measures of volume and size.

30 They are to stand every morning to thank and to praise the LORD, and likewise at evening,

31 and to offer all burnt offerings to the LORD, [a]on the sabbaths, the new moons and [b]the fixed festivals in the number *set* by the ordinance concerning them, continually before the LORD.

32 Thus [a]they are to keep charge of the tent of meeting, and charge of the holy place, and [b]charge of the sons of Aaron their [1]relatives, for the service of the house of the LORD.

Divisions of Levites

24 Now the divisions of the [1]descendants of Aaron *were these:* [a]the sons of Aaron *were* Nadab, Abihu, Eleazar and Ithamar.

2 [a]But Nadab and Abihu died before their father and had no [1]sons. So Eleazar and Ithamar served as priests.

3 David, with [a]Zadok of the sons of Eleazar and Ahimelech of the sons of Ithamar, divided them according to their offices [1]for their ministry.

4 Since more chief men were found from the [1]descendants of Eleazar than the [1]descendants of Ithamar, they divided them thus: *there were* sixteen heads of fathers' households of the [1]descendants of Eleazar

7 [1]In Ex 6:17, *Libni*
10 [1]In v 11, *Zizah*
11 [1]Lit *mustering*
13 [a]Ex 6:20 [b]Ex 28:1 [c]Ex 30:6-10
14 [a]Deut 33:1; Ps 90: title
16 [1]Lit *sons* [2]In ch 24:20, *Shubael*
17 [1]Lit *sons...were*
18 [1]Lit *sons* [2]In ch 24:22, *Shelomoth*
24 [a]Num 10:17, 21
24 [1]Lit *mustered* [2]Lit *heads* [b]1 Chr 23:3
25 [a]1 Chr 22:18
26 [a]Num 4:5, 15; 7:9; Deut 10:8
28 [1]Lit *at the hand of*
29 [a]Lev 24:5-9 [b]Lev 6:20 [c]1 Chr 9:31 [d]Lev 6:21 [e]Lev 19:35, 36
31 [a]Is 1:13, 14 [b]Lev 23:2-4
32 [1]Lit *brothers* [a]Num 1:53; 1 Chr 9:27 [b]Num 3:6-9, 38
24:1 [1]Lit *sons* [a]Ex 6:23
2 [1]Or *children* [a]Lev 10:2
3 [1]Lit *in their service* [a]1 Chr 6:8
4 [1]Lit *sons*

23:24,27 *twenty years old and upward.* See note on v. 3.

23:28–32 See note on 9:28–34. The function of the Levites was to assist the priests. In addition to the care of the precincts and implements, baked goods and music (mentioned as Levitical duties in 9:22–34), the Chronicler adds details on the role of the Levites assisting in sacrifices.

23:30 *morning . . . evening.* See Ex 29:38–41; Num 28:3–8.

24:1–19 There are several lists of priests from the postexilic period (see 6:3–15; 9:10–13; Ezra 2:36–39; Neh 10:1–8; 11:10–12; 12:1–7,12–21).

24:2 *Nadab and Abihu died.* The Chronicler alludes to the events recorded in Lev 10:1–3 (see note on 6:1–3).

24:3 *Zadok . . . Ahimelech.* Zadok and Abiathar had served as David's high priests. Here, late in David's life, Abiathar's son Ahimelech appears to have taken over some of his father's duties (see note on 6:8), but see note on 2 Sam 8:17.

24:4 *sixteen . . . eight.* A total of 24 divisions was selected by lot. This would allow for service either in monthly shifts, as was done by priests in Egyptian mortuary temples, or for two-week shifts once each year as found in NT times. The names of the first, sec-

and eight of the [1]descendants of Ithamar, according to their fathers' households.

5 [a]Thus they were divided by lot, the one as the other; for they were officers of the sanctuary and officers of God, both from the [1]descendants of Eleazar and the [1]descendants of Ithamar.

6 Shemaiah, the son of Nethanel the scribe, from the Levites, recorded them in the presence of the king, the princes, Zadok the priest, [a]Ahimelech the son of Abiathar, and the heads of the fathers' *households* of the priests and of the Levites; one father's household taken for Eleazar and one taken for Ithamar.

7 Now the first lot came out for Jehoiarib, the second for Jedaiah,

8 the third for Harim, the fourth for Seorim,

9 the fifth for Malchijah, the sixth for Mijamin,

10 the seventh for Hakkoz, the eighth for [a]Abijah,

11 the ninth for Jeshua, the tenth for Shecaniah,

12 the eleventh for Eliashib, the twelfth for Jakim,

13 the thirteenth for Huppah, the fourteenth for Jeshebeab,

14 the fifteenth for Bilgah, the sixteenth for Immer,

15 the seventeenth for Hezir, the eighteenth for Happizzez,

16 the nineteenth for Pethahiah, the twentieth for Jehezkel,

17 the twenty-first for Jachin, the twenty-second for Gamul,

18 the twenty-third for Delaiah, the twenty-fourth for Maaziah.

19 [a]These were their offices for their ministry when *they* came in to the house of the LORD according to the ordinance *given* to them through Aaron their father, just as the LORD God of Israel had commanded him.

20 Now for the rest of the sons of Levi: of the sons of Amram, [1]Shubael; of the sons of Shubael, Jehdeiah.

21 Of Rehabiah: of the sons of Rehabiah, Isshiah the first.

22 Of the Izharites, [1]Shelomoth; of the sons of Shelomoth, Jahath.

23 The sons [a]*of Hebron:* Jeriah *the first,* Amariah the second, Jahaziel the third, Jekameam the fourth.

24 *Of* the sons of Uzziel, Micah; of the sons of Micah, Shamir.

25 The brother of Micah, Isshiah; of the sons of Isshiah, Zechariah.

26 The sons of Merari, Mahli and Mushi; the sons of Jaaziah, Beno.

27 The sons of Merari: by Jaaziah *were* Beno, Shoham, Zaccur and Ibri.

28 By Mahli: Eleazar, who had no sons.

29 By Kish: the sons of Kish, Jerahmeel.

30 The sons of Mushi: Mahli, Eder and Jerimoth. These *were* the sons of the Levites according to their fathers' households.

31 [a]These also cast lots just as their [1]relatives the sons of Aaron in the presence of David the king, [b]Zadok, Ahimelech, and the heads of the fathers' *households* of the priests and of the Levites—the head of fathers' *households* as well as those of his younger brother.

Number and Services of Musicians

25 Moreover, David and the commanders of the army set apart for the service *some* of the sons of [a]Asaph and of Heman and of Jeduthun, who *were* to [b]prophesy with lyres, [c]harps and cymbals; and the number of [1]those who performed their service was:

2 Of the sons of Asaph: Zaccur, Joseph, Nethaniah and [1]Asharelah; the sons of Asaph *were* under the [2]direction of Asaph, who prophesied under the [2]direction of the king.

3 [a]Of Jeduthun, the sons of Jeduthun: Gedaliah, [1]Zeri, Jeshaiah, [2]Shimei, Hashabiah and Mattithiah, six, under the [3]direction of their father Jeduthun with the harp, who prophesied in giving thanks and praising the LORD.

4 Of Heman, the sons of Heman: Bukkiah, Mattaniah, [1]Uzziel, [2]Shebuel and Jerimoth, Hananiah, Hanani, Eliathah, Giddalti and Romamti-ezer, Joshbekashah, Mallothi, Hothir, Mahazioth.

5 All these *were* the sons of Heman [a]the king's seer to [1]exalt him according to the

4 [1]Lit *sons*
5 [1]Lit *sons* [a]1 Chr 24:31
6 [a]1 Chr 18:16
10 [a]Neh 12:4; Luke 1:5
19 [a]1 Chr 9:25
20 [1]In 23:16, *Shebuel*
22 [1]In 23:18, *Shelomith*
23 [a]1 Chr 23:19
31 [1]Lit *brothers* [a]1 Chr 24:5, 6 [b]1 Chr 24:6
25:1 [1]Lit *workmen according to their service* [a]1 Chr 6:33, 39 [b]2 Kin 3:15 [c]1 Chr 15:16
2 [1]In v 14, *Jesharelah* [2]Lit *hand(s)*
3 [1]In v 11, *Izri* [2]So with mss and ancient versions, cf v 17 [3]Lit *hands* [a]1 Chr 16:41, 42
4 [1]In v 18, *Azarel* [2]In v 20, *Shubael*
5 [1]Lit *lift up the horn* [a]2 Sam 24:11; 1 Chr 21:9

ond, fourth, ninth and 24th divisions have been found in a Dead Sea scroll from the fourth cave at Qumran (see essay, p. 1356).
24:7 *Jehoiarib.* Mattathias, father of the Maccabees, was a member of the Jehoiarib division (in the Apocrypha see 1 Maccabees 2:1).
24:10 *Abijah.* The father of John the Baptist was "of the division of Abijah" (Luke 1:5).
24:15 *Hezir.* The division from the family of Hezir was prominent in intertestamental times; the name appears on one of the large tombs in the Kidron Valley, east of Jerusalem.
24:20–31 This list supplements 23:7–23 by extending some of the lines mentioned there.
25:1 *commanders of the army.* David often sought the counsel of military leaders (11:10; 12:32; 28:1), even in cultic affairs (13:1; 15:25). *Asaph . . . Heman . . . Jeduthun.* See note on 6:31–48. *to prophesy.* There are several passages in Chronicles, largely in portions unique to these books, where cultic personnel are designated prophets (here; 2 Chr 20:14–17; 29:30; 35:15; cf. 2 Kin 23:2; 2 Chr 34:30). Zechariah the priest also appears to function as a prophet, though he is not so named (2 Chr 24:19–22). This may reflect postexilic interest in the prophet-priest-king figure of Messianic expectation: In Chronicles not only do priests prophesy, but kings also function as priests (see notes on 15:27; 16:1–3). David's organizing of the temple musicians may reflect his overall interest in music (1 Sam 16:23; 18:10; 19:9; 2 Sam 1:17–27; 6:5,14).

words of God, for God gave fourteen sons
and three daughters to Heman.
6 All these were under the [1]direction of
their father to sing in the house of the LORD,
[a]with cymbals, harps and lyres, for the service
of the house of God. [b]Asaph, Jeduthun and
Heman *were* under the [1]direction of the king.
7 Their number who were trained in
singing to the LORD, with their [1]relatives, all
who were skillful, *was* [a]288.

Divisions of Musicians

8 [a]They cast lots for their duties, all
alike, the small as well as the great, the
teacher *as well* as the pupil.
9 Now the first lot came out for Asaph to
Joseph, the second for Gedaliah, he with his
relatives and sons *were* twelve;
10 the third to Zaccur, his sons and his relatives, twelve;
11 the fourth to [1]Izri, his sons and his relatives, twelve;
12 the fifth to Nethaniah, his sons and his
relatives, twelve;
13 the sixth to Bukkiah, his sons and his
relatives, twelve;
14 the seventh to [1]Jesharelah, his sons
and his relatives, twelve;
15 the eighth to Jeshaiah, his sons and his
relatives, twelve;
16 the ninth to Mattaniah, his sons and
his relatives, twelve;
17 the tenth to Shimei, his sons and his
relatives, twelve;
18 the eleventh to Azarel, his sons and his
relatives, twelve;
19 the twelfth to Hashabiah, his sons and
his relatives, twelve;
20 for the thirteenth, Shubael, his sons
and his relatives, twelve;
21 for the fourteenth, Mattithiah, his sons
and his relatives, twelve;
22 for the fifteenth to Jeremoth, his sons
and his relatives, twelve;
23 for the sixteenth to Hananiah, his sons
and his relatives, twelve;
24 for the seventeenth to Joshbekashah,
his sons and his relatives, twelve;
25 for the eighteenth to Hanani, his sons
and his relatives, twelve;
26 for the nineteenth to Mallothi, his sons
and his relatives, twelve;
27 for the twentieth to Eliathah, his sons
and his relatives, twelve;
28 for the twenty-first to Hothir, his sons
and his relatives, twelve;
29 for the twenty-second to Giddalti, his
sons and his relatives, twelve;
30 for the twenty-third to Mahazioth, his
sons and his relatives, twelve;
31 for the twenty-fourth to Romamti-ezer,
his sons and his relatives, twelve.

Divisions of the Gatekeepers

26 For the divisions of the gatekeepers
there were of the Korahites, [1]Meshele-
miah the son of Kore, of the sons of [2]Asaph.
2 Meshelemiah had sons: Zechariah the
firstborn, Jediael the second, Zebadiah the
third, Jathniel the fourth,
3 Elam the fifth, Johanan the sixth,
Eliehoenai the seventh.
4 [a]Obed-edom had sons: Shemaiah the
firstborn, Jehozabad the second, Joah the
third, Sacar the fourth, Nethanel the fifth,
5 Ammiel the sixth, Issachar the seventh
and Peullethai the eighth; God had indeed
blessed him.
6 Also to his son Shemaiah sons were
born who ruled over the house of their
father, for they were mighty men of valor.
7 The sons of Shemaiah *were* Othni,
Rephael, Obed and Elzabad, whose brothers,
Elihu and Semachiah, were valiant men.
8 All these *were* of the sons of Obed-
edom; they and their sons and their [1]rela-
tives *were* able men with strength for the service, 62 from Obed-edom.
9 Meshelemiah had sons and relatives,
18 valiant men.
10 Also [a]Hosah, *one* of the sons of Merari
had sons: Shimri the first (although he was
not the firstborn, his father made him first),
11 Hilkiah the second, Tebaliah the third,
Zechariah the fourth; all the sons and relatives of Hosah *were* 13.
12 To these divisions of the gatekeepers,
the chief men, *were given* duties like their
relatives to minister in the house of the LORD.
13 [a]They cast lots, the small and the great
alike, according to their fathers' households,
for every gate.
14 The lot to the east fell to [1]Shelemiah.
Then they cast lots *for* his son Zechariah, a
counselor with insight, and his lot came out
to the north.
15 For Obed-edom *it fell* to the south, and
to his sons went the storehouse.

6 [1]Lit *hands* [a]1 Chr 15:16 [b]1 Chr 15:19
7 [1]Lit *brothers,* and so throughout the ch [a]1 Chr 23:5
8 [a]1 Chr 26:13
11 [1]In v 3, *Zeri*
14 [1]In v 2, *Asherelah*

26:1 [1]In v 14, *Shelemiah* [2]In 9:19, *Ebiasaph*
4 [a]2 Sam 6:11; 1 Chr 13:14
8 [1]Lit *brothers,* and so throughout the ch
10 [a]1 Chr 16:38
13 [a]1 Chr 24:5, 31; 25:8
14 [1]In 9:17, *Shallum*

25:5 *fourteen sons and three daughters.* Numerous progeny are a sign of divine blessing (see Job 1:2; 42:13). This is specifically stated for Heman as the result of the promises of God to exalt him. See 3:1–9; 14:2–7; 26:4–5; 2 Chr 11:18–21; 13:21; 21:2; 24:3.

26:1–19 The most extensive of the Chronicler's lists of gatekeepers (see 9:17–27; 16:37–38). A list of gatekeepers in the postexilic period is found in Ezra 2:42 (Neh 7:45).

26:1 *Asaph.* This name appears to be an abbreviation of Ebiasaph (6:23; 9:19); he should not be confused with the temple musician (25:1–2,6).

26:4–5 Numerous sons are again a sign of divine blessing (see note on 25:5).

26:4 *Obed-edom.* Had cared for the ark when it was left at his house (see note on 13:13).

26:12 *duties.* Elaborated in 9:22–29.

26:14 *to the east.* The east gate was the main entrance; it had six guard posts, as opposed to four at the other gates (v. 17).

26:15 *to the south.* The palaces of David and Solomon were south of the temple mount. The southern gate would be the main one used by the king, and this assignment probably

16 For Shuppim and Hosah *it was* to the west, by the gate of Shallecheth, on the ascending highway. Guard corresponded to guard.

17 On the east there were six Levites, on the north four daily, on the south four daily, and at the storehouse two by two.

18 At the [1][a]Parbar on the west *there were* four at the highway and two at the Parbar.

19 These were the divisions of the gatekeepers of the sons of Korah and of the sons of Merari.

Keepers of the Treasure

20 [1]The Levites, their relatives, [2]had [a]charge of the treasures of the house of God and of the treasures of the dedicated gifts.

21 The sons of Ladan, the sons of the Gershonites belonging to Ladan, *namely,* the Jehielites, *were* the heads of the fathers' *households,* belonging to Ladan the Gershonite.

22 The sons of Jehieli, Zetham and Joel his brother, [1]had charge of the treasures of the house of the LORD.

23 As for the Amramites, the Izharites, the Hebronites and the Uzzielites,

24 Shebuel the son of Gershom, the son of Moses, was officer over the treasures.

25 His relatives by Eliezer *were* Rehabiah his son, Jeshaiah his son, Joram his son, Zichri his son and Shelomoth his son.

26 This Shelomoth and his relatives [1]had charge of all the treasures of the dedicated gifts [a]which King David and the heads of the fathers' *households,* the commanders of thousands and hundreds, and the commanders of the army, had dedicated.

27 They dedicated [1]part of the spoil won in battles to repair the house of the LORD.

28 And all that Samuel the seer had dedicated and Saul the son of Kish, Abner the son of Ner and Joab the son of Zeruiah, everyone who had dedicated *anything, all of this* was [1]in the care of [2]Shelomoth and his relatives.

Outside Duties

29 As for the Izharites, Chenaniah and his sons [a]were *assigned* to outside duties for Israel, as [b]officers and judges.

30 As for the Hebronites, [a]Hashabiah and his relatives, 1,700 capable men, had charge of the affairs of Israel [1]west of the Jordan, for all the work of the LORD and the service of the king.

31 As for the Hebronites, [a]Jerijah the chief [1](these Hebronites were investigated according to their genealogies and fathers' *households,* in the fortieth year of David's reign, and men of outstanding capability were found among them at [b]Jazer of Gilead)

32 and his relatives, capable men, *were* 2,700 in number, heads of fathers' *households.* And King David made them overseers of the Reubenites, the Gadites and the half-tribe of the Manassites [a]concerning [1]all the affairs of God and of the king.

Commanders of the Army

27 Now *this is* the enumeration of the sons of Israel, the heads of fathers' *households,* the commanders of thousands and of hundreds, and their officers who served the king in all the affairs of the divisions which came in and went out month by month throughout all the months of the year, each division *numbering* 24,000:

2 Jashobeam the son of Zabdiel [1][a]had charge of the first division for the first month; and in his division *were* 24,000.

3 *He was* from the sons of Perez, *and was*

18 [1]Possibly *court* or *colonnade* [a]2 Kin 23:11
20 [1]So Gr; Heb *As for the Levites, Ahijah had* [2]Lit *were over* [a]1 Chr 26:22, 24, 26; 28:12; Ezra 2:69
22 [1]Lit *were over*
26 [1]Lit *were over* [a]2 Sam 8:11
27 [1]Heb *from the battles and from the spoil*
28 [1]Lit *under the hand* [2]Heb *Shelomith*
29 [a]Neh 11:16 [b]1 Chr 23:4
30 [1]Lit *beyond the Jordan westward* [a]1 Chr 27:17
31 [1]Heb *according to the Hebronites... father's households* [a]1 Chr 23:19 [b]1 Chr 6:81
32 [1]Lit *every matter of God and matter of the king* [a]2 Chr 19:11
27:2 [1]Lit *was over,* and so throughout the ch [a]2 Sam 23:8-30; 1 Chr 11:11-31

reflects a particular honor for Obed-edom (see notes on 26:4–5; see also Ezek 46:1–10).

26:16 *gate of Shallecheth.* The only reference to a gate by this name; presumably it was on the western side. The Chronicler writes to an audience familiar with these topographical details.

26:20 *treasures of the house of God.* The Levites in charge of these treasuries received the offerings of the people and cared for the valuable temple equipment (9:28–29). *treasures of the dedicated gifts.* The plunder from warfare (vv. 27–28). Texts from Mesopotamian temples confirm the presence of temple officers who served as assayers to handle and refine the precious metals received as revenue and offerings. The procedure with reference to the offerings of the people may be seen in the reign of Joash (2 Chr 24:4–14; 2 Kin 12:4–16). Numerous passages reflect on the wealth collected in the temple (see, e.g., 29:1–9; 2 Chr 4:1–22; 34:9–11; 36:7,10,18–19; 1 Kin 14:25–28; 15:15,18; 2 Kin 12:4–18; 14:14; 16:8; 25:13–17).

26:26 *gifts which King David. . . had dedicated.* See note on 18:1–20:8; see also 2 Chr 5:1.

26:27 *They dedicated part of the spoil won in battles.* Cf. Gen 14:17–20.

26:29–32 These verses designate the 6,000 officials and judges (23:4) who would work outside Jerusalem; they are drawn from two sub-clans of Kohath (6:18). Deut 17:8–13 envisages a judicial function for the priests and Levites (see 2 Chr 19:4–11).

26:30,32 *for all the work of the LORD and the service of the king . . concerning all the affairs of God and of the king.* In the theocracy (kingdom of God) there is no division between secular and sacred, no tension in serving God and the king (cf. Matt 22:15–22; Luke 16:10–13; Rom 13:1–7; 1 Tim 2:1–4; 1 Pet 2:13–17).

26:31 *fortieth year.* The last year of David's reign.

27:1–15 The names of the commanders of David's army are the same as those found in the list of his mighty men (see 11:11–47; see also 2 Sam 23:8–39 and notes). Those who had served David while he fled from Saul became commanders in the regular army.

27:1 *24,000.* See note on 12:23–37. Although a national militia consisting of 12 units of 24,000 each (a total of 288,000) is not unreasonable, the stress in this passage on unit commanders and divisions suggests that here too the Hebrew word for "1,000" should perhaps be taken as the designation of a military unit. To designate a division as "1,000" would be to give the upper limit of the number of men in such a unit, though such units would ordinarily not have a full complement of men. If this approach is followed, the figures in the following verses would be read as "24 units" instead of 24,000.

27:2 *Jashobeam.* See 11:11.

chief of all the commanders of the army for the first month.

4 Dodai the Ahohite and his division had charge of the division for the second month, Mikloth *being* the chief officer; and in his division *were* 24,000.

5 The third commander of the army for the third month *was* Benaiah, the son of Jehoiada the priest, *as* chief; and in his division *were* 24,000.

6 This Benaiah *was* the mighty man of the thirty, and had charge of thirty; and over his division was Ammizabad his son.

7 The fourth for the fourth month *was* Asahel the brother of Joab, and Zebadiah his son after him; and in his division *were* 24,000.

8 The fifth for the fifth month *was* the commander Shamhuth the Izrahite; and in his division *were* 24,000.

9 The sixth for the sixth month *was* Ira the son of Ikkesh the Tekoite; and in his division *were* 24,000.

10 The seventh for the seventh month *was* Helez the Pelonite of the sons of Ephraim; and in his division *were* 24,000.

11 The eighth for the eighth month *was* Sibbecai the Hushathite of the Zerahites; and in his division *were* 24,000.

12 The ninth for the ninth month *was* Abiezer the Anathothite of the Benjamites; and in his division *were* 24,000.

13 The tenth for the tenth month *was* Maharai the Netophathite of the Zerahites; and in his division *were* 24,000.

14 The eleventh for the eleventh month *was* Benaiah the Pirathonite of the sons of Ephraim; and in his division *were* 24,000.

15 The twelfth for the twelfth month *was* Heldai the Netophathite of Othniel; and in his division *were* 24,000.

Chief Officers of the Tribes

16 Now in charge of the tribes of Israel: chief officer for the Reubenites was Eliezer the son of Zichri; for the Simeonites, Shephatiah the son of Maacah;

17 for Levi, Hashabiah the son of Kemuel; for Aaron, Zadok;

18 for Judah, Elihu, *one* of David's brothers; for Issachar, Omri the son of Michael;

19 for Zebulun, Ishmaiah the son of Obadiah; for Naphtali, Jeremoth the son of Azriel;

20 for the sons of Ephraim, Hoshea the son of Azaziah; for the half-tribe of Manasseh, Joel the son of Pedaiah;

21 for the half-tribe of Manasseh in Gilead, Iddo the son of Zechariah; for Benjamin, Jaasiel the son of Abner;

22 for Dan, Azarel the son of Jeroham. [a]These *were* the princes of the tribes of Israel.

23 But David did not [1]count those twenty years of age and under, [a]because the LORD had said He would multiply Israel [b]as the stars of heaven.

24 Joab the son of Zeruiah had begun to count *them*, but did not finish; and because of [a]this, wrath came upon Israel, and the number was not included in the account of the chronicles of King David.

Various Overseers

25 Now Azmaveth the son of Adiel had charge of the king's storehouses. And Jonathan the son of Uzziah had charge of the storehouses in the country, in the cities, in the villages and in the towers.

26 Ezri the son of Chelub had charge of the [1]agricultural workers who tilled the soil.

27 Shimei the Ramathite had charge of the vineyards; and Zabdi the Shiphmite had charge of the [1]produce of the vineyards *stored* in the wine cellars.

28 Baal-hanan the Gederite had charge of the olive and [a]sycamore trees in the [1]Shephelah; and Joash had charge of the stores of oil.

29 Shitrai the Sharonite had charge of the cattle which were grazing in [a]Sharon; and Shaphat the son of Adlai had charge of the cattle in the valleys.

22 [a]1 Chr 28:1
23 [1]Lit *take their number from* [a]1 Chr 21:2-5 [b]Gen 15:5; 22:17; 26:4
24 [a]2 Sam 24:12-15; 1 Chr 21:1-7
26 [1]Lit *doers of the work of the field for the tilling of...*
27 [1]Lit *what was in the vineyards of the storehouses of wine*
28 [1]Or *lowlands* [a]1 Kin 10:27; 2 Chr 1:15
29 [a]1 Chr 5:16

27:4 *Dodai.* See 11:12.

27:5 *Benaiah.* See 11:22–25; 18:17.

27:7 *Asahel.* See 11:26; 2 Sam 2:18–23.

27:9–15 The remainder of the commanders were selected from among the thirty (see 11:25 and the names listed in 11:27–31).

27:16–22 The Chronicler's interest in "all Israel" appears in this list of officers who were over the 12 tribes (see Introduction: Purpose and Themes). The number is kept at 12 by omitting Gad and Asher (see note on 2:1–2).

27:17 *Zadok.* See note on 6:8; see also 12:28; 16:39.

27:18 *Elihu.* Not named elsewhere among the brothers of David. Perhaps he is the unnamed son from the list in 2:10–17 (see note there). Elihu could also be a variant of the name of Jesse's oldest son, Eliab, or the term "brother" could be taken in the sense of "relative," in which case Elihu would be a more distant kinsman.

27:21 *Abner.* A relative of King Saul (see 26:28; 1 Sam 14:50–51; 17:55–58; 26:5–16; 2 Sam 2:8–4:1).

27:23–24 *count . . . the number.* Refers to the census narrative in ch. 21 (2 Sam 24).

27:23 *twenty years of age and under.* The figures reported in ch. 21 and 2 Sam 24 were the numbers of those older than 20 years. *said He would multiply Israel as the stars.* The patriarchal promises of numerous descendants (Gen 12:2; 13:16; 15:5; 22:17) appear to have been the basis for the objections of Joab (v. 24) to the taking of a census (21:3; 2 Sam 24:3).

27:24 *did not finish.* Joab did not count those under age 20, nor did he include the tribes of Levi and Benjamin (21:6).

27:25–31 A list of the administrators of David's property (v. 31). The large cities of the ancient Near East had three basic economic sectors: (1) royal, (2) temple and (3) private. There is no evidence of direct taxation during the reign of David; his court appears to have been financed by extensive landholdings, commerce, plunder from his many wars, and tribute from subjugated kingdoms.

30 Obil the Ishmaelite had charge of the
camels; and Jehdeiah the Meronothite had
charge of the donkeys.
31 Jaziz the [a]Hagrite had charge of the
flocks. All these were [1]overseers of the property which belonged to King David.

Counselors

32 Also Jonathan, David's uncle, *was* a
counselor, a man of understanding, and a
scribe; and Jehiel the son of Hachmoni
[1]tutored the king's sons.
33 [a]Ahithophel *was* counselor to the king;
and [b]Hushai the Archite *was* the king's
friend.
34 Jehoiada the son of [a]Benaiah, and
[b]Abiathar [1]succeeded Ahithophel; and Joab
was the [c]commander of the king's army.

David's Address about the Temple

28 Now [a]David assembled at Jerusalem all
the officials of Israel, the princes of the
tribes, and the commanders of the divisions
that served the king, and the commanders of
thousands, and the commanders of hundreds, and the overseers of all the property
and livestock belonging to the king and his
sons, with the officials and [b]the mighty men,
even all the valiant men.
2 Then King David rose to his feet and
said, "Listen to me, my brethren and my people; I [a]*had* [1]intended to build a [2]permanent
home for the ark of the covenant of the LORD
and for [b]the footstool of our God. So I had
made preparations to build *it.*
3 "But God said to me, '[a]You shall not
build a house for My name because you are
a man of war and have shed blood.'
4 "Yet, the LORD, the God of Israel, [a]chose
me from all the house of my father to be king
over Israel [b]forever. For [c]He has chosen
Judah to be a leader; and [d]in the house of
Judah, my father's house, and among the
sons of my father He took pleasure in me to
make *me* king over all Israel.
5 "[a]Of all my sons (for the LORD has given
me many sons), [b]He has chosen my son
Solomon to sit on the throne of the kingdom
of the LORD over Israel.
6 "He said to me, 'Your son [a]Solomon is
the one who shall build My house and My
courts; for I have chosen him to be a son to
Me, and I will be a father to him.
7 'I will establish his kingdom forever [a]if
he resolutely performs My commandments
and My ordinances, as [1]is done now.'
8 "So now, in the sight of all Israel, the
assembly of the LORD, and in the hearing of
our God, observe and seek after all the commandments of the LORD your God so that you
may possess the good land and bequeath *it*
to your sons after you forever.
9 "As for you, my son Solomon, know the
God of your father, and [a]serve Him with [1]a
whole heart and a willing [2]mind; [b]for the
LORD searches all hearts, and understands
every intent of the thoughts. [c]If you seek
Him, He will let you find Him; but if you forsake Him, He will reject you forever.
10 "Consider now, for the LORD has chosen
you to build a house for the sanctuary; [a]be
courageous and act."
11 Then David gave to his son Solomon
[a]the plan of [b]the porch *of the temple,* its
buildings, its storehouses, its upper rooms,
its inner rooms and [c]the room for the mercy
seat;
12 and the plan of all that he had in
[1]mind, for the courts of the house of the
LORD, and for all the surrounding rooms, for
[a]the storehouses of the house of God and for
the storehouses of the dedicated things;
13 also for [a]the divisions of the priests and
[b]the Levites and for all the work of the service of the house of the LORD and for all the
utensils of service in the house of the LORD;
14 for the golden *utensils,* the weight of
gold for all utensils for every kind of service;
for the silver utensils, the weight *of silver* for
all utensils for every kind of service;

31 [1]Or *rulers* [a]1 Chr 5:10
32 [1]Lit *was with*
33 [a]2 Sam 15:12 [b]2 Sam 15:32, 37
34 [1]Lit *after* [a]1 Chr 27:5 [b]1 Kin 1:7 [c]1 Chr 11:6
28:1 [a]1 Chr 23:2; 27:1-31 [b]1 Chr 11:10-47
2 [1]Lit *in my heart* [2]Lit *house of rest* [a]1 Chr 17:1, 2 [b]Ps 132:7; Is 66:1
3 [a]1 Chr 22:8
4 [a]1 Sam 16:6-13 [b]1 Chr 17:23, 27 [c]Gen 49:8-10; 1 Chr 5:2 [d]1 Sam 16:1
5 [a]1 Chr 3:1-9; 14:3-7 [b]1 Chr 22:9, 10
6 [a]2 Sam 7:13, 14
7 [1]Lit *at this day* [a]1 Chr 22:13
9 [1]Or *the same* [2]Lit *soul* [a]1 Kin 8:61; 1 Chr 29:17-19 [b]1 Sam 16:7 [c]2 Chr 15:2; Jer 29:13
10 [a]1 Chr 22:13
11 [a]Ex 25:40; 1 Chr 28:12, 19 [b]1 Kin 6:3 [c]Ex 25:17-22
12 [1]Lit *the spirit with him* [a]1 Chr 26:20, 28
13 [a]1 Chr 24:1 [b]1 Chr 23:6

27:32–34 A list of David's cabinet members, supplementary to that in 18:14–17.
27:33 *Ahithophel.* Was replaced after he committed suicide, following his support of Absalom's rebellion (2 Sam 15:12, 31–37; 16:20–17:23).
27:34 *Benaiah.* See v. 5.
28:1–29:30 The account of the transition from the reign of David to that of Solomon is one of the clearest demonstrations of the Chronicler's idealization of their reigns when it is compared with the succession account in 1 Kin 1–2. The Chronicler makes no mention of the infirmities of the aged David (1 Kin 1:1–4), the rebellion of Adonijah and the king's sons (1 Kin 1:5–10), the court intrigue to secure Solomon's succession (1 Kin 1:11–31) or David's charge to Solomon to punish his enemies after his death (1 Kin 2:1–9). His selection of material presents a transition of power that is smooth and peaceful and receives the support of "all Israel" (29:25), the officials and the people (28:1–2; 29:6–9,21–25). Instead of the bedridden David who sends others to anoint Solomon (1 Kin 1:32–35), David himself is present and in charge of the ceremonies (see 23:1 and note).
28:1 The assembly is composed largely of the groups named in ch. 27. This public announcement (v. 5) follows the private announcement of Solomon's succession in ch. 22 (see note on 22:2–19).
28:3 *you are a man of war and have shed blood.* See note on 22:8–9.
28:5 *chosen my son Solomon.* See vv. 6,10; 29:1. These are the only uses in the OT of the Hebrew verb for "chosen" with reference to any king after David (see Introduction: Purpose and Themes). The Chronicler's application of this term to Solomon is consistent with his depiction of that king. *kingdom of the LORD.* See note on 17:14.
28:6 *a son to Me.* See 17:12–14 and note; see also 22:10.
28:8–9 See Introduction: Portrait of David and Solomon.
28:12 David provides Solomon with the plans for the temple. This reflects the Chronicler's modeling David after Moses: Just as Moses received the plans for the tabernacle from God (Ex 25–30), so also David received the plans for the temple.

15 and the weight *of gold* for the [a]golden lampstands and their golden lamps, with the weight of each lampstand and its lamps; and *the weight of silver* for the silver lampstands, with the weight of each lampstand and its lamps according to the use of each lampstand;

16 and the gold by weight for the tables of showbread, for each table; and silver for the silver tables;

17 and the forks, the basins, and the pitchers of pure gold; and for the golden bowls with the weight for each bowl; and for the silver bowls with the weight for each bowl;

18 and for [a]the altar of incense refined gold by weight; and gold for the model of the chariot, *even* [b]the cherubim that spread out *their wings* and covered the ark of the covenant of the LORD.

19 "All *this*," *said David*, "the LORD made me understand in writing by His hand upon me, [a]all the [1]details of this pattern."

20 Then David said to his son Solomon, "[a]Be strong and courageous, and act; do not fear nor be dismayed, for the LORD God, my God, is with you. [b]He will not fail you nor forsake you until all the work for the service of the house of the LORD is finished.

21 "Now behold, [a]*there are* the divisions of the priests and the Levites for all the service of the house of God, and [b]every willing man of any skill will be with you in all the work for all kinds of service. The officials also and all the people will be entirely at your command."

Offerings for the Temple

29 Then King David said to the entire assembly, "My son Solomon, whom alone God has chosen, [a]is still young and inexperienced and the work is great; for [b]the [1]temple is not for man, but for the LORD God.

2 "Now [a]with all my ability I have provided for the house of my God the gold for the *things of* gold, and the silver for the *things of* silver, and the bronze for the *things of* bronze, the iron for the *things of* iron, and wood for the *things of* wood, onyx stones and inlaid *stones*, stones of antimony and stones of various colors, and all kinds of precious stones and alabaster in abundance.

3 "Moreover, in my delight in the house of my God, the treasure I have of gold and silver, I give to the house of my God, over and above all that I have already provided for the holy [1]temple,

4 *namely*, [a]3,000 talents of gold, of [b]the gold of Ophir, and 7,000 talents of refined silver, to overlay the walls of the [1]buildings;

5 of gold for the *things of* gold and of silver for the *things of* silver, that is, for all the work [1]done by the craftsmen. Who then is willing [2]to consecrate himself this day to the LORD?"

6 Then [a]the rulers of the fathers' *households*, and the princes of the tribes of Israel, and the commanders of thousands and of hundreds, with [b]the overseers over the king's work, offered willingly;

7 and for the service for the house of God they gave 5,000 talents and 10,000 [a]darics of gold, and 10,000 talents of silver, and 18,000 talents of brass, and 100,000 talents of iron.

8 [1]Whoever possessed *precious* stones gave them to the treasury of the house of the LORD, [2]in care of [a]Jehiel the Gershonite.

9 Then the people rejoiced because they had offered so willingly, for they made their offering to the LORD [a]with a whole heart, and King David also rejoiced greatly.

David's Prayer

10 So David blessed the LORD in the sight of all the assembly; and David said, "Blessed are You, O LORD God of Israel our father, forever and ever.

11 "[a]Yours, O LORD, is the greatness and the power and the glory and the victory and the majesty, indeed everything that is in the heavens and the earth; Yours is the dominion, O LORD, and You exalt Yourself as head over all.

12 "[a]Both riches and honor *come* from You, and You rule over all, and [b]in Your hand is power and might; and it lies in Your hand to make great and to strengthen everyone.

13 "Now therefore, our God, we thank You, and praise Your glorious name.

14 "But who am I and who are my people that we should [1]be able to offer as generously as this? For all things come from You, and from Your hand we have given You.

15 "For [a]we are sojourners before You, and tenants, as all our fathers were; [b]our days on the earth are like a shadow, and there is no hope.

16 "O LORD our God, all this abundance that we have provided to build You a house for Your holy name, it is from Your hand, and all is Yours.

17 "Since I know, O my God, that [a]You try

15 [a]Ex 25:31-39 **18** [a]Ex 30:1-10 [b]Ex 25:18-22 **19** [1]Lit *works* [a]1 Chr 28:11, 12 **20** [a]1 Chr 22:13 [b]Josh 1:5; Heb 13:5 **21** [a]1 Chr 28:13 [b]Ex 35:25-35; 36:1, 2 **29:1** [1]Lit *palace* [a]1 Chr 22:5 [b]1 Chr 29:19 **2** [a]1 Chr 22:3-5 **3** [1]Lit *house*

4 [1]Lit *houses* [a]1 Chr 22:14 [b]1 Kin 9:28 **5** [1]Lit *by the hand of the craftsmen* [2]Lit *to fill his hand* **6** [a]1 Chr 27:1; 28:1 [b]1 Chr 27:25-31 **7** [a]Ezra 2:69; Neh 7:70 **8** [1]Lit *those with whom were found* [2]Lit *under the hand of* [a]1 Chr 23:8 **9** [a]1 Kin 8:61; 2 Cor 9:7 **11** [a]Matt 6:13; Rev 5:13 **12** [a]2 Chr 1:12 [b]2 Chr 20:6 **14** [1]Lit *retain strength* **15** [a]Lev 25:23 [b]Job 14:2, 10-12 **17** [a]1 Chr 28:9

28:19 *in writing by His hand upon me.* The Chronicler may intend no more than the ordinary process of inspiration whereby David wrote under divine influence. On the other hand, he may imply a parallel with Moses, who also received documents from the hand of the Lord (Ex 25:40; 27:8; 31:18; 32:16).
28:20 See Introduction: Portrait of David and Solomon.
29:1 *chosen.* See note on 28:5. *young.* See note on 22:5.
29:2–9 After donating his personal fortune to the construction of the temple, David appeals to the people for their voluntary gifts. The Chronicler again appears to be modeling his account of David on events from the life of Moses (Ex 25:1–8; 35:4–9,20–29). The willing response of the people aided the building of both tabernacle and temple.
29:7 *darics.* The daric was a Persian coin, apparently named for Darius I (522–486 B.C.) in whose reign it first appears (see Ezra 8:27). Since the Chronicler's readers were familiar with it, he could use it as an up-to-date standard of value for an earlier treasure of gold.

the heart and [b]delight in uprightness, I, in
the integrity of my heart, have willingly
offered all these *things;* so now with joy I
have seen Your people, who are present here,
make *their* offerings willingly to You.
18 "O LORD, the God of Abraham, Isaac and
Israel, our fathers, preserve this forever in
the [1]intentions of the heart of Your people,
and direct their heart to You;
19 and [a]give to my son Solomon a perfect
heart to keep Your commandments, Your testimonies and Your statutes, and to do *them*
all, and [b]to build the [1]temple, for which I
have made provision."
20 Then David said to all the assembly,
"Now bless the LORD your God." And [a]all the
assembly blessed the LORD, the God of their
fathers, and [b]bowed low and did homage to
the LORD and to the king.

Sacrifices

21 On the next day [a]they [1]made sacrifices
to the LORD and offered burnt offerings to the
LORD, 1,000 bulls, 1,000 rams *and* 1,000
lambs, with their drink offerings and sacrifices in abundance for all Israel.
22 So they ate and drank that day before
the LORD with great gladness.

Solomon Again Made King

And they made Solomon the son of David
king [a]a second time, and they [b]anointed *him*
as ruler for the LORD and Zadok as priest.
23 Then [a]Solomon sat on the throne of the
LORD as king instead of David his father; and
he prospered, and all Israel obeyed him.
24 All the officials, the mighty men, and
also all the sons of King David [1]pledged allegiance to King Solomon.
25 [a]The LORD highly exalted Solomon in
the sight of all Israel, and [b]bestowed on him
royal majesty which had not been on any
king before him in Israel.
26 Now [a]David the son of Jesse reigned
over all Israel.
27 [a]The period which he reigned over
Israel *was* forty years; he reigned in Hebron
seven years and [1]in Jerusalem thirty-three
years.

Death of David

28 Then he died in [a]a [1]ripe old age, [b]full
of days, riches and honor; and his son
Solomon reigned in his place.
29 "Now the acts of King David, from first
to last, are written in the chronicles of [a]Sam-
uel the seer, in the chronicles of [b]Nathan the
prophet and in the chronicles of [c]Gad the
seer,
30 with all his reign, his power, and the
circumstances which came on him, on Israel,
and on all the kingdoms of the lands.

17 [b]Ps 15:2
18 [1]Lit *intent of the thoughts of the heart*
19 [1]Lit *palace* [a]1 Chr 28:9; Ps 72:1 [b]1 Chr 29:1, 2
20 [a]Josh 22:33 [b]Ex 4:31
21 [1]Lit *sacrificed* [a]1 Kin 8:62, 63
22 [a]1 Chr 23:1 [b]1 Kin 1:33-39
23 [a]1 Kin 2:12
24 [1]Lit *put a hand under Solomon*
25 [a]2 Chr 1:1 [b]1 Kin 3:13; 2 Chr 1:12
26 [a]1 Chr 18:14
27 [1]Lit *he reigned in* [a]2 Sam 5:4, 5; 1 Kin 2:11; 1 Chr 3:4
28 [1]Lit *good* [a]Gen 15:15; Acts 13:36 [b]1 Chr 23:1
29 [a]1 Sam 9:9 [b]2 Sam 7:2-4; 12:1-7 [c]1 Sam 22:5

29:22 *ate and drank.* See 12:38–40 and note. The anointing of both Solomon and Zadok portrays the harmony between them (see Zech 4:14; 6:13 and notes). *second time.* Perhaps the first time was Solomon's anointing recorded in 1 Kin 1:32–36, but omitted by the Chronicler (see note on 28:1–29:30). However, the phrase "second time" is missing in the Septuagint, suggesting that it may have been an addition to the Hebrew text of this passage by an ancient scribe after the Septuagint had already been translated, in order to harmonize the Chronicles account with Kings. Multiple anointings are found in the cases of both Saul (1 Sam 10:1,24; 11:14–15) and David (1 Sam 16:13; 2 Sam 2:4; 5:3).
29:24 *All . . . pledged allegiance.* But compare the rebellion of Adonijah, in which the officers and sons of the king had assisted the attempted coup (1 Kin 1:9,19,25). Again the Chronicler has bypassed a negative event that would tarnish his image of David and Solomon.
29:25 *all Israel.* See 11:1,10; 12:38–40; see also Introduction: Purpose and Themes.
29:27 See note on 3:1–9.
29:28 *full of days, riches and honor.* As a feature of the Chronicler's theme of immediate retribution (see Introduction: Purpose and Themes), the righteous enjoy these blessings (cf. Ps 128; Prov 3:2,4,9–10,16,22,33–35).
29:29 See Introduction: Author, Date and Sources.
29:30 *all the kingdoms of the lands.* Those immediately surrounding David's kingdom.

2 Chronicles

INTRODUCTION

See Introduction to 1 Chronicles.

The Building of the Temple in Chronicles

The Chronicler has used the Pentateuchal history as a model for his account of the reigns of David and Solomon. Similarly, the Pentateuchal record of the building of the tabernacle affects his account of the building of the temple:

1. The building of the tabernacle was entrusted to Bezalel and Oholiab (Ex 35:30 — 36:7), and they provide the Chronicler's model for the relationship of Solomon and Huram-abi (2 Chr 2:13). It is significant that the only references to Bezalel outside the book of Exodus are in Chronicles (1 Chr 2:20; 2 Chr 1:5).

Solomon is the new Bezalel: (1) Both Solomon and Bezalel are designated by name for their tasks by God; they are the only workers on their projects to be chosen by name (Ex 31:2; 35:30 — 36:2; 38:22 – 23; 1 Chr 28:6). (2) Both are from the tribe of Judah (Ex 31:2; 35:30; 1 Chr 2:20; 3:10). (3) Both receive the Spirit to endow them with wisdom (Ex 31:3; 35:30 – 31; 2 Chr 1:1 – 13), and Solomon's vision at Gibeon (2 Chr 1:3 – 13) dominates the preface to the account of the temple construction (2 Chr 2 — 7). (4) Both build a bronze altar for the sanctuary (2 Chr 1:5; 4:1; 7:7) — significantly, the bronze altar is not mentioned in the summary list of Huram-abi's work (4:12 – 16). (5) Both make the sanctuary furnishings (Ex 31:1 – 10; 37:10 – 29; 2 Chr 4:19 – 22).

Similarly, Huram-abi becomes the new Oholiab: (1) In the account of the temple building in Kings, Huram-abi is not mentioned until after the story of the main construction of temple and palace has been told (1 Kin 7:13 – 45); in Chronicles he is introduced as being involved in the building work from the beginning, just as Oholiab worked on the tabernacle from the beginning (Ex 31:6; 2 Chr 2:13). (2) Kings speaks only of Huram-abi's skill in casting bronze (1 Kin 7:14); in Chronicles, however, his list of skills is the same as Oholiab's (Ex 31:1 – 6; 35:30 – 36:2; 38:22 – 23; 2 Chr 2:14). (3) Kings reports that the mother of Huram-abi was a widow from the tribe of Naphtali (1 Kin 7:14); Chronicles, however, states that she was a widow from the tribe of Dan (2 Chr 2:14), thus giving Huram-abi the same ancestry as Oholiab (Ex 31:6; 35:34; 38:23). See note on 2 Chr 2:13.

2. The plans for both tabernacle and temple are given by God (Ex 25:1 — 30:37; see Ex 25:9,40; 27:8; see also 1 Chr 28:11 – 19 — not mentioned in Samuel and Kings).

3. The spoils of war are used as building materials for both tabernacle and temple (Ex 3:21 – 22; 12:35 – 36; see 1 Chr 18:6 – 11 — not mentioned in Samuel and Kings).

4. The people contribute willingly and generously for both structures (Ex 25:1 – 7; 36:3 – 7; see 1 Chr 29:1 – 9 — not mentioned in Samuel and Kings).

5. The glory cloud appears at the dedication of both structures (Ex 40:34 – 35; 2 Chr 7:1 – 3).

Solomon Worships at Gibeon

1 Now [a]Solomon the son of David established himself securely over his kingdom, and the LORD his God *was* with him and [b]exalted him greatly.

2 Solomon spoke to all Israel, [a]to the commanders of thousands and of hundreds and to the judges and to every leader in all Israel, the heads of the fathers' *households.*

3 Then Solomon and all the assembly with him went to [a]the high place which was at Gibeon, [b]for God's tent of meeting was there, which Moses the servant of the LORD had made in the wilderness.

4 However, David had brought up [a]the ark of God from Kiriath-jearim [1]to [b]the place he had prepared for it, for he had pitched a tent for it in Jerusalem.

5 Now [a]the bronze altar, which Bezalel the son of Uri, the son of Hur, had made, [1]was there before the tabernacle of the LORD, and Solomon and the assembly sought it out.

6 Solomon went up there before the LORD to the bronze altar which *was* at the tent of meeting, and [a]offered a thousand burnt offerings on it.

7 [a]In that night God appeared to Solomon and said to him, "Ask what I shall give you."

Solomon's Prayer for Wisdom

8 Solomon said to God, "You have dealt with my father David with great lovingkindness, and [a]have made me king in his place.

9 "Now, O LORD God, [a]Your [1]promise to my father David is fulfilled, for You have made me king over [b]a people as numerous as the dust of the earth.

10 "[a]Give me now wisdom and knowledge, [b]that I may go out and come in before this people, for who can rule this great people of Yours?"

11 [a]God said to Solomon, "Because [1]you had this in mind, and did not ask for riches, wealth or honor, or the life of those who hate you, nor have you even asked for long life, but you have asked for yourself wisdom and knowledge that you may rule My people over whom I have made you king,

12 wisdom and knowledge have been granted to you. And [a]I will give you riches and wealth and honor, [1]such as none of the kings who were before you has possessed nor those who will [2]come after you."

13 [a]So Solomon went [1]from the high place which was at Gibeon, from the tent of meeting, to Jerusalem, and he reigned over Israel.

Solomon's Wealth

14 [a]Solomon amassed chariots and horsemen. [b]He had 1,400 chariots and 12,000 horsemen, and he stationed them in [c]the chariot cities and with the king at Jerusalem.

15 [a]The king made [b]silver and gold as plentiful in Jerusalem as stones, and he made cedars as plentiful as sycamores in the [1]lowland.

16 Solomon's [a]horses were imported from Egypt and from Kue; the king's traders procured them from Kue for a price.

17 They [1]imported chariots from Egypt for 600 *shekels* of silver apiece and horses for 150 apiece, and [2]by the same means they [3]exported them to all the kings of the Hittites and the kings of Aram.

Solomon Will Build a Temple and Palace

2 [1a]Now Solomon [2]decided to build a house for the name of the LORD and a [3]royal palace for himself.

2 [1]So [a]Solomon [2]assigned 70,000 men to carry loads and 80,000 men to quarry *stone* in the mountains and 3,600 to supervise them.

3 [a]Then Solomon sent *word* to [1]Huram

1:1 [a]1 Kin 2:12, 46 [b]1 Chr 29:25 **2** [a]1 Chr 28:1 **3** [a]1 Kin 3:4 [b]Ex 36:8 **4** [1]Lit *where David had prepared for it* [a]1 Chr 15:25-28 [b]2 Chr 6:2 **5** [1]Lit *he put* [a]Ex 31:9; 38:1-7 **6** [a]1 Kin 3:4 **7** [a]1 Kin 3:5-14 **8** [a]1 Chr 28:5 **9** [1]Lit *word* [a]2 Sam 7:12-16 [b]Gen 13:16; 22:17; 28:14 **10** [a]1 Kin 3:9 [b]Num 27:17; 2 Sam 5:2

11 [1]Lit *this was in your heart* [a]1 Kin 3:11 **12** [1]Lit *which was not so to the kings who were before you* [2]Lit *be* [a]1 Chr 29:25; 2 Chr 9:22 **13** [1]Lit *to* [a]2 Chr 1:3 **14** [a]1 Kin 10:26-29 [b]1 Kin 4:26 [c]1 Kin 9:19 **15** [1]Heb *shephelah* [a]1 Kin 10:27 [b]Deut 17:17 **16** [a]Deut 17:16 **17** [1]Lit *brought up and brought out* [2]Lit *and in like manner by their hand* [3]Lit *brought out* **2:1** [1]Ch 1:18 in Heb [2]Lit *said* [3]Lit *house for his royalty* [a]1 Kin 5:5 **2** [1]Ch 2:1 in Heb [2]Lit *numbered* [a]1 Kin 5:15, 16; 2 Chr 2:18 **3** [1]In 1 Kin 5:18, *Hiram* [a]1 Kin 5:2-11

1:1–9:31 The account of the reign of Solomon is primarily devoted to his building of the temple (chs. 2–7); his endowment with wisdom is mainly to facilitate the building work. Much of the material in Kings that does not bear on building the temple is omitted by the Chronicler; e.g., he does not mention the judgment between the prostitutes (1 Kin 3:16–28) or the building of the royal palace (1 Kin 7:1–12).

1:1 *established himself.* This expression, or a variation of it, is common in Chronicles (12:13; 13:7–8,21; 15:8; 16:9; 17:1; 21:4; 23:1; 25:11; 27:6; 32:5; 1 Chr 11:10; 19:13). Here and in 21:4 it includes the elimination of enemies and rivals to the throne (see 1 Kin 2, especially v. 46).

1:2–13 See 1 Kin 3:4–15 and notes. Verses 2–6 are largely unique to Chronicles and show some of the writer's concerns: 1. The support of "all Israel" (v. 2) is emphasized (see Introduction to 1 Chronicles: Purpose and Themes). 2. While the writer of Kings is somewhat apologetic about Solomon's visit to a high place (1 Kin 3:3), the Chronicler adds the note that this was the location of the tabernacle made by Moses in the wilderness (v. 3), bringing Solomon's action into line with the provisions of the law (Lev 17:8–9).

1:5 *Bezalel.* See Introduction: The Building of the Temple in Chronicles. It is specifically in connection with his offering on the altar built by Bezalel (Ex 31:1–11; 38:1–2) that Solomon receives the wisdom from God to reign. In the account that follows, Solomon devotes his gift of wisdom primarily to building the temple, just as Bezalel had been gifted by God to serve as the master craftsman of the tabernacle.

1:7 *God . . . said to him.* Both David and Solomon function as prophets (7:1; 29:25; 1 Chr 22:8; 28:6,19).

1:9 *numerous as the dust.* In provisional fulfillment of the promise to Abraham (Gen 13:16; 22:17; see note on 1 Chr 27:23; cf. Gen 28:14).

1:14–17 The Chronicler does not include the material in 1 Kin 3:16–4:34. He moves rather to the account of Solomon's wealth in 1 Kin 10:26–29; part of this material is repeated in 2 Chr 9:25–28. Recounting Solomon's wealth at this point shows the fulfillment of God's promise (v. 12).

1:16 *Egypt.* See note on 1 Kin 10:29.

2:1 *palace.* Although the Chronicler frequently mentions the palace Solomon built (7:11; 8:1; 9:11), he gives no details of its construction (see 1 Kin 7:1–12).

2:2 See vv. 17–18.

2:3–10 The Chronicler's theological interests appear in his handling of Solomon's correspondence with Huram (a variant of

the king of Tyre, saying, "[b]As you dealt with
David my father and sent him cedars to build
him a house to dwell in, so do for me.
4 "Behold, I am about to build a house for
the name of the LORD my God, dedicating it
to Him, [a]to burn fragrant incense before Him
and *to set out* [b]the showbread continually,
and to offer [c]burnt offerings morning and
evening, [d]on sabbaths and on new moons
and on the appointed feasts of the LORD our
God, this *being required* forever in Israel.
5 "The house which I am about to build
will be great, for [a]greater is our God than all
the gods.
6 "But [a]who is able to build a house for
Him, for the heavens and the highest heavens cannot contain Him? So who am I, that I
should build a house for Him, except to
[1]burn *incense* before Him?
7 "Now [a]send me a skilled man to work in
gold, silver, brass and iron, and in purple,
crimson and violet *fabrics,* and who knows
how to make engravings, to *work* with the
skilled men [1b]whom I have in Judah and
Jerusalem, whom David my father provided.
8 "[a]Send me also cedar, cypress and
algum timber from Lebanon, for I know that
your servants know how to cut timber of
Lebanon; and indeed [b]my servants *will work*
with your servants,
9 to prepare timber in abundance for me,
for the house which I am about to build *will
be* great and wonderful.
10 "Now behold, [a]I will give to your servants, the woodsmen who cut the timber,
20,000 [1]kors of crushed wheat and 20,000
[1]kors of barley, and 20,000 baths of wine and
20,000 baths of oil."

Huram to Assist

11 Then Huram, king of Tyre, [1]answered
in a letter sent to Solomon: "[a]Because the
LORD loves His people, He has made you king
over them."
12 Then Huram [1]continued, "Blessed be
[a]the LORD, the God of Israel, who has made
heaven and earth, who has given King David
a wise son, [2]endowed with discretion and
understanding, [b]who will build a house for
the LORD and a [3]royal palace for himself.
13 "Now I am sending Huram-abi, a skilled
man, [1]endowed with understanding,
14 [a]the son of a [1]Danite woman and [2]a
Tyrian father, who knows how to work in
gold, silver, bronze, iron, stone and wood,
and in purple, violet, linen and crimson fabrics, and *who knows how* to make all kinds
of engravings and to [3]execute any design
which may be assigned to him, *to work* with
your skilled men and with [4]those of my lord
David your father.
15 "Now then, let my lord send to his servants wheat and barley, oil and wine, of
[a]which he has spoken.
16 "[a]We will cut whatever timber you need
from Lebanon and bring it to you on rafts by
sea to Joppa, so that you may carry it up to
Jerusalem."
17 Solomon numbered all the aliens who
were in the land of Israel, [a]following the
[1]census which his father David had [2]taken;
and 153,600 were found.
18 [a]He appointed 70,000 of them to carry
loads and 80,000 to quarry *stones* in the
mountains and 3,600 supervisors to make
the people work.

The Temple Construction in Jerusalem

3 [a]Then Solomon began to build the house
of the LORD in Jerusalem on Mount Moriah, where *the LORD* had appeared to his
father David, at the place that David had pre-

3 [b]1 Chr 14:1 **4** [a]Ex 30:7 [b]Ex 25:30 [c]Ex 29:38-42 [d]Num 28:9, 10 **5** [a]Ex 15:11; 1 Chr 16:25 **6** [1]Lit *offer up in smoke* [a]1 Kin 8:27; 2 Chr 6:18 **7** [1]Lit *who are with me* [a]Ex 31:3-5; 2 Chr 2:13, 14 [b]1 Chr 22:15 **8** [a]1 Kin 5:6 [b]2 Chr 9:10, 11 **10** [1]I.e. One kor equals approx 10 bu [a]1 Kin 5:11 **11** [1]Lit *said...and he sent*

11 [a]1 Kin 10:9; 2 Chr 9:8 **12** [1]Lit *said* [2]Lit *knowing discretion* [3]Lit *house for his royalty* [a]Ps 33:6; 102:25 [b]2 Chr 2:1 **13** [1]Lit *knowing understanding* **14** [1]Lit *a woman of the daughters of Dan* [2]Lit *whose father is a Tyrian man* [3]Lit *devise any device* [4]Lit *skilled men* [a]1 Kin 7:14 **15** [a]2 Chr 2:10 **16** [a]1 Kin 5:8, 9 **17** [1]Lit *numbering* [2]Lit *numbered of them* [a]1 Chr 22:2 **18** [a]2 Chr 2:2 **3:1** [a]1 Kin 6:1

Hiram) of Tyre. In the Kings account the correspondence was initiated by Huram (1 Kin 5:1). The Chronicler omits this (and also the material in 1 Kin 5:3–5) but adds his own material, reflecting his concerns with the temple worship in vv. 3–7.

2:4 See 1 Chr 23:28–31.

2:7 See Introduction: The Building of the Temple in Chronicles. In the Kings account Solomon's request for a master craftsman is found late in the narrative (1 Kin 7:13); to carry out his parallel between Oholiab and Huram-abi, the Chronicler includes it in the initial correspondence. Furthermore, here and in vv. 13–14 the list of Huram-abi's skills is expanded and matches that of Bezalel and Oholiab (Kings is concerned only with casting bronze).

2:10 The payment here differs from that reported in 1 Kin 5:11, but the texts speak of two different payments: In Kings the payment is an annual sum delivered to the royal household of Hiram, while Chronicles speaks of one payment to the woodsmen. The goods paid are also not identical; the oil specified in Kings is of a finer quality.

2:11–16 See 1 Kin 5:7–9; 7:13–14 and notes.

2:13 *Huram-abi.* See note on v. 7. Kings reports that the ancestry of Huram-abi was through a widow of Naphtali (1 Kin 7:14); Chronicles strengthens the parallel between Huram-abi and Oholiab by assigning him Danite ancestry. These statements are not necessarily contradictory: (1) The mother's ancestry may have been Danite, though she lived in the territory of Naphtali; or (2) her parents may have been from Dan and Naphtali, allowing her descent to be reckoned to either. The Danites had been previously associated with the Phoenicians (Judg 18:7).

2:17–18 See 1 Kin 5:13–18 and notes. The Chronicler specifies that this levy of forced laborers was from aliens resident in the land, not from Israelites. This is not stated in the parallel passage in Kings, though 1 Kin 9:20–22 confirms that alien labor was used (see 8:8).

2:18 *3,600 supervisors.* See v. 2. The number given in 1 Kin 5:16 is 3,300; however, some manuscripts of the Septuagint (the Greek translation of the OT) also have 3,600. The Chronicler may have been following a different text of Kings from the present Masoretic (traditional Hebrew) text at this point (but see note on 1 Kin 5:16).

3:1–17 The Chronicler has considerably curtailed the description of the temple's construction found in Kings, omitting completely 1 Kin 6:4–20. This abridgment probably indicates that the Chronicler's audience was familiar with the details of the earlier history and that the temple of the restoration period was less elaborate than the original Solomonic structure (Hag 2:3). On the other hand, the Chronicler goes into more detail on the furnishings and implements (3:6–9; 4:1,6–9).

3:1 *Mount Moriah.* The only passage in the OT where Mount

pared [b]on the threshing floor of [1]Ornan the Jebusite.

2 He began to build on the second *day* in the second month [1]of the fourth year of his reign.

Dimensions and Materials of the Temple

3 Now these are the [1]foundations which [a]Solomon laid for building the house of God. The length in [2]cubits, according to the old standard *was* sixty cubits, and the width twenty cubits.

4 The porch which was in front of the house [a]was as long as the width of the house, twenty cubits, and the height 120; and inside he overlaid it with pure gold.

5 He overlaid [a]the [1]main room with cypress wood and overlaid it with fine gold, and [2]ornamented it with palm trees and chains.

6 Further, he [1]adorned the house with precious stones; and the gold was gold from [2]Parvaim.

7 [a]He also overlaid the house with gold—the beams, the thresholds and its walls and its doors; and he [b]carved cherubim on the walls.

8 Now he made [a]the [1]room of the holy of holies: its length across the width of the house *was* twenty cubits, and its width *was* twenty cubits; and he overlaid it with fine gold, *amounting* to 600 talents.

9 The weight of the nails was fifty shekels of gold. He also overlaid [a]the upper rooms with gold.

10 [a]Then he made two [1]sculptured cherubim in the room of the holy of holies and overlaid them with gold.

11 The wingspan of the cherubim *was* twenty cubits; the wing of one, of five cubits, touched the wall of the house, and *its* other wing, of five cubits, touched the wing of the other cherub.

12 The wing of the other cherub, of five cubits, touched the wall of the house; and *its* other wing of five cubits was attached to the wing of the [1]first cherub.

13 The wings of these cherubim extended twenty cubits, and they stood on their feet [1]facing the *main* room.

14 [a]He made the veil of violet, purple, crimson and fine linen, and he worked cherubim on it.

15 [a]He also made two pillars for the front of the house, thirty-five cubits [1]high, and the capital on the top of each *was* five cubits.

16 He made chains in the inner sanctuary and placed *them* on the tops of the pillars; and he made one hundred pomegranates and placed *them* on the chains.

17 [a]He erected the pillars in front of the temple, one on the right and the other on the left, and named the one on the right Jachin and the one on the left Boaz.

Furnishings of the Temple

4 Then [a]he made a bronze altar, twenty cubits in length and twenty cubits in width and ten cubits in height.

2 [a]Also he made the cast *metal* sea, ten cubits from brim to brim, circular in form, and its height *was* five cubits and [1]its circumference thirty cubits.

3 Now figures like oxen *were* under it *and* all around it, ten cubits, entirely encircling the sea. The oxen *were* in two rows, cast [1]in one piece.

4 It stood on twelve oxen, three facing

3:1 [1]In 2 Sam 24:18, *Araunah* [b]1 Chr 21:18
2 [1]Lit *in*
3 [1]Lit *founding of Solomon to build* [2]I.e. One cubit equals approx 18 in. [a]1 Kin 6:2
4 [a]1 Kin 6:3
5 [1]Lit *great house* [2]Lit *put on it palm trees* [a]1 Kin 6:17
6 [1]Lit *overlaid...for beauty* [2]Or *country of gold*
7 [a]1 Kin 6:20-22 [b]1 Kin 6:29-35
8 [1]Lit *house* [a]Ex 26:33; 1 Kin 6:16
9 [a]1 Chr 28:11
10 [1]Lit *cherubim of sculptured work* [a]Ex 25:18-20; 1 Kin 6:23-28
12 [1]Lit *other*
13 [1]Lit *and their faces to*
14 [a]Ex 26:31
15 [1]Lit *long* [a]1 Kin 7:15-20
17 [a]1 Kin 7:21
4:1 [a]Ex 27:1, 2; 2 Kin 16:14
2 [1]Lit *a line of 30 cubits encircling it round about* [a]1 Kin 7:23-26
3 [1]Lit *in its casting*

Zion is identified with Mount Moriah, the place where Abraham was commanded to offer Isaac (Gen 22:2,14). *the place that David had prepared.* See 1 Chr 21:18–22:1.

3:2 *second month of the fourth year.* In the spring of 966 B.C. (see note on 1 Kin 6:1).

3:4 *overlaid.* Or "inlaid," which perhaps gives a more correct picture: not that the entire interior was covered with gold leaf, but that designs (palm trees, chains) were inlaid with gold leaf (v. 5).

3:6 *Parvaim.* Designates either the source of the gold (perhaps southeast Arabia) or a particular quality of fine gold.

3:7 *cherubim.* See vv. 10–14; see also notes on Gen 3:24; Ezek 1:5.

3:8 *length . . . was twenty cubits, and its width was twenty cubits.* It was also 20 cubits high (1 Kin 6:20), making the dimensions of the holy of holies a perfect cube, as probably also in the tabernacle. In the New Jerusalem there is no temple (Rev 21:22); rather, the whole city is in the shape of a cube (Rev 21:16), for the whole city becomes "the holy of holies."

3:9 *nails . . . of gold.* The fact that gold is such a soft metal would make it unlikely that nails were made of this substance. It is probable that this small amount (only 1 1/4 pounds) represents gold leaf or sheeting used to gild the nail heads.

3:10–13 See 1 Kin 6:23–27 and notes.

3:14 *veil.* Also separated the two rooms of the tabernacle (Ex 26:31). Wooden doors could also be closed across the opening (4:22; 1 Kin 6:31–32; cf. Matt 27:51; Heb 9:8).

3:15 *thirty-five cubits high.* Since 1 Kin 7:15 indicates the pillars were each 18 cubits high (confirmed by 2 Kin 25:17; Jer 52:21, though the Septuagint at Jer 52:21 has 35), 35 here probably refers to the combined height of both. Alternatively, 35 may be the result of a copyist's mistake.

3:17 *pillars.* Remains of such pillars have been found in the excavations of numerous temples in the Holy Land. Cf. Rev 3:12. *Jachin . . . Boaz.* Jachin probably means "He establishes," and Boaz probably means "in Him is strength."

4:1 *bronze altar.* The parallel text in Kings does not mention the main altar of the temple described here (1 Kin 7:22–23), though several other passages in Kings do refer to it (1 Kin 8:64; 9:25; 2 Kin 16:14). The main altar of Solomon's temple was similar to the altar with steps that is described in Ezek 43:13–17.

4:2 *cast metal sea.* Replaced the bronze basin of the tabernacle (Ex 30:18); it was used by the priests for their ceremonial washing (v. 6; Ex 30:21). The NT views these rituals as foreshadowing the cleansing provided by Christ (Titus 3:5; Heb 9:11–14). In the temple of Ezekiel, the sea, which was on the south side in front of the temple (v. 10), has been replaced by a life-giving river that flows from the south side of the temple (Ezek 47:1–12; cf. Joel 3:18; Zech 14:8; John 4:9–15; Rev 22:1–2).

4:3 *oxen.* 1 Kin 7:24 has "gourds." The Hebrew for the two words is very similar, so the difference may well be due to a copyist's mistake.

4:4 *twelve oxen.* Possibly symbolic of the 12 tribes, which also

the north, three facing west, three facing
south and three facing east; and the sea *was*
set on top of them and all their hindquarters
turned inwards.
5 It was a handbreadth thick, and its
brim was made like the brim of a cup, *like* a
lily blossom; it [a]could hold 3,000 baths.
6 [a]He also made ten basins in which to
wash, and he set five on the right side and
five on the left [1]to rinse things for the burnt
offering; but the sea *was* for the priests to
wash in.
7 Then [a]he made the ten golden lampstands in the way prescribed for them and
he set them in the temple, five on the right
side and five on the left.
8 He also made [a]ten tables and placed
them in the temple, five on the right side and
five on the left. And he made one hundred
golden bowls.
9 Then he made [a]the court of the priests
and [b]the great court and doors for the court,
and overlaid their doors with bronze.
10 [a]He set the sea on the right [1]side *of the*
house toward the southeast.
11 [a]Huram also made the pails, the shovels and the bowls. So Huram finished doing
the work which he performed for King
Solomon in the house of God:
12 the two pillars, the bowls and the two
capitals on top of the pillars, and the two
networks to cover the two bowls of the capitals which were on top of the pillars,
13 and [a]the four hundred pomegranates
for the two networks, two rows of pomegranates for each network to cover the two bowls
of the capitals which were on the pillars.
14 [a]He also made the stands and he made
the basins on the stands,
15 *and* the one sea with the twelve oxen
under it.
16 The pails, the shovels, the forks and all
its utensils, [a]Huram-abi made of polished
bronze for King Solomon for the house of the
LORD.
17 On the plain of the Jordan the king cast
them in the clay ground between Succoth
and Zeredah.

5 [a]1 Kin 7:26
6 [1]Lit *in which to* [a]Ex 30:17-21; 1 Kin 7:38, 40
7 [a]Ex 25:31-40; 1 Kin 7:49
8 [a]1 Kin 7:48
9 [a]1 Kin 6:36 [b]2 Kin 21:5
10 [1]Lit *shoulder* [a]1 Kin 7:39
11 [a]1 Kin 7:40-51
13 [a]1 Kin 7:20
14 [a]1 Kin 7:27-43
16 [a]1 Kin 7:14; 2 Chr 2:13

18 [a]Thus Solomon made all these utensils
in great quantities, for the weight of the
bronze could not be found out.
19 Solomon also made all the things that
were in the house of God: even the golden
altar, [a]the tables with the bread of the Presence on them,
20 the lampstands with their lamps of
pure gold, [a]to burn in front of the inner sanctuary in the way prescribed;
21 the flowers, the lamps, and the tongs of
gold, of purest gold;
22 and the snuffers, the bowls, the spoons
and the firepans of pure gold; and the
entrance of the house, its inner doors for the
holy of holies and the doors of the house,
that is, of the nave, of gold.

The Ark Is Brought into the Temple

5 [a]Thus all the work that Solomon performed for the house of the LORD was finished. And Solomon brought in the [1b]things
that David his father had dedicated, even the
silver and the gold and all the utensils, *and*
put *them* in the treasuries of the house of
God.
2 [a]Then Solomon assembled to Jerusalem the elders of Israel and all the heads of
the tribes, the leaders of the fathers' *house-*
holds of the sons of Israel, [b]to bring up the
ark of the covenant of the LORD out of the
city of David, which is Zion.
3 [a]All the men of Israel assembled themselves to the king at [b]the feast, that is *in* the
seventh month.
4 Then all the elders of Israel came, and
[a]the Levites took up the ark.
5 They brought up the ark and the tent of
meeting and all the holy utensils which *were*
in the tent; the Levitical priests brought them
up.
6 And King Solomon and all the congregation of Israel who were assembled with
him before the ark, were sacrificing [1]so
many sheep and oxen that they could not be
counted or numbered.
7 Then the priests brought the ark of the
covenant of the LORD to its place, into the

18 [a]1 Kin 7:47
19 [a]2 Chr 4:8
20 [a]Ex 25:31-37; 2 Chr 5:7
5:1 [1]Lit *dedicated things of David,* [a]1 Kin 7:51 [b]2 Sam 8:11; 1 Chr 18:11
2 [a]1 Kin 8:1-9 [b]2 Sam 6:12-15; 1 Chr 15:25-28; 2 Chr 1:4
3 [a]1 Kin 8:2 [b]2 Chr 7:8-10
4 [a]Josh 3:6; 2 Chr 5:7
6 [1]Lit *sheep... numbered for multitude*

---

encamped three on each side of the tabernacle during the wilderness journeys (Num 2; cf. Ezek 48:30–35).

4:5 *3,000 baths.* 1 Kin 7:26 has 2,000 baths. These figures could easily have been misread by the ancient scribes.

4:6 *ten basins.* See 1 Kin 7:38–39.

4:7 *ten golden lampstands.* Instead of one, as in the tabernacle (Ex 25:31–40). *prescribed.* See 1 Chr 28:15. These lamps were not necessarily of the same shape as described in Ex 25:31–40, but could have resembled the style of lamp depicted in Zech 4:2–6.

4:8 *ten tables.* Instead of one, as in the tabernacle (Ex 25:23–30; 40:4; Lev 24:5–9; 1 Sam 21:1–6; Ezek 41:22; Heb 9:2; cf. 2 Chr 13:11; 29:18).

4:11–16 See 1 Kin 7:40–45.

4:17–22 See 1 Kin 7:46–50.

4:17 *clay ground.* The clay beds of the Jordan plain made it possible to dig molds for these bronze castings.

5:1 *things that David his father had dedicated.* See notes on 1 Chr 18:1–20:8; 22:2–16; 29:2–5; see also 1 Chr 26:26.

5:2–14 See 1 Kin 8:1–11 and notes.

5:2 *ark.* Had been in a tent provided for it 40 years earlier when David brought it to Jerusalem (1 Chr 15:1–16:6).

5:3 *feast . . . in the seventh month.* The Feast of Booths. The month is designated by its Canaanite name Ethanim in 1 Kin 8:2; the Hebrew name is Tishri. According to 1 Kin 6:38 the temple was completed in the eighth month of Solomon's 11th year, i.e., September-October, 959 B.C. This celebration of dedication took place either a month before the completion of the work or 11 months after, probably the latter (see note on 1 Kin 8:2).

5:6 Cf. David's bringing of the ark to Jerusalem (1 Chr 15:26; 16:1–3).

inner sanctuary of the house, to the holy of
holies, under the wings of the cherubim.
8 For the cherubim spread their wings
over the place of the ark, so that the cherubim
made a covering over the ark and its [1]poles.
9 The poles were so long that [a]the ends
of the poles of the ark could be seen in front
of the inner sanctuary, but they could not be
seen outside; and [1]they are there to this day.
10 [a]There was nothing in the ark except
the two tablets which Moses put *there* at
Horeb, where the LORD made a covenant
with the sons of Israel, when they came out
of Egypt.

The Glory of God Fills the Temple

11 When the priests came forth from the
holy place (for all the priests who were present had sanctified themselves, without
regard [a]to divisions),
12 and all the Levitical singers, [a]Asaph,
Heman, Jeduthun, and their sons and kinsmen, clothed in fine linen, [b]with cymbals,
harps and lyres, standing east of the altar,
and with them one hundred and twenty
priests [c]blowing trumpets
13 in unison when the trumpeters and the
singers were to make themselves heard with
one voice to praise and to glorify the LORD,
and when they lifted up their voice [a]accom-
panied by trumpets and cymbals and instruments of music, and when they praised the
LORD *saying,* "[b]*He* indeed is good for His lovingkindness is everlasting," then the house,
the house of the LORD, was filled with a
cloud,
14 so that the priests could not stand to
minister because of the cloud, for [a]the glory
of the LORD filled the house of God.

Solomon's Dedication

6 [a]Then Solomon said,
"The LORD has said that He would
dwell in the thick cloud.
2 "I have built You a lofty house,
And a place for Your dwelling
forever."
3 Then the king [1]faced about and blessed
all the assembly of Israel, while all the
assembly of Israel was standing.
4 He said, "Blessed be the LORD, the God
of Israel, who spoke with His mouth to my

8 [1]Lit *poles above*
9 [1]Lit *it is*
[a]1 Kin 8:8, 9
10 [a]Deut 10:2-5; Heb 9:4
11 [a]1 Chr 24:1-5
12 [a]1 Chr 25:1-4 [b]1 Chr 13:8; 15:16, 24 [c]2 Chr 7:6
13 [a]1 Chr 16:42 [b]1 Chr 16:34; 2 Chr 7:3; Ezra 3:11; Ps 100:5; Jer 33:11
14 [a]Ex 40:35; 1 Kin 8:11
6:1 [a]1 Kin 8:12-50
3 [1]Lit *turned his face about*

6 [a]2 Chr 12:13 [b]1 Chr 28:4
7 [1]Lit *with* [a]1 Kin 5:3; 1 Chr 28:2
8 [1]Lit *with*
9 [1]Lit *will come forth from your loins*
10 [1]Lit *spoke*
11 [a]2 Chr 5:7, 10
13 [a]Neh 8:4 [b]1 Kin 8:54
14 [a]Ex 15:11; Deut 3:24 [b]Deut 7:9
15 [1]Lit *spoken to* [a]1 Chr 22:9, 10

father David and has fulfilled *it* with His
hands, saying,
5 'Since the day that I brought My people
from the land of Egypt, I did not choose a
city out of all the tribes of Israel *in which* to
build a house that My name might be there,
nor did I choose any man for a leader over
My people Israel;
6 but [a]I have chosen Jerusalem that My
name might be there, and I [b]have chosen
David to be over My people Israel.'
7 "[a]Now it was [1]in the heart of my father
David to build a house for the name of the
LORD, the God of Israel.
8 "But the LORD said to my father David,
'Because it was [1]in your heart to build a
house for My name, you did well that it was
[1]in your heart.
9 'Nevertheless you shall not build the
house, but your son who [1]will be born to
you, he shall build the house for My name.'
10 "Now the LORD has fulfilled His word
which He spoke; for I have risen in the place
of my father David and sit on the throne of
Israel, as the LORD [1]promised, and have built
the house for the name of the LORD, the God
of Israel.
11 "There I have set the ark [a]in which is
the covenant of the LORD, which He made
with the sons of Israel."

Solomon's Prayer of Dedication

12 Then he stood before the altar of the
LORD in the presence of all the assembly of
Israel and spread out his hands.
13 [a]Now Solomon had made a bronze
platform, five cubits long, five cubits wide
and three cubits high, and had set it in the
midst of the court; and he stood on it, [b]knelt
on his knees in the presence of all the assembly of Israel and spread out his hands toward
heaven.
14 He said, "O LORD, the God of Israel,
[a]there is no god like You in heaven or on
earth, [b]keeping covenant and *showing* lovingkindness to Your servants who walk
before You with all their heart;
15 [a]who has kept with Your servant
David, my father, that which You have
[1]promised him; indeed You have spoken
with Your mouth and have fulfilled it with
Your hand, as it is this day.

5:9 *there to this day.* See note on 1 Kin 8:8; see also 8:8; 10:19; 20:26; 21:10; 35:25; 1 Chr 4:41,43; 5:26; 13:11; 17:5.
5:10 *two tablets.* See Ex 31:18 and note; see also Ex 32:15–16. The ark had earlier contained also the gold jar of manna (Ex 16:32–34) and Aaron's staff (Num 17:10–11; Heb 9:4). These items were presumably lost, perhaps while the ark was in Philistine hands.
5:12 *fine linen.* See 1 Chr 15:27 and note.
5:14 *cloud . . . glory of the LORD.* Cf. 7:1–3. The glory cloud represented the presence of God. It had guided Israel out of Egypt and through the wilderness, and was present above the tabernacle (Ex 13:21–22; 40:34–38; cf. Ezek 43:1–5; Hag 2:9; Zech 1:16; 2:10; 8:3).
6:1–11 See notes on 1 Kin 8:12–21.
6:8–9 Cf. David's speech in 1 Chr 28:2–3.
6:12–21 See notes on 1 Kin 8:22–30.
6:13 Not in 1 Kin 8. Some think that the Chronicler may have wished to clarify the fact that Solomon was not "before the altar" (v. 12) exercising priestly duties. On the other hand, the verse may have been dropped from Kings by a copying error: The phrase "spread out his hands" occurs in vv. 12–13; it is possible that the scribe copying Kings looked back to the second occurrence of the phrase, thus omitting the verse. The verse would then be present in Chronicles because it was in the particular text of Kings used by the Chronicler.

16 "Now therefore, O LORD, the God of Israel, keep with Your servant David, my father,
that which You have [1]promised him, saying,
'[2][a]You shall not lack a man to sit on the
throne of Israel, if only your sons take heed
to their way, to walk in My law as you have
walked before Me.'
17 "Now therefore, O LORD, the God of Israel, let Your word be confirmed which You
have spoken to Your servant David.
18 "But [a]will God indeed dwell with
mankind on the earth? Behold, [b]heaven and
the [1]highest heaven cannot contain You;
how much less this house which I have built.
19 "Yet have regard to the prayer of Your
servant and to his supplication, O LORD my
God, to listen to the cry and to the prayer
which Your servant prays before You;
20 that Your [a]eye may be open toward this
house day and night, toward [b]the place of
which You have said that *You would* put Your
name there, to listen to the prayer which
Your servant shall pray toward this place.
21 "Listen to the supplications of Your servant and of Your people Israel when they pray
toward this place; hear from Your dwelling
place, from heaven; [a]hear and forgive.
22 "If a man sins against his neighbor and
is made to take an oath, and he comes *and*
takes an oath before Your altar in this house,
23 then hear from heaven and act and
judge Your servants, [1][a]punishing the wicked
by bringing his way on his own head and
justifying the righteous by giving him
according to his righteousness.
24 "If Your people Israel [1]are defeated
before an enemy because [a]they have sinned
against You, and they return *to You* and confess Your name, and pray and make supplication before You in this house,
25 then hear from heaven and forgive the
sin of Your people Israel, and bring them
back to the land which You have given to
them and to their fathers.
26 "When the [a]heavens are shut up and
there is no rain because they have sinned
against You, and they pray toward this place
and confess Your name, and turn from their
sin when You afflict them;
27 then hear in heaven and forgive the sin
of Your servants and Your people Israel,
indeed, [a]teach them the good way in which
they should walk. And send rain on Your
land which You have given to Your people
for an inheritance.
28 "If there is [a]famine in the land, if there is
pestilence, if there is blight or mildew, if there
is locust or grasshopper, if their enemies
besiege them in the land of their [1]cities, whatever plague or whatever sickness *there is*,
29 whatever prayer or supplication is
made by any man or by all Your people Israel, [1]each knowing his own affliction and his
own pain, and spreading his hands toward
this house,
30 then hear from heaven Your dwelling
place, and forgive, and render to each
according to all his ways, whose heart You
know [a]for You alone know the hearts of the
sons of men,
31 that they may [1]fear You, to walk in
Your ways [2]as long as they live in the land
which You have given to our fathers.
32 "Also concerning [a]the foreigner who is
not from Your people Israel, when he comes
from a far country for Your great name's sake
and Your mighty hand and Your outstretched
arm, when they come and pray toward this
house,
33 then hear from heaven, from Your
dwelling place, and do according to all for
which the foreigner calls to You, in order that
all the peoples of the earth may know Your
name, and [1]fear You as *do* Your people Israel, and that they may know that [2]this house
which I have built is [a]called by Your name.
34 "When Your people go out to battle
against their enemies, by whatever way You
shall send them, and they pray to You toward
this city which You have chosen and the
house which I have built for Your name,
35 then hear from heaven their prayer and
their supplication, and maintain their cause.
36 "When they sin against You ([a]for there
is no man who does not sin) and You are
angry with them and deliver them to an enemy, so that [1]they take them away captive to
a land far off or near,
37 if they [1]take thought in the land where
they are taken captive, and repent and make
supplication to You in the land of their captivity, saying, 'We have sinned, we have committed iniquity and have acted wickedly';
38 [a]if they return to You with all their
heart and with all their soul in the land of
their captivity, where they have been taken
captive, and pray toward their land which
You have given to their fathers and the city
which You have chosen, and toward the
house which I have built for Your name,
39 then hear from heaven, from Your
dwelling place, their prayer and supplica-

16 [1]Lit *spoken to* [2]Lit *There shall not be cut off to you a man from before Me* [a]1 Kin 2:4; 2 Chr 7:18
18 [1]Lit *heaven of heavens* [a]Ps 113:5, 6 [b]2 Chr 2:6; Is 66:1; Acts 7:49
20 [a]Ps 33:18; 34:15 [b]Deut 12:11
21 [a]Is 43:25; 44:22; Mic 7:18
23 [1]Lit *returning* [a]Is 3:11; Rom 2:8, 9
24 [1]Lit *smitten* [a]Ps 51:4
26 [a]1 Kin 17:1
27 [a]Ps 94:12
28 [a]2 Chr 20:9

28 [1]Lit *gates*
29 [1]Lit *whoever shall know*
30 [a]1 Sam 16:7; 1 Chr 28:9
31 [1]Or *reverence* [2]Lit *all the days that they live on the face of the land*
32 [a]Is 56:3-8
33 [1]Or *reverence* [2]Lit *Your name is called upon this house* [a]2 Chr 7:14
36 [1]Lit *their captors take them captive* [a]Job 15:14-16; James 3:2; 1 John 1:8-10
37 [1]Lit *return to their heart*
38 [a]Jer 29:12, 13

6:18 Cf. 2:6.
6:22–39 See notes on 1 Kin 8:31–46.
6:22–23 See Ex 22:10–11; Lev 6:3–5.
6:24–25 See Lev 26:17,23; Deut 28:25,36–37,48–57,64; Josh 7:11–12.
6:26–27 See Lev 26:19; Deut 11:10–15; 28:18,22–24.
6:28–31 See Lev 26:16,20,25–26; Deut 28:20–22,27–28,35,42.
6:32–33 The prophets also envisaged the Gentiles as coming to Jerusalem to worship the Lord (Is 56:6–8; Zech 8:20–23; 14:16–21; cf. Ps 87).
6:34–35 See Lev 26:7–8; Deut 28:6–7. The Chronicler repeatedly demonstrates God's answer to prayer in time of battle (ch. 13; 14:9–15; 18:31; 20:1–29; 25:5–13; 32:20–22).
6:36 *no man who does not sin.* See Jer 13:23; Rom 3:23. *captive to a land far off.* See 36:15–20; Lev 26:33,44–45; Deut 28:49–52; 2 Kin 17:7–20; 25:1–21.

tions, and maintain their cause and forgive Your people who have sinned against You.

40 "Now, O my God, I pray, [a]let Your eyes be open and [b]Your ears attentive to the prayer *offered* in this place.

41 "[a]Now therefore arise, O LORD God, to Your resting place, You and the ark of Your might; let Your priests, O LORD God, be clothed with salvation and let Your godly ones rejoice in what is good.

42 "O LORD God, do not turn away the face of Your anointed; [a]remember *Your* lovingkindness to Your servant David."

The Shekinah Glory

7 [a]Now when Solomon had finished praying, [b]fire came down from heaven and consumed the burnt offering and the sacrifices, and the glory of the LORD filled the house.

2 [a]The priests could not enter into the house of the LORD because the glory of the LORD filled the LORD's house.

3 All the sons of Israel, seeing the fire come down and the glory of the LORD upon the house, bowed down on the pavement with their faces to the ground, and they worshiped and gave praise to the LORD, *saying,* "[a]Truly He is good, truly His lovingkindness is everlasting."

Sacrifices Offered

4 [a]Then the king and all the people offered sacrifice before the LORD.

5 King Solomon offered a sacrifice of 22,000 oxen and 120,000 sheep. Thus the king and all the people dedicated the house of God.

6 The priests stood at their posts, and [a]the Levites also, with the instruments of music to the LORD, which King David had made for giving praise to the LORD—"for His lovingkindness is everlasting"—whenever [1]he gave praise by their [2]means, while [b]the priests on the other side blew trumpets; and all Israel was standing.

7 [a]Then Solomon consecrated the middle of the court that *was* before the house of the LORD, for there he offered the burnt offerings and the fat of the peace offerings because the bronze altar which Solomon had made was not able to contain the burnt offering, the grain offering and the fat.

The Feast of Dedication

8 So [a]Solomon observed the feast at that time for seven days, and all Israel with him, a very great assembly *who came* from the entrance of Hamath to the [b]brook of Egypt.

9 On the eighth day they held [a]a solemn assembly, for the dedication of the altar they observed seven days and the feast seven days.

10 Then on the twenty-third day of the seventh month he sent the people to their tents, rejoicing and happy of heart because of the goodness that the LORD had shown to David and to Solomon and to His people Israel.

God's Promise and Warning

11 [a]Thus Solomon finished the house of the LORD and the king's palace, and successfully completed all that [1]he had planned on doing in the house of the LORD and in his palace.

12 Then the LORD appeared to Solomon at night and said to him, "I have heard your prayer and [a]have chosen this place for Myself as a house of sacrifice.

13 "[a]If I shut up the heavens so that there is no rain, or if I command the locust to devour the land, or if I send pestilence among My people,

14 [a]and My people [1]who are called by My name humble themselves and pray and seek My face and turn from their wicked ways, then I will hear from heaven, will forgive their sin and will heal their land.

40 [a]2 Chr 7:15; Neh 1:6, 11 [b]Ps 17:1
41 [a]Ps 132:8, 9
42 [a]Ps 89:24, 28; 132:10-12; Is 55:3
7:1 [a]1 Kin 8:54 [b]Lev 9:23f; 1 Kin 18:24, 38
2 [a]2 Chr 5:14
3 [a]2 Chr 5:13; 20:21
4 [a]1 Kin 8:62, 63
6 [1]Lit *David* [2]Lit *hand* [a]1 Chr 15:16-21 [b]2 Chr 5:12
7 [a]1 Kin 8:64-66
8 [a]1 Kin 8:65 [b]Gen 15:18
9 [a]Lev 23:36
11 [1]Lit *came upon the heart of Solomon to do* [a]1 Kin 9:1-9
12 [a]Deut 12:5, 11
13 [a]2 Chr 6:26-28
14 [1]Lit *over whom My name is called* [a]2 Chr 6:37-39; James 4:10

6:40–42 The Chronicler replaces the ending of Solomon's prayer in Kings (1 Kin 8:50–53) with a repetition of Ps 132:8–10, a psalm that deals with bringing the ark to the temple, the theme of this section in Chronicles (5:2–14). The prayer in Kings ends with an appeal to the exodus deliverance under Moses, while in Chronicles the appeal is on the basis of the eternal promises to David.

7:1–22 See 1 Kin 8:54–9:9 and notes.

7:1–3 Not found in 1 Kin 8. The addition of the fire descending from heaven to consume the sacrifices provides the same sign of divine acceptance as was given at the dedication of the tabernacle (Lev 9:23–24) and David's offering at the threshing floor of Ornan (a variant of Araunah; see 2 Sam 24:16) the Jebusite (1 Chr 21:26; cf. 1 Kin 18:38). While vv. 1–3 are unique to Chronicles, the Chronicler has omitted Solomon's blessing of the congregation (1 Kin 8:55–61).

7:1 *glory of the LORD.* See 5:14 and note.

7:3 *He is good . . . everlasting.* See v. 6; 5:13.

7:6 The verse is unique to Chronicles and reflects the author's overall interest in the Levites, especially the musicians (cf. 29:26–27; see note on 1 Chr 6:31–48). *all Israel.* See Introduction to 1 Chronicles: Purpose and Themes.

7:8 *from the entrance of Hamath to the brook of Egypt.* Not only were the patriarchal promises of descendants provisionally fulfilled under David and Solomon (see 1:9; 1 Chr 27:23–24 and notes), but also the promises of land (Gen 15:18–21).

7:9 *eighth day.* The final day of the Feast of Booths (see 5:3 and note; Lev 23:36; Num 29:35). *seven days . . . seven days.* The dedication had run from the 8th to the 14th day of the month, and the Feast of Booths from the 15th to the 22nd day. The day of atonement was on the 10th day of the 7th month (Lev 16; cf. 1 Kin 8:65–66).

7:12 *appeared to Solomon.* The second time God appeared to Solomon; the first was at Gibeon (1:3–13; 1 Kin 9:2).

7:13–15 Unique to Chronicles. These verses illustrate the writer's emphasis on immediate retribution (see Introduction to 1 Chronicles: Purpose and Themes). The Chronicler subsequently portrays the kings in a way that demonstrates this principle (see v. 22).

7:14 See, e.g., 12:6–7,12.

15 "[a]Now My eyes will be open and My ears attentive to the [1]prayer *offered* in this place.

16 "For [a]now I have chosen and consecrated this house that My name may be there forever, and My eyes and My heart will be there perpetually.

17 "As for you, if you walk before Me as your father David walked, even to do according to all that I have commanded you, and will keep My statutes and My ordinances,

18 then I will establish your royal throne as I covenanted with your father David, saying, '[1][a]You shall not lack a man *to be* ruler in Israel.'

19 "[a]But if you turn away and forsake My statutes and My commandments which I have set before you, and go and serve other gods and worship them,

20 [a]then I will uproot you from My land which I have given [1]you, and this house which I have consecrated for My name I will cast out of My sight and I will make it [b]a proverb and a byword among all peoples.

21 "As for this house, which was exalted, everyone who passes by it will be astonished and say, '[a]Why has the LORD done thus to this land and to this house?'

22 "And they will say, 'Because [a]they forsook the LORD, the God of their fathers who brought them from the land of Egypt, and they adopted other gods and worshiped them and served them; therefore He has brought all this adversity on them.' "

Solomon's Activities and Accomplishments

8 [a]Now it came about at the end of the twenty years in which Solomon had built the house of the LORD and his own house

2 that he built the cities which Huram had given to [1]him, and settled the sons of Israel there.

3 Then Solomon went to Hamath-zobah and captured it.

4 He built Tadmor in the wilderness and all the storage cities which he had built in Hamath.

5 He also built upper [a]Beth-horon and lower Beth-horon, [b]fortified cities *with* walls, gates and bars;

6 and Baalath and all the storage cities that Solomon had, and all the cities for [1]his chariots and cities for [1]his horsemen, and all that it pleased Solomon to build in Jerusalem, in Lebanon, and in all the land [2]under his rule.

7 [a]All of the people who were left of the Hittites, the Amorites, the Perizzites, the Hivites and the Jebusites, who were not of Israel,

8 *namely,* from their descendants who were left after them in the land whom the sons of Israel had not destroyed, [a]them Solomon raised as forced laborers to this day.

9 But Solomon did not make slaves for his work from the sons of Israel; they were men of war, his chief captains and commanders of his chariots and his horsemen.

10 These were the chief [1]officers of King Solomon, two hundred and fifty who ruled over the people.

11 [a]Then Solomon brought Pharaoh's daughter up from the city of David to the house which he had built for her, for he said, "My wife shall not dwell in the house of David king of Israel, because [1]the places are holy where the ark of the LORD has entered."

12 Then Solomon offered burnt offerings to the LORD on [a]the altar of the LORD which he had built before the porch;

13 and [a]*did so* according to the daily rule, offering *them* up [b]according to the commandment of Moses, for [c]the sabbaths, [d]the new moons and the [e]three annual feasts—the Feast of Unleavened Bread, the Feast of Weeks and the Feast of Booths.

14 Now according to the ordinance of his father David, he appointed [a]the divisions of the priests for their service, and [b]the Levites for their duties of praise and ministering before the priests according to the daily rule, and [c]the gatekeepers by their divisions at every gate; for [d]David the man of God had so commanded.

15 [1]Lit *prayer of this place* [a]2 Chr 6:20, 40
16 [a]2 Chr 7:12
18 [1]Lit *There shall not be cut off to you a man* [a]1 Kin 2:4; 2 Chr 6:16
19 [a]Lev 26:14, 33; Deut 28:15
20 [1]Ancient versions and Heb read *them* [a]Deut 29:28; 1 Kin 14:15 [b]Deut 28:37
21 [a]Deut 29:24-27
22 [a]Judg 2:13
8:1 [a]1 Kin 9:10-28
2 [1]Lit *Solomon*
5 [a]1 Chr 7:24 [b]2 Chr 14:7
6 [1]Lit *the* [2]Lit *of*
7 [a]Gen 15:18-21; 1 Kin 9:20
8 [a]1 Kin 4:6; 9:21
10 [1]Or *deputies*
11 [1]Lit *they are* [a]1 Kin 3:1; 7:8
12 [a]2 Chr 4:1
13 [a]Ex 29:38-42 [b]Num 28:3 [c]Num 28:9, 10 [d]Num 28:11 [e]Ex 23:14-17; 34:22, 23; Deut 16:16
14 [a]1 Chr 24:1 [b]1 Chr 25:1 [c]1 Chr 26:1 [d]Neh 12:24, 36

7:17–18 See 1 Kin 9:4–5. Such words as these reinforced ancient Israel's Messianic hopes.

7:19–22 See 1 Kin 9:6–9.

8:1–18 See 1 Kin 9:10–18 and notes. Verses 13–16 are unique to Chronicles and underscore the Chronicler's concern to show continuity with the past and his association of David with Moses (see Introduction to 1 Chronicles: Purpose and Themes).

8:1–2 In 1 Kin 9:10–14 the cities were given to Hiram by Solomon, whereas in Chronicles the reverse is true. Perhaps as part of his effort to idealize Solomon, the Chronicler does not record the fact that Hiram found these cities unacceptable payment (1 Kin 9:11–13); he mentions only the sequel to the story, the return of the cities to Solomon and their subsequent improvement. They may also have served as a kind of collateral against the monies owed Hiram, who returned them when the debt was satisfied (see note on 1 Kin 9:11). The Chronicler also says nothing about Pharaoh's gift of Gezer to Solomon (1 Kin 9:16).

8:3–4 The Chronicler records an additional military campaign to the north, not mentioned in Kings. David had also campaigned in the north against Zobah (1 Chr 18:3–9; 19:6; 2 Sam 8:3–12; 10:6–8; cf. 1 Kin 11:23–24).

8:5 The two Beth-horons were situated on a strategic road from the coastal plain to the area just north of Jerusalem.

8:7 *not of Israel.* See 2:17; 1 Chr 22:2; 1 Kin 9:21.

8:8 *to this day.* See note on 5:9.

8:11 *holy.* Both 1 Kin 9:24 and Chronicles record the transfer of Pharaoh's daughter to special quarters, but only Chronicles adds the reason: Not only the temple but also David's palace was regarded as holy, because of the presence of the ark.

8:12–16 In line with his overall interests, the Chronicler considerably elaborates on the sacrificial and temple provisions made by Solomon. While 1 Kin 9:25 mentions only the sacrifices at the three annual feasts, the Chronicler adds the offerings on sabbaths and new moons to conform these provisions fully to Mosaic prescription (Lev 23:1–37; Num 28–29).

15 And they did not depart from the commandment of the king to the priests and Levites in any manner or concerning the storehouses.

16 Thus all the work of Solomon was carried out [1]from the day of the foundation of the house of the LORD, and until it was finished. So the house of the LORD was completed.

17 Then Solomon went to [a]Ezion-geber and to [b]Eloth on the seashore in the land of Edom.

18 And Huram by his servants sent him ships and servants who knew the sea; and they went with Solomon's servants to Ophir, and [a]took from there four hundred and fifty talents of gold and brought them to King Solomon.

Visit of the Queen of Sheba

9 [a]Now when the queen of Sheba heard of the fame of Solomon, she came to Jerusalem to test Solomon with difficult questions. She had a very large retinue, with camels carrying spices and a large amount of gold and precious stones; and when she came to Solomon, she spoke with him about all that was on her heart.

2 Solomon [1]answered all her questions; nothing was hidden from Solomon which he did not [2]explain to her.

3 When the queen of Sheba had seen the wisdom of Solomon, the house which he had built,

4 the food at his table, the seating of his servants, the attendance of his ministers and their attire, his cupbearers and their attire, and [1]his stairway by which he went up to the house of the LORD, she was breathless.

5 Then she said to the king, "It was a true report which I heard in my own land about your words and your wisdom.

6 "Nevertheless I did not believe their reports until I came and my eyes had seen it. And behold, the half of the greatness of your wisdom was not told me. You surpass the report that I heard.

7 "How [1]blessed are your men, how [1]blessed are these your servants who stand before you continually and hear your wisdom.

8 "Blessed be the LORD your God who delighted in you, [a]setting you on His throne as king for the LORD your God; [b]because your God loved Israel establishing them forever, therefore He made you king over them, to do justice and righteousness."

9 Then she gave the king one hundred and twenty talents of gold and a very great *amount of* spices and precious stones; there had never been spice like that which the queen of Sheba gave to King Solomon.

10 The servants of Huram and the servants of Solomon [a]who brought gold from Ophir, also brought algum trees and precious stones.

11 From the algum trees the king made steps for the house of the LORD and for the king's palace, and lyres and harps for the singers; and none like that was seen before in the land of Judah.

12 King Solomon gave to the queen of Sheba all her desire which she requested besides *a return for* what she had brought to the king. Then she turned and went to her own land with her servants.

Solomon's Wealth and Power

13 [a]Now the weight of gold which came to Solomon in one year was 666 talents of gold,

14 besides that which the traders and merchants brought; and all [a]the kings of Arabia and the governors of the country brought gold and silver to Solomon.

15 King Solomon made 200 large shields of beaten gold, [1]using 600 *shekels of* beaten gold on each large shield.

16 *He made* 300 shields of beaten gold, [1]using three hundred shekels of gold on each shield, and the king put them in the house of the forest of Lebanon.

17 Moreover, the king made a great throne of ivory and overlaid it with pure gold.

18 *There were* six steps to the throne and a footstool in gold attached to the throne, and [1]arms [2]on each side of the seat, and two lions standing beside the [1]arms.

19 Twelve lions were standing there on the six steps on the one side and on the other; nothing like *it* was made for any *other* kingdom.

20 All King Solomon's drinking vessels *were* of gold, and all the vessels of the house of the forest of Lebanon *were* of pure gold; silver was not considered [1]valuable in the days of Solomon.

16 [1]So ancient versions; M.T. *as far as*
17 [a]1 Kin 9:26 [b]2 Kin 14:22
18 [a]2 Chr 9:10, 13
9:1 [a]1 Kin 10:1-13; Matt 12:42; Luke 11:31
2 [1]Lit *told her all her words* [2]Lit *tell*
4 [1]Or *his burnt offering which he offered*
7 [1]Or *happy*
8 [a]1 Chr 28:5; 29:23 [b]Deut 7:8; 2 Chr 2:11
10 [a]1 Kin 10:11; 2 Chr 8:18
13 [a]1 Kin 10:14-28
14 [a]Ps 68:29; 72:10
15 [1]Lit *he brought up*
16 [1]Lit *he brought up*
18 [1]Lit *hands* [2]Lit *on this side and on this at the place of the seat*
20 [1]Lit *anything*

8:17–18 See 1 Kin 9:26–28. This joint venture between Solomon and Huram secured for these kings the lucrative trade routes through the Mediterranean to the south Arabian peninsula; Solomon became the middleman between these economic spheres.

8:18 *Huram . . . sent him ships.* Presumably ships crafted in Phoenicia and assembled at the port of Ezion-geber after being shipped overland (see 9:21).

9:1–12 See 1 Kin 10:1–13 and notes. The visit of the queen of Sheba portrays the fulfillment of God's promise to give Solomon wisdom and wealth (1:12). Although the themes of Solomon's wisdom and wealth are here put to the fore, a major motive for the queen's visit may have been commercial, perhaps prompted by Solomon's naval operations toward south Arabia (8:17–18).

9:1 *Sheba.* See note on 1 Kin 10:1; see also Job 1:15; 6:19; Ps 72:10–11,15; Is 60:6; Jer 6:20; Ezek 27:22; 38:13; Joel 3:8.

9:8 *His throne.* The most significant variation from the account of the queen's visit in 1 Kings (10:9) is found here. The queen's speech becomes the vehicle for the Chronicler's conviction that the throne of Israel is the throne of God, for whom the king ruled (see 13:18; see also note on 1 Chr 17:14).

21 [a]For the king had ships which went to
Tarshish with the servants of Huram; once
every three years the ships of Tarshish came
bringing gold and silver, ivory and apes and
peacocks.
22 [a]So King Solomon became greater than
all the kings of the earth in riches and wisdom.
23 And all the kings of the earth were
seeking the presence of Solomon, to hear his
wisdom which God had put in his heart.
24 [a]They brought every man his gift, articles of silver and gold, garments, weapons,
spices, horses and mules, so much year by
year.
25 Now Solomon had [a]4,000 stalls for
horses and chariots and 12,000 horsemen,
and he stationed them in the chariot cities
and with the king in Jerusalem.
26 [a]He was the ruler over all the kings from
the Euphrates River even to the land of the
Philistines, and as far as the border of Egypt.
27 [a]The king made silver *as common* as
stones in Jerusalem, and he made cedars as
plentiful as sycamore trees that are in the
[1]lowland.
28 [a]And they were bringing horses for
Solomon from Egypt and from all countries.
29 [a]Now the rest of the acts of Solomon,
from first to last, [b]are they not written in the
[1]records of Nathan the prophet, and in the
prophecy of Ahijah the Shilonite, and in
the visions of [2]Iddo the seer concerning Jeroboam the son of Nebat?
30 [a]Solomon reigned forty years in
Jerusalem over all Israel.

Death of Solomon

31 And Solomon slept with his fathers and
was buried in [a]the city of his father David;
and his son Rehoboam reigned in his place.

Rehoboam's Reign of Folly

10 [a]Then Rehoboam went to Shechem, for
all Israel had come to Shechem to make
him king.
2 When Jeroboam the son of Nebat
heard *of it* (for [a]he was in Egypt where he
had fled from the presence of King Solomon), Jeroboam returned from Egypt.

21 [a]2 Chr 20:36, 37
22 [a]1 Kin 3:13; 2 Chr 1:12
24 [a]Ps 72:10
25 [a]Deut 17:16; 1 Kin 4:26; 10:26; 2 Chr 1:14
26 [a]Gen 15:18; 1 Kin 4:21, 24
27 [1]Heb *shephelah* [a]2 Chr 1:15-17
28 [a]2 Chr 1:16
29 [1]Lit *words* [2]Heb *Jedo* [a]1 Kin 11:41-43 [b]1 Chr 29:29
30 [a]1 Kin 11:42, 43
31 [a]1 Kin 2:10
10:1 [a]1 Kin 12:1-20
2 [a]1 Kin 11:40

3 So they sent and summoned him.
When Jeroboam and all Israel came, they
spoke to Rehoboam, saying,
4 "Your father made our [a]yoke hard; now
therefore lighten the hard service of your
father and his heavy yoke which he put on
us, and we will serve you."
5 He said to them, "Return to me again in
three days." So the people departed.
6 Then King Rehoboam [a]consulted with
the elders who had [1]served his father Solomon while he was still alive, saying, "How
do you counsel *me* to answer this people?"
7 They spoke to him, saying, "If you will
be kind to this people and please them and
[a]speak good words to them, then they will
be your servants forever."
8 But he [a]forsook the counsel of the elders which they had given him, and consulted with the young men who grew up with
him [1]and served him.
9 So he said to them, "What counsel do
you give that we may answer this people,
who have spoken to me, saying, 'Lighten the
yoke which your father put on us'?"
10 The young men who grew up with him
spoke to him, saying, "Thus you shall say to
the people who spoke to you, saying, 'Your
father made our yoke heavy, but you make it
lighter for us.' Thus you shall say to them,
'My little finger is thicker than my father's
loins!
11 'Whereas my father loaded you with a
heavy yoke, I will add to your yoke; my
father disciplined you with whips, but I *will
discipline you* with scorpions.' "
12 So Jeroboam and all the people came to
Rehoboam on the third day as the king had
[1]directed, saying, "Return to me on the third
day."
13 The king answered them harshly, and
King Rehoboam forsook the counsel of the
elders.
14 He spoke to them according to the
advice of the young men, saying, "[1]My
father made your yoke heavy, but I will add
to it; my father disciplined you with whips,
but I *will discipline you* with scorpions."
15 So the king did not listen to the people,
[a]for it was a turn *of events* from God [b]that

4 [a]1 Kin 5:13-16
6 [1]Lit *stood before* [a]Job 8:8, 9; 32:7
7 [a]Prov 15:1
8 [1]Lit *who stood before* [a]2 Sam 17:14; Prov 13:20
12 [1]Lit *spoken*
14 [1]Many mss read *I have made*
15 [a]2 Chr 25:16-20 [b]1 Kin 11:29-39

9:26 See 7:8 and note.
9:27 See 1:15.
9:28 The Chronicler omits the accounts of Solomon's wives and the rebellions at the end of his reign (1 Kin 11:1–40), both of which would detract from his uniformly positive portrayal of Solomon. *horses . . . Egypt.* See note on 1:16.
9:29–31 See 1 Kin 11:41–43.
10:1–36:23 The material covering the divided monarchy in Chronicles is considerably shorter than that in Kings: 27 chapters compared to 36 (1 Kin 12–2 Kin 25). Moreover, about half of this material is unique to Chronicles and shows no dependence on Kings. The most obvious reason for this is that the Chronicler has written a history of the Davidic dynasty in Judah; the history of the northern kingdom is passed over in silence except where it impinges on that of Judah. At least two considerations prompt this treatment of the divided kingdom: 1. The Chronicler is concerned to trace God's faithfulness to His promise to give David an unbroken line of descent on the throne of Israel. 2. At the time of the Chronicler the restored community was confined to the returnees of the kingdom of Judah, who were actually the remnant of all Israel (see Introduction to 1 Chronicles: Purpose and Themes).
10:1–19 See 1 Kin 12:1–20 and notes. Somewhat in line with his idealization of Solomon, the Chronicler places most of the blame for the schism on the rebellious Jeroboam (cf. 13:6–7).
10:1 *Rehoboam.* Reigned 930–913 B.C.
10:2 *Jeroboam.* His second mention in Chronicles (see 9:29). The Chronicler assumes the reader's familiarity with 1 Kin 11:26–40.

the LORD might establish His word, which He
spoke through Ahijah the Shilonite to Jeroboam the son of Nebat.
16 When all Israel *saw* that the king did
not listen to them the people answered the
king, saying,
"[a]What portion do we have in David?
We have no inheritance in the son of
Jesse.
Every man to your tents, O Israel;
Now look after your own house,
David."
[b]So all Israel departed to their tents.
17 But as for the sons of Israel who lived
in the cities of Judah, Rehoboam reigned
over them.
18 Then King Rehoboam sent Hadoram,
who was [a]over the forced labor, and the sons
of Israel stoned him [1]to death. And King
Rehoboam made haste to mount his chariot
to flee to Jerusalem.
19 So [a]Israel has been in rebellion against
the house of David to this day.

Rehoboam Reigns over Judah and Builds Cities

11 [a]Now when Rehoboam had come to
Jerusalem, he assembled the house of
Judah and Benjamin, 180,000 chosen men
who were warriors, to fight against Israel to
restore the kingdom to Rehoboam.
2 But the word of the LORD came to [a]She-
maiah the man of God, saying,
3 "Speak to Rehoboam the son of Solomon, king of Judah, and to all Israel in Judah
and Benjamin, saying,
4 'Thus says the LORD, "You shall not go
up or fight against [a]your [1]relatives; return
every man to his house, [b]for this thing is
from Me."'" So they listened to the words
of the LORD and returned from going against
Jeroboam.
5 Rehoboam lived in Jerusalem and
[a]built cities for defense in Judah.
6 Thus he built Bethlehem, Etam, Tekoa,
7 Beth-zur, Soco, Adullam,
8 Gath, Mareshah, Ziph,
9 Adoraim, Lachish, Azekah,
10 Zorah, Aijalon and Hebron, which are
fortified cities in Judah and in Benjamin.
11 He also strengthened the fortresses and
put officers in them and stores of food, oil
and wine.
12 *He put* shields and spears in every city
and strengthened them greatly. So he held
Judah and Benjamin.
13 Moreover, the priests and the Levites
who were in all Israel stood with him from
all their districts.

Jeroboam Appoints False Priests

14 For [a]the Levites left their pasture lands
and their property and came to Judah and
Jerusalem, for [b]Jeroboam and his sons had
excluded them from serving as priests to the
LORD.
15 [a]He set up priests of his own for the
high places, for the satyrs and for the calves
which he had made.
16 [a]Those from all the tribes of Israel who
set their hearts on seeking the LORD God of
Israel [1]followed them to Jerusalem, to sacrifice to the LORD God of their fathers.
17 [a]They strengthened the kingdom of
Judah and supported Rehoboam the son of
Solomon for three years, for they walked in
the way of David and Solomon for three
years.

Rehoboam's Family

18 Then Rehoboam took as a wife Mahalath the daughter of Jerimoth the son of
David *and of* Abihail the daughter of [a]Eliab
the son of Jesse,
19 and she bore him sons: Jeush, Shemariah and Zaham.
20 After her he took [a]Maacah the daugh-

16 [a]2 Sam 20:1 [b]2 Chr 10:19
18 [1]Lit *with stones that he died* [a]1 Kin 4:6; 5:14
19 [a]1 Kin 12:19
11:1 [a]1 Kin 12:21-24
2 [a]2 Chr 12:5-7, 15
4 [1]Lit *brothers* [a]2 Chr 28:8-11 [b]2 Chr 10:15
5 [a]2 Chr 8:2-6; 11:23

14 [a]Num 35:2-5 [b]1 Kin 12:28-33; 2 Chr 13:9
15 [a]1 Kin 12:31; 13:33
16 [1]Lit *came after* [a]2 Chr 15:9
17 [a]2 Chr 12:1
18 [a]1 Sam 16:6
20 [a]1 Kin 15:2; 2 Chr 13:2

10:15 *Ahijah.* The Chronicler assumes the reader's familiarity with 1 Kin 11:29–33.
10:18 *Hadoram . . . over the forced labor.* Had held the same office under Solomon (see 1 Kin 4:6; 5:14, where he is called Adoniram).
10:19 *to this day.* See note on 5:9.
11:1–23 Verses 1–4 are parallel to 1 Kin 12:21–24; vv. 5–23 are largely unique to Chronicles. The Chronicler's account of Rehoboam is a good example of his emphasis on immediate retribution (see Introduction to 1 Chronicles: Purpose and Themes). Ch. 11 traces the rewards for obedience to the command of God (vv. 1–4): Rehoboam enjoys prosperity and power (vv. 5–12), popular support (vv. 13–17) and progeny (vv. 18–23). Ch. 12 demonstrates the reverse: Disobedience brings judgment.
11:2 *Shemaiah.* The function of the prophets as guardians of the theocracy (God's kingdom) is prominent in Chronicles; most of Judah's kings are portrayed as receiving advice from prophets (see Introduction to 1 Chronicles: Purpose and Themes).
11:3 *all Israel in Judah and Benjamin.* A variation from the wording found in 1 Kin 12:23, in accordance with the Chronicler's interest in "all Israel."
11:4 *from Me.* See 10:15.
11:5–10 This list of cities is not found in Kings. Rehoboam fortified his eastern, western and southern borders, but not the north, perhaps demonstrating his hope of reunification of the kingdoms, as well as the threat of invasion from Egypt.
11:13–17 The Chronicler assumes the reader's familiarity with 1 Kin 12:26–33. This material is unique to Chronicles and reflects the author's concern both with the temple and its personnel and with showing that the kingdom of Judah was the remnant of all Israel.
11:14 *pasture lands and their property.* See 1 Chr 6:54–80; Lev 25:32–34; Num 35:1–5; see also Introduction to 1 Chronicles: Purpose and Themes.
11:15 *satyrs and . . . calves.* The account in Kings mentions only the golden calves (for the worship of goat idols or satyrs see Lev 17:7).
11:17 *way of David and Solomon.* Characteristic of the Chronicler's idealization of Solomon; contrast the portrait of Solomon in 1 Kin 11:1–13. *three years.* See note on 12:2.
11:18–22 The report on the size of Rehoboam's family is placed here as part of the Chronicler's effort to show God's blessing on his obedience (see note on 11:1–23). The material is not in chronological sequence with the surrounding context

ter of [1]Absalom, and she bore him Abijah,
Attai, Ziza and Shelomith.
21 Rehoboam loved Maacah the daughter
of Absalom more than all his *other* wives and
concubines. For [a]he had taken eighteen
wives and sixty concubines and fathered
twenty-eight sons and sixty daughters.
22 [a]Rehoboam appointed Abijah the son
of Maacah as head and leader among his
brothers, for he *intended* to make him king.
23 He acted wisely and distributed [1]some
of his sons through all the territories of
Judah and Benjamin to all the fortified cities,
and he gave them food in abundance. And
he sought many wives *for them*.

Shishak of Egypt Invades Judah

12 [a]When the kingdom of Rehoboam was
established and strong, [b]he and all Israel with him forsook the law of the LORD.
2 [a]And it came about in King Rehoboam's fifth year, because they had been
unfaithful to the LORD, that [b]Shishak king of
Egypt came up against Jerusalem
3 with 1,200 chariots and 60,000 horsemen. And the people who came with him
from Egypt were without number: [a]the
Lubim, the Sukkiim and the Ethiopians.
4 He captured [a]the fortified cities of
Judah and came as far as Jerusalem.
5 Then [a]Shemaiah the prophet came to
Rehoboam and the princes of Judah who
had gathered at Jerusalem because of Shishak, and he said to them, "Thus says the
LORD, '[b]You have forsaken Me, so I also have
forsaken you [1]to Shishak.' "
6 So the princes of Israel and the king
humbled themselves and said, "The [a]LORD is
righteous."
7 When the LORD saw that they humbled
themselves, the word of the LORD came to
Shemaiah, saying, "[a]They have humbled
themselves *so* I will not destroy them, but I
will grant them some *measure* of deliverance, and [b]My wrath shall not be poured out
on Jerusalem by means of Shishak.
8 "But they will become his slaves so
[a]that they may learn *the difference between*
My service and the service of the kingdoms
of the countries."

Plunder Impoverishes Judah

9 [a]So Shishak king of Egypt came up
against Jerusalem, and took the treasures of
the house of the LORD and the treasures of
the king's palace. He took everything; [b]he
even took the golden shields which Solomon
had made.
10 Then King Rehoboam made shields of
bronze in their place and committed them to
the [1]care of the commanders of the [2]guard
who guarded the door of the king's house.
11 As often as the king entered the house
of the LORD, the [1]guards came and carried
them and *then* brought them back into the
[1]guards' room.
12 And [a]when he humbled himself, the
anger of the LORD turned away from him, so
as not to destroy *him* completely; and also
conditions [b]were good in Judah.
13 [a]So King Rehoboam strengthened himself in Jerusalem and reigned. Now Rehoboam was forty-one years old when he began
to reign, and he reigned seventeen years in
Jerusalem, the city which the LORD had chosen from all the tribes of Israel, to put His
name there. And his mother's name was
Naamah the Ammonitess.
14 He did evil [a]because he did not set his
heart to seek the LORD.
15 [a]Now the acts of Rehoboam, from first
to last, are they not written in the [1]records of
[b]Shemaiah the prophet and of [c]Iddo the seer,
according to genealogical enrollment? And

20 [1]In 1 Kin 15:2, *Abishalom* **21** [a]Deut 17:17 **22** [a]Deut 21:15-17 **23** [1]Lit *from all* **12:1** [a]2 Chr 11:17; 12:13 [b]2 Chr 26:13-16 **2** [a]1 Kin 14:25 [b]1 Kin 11:40 **3** [a]2 Chr 16:8; Nah 3:9 **4** [a]2 Chr 11:5-12 **5** [1]Lit *in the hand of* [a]2 Chr 11:2 [b]Deut 28:15; 2 Chr 15:2 **6** [a]Ex 9:27; Dan 9:14 **7** [a]1 Kin 21:29 **7** [b]2 Chr 34:25-27; Ps 78:38 **8** [a]Deut 28:47, 48 **9** [a]1 Kin 14:26-28 [b]1 Kin 10:16, 17; 2 Chr 9:15, 16 **10** [1]Lit *hands* [2]Lit *runners* **11** [1]Lit *runners* **12** [a]2 Chr 12:6, 7 [b]2 Chr 19:3 **13** [a]1 Kin 14:21 **14** [a]2 Chr 19:3 **15** [1]Lit *words* [a]1 Kin 14:29 [b]2 Chr 12:5 [c]2 Chr 9:29

but summarizes events throughout his reign. The Chronicler uses numerous progeny as a sign of divine blessing (see 13:21; see also notes on 21:2; 1 Chr 25:5).

11:20 *Maacah the daughter of Absalom.* See note on 1 Kin 15:2. She was likely the granddaughter of Absalom, through his daughter Tamar (2 Sam 14:27; 18:18), who was married to Uriel (2 Chr 13:2).

11:21–22 These verses explain why the eldest son was not appointed Rehoboam's successor.

11:23 *distributed some of his sons.* Rehoboam may have sought to secure the succession of Abijah by assigning other sons to outlying posts, perhaps to avoid the difficulties faced by David, whose sons at court (Adonijah and Absalom) had attempted to seize power.

12:1–14 See note on 11:1–23. Whereas obedience to the prophetic word (11:1–4) had brought blessing (11:5–23), now the prophet comes to announce judgment for disobedience (see 1 Kin 14:25–28). While the writer of Kings also reports the attack of Shishak, the Chronicler alone adds the rationale that the invasion was because of forsaking the commands of God (vv. 1–2,5).

12:1 *all Israel.* Used in a variety of ways in 2 Chronicles: (1) of both kingdoms (9:30), (2) of the northern kingdom (10:16; 11:13) or (3) of the southern kingdom alone (as here; 11:3). *forsook.* The opposite of seeking the LORD (v. 14); see v. 5; see also note on 24:18,20,24.

12:2 *fifth year.* 925 B.C. The Chronicler often introduces chronological notes not found in Kings (e.g., 11:17; 15:10,19; 16:1, 12–13; 17:7; 21:20; 24:15,17,23; 26:16; 27:5,8; 29:3; 34:3; 36:21). These become a vehicle for his emphasis on immediate retribution by dividing the reigns of individual kings into cycles of obedience-blessing and disobedience-punishment. This sequence is clear for Rehoboam: Three years of obedience and blessing (11:17) are followed by rebellion, presumably in the fourth year (12:1), and punishment in the fifth (here). *Shishak.* Founder of the 22nd dynasty of Egypt, he ruled c. 945–924 B.C. The Bible mentions this invasion only as it affected Jerusalem, but Shishak's own inscription on the wall of the temple of Amun at Karnak (Thebes) indicates that his armies also swept as far north as the plain of Jezreel and Megiddo.

12:3 *Sukkiim.* Probably a group of mercenary soldiers of Libyan origin who are known from Egyptian texts.

12:5 See notes on vv. 1–14; v. 1.

12:6–7 See v. 12. The Chronicler has in mind God's promise in 7:14.

12:13 *seventeen years.* See note on 10:1.

12:15–16 See 1 Kin 14:29–31.

there were wars between Rehoboam and Jeroboam continually.

16 And Rehoboam slept with his fathers and was buried in the city of David; and his son [a]Abijah became king in his place.

Abijah Succeeds Rehoboam

13 [a]In the eighteenth year of King Jeroboam, Abijah became king over Judah.

2 He reigned three years in Jerusalem; and his mother's name was Micaiah the daughter of Uriel of Gibeah.

[a]Now there was war between Abijah and Jeroboam.

3 Abijah began the battle with an army of valiant warriors, 400,000 chosen men, while Jeroboam drew up in battle formation against him with 800,000 chosen men *who were* valiant warriors.

Civil War

4 Then Abijah stood on Mount [a]Zemaraim, which is in the hill country of Ephraim, and said, "Listen to me, Jeroboam and all Israel:

5 "Do you not know that [a]the LORD God of Israel gave the rule over Israel forever to David [1]and his sons by [b]a covenant of salt?

6 "Yet [a]Jeroboam the son of Nebat, the servant of Solomon the son of David, rose up and rebelled against his [1]master,

7 and worthless men gathered about him, scoundrels, who proved too strong for Rehoboam, the son of Solomon, when [1a]he was young and timid and could not hold his own against them.

8 "So now you intend to resist the kingdom of the LORD [1]through the sons of David, [2]being a great multitude and *having* with you [a]the golden calves which Jeroboam made for gods for you.

9 "[a]Have you not driven out the priests of the LORD, the sons of Aaron and the Levites, and made for yourselves priests like the peoples of *other* lands? Whoever comes [b]to consecrate himself with a young bull and seven rams, even he may become a priest of *what are* [c]no gods.

10 "But as for us, the LORD is our God, and we have not forsaken Him; and the sons of Aaron are ministering to the LORD as priests, and the Levites [1]attend to their work.

11 "Every morning and evening [a]they [1]burn to the LORD burnt offerings and fragrant incense, and [b]the showbread is *set* on the clean table, and the golden lampstand with its lamps is *ready* to light every evening; for we keep the charge of the LORD our God, but you have forsaken Him.

12 "Now behold, God is with us at *our* head and [a]His priests with the signal trumpets to sound the alarm against you. O sons of Israel, do not fight against the LORD God of your fathers, for you will not succeed."

13 But Jeroboam [a]had set an ambush to come from the rear, so that *Israel* was in front of Judah and the ambush was behind them.

14 When Judah turned around, behold, [1]they were attacked both front and rear; so [a]they cried to the LORD, and the priests blew the trumpets.

15 Then the men of Judah raised a war cry, and when the men of Judah raised the war cry, then it was that God [1a]routed Jeroboam and all Israel before Abijah and Judah.

16 When the sons of Israel fled before Judah, [a]God gave them into their hand.

17 Abijah and his people defeated them with a great slaughter, so that 500,000 chosen men of Israel fell slain.

18 Thus the sons of Israel were subdued at that time, and the sons of Judah [1]conquered [a]because they trusted in the LORD, the God of their fathers.

19 Abijah pursued Jeroboam and captured from him *several* cities, Bethel with its villages, Jeshanah with its villages and [1]Ephron with its villages.

Death of Jeroboam

20 Jeroboam did not again recover strength in the days of Abijah; and the [a]LORD struck him and [b]he died.

16 [a]2 Chr 11:20 **13:1** [a]1 Kin 15:1, 2 **2** [a]1 Kin 15:7 **4** [a]Josh 18:22 **5** [1]Lit *to him and to his sons* [a]2 Sam 7:12-16 [b]Lev 2:13; Num 18:19 **6** [1]Or *lord* [a]1 Kin 11:26 **7** [1]Lit *Rehoboam* [a]2 Chr 12:13 **8** [1]Lit *in the hands of* [2]Lit *and you are a* [a]1 Kin 12:28; 2 Chr 11:15 **9** [a]2 Chr 11:14, 15 [b]Ex 29:29-33 [c]Jer 2:11; 5:7 **10** [1]Lit *in the work* **11** [1]Lit *offer up in smoke* [a]Ex 29:38; 2 Chr 2:4 [b]Ex 25:30-39; Lev 24:5-9 **12** [a]Num 10:8, 9 **13** [a]Josh 8:4-9 **14** [1]Lit *the battle was before and behind them* [a]2 Chr 14:11 **15** [1]Lit *smote* [a]2 Chr 14:12 **16** [a]2 Chr 16:8 **18** [1]Lit *were strong* [a]2 Chr 14:11 **19** [1]Another reading is *Ephrain* **20** [a]1 Sam 25:38 [b]1 Kin 14:20

13:1–14:1 The Chronicler's account of Abijah's reign is about three times longer than that in 1 Kin 15:1–8, largely due to Abijah's lengthy speech (13:4–12; see note on 28:1–27). The most striking difference in the accounts of Abijah's reign in Kings and in Chronicles is the evaluation given in each: Kings offers a negative evaluation (1 Kin 15:3), for which there was no doubt warrant, while the assessment in Chronicles is positive, in view of what the Chronicler is able to report of him. The kings' reigns, like the lives of common people, were often a mixture of good and evil.

13:2 *three years.* 913–910 B.C. *Macaiah.* A variant of Maacah (see note on 11:20).

13:3 *400,000 . . . 800,000.* Surprisingly large figures but in line with those in 1 Chr 21:5 (see note there). Apparently this was all-out war.

13:4 *Mount Zemaraim.* Location uncertain. The town Zemaraim was in the territory of Benjamin (Josh 18:22); presumably the battle was along the common border of Benjamin and Israel. *all Israel.* See note on 12:1; here and in v. 15 the reference is to the northern kingdom.

13:5 See 7:17–18; 1 Chr 17:13–14. *covenant of salt.* See notes on Num 18:19; 2 Kin 2:20.

13:6 See note on 10:1–19.

13:7 Not all in the northern kingdom are rebuked, only the leadership—a subtle appeal to those in the north who had been led into rebellion. *worthless men.* See note on Deut 13:13. *young and timid.* Cf. 1 Chr 22:5; 29:1. Rehoboam was 41 years old at the time of the schism (12:13).

13:8 *kingdom of the LORD.* The house of David represents the kingdom of God (see 9:8 and note).

13:9 See 1 Kin 12:25–33. *consecrate himself.* Cf. Ex 29:1.

13:10–12 The Chronicler's concern with acceptable worship focuses on the legitimate priests and the observance of prescribed worship (cf. 1 Chr 23:28–31).

21 But Abijah became powerful; and took fourteen wives to himself, and became the father of twenty-two sons and sixteen daughters.

22 Now the rest of the acts of Abijah, and his ways and his words are written in [a]the [1]treatise of [b]the prophet Iddo.

Asa Succeeds Abijah in Judah

14 [1a]So Abijah slept with his fathers, and they buried him in the city of David, and his son Asa became king in his place. The land was undisturbed for ten years during his days.

2 [1]Asa did good and right in the sight of the LORD his God,

3 for he removed [a]the foreign altars and [b]high places, tore down the *sacred* pillars, cut down the [1c]Asherim,

4 and commanded Judah to seek the LORD God of their fathers and to observe the law and the commandment.

5 He also removed the high places and the [a]incense altars from all the cities of Judah. And the kingdom was undisturbed under him.

6 [a]He built fortified cities in Judah, since the land was undisturbed, and [1]there was no one at war with him during those years, [b]because the LORD had given him rest.

7 For he said to Judah, "[a]Let us build these cities and surround *them* with walls and towers, gates and bars. The land is still [1]ours because we have sought the LORD our God; we have sought Him, and He has given us rest on every side." So they built and prospered.

8 Now Asa had an army of [a]300,000 from Judah, bearing large shields and spears, and 280,000 from Benjamin, bearing shields and wielding bows; all of them were valiant warriors.

9 Now Zerah the Ethiopian [a]came out against them with an army of a million men and 300 chariots, and he came to [b]Mareshah.

10 So Asa went out [1]to meet him, and they drew up in battle formation in the valley of Zephathah at Mareshah.

11 Then Asa [a]called to the LORD his God and said, "LORD, there is no one besides You to help *in the battle* between the powerful and those who have no strength; so help us, O LORD our God, [b]for we trust in You, and in Your name have come against this multitude. O LORD, You are our God; let not man prevail against You."

12 So [a]the LORD [1]routed the Ethiopians before Asa and before Judah, and the Ethiopians fled.

13 Asa and the people who *were* with him pursued them as far as [a]Gerar; and so many Ethiopians fell that [1]they could not recover, for they were shattered before the LORD and before His army. And they carried away very much plunder.

14 They [1]destroyed all the cities around Gerar, [a]for the dread of the LORD had fallen on them; and they despoiled all the cities, for there was much plunder in them.

15 They also struck down [1]those who owned livestock, and they carried away large numbers of sheep and camels. Then they returned to Jerusalem.

22 [1]Heb *midrash* [a]2 Chr 24:27 [b]2 Chr 9:29
14:1 [1]Ch 13:23 in Heb [a]1 Kin 15:8
2 [1]Ch 14:1 in Heb
3 [1]I.e. wooden symbols of a female deity [a]Deut 7:5 [b]1 Kin 15:12-14 [c]Ex 34:13
5 [a]2 Chr 34:4, 7
6 [1]Lit *there was not with him war* [a]2 Chr 11:5 [b]2 Chr 15:15
7 [1]Lit *before us* [a]2 Chr 8:5
8 [a]2 Chr 13:3
9 [a]2 Chr 12:2, 3; 16:8 [b]2 Chr 11:8
10 [1]Lit *before him*
11 [a]2 Chr 13:14 [b]2 Chr 13:18
12 [1]Lit *struck* [a]2 Chr 13:15
13 [1]Or *there was none left alive* [a]Gen 10:19
14 [1]Lit *smote* [a]2 Chr 17:10
15 [1]Lit *tents of livestock*

13:21 See note on 11:18–22.

14:1 *undisturbed for ten years.* For the Chronicler peace and prosperity go hand in hand with righteous rule. This first decade of Asa's reign (910–900 B.C.) preceded the invasion by Zerah (14:9–15) and was followed by 20 more years of peace, from the 15th (15:10) to the 35th years (15:19). Contrast this account with the statement that there was war between Asa and Baasha throughout their reigns (see 1 Kin 15:16 and note). The tensions between the two kingdoms may have accounted for Asa's fortifications (14:7–8), though actual combat was likely confined to raids until the major campaign was launched in Asa's 36th year (16:1). See 15:8 and note.

14:2–16:14 The account of Asa's reign (910–869 B.C.) here is greatly expanded over the one in 1 Kin 15:9–24. The expansions characteristically express the Chronicler's view concerning the relationship between obedience and blessing, disobedience and punishment. The author introduces chronological notes into his account to divide Asa's reign into these periods (see note on 12:2): For ten years Asa did what was right and prospered (14:1–7), and an invasion by a powerful Cushite (Ethiopian) force was repulsed because he called on the Lord (14:8–15). There followed further reforms (15:1–9) and a covenant renewal in Asa's 15th year (15:10–18), and so he enjoyed peace until his 35th year (15:19). But then came a change: When confronted by an invasion from the northern kingdom in his 36th year (16:1), he hired Aramean reinforcements rather than trusting in the Lord (16:2–6), and imprisoned the prophet who rebuked him (16:7–10). In his 39th year he was afflicted with a disease (16:12), but still steadfastly refused to seek the Lord. In his 41st year he died (16:13).

14:3 *sacred pillars.* See note on 1 Kin 14:23. *Asherim.* Wooden symbols of the goddess Asherah (here and throughout 2 Chronicles).

14:5 *removed the high places.* 1 Kin 15:14 states that Asa did not remove the high places. This difficulty is best resolved by the Chronicler's own statement in 15:17, which is properly parallel to 1 Kin 15:14: Early in his reign Asa did attempt to remove the high places, but pagan worship was extremely resilient, and ultimately his efforts were unsuccessful (15:17). Statements that the high places both were and were not removed are also found in the reign of Jehoshaphat (17:6; 20:33). Cf. Deut 12:2–3.

14:7 *rest on every side.* See note on 20:30.

14:9 *Zerah the Ethiopian.* Lit. "Zerah the Cushite." Many identify him with Pharaoh Osorkon I, second pharaoh of the 22nd Egyptian dynasty. However, since he is not called "king" or "pharaoh," and is known as the "Cushite" or "Nubian," some prefer to identify him as an otherwise unknown general serving the pharaoh. The invasion appears to have been an attempt to duplicate the attack of Shishak 30 years earlier (12:1–12), but the results against Asa were quite different.

14:10 *valley of Zephathah.* Marked the entrance to a road leading to the hills of Judah and Jerusalem. *Mareshah.* Earlier fortified by Rehoboam (11:8) to protect the route mentioned here.

14:13 *Gerar.* See note on Gen 20:1. *plunder.* Much of this booty (v. 14) made its way to the storehouses of the temple (15:18; see note on 1 Chr 18:1–20:8).

14:14 *dread of the LORD.* See note on 1 Chr 14:17.

The Prophet Azariah Warns Asa

15 Now [a]the Spirit of God came on Azariah the son of Oded,

2 and he went out [1]to meet Asa and said to him, "Listen to me, Asa, and all Judah and Benjamin: [a]the LORD is with you when you are with Him. And [b]if you seek Him, He will let you find Him; but if you forsake Him, He will forsake you.

3 "[a]For many days Israel was without the true God and without [b]a teaching priest and without law.

4 "But [a]in their distress they turned to the LORD God of Israel, and they sought Him, and He let them find Him.

5 "[a]In those times there was no peace to him who went out or to him who came in, for many disturbances [1]afflicted all the inhabitants of the lands.

6 "[a]Nation was crushed by nation, and city by city, for God troubled them with every kind of distress.

7 "But you, [a]be strong and do not [1]lose courage, for there is [b]reward for your work."

Asa's Reforms

8 Now when Asa heard these words and the [1]prophecy which Azariah the son of Oded the prophet spoke, he took courage and removed the abominable idols from all the land of Judah and Benjamin and from [a]the cities which he had captured in the hill country of Ephraim. [b]He then restored the altar of the LORD which was in front of the porch of the LORD.

9 He gathered all Judah and Benjamin and those from Ephraim, Manasseh and Simeon [a]who resided with them, for many defected to him from Israel when they saw that the LORD his God was with him.

10 So they assembled at Jerusalem in the third month of the fifteenth year of Asa's reign.

11 [a]They sacrificed to the LORD that day 700 oxen and 7,000 sheep from the spoil they had brought.

12 [a]They entered into the covenant to seek the LORD God of their fathers with all their heart and soul;

13 and whoever would not seek the LORD God of Israel [a]should be put to death, whether small or great, man or woman.

14 Moreover, they made an oath to the LORD with a loud voice, with shouting, with trumpets and with horns.

15 All Judah rejoiced concerning the oath, for they had sworn with their whole heart and had sought Him [1]earnestly, and He let them find Him. So [a]the LORD gave them rest on every side.

16 [a]He also removed Maacah, the mother of King Asa, from the *position of* queen mother, because she had made a horrid image [1]as [b]an Asherah, and [c]Asa cut down her horrid image, crushed *it* and burned *it* at the brook Kidron.

17 But the high places were not removed from Israel; nevertheless Asa's heart was blameless all his days.

18 He brought into the house of God the dedicated things of his father and his own dedicated things: silver and gold and utensils.

19 And there was no more war until the thirty-fifth year of Asa's reign.

Asa Wars against Baasha

16 In the thirty-sixth year of Asa's reign [a]Baasha king of Israel came up against Judah and [1]fortified Ramah in order to prevent *anyone* from going out or coming in to Asa king of Judah.

2 Then Asa brought out silver and gold

15:1 [a]2 Chr 20:14; 24:20
2 [1]Lit *before Asa* [a]2 Chr 20:17 [b]2 Chr 15:4, 15
3 [a]1 Kin 12:28-33 [b]Lev 10:8-11; 2 Chr 17:9
4 [a]Deut 4:29
5 [1]Lit *were on* [a]Judg 5:6
6 [a]Matt 24:7
7 [1]Lit *let your hands drop* [a]Josh 1:7, 9 [b]Ps 58:11
8 [1]With several ancient versions; Heb *the prophecy, Oded the prophet* [a]2 Chr 13:19 [b]2 Chr 4:1; 8:12
9 [a]2 Chr 11:16
11 [a]2 Chr 14:13-15
12 [a]2 Chr 23:16
13 [a]Ex 22:20; Deut 13:6-9
15 [1]Lit *with their whole desire* [a]2 Chr 14:7
16 [1]Or for *Asherah* [a]1 Kin 15:13-15 [b]Ex 34:13 [c]2 Chr 14:2-5
16:1 [1]Lit *built* [a]1 Kin 15:17-22

15:1–19 This chapter appears to recount a second stage in the reforms introduced by Asa, beginning with the victory over Zerah and encouraged by the preaching of Azariah (v. 1).
15:3 *teaching priest.* The duties of the priests were not only to officiate at the altar, but also to teach the law (see 17:7–9; Lev 10:11).
15:8 *cities which he had captured in . . . Ephraim.* A tacit admission that there had been some fighting between Baasha and Asa prior to Asa's 36th year (16:1); see 17:1.
15:9 *many defected to him.* Cf. the defection from the northern kingdom that also occurred under Rehoboam (11:13–17).
15:10 *third month of the fifteenth year.* Spring, 895 B.C., the year after Zerah's invasion (v. 19). The Feast of Weeks (or Pentecost) was held in the third month (Lev 23:15–21) and may have been the occasion for this assembly.
15:12 *covenant.* A renewal of the covenant made at Sinai, similar to the covenant renewals on the plain of Moab (Deut 29:1), at Mount Ebal (Josh 8:30–35), at Shechem (Josh 24:25) and at Gilgal (1 Sam 11:14; see note there). Later the priest Jehoiada (23:16), as well as Hezekiah (29:10) and Josiah (34:31), would also lead in renewals of the covenant—events of primary significance in the view of the Chronicler.
15:13 *would not seek the LORD.* Would turn to other gods. *should be put to death.* In accordance with basic covenant law (Ex 22:20; Deut 13:6–9).
15:15 *rest.* See note on 20:30.
15:16 *Asherah.* See note on 14:3.
15:17 *high places were not removed.* See 14:5 and note.
16:1 *thirty-sixth year of Asa's reign Baasha.* According to Kings, Baasha ruled for 24 years and was succeeded by Elah in the 26th year of Asa (1 Kin 15:33; 16:8). Obviously Baasha could not have been alive in the 36th year of Asa, where this passage places him—he had been dead for a decade. In order to solve this difficulty, some suggest that the Chronicler here and in 15:19 is dating from the schism in Israel rather than from the year number of Asa's reign: Since Rehoboam had reigned 17 years and Abijah 3, 20 years are deducted with the result that the 35th and 36th years of Asa are in fact the 15th and 16th years of his reign. This would make Baasha's attack come as a possible response to the defections from the northern kingdom (15:9). While this solution may be possible, it has not met with general acceptance. The action described here is not dated in 1 Kin 15:17. Perhaps the dates here and in 15:19 are the result of a copyist's error (possibly for an original 25th and 26th).
16:2–9 Hiring foreign troops brought Asa into a foreign alliance, which showed lack of trust in the Lord. Other examples

from the treasuries of the house of the LORD and the king's house, and sent them to Ben-hadad king of Aram, who lived in Damascus, saying,

3 "*Let there be* a treaty between [1]you and me, *as* between my father and your father. Behold, I have sent you silver and gold; go, break your treaty with Baasha king of Israel so that he will withdraw from me."

4 So Ben-hadad listened to King Asa and sent the commanders of his armies against the cities of Israel, and they [1]conquered Ijon, Dan, Abel-maim and all [a]the [2]store cities of Naphtali.

5 When Baasha heard *of it,* he ceased [1]fortifying Ramah and stopped his work.

6 Then King Asa brought all Judah, and they carried away the stones of Ramah and its timber with which Baasha had been building, and with them he [1]fortified Geba and Mizpah.

Asa Imprisons the Prophet

7 At that time [a]Hanani the seer came to Asa king of Judah and said to him, "[b]Because you have relied on the king of Aram and have not relied on the LORD your God, therefore the army of the king of Aram has escaped out of your hand.

8 "Were not [a]the Ethiopians and the Lubim [b]an immense army with very many chariots and horsemen? Yet [c]because you relied on the LORD, He delivered them into your hand.

9 "For [a]the eyes of the LORD move to and fro throughout the earth that He may strongly support those [b]whose heart is completely His. You have acted foolishly in this. Indeed, from now on you will surely have wars."

10 Then Asa was angry with the seer and put him in [1]prison, for he was enraged at him for this. And Asa oppressed some of the people at the same time.

11 [a]Now, the acts of Asa from first to last, behold, they are written in the Book of the Kings of Judah and Israel.

12 In the thirty-ninth year of his reign Asa became diseased in his feet. His disease was severe, yet even in his disease he [a]did not seek the LORD, but the physicians.

13 So Asa slept with his fathers, [1]having died in the forty-first year of his reign.

14 They buried him in his own tomb which he had cut out for himself in the city of David, and they laid him in the resting place which he had filled [a]with spices of various kinds blended by the perfumers' art; and [b]they made a very great fire for him.

Jehoshaphat Succeeds Asa

17 [a]Jehoshaphat his son then became king in his place, and made his position over Israel firm.

2 He placed troops in all [a]the fortified cities of Judah, and set garrisons in the land of Judah and in the cities of Ephraim [b]which Asa his father had captured.

His Good Reign

3 The LORD was with Jehoshaphat because he [1]followed the example of his father David's earlier days and did not seek the Baals,

4 but sought the God of his father, [1]followed His commandments, [a]and did not act as Israel did.

5 So the LORD established the kingdom in his [1]control, and all Judah brought tribute to Jehoshaphat, and [a]he had great riches and honor.

6 [1]He took great pride in the ways of the LORD and again [a]removed the high places and the Asherim from Judah.

7 Then in the third year of his reign he sent his officials, Ben-hail, Obadiah, Zechariah, Nethanel and Micaiah, [a]to teach in the cities of Judah;

8 and with them [a]the Levites, Shemaiah, Nethaniah, Zebadiah, Asahel, Shemiramoth, Jehonathan, Adonijah, Tobijah and Tobadonijah, the Levites; and with them Elishama and Jehoram, the priests.

9 They taught in Judah, *having* [a]the book of the law of the LORD with them; and they went throughout all the cities of Judah and taught among the people.

3 [1]Lit *me and you*
4 [1]Lit *smote* [2]Lit *storage places of the cities* [a]Ex 1:11
5 [1]Lit *building*
6 [1]Lit *built*
7 [a]1 Kin 16:1; 2 Chr 19:2 [b]2 Chr 14:11; 32:7, 8
8 [a]2 Chr 14:9 [b]2 Chr 12:3 [c]2 Chr 13:16, 18
9 [a]Prov 15:3; Jer 16:17; Zech 4:10 [b]2 Chr 15:17
10 [1]Lit *the house of the stocks*
11 [a]1 Kin 15:23, 24
12 [a]Jer 17:5
13 [1]Lit *and*
14 [a]Gen 50:2; John 19:39, 40 [b]2 Chr 21:19
17:1 [a]1 Kin 15:24
2 [a]2 Chr 11:5 [b]2 Chr 15:8
3 [1]Lit *walked in the earlier ways of his father*
4 [1]Lit *walked in* [a]1 Kin 12:28
5 [1]Lit *hand* [a]2 Chr 18:1
6 [1]Lit *his heart was high* [a]2 Chr 15:17
7 [a]2 Chr 15:3; 35:3
8 [a]2 Chr 19:8
9 [a]Deut 6:4-9

---

of condemned foreign alliances are found in the reigns of Jehoshaphat (20:35–37), Ahaziah (22:1–9) and Ahaz (28:16–21). By hiring Ben-hadad to the north, Asa opened a two-front war for Baasha and forced his withdrawal.

16:12 *diseased in his feet.* For other examples of disease as punishment for sin see 21:16–20; 26:16–23; Acts 12:23. Cf. 2 Kin 15:5.

17:1–21:3 The Chronicler's account of Jehoshaphat's reign is more than twice as long as that in Kings, where the interest in Ahab and Elijah overshadows the space allotted to Jehoshaphat (1 Kin 22:1–46). The Chronicler has also used Jehoshaphat's reign to emphasize immediate retribution. This theme is specifically announced in 19:10 and is illustrated in the blessing of Jehoshaphat's obedient faith and in the reproof for his wrongdoing (19:2–3; 20:35–37). Jehoshaphat reigned 872–848 B.C., from 872 to 869 likely as co-regent with his father Asa (see 20:31 and note). The details of his reign may not be in chronological order; the teaching mission of 17:7–9 may have been part of the reforms noted in 19:4–11.

17:2 *cities of Judah . . . cities of Ephraim.* See note on 15:8. Abijah (13:19), Asa (15:8) and now Jehoshaphat had managed to hold these cities; they would be lost under Amaziah (25:17–24).

17:6 *removed the high places.* Just as his father Asa had attempted to remove the high places, only to have them be restored (14:5; 15:17), so also Jehoshaphat removed them initially, only to have them revive and persist (20:33; cf. 1 Kin 22:43). But see notes on 1 Kin 3:2; 15:14. *Asherim.* See note on 14:3.

17:7–9 This incident may be part of the reform more fully detailed in 19:4–11. In the theocracy, the law of the Lord was supposed to be an integral part of the law of the land; the king and his officials, as well as the priests and prophets, were representatives of the Lord's kingship over His people.

17:7 *third year.* Perhaps the first year of his sole reign after a co-regency of three years with his father Asa (see 20:31 and note).

10 Now [a]the dread of the LORD was on all the kingdoms of the lands which *were* around Judah, so that they did not make war against Jehoshaphat.

11 Some of the Philistines [a]brought gifts and silver as tribute to Jehoshaphat; the Arabians also brought him flocks, 7,700 rams and 7,700 male goats.

12 So Jehoshaphat grew greater and greater, and he built fortresses and store cities in Judah.

13 He had large supplies in the cities of Judah, and warriors, valiant men, in Jerusalem.

14 This was their muster according to their fathers' households: of Judah, commanders of thousands, Adnah *was* the commander, and with him 300,000 valiant warriors;

15 and next to him *was* Johanan the commander, and with him 280,000;

16 and next to him Amasiah the son of Zichri, [a]who volunteered for the LORD, and with him 200,000 valiant warriors;

17 and of Benjamin, Eliada a valiant warrior, and with him 200,000 armed with bow and shield;

18 and next to him Jehozabad, and with him 180,000 equipped for war.

19 These are they who served the king, apart from [a]those whom the king put in the fortified cities through all Judah.

Jehoshaphat Allies with Ahab

18 Now [a]Jehoshaphat had great riches and honor; and he allied himself by marriage with Ahab.

2 [a]Some years later he went down to *visit* Ahab at Samaria. And Ahab slaughtered many sheep and oxen for him and the people who were with him, and induced him to go up against Ramoth-gilead.

3 Ahab king of Israel said to Jehoshaphat king of Judah, "Will you go with me *against* Ramoth-gilead?" And he said to him, "I am as you are, and my people as your people, and *we will be* with you in the battle."

4 Moreover, Jehoshaphat said to the king of Israel, "Please inquire [1]first for the word of the LORD."

5 Then the king of Israel assembled the prophets, four hundred men, and said to them, "Shall we go against Ramoth-gilead to battle, or shall I refrain?" And they said, "Go up, for God will give *it* into the hand of the king."

6 But Jehoshaphat said, "Is there not yet a prophet of the LORD here that we may inquire of him?"

7 The king of Israel said to Jehoshaphat, "There is yet one man by whom we may inquire of the LORD, but I hate him, for he never prophesies good concerning me but always evil. He is Micaiah, son of Imla." But Jehoshaphat said, "Let not the king say so."

Ahab's False Prophets Assure Victory

8 Then the king of Israel called an officer and said, "[1]Bring quickly Micaiah, Imla's son."

9 Now the king of Israel and Jehoshaphat the king of Judah were sitting each on his throne, arrayed in *their* robes, and *they* were sitting [a]at the threshing floor at the entrance of the gate of Samaria; and all the prophets were prophesying before them.

10 Zedekiah the son of Chenaanah made horns of iron for himself and said, "Thus says the LORD, 'With these you shall gore the Arameans until they are consumed.' "

11 All the prophets were prophesying thus, saying, "Go up to Ramoth-gilead and succeed, for the LORD will give *it* into the hand of the king."

Micaiah Brings Word from God

12 Then the messenger who went to summon Micaiah spoke to him saying, "Behold, the words of the prophets are uniformly favorable to the king. So please let your word be like one of them and speak favorably."

13 But Micaiah said, "As the LORD lives, [a]what my God says, that I will speak."

14 When he came to the king, the king said to him, "Micaiah, shall we go to Ramoth-gilead to battle, or shall I refrain?" He said, "Go up and succeed, for they will be given into your hand."

15 Then the king said to him, "How many times must I adjure you to speak to me nothing but the truth in the name of the LORD?"

16 So he said,
"I saw all Israel

10 [a]2 Chr 14:14
11 [a]2 Chr 9:14; 26:8
16 [a]Judg 5:2, 9; 1 Chr 29:9
19 [a]2 Chr 17:2
18:1 [a]2 Chr 17:5
2 [a]1 Kin 22:2-35
4 [1]Lit *as the day*
8 [1]Lit *Hasten*
9 [a]Ruth 4:1
13 [a]Num 22:18-20, 35

17:10–11 See note on 1 Chr 18:1–20:8.
17:10 *dread of the LORD.* See note on 1 Chr 14:17.
17:14–18 *300,000 . . . 280,000 . . . 200,000 . . . 200,000 . . . 180,000.* Or "300 units . . . 280 units . . . 200 units . . . 200 units . . . 180 units" (see notes on 1 Chr 12:23–37; 27:1).
18:1–19:3 See 1 Kin 22:1–40 and notes. To conform with his interest in the southern kingdom and Jehoshaphat, the Chronicler omits elaboration on the death of Ahab and his succession (1 Kin 22:36–40) and adds the material on the prophetic condemnation of Jehoshaphat's involvement (19:1–3).
18:1 Not found in 1 Kin 22. The verse enhances the status of Jehoshaphat by mentioning the blessing of wealth for his fidelity, and also sets the stage for an entangling foreign alliance condemned by the prophet in 19:2–3. *allied himself by marriage with Ahab.* This marriage alliance to Athaliah, daughter of Ahab, resulted later in an attempt to exterminate the Davidic line (22:10–23:21).
18:2 The Chronicler further enhances the status of Jehoshaphat by noting the large number of animals Ahab slaughtered in his honor, a note not found in 1 Kin 22. *induced him.* Also not found in the parallel text. The Hebrew for this verb is often used in the sense of inciting to evil (e.g., 1 Chr 21:1) and may express the Chronicler's attitude toward Jehoshaphat's involvement.
18:4 *inquire first for the word of the LORD.* This request fits the Chronicler's overall positive portrait of Jehoshaphat.

Scattered on the mountains,
[a]Like sheep which have no shepherd;
And the LORD said,
'These have no master.
Let each of them return to his house
in peace.' "
17 Then the king of Israel said to Jehoshaphat, "Did I not tell you that he would not
prophesy good concerning me, but evil?"
18 Micaiah said, "Therefore, hear the
word of the LORD. [a]I saw the LORD sitting on
His throne, and all the host of heaven standing on His right and on His left.
19 "The LORD said, 'Who will entice Ahab
king of Israel to go up and fall at Ramoth-gilead?' And one said this while another said
that.
20 "Then a [a]spirit came forward and stood
before the LORD and said, 'I will entice him.'
And the LORD said to him, 'How?'
21 "He said, 'I will go and be [a]a deceiving
spirit in the mouth of all his prophets.' Then
He said, 'You are to entice *him* and prevail
also. Go and do so.'
22 "Now therefore, behold, [a]the LORD has
put a deceiving spirit in the mouth of these
your prophets, for the LORD has proclaimed
disaster against you."
23 Then Zedekiah the son of Chenaanah
came near and [a]struck Micaiah on the cheek
and said, "[1]How did the Spirit of the LORD
pass from me to speak to you?"
24 Micaiah said, "Behold, you will see on
that day when you enter an inner room to
hide yourself."
25 Then the king of Israel said, "[a]Take
Micaiah and return him to Amon [b]the governor of the city and to Joash the king's son;
26 and say, 'Thus says the king, "[a]Put this
man in prison and feed him [1]sparingly with
bread and water until I return safely." ' "
27 Micaiah said, "If you indeed return
safely, the LORD has not spoken by me." And
he said, "[a]Listen, all you people."

Ahab's Defeat and Death

28 So the king of Israel and Jehoshaphat
king of Judah went up against Ramoth-
gilead.
29 The king of Israel said to Jehoshaphat,
"I will disguise myself and go into battle, but
you put on your robes." So the king of Israel
disguised himself, and they went into battle.
30 Now the king of Aram had commanded
the captains of his chariots, saying, "Do not
fight with small or great, but with the king of
Israel alone."
31 So when the captains of the chariots
saw Jehoshaphat, they said, "It is the king of
Israel," and they turned aside to fight against
him. But Jehoshaphat [a]cried out, and the
LORD helped him, and God diverted them
from him.
32 When the captains of the chariots saw
that it was not the king of Israel, they turned
back from pursuing him.
33 A certain man drew his bow at random
and struck the king of Israel [1]in a joint of the
armor. So he said to the driver of the chariot,
"Turn [2]around and take me out of the [3]fight,
for I am severely wounded."
34 The battle raged that day, and the king
of Israel propped himself up in his chariot in
front of the Arameans until the evening; and
at sunset he died.

Jehu Rebukes Jehoshaphat

19 Then Jehoshaphat the king of Judah
returned in safety to his house in Jerusalem.
2 [a]Jehu the son of Hanani the seer went
out to meet him and said to King Jehoshaphat, "[b]Should you help the wicked and love
those who hate the LORD and [1c]so *bring*
wrath on yourself from the LORD?
3 "But [1a]there is *some* good in you, for
[b]you have removed the [2]Asheroth from the
land and you [c]have set your heart to seek
God."
4 So Jehoshaphat lived in Jerusalem and
went out again among the people from Beersheba to the hill country of Ephraim and
[a]brought them back to the LORD, the God of
their fathers.

Reforms Instituted

5 He appointed [a]judges in the land in all
the fortified cities of Judah, city by city.
6 He said to the judges, "Consider what
you are doing, for [a]you do not judge for man
but for the LORD who is with you [1]when you
render judgment.

16 [a]Num 27:17; 1 Kin 22:17; Ezek 34:5; 35:4-8; Matt 9:36; Mark 6:34
18 [a]Is 6:1-5; Dan 7:9, 10
20 [a]Job 1:6; 2 Thess 2:9
21 [a]John 8:44
22 [a]Is 19:14; Ezek 14:9
23 [1]Lit *Which way* [a]Jer 20:2; Mark 14:65; Acts 23:2
25 [a]2 Chr 18:8 [b]2 Chr 34:8
26 [1]Lit *with bread of affliction and water of affliction* [a]2 Chr 16:10
27 [a]Mic 1:2
31 [a]2 Chr 13:14, 15
33 [1]Lit *between the scale-armor and the breastplate* [2]Lit *your hand* [3]Lit *camp*
19:2 [1]Lit *by this* [a]1 Kin 16:1; 2 Chr 20:34 [b]2 Chr 18:1, 3 [c]2 Chr 24:18
3 [1]Lit *good things are found* [2]I.e. wooden pillars [a]2 Chr 12:12 [b]2 Chr 17:6 [c]2 Chr 12:14
4 [a]2 Chr 15:8-13
5 [a]Deut 16:18-20
6 [1]Lit *in the word of judgment* [a]Lev 19:15; Deut 1:17

18:29 The fact that Ahab disguises himself while directing Jehoshaphat into battle in royal regalia, thus making Jehoshaphat the logical target for attack, is consistent with Israel's dominant position at this time.
18:31 *the LORD helped him, and God diverted them from him.* Not found in 1 Kin 22:32. However, some Septuagint (the Greek translation of the OT) manuscripts of Kings do contain the statement that "the LORD helped him," suggesting that the Chronicler was following a Hebrew text of Kings that had these words.
19:1–3 Not found in 1 Kin 22.
19:2 *Should you help the wicked . . . ?* Jehu's father Hanani had earlier given Jehoshaphat's father Asa the same warning (see 16:7–9). Jehoshaphat later committed the same sin again and suffered for it (20:35–37).
19:3 *Asheroth.* See note on 14:3.
19:4 *Jehoshaphat . . . went . . . among the people.* The king traveled throughout the realm personally to promote religious reformation.
19:5 *appointed judges.* The name Jehoshaphat (meaning "The LORD judges") is appropriate for the king who instituted this judicial reform. The arrangement of the courts under Jehoshaphat (vv. 5–11) would be of particular interest to the Chronicler's audience in the postexilic period, when the courts of the restored community would have their own existence and structure legitimized by this precedent.
19:6 Cf. Deut 16:18–20; 17:8–13.

7 “Now then let the fear of the LORD be upon you; [1]be very careful what you do, for [2]the LORD our God will [a]have no part in unrighteousness [b]or partiality or the taking of a bribe.”

8 In Jerusalem also Jehoshaphat appointed some [a]of the Levites and priests, and some of the heads of the fathers’ *households* of Israel, for the judgment of the LORD and to judge [1]disputes among the inhabitants of Jerusalem.

9 Then he charged them saying, “Thus you shall do in the fear of the LORD, faithfully and wholeheartedly.

10 “[a]Whenever any dispute comes to you from your brethren who live in their cities, between blood and blood, between law and commandment, statutes and ordinances, you shall warn them so that they may not be guilty before the LORD, and [b]wrath may *not* come on you and your brethren. Thus you shall do and you will not be guilty.

11 “Behold, Amariah the chief priest will be over you in [1a]all that pertains to the LORD, and Zebadiah the son of Ishmael, the ruler of the house of Judah, in [1]all that pertains to the king. Also the Levites shall be officers before you. [2b]Act resolutely, and the LORD be with the upright.”

Judah Invaded

20 Now it came about after this that the sons of Moab and the sons of Ammon, together with some of the [1a]Meunites, came to make war against Jehoshaphat.

2 Then some came and reported to Jehoshaphat, saying, “A great multitude is coming against you from beyond the sea, out of [1]Aram and behold, they are in [a]Hazazon-tamar (that is Engedi).”

3 Jehoshaphat was afraid and [1a]turned his attention to seek the LORD, and [b]proclaimed a fast throughout all Judah.

4 So Judah gathered together to [a]seek help from the LORD; they even came from all the cities of Judah to seek the LORD.

Jehoshaphat’s Prayer

5 Then Jehoshaphat stood in the assembly of Judah and Jerusalem, in the house of the LORD before the new court,

6 and he said, “O LORD, the God of our fathers, [a]are You not God in the heavens? And [b]are You not ruler over all the kingdoms of the nations? Power and might are in Your hand so that no one can stand against You.

7 “Did You not, O our God, drive out the inhabitants of this land before Your people Israel and [a]give it to the descendants of [b]Abraham Your friend forever?

8 “They have lived in it, and have built You a sanctuary there for Your name, saying,

9 ‘[a]Should evil come upon us, the sword, *or* judgment, or pestilence, or famine, we will stand before this house and before You (for [b]Your name is in this house) and cry to You in our distress, and You will hear and deliver *us*.’

10 “Now behold, [a]the sons of Ammon and Moab and [1]Mount Seir, [b]whom You did not let Israel invade when they came out of the land of Egypt (they turned aside from them and did not destroy them),

11 see *how* they are rewarding us by [a]coming to drive us out from Your possession which You have given us as an inheritance.

12 “O our God, [a]will You not judge them? For we are powerless before this great multitude who are coming against us; nor do we know what to do, but [b]our eyes are on You.”

13 All Judah was standing before the LORD, with their infants, their wives and their children.

Jahaziel Answers the Prayer

14 Then in the midst of the assembly [a]the Spirit of the LORD came upon Jahaziel the

7 [1]Lit *be careful and do* [2]Lit *there is not with the LORD our God* [a]Gen 18:25; Deut 32:4 [b]Deut 10:17, 18
8 [1]So the versions; Heb reads *disputes. And they returned to Jerusalem,* or *And they lived in Jerusalem* [a]2 Chr 17:8, 9
10 [a]Deut 17:8 [b]2 Chr 19:2
11 [1]Lit *every matter of* [2]Lit *Be strong and do* [a]2 Chr 19:8 [b]1 Chr 28:20
20:1 [1]So with Gr; Heb *Ammonites* [a]1 Chr 4:41; 2 Chr 26:7
2 [1]Another reading is *Edom* [a]Gen 14:7
3 [1]Lit *set his face* [a]2 Chr 19:3 [b]1 Sam 7:6; Ezra 8:21
4 [a]Joel 1:14
6 [a]Deut 4:39 [b]1 Chr 29:11
7 [a]Is 41:8 [b]James 2:23
9 [a]2 Chr 6:28-30 [b]2 Chr 6:20
10 [1]I.e. Edom [a]2 Chr 20:1, 22 [b]Num 20:17-21
11 [a]Ps 83:12
12 [a]Judg 11:27 [b]Ps 25:15; 121:1, 2
14 [a]2 Chr 15:1; 24:20

19:7 *let the fear of the LORD be upon you.* Let a terrifying sense of God’s presence restrain you from any injustice (see note on 1 Chr 14:17).

19:8 *Levites and priests . . . for the judgment of the LORD.* See note on 1 Chr 26:29–32. One effect of this judicial reform appears to be the bringing of the traditional system of justice administered by the elders of the city under closer royal and priestly supervision.

19:11 *all that pertains to the LORD . . . all that pertains to the king.* This division into the affairs of religion and the affairs of the king reflects the postexilic structure of the Chronicler’s day. Cf. the anointing of Solomon and Zadok (1 Chr 29:22) and the administration of the postexilic community by Zerubbabel, a Davidic descendant, and Joshua, the high priest (Zech 4:14; 6:9–15).

20:1–30 This episode held special interest for the Chronicler since the restored community was being harassed by the descendants of these same peoples (see Neh 2:19; 4:1–3,7–9; 6:1–4; 13). He uses it to encourage his contemporaries to trust in the Lord and His prophets, as Jehoshaphat son of David had exhorted (v. 20). The account is significantly structured. Apart from the outer frame, which highlights the reversal of circumstances (vv. 1–4,28–30), it falls into three divisions: (1) Jehoshaphat’s prayer (vv. 5–13), (2) the Lord’s response (vv. 14–19), (3) the great victory (vv. 20–27). At the center of each is its crucial statement, and these are all linked by a key word: v. 9, “we will stand before this house and before You”; v. 17, “stand and see the salvation of the LORD on your behalf”; v. 23, “The sons of Ammon and Moab rose up (lit. ‘stood up’) against the inhabitants of Mount Seir destroying them.”

20:1 *Meunites.* A people from the region of Mount Seir in Edom (26:7; 1 Chr 4:41; cf. 2 Chr 20:10,22–23).

20:2 *Aram.* The Arameans are well to the north and not mentioned among the attackers named in v. 1, so “Edom” may be the correct reading (supported in some manuscripts). The difference between “Aram” and “Edom” in Hebrew is only one letter, which is very similar in shape and was often confused in the process of copying manuscripts.

20:5–12 Jehoshaphat’s prayer shows him to be a true theocratic king, a worthy son of David and type (foreshadowing) of the awaited Messiah (see Introduction to 1 Chronicles: Purpose and Themes).

20:9 An apparent reference to Solomon’s prayer and the divine promise of response (6:14–42; 7:12–22).

son of Zechariah, the son of Benaiah, the son
of Jeiel, the son of Mattaniah, the Levite of
the sons of Asaph;
15 and he said, "Listen, all Judah and the
inhabitants of Jerusalem and King Jehoshaphat: thus says the LORD to you, '[a]Do not
fear or be dismayed because of this great
multitude, for [b]the battle is not yours but
God's.
16 'Tomorrow go down against them.
Behold, they will come up by the ascent of
Ziz, and you will find them at the end of the
valley in front of the wilderness of Jeruel.
17 'You *need* not fight in this *battle;* station
yourselves, [a]stand and see the salvation of
the LORD on your behalf, O Judah and Jerusalem.' Do not fear or be dismayed; tomorrow go out to face them, [b]for the LORD is
with you."
18 Jehoshaphat [a]bowed his head with *his*
face to the ground, and all Judah and the
inhabitants of Jerusalem fell down before the
LORD, worshiping the LORD.
19 The Levites, from the sons of the
Kohathites and of the sons of the Korahites,
stood up to praise the LORD God of Israel,
with a very loud voice.

Enemies Destroy Themselves

20 They rose early in the morning and
went out to the wilderness of Tekoa; and
when they went out, Jehoshaphat stood and
said, "Listen to me, O Judah and inhabitants
of Jerusalem, [a]put your trust in the LORD
your God and you will be established. Put
your trust in His prophets and succeed."
21 When he had consulted with the people, he appointed those who sang to the LORD
and those who [a]praised *Him* in holy attire, as
they went out before the army and said,
"[b]Give thanks to the LORD, for His lovingkindness is everlasting."
22 When they began singing and praising,
the LORD [a]set ambushes against the sons of
[b]Ammon, Moab and Mount Seir, who had
come against Judah; so they were [1]routed.
23 For the sons of Ammon and Moab rose
up against the inhabitants of Mount Seir
destroying *them* completely; and when they
had finished with the inhabitants of Seir,
[a]they helped to destroy one another.
24 When Judah came to the lookout of the
wilderness, they looked toward the multitude, and behold, they *were* corpses lying on
the ground, and no one had escaped.
25 When Jehoshaphat and his people
came to take their spoil, they found much
among them, *including* goods, [1]garments
and valuable things which they took for
themselves, more than they could carry. And
they were three days taking the spoil because
there was so much.

Triumphant Return to Jerusalem

26 Then on the fourth day they assembled
in the valley of Beracah, for there they
blessed the LORD. Therefore they have named
that place "The Valley of [1]Beracah" until
today.
27 Every man of Judah and Jerusalem
returned with Jehoshaphat at their head,
returning to Jerusalem with joy, [a]for the
LORD had made them to rejoice over their
enemies.
28 They came to Jerusalem with harps,
lyres and trumpets to the house of the LORD.
29 And [a]the dread of God was on all the
kingdoms of the lands when they heard that
the LORD had fought against the enemies of
Israel.
30 So the kingdom of Jehoshaphat was at
peace, [a]for his God gave him rest on all
sides.
31 [a]Now Jehoshaphat reigned over Judah.
He *was* thirty-five years old when he became
king, and he reigned in Jerusalem twenty-
five years. And his mother's name *was* Azubah the daughter of Shilhi.
32 He walked in the way of his father Asa
and did not depart from it, doing right in the
sight of the LORD.
33 [a]The high places, however, were not
removed; [b]the people had not yet directed
their hearts to the God of their fathers.
34 Now the rest of the acts of Jehoshaphat,
first [1]to last, behold, they are written in the
annals of [a]Jehu the son of Hanani, which is
[2]recorded in the Book of the Kings of Israel.

15 [a]Ex 14:13; Deut 20:1-4; 2 Chr 32:7, 8 [b]1 Sam 17:47
17 [a]Ex 14:13 [b]2 Chr 15:2
18 [a]Ex 4:31
20 [a]Is 7:9
21 [a]1 Chr 16:29; Ps 29:2 [b]1 Chr 16:34
22 [1]Lit *struck down* [a]2 Chr 13:13 [b]2 Chr 20:10
23 [a]Judg 7:22; 1 Sam 14:20
25 [1]So several ancient mss; others read *corpses*
26 [1]I.e. blessing
27 [a]Neh 12:43
29 [a]2 Chr 14:14; 17:10
30 [a]2 Chr 14:6, 7; 15:15
31 [a]1 Kin 22:41-43
33 [a]2 Chr 17:6 [b]2 Chr 19:3
34 [1]Lit *and* [2]Lit *taken up* [a]2 Chr 19:2

20:15 See Ex 14:13–14.
20:16 *ascent of Ziz.* Began seven miles north of Engedi and wound inland, emerging west of Tekoa. *Jeruel.* Southeast of Tekoa.
20:19 *Levites.* The Chronicler's interest in the priests and Levites is apparent throughout the account (vv. 14,21–22,28).
20:20 *put your trust in the LORD your God and . . . in His prophets.* A particularly apt word for the Chronicler's contemporaries to hear from this son of David—at a time when their only hope for the future lay with the Lord and the reassuring words of His prophets.
20:21 *in holy attire.* See note on Ps 29:2.
20:22 *ambushes.* The nature of this "ambush" is indicated in v. 23: Israel's foes destroyed each other in the confusion of battle, similar to the victory under Gideon (Judg 7:22).
20:26 *until today.* See note on 5:9.
20:29 *the dread of God.* See note on 1 Chr 14:17.
20:30 *rest on all sides.* Rest from enemies is part of God's blessing for obedience in Chronicles (14:5–7; 15:15; 1 Chr 22:8–9,18). Righteous kings have victory in warfare (Abijah, Asa, Jehoshaphat, Uzziah, Hezekiah), while wicked rulers experience defeat (Jehoram, Ahaz, Joash, Zedekiah).
20:31 *twenty-five years.* Kings reports 22 (18 in 2 Kin 3:1, and 4 more in 8:16). These figures are reconciled by suggesting a co-regency with his father Asa for three years, probably due to the severity of his father's illness and the need to arrange for a secure succession (16:10–14). The author of Kings speaks only of his years of sole reign after his father's death.
20:33 *high places . . . were not removed.* See note on 17:6.
20:34 *Jehu the son of Hanani.* See note on 19:2.

Alliance Displeases God

35 [a]After this Jehoshaphat king of Judah
allied himself with Ahaziah king of Israel. He
acted wickedly [1]in so doing.
36 So he allied himself with him to make
ships to go [a]to Tarshish, and they made the
ships in Ezion-geber.
37 Then Eliezer the son of Dodavahu of
Mareshah prophesied against Jehoshaphat
saying, "Because you have allied yourself
with Ahaziah, the LORD has destroyed your
works." So the ships were broken and could
not go to Tarshish.

Jehoram Succeeds Jehoshaphat in Judah

21 [a]Then Jehoshaphat slept with his
fathers and was buried with his fathers
in the city of David, and Jehoram his son
became king in his place.
2 He had brothers, the sons of Jehoshaphat: Azariah, Jehiel, Zechariah, [1]Azaryahu,
Michael and Shephatiah. All these *were* the
sons of Jehoshaphat king [a]of Israel.
3 Their father gave them many gifts of
silver, gold and precious things, [a]with fortified cities in Judah, but he gave the kingdom
to Jehoram because he was the firstborn.
4 Now when Jehoram had [1]taken over
the kingdom of his father and made himself
[2]secure, he [a]killed all his brothers with the
sword, and some of the rulers of Israel also.
5 [a]Jehoram *was* thirty-two years old
when he became king, and he reigned eight
years in Jerusalem.
6 [a]He walked in the way of the kings of
Israel, just as the house of Ahab did ([b]for
Ahab's daughter was his wife), and he did
evil in the sight of the LORD.
7 Yet the LORD was not willing to destroy
the house of David because of the covenant
which He had made with David, [a]and since
He had promised to give a lamp to him and
his sons forever.

Revolt against Judah

8 In his days [a]Edom revolted [1]against the
rule of Judah and set up a king over themselves.
9 Then Jehoram crossed over with his
commanders and all his chariots with him.
And he arose by night and struck down the
Edomites who were surrounding him and
the commanders of the chariots.
10 So Edom revolted [1]against Judah to this
day. Then Libnah revolted at the same time
[2]against his rule, because he had forsaken
the LORD God of his fathers.
11 Moreover, [a]he made high places in the
mountains of Judah, and caused the inhabitants of Jerusalem [b]to play the harlot and led
Judah astray.
12 Then a letter came to him from Elijah
the prophet saying, "Thus says the LORD God
of your father David, 'Because [a]you have not
walked in the ways of Jehoshaphat your
father [b]and the ways of Asa king of Judah,
13 but [a]have walked in the way of the
kings of Israel, and have caused Judah and
the inhabitants of Jerusalem to play the harlot [b]as the house of Ahab played the harlot,
and you [c]have also killed your brothers,
[1]your own family, who were better than you,
14 behold, the LORD is going to strike your
people, your sons, your wives and all your
possessions with a great [1]calamity;
15 and [a]you will suffer [1]severe sickness, a
disease of your bowels, until your bowels

35 [1]Lit *to do* [a]1 Kin 22:48, 49 **36** [a]2 Chr 9:21 **21:1** [a]1 Kin 22:50 **2** [1]Or *Azariah* [a]2 Chr 12:6; 23:2 **3** [a]2 Chr 11:5 **4** [1]Lit *risen up* [2]Lit *strong* [a]Gen 4:8; Judg 9:5 **5** [a]2 Kin 8:17-22 **6** [a]1 Kin 12:28-30 [b]2 Chr 18:1
7 [a]2 Sam 7:12-17; 1 Kin 11:13, 36 **8** [1]Lit *from under the hand of* [a]2 Chr 20:22, 23; 21:10 **10** [1]Lit *from under the hand of* [2]Lit *from under his hand* **11** [a]1 Kin 11:7 [b]Lev 20:5 **12** [a]2 Chr 17:3, 4 [b]2 Chr 14:2-5 **13** [1]Lit *your father's house* [a]2 Chr 21:6 [b]1 Kin 16:31-33 [c]2 Chr 21:4 **14** [1]Lit *blow* **15** [1]Lit *in many sicknesses* [a]2 Chr 21:18, 19

20:35–37 See 1 Kin 22:48–49. The lucrative maritime trade through the Gulf of Aqaba no doubt tempted Jehoshaphat to enter into this improper alliance (see 19:2 and note). Solomon's earlier alliance for the same purpose had been with a non-Israelite king (8:17–18).
20:35 *Ahaziah.* Reigned 853–852 B.C. (see 1 Kin 22:51–2 Kin 1:18 for the account of his reign).
21:2 *sons of Jehoshaphat.* The Chronicler shows the blessing of God on Jehoshaphat by mentioning his large family, particularly his seven sons (see 11:18–22; 1 Chr 25:5 and notes). Jehoshaphat's large number of sons is in striking contrast to the wicked Jehoram who, after murdering his brothers (v. 4), is left with but one son (v. 17). Jehoram's wife Athaliah would later perform a similar slaughter (22:10).
21:3 Cf. the similar actions of Rehoboam (11:23).
21:4–20 See 2 Kin 8:16–24.
21:4 This bloody assassination of all potential rivals is not reported in Kings, but it fits the pattern of the northern kings (see v. 6). The princes of Israel were probably leading men in the southern kingdom who opposed having a king married to a daughter of Ahab. For this use of "Israel" see note on 12:1.
21:5 *eight years.* 848–841 B.C. The period 853–848 was probably a co-regency of Jehoram with his father Jehoshaphat—Jehoshaphat's 18th year was also Jehoram's second year (cf. 2 Kin 1:17; 3:1).
21:6 *Ahab's daughter was his wife.* Probably the marriage referred to in 18:1, used to cement the alliance between Jehoshaphat and Ahab. Such political marriages were common. Many of Solomon's marriages sealed international relationships, as did Ahab's marriage to Jezebel.
21:8–10 The pious Jehoshaphat had enjoyed victory over Edom (20:1–30), while the wicked Jehoram is defeated in his attempt to keep Edom in subjection to Judah (see note on 20:30).
21:10 *To this day.* See note on 5:9. *Libnah.* Located between Judah and Philistia. *because he had forsaken the LORD.* Not found in 2 Kin 8:22. The Chronicler introduces this judgment as an indication of immediate retribution (see notes on 12:1–14; 12:2; see also Introduction to 1 Chronicles: Purpose and Themes).
21:12–20a Not found in the parallel text in 2 Kin 8.
21:12–15 This reference to a letter from Elijah is the only mention in Chronicles of that prophet, to whom the books of Kings give so much attention (1 Kin 17–2 Kin 2). Elijah's letter specifically announces the immediate consequences of Jehoram's disobedience—further defeat in war, which will cost Jehoram his wives and sons; and disease, which will lead to his death (see note on 16:12). Cf. also the foot disease of Asa (16:12–14) and the leprosy of Uzziah (26:16–23). Kings does not mention the nature of Jehoram's death. Some have argued that this letter could not be authentic because, they claim, Elijah was taken to heaven before Jehoram became king. But this is not a neces-

come out because of the sickness, day by
day.' "
16 Then [a]the LORD stirred up against Jehoram the spirit of the Philistines and [b]the
Arabs who [1]bordered the Ethiopians;
17 and they came against Judah and
invaded it, and carried away all the possessions found in the king's house together with
his sons and his wives, so that no son was
left to him except [1][a]Jehoahaz, the youngest
of his sons.
18 So after all this the LORD smote him [a]in
his bowels with an incurable sickness.
19 Now it came about in the course of
time, at the end of two years, that his bowels
came out because of his sickness and he died
in great pain. And his people made no fire
for him like [a]the fire for his fathers.
20 He was thirty-two years old when he
became king, and he reigned in Jerusalem
eight years; and he departed [1][a]with no one's
regret, and they buried him in the city of
David, [b]but not in the tombs of the kings.

Ahaziah Succeeds Jehoram in Judah

22 [a]Then the inhabitants of Jerusalem
made [1]Ahaziah, his youngest son, king
in his place, for the band of men who came
with [b]the Arabs to the camp had slain all the
older *sons*. So Ahaziah the son of Jehoram
king of Judah began to reign.
2 Ahaziah *was* [1]twenty-two years old
when he became king, and he reigned one
year in Jerusalem. And his mother's name
was Athaliah, the [2]granddaughter of Omri.
3 He also walked in the ways of the
house of Ahab, for his mother was his counselor to do wickedly.
4 He did evil in the sight of the LORD like
the house of Ahab, for they were his counselors after the death of his father, to [a]his
destruction.

Ahaziah Allies with Jehoram of Israel

5 He also walked according to their counsel, and went with Jehoram the son of Ahab
king of Israel to wage war against Hazael
king of Aram at Ramoth-gilead. But the
[1][a]Arameans [2]wounded [3]Joram.
6 So he returned to be healed in Jezreel
of the wounds [1]which they had inflicted on
him at Ramah, when he fought against Hazael king of Aram. And [2]Ahaziah, the son of
Jehoram king of Judah, went down to see
Jehoram the son of Ahab in Jezreel, because
he was sick.
7 Now [a]the destruction of Ahaziah was
from God, in that [1]he went to Joram. For
when he came, [b]he went out with Jehoram
against Jehu the son of Nimshi, [c]whom the
LORD had anointed to cut off the house of
Ahab.

Jehu Murders Princes of Judah

8 [a]It came about when Jehu was executing judgment on the house of Ahab, he
found the princes of Judah and the sons of
Ahaziah's brothers ministering to Ahaziah,
and slew them.
9 [a]He also sought Ahaziah, and they
caught him while he was hiding in Samaria;
they brought him to Jehu, put him to death

16 [1]Lit *were at the hand of* [a]2 Chr 33:11 [b]2 Chr 17:11; 22:1
17 [1]In 2 Chr 22:1, *Ahaziah* [a]2 Chr 25:23
18 [a]2 Chr 21:15
19 [a]2 Chr 16:14
20 [1]Lit *without desire* [a]Jer 22:18, 28 [b]2 Chr 24:25; 28:27
22:1 [1]In 2 Chr 21:17, *Jehoahaz* [a]2 Kin 8:24-29 [b]2 Chr 21:16
2 [1]So some versions and 2 Kin 8:26; Heb *42 years* [2]Lit *daughter*
4 [a]Prov 13:20
5 [1]Heb *archers* [2]Lit *smote* [3]I.e. Jehoram [a]2 Kin 8:28
6 [1]Lit *with which...smitten* [2]So with 2 Kin 8:29; Heb *Azariah*
7 [1]Lit *to go* [a]2 Chr 10:15 [b]2 Kin 9:21 [c]2 Kin 9:6, 7
8 [a]2 Kin 10:11-14
9 [a]2 Kin 9:27

sary conclusion (see 2 Kin 1:17; see also note on 2 Kin 3:11). Elijah's translation may well have taken place as late as 848 B.C.

21:16 *Ethiopians.* Lit. "Cushites," people from the upper Nile region.

21:20 *eight years.* See note on v. 5. This is the first time that the Chronicler does not refer his readers to other sources for additional details on the reign of a king. *not in the tombs of the kings.* Only the Chronicler mentions the refusal of the people to accord Jehoram the customary burial honors of a tomb with the other kings of Judah (cf. 24:25).

22:1–9 The Chronicler's account of Ahaziah's reign is much shorter than the parallel in 2 Kin 8:24–9:29, probably due to the fact that the Kings account focuses on the rebellion of Jehu and the downfall of the dynasty of Omri (see 2 Kin 8:26; see also 1 Kin 16:21–28)—events in the northern kingdom, in which the Chronicler is not interested. The Chronicler's account again shows his interest in immediate retribution: Ahaziah's personal wickedness and his involvement in a foreign alliance result in immediate judgment and a reign of only one year (see note on 16:2–9; see also Introduction to 1 Chronicles: Purpose and Themes).

22:1 *had slain all the older sons.* Emphasizes divine retribution: Jehoram, who murdered all his brothers, had to watch the death of his own sons (21:4,13,16–17).

22:2 *twenty-two.* See NASB marg. The Hebrew reading of "42" would make Ahaziah older than his father (21:20). *one year.* 841 B.C.

22:3–4 The great influence of the dynasty of Omri in Judah is indicated by the power of Athaliah and the presence of advisers from the northern kingdom (see note on 18:29).

22:5 *went with Jehoram . . . to wage war.* An action similar to that for which Jehoshaphat had been rebuked (see 19:2 and note). *Hazael.* Had been anointed by Elisha; he later killed his master in a coup to seize the throne (2 Kin 8:13–15; cf. 1 Kin 19:15 and note). *Ramoth-gilead.* Located in the Transjordan border area between Israel and Aram. More than ten years earlier Jehoshaphat had participated with Ahab in a battle there that cost Ahab his life (ch. 18; 1 Kin 22).

22:6 *returned to . . . Jezreel.* Jehoram apparently recovered Ramoth-gilead and left Jehu in charge (2 Kin 8:28–9:28).

22:7 *destruction of Ahaziah was from God.* The Chronicler assumes that the reader is familiar with the account of Jehu's anointing and the additional details of the coup, which resulted in the deaths of Jehoram and Ahaziah (2 Kin 8:28–9:28). While the writer of Kings primarily portrays the end of the dynasty of Omri as a result of the judgment of God (1 Kin 21:20–29; 2 Kin 9:24–10:17), the Chronicler notes that the assassination of Ahaziah was also brought about by God.

22:9 The account of Ahaziah's death appears to be somewhat different in the two histories (cf. 2 Kin 9:21–27; 10:12–14). Since the writer of Chronicles presumes the reader's familiarity with the other account (see note on v. 7), it is best to take the details of Chronicles as supplementary to Kings, not contradictory, though it is difficult to know the precise sequence and location of events. Apart from the Chronicler's statement that Ahaziah received a decent burial because of his father's piety rather than his own, the apparent differences in the two accounts do not appear to be theologically motivated. There is no summary statement about the reign of Ahaziah in either history.

[b]and buried him. For they said, "He is the son of Jehoshaphat, [c]who sought the LORD with all his heart." So there was no one of the house of Ahaziah to retain the power of the kingdom.

10 [a]Now when Athaliah the mother of Ahaziah saw that her son was dead, she rose and destroyed all the royal [1]offspring of the house of Judah.

11 But Jehoshabeath the king's daughter took Joash the son of Ahaziah, and stole him from among the king's sons who were being put to death, and placed him and his nurse in the bedroom. So Jehoshabeath, the daughter of King Jehoram, the wife of Jehoiada the priest (for she was the sister of Ahaziah), hid him from Athaliah so that she would not put him to death.

12 He was hidden with them in the house of God six years while Athaliah reigned over the land.

Jehoiada Sets Joash on the Throne of Judah

23 [a]Now in the seventh year Jehoiada strengthened himself, and took captains of hundreds: Azariah the son of Jeroham, Ishmael the son of Johanan, Azariah the son of Obed, Maaseiah the son of Adaiah, and Elishaphat the son of Zichri, *and they entered* into a covenant with him.

2 They went throughout Judah and gathered the Levites from all the cities of Judah, and the heads of the fathers' *households* of [a]Israel, and they came to Jerusalem.

3 Then all the assembly made a covenant with the king in the house of God. And [1]Jehoiada said to them, "Behold, the king's son shall reign, [a]as the LORD has spoken concerning the sons of David.

4 "This is the thing which you shall do: one third of you, of the priests and Levites [a]who come in on the sabbath, *shall be* gatekeepers,

5 and one third *shall be* at the king's house, and a third at the Gate of the Foundation; and all the people *shall be* in the courts of the house of the LORD.

6 "But let no one enter the house of the LORD except the priests and [a]the ministering Levites; they may enter, for they are holy. And let all the people keep the charge of the LORD.

7 "The Levites will surround the king, each man with his weapons in his hand; and whoever enters the house, let him be killed. Thus be with the king when he comes in and when he goes out."

8 So the Levites and all Judah did according to all that Jehoiada the priest commanded. And each one of them took his men who were to come in on the sabbath, with those who were to go out on the sabbath, for Jehoiada the priest did not dismiss *any of* [a]the divisions.

9 Then Jehoiada the priest gave to the captains of hundreds the spears and the large and small shields which had been King David's, which were in the house of God.

10 He stationed all the people, each man with his weapon in his hand, from the right [1]side of the house to the left [1]side of the house, by the altar and by the house, around the king.

11 Then they brought out the king's son and put the crown on him, and *gave him* [a]the testimony and made him king. And Jehoiada and his sons anointed him and said, "[b]*Long* live the king!"

Athaliah Murdered

12 When Athaliah heard the noise of the people running and praising the king, she came into the house of the LORD to the people.

9 [b]2 Kin 9:28 [c]2 Chr 17:4
10 [1]Lit *seed* [a]2 Kin 11:1-3
23:1 [a]2 Kin 11:4-20
2 [a]2 Chr 11:13-17; 21:2
3 [1]Lit *he* [a]2 Sam 7:12; 2 Chr 21:7
4 [a]1 Chr 9:25
6 [a]1 Chr 23:28-32
8 [a]1 Chr 24:1
10 [1]Lit *shoulder*
11 [a]Ex 25:16, 21 [b]1 Sam 10:24

22:10–12 See 2 Kin 11:1–3. In the history of Judah, Athaliah represents the only break in the continuity of the Davidic dynasty; she is the only queen of Judah to rule in her own name (841–835 B.C.). Her attempt to wipe out the royal family repeated the action of her husband Jehoram (21:4). It threatened the continuity of the Davidic dynasty, and if she had succeeded, Judah may have been claimed by the dynasty of Omri in the north since Athaliah was from that dynasty and had no living son and heir.

22:11 *wife of Jehoiada the priest.* Not noted in Kings.

23:1–24:27 See 2 Kin 11:4–12:21 and notes. The Chronicler divides the reign of Joash (835–796 B.C.) into three parts: (1) the recovery of the throne for the house of David (ch. 23); (2) Joash and Jehoiada—the good years (24:1–16); (3) Joash alone—the bad years (24:17–27). The last section is largely unique to Chronicles and further develops the theme of immediate retribution: Once again chronological notes provide the framework for cycles of obedience and disobedience (24:15–17,23); see notes on 12:2; 14:2–16:14.

23:1–21 See 2 Kin 11:4–20. The Chronicler has followed his source rather closely but has introduced material reflecting his own concerns in three areas: 1. The account in Kings has more to say about the participation of the military in the coup; the Chronicler adds material emphasizing the presence of temple officials and their role (vv. 2,6,8,13,18–19). 2. The Chronicler stresses the widespread popular support for the coup by mentioning the presence of large groups of people, such as "all the people" or "the whole assembly" (vv. 3,5–6,8,10,16–17). 3. The Chronicler shows additional concern for the sanctity of the temple area by inserting notes showing the steps taken to ensure that only qualified personnel enter the temple precincts (vv. 5–6,19).

23:1 *Azariah . . . Elishaphat.* The Chronicler names the commanders, which was not done in Kings, but he does not mention the Carites, mercenaries who served as a royal guard (see note on 2 Kin 11:4). Verse 20 exhibits the same omission (cf. 2 Kin 11:19), the motive for which may have been the Chronicler's concern that only authorized persons enter the temple precincts.

23:2 *the Levites . . . and the heads of the . . . households of Israel.* Reflects both the Chronicler's concerns with the temple personnel and the widespread support for the coup against Athaliah.

23:3 *as the LORD has spoken.* See 2 Sam 7:11–16.

23:11 *the testimony.* May refer to the covenant sworn by the assembly (vv. 1,3; cf. v. 16) or to the law of God, by which the king was to rule (see Deut 17:18–20). See note on 2 Kin 11:12.

13 She looked, and behold, the king was standing by his pillar at the entrance, and the captains and the [1]trumpeters *were* beside the king. And all the people of the land rejoiced and blew trumpets, the singers with *their* musical instruments [2]leading the praise. Then Athaliah tore her clothes and said, "Treason! Treason!"

14 Jehoiada the priest brought out the captains of hundreds who were appointed over the army and said to them, "Bring her out [1]between the ranks; and whoever follows her, put to death with the sword." For the priest said, "Let her not be put to death in the house of the LORD."

15 So they [1]seized her, and when she arrived at the entrance of [a]the Horse Gate of the king's house, they [b]put her to death there.

Reforms Carried Out

16 Then [a]Jehoiada made a covenant between himself and all the people and the king, that they would be the LORD's people.

17 And all the people went to the house of Baal and tore it down, and they broke in pieces his altars and his images, and [a]killed Mattan the priest of Baal before the altars.

18 Moreover, Jehoiada placed the offices of the house of the LORD under the [1]authority of [a]the Levitical priests, [b]whom David had assigned over the house of the LORD, to offer the burnt offerings of the LORD, as it is written in the law of Moses—[c]with rejoicing and singing according to the [2]order of David.

19 He stationed [a]the gatekeepers of the house of the LORD, so that no one would enter *who was* in any way unclean.

20 [a]He took the captains of hundreds, the nobles, the rulers of the people and all the people of the land, and brought the king down from the house of the LORD, and came through the upper gate to the king's house. And they placed the king upon the royal throne.

21 So [a]all of the people of the land rejoiced and the city was quiet. For they had put Athaliah to death with the sword.

13 [1]Lit *trumpets* [2]Lit *and leading for praising*
14 [1]Lit *from within*
15 [1]Lit *placed hands to her* [a]Neh 3:28; Jer 31:40 [b]2 Chr 22:10
16 [a]2 Kin 11:17
17 [a]Deut 13:6-9; 1 Kin 18:40
18 [1]Lit *hand* [2]Lit *hands of* [a]2 Chr 5:5 [b]1 Chr 23:6, 25-31 [c]1 Chr 25:1
19 [a]1 Chr 9:22
20 [a]2 Kin 11:19
21 [a]2 Kin 11:20

Young Joash Influenced by Jehoiada

24 [a]Joash *was* seven years old when he became king, and he reigned forty years in Jerusalem; and his mother's name *was* Zibiah from Beersheba.

2 [a]Joash did what was right in the sight of the LORD all the days of Jehoiada the priest.

3 Jehoiada took two wives for him, and he became the father of sons and daughters.

Faithless Priests

4 Now it came about after this that Joash [1]decided [a]to restore the house of the LORD.

5 He gathered the priests and Levites and said to them, "Go out to the cities of Judah and collect money from all [a]Israel to [1]repair the house of your God [2]annually, and you shall do the matter quickly." But the Levites did not act quickly.

6 So the king summoned Jehoiada the chief *priest* and said to him, "Why have you not required the Levites to bring in from Judah and from Jerusalem [a]the levy *fixed by* Moses the servant of the LORD on the congregation of Israel [b]for the tent of the testimony?"

7 For [a]the sons of the wicked Athaliah had broken into the house of God and even [1]used the holy things of the house of the LORD for the Baals.

Temple Repaired

8 So the king commanded, and [a]they made a chest and set it outside by the gate of the house of the LORD.

9 [a]They made a proclamation in Judah and Jerusalem to bring to the LORD [b]the levy *fixed by* Moses the servant of God on Israel in the wilderness.

10 All the officers and all the people rejoiced and brought in their levies and [1]dropped *them* into the chest until they had finished.

11 It came about whenever the chest was brought in to the king's officer by the Levites, and when [a]they saw that there was much money, then the king's scribe and the chief priest's officer would come, empty the

24:1 [a]2 Kin 11:21; 12:1-15
2 [a]2 Chr 26:4, 5
4 [1]Lit *was with a heart* [a]2 Chr 24:7
5 [1]Lit *to strengthen* [2]Lit *from year to year* [a]2 Chr 21:2
6 [a]Ex 30:12-16 [b]Num 1:50
7 [1]Lit *made* [a]2 Chr 21:17
8 [a]2 Kin 12:9
9 [a]2 Chr 36:22 [b]2 Chr 24:6
10 [1]Lit *threw*
11 [a]2 Kin 12:10

23:13 *singers with their musical instruments.* The Chronicler adds a note (not found in 2 Kin 11:14) about the presence of Levitical musicians, who were leading the praises (see note on 1 Chr 6:31–48).

23:18–19 The Chronicler adds information on the cultic ritual and the guards at the gates (see note on vv. 1–21).

23:20 See note on v. 1.

24:1–14 See 2 Kin 12:1–17.

24:1 *forty years.* 835–796 B.C.

24:2 Provides the outline for the Chronicler's treatment of Joash—the good years while Jehoiada was alive (vv. 1–16), and the turn to evil after his death (vv. 17–27). See note on 25:2.

24:3 Another expression of the Chronicler's conviction that large families represent the blessing of God (see v. 27; see also note on 1 Chr 25:5).

24:4 *restore the house of the LORD.* The vandalism and atrocities of Athaliah (v. 7) required the refurbishing of the temple.

24:5 The writer of 2 Kings speaks of three different sources of revenue (2 Kin 12:4–5), whereas the Chronicler mentions only the census tax (see Ex 30:14; 38:26; Matt 17:24). The reason for the tardiness of the priests is not stated (see 2 Kin 12:6–8). The writer of Kings notes that the audience with the priests takes place in the 23rd year of Joash's reign, when he is presumably no longer the ward of Jehoiada. Resistance on the part of the priests to the reassignment of the temple revenues for repair work may be the underlying cause.

24:8 *chest.* Mesopotamian texts speak of a similar offering box placed in temples. Representatives of both the king and the temple officials administered temple revenues (see note on 1 Chr 26:20).

chest, take it, and return it to its place. Thus they did daily and collected much money.

12 The king and Jehoiada gave it to those who did the work of the service of the house of the LORD; and they hired masons and carpenters to restore the house of the LORD, and also workers in iron and bronze to [1]repair the house of the LORD.

13 So the workmen labored, and the repair work progressed in their hands, and they [1]restored the house of God [2]according to its specifications and strengthened it.

14 When they had finished, they brought the rest of the money before the king and Jehoiada; and it was made into utensils for the house of the LORD, utensils for the service and the burnt offering, and pans and utensils of gold and silver. And they offered burnt offerings in the house of the LORD continually all the days of Jehoiada.

15 Now when Jehoiada [1]reached a ripe old age he died; he was one hundred and thirty years old at his death.

16 They buried him [a]in the city of David among the kings, because he had done well in [b]Israel and [1]to God and His house.

17 But after the death of Jehoiada the officials of Judah came and bowed down to the king, and the king listened to them.

18 They abandoned [a]the house of the LORD, the God of their fathers, and [b]served the [1]Asherim and the idols; so [c]wrath came upon Judah and Jerusalem for this their guilt.

19 Yet [a]He sent prophets to them to bring them back to the LORD; though they testified against them, they would not listen.

Joash Murders Son of Jehoiada

20 [a]Then the Spirit of God [1]came on Zechariah the son of Jehoiada the priest; and he stood above the people and said to them, "Thus God has said, '[b]Why do you transgress the commandments of the LORD and do not prosper? [c]Because you have forsaken the LORD, He has also forsaken you.' "

21 So [a]they conspired against him and at the command of the king they stoned him [1]to death in the court of the house of the LORD.

22 Thus Joash the king did not remember the kindness which his father Jehoiada had shown him, but he murdered his son. And as he died he said, "May [a]the LORD see and [1]avenge!"

Aram Invades and Defeats Judah

23 Now it happened at the turn of the year that [a]the army of the Arameans came up against him; and they came to Judah and Jerusalem, destroyed all the officials of the people from among the people, and sent all their spoil to the king of Damascus.

24 Indeed the army of the Arameans came with a small number of men; yet [a]the LORD delivered a very great army into their hands, [b]because they had forsaken the LORD, the God of their fathers. Thus they executed judgment on Joash.

25 [a]When they had departed from him (for they left him very sick), his own servants conspired against him because of the blood of the [1]son of Jehoiada the priest, and murdered him on his bed. So he died, and they buried him in the city of David, but they did not bury him in the tombs of the kings.

26 Now these are those who conspired against him: Zabad the son of Shimeath the Ammonitess, and Jehozabad the son of Shimrith the Moabitess.

27 As to his sons and the many [1]oracles against him and [a]the [2]rebuilding of the house of God, behold, they are written in the [3b]treatise of the Book of the Kings. Then Amaziah his son became king in his place.

Amaziah Succeeds Joash in Judah

25 [a]Amaziah was twenty-five years old when he became king, and he reigned twenty-nine years in Jerusalem. And his mother's name was Jehoaddan of Jerusalem.

12 [1]Lit *to strengthen*
13 [1]Lit *set up* [2]Lit *upon its proportion*
15 [1]Lit *became old and satisfied with days*
16 [1]Lit *with* [a]2 Chr 21:20 [b]2 Chr 21:2
18 [1]I.e. wooden symbols of a female deity [a]2 Chr 24:4 [b]Ex 34:12-14 [c]Josh 22:20
19 [a]Jer 7:25
20 [1]Lit *clothed* [a]2 Chr 20:14 [b]Num 14:41 [c]2 Chr 15:2
21 [1]Lit *with stones* [a]Neh 9:26; Matt 23:34, 35
22 [1]Lit *seek*, or *require* [a]Gen 9:5
23 [a]2 Kin 12:17
24 [a]2 Chr 16:7, 8 [b]2 Chr 24:20
25 [1]So some ancient versions; Heb *sons* [a]2 Kin 12:20, 21
27 [1]Or *burdens upon* [2]Lit *founding* [3]Heb *midrash* [a]2 Chr 24:12 [b]2 Chr 13:22
25:1 [a]2 Kin 14:1-6

24:14 See 2 Kin 12:13–14. *all the days of Jehoiada.* An additional note on the part of the Chronicler to introduce the turn to the worse in the reign of Joash upon Jehoiada's death (vv. 15–16).

24:15–22 This section is unique to the Chronicler and shows his emphasis on immediate retribution (see note on 23:1–24:27). After a period of righteous rule until the death of Jehoiada, Joash turns to idolatry and murders Jehoiada's son. In the following year he is invaded and defeated by Aram because Judah, under his leadership, "had forsaken the LORD" (v. 24).

24:18,20,24 *abandoned . . . forsaken . . . forsaken . . . forsaken.* The Hebrew word is the same in these verses; it is a verb frequently used by the Chronicler to denote the reason for divine punishment (see note on 12:1; see also 7:19,22; 12:5; 13:10–11; 15:2; 21:10; 24:18,20,24; 28:6; 29:6; 34:25; 1 Chr 28:9,20).

24:19 *Yet He sent prophets.* Israel's failure to heed the Lord's prophets ultimately led to her destruction (see 36:16; cf. 20:20; see also Introduction to 1 Chronicles: Purpose and Themes).

24:20 *Zechariah.* See note on Matt 23:35.

24:24 *small number of men.* Just as God had helped the small army of Judah against overwhelming odds when the king and people were faithful to Him (14:8–9; 20:2,12), so now in their unfaithfulness they are defeated by a much smaller force of invaders (see note on 20:30).

24:25 *servants . . . because of the blood of the son . . . murdered him.* Only the Chronicler mentions that this assassination was revenge for the murder of Zechariah. *did not bury him in the tombs of the kings.* Burial in the tombs of the kings was an honor accorded to Jehoiada (v. 16), but withheld from his rebellious ward Joash (see note on 21:20).

24:26 *the Ammonitess. . . the Moabitess.* Information not given in Kings but important to the Chronicler (see note on 20:1–30).

25:1–28 Typically, the Chronicler has divided the reign of Amaziah into two parts: (1) the good years, marked by obedience, divine blessing and victory (vv. 1–13), and (2) the bad years of idolatry, defeat and regicide (vv. 14–28). See 2 Kin 14:1–20 and notes.

25:1 *twenty-nine years.* 796–767 B.C.

2 He did right in the sight of the LORD,
[a]yet not with a whole heart.
3 Now [a]it came about as soon as the kingdom was [1]firmly in his grasp, that he killed
his servants who had slain his father the king.
4 However, he did not put their children
to death, but *did* as it is written in the law in
the book of Moses, which the LORD commanded, saying, "[a]Fathers shall not be put to
death for sons, nor sons be put to death for
fathers, but each shall be put to death for his
own sin."

Amaziah Defeats Edomites

5 Moreover, Amaziah assembled Judah
and appointed them according to *their*
fathers' households under commanders of
thousands and commanders of hundreds
throughout Judah and Benjamin; and he
[1]took a census of those [a]from twenty years
old and upward and found them to be
[b]300,000 choice men, *able* to go to war *and*
handle spear and shield.
6 He hired also 100,000 valiant warriors
out of Israel for one hundred talents of silver.
7 But [a]a man of God came to him saying,
"O king, do not let the army of Israel go with
you, for the LORD is not with Israel *nor with*
any of the sons of Ephraim.
8 "But if you do go, do *it*, be strong for the
battle; *yet* God will [1]bring you down before
the enemy, [a]for God has power to help and
to [1]bring down."
9 Amaziah said to the man of God, "But
what *shall we* do for the hundred talents
which I have given to the troops of Israel?"
And the man of God answered, "[a]The LORD
has much more to give you than this."
10 Then Amaziah [1]dismissed them, the
troops which came to him from Ephraim, to
go home; so their anger burned against Judah
and they returned [2]home in fierce anger.
11 Now Amaziah strengthened himself
and led his people forth, and went to [a]the
Valley of Salt and struck down 10,000 of the
sons of Seir.
12 The sons of Judah also captured 10,000
alive and brought them to the top of the cliff
and threw them down from the top of the
cliff, so that they were all dashed to pieces.
13 But the [1]troops whom Amaziah sent
back from going with him to battle, raided
the cities of Judah, from Samaria to Beth-
horon, and struck down 3,000 of them and
plundered much spoil.

Amaziah Rebuked for Idolatry

14 Now after Amaziah came from slaughtering the Edomites, [a]he brought the gods of
the sons of Seir, set them up as his gods,
bowed down before them and burned
incense to them.
15 Then the anger of the LORD burned
against Amaziah, and He sent him a prophet
who said to him, "Why have you sought the
gods of the people [a]who have not delivered
their own people from your hand?"
16 As he was talking with him, [1]the king
said to him, "Have we appointed you a royal
counselor? Stop! Why should you be struck
down?" Then the prophet stopped and said,
"I know that God has planned to destroy
you, because you have done this and have
not listened to my counsel."

Amaziah Defeated by Joash of Israel

17 [a]Then Amaziah king of Judah took
counsel and sent to Joash the son of Jehoahaz the son of Jehu, the king of Israel, saying, "Come, let us face each other."
18 Joash the king of Israel sent to Amaziah king of Judah, saying, "[a]The thorn bush
which was in Lebanon sent to the cedar
which was in Lebanon, saying, 'Give your
daughter to my son in marriage.' But there
passed by a wild beast that was in Lebanon
and trampled the thorn bush.
19 "You said, 'Behold, you have [1]defeated
Edom.' And [a]your heart has [2]become proud
in boasting. Now stay at home; for why
should you provoke trouble so that you, even
you, would fall and Judah with you?"
20 But Amaziah would not listen, for it
was from God, that He might deliver them

2 [a]2 Chr 25:14
3 [1]Lit *firm upon him* [a]2 Kin 14:5
4 [a]Deut 24:16
5 [1]Lit *mustered* [a]Num 1:3 [b]2 Chr 26:13
7 [a]2 Kin 4:9
8 [1]Lit *cause to stumble* [a]2 Chr 14:11; 20:6
9 [a]Deut 8:18; Prov 10:22
10 [1]Lit *separated* [2]Lit *to their own place*
11 [a]2 Kin 14:7
13 [1]Lit *sons of the troops*
14 [a]2 Chr 28:23
15 [a]2 Chr 25:11, 12
16 [1]Lit *he*
17 [a]2 Kin 14:8-14
18 [a]Judg 9:8-15
19 [1]Lit *smitten* [2]Lit *lifted you up to boast* [a]2 Chr 26:16; 32:25

25:2 The Chronicler does not indicate that Amaziah failed to remove the high places, which continued to be used as places for sacrifice by the people (see 2 Kin 14:4). Also compare 24:2 with 2 Kin 12:4, and 26:4 with 2 Kin 15:4. The writer appears to be motivated by his outline, which covered the good years first and then the reversion to evil. Negative comments about these kings are held to the second half of the account of their reigns, whereas in Kings the summary judgment about their reigns and the high places is given immediately.

25:5–16 An expansion of 2 Kin 14:7. The author of Kings mentions the successful war with Edom only as a prelude to Amaziah's challenge to Joash, but the Chronicler sets it in the framework of his emphasis on immediate retribution: Obedience brings victory over Edom, while the subsequent idolatry (vv. 14–16) brings defeat in the campaign against Israel. By expanding his account the Chronicler gives the theological reason for both the victory over Edom and the defeat before Israel.

25:7 *do not let the army of Israel go with you.* Another instance of the Chronicler's condemnation of alliances that imply lack of trust in the Lord (see notes on 16:2–9; 22:5). Cf. other prophetic speeches that call on the people to trust in God (20:15–17,20; 32:7–8).

25:13 This may be the inciting incident for the later war with the north. *Samaria.* A town by this name in the southern kingdom is not otherwise known. The reference may be a copyist's error.

25:14–25 The Chronicler's account of the war with the north is close to the parallel in 2 Kin 14:8–14, except for some additions in line with his theme of immediate retribution. The Chronicler mentions Amaziah's foolish idolatry and the prophetic speech of judgment, neither of which is found in Kings. He also adds notes in vv. 20,27 to emphasize that the idolatry of Amaziah was being punished.

25:18 Cf. the parable in Judg 9:7–15.

into the hand *of Joash* because they had
sought the gods of Edom.
21 So Joash king of Israel went up, and he
and Amaziah king of Judah faced each other
at Beth-shemesh, which belonged to Judah.
22 Judah was defeated [1]by Israel, and they
fled each to his tent.
23 Then Joash king of Israel captured
Amaziah king of Judah, the son of Joash the
son of [a]Jehoahaz, at Beth-shemesh, and
brought him to Jerusalem and tore down the
wall of Jerusalem from the Gate of Ephraim
to the Corner Gate, 400 [1]cubits.
24 *He took* all the gold and silver and all
the utensils which were found in the house
of God with [a]Obed-edom, and the treasures
of the king's house, the hostages also, and
returned to Samaria.
25 [a]And Amaziah, the son of Joash king
of Judah, lived fifteen years after the death of
Joash, son of Jehoahaz, king of Israel.
26 Now the rest of the acts of Amaziah,
from first to last, behold, are they not written
in the Book of the Kings of Judah and Israel?
27 From the time that Amaziah turned
away from following the LORD they conspired
against him in Jerusalem, and he fled to
Lachish; but they sent after him to Lachish
and killed him there.
28 Then they brought him on horses and
buried him with his fathers in the city of
Judah.

Uzziah Succeeds Amaziah in Judah

26 And all the people of Judah took [1]Uzzi-
ah, who *was* sixteen years old, and
made him king in the place of his father
Amaziah.
2 He built Eloth and restored it to Judah
after the king slept with his fathers.
3 Uzziah was [a]sixteen years old when he
became king, and he reigned fifty-two years
in Jerusalem; and his mother's name was
[1]Jechiliah of Jerusalem.
4 He did right in the sight of the LORD
according to all that his father Amaziah had
done.
5 [a]He continued to seek God in the days
of Zechariah, [b]who had understanding
[1]through the vision of God; and [2c]as long as
he sought the LORD, God prospered him.

Uzziah Succeeds in War

6 Now he went out and [a]warred against
the Philistines, and broke down the wall of
Gath and the wall of Jabneh and the wall of
Ashdod; and he built cities in *the area of*
Ashdod and among the Philistines.
7 [a]God helped him against the Philistines, and against the Arabians who lived in
Gur-baal, and the Meunites.
8 The Ammonites also gave [a]tribute to
Uzziah, and his [1]fame extended to the border of Egypt, for he became very strong.
9 Moreover, Uzziah built towers in Jerusalem at [a]the Corner Gate and at the [b]Valley
Gate and at the corner buttress and fortified
them.
10 He built towers in the wilderness and
[a]hewed many cisterns, for he had much livestock, both in the [1]lowland and in the plain.
He also had plowmen and vinedressers in
the hill country and the fertile fields, for he
loved the soil.
11 Moreover, Uzziah had an army ready
for battle, which [1]entered combat by divi-

22 [1]Lit *before*
23 [1]I.e. One cubit equals approx 18 in. [a]2 Chr 21:17; 22:1
24 [a]1 Chr 26:15
25 [a]2 Kin 14:17-22
26:1 [1]In 2 Kin 14:21, *Azariah*
3 [1]In 2 Kin 15:2, *Jecoliah* [a]2 Kin 15:2, 3
5 [1]Many mss read *in the fear of God* [2]Lit *in the days of his seeking* [a]2 Chr 24:2 [b]Dan 1:17 [c]2 Chr 15:2
6 [a]Is 14:29
7 [a]2 Chr 21:16
8 [1]Lit *name went to the entering of Egypt* [a]2 Chr 17:11
9 [a]2 Chr 25:23 [b]Neh 2:13, 15; 3:13
10 [1]Heb *shephelah* [a]Gen 26:18-21
11 [1]Lit *goes out to*

25:23 *Gate of Ephraim to the Corner Gate.* Both gates were located in the northern wall of the city, the Ephraim Gate at the northwest and the Corner Gate at the northeast.

25:24 The family of Obed-edom was the Levitical family into whose care the temple storehouse had been entrusted (1 Chr 26:15).

25:27 See note on vv. 14–25.

26:1–23 See 2 Kin 15:1–7 and notes. The Chronicler has characteristically divided his account of Uzziah's reign into two parts: the good years, then the bad; cf. his treatment of Uzziah's father Amaziah and his grandfather Joash (see notes on 24:2; 25:1–28). The Chronicler elaborates on the blessings and divine help that flowed from Uzziah's obedience and fidelity (vv. 4–15), whereas the author of Kings only alludes to his fidelity (2 Kin 15:3). Where Kings only mentions Uzziah's leprosy (2 Kin 15:5), the Chronicler gives additional details to show that the disease was a result of unfaithfulness (vv. 16–21). Under Uzziah and his contemporary in the north, Jeroboam II, the borders of Israel and Judah briefly reached the extent they had attained under David and Solomon (vv. 6–8; 2 Kin 14:25). In part, this flourishing of the two kingdoms was facilitated by the removal of the Aramean threat by Assyria under Adadnirari III (802 B.C.), following which Assyria herself went into a period of weakness.

26:1 *Uzziah.* Also called Azariah (see, e.g., 2 Kin 15:6–7; 1 Chr 3:12). It is likely that Uzziah was a throne name, while Azariah was his personal name.

26:3 *fifty-two years.* 792–740 B.C., including a co-regency with Amaziah from 792 to 767.

26:4 The Chronicler has constructed his account of Uzziah's reign to give it the same outline as that for Amaziah and Joash (see note on vv. 1–23). He has also once again bypassed the statement in the parallel account that the king did not remove the high places (2 Kin 15:4), just as he did in the accounts of the other two kings (see note on 25:2).

26:5 *days of Zechariah.* The author again uses chronological notes to portray the cycles of blessing and judgment associated with the individual king's response to God's commands (see note on 12:2).

26:6–8 Uzziah's conquests were toward the southeast and the southwest; Israel's powerful Jeroboam II was in control to the north of Judah.

26:7 *Meunites.* See note on 20:1.

26:9 *Corner Gate . . . Valley Gate.* Found at the northeast and southwest portions of the walls. *fortified.* This construction along the wall of Jerusalem may reflect, in part, repair of the damage done by Joash during the reign of Amaziah (25:23).

26:10 *towers . . . cisterns.* Towers and cisterns have been found in several excavations (Qumran, Gibeah, Beersheba). A seal bearing Uzziah's name has been found in a cistern at Tell Beit Mirsim.

26:11 *Uzziah had an army ready for battle.* Tiglath-pileser III of Assyria states that he was opposed in his advance toward the west (743 B.C.) by a coalition headed by "Azriau of Yaudi," perhaps Azariah (Uzziah) of Judah.

sions according to the number of their
muster, [2]prepared by Jeiel the scribe and
Maaseiah the official, under the direction of
Hananiah, one of the king's officers.
12 The total number of the heads of the
[1]households, of valiant warriors, was 2,600.
13 Under their direction was an [1]elite
army of [a]307,500, who could wage war with
great power, to help the king against the enemy.
14 Moreover, Uzziah prepared [1]for all the
army shields, spears, helmets, body armor,
bows and sling stones.
15 In Jerusalem he made engines *of war*
invented by skillful men to be on the towers
and on the corners for the purpose of shooting arrows and great stones. Hence his [1]fame
spread afar, for he was marvelously helped
until he *was* strong.

Pride Is Uzziah's Undoing

16 But [a]when he became strong, his heart
was so [1]proud that he acted corruptly, and
he was unfaithful to the LORD his God, for
[b]he entered the temple of the LORD to burn
incense on the altar of incense.
17 Then [a]Azariah the priest entered after
him and with him eighty priests of the LORD,
valiant men.
18 [a]They opposed Uzziah the king and
said to him, "[b]It is not for you, Uzziah, to
burn incense to the LORD, [c]but for the priests,
the sons of Aaron who are consecrated to
burn incense. Get out of the sanctuary, for
you have been unfaithful and will have no
honor from the LORD God."
19 But Uzziah, with a censer in his hand
for burning incense, was enraged; and while
he was enraged with the priests, [a]the leprosy
broke out on his forehead before the priests
in the house of the LORD, beside the altar of
incense.
20 Azariah the chief priest and all the
priests looked at him, and behold, he *was*
leprous on his forehead; and they hurried
him out of there, and he himself also hastened to get out because the LORD had smitten him.
21 [a]King Uzziah was a leper to the day of
his death; and he lived in [b]a separate house,
being a leper, for he was cut off from the
house of the LORD. And Jotham his son *was*
over the king's house judging the people of
the land.
22 Now the rest of the acts of Uzziah, first
to last, the prophet [a]Isaiah, the son of Amoz,
has written.
23 So Uzziah slept with his fathers, and
they buried him with his fathers [a]in the field
of the grave which belonged to the kings, for
they said, "He is a leper." And Jotham his
son became king in his place.

Jotham Succeeds Uzziah in Judah

27 [a]Jotham was twenty-five years old
when he became king, and he reigned
sixteen years in Jerusalem. And his mother's
name was Jerushah the daughter of Zadok.
2 He did right in the sight of the LORD,
according to all that his father Uzziah had
done; [a]however he did not enter the temple
of the LORD. But the people continued acting
corruptly.
3 He built the upper gate of the house of
the LORD, and he built extensively the wall of
[a]Ophel.
4 Moreover, he built [a]cities in the hill
country of Judah, and he built fortresses and
towers on the wooded *hills*.
5 He fought also with the king of the
Ammonites and prevailed over them so that
the Ammonites gave him during that year
one hundred talents of silver, ten thousand
[1]kors of wheat and ten thousand of barley.
The Ammonites also paid him this *amount*
in the second and in the third year.
6 [a]So Jotham became mighty because he
ordered his ways before the LORD his God.
7 [a]Now the rest of the acts of Jotham,
even all his wars and his acts, behold, they
are written in the Book of the Kings of Israel
and Judah.

11 [2]Lit *by the hand of*
12 [1]Lit *fathers*
13 [1]Lit *powerful* [a]2 Chr 25:5
14 [1]Lit *for them, for all*
15 [1]Lit *name*
16 [1]Lit *lifted up* [a]Deut 32:15; 2 Chr 25:19 [b]1 Kin 13:1-4
17 [a]1 Chr 6:10
18 [a]2 Chr 19:2 [b]Num 3:10; 16:39, 40 [c]Ex 30:7, 8
19 [a]2 Kin 5:25-27

21 [a]2 Kin 15:5-7 [b]Lev 13:46
22 [a]Is 1:1
23 [a]2 Chr 21:20; 28:27; Is 6:1
27:1 [a]2 Kin 15:33-35
2 [a]2 Chr 26:16
3 [a]2 Chr 33:14; Neh 3:26
4 [a]2 Chr 11:5
5 [1]I.e. One kor equals approx 10 bu
6 [a]2 Chr 26:5
7 [a]2 Kin 15:36

26:15 *engines . . . for the purpose of shooting arrows and great stones.* Since the catapult was not known in the military technology of the period, and since torsion-operated devices for shooting arrows did not appear for approximately another three centuries, the devices mentioned here may refer to defensive constructions to protect those shooting arrows and hurling stones from the tops of the walls.

26:16 *when he became strong.* See note on v. 5.

26:19 *leprosy.* For disease as a punishment for sin see notes on 16:12; 21:12–15.

26:21 *his death.* See Is 6:1 and note. *separate house.* Or "house where he was relieved of responsibilities"; the same phrase in the Canaanite texts from Ugarit suggests a kind of quarantine or separation.

26:22 *Isaiah . . . has written.* Not a reference to the canonical book but to some other work no longer in existence.

26:23 *buried . . . in the field . . . which belonged to the kings.* Cf. 2 Kin 15:7. Apparently due to his leprosy, Uzziah was buried in a cemetery belonging to the kings, though not in the tombs of the kings.

27:1–9 See 2 Kin 15:32–38 and notes.

27:1 *sixteen years.* 750–735 B.C., including a co-regency with Uzziah (750–740). His reign also overlapped that of his successor Ahaz from 735 to 732.

27:2 *did not enter the temple.* The Chronicler commends Jotham for not making the same error Uzziah did (26:16). *acting corruptly.* Appears to refer to the flourishing high places (2 Kin 15:35).

27:3–6 Unique to the Chronicler and an elaboration of his thesis that fidelity to God's commands brings blessing: in construction, military victory and prosperity—all "because he ordered his ways before the LORD" (v. 6). Judah's relationship with the Ammonites held particular interest for the Chronicler (see notes on 20:1–30; 24:26).

27:7 *all his wars.* See, e.g., 2 Kin 15:37.

8 He was [a]twenty-five years old when he
became king, and he reigned sixteen years in
Jerusalem.
9 And Jotham slept with his fathers, and
they buried him in the city of David; and
Ahaz his son became king in his place.

Ahaz Succeeds Jotham in Judah

28 [a]Ahaz *was* twenty years old when he
became king, and he reigned sixteen
years in Jerusalem; and [b]he did not do right
in the sight of the LORD as David his father
had done.
2 [a]But he walked in the ways of the kings
of Israel; he also [b]made molten images for
the Baals.
3 Moreover, [a]he burned incense in the
valley of Ben-hinnom and [b]burned his sons
in fire, [c]according to the abominations of the
nations whom the LORD had driven out
before the sons of Israel.
4 He sacrificed and [a]burned incense on
the high places, on the hills and under every
green tree.

Judah Is Invaded

5 Wherefore, [a]the LORD his God delivered
him into the hand of the king of Aram; and
they [1]defeated him and carried away from
him a great number of captives and brought
them to Damascus. And he was also delivered into the hand of the king of Israel, who
[2]inflicted him with heavy casualties.
6 For [a]Pekah the son of Remaliah slew in
Judah 120,000 in one day, all valiant men,
because they had forsaken the LORD God of
their fathers.
7 And Zichri, a mighty man of Ephraim,
slew Maaseiah the king's son and Azrikam
the ruler of the house and Elkanah the second to the king.
8 [a]The sons of Israel carried away captive of [b]their brethren 200,000 women, sons
and daughters; and they [1]took also a great
deal of spoil from them, and brought the
spoil to Samaria.
9 But a prophet of the LORD was there,
whose name *was* Oded; and [a]he went out to
meet the army which came to Samaria and
said to them, "Behold, because the LORD, the
God of your fathers, [b]was angry with Judah,
He has delivered them into your hand, and
you have slain them in a rage [c]*which* has
even reached heaven.
10 "Now you are proposing to [a]subjugate
for yourselves the people of Judah and
Jerusalem for male and female slaves. Surely, *do* you not *have* transgressions of your
own against the LORD your God?
11 "Now therefore, listen to me and return
the captives [a]whom you captured from your
brothers, [b]for the burning anger of the LORD
is against you."
12 Then some of the heads of the sons of
Ephraim—Azariah the son of Johanan,
Berechiah the son of Meshillemoth, Jehizki-
ah the son of Shallum, and Amasa the son of
Hadlai—arose against those who were coming from the battle,
13 and said to them, "You must not bring
the captives in here, for you are proposing *to*
bring upon us guilt against the LORD adding
to our sins and our guilt; for our guilt is
great so that *His* burning anger is against
Israel."
14 So the armed men left the captives and
the spoil before the officers and all the
assembly.
15 Then [a]the men who were designated
by name arose, took the captives, and they
clothed all their naked ones from the spoil;
and they gave them clothes and sandals, fed
them and [b]gave them drink, anointed them
with oil, led all their feeble ones on donkeys,
and brought them to Jericho, [c]the city of
palm trees, to their brothers; then they
returned to Samaria.

8 [a]2 Chr 27:1 **28:1** [a]2 Kin 16:2-4 [b]2 Chr 27:2 **2** [a]2 Chr 22:3 [b]Ex 34:17 **3** [a]Josh 15:8 [b]Lev 18:21; 2 Chr 33:6 [c]2 Chr 33:2 **4** [a]2 Chr 28:25 **5** [1]Lit *smote* [2]Lit *smote him with a great smiting* [a]2 Kin 16:5; 2 Chr 24:24; Is 7:1 **6** [a]2 Kin 16:5 **8** [a]Deut 28:25, 41 [b]2 Chr 11:4

8 [1]Lit *plundered* **9** [a]2 Chr 25:15 [b]Is 47:6 [c]Ezra 9:6; Rev 18:5 **10** [a]Lev 25:39 **11** [a]2 Chr 28:8 [b]James 2:13 **15** [a]2 Chr 28:12 [b]2 Kin 6:22; Prov 25:21, 22 [c]Deut 34:3

28:1–27 See 2 Kin 16:1–20 and notes, though only the introduction and conclusion in the two accounts are strictly parallel. The reign of Ahaz is the only one for which the Chronicler does not mention a single redeeming feature. In his account the Chronicler appears to adopt explicit parallels from the speech of Abijah condemning the northern kingdom (ch. 13) in order to show that under Ahaz the southern kingdom had sunk to the same depths of apostasy. Judah's religious fidelity, of which Abijah had boasted, was completely overthrown under Ahaz.

28:1 *sixteen years.* 732–715 B.C., not including the co-regency with Jotham (735–732).

28:2 *made molten images.* Cf. 13:8.

28:3 *valley of Ben-hinnom.* Cf. 33:6. Josiah put an end to the pagan practices observed there (2 Kin 23:10). *burned his sons in fire.* See Lev 20:1–5; Jer 7:31–32. 2 Kin 16:3 has the singular "son." Some have regarded the plural as a deliberate inflation on the part of the Chronicler to heighten the wickedness of Ahaz. However, some manuscripts of the Septuagint (the Greek translation of the OT) also have a plural in 2 Kin 16:3, suggesting that the Chronicler may have faithfully copied the text before him.

28:5 Cf. 13:16–17. *God delivered him into the hand of.* According to the Chronicler's view on immediate retribution, defeat in war is one of the results of disobedience (see note on 20:30). *also delivered into the hand of the king of Israel.* 2 Kin 16:5–6 and Is 7 make it clear that Rezin (king of Aram) and Pekah acted together against Judah. The Chronicler has chosen either to treat them separately or to report on two different episodes of the Aram-Israel coalition.

28:6 *Pekah.* Reigned over the northern kingdom 752–732 B.C. (see 2 Kin 15:27–31). *had forsaken the LORD.* The same charge Abijah made against the northern kingdom (13:11).

28:9–15 The kindness of the northern captors to their captives from Judah, especially as recorded in vv. 14–15, may be the background for Jesus' parable of the Good Samaritan (Luke 10:25–37). Oded's attitude to the north is shown by his willingness to call them "brothers" (v. 11). In this case, too, the record of ch. 13 has been reversed: The northern tribes are more righteous than the south.

Compromise with Assyria

16 [a]At that time King Ahaz sent to the
[1]kings of Assyria for help.
17 [a]For again the Edomites had come and
attacked Judah and carried away captives.
18 [a]The Philistines also had invaded the
cities of the [1]lowland and of the Negev of
Judah, and had taken Beth-shemesh, Aijalon, Gederoth, and Soco with its villages,
Timnah with its villages, and Gimzo with its
villages, and they settled there.
19 For the LORD humbled Judah because
of Ahaz king of [a]Israel, for he had brought
about a lack of restraint in Judah and was
very unfaithful to the LORD.
20 So [a]Tilgath-pilneser king of Assyria
came against him and afflicted him instead
of strengthening him.
21 [a]Although Ahaz took a portion out of
the house of the LORD and out of the palace
of the king and of the princes, and gave *it* to
the king of Assyria, it did not help him.
22 Now in the time of his distress this
same King Ahaz [a]became yet more unfaithful to the LORD.
23 [a]For he sacrificed to the gods of
Damascus which had [1]defeated him, and
said, "[b]Because the gods of the kings of
Aram helped them, I will sacrifice to them
that they may help me." But they became the
[2]downfall of him and all Israel.

16 [1]Ancient versions read *king* [a]2 Kin 16:7
17 [a]Obad 10, 14
18 [1]Heb *shephelah* [a]Ezek 16:57
19 [a]2 Chr 21:2
20 [a]1 Chr 5:26
21 [a]2 Kin 16:8, 9
22 [a]Is 1:5; Jer 5:3; Rev 16:11
23 [1]Lit *smitten* [2]Lit *stumbling* [a]2 Chr 25:14 [b]Jer 44:17, 18
24 [a]2 Kin 16:17 [b]2 Chr 29:7 [c]2 Chr 30:14; 33:3-5
26 [a]2 Kin 16:19, 20
27 [a]2 Kin 16:20; 2 Chr 24:25; Is 14:28 [b]2 Chr 21:2
29:1 [a]2 Kin 18:1-3
2 [a]2 Chr 28:1; 34:2
3 [a]2 Chr 28:24; 29:7

24 Moreover, when Ahaz gathered together the utensils of the house of God, he [a]cut
the utensils of the house of God in pieces;
and he [b]closed the doors of the house of the
LORD and [c]made altars for himself in every
corner of Jerusalem.
25 In every city of Judah he made high
places to burn incense to other gods, and
provoked the LORD, the God of his fathers, to
anger.
26 [a]Now the rest of his acts and all his
ways, from first to last, behold, they are written in the Book of the Kings of Judah and
Israel.
27 [a]So Ahaz slept with his fathers, and
they buried him in the city, in Jerusalem, for
they did not bring him into the tombs of the
kings of [b]Israel; and Hezekiah his son
reigned in his place.

Hezekiah Succeeds Ahaz in Judah

29 [a]Hezekiah became king *when he was*
twenty-five years old; and he reigned
twenty-nine years in Jerusalem. And his
mother's name *was* Abijah, the daughter of
Zechariah.
2 [a]He did right in the sight of the LORD,
according to all that his father David had
done.
3 In the first year of his reign, in the first
month, he [a]opened the doors of the house of
the LORD and repaired them.

28:17–18 *Edomites . . . attacked Judah . . . Philistines also had invaded.* Foreign alliances (v. 16) led to further defeats for Ahaz (see note on 16:2–9).
28:19 *The LORD humbled Judah because of Ahaz.* The same formula used to describe the defeat of the northern tribes in 13:18, though under Ahaz it is Judah that is subdued.
28:20 *Tilgath-pilneser.* A variant of Tiglath-pileser, king of Assyria 745–727 B.C. (see 1 Chr 5:26 and note). *afflicted him instead of strengthening him.* Appears on the surface to contradict the statement in 2 Kin 16:9 that Tiglath-pileser III responded to Ahaz's request by attacking and capturing Damascus, exiling its population and killing Rezin. The Chronicler assumes the reader's familiarity with the other account and knows of the temporary respite for Judah gained by Assyrian intervention against Damascus and the northern kingdom of Israel. But he focuses on the long-range results, in which Judah herself was reduced to vassalage to Assyria.
28:22–23 The Chronicler presumes the reader's familiarity with Ahaz's trip to Damascus and his copying of the altar and practices there (2 Kin 16:10–16).
28:24–25 Additional details on Ahaz's alterations are found in 2 Kin 16:17–18. The Chronicler also adds details in his description of Hezekiah's reforming activities to correct some of the abuses under Ahaz: Not only had the doors been shut, but also the lamps were put out and offerings were not made at the sanctuary (29:7); the altar and utensils were desecrated, and the table for the consecrated bread was neglected (29:18–19). It is precisely these accoutrements of proper temple service about which Abijah had boasted when he proclaimed the faithfulness of Judah in contrast to that of the northern kingdom (13:11). Now these orthodox furnishings are lacking under Ahaz and make the southern kingdom just like the north (see note on vv. 1–27).
28:27 *did not bring him into the tombs of the kings.* The third king whose wickedness resulted in the loss of this honor at death. The others were Jehoram (21:20) and Joash (24:25). Uzziah's sin and leprosy brought the same result, though it is not reported in exactly the same terms (26:23). Cf. also Manasseh (33:20).
29:1–32:33 The Chronicler devotes more attention to Hezekiah than to any other post-Solomonic king. Although the parallel text (2 Kin 18–20) has about the same amount of material, only about a fourth of the total relates the same or similar material; only a few verses are strict literary parallels (29:1–2; 32:32–33). In Kings preeminence among the post-Solomonic kings is given to Josiah (2 Kin 22–23; cf. 1 Kin 13:2), and the record of Hezekiah is primarily devoted to his confrontation with Sennacherib of Assyria. By contrast, the Chronicler highlights almost exclusively Hezekiah's religious reform and his devotion to matters of ceremony and ritual. The parallel passage (2 Kin 18:1–6) touches the religious reform only briefly. The numerous parallels in these chapters with the account of Solomon's reign suggest that the Chronicler viewed Hezekiah as a "second Solomon" in his celebration of the Passover (30:2,5,23,25–26), his cultic arrangements (29:7,18,35; 31:2–3), his wealth (32:27–29), the honor accorded him by the Gentiles (32:23) and the extent of his dominion (30:25).
29:1 *twenty-nine years.* 715–686 B.C. (but see note on Is 36:1), including a 15-year extension of life granted by God (2 Kin 20:6) but not mentioned by the Chronicler.
29:3–30:27 Not found in Kings.
29:3 *first year.* 715 B.C., another example of the Chronicler's practice of introducing chronological materials into his narrative (see note on 12:2). *opened the doors of the house of the LORD.* Necessary after the actions of Ahaz (28:24). *repaired them.* The repairs to the doors included new gold overlay (2 Kin 18:16).

4 He brought in the priests and the Levites and gathered them into the square on the east.

Reforms Begun

5 Then he said to them, "Listen to me, O Levites. [a]Consecrate yourselves now, and consecrate the house of the LORD, the God of your fathers, and carry the uncleanness out from the holy place.

6 "For our fathers have been unfaithful and have done evil in the sight of the LORD our God, and have forsaken Him and [a]turned their faces away from the dwelling place of the LORD, and have [1]turned *their* backs.

7 "They have also [a]shut the doors of the porch and put out the lamps, and have not burned incense or offered burnt offerings in the holy place to the God of Israel.

8 "Therefore [a]the wrath of the LORD was against Judah and Jerusalem, and He has made them an object of terror, of horror, and of [b]hissing, as you see with your own eyes.

9 "For behold, [a]our fathers have fallen by the sword, and our sons and our daughters and our wives are in captivity for this.

10 "Now it is in my heart [a]to make a covenant with the LORD God of Israel, that His burning anger may turn away from us.

11 "My sons, do not be negligent now, for [a]the LORD has chosen you to stand before Him, to minister to Him, and to be His ministers and burn incense."

12 Then the Levites arose: [a]Mahath, the son of Amasai and Joel the son of Azariah, from the sons of [b]the Kohathites; and from the sons of Merari, Kish the son of Abdi and Azariah the son of Jehallelel; and from the Gershonites, Joah the son of Zimmah and Eden the son of Joah;

13 and from the sons of Elizaphan, Shimri and [1]Jeiel; and from the sons of Asaph, Zechariah and Mattaniah;

14 and from the sons of Heman, [1]Jehiel and Shimei; and from the sons of Jeduthun, Shemaiah and Uzziel.

15 They assembled their brothers, [a]consecrated themselves, and went in [b]to cleanse the house of the LORD, according to the commandment of the king [c]by the words of the LORD.

16 So the priests went in to the inner part of the house of the LORD to cleanse *it,* and every unclean thing which they found in the temple of the LORD they brought out to the court of the house of the LORD. Then the Levites received *it* to carry out to [a]the Kidron [1]valley.

17 Now they began [1]the consecration [a]on the first *day* of the first month, and on the eighth day of the month they entered the porch of the LORD. Then they consecrated the house of the LORD in eight days, and finished on the sixteenth day of the first month.

18 Then they went in to King Hezekiah and said, "We have cleansed the whole house of the LORD, the altar of burnt offering with all of its utensils, and the table of showbread with all of its utensils.

19 "Moreover, [a]all the utensils which King Ahaz had discarded during his reign in his unfaithfulness, we have prepared and consecrated; and behold, they are before the altar of the LORD."

Hezekiah Restores Temple Worship

20 Then King Hezekiah arose early and assembled the princes of the city and went up to the house of the LORD.

21 They brought seven bulls, seven rams, seven lambs and seven male goats [a]for a sin offering for the kingdom, the sanctuary, and Judah. And he ordered the priests, the sons of Aaron, to offer *them* on the altar of the LORD.

22 So they slaughtered the bulls, and the priests took the blood and sprinkled it on the altar. They also slaughtered the rams and sprinkled the blood on the altar; they slaughtered the lambs also and [a]sprinkled the blood on the altar.

23 Then they brought the male goats of the sin offering before the king and the assembly, and [a]they laid their hands on them.

24 The priests slaughtered them and purged the altar with their blood [a]to atone for all Israel, for the king ordered the burnt offering and the sin offering for all Israel.

25 [a]He then stationed the Levites in the house of the LORD with cymbals, with harps and with lyres, [b]according to the command of David and of [c]Gad the king's seer, and of

5 [a]2 Chr 29:15, 34; 35:6 **6** [1]Lit *given* [a]Ezek 8:16 **7** [a]2 Chr 28:24 **8** [a]2 Chr 24:20 [b]Jer 25:9, 18 **9** [a]2 Chr 28:5-8, 17 **10** [a]2 Chr 23:16 **11** [a]Num 3:6; 8:6 **12** [a]2 Chr 31:13 [b]Num 3:19, 20 **13** [1]Or *Jeuel* **14** [1]Or *Jehuel,* 1 Chr 15:18, 20 **15** [a]2 Chr 29:5 [b]1 Chr 23:28 [c]2 Chr 30:12

16 [1]Or *wadi* [a]2 Chr 15:16 **17** [1]Lit *to consecrate* [a]2 Chr 29:3 **19** [a]2 Chr 28:24 **21** [a]Lev 4:3-14 **22** [a]Lev 4:18 **23** [a]Lev 4:15 **24** [a]Lev 4:26 **25** [a]1 Chr 25:6 [b]2 Chr 8:14 [c]2 Sam 24:11

29:5–11 Hezekiah's speech demonstrates again the Chronicler's convictions about the coherence of action and effect: The sins of the past brought difficulty and judgment, but renewed fidelity brings relief.

29:7 Hezekiah reinstitutes these temple arrangements—following the pattern of Solomon (2:4; 4:7).

29:8 *object of terror, of horror, and of hissing.* Echoes the language of the prophets, especially Jeremiah (see Jer 19:8; 25:9,18; 29:18; 51:37). Reference is to the Assyrian devastation of the northern kingdom and much of Judah.

29:12 *Kohathites . . . sons of Merari . . . Gershonites.* The three clans of Levi (1 Chr 6:1).

29:13–14 *Asaph . . . Heman . . . Jeduthun.* Founders of the three families of Levitical musicians (1 Chr 6:31–48; 25:1–31).

29:13 *Elizaphan.* A leader of the Kohathites (Num 3:30), whose family had achieved status almost as a sub-clan (see 1 Chr 15:8 and note on 1 Chr 15:4–10).

29:16 *carry out to the Kidron Valley.* Asa also burned pagan cult objects there (15:16; cf. 30:14).

29:18 These actions under Hezekiah mirror those of Solomon (2:4).

29:21 *sin offering.* See Lev 4:1–5:13.

29:22 *sprinkled the blood.* See Lev 17:6; Num 18:17.

29:23 *laid their hands on them.* See Lev 4:13–15; 8:14–15; Num 8:12.

29:25 *David and of Gad . . . and of Nathan . . . prophets.* The

[d]Nathan the prophet; for the command was
from the LORD through His prophets.
26 The Levites stood with [a]the *musical*
instruments of David, and [b]the priests with
the trumpets.
27 Then Hezekiah gave the order to offer
the burnt offering on the altar. When the
burnt offering began, [a]the song to the LORD
also began with the trumpets, [1]*accompanied*
by the instruments of David, king of Israel.
28 While the whole assembly worshiped,
the singers also sang and the trumpets
sounded; all this *continued* until the burnt
offering was finished.
29 Now at the completion of the burnt
offerings, [a]the king and all who were present
with him bowed down and worshiped.
30 Moreover, King Hezekiah and the officials ordered the Levites to sing praises to
the LORD with the words of David and Asaph
the seer. [a]So they sang praises with joy, and
bowed down and worshiped.
31 Then Hezekiah said, "[a]Now *that* you
have [1]consecrated yourselves to the LORD,
come near and bring sacrifices and thank
offerings to the house of the LORD." And the
assembly brought sacrifices and thank offerings, and [b]all those who were [2]willing
brought burnt offerings.
32 The number of the burnt offerings
which the assembly brought was 70 bulls,
100 rams, and 200 lambs; all these were for a
burnt offering to the LORD.
33 The consecrated things were 600 bulls
and 3,000 sheep.
34 But the priests were too few, so that they
were unable to skin all the burnt offerings;
[a]therefore their brothers the Levites helped
them until the work was completed and until
the *other* priests had consecrated themselves.
For [b]the Levites were more [1]conscientious to
consecrate themselves than the priests.
35 There *were* also [1][a]many burnt offerings
with [b]the fat of the peace offerings and with
[c]the libations for the burnt offerings. Thus
the service of the house of the LORD was
established *again*.
36 Then Hezekiah and all the people
rejoiced over what God had prepared for the
people, because the thing came about suddenly.

All Israel Invited to the Passover

30 Now Hezekiah sent to all Israel and
Judah and wrote letters also to Ephraim
and Manasseh, that they should come to the
house of the LORD at Jerusalem to [1]celebrate
the Passover to the LORD God of Israel.
2 For the king and his princes and all the
assembly in Jerusalem had decided [a]to celebrate the Passover in the second month,
3 since they could not celebrate it [a]at
that time, because the priests had not consecrated themselves in sufficient numbers, nor
had the people been gathered to Jerusalem.
4 Thus the thing was right in the sight of
the king and [1]all the assembly.
5 So they established a decree to circulate a [1]proclamation throughout all Israel
[a]from Beersheba even to Dan, that they
should come to celebrate the Passover to the
LORD God of Israel at Jerusalem. For they had
not celebrated *it* in great numbers as it was
[2]prescribed.
6 [a]The [1]couriers went throughout all
Israel and Judah with the letters from the
hand of the king and his princes, even
according to the command of the king, saying, "O sons of Israel, return to the LORD God
of Abraham, Isaac and Israel, that He may
return to those of you who escaped *and* are
left from [b]the [2]hand of the kings of Assyria.
7 "[a]Do not be like your fathers and your
brothers, who were unfaithful to the LORD
God of their fathers, so that [b]He made them
a horror, as you see.

25 [d]2 Sam 7:2
26 [a]1 Chr 23:5 [b]2 Chr 5:12
27 [1]Lit *and according to the authority of the instruments* [a]2 Chr 23:18
29 [a]2 Chr 20:18
30 [a]Ps 100:1; 106:12
31 [1]Lit *filled your hands* [2]Lit *willing of heart* [a]2 Chr 13:9 [b]Ex 35:5, 22
34 [1]Lit *upright of heart* [a]2 Chr 35:11 [b]2 Chr 30:3
35 [1]Lit *the burnt offerings to an abundance* [a]2 Chr 29:32
35 [b]Lev 3:16 [c]Num 15:5-10
30:1 [1]Lit *do*, so in vv 2, 3, 5, 13, 21, 23
2 [a]Num 9:10, 11; 2 Chr 30:13, 15
3 [a]2 Chr 29:17, 34
4 [1]Lit *in the sight of all*
5 [1]Lit *voice* [2]Lit *written* [a]Judg 20:1
6 [1]Lit *runners* [2]Lit *palm* [a]Esth 8:14; Job 9:25; Jer 51:31 [b]2 Chr 28:20
7 [a]Ezek 20:13 [b]2 Chr 29:8

Chronicler considers David among the prophets (see notes on 1:7; 1 Chr 28:19).

29:26 *instruments of David.* See 1 Chr 23:5.

29:35 *many burnt offerings . . . peace offerings . . . libations.* Reminiscent of the dedication of the temple under Solomon (7:4–6). For the laws regarding the peace offerings see Lev 3; 7:11–21; for the "libations for the burnt offerings" see Num 15:1–12. *service of the house of the LORD was established again.* Similar to the formula used in 8:16 with reference to Solomon's work.

30:1–27 Unique to the Chronicler; cf. the famous Passover under Josiah (35:1–19; 2 Kin 23:21–23). Hezekiah allowed two deviations from the law (Ex 12; Deut 16:1–8) in this observance: (1) the date in the second month (v. 2) and (2) exemption from some ritual requirements (vv. 18–19).

30:1 *all Israel and Judah.* See Introduction to 1 Chronicles: Purpose and Themes. With the northern kingdom now ended as the result of the Assyrian invasion and deportation (which surprisingly is not mentioned), the Chronicler shows "all Israel" once again united around the Davidic king and the temple (see vv. 5,18–19,25).

30:2 *second month.* After the division of the kingdom, Jeroboam deferred the sacral calendar of the northern kingdom by one month (1 Kin 12:32), possibly to further wean the subjects in the north away from devotion to Jerusalem. By delaying the celebration of Passover one month, Hezekiah not only allows time for the priests to consecrate themselves (v. 3) and for the people to gather (vv. 3,13), but also achieves unity between the kingdoms on the date of the Passover for the first time since the schism more than two centuries earlier. Delaying the date reflects Hezekiah's concern to involve "all Israel." For the first time since Solomon the entire nation observes Passover together, reflecting the Chronicler's view that Hezekiah is a "second Solomon." Passover was prescribed for the 14th day of the first month (Ex 12:2,6; Deut 16:1–8), but could not be celebrated at that time due to the defilement of the temple and the purification rites under way (29:3,17). For celebration of Passover by the restored community shortly after the dedication of the rebuilt temple see Ezra 6:16–22.

30:5 *great numbers.* Another comparison with the time of Solomon (see v. 26). At the time of its inception, Passover was primarily a family observance (Ex 12). It later became a national celebration at the temple (v. 8; see Deut 16:1–8).

8 "Now do not [a]stiffen your neck like your fathers, but [1]yield to the LORD and enter His sanctuary which He has consecrated forever, and serve the LORD your God, [b]that His burning anger may turn away from you.

9 "For [a]if you return to the LORD, your brothers and your sons *will find* compassion before those who led them captive and will return to this land. [b]For the LORD your God is gracious and compassionate, and will not turn *His* face away from you if you return to Him."

10 So the [1]couriers passed from city to city through the country of Ephraim and Manasseh, and as far as Zebulun, but [a]they laughed them to scorn and mocked them.

11 Nevertheless [a]some men of Asher, Manasseh and Zebulun humbled themselves and came to Jerusalem.

12 The [a]hand of God was also on Judah to give them one heart to do what the king and the princes commanded by the word of the LORD.

Passover Reinstituted

13 Now many people were gathered at Jerusalem to celebrate the Feast of Unleavened Bread [a]in the second month, a very large assembly.

14 They arose and removed the altars which *were* in Jerusalem; they also [a]removed all the incense altars and [b]cast *them* into the brook Kidron.

15 Then [a]they slaughtered the Passover *lambs* on the fourteenth of the second month. And [b]the priests and Levites were ashamed of themselves, and consecrated themselves and brought burnt offerings to the house of the LORD.

16 [a]They stood at their stations after their custom, according to the law of Moses the man of God; the priests sprinkled the blood *which they received* from the hand of the Levites.

17 For *there were* many in the assembly who had not consecrated themselves; therefore, [a]the Levites *were* over the slaughter of the Passover *lambs* for everyone who *was* unclean, in order to consecrate *them* to the LORD.

18 For a multitude of the people, [a]*even* many from Ephraim and Manasseh, Issachar and Zebulun, had not purified themselves, [b]yet they ate the Passover [c]otherwise than [1]prescribed. For Hezekiah prayed for them, saying, "May the good LORD pardon

19 [a]everyone who prepares his heart to seek God, the LORD God of his fathers, though not according to the purification *rules* of the sanctuary."

20 So the LORD heard Hezekiah and [a]healed the people.

21 The sons of Israel present in Jerusalem [a]celebrated the Feast of Unleavened Bread *for* seven days with great joy, and the Levites and the priests praised the LORD day after day with loud instruments to the LORD.

22 Then Hezekiah [a]spoke [1]encouragingly to all the Levites who showed good insight *in the things* of the LORD. So they ate for the appointed seven days, sacrificing peace offerings and [b]giving thanks to the LORD God of their fathers.

23 Then the whole assembly [a]decided to celebrate *the feast* another seven days, so they celebrated the seven days with joy.

24 For [a]Hezekiah king of Judah had contributed to the assembly 1,000 bulls and 7,000 sheep, and the princes had contributed to the assembly 1,000 bulls and 10,000 sheep; and [b]a large number of priests consecrated themselves.

25 All the assembly of Judah rejoiced, with the priests and the Levites and [a]all the assembly that came from Israel, both the sojourners who came from the land of Israel and those living in Judah.

26 So there was great joy in Jerusalem, because there was nothing like this in Jerusalem [a]since the days of Solomon the son of David, king of Israel.

27 Then [a]the Levitical priests arose and [b]blessed the people; and their voice was heard and their prayer came to [c]His holy dwelling place, to heaven.

8 [1]Lit *give a hand* [a]Ex 32:9 [b]2 Chr 29:10
9 [a]Deut 30:2 [b]Ex 34:6, 7; Mic 7:18
10 [1]Lit *runners* [a]2 Chr 36:16
11 [a]2 Chr 30:18, 21, 25
12 [a]2 Cor 3:5; Phil 2:13; Heb 13:20, 21
13 [a]2 Chr 30:2
14 [a]2 Chr 28:24 [b]2 Chr 29:16
15 [a]2 Chr 30:2, 3 [b]2 Chr 29:34
16 [a]2 Chr 35:10, 15
17 [a]2 Chr 29:34
18 [1]Lit *written* [a]2 Chr 30:11, 25 [b]Num 9:10 [c]Ex 12:43-49
19 [a]2 Chr 19:3
20 [a]James 5:16
21 [a]Ex 12:15; 13:6
22 [1]Lit *to the heart of* [a]2 Chr 32:6 [b]Ezra 10:11
23 [a]1 Kin 8:65
24 [a]2 Chr 35:7, 8 [b]2 Chr 29:34; 30:3
25 [a]2 Chr 30:11, 18
26 [a]2 Chr 7:8-10
27 [a]2 Chr 23:18 [b]Num 6:23 [c]Deut 26:15; Ps 68:5

30:8 *enter His sanctuary.* Passover was one of three annual pilgrim feasts requiring attendance at the temple (see Num 28:9–29:39).
30:9 *find compassion before those who led them captive.* In Solomon's prayer in 6:39 the Chronicler omitted the phrase found in the parallel account (1 Kin 8:50) that their conquerors would "have compassion on them." Here the phrase is found in the speech of Hezekiah, again portraying him as a kind of "second Solomon" (see Lev 26:40–42). *will return to this land.* Those who repent will have hope of return, even those from the Assyrian captivity.
30:14 *cast them into the brook Kidron.* See 29:16 and note.
30:15 *the priests and Levites . . . consecrated themselves.* The reproach previously directed against the priests (v. 3; 29:34) is here broadened to include also the Levites—an exhortation to the priests and Levites of the restored community to be faithful.
30:17 *Levites were over the slaughter of the Passover lambs.* See Ex 12:6; Deut 16:6. According to the law the heads of families were to slay the Passover sacrifice. The Levites perhaps acted for the recent arrivals from the northern kingdom who were not ceremonially clean. Cf. John 11:55.
30:18–19 Faith and obedience take precedence over ritual (see Mark 7:1–23; John 7:22–23; 9:14–16).
30:20 The response to Hezekiah's prayer recalls the prayer of Solomon (7:14).
30:23 *another seven days.* The festival was observed for two weeks, just as the observance of the dedication of Solomon's temple had been (7:8–9).
30:26 *since the days of Solomon.* An explicit indication of the Chronicler's modeling of the reign of Hezekiah after that of Solomon (see note on 29:1–32:33).
30:27 *prayer came to His holy dwelling place, to heaven.* Another echo of Solomon's dedication prayer (6:21,30,33,39).

Idols Are Destroyed

31 Now when all this was finished, all Israel who were present went out to the cities of Judah, [a]broke the pillars in pieces, cut down the [1]Asherim and pulled down the high places and the altars throughout all Judah and Benjamin, as well as in Ephraim and Manasseh, [2]until they had destroyed them all. Then all the sons of Israel returned to their cities, each to his possession.

2 And Hezekiah appointed [a]the divisions of the priests and the Levites by their divisions, each according to his service, *both* the priests and the Levites, [b]for burnt offerings and for peace offerings, to minister and to give thanks and to praise in the gates of the camp of the LORD.

Reforms Continued

3 *He* also *appointed* [a]the king's portion of his goods for the burnt offerings, *namely,* for the morning and evening burnt offerings, and the burnt offerings for the sabbaths and for the new moons and for the fixed festivals, [b]as it is written in the law of the LORD.

4 Also he [1]commanded the people who lived in Jerusalem to give [a]the portion due to the priests and the Levites, that they might devote themselves to [b]the law of the LORD.

5 As soon as the [1]order spread, the sons of Israel provided in abundance the first fruits of grain, new wine, oil, honey and of all the produce of the field; and they brought in abundantly [a]the tithe of all.

6 The sons of Israel and Judah who lived in the cities of Judah also brought in the tithe of oxen and sheep, and [a]the tithe of [1]sacred gifts which were consecrated to the LORD their God, and placed *them* in heaps.

7 In the third month they began to [1]make the heaps, and finished *them* by the seventh month.

8 When Hezekiah and the rulers came and saw the heaps, they blessed the LORD and [a]His people Israel.

9 Then Hezekiah questioned the priests and the Levites concerning the heaps.

10 Azariah the chief priest [a]of the house of Zadok said to [1]him, "[b]Since the contributions began to be brought into the house of the LORD, we have had enough to eat with plenty left over, for the LORD has blessed His people, and this great quantity is left over."

11 Then Hezekiah commanded *them* to prepare [a]rooms in the house of the LORD, and they prepared *them.*

12 They faithfully brought in the contributions and the tithes and the consecrated things; and Conaniah the Levite *was* the officer in charge [a]of them and his brother Shimei *was* second.

13 Jehiel, Azaziah, Nahath, Asahel, Jerimoth, Jozabad, Eliel, Ismachiah, Mahath and Benaiah *were* overseers [1]under the authority of Conaniah and Shimei his brother by the appointment of King Hezekiah, and [a]Azariah *was* the *chief* officer of the house of God.

14 Kore the son of Imnah the Levite, the keeper of the eastern *gate, was* over the freewill offerings of God, to apportion the contributions for the LORD and the most holy things.

15 [1]Under his authority *were* [a]Eden, Miniamin, Jeshua, Shemaiah, Amariah and Shecaniah in [b]the cities of the priests, to distribute faithfully *their portions* to their brothers by divisions, whether great or small,

16 without regard to their genealogical enrollment, to the males from [1a]thirty years old and upward—everyone who entered the house of the LORD [b]for his daily obligations—for their work in their duties according to their divisions;

17 as well as the priests who were enrolled genealogically according to their fathers' households, and the Levites [a]from twenty years old and upwards, by their duties *and* their divisions.

18 The genealogical enrollment *included* [1]all their little children, their wives, their sons and their daughters, for the whole assembly, for they consecrated themselves [2]faithfully in holiness.

19 Also for the sons of Aaron the priests *who were* in [a]the pasture lands of their cities, or in each and every city, [b]*there were* men who were designated by name to distribute

31:1 [1]I.e. wooden symbols of a female deity [2]Lit *even to completion* [a]2 Kin 18:4
2 [a]1 Chr 24:1 [b]1 Chr 23:28-31
3 [a]2 Chr 35:7 [b]Num 28:1-29:40
4 [1]Lit *said to* [a]Num 18:8 [b]Mal 2:7
5 [1]Lit *word* [a]Neh 13:12
6 [1]Lit *consecrated things* [a]Lev 27:30; Deut 14:28
7 [1]Lit *found*
8 [a]Deut 33:29; Ps 33:12; 144:15
10 [1]Lit *him, and he said* [a]1 Chr 6:8, 9 [b]Mal 3:10
11 [a]1 Kin 6:5, 8
12 [a]2 Chr 35:9
13 [1]Lit *from the hand of* [a]2 Chr 31:10
15 [1]Lit *under his hand* [a]2 Chr 29:12 [b]Josh 21:9-19
16 [1]Heb *three* [a]1 Chr 23:3 [b]Ezra 3:4
17 [a]1 Chr 23:24
18 [1]Lit *with all* [2]Lit *in their faithfulness*
19 [a]Lev 25:34; Num 35:2-5 [b]2 Chr 31:12-15

31:1–21 Apart from the first verse, which parallels 2 Kin 18:4, the material of this chapter is unique to the Chronicler, whose interest in the Levites and the temple predominates. Hezekiah's efforts to ensure the material support of the Levites (v. 4) probably had relevance to the postexilic audience for whom the Chronicler wrote.

31:1 *all Israel . . . all the sons of Israel.* The Chronicler's interest in "all Israel" as united under Hezekiah is again apparent. *pillars.* See note on 1 Kin 14:23. *Asherim.* See note on 14:3.

31:2 Echoes 8:14. The Chronicler continues to model Hezekiah as a "second Solomon" (see notes on 29:7,18).

31:3 *appointed the king's portion.* The king's giving from his own wealth prompted a generous response from the people, as it had also under David (1 Chr 29:3–9).

31:5–6 See Deut 12:5–19; 14:22–27. The grain, new wine and oil had to be brought to the temple (Deut 12:17). Those coming from a distance, however, could bring the value of their offerings and purchase them on arrival (Deut 14:24). Only those who actually lived in Judah brought the tithe of their herds and flocks, a difficult procedure for those who lived farther away. For the restored community's commitment to bring their first fruits, tithes and offerings see Neh 10:35–39. For their failure to do so see Neh 13:10–13; Mal 3:8–10.

31:7 *third month.* May-June, the time of the Feast of Pentecost and the grain harvest. *seventh month.* September-October, the time of the Feast of Booths and the fruit and vine harvest (see Ex 23:16).

31:16 *thirty years.* Though all ancient manuscripts read "three years," that is probably a copyist's mistake for "30 years," the age at which duties were assigned in the temple (1 Chr 23:3).

portions to every male among the priests and to everyone genealogically enrolled among the Levites.

20 Thus Hezekiah did throughout all Judah; and [a]he did what *was* good, right and true before the LORD his God.

21 Every work which he began in the service of the house of God in law and in commandment, seeking his God, he did with all his heart and [a]prospered.

Sennacherib Invades Judah

32 After these [1]acts of faithfulness [a]Sennacherib king of Assyria came and invaded Judah and besieged the fortified cities, and [2]thought to break into them for himself.

2 Now when Hezekiah saw that Sennacherib had come and that [1]he intended to make war on Jerusalem,

3 he decided with his officers and his warriors to cut off the *supply of* water from the springs which *were* outside the city, and they helped him.

4 So many people assembled [a]and stopped up all the springs and [b]the stream which flowed [1]through the region, saying, "Why should the kings of Assyria come and find abundant water?"

5 And he took courage and [a]rebuilt all the wall that had been broken down and [1]erected towers on it, and *built* [b]another outside wall and strengthened the [c]Millo *in* the city of David, and made weapons and shields in great number.

6 He appointed military officers over the people and gathered them to him in the square at the city gate, and [a]spoke [1]encouragingly to them, saying,

7 "[a]Be strong and courageous, do not fear or be dismayed because of the king of Assyria nor because of all the horde that is with him; [b]for the one with us is greater than the one with him.

8 "With him is *only* [a]an arm of flesh, but [b]with us is the LORD our God to help us and to fight our battles." And the people relied on the words of Hezekiah king of Judah.

20 [a]2 Kin 20:3; 22:2
21 [a]Deut 29:9; Prov 3:9, 10
32:1 [1]Lit *things and this faithfulness* [2]Lit *said* [a]2 Kin 18:13-19, 37; Is 36:1-37:38
2 [1]Lit *his face for war against*
4 [1]Lit *in the midst of the land* [a]2 Kin 20:20 [b]2 Chr 32:30
5 [1]Lit *raised on the towers* [a]2 Chr 25:23 [b]2 Kin 25:4 [c]1 Kin 9:24
6 [1]Lit *upon their hearts* [a]2 Chr 30:22
7 [a]1 Chr 22:13 [b]2 Kin 6:16
8 [a]Jer 17:5 [b]2 Chr 20:17

Sennacherib Undermines Hezekiah

9 After this [a]Sennacherib king of Assyria sent his servants to Jerusalem while he *was* [1]besieging Lachish with all his forces with him, against Hezekiah king of Judah and against all Judah who *were* at Jerusalem, saying,

10 "Thus says Sennacherib king of Assyria, 'On what are you trusting that you are remaining in Jerusalem under siege?

11 'Is not Hezekiah misleading you to give yourselves over to die by hunger and by thirst, saying, "The LORD our God will deliver us from the [1]hand of the king of Assyria"?

12 '[a]Has not the same Hezekiah taken away His high places and His altars, and said to Judah and [1]Jerusalem, "You shall worship before one altar, and on it you shall [2]burn incense"?

13 'Do you not know what I and my fathers have done to all the peoples of the lands? [a]Were the gods of the nations of the lands able at all to deliver their land from my hand?

14 '[a]Who *was there* among all the gods of those nations which my fathers utterly destroyed who could deliver his people out of my hand, that your God should be able to deliver you from my hand?

15 'Now therefore, do not let Hezekiah deceive you or mislead you like this, and do not believe him, for [a]no god of any nation or kingdom was able to deliver his people from my hand or from the hand of my fathers. How much less will your God deliver you from my hand?' "

16 His servants spoke further against the LORD God and against His servant Hezekiah.

17 He also wrote letters to insult the LORD God of Israel, and to speak against Him, saying, "[a]As the gods of the nations of the lands [1]have not delivered their people from my hand, so the God of Hezekiah will not deliver His people from my hand."

18 [a]They called this out with a loud voice in the language of Judah to the people of Jerusalem who were on the wall, to frighten and terrify them, so that they might take the city.

9 [1]Lit *against* [a]2 Kin 18:17
11 [1]Lit *palm*
12 [1]Lit *Jerusalem, saying,* [2]Lit *offer up in smoke* [a]2 Chr 31:1
13 [a]2 Kin 18:33-35
14 [a]Is 10:9-11
15 [a]Ex 5:2; Is 36:18-20; Dan 3:15
17 [1]Lit *who have* [a]2 Chr 32:14
18 [a]2 Kin 18:28

31:20–21 Another brief indication of the Chronicler's emphasis on immediate retribution: Not only does disobedience bring immediate chastening, but obedience and seeking God bring prosperity.

32:1–23 The record of Sennacherib's invasion is much more detailed in 2 Kings and Isaiah (see note on 29:1–32:33).

32:1 The Chronicler omits the date of the invasion (701 B.C., Hezekiah's 14th year; see 2 Kin 18:13; Is 36:1).

32:2–8 Unique to the Chronicler, but normal preparations for invasion.

32:3–4 See v. 30.

32:9 The Chronicler bypasses 2 Kin 18:14–16, which records Hezekiah's suit for peace with its accompanying bribe stripped from the temple treasures. These acts were apparently out of accord with the Chronicler's portrait of Hezekiah. He also omits 2 Kin 18:17b–18.

32:10 The Chronicler omits 2 Kin 18:20–21 (and Is 36:5–6), containing a portion of the Assyrian commander's speech ridiculing Hezekiah and the citizens of Jerusalem for trusting in Egypt and Pharaoh. This, too, may be theologically motivated, in light of the Chronicler's attitude toward foreign alliances (see note on 16:2–9). The same concern with foreign alliances is also likely the reason for the omission of the material in 2 Kin 18:23–27 (and Is 36:8–12), where mention is again made of the hope of Egyptian intervention (see 2 Kin 19:9 for the incursion of Tirhakah).

32:16 *spoke further.* The Chronicler appears to assume his reader's familiarity with the longer account of the Assyrian taunts found in Kings and Isaiah.

32:18 *called this out . . . in the language of Judah.* Assumes knowledge of the fuller story (2 Kin 18:26–28; Is 36:11–13).

19 They spoke [1]of the God of Jerusalem as of [a]the gods of the peoples of the earth, the work of men's hands.

Hezekiah's Prayer Is Answered

20 But King Hezekiah and Isaiah the prophet, the son of Amoz, prayed about this and cried out to heaven.

21 And the LORD sent an angel who destroyed every mighty warrior, commander and officer in the camp of the king of Assyria. So he returned [1]in shame to his own land. And when he had entered the temple of his god, some of his own children killed him there with the sword.

22 So the LORD [a]saved Hezekiah and the inhabitants of Jerusalem from the hand of Sennacherib the king of Assyria and from the hand of all *others,* and [1]guided them on every side.

23 And [a]many were bringing gifts to the LORD at Jerusalem and choice presents to Hezekiah king of Judah, so that [b]he was exalted in the sight of all nations thereafter.

24 [a]In those days Hezekiah became [1]mortally ill; and he prayed to the LORD, and [2]the LORD spoke to him and gave him a sign.

25 But Hezekiah gave no return for the benefit [1]he received, [a]because his heart was [2]proud; [b]therefore wrath came on him and on Judah and Jerusalem.

26 However, [a]Hezekiah [1]humbled the pride of his heart, both he and the inhabitants of Jerusalem, so that the wrath of the LORD did not come on them in the days of Hezekiah.

27 Now Hezekiah had immense riches and honor; and he made for himself treasuries for silver, gold, precious stones, spices, shields and all kinds of valuable articles,

28 storehouses also for the produce of grain, wine and oil, pens for all kinds of cattle and [1]sheepfolds for the flocks.

29 He made cities for himself and acquired flocks and herds in abundance, for [a]God had given him very great [1]wealth.

30 It was Hezekiah who [a]stopped the upper outlet of the waters of [b]Gihon and directed them to the west side of the city of David. And Hezekiah prospered in all that he did.

31 Even *in the matter of* [a]the envoys of the rulers of Babylon, who sent to him to inquire of [b]the wonder that had happened in the land, God left him *alone only* [c]to test him, that He might know all that was in his heart.

32 Now the rest of the acts of Hezekiah and his deeds of devotion, behold, they are written in the vision of Isaiah the prophet, the son of Amoz, in the Book of the Kings of Judah and Israel.

33 So Hezekiah slept with his fathers, and they buried him in the [1]upper section of the tombs of the sons of David; and all Judah and the inhabitants of Jerusalem [a]honored him at his death. And his son Manasseh became king in his place.

Manasseh Succeeds Hezekiah in Judah

33 [a]Manasseh was twelve years old when he became king, and he reigned fifty-five years in Jerusalem.

2 [a]He did evil in the sight of the LORD according to the abominations of the nations whom the LORD dispossessed before the sons of Israel.

3 For [a]he rebuilt the high places which Hezekiah his father had broken down; [b]he also erected altars for the Baals and made [1]Asherim, and worshiped all the host of heaven and served them.

4 [a]He built altars in the house of the LORD of which the LORD had said, "My name shall be [b]in Jerusalem forever."

5 For he built altars for all the host of

19 [1]Lit *to* [a]Ps 115:4-8 **21** [1]Lit *in shame of face* **22** [1]Another reading is *gave them rest* [a]Is 31:5 **23** [a]2 Sam 8:10 [b]2 Chr 1:1 **24** [1]Lit *sick to the point of death* [2]Lit *He* [a]2 Kin 20:1-11; Is 38:1-8 **25** [1]Lit *to him* [2]Lit *high* [a]2 Chr 26:16; 32:31 [b]2 Chr 24:18 **26** [1]Lit *humbled himself in* [a]Jer 26:18, 19 **28** [1]So ancient versions; Heb *flocks for the sheepfolds*

29 [1]Lit *possessions, property* [a]1 Chr 29:12 **30** [a]2 Kin 20:20 [b]1 Kin 1:33 **31** [a]2 Kin 20:12; Is 39:1 [b]2 Chr 32:24; Is 38:7, 8 [c]Deut 8:16 **33** [1]Or *ascent to* [a]Ps 112:6; Prov 10:7 **33:1** [a]2 Kin 21:1-9 **2** [a]2 Chr 28:3; Jer 15:4 **3** [1]I.e. wooden symbols of a female deity [a]2 Chr 31:1 [b]Deut 16:21; 2 Kin 23:5, 6 **4** [a]2 Chr 28:24 [b]2 Sam 7:13; 2 Chr 7:16

32:20 This brief reference to the prayers of Hezekiah and Isaiah abridges the much longer narrative in 2 Kin 19:1–34 (and Is 37:1–35).

32:21 See 2 Kin 19:35–37; Is 37:36–38. The Chronicler and the parallel accounts telescope events somewhat: Sennacherib's invasion of Judah was in 701 B.C., while his death at the hand of his sons was in 681.

32:23 *exalted in the sight of all nations.* Another effort to compare Hezekiah with Solomon (see 9:23–24).

32:24 The Chronicler again abridges the narrative in 2 Kin 20:1–11 (and Is 38:1–8), assuming the reader's familiarity with the role of Isaiah and the miraculous sign of the shadow reversing ten steps.

32:25–30 Not found in the parallel texts.

32:25–26 *proud . . . pride.* The Chronicler does not specify the nature of Hezekiah's pride (however, see v. 31; 2 Kin 20:12–13; Is 39:1–2). Even for a "second Solomon" like Hezekiah, disobedience brings anger from the Lord.

32:27–29 The Chronicler likens Hezekiah to Solomon also by recounting his wealth (9:13–14).

32:30 See vv. 2–4; 2 Kin 20:20.

32:31 See v. 25. The Chronicler assumes the reader's knowledge of the fuller account in 2 Kin 20:12–19 (and Is 39:1–8). The envoys from Babylon were apparently interested in joint efforts against the Assyrians, hoping to open two fronts against them simultaneously.

33:1–20 See 2 Kin 21:1–18 and notes. Manasseh had the longest reign of any of the kings of Judah, a total of 55 years (v. 1). The emphasis in the two accounts differs: While both histories report at length the evil done in Manasseh's reign, only the Chronicler mentions his journey to Babylon and his repentance and restoration to rule. For the writer of Kings, the picture is only a bad one in which Manasseh could be considered almost single-handedly the cause of the exile (2 Kin 21:10–15; 23:26). Some scholars regard the record of Manasseh's repentance in Chronicles as motivated by the author's emphasis on immediate retribution: Length of reign is viewed as a blessing for obedience, so that the Chronicler deliberately records some good in Manasseh as a ground for his long reign. However, it must be noted that length of reign is not elsewhere used by the Chronicler as an indication of divine blessing. The usual indicators for such blessing in his account are peace and prosperity, building projects, success in warfare and large families.

33:1 *fifty-five years.* 697–642 B.C.

33:3 *Asherim.* See note on 14:3.

heaven in [a]the two courts of the house of the
LORD.
6 [a]He made his sons pass through the
fire in the valley of Ben-hinnom; and he
practiced witchcraft, used divination, practiced sorcery and [b]dealt with mediums and
spiritists. He did much evil in the sight of the
LORD, provoking Him *to anger.*
7 Then he put [a]the carved image of the
idol which he had made in the house of God,
of which God had said to David and to
Solomon his son, "[b]In this house and in
Jerusalem, which I have chosen from all the
tribes of Israel, I will put My name forever;
8 and I will not again remove the foot of
Israel from the land [a]which I have appointed
for your fathers, if only they will observe to
do all that I have commanded them according to all the law, the statutes and the ordinances *given* through Moses."
9 Thus Manasseh misled Judah and the
inhabitants of Jerusalem to do more evil
than the nations whom the LORD destroyed
before the sons of Israel.

Manasseh's Idolatry Rebuked

10 The LORD spoke to Manasseh and his
people, but [a]they paid no attention.
11 [a]Therefore the LORD brought the commanders of the army of the king of Assyria
against them, and they captured Manasseh
with [1]hooks, [b]bound him with bronze *chains*
and took him to Babylon.
12 When [a]he was in distress, he entreated
the LORD his God and [b]humbled himself
greatly before the God of his fathers.
13 When he prayed to Him, [a]He was
moved by his entreaty and heard his supplication, and brought him again to Jerusalem
to his kingdom. Then Manasseh [b]knew that
the LORD *was* God.
14 Now after this he built the outer wall of
the city of David on the west side of [a]Gihon,
in the valley, even to the entrance of the
[b]Fish Gate; and he encircled the [c]Ophel *with
it* and made it very high. Then he put army
commanders in all the fortified cities of
Judah.
15 He also [a]removed the foreign gods and
the idol from the house of the LORD, as well
as all the altars which he had built on the
mountain of the house of the LORD and in
Jerusalem, and he threw *them* outside the
city.
16 He set up the altar of the LORD and sacrificed [a]peace offerings and thank offerings
on it; and he ordered Judah to serve the LORD
God of Israel.
17 Nevertheless [a]the people still sacrificed
in the high places, *although* only to the LORD
their God.
18 Now the rest of the acts of Manasseh
even [a]his prayer to his God, and the words of
[b]the seers who spoke to him in the name of
the LORD God of Israel, behold, they are
among the records of the kings of [c]Israel.
19 His prayer also and [a]*how God* was
entreated by him, and all his sin, his unfaithfulness, and [b]the sites on which he built high
places and erected the Asherim and the
carved images, before he humbled himself,
behold, they are written in the records of the
[1]Hozai.
20 So Manasseh slept with his fathers, and
they buried him in his own house. And
Amon his son became king in his place.

Amon Becomes King in Judah

21 [a]Amon *was* twenty-two years old when
he became king, and he reigned two years in
Jerusalem.
22 He did evil in the sight of the LORD as
Manasseh his father [a]had done, and Amon
sacrificed to all [b]the carved images which his
father Manasseh had made, and he served
them.

5 [a]2 Chr 4:9
6 [a]2 Chr 28:3 [b]Lev 19:31; 20:27
7 [a]2 Chr 33:15 [b]1 Kin 9:3-5; 2 Chr 7:16; 33:4
8 [a]2 Sam 7:10
10 [a]Neh 9:29; Jer 25:4
11 [1]I.e. thongs put through the nose [a]Deut 28:36 [b]2 Chr 36:6
12 [a]Ps 118:5; 120:1; 130:1, 2 [b]2 Chr 32:26
13 [a]1 Chr 5:20; Ezra 8:23 [b]Dan 4:32
14 [a]1 Kin 1:33
14 [b]Neh 3:3 [c]2 Chr 27:3
15 [a]2 Chr 33:3-7
16 [a]Lev 7:11-18
17 [a]2 Chr 32:12
18 [a]2 Chr 33:12, 13 [b]2 Chr 33:10 [c]2 Chr 21:2
19 [1]Gr reads *seers* [a]2 Chr 33:13 [b]2 Chr 33:3
21 [a]2 Kin 21:19-24
22 [a]2 Chr 33:2-7 [b]2 Chr 34:3, 4

33:6 *made his sons pass through the fire.* See 28:3–4.

33:10 See note on vv. 1–20. The Chronicler abridges what the Lord said to Manasseh and the people through the prophets; the fuller record is found in 2 Kin 21:10–15.

33:11–17 Unique to the Chronicler, showing his stress on immediate retribution: Manasseh's evil brings invasion and defeat, while his repentance brings restoration to rule.

33:11 *took him to Babylon.* In extant non-Biblical records there is no reference as yet to Manasseh being taken to Babylon by an Assyrian king. Esarhaddon (681–669 B.C.) lists him among 22 kings required to forward materials for his building projects, and Ashurbanipal (669–627) names him as one of a number of vassals supporting his campaign against Egypt. The fact that an Assyrian king would have him taken to Babylon suggests that this incident may have taken place during the rebellion of Shamash-shum-ukin against his brother and overlord Ashurbanipal. This rebellion lasted from 652 to 648, and Manasseh may have joined or at least have been suspected of assisting in the Babylonian defection from Assyria. Manasseh may have been found innocent, or he may have been pardoned on the basis of a renewed pledge of loyalty. Egypt had also bolted from the Assyrian yoke under the new 26th dynasty, and the return of Manasseh to rule may reflect the Assyrian need of a vassal near the border of Egypt.

33:12 The language is reminiscent of Solomon's prayer (7:14).

33:14 *built the outer wall.* For the Chronicler such building programs are a sign of divine blessing (8:1–6; 11:5–12; 14:6–7; 26:9–10,14–15; 32:1–5,27–30; 1 Chr 11:7–9; 15:1).

33:15–16 Whatever the precise nature of Manasseh's reforms, Josiah would later still need to remove "the altars which Manasseh had made in the two courts of the house of the LORD" (2 Kin 23:12).

33:19 *Asherim.* See note on 14:3.

33:20 *buried him in his own house.* Cf. 2 Kin 21:18. His burial in the palace garden makes Manasseh the fifth king the Chronicler names who was not buried in the tombs of the kings (see note on 28:27).

33:21–25 See 2 Kin 21:19–26. The Chronicler's account of the reign of Amon (642–640 B.C.) is quite similar to that in Kings, apart from (1) the additional note that Amon was not repentant like his father Manasseh, a note based on a passage unique to the Chronicler (vv. 12–13), and (2) the absence of the death formula.

23 Moreover, he did not humble himself before the LORD [a]as his father Manasseh had [1]done, but Amon multiplied guilt.

24 Finally [a]his servants conspired against him and put him to death in his own house.

25 But the people of the land [1]killed all the conspirators against King Amon, and the people of the land made Josiah his son king in his place.

Josiah Succeeds Amon in Judah

34 [a]Josiah *was* eight years old when he became king, and he reigned thirty-one years in Jerusalem.

2 [a]He did right in the sight of the LORD, and walked in the ways of his father David and did not turn aside to the right or to the left.

3 For in the eighth year of his reign while he was still a youth, he began to [a]seek the God of his father David; and in the twelfth year he began [b]to purge Judah and Jerusalem of the high places, the Asherim, the carved images and the molten images.

4 They tore down the altars of the Baals in his presence, and [a]the incense altars that were high above them he chopped down; also the Asherim, the carved images and the molten images he broke in pieces and [b]ground to powder and scattered *it* on the graves of those who had sacrificed to them.

5 Then [a]he burned the bones of the priests on their altars and purged Judah and Jerusalem.

6 [a]In the cities of Manasseh, Ephraim, Simeon, even as far as Naphtali, in their surrounding ruins,

7 he also tore down the altars and [a]beat the Asherim and the carved images into powder, and chopped down all the incense altars throughout the land of Israel. Then he returned to Jerusalem.

Josiah Repairs the Temple

8 [a]Now in the eighteenth year of his reign, when he had purged the land and the house, he sent Shaphan the son of Azaliah, and Maaseiah [b]an official of the city, and Joah the son of Joahaz the recorder, to repair the house of the LORD his God.

9 They came to [a]Hilkiah the high priest and delivered the money that was brought into the house of God, which the Levites, the [1]doorkeepers, had collected [2]from [b]Manasseh and Ephraim, and from all the remnant of Israel, and from all Judah and Benjamin and the inhabitants of Jerusalem.

10 Then they gave *it* into the hands of the workmen who had the oversight of the house of the LORD, and the workmen who were working in the house of the LORD [1]used it to restore and repair the house.

11 They in turn gave *it* to the carpenters and to the builders to buy quarried stone and timber for couplings and to make beams for the houses [a]which the kings of Judah had let go to ruin.

12 [a]The men did the work faithfully with foremen over them to supervise: Jahath and Obadiah, the Levites of the sons of Merari, Zechariah and Meshullam of the sons of the Kohathites, and [b]the Levites, all who were skillful with musical instruments.

13 *They were* also over [a]the burden bear-

23 [1]Lit *humbled himself* [a]2 Chr 33:12, 19
24 [a]2 Chr 25:27
25 [1]Lit *smote*
34:1 [a]2 Kin 22:1, 2; Jer 1:2; 3:6
2 [a]2 Chr 29:2
3 [a]2 Chr 15:2; Prov 8:17 [b]1 Kin 13:2; 2 Chr 33:22
4 [a]2 Kin 23:4, 5, 11 [b]Ex 32:20
5 [a]1 Kin 13:2; 2 Kin 23:20
6 [a]2 Kin 23:15, 19
7 [a]2 Chr 31:1
8 [a]2 Kin 22:3-20 [b]2 Chr 18:25
9 [1]Lit *guardians of the threshold* [2]Lit *from the hand of* [a]2 Chr 35:8 [b]2 Chr 30:10, 18
10 [1]Lit *gave*
11 [a]2 Chr 33:4-7
12 [a]2 Kin 12:15 [b]1 Chr 25:1
13 [a]Neh 4:10

34:1–36:1 See 2 Kin 22:1–23:30 and notes. Both accounts of Josiah's reign are about the same length and treat the same subjects, but with considerable variation in emphasis. Both deal with three different aspects of Josiah's reform: (1) the removal of foreign cults, (2) the finding of the book of the law and the covenant renewal that followed and (3) the celebration of Passover. On the second item the two histories are quite similar. On the first item the writer of Kings goes to great lengths (2 Kin 23:4–20), while the Chronicler summarizes it only briefly (34:3–7,33). The account of the Passover is greatly expanded in Chronicles (35:1–19), while only alluded to in 2 Kings (23:21–23). Not only are these items treated at different lengths, but the order is also changed. In Kings the finding of the book of the law in the temple in Josiah's 18th year is the first incident mentioned. The writer appears to have organized his material geographically, i.e., beginning with the temple and spreading through the city, then into the rest of the nation. The Chronicler, on the other hand, has arranged the incidents in order of their occurrence and has characteristically introduced a number of chronological notes into the text: 34:3 (two notes without parallel in Kings); 34:8 (see 2 Kin 22:3); 35:19 (see 2 Kin 23:23; see also note on 2 Chr 12:2). Chronicles makes it clear that the reform began in Josiah's 12th year (34:3), six years before the discovery of the book of the law.

34:1–2 See 2 Kin 22:1–2.

34:1 *thirty-one years.* 640–609 B.C.

34:3–7 The writer of Kings covers this aspect of Josiah's reform in much greater detail (2 Kin 23:4–20). He also delays his account of the removal of pagan cults until after the discovery of the book of the law, while the Chronicler places it before.

34:3 Some scholars have sought to tie the events of Josiah's 8th (v. 3), 12th (v. 3) and 18th (v. 8) years to stages in the progressive decline and fall of the Assyrian empire, which had dominated the area for about two centuries. The demise of Assyrian control in Aram and Israel undoubtedly facilitated and encouraged Josiah's reassertion of Davidic authority over former Assyrian provinces (vv. 6–7). However, one must not undercut religious motives in Josiah's reforms. Otherwise, the reform is reduced to merely a religious expression of an essentially political rebellion. *Asherim.* See note on 14:3.

34:6 *Manasseh, Ephraim, Simeon, even as far as Naphtali.* The Chronicler's concern for "all Israel" (see Introduction to 1 Chronicles: Purpose and Themes) is apparent in his recording the involvement of the northern tribes in Josiah's reform (see also vv. 9,21,33). The Chronicler again shows all Israel united under a Davidic king, just as he did under Hezekiah (see note on 30:1). *Simeon.* Perhaps some Simeonites had migrated from Judah to the north.

34:7 *throughout the land of Israel.* Defined by the list of tribes in v. 6.

34:8–21 See 2 Kin 22:3–13 and notes.

34:9 *Manasseh and Ephraim, and from all the remnant of Israel.* Again as part of his concern with "all Israel," the Chronicler notes that worshipers from the north also brought gifts to the temple (not explicitly indicated in 2 Kin 22:4).

34:10–13 Cf. 24:8–12.

ers, and supervised all the workmen from job to job; and *some* of the Levites *were* scribes and officials and gatekeepers.

Hilkiah Discovers Lost Book of the Law

14 When they were bringing out the money which had been brought into the house of the LORD, [a]Hilkiah the priest found the book of the law of the LORD *given* by Moses.

15 Hilkiah responded and said to Shaphan the scribe, "I have found the book of the law in the house of the LORD." And Hilkiah gave the book to Shaphan.

16 Then Shaphan brought the book to the king and [1]reported further word to the king, saying, "Everything that was [2]entrusted to your servants they are doing.

17 "They have also emptied out the money which was found in the house of the LORD, and have delivered it into the hands of the supervisors and the workmen."

18 Moreover, Shaphan the scribe told the king saying, "Hilkiah the priest gave me a book." And Shaphan read from it in the presence of the king.

19 When the king heard [a]the words of the law, [b]he tore his clothes.

20 Then the king commanded Hilkiah, Ahikam the son of Shaphan, [1]Abdon the son of Micah, Shaphan the scribe, and Asaiah the king's servant, saying,

21 "Go, inquire of the LORD for me and for those who are left in Israel and in Judah, concerning the words of the book which has been found; for [a]great is the wrath of the LORD which is poured out on us because our fathers have not observed the word of the LORD, to do according to all that is written in this book."

Huldah, the Prophetess, Speaks

22 So Hilkiah and *those* whom the king [1]had told went to Huldah the prophetess, the wife of Shallum the son of [2]Tokhath, the son of Hasrah, the keeper of the wardrobe (now she lived in Jerusalem in the Second Quarter); and they spoke to her regarding this.

23 She said to them, "Thus says the LORD, the God of Israel, 'Tell the man who sent you to Me,

24 thus says the LORD, "Behold, [a]I am bringing evil on this place and on its inhabitants, *even* all [b]the curses written in the book which they have read in the presence of the king of Judah.

25 "[a]Because they have forsaken Me and have burned incense to other gods, that they might provoke Me to anger with all the works of their hands; therefore My wrath will be poured out on this place and it shall not be quenched." '

26 "But to the king of Judah who sent you to inquire of the LORD, thus you will say to him, 'Thus says the LORD God of Israel *regarding* the words which you have heard,

27 "[a]Because your heart was tender and you humbled yourself before God when you heard His words against this place and against its inhabitants, and *because* you humbled yourself before Me, tore your clothes and wept before Me, I truly have heard you," declares the LORD.

28 "Behold, I will gather you to your fathers and you shall be gathered to your grave in peace, so your eyes will not see all the evil which I will bring on this place and on its inhabitants." ' " And they brought back word to the king.

29 [a]Then the king sent and gathered all the elders of Judah and Jerusalem.

30 The king went up to the house of the LORD and [a]all the men of Judah, the inhabitants of Jerusalem, the priests, the Levites and all the people, from the greatest to the least; and he read in their hearing all the words of the book of the covenant which was found in the house of the LORD.

Josiah's Good Reign

31 Then the king [a]stood in his place and [b]made a covenant before the LORD to walk after the LORD, and to keep His commandments and His testimonies and His statutes with all his heart and with all his soul, to perform the words of the covenant written in this book.

32 Moreover, he made all who were present in Jerusalem and Benjamin to stand *with him.* So the inhabitants of Jerusalem did according to the covenant of God, the God of their fathers.

33 Josiah [a]removed all the abominations from all the lands belonging to the sons of Israel, and made all who were present in Israel to serve the LORD their God. Throughout his [1]lifetime they did not turn from following the LORD God of their fathers.

The Passover Observed Again

35 Then Josiah [a]celebrated the Passover to the LORD in Jerusalem, and [b]they slaughtered the Passover *animals* on the fourteenth *day* of the first month.

2 He set the priests in their offices and

14 [a]2 Chr 34:9
16 [1]Lit *returned* [2]Lit *given into the hand of*
19 [a]Deut 28:3-68 [b]Josh 7:6
20 [1]In 2 Kin 22:12, *Achbor, son of Micaiah*
21 [a]2 Chr 29:8
22 [1]So with Gr [2]In 2 Kin 22:14 *Tikvah, son of Harhas*
24 [a]2 Chr 36:14-20 [b]Deut 28:15-68
25 [a]2 Chr 33:3
27 [a]2 Kin 22:19; 2 Chr 12:7; 32:26
29 [a]2 Kin 23:1-3
30 [a]Neh 8:1-3
31 [a]2 Kin 11:14; 23:3; 2 Chr 30:16 [b]2 Chr 23:16; 29:10
33 [1]Lit *days* [a]2 Chr 34:3-7
35:1 [a]2 Kin 23:21 [b]Ex 12:6; Num 9:3

34:22–28 See 2 Kin 22:14–20 and notes.

34:28 *gathered to your grave in peace.* See the death and burial account (35:20–25).

34:29–31 See 2 Kin 23:1–3.

34:30 *the priests, the Levites.* Cf. 2 Kin 23:2, which has "the priests and the prophets."

34:33 *all the lands belonging to the sons of Israel . . . all who were present in Israel.* See note on v. 6.

35:1–19 The Chronicler gives much more extensive coverage to Josiah's Passover celebration than is found in the brief allusion in Kings (2 Kin 23:21–23).

35:1 *first month.* The traditional month; contrast the Passover of Hezekiah (see note on 30:2).

[a]encouraged them in the service of the house
of the LORD.
3 He also said to [a]the Levites who taught
all Israel *and* who were holy to the LORD,
"Put the holy ark in the house which
Solomon the son of David king of Israel built;
[b]it will be a burden on *your* shoulders no
longer. Now serve the LORD your God and
His people Israel.
4 "[a]Prepare *yourselves* by your fathers'
households in your divisions, according to
the writing of David king of Israel and
[b]according to the writing of his son Solomon.
5 "Moreover, [a]stand in the holy place
according to the sections of the fathers'
households of your brethren the [1]lay people,
and according to the Levites, by division of a
father's household.
6 "Now [a]slaughter the Passover *animals*,
[b]sanctify yourselves and prepare for your
brethren to do according to the word of the
LORD by Moses."
7 Josiah contributed to the lay people, to
all who were present, flocks of lambs and
young goats, all for the Passover offerings,
numbering 30,000 plus 3,000 bulls; these
were from the king's possessions.
8 His officers also contributed a freewill
offering to the people, the priests and the
Levites. Hilkiah and Zechariah and Jehiel,
[a]the officials of the house of God, gave to the
priests for the Passover offerings 2,600 *from
the flocks* and 300 bulls.
9 [a]Conaniah also, and Shemaiah and
Nethanel, his brothers, and Hashabiah and
Jeiel and Jozabad, the officers of the Levites,
contributed to the Levites for the Passover
offerings 5,000 *from the flocks* and 500 bulls.
10 So the service was prepared, and [a]the
priests stood at their stations and the Levites
by their divisions according to the king's
command.
11 [1][a]They slaughtered the Passover *animals*, and while [b]the priests sprinkled [2]the
blood *received* from their hand, [c]the Levites
skinned *them*.
12 Then they removed the burnt offerings
that *they* might give them to the sections of
the fathers' households of the lay people to
present to the LORD, as it is written in the
book of Moses. *They did* this also with the
bulls.
13 So [a]they roasted the Passover *animals*
on the fire according to the ordinance, and
they boiled [b]the holy things in pots, in ket-
tles, in pans, and carried *them* speedily to all
the lay people.
14 Afterwards they prepared for themselves and for the priests, because the
priests, the sons of Aaron, *were* offering the
burnt offerings and the fat until night; therefore the Levites prepared for themselves and
for the priests, the sons of Aaron.
15 The singers, the sons of Asaph, *were*
also at their stations [a]according to the command of David, Asaph, Heman, and Jeduthun the king's seer; and [b]the gatekeepers at
each gate did not have to depart from their
service, because the Levites their brethren
prepared for them.
16 So all the service of the LORD was prepared on that day to celebrate the Passover,
and to offer burnt offerings on the altar of
the LORD according to the command of King
Josiah.
17 Thus [a]the sons of Israel who were present celebrated the Passover at that time, and
the Feast of Unleavened Bread seven days.
18 [a]There had not been celebrated a
Passover like it in Israel since the days of
Samuel the prophet; nor had any of the kings
of Israel celebrated such a Passover as Josiah
did with the priests, the Levites, all Judah
and Israel who were present, and the inhabitants of Jerusalem.
19 In the eighteenth year of Josiah's reign
this Passover was celebrated.

Josiah Dies in Battle

20 [a]After all this, when Josiah had set the
[1]temple in order, Neco king of Egypt came
up to make war at [b]Carchemish on the
Euphrates, and Josiah went out to engage
him.
21 But [1]Neco sent messengers to him, saying, "[a]What have we to do with each other,
O King of Judah? *I am* not *coming* against
you today but against the house with which
I am at war, and God has ordered me to hurry. Stop for your own sake from *interfering*

2 [a]2 Chr 29:11
3 [a]2 Chr 17:8, 9; Neh 8:7 [b]1 Chr 23:26
4 [a]1 Chr 9:10-13 [b]2 Chr 8:14
5 [1]Lit *sons of the people*, and so throughout the ch [a]Ezra 6:18
6 [a]2 Chr 35:1 [b]2 Chr 29:5
8 [a]2 Chr 31:13
9 [a]2 Chr 31:12
10 [a]2 Chr 35:5
11 [1]I.e. the Levites [2]So with Gr [a]2 Chr 35:1, 6 [b]2 Chr 29:22 [c]2 Chr 29:34
13 [a]Ex 12:8, 9 [b]Lev 6:28
15 [a]1 Chr 25:1 [b]1 Chr 26:12-19
17 [a]Ex 12:1-20; 2 Chr 30:21
18 [a]2 Kin 23:21; 2 Chr 30:5
20 [1]Lit *house* [a]2 Kin 23:29, 30 [b]Is 10:9; Jer 46:2
21 [1]Lit *he* [a]2 Chr 25:19

35:3 *Put the holy ark in the house.* Implies that it had been removed, perhaps for protection during the evil reigns of Manasseh and Amon, who preceded Josiah.
35:4 *David . . . Solomon.* The Chronicler specifically parallels David and Solomon in three cases: 7:10 (contrast 1 Kin 8:66, where only David is mentioned); 11:17; and here. This tendency reflects his glorification and idealization of both (see Introduction to 1 Chronicles: Portrait of David and Solomon).
35:7–9 The emphasis in Chronicles on voluntary and joyful giving (24:8–14; 29:31–36; 31:3–21; 1 Chr 29:3–9) presumably had direct relevance to the postexilic readers for whom the Chronicler wrote.
35:18 *since the days of Samuel the prophet.* Instead of "from the days of the judges" (2 Kin 23:22).
35:19 *eighteenth year.* The same year as the discovery of the book of the law (34:8,14).
35:20–27 See 2 Kin 23:28–30. In 609 B.C. Pharaoh Neco "went up to the king of Assyria to the river Euphrates" (2 Kin 23:29) against the Babylonians.
35:20 *at Carchemish.* Not found in Kings.
35:21–22 Unique to the Chronicler, showing his view on retribution once again: Josiah's death in battle comes as a result of his disobedience to the word of God as heard even in the mouth of the pagan pharaoh.
35:21 *house with which I am at war.* A reference to the Babylonians; Nabopolassar was on the throne of Babylon, while his son Nebuchadnezzar was commanding the armies in the field. Nebuchadnezzar would succeed his father after another battle

with God who is with me, so that He will not
destroy you."
22 However, Josiah would not turn [1]away
from him, but [a]disguised himself in order to
make war with him; nor did he listen to the
words of Neco [b]from the mouth of God, but
came to make war on the plain of [c]Megiddo.
23 The archers shot King Josiah, and the
king said to his servants, "Take me away, for
I am badly wounded."
24 So his servants took him out of the
chariot and carried him in the second chariot which he had, and brought him to
Jerusalem [1]where he died and was buried in
the tombs of his fathers. [a]All Judah and
Jerusalem mourned for Josiah.
25 Then [a]Jeremiah chanted a lament for
Josiah. And all the male and female singers
speak about Josiah in their lamentations to
this day. And they made them an ordinance
in Israel; behold, they are also written in the
Lamentations.
26 Now the rest of the acts of Josiah and
his deeds of devotion as written in the law of
the LORD,
27 and his acts, first to last, behold, they
are written in the Book of the Kings of Israel
and Judah.

Jehoahaz, Jehoiakim, then Jehoiachin Rule

36 [a]Then the people of the land took
[1b]Joahaz the son of Josiah, and made
him king in place of his father in Jerusalem.
2 Joahaz was twenty-three years old
when he became king, and he reigned three
months in Jerusalem.
3 Then the king of Egypt deposed him at
Jerusalem, and imposed on the land a fine of
one hundred talents of silver and one talent
of gold.
4 The king of Egypt made Eliakim his
brother king over Judah and Jerusalem, and
changed his name to Jehoiakim. But [a]Neco
took Joahaz his brother and brought him to
Egypt.
5 [a]Jehoiakim was twenty-five years old
when he became king, and he reigned eleven
years in Jerusalem; and he did evil in the
sight of the LORD his God.
6 Nebuchadnezzar king of Babylon came
up [a]against him and [b]bound him with
bronze *chains* to take him to Babylon.
7 [a]Nebuchadnezzar also brought *some* of
the articles of the house of the LORD to Babylon and put them in his temple at Babylon.
8 [a]Now the rest of the acts of Jehoiakim
and [1]the abominations which he did, and
what was found against him, behold, they
are written in the Book of the Kings of Israel
and Judah. And Jehoiachin his son became
king in his place.
9 [a]Jehoiachin was eight years old when
he became king, and he reigned three
months and ten days in Jerusalem, and he
did evil in the sight of the LORD.

Captivity in Babylon Begun

10 [a]At the turn of the year King Nebuchadnezzar sent and brought him to Babylon
with the valuable articles of the house of the
LORD, and he made his kinsman [b]Zedekiah
king over Judah and Jerusalem.

Zedekiah Rules in Judah

11 [a]Zedekiah was twenty-one years old
when he became king, and he reigned eleven
years in Jerusalem.
12 He did evil in the sight of the LORD his
God; [a]he did not humble himself [b]before Jeremiah the prophet [1]who spoke for the LORD.
13 [a]He also rebelled against King Nebuchadnezzar who had made him swear *alle-*

22 [1]Lit *his face* [a]2 Chr 18:29 [b]2 Chr 35:21 [c]Judg 5:19
24 [1]Lit *and* [a]Zech 12:11
25 [a]Jer 22:10; Lam 4:20
36:1 [1]I.e. short form of Jehoahaz [a]2 Kin 23:30-34 [b]Jer 22:11
4 [a]Jer 22:10-12
5 [a]2 Kin 23:36, 37; Jer 22:13-19; 26:1; 35:1
6 [a]2 Kin 24:1; Jer 25:1-9 [b]2 Chr 33:11
7 [a]2 Kin 24:13
8 [1]Lit *his* [a]2 Kin 24:5
9 [a]2 Kin 24:8-17
10 [a]2 Sam 11:1; Jer 22:25; 24:1; 29:1; Ezek 17:12 [b]Jer 37:1
11 [a]2 Kin 24:18-20; Jer 27:1; 28:1; 52:1
12 [1]Lit *from the mouth of the LORD* [a]2 Chr 33:23 [b]Jer 21:3-7
13 [a]Jer 52:3; Ezek 17:15

---

at Carchemish against Egypt in 605 B.C. Josiah may have been an ally of Babylon (see 32:31; 33:11 and notes).

35:22 *disguised himself.* Cf. Ahab and Jehoshaphat (see 18:29 and note). *plain of Megiddo.* See note on Judg 5:19.

35:24b–25 Unique to Chronicles.

35:25 *Jeremiah chanted a lament for Josiah.* Jeremiah held Josiah in high esteem (Jer 22:15–16). The laments he composed are no longer extant. The statement that he composed laments is one of the reasons the book of Lamentations has been traditionally associated with him. *to this day.* See note on 5:9.

36:2–14 Josiah is the only king of Judah to be succeeded by three of his sons (Jehoahaz, Jehoiakim and Zedekiah). The Chronicler's account of the reigns of the remaining kings of Judah is quite brief.

36:2 See 2 Kin 23:31–35. With the death of Josiah at the hands of Pharaoh Neco, Judah slipped into a period of Egyptian domination (vv. 3–4). *three months.* In 609 B.C. Neco's assertion of authority over Judah ended the brief 20 years of Judahite independence under Josiah. The Chronicler makes no moral judgment on this brief reign, though the author of Kings does (2 Kin 23:32).

36:4 Just as Neco took Jehoahaz into captivity and replaced him with Eliakim, whose name he changed to Jehoiakim, so also Nebuchadnezzar would later take Jehoiachin to Babylon, replacing him with Mattaniah, whose name he changed to Zedekiah (2 Kin 24:15–17). Each conqueror wanted to place his own man on the throne; the change of name implied authority over him.

36:5–8 See 2 Kin 23:36–24:7. Jehoiakim persecuted the prophets and is the object of scathing denunciation by Jeremiah (Jer 25–26; 36). After the Egyptian defeat at Carchemish (Jer 46:2) in 605 B.C., Jehoiakim transferred allegiance to Nebuchadnezzar of Babylon. When he later rebelled and again allied himself with Egypt, Nebuchadnezzar sent a punitive army against him. But Jehoiakim died before the army arrived, and Nebuchadnezzar took his son Jehoiachin into captivity.

36:5 *eleven years.* 609–598 B.C.

36:9–10 See 2 Kin 24:8–17; see also Jer 22:24–28; 24:1; 29:2; 52:31. Although Jehoiachin was taken into captivity (597 B.C.) with a large retinue, including the queen mother and high officials, and was succeeded by Zedekiah, the exiles continued to date in terms of his reign (Jer 52:31; Ezek 1:2; cf. Esth 2:5–6).

36:9 *three months and ten days.* 598–597 B.C.

36:11–14 See 2 Kin 24:18–20; Jer 52:1–3. Verses 13b–14 are unique to the Chronicler (cf. Jer 1:3; 21:1–7; 24:8; 27:1–15; 32:1–5; 34:1–7,21; 37:1–39:7). Zedekiah succumbed to the temptation to look to Egypt for help and rebelled against Nebuchadnezzar. Babylonian reaction was swift. Jerusalem was besieged (Jer 21:3–7) in 588 B.C. and held out for over two years before being destroyed in the summer of 586.

giance by God. But [b]he stiffened his neck
and hardened his heart against turning to the
LORD God of Israel.
14 Furthermore, all the officials of the
priests and the people were very unfaithful
following all the abominations of the nations;
and they defiled the house of the LORD which
He had sanctified in Jerusalem.
15 The LORD, the God of their fathers,
[a]sent *word* to them again and again by His
messengers, because He had compassion on
His people and on His dwelling place;
16 but they *continually* [a]mocked the messengers of God, [b]despised His words and
scoffed at His prophets, [c]until the wrath of
the LORD arose against His people, until there
was no remedy.
17 [a]Therefore He brought up against them
the king of the Chaldeans who slew their
young men with the sword in the house of
their sanctuary, and had no compassion on
young man or virgin, old man or infirm; He
gave *them* all into his hand.
18 [a]All the articles of the house of God,
great and small, and the treasures of the
house of the LORD, and the treasures of the
king and of his officers, he brought *them* all
to Babylon.

13 [b]2 Chr 30:8 **15** [a]Jer 7:13; 25:3 **16** [a]2 Chr 30:10; Jer 5:12, 13 [b]Prov 1:24-32 [c]Ezra 5:12 **17** [a]2 Kin 25:1-7; Jer 21:1-10 **18** [a]2 Chr 36:7, 10

19 Then [a]they burned the house of God
and broke down the wall of Jerusalem, and
burned all its fortified buildings with fire and
destroyed all its valuable articles.
20 Those who had escaped from the
sword he [a]carried away to Babylon; and
[b]they were servants to him and to his sons
until the rule of the kingdom of Persia,
21 [a]to fulfill the word of the LORD by the
mouth of Jeremiah, until [b]the land had
enjoyed its sabbaths. [c]All the days of its desolation it kept sabbath [1d]until seventy years
were complete.

Cyrus Permits Return

22 [a]Now in the first year of Cyrus king of
Persia—in order to fulfill the word of the LORD
[b]by the mouth of Jeremiah—the LORD [c]stirred
up the spirit of Cyrus king of Persia, so that
he sent a proclamation throughout his kingdom, and also *put it* in writing, saying,
23 "Thus says Cyrus king of Persia, 'The
LORD, the God of heaven, has given me all
the kingdoms of the earth, and He has
appointed me to build Him a house in
Jerusalem, which is in Judah. Whoever there
is among you of all His people, may the LORD
his God be with him, and let him go up!' "

19 [a]1 Kin 9:8; 2 Kin 25:9; Jer 52:13 **20** [a]2 Kin 25:11 [b]Jer 27:7 **21** [1]Lit *to fulfill seventy years* [a]Jer 29:10 [b]Lev 26:34 [c]Lev 25:4 [d]Jer 25:11 **22** [a]Ezra 1:1-3 [b]Jer 25:12; 29:10 [c]Is 44:28

36:11 *eleven years.* 597–586 B.C.

36:15–16 See 24:19 and note.

36:20–21 The conclusion of the two Biblical histories is interestingly different: The writer(s) of Samuel and Kings had sought to show why the exile occurred and had traced the sad history of Israel's disobedience to the exile, the time in which the writer(s) of those books lived. With the state at an end, he could still show God's faithfulness to His promises to David (2 Kin 25:27–30) by reporting the favor bestowed on his descendants. The Chronicler, whose vantage point was after the exile, was able to look back to the exile not only as judgment, but also as containing hope for the future. For him the purified remnant had returned to a purified land (vv. 22–23), and a new age was beginning. The exile was not judgment alone, but also blessing, for it allowed the land to catch up on its sabbath rests (Lev 26:40–45). And God had remembered His covenant (Lev 26:45) and restored His people to the land (see next note).

36:22–23 The writer of Kings concluded his history before the restoration; so this text is not paralleled in his account. It is repeated, however, at the beginning of Ezra (1:1–4), which resumes the history at the point where Chronicles ends—indicating that Chronicles and Ezra may have been written by the same author. See the prophecy of Jeremiah (Jer 25:1–14; cf. Dan 9). Cyrus also issued decrees for other captive peoples, allowing them to return to their lands. Under God's sovereignty, this effort by a Persian king to win the favor of peoples treated harshly by the Babylonians also inaugurated the restoration period. See notes on Ezra 1:1–4.

Ezra

INTRODUCTION

Ezra and Nehemiah

Although the caption to Neh 1:1, "The words of Nehemiah the son of Hacaliah," indicates that Ezra and Nehemiah were originally two separate compositions, they were combined as one in the earliest Hebrew manuscripts. Josephus (c. A.D. 37 – 100) and the Jewish Talmud refer to the book of Ezra but not to a separate book of Nehemiah. The oldest manuscripts of the Septuagint (the Greek translation of the OT) also treat Ezra and Nehemiah as one book.

Origen (A.D. 185 – 253) is the first writer known to distinguish between two books, which he called I Ezra and II Ezra. In translating the Latin Vulgate (A.D. 390 – 405), Jerome called Nehemiah the second book of Esdrae (Ezra). The English translations by Wycliffe (1382) and Coverdale (1535) also called Ezra "I Esdras" and Nehemiah "II Esdras." The same separation first appeared in a Hebrew manuscript in 1448.

Literary Form and Authorship

As in the closely related books of 1 and 2 Chronicles, one notes the prominence of various lists in Ezra and Nehemiah, which have evidently been obtained from official sources. Included are lists of (1) the temple articles (Ezra 1:9 – 11), (2) the returned exiles (Ezra 2, which is virtually the same as Neh 7:6 – 73), (3) the genealogy of Ezra (Ezra 7:1 – 5), (4) the heads of the clans (Ezra 8:1 – 14), (5) those involved in mixed marriages (Ezra 10:18 – 43), (6) those who helped rebuild the wall (Neh 3), (7) those who sealed the covenant (Neh 10:1 – 27), (8) residents of Jerusalem and other towns (Neh 11:3 – 36) and (9) priests and Levites (Neh 12:1 – 26).

Also included in Ezra are seven official documents or letters (all in Aramaic except the first, which is in Hebrew): (1) the decree of Cyrus (1:2 – 4), (2) the accusation of Rehum and others against the Jews (4:11 – 16), (3) the reply of Artaxerxes I (4:17 – 22), (4) the report from Tattenai (5:7 – 17), (5) the memorandum of Cyrus's decree (6:2b-5), (6) Darius's reply to Tattenai (6:6 – 12) and (7) the authorization given by Artaxerxes I to Ezra (7:12 – 26). The documents compare favorably with contemporary non-Biblical documents of the Persian period.

Certain materials in Ezra are first-person extracts from his memoirs: 7:27 – 28; 8:1 – 34; 9. Other sections are written in the third person: 7:1 – 26; 10; see also Neh 8. Linguistic analysis has shown that the first-person and third-person extracts resemble each other, making it likely that the same author wrote both.

Most scholars conclude that the author/compiler of Ezra and Nehemiah was also the author of 1,2 Chronicles. This viewpoint is based on certain characteristics common to both Chronicles and Ezra-Nehemiah. The verses at the end of Chronicles and at the beginning of Ezra are virtually identical. Both Chronicles and Ezra-Nehemiah exhibit a fondness for lists, for the description of religious festivals and for such phrases as "heads of fathers' households" and "the house of God." Especially striking in these books is the prominence of Levites and temple personnel. The words for "singer," "gatekeeper" and "temple servants" are used almost exclusively in Ezra-Nehemiah and Chronicles. See Introduction to 1 Chronicles: Author, Date and Sources.

Date

We may date the composition of Ezra c. 440 B.C. and the Nehemiah memoirs c. 430.

The Order of Ezra and Nehemiah

According to the traditional view, Ezra arrived in Jerusalem in the seventh year (Ezra 7:8) of Artaxerxes I (458 B.C.), followed by Nehemiah, who arrived in the king's 20th year (445; Neh 2:1).

Some have proposed a reverse order in which Nehemiah arrived in 445 B.C., while Ezra arrived in the seventh year of Artaxerxes II (398). By amending "seventh" (Ezra 7:8) to either "27th" or "37th," others place Ezra after Nehemiah but maintain that they were contemporaries.

These alternative views, however, present more problems than the traditional position. As the text stands, Ezra arrived before Nehemiah and they are found together in Neh 8:9 (at the reading of the Law) and Neh 12:26,36 (at the dedication of the wall). See chart, p. 637.

Languages

Ezra and Nehemiah were written in a form of late Hebrew with the exception of Ezra 4:8—6:18; 7:12–26, which were written in Aramaic, the international language during the Persian period. Of these 67 Aramaic verses, 52 are in records or letters. Ezra evidently found these documents in Aramaic and copied them, inserting connecting verses in Aramaic.

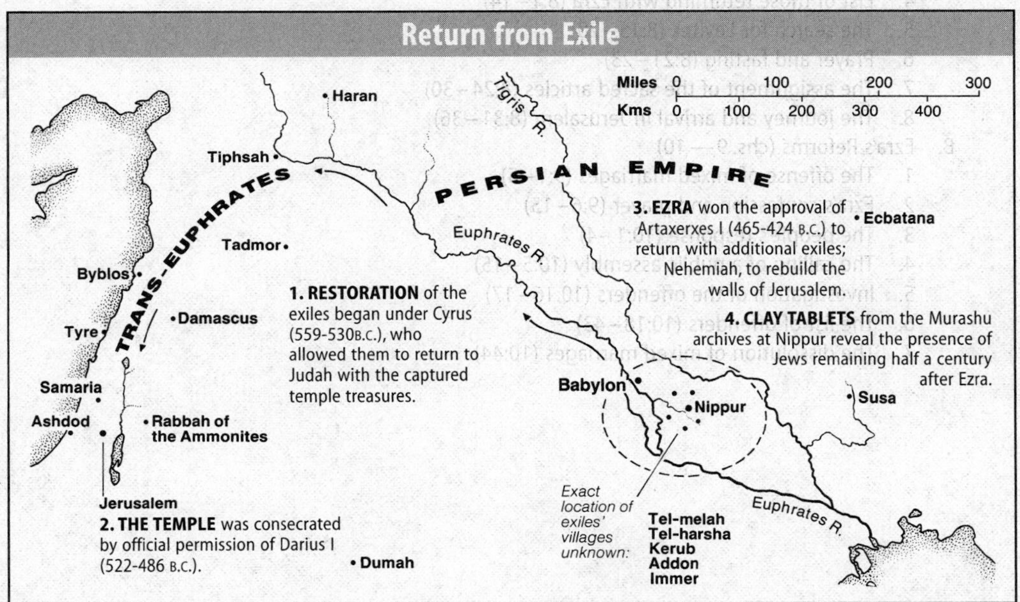
Return from Exile
Miles 0 100 200 300
Kms 0 100 200 300 400
Haran
Tigris R.
Tiphsah
TRANS-EUPHRATES
PERSIAN EMPIRE
Euphrates R.
Tadmor
Byblos
Tyre
Damascus
Samaria
Ashdod
Rabbah of the Ammonites
Jerusalem
Dumah
Babylon
Nippur
Susa
Ecbatana
1. RESTORATION of the exiles began under Cyrus (559-530B.C.), who allowed them to return to Judah with the captured temple treasures.
2. THE TEMPLE was consecrated by official permission of Darius I (522-486 B.C.).
3. EZRA won the approval of Artaxerxes I (465-424 B.C.) to return with additional exiles; Nehemiah, to rebuild the walls of Jerusalem.
4. CLAY TABLETS from the Murashu archives at Nippur reveal the presence of Jews remaining half a century after Ezra.
Exact location of exiles' villages unknown:
Tel-melah
Tel-harsha
Kerub
Addon
Immer

Outline

I. First Return from Exile and Rebuilding of the Temple (chs. 1—6)
   A. First Return of the Exiles (ch. 1)
      1. The edict of Cyrus (1:1–4)
      2. The return under Sheshbazzar (1:5–11)
   B. List of Returning Exiles (ch. 2)
   C. Revival of Temple Worship (ch. 3)
      1. The rebuilding of the altar (3:1–3)
      2. The Feast of Booths (3:4–6)
      3. The beginning of temple reconstruction (3:7–13)
   D. Opposition to Rebuilding (4:1–23)
      1. Opposition during the reign of Cyrus (4:1–5)
      2. Opposition during the reign of Ahasuerus (4:6)
      3. Opposition during the reign of Artaxerxes (4:7–23)
   E. Completion of the Temple (4:24—6:22)
      1. Resumption of work under Darius (4:24)

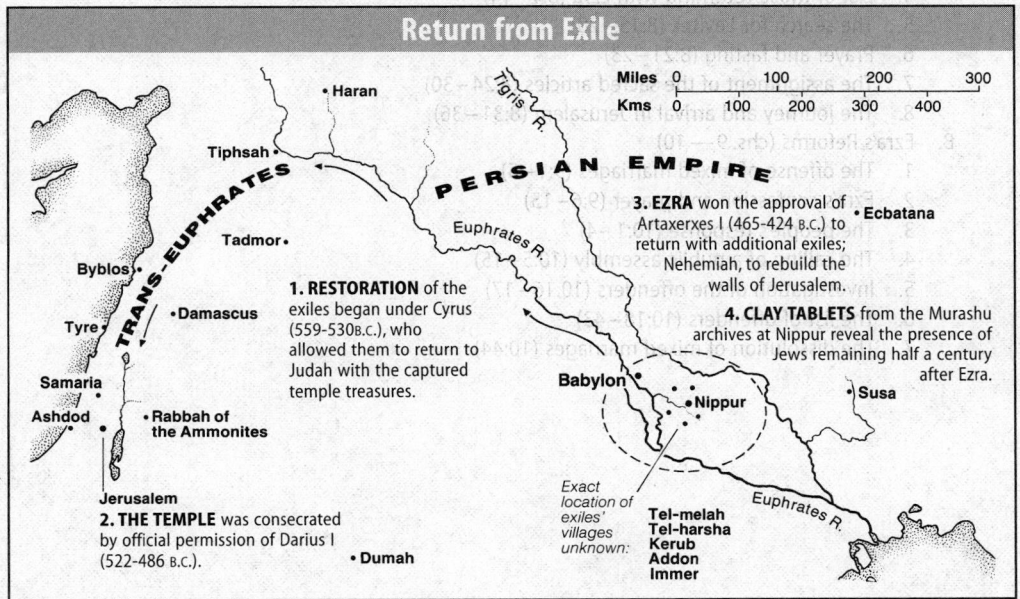

2. A new beginning inspired by Haggai and Zechariah (5:1–2)
3. Intervention of the governor, Tattenai (5:3–5)
4. Report to Darius (5:6–17)
5. Search for the decree of Cyrus (6:1–5)
6. Darius's order for the rebuilding of the temple (6:6–12)
7. Completion of the temple (6:13–15)
8. Dedication of the temple (6:16–18)
9. Celebration of Passover (6:19–22)

II. Ezra's Return and Reforms (chs. 7—10)

A. Ezra's Return to Jerusalem (chs. 7—8)

1. Introduction (7:1–10)
2. The authorization by Artaxerxes (7:11–26)
3. Ezra's doxology (7:27–28)
4. List of those returning with Ezra (8:1–14)
5. The search for Levites (8:15–20)
6. Prayer and fasting (8:21–23)
7. The assignment of the sacred articles (8:24–30)
8. The journey and arrival in Jerusalem (8:31–36)

B. Ezra's Reforms (chs. 9—10)

1. The offense of mixed marriages (9:1–5)
2. Ezra's confession and prayer (9:6–15)
3. The people's response (10:1–4)
4. The calling of a public assembly (10:5–15)
5. Investigation of the offenders (10:16–17)
6. The list of offenders (10:18–43)
7. The dissolution of mixed marriages (10:44)

Cyrus's Proclamation

1 [a]Now in the first year of Cyrus king of
Persia, in order to fulfill the word of the
LORD by the mouth of Jeremiah, the LORD
stirred up the spirit of Cyrus king of Persia,
so that he [b]sent a proclamation throughout
all his kingdom, and also *put it* in writing,
saying:
2 "Thus says Cyrus king of Persia, 'The
LORD, the God of heaven, has given me all
the kingdoms of the earth and [a]He has
appointed me to build Him a house in Jerusalem, which is in Judah.
3 'Whoever there is among you of all His
people, may his God be with him! Let him go
up to Jerusalem which is in Judah and
rebuild the house of the LORD, the God of
Israel; [a]He is the God who is in Jerusalem.
4 'Every survivor, at whatever place he
may [1]live, let the men of [2]that place support
him with silver and gold, with goods and
cattle, together with a freewill offering for
the house of God which is in Jerusalem.' "

Holy Vessels Restored

5 Then the heads of fathers' *households*
of Judah and Benjamin and the priests and
the Levites arose, [a]even everyone whose
spirit God had stirred to go up and rebuild
the house of the LORD which is in Jerusalem.
6 All those about them [1a]encouraged
them with articles of silver, with gold, with
goods, with cattle and with valuables, aside
from all that was given as a freewill offering.
7 [a]Also King Cyrus brought out the articles of the house of the LORD, [b]which Nebuchadnezzar had carried away from Jerusalem and put in the house of his gods;
8 and Cyrus, king of Persia, had them
brought out by the hand of Mithredath the
treasurer, and he counted them out to
[a]Sheshbazzar, the prince of Judah.
9 Now this *was* their number: 30 [a]gold
dishes, 1,000 silver dishes, 29 [1]duplicates;
10 30 gold bowls, 410 silver bowls of a
second *kind and* 1,000 other articles.
11 All the articles of gold and silver *num-*

1:1 [a]2 Chr 36:22; Jer 25:12; 29:10 [b]Ezra 5:13
2 [a]Is 44:28; 45:1, 12, 13
3 [a]1 Kin 8:23; 18:39; Is 37:16; Dan 6:26
4 [1]Or *reside as an alien* [2]Lit *his*
5 [a]Ezra 1:1, 2
6 [1]Lit *strengthened their hands* [a]Neh 6:9; Is 35:3
7 [a]Ezra 5:14; 6:5 [b]2 Kin 24:13; 2 Chr 36:7
8 [a]Ezra 5:14
9 [1]Heb obscure; other possible meanings are *knives, censers* [a]Ezra 8:27

1:1–3a Virtually identical with the last two verses of 2 Chronicles. This fact has been used to argue that Chronicles and Ezra-Nehemiah were written and/or edited by the same person, the so-called Chronicler. However, the repetition may have been a device of the author of Chronicles (or less probably of Ezra) to dovetail the narratives chronologically.

1:1 *first year.* Of the reign of Cyrus over Babylon, beginning in March, 538 B.C., after he captured Babylon in October, 539. Cyrus, the founder of the Persian empire, reigned over the Persians from 559 until 530. Is 44:28; 45:1 speak of him as the Lord's "shepherd" and His "anointed." *to fulfill the word of the LORD by the mouth of Jeremiah.* Jeremiah prophesied a 70-year Babylonian captivity (Jer 25:11–12; 29:10). The first deportation began in 605, the third year of Jehoiakim (Dan 1:1); in 538, approximately 70 years later, the people began to return.

1:2–4 This oral proclamation of Cyrus's decree was written in Hebrew, the language of the Israelite captives, in contrast to the copy of the decree in 6:3–5, which was an Aramaic memorandum for the archives.

1:2 *God of heaven.* Of the 22 OT occurrences of the phrase, 17 occur in Ezra, Nehemiah and Daniel. *house in Jerusalem.* Jerusalem and the house of God are prominent subjects in Ezra and Nehemiah.

1:3 Cyrus instituted the policy of placating the gods of his subject peoples instead of carrying off their cult images as the Assyrians and the Babylonians had done earlier. His generosity to the Jews was paralleled by his benevolence to the Babylonians.

1:4 *Every survivor, at whatever place he may live.* Probably designates the many Jews who did not wish to leave Mesopotamia. *freewill offering.* A key to the restoration of God's temple and its services (see 2:68; 3:5; 8:28).

1:5 *heads of fathers' households.* In ancient times families were extended families—more like clans than modern nuclear families. The authority figure was the patriarch, who was the "head of the household." See 10:16; see also 2:59; Neh 7:61; 10:34. *Judah and Benjamin.* The two main tribes of the kingdom of Judah, which the Babylonians had exiled. *Levites.* See Introduction to Leviticus: Title.

1:7 It was the custom for conquerors to carry off the images of the gods of conquered cities. Since the Jews did not have an image of the Lord (see note on Ex 20:4), Nebuchadnezzar carried away only the temple articles.

1:8 *Mithredath.* A Persian name meaning "given by/to Mithra," a Persian god who became popular among Roman soldiers in the second century A.D. *Sheshbazzar.* A Babylonian name meaning either "Sin, protect the father" or "Shamash/Shashu, protect the father." Sin was the moon-god, and Shamash (Shashu is a variant) was the sun-god. In spite of his Babylonian name, Sheshbazzar was probably a Jewish official who served as a deputy governor of Judah under the satrap in Samaria (see 5:14). Some believe that Sheshbazzar and Zerubbabel were the same person and give the following reasons: 1. Both were governors (5:14; Hag 1:1; 2:2). 2. Both are said to have laid the foundation of the temple (3:2–8; 5:16; Hag 1:14–15; Zech 4:6–10). 3. Jews in Babylon were often given "official" Babylonian names (cf. Dan 1:7). 4. Josephus (*Antiquities,* 11.1.3) seems to identify Sheshbazzar with Zerubbabel.

Others point out, however, that the Apocrypha distinguishes between the two men (1 Esdras 6:18). Furthermore, it is likely that Sheshbazzar was an elderly man at the time of the return, while Zerubbabel was probably a younger contemporary. Sheshbazzar also may have been viewed as the official governor, while Zerubbabel served as the popular leader (3:8–11). Whereas the high priest Jeshua is associated with Zerubbabel, no priest is associated with Sheshbazzar. Although Sheshbazzar presided over the foundation of the temple in 536 B.C., so little was accomplished that Zerubbabel had to preside over a second foundation some 16 years later (see Hag 1:14–15; Zech 4:6–10).

Still others hold that Sheshbazzar is to be identified with Shenazzar (1 Chr 3:18), the fourth son of King Jeconiah. Zerubbabel would then have been Sheshbazzar's nephew (compare 3:2 with 1 Chr 3:18).

1:9–11 When Assyrian and Babylonian conquerors carried off plunder, their scribes made a careful inventory of all the goods seized. The total of the figures in vv. 9–10 adds up to 2,499 rather than the 5,400 of v. 11. It may be that only the larger and more valuable vessels were specified.

1:11 We are not told anything about the details of Sheshbazzar's journey, which probably took place in 537 B.C. Judging from Ezra's later journey (7:8–9), the trip took about four months. See map No. 7b at the end of the study Bible; see also map, p. 633.

bered 5,400. Sheshbazzar brought them all
up with the exiles who went up from Babylon to Jerusalem.

Number of Those Returning

2 [a]Now these are the [1]people of the province who came up out of the captivity of
the exiles whom Nebuchadnezzar the king
of Babylon had carried away to Babylon, and
returned to Jerusalem and Judah, each to his
city.

2 [1]These came with Zerubbabel, Jeshua,
Nehemiah, [2]Seraiah, [3]Reelaiah, Mordecai,
Bilshan, [4]Mispar, Bigvai, [5]Rehum *and* Baa-
nah.

The number of the men of the people of
Israel:

3 the sons of Parosh, 2,172;
4 the sons of Shephatiah, 372;
5 the sons of [a]Arah, 775;
6 the sons of [a]Pahath-moab of the sons
of Jeshua *and* Joab, 2,812;
7 the sons of Elam, 1,254;
8 the sons of Zattu, 945;
9 the sons of Zaccai, 760;
10 the sons of [1]Bani, 642;
11 the sons of Bebai, 623;
12 the sons of Azgad, 1,222;
13 the sons of [a]Adonikam, 666;
14 the sons of Bigvai, 2,056;
15 the sons of Adin, 454;
16 the sons of Ater of Hezekiah, 98;
17 the sons of Bezai, 323;
18 the sons of [1]Jorah, 112;
19 the sons of Hashum, 223;
20 the sons of [1]Gibbar, 95;
21 the [1]men of [a]Bethlehem, 123;
22 the men of Netophah, 56;
23 the men of Anathoth, 128;
24 the sons of [1]Azmaveth, 42;
25 the sons of [1]Kiriath-arim, Chephirah
and Beeroth, 743;
26 the sons of [a]Ramah and Geba, 621;
27 the men of Michmas, 122;
28 the men of Bethel and Ai, 223;
29 the sons of Nebo, 52;
30 the sons of Magbish, 156;
31 the sons of the other Elam, 1,254;
32 the sons of Harim, 320;
33 the sons of Lod, Hadid and Ono, 725;
34 the [1]men of [a]Jericho, 345;
35 the sons of Senaah, 3,630.

Priests Returning

36 [a]The priests: the sons of Jedaiah of the
house of Jeshua, 973;
37 the sons of [a]Immer, 1,052;
38 [a]the sons of Pashhur, 1,247;
39 the sons of [a]Harim, 1,017.

Levites Returning

40 The Levites: the sons of Jeshua and
Kadmiel, of the sons of [1]Hodaviah, 74.
41 The singers: the sons of Asaph, 128.

2:1 [1]Lit *sons* [a]2 Kin 24:14-16; 25:11; 2 Chr 36:20; Neh 7:6-73
2 [1]Lit *who* [2]In Neh 7:7, *Azariah* [3]In Neh 7:7, *Raamiah* [4]In Neh 7:7, *Mispereth* [5]In Neh 7:7, *Nehum*
5 [a]Neh 7:10
6 [a]Neh 7:11
10 [1]In Neh 7:15, *Binnui*
13 [a]Ezra 8:13
18 [1]In Neh 7:24, *Hariph*
20 [1]In Neh 7:25, *Gibeon*
21 [1]Lit *sons* [a]Gen 35:19; Matt 2:6
24 [1]In Neh 7:28, *Beth-azmaveth*
25 [1]In Neh 7:29, *Kiriath-jearim*
26 [a]Josh 18:25
34 [1]Lit *sons* [a]1 Kin 16:34; 2 Chr 28:15
36 [a]1 Chr 24:7-18
37 [a]1 Chr 24:14
38 [a]1 Chr 9:12
39 [a]1 Chr 24:8
40 [1]In Ezra 3:9, *Judah;* in Neh 7:43, *Hodevah*

2:1–70 The list of returning exiles in ch. 2 almost exactly parallels the list in Neh 7:6–73 (see also 1 Esdras 5:4–46 in the Apocrypha). The list of localities indicates that people retained the memories of their homes and that exiles from a wide background of tribes, villages and towns returned. In comparing the list here with that in Neh 7, one notes many differences in the names and numbers listed. About 20 percent of the numbers, e.g., are not the same in Ezra and Nehemiah. Many of these differences may be explained, however, by assuming that a cipher notation was used with vertical strokes for units and horizontal strokes for tens, which led to copying errors.

2:1 *province.* Probably Judah (cf. 5:8, where the Aramaic word for "province" occurs; see also Neh 1:3).

2:2 *Zerubbabel.* See notes on 3:2; 5:2. *Jeshua.* Means "The LORD saves" and is an Aramaic variant of Hebrew "Joshua." The Greek form is "Jesus" (see note on Matt 1:21). Jeshua is the same as the Joshua of Hag 1:1, the son of the high priest Jehozadak (Jozadak, Ezra 3:2), who was taken into exile (1 Chr 6:15). *Nehemiah.* Not the Nehemiah of the book by that name. *Mordecai.* A Babylonian name based on that of Marduk the god of Babylon (cf. Jer 50:2). Esther's cousin had the same name (Esth 2:7).

2:3 *Parosh.* Means "flea" (Israelites were often named after insects and animals). Members of this family, as well as of several other families named in vv. 6–14, also returned with Ezra (8:3–14).

2:5 *Arah.* Probably means "wild ox." Since the name is rare in the OT and has been found in documents from Mesopotamia, it may have been adopted during the exile.

2:6 *Pahath-moab.* Means "governor of Moab" and may have once designated an official title.

2:12 *Azgad.* Cf. 8:12; means "Gad is strong." It is a reference either to Gad (the god of fortune, referred to in Is 65:11) or to the Transjordanian tribe of Gad.

2:16 *Ater.* Means "left-handed," as in Judg 3:15; 20:16.

2:21–35 Whereas the names in vv. 3–20 are of families, vv. 21–35 present a series of villages and towns, many of which were in Benjamite territory north of Jerusalem. It is significant that there are no references to towns in the Negev, south of Judah. When Nebuchadnezzar overran Judah in 597 B.C. (Jer 13:19), the Edomites (see the book of Obadiah) took advantage of the situation and occupied that area.

2:21 *men of Bethlehem.* The ancestors of Jesus may have been among the returnees (see 1 Sam 17:12; 20:6; Mic 5:2; Luke 2:4).

2:23 *Anathoth.* See note on Jer 1:1.

2:28 *Bethel.* See note on Gen 12:8. Towns such as Bethel, Mizpah, Gibeon and Gibeah seem to have escaped the Babylonian assault. Bethel, however, was destroyed in the transition between the Babylonian and Persian periods. Archaeological excavations reveal that there was a small town on the site in Ezra's day.

2:31 See v. 7.

2:33 *Lod.* Modern Lydda.

2:35 *Senaah.* The largest number of returnees—3,630 (3,930 in Neh 7:38)—is associated with Senaah. It has therefore been suggested that they did not come from a specific locality or family, but represented the poorer and lower classes of people, as inferred from the meaning of the name ("the hated one").

2:36–39 Four clans of priests numbering 4,289, about a tenth of the total.

2:40 *Levites.* See Introduction to Leviticus: Title. *74.* The number of Levites who returned was relatively small (cf. 8:15). Since the Levites had been entrusted with the menial tasks of temple service, many of them may have found a more comfortable way of life in exile.

2:41 *Asaph.* One of the three Levites appointed by David over the temple singers (1 Chr 25:1; 2 Chr 5:12; 35:15), whose duties are detailed in 1 Chr 15:16–24.

Chronology: Ezra–Nehemiah

Dates below are given according to a Nisan-to-Nisan Jewish calendar (see chart, p. 92). Roman numerals represent months; Arabic numerals represent days.

540 B.C. — 530 — 520 — 510 — 500 — 490 — 480 — 470 — 460 — 450 — 440 — 430 B.C.

YEAR	MONTH	DAY	EVENT	REFERENCE
539 B.C.	Oct.	12	Capture of Babylon	Dan 5:30
538 **537**	Mar. to Mar.	24 11	Cyrus's first year	Ezra 1:1-4
537(?)			Return under Sheshbazzar	Ezra 1:11
537	VII		Building of altar	Ezra 3:1
536	II		Work on temple begun	Ezra 3:8
536-530			Opposition during Cyrus's reign	Ezra 4:1-5
530-520			Work on temple ceased	Ezra 4:24
520	VI =Sept.	24 21	Work on temple renewed under Darius	Ezra 5:2; Hag 1:14
516	XII =Mar.	3 12	Temple completed	Ezra 6:15
458	I =Apr.	1 8	Ezra departs from Babylon	Ezra 7:6-9
	V =Aug.	1 4	Ezra arrives in Jerusalem	Ezra 7:8-9
	IX =Dec.	20 19	People assemble	Ezra 10:9
	X =Dec.	1 29	Committee begins investigation	Ezra 10:16
457	I =Mar.	1 27	Committee ends investigation	Ezra 10:17
445 **444**	Apr to Apr.	13 2	20th year of Artaxerxes I	Neh 1:1
445	I =Mar.–Apr.		Nehemiah approaches king	Neh 2:1
	Aug.(?)		Nehemiah arrives in Jerusalem	Neh 2:11
	VI =Oct.	25 2	Completion of wall	Neh 6:15
	VII=Oct. to Nov.	8 5	Public assembly	Neh 7:73–8:1
	VII =Oct.	15-22 22-28	Feast of Booths	Neh 8:14
	VII =Oct.	24 30	Fast	Neh 9:1
433 **432**	Apr. to Apr.	1	32nd year of Artaxerxes; Nehemiah's recall and return	Neh 5:14; 13:6

42 The sons of the gatekeepers: the sons
of Shallum, the sons of Ater, the sons of Talmon, the sons of Akkub, the sons of Hatita,
the sons of Shobai, in all 139.
43 The [a]temple servants: the sons of Ziha,
the sons of Hasupha, the sons of Tabbaoth,
44 the sons of Keros, the sons of [1]Siaha,
the sons of Padon,
45 the sons of Lebanah, the sons of Haga-
bah, the sons of Akkub,
46 the sons of Hagab, the sons of Shalmai,
the sons of Hanan,
47 the sons of Giddel, the sons of Gahar,
the sons of Reaiah,
48 the sons of Rezin, the sons of Nekoda,
the sons of Gazzam,
49 the sons of Uzza, the sons of Paseah,
the sons of Besai,
50 the sons of Asnah, the sons of Meunim,
the sons of [1]Nephisim,
51 the sons of Bakbuk, the sons of Haku-
pha, the sons of Harhur,
52 the sons of [1]Bazluth, the sons of Mehi-
da, the sons of Harsha,
53 the sons of Barkos, the sons of Sisera,
the sons of Temah,
54 the sons of Neziah, the sons of Hatipha.
55 The sons of [a]Solomon's servants: the
sons of Sotai, the sons of [1]Hassophereth, the
sons of [2]Peruda,
56 the sons of Jaalah, the sons of Darkon,
the sons of Giddel,
57 the sons of Shephatiah, the sons of
Hattil, the sons of Pochereth-hazzebaim, the
sons of [1]Ami.
58 All the [a]temple servants and the sons
of [b]Solomon's servants were 392.
59 Now these are those who came up
from Tel-melah, Tel-harsha, Cherub, [1]Addan
and Immer, but they were not able to [2]give
evidence of their fathers' households and
their [3]descendants, whether they were of
Israel:
60 the sons of Delaiah, the sons of Tobiah,
the sons of Nekoda, 652.

Priests Removed

61 Of the sons of the priests: the sons of
[1]Habaiah, the sons of Hakkoz, the sons of
[a]Barzillai, who took a wife from the daughters of Barzillai the Gileadite, and he was
called by their name.
62 These searched *among* their ancestral
registration, but they could not be located;
[a]therefore they were considered unclean *and*
excluded from the priesthood.
63 The [1]governor said to them [a]that they
should not eat from the most holy things until
a priest stood up with [b]Urim and Thummim.
64 The whole assembly [1]numbered 42,360,
65 besides their male and female servants
[1]who numbered 7,337; and they had 200
[a]singing men and women.
66 Their horses were 736; their mules,
245;

43 [a]1 Chr 9:2 **44** [1]In Neh 7:47, *Sia* **50** [1]In Neh 7:52, *Nephushesim* **52** [1]In Neh 7:54, *Bazlith* **55** [1]In Neh 7:57, *Sophereth* [2]In Neh 7:57, *Perida* [a]1 Kin 9:21
57 [1]In Neh 7:59, *Amon* **58** [a]1 Chr 9:2 [b]1 Kin 9:21 **59** [1]In Neh 7:61, *Addon* [2]Lit *tell* [3]Lit *seed* **61** [1]In Neh 7:63, *Hobaiah* [a]2 Sam 17:27; 1 Kin 2:7 **62** [a]Num 16:39, 40 **63** [1]Heb *Tirshatha,* a Persian title [a]Lev 2:3, 10 [b]Ex 28:30; Num 27:21 **64** [1]Lit *together was* **65** [1]Lit *they were* [a]2 Chr 35:25

2:42 *gatekeepers.* Usually Levites (1 Chr 9:26; 2 Chr 23:4; 35:15; Neh 12:25; 13:22). They are mentioned 16 times in Ezra-Nehemiah and 19 times in Chronicles. Their primary function was to tend the doors and gates of the temple (1 Chr 9:17–27) and to perform other menial tasks (1 Chr 9:28–32; 2 Chr 31:14).
2:43–57 The temple servants and the descendants of Solomon's servants together numbered 392 (v. 58), which was more than the total of the Levites, singers and gatekeepers together (vv. 40–42).
2:46 *Hanan.* Means "(God) is gracious." The verb "to be gracious" and its derivatives are the components of numerous personal names in the OT—e.g., Johanan ("The LORD is gracious"; see 8:12), which has given us the English name John.
2:51 *Bakbuk.* Means "jar." It may have originally been a nickname for a fat man with a protruding belly. Cf. Jer 19:1,10, where the same Hebrew word is translated "jar"; see Jer 19:7, where the Hebrew for "make a void" means lit. "pour out" and sounds like the Hebrew for "jar."
2:53 *Barkos.* Means "son of Kos" (or Qos, an Edomite god).
2:55,58 *sons of Solomon's servants.* The phrase occurs only here and in Neh 7:57,60; 11:3. These may be the descendants of the Canaanites whom Solomon enslaved (1 Kin 9:20–21).
2:55 *Hassophereth.* Probably means "the scribal office/function" and may have once been an official title.
2:59–63 Individuals who lacked evidence of their ancestry.
2:59 *Tel-melah . . . Immer.* Places in Mesopotamia where the Jews were settled by their Babylonian captors. *Tel-melah.* Means "mound of salt," possibly a mound on which salt had been scattered (see Judg 9:45 and note). The Hebrew word *tel* designates a hill-like mound (see note on Josh 11:13) formed by the remains of a ruined city. The Jewish exiles had been settled along the Chebar River (Ezek 1:1), perhaps near Nippur, a city in southern Mesopotamia that was the stronghold of rebels. The Jews had probably been settled on the mounds of ruined cities that had been depopulated by the Babylonians.
2:61 *Barzillai.* Means "man of iron." For another Barzillai see 2 Sam 17:27–29; 19:31–39; 1 Kin 2:7.
2:63 *governor.* Probably either Sheshbazzar or Zerubbabel (see note on 1:8). *Urim and Thummim.* See note on Ex 28:30.
2:64 *42,360.* Considerably more than the sum of the other figures given:

Categories	*Ezra*	*Nehemiah*	*1 Esdras*
Men of Israel	24,144	25,406	25,947
Priests	4,289	4,289	5,288
Levites, singers, gatekeepers	341	360	341
Temple servants, descendants of Solomon's servants	392	392	372
Men of unproven origin	652	642	652
Totals	29,818	31,089	32,600

It is difficult to account for the difference of about 10,000–12,000. The figure may refer to an unspecified 10,000–12,000 women and/or children, and it doubtless includes the priests of unproven origin referred to in vv. 61–63. Some suggest that the groups explicitly counted were returnees from Judah and Benjamin, while the remainder were from other tribes.
2:65 *male and female servants.* The ratio of servants to others (one to six) is relatively high. The fact that so many returned with their masters speaks highly of the benevolent treatment of servants by the Jews. *singing men and women.* The men and women singers listed here may be secular singers who sang at social events such as weddings and funerals (2 Chr 35:25), as distinct from the temple singers of v. 41, who were all male.
2:66 *horses.* Perhaps a donation from Cyrus for the nobility. *mules.* Often used by royalty and the wealthy (1 Kin 1:33; Is 66:20).

67 their camels, 435; *their* donkeys, 6,720.
68 Some of the heads of fathers' *households,* when they arrived at the house of the
LORD which is in Jerusalem, offered willingly
for the house of God to [1]restore it on its
foundation.
69 According to their ability they gave [a]to
the treasury for the work 61,000 gold drachmas and 5,000 silver minas and 100 priestly
[1]garments.
70 [a]Now the priests and the Levites, some
of the people, the singers, the gatekeepers
and the temple servants lived in their cities,
and all Israel in their cities.

Altar and Sacrifices Restored

3 Now when the seventh month came, and
[a]the sons of Israel *were* in the cities, the
people gathered together as one man to Jerusalem.
2 Then [a]Jeshua the son of Jozadak and
his brothers the priests, and [b]Zerubbabel the
son [c]of Shealtiel and his brothers arose and
[d]built the altar of the God of Israel to offer
burnt offerings on it, [e]as it is written in the
law of Moses, the man of God.
3 So they set up the altar on its foundation, for [1a]they were terrified because of the
peoples of the lands; and they [b]offered burnt
offerings on it to the LORD, burnt offerings
morning and evening.
4 They celebrated the [a]Feast of [1]Booths,
[b]as it is written, and *offered* [2]the fixed number of burnt offerings daily, [c]according to the
ordinance, as each day required;
5 and afterward *there was* a [a]continual
burnt offering, also [b]for the new moons and
[c]for all the fixed festivals of the LORD that
were consecrated, and from everyone who
offered a freewill offering to the LORD.
6 From the first day of the seventh month
they began to offer burnt offerings to the
LORD, but the foundation of the temple of the
LORD had not been laid.
7 Then they gave money to the masons
and carpenters, and [a]food, drink and oil to
the Sidonians and to the Tyrians, [b]to bring
cedar wood from Lebanon to the sea at [c]Jop-
pa, according to the permission they had
[1]from [d]Cyrus king of Persia.

Temple Restoration Begun

8 Now in the second year of their coming
to the house of God at Jerusalem in the second month, [a]Zerubbabel the son of Shealtiel
and Jeshua the son of Jozadak and the rest
of their brothers the priests and the Levites,
and all who came from the captivity to
Jerusalem, began *the work* and [b]appointed
the Levites from twenty years and older to
oversee the work of the house of the LORD.
9 Then [a]Jeshua *with* his sons and brothers stood united *with* Kadmiel and his sons,
the sons of [1]Judah *and* the sons of Henadad
with their sons and brothers the Levites, to
oversee the workmen in the temple of God.
10 Now when the builders had [a]laid the
foundation of the temple of the LORD, [1]the
priests stood in their apparel with trumpets,
and the Levites, the sons of Asaph, with
cymbals, to praise the LORD [b]according to the
[2]directions of King David of Israel.
11 [a]They sang, praising and giving thanks
to the LORD, *saying,* "[b]For He is good, for His

68 [1]Lit *establish*
69 [1]Or *tunics* [a]Ezra 8:25-34
70 [a]1 Chr 9:2; Neh 11:3
3:1 [a]Neh 7:73; 8:1
2 [a]Neh 12:1, 8 [b]Ezra 2:2; Hag 1:1; 2:2 [c]1 Chr 3:17 [d]Ex 27:1 [e]Deut 12:5, 6
3 [1]Lit *terror* was *upon them* [a]Ezra 4:4 [b]Num 28:2
4 [1]Or *Tabernacles* [2]Lit *by number* [a]Neh 8:14; Zech 14:16 [b]Ex 23:16 [c]Num 29:12
5 [a]Ex 29:38; Num 28:3 [b]Num 28:11
5 [c]Num 29:39
7 [1]Lit *of* [a]2 Chr 2:10; Acts 12:20 [b]2 Chr 2:16 [c]Acts 9:36 [d]Ezra 1:2; 6:3
8 [a]Ezra 3:2; 4:3 [b]1 Chr 23:4, 24
9 [1]In Ezra 2:40, *Hodaviah* [a]Ezra 2:40
10 [1]So with the Gr and some mss; M.T. *they set the priests* [2]Lit *hands* [a]Zech 4:6-10 [b]1 Chr 6:31; 25:1
11 [a]2 Chr 7:3; Neh 12:24, 40 [b]1 Chr 16:34; 2 Chr 5:13; Ps 100:5; 106:1; 107:1; 118:1; 131:1; Jer 33:11

2:67 *donkeys.* Were used to carry loads, women or children. Sheep, goats and cattle are not mentioned. They would have slowed the caravan.
2:68 *arrived . . . Jerusalem.* For the route of the return from exile see map No. 7b at the end of the study Bible.
2:69 The parallel passage (Neh 7:70–72) gives a fuller description than the account in Ezra. In Ezra the gifts come from the heads of the families (v. 68), while in Nehemiah the gifts are credited to three sources: the governor, the heads of the families, and the rest of the people. *drachmas.* The drachma was a Greek silver coin. Some believe that the coin intended here was the Persian *daric,* a gold coin. *minas.* In the sexagesimal system (based on the number 60) that originated in Mesopotamia, there were 60 shekels in a mina and 60 minas in a talent. A shekel, which was about two-fifths of an ounce of silver, was the average wage for a month's work. Thus a mina would be the equivalent of five years' wages, and a talent would be 300 years' wages.
2:70 Later, Nehemiah (11:1–2) would be compelled to move people by lot to reinforce the population of Jerusalem.
3:1 *seventh month.* Tishri (September-October), about three months after the arrival of the exiles in Judah (in 537 B.C.). Tishri was one of the most sacred months of the Jewish year (see Lev 23:23–43 and notes).
3:2 *Jeshua . . . Zerubbabel.* The priest takes precedence over the civil leader in view of the nature of the occasion (contrast 3:8; 4:3; 5:2; Hag 1:1).
3:4 *Feast of Booths.* See Lev 23:33–43 and notes.
3:5 *new moons.* See note on 1 Sam 20:5. *festivals . . . that were consecrated.* See note on Lev 23:2. *freewill offering.* See note on 1:4. It is noteworthy that the restoration of the sacrifices preceded the erection of the temple itself.
3:7 *cedar wood.* As in the case of the first temple, the Phoenicians cooperated by sending timber and workmen (1 Kin 5:6–12).
3:8 *second year.* Since the Jews probably returned to Judah in the spring of 537 B.C., the second year would be the spring of 536. *second month.* The same month (April-May) in which Solomon had begun his temple (1 Kin 6:1). *twenty years.* In earlier times the lower age limit for Levites was 30 (Num 4:3) or 25 years (Num 8:24). It was later reduced to 20 (1 Chr 23:24,27; 2 Chr 31:17), probably because there were so few Levites.
3:10 *trumpets.* Made of hammered silver (see Num 10:2 and note). According to Josephus (*Antiquities,* 3.12.6—written C. A.D. 93), the trumpet was "in length a little short of a cubit; it is a narrow tube, slightly thicker than a flute." With the possible exception of their use at the coronation of Joash (2 Kin 11:14; 2 Chr 23:13), the trumpets were always blown by priests. They were most often used on joyous occasions, such as here and at the dedication of the rebuilt walls of Jerusalem (Neh 12:35; cf. 2 Chr 5:13; Ps 98:6). *cymbals.* The Hebrew for this word occurs 13 times in the OT, all in Chronicles except here and Neh 12:27.
3:11 *sang.* May mean "sang responsively," referring to antiphonal singing by a choir divided into two groups. *He is good . . . His lovingkindness is . . . forever.* See, e.g., 1 Chr 16:34;

lovingkindness is upon Israel forever." And
all the people shouted with a great shout
when they praised the LORD because the
foundation of the house of the LORD was laid.
12 Yet many of the priests and Levites and
heads of fathers' *households,* [a]the old men
who had seen the first [1]temple, wept with a
loud voice when the foundation of this
house was laid before their eyes, while many
shouted aloud for joy,
13 so that the people could not distinguish
the sound of the shout of joy from the sound
of the weeping of the people, for the people
shouted with a loud shout, and the sound
was heard far away.

12 [1]Lit *house* [a]Hag 2:3
4:1 [a]Ezra 4:7-10 [b]Ezra 1:11
2 [a]2 Kin 17:32 [b]2 Kin 19:37

Adversaries Hinder the Work

4 Now when [a]the enemies of Judah and
Benjamin heard that [b]the people of the
exile were building a temple to the LORD God
of Israel,
2 they approached Zerubbabel and the
heads of fathers' *households,* and said to
them, "Let us build with you, for we, like
you, seek your God; [a]and we have been sacrificing to Him since the days of [b]Esarhad-

---

2 Chr 5:13; Ps 100:5. *great shout.* See Josh 6:5,20; 1 Sam 4:5; Ps 95:1.
3:13 *shout of joy . . . sound of the weeping.* The people of Israel were accustomed to showing their emotions in visible and audible ways (10:1; Neh 1:4; 8:9). The same God who had permitted judgment had now brought them back and would enable them to complete the project. A Babylonian cornerstone reads: "I started the work weeping, I finished it rejoicing." Cf. Ps 126:5–6.
4:1–23 A summary of various attempts to thwart the efforts of the Jews. In vv. 1–5 the author describes events in the reign of Cyrus (559–530 B.C.), in v. 6 the reign of Ahasuerus (486–465) and in vv. 7–23 the reign of Artaxerxes I (465–424). He then reverts in v. 24 to the time of Darius I (522–486), during whose reign the temple was completed (see 5:1–2; 6:13–15; Haggai; Zech 1:1–17; 4:9).
4:1 *enemies.* The people who offered their "help" (v. 2) were from Samaria. *Judah and Benjamin.* See notes on 1:5; 1 Kin 12:21.
4:2 After the fall of Samaria in 722–721 B.C., the Assyrian kings brought in people from Mesopotamia and Aram. These people served their own gods but also took up the worship of the Lord as the god of the land (2 Kin 17:24–41). *Esarhaddon.* See note on 2 Kin 19:37.

Zerubbabel's Temple

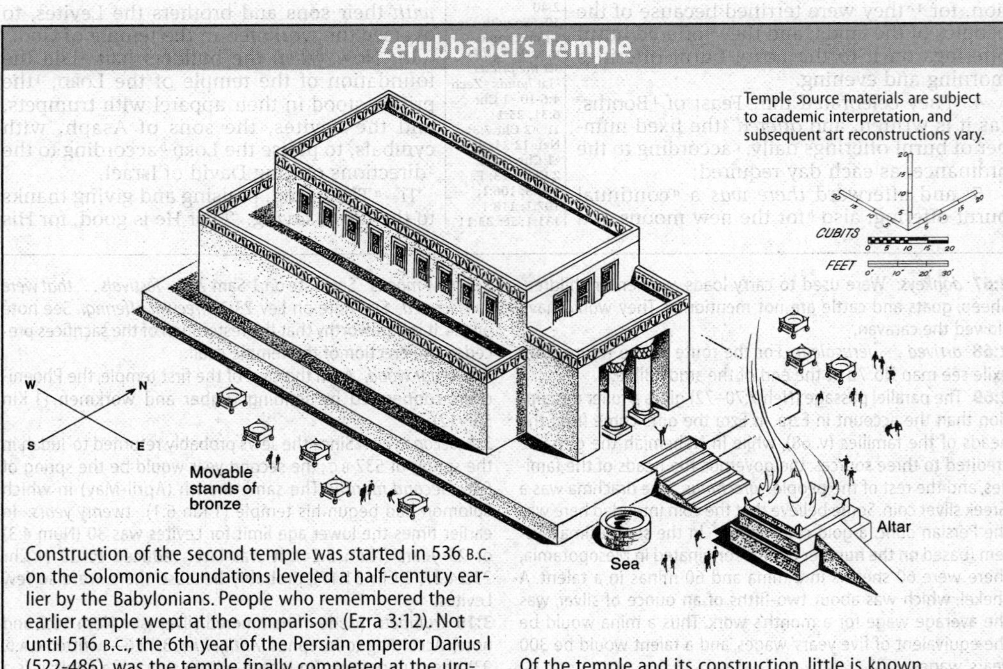
Temple source materials are subject to academic interpretation, and subsequent art reconstructions vary.
CUBITS
0 5 10 15 20
FEET
0' 10' 20' 30'
W
N
S
E
Movable stands of bronze
Altar
Sea

Construction of the second temple was started in 536 B.C. on the Solomonic foundations leveled a half-century earlier by the Babylonians. People who remembered the earlier temple wept at the comparison (Ezra 3:12). Not until 516 B.C., the 6th year of the Persian emperor Darius I (522-486), was the temple finally completed at the urging of Haggai and Zechariah (Ezra 6:13-15).

Archaeological evidence confirms that the Persian period in the Holy Land was a comparatively impoverished one in terms of material culture. Later Aramaic documents from Elephantine in Upper Egypt illustrate the official process of gaining permission to construct a Jewish place of worship, and the opposition engendered by the presence of various foes during this period.

Of the temple and its construction, little is known. Among the few contemporary buildings, the Persian palace at Lachish and the Tobiad monument at Iraq el-Amir may be compared in terms of technique.

Unlike the more famous structures razed in 586 B.C. and A.D. 70, the temple begun by Zerubbabel suffered no major hostile destruction, but was gradually repaired and reconstructed over a long period. Eventually it was replaced entirely by Herod's magnificent edifice.

©1981 Hugh Claycombe

don king of Assyria, who brought us up
here."
3 But Zerubbabel and Jeshua and the rest
of the heads of fathers' *households* of Israel
said to them, "[a]You have nothing in common
with us in building a house to our God; but
we ourselves will together build to the LORD
God of Israel, [b]as King Cyrus, the king of Persia has commanded us."
4 Then [a]the people of the land [1]discour-
aged the people of Judah, and frightened
them from building,
5 and hired counselors against them to
frustrate their counsel all the days of Cyrus
king of Persia, even until the reign of Darius
king of Persia.
6 Now in the reign of [1][a]Ahasuerus, in the
beginning of his reign, they wrote an accusation against the inhabitants of Judah and
Jerusalem.
7 And in the days of [1]Artaxerxes, Bish-
lam, Mithredath, Tabeel and the rest of his
colleagues wrote to Artaxerxes king of Persia; and the [2]text of the letter was written in
Aramaic and translated [a]*from* Aramaic.

The Letter to King Artaxerxes

8 [1]Rehum the commander and Shimshai
the scribe wrote a letter against Jerusalem to
King Artaxerxes, as follows—

9 then *wrote* Rehum the commander and
Shimshai the scribe and [a]the rest of their colleagues, the judges and [b]the lesser governors, the officials, the secretaries, the men of
Erech, the Babylonians, the men of Susa,
that is, the Elamites,
10 and the rest of the nations which the
great and honorable [1]Osnappar deported and
settled in the city of Samaria, and in the rest
of the region beyond the [2]River. [a]Now
11 this is the copy of the letter which they
sent to him:
"To King Artaxerxes: Your servants, the
men in the region beyond the River, and now
12 let it be known to the king that the
Jews who came up from you have come to
us at Jerusalem; they are rebuilding [a]the
rebellious and evil city and [b]are finishing the
walls and repairing the foundations.
13 "Now let it be known to the king, that if
that city is rebuilt and the walls are finished,
[a]they will not pay tribute, custom or toll, and
it will damage the revenue of the kings.
14 "Now because we [1]are in the service of
the palace, and it is not fitting for us to see
the king's dishonor, therefore we have sent
and informed the king,
15 so that a search may be made in the
record books of your fathers. And you will
discover in the record books and learn that

3 [a]Neh 2:20 [b]Ezra 1:1, 2
4 [1]Lit *weakened the hands of* [a]Ezra 3:3
6 [1]Or *Xerxes;* Heb *Ahash-verosh* [a]Esth 1:1; Dan 9:1
7 [1]Heb *Artah-shashta* [2]Lit *writing* [a]2 Kin 18:26; Dan 2:4
8 [1]Ch 4:8-6:18 is in Aram
9 [a]2 Kin 17:24 [b]Ezra 5:6; 6:6
10 [1]I.e. probably Ashurbanipal [2]I.e. Euphrates River, and so throughout the ch [a]Ezra 4:11, 17; 7:12
12 [a]2 Chr 36:13 [b]Ezra 5:3, 9
13 [a]Ezra 4:20; 7:24
14 [1]Lit *eat the salt*

4:4 *people of the land.* Josephus (*Antiquities,* 11.2.1) singles out especially the Cutheans (see 2 Kin 17:24,30). *frightened them.* The Hebrew for this verb often describes the fear aroused in a battle situation (Judg 20:41; 2 Sam 4:1; 2 Chr 32:18).
4:5 *hired.* Cf. the hiring of Balaam (Deut 23:4–5; Neh 13:2) and the hiring of a prophet to intimidate Nehemiah (Neh 6:12–13).
4:6 *Ahasuerus.* See the book of Esther. When Darius died in 486 B.C., Egypt rebelled, and Ahasuerus, the son of Darius, had to march west to suppress the revolt.
4:7 *Artaxerxes.* Three Persian kings bore this name: Artaxerxes I (465–424 B.C.), II (404–358) and III (358–338). The king here is Artaxerxes I. *Mithredath.* See 1:8 and note. *Tabeel.* An Aramaic name (see Is 7:6 and note). *wrote.* Near Eastern kings employed an elaborate system of informers and spies. Egyptian sources speak of the "ears and eyes" of Pharaoh. Sargon II of Assyria had agents in Urartu whom he ordered: "Write me whatever you see and hear." The King's Eye and the King's Ear were two officials who reported to the Persian monarch.
4:8–6:18 For this passage the author draws upon Aramaic documents. In the original text of Ezra, this section is written in Aramaic; a further Aramaic section is 7:12–26.
4:8 *commander.* An official who had the role of a chancellor or commissioner. Perhaps Rehum dictated, and Shimshai wrote the letter in Aramaic. (Alternatively, Shimshai may have been a high official rather than a scribe.) The letter would then be read in a Persian translation before the king (v. 18). According to Herodotus (3.128), royal scribes were attached to each governor to report directly to the Persian king.
4:9 *colleagues.* See vv. 17,23; 5:3,6; 6:6,13. One of the striking characteristics of Persian bureaucracy was that each responsibility was shared among colleagues. *Erech.* See note on Gen 10:10. *Babylonians.* During the reign of the Assyrian king Ashurbanipal (669–627 B.C.), a major revolt had taken place (652–648), involving Shamash-shum-ukin, the brother of the king and the ruler over Babylonia. After a long siege Shamash-shum-ukin hurled himself into the flames. Doubtless these men of Babylon and the other cities mentioned were the descendants of the rebels, whom the Assyrians deported to the west. *Susa.* The major city of Elam (in southwest Iran). Because of Susa's part in the revolt, Ashurbanipal brutally destroyed it in 640 (two centuries before Rehum's letter).
4:10 *Osnappar.* The last great Assyrian king, famed for his library at Nineveh. He is not named elsewhere in the Bible, but he is probably the king who freed Manasseh from exile (2 Chr 33:11–13). *deported.* Osnappar (a variant of Ashurbanipal) may be the unnamed Assyrian king who brought people to Samaria according to 2 Kin 17:24. It is characteristic of such deportations that the descendants of populations that had been removed from their homelands nearly two centuries earlier should still stress their origins. *Samaria.* The murder of Amon king of Judah (642–640 B.C.; see 2 Kin 21:23; 2 Chr 33:24) was probably the result of an anti-Assyrian movement inspired by the revolt in Elam and Babylonia. The Assyrians may then have deported the rebellious Samaritans and replaced them with the rebellious Elamites and Babylonians. *beyond the River.* That is, the Euphrates River. From Israel's point of view the land "beyond the River" was Mesopotamia (Josh 24:2–3,14–15; 2 Sam 10:16). From the Mesopotamian point of view the land "beyond the River" included the areas of Aram, Phoenicia and Israel (1 Kin 4:24). The Persians also called this area Athura.
4:12 *finishing the walls and repairing the foundations.* As Isaiah had foretold (see Is 58:12 and note).
4:13 Most of the gold and silver coins that came into Persia's treasury were melted down to be stored as bullion. Very little of the taxes returned to benefit the provinces.
4:14 *we are in the service of the palace.* Lit. "we eat the salt of the palace." Salt was made a royal monopoly by the Ptolemies in Egypt, and perhaps by the Persians as well.
4:15 *record books.* See 5:17; 6:1; Esth 2:23; 6:1–2. There were several repositories of such documents at the major capitals.

that city is a rebellious city and damaging to kings and provinces, and that they have incited revolt within it in past days; therefore that city was laid waste.

16 "We inform the king that if that city is rebuilt and the walls finished, as a result you will have no possession in *the province* beyond the River."

The King Replies and Work Stops

17 *Then* the king sent an answer to Rehum the commander, to Shimshai the scribe, and to the rest of their colleagues who live in Samaria and in the rest of *the provinces* beyond the River: "Peace. And now

18 the document which you sent to us has been [1][a]translated and read before me.

19 "A decree has been [1]issued by me, and a search has been made and it has been discovered that that city has risen up against the kings in past days, that rebellion and revolt have been perpetrated in it,

20 [a]that mighty kings have [1]ruled over Jerusalem, governing all *the provinces* [b]beyond the River, and that [c]tribute, custom and toll were paid to them.

21 "So, now issue a decree to make these men stop *work,* that this city may not be rebuilt until a decree is issued by me.

22 "Beware of being negligent in carrying out this *matter;* why should damage increase to the detriment of the kings?"

23 Then as soon as the copy of King Artaxerxes' document was read before Rehum and Shimshai the scribe and their colleagues, they went in haste to Jerusalem to the Jews and stopped them by force of arms.

24 Then work on the house of God in Jerusalem ceased, and it was stopped until the second year of the reign of Darius king of Persia.

Temple Work Resumed

5 When the prophets, [a]Haggai the prophet and [b]Zechariah the son of Iddo, prophesied to the Jews who were in Judah and Jerusalem in the name of the God of Israel, who was over them,

2 then [a]Zerubbabel the son of Shealtiel and Jeshua the son of Jozadak arose and began to rebuild the house of God which is in Jerusalem; and [b]the prophets of God were with them supporting them.

3 At that time [a]Tattenai, the governor of *the province* beyond the [1]River, and Shethar-bozenai and their colleagues came to them and spoke to them thus, "[b]Who issued you a decree to rebuild this [2]temple and to finish this structure?"

4 [a]Then we told them accordingly what the names of the men were who were reconstructing this building.

5 But [a]the eye of their God was on the elders of the Jews, and they did not stop them until a report could come to Darius, and then a written reply be returned concerning it.

Adversaries Write to Darius

6 *This is* the copy of the letter which [a]Tattenai, the governor of *the province* beyond the River, and Shethar-bozenai and his colleagues [b]the officials, who were beyond the River, sent to Darius the king.

7 They sent a report to him in which it was written thus: "To Darius the king, all peace.

8 "Let it be known to the king that we have gone to the province of Judah, to the

18 [1]Lit *plainly read before* [a]Neh 8:8
19 [1]Lit *put forth*
20 [1]Lit *been* [a]1 Kin 4:21; 1 Chr 18:3 [b]Gen 15:18; Josh 1:4 [c]Ezra 4:13; 7:24

5:1 [a]Hag 1:1 [b]Zech 1:1
2 [a]Ezra 3:2; Hag 1:12; Zech 4:6-9 [b]Ezra 6:14; Hag 2:4; Zech 3:1
3 [1]I.e. Euphrates River, and so throughout the ch [2]Lit *house,* and so in vv 9, 11, 12 [a]Ezra 6:6, 13 [b]Ezra 1:3; 5:9
4 [a]Ezra 5:10
5 [a]Ezra 7:6, 28
6 [a]Ezra 5:3 [b]Ezra 4:9

These royal archives preserved documents for centuries. In the third century B.C. the Babylonian priest Berossus made use of the Babylonian Chronicles in his history of Babylon, which covered events from the Assyrian to the Hellenistic (beginning with Alexander's conquest of Babylon in 330 B.C.) eras.

4:18 *translated.* From Aramaic into Persian (see note on 4:8–6:18). *read.* Since the king probably could not read Aramaic, he would have had the document read to him.

4:19 *rebellion.* There is some truth in the accusation. Jerusalem had rebelled against the Assyrians in 701 B.C. (2 Kin 18:7) and against the Babylonians in 600 and 589 (2 Kin 24:1,20).

4:21–23 As a result of the intervention of the provincial authorities, Artaxerxes I (see v. 11 and note on v. 7) ordered that the Jews stop rebuilding the walls of Jerusalem (see note on Neh 1:3). The events of vv. 7–23 probably occurred prior to 445 B.C.. The forcible destruction of these recently rebuilt walls rather than the destruction by Nebuchadnezzar would then be the basis of the report made to Nehemiah (Neh 1:3).

4:24 After this long digression describing the opposition to Jewish efforts, the writer returns to his original subject of the rebuilding of the temple (vv. 1–5). *second year of the reign of Darius.* According to Persian reckoning, the second regnal year of Darius I began on Nisan 1 (Apr. 3), 520 B.C., and lasted until Feb. 21, 519. In that year the prophet Haggai (Hag 1:1–5) exhorted Zerubbabel to begin rebuilding the temple on the first day of the sixth month (Aug. 29). Work began on the temple on the 24th day of the month, Sept. 21 (Hag 1:15). During his first two years, Darius had to establish his right to the throne by fighting numerous rebels, as recounted in his famous Behistun (Bisitun) inscription. It was only after the stabilization of the Persian empire that efforts to rebuild the temple could be permitted.

5:1 *Haggai . . . Zechariah.* Beginning on Aug. 29, 520 B.C. (Hag 1:1), and continuing until Dec. 18 (Hag 2:1,10,20), the prophet Haggai delivered a series of messages to stir up the people to resume work on the temple. Two months after Haggai's first speech, Zechariah joined him (Zech 1:1).

5:2 *Zerubbabel.* A Babylonian name meaning "offspring of Babylon," referring to his birth in exile. He was the son of Shealtiel and the grandson of Jeconiah (1 Chr 3:17), the next-to-last king of Judah. Zerubbabel was the last of the Davidic line to be entrusted with political authority by the occupying powers. He was also an ancestor of Jesus (Matt 1:12–13; Luke 3:27). *Jeshua.* See note on 2:2.

5:3 *Tattenai.* Probably a Babylonian name. *Shethar-bozenai.* Perhaps a Persian official.

5:5 *did not stop.* The Persian governor gave the Jews the benefit of the doubt by not stopping the work while the inquiry was proceeding.

5:6–7 *sent to Darius the king . . . to him.* Texts found in the royal city of Persepolis vividly confirm that such inquiries were sent directly to the king himself, revealing the close attention he paid to minute details.

house of the great God, which is being built
with huge stones, and [1]beams are being laid
in the walls; and this work is going on with
great care and is succeeding in their hands.
9 "Then we asked those elders and said to
them thus, 'Who issued you a decree to
rebuild this temple and to finish this structure?'
10 "We also asked them their names so as
to inform you, and that we might write down
the names of the men who were at their
head.
11 "Thus they [1]answered us, saying, 'We
are the servants of the God of heaven and
earth and are rebuilding the temple that was
built many years ago, [a]which a great king of
Israel built and finished.
12 'But [a]because our fathers had provoked
the God of heaven to wrath, [b]He gave them
into the hand of Nebuchadnezzar king of
Babylon, the Chaldean, *who* destroyed this
temple and deported the people to Babylon.
13 'However, [a]in the first year of Cyrus
king of Babylon, King Cyrus [b]issued a decree
to rebuild this house of God.
14 'Also [a]the gold and silver utensils of the
house of God which Nebuchadnezzar had
taken from the temple [1]in Jerusalem, and
brought them to the temple of Babylon,
these King Cyrus took from the temple of
Babylon and they were given to one [b]whose
name was Sheshbazzar, whom he had
appointed governor.
15 'He said to him, "Take these utensils, go
and deposit them in the temple [1]in
Jerusalem and let the house of God be rebuilt
in its place."
16 'Then that Sheshbazzar came *and* [a]laid
the foundations of the house of God [1]in
Jerusalem; and from then until now it has
been under construction and it is [b]not *yet*
completed.'
17 "Now if it pleases the king, [a]let a search
be conducted in the king's treasure house,
which is there in Babylon, if it be that a
decree was issued by King Cyrus to rebuild
this house of God at Jerusalem; and let the
king send to us his decision concerning this
matter."

Darius Finds Cyrus's Decree

6 Then King Darius issued a decree, and
[a]search was made in the [1]archives, where
the treasures were stored in Babylon.
2 In [1]Ecbatana in the fortress, which is
[a]in the province of Media, a scroll was found
and there was written in it as follows: "Memorandum—
3 "[a]In the first year of King Cyrus, Cyrus
the king issued a decree: '*Concerning* the
house of God at Jerusalem, let the [1]temple,
the place where sacrifices are offered, be
rebuilt and let its foundations be [2]retained,
its height being 60 cubits and its width 60
cubits;
4 [a]with three layers of huge stones and
[1]one layer of timbers. And let the cost be
paid from the [2]royal treasury.
5 'Also let [a]the gold and silver utensils of
the house of God, which Nebuchadnezzar
took from the temple in Jerusalem and
brought to Babylon, be returned and
[1]brought to their places in the temple in
Jerusalem; and you shall put *them* in the
house of God.'
6 "Now *therefore,* [a]Tattenai, governor of
the province beyond the [1]River, Shethar-bozenai and [2]your colleagues, the officials of *the
provinces* beyond the [1]River, [3]keep away
from there.

8 [1]Lit *timber is*
11 [1]Lit *returned us the word* [a]1 Kin 6:1, 38
12 [a]2 Chr 36:16, 17 [b]2 Kin 25:8-11; Jer 52:12-15
13 [a]Ezra 1:1 [b]Ezra 1:1-4
14 [1]Lit *that was in* [a]Ezra 1:7; 6:5; Dan 5:2 [b]Ezra 1:8; 5:16
15 [1]Lit *that is in*
16 [1]Lit *that is in* [a]Ezra 3:8, 10 [b]Ezra 6:15
17 [a]Ezra 6:1, 2
6:1 [1]Lit *house of the books* [a]Ezra 5:17
2 [1]Aram *Achmetha* [a]2 Kin 17:6
3 [1]Lit *house* [2]Or *fixed, laid* [a]Ezra 1:1; 5:13
4 [1]So Gr; Aram *a layer of new timber* [2]Lit *king's house* [a]1 Kin 6:36
5 [1]Lit *go* [a]Ezra 1:7; 5:14
6 [1]I.e. Euphrates River, and so throughout the ch [2]Aram *their* [3]Lit *be distant* [a]Ezra 5:3; 6:13

5:8 *beams.* May refer to interior paneling (1 Kin 6:15–18) or to logs alternating with the brick or stone layers in the walls (see note on 6:4).

5:11 *great king of Israel.* According to 1 Kin 6:1 Solomon began building the temple in the fourth year of his reign (966 B.C.). The project lasted seven years (1 Kin 6:38).

5:12 *Chaldean.* The Chaldeans were the inhabitants of the southern regions of Mesopotamia who established the Neo-Babylonian empire (612–539 B.C.). Their origins are obscure. In the late seventh century B.C. the Chaldeans, led by Nebuchadnezzar's father Nabopolassar, overthrew the Assyrians.

5:14 *Sheshbazzar . . . governor.* See note on 1:8.

6:1 *archives, where the treasures were stored in Babylon.* Many documents have also been found in the so-called "treasury" area of Persepolis (see map, p. 545).

6:2 *Ecbatana.* One of the four capitals (along with Babylon, Persepolis and Susa) of the Persian empire. Located in what is today the Iranian city of Hamadan, its remains have not yet been excavated. This is the only reference to the site in the OT, though there are numerous references in the Apocryphal books (Judith 1:1–4; Tobit 3:7; 7:1; 14:12–14; 2 Maccabees 9:3). *Media.* The homeland of the Medes in northwestern Iran. The Medes were an Indo-European tribe related to the Persians. After the rise of Cyrus in 550 B.C., they became subordinate to the Persians. The name of the area was retained as late as the NT era (Acts 2:9).

6:3–5 Compare this Aramaic memorandum of the decree of Cyrus with the Hebrew version in 1:2–4. The Aramaic is written in a more sober administrative style without any reference to the Lord (Yahweh). A similar memorandum dealing with permission to rebuild the Jewish temple at Elephantine in Upper Egypt was found among fifth-century B.C. Aramaic papyri recovered at that site.

6:3 *height being 60 cubits and its width 60 cubits.* These dimensions, which contrast with those of Solomon's temple (see 1 Kin 6:2 and note), are probably not specifications of the temple as built but of the outer limits of a building the Persians were willing to subsidize. The second temple was not as grandiose as the first (3:12; Hag 2:3).

6:4 *huge stones . . . timbers.* See 5:8. The same kind of construction is mentioned in 1 Kin 6:36; 7:12. Such a design was possibly intended to cushion the building against earthquake shocks. *let the cost be paid from the royal treasury.* In 1973 archaeologists discovered at Xanthos in southwest Turkey a religious foundation charter from the late Persian period that provides some striking parallels with this decree of Cyrus. As in Ezra, amounts of sacrifices, names of priests and the responsibility for the upkeep of the cult are specified. The Persian king seems to have known details of the cult.

7 "Leave this work on the house of God
alone; let the governor of the Jews and the
elders of the Jews rebuild this house of God
on its site.
8 "Moreover, [a]I issue a decree concerning
what you are to do for these elders of Judah
in the rebuilding of this house of God: the
full cost is to be paid to these people from
the royal treasury out of the taxes of *the
provinces* beyond the River, and that without
delay.
9 "Whatever is needed, both young bulls,
rams, and lambs for a burnt offering to the
God of heaven, and wheat, salt, wine and
anointing oil, as the priests in Jerusalem
request, *it* is to be given to them daily without fail,
10 that they may offer [1]acceptable sacrifices to the God of heaven and [a]pray for the
life of the king and his sons.
11 "And I issued a decree that [a]any man
who violates this edict, a timber shall be
drawn from his house and he shall be
impaled on it and [b]his house shall be made a
refuse heap on account of this.
12 "May the God who [a]has caused His
name to dwell there overthrow any king or
people who [1]attempts to change *it*, so as to
destroy this house of God in Jerusalem. I,
Darius, have issued *this* decree, let *it* be carried out with all diligence!"

The Temple Completed and Dedicated

13 Then [a]Tattenai, the governor of *the
province* beyond the River, Shethar-bozenai
and their colleagues carried out *the decree*
with all diligence, just as King Darius had
sent.
14 And [a]the elders of the Jews [1]were successful in building through the prophesying
of Haggai the prophet and Zechariah the son
of Iddo. And [2]they finished building according to the command of the God of Israel and
the decree [b]of Cyrus, [c]Darius, and [d]Artax-
erxes king of Persia.
15 This [1]temple was completed [2]on the
third day of the [a]month Adar; it was the
sixth year of the reign of King Darius.
16 And the sons of Israel, the priests, the
Levites and the rest of the [1]exiles, [a]celebrat-
ed the dedication of this house of God with
joy.
17 They offered for the dedication of this
temple of God 100 bulls, 200 rams, 400
lambs, and as a sin offering for all Israel [a]12
male goats, corresponding to the number of
the tribes of Israel.
18 Then they appointed the priests to

8 [a]Ezra 6:4; 7:14-22 **10** [1]Lit *pleasing;* or *sweet-smelling sacrifices* [a]Ezra 7:23; Jer 29:7; 1 Tim 2:1, 2 **11** [a]Ezra 7:26 [b]Dan 2:5; 3:29 **12** [1]Lit *sends his hand* [a]Deut 12:5, 11; 1 Kin 9:3

13 [a]Ezra 6:6 **14** [1]Lit *were building and succeeding* [2]Lit *built and finished* [a]Ezra 5:1, 2 [b]Ezra 1:1; 5:13 [c]Ezra 4:24; 6:12 [d]Ezra 7:1 **15** [1]Lit *house* [2]Lit *until* [a]Esth 3:7 **16** [1]Lit *sons of the captivity* [a]1 Kin 8:63; 2 Chr 7:5 **17** [a]Ezra 8:35

6:8 *paid . . . from the royal treasury.* It was a consistent policy of Persian kings to help restore sanctuaries in their empire. For example, a memorandum concerning the rebuilding of the Jewish temple at Elephantine was written by the Persian governors of Judah and Samaria. Also from non-Biblical sources we learn that Cyrus repaired temples at Uruk (Erech) and Ur. Cambyses, successor to Cyrus, gave funds for the temple at Sais in Egypt. The temple of Amun in the Khargah Oasis was rebuilt by order of Darius.

6:9 That the Persian monarchs were interested in the details of foreign religions is shown clearly by the ordinances of Cambyses and Darius I, regulating the temples and priests in Egypt. On the authority of Darius II (423–404 B.C.) a letter was written to the Jews at Elephantine concerning the keeping of the Feast of Unleavened Bread.

6:10 *pray for the life of the king and his sons.* In the inscription on the Cyrus Cylinder (made of baked clay), the king asks: "May all the gods whom I have resettled in their sacred cities ask Bel and Nebo daily for a long life for me." The Jews of Elephantine offered to pray for the Persian governor of Judah. The daily synagogue services included a prayer for the royal family (cf. 1 Tim 2:1–2).

6:11 *any man who violates this edict.* It was customary at the end of decrees and treaties to append a long list of curses against anyone who might disregard them. *impaled.* According to Herodotus (3.159), Darius I impaled 3,000 Babylonians when he took the city of Babylon. See Esth 2:23 and note.

6:12 *May the God . . . overthrow any king or people.* At the end of his famous Behistun (Bisitun) inscription Darius I warned: "If you see this inscription or these sculptures, and destroy them and do not protect them as long as you have strength, may Ahuramazda strike you, and may you not have a family, and what you do . . . may Ahuramazda utterly destroy." *caused His name to dwell.* See note on Deut 12:5.

6:13–14 Work on the temple had made little progress not only because of opposition but also because of the preoccupation of the returnees with their own homes (Hag 1:2–9). Because they had placed their own interests first, God sent them famine as a judgment (Hag 1:5–6,10–11). Spurred by the preaching of Haggai and Zechariah, and under the leadership of Zerubbabel and Jeshua, a new effort was begun (Hag 1:12–15).

6:14 *Artaxerxes.* The reference to him seems out of place, because he did not contribute to rebuilding the temple. He may have been inserted here since he contributed to the work of the temple at a later date under Ezra (7:21–24).

6:15 *temple was completed.* On Mar. 12, 516 B.C., almost 70 years after its destruction. The renewed work on the temple had begun on Sept. 21, 520 (Hag 1:15), and sustained effort had continued for almost three and a half years. According to Hag 2:3, the older members who could remember the splendor of Solomon's temple were disappointed when they saw the smaller size of Zerubbabel's temple (cf. Ezra 3:12). Yet in the long run the second temple, though not as grand as the first, enjoyed a much longer life. The general plan of the second temple was similar to that of Solomon's, but the most holy place was left empty because the ark of the covenant had been lost through the Babylonian conquest. According to Josephus, on the Day of Atonement the high priest placed his censer on the slab of stone that marked the former location of the ark. The holy place was furnished with a table for the bread of the Presence, the incense altar, and one lampstand (in the Apocrypha cf. 1 Maccabees 1:21–22; 4:49–51) instead of Solomon's ten (1 Kin 7:49).

6:16 *exiles . . . dedication.* Cf. the dedication of Solomon's temple (1 Kin 8). The leaders of those who returned from exile were responsible for the completion of the temple. "Dedication" translates the Aramaic word *ḥanukkah.* The Jewish holiday in December that celebrates the recapture of the temple from the Seleucids and its rededication (165 B.C.) is also known as Hanukkah.

6:17 *100 . . . 200 . . . 400.* The number of animals sacrificed was small in comparison with similar services in the reigns of Solomon (1 Kin 8:5,63), Hezekiah (2 Chr 30:24) and Josiah (2 Chr 35:7), when thousands rather than hundreds were offered.

[a]their divisions and the Levites in [b]their
orders for the service of God [1]in Jerusalem,
[c]as it is written in the book of Moses.

The Passover Observed

19 [a]The exiles observed the Passover on
[b]the fourteenth of the first month.
20 [a]For the priests and the Levites had
purified themselves together; all of them
were pure. Then [b]they slaughtered the
Passover *lamb* for all the exiles, both for
their brothers the priests and for themselves.
21 The sons of Israel who returned from
exile and [a]all those who had separated themselves from [b]the impurity of the nations of
the land to *join* them, to seek the LORD God
of Israel, ate *the Passover.*
22 And [a]they observed the Feast of
Unleavened Bread seven days with joy, for
the LORD had caused them to rejoice, and
[b]had turned the heart of [c]the king of Assyria
toward them to [1]encourage them in the work
of the house of God, the God of Israel.

Ezra Journeys from Babylon to Jerusalem

7 [a]Now after these things, in the reign of
[b]Artaxerxes king of Persia, *there went up*
Ezra son of Seraiah, son of Azariah, son of
Hilkiah,
2 son of Shallum, son of Zadok, son of
Ahitub,
3 son of Amariah, son of Azariah, son of
Meraioth,
4 son of Zerahiah, son of Uzzi, son of
Bukki,
5 son of Abishua, son of Phinehas, son
of Eleazar, son of Aaron the chief priest.
6 This Ezra went up from Babylon, and
he was a [a]scribe skilled in the law of Moses,
which the LORD God of Israel had given; and
the king granted him all [1]he requested
[b]because the hand of the LORD his God *was*
upon him.
7 [a]Some of the sons of Israel and some of
the priests, the Levites, the singers, the gatekeepers and the temple servants went up to
Jerusalem in the seventh year of King Artaxerxes.
8 He came to Jerusalem in the fifth
month, which was in the seventh year of the
king.
9 For on the first of the first month [1]he
began to go up from Babylon; and on the
first of the fifth month he came to Jerusalem,

18 [1]Lit *which is in* [a]1 Chr 24:1; 2 Chr 35:5 [b]1 Chr 23:6 [c]Num 3:6; 8:9 **19** [a]Ezra 1:11 [b]Ex 12:6 **20** [a]2 Chr 29:34; 30:15 [b]2 Chr 35:11 **21** [a]Neh 9:2; 10:28 [b]Ezra 9:11 **22** [1]Lit *strengthen their hands* [a]Ex 12:15 [b]Ezra 7:27; Prov 21:1 [c]Ezra 1:1; 6:1 **7:1** [a]1 Chr 6:4-14 [b]Ezra 7:12, 21; Neh 2:1

6 [1]Lit *his request* [a]Ezra 7:11, 12, 21 [b]Ezra 7:9, 28; 8:22 **7** [a]Ezra 8:1-20 **9** [1]Lit *was the foundation*

6:18 *divisions.* The priests were separated into 24 divisions (1 Chr 24:1–19), each of which served at the temple for a week at a time (cf. Luke 1:5,8). In 1962 fragments of a synagogue inscription listing the 24 divisions were found at Caesarea. *written in the book of Moses.* Perhaps referring to such passages as Ex 29; Lev 8; Num 3; 8:5–26; 18.
6:19 *Passover on the fourteenth of the first month.* The date would have been about Apr. 21, 516 B.C.
6:20 *purified themselves . . . pure.* See note on Lev 4:12. Priests and Levites had to be ceremonially clean to fulfill their ritual functions.
6:21 *all those who had separated themselves.* The returning exiles were willing to accept those who separated themselves from the paganism of the foreigners who had been introduced into the area by the Assyrians.
6:22 *king of Assyria.* A surprising title for Darius, the Persian king. But even after the fall of Nineveh in 612 B.C., the term "Assyria" continued to be used for former territories the Assyrians had occupied (even Syria is an abbreviation of Assyria). Persian kings adopted a variety of titles, including "king of Babylon" (cf. 5:13; Neh 13:6).
7:1–5 The genealogy of Ezra given here lists 16 ancestors back to Aaron, the brother of Moses.
7:1 *after these things.* The events of the preceding chapter concluded with the completion of the temple in 516 B.C. *Artaxerxes.* The identity of the king mentioned in this chapter has been disputed. If this was Artaxerxes I, which seems likely, Ezra would have arrived in Judah in 458, and there would be a gap of almost 60 years between the events of ch. 6 and those of ch. 7. The only recorded event during this interval is the opposition to the rebuilding of Jerusalem in the reign of Ahasuerus (486–465) in 4:6. *Ezra.* Perhaps a shortened form of Azariah, a name that occurs twice in the list of his ancestors. The Greek form is Esdras, as in the Apocrypha. *Seraiah.* Means "The LORD is prince." He was the high priest under Zedekiah who was killed in 586 by Nebuchadnezzar (2 Kin 25:18–21) some 128 years before Ezra's arrival. He was therefore the ancestor rather than the father of Ezra; "son" often means "descendant" (see 1 Chr 6:14–15). *Azariah.* Means "The LORD helps." *Hilkiah.* Means "My portion is the LORD." He was the high priest under Josiah (2 Kin 22:4).
7:2 *Zadok.* Means "righteous." He was a priest under David (2 Sam 8:17). Solomon appointed Zadok as high priest in place of Abiathar, who supported the rebel Adonijah (1 Kin 1:7–8; 2:35). Ezekiel regarded the Zadokites as free from idolatry (Ezek 44:15). They held the office of high priest until 171 B.C. The Sadducees may have been named after Zadok, and the Qumran community (see essay, p. 1356) looked for the restoration of the Zadokite priesthood. *Ahitub.* Probably means "My (divine) brother is good." He was actually the grandfather of Zadok (Neh 11:11).
7:5 *Eleazar.* Means "God helps." The Greek form of the name is Lazarus (John 11:1).
7:6 *scribe.* See Neh 8:1,4,9,13; 12:26,36. Earlier, scribes served kings as secretaries, such as Seraiah under David (2 Sam 8:17, where the Hebrew word for "scribe" is translated "secretary"; see note there). Other scribes took dictation—such as Baruch, who wrote down what Jeremiah spoke (Jer 36:32). From the exilic period on, the "scribes" were scholars who studied and taught the Scriptures (cf. the "teachers of the law" and "scribes" in the NT; see notes on Matt 2:4; Luke 5:17). In the NT period they were addressed as "rabbis" (cf. Matt 23:7). *skilled.* The Hebrew for this phrase is translated "ready" in Ps 45:1 and "skilled" in Prov 22:29. *hand of the LORD.* For this striking description of God's power and favor cf. also vv. 9,28; 8:18,22,31; Neh 2:8,18.
7:7–9 *seventh year . . . first of the first month . . . first of the fifth month.* Ezra began his journey on the first of Nisan (Apr. 8, 458 B.C.) and arrived in Jerusalem on the first of Ab (Aug. 4, 458). The journey took four months, including an 11-day delay indicated by the comparison of v. 9 with 8:31. The spring was the most auspicious time for such journeys; most armies went on campaigns at this time of the year. Although the actual distance between Babylon and Jerusalem is about 500 miles, the travelers had to cover a total of about 900 miles, going northwest along the Euphrates River and then south. The relatively slow pace was caused by the presence of the elderly and the children. See map No. 7b at the end of the study Bible.

[a]because the good hand of his God *was* upon
him.
10 For Ezra had set his heart to [1]study the
law of the LORD and to practice *it,* and [a]to
teach *His* statutes and ordinances in Israel.

King's Decree on Behalf of Ezra

11 Now this is the copy of the decree
which King Artaxerxes gave to Ezra the
priest, the scribe, [1]learned in the words of
the commandments of the LORD and His statutes to Israel:
12 "[1]Artaxerxes, [a]king of kings, to Ezra the
priest, the scribe of the law of the God of
heaven, perfect *peace.* And now
13 [a]I have issued a decree that any of the
people of Israel and their priests and the
Levites in my kingdom who are willing to go
to Jerusalem, may go with you.
14 "Forasmuch as you are sent [1]by the king
and his [a]seven counselors to inquire concerning Judah and Jerusalem according to
the law of your God which is in your hand,
15 and to bring the silver and gold, which
the king and his counselors have freely
offered to the God of Israel, [a]whose dwelling
is in Jerusalem,
16 with [a]all the silver and gold which you
find in the whole province of Babylon, along
[b]with the freewill offering of the people and
of the priests, who [c]offered willingly for the
house of their God which is in Jerusalem;

9 [a]Ezra 7:6; Neh 2:8 **10** [1]Lit *seek* [a]Deut 33:10; Ezra 7:25; Neh 8:1 **11** [1]Lit *the scribe of* **12** [1]Ch 7:12-26 is in Aram [a]Ezek 26:7; Dan 2:37 **13** [a]Ezra 6:1 **14** [1]Lit *from before* [a]Ezra 7:15, 28; 8:25 **15** [a]2 Chr 6:2; Ezra 6:12; Ps 135:21 **16** [a]Ezra 8:25 [b]Ezra 1:4, 6 [c]1 Chr 29:6

17 [a]Num 15:4-13 [b]Deut 12:5-11 **20** [a]Ezra 6:4 **21** [1]I.e. Euphrates River, and so throughout the ch [a]Ezra 7:6 **22** [1]I.e. One kor equals approx ten bu [2]Lit *without prescription* **23** [1]Lit *from the decree of* [a]Ezra 6:10 **24** [1]Lit *throw on them* [a]Ezra 4:13, 20 [b]Ezra 7:7

17 with this money, therefore, you shall
diligently buy bulls, rams and lambs, [a]with
their grain offerings and their drink offerings
and [b]offer them on the altar of the house of
your God which is in Jerusalem.
18 "Whatever seems good to you and to
your brothers to do with the rest of the silver
and gold, you may do according to the will of
your God.
19 "Also the utensils which are given to
you for the service of the house of your God,
deliver in full before the God of Jerusalem.
20 "The rest of the needs for the house of
your God, for which you may have occasion
to provide, [a]provide *for it* from the royal
treasury.
21 "I, even I, King Artaxerxes, issue a
decree to all the treasurers who are *in the
provinces* beyond the [1]River, that whatever
Ezra the priest, [a]the scribe of the law of the
God of heaven, may require of you, it shall
be done diligently,
22 *even* up to 100 talents of silver, 100
[1]kors of wheat, 100 baths of wine, 100 baths
of oil, and salt [2]as needed.
23 "Whatever is [1]commanded by the God
of heaven, let it be done with zeal for the
house of the God of heaven, [a]so that there
will not be wrath against the kingdom of the
king and his sons.
24 "We also inform you that [a]it is not
allowed to [1]impose tax, tribute or toll [b]*on* any

7:10 *study . . . practice . . . teach.* See Neh 8.

7:11 *decree.* Many regard the letter of Artaxerxes I as the beginning point of Daniel's first 69 "weeks" (Dan 9:24–27). Others regard the commission of Nehemiah by the same king as the starting point of this prophecy (Neh 1:1,11; 2:1–8). By using either a solar calendar with the former date (458 B.C.) or a lunar calendar with the latter date (445), one can arrive remarkably close to the date of Jesus' public ministry.

7:12 The text of vv. 12–26 is in Aramaic (see note on 4:18–6:18). *king of kings.* The phrase was originally used by Assyrian kings, since their empires incorporated many kingdoms. It was then used by the later Babylonian (Ezek 26:7; Dan 2:37) and Persian kings. Cf. 1 Tim 6:15; Rev 17:14; 19:16.

7:13 *people of Israel.* It is noteworthy that "Israel" is used rather than "Judah." It was Ezra's aim to make one Israel of all who returned. The markedly Jewish coloring of this decree may have resulted from the king's use of Jewish officials, quite possibly Ezra himself, to help him compose it.

7:14 *seven counselors.* Cf. Esth 1:14, which refers to the seven princes who "had access to the king's presence." This corresponds with Persian practice as reported by the early Greek historians Herodotus and Xenophon. *law of your God.* Perhaps the complete Pentateuch (the five books of Moses) in its present form (see v. 6).

7:15 *silver and gold.* Cf. Hag 2:8. *freely offered.* The Persian treasury had ample funds, and benevolence was a well-attested policy of Persian kings.

7:16 *offering of the people.* The custom of sending gifts to Jerusalem from the Jews who lived outside the Holy Land continued until the Jewish-Roman War, when the Romans forced the Jews to send such contributions to the temple of Jupiter instead (Josephus, *Antiquities,* 18.9.1). There are close parallels to such directives in the contemporary letters from the Jewish garrison at Elephantine in Egypt, including a papyrus in which Darius II ordered: "Let grain offering, incense and burnt offering be offered" on the altar of the god Yahu "in your name."

7:20 *provide for it from the royal treasury.* Texts from the treasury at Persepolis also record the disbursement of supplies and funds from the royal purse.

7:22 *100 talents.* An enormous amount (about three and three-fourths tons). *100 kors.* The total was relatively small (about 600 bushels). The wheat would be used in grain offerings. *salt as needed.* See note on 4:14. A close parallel is the benefaction of Antiochus III as recorded by Josephus (*Antiquities,* 12.3.3): "In the first place we have decided, on account of their piety, to furnish for their sacrifices an allowance of sacrificial animals, wine, oil and frankincense to the value of 20,000 pieces of silver, and sacred artabae of fine flour in accordance with their native law, and 1,460 medimni of wheat and 375 medimni of salt."

7:23 *wrath against the kingdom of the king.* Egypt had revolted against the Persians in 460 B.C. and had expelled the Persians with the help of the Athenians in 459. In 458, when Ezra traveled to Jerusalem, the Persians were involved in suppressing this revolt. *his sons.* We do not know how many sons the king had at this time, but he ultimately had 18, according to Ctesias (a Greek physician who wrote an extensive history of Persia).

7:24 *not . . . to impose tax . . . or toll on . . . the priests . . . or servants.* Priests and other temple personnel were often given exemptions from enforced labor or taxes. A close parallel is found in the Gadates Inscription of Darius I to a governor in western Turkey, granting exemptions to the priests of Apollo. Antiochus III granted similar exemptions to the Jews: "The priests, the scribes of the temple and the temple singers shall be relieved from the poll tax, the crown tax and the salt tax that they pay" (Josephus, *Antiquities,* 12.3.3).

of the priests, Levites, singers, doorkeepers, Nethinim or servants of this house of God.

25 "You, Ezra, according to the wisdom of your God which is in your hand, [a]appoint magistrates and judges that they may judge all the people who are in *the province* beyond the River, *even* all those who know the laws of your God; and you may [b]teach anyone who is ignorant *of them.*

26 "[a]Whoever will not observe the law of your God and the law of the king, let judgment be executed upon him strictly, whether for death or for [1]banishment or for confiscation of goods or for imprisonment."

The King's Kindness

27 Blessed be the LORD, the God of our fathers, [a]who has put *such a thing* as this in the king's heart, to adorn the house of the LORD which is in Jerusalem,

28 and [a]has extended lovingkindness to me before the king and his counselors and before all the king's mighty princes. Thus I was strengthened according to [b]the hand of the LORD my God upon me, and I gathered [1]leading men from Israel to go up with me.

People Who Went with Ezra

8 Now these are the heads of their fathers' *households* and the genealogical enrollment of those who went up with me from Babylon in the reign of King Artaxerxes:

2 of the sons of Phinehas, Gershom; of the sons of Ithamar, Daniel; of the sons of David, [a]Hattush;

3 of the sons of Shecaniah *who was* of the sons of [a]Parosh, Zechariah and with him 150 males *who were in* the genealogical list;

4 of the sons of Pahath-moab, Eliehoenai the son of Zerahiah and 200 males with him;

5 of the sons of Zattu, Shecaniah, the son of Jahaziel and 300 males with him;

6 and of the sons of [a]Adin, Ebed the son of Jonathan and 50 males with him;

7 and of the sons of Elam, Jeshaiah the son of Athaliah and 70 males with him;

8 and of the sons of Shephatiah, Zebadiah the son of Michael and 80 males with him;

9 of the sons of Joab, Obadiah the son of Jehiel and 218 males with him;

10 and of the sons of Bani, Shelomith, the son of Josiphiah and 160 males with him;

11 and of the sons of Bebai, Zechariah the son of Bebai and 28 males with him;

12 and of the sons of Azgad, Johanan the son of Hakkatan and 110 males with him;

13 and of the sons of Adonikam, the last ones, these being their names, Eliphelet, Jeuel and Shemaiah, and 60 males with them;

14 and of the sons of Bigvai, Uthai and [1]Zabbud, and 70 males with [2]them.

Ezra Sends for Levites

15 Now I assembled them at [a]the river that runs to Ahava, where we camped for three days; and when I observed the people and the priests, I [b]did not find any Levites there.

16 So I sent for Eliezer, Ariel, Shemaiah, Elnathan, Jarib, Elnathan, Nathan, Zechari-

25 [a]Ex 18:21; Deut 16:18 [b]Ezra 7:10; Mal 2:7; Col 1:28
26 [1]Lit *rooting out* [a]Ezra 6:11, 12
27 [a]Ezra 6:22
28 [1]Lit *heads* [a]Ezra 9:9 [b]Ezra 5:5
8:2 [a]1 Chr 3:22
3 [a]Ezra 2:3
6 [a]Ezra 2:15; Neh 7:20; 10:16
14 [1]Or *Zakkur* [2]Or *him*
15 [a]Ezra 8:21, 31 [b]Ezra 7:7; 8:2

7:26 *Whoever will not observe . . . let judgment be executed.* The extensive powers given to Ezra are striking and extend to secular fields. Perhaps the implementation of these provisions involved Ezra in a great deal of traveling, which would explain the silence about his activities between his arrival and the arrival of Nehemiah 13 years later. A close parallel to the king's commission of Ezra may be found in an earlier commission by Darius I, who sent Udjahorresenet, a priest and scholar, back to Egypt. He ordered the codification of the Egyptian laws by the chief men of Egypt—a task that took from 518 to 503 B.C.

7:28 *me.* The first occurrence of the first person for Ezra—a trait that characterizes the "Ezra Memoirs," which begin in v. 27 and continue to the end of ch. 9.

8:1–21 In vv. 1–14 Ezra lists those who accompanied him in his return from Mesopotamia, including the descendants of 15 individuals. The figures of the men given total 1,496 in addition to the individuals named. There were also women and children (see note on v. 21). About 40 Levites (vv. 18–19) are also included, as are 220 "temple servants" (v. 20).

8:2 *Gershom.* Also the name of the firstborn son of Moses and Zipporah. "Gershom" sounds like the Hebrew for "a sojourner there" (see Ex 2:22). *Ithamar.* Also the name of the fourth son of Aaron (Ex 6:23).

8:3 *Zechariah.* Cf. v. 11. The name means "The LORD remembers"; it was the name of about 30 individuals mentioned in the Bible, including both the OT prophet and the father of John the Baptist (Luke 1:5–67).

8:4 *Eliehoenai.* Means "On the LORD are my eyes"; the name occurs only here and in 1 Chr 26:3. Cf. Ps 25:15.

8:6 *Ebed.* May be a shortened form of Obadiah (cf. v. 9), meaning "servant of the LORD." *Jonathan.* Means "The LORD gives"; it was the name of 15 OT individuals.

8:7 *Athaliah.* Also the name of a famous queen, daughter of Ahab (2 Kin 11).

8:8 *Michael.* Means "Who is like God?" It was the name of ten other Biblical personages, including the archangel (Dan 10:13; Jude 9; Rev 12:7).

8:10 *Shelomith.* Although it is a feminine form (see also note on Song 6:13), it is often a man's name, as here. The Greek equivalent is Salome.

8:12 *Azgad.* See note on 2:12. *Johanan.* See note on 2:46. *Hakkatan.* Means "the little one"; the name occurs only here.

8:15 *river that runs to Ahava.* Probably a canal that flows into either the Euphrates or the Tigris (the Chebar "River" in Ezek 1:1 was also a canal). *three days.* Perhaps from the 9th to the 12th day of Nisan; the journey began on the 12th (see v. 31). *did not find any Levites.* Since they were entrusted with many menial tasks, they may have found a more comfortable way of life in exile. A rabbinic midrash (comment) on Ps 137 relates the legend that Levites were in the caravan but that they were not qualified to officiate because when Nebuchadnezzar had ordered them to sing for him the songs of Zion, "they refused and bit off the ends of their fingers, so that they could not play on the harps." In the Hellenistic era (following Alexander's conquest of the Holy Land in 333 B.C.) the role of the Levites declined sharply, though the "Temple Scroll" among the Dead Sea Scrolls from Qumran (see essay, p. 1356) assigns important roles to them.

8:16 *Ariel.* Means "lion of God" or "altar hearth" (see note on Is 29:1,2,7). It occurs only here as a personal name. *Meshullam.* Perhaps means "rewarded." Some assume that he is the same

ah and Meshullam, [1]leading men, and for
Joiarib and Elnathan, teachers.
17 I sent them to Iddo the [1]leading man at
the place Casiphia; and I [2]told them what to
say to [3]Iddo *and* his brothers, [a]the temple servants at the place Casiphia, *that is,* to bring
ministers to us for the house of our God.
18 [a]According to the good hand of our
God upon us they brought us a [b]man of
insight of the sons of Mahli, the son of Levi,
the son of Israel, namely Sherebiah, and his
sons and brothers, 18 men;
19 and Hashabiah and [1]Jeshaiah of the
sons of Merari, with his brothers and their
sons, 20 men;
20 and 220 of [a]the temple servants, whom
David and the princes had given for the service of the Levites, all of them designated by
name.

Protection of God Invoked

21 Then I proclaimed [a]a fast there at [b]the
river of Ahava, that we might [c]humble ourselves before our God to seek from Him a
[1]safe journey for us, our little ones, and all
our possessions.
22 For I was ashamed to request from the
king troops and horsemen to [1]protect us
from the enemy on the way, because we had
said to the king, "[a]The hand of our God is
[2]favorably disposed to all those who seek
Him, but [b]His power and His anger are
against all those who [c]forsake Him."
23 So we fasted and sought our God concerning this *matter,* and He [1][a]listened to our
entreaty.
24 Then I set apart twelve of the leading
priests, [a]Sherebiah, Hashabiah, and with
them ten of their brothers;
25 and I [a]weighed out to them [b]the silver,
the gold and the utensils, the offering for the

16 [1]Lit *heads* **17** [1]Lit *head* [2]Lit *put words in their mouth to say* [3]So Gr; Heb *Iddo his brother* [a]Ezra 2:43 **18** [a]Ezra 7:6, 28 [b]2 Chr 30:22 **19** [1]So Gr; Heb *with him Jeshaiah* **20** [a]Ezra 2:43; 7:7 **21** [1]Lit *straight way* [a]1 Sam 7:6; 2 Chr 20:3 [b]Ezra 8:15, 31 [c]Lev 16:29; 23:29; Is 58:3, 5 **22** [1]Lit *help* [2]Lit *upon all...for good* [a]Ezra 7:6, 9, 28 [b]Josh 22:16 [c]2 Chr 15:2 **23** [1]Lit *was entreated by us* [a]1 Chr 5:20; 2 Chr 33:13 **24** [a]Ezra 8:18, 19 **25** [a]Ezra 8:33 [b]Ezra 7:15, 16

25 [c]Ezra 7:14 **26** [a]Ezra 1:9-11 **28** [a]Lev 21:6-8 [b]Lev 22:2, 3 **29** [a]Ezra 8:33, 34 **30** [a]Ezra 1:9 **31** [a]Ezra 8:15, 21 [b]Ezra 7:9 [c]Ezra 8:22 **32** [a]Neh 2:11 **33** [a]Ezra 8:30 [b]Neh 3:4, 21

house of our God which the king and [c]his
counselors and his princes and all Israel
present *there* had offered.
26 [a]Thus I weighed into their hands 650
talents of silver, and silver utensils *worth* 100
talents, *and* 100 gold talents,
27 and 20 gold bowls *worth* 1,000 darics,
and two utensils of fine shiny bronze, precious as gold.
28 Then I said to them, "[a]You are holy to
the LORD, and the [b]utensils are holy; and the
silver and the gold are a freewill offering to
the LORD God of your fathers.
29 "Watch and keep *them* [a]until you weigh
them before the leading priests, the Levites
and the heads of the fathers' *households* of
Israel at Jerusalem, *in* the chambers of the
house of the LORD."
30 So the priests and the Levites [a]accepted
the weighed out silver and gold and the
utensils, to bring *them* to Jerusalem to the
house of our God.
31 Then we journeyed from [a]the river
Ahava on [b]the twelfth of the first month to
go to Jerusalem; and [c]the hand of our God
was over us, and He delivered us from the
hand of the enemy and the ambushes by the
way.
32 [a]Thus we came to Jerusalem and
remained there three days.

Treasure Placed in the Temple

33 On the fourth day the silver and the
gold and the utensils [a]were weighed out in
the house of our God into the hand of [b]Mer-
emoth the son of Uriah the priest, and with
him *was* Eleazar the son of Phinehas; and
with them *were* the Levites, Jozabad the son
of Jeshua and Noadiah the son of Binnui.
34 Everything *was* numbered and weighed,
and all the weight was recorded at that time.

---

as the Meshullam who opposed the marriage reforms (10:15). *teachers.* Lit. "those who cause to understand." The Hebrew for this word is translated "explained" in Neh 8:7.

8:17 *Casiphia.* Some have located it at the site that was later to become the Parthian capital of Ctesiphon on the Tigris River, north of Babylon.

8:18–19 *18 men . . . 20 men.* Only about 40 Levites from two families were found who were willing to join Ezra's caravan.

8:20 *temple servants.* See note on 2:43–57.

8:21 *safe journey.* Lit. "straight way"—unimpeded by obstacles and dangers (see v. 31; cf. Prov 3:6). *possessions.* The vast treasures they were carrying with them offered a tempting bait for robbers.

8:22 *I was ashamed.* Scripture speaks often of unholy shame (Jer 48:13; 49:23; Mic 3:7) and on occasion, as here, of holy shame. Ezra was quick to blush with such shame (see also 9:6). Having proclaimed his faith in God's ability to protect the caravan, he was embarrassed to ask for human protection. Grave dangers faced travelers going the great distance between Mesopotamia and the Holy Land. Some 13 years later Nehemiah was accompanied by an armed escort. The difference, however, does not mean that Nehemiah was a man of lesser faith (see note on Neh 2:9).

8:23 *fasted and sought our God.* For the association of fasting and prayer see Neh 1:4; Dan 9:3; Matt 17:21; Acts 14:23.

8:25 *offering.* Lit. "what is lifted," i.e., dedicated (cf. Ex 25:2; 35:5; Lev 7:14). In Deut 12:6 the Hebrew for this word is translated "the contribution of your hand."

8:26 *650 talents . . . 100 talents.* Enormous sums, worth millions of dollars today. See also note on 7:22.

8:27 *1,000 darics.* About 19 pounds. The word occurs only here and in 1 Chr 29:7 (but see note on 2:69). *shiny.* This kind of bronze may have been orichalc, a bright yellow (the Hebrew for "yellowish" in Lev 13:30,32,36 is related to the Hebrew for "shiny" here) alloy of copper, which resembles gold and was highly prized in ancient times.

8:31 *twelfth.* See notes on v. 15; 7:7–9.

8:32 *remained there three days.* Nehemiah also took a similar rest period after his arrival in Jerusalem (Neh 2:11).

8:33 *Meremoth the son of Uriah.* Probably the same as the man who repaired two sections of the wall (Neh 3:4,21).

8:34 *recorded.* According to Babylonian practice (e.g., in the Code of Hammurapi; see chart, p. xix) almost every transaction, including sales and marriages, had to be recorded in writing. Ezra may have had to send back to Artaxerxes a signed certification of the delivery of the treasures.

35 [a]The exiles who had come from the
captivity offered burnt offerings to the God
of Israel: [b]12 bulls for all Israel, 96 rams, 77
lambs, 12 male goats for a sin offering, all as
a burnt offering to the LORD.
36 Then [a]they delivered the king's edicts
to [b]the king's satraps and to the governors *in
the provinces* beyond the [1]River, and they
supported the people and the house of God.

Mixed Marriages

9 Now when these things had been completed,
the princes approached me, saying,
"The people of Israel and the priests and
the Levites have not [a]separated themselves
from the peoples of the lands, [b]according to
their abominations, *those* of the Canaanites,
the Hittites, the Perizzites, the Jebusites, the
Ammonites, the Moabites, the Egyptians and
the Amorites.
2 "For [a]they have taken some of their
daughters *as wives* for themselves and for
their sons, so that [b]the holy [1]race has [c]intermingled
with the peoples of the lands;
indeed, the hands of the princes and the
rulers have been foremost in this unfaithfulness."
3 When I heard about this matter, I [a]tore
my garment and my robe, and pulled some
of the hair from my head and my beard, and
[b]sat down appalled.
4 Then [a]everyone who trembled at the
words of the God of Israel on account of the
unfaithfulness of the exiles gathered to me,
and I sat appalled until [b]the evening offering.

Prayer of Confession

5 But at the evening offering I arose from
my [1]humiliation, even with my garment and
my robe torn, and I fell on my knees and
[a]stretched out my [2]hands to the LORD my
God;
6 and I said, "O my God, I am ashamed
and embarrassed to lift up my face to You,
my God, for our iniquities have [1]risen above
our heads and our [a]guilt has grown even to
the heavens.
7 "[a]Since the days of our fathers to this
day we *have been* in great guilt, and on
account of our iniquities we, our kings *and*
our priests have been given into the hand of
the kings of the lands, to the sword, to captivity
and to plunder and to [1b]open shame,
as *it is* this day.
8 "But now for a brief moment grace has
been *shown* from the LORD our God, [a]to leave
us an escaped remnant and to give us a [b]peg
in His holy place, that our God may [c]enlight-

35 [a]Ezra 2:1 [b]Ezra 6:17 **36** [1]I.e. Euphrates River [a]Ezra 7:21-24 [b]Ezra 4:7; 5:6 **9:1** [a]Ezra 6:21; Neh 9:2 [b]Lev 18:24-30 **2** [1]Lit *seed* [a]Deut 7:3; Ezra 10:2, 18 [b]Ex 22:31; Deut 14:2; 2 Cor 6:14 [c]Neh 13:3 **3** [a]2 Kin 18:37 **3** [b]Neh 1:4 **4** [a]Ezra 10:3; Is 66:2 [b]Ex 29:39 **5** [1]Or *fasting* [2]Lit *palms* [a]Ex 9:29 **6** [1]Lit *multiplied over the head* [a]2 Chr 28:9; Ezra 9:13, 15; Rev 18:5 **7** [1]Lit *shame of faces* [a]2 Chr 29:6; Ps 106:6 [b]Dan 9:7 **8** [a]Ezra 9:13-15 [b]Is 22:23 [c]Ps 13:3

8:35 *offered.* Except for the identical number of male goats, the offerings here were far fewer than those presented by the returnees under Zerubbabel (6:17), who brought with him a far greater number of families.

9:1 *when these things had been completed . . . have not separated themselves.* Ezra had reached Jerusalem in the fifth month (7:9). The measures dealing with the problem of intermarriage were announced in the ninth month (10:9), or four months after his arrival. Those who brought Ezra's attention to the problem were probably the ordinary members of the community rather than the leaders, who were themselves guilty (v. 2). Malachi, who prophesied about the same time as Ezra's mission, indicates that some Jews had broken their marriages to marry daughters of a foreign god (Mal 2:10–16), perhaps the daughters of influential landholders. One of the reasons for such intermarriages may have been the shortage of returning Jewish women who were available. What happened to a Jewish community that was lax concerning intermarriage can be seen in the example of the Elephantine settlement in Egypt, which was contemporary with Ezra and Nehemiah. There the Jews who married pagan spouses expressed their devotion to pagan gods in addition to the Lord. The Elephantine community was gradually assimilated and disappeared. *peoples of the lands.* The eight groups mentioned are representative of the original inhabitants of Canaan before the Israelite conquest (see note on Ex 3:8). Only the Ammonites, Moabites and Egyptians were still living there in the postexilic period (cf. 2 Chr 8:7–8). *Canaanites.* See note on Gen 10:6. *Hittites.* See note on Gen 10:15. *Perizzites.* See note on Gen 13:7. *Jebusites.* See note on Gen 10:16. *the Ammonites, the Moabites.* See note on Gen 19:36–38. *Amorites.* See note on Gen 10:16.

9:2 *holy race.* The Hebrew for this phrase is translated "holy seed" in Is 6:13. *been foremost.* In the wrong direction (see 10:18). *unfaithfulness.* See 10:6; Josh 22:16; Dan 9:7. Marrying those who did not belong to the Lord was an act of infidelity for the people of Israel.

9:3 *tore my garment and my robe.* A common way to express grief or distress (see v. 5; Gen 37:29,34; Josh 7:6; Judg 11:35; 2 Sam 13:19; 2 Chr 34:27; Esth 4:1; Job 1:20; Is 36:22; Jer 41:5; Matt 26:65). *pulled some of the hair from my head and my beard.* Unique in the Bible. Elsewhere we read about the shaving of one's head and/or beard (Job 1:20; Jer 41:5; 47:5; Ezek 7:18; Amos 8:10). When Nehemiah was confronted with the same problem of intermarriage, instead of pulling out his own hair he pulled out the hair of the offending parties (Neh 13:25).

9:4 *everyone who trembled.* Cf. Ex 19:16; Is 66:2; Heb 12:21. *appalled.* See v. 3; cf. Dan 4:19; 8:27. *evening offering.* See Ex 12:6. The informants had probably visited Ezra in the morning, so that he must have sat appalled for many hours. The time of the evening sacrifice, usually about 3:00 P.M., was also the appointed time for prayer and confession (Acts 3:1).

9:5 *humiliation.* The Hebrew for this word later meant "fasting." See note on Lev 16:29,31. *fell on my knees.* Cf. 1 Kin 8:54; Ps 95:6; Dan 6:10. *stretched out my hands.* See note on Ex 9:29. Ezra's prayer (vv. 6–15) may be compared with those of Nehemiah (Neh 9:5–37) and Daniel (Dan 9:4–19).

9:6 *ashamed and embarrassed.* See 8:22 and note; Luke 18:13. Ezra felt both an inner shame before God and an outward humiliation before people for his own sins and the sins of his people. The two Hebrew verbs often occur together; see Ps 35:4; Is 45:16; Jer 31:19 ("ashamed and also humiliated"). *our iniquities . . . our guilt.* Cf. also vv. 7,13,15; 10:10,19; 1 Chr 21:3; 2 Chr 24:18; Ps 38:4. *has grown even to the heavens.* But God's love is more than a match for our guilt (Ps 103:11–12).

9:7 *Since the days of our fathers.* Israelites were conscious of their corporate solidarity with their ancestors. *sword.* Cf. Neh 4:13. In Ezek 21 "the sword of the king of Babylon" (21:19) is described as an instrument of divine judgment. *open shame.* Cf. Dan 9:7–8; 2 Chr 32:21.

9:8 *remnant.* See Gen 45:7; Is 1:9; 10:20–22 and notes. *peg.* Or "nail," like a nail driven into a wall (see Is 22:23 and note) or a tent peg driven into the ground (Is 33:20; 54:2). *enlight-*

en our eyes and grant us a little reviving in our bondage.

9 "[a]For we are slaves; yet in our bondage our God has not forsaken us, but [b]has extended lovingkindness to us in the sight of the kings of Persia, to give us reviving to raise up the house of our God, to restore its ruins and to give us a wall in Judah and Jerusalem.

10 "Now, our God, what shall we say after this? For we have forsaken Your commandments,

11 which You have commanded by Your servants the prophets, saying, 'The land which you are entering to possess is an unclean land with the uncleanness of the peoples of the lands, with their abominations which have filled it from end to end *and* [a]with their impurity.

12 'So now do not [a]give your daughters to their sons nor take their daughters to your sons, and [b]never seek their peace or their prosperity, that you may be strong and eat the good *things* of the land and [c]leave *it* as an inheritance to your sons forever.'

13 "After all that has come upon us for our evil deeds and [a]our great guilt, since You our God have requited *us* less than our iniquities *deserve,* and have given us [b]an escaped remnant as this,

14 [a]shall we again break Your commandments and intermarry with the peoples [1]who commit these abominations? [b]Would You not be angry with us [2]to the point of destruction, until there is no remnant nor any who escape?

15 "O LORD God of Israel, [a]You are righteous, for we have been left an escaped remnant, as *it is* this day; behold, we are before You in [b]our guilt, for [c]no one can stand before You because of this."

Reconciliation with God

10 Now [a]while Ezra was praying and making confession, weeping and prostrating himself [b]before the house of God, a very large assembly, men, women and children, gathered to him from Israel; for the people wept bitterly.

2 Shecaniah the son of Jehiel, one of the sons of Elam, said to Ezra, "[a]We have been unfaithful to our God and have [1]married foreign women from the peoples of the land; yet now there is hope for Israel in spite of this.

3 "So now [a]let us make a covenant with our God to put away all the wives and [1b]their children, according to the counsel of [2]my lord and of [c]those who tremble at the commandment of our God; and let it be done [d]according to the law.

4 "Arise! For *this* matter is [1]your responsibility, but we will be with you; [a]be courageous and act."

5 Then Ezra rose and [a]made the leading priests, the Levites and all Israel, take oath that they would do according to this [1]proposal; so they took the oath.

6 Then Ezra [a]rose from before the house of God and went into the chamber of Jehohanan the son of Eliashib. Although he went there, [b]he did not eat bread nor drink water, for he was mourning over the unfaithfulness of the exiles.

7 They made a proclamation throughout

9 [a]Neh 9:36 [b]Ezra 7:28
11 [a]Ezra 6:21
12 [a]Ex 34:15, 16; Deut 7:3; Ezra 9:2 [b]Deut 23:6 [c]Prov 13:22
13 [a]Ezra 9:6, 7 [b]Ezra 9:8
14 [1]Lit *of these abominations* [2]Lit *to destroy* [a]Ezra 9:2 [b]Deut 9:8, 14
15 [a]Neh 9:33; Dan 9:7
15 [b]Ezra 9:6 [c]Job 9:2; Ps 130:3
10:1 [a]Dan 9:4, 20 [b]2 Chr 20:9
2 [1]Lit *given dwelling to* [a]Ezra 9:2; Neh 13:27
3 [1]Lit *that which is born of them* [2]Or *the Lord* [a]2 Chr 34:31 [b]Ezra 10:44 [c]Ezra 9:4 [d]Deut 7:2, 3
4 [1]Lit *upon you* [a]1 Chr 28:10
5 [1]Lit *word, thing* [a]Neh 5:12; 13:25
6 [a]Ezra 10:1 [b]Deut 9:18

en our eyes. An increase in light means vitality and joy (Ps 13:3; 19:8; Eccl 8:1).

9:9 *kings of Persia.* The Achaemenid Persian kings were favorably disposed to the Jews: Cyrus (539–530 B.C.) gave them permission to return (ch. 1); his son Cambyses (530–522), though not named in the Bible, also favored the Jews, as we learn from Elephantine papyri; Darius I (522–486) renewed the decree of Cyrus (ch. 6); his son Ahasuerus (486–465) granted privileges and protection to Jews (Esth 8–10); his son Artaxerxes I (465–424) gave authorizations to Ezra (ch. 7) and to Nehemiah (Neh 2). *restore its ruins.* Isaiah had prophesied that the Lord would restore Jerusalem's ruins (Is 44:26), which would burst into singing (Is 52:9; cf. 58:12; 61:4). *wall.* Used of a city wall only in Mic 7:11. The use here is metaphorical (cf. Zech 2:4–5).

9:11–12 The references are not to a single OT passage but to several passages, such as Deut 11:8–9; Is 1:19; Ezek 37:25.

9:11 *Your servants the prophets.* See notes on Jer 7:25; Zech 1:6. *uncleanness.* Of Canaanite idolatry and the immoral practices associated with it (Lev 18:3; 2 Chr 29:5; Lam 1:17; Ezek 7:20; 36:17). The degrading practices and beliefs of the Canaanites are described in texts from ancient Ugarit (see chart, p. xix).

9:14 *be angry.* God's anger came upon the Israelites because they had violated His covenant with them (Deut 7:4; 11:16–17; 29:26–28; Josh 23:16; Judg 2:20).

9:15 *You are righteous.* See note on Ps 4:1. *our guilt.* A proper sense of God's holiness makes us aware of our unworthiness. See Is 6:1–5; Luke 5:8. For comparable passages of national lament see Ps 44; 60; 74; 79–80; 83; 85; 90; 108; 126; 129; 137.

10:1 *weeping.* Not silently but out loud (see 3:13 and note; Neh 1:4; Joel 2:12). *prostrating himself.* The prophets and other leaders used object lessons, even bizarre actions, to attract people's attention (Is 7:3; 8:1–4,18; Jer 13:1–11; 19; 27:2–12; Ezek 4:1–5:4).

10:2 Ezra, as a wise teacher, waited for his audience to draw their own conclusions about what should be done. *Shecaniah.* Perhaps his father Jehiel is the Jehiel mentioned in v. 26 since he was also of the family of Elam. If so, Shecaniah was doubtless grieved that his father had married a non-Jewish woman. Six members of the clan of Elam were involved in intermarriage (v. 26).

10:3 *make a covenant.* Lit. "cut a covenant" (see note on Gen 15:18). *wives and their children.* Mothers were given custody of their children when marriages were dissolved. When Hagar was dismissed, Ishmael was sent with her (Gen 21:14). In Babylonia divorced women were granted their children and had to wait for them to grow up before remarrying, according to the Code of Hammurapi (see chart, p. xix). In Greece, however, children from broken homes remained with their fathers.

10:4 *Arise!* Cf. David's exhortation (1 Chr 22:16).

10:5 *oath.* The implied curse attendant upon nonfulfillment of a Biblical oath is often expressed in the vague statement, "May God do so to you, and more also, if . . ." (see note on 1 Sam 3:17). On rare occasions the full implications of the curse are spelled out (Num 5:19–22; Job 31; Ps 7:4–5; 137:5–6).

10:6 *chamber.* Such temple chambers were used as storerooms (8:29; Neh 13:4–5). *did not eat bread nor drink water.* Complete fasting from both food and drink was rare. Moses did it twice (Ex 34:28; Deut 9:18), and the Ninevites also did it (Jon

Judah and Jerusalem to all the exiles, that they should assemble at Jerusalem,

8 and that whoever would not come within three days, according to the counsel of the leaders and the elders, all his possessions should be forfeited and he himself excluded from the assembly of the exiles.

9 So all the men of Judah and Benjamin assembled at Jerusalem within the three days. It was the ninth month on the twentieth of the month, and all the people sat in the open square *before* the house of God, [a]trembling because of this matter and the heavy rain.

10 Then Ezra the priest stood up and said to them, "You have been unfaithful and have married foreign wives adding to the guilt of Israel.

11 "Now therefore, [a]make confession to the LORD God of your fathers and [b]do His will; and [c]separate yourselves from the peoples of the land and from the foreign wives."

12 Then all the assembly replied with a loud voice, "That's right! As you have said, so it is [1]our duty to do.

13 "But there are many people; it is the rainy season and we are not able to stand in the open. Nor *can* the task *be done* in one or two days, for we have transgressed greatly in this matter.

14 "Let our leaders [1]represent the whole assembly and let all those in our cities who have married foreign wives come at appointed times, together with the elders and judges of each city, until the [a]fierce anger of our God on account of this matter is turned away from us."

15 Only Jonathan the son of Asahel and Jahzeiah the son of Tikvah [1]opposed this, with Meshullam and Shabbethai the Levite supporting them.

16 But the exiles did so. And [1]Ezra the priest selected men *who were* heads of fathers' *households* for *each of* their father's households, all of them by name. So they [2]convened on the first day of the tenth month to investigate the matter.

17 They finished *investigating* all the men who had married foreign wives by the first day of the first month.

List of Offenders

18 Among the sons of the priests who had married foreign wives were found of the sons of [a]Jeshua the son of Jozadak, and his brothers: Maaseiah, Eliezer, Jarib and Gedaliah.

19 They [1]pledged to put away their wives, and being guilty, [a]*they offered* a ram of the flock for their offense.

20 Of the sons of Immer *there were* Hanani and Zebadiah;

21 and of the sons of Harim: Maaseiah, Elijah, Shemaiah, Jehiel and Uzziah;

22 and of the sons of Pashhur: Elioenai, Maaseiah, Ishmael, Nethanel, Jozabad and Elasah.

23 Of Levites *there were* Jozabad, Shimei, Kelaiah (that is, Kelita), Pethahiah, Judah and Eliezer.

24 Of the singers *there was* Eliashib; and of the gatekeepers: Shallum, Telem and Uri.

25 Of Israel, of the sons of [a]Parosh *there were* Ramiah, Izziah, Malchijah, Mijamin, Eleazar, Malchijah and Benaiah;

9 [a]1 Sam 12:18; Ezra 9:4; 10:3
11 [a]Lev 26:40; Prov 28:13 [b]Rom 12:2 [c]Ezra 10:3
12 [1]Lit *upon us*
14 [1]Lit *stand for* [a]2 Kin 23:26; 2 Chr 28:11-13; 29:10; 30:8
15 [1]Lit *stood against*
16 [1]Heb reads *there were set apart Ezra the priest, men...* [2]Lit *sat*
18 [a]Ezra 5:2; Hag 1:1, 12; 2:4; Zech 3:1; 6:11
19 [1]Lit *gave their hand* [a]Lev 5:15; 6:6
25 [a]Ezra 2:3; 8:3; Neh 7:8

3:7). Ordinarily, fasting involved abstaining only from eating (1 Sam 1:7; 2 Sam 3:35). *mourning.* The Hebrew for this word often describes the reaction of those aware of the threat of deserved judgment (Ex 33:4; Num 14:39).

10:7–8 While Ezra continued to fast and pray, the officials and elders ordered all the exiles to assemble in Jerusalem. Although Ezra had been invested with great authority (7:25–26), he used it sparingly and influenced the people by his example.

10:8 *within three days.* Since the territory of Judah had been much reduced, the most distant people would not be more than 50 miles from Jerusalem. The borders were Bethel in the north, Beersheba in the south, Jericho in the east and Ono in the west (cf. Neh 7:26–38; 11:25–35). *forfeited.* The Hebrew for this word means "to ban from profane use and to devote to the Lord," either by destruction (see Ex 22:20; Num 21:2; Deut 2:34; 13:12–18 and notes) or by giving it to the Lord's treasury (cf. Lev 27:28; Josh 6:19; 7:1–15).

10:9,16–17 See chart, p. 637.

10:9 *Judah and Benjamin.* See note on 1:5. *open square.* Either the outer court of the temple or the open space before the Water Gate (Neh 8:1). *rain.* The Hebrew for this word is a plural of intensity, indicating heavy torrential rains. The ninth month, Kislev (November-December), is in the middle of the "rainy season" (v. 13), which begins with light showers in October and lasts to mid-April. December and January are also cold months, with temperatures in the 50s and even 40s in Jerusalem. The people shivered not only because they were drenched, but perhaps also because they sensed divine displeasure in the heavy rains (see 1 Sam 12:17–18; Ezek 13:11,13).

10:10 *adding to the guilt of Israel.* See Ex 9:34; Judg 3:12; 4:1; 2 Chr 28:13. The sins and failures of the exiles were great enough, but they added insult to injury by marrying pagan women.

10:11 *separate yourselves.* See Num 16:21; 2 Cor 6:14.

10:12 *with a loud voice.* See Neh 9:4.

10:14 *elders and judges of each city.* See Deut 16:18; 19:12; 21:3,19; Ruth 4:2.

10:15 Perhaps these four men opposed the measure because they wanted to protect themselves or their relatives, or they may have viewed it as being too harsh. *Jahzeiah.* Means "May the LORD see" (the name is found only here). *Tikvah.* Means "hope" (found elsewhere only in 2 Kin 22:14). *Meshullam.* See note on 8:16. If he is the Meshullam of v. 29, he himself had married a pagan wife. *Shabbethai.* Occurs only here and in Neh 8:7; 11:16; perhaps means "one born on the Sabbath."

10:16–17 The committee completed its work in three months, discovering that about 110 men were guilty of marrying pagan wives.

10:18–22 See 2:36–39.

10:19 *pledged.* For the symbolic use of the handshake (see NASB marg.) see 2 Kin 10:15; Ezek 17:18. *ram.* Guilt offerings were to be made for sins committed unintentionally (Lev 5:14–19) as well as intentionally (Lev 6:1–7), and a ram was the appropriate offering in either case (Lev 5:15; 6:6).

10:24 It is striking that only one singer and three gatekeepers were involved. No temple servants (2:43–54) or descendants of Solomon's servants (2:55–57) sinned through intermarriage.

26 and of the sons of Elam: Mattaniah,
Zechariah, Jehiel, Abdi, Jeremoth and Elijah;
27 and of the sons of [a]Zattu: Elioenai, Eliashib, Mattaniah, Jeremoth, Zabad and Azi-
za;
28 and of the sons of Bebai: Jehohanan,
Hananiah, Zabbai *and* Athlai;
29 and of the sons of Bani: Meshullam,
Malluch and Adaiah, Jashub, Sheal *and* Jeremoth;
30 and of the sons of Pahath-moab: Adna,
Chelal, Benaiah, Maaseiah, Mattaniah, Bezalel, Binnui and Manasseh;
31 and *of* the sons of Harim: Eliezer, Isshi-
jah, [a]Malchijah, Shemaiah, Shimeon,
32 Benjamin, Malluch *and* Shemariah;
33 of the sons of Hashum: Mattenai, Mat-
tattah, Zabad, Eliphelet, Jeremai, Manasseh
and Shimei;
34 of the sons of Bani: Maadai, Amram,
Uel,
35 Benaiah, Bedeiah, Cheluhi,
36 Vaniah, Meremoth, Eliashib,
37 Mattaniah, Mattenai, Jaasu,
38 Bani, Binnui, Shimei,
39 Shelemiah, Nathan, Adaiah,
40 Machnadebai, Shashai, Sharai,
41 Azarel, Shelemiah, Shemariah,
42 Shallum, Amariah *and* Joseph.
43 Of the sons of [a]Nebo *there were* Jeiel,
Mattithiah, Zabad, Zebina, Jaddai, Joel *and*
Benaiah.
44 All these had married [a]foreign wives,
and some of them had wives *by whom* they
had children.

27 [a]Ezra 2:8; Neh 7:13
31 [a]Neh 3:11
43 [a]Num 32:38; Ezra 2:29
44 [a]1 Kin 11:1-3; Ezra 10:3

10:25–43 See 2:3–20.
10:30 *Bezalel.* Cf. Ex 31:2.
10:31 *Shimeon.* Probably means "one who hears." The Hebrew for this name is the same as that for Simeon, Jacob's second son. In Greek the name became Simon (e.g., Matt 4:18).
10:43 *Nebo.* The Hebrew equivalent of the name of the Babylonian god Nabu (see Is 46:1); found only here as a personal name.
10:44 Some of the marriages had produced children, but this was not accepted as a reason for halting the divorce proceedings.

Nehemiah

INTRODUCTION

See Introduction to Ezra.

Outline

I. Nehemiah's First Administration (chs. 1—12)
   A. Nehemiah's Response to the Situation in Jerusalem (ch. 1)
      1. News of the plight of Jerusalem (1:1–4)
      2. Nehemiah's prayer (1:5–11)
   B. Nehemiah's Journey to Jerusalem (ch. 2)
      1. The king's response (2:1–8)
      2. The journey itself (2:9–10)
      3. Nehemiah's nocturnal inspection of the walls (2:11–16)
      4. His exhortation to rebuild (2:17–18)
      5. The opposition of Sanballat, Tobiah and Geshem (2:19–20)
   C. List of the Builders of the Wall (ch. 3)
      1. The northern section (3:1–7)
      2. The western section (3:8–13)
      3. The southern section (3:14)
      4. The eastern section (3:15–32)
   D. Opposition to Rebuilding the Wall (ch. 4)
      1. The derision of Sanballat and Tobiah (4:1–5)
      2. The threat of attack (4:6–15)
      3. Rebuilding the wall (4:16–23)
   E. Social and Economic Problems (ch. 5)
      1. The complaints of the poor (5:1–5)
      2. The cancellation of debts (5:6–13)
      3. Nehemiah's unselfish example (5:14–19)
   F. The Wall Rebuilt Despite Opposition (ch. 6)
      1. Attempts to snare Nehemiah (6:1–9)
      2. The hiring of false prophets (6:10–14)
      3. The completion of the wall (6:15–19)
   G. List of Exiles (7:1–73a)
      1. Provisions for the protection of Jerusalem (7:1–3)
      2. Nehemiah's discovery of the list of returnees (7:4–5)
      3. The returnees delineated (7:6–72)
      4. Settlement of the exiles (7:73a)
   H. Ezra's Preaching and the Outbreak of Revival (7:73b—10:39)
      1. The public exposition of the Scriptures (7:73b—8:12)
      2. The Feast of Booths (8:13–18)
      3. A day of fasting, confession and prayer (9:1–5a)
      4. A recital of God's dealings with Israel (9:5b-31)
      5. Confession of sins (9:32–37)
      6. A binding agreement (9:38)
      7. A list of those who sealed it (10:1–29)

        8. Provisions of the agreement (10:30–39)
    I. New Residents of Judah and Jerusalem (ch. 11)
        1. New residents for Jerusalem (11:1–24)
            a. Introductory remarks (11:1–4a)
            b. Residents from Judah (11:4b-6)
            c. From Benjamin (11:7–9)
            d. From the priests (11:10–14)
            e. From the Levites (11:15–18)
            f. From the temple staff (11:19–24)
        2. New residents for Judah (11:25–36)
            a. Places settled by those from Judah (11:25–30)
            b. Places settled by those from Benjamin (11:31–35)
            c. Transfer of Levites from Judah to Benjamin (11:36)
    J. Lists of Priests and the Dedication of the Wall (ch. 12)
        1. Priests and Levites from the first return (12:1–9)
        2. High priests and Levites since Joiakim (12:10–26)
        3. Dedication of the wall of Jerusalem (12:27–43)
        4. Regulation of the temple offerings and services (12:44–47)
II. Nehemiah's Second Administration (ch. 13)
    A. Abuses during His Absence (13:1–5)
        1. Mixed marriages (13:1–3)
        2. Tobiah's occupation of the temple quarters (13:4–5)
    B. Nehemiah's Return (13:6–9)
        1. His arrival (13:6–7)
        2. His expulsion of Tobiah (13:8–9)
    C. Reorganization and Reforms (13:10–31)
        1. Offerings for the temple staff (13:10–14)
        2. The abuse of the Sabbath (13:15–22)
        3. Mixed marriages (13:23–29)
        4. Provisions of wood and first fruits (13:30–31)

Nehemiah's Grief for the Exiles

1 The words of [a]Nehemiah the son of Hacaliah.
Now it happened in [b]the month Chislev,
[c]*in* the twentieth year, while I was in [d]Susa
the [1]capitol,
2 that [a]Hanani, one of my brothers, and
[1]some men from Judah came; and I asked
them concerning the Jews who had escaped
and had survived the captivity, and about
Jerusalem.
3 They said to me, "The remnant there in
the [a]province who survived the captivity are
in great distress and [b]reproach, and [b]the wall
of Jerusalem is broken down and [c]its gates
are burned with fire."
4 When I heard these words, [a]I sat down
and wept and mourned for days; and I was
fasting and praying before [b]the God of heaven.
5 I said, "I beseech You, O LORD God of
heaven, [a]the great and awesome God, [b]who
preserves the covenant and lovingkindness
for those who love Him and keep His commandments,
6 [a]let Your ear now be attentive and Your
eyes open to hear the prayer of Your servant
which I am praying before You now, day and
night, on behalf of the sons of Israel Your
servants, [b]confessing the sins of the sons of
Israel which we have sinned against You; [c]I
and my father's house have sinned.
7 "[a]We have acted very corruptly against
You and have not kept the commandments,
nor the statutes, nor the ordinances [b]which
You commanded Your servant Moses.
8 "Remember the word which You commanded Your servant Moses, saying, '[a]If you
are unfaithful I will scatter you among the
peoples;
9 [a]but *if* you return to Me and keep My
commandments and do them, though those
of you who have been scattered were in the
most remote part of the heavens, I [b]will gather them from there and will bring them [c]to
the place where I have chosen to cause My
name to dwell.'
10 "[a]They are Your servants and Your people whom You redeemed by Your great power and by Your strong hand.
11 "O Lord, I beseech You, [a]may Your ear
be attentive to the prayer of Your servant and
the prayer of Your servants who delight to
[1]revere Your name, and make Your servant
successful today and grant him compassion
before this man."
Now I was the [b]cupbearer to the king.

1:1 [1]Or *palace or citadel* [a]Neh 10:1 [b]Zech 7:1 [c]Neh 2:1 [d]Esth 1:2; Dan 8:2 **2** [1]Lit *he and some* [a]Neh 7:2 **3** [a]Neh 7:6 [b]Neh 2:17 [c]Neh 2:3 **4** [a]Ezra 9:3; 10:1 [b]Neh 2:4 **5** [a]Neh 4:14; 9:32; Dan 9:4 [b]Ex 20:6; Ps 89:2, 3 **6** [a]Dan 9:17 **6** [b]Ezra 10:1; Dan 9:20 [c]2 Chr 29:6 **7** [a]Dan 9:5 [b]Deut 28:14 **8** [a]Lev 26:33 **9** [a]Deut 30:2, 3 [b]Deut 30:4 [c]Deut 12:5 **10** [a]Ex 32:11; Deut 9:29 **11** [1]Or *fear* [a]Neh 1:6 [b]Gen 40:21; Neh 2:1

1:1 *The words of.* Originally an introduction to the title of a separate composition (see Jer 1:1; Amos 1:1), though the books of Ezra and Nehemiah appear as a single work from earliest times (see Introduction to Ezra: Ezra and Nehemiah). *Nehemiah.* Means "The LORD comforts." *Hacaliah.* Perhaps means "Wait for the LORD," though an imperative in a Hebrew name is quite unusual. The name occurs only here and in 10:1. *Chislev . . . twentieth year.* November-December, 445 B.C. See chart, p. 637. *Susa.* See note on Ezra 4:9.
1:2 *Hanani.* Probably a shortened form of Hananiah, which means "The LORD is gracious." *one of my brothers.* See 7:2. The Elephantine papyri mention a Hananiah who was the head of Jewish affairs in Jerusalem. Many believe that he is to be identified with Nehemiah's brother, and that he may have governed between Nehemiah's first and second terms (see note on 7:2). *Jews who had escaped.* See Ezra 9:8 and notes on Gen 45:7; 2 Kin 19:30–31; Is 1:9; 10:20–22.
1:3 *province.* See note on Ezra 2:1. *wall of Jerusalem is broken down.* The lack of a city wall meant that the people were defenseless against their enemies. Thucydides (1.89) describes the comparable condition of Athens after its devastation by the Persians in 480–479 B.C. Excavations at Jerusalem during 1961–67 revealed that the lack of a wall on the eastern slopes also meant the disintegration of the terraces there. When Nebuchadnezzar assaulted Jerusalem, he battered and broke down the walls around it (2 Kin 25:10). Most, however, do not believe that Nehemiah's distress was caused by Nebuchadnezzar's destruction in 586 but by the episode of Ezra 4:7–23. The Jews had attempted to rebuild the walls earlier in the reign of Artaxerxes I; but after the protest of Rehum and Shimshai, the king ordered the Jews to desist. See note on Ezra 4:21–23.
1:4 *sat down.* Cf. Ezra 9:3; Job 2:13. *wept.* See 8:9; Ezra 3:13 and note; 10:1; Esth 8:3. *mourned.* See Ezra 10:6; Dan 10:2. *fasting and praying.* See note on Ezra 8:23. During the exile, fasting became a common practice, including solemn fasts to commemorate the fall of Jerusalem and the murder of Gedaliah (see note on Zech 8:19; see also Esth 4:16; Dan 9:3; 10:3; Zech 7:3–7). *God of heaven.* See note on Ezra 1:2.
1:5 *lovingkindness.* Or "faithful love," the quality that honors a covenant through thick and thin.
1:6 *praying before You now, day and night.* Cf. Ps 42:3; 88:1; Jer 9:1; 14:17; Lam 2:18; Luke 2:37; 1 Thess 3:10; 1 Tim 5:5; 2 Tim 1:3. *sins . . . I and my father's house.* Nehemiah does not exclude himself or members of his own family in his confession of sins. A true sense of the awesome holiness of God reveals the depths of our own sinfulness (Is 6:1–5; Luke 5:8).
1:7 *commandments . . . statutes . . . ordinances.* See note on Gen 26:5. *Moses.* For the prominence of the law of Moses in Ezra and Nehemiah see Ezra 3:2; 6:18; 7:6; Neh 1:8; 8:1,14; 9:14; 10:29; 13:1.
1:8 *Remember.* See note on 13:31; a key word in the book (4:14; 5:19; 6:14; 13:14,22,29,31). *unfaithful . . . scatter.* Dispersion was the inescapable consequence of the people's unfaithfulness. By the NT period there were still more Jews in the Diaspora (dispersion) than in the Holy Land.
1:9 *I will gather them.* See Deut 30:1–5; a frequent promise, especially in the prophets (e.g., Is 11:12; Jer 23:3; 31:8–10; Ezek 20:34,41; 36:24; Mic 2:12). *chosen to cause My name to dwell.* See Deut 12:5 and note; Ps 132:13.
1:10 *Your people . . . You redeemed.* Although they had sinned and failed, they were still God's people by virtue of His redeeming them (see Deut 4:34; 9:29).
1:11 *make Your servant successful today.* Cf. Gen 24:12. *cupbearer.* Lit. "one who gives (someone) something to drink." The Hebrew for this word occurs 11 other times in the OT in the sense of "cupbearer" (Gen 40:1–2,5,9,13,20–21,23; 41:9; 1 Kin 10:5; 2 Chr 9:4). According to the Greek historian Xenophon (*Cyropaedia,* 1.3.9), one of the cupbearer's duties was to choose and taste the king's wine to make certain that it was not poisoned (see 2:1). Thus Nehemiah had to be a man who enjoyed the unreserved confidence of the king. The need for trustworthy court attendants is underscored by the intrigues that characterized the Achaemenid court of Persia. Ahasuerus, the father of Artaxerxes I, was killed in his own bedchamber by a courtier.

Nehemiah's Prayer Answered

2 And it came about in the month Nisan,
[a]in the twentieth year of King [b]Artaxerx-
es, that wine *was* before him, and [c]I took up
the wine and gave it to the king. Now I had
not been sad in his presence.
2 So the king said to me, "Why is your
face sad though you are not sick? [a]This is
nothing but sadness of heart." Then I was
very much afraid.
3 I said to the king, "[a]Let the king live
forever. Why should my face not be sad
[b]when the city, the place of my fathers'
tombs, lies desolate and its gates have been
consumed by fire?"
4 Then the king said to me, "What would
you request?" [a]So I prayed to the God of
heaven.
5 I said to the king, "If it please the king,
and if your servant has found favor before
you, send me to Judah, to the city of my
fathers' tombs, that I may rebuild it."
6 Then the king said to me, the queen sitting beside him, "How long will your journey
be, and when will you return?" So it pleased
the king to send me, and [a]I gave him a definite time.
7 And I said to the king, "If it please the
king, let letters be given me [a]for the governors *of the provinces* beyond the River, that
they may allow me to pass through until I
come to Judah,
8 and a letter to Asaph the keeper of the
king's [a]forest, that he may give me timber to
make beams for the gates of [b]the fortress
which is by the [1]temple, for the wall of the
city and for the house to which I will go."
And the king granted *them* to me because
[c]the good hand of my God *was* on me.
9 Then I came to [a]the governors *of the
provinces* beyond the River and gave them
the king's letters. Now [b]the king had sent
with me officers of the army and horsemen.
10 When [a]Sanballat the Horonite and
Tobiah the Ammonite [1]official heard *about
it,* it was very displeasing to them that some-

2:1 [a]Neh 1:1 [b]Ezra 7:1 [c]Neh 1:11
2 [a]Prov 15:13
3 [a]Dan 2:4 [b]2 Kin 25:8-10; 2 Chr 36:19; Neh 1:3; Jer 52:12-14
4 [a]Neh 1:4
6 [a]Neh 13:6
7 [a]Ezra 7:21; 8:36
8 [1]Lit *house* [a]Eccl 2:5, 6 [b]Neh 7:2 [c]Ezra 7:6; Neh 2:18
9 [a]Neh 2:7 [b]Ezra 8:22
10 [1]Lit *servant* [a]Neh 2:19; 4:1

2:1 *Nisan . . . twentieth year.* March-April, 444 B.C. (see chart, p. 637). There was a delay of four months from Chislev, when Nehemiah first heard the news (1:1), to Nisan, when he approached the king. Various reasons have been suggested: 1. The king may have been in his other winter palace at Babylon. 2. Perhaps the king was not in the right mood. 3. Even though Nehemiah was a favorite of the king, he would not have rashly blurted out his request. *sad in his presence.* No matter what one's personal problems were, the king's servants were expected to keep their feelings to themselves and to display a cheerful disposition before him.

2:3 *Let the king live forever.* A common form of address to kings. *city.* Nehemiah does not mention Jerusalem by name (see v. 5); he may have wished to arouse the king's sympathy by stressing first the desecration of ancestral tombs.

2:4 *I prayed to the God of heaven.* Before turning to answer the king, Nehemiah utters a brief, spontaneous prayer to God. One of Nehemiah's striking characteristics is his frequent recourse to prayer (1:4; 4:4,9; 5:19; 6:9,14; 13:14,22,29,31).

2:6 *queen.* The Hebrew for this word is used only here and in Ps 45:9. It is a loanword from Akkadian and means lit. "(woman) of the palace." The Aramaic equivalent is found only in Dan 5:2–3,23, where it is translated "wives." Ctesias, a Greek who lived at the Achaemenid court, informs us that the name of Artaxerxes's queen was Damaspia and that he had at least three concubines. Like Esther, Damaspia may have used her influence with the king (Esth 5). The Achaemenid court was notorious for the great influence exercised by the royal women. Especially domineering was Amestris, the cruel wife of Ahasuerus and mother of Artaxerxes I. *How long will your journey be . . . ?* Nehemiah probably asked for a brief leave of absence, which he then had extended. We can infer from 5:14 that he spent 12 years on his first term as governor of Judah. In the 32nd year of Artaxerxes, Nehemiah returned to report to the king and then came back to Judah for a second term (13:6–7).

2:7 *letters.* A contemporary document from Arsames, the satrap of Egypt who was at the Persian court, to one of his officers who was returning to Egypt orders Persian officials to provide him with food and drink on the stages of his journey. *beyond the River.* See note on Ezra 4:10.

2:8 *forest.* The Hebrew for this word is *pardes*, a loanword from Old Persian meaning "enclosure," a pleasant retreat or park. The word occurs elsewhere in the OT only in Eccl 2:5 ("parks") and Song 4:13 ("orchard"). In the Septuagint (the Greek translation of the OT) the Greek transliteration *paradeisos* is used here. In the period between the OT and the NT, the word acquired the sense of the abode of the blessed dead, i.e., "paradise." It appears three times in the NT (Luke 23:43; 2 Cor 12:4; Rev 2:7). As to the location of the "king's forest," some believe that it was in Lebanon, which was famed for its forests of cedars and other coniferous trees (see notes on Judg 9:15; Ezra 3:7). But a more plausible suggestion is that it should be identified with Solomon's gardens at Etham, about six miles south of Jerusalem (see Josephus, *Antiquities,* 8.7.3). For city gates, costly imported cedars from Lebanon would not be used but rather indigenous oak, poplar or terebinth (Hos 4:13). *fortress.* Probably refers to the fortress north of the temple, the forerunner of the Antonia fortress built by Herod the Great (Josephus, *Antiquities,* 15.11.4; see Acts 21:34,37; 22:24).

2:9 *officers of the army and horsemen.* In striking contrast to Ezra (see note on Ezra 8:22), Nehemiah was accompanied by an armed escort since he was officially Judah's governor.

2:10 *Sanballat.* A Babylonian name, meaning "Sin (the moon-god) has given life." *Horonite.* Identifies him as coming from (1) Hauran (Ezek 47:16,18), east of the Sea of Galilee, (2) Horonaim, in Moab (Jer 48:34), or, most probably, (3) either Upper or Lower Beth Horon, two key cities 12 miles northwest of Jerusalem, which guarded the main road to Jerusalem (Josh 10:10; 16:3,5; 1 Maccabees 3:16; 7:39). Sanballat was the chief political opponent of Nehemiah (v. 19; 4:1,7; 6:1–2,5,12,14; 13:28). He held the position of governor over Samaria (cf. 4:1–2). An Elephantine papyrus letter of the late fifth century B.C. to Bagohi (Bigvai), governor of Judah, refers to "Delaiah and Shelemiah, the sons of Sanballat, governor of Samaria." In 1962 a fourth-century B.C. papyrus was found in a cave north of Jericho, listing the name Sanballat, probably a descendant of Nehemiah's contemporary. *Tobiah.* Means "The LORD is good." He was probably a worshiper of the Lord (Yahweh), as indicated not only by his name but also by that of his son Jehohanan (6:17–18), meaning "The LORD is gracious." Jehohanan was married to the daughter of Meshullam son of Berechiah, the leader of one of the groups repairing the wall (3:4,30; 6:18). Tobiah also had a close relationship with Eliashib the priest (13:4–7). *Ammonite.* See Ezra 9:1; see also note on Gen 19:36–38. Tobi-

one had come to seek the welfare of the sons
of Israel.

Nehemiah Inspects Jerusalem's Walls

11 So I [a]came to Jerusalem and was there
three days.
12 And I arose in the night, I and a few
men with me. I did not tell anyone what my
God was putting into my [1]mind to do for
Jerusalem and there was no animal with me
except the animal on which I was riding.
13 So I went out at night by [a]the Valley
Gate in the direction of the Dragon's Well and
on to the [1]Refuse Gate, inspecting the walls of
Jerusalem [b]which were broken down and its
[c]gates which were consumed by fire.
14 Then I passed on to [a]the Fountain Gate
and [b]the King's Pool, but there was no place
for [1]my mount to pass.
15 So I went up at night by the [a]ravine
and inspected the wall. Then I entered the
Valley Gate again and returned.
16 The officials did not know where I had
gone or what I had done; nor had I as yet
told the Jews, the priests, the nobles, the officials or the rest who did the work.
17 Then I said to them, "You see the bad
situation we are in, that [a]Jerusalem is deso-

11 [a]Ezra 8:32
12 [1]Lit *heart*
13 [1]Lit *Gate of Ash-heaps* [a]Neh 3:13
13 [b]Neh 1:3 [c]Neh 2:3, 17
14 [1]Lit *the animal under me* [a]Neh 3:15 [b]2 Kin 20:20
15 [a]John 18:1
17 [a]Neh 1:3

ah was probably governor of Transjordan under the Persians. In later generations a prominent family bearing the name of Tobiah was sometimes associated with the region of Ammon in non-Biblical texts. *very displeasing.* The reasons for the opposition of Sanballat and Tobiah were not basically religious but political. The authority of the Samaritan governor in particular was threatened by Nehemiah's arrival.

2:11 *three days.* See note on Ezra 8:32.

2:12 Nehemiah was cautious and discreet as he inspected the city's fortifications. *animal on which I was riding.* Probably a mule or donkey.

2:13 Nehemiah did not make a complete circuit of the walls, but only of the southern area (see map below). Jerusalem was always attacked from the north because it was most vulnerable there, so the walls had probably been completely destroyed in that part of the city. *Valley Gate.* See 3:13. According to 2 Chr 26:9 Uzziah fortified towers in the west wall, which overlooked the Tyropoeon Valley, i.e., the central valley between the Hinnom and Kidron valleys. Excavations in 1927–28 uncovered the remains of a gate from the Persian period, which has been identified as the Valley Gate. *Dragon's Well.* Many scholars suggest that this was En-rogel (Josh 15:7–8; 18:16; 2 Sam 17:17; 1 Kin 1:9), a well situated at the junction of the Hinnom and Kidron valleys, 250 yards south of the southeast ridge of Jerusalem. Others suggest that it was the Pool of Siloam. *Refuse Gate.* Perhaps the gate leading to the rubbish dump in the Hinnom Valley (cf. 3:13–14; 12:31; 2 Kin 23:10). It was situated about 500 yards south of the Valley Gate (3:13).

2:14 *Fountain Gate.* Possibly in the southeast wall facing toward En-rogel (see 3:15; 12:37). *King's Pool.* Hezekiah may have diverted the overflow from his Siloam tunnel (cf. 2 Kin 20:20; 2 Chr 32:30) to irrigate the royal gardens (2 Kin 25:4) located outside the city walls at the junction of the Kidron and Hinnom valleys. The King's Pool was probably therefore the Pool of Siloam (3:15) or the adjacent Birket el-Hamra. *no place . . . to pass.* Possibly because of the collapse of the supporting terraces (cf. 2 Sam 5:9; 1 Kin 9:15,24) on the east side of the city.

2:15 *ravine.* The Kidron.

2:16 *nobles.* The Hebrew root for this word means "free" (see 4:14,19; 5:7; 6:17; 7:5; 13:17; see also note on 3:5).

2:17 *desolate.* The condition of the walls and gates of the city since their destruction by Nebuchadnezzar in 586 B.C., in spite of abortive attempts to rebuild them. The leaders and people had evidently become reconciled to this sad state of affairs. It took an outsider to assess the situation and to rally them to renewed efforts.

Jerusalem of the Returning Exiles

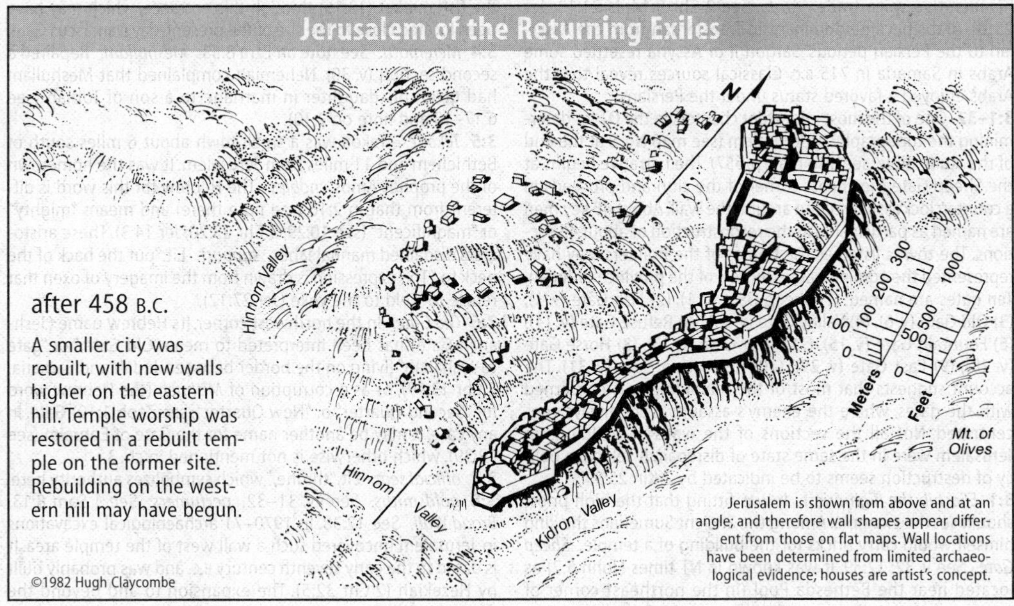
N
Hinnom Valley
Hinnom Valley
Kidron Valley
Mt. of Olives
Meters
0
100
200
300
Feet
0
500
1000

after 458 B.C.

A smaller city was rebuilt, with new walls higher on the eastern hill. Temple worship was restored in a rebuilt temple on the former site. Rebuilding on the western hill may have begun.

Jerusalem is shown from above and at an angle; and therefore wall shapes appear different from those on flat maps. Wall locations have been determined from limited archaeological evidence; houses are artist's concept.

©1982 Hugh Claycombe

late and its gates burned by fire. Come, let us rebuild the wall of Jerusalem so that we will no longer be a reproach."

18 I told them how the hand of my God had been favorable to me and also about the king's words which he had spoken to me. Then they said, "Let us arise and build." [a]So they put their hands to the good *work.*

19 But when Sanballat the Horonite and Tobiah the Ammonite [1]official, and [a]Geshem the Arab heard *it,* [b]they mocked us and despised us and said, "What is this thing you are doing? [a]Are you rebelling against the king?"

20 So I answered them and said to them, "[a]The God of heaven will give us success; therefore we His servants will arise and build, [b]but you have no portion, right or memorial in Jerusalem."

Builders of the Walls

3 Then [a]Eliashib the high priest arose with his brothers the priests and built [b]the Sheep Gate; they consecrated it and [c]hung its doors. They consecrated [1]the wall to [d]the Tower of the Hundred *and* [e]the Tower of Hananel.

2 Next to him [a]the men of Jericho built, and next to [1]them Zaccur the son of Imri built.

3 Now the sons of Hassenaah built [a]the Fish Gate; they laid its beams and hung its doors with its bolts and bars.

4 Next to them Meremoth the son of Uriah the son of Hakkoz made repairs. And next to him Meshullam the son of Berechiah the son of Meshezabel made repairs. And next to [1]him Zadok the son of Baana *also* made repairs.

5 Moreover, next to [1]him the Tekoites made repairs, but their nobles did not [2]support the work of their masters.

6 Joiada the son of Paseah and Meshullam the son of Besodeiah repaired [a]the Old Gate; they laid its beams and hung its doors with its bolts and its bars.

7 Next to them Melatiah the Gibeonite and Jadon the Meronothite, the men of Gibeon and of Mizpah, [1]also made repairs for the official seat of the [a]governor *of the province* beyond the River.

8 Next to him Uzziel the son of Harhaiah of the [a]goldsmiths made repairs. And next to him Hananiah, one of the perfumers, made

18 [a]2 Sam 2:7
19 [1]Lit *servant* [a]Neh 6:6 [b]Neh 4:1
20 [a]Ezra 4:3 [b]Neh 2:4; Acts 8:21
3:1 [1]Lit *it* [a]Neh 3:20; 13:28 [b]Neh 3:32; 12:39 [c]Neh 6:1; 7:1 [d]Neh 12:39 [e]Jer 31:38
2 [1]Lit *him* [a]Neh 7:36
3 [a]Neh 12:39
4 [1]Lit *them*
5 [1]Lit *them* [2]Lit *bring their neck to*
6 [a]Neh 12:39
7 [1]Or *which was under the jurisdiction of the governor* of the province *beyond the River, also made repairs* [a]Neh 2:7
8 [a]Neh 3:31, 32

2:18 *my God . . . and . . . the king's words.* Nehemiah could personally attest that God was alive and active in his behalf and that he (Nehemiah) had come with royal sanction and authority.

2:19 *Sanballat . . . Tobiah.* See note on v. 10. *Geshem.* Inscriptions from Dedan in northwest Arabia and from Tell el-Maskhutah near Ismailia in Egypt bear the name of Geshem, who may have been in charge of a north Arabian confederacy that controlled vast areas from northeast Egypt to northern Arabia, including the southern part of the Holy Land. Geshem may have been opposed to Nehemiah's development of an independent kingdom because he feared that it might interfere with his lucrative spice trade. *Arab.* See 2 Chr 9:14; Is 21:13; Jer 25:24. Arabs became dominant in Transjordan from the Assyrian to the Persian periods. Sargon II of Assyria resettled some Arabs in Samaria in 715 B.C. Classical sources reveal that the Arabs enjoyed a favored status under the Persians.

3:1–32 One of the most important chapters in the OT for determining the topography of Jerusalem (see map No. 8 at the end of the study Bible; see also map, p. 657). The narrative begins at the Sheep Gate (northeast corner of the city) and proceeds in a counterclockwise direction around the wall. About 40 key men are named as participants in the reconstruction of about 45 sections. The towns listed as the homes of the builders may have represented the administrative centers of the province of Judah. Ten gates are named: (1) Sheep Gate (v. 1), (2) Fish Gate (v. 3), (3) Old Gate (v. 6), (4) Valley Gate (v. 13), (5) Refuse Gate (v. 14), (6) Fountain Gate (v. 15), (7) Water Gate (v. 26), (8) Horse Gate (v. 28), (9) East Gate (v. 29), (10) Inspection Gate (v. 31). The account suggests that most of the rebuilding was concerned with the gates, where the enemy's assaults were always concentrated. Not all the sections of the walls or buildings in Jerusalem were in the same state of disrepair. A selective policy of destruction seems to be indicated by 2 Kin 25:9.

3:1 *Eliashib the high priest.* It was fitting that the high priest should set the example. Among the ancient Sumerians the king himself would carry bricks for the building of a temple. *Sheep Gate.* See v. 32; 12:39. It was known in NT times (John 5:2) as located near the Bethesda Pool (in the northeast corner of Jerusalem). Even today a sheep market is held periodically near this area. The Sheep Gate may have replaced the earlier Gate of Benjamin (Jer 37:13; 38:7; Zech 14:10). *Tower of the Hundred.* See 12:39. "Hundred" may refer to (1) its height (100 cubits), (2) the number of its steps or (3) a military unit (cf. Deut 1:15). *Tower of Hananel.* The towers were associated with the "fortress which is by the temple" (2:8) in protecting the vulnerable northern approaches to the city.

3:3 *Fish Gate.* See 12:39. During the days of the first temple, it was one of Jerusalem's main entrances (2 Chr 33:14; Zeph 1:10). Merchants brought fish from either Tyre or the Sea of Galilee to the fish market (13:16) through this entrance, which may have been located close to the site of the present-day Damascus Gate.

3:4 *Meremoth.* See note on Ezra 8:33. *Meshullam.* Repaired a second section (v. 30). Nehemiah complained that Meshullam had given his daughter in marriage to a son of Tobiah (see 6:17–18 and note on 2:10).

3:5 *Tekoites.* Tekoa was a small town about 6 miles south of Bethlehem and 11 miles from Jerusalem. It was the hometown of the prophet Amos. *nobles.* The Hebrew for this word is different from that in 2:16 (see note there) and means "mighty" or "magnificent" (see 10:29; 2 Chr 23:20; Jer 14:3). These aristocrats disdained manual labor. *support.* Lit. "put the back of the neck to." The expression is drawn from the imagery of oxen that refuse to yield to the yoke (Jer 27:12).

3:6 *Old Gate.* In the northwest corner. Its Hebrew name (Jeshanah Gate) has been interpreted to mean "Old Gate," or "gate to Jeshanah" (lying on the border between Judah and Samaria, 2 Chr 13:19), or as a corruption of *Mishneh* (the Hebrew word for "Second Quarter" or "New Quarter"; see Zeph 1:10) Gate. In any case, it may be another name for the Gate of Ephraim (see 12:39), which otherwise is not mentioned in ch. 3.

3:7 *official seat.* Lit. "throne," which symbolizes authority here.

3:8 *goldsmiths.* See vv. 31–32. *perfumers.* See 1 Sam 8:13. *Broad Wall.* See 12:38. In 1970–71 archaeological excavations in Jerusalem uncovered such a wall west of the temple area. It is dated to the early seventh century B.C. and was probably built by Hezekiah (2 Chr 32:5). The expansion to and beyond the

repairs, and they restored Jerusalem as far as
[b]the Broad Wall.
9 Next to them Rephaiah the son of Hur,
[a]the official of half the district of Jerusalem,
made repairs.
10 Next to them Jedaiah the son of Haru-
maph made repairs opposite his house. And
next to him Hattush the son of Hashabneiah
made repairs.
11 Malchijah the son of Harim and Hasshub the son of Pahath-moab repaired
another section and [a]the Tower of Furnaces.
12 Next to him Shallum the son of Hallohesh, [a]the official of half the district of Jerusalem, made repairs, he and his daughters.
13 Hanun and the inhabitants of Zanoah
repaired [a]the Valley Gate. They built it and
hung its doors with its bolts and its bars, and
a thousand cubits of the wall to the [1]Refuse
Gate.
14 Malchijah the son of Rechab, the official of the district of [a]Beth-haccherem
repaired the [1b]Refuse Gate. He built it and
hung its doors with its bolts and its bars.
15 Shallum the son of Col-hozeh, the official of the district of Mizpah, [a]repaired the
Fountain Gate. He built it, covered it and
hung its doors with its bolts and its bars, and
the wall of the Pool of Shelah at [b]the king's
garden as far as [c]the steps that descend from
the city of David.
16 After him Nehemiah the son of Azbuk,
[a]official of half the district of Beth-zur, made
repairs as far as *a point* opposite the tombs
of David, and as far as [b]the artificial pool and
the house of the mighty men.
17 After him the Levites carried out
repairs *under* Rehum the son of Bani. Next to
him Hashabiah, the official of half the district of Keilah, carried out repairs for his district.
18 After him their brothers carried out
repairs *under* Bavvai the son of Henadad,
official of *the other* half of the district of Keilah.
19 Next to him Ezer the son of Jeshua,
[a]the official of Mizpah, repaired [1]another
section in front of the ascent of the armory
[b]at the Angle.
20 After him Baruch the son of Zabbai
zealously repaired another section, from the
Angle to the doorway of the house of [a]Elia-
shib the high priest.
21 After him Meremoth the son of Uriah
the son of Hakkoz repaired another section,
from the doorway of Eliashib's house even
as far as the end of [1]his house.
22 After him the priests, [a]the men of the
[1]valley, carried out repairs.
23 After [1]them Benjamin and Hasshub
carried out repairs in front of their house.
After [1]them Azariah the son of Maaseiah,
son of Ananiah, carried out repairs beside
his house.
24 After him Binnui the son of Henadad
repaired another section, from the house of
Azariah as far as [a]the Angle and as far as the
corner.
25 Palal the son of Uzai *made repairs* in
front of the Angle and the tower projecting
from the upper house of the king, which is
by [a]the court of the guard. After him Pedaiah
the son of Parosh *made repairs.*
26 [a]The temple servants living in [b]Ophel
made repairs as far as the front of [c]the Water
Gate toward the east and the projecting tower.

8 [b]Neh 12:38
9 [a]Neh 3:12, 17
11 [a]Neh 12:38
12 [a]Neh 3:9
13 [1]Lit *Gate of Ash-heaps* [a]Neh 2:13
14 [1]Lit *Gate of Ash-heaps* [a]Jer 6:1 [b]Neh 2:13
15 [a]Neh 2:17 [b]2 Kin 25:4 [c]Neh 12:37
16 [a]Neh 3:9, 12, 17 [b]2 Kin 20:20; Is 7:3
19 [1]Lit *a second measure,* and so in vv 20, 21, 24, 30 [a]Neh 3:15 [b]2 Chr 26:9
20 [a]Neh 3:1
21 [1]Lit *Eliashib's*
22 [1]Lit *circle;* i.e. lower Jordan valley [a]Neh 12:28
23 [1]Lit *him*
24 [a]Neh 3:19
25 [a]Jer 32:2
26 [a]Neh 7:46 [b]Neh 11:21 [c]Neh 8:1

Broad Wall may have become necessary because of the influx of refugees fleeing from the fall of Samaria in 722–721.

3:10 *Jedaiah . . . made repairs opposite his house.* See vv. 23,28–30. It made sense to have him and others repair the sections of the wall nearest their homes.

3:11 *Tower of Furnaces.* It was on the western wall, perhaps in the same location as one built by Uzziah (2 Chr 26:9). The furnaces may have been those situated in the "bakers' street " (Jer 37:21).

3:12 *daughters.* A unique reference to women working on the wall. When the Athenians attempted to rebuild their walls after the Persians had destroyed them, it was decreed that "the whole population of the city—men, women and children—should take part in the wall-building" (Thucydides, 1.90.3).

3:13 *Valley Gate.* See note on 2:13. *a thousand cubits.* Five hundred yards, an extraordinary length; probably most of the section was relatively intact. *Refuse Gate.* See note on 2:13.

3:14 *Beth-haccherem.* Means "house of the vineyard." It was a fire-signal point (Jer 6:1) and is identified with Ramat Rahel, two miles south of Jerusalem. It may have been the residence of a district governor in the Persian period.

3:15 *Fountain Gate.* See note on 2:14. *Pool of Shelah.* Shelah is a variant of Shiloah, i.e., Siloam, perhaps the lower Pool of Is 22:9 (see note on Is 8:6). *king's garden.* See note on 2:14. *city of David.* See 12:37; see also note on 2 Sam 5:7.

3:16 *Beth-zur.* A district capital, 13 miles south of Jerusalem. Excavations in 1931 and 1957 revealed that occupation was sparse during the early Persian period but was resumed in the fifth century B.C. *tombs of David.* Cf. 2:5. David was buried in the city area (1 Kin 2:10; 2 Chr 21:20; 32:33; Acts 2:29). The so-called Tomb of David on Mount Zion venerated today by Jewish pilgrims is in the Coenaculum building, erected in the 14th century A.D. Such a site for David's tomb is mentioned no earlier than the ninth century A.D. *house of the mighty men.* May have been the house of David's mighty men (see 2 Sam 23:8–39), which perhaps served later as the barracks or armory.

3:17–18 *Keilah.* Located about 15 miles southwest of Jerusalem, it played an important role in David's early history (1 Sam 23:1–13).

3:19 *armory.* See note on v. 16.

3:20–21 The residences of the high priest and his fellow priests were located inside the city along the eastern wall.

3:25 *upper house of the king.* Perhaps the old palace of David (see 12:37). Like Solomon's palace, it would have had a guardhouse (Jer 32:2).

3:26 *Ophel.* See v. 27. The word means "swelling" or "bulge," hence a "hill" (as in Mic 4:8), specifically the northern part of the southeastern hill of Jerusalem, which formed the original City of David, just south of the temple area (2 Chr 27:3). *Water Gate.* So called because it led to the main source of Jerusalem's water, the Gihon spring. It must have opened onto a large area, for the reading of the Law took place there (8:1,3,16; 12:37). *projecting tower.* Perhaps the large tower whose ruins were discovered by archaeologists on the crest of the Ophel hill in

27 After [1]them [a]the Tekoites repaired another section in front of the great projecting tower and as far as the wall of Ophel.

28 Above [a]the Horse Gate the priests carried out repairs, each in front of his house.

29 After [1]them Zadok the son of Immer carried out repairs in front of his house. And after him Shemaiah the son of Shecaniah, the keeper of the East Gate, carried out repairs.

30 After him Hananiah the son of Shelemiah, and Hanun the sixth son of Zalaph, repaired another section. After him Meshullam the son of Berechiah carried out repairs in front of his own [1]quarters.

31 After him Malchijah, [1]one of [a]the goldsmiths, carried out repairs as far as the house of the temple servants and of the merchants, in front of the [2]Inspection Gate and as far as the upper room of the corner.

32 Between the upper room of the corner and [a]the Sheep Gate the goldsmiths and the merchants carried out repairs.

Work Is Ridiculed

4 [1]Now it came about that when [a]Sanballat heard that we were rebuilding the wall, he became furious and very angry and mocked the Jews.

2 He spoke in the presence of his brothers and [a]the [1]wealthy *men* of Samaria and said, "What are these feeble Jews doing? Are they going to restore *it* for themselves? Can they offer sacrifices? Can they finish in a day? Can they revive the stones from the [2b]dusty rubble even the burned ones?"

3 Now Tobiah the Ammonite *was* near him and he said, "Even what they are building—[a]if a fox should [1]jump on *it,* he would break their stone wall down!"

4 [a]Hear, O our God, how we are despised! [b]Return their reproach on their own heads and give them up for plunder in a land of captivity.

5 Do not [1a]forgive their iniquity and let not their sin be blotted out before You, for they have [2]demoralized the builders.

6 So we built the wall and the whole wall was joined together to half its *height,* for the people had a [1]mind to work.

7 [1]Now when Sanballat, Tobiah, the Arabs, the Ammonites and the Ashdodites heard that the [2]repair of the walls of Jerusalem went on, *and* that the breaches began to be closed, they were very angry.

8 All of them [a]conspired together to come *and* fight against Jerusalem and to cause a disturbance in it.

Discouragement Overcome

9 But we prayed to our God, and because of them we [a]set up a guard against them day and night.

10 Thus [1]in Judah it was said,

"The strength of the burden bearers is failing,
Yet there is much [2]rubbish;
And we ourselves are unable
To rebuild the wall."

11 Our enemies said, "They will not know or see until we come among them, kill them and put a stop to the work."

12 When the Jews who lived near them came and told us ten times, "[1]They will come up against us from every place where you may turn,"

13 then I stationed *men* in the lowest parts of the space behind the wall, the [1]exposed places, and I [a]stationed the people in families with their swords, spears and bows.

14 When I saw *their fear,* I rose and spoke to the nobles, the officials and the rest of the people: "[a]Do not be afraid of them; remember the Lord who is great and awesome, and [b]fight for your brothers, your sons, your daughters, your wives and your houses."

15 When our enemies heard that it was

27 [1]Lit *him* [a]Neh 3:5
28 [a]2 Kin 11:16; 2 Chr 23:15; Jer 31:40
29 [1]Lit *him*
30 [1]Or *cell*
31 [1]Lit *son of* [2]Or *Mustering* [a]Neh 3:8, 32
32 [a]Neh 3:1; 12:39
4:1 [1]Ch 3:33 in Heb [a]Neh 2:10
2 [1]Or *army* [2]Lit *heaps of dust* [a]Ezra 4:9, 10 [b]Neh 4:10
3 [1]Lit *go up* [a]Lam 5:18
4 [a]Ps 123:3, 4 [b]Ps 79:12
5 [1]Lit *cover* [2]Lit *offended against* [a]Ps 69:27, 28; Jer 18:23
6 [1]Lit *heart*
7 [1]Ch 4:1 in Heb [2]Lit *healing*
8 [a]Ps 83:3
9 [a]Neh 4:11
10 [1]Lit *Judah said* [2]Lit *dust*
12 [1]So Gr; Heb omits *they...up*
13 [1]Lit *bare* [a]Neh 4:17, 18
14 [a]Num 14:9; Deut 1:29, 30 [b]2 Sam 10:12

1923–25. Excavations at the base of the tower in 1978 revealed a level dating to the Persian era.

3:27 *Tekoites.* The common people of Tekoa did double duty, whereas the nobles of Tekoa shirked their responsibility (see note on v. 5).

3:28 *Horse Gate.* Where Athaliah was slain (2 Chr 23:15). It may have been the easternmost point in the city wall—a gate through which one could reach the Kidron Valley (Jer 31:40).

3:29 *East Gate.* May have been the predecessor of the present Golden Gate.

3:31 *goldsmiths.* See v. 8. *Inspection Gate.* In the northern part of the eastern wall.

3:32 *Sheep Gate.* Back to the point of departure (see v. 1).

4:2 *He . . . said.* Disputes between rival Persian governors were frequent. Sanballat asked several derisive questions to taunt the Jews and to discourage them in their efforts. *burned.* Fire had damaged the stones, which were probably limestone, and had caused many of them to crack and crumble.

4:3 *fox.* See Judg 15:4; Song 2:15. The Hebrew for this word may also mean "jackal." The jackal normally hunts in packs, whereas the fox is usually a nocturnal and solitary animal.

4:4–5 As in the so-called imprecatory psalms (Ps 79:12; 83; 94:1–3; 109:14; 137:7–9), Nehemiah does not himself take action against his opponents but calls down on them redress from God. In v. 5 Nehemiah's prayer echoes the language of Jer 18:23.

4:7 *Ashdodites.* See note on Is 20:1. Ashdod became a district capital under Persian rule.

4:9 *prayed . . . set up a guard.* Prayer and watchfulness blend faith and action, and also emphasize both the divine side and the human side.

4:10 *failing.* The picture is of a worker staggering under the weight of his load and ready to fall at any step.

4:11 *Our enemies said.* Either Nehemiah had friendly informants, or the enemy was spreading unsettling rumors.

4:12 *ten times.* Many times.

4:13 *lowest parts . . . exposed places.* Nehemiah posted men conspicuously in the areas that were the most vulnerable along the wall. *spears.* Used as thrusting weapons (Num 25:7–8; 1 Kin 18:28).

4:14 *Do not be afraid of them; remember the Lord.* See note on 1:8. The best way to dispel fear is to remember the Lord, who alone is to be feared (see Deut 3:22; 20:3; 31:6).

known to us, and that [a]God had frustrated
their plan, then all of us returned to the wall,
each one to his work.
16 From that day on, half of my servants
carried on the work while half of them held
the spears, the shields, the bows and the
breastplates; and the captains *were* behind
the whole house of Judah.
17 Those who were rebuilding the wall
and those who carried burdens took *their*
load with one hand doing the work and the
other holding a weapon.
18 As for the builders, each *wore* his
sword girded at his side as he built, while
[1]the trumpeter *stood* near me.
19 I said to the nobles, the officials and
the rest of the people, "The work is great and
extensive, and we are separated on the wall
far from one another.
20 "At whatever place you hear the sound
of the trumpet, [1]rally to us there. [a]Our God
will fight for us."
21 So we carried on the work with half of
them holding spears from [1]dawn until the
stars [2]appeared.
22 At that time I also said to the people,
"Let each man with his servant spend the
night within Jerusalem so that they may be a
guard for us by night and a laborer by day."
23 So neither I, my brothers, my servants,
nor the men of the guard who followed me,
none of us removed our clothes, each *took*
his weapon *even to* the water.

Usury Abolished

5 Now [a]there was a great outcry of the
people and of their wives against their
[b]Jewish brothers.
2 For there were those who said, "We, our
sons and our daughters are many; therefore
let us [a]get grain that we may eat and live."
3 There were others who said, "We are
mortgaging our fields, our vineyards and our
houses that we might get grain because of
the famine."
4 Also there were those who said, "We
have borrowed money [a]for the king's tax *on*
our fields and our vineyards.
5 "Now [a]our flesh is like the flesh of our
brothers, our children like their children. Yet
behold, [b]we are forcing our sons and our
daughters to be slaves, and some of our

15 [a]2 Sam 17:14 **18** [1]Lit *he who sounded the trumpet* **20** [1]Lit *assemble yourselves* [a]Ex 14:14; Deut 1:30 **21** [1]Lit *rising of the dawn* [2]Lit *came out*

5:1 [a]Lev 25:35 [b]Deut 15:7 **2** [a]Hag 1:6 **4** [a]Ezra 4:13; 7:24 **5** [a]Gen 37:27 [b]Lev 25:39

4:16 *shields.* Made primarily of wood or wickerwork and therefore combustible (Ezek 39:9). *breastplates.* The Hebrew for this word designated primarily a breastplate of metal or a coat of mail (see 2 Chr 18:33).
4:17 *with one hand doing the work and the other holding a weapon.* Means either that the workers carried their materials with one hand and their weapons with the other, or simply that the weapons were kept close at hand.
4:18 *trumpeter.* See note on Is 18:3; see also Josh 6:4,6,8,13.
4:20 *Our God will fight for us.* For the concept of holy war, in which God fights for His people, see Josh 10:14,42; Judg 4:14; 20:35; 2 Sam 5:24; see also essay, p. 271.
4:21 *until the stars appeared.* Indicates the earnestness of their efforts, since the usual time to stop working was at sunset (Deut 24:15; Matt 20:8).
4:22 *guards for us by night.* Even men from outside Jerusalem stayed in the city at night so that some of them could serve as sentries.
4:23 Constant preparedness was the rule. According to Josephus (*Antiquities,* 11.5.8), Nehemiah "himself made the rounds of the city by night, never tiring either through work or lack of food and sleep, neither of which he took for pleasure but as a necessity."
5:1–19 During his major effort to rebuild the walls of Jerusalem, Nehemiah faced an economic crisis. Since the building of the wall took only 52 days (6:15), it is surprising that Nehemiah called a "great assembly" (v. 7) in the midst of such a project. Perhaps the economic pressures created by the rebuilding program brought to light problems that had long been simmering and that had to be dealt with before work could proceed. Among the classes affected by the economic crisis were (1) the landless, who were short of food (v. 2); (2) the landowners, who were compelled to mortgage their properties (v. 3); (3) those forced to borrow money at exorbitant interest rates and sell their children into slavery (vv. 4–5).
5:1 *wives.* The situation was so serious that the wives joined in the protest as they ran short of funds and supplies to feed their families. They complained not against the foreign authorities but against their own countrymen who were taking advantage of their poorer brothers at a time when all were needed for the defense of the country.
5:2 *grain.* About six to seven bushels would be needed for a man to feed his family for a month.
5:3 *mortgaging.* Even those who had considerable property were forced to mortgage it, benefiting the wealthy few (cf. Is 5:8). In times of economic stress the rich got richer, and the poor got poorer. *famine.* The economic situation was aggravated by the natural conditions that had produced a famine. Some 75 years earlier the prophet Haggai had referred to a time of drought, when food was insufficient (Hag 1:5–11). Such times of distress were considered to be expressions of God's judgment (Is 51:19; Jer 14:13–18; Amos 4:6). Famines were common in Canaan. They occurred in the time of Abraham (Gen 12:10), Isaac (Gen 26:1), Joseph (Gen 41:27,54), Ruth (Ruth 1:1), David (2 Sam 21:1), Elijah (1 Kin 18:2), Elisha (2 Kin 4:38) and Claudius (Acts 11:28).
5:4 *tax.* It is estimated that the Persian king collected the equivalent of 20 million darics a year in taxes. Little was ever returned to benefit the provinces, because most of it was melted down and stored as bullion. Alexander the Great found at Susa alone 9,000 talents (about 340 tons) of coined gold and 40,000 talents (about 1,500 tons) of silver stored as bullion. As coined money was increasingly taken out of circulation by taxes, poverty increased dramatically. The acquisition of land by the Persians and its removal from production also helped produce a 50 percent rise in prices during the Persian period.
5:5 *slaves.* In times of economic distress families would borrow funds, using family members as collateral. If a man could not repay the loan and its interest, his children, his wife, or even the man himself could be sold into bondage. An Israelite who fell into debt, however, would serve his creditor as a "hired man" (Lev 25:39–40). He was to be released in the seventh year (Deut 15:12–18), unless he chose to stay voluntarily. During the seven-year famine in Egypt, Joseph was approached by people who asked him to accept their land and their bodies in exchange for food (Gen 47:18–19). The irony for the Israelites was that at least as exiles in Mesopotamia their families were together, but now, because of dire economic necessity, their children were being sold into slavery.

daughters are forced into bondage *already,* and [1]we are helpless because our fields and vineyards belong to others."

6 Then I was very [a]angry when I had heard their outcry and these words.

7 I consulted with myself and contended with the nobles and the rulers and said to them, "[a]You are exacting usury, each from his brother!" Therefore, I held a great assembly against them.

8 I said to them, "We according to our ability [a]have [1]redeemed our Jewish brothers who were sold to the nations; now would you even sell your brothers that they may be sold to us?" Then they were silent and could not find a word *to say.*

9 Again I said, "The thing which you are doing is not good; should you not walk in the fear of our God because of [a]the reproach of the nations, our enemies?

10 "And likewise I, my brothers and my servants are lending them money and grain. Please, let us leave off this usury.

11 "Please, give back to them this very day their fields, their vineyards, their olive groves and their houses, also the hundredth *part* of the money and of the grain, the new wine and the oil that you are exacting from them."

12 Then they said, "We [a]will give *it* back and [b]will require nothing from them; we will do exactly as you say." So I called the priests and [c]took an oath from them that they would do according to this [1]promise.

13 I [a]also shook out the [1]front of my garment and said, "Thus may God shake out every man from his house and from his possessions who does not fulfill this [2]promise; even thus may he be shaken out and emptied." And [b]all the assembly said, "Amen!" And they praised the LORD. Then the people did according to this [2]promise.

Nehemiah's Example

14 Moreover, from the day that I was appointed to be their governor in the land of Judah, from [a]the twentieth year to the [b]thirty-second year of King Artaxerxes, *for* twelve years, neither I nor my [1]kinsmen have eaten the governor's food *allowance.*

15 But the former governors who were before me [1]laid burdens on the people and took from them bread and wine besides forty shekels of silver; even their servants domineered the people. But I did not do so [a]because of the fear of God.

16 I also [1]applied myself to the work on this wall; we did not buy any land, and all my servants were gathered there for the work.

17 Moreover, [a]*there were* at my table one hundred and fifty Jews and officials, besides those who came to us from the nations that were around us.

18 Now [a]that which was prepared for each day was one ox *and* six choice sheep, also birds were prepared for me; and once in ten days all sorts of wine *were furnished* in

5 [1]Lit *there is not the power in our hands*
6 [a]Ex 11:8
7 [a]Ex 22:25; Lev 25:36; Deut 23:19, 20
8 [1]Lit *bought* [a]Lev 25:48
9 [a]Neh 4:4
12 [1]Lit *word* [a]2 Chr 28:15 [b]Neh 10:31 [c]Ezra 10:5
13 [1]Lit *bosom* [2]Lit *word* [a]Acts 18:6 [b]Neh 8:6
14 [1]Lit *brothers* [a]Neh 1:1 [b]Neh 13:6
15 [1]Lit *made heavy* [a]Neh 5:9; Job 31:23
16 [1]Or *held fast*
17 [a]1 Kin 18:19
18 [a]1 Kin 4:22, 23

5:6 *I was very angry.* Sometimes it becomes necessary to express indignation against social injustice (cf. Mark 11:15–18; Eph 4:26).
5:7 *usury.* See notes on Ex 22:25–27; Lev 25:36; Deut 23:20. Josephus (*Antiquities,* 4.8.25) explains: "Let it not be permitted to lend upon usury to any Hebrew either meat or drink; for it is not just to draw a revenue from the misfortunes of a fellow countryman. Rather, in consoling him in his distress, you should reckon as gain the gratitude of such persons and the recompense that God has in store for an act of generosity."
5:8 *Jewish brothers who were sold.* An impoverished brother could be hired as a servant, but he was not to be sold as a slave (Lev 25:39–42). *to the nations.* The sale of fellow Hebrews as slaves to foreigners was forbidden (Ex 21:8). *were silent.* Their guilt was so obvious that they had no rebuttal or excuse (cf. John 8:7–10).
5:9 *not good.* Failure to treat others, especially fellow believers, with compassion is an insult to our Maker and a blot on our testimony (cf. Prov 14:31; 1 Pet 2:12–15).
5:10 *let us leave off this usury.* The OT condemns the greed that seeks a profit at the expense of people (Ps 119:36; Is 56:9–12; 57:17; Jer 6:13; 8:10; 22:13–17; Ezek 22:12–13; 33:31). In view of the economic crisis facing his people, Nehemiah urges the creditors to relinquish their rights to repayment with interest.
5:11 *grain, the new wine and the oil.* See notes on 10:37; Deut 7:13.
5:13 *shook out the front of my garment.* Symbolizing the solemnity of an oath and reinforcing the attendant curses for its nonfulfillment. *Amen!* See 8:6; Num 5:22; see also note on Deut 27:15.
5:14 *thirty-second year.* From Apr. 1, 433 B.C., to Apr. 19, 432. Nehemiah served his first term as governor for 12 years before being recalled to court (13:6), after which he returned to Jerusalem (13:7) for a second term whose length cannot be determined. *governor's food allowance.* See v. 18. Provincial governors normally assessed the people in their provinces for their support. But Nehemiah, like Paul (1 Cor 9; 2 Thess 3:8–9), sacrificed even what was normally his in order to serve as an example to the people.
5:15 *governors.* The Hebrew for this word is used of Sheshbazzar (Ezra 5:14) and Zerubbabel (Hag 1:1,14; 2:2) as well as of various Persian officials (Ezra 5:3,6; 6:6–7,13; 8:36; Neh 2:7,9; 3:7). Nehemiah was not referring here to men of the caliber of Zerubbabel. Some believe that Judah did not have governors before Nehemiah and that the reference here is to governors of Samaria. But new archaeological evidence, in the form of seals and seal impressions, confirms the reference to the previous governors of Judah. *burdens.* It was customary Persian practice to exempt temple personnel from taxation, which increased the burden on lay people. *servants.* If the governors themselves used extortion, their underlings often proved even more oppressive (cf. Matt 18:21–35; 20:25–28). *fear of God.* Those in high positions are in danger of abusing their authority over their subordinates if they forget that they themselves are servants of a superior "Master in heaven" (Col 4:1; cf. Gen 39:9; 2 Cor 5:11).
5:16 *did not buy any land.* Nehemiah's behavior as governor was guided by principles of service rather than by opportunism.
5:17 *at my table.* As part of his social responsibility, a ruler or governor was expected to entertain lavishly. A text found at Nimrud has Ashurnasirpal II feeding 69,574 guests at a banquet for ten days. When Solomon dedicated the temple, he sacrificed 22,000 cattle and 120,000 sheep and goats, and held a great festival for the assembly for 14 days (1 Kin 8:62–65). We are not told how many he fed (cf. 1 Kin 4:27).
5:18 *each day.* The meat listed here would provide one meal

abundance. Yet for all this [b]I did not demand
the governor's food *allowance*, because the
servitude was heavy on this people.
19 [a]Remember me, O my God, for good,
according to all that I have done for this people.

The Enemy's Plot

6 Now when it was reported to Sanballat,
Tobiah, to Geshem the Arab and to the
rest of our enemies that I had rebuilt the
wall, and *that* no breach remained in it,
[a]although at that time I had not set up the
doors in the gates,
2 then Sanballat and Geshem sent *a message* to me, saying, "Come, let us meet
together at [1]Chephirim in the plain of [a]Ono."
But they were planning to [2]harm me.
3 So I sent messengers to them, saying,
"I am doing a great work and I cannot come
down. Why should the work stop while I
leave it and come down to you?"
4 They sent *messages* to me four times in
this manner, and I answered them in the
same way.
5 Then Sanballat sent his servant to me
in the same manner a fifth time with an open
letter in his hand.
6 In it was written, "It is reported among
the nations, and [1]Gashmu says, that [a]you
and the Jews are planning to rebel; therefore
you are rebuilding the wall. And you are to
be their king, according to these reports.
7 "You have also appointed prophets to
proclaim in Jerusalem concerning [1]you, 'A
king is in Judah!' And now it will be reported to the king according to these reports. So
come now, let us take counsel together."
8 Then I sent *a message* to him saying,
"Such things as you are saying have not been
done, but you are [a]inventing them [1]in your
own mind."
9 For all of them were *trying* to frighten
us, [1]thinking, "[2]They will become discouraged with the work and it will not be done."
But now, [a]*O God,* strengthen my hands.
10 When I entered the house of Shemaiah
the son of Delaiah, son of Mehetabel, [a]who
was [1]confined at home, he said, "Let us meet
together in the house of God, within the temple, and let us close the doors of the temple,
for they are coming to kill you, and they are
coming to kill you at night."
11 But I said, "[a]Should a man like me flee?
And could one such as I go into the temple
[1]to save his life? I will not go in."
12 Then I perceived [1]that surely God had
not sent him, but he uttered *his* prophecy
against me because Tobiah and Sanballat
had hired him.
13 He was hired for this reason, [a]that I
might become frightened and act according-

18 [b]2 Thess 3:8
19 [a]Neh 13:14, 22, 31
6:1 [a]Neh 3:1, 3
2 [1]Another reading is, one of *the villages* [2]Lit *do evil to me* [a]1 Chr 8:12
6 [1]In v 1 and elsewhere, *Geshem* [a]Neh 2:19
7 [1]Lit *you, saying*
8 [1]Lit *from your heart* [a]Job 13:4; Ps 52:2
9 [1]Lit *saying,* [2]Lit *Their hands will drop from* [a]Ps 138:3
10 [1]Lit *shut up* [a]Jer 36:5
11 [1]Lit *and live* [a]Prov 28:1
12 [1]Lit *and behold God*
13 [a]Neh 6:6

for 600–800 persons, including the 150 Jews and officials of v. 17. Cf. Solomon's provisions for one day (1 Kin 4:22–23). *choice sheep.* Cf. Mal 1:8. *birds.* Poultry. Chickens were domesticated in the Indus River Valley by 2000 B.C. and were brought to Egypt by the time of Thutmose III (15th century B.C.). They were known in Mesopotamia and in Greece by the eighth century B.C. The earliest inscriptional evidence for poultry in the land of Canaan is the seal of Jaazaniah (dated c. 600 B.C.), which depicts a fighting rooster.

5:19 *Remember me.* See note on 1:8; cf. Heb 6:10. Perhaps Nehemiah's memoirs (see Introduction to Ezra: Literary Form and Authorship) were inscribed as a memorial that was set up in the temple. A striking parallel to Nehemiah's prayer is found in a prayer of Nebuchadnezzar: "O Marduk, my lord, do remember my deeds favorably as good [deeds]; may (these) my good deeds be always before your mind."

6:1 *Sanballat, Tobiah, to Geshem.* See notes on 2:10,19.

6:2 *Ono.* Located about seven miles southeast of Joppa near Lod (Lydda; see note on Ezra 2:33), in the westernmost area settled by the returning Jews (Neh 7:37; 11:35). It may have been proposed as neutral territory, but Nehemiah recognized the invitation as a trap (cf. Gen 4:8; Jer 41:1–3).

6:3 Nehemiah's sharp reply may seem like a haughty response to a reasonable invitation, but he correctly discerned the insincerity of his enemies. He refused to be distracted by matters that would divert his energies from rebuilding Jerusalem's wall.

6:4 *four times.* Nehemiah's foes were persistent, but he was equally persistent in resisting them.

6:5 *open letter.* During this period a letter was ordinarily written on a papyrus or leather sheet, which was rolled up, tied with a string and sealed with a clay bulla (seal impression) to guarantee the letter's authenticity. Sanballat apparently wanted the contents of his letter to be made known to the public at large.

6:6 *their king.* The Persian kings did not tolerate the claims of pretenders to kingship, as we can see from the Behistun (Bisitun) inscription of Darius I. In NT times the Roman emperor was likewise suspicious of any unauthorized claims to royalty (John 19:12; cf. Matt 2:1–13).

6:8 *Such things . . . you are inventing.* Nehemiah does not mince words. He calls the report a lie. He may have sent his own messenger to the Persian king to assure him of his loyalty.

6:9 *They will become discouraged with the work.* Lit. "Their hands will get too weak for the work," figurative language to express the idea of discouragement. The Hebrew for this phrase is used also in Ezra 4:4; Jer 38:4, as well as on an ostracon from Lachish dated c. 588 B.C.

6:10 *Shemaiah . . . was confined.* Perhaps as a symbolic action to indicate that his own life was in danger and to suggest that both Nehemiah and he must flee to the temple (for other symbolic actions see 1 Kin 22:11; Is 20:2–4; Jer 27:2–7; 28:10–11; Ezek 4:1–17; 12:3–11; Acts 21:11). Since Shemaiah had access to the temple, he may have been a priest. He was clearly a friend of Tobiah (cf. v. 12), and therefore Nehemiah's enemy. It was at least credible for Shemaiah to propose that Nehemiah take refuge in the temple area at the altar of asylum (see Ex 21:13–14 and notes), but not in the "house of God," the temple building itself.

6:11 Even if the threat against his life was real, Nehemiah was not a coward who would run into hiding. Nor would he transgress the law to save his life. As a layman, he was not permitted to enter the sanctuary (Num 18:7). When King Uzziah entered the temple to burn incense, he was punished by being afflicted with leprosy (2 Chr 26:16–21).

6:12 The fact that Shemaiah proposed a course of action contrary to God's word revealed him as a false prophet (cf. Deut 18:20; Is 8:19–20; see note on Deut 13:1–5).

6:13 If Nehemiah had wavered in the face of the threat against him, his leadership would have been discredited and morale among the people would have plummeted.

ly and sin, so that they might have an evil report in order that they could reproach me.

14 [a]Remember, O my God, Tobiah and Sanballat according to these works of theirs, and also Noadiah [b]the prophetess and the rest of the prophets who were *trying* to frighten me.

The Wall Is Finished

15 So [a]the wall was completed on the twenty-fifth of *the month* Elul, in fifty-two days.

16 [a]When all our enemies heard *of it,* and all the nations surrounding us saw *it,* they [1]lost their confidence; for [b]they recognized that this work had been accomplished [2]with the help of our God.

17 Also in those days many letters went from the nobles of Judah to Tobiah, and Tobiah's *letters* came to them.

18 For many in Judah were bound by oath to him because he was the son-in-law of Shecaniah the son of Arah, and his son Jehohanan had married the daughter of Meshullam the son of Berechiah.

19 Moreover, they were speaking about his good deeds in my presence and reported my words to him. Then Tobiah sent letters to frighten me.

Census of First Returned Exiles

7 Now when [a]the wall was rebuilt and I had set up the doors, and the gatekeepers and the singers and the Levites were appointed,

2 then I put [a]Hanani my brother, and [b]Hananiah the commander of [c]the fortress, in charge of Jerusalem, for he was [d]a faithful man and feared God more than many.

3 Then I said to them, "Do not let the gates of Jerusalem be opened until the sun is hot, and while they are standing *guard,* let them shut and bolt the doors. Also appoint guards from the inhabitants of Jerusalem, each at his post, and each in front of his own house."

4 Now the city was large and spacious, but the people in it were few and the houses were not built.

5 [a]Then my God put it into my heart to assemble the nobles, the officials and the people to be enrolled by genealogies. Then I found the book of the genealogy of those who came up first [1]in which I found the following record:

6 [a]These are the [1]people of the province who came up from the captivity of the exiles whom Nebuchadnezzar the king of Babylon had carried away, and who returned to Jerusalem and Judah, each to his city,

7 who came with Zerubbabel, Jeshua, Nehemiah, [1]Azariah, [2]Raamiah, Nahamani, Mordecai, Bilshan, [3]Mispereth, Bigvai, [4]Nehum, Baanah.

The number of men of the people of Israel:

8 the sons of Parosh, 2,172;

9 the sons of Shephatiah, 372;

10 the sons of Arah, 652;

11 the sons of Pahath-moab of the sons of Jeshua and Joab, 2,818;

12 the sons of Elam, 1,254;

13 the sons of Zattu, 845;

14 the sons of Zaccai, 760;

15 the sons of [1]Binnui, 648;

16 the sons of Bebai, 628;

17 the sons of Azgad, 2,322;

18 the sons of Adonikam, 667;

19 the sons of Bigvai, 2,067;

20 the sons of Adin, 655;

21 the sons of Ater, of Hezekiah, 98;

22 the sons of Hashum, 328;

23 the sons of Bezai, 324;

24 the sons of [1]Hariph, 112;

25 the sons of [1]Gibeon, 95;

26 the men of Bethlehem and Netophah, 188;

27 the men of Anathoth, 128;

28 the men of [1]Beth-azmaveth, 42;

29 the men of [1]Kiriath-jearim, Chephirah and Beeroth, 743;

30 the men of Ramah and Geba, 621;

31 the men of Michmas, 122;

32 the men of Bethel and Ai, 123;

33 the men of the other Nebo, 52;

34 the sons of the other Elam, 1,254;

35 the sons of Harim, 320;

36 the [1]men of Jericho, 345;

37 the sons of Lod, Hadid and Ono, 721;

38 the sons of Senaah, 3,930.

39 The priests: the sons of Jedaiah of the house of Jeshua, 973;

14 [a]Neh 13:29 [b]Ezek 13:17
15 [a]Neh 4:1, 2
16 [1]Lit *fell exceedingly in their own eyes* [2]Lit *from our God* [a]Neh 2:10; 4:1, 7 [b]Ex 14:25
7:1 [a]Neh 6:1, 15
2 [a]Neh 1:2 [b]Neh 10:23 [c]Neh 2:8 [d]Neh 13:13
5 [a]Prov 2:6; 3:6

5 [1]Lit *and I found written in it*
6 [1]Lit *sons* [a]Ezra 2:1-70
7 [1]In Ezra 2:2, *Seraiah* [2]In Ezra 2:2, *Reelaiah* [3]In Ezra 2:2, *Mispar* [4]In Ezra 2:2, *Rehum*
15 [1]In Ezra 2:10, *Bani*
24 [1]In Ezra 2:18, *Jorah*
25 [1]In Ezra 2:20, *Gibbar*
28 [1]In Ezra 2:24, *Azmaveth*
29 [1]In Ezra 2:25, *Kiriath-arim*
36 [1]Lit *sons*

6:14 *Remember.* See note on 1:8. *prophetess.* See note on Ex 15:20.

6:15 *twenty-fifth of the month Elul.* Oct. 2, 444 B.C. *fifty-two days.* The walls that lay in ruins for nearly a century and a half were rebuilt in less than two months once the people were galvanized into action by Nehemiah's leadership. Archaeological investigations have shown that the circumference of the wall in Nehemiah's day was much reduced. Josephus states (*Antiquities,* 11.5.8) that the rebuilding of the wall took two years and four months, but he is doubtless including such additional tasks as further strengthening of various sections, embellishing and beautifying, and the like. The dedication of the wall is described in 12:27–47.

6:17–18 Tobiah was related to an influential family in Judah, since his son Jehohanan was married to the daughter of Meshullam, who had helped repair the wall of Jerusalem (3:4,30).

7:2 *Hanani my brother, and Hananiah.* Or "Hanani my brother, that is, Hananiah" (see note on 1:2). *fortress.* See notes on 2:8;3:1. *in charge of Jerusalem.* Over Rephaiah and Shallum, who were over sections of the city (3:9,12).

7:3 *until the sun is hot.* Normally the gates would be opened at dawn, but their opening was to be delayed until the sun was high in the heavens to prevent the enemy from making a surprise attack before most of the people were up.

7:6–73 Essentially the same as Ezra 2. See notes there for the nature of the list and the reasons for the numerous variations in names and numbers between the two lists.

7:7 *Nahamani.* Does not occur in Ezra 2:2.

40 the sons of Immer, 1,052;
41 the sons of Pashhur, 1,247;
42 the sons of Harim, 1,017.
43 The Levites: the sons of Jeshua, of Kadmiel, of the sons of [1]Hodevah, 74.
44 The singers: the sons of Asaph, 148.
45 The gatekeepers: the sons of Shallum,
the sons of Ater, the sons of Talmon, the sons
of Akkub, the sons of Hatita, the sons of Shobai, 138.
46 The temple servants: the sons of Ziha,
the sons of Hasupha, the sons of Tabbaoth,
47 the sons of Keros, the sons of [1]Sia, the
sons of Padon,
48 the sons of Lebana, the sons of Haga-
ba, the sons of Shalmai,
49 the sons of Hanan, the sons of Giddel,
the sons of Gahar,
50 the sons of Reaiah, the sons of Rezin,
the sons of Nekoda,
51 the sons of Gazzam, the sons of Uzza,
the sons of Paseah,
52 the sons of Besai, the sons of Meunim,
the sons of [1]Nephushesim,
53 the sons of Bakbuk, the sons of Haku-
pha, the sons of Harhur,
54 the sons of [1]Bazlith, the sons of Mehi-
da, the sons of Harsha,
55 the sons of Barkos, the sons of Sisera,
the sons of Temah,
56 the sons of Neziah, the sons of Hatipha.
57 The sons of Solomon's servants: the
sons of Sotai, the sons of [1]Sophereth, the
sons of [2]Perida,
58 the sons of Jaala, the sons of Darkon,
the sons of Giddel,
59 the sons of Shephatiah, the sons of
Hattil, the sons of Pochereth-hazzebaim, the
sons of [1]Amon.
60 All the temple servants and the sons of
Solomon's servants *were* 392.
61 These *were* they who came up from
Tel-melah, Tel-harsha, Cherub, [1]Addon and
Immer; but they could not show their
fathers' houses or their [2]descendants,
whether they were of Israel:
62 the sons of Delaiah, the sons of Tobiah,
the sons of Nekoda, 642.
63 Of the priests: the sons of [1]Hobaiah,
the sons of Hakkoz, the sons of Barzillai,
who took a wife of the daughters of Barzillai,
the Gileadite, and was named after them.
64 These searched *among* their ancestral
registration, but it could not be located;
therefore they were considered unclean *and*
excluded from the priesthood.
65 [a]The [1]governor said to them that they
should not eat from the most holy things
until a priest arose with [b]Urim and Thummim.

Total of People and Gifts

66 The whole assembly together *was*
42,360,
67 besides their male and their female servants, [1]of whom *there were* 7,337; and they
had 245 male and female singers.
68 [1a]Their horses were 736; their mules,
245;
69 *their* camels, 435; *their* donkeys, 6,720.
70 Some from among the heads of fathers'
households gave to the work. The [1a]governor
gave to the treasury 1,000 gold drachmas, 50
basins, 530 priests' garments.
71 Some of the heads of fathers' *house-*
holds gave into the treasury of the work
20,000 gold drachmas and 2,200 silver
minas.
72 That which the rest of the people gave
was 20,000 gold drachmas and 2,000 silver
minas and 67 priests' garments.
73 Now [a]the priests, the Levites, the gatekeepers, the singers, some of the people, the
temple servants and all Israel, lived in their
cities.
[b]And when the seventh month came, the
sons of Israel *were* in their cities.

Ezra Reads the Law

8 And all the people gathered as one man at
the square which was in front of [a]the
Water Gate, and they [1]asked [b]Ezra the scribe
to bring [c]the book of the law of Moses which
the LORD had [2]given to Israel.
2 Then [a]Ezra the priest brought the law
before the assembly of men, women and all
who *could* listen with understanding, on [b]the
first day of the seventh month.
3 He read from it before the square
which was in front of [a]the Water Gate from

43 [1]In Ezra 2:40, *Hodaviah* **47** [1]In Ezra 2:44, *Siaha* **52** [1]In Ezra 2:50, *Nephisim* **54** [1]In Ezra 2:52, *Bazluth* **57** [1]In Ezra 2:55, *Hassophereth* [2]In Ezra 2:55, *Peruda* **59** [1]In Ezra 2:57, *Ami* **61** [1]In Ezra 2:59, *Addan* [2]Lit *seed* **63** [1]In Ezra 2:61, *Habaiah*

65 [1]Heb *Tirshatha*, a Persian title [a]Neh 8:9; 10:1 [b]Ex 28:30; Deut 33:8 **67** [1]Lit *these* **68** [1]So with some ancient mss and Gr [a]Ezra 2:66 **70** [1]Heb *Tirshatha*, a Persian title [a]Neh 7:65; 8:9 **73** [a]1 Chr 9:2 [b]Ezra 3:1 **8:1** [1]Lit *said to* [2]Lit *commanded* [a]Neh 3:26 [b]Ezra 7:6 [c]2 Chr 34:15 **2** [a]Deut 31:9-11; Neh 8:9 [b]Lev 23:24 **3** [a]Neh 8:1

7:43 *74.* See note on Ezra 2:40.
7:70 *drachmas.* See note on Ezra 2:69.
7:73 *lived in their cities.* See note on Ezra 2:70. *seventh month.* October-November, 444 B.C.
8:1–18 According to the traditional view, the reading of the Law by Ezra would be the first reference to him in almost 13 years since his arrival in 458 B.C. Since he was commissioned to teach the Law (Ezra 7:6,10,14,25–26), it is surprising that there was such a long delay in its public proclamation.
8:1 *all the people gathered.* See Ezra 3:1, which also refers to an assembly called in the seventh month (Tishri), the beginning of the civil year (see chart, p. 92). *square . . . in front of the Water Gate.* See vv. 3,16; see also notes on 3:26; Ezra 10:9. Squares were normally located near a city gate (2 Chr 32:6). *scribe.* See note on Ezra 7:6. *book of the law of Moses.* Cf. vv. 2–3,5,8–9,13–15,18. Four views have been proposed concerning the extent of this book: (1) a collection of legal materials, (2) the priestly laws of Exodus and Leviticus, (3) the laws of Deuteronomy, (4) the Pentateuch. Surely Ezra could have brought back with him the Torah, i.e., the entire Pentateuch.
8:2 *women.* See 10:28. Women did not usually participate in assemblies (see note on Ex 10:11), but were brought, together with children, on such solemn occasions (Deut 31:12; Josh 8:35; 2 Kin 23:2). *first day of the seventh month.* Oct. 8, 444 B.C.; the New Year's Day of the civil calendar (see note on Lev 23:24), celebrated as the Feast of Trumpets (Num 29:1–6), with cessation of labor and a sacred assembly.
8:3 *read from it.* See Ex 24:7; Acts 8:30. *from early morning until*

[1]early morning until midday, in the presence of men and women, those who could understand; and all the people were attentive to the book of the law.

4 Ezra the scribe stood at a wooden podium which they had made for the purpose. And beside him stood Mattithiah, Shema, Anaiah, Uriah, Hilkiah, and Maaseiah on his right hand; and Pedaiah, Mishael, Malchijah, Hashum, Hashbaddanah, Zechariah *and* Meshullam on his left hand.

5 Ezra opened [a]the book in the sight of all the people for he was standing above all the people; and when he opened it, all the people [b]stood up.

6 Then Ezra blessed the LORD the great God. And all the people answered, "[a]Amen, Amen!" while lifting up their hands; then [b]they bowed low and worshiped the LORD with *their* faces to the ground.

7 Also Jeshua, Bani, Sherebiah, Jamin, Akkub, Shabbethai, Hodiah, Maaseiah, Kelita, Azariah, Jozabad, Hanan, Pelaiah, the Levites, explained the law to the people while the people *remained* in their place.

8 They read from the book, from the law of God, [1]translating to give the sense so that they understood the reading.

"This Day Is Holy"

9 Then Nehemiah, who was the [1a]governor, and Ezra [b]the priest *and* scribe, and the Levites who taught the people said to all the people, "[c]This day is holy to the LORD your God; [d]do not mourn or weep." For all the people were weeping when they heard the words of the law.

10 Then he said to them, "Go, eat of the fat, drink of the sweet, and [a]send portions to him who has nothing prepared; for this day is holy to our Lord. Do not be grieved, for the joy of the LORD is your strength."

11 So the Levites calmed all the people, saying, "Be still, for the day is holy; do not be grieved."

12 All the people went away to eat, to drink, [a]to send portions and to [1]celebrate a great festival, [b]because they understood the words which had been made known to them.

Feast of Booths Restored

13 Then on the second day the heads of fathers' *households* of all the people, the priests and the Levites were gathered to Ezra the scribe that they might gain insight into the words of the law.

14 They found written in the law how the LORD had commanded through Moses that the sons of Israel [a]should live in booths during the feast of the seventh month.

15 [1a]So they proclaimed and circulated a proclamation in all their cities and [b]in Jerusalem, saying, "[c]Go out to the hills, and bring olive branches and [2]wild olive branches, myrtle branches, palm branches and branches of *other* leafy trees, to make booths, as it is written."

3 [1]Lit *the light*
5 [a]Neh 8:3 [b]Judg 3:20; 1 Kin 8:12-14
6 [a]Neh 5:13 [b]Ex 4:31
8 [1]Or *explaining*
9 [1]Heb *Tirshatha*, a Persian title [a]Neh 7:65, 70 [b]Neh 12:26 [c]Neh 8:2
9 [a]Deut 12:7, 12
10 [a]Deut 26:11-13
12 [1]Lit *make a great rejoicing* [a]Neh 8:10 [b]Neh 8:7, 8
14 [a]Lev 23:34, 40, 42
15 [1]Lit *And that they will cause to be heard* [2]Lit *oil tree*, species unknown [a]Lev 23:4 [b]Deut 16:16 [c]Lev 23:40

midday. The people evidently stood (vv. 5,7) for five or six hours, listening attentively to the reading and exposition (vv. 7–8,12) of the Scriptures.

8:5 *book.* Scroll (see note on Ex 17:14). *all the people stood up.* The rabbis deduced from this verse that the congregation should stand for the reading of the Torah. It is customary in Eastern Orthodox churches for the congregation to stand throughout the service.

8:6 *lifting up their hands.* See Ex 9:29 and note; Ps 28:2; 134:2; 1 Tim 2:8. *Amen, Amen!* See notes on Deut 27:15; Rom 1:25. The repetition conveys the intensity of feeling behind the affirmation (for other repetitions see Gen 22:11 and note; cf. 2 Kin 11:14; Luke 23:21). *worshiped.* In its original sense the Hebrew for this verb meant "to prostrate oneself on the ground," as the frequently accompanying phrase "to the ground" indicates. Private acts of worship often involved prostration "to the ground," as in the case of Abraham's servant (Gen 24:52), Moses (Ex 34:8), Joshua (Josh 5:14) and Job (Job 1:20). There are three cases of spontaneous communal worship in Exodus (4:31; 12:27; 33:10). In 2 Chr 20:18 Jehoshaphat and the people "fell down before the LORD, worshiping the LORD" when they heard His promise of victory.

8:7 *explained.* See v. 8; Ezra 8:16 and note; Ps 119:34,73,130; Is 40:14.

8:8 *read.* See note on v. 3. *translating.* Rabbinic tradition understands the Hebrew for this expression as referring to translation from Hebrew into an Aramaic Targum. But there is no evidence of Targums (free Aramaic translations of OT books or passages) from such an early date. The earliest extensive Targum is one on Job from Qumran, dated c. 150–100 B.C. Targums exist for every book of the OT except Daniel and Ezra-Nehemiah. *understood.* See v. 12.

8:9 *Nehemiah . . . Ezra.* An explicit reference showing that they were contemporaries (see 12:26,36). *do not mourn.* See Ezra 10:6 and note; Esth 9:22; Is 57:18–19; Jer 31:13. *weep.* See 1:4; Ezra 3:13 and note; 10:1.

8:10 *eat of the fat.* Delicious festive food prepared with much fat. The fat of sacrificial animals was offered to God as the tastiest element of the burnt offering (Lev 1:8,12), the peace offering (Lev 3:9–10), the sin offering (Lev 4:8–10) and the guilt offering (Lev 7:3–4). The fat was not to be eaten in these cases. *send portions to him who has nothing.* It was customary for God's people to remember the less fortunate on joyous occasions (2 Sam 6:19; Esth 9:22; contrast 1 Cor 11:20–22; James 2:14–16).

8:14 *booths.* See notes on Ex 23:16; Lev 23:34,42; John 7:37.

8:15 *olive.* Widespread in Mediterranean countries. It was growing in Canaan before the conquest (Deut 8:8). Because it takes an olive tree 30 years to mature, its cultivation requires peaceful conditions. *wild olive branches.* Lit. "tree of oil," commonly regarded as the wild olive tree. But this is questionable since the "tree of oil" was used as timber (1 Kin 6:23,31–33), whereas the wood of the wild olive tree would have been of little value for use in the temple's furniture. Also, the wild olive tree contains very little oil. The phrase may refer to a resinous tree like the fir. *myrtle.* Evergreen bushes with a pleasing odor (Is 41:19; 55:13; Zech 1:8,10–11). *palm.* The date palm was common around Jericho (Deut 34:3; 2 Chr 28:15). *other leafy trees.* Cf. Ezek 6:13; 20:28. Later Jewish celebrations of the Feast of Tabernacles include waving the *lulav* (made of branches of palms, myrtles and willows) with the right hand and holding branches of the *ethrog* (a citrus native to Canaan) in the left.

16 So the people went out and brought *them* and made booths for themselves, each [a]on his roof, and in their courts and in the courts of the house of God, and in the square at [b]the Water Gate and in the square at [c]the Gate of Ephraim.

17 The entire assembly of those who had returned from the captivity made booths and lived in [1]them. The sons of Israel [a]had indeed not done so from the days of Joshua the son of Nun to that day. And [b]there was great rejoicing.

18 [a]He read from the book of the law of God daily, from the first day to the last day. And they [b]celebrated the feast seven days, and on [c]the eighth day *there was* a solemn assembly according to the ordinance.

The People Confess Their Sin

9 Now on the twenty-fourth day of [a]this month the sons of Israel assembled [b]with fasting, in sackcloth and with [c]dirt upon them.

2 The [1a]descendants of Israel separated themselves from all foreigners, and stood and [b]confessed their sins and the iniquities of their fathers.

3 While [a]they stood in their place, they read from the book of the law of the LORD their God for a fourth of the day; and for *another* fourth they confessed and worshiped the LORD their God.

4 [a]Now on the Levites' platform stood Jeshua, Bani, Kadmiel, Shebaniah, Bunni, Sherebiah, Bani *and* Chenani, and they cried with a loud voice to the LORD their God.

5 Then the Levites, Jeshua, Kadmiel, Bani, Hashabneiah, Sherebiah, Hodiah, Shebaniah *and* Pethahiah, said, "Arise, bless the LORD your God forever and ever!

O may Your glorious name be blessed
And exalted above all blessing and praise!
6 "[a]You alone are the LORD.
[b]You have made the heavens,
The heaven of heavens with all their host,
The earth and all that is on it,
The seas and all that is in them.
[c]You give life to all of them
And the heavenly host bows down before You.
7 "You are the LORD God,
[a]Who chose Abram
And brought him out from [b]Ur of the Chaldees,
And [c]gave him the name Abraham.
8 "You found [a]his heart faithful before You,
And made a covenant with him
To give *him* the land of the Canaanite,
Of the Hittite and the Amorite,
Of the Perizzite, the Jebusite and the Girgashite—
To give *it* to his [1]descendants.
And You [b]have fulfilled Your promise,
For You are righteous.

9 "[a]You saw the affliction of our fathers in Egypt,
And [b]heard their cry by the [1]Red Sea.
10 "Then You performed [a]signs and wonders against Pharaoh,
Against all his servants and all the people of his land;
For You knew that [b]they acted arrogantly toward them,
And [c]made a name for Yourself as *it is* this day.

16 [a]Jer 32:29 [b]Neh 8:1 [c]2 Kin 14:13; Neh 12:39
17 [1]Lit *the booths* [a]2 Chr 7:8; 8:13 [b]2 Chr 30:21
18 [a]Deut 31:11 [b]Lev 23:36 [c]Num 29:35
9:1 [a]Neh 8:2 [b]Ezra 8:23 [c]1 Sam 4:12
2 [1]Lit *seed* [a]Ezra 10:11; Neh 13:3 [b]Prov 28:13; Jer 3:13
3 [a]Neh 8:4
4 [a]Neh 8:7
6 [a]Deut 6:4; 2 Kin 19:15 [b]Gen 1:1 [c]Col 1:16f
7 [a]Gen 12:1 [b]Gen 11:31 [c]Gen 17:5
8 [1]Lit *seed* [a]Gen 15:6, 18-21 [b]Josh 21:43-45
9 [1]Lit *Sea of Reeds* [a]Ex 3:7 [b]Ex 14:10-14, 31
10 [a]Ex 7:8-12:32 [b]Ex 5:2 [c]Ex 9:16

8:16 *courts of the house of God.* See note on 13:7. The temple that Ezekiel saw in his visions had an outer and an inner court (see diagram, p. 1212). Ezekiel's temple was to some extent patterned after Solomon's, which had an inner court of priests and an outer court (1 Kin 6:36; 7:12; 2 Kin 21:5; 23:12; 2 Chr 4:9; 33:5). The temple of the NT era had a court of the Gentiles and an inner court, which was subdivided into courts of the women, of Israel and of the priests. The Temple Scroll from Qumran has God setting forth in detail an ideal temple. Columns 40–46 describe the outer court as follows: "On the roof of the third story are columns for the constructing of booths for the Feast of Tabernacles, to be occupied by the elders, tribal chieftains and commanders of thousands and hundreds." *Gate of Ephraim.* A gate of the oldest rampart of Jerusalem (see note on 3:6; see also 2 Kin 14:13). It was restored by Nehemiah (12:39).

8:17 *from the days of Joshua . . . to that day.* The phrase does not mean that the Feast of Booths had not been celebrated since Joshua's time, because such celebrations took place after the dedication of Solomon's temple (2 Chr 7:8–10) and after the return of the exiles (Ezra 3:4). What apparently is meant is that the feast had not been celebrated before with such great joy (cf. 2 Chr 30:26; 35:18).

8:18 *assembly.* See Num 29:35.

9:1–37 The ninth chapters of Ezra, Nehemiah and Daniel are devoted to confessions of national sin and to prayers for God's grace.

9:1 *twenty-fourth day.* Oct. 30, 444 B.C.; a day of penance in the spirit of the day of atonement, which was held on the tenth day (Lev 16:29–30). *fasting . . . sackcloth . . . dirt.* See notes on Gen 37:34; Ezra 8:23; 10:6; Joel 1:13–14.

9:3 *fourth of the day.* About three hours.

9:5–37 One of the most beautiful prayers outside the Psalms, it reviews God's grace and power (1) in creation (v. 6), (2) in the Abrahamic covenant (vv. 7–8), (3) in Egypt and at the Red Sea (vv. 9–11), (4) in the wilderness and at Sinai (vv. 12–21), (5) during the conquest of Canaan (vv. 22–25), (6) through the judges (vv. 26–28), (7) through the prophets (vv. 29–31) and (8) in the present situation (vv. 32–37). Cf. Ps 78; 105–106.

9:6 *You alone are the LORD.* Though not in the words of Deut 6:4, which expresses the central monotheistic conviction of Israel's faith, the prayer begins with a similar affirmation (cf. 2 Kin 19:15; Ps 86:10). *heaven of heavens.* See Deut 10:14; 1 Kin 8:27; 2 Chr 2:6; Ps 148:4. *heavenly host bows down before You.* See Ps 89:5–7.

9:7 *Ur of the Chaldees.* See note on Gen 11:28. *gave him the name Abraham.* See note on Gen 17:5.

9:8 *faithful.* Compare Rom 4:16–22 with James 2:21–23. *made a covenant with him.* See note on Gen 15:18. *Canaanite . . . Girgashite.* See notes on Gen 10:6,15–18; 13:7; Ex 3:8; Ezra 9:1.

9:9 *Red Sea.* See notes on Ex 13:18; 14:2.

11 "[a]You divided the sea before them,
So they passed through the midst of the sea on dry ground;
And [b]their pursuers You hurled into the depths,
Like a stone into [1]raging waters.
12 "And with a pillar of cloud [a]You led them by day,
And with a pillar of fire by night
To light for them the way
In which they were to go.
13 "Then [a]You came down on Mount Sinai,
And [b]spoke with them from heaven;
You gave them [c]just ordinances and true laws,
Good statutes and commandments.
14 "So You made known to them [a]Your holy sabbath,
And laid down for them commandments, statutes and law,
Through Your servant Moses.
15 "You [a]provided bread from heaven for them for their hunger,
You [b]brought forth water from a rock for them for their thirst,
And You [c]told them to enter in order to possess
The land which You [1]swore to give them.

16 "But they, our fathers, [a]acted arrogantly;
They [1b]became stubborn and would not listen to Your commandments.
17 "They refused to listen,
And [a]did not remember Your wondrous deeds which You had performed among them;
So they became stubborn and [b]appointed a leader to return to their slavery [1]in Egypt.
But You are a God [c]of forgiveness,
Gracious and compassionate,
Slow to anger and abounding in lovingkindness;
And You did not forsake them.
18 "Even when they [a]made for themselves
A calf of molten metal
And said, 'This is your God
Who brought you up from Egypt,'
And committed great [1]blasphemies,
19 [a]You, in Your great compassion,
Did not forsake them in the wilderness;
[b]The pillar of cloud did not leave them by day,
To guide them on their way,
Nor the pillar of fire by night, to light for them the way in which they were to go.
20 "[a]You gave Your good Spirit to instruct them,
Your manna You did not withhold from their mouth,
And You gave them water for their thirst.
21 "Indeed, [a]forty years You provided for them in the wilderness *and* they were not in want;
Their clothes did not wear out, nor did their feet swell.
22 "You also gave them kingdoms and peoples,
And allotted *them* to them as a [1]boundary.
[a]They took possession of the land of Sihon [2]the king of Heshbon
And the land of Og the king of Bashan.
23 "You made their sons numerous as [a]the stars of heaven,
And You brought them into the land
Which You had told their fathers to enter and possess.
24 "[a]So their sons entered and possessed the land.
And [b]You subdued before them the inhabitants of the land, the Canaanites,
And You gave them into their hand, with their kings and the peoples of the land,
To do with them [1]as they desired.
25 "[a]They captured fortified cities and a [1b]fertile land.
They took possession of [c]houses full of every good thing,
Hewn cisterns, vineyards, olive groves,

11 [1]Lit *strong, mighty* [a]Ex 14:21 [b]Ex 15:1, 5, 10
12 [a]Ex 13:21, 22
13 [a]Ex 19:11, 18-20 [b]Ex 20:1 [c]Ps 19:7-9
14 [a]Ex 16:23; 20:8
15 [1]Lit *lifted up Your hand* [a]Ex 16:4, 14, 15 [b]Ex 17:6; Num 20:7-13 [c]Deut 1:8, 21
16 [1]Lit *stiffened their neck;* so also v 17 [a]Neh 9:10 [b]Deut 1:26-33; 31:27; Neh 9:29
17 [1]So Gr and some Heb mss; Heb reads *in their rebellion* [a]Ps 78:11, 42-55 [b]Num 14:4 [c]Ex 34:6, 7; Num 14:18
18 [a]Ex 32:4-8, 31

18 [1]Lit *acts of contempt*
19 [a]Deut 8:2-4; Neh 9:27, 31 [b]Neh 9:12
20 [a]Num 11:17; Neh 9:30; Is 63:11-14
21 [a]Deut 2:7
22 [1]Lit *side, corner* [2]So the Gr and the Latin; Heb reads *and the land of the king of Heshbon* [a]Num 21:21-35
23 [a]Gen 15:5; 22:17
24 [1]Lit *according to their desire* [a]Josh 11:23; 21:43 [b]Josh 18:1
25 [1]Lit *fat* [a]Deut 3:5 [b]Num 13:27 [c]Deut 6:11

9:11 *divided the sea.* See Ex 14:21–22; 1 Cor 10:1.
9:13 *laws.* The singular form of the Hebrew for this word is *Torah,* which means "instruction," "law," and later the Pentateuch, the five books of Moses.
9:14 *holy sabbath.* According to the rabbis, "the Sabbath outweighs all the commandments of the Torah." See 10:31–33; 13:15–22.
9:15 *bread from heaven.* See note on Ex 16:4. *water from a rock.* See note on Ex 17:6. *swore.* See Gen 14:22 and note; 22:15–17; Ex 6:8; Ezek 20:6; 47:14.
9:16 *stubborn.* See vv. 17,29; see also notes on 3:5; Ex 32:9.
9:17 *appointed a leader.* Their intention to do so is recorded in Num 14:4. *Gracious . . . abounding in lovingkindness.* See note on Ex 34:6–7.
9:18 *blasphemies.* See v. 26; Ex 32:4; Ezek 35:12.
9:19 *compassion.* See vv. 27–28; a tender, maternal kind of love (see note on Zech 1:16).
9:20 *Spirit to instruct.* See Ex 31:3.
9:21 *clothes did not wear out.* Evidence of the special providence of God (see Deut 8:4; 29:5; contrast Josh 9:13). *swell.* Or "blister"; the Hebrew for this word occurs only here and in Deut 8:4.
9:22 *Sihon . . . Og.* See Num 21:21–35.
9:23 *numerous as the stars.* See notes on Gen 13:16; 15:5; 22:17.
9:25 See Deut 6:10–12 and note; Josh 24:13. *fertile.* See v. 35; cf. Num 14:7; Deut 8:7; Josh 23:13. *Hewn cisterns.* Because of the lack of rainfall during much of the year, almost every house had its own well or cistern in which to store water from the rainy seasons (2 Kin 18:31; Prov 5:15). By 1200 B.C. the technique

Fruit trees in abundance.
So they ate, were filled and [d]grew fat,
And [e]reveled in Your great goodness.

26 "[a]But they became disobedient and
rebelled against You,
And [b]cast Your law behind their backs
And [c]killed Your prophets who had
[d]admonished them
So that they might return to You,
And [e]they committed great
[1]blasphemies.
27 "Therefore You [a]delivered them into
the hand of their oppressors who
oppressed them,
But when they cried to You [b]in the
time of their distress,
You heard from heaven, and according
to Your great compassion
You [c]gave them deliverers who
delivered them from the hand of
their oppressors.
28 "But [a]as soon as they had rest, they did
evil again before You;
Therefore You abandoned them to the
hand of their enemies, so that they
ruled over them.
When they cried again to You, You
heard from heaven,
And [b]many times You rescued them
according to Your compassion,
29 And [a]admonished them in order to
turn them back to Your law.
Yet [b]they acted arrogantly and did not
listen to Your commandments but
sinned against Your ordinances,
By [c]which if a man observes them he
shall live.
And they [1d]turned a stubborn
shoulder and stiffened their neck,
and would not listen.
30 "[a]However, You bore with them for
many years,
And [b]admonished them by [c]Your
Spirit through Your prophets,
Yet they would not give ear.
Therefore You gave them into the
hand of the peoples of the lands.
31 "Nevertheless, in Your great
compassion You [a]did not make an
end of them or forsake them,
For You are [b]a gracious and
compassionate God.

32 "Now therefore, our God, [a]the great, the
mighty, and the awesome God, who
keeps covenant and lovingkindness,
Do not let all the hardship seem
insignificant before You,
Which has come upon us, our kings,
our princes, our priests, our
prophets, our fathers and on all
Your people,
[b]From the days of the kings of Assyria
to this day.
33 "However, [a]You are just in all that has
come upon us;
For You have dealt faithfully, but we
have acted wickedly.
34 "For our kings, our leaders, our priests
and our fathers have not kept Your
law
Or paid attention to Your
commandments and Your
[1]admonitions with which You have
[2]admonished them.
35 "But [a]they, in their own kingdom,
[b]With Your great goodness which You
gave them,
With the broad and rich land which
You set before them,
Did not serve You or turn from their
evil deeds.
36 "Behold, [a]we are slaves today,
And as to the land which You gave to
our fathers to eat of its fruit and its
bounty,
Behold, we are slaves in it.
37 "[a]Its abundant produce is for the kings
Whom You have set over us because
of our sins;
They also rule over our bodies
And over our cattle as they please,
So we are in great distress.

A Covenant Results

38 "[1]Now because of all this
[a]We are making an agreement in
writing;
And on the [b]sealed document *are the
names of* our leaders, our Levites
and our priests."

Signers of the Document

10 [1]Now on the [a]sealed document *were
the names of:* Nehemiah the [2]governor,
the son of Hacaliah, and Zedekiah,

25 [d]Deut 32:15 [e]1 Kin 8:66
26 [1]Lit *acts of contempt* [a]Judg 2:11 [b]1 Kin 14:9 [c]2 Chr 36:16 [d]Neh 9:30 [e]Neh 9:18
27 [a]Judg 2:14 [b]Deut 4:29 [c]Judg 2:16
28 [a]Judg 3:11 [b]Ps 106:43
29 [1]Lit *gave* [a]Neh 9:26, 30 [b]Neh 9:10, 16 [c]Lev 18:5 [d]Zech 7:11
30 [a]Ps 95:10; Acts 13:18 [b]2 Kin 17:13-18; 2 Chr 36:15, 16; Neh 9:26, 29 [c]Neh 9:20
31 [a]Jer 4:27 [b]Neh 9:17
32 [a]Neh 1:5 [b]2 Kin 15:19, 29; 2 Kin 17:3-6; Ezra 4:2, 10
33 [a]Gen 18:25; Jer 12:1
34 [1]Lit *testimonies* [2]Or *witnessed*
35 [a]Deut 28:47 [b]Neh 9:25
36 [a]Deut 28:48
37 [a]Deut 28:33
38 [1]Ch 10:1 in Heb [a]Neh 10:29 [b]Neh 10:1
10:1 [1]Ch 10:2 in Heb [2]Heb *Tirshatha,* a Persian title [a]Neh 9:38

of waterproofing cisterns was developed, permitting greater occupation of the central hills of Judah. *vineyards, olive groves, Fruit trees.* Cf. Deut 8:8. The Egyptian story of Sinuhe (c. 2000 B.C.) describes Canaan as follows: "Figs were in it, and grapes. It had more wine than water. Plentiful was its honey, abundant its olives. Every (kind of) fruit was on its trees." *grew fat.* Elsewhere the Hebrew for this word always implies physical fullness and spiritual insensitivity.
9:26–28 See note on Judg 2:6–3:6.
9:27 *deliverers.* See Introduction to Judges: Title.
9:29 *if a man observes them he shall live.* See note on Lev 18:5. *they turned a stubborn shoulder.* See Zech 7:11; cf. the similar expressions in v. 16; 3:5; Hos 4:16.
9:32 *kings of Assyria.* Including Tiglath-pileser III, also known as Pul (1 Chr 5:26); Shalmaneser V (2 Kin 18:9); Sargon II (Is 20:1); Sennacherib (2 Kin 18:13); Esarhaddon (Ezra 4:2); and Ashurbanipal (Ezra 4:10).
9:37 *rule over our bodies.* See 1 Sam 8:11–13. The Persian rulers drafted their subjects into military service. Some Jews may have accompanied Xerxes on his invasion of Greece in 480 B.C.
10:1–27 A legal list, bearing the official seal and containing a roster of 84 names.

2 Seraiah, Azariah, Jeremiah,
3 Pashhur, Amariah, Malchijah,
4 Hattush, Shebaniah, Malluch,
5 Harim, Meremoth, Obadiah,
6 Daniel, Ginnethon, Baruch,
7 Meshullam, Abijah, Mijamin,
8 Maaziah, Bilgai, Shemaiah. These *were* the priests.

9 And the Levites: Jeshua the son of Azaniah, Binnui of the sons of Henadad, Kadmiel;

10 also their brothers Shebaniah, Hodiah, Kelita, Pelaiah, Hanan,
11 Mica, Rehob, Hashabiah,
12 Zaccur, Sherebiah, Shebaniah,
13 Hodiah, Bani, Beninu.

14 The leaders of the people: Parosh, Pahath-moab, Elam, Zattu, Bani,
15 Bunni, Azgad, Bebai,
16 Adonijah, Bigvai, Adin,
17 Ater, Hezekiah, Azzur,
18 Hodiah, Hashum, Bezai,
19 Hariph, Anathoth, Nebai,
20 Magpiash, Meshullam, Hezir,
21 Meshezabel, Zadok, Jaddua,
22 Pelatiah, Hanan, Anaiah,
23 Hoshea, Hananiah, Hasshub,
24 Hallohesh, Pilha, Shobek,
25 Rehum, Hashabnah, Maaseiah,
26 Ahiah, Hanan, Anan,
27 Malluch, Harim, Baanah.

Obligations of the Document

28 Now [a]the rest of the people, the priests, the Levites, the gatekeepers, the singers, the temple servants and [b]all those who had separated themselves from the peoples of the lands to the law of God, their wives, their sons and their daughters, all those who had knowledge and understanding,

29 are joining with their [1]kinsmen, their nobles, and are [2][a]taking on themselves a curse and an oath to walk in God's law, which was given through Moses, God's servant, and to keep and to observe all the commandments of [3]GOD our Lord, and His ordinances and His statutes;

30 and [a]that we will not give our daughters to the peoples of the land or take their daughters for our sons.

31 As [a]for the peoples of the land who bring wares or any grain on the sabbath day to sell, we will not buy from them on the sabbath or a holy day; and we will forego *the crops* the [b]seventh year and the [c]exaction of every debt.

32 We also [1]placed ourselves under obligation to contribute yearly [a]one third of a shekel for the service of the house of our God:

33 for the [a]showbread, for the continual grain offering, for the continual burnt offering, the sabbaths, the new moon, for the appointed times, for the holy things and for the sin offerings to make atonement for Israel, and all the work of the house of our God.

34 Likewise [a]we cast lots [b]for the supply of wood *among* the priests, the Levites and the people so that they might bring it to the house of our God, according to our fathers' households, at fixed times annually, to burn on the altar of the LORD our God, as it is written in the law;

35 and that they might bring the first fruits of our ground and [a]the first fruits of all the fruit of every tree to the house of the LORD annually,

36 and [a]bring to the house of our God the firstborn of our sons and of our cattle, and the firstborn of our herds and our flocks as it is written in the law, for the priests who are ministering in the house of our God.

37 [a]We will also bring the first of our [1]dough, our contributions, the fruit of every

28 [a]Ezra 2:36-58 [b]Neh 9:2 **29** [1]Lit *brothers* [2]Lit *entering into a* [a]Neh 5:12 **29** [3]Heb *YHWH,* usually rendered *LORD* **30** [a]Ex 34:16; Deut 7:3 **31** [a]Neh 13:15-22 [b]Ex 23:10, 11; Lev 25:1-7 [c]Deut 15:1, 2 **32** [1]Lit *imposed commandments on us* [a]Ex 30:11-16; Matt 17:24 **33** [a]Lev 24:5, 6; 2 Chr 2:4 **34** [a]Neh 11:1 [b]Neh 13:31 **35** [a]Ex 23:19; 34:26; Deut 26:2 **36** [a]Ex 13:2 **37** [1]Or *coarse meal* [a]Lev 23:17

10:2–8 About half of these names occur again in 12:1–7.
10:9–13 Most of these names appear also in the lists of Levites in 8:7; 9:4–5.
10:14–27 Almost half of the names in this category are also found in the lists of 7:6–63; Ezra 2:1–61.
10:28 *Levites.* See Introduction to Leviticus: Title. *gatekeepers.* See note on Ezra 2:42. *wives . . . sons . . . daughters.* See note on 8:2.
10:31–33 Perhaps a code drawn up by Nehemiah to correct the abuses listed in 13:15–22.
10:31 *on the sabbath day to sell.* Though Ex 20:8–11; Deut 5:12–15 do not explicitly prohibit trading on the sabbath, see Jer 17:19–27; Amos 8:5 and note. *forego the crops the seventh year and . . . every debt.* See note on Lev 25:4. The Romans misrepresented the sabbath and the sabbath year as caused by laziness. According to Tacitus, the Jews "were led by the charms of indolence to give over the seventh year as well to inactivity."
10:32 *third of a shekel.* Ex 30:13–14 speaks of "half a shekel" as a "contribution to the LORD" from each man who was 20 years old or more as a symbolic ransom. Later Joash used the annual contributions for the repair of the temple (2 Chr 24:4–14). In the NT period Jewish men from everywhere sent an offering of a half shekel (actually two drachmas, its equivalent; see Josephus, *Antiquities,* 3.8.2) for the temple in Jerusalem (Matt 17:24). The pledge of a third of a shekel in Nehemiah's time may have been due to economic circumstances.
10:33 *showbread.* See note on Lev 24:8.
10:34 *cast lots.* See notes on 11:1; Jon 1:7. *supply of wood.* Though there is no specific reference to a wood offering in the Pentateuch, the perpetual burning of fire on the sanctuary altar (Lev 6:12–13) would have required a continual supply of wood. Josephus mentions "the festival of wood offering" on the 14th day of the fifth month (Ab). The Jewish Mishnah (rabbinic interpretations and applications of Pentateuchal laws) lists nine times when certain families brought wood, and stipulates that all kinds of wood were suitable except the vine and the olive. The Temple Scroll from Qumran describes the celebration of a wood offering festival for six days following a new oil festival.
10:35 *first fruits.* Brought to the sanctuary to support the priests and Levites (Ex 23:19; Num 18:13; Deut 26:1–11; Ezek 44:30).
10:36 *firstborn.* See note on Ex 13:13.
10:37 *new wine.* See note on Deut 7:13. Though the Hebrew for this term can refer to freshly pressed grape juice (Is 65:8; Mic 6:15), it can also be used of intoxicating wine (Hos 4:11).

tree, the new wine and the oil [b]to the priests
at the chambers of the house of our God, and
the [c]tithe of our ground to the Levites, for
the Levites are they who receive the tithes in
all the rural towns.
38 [a]The priest, the son of Aaron, shall be
with the Levites when the Levites receive
tithes, and the Levites shall bring up the
tenth of the tithes to the house of our God, to
the chambers of [b]the storehouse.
39 For the sons of Israel and the sons of
Levi shall bring the [a]contribution of the
grain, the new wine and the oil to the chambers; there are the utensils of the sanctuary,
the priests who are ministering, the gatekeepers and the singers. Thus [b]we will not
[1]neglect the house of our God.

Time Passes; Heads of Provinces

11 Now [a]the leaders of the people lived in
Jerusalem, but the rest of the people
[b]cast lots to bring one out of ten to live in
Jerusalem, [c]the holy city, while nine-tenths
remained in the *other* cities.
2 And the people blessed all the men
who [a]volunteered to live in Jerusalem.
3 [a]Now these are the heads of the
provinces who lived in Jerusalem, but in the
cities of Judah [b]each lived on his own property in their cities—the [1]Israelites, the
priests, the Levites, the [2c]temple servants
and the [3d]descendants of Solomon's servants.
4 Some of the sons of Judah and some of
the sons of Benjamin lived in Jerusalem.
From the sons of Judah: Athaiah the son of
Uzziah, the son of Zechariah, the son of Amariah, the son of Shephatiah, the son of
Mahalalel, of the sons of Perez;
5 and Maaseiah the son of Baruch, the
son of Col-hozeh, the son of Hazaiah, the
son of Adaiah, the son of Joiarib, the son of
Zechariah, the son of the Shilonite.
6 All the sons of Perez who lived in
Jerusalem were 468 able men.
7 Now these are the sons of Benjamin:
Sallu the son of Meshullam, the son of Joed,
the son of Pedaiah, the son of Kolaiah, the
son of Maaseiah, the son of Ithiel, the son of
Jeshaiah;
8 and after him Gabbai *and* Sallai, 928.
9 Joel the son of Zichri was their overseer, and Judah the son of Hassenuah was
second [1]in command of the city.
10 From the priests: Jedaiah the son of Joiarib, Jachin,
11 Seraiah the son of Hilkiah, the son of
Meshullam, the son of Zadok, the son of
Meraioth, the son of Ahitub, the leader of the
house of God,
12 and their [1]kinsmen who performed the
work of the [2]temple, 822; and Adaiah the son
of Jeroham, the son of Pelaliah, the son of
Amzi, the son of Zechariah, the son of Pashhur, the son of Malchijah,
13 and his kinsmen, heads of fathers'
households, 242; and Amashsai the son of
Azarel, the son of Ahzai, the son of Meshillemoth, the son of Immer,
14 and their brothers, valiant warriors,
128. And their overseer was Zabdiel, the son
of [1]Haggedolim.
15 Now from the Levites: Shemaiah the
son of Hasshub, the son of Azrikam, the son
of Hashabiah, the son of Bunni;
16 and Shabbethai and Jozabad, from the
[1]leaders of the Levites, who were [2]in charge
of [a]the outside work of the house of God;
17 and Mattaniah the son of Mica, the son
of [1]Zabdi, the son of Asaph, who was the
[2]leader in beginning the thanksgiving at
prayer, and Bakbukiah, the second among
his brethren; and [3]Abda the son of [4]Sham-
mua, the son of Galal, the son of Jeduthun.
18 All the Levites in [a]the holy city *were*
284.
19 Also the gatekeepers, Akkub, Talmon
and their brethren who kept watch at the
gates, *were* 172.

Outside Jerusalem

20 The rest of Israel, of the priests *and* of

37 [b]Neh 13:5, 9 [c]Lev 27:30; Num 18:21
38 [a]Num 18:26 [b]Neh 13:12, 13
39 [1]Lit *forsake* [a]Deut 12:6 [b]Neh 13:10, 11
11:1 [a]Neh 7:4 [b]Neh 10:34 [c]Neh 11:18; Is 48:2
2 [a]Judg 5:9
3 [1]Lit *Israel* [2]Heb *Nethinim* [3]Lit *sons* [a]1 Chr 9:2-34 [b]Neh 7:73; 11:20 [c]Ezra 2:43 [d]Neh 7:57

9 [1]Lit *over*
12 [1]Lit *brothers*, and so throughout the ch [2]Lit *house*
14 [1]Or *the great ones*
16 [1]Lit *heads* [2]Lit *over* [a]1 Chr 26:29
17 [1]In 1 Chr 9:15, *Zichri* [2]Lit *head* [3]In 1 Chr 9:16, *Obadiah* [4]In 1 Chr 9:16, *Shemaiah*
18 [a]Neh 11:1

tithe. See notes on Gen 14:20; 28:22; Lev 27:30; Amos 4:4. *chambers.* Rooms in the courts of the temple were used as storage areas for silver, gold and sacred articles (cf. vv. 38–39; 12:44; 13:4–5,9; Ezra 8:28–30). *Levites.* Tithes were meant for their support (13:12–13; Num 18:21–32).

10:39 See 13:11. *we will not neglect.* Haggai (Hag 1:4–9) had accused the people of neglecting the temple.

11:1 *cast lots.* See 10:34. Lots were usually made out of small stones or pieces of wood. Sometimes arrows were used (Ezek 21:21). *one out of ten to live in Jerusalem.* Josephus (*Antiquities,* 11.5.8) asserts: "But Nehemiah, seeing that the city had a small population, urged the priests and Levites to leave the countryside and move to the city and remain there, for he had prepared houses for them at his own expense." The practice of redistributing populations was also used to establish Greek and Hellenistic cities. It involved the forcible transfer from rural settlements to urban centers. Tiberias on the Sea of Galilee was populated with Gentiles by such a process by Herod Antipas in A.D. 18. *holy city.* See Is 48:2 and note; Dan 9:24; Matt 4:5; 27:53; Rev 11:2; cf. Joel 3:17.

11:2 In addition to those chosen by lot (v. 1), some volunteered out of a sense of duty. But evidently most preferred to stay in their hometowns.

11:3–19 A census roster that parallels 1 Chr 9:2–21, a list of the first residents in Jerusalem after the return from Babylonia. About half the names in the two lists are the same.

11:8 *928.* The men of Benjamin provided twice as many men as Judah (v. 6) to live in and protect the city of Jerusalem.

11:9 *second in command.* See 2 Chr 34:22 (in Zeph 1:10 the Hebrew for this phrase is translated "Second Quarter").

11:16 *outside work.* Duties outside the temple (cf. 1 Chr 26:29) but connected with it.

11:17 *Asaph.* See note on Ezra 2:41; see also titles of Ps 50; 73–83. *Jeduthun.* See 1 Chr 16:42; 25:1,3; 2 Chr 5:12; titles of Ps 39; 62; 77.

11:18 *284.* The relatively small number of Levites, compared

the Levites, *were* in all the cities of Judah,
each [a]on his own inheritance.
21 But [a]the temple servants were living in
Ophel, and Ziha and Gishpa were [1]in charge
of the temple servants.
22 Now [a]the overseer of the Levites in
Jerusalem was Uzzi the son of Bani, the son
of Hashabiah, the son of Mattaniah, the son
of Mica, from the sons of Asaph, who were
the singers for the [1]service of the house of
God.
23 [a]For *there was* a commandment from
the king concerning them and a firm regulation for the song leaders [b]day by day.
24 Pethahiah the son of Meshezabel, of
the sons [a]of Zerah the son of Judah, was the
[b]king's [1]representative in all matters concerning the people.
25 Now as for the villages with their
fields, some of the sons of Judah lived in
[a]Kiriath-arba and its [1]towns, in [b]Dibon and
its [1]towns, and in Jekabzeel and its villages,
26 and in Jeshua, in Moladah and Beth-
pelet,
27 and in Hazar-shual, in Beersheba and
its towns,
28 and in Ziklag, in Meconah and in its
towns,
29 and in En-rimmon, in Zorah and in Jarmuth,
30 Zanoah, Adullam, and their villages,
Lachish and its fields, Azekah and its towns.
So they encamped from Beersheba as far as
the valley of Hinnom.
31 The sons of Benjamin also *lived* from
Geba *onward,* at Michmash and Aija, at
Bethel and its towns,
32 at Anathoth, Nob, Ananiah,
33 Hazor, Ramah, Gittaim,
34 Hadid, Zeboim, Neballat,
35 Lod and Ono, the valley of craftsmen.
36 From the Levites, *some* divisions in
Judah belonged to Benjamin.

Priests and Levites Who Returned to Jerusalem with Zerubbabel

12 Now these are [a]the priests and the
Levites who came up with Zerubbabel
the son of Shealtiel, and Jeshua: Seraiah, Jeremiah, Ezra,
2 Amariah, Malluch, Hattush,
3 Shecaniah, Rehum, Meremoth,
4 Iddo, Ginnethoi, Abijah,
5 Mijamin, Maadiah, Bilgah,
6 Shemaiah and Joiarib, Jedaiah,
7 Sallu, Amok, Hilkiah and Jedaiah.
These were the heads of the priests and their
[1]kinsmen in the days of Jeshua.
8 The Levites *were* Jeshua, Binnui, Kadmiel, Sherebiah, Judah, *and* Mattaniah *who*

20 [a]Neh 11:3
21 [1]Lit *over* [a]Neh 3:26
22 [1]Or *work* [a]Neh 11:9, 14
23 [a]Ezra 6:8; 7:20 [b]Neh 12:47
24 [1]Lit *hand* [a]Gen 38:30 [b]1 Chr 18:17
25 [1]Lit *daughters,* and so throughout the ch [a]Josh 14:15 [b]Josh 13:9, 17
12:1 [a]Ezra 2:1; 7:7
7 [1]Lit *brothers*

with 1,192 priests (the total of 822, 242 and 128 in vv. 12–13), is striking (see note on Ezra 2:40).

11:20 *his own inheritance.* Ancestral property—including land, buildings and movable goods—acquired by either conquest or inheritance (Gen 31:14; Num 18:21; 27:7; 34:2; 36:3; 1 Kin 21:1–4).

11:21 *Ophel.* See note on 3:26.

11:23 *commandment from the king.* David had regulated the services of the Levites, including the singers (1 Chr 25). The Persian king, Darius I, gave a royal stipend so that the Jewish elders might "pray for the life of the king and his sons" (Ezra 6:10). Artaxerxes I may have done much the same for the Levite choir.

11:25–30 An important list, corresponding to earlier lists of towns in Judah. All these names also appear in Josh 15 with the exception of Dibon, Jekabzeel (but see Kabzeel in Josh 15:21), Jeshua, Meconah and En-rimmon (but see Ain and Rimmon in Josh 15:32). The list, however, is not comprehensive, since a number of towns listed in ch. 3; Ezra 2:21–22 are lacking. No Judean coins have been found outside the area designated by vv. 25–30.

11:25 *Kiriath-arba.* See note on Gen 23:2. In the Hellenistic era it fell to the Idumeans, together with other Judean towns.

11:26 *Moladah.* Near Beersheba; later occupied by the Idumeans. *Beth-pelet.* Means "house of refuge," a site near Beersheba.

11:27 *Hazar-shual.* Means "enclosure of a fox" (see 1 Chr 4:28). *Beersheba.* See note on Gen 21:31. Archaeological excavations reveal that the city was destroyed by Sennacherib in 701 B.C. and only resettled in the Persian period.

11:28 *Ziklag.* Given to David by Achish, king of Gath (1 Sam 27:6), and taken by the Amalekites (1 Sam 30:1); see Josh 15:31.

11:29 *En-rimmon.* Means "spring of the pomegranate," probably Khirbet Umm er-Ramamin, nine miles north-northeast of Beersheba (see Josh 15:32). *Zorah.* See note on Judg 13:2. *Jarmuth.* Eight miles north-northeast of Eleutheropolis (Beit Jibrin), it was one of five Canaanite cities in the south that attempted to halt Joshua's invasion (Josh 10:3–5).

11:30 *Zanoah.* A village in the Shephelah district of low hills between Judah and Philistia. The men of Zanoah repaired the Valley Gate (3:13). The site has been identified with Khirbet Zanu, three miles south-southeast of Beth Shemesh. *Adullam.* See note on Gen 38:1. *Lachish.* See Josh 10:3; see also notes on Is 36:2; Mic 1:13. *Azekah.* See note on Jer 34:7. *Hinnom.* The valley west and south of Jerusalem; Gehenna in the NT.

11:31–35 Most of the Benjamite towns listed here appear also in 7:26–38; Ezra 2:23–35.

11:31 *Geba.* See 12:29; see also note on 1 Sam 13:3. *Michmash.* See note on 1 Sam 13:2. *Aija.* An alternate name for Ai (see note on Josh 7:2). *Bethel.* See notes on Gen 12:8; Josh 7:2; Ezra 2:28; Amos 4:4.

11:32 *Anathoth.* See note on Jer 1:1. *Nob.* See note on 1 Sam 21:1. *Ananiah.* Probably Bethany, meaning "house of Ananiah" (see note on Matt 21:17).

11:33 *Gittaim.* Its location is not known.

11:34 *Hadid.* Three to four miles northeast of Lod (see 7:37; Ezra 2:33).

11:35 *Lod.* See note on Ezra 2:33. *Ono.* See note on 6:2. *valley of craftsmen. Ge-harashim* in Hebrew (see 1 Chr 4:14). It may be the broad valley between Lod and Ono. The name may preserve the memory of the Philistine iron monopoly (1 Sam 13:19–20).

12:1 *Zerubbabel the son of Shealtiel.* See Ezra 3:2,8; 5:2; see also note on Hag 1:1. *Jeshua.* Returned from Babylonian exile in 538 B.C. (see vv. 10,26; 7:7; Ezra 2:2 and note; Hag 1:1; Zech 3:1 and note). *Ezra.* Not the Ezra of the book, who was the leader of the exiles who returned 80 years later.

12:7 *heads of the priests.* The rotation of 24 priestly houses was established at the time of David (1 Chr 24:3,7–19). Twenty-two heads of priestly houses are mentioned in vv. 1–7. Inscriptions listing the 24 divisions of the priests probably hung

was [1]in charge of the songs of thanksgiving, he and his brothers.

9 Also Bakbukiah and Unni, their brothers, stood opposite them [a]in *their* service divisions.

10 Jeshua [1]became the father of Joiakim, and Joiakim [1]became the father of Eliashib, and Eliashib [1]became the father of Joiada,

11 and Joiada became the father of Jonathan, and Jonathan became the father of Jaddua.

12 Now in the days of Joiakim, the priests, the heads of fathers' *households* were: of Seraiah, Meraiah; of Jeremiah, Hananiah;

13 of Ezra, Meshullam; of Amariah, Jehohanan;

14 of [1]Malluchi, Jonathan; of Shebaniah, Joseph;

15 of Harim, Adna; of Meraioth, Helkai;

16 of Iddo, Zechariah; of Ginnethon, Meshullam;

17 of Abijah, Zichri; of Miniamin, of Moadiah, Piltai;

18 of Bilgah, Shammua; of Shemaiah, Jehonathan;

19 of Joiarib, Mattenai; of Jedaiah, Uzzi;

20 of Sallai, Kallai; of Amok, Eber;

21 of Hilkiah, Hashabiah; of Jedaiah, Nethanel.

The Chief Levites

22 As for the Levites, the heads of fathers' *households* were registered in the days of Eliashib, Joiada, and Johanan and Jaddua; so *were* the priests in the reign of Darius the Persian.

23 The sons of Levi, the heads of fathers' *households,* were registered in the Book of the Chronicles up to the days of Johanan the son of Eliashib.

24 The heads of the Levites *were* Hashabiah, Sherebiah and Jeshua the son of Kadmiel, with their brothers opposite them, [a]to praise *and* give thanks, [1]as prescribed by David the man of God, [b]division corresponding to division.

25 Mattaniah, Bakbukiah, Obadiah, Meshullam, Talmon *and* Akkub *were* gatekeepers keeping watch at [a]the storehouses of the gates.

26 These *served* in the days of Joiakim the son of Jeshua, the son of Jozadak, and in the days of [a]Nehemiah the governor and of Ezra the priest *and* scribe.

Dedication of the Wall

27 Now at the dedication of the wall of Jerusalem they sought out the Levites from all their places, to bring them to Jerusalem so that they might celebrate the dedication with gladness, with hymns of thanksgiving and with songs [a]*to the accompaniment* of cymbals, harps and lyres.

28 So the sons of the singers were assembled from the district around Jerusalem, and from [a]the villages of the Netophathites,

29 from Beth-gilgal and from *their* fields in Geba and Azmaveth, for the singers had built themselves villages around Jerusalem.

30 The priests and the Levites [a]purified themselves; they also purified the people, the gates and the wall.

8 [1]Lit *over*
9 [a]Neh 12:24
10 [1]Lit *begot,* and so in vv 11, 12
14 [1]In Neh 12:2, *Malluch*

24 [1]Lit *in the commandment of* [a]Neh 11:17 [b]Neh 12:9
25 [a]1 Chr 26:15
26 [a]Neh 8:9
27 [a]1 Chr 15:16, 28
28 [a]1 Chr 9:16
30 [a]Neh 13:22, 30

in many synagogues in the Holy Land. So far, only fragments of two such inscriptions have been recovered—from Ashkelon in the 1920s and from Caesarea in the 1960s (dated to the third and fourth centuries A.D.).

12:9 *opposite them.* See v. 24; Ezra 3:11 and note; cf. 2 Chr 7:6. The singing was antiphonal, with two sections of the choir standing opposite each other. *service divisions.* The Hebrew for this word (*Mishmarot*) is the title of a work from Qumran, which discusses in detail the rotation of the priestly families' service in the temple according to the sect's solar calendar and synchronized with the conventional lunar calendar.

12:10 *Jeshua.* See note on v. 1. *Joiakim.* See vv. 12,26. *Eliashib.* See vv. 22–23; the high priest who assisted in rebuilding the wall (3:1,20–21; 13:28). A priest named Eliashib was guilty of defiling the temple by assigning rooms to Tobiah the Ammonite (13:4,7). It is not known whether this Eliashib was the same as the high priest.

12:11 *Jonathan.* Since v. 22 mentions a Johanan after Joiada and before Jaddua, and v. 23 identifies Johanan as "son" of Eliashib, some believe that "Jonathan" is an error for "Johanan." Further complicating the identification are attempts to identify this high priest with a "Johanan" mentioned in the Elephantine papyri and in Josephus (*Antiquities,* 11.7.1). Such an identification, however, is disputable.

12:12–21 All but one (Hattush, v. 2) of the 22 priestly families listed in vv. 1–7 are repeated (Rehum, v. 3, is a variant of Harim, v. 15; Mijamin, v. 5, is a variant of Miniamin, v. 17) in this later list, which dates to the time of Joiakim (v. 12), high priest in the late sixth and/or early fifth centuries B.C.

12:22 *Darius the Persian.* Either Darius II Nothus (423–404 B.C.) or Darius III Codomannus (336–331).

12:23 *Book of the Chronicles.* Cf. 7:5. This may have been the official temple chronicle, containing various lists and records. Cf. the annals of the Persian kings (Ezra 4:15; Esth 2:23; 6:1; 10:2); cf. also the "Book of the Chronicles of the Kings," mentioned frequently in 1, 2 Kings.

12:26 *Nehemiah . . . Ezra.* See note on 8:9.

12:27 *dedication.* See note on Ezra 6:16. *cymbals.* See note on Ezra 3:10. Cymbals were used in religious ceremonies (1 Chr 16:42; 25:1; 2 Chr 5:12; 29:25). Ancient examples have been found at Beth-shemesh and Tell Abu Hawam. *harps.* See note on Gen 31:27; used mainly in religious ceremonies (1 Sam 10:5; 2 Sam 6:5; Ps 150:3). Ancient harps have been reconstructed from information derived from the remains of harps at Ur, pictures of harps, and cuneiform texts describing in detail the tuning of harps. *lyres.* Had strings of the same length but of different diameters and tensions (see 1 Chr 15:16; Dan 3:5).

12:28 *Netophathites.* From Netophah, a town near Bethlehem (7:26).

12:29 *Beth-gilgal.* Perhaps the Gilgal near Jericho (see note on Josh 4:19), or the Gilgal of Elijah (2 Kin 2:1), about seven miles north of Bethel.

12:30 *purified.* See note on Lev 4:12. The Levites are said to have purified all that was sacred in the temple (1 Chr 23:28) and the temple itself (2 Chr 29:15) during times of revival. Ritual purity was intended to teach God's holiness and moral purity (Lev 16:30).

Procedures for the Temple

31 Then I had the leaders of Judah come up on top of the wall, and I appointed two great [1]choirs, [2a]the first proceeding to the right on top of the wall toward [b]the Refuse Gate.

32 Hoshaiah and half of the leaders of Judah followed them,

33 with Azariah, Ezra, Meshullam,

34 Judah, Benjamin, Shemaiah, Jeremiah,

35 and some of the sons of the priests with trumpets; *and* Zechariah the son of Jonathan, the son of Shemaiah, the son of Mattaniah, the son of Micaiah, the son of Zaccur, the son of Asaph,

36 and his [1]kinsmen, Shemaiah, Azarel, Milalai, Gilalai, Maai, Nethanel, Judah *and* Hanani, [a]with the musical instruments of David the man of God. And Ezra the scribe went before them.

37 At [a]the Fountain Gate they went directly up [b]the steps of the city of David by the stairway of the wall above the house of David to [c]the Water Gate on the east.

38 [a]The second [1]choir proceeded to the [2]left, while I followed them with half of the people on the wall, [b]above the Tower of Furnaces, to [c]the Broad Wall,

39 and above [a]the Gate of Ephraim, by [b]the Old Gate, by the [c]Fish Gate, [d]the Tower of Hananel and the Tower of the Hundred, as far as the Sheep Gate; and they stopped at [e]the Gate of the Guard.

40 Then the two choirs took their stand in the house of God. So did I and half of the officials with me;

41 and the priests, Eliakim, Maaseiah, Miniamin, Micaiah, Elioenai, Zechariah and Hananiah, with the trumpets;

42 and Maaseiah, Shemaiah, Eleazar, Uzzi, Jehohanan, Malchijah, Elam and Ezer. And the singers [1]sang, with Jezrahiah *their* leader,

43 and on that day they offered great sacrifices and rejoiced because [a]God had given them great joy, even the women and children rejoiced, so that the joy of Jerusalem was heard from afar.

44 On that day [a]men were also appointed over the chambers for the stores, the contributions, the first fruits and the tithes, to gather into them from the fields of the cities the portions required by the law for the priests and Levites; for Judah rejoiced over the priests and Levites who [1]served.

45 For they performed the [1]worship of their God and the service of purification, together with the singers and the gatekeepers [a]in accordance with the command of David *and* of his son Solomon.

46 For in the days of David and [a]Asaph, in ancient times, *there were* [1b]leaders of the singers, songs of praise and hymns of thanksgiving to God.

47 So all Israel in the days of Zerubbabel and Nehemiah gave the portions due the singers and the gatekeepers [a]as each day required, and [b]set apart the consecrated *portion* for the Levites, and the Levites set apart the consecrated *portion* for the sons of Aaron.

Foreigners Excluded

13 On that day [a]they read aloud from the book of Moses in the hearing of the people; and there was found written in it that [b]no Ammonite or Moabite should ever enter the assembly of God,

2 because they did not meet the sons of Israel with bread and water, but [a]hired Balaam against them to curse them. However, [b]our God turned the curse into a blessing.

3 So when they heard the law, [a]they excluded [b]all foreigners from Israel.

Tobiah Expelled and the Temple Cleansed

4 Now prior to this, Eliashib the priest, [a]who was appointed over the chambers of the house of our God, being [1]related to [b]Tobiah,

5 had prepared a large [1]room for him, where formerly they put the grain offerings,

31 [1]Lit *thanksgiving choirs* [2]Heb *and processions to the right* [a]Neh 12:38 [b]Neh 2:13
36 [1]Lit *brothers* [a]Neh 12:24
37 [a]Neh 2:14 [b]Neh 3:15 [c]Neh 3:26
38 [1]Lit *thanksgiving choir* [2]Lit *front* [a]Neh 12:31 [b]Neh 3:11 [c]Neh 3:8
39 [a]Neh 8:16 [b]Neh 3:6 [c]Neh 3:3 [d]Neh 3:1 [e]Neh 3:25
42 [1]Lit *caused their voices to be heard*
43 [a]Ps 9:2; 92:4
44 [1]Lit *stood* [a]Neh 13:4, 5, 12, 13
45 [1]Lit *service* [a]1 Chr 25:1
46 [1]Lit *heads* [a]2 Chr 29:30 [b]1 Chr 9:33
47 [a]Neh 11:23 [b]Num 18:21
13:1 [a]Neh 9:3 [b]Deut 23:3-5; Neh 13:23
2 [a]Num 22:3-11 [b]Deut 23:5
3 [a]Neh 9:2; 10:28 [b]Ex 12:38
4 [1]Lit *close to* [a]Neh 12:44 [b]Neh 2:10; 6:1, 17, 18
5 [1]Or *chamber*

12:31 *two great choirs.* See note on v. 38. The two great processions probably started from the area of the Valley Gate (2:13,15; 3:13) near the center of the western section of the wall. The first procession, led by Ezra (v. 36), moved in a counterclockwise direction upon the wall; the second, with Nehemiah (v. 38), moved in a clockwise direction. Both met between the Water Gate (v. 37) and the Gate of the Guard (v. 39), then entered the temple area. Cf. Ps 48:12–13. *to the right.* Or "to the south." The Semite oriented himself facing east, so the right hand represented the south (see Josh 17:7; 1 Sam 23:24; Job 23:9). *Refuse Gate.* See note on 2:13.

12:35 *trumpets.* See note on Ezra 3:10. Each choir had priests blowing trumpets, as well as Levites playing other musical instruments. *Asaph.* See note on 11:17.

12:36 *Ezra the scribe.* See notes on Ezra 7:1,6.

12:37 *Fountain Gate.* See note on 2:14. *city of David.* See 3:15; see also note on 2 Sam 5:7. *Water Gate.* See note on 3:26.

12:38 *choir.* Lit. "thanks," i.e., "thanksgiving choir" (see v. 40). *Tower of Furnaces.* See note on 3:11. *Broad Wall.* See note on 3:8.

12:39 *Gate of Ephraim.* See notes on 3:6; 8:16. *Old Gate.* See note on 3:6. *Fish Gate.* See note on 3:3. *Tower of Hananel . . . Tower of the Hundred . . . Sheep Gate.* See note on 3:1. *Gate of the Guard.* Cf. Jer 32:2.

12:43 *God had given them great joy.* See 1 Chr 29:9; Jon 4:6. *women.* See 8:2; Ex 15:20 and notes. *heard from afar.* See note on Ezra 3:13; cf. 1 Kin 1:40; 2 Kin 11:13.

12:44 *Judah rejoiced.* The people cheerfully contributed their offerings to support the priests and Levites (cf. 2 Cor 9:7). *who served.* See Deut 10:8.

12:46 *Asaph.* See note on 11:17.

12:47 *gave.* The Hebrew for this verb implies continued giving.

13:1–2 See Deut 23:3–6.

13:2 *Balaam.* See note on Num 22:5. An Aramaic inscription of the sixth century B.C. found at Deir 'Alla in Transjordan refers to Balaam.

13:4 *Eliashib.* See note on 12:10. *Tobiah.* See note on 2:10.

13:5 *prepared a large room.* During Nehemiah's absence from

the frankincense, the utensils and the tithes
of grain, wine and oil [a]prescribed for the
Levites, the singers and the gatekeepers, and
the [2]contributions for the priests.
6 But during all this *time* I was not in
Jerusalem, for in [a]the thirty-second year of
[b]Artaxerxes king of Babylon I had gone to
the king. After some time, however, I asked
leave from the king,
7 and I came to Jerusalem and [1]learned
about the evil that Eliashib had done for
Tobiah, [a]by preparing a [2]room for him in the
courts of the house of God.
8 It was very displeasing to me, so I
[a]threw all of Tobiah's household goods out
of the room.
9 Then I gave an order and [a]they
cleansed the rooms; and I returned there the
utensils of the house of God with the grain
offerings and the frankincense.

Tithes Restored

10 I also [1]discovered that [a]the portions of
the Levites had not been given *them,* so that
the Levites and the singers who performed
the service had [2]gone away, [b]each to his own
field.
11 So I [1a]reprimanded the officials and
said, "[b]Why is the house of God forsaken?"
Then I gathered them together and restored
them to their posts.
12 All Judah then brought [a]the tithe of the
grain, wine and oil into the storehouses.
13 In charge of the storehouses I appointed Shelemiah the priest, Zadok the scribe,
and Pedaiah of the Levites, and in addition to
them was Hanan the son of Zaccur, the son
of Mattaniah; for [a]they were considered reliable, and it was [1]their task to distribute to
their [2]kinsmen.
14 [a]Remember me for this, O my God, and
do not blot out my loyal deeds which I have
performed for the house of my God and its
services.

Sabbath Restored

15 In those days I saw in Judah some who
were treading wine presses [a]on the sabbath,
and bringing in sacks of grain and loading
them on donkeys, as well as wine, grapes,
figs and all kinds of loads, [b]and they brought
them into Jerusalem on the sabbath day. So
[c]I admonished *them* on the day they sold
food.
16 Also men of Tyre were living [1]there
who imported fish and all kinds of merchandise, and sold *them* to the sons of Judah on
the sabbath, even in Jerusalem.
17 Then [a]I [1]reprimanded the nobles of
Judah and said to them, "What is this evil
thing you are doing, [2]by profaning the sabbath day?
18 "[a]Did not your fathers do the same, so
that our God brought on us and on this city
all this trouble? Yet you are adding to the
wrath on Israel by profaning the sabbath."

5 [2]Lit *heave offerings* [a]Num 18:21
6 [a]Neh 5:14 [b]Ezra 6:22
7 [1]Or *understood* [2]Or *chamber,* and so in vv 8, 9 [a]Neh 13:5
8 [a]John 2:13-16
9 [a]2 Chr 29:5, 15, 16
10 [1]Or *knew* [2]Lit *fled* [a]Deut 12:19; Neh 10:37 [b]Neh 12:28, 29
11 [1]Or *contended with* [a]Neh 13:17, 25 [b]Neh 10:39
12 [a]Neh 10:37; 12:44; Mal 3:10
13 [1]Lit *on them to* [2]Lit *brothers* [a]Neh 7:2
14 [a]Neh 5:19; 13:22, 31
15 [a]Ex 20:8; 34:21; Deut 5:12-14; Jer 17:22 [b]Neh 10:31; Jer 17:21 [c]Neh 9:29; 13:21
16 [1]Lit *in it*
17 [1]Or *contended with* [2]Lit *and* [a]Neh 13:11, 25
18 [a]Ezra 9:13; Jer 17:21

the city to return to the Persian king's court, Tobiah, one of his archenemies, had used his influence with Eliashib to gain entrance into a chamber ordinarily set aside for the storage of tithes and other offerings (see 10:37 and note; cf. Num 18:21–32; Deut 14:28–29; 26:12–15). Elsewhere we read of the chamber of Meshullam (3:30) and of Jehohanan (Ezra 10:6).

13:6 *thirty-second year of Artaxerxes.* See note on 5:14. *king of Babylon.* The title was assumed by Cyrus after his conquest of Babylon (see Ezra 5:13) and was adopted by subsequent Achaemenid (Persian) kings.

13:7 *came to Jerusalem.* Nehemiah's second term must have ended before 407 B.C., when Bagohi (Bigvai) was governor of Judah according to the Elephantine papyri. Some have suggested that after Nehemiah's first term he was succeeded by his brother Hanani (see note on 1:2). *courts.* See note on 8:16. Zerubbabel's temple had two courtyards (Zech 3:7; cf. Is 62:9).

13:8 *displeasing . . . threw.* Nehemiah expressed his indignation by taking action (cf. vv. 24–25; 5:6–7). Contrast the reaction of Ezra, who "sat down appalled" (Ezra 9:3). Nehemiah's action reminds us of Christ's expulsion of the moneychangers from the temple area (Matt 21:12–13).

13:9 *rooms.* Though only a single chamber was mentioned in vv. 5–8, additional rooms were involved. A parallel to the occupation and desecration of the temple by Tobiah comes from a century earlier in Egypt, where Greek mercenaries had occupied the temple of Neith at Sais. Upon the appeal of the Egyptian priest, Udjahorresnet, the Persian king had the squatters driven out and the temple's ceremonies, processions and revenues restored: "And His Majesty commanded that all the foreigners who had settled in the temple of Neith should be driven out and that all their houses and all their superfluities that were in this temple should be thrown down, and that all their own baggage should be carried for them outside the wall of this temple."

13:10 Nehemiah was apparently correcting an abuse of long standing. Strictly speaking, the Levites had no holdings (Num 18:20,23–24; Deut 14:29; 18:1), but some may have had private income (Deut 18:8). Therefore the Levites were dependent on the faithful support of the people. This may explain the reluctance of great numbers of Levites to return from exile (see Ezra 8:15–20). For the complaints of those who found little material advantage in serving the Lord see Mal 2:17; 3:13–15.

13:11 *forsaken.* See note on 10:39.

13:12 *tithe.* See 12:44. Temples in Mesopotamia also levied tithes for the support of their personnel.

13:13 Of the four treasurers, one was a priest, one a Levite, one a scribe and one a layman of rank. *reliable.* Nehemiah appointed honest men to make sure that supplies were distributed equitably, just as the church appointed deacons for this purpose (Acts 6:1–5).

13:15 *treading wine presses.* See notes on Is 5:2; 16:10. *sabbath.* The temptation to violate the sabbath rest was especially characteristic of non-Jewish merchants (see 10:31; Is 56:1–8). On the other hand, the high regard that many had for the sabbath was expressed by parents who called their children Shabbethai (see 8:7; 11:16; Ezra 10:15).

13:16 *Tyre.* See note on Is 23:1. *fish.* Most of the fish exported by the Tyrians (Ezek 26:4–5,14) was dried, smoked or salted. Fish, much of it from the Sea of Galilee, was an important part of the Israelites' diet (Lev 11:9; Num 11:5; Matt 15:34; Luke 24:42; John 21:5–13). It was sold at the market near the Fish Gate (see note on 3:3).

13:17 *reprimanded the nobles.* Because they were the leaders. *profaning.* Turning what is sacred into common use and so profaning it (see Mal 2:10–11).

19 [a]It came about that just as it grew dark
at the gates of Jerusalem before the sabbath,
I commanded that the doors should be shut
[1]and that they should not open them until
after the sabbath. Then I stationed some of
my servants at the gates *so that* no load
would enter on the sabbath day.
20 Once or twice the traders and merchants of every kind of merchandise spent
the night outside Jerusalem.
21 Then [a]I [1]warned them and said to
them, "Why do you spend the night in front
of the wall? If you do so again, I will [2]use
force against you." From that time on they
did not come on the sabbath.
22 And I commanded the Levites that
[a]they should purify themselves and come as
gatekeepers to sanctify the sabbath day. *For*
this also [b]remember me, O my God, and
have compassion on me according to the
greatness of Your lovingkindness.

Mixed Marriages Forbidden

23 In those days I also saw that the Jews
had [1a]married women from [b]Ashdod,
[c]Ammon *and* Moab.
24 As for their children, half spoke in the
language of Ashdod, and none of them was
able to speak the language of Judah, but [1]the
language of his own people.
25 So [a]I contended with them and cursed
them and [b]struck some of them and pulled
out their hair, and [c]made them swear by
God, "You shall not give your daughters to
their sons, nor take of their daughters for
your sons or for yourselves.
26 "[a]Did not Solomon king of Israel sin
regarding these things? [b]Yet among the many
nations there was no king like him, and [c]he
was loved by his God, and God made him
king over all Israel; nevertheless the foreign
women caused even him to sin.
27 "[1]Do we then hear about you that you
have committed all this great evil [a]by acting
unfaithfully against our God by [2]marrying
foreign women?"
28 Even one of the sons of Joiada, the son
of Eliashib the high priest, was a son-in-law
of [a]Sanballat the Horonite, so I drove him
away from me.
29 [a]Remember them, O my God, [1]be-
cause they have defiled the priesthood and
the [b]covenant of the priesthood and the
Levites.
30 [a]Thus I purified them from everything
foreign and appointed duties for the priests
and the Levites, each in his task,
31 and *I arranged* [a]for the supply of wood
at appointed times and for the first fruits.
[b]Remember me, O my God, for good.

19 [1]Lit *and commanded* [a]Lev 23:32
21 [1]Lit *witnessed against* [2]Lit *send a hand against* [a]Neh 13:15
22 [a]1 Chr 15:12; Neh 12:30 [b]Neh 13:14, 31
23 [1]Lit *given dwelling to* [a]Ex 34:11-16; Deut 7:1-5; Ezra 9:2; Neh 10:30 [b]Neh 4:7 [c]Ezra 9:1; Neh 13:1
24 [1]Lit *according to the tongue of people and people*
25 [a]Neh 13:11, 17 [b]Deut 25:2 [c]Neh 10:29, 30
26 [a]1 Kin 11:1 [b]1 Kin 3:13; 2 Chr 1:12 [c]2 Sam 12:24, 25
27 [1]Or *Is it reported* [2]Lit *giving dwelling to* [a]Ezra 10:2; Neh 13:23
28 [a]Neh 2:10, 19; 4:1
29 [1]Lit *for the defilings of* [a]Neh 6:14 [b]Num 25:13
30 [a]Neh 10:30
31 [a]Neh 10:34 [b]Neh 13:14, 22

13:19 *just as it grew dark.* Before sunset, when the sabbath began. The Israelites, like the Babylonians, counted their days from sunset to sunset (the Egyptians reckoned theirs from dawn to dawn). The precise moment when the sabbath began was heralded by the blowing of a trumpet by a priest. According to the Jewish Mishnah, "On the eve of sabbath they used to blow six more blasts, three to cause the people to cease from work and three to mark the break between the sacred and the profane." Josephus (*Jewish Wars,* 4.9.12) speaks of the location on the parapet of the temple where the priests "gave a signal beforehand, with a trumpet, at the beginning of every seventh day, in the evening twilight, and also at the evening when that day was finished, announcing to the people the respective hours for ceasing work and for resuming their labors." Excavators at the temple mount recovered a stone from the southwest corner of the parapet, which had fallen to the ground in Titus's siege, with the inscription "for the place of the blowing (of the trumpet)."
13:22 *remember me.* See note on 1:8.
13:23 Ezra had dealt with the same problem of intermarriage some 25 years before (see note on Ezra 9:1). *Ashdod.* See 4:7; Is 20:1 and notes. *Ammon and Moab.* See note on Gen 19:36–38.
13:24 The Israelites recognized other people as foreigners by their languages (see Deut 3:9; Judg 12:6; Ps 114:1; Is 33:19; Ezek 3:5–6).
13:25 *pulled out their hair.* See Ezra 9:3; Is 50:6 and notes. *You shall not give.* Nehemiah's action was designed to prevent future intermarriages, whereas Ezra dissolved the existing unions.
13:26 *Solomon.* Israel's outstanding king in terms of wealth and political achievements (1 Kin 3:13; 2 Chr 1:12). Solomon began his reign by humbly asking for wisdom from the Lord (1 Kin 3:5–9). *caused even him to sin.* In later years his foreign wives led him to worship other gods, so that he built a high place for Chemosh, the god of the Moabites (1 Kin 11:7).
13:28 *son-in-law of Sanballat.* According to Lev 21:14 the high priest was not to marry a foreigner. The expulsion of Joiada's son followed either this special ban or the general prohibition against intermarriage. The union described in this verse was especially rankling to Nehemiah in the light of Sanballat's enmity (see 2:10). Josephus (*Antiquities,* 11.7.2) records that an almost identical episode, involving a marriage between the daughter of a Sanballat of Samaria and the brother of the Jewish high priest, took place a little over a century later in the time of Alexander the Great.
13:30 *duties.* Or "divisions," referring to the assignment of particular duties to groups of priests and Levites, possibly on a rotating basis (see note on 12:9).
13:31 *wood.* See note on 10:34. *first fruits.* See note on 10:35. *Remember me . . . for good.* The last recorded words of Nehemiah recapitulate a theme running through the final chapter (vv. 14,22; see note on 1:8). His motive throughout his ministry was to please and to serve his divine Sovereign.

Esther

INTRODUCTION

Author and Date

Although we do not know who wrote the book of Esther, from internal evidence it is possible to make some inferences about the author and the date of composition. It is clear that the author was a Jew, both from his emphasis on the origin of a Jewish festival and from the Jewish nationalism that permeates the story. The author's knowledge of Persian customs, the setting of the story in the city of Susa and the absence of any reference to the land of Judah or to Jerusalem suggest that he was a resident of a Persian city. The earliest date for the book would be shortly after the events narrated, i.e., c. 460 B.C. (before Ezra's return to Jerusalem; see note on 8:12). Internal evidence also suggests that the festival of Purim had been observed for some time prior to the writing of the book (9:19). Several scholars have dated the book in the Hellenistic period; the absence of Greek words and the style of the author's Hebrew dialect, however, suggest that the book must have been written before the Persian empire fell to Greece in 331.

Purpose, Themes and Literary Features

The author's central purpose was to record the institution of the annual festival of Purim and to keep alive for later generations the memory of the great deliverance of the Jewish people during the reign of Ahasuerus. The book accounts for both the initiation of that observance and the obligation for its perpetual commemoration (see 3:7; 9:24,28 – 32; see also chart, p. 164).

Throughout much of the story the author calls to mind the ongoing conflict of Israel with the Amalekites (see notes on 2:5; 3:1 – 6; 9:5 – 10), a conflict that began during the exodus (Ex 17:8 – 16; Deut 25:17 – 19) and continued through Israel's history (1 Sam 15; 1 Chr 4:43; and, of course, Esther). As the first to attack Israel after their deliverance from Egypt, the Amalekites were viewed — and the author of Esther views them — as the epitome of all the powers of the world arrayed against God's people (see Num 24:20; 1 Sam 15:1 – 3; 28:18). Now that Israel has been released from captivity, Haman's edict is the final major effort in the OT period to destroy them.

Closely associated with the conflict with the Amalekites is the rest that is promised to the people of God (see Deut 25:19). With Haman's defeat the Jews enjoy rest from their enemies (9:16,22).

The author also draws upon the remnant motif that recurs throughout the Bible (natural disasters, disease, warfare or other calamities threaten God's people; those who survive constitute a remnant). Events in the Persian city of Susa threatened the continuity of God's purposes in redemptive history. The future existence of God's chosen people, and ultimately the appearance of the Redeemer-Messiah, were jeopardized by Haman's edict to destroy the Jews. The author of Esther patterned much of his material on the events of the Joseph story (see notes on 2:3 – 4,9,21 – 23; 3:4; 4:14; 6:1,8,14; 8:6), in which the remnant motif is also central to the narrative (Gen 45:7).

Feasting is another prominent theme in Esther, as shown in the outline below. Banquets provide the setting for important plot developments. There are ten banquets: (1) 1:3 – 4, (2) 1:5 – 8, (3) 1:9, (4) 2:18, (5) 3:15, (6) 5:1 – 8, (7) 7:1 – 10, (8) 8:17, (9) 9:17, (10) 9:18 – 32. The three pairs of banquets that mark the beginning, middle and end of the story are particularly prominent: the two banquets given by Ahasuerus, the two prepared by Esther and the double celebration of Purim.

Recording duplications appears to be one of the favorite compositional techniques of the writer. In addition to the three groups of banquets that come in pairs there are two lists of the king's servants (1:10,14), two reports that Esther concealed her identity (2:10,20), two gatherings of the women (2:8,19), two houses for the women (2:12 – 14), two fasts (4:3,16), two consultations of Haman with his wife and friends (5:14; 6:13), two unscheduled appearances of Esther before the king (5:2; 8:3), two investitures for Mordecai (6:7 – 11;

8:15), two coverings of Haman's face (6:12; 7:8), two references to Haman's sons (5:11; 9:6–10, 13–14), two appearances of Harbona (1:10; 7:9), two royal edicts (3:12–14; 8:1–13), two references to the subsiding of the king's anger (2:1; 7:10), two references to the irrevocability of the Persian laws (1:19; 8:8), two days for the Jews to take vengeance (9:5–15) and two letters instituting the commemoration of Purim (9:20–32).

An outstanding feature of this book — one that has given rise to considerable discussion — is the complete absence of any explicit reference to God, worship, prayer, or sacrifice. This "secularity" has produced many detractors who have judged the book to be of little religious value. However, it appears that the author has deliberately refrained from mentioning God or any religious activity as a literary device to heighten the fact that it is God who controls and directs all the seemingly insignificant coincidences (see, e.g., note on 6:1) that make up the plot and issue in deliverance for the Jews. God's sovereign rule is assumed at every point (see note on 4:12–16), an assumption made all the more effective by the total absence of reference to Him.

Outline

- I. The Feasts of Ahasuerus (1:1 — 2:18)
  - A. Vashti Deposed (ch. 1)
  - B. Esther Made Queen (2:1–18)
- II. The Feasts of Esther (2:19 — 7:10)
  - A. Mordecai Uncovers a Plot (2:19–23)
  - B. Haman's Plot (ch. 3)
  - C. Mordecai Persuades Esther to Help (ch. 4)
  - D. Esther's Request to the King: The First Banquet (5:1–8)
  - E. A Sleepless Night (5:9 — 6:14)
  - F. Haman Hanged: The Second Banquet (ch. 7)
- III. The Feasts of Purim (chs. 8 — 10)
  - A. The King's Edict in Behalf of the Jews (ch. 8)
  - B. The Institution of Purim (ch. 9)
  - C. The Promotion of Mordecai (ch. 10)

The Banquets of the King

1 Now it took place in the days of [a]Ahasuerus, the Ahasuerus who reigned [b]from India to [1]Ethiopia over [c]127 provinces,

2 in those days as King Ahasuerus [a]sat on his royal throne which *was* at the citadel in [b]Susa,

3 in the third year of his reign [a]he gave a banquet for all his princes and attendants, the army *officers* of Persia and Media, the nobles and the princes of his provinces being in his presence.

4 [1]And he displayed the riches of his royal glory and the splendor of his great majesty for many days, 180 days.

5 When these days were completed, the king gave a banquet lasting seven days for all the people who were present at the citadel in Susa, from the greatest to the least, in the court of [a]the garden of the king's palace.

6 *There were hangings of* fine white and violet linen held by cords of fine purple linen on silver rings and marble columns, *and* [a]couches of gold and silver on a mosaic pavement of porphyry, marble, mother-of-pearl and precious stones.

7 Drinks were served in golden vessels of various kinds, and the royal wine was plentiful [a]according to the king's [1]bounty.

8 The drinking was *done* according to the law, there was no compulsion, for so the king had given orders to each official of his household that he should do according to the desires of each person.

9 Queen Vashti also gave a banquet for the women in the [1]palace which belonged to King Ahasuerus.

Queen Vashti's Refusal

10 On the seventh day, when the heart of the king was [a]merry with wine, he commanded Mehuman, Biztha, Harbona, Bigtha, Abagtha, Zethar and Carkas, the seven eunuchs who served in the presence of King Ahasuerus,

11 to bring Queen Vashti before the king with *her* royal [a]crown in order to display her beauty to the people and the princes, for she was beautiful.

12 But Queen Vashti refused to come at the king's command delivered by the eunuchs. Then the king became very angry and his wrath burned within him.

13 Then the king said to [a]the wise men [b]who understood the times—for it was the custom of the king so *to speak* before all who knew law and justice

14 and were close to him: Carshena, Shethar, Admatha, Tarshish, Meres, Marsena and Memucan, the seven princes of Persia and Media [a]who [1]had access to the king's presence and sat in the first place in the kingdom—

15 "According to law, what is to be done with Queen Vashti, because she did not [1]obey the command of King Ahasuerus *delivered* by the eunuchs?"

16 In the presence of the king and the princes, Memucan said, "Queen Vashti has wronged not only the king but *also* all the princes and all the peoples who are in all the provinces of King Ahasuerus.

17 "For the queen's conduct will [1]become known to all the women causing them [2]to look with contempt on their husbands by saying, 'King Ahasuerus commanded Queen Vashti to be brought in to his presence, but she did not come.'

18 "This day the ladies of Persia and Media who have heard of the queen's conduct will speak in *the same way* to all the king's

1:1 [1]Lit *Cush* [a]Ezra 4:6; Dan 9:1 [b]Esth 8:9 [c]Esth 9:30
2 [a]1 Kin 1:46 [b]Neh 1:1; Dan 8:2
3 [a]Esth 2:18
4 [1]Lit *When*
5 [a]Esth 7:7, 8
6 [a]Ezek 23:41; Amos 6:4
7 [1]Lit *hand* [a]Esth 2:18
9 [1]Lit *royal house*
10 [a]Judg 16:25
11 [a]Esth 2:17; 6:8
13 [a]Jer 10:7; Dan 2:2 [b]1 Chr 12:32
14 [1]Lit *saw the face of the king* [a]2 Kin 25:19; Matt 18:10
15 [1]Lit *do*
17 [1]Lit *go forth* [2]Lit *to despise...in their eyes*

1:1 *Ahasuerus.* Also known as "Xerxes," a Greek form of the Persian name Khshayarshan. Ahasuerus succeeded his father Darius and ruled 486–465 B.C. *127 provinces.* See 8:9. The Greek historian Herodotus (3.89) records that Ahasuerus's father Darius had organized the empire into 20 satrapies. (Satraps, the rulers of the satrapies, are mentioned in 3:12; 8:9; 9:3.) The provinces were smaller administrative units.

1:2 *citadel in Susa.* The fortified acropolis and palace complex; it is distinguished from the surrounding city in 3:15; 4:1–2,6; 8:15. Several archaeological investigations have been made at the site since the mid–19th century. Ahasuerus had made extensive renovations in the palace structures. *Susa.* The winter residence of the Persian kings; the three other capitals were Ecbatana (Ezra 6:2), Babylon and Persepolis. One of Daniel's visions was set in Susa (Dan 8:2); Nehemiah also served there (Neh 1:1).

1:3–4 The year (483–482 B.C.), the persons in attendance and the length of the meeting suggest that the purpose of the gathering may have been to plan for the disastrous campaigns of 482–479 against Greece. Herodotus (7.8) possibly describes this assembly.

1:3 *banquet.* Feasting is a prominent theme in Esther (see Introduction: Purpose, Themes and Literary Features).

1:5–6 The excavations at Susa have unearthed a text in which Ahasuerus's father Darius describes in some detail the building of his palace. Ahasuerus continued the work his father had begun.

1:9 *Queen Vashti.* Deposed in 484/483 B.C.; Esther became queen in 479/478 (2:16–17). The Greek historians call Ahasuerus's queen Amestris; they record her influence during the early part of his reign and as queen mother during the following reign of her son Artaxerxes (Ezra 7:1,7,11–12,21; 8:1; Neh 2:1; 5:14; 13:6) until the time of her own death c. 424. Artaxerxes came to the throne when he was 18 years old; therefore he was born c. 484/483, approximately at the time of Vashti's deposal. Since he was the third son of Amestris, the name Amestris cannot be identified with Esther and must be viewed as a Greek version of the name Vashti. Comparatively little is known of the late portions of Ahasuerus's reign, nor is it possible to determine the subsequent events of the life of Esther. Apparently after Esther's death or her fall from favor, Vashti was able to reassert her power and to exercise a controlling influence over her son.

1:13–14 Ezra 7:14 and the Greek historian Herodotus indicate that seven men functioned as the immediate advisers to the king.

1:13 *wise men who understood the times.* Court astrologers.

princes, and there will be plenty of contempt
and anger.
19 "If it pleases the king, let a royal [1]edict
be issued by him and let it be written in the
laws of Persia and Media so [a]that it cannot
[2]be repealed, that Vashti may no longer
come into the presence of King Ahasuerus,
and let the king give her royal position to
[3]another who is more worthy than she.
20 "When the king's edict which he will
make is heard throughout all his kingdom,
[1]great as it is, then [a]all women will give hon-
or to their husbands, great and small."
21 *This* word pleased the king and the
princes, and the king did [1]as Memucan proposed.
22 So he sent letters to all the king's
provinces, [a]to each province according to its
script and to every people according to their
language, that every man should [b]be the
master in his own house and the one who
speaks in the language of his own people.

Vashti's Successor Sought

2 After these things [a]when the anger of
King Ahasuerus had subsided, he remembered Vashti and what she had done and
[b]what had been decreed against her.
2 Then the king's attendants, who served
him, said, "[a]Let beautiful young virgins be
sought for the king.
3 "Let the king appoint overseers in [a]all
the provinces of his kingdom that they may
gather every beautiful young virgin to the
citadel of Susa, to the harem, into the custody of [b]Hegai, the king's eunuch, who is in
charge of the women; and [c]let their cosmetics be given *them*.
4 "Then let the young lady who pleases
the king be queen in place of Vashti." And
the matter pleased the king, and he did
accordingly.
5 *Now* there was at the citadel in Susa a
Jew whose name was [a]Mordecai, the son of
Jair, the son of Shimei, the son of Kish, a
Benjamite,
6 [a]who had been taken into exile from
Jerusalem with the captives who had been
exiled with Jeconiah king of Judah, whom
Nebuchadnezzar the king of Babylon had
exiled.
7 He was bringing up Hadassah, that is
[a]Esther, his uncle's daughter, for she had no
father or mother. Now the young lady was
beautiful of form and [1]face, and when her
father and her mother died, Mordecai took
her as his own daughter.

Esther Finds Favor

8 So it came about when the command
and decree of the king were heard and
[a]many young ladies were gathered to the
citadel of Susa into the custody of [b]Hegai,
that Esther was taken to the king's [1]palace

19 [1]Lit *word go forth from* [2]Lit *pass away* [3]Lit *her neighbor* [a]Esth 8:8; Dan 6:8
20 [1]Lit *for great is it* [a]Eph 5:22; Col 3:18
21 [1]Lit *according to the word of*
22 [a]Esth 3:12; 8:9 [b]Eph 5:22-24
2:1 [a]Esth 7:10 [b]Esth 1:19, 20
2 [a]1 Kin 1:2
3 [a]Esth 1:1, 2 [b]Esth 2:8, 15 [c]Esth 2:9, 12
5 [a]Esth 3:2
6 [a]2 Kin 24:14, 15; 2 Chr 36:10
7 [1]Lit *good of appearance* [a]Esth 2:15
8 [1]Lit *house* [a]Esth 2:3 [b]Esth 2:3, 15

1:19 *cannot be repealed.* The irrevocability of the Persian laws is mentioned in 8:8 and Dan 6:8. *no longer come into.* The punishment corresponds to the crime: Since Vashti refused to appear before the king, it is decreed that she never appear before him again. Furthermore, from this point on she is no longer given the title "Queen" in the book of Esther.
1:22 *that . . . people.* The king's example of deposing Vashti, plus the elevation of the husband's language in ethnically mixed marriages, served to strengthen the husband's role as ruler in the home and reinforced the common language base in the empire (see Neh 13:23–24).
2:1 *After these things.* Esther was taken to Ahasuerus "in the seventh year of his reign" (v. 16), i.e., in December, 479 B.C., or January, 478. The Greek wars intervened before a new queen was sought (see note on 1:3–4).
2:2 *virgins . . . for the king.* To add to his harem.
2:3–4 The phraseology here is similar to that in Gen 41:34–37. This and numerous other parallels suggest that the author of Esther modeled his work after the Joseph story. Both accounts are set in the courts of foreign monarchs and portray Israelite heroes who rise to prominence and provide the means by which their people are saved (see notes on vv. 9,21–23; 3:4; 4:14; 6:1,8,14; 8:6).
2:5 *at the citadel in Susa a Jew.* As far back as the fall of the northern kingdom in 722–721 B.C. Israelites had been exiled among the cities of the Medes (2 Kin 17:6). After the conquest of Babylon by King Cyrus of Persia in 539, some of the Jewish population taken there by the Babylonians (605–586) probably moved eastward into the cities of Medo-Persia. Only 50,000 returned to Israel in the restoration of 538 (Ezra 2:64–67). The presence of a large Jewish population in Medo-Persia is confirmed by the discovery of an archive of texts in Nippur (southern Mesopotamia) from the period of Artaxerxes I (465–424) and Darius II (424–405). This archive contains the names of about 100 Jews who lived in that city. Some had attained positions of importance and wealth. Similar Jewish populations are probable in many other Medo-Persian cities. *Mordecai.* The name is derived from that of the Babylonian deity Marduk. There are numerous examples in the Bible of Jews having double names—a Hebrew name and a "Gentile" name. Mordecai likely had a Hebrew name, as did Esther (v. 7), Daniel and his friends (Dan 1:6–7), Joseph (Gen 41:45) and others, but the text does not mention Mordecai's Hebrew name. A cuneiform tablet from Borsippa near Babylon mentions a scribe by the name of Mardukaya; he was an accountant or minister at the court of Susa in the early years of Ahasuerus. Many scholars identify him with Mordecai. *son of Jair, the son of Shimei, the son of Kish.* The persons named could be immediate ancestors, in which case Mordecai would be the great-grandson of Kish, who was among the exiles with Jehoiachin in 597 B.C. It is more likely, however, that the names refer to remote ancestors in the tribe of Benjamin (see 2 Sam 16:5–14 for Shimei, 1 Sam 9:1 for Kish). This association with the tribe and family of King Saul sets the stage for the ongoing conflict between Israel and the Amalekites (see notes on 3:1–6). If the names are those of remote ancestors, the clause "who had been carried into exile" (v. 6) would not apply to Mordecai, who would have been over 100 years old in that case; rather, it would have to be taken as an elliptical construction in the sense "whose family had been taken into exile."
2:6 *Jeconiah king of Judah.* See 2 Kin 24:8–17; 2 Chr 36:9–10.
2:7 *Hadassah.* Esther's Hebrew name, meaning "myrtle." The name Esther is likely derived from the Persian word for "star," though some derive it from the name of the Babylonian goddess Ishtar (see note on Jer 7:18).
2:8 *Esther was taken.* Neither she nor Mordecai would have had any choice in the matter (cf. 2 Sam 11:4).

into the custody of Hegai, who was in charge
of the women.
9 Now the young lady pleased him and
found favor with him. So he quickly provided her with her [a]cosmetics and [1]food, gave
her seven choice maids from the king's
palace and transferred her and her maids to
the best place in the harem.
10 [a]Esther did not make known her people or her kindred, for Mordecai had instructed her that she should not make *them*
known.
11 Every day Mordecai walked back and
forth in front of the court of the harem to
learn how Esther was and how she fared.
12 Now when the turn of each young lady
came to go in to King Ahasuerus, after the
end of her twelve months under the regulations for the women—for the days of their
beautification were completed as follows: six
months with oil of myrrh and six months
with spices and the cosmetics for women—
13 the young lady would go in to the king
in this way: anything that she [1]desired was
given her to take with her from the harem to
the king's palace.
14 In the evening she would go in and in
the morning she would return to the second
harem, to the [1]custody of Shaashgaz, the
king's eunuch who was in charge of the concubines. She would not again go in to the
king unless the king delighted in her and she
was summoned by name.
15 Now when the turn of Esther, [a]the
daughter of Abihail the uncle of Mordecai
who had taken her as his daughter, came to
go in to the king, she did not request anything except what [b]Hegai, the king's eunuch
who was in charge of the women, [1]advised.
And Esther found favor in the eyes of all who
saw her.
16 So Esther was taken to King Ahasuerus
to his royal palace in the tenth month which
is the month Tebeth, in the seventh year of
his reign.

Esther Becomes Queen

17 The king loved Esther more than all the
women, and she found favor and kindness
with him more than all the virgins, so that
[a]he set the royal crown on her head and
made her queen instead of Vashti.
18 Then [a]the king gave a great banquet,
Esther's banquet, for all his princes and his
servants; he also made a holiday for the
provinces and gave gifts [b]according to the
king's bounty.
19 [a]When the virgins were gathered
together the second time, then Mordecai
[b]was sitting at the king's gate.
20 [a]Esther had not yet made known her
kindred or her people, even as Mordecai had
commanded her; for Esther did [1]what Mordecai told her as she had done [b]when under
his care.

Mordecai Saves the King

21 In those days, while Mordecai was sitting at the king's gate, [a]Bigthan and Teresh,
two of the king's officials from those who
guarded the door, became angry and sought
to [1]lay hands on King Ahasuerus.
22 But the [1]plot became known to Mordecai and [a]he told Queen Esther, and Esther
[2]informed the king in Mordecai's name.
23 Now when the plot was investigated
and found *to be so,* they were both hanged
on a [1]gallows; and it was written in [a]the

9 [1]Lit *portions* [a]Esth 2:3, 12
10 [a]Esth 2:20
13 [1]Lit *said*
14 [1]Lit *hand*
15 [1]Lit *said* [a]Esth 2:7; 9:29 [b]Esth 2:3, 8

17 [a]Esth 1:11
18 [a]Esth 1:3 [b]Esth 1:7
19 [a]Esth 2:3, 4 [b]Esth 2:21; 3:2
20 [1]Lit *the word of Mordecai* [a]Esth 2:10 [b]Esth 2:7
21 [1]Lit *send a hand against* [a]Esth 6:2
22 [1]Lit *matter,* so also v 23 [2]Lit *told* [a]Esth 6:1, 2
23 [1]Lit *tree* [a]Esth 10:2

2:9 *food.* Lit."her portions." Unlike Daniel and his friends (Dan 1:5–10), Esther does not observe the dietary laws, perhaps in part to conceal her Jewish identity (vv. 10,20). Giving such portions is a sign of special favor (1 Sam 9:22–24; 2 Kin 25:29–30; Dan 1:1–10; negatively, Jer 13:25); in the Joseph narrative cf. Gen 43:34. The motif of giving portions appears later as a practice in observing Purim (9:19,22).
2:10 The fact that Esther concealed her identity is reported twice—here and in v. 20 (for the author's use of duplications see Introduction: Purpose, Themes and Literary Features).
2:14 *to the second harem.* To the chambers of the concubines.
2:16 *tenth month . . . seventh year.* December, 479 B.C., or January, 478 (see notes on 1:3–4; 2:1). Esther's tenure as queen continued through the events of the book, i.e., through 473 (see 3:7 and note; see also 8:9–13; 9:1). She may have died or fallen from favor shortly thereafter (see note on 1:9).
2:18 *holiday.* The Hebrew for this word, unique to this verse, may imply a remission of taxes, an emancipation of slaves, a cancellation of debts or a remission of obligatory military service.
2:19 See Introduction: Purpose, Themes and Literary Features. The enlargement of the harem apparently continued unabated. Perhaps there is a causal connection between the second gathering of women and the assassination plot (vv. 21–23); some have suggested that it reflects palace intrigue in support of the deposed Vashti. *king's gate.* The gate of an ancient city was its major commercial and legal center. Markets were held in the gate; the court sat there to transact its business (see Deut 21:18–20; Josh 20:4; Ruth 4:1–11; Ps 69:12). A king might hold an audience at the gate (see 2 Sam 19:8; 1 Kin 22:10). Daniel was at the king's gate (NASB "king's court") as ruler over all Babylon (Dan 2:48–49). Mordecai's sitting at the king's gate confirms his holding a high position in the civil service of the empire (see note on v. 5). From this vantage point he might overhear plans for the murder of the king.
2:21–23 Another point of comparison with the Joseph narrative is the involvement of two chamberlains (Gen 40:1–3; see note on vv. 3–4).
2:23 *hanged on a gallows.* Or "impaled on poles." Among the Persians this form of execution was impalement, as is confirmed in pictures and statues from the ancient Near East and in the comments of the Greek historian Herodotus (3.125,129; 4.43). According to Herodotus (3.159) Darius I impaled 3,000 Babylonians when he took Babylon, an act that Darius himself recorded in his Behistun (Bisitun) inscription. In Israelite and Canaanite practice, hanging was an exhibition of the corpse and not the means of execution itself (Deut 21:22–23; Josh 8:29; 10:26; 1 Sam 31:8–10; 2 Sam 4:12; 21:9–10). The execution of a chamberlain in the Joseph narrative also appears to have been by impalement (Gen 40:19). The sons of Haman were killed by the sword, and then their corpses were displayed in this way (9:5–14). *Chronicles.* The concern of the author of Esther with rhetorical symmetry is seen in the fact that the Chronicles are

Book of the Chronicles in the king's presence.

Haman's Plot against the Jews

3 After these events King Ahasuerus [a]promoted Haman, the son of Hammedatha [b]the Agagite, and [a]advanced him and [1]established his authority over all the princes who *were* with him.

2 All the king's servants who were at the king's gate bowed down [1]and paid homage to Haman; for so the king had commanded concerning him. But [a]Mordecai neither bowed down nor paid homage.

3 Then the king's servants who were at [a]the king's gate said to Mordecai, "[b]Why are you transgressing the king's command?"

4 Now it was when they had spoken daily to him and he would not listen to them, that they told Haman to see whether Mordecai's reason would stand; for he had told them that he was a Jew.

5 When Haman saw that [a]Mordecai neither bowed down nor paid homage to him, Haman was filled with rage.

6 But he [1]disdained to [2]lay hands on Mordecai alone, for they had told him *who* the people of Mordecai *were;* therefore Haman [a]sought to destroy all the Jews, the people of Mordecai, who *were* throughout the whole kingdom of Ahasuerus.

7 In the first month, which is the month Nisan, in the twelfth year of King Ahasuerus, [1]Pur, that is the lot, was [a]cast before Haman from day to day and from month *to month,* [2]until the twelfth month, that is [b]the month Adar.

8 Then Haman said to King Ahasuerus, "There is a certain people scattered and dispersed among the peoples in all the provinces of your kingdom; [a]their laws are different from *those* of all *other* people and they do not observe the king's laws, so it is not in the king's interest to let them remain.

9 "If it is pleasing to the king, let it be [1]decreed that they be destroyed, and I will pay ten thousand talents of silver into the hands of those who carry on the *king's* business, to put into the king's treasuries."

10 Then [a]the king took his signet ring from his hand and gave it to Haman, the son of Hammedatha [b]the Agagite, [c]the enemy of the Jews.

11 The king said to Haman, "The silver is [1]yours, and the people *also,* to do with them as you please."

12 [a]Then the king's scribes were summoned on the thirteenth day of the first month, and it was written just as Haman commanded to [b]the king's satraps, to the governors who were over each province and to the princes of each people, each province

3:1 [1]Lit *set his seat* [a]Esth 5:11 [b]Esth 3:10; 8:3
2 [1]Lit *and prostrated themselves before* [a]Esth 2:19; 5:9
3 [a]Esth 2:19 [b]Esth 3:2
5 [a]Esth 5:9
6 [1]Lit *despised in his eyes* [2]Lit *send a hand against* [a]Ps 83:4
7 [1]Lit *he cast Pur...before* [2]Gr *and the lot fell on the thirteenth day of* [a]Esth 9:24-26 [b]Ezra 6:15
8 [a]Ezra 4:12-15; Acts 16:20, 21
9 [1]Lit *written*
10 [a]Gen 41:42; Esth 8:2 [b]Esth 3:1 [c]Esth 7:6
11 [1]Lit *given to you*
12 [a]Esth 8:9 [b]Ezra 8:36

mentioned in the beginning (here), middle (6:1) and end (10:2) of the narrative. The episode dealing with the plot of Bigthana and Teresh is a good example of the many "coincidences" in the book that later take on crucial significance for the story.

3:1 *After these events.* Four years have elapsed since Esther's selection as queen (v. 7; 2:16–17). The fact that no reason is given for the promotion of Haman provides an ironic contrast between the unrewarded merit of Mordecai (2:21–23; see 6:3) and the unmerited reward of Haman. *son of Hammedatha the Agagite.* There is some debate about the ancestry of Haman. The name Hammedatha appears to be Persian and probably refers to an immediate ancestor. The title "Agagite" could refer to some other immediate ancestor or to an unknown place; however, it is far more likely that it refers to Agag, king of Amalek (1 Sam 15:20). The Amalekites had attacked Israel after she fled from Egypt (Ex 17:8–16; 1 Sam 14:47–48); for this reason the Lord would "have war against Amalek from generation to generation" (Ex 17:16). Israel was not to forget, but must "blot out the memory of Amalek from under heaven" (Deut 25:17–19). Saul's attack on Amalek (1 Sam 15) resulted in the death of most, though not all (1 Chr 4:42–43), of the city's population and later in the death of King Agag. In Esther, about 500 years after the battle led by the Benjamite Saul, the Benjamite Mordecai (see note on 2:5) continues the war with the Amalekites.

3:2–6 Obedience to the second commandment (Ex 20:4) is not the issue in Mordecai's refusal to bow down to Haman, for the Jews were willing to bow down to kings (see 1 Sam 24:8; 2 Sam 14:4; 1 Kin 1:16) and to other persons (see Gen 23:7; 33:3; 44:14). Only the long-standing enmity between the Jews and the Amalekites accounts both for Mordecai's refusal and for Haman's intent to destroy all the Jews (vv. 5–6). The threat against the Jews "throughout the whole kingdom" (v. 6) is a threat against the ultimate issue of redemptive history (see Introduction: Purpose, Themes and Literary Features).

3:4 Compare the phraseology with that in the Joseph story (Gen 39:10).

3:7 *first month . . . twelfth year.* April or May, 474 B.C., the fifth year of Esther's reign. *Pur.* See 9:24,26. This word is found in Akkadian texts with the meaning "lot" (as here). The celebration known as Purim takes its name from the plural of this noun (see 9:23–32). There is irony in the fact that the month of the Jews' celebration of the Passover deliverance from Egypt is also the month that Haman begins plotting their destruction (Ex 12:1–11). *was cast.* Perhaps by the astrologers who assisted Haman (5:10,14; 6:12–13). *twelfth month.* An 11-month delay is contemplated between the securing of the decree and the execution of it in the month Adar (February-March).

3:8–9 The name of the people Haman wishes to destroy is slyly omitted in this blend of the true and the false: The Jews did have their own customs and laws, but they were not disobedient to the king (Jer 29:7).

3:8 *scattered and dispersed.* See 8:11,17; 9:2, 12,16,19–20,28.

3:9 *ten thousand talents.* Herodotus (3.95) records that the annual income of the Persian empire was 15,000 talents. If this figure is correct, Haman offers two-thirds of that amount—a huge sum. Presumably the money would have come from the plundered wealth of the victims of the decree. Verse 13 implies that those who would take part in the massacre were to be allowed to keep the plunder, perhaps adding financial incentive to the execution of the decree since Ahasuerus disavows taking the money (v. 11). On the other hand, 4:7 and 7:4 may imply that the king had planned on collecting some of the money. *those who carry on the king's business.* This clause may represent the title of revenue officers who would bring the money to the treasury, or it could refer to those who carry out the decree. The Amalekites had once before plundered Israel (see note on v. 1); Haman plans a recurrence.

3:12 *thirteenth day . . . first month.* In the 12th year of

according to its script, each people according
to its language, being written [c]in the name of
King Ahasuerus and sealed with the king's
signet ring.
13 Letters were sent by [a]couriers to all the
king's provinces [b]to destroy, to kill and to
annihilate all the Jews, both young and old,
women and children, [c]in one day, the thirteenth *day* of the twelfth month, which is the
month Adar, and to [d]seize their possessions
as plunder.
14 [a]A copy of the edict to be [1]issued as
law in every province was published to all
the peoples so that they should be ready for
this day.
15 The couriers went out impelled by the
king's command while the decree was
[1]issued at the citadel in Susa; and while the
king and Haman sat down to drink, [a]the city
of Susa was in confusion.

Esther Learns of Haman's Plot

4 When Mordecai learned [a]all that had been
done, [1]he tore his clothes, put on sackcloth and ashes, and went out into the midst
of the city and wailed loudly and bitterly.
2 He went as far as the king's gate, for no
one was to enter the king's gate clothed in
sackcloth.
3 In each and every province where the
command and decree of the king came, there
was great mourning among the Jews, with
[a]fasting, weeping and wailing; and many lay
on sackcloth and ashes.
4 Then Esther's maidens and her
eunuchs came and told her, and the queen
writhed in great anguish. And she sent garments to clothe Mordecai that he might
remove his sackcloth from him, but he did
not accept *them*.
5 Then Esther summoned Hathach from
the king's eunuchs, whom [1]the king had
appointed to attend her, and ordered him *to
go* to Mordecai to learn what this *was* and
why it *was*.

12 [c]1 Kin 21:8; Esth 8:8, 10 **13** [a]2 Chr 30:6; Esth 8:10, 14 [b]Esth 7:4 [c]Esth 8:12 [d]Esth 8:11; 9:10 **14** [1]Lit *given* [a]Esth 8:13, 14 **15** [1]Lit *given* [a]Esth 8:15 **4:1** [1]Lit *Mordecai* [a]2 Sam 1:11; Esth 3:8-10; Jon 3:5,6 **3** [a]Esth 4:16 **5** [1]Lit *he*

7 [a]Esth 3:9 **8** [a]Esth 3:14 **11** [a]Esth 5:1; 6:4 [b]Dan 2:9 [c]Esth 5:2; 8:4 **14** [a]Lev 26:42; 2 Kin 13:5 **16** [a]Joel 1:14; 2:12 [b]Esth 5:1

6 So Hathach went out to Mordecai to
the city square in front of the king's gate.
7 Mordecai told him all that had happened to him, and [a]the exact amount of
money that Haman had promised to pay to
the king's treasuries for the destruction of
the Jews.
8 He also gave him [a]a copy of the text of
the edict which had been issued in Susa for
their destruction, that he might show Esther
and inform her, and to order her to go in to
the king to implore his favor and to plead
with him for her people.
9 Hathach came back and related Mordecai's words to Esther.
10 Then Esther spoke to Hathach and
ordered him *to reply* to Mordecai:
11 "All the king's servants and the people
of the king's provinces know that for any
man or woman who [a]comes to the king to
the inner court who is not summoned, [b]he
has but one law, that he be put to death,
unless the king holds out [c]to him the golden
scepter so that he may live. And I have not
been summoned to come to the king for
these thirty days."
12 They related Esther's words to Mordecai.
13 Then Mordecai told *them* to reply to
Esther, "Do not imagine that you in the
king's palace can escape any more than all
the Jews.
14 "For if you remain silent at this time,
relief and [a]deliverance will arise for the Jews
from another place and you and your
father's house will perish. And who knows
whether you have not attained royalty for
such a time as this?"

Esther Plans to Intercede

15 Then Esther told *them* to reply to Mordecai,
16 "Go, assemble all the Jews who are
found in Susa, and fast for me; [a]do not eat or
drink for [b]three days, night or day. I and my

Ahasuerus's reign (v. 7), i.e., Apr. 17, 474 B.C.

3:13 Haman's decree against Israel is the same destruction that had earlier been decreed against Amalek (1 Sam 15:3). *thirteenth day . . . twelfth month.* Mar. 7, 473 B.C. (see 8:12).

3:15 Haman and the king will drink together again in the story when the fate of the Jews is once again being decided (7:1–2), but then it will be at the dissolution of their relationship and the reversal of the decree here celebrated. The celebration here is in sharp contrast to the fasting and mourning of the Jews (4:1–3,15–16).

4:2 *king's gate.* See note on 2:19.

4:3 See note on 3:15. The prominence of feasting throughout the book of Esther sets the fasts of vv. 3,16 in sharp relief; a pair of fasts matches the prominent pairs of banquets (see Introduction: Purpose, Themes and Literary Features; see also note on 9:31).

4:4–12 The fact that the dialogue of Esther and Mordecai is mediated by Hathach reflects the prohibition against Mordecai's entering the royal citadel dressed in mourning (v. 2) and the isolation of Esther in the harem quarters.

4:7 See note on 3:9. That Mordecai is aware of the amount Haman promised to the king is a reminder of his high position in the bureaucracy at Susa (2:21–23).

4:11 Herodotus (3.118,140) also notes that anyone approaching the Persian king unsummoned would be killed unless the king gave immediate pardon.

4:12–16 The themes of the book of Esther are most clearly expressed in this passage. Mordecai's confidence for the Jews' deliverance is based on God's sovereignty in working out His purposes and fulfilling His promises. Their deliverance will come, even if through some means other than Esther. Yet that sovereignty is not fatalistic: Unless Esther exercises her individual responsibility, she and her family will perish. Cf. Matt 26:24; Acts 2:23 for similar treatments of the relationship between divine sovereignty and human responsibility.

4:14 *such a time as this.* Cf. Gen 45:5–7 in the Joseph narrative.

4:16 *fast.* See note on v. 3. Prayer, which usually accompanied such fasting, was presumably a part of this fast as well (see Judg

maidens also will fast in the same way. And thus I will go in to the king, which is not according to the law; and if I perish, I perish."

17 So Mordecai went away and did just as Esther had commanded him.

Esther Plans a Banquet

5 Now it came about [a]on the third day that Esther put on her royal robes and stood [b]in the inner court of the king's palace in front of the king's [1]rooms, and the king was sitting on his royal throne in the [2]throne room, opposite the entrance to the palace.

2 When the king saw Esther the queen standing in the court, [a]she obtained favor in his sight; and [b]the king extended to Esther the golden scepter which *was* in his hand. So Esther came near and touched the top of the scepter.

3 Then the king said to her, "What is *troubling* you, Queen Esther? And what is your request? [a]Even to half of the kingdom it shall be given to you."

4 Esther said, "If it pleases the king, may the king and Haman come this day to the banquet that I have prepared for him."

5 Then the king said, "[a]Bring Haman quickly that we may do [1]as Esther desires." So the king and Haman came to the banquet which Esther had prepared.

6 [1]As they drank their wine at the banquet, [a]the king said to Esther, "[b]What is your petition, for it shall be granted to you. And what is your request? Even to half of the kingdom it shall be done."

7 So Esther replied, "My petition and my request is:

8 [a]if I have found favor in the sight of the king, and if it pleases the king to grant my petition and do [1]what I request, may the king and Haman come to [b]the banquet which I will prepare for them, and tomorrow I will do [2]as the king says."

Haman's Pride

9 Then Haman went out that day glad and pleased of heart; but when Haman saw Mordecai [a]in the king's gate and [b]that he did not stand up or [1]tremble before him, Haman was filled with anger against Mordecai.

10 Haman controlled himself, however, went to his house and [1]sent for his friends and his wife [a]Zeresh.

11 Then Haman recounted to them the glory of his riches, and the [1a]number of his sons, and every *instance* where the king had magnified him and how he had [2b]promoted him above the princes and servants of the king.

12 Haman also said, "Even Esther the queen let no one but me come with the king to the banquet which she had prepared; and [a]tomorrow also I am [1]invited by her with the king.

13 "Yet all of this [1]does not satisfy me every time I see Mordecai the Jew sitting at [a]the king's gate."

14 Then Zeresh his wife and all his friends said to him, "[a]Have a [1]gallows fifty cubits high made and in the morning ask the king to have Mordecai hanged on it; then go joyfully with the king to the banquet." And the [2]advice pleased Haman, so he had the gallows made.

The King Plans to Honor Mordecai

6 During that night [1]the king [a]could not sleep so he gave an order to bring [b]the book of records, the chronicles, and they were read before the king.

2 It was found written what [a]Mordecai had reported concerning Bigthana and

5:1 [1]Lit *house* [2]Lit *royal house* [a]Esth 4:16 [b]Esth 4:11; 6:4
2 [a]Esth 2:9 [b]Esth 4:11; 8:4
3 [a]Esth 7:2; Mark 6:23
5 [1]Lit *the word of Esther* [a]Esth 6:14
6 [1]Lit *at the banquet of wine* [a]Esth 7:2 [b]Esth 5:3
8 [1]Lit *my request* [a]Esth 7:3; 8:5 [b]Esth 6:14
8 [2]Lit *according to the word of the king*
9 [1]Or *move for* [a]Esth 2:19 [b]Esth 3:5
10 [1]Lit *sent and brought* [a]Esth 6:13
11 [1]Lit *multitude* [2]Lit *lifted* [a]Esth 9:7-10 [b]Esth 3:1
12 [1]Lit *summoned to her* [a]Esth 5:8
13 [1]Lit *is not suitable to me* [a]Esth 5:9
14 [1]Lit *tree* [2]Lit *thing* [a]Esth 6:4; 7:9, 10
6:1 [1]Lit *the king's sleep fled* [a]Dan 6:18 [b]Esth 2:23; 10:2
2 [a]Esth 2:21, 22

20:26; 1 Sam 7:6; 2 Sam 12:16; Ezra 8:21–23; Neh 9:1–3; Is 58:3; Jer 14:12; Joel 1:14; 2:12–17; Jon 3:6–9). The omission of any reference to prayer or to God is consistent with the author's intention; absence of any distinctively religious concepts or vocabulary is a rhetorical device used to heighten the fact that it is indeed God who has been active in the whole narrative (see Introduction: Purpose, Themes and Literary Features). *I and my maidens also will fast.* Note the rhetorical symmetry: Where once Esther and her maids had received special foods (2:9), now they share a fast. *if I perish.* Cf. the similar formulation in the Joseph narrative (Gen 43:14).

5:2 See Prov 21:1.

5:6–7 One can only speculate regarding Esther's reasons for delaying her answer to the king's question until he had asked it a third time (vv. 3,6; 7:2). The author uses these delays as plot retardation devices that sustain the tension and permit the introduction of new material on Haman's self-aggrandizement (vv. 11–12) and Mordecai's reward (6:6–11).

5:9 Haman's rage is kindled when Mordecai does not rise in his presence—an ironic contrast to his earlier refusal to bow (3:2–6).

5:11 *the number of his sons.* Haman had ten sons (9:7–10). Herodotus (1.136) reports that the Persians prized a large number of sons second only to valor in battle; the Persian king sent gifts to the subject with the most sons (cf. Ps 127:3–5).

5:12–13 See Prov 16:18; 29:23.

5:14 *fifty cubits high.* There may be a note of hyperbole in the height of the gallows (75 feet). Others have suggested that the gallows was erected atop some other structure to achieve this height, e.g., the city wall (see 1 Sam 31:10). *hanged.* See note on 2:23.

6:1 This verse marks the literary center of the narrative. When things could not look worse, a series of seemingly trivial coincidences marks a critical turn that brings resolution to the story. The king's inability to sleep, his requesting the reading of the Chronicles, the reading of the passage reporting Mordecai's past kindness, Haman's noisy carpentry in the early hours of the morning (5:14), his sudden entry into the outer court and his assumption that he was the man the king wished to honor—all are events testifying to the sovereignty of God over the events of the narrative. Circumstances that seemed incidental earlier in the narrative take on crucial significance. Just as in the Joseph story (Gen 41:1–45), the hero's personal fortunes are reversed because of the monarch's disturbed sleep (cf. Dan 2:1; 6:18).

6:2 The scribe was reading at the time from the Chronicles that recorded events five years earlier (compare 3:7 with 2:16).

Teresh, two of the king's eunuchs who were doorkeepers, that they had sought to lay hands on King Ahasuerus.

3 The king said, "What honor or dignity has been bestowed on Mordecai for this?" Then the king's servants who attended him said, "Nothing has been done for him."

4 So the king said, "Who is in the court?" Now Haman had just [a]entered the outer court of the king's palace in order to speak to the king about [b]hanging Mordecai on the gallows which he had prepared for him.

5 The king's servants said to him, "Behold, Haman is standing in the court." And the king said, "Let him come in."

6 So Haman came in and the king said to him, "What is to be done for the man [a]whom the king desires to honor?" And Haman said [1]to himself, "Whom would the king desire to honor more than me?"

7 Then Haman said to the king, "For the man whom the king desires to honor,

8 let them bring a royal robe which the king has worn, and [a]the horse on which the king has ridden, and on whose head [b]a royal crown has been placed;

9 and let the robe and the horse be handed over to one of the king's most noble princes and let them array the man whom the king desires to honor and lead him on horseback through the city square, [a]and proclaim before him, 'Thus it shall be done to the man whom the king desires to honor.' "

Haman Must Honor Mordecai

10 Then the king said to Haman, "Take quickly the robes and the horse as you have said, and do so for Mordecai the Jew, who is sitting at the king's gate; do not fall short in anything of all that you have said."

11 So Haman took the robe and the horse, and arrayed Mordecai, and led him *on horseback* through the city square, and proclaimed before him, "Thus it shall be done to the man whom the king desires to honor."

12 Then Mordecai returned to the king's gate. But Haman hurried home, mourning, [a]with *his* head covered.

13 Haman recounted [a]to Zeresh his wife and all his friends everything that had happened to him. Then his wise men and Zeresh his wife said to him, "If Mordecai, before whom you have begun to fall, is [1]of Jewish origin, you will not overcome him, but will surely fall before him."

14 While they were still talking with him, the king's eunuchs arrived and hastily [a]brought Haman to the banquet which Esther had prepared.

4 [a]Esth 4:11 [b]Esth 5:14
6 [1]Lit *in his heart* [a]Esth 6:7, 9, 11
8 [a]1 Kin 1:33 [b]Esth 1:11; 2:17
9 [a]Gen 41:43
12 [a]2 Sam 15:30
13 [a]Esth 5:10

Esther's Plea

7 Now the king and Haman came to drink *wine* with Esther the queen.

2 And the king said to Esther on the second day also [1]as they drank their wine at the banquet, "[a]What is your petition, Queen Esther? It shall be granted you. And what is your request? [b]Even to half of the kingdom it shall be done."

3 Then Queen Esther replied, "[a]If I have found favor in your sight, O king, and if it pleases the king, let my life be given me as my petition, and my people as my request;

4 for [a]we have been sold, I and my people, to be destroyed, [b]to be killed and to be annihilated. Now if we had only been sold as slaves, men and women, I would have remained silent, for the [1]trouble would not be commensurate with the [2]annoyance to the king."

5 Then King Ahasuerus [1]asked Queen Esther, "Who is he, and where is he, [2]who would presume to do thus?"

6 Esther said, "[a]A foe and an enemy is this wicked Haman!" Then Haman became terrified before the king and queen.

Haman Is Hanged

7 The king arose [a]in his anger from [1]drinking wine *and went* into [b]the palace garden; but Haman stayed to beg for his life from Queen Esther, for he saw that harm had been determined against him by the king.

8 Now when the king returned from the palace garden into the [1]place where they were drinking wine, Haman was falling on [a]the couch where Esther was. Then the king said, "Will he even assault the queen with

13 [1]Lit *from the seed of the Jews*
14 [a]Esth 5:8
7:2 [1]Lit *at the banquet of wine* [a]Esth 5:6; 9:12 [b]Esth 5:3
3 [a]Esth 5:8; 8:5
4 [1]Or *enemy could not compensate for the loss* [2]Or *damage* [a]Esth 3:9 [b]Esth 3:13
5 [1]Lit *said and said to* [2]Lit *whose heart has been filled*
6 [a]Esth 3:10
7 [1]Lit *the banquet of wine* [a]Esth 1:12 [b]Esth 1:5
8 [1]Lit *house of the banquet of wine* [a]Esth 1:6

6:4–6 Again, the irony is evident: Just as Haman had withheld from the king the identity of the "certain people" (3:8), so now the king unintentionally keeps from Haman the identity of the "man whom the king desires to honor" (v. 6).
6:8 *royal robe which the king has worn.* See 8:15; see also Introduction: Purpose, Themes and Literary Features. Cf. in the Joseph story Gen 41:41–43. Great significance was attached to the king's garment in ancient times; wearing his garments was a sign of unique favor (1 Sam 18:4). To wear another's garments was to partake of his power, stature, honor or sanctity (2 Kin 2:13–14; Is 61:3,10; Zech 3; Mark 5:27). Haman's suggestion is not only a great honor to the recipient, but it is also considerably flattering to the king: Wearing his garment was chosen instead of wealth.
6:13 See Introduction: Purpose, Themes and Literary Features.
6:14 Guests were usually escorted to feasts (see in the Joseph narrative Gen 43:15–26; cf. Matt 22:1–14).
7:2 See 5:3,6.
7:3 See 2:15,17.
7:4 *sold.* Esther refers to the bribe Haman offered to the king (3:9; 4:7); she also paraphrases Haman's edict (3:13). *for the trouble . . . king.* The statement probably means either (1) that the affliction of the Jews would be less injurious to the king if slavery was all that was involved, or (2) that Esther would not trouble the king if slavery was the only issue.
7:8 *falling on the couch where Esther was.* Meals were customarily taken reclining on a couch (Amos 6:4–7; John 13:23). It is ironic that Haman, who became angry when the Jew Mordecai would not bow down (which set the whole story in motion), now falls before the Jewess Esther (see 6:13). The king's

me in the house?" As the word went out of the king's mouth, they covered Haman's face.

9 Then Harbonah, one of the eunuchs who *were* before the king said, "Behold indeed, [a]the gallows standing at Haman's house fifty cubits high, which Haman made for Mordecai [b]who spoke good on behalf of the king!" And the king said, "Hang him on it."

10 [a]So they hanged Haman on the [1]gallows which he had prepared for Mordecai, [b]and the king's anger subsided.

Mordecai Promoted

8 On that day King Ahasuerus gave the house of Haman, [a]the enemy of the Jews, to Queen Esther; and Mordecai came before the king, for Esther had disclosed [b]what he was to her.

2 [a]The king took off his signet ring which he had taken away from Haman, and gave it to Mordecai. And Esther set Mordecai over the house of Haman.

3 Then Esther spoke again to the king, fell at his feet, wept and implored him to avert the evil *scheme* of Haman the Agagite and his plot which he had devised against the Jews.

4 [a]The king extended the golden scepter to Esther. So Esther arose and stood before the king.

5 Then she said, "[a]If it pleases the king and if I have found favor before him and the matter *seems* proper to the king and I am pleasing in his sight, let it be written to revoke the [b]letters devised by Haman, the son of Hammedatha the Agagite, which he wrote to destroy the Jews who are in all the king's provinces.

6 "For [a]how can I endure to see the calamity which will befall my people, and how can I endure to see the destruction of my kindred?"

9 [a]Esth 5:14 [b]Esth 2:22
10 [1]Lit *tree* [a]Ps 7:16; 94:23 [b]Esth 7:7, 8
8:1 [a]Esth 7:6 [b]Esth 2:7, 15
2 [a]Esth 3:10
4 [a]Esth 4:11; 5:2
5 [a]Esth 5:8; 7:3 [b]Esth 3:13
6 [a]Esth 7:4; 9:1

7 [a]Esth 8:1
8 [1]Lit *according to the good in your eyes* [a]Esth 3:12; 8:10 [b]Esth 1:19
9 [1]Lit *in it* [2]Lit *Cush* [a]Esth 3:12 [b]Esth 1:1 [c]Esth 1:22; 3:12
10 [a]1 Kin 4:28
11 [1]Lit *Which* [a]Esth 9:2 [b]Esth 3:13 [c]Esth 9:10
12 [a]Esth 3:13; 9:1
13 [1]Lit *given* [a]Esth 3:14

7 So King Ahasuerus said to Queen Esther and to Mordecai the Jew, "Behold, [a]I have given the house of Haman to Esther, and him they have hanged on the gallows because he had stretched out his hands against the Jews.

The King's Decree Avenges the Jews

8 "Now you write to the Jews [1]as you see fit, in the king's name, and [a]seal *it* with the king's signet ring; for a decree which is written in the name of the king and sealed with the king's signet ring [b]may not be revoked."

9 [a]So the king's scribes were called at that time in the third month (that is, the month Sivan), on the twenty-third [1]day; and it was written according to all that Mordecai commanded to the Jews, the satraps, the governors and the princes of the provinces which *extended* [b]from India to [2]Ethiopia, 127 provinces, to [c]every province according to its script, and to every people according to their language as well as to the Jews according to their script and their language.

10 He wrote in the name of King Ahasuerus, and sealed it with the king's signet ring, and sent letters by couriers on [a]horses, riding on steeds sired by the royal stud.

11 [1]In them the king granted the Jews who were in each and every city *the right* [a]to assemble and to defend their lives, [b]to destroy, to kill and to annihilate the entire army of any people or province which might attack them, including children and women, and [c]to plunder their spoil,

12 on [a]one day in all the provinces of King Ahasuerus, the thirteenth *day* of the twelfth month (that is, the month Adar).

13 [a]A copy of the edict to be [1]issued as law in each and every province was published to all the peoples, so that the Jews would be ready for this day to avenge themselves on their enemies.

---

leaving the room sets the stage for the final twist that would seal Haman's fate. *covered Haman's face.* See 6:12; see also Introduction: Purpose, Themes and Literary Features.

7:9 Before this moment there is no evidence that Esther had known of Mordecai's triumph earlier in the day (ch. 6); she has pleaded for the life of her people. Harbona's reference to the gallows in effect introduces a second charge against Haman—his attempt to kill the king's benefactor. *Harbonah.* See Introduction: Purpose, Themes and Literary Features. He had been sent earlier to bring Vashti and thus set in motion the events that would lead to her fall and the choice of Esther (1:10); now he is instrumental in the fall of Haman and the rise of Mordecai.

7:10 *subsided.* See 2:1; see also Introduction: Purpose, Themes and Literary Features.

8:1–17 The author achieves considerable literary symmetry by recapitulating much of 3:1–4:3 in almost identical terms.

8:1 *gave the house of Haman . . . to Queen Esther.* Herodotus (3.128–129) and Josephus (*Antiquities*, 11.17) confirm that the property of a traitor reverted to the crown; Ahasuerus presents Haman's wealth (5:11) to Esther.

8:2 Cf. 3:10, where the king's offer of his ring includes Haman's keeping the money; here Mordecai receives the office and the estate of Haman.

8:3–6 Esther and Mordecai are secure (7:4–5), but the irrevocable decree is still a threat to the rest of the Jews.

8:3 *Agagite.* See note on 3:1.

8:5 *favor.* See 4:11; 5:2.

8:6 Cf. the Joseph story (Gen 44:34).

8:8 See 1:19; see also Introduction: Purpose, Themes and Literary Features. The dilemma is the same as the one that confronted Darius the Mede in Daniel (Dan 6:8,12,15). The solution is to issue another decree that in effect counters the original decree of Haman without formally revoking it (see note on 9:2–3).

8:9–13 The phraseology is taken from the parallel in 3:12–14. The extent of the destruction is the same as that earlier decreed against Amalek (see note on 3:13).

8:9 *third month . . . twenty-third day.* In Ahasuerus's 12th year, i.e., June 25, 474 B.C., two months and ten days after the proclamation of Haman's edict (see note on 3:13).

8:12 *thirteenth day . . . twelfth month.* Mar. 7, 473 B.C. (see 3:13). Some 15 years after this first Purim, Ezra would lead his expedition to Jerusalem (Ezra 7:9).

14 The couriers, hastened and impelled by the king's command, went out, riding on the royal steeds; and the decree was given out at the citadel in Susa.

15 Then Mordecai went out from the presence of the king [a]in royal robes of [1]blue and white, with a large crown of gold and [b]a garment of fine linen and purple; and [c]the city of Susa shouted and rejoiced.

16 For the Jews there was [a]light and gladness and joy and honor.

17 In each and every province and in each and every city, wherever the king's commandment and his decree arrived, there was gladness and joy for the Jews, a feast and a [1][a]holiday. And [b]many among the peoples of the land became Jews, for the dread of the Jews had fallen on them.

The Jews Destroy Their Enemies

9 Now [a]in the twelfth month (that is, the month Adar), on [b]the thirteenth [1]day [c]when the king's command and edict [2]were about to be executed, on the day when the enemies of the Jews hoped to gain the mastery over them, it was turned to the contrary so that the Jews themselves gained the mastery over those who hated them.

2 [a]The Jews assembled in their cities throughout all the provinces of King Ahasuerus to lay hands on those who sought their harm; and no one could stand before them, [b]for the dread of them had fallen on all the peoples.

3 Even all the princes of the provinces, [a]the satraps, the governors and those who were doing the king's business [1]assisted the Jews, because the dread of Mordecai had fallen on them.

4 Indeed, Mordecai was great in the king's house, and his fame spread throughout all the provinces; for the man Mordecai [a]became greater and greater.

5 Thus [a]the Jews struck all their enemies with [1]the sword, killing and destroying; and they did what they pleased to those who hated them.

6 At the citadel in Susa the Jews killed and destroyed five hundred men,

7 and Parshandatha, Dalphon, Aspatha,

8 Poratha, Adalia, Aridatha,

9 Parmashta, Arisai, Aridai and Vaizatha,

10 [a]the ten sons of Haman the son of Hammedatha, the Jews' enemy; but [b]they did not lay their hands on the plunder.

11 On that day the number of those who were killed at the citadel in Susa [1]was reported to the king.

12 The king said to Queen Esther, "The Jews have killed and destroyed five hundred men and the ten sons of Haman at the citadel in Susa. What then have they done in the rest of the king's provinces! [a]Now what is your petition? It shall even be granted you. And what is your further request? It shall also be done."

13 Then said Esther, "If it pleases the king, [a]let tomorrow also be granted to the Jews who are in Susa to do according to the edict of today; and let Haman's ten sons be hanged on the gallows."

14 So the king commanded that it should be done so; and an edict was issued in Susa, and Haman's ten sons were hanged.

15 The Jews who were in Susa assembled also on the fourteenth day of the month Adar and killed [a]three hundred men in Susa, but [b]they did not lay their hands on the plunder.

16 Now [a]the rest of the Jews who *were* in the king's provinces [b]assembled, to defend their lives and [1]rid themselves of their enemies, and kill 75,000 of those who hated them; but they did not lay their hands on the plunder.

17 *This was done* on [a]the thirteenth day of the month Adar, and [b]on the fourteenth [1]day they rested and made it a day of feasting and rejoicing.

18 But the Jews who were in Susa [a]assembled on the thirteenth and [b]the fourteenth

15 [1]Or *violet* [a]Esth 5:11 [b]Gen 41:42 [c]Esth 3:15
16 [a]Ps 97:11; 112:4
17 [1]Lit *good day* [a]Esth 9:19 [b]Esth 9:27
9:1 [1]Lit *day in it* [2]Lit *drew near* [a]Esth 8:12 [b]Esth 9:17 [c]Esth 3:13
2 [a]Esth 8:11; 9:15-18 [b]Esth 8:17
3 [1]Lit *lifted up* [a]Ezra 8:36
4 [a]2 Sam 3:1; 1 Chr 11:9
5 [1]Lit *the stroke of* [a]Esth 3:13
10 [a]Esth 5:11 [b]Esth 8:11
11 [1]Lit *came*
12 [a]Esth 5:6; 7:2
13 [a]Esth 8:11; 9:15
15 [a]Esth 9:12 [b]Esth 9:10
16 [1]Lit *have rest from* [a]Esth 9:2 [b]Lev 26:7, 8; Esth 8:11
17 [1]Lit *in it* [a]Esth 9:1 [b]Esth 9:21
18 [a]Esth 8:11; 9:2 [b]Esth 9:21

8:14–17 The phraseology is taken from 3:15–4:3.

8:15 *royal robes.* Mordecai's second investiture (see Introduction: Purpose, Themes and Literary Features; see also note on 6:8).

9:1 See notes on 8:9–13. The Jews carry out the edict of Mordecai eight months and 20 days later. *turned to the contrary.* The statement that the opposite happened points to the author's concern with literary symmetry: He balances most of the details from the first half of the story with their explicit reversal in the second half.

9:2–3 An illustration of Gen 12:3. Confronted with two conflicting edicts issued in the king's name—the edict of Haman and the edict of Mordecai—the governors follow the edict of the current regime.

9:5–10 The Jews attend to the unfinished business of "blotting out the name of the Amalekites" (Ex 17:16; Deut 25:17–19; see notes on 3:1–6). This incident is presented as the antithesis of 1 Sam 15: The narrator is emphatic that the Jews did not take plunder, in spite of the king's permission to do so (8:11). Seizing the plunder 500 years earlier in the battle against Amalek had cost Saul his kingship (1 Sam 15:17–19); here, not taking the plunder brings royal power to Mordecai (vv. 20–23). See vv. 15–16; cf. Gen 14:22–24.

9:10 *sons of Haman.* The second reference to Haman's sons (see 5:11; see also Introduction: Purpose, Themes and Literary Features).

9:12 See 5:3,6; 7:2.

9:13 The reference to hanging in this case is to the display of the corpses, not to the means of the execution (see vv. 7–10 and note on 2:23).

9:15–16 See note on vv. 5–10.

9:16,22 *rid themselves of their enemies.* Closely associated with the vengeance on their enemies is the rest promised to Israel (Deut 25:19). The defeat of Haman brings rest to the Jews. Cf. 1 Chr 22:6–10; Ps 95:8–11; Is 32:18; Heb 3:11–4:11.

9:18–19 The author accounts for the tradition of observing Purim on two different days: It is observed on the 14th in most towns, but the Jews of Susa observed it on the 15th. Today it is observed on the 14th except in Jerusalem, where it is observed on the 15th.

[1]of the same month, and they rested on the
fifteenth [1]day and made it a day of feasting
and rejoicing.
19 Therefore the Jews of the rural areas,
who live in [a]the rural towns, make the fourteenth day of the month Adar *a* [1][b]holiday for
rejoicing and feasting and [c]sending portions
of food to one another.

The Feast of Purim Instituted

20 Then Mordecai recorded these events,
and he sent letters to all the Jews who were
in all the provinces of King Ahasuerus, both
near and far,
21 obliging them to celebrate the fourteenth day of the month Adar, and the fifteenth day [1]of the same month, annually,
22 because on those days the Jews [1]rid
themselves of their enemies, and *it was a*
month which was [a]turned for them from sorrow into gladness and from mourning into a
[2]holiday; that they should make them days of
feasting and rejoicing and [b]sending portions
of food to one another and gifts to the poor.
23 Thus the Jews undertook what they
had started to do, and what Mordecai had
written to them.
24 For Haman the son of Hammedatha,
the Agagite, the adversary of all the Jews,
had schemed against the Jews to destroy
them and [a]had cast Pur, that is the lot, to disturb them and destroy them.
25 But [a]when it came [1]to the king's attention, he commanded by letter [b]that his
wicked scheme which he had [2]devised
against the Jews, [c]should return on his own
head and that he and his sons should be
hanged on the [3]gallows.
26 Therefore they called these days Purim
after the name of Pur. [1]And [a]because of the
instructions in this letter, both what they had
seen in this regard and what had happened
to them,
27 the Jews established and [1]made a custom for themselves and for their [2]descen-
dants and for [a]all those who allied themselves with them, so that [3]they would not
fail [b]to celebrate these two days according to
their [4]regulation and according to their
appointed time annually.
28 So these days were to be remembered
and celebrated throughout every generation,
every family, every province and every city;
and these days of Purim were not to [1]fail
from among the Jews, or their memory [2]fade
from their [3]descendants.
29 Then Queen Esther, [a]daughter of Abihail, with Mordecai the Jew, wrote with full
authority to confirm [b]this second letter about
Purim.
30 He sent letters to all the Jews, [a]to the
127 provinces of the kingdom of Ahasuerus,
namely, words of peace and truth,
31 to establish these days of Purim at their
appointed times, just as Mordecai the Jew
and Queen Esther had established for them,
and just as they had established for themselves and for their [1]descendants with
[2]instructions [a]for their times of fasting and
their lamentations.
32 The command of Esther established
these [1]customs for [a]Purim, and it was written in the book.

Mordecai's Greatness

10 Now King Ahasuerus laid a tribute on
the land and on the [a]coastlands of the
sea.
2 And all the [1]accomplishments of his
authority and strength, and the full account
of the greatness of Mordecai [a]to which the
king [2]advanced him, are they not written in
[b]the Book of the Chronicles of the Kings of
Media and Persia?
3 For Mordecai the Jew was [a]second *only*
to King Ahasuerus, and great among the
Jews and in favor with his many kinsmen,
[b]one who sought the good of his people and
one who spoke for the welfare of his whole
nation.

18 [1]Lit *in it*
19 [1]Lit *rejoicing and feasting and a good day and sending* [a]Deut 3:5; Zech 2:4 [b]Esth 9:22 [c]Neh 8:10
21 [1]Lit *in it*
22 [1]Lit *had rest from* [2]Lit *good day* [a]Ps 30:11 [b]Neh 8:12
24 [a]Esth 3:7
25 [1]Lit *before the king, he* [2]Lit *schemed* [3]Lit *tree* [a]Esth 7:4-10 [b]Esth 3:6-15 [c]Ps 7:16
26 [1]Lit *Therefore because of all the words* [a]Esth 9:20
27 [1]Lit *received* [2]Lit *seed*
27 [3]Lit *it should not pass away* [4]Lit *writing* [a]Esth 8:17 [b]Esth 9:20, 21
28 [1]Lit *pass away* [2]Lit *end* [3]Lit *seed*
29 [a]Esth 2:15 [b]Esth 9:20, 21
30 [a]Esth 1:1
31 [1]Lit *seed* [2]Lit *words* [a]Esth 4:3
32 [1]Lit *words* [a]Esth 9:26
10:1 [a]Is 11:11; 24:15
2 [1]Lit *doings* [2]Lit *made him great* [a]Esth 8:15; 9:4 [b]Esth 2:23
3 [a]Gen 41:43, 44 [b]Neh 2:10

9:20 *Mordecai recorded these events.* Some take this as indicating that Mordecai wrote the book of Esther; however, the more natural understanding is that he recorded the events in the letters he sent.
9:22 *portions of food.* See note on 2:9; cf. Neh 8:10,12.
9:24,26 *Pur.* See note on 3:7.
9:27 *all those who allied themselves with them.* Some refer this phrase to a period of Jewish proselytism and regard it as important to dating the book. It is more likely that it refers to those mentioned in 8:17.
9:31 *fasting.* See notes on 4:3,16. No date is assigned for this fast. Jews traditionally observe the 13th of Adar, Haman's propitious day (see 3:7,13), as a fast ("the fast of Esther") before the celebration of Purim. These three days of victory celebration on the 13th–15th days of Adar rhetorically balance the three days of Esther's fasting prior to interceding with the king (4:16).
10:1–2 The reference to this taxation may represent material in the author's source, to which he directs the reader for additional information and confirmation (see note on 2:23).

Wisdom Literature

The Jews sometimes speak of the OT as the Law, the Prophets and the Writings. Included within the third division are Psalms and wisdom materials such as Job, Proverbs and Ecclesiastes. These wisdom books are associated with a class of people called "wise men" or "sages" who are listed with priests and prophets as an important force in Israelite society (Jer 18:18). Wise men were called on to give advice to kings and to instruct the young. Whereas the priests and prophets dealt more with the religious side of life, wise men were concerned about practical and philosophical matters. Some of their writings, like Proverbs, were optimistic, as they showed the young how to behave in order to live prosperous and happy lives. Other materials, such as Job and Ecclesiastes, were more pessimistic as they wrestled with difficult philosophical and theological questions such as the problem of evil and the prosperity of the wicked (see also Ps 37; 73). Both viewpoints—the optimistic and the pessimistic—are also found in the literature of other nations in the ancient Near East.

Because of the nature of Proverbs, we must not interpret it as prophecy or its statements about certain effects and results as promises. For instance, 10:27 says that the years of the wicked are cut short, while the righteous live long and prosperous lives (see 3:2 and note). The righteous have abundant food (10:3), but the wicked will go hungry (13:25). While such verses are generally true, there are enough exceptions to indicate that sometimes the righteous suffer and the wicked prosper. Normally the righteous and wicked "are rewarded in the earth" (11:31), but at other times reward and punishment lie beyond the grave.

Job

INTRODUCTION

Author

Although most of the book consists of the words of Job and his counselors, Job himself was not the author. We may be sure that the author was an Israelite, since he (not Job or his friends) frequently uses the Israelite covenant name for God (*Yahweh;* NASB "the LORD"). In the prologue (chs. 1—2), divine discourses (38:1—42:6) and epilogue (42:7–17) "LORD" occurs a total of 25 times, while in the rest of the book (chs. 3—37) it appears only once (12:9).

The unknown author probably had access to oral and/or written sources from which, under divine inspiration, he composed the book that we now have. Of course the subject matter of the prologue had to be divinely revealed to him, since it contains information only God could know. While the author preserves much of the archaic and non-Israelite flavor in the language of Job and his friends, he also reveals his own style as a writer of wisdom literature. The literary structures and the quality of the rhetoric used display the author's literary genius.

Date

Two dates are involved: (1) the date of the man Job and his historical setting, and (2) the date of the inspired writer who composed the book. The latter could be dated anytime from the reign of Solomon to the exile. Although the writer was an Israelite, he mentions nothing of Israelite history. He had a written and/or oral account about the non-Israelite sage Job (1:1), whose setting appears to be during the second millennium B.C. (2000–1000), and probably late in that millennium (see note on 19:24). Like the Hebrew patriarchs, Job lived more than 100 years (42:16). His wealth was measured in cattle (1:3), and he acted as priest for his family (1:5). The raiding of Sabean (1:15) and Chaldean (1:17) tribes fits the second millennium, as does the mention of the *qesitah,* a "piece of money," in 42:11 (see Gen 33:19; Josh 24:32). The discovery of a Targum (Aramaic paraphrase) on Job from the first or second century B.C. (the earliest written Targum) makes a very late date for authorship highly unlikely.

Language and Text

In many places Job is difficult to translate because of its many unusual words and its style. For that reason, modern translations frequently differ widely. Even the early translator(s) of Job into Greek (the Septuagint) seems often to have been perplexed. The Septuagint of Job is about 400 lines shorter than the accepted Hebrew text, and it may be that the translator(s) simply omitted lines he (they) did not understand. The early Syriac (Peshitta), Aramaic (Targum) and Latin (Vulgate) translators had similar difficulties.

Theme and Message

The book provides a profound statement on the subject of theodicy (the justice of God in light of human suffering). But the manner in which the problem of theodicy is conceived and the solution offered (if it may be called that) is uniquely Israelite. The theodicy question in Greek and later Western thought has been: How can the justice of an almighty God be defended in the face of evil, especially human suffering—and, even more particularly, the suffering of the innocent? In this form of the question, three possible assumptions are left open: (1) that God is not almighty, (2) that God is not just (that there is a "demonic" element in His being) and (3) that man may be innocent. In ancient Israel, however, it was indisputable that God is almighty, that He is perfectly just and that no human is wholly innocent in His sight. These three assumptions were also fundamental to the theology of Job and his friends. Simple logic then dictated the conclusion: Every person's suffering is indicative of the measure of his guilt in the eyes of God. In the abstract, this conclusion appeared

inescapable, logically imperative and theologically satisfying. Hence, in the context of such a theology, theodicy was not a problem because its solution was self-evident.

But what was thus theologically self-evident and unassailable in the abstract was often, as in the case of Job, in radical tension with actual human experience. There were those whose godliness was genuine, whose moral character was upright and who, though not sinless, had kept themselves from great transgression, but who nonetheless were made to suffer bitterly. For these the self-evident theology brought no consolation and offered no guidance. It only gave rise to a great enigma. And the God to whom the sufferer was accustomed to turn in moments of need and distress became Himself the overwhelming enigma. In the speeches of chs. 3—37, we hear on the one hand the flawless logic but wounding thrusts of those who insisted on the "orthodox" theology, and on the other hand the writhing of soul of the righteous sufferer who struggles with the great enigma. In addition he suffers from the wounds inflicted by his well-intended friends (see note on 5:27). Here, then, we have a graphic portrayal of the unique form of the problem of theodicy as experienced by righteous sufferers within orthodox Israel.

The "solution" offered is also uniquely Israelite—or, better said, Biblical. The relationship between God and man is not exclusive and closed. A third party intrudes, the great adversary (see chs. 1—2). Incapable of contending with God hand to hand, power pitted against power, he is bent on frustrating God's enterprise embodied in the creation and centered on the God-man relationship. As tempter he seeks to alienate man from God (see Gen 3; Matt 4:1); as accuser (one of the names by which he is called, *śaṭan*, means "accuser") he seeks to alienate God from man (see Zech 3:1; Rev 12:9–10). His all-consuming purpose is to drive an irremovable wedge between God and man, to effect an alienation that cannot be reconciled.

In the story of Job, the author portrays the adversary in his boldest and most radical assault on God and the godly man in the special and intimate relationship that is dearest to them both. When God calls up the name of Job before the accuser and testifies to the righteousness of this one on the earth—this man in whom God delights—Satan attempts with one crafty thrust both to assail God's beloved and to show up God as a fool. True to one of his modes of operation, he accuses Job before God. He charges that Job's godliness is evil. The very godliness in which God takes delight is void of all integrity; it is a terrible sin. Job's godliness is self-serving; he is righteous only because it pays. If God will only let Satan tempt Job by breaking the link between righteousness and blessing, he will expose the righteous man for the sinner he is.

It is the adversary's ultimate challenge. For if the godliness of the righteous man in whom God delights can be shown to be a terrible sin, then a chasm of alienation stands between them that cannot be bridged. Then even redemption is unthinkable, for the godliest of men will be shown to be the most ungodly. God's whole enterprise in creation and redemption will be shown to be radically flawed, and God can only sweep it all away in awful judgment.

The accusation, once raised, cannot be removed, not even by destroying the accuser. So God lets the adversary have his way with Job (within specified limits) so that God and the righteous Job may be vindicated and the great accuser silenced. Thus comes the anguish of Job, robbed of every sign of God's favor so that God becomes for him the great enigma. Also his righteousness is assailed on earth through the logic of the "orthodox" theology of his friends. Alone he agonizes. But he knows in his heart that his godliness has been authentic and that someday he will be vindicated (see 13:18; 14:13–17; 16:19; 19:25–27). And in spite of all, though he may curse the day of his birth (ch. 3) and chide God for treating him unjustly (9:28–35)—the uncalculated outcry of a distraught spirit—he will not curse God (as his wife, the human nearest his heart, proposes; see 2:9). In fact, what pains him most is God's apparent alienation from him.

In the end the adversary is silenced. And the astute theologians, Job's friends, are silenced. And Job is silenced. But God is not. And when He speaks, it is to Job that He speaks, bringing the silence of regret for hasty speech in days of suffering and the silence of repose in the ways of the Almighty (see 38:1—42:6). Furthermore, as his heavenly friend, God hears Job's intercessions for his associates (42:8–10), and He restores Job's beatitude (42:10–17).

In summary, the author's pastoral word to the godly sufferer is that his righteousness has such supreme value that God treasures it more than all. And the great adversary knows that if he is to thwart the purposes of God he must assail the righteousness of man (see 1:21–22; 2:9–10; 23:8, 10; cf. Gen 15:6). At stake in the suffering of the truly godly is the outcome of the struggle in heaven between the great adversary and God,

with the all-encompassing divine purpose in the balance. Thus the suffering of the righteous has a meaning and value commensurate with the titanic spiritual struggle of the ages.

Literary Form and Structure

Like some other ancient compositions, the book of Job has a sandwich literary structure: prologue (prose), main body (poetry), and epilogue (prose), revealing a creative composition, not an arbitrary compilation. Some of Job's words are lament (cf. ch. 3 and many shorter poems in his speeches), but the form of lament is unique to Job and often unlike the regular format of most lament psalms (except Ps 88). Much of the book takes the form of legal disputation. Although the friends come to console him, they end up arguing over the reason for Job's suffering. The argument breaks down in ch. 27, and Job then proceeds to make his final appeal to God for vindication (chs. 29—31). The wisdom poem in ch. 28 appears to be the words of the author, who sees the failure of the dispute as evidence of a lack of wisdom. So in praise of true wisdom he centers his structural apex between the three cycles of dialogue-dispute (chs. 3—27) and the three monologues: Job's (chs. 29—31), Elihu's (chs. 32—37) and God's (38:1—42:6). Job's monologue turns directly to God for a legal decision: that he is innocent of the charges his counselors have leveled against him. Elihu's monologue—another human perspective on why people suffer—rebukes Job but moves beyond the punishment theme to the value of divine chastening and God's redemptive purpose in it. God's monologue gives the divine perspective: Job is not condemned, but neither is a logical or legal answer given to why Job has suffered. That remains a mystery to Job, though the reader is ready for Job's restoration in the epilogue because he has had the heavenly vantage point of the prologue all along. So the literary structure and the theological significance of the book are beautifully tied together.

Outline

- I. Prologue (chs. 1—2)
  - A. Job's Happiness (1:1–5)
  - B. Job's Testing (1:6—2:13)
    1. Satan's first accusation (1:6–12)
    2. Job's faith despite loss of family and property (1:13–22)
    3. Satan's second accusation (2:1–6)
    4. Job's faith during personal suffering (2:7–10)
    5. The coming of the three friends (2:11–13)
- II. Dialogue-Dispute (chs. 3—27)
  - A. Job's Opening Lament (ch. 3)
  - B. First Cycle of Speeches (chs. 4—14)
    1. Eliphaz (chs. 4—5)
    2. Job's reply (chs. 6—7)
    3. Bildad (ch. 8)
    4. Job's reply (chs. 9—10)
    5. Zophar (ch. 11)
    6. Job's reply (chs. 12—14)
  - C. Second Cycle of Speeches (chs. 15—21)
    1. Eliphaz (ch. 15)
    2. Job's reply (chs. 16—17)
    3. Bildad (ch. 18)
    4. Job's reply (ch. 19)
    5. Zophar (ch. 20)
    6. Job's reply (ch. 21)
  - D. Third Cycle of Speeches (chs. 22—26)
    1. Eliphaz (ch. 22)
    2. Job's reply (chs. 23—24)
    3. Bildad (ch. 25)

        4. Job's reply (ch. 26)
    E. Job's Closing Discourse (ch. 27)
III. Interlude on Wisdom (ch. 28)
IV. Monologues (29:1 — 42:6)
    A. Job's Call for Vindication (chs. 29 — 31)
        1. His past honor and blessing (ch. 29)
        2. His present dishonor and suffering (ch. 30)
        3. His protestations of innocence and final oath (ch. 31)
    B. Elihu's Speeches (chs. 32 — 37)
        1. Introduction (32:1 – 5)
        2. The speeches themselves (32:6 — 37:24)
            a. First speech (32:6 — 33:33)
            b. Second speech (ch. 34)
            c. Third speech (ch. 35)
            d. Fourth speech (chs. 36 — 37)
    C. Divine Discourses (38:1 — 42:6)
        1. God's first discourse (38:1 — 40:2)
        2. Job's response (40:3 – 5)
        3. God's second discourse (40:6 — 41:34)
        4. Job's repentance (42:1 – 6)
V. Epilogue (42:7 – 17)
    A. God's Verdict (42:7 – 9)
    B. Job's Restoration (42:10 – 17)

Job's Character and Wealth

1 There was a man in the [a]land of Uz whose name was [b]Job; and that man was [c]blameless, upright, [d]fearing God and [e]turning away from evil.

2 [a]Seven sons and three daughters were born to him.

3 [a]His possessions also were 7,000 sheep, 3,000 camels, 500 yoke of oxen, 500 female donkeys, and very many servants; and that man was [b]the greatest of all the [1]men of the east.

4 His sons used to go and hold a feast in the house of each one on his day, and they would send and invite their three sisters to eat and drink with them.

5 When the days of feasting had completed their cycle, Job would send and consecrate them, rising up early in the morning and offering [a]burnt offerings *according to* the number of them all; for Job said, "[b]Perhaps my sons have sinned and [c]cursed God in their hearts." Thus Job did continually.

6 [a]Now there was a day when the [b]sons of God came to present themselves before the LORD, and [1]Satan also came among them.

7 The LORD said to Satan, "From where do you come?" Then Satan answered the LORD and said, "[a]From roaming about on the earth and walking around on it."

8 The LORD said to Satan, "Have you [1]considered [a]My servant Job? For there is no one like him on the earth, [b]a blameless and upright man, [2]fearing God and turning away from evil."

9 Then [a]Satan answered the [1]LORD, "Does Job fear God for nothing?

10 "[a]Have You not made a hedge about him and his house and all that he has, on every side? [b]You have blessed the work of his hands, and his [c]possessions have increased in the land.

11 "[a]But put forth Your hand now and [b]touch all that he has; he will surely curse You to Your face."

12 Then the LORD said to Satan, "Behold, all that he has is in your [1]power, only do not put forth your hand on him." So Satan departed from the presence of the LORD.

Satan Allowed to Test Job

13 Now on the day when his sons and his daughters were eating and drinking wine in their oldest brother's house,

14 a messenger came to Job and said, "The oxen were plowing and the [1]donkeys feeding beside them,

15 and [1]the [a]Sabeans [2]attacked and took them. They also [3]slew the servants with the edge of the sword, and [4]I alone have escaped to tell you."

16 While he was still speaking, another also came and said, "[a]The fire of God fell from heaven and burned up the sheep and the servants and consumed them, and I alone have escaped to tell you."

17 While he was still speaking, another also came and said, "The [a]Chaldeans formed three bands and made a raid on the camels and took them and [1]slew the servants with

1:1 [a]Jer 25:20; Lam 4:21 [b]Ezek 14:14, 20; James 5:11 [c]Gen 6:9; 17:1; Deut 18:13 [d]Gen 22:12; 42:18; Ex 18:21; Prov 8:13 [e]Job 28:28
2 [a]Job 42:13
3 [1]Lit *sons* [a]Job 42:12 [b]Job 29:25
5 [a]Gen 8:20; Job 42:8 [b]Job 8:4 [c]1 Kin 21:10, 13
6 [1]I.e. the adversary, and so throughout chs 1 and 2 [a]Job 2:1 [b]Job 38:7
7 [a]1 Pet 5:8
8 [1]Lit *set your heart to* [2]Or *revering* [a]Num 12:7; Josh 1:2, 7; Job 42:7, 8 [b]Job 1:1
9 [1]Lit *LORD and said* [a]Rev 12:9f
10 [a]Job 29:2-6; Ps 34:7 [b]Job 31:25 [c]Job 1:3; 31:25
11 [a]Job 2:5 [b]Job 19:21
12 [1]Lit *hand*
14 [1]Lit *female donkeys*
15 [1]Lit *Sheba* [2]Lit *fell upon* [3]Lit *smote* [4]Lit *only I alone*, and so also vv 16, 17, 19 [a]Gen 10:7; Job 6:19
16 [a]Gen 19:24; Lev 10:2; Num 11:1-3
17 [1]Lit *smote* [a]Gen 11:28, 31

1:1 *land of Uz.* A large territory east of the Jordan (see v. 3), which included Edom in the south (see Gen 36:28; Lam 4:21) and the Aramean lands in the north (see Gen 10:23; 22:21). *blameless, upright.* Spiritually and morally upright. This does not mean that Job was sinless. He later defends his moral integrity but also admits he is a sinner (see 6:24; 7:21). *fearing God.* See 28:28; Prov 3:7; see also note on Gen 20:11.

1:2 *Seven sons.* An ideal number, signifying completeness (see note on Ruth 4:15).

1:3 *7,000 sheep.* See note on 42:12. Job's enormous wealth was in livestock, not land (see Gen 12:16; 13:2; 26:14). *donkeys.* The Hebrew for this word is feminine in form. Donkeys that produced offspring were very valuable. *men of the east.* The Hebrew for this phrase is translated "eastern peoples" in Gen 29:1; Judg 6:3 (see note there).

1:5 *days of feasting.* On special occasions, feasts might last a week (see Gen 29:27; Judg 14:12). *consecrate them.* Make them ceremonially clean in preparation for the sacrifices he offered for them (see Ex 19:10,14). *offering burnt offerings.* Before the ceremonial laws of Moses were introduced, the father of the household acted as priest (see Gen 15:9–10).

1:6 *sons of God came to present themselves.* Angels who came as members of the heavenly council who stand in the presence of God (see 1 Kin 22:19; Ps 89:5–7; Jer 23:18,22). *Satan.* Lit. "the adversary/accuser" (see Rev 12:10). In Job the Hebrew for this word is always preceded by the definite article. In the Hebrew of 1 Chr 21:1 the article is not used, because by then "Satan" had become a proper name.

1:7 *The LORD.* The Israelite covenant name for God (see Introduction: Author; see also note on Gen 2:4).

1:8 *Have you considered . . . Job?* The Lord, not Satan, initiates the dialogue that leads to the testing of Job. He holds up Job as one against whom "the accuser" can lodge no accusation. *My servant.* See 42:7–8 and note; a designation for one who stands in a special relationship with God and is loyal in service (e.g., Moses, Num 12:7; David, 2 Sam 7:5; see Is 42:1; 52:13; 53:11).

1:9 "The accuser" boldly accuses the man God commends: He says Job's righteousness, in which God delights, is self-serving—the heart of Satan's attack on God and His faithful servant in the book of Job.

1:10 *hedge.* Symbolizes protection (see Is 5:5; contrast Job 3:23).

1:11 *put forth Your hand now and touch.* See 4:5.

1:12 Satan, the accuser, is given power to afflict (v. 12a) but is kept on a leash (v. 12b). In all his evil among men (vv. 15,17) or in nature (vv. 16,19), Satan is under God's power (compare 1 Chr 21:1 with 2 Sam 24:1; see 1 Sam 16:14; 2 Sam 24:16; 1 Cor 5:5; 2 Cor 12:7; Heb 2:14). The contest, however, is not a sham. Will Job curse God to His face? If Job does not, the accuser will be proven false and God's delight in Job vindicated.

1:15 *Sabeans.* Probably south Arabians from Sheba, whose descendants became wealthy traders in spices, gold and precious stones (see the account of the queen of Sheba in 1 Kin 10:1–13; see also Ps 72:10,15; Is 60:6; Jer 6:20; Ezek 27:22; Joel 3:8). Job 6:19 calls the Sabeans "travelers" and associates them with Tema (about 350 miles southeast of Jerusalem).

1:16 *fire of God.* Lightning (see Num 11:1; 1 Kin 18:38; 2 Kin 1:12).

1:17 *Chaldeans.* A people who were Bedouin until c. 1000 B.C., when they settled in southern Mesopotamia and later became the nucleus of Nebuchadnezzar's Babylonian empire.

the edge of the sword, and I alone have
escaped to tell you."
18 While he was still speaking, another
also came and said, "Your sons and your
daughters were eating and drinking wine in
their oldest brother's house,
19 and behold, a great wind came from
across the wilderness and struck the four
corners of the house, and it fell on the young
people and they died, and I alone have
escaped to tell you."
20 Then Job arose and [a]tore his robe and
shaved his head, and he fell to the ground
and worshiped.
21 He said,
"[a]Naked I came from my mother's
womb,
And naked I shall return there.
The [b]LORD gave and the LORD has
taken away.
Blessed be the name of the LORD."
22 [a]Through all this Job did not sin nor
did he [1]blame God.

Job Loses His Health

2 [a]Again there was a day when the sons of
God came to present themselves before
the LORD, and Satan also came among them
to present himself before the LORD.
2 The LORD said to Satan, "Where have
you come from?" Then Satan answered the
LORD and said, "From roaming about on the
earth and walking around on it."
3 The LORD said to Satan, "Have you
[1]considered My servant Job? For there is no
one like him on the earth, a blameless and
upright man [2]fearing God and turning away

20 [a]Gen 37:29, 34; Josh 7:6 **21** [a]Eccl 5:15 [b]1 Sam 2:7, 8; Job 2:10 **22** [1]Lit *ascribe unseemliness to* [a]Job 2:10 **2:1** [a]Job 1:6-8 **3** [1]Lit *set your heart to* [2]Or *revering*

3 [3]Lit *swallow him up* [a]Job 27:5, 6 **5** [a]Job 1:11 [b]Job 19:20 **6** [1]Lit *hand* **7** [a]Deut 28:35; Job 7:5; 13:28; 30:17, 18, 30 **8** [a]Job 42:6; Jer 6:26; Ezek 27:30; Jon 3:6 **10** [a]Job 1:21 [b]Job 1:22; Ps 39:1; James 1:12 **11** [a]Gen 36:11; Job 6:19; Jer 49:7 [b]Gen 25:2 [c]Job 42:11; Rom 12:15 **12** [a]Job 1:20 [b]Josh 7:6; Neh 9:1; Lam 2:10; Ezek 27:30 **13** [a]Gen 50:10; Ezek 3:15

from evil. And he still [a]holds fast his integrity, although you incited Me against him to
[3]ruin him without cause."
4 Satan answered the LORD and said,
"Skin for skin! Yes, all that a man has he will
give for his life.
5 "[a]However, put forth Your hand now,
and [b]touch his bone and his flesh; he will
curse You to Your face."
6 So the LORD said to Satan, "Behold, he
is in your [1]power, only spare his life."
7 Then Satan went out from the presence
of the LORD and smote Job with [a]sore boils
from the sole of his foot to the crown of his
head.
8 And he took a potsherd to scrape himself while [a]he was sitting among the ashes.
9 Then his wife said to him, "Do you still
hold fast your integrity? Curse God and die!"
10 But he said to her, "You speak as one of
the foolish women speaks. [a]Shall we indeed
accept good from God and not accept adversity?" [b]In all this Job did not sin with his lips.
11 Now when Job's three friends heard of
all this adversity that had come upon him,
they came each one from his own place, Eliphaz the [a]Temanite, Bildad the [b]Shuhite and
Zophar the Naamathite; and they made an
appointment together to come to [c]sympa-
thize with him and comfort him.
12 When they lifted up their eyes at a distance and did not recognize him, they raised
their voices and wept. And each of them
[a]tore his robe and they [b]threw dust over
their heads toward the sky.
13 [a]Then they sat down on the ground
with him for seven days and seven nights

1:19 *great wind.* Tornado.

1:20 *Then Job arose.* He is silent until his children are killed. *tore his robe and shaved his head.* In mourning (see notes on Gen 37:34; Is 15:2).

1:21 *shall return there.* See Gen 2:7; 3:19 and note. *The LORD gave and the LORD has taken away.* Job's faith leads him to see the sovereign God's hand at work, and that gives him repose even in the face of calamity.

2:1–3 Except for the final sentence, this passage is almost identical to 1:6–8. He who accused Job of having a deceitful motive is now shown to have a deceitful motive himself: to discredit the Lord through Job.

2:3 *you incited Me.* God cannot be stirred up to do things against His will. Though it is not always clear how, everything that happens is part of His divine purpose (see 38:2).

2:4 *Skin for skin!* No doubt a proverb—perhaps originally an expression of willingness to barter one animal skin for another of equal value.

2:5 *touch his bone and his flesh.* See 1:11–12; cf. Gen 2:23; Luke 24:39.

2:6 *spare his life.* Satan is still limited by God. Should Job die, neither God nor Job could be vindicated.

2:7 The precise nature of Job's sickness is uncertain, but its symptoms were painful festering sores over the whole body (7:5), nightmares (7:14), scabs that peeled and became black (30:28,30), disfigurement and revolting appearance (2:12; 19:19), bad breath (19:17), excessive thinness (17:7; 19:20), fever (30:30) and pain day and night (30:17). *boils.* See Ex 9:9; Lev 13:18; 2 Kin 20:7.

2:8 *ashes.* Symbolic of mourning (see 42:6; Esth 4:3; cf. Jon 3:6, which speaks of sitting in dust).

2:9 *Curse God.* The Hebrew for this expression here and in 1:5 employs a euphemism (lit. "Bless God"). Satan is using Job's wife to tempt Job as he used Eve to tempt Adam. *and die.* Since nothing but death is left for Job, his wife wants him to provoke God to administer the final stroke due to all who curse Him (Lev 24:10–16).

2:10 *Shall we indeed accept good from God, and not accept adversity?* A key theme of the book: Trouble and suffering are not merely punishment for sin; for God's people they may serve as a trial (as here) or as a discipline that culminates in spiritual gain (see 5:17; Deut 8:5; 2 Sam 7:14; Ps 94:12; Prov 3:11–12; 1 Cor 11:32; Heb 12:5–11).

2:11 *three friends.* Older than Job (see 15:10). *Eliphaz.* An Edomite name (see Gen 36:11). *Temanite.* Teman was a village in Edom, south of the Dead Sea (see Gen 36:11; Jer 49:7; Ezek 25:13; Amos 1:12; Obad 9). *Shuhite.* Bildad may have been a descendant of Shuah, the youngest son of Abraham and Keturah (Gen 25:2). *Naamathite.* Apart from 11:1; 20:1; 42:9, this word does not occur elsewhere in the Bible.

2:12 *did not recognize him.* Cf. Is 52:14; 53:3. *tore his robe . . . threw dust over their heads.* Visible signs of mourning (see note on 1:20).

2:13 *sat down on the ground with him.* See Ezek 3:15; possibly an expression of sympathy. *seven.* See Gen 50:10; 1 Sam 31:13; the number of completeness (see 1:2; see also note on Ruth

with no one speaking a word to him, for they saw that *his* pain was very great.

Job's Lament

3 Afterward Job opened his mouth and cursed [1]the day of his *birth.*
2 And Job [1]said,
3 "[a]Let the day perish on which I was to
be born,
And the night *which* said, 'A [1]boy is
conceived.'
4 "May that day be darkness;
Let not God above care for it,
Nor light shine on it.
5 "Let [a]darkness and black gloom claim
it;
Let a cloud settle on it;
Let the blackness of the day terrify it.
6 "*As for* that night, let darkness seize it;
Let it not rejoice among the days of
the year;
Let it not come into the number of the
months.
7 "Behold, let that night be barren;
Let no joyful shout enter it.
8 "Let those curse it who curse the day,
Who are [1]prepared to [a]rouse
Leviathan.
9 "Let the stars of its twilight be
darkened;
Let it wait for light but have none,
And let it not see the [1]breaking dawn;
10 Because it did not shut the opening of
my *mother's* womb,
Or hide trouble from my eyes.

11 "[a]Why did I not die [1]at birth,
Come forth from the womb and
expire?
12 "Why did the knees receive me,
And why the breasts, that I should
suck?
13 "For now I [a]would have lain down and
been quiet;
I would have slept then, I would have
been at rest,
14 With [a]kings and *with* [b]counselors of
the earth,
Who rebuilt [c]ruins for themselves;
15 Or with [a]princes [b]who had gold,
Who were filling their houses *with*
silver.
16 "Or like a miscarriage which is
[1]discarded, I would not be,
As infants that never saw light.
17 "There the wicked cease from raging,
And there the [1]weary are at [a]rest.
18 "The prisoners are at ease together;
They do not hear the voice of the
taskmaster.
19 "The small and the great are there,
And the slave is free from his master.

20 "Why is [a]light given to him who
suffers,
And life to the bitter of soul,
21 Who [1a]long for death, but there is
none,
And dig for it more than for [b]hidden
treasures,
22 Who rejoice greatly,
And exult when they find the grave?
23 "*Why is light given* to a man [a]whose
way is hidden,
And whom [b]God has hedged in?
24 "For [a]my groaning comes at the sight
of my food,
And [b]my cries pour out like water.
25 "For [1a]what I fear comes upon me,
And what I dread befalls me.
26 "I [a]am not at ease, nor am I quiet,
And I am not at rest, but turmoil
comes."

Eliphaz: Innocent Do Not Suffer

4 Then Eliphaz the Temanite [1]answered,
2 "If one ventures a word with you, will
you become impatient?
But [a]who can refrain [1]from speaking?
3 "Behold [a]you have admonished many,
And you have strengthened weak
hands.

3:1 [1]Lit *his day*
2 [1]Lit *answered and said*
3 [1]Lit *man-child* [a]Jer 20:14-18
5 [a]Jer 13:16
8 [1]Or *skillful* [a]Job 41:1, 25
9 [1]Lit *eyelids*
11 [1]Lit *from the womb* [a]Job 10:18, 19
13 [a]Job 3:13-19; 7:8-10, 21; 10:21, 22; 14:10-15, 20-22; 16:22; 17:13-16; 19:25-27; 21:13, 23-26; 24:19, 20; 26:5, 6; 34:22
14 [a]Job 12:18 [b]Job 12:17 [c]Job 15:28; Is 58:12
15 [a]Job 12:21 [b]Job 27:16, 17
16 [1]Lit *hidden*
17 [1]Lit *weary of strength* [a]Job 17:16
20 [a]Jer 20:18
21 [1]Lit *wait* [a]Rev 9:6 [b]Prov 2:4
23 [a]Job 19:6, 8, 12 [b]Job 19:8; Ps 88:8; Lam 3:7
24 [a]Job 6:7; 33:20 [b]Job 30:16; Ps 42:4
25 [1]Lit *the fear I fear and* [a]Job 9:28; 30:15
26 [a]Job 7:13, 14
4:1 [1]Lit *answered and said*
2 [1]Lit *in words* [a]Job 32:18-20
3 [a]Job 4:3, 4; 29:15, 16, 21, 25

4:15). *no one speaking a word to him.* A wiser response than their later speeches would prove to be (see 16:2–3).
3:3 *Let the day perish on which I was . . . born.* Job's very existence, which has been a joy to him because of God's favor, is now his intolerable burden. He is as close as he will ever come to cursing God, but he does not do it.
3:4 *May that day be darkness.* God had said in Gen 1:3, "Let there be light." Job, using similar language, would negate God's creative act.
3:8 *those . . . who curse the day.* Eastern soothsayers, like Balaam (see Num 22–24), who pronounced curses on people, objects and days. *Leviathan.* Using vivid, figurative language, Job wishes that "those . . . who curse the day" would arouse the sea monster Leviathan (see note on Is 27:1) to swallow the day-night of his birth.
3:11–12,16,20–23 A series of rhetorical questions.
3:16 Since in fact his birth had taken place, the next possibility would have been a stillbirth. He would then have lived only in the grave (or Sheol), which he envisions as a place of peace and rest (vv. 13–19; see note on Gen 37:35). Such a situation would be much better than his present intolerable condition, in which he can find neither peace nor rest (v. 26).
3:18 *voice of the taskmaster.* As in Egypt (see Ex 5:13–14).
3:21–22 Death has become desirable for Job.
3:23 *whom God has hedged in.* God, who had put a hedge of protection around him (see 1:10 and note), has now, he feels, hemmed him in with turmoil (see v. 26).
4:1 *Eliphaz the Temanite.* See note on 2:11. Teman was an Edomite town noted for wisdom (see Jer 49:7). The speeches of Job's three friends contain elements of truth, but they must be carefully interpreted in context. The problem is not so much with what the friends knew but with what they did not know: God's high purpose in allowing Satan to buffet Job.
4:2 *ventures a word.* Eliphaz seems to be genuinely concerned with Job's well-being and offers a complimentary word (vv. 3–4). *impatient.* See note on 9:2–3.

4 "Your words have [1]helped the tottering
to stand,
And you have strengthened [2]feeble
knees.
5 "But now it has come to you, and you
[a]are impatient;
It [b]touches you, and you are dismayed.
6 "Is not your [1][a]fear *of God* [b]your
confidence,
And the integrity of your ways your
hope?

7 "Remember now, [a]who *ever* perished
being innocent?
Or where were the upright destroyed?
8 "According to what I have seen, [a]those
who plow iniquity
And those who sow trouble harvest it.
9 "By [a]the breath of God they perish,
And [b]by the [1]blast of His anger they
come to an end.
10 "The [a]roaring of the lion and the voice
of the *fierce* lion,
And the teeth of the young lions are
broken.
11 "The [a]lion perishes for lack of prey,
And the [b]whelps of the lioness are
scattered.

12 "Now a word [a]was brought to me
stealthily,
And my ear received a [b]whisper of it.
13 "Amid disquieting [a]thoughts from the
visions of the night,
When deep sleep falls on men,
14 Dread came upon me, and trembling,
And made [1]all my bones shake.
15 "Then a [1]spirit passed by my face;
The hair of my flesh bristled up.
16 "It stood still, but I could not discern
its appearance;
A form *was* before my eyes;
There was silence, then I heard a
voice:
17 'Can [a]mankind be just [1]before God?
Can a man be pure [1]before his [b]Maker?
18 '[a]He puts no trust even in His servants;
And against His angels He charges
error.
19 'How much more those who dwell in
[a]houses of clay,
Whose [b]foundation is in the dust,
Who are crushed before the moth!
20 '[a]Between morning and evening they
are broken in pieces;
Unobserved, they [b]perish forever.
21 'Is not their [a]tent-cord plucked up
within them?
They die, yet [b]without wisdom.'

God Is Just

5 "Call now, is there anyone who will
answer you?
And to which of the [a]holy ones will
you turn?
2 "For [a]anger slays the foolish man,
And jealousy kills the simple.
3 "I have seen the [a]foolish taking root,
And I [b]cursed his abode immediately.
4 "His [a]sons are far from safety,
They are even [1]oppressed in the gate,
And there is no deliverer.
5 "[1]His harvest the hungry devour
And take it to a *place of* thorns,
And the [2][a]schemer is eager for their
wealth.
6 "For [a]affliction does not come from the
dust,
Nor does trouble sprout from the
ground,
7 For [a]man is born for trouble,
As sparks fly upward.

4 [1]Lit *caused* [2]Lit *bowing*
5 [a]Job 6:14 [b]Job 19:21
6 [1]Or *reverence* [a]Job 1:1 [b]Prov 3:26
7 [a]Job 8:20; 36:6, 7; Ps 37:25
8 [a]Job 15:31, 35; Prov 22:8; Hos 10:13; Gal 6:7
9 [1]Lit *wind* [a]Job 15:30; Is 11:4; 30:33; 2 Thess 2:8 [b]Job 40:11-13
10 [a]Job 5:15; Ps 58:6
11 [a]Job 29:17; Ps 34:10 [b]Job 5:4; 20:10; 27:14
12 [a]Job 4:12-17; 33:15-18 [b]Job 26:14
13 [a]Job 33:15
14 [1]Lit *the multitude of*
15 [1]Or *breath passed over*
17 [1]Lit *from* [a]Job 9:2; 25:4 [b]Job 31:15; 32:22; 35:10; 36:3
18 [a]Job 15:15
19 [a]Job 10:9; 33:6 [b]Gen 2:7; 3:19; Job 22:16
20 [a]Job 14:2 [b]Job 14:20; 20:7
21 [a]Job 8:22 [b]Job 18:21; 36:12
5:1 [a]Job 15:15
2 [a]Prov 12:16; 27:3
3 [a]Jer 12:2 [b]Job 24:18; 31:30
4 [1]Lit *crushed* [a]Job 4:11
5 [1]Lit *Whose* [2]Ancient versions read *thirsty* [a]Job 18:8-10; 22:10
6 [a]Job 15:35
7 [a]Job 14:1

4:5 *touches you.* See 1:11; 2:5; 19:21.
4:6–7 Eliphaz counsels Job to be confident that his piety will count with God, that though God is now chastening him for some sin, it is to a good end (see v. 17; 5:17), and he can be assured that God will not destroy him along with the wicked.
4:6 *fear.* See note on 1:1. The word is used only by Eliphaz (see 15:4; 22:4).
4:7–9 If Job is truly innocent, he will not be destroyed.
4:8–11 Just as the strongest lions eventually die (vv. 10–11), so the wicked are eventually destroyed (vv. 8–9).
4:9 *blast of His anger.* See Ex 15:7–8. God's judgment is fearfully severe.
4:12–21 Eliphaz tells of a hair-raising (see v. 15), mystical experience mediated through a dream (see v. 13), through which he claims to have received divine revelation and on which he bases his advice to Job.
4:13 *Amid . . . visions . . . When deep sleep falls on men.* Eliphaz's words are echoed by Elihu in 33:15.
4:14 *all my bones shake.* A sign of great distress (see Jer 23:9; Hab 3:16).
4:17–21 All mortals are sinful; therefore God has a right to punish them. Job should be thankful for the correction God is giving him (see 5:17).
4:18–19 If the angels, who are not made of dust, can be guilty in God's sight, how much more man (see 15:15–16)!
4:18 *servants.* Angels.
4:19 *houses of clay.* Bodies made of dust (see 10:9; 33:6; see also note on Gen 2:7). *moth.* A symbol of fragility (cf. 27:18).
4:20 *Between morning and evening.* A vivid picture of the shortness of life.
4:21 *tent-cord.* A tent was a temporary home, like the human body (see 2 Cor 5:1,4; 2 Pet 1:13). *without wisdom.* Needlessly and senselessly (see v. 20).
5:1 *to which . . . will you turn?* To plead your case with God. The idea of a mediator, someone to arbitrate between God and Job, is an important motif in the book (see 9:33; 16:19–20; see also note on 19:25). *holy ones.* Holy angels, the "sons of God" in the prologue (see 1:6 and note; 2:1).
5:2 Without mentioning him, Eliphaz implies that Job is resentful against God and that harm will follow. *foolish man.* One who pays no attention to God. The Hebrew for "fool" or "foolish" denotes moral deficiency.
5:3 *the foolish taking root.* A wicked man prospering like a tree taking root (see Ps 1:3).
5:6 Unlike a weed, trouble must be sown and cultivated.
5:7 *man is born for trouble.* See 14:1; proof that no one is righteous in the eyes of God (see 4:17–19). Job should stop behaving like a fool (see vv. 1–7) and should humble himself. Then

8 "But as for me, I would [a]seek God,
And I would place my cause before God;
9 Who [a]does great and unsearchable things,
[1]Wonders without number.
10 "He [a]gives rain on the earth
And sends water on the fields,
11 So that [a]He sets on high those who are lowly,
And those who mourn are lifted to safety.
12 "He [a]frustrates the plotting of the shrewd,
So that their hands cannot attain success.
13 "He [a]captures the wise by their own shrewdness,
And the advice of the cunning is quickly thwarted.
14 "By day they [a]meet with darkness,
And grope at noon as in the night.
15 "But He saves from [a]the sword of their mouth,
And [b]the poor from the hand of the mighty.
16 "So the helpless has hope,
And [a]unrighteousness must shut its mouth.

17 "Behold, how [a]happy is the man whom God reproves,
So do not despise the [b]discipline of [1]the Almighty.
18 "For [a]He inflicts pain, and [1]gives relief;
He wounds, and His hands *also* heal.
19 "[1]From six troubles [a]He will deliver you,
Even in seven [b]evil will not touch you.
20 "In [a]famine He will redeem you from death,
And [b]in war from the power of the sword.

8 [a]Job 13:2, 3; Ps 50:15
9 [1]Or *Miracles* [a]Job 9:10; 37:14, 16; 42:3
10 [a]Job 36:27-29; 37:6-11; 38:26
11 [a]Job 22:29; 36:7
12 [a]Ps 33:10
13 [a]Job 37:24; 1 Cor 3:19
14 [a]Job 12:25; 15:30; 18:18; 20:26; 24:13
15 [a]Job 4:10, 11; Ps 35:10 [b]Job 29:17; 34:28; 36:6, 15; 38:15
16 [a]Ps 107:42
17 [1]Heb *Shaddai*, and so throughout ch 6 [a]Ps 94:12 [b]Job 36:15, 16; Prov 3:11; Heb 12:5-11; James 1:12
18 [1]Lit *binds* [a]Deut 32:39; 1 Sam 2:6; Is 30:26; Hos 6:1
19 [1]Lit *In* [a]Ps 34:19 [b]Ps 91:10
20 [a]Ps 33:19; 37:19 [b]Ps 144:10

21 [a]Job 5:15; Ps 31:20 [b]Ps 91:5, 6
22 [1]Lit *beasts of the earth* [a]Job 8:21 [b]Ps 91:13; Ezek 34:25; Hos 2:18
23 [a]Is 11:6-9; 65:25
24 [a]Job 8:6
25 [1]Lit *seed* [a]Ps 112:2 [b]Is 44:3, 4; 48:19
26 [a]Job 42:17
6:1 [1]Lit *answered and said*
2 [a]Job 31:6
3 [a]Job 23:2
4 [1]Lit *Whose* [a]Job 16:13; Ps 38:2 [b]Job 20:16; 21:20 [c]Job 30:15
5 [a]Job 39:5-8

21 "You will be [a]hidden from the scourge of the tongue,
[b]And you will not be afraid of violence when it comes.
22 "You will [a]laugh at violence and famine,
[b]And you will not be afraid of [1]wild beasts.
23 "For you will be in league with the stones of the field,
And [a]the beasts of the field will be at peace with you.
24 "You will know that your [a]tent is secure,
For you will visit your abode and fear no loss.
25 "You will know also that your [1][a]descendants will be many,
And [b]your offspring as the grass of the earth.
26 "You will [a]come to the grave in full vigor,
Like the stacking of grain in its season.
27 "Behold this; we have investigated it, *and* so it is.
Hear it, and know for yourself."

Job's Friends Are No Help

6 Then Job [1]answered,
2 "[a]Oh that my grief were actually weighed
And laid in the balances together with my calamity!
3 "For then it would be [a]heavier than the sand of the seas;
Therefore my words have been rash.
4 "For the [a]arrows of the Almighty are within me,
[1]Their [b]poison my spirit drinks;
The [c]terrors of God are arrayed against me.
5 "Does the [a]wild donkey bray over *his* grass,
Or does the ox low over his fodder?

God would bless, and injustice would shut its mouth (see v. 16). *sparks.* Lit. "sons of Resheph." In Canaanite mythology, Resheph was a god of plague and destruction. "(Sons of) Resheph" is used as a poetic image in the OT for fire (Song 8:6), bolts of lightning (Ps 78:48) and pestilence (Deut 32:24; Hab 3:5).

5:9 Repeated in 9:10.

5:13 Quoted in part in 1 Cor 3:19 (the only clear quotation of Job in the NT).

5:17–26 While the preceding hymn (vv. 8–16) spoke of God's goodness and justice, this poem celebrates the blessedness of the man whom God disciplines (see Prov 1:2,7; 3:12; 23:13,23). Eliphaz believed that discipline is temporary and is followed by healing (v. 18), and that the good man will always be rescued. But with Job's wealth gone and his children dead, these words about security (v. 24) and children (v. 25) must have seemed cruel indeed to him.

5:17 *Almighty.* The first of 31 times that the Hebrew word *Shaddai* is used in Job (see note on Gen 17:1).

5:18–19 See Hos 6:1–2.

5:19 *six . . . seven.* See 33:29; 40:5; Prov 6:16; 30:15,18,21,29; Eccl 11:2; Amos 1:3,6,9,11,13; 2:1,4,6; Mic 5:5. Normally, such number patterns are not to be taken literally but are a poetic way of saying "many."

5:23 *in league with the stones.* A figurative way of saying that stones will "be at peace with you" and will not ruin the crops (see 2 Kin 3:19; Is 5:2; Matt 13:5).

5:25 *as the grass.* As numerous as blades of grass (see note on Gen 13:16).

5:26 Eliphaz's prediction was more accurate than he realized (see 42:16–17).

5:27 *know for yourself.* Eliphaz's conclusion: Job must turn from unrighteousness (4:7) and resentment against God (v. 2) to humility (v. 11) and the acceptance of God's righteous discipline (v. 17). Eliphaz's purpose is to offer theological comfort and counsel to Job (2:11), but instead he wounds him with false accusation.

6:2–3 Job appeals for a sympathetic understanding of the harsh words he spoke in ch. 3.

6:4 *arrows of the Almighty.* Job shares Eliphaz's "orthodox" theology and believes that God is aiming His arrows of judgment at him—though he does not know why (see 7:20; 16:12–13; see also Lam 3:12; cf. Deut 32:23; Ps 7:13; 38:2).

6:5–6 Job claims the right to bray and bellow, since he has been wounded by God and offered tasteless food (words) by his friends.

6 "Can something tasteless be eaten
without salt,
Or is there any taste in the [1]white of
an egg?
7 "My soul [a]refuses to touch *them;*
They are like loathsome food to me.

8 "Oh that my request might come to
pass,
And that God would grant my longing!
9 "Would that God were [a]willing to crush
me,
That He would loose His hand and cut
me off!
10 "But it is still my consolation,
And I rejoice in unsparing pain,
That I [a]have not [1]denied the words of
the Holy One.
11 "What is my strength, that I should
wait?
And what is my end, that I should
[1a]endure?
12 "Is my strength the strength of stones,
Or is my flesh bronze?
13 "Is it that my [a]help is not within me,
And that [1b]deliverance is driven from
me?

14 "For the [a]despairing man *there should
be* kindness from his friend;
So that he does not [b]forsake the [1]fear
of the Almighty.
15 "My brothers have acted [a]deceitfully
like a [1]wadi,
Like the torrents of [1]wadis which
vanish,
16 Which are turbid because of ice
And into which the snow [1]melts.
17 "When [a]they become waterless, they
[1]are silent,
When it is hot, they vanish from their
place.
18 "The [1]paths of their course wind along,
They go up into nothing and perish.
19 "The caravans of [a]Tema looked,
The travelers of [b]Sheba hoped for
them.
20 "They [a]were [1]disappointed for they had
trusted,
They came there and were confounded.
21 "Indeed, you have now become such,
[a]You see a terror and are afraid.
22 "Have I said, 'Give me *something,*'
Or, 'Offer a bribe for me from your
wealth,'
23 Or, 'Deliver me from the hand of the
adversary,'
Or, 'Redeem me from the hand of the
tyrants'?

24 "Teach me, and [a]I will be silent;
And show me how I have erred.
25 "How painful are honest words!
But what does your argument prove?
26 "Do you intend to reprove *my* words,
When the [a]words of one in despair
belong to the wind?
27 "You would even [a]cast *lots* for [b]the
orphans
And [c]barter over your friend.
28 "Now please look at me,
And *see* if I [a]lie to your face.
29 "Desist now, let there be no injustice;
Even desist, [a]my righteousness is yet
in it.
30 "Is there injustice on my tongue?
Cannot [a]my palate discern [1]calamities?

Job's Life Seems Futile

7 "[1]Is not man [a]forced to labor on earth,
And *are not* his days like the days of
[b]a hired man?
2 "As a slave who pants for the shade,
And as a hired man who eagerly waits
for his wages,
3 So am I allotted months of vanity,
And [a]nights of trouble are appointed
me.
4 "When I [a]lie down I say,
'When shall I arise?'
But the night continues,
And I am [1]continually tossing until
dawn.
5 "My [a]flesh is clothed with worms and a
crust of dirt,
My skin hardens and runs.
6 "My days are [a]swifter than a weaver's
shuttle,
And come to an end [b]without hope.
7 "Remember that my life [a]is *but* breath;
My eye will [b]not again see good.

6 [1]Heb *hallamuth,* meaning uncertain. Perhaps the juice of a plant **7** [a]Job 3:24; 33:20 **9** [a]Num 11:15; 1 Kin 19:4; Job 7:16; 9:21; 10:1 **10** [1]Lit *hidden* [a]Job 22:22; 23:11, 12 **11** [1]Lit *prolong my soul* [a]Job 21:4 **13** [1]So ancient versions [a]Job 26:2 [b]Job 26:3 **14** [1]Or *reverence* [a]Job 4:5 [b]Job 1:5; 15:4 **15** [1]Or *brooks* [a]Jer 15:18 **16** [1]Lit *hides itself* **17** [1]Or *cease* [a]Job 24:19 **18** [1]Or *caravans turn from their course, they go up into the waste and perish* **19** [a]Gen 25:15; Is 21:14; Jer 25:23 [b]Job 1:15 **20** [1]Lit *ashamed* [a]Jer 14:3
21 [a]Ps 38:11 **24** [a]Ps 39:1 **26** [a]Job 8:2; 15:2; 16:3 **27** [a]Joel 3:3; Nah 3:10 [b]Job 22:9; 24:3, 9 [c]2 Pet 2:3 **28** [a]Job 27:4; 33:3; 36:4 **29** [a]Job 13:18; 19:6; 23:10; 27:5, 6; 34:5; 42:1-6 **30** [1]Or *words* [a]Job 12:11 **7:1** [1]Lit *Has not man compulsory labor* [a]Job 5:7; 10:17; 14:1, 14 [b]Job 14:6 **3** [a]Job 16:7 **4** [1]Lit *sated with* [a]Deut 28:67; Job 7:13, 14 **5** [a]Job 2:7; 17:14 **6** [a]Job 9:25 [b]Job 13:15; 14:19; 17:15, 16; 19:10 **7** [a]Job 7:16; Ps 78:39; James 4:14 [b]Job 9:25

6:8–9 Job repeats the thoughts of ch. 3.
6:10 *But.* Job has the joy of knowing that he has remained true to God.
6:11–13 With no human resources left, Job considers his condition hopeless.
6:11 *endure.* See note on 9:2–3.
6:14–15 See Gal 6:1. Job needs spiritual help, but his friends are proving to be undependable.
6:15 *brothers.* By calling his friends his "brothers," Job makes their callousness stand out more sharply.
6:19 *Tema.* See note on Is 21:14. *Sheba.* See note on 1:15.
6:22–23 Job has not asked them for anything except what will cost them nothing: their friendship and counsel.
6:25 *honest words.* Job is referring to his own words.
6:26 *wind.* See 8:2.
6:27 In addition to dishonesty, Job accuses his friends of heartless cruelty.
6:29 Job softens his tone, pleading that his friends take back their false accusations.
7:1–21 Having replied to Eliphaz, Job now addresses his complaint toward God.
7:1 *forced to labor.* See 14:14. The Hebrew for this expression sometimes implies military service. It is also used in reference to the Babylonian exile in Is 40:2 (see note there).
7:2 *shade.* End of the workday.
7:5 See note on 2:7.
7:7 *my life is but breath.* As a chronic sufferer he has lost all sense of purpose in life (see v. 3; see also Ps 144:3–4). He does

8 "The [a]eye of him who sees me will
behold me no longer;
Your eyes *will be* on me, but [b]I will
not be.
9 "When a [a]cloud vanishes, it is gone,
So [b]he who goes down to [c]Sheol does
not come up.
10 "He will not return again to his house,
Nor will [a]his place know him
anymore.

11 "Therefore [a]I will not restrain my
mouth;
I will speak in the anguish of my spirit,
I will complain in the bitterness of my
soul.
12 "Am I the sea, or [a]the sea monster,
That You set a guard over me?
13 "If I say, '[a]My bed will comfort me,
My couch will [1]ease my complaint,'
14 Then You frighten me with dreams
And terrify me by visions;
15 So that my soul would choose
suffocation,
Death rather than my [1]pains.
16 "I [1a]waste away; I will not live forever.
Leave me alone, [b]for my days are *but*
a breath.
17 "[a]What is man that You magnify him,
And that You [1]are concerned about
him,
18 That [a]You examine him every morning
And try him every moment?
19 "[1a]Will You never turn Your gaze away
from me,
Nor let me alone until I swallow my
spittle?

8 [a]Job 8:18; 20:9 [b]Job 7:21
9 [a]Job 30:15 [b]Job 3:13-19 [c]2 Sam 12:23; Job 11:8; 14:13; 17:13, 16
10 [a]Job 8:18; 20:9; 27:21, 23
11 [a]Job 10:1; 21:4; 23:2; Ps 40:9
12 [a]Ezek 32:2, 3
13 [1]Lit *bear* [a]Job 7:4; Ps 6:6
15 [1]Lit *bones*
16 [1]Or *loathe* [a]Job 6:9; 9:21; 10:1 [b]Job 7:7
17 [1]Lit *set Your heart on* [a]Job 22:2; Ps 8:4; 144:3; Heb 2:6
18 [a]Job 14:3
19 [1]Lit *How long will You not* [a]Job 9:18; 10:20; 14:6
20 [a]Job 35:3, 6 [b]Ps 36:6
21 [a]Job 9:28; 10:14 [b]Job 10:9 [c]Job 7:8
8:1 [1]Lit *answered and said*
2 [a]Job 6:26
3 [1]Heb *Shaddai* [a]Gen 18:25; Deut 32:4; 2 Chr 19:7; Job 34:10, 12; 36:23; 37:23; Rom 3:5
4 [1]Lit *hand* [a]Job 1:5, 18, 19
5 [1]Heb *Shaddai* [a]Job 5:17-27
6 [1]Lit *place* [a]Job 22:27; 34:28; Ps 7:6 [b]Job 5:24
7 [a]Job 42:12
8 [a]Deut 4:32; 32:7; Job 15:18; 20:4

20 "[a]Have I sinned? What have I done to
You,
O [b]watcher of men?
Why have You set me as Your target,
So that I am a burden to myself?
21 "Why then [a]do You not pardon my
transgression
And take away my iniquity?
For now I will [b]lie down in the dust;
And You will seek me, [c]but I will not
be."

Bildad Says God Rewards the Good

8 Then Bildad the Shuhite [1]answered,
2 "How long will you say these things,
And the [a]words of your mouth be a
mighty wind?
3 "Does [a]God pervert justice?
Or does [1]the Almighty pervert what is
right?
4 "[a]If your sons sinned against Him,
Then He delivered them into the
[1]power of their transgression.
5 "If you would [a]seek God
And implore the compassion of [1]the
Almighty,
6 If you are pure and upright,
Surely now [a]He would rouse Himself
for you
And restore your righteous [1b]estate.
7 "Though your beginning was
insignificant,
Yet your [a]end will increase greatly.

8 "Please [a]inquire of past generations,
And consider the things searched out
by their fathers.

not anticipate healing and sees death as his only escape.
7:8 *Your eyes will be on me, but I will not be.* See v. 21.
7:9 *he who goes down to Sheol does not come up.* Such statements are based on common observation and are not meant to dogmatize about what happens after death. Mesopotamian descriptions of the netherworld refer to it similarly as the "land of no return" (see note on v. 21).
7:11 *not restrain my mouth.* Job is determined to cry out against the apparent injustice of God who, it seems, will not leave him alone (vv. 17–20). *speak in . . . anguish.* See Jer 4:19. *bitterness of . . . soul.* See 10:1; 21:25; 27:2.
7:12 *the sea, or the sea monster.* See 3:8. The boisterous sea monster was a symbol of chaos (see Ps 74:13–14 and note; Is 27:1; 51:9), and Job objects to being treated like him.
7:13–14 He thinks that even the nightmares that disturb his much-needed sleep are from God.
7:16 *I waste away.* See note on 9:21.
7:17 *What is man that You magnify him . . . ?* See Ps 144:3; cf. Ps 8:4–8, where the answer is given that man is created in God's image to have dominion over the world (see Gen 1:27–28). Job's words (vv. 18–21) are a parody on this theme—as if God's only interest in man is to scrutinize him unmercifully and take quick offense at his slightest fault.
7:19 *until I swallow my spittle?* Job's words suggest he is never free from God's gaze—not even long enough to "swallow."
7:20 *Have I sinned? What have I done to you . . . ?* I have not been perfect, but what terrible sin have I committed that deserves this kind of suffering? *watcher.* The Hebrew for this word is used in a favorable sense in Is 27:3, but here Job complains that God is too critical. *set me as Your target.* See note on 6:4. *burden to myself.* Ancient Hebrew scribes report that a change in the text had been made from "you" to "myself" because the reading "you" involved too presumptuous a questioning of God's justice.
7:21 *transgression . . . iniquity.* Job confesses that he is a sinner, but he cannot understand why God refuses to forgive him. *lie down in the dust.* Of the netherworld, as in Mesopotamian descriptions of it (see note on v. 9).
8:2 *How long . . . ?* See 18:2. In contrast to the older Eliphaz, Bildad is impatient.
8:3 *Does God pervert justice?* But Job has not yet blatantly accused God of injustice.
8:5–6 Bildad reasons as follows: God cannot be unjust, so Job and his family must be suffering as a result of sinfulness. Job should plead for mercy, and if he has been upright, God will restore him.
8:6 *If you are pure and upright.* We know God's verdict about Job (see 1:8; 2:3), but Bildad is confident that Job is a hypocrite (see v. 13).
8:7 See v. 21. Bildad spoke more accurately than he realized (see 42:10–17).
8:8 *inquire of past generations.* Eliphaz appealed to revelation from the spirit world (see 4:12–21), while Bildad appeals to the accumulated wisdom of tradition.

9 "For we are *only* of yesterday and know
nothing,
Because [a]our days on earth are as a
shadow.
10 "Will they not teach you *and* tell you,
And bring forth words from their
minds?

11 "Can the papyrus grow up without a
marsh?
Can the rushes grow without water?
12 "While it is still green *and* not cut
down,
Yet it withers before any *other* [1]plant.
13 "So are the paths of [a]all who forget
God;
And the [b]hope of the godless will
perish,
14 Whose confidence is fragile,
And whose trust a [a]spider's [1]web.
15 "He [1]trusts in his [a]house, but it does
not stand;
He holds fast to it, but it does not
endure.
16 "He [1a]thrives before the sun,
And his [b]shoots spread out over his
garden.
17 "His roots wrap around a rock pile,
He [1]grasps a house of stones.
18 "If he is [1]removed from [a]his place,
Then it will deny him, *saying,* '[b]I
never saw you.'
19 "Behold, [a]this is the joy of His way;
And out of the dust others will spring.
20 "Lo, [a]God will not reject *a man of*
integrity,
Nor [b]will He [1]support the evildoers.
21 "He will yet fill [a]your mouth with
laughter
And your lips with shouting.
22 "Those who hate you will be [a]clothed
with shame,
And the [b]tent of the wicked will be no
longer."

9 [a]Job 14:2
12 [1]Lit *reed*
13 [a]Ps 9:17 [b]Job 11:20; 13:16; 15:34; 20:5; 27:8
14 [1]Lit *house* [a]Is 59:5, 6
15 [1]Lit *leans on* [a]Job 8:22; 27:18; Ps 49:11
16 [1]Lit *is lush* [a]Ps 37:35; Jer 11:16 [b]Ps 80:11
17 [1]Heb *sees*
18 [1]Lit *swallowed up* [a]Job 7:10 [b]Job 7:8
19 [a]Job 20:5
20 [1]Lit *strengthen the hand of* [a]Job 4:7 [b]Job 21:30
21 [a]Job 5:22; Ps 126:1, 2
22 [a]Ps 132:18
22 [b]Job 8:15; 15:34; 18:14; 21:28
9:1 [1]Lit *answered and said*
2 [1]Lit *with* [a]Job 4:17; 25:4
3 [a]Job 10:2; 13:19; 23:6; 40:2
4 [1]Lit *stiffened his neck against* [2]Lit *and remained safe* [a]Job 11:6; 12:13; 28:23; 38:36, 37 [b]Job 9:19; 23:6 [c]2 Chr 13:12; Prov 29:1
5 [a]Job 9:5-10; 26:6-14; 41:11
6 [a]Is 2:19, 21; 13:13; Hag 2:6 [b]Ps 75:3
7 [1]Lit *and it does not shine* [a]Is 13:10; Ezek 32:7, 8
8 [1]Lit *treads upon the heights of* [a]Gen 1:1; Job 37:18; Ps 104:2; Is 40:22 [b]Job 38:16; Ps 77:19

Job Says There Is No Arbitrator between God and Man

9 Then Job [1]answered,
2 "In truth I know that this is so;
But how can a [a]man be in the right
[1]before God?
3 "If one wished to [a]dispute with Him,
He could not answer Him once in a
thousand *times.*
4 "[a]Wise in heart and [b]mighty in strength,
Who has [1c]defied Him [2]without harm?
5 "[a]*It is God* who removes the
mountains, they know not *how,*
When He overturns them in His anger;
6 Who [a]shakes the earth out of its
place,
And its [b]pillars tremble;
7 Who commands the [a]sun [1]not to shine,
And sets a seal upon the stars;
8 Who alone [a]stretches out the heavens
And [1b]tramples down the waves of the
sea;
9 Who makes the [a]Bear, Orion and the
Pleiades,
And the [b]chambers of the south;
10 Who [a]does great things,
[1]unfathomable,
And wondrous works without
number.
11 "Were He to pass by me, [a]I would not
see Him;
Were He to move past *me,* I would not
perceive Him.
12 "Were He to snatch away, who could
[a]restrain Him?
Who could say to Him, '[b]What are
You doing?'

9 [a]Job 38:31, 32; Amos 5:8 [b]Job 37:9 10 [1]Lit *until there is no searching out* [a]Job 5:9 11 [a]Job 23:8, 9; 35:14 12 [a]Job 10:7; 11:10 [b]Is 45:9

8:9 *our days . . . are as a shadow.* A common motif in wisdom literature (see 14:2; 1 Chr 29:15; Ps 102:11; 144:4; Eccl 6:12; 8:13).
8:11–19 A practical wisdom poem, giving words of instruction learned from the fathers. It is introduced in v. 10 and applied to Job in vv. 20–22.
8:20 Bildad is blunt about Job's being an evildoer, whereas Eliphaz had resorted to insinuation (see 4:7–9).
8:21 See note on v. 7.
9:2–3 Job does not believe that he is sinless, but he wishes to have his day in court so that he can prove he is innocent of the kind of sin that deserves the suffering he endures. In his despair he voices awful complaints against God (see vv. 16–20,22–24, 29–35; 10:1–7,13–17). Yet he does not abandon God; he does not curse Him (see 10:2,8–12), as Satan said he would (see 1:11; 2:5). Ch. 42 implies that Job persevered, but chs. 9–10 show that he did so with impatience (see 4:2; 6:11; 21:4). Cf. James 5:11, which speaks of Job's endurance, not (as traditionally) his patience.
9:3 *dispute.* See v. 14. Job's speech is filled with the imagery of the courtroom: "answer Him" (vv. 3,14,32), "right . . . implore . . . judge" (v. 15), "summon" (v. 19), "declare me guilty" (v. 20), "judges" (v. 24), "court" (v. 32), "contend with me" (10:2), "witnesses" (10:17). Job argues his innocence, but he feels that because God is so great there is no use in contending with Him (v. 14). Job's innocence does him no good (v. 15).
9:5–10 A beautiful hymn about God's greatness. But Job is not blessed by it, for he does not see that God's power is controlled by goodness and justice.
9:6 *pillars.* See 26:11. The metaphor of the earth resting on a foundation (see 38:6; 1 Sam 2:8; Ps 75:3; 104:5) is changed in 26:7 to a description of the earth suspended over nothing.
9:8 *stretches out the heavens.* Either (1) creates the heavens (see Is 44:24), or perhaps (2) causes the dawn to spread, like a man stretching out a tent (see Ps 104:2). *tramples down the waves.* Canaanite texts describe the goddess Asherah as walking on the sea (or sea-god) to subdue it. Similarly, God "tramples down the waves" to control the boisterous sea.
9:9 *Bear, Orion . . . Pleiades.* These three constellations are mentioned again in 38:31–32, and the last two are mentioned in Amos 5:8 (see note there). Despite their limited knowledge of astronomy, the ancient Israelites were awed by the fact that God had created the constellations.
9:10 The same words are spoken by Eliphaz in 5:9.
9:12 *who could restrain Him?* Job argues that God has an

13 "God will not turn back His anger;
Beneath Him crouch the helpers of [a]Rahab.
14 "How then can [a]I [1]answer Him,
And choose my words [2]before Him?
15 "For [a]though I were right, I could not [1]answer;
I would have to [b]implore the mercy of my judge.
16 "If I called and He answered me,
I could not believe that He was listening to my voice.
17 "For He [a]bruises me with a tempest
And multiplies my wounds without cause.
18 "He will [a]not allow me to get my breath,
But saturates me with [b]bitterness.
19 "If *it is a matter* of power, [a]behold, *He is* the strong one!
And if *it is a matter* of justice, who can summon [1]Him?
20 "[a]Though I am righteous, my mouth will [b]condemn me;
Though I am guiltless, He will declare me guilty.
21 "I am [a]guiltless;
I do not take notice of myself;
I [b]despise my life.
22 "It is *all* one; therefore I say,
'He [a]destroys the guiltless and the wicked.'
23 "If the scourge kills suddenly,
He [a]mocks the despair of the innocent.
24 "The earth [a]is given into the hand of the wicked;
He [b]covers the faces of its judges.
If *it is* not *He,* then who is it?

25 "Now [a]my days are swifter than a runner;
They flee away, [b]they see no good.
26 "They slip by like [a]reed boats,
Like an [b]eagle that swoops on [1]its prey.
27 "Though I say, 'I will forget [a]my complaint,
I will leave off my *sad* countenance and be cheerful,'
28 I am [a]afraid of all my pains,
I know that [b]You will not acquit me.
29 "I am accounted [a]wicked,
Why then should I toil in vain?
30 "If I should [a]wash myself with snow
And cleanse [b]my hands with lye,
31 Yet You would plunge me into the pit,
And my own clothes would abhor me.
32 "For [a]*He is* not a man as I am that [b]I may answer Him,
That we may go to [1]court together.
33 "There is no [a]umpire between us,
Who may lay his hand upon us both.
34 "Let Him [a]remove His rod from me,
And let not dread of Him terrify me.
35 "*Then* I [a]would speak and not fear Him;
But I am not like that in myself.

Job Despairs of God's Dealings

10 "[1][a]I loathe my own life;
I will give full vent to [b]my complaint;
I will speak in the bitterness of my soul.
2 "I will say to God, '[a]Do not condemn me;
Let me know why You contend with me.
3 'Is it [1]right for You indeed to [a]oppress,
To reject [b]the labor of Your hands,
And [2]to look favorably on [c]the schemes of the wicked?
4 'Have You eyes of flesh?
Or do You [a]see as a man sees?

13 [a]Job 26:12; Ps 89:10; Is 30:7; 51:9
14 [1]Or *plead my case* [2]Lit *with* [a]Job 9:3, 32
15 [1]Or *plead my case* [a]Job 9:20, 21; 10:15 [b]Job 8:5
17 [a]Job 16:12, 14; 30:22
18 [a]Job 7:19; 10:20 [b]Job 13:26; 27:2
19 [1]So with Gr; Heb *me* [a]Job 9:4
20 [a]Job 9:15 [b]Job 9:29; 15:6
21 [a]Job 1:1; 12:4; 13:18 [b]Job 7:16
22 [a]Job 10:7, 8
23 [a]Job 24:12
24 [a]Job 10:3; 12:6; 16:11 [b]Job 12:17
25 [a]Job 7:6 [b]Job 7:7
26 [1]Lit *food* [a]Is 18:2 [b]Job 39:29; Hab 1:8
27 [a]Job 7:11
28 [a]Job 3:25 [b]Job 7:21; 10:14
29 [a]Job 10:2; Ps 37:33
30 [a]Jer 2:22 [b]Job 31:7
32 [1]Lit *judgment* [a]Eccl 6:10 [b]Job 9:3; Rom 9:20
33 [a]1 Sam 2:25; Job 9:19; Is 1:18
34 [a]Job 13:21
35 [a]Job 13:22
10:1 [1]Lit *My soul loathes* [a]Job 7:16 [b]Job 7:11
2 [a]Job 9:29
3 [1]Lit *good* [2]Lit *You shine forth* [a]Job 9:22-24; 16:11; 19:6; 27:2 [b]Job 10:8; 14:15; Ps 138:8; Is 64:8 [c]Job 21:16; 22:18
4 [a]1 Sam 16:7; Job 28:24; 34:21

unchallengeable, sovereign freedom that works to accomplish everything He pleases.

9:13 *Rahab.* Not the prostitute Rahab of Josh 2 but a mythical sea monster (see 26:12), elsewhere used as symbolic of Egypt (see Is 30:7 and note). See 3:8; 7:12 and notes.

9:15 *judge.* God's fairness is unimpeachable (see Gen 18:25 and note).

9:17 Job does not know that God has allowed Satan to crush him for a high purpose.

9:20 *mouth will condemn me.* See 15:6.

9:21 *I despise my life.* See 7:16; words of despairing resignation that would be partially echoed in Job's final outpouring of repentance (see 42:6).

9:22–24 God has become Job's great enigma. Job describes a phantom God—one who does not exist, except in Job's mind. The God of the Bible is not morally indifferent (cf. God's words in 38:2; 40:2 and Job's response in 42:3).

9:24 *covers the faces of its judges.* Statues of Lady Justice are blindfolded, implying that she will judge impartially. But Job's accusation against God is that He has blindfolded the judges so that they see neither crimes nor innocence.

9:26 *reed boats.* See note on Ex 2:3.

9:28 *You will not acquit me.* Job wants to stand before God as an innocent man—not sinless, but innocent of any sin commensurate with his suffering.

9:29 *accounted wicked.* As appears from the bitter suffering he is enduring.

9:30 *lye.* A vegetable alkali used as a cleansing agent. The Hebrew underlying this word is translated "soap" in Jer 2:22; Mal 3:2.

9:33 *umpire between us.* See note on 5:1. God is so immense that Job feels he needs someone who can help him, someone who can argue his case in court. Job's call is not directly predicting the mediatorship of Christ, for Job is not looking for one to forgive him but for one who can testify to his innocence (see 16:20–21; 19:25–26).

9:34 See 13:21. *His rod.* Symbolic of divine judgment and wrath (see, e.g., Ps 89:32; Lam 3:1).

10:1 *I loathe my own life.* See note on 9:21. *bitterness of my soul.* Because Job is so bitter, his mind has conjured up a false picture of God.

10:3 Job imagines that God is angry with him, an innocent man (see 9:28 and note), and that He takes delight in the wicked. Such words are a reminder that the sickroom is not the place to argue theology; in times of severe suffering, people may say things that require a response of love and understanding. Job himself will eventually repent, and God will forgive (42:1–6).

10:4 *eyes of flesh.* Imperfect vision, like that of a man.

5 'Are Your days as the days of a mortal,
Or [a]Your years as man's years,
6 That [a]You should seek for my guilt
And search after my sin?
7 'According to Your knowledge [a]I am
indeed not guilty,
Yet there is [b]no deliverance from Your
hand.

8 '[a]Your hands fashioned and made me
[1]altogether,
[b]And would You destroy me?
9 'Remember now, that You have made
me as [a]clay;
And would You [b]turn me into dust
again?
10 'Did You not pour me out like milk
And curdle me like cheese;
11 Clothe me with skin and flesh,
And knit me together with bones and
sinews?
12 'You have [a]granted me life and
lovingkindness;
And Your care has preserved my spirit.
13 'Yet [a]these things You have concealed
in Your heart;
I know that this is within You:
14 If I sin, then You would [a]take note of
me,
And [b]would not acquit me of my guilt.
15 'If [a]I am wicked, woe to me!
And [b]if I am righteous, I dare not lift
up my head.
I am sated with disgrace and
[1]conscious of my misery.
16 'Should *my head* be lifted up, [a]You
would hunt me like a lion;
And again You would show Your
[b]power against me.
17 'You renew [a]Your witnesses against
me
And increase Your anger toward me;
[1b]Hardship after hardship is with me.

18 '[a]Why then have You brought me out
of the womb?
Would that I had died and no eye had
seen me!
19 'I should have been as though I had
not been,
Carried from womb to tomb.'
20 "Would He not let [a]my few days alone?
[1b]Withdraw from me that I may have
a little cheer
21 Before I go—[a]and I shall not return—
[b]To the land of darkness and [c]deep
shadow,
22 The land of utter gloom as darkness
itself,
Of deep shadow without order,
And which shines as the darkness."

Zophar Rebukes Job

11 Then Zophar the Naamathite [1]answered,
2 "Shall a multitude of words go
unanswered,
And a [a]talkative man be acquitted?
3 "Shall your boasts silence men?
And shall you [a]scoff and none rebuke?
4 "For [a]you have said, 'My teaching is
pure,
And [b]I am innocent in your eyes.'
5 "But would that God might speak,
And open His lips against you,
6 And show you the secrets of wisdom!
For sound wisdom [1a]has two sides.
Know then that God [2]forgets a part of
[b]your iniquity.

7 "[a]Can you discover the depths of God?
Can you discover the limits of the
Almighty?
8 "*They are* [a]high as [1]the heavens, what
can you do?
Deeper than [2b]Sheol, what can you
know?

5 [a]Job 36:26
6 [a]Job 14:16
7 [a]Job 9:21; 13:18 [b]Job 9:12; 23:13; 27:22
8 [1]Lit *together round about* [a]Job 10:3; Ps 119:73 [b]Job 9:22
9 [a]Job 4:19; 33:6 [b]Job 7:21
12 [a]Job 33:4
13 [a]Job 23:13
14 [a]Job 7:20 [b]Job 7:21; 9:28
15 [1]Lit *see* [a]Job 10:7; Is 3:11 [b]Job 6:29
16 [a]Is 38:13; Lam 3:10; Hos 13:7 [b]Job 5:9
17 [1]Lit *Changes and warfare are with me* [a]Ruth 1:21; Job 16:8 [b]Job 7:1
18 [a]Job 3:11-13
20 [1]Lit *Put* [a]Job 14:1 [b]Job 7:16, 19
21 [a]2 Sam 12:23; Job 3:13-19; 16:22 [b]Ps 88:12 [c]Job 10:22; 34:22; 38:17; Ps 23:4
11:1 [1]Lit *answered and said*
2 [a]Job 8:2; 15:2; 18:2
3 [a]Job 17:2; 21:3
4 [a]Job 6:10 [b]Job 10:7
6 [1]Lit *is double* [2]Lit *causes to be forgotten for you* [a]Job 9:4 [b]Job 15:5; 22:5
7 [a]Job 33:12, 13; 36:26; 37:5, 23; Rom 11:33
8 [1]Lit *the heights of heaven* [2]I.e. the nether world [a]Job 22:12; 35:5 [b]Job 26:6; 38:17

10:8–17 Job continues to question God as if He were his adversary in court. He wants to know how God, who so wonderfully formed him in the womb, could all the while have planned (see v. 13) to punish him—even though he may be innocent.
10:8–11 A poetic description of God making a baby in the womb (see Ps 139:13–16).
10:8 See Ps 119:73.
10:9 *made me as clay.* See note on 4:19. *turn me into dust.* See note on Gen 3:19.
10:15–16 Job says that whether he is guilty or innocent, the all-powerful God will not treat him justly.
10:17 *witnesses against me.* See note on 9:3.
10:18–22 See notes on ch. 3.
10:21 *shall not return.* See note on 7:9. *land of darkness and deep shadow.* See 38:17. Ancient Mesopotamian documents refer to the netherworld as the "house of darkness."
11:1–20 Like Eliphaz (see 4:7–11) and Bildad (see 8:3–6), Zophar claims that Job's sins have caused his troubles.
11:2–3 Zophar's failure to put himself in Job's place before condemning him shows a lack of compassion. Nor is Zophar entirely correct in his condemnation: Job has sincerely challenged what he perceives to be God's unjust actions (see 9:14–24), but he has not mocked God (as Zophar accuses him of having done).
11:4 *I am innocent.* In 10:7,15 Job had disclaimed being guilty, and in 9:21 he said he was "guiltless," the word God used to describe him in 1:8; 2:3. Zophar, however, implies that Job was claiming absolute purity (sinless perfection), but Job nowhere uses such terms of himself.
11:5 Zophar thought God should speak against Job, but eventually God spoke against Zophar himself (see 42:7).
11:6 *sound wisdom has two sides.* OT wisdom literature (especially Proverbs) makes abundant use of the term *mashal* ("proverb," "riddle," "parable"), which often had a hidden as well as an obvious meaning. Zophar thinks Job is shallow and lacks an understanding of the true nature of God (see vv. 7–9).
11:7 Unwittingly, Zophar anticipates the Lord's discourses in 38:1–42:6.
11:8–9 In the same way that Zophar speaks of the height, depth, length and width of God's knowledge, Paul speaks of Christ's love (see Eph 3:18).
11:8 *what can you do?* Can you climb into the heavens and explore God's knowledge?

9 "Its measure is longer than the earth
And broader than the sea.
10 "If He passes by or shuts up,
Or calls an assembly, [a]who can
restrain Him?
11 "For [a]He knows false men,
And He [b]sees iniquity [1]without
investigating.
12 "[1a]An idiot will become intelligent
When the [2]foal of a [b]wild donkey is
born a man.

13 "[a]If you would [b]direct your heart right
And [c]spread out your hand to Him,
14 If iniquity is in your hand, [a]put it far
away,
And do not let wickedness dwell in
your tents;
15 "Then, indeed, you could [a]lift up your
face without *moral* defect,
And you would be steadfast and [b]not
fear.
16 "For you would [a]forget *your* trouble,
As [b]waters that have passed by, you
would remember *it*.
17 "Your [1]life would be [2a]brighter than
noonday;
Darkness would be like the morning.
18 "Then you would trust, because there
is hope;
And you would look around and rest
securely.
19 "You would [a]lie down and none would
disturb *you*,
And many would [b]entreat your [1]favor.
20 "But the [a]eyes of the wicked will fail,
And [1]there will [b]be no escape for them;
And their [c]hope is [2d]to breathe their
last."

Job Chides His Accusers

12 Then Job [1]responded,
2 "Truly then [a]you are the people,
And with you wisdom will die!
3 "But [a]I have intelligence as well as you;
I am not inferior to you.
And [1]who does not know such things
as these?
4 "I am a [a]joke to [1]my friends,
The one who called on God and He
answered him;
The just *and* [b]blameless *man* is a
joke.
5 "[1]He who is at ease holds calamity in
contempt,
As prepared for those whose feet
slip.
6 "The [a]tents of the destroyers prosper,
And those who provoke God [b]are
secure,
[1]Whom God brings [c]into their power.

7 "But now ask the beasts, and let them
teach you;
And the birds of the heavens, and let
them tell you.
8 "Or speak to the earth, and let it teach
you;
And let the fish of the sea declare to
you.
9 "Who among all these does not know
That [a]the hand of the LORD has done
this,
10 [a]In whose hand is the life of every
living thing,
And [b]the breath of all mankind?
11 "Does not [a]the ear test words,
As the palate [1]tastes its food?
12 "Wisdom is with [a]aged men,
With [1]long life is understanding.

Job Speaks of the Power of God

13 "With Him are [a]wisdom and [a]might;
To Him belong counsel and
[b]understanding.

10 [a]Job 9:12 **11** [1]Or *even He does not consider* [a]Job 34:21-23 [b]Job 24:23; 28:24; 31:4 **12** [1]Lit *A hollow man* [2]Lit *donkey* [a]Ps 39:5, 11; 62:9; 144:4; Eccl 1:2; 11:10 [b]Job 39:5 **13** [a]Job 5:17-27; 11:13-20 [b]1 Sam 7:3; Ps 78:8 [c]Job 22:27; Ps 88:9; 143:6 **14** [a]Job 22:23 **15** [a]Job 22:26 [b]Ps 27:3; 46:2 **16** [a]Is 65:16 [b]Job 22:11 **17** [1]Lit *duration of life* [2]Lit *above noonday* [a]Job 22:26 **19** [1]Lit *face* [a]Lev 26:6; Is 17:2; Mic 4:4; Zeph 3:13 [b]Is 45:14 **20** [1]Lit *escape has perished from them* [2]Lit *the expiring of the soul* [a]Deut 28:65; Job 17:5 [b]Job 27:22; 34:22 [c]Job 8:13 [d]Job 6:9 **12:1** [1]Lit *answered and said* **2** [a]Job 17:10

3 [1]Lit *with whom is there not like these?* [a]Job 13:2 **4** [1]Lit *his* [a]Job 17:6; 30:1, 9, 10; 34:7 [b]Job 6:29 **5** [1]Lit *Contempt for calamity is the thought of him who is at ease* **6** [1]Or *He who brings God into his hand* [a]Job 9:24; 21:7-9 [b]Job 24:23 [c]Job 22:18 **9** [a]Is 41:20 **10** [a]Acts 17:28 [b]Job 27:3; 33:4 **11** [1]Lit *tastes food for itself* [a]Job 34:3 **12** [1]Lit *length of days* [a]Job 15:10; 32:7 **13** [a]Job 9:4 [b]Job 11:6; 26:12; 32:8; 36:5; 38:36

11:11–12 *false . . . idiot.* Zophar claims that it would take a miracle to change Job.
11:13–20 Zophar assumes that Job's problems are rooted in his sin; all Job has to do is to repent, and then his life will become blessed and happy. But God nowhere guarantees a life "brighter than noonday" (v. 17) simply because we are His children. He has higher purposes for us than our physical prosperity, or people courting our favor (v. 19). Zophar's philosophy is in conflict with Ps 73.
11:13 *spread out your hand to Him.* For help (see Prov 1:24; Lam 1:17).
11:15 *lift up your face without moral defect.* Zophar echoes Job's thought in 10:15.
11:20 Bildad ended his speech in a similar way (see 8:22).
12:1–14:22 As before, Job's reply is divided into two parts: He speaks to his three friends (12:2–13:19), then to God (13:20–14:22).
12:2 For the first time, Job reacts with sarcasm to the harshness of his counselors (see v. 20).
12:3 *who does not know . . . ?* See v. 9. The advice of Job's friends is trivial and commonplace.
12:4 *God . . . answered.* In the days before his suffering began (contrast 9:16).
12:5 The prosperous despise those who, like Job, have trouble.
12:6 Such statements (see 9:21–24) irked the counselors and made them brand Job as a man whose feet were slipping (see v. 5).
12:7–12 Job appeals to all creation to prove that God does what He pleases—that He does not use a person's piety as the sole basis for granting freedom from affliction.
12:7 *let them teach you.* That the righteous suffer and the evil are secure.
12:9 *LORD.* The only place in Job's and his friends' speeches (chs. 3–37) where the divine name "LORD" (Hebrew *Yahweh*) is used (see Introduction: Author).
12:11 Echoed by Elihu in 34:3. Cf. 6:6, where Job says that Eliphaz's words are like "something tasteless."
12:12 Job sarcastically chides his counselors for being elders and yet lacking in true wisdom.
12:13–25 The theme of this section is stated in v. 13: God is

14 "Behold, He [a]tears down, and it cannot
be rebuilt;
He [1][b]imprisons a man, and [2]there can
be no release.
15 "Behold, He [a]restrains the waters, and
they dry up;
And He [b]sends them out, and they
[1]inundate the earth.
16 "With Him are strength and sound
wisdom,
The [a]misled and the misleader belong
to Him.
17 "He makes [a]counselors walk [1]barefoot
And makes fools of [b]judges.
18 "He [a]loosens the [1]bond of kings
And binds their loins with a girdle.
19 "He makes priests walk [1]barefoot
And overthrows [a]the secure ones.
20 "He deprives the trusted ones of speech
And [a]takes away the discernment of
the elders.
21 "He [a]pours contempt on nobles
And [b]loosens the belt of the strong.
22 "He [a]reveals mysteries from the
darkness
And brings the deep darkness into
light.
23 "He [a]makes the nations great, then
destroys them;
He [1]enlarges the nations, then leads
them away.
24 "He [a]deprives of intelligence the chiefs
of the earth's people
And makes them wander in a pathless
waste.
25 "They [a]grope in darkness with no light,
And He makes them [b]stagger like a
drunken man.

Job Says His Friends' Proverbs Are Ashes

13 "[a]Behold, my eye has seen all *this,*
My ear has heard and understood it.
2 "[a]What you know I also know;
I am not inferior to you.
3 "But [a]I would speak to [1]the Almighty,
And I desire to [b]argue with God.
4 "But you [a]smear with lies;
You are all [b]worthless physicians.
5 "O that you would [a]be completely silent,
And that it would become your
wisdom!
6 "Please hear my argument
And listen to the contentions of my
lips.
7 "Will you [a]speak what is unjust for
God,
And speak what is deceitful for Him?
8 "Will you [a]show partiality for Him?
Will you contend for God?
9 "Will it be well when He examines you?
Or [a]will you deceive Him as one
deceives a man?
10 "He will surely reprove you
If you secretly [a]show partiality.
11 "Will not [a]His [1]majesty terrify you,
And the dread of Him fall on you?
12 "Your memorable sayings are proverbs
of ashes,
Your defenses are defenses of clay.

Job Is Sure He Will Be Vindicated

13 "[a]Be silent before me so that I may
speak;
Then let come on me what may.
14 "Why should I take my flesh in my
teeth
And [a]put my life in my [1]hands?
15 "[a]Though He slay me,
I will hope in Him.
Nevertheless I [b]will argue my ways
[1]before Him.
16 "This also will be my [a]salvation,
For [b]a godless man may not come
before His presence.
17 "Listen carefully to my speech,
And let my declaration *fill* your ears.
18 "Behold now, I have [a]prepared my case;
I know that [b]I will be vindicated.
19 "[a]Who will contend with me?
For then I would be silent and [b]die.
20 "Only two things do not do to me,
Then I will not hide from Your face:

14 [1]Lit *shuts against* [2]Lit *it is not opened* [a]Job 19:10; Is 25:2 [b]Job 37:7
15 [1]Lit *overturn* [a]Deut 11:17; 1 Kin 8:35; 17:1 [b]Gen 7:11-24
16 [a]Job 13:7, 9
17 [1]Or *stripped* [a]Job 3:14 [b]Job 9:24
18 [1]Or *discipline* [a]Ps 116:16
19 [1]Or *stripped* [a]Job 24:22; 34:24-28; 35:9
20 [a]Job 17:4; 32:9
21 [a]Job 34:19; Ps 107:40 [b]Job 12:18
22 [a]Dan 2:22; 1 Cor 4:5
23 [1]Or *spreads out* [a]Is 9:3; 26:15
24 [a]Job 12:20
25 [a]Job 5:14 [b]Is 24:20
13:1 [a]Job 12:9
2 [a]Job 12:3
3 [1]Heb *Shaddai* [a]Job 13:22; 23:4 [b]Job 13:15
4 [a]Ps 119:69 [b]Jer 23:32
5 [a]Job 13:13; 21:5; Prov 17:28
7 [a]Job 27:4
8 [a]Lev 19:15; Prov 24:23
9 [a]Job 12:16
10 [a]Job 13:8; 32:21; 34:19
11 [1]Lit *exaltation* [a]Job 31:23
13 [a]Job 13:5
14 [1]Lit *palm* [a]Ps 119:109
15 [1]Lit *to His face* [a]Job 7:6 [b]Job 27:5
16 [a]Job 23:7; Is 12:1, 2 [b]Job 34:21-23
18 [a]Job 23:4 [b]Job 9:21; 10:7; 12:4
19 [a]Is 50:8 [b]Job 7:21; 10:8

sovereign in the created world, and especially in history. The rest of the poem dwells on the negative aspects of God's power and wisdom—e.g., the destructive forces of nature (vv. 14–15), how judges become fools (v. 17), how priests become humiliated (v. 19), how trusted advisers are silenced and elders deprived of good sense (v. 20). Contrast the claim of Eliphaz that God always uses His power in ways that make sense (5:10–16).
12:20 See note on v. 2.
12:21a,24b The Hebrew text of these lines is repeated verbatim in Ps 107:40.
12:22 God knows even secret, evil plans.
12:25 *grope in darkness.* Job concludes this section with a parody of Eliphaz's confident assertion in 5:14.
13:1–12 Job feels that his counselors have become completely untrustworthy (see v. 12). He calls them quacks (see v. 4; see also 16:2) and accuses them of showing partiality to God (since God is stronger than Job) by telling lies about Job (see vv. 7–8). Someday God will examine and punish them for their deception (see vv. 9–11).
13:1 *all this.* God's sovereign actions as described in ch. 12.
13:2 See 15:9. *I am not inferior to you.* Repeated from 12:3.
13:5 See v. 13. The friends' silent presence had ministered to Job earlier (see 2:13), but Job's current retort is intended as sarcasm (cf. Prov 17:28).
13:12 *defenses.* Arguments in their defense of God's judgment.
13:15 No matter what happens, Job intends to seek vindication from God and believes that he will receive it (see v. 18).
13:16 *be my salvation.* See Phil 1:19 (perhaps Paul was reflecting on Job's experience).
13:17 Job asks his friends to listen to what he is going to say to God in 13:20–14:22.
13:20 *two things.* Job wants God (1) to withdraw His hand of punishment (v. 21), and (2) to start communicating with him (v. 22).

21 [a]Remove Your [1]hand from me,
And let not the dread of You terrify me.
22 "Then call, and [a]I will answer;
Or let me speak, then reply to me.
23 "[a]How many are my iniquities and sins?
Make known to me my [1]rebellion and my sin.
24 "Why do You [a]hide Your face
And consider me [b]Your enemy?
25 "Will You cause a [a]driven leaf to tremble?
Or will You pursue the dry [b]chaff?
26 "For You write [a]bitter things against me
And [b]make me to inherit the iniquities of my youth.
27 "You [a]put my feet in the stocks
And watch all my paths;
You [1]set a limit for the soles of my feet,
28 While [1]I am decaying like a [a]rotten thing,
Like a garment that is moth-eaten.

Job Speaks of the Finality of Death

14 "[a]Man, who is born of woman,
Is [1]short-lived and [b]full of turmoil.
2 "[a]Like a flower he comes forth and withers.
He also flees like [b]a shadow and does not remain.
3 "You also [a]open Your eyes on him
And [b]bring [1]him into judgment with Yourself.
4 "[a]Who can make the clean out of the unclean?
No one!
5 "Since his days are determined,
The [a]number of his months is with You;
And his limits You have [1]set so that he cannot pass.

21 [1]Lit *palm* [a]Job 9:34; Ps 39:10
22 [a]Job 9:16; 14:15
23 [1]Or *transgression* [a]Job 7:21
24 [a]Ps 13:1; 44:24; 88:14; Is 8:17 [b]Job 19:11; 33:10; Lam 2:5
25 [a]Lev 26:36 [b]Job 21:18
26 [a]Job 9:18 [b]Ps 25:7
27 [1]Lit *carve for* [a]Job 33:11
28 [1]Lit *he is* [a]Job 2:7
14:1 [1]Lit *short of days* [a]Job 5:7 [b]Eccl 2:23
2 [a]Ps 90:5, 6; 103:15; Is 40:6, 7; James 1:10; 1 Pet 1:24 [b]Job 8:9
3 [1]So with some ancient versions; M.T. *me* [a]Ps 8:4; 144:3 [b]Ps 143:2
4 [a]Job 15:14; 25:4; Ps 51:5
5 [1]Lit *made* [a]Job 21:21
6 [1]Lit *cease* [2]Lit *makes acceptable* [a]Job 7:19; Ps 39:13
7 [1]Or *cease*
10 [a]Job 3:13; 14:10-15 [b]Job 13:9
11 [1]Lit *disappears* [a]Is 19:5
12 [1]Lit *They* [2]Lit *their* [a]Job 3:13
13 [1]I.e. the nether world [a]Is 26:20
15 [a]Job 10:3
16 [a]Job 31:4; 34:21; Ps 139:1-3; Prov 5:21 [b]Job 10:6
17 [1]Lit *plaster; or glue together* [a]Deut 32:32-34
18 [1]Lit *withers*

6 "[a]Turn Your gaze from him that he may [1]rest,
Until he [2]fulfills his day like a hired man.
7 "For there is hope for a tree,
When it is cut down, that it will sprout again,
And its shoots will not [1]fail.
8 "Though its roots grow old in the ground
And its stump dies in the dry soil,
9 At the scent of water it will flourish
And put forth sprigs like a plant.
10 "But [a]man dies and lies prostrate.
Man [b]expires, and where is he?
11 "*As* [a]water [1]evaporates from the sea,
And a river becomes parched and dried up,
12 So [a]man lies down and does not rise.
Until the heavens are no longer,
[1]He will not awake nor be aroused out of [2]his sleep.

13 "Oh that You would hide me in [1]Sheol,
That You would conceal me [a]until Your wrath returns *to You,*
That You would set a limit for me and remember me!
14 "If a man dies, will he live *again?*
All the days of my struggle I will wait
Until my change comes.
15 "You will call, and I will answer You;
You will long for [a]the work of Your hands.
16 "For now You [a]number my steps,
You do not [b]observe my sin.
17 "My transgression is [a]sealed up in a bag,
And You [1]wrap up my iniquity.

18 "But the falling mountain [1]crumbles away,
And the rock moves from its place;

13:21 See 9:34.
13:23 Job's words are based on the counselors' point that suffering always implies sinfulness. He does not yet understand that God has a higher purpose in his suffering. *iniquities . . . sins . . . rebellion.* The three most important Hebrew terms for sin lie behind these translations (see Ex 34:7; Is 59:12 and note).
13:24 *hide Your face.* Withhold Your blessing (see note on Ps 13:1).
13:25 *driven leaf . . . dry chaff.* See note on Ps 1:4.
13:26 *iniquities of my youth.* Since Job feels that he is not presently guilty of a sinful life, God must still be holding the sins of his youth against him. *write . . . things against me.* See Ps 130:3; Hos 13:12; contrast 1 Cor 13:5.
13:27 *You put . . . my paths.* Elihu later quotes Job's words (see 33:11). *limit for the soles of my feet.* The Babylonian Code of Hammurapi (18th century B.C.) attests to the practice of putting marks on slaves. Job feels that he is being harassed by a God who has taken him captive and is tormenting him (see v. 25).
13:28–14:1 The introduction to ch. 14, expressing the pessimistic theme that man's legacy is trouble and his destiny is death.
13:28 *garment that is moth-eaten.* See Matt 6:19–20; Luke 12:33.
14:1 See 5:7.
14:2–6 A symmetrical poem centered around v. 4; v. 2 corresponds to v. 5, and v. 3 to v. 6. Job expostulates with God: Given man's insignificance and inherited impurity, why do You take him so seriously (see 13:25)?
14:2 *he . . . withers.* Life at best is brief and fragile (see 8:9; Ps 37:2; Is 40:7,24). *like a shadow.* See note on 8:9.
14:7–12 Man is like a flower that lives its short life and is gone (v. 2), not like a tree that revives even after it has been cut down.
14:7 *sprout.* The Hebrew root underlying this word is translated "change" in v. 14.
14:13–17 Job's spirit now appears to rise above the despair engendered by his rotting body. Although resurrection in the fullest sense is not taught here, Job is saying that if God so desires He is able to hide Job in the grave, then raise him back to life at a time when the divine anger is past.
14:14 *struggle.* See note on 7:1.
14:18–22 Job's pessimism arises not from skepticism about the possibility of resurrection from the dead but rather from God's apparent unwillingness to do something immediately for

19 Water wears away stones,
Its torrents wash away the dust of the earth;
So You [a]destroy man's hope.
20 "You forever overpower him and he [a]departs;
You change his appearance and send him away.
21 "His sons achieve honor, but [a]he does not know *it;*
Or they become insignificant, but he does not perceive it.
22 "But his [1]body pains him,
And he mourns only for himself."

Eliphaz Says Job Presumes Much

15 Then Eliphaz the Temanite [1]responded,
2 "Should a wise man answer with windy knowledge
[a]And fill [1]himself with the east wind?
3 "Should he argue with useless talk,
Or with words which are not profitable?
4 "Indeed, you do away with [1]reverence
And hinder meditation before God.
5 "For [a]your guilt teaches your mouth,
And you choose the language of [b]the crafty.
6 "Your [a]own mouth condemns you, and not I;
And your own lips testify against you.

7 "Were you the first man to be born,
Or [a]were you brought forth before the hills?
8 "Do you hear the [a]secret counsel of God,
And limit wisdom to yourself?
9 "[a]What do you know that we do not know?
What do you understand that [1]we do not?
10 "Both the [a]gray-haired and the aged are among us,
Older than your father.
11 "Are [a]the consolations of God too small for you,
Even the [b]word *spoken* gently with you?
12 "Why does your [a]heart carry you away?
And why do your eyes flash,
13 That you should turn your spirit against God
And allow *such* words to go out of your mouth?
14 "What is man, that [a]he should be pure,
Or [b]he who is born of a woman, that he should be righteous?
15 "Behold, He puts no trust in His [a]holy ones,
And the [b]heavens are not pure in His sight;
16 How much less one who is [a]detestable and corrupt,
Man, who [b]drinks iniquity like water!

What Eliphaz Has Seen of Life

17 "I will tell you, listen to me;
And what I have seen I will also declare;
18 What wise men have told,
And have not concealed from [a]their fathers,
19 To whom alone the land was given,
And no alien passed among them.
20 "The wicked man writhes [a]in pain all *his* days,
And [1]numbered are the years [b]stored up for the ruthless.
21 "[1]Sounds of [a]terror are in his ears;
[b]While at peace the destroyer comes upon him.
22 "He does not believe that he will [a]return from darkness,
And he is destined for [b]the sword.
23 "He wanders about for food, saying, 'Where is it?'

19 [a]Job 7:6 **20** [a]Job 4:20; 20:7 **21** [a]Eccl 9:5 **22** [1]Lit *flesh* **15:1** [1]Lit *answered and said* **2** [1]Lit *his belly* [a]Job 6:26 **4** [1]Lit *fear* **5** [a]Job 22:5 [b]Job 5:12, 13 **6** [a]Job 18:7 **7** [a]Job 38:4, 21; Prov 8:25 **8** [a]Job 29:4; Rom 11:34; 1 Cor 2:11 **9** [1]Lit *is not within us?* [a]Job 12:3; 13:2 **10** [a]Job 12:12; 32:6, 7 **11** [a]Job 5:17-19; 36:15, 16 [b]Job 6:10; 23:12 **12** [a]Job 11:13; 36:13 **14** [a]Job 14:4; Prov 20:9; Eccl 7:20 [b]Job 25:4 **15** [a]Job 5:1 [b]Job 25:5 **16** [a]Ps 14:1 [b]Job 34:7; Prov 19:28 **18** [a]Job 8:8; 20:4 **20** [1]Lit *the number of years are* [a]Job 15:24 [b]Job 24:1; 27:13 **21** [1]Lit *A sound of terrors is* [a]Job 15:24; 18:11; 20:25; 24:17; 27:20 [b]Job 20:21; 1 Thess 5:3 **22** [a]Job 15:30 [b]Job 19:29; 27:14; 33:18; 36:12

a person like him, whose life has become a nightmare of pain and mourning.

15:1–6 Up to this point Eliphaz has been the most sympathetic of the three counselors, but now he has run out of patience with Job and denounces him more severely than before.

15:2 *windy.* The Hebrew word is also used in 16:3, where Job hurls Eliphaz's charges back at him. *east wind.* See 27:21; 38:24; the sirocco that blows in from the desert (see notes on Gen 41:6; Jer 4:11).

15:4 *reverence.* See note on 4:6.

15:5 See Matt 15:11,17–18.

15:6 *mouth condemns you.* See 9:20.

15:7–10 Job, says Eliphaz, presumes to be wise enough to sit among the members of God's council in heaven (see note on 1:6) when in reality he is no wiser than ordinary elders and sages on earth.

15:10 Age, with its tested experience, was equated with wisdom in ancient times—a truism denied by Elihu (see 32:6–9).

15:11–13 Eliphaz chides Job for replying in rage to his friends' attempts to console him with gentle words, which Eliphaz believes come from God Himself (v. 11). But Eliphaz has been guilty of cruel insinuation (ch. 5), and the other two counselors have been even more malicious. Genuine words of comfort for Job have been few indeed (see 4:2–6).

15:14–16 See 25:4–6. Eliphaz repeats what he had already said in 4:17–19, perhaps because he thought the earlier words had come to him through divine revelation (see note on 4:12–21).

15:14 *born of a woman.* An echo of Job's words in 14:1.

15:15 *holy ones.* Angels (see note on 5:1).

15:16 *drinks iniquity like water.* See Elihu's description of Job in 34:7.

15:17–26 Eliphaz now bolsters his earlier advice with traditional wisdom: The wicked man (a caricature of Job) can never escape the suffering he deserves.

15:20–35 A poem on the fate of the wicked (see 8:11–19). Eliphaz's caricature continues with a variety of figures: a belligerent sinner who attacks God (vv. 24–26); a fat, rich wicked man who finally gets what he deserves (vv. 27–32); a grapevine stripped before the fruit is ripe (v. 33a); an olive tree shedding its blossoms (v. 33b). As long as Eliphaz rejects Job's insistence that the wicked go on prospering, he does not have to wrestle with the disturbing corollary: the mystery of why the innocent sometimes suffer.

He knows that a day of [a]darkness is
[1]at hand.
24 "Distress and anguish terrify him,
They overpower him like a king ready
for the attack,
25 Because he has stretched out his hand
against God
And conducts himself [a]arrogantly
against [1]the Almighty.
26 "He rushes [1]headlong at Him
With [2]his massive shield.
27 "For he has [a]covered his face with his
fat
And made his thighs heavy with flesh.
28 "He has [a]lived in desolate cities,
In houses no one would inhabit,
Which are destined to become [1]ruins.
29 "He [a]will not become rich, nor will his
wealth endure;
And his grain will not bend down to
the ground.
30 "He will [a]not [1]escape from darkness;
The [b]flame will wither his shoots,
And by [c]the breath of His mouth he
will go away.
31 "Let him not [a]trust in emptiness,
deceiving himself;
For emptiness will be his [1]reward.
32 "It will be accomplished [a]before his
time,
And his palm [b]branch will not be
green.
33 "He will drop off his unripe grape like
the vine,
And will [a]cast off his flower like the
olive tree.
34 "For the company of [a]the godless is
barren,
And fire consumes [b]the tents of [1]the
corrupt.
35 "They [a]conceive [1]mischief and bring
forth iniquity,
And their [2]mind prepares deception."

Job Says Friends Are Sorry Comforters

16 Then Job [1]answered,
2 "I have heard many such things;
[1a]Sorry comforters are you all.
3 "Is there *no* limit to [a]windy words?
Or what plagues you that you answer?
4 "I too could speak like you,
If [1]I were in your place.

23 [1]Lit *ready at his hand* [a]Job 15:22, 30
25 [1]Heb *Shaddai* [a]Job 36:9
26 [1]Lit *with a stiff neck* [2]Lit *the thick-bossed shields*
27 [a]Ps 73:7; 119:70
28 [1]Or *heaps* [a]Job 3:14; Is 5:8, 9
29 [a]Job 27:16, 17
30 [1]Lit *turn aside* [a]Job 5:14; 15:22 [b]Job 15:34; 20:26; 22:20; 31:12 [c]Job 4:9
31 [1]Lit *exchange* [a]Job 35:13; Is 59:4
32 [a]Job 22:16; Eccl 7:17 [b]Job 18:16
33 [a]Job 14:2
34 [1]Lit *a bribe* [a]Job 8:13 [b]Job 8:22
35 [1]Or *pain* [2]Lit *belly* [a]Ps 7:14; Is 59:4
16:1 [1]Lit *answered and said*
2 [1]Lit *Comforters of trouble* [a]Job 13:4; 21:34
3 [a]Job 6:26
4 [1]Lit *your soul were in place of my soul*

4 [a]Ps 22:7; 109:25; Zeph 2:15; Matt 27:39
6 [a]Job 9:27, 28
7 [a]Job 7:3 [b]Job 16:20; 19:13-15
8 [a]Job 10:17 [b]Job 19:20; Ps 109:24
9 [1]Lit *borne a grudge against me* [2]Lit *sharpens his eyes* [a]Job 19:11; Hos 6:1 [b]Ps 35:16; Lam 2:16; Acts 7:54 [c]Job 13:24; 33:10
10 [1]Lit *struck* [a]Ps 22:13 [b]Is 50:6; Lam 3:30; Acts 23:2 [c]Job 30:12; Ps 35:15
12 [a]Job 9:17 [b]Job 7:20; Lam 3:12
13 [a]Job 6:4; 19:12; 25:3 [b]Job 20:25

I could compose words against you
And [a]shake my head at you.
5 "I could strengthen you with my
mouth,
And the solace of my lips could lessen
your pain.

Job Says God Shattered Him

6 "If I speak, [a]my pain is not lessened,
And if I hold back, what has left me?
7 "But now He has [a]exhausted me;
You have laid [b]waste all my company.
8 "You have shriveled me up,
[a]It has become a witness;
And my [b]leanness rises up against me,
It testifies to my face.
9 "His anger has [a]torn me and [1]hunted
me down,
He has [b]gnashed at me with His
teeth;
My [c]adversary [2]glares at me.
10 "They have [a]gaped at me with their
mouth,
They have [1b]slapped me on the cheek
with contempt;
They have [c]massed themselves against
me.
11 "God hands me over to ruffians
And tosses me into the hands of the
wicked.
12 "I was at ease, but [a]He shattered me,
And He has grasped me by the neck
and shaken me to pieces;
He has also set me up as His [b]target.
13 "His [a]arrows surround me.
Without mercy He splits my kidneys
open;
He pours out [b]my gall on the ground.
14 "He [a]breaks through me with breach
after breach;
He [b]runs at me like a warrior.
15 "I have sewed [a]sackcloth over my skin
And [b]thrust my horn in the dust.
16 "My face is flushed from [a]weeping,
[b]And deep darkness is on my eyelids,
17 Although there is no [a]violence in my
hands,
And [b]my prayer is pure.

18 "O earth, do not cover my blood,

14 [a]Job 9:17 [b]Joel 2:7 **15** [a]Gen 37:34; Ps 69:11 [b]Ps 7:5
16 [a]Job 16:20 [b]Job 24:17 **17** [a]Is 59:6; Jon 3:8 [b]Job 27:4

15:23,30 *darkness.* Death, characterized by the journey to the netherworld (see note on 10:21).
15:35 *They conceive mischief and bring forth iniquity.* Repeated in Is 59:4 (see note there). Once initiated, sinful thoughts develop quickly into evil acts.
16:2–5 Helpful advice is usually brief and encouraging, not lengthy and judgmental.
16:2 *Sorry comforters.* See note on 13:1–12. Job would eventually be comforted, but not by his three friends (see 42:11).
16:3 *windy.* See note on 15:2.
16:4 *shake . . . head.* A gesture of insult and scorn (see Ps 22:7; Jer 48:27; Matt 27:39).
16:9 The figure here is graphic and disturbing: God, like a ferocious lion (see 10:16), attacks and tears at Job's flesh. *adversary.* The Hebrew for this word is translated "enemy" in 19:11.
16:10–14 Job sees himself as God's target and views his situation as the reverse of Eliphaz's description in 15:25–26.
16:12 *I was at ease, but He shattered me.* See 2:3 and note. *set me up as His target.* See note on 6:4.
16:15–17 Job summarizes his misery: Though innocent, he continues to suffer.
16:15 *sackcloth . . . dust.* Signs of mourning (see notes on Gen 37:34; Jon 3:5–6).
16:18–21 Verse 18 (see v. 22; 17:1) indicates that Job does

And let there be no *resting* place for
my cry.
19 "Even now, behold, [a]my witness is in
heaven,
And my [1]advocate is [b]on high.
20 "My friends are my scoffers;
[a]My eye [1]weeps to God.
21 "O that a man might plead with God
As a man with his neighbor!
22 "For when a few years are past,
I shall go the way [a]of no return.

Job Says He Has Become a Byword

17 "My spirit is broken, my days are
extinguished,
The [1a]grave is *ready* for me.
2 "[a]Surely mockers are with me,
And my eye [1]gazes on their
provocation.

3 "Lay down, now, a pledge [a]for me with
Yourself;
Who is there that will [1]be my
guarantor?
4 "For You have [1a]kept their heart from
understanding,
Therefore You will not exalt *them.*
5 "He who [a]informs against friends for a
share *of the spoil,*
The [b]eyes of his children also will
languish.

6 "But He has made me a [a]byword of the
people,
And I am [1]one at whom men [b]spit.
7 "My eye has also grown [a]dim because
of grief,
And all my [b]members are as a
shadow.
8 "The upright will be appalled at this,
And the [a]innocent will stir up himself
against the godless.

19 [1]Or *witness* [a]Gen 31:50; Job 19:25-27; Rom 1:9; Phil 1:8; 1 Thess 2:5 [b]Job 31:2
20 [1]Or *drips* [a]Job 17:7
22 [a]Job 3:13
17:1 [1]Lit *graves* [a]Ps 88:3, 4
2 [1]Lit *lodges* [a]Job 12:4; 17:6
3 [1]Lit *strike hands with me* [a]Ps 119:122; Is 38:14
4 [1]Lit *hidden* [a]Job 12:20
5 [a]Lev 19:13, 16 [b]Job 11:20
6 [1]Lit *a spitting to the faces* [a]Job 17:2 [b]Job 30:10
7 [a]Job 16:16 [b]Job 16:8
8 [a]Job 22:19

9 [a]Prov 4:18 [b]Job 22:30; 31:7
10 [1]With some ancient mss and versions; M.T. *them* [a]Job 12:2
11 [a]Job 7:6
13 [1]Lit *spread out* [a]Job 3:13
14 [a]Job 7:5; 13:28; 30:30 [b]Job 21:26; 25:6
15 [a]Job 7:6
16 [1]So the Gr; Heb possibly *Let my* limbs *sink down to Sheol, since there is rest in the dust for all* [a]Job 3:17; 21:33
18:1 [1]Lit *answered and said*
3 [a]Ps 73:22
4 [1]Lit *he...tears himself...his*
5 [1]Lit *spark* [a]Job 21:17; Prov 13:9; 20:20; 24:20

9 "Nevertheless [a]the righteous will hold
to his way,
And [b]he who has clean hands will
grow stronger and stronger.
10 "But come again all of [1]you now,
For I [a]do not find a wise man among
you.
11 "My [a]days are past, my plans are torn
apart,
Even the wishes of my heart.
12 "They make night into day, *saying,*
'The light is near,' in the presence of
darkness.
13 "If I look for [a]Sheol as my home,
I [1]make my bed in the darkness;
14 If I call to the [a]pit, 'You are my father';
To the [b]worm, 'my mother and my
sister';
15 Where now is [a]my hope?
And who regards my hope?
16 "[1]Will it go down with me to Sheol?
Shall we together [a]go down into the
dust?"

Bildad Speaks of the Wicked

18 Then Bildad the Shuhite [1]responded,
2 "How long will you hunt for words?
Show understanding and then we can
talk.
3 "Why are we [a]regarded as beasts,
As stupid in your eyes?
4 "O [1]you who tear yourself in your
anger—
For your sake is the earth to be
abandoned,
Or the rock to be moved from its
place?

5 "Indeed, the [a]light of the wicked goes
out,
And the [1]flame of his fire gives no
light.

---

not think he will live long enough to be vindicated before his peers. His only hope is that in heaven he has a friend (v. 20), a holy one (see 5:1), who will be his "witness," his "advocate," one who will plead with God on his behalf (v. 21; see 9:33 and note).
16:18 *blood . . . cry.* Job felt that his blood, like Abel's (see Gen 4:10 and note), was innocent and would therefore cry out from the ground after his death.
16:22 *when a few years are past.* Job does not expect his death immediately. *way of no return.* To the netherworld (see notes on 7:9; 10:21).
17:1 *The grave is ready for me.* See note on vv. 10–16.
17:3 *Lay down . . . a pledge for me with Yourself.* Job is asking God for a guarantee that he is right, that he is not guilty of sins that deserve punishment (as his counselors have said).
17:4 *their heart.* Those of his three friends.
17:5 Job quotes a proverb to counter the false accusations of his friends.
17:6–9 The guarantee Job asked for is not provided, so he feels that God is responsible for making him an object of scorn. If the tone of vv. 8–9 is intended as sarcastic (as v. 10 would seem to indicate), the "upright" and "innocent" are the counselors (v. 8).
17:6 *byword.* See 30:9; an object of scorn and ridicule (see the covenant curse in Deut 28:37). *one at whom men spit.* See 30:10.
17:7 *members are as a shadow.* See note on 2:7.
17:10–16 Zophar had promised that Job's repentance would turn his darkness into light (11:17). Job now makes a parody on such advice (vv. 12–16). His only hope is the grave (see v. 1), which will not be as his home had been (vv. 13–15).
17:13 *home.* See Eccl 12:5. *darkness.* See 18:18; the netherworld (see note on 10:21).
17:14 In the grave, one's family consists only of decomposition and maggots.
17:15 *Where . . . is my hope?* See 14:19.
17:16 *Sheol.* See 38:17; Matt 16:18. See note on Gen 37:35. *dust.* See note on 7:21.
18:1–4 Bildad resents what he perceives to be a belittling attitude. He considers Job's emotional reaction as self-centered and irrational.
18:5–21 Another poem on the fate of the wicked (see 8:11–19; 15:20–35). Bildad wants to convince Job that he is wrong when he claims that the righteous suffer and the wicked prosper. Bildad is absolutely certain that every wicked person gets paid in full, in this life, for his wicked deeds.
18:5 *the light of the wicked goes out.* See 21:17; repeated in Prov 13:9. Life, symbolized by light, is extinguished.

6 "The light in his tent is [a]darkened,
And his lamp goes out above him.
7 "His [1]vigorous stride is shortened,
And his [a]own scheme brings him down.
8 "For he is [a]thrown into the net by his own feet,
And he steps on the webbing.
9 "A snare seizes *him* by the heel,
And a trap snaps shut on him.
10 "A noose for him is hidden in the ground,
And a trap for him on the path.
11 "All around [a]terrors frighten him,
And [b]harry him at every step.
12 "His strength is [a]famished,
And calamity is ready at his side.
13 "[1]His skin is devoured by disease,
The firstborn of death [a]devours his [2]limbs.
14 "He is [a]torn from [1]the security of his tent,
And [2]they march him before the king of [b]terrors.
15 "[1]There dwells in his tent nothing of his;
[a]Brimstone is scattered on his habitation.
16 "His [a]roots are dried below,
And his [b]branch is cut off above.
17 "[a]Memory of him perishes from the earth,
And he has no name abroad.
18 "[1]He is driven from light [a]into darkness,
And [b]chased from the inhabited world.
19 "He has no [a]offspring or posterity among his people,
Nor any survivor where he sojourned.
20 "Those [1]in the west are appalled at [a]his [2]fate,
And those [3]in the east are seized with horror.
21 "Surely such are the [a]dwellings of the wicked,
And this is the place of him who does not know God."

Job Feels Insulted

19 Then Job [1]responded,
2 "How long will you torment [1]me
And crush me with words?
3 "These ten times you have insulted me;
You are not ashamed to wrong me.
4 "Even if I have truly erred,
My error lodges with me.
5 "If indeed you [a]vaunt yourselves against me
And prove my disgrace to me,
6 Know then that [a]God has wronged me
And has closed [b]His net around me.

Everything Is against Him

7 "Behold, [a]I cry, 'Violence!' but I get no answer;
I shout for help, but there is no justice.
8 "He has [a]walled up my way so that I cannot pass,
And He has put [b]darkness on my paths.
9 "He has [a]stripped my honor from me
And removed the [b]crown from my head.
10 "He [a]breaks me down on every side, and I am gone;
And He has uprooted my [b]hope [c]like a tree.
11 "He has also [a]kindled His anger against me
And [b]considered me as His enemy.
12 "His [a]troops come together,
And [b]build up their [1]way against me
And camp around my tent.

13 "He has [a]removed my brothers far from me,

6 [a]Job 12:25
7 [1]Lit *steps of his strength* [a]Job 15:6
8 [a]Job 22:10; Ps 9:15; 35:8; Is 24:17, 18
11 [a]Job 15:21 [b]Job 18:18; 20:8
12 [a]Is 8:21
13 [1]Heb *It eats parts of his skin* [2]Or *parts* [a]Zech 14:12
14 [1]Lit *his tent his trust* [2]Or *you or she shall march* [a]Job 8:22; 18:6 [b]Job 15:21
15 [1]A suggested reading is *Fire dwells in his tent* [a]Ps 11:6
16 [a]Is 5:24; Hos 9:16; Amos 2:9; Mal 4:1 [b]Job 15:30, 32
17 [a]Job 24:20; Ps 34:16; Prov 10:7
18 [1]Lit *They drive him...And chase him* [a]Job 5:14; Is 8:22 [b]Job 20:8; 27:21-23
19 [a]Job 27:14, 15; Is 14:22
20 [1]Lit *who come after* [2]Lit *day* [3]Lit *who have gone before* [a]Ps 37:13; Jer 50:27; Obad 12
21 [a]Job 21:28

19:1 [1]Lit *answered and said*
2 [1]Lit *my soul*
5 [a]Ps 35:26; 38:16; 55:12, 13
6 [a]Job 16:11; 27:2 [b]Job 18:8-10; Ps 66:11; Lam 1:13
7 [a]Job 9:24; 30:20, 24; Hab 1:2
8 [a]Job 3:23; Lam 3:7, 9 [b]Job 30:26
9 [a]Job 12:17, 19; Ps 89:44 [b]Job 16:15; Ps 89:39; Lam 5:16
10 [a]Job 12:14 [b]Job 7:6 [c]Job 24:20 **11** [a]Job 16:9 [b]Job 13:24; 33:10 **12** [1]I.e. siegework [a]Job 16:13 [b]Job 30:12 **13** [a]Job 16:7; Ps 69:8

18:13 *firstborn of death.* See 5:7.
18:14 *king of terrors.* A vivid figure of speech referring to death, which is personified in v. 13. Canaanite literature pictured death as the devouring god Mot. Isaiah reverses the figure and envisions the Lord as swallowing up death forever (Is 25:8; see 1 Cor 15:54).
18:15 *Brimstone.* Reminiscent of the destruction of Sodom and Gomorrah (see Gen 19:24).
18:16 *roots . . . And . . . branch.* Cf. Amos 2:9; figurative for descendants (see, e.g., Is 11:1,10) and/or ancestors (see, e.g., Judg 5:14; Is 14:29).
18:17 *Memory of him perishes.* Apparently Bildad knows nothing of punishment in the realm of death. The only retribution beyond the grave is having one's memory (name) cut off by not leaving any heirs (see v. 19).
18:18 *darkness.* See 17:13; the netherworld (see note on 10:21).
18:21 *the wicked . . . does not know God.* Having no intimate knowledge of God is synonymous with being wicked (see Hos 4:1–2,6).
19:3 *ten times.* Several times. Ten is often used as a round number (see, e.g., Gen 31:41; 1 Sam 1:8).
19:4 *lodges with me.* If Job has erred, it is his responsibility. His friends have no right to interfere or to behave as if they were God (see v. 22).
19:6 *wronged.* Cf. 40:8. The Hebrew for this verb is twice translated "pervert" in 8:3, where Bildad denied that God perverts justice. But Job, struggling with the enigma of his suffering, can only conclude that God is his enemy, though in fact He is his friend who delights in him (see 1:8; 2:3). Job's true enemy, of course, is the Accuser. *closed His net.* The wicked may get themselves into trouble, as Bildad had pointed out (see 18:8–10), but Job here attributes his suffering to God.
19:7 *I cry, 'Violence!'* See Hab 1:2.
19:8–12 In Job's mind, God is at war with him (see 16:12–14).
19:10 *uprooted my hope like a tree.* See 24:20; unlike 14:7–9, where Job had used as a symbol of hope a tree that is cut down but later sprouts again.
19:12 *their way.* See 30:12.
19:13–19 See Jer 12:6. Nothing in life hurts more than rejec-

And my [b]acquaintances are
completely estranged from me.
14 "My relatives have failed,
And my [a]intimate friends have
forgotten me.
15 "Those who live in my house and my
maids consider me a stranger.
I am a foreigner in their sight.
16 "I call to my servant, but he does not
answer;
I have to implore him with my mouth.
17 "My breath is [1]offensive to my wife,
And I am loathsome to my own
brothers.
18 "Even young children despise me;
I rise up and they speak against me.
19 "All [1]my [a]associates abhor me,
And those I love have turned against
me.
20 "My [a]bone clings to my skin and my
flesh,
And I have escaped *only* by the skin of
my teeth.
21 "Pity me, pity me, O you my friends,
For the [a]hand of God has struck me.
22 "Why do you [a]persecute me as God
does,
And are not satisfied with my flesh?

Job Says, "My Redeemer Lives"

23 "Oh that my words were written!
Oh that they were [a]inscribed in a
book!
24 "That with an iron stylus and lead
They were engraved in the rock forever!
25 "As for me, I know that [a]my [1]Redeemer
lives,
And [2]at the last He will take His stand
on the [3]earth.
26 "Even after my skin [1]is destroyed,
Yet from my flesh I shall [a]see God;
27 Whom I [1]myself shall behold,
And whom my eyes will see and not
another.
My [2]heart [a]faints [3]within me!
28 "If you say, 'How shall we [a]persecute
him?'
And '[1]What pretext for a case against
him can we find?'
29 "*Then* be afraid of [a]the sword for
yourselves,
For wrath *brings* the punishment of
the sword,
So that you may know [b]there is
judgment."

13 [b]Job 16:20; Ps 88:8, 18 **14** [a]Job 19:19 **17** [1]Lit *strange* **19** [1]Lit *the men of my council* [a]Ps 38:11; 55:12, 13 **20** [a]Job 16:8; 33:21; Ps 102:5; Lam 4:8 **21** [a]Job 1:11; Ps 38:2 **22** [a]Job 13:24, 25; 16:11; 19:6; Ps 69:26 **23** [a]Is 30:8; Jer 36:2 **25** [1]Or *Vindicator, defender;* lit *kinsman* [a]Job 16:19; Ps 78:35; Prov 23:11; Is 43:14; Jer 50:34

25 [2]Or *as the Last* [3]Lit *dust* **26** [1]Lit *which they have cut off* [a]Ps 17:15; Matt 5:8; 1 Cor 13:12; 1 John 3:2 **27** [1]Or *on my side* [2]Lit *kidneys* [3]Lit *in my loins* [a]Ps 73:26 **28** [1]Or *the root of the matter is found in him* [a]Job 19:22 **29** [a]Job 15:22 [b]Job 22:4; Ps 1:5; 9:7; Eccl 12:14 **20:1** [1]Lit *answered and said* **2** [1]Lit *return* [2]Lit *haste within me* **3** [a]Job 19:3 **4** [a]Job 8:8

Zophar Says, "The Triumph of the Wicked Is Short"

20 Then Zophar the Naamathite [1]answered,
2 "Therefore my disquieting thoughts
make me [1]respond,
Even because of my [2]inward agitation.
3 "I listened to [a]the reproof which insults
me,
And the spirit of my understanding
makes me answer.
4 "Do you know this from [a]of old,
From the establishment of man on
earth,
5 That the [a]triumphing of the wicked is
short,
And [b]the joy of the godless momentary?

5 [a]Job 8:12, 13; Ps 37:35, 36 [b]Job 8:13

tion by one's family and friends. Job's children are gone, and his wife, brothers, friends and servants find him repulsive.
19:17 *breath is offensive.* See note on 2:7.
19:18 *young children despise me.* An intolerable insult in a patriarchal society, where one's elders were to be honored and respected (see Ex 20:12 and note).
19:20 *my skin and my flesh.* See note on 2:7. *skin of my teeth.* It is possible that the Hebrew for "only by the skin of my teeth" refers to gums ("with only my gums"), implying that Job's teeth are gone.
19:21 *hand of God has struck me.* See 1:11; 2:4–6; see also note on v. 6.
19:23–27 Probably the best-known and most-loved passage in the book of Job, reaching a high point in Job's understanding of his own situation and of his relationship to God. Its position between two sections in which Job pleads with (vv. 21–22) and then warns (vv. 28–29) his friends causes it to stand out even more boldly.
19:23 *my words.* Job would have his complaint and defense recorded so that even after his death they would endure until he is finally vindicated. *book.* See note on Ex 17:14.
19:24 *iron.* See also 20:24; 28:2; 40:18; 41:27. Iron did not come into common use in the ancient Near East until the 12th century B.C.
19:25 *I know that my Redeemer lives.* This staunch confession of faith has been appropriated by generations of Christians, especially through the medium of Handel's *Messiah.* But these celebrate redemption from guilt and judgment; Job had something else in mind. Although in other contexts he desires a defender as an advocate in heaven who would plead with God on his behalf (see 9:33–34; 16:18–21 and notes; see also note on 5:1), here the Redeemer seems to be none other than God Himself (see note on Ruth 2:20). Job expresses confidence that ultimately God will vindicate His faithful servants in the face of all false accusations. *at the last.* Lit. "afterward" (after Job's life has ended). *He will take His stand.* To defend and vindicate me (see 42:7–10).
19:26 *my skin is destroyed.* Job senses that the ravages of his disease will eventually bring about his death. *I shall see God.* He is absolutely certain, however, that death is not the end of existence and that someday he will stand in the presence of his Redeemer and see Him with his own eyes (see v. 27; see also Matt 5:8; 1 John 3:2). See note on 42:5.
19:28 *persecute.* Job's tirade against the counselors is being resumed after the intervening section (vv. 23–27).
20:1–29 Yet another poem on the fate of the wicked as held by the "orthodox" theology of Job's friends (see 8:11–19; 15:20–35; 18:5–21).
20:2–3 Zophar takes Job's words, especially his closing words in 19:28–29, as a personal affront. Job has dared to assert that on Zophar's theory of retribution Zophar himself is due for punishment.
20:4–11 Zophar is proud that he is a healthy and prosperous man, for, in his view, that in itself is proof of his goodness and righteousness. But the joy and vigor of the wicked will always be brief and elusive (see Ps 73:18–20 and note).

6 "Though his loftiness [1][a]reaches the
heavens,
And his head touches the clouds,
7 He [a]perishes forever like his refuse;
Those who have seen him [b]will say,
'Where is he?'
8 "He flies away like a [a]dream, and they
cannot find him;
Even like a vision of the night he is
[b]chased away.
9 "The [a]eye which saw him sees him no
longer,
And [b]his place no longer beholds him.
10 "His [a]sons [1]favor the poor,
And his hands [b]give back his wealth.
11 "His [a]bones are full of his youthful
vigor,
But it lies down with him [1]in the dust.

12 "Though [a]evil is sweet in his mouth
And he hides it under his tongue,
13 *Though* he [1]desires it and will not let
it go,
But holds it [a]in his [2]mouth,
14 *Yet* his food in his stomach is changed
To the [1]venom of cobras within him.
15 "He swallows riches,
But will [a]vomit them up;
God will expel them from his belly.
16 "He sucks [a]the poison of cobras;
The viper's tongue slays him.
17 "He does not look at [a]the streams,
The rivers flowing with honey and
curds.
18 "He [a]returns what he has attained
And cannot swallow *it;*
As to the riches of his trading,
He cannot even enjoy *them.*
19 "For he has [a]oppressed *and* forsaken
the poor;
He has seized a house which he has
not built.

20 "Because he knew no quiet [1]within
him,
He does [a]not retain anything he
desires.
21 "Nothing remains [1]for him to devour,
Therefore [a]his prosperity does not
endure.
22 "In the fullness of his plenty he will be
cramped;
The [a]hand of everyone who suffers
will come *against* him.
23 "When he [a]fills his belly,
God will send His fierce anger on him
And will [b]rain *it* on him [1]while he is
eating.
24 "He may [a]flee from the iron weapon,
But the bronze bow will pierce him.
25 "It is drawn forth and comes out of his
back,
Even the glittering point from [a]his
gall.
[b]Terrors come upon him,
26 Complete [a]darkness is held in reserve
for his treasures,
And unfanned [b]fire will devour him;
It will consume the survivor in his
tent.
27 "The [a]heavens will reveal his iniquity,
And the earth will rise up against him.
28 "The [a]increase of his house will depart;
His possessions will flow away [b]in the
day of His anger.
29 "This is the wicked man's [a]portion
from God,
Even the heritage decreed to him by
God."

Job Says God Will Deal with the Wicked

21 Then Job [1]answered,
2 "Listen carefully to my speech,
And let this be your *way of*
consolation.
3 "Bear with me that I may speak;
Then after I have spoken, you may
[a]mock.
4 "As for me, is [a]my complaint [1]to man?
And [b]why should [2]I not be impatient?
5 "Look at me, and be astonished,
And [a]put *your* hand over *your* mouth.
6 "Even when I remember, I am
disturbed,
And [a]horror takes hold of my flesh.

6 [1]Lit *goes up to* [a]Is 14:13, 14; Obad 3, 4
7 [a]Job 4:20; 14:20 [b]Job 7:10; 8:18
8 [a]Ps 73:20; 90:5 [b]Job 18:18; 27:21-23
9 [a]Job 7:8; 8:18 [b]Job 7:10
10 [1]Or *seek the favor of* [a]Job 5:4; 27:14 [b]Job 20:18; 27:16, 17
11 [1]Lit *on* [a]Job 21:23, 24
12 [a]Job 15:16
13 [1]Lit *has compassion on* [2]Lit *palate* [a]Num 11:18-20, 33; Job 20:23
14 [1]Lit *gall*
15 [a]Job 20:10, 20, 21
16 [a]Deut 32:24, 33
17 [a]Deut 32:13, 14; Job 29:6
18 [a]Job 20:10, 15
19 [a]Job 24:2-4; 35:9
20 [1]Lit *in his belly* [a]Eccl 5:13-15
21 [1]Or *of what he devours*
21 [a]Job 15:29
22 [a]Job 5:5
23 [1]Or *as his food* [a]Job 20:13, 14 [b]Num 11:18-20, 33; Ps 78:30, 31
24 [a]Is 24:18; Amos 5:19
25 [a]Job 16:13 [b]Job 18:11, 14
26 [a]Job 18:18 [b]Job 15:30; Ps 21:9
27 [a]Deut 31:28; Is 26:21
28 [a]Deut 28:31 [b]Job 20:15; 21:30
29 [a]Job 27:13; 31:2, 3
21:1 [1]Lit *answered and said*
3 [a]Job 11:3; 17:2
4 [1]Or *against* [2]Lit *my spirit* [a]Job 7:11 [b]Job 6:11
5 [a]Judg 18:19; Job 13:5; 29:9; 40:4 **6** [a]Ps 55:5

20:6 *loftiness reaches the heavens.* See Gen 11:4 and note.
20:7 *refuse.* A symbol of what is temporary and worthless (see 1 Kin 14:10).
20:10,19 Oppression of the poor is the mark of the truly wicked (see, e.g., Amos 2:6–8; 8:4–8). On this subject, Job had no quarrel with Zophar (see 31:16–23).
20:11 *dust.* See note on 7:21.
20:12–15 An evil man's wicked deeds are like tasty food that pleases his palate but turns sour in his stomach.
20:15 *He swallows riches.* After taking what belonged to the poor (see note on vv. 10,19).
20:18 *what he has attained . . . He cannot even enjoy.* A common theme in wisdom literature (see, e.g., Eccl 2:18–23).
20:20–25 Although a wicked man may fill his belly, when God vents His anger against him there will be nothing for him to eat.
20:24 *iron.* See note on 19:24.
20:26 *darkness.* See note on 10:21.
20:27 See Deut 30:19 and note.
20:29 Like Bildad in 18:21, Zophar concludes his speech with a summary statement in which he claims that all he has said is in accord with God's plans for judging sinners. *This is the wicked man's portion from God.* Repeated almost verbatim by Job in 27:13.
21:2 *your way of consolation.* See v. 34 ("you . . . comfort me"), which, with v. 2, frames Job's reply to Zophar.
21:4 *is my complaint to man?* No, says Job, I am complaining to God, because He is responsible for my condition—at least Job so perceived it. *impatient.* See note on 9:2–3.
21:5 *Look at me.* Job addresses his three friends.
21:6 *when I remember.* His complaint to God (see note on v.4). *I am disturbed.* To contemplate the morally upside-down situation in which the wicked flourish.

7 "Why [a]do the wicked *still* live,
Continue on, also become very
[b]powerful?
8 "Their [1a]descendants are established
with them in their sight,
And their offspring before their eyes,
9 Their houses [a]are safe from fear,
And the rod of God is not on them.
10 "His ox mates [1]without fail;
His cow calves and does not abort.
11 "They send forth their little ones like
the flock,
And their children skip about.
12 "They [1]sing to the timbrel and harp
And rejoice at the sound of the flute.
13 "They [a]spend their days in prosperity,
And [1]suddenly they go down to [2]Sheol.
14 "They say to God, '[a]Depart from us!
We do not even desire the knowledge
of Your ways.
15 '[1]Who is [2]the Almighty, that we should
serve Him,
And [a]what would we gain if we
entreat Him?'
16 "Behold, their prosperity is not in their
hand;
The [a]counsel of the wicked is far from
me.

17 "How often is [a]the lamp of the wicked
put out,
Or does their [b]calamity fall on them?
Does [1]God apportion destruction in
His anger?
18 "Are they as [a]straw before the wind,
And like [b]chaff which the storm
carries away?
19 "*You say,* '[a]God stores away [1]a man's
iniquity for his sons.'
Let [2]God repay him so that he may
know *it.*
20 "Let his [a]own eyes see his decay,
And let him [b]drink of the wrath of
[1]the Almighty.
21 "For what does he care for his
household [1]after him,
When the number of his months is cut
off?

22 "Can anyone [a]teach God knowledge,
In that He [b]judges those on high?
23 "One [a]dies in his full strength,
Being wholly at ease and [1]satisfied;
24 His [1]sides are filled out with fat,
And the [a]marrow of his bones is moist,
25 While another dies with a bitter soul,
Never even [1]tasting *anything* good.
26 "Together they [a]lie down in the dust,
And [b]worms cover them.

27 "Behold, I know your thoughts,
And the plans by which you would
wrong me.
28 "For you say, 'Where is the house of
[a]the nobleman,
And where is the [b]tent, the dwelling
places of the wicked?'
29 "Have you not asked wayfaring men,
And do you not recognize their
[1]witness?
30 "For the [a]wicked is reserved for the day
of calamity;
They will be led forth at [b]the day of
fury.
31 "Who will [1]confront him with his
actions,
And who will repay him for what he
has done?
32 "While he is carried to the grave,
Men will keep watch over *his* tomb.
33 "The [a]clods of the valley will [1]gently
cover him;
Moreover, [b]all men will [2]follow after
him,
While countless ones *go* before him.
34 "How then will you vainly [a]comfort me,
For your answers remain *full of*
[1]falsehood?"

Eliphaz Accuses and Exhorts Job

22 Then Eliphaz the Temanite [1]responded,
2 "Can a vigorous [a]man be of use to
God,
Or a wise man be useful to himself?

7 [a]Job 9:24; Ps 73:3; Jer 12:1; Hab 1:13 [b]Job 12:19 **8** [1]Lit *seed* [a]Ps 17:14 **9** [a]Job 12:6 **10** [1]Lit *and does not fail* **12** [1]Lit *lifted up the voice* **13** [1]So with most versions; M.T. *are shattered by Sheol* [2]I.e. the nether world [a]Job 21:23; 36:11 **14** [a]Job 22:17 **15** [1]Lit *What* [2]Heb *Shaddai* [a]Job 22:17; 34:9 **16** [a]Job 22:18 **17** [1]Lit *He* [a]Job 18:5, 6 [b]Job 31:2, 3 **18** [a]Job 13:25; Ps 83:13 [b]Ps 1:4; 35:5; Is 17:13; Hos 13:3 **19** [1]Lit *his* [2]Lit *Him* [a]Ex 20:5; Jer 31:29; Ezek 18:2 **20** [1]Heb *Shaddai* [a]Num 14:28-32; Jer 31:30; Ezek 18:4 [b]Ps 60:3; Is 51:17; Jer 25:15; Rev 14:10 **21** [1]I.e. after he dies

22 [a]Job 35:11; 36:22; Is 40:14; Rom 11:34 [b]Job 4:18; 15:15; Ps 82:1 **23** [1]Or *quiet* [a]Job 20:11; 21:13 **24** [1]So with Syr; Heb uncertain. Some render as, *his pails are full of milk* [a]Prov 3:8 **25** [1]Lit *eating* **26** [a]Job 3:13; 20:11; Eccl 9:2 [b]Job 24:20; Is 14:11 **28** [a]Job 1:3; 31:37 [b]Job 8:22; 18:21 **29** [1]Lit *signs* **30** [a]Job 20:29; Prov 16:4; 2 Pet 2:9 [b]Job 21:17, 20; 40:11 **31** [1]Lit *declare* *his way to his face* **33** [1]Lit *be sweet to him* [2]Lit *draw* [a]Job 3:22; 17:16 [b]Job 3:19; 24:24 **34** [1]Or *faithlessness* [a]Job 16:2

22:1 [1]Lit *answered and said* **2** [a]Job 35:7; Luke 17:10

21:7–15 Job's counselors have elaborated on the fate of the wicked (see 8:11–19; 15:20–35; 18:5–21; ch. 20), but Job insists that experience shows just the reverse of what his friends have said. The wicked, who want to know nothing of God's ways and who even consider prayer a useless exercise (vv. 14–15), flourish in all they do. Far from dying prematurely, as Zophar assumed concerning them (see 20:11), they live long and increase in power (v. 7). Bildad's claim that the wicked have no offspring or descendants (see 18:19) Job flatly denies (vv. 8, 11).
21:9 *rod of God.* See note on 9:34.
21:13 *suddenly.* Or "quietly." The Hebrew root underlying this word is translated "those who live quietly" in Ps 35:20.
21:16 See 22:18. Job disavows the unholy counsel of the wicked and knows that God is in control (see v. 17), but such knowledge makes God all the more of an enigma to him.
21:17 *lamp of the wicked put out.* See 18:5 and note.
21:18 *straw . . . chaff.* See 13:25; see also note on Ps 1:4.
21:20 *drink . . . wrath of the Almighty.* See note on Is 51:17.
21:22 *Can anyone teach God . . . ?* See Is 40:14. On the contrary, God is the one who does the teaching (see 35:11; 36:22; chs. 38–41).
21:26 *dust.* See note on 7:21.
21:34 *How then will you . . . comfort me . . . ?* See 16:2 and note.
22:1–26:14 The third cycle of speeches, unlike the first (chs. 4–14) and second (chs. 15–21), is truncated and abbreviated. Bildad's speech is very brief (25:1–6), and Zophar does not speak at all. The dialogue between Job and his friends comes to an end because the friends cannot convince Job of his guilt—Job cannot acknowledge what is not true.
22:2–4 Eliphaz's odd reasoning is as follows: Since all things have their origin in God, man's giving back what God has given him does not enhance God in any way. Indeed, God is indif-

3 "Is there any pleasure to [1]the Almighty if you are righteous,
Or profit if you make your ways perfect?
4 "Is it because of your [1]reverence that He reproves you,
That He [a]enters into judgment against you?
5 "Is not [a]your wickedness great,
And your iniquities without end?
6 "For you have [a]taken pledges of your brothers without cause,
And [b]stripped [1]men naked.
7 "To the weary you have [a]given no water to drink,
And from the hungry you have [b]withheld bread.
8 "But the earth [a]belongs to the [b]mighty man,
And [c]the honorable man dwells in it.
9 "You have sent [a]widows away empty,
And the [1]strength of the [b]orphans has been crushed.
10 "Therefore [a]snares surround you,
And sudden [b]dread terrifies you,
11 Or [a]darkness, so that you cannot see,
And an [b]abundance of water covers you.

12 "Is not God [a]*in* the height of heaven?
Look also at the [1]distant stars, how high they are!
13 "You say, '[a]What does God know?
Can He judge through the thick darkness?
14 '[a]Clouds are a hiding place for Him, so that He cannot see;
And He walks on the [1]vault of heaven.'
15 "Will you keep to the ancient path
Which [a]wicked men have trod,
16 Who were snatched away [a]before their time,
Whose [b]foundations were [1]washed away by a river?
17 "They [a]said to God, 'Depart from us!'
And 'What can [1]the Almighty do to them?'
18 "Yet He [a]filled their houses with good *things;*
But [b]the counsel of the wicked is far from me.
19 "The [a]righteous see and are glad,
And the innocent mock them,
20 *Saying,* 'Truly our adversaries are cut off,
And their [1]abundance [a]the fire has consumed.'

21 "[1][a]Yield now and be at peace with Him;
Thereby good will come to you.
22 "Please receive [1][a]instruction from His mouth
And establish His words in your heart.
23 "If you [a]return to [1]the Almighty, you will be [2]restored;
If you [b]remove unrighteousness far from your tent,
24 And [a]place *your* [1]gold in the dust,
And *the gold of* Ophir among the stones of the brooks,
25 Then [1]the Almighty will be your [2]gold
And choice silver to you.
26 "For then you will [a]delight in [1]the Almighty
And lift up your face to God.
27 "You will [a]pray to Him, and [b]He will hear you;
And you will pay your vows.
28 "You will also decree a thing, and it will be established for you;
And [a]light will shine on your ways.

3 [1]Heb *Shaddai* **4** [1]Or *fear* [a]Job 14:3; 19:29 **5** [a]Job 11:6; 15:5 **6** [1]Lit *clothing of the naked* [a]Ex 22:26; Deut 24:6, 17; Job 24:3, 9; Ezek 18:16 [b]Job 31:19, 20 **7** [a]Job 31:16, 17 [b]Job 31:31 **8** [a]Job 9:24 [b]Job 12:19 [c]Is 3:3; 9:15 **9** [1]Lit *arms* [a]Job 24:3, 21; 29:13; 31:16, 18 [b]Job 6:27 **10** [a]Job 18:8 [b]Job 15:21 **11** [a]Job 5:14 [b]Job 38:34; Ps 69:2; 124:5; Lam 3:54 **12** [1]Lit *head, top-most* [a]Job 11:7-9 **13** [a]Ps 10:11; 59:7; 64:5; 94:7; Is 29:15; Ezek 8:12 **14** [1]Lit *circle* [a]Job 26:9 **15** [a]Job 34:36 **16** [a]Job 15:32; 21:13, 18 **16** [1]Lit *poured out* [b]Job 14:19; Ps 90:5; Is 28:2; Matt 7:26, 27 **17** [1]Heb *Shaddai* [a]Job 21:14, 15 **18** [a]Job 12:6 [b]Job 21:16 **19** [a]Ps 52:6; 58:10; 107:42 **20** [1]Or *excess* [a]Job 15:30 **21** [1]Or *Know intimately* [a]Ps 34:10 **22** [1]Or *law* [a]Job 6:10; 23:12; Prov 2:6 **23** [1]Heb *Shaddai* [2]Lit *built up* [a]Job 8:5; 11:13; Is 19:22; 31:6; Zech 1:3 [b]Job 11:14

24 [1]Lit *ore* [a]Job 31:24, 25 **25** [1]Heb *Shaddai* [2]Lit *ore* **26** [1]Heb *Shaddai* [a]Job 27:10; Ps 37:4; Is 58:14 **27** [a]Job 11:13; 33:26; Is 58:9 [b]Job 34:28 **28** [a]Job 11:17; Ps 112:4

ferent to man's goodness, because goodness is expected of him. It is when man becomes wicked that God is aroused (v. 4).

22:4 *reverence.* See note on 4:6. *enters into judgment.* See note on 9:3.

22:5–11 In his earlier speeches, Eliphaz was the least caustic and at first even offered consolation (4:6; 5:17). But despite what he said in 4:3–4, Eliphaz now reprimands Job for gross social sins against the needy, who are naked and hungry (vv. 6–7), and against widows and the fatherless (v. 9). The only proof Eliphaz has for Job's alleged wickedness is his present suffering (vv. 10–11). In ch. 29 Job emphatically denies the kind of behavior of which Eliphaz accuses him.

22:6 *taken pledges . . . stripped men naked.* Sins condemned by the prophets (see, e.g., Amos 2:8 and note).

22:9 *widows . . . orphans.* See 24:3; Is 1:17 and note; James 1:27. *strength.* Lit. "arms" (as in 38:15).

22:10 *snares.* See 19:6 and note.

22:11 *darkness . . . abundance of water.* Two common figures of trouble and distress (see Ps 42:7 and note; Is 8:7–8,22; 43:2).

22:12–20 Eliphaz finally appears to support the argument of Bildad and Zophar, who were fully convinced that Job was a wicked man. Eliphaz makes a severe accusation: Job follows the path of the ungodly (v. 15), who defy God's power and say, "What can the Almighty do to them?" (v. 17; see vv. 13–14). They even have contempt for God's goodness (v. 18).

22:18 See 21:16 and note.

22:21–30 Eliphaz makes one last attempt to reach Job. In many ways it is a commendable call to repentance: Submit to God (v. 21), establish God's words in your heart (v. 22), return to the Almighty and forsake wickedness (v. 23), find your delight in God rather than in gold (vv. 24–26), pray and obey (v. 27) and become concerned about sinners (vv. 29–30). But Eliphaz's advice assumes (1) that Job is a very wicked man and (2) that Job's major concern is the return of his prosperity (see v. 21). Job had already made it clear in 19:25–27 that he deeply yearned to see God and be His friend.

22:22 See Job's response in 23:12. *establish His words in your heart.* See Ps 119:11.

22:24 *gold of Ophir.* See 28:16; the finest gold (see notes on 1 Kin 9:28; 10:11; Ps 45:9; Is 13:12).

22:28 *light will shine on your ways.* Through obedience to the word of God (see vv. 22,27; 29:3; Ps 119:105).

29 "When [1]you are cast down, you will
speak with [2]confidence,
And the [3][a]humble person He will save.
30 "He will deliver one who is not
innocent,
And he will be [a]delivered through the
cleanness of your hands."

Job Says He Longs for God

23 Then Job [1]replied,
2 "Even today my [a]complaint is
rebellion;
[1]His hand is [b]heavy despite my
groaning.
3 "Oh that I knew where I might find
Him,
That I might come to His seat!
4 "I would [a]present *my* case before Him
And fill my mouth with arguments.
5 "I would learn the words *which* He
would [1]answer,
And perceive what He would say to
me.
6 "Would He contend with me by [a]the
greatness of *His* power?
No, surely He would pay attention to
me.
7 "There the upright would [a]reason with
Him;
And I [1]would be [b]delivered forever
from my Judge.

8 "Behold, I go forward but He is not
there,
And backward, but I [a]cannot perceive
Him;
9 When He acts on the left, I cannot
behold *Him;*
He turns on the right, I cannot see
Him.
10 "But He knows the [1]way I take;
When He has [a]tried me, I shall come
forth as gold.
11 "My foot has [a]held fast to His path;
I have kept His way and not turned
aside.
12 "I have not departed from the
command of His lips;
I have treasured the [a]words of His
mouth [1]more than my [2]necessary
food.
13 "But He is unique and who can turn
Him?
And *what* His soul desires, that He
does.
14 "For He performs what is appointed for
me,
And many such *decrees* are with Him.
15 "Therefore, I would be dismayed at His
presence;
When I consider, I am terrified of Him.
16 "*It is* God *who* has made my [a]heart
faint,
And the Almighty *who* has dismayed
me,
17 But I [a]am not silenced by the
darkness,
Nor [b]deep gloom *which* covers me.

Job Says God Seems to Ignore Wrongs

24 "[a]Why are [1]times not stored up by the
Almighty,
And why do those who know Him not
see [b]His days?
2 "[1]Some [a]remove the landmarks;
They seize and [2]devour flocks.
3 "They drive away the donkeys of the
[a]orphans;
They take the [b]widow's ox for a
pledge.

29 [1]Lit *they cast you down* [2]Lit *pride* [3]Lit *lowly of eyes* [a]Job 5:11; 36:7; Matt 23:12; James 4:6; 1 Pet 5:5
30 [a]Job 42:7, 8; Ps 18:20; 24:3, 4
23:1 [1]Lit *answered and said*
2 [1]So with Gr and Syr; M.T. *My* [a]Job 7:11 [b]Job 6:2, 3; Ps 32:4
4 [a]Job 13:18
5 [1]Lit *answer me*
6 [a]Job 9:4
7 [1]Or *bring forth my justice forever* [a]Job 13:3 [b]Job 13:16; 23:10
8 [a]Job 9:11; 35:14
10 [1]Lit *way with me* [a]Job 7:18; Ps 7:9; 11:5; 66:10; Zech 13:9; 1 Pet 1:7
11 [a]Job 31:7; Ps 17:5; 44:18
12 [1]Or with some versions, *in my breast* [2]Lit *prescribed portion* [a]Job 6:10; 22:22
16 [a]Deut 20:3; Job 27:2; Jer 51:46
17 [a]Job 10:18, 19 [b]Job 19:8
24:1 [1]I.e. times of judgment [a]Acts 1:7 [b]Is 2:12; Jer 46:10; Obad 15; Zeph 1:7
2 [1]Lit *They* [2]Or *pasture* [a]Deut 19:14; 27:17; Prov 23:10
3 [a]Job 6:27 [b]Deut 24:17; Job 22:9

22:30 *cleanness of your hands.* See note on Ps 24:4.
23:2 *my complaint.* See 21:4 and note. *His hand is heavy.* See 33:7; see also note on 1 Sam 5:6.
23:3 *where I might find Him.* See note on vv. 8–9.
23:6 *pay attention to me.* Job is seeking a fair trial. In 9:14–20 Job was fearful that he could not find words to argue with God. Now he is confident that if God would give him a hearing, he would be acquitted (see 13:13–19; see also Ps 17:1–3; 26:1–3 and notes).
23:8–9 *forward . . . backward . . . left . . . right.* Whatever direction Job went, he could not find God (contrast Ps 139:7–10).
23:8,10 *I cannot perceive Him . . . But He knows the way I take.* Job is frustrated over his apparent inability to have an audience with God, who knows that he is an upright man. Job is here answering Eliphaz's admonition beginning in 22:21: "Yield now and . . . good will come." Job replies that this is what he has always done (vv. 11–12). He treasures God's words more than his daily food. He admits that God is testing him—not to purge away his sinful dross, but to show that Job is pure gold (see Ps 119:11,101,168; 1 Pet 1:7).
23:12 Job's response to the advice offered by Eliphaz in 22:22. *words . . . more than my necessary food.* See Deut 8:3.
23:13 *He is unique.* Lit. "He is one." Though Job is not an Israelite, he worships the one true God—there is no other (see Deut 6:4 and note). *what His soul desires, that He does.* He is sovereign (see Ps 115:3; 135:6; Luke 10:21).
23:15 *I would be dismayed.* See note on 21:6. A necessary part of Job's faith is fear of a God who does what He pleases. By contrast, the counselors tried to make God predictable.
23:17 *I am not silenced by the darkness.* Job responds to Eliphaz's accusation in 22:11 (see note there).
24:1–12 Job describes the terrible injustice that often exists in the world. Robbery of both the "haves" (see v. 2) and the "have-nots" (see vv. 3–4) is equally obnoxious to him. But perhaps his suffering has enabled him to empathize with the poor, who must forage for food (v. 5) and "glean the vineyard of the wicked" (v. 6). The scene he depicts is heart-rending: The naked shiver in the cold of night (vv. 7–8), fatherless infants are snatched from the breast (v. 9), field hands harvest food but go hungry (v. 10), vineyard workers make wine but suffer thirst (v. 11), groans rise from the dying and wounded (v. 12). Job cannot understand why God is silent and indifferent (vv. 1,12) in the face of such misery, but the fact that God waits disproves the counselors' theory of suffering. Job is no more out of God's favor as one of the victims than the criminal in vv. 13–17 is in God's favor because of God's inaction.
24:1 See note on vv. 21–24.
24:2 *remove the landmarks.* A serious crime in ancient times (see note on Deut 19:14).
24:3 *orphans . . . widow's.* See 22:9; Is 1:17 and note; James 1:27.

4 "They push [a]the needy aside from the road;
The [b]poor of the land are made to hide themselves altogether.
5 "Behold, as [a]wild donkeys in the wilderness
They [b]go forth seeking food in their activity,
As [1]bread for *their* children in the desert.
6 "They harvest their fodder in the field
And glean the vineyard of the wicked.
7 "[a]They spend the night naked, without clothing,
And have no covering against the cold.
8 "They are wet with the mountain rains
And hug the rock for want of a shelter.
9 "[1]Others snatch the [a]orphan from the breast,
And against the poor they take a pledge.
10 "They cause *the poor* to go about naked without clothing,
And they take away the sheaves from the hungry.
11 "Within the walls they produce oil;
They tread wine presses but thirst.
12 "From the city men groan,
And the souls of the wounded cry out;
Yet God [a]does not pay attention to folly.

13 "[1]Others have been with those who rebel against the light;
They do not want to know its ways
Nor abide in its paths.
14 "The murderer [a]arises at dawn;
He [b]kills the poor and the needy,
And at night he is as a thief.
15 "The eye of the [a]adulterer waits for the twilight,
Saying, 'No eye will see me.'
And he [1]disguises his face.
16 "In the dark they [a]dig into houses,
They [b]shut themselves up by day;
They do not know the light.
17 "For the morning is the same to him as thick darkness,
For he is familiar with the [a]terrors of thick darkness.

18 "They are [1][a]insignificant on the surface of the water;
Their portion is [b]cursed on the earth.
They do not turn [2]toward the [c]vineyards.
19 "Drought and heat [1][a]consume the snow waters,
So does [2][b]Sheol *those who* have sinned.
20 "A [1][a]mother will forget him;
The [b]worm feeds sweetly till he is [c]no longer remembered.
And wickedness will be broken [d]like a tree.
21 "He wrongs the [1]barren woman
And does no good for [a]the widow.
22 "But He drags off the valiant by [a]His power;
He rises, but [b]no one has assurance of life.
23 "He provides them [a]with security, and they are supported;
And His [b]eyes are on their ways.
24 "They are exalted a [a]little while, then they are gone;
Moreover, they are [b]brought low and like everything gathered up;
Even like the heads of grain they are cut off.
25 "Now if it is not so, [a]who can prove me a liar,
And make my speech worthless?"

Bildad Says Man Is Inferior

25 Then Bildad the Shuhite [1]answered,
2 "[a]Dominion and awe [1]belong to Him
Who establishes peace in [b]His heights.
3 "Is there any number to [a]His troops?
And upon whom does His light not rise?
4 "How then can a man be [a]just with God?
Or how can he be [b]clean who is born of woman?

4 [a]Job 24:14; 29:16; 30:25; 31:19 [b]Job 29:12; Ps 41:1; Prov 14:31; 28:28; Amos 8:4
5 [1]Lit *his bread* [a]Job 39:5-8 [b]Ps 104:23
7 [a]Ex 22:26; Job 22:6
9 [1]Lit *They* [a]Job 6:27
12 [a]Job 9:23, 24
13 [1]Lit *They*
14 [a]Mic 2:1 [b]Ps 10:8
15 [1]Or *puts a covering on his face* [a]Prov 7:9
16 [a]Ex 22:2; Matt 6:19 [b]John 3:20
17 [a]Job 15:21
18 [1]Or *light* or *swift* [2]Lit *to the path of* [a]Job 22:11, 16; 27:20 [b]Job 5:3 [c]Job 24:6, 11
19 [1]Lit *seize* [2]I.e. nether world [a]Job 6:16, 17 [b]Job 21:13
20 [1]Lit *womb* [a]Is 49:15 [b]Job 21:26 [c]Job 18:17; Ps 34:16; Prov 10:7 [d]Job 19:10; Dan 4:14
21 [1]Lit *barren who does not bear* [a]Job 22:9
22 [a]Job 9:4 [b]Job 18:20
23 [a]Job 12:6 [b]Job 10:4; 11:11
24 [a]Ps 37:10 [b]Job 14:21
25 [a]Job 6:28; 27:4
25:1 [1]Lit *answered and said*
2 [1]Lit *are with Him* [a]Job 9:4; 36:5, 22; 37:23; 42:2 [b]Job 16:19; 31:2
3 [a]Job 16:13
4 [a]Job 4:17; 9:2 [b]Job 14:4

24:5 *wild donkeys.* See 39:5–8.
24:6 *glean.* See note on Ruth 1:22.
24:7,10 Job implicitly denies the accusation of Eliphaz (see 22:6).
24:13–17 A description of those who cause the suffering depicted in vv. 2–12: the murderer (v. 14), the adulterer (v. 15), the robber (v. 16). Darkness is their element, the medium in which they thrive (see vv. 14–17). By contrast, God's law is the light against which they rebel (see v. 13; see also note on 22:28).
24:18–20 Job seems to agree with the counselors here. But it is also legitimate to translate the verses as Job's call for redress against evildoers: "May their portion of the earth be cursed . . . may Sheol consume . . . May their mother forget them; may the worm feed sweetly till they are no longer remembered and their wickedness is broken like a tree."
24:20 *worm feeds sweetly.* See 21:26; Is 14:11. *broken like a tree.* See note on 19:10.
24:21–24 By way of summary, Job says that God judges the wicked, but He does so in His own good time. Job wishes, however, that God would give the righteous the satisfaction of seeing it happen (v. 1).
24:24 *like the heads of grain they are cut off*. A symbol of judgment (see note on Is 17:5).
25:1–6 See note on 22:1–26:14. Bildad adds nothing new here, and Zophar, who has already admitted how emotionally disturbed he was (see 20:2), doesn't even comment.
25:2 *establishes peace in His heights.* Bildad apparently considered heaven as a place of warfare, where God must use His celestial troops (see v. 3) to establish order.
25:3 *His troops.* Angels. *His light.* The sun. All that is under God's dominion pales before Him.
25:4–6 Bildad echoes Eliphaz's earlier statements about human depravity (4:17–19; 15:14–16).

5 "If even [a]the moon has no brightness
And the [b]stars are not pure in His sight,
6 How much less [a]man, *that* [b]maggot,
And the son of man, *that* worm!"

Job Rebukes Bildad

26 Then Job [1]responded,
2 "What a help you are to [1a]the weak!
How you have saved the arm [b]without strength!
3 "What counsel you have given to *one* without wisdom!
What helpful insight you have abundantly [1]provided!
4 "To whom have you uttered words?
And whose [1]spirit was expressed through you?

The Greatness of God

5 "The [1a]departed spirits tremble
Under the waters and their inhabitants.
6 "Naked is [1a]Sheol before Him,
And [2b]Abaddon has no covering.
7 "He [a]stretches out the north over empty space
And hangs the earth on nothing.
8 "He [a]wraps up the waters in His clouds,
And the cloud does not burst under them.
9 "He [1a]obscures the face of the [2]full moon
And spreads His cloud over it.
10 "He has inscribed a [a]circle on the surface of the waters
At the [b]boundary of light and darkness.
11 "The pillars of heaven tremble
And are amazed at His rebuke.
12 "He [a]quieted the sea with His power,
And by His [b]understanding He shattered [c]Rahab.
13 "By His breath the [a]heavens are [1]cleared;
His hand has pierced [b]the fleeing serpent.
14 "Behold, these are the fringes of His ways;
And how faint [a]a word we hear of Him!
But His mighty [b]thunder, who can understand?"

Job Affirms His Righteousness

27 Then Job [1]continued his [a]discourse and said,
2 "As God lives, [a]who has taken away my right,
And the Almighty, [b]who has embittered my soul,
3 For as long as [1]life is in me,
And the [2a]breath of God is in my nostrils,
4 My lips certainly will not speak unjustly,
Nor will [a]my tongue mutter deceit.
5 "Far be it from me that I should declare you right;
Till I die [a]I will not put away my integrity from me.
6 "I [a]hold fast my righteousness and will not let it go.
My heart does not reproach any of my days.

The State of the Godless

7 "May my enemy be as the wicked
And [1]my opponent as the unjust.

5 [a]Job 31:26 [b]Job 15:15
6 [a]Job 7:17 [b]Job 17:14
26:1 [1]Lit *responded and said*
2 [1]Lit *no power* [a]Job 6:11, 12 [b]Ps 71:9
3 [1]Lit *made known*
4 [1]Lit *breath has gone forth*
5 [1]Or *shades;* Heb *Rephaim* [a]Job 3:13; Ps 88:10
6 [1]I.e. the nether world [2]I.e. place of destruction [a]Job 9:5-10; 26:6-14; 38:17; 41:11 [b]Job 28:22; 31:12
7 [a]Job 9:8
8 [a]Job 37:11; Prov 30:4
9 [1]Lit *covers* [2]Or *throne* [a]Job 22:14; Ps 97:2; 105:39
10 [a]Job 38:1-11; Prov 8:29 [b]Job 38:19, 20, 24
12 [a]Is 51:15; Jer 31:35 [b]Job 12:13 [c]Job 9:13
13 [1]Lit *made beautiful* [a]Job 9:8 [b]Is 27:1
14 [a]Job 4:12 [b]Job 36:29; 37:4, 5
27:1 [1]Or *again took up* [a]Job 13:12; 29:1
2 [a]Job 16:11; 34:5 [b]Job 9:18
3 [1]Lit *breath* [2]Or *spirit* [a]Job 32:8; 33:4
4 [a]Job 6:28; 33:3
5 [a]Job 6:29
6 [a]Job 2:3; 13:18

7 [1]Lit *he who rises up against me*

26:2–4 With biting sarcasm, Job responds to Bildad alone (the Hebrew for the word "you" in these verses is singular rather than plural), indicating that Eliphaz and Zophar have already been silenced.
26:2 *saved the arm without strength.* See 4:3–4; Is 35:3; Heb 12:12.
26:5–14 Job's poem about the vast power of God, the theme of Bildad's final speech (ch. 25), is written in colorful language that is often highly figurative.
26:5 *The departed spirits.* The Hebrew for this expression is translated "the dead" in Prov 2:18, "spirits of the dead" in Is 14:9 and "departed spirits" in Is 26:14. The term is used figuratively of the deceased who inhabit the netherworld (see 3:13–15, 17–19; see also note on 3:16). *waters.* Part of the world inhabited by living beings, and therefore above the netherworld.
26:6 *Sheol.* Personified elsewhere as the "king of terrors" (see 18:14 and note). *Abaddon.* See 28:22; 31:12; Prov 15:11. In Rev 9:11, Abaddon is the name of the "angel of the abyss" (see note there).
26:7 *He.* God. *stretches out the north.* See 37:18. *empty space.* The Hebrew for this word is translated "formless" in Gen 1:2. *nothing.* See note on 9:6.
26:11 *pillars of heaven.* See note on 9:6.
26:12 *Rahab.* See note on 9:13.
26:13 *fleeing serpent.* A description of the sea monster Leviathan (see notes on 3:8; Is 27:1).
26:14 *these are the fringes of His ways.* What God has revealed of His dominion over natural and supernatural forces amounts to no more than a whisper. Job is impressed with the severely limited character of human understanding. Zophar had chided Job about his inability to fathom the mysteries of God (11:7–9), but the knowledge possessed by Job's friends was not superior to that of Job himself (see 12:3; 13:2). *His mighty thunder.* If it is difficult for us to comprehend the little that we know about God, how much more impossible it would be to understand the full extent of His might!
27:1–23 The dialogue-dispute section of the book begins with Job's opening lament (ch. 3), continues with the three cycles of speeches (chs. 4–14; 15–21; 22–26) and concludes with Job's closing discourse (ch. 27), in which he reasserts his own innocence (vv. 2–6) and eloquently describes the ultimate fate of the wicked (vv. 13–23).
27:2 *As God lives.* The most solemn of oaths (see note on Gen 42:15). Job's faith in God continued despite his perception of denied justice.
27:5 *you.* The Hebrew for this word is plural. In his summary statement, Job once again speaks to his three friends as a group.
27:6 *hold fast my righteousness.* God had spoken similarly of Job (see 2:3).
27:7 *May my enemy be as the wicked.* Job calls for his friends,

8 "For what is [a]the hope of the godless
[1]when he is cut off,
When God requires [b]his [2]life?
9 "Will God [a]hear his cry
When [b]distress comes upon him?
10 "Will he take [a]delight in the Almighty?
Will he call on God at all times?
11 "I will instruct you in the [1]power of God;
What is with the Almighty I will not conceal.
12 "Behold, all of you have seen *it;*
Why then do you [1]act foolishly?

13 "This is [a]the portion of a wicked man from God,
And the inheritance *which* [b]tyrants receive from the Almighty.
14 "Though his sons are many, [1]they are destined [a]for the sword;
And his [b]descendants will not be satisfied with bread.
15 "His survivors will be buried because of the plague,
And [1]their [a]widows will not be able to weep.
16 "Though he piles up silver like dust
And prepares garments as *plentiful as* the clay,
17 He may prepare *it,* [a]but the just will wear *it*
And the innocent will divide the silver.
18 "He has built his [a]house like the [1]spider's web,
Or as a hut *which* the watchman has made.
19 "He lies down rich, but never [1]again;
He opens his eyes, and [a]it is no longer.
20 "[a]Terrors overtake him like a flood;
A tempest steals him away [b]in the night.
21 "The east [a]wind carries him away, and he is gone,
For it whirls him [b]away from his place.
22 "For it will hurl at him [a]without sparing;
He will surely try to [b]flee from its [1]power.
23 "*Men* will clap their hands at him
And will [a]hiss him from his place.

Job Tells of Earth's Treasures

28 "Surely there is a [1]mine for silver
And a place [2]where they refine gold.
2 "Iron is taken from the dust,
And copper is smelted from rock.
3 "*Man* puts an end to darkness,
And [a]to the farthest limit he searches out
The rock in gloom and deep shadow.
4 "He [1]sinks a shaft far from [2]habitation,
Forgotten by the foot;
They hang and swing to and fro far from men.
5 "The earth, from it comes food,
And underneath it is turned up as fire.
6 "Its rocks are the [1]source of sapphires,
And its dust *contains* gold.
7 "The path no bird of prey knows,
Nor has the falcon's eye caught sight of it.
8 "The [1]proud beasts have not trodden it,
Nor has the *fierce* lion passed over it.
9 "He puts his hand on the flint;
He overturns the mountains at the [1]base.
10 "He hews out channels through the rocks,
And his eye sees anything precious.
11 "He dams up the streams from [1]flowing,
And what is hidden he brings out to the light.

8 [1]Or *though he gains* [2]Lit *soul* [a]Job 8:13; 11:20 [b]Job 12:10
9 [a]Job 35:12, 13; Ps 18:41; Prov 1:28; Is 1:15; Jer 14:12; Mic 3:4 [b]Prov 1:27
10 [a]Job 22:26, 27; Ps 37:4; Is 58:14
11 [1]Lit *hand*
12 [1]Or *speak vanity*
13 [a]Job 20:29 [b]Job 15:20
14 [1]Lit *the sword is for them* [a]Job 15:22; 18:19 [b]Job 20:10
15 [1]So ancient versions; Heb *his* [a]Ps 78:64
17 [a]Job 20:18-21
18 [1]So ancient versions; Heb *moth* [a]Job 8:15; 18:14
19 [1]So ancient versions; Heb *will be gathered* [a]Job 7:8, 21; 20:7
20 [a]Job 15:21 [b]Job 20:8; 34:20
21 [a]Job 21:18 [b]Job 7:10
22 [1]Lit *hand* [a]Jer 13:14; Ezek 5:11; 24:14 [b]Job 11:20
23 [a]Job 18:18; 20:8
28:1 [1]Or *source* [2]Lit *for gold they refine*
3 [a]Eccl 1:13
4 [1]Lit *breaks open* [2]Lit *sojourning*
6 [1]Or *place*
8 [1]Lit *sons of pride*
9 [1]Lit *roots*
11 [1]Lit *weeping*

who had falsely accused him of being wicked, to be treated as though they themselves were wicked men (cf. Ps 109:6–15; 137:8–9).

27:11 *I will instruct you.* Job is about to remind his counselors about an issue on which they all agree: that the truly wicked deserve God's wrath (vv. 13–23). The three friends had falsely put Job in that category.

27:13–23 A poem that dramatizes the effect of Job's earlier call for redress (v. 7).

27:13 Job echoes the words of Zophar in 20:29 (see note there).

27:18 *web . . . hut.* Symbols of fragility (see note on 4:19; Is 1:8 and note; 24:20).

27:21 *east wind.* See note on 15:2.

28:1–28 Job's friends' application of traditional wisdom to human suffering has been even more unsatisfactory than Job's untraditional response. Both attempts to penetrate the mystery have failed, and the dialogue has come to an unsatisfactory conclusion. Therefore Job, or perhaps the unknown author of the book, inserts a striking wisdom poem that answers the question, "Where can wisdom be found?" (v. 12; see v. 20). The poem consists of three parts: (1) precious stones and metals are found in the deepest mines (vv. 1–11); (2) wisdom is not found in mines, nor can it be bought with precious stones or metals (vv. 12–19); (3) wisdom is found only in God and in the fear of Him (vv. 20–28). The chapter, then, anticipates the theme of God's speeches (38:1–42:6): God alone is the answer to the mystery that Job and his friends have sought to fathom.

28:1–11 A fascinating, lyrical description of ancient mining techniques.

28:2 *Iron.* See note on 19:24.

28:3 *puts an end to darkness.* By using an artificial source of light, such as a torch or lamp.

28:4 *hang and swing.* Mining, then as now, is difficult and dangerous work. Men will hazard everything to dig the earth's treasures.

28:6 *sapphires.* See v. 16; see also notes on Song 5:14; Is 54:11.

28:9 *mountains at the base.* A poetic expression emphasizing great depth (cf. Jon 2:6).

28:10 *channels through the rocks.* An eighth-century B.C. inscription found at Jerusalem's Pool of Siloam testifies to the sophistication of ancient tunneling technology.

The Search for Wisdom Is Harder

12 "But [a]where can wisdom be found?
And where is the place of
understanding?
13 "[a]Man does not know its value,
Nor is it found in the land of the living.
14 "The deep says, 'It is not in me';
And the sea says, 'It is not with me.'
15 "[a]Pure gold cannot be given in
exchange for it,
Nor can silver be weighed as its price.
16 "It cannot be valued in the gold of
Ophir,
In precious onyx, or sapphire.
17 "[a]Gold or glass cannot equal it,
Nor can it be exchanged for articles of
fine gold.
18 "Coral and crystal are not to be
mentioned;
And the acquisition of [a]wisdom is
above *that of* pearls.
19 "The topaz of Ethiopia cannot equal it,
Nor can it be valued in [a]pure gold.
20 "[a]Where then does wisdom come
from?
And where is the place of
understanding?
21 "Thus it is hidden from the eyes of all
living
And concealed from the birds of the
sky.
22 "[1a]Abaddon and Death say,
'With our ears we have heard a report
of it.'

23 "[a]God understands its way,
And He knows its place.
24 "For He [a]looks to the ends of the earth
And sees everything under the
heavens.
25 "When He imparted [a]weight to the
wind
And [b]meted out the waters by measure,
26 When He set a [a]limit for the rain
And a course for the [b]thunderbolt,
27 Then He saw it and declared it;
He established it and also searched it
out.
28 "And to man He said, 'Behold, the
[a]fear of the Lord, that is wisdom;
And to depart from evil is
understanding.' "

Job's Past Was Glorious

29 And Job again took up his [a]discourse
and said,
2 "Oh that I were as in months gone by,
As in the days when God [a]watched
over me;
3 When [a]His lamp shone over my head,
And [b]by His light I walked through
darkness;
4 As I was in [1]the prime of my days,
When the [2a]friendship of God *was*
over my tent;
5 When [1]the Almighty was yet with me,
And my children were around me;
6 When my steps were bathed in
[a]butter,
And the [b]rock poured out for me
streams of oil!
7 "When I went out to [a]the gate of the
city,
When I [1]took my seat in the square,
8 The young men saw me and hid
themselves,
And the old men arose *and* stood.
9 "The princes [a]stopped talking
And [b]put *their* hands on their mouths;
10 The voice of the nobles was [1a]hushed,
And their [b]tongue stuck to their
palate.
11 "For when [a]the ear heard, it called me
blessed,
And when the eye saw, it gave witness
of me,

12 [a]Job 28:23, 28; Eccl 7:24
13 [a]Matt 13:44-46
15 [a]Prov 3:13, 14; 8:10, 11; 16:16
17 [a]Prov 8:10; 16:16
18 [a]Prov 8:11
19 [a]Prov 8:19
20 [a]Job 28:23, 28
22 [1]I.e. Destruction [a]Job 26:6; Prov 8:32-36
23 [a]Job 9:4; Prov 8:22-36
24 [a]Ps 11:4; 33:13, 14; 66:7; Prov 15:3
25 [a]Ps 135:7 [b]Job 12:15; 38:8-11
26 [a]Job 37:6, 11, 12; 38:26-28 [b]Job 37:3; 38:25
28 [a]Ps 111:10; Prov 1:7; 9:10; Eccl 12:13
29:1 [a]Num 23:7; 24:3; Job 13:12; 27:1
2 [a]Jer 31:28
3 [a]Job 18:6 [b]Job 11:17
4 [1]Lit *the days of my autumn* [2]Lit *counsel* [a]Job 15:8; Ps 25:14; Prov 3:32
5 [1]Heb *Shaddai*
6 [a]Deut 32:14; Job 20:17 [b]Deut 32:13; Ps 81:16
7 [1]Lit *set up* [a]Job 31:21
9 [a]Job 29:21 [b]Job 21:5
10 [1]Lit *hidden* [a]Job 29:22 [b]Ps 137:6
11 [a]Job 4:3, 4

28:12 The questions, repeated almost verbatim in v. 20, are answered in v. 28.
28:16 *gold of Ophir.* See 22:24 and note.
28:18 *the acquisition of wisdom is above . . . pearls.* Cf. the value of an "excellent wife" (Prov 31:10), who fears the Lord (Prov 31:30) and is therefore wise (see v. 28).
28:19 *Ethiopia.* The Hebrew term (Cush) actually includes the entire upper Nile region, south of Egypt.
28:21 *hidden . . . from the birds.* As are precious stones and metals (see v. 7).
28:22 *Abaddon and Death.* See note on 26:6.
28:25–27 Wisdom has been with God from the time of creation itself (see Prov 8:22–31).
28:28 *fear of the Lord . . . depart from evil.* See the description of Job's character in 1:1,8; 2:3. *that is wisdom.* "The fear of the LORD is the beginning of wisdom" (Ps 111:10; Prov 9:10; see Prov 1:7).
29:1–31:40 Like a lawyer submitting his final brief, Job presents a three-part summation: Part one (ch. 29) is a nostalgic review of his former happiness, wealth and honor; part two (ch. 30) is a lament over the loss of everything, especially his honor; part three (ch. 31) is a final protestation of his innocence.
29:1–25 A classic example of Semitic rhetoric, using the following symmetrical pattern: blessing (vv. 2–6), honor (vv. 7–10), benevolence (vv. 11–17), blessing (vv. 18–20), honor (vv. 21–25).
29:2–6 Words charged with emotion. In earlier days, God had been Job's friend and companion.
29:3 *by His light I walked.* See note on 22:28.
29:4 *When the friendship of God was over my tent.* Lit. "When God's council was by my tent," or "When God was an intimate in my tent." The clause evokes a situation similar to that in Gen 18, where God and two members of His heavenly council eat and drink at Abraham's tent—and there God discloses to His friend the imminent birth of the promised son and God's intentions concerning Sodom and Gomorrah.
29:5 *my children were around me.* See 1:2.
29:6 *butter . . . oil.* Symbols of richness and luxury (see 20:17; Ezek 16:19).
29:7 *gate of the city.* Where the most important business was conducted and the most significant legal cases were tried (see note on Ruth 4:1). *took my seat.* As a city elder, a member of the ruling council (see note on Gen 19:1).

12 Because I delivered [a]the poor who cried for help,
And the [b]orphan who had no helper.
13 "The blessing of the one [a]ready to perish came upon me,
And I made the [b]widow's heart sing for joy.
14 "I [a]put on righteousness, and it clothed me;
My justice was like a robe and a turban.
15 "I was [a]eyes to the blind
And feet to the lame.
16 "I was a father to [a]the needy,
And I investigated the case which I did not know.
17 "I [a]broke the jaws of the wicked
And snatched the prey from his teeth.
18 "Then I [1]thought, 'I shall die [2]in my nest,
And I shall multiply *my* days as the sand.
19 'My [a]root is spread out to the waters,
And [b]dew lies all night on my branch.
20 'My glory is *ever* new with me,
And my [a]bow is renewed in my hand.'

21 "To me [a]they listened and waited,
And kept silent for my counsel.
22 "After my words they did not [a]speak again,
And [b]my speech dropped on them.
23 "They waited for me as for the rain,
And opened their mouth as for the spring rain.
24 "I smiled on them when they did not believe,
And the light of my face they did not cast down.
25 "I chose a way for them and sat as [a]chief,
And dwelt as a king among the troops,
As one who [b]comforted the mourners.

Job's Present State Is Humiliating

30 "But now those younger than I [a]mock me,
Whose fathers I disdained to put with the dogs of my flock.

12 [a]Job 24:4, 9; 34:28; Ps 72:12; Prov 21:13 [b]Job 31:17, 21
13 [a]Job 31:19 [b]Job 22:9
14 [a]Job 27:5, 6; Ps 132:9; Is 59:17; 61:10; Eph 6:14
15 [a]Num 10:31
16 [a]Job 24:4; Prov 29:7
17 [a]Ps 3:7
18 [1]Lit *said* [2]Lit *with*
19 [a]Jer 17:8 [b]Hos 14:5
20 [a]Gen 49:24; Ps 18:34
21 [a]Job 4:3; 29:9
22 [a]Job 29:10 [b]Deut 32:2
25 [a]Job 1:3; 31:37 [b]Job 4:4; 16:5
30:1 [a]Job 12:4

2 "Indeed, what *good was* the strength of their hands to me?
Vigor had perished from them.
3 "From want and famine they are gaunt
Who gnaw the dry ground by night in waste and desolation,
4 Who pluck [1]mallow by the bushes,
And whose food is the root of the broom shrub.
5 "They are driven from the community;
They shout against them as *against* a thief,
6 So that they dwell in dreadful [1]valleys,
In holes of the earth and of the rocks.
7 "Among the bushes they [1]cry out;
Under the nettles they are gathered together.
8 "[1]Fools, even [2]those without a name,
They were scourged from the land.

9 "And now I have become their [1][a]taunt,
I have even become a [b]byword to them.
10 "They abhor me *and* stand aloof from me,
And they do not [1]refrain from [a]spitting at my face.
11 "Because [1]He has loosed [2]His [3]bowstring and [a]afflicted me,
They have cast off [b]the bridle before me.
12 "On the right hand their [1]brood arises;
They [a]thrust aside my feet [b]and build up against me their ways of destruction.
13 "They [a]break up my path,
They profit [1]from my destruction;
No one restrains them.
14 "As *through* a wide breach they come,
[1]Amid the tempest they roll on.
15 "[a]Terrors are turned against me;
They pursue my [1]honor as the wind,
And my [2]prosperity has passed away [b]like a cloud.

16 "And now [a]my soul is poured out [1]within me;
Days of affliction have seized me.
17 "At night it pierces [a]my bones [1]within me,
And my gnawing *pains* take no rest.

4 [1]I.e. plant of the salt marshes
6 [1]Or *wadis*
7 [1]Or *bray*
8 [1]Lit *Sons of fools* [2]Lit *sons*
9 [1]Lit *song* [a]Job 12:4 [b]Job 17:6; Ps 69:11; Lam 3:14, 63
10 [1]Lit *withhold spit from my face* [a]Num 12:14; Deut 25:9; Job 17:6; Is 50:6; Matt 26:67
11 [1]Or *they* [2]Some mss read *my* [3]Or *cord* [a]Ruth 1:21; Ps 88:7 [b]Ps 32:9
12 [1]Possibly *sprout* or *offspring* [a]Ps 140:4, 5 [b]Job 19:12
13 [1]Lit *for* [a]Is 3:12
14 [1]Lit *Under*
15 [1]Or *nobility* [2]Or *welfare* [a]Job 3:25; 31:23; Ps 55:3-5 [b]Job 7:9; Hos 13:3
16 [1]Lit *upon* [a]1 Sam 1:15; Job 3:24; Ps 22:14; 42:4; Is 53:12
17 [1]Lit *from upon* [a]Job 30:30

29:12–13 *I delivered . . . the orphan . . . I made the widow's heart sing.* Implicitly responding to Eliphaz's accusation in 22:9, Job expresses his concern for the helpless and unfortunate (see 24:9; 31:16–18,21).
29:14 *I put on righteousness . . . justice was like a robe.* For similar imagery see Is 59:17; 61:10; Eph 6:14,17.
29:18 *I thought.* Job muses on what might have been the course of his life.
29:21–25 His counsel was valued (vv. 21–23), his approval sought (v. 24) and his civic leadership accepted with gratitude (v. 25).
30:1–31 In contrast to the positive notes of blessing and honor sounded in ch. 29, Job now bemoans the suffering and dishonor he has been forced to undergo. God has heaped overwhelming terrors on him (v. 15). His final, forlorn lament (see v. 31) over his condition shows that his rage has not yet subsided.
30:1,9 *now . . . their taunt.* Earlier both young and old had deferred to him (see 29:8–11,21–25).
30:4 *mallow.* Probably saltwort, which grows in otherwise infertile areas, including the regions east of Sinai where Job and his friends lived. Cf. 39:6. *broom shrub.* A large bush that grows in the deserts of the Middle East (see 1 Kin 19:4; Ps 120:4).
30:9 *byword.* See note on 17:6.
30:11 *He has loosed His bowstring.* Cf. 29:20.
30:12 *ways of destruction.* See 19:12.
30:14 *breach.* In a city wall.
30:15 *pursue my honor as the wind.* See v. 22.
30:17 *gnawing pains.* See note on 2:7.

18 "By a great force my garment is
[a]distorted;
It binds me about as the collar of my
coat.
19 "He has cast me into the [a]mire,
And I have become like dust and
ashes.
20 "I [a]cry out to You for help, but You do
not answer me;
I stand up, and You turn Your
attention against me.
21 "You have [1]become cruel to me;
With the might of Your hand You
[a]persecute me.
22 "You [a]lift me up to the wind *and* cause
me to ride;
And You dissolve me in a storm.
23 "For I know that You [a]will bring me to
death
And to the [b]house of meeting for all
living.

24 "Yet does not one in a heap of ruins
stretch out *his* hand,
Or in his disaster therefore [a]cry out for
help?
25 "Have I not [a]wept for the [1]one whose
life is hard?
Was not my soul grieved for [b]the
needy?
26 "When I [a]expected good, then evil
came;
When I waited for light, [b]then
darkness came.
27 "[1]I am seething [a]within and cannot
relax;
Days of affliction confront me.
28 "I go about [1a]mourning without
comfort;
I stand up in the assembly *and* [b]cry
out for help.
29 "I have become a brother to [a]jackals
And a companion of ostriches.
30 "My [a]skin turns black [1]on me,
And my [b]bones burn with [2]fever.
31 "Therefore my [a]harp [1]is turned to
mourning,
And my flute to the sound of those
who weep.

Job Asserts His Integrity

31 "I have made a covenant with my
[a]eyes;
How then could I gaze at a virgin?
2 "And what is [a]the portion of God from
above
Or the heritage of the Almighty from
on high?
3 "Is it not [a]calamity to the unjust
And disaster to [b]those who work
iniquity?
4 "Does He not [a]see my ways
And [b]number all my steps?

5 "If I have [a]walked with falsehood,
And my foot has hastened after deceit,
6 Let Him [a]weigh me with [1]accurate
scales,
And let God know [b]my integrity.
7 "If my step has [a]turned from the way,
Or my heart [1]followed my eyes,
Or if any [b]spot has stuck to my hands,
8 Let me [a]sow and another eat,
And let my [1b]crops be uprooted.

9 "If my heart has been [a]enticed by a
woman,
Or I have lurked at my neighbor's
doorway,
10 May my wife [a]grind for another,
And let [b]others [1]kneel down over her.
11 "For that would be a [a]lustful crime;
Moreover, it would be [b]an iniquity
punishable by judges.
12 "For it would be [a]fire that consumes to
[1b]Abaddon,
And would [c]uproot all my [2]increase.

18 [a]Job 2:7 **19** [a]Ps 69:2, 14 **20** [a]Job 19:7 **21** [1]Lit *turned to be* [a]Job 10:3; 16:9, 14; 19:6, 22 **22** [a]Job 9:17; 27:21 **23** [a]Job 9:22; 10:8 [b]Job 3:19; Eccl 12:5 **24** [a]Job 19:7 **25** [1]Lit *hard of day* [a]Ps 35:13, 14; Rom 12:15 [b]Job 24:4 **26** [a]Job 3:25, 26; Jer 8:15 [b]Job 19:8 **27** [1]Lit *My inward parts are boiling* [a]Lam 2:11 **28** [1]Or *blackened, but not by the heat of the sun* [a]Job 30:31; Ps 38:6; 42:9; 43:2 [b]Job 19:7 **29** [a]Ps 44:19; Mic 1:8 **30** [1]Lit *from upon* [2]Lit *heat* [a]Job 2:7 [b]Ps 102:3

31 [1]Lit *becomes* [a]Is 24:8 **31:1** [a]Matt 5:28 **2** [a]Job 20:29 **3** [a]Job 18:12; 21:30 [b]Job 34:22 **4** [a]2 Chr 16:9; Job 24:23; 28:24; 34:21; 36:7; Prov 5:21; 15:3 [b]Job 14:16; 31:37 **5** [a]Job 15:31; Mic 2:11 **6** [1]Lit *just* [a]Job 6:2, 3 [b]Job 23:10; 27:5, 6 **7** [1]Lit *walked after* [a]Job 23:11 [b]Job 9:30 **8** [1]Or *offspring* [a]Lev 26:16; Job 20:18; Mic 6:15 [b]Job 31:12 **9** [a]Job 24:15; 31:1 **10** [1]I.e. sexual relations [a]Is 47:2 [b]Deut 28:30; Jer 8:10

11 [a]Lev 20:10; Deut 22:24 [b]Job 31:28 **12** [1]I.e. place of destruction [2]Or *yield* [a]Job 15:30 [b]Job 26:6 [c]Job 20:28; 31:8

30:19 *dust and ashes.* Symbolic of humiliation and insignificance (see note on Gen 18:27). Job would someday use "dust and ashes" to symbolize repentance (42:6).

30:20–23 Job now directs his thoughts away from men and toward God. He accuses God of abusing His power by attacking him despite his pleas for mercy.

30:24 Job feels that he has been treated unjustly, whether by God or by man.

30:26 Cf. Is 5:2,7.

30:28 *mourning.* See v. 30; see also note on 2:7.

30:29 *brother to jackals . . . companion of ostriches.* The prophet Micah uses similar imagery of himself in Mic 1:8.

30:30 *fever.* See note on 2:7.

31:1–40 The climactic section of Job's three-part summation (see note on 29:1–31:40). It is negative in the sense that Job denies all the sins listed, but it has the positive purpose of attesting loyalty to God as his sovereign Lord. In the strongest legal terms, using a series of self-maledictory oaths, Job completes his defense. No more can be said (v. 40). He now affixes his signature to the document (v. 35), and the burden of proof that he is a wretched sinner rests with God. Job's call for vindication had reached a climax in 27:2–6. Now he amplifies that statement with the details of his godly life. Each disavowal (vv. 5–7,9,13,16–21,24–27,29–34,38–39) is accompanied by an oath that calls for the punishment the offense deserves (vv. 8,10–12,14–15,22–23,28,40). The principle at work is the so-called "law of retaliation" (see Ex 21:23–25 and note).

31:1–12 Job begins with sins of the heart, especially sexual lust (vv. 1–4), cheating in business (vv. 5–8) and marital infidelity (vv. 9–12).

31:1 *gaze at a virgin.* To do so is to sin (see Matt 5:28).

31:4 Echoed by Elihu in 34:21.

31:6 *Him weigh me with accurate scales.* See 6:2; Prov 16:12; 21:2; 24:12. *integrity.* Does not imply sinless perfection (see note on 1:1).

31:12 *Abaddon.* See note on 26:6.

13 "If I have [a]despised the claim of my
male or female slaves
When they filed a complaint against
me,
14 What then could I do when God arises?
And when He calls me to account,
what will I answer Him?
15 "Did not [a]He who made me in the
womb make him,
And the same one fashion us in the
womb?

16 "If I have kept [a]the poor from *their*
desire,
Or have caused the eyes of [b]the
widow to fail,
17 Or have [a]eaten my morsel alone,
And [b]the orphan has not [1]shared it
18 (But from my youth he grew up with
me as with a father,
And from [1]infancy I guided her),
19 If I have seen anyone perish [a]for lack
of clothing,
Or that [b]the needy had no covering,
20 If his loins have not [1]thanked me,
And if he has not been warmed with
the fleece of my sheep,
21 If I have lifted up my hand against
[a]the orphan,
Because I saw [1]I had support [b]in the
gate,
22 Let my shoulder fall from the [1]socket,
And my [a]arm be broken off [2]at the
elbow.
23 "For [a]calamity from God is a terror to
me,
And because of [b]His [1]majesty I can do
nothing.

24 "If I have put my confidence *in* [a]gold,
And called fine gold my trust,
25 If I have [a]gloated because my wealth
was great,
And because my hand had secured *so*
much;
26 If I have [a]looked at the [1]sun when it
shone
Or the moon going in splendor,
27 And my heart became secretly
enticed,
And my hand [1]threw a kiss from my
mouth,
28 That too would have been [a]an iniquity
calling for [1]judgment,
For I would have [b]denied God above.

29 "Have I [a]rejoiced at the extinction of
my enemy,
Or [1]exulted when evil befell him?
30 "[1]No, [a]I have not [2]allowed my mouth
to sin
By asking for his life in [b]a curse.
31 "Have the men of my tent not said,
'Who can [1]find one who has not been
[a]satisfied with his meat'?
32 "The alien has not lodged outside,
For I have opened my doors to the
[1]traveler.
33 "Have I [a]covered my transgressions like
[1]Adam,
By hiding my iniquity in my bosom,
34 Because I [a]feared the great multitude,
And the contempt of families terrified
me,
And kept silent and did not go out of
doors?
35 "Oh that I had one to hear me!
Behold, here is my [1]signature;
[a]Let the Almighty answer me!
And the indictment which my
[b]adversary has written,
36 Surely I would carry it on my
shoulder,
I would bind it to myself like a crown.
37 "I would declare to Him [a]the number
of my steps;
Like [b]a prince I would approach Him.

38 "If my [a]land cries out against me,
And its furrows weep together;
39 If I have [a]eaten its [1]fruit without
money,
Or have [b]caused [2]its owners to lose
their lives,

13 [a]Deut 24:14, 15 **15** [a]Job 10:3 **16** [a]Job 5:16; 20:19 [b]Ex 22:22-24; Job 22:9 **17** [1]Lit *eaten from it* [a]Job 22:7 [b]Job 29:12 **18** [1]Lit *my mother's womb* **19** [a]Job 22:6; 29:13 [b]Job 24:4 **20** [1]Lit *blessed* **21** [1]Lit *my help* [a]Job 29:12; 31:17 [b]Job 29:7 **22** [1]Lit *shoulder;* or *back* [2]Lit *from the bone of the upper arm* [a]Job 38:15 **23** [1]Lit *exaltation* [a]Job 31:3 [b]Job 13:11 **24** [a]Job 22:24; Mark 10:23-25 **25** [a]Job 1:3, 10; Ps 62:10 **26** [1]Lit *light* [a]Deut 4:19; 17:3; Ezek 8:16

27 [1]Lit *kissed my mouth* **28** [1]Lit *judges* [a]Deut 17:2-7; Job 31:11 [b]Josh 24:27; Is 59:13 **29** [1]Lit *lifted myself up* [a]Prov 17:5; 24:17; Obad 12 **30** [1]Lit *And* [2]Lit *given my palate* [a]Ps 7:4 [b]Job 5:3 **31** [1]Lit *give* [a]Job 22:7 **32** [1]M.T. *way* **33** [1]Or *mankind* [a]Gen 3:10; Prov 28:13 **34** [a]Ex 23:2 **35** [1]Lit *mark* [a]Job 19:7; 30:20, 24, 28; 35:14 [b]Job 27:7 **37** [a]Job 31:4 [b]Job 1:3; 29:25 **38** [a]Job 24:2 **39** [1]Lit *strength* [2]Lit *the soul of its owners to expire* [a]Job 24:6, 10-12; James 5:4 [b]1 Kin 21:19

31:13–23 Job reveals genuine understanding concerning matters of social justice: Human equality is based on creation (vv. 13–15), compassion toward those in need is essential (vv. 16–20), and power and influence must not be abused (vv. 21–23).
31:16–17 *widow . . . orphan.* See note on 29:12–13.
31:24–28 Covetous greed (vv. 24–25) and idolatry (vv. 26–27) are equally reprehensible in the eyes of God (v. 28; see Matt 6:19–24; Col 3:5).
31:25 *my wealth was great.* See 1:3,10.
31:26–28 The sun and moon are not to be objects of worship (see Deut 4:19; 17:3; Ezek 8:16–17).
31:27 *kiss.* An ancient gesture of worship (see 1 Kin 19:18; Hos 13:2).
31:29–32 The sin of gloating over one's enemy was condemned by Moses (Ex 23:4–5) and by Christ (Matt 5:43–47).
31:33–34 A strong denial of hypocrisy.
31:33 *like Adam.* See Gen 3:8–10; Hos 6:7.
31:35–37 Job's final call for justice. His signature endorses every word of the oaths he has just taken.
31:35 *one to hear me.* See notes on 5:1; 9:33; 16:18–21; 19:25. *Let the Almighty answer me!* See note on 38:1. *adversary.* The Hebrew for this word is not the same as that for "Satan" (see note on 1:6). Here Job's accuser is either (1) a human adversary (perhaps one of the three friends) or (2) God Himself. In any event, Job assumes that accusations have been lodged against him before the court of heaven to which God has responded with judgments.
31:36 *shoulder.* Inscriptions were sometimes worn on the shoulder as a perpetual reminder of their importance (see Ex 28:12).
31:38–40 A climactic oath that completes an earlier theme and creates a unique emphasis. Job calls for a curse on his land if he has not been fully committed to social justice (see also vv. 13–15).

40 Let [a]briars [1]grow instead of wheat,
And stinkweed instead of barley."
The words of Job are ended.

Elihu in Anger Rebukes Job

32 Then these three men ceased answering Job, because he was [a]righteous in
his own eyes.
2 But the anger of Elihu the son of
Barachel the [a]Buzite, of the family of Ram
burned; against Job his anger burned
[b]because he justified himself [1c]before God.
3 And his anger burned against his three
friends because they had found no answer,
and yet had condemned Job.
4 Now Elihu had waited [1]to speak to Job
because they were years older than he.
5 And when Elihu saw that there was no
answer in the mouth of the three men his
anger burned.
6 So Elihu the son of Barachel the Buzite
[1]spoke out and said,

"I am young in years and you are [a]old;
Therefore I was shy and afraid to tell
you [2]what I think.
7 "I [1]thought [2a]age should speak,
And [3]increased years should teach
wisdom.
8 "But it is a spirit in man,
And the [a]breath of the Almighty gives
them [b]understanding.
9 "The [1]abundant *in years* may not be
wise,
Nor may [a]elders understand justice.
10 "So I [1]say, 'Listen to me,
I too will tell [2]what I think.'

11 "Behold, I waited for your words,
I listened to your reasonings,
While you [1]pondered what to say.
12 "I even paid close attention to you;
[1]Indeed, there was no one who
refuted Job,
Not one of you who answered his
words.
13 "Do not say,
'[a]We have found wisdom;
God will [1]rout him, not man.'
14 "For he has not arranged *his* words
against me,
Nor will I reply to him with your
[1]arguments.

15 "They are dismayed, they no longer
answer;
Words have [1]failed them.
16 "Shall I wait, because they do not
speak,
Because they [1]stop *and* no longer
answer?
17 "I too will answer my share,
I also will tell my opinion.
18 "For I am full of words;
The spirit within me constrains me.
19 "Behold, my belly is like unvented
wine,
Like new wineskins it is about to
burst.
20 "Let me speak that I may get relief;
Let me open my lips and answer.
21 "Let me now [a]be partial to no one,
Nor flatter *any* man.
22 "For I do not know how to flatter,
Else my Maker would soon take me
away.

Elihu Claims to Speak for God

33 "However now, Job, please [a]hear my
speech,
And listen to all my words.
2 "Behold now, I open my mouth,
My tongue in my [1]mouth speaks.

40 [1]Lit *come forth* [a]Job 32:13; Is 5:6
32:1 [a]Job 10:7; 13:18; 27:5, 6; 31:6
2 [1]Or *more than* [a]Gen 22:21 [b]Job 27:5, 6 [c]Job 30:21
4 [1]Lit *for Job with words;* or possibly *while they were speaking with Job*
6 [1]Lit *answered* [2]Lit *my knowledge* [a]Job 15:10
7 [1]Lit *said* [2]Lit *days* [3]Lit *many* [a]Job 8:8, 9
8 [a]Job 33:4 [b]Job 38:36
9 [1]Or *nobles* [a]Job 32:7
10 [1]Or *said* [2]Lit *my knowledge*
11 [1]Lit *searched out words*
12 [1]Lit *Behold*
13 [1]Lit *drive away* [a]Jer 9:23
14 [1]Lit *words*
15 [1]Lit *moved away from*
16 [1]Lit *stand*
21 [a]Lev 19:15; Job 13:8, 10; 34:19
33:1 [a]Job 13:6
2 [1]Lit *palate*

31:40 *The words of Job are ended.* His complaints and arguments are now over. He will only make brief statements of contrition (40:4–5; 42:2–6) following the divine discourses.
32:1–37:24 A fourth counselor, named Elihu and younger than the other three (32:4,6–7,9), has been standing on the sidelines, giving deference to age and listening to the dialogue-dispute. But now he declares himself ready to show that both Job and the three other counselors are in the wrong. Elihu's four poetic speeches (32:5–33:33; ch. 34; ch. 35; chs. 36–37) are preceded by a prose introduction (32:1–4) written by the author of the book.
32:1 *righteous in his own eyes.* He insisted on his innocence in spite of the terrible suffering that he was experiencing.
32:2–3 *anger.* Elihu considers Job's emphasis on vindicating himself rather than God reprehensible, but he also believes that the friends' inability to refute Job was tantamount to condemning God.
32:2 *Buzite.* An inhabitant of Buz, a desert region in the east (see Jer 25:23).
32:6,10 *tell . . . what I think.* See v. 17. Elihu is eager to share his thoughts and assumes that he can communicate them effectively (see note on 36:4).
32:6 *young . . . afraid.* See Jer 1:6–8; 1 Tim 4:12; 2 Tim 1:7.
32:8 *breath of the Almighty.* See 33:4.
32:14 *Nor will I reply to him with your arguments.* Elihu feels that something important has been left out and, where the wisdom of age has failed, he has the understanding to supply the right answers.
32:15–22 Elihu delivers a soliloquy to himself, but it is also for the benefit of those who may be listening.
32:15–16 *Words have failed them . . . they stop and no longer answer.* See v. 5. The breakdown of the third cycle in the dialogue-dispute cut short Bildad's last word and left Zophar without a third speech (see note on 22:1–26:14).
32:18 *I am full of words.* Elihu's speeches continue unabated through ch. 37. He has a genuine contribution to make, however, to the problems Job is facing. At the same time, he does not stoop to false accusation about Job's earlier life but usually confines his criticism of Job to quotations from Job himself. This is perhaps the reason that God, in the epilogue, does not condemn Elihu along with Job's three friends (see 42:7).
32:19 *new wineskins . . . about to burst.* Old wineskins might be expected to crack or break (see Matt 9:17), but not new ones. Elihu is obviously eager to speak.
33:1–33 Elihu turns to Job and speaks directly to him. Unlike the three friends, he addresses Job by name (vv. 1,31; see 37:14).
33:1 *listen to all my words.* He is thoroughly convinced of the importance and wisdom of the advice he is about to give (see vv. 31,33).

3 "My words are *from* the uprightness of
my heart,
And my lips speak [a]knowledge
sincerely.
4 "The [a]Spirit of God has made me,
And the [b]breath of [1]the Almighty
gives me life.
5 "[a]Refute me if you can;
Array yourselves before me, take your
stand.
6 "Behold, I belong to God like you;
I too have been [1]formed out of the
[a]clay.
7 "Behold, [a]no fear of me should terrify
you,
Nor should my pressure weigh heavily
on you.

8 "Surely you have spoken in my
hearing,
And I have heard the sound of *your*
words:
9 'I am [a]pure, [b]without transgression;
I am innocent and there [c]is no guilt in
me.
10 'Behold, He [1]invents pretexts against
me;
He [a]counts me as His enemy.
11 'He [a]puts my feet in the stocks;
He watches all my paths.'
12 "Behold, let me [1]tell you, [a]you are not
right in this,
For God is greater than man.

13 "Why do you [a]complain against Him
That He does not give an account of
all His doings?
14 "Indeed [a]God speaks once,
Or twice, *yet* no one notices it.

3 [a]Job 6:28; 27:4; 36:4
4 [1]Heb *Shaddai* [a]Gen 2:7; Job 10:3; 32:8 [b]Job 27:3
5 [a]Job 33:32
6 [1]Lit *cut out of* [a]Job 4:19
7 [a]Job 13:21
9 [a]Job 9:21; 10:7; 13:18; 16:17 [b]Job 7:21; 13:23; 14:17 [c]Job 10:14
10 [1]Lit *finds* [a]Job 13:24
11 [a]Job 13:27
12 [1]Lit *answer* [a]Eccl 7:20
13 [a]Job 40:2; Is 45:9
14 [a]Job 33:29; 40:5; Ps 62:11
15 [a]Job 4:12-17; 33:15-18
16 [a]Job 36:10, 15
17 [1]Lit *hide*
18 [1]M.T. *perishing by the sword* [a]Job 33:22, 24, 28, 30 [b]Job 15:22
19 [1]Lit *He* [a]Job 30:17
20 [a]Job 3:24; 6:7; Ps 107:18
21 [a]Job 16:8 [b]Job 19:20; Ps 22:17; 102:5
22 [a]Job 33:18, 28
23 [1]Lit *his uprightness* [a]Gen 40:8
24 [a]Job 33:18, 28; Is 38:17 [b]Job 36:18; Ps 49:7

15 "In a [a]dream, a vision of the night,
When sound sleep falls on men,
While they slumber in their beds,
16 Then [a]He opens the ears of men,
And seals their instruction,
17 That He may turn man aside *from his*
conduct,
And [1]keep man from pride;
18 He [a]keeps back his soul from the pit,
And his life from [1]passing over [b]into
Sheol.

19 "[1]Man is also chastened with [a]pain on
his bed,
And with unceasing complaint in his
bones;
20 So that his life [a]loathes bread,
And his soul favorite food.
21 "His [a]flesh wastes away from sight,
And his [b]bones which were not seen
stick out.
22 "Then [a]his soul draws near to the pit,
And his life to those who bring
death.

23 "If there is an angel *as* [a]mediator for
him,
One out of a thousand,
To remind a man what is [1]right for
him,
24 Then let him be gracious to him, and
say,
'Deliver him from [a]going down to the
pit,
I have found a [b]ransom';
25 Let his flesh become fresher than in
youth,
Let him return to the days of his
youthful vigor;

33:4 *Spirit of God has made me.* See Gen 1:2 and note. *breath of the Almighty.* See 32:8. *gives me life.* See 27:3; see also Gen 2:7 and note.
33:5 *Refute me.* He opens and closes his speech (see v. 32) with the same plea. *if you can.* His attitude of superiority shows through.
33:6 *I . . . have been formed out of the clay.* See note on 4:19.
33:7 *my pressure weigh heavily on you.* The idiom is elsewhere used only of God (see 23:2; see also note on 1 Sam 5:6).
33:8 *Surely you have spoken.* Elihu's method is to quote Job (vv. 9–11; 34:5–6,9; 35:2–3) and then show him where and how he is wrong. The quotations are not always verbatim, which indicates that Elihu is content simply to repeat the substance of Job's arguments.
33:11 Elihu quotes Job's words almost verbatim here (see 13:27).
33:12 *you are not right.* Elihu feels that Job needs to be corrected. Certainly Job's perception of God as his enemy (see v. 10; 13:24; 19:11) is wrong, but Elihu is also offended by what he considers Job's claim to purity (see v. 9). Job, however, had never claimed to be "pure, without transgression," though some of his words were also understood that way by Eliphaz (see 15:14–16). Job admits being a sinner (7:21; 13:26) but disclaims the outrageous sins for which he thinks he is being punished. His complaints about God's silence (see v. 13) are also an offense to Elihu. But he imputes to Job the blanket statement that God never speaks to man, whereas Job's point is that God is silent in his present experience.
33:15 *In a dream . . . When sound sleep falls on men.* Elihu echoes Eliphaz (see 4:13).
33:18 *pit.* See vv. 22,24,28,30; a metaphor for the grave, as often in the Psalms. *passing over into Sheol.* See NASB marg. and 36:12.
33:19 *Man is also chastened with pain on his bed.* Dreams and visions (see v. 15) are not the only ways in which God speaks. He can talk to us in ways that we do not perceive (see v. 14). Elihu rightly states that God speaks to man in order to turn him from sin. But he overlooks Job's reason for wanting an audience with God: to find out what sins he is being accused of (see 13:22–23).
33:23–28 Having emphasized the importance of the chastening aspect of suffering, a point mentioned only briefly by Eliphaz (see 5:17), Elihu now moves on to the possibility of redemption based on a mediator (see note on 5:1). He further allows for God's gracious response of forgiveness where sincere repentance is present (vv. 27–28). But Elihu is still ignorant of the true nature of Job's relationship to God, known only in the divine council (chs. 1–2).
33:24 *Deliver him from going down to the pit.* See Is 38:17. *ransom.* See Ps 49:7–9 and note.
33:25 *flesh become fresher than in youth . . . return.* Similar phrases are used in 2 Kin 5:14 with reference to healing from leprosy.

26 Then he will [a]pray to God, and He
will accept him,
That [b]he may see His face with joy,
And He may restore His righteousness
to man.
27 "He will sing to men and say,
'I [a]have sinned and perverted what is
right,
And it is not [b]proper for me.
28 'He has redeemed my soul from going
to the pit,
And my life shall [a]see the light.'

29 "Behold, God does [a]all these
[1]oftentimes with men,
30 To [a]bring back his soul from the pit,
That he may be enlightened with the
light of life.
31 "Pay attention, O Job, listen to me;
Keep silent, and let me speak.
32 "*Then* if [1]you have anything to say,
answer me;
Speak, for I desire to justify you.
33 "If not, [a]listen to me;
Keep silent, and I will teach you
wisdom."

Elihu Vindicates God's Justice

34 Then Elihu continued and said,
2 "Hear my words, you wise men,
And listen to me, you who know.
3 "For [a]the ear tests words
As the palate tastes food.
4 "Let us choose for ourselves what is
right;
Let us know among ourselves what is
good.
5 "For Job has said, '[a]I am righteous,
But [b]God has taken away my right;

26 [a]Job 22:27; 34:28; Ps 50:14, 15 [b]Job 22:26
27 [a]2 Sam 12:13; Luke 15:21 [b]Rom 6:21
28 [a]Job 22:28
29 [1]Lit *twice, three times* [a]Eph 1:11; Phil 2:13
30 [a]Job 33:18; Zech 9:11
32 [1]Lit *there are words*
33 [a]Ps 34:11
34:3 [a]Job 12:11
5 [a]Job 13:18; 33:9 [b]Job 27:2

6 [1]Or *Although I am right I am accounted a liar* [2]Lit *arrow* [a]Job 6:4
7 [a]Job 15:16
8 [a]Job 22:15
9 [1]Or *takes delight in God* [a]Job 21:15; 35:3; Ps 50:18
10 [a]Gen 18:25; Deut 32:4; Job 8:3; 34:12; Rom 9:14
11 [1]Lit *a man* [a]Job 34:25; Ps 62:12; Prov 24:12; Jer 32:19; Ezek 33:20; Matt 16:27; Rom 2:6; 2 Cor 5:10; Rev 22:12
12 [a]Job 34:10
13 [a]Job 38:4 [b]Job 38:5
14 [1]Lit *set His mind on Himself* [a]Job 12:10; Ps 104:29; Eccl 12:7
15 [a]Gen 7:21; Job 9:22 [b]Gen 3:19; Job 10:9
17 [a]2 Sam 23:3; Job 34:30 [b]Job 40:8

6 [1]Should I lie concerning my right?
My [2][a]wound is incurable, *though I am*
without transgression.'
7 "What man is like Job,
Who [a]drinks up derision like water,
8 Who goes [a]in company with the
workers of iniquity,
And walks with wicked men?
9 "For he has said, '[a]It profits a man
nothing
When he [1]is pleased with God.'

10 "Therefore, listen to me, you men of
understanding.
Far be it from God to [a]do wickedness,
And from the Almighty to do wrong.
11 "For He pays a man according to [a]his
work,
And makes [1]him find it according to
his way.
12 "Surely, [a]God will not act wickedly,
And the Almighty will not pervert
justice.
13 "Who [a]gave Him authority over the
earth?
And who [b]has laid *on Him* the whole
world?
14 "If He should [1]determine to do so,
If He should [a]gather to Himself His
spirit and His breath,
15 All [a]flesh would perish together,
And man would [b]return to dust.

16 "But if *you have* understanding, hear
this;
Listen to the sound of my words.
17 "Shall [a]one who hates justice rule?
And [b]will you condemn the righteous
mighty One,

33:26 *see His face.* Not literally (see note on Gen 16:13).
33:30 *To bring back his soul from the pit.* Elihu teaches that God's apparent cruelty in chastening human beings is in reality an act of love, since man is never punished in this life in keeping with what he fully deserves (see v. 27). *light of life.* Spiritual well-being (see Ps 49:19; see also Ps 27:1 and note). In some contexts, the phrase refers to resurrection (see note on Is 53:11).
33:32 *I desire to justify you.* But this will happen, Elihu insists, only if Job repents.
34:1–37 The second of Elihu's four speeches (see note on 32:1–37:24), divided into three sections: (1) addressed to a group of wise men (vv. 2–15), doubtless including the three friends; (2) addressed to Job (vv. 16–33); (3) addressed to himself (vv. 34–37), as in 32:15–22 (see note there).
34:2,10 *listen to me.* Although it is possible that Elihu is overly impressed with his own wisdom, it is more likely that he considered himself a messenger of God (see 32:8; 33:4), especially in the light of his humble attitude in v. 4.
34:2 *wise men . . . you who know.* Also referred to as "men of understanding" (vv. 10,34).
34:3 Elihu echoes the words of Job in 12:11 (see note there).
34:5,9 *Job has said . . . For he has said.* Elihu again quotes Job and then goes on to defend God's justice against what he considers to be Job's false theology (e.g., 9:14–24; 16:11–17; 19:7; 21:17–18; 24:1–12; 27:2). The substance of the quotation in v. 5 is accurate (cf. 12:4; 13:18; 27:6), and much of v. 6 represents Job fairly (see 21:34; 27:5; see also 6:4 and note)—though Job had never claimed to be completely guiltless. Verse 9 is not a direct quotation from Job, who had only imagined the wicked saying something similar (see 21:15). But perhaps Elihu derives it from Job's repeated statement that God treats the righteous and the wicked in the same way (cf. 9:22; 21:17; 24:1–12), leading to the conclusion that it does not pay to please God.
34:7 *drinks up derision like water.* See Eliphaz's description of man in 15:16.
34:10 *Far be it from God to do wickedness.* See Gen 18:25 and note. Elihu's concern that Job was making God the author of evil is commendable. Job, in his frustration, has come perilously close to charging God with wrongdoing (12:4–6; 24:1–12). He has suggested that this is the only conclusion he can reach on the basis of his knowledge and experience (9:24).
34:11 See 2 Cor 5:10.
34:13–15 Elihu is zealous for God's glory as the sovereign Sustainer who demonstrates His grace every moment by granting life and breath to man.
34:15 *return to dust.* See Eccl 12:7; see also Gen 3:19 and note.
34:16 *hear . . . Listen.* The Hebrew for these verbs is singular, addressed to Job. Elihu is concerned that Job's attitude about God's justice be corrected (see v. 17), so he stresses God's impartial rule as Lord of all, especially in meting out justice to the wicked in high places (see vv. 18–20).

18 Who says to a king, 'Worthless one,'
To nobles, 'Wicked ones';
19 Who shows no [a]partiality to princes
Nor regards the rich above the poor,
For they all are the [b]work of His hands?
20 "In a moment they die, and [a]at midnight
People are shaken and pass away,
And [b]the mighty are taken away
without a hand.

21 "For [a]His eyes are upon the ways of a
man,
And He sees all his steps.
22 "There is [a]no darkness or deep shadow
Where the workers of iniquity may
hide themselves.
23 "For He does not [a]*need to* consider a
man further,
That he should go before God in
judgment.
24 "He breaks in pieces [a]mighty men
without inquiry,
And sets others in their place.
25 "Therefore He [a]knows their works,
And [b]He overthrows *them* in the night,
And they are crushed.
26 "He [a]strikes them like the wicked
[1]In a public place,
27 Because they [a]turned aside from
following Him,
And [b]had no regard for any of His
ways;
28 So that they caused [a]the cry of the
poor to come to Him,
And that He might [b]hear the cry of the
afflicted—
29 When He keeps quiet, who then can
condemn?
And when He hides His face, who
then can behold Him,
That is, in regard to both nation and
man?—
30 So that [a]godless men would not rule
Nor be snares of the people.

31 "For has anyone said to God,
'I have borne *chastisement;*
I will not offend *anymore;*
32 Teach me what I do not see;
If I have [a]done iniquity,
I will not do it again'?
33 "Shall He [a]recompense on your terms,
because you have rejected *it?*
For you must choose, and not I;
Therefore declare what you know.
34 "Men of understanding will say to me,
And a wise man who hears me,
35 'Job [a]speaks without knowledge,
And his words are without wisdom.
36 'Job ought to be tried [1]to the limit,
Because he answers [a]like wicked men.
37 'For he adds [a]rebellion to his sin;
He [b]claps his hands among us,
And multiplies his words against
God.' "

Elihu Sharply Reproves Job

35 Then Elihu continued and said,
2 "Do you think this is according to
[a]justice?
Do you say, 'My righteousness is more
than God's'?
3 "For you say, '[a]What advantage will it
be to [1]You?
[b]What profit will I have, more than if I
had sinned?'
4 "I will answer you,
And your friends with you.
5 "[a]Look at the heavens and see;
And behold [b]the clouds—they are
higher than you.
6 "If you have sinned, [a]what do you
accomplish against Him?
And if your transgressions are many,
what do you do to Him?
7 "If you are righteous, [a]what do you
give to Him,
Or what does He receive from your
hand?
8 "Your wickedness is for a man like
yourself,
And your righteousness is for a son of
man.

9 "Because of the [a]multitude of
oppressions they cry out;
They cry for help because of the arm
[b]of the mighty.

19 [a]Lev 19:15; Deut 10:17; 2 Chr 19:7; Acts 10:34; Rom 2:11; Gal 2:6; Eph 6:9; Col 3:25; 1 Pet 1:17 [b]Job 10:3
20 [a]Ex 12:29; Job 34:25; 36:20 [b]Job 12:19
21 [a]Job 24:23; 31:4; Prov 5:21; 15:3; Jer 16:17
22 [a]Ps 139:11, 12; Amos 9:2, 3
23 [a]Job 11:11
24 [a]Job 12:19
25 [a]Job 34:11 [b]Job 34:20
26 [1]Lit *In the place of the ones seeing* [a]Ps 9:5; 11:5
27 [a]1 Sam 15:11 [b]Job 21:14
28 [a]Job 35:9; James 5:4 [b]Ex 22:23; Job 22:27
30 [a]Job 5:15; 20:5; 34:17; Prov 29:2-12
32 [a]Job 33:27
33 [a]Job 41:11
35 [a]Job 35:16; 38:2
36 [1]Or *to the end* [a]Job 22:15
37 [a]Job 23:2 [b]Job 27:23
35:2 [a]Job 27:2
3 [1]Or *you* [a]Job 34:9 [b]Job 9:30, 31
5 [a]Gen 15:5; Ps 8:3 [b]Job 22:12
6 [a]Job 7:20; Prov 8:36; Jer 7:19
7 [a]Job 22:2, 3; Prov 9:12; Luke 17:10; Rom 11:35
9 [a]Ex 2:23 [b]Job 12:19

34:18 *Worthless.* See note on Deut 13:13.
34:21–28 God's omniscience guarantees that He will not make any mistakes when He punishes evildoers. It is not necessary for Him to set times to examine people for judgment (see v. 23; contrast 24:1).
34:21 Elihu echoes the words of Job in 31:4.
34:29 *When He keeps quiet, who then can condemn?* Elihu attempts to answer Job's complaint about God's silence (ch. 23). God watches over men and nations to see that right is done (vv. 29–30).
34:31–33 First indirectly (vv. 31–32) and then more directly (v. 33), Elihu condemns Job and calls for his repentance.
34:35 *Job speaks without knowledge.* A motif in the first discourse of the Lord (see 38:2) and the final response of Job (see 42:3).
35:1–16 Elihu's third speech (see note on 32:1–37:24), addressed to Job.
35:2 *My righteousness.* Elihu thinks that it is unjust and inconsistent for Job to expect vindication from God and at the same time imply that God does not care whether we are righteous (see v. 3). But allowance must be made for a person to express his feelings. The psalmist who thirsted for God (Ps 42:1–2) also questioned why God had forgotten him (Ps 42:9) and rejected him (Ps 43:2).
35:5 *Look at the heavens and see.* Elihu asserts that God is so far above man that there is really nothing man can do, good or bad, that will affect God's essential nature (see v. 6).
35:9 *they cry out; They cry for help.* Elihu states that those like Job who pray for help when suffering innocently never seem to get around to trusting the justice and goodness of their Mak-

10 "But [a]no one says, 'Where is God my
Maker,
Who [b]gives songs in the night,
11 Who [a]teaches us more than the beasts
of the earth
And makes us wiser than the birds of
the heavens?'
12 "There [a]they cry out, but He does not
answer
Because of the pride of evil men.
13 "Surely [a]God will not listen to [1]an
empty *cry,*
Nor will the Almighty regard it.
14 "How much less when [a]you say you do
not behold Him,
The [b]case is before Him, and you
must wait for Him!
15 "And now, because He has not visited
in His anger,
Nor has He acknowledged
[1]transgression well,
16 So Job opens his mouth [1]emptily;
He multiplies words [a]without
knowledge."

Elihu Speaks of God's Dealings with Men

36 Then Elihu continued and said,
2 "Wait for me a little, and I will show
you
That there [1]is yet more to be said in
God's behalf.
3 "I will fetch my knowledge from afar,
And I will ascribe [a]righteousness to
my Maker.
4 "For truly [a]my words are not false;
One who is [b]perfect in knowledge is
with you.
5 "Behold, God is mighty but does not
[a]despise *any;*
He is [b]mighty in strength of
understanding.
6 "He does not [a]keep the wicked alive,
But gives justice to [b]the afflicted.
7 "He does not [a]withdraw His eyes from
the righteous;
But [b]with kings on the throne
He has seated them forever, and they
are exalted.
8 "And if they are bound in fetters,
And are caught in the cords of
[a]affliction,
9 Then He declares to them their work
And their transgressions, that they
have [a]magnified themselves.
10 "[a]He opens their ear to instruction,
And [b]commands that they return from
evil.
11 "If they hear and serve *Him,*
They will [a]end their days in prosperity
And their years in [b]pleasures.
12 "But if they do not hear, they shall
[1]perish [a]by the sword
And they will [b]die without knowledge.
13 "But the godless in heart lay up anger;
They do not cry for help when He
binds them.
14 "[1]They die in youth,
And their life *perishes* among the [a]cult
prostitutes.
15 "He delivers the afflicted in [1]their
[a]affliction,
And [b]opens their ear [2]in *time of*
oppression.
16 "Then indeed, He [a]enticed you from
the mouth of distress,
Instead of it, a broad place with no
constraint;
And that which was set on your table
was full of [1]fatness.
17 "But you were full of [a]judgment on the
wicked;
Judgment and justice take hold
of you.

10 [a]Job 21:14; 27:10; 36:13; Is 51:13 [b]Job 8:21; Ps 42:8; 77:6; 149:5; Acts 16:25
11 [a]Job 36:22; Ps 94:12; Jer 32:33
12 [a]Prov 1:28
13 [1]Or *falsehood* [a]Job 27:9; Prov 15:29; Is 1:15; Jer 11:11; Mic 3:4
14 [a]Job 9:11; 23:8, 9 [b]Job 31:35
15 [1]Or *arrogance*
16 [1]Lit *vainly* [a]Job 34:35; 38:2
36:2 [1]Lit *are yet words for God*
3 [a]Job 8:3; 37:23
4 [a]Job 33:3 [b]Job 37:16
5 [a]Ps 22:24; 69:33; 102:17 [b]Job 12:13
6 [a]Job 8:22; 34:26
6 [b]Job 5:15
7 [a]Ps 33:18; 34:15 [b]Job 5:11; Ps 113:8
8 [a]Job 36:15, 21
9 [a]Job 15:25
10 [a]Job 33:16; 36:15 [b]2 Kin 17:13; Job 36:21; Jon 3:8
11 [a]1 Tim 4:8 [b]Ps 16:11
12 [1]Lit *pass away* [a]Job 15:22 [b]Job 4:21
14 [1]Or *Their soul dies* [a]Deut 23:17
15 [1]Lit *his* [2]Or *in adversity* [a]Job 36:8, 21 [b]Job 36:10
16 [1]Or *rich food* [a]Hos 2:14
17 [a]Job 22:5, 10, 11

er, who is also the author of wisdom and joy (see vv. 10–11). Such failure is a sign of arrogance (see v. 12), so Job's complaint against God's justice and about God's silence is meaningless talk (see vv. 13–16).
35:10–11 *gives songs . . . teaches . . . makes us wiser.* God chooses to condescend, to reach out to man in love.
35:12 Since men are arrogant, God does not listen (see v. 13). Job himself might not be wicked, but he shares their arrogance. He too receives no answer, because he does not ask rightly (see v. 14).
35:16 The reference here to Job in the third person does not necessarily mean that someone other than Job is being addressed (see note on vv. 1–16). *multiplies words.* Against God (see 34:37). *without knowledge.* See 38:2 and note.
36:1–37:24 Elihu's fourth and final (see 36:2) speech (see note on 32:1–37:24), addressed for the most part to Job (but see note on 37:2).
36:2–4 Elihu desires to strengthen the case for God's goodness and justice.
36:4 *perfect in knowledge.* Here Elihu applies the phrase to himself, while in 37:16 he applies it to God—thus appearing to make himself equal to God. But the Hebrew for "knowledge" is not quite the same here as in 37:16. Elihu is probably referring to his ability as a communicator, i.e., he claims perfection in the knowledge of speech (see note on 32:6,10,17).
36:5 God's power assures the fulfillment of His purpose.
36:6–9 A classic statement of God's justice in rewarding the righteous and punishing sinners (in contrast to what Job has been claiming). In v. 7 Elihu perhaps has in mind Job's complaint that God will not leave him alone (see 7:17–19), and in v. 9 he may be thinking of Job's charge that God will not present His indictment against him (see 31:35–36).
36:10 *opens their ear to instruction.* Elihu states that God uses trouble to gain man's attention.
36:12 See note on 33:18.
36:13–15 Elihu understands that the basic spiritual need of man stems from his hardness of heart—his refusal to yield to God, to cry out to God in his distress (see Ps 107), or to hear the voice of God in suffering.
36:14 *cult prostitutes.* See note on 1 Kin 14:24.
36:16–21 Elihu warns Job to respond to God's discipline by turning away from evil (see v. 21). Verse 16 shows that he still views Job as a man for whom there is hope.
36:16 *He enticed you.* With tender compassion, God brings His people back to Himself (see Hos 2:14).

18 "*Beware* that [a]wrath does not entice
you to scoffing;
And do not let the greatness of the
[b]ransom turn you aside.
19 "Will your [1]riches keep you from
distress,
Or all the forces of *your* strength?
20 "Do not long for [a]the night,
When people [1]vanish in their place.
21 "Be careful, do [a]not turn to evil,
For you have preferred this to
[b]affliction.
22 "Behold, God is exalted in His power;
Who is a [a]teacher like Him?
23 "Who has appointed Him His way,
And who has said, '[a]You have done
wrong'?

24 "Remember that you should [a]exalt His
work,
Of which men have [b]sung.
25 "All men have seen it;
Man beholds from afar.
26 "Behold, God is [a]exalted, and [b]we do
not know *Him;*
The [c]number of His years is
unsearchable.
27 "For [a]He draws up the drops of water,
They distill rain from [1]the [2]mist,
28 Which the clouds pour down,
They drip upon man abundantly.
29 "Can anyone understand the
[a]spreading of the clouds,
The [b]thundering of His [1]pavilion?
30 "Behold, He spreads His [1]lightning
about Him,
And He covers the depths of the sea.
31 "For by these He [a]judges peoples;
He [b]gives food in abundance.
32 "He covers *His* hands with the [1]lightning,
And [a]commands it to strike the mark.
33 "Its [a]noise declares [1]His presence;
The cattle also, concerning what is
coming up.

Elihu Says God Is Back of the Storm

37 "At this also my heart trembles,
And leaps from its place.
2 "Listen closely to the [a]thunder of His
voice,
And the rumbling that goes out from
His mouth.
3 "Under the whole heaven He lets it
loose,
And His [1]lightning to the [a]ends of the
earth.
4 "After it, a voice roars;
He thunders with His majestic voice,
And He does not restrain [1]the
lightnings when His voice is heard.
5 "God [a]thunders with His voice
wondrously,
Doing [b]great things which we cannot
comprehend.
6 "For to [a]the snow He says, 'Fall on the
earth,'
And to the [1b]downpour and the rain,
'Be strong.'
7 "He [a]seals the hand of every man,
That [b]all men may know His work.
8 "Then the beast goes into its [a]lair
And remains in its [1]den.
9 "Out of the [1a]south comes the storm,
And out of the [2]north the cold.
10 "From the breath of God [a]ice is made,
And the expanse of the waters is
frozen.
11 "Also with moisture He [a]loads the thick
cloud;
He [b]disperses [c]the cloud of His
[1]lightning.
12 "It changes direction, turning around
by His guidance,
That [1]it may do whatever He
[a]commands [2]it
On the [b]face of the inhabited earth.
13 "Whether for [1a]correction, or for [b]His
world,
Or for [c]lovingkindness, He causes it to
[2]happen.

14 "Listen to this, O Job,
Stand and consider the wonders of
God.

18 [a]Jon 4:4, 9 [b]Job 33:24 **19** [1]Or *cry* **20** [1]Lit *go up* [a]Job 34:20, 25 **21** [a]Job 36:10; Ps 31:6; 66:18 [b]Job 36:8, 15; Heb 11:25 **22** [a]Job 35:11 **23** [a]Deut 32:4; Job 8:3 **24** [a]Ps 92:5; Rev 15:3 [b]Ex 15:1; Judg 5:1; 1 Chr 16:9; Ps 59:16; 138:5 **26** [a]Job 11:7-9; 37:23 [b]1 Cor 13:12 [c]Job 10:5; Ps 90:2; 102:24, 27; Heb 1:12 **27** [1]Lit *its* [2]Or *flood* [a]Job 5:10; 36:26-29; 37:6, 11; 38:28; Ps 147:8 **29** [1]Lit *booth* [a]Job 37:11, 16 [b]Job 26:14 **30** [1]Lit *light* **31** [a]Job 37:13 [b]Ps 104:27; 136:25; Acts 14:17 **32** [1]Lit *light* [a]Job 37:11, 12, 15 **33** [1]Lit *concerning Him* [a]Job 37:2

37:2 [a]Job 36:33; 37:4, 5; Ps 29:3-9 **3** [1]Lit *light* [a]Job 28:24; 37:11, 12; 38:13 **4** [1]Lit *them* **5** [a]Job 26:14 [b]Job 5:9; 37:14, 16, 23 **6** [1]Lit *shower of rain and shower of rains* [a]Job 38:22 [b]Job 36:27 **7** [a]Job 12:14 [b]Ps 111:2 **8** [1]Lit *dens* [a]Job 38:40; Ps 104:21, 22 **9** [1]Lit *chamber* [2]Lit *scattering winds* [a]Job 9:9 **10** [a]Job 38:29; Ps 147:17 **11** [1]Lit *light* [a]Job 36:27 [b]Job 36:29 [c]Job 37:15 **12** [1]Lit *they* [2]Lit *them* [a]Job 36:32; Ps 148:8 [b]Is 14:21; 27:6

13 [1]Lit *the rod* [2]Lit *be found* [a]Ex 9:18, 23; 1 Sam 12:18, 19 [b]Job 38:26, 27 [c]1 Kin 18:41-46

36:21 *Be careful, do not turn to evil.* Elihu's evaluation of Job is the opposite of God's (see 1:8; 2:3).
36:22–33 Elihu anticipates some of God's statements in the discourses of chs. 38–41.
36:24 *His work, Of which men have sung.* See, e.g., Ex 15:1; Judg 5:1.
36:26 *we do not know Him.* See 37:5. That God's ways and thoughts are infinitely higher than ours is an important theme in chs. 38–41.
36:30 *covers.* Here in the sense of "lighting up" the depths of the sea.
36:31 *judges.* The verb can be translated "nourishes," meaning the Lord nourishes the peoples with the showers mentioned in vv. 27–30.
36:32 *His hands.* Lit. "both hands." God works with equal effectiveness with either hand (cf. 1 Chr 12:2).
37:1–13 A continuation of Elihu's hymnic description of God's marvels exhibited in the earth's atmosphere, beginning in 36:27. His heart pounds at the awesome display (see v. 1). The passage reveals a sophisticated observation of atmospheric conditions and their effects: the evaporation and distillation of water for rain (see 36:27), the clouds as holders of moisture (see 36:28; 37:11) and the cyclonic behavior of clouds (see v. 12). Such forces originate from God's command and always perform His will for mankind, whether for good or for ill (v. 13).
37:2 *Listen.* The Hebrew for this verb is plural, indicating that others (including the three friends) besides Job are being addressed here (see note on 36:1–37:24). *thunder of His voice . . . rumbling.* Thunder (see v. 4).
37:5 *we cannot comprehend.* See note on 36:26.
37:10 *breath of God.* Here a metaphor for a chilling wind.
37:14–18 Job is challenged to ponder God's power over the

15 "Do you know how God establishes them,
And makes the [1]lightning of His cloud to shine?
16 "Do you know about the layers of the thick clouds,
The [a]wonders of one [b]perfect in knowledge,
17 You whose garments are hot,
When the land is still because of the south wind?
18 "Can you, with Him, [a]spread out the skies,
Strong as a molten mirror?
19 "Teach us what we shall say to Him;
We [a]cannot arrange *our case* because of darkness.
20 "Shall it be told Him that I would speak?
[1]Or should a man say that he would be swallowed up?

21 "Now [1]men do not see the light which is bright in the skies;
But the wind has passed and cleared them.
22 "Out of the north comes golden *splendor;*
Around God is awesome majesty.
23 "The Almighty—[a]we cannot find Him;
He is [b]exalted in power
And [c]He will not do violence [d]to justice and abundant righteousness.
24 "Therefore men [a]fear Him;
He does not [b]regard any who are wise of heart."

15 [1]Lit *light*
16 [a]Job 37:5, 14, 23 [b]Job 36:4
18 [a]Job 9:8; Ps 104:2; Is 44:24; 45:12; Jer 10:12; Zech 12:1
19 [a]Job 9:14; Rom 8:26
20 [1]Or *If a man speak, surely he shall be swallowed up*
21 [1]Lit *they*
23 [a]Job 11:7, 8; Rom 11:33; 1 Tim 6:16 [b]Job 9:4; 36:5 [c]Is 63:9; Lam 3:33; Ezek 18:23, 32; 33:11 [d]Job 8:3
24 [a]Matt 10:28 [b]Job 5:13; Matt 11:25; 1 Cor 1:26

38:1 [a]Job 40:6
2 [a]Job 35:16; 42:3
3 [a]Job 40:7 [b]Job 42:4
4 [1]Lit *know understanding* [a]Job 15:7; Ps 104:5; Prov 8:29; 30:4
5 [a]Prov 8:29; Is 40:12
6 [a]Job 26:7
7 [a]Job 1:6
8 [a]Gen 1:9; Ps 104:6-9; Prov 8:29; Jer 5:22
10 [1]Lit *broke My decree on it* [a]Gen 1:9; Ps 33:7; 104:9; Prov 8:29; Jer 5:22
12 [1]Lit *from your days*

God Speaks Now to Job

38 Then the LORD [a]answered Job out of the whirlwind and said,
2 "Who is this that [a]darkens counsel
By words without knowledge?
3 "Now [a]gird up your loins like a man,
And [b]I will ask you, and you instruct Me!

4 "Where were you [a]when I laid the foundation of the earth?
Tell *Me,* if you [1]have understanding,
5 Who set its [a]measurements? Since you know.
Or who stretched the line on it?
6 "On what [a]were its bases sunk?
Or who laid its cornerstone,
7 When the morning stars sang together
And all the [a]sons of God shouted for joy?

8 "Or *who* [a]enclosed the sea with doors
When, bursting forth, it went out from the womb;
9 When I made a cloud its garment
And thick darkness its swaddling band,
10 And I [1a]placed boundaries on it
And set a bolt and doors,
11 And I said, 'Thus far you shall come, but no farther;
And here shall your proud waves stop'?

God's Mighty Power

12 "Have you [1]ever in your life commanded the morning,
And caused the dawn to know its place,

elements. The question format is also used in the divine discourses (chs. 38–41).
37:16 *perfect in knowledge.* See note on 36:4.
37:18 *spread out the skies.* See 26:7. *Strong as . . . mirror.* Ancient mirrors were made out of bronze, so they were very hard. In Deut 28:23, a bronze sky symbolizes unremitting heat (see note there; see also Deut 28:22).
37:19 *We cannot arrange our case.* Job had dared to sign his defense and call for an audience with God (see 31:35). For this, Elihu seeks to shame him. But he softens his tone by including himself as one equally vulnerable to God's majesty.
37:22 *Out of the north comes golden splendor.* See note on Ps 48:2. *awesome majesty.* Elihu prepares Job for the appearance of God in the storm (chs. 38–41).
37:24 *fear.* See 28:28; Gen 20:11 and notes.
38:1–42:6 The theophany (appearance of God) to Job, consisting of two discourses by the Lord (38:1–40:2; 40:6–41:34), each of which receives a brief response from Job (40:3–5; 42:1–6).
38:1 *the LORD.* The Israelite covenant name for God (see Introduction: Author). *whirlwind.* See 40:6. Elihu had imagined the appearance of the divine presence as a display of "golden splendor" and "awesome majesty" (37:22). He also had anticipated the storm or whirlwind (see note on 37:22), from which Job would hear the voice of God. Job had said, "Let the Almighty answer me" (31:35). He now receives the Lord's answer.
38:2 See 35:16. In 42:3, Job echoes the Lord's words. God states that Job's complaining and raging against Him are unjustified and proceed from limited understanding.
38:3 Repeated in 40:7 (see also 42:4). The format of God's response is to ply Job with rhetorical questions, to each of which Job must plead ignorance. God says nothing about Job's suffering, nor does He address Job's problem about divine justice. Job gets neither a bill of indictment nor a verdict of innocence. But, more important, God does not humiliate or condemn him—which surely would have been the case if the counselors had been right. So by implication Job is vindicated, and later his vindication is directly affirmed (see 42:7–8). The divine discourses, then, succeed in bringing Job to complete faith in God's goodness without his receiving a direct answer to his questions.
38:4–38 Inanimate creation testifies to God's sovereignty and power (the earth, vv. 4–7,18; the sea, vv. 8–11,16; the sun, vv. 12–15; the netherworld, v. 17; light and darkness, vv. 19–20; the weather, vv. 22–30,34–38; the constellations, vv. 31–33). See note on 38:39–39:30.
38:4–5 See the similar questions of Agur, and the similar irony in his demand for a response (Prov 30:4).
38:7 See Ps 148:2–3; see also note on Ps 65:13. When the earth was created, the angels were there to sing the praises of the Creator, but Job was not (see vv. 4–5). He should therefore not expect to be able to understand even lesser aspects of God's plans for the world and for mankind. *sons of God.* See 1:6 and note.
38:10–11 See Ps 33:7; Jer 5:22.
38:11 *And I said.* God the Father controls the sea by speaking to it, as does God the Son (see Luke 8:24–25).
38:12–13 The arrival of the dawn sends the wicked scurrying for cover.

13 That it might take hold of [a]the ends of
the earth,
And [b]the wicked be shaken out of it?
14 "It is changed like clay *under* the seal;
And they stand forth like a garment.
15 "[a]From the wicked their light is
withheld,
And the [b]uplifted arm is broken.

16 "Have you entered into [a]the springs of
the sea
Or walked [1]in the recesses of the deep?
17 "Have the gates of death been revealed
to you,
Or have you seen the gates of [a]deep
darkness?
18 "Have you understood the [1]expanse of
[a]the earth?
Tell *Me,* if you know all this.

19 "Where is the way to the dwelling of
light?
And darkness, where is its place,
20 That you may take it to [a]its territory
And that you may discern the paths to
its [1]home?
21 "You know, for [a]you were born then,
And the number of your days is great!
22 "Have you entered the storehouses [a]of
the snow,
Or have you seen the storehouses of
the [b]hail,
23 Which I have reserved for the time of
distress,
For the day of war and battle?
24 "Where is the way that [a]the light is
divided,
Or the east wind scattered on the
earth?

25 "Who has cleft a channel for the flood,
Or a way for the thunderbolt,
26 To bring [a]rain on a land without
[1]people,
On a desert without a man in it,
27 To [a]satisfy the waste and desolate land
And to make the [1]seeds of grass to
sprout?
28 "Has [a]the rain a father?
Or who has begotten the drops of
dew?
29 "From whose womb has come the [a]ice?
And the frost of heaven, who has
given it birth?
30 "Water [1]becomes hard like stone,
And the surface of the deep is
imprisoned.

31 "Can you bind the chains of the
[a]Pleiades,
Or loose the cords of Orion?
32 "Can you lead forth a [1]constellation in
its season,
And guide the Bear with her [2]satellites?
33 "Do you know the [a]ordinances of the
heavens,
Or fix their rule over the earth?

34 "Can you lift up your voice to the
clouds,
So that an [a]abundance of water will
cover you?
35 "Can you [a]send forth lightnings that
they may go
And say to you, 'Here we are'?
36 "Who has [a]put wisdom in the
innermost being
Or given [b]understanding to the [1]mind?
37 "Who can count the clouds by wisdom,
Or [a]tip the water jars of the heavens,
38 When the dust hardens into a mass
And the clods stick together?

39 "Can you hunt the [a]prey for the lion,
Or satisfy the appetite of the young
lions,
40 When they [a]crouch in *their* dens
And lie in wait in *their* lair?
41 "Who prepares for [a]the raven its
nourishment
When its young cry to God
And wander about without food?

13 [a]Job 28:24; 37:3 [b]Job 34:25, 26; 36:6
15 [a]Job 5:14 [b]Num 15:30; Ps 10:15; 37:17
16 [1]Or *in search of* [a]Gen 7:11; 8:2; Prov 8:24, 28
17 [a]Job 10:21; 26:6; 34:22
18 [1]Or *width* [a]Job 28:24
20 [1]Lit *house* [a]Job 26:10
21 [a]Job 15:7
22 [a]Job 37:6 [b]Ex 9:18; Josh 10:11; Is 30:30; Ezek 13:11, 13; Rev 16:21
24 [a]Job 26:10
26 [1]Lit *man* [a]Job 36:27
27 [1]Or *growth* [a]Ps 104:13, 14; 107:35
28 [a]Job 36:27, 28; Ps 147:8; Jer 14:22
29 [a]Job 37:10; Ps 147:17
30 [1]Lit *hides itself*
31 [a]Job 9:9; Amos 5:8
32 [1]Heb *Mazzaroth* [2]Lit *sons*
33 [a]Ps 148:6; Jer 31:35, 36
34 [a]Job 22:11; 36:27, 28; 38:37
35 [a]Job 36:32; 37:3
36 [1]Or *rooster* [a]Job 9:4; Ps 51:6; Eccl 2:26 [b]Job 32:8
37 [a]Job 38:34
39 [a]Ps 104:21
40 [a]Job 37:8
41 [a]Ps 147:9; Matt 6:26; Luke 12:24
39:1 [1]Lit *goats of the rock* [a]Deut 14:5; 1 Sam 24:2; Ps 104:18 [b]Ps 29:9

God Speaks of Nature and Its Beings

39 "Do you know the time the
[1a]mountain goats give birth?
Do you observe the calving of the
[b]deer?
2 "Can you count the months they fulfill,
Or do you know the time they give
birth?
3 "They kneel down, they bring forth
their young,
They get rid of their labor pains.

38:14 *clay under the seal.* Either a cylinder seal (see note on Gen 38:18) or a stamp seal.
38:15 *their light.* The night is when the wicked are active (see John 3:19; for the imagery cf. Luke 11:35). *uplifted arm is broken.* See 22:9 and note.
38:16 *springs of the sea.* See Gen 7:11; 8:2.
38:17 *gates of death.* See note on 17:16; see also 26:5–6.
38:22–23 *hail . . . For the day of war.* See, e.g., Josh 10:11; Is 28:2 and note.
38:24 *east wind.* See note on 15:2.
38:31–32 *Pleiades . . . Orion . . . Bear.* See note on 9:9.
38:36 *innermost being . . . mind.* It is possible that the first word should be translated "ibis" and the second "rooster," two birds whose habits were sometimes observed by people who wished to forecast the weather. If so, the words would serve as a transition to the next major section of the first divine discourse.
38:39–39:30 Animate creation testifies to God's sovereignty, power and loving care (the lion, 38:39–40; the raven, 38:41; the mountain goat, 39:1–4; the wild donkey, vv. 5–8; the wild ox, vv. 9–12; the ostrich, vv. 13–18; the horse, vv. 19–25; the hawk, v. 26; the eagle, vv. 27–30). See note on 38:4–38.
38:41 *prepares for the raven its nourishment.* God cares for and feeds all the birds, of which the raven is representative (e.g., compare Luke 12:24 with Matt 6:26).

4 "Their offspring become strong, they grow up in the open field;
They leave and do not return to them.

5 "Who sent out the [a]wild donkey free?
And who loosed the bonds of the swift donkey,
6 To whom I gave [a]the wilderness for a home
And the salt land for his dwelling place?
7 "He scorns the tumult of the city,
The shoutings of the driver he does not hear.
8 "He explores the mountains for his pasture
And searches after every green thing.
9 "Will the [a]wild ox consent to serve you,
Or will he spend the night at your manger?
10 "Can you bind the wild ox in a furrow with [1]ropes,
Or will he harrow the valleys after you?
11 "Will you trust him because his strength is great
And leave your labor to him?
12 "Will you have faith in him that he will return your [1]grain
And gather *it from* your threshing floor?

13 "The ostriches' wings flap joyously
With the pinion and plumage of [1]love,
14 For she abandons her eggs to the earth
And warms them in the dust,
15 And she forgets that a foot may crush [1]them,
Or that a wild beast may trample [1]them.
16 "She treats her young [a]cruelly, as if *they* were not hers;
Though her labor be in vain, *she is* [1]unconcerned;
17 Because God has made her forget wisdom,
And has not given her a share of understanding.
18 "When she lifts herself [1]on high,
She laughs at the horse and his rider.

19 "Do you give the horse *his* might?
Do you clothe his neck with a mane?
20 "Do you make him [a]leap like the locust?
His majestic [b]snorting is terrible.
21 "[1]He paws in the valley, and rejoices in *his* strength;
He [a]goes out to meet the weapons.
22 "He laughs at fear and is not dismayed;
And he does not turn back from the sword.
23 "The quiver rattles against him,
The flashing spear and javelin.
24 "With shaking and rage he [1]races over the ground,
And he does not stand still at the voice of the trumpet.
25 "As often as the trumpet *sounds* he says, 'Aha!'
And he scents the battle from afar,
And the thunder of the captains and the war cry.

26 "Is it by your understanding that the hawk soars,
Stretching his wings toward the south?
27 "Is it at your [1]command that the eagle mounts up
And makes [a]his nest on high?
28 "On the cliff he dwells and lodges,
Upon the rocky crag, an inaccessible place.
29 "From there he [a]spies out food;
His eyes see *it* from afar.
30 "His young ones also suck up blood;
And [a]where the slain are, there is he."

Job: What Can I Say?

40 Then the LORD said to Job,
2 "Will the faultfinder [a]contend with the Almighty?
Let him who [b]reproves God answer it."

3 Then Job answered the LORD and said,

5 [a]Job 6:5; 11:12; 24:5; Ps 104:11 **6** [a]Job 24:5; Jer 2:24; Hos 8:9 **9** [a]Num 23:22; Deut 33:17; Ps 22:21; 29:6; 92:10; Is 34:7 **10** [1]Lit *his rope* **12** [1]Lit *seed* **13** [1]Or *a stork* **15** [1]Lit *it* **16** [1]Lit *without fear* [a]Lam 4:3

18 [1]Or *to flee* **20** [a]Joel 2:5 [b]Jer 8:16 **21** [1]Lit *They paw* [a]Jer 8:6 **24** [1]Or *swallows up* **27** [1]Lit *mouth* [a]Jer 49:16; Obad 4 **29** [a]Job 9:26 **30** [a]Matt 24:28; Luke 17:37 **40:2** [a]Job 9:3; 10:2; 33:13; Is 45:9 [b]Job 13:3; 23:4; 31:35

39:5 *wild donkey.* See 24:5; see also the description of Ishmael in Gen 16:12 and note there.
39:9–12 As there was an implied contrast between the wild donkey and the domestic donkey (see v. 7), here there is a more explicit contrast between the wild ox and the domestic ox.
39:11 *strength is great.* In the OT, the wild ox (the now virtually extinct aurochs) often symbolizes strength (see, e.g., Num 23:22; 24:8; Deut 33:17; Ps 29:6). Next to the elephant and rhinoceros, the wild ox was the largest and most powerful land animal of the OT world.
39:13–18 This stanza is unique in the discourses, because in it the Lord asks Job no questions. Could it be because the ostrich is so amusing?
39:13 *pinion and plumage of love.* The Hebrew for "love" can be translated "a stork" (see NASB marg.). A stork's wings were particularly impressive (see Zech 5:9).
39:18 *horse and his rider.* Forms a transition to the next paragraph.
39:19–25 The horse is the only domestic animal in the discourses. This fact, though unexpected, serves the Lord's purpose, since it is specifically the war horse that is in view.
39:20 *like the locust.* Horses and locusts are compared also in Jer 51:27; Rev 9:7; cf. Joel 2:4.
39:26 *hawk.* The sparrow hawk, not resident to the Holy Land, stops there in its migration south for the winter.
39:27 *eagle.* Or possibly "vulture" (see v. 30).
40:1–2 The conclusion of the first divine discourse. Once again, God challenges Job to answer Him.
40:3–5 Job, duly chastened and no longer "like a prince" (31:37), is unwilling to speak another word of complaint.

4 "Behold, I am insignificant; what can I reply to You?
I [a]lay my hand on my mouth.
5 "Once I have spoken, and [a]I will not answer;
Even twice, and I will add nothing more."

God Questions Job

6 Then the [a]LORD answered Job out of
the storm and said,
7 "Now [a]gird up your loins like a man;
I will [b]ask you, and you instruct Me.
8 "Will you really [a]annul My judgment?
Will you [b]condemn Me [c]that you may be justified?
9 "Or do you have an arm like God,
And can you [a]thunder with a voice like His?

10 "[a]Adorn yourself with eminence and dignity,
And clothe yourself with honor and majesty.
11 "Pour out [a]the overflowings of your anger,
And look on everyone who is [b]proud, and make him low.
12 "Look on everyone who is proud, *and* [a]humble him,
And [b]tread down the wicked [1]where they stand.
13 "[a]Hide them in the dust together;
Bind [1]them in the hidden *place.*
14 "Then I will also [1]confess to you,
That your own right hand can save you.

God's Power Shown in Creatures

15 "Behold now, [1]Behemoth, which [a]I made [2]as well as you;
He eats grass like an ox.
16 "Behold now, his strength in his loins
And his power in the muscles of his belly.
17 "He bends his tail like a cedar;
The sinews of his thighs are knit together.
18 "His bones are tubes of bronze;
His [1]limbs are like bars of iron.

19 "He is the [a]first of the ways of God;
Let his [b]maker bring near his sword.
20 "Surely the mountains [a]bring him food,
And all the beasts of the field [b]play there.
21 "Under the lotus plants he lies down,
In the covert of the reeds and the marsh.
22 "The lotus plants cover him with [1]shade;
The willows of the brook surround him.
23 "If a river [1]rages, he is not alarmed;
He is confident, though the [a]Jordan rushes to his mouth.
24 "Can anyone capture him [1]when he is on watch,
With [2]barbs can anyone pierce *his* nose?

God's Power Shown in Creatures

41 "[1]Can you draw out [2][a]Leviathan with a fishhook?
Or press down his tongue with a cord?
2 "Can you [a]put a [1]rope in his nose
Or pierce his jaw with a [2]hook?

4 [a]Job 21:5; 29:9
5 [a]Job 9:3, 15
6 [a]Job 38:1
7 [a]Job 38:3 [b]Job 38:3; 42:4
8 [a]Rom 3:4 [b]Job 10:3, 7; 16:11; 19:6; 27:2 [c]Job 13:18; 27:6
9 [a]Job 37:5; Ps 29:3
10 [a]Ps 93:1; 104:1
11 [a]Is 42:25; Nah 1:6, 8 [b]Is 2:12; Dan 4:37
12 [1]Lit *under them* [a]1 Sam 2:7; Is 2:12; 13:11; Dan 4:37 [b]Is 63:3
13 [1]Or *their faces* [a]Is 2:10-12
14 [1]Or *praise you*
15 [1]Or *the hippopotamus* [2]Lit *with* [a]Job 40:19
18 [1]Lit *bones*
19 [a]Job 41:33 [b]Job 40:15
20 [a]Ps 104:14 [b]Ps 104:26
22 [1]Lit *his shade*
23 [1]Or *oppresses* [a]Gen 13:10
24 [1]Lit *in his eyes* [2]Lit *snares*
41:1 [1]Ch 40:25 in Heb [2]Or *the crocodile* [a]Job 3:8; Ps 74:14; 104:26; Is 27:1
2 [1]Lit *rope of rushes* [2]Or *thorn* or *ring* [a]2 Kin 19:28; Is 37:29

40:4 *insignificant.* The Hebrew for this word can also mean "small" or "unworthy."
40:5 *Once . . . twice.* See note on 5:19.
40:6 See 38:1 and note.
40:7 Repeated from 38:3 (see note there).
40:8–14 The prologue to the second divine discourse, which ends at 41:34. Unlike the first discourse, God here addresses the issues of His own justice and Job's futile attempt at self-justification. In chs. 21 and 24, Job had complained about God's indifference toward the wickedness of evil men. Here the Lord asserts His ability and determination to administer justice—a matter over which Job has no control. Therefore by implication Job is admonished to leave all this, including his own vindication (see v. 14), under the power of God's strong arm (see v. 9).
40:8 *Will you condemn Me that you may be justified?* In 19:6, Job had said, "God has wronged me."
40:10 *clothe yourself with honor and majesty.* The Hebrew underlying this clause describes God in Ps 104:1: "You are clothed with splendor and majesty." The Lord here challenges Job to take on the appearance of deity—if he can.
40:11–12 See Is 13:11, where the Lord describes Himself as doing these things.
40:13 *dust.* See note on 7:21.
40:14 *your own right hand can save you.* Contrast Ps 49:7–9 (see note there).
40:15–24 The first of two poems (ch. 41 constitutes the second) in this discourse, each describing a huge beast and resuming the animal theme of ch. 39.
40:15 *Behemoth.* The word is Hebrew and means "beast par excellence," referring to a large land animal (possibly the hippopotamus or the elephant). Much of the language used to describe him in vv. 16–24 is highly poetic and hyperbolic. *which I made.* He is one of God's creatures, not a mythical being.
40:18 *iron.* See note on 19:24.
40:19 *first of the ways of God.* The Hebrew underlying this phrase is translated "beginning of His way" in Prov 8:22 with reference to the creation of wisdom (see Prov 8:12). Here the descriptive phrase stresses the importance of the Behemoth as an example of a huge animal under the control of a sovereign God.
40:21–23 *reeds and the marsh . . . willows . . . Jordan.* The area described is probably the Huleh region, north of the Sea of Galilee.
40:24 The proposal to capture the Behemoth forms a transition to the similar proposal concerning the Leviathan in 41:1.
41:1–34 The second of two poems in the Lord's final discourse (see note on 40:15–24).
41:1 *Leviathan.* The OT uses the word in both a figurative and a literal sense. For its figurative usage see note on 3:8. Literally, the Leviathan was a large marine animal (see Ps 104:26), here perhaps a crocodile (see NASB marg.). His description in ch. 41 indicates that he is even more terrifying than the Behemoth in ch. 40.

3 "Will he make many supplications to you,
Or will he speak to you soft words?
4 "Will he make a covenant with you?
Will you take him for a servant forever?
5 "Will you play with him as with a bird,
Or will you bind him for your maidens?
6 "Will the [1]traders bargain over him?
Will they divide him among the merchants?
7 "Can you fill his skin with harpoons,
Or his head with fishing spears?
8 "Lay your hand on him;
Remember the battle; [1]you will not do it again!
9 "[1]Behold, [2]your expectation is false;
Will [3]you be laid low even at the sight of him?
10 "No one is so fierce that he dares to [a]arouse him;
Who then is he that can stand before Me?
11 "Who has [1a]given to Me that I should repay *him?*
Whatever is [b]under the whole heaven is Mine.

12 "I will not keep silence concerning his limbs,
Or his mighty strength, or his [1]orderly frame.
13 "Who can [1]strip off his outer armor?
Who can come within his double [2]mail?
14 "Who can open the doors of his face?
Around his teeth there is terror.
15 "*His* [1]strong scales are *his* pride,
Shut up *as with* a tight seal.
16 "One is so near to another
That no air can come between them.
17 "They are joined one to another;
They clasp each other and cannot be separated.
18 "His sneezes flash forth light,
And his eyes are like the [a]eyelids of the morning.
19 "Out of his mouth go burning torches;
Sparks of fire leap forth.
20 "Out of his nostrils smoke goes forth
As *from* a boiling pot and *burning* rushes.
21 "His breath kindles coals,
And a flame goes forth from his mouth.
22 "In his neck lodges strength,
And dismay leaps before him.
23 "The folds of his flesh are joined together,
Firm on him and immovable.
24 "His heart is as hard as a stone,
Even as hard as a lower millstone.
25 "When he raises himself up, the [1]mighty fear;
Because of the crashing they are bewildered.
26 "The sword that reaches him cannot avail,
Nor the spear, the dart or the javelin.
27 "He regards iron as straw,
Bronze as rotten wood.
28 "The [1]arrow cannot make him flee;
Slingstones are turned into stubble for him.
29 "Clubs are regarded as stubble;
He laughs at the rattling of the javelin.
30 "His underparts are *like* sharp potsherds;
He [1]spreads out *like* a threshing sledge on the mire.
31 "He makes the depths boil like a pot;
He makes the sea like a jar of ointment.
32 "Behind him he makes a wake to shine;
One would think the deep to be gray-haired.
33 "[a]Nothing on [1]earth is like him,
One made without fear.
34 "[1]He looks on everything that is high;
He is king over all the [a]sons of pride."

Job's Confession

42 Then Job answered the LORD and said,
2 "I know that [a]You can do all things,
And that no purpose of Yours can be thwarted.
3 'Who is this that [a]hides counsel without knowledge?'
"Therefore I have declared that which I did not understand,
Things [b]too wonderful for me, which I did not know."
4 'Hear, now, and I will speak;
I will [a]ask You, and You instruct me.'
5 "I have [a]heard of You by the hearing of the ear;
But now my [b]eye sees You;

6 [1]Lit *partners* 8 [1]Lit *do not add* 9 [1]Ch 41:1 in Heb [2]Lit *his* [3]Lit *he* 10 [a]Job 3:8 11 [1]Lit *anticipated* [a]Rom 11:35 [b]Ex 19:5; Deut 10:14; Job 9:5-10; 26:6-14; 28:24; Ps 24:1; 50:12; 1 Cor 10:26 12 [1]Or *graceful* 13 [1]Lit *uncover the face of his garment* [2]So Gr; Heb *bridle* 15 [1]Lit *rows of shields* 18 [a]Job 3:9

25 [1]Or *gods* 28 [1]Lit *son of the bow* 30 [1]Or *moves across* 33 [1]Lit *dust* [a]Job 40:19 34 [1]Ch 41:26 in Heb [a]Job 28:8 42:2 [a]Gen 18:14; Matt 19:26 3 [a]Job 38:2 [b]Ps 40:5; 131:1; 139:6 4 [a]Job 38:3; 40:7 5 [a]Job 26:14; Rom 10:17 [b]Is 6:5; Eph 1:17, 18

41:10 The Leviathan is mighty, but God is infinitely more powerful.
41:11 Perhaps alluded to, though not directly quoted, by Paul in Rom 11:35.
41:14–15 *doors of his face . . . teeth . . . strong scales.* Characteristic of the crocodile (see note on v. 1).
41:18–21 Highly figurative, exaggerated poetic imagery.
41:27 *iron.* See note on 19:24.
41:30 *sharp potsherds.* Broken pottery fragments.
41:34 *king over all the sons of pride.* The Lord alone can humble such creatures. Job cannot be expected to do so, though God challenges him to attempt it—if he so desires (see 40:11–12).
42:1–6 Job's last recorded words are his response to the Lord's second discourse.
42:2 Job finally sees that God and His purposes are supreme.
42:3 Job quotes the Lord's words in 38:2.
42:4 Job quotes the Lord's words in 38:3; 40:7.
42:5 Job—and his three friends, and Elihu—had only heard of God, but now Job has seen God (see Is 6:5) with the eyes of

6 Therefore I retract,
And I repent in dust and ashes."

God Displeased with Job's Friends

7 It came about after the LORD had spoken these words to Job, that the LORD said to
Eliphaz the Temanite, "My wrath is kindled
against you and against your two friends,
because you have not spoken of Me what is
right [a]as My servant Job has.
8 "Now therefore, take for yourselves
[a]seven bulls and seven rams, and go to My
servant Job, and offer up a [b]burnt offering
for yourselves, and My servant Job will [c]pray
for you. [d]For I will [1]accept him so that I may
not do with you *according to your* folly,
because you have not spoken of Me what is
right, as My servant Job has."
9 So Eliphaz the Temanite and Bildad the
Shuhite *and* Zophar the Naamathite went
and did as the LORD told them; and the LORD
[1]accepted Job.

God Restores Job's Fortunes

10 The LORD [a]restored the fortunes of Job
when he prayed for his friends, and the LORD
increased all that Job had twofold.
11 Then all his [a]brothers and all his sisters and all who had known him before
came to him, and they ate bread with him in
his house; and they [b]consoled him and comforted him for all the adversities that the
LORD had brought on him. And each one
gave him one [1]piece of money, and each a
ring of gold.
12 [a]The LORD blessed the latter *days* of Job
more than his beginning; [b]and he had 14,000
sheep and 6,000 camels and 1,000 yoke of
oxen and 1,000 female donkeys.
13 [a]He had seven sons and three daughters.
14 He named the first Jemimah, and the
second Keziah, and the third Keren-happuch.
15 In all the land no women were found
so fair as Job's daughters; and their father
gave them inheritance among their brothers.
16 After this, Job lived 140 years, and saw
his sons and his grandsons, four generations.
17 [a]And Job died, an old man and full of
days.

7 [a]Job 40:3-5; 42:1-6
8 [1]Lit *lift up his face* [a]Num 23:1 [b]Job 1:5 [c]Gen 20:17; James 5:16; 1 John 5:16 [d]Job 22:30
9 [1]Lit *lifted up the face of*
10 [a]Deut 30:3; Job 1:2, 3; Ps 14:7; 85:1-3; 126:1-6
11 [1]Heb *qesitah* [a]Job 19:13 [b]Job 2:11
12 [a]Job 1:10; 8:7; James 5:11 [b]Job 1:3
13 [a]Job 1:2
17 [a]Gen 15:15; 25:8; Job 5:26

faith and spiritual understanding. He can therefore accept God's plan for his life (see v. 2)—which includes suffering. *my eye sees You.* A down payment on the hope expressed in 19:26 (see note there).

42:6 *I retract.* See note on 9:21. To his humility (see 40:4–5) Job adds repentance for the presumptuous words he had spoken to God. *dust and ashes.* See 30:19 and note.

42:7–9 Despite Job's mistakes in word and attitude while he suffered, he is now commended and the counselors are rebuked. Why? Because even in his rage, even when he challenged God, he was determined to speak honestly before Him. The counselors, on the other hand, mouthed many correct and often beautiful creedal statements, but without living knowledge of the God they claimed to honor. Job spoke to God; they only spoke about God. Even worse, their spiritual arrogance caused them to claim knowledge they did not possess. They presumed to know why Job was suffering.

42:7–8 *My servant Job.* The phrase is used four times in these two verses (see note on 1:8).

42:10 Job's prayer for those who had abused him is a touching OT illustration of the high Christian virtue our Lord taught in Matt 5:44. Job's prayer marked the turning point back to prosperity for him.

42:11 Contrast 16:2; 19:13. *piece of money.* The Hebrew for this phrase is found elsewhere in the OT only in Gen 33:19 (see note there); Josh 24:32.

42:12–16 The cosmic contest with the Accuser is now over, and Job is restored. No longer is there a reason for Job to experience suffering—unless he was sinful and deserved it, which is not the case. God does not allow us to suffer for no reason, and even though the reason may be hidden in the mystery of His divine purpose (see Is 55:8–9)—never for us to know in this life—we must trust in Him as the God who does only what is right.

42:12 The number of animals is in each case twice as many (see v. 10) as Job had owned before (see 1:3).

42:13 *seven sons and three daughters.* To replace the children he had lost earlier (see 1:2,18–19).

42:14 *Jemimah.* Means "dove." *Keziah.* Means "cinnamon." *Keren-happuch.* Means "container of antimony," a highly prized eyeshadow (see note on Jer 4:30).

42:15 *gave them inheritance among their brothers.* Contrast Num 27:8.

42:16 *lived 140 years.* The longevity of a true patriarch (see note on Ex 6:16). *saw . . . four generations.* See Gen 50:23.

42:17 *old man and full of days.* See 5:26 and note; Gen 25:8.

Psalms

INTRODUCTION

Title

The titles "Psalms" and "Psalter" come from the Septuagint (the Greek translation of the OT), where they originally referred to stringed instruments (such as harp, lyre and lute), then to songs sung with their accompaniment. The traditional Hebrew title is *tehillim* (meaning "praises"; see note on Ps 145 title), even though many of the psalms are *tephillot* (meaning "prayers"). In fact, one of the first collections included in the book was titled "the prayers of David the son of Jesse" (72:20).

Collection, Arrangement and Date

The Psalter is a collection of collections and represents the final stage in a process that spanned centuries. It was put into its final form by postexilic temple personnel, who completed it probably in the third century B.C. As such, it served as the prayer book (book of prayer, praise and religious instruction) for the second (Zerubbabel's and Herod's) temple and for use in the synagogues. By the first century A.D. it was referred to as the "book of Psalms" (Luke 20:42; Acts 1:20). At that time also Psalms was used as a title for the entire section of the Hebrew OT canon known as the "Writings" (see Luke 24:44).

Many collections preceded this final compilation of the Psalms. In fact, the formation of psalters probably goes back to the early days of the first (Solomon's) temple (or even to the time of David), when the temple liturgy began to take shape. Reference has already been made to "the prayers of David." Additional collections expressly referred to in the present Psalter titles are: (1) the songs and/or psalms "of the sons of Korah" (Ps 42—49; 84—85; 87—88), (2) the psalms and/or songs "of Asaph" (Ps 50; 73—83) and (3) the songs "of Ascents" (Ps 120—134).

Other evidence points to further compilations. Ps 1—41 (Book 1) make frequent use of the divine name *Yahweh* ("the LORD"), while Ps 42—72 (Book 2) make frequent use of *Elohim* ("God"). The reason for the *Elohim* collection in distinction from the *Yahweh* collection remains unexplained, but both of them date, at least essentially in their present form, from the period of the monarchy. Moreover, Ps 93—100 appear to be a traditional collection (see "The LORD reigns" in 93:1; 96:10; 97:1; 99:1). Other apparent groupings include Ps 111—118 (a series of Hallelujah, "Praise the LORD" psalms), Ps 138—145 (all of which include "of David" in their titles) and Ps 146—150 (with their frequent "Praise the LORD"; see NASB marg. note on 111:1). Whether the "Great Hallel" (Ps 120—136) was already a recognized unit is not known. (The seven "penitential psalms" get their name from Christian liturgical usage and so were never a unit in the Jewish Psalter tradition; see introduction to Ps 6.)

In its final edition, the Psalter contained 150 psalms. On this the Septuagint and Hebrew texts agree, though they arrive at this number differently. The Septuagint has an extra psalm at the end (but not numbered separately as Ps 151); it also unites Ps 9—10 (see note on Ps 9) and Ps 114—115 and divides Ps 116 and Ps 147 each into two psalms. Strangely, both the Septuagint and Hebrew texts number Ps 42—43 as two psalms whereas they were evidently originally one (see note on Ps 42—43).

The Psalter was divided into five Books (Ps 1—41; 42—72; 73—89; 90—106; 107—150), and each was provided with an appropriate concluding doxology (see 41:13; 72:18–19; 89:52; 106:48; 150). The first two of these Books, as already noted, were probably preexilic. The division of the remaining psalms into three Books, thus attaining the number five, was possibly in imitation of the five books of Moses (otherwise known simply as the Law). At least one of these divisions (between Ps 106—107) seems arbitrary (see introduction to Ps 107). In spite of this five-book division, the Psalter was clearly thought of as a whole, with an introduction (Ps 1—2) and a conclusion (Ps 146—150). Notes throughout the Psalms give additional indications of conscious arrangement.

Authorship and Titles (or Superscriptions)

Of the 150 psalms, only 34 lack superscriptions of any kind (only 17 in the Septuagint). These so-called "orphan" psalms are found mainly in Books 3–5, where they tend to occur in clusters: Ps 91; 93—97; 99; 104—107; 111—119; 135—137; 146—150. (In Books 1–2, only Ps 1—2; 10; 33; 43; 71 lack titles, and Ps 10; 43 are actually continuations of the preceding psalms.)

The contents of the superscriptions vary but fall into a few broad categories: (1) author, (2) name of collection, (3) type of psalm, (4) musical notations, (5) liturgical notations and (6) brief indications of occasion for composition. For details see notes on the titles of the various psalms.

Students of the Psalms are not agreed on the antiquity and reliability of these superscriptions. That many of them are at least preexilic appears evident from the fact that the Septuagint translators were no longer clear as to their meaning. Furthermore, the practice of attaching titles, including the name of the author, is ancient. On the other hand, comparison between the Septuagint and the Hebrew texts shows that the content of some titles was still subject to change well into the postexilic period. Most discussion centers on categories 1 and 6 above.

As for the superscriptions regarding occasion of composition, many of these brief notations of events read as if they had been taken from 1,2 Samuel. Moreover, they are sometimes not easily correlated with the content of the psalms they head. The suspicion therefore arises that they are later attempts to fit the psalms into the real-life events of history. But then why the limited number of such notations, and why the apparent mismatches? The arguments cut both ways.

Regarding authorship, opinions are even more divided. The notations themselves are ambiguous since the Hebrew phraseology used, meaning in general "belonging to," can also be taken in the sense of "concerning" or "for the use of" or "dedicated to." The name may refer to the title of a collection of psalms that had been gathered under a certain name (as "Of Asaph" or "Of the sons of Korah"). As for Davidic authorship, there can be little doubt that the Psalter contains psalms composed by that noted singer and musician and that there was at one time a "Davidic" psalter. This, however, may have also included psalms written concerning David, or concerning one of the later Davidic kings, or even psalms written in the manner of those he authored. It is also true that the tradition as to which psalms are "Davidic" remains somewhat indefinite, and some "Davidic" psalms seem clearly to reflect later situations (see, e.g., Ps 30 title—but see also note there; and see introduction to Ps 69 and note on Ps 122 title). Moreover, "David" is sometimes used elsewhere as a collective for the kings of his dynasty, and this could also be true in the psalm titles.

The word *Selah* is found in 39 psalms, all but two of which (Ps 140; 143, both "Davidic") are in Books 1–3. It is also found in Hab 3, a psalm-like poem. Suggestions as to its meaning abound, but honesty must confess ignorance. Most likely, it is a liturgical notation. The common suggestions that it calls for a brief musical interlude or for a brief liturgical response by the congregation are plausible (the former may be supported by the Septuagint rendering). In some instances its present placement in the Hebrew text is highly questionable.

Psalm Types

Superscriptions to the Psalms acquaint us with an ancient system of classification: (1) *mizmor* ("psalm"); (2) *Shiggaion* (see note on Ps 7 title); (3) *Mikhtam* (see note on Ps 16 title); (4) *shir* ("song"); (5) *Maskil* (see note on Ps 32 title); (6) *tephillah* ("prayer"); (7) *tehillah* ("praise"); (8) *lehazkir* ("for being remembered"—i.e., before God, a petition); (9) *letodah* ("for praising" or "for giving thanks"); (10) *lelammed* ("for teaching"); and (11) *shir yedidot* ("song of loves"—i.e., a wedding song). The meaning of many of these terms, however, is uncertain. In addition, some titles contain two of these (especially *mizmor* and *shir*), indicating that the types are diversely based and overlapping.

Analysis of content has given rise to a different classification that has proven useful for study of the Psalms. The main types that can be identified are: (1) prayers of the individual (e.g., Ps 3; 7–8); (2) praise from the individual for God's saving help (e.g., Ps 30; 34); (3) prayers of the community (e.g., Ps 12; 44; 79); (4) praise from the community for God's saving help (e.g., Ps 66; 75); (5) confessions of confidence in the Lord (e.g., Ps 11; 16; 52); (6) hymns in praise of God's majesty and virtues (e.g., Ps 8; 19; 29; 65); (7) hymns celebrating God's universal reign (Ps 47; 93—99); (8) songs of Zion, the city of God (Ps 46; 48; 76; 84; 122; 126; 129; 137);

(9) royal psalms — by, for or concerning the king, the Lord's anointed (e.g., Ps 2; 18; 20; 45; 72; 89; 110); (10) pilgrimage songs (Ps 120 — 134); (11) liturgical songs (e.g., Ps 15; 24; 68); (12) didactic (instructional) songs (e.g., Ps 1; 34; 37; 73; 112; 119; 128; 133).

This classification also involves some overlapping. For example, "prayers of the individual" may include prayers of the king (in his special capacity as king) or even prayers of the community speaking in the collective first person singular. Nevertheless, it is helpful to study a psalm in conjunction with others of the same type. Attempts to fix specific liturgical settings for each type have not been very convincing. For those psalms about which something can be said in this regard see the introductions to the individual psalms.

Of all these psalm types, the prayers (both of the individual and of the community) are the most complex. Several modes of speech combine to form these appeals to God: (1) address to God: "O Lord," "my God," "my deliverer"; (2) initial appeal: "Arise," "Answer me," "Help," "Save me"; (3) description of distress: "Many are rising up against me," "[The wicked] attack," "I am in distress"; (4) complaint against God: "Why have You forsaken me?" "How long will You hide Your face from me?"; (5) petition: "Do not be far from me," "Vindicate me"; (6) motivation for God to hear: "for I take refuge in You," "for Your name's sake"; (7) accusation against the adversary: "Whose mouths speak deceit," "Violent men have sought my life" ("the wicked" are often quoted); (8) call for redress: "Let the wicked be put to shame," "Seek out [the wickedness of the wicked]"; (9) claims of innocence: "Vindicate me . . . according to my righteousness and my integrity," "Princes persecute me without cause"; (10) confessions of sin: "I have sinned against You," "I confess my iniquity"; (11) professions of trust: "You are a shield about me," "You will answer me"; (12) vows to praise for deliverance: "We will sing and praise Your power," "My mouth offers praise with joyful lips"; (13) calls to praise: "Magnify the LORD with me," "Sing praise to the LORD"; (14) motivations for praise: "for You have delivered my soul," "for the LORD hears the needy."

Though not all these appear in every prayer, they all belong to the conventions of prayer in the Psalter, with petition itself being but one (usually brief) element among the rest. On the whole they reflect the conventions of the court, the psalmist(s) presenting his/their case before the heavenly King/Judge. When beset by wicked adversaries, the petitioner describes his situation, pleads his innocence ("righteousness"), lodges accusation against his adversaries, and appeals for deliverance and judicial redress. When suffering at the hands of God (when God is his adversary), he confesses his guilt and pleads for mercy. Giving attention to the various modes of speech in the prayers and to their functions in the judicial appeals they present will significantly aid the reader.

Literary Features

The Psalter is from first to last poetry, even though it contains many prayers and not all OT prayers were poetic (see 1 Kin 8:23 – 53; Ezra 9:6 – 15; Neh 9:5 – 37; Dan 9:4 – 19) — nor was all praise poetic, for that matter (see 1 Kin 8:15 – 21). The Psalms are impassioned, vivid and concrete; they are rich in images, in simile and metaphor. Assonance, alliteration and wordplays abound in the Hebrew text. Effective use of repetition and the piling up of synonyms and complements to fill out the picture are characteristic. Key words frequently highlight major themes in prayer or song. Enclosure (repetition of a significant word or phrase at the end that occurs at the beginning) frequently wraps up a composition or a unit within it. The notes on the structure of the individual psalms often call attention to literary frames within which the psalm has been set.

Hebrew poetry lacks rhyme and regular meter. Its most distinctive and pervasive feature is parallelism. Most poetic lines are composed of two (sometimes three) balanced segments (the balance is often loose, with the second segment commonly somewhat shorter than the first). The second segment either echoes (synonymous parallelism), contrasts (antithetic parallelism) or syntactically completes (synthetic parallelism) the first. These three types are generalizations and are not wholly adequate to describe the rich variety that the creativity of the poets has achieved within the basic two-segment line structure. They can serve, however, as rough distinctions that will assist the reader.

Determining where the Hebrew poetic lines or line segments begin or end (scanning) is sometimes an uncertain matter. Even the Septuagint at times scans the lines differently from the way the Hebrew texts now available to us do. It is therefore not surprising that modern translations occasionally differ.

A related problem is the extremely concise, often elliptical writing style of the Hebrew poets. The syntactical connection of words must at times be inferred simply from context. Where more than one possibility

presents itself, the translator is confronted with ambiguity. He is not always sure with which line segment a border word or phrase is to be read.

The stanza structure of Hebrew poetry is also a matter of dispute. Occasionally, recurring refrains mark off stanzas (see Ps 42—43; 57). In Ps 110 two balanced stanzas are divided by their introductory oracles (see also introduction to Ps 132), while Ps 119 devotes eight lines to each letter of the Hebrew alphabet. For the most part, however, no such obvious indicators are present. The NASB has used spaces to mark off poetic paragraphs (called "stanzas" in the notes). Usually this could be done with some confidence, and the reader is advised to be guided by them. But there are a few places where these divisions are questionable—and are challenged in the notes.

Close study of the Psalms discloses that the authors often composed with an overall design in mind. This is true of the alphabetic acrostics, in which the poet devoted to each letter of the Hebrew alphabet one line segment (as in Ps 111—112), or a single line (as in Ps 25; 34; 145), or two lines (as in Ps 37), or eight lines (as in Ps 119). In addition Ps 33; 38; 103 each have 22 lines in the Hebrew, no doubt because of the number of letters in the Hebrew alphabet (see Introduction to Lamentations: Literary Features). The oft-voiced notion that this device was used as a memory aid seems culturally prejudiced and quite unwarranted. Actually people of that time were able to memorize far more readily than most people today. It is much more likely that the alphabet—which was relatively recently invented as a simple system of symbols capable of representing in writing the rich and complex patterns of human speech and therefore of inscribing all that man can put into words (one of the greatest intellectual achievements of all time)—commended itself as a framework on which to hang significant phrases.

Other forms were also used. Ps 44 is a prayer fashioned after the design of a ziggurat (a Babylonian stepped pyramid; see note on Gen 11:4). A sense of symmetry is pervasive. Many Psalms begin and end with the same call to praise ("Praise the Lord," Ps 113; 135; "O LORD, our Lord . . . ," Ps 8). A particularly interesting device is to place a key thematic line at the very center, sometimes constructing the whole or part of the poem around that center (see note on 6:6). Still other design features are pointed out in the notes. The authors of the psalms crafted their compositions very carefully. They were heirs of an ancient art (in many details showing that they had inherited a poetic tradition that goes back hundreds of years), and they developed it to a state of high sophistication. Their works are best appreciated when carefully studied and pondered.

Theology

The Psalter is for the most part a book of prayer and praise. It speaks to God in prayer and it speaks of God in praise—also in professions of faith and trust. Although occasionally didactic (instructional) in form and purpose (teaching the way of godliness), the Psalter is not a catechism of doctrine. Its "theology" is therefore not abstract or systematic but confessional and doxological. So a summation of that "theology" impoverishes it by translating it into an objective mode.

Furthermore, any summation faces a still greater problem. The Psalter is a large collection of independent pieces of many kinds, serving different purposes and written over the course of many centuries. Not only must a brief summary of its "theology" be selective and incomplete; it will also of necessity be somewhat artificial. It will suggest that each psalm reflects or at least presupposes the "theology" outlined, that there is no "theological" tension or progression within the Psalter. Manifestly this is not so.

Still, the final editors of the Psalter were obviously not eclectic in their selection. They knew that many voices from many times spoke here, but none that in their judgment was incompatible with the Law and the Prophets. No doubt they also assumed that each psalm was to be understood in the light of the collection as a whole. That assumption we may share. Hence something, after all, can be said concerning major theological themes that, while admittedly a bit artificial, need not seriously distort and can be helpful to the student of the Psalms.

At the core of the theology of the Psalter is the conviction that the gravitational center of life (of right human understanding, trust, hope, service, morality, adoration), but also of history and of the whole creation (heaven and earth), is God (*Yahweh,* "the LORD"). He is the Great King over all, the One to whom all things are subject. He created all things and preserves them; they are the robe of glory with which He has clothed Himself. Because He ordered them, they have a well-defined and "true" identity (no chaos there). Because He main-

tains them, they are sustained and kept secure from disruption, confusion or annihilation. Because He alone is the sovereign God, they are governed by one hand and held in the service of one divine purpose. Under God creation is a cosmos — an orderly and systematic whole. What we distinguish as "nature" and history had for them one Lord, under whose rule all things worked together. Through the creation the Great King's majestic glory is displayed. He is good (wise, righteous, faithful, amazingly benevolent and merciful — evoking trust), and He is great (His knowledge, thoughts and works are beyond human comprehension — evoking reverent awe). By His good and lordly rule He is shown to be the Holy One.

As the Great King by right of creation and enduring absolute sovereignty, He ultimately will not tolerate any worldly power that opposes or denies or ignores Him. He will come to rule the nations so that all will be compelled to acknowledge Him. This expectation is no doubt the root and broadest scope of the psalmists' long view of the future. Because the Lord is the Great King beyond all challenge, His righteous and peaceable kingdom will come, overwhelming all opposition and purging the creation of all rebellion against His rule — such will be the ultimate outcome of history.

As the Great King on whom all creatures depend, He opposes the "proud," those who rely on their own resources (and/or the gods they have contrived) to work out their own destiny. These are the ones who ruthlessly wield whatever power they possess to attain worldly wealth, status and security; who are a law to themselves and exploit others as they will. In the Psalter, this kind of "pride" is the root of all evil. Those who embrace it, though they may seem to prosper, will be brought down to death, their final end. The "humble," the "poor and needy," those who acknowledge their dependence on the Lord in all things — these are the ones in whom God delights. Hence the "fear of the LORD" — i.e., humble trust in and obedience to the Lord — is the "beginning" of all wisdom (111:10). Ultimately, those who embrace it will inherit the earth. Not even death can hinder their seeing the face of God.

The psalmists' hope for the future — the future of God and His kingdom and the future of the godly — was firm, though somewhat generalized. None of the psalmists gives expression to a two-age vision of the future (the present evil age giving way to a new age of righteousness and peace on the other side of a great eschatological divide). Such a view began to appear in the intertestamental literature — a view that had been foreshadowed by Daniel (see especially 12:2 – 3) and by Isaiah (see 65:17 – 25; 66:22 – 24) — and it later received full expression in the teaching of Jesus and the apostles. But this revelation was only a fuller development consistent with the hopes the psalmists lived by.

Because God is the Great King, He is the ultimate Executor of justice among men (to avenge oneself is an act of the "proud"). God is the court of appeal when persons are threatened or wronged — especially when no earthly court that He has established has jurisdiction (as in the case of international conflicts) or is able to judge (as when one is wronged by public slander) or is willing to act (out of fear or corruption). He is the mighty and faithful Defender of the defenseless and the wronged. He knows every deed and the secrets of every heart. There is no escaping His scrutiny. No false testimony will mislead Him in judgment. And He hears the pleas brought to Him. As the good and faithful Judge, He delivers those who are oppressed or wrongfully attacked and redresses the wrongs committed against them (see note on 5:10). This is the unwavering conviction that accounts for the psalmists' impatient complaints when they boldly, yet as "poor and needy," cry to Him, "Why (have you not yet delivered me)?" "How long, O LORD (before you act)?"

As the Great King over all the earth, the Lord has chosen Israel to be His servant people, His "inheritance" among the nations. He has delivered them by mighty acts out of the hands of the world powers, He has given them a land of their own (territory that He took from other nations to be His own "inheritance" in the earth), and He has united them with Himself in covenant as the initial embodiment of His redeemed kingdom. Thus both their destiny and His honor came to be bound up with this relationship. To them He also gave His word of revelation, which testified of Him, made specific His promises and proclaimed His will. By God's covenant, Israel was to live among the nations, loyal only to her heavenly King. She was to trust solely in His protection, hope in His promises, live in accordance with His will and worship Him exclusively. She was to sing His praises to the whole world — which in a special sense revealed Israel's anticipatory role in the evangelization of the nations.

As the Great King, Israel's covenant Lord, God chose David to be His royal representative on earth. In this capacity, David was the Lord's "servant" — i.e., a member of the Great King's administration. The Lord Himself

anointed him and adopted him as His royal "son" to rule in His name. Through him God made His people secure in the promised land and subdued all the powers that threatened them. What is more, He covenanted to preserve the Davidic dynasty. Henceforth the kingdom of God on earth, while not dependent on the house of David, was linked to it by God's decision and commitment. In its continuity and strength lay Israel's security and hope as she faced a hostile world. And since the Davidic kings were God's royal representatives in the earth, in concept seated at God's right hand (110:1), the scope of their rule was potentially worldwide (see Ps 2).

The Lord's anointed, however, was more than a warrior king. He was to be endowed by God to govern His people with godlike righteousness: to deliver the oppressed, defend the defenseless, suppress the wicked, and thus bless the nation with internal peace and prosperity. He was also an intercessor with God in behalf of the nation, the builder and maintainer of the temple (as God's earthly palace and the nation's house of prayer) and the foremost voice calling the nation to worship the Lord. It is perhaps with a view to these last duties that he is declared to be not only king, but also "priest" (see Ps 110 and notes).

As the Great King, Israel's covenant Lord, God (who had chosen David and his dynasty to be His royal representatives) also chose Jerusalem (the City of David) as His own royal city, the earthly seat of His throne. Thus Jerusalem (Zion) became the earthly capital (and symbol) of the kingdom of God. There in His palace (the temple) He sat enthroned among His people. There His people could meet with Him to bring their prayers and praise, and to see His power and glory. From there He brought salvation, dispensed blessings and judged the nations. And with Him as the city's great Defender, Jerusalem was the secure citadel of the kingdom of God, the hope and joy of God's people.

God's goodwill and faithfulness toward His people were most strikingly symbolized by His pledged presence among them at His temple in Jerusalem, the "city of the great King" (48:2). But no manifestation of His benevolence was greater than His readiness to forgive the sins of those who humbly confessed them and whose hearts showed Him that their repentance was genuine and that their professions of loyalty to Him had integrity. As they anguished over their own sinfulness, the psalmists remembered the ancient testimony of their covenant Lord: I am *Yahweh* ("the LORD"), "the LORD God, compassionate and gracious, slow to anger, and abounding in lovingkindness and truth, who keeps lovingkindness for thousands, forgives inquity, transgression and sin" (Ex 34:6–7). Only so did they dare to submit to Him as His people, to "fear" Him (see 130:3–4).

Unquestionably the supreme kingship of Yahweh (in which He displays His transcendent greatness and goodness) is the most basic metaphor and most pervasive theological concept in the Psalter—as in the OT generally. It provides the fundamental perspective in which man is to view Himself, the whole creation, events in "nature" and history, and the future. The whole creation is His one kingdom. To be a creature in the world is to be a part of His kingdom and under His rule. To be a human being in the world is to be dependent on and responsible to Him. To proudly deny that fact is the root of all wickedness—the wickedness that now pervades the world.

God's election of Israel and subsequently of David and Zion, together with the giving of His word, represent the renewed inbreaking of God's righteous kingdom into this world of rebellion and evil. It initiates the great divide between the righteous nation and the wicked nations, and on a deeper level between the righteous and the wicked, a more significant distinction that cuts even through Israel. In the end this divine enterprise will triumph. Human pride will be humbled, and wrongs will be redressed. The humble will be given the whole earth to possess, and the righteous and peaceable kingdom of God will come to full realization. These theological themes, of course, have profound religious and moral implications. Of these, too, the psalmists spoke.

One question that ought yet to be addressed is: Do the Psalms speak of the Christ? Yes, but in a variety of ways—and not as the prophets do. The Psalter is not a book of prophetic oracles and was never numbered among the prophetic books.

When the Psalms speak of the king on David's throne, they speak of the king who is being crowned (as in Ps 2; 72; 110—though some think 110 is an exception) or is reigning (as in Ps 45) at the time. They proclaim his status as God's anointed and declare what God will accomplish through him and his dynasty. Thus they also speak of the sons of David to come—and in the exile and the postexilic era, when there was no reigning king, they spoke to Israel only of the great Son of David whom the prophets had announced as the

one in whom God's covenant with David would yet be fulfilled. So the NT quotes these psalms as testimonies to Christ, which in their unique way they are. In Him they are truly fulfilled.

When in the Psalms righteous sufferers — who are "righteous" because they are innocent, not having provoked or wronged their adversaries, and because they are among the "humble" who trust in the Lord — cry out to God in their distress (as in Ps 22; 69), they give voice to the sufferings of God's servants in a hostile and evil world.

These cries became the prayers of God's oppressed "saints," and as such they were taken up into Israel's book of prayers. When Christ came in the flesh, He identified Himself with God's "humble" people in the world. He became for them God's righteous servant par excellence, and He shared their sufferings at the hands of evil men. Thus these prayers became His prayers also — uniquely His prayers. In Him the suffering and deliverance of which these prayers speak are fulfilled (though they continue to be the prayers also of those who take up their cross and follow Him).

Similarly, in speaking of God's covenant people, of the city of God, and of the temple in which God dwells, the Psalms ultimately speak of Christ's church. The Psalter is not only the prayer book of the second temple; it is also the enduring prayer book of the people of God. Now, however, it must be used in the light of the new era of redemption that dawned with the first coming of the Messiah and that will be consummated at His second coming.

The following expressions occur often in the Psalms:

Selah	May mean *Pause, Crescendo* or *Musical Interlude*
Maskil	Possibly, *Contemplative*, or *Didactic*, or *Skillful Psalm*
Mikhtam	Possibly, *Epigrammatic Poem*, or *Atonement Psalm*
Sheol	The nether world

BOOK 1

Psalm 1

1 How blessed is the man who [a]does
not walk in the [b]counsel of the
wicked,
Nor stand in the [1][c]path of sinners,
Nor [d]sit in the seat of scoffers!
2 But his [a]delight is [b]in the law of the
LORD,
And in His law he meditates [c]day and
[d]night.
3 He will be like [a]a tree *firmly* planted
by [1]streams of water,
Which yields its fruit in its season
And its [2]leaf does not wither;
And [3]in whatever he does, [b]he
prospers.

4 The wicked are not so,
But they are like [a]chaff which the
wind drives away.
5 Therefore [a]the wicked will not stand
in the [b]judgment,
Nor sinners in [c]the assembly of the
righteous.
6 For the LORD [1][a]knows the way of the
righteous,
But the way of [b]the wicked will
perish.

Psalm 2

1 Why are [a]the [1]nations in an uproar
And the peoples [b]devising a vain
thing?
2 The [a]kings of the earth take their
stand
And the rulers take counsel together
[b]Against the LORD and against His
[1][c]Anointed, saying,

1:1 [1]Or *way* [a]Prov 4:14 [b]Ps 5:9, 10; 10:2-11; 36:1-4 [c]Ps 17:4; 119:104 [d]Ps 26:4, 5; Jer 15:17
2 [a]Ps 119:14, 16, 35 [b]Josh 1:8 [c]Ps 25:5 [d]Ps 63:5, 6
3 [1]Or *canals* [a]Ps 92:12-14; Jer 17:8; Ezek 19:10
3 [2]Or *foliage* [3]Or *all that he does prospers* [b]Gen 39:2, 3, 23; Ps 128:2
4 [a]Job 21:18; Ps 35:5; Is 17:13
5 [a]Ps 5:5 [b]Ps 9:7, 8, 16 [c]Ps 89:5, 7
6 [1]Or *approves* or *has regard to* [a]Ps 37:18; Nah 1:7; John 10:14; 2 Tim 2:19 [b]Ps 9:5, 6; 11:6
2:1 [1]Or *Gentiles* [a]Ps 46:6; 83:2-5; Acts 4:25, 26 [b]Ps 21:11
2 [1]Or *Messiah* [a]Ps 48:4-6 [b]Ps 74:18, 23 [c]John 1:41

Ps 1 Author and date unknown. Godly wisdom here declares the final outcome of the two "ways": "the path of sinners" (v. 1) and "the way of the righteous" (v. 6). See 34:19–22; 37; essay, p. 689. As an introduction to the book, this psalm reminds the reader (1) that those of whom the Psalms speak (using various terms) as the people of God, those whom He receives in His presence and favors with His salvation and blessing, must be characterized by righteousness—sinners have no place among them (v. 5; see Ps 15; 24)—and (2) that the godly piety that speaks in the Psalms is a faithful response to God's revealed (and written) directives for life—which is the path that leads to blessedness.
1:1 Speaks progressively of association with the ungodly and participation in their ungodly ways. *Blessed.* The happy condition of those who revere the Lord and do His will (see 94:12; 112:1; 119:1–2; 128:1; Prov 29:18; cf. Ps 41:1; 106:3; Prov 14:21; Is 56:2), who put their trust in Him (see 40:4; 84:5,12; 144:15; 146:5; Prov 16:20; Is 30:18; Jer 17:7; cf. Ps 2:12; 34:8), and so are blessed by God (see especially 41:1–3; 144:12–14; see also Matt 5:3–12). The Psalter begins by proclaiming the blessedness of the godly and ends by calling all living things to praise God in His earthly and heavenly sanctuaries (Ps 150). *walk in.* Order his life according to. *counsel.* Deliberations and advice (see Prov 1:10–19). *stand.* Station oneself. *sinners.* See v. 5; those for whom evil is habitual, for whom wickedness is a way of life. *sit.* Settle oneself. *scoffers!* Those who ridicule God and defiantly reject His law (see Prov 1:22).
1:2 *in His law he meditates.* Seeking guidance for life in God's law rather than in the deliberations of the wicked. *day and night.* See Josh 1:8.
1:3 *like a tree . . . does not wither.* See Jer 17:8; a simile of the blessedness of the righteous. Such a tree withstands the buffeting of the winds and, flourishing, it blesses man, animals and birds with its unfailing fruit and shade.
1:4 *like chaff . . . drives away.* A simile of the wretchedness of the wicked. Chaff is carried away by the lightest wind, and its removal brings about cleansing by extracting what is utterly useless (see note on Ruth 1:22).
1:5 *will not stand in the judgment.* Will not be able to withstand God's wrath when He judges (see 76:7; 130:3; Ezra 9:15; Mal 3:2; Matt 25:31–46; Rev 6:17). *assembly.* The worshiping assembly at God's sanctuary (as in 22:25; 26:12; 35:18; 40:9–10; 111:1; 149:1; see Ps 15; 24). *righteous.* One of several terms in the OT for God's people; it presents them as those who honor God and order their lives in all things according to His will. In every human relationship they faithfully fulfill the obligations that the relationship entails, remembering that power and authority (of whatever sort: domestic, social, political, economic, religious, intellectual) are to be used to bless, not to exploit.
1:6 *way . . . way.* Implicit in the destinies of the two lifestyles are also the destinies of those who choose them.
Ps 2 Author and date unknown (Peter and John ascribed it to David in Acts 4:25—possibly in accordance with the Jewish practice of honoring David as the primary author of the Psalter). A royal psalm, it was originally composed for the coronation of Davidic kings, in light of the Lord's covenant with David (see 2 Sam 7). Later, prophetic words of judgment against the house of David and announcements of God's future redemption of His people through an exalted royal son of David highlighted the Messianic import of this psalm. As the second half of a two-part introduction to the Psalms, it proclaims the blessedness of all who acknowledge the lordship of God and His anointed and "take refuge in Him" (v. 12; see note on 1:1)—as does the godly piety that speaks in the Psalms. This psalm is frequently quoted in the NT, where it is applied to Christ as the great Son of David and God's Anointed.
2:1–3 The nations rebel. In the ancient Near East the coronation of a new king was often the occasion for the revolt of peoples and kings who had been subject to the crown. The newly anointed king is here pictured as ruler over an empire.
2:1–2 For a NT application see Acts 4:25–28.
2:1 *Why . . . ?* A rhetorical question that implies "How dare they!"
2:2 *LORD . . . His Anointed.* To rebel against the Lord's Anointed is also to rebel against the One who anointed Him. *Anointed.* The psalm refers to the Davidic king and is ultimately fulfilled in Christ. The English word "Messiah" comes from the Hebrew word for "anointed one," and the English word "Christ" from the Greek word for "anointed one."

3 "Let us [a]tear their fetters apart
And cast away their cords from us!"

4 He who [1]sits in the heavens [a]laughs,
The Lord [b]scoffs at them.
5 Then He will speak to them in His
[a]anger
And [b]terrify them in His fury, saying,
6 "But as for Me, I have [1]installed [a]My
King
Upon Zion, [b]My holy mountain."

7 "I will surely tell of the [1]decree of the
LORD:
He said to Me, 'You are [a]My Son,
Today I have begotten You.
8 'Ask of Me, and [a]I will surely give [b]the
[1]nations as Your inheritance,
And the *very* [c]ends of the earth as
Your possession.
9 'You shall [1a]break them with a [2]rod of
iron,
You shall [b]shatter them like
[3]earthenware.'"

10 Now therefore, O kings, [a]show
discernment;
Take warning, O [1]judges of the earth.
11 [1]Worship the LORD with [2a]reverence
And rejoice with [b]trembling.
12 [1]Do homage to [a]the Son, that He not
become angry, and you perish *in*
the way,
For [b]His wrath may [2]soon be kindled.
How blessed are all who [c]take refuge
in Him!

Psalm 3

A Psalm of David, when [†]he fled from
Absalom his son.

1 O LORD, how [a]my adversaries have
increased!
Many are rising up against me.
2 Many are saying [1]of my soul,
"There is no [2a]deliverance for him
in God." [3]Selah.

3 But You, O LORD, are [a]a shield about
me,
My [b]glory, and the One who [c]lifts my
head.
4 I was crying to the LORD with my
voice,

3 [a]Jer 5:5
4 [1]Or *is enthroned* [a]Ps 37:13 [b]Ps 59:8
5 [a]Ps 21:8, 9; 76:7 [b]Ps 78:49, 50
6 [1]Or *consecrated* [a]Ps 45:6 [b]Ps 48:1, 2
7 [1]Or *decree: The LORD said to Me* [a]Acts 13:33; Heb 1:5; 5:5
8 [1]Or *Gentiles* [a]Ps 21:1, 2 [b]Ps 22:27 [c]Ps 67:7
9 [1]Another reading is *rule* [2]Or *scepter* or *staff* [3]Lit *potter's ware* [a]Ps 89:23; 110:5, 6; Rev 2:26, 27; 12:5; 19:15 [b]Ps 28:5; 52:5; 72:4
10 [1]Or *leaders* [a]Prov 8:15; 27:11
11 [1]Or *Serve* [2]Or *fear* [a]Ps 5:7
11 [b]Ps 119:119, 120
12 [1]Lit *Kiss;* some ancient versions read *Do homage purely,* or, *Lay hold of instruction* [2]Or *quickly, suddenly, easily* [a]Ps 2:7 [b]Rev 6:16, 17 [c]Ps 5:11; 34:22
3:1 [†]2 Sam 15:13-17, 29 [a]2 Sam 15:12; Ps 69:4
2 [1]Or *to* [2]Or *salvation* [3]*Selah* may mean: *Pause, Crescendo* or *Musical interlude* [a]Ps 22:7, 8; 71:11
3 [a]Ps 5:12; 28:7 [b]Ps 62:7 [c]Ps 9:13; 27:6

2:4–6 The Lord mocks the rebels. With derisive laughter the Lord meets the confederacy of rebellious world powers with the sovereign declaration that it is He who has established the Davidic king in His own royal city of Zion (Jerusalem).

2:4 See 59:8.

2:5 *anger . . . fury.* God's anger is always an expression of His righteousness (see 7:11; see also note on 4:1).

2:6 *holy mountain.* The site of the Jerusalem temple (see 2 Chr 33:15); see also 3:4; 15:1; 43:3; 99:9 ("holy hill").

2:7–9 The Lord's Anointed proclaims the Lord's coronation decree. For NT application to Jesus' resurrection see Acts 13:33; to His superiority over angels see Heb 1:5; to His appointment as high priest see Heb 5:5.

2:7 *Son . . . begotten You.* In the ancient Near East the relationship between a great king and one of his subject kings, who ruled by his authority and owed him allegiance, was expressed not only by the words "lord" and "servant" but also by "father" and "son." The Davidic king was the Lord's "servant" and His "son" (2 Sam 7:5,14).

2:8 *Your inheritance.* Your domain—as the promised land was the Lord's "inheritance" (Ex 15:17; see Josh 22:19; Ps 28:9; 79:1; 82:8). *ends of the earth.* Ultimately the rule of the Lord's Anointed will extend as far as the rule of God Himself.

2:9 According to Rev 12:5; 19:15 this word will be fulfilled in the triumphant reign of Christ; in Rev 2:26–27 Christ declares that He will appoint those who remain faithful to Him to share in His subjugating rule over the nations. *shatter them like earthenware.* See Jer 19:11.

2:10–12 The rebellious rulers are warned.

2:11 *rejoice.* Hail the Lord as King with joy. *trembling.* Awe and reverence.

2:12 *Do homage to.* Lit. "Kiss," as a sign of submission (see 1 Sam 10:1; 1 Kin 19:18; Hos 13:2; see also note on Gen 41:40). Submission to an Assyrian king was expressed by kissing his feet. *perish in the way.* See 1:6 and note. *blessed.* See 1:1 and note.

Ps 3 Though threatened by many foes, the psalmist prays confidently to the Lord. Ps 3 and 4 are linked by references to glory (see v. 3; 4:2) and to the psalmist's sleep at night (see v. 5; 4:8). In v. 5 David speaks of the assurance of his waking in the morning because the Lord will keep him while he sleeps; in 4:8 he speaks of the inner quietness with which he goes to sleep because of the Lord's care. This juxtaposition of prayers with references to waking (morning) and sleeping (evening) at the beginning of the Psalter suggests that God's faithful care sustains the godly day and night whatever the need or circumstances, many of which will be mentioned in this book of prayers.

3 title *when he fled.* See 2 Sam 15:13–17:22. References to events in David's life stand in the superscriptions of 13 psalms (3; 7; 18; 34; 51–52; 54; 56–57; 59–60; 63; 142), all but one (Ps 142) in Books 1 and 2. See Introduction: Authorship and Titles (or Superscriptions).

3:1–2 David's need: threatened by many foes.

3:2 See 22:7–8; 71:10–11. The psalmists frequently quote their wicked oppressors in order to portray how they mock (see note on 1:1) God and His servants (see note on 10:11). *Selah.* A word of uncertain meaning, occurring frequently in the Psalms—possibly a musical term; see Introduction: Authorship and Titles (or Superscriptions).

3:3–4 David's confidence in God, who does not fail to answer his prayers.

3:3 *shield.* That one's king is his shield (protector) was a common concept in ancient Israel (see 7:10; 47:9; 59:11; 84:9; 89:18; Gen 15:1). That the Lord is the shield of His people is frequently asserted (see 84:11; 91:4; 115:9–11; Deut 33:29; Prov 30:5) or claimed (see 18:2,30; 28:7; 33:20; 119:114; 144:2). *My glory.* The psalmist rejoices in the Lord as his royal provider and protector (see note on 2:11). *lifts my head.* In victory over his enemies (see 110:7).

And He [a]answered me from [b]His
holy [1]mountain. Selah.
5 [1]I [a]lay down and slept;
I awoke, for the LORD sustains me.
6 I will [a]not be afraid of ten thousands
of people
Who have [b]set themselves against me
round about.

7 [a]Arise, O LORD; [b]save me, O my God!
For You [1]have [c]smitten all my enemies
on the [2]cheek;
You [3]have [d]shattered the teeth of the
wicked.
8 [1a]Salvation belongs to the LORD;
Your [b]blessing [2]*be* upon Your
people! Selah.

Psalm 4

[†]For the choir director; on stringed instruments.
A Psalm of David.

1 [a]Answer me when [b]I call, O God [1]of
my righteousness!
You have [2c]relieved me in my distress;
Be [d]gracious to me and [e]hear my
prayer.
2 O sons of men, how long will [a]my
[1]honor become [b]a reproach?
How long will you love [c]what is
worthless and aim at [d]deception?
[2]Selah.
3 But know that the LORD has [1a]set
apart the [b]godly man for Himself;
The LORD [c]hears when I call to Him.

4 [1a]Tremble, [2b]and do not sin;
[3c]Meditate in your heart upon your
bed, and be still. Selah.
5 Offer [1]the [a]sacrifices of
righteousness,
And [b]trust in the LORD.

6 Many are saying, "[a]Who will show us
any good?"
[b]Lift up the light of Your countenance
upon us, O LORD!
7 You have put [a]gladness in my
heart,
More than when their grain and new
wine abound.

4 [1]Or *hill* [a]Ps 4:3; 34:4 [b]Ps 2:6; 15:1; 43:3 **5** [1]Or *As for me, I* [a]Lev 26:6; Ps 4:8; Prov 3:24 **6** [a]Ps 23:4; 27:3 [b]Ps 118:10-13 **7** [1]Or *smite* [2]Or *jaw* [3]Or *shatter* [a]Ps 7:6 [b]Ps 6:4; 22:21 [c]Job 16:10 [d]Ps 57:4; 58:6 **8** [1]Or *Deliverance* [2]Or *is* [a]Ps 28:8; 35:3; Is 43:11 [b]Ps 29:11 **4:1** [†]I.e. Belonging to the choir director's anthology [1]I.e. who maintains my right [2]Lit *made room for* [a]Ps 3:4; 17:6 [b]Ps 18:6 [c]Ps 18:18, 19 [d]Ps 25:16 [e]Ps 17:6; 39:12

2 [1]Or *glory* [2]*Selah* may mean: *Pause, Crescendo* or *Musical interlude* [a]Ps 3:3 [b]Ps 69:7-10, 19, 20 [c]Ps 12:2; 31:6 [d]Ps 31:18 **3** [1]Another reading is *dealt wonderfully with* [a]Ps 135:4 [b]Ps 31:23; 50:5; 79:2 [c]Ps 6:8, 9; 17:6 **4** [1]I.e. with anger or fear [2]Or *but* [3]Lit *Speak* [a]Ps 99:1 [b]Ps 119:11; Eph 4:26 [c]Ps 77:6 **5** [1]Or *righteous sacrifices* [a]Deut 33:19; Ps 51:19 [b]Ps 37:3, 5; 62:8 **6** [a]Job 7:7; 9:25 [b]Num 6:26; Ps 80:3, 7, 19 **7** [a]Ps 97:11, 12; Is 9:3; Acts 14:17

3:4 *holy mountain.* The place of the Lord's sanctuary, the earthly counterpart of His heavenly throne room (see note on 2:6).

3:5–6 David's sense of security.

3:5 Even while his own watchfulness is surrendered to sleep, the watchful Lord preserves him (see 4:8).

3:7–8 David's prayer.

3:7 *Arise . . . save.* Hebrew idiom frequently prefaces an imperative calling for immediate action with the call to arise (see Ex 12:31, "Rise up"; Deut 2:13; Judg 7:9, "Arise"). In poetry the two imperatives of the idiom are often distributed between the two halves of the poetic line. Hence the psalmist's prayer is: "Arise (and) save me." *LORD . . . my God.* That is, LORD my God; the two elements of a compound divine name are also frequently distributed between the two halves of a poetic line. *shattered the teeth.* Probably likening the enemies to wild animals (see note on 7:2).

3:8 *Salvation belongs to the LORD.* A common feature in the prayers of the Psalter is a concluding expression of confidence that the prayer will be or has been heard (as in 6:8–10; 7:10–17; 10:16–18; 12:7; 13:5–6 and often elsewhere; see note on 12:5–6). Here David's confidence becomes a testimony to God's people. *Your blessing be upon Your people!* See 25:22; 28:8–9; 51:18. The psalmists stood before God, the royal King, as His servants responsible for the well-being of His people.

Ps 4 Perhaps a prayer for relief when some calamity (possibly drought; see v. 7) has fallen and many are turning from the Lord to the gods of Canaan, from whom they hope to receive better. See introduction to Ps 3.

4 title See Hab 3:19. *For the choir director.* Probably a liturgical notation, indicating either that the psalm was to be added to the collection of works to be used by the choir director in Israel's worship services, or that when the psalm was used in the temple worship it was to be spoken by the leader of the Levitical choir—or by the choir itself (see 1 Chr 23:5,30; 25; Neh 11:17). In this liturgical activity the Levites functioned as representatives of the worshiping congregation. Following their lead the people probably responded with "Amen" and "Praise the LORD" (Hallelujah); see 1 Chr 16:36; Neh 5:13; cf. 1 Cor 14:16; Rev 5:14; 7:12; 19:4. *on stringed instruments.* See Ps 6; 54–55; 61; 67; 76 titles. This is a liturgical notation, indicating that the Levites (see previous note) were to accompany the psalm with harp and lyre (see 1 Chr 23:5; 25:1,3,6; cf. Ps 33:2; 43:4; 71:22; see also notes on Ps 39; 42 titles).

4:1 Initial request to be heard. *You have relieved me.* Lit. "You have made a spacious place for me" (see 18:19 and note).

4:2–3 David rebukes those who turn away from his God to seek relief from the counterfeit gods; he assures them that the Lord will hear him.

4:2 *how long . . . ?* See Introduction: Theology; see also note on 6:3. *my honor.* Or "my glory." David's special relationship with the Lord is the source of his glory—or perhaps he here speaks directly of God ("my Glorious One become a reproach"). *Selah.* See note on 3:2; see also Introduction: Authorship and Titles (or Superscriptions).

4:3 *godly.* Hebrew *ḥasid,* which occurs 26 times in the Psalms (once of God: 145:17, "kind"; cf. 18:25) and is usually rendered (in the plural) in the NASB as "godly ones." It is one of several Hebrew words for God's people, referring to them as people who are or should be devoted to God and faithful to Him.

4:4–5 An exhortation not to give way to exasperation or anxiety (see NASB marg.) but to look to the Lord.

4:4 *Tremble, and do not sin.* Paul uses these words in a different context (see Eph 4:26).

4:6 In the face of widespread uncertainty, David prays for the Lord to bless. *Who . . . ?* Which of the gods . . . ? *countenance upon us.* See note on 13:1; a common expression for favor, reminiscent of the Aaronic benediction (see Num 6:25–26).

4:7–8 David's confidence (see note on 3:8).

4:7 *heart.* In Biblical language the center of the human spirit, from which spring emotions, thought, motivations, courage and action—"the springs of life" (Prov 4:23).

8 In peace I will [1]both [a]lie down and
sleep,
For You alone, O LORD, make me to
[b]dwell in safety.

Psalm 5

For the choir director; for [†]flute accompaniment.
A Psalm of David.

1 [a]Give ear to my words, O LORD,
Consider my [1][b]groaning.
2 Heed [a]the sound of my cry for help,
[b]my King and my God,
For to You I pray.
3 In the morning, O LORD, [1]You will hear
my voice;
In the [a]morning I will order *my*
[2]*prayer* to You and *eagerly* [b]watch.

4 For You are not a God [a]who takes
pleasure in wickedness;
[b]No evil [1]dwells with You.
5 The [a]boastful shall not [b]stand before
Your eyes;
You [c]hate all who do iniquity.
6 You [a]destroy those who speak
falsehood;
The LORD abhors [b]the man of
bloodshed and deceit.
7 But as for me, [a]by Your abundant
lovingkindness I will enter Your
house,
[1]At Your holy temple I will [b]bow in
[c]reverence for You.

8 O LORD, [a]lead me [b]in Your
righteousness [c]because of [1]my foes;
Make Your way [2]straight before me.
9 There is [a]nothing [1]reliable in [2]what
they say;
Their [b]inward part is destruction *itself*.
Their [c]throat is an open grave;
They [3]flatter with their tongue.
10 Hold them guilty, O God;
[a]By their own devices let them fall!
In the multitude of their
transgressions [b]thrust them out,
For they are [c]rebellious against You.

11 But let all who [a]take refuge in You [b]be
glad,
Let them ever sing for joy;
And [1]may You [c]shelter them,
That those who [d]love Your name may
exult in You.

8 [1]Or *at the same time* [a]Job 11:19; Ps 3:5 [b]Lev 25:18; Deut 12:10; Ps 16:9
5:1 [†]Heb *Nehiloth* [1]Or *meditation* [a]Ps 54:2 [b]Ps 104:34
2 [a]Ps 140:6 [b]Ps 84:3
3 [1]Or *May You hear* [2]Or sacrifice [a]Ps 88:13 [b]Ps 130:5
4 [1]Lit *sojourns* [a]Ps 11:5; 34:16 [b]Ps 92:15
5 [a]Ps 73:3; 75:4 [b]Ps 1:5 [c]Ps 11:5; 45:7
6 [a]Ps 52:4, 5 [b]Ps 55:23
7 [1]Or *Toward* [a]Ps 69:13 [b]Ps 138:2 [c]Ps 115:11, 13
8 [1]Or *those who lie in wait for me* [2]Or *smooth* [a]Ps 31:3 [b]Ps 31:1 [c]Ps 27:11
9 [1]Or *true* [2]Lit *his mouth* [3]Or *make their tongue smooth* [a]Ps 52:3 [b]Ps 7:14 [c]Rom 3:13
10 [a]Ps 9:16 [b]Ps 36:12 [c]Ps 107:10, 11
11 [1]Or *You shelter* [a]Ps 2:12 [b]Ps 33:1; 64:10 [c]Ps 12:7 [d]Ps 69:36

4:8 See 3:5–6. *In peace.* Without anxiety.
Ps 5 This morning prayer, perhaps offered at the time of the morning sacrifice, is the psalmist's cry for help when his enemies spread malicious lies to destroy him.
5 title *For the choir director.* See note on Ps 4 title. *flute.* The Hebrew for this word occurs only here; meaning uncertain.
5:1–3 Initial appeal to be heard.
5:2 *King.* See Introduction: Theology.
5:4–6 An appeal to the righteousness of God's rule over mankind.
5:5 *The boastful.* See note on 31:23.
5:7–8 The psalmist presents his plea to the Lord in humble reverence (v. 7), trusting in the Lord's great mercy (v. 7) and righteousness (v. 8).
5:7 *abundant lovingkindness.* See note on 6:4.
5:8 *lead me.* As a shepherd (see 23:3). *Your righteousness.* Very often the "righteousness" of God in the Psalms (and frequently elsewhere in the OT) refers to the faithfulness with which He acts. This faithfulness is in full accordance with His commitments (both expressed and implied) to His people and with His status as the divine King—to whom the powerless may look for protection, the oppressed for redress and the needy for help. *Make Your way straight* . May the way down which You lead me be straight, level and smooth, free from obstacles and temptations. The psalmist prays that God will so direct him that his enemies will have no grounds for their malicious accusations (see 25:4; 27:11; 139:24; 143:8–10).
5:9–10 Accusation (a common element in the prayers of the Psalter) and call for redress.
5:9 *what they say.* The most frequent weapon used against the psalmists is the tongue (for a striking example see Ps 12; see also note on 10:7). The psalmists experienced that the tongue is as deadly as the sword (see 57:4; 64:3–4). Perhaps appeals to God against those who maliciously wield the tongue are frequent in the Psalms because only in God's courtroom can a person experience redress for such attacks. *inward part.* See note on 4:7. *throat . . . grave.* See note on 49:14. *they flatter.* For the plots and intrigues of enemies, usually involving lies to discredit the king and bring him down, see Ps 17; 25; 27–28; 31; 35; 41; 52; 54–57; 59; 63–64; 71; 86; 109; 140–141—all ascribed to David. Frequently such attacks came when the king was "low" and seemingly abandoned by God (as in Ps 25; 35; 41; 71; 86; 109). In that case he was viewed as no longer fit to be king—God was no longer with him (and so he could no longer secure the safety of the nation; see 1 Sam 8:20; 11:12; 12:12; 25:28; 2 Sam 3:18; 7:9–11). In any event, he was an easy prey (see 3:2; 22:7–8; 71:11). See note on 86:17. See also Paul's use of this verse in Rom 3:13.
5:10 The presence of so-called "imprecations" (curses) in the Psalms has occasioned endless discussion and has caused many Christians to wince, in view of Jesus' instructions to turn the other cheek and to pray for one's enemies (see Matt 5:39,44), and His own example on the cross (see Luke 23:34). Actually, these "imprecations" are not that at all; rather, they are appeals to God to redress wrongs perpetrated against the psalmists by imposing penalties commensurate with the violence done (see 28:4)—in accordance also with normal judicial procedure in human courts (see Deut 25:1–3). The psalmists knew that he who has been wronged is not to right that wrong by his own hand but is to leave redress to the Lord, who says, "Vengeance is Mine, and retribution" (Deut 32:35; see Prov 20:22; Rom 12:19). Therefore they appeal their cases to the divine Judge (see Jer 15:15). *thrust them out.* From God's presence, thus from the source of blessing and life (see Gen 3:23). *rebellious against You.* By their attacks on the psalmist.
5:11 The psalmist expands his prayer to include all the godly (see note on 3:8). *Your name.* The name of the Lord is the manifestation of His character (see notes on Ex 3:14–15; 34:6–7). It has no separate existence apart from the Lord, but is synonymous with the Lord Himself in His gracious manifestation and accessibility to His people. Hence the Jerusalem

12 For it is You who [a]blesses the
righteous man, O LORD,
You [b]surround him with favor as with
a shield.

Psalm 6

For the choir director; with stringed instruments, †upon an eight-string lyre. A Psalm of David.

1 O LORD, [a]do not rebuke me in Your
anger,
Nor chasten me in Your wrath.
2 Be gracious to me, O LORD, for I *am*
[a]pining away;
[b]Heal me, O LORD, for [c]my bones are
dismayed.
3 And my [a]soul is greatly dismayed;
But You, O LORD—[b]how long?

4 Return, O LORD, [a]rescue my [1]soul;
Save me because of Your
lovingkindness.
5 For [a]there is no [1]mention of You in
death;
In [2]Sheol who will give You thanks?

6 I am [a]weary with my sighing;
Every night I make my bed swim,
I dissolve my couch with [b]my tears.
7 My [a]eye has wasted away with grief;
It has become old because of all my
adversaries.

8 [a]Depart from me, all you who do
iniquity,
For the LORD [b]has heard the voice of
my weeping.

12 [a]Ps 29:11 [b]Ps 32:7, 10 **6:1** †Or *according to a lower octave* (Heb *Sheminith*) [a]Ps 38:1; 118:18 **2** [a]Ps 102:4, 11 [b]Ps 41:4; 147:3; Hos 6:1 [c]Ps 22:14; 31:10 **3** [a]Ps 88:3; John 12:27 [b]Ps 90:13 **4** [1]Or *life* [a]Ps 17:13 **5** [1]Or *remembrance* [2]I.e. the nether world [a]Ps 30:9; 88:10-12; 115:17; Eccl 9:10; Is 38:18 **6** [a]Ps 69:3 [b]Ps 42:3 **7** [a]Job 17:7; Ps 31:9; 38:10 **8** [a]Ps 119:115; Matt 7:23; Luke 13:27 [b]Ps 3:4; 28:6

temple is the earthly residence of His name among His people (see 74:7; Deut 12:5,11; 2 Sam 7:13), and His people can pray to Him by calling on His name (see 79:6; 80:18; 99:6; 105:1; 116:4,13,17). The name of the Lord protects (see 20:1; Prov 18:10); the Lord saves by His name (see 54:1); and His saving acts testify that His name is near (see 52:9). Accordingly, the godly "trust in" His name (20:7; 33:21), hope in His name (see 52:9), "sing praise" to His name (7:17; 9:2; 18:49) and "rejoice in" His name (89:16). Both the "love" and the "fear" that belong alone to God are similarly directed toward His name (love: 69:36; 119:132; fear: 61:5; 86:11; 102:15).

5:12 See note on 3:8. *righteous.* See note on 1:5.

Ps 6 A prayer in time of severe illness, an occasion seized upon by David's enemies to vent their animosity. In early Christian liturgical tradition it was numbered with the seven penitential psalms (the others: Ps 32; 38; 51; 102; 130; 143).

6 title See note on Ps 4 title. *upon.* Represents a Hebrew preposition of varied usage such as "on" and "according to" (also found in the titles of Ps 8; 12; 46; 53; 81; 84; 88). *eight-string lyre.* Occurs also in Ps 12 title and in 1 Chr 15:21.

6:1–3 Initial appeal for mercy. Though the Lord has sent him illness to chastise him for his sin (see 32:3–5; 38:1–8,17–18), the psalmist asks that God would not in anger impose the full measure of the penalty for sin, for then death must come (see v. 5; see also 130:3).

6:1 Ps 38 begins similarly. *rebuke . . . chasten.* That is, rebuke-and-chasten (see 39:11; see also note on 3:7). *anger . . . wrath.* See note on 2:5.

6:2 *bones.* As the inner skeleton, they here represent the whole body.

6:3 *soul.* Not a spiritual aspect in distinction from the physical, nor the psalmist's "inner" being in distinction from his "outer" being, but his very self as a living, conscious, personal being. Its use in conjunction with "bones" (also in 35:9–10: "soul" and "all my bones") did not for the Hebrew writer involve reference to two distinct entities but constituted for him two ways of referring to himself, as is the case also in the combination "soul" and "body" (31:9) "soul" and "flesh" (63:1). *But You . . . how long?* See Introduction: Theology. Such language of impatience and complaint is found frequently in the prayers of the Psalter (usually "how long?" or "when?" or "why?"). It expresses the anguish of relief not (yet) granted and exhibits the boldness with which the psalmists wrestled with God on the basis of their relationship with Him and their conviction concerning His righteousness (see note on 5:8).

6:4–5 Earnest prayer for deliverance from death.

6:4 *lovingkindness.* The Hebrew for this phrase denotes befriending. Appeal to God's "(unfailing) love, kindness, mercy" is frequent in the OT since it summarizes all that the Lord covenanted to show to Israel (see Deut 7:9,12) as well as to David and his dynasty (see 89:24,28,33; 2 Sam 7:15; Is 55:3).

6:5 The psalmist urges that God's praise is at stake. It is the living, not the dead, who remember God's mercies and celebrate His deliverances. The Israelites usually viewed death as they saw it—the very opposite of life. And resurrection was not yet a part of their communal experience with God. The grave brought no escape from God (see 139:8), but just how they viewed the condition of the godly dead is not clear. (Non-Biblical documents from the ancient Near East indicate a general conception that immortality was reserved for the gods but that the dead continued to have some kind of shadowy existence in the dismal nether world.) The OT writers knew that man was created for life, that God's will for His people was life and that He had power over death. They also knew that death was every man's lot, and at its proper time the godly rested in God and accepted it with equanimity (see Gen 15:15; 25:8; 47:30; 49:33; 1 Kin 2:2). Death could even be a blessing for the righteous, affording escape from the greater evil that would overtake the living (see 2 Kin 22:20; Is 57:1–2). Furthermore, the death of the righteous was reputedly better than that of the wicked (see Num 23:10). It seems clear that there was even an awareness that death (as observed) was not the end of hope for the righteous, that God had more in store for them (see especially 16:9–11; 17:15; 49:14–15; 73:24; see also note on Gen 5:24). But when the psalmists wrestled with God for the preservation of life, it was death as they saw it, in its radical contradiction to life, that was evoked.

6:6–7 Anguish at night because of the prolongation of the illness and the barbs of the enemies.

6:6 *I am weary with my sighing.* The very center of the poem—thus underscoring the pathos of this prayer. This literary device—of placing a key thematic line at the very center of the psalm—was frequently used (see notes on 8:4; 21:7; 23:4; 34:8–14; 42:8; 47:5–6; 48:8; 54:4; 71:14; 74:12; 76:7; 82:5a; 86:9; 92:8; 97:7; 113:5; 138:4–5; 141:5; see also Introduction: Literary Features).

6:7 *eye has wasted away . . . old.* In the vivid language of the OT the eyes are dimmed by failing strength (see 38:10; 1 Sam 14:27,29; Jer 14:6), by grief (often associated with affliction: 31:9; 88:9; Job 17:7; Lam 2:11) and by longings unsatisfied or hope deferred (see 69:3; 119:82,123; Deut 28:32; Is 38:14). *because of all my adversaries.* See note on 5:9.

9 The LORD [a]has heard my supplication,
The LORD [b]receives my prayer.
10 All my enemies will [a]be ashamed and
greatly dismayed;
They shall [1]turn back, they will
[b]suddenly be ashamed.

Psalm 7

A [†]Shiggaion of David, which he sang to the LORD [•]concerning Cush, a Benjamite.

1 O LORD MY GOD, [a]in You I have taken
refuge;
Save me from all those who pursue
me, and [b]deliver me,
2 Or he will tear [1]my soul [a]like a lion,
[2]Dragging me away, while there is
none to deliver.

3 O LORD my God, if I have done this,
If there is [a]injustice in my hands,
4 If I have [a]rewarded evil to [1]my friend,
Or have [b]plundered [2]him who without
cause was my adversary,
5 Let the enemy pursue [1]my soul and
overtake [2]*it;*
And let him trample my life down to
the ground
And lay my glory in the dust. [3]Selah.

6 [a]Arise, O LORD, in Your anger;
[b]Lift up Yourself against [c]the rage of
my adversaries,
And [d]arouse Yourself [1]for me; You
have appointed judgment.
7 Let the assembly of the [a]peoples
encompass You,
And over [1]them return on high.
8 The LORD [a]judges the peoples;
[1][b]Vindicate me, O LORD, according to
my righteousness and my integrity
that is in me.
9 O let [a]the evil of the wicked come to
an end, but [b]establish the righteous;
For the righteous God [c]tries the hearts
and [1]minds.
10 My [a]shield is [1]with God,
Who [b]saves the upright in heart.
11 God is a [a]righteous judge,
And a God who has [b]indignation
every day.

12 If [1]a man [a]does not repent, He will
[b]sharpen His sword;
He has [c]bent His bow and [2]made it
ready.
13 He has also prepared [1]for Himself
deadly weapons;
He makes His [a]arrows fiery shafts.
14 Behold, he travails with wickedness,
And he [a]conceives mischief and
brings forth falsehood.
15 He has dug a pit and hollowed it out,
And has [a]fallen into the hole which he
made.
16 His [a]mischief will return upon his
own head,
And his [b]violence will descend upon
[1]his own pate.

17 I will give thanks to the LORD
[a]according to His righteousness
And will [b]sing praise to the name of
the LORD Most High.

9 [a]Ps 116:1 [b]Ps 66:19, 20 **10** [1]Or *again be ashamed suddenly* [a]Ps 71:13, 24 [b]Ps 73:19 **7:1** [†]I.e. Dithyrambic rhythm; or wild passionate song [•]Or *concerning the words of* [a]Ps 31:1; 71:1 [b]Ps 31:15 **2** [1]Or *me* [2]Or *Rending it in pieces, while* [a]Ps 57:4; Is 38:13 **3** [a]1 Sam 24:11 **4** [1]Lit *him who was at peace with me* [2]Or *my adversary without cause* [a]Ps 109:4, 5 [b]1 Sam 24:7; 26:9 **5** [1]Or *me* [2]Or me [3]*Selah* may mean: *Pause, Crescendo* or *Musical interlude* **6** [1]One ancient version reads *O my God* [a]Ps 3:7 [b]Ps 94:2 [c]Ps 138:7 [d]Ps 35:23; 44:23 **7** [1]Lit *it* [a]Ps 22:27 **8** [a]Ps 96:13; 98:9

8 [1]Lit *Judge* [b]Ps 18:20; 26:1; 35:24; 43:1 **9** [1]Lit *kidneys,* figurative for inner man [a]Ps 34:21; 94:23 [b]Ps 37:23; 40:2 [c]Ps 11:4, 5; Jer 11:20; Rev 2:23 **10** [1]Lit *upon* [a]Ps 18:2, 30 [b]Ps 97:10, 11; 125:4

11 [a]Ps 50:6 [b]Ps 90:9 **12** [1]Lit *he* [2]Lit *fixed it* [a]Ps 58:5 [b]Deut 32:41 [c]Ps 64:7 **13** [1]Or *His deadly weapons* [a]Ps 18:14; 45:5 **14** [a]Job 15:35; Is 59:4; James 1:15 **15** [a]Job 4:8; Ps 57:6 **16** [1]I.e. the crown of his own head [a]Esth 9:25; Ps 140:9 [b]Ps 140:11 **17** [a]Ps 71:15, 16 [b]Ps 9:2; 66:1, 2, 4

6:8–10 Concluding expression of buoyant confidence (see note on 3:8).

6:10 At the psalmist's restoration, his enemies will be disgraced.

Ps 7 An appeal to the Lord's court of justice when enemies attack.

7 title *Shiggaion.* See NASB marg. The word occurs only here (but see its plural in Hab 3:1). *Cush.* Not otherwise known, but as a Benjamite he was probably a supporter of Saul. Hence the title associates the psalm with Saul's determined attempts on David's life. See Introduction: Authorship and Titles (or Superscriptions).

7:1–2 Initial summation of David's appeal.

7:2 *like a lion.* As a young shepherd, David had been attacked by lions (see 1 Sam 17:34–35). But it is also a convention in the Psalms to liken the attack of enemies to that of ferocious animals, especially the lion (see 10:9; 17:12; 22:12–13,16,20–21; 35:17; 57:4; 58:6; 124:6).

7:3–5 David pleads his own innocence; he has given his enemy no cause to attack him.

7:5 *my soul.* Lit. "my glory," a way of referring to the core of one's being (see 16:9; 30:12; 57:8; 108:1 and notes).

7:6–9 An appeal to the Judge of all the earth to execute His judgment over all peoples, and particularly to adjudicate David's cause.

7:6 *Arise . . . Lift up.* See note on 3:7. *anger.* See v. 11 and note on 2:5. *arouse.* The Lord does not sleep (see 121:4) while evil triumphs and the oppressed cry to Him in vain (as they do to Baal; see 1 Kin 18:27). But the psalmists' language of urgent prayer vividly expresses their anguished impatience with God's inaction in the face of their great need (see 80:2; see also 78:65; Is 51:9).

7:8 *my righteousness.* See vv. 3–5.

7:9 *the righteous.* See note on 1:5. *righteous.* See note on 5:8. *hearts and minds.* Lit. "hearts and kidneys." The Israelites used the words as virtual synonyms (but "heart" most often) to refer to man's innermost center of conscious life (see note on 4:7). To search mind and heart was a conventional expression for God's examination of man's hidden character and motives (see Jer 11:20; 17:10; 20:12).

7:10–13 David's confidence that his prayer will be heard (see note on 3:8).

7:10 *shield.* See note on 3:3. *heart.* See note on 4:7.

7:11 *every day.* God's judgments are not all kept in store for some future day.

7:14–16 David comforts himself with the common wisdom that under God's rule "crime does not pay."

7:17 A vow to praise. Many prayers in the Psalter include such vows in anticipation of the expected answer to prayer. They reflect Israel's religious consciousness that praise must follow deliverance as surely as prayer springs from need—if God is to be truly honored. Such praise was usually offered with thank

Psalm 8

For the choir director; on the Gittith.
A Psalm of David.

1 O LORD, our Lord,
How majestic is Your name in all the earth,
Who have [1a]displayed Your splendor above the heavens!
2 [a]From the mouth of infants and nursing babes You have established [1b]strength
Because of Your adversaries,
To make [c]the enemy and the revengeful cease.

3 When I [1a]consider [b]Your heavens, the work of Your fingers,
The [c]moon and the stars, which You have [2]ordained;
4 [a]What is man that You [1]take thought of him,
And the son of man that You care for him?
5 Yet You have made him a [a]little lower than [1]God,
And [b]You crown him with [c]glory and majesty!
6 You make him to [a]rule over the works of Your hands;
You have [b]put all things under his feet,
7 All sheep and oxen,
And also the [1]beasts of the field,
8 The birds of the heavens and the fish of the sea,
Whatever passes through the paths of the seas.

9 [a]O LORD, our Lord,
How majestic is Your name in all the earth!

Psalm 9

For the choir director; on [†]Muth-labben.
A Psalm of David.

1 I will give thanks to the LORD with all [a]my heart;
I will [b]tell of all Your [1]wonders.
2 I will be glad and [a]exult in You;
I will [b]sing praise to Your name,
O [c]Most High.

8:1 [1]Or *set* [a]Ps 57:5, 11; 113:4; 148:13
2 [1]Or *a bulwark* [a]Matt 21:16; 1 Cor 1:27 [b]Ps 29:1; 118:14 [c]Ps 44:16
3 [1]Or *see* [2]Or *appointed, fixed* [a]Ps 111:2 [b]Ps 89:11; 144:5 [c]Ps 136:9
4 [1]Or *remember him* [a]Job 7:17; Ps 144:3; Heb 2:6-8
5 [1]Or *the angels;* Heb *Elohim* [a]Gen 1:26; Ps 82:6
5 [b]Ps 103:4 [c]Ps 21:5
6 [a]Gen 1:26, 28 [b]1 Cor 15:27; Eph 1:22; Heb 2:8
7 [1]Or *animals*
9 [a]Ps 8:1
9:1 [†]I.e. "Death to the Son" [1]Or *miracles* [a]Ps 86:12 [b]Ps 26:7
2 [a]Ps 5:11; 104:34 [b]Ps 66:2, 4 [c]Ps 83:18; 92:1

offerings and involved celebrating God's saving act in the presence of those assembled at the temple (see 50:14–15,23; see also note on 9:1). *name of the LORD.* See note on 5:11. *Most High.* See note on Gen 14:19.

Ps 8 In praise of the Creator (not of man—as is evident from the doxology that encloses it, vv. 1,9; see also note on 9:1) out of wonder over His sovereign ordering of the creation. Gen 1 (particularly vv. 26–28) clearly provides the spectacles, but David speaks out of his present experience of reality (perhaps on a bright, clear night when the vast host of the heavenly lights, stretching from horizon to horizon, erased from his musings small everyday affairs and engaged his mind with deeper thoughts). Two matters especially impressed him: (1) the glory of God reflected in the starry heavens, and (2) the astonishing condescension of God to be mindful of puny man, to crown him with glory almost godlike and to grant him lordly power over His creatures.

8 title *For the choir director.* See note on Ps 4 title. *on.* See note on Ps 6 title. *Gittith.* See Ps 81; 84 titles. The Hebrew word perhaps refers to either the wine press ("song of the wine press") or the Philistine city of Gath ("Gittite lyre or music"; see 2 Sam 15:18).

8:1a *name.* See note on 5:11.

8:1b–2 The mighty God, whose glory is displayed across the face of the heavens, appoints (and evokes) the praise of little children to silence the dark powers arrayed against Him (for a NT application see Matt 21:16).

8:2 *revengeful.* See 44:16; one who strikes back in malicious revenge (not as in 9:12).

8:3–5 The vastness and majesty of the heavens as the handiwork of God (see 19:1–6; 104:19–23) evoke wonder for what their Maker has done for little man, who is here today and gone tomorrow (see 144:3–4). (See Job 7:17–21 for Job's complaint that God takes man too seriously.)

8:3 *fingers.* See note on Ex 8:19.

8:4–6 Heb 2:6–8, quoting the Septuagint (the Greek translation of the OT), applies these verses to Jesus, who as the incarnate Son of God is both the representative man and the one in whom man's appointed destiny will be fully realized. The author of Hebrews thus makes use of the eschatological implications of these words in his testimony to Christ. Paul does the same with v. 6 in 1 Cor 15:27 (see also Eph 1:22).

8:4 *What.* The Hebrew for this word is translated "how" in vv. 1,9 and begins the line that serves as the center of the psalm (see note on 6:6). *take thought of.* Lit. "remember" (see note on Gen 8:1). *son of man.* Often a poetic synonym for "man" (see 80:17; 144:3; see also note on Ezek 2:1).

8:5 *God.* The Hebrew can be translated "God" or "angels."

8:6–8 See Gen 1:26–27. Man's rule is real—a part of his "glory and majesty" (v. 5)—and it is his destiny (the eschatological import drawn on by Paul and the author of Hebrews; see note on vv. 4–6). But it is not absolute or independent. It is participation, as a subordinate, in God's rule; and it is a gift, not a right.

8:9 Repeated verbatim from v. 1a (see note there).

Ps 9 That Ps 9 and 10 were sometimes viewed (or used) as one psalm is known from the Septuagint (the Greek translation of the OT). Whether they were originally composed as one psalm is not known, though a number of indicators point in that direction. Ps 10 is the only psalm from Ps 3 to 32 that has no superscription, and the Hebrew text of the two psalms together appears to reflect an incomplete (or broken) acrostic structure. The first letter of each verse or pair of verses tends to follow the order of the Hebrew alphabet near the beginning of Ps 9 and again near the end of Ps 10. The thoughts also tend to be developed in two-verse units throughout. Ps 9 is predominantly praise (by the king) for God's deliverance from hostile nations (the specific occasion is unknown, but since there is no reference to victories on the part of Israel, God's destruction of the nations may have come by other means). It concludes with a short prayer for God's continuing righteous judgments (see v. 4) on the haughty nations. Ps 10 is predominantly prayer against the rapacity of unscrupulous men within the realm—as arrogant and wicked in their dealings with the "afflicted" (v. 2) as the nations were in their attacks on Israel (vv. 2–11 can serve equally as a description of both). The conjunction of these two within a single psalm is not unthinkable since the attacks of "the wicked" (9:5; 10:4), whether from within or from without, on the godly community are equally threatening to true Israel.

3 When my enemies turn back,
They stumble and [a]perish before You.
4 For You have [a]maintained [1]my just
cause;
You have sat on the throne [2][b]judging
righteously.
5 You have [a]rebuked the nations, You
have destroyed the wicked;
You have [b]blotted out their name
forever and ever.
6 [1]The enemy has come to an end in
perpetual ruins,
And You have uprooted the cities;
The very [a]memory of them has
perished.

7 But the [a]LORD [1]abides forever;
He has established His [b]throne for
judgment,
8 And He will [a]judge the world in
righteousness;
He will execute judgment for the
peoples with equity.
9 [1]The LORD also will be a [a]stronghold
for the oppressed,
A stronghold in times of trouble;
10 And [1]those who [a]know Your name
will put their trust in You,
For You, O LORD, have not [b]forsaken
those who seek You.

11 Sing praises to the LORD, who [a]dwells
in Zion;
[b]Declare among the peoples His
deeds.
12 For [a]He who [1]requires blood
remembers them;
He does not forget [b]the cry of the
afflicted.
13 Be gracious to me, O LORD;
See my affliction from those [a]who
hate me,
You who [b]lift me up from the gates of
death,
14 That I may tell of [a]all Your praises,
That in the gates of the daughter of
Zion
I may [b]rejoice in Your [1]salvation.
15 The nations have sunk down [a]in the
pit which they have made;
In the [b]net which they hid, their own
foot has been caught.
16 The LORD has [a]made Himself known;
He has [b]executed judgment.
In the work of his own hands the
wicked is snared. [1]Higgaion [2]Selah.

17 The wicked will [1][a]return to [2]Sheol,
Even all the nations who [b]forget God.
18 For the [a]needy will not always be
forgotten,
Nor the [b]hope of the afflicted perish
forever.

3 [a]Ps 27:2
4 [1]Lit *my right and my cause* [2]Or *a righteous Judge* [a]Ps 140:12 [b]Ps 50:6
5 [a]Ps 119:21 [b]Ps 69:28; Prov 10:7
6 [1]Or *O enemy, desolations are finished forever; And their cities You have plucked up* [a]Ps 34:16
7 [1]Or *sits* as king [a]Ps 10:16 [b]Ps 89:14
8 [a]Ps 96:13; 98:9
9 [1]Or *Let the* LORD *also be* [a]Ps 32:7; 59:9, 16, 17
10 [1]Or *let those...name put* [a]Ps 91:14 [b]Ps 37:28; 94:14
11 [a]Ps 76:2
11 [b]Ps 105:1; 107:22
12 [1]I.e. avenges bloodshed [a]Gen 9:5; Ps 72:14 [b]Ps 9:18
13 [a]Ps 38:19 [b]Ps 30:3; 86:13
14 [1]Or *deliverance* [a]Ps 106:2 [b]Ps 13:5; 20:5; 35:9; 51:12
15 [a]Ps 7:15, 16 [b]Ps 57:6
16 [1]Perhaps, resounding music or meditation [2]*Selah* may mean: *Pause, Crescendo* or *Musical interlude* [a]Ex 7:5 [b]Ps 9:4
17 [1]Or *turn* [2]I.e. the nether world [a]Ps 49:14 [b]Job 8:13; Ps 50:22
18 [a]Ps 9:12; 12:5 [b]Ps 62:5; 71:5; Prov 23:18

Praise of God's past deliverances is often an integral part of prayer in the Psalter (see 3:3–4,8 and notes; 25:6; 40:1–5), as also in other ancient Near Eastern prayers. Such praise expressed the ground of the psalmist's hope that his present prayer would be heard, and it also functioned to motivate the Lord to act once more in His people's (or His servant's) behalf. For other lengthy prefaces to prayer see Ps 40; 44; 89. Probably Ps 9–10 came to be separated for the purpose of separate liturgical use, as did Ps 42–43 (see introduction there).

9 title *For the choir director.* See note on Ps 4 title. *on.* See titles of Ps 22; 45; 56–60; 69; 75; 80. The Hebrew for this word (also translated "upon," "set to," or "according to") may indicate that these were tune titles.

9:1–2 Initial announcement of praise.

9:1 *heart.* See note on 4:7. *tell of.* The praise of God in the Psalter is rarely a private matter between the psalmist and the Lord. It is usually a public (at the temple) celebration of God's holy virtues or of His saving acts or gracious bestowal of blessings. In his praise the psalmist proclaims to the assembled throng God's glorious attributes or His righteous (see note on 5:8) deeds (see, e.g., 22:22–31; 56:12–13; 61:8; 65:1; 69:30–33). To this is usually added a call to praise, summoning all who hear to take up the praise—to acknowledge and joyfully celebrate God's glory, His goodness and all His righteous acts. This aspect of praise in the Psalms has rightly been called the OT anticipation of NT evangelism. *wonders.* God's saving acts, sometimes involving miracles—as in the exodus from Egypt, the wilderness wanderings and the entrance into the promised land—and sometimes not, but always involving the manifestation of God's sovereign lordship over events. Here reference is to the destruction of the enemies celebrated in this psalm.

9:2,10 *Your name.* See note on 5:11.

9:2 *Most High.* See note on Gen 14:19.

9:3–6 In destroying the enemies, God has redressed the wrongs committed by them against David (and Israel).

9:4 *throne.* See note on v. 7.

9:5 *blotted out their name.* As if from a register of mankind written on a papyrus scroll (see Num 5:23; see also Deut 9:14; 25:19; 29:20; 2 Kin 14:27).

9:7–10 Celebration of the righteous rule of God (see note on 5:8), which evokes trust in those who look to the Lord.

9:7 *His throne.* In heaven (see 11:4). See also v. 4.

9:8 See Acts 17:31.

9:11–12 A call to the assembly at the temple to take up the praise of God for His righteous judgments (see note on v. 1).

9:11 *dwells in Zion.* God's heavenly throne (see v. 7) has its counterpart on earth in His temple at Jerusalem, from which center He rules the world (see 2:6; 3:4 and notes; 20:2). For God's election of Zion as the seat of His rule see 132:13.

9:12 *He who requires blood.* See Deut 32:41,43.

9:13–14 Perhaps a recollection of David's prayer ("the cry of the afflicted," v. 12), which the Lord has now answered.

9:13 *gates of death.* See Job 17:16 and note.

9:14 *tell.* See notes on v. 1; 7:17. *gates.* Having been thrust down by the attacks of his enemies to "the gates of death" (v. 13), David prayed to be lifted up so he could celebrate his deliverance (see note on v. 1) in "the gates of . . . Zion." *daughter of Zion.* A personification of Jerusalem and its inhabitants.

9:15–18 Under the Lord's just rule, those who wickedly attack others bring destruction on themselves (see 7:14–16 and note) and their end will be the grave. But those who are attacked ("the needy," v. 18) will not trust in the Lord in vain.

9:17 *forget.* Take no account of.

9:18 *needy . . . afflicted.* In this psalm David and Israel are

19 [a]Arise, O LORD, do not let man prevail;
Let the nations be [b]judged before You.
20 Put them [a]in fear, O LORD;
Let the nations know that they are
[b]but men. Selah.

Psalm 10

1 Why [a]do You stand afar off, O LORD?
Why [b]do You hide [1]*Yourself* in times
of trouble?
2 In [a]pride the wicked [1]hotly pursue the
afflicted;
[2]Let them be [b]caught in the plots
which they have devised.

3 For the wicked [a]boasts of his [b]heart's
desire,
And [1]the greedy man curses *and*
[c]spurns the LORD.
4 The wicked, in the haughtiness of his
countenance, [a]does not seek *Him.*
All his [1]thoughts are, "[b]There is no
God."

5 His ways [1a]prosper at all times;
Your judgments are on high, [b]out of
his sight;
As for all his adversaries, he snorts at
them.
6 He says to himself, "[a]I will not be
moved;
[1]Throughout all generations [b]I will not
be in adversity."
7 His [a]mouth is full of curses and deceit
and [b]oppression;
[c]Under his tongue is mischief and
wickedness.
8 He sits in the [a]lurking places of the
villages;
In the hiding places he [b]kills the
innocent;
His eyes [1]stealthily watch for the
[2c]unfortunate.
9 He lurks in a hiding place as [a]a lion in
his [1]lair;
He [b]lurks to catch [c]the afflicted;
He catches the afflicted when he
draws him into his [d]net.
10 He [1]crouches, he [2]bows down,
And the [3]unfortunate fall [4]by his
mighty ones.
11 He [a]says to himself, "God has
forgotten;
He has hidden His face; He will never
see it."

12 Arise, O LORD; O God, [a]lift up Your
hand.
[b]Do not forget the afflicted.
13 Why has the wicked [a]spurned God?
He has said to himself, "You will not
require *it.*"
14 You have seen *it,* for You have beheld
[a]mischief and vexation to [1]take it
into Your hand.
The [2b]unfortunate commits *himself* to
You;
You have been the [c]helper of the
orphan.
15 [a]Break the arm of the wicked and the
evildoer,
[1b]Seek out his wickedness until You
find none.

16 The LORD is [a]King forever and ever;

19 [a]Num 10:35 [b]Ps 9:5
20 [a]Ps 14:5 [b]Ps 62:9
10:1 [1]Or Your eyes [a]Ps 22:1 [b]Ps 13:1; 55:1
2 [1]Lit *burn* [2]Or *They will be caught* [a]Ps 73:6, 8 [b]Ps 7:16; 9:16
3 [1]Or *blesses the greedy man* [a]Ps 49:6; 94:3, 4 [b]Ps 112:10 [c]Ps 10:13
4 [1]Or *plots* [a]Ps 10:13; 36:2 [b]Ps 14:1; 36:1
5 [1]Lit *are strong* [a]Ps 52:7 [b]Ps 28:5
6 [1]Lit *To* [a]Ps 49:11; Eccl 8:11 [b]Rev 18:7
7 [a]Rom 3:14 [b]Ps 73:8 [c]Job 20:12; Ps 140:3
8 [1]Lit *lie in wait* [2]Or *poor* [a]Ps 11:2 [b]Ps 94:6 [c]Ps 72:12
9 [1]Or *thicket* [a]Ps 17:12 [b]Ps 59:3; Mic 7:2 [c]Ps 10:2 [d]Ps 140:5
10 [1]Or *is crushed* [2]Or *is bowed down* [3]Or *poor* [4]Or *into his claws*
11 [a]Ps 10:4
12 [a]Ps 17:7; Mic 5:9 [b]Ps 9:12
13 [a]Ps 10:3
14 [1]Lit *put, give* [2]Or *poor* [a]Ps 10:7 [b]Ps 22:11 [c]Ps 68:5
15 [1]Or *May You seek* [a]Ps 37:17 [b]Ps 140:11
16 [a]Ps 29:10

counted among them because of the threat from the enemies. *not . . . forgotten.* Those who forget God will come to nothing, but the needy and afflicted will not be forgotten by God (see v. 12).

9:19–20 A prayer at the conclusion of praise, asking that the Lord may ever rule over the nations as He has done in the event here celebrated—that those who "forget God" (v. 17) may know that they are only men, not gods, and cannot withstand the God of Israel (see 10:18).

9:19 *Arise.* See note on 3:7.

Ps 10 A prayer for rescue from the attacks of unscrupulous men—containing a classic OT portrayal of "the wicked." See introduction to Ps 9.

10:1 See note on 6:3; see also Introduction: Theology.

10:2–11 Accusation lodged against the oppressors (see note on 5:9–10). In the Hebrew the interchange of singular and plural indicates that these accusations are being lodged against wicked oppressors in general. Their deeds betray the arrogance (see vv. 2–5—so long as they prosper, v. 5) with which they defy God (see vv. 3–4,13; see especially their words in vv. 6,11,13). They greedily seek to glut their unrestrained appetites (see v. 3) by victimizing others, taking account of neither God (see v. 4) nor His law (see v. 5).

10:2 *pursue . . . caught.* The psalmists often use imagery from the hunt (see vv. 8–9).

10:3 *heart's.* See note on 4:7.

10:4 The wicked man does not consider that he has God to contend with (see note on v. 11; see also 14:1; 36:1; 53:1).

10:6 See vv. 11,13 and note on 3:2. *to himself.* Lit. "in his heart" (also in vv. 11,13); see note on 4:7. *I will not be moved.* Nothing will disturb my well-being, unsettle my security.

10:7 *curses and deceit and oppression.* The three most common weapons of the tongue in Israel's experience (see note on 5:9). *curses.* The ancient Near Eastern peoples thought that by pronouncing curses on someone they could bring down the power of the gods (or other mysterious powers) on that person. They had a large conventional stock of such curses. *deceit.* Slander and false testimony for malicious purposes (see, e.g., 1 Kin 21:8–15).

10:9 See note on 7:2.

10:11 See note on 3:2. The arrogance with which the wicked speak (see 17:10), especially their easy dismissal of God's knowledge of their evil acts and His unfailing prosecution of their malicious deeds, is frequently noted by the psalmists (see v. 13; 12:4; 42:3,10; 59:7; 64:5; 71:11; 73:11; 94:7; 115:2; see also Is 29:15; Ezek 8:12).

10:12–15 Prayer that God will call the wicked to account.

10:12 *Arise.* See note on 3:7. *forget.* See 9:18. *afflicted.* Those at the mercy of the oppressors (see v. 9).

10:13 *Why . . . ? He.* See note on 6:3.

10:14 Appeal to God's righteous rule (see 5:4–6).

10:15 *Break the arm.* Destroy the power to oppress. *Seek out his wickedness.* Humble his arrogance (see v. 13) with Your righteous judgment.

[b]Nations have perished from His land.
17 O LORD, You have heard the [a]desire of
the [1]humble;
You will [b]strengthen their heart, [c]You
will incline Your ear
18 To [1]vindicate the [a]orphan and the
[b]oppressed,
So that man who is of the earth will
no longer cause [c]terror.

Psalm 11

For the choir director. *A Psalm* of David.

1 In the LORD I [a]take refuge;
How can you say to my soul, "Flee *as*
a bird to your [b]mountain;
2 For, behold, the wicked [a]bend the bow,
They [1b]make ready their arrow upon
the string
To [c]shoot in darkness at the upright in
heart.
3 If the [a]foundations are destroyed,
What can the righteous do?"
4 The LORD is in His [a]holy temple; the
[1]LORD's [b]throne is in heaven;
His [c]eyes behold, His eyelids test the
sons of men.
5 The LORD [a]tests the righteous and [b]the
wicked,
And the one who loves violence His
soul hates.
6 Upon the wicked He will [a]rain
[1]snares;
[b]Fire and brimstone and [c]burning wind
will be the portion of [d]their cup.
7 For the LORD is [a]righteous, [b]He loves
[1]righteousness;
The upright will [c]behold His face.

Psalm 12

For the choir director; [†]upon an eight-stringed
lyre. A Psalm of David.

1 Help, LORD, for [a]the godly man ceases
to be,
For the faithful disappear from among
the sons of men.
2 They [a]speak [1]falsehood to one
another;
With [b]flattering [2]lips and with a
double heart they speak.
3 May the LORD cut off all flattering lips,
The tongue that [a]speaks great things;
4 Who [a]have said, "With our tongue we
will prevail;
Our lips are [1]our own; who is lord
over us?"

3 [a]Dan 7:8; Rev 13:5 **4** [1]Lit *with us* [a]Ps 73:8, 9

16 [b]Deut 8:20
17 [1]Or *afflicted* [a]Ps 9:18 [b]1 Chr 29:18 [c]Ps 34:15
18 [1]Lit *judge* [a]Ps 146:9 [b]Ps 9:9; 74:21 [c]Is 29:20
11:1 [a]Ps 2:12 [b]Ps 121:1
2 [1]Or *fixed* [a]Ps 7:12; 37:14 [b]Ps 64:3 [c]Ps 64:4
3 [a]Ps 82:5; 87:1; 119:152
4 [1]Lit LORD, His throne [a]Ps 18:6; Mic 1:2; Hab 2:20 [b]Ps 103:19; Is 66:1; Matt 5:34; Rev 4:2 [c]Ps 33:18; 34:15, 16
5 [a]Gen 22:1; Ps 34:19; James 1:12 [b]Ps 5:5
6 [1]Or *coals of fire* [a]Ps 18:13, 14 [b]Gen 19:24; Ezek 38:22 [c]Jer 4:11, 12 [d]Ps 75:8
7 [1]Or *righteous deeds* [a]Ps 7:9, 11 [b]Ps 33:5; 45:7 [c]Ps 16:11; 17:15
12:1 [†]Or *according to a lower octave* (Heb *Sheminith*) [a]Is 57:1; Mic 7:2
2 [1]Or *emptiness* [2]Lit *lip* [a]Ps 10:7; 41:6 [b]Ps 28:3; 55:21; Jer 9:8; Rom 16:18

10:16–18 The psalmist's confidence in the righteous reign of the Lord (see note on 3:8). Reference to the nations (v. 16) and to the humbling of proud man (see v. 18; see also 9:19–20) suggests links with Ps 9. As the conclusion to Ps 10, this stanza expands the vision of God's just rule to its universal scope and sets the purging of the Lord's land of all nations that do not acknowledge Him (see v. 16) alongside God's judicial dealing with the wicked oppressors. Both belong to God's assertion of His righteous rule in the face of man's arrogant denial of it.

10:18 *who is of the earth.* Who is not God and so constitutes no ultimate threat (see 49:12,20; 56:4,11; 62:9; 78:39; 103:14–16; 118:6,8–9; 144:4; Is 31:3; Jer 17:5).

Ps 11 A confession of confident trust in the Lord's righteous rule, at a time when wicked adversaries seem to have the upper hand.

11 title *For the choir director.* See note on Ps 4 title.

11:1–3 David testifies of his unshakable trust in the Lord (his refuge) to apprehensive people around him. These people, seeing the power and underhandedness of the enemy (they "shoot in darkness," v. 2), fear that the foundations (v. 3) are crumbling and that flight to a mountain refuge is the only recourse. He dismisses their fearful advice with disdain.

11:2 It is not clear whether those who wield the bows and arrows are archers or false accusers (see 57:4; 64:4; see also note on 5:9). *heart.* See note on 4:7.

11:3 *foundations.* Of the world order (see 82:5). To those who counsel flight, the powerful upsurge of evil appears to indicate that the righteous can no longer count on a world order in which good triumphs over evil. *righteous.* See note on 1:5.

11:4–7 Reply to the fearful: The Lord is still securely on His heavenly throne. And the righteous Lord (see v. 7) discerns the righteous (see v. 5) to give them a place in His presence (see v. 7), while His judgment will "rain" (v. 6) on the wicked.

11:4 *The LORD is in His holy temple.* Repeated verbatim in Hab 2:20. Here reference is to His heavenly temple.

11:6 Perhaps recalling God's judgment on Sodom and Gomorrah (see Gen 19:24,28; see also Rev 14:10; 20:10; 21:8). *their cup.* See 75:8 and note on 16:5).

11:7 *righteous.* See note on 5:8. *The upright.* Those concerning whom the fearful despaired (see v. 2). *behold His face.* The Hebrew for "see the king's face" was an expression denoting access to the king (see Gen 43:3,5; 44:23,26; 2 Sam 3:13, "see my face . . . when you come to see me"; 14:24,28,32). Sometimes it referred to those who served before the king (see 2 Kin 25:19, "king's advisers"; Esth 1:14, those "who had access to the king's presence"). Here David speaks of special freedom of access before the heavenly King. Reference is no doubt to His presence at the temple (God's earthly royal house), but that is still the presence of the One who sits on the heavenly throne. Ultimate access to the heavenly temple may also be implied (see 16:11; 17:15; see also 23:6; 140:13). Even the pagan peoples surrounding Israel believed that man continued after death, though only in some kind of shadowy existence in the nether world (see Is 14:9–17).

Ps 12 A prayer for help when it seems that all men are faithless and every tongue false (see Mic 7:1–7).

12 title *For the choir director.* See note on Ps 4 title. *upon.* See note on Ps 6 title.

12:1–2 Initial appeal, with description of the cause of distress.

12:1 *godly.* See note on 4:3. *the faithful.* Those who maintain moral integrity.

12:2 See 5:9 and note.

12:3–4 The prayer.

12:3 *cut off.* Put an end to (physical mutilation is not in view). *speaks great things.* See note on 10:2–11.

12:4 See notes on 3:2; 10:11.

5 "Because of the [a]devastation of the afflicted, because of the groaning of the needy,
Now [b]I will arise," says the LORD; "I will [c]set him in the safety for which he longs."
6 The [a]words of the LORD are pure words;
As silver [b]tried in a furnace on the earth, refined seven times.
7 You, O LORD, will keep them;
You will [a]preserve him from this generation forever.
8 The [a]wicked strut about on every side
When [1b]vileness is exalted among the sons of men.

Psalm 13

For the choir director. A Psalm of David.

1 How long, O LORD? Will You [a]forget me forever?
How long [b]will You hide Your face from me?
2 How long shall I [a]take counsel in my soul,
Having [b]sorrow in my heart all the day?
How long will my enemy be exalted over me?

3 [a]Consider *and* answer me, O LORD my God;
[b]Enlighten my eyes, or I will [c]sleep the *sleep of* death,
4 And my enemy will [a]say, "I have overcome him,"
And [b]my adversaries will rejoice when I am shaken.

5 But I have [a]trusted in Your lovingkindness;
My heart shall [b]rejoice in Your salvation.
6 I will [a]sing to the LORD,
Because He has [b]dealt bountifully with me.

Psalm 14

For the choir director. *A Psalm* of David.

1 The fool has [a]said in his heart, "There is no God."
They are corrupt, they have committed abominable [1]deeds;
There is [b]no one who does good.
2 The LORD has [a]looked down from heaven upon the sons of men
To see if there are any who [1b]understand,
Who [c]seek after God.

12:5 [a]Ps 9:9; 10:18 [b]Is 33:10 [c]Ps 34:6; 35:10 **6** [a]2 Sam 22:31; Ps 18:30; 19:8, 10; 119:140 [b]Prov 30:5 **7** [a]Ps 37:28; 97:10 **8** [1]Or *worthlessness* [a]Ps 55:10, 11 [b]Is 32:5 **13:1** [a]Ps 44:24 [b]Job 13:24; Ps 89:46 **2** [a]Ps 42:4 [b]Ps 42:9

3 [a]Ps 5:1 [b]1 Sam 14:29; Ezra 9:8; Job 33:30; Ps 18:28 [c]Jer 51:39 **4** [a]Ps 12:4 [b]Ps 25:2; 38:16 **5** [a]Ps 52:8 [b]Ps 9:14 **6** [a]Ps 96:1, 2 [b]Ps 116:7; 119:17; 142:7 **14:1** [1]Lit *doings* [a]Ps 10:4; 53:1 [b]Ps 14:1-3; 130:3; Rom 3:10-12 **2** [1]Or *act wisely* [a]Ps 33:13, 14; 102:19 [b]Ps 92:6 [c]1 Chr 22:19

12:5–6 A reassuring word from the Lord. Such words of assurance following prayer in the Psalms were perhaps spoken by a priest (see 1 Sam 1:17) or a prophet (see 51:8 and note; 2 Sam 12:13). It may be that abrupt transitions from prayer to confidence in the Psalms (see note on 3:8) presuppose such priestly or prophetic words, even when they are not contained in the psalm. Here it is possible that David merely recalls this appropriate word from the Lord; notice that it is a general reassurance concerning the righteous rule of God (see note on 4:1).

12:5 *Now I will arise.* See Is 33:10.

12:6 *words of the LORD.* Set in sharp contrast with the boastful words of the adversaries; they are as flawless as thoroughly refined silver. *furnace on the earth.* See note on Deut 4:20. *seven.* Signifies fullness or completeness—here thoroughness of refining.

12:7–8 Concluding expression of confidence (see note on 3:8).

12:8 David is confident, even though at the present time the wicked think they have the upper hand (see vv. 1–4).

Ps 13 A cry to the Lord for deliverance from a serious illness that threatens death (see v. 3), which would give David's enemies just what they wanted. See introduction to Ps 6.

13 title *For the choir director.* See note on Ps 4 title.

13:1–2 An anguished complaint concerning a prolonged serious illness.

13:1 *How long . . . ?* See note on 6:3; see also Introduction: Theology. *forget.* Ignore. *hide Your face.* For use in combination with "forget" see 44:24. In moments of need the psalmists frequently ask God why He hides His face (see 30:7; 44:24; 88:14), or they plead with Him not to do so (see 27:9; 69:17; 102:2; 143:7). When He does hide His face, those who depend on Him can only despair (see 30:7; 104:29). When His face shines on a person, blessing and deliverance come (see 4:6 and note; 31:16; 67:1; 80:3,7,19; 119:135).

13:2 *heart.* See note on 4:7.

13:3–4 Appeal for deliverance from death.

13:3 *Enlighten my eyes.* Restore me (see note on 6:7).

13:4 See notes on 3:2; 5:9. *shaken.* Referring to death (as in 18:38; 82:7; 106:26; Judg 5:27; 2 Sam 1:19; Job 18:12).

13:5–6 Concluding expression of confidence (see note on 3:8).

13:5 *lovingkindness.* See note on 6:4. *heart.* See note on 4:7. *shall rejoice.* It is David who will rejoice, not his enemies.

13:6 See note on 7:17.

Ps 14 A testimony concerning the folly of evil men. This psalm has many links with Ps 10; 12. It shares the view of Ps 11 that the righteous Lord is on the throne, and it stands in contrast with Ps 15, which describes those who are acceptable to God. Ps 53 is a somewhat revised duplicate of this psalm.

14 title *For the choir director.* See note on Ps 4 title.

14:1–3 Characterization of the wicked. For Paul's use of these verses in a different context see Rom 3:10–12.

14:1 Not intended as a definition of the "fool"; see previous note. The Hebrew words rendered "fool" in Psalms denote one who is morally deficient. *has said.* See note on 3:2. *heart.* See note on 4:7. *no God.* A practical atheism (see 10:4,6,11,13; 36:1; see also note on 10:4). *no one who does good.* Mankind in general is corrupt. Here the reference is to those who take no account of God and do not hesitate to show their malice toward "the righteous generation" (see vv. 4–5)—as in 9:19–20; 10:2–11,13,18; 12:1–4,7–8 (this is also the situation that Ps 11 describes). Elsewhere the psalmists included themselves among those who are not righteous in God's eyes (see 130:3; 143:2; see also 1 Kin 8:46; Job 9:2; Eccl 7:20).

14:2 *The LORD.* Emphatically contrasted with "the fool" (v. 1). *Who seek after God.* Those who truly seek God are described in Ps 15.

3 They have all [a]turned aside, together
they have become corrupt;
There is [b]no one who does good, not
even one.

4 Do all the workers of wickedness [a]not
know,
Who [b]eat up my people *as* they eat
bread,
And [c]do not call upon the Lord?
5 There they are in great dread,
For God is with the [a]righteous
generation.
6 You would put to shame the counsel
of the afflicted,
But the LORD is his [a]refuge.

7 Oh, that [a]the salvation of Israel
[1]would come out of Zion!
When the LORD [2b]restores His captive
people,
Jacob will rejoice, Israel will be glad.

Psalm 15

A Psalm of David.

1 O LORD, who may [1]abide [a]in Your tent?
Who may dwell on Your [b]holy hill?
2 He who [a]walks with integrity, and
works righteousness,
And [b]speaks truth in his heart.
3 He [a]does not slander [1]with his tongue,
Nor [b]does evil to his neighbor,
Nor [c]takes up a reproach against his
friend;
4 In [1]whose eyes a reprobate is despised,
But [2]who [a]honors those who fear the
LORD;
He [b]swears to his own hurt and does
not change;
5 He [a]does not put out his money [1]at
interest,
Nor [b]does he take a bribe against the
innocent.
[c]He who does these things will never
be shaken.

Psalm 16

A [†]Mikhtam of David.

1 [a]Preserve me, O God, for [b]I take
refuge in You.
2 [1]I said to the LORD, "You are [2]my Lord;
I [a]have no good besides You."
3 As for the [1a]saints who are in the earth,
[2]They are the majestic ones [b]in whom
is all my delight.
4 The [1a]sorrows of those who have
[2]bartered for another *god* will be
multiplied;
I shall not pour out their drink
offerings of [b]blood,
Nor will I [c]take their names upon my
lips.

5 The LORD is the [a]portion of my
inheritance and my [b]cup;

3 [a]Ps 58:3 [b]Ps 143:2
4 [a]Ps 82:5 [b]Ps 27:2; Jer 10:25; Mic 3:3 [c]Ps 79:6; Is 64:7
5 [a]Ps 73:15; 112:2
6 [a]Ps 9:9; 40:17; 46:1; 142:5
7 [1]Lit *would be* [2]Or *restores the fortunes of His people* [a]Ps 53:6 [b]Ps 85:1, 2
15:1 [1]Lit *sojourn* [a]Ps 27:5, 6; 61:4 [b]Ps 24:3
2 [a]Ps 24:4; Is 33:15 [b]Zech 8:16; Eph 4:25
3 [1]Lit *according to* [a]Ps 50:20 [b]Ps 28:3 [c]Ex 23:1
4 [1]Lit *his* [2]Lit *he* [a]Acts 28:10 [b]Judg 11:35
5 [1]I.e. to a fellow Israelite [a]Ex 22:25; Lev 25:36; Deut 23:20; Ezek 18:8 [b]Ex 23:8; Deut 16:19 [c]2 Pet 1:10
16:1 [†]Possibly *Epigrammatic Poem* or *Atonement Psalm* [a]Ps 17:8 [b]Ps 7:1
2 [1]Or *O my soul, you said* [2]Or *the Lord* [a]Ps 73:25
3 [1]Lit *holy ones;* i.e. the godly [2]Lit *And the majestic ones...delight* [a]Ps 101:6 [b]Ps 119:63

4 [1]I.e. sorrows due to idolatry [2]Or *hastened to* [a]Ps 32:10 [b]Ps 106:37, 38 [c]Ex 23:13; Josh 23:7 **5** [a]Ps 73:26; 119:57; 142:5; Lam 3:24 [b]Ps 23:5

14:3 *turned aside.* From God and goodness.
14:4–6 The folly of the wicked exposed.
14:4 *eat up . . . do not call upon the LORD.* Renewed characterization of the wicked: They live by the violence of their own hands and do not rely on the Lord (see 10:2–4).
14:5 Even God's mighty defense of the righteous teaches them nothing. *righteous.* See note on 1:5.
14:6 *afflicted.* God's people as the victims of injustice. *refuge.* See note on 4:1.
14:7 The psalmist longs for Israel's complete deliverance from her enemies—which will come when God deals with the wicked in defense of their victims. For a similar expansion of scope see 10:16–18 and note. *Zion.* See note on 9:11. *Jacob . . . Israel.* Synonyms (see Gen 32:28).
Ps 15 Instruction to those who wish to have access to God at His temple (see 24:3–6; Is 33:14–16). See also introduction to Ps 14.
15:1 *abide . . . dwell on.* Not as a priest but as God's guest in His holy, royal house, the temple (see 23:6; 27:4–6; 61:4; 84:10; 2 Sam 12:20). *holy hill.* See note on 2:6.
15:2–5 Not sacrifices or ritual purity (as among the religions of the ancient Near East) but moral righteousness gives access to the Lord, the God of Israel (see the basic covenantal law: Ex 20:1–17; see also Is 1:10–17; 33:14–16; 58:6–10; Jer 7:2–7; Ezek 18:5–9; Hos 6:6; Amos 5:14–15,21–24; Mic 6:6–8; Zech 7:9–10; 8:16–17).
15:2 *integrity.* See Gen 17:1 and note. *works righteousness.* See note on 1:5. *heart.* See note on 4:7.
15:3 *tongue.* See note on 5:9.
15:4 *those who fear the LORD.* Those who honor God and order their lives in accordance with His will (see note on Gen 20:11) because of their reverence for Him.
15:5 *interest.* See note on Ex 22:25–27. *be shaken.* See note on 10:6.
Ps 16 A prayer for safekeeping (the petition element in prayer psalms is often relatively short; see 3:7; 22:19–21; 44:23–26), pleading for the Lord's protection against the threat of death. It could also be called a psalm of trust.
16 title *Mikhtam.* The term remains unexplained, though it always stands in the superscription of Davidic prayers occasioned by great danger (see Ps 56–60).
16:1 The petition and the basis for it. The rest of the psalm elaborates on the latter element.
16:2–4 The Lord is David's one and only good thing (see 73:25,28); David will have nothing to do with the counterfeit gods to whom others pour out their libations (see 4:2).
16:3 See Ps 101.
16:4 *sorrows . . . will be multiplied.* In contrast with David's good "portion" (v. 5; see note on 11:6), which affords him much joy (see 73:18–20). *drink offerings of blood.* Blood of sacrifices poured on altars. *take their names upon.* Appeal to or worship them (see Josh 23:7).
16:5–6 Joy over the inheritance received from the Lord. David refers to what the Lord bestowed on His people in the promised land, either to the gift of fields there (see Num 16:14) or to the Lord Himself (as in 73:26; 119:57; 142:5; Lam 3:24), who was the inheritance of the priests (see Num 18:20) and the Levites (see Deut 10:9).
16:5 *cup.* A metaphor referring to what the host offers his guests to drink. To the godly the Lord offers a cup of blessings

You support my [c]lot.
6 The [a]lines have fallen to me in pleasant places;
Indeed, my heritage is [b]beautiful to me.

7 I will bless the LORD who has [a]counseled me;
Indeed, my [1b]mind instructs me in the night.
8 [a]I have [b]set the LORD continually before me;
Because He is [c]at my right hand, [d]I will not be shaken.
9 Therefore [a]my heart is glad and [b]my glory rejoices;
My flesh also will [c]dwell securely.
10 For You [a]will not abandon my soul to [1]Sheol;
Nor will You [2b]allow Your [3]Holy One to [4]undergo decay.
11 You will make known to me [a]the path of life;
In [b]Your presence is fullness of joy;
In Your right hand there are [c]pleasures forever.

Psalm 17

A Prayer of David.

1 Hear a [a]just cause, O LORD, [b]give heed to my cry;
[c]Give ear to my prayer, which is not from [d]deceitful lips.

5 [c]Ps 125:3 mg **6** [a]Ps 78:55 [b]Jer 3:19 **7** [1]Lit *kidneys,* figurative for inner man [a]Ps 73:24 [b]Ps 77:6 **8** [a]Ps 16:8-11; Acts 2:25-28 [b]Ps 27:8; 123:1, 2 [c]Ps 73:23; 110:5; 121:5 [d]Ps 112:6 **9** [a]Ps 4:7; 13:5 [b]Ps 30:12; 57:8; 108:1 [c]Ps 4:8 **10** [1]I.e. the nether world [2]Lit *give* [3]Or *godly one* [4]Or *see corruption* or *the pit* [a]Ps 49:15; 86:13 [b]Acts 13:35 **11** [a]Ps 139:24; Matt 7:14 [b]Ps 21:6; 43:4 [c]Job 36:11; Ps 36:7, 8; 46:4 **17:1** [a]Ps 9:4 [b]Ps 61:1; 142:6 [c]Ps 88:2 [d]Is 29:13

2 [1]I.e. vindication [a]Ps 103:6 [b]Ps 98:9; 99:4 **3** [1]Or *no evil device in me; My mouth* [a]Ps 26:1, 2 [b]Job 23:10; Ps 66:10; Zech 13:9; 1 Pet 1:7 [c]Jer 50:20 [d]Ps 39:1 **4** [a]Ps 119:9, 101 [b]Ps 10:5-11 **5** [1]Lit *tracks* [a]Job 23:11; Ps 44:18; 119:133 [b]Ps 18:36; 37:31

2 Let [a]my [1]judgment come forth from Your presence;
Let Your eyes look with [b]equity.
3 You have [a]tried my heart;
You have visited *me* by night;
You have [b]tested me and [c]You find [1]nothing;
I have [d]purposed that my mouth will not transgress.
4 As for the deeds of men, [a]by the word of Your lips
I have kept from the [b]paths of the violent.
5 My [a]steps have held fast to Your [1]paths.
My [b]feet have not slipped.

6 I have [a]called upon You, for You will answer me, O God;
[b]Incline Your ear to me, hear my speech.
7 [a]Wondrously show Your lovingkindness,
O [b]Savior of those who take refuge [1]at Your right hand
From those who rise up *against them.*
8 Keep me as [1]the [a]apple of the eye;
Hide me [b]in the shadow of Your wings
9 From the [a]wicked who despoil me,
My [b]deadly enemies who surround me.

6 [a]Ps 86:7; 116:2 [b]Ps 88:2 **7** [1]Or *from those who rise up...at Your right hand* [a]Ps 31:21 [b]Ps 20:6 **8** [1]Lit *the pupil, the daughter of the eye* [a]Deut 32:10; Zech 2:8 [b]Ruth 2:12; Ps 36:7; 57:1; 61:4; 63:7; 91:1, 4 **9** [a]Ps 31:20 [b]Ps 27:12

(see 23:5) or salvation (see 116:13); He makes the wicked drink from a cup of wrath (see Jer 25:15; Rev 14:10; 16:19). *support my lot.* Just as each Israelite's family inheritance in the promised land was to be secure (see Lev 25; Num 36:7).

16:7–8 Praise of the Lord who counsels and keeps.

16:7 *counseled.* Shown the way that leads to life (see v. 11). *mind.* Lit. "kidneys" (see note on 7:9).

16:8 *He is at my right hand.* As sustainer and protector (see 73:23; 109:31; 110:5; 121:5); complemented by the reference to the Lord's right hand in v. 11. *not be shaken.* See note on 10:6.

16:9–11 Describes the joy of total security. David speaks here, as in the rest of his psalms, first of all of himself and of the life he now enjoys by the gracious provision and care of God. The Lord, in whom the psalmist takes refuge, wills life for him (hence he made known to him the path of life, v. 11) and will not abandon him to the grave, even though "flesh and . . . heart . . . fail" (73:26). But implicit in these words of assurance (if not actually explicit) is the confidence that, with the Lord as his refuge, even the grave cannot rob him of life (see 17:15; 73:24; see also note on 11:7). If this could be said of David, how much more of David's promised Son! So Peter quotes vv. 8–11 and declares that with these words David prophesied of Christ and His resurrection (Acts 2:25–28; see Paul's similar use of v. 10b in Acts 13:35). See also note on 6:5.

16:9 *heart.* See note on 4:7. *glory.* See note on 7:5.

16:10 *Holy One.* Hebrew *ḥasid* (see note on 4:3). Reference is first of all to David (see note on 2:2), but the psalm is ultimately fulfilled in Christ.

16:11 *path of life.* See Prov 15:24. *Your right hand.* See note on v. 8.

Ps 17 The psalmist appeals to the Lord as Judge, when under attack by ungodly foes. The psalm reflects many of the Hebrew conventions of lodging a judicial appeal before the king.

17 title *A Prayer.* See titles of Ps 86; 90; 102; 142; see also 72:20.

17:1–2 The initial appeal for justice.

17:1 *Hear a just cause . . . my cry.* His case is truly just, not a clever misrepresentation by deceitful lips (for a similar situation see 1 Sam 24:15).

17:3–5 David's claim of innocence in support of the rightness of his case. He is not guilty of the ungodly ways of his attackers—let God examine him (cf. 139:23–24).

17:3 *heart.* See note on 4:7.

17:4 *word of Your lips.* God's revealed will, by which He has made known the "paths" (v. 5) that people are to walk.

17:6–9 The petition: what the Lord is to do for him—motivated by David's trust in Him ("for You will answer me," v. 6) and the Lord's unfailing righteousness (see v. 7).

17:7 *Wondrously.* See note on 9:1. *lovingkindness.* See note on 6:4.

17:8 *apple of the eye.* See note on Deut 32:10. *shadow.* A conventional Hebrew metaphor for protection against oppression—as shade protects from the oppressive heat of the hot desert sun. Kings were spoken of as the "shade" of those dependent on them for protection (as in Num 14:9, "protection"—lit. "shade"; Lam 4:20; Ezek 31:6,12,17). Similarly, the Lord is the protective "shade" of his people (see 91:1; 121:5; Is 25:4; 49:2; 51:16). *wings.* Metaphor for the protective outreach of God's power (see 36:7; 57:1; 61:4; 63:7; 91:4; Ruth 2:12; see also Matt 23:37).

17:10–12 The accusation lodged against the vicious adversaries (see note on 5:9–10).

17:10 *mouth.* See note on 5:9. *speak proudly.* See note on 10:11.

10 They have [a]closed their [1]unfeeling
heart,
With their mouth they [b]speak proudly.
11 They have now [a]surrounded us in our
steps;
They set their eyes [b]to cast *us* down to
the ground.
12 He is [a]like a lion that is eager to tear,
And as a young lion [b]lurking in hiding
places.

13 [a]Arise, O LORD, confront him, [b]bring
him low;
[c]Deliver my soul from the wicked with
[d]Your sword,
14 From men with [a]Your hand, O LORD,
From men [1]of the world, [b]whose
portion is in *this* life,
And whose belly You [c]fill with Your
treasure;
They are satisfied with children,
And leave their abundance to their
babes.
15 As for me, I shall [a]behold Your face in
righteousness;
[b]I will be satisfied [1]with Your [c]likeness
when I awake.

Psalm 18

For the choir director. A *Psalm* of David the servant of the LORD, [†]who spoke to the LORD the words of this song in the day that the LORD delivered him from the hand of all his enemies and from the hand of Saul. And he said,

1 "I love You, O LORD, [a]my strength."

10 [1]Lit *fat* [a]Job 15:27; Ps 73:7 [b]1 Sam 2:3; Ps 31:18; 73:8
11 [a]Ps 88:17 [b]Ps 37:14
12 [a]Ps 7:2 [b]Ps 10:9
13 [a]Ps 3:7 [b]Ps 55:23 [c]Ps 22:20 [d]Ps 7:12
14 [1]Or *whose portion in life is of the world* [a]Ps 17:7 [b]Ps 73:3-7; Luke 16:25 [c]Ps 49:6
15 [1]Or *with* beholding [a]Ps 11:7; 16:11; 140:13; 1 John 3:2 [b]Ps 4:6, 7 [c]Num 12:8
18:1 [†]2 Sam 22:1-51 [a]Ps 59:17

2 [1]Or *crag* [a]Deut 32:18; 1 Sam 2:2; Ps 18:31, 46; 28:1; 31:3; 42:9; 71:3; 78:15 [b]Ps 144:2 [c]Ps 19:14 [d]Ps 28:7; 33:20; 59:11; 84:9, 11; Prov 30:5 [e]Ps 75:10 [f]Ps 59:9
3 [a]Ps 48:1; 96:4; 145:3 [b]Ps 34:6
4 [1]Or *destruction;* Heb *Belial* [2]Or *were assailing* or *terrifying* [a]Ps 116:3 [b]Ps 69:2; 124:3, 4
5 [1]I.e. the nether world [a]Ps 116:3
6 [a]Ps 50:15; 120:1 [b]Ps 3:4 [c]Ps 34:15

2 The LORD is [a]my [1]rock and [b]my
fortress and my [c]deliverer,
My God, my rock, in whom I take
refuge;
My [d]shield and the [e]horn of my
salvation, my [f]stronghold.
3 I call upon the LORD, who is [a]worthy
to be praised,
And I am [b]saved from my enemies.

4 The [a]cords of death encompassed me,
And the [b]torrents of [1]ungodliness
[2]terrified me.
5 The [a]cords of [1]Sheol surrounded me;
The snares of death confronted me.
6 In my [a]distress I called upon the LORD,
And cried to my God for help;
He heard my voice [b]out of His temple,
And my [c]cry for help before Him came
into His ears.

7 Then the [a]earth shook and quaked;
And the [b]foundations of the
mountains were trembling
And were shaken, because He was
angry.
8 Smoke went up [1]out of His nostrils,
And [a]fire from His mouth devoured;
Coals were kindled by it.
9 He [a]bowed the heavens also, and
came down
With thick [b]darkness under His feet.
10 He rode upon a [a]cherub and flew;

7 [a]Judg 5:4; Ps 68:7, 8; Is 13:13; Hag 2:6 [b]Ps 114:4, 6 **8** [1]Or *in His wrath* [a]Ps 50:3 **9** [a]Ps 144:5 [b]Ps 97:2 **10** [a]Ps 80:1; 99:1

17:12 *lion.* See note on 7:2.
17:13–14a Petition: how the Lord is to deal with the two parties in the conflict.
17:13 *Arise.* See note on 3:7. *bring him low.* See note on 5:10.
17:14 *men.* See 9:19–20; 10:18; 12:1–4,8; 14:1–3.
17:14b–15 Concluding confession of confidence (see note on 3:8).
17:15 *in righteousness.* The righteous Judge (see note on 5:8) will acknowledge and vindicate the innocence (righteousness) of the petitioner. *behold Your face.* See note on 11:7. *when I awake.* From the night of death (see note on 11:7)—in radical contrast to the destiny of the "men of the world" (v. 14; see notes on 6:5; 16:9–11). *behold . . . Your likeness.* As Moses the servant of the Lord had seen it (see Num 12:8).
Ps 18 This song of David occurs also (with minor variations) in 2 Sam 22 (see notes there). In its structure, apart from the introduction (vv. 1–3) and the conclusion (vv. 46–50), the song is composed of three major divisions: (1) the Lord's deliverance of David from his mortal enemies (vv. 4–19); (2) the moral grounds for the Lord's saving help (vv. 20–29); (3) the Lord's help recounted (vv. 30–45).
18 title *For the choir director.* See note on Ps 4 title. *servant of the LORD.* See 78:70; 89:3,20,39; 132:10; 144:10. The title designates David in his royal office as, in effect, an official in the Lord's own kingly rule over His people (see 2 Sam 7:5)—as were Moses (see Ex 14:31 and note), Joshua (see Josh 24:29) and the prophets (Elijah, 2 Kin 9:36; Jonah, 2 Kin 14:25; Isaiah, Is 20:3; Daniel, Dan 6:20). *song.* See note on Ps 30 title. *day that the LORD delivered him.* It is possible that David composed his song shortly after his victories over his foreign enemies (2 Sam 8:1–14), but it may have been later in his life.
18:1–3 A prelude of praise.
18:1 Does not occur in 2 Sam 22. *I love You.* From an unusual Hebrew expression that emphasizes the fervor of David's love.
18:2 *rock . . . rock.* The translation of two different Hebrew words. "Rock" is a common poetic figure for God (or the gods: Deut 32:31,37; Is 44:8), symbolizing His unfailing (see Is 26:4) strength as a fortress refuge (see vv. 31,46; 31:2–3; 42:9; 62:7; 71:3; 94:22; Is 17:10) or as deliverer (see 19:14; 62:2; 78:35; 89:26; 95:1; Deut 32:15). It is a figure particularly appropriate for David's experience (see 1 Sam 23:14,25; 24:2,22; 26:20), for the Lord was his true security. *fortress.* See note on 2 Sam 22:2. *shield.* See note on 3:3. *horn.* Here symbolizes strength (see Deut 33:17; Jer 48:25).
18:4–6 God heard his cry for help.
18:4–5 David depicts his experiences in poetic figures of mortal danger.
18:4 *cords.* 2 Sam 22:5 has "waves." *torrents of ungodliness.* See note on 30:1.
18:5 *cords of Sheol . . . snares of death.* See 116:3. He had, as it were, been snared by death (personified) and bound as a prisoner of the grave (see Job 36:8).
18:6 *temple.* God's heavenly abode, where He sits enthroned (see 11:4; 113:5; Is 6:1; 40:22).
18:7–15 The Lord came to the aid of His servant—depicted as a fearful theophany (divine manifestation) of the heavenly Warrior descending in wrathful attack upon David's enemies (see 5:4–5; 68:1–8; 77:16–19; Mic 1:3–4; Nah 1:2–6; Hab 3:3–15).

And He sped upon the [b]wings of the
wind.
11 He made [a]darkness His hiding place,
[b]His [1]canopy around Him,
Darkness of waters, thick clouds of
the skies.
12 From the [a]brightness before Him
passed His thick clouds,
Hailstones and [b]coals of fire.
13 The LORD also [a]thundered in the
heavens,
And the Most High uttered His voice,
Hailstones and coals of fire.
14 He [a]sent out His arrows, and scattered
them,
And lightning flashes in abundance,
and [1]routed them.
15 Then the [a]channels of water appeared,
And the foundations of the world
were [1]laid bare
At Your [b]rebuke, O LORD,
At the blast of the [c]breath of Your
nostrils.

16 He [a]sent from on high, He took me;
He drew me out of [b]many waters.
17 He [a]delivered me from my strong
enemy,
And from those who hated me, for
they were [b]too mighty for me.
18 They confronted me in [a]the day of my
calamity,
But [b]the LORD was my stay.
19 He brought me forth also into a
[a]broad place;
He rescued me, because [b]He delighted
in me.

20 The LORD has [a]rewarded me according
to my righteousness;
According to the [b]cleanness of my
hands He has recompensed me.
21 For I have [a]kept the ways of the LORD,
And have [b]not wickedly departed from
my God.
22 For all [a]His ordinances were before
me,
And I did not put away His [b]statutes
from me.
23 I was also [1a]blameless with Him,
And I [b]kept myself from my iniquity.
24 Therefore the LORD has [a]recompensed
me according to my righteousness,
According to the cleanness of my
hands in His eyes.

25 With [a]the kind You show Yourself
kind;
With the [1]blameless [b]You show
Yourself blameless;
26 With the pure You show Yourself
[a]pure,
And with the crooked [b]You show
Yourself [1]astute.
27 For You [a]save an afflicted people,
But [b]haughty eyes You abase.
28 For You [a]light my lamp;
The LORD my God [b]illumines my
darkness.
29 For by You I can [1a]run upon a troop;
And by my God I can [b]leap over a
wall.

30 As for God, His way is [1a]blameless;
The [b]word of the LORD is tried;
He is a [c]shield to all who take refuge
in Him.

10 [b]Ps 104:3 **11** [1]Or *pavilion* [a]Deut 4:11 [b]Ps 97:2 **12** [a]Ps 104:2 [b]Ps 97:3; 140:10; Hab 3:4 **13** [a]Ps 29:3; 104:7 **14** [1]Lit *confused* [a]Ps 144:6; Hab 3:11 **15** [1]Or *uncovered* [a]Ps 106:9 [b]Ps 76:6 [c]Ps 18:8 **16** [a]Ps 144:7 [b]Ps 32:6 **17** [a]Ps 59:1 [b]Ps 35:10; 142:6 **18** [a]Ps 59:16 [b]Ps 16:8 **19** [a]Ps 4:1; 31:8; 118:5 [b]Ps 37:23; 41:11 **20** [a]1 Sam 24:19; Job 33:26; Ps 7:8 **20** [b]Job 22:30; Ps 24:4 **21** [a]Ps 37:34; 119:33; Prov 8:32 [b]2 Chr 34:33; Ps 119:102 **22** [a]Ps 119:30 [b]Ps 119:83 **23** [1]Lit *complete;* or *having integrity;* or *perfect* [a]Ps 18:32 [b]Ps 19:12, 13; 25:11; 66:18 **24** [a]1 Sam 26:23; Ps 18:20 **25** [1]V 23, note 1 [a]1 Kin 8:32; Ps 62:12; Matt 5:7 [b]Ps 18:30 **26** [1]Lit *twisted* [a]Job 25:5; Hab 1:13 [b]Lev 26:23, 24, 27, 28; Prov 3:34 **27** [a]Ps 72:12 [b]Ps 101:5; Prov 6:17 **28** [a]1 Kin 15:4; Job 18:6; Ps 132:17 [b]Ps 27:1 **29** [1]Or *crush a troop* [a]Ps 118:10-12 [b]Ps 18:33; 40:2 **30** [1]V 23, note 1 [a]Deut 32:4; Ps 19:7; 145:17; Rev 15:3 [b]Ps 12:6 [c]Ps 17:7; 91:4

He sweeps down upon them like a fierce thunderstorm (see Josh 10:11; Judg 5:20–22; 1 Sam 2:10; 7:10; 2 Sam 5:24; Is 29:6).
18:8 God's fierce majesty is portrayed in terms similar to those applied to the awesome Leviathan (Job 41:19–21).
18:9 *bowed the heavens also, and came down.* See Is 64:1 and note.
18:10 *cherub.* A symbol of royalty (see 80:1; 99:1; see also notes on Gen 3:24; Ex 25:18). In Ezek 1; 10, cherubim appear as the bearers of the throne-chariot of God.
18:13 *Most High.* See note on Gen 14:19. *voice.* For thunder as the voice of God see Ps 29; Job 37:2–5.
18:14 *arrows.* For shafts of lightning as the arrows of God see 77:17; 144:6; Hab 3:11.
18:15 Perhaps recalls the great deed of the heavenly Warrior when He defeated Israel's enemy at the Red Sea (see Ex 15:1–12).
18:16–19 The deliverance.
18:16 *many waters.* See note on 32:6.
18:19 *broad place.* See 4:1 and note; where he is free to roam unconfined by the threats and dangers that had hemmed him in (vv. 4–6,16–18). To be afflicted or oppressed is like being bound by fetters (Job 36:8,13). To be delivered is to be set free (Job 36:16). *delighted in me.* God was pleased with David as "a man after His own heart" (1 Sam 13:14; see also 1 Sam 15:28; 1 Kin 14:8; 15:5), a man with whom He had made a covenant assuring him of an enduring dynasty (2 Sam 7). The thought is further elaborated in vv. 20–29.
18:20–24 David's righteousness rewarded. David's assertion of his righteousness (like that of Samuel, 1 Sam 12:3; Hezekiah, 2 Kin 20:3; Job, Job 13:23; 27:6; 31; see also Ps 17:3–5; 26; 44:17–18; 101) is not a pretentious boast of sinless perfection (see 51:5). Rather, it is a claim that, in contrast to his enemies, he has devoted himself heart and life to the service of the Lord, that his has been a godliness with integrity—itself the fruit of God's gracious working in his heart (see 51:10–12).
18:20 *my righteousness.* See note on 1:5. *rewarded me.* As a king benevolently rewards those who loyally serve him.
18:21 *ways of the LORD.* See 25:4 and note.
18:25–29 Because God responds to man in kind (see Job 34:1; Prov 3:34), David has experienced the Lord's favor.
18:26 *crooked.* Deviating from the straight path of truth and righteousness. *astute.* God responds to their perverse dealings thrust for thrust, like a wrestler countering his opponent.
18:27 The thought of this verse fits well with David's and Saul's reversals of status. It also echoes the central theme of Hannah's song, which the author of Samuel uses to highlight a major thesis of his account of the ways of God as He brings about His kingdom.
18:28 *light my lamp.* God causes his life and undertakings to flourish (see especially Job 18:5–6; 21:17). *illumines.* See note on 27:1.
18:30–36 By God's blessing David the king has thrived.

31 For [a]who is God, but the LORD?
And who is a [b]rock, except our God,
32 The God who [a]girds me with strength
And [1]makes my way [2b]blameless?
33 He [a]makes my feet like hinds' *feet*,
And [b]sets me upon my high places.
34 He [a]trains my hands for battle,
So that my arms can [b]bend a bow of bronze.
35 You have also given me [a]the shield of Your salvation,
And Your [b]right hand upholds me;
And [c]Your [1]gentleness makes me great.
36 You [a]enlarge my steps under me,
And my [1b]feet have not slipped.

37 I [a]pursued my enemies and overtook them,
And I did not turn back [b]until they were consumed.
38 I shattered them, so that they were [a]not able to rise;
They fell [b]under my feet.
39 For You have [a]girded me with strength for battle;
You have [1b]subdued under me those who rose up against me.
40 You have also made my enemies [a]turn their backs to me,
And I [1b]destroyed those who hated me.
41 They cried for help, but there was [a]none to save,
Even to the LORD, but [b]He did not answer them.
42 Then I beat them fine as the [a]dust before the wind;
I emptied them out as the mire of the streets.

43 You have delivered me from the [a]contentions of the people;
You have placed me as [b]head of the nations;
A [c]people whom I have not known serve me.
44 As soon as they hear, they obey me;
Foreigners [1a]submit to me.
45 Foreigners [a]fade away,
And [b]come trembling out of their [1]fortresses.

46 The LORD [a]lives, and blessed be [b]my rock;
And exalted be [c]the God of my salvation,
47 The God who [a]executes vengeance for me,
And [b]subdues peoples under me.
48 He [a]delivers me from my enemies;
Surely You [b]lift me above those who rise up against me;
You rescue me from the [c]violent man.
49 Therefore I will [a]give thanks to You among the nations, O LORD,
And I will [b]sing praises to Your name.
50 He gives great [1a]deliverance to His king,
And shows lovingkindness to [b]His anointed,
To David and [c]his [2]descendants forever.

Psalm 19

For the choir director. A Psalm of David.

1 The [a]heavens are telling of the glory of God;
And their [b]expanse is declaring the work of His hands.
2 Day to [a]day pours forth speech,
And [b]night to night reveals knowledge.

31 [a]Deut 32:39; 1 Sam 2:2; Ps 86:8-10; Is 45:5 [b]Deut 32:31; Ps 18:2; 62:2 **32** [1]Or *has made* [2]Lit *complete;* or *having integrity* [a]Ps 18:39; Is 45:5 [b]Ps 18:23 **33** [a]Hab 3:19 [b]Deut 32:13 **34** [a]Ps 144:1 [b]Job 29:20 **35** [1]Or *condescension* [a]Ps 33:20 [b]Ps 63:8; 119:117 [c]Ps 138:6 **36** [1]Lit *ankles* [a]Ps 18:33 [b]Ps 66:9; Prov 4:12 **37** [a]Ps 44:5 [b]Ps 37:20 **38** [a]Ps 36:12 [b]Ps 47:3 **39** [1]Lit *caused to bow down* [a]Ps 18:32 [b]Ps 18:47 **40** [1]Or *silenced* [a]Ps 21:12 [b]Ps 94:23 **41** [a]Ps 50:22 [b]Job 27:9; Prov 1:28 **42** [a]Ps 83:13 **43** [a]2 Sam 3:1; 19:9; Ps 35:1 **43** [b]2 Sam 8:1-18; Ps 89:27 [c]Is 55:5 **44** [1]Lit *deceive me;* i.e. give feigned obedience [a]Ps 66:3 **45** [1]Lit *fastnesses* [a]Ps 37:2 [b]Mic 7:17 **46** [a]Job 19:25 [b]Ps 18:2 [c]Ps 51:14 **47** [a]Ps 94:1 [b]Ps 18:43; 47:3; 144:2 **48** [a]Ps 3:7 [b]Ps 27:6; 59:1 [c]Ps 11:5 **49** [a]Rom 15:9 [b]Ps 108:1 **50** [1]I.e. victories; lit *salvations* [2]Lit *seed* [a]Ps 21:1; 144:10 [b]Ps 28:8 [c]Ps 89:4 **19:1** [a]Ps 8:1; 50:6; Rom 1:19, 20 [b]Gen 1:6, 7 **2** [a]Ps 74:16 [b]Ps 139:12

18:30 *is blameless.* Does not fail—and so, because of His blessing, David's way has not failed (see v. 32). *word of the LORD.* While the reference is general, it applies especially to God's promise to David (see 2 Sam 7:8–16). *tried.* See note on 12:6. *shield.* See note on 3:3.
18:37–42 With God's help David has crushed all his foes.
18:43–45 God has made David the head of nations (see 2 Sam 5; 8; 10)—he who had been, it seemed, on the brink of death (see vv. 4–5), sinking into the depths (see v. 16).
18:43 *contentions of the people.* All the threats he had endured from his own people in the days of Saul, and perhaps also in the time of Absalom's rebellion. *people whom I have not known.* Those with whom he had had no previous relations.
18:46–50 Concluding doxology.
18:46 *The LORD lives.* God's interventions and blessings in David's behalf have shown Him to be the living God (see Deut 5:26).
18:47 *executes vengeance for me.* Redresses the wrongs committed against me (see Deut 32:41).
18:49 David vows to praise the Lord among the nations (see note on 9:1). *name.* See note on 5:11.
18:50 *his king . . . his anointed.* David views himself as the Lord's chosen and anointed king (see 1 Sam 16:13; see also notes on 1 Sam 10:25; 12:14–15). *shows lovingkindness.* David's final words recall the Lord's covenant with him (see 2 Sam 7:8–16). The whole song is to be understood in the context of David's official capacity and the Lord's covenant with him. What David claims in this grand conclusion—as, indeed, in the whole psalm—has been and is being fulfilled in Jesus Christ, David's great descendant.
Ps 19 A hymn extolling "the glory of God" (v. 1) as revealed to all by the starry heavens (see vv. 1–6) and "the law of the LORD" (v. 7), which has been given to Israel (see vv. 7–13). Placed next to Ps 18, it completes the cycle of praise—for the Lord's saving acts, for His glory reflected in creation and for His law.
19 title *For the choir director.* See note on Ps 4 title.
19:1–4a The silent heavens speak, declaring the glory of their Maker to all who are on the earth (see 148:3). The heavenly lights are not divine (see Deut 4:19; 17:3), nor do they control or disclose man's destiny (see Is 47:13; Jer 10:2; Dan 4:7). Their glory testifies to the righteousness and faithfulness of the Lord who created them (see 50:6; 89:5–8; 97:6; see also Rom 1:19–20).

3 There is no speech, nor are there words;
Their voice is not heard.
4 Their [1][a]line has gone out through all the earth,
And their utterances to the end of the world.
In them He has [b]placed a tent for the sun,
5 Which is as a bridegroom coming out of his chamber;
It rejoices as a strong man to run his course.
6 Its [a]rising is from [1]one end of the heavens,
And its circuit to the [2]other end of them;
And there is nothing hidden from its heat.

7 [a]The law of the LORD is [1][b]perfect, [c]restoring the soul;
The testimony of the LORD is [d]sure, making [e]wise the simple.
8 The precepts of the LORD are [a]right, [b]rejoicing the heart;
The commandment of the LORD is [c]pure, [d]enlightening the eyes.
9 The fear of the LORD is clean, enduring forever;
The judgments of the LORD are [a]true; they are [b]righteous altogether.
10 They are more desirable than [a]gold, yes, than much fine gold;
[b]Sweeter also than honey and the drippings of the honeycomb.
11 Moreover, by them [a]Your servant is warned;
In keeping them there is great [b]reward.

4 [1]Another reading is *sound* [a]Rom 10:18 [b]Ps 104:2
6 [1]Lit *the* [2]Lit *the ends* [a]Ps 113:3; Eccl 1:5
7 [1]I.e. blameless [a]Ps 111:7 [b]Ps 119:160 [c]Ps 23:3 [d]Ps 93:5 [e]Ps 119:98-100
8 [a]Ps 119:128 [b]Ps 119:14 [c]Ps 12:6 [d]Ps 36:9
9 [a]Ps 119:142 [b]Ps 119:138
10 [a]Ps 119:72, 127 [b]Ps 119:103
11 [a]Ps 17:4 [b]Ps 24:5, 6; Prov 29:18
12 [a]Ps 40:12; 139:6 [b]Ps 51:1, 2 [c]Ps 90:8; 139:23, 24
13 [1]Lit *complete* [a]Num 15:30 [b]Ps 119:133 [c]Ps 18:32 [d]Ps 25:11
14 [a]Ps 104:34 [b]Ps 18:2 [c]Ps 31:5; Is 47:4
20:1 [a]Ps 50:15 [b]Ps 91:14 [c]Ps 46:7, 11
2 [a]Ps 3:4 [b]Ps 110:2
3 [1]Lit *fat* [2]*Selah* may mean: *Pause, Crescendo* or *Musical interlude* [a]Acts 10:4 [b]Ps 51:19
4 [1]Or *purpose* [a]Ps 21:2 [b]Ps 145:19
5 [1]Or *Let us sing* [2]Or *salvation* [a]Ps 9:14 [b]Ps 60:4 [c]1 Sam 1:17
6 [a]Ps 41:11

12 Who can [a]discern *his* errors? [b]Acquit me of [c]hidden *faults.*
13 Also keep back Your servant [a]from presumptuous *sins;*
Let them not [b]rule over me;
Then I will be [1][c]blameless,
And I shall be acquitted of [d]great transgression.
14 Let the words of my mouth and [a]the meditation of my heart
Be acceptable in Your sight,
O LORD, [b]my rock and my [c]Redeemer.

Psalm 20

For the choir director. A Psalm of David.

1 May the LORD answer you [a]in the day of trouble!
May the [b]name of the [c]God of Jacob set you *securely* on high!
2 May He send you help [a]from the sanctuary
And [b]support you from Zion!
3 May He [a]remember all your meal offerings
And [b]find your burnt offering [1]acceptable! [2]Selah.

4 May He grant you your [a]heart's desire
And [b]fulfill all your [1]counsel!
5 [1]We will [a]sing for joy over your [2]victory,
And in the name of our God we will [b]set up our banners.
May the LORD [c]fulfill all your petitions.

6 Now [a]I know that the LORD saves His anointed;

19:4 Interpreting this heavenly proclamation eschatologically in the light of Christ, Paul applies this verse to the proclamation of the gospel in his own day (see Rom 10:18). He thus associates these two universal proclamations.
19:4b–6 The heavens are the divinely pitched "tent" for the lordly sun—widely worshiped in the ancient Near East (cf. Deut 4:19; 17:3; 2 Kin 23:5,11; Jer 8:2; Ezek 8:16), but here, as in 136:7–8; Gen 1:16, a mere creature of God. Of the created realm, the sun is the supreme metaphor of the glory of God (see 84:11; Is 60:19–20), as it makes its daily triumphant sweep across the whole extent of the heavens and pours out its heat (felt presence) on every creature.
19:7–10 Stately, rhythmic celebration of the life-nurturing effects of the Lord's revealed law (see Ps 119).
19:7 *the simple.* The childlike, those whose understanding and judgment have not yet matured (see 119:98–100; Prov 1:4; cf. 2 Tim 3:15; Heb 5:13–14).
19:8 *heart.* See note on 4:7.
19:9 *fear of the LORD.* The sum of what the law requires (see note on 15:4).
19:10 *Sweeter also than honey.* By contrast, those who abandon the law turn justice into bitterness (see Amos 5:7; 6:12).
19:11–13 The law marks the way that leads to life (see Deut 5:33). But man's moral consciousness remains flawed and imperfect; hence he errs without realizing it and has reason to seek pardon for hidden faults (v. 12; see Lev 5:2–4). Willful sins (v. 13), however, are open rebellion; they are the great transgression (v. 13) that leads to being cut off from God's people (see Num 15:30–31).
19:11,13 *Your servant.* The psalmist himself.
19:14 The psalmist presents this hymn as a praise offering to the Lord. *heart.* See note on 4:7. *rock . . . Redeemer.* See 78:35. *rock.* See notes on 18:2; Gen 49:24. *Redeemer.* See note on Ex 6:6.
Ps 20 A liturgy of prayer for the king just before he goes out to battle against a threatening force (see 2 Chr 20:1–30).
20 title *For the choir director.* See note on Ps 4 title.
20:1–5 The people (perhaps his assembled army) address the king, adding their prayers to his prayer for victory.
20:1 *answer you.* Hear your prayers, offered in the present distress, accompanied by "offerings" (v. 3); see v. 9. *name.* See vv. 5,7; see also note on 5:11. *Jacob.* See note on 14:7. *set you . . . on high.* Lit. "raise you to a high, secure place."
20:2 *Zion.* See note on 9:11.
20:4 *heart's desire.* See note on 4:7.
20:5 *We will sing . . . name of our God.* See note on 7:17. *banners.* Probably the troop standards around which the units rallied.
20:6 A participant in the liturgy (perhaps a Levite; see 2 Chr 20:14) announces assurance that the king's prayer will be heard. *His anointed.* The king appointed by the Lord to rule in His name (see 2:2 and note).

He will [b]answer him from His holy
heaven
With the [1c]saving strength of His right
hand.
7 Some [1]*boast* in chariots and some in
[a]horses,
But [b]we [2]will boast in the name of the
LORD, our God.
8 They have [a]bowed down and fallen,
But we have [b]risen and stood
upright.
9 [1a]Save, O LORD;
May the [b]King answer us in the day
we call.

Psalm 21

For the choir director. A Psalm of David.

1 O LORD, in Your strength the king will
[a]be glad,
And in Your [1]salvation how greatly he
will rejoice!
2 You have [a]given him his heart's
desire,
And You have not withheld the
request of his lips. [1]Selah.
3 For You [a]meet him with the blessings
of good things;
You set a [b]crown of fine gold on his
head.
4 He asked life of You,
You [a]gave it to him,
[b]Length of days forever and ever.
5 His [a]glory is great through Your
[1]salvation,
[b]Splendor and majesty You place upon
him.
6 For You make him [1]most [a]blessed
forever;
You make him joyful [b]with gladness in
Your presence.
7 For the king [a]trusts in the LORD,
And through the lovingkindness of the
Most High [b]he will not be shaken.
8 Your hand will [a]find out all your
enemies;
Your right hand will find out those
who hate you.
9 You will make them [a]as a fiery oven in
the time [1]of your anger;
The LORD will [b]swallow them up in
His wrath,
And [c]fire will devour them.
10 Their [1]offspring You will destroy from
the earth,
And their [2a]descendants from among
the sons of men.
11 Though they [1a]intended evil against
You
And [b]devised a plot,
They will not succeed.
12 For You will [a]make them turn their
back;
You will [1]aim [b]with Your bowstrings
at their faces.
13 Be exalted, O LORD, in Your strength;
We will [a]sing and praise Your power.

6 [1]Or *mighty deeds of the victory of His right hand* [b]Is 58:9 [c]Ps 28:8
7 [1]Or praise *chariots,* or trust, or are strong *through* [2]Lit *make mention of;* or *praise the name* [a]Ps 33:17 [b]2 Chr 32:8
8 [a]Is 2:11, 17 [b]Ps 37:24; Mic 7:8
9 [1]Or *O LORD, save the king; answer us* [a]Ps 3:7 [b]Ps 17:6
21:1 [1]Or *victory* [a]Ps 59:16, 17
2 [1]*Selah* may mean: *Pause, Crescendo* or *Musical interlude* [a]Ps 20:4; 37:4
3 [a]Ps 59:10 [b]2 Sam 12:30
4 [a]Ps 61:6; 133:3 [b]Ps 91:16
5 [1]Or *victory* [a]Ps 9:14; 20:5
5 [b]Ps 8:5; 96:6
6 [1]Lit *blessings* [a]1 Chr 17:27 [b]Ps 43:4
7 [a]Ps 125:1 [b]Ps 112:6
8 [a]Is 10:10
9 [1]Or *of your presence* [a]Mal 4:1 [b]Lam 2:2 [c]Ps 50:3
10 [1]Lit *fruit* [2]Lit *seed* [a]Ps 37:28
11 [1]Lit *stretched out* [a]Ps 2:1-3 [b]Ps 10:2
12 [1]Lit *make ready* [a]Ps 18:40 [b]Ps 7:12, 13
13 [a]Ps 59:16; 81:1

20:7–8 The army's confession of trust in the Lord rather than in a chariot corps (cf. 33:16–17)—the enemy perhaps came reinforced by such a prized corps. See David's similar confession of confidence when he faced Goliath (1 Sam 17:45–47).
20:9 The army's concluding petition. *answer us.* See note on v. 1. The psalm ends as it began.
Ps 21 A psalm of praise for victories granted to the king. It is thus linked with Ps 20, but whether both were occasioned by the same events is unknown. Here the people's praise follows that of the king (see v. 1); there (Ps 20) the people's prayer was added to the king's. In its structure, the psalm is framed by vv. 1,13 ("O LORD, in Your strength" is in both verses) and is centered around v. 7, which proclaims the king's trust in the Lord and the security afforded him by God's unfailing love (see Introduction: Literary Features).
21 title *For the choir director.* See note on Ps 4 title.
21:2–6 The people celebrate the Lord's many favors to the king: all "his heart's desire" (v. 2). Verse 2 announces the theme; vv. 3–5 develop the theme; v. 6 climactically summarizes the theme.
21:2 *heart's desire.* See note on 4:7.
21:3 *meet him.* Welcome him back from the battles. *set a crown . . . on his head.* Exchange the warrior's helmet for the ceremonial emblem of royalty—possibly the captured crown of the defeated king (see 2 Sam 12:30).
21:4 The king's life has been spared—to live for ever and ever (see 1 Kin 1:31; Dan 2:4; 3:9; see also 1 Sam 10:24; 1 Kin 1:25, 34,39).
21:5 *glory . . . Splendor and majesty.* See 45:3; like that of his heavenly Overlord (see 96:3).
21:6 *blessed forever.* Either (1) blessings of enduring value or (2) an unending flow of blessings. *Your presence.* Your favor, which is the supreme cause of joy because it is the greatest blessing and the wellspring of all other blessings.
21:7 The center of the psalm (see note on 6:6). A participant in the liturgy (perhaps a priest or Levite) proclaims the reasons for the king's security. *LORD . . . Most High.* That is, LORD Most High (see 7:17; see also note on 3:7). *lovingkindness.* See note on 6:4. *Most High.* See note on Gen 14:19. *shaken.* See note on 10:6.
21:8–12 The people hail the future victories of their triumphant king. Verse 8 announces the theme; vv. 9–11 develop the theme; v. 12 summarizes the theme.
21:9 *The LORD . . . in His wrath .* Credits the king's victories to the Lord's wrath (see note on 2:5).
21:10 The king's royal enemies will be left no descendants to rise against him again.
21:13 Conclusion—and return to the beginning: Lord, assert Your strength, in which "the king will be glad" (v. 1; see also v. 7), and we will ever praise Your might.
Ps 22 The anguished prayer of David as a godly sufferer victimized by the vicious and prolonged attacks of enemies whom he has not provoked and from whom the Lord has not (yet) delivered him. It has many similarities with Ps 69, but contains no calls for redress (see note on 5:10) such as are found in 69:22–28. No other psalm fitted quite so aptly the circumstances of Jesus at His crucifixion. Hence on the cross He took it to His lips (see Matt 27:46 and parallels), and the Gospel writers, especially Matthew and John, frequently alluded to it (as

Psalm 22

For the choir director; upon [†]Aijeleth Hashshahar.
A Psalm of David.

1 [a]My God, my God, why have You
forsaken me?
[1b]Far from my deliverance are the
words of my [2c]groaning.
2 O my God, I [a]cry by day, but You do
not answer;
And by night, but [1]I have no rest.
3 Yet [a]You are holy,
O You who [1]are enthroned upon [b]the
praises of Israel.
4 In You our fathers [a]trusted;
They trusted and You [b]delivered them.
5 To You they cried out and were
delivered;
[a]In You they trusted and were not
[1]disappointed.

6 But I am a [a]worm and not a man,
A [b]reproach of men and [c]despised by
the people.
7 All who see me [1a]sneer at me;
They [2]separate with the lip, they [b]wag
the head, *saying,*
8 "[1]Commit *yourself* to the LORD; [a]let
Him deliver him;
Let Him rescue him, because He
delights in him."

9 Yet You are He who [a]brought me forth
from the womb;
You made me trust *when* upon my
mother's breasts.
10 Upon You I was cast [a]from [1]birth;
You have been my God from my
mother's womb.

11 [a]Be not far from me, for [1]trouble is
near;
For there is [b]none to help.
12 Many [a]bulls have surrounded me;
Strong *bulls* of [b]Bashan have encircled
me.
13 They [a]open wide their mouth at me,
As a ravening and a roaring [b]lion.
14 I am [a]poured out like water,
And all my [b]bones are out of joint;
My [c]heart is like wax;
It is melted within [1]me.
15 My [a]strength is dried up like a
potsherd,
And [b]my tongue cleaves to my jaws;
And You [c]lay me [1]in the dust of death.
16 For [a]dogs have surrounded me;
[1]A band of evildoers has encompassed
me;
[2]They [b]pierced my hands and my feet.
17 I can count all my bones.
[a]They look, they stare at me;
18 They [a]divide my garments among them,
And for my clothing they cast lots.

19 But You, O LORD, [a]be not far off;
O You my help, [b]hasten to my
assistance.
20 Deliver my [1]soul from [a]the sword,
My [b]only *life* from the [2]power of the
dog.
21 Save me from the [a]lion's mouth;
From the horns of the [b]wild oxen You
[c]answer me.

22:1 [†]Lit *the hind of the morning* [1]Or *Why are You so far from helping me,* and from *the words of my groaning?* [2]Lit *roaring* [a]Matt 27:46; Mark 15:34 [b]Ps 10:1 [c]Job 3:24; Ps 6:6; 32:3; 38:8
2 [1]Lit *there is no silence for me* [a]Ps 42:3; 88:1
3 [1]Or *inhabit the praises* [a]Ps 99:9 [b]Deut 10:21; Ps 148:14
4 [a]Ps 78:53 [b]Ps 107:6
5 [1]Or *ashamed* [a]Is 49:23
6 [a]Job 25:6; Is 41:14 [b]Ps 31:11 [c]Is 49:7; 53:3
7 [1]Or *mock me* [2]I.e. make mouths at me [a]Ps 79:4; Is 53:3; Luke 23:35 [b]Matt 27:39; Mark 15:29
8 [1]Lit *Roll;* another reading is *He committed* himself [a]Ps 91:14; Matt 27:43
9 [a]Ps 71:5, 6
10 [1]Lit a *womb* [a]Is 46:3; 49:1
11 [1]Or *distress* [a]Ps 71:12 [b]2 Kin 14:26; Ps 72:12; Is 63:5
12 [a]Ps 22:21; 68:30 [b]Deut 32:14; Amos 4:1
13 [a]Job 16:10; Ps 35:21; Lam 2:16; 3:46 [b]Ps 10:9; 17:12
14 [1]Lit *my inward parts* [a]Job 30:16 [b]Ps 31:10; Dan 5:6 [c]Josh 7:5; Job 23:16; Ps 73:26; Nah 2:10
15 [1]Lit *to* [a]Ps 38:10 [b]John 19:28 [c]Ps 104:29
16 [1]Or *An assembly* [2]Another reading is *Like a lion, my...* [a]Ps 59:6, 7 [b]Matt 27:35; John 20:25
17 [a]Luke 23:27, 35
18 [a]Matt 27:35; Mark 15:24; Luke 23:34; John 19:24
19 [a]Ps 22:11 [b]Ps 70:5
20 [1]Or *life* [2]Lit *paw* [a]Ps 37:14 [b]Ps 35:17
21 [a]Ps 22:13 [b]Ps 22:12 [c]Ps 34:4; 118:5; 120:1

---

they did to Ps 69) in their accounts of Christ's passion (Matt 27:35,39,43; John 19:23–24,28). They saw in the passion of Jesus the fulfillment of this cry of the righteous sufferer. The author of Hebrews placed the words of v. 22 on Jesus' lips (see Heb 2:12 and note). No psalm is quoted more frequently in the NT.
22 title See notes on Ps 4; 9 titles.
22:1 *why . . . ?* See note on 6:3; see also Introduction: Theology.
22:1a Quoted by Jesus in Matt 27:46; Mark 15:34.
22:3–5 Recollection of what the Lord has been for Israel (see note on vv. 9–10).
22:3 *enthroned.* See note on 9:11. *praises of Israel.* The one Israel praises for His saving acts in her behalf (see 148:14; Deut 10:21; Jer 17:14).
22:6 *a worm and not a man.* See Job 25:6; Is 41:14.
22:7 *separate with the lip . . . wag the head.* See Matt 27:39; Mark 15:29; see also note on 5:9.
22:8 Quoted in part in Matt 27:43; see note on 3:2.
22:9–10 Recollection of what the Lord has been for him (see note on vv. 3–5).
22:12–18 The psalmist's deep distress. In vv. 12–13,16–18 he uses four figures to portray the attacks of his enemies; in vv. 14–15 he describes his inner sense of powerlessness under their fierce attacks.
22:12–13,16 *bulls . . . lion . . . dogs.* Metaphors for the enemies (see note on 7:2).
22:12 *Bashan.* Noted for its good pasturage, and hence for the size and vigor of its animals (see Deut 32:14, Ezek 39:18 and note; Amos 4:1).
22:14 *bones . . . heart.* See note on 102:4. *heart.* See note on 4:7.
22:15 See John 19:28 and note. *dust of death.* See v. 29; see also Job 7:21 and note.
22:16 *pierced my hands and my feet.* The dogs and/or evil men wound his limbs as he seeks to ward off their attacks. But see also Is 53:5; Zech 12:10; John 19:34,37.
22:17 *I can count all my bones.* Perhaps better, "I must display all my bones." The figure may be of one attacked by highway robbers or enemy soldiers, who strip him of his garments (see v. 18; see also note on vv. 20–21).
22:18 See introduction to this psalm; see also John 19:23–24.
22:20–21 The psalmist's prayer recalls in reverse order the four figures by which he portrayed his attackers in vv. 12–13,16–18: "sword," "dog," "lion," "wild oxen." Here "sword" may evoke the scene described in vv. 16b–18, and thus many interpret it as an attack by robbers or enemy soldiers, though "sword" is often used figuratively of any violent death.
22:21 *You answer me.* The psalmist experiences the assurance of having been heard. The sense is: You have heard my petition and will answer me by delivering me from death at the hands of my enemies (see note on 3:8). *wild oxen.* Aurochs, wild ancestors of domestic cattle; or possibly oryxes, large straight-horned antelopes.

22 I will [a]tell of Your name to my
brethren;
In the midst of the assembly I will
praise You.
23 [a]You who fear the LORD, praise Him;
All you [1]descendants of Jacob, [b]glorify
Him,
And [c]stand in awe of Him, all you
[1]descendants of Israel.
24 For He has [a]not despised nor abhorred
the affliction of the afflicted;
Nor has He [b]hidden His face from
him;
But [c]when he cried to Him for help,
He heard.

25 From You *comes* [a]my praise in the
great assembly;
I shall [b]pay my vows before those
who fear Him.
26 The [1]afflicted will eat and [a]be
satisfied;
Those who seek Him will [b]praise the
LORD.
Let your [c]heart live forever!
27 All the [a]ends of the earth will
remember and turn to the LORD,
And all the [b]families of the nations
will worship before [1]You.
28 For the [a]kingdom is the LORD's
And He [b]rules over the nations.

29 All the [1a]prosperous of the earth will
eat and worship,
All those who [b]go down to the dust
will bow before Him,
Even he who [2c]cannot keep his soul
alive.
30 [1a]Posterity will serve Him;
It will be told of the Lord to [b]the
coming generation.
31 They will come and [a]will declare His
righteousness
To a people [b]who will be born, that
He has performed *it*.

Psalm 23

A Psalm of David.

1 The LORD is my [a]shepherd,
I [1]shall [b]not want.
2 He makes me lie down in [a]green
pastures;
He [b]leads me beside [1c]quiet waters.
3 He [a]restores my soul;
He [b]guides me in the [1c]paths of
righteousness
For His name's sake.

4 Even though I [a]walk through the
[1]valley of the shadow of death,

22 [a]Ps 40:10; Heb 2:12
23 [1]Lit *seed* [a]Ps 135:19, 20 [b]Ps 86:12 [c]Ps 33:8
24 [a]Ps 69:33 [b]Ps 27:9; 69:17; 102:2 [c]Ps 31:22; Heb 5:7
25 [a]Ps 35:18; 40:9, 10 [b]Ps 61:8; Eccl 5:4
26 [1]Or *poor* [a]Ps 107:9 [b]Ps 40:16 [c]Ps 69:32
27 [1]Some versions read *Him* [a]Ps 2:8; 82:8 [b]Ps 86:9
28 [a]Ps 47:7; Obad 21; Zech 14:9; Matt 6:13 [b]Ps 47:8
29 [1]Lit *fat ones* [2]Or *did not* [a]Ps 17:10; 45:12; Hab 1:16 [b]Ps 28:1; Is 26:19 [c]Ps 89:48
30 [1]Lit *A seed* [a]Ps 102:28 [b]Ps 102:18
31 [a]Ps 40:9; 71:18 [b]Ps 78:6
23:1 [1]Or *do* [a]Ps 78:52; 80:1; Is 40:11; Jer 31:10; Ezek 34:11-13; John 10:11; 1 Pet 2:25 [b]Ps 34:9, 10; Phil 4:19
2 [1]Lit *waters of rest* [a]Ps 65:11-13; Ezek 34:14 [b]Rev 7:17 [c]Ps 36:8; 46:4 8:20
3 [1]Lit *tracks* [a]Ps 19:7 [b]Ps 5:8; 31:3 [c]Ps 85:13; Prov 4:11;
4 [1]Or *valley of deep darkness* [a]Job 10:21, 22; Ps 107:14

22:22–31 Vows to praise the Lord when the Lord's sure deliverance comes (see note on 7:17). The vows proper appear in vv. 22,25. Verses 23–24 anticipate the calls to praise that will accompany the psalmist's praise (see note on 9:1). Verses 26–31 describe the expanding company of those who will take up the praise—a worldwide company of persons from every station in life and continuing through the generations. No psalm or prophecy contains a grander vision of the scope of the throng of worshipers who will join in the praise of God's saving acts.
22:22 See Heb 2:12 and note. *name.* See note on 5:11.
22:23 *fear the LORD.* See v. 25; see also note on 15:4.
22:25 *assembly.* See note on 1:5.
22:26 *will eat and be satisfied.* As they share in the ceremonial festival of praise (see Lev 7:11–27).
22:27 *All the ends of the earth.* They too will be told of God's saving acts (see 18:49 and note on 9:1). The good news that the God of Israel hears the prayers of His people and saves them will move them to turn from their idols to the true God.
22:28 The rule of the God of Israel is universal, and the nations will come to recognize that fact through what He does in behalf of His people (see Ps 47; Gen 12:2–3; see also Deut 32:21; Rom 10:19; 11:13–14).
22:29 *All the prosperous . . . All those who go down.* The most prosperous and those on the brink of death, and all those whose life situation falls in between these two extremes. *dust.* See v. 15; see also Job 7:21 and note.
22:31 *righteousness.* See note on 4:1.
Ps 23 A profession of joyful trust in the Lord as the good Shepherd-King. The psalm may have accompanied a festival of praise at "the house of the LORD" (v. 6) following a deliverance, such as is contemplated in 22:25–31 (see note on 7:17). The psalm can be divided into two balanced stanzas, each having four couplets (a couplet is one line of Hebrew poetry): (1) stanza one: vv. 1–2a,2b–3a,3b-c,4a-c (v. 4a-b is metrically a half-couplet); (2) stanza two: vv. 5a-b,5c-d,6a-b,6c-d. The triplet in the middle (v. 4d-f) is then a centering line (see note on 6:6), focusing on the Shepherd-King's reassuring presence with His people. It serves as a transition between the two stanzas, concluding the shepherd-sheep motif of the first and introducing the direct address ("you") of the second. The psalm is framed by the first and last couplets, each of which refers to "the LORD."
23:1 *shepherd.* A widely used metaphor for kings in the ancient Near East, and also in Israel (see 78:71–72; 2 Sam 5:2; Is 44:28; Jer 3:15; 23:1–4; Mic 5:4). For the Lord as the shepherd of Israel see 28:9; 79:13; 80:1; 95:7; 100:3; Gen 48:15; Is 40:11; Jer 17:16; 31:10; 50:19; Ezek 34:11–16. Here David the king acknowledges that the Lord is his Shepherd-King. For Jesus as the shepherd of His people see John 10:11,14; Heb 13:20; 1 Pet 5:4; Rev 7:17. *not want.* On the contrary, he will enjoy "goodness" all his life (v. 6).
23:2 *lie down.* For flocks lying down in contented and secure rest see Is 14:30; 17:2; Jer 33:12; Ezek 34:14–15; Zeph 2:7; 3:13. *green pastures.* Metaphor for all that makes life to flourish (see Ezek 34:14; John 10:9). *leads me.* Like a shepherd (see Is 40:11). *quiet waters.* Lit. "waters of resting places," i.e., restful waters—waters that provide refreshment and well-being (see Is 49:10).
23:3 *restores my soul.* Revives me, refreshes my spirit (see 19:7; Ruth 4:15; Prov 25:13; Lam 1:16). *guides me in the paths of righteousness.* As a shepherd leads his sheep (see 77:20; 78:72) in paths that offer safety and well-being, so David's Shepherd-King guides him in ways that cause him to be secure and prosperous. For this meaning of "righteousness" see Prov 8:18; 21:21; Is 48:18; see also Prov 8:20–21. It is also possible that "paths of righteousness" refers to the paths that conform to God's moral will. *for His name's sake.* The prosperity of the Lord's servant brings honor to the Lord's name (see 1 Kin 8:41–42; Is 48:9; Jer 14:21; Ezek 20:9,14,22).

I [b]fear no [2]evil, for [c]You are with me;
Your [d]rod and Your staff, they comfort
me.
5 You [a]prepare a table before me in the
presence of my enemies;
You [1]have [b]anointed my head with oil;
My [c]cup overflows.
6 [1]Surely [a]goodness and lovingkindness
will follow me all the days of my
life,
And I will [2b]dwell in the house of the
LORD [3]forever.

Psalm 24

A Psalm of David.

1 The [a]earth is the LORD's, and [1]all it
contains,
The [b]world, and those who dwell
in it.
2 For He has [a]founded it upon the seas
And established it upon the rivers.
3 Who may [a]ascend into the [b]hill of the
LORD?
And who may stand in His holy
[c]place?
4 He who has [a]clean hands and a [b]pure
heart,
Who has not [c]lifted up his soul [1]to
falsehood
And has not [d]sworn deceitfully.
5 He shall receive a [a]blessing from the
LORD
And [1b]righteousness from the God of
his salvation.
6 [1]This is the generation of those who
[a]seek Him,
Who seek Your face—*even* Jacob.
[2]Selah.
7 [a]Lift up your heads, O gates,
And be lifted up, O [1]ancient doors,
That the King of [b]glory may come in!
8 Who is the King of glory?
The LORD [a]strong and mighty,
The LORD [b]mighty in battle.
9 Lift up your heads, O gates,
And lift *them* up, O [1]ancient doors,
That the King of [a]glory may come in!

4 [2]Or *harm* [b]Ps 3:6; 27:1 [c]Ps 16:8; Is 43:2 [d]Mic 7:14
5 [1]Or *anoint* [a]Ps 78:19 [b]Ps 92:10; Luke 7:46 [c]Ps 16:5
6 [1]Or *Only* [2]Another reading is *return to* [3]Lit *for length of days* [a]Ps 25:7, 10 [b]Ps 27:4-6
24:1 [1]Lit *its fullness* [a]1 Cor 10:26 [b]Ps 89:11
2 [a]Ps 104:3, 5; 136:6
3 [a]Ps 15:1 [b]Ps 2:6 [c]Ps 65:4
4 [1]Or *in vain* [a]Job 17:9; Ps 22:30; 26:6 [b]Ps 51:10; 73:1; Matt 5:8 [c]Ezek 18:15 [d]Ps 15:4
5 [1]I.e. as vindicated [a]Ps 115:13 [b]Ps 36:10
6 [1]Or *Such* [2]*Selah* may mean: *Pause, Crescendo* or *Musical interlude* [a]Ps 27:4, 8
7 [1]Lit *everlasting* [a]Ps 118:20; Is 26:2 [b]Ps 29:2, 9; 97:6; Acts 7:2; 1 Cor 2:8
8 [a]Deut 4:34; Ps 96:7 [b]Ex 15:3, 6; Ps 76:3-6
9 [1]Lit *everlasting* [a]Ps 26:8; 57:11

23:4 *for You . . . comfort me.* The very center of the psalm; see introductory note above. *with me.* See 16:8 and note; see also Deut 31:6,8; Matt 28:20. *rod.* Instrument of authority (as in 2:9; 45:6; Ex 21:20; 2 Sam 7:14; Job 9:34); used also by shepherds for counting, guiding, rescuing and protecting sheep (see Lev 27:32; Ezek 20:37). *staff.* Instrument of support (as in Ex 21:19; Judg 6:21; 2 Kin 4:29; Zech 8:4). *comfort me.* Reassure me (as in 71:21; 86:17; Ruth 2:13; Is 12:1; 40:1; 49:13).

23:5 The heavenly Shepherd-King receives David at His table as his vassal king and takes him under His protection. In the ancient Near East, covenants were often concluded with a meal expressive of the bond of friendship (see 41:9; Gen 31:54; Obad 7); in the case of vassal treaties or covenants, the vassal was present as the guest of the overlord (see Ex 24:8–12). *anointed my head with oil.* Customary treatment of an honored guest at a banquet (see Luke 7:46; see also 2 Sam 12:20; Eccl 9:8; Dan 10:3). *cup.* Of the Lord's banquet (see note on 16:5).

23:6 *goodness and lovingkindness.* Both frequently refer to covenant benefits (see note on 6:4); here they are personified (see 25:21; 43:3; 79:8; 89:14). *follow.* Lit. "pursue." *dwell in the house of the LORD.* See note on 15:1. *forever.* The Hebrew for this word suggests "throughout the years." But see also notes on 11:7; 16:9–11.

Ps 24 A processional liturgy (see Ps 47; 68; 118; 132) celebrating the Lord's entrance into Zion—composed either for the occasion when David brought the ark to Jerusalem (see 2 Sam 6) or for a festival commemorating the event. It was probably placed next to Ps 23 because it prescribes who may enter the sanctuary (see 23:6). The church has long used this psalm in celebration of Christ's ascension into the heavenly Jerusalem—and into the sanctuary on high (see introduction to Ps 47).

24:1–2 The prelude (perhaps spoken by a Levite), proclaiming the Lord as the Creator, Sustainer and Possessor of the whole world, and therefore worthy of worship and reverent loyalty as "the King of glory" (vv. 7–10; see Ps 29; 33:6–11; 89:5–18; 93; 95:3–5; 104).

24:1 *The earth . . . all it contains.* For Paul's use of this declaration see 1 Cor 10:25–26.

24:2 An echo of Gen 1:1–10. *founded . . . established.* A metaphor taken from the founding of a city (see Josh 6:26; 1 Kin 16:24; Is 14:32) or of a temple (see 1 Kin 5:17; 6:37; Ezra 3:6–12; Is 44:28; Hag 2:18; Zech 4:9; 8:9). Like a temple, the earth was depicted as having foundations (see 18:15; 82:5; 1 Sam 2:8; Prov 8:29; Is 24:18) and pillars (see 75:3; Job 9:6). In the ancient Near East, temples were thought of as microcosms of the created world, so language applicable to a temple could readily be applied to the earth. *upon.* Or "above" (see 104:5–9; Gen 1:9; 49:25; Ex 20:4; Deut 33:13).

24:3–6 Instruction concerning those who may enter the sanctuary (probably spoken by a priest); see Ps 15 and introduction.

24:3 *hill of the LORD.* See 2:6 and note.

24:4 *clean hands.* Guiltless actions. *pure heart.* Right attitudes and motives. Jesus said that the "pure in heart . . . shall see God" (Matt 5:8). *heart.* See note on 4:7. *lifted up his soul to.* Worshiped or put his trust in (see 25:1–2). *soul.* See note on 6:3. *sworn deceitfully.* Thus it includes perjury (for the same concern see Ex 20:16; Lev 19:12; Jer 5:2; 7:9; Zech 5:4; Mal 3:5).

24:5 *righteousness.* That is, the fruits of vindication, such as righteous treatment from a faithful God; hence, here a synonym of "blessing" (see 23:3 and note).

24:6 *generation.* See note on 78:8. *Jacob.* See note on 14:7.

24:7–10 Heralding the approach of the King of glory (perhaps spoken by the king at the head of the assembled Israelites, with responses by the keepers of the gates). The Lord's arrival at His sanctuary in Zion completes His march from Egypt. "The LORD of hosts" (v. 10), "the LORD mighty in battle" (v. 8; see Ex 15:1–18), has triumphed over all His enemies and comes now in victory to His own city (see Ps 46; 48; 76; 87), His "resting place" (132:8,14; see 68:7–8; Judg 5:4–5; Hab 3:3–7). Henceforth Jerusalem is the royal city of the kingdom of God (see note on 9:11).

24:7 *Lift up your heads . . . be lifted up.* In jubilant reception of the victorious King of glory (see 3:3; 27:6; 110:7). *gates.* Reference could be to the gates of either the city or the sanctuary. *doors.* A synonym for "gates," not in this case the doors of the gates (as in Judg 16:3; 1 Sam 21:13). The gates are personified for dramatic effect, as in Is 14:31.

10 Who is this King of glory?
The LORD of [a]hosts,
He is the King of glory. Selah.

Psalm 25

A Psalm of David.

1 To You, O LORD, I [a]lift up my soul.
2 O my God, in You [a]I trust,
Do not let me [b]be ashamed;
Do not let my [c]enemies exult over me.
3 Indeed, [a]none of those who wait for
You will be ashamed;
[1]Those who [b]deal treacherously
without cause will be ashamed.

4 [a]Make me know Your ways, O LORD;
Teach me Your paths.
5 Lead me in [a]Your truth and teach me,
For You are the [b]God of my salvation;
For You I [c]wait all the day.
6 [a]Remember, O LORD, Your compassion
and Your lovingkindnesses,
For they have been [1b]from of old.
7 Do not remember the [a]sins of my
youth or my transgressions;
[b]According to Your lovingkindness
remember me,
For Your [c]goodness' sake, O LORD.

8 [a]Good and [b]upright is the LORD;
Therefore He [c]instructs sinners in the
way.
9 He [a]leads the [1]humble in justice,
And He [b]teaches the [1]humble His way.

10 [a]Gen 32:2; Josh 5:14; 2 Sam 5:10; Neh 9:6
25:1 [a]Ps 86:4; 143:8
2 [a]Ps 31:1 [b]Ps 25:20; 31:1 [c]Ps 13:4; 41:11
3 [1]Or *Let those...be ashamed* [a]Ps 37:9; 40:1; Is 49:23 [b]Ps 119:158; Is 21:2; Hab 1:13
4 [a]Ex 33:13; Ps 27:11; 86:11
5 [a]Ps 25:10; 43:3 [b]Ps 79:9 [c]Ps 40:1
6 [1]Or *everlasting* [a]Ps 98:3 [b]Ps 103:17
7 [a]Job 13:26; 20:11 [b]Ps 51:1 [c]Ps 31:19
8 [a]Ps 86:5 [b]Ps 92:15 [c]Ps 32:8
9 [1]Or *afflicted* [a]Ps 23:3 [b]Ps 27:11

10 [a]Ps 40:11 [b]Ps 103:18
11 [a]Ps 31:3; 79:9 [b]Ex 34:9
12 [a]Ps 31:19 [b]Ps 25:8; 37:23
13 [1]Lit *good* [2]Lit *seed* [3]Or *earth* [a]Prov 1:33; Jer 23:6 [b]Ps 37:11; 69:36; Matt 5:5
14 [1]Or *counsel* or *intimacy* [2]Or *And His covenant, to make them know it* [a]Prov 3:32; John 7:17 [b]Gen 17:1, 2

10 All the paths of the LORD are
[a]lovingkindness and truth
To [b]those who keep His covenant and
His testimonies.
11 For [a]Your name's sake, O LORD,
[b]Pardon my iniquity, for it is great.

12 Who is the man who [a]fears the
LORD?
He will [b]instruct him in the way he
should choose.
13 His soul will [a]abide in [1]prosperity,
And his [2]descendants will [b]inherit the
[3]land.
14 The [1a]secret of the LORD is for those
who fear Him,
[2]And He will [b]make them know His
covenant.
15 My [a]eyes are continually toward the
LORD,
For He will [1b]pluck my feet out of the
net.

16 [a]Turn to me and be gracious to me,
For I am [b]lonely and afflicted.
17 [1]The [a]troubles of my heart are
enlarged;
Bring me [b]out of my distresses.
18 [a]Look upon my affliction and my
[1]trouble,
And [b]forgive all my sins.

15 [1]Lit *bring out* [a]Ps 123:2; 141:8 [b]Ps 31:4; 124:7 **16** [a]Ps 69:16 [b]Ps 143:4 **17** [1]Some commentators read *Relieve the troubles of my heart* [a]Ps 40:12 [b]Ps 107:6 **18** [1]Lit *toil* [a]2 Sam 16:12; Ps 31:7 [b]Ps 103:3

24:10 *LORD of hosts.* See note on 1 Sam 1:3. Here it stands in climactic position.

Ps 25 The psalmist prays for God's covenant mercies when suffering affliction for sins and when enemies seize the occasion to attack, perhaps by trying to discredit the king through false accusations (see note on 5:9). Appealing to God's covenant benevolence (His compassion, lovingkindess, goodness, uprightness, truth and grace; see vv. 6–8,10,16) and to his own reliance on the Lord (see vv. 1,5,15,20–21), he prays for deliverance from his enemies (see vv. 2,19), for guidance in God's will (see vv. 4–5,21; see also vv. 8–10,12), for the forgiveness of his sins (see vv. 7,11,18) and for relief from his affliction (see vv. 2,16–18,20). These are related: God's forgiveness will express itself in removing his affliction, and then his enemies will no longer have occasion to slander him. And with God guiding him in "His way" (v. 9)—i.e., in "His covenant and His testimonies" (v. 10)—he will no longer wander into "transgressions" (v. 7). This psalm is linked with Ps 24 by its reference to "lifting up the soul" in reliance on God (see v. 1; 24:4). Structurally, the psalm is an alphabetic acrostic (somewhat irregular, with an additional, concluding verse that extends the lines beyond the alphabet). It is composed of four unequal stanzas (of three, four, eight and seven verses). The first and fourth stanzas are thematically related, as are the second and third (an *a-b/b-a* pattern).

25:1–3 Prayer for relief from distress or illness and the slander of his enemies that it occasions.

25:3 *without cause.* David has given no cause for the hostility of his adversaries.

25:4–7 Prayer for guidance and pardon.

25:4 *Your ways . . . Your paths.* Metaphors for "His covenant and His testimonies" (v. 10; see Deut 8:6; 10:12–13; 26:17; 30:16; Josh 22:5; see also vv. 8–9; 18:21; 51:13; 81:13; 95:10; 119:3,15; 128:1).

25:5 *Your truth.* A life of faithfulness to the Lord.

25:6–7 *Remember . . . Do not remember.* Remember your longstanding ("from of old") "compassion and . . . lovingkindnesses," but do not remember my long-standing sins (those "of my youth"). *lovingkindness.* See v. 10 and note on 6:4.

25:8–15 Confidence in the Lord's covenant favors. In this context of prayer for pardon, David implicitly identifies himself with sinners (v. 8) as well as with the humble (v. 9)—those who keep God's covenant (see vv. 10,14) and those who fear the Lord (see vv. 12,14). As sinner he is in need of forgiveness; as humble servant of the Lord he hopefully awaits God's pardon and guidance in covenant faithfulness.

25:9 *humble.* Those who acknowledge that they are without resources.

25:10 *paths of the LORD.* The Lord's benevolent dealings (see 103:7; 138:5) with those who are true to His ways (see note on v. 4).

25:11 *For Your name's sake.* See note on 23:3; see also 1 John 2:12. *name's.* See note on 5:11.

25:12 *the way he should choose.* Or "the way chosen for him."

25:13 *inherit the land.* Retain their family portion in the promised land (see 37:9,11,18,22,29,34; 69:36; Is 60:21).

25:14 *secret of the LORD.* The Lord takes into His confidence as friends those who fear Him (see Gen 18:17–19; Job 29:4). *fear.* See note on 15:4.

25:16–21 Prayer for relief from distress or illness and the attacks of his enemies.

25:17 *heart.* See note on 4:7.

19 Look upon my enemies, for they [a]are many,
And they [b]hate me with violent hatred.
20 [a]Guard my soul and deliver me;
Do not let me [b]be ashamed, for I take refuge in You.
21 Let [a]integrity and uprightness preserve me,
For [b]I wait for You.
22 [a]Redeem Israel, O God,
Out of all his troubles.

Psalm 26

A Psalm of David.

1 [1a]Vindicate me, O LORD, for I have [b]walked in my integrity,
And I have [c]trusted in the LORD [2d]without wavering.
2 [a]Examine me, O LORD, and try me;
[b]Test my [1]mind and my heart.
3 For Your [a]lovingkindness is before my eyes,
And I have [b]walked in Your [1]truth.
4 I do not [a]sit with [1]deceitful men,
Nor will I go with [2b]pretenders.
5 I [a]hate the assembly of evildoers,
And I will not sit with the wicked.
6 I shall [a]wash my hands in innocence,
And I will go about [b]Your altar, O LORD,
7 That I may proclaim with the voice of [a]thanksgiving
And declare all Your [1]wonders.

8 O LORD, I [a]love the habitation of Your house
And the place [1]where Your [b]glory dwells.
9 [a]Do not [1]take my soul away *along* with sinners,
Nor my life with [b]men of bloodshed,
10 In whose hands is a [a]wicked scheme,
And whose right hand is full of [b]bribes.
11 But as for me, I shall [a]walk in my integrity;
[b]Redeem me, and be gracious to me.
12 [a]My foot stands on a [b]level place;
In the [c]congregations I shall bless the LORD.

Psalm 27

A Psalm of David.

1 The LORD is my [a]light and my [b]salvation;

19 [a]Ps 3:1 [b]Ps 9:13 **20** [a]Ps 86:2 [b]Ps 25:2 **21** [a]Ps 41:12 [b]Ps 25:3 **22** [a]Ps 130:8 **26:1** [1]Lit *Judge* [2]Lit *I do not slide* [a]Ps 7:8 [b]2 Kin 20:3; Prov 20:7 [c]Ps 13:5; 28:7 [d]Heb 10:23 **2** [1]Lit *kidneys,* figurative for inner man [a]Ps 17:3; 139:23 [b]Ps 7:9 **3** [1]Or *faithfulness* [a]Ps 48:9 [b]2 Kin 20:3; Ps 86:11 **4** [1]Or *worthless men;* lit *men of falsehood* [2]Or *dissemblers, hyprocrites* [a]Ps 1:1 [b]Ps 28:3 **5** [a]Ps 31:6; 139:21 **6** [a]Ps 73:13

6 [b]Ps 43:3, 4 **7** [1]Or *miracles* [a]Ps 9:1 **8** [1]Lit *of the tabernacle of Your glory* [a]Ps 27:4 [b]Ps 24:7 **9** [1]Lit *gather* [a]Ps 28:3 [b]Ps 139:19 **10** [a]Ps 37:7 [b]Ps 15:5

11 [a]Ps 26:1 [b]Ps 44:26; 69:18 **12** [a]Ps 40:2 [b]Ps 27:11 [c]Ps 22:22
27:1 [a]Ps 18:28; Is 60:20; Mic 7:8 [b]Ex 15:2; Ps 62:7; 118:14; Is 33:2; Jon 2:9

25:21 *integrity and uprightness.* Personified virtues (see 23:6 and note). Pardon is not enough; David prays that God will enable him to live a life of unmarred moral rectitude—even as God is "good and upright" (v. 8; see 51:10–12).

25:22 A concluding prayer in behalf of all God's people (see 3:8 and note). *Redeem.* Here, as often, a synonym for "deliver."

Ps 26 A prayer for God's discerning mercies—to spare His faithful and godly servant from the death that overtakes the wicked and ungodly. The prayer for vindication (see v. 1) suggests that the king is threatened by the "deceitful" (v. 4) and "men of bloodshed" (v. 9) to whom he refers (as in Ps 23; 25; 27–28). This psalm is linked with Ps 27–28 (see also Ps 23–24) by the theme of the Lord's house: Here David's "love" (v. 8) for the temple (or tabernacle) testifies to the authenticity of his piety; in Ps 27 the Lord's temple is David's sanctuary from his enemies; in Ps 28 David directs his cry for help to the Lord's throne room ("Your holy sanctuary," 28:2) in the temple.

26:1–8 An appeal for God to take account of David's moral integrity, his unwavering trust and his genuine delight in the Lord—not a boast of self-righteousness, such as that of the Pharisee (Luke 18:9–14).

26:1 *walked in my integrity.* See v. 11 and note; a claim of moral integrity (see vv. 2–5), not sinless perfection (see 7:8; 41:12; 101:2; and especially 1 Kin 9:4). *trusted.* Obedience and trust are the two sides of godliness, as the Abraham story exemplifies (see Gen 12:4 and note; 22:12; see also Ps 34:8–14 and note).

26:2 *mind . . . heart.* See note on 7:9.

26:3 *Your lovingkindness . . . Your truth.* That is, your lovingkindness-and-truth (see 40:10). David keeps his eye steadfastly on the Lord's lovingkindness (see note on 6:4) and truth (faithfulness; see 25:10), which are pledged to those "who keep His covenant and His testimonies" (25:10). *have walked.* In order to receive the covenant benefits.

26:4–5 *sit with.* David refuses to settle in or associate himself with that company he describes as "deceitful men," "pretenders," "evildoers," "the wicked" (see 1:1 and note; see also Ps 101).

26:4 *pretenders.* Context may suggest those who deal fraudulently—or people like those described in Prov 6:12–14.

26:6 *wash my hands in innocence.* Reference appears to be to a ritual claiming innocence. "Clean hands and a pure heart" are requisite for those who come to God (see 24:4 and note). *go about Your altar.* To vocally celebrate God's saving acts beside His altar was a public act of devotion in which one also invited all the assembled worshipers to praise (see 43:4).

26:7 *proclaim with . . . thanksgiving . . . declare . . . Your wonders.* See note on 9:1.

26:8 *where Your glory dwells.* The presence of God's glory signaled the presence of God Himself (see Ex 24:16; 33:22). His glory dwelling in the tabernacle (see Ex 40:35), and later the temple (see 1 Kin 8:11), assured Israel of the Lord's holy, yet gracious, presence among them. John 1:14 announces that same presence in the Word who became flesh and who "dwelt among us."

26:9–11 An appeal that God will not bring on David the end (death) that awaits the wicked.

26:9 *soul.* See note on 6:3.

26:11 *walk in my integrity.* A return to the appeal with which David began (see v. 1). *Redeem.* See note on 25:22.

26:12 A concluding confession of confidence (see note on 3:8) and a vow to praise (see note on 7:17). *level place.* Where the going is smooth and free from the danger of falling (see 143:10; Is 40:4; 42:16). *congregations.* See note on 1:5. *bless.* That is, "praise" (see note on 9:1).

Ps 27 David's triumphantly confident prayer to God to deliver him from all those who conspire to bring him down. The prayer presupposes the Lord's covenant with David (see 2 Sam 7). Faith's soliloquy (in two stanzas: vv. 1–3, 4–6), which publicly testifies to the king's confident reliance on the Lord, introduces the prayer of vv. 7–12. The conclusion (vv. 13–14) echoes the confidence of vv. 1–6 and adds faith's dialogue with itself—faith exhorting faith to wait patiently for that which is sure,

Whom shall I fear?
The LORD is the [1c]defense of my life;
[d]Whom shall I dread?
2 When evildoers came upon me to
[a]devour my flesh,
My adversaries and my enemies, they
[b]stumbled and fell.
3 Though a [a]host encamp against me,
My heart will not fear;
Though war arise against me,
In *spite of* this I [1]shall be [b]confident.

4 [a]One thing I have asked from the
LORD, that I shall seek:
That I may [b]dwell in the house of the
LORD all the days of my life,
To behold [c]the [1]beauty of the LORD
And to [2d]meditate in His temple.
5 For in the [a]day of trouble He will
[b]conceal me in His [1]tabernacle;
In the secret place of His tent He will
[c]hide me;
He will [d]lift me up on a rock.
6 And now [a]my head will be lifted up
above my enemies around me,
And I will offer in His tent [b]sacrifices
[1]with shouts of joy;
I will [c]sing, yes, I will sing praises to
the LORD.

7 [a]Hear, O LORD, when I cry with my
voice,
And be gracious to me and [b]answer
me.
8 *When You said,* "[a]Seek My face," my
heart said to You,
"Your face, O LORD, [b]I shall seek."
9 [a]Do not hide Your face from me,
Do not turn Your servant away in
[b]anger;

27:1 [1]Or *refuge* [c]Ps 28:8 [d]Ps 118:6
2 [a]Ps 14:4 [b]Ps 9:3
3 [1]Lit *am confident* [a]Ps 3:6 [b]Job 4:6
4 [1]Lit *delightfulness* [2]Lit *inquire* [a]Ps 26:8 [b]Ps 23:6 [c]Ps 90:17 [d]Ps 18:6
5 [1]Or *shelter* [a]Ps 50:15 [b]Ps 31:20 [c]Ps 17:8 [d]Ps 40:2
6 [1]Lit *of shouts* [a]Ps 3:3 [b]Ps 107:22 [c]Ps 13:6
7 [a]Ps 4:3; 61:1 [b]Ps 13:3
8 [a]Ps 105:4; Amos 5:6 [b]Ps 34:4
9 [a]Ps 69:17 [b]Ps 6:1

9 [c]Ps 40:17 [d]Ps 94:14 [e]Ps 37:28
10 [1]Or *If my father...forsake me, Then the* LORD [a]Is 49:15 [b]Is 40:11
11 [1]Or *those who lie in wait for me* [a]Ps 25:4; 86:11 [b]Ps 5:8; 26:12
12 [1]Lit *soul* [a]Ps 41:2 [b]Deut 19:18; Ps 35:11; Matt 26:60 [c]Acts 9:1
13 [1]Or *Surely I believed* [a]Ps 31:19 [b]Job 28:13; Ps 52:5; 116:9; 142:5; Is 38:11; Jer 11:19; Ezek 26:20
14 [a]Ps 25:3; 37:34; 40:1; 62:5; 130:5; Prov 20:22; Is 25:9 [b]Ps 31:24
28:1 [a]Ps 18:2

You have been [c]my help;
[d]Do not abandon me nor [e]forsake
me,
O God of my salvation!
10 [1]For my father and [a]my mother have
forsaken me,
But [b]the LORD will take me up.

11 [a]Teach me Your way, O LORD,
And lead me in a [b]level path
Because of [1]my foes.
12 Do not deliver me over to the [1a]desire
of my adversaries,
For [b]false witnesses have risen against
me,
And such as [c]breathe out violence.
13 [1]*I would have despaired* unless I had
believed that I would see the
[a]goodness of the LORD
In the [b]land of the living.
14 [a]Wait for the LORD;
Be [b]strong and let your heart take
courage;
Yes, wait for the LORD.

Psalm 28

A Psalm of David.

1 To You, O LORD, I call;
My [a]rock, do not be deaf to me,
For if You [b]are silent to me,
I will become like those who [c]go
down to the pit.
2 Hear the [a]voice of my supplications
when I cry to You for help,
When I [b]lift up my hands [c]toward
[1]Your holy [d]sanctuary.

[b]Ps 35:22; 39:12; 83:1 [c]Ps 88:4; 143:7; Prov 1:12 **2** [1]Lit *the innermost place of Your sanctuary* [a]Ps 140:6 [b]Ps 134:2; 141:2; Lam 2:19; 1 Tim 2:8 [c]Ps 5:7; 138:2 [d]1 Kin 6:5

though not yet seen (see Ps 42–43; Heb 11:1). See further the introduction to Ps 26.

27:1–3 The king's security in the Lord in the face of all that his enemies can do (see Ps 2).

27:1 *light.* Often symbolizes well-being (see 97:11; Job 18:5–6; 22:28; 29:3; Prov 13:9; Lam 3:2) or life and salvation (see 18:28; Is 9:2; 49:6; 58:8; 59:9; Jer 13:16; Amos 5:18–20). To say "The LORD is my light" is to confess confidence in Him as the source of these benefits (see Is 10:17; 60:1–2,19–20; Mic 7:8–9). *my salvation.* My Savior (see v. 9).

27:2 *devour my flesh.* See 7:2 and note.

27:3 *heart.* See note on 4:7.

27:4–6 The Lord's temple (or tabernacle) is the king's stronghold—because the Lord Himself is his stronghold (see v. 1; see notes on 9:11; 18:2).

27:4 *dwell in.* See note on 15:1. *beauty of the LORD.* His unfailing benevolence (see 90:17: "favor of the Lord").

27:5 *secret place of His tent.* See 31:20; 32:7; 61:4; 91:1.

27:6 *will offer . . . sacrifices.* See note on 7:17. *I will sing.* See note on 9:1.

27:7–12 Prayer for deliverance from treacherous enemies. These remain unspecified, whether from inside or outside the kingdom or both. Their chief weapon is false charges intent on discrediting the king (see note on 5:9).

27:9 *hide Your face.* See note on 13:1. *anger.* See note on 2:5. *You have been my help.* Or "Be my helper."

27:10 *the LORD will take me up.* Or "may the LORD receive me."

27:11 *Teach me Your way.* Only those who know and do the Lord's will can expect to receive favorable response to their prayers (see Ps 24–26; see also 2 Sam 7:14). *lead me in a level path.* See 5:8 and note.

27:13–14 Concluding note of confidence (see note on 3:8).

27:13 *goodness of the LORD.* The "good" things promised in the Lord's covenant with David (see 2 Sam 7:28; see also 31:19 and note). *land of the living.* This life.

27:14 *Wait for the LORD.* Faith encouraging faith (see 42:5,11; 43:5; 62:5).

Ps 28 A prayer for deliverance from deadly peril at the hands of malicious and God-defying enemies. As with Ps 25, the prayer ends with intercession for all the people of the Lord (see 3:8 and note). Reference in the last verse to the Lord as the shepherd of His people connects this psalm with Ps 23 and probably marks off Ps 23–28 as a collection linked by many common themes. See introductions to Ps 26; 29.

28:1–2 Initial appeal to be heard.

28:1 *rock.* See note on 18:2. *are silent.* Do not act in my behalf. *pit.* Metaphor for the grave (see note on 30:1).

28:2 *lift up my hands.* In worship and prayer (see 63:4; 134:2; 141:2). *Your holy sanctuary.* The inner sanctuary of the temple (see 1 Kin 6:5), where the ark of the covenant stood (see

3 [a]Do not drag me away with the wicked
And with those who work iniquity,
Who [b]speak peace with their neighbors,
While evil is in their hearts.
4 Requite them [a]according to their work and according to the evil of their practices;
Requite them according to the deeds of their hands;
Repay them their [1]recompense.
5 Because they [a]do not regard the works of the LORD
Nor the deeds of His hands,
He will tear them down and not build them up.

6 Blessed be the LORD,
Because He [a]has heard the voice of my supplication.
7 The LORD is my [a]strength and my [b]shield;
My heart [c]trusts in Him, and I am helped;
Therefore [d]my heart exults,
And with [e]my song I shall thank Him.
8 The LORD is [1]their [a]strength,
And He is a [2b]saving defense to His anointed.
9 [a]Save Your people and bless [b]Your inheritance;
Be their [c]shepherd also, and [d]carry them forever.

3 [a]Ps 26:9 [b]Ps 12:2; 55:21; 62:4; Jer 9:8
4 [1]Or *dealings* [a]Ps 62:12; 2 Tim 4:14; Rev 18:6; 22:12
5 [a]Is 5:12
6 [a]Ps 28:2
7 [a]Ps 18:2; 59:17 [b]Ps 3:3 [c]Ps 13:5; 112:7 [d]Ps 16:9 [e]Ps 40:3; 69:30
8 [1]A few mss and ancient versions read *the strength of His people* [a]Ps 20:6; 89:17
8 [2]Or *refuge of salvation* [b]Ps 27:1; 140:7
9 [a]Ps 106:47 [b]Deut 9:29; 32:9; 1 Kin 8:51; Ps 33:12; 106:40 [c]Ps 80:1 [d]Deut 1:31; Is 40:11; 46:3; 63:9
29:1 [1]Or *sons of gods* [a]1 Chr 16:28, 29; Ps 96:7-9
2 [1]Lit *of His name* [2]Or *the majesty of holiness* [a]2 Chr 20:21; Ps 110:3

Psalm 29

A Psalm of David.

1 [a]Ascribe to the LORD, O [1]sons of the mighty,
Ascribe to the LORD glory and strength.
2 Ascribe to the LORD the glory [1]due to His name;
Worship the LORD [a]in [2]holy array.

3 The [a]voice of the LORD is upon the waters;
The God of glory [b]thunders,
The LORD is over [1c]many waters.
4 The voice of the LORD is [a]powerful,
The voice of the LORD is majestic.
5 The voice of the LORD breaks the cedars;
Yes, the LORD breaks in pieces [a]the cedars of Lebanon.

3 [1]Or *great* [a]Ps 104:7 [b]Job 37:4, 5; Ps 18:13 [c]Ps 18:16; 107:23
4 [a]Ps 68:33 **5** [a]Judg 9:15; 1 Kin 5:6; Ps 104:16; Is 2:13; 14:8

1 Kin 8:6–8); it was God's throne room on earth.

28:3–5 Prayer for the Lord, enthroned in the temple, to deliver His servant and deal in judgment with those who harbor malice toward the king and God's people and defy God Himself.

28:3 *evil is in their hearts.* See note on 5:9. *hearts.* See note on 4:7.

28:4 *Requite them.* See note on 5:10; see also Matt 16:27; 2 Tim 4:14; Rev 20:12–13; 22:12.

28:5 *works of the LORD.* His redemption of Israel, the establishment of Israel as His kingdom (by covenant, Ex 19–24), and the appointment of the house of David (also by covenant, 2 Sam 7) as His earthly regent over His people. *deeds of His hands.* By "the deeds of their hands" (v. 4), "the wicked" (v. 3) show that they do not acknowledge Israel and David's regency as the work of God's hands. *He will tear.* Or "May He tear."

28:6–7 Joyful praise, in confidence of being heard (see note on 3:8).

28:7 *shield.* See note on 3:3. *heart.* See note on 4:7. *I shall thank.* See note on 7:17.

28:8–9 The Lord and His people (see note on 3:8).

28:8 *their . . . His anointed.* See NASB marg.; these constitute a unity (see note on 2:2).

28:9 *Save . . . bless.* God's two primary acts by which He effects His people's well-being: He saves from time to time as circumstances require; He blesses day by day to make their lives and labors fruitful. *Your inheritance.* See Deut 9:29. *shepherd.* See introduction; see also 80:1; Is 40:11; Jer 31:10; Ezek 34; Mic 5:4. The answer to this prayer—the last, full answer—has come in the ministry of the "good shepherd" (John 10:11,14).

Ps 29 A hymn in praise of the King of creation, whose majesty and power are trumpeted by the thunderbolts of the rainstorm—as the storm rose above the Mediterranean ("thunders . . . over many waters," v. 3), swept across the Lebanon range (see vv. 5–6) and rolled over the wilds of Kadesh (northern Kadesh, on the upper reaches of the Orontes River, v. 8). The glory of the Lord is not only visible in the creation (19:1–6; 104 and often elsewhere); it is also audible in creation's most awesome voice. This hymn to Yahweh ("the LORD") served also as a testimony and protest against the worship of the Canaanite god Baal, who was thought to be the divine power present in the thunderstorm. Its climactic word (that "in His temple everything says, 'Glory!' ") suggests that in its present location it was intended to serve as a conclusion to the small collection, Ps 23–28 (see introductions to Ps 26; 28). In its structure, a two-verse introduction and a two-verse conclusion enclose a seven-verse stanza. In both the introduction and the conclusion the name Yahweh ("the LORD") is sounded four times; in the body of the psalm it is heard ten times. "The voice of the LORD" is repeated seven times—the seven thunders of God. (The numbers four, seven and ten often signified completeness in OT number symbolism.)

29:1–2 A summons to all beings in the divine realm (see note on v. 1) to worship the Lord—adapted from a conventional call to praise in the liturgy of the temple (see 96:7–9; 1 Chr 16:28–29).

29:1 *sons of the mighty.* Lit. "sons of god(s)." Perhaps reference is to the angelic host (see 103:20; 148:2; Job 1:6 and note; 2:1; Is 6:2), or possibly to all those foolishly thought to be gods—as in Ps 97 (see v. 7), which has several thematic links with this psalm. The Lord alone must be acknowledged as the divine King.

29:2 *name.* See note on 5:11. *in holy array.* Lit. "in the splendor of holiness." It is uncertain whether the phrase describes God Himself or the sanctuary or the (priestly) garb the worshipers are to wear when they approach God. The use of an almost identical Hebrew phrase in 110:3 (translated "in holy array") may give support for the last alternative; see NASB marg.

29:3–9 Praise of the Lord, whose voice the crashing thunder is (see 68:4,33). The sound and fury of creation's awesome displays of power proclaim the glory of Israel's God.

29:5 *cedars of Lebanon.* The mightiest of trees (see Is 2:13 and note).

6 He makes Lebanon [a]skip like a calf,
And [b]Sirion like a young wild ox.
7 The voice of the LORD hews out
[1]flames of fire.
8 The voice of the LORD [1]shakes the
wilderness;
The LORD shakes the wilderness of
[a]Kadesh.
9 The voice of the LORD makes [a]the deer
to calve
And strips the forests bare;
And [b]in His temple everything says,
"Glory!"

10 The LORD sat *as King* at the [a]flood;
Yes, the LORD sits as [b]King forever.
11 [1]The LORD will give [a]strength to His
people;
[2]The LORD will bless His people with
[b]peace.

Psalm 30

A Psalm; a Song at the Dedication of the House.
A Psalm of David.

1 I will [a]extol You, O LORD, for You have
[b]lifted me up,
And have not let my [c]enemies rejoice
over me.
2 O LORD my God,
I [a]cried to You for help, and You
[b]healed me.
3 O LORD, You have [a]brought up my
soul from [1]Sheol;
You have kept me alive, [2]that I would
not [b]go down to the pit.
4 [a]Sing praise to the LORD, you [b]His
godly ones,
And [c]give thanks to His holy [1][d]name.
5 For [a]His anger is but for a moment,
His [b]favor is for a lifetime;
Weeping may [c]last for the night,
But a shout of joy *comes* in the
morning.

6 Now as for me, I said in my prosperity,
"I will [a]never be moved."
7 O LORD, by Your favor You have made
my mountain to stand strong;
You [a]hid Your face, I was dismayed.
8 To You, O LORD, I called,
And to the Lord I made supplication:

6 [a]Ps 114:4, 6 [b]Deut 3:9
7 [1]I.e. lightning
8 [1]Or *causes...to whirl* [a]Num 13:26
9 [a]Job 39:1 [b]Ps 26:8
10 [a]Gen 6:17 [b]Ps 10:16
11 [1]Or *May the LORD give* [2]Or *May the LORD bless* [a]Ps 28:8; 68:35; Is 40:29 [b]Ps 37:11; 72:3
30:1 [a]Ps 118:28; 145:1 [b]Ps 3:3
30:1 [c]Ps 25:2; 35:19, 24
2 [a]Ps 88:13 [b]Ps 6:2; 103:3; Is 53:5
3 [1]I.e. the nether world [2]Some mss read *from among those who go down* [a]Ps 86:13 [b]Ps 28:1
4 [1]Lit *memorial* [a]Ps 149:1 [b]Ps 50:5 [c]Ps 97:12 [d]Ex 3:15; Ps 135:13; Hos 12:5
5 [a]Ps 103:9; Is 26:20; 54:7, 8 [b]Ps 118:1 [c]Ps 126:5; 2 Cor 4:17
6 [a]Ps 10:6; 62:2, 6
7 [a]Deut 31:17; Ps 104:29; 143:7

29:6 *skip.* See 114:4 and note.
29:9 *temple.* A primary thematic link with Ps 23–28. Reference may be to the temple in Jerusalem or to God's heavenly temple, where He sits enthroned (see 2:4; 11:4; 113:5; Is 6:1; 40:22) as the Lord of all creation. But perhaps it is the creation itself that here is named God's temple (see note on 24:2). Then the "everything" (that which cries "Glory!") is absolutely all—all creation shouts His praise (cf. 150:6). *Glory!* See note on 26:8.
29:10–11 The Lord's absolute and everlasting rule is committed to His people's complete salvation and unmixed blessedness—the crowning comfort in a world where threatening tides seem to make everything uncertain.
29:10 *at the flood.* As the One who by His word brought the ordered creation out of the formless "deep" (Gen 1:2,6–10); or the reference may be to the Noahic flood (see Gen 6:17).
Ps 30 A song of praise publicly celebrating the Lord's deliverance from the threat of death, probably brought on by illness ("You healed me," v. 2; see note on 7:17). The psalm is framed by commitments to praise (see vv. 1,12).
30 title *A Song.* See titles of Ps 18; 45–46; 48; 65–68; 75–76; 83; 87–88; 92; 108—all psalms of praise except 83; 88. In addition there are the songs "of Ascents" (Ps 120–134). *at the Dedication of the House. A Psalm of David.* If "of David" indicates authorship, the most probable occasion for the psalm is recorded in 1 Chr 21:1–22:6. In 1 Chr 22:1–6 David dedicated both property and building materials for the temple, and he may well have intended that Ps 30 be used at the dedication of the temple itself. If this is the case, vv. 2–3 would refer to David's predicament in 1 Chr 21:17–30. The "favor" of v. 5 would be an echo of the "mercies" of 1 Chr 21:13, and v. 6 would refer to his sin of misplaced trust in a large, superior army (see 1 Chr 21:1–8). Later, the psalm came to be applied to the exile experience of Israel. In Jewish liturgical practice dating from Talmudic times it is chanted at Hanukkah, the feast that celebrates the rededication of the temple by Judas Maccabeus (165 B.C.) after its desecration by Antiochus Epiphanes (168). In such communal use, the "I" of the psalm becomes the corporate "person" of Israel—a common mode of speaking in the OT.
30:1–3 Introductory announcement of the occasion for praise.
30:1 *lifted me up.* The vivid imagery that associates distress with the need to be "lifted" out of trouble—so expressive of universal human experience—is common in OT poetry (see 69:2,15; 71:20; 88:6; 130:1; Lam 3:55; Jon 2:2). The depths are often linked, as here, with Sheol and "the pit" (v. 3), together with a cluster of related associations: silence (see 31:17; 94:17; 115:17; 1 Sam 2:9), darkness (see 88:6,12; 143:3; Job 10:21–22; 17:13; Eccl 6:4; Lam 3:6), death and destruction (see v. 9; 18:4; 55:23, 88:11; Is 38:17; Hos 13:14), dust (see v. 9; 7:5; 22:15,29; Job 17:16; 40:13; Is 26:19; 29:4), mire (see 40:2; 69:2,14; 40:2) and mud (see 40:2; Job 30:19). See also note on 49:14. *my enemies rejoice over me.* See introduction to Ps 6.
30:3 *Sheol.* Figurative of a "brink-of-death" experience, as in 18:5; Jon 2:2. *pit.* See note on 28:1.
30:4–5 Call to the gathered worshipers to take up the praise of God (see note on 9:1).
30:4 *godly ones.* See note on 4:3. *name.* Lit. "memorial" (see Is 26:8; Hos 12:5).
30:5 *anger.* See note on 2:5. *but for a moment.* See Is 54:7. *last for the night.* Lit. "come in at evening to lodge." The figure is that of a guest lodging for only one night.
30:6–10 Expanded recollection of the Lord's gracious deliverance.
30:6–7 In his security he had grown arrogant, forgetful of who had made his "mountain to stand strong," but the Lord reminded him.
30:6 *never be moved.* He spoke as do the wicked (see 10:6), hence lost the blessing of the righteous (see 15:5). *moved.* See note on 10:6.
30:7 *made my mountain to stand strong.* Reference may be to David's security in his mountain fortress, Zion; or that mountain fortress may here serve as a metaphor for David's state as a vigorous and victorious king, the "mountain" on which he sat with such secure confidence in God. *hid Your face.* See note on 13:1.
30:8–10 Shattered strength swept away all self-reliance; at the brink of death his cries for God's mercy rose.

9 "What profit is there in my blood, if I
[a]go down to the pit?
Will the [b]dust praise You? Will it
declare Your faithfulness?

10 "[a]Hear, O LORD, and be gracious to me;
O LORD, be my [b]helper."
11 You have turned for me [a]my mourning
into dancing;
You have [b]loosed my sackcloth and
girded me with [c]gladness,
12 That *my* [1a]soul may sing praise to You
and not be silent.
O LORD my God, I will [b]give thanks to
You forever.

Psalm 31

For the choir director. A Psalm of David.

1 [a]In You, O LORD, I have taken refuge;
Let me never [b]be ashamed;
[c]In Your righteousness deliver me.
2 [a]Incline Your ear to me, rescue me
quickly;
Be to me a [b]rock of [1]strength,
A stronghold to save me.
3 For You are my [1]rock and [a]my
fortress;
For [b]Your name's sake You will lead
me and guide me.
4 You will [a]pull me out of the net which
they have secretly laid for me,
For You are my [b]strength.
5 [a]Into Your hand I commit my spirit;
You have [b]ransomed me, O LORD,
[c]God of [1]truth.

6 I hate those who [a]regard [1]vain idols,

9 [a]Ps 28:1 [b]Ps 6:5
10 [a]Ps 4:1; 27:7 [b]Ps 27:9; 54:4
11 [a]Eccl 3:4; Jer 31:4, 13 [b]Is 20:2 [c]Ps 4:7
12 [1]Lit *glory* [a]Ps 16:9; 57:8; 108:1 [b]Ps 44:8
31:1 [a]Ps 31:1-3; 71:1-3 [b]Ps 25:2 [c]Ps 143:1
2 [1]Or *refuge, protection* [a]Ps 17:6; 71:2; 86:1; 102:2 [b]Ps 18:2; 71:3
3 [1]Or *crag* [a]Ps 18:2 [b]Ps 23:3; 25:11
4 [a]Ps 25:15 [b]Ps 46:1
5 [1]Or *faithfulness* [a]Luke 23:46; Acts 7:59 [b]Ps 55:18; 71:23 [c]Deut 32:4; Ps 71:22
6 [1]Lit *empty vanities* [a]Jon 2:8

6 [b]Ps 52:8
7 [a]Ps 90:14 [b]Ps 10:14
8 [a]Deut 32:30; Ps 37:33
9 [a]Ps 66:14; 69:17 [b]Ps 6:7 [c]Ps 63:1
10 [1]Or *bones, substance* [a]Ps 13:2 [b]Ps 39:11 [c]Ps 32:3; 38:3; 102:3
11 [a]Ps 69:19 [b]Job 19:13; Ps 38:11; 88:8, 18
12 [a]Ps 88:5
13 [1]Lit *whispering* [a]Ps 50:20; Jer 20:10 [b]Lam 2:22 [c]Ps 62:4; Matt 27:1 [d]Ps 41:7
14 [a]Ps 140:6

But I [b]trust in the LORD.
7 I will [a]rejoice and be glad in Your
lovingkindness,
Because You have [b]seen my affliction;
You have known the troubles of my
soul,
8 And You have not [a]given me over into
the hand of the enemy;
You have set my feet in a large place.

9 Be gracious to me, O LORD, for [a]I am
in distress;
My [b]eye is wasted away from grief,
[c]my soul and my body *also.*
10 For my life is spent with [a]sorrow
And my years with sighing;
My [b]strength has failed because of my
iniquity,
And [c]my [1]body has wasted away.
11 Because of all my adversaries, I have
become a [a]reproach,
Especially to my [b]neighbors,
And an object of dread to my
acquaintances;
Those who see me in the street flee
from me.
12 I am [a]forgotten as a dead man, out of
mind;
I am like a broken vessel.
13 For I have heard the [1a]slander of
many,
[b]Terror is on every side;
While they [c]took counsel together
against me,
They [d]schemed to take away my life.

14 But as for me, I trust in You, O LORD,
I say, "[a]You are my God."

30:9 See note on 6:5. *Your faithfulness.* To your covenant.
30:11–12 God answered—and David vows to prolong his praise forever (see note on 7:17). Dancing and joy replace wailing and sackcloth so that songs of praise, not silence, may attend the acts of God.
30:11 *sackcloth.* A symbol of mourning (see 35:13; Gen 37:34).
30:12 *soul.* Lit. "glory" (see note on 7:5).
Ps 31 A prayer for deliverance when confronted by a conspiracy so powerful and open that all David's friends abandoned him. According to Luke 23:46, Jesus on the cross applied Ps 31:5 to His own circumstances; thus those who share in His sufferings at the hands of anti-Christian forces are encouraged to hear and use this psalm in a new light (see Acts 7:59; 1 Pet 4:19). No psalm expresses a more sturdy trust in the Lord when powerful human forces threaten. The heart of the prayer itself is found in vv. 9–18, which is both preceded and followed by eight Hebrew poetic lines—stanzas that resound with the theme of trust (see v. 14). Verse 13, at the center of the psalm, expresses most clearly the prayer's occasion.
31 title *For the choir director.* See note on Ps 4 title.
31:1–5 Initial appeal to the Lord, the faithful refuge.
31:1 *righteousness.* See note on 4:1.
31:2 *rock.* See note on 18:2.
31:3 *for Your name's sake.* God's honor is at stake in the safety of His servant now under attack (see note on 23:3). *name's.* See note on 5:11. *lead me and guide me.* As a shepherd (see 23:2–3 and notes).
31:4 *net . . . secretly laid for me.* By his enemies (see v. 11).
31:5 *Into Your hand I commit my spirit.* The climactic expression of trust in the Lord—quoted by Jesus in Luke 23:46. *commit.* Lit. "deposit" (as in Jer 36:20), here in the very hands of God, thus entrusting to God's care (see Lev 6:4; 1 Kin 14:27). *my spirit.* His very life. *ransomed.* See note on 25:22 ("Redeem"). *God of truth.* The faithful, trustworthy God (see note on 30:9).
31:6–8 Confession of loyal trust in the Lord, whose past mercies to David when enemies threatened are joyfully recalled.
31:6 *hate.* Refuse to be associated with.
31:7 *lovingkindness.* See vv. 16,21; see also note on 6:4. *soul.* See note on 6:3.
31:8 *large place.* See note on 18:19.
31:9–13 The distress described: He is utterly drained physically and emotionally (see vv. 9–10; see also 22:14–15); all his friends have abandoned him like a piece of broken pottery (see vv. 11–12); and all this because the conspiracy against him is so strong (v. 13).
31:9 *eye is wasted.* See note on 13:3. *soul.* See note on 6:3.
31:10 *body.* See note on 6:2.
31:11–12 Abandonment by friends was a common experience at a time when God seemed to have withdrawn His favor (see 38:11; 41:9; 69:8; 88:8,18; Job 19:13–19; Jer 12:6; 15:17).
31:13 *slander.* See note on 5:9. *Terror is on every side.* See notes on Jer 6:25; 20:3.
31:14–18 His trust in the Lord is unwavering; his defense

15 My [a]times are in Your hand;
[b]Deliver me from the hand of my
enemies and from those who
persecute me.
16 Make Your [a]face to shine upon Your
servant;
[b]Save me in Your lovingkindness.
17 Let me not be [a]put to shame, O LORD,
for I call upon You;
Let the [b]wicked be put to shame, let
them [c]be silent in [1]Sheol.
18 Let the [a]lying lips be mute,
Which [b]speak arrogantly against the
righteous
With pride and contempt.

19 How great is Your [a]goodness,
Which You have stored up for those
who fear You,
Which You have wrought for those
who [b]take refuge in You,
[c]Before the sons of men!
20 You hide them in the [a]secret place of
Your presence from the
[b]conspiracies of man;
You keep them secretly in a [1]shelter
from the [c]strife of tongues.
21 [a]Blessed be the LORD,
For He has made [b]marvelous His
lovingkindness to me in a besieged
[c]city.
22 As for me, [a]I said in my alarm,
"I am [b]cut off from before Your eyes";
Nevertheless You [c]heard the voice of
my supplications
When I cried to You.

23 O love the LORD, all you [a]His godly
ones!
The LORD [b]preserves the faithful
And fully [c]recompenses the proud
doer.
24 [a]Be strong and let your heart take
courage,
All you who [1]hope in the LORD.

Psalm 32

A Psalm of David. A [†]Maskil.

1 [a]How blessed is he whose
transgression is forgiven,
Whose sin is covered!
2 How blessed is the man to whom the
LORD [a]does not impute iniquity,
And in whose spirit there is [b]no
deceit!

3 When [a]I kept silent *about my sin,* [b]my
[1]body wasted away
Through my [2c]groaning all day long.
4 For day and night [a]Your hand was
heavy upon me;

15 [a]Job 14:5; 24:1 [b]Ps 143:9 **16** [a]Num 6:25; Ps 4:6; 80:3 [b]Ps 6:4 **17** [1]I.e. the nether world [a]Ps 25:2, 20 [b]Ps 25:3 [c]1 Sam 2:9; Ps 94:17; 115:17 **18** [a]Ps 109:2; 120:2 [b]1 Sam 2:3; Ps 94:4; Jude 15 **19** [a]Ps 65:4; 145:7; Is 64:4; Rom 2:4; 11:22 [b]Ps 5:11 [c]Ps 23:5 **20** [1]Or *pavilion* [a]Ps 27:5 [b]Ps 37:12 [c]Job 5:21; Ps 31:13 **21** [a]Ps 28:6 [b]Ps 17:7 [c]1 Sam 23:7; Ps 87:5 **22** [a]Ps 116:11 **22** [b]Ps 88:5; Is 38:11, 12; Lam 3:54 [c]Ps 18:6; 66:19; 145:19 **23** [a]Ps 30:4; 37:28; 50:5 [b]Ps 145:20; Rev 2:10 [c]Deut 32:41; Ps 94:2 **24** [1]Or *wait for* [a]Ps 27:14 **32:1** [†]Possibly *Contemplative,* or *Didactic,* or *Skillful Psalm* [a]Ps 85:2; 103:3; Rom 4:7, 8 **2** [a]2 Cor 5:19 [b]John 1:47 **3** [1]Or *bones, substance* [2]Lit *roaring* [a]Ps 39:2, 3 [b]Ps 31:10 [c]Ps 38:8 **4** [a]1 Sam 5:6; Job 23:2; 33:7; Ps 38:2; 39:10

against his powerful enemies is his reliance on God's faithfulness and discerning judgment.

31:14 Cf. v. 22.

31:15 *My times are in Your hand.* All the events and circumstances of life are in the hands of the Lord, "my God" (v. 14).

31:16 *face to shine.* See note on 13:1.

31:17–18 *Let the wicked . . . be mute.* See note on 5:10.

31:18 *lying lips.* See note on 5:9. *righteous.* See note on 1:5.

31:19–20 Confident anticipation of God's saving help (see note on 3:8).

31:19 *stored up.* David deposits his life in the hands of God to share in the covenant benefits that God has stored up for His faithful servants ("goodness"; see Ex 18:9; Num 10:29,32; Deut 26:11; Josh 21:45; 23:14–15; 2 Chr 6:41; Neh 9:25,35; Is 63:7; Jer 33:9; see also Jer 31:12,14, "bounty"). *fear.* See note on 15:4. *wrought . . . Before the sons of men!* Thus showing the Lord's approval of and His standing with His faithful servants in contrast to the accusations of their adversaries (see 86:17).

31:20 *secret place of Your presence.* See note on 27:5. *strife of tongues.* See "slander" (v. 13) and "lying lips" (v. 18).

31:21–22 Praise anticipating deliverance (see note on 12:5–6).

31:21 *besieged city.* Metaphor for the threat he had experienced.

31:22 *cut off from before Your eyes.* See note on 13:1.

31:23–24 Praise culminates by encouraging the saints (see 62:8).

31:23 *godly ones.* See note on 4:3. *the faithful.* Those who maintain moral integrity. *the proud.* Those who refuse to live in humble reliance on the Lord. They arrogantly try to make their way in the world either as a law to themselves (see, e.g., v. 18; 10:2–11; 73:6; 94:2–7; Deut 8:14; Is 2:17; Ezek 28:2,5; Hos 13:6) or by relying on false gods (see Jer 13:9–10). Hence "the proud" is often equivalent to "the wicked."

Ps 32 A grateful testimony of joy for God's gift of forgiveness toward those who with integrity confess their sins and are receptive to God's rule in their lives. The psalm appears to be a liturgical dialogue between David and God in the presence of the worshipers at the sanctuary. In vv. 1–2 and again in v. 11 David speaks to the assembly; in vv. 3–7 he speaks to God (in their hearing); in vv. 8–10 he is addressed by one of the Lord's priests (but see note on vv. 8–10). In traditional Christian usage the psalm has been numbered among the penitential psalms (see introduction to Ps 6).

32 title *Maskil.* Occurs also in the titles of Ps 42; 44–45; 52–55; 74; 78; 88–89; 142. The Hebrew word perhaps indicates that these psalms contain instruction in godliness (see 41:1, "he who considers"; 14:2; 53:2, "anyone who understands"; but see also 47:7, which uses *Maskil* to refer to a "skillful psalm").

32:1–2 Exuberant proclamation of the happy state of those who experience God's forgiveness. *blessed . . . blessed.* See note on 1:1. Repetition underscores. *is forgiven . . . is covered . . . does not impute.* Repetition with variation emphasizes and illumines. For Paul's use of these verses see Rom 4:6–8.

32:2 *in whose spirit there is no deceit.* Only those honest with God receive pardon.

32:3–5 Testimony to a personal experience of God's pardon. God's heavy hand, brought down "day and night" on the stubborn silence of unacknowledged sin, filled life with groaning, but full confession brought blessed relief. Neither the sin nor the form of suffering is identified, other than that the latter was physically and psychologically devastating. But it would be uncharacteristic of the Psalms to speak of mere emotional disturbance brought on by suppressed guilt. Some affliction, perhaps illness, was the instrument of God's chastisement (see Ps 38).

My [1][b]vitality was drained away *as*
with the fever heat of summer.
[2]Selah.

5 I [a]acknowledged my sin to You,
And my iniquity I [b]did not hide;
I said, "[c]I will confess my
transgressions to the LORD";
And You [d]forgave the [1]guilt of my sin.
Selah.

6 Therefore, let everyone who is godly
pray to You [1][a]in a time when You
may be found;
Surely [b]in a flood of great waters they
will not reach him.

7 You are [a]my hiding place; You
[b]preserve me from trouble;
You surround me with [1][c]songs of
deliverance. Selah.

8 I will [a]instruct you and teach you in
the way which you should go;
I will counsel you [b]with My eye upon
you.

9 Do not be [a]as the horse or as the mule
which have no understanding,
Whose trappings include bit and
bridle to hold them in check,
Otherwise they will not come near to
you.

10 Many are the [a]sorrows of the wicked,
But [b]he who trusts in the LORD,
lovingkindness shall surround him.

11 Be [a]glad in the LORD and rejoice, you
righteous ones;
And shout for joy, all you who are
[b]upright in heart.

Psalm 33

1 [a]Sing for joy in the LORD, O you
righteous ones;
Praise is [b]becoming to the upright.

2 Give thanks to the LORD with the
[a]lyre;
Sing praises to Him with a [b]harp of
ten strings.

3 Sing to Him a [a]new song;
Play skillfully with [b]a shout of joy.

4 [1]Lit *life juices were turned into the drought of summer* [2]*Selah* may mean: *Pause, Crescendo* or *Musical interlude* [b]Ps 22:15
5 [1]Or *iniquity* [a]Lev 26:40 [b]Job 31:33 [c]Ps 38:18; Prov 28:13; 1 John 1:9 [d]Ps 103:12
6 [1]Lit *in a time of finding out* [a]Ps 69:13; Is 55:6 [b]Ps 46:1-3; 69:1; 124:5; 144:7; Is 43:2
7 [1]Or *shouts* [a]Ps 9:9; 31:20; 91:1; 119:114 [b]Ps 121:7 [c]Ex 15:1; Judg 5:1; Ps 40:3
8 [a]Ps 25:8 [b]Ps 33:18
9 [a]Prov 26:3
10 [a]Ps 16:4; Prov 13:21; Rom 2:9 [b]Ps 5:11, 12; Prov 16:20
11 [a]Ps 64:10; 68:3; 97:12 [b]Ps 7:10; 64:10
33:1 [a]Ps 32:11; Phil 3:1; 4:4 [b]Ps 92:1; 147:1
2 [a]Ps 71:22; 147:7 [b]Ps 144:9
3 [a]Ps 40:3; 96:1; 98:1; 144:9; Is 42:10; Rev 5:9 [b]Ps 98:4

32:4 *vitality was drained.* Under God's heavy hand he wilted like a plant in the heat of summer.
32:5 Again repetition is used (see note on vv. 1–2). *sin . . . iniquity . . . transgressions.* See 51:1–2; the three most common OT words for evil thoughts and actions (see Is 59:12 and note). *confess.* See Ps 51; 2 Sam 12:13.
32:6–7 A chastened confession that life is secure only with God.
32:6 Though addressed to God as confession, it is also intended for the ears of the fellow worshipers. He admonishes them to "seek the LORD while He may be found . . . while He is near" (Is 55:6) and not to foolishly provoke His withdrawal—and the coming near of His heavy hand—as David had done. A God who forgives is a God to whom one can entrust and devote his life (see 130:4). *godly.* See note on 4:3. *flood of great waters.* Powerful imagery for threatening forces or circumstances. This and related imagery was borrowed from ancient Near Eastern creation myths. In many of these a primal mass of chaotic waters (their threatening and destructive forces were often depicted as a many-headed monster of the deep; see 74:13–14 and note) had to be subdued by the creator-god before he could fashion the world and/or rule as the divine king over the earth. Though in these myths the chaotic waters were subdued when the present world was created, they remained a constant threat to the security and well-being of the present order in the earth (the world in which man lives). Hence by association they were linked with anything that in human experience endangered or troubled that order. They were also associated with the sea, whose angry waves seemed determined at times to engulf the land. Since in Canaanite mythology Sea and Death were the two great enemies of Baal ("lord" of earth), imagery drawn from both realms was used by OT poets, sometimes side by side, to depict threats and distress (see 18:4–5,16; 42:7; 65:7; 74:12–14; 77:16,19; 89:9–10; 93:3–4; 124:4–5; 144:7–8; Job 7:12; 26:12; 38:8–11; Is 5:30; 8:7–8; 17:12–14; 51:9–10; Jer 5:22; 47:2; 51:55; Hab 3:8–10; see also note on Song 8:7). For imagery associated with the realm of death see notes on 30:1; 49:14.
32:7 *surround me with songs of deliverance.* Because of Your help, I will be surrounded by people celebrating Your acts of deliverance, as I bring my thank offerings to You (see notes on 7:17; 9:1; see also 35:27; 51:8).
32:8–10 A priestly word of godly instruction, either to David (do not be foolish toward God again) or to those who have just been exhorted to trust in the Lord (to trust add obedience). Some believe that the psalmist himself here turns to others to warn them against the ways into which he had fallen (see 51:13).
32:9 God's servant must be wiser than beasts, more open to God's will than horses and mules are to the will of their masters (see Is 1:3).
32:10 *lovingkindness.* See note on 6:4.
32:11 A final word to the assembled worshipers—let the praise of God resound (see note on 9:1). See also note on 1:5. *heart.* See note on 4:7.
Ps 33 A liturgy in praise of the Lord, the sovereign God of Israel. In the Psalms, calls to praise (as in vv. 1–3) and motivations for praise (as in vv. 4–19) belong to the language of praise (see note on 9:1). Most likely the voices of the Levitical choir (see 1 Chr 16:7–36; 25:1) are heard in this psalm. Perhaps the choir leader spoke vv. 1–3, the choir vv. 4–19, and the people responded with the words of vv. 20–22. The original occasion is unknown, but reference to a "new song" (see note on v. 3) suggests a national deliverance, such as Judah experienced in the time of Jehoshaphat (see 2 Chr 20) or Hezekiah (see 2 Kin 19); see vv. 10–11,16–17. Along with Ps 1–2; 10 (but see introduction to Ps 9), this is one of the only four psalms in Book I without a superscription. Although structurally not an alphabetic acrostic like the psalm that follows it, the length of the psalm (22 verses) has been determined by the length of the Hebrew alphabet (22 letters); see Ps 38; 103; Lam 5. The body of the psalm is framed by a three-verse introduction (call to praise) and a three-verse conclusion (response to praise). In vv. 4–19 are heard the praise of the Lord, developed in two parts of eight verses each (vv. 4–11, 12–19).
33:1–3 The call to praise. Cf. Eph 5:19.
33:1 *righteous.* The assembly of worshipers (see note on 1:5).
33:3 *new song.* Celebrating God's saving act, as in 40:3; 96:1; 98:1; 144:9; 149:1; see Is 42:10; Rev 5:9; 14:3; see also note on 7:17.

4 For the word of the LORD [a]is upright,
And all His work is *done* [b]in
faithfulness.
5 He [a]loves righteousness and justice;
The [b]earth is full of the
lovingkindness of the LORD.

6 By the [a]word of the LORD the heavens
were made,
And [b]by the breath of His mouth [c]all
their host.
7 He gathers the [a]waters of the sea
together [1]as a heap;
He lays up the deeps in storehouses.
8 Let [a]all the earth fear the LORD;
Let all the inhabitants of the world
[b]stand in awe of Him.
9 For [a]He spoke, and it was done;
He commanded, and it [1]stood fast.
10 The LORD [a]nullifies the counsel of the
nations;
He frustrates the plans of the peoples.
11 The [a]counsel of the LORD stands
forever,
The [b]plans of His heart from
generation to generation.
12 Blessed is the [a]nation whose God is
the LORD,
The people whom He has [b]chosen for
His own inheritance.

13 The LORD [a]looks from heaven;
He [b]sees all the sons of men;
14 From [a]His dwelling place He looks
out
On all the inhabitants of the earth,
15 He who [a]fashions [1]the hearts of them
all,
He who [b]understands all their works.
16 [a]The king is not saved by a mighty
army;
A warrior is not delivered by great
strength.
17 A [a]horse is a false hope for victory;
Nor does it deliver anyone by its great
strength.

18 Behold, [a]the eye of the LORD is on
those who fear Him,
On those who [1][b]hope for His
lovingkindness,
19 To [a]deliver their soul from death
And to keep them alive [b]in famine.
20 Our soul [a]waits for the LORD;
He is our [b]help and our shield.
21 For our [a]heart rejoices in Him,
Because we trust in His holy name.
22 Let Your lovingkindness, O LORD, be
upon us,
According as we have [1]hoped in You.

4 [a]Ps 19:8 [b]Ps 119:90
5 [a]Ps 11:7; 37:28 [b]Ps 119:64
6 [a]Gen 1:6; Ps 148:5; Heb 11:3 [b]Ps 104:30 [c]Gen 2:1
7 [1]Some versions read *in a water skin;* i.e. container [a]Ex 15:8; Josh 3:16; Ps 78:13
8 [a]Ps 67:7 [b]Ps 96:9
9 [1]Or *stood forth* [a]Gen 1:3; Ps 148:5
10 [a]Ps 2:1-3; Is 8:10; 19:3
11 [a]Job 23:12; Prov 19:21 [b]Ps 40:5; 92:5; 139:17; Is 55:8
12 [a]Ps 144:15 [b]Ex 19:5; Deut 7:6; Ps 28:9
13 [a]Job 28:24; Ps 14:2 [b]Ps 11:4
14 [a]1 Kin 8:39, 43; Ps 102:19
15 [1]Or *their heart together* [a]Job 10:8; Ps 119:73 [b]2 Chr 16:9; Job 34:21; Jer 32:19
16 [a]Ps 44:6; 60:11
17 [a]Ps 20:7; 147:10; Prov 21:31
18 [1]Or *wait* [a]Job 36:7; Ps 32:8; 34:15; 1 Pet 3:12 [b]Ps 32:10; 147:11
19 [a]Ps 56:13; Acts 12:11 [b]Job 5:20; Ps 37:19
20 [a]Ps 62:1; 130:6; Is 8:17
[b]Ps 115:9 **21** [a]Ps 13:5; 28:7; Zech 10:7; John 16:22 **22** [1]Or *waited for*

Psalm 34

A Psalm of David when he †feigned madness before •Abimelech, who drove him away and he departed.

1 I will [a]bless the LORD at all times;
His [b]praise shall continually be in my
mouth.

34:1 †Or *changed his behavior* •Possibly a title of King Achish of Gath, see 1 Sam 21:10-15 [a]Eph 5:20; 1 Thess 5:18 [b]Ps 71:6

33:4–19 The praise, in two eight-verse parts.
33:4–11 Because the Lord is the Creator, who by His power imposed His order on the creation (see Gen 1), no power or combination of powers can thwart His plan and purpose to save His people. (Hence His chosen people are the blessed nation; see vv. 12–19.)
33:4 *word.* God's royal word by which He governs all things (see 107:20; 147:15,18). *upright.* Not chaotic, devious or erratic. Under the Lord's rule in the creation there is goodness, order and dependability.
33:5 *loves.* Delights in doing. *righteousness and justice.* See note on 5:8. *lovingkindness of the LORD.* Here, His goodness to all His creatures (see 36:5–9; 104:27–28; see also note on 6:4).
33:6 *word.* God's creating word (see v. 9; 104:7; 119:89; Gen 1; Job 38:8–11; Heb 11:3).
33:7 *as a heap . . . storehouses.* Like a householder storing up his olive oil and grain (see 104:9; Gen 1:9–10; Job 38:8–11; Prov 8:29; Jer 5:22).
33:8 *all the earth . . . all the inhabitants.* Not only Israel, but all mankind, for all experience the goodness of His sovereign rule (see note on 9:1)—but He foils all their contrary designs (vv. 10–11). *fear the LORD.* See v. 18; see also note on 15:4.
33:11 *heart.* See note on 4:7.
33:12–19 Israel is safe and secure under God's protective rule.
33:12 *Blessed.* See note on 1:1. *people whom He has chosen for His own inheritance.* Israel (see Deut 9:29).
33:16 *king.* Nation (see v. 12) and king constitute an organic social unit (see 28:8 and note).
33:18–19 The concluding couplet of the second eight-verse stanza of praise contrasts with the concluding couplet of the first (vv. 10–11); both are climactic and together they voice the heart of the praise.
33:18,22 *lovingkindness.* Here, His covenant favor toward Israel (see note on 6:4).
33:20–22 The people's response: faith's commitment expressed in confession (vv. 20–21) and petition (v. 22).
33:20 *shield.* See note on 3:3.
33:21 *heart.* See note on 4:7. *name.* See note on 5:11.
Ps 34 Praise of the Lord for deliverance in answer to prayer, and instruction in godliness. In the Psalms, praise commonly leads to a call to praise, as in v. 3 (see note on 9:1). Here, uniquely (but see also Ps 92), praise (vv. 1–7) leads into godly instruction (vv. 8–22) in the manner of the wisdom teachers (see essay, p. 689). Structurally, the psalm is a somewhat irregular alphabetic acrostic (it lacks a verse for one Hebrew letter and adds a verse at the end). It develops four major themes (see following notes).
34 title The superscription assigns this psalm to the occasion in David's life (see note on Ps 3 title) narrated in 1 Sam 21:10–15—but note "Abimelech" rather than "Achish" (perhaps Abimelech was a traditional dynastic name or title for Philistine kings; see Gen 20; 21:22–34; 26). Not all agree with this tradition, however; they feel that it is more likely that early Hebrew editors of the Psalms linked 1 Sam 21 with Ps 34 on the basis of word association (the Hebrew for "disguised his sanity," 1 Sam 21:13, comes from the same root as the Hebrew used here for "taste," v. 8).
34:1–7 Praise for the Lord's deliverance in answer to prayer.

2 My soul will [a]make its boast in the LORD;
The [b]humble will hear it and rejoice.
3 O [a]magnify the LORD with me,
And let us [b]exalt His name together.

4 I [a]sought the LORD, and He answered me,
And [b]delivered me from all my fears.
5 They [a]looked to Him and were radiant,
And their faces will [b]never be ashamed.
6 This [1]poor man cried, and [a]the LORD heard him
And saved him out of all his troubles.
7 The [a]angel of the LORD encamps around those who fear Him,
And rescues them.

8 O [a]taste and see that the LORD is good;
How [b]blessed is the man who takes refuge in Him!
9 O fear the LORD, you [a]His saints;
For to those who fear Him there is [b]no want.
10 The young lions do lack and suffer hunger;
But they who seek the LORD shall [a]not be in want of any good thing.
11 [a]Come, you children, listen to me;
[b]I will teach you [c]the fear of the LORD.
12 [a]Who is the man who desires life
And loves *length of* days that he may [b]see good?

13 Keep [a]your tongue from evil
And your lips from speaking [b]deceit.
14 [a]Depart from evil and do good;
Seek peace and [b]pursue it.

15 The [a]eyes of the LORD are toward the righteous
And His ears are *open* to their cry.
16 The [a]face of the LORD is against evildoers,
To [b]cut off the memory of them from the earth.
17 *The righteous* [a]cry, and the LORD hears
And delivers them out of all their troubles.
18 The LORD [a]is near to the [b]brokenhearted
And saves those who are [1c]crushed in spirit.

19 [a]Many are the [b]afflictions of the righteous,
But the LORD [c]delivers him out of them all.
20 He keeps all his bones,
[a]Not one of them is broken.
21 [a]Evil shall slay the wicked,
And those who hate the righteous will be [1]condemned.
22 The LORD [a]redeems the soul of His servants,
And none of those who [b]take refuge in Him will be [1]condemned.

2 [a]Ps 44:8; Jer 9:24; 1 Cor 1:31 [b]Ps 69:32 **3** [a]Ps 35:27; 69:30; Luke 1:46 [b]Ps 18:46 **4** [a]2 Chr 15:2; Ps 9:10; Matt 7:7 [b]Ps 34:6, 17, 19 **5** [a]Ps 36:9; Is 60:5 [b]Ps 25:3 **6** [1]Or *afflicted* [a]Ps 34:4 **7** [a]Ps 91:11; Dan 6:22 **8** [a]Ps 119:103; Heb 6:5; 1 Pet 2:3 [b]Ps 2:12 **9** [a]Ps 31:23 [b]Ps 23:1 **10** [a]Ps 84:11 **11** [a]Ps 66:16 [b]Ps 32:8 [c]Ps 111:10 **12** [a]Ps 34:12-16; 1 Pet 3:10-12 [b]Eccl 3:13
13 [a]Ps 141:3; Prov 13:3; James 1:26 [b]1 Pet 2:22 **14** [a]Ps 37:27; Is 1:16, 17 [b]Rom 14:19; Heb 12:14 **15** [a]Job 36:7; Ps 33:18 **16** [a]Lev 17:10; Jer 44:11; Amos 9:4 [b]Job 18:17; Ps 9:6; 109:15; Prov 10:7 **17** [a]Ps 34:6; 145:19 **18** [1]Or *contrite* [a]Ps 145:18 [b]Ps 147:3; Is 61:1 [c]Ps 51:17; Is 57:15 **19** [a]Prov 24:16 [b]Ps 71:20; 2 Tim 3:11f [c]Ps 34:4, 6, 17

20 [a]John 19:33, 36 **21** [1]Or *held guilty* [a]Ps 94:23; 140:11; Prov 24:16 **22** [1]V 21, note 1 [a]1 Kin 1:29; Ps 71:23 [b]Ps 37:40

34:1–3 Commitment to continual praise—to the encouragement of the godly who are afflicted (v. 2; see the instruction in vv. 8–22).
34:2 *soul.* See note on 6:3.
34:3 *name.* See note on 5:11.
34:4–7 The occasion: God's saving answer to prayer.
34:5 *radiant.* With joy (see Is 60:5).
34:6 *poor.* Here, as often in the Psalms, "poor" characterizes not necessarily one who has no possessions, but one who is (and recognizes that he is) without resources to effect his own deliverance (or secure his own life, safety or well-being)—and so is dependent on God.
34:7 *angel of the LORD.* God's heavenly representative, His "messenger," sent to effect His will on earth (see 35:5–6; see also note on Gen 16:7). *encamps around.* The line speaks of the security with which the Lord surrounds His people, individually and collectively; it does not teach a doctrine of individual "guardian angels." *those who fear Him.* Those described in vv. 8–14.
34:8–14 Instruction in "the fear of the LORD." The title line (v. 11) is at the center of the stanza—Hebrew authors often centered key lines (see note on 6:6). Note the pattern of the imperatives: "taste" (v. 8), "fear" (v. 9), "Come" (v. 11), "Keep" (v. 13), "Depart" (v. 14). A symmetrical development of the theme "good" dominates the stanza: Because the Lord is good (v. 8), those who trust in Him will lack nothing good (v. 10); but in order to experience good days (v. 12), they must shun evil and do good (v. 14). To trust and obey—that is "the fear of the LORD." On the instruction of this stanza see Ps 37. For Peter's use of vv. 12–16 see 1 Pet 3:8–12.
34:8 *blessed.* See note on 1:1.
34:9 *fear the LORD.* See v. 11; see also note on 15:4. *saints.* See note on 4:3.
34:11 *Come, you children.* Conventional language of the wisdom teachers (see Introduction to Proverbs: Purpose and Teaching).
34:13 See 15:2–3; James 3:5–10. For the tongue as a weapon see note on 5:9.
34:14 *Seek peace.* See 37:37; 120:7; Prov 12:20; Zech 8:19 (also Zech 8:16–17); Matt 5:9; Rom 12:18; 1 Cor 7:15; 2 Cor 13:11; 1 Thess 5:13; Heb 12:14; James 3:17–18.
34:15–18 Assurance that the Lord hears the prayers of the righteous. He so thoroughly thwarts those who do evil that they are forgotten (v. 16).
34:15 *righteous.* See vv. 8–14; see also note on 1:5.
34:16 *face of the LORD.* See note on 13:1.
34:17–18 See especially 51:17.
34:19–22 Assurance that the Lord is the unfailing deliverer of the righteous—and condemns the wicked for their hostility toward the righteous (see v. 21).
34:20 *all his bones.* His whole being (see note on 6:2). *Not one of them is broken.* Perhaps John's Gospel applies this word to Jesus (John 19:36; see also Ex 12:46; Num 9:12)—as the one above all others who could be called "righteous" (v. 19).
34:21–22 *condemned.* Dealt with as guilty.
34:22 *redeems.* See note on 25:22.
Ps 35 An appeal to the heavenly King, as divine Warrior and Judge, to come to the defense of "His servant" (v. 27) who is being maliciously slandered by those toward whom he had shown only the most tender friendship. The attack seems to

Psalm 35

A Psalm of David.

1 Contend, O LORD, with those who [a]contend with me;
Fight against those who [b]fight against me.
2 Take hold of [1a]buckler and shield
And rise up for [b]my help.
3 Draw also the spear and [1]the battle-axe to meet those who pursue me;
Say to my soul, "I am [a]your salvation."
4 Let those be [a]ashamed and dishonored who seek my [1]life;
Let those be [b]turned back and humiliated who devise evil against me.
5 Let them be [a]like chaff before the wind,
With the angel of the LORD driving *them* on.
6 Let their way be dark and [a]slippery,
With the angel of the LORD pursuing them.
7 For [a]without cause they [b]hid their net for me;
Without cause they dug a [1]pit for my soul.
8 Let [a]destruction come upon him unawares,
And [b]let the net which he hid catch himself;
Into that very [c]destruction let him fall.

9 And my soul shall [a]rejoice in the LORD;
It shall [b]exult in His salvation.
10 All my [a]bones will say, "LORD, [b]who is like You,
Who delivers the afflicted from him [c]who is too strong for him,
And [d]the afflicted and the needy from him who robs him?"

11 [a]Malicious witnesses rise up;
They ask me of things that I do not know.
12 They [a]repay me evil for good,
To the bereavement of my soul.
13 But as for me, [a]when they were sick, my [b]clothing was sackcloth;
I [c]humbled my soul with fasting,
And my [d]prayer kept returning to my bosom.
14 I went about as though it were my friend or brother;
I [a]bowed down [1]mourning, as one who sorrows for a mother.
15 But [a]at my [1]stumbling they rejoiced and gathered themselves together;
The [2b]smiters whom I did not know gathered together against me,
They [3c]slandered me without ceasing.
16 Like godless jesters at a feast,
They [a]gnashed at me with their teeth.

17 Lord, [a]how long will You look on?
Rescue my soul [b]from their ravages,
My [c]only *life* from the lions.
18 I will [a]give You thanks in the great congregation;
I will [b]praise You among a mighty throng.
19 [a]Do not let those who are wrongfully [b]my enemies rejoice over me;
Nor let those [c]who hate me without cause [1d]wink maliciously.
20 For they do not speak peace,
But they devise [a]deceitful words against those who are quiet in the land.
21 They [a]opened their mouth wide against me;
They said, "[b]Aha, aha, our eyes have seen it!"

35:1 [a]Ps 18:43; Is 49:25 [b]Ps 56:2 **2** [1]I.e. small shield [a]Ps 91:4 [b]Ps 44:26 **3** [1]Or *close up the path against those* [a]Ps 62:2 **4** [1]Or *soul* [a]Ps 70:2 [b]Ps 40:14; 129:5 **5** [a]Job 21:18; Ps 83:13; Is 29:5 **6** [a]Ps 73:18; Jer 23:12 **7** [1]*Pit* has been transposed from line above [a]Ps 69:4; 109:3; 140:5 [b]Ps 9:15 **8** [a]Ps 55:23; Is 47:11; 1 Thess 5:3 [b]Ps 9:15 [c]Ps 73:18 **9** [a]Is 61:10 [b]Ps 9:14; 13:5; Luke 1:47 **10** [a]Ps 51:8 [b]Ex 15:11; Ps 86:8; Mic 7:18 [c]Ps 18:17 [d]Ps 37:14; 109:16

11 [a]Ps 27:12 **12** [a]Ps 38:20; 109:5; Jer 18:20; John 10:32 **13** [a]Job 30:25 [b]Ps 69:11 [c]Ps 69:10 [d]Matt 10:13; Luke 10:6 **14** [1]Or *dressed in black* [a]Ps 38:6 **15** [1]Or *limping* [2]Or *smitten ones* [3]Lit *tore* [a]Obad 12 [b]Job 30:1, 8, 12 [c]Ps 7:2 **16** [a]Job 16:9; Ps 37:12; Lam 2:16 **17** [a]Ps 13:1; Hab 1:13 [b]Ps 35:7 [c]Ps 22:20, 21 **18** [a]Ps 22:22 [b]Ps 22:25 **19** [1]Or *wink the eye* [a]Ps 13:4; 30:1; 38:16 [b]Ps 38:19; 69:4 [c]John 15:25 [d]Prov 6:13; 10:10

20 [a]Ps 55:21; Jer 9:8; Mic 6:12 **21** [a]Job 16:10; Ps 22:13 [b]Ps 40:15; 70:3

have been occasioned by some "distress" (v. 26) that had overtaken the king (see vv. 15,19,21,25), perhaps an illness (see v. 13; see also introduction to Ps 6). Ps 35 exemplifies such a "cry" to the Lord in expectation of vindication as that spoken of in 34:15–22—except that here the author does not expressly identify himself as one of the "righteous" (34:21); he appeals to the Lord rather as innocent victim of an unmotivated attack. Regarding structure, after an initial appeal to the Lord as divine Warrior (vv. 1–3) there follows a threefold elaboration of David's petition to the divine Judge, each concluding with a vow to praise (vv. 4–10, 11–18, 19–28); see note on 7:17.
35:1–3 Appeal to the Lord as Warrior-King (see Ex 15:1–18), David's Overlord.
35:2 *rise up.* See note on 3:7.
35:3 *soul.* See note on 6:3.
35:4–10 Appeal to the Lord to deal with the attackers, matching judgment with their violent intent (see note on 5:10).
35:4 *devise evil against me.* See note on 5:9.
35:5–6 *angel of the LORD.* See 34:7 and note.
35:5 *like chaff.* See note on 1:4.
35:9–10 See note on 7:17.
35:9 *soul.* See note on 6:3.
35:10 *afflicted and . . . needy.* See 34:6 and note.
35:11–18 The accusation—they repaid my friendship with malicious slander—with a renewed petition (v. 17) and a vow to praise (v. 18).
35:12 *soul.* See note on 6:3.
35:13 *sackcloth.* A symbol of mourning (see 30:11; Gen 37:34). *fasting.* An act of mourning (see 69:10).
35:15 *stumbling.* Not morally. He was brought low by circumstances (see 9:3; 27:2; 37:24; 56:13; 119:165).
35:16 *gnashed . . . their teeth.* In malice (see 37:12; Lam 2:16).
35:17 *how long . . . ?* See note on 6:3 (see also Introduction: Theology). *lions.* See note on 7:2.
35:18 *congregation.* See note on 1:5.
35:19–28 Renewed appeal for judgment, with a concluding vow to praise (v. 28).
35:19 *wrongfully my enemies.* See vv. 11–17; an experience frequently reflected also elsewhere in the Psalter (see 38:19; 69:4; 109:3; 119:78,86,161). See also Lam 3:52. *hate me without cause.* See 69:4. It is not known which of these passages is referred to in John 15:25. Both psalms reflect circumstances applicable also to Jesus' experience (but see introduction to Ps 69).
35:21 *Aha, aha.* See v. 25; see also note on 3:2.

22 [a]You have seen it, O LORD, [b]do not keep silent;
O Lord, [c]do not be far from me.
23 [a]Stir up Yourself, and awake to my right
And to my cause, my God and my Lord.
24 [a]Judge me, O LORD my God, according to Your righteousness,
And [b]do not let them rejoice over me.
25 Do not let them say in their heart,
"[a]Aha, our desire!"
Do not let them say, "We have [b]swallowed him up!"
26 Let [a]those be ashamed and humiliated altogether who rejoice at my distress;
Let those be [b]clothed with shame and dishonor who [c]magnify themselves over me.

27 Let them [a]shout for joy and rejoice, who favor [b]my vindication;
And [c]let them say continually, "The LORD be magnified,
Who [d]delights in the prosperity of His servant."
28 And [a]my tongue shall declare Your righteousness
And Your praise all day long.

Psalm 36

For the choir director. *A Psalm* of David the servant of the LORD.

1 Transgression speaks to the ungodly within [1]his heart;
There is [a]no fear of God before his eyes.
2 For [1]it [a]flatters him in his *own* eyes
Concerning the discovery of his iniquity *and* the hatred *of it*.
3 The [a]words of his mouth are wickedness and deceit;
He has [b]ceased to [1]be wise *and* to do good.
4 He [a]plans wickedness upon his bed;
He sets himself on a [b]path that is not good;
He [c]does not despise evil.

5 Your [a]lovingkindness, O LORD, [1]extends to the heavens,
Your faithfulness *reaches* to the skies.
6 Your [a]righteousness is like the [1]mountains of God;
Your [b]judgments are *like* a great deep.
O LORD, You [c]preserve man and beast.
7 How [a]precious is Your lovingkindness, O God!
And the children of men [b]take refuge in the shadow of Your wings.
8 They [a]drink their fill of the [1]abundance of Your house;
And You give them to drink of the [b]river of Your delights.
9 For with You is the [a]fountain of life;
In Your light we see light.

22 [a]Ex 3:7; Ps 10:14 [b]Ps 28:1 [c]Ps 10:1; 22:11; 38:21; 71:12
23 [a]Ps 7:6; 44:23; 59:4; 80:2
24 [a]Ps 9:4; 26:1; 43:1 [b]Ps 35:19
25 [a]Ps 35:21 [b]Ps 56:1; 124:3; Prov 1:12; Lam 2:16
26 [a]Ps 40:14 [b]Ps 109:29 [c]Job 19:5; Ps 38:16
27 [a]Ps 32:11 [b]Ps 9:4 [c]Ps 40:16; 70:4 [d]Ps 147:11; 149:4
28 [a]Ps 51:14; 71:15, 24
36:1 [1]Another reading is *my heart*

36:1 [a]Rom 3:18
2 [1]Or *he flatters himself* [a]Deut 29:19; Ps 10:11; 49:18
3 [1]Or *understand to do good* [a]Ps 10:7; 12:2 [b]Ps 94:8; Jer 4:22
4 [a]Prov 4:16; Mic 2:1 [b]Is 65:2 [c]Ps 52:3; Rom 12:9
5 [1]Lit *is in* [a]Ps 57:10; 103:11; 108:4
6 [1]Or *mighty mountains* [a]Ps 71:19 [b]Job 11:8; Ps 77:19; Rom 11:33 [c]Neh 9:6; Ps 104:14, 15; 145:16
7 [a]Ps 40:5; 139:17 [b]Ruth 2:12; Ps 17:8; 57:1; 91:4 **8** [1]Lit *fatness* [a]Ps 63:5; 65:4; Is 25:6; Jer 31:12-14 [b]Job 20:17; Ps 46:4; Rev 22:1 **9** [a]Jer 2:13

35:22 *do not keep silent.* Do not remain inactive (see 28:1 and note; 83:1; 109:1).
35:23 *Stir up Yourself.* See note on 7:6. *awake.* See note on 3:7.
35:24 *righteousness.* See note on 4:1.
35:25 *swallowed.* See 124:3.
35:26 Once again: May their judgment match their evil intent (see vv. 4–10).
35:27 May all who are faithful supporters of the Lord's "servant" (here no doubt equivalent to His "anointed"; see note on 2:2) have reason to rejoice and praise the Lord.
35:28 *righteousness.* See note on 4:1.
Ps 36 A prayer for God's unfailing protection, as the psalmist reflects on the godlessness of the wicked and the goodness of God. In Jewish practice, vv. 7–10 form part of the morning prayer.
36 title *For the choir director.* See note on Ps 4 title. *servant of the LORD.* His royal servant (see notes on Ps 18 title; 35:27; see also 2 Sam 7:20).
36:1–4 The foolish and haughty godlessness of the wicked.
36:1 *heart.* See note on 4:7. *no fear of God.* See 55:19. They take no account of His all-seeing eye, His righteous judgment and His power to deal with them (see note on 10:11). For Paul's use of this verse see Rom 3:18.
36:2 *flatters him.* Out of the smug, conceited notion that he is accountable to no one.
36:3 *words of his mouth.* See note on 5:9. *ceased to be wise.* See 94:8–11; Prov 2:9–11. *do good.* See 34:8–14 and note.
36:4 *upon his bed.* When one's thoughts are free to range, and to set the course for the activities of the day. The wicked do not meditate on God's law "day and night" (1:2; see 119:55), or let a godly heart instruct them at night (see 16:7), or at night commune with God (see 42:8), think of Him (see 63:6) and reflect on His promises (see 119:148).
36:5–9 The goodness of the Lord—His benevolence toward all His creatures (see 33:4–5).
36:5 *lovingkindness . . . faithfulness.* That is, lovingkindness-and-faithfulness (as in 57:3; 61:7; 85:10; 86:15; 89:14; 115:1; 138:2; Prov 3:3; 14:22; 16:6; 20:28; see note on 3:7). *extends to the heavens . . . to the skies.* Encompasses all the realms of creaturely existence (see 57:10; 108:4).
36:6 *righteousness . . . judgments.* That is, righteousness-and-judgments (as in 33:5; 89:14; 97:2; Hos 2:19; see also Is 9:7; 33:5; Jer 9:24). *righteousness.* See note on 5:8. *mountains of God . . . great deep.* As high as the mountains, as deep as the sea.
36:7 *lovingkindness.* See v. 5; see also note on 6:4. *children of men.* All categories of men. *shadow of Your wings.* See 17:8 and note.
36:8 *drink . . . drink.* Life-giving water. *house.* Here, God's whole estate or realm—i.e., the earth, from which springs the abundance of food for all living things (see note on 24:2). *river.* The "channel" (Job 38:25) by which God brings forth the rain out of His "storehouses" (33:7; see Job 38:8–11,22,37; Jer 10:13) in His "upper chambers" (104:13; see 65:9; Is 30:25 and the references to "blessings" from heaven in Gen 49:25; Deut 33:23). This vivid imagery, depicting God's control over, and gift of, the waters from heaven, which feed the rivers and streams of earth to give life and health wherever they flow, is the source of the symbol of the "river of the water of life" that flows from the temple of God (Rev 22:1–2; see also Ezek 47:1–12). *of Your delights.* Furnishing many sources of joy.
36:9 The climax and summation of vv. 5–9. *fountain of life.*

10 O continue Your lovingkindness to
[a]those who know You,
And Your [b]righteousness to the
upright in heart.
11 Let not the foot of pride come upon
me,
And let not the hand of the wicked
drive me away.
12 There the doers of iniquity have fallen;
They have been thrust down and
[a]cannot rise.

Psalm 37

A Psalm of David.

1 [a]Do not fret because of evildoers,
Be not [b]envious toward wrongdoers.
2 For they will [a]wither quickly like the
grass
And [b]fade like the green herb.
3 [a]Trust in the LORD and do good;
[b]Dwell in the land and [1c]cultivate
faithfulness.
4 [a]Delight yourself in the LORD;
And He will [b]give you the desires of
your heart.
5 [a]Commit your way to the LORD,
Trust also in Him, and He will do it.
6 He will bring forth [a]your
righteousness as the light
And your judgment [b]as the noonday.

7 [1]Rest in the LORD and [a]wait [2]patiently
for Him;
[b]Do not fret because of him who
[c]prospers in his way,
Because of the man who carries out
wicked schemes.
8 Cease from anger and [a]forsake wrath;
Do not fret; *it leads* only to evildoing.
9 For [a]evildoers will be cut off,
But those who wait for the LORD, they
will [b]inherit the land.
10 Yet [a]a little while and the wicked man
will be no more;
And you will look carefully for [b]his
place and he will not be *there*.
11 But [a]the humble will inherit the land
And will delight themselves in
[b]abundant prosperity.

12 The wicked [a]plots against the
righteous
And [b]gnashes at him with his teeth.
13 The Lord [a]laughs at him,
For He sees [b]his day is coming.
14 The wicked have drawn the sword
and [a]bent their bow

10 [a]Jer 22:16 [b]Ps 24:5 **12** [a]Ps 140:10; Is 26:14 **37:1** [a]Prov 23:17; 24:19 [b]Ps 73:3; Prov 3:31 **2** [a]Job 14:2; Ps 90:6; 92:7; James 1:11 [b]Ps 129:6 **3** [1]Or *feed securely* or *feed on His faithfulness* [a]Ps 62:8 [b]Deut 30:20 [c]Is 40:11; Ezek 34:13, 14 **4** [a]Job 22:26; Ps 94:19; Is 58:14 [b]Ps 21:2; 145:19; Matt 7:7, 8 **5** [a]Ps 55:22; Prov 16:3; 1 Pet 5:7 **6** [a]Ps 97:11; Is 58:8, 10; Mic 7:9 **6** [b]Job 11:17 **7** [1]Or *Be still* [2]Or *longingly* [a]Ps 40:1; 62:5; Lam 3:26 [b]Ps 37:1, 8 [c]Jer 12:1 **8** [a]Eph 4:31; Col 3:8 **9** [a]Ps 37:2, 22 [b]Ps 25:13; Prov 2:21; Is 57:13; 60:21; Matt 5:5 **10** [a]Job 24:24 [b]Job 7:10; Ps 37:35, 36

11 [a]Matt 5:5 [b]Ps 72:7 **12** [a]Ps 31:13, 20 [b]Ps 35:16 **13** [a]Ps 2:4 [b]1 Sam 26:10; Job 18:20 **14** [a]Ps 11:2; Lam 2:4

See Jer 2:13; 17:13. Ultimately, for sinners, God provides the water of life through Jesus Christ (John 4:10,14). *Your light.* See 27:1 and note. *see.* Experience, have, enjoy, as in 16:10; 27:13; 34:8,12; 49:9,19; 89:48; 90:15; 106:5; Job 9:25; 42:5; Eccl 1:16 ("observed"); 3:13; 6:6 ("enjoy"); 8:16; Is 53:10; Lam 3:1. *light.* Life in its fullness as it was created to be. For the association of light with life see 49:19; 56:13; Job 3:20; 33:30; Is 53:11 (see NASB marg. there).

36:10–11 The prayer: Your "lovingkindness" (v. 5) and "righteousness" (v. 6), which you display in all creation—show these to all who know (acknowledge) you and are upright (the people of God). But keep the wicked, "foot" and "hand," from success against me (the king; see note on 33:16).

36:10 *lovingkindness.* See note on 6:4. *righteousness.* See note on 4:1.

36:11 *pride.* See note on 31:23.

36:12 Confidence (see note on 3:8). *have fallen.* Perhaps in death (see note on 13:4).

Ps 37 Instruction in godly wisdom. (For other "wisdom" psalms see 34:8–22; 49; 112; others closely related are Ps 1; 73; 91; 92:6–9,12–15; 111; 119; 127–128; 133; see essay, p. 689.) This psalm's dominant theme is related to the contrast between the wicked and the righteous reflected in Ps 36. The central issue addressed is: Who will "inherit the land" (vv. 9,11,22,29), i.e., live on to enjoy the blessings of the Lord in the promised land? Will the wicked, who plot (v. 12), scheme (vv. 7,32), default on debts (v. 21), use raw power to gain advantage (v. 14) and seem thereby to flourish (vv. 7,16,35)? Or will the righteous, who trust in the Lord (vv. 3,5,7,34) and are humble (v. 11), blameless (vv. 18,37), generous (vv. 21,26), upright (v. 37) and peaceable (v. 37), and from whose mouth is heard the moral wisdom that reflects meditation on God's law (vv. 30–31)? For a similar characterization of the wicked see 10:2–11; 73:4–12. For a similar characterization of the righteous see Ps 112. For a similar statement concerning the transitoriness of the wicked see Ps 49; 73:18–20. Structurally, in this alphabetic acrostic, two verses are devoted to each letter of the alphabet, though with some irregularity. The main theme is developed in vv. 1–11, then further elaborated in the rest of the psalm. The whole is framed by statements contrasting the brief career of the wicked (vv. 1–2) and the Lord's sustaining help of the righteous (vv. 39–40).

37:1–2 See v. 7; Ps 73.

37:2 See note on v. 20.

37:3 See 34:8–14 and note.

37:4 *heart.* See note on 4:7.

37:5 *Commit.* See 1 Pet 5:7.

37:6 *righteousness . . . judgment.* That is, righteousness-and-judgment (see note on 36:6). *righteousness.* See note on 1:5.

37:8 *anger . . . wrath.* Evidence of fretting over the wicked's prosperity, gained to the disadvantage of and even at the expense of the righteous.

37:9 *inherit the land.* Receive from the Lord secure entitlement (for them and their children) to the promised land as the created and redeemed sphere and bountiful source of provision for the life of God's people. Those who hope in the Lord—i.e., trustfully look to Him to bestow life and its blessings as a gift—will inherit the land, not those who apart from God and by evil means try to take possession of it and its wealth (see vv. 11,22,29; cf. Josh 7).

37:10 *a little while.* Shortness of time is here a figure for certainty of event (see 58:9; Job 20:5–11; Hag 2:6).

37:11 See Matt 5:5. *humble.* Those who humbly acknowledge their dependence on the goodness and grace of God and betray no arrogance toward their fellowman. *abundant prosperity.* Unmixed blessedness.

37:12 *righteous.* See note on 1:5. *gnashes . . . his teeth.* See 35:16 and note.

37:13 *Lord laughs.* See 2:4. *sees his day is coming.* Strikingly, the psalmist nowhere speaks of God's active involvement in bringing the wicked down—though he hints at it in v. 22. The

To cast down the [b]afflicted and the
needy,
To [c]slay those who are upright in
conduct.
15 Their sword will enter their own heart,
And their [a]bows will be broken.

16 [a]Better is the little of the righteous
Than the abundance of many wicked.
17 For the [a]arms of the wicked will be
broken,
But the LORD [b]sustains the righteous.
18 The LORD [a]knows the days of the
[1]blameless,
And their [b]inheritance will be forever.
19 They will not be ashamed in the time
of evil,
And [a]in the days of famine they will
have abundance.
20 But the [a]wicked will perish;
And the enemies of the LORD will be
like the [1]glory of the pastures,
They vanish—[b]like smoke they vanish
away.
21 The wicked borrows and does not pay
back,
But the righteous [a]is gracious and
gives.
22 For [a]those blessed by Him will
[b]inherit the land,
But those [c]cursed by Him will be cut
off.

23 [a]The steps of a man are established by
the LORD,
And He [b]delights in his way.
24 When [a]he falls, he will not be hurled
headlong,
Because [b]the LORD is the One [1]who
holds his hand.
25 I have been young and now I am old,
Yet [a]I have not seen the righteous
forsaken
Or [b]his [1]descendants begging bread.
26 All day long [a]he is gracious and lends,
And [b]his [1]descendants are a blessing.

27 [a]Depart from evil and do good,
[1]So you will abide [b]forever.

14 [b]Ps 35:10; 86:1 [c]Ps 11:2 **15** [a]1 Sam 2:4; Ps 46:9 **16** [a]Prov 15:16; 16:8 **17** [a]Job 38:15; Ps 10:15; Ezek 30:21 [b]Ps 71:6; 145:14 **18** [1]Lit *complete;* or *perfect* [a]Ps 1:6; 31:7 [b]Ps 37:27, 29 **19** [a]Job 5:20; Ps 33:19 **20** [1]I.e. flowers [a]Ps 73:27 [b]Ps 68:2; 102:3 **21** [a]Ps 112:5, 9 **22** [a]Prov 3:33 [b]Ps 37:9 [c]Job 5:3 **23** [a]1 Sam 2:9; Ps 40:2; 66:9; 119:5 [b]Ps 147:11 **24** [1]Or *who sustains him with His hand* [a]Ps 145:14; Prov 24:16; Mic 7:8 [b]Ps 147:6 **25** [1]Lit *seed* [a]Ps 37:28; Is 41:17; Heb 13:5 [b]Ps 109:10 **26** [1]Lit *seed* [a]Deut 15:8; Ps 37:21 [b]Ps 147:13 **27** [1]Or *And dwell forever* [a]Ps 34:14 [b]Ps 37:18; 102:28

28 [1]Lit *judgment* [2]Lit *seed* [a]Ps 11:7; 33:5 [b]Ps 37:25 [c]Ps 31:23 [d]Ps 21:10; 37:9; Prov 2:22; Is 14:20 **29** [a]Ps 37:9; Prov 2:21 [b]Ps 37:18 **30** [a]Ps 49:3; Prov 10:13 [b]Ps 101:1; 119:13 **31** [a]Deut 6:6; Ps 40:8; 119:11; Is 51:7; Jer 31:33 [b]Ps 26:1; 37:23 **32** [a]Ps 10:8; 17:11 [b]Ps 37:14 **33** [a]Ps 31:8; 2 Pet 2:9 [b]Ps 34:22; 109:31 **34** [a]Ps 27:14; 37:9 [b]Ps 52:5, 6; 91:8 **35** [1]Lit *native;* Heb obscure

28 For the LORD [a]loves [1]justice
And [b]does not forsake His godly ones;
They are [c]preserved forever,
But the [2d]descendants of the wicked
will be cut off.
29 The righteous will [a]inherit the land
And [b]dwell in it forever.
30 The mouth of the righteous [a]utters
wisdom,
And his tongue [b]speaks justice.
31 The [a]law of his God is in his heart;
His [b]steps do not slip.
32 The [a]wicked spies upon the righteous
And [b]seeks to kill him.
33 The LORD will [a]not leave him in his
hand
Or [b]let him be condemned when he is
judged.
34 [a]Wait for the LORD and keep His way,
And He will exalt you to inherit the
land;
When the [b]wicked are cut off, you will
see it.

35 I have [a]seen a wicked, violent man
Spreading himself like a [b]luxuriant
tree in its native soil.
36 Then [1]he passed away, and lo, he
[a]was no more;
I sought for him, but he could not be
found.
37 Mark the [1a]blameless man, and
behold the [b]upright;
For the man of peace will have a
[2c]posterity.
38 But transgressors will be altogether
[a]destroyed;
The [1]posterity of the wicked will be
[b]cut off.
39 But the [a]salvation of the righteous is
from the LORD;
He is their strength [b]in time of trouble.
40 [a]The LORD helps them and delivers
them;

[a]Job 5:3; Jer 12:2 [b]Job 8:16 **36** [1]Ancient versions read *I passed by* [a]Job 20:5; Ps 37:10 **37** [1]Lit *complete;* or *perfect* [2]Lit *an end* [a]Ps 37:18 [b]Ps 7:10 [c]Is 57:1, 2 **38** [1]Lit *end* [a]Ps 1:4-6; 37:20, 28 [b]Ps 37:9; 73:17 **39** [a]Ps 3:8; 62:1 [b]Ps 9:9; 37:19 **40** [a]Ps 54:4

---

certainty that the life of the wicked "will be cut off" is frequently asserted (vv. 9,22,28,34,38; cf. vv. 2,8,10,15,17,20,36,38)—and the Lord also knows it—but God's positive action is here reserved for His care for and protection of the righteous. *his day.* The time for each of them, when he will be "cut off," as in 1 Sam 26:10; Job 18:20 ("his fate").

37:14 *afflicted and the needy.* See 34:6 and note.

37:15 *enter . . . heart.* See 45:5.

37:16–17 *righteous.* See note on 1:5.

37:18 *blameless.* See v. 37; 15:2; see also note on 26:1.

37:20 *glory.* The grass and flowers (cf. v. 2; 90:5–6; 102:11; 103:15–16; Job 14:2; Is 40:6–8; see James 1:10–11).

37:21 See Deut 15:6; 28:12,44).

37:24 See Prov 24:16.

37:26 See note on v. 21.

37:28 *godly ones.* See note on 4:3.

37:29 *forever.* They and their children and children's children, in contrast to the wicked (see v. 28).

37:30 *wisdom.* See 119:98,130; Deut 4:6.

37:31 *heart.* See note on 4:7. *do not slip.* From the right path (see 17:5).

37:32 *spies upon.* See 10:8–9; see also note on 7:2. *seeks to kill him.* Attempting to seize by false charges at court (see v. 33) the very livelihood of their intended victims.

37:35–36 Cf. vv. 25–26.

37:37–38 The great contrast: hope for the one, no hope for the other.

37:37 *blameless.* See note on v. 18.

37:39–40 *the righteous . . . them.* They are not at the mercy of the wicked: The Lord is their refuge, and in spite of all that the wicked do, the Lord makes secure their inheritance in the promised land.

He [b]delivers them from the wicked
and saves them,
Because they [c]take refuge in Him.

Psalm 38

A Psalm of David, for a memorial.

1 O LORD, [a]rebuke me not in Your wrath,
And chasten me not in Your burning
anger.
2 For Your [a]arrows have sunk deep into
me,
And [b]Your hand has pressed down on
me.
3 There is [a]no soundness in my flesh
[b]because of Your indignation;
There is no health [c]in my bones
because of my sin.
4 For my [a]iniquities are gone over my
head;
As a heavy burden they weigh too
much for me.
5 My [1]wounds grow foul *and* fester
Because of [a]my folly.
6 I am bent over and [a]greatly bowed
down;
I [b]go mourning all day long.
7 For my loins are filled with [a]burning,
And there is [b]no soundness in my
flesh.
8 I am [a]benumbed and [1]badly crushed;
I [2b]groan because of the [3]agitation of
my heart.

9 Lord, all [a]my desire is [1]before You;
And my [b]sighing is not hidden from
You.
10 My heart throbs, [a]my strength fails
me;
And the [b]light of my eyes, even [1]that
[2]has gone from me.
11 My [1a]loved ones and my friends stand
aloof from my plague;
And my kinsmen [b]stand afar off.
12 Those who [a]seek my life [b]lay snares
for me;
And those who [c]seek to injure me
have [1]threatened destruction,
And they [d]devise treachery all day
long.

13 But I, like a deaf man, do not hear;
And *I am* like a [a]mute man who does
not open his mouth.
14 Yes, I am like a man who does not
hear,
And in whose mouth are no
arguments.
15 For [a]I [1]hope in You, O LORD;
You [b]will answer, O Lord my God.
16 For I said, "May they not rejoice over
me,
Who, when my foot slips, [a]would
magnify themselves against me."
17 For I am [a]ready to fall,
And [b]my [1]sorrow is continually before
me.
18 For I [1a]confess my iniquity;
I am full of [b]anxiety because of my
sin.
19 But my [a]enemies are vigorous *and*
[1]strong,
And many are those who [b]hate me
wrongfully.
20 And those who [a]repay evil for good,
They [b]oppose me, because I follow
what is good.
21 Do not forsake me, O LORD;
O my God, [a]do not be far from me!
22 Make [a]haste to help me,
O Lord, [b]my salvation!

40 [b]Ps 22:4; Is 31:5; Dan 3:17; 6:23 [c]1 Chr 5:20; Ps 34:22
38:1 [a]Ps 6:1
2 [a]Job 6:4 [b]Ps 32:4
3 [a]Is 1:6 [b]Ps 102:10 [c]Job 33:19; Ps 6:2; 31:10
4 [a]Ezra 9:6; Ps 40:12
5 [1]Or *stripes* [a]Ps 69:5
6 [a]Ps 35:14 [b]Job 30:28; Ps 42:9; 43:2
7 [a]Ps 102:3 [b]Ps 38:3
8 [1]Or *greatly* [2]Lit *roar* [3]Lit *growling* [a]Lam 1:13, 20f; 2:11; 5:17 [b]Job 3:24; Ps 22:1; 32:3
9 [1]Or known *to You* [a]Ps 10:17 [b]Ps 6:6; 102:5
10 [1]Lit *they have* [2]Lit *is not with me* [a]Ps 31:10 [b]Ps 6:7; 69:3; 88:9
11 [1]Or *lovers* [a]Ps 31:11; 88:18 [b]Luke 23:49
12 [1]Lit *spoken* [a]Ps 54:3 [b]Ps 140:5 [c]Ps 35:4 [d]Ps 35:20
13 [a]Ps 39:2, 9
15 [1]Or *wait for* [a]Ps 39:7 [b]Ps 17:6
16 [a]Ps 35:26
17 [1]Lit *pain* [a]Ps 35:15 [b]Ps 13:2
18 [1]Or *declare* [a]Ps 32:5 [b]2 Cor 7:9, 10
19 [1]Or *numerous* [a]Ps 18:17 [b]Ps 35:19
20 [a]Ps 35:12 [b]Ps 109:5; 1 John 3:12
21 [a]Ps 22:19; 35:22
22 [a]Ps 40:13, 17 [b]Ps 27:1

Ps 38 An urgent appeal for relief from a severe and painful illness, God's "rebuke" for a sin David has committed. Neither the specific occasion nor the illness can be identified. David's suffering is aggravated by the withdrawal of his friends (see v. 11) and the unwarranted efforts of his enemies to seize this opportunity to bring him down (vv. 12,16,19–20). See introductions to Ps 39–41. In traditional Christian usage, this is one of seven penitential psalms (see introduction to Ps 6). Like Ps 33 (see introductory note on its structure), its length (22 verses) is based on the number of letters in the Hebrew alphabet. The psalm can be analyzed as composed of five stanzas of four verses each, with a two-verse conclusion.
38 title *a memorial.* Occurs elsewhere only in the title of Ps 70.
38:1–4 Plea for relief from the Lord's rebuke.
38:1 *rebuke . . . chasten.* That is, rebuke-and-chasten (see 39:11; see also note on 3:7). *wrath . . . anger.* See note on 2:5.
38:2 *arrows.* A vivid metaphor for God's blows (see Job 6:4; 34:6; Lam 3:12; Ezek 5:16). *Your hand has pressed down on me.* See 32:4 and note on 32:3–5.
38:3 *bones.* See note on 6:2.
38:4 *burden.* Not only a psychological "burden of guilt," but the heavy burden of suffering described in vv. 5–8.
38:5–8 The devastating physical and psychological effects of his illness.
38:8 *heart.* See note on 4:7.
38:9–12 Renewed appeal, with further elaboration of his troubles: his illness (v. 10), abandonment by his friends (v. 11) and the hostility of his enemies (v. 12).
38:10 *light of my eyes . . . has gone from me.* See note on 13:3.
38:11 See note on 31:11–12.
38:12 See note on 5:9.
38:13–16 Let the Lord answer (v. 15) my enemies. Like a deaf-mute, David will not reply to his enemies (vv. 13–14); he waits for the Lord to act in his behalf (vv. 15–16). See 1 Sam 25:32–39; 2 Sam 16:10,12.
38:16 *when my foot slips.* When he experiences a personal blow to health or circumstance—here referring to his illness (see 66:9; 94:18; 121:3).
38:17–20 As health declines, the vigor of his many enemies increases.
38:17 *ready to fall.* Death seems near (see note on 13:4).
38:18 See vv. 3–4; Ps 32.
38:19–20 He has sinned against the Lord, but he is innocent of any wrong against those attacking him (see note on 35:19).
38:20 *oppose.* Accuse (falsely), as in 71:13; 109:4,20,29; Zech 3:1. *because.* Or "though." *good.* Morally good (see 34:14).
38:21–22 In conclusion, a renewed appeal.

Psalm 39

For the choir director, for [†]Jeduthun.
A Psalm of David.

1 I said, "I will [a]guard my ways
That I [b]may not sin with my tongue;
I will guard [c]my mouth as with a muzzle
While the wicked are in my presence."

2 I was [a]mute [1]and silent,
I [2]refrained *even* from good,
And my [3]sorrow grew worse.
3 My [a]heart was hot within me,
While I was musing the fire burned;
Then I spoke with my tongue:
4 "LORD, make me to know [a]my end
And what is the extent of my days;
Let me know how [b]transient I am.
5 "Behold, You have made [a]my days *as* handbreadths,
And my [b]lifetime as nothing in Your sight;
Surely every man [1]at his best is [2]a mere [c]breath. [3]Selah.
6 "Surely every man [a]walks about as [1]a phantom;
Surely they make an [b]uproar for nothing;
He [c]amasses *riches* and does not know who will gather them.

7 "And now, Lord, for what do I wait?
My [a]hope is in You.
8 "[a]Deliver me from all my transgressions;
Make me not the [b]reproach of the foolish.
9 "I have become [a]mute, I do not open my mouth,
Because it is [b]You who have done *it.*
10 "[a]Remove Your plague from me;
Because of [b]the opposition of Your hand I am [1]perishing.
11 "With [a]reproofs You chasten a man for iniquity;
You [b]consume as a moth what is precious to him;
Surely [c]every man is a mere breath. Selah.

12 "[a]Hear my prayer, O LORD, and give ear to my cry;
Do not be silent [b]at my tears;
For I am [c]a stranger with You,
A [d]sojourner like all my fathers.
13 "[a]Turn Your gaze away from me, that I may [1]smile *again*
Before I depart and am no more."

Psalm 40

For the choir director. A Psalm of David.

1 I [a]waited [1]patiently for the LORD;
And He inclined to me and [b]heard my cry.

39:1 [†]1 Chr 16:41 [a]1 Kin 2:4; 2 Kin 10:31; Ps 119:9 [b]Job 2:10; Ps 34:13; James 3:5-12 [c]Ps 141:3; James 3:2
2 [1]Lit *with silence* [2]Lit *kept silence* [3]Lit *pain* [a]Ps 38:13
3 [a]Ps 32:4; Jer 20:9; Luke 24:32
4 [a]Job 6:11; Ps 90:12; 119:84 [b]Ps 78:39; 103:14
5 [1]Lit *standing firm* [2]Or *altogether vanity* [3]*Selah* may mean: *Pause, Crescendo* or *Musical interlude* [a]Ps 89:47 [b]Ps 144:4 [c]Job 14:2; Ps 62:9; Eccl 6:12
6 [1]Lit *an image* [a]1 Cor 7:31; James 1:10, 11; 1 Pet 1:24 [b]Ps 127:2; Eccl 5:17 [c]Ps 49:10; Eccl 2:26; 5:14; Luke 12:20
7 [a]Ps 38:15
8 [a]Ps 51:9, 14; 79:9 [b]Ps 44:13; 79:4; 119:22
9 [a]Ps 39:2 [b]2 Sam 16:10; Job 2:10
10 [1]Or *wasting away* [a]Job 9:34; 13:21 [b]Ps 32:4
11 [a]Ezek 5:15; 2 Pet 2:16 [b]Job 13:28; Ps 90:7; Is 50:9 [c]Ps 39:5
12 [a]Ps 102:1; 143:1 [b]2 Kin 20:5; Ps 56:8 [c]Lev 25:23; 1 Chr 29:15; Ps 119:19; Heb 11:13; 1 Pet 2:11 [d]Gen 47:9 **13** [1]Or *become cheerful* [a]Job 7:19; 10:20, 21; 14:6; Ps 102:24 **40:1** [1]Or *intently* [a]Ps 25:5; 27:14; 37:7 [b]Ps 34:15

Ps 39 The poignant prayer of a soul deeply troubled by the fragility of human life. He is reminded of this by the present illness through which God is rebuking him (vv. 10–11) for his "transgressions" (v. 8). Ps 38 speaks of silence before the enemy, Ps 39 of silence before God. Both are prayers in times of illness (God's "reproofs," v. 11; 38:1); both acknowledge sin, and both express deep trust in God. See introduction to Ps 40. In addition, this psalm has many links with Ps 90; see also Ps 49.
39 title *For the choir director.* See note on Ps 4 title. *Jeduthun.* One of David's three choir leaders (1 Chr 16:41–42; 25:1,6; 2 Chr 5:12; called his "seer" in 2 Chr 35:15). Jeduthun is probably also the Ethan of 1 Chr 6:44; 15:19; if so, he represented the family of Merari, even as Asaph did the family of Gershon and Heman the family of Kohath, the three sons of Levi (see 1 Chr 6:16,33,39,43–44). See titles of Ps 62; 77; 89.
39:1–3 Introduction: Having determined to keep silent, he could finally no longer suppress his anguish.
39:1 He had kept a muzzle on his mouth for fear that rebellious words would escape in the hearing of the wicked (see Ps 73).
39:2–3 Suppressed anguish only intensified the agony (see Jer 20:9).
39:4–6 A prayer for understanding and patient acceptance of the brief span of human life.
39:4 *how transient I am.* See 78:39 and note on 37:20.
39:5 *as nothing in Your sight.* See 90:4. *a mere breath.* See v. 11; 144:4; Job 14:2; Eccl 6:12.
39:6 Could almost serve as a summary of Ecclesiastes.
39:7–11 A modest prayer: Only grant me relief from your present rebuke.
39:8 *Deliver me.* As from an enemy. *reproach of the foolish.* If the Lord does not restore him, he will be mocked (see 22:7–8; 69:6–12) by godless fools (see 14:1).
39:10 *opposition of Your hand.* See 32:4; 38:2.
39:11 *reproofs . . . chasten.* See 6:1; 38:1. *a mere breath.* See note on v. 5.
39:12–13 The modest prayer repeated even more modestly.
39:12 *a stranger . . . A sojourner.* He lives this life before God only as a pilgrim passing through.
39:13 *Turn Your gaze away from me.* See Job 7:17–19; 10:20–21; 14:6. *smile again.* See Job 9:27; 10:20. *am no more.* Here there is no glimpse of what lies beyond the horizon of death (see note on 6:5).
Ps 40 A prayer for help when troubles abound. The causes of distress are not specified, but David acknowledges that they are occasioned by his sin (see v. 12), as in Ps 38–39; 41 (see introductions to Ps 39; 41). They are aggravated by the gloating of his enemies, a theme also present in Ps 38–39; 41 (see introduction to Ps 6). The prayer begins with praise of God for His past mercies (vv. 1–5) and a testimony to the king's own faithfulness to the Lord (vv. 6–10). These form the grounds for his present appeal for help (vv. 11–17). See also the lengthy prefaces to prayer in Ps 44; 89. Ps 70 is a somewhat revised duplicate of vv. 13–17 of this psalm.
40 title *For the choir director.* See note on Ps 4 title.
40:1–5 Praise of the Lord for past mercies (see introduction to Ps 9).
40:1–3 David's experience of God's past help in time of trouble, which moved him to praise and others to faith (see notes on 7:17; 9:1).

2 He brought me up out of the [a]pit of
destruction, out of the [1]miry clay,
And [b]He set my feet upon a rock
[c]making my footsteps firm.
3 He put a [a]new song in my mouth, a
song of praise to our God;
Many will [b]see and fear
And will trust in the LORD.

4 How [a]blessed is the man who has
made the LORD his trust,
And [b]has not [1]turned to the proud,
nor to those who [c]lapse into
falsehood.
5 Many, O LORD my God, are [a]the
wonders which You have done,
And Your [b]thoughts toward us;
There is none to compare with You.
If I would declare and speak of them,
They [c]would be too numerous to count.

6 [1][a]Sacrifice and meal offering You have
not desired;
My ears You have [2]opened;
Burnt offering and sin offering You
have not required.
7 Then I said, "Behold, I come;
In the scroll of the book it is [1]written
of me.
8 [a]I delight to do Your will, O my God;
[b]Your Law is within my heart."

9 I have [a]proclaimed glad tidings of
righteousness in the great
congregation;
Behold, I will [b]not restrain my lips,
O LORD, [c]You know.

2 [1]Lit *mud of the mire* [a]Ps 69:2, 14; Jer 38:6 [b]Ps 27:5 [c]Ps 37:23
3 [a]Ps 32:7; 33:3 [b]Ps 52:6; 64:9
4 [1]Lit *regard* [a]Ps 34:8; 84:12 [b]Job 37:24 [c]Ps 125:5
5 [a]Job 5:9; Ps 136:4 [b]Ps 139:17; Is 55:8 [c]Ps 71:15; 139:18
6 [1]I.e. Blood sacrifice [2]Lit *dug;* or possibly *pierced* [a]1 Sam 15:22; Ps 51:16; Is 1:11; Jer 6:20; 7:22, 23; Amos 5:22; Mic 6:6-8; Heb 10:5-7
7 [1]Or *prescribed for*
8 [a]John 4:34 [b]Ps 37:31; Jer 31:33; 2 Cor 3:3
9 [a]Ps 22:22, 25 [b]Ps 119:13 [c]Josh 22:22; Ps 139:4
10 [a]Acts 20:20, 27 [b]Ps 89:1
11 [1]Or *May...preserve* [a]Ps 43:3; 57:3; 61:7; Prov 20:28
12 [1]Lit *forsaken* [a]Ps 18:5; 116:3 [b]Ps 38:4; 65:3 [c]Ps 69:4 [d]Ps 73:26
13 [a]Ps 70:1 [b]Ps 22:19; 71:12
14 [1]Or *soul* [2]Or *to injure me* [a]Ps 35:4, 26; 70:2; 71:13 [b]Ps 63:9
15 [1]Or *desolated* [a]Ps 70:3 [b]Ps 35:21; 70:3

10 I have [a]not hidden Your righteousness
within my heart;
I have [b]spoken of Your faithfulness
and Your salvation;
I have not concealed Your
lovingkindness and Your truth from
the great congregation.

11 You, O LORD, will not withhold Your
compassion from me;
[1]Your [a]lovingkindness and Your truth
will continually preserve me.
12 For evils beyond number have
[a]surrounded me;
My [b]iniquities have overtaken me, so
that I am not able to see;
They are [c]more numerous than the
hairs of my head,
And my [d]heart has [1]failed me.

13 [a]Be pleased, O LORD, to deliver me;
Make [b]haste, O LORD, to help me.
14 Let those be [a]ashamed and humiliated
together
Who [b]seek my [1]life to destroy it;
Let those be turned back and
dishonored
Who delight [2]in my hurt.
15 Let those [a]be [1]appalled because of
their shame
Who [b]say to me, "Aha, aha!"
16 [a]Let all who seek You rejoice and be
glad in You;
Let those who love Your salvation [b]say
continually,
"The LORD be magnified!"

16 [a]Ps 70:4 [b]Ps 35:27

40:2 See 30:1 and note.
40:3 *new song.* See note on 33:3. *Many will see.* As a result of David's praise (see 18:49; 22:22–31; see also note on 9:1). *fear.* See note on 34:8–14.
40:4–5 The Lord's benevolence to others: to all who trust in the Lord (v. 4), and to His people Israel (v. 5).
40:4 See Jer 17:7; praise of the Lord for the blessedness of those who trust in Him (see 32:1–2; 146:5). *blessed.* See note on 1:1. *proud.* See note on 31:23.
40:5 *wonders.* See note on 9:1. *thoughts toward us.* God's actions in behalf of Israel are according to His predetermined purpose (see Is 25:1; 46:10–11).
40:6–8 David's commitment to God's will. Heb 10:5–10 applies these verses to Christ (see notes there).
40:6 *have not desired . . . not required.* More important is obedience (see 1 Sam 15:22), especially to God's moral law (see Is 1:10–17; Amos 5:21–24; Mic 6:6–8)—i.e., the ten basic commandments of His covenant (see Ex 20:3–17; Deut 5:7–21). *opened.* Lit. "dug." Translated "opened" (see NASB marg.), it refers to ears made able and eager to hear God's law (see Prov 28:9; Is 48:8; 50:4–5). If, however, it is translated "pierced," it probably refers to the sign by which a servant pledged lifelong service to his beloved master (see Ex 21:6; Deut 15:17).
40:7 *Behold, I come.* Probably refers to David's commitment to the Lord at the time of his enthronement. *in the scroll . . . it is written of me.* Some take this to be a reference to a prophecy, perhaps Deut 17:14–15. The context, however, strongly suggests that the "scroll" refers to the personal copy of the law that the king is to take at the time of his enthronement to serve as the covenant charter of his administration (see Deut 17:18–20; 2 Kin 11:12; cf. 1 Kin 2:3).
40:8 *I delight.* I desire whatever is in full accord with God's "desire" (v. 6)—a claim that frames the stanza.
40:9–10 David's life is filled with praise, proclaiming God's faithful and loving acts in behalf of His people. This, too, God desires more than animal sacrifices (see 50:7–15,23).
40:9 *proclaimed.* See 68:11; 96:2; as good tidings (see 1 Kin 1:42; Is 40:9; 41:27; 52:7; 61:1). *righteousness.* See note on 5:8. *in the great congregation.* See notes on 1:5; 9:1. *not restrain my lips.* He is not silent about God's praise (see 38:13–16; 39:1 and notes).
40:10 *heart.* See note on 4:7. *Your lovingkindness and Your truth.* See note on 26:3.
40:11–17 The prayer for help.
40:11 *Your lovingkindness and Your truth.* Which he has been proclaiming to all at the temple (see v. 10 and note).
40:12 *iniquities have overtaken me.* In the form of the "evils beyond number" that burden him (see Ps 38–39 and their introductions). *not able to see.* See note on 13:3. *more . . . than the hairs of my head.* See Matt 10:30; Luke 12:7. *heart.* See note on 4:7.
40:14–15 In the midst of his troubles his enemies harass him, as in 38:12; 39:8; 41:5,7 and often in the Psalms (see note on 5:9). May those who wish to put him to shame be put to shame themselves (see note on 5:10).
40:15 *Aha, aha!* See note on 3:2.

17 Since [a]I am afflicted and needy,
[1b]Let the Lord be mindful of me.
You are my help and my deliverer;
Do not delay, O my God.

Psalm 41

For the choir director. A Psalm of David.

1 How blessed is he who [a]considers the [1]helpless;
The LORD will deliver him [b]in a day of [2]trouble.
2 The LORD will [a]protect him and keep him alive,
And he shall [1]be called [b]blessed upon the earth;
And [c]do not give him over to the desire of his enemies.
3 The LORD will sustain him upon his sickbed;
In his illness, You [1]restore him to health.

4 As for me, I said, "O LORD, be gracious to me;
[a]Heal my soul, for [b]I have sinned against You."
5 My enemies [a]speak evil against me,
"When will he die, and his name perish?"
6 And [1]when he comes to see *me*, he [a]speaks [2]falsehood;
His heart gathers wickedness to itself;
When he goes outside, he tells it.
7 All who hate me whisper together against me;
Against me they [a]devise my hurt, *saying*,

17 [1]Or *The Lord is mindful* [a]Ps 70:5; 86:1; 109:22 [b]Ps 40:5; 1 Pet 5:7
41:1 [1]Or *poor* [2]Or *evil* [a]Ps 82:3, 4; Prov 14:21 [b]Ps 27:5; 37:19
2 [1]Or *be blessed* [a]Ps 37:28 [b]Ps 37:22 [c]Ps 27:12
3 [1]Lit *turn all his bed*
4 [a]Ps 6:2; 103:3; 147:3 [b]Ps 51:4
5 [a]Ps 38:12
6 [1]Or *if he* [2]Or *emptiness* [a]Ps 12:2; 62:4; Prov 26:24-26
7 [a]Ps 56:5
8 [1]Or *within* [a]Ps 71:10, 11
9 [a]2 Sam 15:12; Job 19:13, 19; Ps 55:12, 13, 20; Jer 20:10; Mic 7:5; Matt 26:23; Luke 22:21; John 13:18
10 [a]Ps 3:3
11 [a]Ps 37:23; 147:11 [b]Ps 25:2
12 [a]Ps 18:32; 37:17; 63:8 [b]Job 36:7; Ps 21:6
13 [a]Ps 72:18, 19; 89:52; 106:48; 150:6
42:1 [†]Possibly *Contemplative*, or *Didactic*, or *Skillful Psalm* [1]Lit *longs for* [a]Ps 119:131
2 [a]Ps 63:1; 84:2; 143:6 [b]Josh 3:10; Ps 84:2; Jer 10:10; Dan 6:26; Matt 26:63; Rom 9:26; 1 Thess 1:9

8 "A wicked thing is poured out [1]upon him,
That when he lies down, he will [a]not rise up again."
9 Even my [a]close friend in whom I trusted,
Who ate my bread,
Has lifted up his heel against me.

10 But You, O LORD, be gracious to me and [a]raise me up,
That I may repay them.
11 By this I know that [a]You are pleased with me,
Because [b]my enemy does not shout in triumph over me.
12 As for me, [a]You uphold me in my integrity,
And You set me [b]in Your presence forever.

13 [a]Blessed be the LORD, the God of Israel,
From everlasting to everlasting.
Amen and Amen.

BOOK 2

Psalm 42

For the choir director. A [†]Maskil of the sons of Korah.

1 As the deer [1]pants for the water brooks,
So my soul [1a]pants for You, O God.
2 My soul [a]thirsts for God, for the [b]living God;

40:17 *afflicted and needy.* In need of God's help (see note on 34:6).

Ps 41 David's prayer for mercy when seriously ill. He acknowledges that his illness is related to his sin (v. 4). See the introductions to Ps 38–40. His enemies greet the prospect of his death with malicious glee (see note on 5:9), and even his "close friend" (v. 9) betrays his friendship (see note on 31:11–12). This psalm concludes a collection of four psalms connected by common themes, and also forms the conclusion to Book 1. (Book 1 begins and ends with a "Blessed" psalm.) In its structure, the psalm is very symmetrical. The first and third stanzas frame the prayer with a note of confidence; the middle stanza elaborates the prayer. Verse 13 is actually not part of the psalm but the doxology that closes Book 1 (see note on v. 13).

41 title *For the choir director.* See note on Ps 4 title.

41:1–3 Confidence that the Lord will restore.

41:1 *How blessed is he who considers the helpless.* Especially if he is king, whose duty it is to defend the powerless (see 72:2,4,12–14; 82:3–4; Prov 29:14; 31:8–9; Is 11:4; Jer 22:16). *Blessed.* See note on 1:1.

41:4–6 Prayer for God to show mercy and to heal.

41:4 *sinned.* See note on 32:3–5.

41:5 *When will he die . . . ?* See note on 3:2. *his name perish.* See note on 9:5.

41:6 *see me.* Visit him in his sickness. *speaks falsehood.* Speaks as if he were a friend. *heart.* See note on 4:7.

41:7–9 His enemies and his friend.

41:9 *close friend . . . Who ate my bread.* One who shared the king's table—i.e., was an honored, as well as trusted, friend (see note on 31:11–12). Reference may be to one who had sealed his friendship by a covenant (see note on 23:5). For Jesus' use of this verse in application to Himself see John 13:18. In fulfilling the role of His royal ancestor as God's anointed king over Israel, the great Son of David also experienced the hostility of men and the betrayal of a trusted associate, and thus fulfilled His forefather's lament.

41:10–12 Prayer, with confidence.

41:10 *That I may repay them.* That I (as king) may call them to account.

41:12 *set.* Establish. *in Your presence.* As the royal servant of Israel's heavenly King. (For the idiom see 101:7; 1 Sam 16:22, "stand before me"; 1 Kin 10:8, "before you"; 17:1, "before whom I stand.") *forever.* Never to be rejected (see 2 Sam 7:15–16).

41:13 The doxology with which the worshiping community is to respond to the contents of Book 1 (see 72:18–19; 89:52; 106:48; 150).

Ps 42–43 A prayer for deliverance from the "oppression of the enemy" (42:9; 43:2) and for restoration to the presence of God at His temple. That these two psalms form a single prayer (though they are counted as two psalms also in the Septuagint) is evident from its unique structure (see below) and the development of common themes. Ps 43 may have come to be separated from Ps 42 for a particular liturgical purpose (see introduction to Ps 9). The speaker may have been a leading member

When shall I come and [1c]appear
before God?
3 My [a]tears have been my food day and
night,
While *they* [b]say to me all day long,
"Where is your God?"
4 These things I remember and I [a]pour
out my soul within me.
For I [b]used to go along with the
throng *and* [1]lead them in
procession to the house of God,
With the voice of [c]joy and
thanksgiving, a multitude keeping
festival.

5 [a]Why are you [1b]in despair, O my soul?
And *why* have you become [c]disturbed
within me?
[2d]Hope in God, for I shall [3]again
praise [4]Him
For the [5e]help of His presence.
6 O my God, my soul is [1]in despair
within me;
Therefore I [a]remember You from [b]the
land of the Jordan
And the [2]peaks of [c]Hermon, from
Mount Mizar.
7 Deep calls to deep at the sound of
Your waterfalls;
All Your [a]breakers and Your waves
have rolled over me.
8 The LORD will [a]command His
lovingkindness in the daytime;

2 [1]Some mss read *see the face of God* [c]Ex 23:17; Ps 43:4; 84:7
3 [a]Ps 80:5; 102:9 [b]Ps 79:10; 115:2; Joel 2:17; Mic 7:10
4 [1]Or *move slowly with them* [a]1 Sam 1:15; Job 30:16; Ps 62:8; Lam 2:19 [b]Ps 55:14; 122:1; Is 30:29 [c]Ps 100:4
5 [1]Or *sunk down* [a]Ps 42:11; 43:5 [b]Ps 38:6; Matt 26:38 [c]Ps 77:3
5 [2]Or *Wait for* [3]Or *still* [4]Some ancient versions read *Him, the help of my countenance and my God* [5]Or *saving acts of* [d]Ps 71:14; Lam 3:24 [e]Ps 44:3
6 [1]Or *sunk down* [2]Lit *Hermons* [a]Ps 61:2 [b]2 Sam 17:22 [c]Deut 3:8
7 [a]Ps 69:1, 2; 88:7; Jon 2:3
8 [a]Ps 57:3; 133:3

of the Korahites whose normal duties involved him in the liturgical activities of the temple (see especially 42:4 and note on Ps 42 title). It may be that the "ungodly nation" (43:1) referred to was the Arameans of Damascus and that the author had been taken captive by the Arameans during one of their incursions into Judah, such as that of Hazael (see 2 Kin 12:17–18). (This attack by Hazael affected especially the area in which the Korahites, descendants of Kohath, had been assigned cities; see Josh 21:4,9–19.) See also notes below. This psalm begins Book 2 of the Psalter, a collection that is distinguished from Book 1 primarily by the fact that the Hebrew word for "God" (*Elohim*) predominates, whereas in the first book the Hebrew word for "the LORD" (*Yahweh*) predominates.

Structurally, the stanzas of this psalm are followed by the same refrain (42:5,11; 43:5). The middle stanza, however, has a verse (42:8) that interrupts the developing thought and injects a note of confidence, such as comes to expression also in the threefold refrain. Apart from the refrains, the prayer is framed by an expression of longing for God's presence (42:1) and a vow to praise God at His altar (43:4). For other psalms with recurring refrains see Ps 46; 49; 59; 80; 107.

42 title *For the choir director.* See note on Ps 4 title. *Maskil.* See note on Ps 32 title. *of the sons of Korah.* Or "for the sons of Korah"; see "for Jeduthun" in Ps 39 title. "Sons of Korah" refers to the Levitical choir made up of the descendants of Korah appointed by David to serve in the temple liturgy. The Korahites represented the Levitical family of Kohath son of Levi. Their leader in the days of David was Heman (see Ps 88 title)—just as Asaph led the choir of the Gershonites and Jeduthun (Ethan) the choir of the Merarites (see 1 Chr 6:31–47 and note on Ps 39 title). This is the first of a collection of seven psalms ascribed to the "sons of Korah" (Ps 42–49); four more occur in Book 3 (Ps 84–85; 87–88).

42:1–4 Longing to be with God at the temple.

42:1 *deer pants for . . . water.* Because its life depends on water—especially when being pressed by hunters, as the psalmist was by his oppressors. *soul.* See note on 6:3.

42:2 *living God.* See Deut 5:26. *When . . . ?* Circumstances (see v. 9; 43:1–2) now prevent him from being at the temple. *appear before God.* Enter His presence to commune with Him (see Ex 19:17; 29:42–43; 30:6,36).

42:3 *day and night.* See vv. 8,10. *Where is your God?* See note on 10:11.

42:4 *soul.* See note on 6:3. *lead them in procession.* Suggests that the author normally had a leading role in the liturgy of the temple.

42:5 The refrain: faith encouraging faith (see 27:13–14 and introduction to Ps 27). *praise Him.* For His saving help (see notes on 7:17; 9:1; see also 43:4).

42:6–10 The cause and depth of the trouble of his soul.

42:6 *soul is in despair.* See vv. 5,11; 43:5. *Therefore I remember You.* As he remembers (v. 4) in his exile the joy of his past intimacy with God, so now in his exile he remembers God and painfully wonders (vv. 7,9–10), yet not without hope (v. 8). (But some believe that the clause should be rendered "because I remember You.") *from the land . . . from Mount Mizar.* Probably indicating that the author speaks from exile outside the contemporary boundaries of Israel and Judah. Some think the author locates himself at Mount Mizar (a small peak or village, not otherwise known) on the flanks of Mount Hermon somewhere near the headwaters of the Jordan. Others translate the Hebrew for "from" as "far from" and understand "the land of the Jordan" to refer to the promised land (which lies along the Jordan and from which the author was separated). The mention of "the peaks of Hermon" may then be a reference to the high peak that marked the northern border of the land (see Deut 3:8; Josh 11:17; 13:11; 1 Chr 5:23) and looked down upon it (see 133:3; Song 4:8). Some have suggested that "Mount Mizar" is an additional reference to "the peaks of Hermon," calling that high peak the "little mountain" (literal translation) in comparison with Mount Zion (see 68:15–16).

42:7 *Deep calls . . . Your waterfalls.* Often taken to be an allusion to the cascading waters of the upper Jordan as they rush down from Mount Hermon. It is more likely, however, that this is a literary allusion to the "waterfalls" by which the waters from God's storehouse of water above (see note on 36:8)—the "deep" above—pour down into the streams and rivers that empty into the seas—the "deep" below. It pictures the great distress the author suffers, and the imagery is continued in the following reference to God's "waves" and "breakers" sweeping over him (see 69:1–2; 88:7; Jon 2:3,5; see also note on 32:6). God's hand is involved in the psalmist's suffering, at least to the extent that He has allowed this catastrophe. He seems to the psalmist to have "forgotten" (v. 9)—to have "rejected" (43:2)—him. But he makes no link between this and any sin in his life (see Ps 44; 77).

42:8 The center: confession of hope in all the trouble. That is, "Day-and-night [cf. v. 3] the LORD directs His love, and His song is with me" (see note on 3:7). *the LORD.* Only here at the center in this psalm (see introduction). *command His lovingkindness.* Send forth His love, like a messenger to do His will (see 43:3). *lovingkindness.* See note on 6:4. *His song.* A song con-

And His song will be with me [b]in the
night,
A prayer to [c]the God of my life.

9 I will say to God [a]my rock, "Why have
You forgotten me?
Why do I go [b]mourning [1]because of
the [c]oppression of the enemy?"
10 As a shattering of my bones, my
adversaries revile me,
While they [a]say to me all day long,
"Where is your God?"
11 [a]Why are you [1]in despair, O my soul?
And why have you become disturbed
within me?
[2]Hope in God, for I shall yet praise
Him,
The [3]help of my countenance and my
God.

Psalm 43

1 [a]Vindicate me, O God, and [b]plead my
case against an ungodly nation;
[1]O deliver me from [c]the deceitful and
unjust man!
2 For You are the [a]God of my strength;
why have You [b]rejected me?
Why do I go [c]mourning [1]because of
the oppression of the enemy?

3 O send out Your [a]light and Your truth,
let them lead me;
Let them bring me to Your [b]holy hill
And to Your [c]dwelling places.
4 Then I will go to [a]the altar of God,
To God [1]my exceeding [b]joy;
And upon the [c]lyre I shall praise You,
O God, my God.

5 [a]Why are you [1]in despair, O my soul?
And why are you disturbed within me?
[2]Hope in God, for I shall [3]again praise
Him,
The [4]help of my countenance and my
God.

Psalm 44

For the choir director. A [†]Maskil of
the sons of Korah.

1 O God, we have heard with our ears,
Our [a]fathers have told us
The [b]work that You did in their days,
In the [c]days of old.
2 You with Your own hand [a]drove out
the nations;
Then You [b]planted them;
You [c]afflicted the peoples,
Then You [d]spread them abroad.
3 For by their own sword they [a]did not
possess the land,
And their own arm did not save them,
But Your right hand and Your [b]arm
and the [c]light of Your presence,
For You [d]favored them.

4 You are [a]my King, O God;
[b]Command [1]victories for Jacob.
5 Through You we will [a]push back our
adversaries;
Through Your name we will [b]trample
down those who rise up against us.
6 For I will [a]not trust in my bow,
Nor will my sword save me.
7 But You [a]have saved us from our
adversaries,
And You have [b]put to shame those
who hate us.
8 In God we have [a]boasted all day long,

8 [b]Job 35:10; Ps 16:7; 63:6; 77:6; 149:5 [c]Eccl 5:18; 8:15
9 [1]Or *while the enemy oppresses* [a]Ps 18:2 [b]Ps 38:6 [c]Ps 17:9
10 [a]Ps 42:3; Joel 2:17
11 [1]Or *sunk down* [2]Or *Wait for* [3]Or *saving acts of* [a]Ps 42:5; 43:5
43:1 [1]Or *May You* [a]Ps 26:1; 35:24 [b]1 Sam 24:15; Ps 35:1 [c]Ps 5:6; 38:12
2 [1]Or *while the enemy oppresses* [a]Ps 18:1; 28:7; 31:4 [b]Ps 44:9; 88:14 [c]Ps 42:9
3 [a]Ps 36:9 [b]Ps 2:6; 3:4; 42:4; 46:4 [c]Ps 84:1
4 [1]Lit *the gladness of my joy* [a]Ps 26:6 [b]Ps 21:6 [c]Ps 33:2; 49:4; 57:8; 71:22
5 [1]Or *sunk down* [a]Ps 42:5, 11
5 [2]Or *Wait for* [3]Or *still* [4]Or *saving acts of*
44:1 [†]Possibly *Contemplative,* or *Didactic,* or *Skillful Psalm* [a]Ex 12:26, 27; Deut 6:20; Judg 6:13; Ps 78:3 [b]Ps 78:12 [c]Deut 32:7; Ps 77:5; Is 51:9; 63:9
2 [a]Josh 3:10; Neh 9:24; Ps 78:55; 80:8 [b]Ex 15:17; 2 Sam 7:10; Jer 24:6; Amos 9:15 [c]Ps 135:10-12 [d]Ps 80:9-11; Zech 2:6
3 [a]Deut 8:17, 18; Josh 24:12 [b]Ps 77:15 [c]Ps 4:6; 89:15 [d]Deut 4:37; 7:7, 8; 10:15; Ps 106:4
4 [1]Lit *salvation* [a]Ps 74:12 [b]Ps 42:8
5 [a]Deut 33:17; Ps 60:12; Dan 8:4 [b]Ps 108:13; Zech 10:5
6 [a]1 Sam 17:47; Ps 33:16; Hos 1:7
7 [a]Ps 136:24 [b]Ps 53:5
8 [a]Ps 34:2

cerning Him. *prayer.* Praise and prayer belong together in the thought of the psalmist.

42:9 Echoed in 43:2. *rock.* See note on 18:2. *Why . . . ? Why . . . ?* See note on 6:3 (see also Introduction: Theology).

42:10 See v. 3. *bones.* See note on 6:2.

43:1–4 Prayer for deliverance from the enemy and for restoration to God's presence.

43:1 A plea in the language of the court (see introduction to Ps 17).

43:2 Echoes 42:9.

43:3 *Your light and Your truth.* Personified as God's messengers who work out (1) His salvation (light; see note on 27:1) and (2) His faithful care in behalf of His own (truth; see 26:3; 30:9; 40:10). May these guide me back to Your temple. *holy hill.* See note on 2:6.

43:4 See note on 7:17. *to the altar.* See 26:6 and note.

Ps 44 Israel's cry for help after suffering a devastating defeat at the hand of an enemy. In the light of vv. 17–22, it is difficult to associate this psalm with any of those defeats announced by the prophets as judgments on Israel's covenant unfaithfulness. It probably relates to an experience of the kingdom of Judah (which as a nation did not break covenant with the Lord until late in her history), perhaps during the reign of Jehoshaphat or Hezekiah. Structurally, three thematic developments rise one upon the other as the psalm advances to the prayer in the closing verses. Its structure is like the stages of a ziggurat (a stepped pyramidal structure that the Babylonians built as a mountain-like base for some of their temples; see Gen 11:4 and note) leading to the temple that crowns it. First there is praise of the Lord for past victories (vv. 1–8), second a description of the present defeat and its consequences (vv. 9–16), third a plea of innocence (vv. 17–22), then finally the prayer (vv. 23–26). Each of the themes (recalling of past mercies, description of the present distress, and claim of covenant loyalty) in its own way functions as a ground for the appeal for help (see Ps 40 and its introduction; see also the lengthy prefaces to prayer in Ps 40; 89).

44 title See note on Ps 42 title.

44:1–8 Praise to God for past victories: (1) those by which Israel became established in the land (vv. 1–3); (2) those by which Israel has been kept secure in the land (vv. 4–8).

44:1 See 78:3.

44:3 *light of Your presence.* See notes on 4:6; 13:1.

44:4 *my.* Here and elsewhere in this psalm the first-person singular pronoun refers to the nation corporately (see note on Ps 30 title). *Jacob.* See note on 14:7.

44:5,8 *Your name.* See v. 20; see also note on 5:11.

And we will [b]give thanks to Your
name forever. [1]Selah.

9 Yet You [a]have rejected *us* and brought
us to [b]dishonor,
And [c]do not go out with our armies.
10 You cause us to [a]turn back from the
adversary;
And those who hate us [b]have taken
spoil for themselves.
11 You give us as [a]sheep [1]to be eaten
And have [b]scattered us among the
nations.
12 You [a]sell Your people [1]cheaply,
And have not [2]profited by their sale.
13 You make us a [a]reproach to our
neighbors,
A scoffing and a [b]derision to those
around us.
14 You make us [a]a byword among the
nations,
A [1b]laughingstock among the peoples.
15 All day long my dishonor is before me
And [1]my [a]humiliation has
overwhelmed me,
16 Because of the voice of him who
[a]reproaches and reviles,
Because of the presence of the [b]enemy
and the avenger.

17 All this has come upon us, but we
have [a]not forgotten You,
And we have not [b]dealt falsely with
Your covenant.
18 Our heart has not [a]turned back,
And our steps [b]have not deviated from
Your way,
19 Yet You have [a]crushed us in a place of
[b]jackals
And covered us with [c]the shadow of
death.
20 If we had [a]forgotten the name of our
God
Or extended our [1]hands to [b]a strange
god,
21 Would not God [a]find this out?
For He knows the secrets of the heart.
22 But [a]for Your sake we are killed all
day long;
We are considered as [b]sheep to be
slaughtered.
23 [a]Arouse Yourself, why [b]do You sleep,
O Lord?
Awake, [c]do not reject us forever.
24 Why do You [a]hide Your face
And [b]forget our affliction and our
oppression?
25 For our [a]soul has sunk down into the
dust;
Our body cleaves to the earth.
26 [a]Rise up, be our help,
And [b]redeem us for the sake of Your
lovingkindness.

8 [1]*Selah* may mean: *Pause, Crescendo* or *Musical interlude* [b]Ps 30:12
9 [a]Ps 43:2; 60:1, 10; 74:1; 89:38; 108:11 [b]Ps 69:19 [c]Ps 60:10; 108:11
10 [a]Lev 26:17; Josh 7:8, 12; Ps 89:43 [b]Ps 89:41
11 [1]Lit *for food* [a]Ps 44:22; Rom 8:36 [b]Lev 26:33; Deut 4:27; 28:64; Ps 106:27; Ezek 20:23
12 [1]Lit *for no wealth* [2]Or *set a high price on them* [a]Deut 32:30; Judg 2:14; 3:8; Is 52:3, 4; Jer 15:13
13 [a]Deut 28:37; Ps 79:4; 89:41 [b]Ps 80:6; Ezek 23:32
14 [1]Lit *shaking of the head* [a]Job 17:6; Ps 69:11; Jer 24:9 [b]2 Kin 19:21; Ps 109:25
15 [1]Lit *the shame of my face has covered me* [a]2 Chr 32:21; Ps 69:7
16 [a]Ps 74:10 [b]Ps 8:2
17 [a]Ps 78:7; 119:61, 83, 109, 141, 153, 176 [b]Ps 78:57
18 [a]Ps 78:57 [b]Job 23:11; Ps 119:51, 157
19 [a]Ps 51:8; 94:5 [b]Job 30:29; Is 13:22; Jer 9:11 [c]Job 3:5; Ps 23:4
20 [1]Lit *palms* [a]Ps 78:11 [b]Deut 6:14; Ps 81:9
21 [a]Ps 139:1, 2; Jer 17:10
22 [a]Rom 8:36 [b]Is 53:7; Jer 12:3
23 [a]Ps 7:6 [b]Ps 78:65 [c]Ps 77:7
24 [a]Job 13:24; Ps 88:14 [b]Ps 42:9; Lam 5:20
25 [a]Ps 119:25
26 [a]Ps 35:2 [b]Ps 6:4; 25:22
45:1 [†]Or possibly *Lilies* [•]Possibly *Contemplative*, or *Didactic*, or *Skillful Psalm* [1]Lit *is astir* [2]Lit *am saying* [3]Lit *works* [4]Probably refers to Solomon as a type of Christ

Psalm 45

For the choir director; according to the [†]Shoshannim. A [•]Maskil of the sons of Korah. A Song of Love.

1 My heart [1]overflows with a good
theme;
I [2]address my [3]verses to the [4]King;

44:9–16 But now You have forsaken us: (1) You have caused us to suffer defeat (vv. 9–12); (2) You have shamed us before our enemies (vv. 13–16).
44:11 *give us as sheep to be eaten.* Have not protected us as our Shepherd-King (see v. 4 and note on 23:1).
44:12 *sell Your people.* Like chattel no longer valued (see Deut 32:30; Judg 2:14). *cheaply.* For nothing of value (see Is 52:3; Jer 15:13; cf. Is 43:3–4).
44:14 *laughingstock.* See NASB marg. and 64:8.
44:16 *the avenger.* See 8:2 and note.
44:17–22 And we have not been disloyal to You: (1) We have not been untrue to Your covenant (vv. 17–19); (2) You are our witness that we have not turned to another god (vv. 20–22).
44:17 *Your covenant.* See Ex 19–24.
44:18 *heart.* See note on 4:7. *Your way.* The way marked out in God's covenant (see note on 5:8).
44:19 *You have crushed us.* But that cannot be used as evidence that we have been disloyal. *place of jackals.* A desolate place, uninhabited by man (see Is 13:22; Jer 9:11). *shadow of death.* The absence of all that was associated with the metaphor "light" (see notes on 30:1; 36:9).
44:20 *extended our hands.* Prayed (see Ex 9:29).
44:22 *But.* Or "As a matter of fact" or "As you, O God, know." From the time of her stay in Egypt (see Ex 1), Israel has suffered the hostility of the nations because of her relationship with the Lord (see Matt 10:34). For Paul's application of this verse to the Christian community in the light of Christ's death and resurrection see Rom 8:36.
44:23–26 The appeal for help: (1) Awake to our need (vv. 23–24); (2) arise to our help (vv. 25–26; see introduction to Ps 16).
44:23 *Arouse Yourself.* See note on 7:6. *why . . . ?* See note on 6:3 (see also Introduction: Theology).
44:24 *hide Your face.* See note on 13:1.
44:25 *has sunk down into the dust.* Is about to sink into death (see 22:29 and note; see also note on 30:1).
44:26 *Rise up.* See note on 3:7. *redeem.* See note on 25:22. *lovingkindness.* See note on 6:4.
Ps 45 A song in praise of the king on his wedding day (see title). He undoubtedly belonged to David's dynasty, and the song was probably used at more than one royal wedding. Since the bride is a foreign princess (see vv. 10,12), the wedding reflects the king's standing as a figure of international significance (see note on v. 9). Accordingly he is addressed as one whose reign is to be characterized by victories over the nations (vv. 3–5; cf. Ps 2; 110). As a royal son of David, he is a type (foreshadowing) of Christ. After the exile this psalm was applied to the Messiah, the promised Son of David who would sit on David's throne (for the application of vv. 6–7 to Christ see Heb 1:8–9). The superscription implies that it was composed and sung by a member of the Levitical temple choir, a fact not surprising in view of the close link between the temple (housing the earthly throne room of Israel's heavenly King) and the

My tongue is the pen of [a]a ready
writer.
2 You are fairer than the sons of men;
[a]Grace is poured [1]upon Your lips;
Therefore God has [b]blessed You
forever.

3 Gird [a]Your sword on *Your* thigh,
O [1][b]Mighty One,
In Your splendor and Your majesty!
4 And in Your majesty ride on
victoriously,
For the cause of truth and [a]meekness
and righteousness;
Let Your [b]right hand teach You
[1]awesome things.
5 Your [a]arrows are sharp;
The [b]peoples fall under You;
Your arrows are [c]in the heart of the
King's enemies.

6 [a]Your throne, O God, is forever and
ever;
A scepter of [b]uprightness is the
scepter of Your kingdom.

45:1 [a]Ezra 7:6
2 [1]Or *through* [a]Luke 4:22 [b]Ps 21:6
3 [1]Or *warrior* [a]Heb 4:12; Rev 1:16 [b]Is 9:6
4 [1]Or *fearful* [a]Zeph 2:3 [b]Ps 21:8
5 [a]Ps 18:14; 120:4; Is 5:28; 7:13 [b]Ps 92:9 [c]2 Sam 18:14
6 [a]Ps 93:2; Heb 1:8, 9 [b]Ps 98:9
7 [a]Ps 11:7; 33:5 [b]Ps 2:2
8 [a]Song 4:14; John 19:39 [b]Ps 150:4
9 [a]Song 6:8 [b]1 Kin 2:19 [c]1 Kin 9:28; Is 13:12
10 [a]Deut 21:13; Ruth 1:16, 17
11 [a]Gen 18:12; 1 Pet 3:6 [b]Eph 5:33
12 [a]Ps 87:4 [b]Ps 22:29; 68:29; 72:10, 11; Is 49:23

7 You have [a]loved righteousness and
hated wickedness;
Therefore God, Your God, has
[b]anointed You
With the oil of joy above Your fellows.
8 All Your garments are *fragrant with*
[a]myrrh and aloes *and* cassia;
Out of ivory palaces [b]stringed
instruments have made You glad.
9 Kings' daughters are among [a]Your
noble ladies;
At Your [b]right hand stands the queen
in [c]gold from Ophir.

10 Listen, O daughter, give attention and
incline your ear:
[a]Forget your people and your father's
house;
11 Then the King will desire your beauty.
Because He is your [a]Lord, [b]bow down
to Him.
12 The daughter of [a]Tyre *will come* with
a gift;
The [b]rich among the people will seek
your favor.

Davidic dynasty (the Lord's appointed regents over His people, described throughout the books of Samuel, Kings and Chronicles). As a word from one of the temple personnel, the song was no doubt received as a word from the temple—and from the One who sat enthroned there. In its structure, the song is framed by vv. 1,17 while vv. 2,16 constitute a secondary frame within them—all addressed to the king. The body of the song falls into two parts: (1) words addressed to the king (vv. 3–9) and (2) words addressed to the royal bride (vv. 10–15). These in turn each contain two parts, reflecting a similar pattern: (1) (a) exhortations to the king (vv. 3–5), (b) the glory of the king (vv. 6–9); (2) (a) exhortations to the bride (vv. 10–11), (b) the glory of the bride (vv. 12–15).

45 title *For the choir director.* See note on Ps 4 title. *according to.* See note on Ps 9 title. *Shoshannim.* Means "Lilies" (see Ps 69 title). "Lilies" may be an abbreviated form of "The Lily (Lilies) of the Covenant" found in the titles of Ps 60; 80. *Maskil.* See note on Ps 32 title. *of the sons of Korah.* See note on Ps 42 title. *Song.* See note on Ps 30 title.

45:1 See v. 17, where the speaker pledges (perhaps by means of this song) to perpetuate the king's memory throughout the generations and awaken the praise of the nations. *heart.* See note on 4:7.

45:2 *fairer than the sons of men.* One who excels in manly traits and beauty, as a king should (see 1 Sam 9:2; 16:18)—but he is so beyond ordinary men as to be almost Godlike (see note on v. 6). *Grace is poured upon Your lips.* See Prov 22:11; Eccl 10:12; cf. Is 50:4; Luke 4:22; see also v. 16, where it is suggested that such a king will be perpetuated in his sons. *forever.* See note on v. 6.

45:3–5 Go forth with your sword victoriously in the service of all that is right, and clothe yourself thereby with glory—make your reign adorn you more truly than the wedding garb with which you are now arrayed (v. 8).

45:3 *splendor and . . . majesty.* See 21:5 and note.

45:4 *righteousness.* See note on 1:5. *awesome things.* See 66:5; 106:22; 145:6.

45:5 *peoples fall under You.* See 2:8–9; 110:1–2,5–6.

45:6–9 The glory of the king's reign: justice and righteousness (see Ps 72).

45:6 *O God.* Possibly the king's throne is called God's throne because he is God's appointed regent. But it is also possible that the king himself is addressed as "god." The Davidic king (the "LORD's anointed," 2 Sam 19:21), because of his special relationship with God, was called at his enthronement the "son" of God (see 2:7; 2 Sam 7:14; 1 Chr 28:6; cf. 89:27). In this psalm, which praises the king and especially extols his "splendor and . . . majesty" (v. 3), it is not unthinkable that he was called "god" as a title of honor (cf. Is 9:6). Such a description of the Davidic king attains its fullest meaning when applied to Christ, as the author of Hebrews does (Heb 1:8–9). (The pharaohs of Egypt were sometimes addressed as "my god" by their vassal kings in Canaan, as evidenced by the Amarna letters; see chart, p. xix.) *forever and ever.* See vv. 2,17. Such was the language used with respect to kings (see note on 21:4). It here gains added significance in the light of God's covenant with David (see 89:4,29,36; 132:12; 2 Sam 7:16). In Christ, the Son of David, it is fulfilled.

45:7 *fellows.* The noble guests of the king, perhaps from other lands. *oil of joy.* God has anointed him with a more delightful oil than the aromatic oils with which his head and body were anointed on his wedding day—namely, with joy (see 23:5; Is 61:3).

45:8–9 The glory of the king's wedding.

45:8 *myrrh.* See notes on Gen 37:25; Song 1:13. *aloes.* See note on Song 4:14. *cassia.* See note on Ex 25:6. *ivory palaces.* See 1 Kin 22:39; Amos 3:15; 6:4.

45:9 *Kings' daughters.* Whether members of his royal harem (see 1 Kin 11:1–3) or guests at his wedding, they represent international recognition of the king. *in gold from Ophir.* Adorned with jewels of finest gold (see notes on Gen 10:29; 1 Kin 9:28) and all the finery associated with it.

45:10–15 The word to the royal bride.

45:10–11 Be totally loyal to your adoring king.

45:12–15 The royal bride's glory.

45:12 *daughter of Tyre.* A personification of the city of Tyre and its inhabitants (see note on 2 Kin 19:21). The king of Tyre was the first foreign ruler to recognize the Davidic dynasty (see 2 Sam 5:11), and Solomon maintained close relations with that city-state (see 1 Kin 5; 9:10–14,26–28). As a great trading center on the Mediterranean coast, Tyre was world-renowned for its wealth (see Is 23; Ezek 26:1–28:19). *the rich.* Such as those

13 The King's daughter is all glorious within;
Her clothing is [a]interwoven with gold.
14 She will be [a]led to the King [b]in embroidered work;
The [c]virgins, her companions who follow her,
Will be brought to You.
15 They will be led forth with gladness and rejoicing;
They will enter into the King's palace.

16 In place of your fathers will be your sons;
You shall make them princes in all the earth.
17 I will cause [a]Your name to be remembered in all generations;
Therefore the peoples [b]will give You thanks forever and ever.

Psalm 46

For the choir director. *A Psalm* of the sons of Korah, †set to Alamoth. A Song.

1 God is our [a]refuge and strength,
[1]A very [b]present help [c]in [2]trouble.
2 Therefore we will [a]not fear, though [b]the earth should change
And though [c]the mountains slip into the heart of the [1]sea;
3 Though its [a]waters roar *and* foam,
Though the mountains quake at its swelling pride. [1]Selah.

4 There is a [a]river whose streams make glad the [b]city of God,
The holy [c]dwelling places of the Most High.
5 God is [a]in the midst of her, she will not be moved;
God will [b]help her [1]when morning dawns.
6 The [1]nations [a]made an uproar, the kingdoms tottered;
He [2b]raised His voice, the earth [c]melted.
7 The LORD of hosts [a]is with us;
The God of Jacob is [b]our stronghold. Selah.

8 Come, [a]behold the works of the LORD,
[1]Who has wrought [b]desolations in the earth.
9 He [a]makes wars to cease to the end of the earth;

13 [a]Ex 39:2, 3 **14** [a]Song 1:4 [b]Judg 5:30; Ezek 16:10 [c]Ps 45:9 **17** [a]Mal 1:11 [b]Ps 138:4 **46:1** †Possibly *for soprano voices* [1]Or *Abundantly available for help* [2]Or *tight places* [a]Ps 14:6; 62:7, 8 [b]Deut 4:7; Ps 145:18 [c]Ps 9:9 **2** [a]Ps 23:4; 27:1 [b]Ps 82:5

2 [1]Lit *seas* [c]Ps 18:7 **3** [1]*Selah* may mean: *Pause, Crescendo* or *Musical interlude* [a]Ps 93:3, 4; Jer 5:22 **4** [a]Ps 36:8; 65:9; Is 8:6; Rev 22:1 [b]Ps 48:1; 87:3; 101:8; Is 60:14; Rev 3:12 [c]Ps 43:3 **5** [1]Lit *at the turning of the morning* [a]Deut 23:14; Is 12:6; Ezek 43:7, 9; Hos 11:9; Joel 2:27; Zech 2:5 [b]Ps 37:40; Is 41:14; Luke 1:54 **6** [1]Or *Gentiles* [2]Lit *gave forth* [a]Ps 2:1, 2 [b]Ps 18:13; 68:33; Jer 25:30; Joel 2:11; Amos 1:2 [c]Amos 9:5; Mic 1:4; Nah 1:5 **7** [a]Num 14:9; 2 Chr 13:12 [b]Ps 9:9; 48:3 **8** [1]Or *Which He has wrought as desolations* [a]Ps 66:5 [b]Is 61:4; Jer 51:43 **9** [a]Is 2:4; Mic 4:3

from your homeland. *seek your favor.* Desire to be in your good graces as the wife of this king.
45:14 *virgins, her companions.* She too has "fellows" (see v. 7), perhaps her permanent attendants. *to You.* To the king.
45:16 *your.* The king's. *In place of your fathers.* As the family line continues (dynastic succession). Perhaps it is also hinted that they will surpass the fathers in honor (see note on v. 2).
45:17 See note on v. 1. *forever and ever.* See note on v. 6.
Ps 46 A celebration of the security of Jerusalem as the city of God (the inspiration of Martin Luther's great hymn, "A Mighty Fortress Is Our God"). Thematically this psalm is closely related to Ps 48 (see also Ps 76; 87), while Ps 47 celebrates God's victorious reign over all the earth. It probably predates the exile. However, as a song concerning the "city of God" (v. 4), the royal city of His kingdom on earth (see Ps 48), it remained for Israel a song of hope celebrating the certain triumph of God's kingdom. It was originally liturgical and sung at the temple: The citizens of Jerusalem (or the Levitical choir in their stead) apparently sang the opening stanza (vv. 1–3) and the responses (vv. 7,11), while the Levitical leader of the liturgy probably sang the second and third stanzas (vv. 4–6,8–10). In its structure, apart from the refrains (vv. 7,11), the psalm is composed of three symmetrical stanzas, each containing three verses. For other psalms with recurring refrains see introduction to Ps 42–43.
46 title *For the choir director.* See note on Ps 4 title. *of the sons of Korah.* See note on Ps 42 title. *set to.* Or "upon." See note on Ps 6 title. *Alamoth.* Probably a musical term. Since the Hebrew word appears to mean "maidens," the phrase "set to *alamoth*" may refer to the "maidens playing tambourines" who accompanied the singers as the liturgical procession made its way to the temple (68:25). *A Song.* See note on Ps 30 title.
46:1–3 A triumphant confession of fearless trust in God, though the continents break up and sink beneath the resurging waters of the seas—i.e., though the creation itself may seem to become uncreated (see 104:6–9; Gen 1:9–10) and all may appear to be going down before the onslaught of the primeval deep. The described upheaval is probably imagery for great threats to Israel's existence (see note on 32:6), especially from her enemies (see vv. 6,8–10; 65:5–8).
46:4–6 A description of blessed Zion—a comforting declaration of God's mighty, sustaining presence in His city.
46:4 *river.* Jerusalem had no river, unlike Thebes (Nah 3:8), Damascus (2 Kin 5:12), Nineveh (Nah 2:6,8) or Babylon (137:1), yet she had a "river." Here the "river" of 36:8 (see note there) serves as a metaphor for the continual outpouring of the sustaining and refreshing blessings of God, which make the city of God like the Garden of Eden (see Gen 2:10; Is 33:21; 51:3; cf. also Ezek 31:4–9). *city of God.* See v. 5; see especially Ps 48. *God . . . Most High.* That is, God Most High (see 57:2; see also note on 3:7). *dwelling places.* See note on 9:11. *Most High.* See note on Gen 14:19.
46:5 *when morning dawns.* When attacks against cities were likely to be launched. His help brings on the dawn of deliverance, dispelling the night of danger (see 44:19 and note; cf. Is 37:36 for an example).
46:6 *nations . . . tottered.* Because of God's victory (see vv. 8–9; 48:4–7). *an uproar.* See v. 3 and note on vv. 1–3; see also 2:1–3; Rev 11:18. *raised His voice.* See 2:5; 9:5; Jer 25:30; Amos 1:2; see also 104:7. God's thunder is evoked (see introduction to Ps 29), the thunder of His wrath (see 18:13; Is 2:10). *earth melted.* As though struck by lightning (see 97:4–5).
46:7 The people's glad response (also v. 11). *LORD of hosts.* See note on 1 Sam 1:3. *Jacob.* See note on 14:7.
46:8–10 A declaration of the blessed effects of God's triumph over the nations.
46:8 *Come, behold.* An invitation to see God's victories in the world (see 48:8 and note). *the LORD.* Emphatic because of its rare use in Book 2 of the Psalter. *in the earth.* Among the hostile nations.
46:9 No more attacks against His city. The verse probably speaks of universal peace (see note on 65:6–7). *breaks . . . cuts*

He [b]breaks the bow and cuts the spear
in two;
He [c]burns the chariots with fire.
10 "[1]Cease *striving* and [a]know that I am
God;
I will be [b]exalted among the [2]nations,
I will be exalted in the earth."
11 The LORD of hosts is with us;
The God of Jacob is our stronghold.
Selah.

Psalm 47

For the choir director. A Psalm of the sons of Korah.

1 O [a]clap your hands, all peoples;
[b]Shout to God with the voice of [1]joy.
2 For the LORD Most High is to be
[a]feared,
A [b]great King over all the earth.
3 He [a]subdues peoples under us
And nations under our feet.
4 He chooses our [a]inheritance for us,
The [b]glory of Jacob whom He loves.
[1]Selah.

9 [b]1 Sam 2:4; Ps 76:3 [c]Is 9:5; Ezek 39:9 **10** [1]Or *Let go, relax* [2]Or *Gentiles* [a]Ps 100:3 [b]Is 2:11, 17 **47:1** [1]Or *a ringing cry* [a]Ps 98:8 [b]Ps 106:47 **2** [a]Deut 7:21; Neh 1:5; Ps 66:3, 5; 68:35 [b]Mal 1:14 **3** [a]Ps 18:47 **4** [1]*Selah* may mean: *Pause, Crescendo* or *Musical interlude* [a]1 Pet 1:4 [b]Amos 6:8; 8:7; Nah 2:2 **5** [1]Or *amid* [a]Ps 68:18 [b]Ps 98:6 **6** [a]Ps 68:4 [b]Ps 89:18 **7** [1]Heb *Maskil* [a]Zech 14:9 [b]1 Cor 14:15 **8** [1]Or *has taken His seat* [a]1 Chr 16:31; Ps 22:28 [b]Ps 97:2 **9** [1]Or *nobles* [2]Lit *has greatly* *exalted Himself* [a]Ps 72:11; 102:22; Is 49:7, 23 [b]Rom 4:11, 12 [c]Ps 89:18 [d]Ps 97:9 **48:1** [a]1 Chr 16:25; Ps 96:4; 145:3

5 God has [a]ascended [1]with a shout,
The LORD, [1]with the [b]sound of a
trumpet.
6 [a]Sing praises to God, sing praises;
Sing praises to [b]our King, sing
praises.
7 For God is the [a]King of all the earth;
Sing praises [b]with a [1]skillful psalm.
8 God [a]reigns over the nations,
God [1]sits on [b]His holy throne.
9 The [1a]princes of the people have
assembled themselves *as* the
[b]people of the God of Abraham,
For the [c]shields of the earth belong to
God;
He [2]is [d]highly exalted.

Psalm 48

A Song; a Psalm of the sons of Korah.

1 [a]Great is the LORD, and greatly to be
praised,

. . . *burns.* See 76:3; see also 1 Sam 2:4. For the Messiah's universal victory over Israel's enemies see Is 9:2–7.
46:10 God's voice breaks through, as He addresses the nations (see v. 6)—the climax. *Cease striving.* Here, the Hebrew for this phrase probably means "Enough!" as in 1 Sam 15:16 ("Wait"). *know.* Acknowledge. *I will be exalted . . . in the earth.* God's mighty acts in behalf of His people will bring Him universal recognition, a major theme in the Psalter (see 22:27; 47:9; 57:5,11; 64:9; 65:8; 66:1–7; 67:2–5; 86:9; 98:2–3; 99:2–3; 102:15) and elsewhere in the OT (see Ex 7:5; 14:4,18; Lev 26:45; Num 14:15; 1 Sam 17:46; 1 Kin 8:41–43; 2 Kin 19:19; Ezek 20:41; 28:25; 36:23; Hab 2:14). This has proven to be supremely true of God's climactic saving act in the birth, life, death, resurrection and glorification of Jesus Christ—yet to be brought to complete fruition at His return.
46:11 See note on v. 7.
Ps 47 Celebration of the universal reign of Israel's God: a testimony to the nations. This psalm belongs to a group of hymns to the Great King found elsewhere clustered in Ps 92–100. Here it serves to link Ps 46 and 48, identifying the God who reigns in Zion as "a great King over all the earth" (v. 2; see v. 7; 48:2). It dates from the period of the monarchy and was composed for use in the temple liturgy on one of the high festival days. The specific setting is perhaps the Feast of Booths (see Lev 23:34), which was also the festival for which Solomon waited to dedicate the temple (see 1 Kin 8:2). A liturgical procession is presupposed (v. 5), similar to that indicated in Ps 24; 68. Later Jewish usage employed this psalm in the synagogue liturgy for *Rosh Hashanah* (the New Year festival). The Christian church has appropriately employed it in the celebration of Christ's ascension (see v. 5). Structurally, vv. 5–6 form a centered (see note on 6:6) couplet between two four-line stanzas (in Hebrew). This center may represent a different voice in the liturgy.
47 title See note on Ps 42 title.
47:1–4 The nations are called to rejoice in the God of Israel, the Lord over all the earth—OT anticipation of the evangelization of the nations (see notes on v. 9; 9:1).
47:1 *clap your hands.* As at the enthronement of a king (see 2 Kin 11:12; see also 98:8) or at other times of rejoicing (see Is 55:12). *voice of joy.* See 1 Kin 1:40; 2 Kin 11:14.
47:2–3 The Lord of all the earth has shaped the destiny of His people Israel (see 105:6; 135:4; Ex 9:29; 15:1–18; 19:5–6; Deut 7:6; 14:2; Is 41:8).
47:2 *to be feared* See 68:35; 89:7; 99:3; 111:9; see also note on 45:4. *Most High.* See note on Gen 14:19. *great King.* A title often used by the imperial rulers of Assyria (see note on 2 Kin 18:19).
47:3 See 2 Sam 5:17–25; 8:1–14; 10.
47:4 *inheritance.* The promised land (see Gen 12:7; 17:8; Ex 3:8; Deut 1:8; Jer 3:18). *glory.* That in which Jacob took supreme delight. *Jacob.* See note on 14:7.
47:5–6 The center of the poem (see note on 6:6). These verses portray the liturgical ascension of God to the temple—perhaps represented by the processional bearing of the ark into the temple. The ark is symbolic of God's throne; the temple is the earthly symbol of His heavenly palace (see Ps 24; 68).
47:5 *a shout . . . sound of a trumpet.* See note on v. 1. *trumpet.* The ram's horn, here announcing the presence of God as King (see 98:6; Ex 19:16,19; Josh 6:4).
47:7–9 The liturgical enthronement of God as world ruler.
47:7 *God is the King of all the earth.* See 2 Sam 15:10; 2 Kin 9:13; Is 52:7. *skillful psalm.* A *Maskil* (see note on Ps 32 title).
47:8 *sits on His holy throne.* In the most holy place of the temple, where He takes the reins of world rule into His hands (see Jer 17:12). This verse is frequently echoed in Revelation (see Rev 4:9,10; 5:1,7,13; 6:16; 7:10,15; 19:4).
47:9 The nations acknowledge the God of Israel to be the Great King—anticipated as the final effect of God's rule (see note on 46:10). *as the people of the God of Abraham.* Thus the promises to Abraham will be fulfilled (see Gen 12:2–3; 17:4–6; 22:17–18). *shields.* See note on 3:3; cf. Is 2:2; 56:7.
Ps 48 A celebration of the security of Zion (as viewed with the eyes of faith) in that it is the city of the Great King (see introductions to Ps 46–47). It may have been sung by the Levitical choir on behalf of the assembled worshipers at the temple. Structure and theme are beautifully matched. The first and last verses combine to frame the whole with a comforting confession concerning Zion's God. The center, v. 8 (see note on 6:6), summarizes the main theme of the body of the psalm. The Hebrew follows a symmetrical pattern: three lines, four lines, four lines, three lines, and develops the theme: (1) the beauty of Zion as God's

In the [b]city of our God, His [c]holy
mountain.
2 [a]Beautiful in elevation, [b]the joy of the
whole earth,
Is Mount Zion *in* the far north,
The [c]city of the great King.
3 God, in her palaces,
Has made Himself known as a
[a]stronghold.

4 For, lo, the [a]kings assembled
themselves,
They passed by together.
5 They saw *it,* then they were amazed;
They were [a]terrified, they [1]fled in
alarm.
6 [1]Panic seized them there,
Anguish, as of [a]a woman in childbirth.
7 With the [a]east wind
You [b]break the [c]ships of Tarshish.
8 As we have heard, so have we seen
In the city of the LORD of hosts, in the
city of our God;
God will [a]establish her forever. [1]Selah.

9 We have thought on [a]Your
lovingkindness, O God,
In the midst of Your temple.
10 As is Your [a]name, O God,
So is Your [b]praise to the ends of the
earth;
Your [c]right hand is full of
righteousness.
11 Let Mount [a]Zion be glad,
Let the [a]daughters of Judah rejoice
Because of Your judgments.
12 Walk about Zion and go around her;
Count her [a]towers;
13 Consider her [a]ramparts;
Go through her palaces,
That you may [b]tell *it* to the next
generation.
14 For [1]such is God,
Our God forever and ever;
He will [a]guide us [2]until death.

Psalm 49

For the choir director. A Psalm of
the sons of Korah.

1 [a]Hear this, all peoples;
Give ear, all [b]inhabitants of the world,

48:1 [b]Ps 46:4 [c]Ps 2:6; 87:1; Is 2:3; Mic 4:1; Zech 8:3
2 [a]Ps 50:2 [b]Lam 2:15 [c]Matt 5:35
3 [a]Ps 46:7
4 [a]2 Sam 10:6-19
5 [1]Lit *were hurried away* [a]Ex 15:15
6 [1]Lit *Trembling* [a]Is 13:8
7 [a]Jer 18:17 [b]1 Kin 22:48 [c]1 Kin 10:22; Ezek 27:25
8 [1]*Selah* may mean: *Pause, Crescendo* or *Musical interlude* [a]Ps 87:5
9 [a]Ps 26:3; 40:10
10 [a]Deut 28:58; Josh 7:9; Mal 1:11 [b]Ps 65:1, 2; 100:1 [c]Is 41:10
11 [a]Ps 97:8
12 [a]Neh 3:1, 11, 25-27
13 [a]Ps 122:7 [b]Ps 78:5-7
14 [1]Lit *this* [2]Lit *upon;* some mss and the Gr read *forever* [a]Ps 23:4; Is 58:11
49:1 [a]Ps 78:1; Is 1:2; Mic 1:2 [b]Ps 33:8

impregnable citadel (vv. 2–3); (2) the futility of all enemy attacks (vv. 4–7); (3) Zion's joy over God's saving acts (vv. 9–11)—related to the second stanza; (4) Zion as impregnable citadel (vv. 12–13)—related to the first stanza. Regularly distributed between the four main stanzas are allusions to the four primary directions (see notes on vv. 2,7,10,13)—suggesting that the city is secure from all points of attack.

48 title *Song.* See note on Ps 30 title. *of the Sons of Korah.* See note on Ps 42 title.

48:1 *In the city of our God, His holy mountain.* See 46:4. *our God.* Occurs in this psalm only here, in the center (v. 8) and at the end (v. 14). *holy mountain.* See 43:3; see also note on 2:6.

48:2–3 Describes the lofty impregnability of Mount Zion.

48:2 *Beautiful.* Its loftiness and secure position are its beauty (see note on 27:4). *elevation.* Although not the highest ridge in its environment, in its significance as the mountain of God it is the "highest" mountain in the world (see 68:15–16 and note; Is 2:2). *joy of the whole earth.* Perhaps referring to admiration from other nations, like that expressed by the queen of Sheba (see 1 Kin 10:1–13). *great King.* See note on 47:2.

48:3 God Himself, not her walls, was Zion's defense, a fact on which the next stanza elaborates (see note on vv. 12–13). *her palaces.* See v. 13.

48:4–7 The futile attacks of hostile nations—they fled in panic when they saw that the Great King was in Zion. Such events as the destruction of the confederacy in the days of Jehoshaphat (see 2 Chr 20) or the slaughter of the Assyrians in the time of Hezekiah (see 2 Kin 19:35–36) may have been in the psalmist's mind.

48:7 *ships of Tarshish.* Great merchant ships of the Mediterranean (see 1 Kin 10:22 and note). *With the east wind You break.* See Acts 27:14; see also 1 Kin 22:48. *east.* See introduction above.

48:8 The central verse and theme (see note on 6:6). *heard . . . seen.* "Seen" is climactic, as in Job 42:5. They had heard because "Our fathers have told us The work that You did in their days" (44:1; see 78:3), but now in the liturgical experience of God at His temple they have "seen" how secure the city of God is. *LORD of hosts.* See note on 1 Sam 1:3. *our God.* See note on v. 1.

48:9–11 The worshipers meditate at the temple with joy because of God's mighty acts in Zion's behalf.

48:9 *In the midst of Your temple.* In the temple courts. *lovingkindness.* See note on 6:4. As is clear from vv. 10–11, reference here is to God's saving acts by which He has expressed His covenant love for His people (see 31:21; 40:9–10).

48:10 *name.* See note on 5:11. *So is Your praise.* Praise of God reaches from the temple to the ends of the earth (see 9:11; 22:27). *right hand.* In Hebrew idiom a subtle reference to the south. *righteousness.* Righteous acts (see 40:9–10 and note; see also note on 4:1).

48:11 *judgments.* God's righteous judgments by which He has acted in defense of Zion.

48:12–13 The people contemplate Zion's defense, viewed from the perspective of what they have "seen" (v. 8) at the temple. The strength of Zion's "towers," "ramparts" and "palaces" is the presence of God.

48:13 *next generation.* Lit. "the generation behind"; in Hebrew idiom "behind" is a subtle reference to the west.

48:14 *Our God.* See note on v. 1. *guide.* See notes on 23:1,3.

Ps 49 A word of instruction from the temple following upon Ps 46–48 (see introductions to those psalms). It concerns rich fools who proudly rely on their great wealth and on themselves to assure their security in the world (see Ps 52). The Levitical author knows what it is to be without wealth (see Num 18:21–24; Deut 14:27–29) and has observed the attitudes of many of the rich (see vv. 5–6). He has seen through their folly, however, and offers his wisdom for all to hear (vv. 1–2), so that those who are awed by the rich may be freed from their spell. Inescapable death is their undoing and their destiny, and in the end the "upright will rule over them" (v. 14). The date of this psalm may well be postexilic. See introduction to Ps 37.

49 title See note on Ps 42 title.

49:1–4 Introduction.

49:1–2 More like the address of the prophets (see 1 Kin 22:28; Is 34:1; Mic 1:2) than that of the wisdom teachers (see 34:11; Prov 1:8,10; 2:1).

2 Both [a]low and high,
Rich and poor together.
3 My mouth will [a]speak wisdom,
And the meditation of my heart *will be* [b]understanding.
4 I will incline my ear to [a]a proverb;
[b]I will [1]express my [c]riddle on the harp.

5 Why should I [a]fear in days of adversity,
When the iniquity of my [1]foes surrounds me,
6 Even those who [a]trust in their wealth
And boast in the abundance of their riches?
7 No man can by any means [a]redeem *his* brother
Or give to God a [b]ransom for him—
8 For [a]the redemption of [1]his soul is costly,
And he should cease *trying* forever—
9 That he should [a]live on eternally,
That he should not [1][b]undergo decay.

10 For he sees *that even* [a]wise men die;
The [b]stupid and the senseless alike perish
And [c]leave their wealth to others.
11 Their [1][a]inner thought is *that* their houses [b]are forever
And their dwelling places to all generations;
They have [c]called their lands after their own names.
12 But [a]man in *his* [1]pomp will not endure;
He is like the [2]beasts that [3]perish.

13 This is the [a]way of those who are foolish,
And of those after them who [b]approve their words. [1]Selah.
14 As sheep they are appointed [a]for [1]Sheol;
Death shall be their shepherd;
And the [b]upright shall rule over them in the morning,
And their form shall be for [1]Sheol [c]to consume
[2]So that they have no habitation.
15 But God will [a]redeem my soul from the [1]power of [2]Sheol,
For [b]He will receive me. Selah.

16 Do not be afraid [a]when a man becomes rich,
When the [1]glory of his house is increased;
17 For when he dies he will [a]carry nothing away;
His [1]glory will not descend after him.
18 Though while he lives he [a]congratulates [1]himself—
And though *men* praise you when you do well for yourself—
19 [1]He shall [a]go to the generation of his fathers;
They will never see [b]the light.
20 [a]Man in *his* [1]pomp, yet without understanding,
Is [b]like the [2]beasts that [3]perish.

2 [a]Ps 62:9 **3** [a]Ps 37:30 [b]Ps 119:130 **4** [1]Lit *open up* [a]Ps 78:2 [b]2 Kin 3:15 [c]Num 12:8 **5** [1]Lit *supplanters* [a]Ps 23:4; 27:1 **6** [a]Job 31:24; Ps 52:7; Prov 11:28; Mark 10:24 **7** [a]Matt 25:8, 9 [b]Job 36:18, 19 **8** [1]Lit *their* [a]Matt 16:26 **9** [1]Or *see corruption* or *the pit* [a]Ps 22:29 [b]Ps 16:10; 89:48 **10** [a]Eccl 2:16 [b]Ps 92:6; 94:8 [c]Ps 39:6; Eccl 2:18, 21; Luke 12:20 **11** [1]Some versions read *graves are their houses* [a]Ps 64:6 [b]Ps 10:6 [c]Gen 4:17; Deut 3:14 **12** [1]Lit *honor* [2]Or *animals* [3]Lit *are destroyed* [a]Ps 49:20

13 [1]*Selah* may mean: *Pause, Crescendo* or *Musical interlude* [a]Jer 17:11 [b]Ps 49:18 **14** [1]I.e. the nether world [2]Lit *Away from his habitation* [a]Ps 9:17 [b]Dan 7:18; Mal 4:3; 1 Cor 6:2; Rev 2:26 [c]Job 24:19 **15** [1]Lit *hand* [2]I.e. the nether world [a]Ps 16:10; 56:13; Hos 13:14 [b]Gen 5:24; Ps 16:11; 73:24 **16** [1]Or *wealth* [a]Ps 37:7 **17** [1]Or *wealth* [a]Ps 17:14; 1 Tim 6:7 **18** [1]Lit *his soul* [a]Deut 29:19; Ps 10:3, 6; Luke 12:19 **19** [1]Lit *You;* or *It* [a]Gen 15:15 [b]Job 33:30; Ps 56:13 **20** [1]Lit *honor* [2]Or *animals* [3]Lit *are destroyed* [a]Ps 49:12 [b]Eccl 3:19

49:3 See Matt 12:34. *wisdom.* See essay, p. 689. *heart.* See note on 4:7.
49:4 *incline my ear.* The wisdom he is about to speak first had to be "heard" by him—all true wisdom is from God (see Job 28). *on the harp.* Another hint of the author's sense of inspiration (see 1 Sam 10:5–6; 2 Kin 3:15).
49:5–11 Those of little means or power need not be unsettled when surrounded by rich fools who threaten and strut; death is their destiny.
49:7–9 Wealth cannot buy escape from death—not even one's "redeemer" can accomplish it (cf. Ex 21:30; Lev 25:47–49). Only God Himself can redeem a life from the grave (see v. 15 and note).
49:10 Anyone whose "eyes are in his head" (Eccl 2:14) can see that even the wise die (see Eccl 7:2; 9:5) and leave their wealth to others (see Eccl 2:18,21). How much more the fool (see 73:18–20; 92:6–7)! See also 89:48; Job 30:23; Eccl 2:14–16. *wise men . . . stupid.* Essentially the "righteous" and the "wicked" of Ps 37. *wealth.* Often gotten by devious means that their foolish "wisdom" had contrived (v. 5). *to others.* But not to their children (see note on 37:29; see also 39:6; Luke 12:20–21).
49:11 Though they lavish wealth on their tombs (see NASB marg.) and try at least to perpetuate their memory by putting their names to their large landholdings (see Num 32:41) as an enduring memorial, they only suffer the bitter irony of having their graves as their "eternal home" (Eccl 12:5).
49:12 Their epitaph (see note on 10:18; see also Eccl 3:19; 7:2) and the psalm's refrain (see introduction to Ps 42–43).
49:13–15 Their fate and mine—so "why should I fear?" (v. 5).
49:13 *foolish.* Foolish by trusting in themselves and their wealth, as those who have "succeeded" (see v. 6).
49:14 *As sheep.* Death is already their shepherd, "guiding" them to the grave. *Death shall be their shepherd.* Or "Death will feed on them." For the imagery of death (or the grave) as an insatiable monster feeding on its victims see 69:15; 141:7; Prov 1:12; 27:20; 30:15–16; Is 5:14; Jon 2:2 ("depth"; lit. "belly"); Hab 2:5. The imagery is borrowed from Canaanite mythology, which so depicts the god Mot (death). As one Canaanite document reads, "Do not approach divine Mot, lest he put you like a lamb into his mouth." *rule over.* See Lev 26:17; Is 14:2; perhaps "prevail over" in contrast to the situation referred to in v. 5. *in the morning.* See vv. 15,19 and notes on 6:5; 11:7; 16:9–11; 17:15. But see also introduction to Ps 57.
49:15 See note on vv. 7–9. *redeem my soul from. . . Sheol.* While this may refer to saving (for a while) from the universal prospect of death (as in Job 5:20; see 116:8), the context strongly suggests that the author, as one of the upright, speaks of his final destiny. Perhaps the thought is of being conveyed into the presence of God in His heavenly temple, analogous to the later Jewish thought of being conveyed to "Abraham's bosom" (Luke 16:22; see notes on 6:5; 11:7; 16:9–11; 17:15). *my soul.* See note on 6:3). *He will receive me.* See 73:24 and note; see also Gen 5:24 and note.
49:16–19 So do not let the present state of the wealthy captivate you.
49:16 *his house.* His whole estate (see Ex 20:17).
49:19 *light.* See notes on 27:1; Is 53:11.
49:20 The last word. See note on v. 12.

Psalm 50

A Psalm of [†]Asaph.

1 [a]The Mighty One, God, the LORD, has spoken,
And summoned the earth [b]from the rising of the sun to its setting.
2 Out of Zion, [a]the perfection of beauty,
God [b]has shone forth.
3 May our God [a]come and not keep silence;
[b]Fire devours before Him,
And it is very [c]tempestuous around Him.
4 He [a]summons the heavens above,
And the earth, to judge His people:
5 "Gather My [a]godly ones to Me,
Those who have made a [b]covenant with Me by [c]sacrifice."
6 And the [a]heavens declare His righteousness,
For [b]God Himself is judge. [1]Selah.

7 "[a]Hear, O My people, and I will speak;
O Israel, I will testify [1]against you;
I am God, [b]your God.
8 "I do [a]not reprove you for your sacrifices,
And your burnt offerings are continually before Me.
9 "I shall take no [a]young bull out of your house
Nor male goats out of your folds.
10 "For [a]every beast of the forest is Mine,
The cattle on a thousand hills.
11 "I know every [a]bird of the mountains,
And everything that moves in the field is [1]Mine.
12 "If I were hungry I would not tell you,
For the [a]world is Mine, and [1]all it contains.
13 "Shall I eat the flesh of [1a]bulls
Or drink the blood of male goats?
14 "Offer to God [a]a sacrifice of thanksgiving

50:1 [†]1 Chr 15:17; 2 Chr 29:30 [a]Josh 22:22 [b]Ps 113:3 **2** [a]Ps 48:2; Lam 2:15 [b]Deut 33:2; Ps 80:1; 94:1 **3** [a]Ps 96:13 [b]Lev 10:2; Num 16:35; Ps 97:3; Dan 7:10 [c]Ps 18:12, 13 **4** [a]Deut 4:26; 31:28; 32:1; Is 1:2 **5** [a]Ps 30:4; 37:28; 52:9 [b]Ex 24:7; 2 Chr 6:11; Ps 25:10 [c]Ps 50:8 **6** [1]*Selah* may mean: *Pause, Crescendo* or *Musical interlude* [a]Ps 89:5; 97:6 [b]Ps 75:7; 96:13 **7** [a]Ps 49:1; 81:8

7 [1]Or *to* [b]Ex 20:2; Ps 48:14 **8** [a]Ps 40:6; 51:16; Is 1:11; Hos 6:6 **9** [a]Ps 69:31 **10** [a]Ps 104:24 **11** [1]Or *in My mind;* lit *with Me* [a]Matt 6:26 **12** [1]Lit *its fullness* [a]Ex 19:5; Deut 10:14; Ps 24:1; 1 Cor 10:26 **13** [1]Lit *strong ones* [a]Ps 50:9 **14** [a]Ps 27:6; 69:30; 107:22; 116:17; Hos 14:2; Rom 12:1; Heb 13:15

Ps 50 The Lord calls His covenant people to account as they meet before Him in worship at the temple. (Thus the psalm has links with Ps 46–49; see introductions to those psalms.) The psalm appears to have been composed for a temple liturgy in which Israel reaffirms her commitment to God's covenant. A leader of the Levitical choir addresses Israel on behalf of the Lord (see Ps 15; 24, either of which may have been spoken earlier in the same liturgy). This liturgy was possibly related to the Feast of Booths (see Deut 31:9–13; see also introduction to Ps 47). In its rebuke of a false understanding of sacrifice the psalm has affinity with the prophecies of Amos, Micah and Isaiah and so may date from the late eighth and/or early seventh centuries B.C. Others find a closer relationship with the reformation of Josiah (2 Kin 22:1–23:25) and the ministry of Jeremiah. Structurally, the psalm has three parts: (1) the announcement of the "coming" of Israel's covenant Lord to call His people to account (vv. 1–6); (2) the Lord's words of correction for those of honest intent (vv. 7–15); (3) His sharp rebuke of "the wicked" among them (vv. 16–23).

50 title A traditional ascription of the psalm to Asaph; or it may mean "for Asaph" (see "for Jeduthun" in Ps 39 title) or for the descendants of Asaph who functioned in his place. This psalm may have been separated from the other psalms of Asaph (73–83) because of its thematic links with Ps 46–49. Asaph was one of David's three choir leaders (see note on Ps 39 title).

50:1–6 The Lord comes (v. 3) in the temple worship to correct and rebuke His people: Israel must know that the God of Zion is the God of Sinai (see Ex 19:16–20).

50:1 *The Mighty One, God, the LORD.* A sequence found elsewhere only in Josh 22:22 (see note there). Ps 50 is noteworthy for its use of numerous names and titles for God (seven in all: three in v. 1, four in the rest of the psalm; see notes on vv. 6,14,21–22). *the earth.* See "the heavens . . . the earth" (v. 4) and "the heavens" (v. 6). When Moses renewed the covenant between the Lord and Israel on the plains of Moab, he called upon heaven and earth to serve as third-party witnesses to the covenant (Deut 30:19; 31:28). The Lord now summons these to testify that His present word to His people is in complete accord with that covenant (see Is 1:2).

50:2 *perfection of beauty.* Because God resides there (cf. Ezek 27:3–4,11; 28:12). *shone forth.* Manifested His glory as He has come to act (see 80:1; 94:1; Deut 33:2; cf. Ezek 28:7,17), now confronting His people, but not yet announcing judgment as in Is 1 or Mic 1.

50:3 *May our God come.* Or "Our God comes" from His enthronement between the cherubim (see 80:1; 99:1; see also 1 Sam 4:4; 2 Sam 6:2; 2 Kin 19:15) in the most holy place of the temple (see note on 28:2; see also Is 26:21; Mic 1:3). *not keep silence.* No longer (see v. 21) will He let their sins go unrebuked. *Fire . . . tempestuous.* See Ex 19:16,18.

50:4 *judge.* Call them to account in accordance with His covenant.

50:5 *godly ones.* See note on 4:3. *by sacrifice.* Sacrifices were a part of the ritual that sealed the covenant (see Ex 24:4–8) and continued to be an integral part of Israel's expression of covenant commitment to the Lord.

50:6 *declare.* See note on v. 1. *righteousness.* See note on 5:8. *judge.* Lord over His people (the Hebrew for "judge" and that for "king" are sometimes used synonymously; see, e.g., Is 33:22). "Judge" occurs as a title for God (see note on v. 1) in, e.g., 94:2; Gen 18:25; Judg 11:27.

50:7–15 The Lord corrects His people.

50:7 *My people.* "Our God" (v. 3) and "your God" (here) reflect the covenant bond. *I am God, your God.* See Ex 19:3–6; Lev 19:2–4,10,25,31,34,36; 20:7,24; 22:33; 23:22.

50:8–13 Israel had not failed to bring enough sacrifices (v. 8), but she was ever tempted to think that sacrifices were of first importance to God, as though He was dependent on them. This notion was widespread among Israel's pagan neighbors. See note on 40:6.

50:10 *thousand.* Used here figuratively for a very large number.

50:12 *the world . . . contains.* See 24:1 and note.

50:14–15 God wants Israel to acknowledge her dependence on Him, by giving thank offerings for His mercies (v. 14) and by praying to Him in times of need (v. 15; see 116:17–19). Those who do so may expect God's gracious answer to their prayers (stated more directly in v. 23). God also desires obedience to His moral law (see vv. 16–21 and note on 40:6).

50:14 *sacrifice of thanksgiving.* See Lev 7:12–13. *God . . . Most High.* That is, God Most High (see 57:2 and note on 3:7). *your vows.* Vows that accompanied prayer in times of need, usually involving thank offerings (see 66:13–15), always involving praise of the Lord for His answer to prayer (see note on 7:17). See also

And [b]pay your vows to the Most High;
15 [a]Call upon Me in the day of trouble;
I shall [b]rescue you, and you will
[c]honor Me."

16 But to the wicked God says,
"What right have you to tell of My
statutes
And to take [a]My covenant in your
mouth?
17 "For you [a]hate discipline,
And you [b]cast My words behind you.
18 "When you see a thief, you [1a]are
pleased with him,
And [2]you [b]associate with adulterers.
19 "You [1a]let your mouth loose in evil
And your [b]tongue frames deceit.
20 "You sit and [a]speak against your
brother;
You slander your own mother's son.
21 "These things you have done and [a]I
kept silence;
You thought that I was just like you;
I will [b]reprove you and state *the case*
in order before your eyes.

22 "Now consider this, you who [a]forget
God,
Or I will [b]tear *you* in pieces, and there
will be none to deliver.
23 "He who [a]offers a sacrifice of
thanksgiving honors Me;
And to him who [1b]orders *his* way
aright
I shall [c]show the salvation of God."

14 [b]Num 30:2; Deut 23:21; Ps 22:25; 56:12; 61:8; 65:1; 76:11 **15** [a]Ps 91:15; 107:6, 13; Zech 13:9 [b]Ps 81:7 [c]Ps 22:23 **16** [a]Is 29:13 **17** [a]Prov 5:12; 12:1; Rom 2:21, 22 [b]1 Kin 14:9; Neh 9:26 **18** [1]Some ancient versions read *run together* [2]Lit *your part is with* [a]Rom 1:32 [b]1 Tim 5:22 **19** [1]Lit *send* [a]Ps 10:7 [b]Ps 36:3; 52:2 **20** [a]Job 19:18; Matt 10:21 **21** [a]Eccl 8:11; Is 42:14; 57:11 [b]Ps 90:8 **22** [a]Job 8:13; Ps 9:17 [b]Ps 7:2 **23** [1]Lit *sets* [a]Ps 50:14 [b]Ps 85:13 [c]Ps 91:16

51:1 [†]2 Sam 12:1 [a]Ps 4:1; 109:26 [b]Ps 69:16; 106:45 [c]Ps 51:9; Is 43:25; 44:22; Acts 3:19; Col 2:14 **2** [a]Ps 51:7; Is 1:16; 4:4; Jer 4:14; Acts 22:16; Rev 1:5 [b]Jer 33:8; Ezek 36:33; Heb 9:14; 1 John 1:7, 9 **3** [1]Or *I myself know* [a]Is 59:12 **4** [1]Or *may be in the right* [2]Many mss read *in Your words* [3]Lit *pure* [a]Gen 20:6; 39:9; 2 Sam 12:13; Ps 41:4 [b]Luke 15:21 [c]Rom 3:4 **5** [a]Job 14:4; 15:14; Ps 58:3; Eph 2:3 **6** [1]Or *inward parts* [a]Job 38:36; Ps 15:2 [b]Prov 2:6; Eccl 2:26; James 1:5 **7** [1]Or *May You purify... that I may be clean* [a]Ex 12:22; Lev 14:4; Num 19:18; Heb 9:19

Psalm 51

For the choir director. A Psalm of David, when [†]Nathan the prophet came to him, after he had gone in to Bathsheba.

1 [a]Be gracious to me, O God, according
to Your lovingkindness;
According to the greatness of [b]Your
compassion [c]blot out my
transgressions.
2 [a]Wash me thoroughly from my
iniquity
And [b]cleanse me from my sin.
3 For [1]I [a]know my transgressions,
And my sin is ever before me.
4 [a]Against You, You only, I have
sinned
And done what is [b]evil in Your sight,
So that [c]You [1]are justified [2]when You
speak
And [3]blameless when You judge.
5 Behold, I was [a]brought forth in
iniquity,
And in sin my mother conceived me.
6 Behold, You desire [a]truth in the
[1]innermost being,
And in the hidden part You will [b]make
me know wisdom.
7 [1]Purify me [a]with hyssop, and I shall
be clean;

Heb 13:15. *Most High.* See note on v. 1; see also note on Gen 14:19.

50:15 *honor Me.* With praise in the fulfillment of the vows (see v. 23)—and, implicitly, with obedience to His covenant law (see following verses).

50:16–23 The Lord's rebuke of the wicked.

50:16 *tell of My statutes.* Apparently a part of the liturgy of covenant commitment.

50:17 *you hate discipline.* They formally participate in the holy ritual but reject God's law as the rule for life outside the ritual.

50:19 *let your mouth loose in evil.* See note on 5:9.

50:21 God's merciful and patient "silence" is distorted by the wicked into bad and self-serving theology (see Eccl 8:11; Is 42:14; 57:11). *thought that I was.* Or "thought the 'I AM' was"; see Ex 3:14 and note (see also note on v. 1). *state the case . . . before your eyes.* Set forth the particulars of My indictment before your eyes.

50:22 *God.* A relatively rare word for "God" (Hebrew *Eloah*), though common in Job. See note on v. 1.

50:23 See note on vv. 14–15.

Ps 51 David's humble prayer for forgiveness and cleansing. As the prayer of a contrite sinner, it represents a proper response to the Lord's confrontation of His people in Ps 50 (compare v. 16 with 50:8–15). This psalm has many points of contact with Ps 25. In traditional Christian usage it is one of seven penitential psalms (see introduction to Ps 6). The psalm is constructed symmetrically: An introduction (vv. 1–2) balances a two-verse conclusion, and the stanzas in Hebrew consist of five lines, three lines, three lines and five lines respectively. The whole is framed by David's prayer for himself (vv. 1–2) and for Zion (vv. 18–19). The well-being of the king and the city stand and fall together (see 28:8 and note on 3:8).

51 title *For the choir director.* See note on Ps 4 title. *when.* For the event referred to see 2 Sam 11:1–12:25; see also note on Ps 3 title.

51:1–2 In mercy grant pardon (see Luke 18:13). Note the piling up of synonyms: gracious, lovingkindness, compassion; blot out, wash, cleanse; transgressions, iniquity, sin (for this last triad see note on 32:5).

51:1 *lovingkindness.* See note on 6:4. *blot out.* See v. 9. The image is that of a papyrus scroll (see note on 9:5) on which God had recorded David's deeds. The "blotting out" of sins pictures forgiveness (Jer 18:23; see Is 43:25). For the imagery of God's keeping records of the events in His realm in the way that earthly kings do, see 56:8; 87:6; 130:3; 139:16; Neh 13:14; Dan 7:10; see also Ex 32:32–33.

51:2 See v. 7. *Wash.* As a filthy garment. *cleanse me.* Make me clean in Your sight (see Lev 11:32).

51:3–6 Confession of sin (cf. Prov 28:13; 1John 1:9).

51:3 *before me.* On my mind.

51:4 *Against You . . . only.* David acknowledges that his sin was preeminently against God (see 2 Sam 12:13; cf. Gen 20:6; 39:9; Luke 15:18). He had violated specific covenant stipulations (Ex 20:13–14,17). *when You speak . . . when You judge.* As the Lord did through Nathan the prophet (2 Sam 12:7–12). For a NT application see Rom 3:4.

51:5 He cannot plead that this sin was a rare aberration in his life; it sprang from what he is and has been (in his "innermost being," v. 6) from birth (see 58:3; Gen 8:21; cf. John 9:34; Eph 2:3). The apparently similar statements in Job 14:4; 15:14;

[2]Wash me, and I shall be [b]whiter than snow.
8 [1]Make me to hear [a]joy and gladness,
Let the [b]bones which You have broken rejoice.
9 [a]Hide Your face from my sins
And blot out all my iniquities.

10 [a]Create [1]in me a [b]clean heart, O God,
And renew [2]a [c]steadfast spirit within me.
11 [a]Do not cast me away from Your presence
And do not take Your [b]Holy Spirit from me.
12 Restore to me the [a]joy of Your salvation
And sustain me with a [b]willing spirit.
13 *Then* I will [a]teach transgressors Your ways,
And sinners will [1]be [b]converted to You.

14 Deliver me from [a]bloodguiltiness, O God, [b]the God of my salvation;
Then my [c]tongue will joyfully sing of Your righteousness.
15 O Lord, [1a]open my lips,
That my mouth may [b]declare Your praise.
16 For You [a]do not delight in sacrifice, otherwise I would give it;
You are not pleased with burnt offering.
17 The sacrifices of God are a [a]broken spirit;
A broken and a contrite heart, O God, You will not despise.

18 [a]By Your favor do good to Zion;
[1b]Build the walls of Jerusalem.
19 Then You will delight in [1a]righteous sacrifices,
In [b]burnt offering and whole burnt offering;
Then [2]young bulls will be offered on Your altar.

7 [2]Or *May You wash* [b]Is 1:18
8 [1]Or *May You make* [a]Is 35:10; Joel 1:16 [b]Ps 35:10
9 [a]Jer 16:17
10 [1]Lit *for* [2]Or *an upright* [a]Ezek 18:31; Eph 2:10 [b]Ps 24:4; Matt 5:8; Acts 15:9 [c]Ps 78:37
11 [a]2 Kin 13:23; 24:20; Jer 7:15 [b]Is 63:10, 11
12 [a]Ps 13:5 [b]Ps 110:3
13 [1]Or *turn back* [a]Acts 9:21, 22 [b]Ps 22:27
14 [a]2 Sam 12:9; Ps 26:9 [b]Ps 25:5 [c]Ps 35:28; 71:15
15 [1]Or *may You open* [a]Ex 4:15 [b]Ps 9:14
16 [a]1 Sam 15:22; Ps 40:6
17 [a]Ps 34:18
18 [1]Or *May You build* [a]Ps 69:35; Is 51:3 [b]Ps 102:16; 147:2
19 [1]Or *sacrifices of righteousness* [2]Lit *they will offer young bulls* [a]Ps 4:5 [b]Ps 66:13, 15

Psalm 52

For the choir director. A [†]Maskil of David, [•]when Doeg the Edomite came and told Saul and said to him, "David has come to the house of Ahimelech."

1 Why do you [a]boast in evil, O mighty man?
The [b]lovingkindness of God *endures* all day long.

52:1 [†]Possibly *Contemplative*, or *Didactic*, or *Skillful Psalm* [•]1 Sam 22:9 [a]Ps 94:4 [b]Ps 52:8

25:4–6 rise from a different motivation.
51:6 The great contrast: He has acted absolutely contrary to what God desires and to what God has been teaching him "in the hidden part." But it is just this "desire" of God and this "teaching" of God that are his hope—what he pleads for in vv. 7,10. *truth.* Moral integrity. *innermost being.* See 139:13–16; Job 38:36. *hidden part.* The most secret place within. *wisdom.* Whoever gives himself over to sin is a fool; he who has God's law in his heart is wise (see 37:30–31).
51:7–9 Renewed prayer for pardon.
51:7 *Purify me.* Lit. "Un-sin me." *hyssop.* Used in ritual cleansing; see note on Ex 12:22. *be clean.* The Hebrew root for this phrase is the same as that for "cleanse" in v. 2. *whiter than snow.* Like a filthy garment, he needs washing (see note on v. 2); but if God washes him, he will be so pure that there is no figurative word that can describe him (see Is 1:18; Dan 7:9; Rev 7:14; 19:14).
51:8 *Make me to hear joy.* Let me be surrounded by joy (see 32:7 and note; see also 35:27), or let me hear a prophetic oracle of forgiveness that will result in joy—from the assurance of sins forgiven (see 2 Sam 12:13). *bones.* See note on 6:2.
51:9 *Hide Your face.* From what is "ever before me" (v. 3). *blot out.* See note on v. 1.
51:10–12 Prayer for purity—for a pure heart, a steadfast spirit of faithfulness and a willing spirit of service. These can be his only if God does not reject him and take His Holy Spirit from him. If granted, the joy of God's salvation will return to gladden his troubled soul.
51:10 *Create.* As something new, which cannot emerge from what now is (see v. 5), and which only God can fashion (see Gen 1:1; Is 65:17; Jer 31:22). *heart.* See note on 4:7.
51:11 The two requests are essentially one (see 139:7; Ezek 39:29). David's prayer recalls the rejection of Saul (see 1 Sam 16:1,14; 2 Sam 7:15) and pleads for God not to take away His Spirit, by which He had equipped and qualified him for his royal office (see 1 Sam 16:13; cf. 2 Sam 23:1–2). *Holy Spirit.* The phrase is found elsewhere in the OT only in Is 63:10–11. By His Spirit, God effected His purposes in creation (see 104:30; Gen 1:2; Job 33:4) and redemption (see Is 32:15; 44:3; 63:11,14; Hag 2:5), equipped His servants for their appointed tasks (see Ex 31:3; Num 11:29; Judg 3:10; 1 Sam 10:6; 16:13; Is 11:2; 42:1), inspired His prophets (see Num 24:2–3; 2 Sam 23:2; Neh 9:30; Is 59:21; 61:1; Ezek 11:5; Mic 3:8; Zech 7:12) and directed their ministries (see 1 Kin 18:12; 2 Kin 2:16; Is 48:16; Ezek 2:2; 3:14). And it is by His Spirit that God gives His people a "new heart and . . . a new spirit" to live by His will (see Ezek 36:26–27; see also Jer 24:7; 32:39; Ezek 11:19; 18:31).
51:13–17 The vow to praise (see note on 7:17).
51:13 His praise for God's forgiveness and purification will be accompanied by instruction for sinners (see Ps 34 and note on 32:8–10). *Your ways.* See 25:4 and note.
51:14 If God will only forgive, praise will follow. *righteousness.* See note on 4:1.
51:15 *open my lips.* By granting the forgiveness and cleansing I seek.
51:16 See note on 40:6.
51:17 *broken spirit; A broken and contrite heart.* What pleases God more than sacrifices is a humble heart that looks to Him when troubles crush and penitently pleads for mercy when sin has been committed (see 50:7–15 and notes; see also 34:17–18).
51:18–19 Prayer for Zion (see note on 3:8).
51:19 *righteous sacrifices.* Such as are pleasing to God; here, sacrifices accompanied by praise for God's mercies (see 50:14–15 and notes).
Ps 52 Fearless confidence in God when under attack by an arrogant and evil enemy. David stands in the presence of God and from the high tower of that refuge hurls his denunciation (much like the prophetic denunciation in Is 22:15–19) into the face of his attacker. Though not a wisdom psalm, it has much in common with Ps 49. The extended depiction of David's enemy forms a sharp contrast with the spirit of Ps 51. See also David's denunciation of Goliath (1 Sam 17:45–47).
52 title *For the choir director.* See note on Ps 4 title. *Maskil.*

2 Your tongue devises [a]destruction,
Like a [b]sharp razor, [c]O worker of deceit.
3 You [a]love evil more than good,
[b]Falsehood more than speaking what is right. [1]Selah.
4 You love all words that devour,
O [a]deceitful tongue.

5 [1]But God will break you down forever;
He will snatch you up and [a]tear you away from *your* tent,
And [b]uproot you from the [c]land of the living. Selah.
6 The righteous will [a]see and fear,
And will [b]laugh at him, *saying,*
7 "Behold, the man who would not make God his refuge,
But [a]trusted in the abundance of his riches
And [b]was strong in [1]his *evil* desire."

8 But as for me, I am like a [a]green olive tree in the house of God;
I [b]trust in the lovingkindness of God forever and ever.
9 I will [a]give You thanks forever, because You have done *it,*
And I will wait on Your name, [b]for *it is* good, in the presence of Your godly ones.

2 [a]Ps 5:9 [b]Ps 57:4; 59:7 [c]Ps 101:7
3 [1]*Selah* may mean: *Pause, Crescendo* or *Musical interlude* [a]Ps 36:4 [b]Ps 58:3; Jer 9:5
4 [a]Ps 120:3
5 [1]Or *Also* [a]Is 22:18, 19 [b]Prov 2:22 [c]Ps 27:13
6 [a]Ps 37:34; 40:3 [b]Job 22:19
7 [1]Or *his destruction* [a]Ps 49:6 [b]Ps 10:6
8 [a]Ps 92:12; 128:3; Jer 11:16 [b]Ps 13:5
9 [a]Ps 30:12 [b]Ps 54:6

53:1 [†]I.e. sickness, a sad tone [•]Possibly *Contemplative,* or *Didactic,* or *Skillful Psalm* [a]Ps 10:4; 14:1-7; 53:1-6 [b]Rom 3:10
2 [1]Or *acts wisely* [a]Rom 3:11 [b]2 Chr 15:2
3 [a]Rom 3:12
4 [a]Jer 4:22
5 [1]Or *dread* [2]Or possibly *those* [a]Lev 26:17, 36; Prov 28:1 [b]Ps 141:7; Jer 8:1, 2; Ezek 6:5 [c]Ps 44:7 [d]2 Kin 17:20; Jer 6:30; Lam 5:22
6 [1]Lit *would be* [a]Ps 14:7

Psalm 53

For the choir director; according to [†]Mahalath.
A [•]Maskil of David.

1 [a]The fool has said in his heart, "There is no God,"
They are corrupt, and have committed abominable injustice;
[b]There is no one who does good.
2 God has looked down from heaven upon the sons of men
To see if there is [a]anyone who [1]understands,
Who [b]seeks after God.
3 [a]Every one of them has turned aside; together they have become corrupt;
There is no one who does good, not even one.

4 Have the workers of wickedness [a]no knowledge,
Who eat up My people *as though* they ate bread
And have not called upon God?
5 There they were in great [1]fear [a]*where* no [1]fear had been;
For God [b]scattered the bones of [2]him who encamped against you;
You [c]put *them* to shame, because [d]God had rejected them.
6 Oh, that [a]the salvation of Israel [1]would come out of Zion!

See note on Ps 32 title. *when.* See note on Ps 3 title. For the event referred to see 1 Sam 22:9–10.

52:1–4 The enemy castigated.

52:1 *Why . . . ?* By what right? See 50:16; Is 3:15. *boast.* By act as well as by word (see 75:4–5). *mighty man.* In his own estimation (see Is 22:17).

52:2 *Your tongue.* See v. 4; see also note on 5:9.

52:3 Your whole moral sense is perverted. *love.* Prefer.

52:4 *tongue.* See note on v. 2.

52:5–7 The enemy's end announced (implicitly a prayer): God will slay you, and the righteous will mock you.

52:5 Note the triple imagery: "break you down," "snatch you up," "uproot you." The arrogant enemy will meet the same end as the rich fools of Ps 49. *from your tent.* See Job 18:14. *uproot you.* Contrast v. 8.

52:6 *righteous.* See note on 1:5. *fear.* Learn from your downfall (see 40:3 and note on 34:8–14).

52:7 See Ps 49.

52:8–9 David's security is God.

52:8 *like a green olive tree.* Which lives for hundreds of years. *green.* See 1:3. It will not be uprooted (see v. 5). *in the house of God.* Olive trees were not planted in the temple courts, but David had access to God's temple as his refuge (see 15:1; 23:6; 27:4; 61:4 and note), where he was kept safe (see 27:5 and note). *lovingkindness.* See note on 6:4.

52:9 A vow to praise (see note on 7:17). *name.* See note on 5:11. *godly ones.* See note on 4:3.

Ps 53 A testimony concerning the folly of evil men, a somewhat revised duplicate of Ps 14; see introduction there. (The main difference between the two psalms is that here the word "God" is used instead of "the LORD"; see also note on v. 5.) The original psalm may have been revised in the light of an event such as is narrated in 2 Chr 20. Here it also serves as a further commentary on the kind of arrogant fool denounced in Ps 52.

53 title *For the choir director.* See note on Ps 4 title. *according to.* See note on Ps 6 title. *Mahalath.* Possibly the name of a tune (see note on Ps 9 title). The Hebrew appears to be the word for "suffering" or "sickness" (see Ps 88 title and note). Perhaps the Hebrew phrase indicates here that the psalm is to be used in a time of affliction, when the godless mock (see Ps 102; see also note on 5:9). *Maskil.* See note on Ps 32 title.

53:1–4 See notes on 14:1–4.

53:5 Differs considerably from 14:5–6, though the basic thought remains the same: God overwhelms the godless who attack His people. Here the verbs are in the past tense (perhaps to express the certainty of their downfall). *where no fear had been.* They fell victim to fear when, humanly speaking, they were not even threatened. God's curse fell on them rather than on Israel (see Lev 26:36–37; see also Judg 7:21; 2 Kin 3:22–23; 7:6–7; Prov 28:1). *scattered the bones.* Over the battlefield of their defeat, their bodies left unburied like something loathsome (see Is 14:18–20; Jer 8:2 and note). *God had rejected them.* As they had rejected Him.

53:6 See note on 14:7.

Ps 54 A prayer for deliverance from enemies who want to have David killed. The prayer is short, like that of Ps 3; 4; 13; yet it is one of the most typical prayers of the Psalter. Completely symmetrical, the prayer is framed by David's cry for vindication (v. 1) and his statement of assurance that he will look in triumph on his foes (v. 7). A confession of confidence (v. 4) centers the prayer (see 42:8 and note on 6:6). Verses 3,5

When God [2]restores His captive people,
[3]Let Jacob rejoice, let Israel be glad.

Psalm 54

For the choir director; on stringed instruments. A [†]Maskil of David, [•]when the Ziphites came and said to Saul, "Is not David hiding himself among us?"

1 Save me, O God, by [a]Your name,
And [1]vindicate me by [b]Your power.
2 [a]Hear my prayer, O God;
[b]Give ear to the words of my mouth.
3 For strangers have [a]risen against me
And [b]violent men have [c]sought my [1]life;
They have [d]not set God before them. [2]Selah.

4 Behold, [a]God is my helper;
The Lord is [1]the [b]sustainer of my soul.
5 [1]He will [a]recompense the evil to [2]my foes;
[3b]Destroy them [c]in Your [4]faithfulness.

6 [1a]Willingly I will sacrifice to You;
I will give [b]thanks to Your name,
O LORD, for it is good.
7 For [1]He has [a]delivered me from all [2]trouble,
And my eye has [b]looked *with satisfaction* upon my enemies.

Psalm 55

For the choir director; on stringed instruments. A [†]Maskil of David.

1 [a]Give ear to my prayer, O God;
And [b]do not hide Yourself from my supplication.
2 Give [a]heed to me and answer me;
I am restless in my [b]complaint and [1c]am surely distracted,
3 Because of the voice of the enemy,
Because of the [a]pressure of the wicked;
For they [b]bring down [1]trouble upon me
And in anger they [c]bear a grudge against me.

4 My [a]heart is in anguish within me,
And the terrors of [b]death have fallen upon me.
5 Fear and [a]trembling come upon me,
And [1b]horror has overwhelmed me.
6 I said, "Oh, that I had wings like a dove!
I would fly away and [1a]be at rest.
7 "Behold, I would wander far away,
I would [a]lodge in the wilderness. [1]Selah.
8 "I would hasten to my place of refuge
From the [a]stormy wind *and* tempest."

9 [1]Confuse, O Lord, [a]divide their tongues,
For I have seen [b]violence and strife in the city.
10 Day and night they go around her upon her walls,
And iniquity and mischief are in her midst.
11 [a]Destruction is in her midst;
[b]Oppression and deceit do not depart from her [1]streets.

12 For it is [a]not an enemy who reproaches me,

6 [2]Or *restores the fortunes of His people* [3]Or *Jacob will rejoice, Israel will be glad*
54:1 [†]Possibly *Contemplative*, or *Didactic*, or *Skillful Psalm* [•]1 Sam 23:19; 26:1 [1]Lit *judge* [a]Ps 20:1 [b]2 Chr 20:6
2 [a]Ps 17:6; 55:1 [b]Ps 5:1
3 [1]Or *soul* [2]*Selah* may mean: *Pause, Crescendo* or *Musical interlude* [a]Ps 86:14 [b]Ps 18:48; 86:14; 140:1, 4, 11 [c]1 Sam 20:1; 25:29; Ps 40:14; 63:9; 70:2 [d]Ps 36:1
4 [1]Lit *as those who sustain* [a]Ps 30:10; 37:40; 118:7 [b]Ps 37:17, 24; 41:12; 51:12; 145:14; Is 41:10
5 [1]Lit *The evil will return* [2]Or *those who lie in wait for me* [3]Or *Put to silence* [4]Or *truth* [a]Ps 94:23 [b]Ps 143:12 [c]Ps 89:49; 96:13; Is 42:3
6 [1]Or *With a freewill offering* [a]Num 15:3; Ps 116:17 [b]Ps 50:14
7 [1]Or *it;* i.e. His name [2]Or *distress* [a]Ps 34:6 [b]Ps 59:10; 92:11; 112:8; 118:7
55:1 [†]Possibly *Contemplative*, or *Didactic*, or *Skillful Psalm* [a]Ps 54:2; 61:1; 86:6 [b]Ps 27:9
2 [a]Ps 66:19; 86:6, 7

2 [1]Or *I must moan* [b]1 Sam 1:16; Job 9:27; Ps 64:1; 77:3; 142:2 [c]Is 38:14; 59:11; Ezek 7:16 **3** [1]Or *wickedness* [a]Ps 17:9 [b]2 Sam 16:7, 8 [c]Ps 71:11; 143:3 **4** [a]Ps 38:8 [b]Ps 18:4, 5; 116:3
5 [1]Lit *shuddering* [a]Ps 119:120 [b]Job 21:6; Is 21:4; Ezek 7:18
6 [1]Lit *settle down* [a]Job 3:13 **7** [1]*Selah* may mean: *Pause, Crescendo* or *Musical interlude* [a]1 Sam 23:14 **8** [a]Is 4:6; 25:4; 29:6 **9** [1]Lit *Swallow up* [a]Gen 11:9 [b]Ps 11:5; Jer 6:7 **11** [1]Or *plaza* [a]Ps 5:9 [b]Ps 10:7; 17:9 **12** [a]Ps 41:9

each form a separate element in the prayer.

54 title *For the choir director.* See note on Ps 4 title. *on stringed instruments.* See note on Ps 4 title. *Maskil.* See note on Ps 32 title. *when.* For the event referred to see 1 Sam 23:19; see also note on Ps 3 title.

54:1–2 Prayer for God to judge his case (see Ps 17).

54:1 *name.* See v. 6; see also note on 5:11.

54:3 The case against his enemies. *have not set God before them.* Like those of Ps 53.

54:4 The confession of confidence and the center of the poem (see 42:8 and note).

54:5 The call for redress (see note on 5:10).

54:6 The vow to praise (see note on 7:17). *name.* See v. 1; see also note on 5:11.

54:7 Assurance of being heard (see note on 3:8).

Ps 55 A prayer for God's help when threatened by a powerful conspiracy in Jerusalem under the leadership of a former friend. The situation described is like that of Absalom's conspiracy against the king (see 2 Sam 15–17): The city is in turmoil; danger is everywhere; there is uncertainty as to who can be trusted; rumors, false reports and slander are circulating freely. Under such circumstances David longs for a quiet retreat to escape it all (vv. 6–8). That being out of the question, he casts his cares on the Lord, whom he knows he can trust. In its structure, the prayer is framed by a plea for help (v. 1) and a simple confession of faith: "I will trust in You" (v. 23).

55 title *For the choir director.* See note on Ps 4 title. *on stringed instruments.* See note on Ps 4 title. *Maskil.* See note on Ps 32 title.

55:1–3 Initial appeal for God to hear.

55:4–8 His heart's anguish.

55:4–5 Danger is everywhere (see 31:13), a danger so great that it is as if death itself were stalking him (see 18:4–5; 116:3).

55:4 *heart.* See note on 4:7. *terrors of death.* See 1 Sam 5:11; 15:32; 28:5; Job 18:14.

55:6–8 He longs for a quiet retreat, away from treacherous and conniving people (see similarly Jer 9:2–6).

55:9–11 Prayer for God to foil the plots of his enemies.

55:9 *Confuse . . . divide their tongues.* Paralyze the conspirators with conflicting designs, as at Babel (Gen 11:5–9; see 2 Sam 17:1–14). *the city.* See v. 11; Jerusalem.

55:10 *iniquity and mischief.* Like watchmen on the walls (see 127:1; 130:6; Song 5:7).

55:11 *Oppression and deceit.* Like watchmen who patrol the city streets (see Song 3:3).

55:12–14 The insults and plots of an enemy can be endured—but those of a treacherous friend?

Then I could bear *it;*
Nor is it one who hates me who [b]has
exalted himself against me,
Then I could hide myself from him.
13 But it is you, a man [1]my equal,
My [a]companion and my [2][b]familiar
friend;
14 We who had sweet [1]fellowship
together
[a]Walked in the house of God in the
throng.
15 Let [1]death come [a]deceitfully upon
them;
Let them [b]go down alive to [2]Sheol,
For evil is in their dwelling, in their
midst.

16 As for me, I shall [a]call upon God,
And the LORD will save me.
17 [a]Evening and [b]morning and at [c]noon,
I will complain and murmur,
And He will hear my voice.
18 He will [a]redeem my soul in peace
[1]from the battle *which is* against me,
For they are [b]many *who strive* with
me.
19 God will [a]hear and [1]answer them—
Even the one [b]who [2]sits enthroned
from of old— Selah.
With whom there [3]is no change,
And who [c]do not fear God.
20 He has put forth his hands against
[a]those who were at peace with him;
He has [1][b]violated his covenant.
21 His [1]speech was [a]smoother than
butter,
But his heart was war;
His words were [a]softer than oil,
Yet they were drawn [b]swords.

22 [a]Cast [1]your burden upon the LORD and
He will sustain you;
[b]He will never allow the righteous to
[2][c]be shaken.
23 But You, O God, will bring them down
to the [1][a]pit of destruction;
[b]Men of bloodshed and deceit will
[c]not live out half their days.
But I will [d]trust in You.

Psalm 56

For the choir director; according to [†]Jonath elem rehokim. A [•]Mikhtam of David, [^]when the Philistines seized him in Gath.

1 Be gracious to me, O God, for man has
[1][a]trampled upon me;
[2]Fighting all day long he [b]oppresses
me.
2 My foes have [1][a]trampled upon me all
day long,
For [2]they are many who [b]fight proudly
against me.
3 [1]When I am [a]afraid,
[2]I will [b]put my trust in You.
4 [a]In God, whose word I praise,
In God I have put my trust;
I shall not be afraid.
[b]What can *mere* [1]man do to me?
5 All day long they [1][a]distort my
words;
All their [2][b]thoughts are against me for
evil.

12 [b]Ps 35:26 **13** [1]Lit *according to my valuation* [2]Or *acquaintance* [a]2 Sam 15:12 [b]Job 19:14; Ps 41:9 **14** [1]Lit *counsel;* or *intimacy* [a]Ps 42:4 **15** [1]Another reading is *desolations be upon them* [2]I.e. the nether world [a]Ps 64:7; Prov 6:15; Is 47:11; 1 Thess 5:3 [b]Num 16:30, 33 **16** [a]Ps 57:2, 3 **17** [a]Ps 141:2; Dan 6:10; Acts 3:1; 10:3, 30 [b]Ps 5:3; 88:13; 92:2 [c]Acts 10:9 **18** [1]Or *so that none may approach me* [a]Ps 103:4 [b]Ps 56:2 **19** [1]Or *afflict* [2]Or *abides from* [3]Lit *are no changes* [a]Ps 78:59 [b]Deut 33:27; Ps 90:2; 93:2 [c]Ps 36:1 **20** [1]Lit *profaned* [a]Ps 7:4; 120:7 [b]Num 30:2; Ps 89:34 **21** [1]Lit *mouth* [a]Ps 12:2; 28:3; Prov 5:3, 4 [b]Ps 57:4; 59:7

22 [1]Or *what He has given you* [2]Or *totter* [a]Ps 37:5; 1 Pet 5:7 [b]Ps 37:24 [c]Ps 15:5; 112:6 **23** [1]Or *lowest pit* [a]Ps 73:18; Is 38:17; Ezek 28:8 [b]Ps 5:6 [c]Job 15:32; Prov 10:27 [d]Ps 25:2; 56:3

56:1 [†]Or *The silent dove of those who are far off,* or, *The dove of the distant terebinths* [•]Possibly *Epigrammatic Poem,* or *Atonement Psalm* [^]1 Sam 21:10, 11 [1]Or *snapped at* [2]Or *A fighting man* [a]Ps 57:3 [b]Ps 17:9 **2** [1]Or *snapped at* [2]Or *many are fighting* [a]Ps 35:25; 57:3; 124:3 [b]Ps 35:1 **3** [1]Lit *In the day* [2]Or *I am one who puts* [a]Ps 55:4, 5 [b]Ps 11:1 **4** [1]Lit *flesh* [a]Ps 56:10, 11 [b]Ps 118:6; Heb 13:6 **5** [1]Or *trouble my affairs* [2]Or *purposes* [a]2 Pet 3:16 [b]Ps 41:7

55:13 *My companion . . . my familiar friend.* See v. 20; see also 41:9 and note.
55:14 *in the house of God.* Their ties of friendship had been a bond hallowed by common commitment to the Lord and sealed by its public display in the presence of God and the worshipers at the temple.
55:15 Prayer for redress (see note on 5:10). *Let death come deceitfully upon them.* The conspirators were seeking his death. *alive to Sheol.* May they go to the grave before life has run its normal course (see v. 23; Num 16:29–33; Prov 1:12; Is 5:14).
55:16–19 Assurance of being heard (see note on 3:8).
55:17 *Evening and morning and at noon, I will complain.* Cf. Dan 6:10.
55:18 *redeem.* Here a synonym for "rescue" (see Is 50:2; Jer 31:11).
55:19 He who is the eternal King will deal with those "With whom there is no change, And who do not fear God" (see 36:1 and note; see also Ps 14; 53).
55:20–21 Further sorrowful (or angry) reflection over the treachery of his former friend.
55:20 *those who were at peace with him.* See 7:4.
55:21 See 28:3; Prov 5:3–4; see also note on 5:9. *heart.* See note on 4:7.
55:22–23 Once more, assurance of being heard.
55:22 A testimony to all who are assembled at the temple. 1 Pet 5:7 echoes this assurance. *righteous.* See note on 1:5.
55:23 *pit of destruction.* The grave (see note on 30:1). *not live out half their days.* See note on v. 15.
Ps 56 A prayer for help when the psalmist is attacked by enemies and his very life is threatened. It is marked by consoling trust in the face of unsettling fear. Structurally, the prayer is framed by an urgent appeal to God (vv. 1–2) and a word of confident assurance (vv. 12–13). An inner frame, vv. 3–4 and vv. 10–11, confesses a sure trust in God in a form that is almost a refrain. The prayer itself is developed in the intervening verses (vv. 5–9).
56 title *For the choir director.* See note on Ps 4 title. *according to.* See note on Ps 9 title. *Mikhtam.* See note on Ps 16 title. *when.* See note on Ps 3 title. For the event referred to see 1 Sam 21:10–15; see also Ps 34 title and note. *seized.* Or "were about to seize."
56:1–2 Initial appeal for God's help.
56:2 *proudly.* Confident in their position of strength, they take no account of David's God (see notes on 3:2; 5:9; 10:11).
56:3–4 See vv. 10–11; confession of trust in the face of fear.
56:4 *word.* God's reassuring promise that He will be the God of His people and will come to their aid when they appeal to Him (see 50:15; 91:15; see also 119:74,81; 130:5). *mere man.* Lit. "flesh"—i.e., man's feebleness compared with God's power (see note on 10:18).
56:5–7 Accusation and call for redress (see note on 5:9–10).
56:5 *distort my words.* See v. 2.

6 They [1][a]attack, they lurk,
They [b]watch my [2]steps,
As they have [c]waited *to take* my [3]life.
7 Because of wickedness, [1][a]cast them
forth,
In anger [b]put down the peoples, O God!

8 You [a]have taken account of my
wanderings;
Put my [b]tears in Your bottle.
Are *they* not in [c]Your book?
9 Then my enemies will [a]turn back [b]in
the day when I call;
This I know, [1]that [c]God is for me.
10 In God, *whose* word I praise,
In the LORD, *whose* word I praise,
11 In God I have put my [1]trust, I shall
not be afraid.
What can man do to me?
12 Your [a]vows are *binding* upon me,
O God;
I will render thank offerings to You.
13 For You have [a]delivered my soul from
death,
[1]Indeed [b]my feet from stumbling,
So that I may [c]walk before God
In the [d]light of the [2]living.

Psalm 57

For the choir director; *set to* [†]Al-tashheth.
A [•]Mikhtam of David, [^]when he fled from Saul
in the cave.

1 Be gracious to me, O God, be gracious
to me,
For my soul [a]takes refuge in You;
And in the [b]shadow of Your wings I
will take refuge
Until destruction [c]passes by.
2 I will cry to God Most High,
To God who [a]accomplishes *all things*
for me.
3 He will [a]send from heaven and save
me;
He reproaches him who [1][b]tramples
upon me. [2]Selah.
God will send forth His
[c]lovingkindness and His [3]truth.

4 My soul is among [a]lions;
I must lie among those who breathe
forth fire,
Even the sons of men, whose [b]teeth
are spears and arrows
And their [c]tongue a sharp sword.
5 [a]Be exalted above the heavens,
O God;
Let Your glory *be* above all the earth.
6 They have [1]prepared a [a]net for my
steps;
My soul is [b]bowed down;
They [c]dug a pit before me;
They *themselves* have [d]fallen into the
midst of it. Selah.

7 [a]My [b]heart is steadfast, O God, my
heart is steadfast;
I will sing, yes, I will sing praises!

6 [1]Or *stir up strife* [2]Lit *heels* [3]Lit *soul* [a]Ps 59:3; 140:2; Is 54:15 [b]Ps 17:11 [c]Ps 71:10
7 [1]Or *will they have escape?* [a]Ps 36:12; Prov 19:5; Ezek 17:15; Rom 2:3 [b]Ps 55:23
8 [a]Ps 139:3 [b]2 Kin 20:5; Ps 39:12 [c]Mal 3:16
9 [1]Or *because* [a]Ps 9:3 [b]Ps 102:2 [c]Ps 41:11; 118:6; Rom 8:31
11 [1]Or *trust without fear*
12 [a]Ps 50:14
13 [1]Or *have You not delivered* [2]Or *life* [a]Ps 33:19; 49:15; 86:13 [b]Ps 116:8 [c]Ps 116:9 [d]Job 33:30
57:1 [†]Lit *Do Not Destroy* [•]Possibly, *Epigrammatic Poem* or *Atonement Psalm* [^]1 Sam 22:1; 24:3 [a]Ps 2:12; 34:22

57:1 [b]Ruth 2:12; Ps 17:8; 36:7; 63:7; 91:4 [c]Is 26:20
2 [a]Ps 138:8
3 [1]Or *snaps at* [2]*Selah* may mean: *Pause, Crescendo* or *Musical interlude* [3]Or *faithfulness* [a]Ps 18:16; 144:5, 7 [b]Ps 56:2 [c]Ps 25:10; 40:11

4 [a]Ps 35:17; 58:6 [b]Prov 30:14 [c]Ps 55:21; 59:7; 64:3; Prov 12:18
5 [a]Ps 57:11; 108:5 **6** [1]Or *spread* [a]Ps 10:9; 31:4; 35:7; 140:5 [b]Ps 145:14 [c]Ps 7:15 [d]Prov 26:27; 28:10; Eccl 10:8 **7** [a]Ps 57:7-11; 108:1-5 [b]Ps 112:7

56:7 See note on 5:10. *anger.* See note on 2:5.
56:8–9 Appeal for God to take special note of the psalmist's troubles.
56:8 *taken account . . . in Your book.* Recorded my troubles in Your heavenly royal records as matters calling for Your action (see note on 51:1).
56:9 If God takes such note of his tears that He records them in His book, He will surely respond to David's call for help.
56:10–11 Renewed confession of trust in the face of fear (see vv. 3–4).
56:12–13 Assurance of being heard (see note on 3:8).
56:12 *Your vows are binding.* Speaking as if his prayer has already been heard, David acknowledges that now he must keep the vows he made to God when he was in trouble (see 66:14 and note on 7:17).
56:13 *my soul.* See note on 6:3. *stumbling.* See note on 35:15. *before God.* See note on 11:7. *light of the living.* The full blessedness of life (see note on 36:9).
Ps 57 A prayer for deliverance when threatened by fierce enemies (it has many links with Ps 56). The psalm appears to reflect the imagery of the night of danger (v. 4: "I must lie [down] among") followed by the morning of salvation (v. 8: "I will awaken the dawn"). For other instances of these associations see 30:5; 46:5; 59:6,14,16; 63:1,6; 90:14. Verses 7–11 are used again in 108:1–5. The psalm is composed of two parts (vv. 1–5 and vv. 6–11) that are alike in structure—both contain three Hebrew couplets and end with an identical refrain. (For the use of refrains elsewhere see introduction to Ps 42–43.)
57 title See note on Ps 56 title. *Al-tashheth.* Possibly meaning "Do Not Destroy" (see Ps 58; 59; 75 titles). *when.* For the event referred to see 1 Sam 24:1–3; see also Ps 142 title.
57:1–5 The prayer.
57:1 Initial cry for God's merciful help. *my soul.* See note on 6:3. *shadow of Your wings.* See note on 17:8.
57:2–3 Confidence of being heard.
57:2 *Most High.* See note on Gen 14:19. *who accomplishes all things for me.* See 138:8. God will not let David's enemies thwart His divine purposes for anointing him king (see 1 Sam 16:1,12; 2 Sam 7). But the Hebrew can also be translated "who makes an end ⌞of troubles⌟ for me" (see 7:9).
57:3 *He will send.* God sends His love and faithfulness (here personified; see note on 23:6) as His messengers from heaven to save His servant (see note on 43:3). *His lovingkindness and His truth.* See note on 26:3. *lovingkindness.* See note on 6:4.
57:4 The threatening situation. *I must lie.* As a sheep among lions. *those who breathe forth fire.* The psalmists often compare their enemies to ferocious beasts (see note on 7:2). (The use of the metaphor here has no connection with the description of Saul and Jonathan in 2 Sam 1:23.) *tongue.* See note on 5:9.
57:5 A prayer for God to show His exalted power and glory throughout His creation by coming to His servant's rescue (see 7:6–7; 21:13; 46:10; 59:5,8; 113:4–9; cf. Ex 14:4; Is 26:15; 44:23; 59:19; see also note on Ps 46:10).
57:6–11 Praise for God's saving help—confidently anticipating the desired deliverance. For such a sudden transition from prayer to assurance see note on 3:8.
57:6 The threat and its outcome: The enemies suffer the calamity they plotted. *net . . . pit.* They hunted him as if he

8 Awake, [a]my glory!
Awake, [b]harp and lyre!
I will awaken the dawn.
9 [a]I will give thanks to You, O Lord, among the peoples;
I will sing praises to You among the [1]nations.
10 For Your [a]lovingkindness is great to the heavens
And Your [1]truth to the clouds.
11 [a]Be exalted above the heavens, O God;
Let Your glory *be* above all the earth.

Psalm 58

For the choir director; *set to* †Al-tashheth.
A •Mikhtam of David.

1 Do you indeed [1]speak righteousness, O [2]gods?
Do you [a]judge [3]uprightly, O sons of men?
2 No, in heart you [a]work unrighteousness;
On earth you [b]weigh out the violence of your hands.
3 The wicked are estranged [a]from the womb;
These who speak lies [b]go astray from [1]birth.
4 They have venom like the [a]venom of a serpent;
Like a deaf cobra that stops up its ear,
5 So that it [a]does not hear the voice of [1b]charmers,
Or a skillful caster of spells.
6 O God, [a]shatter their teeth in their mouth;
Break out the fangs of the young lions, O LORD.
7 Let them [a]flow away like water that runs off;
When he [1b]aims his arrows, let them be as [2]headless shafts.
8 *Let them be* as a snail which [1]melts away as it goes along,
Like the [a]miscarriages of a woman which never see the sun.
9 Before your [a]pots can feel *the fire of* thorns

8 [a]Ps 16:9; 30:12 [b]Ps 150:3 **9** [1]Lit *peoples* [a]Ps 108:3 **10** [1]Or *faithfulness* [a]Ps 36:5; 103:11; 108:4 **11** [a]Ps 57:5; 108:5 **58:1** †Lit *Do Not Destroy* •Possibly *Epigrammatic Poem* or *Atonement Psalm* [1]Another reading is *speak righteousness in silence* [2]Or *mighty ones* or *judges* [3]Or *uprightly the sons of men* [a]Ps 82:2 **2** [a]Mal 3:15 [b]Ps 94:20; Is 10:1 **3** [a]Ps 51:5; Is 48:8

3 [1]Lit *the womb* [b]Ps 53:3 **4** [a]Deut 32:33; Ps 140:3 **5** [1]Or *whisperers* [a]Jer 8:17 [b]Eccl 10:11 **6** [a]Job 4:10; Ps 3:7

7 [1]Lit *bends* [2]Lit *though they were cut off* [a]Josh 2:11; 7:5; Ps 112:10; Is 13:7; Ezek 21:7 [b]Ps 64:3 **8** [1]I.e. secretes slime [a]Job 3:16; Eccl 6:3 **9** [a]Ps 118:12; Eccl 7:6

were a wild beast, but the "lions" themselves were caught.
57:7 All cause for fear has been removed. *heart.* See note on 4:7. *is steadfast.* Feels secure (see 112:7).
57:8 *Awake . . . Awake.* Greet with joy the dawn of the day of deliverance (see Is 51:9,17; 52:1). *glory.* See note on 7:5. *harp and lyre.* Instruments (here personified) to accompany the praise of the Lord at His temple in celebration of deliverance (see 71:22; 81:2; and note on Ps 4 title). *awaken the dawn.* With joyful cries proclaiming God's saving act. (Dawn, too, is here personified—the Canaanites even deified it.)
57:9–10 The vow to praise (see notes on 7:17; 9:1).
57:10 *lovingkindness.* See note on 6:4. *lovingkindness . . . truth.* That is, lovingkindness-and-truth (see v. 3; note on 36:5; see also note on 3:7). *to the heavens . . . to the clouds.* See note on 36:5.
57:11 The refrain (see v. 5), but now as praise (see 18:46; 30:1; 34:3; 35:27; 40:16; 70:4; 92:8; 97:9; 99:2; 113:4; 148:13).
Ps 58 A prayer for God, the supreme Judge, to set right the affairs of men, judging those rulers who corrupt justice, and championing the cause of the righteous. (The psalm was applied by the early church to Jesus' trial before the Sanhedrin; see Matt 26:57–68 and parallels.) Concern for the just use of judicial power is pervasive throughout the OT. This was the primary agency in the administrative structures of the ancient Near East for the protection of the innocent, usually the poor and powerless, against the assaults of unscrupulous men, usually the rich and powerful. Israelite society was troubled with the corruption of this judicial power from the days of Samuel to the end of the monarchy (see, e.g., 1 Sam 8:3; Is 1:23; 5:23; 10:1–2; Ezek 22:6,12; Amos 5:7,10–13; Mic 3:1–3,9–11; 7:2). Even in David's time all was not well (see 2 Sam 15:1–4). For the central concern of this psalm see Ps 82. Structurally, the psalm is framed by a rhetorical address to the wicked judges in their absence (vv. 1–2) and by a reassuring word to "the righteous" (vv. 9–11). The frame also emphasizes the fact that those who do not judge uprightly (v. 1) will be judged by God (v. 11).
58 title *For the choir director.* See note on Ps 4 title. *set to.* See note on Ps 9 title. *Al-tashheth.* See Ps 57; 59; 75 titles. *Mikhtam.* See note on Ps 16 title.
58:1–5 Accusation against the wicked judges whose mouths, hearts and hands (vv. 1–2) are united in the pursuit of injustice.
58:1 *gods.* See NASB marg.; a title applied to those whose administrative positions called upon them to act as earthly representatives of God's heavenly court (see Ex 22:8–9, where the Hebrew for "gods" is translated "judges"; see also Deut 1:17; 2 Chr 19:6). *speak righteousness.* Make just judicial pronouncements.
58:2 *heart.* See note on 4:7. *weigh out the violence.* Issue decisions that result in cruel injustice.
58:3 *from the womb . . . from birth.* Their corrupt ways are not sporadic; they act in accordance with their nature (see 51:5). Here reference is to the wicked; the author does not make a general statement about all people, as is the case in Gen 6:5; 8:21; Job 14:4; 15:14–16; 25:4–6. *The wicked.* See their description in Ps 10. *speak lies.* They have never been concerned for the truth (see John 8:44).
58:4 *venom.* What issues from their mouths is as cruel and deadly as the venom of snakes (see 140:3; Matt 23:33; James 3:8). *stops up its ear.* They are incorrigible; nothing—neither appeals nor threats—will move them.
58:6–8 Prayer for God to purge the land of such perverse judges. The author uses imagery drawn from conventional curses of the ancient Near East (see note on 5:10).
58:6 Let the weapons of their mouths (see 57:4) be broken and torn out. *lions.* See note on 7:2.
58:7 *water that runs off.* And is absorbed by the ground. *arrows.* Malicious pronouncements (see 57:4 and note on 5:9).
58:8 *snail.* Or "slug," that appears to dry up to nothing as it moves over a stone in the hot sun.
58:9–11 Assurance that God will surely judge them (see note on 3:8).
58:9 The meaning of the Hebrew for this verse is uncertain. The verse may be speaking picturesquely of the speed of God's judgment—speed probably signifying here the inescapable certainty of His judgment (see note on 37:10; see also Luke 18:7–8). *thorns.* Twigs from wild thorn bushes were used as fuel for quick heat (see 118:12; Eccl 7:6). *sweep them away.* As by a storm—God's storm (see Job 27:21).

He will [b]sweep them away with a
whirlwind, the [1]green and the
burning alike.

10 The [a]righteous will rejoice when he
[b]sees the vengeance;
He will [c]wash his feet in the blood of
the wicked.
11 And men will say, "Surely there is a
[1a]reward for the righteous;
Surely there is a God who [b]judges [2]on
earth!"

Psalm 59

For the choir director; *set to* [†]Al-tashheth.
A [•]Mikhtam of David, [^]when Saul sent *men*
and they watched the house in order to kill him.

1 [a]Deliver me from my enemies, O my
God;
[1b]Set me *securely* on high away from
those who rise up against me.
2 Deliver me from [a]those who do
iniquity
And save me from [b]men of bloodshed.
3 For behold, they [a]have [1]set an
ambush for my [2]life;
[3]Fierce men [4a]launch an attack
against me,
[b]Not for my transgression nor for my
sin, O LORD,

9 [1]Lit *living* [b]Job 27:21; Ps 83:15; Prov 10:25
10 [a]Job 22:19; Ps 32:11; 64:10; 107:42 [b]Deut 32:43; Ps 91:8; Jer 11:20; 20:12 [c]Ps 68:23
11 [1]Lit *fruit* [2]Or *in* [a]Ps 18:20; 19:11; Is 3:10; Luke 6:23, 35 [b]Ps 9:8; 67:4; 75:7; 94:2
59:1 [†]Lit *Do Not Destroy* [•]Possibly *Epigrammatic Poem* or *Atonement Psalm* [^]1 Sam 19:11 [1]Or *May You put me in an inaccessibly high place* [a]Ps 143:9 [b]Ps 20:1; 69:29
2 [a]Ps 28:3; 36:12; 53:4; 92:7; 94:16 [b]Ps 26:9; 139:19; Prov 29:10
3 [1]Or *lain in wait* [2]Lit *soul* [3]Or *Strong* [4]Or *stir up strife* [a]Ps 56:6 [b]1 Sam 24:11; Ps 7:3, 4; 69:4
4 [1]Lit *Without guilt* [2]Lit *meet* [a]Ps 35:19 [b]Ps 7:6; 35:23

4 [1a]For no guilt of *mine,* they run and
set themselves against me.
[b]Arouse Yourself to [2]help me, and see!
5 You, [a]O LORD God of hosts, the God of
Israel,
Awake to [1b]punish all the nations;
[c]Do not be gracious to any *who are*
treacherous in iniquity. [2]Selah.
6 They [a]return at evening, they howl
like a [b]dog,
And go around the city.
7 Behold, they [a]belch forth with their
mouth;
[b]Swords are in their lips,
For, *they say,* "[c]Who hears?"
8 But You, O LORD, [a]laugh at them;
You [b]scoff at all the nations.

9 *Because of* [1]his [a]strength I will watch
for You,
For God is my [b]stronghold.
10 [1]My God [a]in His lovingkindness will
meet me;
God will let me [b]look *triumphantly*
upon [2]my foes.

5 [1]Lit *visit* [2]*Selah* may mean: *Pause, Crescendo* or *Musical interlude* [a]Ps 69:6; 80:4; 84:8 [b]Ps 9:5; Is 26:14 [c]Is 2:9; Jer 18:23 **6** [a]Ps 59:14 [b]Ps 22:16 **7** [a]Ps 94:4; Prov 15:2, 28 [b]Ps 57:4; Prov 12:18 [c]Job 22:13; Ps 10:11; 73:11; 94:7 **8** [a]Ps 37:13; Prov 1:26 [b]Ps 2:4 **9** [1]Many mss and some ancient versions read *My strength* [a]Ps 18:17 [b]Ps 9:9; 62:2 **10** [1]Many mss and some ancient versions read *The God of my lovingkindness* [2]Lit *those who lie in wait for me* [a]Ps 21:3 [b]Ps 54:7

58:10 *righteous.* Here a judicial term for those who are in the right but who have been wronged (see note on 1:5). *when he sees the vengeance.* When the wrongs committed against them are redressed. *wash his feet in the blood.* Vivid imagery borrowed from the literary conventions of the ancient Near East (see 68:23). Its origin is the exaggerated language of triumphant reports of victory on the battlefield.

58:11 The climax: When God has judged the unjust "gods" (see note on v. 1), all people will see that right ultimately triumphs under God's just rule (see note on 46:10). No more will people despair, like those in Mal 3:15.

Ps 59 A prayer for deliverance when endangered by enemy attacks. If originally composed by David under the circumstances noted in the superscription, it must have been revised for use by one of David's royal sons when Jerusalem was under siege by a hostile force made up of troops from many nations—as when Hezekiah was besieged by the Assyrians (see 2 Kin 18:19). (Some, however, ascribe it to Nehemiah; see Neh 4.) The enemy weapon most prominent is the tongue, attacking with slander and curses. In this psalm, too, the imagery of the night of danger (vv. 6,14), followed by the morning of deliverance (v. 16), is evoked (see introduction to Ps 57). Regarding the structure, the two halves of the psalm (vv. 1–9,10–17) each conclude with an almost identical refrain (vv. 9,17), preceded by a characterization of the enemies (vv. 6,14). The first half of the psalm is predominantly prayer, the second half predominantly assurance of deliverance. The whole is framed by a cry for protection (v. 1) and a joyful confession that God is the psalmist's "stronghold" (v. 17, in Hebrew the same root as that for "Set me securely" in v. 1).

59 title See note on Ps 56 title. *Al-tashheth.* See Ps 57; 58; 75 titles. *when.* For the event referred to see 1 Sam 19:11.

59:1–2 The cry for deliverance.

59:1 *Set me securely.* Lit. "Raise me to a high, secure place."

59:2 *those who do iniquity . . . men of bloodshed.* Common characterizations of those who attack the psalmists out of malice.

59:3–5 By curses and lies (v. 12) the enemies seek to justify their attacks, but the psalmist protests his innocence and pleads with God to judge those who wrong him (see 58:11).

59:3 *set an ambush.* See 10:8–9 and note on 7:2.

59:4 *Arouse Yourself.* See note on 3:7.

59:5 *LORD God of hosts.* See note on 1 Sam 1:3. *God of Israel.* This appeal to the Lord as the God of Israel to punish the nations makes clear that the attack on the psalmist involves an attack by the nations on Israel. *Awake.* See note on 7:6. *punish . . . Do not be gracious.* See note on 5:10. *treacherous in iniquity.* Whether Israelites had joined in the attack is not clear; the Hebrew indicates only that the enemies were treacherous.

59:6–8 Confidence: Surely God mocks such a pack of dogs (see 22:16–17).

59:6 *around the city.* The enemies besiege the city like dogs at night on the prowl for food (see vv. 14–15).

59:7 *Swords are in their lips.* Their "curses and lies" (v. 12). For the imagery see 57:4; see also note on 5:9. *they say.* See note on 3:2.

59:9 *watch.* Hebrew *shamar* (see note on v. 17). The psalmist watches as one who longingly waits for the morning (of salvation); see 130:6.

59:10–13 The prayer renewed. Confident that the Lord will hear his prayer (v. 10) and will punish the nations (v. 5), the psalmist prays that God will not sweep them away suddenly but will prolong their punishment so that Israel ("my people," v. 11) will not forget God's acts of salvation, as they had done so often before (see 78:11; 106:13). Nevertheless, the psalmist asks God not to allow the enemies to escape the full consequences of their malice (vv. 12–13).

59:10 *lovingkindness.* See note on 6:4.

11 Do not slay them, [a]or my people will
forget;
[1b]Scatter them by Your power, and
bring them down,
O Lord, [c]our shield.
12 [1]*On account of* the [a]sin of their mouth
and the words of their lips,
Let them even be [b]caught in their
pride,
And on account of [c]curses and [2]lies
which they utter.
13 [1a]Destroy *them* in wrath, [1]destroy
them that they may be no more;
That *men* may [b]know that God [2]rules
in Jacob
To the ends of the earth. Selah.
14 They [a]return at evening, they howl
like a dog,
And go around the city.
15 They [a]wander about [1]for food
And [2]growl if they are not satisfied.
16 But as for me, I shall [a]sing of Your
strength;
Yes, I shall [b]joyfully sing of Your
lovingkindness in the [c]morning,
For You have been my [d]stronghold
And a [e]refuge in the day of my
distress.
17 [a]O my strength, I will sing praises to
You;
For God is my [b]stronghold, the [1]God
who shows me lovingkindness.

Psalm 60

For the choir director; according to [†]Shushan Eduth. A [•]Mikhtam of David, to teach; [^]when he struggled with Aram-naharaim and with Aram-zobah, and Joab returned, and smote twelve thousand of Edom in the Valley of Salt.

1 O God, [a]You have rejected us. You
have [1b]broken us;
You have been [c]angry; O, [d]restore us.
2 You have made the [1a]land quake, You
have split it open;
[b]Heal its breaches, for it totters.
3 You have [1a]made Your people
experience hardship;
You have given us [2]wine to [b]drink that
makes us stagger.
4 You have given a [a]banner to those
who fear You,

11 [1]Or *Make them wander* [a]Deut 4:9; 6:12 [b]Ps 106:27; 144:6; Is 33:3 [c]Ps 84:9 **12** [1]Or *The sin of their mouth is the word of their lips,* [2]Lit *lying* [a]Prov 12:13 [b]Zeph 3:11 [c]Ps 10:7 **13** [1]Lit *Bring to an end* [2]Or *is Ruler* [a]Ps 104:35 [b]Ps 83:18 **14** [a]Ps 59:6 **15** [1]Or *to devour* [2]Another reading is *tarry all night* [a]Job 15:23 **16** [a]Ps 21:13 [b]Ps 101:1 [c]Ps 5:3; 88:13 [d]Ps 59:9 [e]2 Sam 22:3; Ps 46:1 **17** [1]Lit *God of my lovingkindness* [a]Ps 59:9 [b]Ps 59:10 **60:1** [†]Lit *The lily of testimony* [•]Possibly, *Epigrammatic Poem* or *Atonement Psalm* [^]2 Sam 8:3, 13; 1 Chr 18:3, 12 [1]Or *broken out upon us* [a]Ps 44:9 [b]2 Sam 5:20 [c]Ps 79:5 [d]Ps 80:3 **2** [1]Or *earth* [a]Ps 18:7 [b]2 Chr 7:14; Is 30:26 **3** [1]Lit *caused Your people to see* [2]Lit *wine of staggering* [a]Ps 66:12; 71:20 [b]Ps 75:8; Is 51:17, 22; Jer 25:15 **4** [a]Ps 20:5; Is 5:26; 11:12; 13:2

59:11 *scatter them.* Like vagabonds, with no place to settle (see Gen 4:12; 2 Sam 15:20; Lam 4:15) and having to hunt for food (like dogs, v. 15; see 109:10; Amos 4:8). *shield.* See note on 3:3.

59:12 See note on v. 7. *caught in their pride.* Let the pride with which they treacherously attack the Lord's servant and his people be the trap that catches them. *curses and lies.* See 10:7 and note.

59:13 *That men may know.* When God has thus dealt with Israel's enemies, all the world will acknowledge that the Judge of all the earth (see 58:11) is the God of Israel. *Jacob.* See note on 14:7.

59:14–16 Assurance of being heard (see note on 3:8). Just as God mocks the defiant pack of dogs (vv. 6–8), so the psalmist will sing for joy at God's triumph over them.

59:16 *strength . . . lovingkindness . . . stronghold.* See the refrain (vv. 9,17). *morning.* See introduction.

59:17 The vow to praise (see note on 7:17). *sing.* Hebrew *zamar* (see note on v. 9). The play on words in the refrain marks an advance from watching during the night of danger to singing in the morning of salvation.

Ps 60 A national prayer for God's help after suffering a severe blow by a foreign nation, presumably Edom (see v. 9). The prayer leader may have been the king (the "me" in v. 9), as in 2 Chr 20. The lament that God has "rejected" (v. 1) His people and no longer accompanies their armies links the psalm with Ps 44. Verses 5–12 appear again in 108:6–13. As for its structure, the prayer is framed by three verses lamenting God's rejection of His people (vv. 1–3) and three verses expressing confidence that the God who has rejected them will yet give them victory (vv. 10–12). This transition from lament to confidence constitutes the overarching movement of the prayer. Verses 4–8 contain the plea for help (v. 5) and the grounds for confidence (vv. 4,6–8).

60 title See note on Ps 56 title. *Shushan Eduth.* Means "The Lily of the Covenant" (see Ps 80 title and note on Ps 45 title). *to teach.* Only here in the psalm titles. For other songs that Israel was to learn see Deut 31:19,21; 2 Sam 1:18. That it was intended for a variety of uses, especially to convey confidence in times of national threat, is illustrated by its use in Ps 108. *when.* For the events referred to see 2 Sam 8; 1 Chr 18 (perhaps also 2 Sam 10). If the tradition that assigns the prayer to these events is correct, it must be supposed that our knowledge of the events is incomplete, since these accounts do not mention Edom. The Israelite war against Edom at this time of great northern battles may have been occasioned by an attack on the part of Edom trying to take advantage of Israel's preoccupation elsewhere, an attack in which Edom succeeded in overrunning the garrisons that guarded Judah's southern borders.

60:1–3 Lament over God's rejection of His people (see 44:9–16; 89:38–45) and prayer for restoration.

60:1 *rejected us.* At least momentarily (see 30:5). Defeat by the enemy is interpreted as a sign of God's anger (though no reason for that anger is noted, and the bond between Israel and God is not broken). *broken us.* Like a flood (see 2 Sam 5:20).

60:2 *made the land quake.* As by a devastating earthquake—such as was occasionally experienced in ancient Canaan.

60:3 *wine . . . that makes us stagger.* God has made them drink from the cup of His wrath rather than from His cup of blessing and salvation (see note on 16:5).

60:4–8 A plea for help, grounded in reasons for confidence.

60:4 *banner.* Banners were used as rallying points for troops in preparation for battle and for leading them into action. This practice is often alluded to in Isaiah (5:26; 11:10,12; 13:2; 18:3; 30:17; 49:22; 62:10) and Jeremiah (4:21, "standard"; 50:2; 51:12,27). It is possible to read v. 4 as a petition, in which case it pleads for God to rally the troops of Israel and lead them against the foe. If, however, it is an expression of confidence (as the NASB renders it), the "banner" must be the reassuring word from God recited in vv. 6–8 (see Ex 17:15). *those who fear You.* Your people, in distinction from the nations (see 61:5; see also note on Gen 20:11).

That it may be displayed because of
the truth. [1]Selah.
5 [a]That Your [b]beloved may be delivered,
[c]Save with Your right hand, and
answer [1]us!

6 God has spoken in His [1a]holiness:
"I will exult, I will portion out
[b]Shechem and measure out the
valley of [c]Succoth.
7 "[a]Gilead is Mine, and Manasseh is Mine;
[b]Ephraim also is the [1]helmet of My
head;
Judah is My [2c]scepter.
8 "[a]Moab is My washbowl;
Over [b]Edom I shall throw My shoe;
Shout loud, O [c]Philistia, because of
Me!"

9 Who will bring me into the besieged
city?
Who [1]will lead me to Edom?
10 Have not You Yourself, O God,
[a]rejected us?
And [b]will You not go forth with our
armies, O God?
11 O give us help against the adversary,
For [a]deliverance [1]by man is in vain.
12 [1]Through God we shall [a]do valiantly,
And it is He who will [b]tread down our
adversaries.

Psalm 61

For the choir director; on a stringed instrument.
A Psalm of David.

1 [a]Hear my cry, O God;
[b]Give heed to my prayer.
2 From the [a]end of the earth I call to
You when my heart is [b]faint;
Lead me to [c]the rock that is higher
than I.
3 For You have been a [a]refuge for me,
A [b]tower of strength [1]against the
enemy.

4 [1]*Selah* may mean: *Pause, Crescendo* or *Musical interlude* **5** [1]Some authorities read *me* [a]Ps 60:5-12; 108:6-13 [b]Deut 33:12; Ps 127:2; Is 5:1; Jer 11:15 [c]Ps 17:7 **6** [1]Or *sanctuary* [a]Ps 89:35 [b]Gen 12:6; 33:18; Josh 17:7 [c]Gen 33:17; Josh 13:27 **7** [1]Lit *protection* [2]Or *lawgiver* [a]Josh 13:31 [b]Deut 33:17 [c]Gen 49:10 **8** [a]2 Sam 8:2 [b]2 Sam 8:14 [c]2 Sam 8:1 **9** [1]Or *has led* **10** [a]Ps 60:1; 108:11 [b]Josh 7:12; Ps 44:9 **11** [1]Lit *of* [a]Ps 146:3 **12** [1]Or *In* or *With* [a]Num 24:18; Ps 118:16 [b]Ps 44:5; Is 63:3 **61:1** [a]Ps 64:1 [b]Ps 86:6 **2** [a]Ps 42:6 [b]Ps 77:3 [c]Ps 18:2; 94:22 **3** [1]Lit *from* [a]Ps 62:7 [b]Ps 59:9; Prov 18:10

60:5 *Your beloved.* The Hebrew for this expression is here a word of special endearment, as in 127:2; 2 Sam 12:25; Jer 11:15.
60:6–8 A comforting oracle from the Lord, perhaps recalling an already ancient word from the time of the conquest. If so, it may have been preserved in the "Book of the Wars of the LORD" (Num 21:14). In any event, the Lord is depicted as Israel's triumphant Warrior-King (see Ex 15:3,13–18).
60:6 *portion out . . . measure out.* Divide His conquered territory among His servant people who were with Him in the battles. *Shechem . . . Succoth.* Places representative of the territory west and east of the Jordan taken over by the Lord and Israel (see Gen 33:17–18; 1 Kin 12:25).
60:7 Israel is the Lord's kingdom—the land conquered and His people established within it. *Gilead . . . Manasseh.* Half of Manasseh was established in Gilead, east of the Jordan, and half of it west of the Jordan, just north of Ephraim (see Josh 13:29–31; 17:5–11). This once again showed that the Lord's kingdom included territory both east and west of the Jordan. *Ephraim . . . Judah.* The two leading tribes of Israel, the one representative of the Rachel tribes (Ephraim) in the north, the other of the Leah tribes (Judah) in the south; see Gen 48:13–20; 49:8–12; Num 2:3,18; Josh 15–16. Together they represented all Israel (Is 11:13; Zech 9:13). *helmet.* As a powerful and aggressive tribe (Deut 33:17; Judg 7:24–8:3; 12:1), Ephraim figuratively represents the Lord's helmet. *scepter.* Called such because from Judah would come (Gen 49:10)—and had now come (1 Sam 16:1–13)—the Lord's chosen earthly regent over His people (see 2 Sam 7).
60:8 *Moab . . . Edom . . . Philistia.* Perpetual enemies on Israel's eastern, southern and western borders respectively (see Ex 15:14–15; see also Ex 13:17; Num 20:14–21; 22–24). *is My washbowl.* Is reduced to a household vessel in which the Lord washes His feet (Gen 18:4). The metaphor is perhaps suggested by the fact that Moab lay along the east shore of the Dead Sea. *throw My shoe.* Perhaps refers to the conventional symbolic act by which one claimed possession of land (cf. Ruth 4:7).
60:9 A rhetorical question following the reassuring oracle and leading to the confidence expressed in vv. 10–12. *me . . . me.* Possibly referring to the king (see introduction), though the praying community may be referring to itself collectively (see note on Ps 30 title). *lead me.* As God went before His people into battle in the desert (Ex 13:21) and during the conquest (Ex 23:27–28; 33:2; Deut 9:3; 31:8).
60:10–12 Confidence of victory (see note on 3:8).
60:10 *rejected.* See v. 1.
60:11 *help.* Lit. "salvation" (see v. 5, "Save"). *by man.* See 33:17.
60:12 *do valiantly.* Lit. "do mighty things." With God's help Israel will achieve in a manner similar to that of the Lord Himself (see 118:15–16) and will triumph over Edom (see Num 24:18, "performs valiantly"). *tread down.* Like a victorious warrior (see Is 14:19, 25; Jer 12:10; Zech 10:5).
Ps 61 A prayer for restoration to God's presence. The circumstances appear to be similar to those referred to in Ps 42–43. Here, however, a king is involved (v. 6), and if the author was David, he may have composed this prayer at the time of his flight from Absalom (see 2 Sam 17:21–29). For another possibility see note on v. 2. Ps 61–64 form a series linked together by the common theme of trust in God when under threat. Structurally, the prayer is framed by a cry to God (v. 1) and a vow to praise (v. 8).
61 title See note on Ps 4 title.
61:1 Initial plea for God to hear.
61:2–3 The prayer.
61:2 *end of the earth.* So it seemed (see 42:6). Possibly the phrase here refers to the brink of the nether world, i.e., the grave (see 63:9); the psalmist feels himself near death. *heart.* See note on 4:7. *Lead me.* See 23:2. *rock.* Secure place (see 27:5; 40:2). *higher than I.* The place of security that he seeks is beyond his reach; only God can bring him to it. Since God is often confessed by the psalmists to be their "rock" ("rock of strength" in 31:2; "rock of habitation" in 71:3; see also 18:2; 62:2,6–7; 94:22), it may be that God Himself is that higher "rock" (the secure refuge) that the psalmist pleads for (see v. 3). Or it may be the secure refuge of God's sanctuary (see v. 4; see also 27:5).
61:3 The reason he appeals to God: God has never failed him as a refuge. *enemy.* If this is a prayer when faced with death, death is the present foe (see 68:20; 141:8; Job 33:22; Is 25:8; 28:15; Jer 9:21; Hos 13:14; see also 1 Cor 15:26). See note on 49:14.

4 Let me [1a]dwell in Your tent forever;
Let me [b]take refuge in the shelter of
Your wings. [2]Selah.

5 For You have heard my [a]vows, O God;
You have given *me* the inheritance of
those who [b]fear Your name.
6 You will [1a]prolong the king's [2]life;
His years will be as many generations.
7 He will [1]abide [a]before God forever;
Appoint [b]lovingkindness and truth
that they may preserve him.
8 So I will [a]sing praise to Your name
forever,
That I may [b]pay my vows day by day.

Psalm 62

For the choir director; [†]according to Jeduthun.
A Psalm of David.

1 [a]My soul *waits* in silence for God only;
From Him [b]is my salvation.
2 He only is my [a]rock and my salvation,
My [b]stronghold; I shall not be greatly
shaken.

3 How long will you assail a man,
That you may murder *him,* all of you,
Like a [a]leaning wall, like a tottering
fence?
4 They have counseled only to thrust
him down from his high position;
They [a]delight in falsehood;
They [b]bless with [1]their mouth,
But inwardly they curse. [2]Selah.

5 My soul, [a]wait in silence for God only,
For my hope is from Him.
6 He only is [a]my rock and my salvation,
My stronghold; I shall not be shaken.
7 On God my [a]salvation and my glory
rest;
The rock of my strength, my [b]refuge is
in God.
8 [a]Trust in Him at all times, O people;
[b]Pour out your heart before Him;
God is a refuge for us. Selah.

9 Men of [a]low degree are only [b]vanity
and men of rank are a [c]lie;
In the [d]balances they go up;
They are together lighter than breath.
10 [a]Do not trust in oppression
And do not [1]vainly hope in [b]robbery;
If riches increase, [c]do not set *your*
heart *upon them.*

11 [1]Once God has [a]spoken;
[2]Twice I have heard this:
That [b]power belongs to God;

4 [1]Or *sojourn* [2]*Selah* may mean: *Pause, Crescendo* or *Musical interlude* [a]Ps 23:6; 27:4 [b]Ps 17:8; 91:4 **5** [a]Job 22:27; Ps 56:12 [b]Deut 28:58; Neh 1:11; Ps 86:11; 102:15; Is 59:19; Mal 2:5; 4:2 **6** [1]Lit *add days to* [2]Lit *days* [a]Ps 21:4 **7** [1]Or *sit enthroned* [a]Ps 41:12 [b]Ps 40:11 **8** [a]Judg 5:3; Ps 30:4; 33:2; 71:22 [b]Ps 65:1; Is 19:21 **62:1** [†]Cf 1 Chr 16:41; 25:1; Ps 39 and 77 titles [a]Ps 33:20 [b]Ps 37:39 **2** [a]Ps 89:26 [b]Ps 59:17; 62:6 **3** [a]Is 30:13

4 [1]Lit *his* [2]*Selah* may mean: *Pause, Crescendo* or *Musical interlude* [a]Ps 4:2 [b]Ps 28:3; 55:21 **5** [a]Ps 62:1 **6** [a]Ps 62:2 **7** [a]Ps 85:9; Jer 3:23 [b]Ps 46:1 **8** [a]Ps 37:3, 5; 52:8; Is 26:4 [b]1 Sam 1:15; Ps 42:4; Lam 2:19

9 [a]Ps 49:2 [b]Job 7:16; Ps 39:5; Is 40:17 [c]Ps 116:11 [d]Is 40:15 **10** [1]Lit *become vain in robbery* [a]Is 30:12 [b]Is 61:8; Ezek 22:29; Nah 3:1 [c]Job 31:25; Ps 49:6; 52:7; Mark 10:24; Luke 12:15; 1 Tim 6:10 **11** [1]Or *One thing* [2]Or *These two things I have heard* [a]Job 33:14; 40:5 [b]Ps 59:17; Rev 19:1

61:4–5 Longing for the security of God's sanctuary (see 27:5 and note).
61:4 *dwell in.* See note on 15:1. *tent.* Residence (see 2 Sam 6:17; 7:2; 1 Kin 1:39; 2:28–30). *shelter of Your wings.* See note on 17:8.
61:5 The reason for his longing: Either (1) because God has been so responsive to him in the past, or (2) confidence that his longing is about to be satisfied. *my vows.* The vows that accompanied his prayers (see 50:14; 66:14; see also note on 7:17). *inheritance.* A place with God's people in the promised land, together with all that the Lord had promised to give and to be to His people (see 16:6; 37:18; 135:12; 136:21–22). *those who fear.* See 60:4 and note. *Your name.* See note on 5:11.
61:6–7 Prayer for the king's long life. The king himself may have made this prayer—such transitions to the third person are known from the literature of the ancient Near East—or it may be the prayer of the people, perhaps voiced by a priest or Levite. Later Jewish interpretations applied these verses to the Messiah. They are fulfilled in Christ, David's great Son.
61:6 May the king live forever (see note on 45:6).
61:7 *abide before God.* See note on 41:12. *lovingkindness and truth.* Personified as God's messengers (see notes on 23:6; 43:3; see also note on 26:3).
61:8 The vow to praise (see note on 7:17).
Ps 62 The psalmist commits himself to God when threatened by the assaults of conspirators who wish to dethrone him. The author surely was a king and, if it was David, the circumstances could well have been the efforts of the family of Saul to topple him. Verse 3 suggests a time of weakness and may indicate advanced age. Implicitly the psalm is an appeal to God to uphold him. No psalm surpasses it in its expression of simple trust in God (see Ps 31 and introduction to Ps 61). The psalm is composed of three parts: vv. 1–4, 5–8, 9–12. The middle stanza (vv. 5–8), which begins by echoing vv. 1–2, constitutes the central expression of trust and hope. The whole is framed by a confession of tranquil resting in God (vv. 1–2) and the reason for such trust (vv. 11–12). The remaining verses (vv. 3–4, 9–10) speak of those who threaten.
62 title See note on Ps 39 title.
62:1–4 Confidence in God in the face of conspiracy.
62:1 *My soul.* See note on 6:3. *waits in silence.* Lit. "is silence," i.e., is in repose.
62:2,6 *shaken.* See note on 10:6.
62:3 Question to the assailants: Will you never give up? *leaning wall . . . tottering fence.* A metaphor for David's fragile condition: either (1) a confession that he has no strength in himself, or (2) an acknowledgment that he is in a weakened condition—or, perhaps, (3) a reflection on how his enemies perceive him, a "pushover."
62:4 *high position.* Throne. *falsehood . . . curse.* See note on 10:7. *bless.* For example, "Long live the king!" (1 Sam 10:24; 2 Sam 16:16; see also 1 Kin 1:25,34,39).
62:5–8 Trust in God: an exhortation to himself (v. 5) and to the people (v. 8).
62:5 *wait in silence.* See note on v. 1; faith encouraging faith (see 27:13–14; 42:5,11; 43:5).
62:8 Exhortation to God's people (see 31:23–24). *Pour out your heart.* In earnest prayer (see Lam 2:19). *heart.* See note on 4:7.
62:9–12 Frail, misguided man; mighty, trustworthy God.
62:9–10 Man, as a threat, is nothing (see note on 10:18).
62:9 *Men of low degree . . . men of rank.* Persons of every condition. *lie . . . breath.* People appear to be much more than a puff of wind, especially the rich and powerful.
62:10 A warning to those (including those conspiring against him) who trust in their own devices to get what they want (by fair means or foul) rather than trusting in God to sustain them—a virtual summary of Ps 49. *heart.* See note on 4:7.

12 And lovingkindness [a]is Yours, O Lord,
For You [b]recompense a man according
to his work.

Psalm 63

A Psalm of David, †when he was in
the wilderness of Judah.

1 O God, [a]You are my God; I shall seek
You [1]earnestly;
My soul [b]thirsts for You, my flesh
[2]yearns for You,
In a [c]dry and weary land where there
is no water.
2 Thus I have [a]seen You in the
sanctuary,
To see Your power and Your glory.
3 Because Your [a]lovingkindness is better
than life,
My lips will praise You.
4 So I will bless You [a]as long as I live;
I will [b]lift up my hands in Your name.
5 My soul is [a]satisfied as with [1]marrow
and fatness,
And my mouth offers [b]praises with
joyful lips.

6 When I remember You [a]on my bed,
I meditate on You in the [b]night
watches,
7 For [a]You have been my help,
And in the [b]shadow of Your wings I
sing for joy.
8 My soul [a]clings [1]to You;
Your [b]right hand upholds me.

9 But those who [a]seek my [1]life to
destroy it,
Will go into the [2b]depths of the
earth.
10 [1]They will be [2a]delivered over to the
power of the sword;
They will be a [3b]prey for foxes.
11 But the [a]king will rejoice in God;
Everyone who [b]swears by Him will
glory,
For the [c]mouths of those who speak
lies will be stopped.

Psalm 64

For the choir director. A Psalm of David.

1 Hear my voice, O God, in [a]my
[1]complaint;
[b]Preserve my life from dread of the
enemy.
2 Hide me from the [a]secret counsel of
evildoers,

12 [a]Ps 86:5; 103:8; 130:7 [b]Job 34:11; Ps 28:4; Jer 17:10; Matt 16:27; Rom 2:6; 1 Cor 3:8; Rev 2:23
63:1 †1 Sam 22:5; 23:14 [1]Lit *early* [2]Lit *faints* [a]Ps 118:28 [b]Ps 42:2; 84:2; Matt 5:6 [c]Ps 143:6
2 [a]Ps 27:4
3 [a]Ps 69:16
4 [a]Ps 104:33; 146:2 [b]Ps 28:2; 143:6
5 [1]Lit *fat* [a]Ps 36:8 [b]Ps 71:23
6 [a]Ps 4:4 [b]Ps 16:7; 42:8; 119:55
7 [a]Ps 27:9 [b]Ps 17:8
8 [1]Lit *after* [a]Num 32:12; Deut 1:36; Hos 6:3 [b]Ps 18:35; 41:12
9 [1]Lit *soul* [2]Lit *lowest places* [a]Ps 40:14 [b]Ps 55:15
10 [1]Lit *They will pour him out* [2]Lit *poured out by* [3]Lit *portion* [a]Jer 18:21; Ezek 35:5 [b]Lam 5:18
11 [a]Ps 21:1 [b]Deut 6:13; Is 45:23; 65:16 [c]Job 5:16; Ps 107:42; Rom 3:19
64:1 [1]Or *concern* [a]Ps 55:2 [b]Ps 140:1
2 [a]Ps 56:6

62:11–12 The climax: recollection of God's reassuring word to His people. *power . . . lovingkindness.* Able to do all that He has promised; committed to His people's salvation and blessedness.
62:11 *Once . . . Twice.* See note on Amos 1:3.
62:12 *lovingkindness.* See note on 6:4. *For.* Ultimately every person will experience God's righteousness (see note on 5:8). *recompense . . . according to.* See notes on Jer 17:10; 32:19.
Ps 63 A confession of longing for God and for the security His presence offers when deadly enemies threaten. That longing is vividly described by the metaphor of thirst (v. 1) and hunger (v. 5; see 42:1–2). Like Ps 62 this psalm is an implicit prayer. It is linked to that psalm also by the advancement from hearing (62:11) to seeing (v. 2; see 48:8 and note). The imagery of the night of danger (v. 6) and the morning of salvation (see note on v. 1) once more occurs (see introduction to Ps 57). This psalm was prescribed for daily public prayers of the early church. In its structure, the initial expression of longing (v. 1) gives way at the end to the expectation of joy (v. 11)—the literary frame of the psalm. What he has seen in the sanctuary (v. 2) he remembers on his bed at night (v. 6), and that reassures him that his enemies will suffer the end they plot for him (vv. 9–10).
63 title See note on Ps 3 title. *when.* If this tradition is correct, the reference is probably to 2 Sam 15:23–28; 16:2,14; 17:16,29 since the psalmist is referred to as king (see v. 11).
63:1 Intense longing for God in a time of need. *earnestly.* Lit. "at dawn," "in the morning." *My soul . . . my flesh.* I, with my whole being (see note on 6:3). *dry and weary land.* A metaphor for his situation of need, in which he does not taste "marrow and fatness" (v. 5) supplied by the "river whose streams make glad the city of God" (see 46:4 and note).
63:2–5 Comforting reflection on what he had seen in the sanctuary; it awakens joyful expectations.
63:2 See 27:4; 48:8 and notes.
63:3 *lovingkindness.* See note on 6:4.
63:4 *name.* See note on 5:11. *lift up my hands.* In praise.
63:5 *soul.* See note on 6:3.
63:6–8 Night reflections, remembering what he had seen "in the sanctuary" (v. 2).
63:6 *on my bed.* At night as he expectantly awaits the dawning of the morning of deliverance. *the night watches.* See note on Judg 7:19; see also 119:148; Lam 2:19.
63:7 *shadow of Your wings.* See note on 17:8.
63:9–10 His enemies will get what they deserve; in seeking his life they forfeit their own (see Gen 9:5; Ex 21:23; Deut 19:21; see also note on Ps 5:10).
63:9 *depths.* See note on 30:1. *earth.* Here, the nether world or grave (see note on 61:2).
63:10 *prey for foxes.* Like bodies of enemies left unburied on the battlefield to add to their disgrace (see note on 53:5).
63:11 *Everyone who swears by Him.* Those who revere and trust God (see Deut 6:13). *mouths of those who speak lies.* Those who live by falsehood.
Ps 64 Prayer to God for protection when threatened by a conspiracy. The circumstances may be similar to those reflected in Ps 62 (see introduction to that psalm), but here there is no allusion to the king's weakened condition, and it is not clear whether the conspirators come from within or outside Israel (see note on v. 2). As so often in the prayers of the Psalter, the enemy's tongue is his main weapon (see note on 5:9). The prayer is framed by a plea for protection (vv. 1–2) and a confident word concerning the effects of God's saving action (vv. 9–10). At the center, vv. 5–6 describe the disdainful confidence of the conspirators. Verses 3–4 relate how the enemies attack with their tongues, while vv. 7–8 proclaim how God will turn their tongues against them.
64 title See note on Ps 4 title.
64:1–2 The prayer for protection.
64:1 *Hear.* In Hebrew a wordplay on the word for "be glad" in v. 10 (see note there).

From the tumult of [b]those who do
iniquity,
3 Who [a]have sharpened their tongue
like a sword.
They [b]aimed bitter speech *as* their
arrow,
4 To [a]shoot [1]from concealment at the
blameless;
Suddenly they shoot at him, and [b]do
not fear.
5 They [1]hold fast to themselves an evil
purpose;
They [2]talk of [a]laying snares secretly;
They say, "[b]Who can see them?"
6 They [1]devise injustices, *saying*,
"We are [2]ready with a well-conceived
plot";
For the [3a]inward thought and the
heart of a man are [4]deep.

7 But [a]God [1]will shoot at them with an
arrow;
Suddenly [2]they will be wounded.
8 So [1]they [2]will [a]make him stumble;
[b]Their own tongue is against them;
All who see them will [c]shake the
head.
9 Then all men [1]will [a]fear,
And they [2]will [b]declare the work of
God,
And [3]will consider [4]what He has done.
10 The righteous man will be [a]glad in the
LORD and will [b]take refuge in Him;
And all the upright in heart will glory.

2 [b]Ps 59:2
3 [a]Ps 140:3 [b]Ps 58:7
4 [1]Lit *in* [a]Ps 10:8; 11:2 [b]Ps 55:19
5 [1]Lit *make firm* [2]Lit *tell of* [a]Ps 140:5 [b]Job 22:13; Ps 10:11
6 [1]Or *search out* [2]Lit *complete* [3]Or *inward part* [4]Or *unsearchable* [a]Ps 49:11
7 [1]Or *shot* [2]Or *they were wounded;* lit *their wounds occurred* [a]Ps 7:12, 13
8 [1]Or *they make their tongue a stumbling for themselves* [2]Or *made* [a]Ps 9:3 [b]Prov 12:13; 18:7 [c]Ps 22:7; 44:14; Jer 18:16; 48:27; Lam 2:15
9 [1]Or *feared* [2]Or *declared* [3]Or *considered* [4]Lit *His work* [a]Ps 40:3 [b]Jer 51:10
10 [a]Job 22:19; Ps 32:11 [b]Ps 11:1; 25:20

65:1 [1]Lit *to* [a]Ps 116:18
2 [1]Lit *flesh* [a]Ps 86:9; 145:21; Is 66:23
3 [1]Lit *Words of iniquities* [2]Lit *cover over, atone for* [a]Ps 38:4; 40:12 [b]Ps 79:9

Psalm 65

For the choir director. A Psalm of David.
A Song.

1 There will be silence [1]before You, *and*
praise in Zion, O God,
And to You the [a]vow will be
performed.
2 O You who hear prayer,
To You [a]all [1]men come.
3 [1a]Iniquities prevail against me;
As for our transgressions, You
[2b]forgive them.
4 How [a]blessed is the one whom You
[b]choose and bring near *to You*
To dwell in Your courts.
We will be [c]satisfied with the
goodness of Your house,
Your holy temple.

5 By [a]awesome *deeds* You answer us in
righteousness, O [b]God of our
salvation,
You who are the trust of all the [c]ends
of the earth and of the farthest
[1d]sea;
6 Who [a]establishes the mountains by
His strength,
Being [b]girded with might;
7 Who [a]stills the roaring of the seas,
The roaring of their waves,

4 [a]Ps 33:12; 84:4 [b]Ps 4:3 [c]Ps 36:8 **5** [1]Or *seas* [a]Ps 45:4; 66:3 [b]Ps 85:4 [c]Ps 22:27; 48:10 [d]Ps 107:23 **6** [a]Ps 95:4 [b]Ps 93:1
7 [a]Ps 89:9; 93:3, 4; 107:29; Matt 8:26

64:2 *tumult.* The Hebrew root underlying this expression is the same as that for "uproar" in 2:1.
64:3–4 The enemy attacks.
64:3 *tongue.* See note on 5:9. *swords . . . arrow.* See 59:7.
64:4 *do not fear.* They feel themselves secure from exposure and retaliation, but see vv. 7–8.
64:5–6 The enemies' contemptuous self-confidence.
64:5 *They say.* See notes on 3:2; 10:11.
64:6 *heart.* See note on 4:7. *deep.* See Prov 18:4; 20:5.
64:7–8 Confidence in God's righteous judgment: He will do to them what they had intended to do to David (see 63:9–10 and note). *shoot . . . arrow, Suddenly . . . tongue.* See vv. 3–4.
64:8 *shake the head.* In scorn (see 44:14 and note).
64:9–10 The happy effects of God's judgment: All mankind will fear, proclaim, ponder (see note on 46:10); the righteous will rejoice, take refuge, praise.
64:9 See 58:11; see also 40:3; 52:6; 65:8.
64:10 *righteous.* See note on 1:5. *be glad.* In Hebrew this is the first word of this verse, and it is a wordplay on the Hebrew for "Hear," which is the first word of the first verse.
Ps 65 A hymn in praise of God's great goodness to His people. In answer to their prayers (1) He pardons their sins so that they continue to enjoy the "goodness" of fellowship with Him at His temple (vv. 3–4); (2) He orders the affairs of the world so that international turbulence is put to rest and Israel is secure in her land (vv. 5–8); and (3) He turns the promised land into a veritable Garden of Eden (vv. 9–13). This hymn begins a series of four that are linked by many common themes.
65 title See notes on Ps 4; 30 titles.
65:1–2 Introductory commitment to praise.
65:1 *silence before You.* Perhaps the imagery is that of praise personified as a permanent resident of the temple, lying quietly at rest, whom the people will awaken when they come to make good their vows (see 57:8). *the vow.* Made in conjunction with their prayers in time of need (see 66:14 and note on 7:17).
65:2 *all men.* Lit. "all flesh," perhaps referring to all God's people, as in Joel 2:28 ("all mankind"). Most interpreters believe (in light of vv. 5,8) that the reference is more universal, as in 64:9; 66:1,4,8; 67:3–5 and elsewhere. *come.* To praise God as the (only) God who hears and graciously answers prayers.
65:3–4 The first and primary blessing.
65:3 *our transgressions, You forgive them.* You accept the atonement sacrifices You appointed and so forgive (make atonement for—see NASB marg.) our sins (see 32:1–2; 78:38; 79:9 and notes on Lev 16:20–22; 17:11; Heb 2:17; 9:5,7).
65:4 *blessed.* See note on 1:1. *the one whom You choose and bring near.* Everyone belonging to Israel as God's chosen people (see, e.g., 33:12; Deut 4:37) and whom God accepts at His temple. *dwell in Your courts.* See note on 15:1; see also 23:6. *goodness of Your house.* All the blessings that flow from God's presence (see 36:8 and note).
65:5–8 God stills the nations and makes Israel secure in answer to her prayers.
65:5 *awesome deeds.* Acts of God such as were associated with His deliverance of Israel from Egypt and the conquest of Canaan, acts of power that made Israel's enemies cringe (see 66:3; see also 106:22; 145:6; Deut 10:21; 2 Sam 7:23; Is 64:3). *righteousness.* Saving acts by which God kept His covenanted promises to Israel (see note on 5:8). *trust of all.* Even though the nations of the world did not yet know it.
65:6–7 The God of creation who by His power brought order

And the [b]tumult of the peoples.
8 They who dwell in the [a]ends *of the earth* stand in awe of Your signs;
You make the [1]dawn and the sunset shout for joy.

9 You visit the earth and [a]cause it to overflow;
You greatly [b]enrich it;
The [1c]stream of God is full of water;
You prepare their [d]grain, for thus You prepare [2]the earth.
10 You water its furrows abundantly,
You [1]settle its ridges,
You soften it [a]with showers,
You bless its growth.
11 You have crowned the year [1]with Your [2a]bounty,
And Your [3]paths [b]drip *with* fatness.
12 [a]The pastures of the wilderness drip,
And the [b]hills gird themselves with rejoicing.
13 The meadows are [a]clothed with flocks
And the valleys are [b]covered with grain;
They [c]shout for joy, yes, they sing.

7 [b]Ps 2:1; 74:23; Is 17:12, 13
8 [1]Lit *the outgoings of the morning and evening* [a]Ps 2:8; 139:9; Is 24:16
9 [1]Or *channel* [2]Lit *it* [a]Lev 26:4; Job 5:10; Ps 68:9; 104:13; 147:8; Jer 5:24 [b]Ps 104:24 [c]Ps 46:4 [d]Ps 104:14; 147:14
10 [1]Or *smooth* [a]Deut 32:2; Ps 72:6; 147:8
11 [1]Lit *of* [2]Or *goodness* [3]I.e. wagon tracks [a]Ps 104:28 [b]Job 36:28; Ps 147:14
12 [a]Job 38:26, 27; Joel 2:22 [b]Ps 98:8; Is 55:12
13 [a]Ps 144:13; Is 30:23 [b]Ps 72:16 [c]Ps 98:8; Is 44:23; 55:12

66:1 [a]Ps 81:1; 95:1; 98:4; 100:1
2 [a]Ps 79:9; Is 42:8 [b]Is 42:12
3 [1]Lit *deceive* [a]Ps 47:2; 65:5; 145:6 [b]Ps 18:44; 81:15
4 [1]*Selah* may mean: *Pause, Crescendo* or *Musical interlude* [a]Ps 22:27; 67:7; 86:9; 117:1; Zech 14:16 [b]Ps 67:4
5 [a]Ps 46:8 [b]Ps 106:22
6 [a]Ex 14:21; Ps 106:9 [b]Josh 3:16; Ps 114:3 [c]Ps 105:43
7 [a]Ps 145:13 [b]Ps 11:4

Psalm 66

For the choir director. A Song. A Psalm.

1 [a]Shout joyfully to God, all the earth;
2 Sing the [a]glory of His name;
Make His [b]praise glorious.
3 Say to God, "How [a]awesome are Your works!
Because of the greatness of Your power Your enemies will [1b]give feigned obedience to You.
4 "[a]All the earth will worship You,
And will [b]sing praises to You;
They will sing praises to Your name."
[1]Selah.

5 [a]Come and see the works of God,
Who is [b]awesome in *His* deeds toward the sons of men.
6 He [a]turned the sea into dry land;
They passed through [b]the river on foot;
There let us [c]rejoice in Him!
7 He [a]rules by His might forever;
His [b]eyes keep watch on the nations;

to the world out of the earlier chaos (see Gen 1) similarly in the redemption of His people establishes a peaceful order among nations (see Is 2:4; 11:6–9; Mic 4:3–4) so that Israel may be at rest in the promised land (see also Ps 33; 46). God's mighty acts in redemption are often compared by OT poets with His mighty acts in creation (see 74:12–17; 89:9–18; Is 27:1; 40:6–14,21–31; 51:9–11), since His power as Creator guaranteed His power as Redeemer. *establishes the mountains . . . stills . . . the seas.* Gives order to the whole creation (see 95:4–5).

65:7 *tumult of the peoples.* God's stilling the turbulence of the nations—which often threatened Israel—is compared to His taming the turbulence of the primeval waters of chaos (see notes on 32:6; 33:7).

65:8 All peoples will (ultimately) see God's saving acts in behalf of His people and will be moved to fear (see note on 46:10). And all creation will rejoice (see v. 13). *signs.* Referring to God's great saving acts, such as those He performed when He delivered Israel out of Egypt (Deut 4:34; see Ps 78:43; 105:27; 135:9). As "signs" they indicated that God was at work (see John 2:11 and note).

65:9–13 God blesses the promised land with all good things in answer to Israel's prayers.

65:9 *stream of God.* See note on 36:8.

65:11 *bounty.* Lit. "goodness" (see 68:10; see also 31:19 and note).

65:13 *They shout for joy, yes, they sing.* In the exuberant language of the psalmists, all creation—even its inanimate elements—joins the human chorus to celebrate the goodness of God in creation, blessing and redemption (see 89:12; 96:11–13; 98:8–9; 103:22; 145:10; 148:3–4,7–10; see also Job 38:7; Is 44:23; 49:13; 55:12).

Ps 66 A psalm of praise for God's answer to prayer. It seems that God has saved the author, probably a king, from an enemy threat, and his deliverance has involved also that of the whole nation. It has often been suggested that the psalm speaks of Judah's remarkable deliverance from the Assyrians (see 2 Kin 19). The praise is offered at the temple in fulfillment of a vow (vv. 13–14; see note on 7:17). Such praise was often climaxed by a call for others to take up the praise (see note on 9:1). Here the psalmist exuberantly begins with that call and, as often elsewhere (e.g., 67:3–5; 68:32; 98:4; 99:3; 100:1; 117:1), addresses it even to the far corners of the earth. This psalm is the second in a series of four (see introduction to Ps 65). The psalm is framed by a call to praise (vv. 1–2) and a declaration of the present occasion for praise (vv. 19–20, in Hebrew involving a play on words—the Hebrew for "Blessed" and "prayer" sound very much alike). The first line of the first stanza of the first sequence (v. 5) begins with "Come and see"; the first line of the second stanza of the second sequence (v. 16) begins with "Come and hear."

66 title See notes on Ps 4; 30 titles.

66:1–4 Calling all the earth to joyful praise.

66:1 *all the earth.* See note on 65:2.

66:2 *name.* See note on 5:11.

66:3 *awesome.* See v. 5; see also note on 65:5. *give feigned obedience.* See 81:15.

66:4 See note on 46:10.

66:5–7 Recollection of God's deliverance of Israel at the Red Sea as a sign of His power to rule over the nations. The psalmist portrays His deliverance (see introduction above) both as similar to this Red Sea rescue in its manifestation of God's saving power (see 65:5–7 for a comparison of God's mighty saving acts with His mighty acts of creation) and as a continuation of God's same saving purposes.

66:5 *Come and see.* God's saving acts of old can still be "seen" at His temple, where they are continually celebrated (see 46:8; 48:8–9 and notes). *toward the sons of men.* Specifically in behalf of His people.

66:6 *river.* Possibly the Jordan, but more likely a parallel reference to the Red Sea.

66:7 *rebellious.* Nations that are in revolt against God's rule (see 68:6).

Let not the rebellious [c]exalt
themselves. Selah.

8 Bless our God, O peoples,
And [1][a]sound His praise abroad,
9 Who [1][a]keeps us in life
And [b]does not allow our feet to [2]slip.
10 For You have [a]tried us, O God;
You have [b]refined us as silver is
refined.
11 You [a]brought us into the net;
You laid an oppressive burden upon
our loins.
12 You made men [a]ride over our heads;
We went through [b]fire and through
water,
Yet You [c]brought us out into *a place of*
abundance.
13 I shall [a]come into Your house with
burnt offerings;
I shall [b]pay You my vows,
14 Which my lips uttered
And my mouth spoke when I was [a]in
distress.
15 I shall [a]offer to You burnt offerings of
fat beasts,
With the smoke of [b]rams;
I shall make *an offering of* [1]bulls with
male goats. Selah.

16 [a]Come *and* hear, all who [1]fear God,
And I will [b]tell of what He has done
for my soul.
17 I cried to Him with my mouth,
And [1]He was [a]extolled with my
tongue.
18 If I [1][a]regard wickedness in my heart,
The [b]Lord [2]will not [3]hear;
19 But certainly [a]God has heard;
He has given heed to the voice of my
prayer.
20 [a]Blessed be God,
Who [b]has not turned away my prayer
Nor His lovingkindness from me.

7 [c]Ps 140:8
8 [1]Lit *cause to hear the sound of His praise* [a]Ps 98:4
9 [1]Lit *puts our soul in life* [2]Or *dodder, stumble* [a]Ps 30:3 [b]Ps 121:3
10 [a]Job 23:10; Ps 7:9; 17:3; 26:2 [b]Is 48:10; Zech 13:9; Mal 3:3; 1 Pet 1:7
11 [a]Lam 1:13; Ezek 12:13
12 [a]Is 51:23 [b]Ps 78:21; Is 43:2 [c]Ps 18:19
13 [a]Ps 96:8; Jer 17:26 [b]Ps 22:25; 116:14; Eccl 5:4
14 [a]Ps 18:6
15 [1]Or *cattle* [a]Ps 51:19 [b]Num 6:14
16 [1]Or *revere* [a]Ps 34:11 [b]Ps 71:15, 24
17 [1]Or *praise was under my tongue* [a]Ps 30:1
18 [1]Or *had regarded* [2]Or *would* [3]Or *have heard* [a]Job 36:21; John 9:31 [b]Job 27:9; Ps 18:41; Prov 1:28; 28:9; Is 1:15; James 4:3
19 [a]Ps 18:6; 116:1, 2
20 [a]Ps 68:35 [b]Ps 22:24

Psalm 67

For the choir director; with stringed instruments.
A Psalm. A Song.

1 God be gracious to us and [a]bless us,
And [b]cause His face to shine [1]upon
us— [2]Selah.
2 That [a]Your way may be known on the
earth,
[b]Your salvation among all nations.
3 Let the [a]peoples praise You, O God;
Let all the peoples praise You.
4 Let the [a]nations be glad and sing for
joy;
For You will [b]judge the peoples with
uprightness
And [c]guide the nations on the earth.
Selah.
5 Let the [a]peoples praise You, O God;
Let all the peoples praise You.

67:1 [1]Lit *with* [2]*Selah* may mean: *Pause, Crescendo* or *Musical interlude* [a]Num 6:25 [b]Ps 4:6; 31:16; 80:3, 7, 19; 119:135
2 [a]Ps 98:2; Acts 18:25; Titus 2:11 [b]Is 52:10 **3** [a]Ps 66:4
4 [a]Ps 100:1, 2 [b]Ps 9:8; 96:10, 13; 98:9 [c]Ps 47:8 **5** [a]Ps 67:3

66:8–12 Proclamation in praise of God's new deliverance of His people.

66:8 *peoples.* Here probably the grateful throng of worshipers (see 2 Chr 20:27–28).

66:9 *feet to slip.* See note on 38:16.

66:10 *have tried . . . have refined.* From one point of view, times of distress constitute a testing of God's people as to their trust in and loyalty to God. The metaphor is borrowed from the technology of refining precious metals, which included heating the metals in a crucible to see if all impurities had been removed (see 12:6; 17:3).

66:11–12 *You . . . You.* God's rule is all-pervasive; even when enemies for malicious purposes attack His people, God is not a mere passive observer but has His own holy purposes in it (see Is 45:7; Amos 3:6). *net . . . burden . . . ride over.* Three metaphors describe their suffering: captives thrown into prison, prisoners of war turned into slaves, defeated troops overrun by a chariot force.

66:12 *fire and . . . water.* Conventional metaphors for severe trials (see Is 43:2). *into a place of abundance.* Lit. "to an overflowing" (see 23:5). They were brought out of a situation of distress into a situation of overflowing well-being.

66:13–15 Announcement of fulfillment of vows: addressed to God (see note on 7:17; see also 50:14; 116:17–19).

66:13 *I.* The king.

66:16–20 Proclamation of what God has done: in praise of God, addressed to the worshiping congregation.

66:16 *fear God.* See note on Gen 20:11.

66:17 *He was extolled.* Prayer and praise belonged together in the OT (see also Phil 4:6; 1 Tim 2:1).

66:20 *Blessed be God.* See v. 8. *lovingkindness.* See note on 6:4.

Ps 67 A communal prayer for God's blessing. Its content, form and brevity suggest that it served as a liturgical prayer of the people at the conclusion of worship, perhaps just prior to (or immediately after) the priestly benediction (see note on v. 1). God's blessing of His people (as well as His saving acts in their behalf) will catch the attention of the nations and move them to praise (see 65:2). This psalm is the third in a series of four (see introduction to Ps 65). It has a symmetrical structure: Two verses at the beginning contain the prayer, while the two concluding verses speak of the effects of God's answer. In the intervening verses, framed by a refrain (vv. 3,5), the people seek to motivate God's answer by referring to the worldwide praise that His mercies to His people will awaken.

67 title See notes on Ps 4; 30 titles.

67:1–2 The prayer.

67:1 The heart of the prayer, anticipating (or echoing) the priestly benediction (see Num 6:24–26). *cause His face to shine.* See notes on 4:6; 13:1.

67:2 May God's favors to His people be so obvious that all the world takes notice (see note on 46:10).

67:3–5 The motivation. Elaborating on v. 2, the people speak of the worldwide praise that will resound to God when He graciously blesses His people. Their wish is twofold: (1) that God's blessings may be so abundant that the people will be moved to praise, and (2) that the nations may indeed add their praise to that of Israel—an appropriate expression at this climax of the liturgy of worship.

67:4 May the nations rejoice in the Lord when they see how benevolent the rule of God is (see 98:4–6; 100:1).

6 The [a]earth has yielded its produce;
God, our God, [b]blesses us.
7 God blesses us,
[1]That [a]all the ends of the earth may
fear Him.

Psalm 68

For the choir director. A Psalm of David. A Song.

1 [1]Let [a]God arise, [2]let His enemies be
scattered,
And [3]let those who hate Him flee
before Him.
2 As [a]smoke is driven away, *so* drive
them away;
As [b]wax melts before the fire,
So let the [c]wicked perish before God.
3 But let the [a]righteous be glad; let
them exult before God;
Yes, let them rejoice with gladness.
4 Sing to God, [a]sing praises to His
name;
[1b]Lift up *a song* for Him who [c]rides
through the deserts,
Whose [d]name is [2]the LORD, and exult
before Him.

5 A [a]father of the fatherless and a
[b]judge [1]for the widows,
Is God in His [c]holy habitation.

6 [a]Lev 26:4; Ps 85:12; Ezek 34:27; Zech 8:12 [b]Ps 29:11; 115:12
7 [1]Or *And let all...earth fear Him* [a]Ps 22:27; 33:8
68:1 [1]Or *God shall* [2]Or *His enemies shall* [3]Or *those who hate Him shall* [a]Num 10:35; Ps 12:5; 132:8
2 [a]Ps 37:20; Is 9:18; Hos 13:3 [b]Ps 22:14; 97:5; Mic 1:4 [c]Ps 9:3; 37:20; 80:16
3 [a]Ps 32:11; 64:10; 97:12
4 [1]Or *Cast up* a highway [2]Heb YAH [a]Ps 66:2 [b]Is 57:14; 62:10 [c]Deut 33:26; Ps 18:10; 68:33; Is 40:3 [d]Ex 6:3; Ps 83:18
5 [1]Lit *of* [a]Ps 10:14; 146:9 [b]Deut 10:18 [c]Deut 26:15
6 [1]Lit *makes the solitary to dwell in a house* [a]Ps 107:4-7; 113:9 [b]Ps 69:33; 102:20; 107:10, 14; 146:7; Acts 12:7; 16:26 [c]Ps 78:17; 107:34, 40

6 God [1a]makes a home for the lonely;
He [b]leads out the prisoners into
prosperity,
Only [c]the rebellious dwell in a
parched land.

7 O God, when You [a]went forth before
Your people,
When You [b]marched through the
wilderness, [1]Selah.
8 The [a]earth quaked;
The [b]heavens also dropped *rain* at the
presence of God;
[1c]Sinai itself *quaked* at the presence of
God, the God of Israel.
9 You [a]shed abroad a plentiful rain,
O God;
You confirmed Your inheritance when
it was [1]parched.
10 Your creatures settled in it;
You [a]provided in Your goodness for
the poor, O God.

11 The Lord gives the [1]command;
The [a]women who proclaim the *good*
tidings are a great host:

7 [1]*Selah* may mean: *Pause, Crescendo* or *Musical interlude* [a]Ex 13:21; Ps 78:14; Hab 3:13 [b]Judg 5:4; Ps 78:52 **8** [1]Lit *This is Sinai* which [a]Ex 19:18; Judg 5:4; 2 Sam 22:8; Ps 77:18; Jer 10:10 [b]Judg 5:4; Ps 18:9; Is 45:8 [c]Ex 19:18; Judg 5:5 **9** [1]Lit *weary* [a]Lev 26:4; Deut 11:11; Job 5:10; Ezek 34:26 **10** [a]Ps 65:9; 74:19; 78:20; 107:9 **11** [1]Lit *word* [a]Ex 15:20; 1 Sam 18:6

67:6–7 The effects of God's blessing His people.
67:6 The promised land will yield its abundance (see 65:9–13).
Ps 68 A processional liturgy celebrating the glorious and triumphant rule of Israel's God (see introductions to Ps 24; 47; 118; 132). Verses 1–18 contain many clear references to God's triumphal march from Mount Sinai (in the days of Moses) to Mount Zion (in the days of David). The events at Mount Sinai marked the birth of the kingdom of God among His people; the establishing of the ark of the covenant, symbol of God's throne, in Jerusalem marked the establishment of God's redemptive kingdom in the earth, with Jerusalem as its royal city. The early church, taking its cue from Eph 4:8–13, understood this psalm to foreshadow the resurrection, ascension and present rule of Christ and the final triumph of His church over the hostile world. Ps 68 is the last in a series of four (see introduction to Ps 65).

The psalm is composed of nine stanzas, with the last line as a concluding doxology. The first stanza indicates the beginning of the liturgical procession, and the last refers to its conclusion—God enthroned in His sanctuary. The seventh (vv. 24–27) speaks expressly of the procession coming into view and entering the sanctuary. In light of these clear references, the third stanza (vv. 7–10) suggests a stage in the procession recalling the wilderness journey from Sinai to the promised land, while the fifth (vv. 15–18) marks that stage in which the Lord ascends Mount Zion. On the other hand, the second stanza (vv. 5–6) reflects on the benevolence of God's rule; the fourth (vv. 11–14) recalls His victories over the kings of Canaan; the sixth (vv. 19–23) speaks reassuringly of God's future victories; and the eighth (vv. 28–31) contains prayers that God may muster His power to subdue the enemy as He had done before.
68 title See notes on Ps 4; 30 titles.
68:1–3 The start of the procession, liturgically recalling the beginning of God's march with his people in army formation from Sinai (see Num 10:33–35).
68:1 *enemies be scattered.* See note on v. 30.
68:3 *righteous.* Israel as the committed people of God in distinction from those opposed to the coming of God's kingdom (the "wicked" of v. 2).
68:4–6 A call to praise God for the benevolence of His rule.
68:4 *name.* See note on 5:11. *who rides through the deserts.* Or "who rides on the clouds." With this reading, an epithet of Baal found in Canaanite literature is used to make the point that the Lord (Yahweh, not Baal) is the exalted One who truly makes the storm cloud His chariot (see v. 33; 18:9; 104:3; Is 19:1; Matt 26:64).
68:5–6 God is the defender of the powerless (see 10:14; 146:7–9; 147:6; Deut 10:18).
68:6 *makes a home for the lonely.* See Ex 1:21; Ruth 4:14–17; 1 Sam 2:5. *leads out the prisoners.* As He led Israel out of Egypt (see 69:33; 107:10,14). *rebellious.* See notes on v. 18; 66:7. *parched land.* A place utterly barren, lacking even soil for vegetation (see Ezek 26:4,14).
68:7–10 Recollection of God's march through the wilderness from Sinai into the promised land (see Judg 5:4–5; Hab 3:3–6).
68:8 *earth quaked.* A reference to the quaking of Mount Sinai (Ex 19:18). *heavens also dropped rain.* The Pentateuch preserves no tradition of rain during the wilderness wanderings, but here (and in Judg 5:4) rain is closely associated with the quaking of the earth as a manifestation of the majesty of God. Perhaps the "thunder and lightning flashes and a thick cloud" over Mount Sinai (Ex 19:16) were accompanied by rain. But see also v. 9, which suggests rains that refreshed the people on their journey.
68:9 *Your inheritance.* The people of Israel (see Deut 9:29).
68:10 *it.* Probably refers to the promised land. *goodness.* See 65:11 and note. *provided.* From the produce of Canaan (see Josh 5:11–12). *poor.* Israel as a people dependent on God.
68:11–14 Recollection of God's victories over the kings of Canaan.
68:11 *gives the command.* God declares beforehand that He would be victorious over the Canaanite kings (see Ex 23:22–23, 27–28,31; Deut 7:10–24; 11:23–25; Josh 1:2–6). *proclaim the*

12 "[a]Kings of armies flee, they flee,
And she who remains at home will
[b]divide the spoil!"
13 [1]When you lie down [a]among the
[2]sheepfolds,
You are like the wings of a dove
covered with silver,
And its pinions with glistening gold.
14 When the Almighty [a]scattered the
kings [1]there,
It was snowing in [b]Zalmon.

15 A [1][a]mountain of God is the mountain
of Bashan;
A mountain *of many* peaks is the
mountain of Bashan.
16 Why do you look with envy, O
mountains with *many* peaks,
At the mountain which God has
[a]desired for His abode?
Surely [b]the LORD will dwell *there*
forever.
17 The [a]chariots of God are [1]myriads,
[b]thousands upon thousands;
[2]The Lord is among them *as at* Sinai,
in holiness.
18 You have [a]ascended on high, You have
[b]led captive *Your* captives;
You have received gifts among
men,
Even *among* the rebellious also, that
[1]the LORD God may dwell *there*.

19 Blessed be the Lord, who daily [a]bears
our burden,
[b]The God *who* is our salvation. Selah.
20 God is to us a [a]God of deliverances;
And [b]to [1]GOD the Lord belong escapes
[2]from death.
21 Surely God will [a]shatter the head of
His enemies,
The hairy crown of him who goes on
in his guilty deeds.
22 The Lord [1]said, "[a]I will bring *them*
back from Bashan.
I will bring *them* back from the depths
of the sea;
23 That [1][a]your foot may shatter *them* in
blood,
The tongue of your [b]dogs *may have* its
portion from *your* enemies."

24 They have seen [a]Your [1]procession,
O God,
The [1]procession of my God, my King,
[2][b]into the sanctuary.
25 The [a]singers went on, the musicians
after *them*,
[1]In the midst of the [b]maidens beating
tambourines.
26 [a]Bless God in the congregations,

12 [a]Josh 10:16; Judg 5:19; Ps 135:11 [b]Judg 5:30; 1 Sam 30:24
13 [1]Lit *If* [2]Or *cooking stones* or *saddle bags* [a]Gen 49:14; Judg 5:16
14 [1]Lit *in it* [a]Josh 10:10 [b]Judg 9:48
15 [1]Or *mighty mountain is* [a]Ps 36:6
16 [a]Deut 12:5; Ps 87:1, 2; 132:13 [b]Ps 132:14
17 [1]Lit *twice ten thousand* [2]Another reading is *The Lord came from Sinai into the sanctuary* [a]2 Kin 6:17; Hab 3:8 [b]Deut 33:2; Dan 7:10
18 [1]Heb YAH [a]Ps 7:7; 47:5; Eph 4:8 [b]Judg 5:12
19 [a]Ps 55:22; Is 46:4 [b]Ps 65:5
20 [1]Heb *YHWH*, usually rendered LORD [2]I.e. in view of; lit *for* [a]Ps 106:43 [b]Deut 32:39; Ps 49:15; 56:13
21 [a]Ps 110:6; Hab 3:13
22 [1]Or *says* [a]Num 21:33; Amos 9:1-3
23 [1]Some versions render, you may *bathe your foot in blood* [a]Ps 58:10 [b]1 Kin 21:19; Jer 15:3
24 [1]Lit *goings* [2]Lit *in the sanctuary;* or *in holiness* [a]Ps 77:13 [b]Ps 63:2
25 [1]Or *The maidens in the midst* [a]1 Chr 13:8; 15:6; Ps 47:6 [b]Ex 15:20; Judg 11:34
26 [a]Ps 22:22, 23; 26:12

good tidings. Celebrate God's victories (see Ex 15:1–21; 1 Sam 18:6–7; 2 Chr 20:26–28). *proclaim.* See 40:9 and note.

68:13 *lie down among the sheepfolds.* Rest in camp (see NASB marg.; see also Gen 49:14; Judg 5:16). *wings of a dove covered with silver.* Israel, God's "dove" (see 74:19 and note; cf. Hos 7:11), is enriched with the silver and gold of plunder from the kings of Canaan even though she still remains in camp. This poetic hyperbole (a figure of speech that uses exaggeration for emphasis) celebrates the fact that God had defeated the kings even before Israel met them in battle (see Josh 2:8–11; 5:1; 6:16; see also 2 Sam 5:24; 2 Kin 7:5–7; 19:35; 2 Chr 20:22–30).

68:14 *Almighty.* Hebrew *Shaddai* (see note on Gen 17:1). *snowing in Zalmon.* Zalmon was a mountain near Shechem (see Judg 9:46–48), but others identify it here as Jebel Druze, a dark volcanic mountain east of Bashan. Its name appears to mean "the dark one"—in distinction from the Lebanon ("the white one") range, composed of limestone—and the figure may involve the contrast of white snow scattered on "Dark Mountain." The reference may then be to abandoned weapons littering the field from which the kings have fled headlong (see 2 Kin 7:15).

68:15–18 Celebration of God's ascent to Mount Zion.

68:15–16 The mountains surrounding Bashan, including the towering Mount Hermon, are portrayed as being jealous because God has chosen Mount Zion as the seat of His rule, making it the "highest" of mountains (see 48:2 and note).

68:17 *chariots of God.* God's great heavenly host, here likened to a vast chariot force (see 2 Kin 6:17; Hab 3:8,15). In the time of the Roman empire Jesus referred to God's host in terms of "legions" (Matt 26:53).

68:18 *ascended on high.* Went up to Your place of enthronement on Mount Zion (see 47:5–6 and note; see also 7:7). *led captive . . . received gifts.* Like a victorious king after triumphs on the field of battle. *rebellious.* Those who had opposed the kingdom of God (see v. 6 and note on 66:7) are compelled to submit to Him and bring tribute. *that the LORD God may dwell there.* Grammatically completes the clause, "You have ascended on high." Paul applies this verse (as translated in the Septuagint) to the ascended Christ (Eph 4:8–13), thereby implying that Christ's ascension was a continuation of, and a fulfillment of, God's establishment of His kingdom in His royal city Jerusalem (see introduction).

68:19–23 Joyous confession of hope that God's victorious campaigns will continue until the salvation of His people is complete.

68:19 *bears our burden.* Releases us from bearing the burdens that enslavement to our enemies would impose on us (see 81:6; Is 9:4; 10:27). But some associate this line with such passages as 55:22; Is 46:4.

68:20 *escapes from death.* At the hand of our enemies—implicitly, perhaps, also from death itself as the last great enemy (see notes on 6:5; 11:7; 16:9–11; 17:15; 49:14–15).

68:21 As God assures the life of His people (see v. 20), so He will crush those who oppose Him. *shatter the head.* See Num 24:17.

68:22 *them.* The enemies who fled at the victorious onward march of God and His host (see vv. 12,17). *Bashan . . . depths of the sea.* The former (see also v. 15) was the high plateau east of the Jordan, the latter the Mediterranean Sea—none of the enemies will escape (see Amos 9:1–4).

68:23 See note on 58:10.

68:24–27 The liturgical procession approaches the temple (see Ps 24; 47).

68:25 *maidens beating tambourines.* See note on Jer 31:4.

Even the LORD, *you who are* of the
[b]fountain of Israel.
27 There is [a]Benjamin, the [1]youngest,
[2]ruling them,
The princes of Judah *in* their throng,
The princes of [b]Zebulun, the princes
of Naphtali.

28 [1]Your God has [a]commanded your
strength;
Show Yourself strong, O God, [b]who
have acted [2]on our behalf.
29 [1]Because of Your temple at Jerusalem
[a]Kings will bring gifts to You.
30 Rebuke the [a]beasts [1]in the reeds,
The herd of [b]bulls with the calves of
the peoples,
Trampling under foot the pieces of
silver;
He has [c]scattered the peoples who
delight in war.
31 Envoys will come out of [a]Egypt;
[1][b]Ethiopia will quickly stretch out her
hands to God.

32 Sing to God, O [a]kingdoms of the
earth,
[b]Sing praises to the Lord, Selah.
33 To Him who [a]rides upon the [1][b]highest
heavens, which are from ancient
times;
Behold, [c]He [2]speaks forth with His
voice, a [d]mighty voice.
34 [a]Ascribe strength to God;
His majesty is over Israel
And [b]His strength is in the [1]skies.
35 [1]O God, *You are* [a]awesome from Your
[2]sanctuary.
The God of Israel Himself [b]gives
strength and power to the people.
[c]Blessed be God!

26 [b]Deut 33:28; Is 48:1 **27** [1]Or *smallest* [2]Or *their ruler* [a]Judg 5:14; 1 Sam 9:21 [b]Judg 5:18 **28** [1]Some mss read *Command, God* [2]Lit *for us* [a]Ps 29:11; 44:4 [b]Is 26:12 **29** [1]Or *From Your temple* [a]1 Kin 10:10, 25; 2 Chr 32:23; Ps 45:12; 72:10; Is 18:7 **30** [1]Lit *of* [a]Job 40:21; Ezek 29:3 [b]Ps 22:12 [c]Ps 18:14; 89:10 **31** [1]Lit *Cush* [a]Is 19:19, 21 [b]Is 45:14; Zeph 3:10 **32** [a]Ps 102:22 [b]Ps 67:4 **33** [1]Lit *heaven of heavens of old* [2]Lit *gives forth* [a]Deut 33:26; Ps 18:10; 104:3 [b]Deut 10:14; 1 Kin 8:27 [c]Ps 46:6 [d]Ps 29:4 **34** [a]Ps 29:1

34 [1]Lit *clouds* [b]Ps 150:1 **35** [1]Or *Awesome is God from your sanctuary* [2]Lit *holy places* [a]Deut 7:21; 10:17; Ps 47:2; 66:5 [b]Ps 29:11; Is 40:29 [c]Ps 66:20; 2 Cor 1:3 **69:1** †Or possibly *Lilies*

Psalm 69

For the choir director; according to †Shoshannim.
A Psalm of David.

1 Save me, O God,
For the [a]waters have [1]threatened my
life.
2 I have sunk in deep [a]mire, and there
is no foothold;
I have come into deep waters, and a
[1][b]flood overflows me.
3 I am [a]weary with my crying; my
throat is parched;
My [b]eyes fail while I wait for my
God.
4 Those [a]who hate me without a cause
are more than the hairs of my head;
Those who would [1]destroy me [b]are
powerful, being wrongfully my
enemies;
[c]What I did not steal, I then have to
restore.

[1]Lit *come to the soul* [a]Job 22:11; Ps 32:6; 42:7; 69:14, 15; Jon 2:5 **2** [1]Lit *flowing stream* [a]Ps 40:2 [b]Jon 2:3 **3** [a]Ps 6:6 [b]Deut 28:32; Ps 38:10; 119:82, 123; Is 38:14 **4** [1]Or *silence* [a]Ps 35:19; John 15:25 [b]Ps 35:19; 38:19; 59:3 [c]Ps 35:11; Jer 15:10

68:27 All Israel is represented, from little Benjamin to powerful Judah, and tribes from the north as well as the south. *Benjamin . . . ruling.* Perhaps reflecting the fact that from the tribe of Benjamin came the first king (Saul), who began the royal victories over Israel's enemies (see 1 Sam 11:11; 14:20–23).

68:28–31 Prayer for God to continue His conquest of the threatening powers.

68:28 *Your God has commanded your strength.* Or, perhaps, "Command Your power to act, O God."

68:29 *Because of Your temple.* Because Your earthly royal house has been established in Jerusalem. *bring gifts to You.* Acknowledge You by bringing tribute, as subjected kings brought tribute to their conquerors (see 2 Sam 8:2,6,10; 2 Kin 3:4).

68:30 *Rebuke.* See note on 76:6. *beast in the reeds.* Pharaoh (see Ezek 29:3). *herd of bulls with the calves.* Powerful princes supporting the pharaoh, and the lesser princes of other nations. Egypt is singled out here as representative of the hostile nations—because of Israel's past experiences with that world power and because at the time the psalm was composed it was the one great empire on Israel's immediate horizons. *scattered the peoples.* See v. 1; so that Israel may have peace (see 46:9; 48:4–7; 65:7; 76:3).

68:32–35 Climax of the liturgical procession: a call for all kingdoms to hail with praise the God of Israel as the God who reigns in heaven and has established His earthly throne in the temple in Jerusalem (see Ps 47).

68:33 See v. 4 and note. *speaks forth with . . . a mighty voice.* See note on 29:3–9.

68:35 *awesome.* See 45:4 and note. *gives strength and power to the people.* The Lord of all has made Israel His people (His "kingdom"; see Ex 19:5–6), and His rule among them makes them participants in His victorious power (see 29:10–11).

Ps 69 A plea for God to have mercy and to save from a host of enemies: the prayer of a godly king when under vicious attack by a widespread conspiracy at a time when God had "wounded" him (see v. 26) for some sin in his life (see v. 5). If, as tradition claims, David authored the original psalm (see the superscription), the occasion is unknown. In its present form the prayer suggests a later son of David who ruled over the southern kingdom of Judah (see v. 35). That king may have been Hezekiah (see 2 Kin 18–20; 2 Chr 29–32). In themes and language this psalm has many links with Ps 32; 35; 38; 40; 109 (all psalms "of David"; see also Ps 18). It begins a series of three prayers for deliverance when threatened by enemies. The authors of the NT viewed this cry of a godly sufferer as foreshadowing the sufferings of Christ; no psalm, except Ps 22, is quoted more frequently in the NT.

69 title *For the choir director.* See note on Ps 4 title. *according to.* See note on Ps 9 title. *Shoshannim.* See note on Ps 45 title.

69:1–4 Initial plea for God to save.

69:1–2 *waters . . . deep mire . . . deep waters . . . flood.* Conventional imagery for great distress (see notes on 30:1; 32:6)—here the results of God's "wounding" (see v. 26), but especially of the attacks of the enemies (see vv. 14–15,29).

69:3 *throat is parched.* See 22:15. *eyes fail.* See 6:7 and note.

69:4 *without a cause . . . wrongfully my enemies.* Those whom he has not wronged are pitted against him (see 35:19 and note). *more than the hairs of my head.* See note on 40:12. *I then have to.* An illustrative way of saying that his enemies are spreading false accusations about him (see 5:9 and note).

5 O God, it is You who knows [a]my folly,
And [b]my wrongs are not hidden from You.
6 May those who wait for You not [a]be ashamed through me, O Lord [1]GOD of hosts;
May those who seek You not be dishonored through me, O God of Israel,
7 Because [a]for Your sake I have borne reproach;
[b]Dishonor has covered my face.
8 I have become [a]estranged [1]from my brothers
And an alien to my mother's sons.
9 For [a]zeal for Your house has consumed me,
And [b]the reproaches of those who reproach You have fallen on me.
10 When I wept [a]in my soul with fasting,
It became my reproach.
11 When I made [a]sackcloth my clothing,
I became [b]a byword to them.
12 Those who [a]sit in the gate talk about me,
And I *am* the [1b]song of the drunkards.

13 But as for me, my prayer is to You,
O LORD, [a]at an acceptable time;
O God, in the [b]greatness of Your lovingkindness,
Answer me with [1]Your saving truth.
14 Deliver me from the [a]mire and do not let me sink;
May I be [b]delivered from [1]my foes and from the [2a]deep waters.
15 May the [1a]flood of water not overflow me
Nor the deep swallow me up,
Nor the [b]pit shut its mouth on me.

16 Answer me, O LORD, for [a]Your lovingkindness is good;
[b]According to the greatness of Your compassion, [c]turn to me,
17 And [a]do not hide Your face from Your servant,
For I am [b]in distress; answer me quickly.
18 Oh draw near to my soul *and* [a]redeem it;
[b]Ransom me because of my enemies!
19 You know my [a]reproach and my shame and my dishonor;
All my adversaries are [1]before You.

20 Reproach has [a]broken my heart and I am so sick.
And [b]I looked for sympathy, but there was none,
And for [c]comforters, but I found none.
21 They also gave me [1a]gall [2]for my food
And for my thirst they [b]gave me vinegar to drink.

22 May [a]their table before them become a snare;
And [1b]when they are in peace, *may it become* a trap.
23 May their [a]eyes grow dim so that they cannot see,

5 [a]Ps 38:5 [b]Ps 44:21
6 [1]Heb *YHWH*, usually rendered LORD [a]2 Sam 12:14
7 [a]Jer 15:15 [b]Ps 44:15; Is 50:6; Jer 51:51
8 [1]Lit *to* [a]Job 19:13-15; Ps 31:11; 38:11
9 [a]Ps 119:139; John 2:17 [b]Ps 89:41, 50; Rom 15:3
10 [a]Ps 35:13
11 [a]1 Kin 20:31; Ps 35:13 [b]1 Kin 9:7; Job 17:6; Ps 44:14; Jer 24:9
12 [1]Lit *songs* [a]Gen 19:1; Ruth 4:1 [b]Job 30:9
13 [1]Or *the faithfulness of Your salvation* [a]Ps 32:6; Is 49:8; 2 Cor 6:2 [b]Ps 51:1
14 [1]Lit *those who hate me* [2]Lit *deep places of water* [a]Ps 69:2 [b]Ps 144:7
15 [1]Lit *stream* [a]Ps 124:4, 5 [b]Num 16:33; Ps 28:1; 141:7
16 [a]Ps 63:3; 109:21 [b]Ps 51:1; 106:45 [c]Ps 25:16; 86:16
17 [a]Ps 27:9; 102:2; 143:7 [b]Ps 31:9; 66:14
18 [a]2 Sam 4:9; Ps 26:11; 49:15 [b]Ps 119:134
19 [1]Or *known to You* [a]Ps 22:6; 31:11
20 [a]Jer 23:9 [b]Ps 142:4; Is 63:5 [c]Job 16:2
21 [1]Or *poison* [2]Or *in* [a]Deut 29:18 [b]Matt 27:34, 48; Mark 15:23, 36; Luke 23:36; John 19:28-30
22 [1]Lit *for those who are secure* [a]Rom 11:9, 10 [b]1 Thess 5:3
23 [a]Is 6:10

69:5–12 Prayer that God's discipline of His godly servant may not bring disgrace on all those who trustingly look to the Lord. The author acknowledges (v. 5) that God's "wounding" of him (see v. 26) has been occasioned by some sin in his life (but he has not sinned against those who have become his enemies). Because of his present suffering, his enemies mock his deep commitment to the Lord (see 22:6–8; 42:3; 79:10; 115:2; Job 2:9). Implicitly he prays that God will restore him again and vindicate his trust in Him.
69:5 *folly.* See note on 14:1.
69:8 Even those nearest him dissociate themselves from him (see 31:11–12 and note).
69:9 *zeal for Your house.* What was true of the author was even more true of Jesus (see John 2:17). *reproaches of those who reproach You.* Those who mock God also mock His servant who trusts in Him (see 74:18,22–23; 2 Kin 18:31–35)—as Christ also experienced (see Rom 15:3).
69:10–11 *wept . . . with fasting . . . made sackcloth my clothing.* As tokens of humbling himself before the Lord in repentance as he prays for God to have mercy and restore him (see 35:13 and note; see also Gen 37:34; 2 Sam 12:16–17; Joel 1:13–14; 2:15–17; Jon 3:5).
69:12 *Those who sit in the gate . . . drunkards.* Everyone, from the elders of the city to the town drunks.
69:13–18 Though they mock, I pray to You.
69:13 *at an acceptable time.* When God is near to save (see 32:6 and note; see also Is 49:8; 61:2; 2 Cor 6:2). *greatness of Your lovingkindness.* See note on 6:4.
69:14–15 *mire . . . deep waters . . . flood of water . . . deep.* See note on vv. 1–2.
69:15 *swallow me.* See note on 49:14. *pit.* See note on 30:1.
69:16 *lovingkindness.* See note on 6:4.
69:17 *hide Your face.* See note on 13:1.
69:18 *redeem.* See note on 25:22.
69:19–21 In my trouble they heaped on scorn instead of bringing comfort (see 35:11–16; see also 142:4; Job 13:4; 16:2; 21:34).
69:20 *heart.* See note on 4:7.
69:21 *gall for my food . . . vinegar to drink.* Vivid metaphors for the bitter scorn they made him eat and drink when his whole being craved for the nourishment and refreshment of comfort. The authors of the Gospels, especially Matthew, suggest that the suffering expressed in this verse foreshadowed Christ's suffering on the cross (see Matt 27:34,48; Mark 15:23,36; Luke 23:36; John 19:29).
69:22–28 Prayer for God to redress the wrongs committed (see note on 5:10).
69:22–23 For Paul's application of these verses to the Jews who rejected the Christ see Rom 11:9–10.
69:22 They had set his table with "gall" and "vinegar" (v. 21). *table before them.* Reference may be to the meal accompanying the sealing of a covenant (see note on 23:5). In that case, this verse alludes to a pact uniting the enemies and calls on God to turn it against them.
69:23 They mocked him for his "wound" (v. 26); now may they experience the same failing of the eyes (see v. 3 and note on 6:7) and bending of the back (from weakness and pain; see

And make their [b]loins shake
continually.
24 [a]Pour out Your indignation on them,
And may Your burning anger overtake
them.
25 May their [1a]camp be desolate;
May none dwell in their tents.
26 For they have [a]persecuted him whom
[b]You Yourself have smitten,
And they tell of the pain of those
whom [c]You have [1]wounded.
27 Add [a]iniquity to their iniquity,
And [b]may they not come into [c]Your
righteousness.
28 May they be [a]blotted out of the [b]book
of life
And may they not be [1c]recorded with
the righteous.

29 But I am [a]afflicted and in pain;
[1]May Your salvation, O God, [b]set me
securely on high.
30 I will [a]praise the name of God with
song
And [b]magnify Him with
[c]thanksgiving.
31 And it will [a]please the LORD better
than an ox
Or a young bull with horns and hoofs.
32 The [a]humble [1]have seen *it and* are
glad;
You who seek God, [b]let your heart
[2]revive.
33 For [a]the LORD hears the needy
And [b]does not despise His *who are*
prisoners.

34 Let [a]heaven and earth praise Him,
The seas and [b]everything that moves
in them.
35 For God will [a]save Zion and [b]build the
cities of Judah,
That they may dwell there and
[c]possess it.
36 The [1a]descendants of His servants will
inherit it,
And those who love His name [b]will
dwell in it.

Psalm 70

For the choir director. *A Psalm* of David;
for a memorial.

1 [a]O God, *hasten* to deliver me;
O LORD, hasten to my help!
2 [a]Let those be ashamed and
humiliated
Who seek my [1]life;
Let those be turned back and
dishonored
Who delight [2]in my hurt.
3 [a]Let those be [1]turned back because of
their shame
Who say, "Aha, aha!"

4 Let all who seek You rejoice and be
glad in You;
And let those who love Your salvation
say continually,
"Let God be magnified."
5 But [a]I am afflicted and needy;
[b]Hasten to me, O God!
You are my help and my deliverer;
O LORD, do not delay.

23 [b]Dan 5:6
24 [a]Ps 79:6; Jer 10:25; Ezek 20:8; Hos 5:10
25 [1]Lit *encampment* [a]Matt 23:38; Luke 13:35; Acts 1:20
26 [1]Lit *pierced* [a]2 Chr 28:9; Zech 1:15 [b]Is 53:4 [c]Ps 109:22
27 [a]Neh 4:5; Ps 109:14; Rom 1:28 [b]Is 26:10 [c]Ps 103:17
28 [1]Lit *written* [a]Ex 32:32, 33; Rev 3:5 [b]Phil 4:3; Rev 13:8; 17:8; 20:15 [c]Ps 87:6; Ezek 13:9; Luke 10:20; Heb 12:23
29 [1]Or *Your salvation, O God, will set...* [a]Ps 70:5 [b]Ps 20:1; 59:1
30 [a]Ps 28:7 [b]Ps 34:3 [c]Ps 50:14
31 [a]Ps 50:13, 14; 51:16
32 [1]Some mss and ancient versions read *will see* [2]Or *live* [a]Ps 34:2 [b]Ps 22:26
33 [a]Ps 12:5 [b]Ps 68:6
34 [a]Ps 96:11; 98:7; 148:1-13; Is 44:23; 49:13
34 [b]Is 55:12
35 [a]Ps 46:5; 51:18 [b]Ps 147:2; Is 44:26 [c]Obad 17
36 [1]Lit *seed* [a]Ps 25:13; 102:28 [b]Ps 37:29
70:1 [a]Ps 40:13-17; 70:1-5

2 [1]Or *soul* [2]Or *to injure me* [a]Ps 35:4, 26 **3** [1]Some mss read *appalled* [a]Ps 40:15 **5** [a]Ps 40:17 [b]Ps 141:1

38:5–8). *May . . . their loins shake.* "Loins" refers to the belly and lower part of the back; they were viewed as the back's center of strength (see 66:11; see also Job 40:16).
69:24 *indignation . . . anger.* See note on 2:5. *overtake them.* Like a flash flood.
69:25 They sought to remove him from his place; may they be removed. Cf. Peter's application of this judgment to Judas (Acts 1:20).
69:26 The great wrong committed by his enemies against him and to which reference has repeatedly been made.
69:27 They have falsely charged him with crimes (v. 4); may their real crimes all be charged against them.
69:28 They had plotted his death; may death be their destiny. *book of life.* God's royal list of the righteous, whom God blesses with life (see 1:3; 7:9; 11:7; 34:12; 37:17,29; 55:22; 75:10; 92:12–14; 140:13). For other references to God's books see notes on 9:5; 51:1. In the NT the "book of life" refers to God's list of those destined for eternal life (see Phil 4:3; Rev 3:5; 13:8; 17:8; 20:12,15; 21:27).
69:29 Renewal of the prayer just prior to the vow to praise.
69:30–33 A vow to praise (see note on 7:17) out of assurance that the prayer will be heard (see note on 3:8).
69:30 *name of God.* See v. 36 and note on 5:11.
69:32 *humble.* See note on 34:6. *have seen it and are glad.* See 22:26 and note. *heart.* See note on 4:7. *revive.* Bubble over with the joy of life, because the Lord does hear the prayers of His people in need—contrary to the mocking of scoffers.
69:34–36 A call to praise (see note on 9:1) in the assurance that God will restore Judah and assure His people's inheritance in the promised land. This stanza appears to indicate that in its final form this royal prayer was used at a time when not only the king was in trouble but the kingdom of Judah had also suffered devastating defeat.
69:34 Let all creation praise Him (see 148:1–13; Is 49:13).
69:35–36 *they . . . descendants.* God's people and their children through the generations, specifically "those who love His name."
69:35 *Zion.* See note on 9:11.
Ps 70 An urgent prayer for God's help when threatened by enemies—a somewhat revised duplicate of 40:13–17 (see notes there). This is the second in a series of three such prayers; its language has many links with that of Ps 71. The prayer is framed by pleas for God to "hasten" with His help (vv. 1,5). The rest of the prayer focuses on the effects of God's saving help: (1) upon those "who seek my life" (vv. 2–3) and (2) for those "who seek You" (v. 4).
70 title See note on Ps 4 title. *A memorial.* See note on Ps 38 title.
70:4 God's deliverance of His servant will give joy to all who trust in the Lord, because they see in it the assurance of their own salvation. *Let God be magnified.* Because His saving help is sure and effective (contrast v. 3).

Psalm 71

1 [a]In You, O LORD, I have taken refuge;
Let me never be ashamed.
2 [a]In Your righteousness deliver me and rescue me;
[b]Incline Your ear to me and save me.
3 [a]Be to me a rock of [b]habitation to which I may continually come;
You have given [c]commandment to save me,
For You are [d]my [1]rock and my fortress.
4 [a]Rescue me, O my God, out of the hand of the wicked,
Out of the [1]grasp of the wrongdoer and ruthless man,
5 For You are my [a]hope;
O Lord [1]GOD, *You are* my [b]confidence from my youth.
6 [1]By You I have been [a]sustained from *my* birth;
You are He who [b]took me from my mother's womb;
My [c]praise is continually [2]of You.

7 I have become a [a]marvel to many,
For You are [b]my strong refuge.
8 My [a]mouth is filled with Your praise
And with [b]Your glory all day long.
9 Do not cast me off in the [a]time of old age;
Do not forsake me when my strength fails.
10 For my enemies have spoken [1]against me;
And those who [a]watch for my [2]life [b]have consulted together,
11 Saying, "[a]God has forsaken him;
Pursue and seize him, for there is [b]no one to deliver."

71:1 [a]Ps 25:2, 3; 31:1-3; 71:1-3 **2** [a]Ps 31:1 [b]Ps 17:6 **3** [1]Or *crag* [a]Ps 31:2, 3 [b]Deut 33:27; Ps 90:1; 91:9 [c]Ps 7:6; 42:8 [d]Ps 18:2 **4** [1]Lit *palm* [a]Ps 140:1, 4 **5** [1]Heb *YHWH,* usually rendered *LORD* [a]Ps 39:7; Jer 14:8; 17:7, 13, 17; 50:7 [b]Ps 22:9 **6** [1]Lit *Upon You I have been supported* [2]Lit *in* [a]Ps 22:10; Is 46:3 [b]Job 10:18; Ps 22:9 [c]Ps 34:1 **7** [a]Is 8:18; 1 Cor 4:9 [b]Ps 61:3 **8** [a]Ps 35:28; 63:5 [b]Ps 96:6; 104:1 **9** [a]Ps 71:18; 92:14; Is 46:4 **10** [1]Lit *with reference to* [2]Lit *soul* [a]Ps 56:6 [b]Ps 31:13; 83:3; Matt 27:1 **11** [a]Ps 3:2 [b]Ps 7:2

12 [a]Ps 10:1; 22:11; 35:22; 38:21 [b]Ps 38:22; 40:13; 70:1, 5 **13** [1]Lit *my injury* [a]Ps 35:4, 26; 40:14 [b]Ps 109:29 [c]Esth 9:2; Ps 71:24 **14** [1]Lit *add upon all Your praise* [a]Ps 130:7 [b]Ps 71:8 **15** [1]Lit *numbers* [a]Ps 35:28 [b]Ps 96:2 [c]Ps 40:5 **16** [1]Heb *YHWH,* usually rendered LORD [a]Ps 106:2 [b]Ps 51:14

12 O God, [a]do not be far from me;
O my God, [b]hasten to my help!
13 Let those who are adversaries of my soul be [a]ashamed *and* consumed;
Let them be [b]covered with reproach and dishonor, who [c]seek [1]to injure me.
14 But as for me, I will [a]hope continually,
And will [1b]praise You yet more and more.
15 My [a]mouth shall tell of Your righteousness
And of [b]Your salvation all day long;
For I [c]do not know the [1]sum *of them.*
16 I will come [a]with the mighty deeds of the Lord [1]GOD;
I will [b]make mention of Your righteousness, Yours alone.

17 O God, You [a]have taught me from my youth,
And I still [b]declare Your wondrous deeds.
18 And even when *I am* [a]old and gray,
O God, do not forsake me,
Until I [b]declare Your [1]strength to *this* generation,
Your power to all who are to come.
19 [1]For Your [a]righteousness, O God,
reaches to the [2]heavens,
You who have [b]done great things;
O God, [c]who is like You?
20 You who have [a]shown [1]me many troubles and distresses
Will [b]revive [1]me again,
And will bring [1]me up again [c]from the depths of the earth.

17 [a]Deut 4:5; 6:7 [b]Ps 26:7; 40:5; 119:27 **18** [1]Lit *arm* [a]Ps 71:9 [b]Ps 22:31; 78:4, 6 **19** [1]Or *And* [2]Lit *height* [a]Ps 36:6; 57:10 [b]Ps 126:2; Luke 1:49 [c]Deut 3:24; Ps 35:10 **20** [1]Another reading is *us* [a]Ps 60:3 [b]Ps 80:18; 85:6; 119:25; 138:7; Hos 6:1, 2 [c]Ps 86:13

Ps 71 A prayer for God's help in old age when enemies threaten because they see that the king's strength is waning (see note on 5:9). The psalm bears no superscription, but it may well be that Ps 70 was viewed by the editors of the Psalms as the introduction to Ps 71, in which case the psalm is ascribed to David (in his old age; see vv. 9,18). This suggestion gains support from the fact that Ps 72 is identified as a prayer by and/or for King Solomon (see introduction to that psalm). This is the third in a series of three prayers; its dominant theme is hope (see v. 14). Formally symmetrical, the psalm has a five-four-five, five-four-five (in Hebrew) line pattern: vv. 1–4 (five lines), vv. 5–8 (four lines), vv. 9–13 (five lines), vv. 15–18 (five lines), vv. 19–21 (four lines), vv. 22–24 (five lines). At the center (v. 14; see note on 6:6) stands a confident confession of hope. The whole is framed by an appeal for help (vv. 1–4) and a vow to praise in anticipation of deliverance (vv. 22–24). The intervening verses are linked by references to the troubles the king has experienced and references to old age.

71:1–4 The initial appeal for God's help.

71:2 *Your righteousness.* See vv. 15–16,19,24; see also note on 5:8.

71:5–8 A confession that the Lord has always been his hope (see vv. 14,19–21).

71:5 *from my youth.* See 22:9.

71:7 *a marvel.* The troubles of his life (see v. 20) have been viewed by others as holding some special significance—especially since the Lord has been his "strong refuge" through them all.

71:9–13 A prayer for God's continuing help in the waning years of his life.

71:10 *enemies have spoken against me.* See notes on 3:2; 5:9.

71:13 A plea for redress (see note on 5:10).

71:14 The centered confession of unfaltering hope (see 42:8; see also notes on 6:6; 42:8).

71:15–18 A vow to praise, accompanying the renewal of his prayer (v. 18); see note on 7:17.

71:16–17 *mighty deeds . . . righteousness . . . wondrous deeds.* God's "mighty deeds" in behalf of His people are expressions of His righteousness; thus they can also be called His "righteousness" (v. 24).

71:16 *come.* To the temple, where God's people assemble for worship.

71:19–21 A confession that the Lord is still his hope, in the face of all his troubles (see vv. 5–8,14).

71:19 *reaches to the heavens.* Is as expansive as all space above the earth (see also 36:5 and note). *O God, who is like You?* See Mic 7:18.

71:20 *revive me again.* He who gave him life (see v. 6) will renew his life. *depths of the earth.* The realm of the dead, of which the grave is the portal (see note on 30:1).

21 May You increase my [a]greatness
And turn *to* [b]comfort me.

22 I will also praise You with [1][a]a harp,
Even Your [2]truth, O my God;
To You I will sing praises with the
[b]lyre,
O [c]Holy One of Israel.
23 My lips will [a]shout for joy when I sing
praises to You;
And my [b]soul, which You have
redeemed.
24 My [a]tongue also will utter Your
righteousness all day long;
For they are [b]ashamed, for they are
humiliated who seek [1]my hurt.

Psalm 72

A Psalm of Solomon.

1 Give the king [a]Your judgments, O God,
And [b]Your righteousness to the king's
son.
2 [1]May [2]he [a]judge Your people with
righteousness
And [3][b]Your afflicted with justice.
3 [1]Let the mountains bring [2][a]peace to
the people,
And the hills, in righteousness.
4 [1]May he [a]vindicate the [2]afflicted of
the people,
Save the children of the needy
And crush the oppressor.

5 [1]Let them fear You [a]while the sun
endures,
And [2]as long as the moon, throughout
all generations.
6 [1]May he come down [a]like rain upon
the mown grass,
Like [b]showers that water the earth.
7 In his days [1]may the [a]righteous
flourish,
And [b]abundance of peace till the
moon is no more.

8 May he also rule [a]from sea to sea
And from the River to the ends of the
earth.
9 [1]Let [a]the nomads of the desert [b]bow
before him,
And his enemies [c]lick the dust.
10 [1]Let the kings of [a]Tarshish and of the
[2][b]islands bring presents;
The kings of [c]Sheba and [d]Seba [e]offer
[3]gifts.
11 [1]And let all [a]kings bow down before
him,
All [b]nations serve him.

12 For he will [a]deliver the needy when
he cries for help,
The [1]afflicted also, and him who has
no helper.
13 He will have [a]compassion on the poor
and needy,

21 [a]Ps 18:35 [b]Ps 23:4; 86:17; Is 12:1; 49:13
22 [1]Lit *an instrument of a harp* [2]Or *faithfulness* [a]Ps 33:2; 81:2; 92:1-3; 144:9 [b]Ps 33:2; 147:7 [c]2 Kin 19:22; Ps 78:41; 89:18; Is 1:4
23 [a]Ps 5:11; 32:11; 132:9, 16 [b]Ps 34:22; 55:18; 103:4
24 [1]Or *to injure me* [a]Ps 35:28 [b]Ps 71:13
72:1 [a]1 Kin 3:9; 1 Chr 22:13 [b]Ps 24:5
2 [1]Or *He* will judge [2]Many of the pronouns in this Psalm may be rendered *He* since the typical reference is to the Messiah [3]Or *Your humble* [a]Is 9:7; 11:2-5; 32:1 [b]Ps 82:3
3 [1]Or *The mountains will bring* [2]Or *prosperity* [a]Is 2:4; 9:5, 6; Mic 4:3, 4; Zech 9:10
4 [1]Or *He will vindicate* [2]Or *humble* [a]Is 11:4
5 [1]Or *They will fear* [a]Ps 72:17; 89:36, 37
5 [2]Lit *before the moon*
6 [1]Or *He will come down* [a]Deut 32:2; 2 Sam 23:4; Hos 6:3 [b]Ps 65:10
7 [1]Or *the righteous will flourish* [a]Ps 92:12 [b]Is 2:4 **8** [a]Ex 23:31; Zech 9:10 **9** [1]Or *The nomads...will bow* [a]Ps 74:14; Is 23:13 [b]Ps 22:29 [c]Is 49:23; Mic 7:17 **10** [1]Or *The kings...will bring* [2]Or *coastlands* [3]Or *tribute* [a]2 Chr 9:21; Ps 48:7 [b]Ps 97:1; Is 42:4, 10; Zeph 2:11 [c]1 Kin 10:1; Job 6:19; Is 60:6 [d]Gen 10:7; Is 43:3 [e]Ps 45:12; 68:29 **11** [1]Or *All kings will bow down* [a]Ps 138:4; Is 49:23 [b]Ps 86:9 **12** [1]Or *humble* [a]Job 29:12; Ps 72:4 **13** [a]Prov 19:17; 28:8

71:22–24 A vow to praise in confident anticipation of God's saving help (see notes on 3:8; 7:17).
71:22 *harp . . . lyre.* See note on 57:8. *Holy One of Israel.* See 78:41; 89:18; see also note on Is 1:4.
71:23 *redeemed.* Here, as often, a synonym for "deliver."
71:24 *righteousness.* God's saving acts in behalf of His people according to His covenant promises.
Ps 72 A prayer for the king, a son of David who rules on David's throne as God's earthly regent over His people. It may have been used at the time of the king's coronation (as were Ps 2; 110). Written as a petition, vv. 2–11, 17 express the desire of the nation that the king's reign will, as a consequence of God's endowment of His servant, be characterized by justice and righteousness, the supreme virtues of kingship. The prayer reflects the ideal concept of the king and the glorious effects of his reign. See Jeremiah's indictment of some of the last Davidic kings (e.g., Jer 22:2–3,13,15) and the prophetic announcement of the Messiah's righteous rule (see Is 9:7; 11:4–5; Jer 23:5–6; 33:15–16; Zech 9:9). Later Jewish tradition saw in this psalm a description of the Messiah, as did the early church. The last three verses do not belong to the prayer (see notes there).
72 title *of Solomon.* Either by him or for him—of course, both may be true. Undoubtedly it was also used by Israel (Judah) as a prayer for later Davidic kings.
72:1 The basic prayer. *judgments . . . righteousness.* May the king be endowed with the gift for and the love of justice and righteousness so that his reign reflects the rule of God Himself. Solomon asked for wisdom (see 1 Kin 3:9,11–12; see also Prov 16:12). *righteousness.* See note on 5:8.
72:2–7 The quality of his reign: May it be righteous, prosperous and enduring.
72:3 Righteousness in the realm will be like fertilizing rain on the land, for then the Lord will bless His people with abundance (see vv. 6–7; 5:12; 65:9–13; 133:3; Lev 25:19; Deut 28:8).
72:5 *while the sun endures.* See 21:4 and note.
72:6 See v. 3 and note; see also v. 7. For another vivid metaphor expressive of the significance of the Lord's anointed for the realm see Lam 4:20.
72:7 *righteous.* See note on 1:5. *flourish.* Because the king supports and protects them, but uses all his royal power to suppress the wicked (see Ps 101).
72:8–14 The extent of his domain (vv. 8–11) as the result of his righteous rule (vv. 12–14).
72:8 His kingdom and his authority will extend to all the world (see vv. 9–11). Ideally and potentially, as God's earthly regent, he possesses royal authority that extends on earth as far as God's—an expectation that is fulfilled in Christ. See Zech 9:10 and note.
72:9 The tribes of the Arabian Desert to the east will yield to him. *lick the dust.* See Mic 7:17.
72:10 The kings whose lands border the Mediterranean Sea to the west will acknowledge him as overlord, as will those who rule in south Arabia and along the eastern African coast. *Tarshish.* A distant Mediterranean seaport, perhaps as far west as modern Spain. *Sheba.* See notes on Gen 10:28; 1 Kin 10:1; Joel 3:8. *Seba.* Elsewhere in the OT associated with Cush (Gen 10:7; Is 43:3); it may refer to a region in modern Sudan, south of Egypt.

And the [1]lives of the needy he will
save.
14 He will [1][a]rescue their [2]life from
oppression and violence,
And their blood will be [b]precious in
his sight;
15 So may he live, and may the [a]gold of
Sheba be given to him;
And let [1]them pray for him
continually;
Let [1]them bless him all day long.

16 May there be abundance of grain in
the earth on top of the mountains;
Its fruit will wave like *the cedars of*
[a]Lebanon;
And may those from the city flourish
like [b]vegetation of the earth.
17 May his [a]name endure forever;
May his name [1]increase [2][b]as long as
the sun *shines;*
And let *men* [c]bless themselves by
him;
[d]Let all nations call him blessed.

18 [a]Blessed be the LORD God, the God of
Israel,
Who alone [b]works wonders.
19 And blessed be His [a]glorious name
forever;
And may the whole [b]earth be filled
with His glory.
[c]Amen, and Amen.

20 The prayers of David the son of Jesse
are ended.

BOOK 3

Psalm 73

A Psalm of Asaph.

1 Surely God is [a]good to Israel,
To those who are [b]pure in heart!
2 But as for me, [a]my feet came close to
stumbling,
My steps [1]had almost slipped.
3 For I was [a]envious of the [1]arrogant
As I saw the [b]prosperity of the
wicked.
4 For there are no pains in their death,
And their [1]body is fat.
5 They are [a]not [1]in trouble *as other* [2]men,
Nor are they [b]plagued [3]like mankind.
6 Therefore pride is [a]their necklace;
The [b]garment of violence covers them.
7 Their eye [1]bulges from [a]fatness;
The imaginations of *their* heart [2]run
riot.
8 They [a]mock and [1]wickedly speak of
oppression;
They [b]speak from on high.
9 They have [a]set their mouth [1]against
the heavens,
And their tongue [2]parades through the
earth.

10 Therefore [1]his people return to this
place,
And waters of [a]abundance are [2]drunk
by them.

13 [1]Lit *souls* **14** [1]Lit *redeem* [2]Lit *soul* [a]Ps 69:18 [b]1 Sam 26:21; Ps 116:15 **15** [1]Lit *him* [a]Is 60:6 **16** [a]Ps 104:16 [b]Job 5:25 **17** [1]Or *sprout forth* [2]Lit *before the sun* [a]Ex 3:15; Ps 135:13 [b]Ps 89:36 [c]Gen 12:3; 22:18 [d]Luke 1:48 **18** [a]1 Chr 29:10; Ps 41:13; 89:52; 106:48 [b]Ex 15:11; Job 5:9; Ps 77:14; 86:10; 136:4 **19** [a]Neh 9:5; Ps 96:8 [b]Num 14:21 [c]Ps 41:13

73:1 [a]Ps 86:5 [b]Ps 24:4; 51:10; Matt 5:8 **2** [1]Lit *were caused to slip* [a]Ps 94:18 **3** [1]Or *boasters* [a]Ps 37:1; Prov 23:17 [b]Job 21:7; Ps 37:7; Jer 12:1 **4** [1]Or *belly* **5** [1]Lit *in the trouble of men* [2]Or *mortals* [3]Lit *with* [a]Job 21:9; Ps 73:12 [b]Ps 73:14 **6** [a]Gen 41:42; Prov 1:9 [b]Ps 109:18 **7** [1]Lit *goes forth* [2]Lit *overflow* [a]Job 15:27; Ps 17:10; Jer 5:28 **8** [1]Or *they speak in wickedness; From on high they speak of oppression* [a]Ps 1:1 [b]Ps 17:10; 2 Pet 2:18; Jude 16 **9** [1]Or *in* [2]Lit *walks* [a]Rev 13:6 **10** [1]Or *His* [2]Lit *drained out* [a]Ps 23:5

72:15–17 Concluding summation: May the king enjoy a long, prosperous, world-renowned reign—one that blesses all the nations.

72:17 *all nations.* The language recalls the promise to Abraham (see Gen 12:3; 22:18) and suggests that it will be fulfilled through the royal son of David—ultimately the Messiah.

72:18–19 A doxology at the conclusion of Book 2 of the Psalter (see 41:13 and note). It is the people's response, their "Amen," to the contents of Book 2 (see note on Ps 4 title).

72:19 *filled with His glory.* See note on 85:9.

72:20 An editorial notation probably carried over from an earlier collection of psalms ascribed exclusively to David. *prayers of David.* See titles of Ps 86; 142.

Ps 73 A word of godly wisdom concerning the destinies of the righteous and the wicked. The editors of the Psalter placed it at the beginning of Book 3, as they did Ps 1 at the beginning of the whole collection (see introduction to Ps 1). Here is addressed one of the most disturbing problems of the OT saints: How is it that the wicked so often prosper while the godly suffer so much? Thematically the psalm has many links with Ps 49 (see introduction to that psalm; see also Ps 37). Its date may be as late as the postexilic era. Thematic development divides the psalm's structure into two halves of 14 verses each. The whole is framed by the sharply etched contrast of v. 1 and v. 27.

73 title The psalm is ascribed to Asaph, leader of one of David's Levitical choirs (see notes on Ps 39; 42; 50 titles). It begins a collection of 11 Asaphite psalms (Ps 73–83), to which Ps 50 at one time probably belonged. In view of the fact that the collection clearly contains prayers from a later date (e.g., Ps 74; 79; 83), references to Asaph in these titles must sometimes include descendants of Asaph who functioned in his place (see note on Ps 50 title). The Asaphite psalms are dominated by the theme of God's rule over His people and the nations. Apart from an introductory word of instruction (Ps 73) the collection is bracketed by prayers for God to rescue His people from foreign oppression (Ps 74; 83). The rest of the collection (Ps 75–82) appears to reflect thematic pairing: 1. The God who brings down the wicked and exalts the righteous (Ps 75) is the God and Savior of Israel (Ps 76). 2. God's saving acts in behalf of His people are remembered (Ps 77–78). 3. God is petitioned for help against the devastating attacks of Israel's enemies (Ps 79–80). 4. God is portrayed as presiding in judgment over His people (Ps 81) and over the world powers (Ps 82).

73:1–14 An almost fatal trial of faith: In the midst of his many troubles a godly man lets his eyes become fixed on the prosperity of the wicked.

73:1 *pure in heart!* See v. 13; see also note on 24:4. *heart.* See note on 4:7.

73:2 *feet came close to stumbling.* From the path of truth and godliness (see 37:31 and note).

73:4–12 A description of the prosperous state of the wicked and the haughty self-reliance such prosperity engenders—hardly an objective account; it is rather the exaggerated picture that envious and troubled eyes perceived (see the description of the wicked in 10:2–11; cf. Job's anguished portrayal of the prosperity of the wicked in Job 21).

73:6 *pride is their necklace.* Contrast Prov 1:9; 3:3,22.

11 They say, "[a]How does God know?
And is there knowledge [1]with the
Most High?"
12 Behold, [a]these are the wicked;
And always [b]at ease, they have
increased *in* wealth.
13 Surely [a]in vain I have [1]kept my heart
pure
And [b]washed my hands in innocence;
14 For I have been stricken [a]all day long
And [1b]chastened every morning.

15 If I had said, "I will speak thus,"
Behold, I would have betrayed the
[a]generation of Your children.
16 When I [a]pondered to understand this,
It was [1]troublesome in my sight
17 Until I came into the [1a]sanctuary of
God;
Then I perceived their [b]end.
18 Surely You set them in [a]slippery places;
You cast them down to [1b]destruction.
19 How they are [1a]destroyed in a
moment!
They are utterly swept away by
[b]sudden terrors!
20 Like a [a]dream when one awakes,
O Lord, when [b]aroused, You will
[c]despise their [1]form.

21 When my [a]heart was embittered
And I was [b]pierced [1]within,
22 Then I was [a]senseless and ignorant;
I was *like* [1]a [b]beast [2]before You.

23 Nevertheless [a]I am continually with
You;
You have taken hold of my right hand.
24 With Your counsel You will [a]guide me,
And afterward [b]receive me [1]to glory.

25 [a]Whom have I in heaven *but You?*
And [1]besides You, I desire nothing on
earth.
26 My [a]flesh and my heart may fail,
But God is the [1]strength of my heart
and my [b]portion forever.
27 For, behold, [a]those who are far from
You will [b]perish;
You have [1]destroyed all those who
[2c]are unfaithful to You.
28 But as for me, [a]the nearness of God is
my good;
I have made the Lord [1]GOD my [b]refuge,
That I may [c]tell of all Your works.

Psalm 74

A [†]Maskil of Asaph.

1 O God, why have You [a]rejected *us*
forever?
Why does Your anger [b]smoke against
the [c]sheep of Your [1]pasture?

11 [1]Lit *in* [a]Job 22:13 **12** [a]Ps 49:6; 52:7 [b]Jer 49:31; Ezek 23:42 **13** [1]Or *cleansed my heart* [a]Job 21:15; 34:9; 35:3 [b]Ps 26:6 **14** [1]Lit *my chastening* [a]Ps 38:6 [b]Job 33:19; Ps 118:18 **15** [a]Ps 14:5 **16** [1]Lit *labor, trouble* [a]Eccl 8:17 **17** [1]Lit *sanctuaries* [a]Ps 27:4; 77:13 [b]Ps 37:38 **18** [1]Lit *ruins* [a]Ps 35:6 [b]Ps 35:8; 36:12 **19** [1]Lit *become a desolation* [a]Num 16:21; Is 47:11 [b]Job 18:11 **20** [1]Or *image* [a]Job 20:8 [b]Ps 78:65 [c]1 Sam 2:30 **21** [1]Lit *in my kidneys* [a]Judg 10:16 [b]Acts 2:37 **22** [1]Or *an animal* [2]Lit *with You* [a]Ps 49:10; 92:6 [b]Job 18:3; Ps 49:20; Eccl 3:18 **23** [a]Ps 16:8 **24** [1]Or *with honor* [a]Ps 32:8; 48:14; Is 58:11 [b]Gen 5:24; Ps 49:15 **25** [1]Or *with* [a]Ps 16:2; Phil 3:8

26 [1]Lit *rock* [a]Ps 38:10; 40:12; 84:2; 119:81 [b]Ps 16:5 **27** [1]Or *silenced* [2]Lit *go to a whoring from* [a]Ps 119:155 [b]Ps 37:20 [c]Ex 34:15; Num 15:39; Ps 106:39; Hos 4:12; 9:1 **28** [1]Heb *YHWH*, usually rendered *LORD* [a]Ps 65:4; Heb 10:22; James 4:8 [b]Ps 14:6; 71:7 [c]Ps 40:5; 107:22; 118:17 **74:1** [†]Possibly, *Contemplative*, or *Didactic*, or *Skillful Psalm* [1]Or *pasturing* [a]Ps 44:9; 77:7 [b]Deut 29:20; Ps 18:8; 89:46 [c]Ps 79:13; 95:7; 100:3

73:11 *God . . . Most High.* That is, God Most High (see 57:2; see also note on 3:7). *Most High.* See note on Gen 14:19.
73:13–14 The thoughts that plagued him when he compared the state of the wicked with his own troubled lot.
73:13 *heart pure.* See note on v. 1.
73:14 *chastened.* As a child by his father to keep him in the right way (see Prov 3:12; 23:13–14).
73:15–28 The renewal of faith: In the temple the godly man sees the destiny God has appointed for the wicked.
73:15 *If I had said.* If he had given public expression to his thoughts as embodying true insight. *Your children.* Those characterized by a humble reliance on and commitment to God.
73:18–20 Though the wicked seem to prosper, God has made their position precarious, and without warning they are swept away. The psalmist does not reflect on their state after death but leaves it as his final word that the wicked fall utterly and inevitably from their state of proud prosperity (see Ps 49; cf. the final state of the godly in v. 24).
73:20 When God arouses Himself as from sleep (see note on 7:6) and deals with the wicked, they vanish like the shadowy characters of a dream.
73:21 *heart.* See note on 4:7. *within.* Lit. "in my kidneys" (see note on 7:9).
73:22 *a beast.* As stupid as a beast (see Job 18:3).
73:23–26 Although he had (almost) fallen to the level of beastly stupidity, God has not, will not, let him go—ever!
73:24 God's counsel has overcome his folly and will guide him through all the pitfalls of life (see 16:7; 32:8; 48:14). *receive me to glory.* At the end of the believer's pilgrimage (see 49:15 and note).
73:25 Though he has envied the prosperity of the wicked, he now confesses that nothing in heaven or earth is more desirable than God.
73:26 *My flesh . . . heart.* My whole being (see 84:2). *heart.* See note on 4:7. *portion.* Since the psalmist was a Levite, the Lord was his portion in the promised land in that he lived by the people's tithes dedicated to the Lord (see Num 18:21–24; Deut 10:9; 18:1–2). Here he confesses more: The Lord Himself is his sustainer, his preserver—his very life.
73:28 *I may tell of all Your works.* A concluding vow to praise God for all His mercies to him (see note on 7:17).
Ps 74 A prayer for God to come to the aid of His people and defend His cause in the face of the mocking of the enemies—the Lord's relation to His people is like that of a king to his nation. The psalm dates from the time of the exile when Israel had been destroyed as a nation, the promised land devastated and the temple reduced to ruins (see Ps 79; Lam 2). Its relationship to the ministries of Jeremiah and Ezekiel is uncertain (see note on v. 9). Thematically the psalm divides into two halves of 11 verses each, with v. 12 (the center line; see note there) highlighting the primary thematic element that unifies the prayer. Verses 1–11 are framed by the "Why's" of the people's complaint (vv. 1,11); the whole psalm is framed by pleas for God to "remember" (vv. 2,22). Note also that the "they's" of vv. 4–8 have their counterpoint in the "You's" of vv. 13–17 (highlighted in the Hebrew by seven emphatic pronouns)—the mighty acts of God are appealed to against the destructive and haughty deeds of the enemies.
74 title *Maskil.* See note on Ps 32 title. *Asaph.* See note on Ps 73 title.
74:1–2 Initial complaint and appeal.
74:1 *why . . . ? Why . . . ?* Cf. "How long . . . ?" (v. 10) and "Why . . . ?" (v. 11). See note on 6:3; see also Introduction:

2 Remember Your congregation, which
You have [a]purchased of old,
Which You have [b]redeemed to be the
[c]tribe of Your inheritance;
And this Mount [d]Zion, where You
have dwelt.
3 [1]Turn Your footsteps toward the
[a]perpetual ruins;
The enemy [b]has damaged everything
within the sanctuary.
4 Your adversaries have [a]roared in the
midst of Your meeting place;
They have set up their [b]own
[1]standards [c]for signs.
5 It seems as if one had lifted up
His [1a]axe in a [2]forest of trees.
6 And now [1]all its [a]carved work
They smash with hatchet and
[2]hammers.
7 They have [1a]burned Your sanctuary
[2]to the ground;
They have [b]defiled the dwelling place
of Your name.
8 They [a]said in their heart, "Let us
[1]completely [2]subdue them."
They have burned all the meeting
places of God in the land.
9 We do not see our [a]signs;
There is [b]no longer any prophet,
Nor is there any among us who knows
[c]how long.
10 How long, O God, will the adversary
[a]revile,
And the enemy [b]spurn Your name
forever?
11 Why [a]do You withdraw Your hand,
even Your right hand?
From within Your bosom, [b]destroy
them!
12 Yet God is [a]my king from of old,
Who works deeds of deliverance in
the midst of the earth.
13 [1]You [a]divided the sea by Your
strength;
[1]You [b]broke the heads of the [c]sea
monsters [2]in the waters.
14 [1]You crushed the heads of
[2a]Leviathan;
[1]You gave him as food for the
[3]creatures [b]of the wilderness.
15 [1]You [a]broke open springs and
torrents;
[1]You [b]dried up ever-flowing streams.
16 Yours is the day, Yours also is the
night;
[1]You have [a]prepared the [2]light and the
sun.
17 [1]You have [a]established all the
boundaries of the earth;
[1]You have [2]made [b]summer and
winter.

2 [a]Ex 15:16; Deut 32:6 [b]Ex 15:13; Ps 77:15; 106:10; Is 63:9 [c]Deut 32:9; Is 63:17; Jer 10:16; 51:19 [d]Ps 9:11; 68:16
3 [1]Lit *Lift up* [a]Is 61:4 [b]Ps 79:1
4 [1]Lit *signs* [a]Lam 2:7 [b]Num 2:2 [c]Ps 74:9
5 [1]Lit *axes* [2]Lit *thicket* [a]Jer 46:22
6 [1]Lit *altogether* [2]Or *axes* [a]1 Kin 6:18, 29, 32, 35
7 [1]Lit *set on fire* [2]Or *To the ground they...* [a]2 Kin 25:9 [b]Ps 89:39; Lam 2:2
8 [1]Lit *altogether* [2]Or *oppress* [a]Ps 83:4
9 [a]Ps 78:43 [b]1 Sam 3:1; Lam 2:9; Ezek 7:26; Amos 8:11 [c]Ps 6:3; 79:5; 80:4
10 [a]Ps 44:16; 79:12; 89:51
10 [b]Lev 24:16
11 [a]Lam 2:3 [b]Ps 59:13
12 [a]Ps 44:4
13 [1]Or *You Yourself* [2]Lit *on* [a]Ex 14:21; Ps 78:13 [b]Is 51:9 [c]Ps 148:7; Jer 51:34
14 [1]Or *You Yourself* [2]Or *sea monster* [3]Lit *people* [a]Job 41:1; Ps 104:26; Is 27:1 [b]Ps 72:9
15 [1]Or *You Yourself* [a]Ex 17:5, 6; Num 20:11; Ps 78:15; 105:41; 114:8; Is 48:21 [b]Ex 14:21, 22; Josh 2:10; 3:13; Ps 114:3
16 [1]Or *You Yourself* [2]Or *luminary* [a]Gen 1:14-18; Ps 104:19; 136:7, 8
17 [1]Or *You Yourself* [2]Or *formed* [a]Deut 32:8; Acts 17:26 [b]Gen 8:22; Ps 147:16-18

Theology. *forever.* So it seemed, since no relief was in sight. *anger.* See note on 2:5. *sheep of Your pasture.* See note on 23:1.
74:2 *purchased.* Or "acquired"; or "created." *redeemed.* Here, as often, a synonym for "deliver." *Mount Zion.* See note on 9:11. This verse recalls the victory song of Ex 15 (see especially vv. 13–17, and compare the center verse of this psalm, v. 12, with the last verse of the song, Ex 15:18) and thus sets the stage for the other exodus recollections that follow. The Babylonian destruction of Zion seems to be the undoing of God's great victory over Egypt when He redeemed His people. *tribe.* Here referring to all Israel. *Your inheritance.* See Deut 9:29.
74:3–8 The Babylonians' high-handed destruction of the Lord's temple.
74:3 *Turn Your footsteps toward.* Hurry to restore.
74:4 *standards.* Probably troop standards (see Num 1:52; Is 31:9; Jer 4:21). *for signs.* Signifying their triumph.
74:6 *carved work.* See 1 Kin 6:15.
74:7 *Your name.* See note on 5:11.
74:8 *They said.* See note on 10:11. *all the meeting places of God.* The reference is uncertain. At the time of the Babylonian attacks there may have been a number of (illegitimate) places in Judah where people went to worship God (see notes on 1 Kin 3:2; 2 Kin 18:4).
74:9–11 The complaint and prayer renewed (see vv. 1–2).
74:9 *not see . . . signs.* As we did at the time of the exodus (see vv. 13–15; 78:43). *no . . . prophet.* Jeremiah had been taken to Egypt (see Jer 43:6–7), but whether Ezekiel was no longer prophesying is unknown. Perhaps this psalm was composed by an Asaphite who remained in Israel, part of a small group overlooked by Johanan when that army officer led the remnant to Egypt (see Jer 43:4–7).
74:10 *revile . . . spurn Your name.* See v. 18; see also v. 22; 2 Kin 18:32–35; Is 37:6,23.
74:12 The center verse (center line in the Hebrew text; see note on 6:6). The whole psalm presupposes the truth confessed here: God is Israel's King, her hope and Savior; Israel is God's people (kingdom). This accounts for both the complaint and the prayer, and why the destruction of Israel brings with it the mocking of God. *my.* Communal use of the singular pronoun (see note on Ps 30 title). *from of old.* From the days of the exodus (see Ex 3:7; 19:5–6).
74:13–17 The Lord is the mighty God of salvation and creation (see 65:6–7 and note).
74:13–14 Recollection of God's mighty acts when He delivered His people from Egypt. The imagery is borrowed from ancient Near Eastern creation myths, in which the primeval chaotic waters were depicted as a many-headed monster that the creator-god overcame, after which he established the world order (see note on 32:6). The poet here interweaves creation and salvation themes to celebrate the fact that the God of Israel has shown by His saving acts (His opening of the Red Sea for His people and His destruction of the Egyptians) that He is able to overcome all hostile powers to redeem His people and establish His new order in the world. For poetic use of this imagery (1) to celebrate God's creation works see 89:10; Job 9:13; 26:12–13; (2) to celebrate the deliverance from Egypt see Is 51:9; (3) to announce a future deliverance of Israel see Is 27:1. Echoes of the same imagery are present in the judgment announced against Egypt in Ezek 29:3–5; 32:2–6.
74:15 Recollection of God's water miracles at the Red Sea, in the wilderness and at the Jordan.
74:16–17 God is the One who established the orders of creation; He (alone) is able to effect redemption and establish His kingdom in the world against all creaturely opposition.

18 Remember this, [1]O LORD, that the
enemy has [a]reviled,
And a [b]foolish people has spurned
Your name.
19 Do not deliver the soul of Your
[a]turtledove to the wild beast;
[b]Do not forget the life of Your afflicted
forever.
20 Consider the [a]covenant;
For the [b]dark places of the land are
full of the habitations of violence.
21 Let not the [a]oppressed return
dishonored;
Let the [b]afflicted and needy praise
Your name.

22 Arise, O God, *and* [a]plead Your own
cause;
Remember [1]how the [b]foolish man
reproaches You all day long.
23 Do not forget the voice of Your
[a]adversaries,
The [b]uproar of those who rise against
You which ascends continually.

Psalm 75

For the choir director; *set to* [†]Al-tashheth.
A Psalm of Asaph, a Song.

1 We [a]give thanks to You, O God, we
give thanks,
For Your name is [b]near;
Men declare [c]Your wondrous works.

18 [1]Or *that the enemy has reviled the LORD* [a]Ps 74:10 [b]Deut 32:6; Ps 14:1; 39:8; 53:1 **19** [a]Song 2:14 [b]Ps 9:18 **20** [a]Gen 17:7; Ps 106:45 [b]Ps 88:6; 143:3 **21** [a]Ps 103:6 [b]Ps 35:10; Is 41:17 **22** [1]Lit *Your reproach from the foolish man* [a]Ps 43:1; Is 3:13; 43:26; Ezek 20:35 [b]Ps 14:1; 53:1; 74:18 **23** [a]Ps 74:10 [b]Ps 65:7 **75:1** [†]Lit *Do Not Destroy* [a]Ps 79:13 [b]Ps 145:18 [c]Ps 26:7; 44:1; 71:17

2 [a]Ps 102:13 [b]Ps 9:8; 67:4; Is 11:4 **3** [1]Or *totter* [2]*Selah* may mean: *Pause, Crescendo* or *Musical interlude* [a]Ps 46:6; Is 24:19 [b]1 Sam 2:8 **4** [a]Zech 1:21 **5** [1]Lit *neck* [a]1 Sam 2:3; Ps 94:4 **6** [1]Or *mountainous desert* [a]Ps 3:3

2 "When I select an [a]appointed time,
It is I who [b]judge with equity.
3 "The [a]earth and all who dwell in it
[1]melt;
It is I who have firmly set its [b]pillars.
[2]Selah.
4 "I said to the boastful, 'Do not boast,'
And to the wicked, '[a]Do not lift up the
horn;
5 Do not lift up your horn on high,
[a]Do not speak with insolent [1]pride.' "

6 For not from the east, nor from the
west,
Nor from the [1a]desert *comes*
exaltation;
7 But [a]God is the Judge;
He [b]puts down one and exalts
another.
8 For a [a]cup is in the hand of the LORD,
and the wine foams;
It is [1b]well mixed, and He pours out of
this;
Surely all the wicked of the earth must
drain *and* [c]drink down its dregs.

9 But as for me, I will [a]declare *it*
forever;
I will sing praises to the God of
Jacob.

7 [a]Ps 50:6 [b]1 Sam 2:7; Ps 147:6; Dan 2:21 **8** [1]Lit *full of mixture* [a]Job 21:20; Ps 11:6; 60:3; Jer 25:15 [b]Prov 23:30 [c]Obad 16 **9** [a]Ps 22:22; 40:10

74:18–23 A prayer for God to defend His cause and restore His people.
74:18 See vv. 2,10. *foolish people.* The "enemies" of v. 10 are here called fools for their contempt of God (see v. 22; see also note on 14:1).
74:19 *Your turtledove.* Israel—probably a figure of endearment (see Song 2:14; 5:2; 6:9; see also Ps 68:13 and note). *wild beast.* See note on 7:2.
74:20 *the covenant.* God's covenant to be the God of Israel, who makes them secure and richly blessed in the promised land (see Ex 19:5–6; 23:27–31; 34:10–11; Lev 26:11–12,42,44–45; Deut 28:1–14; see also Ps 105:8–11; 106:45; 111:5,9; Is 54:10; Jer 14:21; Ezek 16:60).
74:21 *afflicted and needy.* See note on 34:6. *praise Your name.* May they have cause to do so.
74:22 *Arise.* See note on 3:7.
74:23 *voice . . . uproar.* See 64:2.
Ps 75 A song of reassurance when arrogant worldly powers threaten Israel's security. The psalm may date from the time of the Assyrian menace (see 2 Kin 18:13–19:37). See also Ps 11; 76. Thematic parallels to the song of Hannah (1 Sam 2:1–10) are numerous. The worshiping congregation speaks (v. 1), perhaps led in its praise by one of the descendants of Asaph (v. 9). The psalm is framed by thanksgiving (v. 1) and praise (vv. 9–10). Two (Hebrew) stanzas of four lines each form the body of the psalm, and each stanza is composed of two couplets. The first stanza contains a reassuring word from heaven; the second contains a triumphant response from earth.
75 title *For the choir director.* See note on Ps 4 title. *set to.* See note on Ps 9 title. *Al-tashheth.* See note on Ps 57 title; see also Ps 58; 59 titles. *Asaph.* See note on Ps 73 title. *Song.* See note on Ps 30 title.
75:1 The congregation begins with thanksgiving in the form of praise (see 7:17; 28:7; 30:12; 35:18). *name.* See notes on 5:11; 74:7. *wondrous works.* See note on 9:1.
75:2–5 A reassuring word from above: God will not fail to call the arrogant to account. It is not clear whether a new word from the Lord is heard or whether these verses recall (and perhaps summarize) earlier prophetic words (such as those of Isaiah in 2 Kin 19:21–34).
75:2 God will not fail to judge—but in His own time.
75:3 When, because of the upsurge of evil powers, the whole moral order of the world seems to have crumbled, God still guarantees its stability (see note on 11:3). *pillars.* A figure for that which stabilizes the world order (see note on 24:2).
75:4 *boastful . . . wicked.* To the psalmists the wicked are both arrogant (see especially Ps 10; 73:4–12; 94:4; see also note on 31:23) and foolish (see 14:1; 74:18,22; 92:6; 94:8). *lift up the horn.* A figure for defiant opposition, based on the action of attacking bulls. "Horn" (see also v. 10) is a common Biblical metaphor for vigor or strength (see note on 18:2).
75:6–8 Triumphant echo from earth: perhaps spoken by the Levitical song leader in elaboration of the comforting word from God.
75:8 *cup.* See note on 16:5. *well mixed.* Probably mixed with spices to increase the intoxicating effect (see Prov 9:2,5; 23:29–30; Song 8:2; Is 65:11). *drink down its dregs.* Because God pours it out, they have no choice.
75:9 Concluding vow to praise God forever (see note on 7:17) for His righteous judgments. *me.* Probably the Levitical song leader speaking representatively for the people, but the pronoun may be a communal use of the singular, as in 74:12 (see note on Ps 30 title). *Jacob.* A synonym for Israel (see Gen 32:28).

10 And all the [a]horns of the wicked [1]He
will cut off,
But [b]the horns of the righteous will be
lifted up.

Psalm 76

For the choir director; on stringed instruments.
A Psalm of Asaph, a Song.

1 God is [a]known in Judah;
His name is [b]great in Israel.
2 His [1a]tabernacle is in [b]Salem;
His [c]dwelling place also is in Zion.
3 There He [a]broke the [1]flaming arrows,
The shield and the sword and the
[2]weapons of war. [3]Selah.

4 You are resplendent,
[1]More majestic than the mountains of
prey.
5 The [a]stouthearted were plundered,
[1]They sank into sleep;
And none of the [2]warriors could use
his hands.
6 At Your [a]rebuke, O God of Jacob,
Both [1b]rider and horse were cast into
a dead sleep.
7 You, even You, are [a]to be feared;
And [b]who may stand in Your presence
when once [1]You are angry?

8 You caused judgment to be heard from
heaven;
The earth [a]feared and was still
9 When God [a]arose to judgment,
To save all the humble of the earth.
Selah.
10 For the [1a]wrath of man shall praise
You;
With a remnant of wrath You will gird
Yourself.

11 [a]Make vows to the LORD your God and
[b]fulfill *them;*
Let all who are around Him [c]bring
gifts to Him who is to be feared.
12 He will cut off the spirit of princes;
He is [1a]feared by the kings of the
earth.

Psalm 77

For the choir director; [†]according to Jeduthun.
A Psalm of Asaph.

1 My voice *rises* to God, and I will [a]cry
aloud;
My voice *rises* to God, and He will
hear me.

10 [1]Heb *I* [a]Ps 101:8; Jer 48:25 [b]1 Sam 2:1; Ps 89:17; 92:10; 148:14
76:1 [a]Ps 48:3 [b]Ps 99:3
2 [1]Lit *shelter* [a]Ps 27:5; Lam 2:6 [b]Gen 14:18 [c]Ps 9:11; 132:13; 135:21
3 [1]Lit *fiery shafts of the bow* [2]Lit *battle* [3]*Selah* may mean: *Pause, Crescendo* or *Musical interlude* [a]Ps 46:9
4 [1]Or *Majestic from the mountains*
5 [1]Lit *They slumbered their sleep* [2]Lit *men of might have found their hands* [a]Is 10:12; 46:12
6 [1]Lit *chariot* [a]Ps 80:16 [b]Ex 15:1, 21; Ps 78:53
7 [1]Lit *Your anger is* [a]1 Chr 16:25; Ps 89:7; 96:4 [b]Ezra 9:15; Ps 130:3; Nah 1:6; Mal 3:2; Rev 6:17
8 [a]1 Chr 16:30; 2 Chr 20:29, 30; Ps 33:8
9 [a]Ps 9:7, 8; 74:22; 82:8 **10** [1]Lit *wraths* [a]Ex 9:16; Rom 9:17
11 [a]Eccl 5:4-6 [b]Ps 50:14 [c]2 Chr 32:23; Ps 68:29 **12** [1]Lit *awesome to* [a]Ps 47:2 **77:1** [†]1 Chr 16:41 [a]Ps 3:4; 142:1

75:10 *righteous.* See note on 1:5. *lifted up.* See v. 7; see also note on v. 4.

Ps 76 A celebration of the Lord's invincible power in defense of Jerusalem, His royal city. The psalm is thematically related to Ps 46; 48; 87 (see introduction to Ps 46). The ancient tradition may well be correct that the psalm was composed after the Lord's destruction of Sennacherib's army when it threatened Jerusalem (see 2 Kin 19:35). Structurally, the opening (vv. 1–3) and closing (vv. 11–12) stanzas contain the main thematic development. Between them, a seven-verse stanza of praise addressed to God (vv. 4–10) celebrates His awesome act of judgment. The internal structure is notable: Verses 4,7,10 present general reflections, while the intervening verses recall the judgment itself. Verse 7, the center line (see note on 6:6), states the main theme of this stanza.

76 title *For the choir director.* See note on Ps 4 title. *on stringed instruments.* See note on Ps 4 title. *Asaph.* See note on Ps 73 title. *Song.* See note on Ps 30 title.

76:1–3 God's crushing defeat of the enemy in defense of Zion.

76:1 *is known.* Now especially—as a result of His marvelous act. *Israel.* The poet probably does not intend to distinguish between the two kingdoms (Judah and Israel) but only, by joining their names together, to refer to the whole of God's covenant people. Moreover, as a result of the Assyrian invasions, many displaced Israelites from the northern kingdom now resided in and around Jerusalem.

76:2 *tabernacle.* Lit. "booth," referring to the temple. Since the Lord has just achieved a great victory over a menacing army, the poet may have wished to speak of the temple as the Lord's campaign tent (see 2 Sam 11:11; 1 Kin 20:12,16). But see also 18:11 ("canopy"); 31:20 ("shelter"). *Salem.* Jerusalem, as the parallelism makes clear (see note on Gen 14:18). *Zion.* See note on 9:11.

76:4–10 Praise of God's awesome majesty, whose mighty judgment evokes fearful reverence (see introduction).

76:5–6 Perhaps echoes also God's victory over the Egyptians at the Red Sea (see Ex 14:28,30; 15:4–5,10).

76:6 *rebuke.* This word, when predicated of God, usually refers to either (1) the thunder of His fierce majesty by which He wields His sovereign control over cosmic entities (see 18:15; 104:7; 106:9; Job 26:11; Is 50:2; Nah 1:4) or repulses His enemies (as here; see also 9:5; 68:30; Is 17:13), or (2) the thunder of His wrath (see 80:16; Is 51:20; 54:9; 66:15; Mal 2:3). *God of Jacob.* A link with Ps 75 (see 75:9 and note).

76:7 The thematic center of vv. 4–10 (see note on 6:6).

76:8 *from heaven.* Though God is present in Zion (see v. 2), He sovereignly rules from heaven.

76:10 *wrath.* See note on 2:5. *shall praise You.* When His judgments bring deliverance, those rescued praise Him. When men rise against God's kingdom, He crushes them in wrath to His own praise as Victor and Deliverer. The "remnant of wrath" indicates that particular judgments do not exhaust His wrath; a remainder is left to deal with other hostile powers.

76:11–12 Let Israel acknowledge God's help with grateful vows; let the nations acknowledge His sovereign rule with tribute.

76:11 *Make vows.* See note on 50:14.

76:12 *spirit of princes.* Their bold rebelliousness.

Ps 77 Comforting reflections in a time of great distress. The distress appears to be personal rather than national. Comparison of vv. 16–19 with Hab 3:8–10 suggests, but does not prove, a time late in the monarchy. The poetic development advances from anguished bewilderment (vv. 1–9) to comforting recollection (vv. 10–20). A striking and dramatic feature is the insertion of a four-verse section (vv. 16–19) between the third and fourth verses of another four-verse section (vv. 13–15,20).

77 title *For the choir director.* See note on Ps 4 title. *Jeduthun.* See note on Ps 39 title. *Asaph.* See note on Ps 73 title.

77:1–9 Anguished perplexity over God's apparent inaction, when He fails to respond to unceasing and urgent prayers.

2 In the [a]day of my trouble I sought the
Lord;
[b]In the night my [c]hand was stretched
out [1]without weariness;
My soul [d]refused to be comforted.
3 *When* I remember God, then I am
[a]disturbed;
When I [b]sigh, then [c]my spirit grows
faint. [1]Selah.
4 You have held my eyelids *open;*
I am so troubled that I [a]cannot speak.
5 I have considered the [a]days of old,
The years of long ago.
6 I will remember my [a]song in the
night;
I [b]will meditate with my heart,
And my spirit [1]ponders:
7 Will the Lord [a]reject forever?
And will He [b]never be favorable
again?
8 Has His [a]lovingkindness ceased
forever?
Has *His* [1b]promise come to an end
[2]forever?
9 Has God [a]forgotten to be gracious,
Or has He in anger [1]withdrawn His
[b]compassion? Selah.
10 Then I said, "[a]It is my [1]grief,
That the [b]right hand of the Most High
has changed."
11 I shall remember the [a]deeds of [1]the
LORD;
Surely I will [a]remember Your wonders
of old.
12 I will [a]meditate on all Your work
And muse on Your deeds.

2 [1]Lit *and did not grow numb* [a]Ps 50:15; 86:7 [b]Ps 63:6; Is 26:9 [c]Job 11:13; Ps 88:9 [d]Gen 37:35
3 [1]*Selah* may mean: *Pause, Crescendo* or *Musical interlude* [a]Ps 42:5, 11; 43:5 [b]Ps 55:2; 142:2 [c]Ps 61:2; 143:4
4 [a]Ps 39:9
5 [a]Deut 32:7; Ps 44:1; 143:5; Is 51:9
6 [1]Lit *searched* [a]Ps 42:8 [b]Ps 4:4
7 [a]Ps 44:9 [b]Ps 85:1, 5
8 [1]Lit *word* [2]Lit *from generation to generation* [a]Ps 89:49 [b]2 Pet 3:9
9 [1]Lit *shut up* [a]Is 49:15 [b]Ps 25:6; 40:11; 51:1
10 [1]Or *infirmity, the years of the right hand of the Most High* [a]Ps 31:22; 73:14 [b]Ps 44:2, 3
11 [1]Heb YAH [a]Ps 105:5; 143:5
12 [a]Ps 145:5
13 [a]Ps 63:2; 73:17 [b]Ex 15:11; Ps 71:19; 86:8
14 [a]Ps 72:18 [b]Ps 106:8
15 [1]Lit *arm* [a]Ex 6:6; Deut 9:29; Ps 74:2; 78:42 [b]Ps 80:1
16 [a]Ex 14:21; Ps 114:3; Hab 3:8, 10
17 [1]Lit *went* [a]Judg 5:4 [b]Ps 68:33 [c]Ps 18:14

13 Your way, O God, is [a]holy;
[b]What god is great like our God?
14 You are the [a]God who works wonders;
You have [b]made known Your strength
among the peoples.
15 You have by Your [1]power [a]redeemed
Your people,
The sons of Jacob and [b]Joseph. Selah.
16 The [a]waters saw You, O God;
The waters saw You, they were in
anguish;
The deeps also trembled.
17 The [a]clouds poured out water;
The skies [b]gave forth a sound;
Your [c]arrows [1]flashed here and there.
18 The [a]sound of Your thunder was in
the whirlwind;
The [b]lightnings lit up the world;
The [c]earth trembled and shook.
19 Your [a]way was in the sea
And Your paths in the mighty waters,
And Your footprints may not be
known.
20 You [a]led Your people like a flock
By the hand of [b]Moses and Aaron.

Psalm 78

A [†]Maskil of Asaph.

1 [a]Listen, O my people, to my
[1]instruction;
[b]Incline your ears to the words of my
mouth.

18 [a]Ps 18:13; 104:7 [b]Ps 97:4 [c]Judg 5:4; Ps 18:7 **19** [a]Is 51:10; Hab 3:15 **20** [a]Ex 13:21; 14:19; Ps 78:52; 80:1; Is 63:11-13 [b]Ex 6:26; Ps 105:26 **78:1** [†]Possibly, *Contemplative,* or *Didactic,* or *Skillful Psalm* [1]Or *law, teaching* [a]Is 51:4 [b]Is 55:3

77:2 *soul.* See note on 6:3.
77:3–6 Remembrance of God's past mercies intensifies the present perplexity (as also in 22:1–11). God's failure to act now is so troubling that the psalmist cannot sleep (cf. 3:5; 4:8) and words fail (but see vv. 10–20).
77:6 *heart.* See note on 4:7.
77:7–9 Though words fail (v. 4), troubled thoughts will not go away.
77:8 *lovingkindness.* See note on 6:4.
77:9 *anger.* See note on 2:5.
77:10–20 Reassuring recollection of God's mighty acts in behalf of Israel in the exodus.
77:10–12 Faith's decision to look beyond the present troubles—and God's bewildering inactivity—to draw hope anew from God's saving acts of old.
77:10 *Most High.* See note on Gen 14:19.
77:11,14 *wonders.* See note on 9:1.
77:13–20 God's mighty acts in the exodus recalled.
77:13 Appears to echo Ex 15:11. *is holy.* Or "is seen in the sanctuary" (see 63:2).
77:15 *redeemed.* Here, as often, a synonym for "deliver" (see 74:2). *Joseph.* OT authors sometimes refer to the northern kingdom as "Joseph" (or "Ephraim," Joseph's son) in distinction from the southern kingdom of Judah (see 78:67; 2 Sam 19:20; 1 Kin 11:28; Ezek 37:16,19; Amos 5:6,15; 6:6; Zech 10:6). However, here and elsewhere (see 80:1; 81:5; Obad 18) Joseph—the one elevated to the position of firstborn (see Gen 48:5 and note; Josh 16:1–4; 1 Chr 5:2; Ezek 47:13)—represents the whole of his generation and thus also all the descendants of Jacob.
77:16–19 A poetically heightened description of the majesty of God displayed when He opened a way through the Red Sea. Verses 16,19 speak expressly of that event; the intervening verses (vv. 17–18) evoke the majesty of God displayed in the thunderstorm and earthquake. Ex 14:19 speaks only of God's cloud, not of a thunderstorm or earthquake, but the Hebrew poets often associated either or both with the Lord's coming to effect redemption or judgment—no doubt because these were the two most fearsome displays of power known to them (see 18:12–14; 68:8; Judg 5:4–5; Hab 3:6,10). Here the psalmist declares: It was the God of thunderstorm and earthquake who made His majestic way through the mighty waters of the sea to bring His people out of bondage. For Christians the display of God's power in behalf of His people now includes the resurrection of Jesus Christ from the dead (see Matt 28:2; cf. Eph 1:18–23).
77:17 *arrows.* Lightning bolts.
77:20 Completes the thought of v. 15 (see introduction). *led Your people.* Through the Wilderness of Sinai.
Ps 78 A psalm of instruction—of warnings not to repeat Israel's sins of the past but to remember God's saving acts and marvelously persistent grace and, remembering, to keep faith with Him and His covenant. Here as elsewhere (pervasively in the OT), trust in and loyalty to God on the part of God's people are covenant matters. They do not spring from abstract principles

2 I will [a]open my mouth in a parable;
I will utter [b]dark sayings of old,
3 Which we have heard and known,
And [a]our fathers have told us.
4 We will [a]not conceal them from their children,
But [b]tell to the generation to come the praises of the LORD,
And His strength and His [c]wondrous works that He has done.

5 For He established a [a]testimony in Jacob
And appointed a [b]law in Israel,
Which He [c]commanded our fathers
That they should [1][d]teach them to their children,
6 [a]That the generation to come might know, *even* [b]the children *yet* to be born,
That they may arise and [c]tell *them* to their children,
7 That they should put their confidence in God
And [a]not forget the works of God,
But [b]keep His commandments,
8 And [a]not be like their fathers,
A [b]stubborn and rebellious generation,
A generation that [c]did not [1]prepare its heart
And whose spirit was not [d]faithful to God.

9 The sons of Ephraim [1]were [a]archers equipped with bows,
Yet [b]they turned back in the day of battle.
10 They [a]did not keep the covenant of God
And refused to [b]walk in His law;
11 They [a]forgot His deeds
And His [1]miracles that He had shown them.
12 [a]He wrought wonders before their fathers

2 [a]Ps 49:4; Matt 13:35 [b]Prov 1:6 **3** [a]Ps 44:1 **4** [a]Ex 12:26; Deut 6:7; 11:19; Job 15:18; Ps 145:4; Is 38:19; Joel 1:3 [b]Ex 13:8, 14; Ps 22:30 [c]Job 37:16; Ps 26:7; 71:17 **5** [1]Lit *make them known* [a]Ps 19:7; 81:5; Is 8:20 [b]Ps 147:19 [c]Deut 6:4-9 [d]Deut 4:9 **6** [a]Ps 102:18 [b]Ps 22:31 [c]Deut 11:19 **7** [a]Deut 4:9; 6:12; 8:14 [b]Deut 4:2; 5:1, 29; 27:1; Josh 22:5 **8** [1]Or *put right* [a]2 Kin 17:14; 2 Chr 30:7; Ezek 20:18 [b]Ex 32:9; Deut 9:7, 24; 31:27; Judg 2:19; Is 30:9 [c]Job 11:13; Ps 78:37 [d]Ps 51:10

9 [1]Or *being* [a]1 Chr 12:2 [b]Judg 20:39; Ps 78:57 **10** [a]Judg 2:20; 1 Kin 11:11; 2 Kin 17:15; 18:12 [b]Ps 119:1; Jer 32:23; 44:10, 23 **11** [1]Or *wonderful works* [a]Ps 106:13 **12** [a]Ex chs 7-12; Ps 106:22

(such as the formal structure of the God-man relationship) or from general human consciousness (such as feelings of dependence on "God" or a sense of awe in the presence of the "holy"), but they result from remembering God's mighty saving acts. Correspondingly, unfaithfulness is the more blameworthy because it contemptuously disregards all God's wonderful acts in His people's behalf (see Ps 105–106).

The psalm probably dates from the period of the divided monarchy and may have been composed about the time of the prophet Hosea (both Hosea and Isaiah speak frequently of the northern kingdom as Ephraim since it was the dominant tribe of that realm). Israel's unfaithfulness is here epitomized in the sin of Ephraim (v. 9); the psalm concludes by recalling the rejection of "Israel" (v. 59) and the abandonment of Shiloh (v. 60), but the election of Judah and Mount Zion (v. 68). Coming, as may be assumed, from the pen of an Asaphite, the psalm was no doubt a warning to worshipers at Jerusalem not to fall away after the manner of their brothers to the north.

By placing this psalm next to Ps 77, the editors of the Psalter ranged David alongside Moses (and Aaron) as the Lord's shepherd over His people (see vv. 70–72; 77:20) who brought the exodus to its (provisionally) climactic fruition by completing the conquest of the promised land—a perspective apparently shared by the author of the psalm.

The psalm is composed of 77 (Hebrew) lines (72 numbered verses) and seven stanzas—with an 11-line introduction. After the introduction, the structure of the stanzas in Hebrew is symmetrical: 8 lines, 16 lines, 9 lines, 16 lines, 9 lines, 8 lines. The two sequences of 16 lines–9 lines constitute a thematic cycle, while the two 8-line stanzas frame the double cycle and underscore the contrast between the sin of Israel ("Ephraim," vv. 9–16) and the unending mercy of God to His people—mercy that is evidenced in His victory over His enemies and His election of Zion (in Judah) and David (vv. 65–72).

78 title *Maskil.* See note on Ps 32 title. *Asaph.* See note on Ps 73 title.

78:1–8 Our children must hear what our fathers have told us, so that they may be faithful to the Lord.

78:1–2 This introduction is written in the style of a wisdom writer (see essay, p. 689; see also Ps 49:1–4).

78:2 *parable . . . dark sayings.* The Hebrew underlying these two expressions occurs in 49:4 ("proverb," "riddle") and Ezek 17:2 ("riddle," "parable")—which raises the question of whether the author is here influenced by prophetic use of wisdom language. While both terms had specialized uses—those reflected in 49:4—they apparently also became conventionalized more generally for instruction in a wide variety of forms. *of old.* Things for instruction from the past. Matt 13:35 refers to this verse as a prophecy of Jesus' parabolic teaching. Matthew apparently perceived in this psalm a prophetic voice anticipating that of the great Prophet. The "parables" of the psalm are, however, more like the teaching of Stephen (Acts 7) than that of Jesus.

78:4–5 The Lord's saving acts and covenant statutes—both must be taught, and in relationship, for together they remain the focal point for faith and obedience down through the generations (see vv. 7–8).

78:4 *not conceal them.* See Job 15:18.

78:5 *teach . . . their children.* See, e.g., Ex 10:2; 12:26–27; 13:8,14; Deut 4:9; 6:20–21.

78:8 *stubborn and rebellious.* Like a rebellious son (see Deut 9:6–7, 24; 31:27). *generation.* A people with certain characteristics (see 24:6; Deut 32:5,20), thus not limited to the exodus generation (see vv. 9–11,56–64). *heart.* See note on 4:7.

78:9–16 The northern kingdom has violated God's covenant, not remembering His saving acts (a message emphasized by the prophets Amos and Hosea). Israel's history with God has been a long series of rebellions on her part (vv. 9–16,32–39, 56–64), beginning already in the wilderness (vv. 17–31,40–55).

78:9 *sons of Ephraim.* The northern kingdom, dominated by the tribe of Ephraim (see introduction). *turned back.* Neither the tribe of Ephraim nor the northern kingdom had a reputation for cowardice or ineffectiveness in battle (see, e.g., Deut 33:17). This verse is best understood as a metaphor for Israel's betrayal of God's covenant (see v. 10), related to the figure of the "treacherous bow" (v. 57).

78:12–16 A summary reference to the plagues in Egypt and to the water miracles at the Red Sea and in the wilderness. In the two cycles that follow (vv. 17–39,40–64), further elaboration intensifies the indictment.

78:12 See Ex 7–12. *Zoan.* A city in the northeast part of the Nile delta (see v. 43; see also Num 13:22 and note).

In the land of Egypt, in the [b]field of
Zoan.
13 He [a]divided the sea and caused them
to pass through,
And He made the waters stand [b]up
like a heap.
14 Then He led them with the cloud by
[a]day
And all the night with a [b]light of fire.
15 He [a]split the rocks in the wilderness
And gave *them* abundant drink like
the ocean depths.
16 He [a]brought forth streams also from
the rock
And caused waters to run down like
rivers.

17 Yet they still continued to sin against
Him,
To [a]rebel against the Most High in the
desert.
18 And in their heart they [a]put God to
the test
By asking [b]food according to their
desire.
19 Then they spoke against God;
They said, "[a]Can God prepare a table
in the wilderness?
20 "Behold, He [a]struck the rock so that
waters gushed out,
And streams were overflowing;
Can He give bread also?
Will He provide [1b]meat for His
people?"

21 Therefore the LORD heard and [1]was
[a]full of wrath;
And a fire was kindled against Jacob
And anger also mounted against
Israel,
22 Because they [a]did not believe in God
And did not trust in His salvation.
23 Yet He commanded the clouds above
And [a]opened the doors of heaven;
24 He [a]rained down manna upon them to
eat
And gave them [1b]food from heaven.
25 Man did eat the bread of [1]angels;
He sent them [2]food [3a]in abundance.
26 He [a]caused the east wind to blow in
the heavens
And by His [1]power He directed the
south wind.
27 When He rained [1]meat upon them like
the dust,
Even [a]winged fowl like the sand of
the seas,
28 Then He let *them* fall in the midst of
[1]their camp,
Round about their dwellings.
29 So they [a]ate and were well filled,
And their desire He gave to them.
30 [1]Before they had satisfied their desire,
[a]While their food was in their mouths,
31 The [a]anger of God rose against them
And killed [1]some of their [b]stoutest
ones,
And [2]subdued the choice men of
Israel.
32 In spite of all this they [a]still sinned
And [b]did not believe in His wonderful
works.
33 So He brought [a]their days to an end in
[1]futility
And their years in sudden terror.

34 When He killed them, then they
[a]sought Him,
And returned and searched [b]diligently
for God;
35 And they remembered that God was
their [a]rock,
And the Most High God their
[b]Redeemer.

12 [b]Num 13:22; Ps 78:43; Is 19:11; 30:4; Ezek 30:14 **13** [a]Ex 14:21; Ps 74:13; 136:13 [b]Ex 15:8; Ps 33:7 **14** [a]Ex 13:21; Ps 105:39 [b]Ex 14:24 **15** [a]Ex 17:6; Num 20:11; Ps 105:41; 114:8; Is 48:21; 1 Cor 10:4 **16** [a]Num 20:8, 10, 11 **17** [a]Deut 9:22; Is 63:10; Heb 3:16 **18** [a]Ex 17:6; Deut 6:16; Ps 78:41, 56; 95:9; 106:14; 1 Cor 10:9 [b]Num 11:4 **19** [a]Ex 16:3; Num 11:4; 20:3; 21:5; Ps 23:5 **20** [1]Lit *flesh* [a]Num 20:11; Ps 78:15, 16 [b]Num 11:18 **21** [1]Or *became infuriated* [a]Num 11:1 **22** [a]Deut 1:32; 9:23; Heb 3:18 **23** [a]Gen 7:11; Mal 3:10

24 [1]Lit *grain* [a]Ex 16:4 [b]Ps 105:40; John 6:31 **25** [1]Lit *mighty ones* [2]Or *provision* [3]Lit *to satiation* [a]Ex 16:3 **26** [1]Or *strength* [a]Num 11:31 **27** [1]Lit *flesh* [a]Ex 16:13; Ps 105:40 **28** [1]Lit *His* **29** [a]Num 11:19, 20 **30** [1]Lit *They were not estranged from* [a]Num 11:33 **31** [1]Lit *among their fat ones* [2]Lit *caused to bow down* [a]Num 11:33, 34; Job 20:23 [b]Is 10:16 **32** [a]Num chs 14, 16, 17 [b]Num 14:11; Ps 78:11 **33** [1]Lit *vanity, a mere breath* [a]Num 14:29, 35 **34** [a]Num 21:7; Hos 5:15 [b]Ps 63:1 **35** [a]Deut 32:4 [b]Ex 15:13; Deut 9:26; Ps 74:2; Is 41:14

78:13 See Ex 14:1–15:21.
78:15–16 See v. 20; Ex 17:6; Num 20:8,10–11.
78:17–31 Israel's rebelliousness in the wilderness; God's marvelous provision of food—and His anger.
78:17 *continued.* Although no sin in the wilderness has yet been mentioned, the poet probably expected his readers to recall (in conjunction with the miraculous provisions of water just mentioned) how the people grumbled at Marah because of lack of water (see Ex 15:24). *Most High.* See vv. 35,56; see also note on Gen 14:19.
78:18 See Ex 16:2–3. *put God to the test.* See vv. 41,56; see also note on Ex 17:2.
78:19 *Can God prepare a table . . . ?* For a different use of the same imagery see 23:5.
78:20 *bread . . . meat.* The poet is probably combining and compressing two episodes (Ex 16:2–3; Num 11:4).
78:21 *wrath.* See vv. 31,49–50,58–59,62; see also note on 2:5.
78:23 *opened the doors of heaven.* For this imagery see Gen 7:11; 2 Kin 7:2; Mal 3:10.
78:25 *bread of angels.* So called because it came down from heaven. *angels.* Lit. "mighty ones." The Hebrew word is used only here of the angels, but reference is clearly to heavenly beings (see 103:20).
78:26–28 See Ex 16:13; Num 11:31.
78:26 *east wind . . . south wind.* Since the quails were migrating from Egypt at this time, the south wind may have carried them north and the east wind may have diverted them to the wilderness area occupied by the Israelites (the book of Numbers does not provide wind directions).
78:27 *like the dust . . . like the sand.* Similes for a huge number (see note on Gen 13:16).
78:30–31 See Num 11:33.
78:32–39 Rebelliousness, which became Israel's way of life, showed itself early in the wilderness wandering (vv. 17–31) and continued throughout that journey.
78:32 *did not believe.* That God could give them victory over the Canaanites (see Num 14:11).
78:33 The exodus generation was condemned to die in the wilderness (see Num 14:22–23,28–35).
78:34–37 A cycle repeated frequently during the period of the judges.

36 But they [a]deceived Him with their mouth
And [b]lied to Him with their tongue.
37 For their heart was not [a]steadfast toward Him,
Nor were they faithful in His covenant.
38 But He, being [a]compassionate,
[1b]forgave *their* iniquity and did not destroy *them;*
And often He [2c]restrained His anger
And did not arouse all His wrath.
39 Thus [a]He remembered that they were but [b]flesh,
A [1c]wind that passes and does not return.

40 How often they [a]rebelled against Him in the wilderness
And [b]grieved Him in the [c]desert!
41 Again and again they [1a]tempted God,
And pained the [b]Holy One of Israel.
42 They [a]did not remember [b]His [1]power,
The day when He [c]redeemed them from the adversary,
43 When He performed His [a]signs in Egypt
And His [b]marvels in the field of Zoan,
44 And [a]turned their rivers to blood,
And their streams, they could not drink.
45 He sent among them swarms of [a]flies which devoured them,
And [b]frogs which destroyed them.
46 He gave also their crops to the [a]grasshopper
And the product of their labor to the [b]locust.
47 He [1]destroyed their vines with [a]hailstones
And their sycamore trees with frost.
48 He gave over their [a]cattle also to the hailstones
And their herds to bolts of lightning.
49 He [a]sent upon them His burning anger,
Fury and indignation and trouble,
[1]A band of destroying angels.
50 He leveled a path for His anger;
He did not spare their soul from death,
But [a]gave over their life to the plague,
51 And [a]smote all the firstborn in Egypt,
The [b]first *issue* of their virility in the tents of [c]Ham.
52 But He [a]led forth His own people like sheep
And guided them in the wilderness [b]like a flock;
53 He led them [a]safely, so that they did not fear;
But [b]the sea engulfed their enemies.
54 So [a]He brought them to His holy [1]land,
To this [2b]hill country [c]which His right hand had gained.
55 He also [a]drove out the nations before them
And [b]apportioned them for an inheritance by measurement,
And made the tribes of Israel dwell in their tents.
56 Yet they [1a]tempted and [b]rebelled against the Most High God
And did not keep His testimonies,
57 But turned back and [a]acted treacherously like their fathers;
They [b]turned aside like a treacherous bow.
58 For they [a]provoked Him with their [b]high places
And [c]aroused His jealousy with their [d]graven images.
59 When God heard, He [1]was filled with [a]wrath
And greatly [b]abhorred Israel;
60 So that He [a]abandoned the [b]dwelling place at Shiloh,

36 [a]Ex 24:7, 8; Ezek 33:31 [b]Ex 32:7, 8; Is 57:11
37 [a]Ps 51:10; 78:8; Acts 8:21
38 [1]Lit *covered over, atoned for* [2]Lit *turned away* [a]Ex 34:6 [b]Num 14:18-20 [c]Is 48:9
39 [1]Or *breath* [a]Job 10:9; Ps 103:14 [b]Gen 6:3 [c]Job 7:7, 16; Ps 103:14; James 4:14
40 [a]Ps 95:8, 9; 106:43; 107:11; Heb 3:16 [b]Ps 95:10; Is 63:10; Eph 4:30 [c]Ps 106:14
41 [1]Or *put God to the test* [a]Num 14:22 [b]2 Kin 19:22; Ps 89:18
42 [1]Lit *hand* [a]Judg 8:34 [b]Ps 44:3 [c]Ps 106:10
43 [a]Ps 105:27 [b]Ex 4:21; 7:3
44 [a]Ex 7:20; Ps 105:29
45 [a]Ex 8:24; Ps 105:31 [b]Ex 8:6; Ps 105:30
46 [a]1 Kin 8:37; Ps 105:34 [b]Ex 10:14
47 [1]Lit *was killing* [a]Ex 9:23-25; Ps 105:32
48 [a]Ex 9:19
49 [1]Lit *A deputation of angels of evil* [a]Ex 15:7
50 [a]Ex 12:29, 30
51 [a]Ex 12:29; Ps 105:36; 135:8; 136:10 [b]Gen 49:3 [c]Ps 105:23, 27; 106:22
52 [a]Ex 15:22 [b]Ps 77:20
53 [a]Ex 14:19, 20 [b]Ex 14:27, 28; Ps 106:11
54 [1]Lit *border, territory* [2]Or *mountain* [a]Ex 15:17 [b]Ps 68:16; Is 11:9 [c]Ps 44:3
55 [a]Josh 11:16-23; Ps 44:2 [b]Josh 13:7; 23:4; Ps 105:11; 135:12
56 [1]Or *put to the test* [a]Ps 78:18 [b]Judg 2:11-13; Ps 78:40
57 [a]Ezek 20:27, 28 [b]Hos 7:16 **58** [a]Deut 4:25; Judg 2:12; 1 Kin 14:9; Is 65:3 [b]Lev 26:30; 1 Kin 3:2; 2 Kin 16:4; Jer 17:3 [c]Deut 32:16, 21; 1 Kin 14:22 [d]Ex 20:4; Lev 26:1; Deut 4:25
59 [1]Or *became infuriated* [a]Deut 1:34; 9:19; Ps 106:40 [b]Lev 26:30; Deut 32:19; Amos 6:8 **60** [a]1 Sam 4:11; Ps 78:67; Jer 7:12, 14; 26:6 [b]Josh 18:1

78:35 *rock.* See note on 18:2. *Redeemer.* Deliverer (see note on Ex 6:6).
78:36 See Is 29:13.
78:37 *heart.* See note on 4:7.
78:38 See Ex 32:14; Num 14:20. *forgave.* See note on 65:3.
78:39 See 103:14; see also note on 10:18.
78:40–64 The second cycle (the first is vv. 17–39).
78:40–55 Israel's rebelliousness began in the wilderness; she did not remember how she had been delivered from oppression by God's plagues upon Egypt (see v. 12). Yet He brought them through the sea and the wilderness and established them in the promised land.
78:41 *Holy One of Israel.* See 71:22; 89:18; see also note on Is 1:4.
78:44–51 The plagues upon Egypt (see Ex 7–12): The sequence in Exodus is followed only in the first and last; the third, fifth, sixth and ninth plagues are not mentioned.
78:47 *sycamore trees.* See note on Amos 7:14.
78:49 *destroying angels.* The poet personifies God's wrath, indignation and hostility as agents of His anger.
78:51 *tents.* Dwellings. *Ham.* For the association of Ham with Egypt see 105:23,27; 106:21–22; Gen 10:6 and note.
78:53 *sea.* Red Sea.
78:55 Summarizes the story told in Joshua.
78:56–64 Rebelliousness continued to be Israel's way of life in the promised land (a recurring theme of Judges; see also 1 Sam 2:12–7:2), so God rejected Israel (v. 59; see Jer 7:15).
78:57 *treacherous bow.* See note on v. 9.
78:58 *high places.* See note on 1 Sam 9:12. *jealousy.* God's intense reaction to disloyalty to Him (see note on Ex 20:5).
78:59 *greatly abhorred Israel.* Abandoned her to her enemies. The psalmist does not speak of a permanent casting off of Israel, not even of the ten northern tribes.
78:60 *Shiloh.* The center of worship since the time of Joshua (see Josh 18:1,8; 21:1–2; Judg 18:31; 1 Sam 1:3; Jer 7:12), it was located in Ephraim between Bethel and Shechem (see Judg

The tent [1]which He had pitched
among men,
61 And gave up His [a]strength to captivity
And His glory [b]into the hand of the
adversary.
62 He also [a]delivered His people to the
sword,
And [1]was filled with wrath at His
inheritance.
63 [a]Fire devoured [1]His young men,
And [1]His [b]virgins had no wedding
songs.
64 [1]His [a]priests fell by the sword,
And [1]His [b]widows could not weep.

65 Then the Lord [a]awoke as *if from*
sleep,
Like a [b]warrior [1]overcome by wine.
66 He [1a]drove His adversaries backward;
He put on them an everlasting
reproach.
67 He also [a]rejected the tent of Joseph,
And did not choose the tribe of
Ephraim,
68 But chose the tribe of Judah,
Mount [a]Zion which He loved.
69 And He [a]built His sanctuary like the
heights,
Like the earth which He has founded
forever.
70 He also [a]chose David His servant
And took him from the sheepfolds;
71 From [1a]the care of the [2]ewes [b]with
suckling lambs He brought him
To [c]shepherd Jacob His people,
And Israel [d]His inheritance.
72 So he shepherded them according to
the [a]integrity of his heart,
And guided them with his skillful
hands.

Psalm 79

A Psalm of Asaph.

1 O God, the [a]nations have [1]invaded
[b]Your inheritance;
They have defiled Your [c]holy temple;
They have [d]laid Jerusalem in ruins.

60 [1]Some ancient versions read *where He dwelt* **61** [a]Ps 63:2; 132:8 [b]1 Sam 4:17 **62** [1]Or *became infuriated* [a]Judg 20:21; 1 Sam 4:10 **63** [1]Or *their* [a]Num 11:1; 21:28; Is 26:11; Jer 48:45 [b]Jer 7:34; 16:9; Lam 2:21 **64** [1]Or *their* [a]1 Sam 4:17; 22:18 [b]Job 27:15; Ezek 24:23 **65** [1]Or *sobered up from* [a]Ps 44:23; 73:20 [b]Is 42:13 **66** [1]Lit *smote* [a]1 Sam 5:6 **67** [a]Ps 78:60 **68** [a]Ps 87:2; 132:13 **69** [a]1 Kin 6:1-38 **70** [a]1 Sam 16:11, 12 **71** [1]Lit *following* [2]Lit *ewes which gave suck, He...* [a]2 Sam 7:8; Is 40:11 [b]Gen 33:13 [c]2 Sam 5:2; 1 Chr 11:2; Ps 28:9 [d]1 Sam 10:1 **72** [a]1 Kin 9:4 **79:1** [1]Lit *come into* [a]Lam 1:10 [b]Ps 74:2 [c]Ps 74:3, 7 [d]2 Kin 25:9, 10; 2 Chr 36:17-19; Jer 26:18; 52:12-14; Mic 3:12

21:19). Apparently it was destroyed by the Philistines when they captured the ark or shortly afterward (see note on Jer 7:12).

78:61 *His strength . . . His glory.* The ark is here so called because it was the sign of God's kingship in Israel and the focal point for the display of His power and glory (see 26:8; 63:2; 1 Sam 4:3,21–22).

78:62,71 *His inheritance.* See Deut 9:29.

78:63 *Fire.* Often associated with the sword (see vv. 62,64) as the two primary instruments of destruction in ancient warfare. *no wedding songs.* So great was the catastrophe that both the wedding songs of the brides and the wailing of the widows (see v. 64) were silenced in the land.

78:64 *priests fell by the sword.* See 1 Sam 4:11.

78:65–72 The Lord's election of Judah (instead of Ephraim) as the leading tribe in Israel (anticipated in Jacob's deathbed blessing of his sons, Gen 49:8–12), of Mount Zion (instead of Shiloh) as the place of His sanctuary (royal seat), and of David as His regent to shepherd His people. By these acts the Lord established His people securely as His kingdom in the promised land, following the long period of Israel's troubles from the death of Joshua to the death of Saul—by then God's salvation of Israel begun in the exodus reached its climactic (if provisional) fulfillment (see introduction to Ps 68 and the combination of echoes of God's saving act in the exodus and through David in Isaiah's prophecy of Israel's future deliverance, Is 11:11–16).

78:65 *awoke as if from sleep.* Poetic hyperbole to highlight the contrast between God's action in behalf of His people in the days of David and the preceding time of Israel's troubles (see note on 7:6).

78:66–72 The saving events noted have two focal points: (1) God's decisive victory over His enemies (thus securing His realm) and the establishment of Zion as His royal city, and (2) the appointment of David to be the shepherd of His people.

78:67 *tent of Joseph.* A figure for the tribe of Ephraim (for the figurative use of "tent" see v. 51; see also 69:25; 83:6; 84:10; 120:5; Gen 9:27; Deut 33:18; 1 Kin 12:16; Job 8:22; 12:6; Hab 3:7; Mal 2:12).

78:68,70 *chose . . . Mount Zion . . . chose David.* See Ps 132.

78:69 *heights . . . earth.* The verse is subject to two interpretations: (1) The Lord built His sanctuary as impregnable as a mountain fortress and as enduring and unmovable as the age-old earth, or (2) the Lord built His sanctuary as secure and enduring as the heavens and the earth (see note on 24:2) and there manifests Himself as the Lord of glory (see 24:7–10; 26:8; 63:2; 96:6), even as He does in the creation (see 19:1; 29:9; 97:6).

78:70–71 See 1 Sam 16:11–13; 2 Sam 7:8.

78:70 *His servant.* Here an official title marking David as a member of God's royal administration (see notes on Ex 14:31; Ps 18 title; Is 41:8–9; 42:1).

78:71 *shepherd.* See note on 23:1.

78:72 Israel under the care of the Lord's royal shepherd from the house of David was for the prophets the hope of God's people (see Ezek 34:23; 37:24; Mic 5:4—fulfilled in Jesus Christ, Matt 2:6; John 10:11; Rev 7:17).

Ps 79 Israel's prayer for God's forgiveness and help and for His judgment on the nations that have so cruelly destroyed her, showing utter contempt for both the Lord and His people. Like Ps 74, with which it has many thematic links, it dates from the time of the exile. The poignancy of its appeal is heightened by its juxtaposition to Ps 77 (recalling God's saving acts under Moses) and Ps 78 (recalling God's saving acts under David), two psalms with which it is significantly linked by the shepherd-sheep figure and other thematic elements. Israel acknowledges that the Lord has used the nations to punish her for her sins, so she pleads for pardon. But she knows too that the nations have acted out of their hostility to and disdain for God and His people; that warrants her plea for God's judgment on them (see Is 10:5–11; 47:6–7). Daniel's prayer (Dan 9:4–19) contains much that is similar to the elements of penitence in this psalm.

79 title *Asaph.* See note on Ps 73 title.

79:1–4 What the nations have done: They have attacked God's own special domain, violated His temple, destroyed His royal city, slaughtered His people, degraded them in death (by withholding burial—see note on 53:5—and leaving their bodies as carrion for birds and beasts) and reduced them to the scorn of the world.

79:1 *Your inheritance.* Cf. 78:62,71. Here reference is to Israel's homeland as the Lord's domain (see note on 2:8). *holy temple.* See note on 78:69.

2 They have given the [a]dead bodies of
Your servants for food to the birds
of the heavens,
The flesh of Your godly ones to the
beasts of the earth.
3 They have poured out their blood like
water round about Jerusalem;
And there was [a]no one to bury them.
4 We have become a [a]reproach to our
neighbors,
A scoffing and derision to those
around us.
5 [a]How long, O LORD? Will You be angry
forever?
Will Your [b]jealousy [c]burn like fire?
6 [a]Pour out Your wrath upon the
nations which [b]do not know You,
And upon the kingdoms which [c]do
not call upon Your name.
7 For they have [a]devoured Jacob
And [b]laid waste his [1]habitation.
8 [a]Do not remember [1]the iniquities of
our forefathers against us;
Let Your compassion come quickly to
[b]meet us,
For we are [c]brought very low.
9 [a]Help us, O God of our salvation, for
the glory of [b]Your name;
And deliver us and [1][c]forgive our sins
[d]for Your name's sake.
10 [a]Why should the nations say, "Where
is their God?"
Let there be known among the nations
in our sight,
[b]Vengeance for the blood of Your
servants which has been shed.
11 Let [a]the groaning of the prisoner come
before You;
According to the greatness of Your
[1]power preserve [2]those who are
[a]doomed to die.
12 And return to our neighbors
[a]sevenfold [b]into their bosom
[1]The [c]reproach with which they have
reproached You, O Lord.
13 So we Your people and the [a]sheep of
Your [1]pasture
Will [b]give thanks to You forever;
To all generations we will [c]tell of Your
praise.

Psalm 80

For the choir director; *set to* [†]El Shoshannim;
[•]Eduth. A Psalm of Asaph.

1 Oh, give ear, [a]Shepherd of Israel,
You who lead [b]Joseph like a flock;

2 [a]Deut 28:26; Jer 7:33; 16:4; 19:7; 34:20
3 [a]Jer 14:16; 16:4
4 [a]Ps 44:13; 80:6; Dan 9:16
5 [a]Ps 13:1; 74:1, 9, 10; 85:5; 89:46 [b]Deut 29:20; Ezek 36:5; 38:19 [c]Ps 89:46; Zeph 3:8
6 [a]Ps 69:24; Jer 10:25; Ezek 21:31; Zeph 3:8 [b]1 Thess 4:5; 2 Thess 1:8 [c]Ps 14:4; 53:4
7 [1]Lit *pasture* [a]Ps 53:4 [b]2 Chr 36:19; Jer 39:8
8 [1]Or our *former iniquities* [a]Ps 106:6; Is 64:9 [b]Ps 21:3 [c]Deut 28:43; Ps 116:6; 142:6; Is 26:5
9 [1]Lit *cover over, atone for* [a]2 Chr 14:11 [b]Ps 31:3 [c]Ps 25:11; 65:3 [d]Jer 14:7
10 [a]Ps 42:10; 115:2 [b]Ps 94:1, 2
11 [1]Lit *arm* [2]Lit *the children of death* [a]Ps 102:20
12 [1]Lit *Their* [a]Gen 4:15; Lev 26:21, 28; Ps 12:6; 119:164; Prov 6:31; 24:16; Is 30:26 [b]Ps 35:13; Is 65:6, 7; Jer 32:18; Luke 6:38 [c]Ps 74:10, 18, 22
13 [1]Or *pasturing* [a]Ps 74:1; 95:7; 100:3 [b]Ps 44:8 [c]Ps 89:1; Is 43:21
80:1 [†]Possibly, *to the Lilies* [•]Lit *A testimony* [a]Ps 23:1 [b]Ps 77:15; 78:67; Amos 5:15

79:2 *Your servants.* Though banished from the Lord's land for sins that cannot be denied, the exiles plead their special covenant relationship with God (see "Your godly ones," here, and "Your people and the sheep of Your pasture," v. 13). *godly ones.* See note on 4:3.
79:3 *poured out their blood . . . round about Jerusalem.* Cf. 2 Kin 21:16.
79:5–8 A prayer for God to relent and deal with the nations who do not acknowledge Him.
79:5 *How long . . . ?* See note on 6:3 (see also Introduction: Theology). *angry.* See v. 6 ("wrath"); see also note on 2:5. *jealousy.* See note on 78:58. *burn like fire.* See Deut 4:24; 6:15; Zeph 1:18; 3:8.
79:6–7 See Jer 10:25 and note. Perhaps the psalmist is quoting Jeremiah here.
79:6 *Pour out Your wrath.* As they "poured out" (v. 3) the blood of Your people. The exiles plead with God to redress the wrongs committed against them (see note on 5:10).
79:7 *devoured.* Like wild beasts (see 44:11; 74:19 and note on 7:2). *Jacob.* A synonym for Israel (see Gen 32:28).
79:8 *iniquities of our forefathers.* Israel suffered exile because of the accumulated sins of the nation (see 2 Kin 17:7–23; 23:26–27; 24:3–4; Dan 9:4–14), from which she did not repent until the judgment of God had fallen on her. The exiles here pray that God will take notice of their penitence and not continue to hold the sins of past generations against His now repentant people. *compassion.* Here personified as God's agent sent to bring relief (see notes on 23:6; 43:3).
79:9–11 A prayer for God to help and forgive His people and to redress the violent acts of the enemies.
79:9 *for the glory of Your name.* As the desolation of God's people brings reproach to God (see v. 10), so their salvation and prosperity bring Him glory (see note on 23:3). *forgive.* See note on 65:3.
79:10 *Where is their God?* See note on 3:2. *Vengeance.* Redress (see Deut 32:35,43).
79:11 *prisoners . . . those who are doomed to die.* The exiles, as imperial captives in Babylonia (see 102:20)—not actually in prisons, but under threat of death should they seek to return to their homeland.
79:12–13 Concluding prayer and vow to praise.
79:12 *return . . . into their bosom.* See note on Jer 32:18. *sevenfold.* In full measure; the number seven symbolized completeness. *reproach . . . reproached You.* The enemies' violent action against Israel was above all a high-handed reviling of God (see vv. 1,10; 2 Kin 19:10–12,22–23; Is 52:5).
79:13 See note on 7:17. *sheep of Your pasture.* See 74:1; 77:20; 78:72. *To all generations.* See 78:4.
Ps 80 Israel's prayer for restoration when she had been ravaged by a foreign power. It seems likely that "Ephraim and Benjamin and Manasseh" (v. 2) here represent the northern kingdom. If Jeroboam was indeed given ten tribes (see 1 Kin 11:29–36), leaving only one to Rehoboam—Judah (see 1 Kin 12:20), which was actually two tribes because Simeon was located within Judah (see Josh 19:1–9)—then Benjamin belonged to the northern kingdom. However, part of Benjamin must always have remained with the southern kingdom since its territory actually bordered on Jerusalem itself, and the southern kingdom continued to control Jerusalem's environs (see 1 Kin 12:21). This suggests that the disaster suffered was the Assyrian campaign that swept the northern kingdom away (see 2 Kin 17:1–6). Recent archaeological surveys of the Holy Land have shown that Jerusalem and the surrounding countryside experienced at this time a dramatic increase of population, no doubt the result of a massive influx of displaced persons from the north fleeing the Assyrian beast. This could account for the presence of "Ephraim and Benjamin and Manasseh" at the Jerusalem sanctuary, and for a national prayer for restoration with special

You who [c]are enthroned *above* the cherubim, shine forth!
2 Before [a]Ephraim and Benjamin and Manasseh, [b]stir up Your power
And come to save us!
3 O God, [a]restore us
And [b]cause Your face to shine *upon us,* [1]and we will be saved.

4 O [a]LORD God *of* hosts,
[b]How long will You [1]be angry with the prayer of Your people?
5 You have fed them with the [a]bread of tears,
And You have made them to drink tears in [1]large measure.
6 You make us [1]an object of contention [a]to our neighbors,
And our enemies laugh among themselves.
7 O God *of* hosts, restore us
And cause Your face to shine *upon us,*
[1]and we will be saved.

8 You removed a [a]vine from Egypt;
You [b]drove out the [1]nations and [c]planted it.
9 You [a]cleared *the ground* before it,
And it [b]took deep root and filled the land.
10 The mountains were covered with its shadow,
And [1]the cedars of God with its [a]boughs.
11 It was sending out its branches [a]to the sea
And its shoots to the River.
12 Why have You [a]broken down its [1]hedges,
So that all who pass *that* way pick its *fruit?*
13 A boar from the forest [a]eats it away
And whatever moves in the field feeds on it.

14 O God *of* hosts, [a]turn again now, we beseech You;
[b]Look down from heaven and see, and take care of this vine,
15 Even the [1a]shoot which Your right hand has planted,
And on the [2]son whom You have [3]strengthened for Yourself.
16 It is [a]burned with fire, it is cut down;
They perish at the [b]rebuke of Your countenance.
17 Let [a]Your hand be upon the man of Your right hand,
Upon the son of man whom You [b]made strong for Yourself.

80:1 [c]Ex 25:22; 1 Sam 4:4; 2 Sam 6:2; Ps 99:1
2 [a]Num 2:18-24 [b]Ps 35:23
3 [1]Or *that we may* [a]Ps 60:1; 80:7, 19; 85:4; 126:1; Lam 5:21 [b]Num 6:25; Ps 4:6; 31:16
4 [1]Lit *smoke against* [a]Ps 59:5; 84:8 [b]Ps 79:5; 85:5
5 [1]Lit *a third part of a* [a]Ps 42:3; 102:9; Is 30:20
6 [1]Lit *a strife to* [a]Ps 44:13; 79:4
7 [1]Or *that we may*
8 [1]Or *Gentiles* [a]Ps 80:15; Is 5:1, 2, 7; Jer 2:21; 12:10; Ezek 17:6; 19:10 [b]Josh 13:6; 2 Chr 20:7; Ps 44:2; Acts 7:45 [c]Jer 11:17; 32:41; Ezek 17:23; Amos 9:15
9 [a]Ex 23:28; Josh 24:12; Is 5:2 [b]Hos 14:5
10 [1]Or *its boughs are like the cedars of God* [a]Gen 49:22
11 [a]Ps 72:8
12 [1]Or *walls, fences* [a]Ps 89:40; Is 5:5
13 [a]Jer 5:6 **14** [a]Ps 90:13 [b]Ps 102:19; Is 63:15 **15** [1]Or *root* [2]Or figuratively: *branch* [3]Or *secured* [a]Ps 80:8 **16** [a]2 Chr 36:19; Ps 74:8; Jer 52:13 [b]Ps 39:11; 76:6 **17** [a]Ps 89:21 [b]Ps 80:15

focus on these tribes (see notes below).

The prayer has five (Hebrew) stanzas of four lines each. A recurring petition climaxes the first, second and last (for other refrains see introduction to Ps 42–43), with a progressing urgency of appeal: "O God" (v. 3); "O God of hosts" (v. 7); "O LORD God of hosts" (v. 19).

80 title *For the choir director.* See note on Ps 4 title. *set to.* See note on Ps 9 title. *El Shoshannim.* See note on Ps 45 title. *Asaph.* See note on Ps 73 title.

80:1–3 An appeal for God to arouse Himself and go before His people again with all His glory and might as He did in days of old in the wilderness.

80:1 See the shepherd-flock motif in 74:1; 77:20; 78:52,71–72; 79:13. *Joseph.* See note on 77:15. *enthroned above the cherubim.* See note on Ex 25:18. *shine forth!* Let Your glory be seen again, as in the wilderness journey (see Ex 24:16–17; 40:34–35), but now especially through Your new saving act (see 102:15–16; Ex 14:4,17–18; Num 14:22; Is 40:5; 44:23; 60:1–2).

80:2 *Ephraim and Benjamin and Manasseh.* March against the nations as You marched in the midst of Your army from Sinai into the promised land (in that march the ark of the covenant advanced in front of the troops of these three tribes; see Num 10:21–24; see also introduction to Ps 68). *stir up.* See note on 7:6.

80:3 *cause Your face to shine.* See vv. 7,19; an echo of the priestly benediction (see Num 6:25; see also notes on 4:6; 13:1).

80:4–7 A lament over the Lord's severe punishment of His people.

80:4 *LORD . . . of hosts.* See vv. 7,14,19; see also note on 1 Sam 1:3. *How long . . . ?* See note on 6:3 (see also Introduction: Theology). *angry.* See note on 2:5.

80:5 God has now given them tears to eat and tears to drink rather than "the bread of angels" and water from the rock (see 78:20,25).

80:8–16 This use of the vine-vineyard metaphor (here to describe Israel's changed condition) is found also in the prophets (see Is 3:14; 5:1–7; 27:2; Jer 2:21; 12:10; Ezek 17:6–8; 19:10–14; Hos 10:1; 14:7; Mic 7:1; see also Gen 49:22; Matt 20:1–16; Mark 12:1–9; Luke 20:9–16; John 15:1–5).

80:8–11 Israel was once God's flourishing transplanted vine.

80:8 *removed.* See 78:52; here the Hebrew for this verb has the sense of "uprooted" (as in Job 19:10). *drove out the nations and planted.* See 44:2. *planted.* Transplanted.

80:9 *cleared the ground.* See Is 5:2.

80:10 *cedars of God.* Or "mighty cedars." The Hebrew word for "God" is sometimes used in the sense of "mighty" (see, e.g., note on 29:1).

80:11 *sea . . . River.* The "sea" is probably the Mediterranean and the "River" the Euphrates (see Ex 23:31 and note).

80:12–15 A prayer for God to renew His care for His ravaged vine.

80:12 *Why . . . ?* Israel's anguished perplexity over God's abandonment (see note on 6:3). *broken down its hedges.* Taken away its defenses.

80:14 *take care of.* See Ex 3:16. But the Hebrew for this phrase may have the sense here that it has in Ruth 1:6: "visited" for the purpose of giving aid.

80:15 *son.* Israel (see Ex 4:22–23; Hos 11:1). But "son" may sometimes be used also to refer to a vine branch (see NASB marg.; see also note on Gen 49:22). That may be the case here, thus yielding the conventional pair "shoot and branch," a figure for the whole vine (see Job 18:16; 29:19; Ezek 17:7; Mal 4:1; see also Is 5:24; 27:6; 37:31; Ezek 17:9; 31:7; Hos 9:16; Amos 2:9; Rom 11:16). *strengthened.* See v. 17; lit. "made vigorous."

80:16–19 Concluding prayer for restoration.

80:16 *rebuke.* See 9:5 and note on 76:6.

80:17 *Let Your hand be upon.* Show your favor to (see Ezra

18 Then we shall not [a]turn back from
You;
[b]Revive us, and we will call upon Your
name.
19 O LORD God of hosts, [a]restore us;
Cause Your face to shine *upon us,*
[1]and we will be saved.

Psalm 81

For the choir director; [†]on the Gittith.
A Psalm of Asaph.

1 [a]Sing for joy to God our [b]strength;
Shout [c]joyfully to the [d]God of Jacob.
2 Raise a song, strike [a]the timbrel,
The sweet sounding [b]lyre with the
[c]harp.
3 Blow the trumpet at the [a]new moon,
At the full moon, on our [b]feast day.
4 For it is a statute for Israel,
An ordinance of the God of Jacob.
5 He established it for a testimony in
Joseph
When he [1a]went throughout the land
of Egypt.
I heard a [b]language that I did not
know:
6 "I [1a]relieved his shoulder of the burden,
His hands were freed from the [2]basket.
7 "You [a]called in trouble and I rescued
you;
I [b]answered you in the hiding place of
thunder;
I proved you at the [c]waters of
Meribah. [1]Selah.
8 "[a]Hear, O My people, and I will
[1]admonish you;
O Israel, if you [b]would listen to Me!
9 "Let there be no [a]strange god among
you;
Nor shall you worship any foreign god.
10 "[a]I, the LORD, am your God,
Who brought you up from the land of
Egypt;
[b]Open your mouth wide and I will [c]fill
it.

18 [a]Is 50:5 [b]Ps 71:20 **19** [1]Or *that we may* [a]Ps 80:3 **81:1** [†]Or *according to* [a]Ps 51:14; 59:16; 95:1 [b]Ps 46:1 [c]Ps 66:1; 95:2; 98:4 [d]Ps 84:8 **2** [a]Ex 15:20; Ps 149:3 [b]Ps 92:3; 98:5; 147:7 [c]Ps 108:2; 144:9 **3** [a]Num 10:10 [b]Lev 23:24 **5** [1]Lit *went out over* [a]Ex 11:4 **5** [b]Deut 28:49; Ps 114:1; Jer 5:15 **6** [1]Lit *removed his shoulder from* [2]Or *brick load* [a]Is 9:4; 10:27 **7** [1]*Selah* may mean: *Pause, Crescendo* or *Musical interlude* [a]Ex 2:23; 14:10; Ps 50:15 [b]Ex 19:19; 20:18 [c]Ex 17:6, 7; Num 20:13; Ps 95:8

8 [1]Or *bear witness against* [a]Ps 50:7 [b]Ps 95:7 **9** [a]Ex 20:3; Deut 5:7; 32:12; Ps 44:20; Is 43:12 **10** [a]Ex 20:2; Deut 5:6 [b]Job 29:23 [c]Ps 37:4; 78:25; 107:9

7:6,9,28; 8:18,22,31; Neh 2:8,18). *Your right hand.* Reference may be to the Davidic king as the Lord's anointed, seated in the place of honor in God's presence (see 110:1) and the one in whom the hope of the nation rested (see 2:7–9; 72:8–11; 89:21–25). But v. 15 strongly suggests another sense: that "the man" is Jacob/Israel and that he is "of" God's "right hand" in that he has been "planted" and "strengthened" by Him.

80:18 A vow to be loyal to God and to trust in Him alone. It occurs in a place where it would be more common to find a vow to praise (see note on 7:17).

Ps 81 A festival song. But it is unclear whether the festival is Passover/Unleavened Bread (v. 5; see Ex 12:14–17) or the Jewish New Year (v. 3; see Lev 23:24; Num 29:1) or the Feast of Booths (v. 3; see Lev 23:34; Num 29:12). It may have been used at all three. But more likely it was composed for use at both New Year (the first day of the month, "New Moon") and the beginning of Booths (the 15th day of the month, full moon); see notes below. Whether the psalm is preexilic or postexilic cannot be determined, but it clearly shows the grand significance of Israel's annual religious festivals (see chart, pp. 164–165). As memorials of God's saving acts they called Israel to celebration, remembrance and recommitment (see Ps 95). In this psalm Israel is addressed by a Levite, speaking (prophetically) on behalf of God.

The psalm's thematic development follows a symmetrical pattern: two verses, three verses; two verses, three verses; two verses, four verses. Note also the contrast between vv. 6–7 and vv. 11–12, and the thematic link between v. 10c and v. 16.

81 title *For the choir director.* See note on Ps 4 title. *on.* See note on Ps 6 title. *Gittith.* See note on Ps 8 title. *Asaph.* See note on Ps 73 title.

81:1–5 A summons to celebrate the appointed sacred feast.

81:1 *Jacob.* A synonym for Israel (see Gen 32:28).

81:2 *timbrel.* See note on Jer 31:4. *lyre with the harp.* See note on 57:8.

81:3 *trumpet.* The ram's horn trumpet (see Ex 19:13). *our feast.* Probably the Feast of Booths, often called simply "the feast" (see 1 Kin 8:2,65; 12:32; 2 Chr 5:3; 7:8; Neh 8:14,18; Ezek 45:25; see also Deut 16:14). As the great seven-day autumn festival, beginning on the 15th of the month (full moon), it followed shortly after the day of atonement (observed on the tenth of the month, Lev 16:29), recalled God's care for His people during the wilderness journey (see Lev 23:43), served as a feast of thanksgiving for the harvest (see Lev 23:39–40; Deut 16:13–15) and marked the conclusion of the annual cycle of religious festivals that began with Passover and Unleavened Bread six months earlier (see Ex 23:14–17; Lev 23; Deut 16:16). Every seventh year at this festival the covenant law was to be read to all the people (see Deut 31:9–13; Neh 8:2,15). The first day of this month (New Moon) was commemorated with trumpets (see Lev 23:24). It later came to be known as New Year since the seventh month marked the end of harvest and the beginning of the rainy season, when the new crops were planted.

81:4–5 *statute . . . ordinance . . . testimony.* See the passages referred to in note on v. 3.

81:5 *Joseph.* See note on 77:15. *went throughout the land of Egypt.* Some believe this indicates that the festival referred to is Passover and Unleavened Bread (see Ex 12:14,42). More likely it serves as a reference to the whole exodus period, while highlighting especially God's triumph over Egypt by which He had set His people free (see vv. 6–7). *heard a language that I did not know.* Was an alien in a foreign land (see 114:1; see also Deut 28:49; Is 19:18; 33:19; Jer 5:15; Ezek 3:5–6). An alternative translation is "heard a voice that I did not know." In this case, the "voice" is the "thunder" of God's judgment against Egypt (see v. 7), which the Levitical author then proceeds to interpret as to its present reference for the celebrating congregation (vv. 6–16).

81:6–10 God heard and delivered and now summons His people to loyalty.

81:6 *burden . . . basket.* The forced labor to which the Israelites were subjected in Egypt (see Ex 1:11–14).

81:7 *You called . . . I rescued.* See Ex 3:7–10. *in the hiding place of thunder.* See 106:9; Ex 14:21,24; 15:8,10; see also note on 76:6. *I proved you.* See Ex 17:1–7.

81:8–10 God heard His people in their distress (vv. 6–7); now they must listen to Him.

81:9–10 See Ex 19:4–5; 20:2–4; Deut 4:15–20.

81:10 *Open your mouth wide.* Trust in the Lord alone for all of life's needs. *I will fill it.* See v. 16; as He did in the wilderness (see 78:23–29; see also 37:3–4; Deut 11:13–15; 28:1–4).

11 "But My people [a]did not listen to My
voice,
And Israel did not [1]obey Me.
12 "So I [a]gave [1]them over to the
stubbornness of their heart,
To walk in their own devices.
13 "Oh that My people [a]would listen to Me,
That Israel would [b]walk in My ways!
14 "I would quickly [a]subdue their enemies
And [b]turn My hand against their
adversaries.
15 "[a]Those who hate the LORD would
[b]pretend obedience to Him,
And their time *of punishment* would
be forever.
16 "[1]But I would feed you with the
[2a]finest of the wheat,
And with [b]honey from the rock I
would satisfy you."

Psalm 82

A Psalm of Asaph.

1 God takes His [a]stand in [1]His own
congregation;
He [b]judges in the midst of the [2c]rulers.
2 How long will you [a]judge unjustly
And [b]show partiality to the wicked?
[1]Selah.
3 [a]Vindicate the weak and fatherless;
Do justice to the afflicted and destitute.
4 [a]Rescue the weak and needy;
Deliver *them* out of the hand of the
wicked.
5 They [a]do not know nor do they
understand;
They [b]walk about in darkness;
All the [c]foundations of the earth are
shaken.
6 [1]I [a]said, "You are gods,
And all of you are [b]sons of the Most
High.
7 "Nevertheless [a]you will die like men
And fall like *any* [b]one of the princes."
8 [a]Arise, O God, [b]judge the earth!
For it is You who [c]possesses all the
nations.

Psalm 83

A Song, a Psalm of Asaph.

1 O God, [a]do not remain quiet;
[b]Do not be silent and, O God, do not
be still.

11 [1]Lit *yield to* [a]Deut 32:15; Ps 106:25 **12** [1]Lit *him* [a]Job 8:4; Acts 7:42; Rom 1:24, 26 **13** [a]Deut 5:29; Ps 81:8; Is 48:18 [b]Ps 128:1; Is 42:24; Jer 7:23 **14** [a]Ps 18:47; 47:3 [b]Amos 1:8 **15** [a]Rom 1:30 [b]Ps 18:44; 66:3 **16** [1]Lit *He would feed him* [2]Lit *fat* [a]Deut 32:14; Ps 147:14 [b]Deut 32:13 **82:1** [1]Lit *the congregation of God* [2]Lit *gods* [a]Is 3:13 [b]2 Chr 19:6; Ps 58:11 [c]Ex 21:6; 22:8, 28 **2** [1]*Selah* may mean: *Pause, Crescendo* or *Musical interlude* [a]Ps 58:1 [b]Deut 1:17; Prov 18:5 **3** [a]Deut 24:17; Ps 10:18; Is 11:4; Jer 22:16 **4** [a]Job 29:12 **5** [a]Ps 14:4; Jer 4:22; Mic 3:1 [b]Prov 2:13; Is 59:9; Jer 23:12 [c]Ps 11:3

6 [1]Lit *I, on my part* [a]Ps 82:1; John 10:34 [b]Ps 89:26 **7** [a]Job 21:32; Ps 49:12; Ezek 31:14 [b]Ps 83:11 **8** [a]Ps 12:5 [b]Ps 58:11; 96:13 [c]Ps 2:8; Rev 11:15 **83:1** [a]Ps 28:1; 35:22 [b]Ps 109:1

81:11–16 Israel has not listened—if only they would! See Ezek 18:23,32; 33:11.
81:11 See 78:10,17,32,40,56; Deut 9:7,24; Jer 7:24–26.
81:12 It is God who "circumcises" the heart (see Deut 30:6; see also 1 Kin 8:58; Jer 31:33; Ezek 11:19; 36:26). Thus for God to abandon His people to their sins is the most fearful of punishments (see 78:29; Is 6:9–10; 29:10; 63:17; cf. Rom 1:24,26,28).
81:13–16 See the promised covenant blessings outlined in Ex 23:22–27; Lev 26:3–13; Deut 7:12–26; 28:1–14.
81:13 *My ways.* See 25:4 and note.
81:16 *honey from the rock.* See note on Deut 32:13.
Ps 82 A word of judgment on unjust rulers and judges. The Levitical author of this psalm evokes a vision of God presiding over His heavenly court—analogous to the experiences of the prophets (see 1 Kin 22:19–22; Is 6:1–7; Jer 23:18,22; see also Job 15:8). As the Great King (see introduction to Ps 47) and the Judge of all the earth (see 94:2; Gen 18:25; 1 Sam 2:10) who "loves justice" (99:4) and judges the nations in righteousness (see 9:8; 96:13; 98:9), he is seen calling to account those responsible for defending the weak and oppressed on earth. An early rabbinic interpretation (see John 10:34–35) understood the "gods" (v. 6) to be unjust rulers and judges in Israel, of whom there were many (see 1 Sam 8:3; Is 1:16–17; 3:13–15; Jer 21:12; 22:3; Ezek 34:4,21; Mic 3:1–3; 7:3). Today many identify the "gods" as the kings of surrounding nations who encouraged the conceit that they were actually or virtually divine beings but who ruled with lofty disregard for justice—though honoring it as a royal ideal. Others hold that the "gods" are the divine beings in whose names the kings claimed to rule (see 95:3). In any event, rulers and judges here are confronted by their King and Judge (see Ps 58). Structurally, the words of the Levite (vv. 1,6) frame the words of God. At the very center (v. 5a; see note on 6:6) stands the most devastating judgment of all.
82 title See note on Ps 73 title.
82:1 *congregation.* The assembly in the great hall of judgment (cf. 1 Kin 7:7) in heaven (see 89:5; 1 Kin 22:19; Job 1:6; 2:1; Is 6:1–4). As if in a vision, the psalmist sees the rulers and judges gathered before the Great King to give account of their administration of justice. *rulers.* Or "gods" (see NASB marg.; see also v. 6. In the language of the OT—and in accordance with the conceptual world of the ancient Near East—rulers and judges, as deputies of the heavenly King, could be given the honorific title "god" (see note on 45:6; 58:1) or be called "son of God" (see 2:7 and note).
82:3–4 In the OT a first-order task of kings and judges was to protect the powerless against all who would exploit or oppress them (see 72:2,4,12–14; Prov 31:8–9; Is 11:4; Jer 22:3,16).
82:5 *They do not know nor . . . understand.* The center of the poem (see note on 6:6). They ought to have shared in the wisdom of God (see 1 Kin 3:9; Prov 8:14–16; Is 11:2), but they are utterly devoid of true understanding of moral issues or of the moral order that God's rule sustains (see Is 44:19). *foundations . . . are shaken.* When such men are the wardens of justice, the whole world order crumbles (see 11:3; 75:3 and notes).
82:6 *I said.* Those who rule (or judge) do so by God's appointment (see 2:7; Is 44:28) and thus they are His representatives—whether they acknowledge Him or not (see Ex 9:16; Jer 27:6; Dan 2:21; 4:17,32; 5:18; John 19:11; Rom 13:1). *gods.* See note on v. 1. *sons of.* See note on v. 1. *Most High.* See note on Gen 14:19.
82:7 However exalted their position, these corrupt "gods" will be brought low by the same judgment as other men. *fall.* See note on 13:4.
82:8 Having seen the prospect in store, the psalmist prays for God's judgment to hasten and for the perfect reign of God to come quickly to the whole world. *Arise.* See note on 3:7. *possesses.* The nations are Your domain (see note on 79:1).
Ps 83 Israel's prayer for God to crush His enemies when the whole world—or so it seemed—was arrayed against His people. Neither Kings nor Chronicles tells of a confederacy as extensive as that described here. Perhaps only some of the nations mentioned were actually attacking, while the rest of Israel's his-

2 For behold, Your enemies [a]make an
uproar,
And [b]those who hate You have
[1c]exalted themselves.
3 They [a]make shrewd plans against
Your people,
And [1]conspire together against [b]Your
[2]treasured ones.
4 They have said, "Come, and [a]let us
wipe them out [1]as a nation,
That the [b]name of Israel be
remembered no more."
5 For they have [1a]conspired together
with one mind;
Against You they make a covenant:
6 The tents of [a]Edom and the
[b]Ishmaelites,
[c]Moab and the [d]Hagrites;
7 [a]Gebal and [b]Ammon and [c]Amalek,
[d]Philistia with the inhabitants of
[e]Tyre;
8 [a]Assyria also has joined with them;
They have become [1]a help to the
[b]children of Lot. [2]Selah.

9 Deal with them [a]as with Midian,
As [b]with Sisera *and* Jabin at the
torrent of Kishon,
10 Who were destroyed at En-dor,
Who [a]became as dung for the ground.
11 Make their nobles like [a]Oreb and Zeeb
And all their princes like [b]Zebah and
Zalmunna,
12 Who said, "[a]Let us possess for
ourselves
The [b]pastures of God."

13 O my God, make them like the
[1a]whirling dust,
Like [b]chaff before the wind.
14 Like [a]fire that burns the forest
And like a flame that [b]sets the
mountains on fire,
15 So pursue them [a]with Your tempest
And terrify them with Your storm.
16 [a]Fill their faces with dishonor,
That they may seek Your name, O
LORD.
17 Let them be [a]ashamed and dismayed
forever,
And let them be humiliated and
perish,
18 That they may [a]know that [b]You alone,
whose name is the LORD,
Are the [c]Most High over all the earth.

Psalm 84

For the choir director; [†]on the Gittith.
A Psalm of the sons of Korah.

1 How lovely are Your [a]dwelling places,
O LORD of hosts!

2 [1]Lit *lifted up the head* [a]Ps 2:1; Is 17:12 [b]Ps 81:15 [c]Judg 8:28; Zech 1:21 **3** [1]Or *consult* [2]Or *hidden ones* [a]Ps 64:2; Is 29:15 [b]Ps 27:5; 31:20 **4** [1]Lit *from* [a]Esth 3:6; Ps 74:8; Jer 48:2 [b]Ps 41:5; Jer 11:19 **5** [1]Or *consulted* [a]Ps 2:2; Dan 6:7 **6** [a]2 Chr 20:10; Ps 137:7 [b]Gen 25:12-16 [c]2 Chr 20:10 [d]1 Chr 5:10 **7** [a]Josh 13:5; Ezek 27:9 [b]2 Chr 20:10 [c]1 Sam 15:2 [d]1 Sam 4:1; 29:1 [e]Ezek 27:3; Amos 1:9 **8** [1]Lit *an arm* [2]*Selah* may mean: *Pause, Crescendo* or *Musical interlude* [a]2 Kin 15:19 [b]Deut 2:9 **9** [a]Judg 7:1-24 [b]Judg 4:7, 15, 21-24 **10** [a]Zeph 1:17 **11** [a]Judg 7:25 [b]Judg 8:12, 21 **12** [a]2 Chr 20:11 [b]Ps 132:13 **13** [1]Or *tumbleweed* [a]Is 17:13 [b]Job 21:18; Ps 35:5; Is 40:24; Jer 13:24 **14** [a]Is 9:18 [b]Ex 19:18; Deut 32:22 **15** [a]Job 9:17; Ps 58:9 **16** [a]Job 10:15; Ps 109:29; 132:18 **17** [a]Ps 35:4; 70:2 **18** [a]Ps 59:13 [b]Ps 86:10; Is 45:21 [c]Ps 9:2; 18:13; 97:9 **84:1** [†]Or *according to* [a]Ps 43:3; 132:5

toric enemies were more passively supporting the campaign. If so, the occasion may have been that reported in 2 Chr 20, when Moab, Ammon, Edom and their allies were invading Judah. In any event, the psalm must date from sometime after the reign of Solomon and before the great thrust of Assyria in the time of King Menahem (see 2 Kin 15:19).

Each of the two main divisions (vv. 1–8, 9–18) consists of two four-verse stanzas, with the latter division being extended by a two-verse stanza that brings the prayer to its climactic conclusion.

83 title *Song.* See note on Ps 30 title. *Asaph.* See note on Ps 73 title.

83:1–4 An appeal to God to act in the face of Israel's imminent danger.

83:1 *do not remain quiet.* Do not remain inactive (see 35:22; 109:1).

83:4 *They have said.* See note on 3:2. *let us wipe them out.* Israel's very existence is at stake (see v. 12).

83:5–8 The array of nations allied against Israel—threat from every quarter.

83:6 *Hagrites.* Either Ishmaelites (descendants of Hagar) or a group mentioned in Assyrian inscriptions as an Aramean confederacy (see 1 Chr 5:10,18–22; 27:31).

83:7 *Gebal.* See 1 Kin 5:18; Ezek 27:9. Gebal was an important Phoenician city (also called Byblos).

83:8 *Assyria.* Since it is mentioned only as an ally of Moab and Ammon (the descendants of Lot; see note on Gen 19:36–38), Assyria, though distantly active in the region, must not yet have become a major threat in its own right.

83:9–12 A plea for God to destroy His enemies as He did of old in the time of the judges. Those who hurl themselves against the kingdom of God to destroy it from the earth—so that the godless powers are left to shape the destiny of the world as they will—must be crushed if God's kingdom of righteousness and peace is to come and be at rest (see note on 5:10).

83:9 *as with Midian.* In Gideon's great victory (see Judg 7). *as with Sisera and Jabin.* In Barak's defeat of the Canaanite coalition (see Judg 4).

83:10 *En-dor.* See Josh 17:11 and note; northeast of where the main battle was fought—apparently where much of the fleeing army was overtaken and decimated.

83:11 *Oreb and Zeeb . . . Zebah and Zalmunna.* Leaders of the Midianite host destroyed by Gideon.

83:12 See v. 4.

83:13–16 The plea renewed, with vivid imagery of fleeing armies and of God's fearsome power.

83:15 Imagery of the heavenly Warrior attacking His enemies out of the thunderstorm (see 18:7–15; 68:33; 77:17–18; Ex 15:7–10; Josh 10:11; Judg 5:4,20–21; 1 Sam 2:10; 7:10; Is 29:5–6; 33:3). For the storm cloud as God's chariot see 68:4 and note.

83:16 *may seek.* See note on v. 18. *name.* See note on 5:11.

83:17–18 The prayer's climactic conclusion.

83:18 The ultimate goal of God's warfare is not merely the security of Israel and the destruction of Israel's (and God's) enemies but the worldwide acknowledgment of the true God and of His rule, even to the point of seeking Him as His people do (see v. 16; see also 40:9; 47:9; 58:11; 59:13 and notes). *Most High.* See note on Gen 14:19.

Ps 84 A prayer of longing for the house of the Lord. In tone and perspective it stands close to Ps 42 and may reflect similar circumstances. If so, the author (presumably a Levite who normally functioned in the temple service), now barred from access to God's house (perhaps when Sennacherib was ravaging Judah; see 2 Kin 18:13–16), gives voice to his longing for the sweet

2 My [a]soul longed and even yearned for
the courts of the LORD;
My heart and my flesh sing for joy to
the [b]living God.
3 The bird also has found a house,
And the swallow a nest for herself,
where she may lay her young,
Even Your [a]altars, O LORD of hosts,
[b]My King and my God.
4 How [a]blessed are those who dwell in
Your house!
They are [b]ever praising You. [1]Selah.

5 How blessed is the man whose
[a]strength is in You,
In [1]whose heart are the [b]highways *to*
Zion!
6 Passing through the valley of [1]Baca
they make it a [2]spring;
The [a]early rain also covers it with
blessings.
7 They [a]go from strength to strength,
[1]*Every one of them* [b]appears before
God in Zion.

8 O [a]LORD God of hosts, hear my prayer;
Give ear, O [b]God of Jacob! Selah.

2 [a]Ps 42:1, 2; 63:1 [b]Ps 42:2
3 [a]Ps 43:4 [b]Ps 5:2
4 [1]*Selah* may mean: *Pause, Crescendo* or *Musical interlude* [a]Ps 65:4 [b]Ps 42:5, 11
5 [1]Lit *their* [a]Ps 81:1 [b]Ps 86:11; 122:1; Jer 31:6
6 [1]Probably, *Weeping;* or *Balsam trees* [2]Or *place of springs* [a]Ps 107:35; Joel 2:23
7 [1]Some ancient versions read *The God of gods will be seen in Zion* [a]Prov 4:18; Is 40:31; John 1:16; 2 Cor 3:18 [b]Ex 34:23; Deut 16:16; Ps 42:2
8 [a]Ps 59:5; 80:4; 84:1 [b]Ps 81:1
9 [a]Gen 15:1; Ps 3:3; 28:7; 59:11; 115:9-11 [b]1 Sam 16:6; 2 Sam 19:21; Ps 2:2; 132:17
10 [a]Ps 27:4

9 Behold our [a]shield, O God,
And look upon the face of [b]Your
anointed.
10 For [a]a day in Your courts is better than
a thousand *outside.*
I would rather stand at the threshold
of the house of my God
Than dwell in the tents of wickedness.
11 For the LORD God is [a]a sun and [b]shield;
The LORD gives grace and [c]glory;
[d]No good thing does He withhold
[1]from those who walk [2]uprightly.
12 O LORD of hosts,
How [a]blessed is the man who trusts in
You!

Psalm 85

For the choir director. A Psalm of
the sons of Korah.

1 O LORD, You showed [a]favor to Your
land;
You [1][b]restored the captivity of Jacob.

11 [1]Lit *with regard to* [2]Lit *with integrity* [a]Is 60:19, 20; Mal 4:2; Rev 21:23 [b]Gen 15:1 [c]Ps 85:9 [d]Ps 34:9, 10 **12** [a]Ps 2:12; 40:4
85:1 [1]Or *restore the fortunes* [a]Ps 77:7; 106:4 [b]Ezra 1:11; Ps 14:7; 126:1; Jer 30:18; Ezek 39:25; Hos 6:11; Joel 3:1

nearness to God in His temple that he had known in the past. Reference to God and His temple and to the "blessedness" (see vv. 4–5,12) of those having free access to both dominates the psalm and highlights its central themes.

The psalm has three main divisions (vv. 1–4, 5–7, 8–11) and a conclusion (v. 12). In the Hebrew text, a six-line unit precedes and follows a three-line reflection on the blessedness of those free to make pilgrimage to Zion. Each of these six-line divisions contains three references to the "LORD," while the seventh reference (symbolizing completeness or perfection) appears in the conclusion.

84 title *For the choir director.* See note on Ps 4 title. *on.* See note on Ps 6 title. *Gittith.* See note on Ps 8 title. *of the sons of Korah.* See note on Ps 42 title.

84:1–4 A confession of deep longing for the house of the Lord.

84:1 *lovely.* The traditional rendering of the Hebrew here, but perhaps better translated "beloved" or "loved." *LORD of hosts.* See vv. 3,8,12; see also note on 1 Sam 1:3.

84:2 *My soul.* I (see note on 6:3). *courts.* Of the temple (see v. 10; 2 Kin 21:5; 23:11–12). *My heart . . . flesh.* My whole being (see 73:26). *heart.* See note on 4:7. *living God.* See Deut 5:26.

84:3 The psalmist is jealous of the small birds that have such unhindered access to the temple and the altar. They are able even to build their nests there for their young—the place where Israel was to have communion with God.

84:4–5,12 *blessed.* See note on 1:1.

84:4 *who dwell in Your house.* See note on 15:1.

84:5–7 The joyful blessedness of those who are free to make pilgrimage to Zion—them too the psalmist envies.

84:5 *the man whose strength is in You.* The one who has come to know the Lord as his deliverer and the sustainer of his life. *In whose heart are the highways to Zion.* The highways the Israelites took to observe the religious festivals at Jerusalem (Zion, v. 7). *heart.* See note on 4:7.

84:6 *Passing.* On their way to the temple. *Baca.* Means either "weeping" or "balsam trees" (common in arid valleys). The place is unknown and may be figurative (see 23:4) for arid stretches the pilgrims had to traverse. *spring.* The joyful expectations of the pilgrims transform the difficult ways into places of refreshment. *early rain.* The gentle early showers that are harbingers of the later spring rains (see Joel 2:23). *blessings.* The Hebrew for this word may refer to "blessings" or to "pools"; it is likely that both are intended. By God's benevolent care over His pilgrims, the vale of weeping (or balsam trees), already transformed by the glad hearts of the expectant wayfarers, is turned into a valley of praise (see 2 Chr 20:26). God's saints on their hopeful way to Zion experience anew the bountiful hand of God as their ancestors did on their way through the Wilderness of Sinai to the promised land (see 78:15–16; 105:41; 114:8)—and as their descendants would on their return to Zion from Babylonian exile (see Is 41:17–20; 43:19–20; 49:10).

84:7 *from strength to strength.* Whatever the toils and hardships of the journey (see Is 40:31). *Zion.* See 9:11 and note.

84:8–11 A prayer for the king, and its motivation: Only as God blesses the king in Jerusalem will the psalmist once more realize his great desire to return to his accustomed service in the temple (see introduction).

84:8 *LORD God of hosts . . . God of Jacob.* That is, LORD God of Hosts, the God of Jacob (see 59:5; see also note on 3:7). *Jacob.* A synonym for Israel (see Gen 32:28).

84:9 *our shield.* The king in Jerusalem (see note on 3:3). *Your anointed.* God's earthly regent over His people (from David's line); see note on 2:2.

84:10 *stand at the threshold.* Perhaps the psalmist's normal (and humble) service at the temple was that of doorkeeper (see 2 Kin 22:4). *dwell in the tents of wickedness.* Share in the life of those who do not honor the God of Zion.

84:11 *sun.* The glorious source of the light of life (see note on 27:1). *shield.* See note on 3:3. *uprightly.* See 15:2 and note on Gen 17:1.

84:12 The sum of it all (see 40:4).

Ps 85 A communal prayer for the renewal of God's mercies to His people at a time when they are once more suffering distress. Many believe that vv. 1–3 refer to the return from exile and that the troubles experienced are those alluded to by Nehemiah and Malachi. Verse 12 suggests that a drought has ravaged the land and may reflect the drought with which the Lord chastened His people in the time of Haggai (see Hag 1:5–11).

2 You [a]forgave the iniquity of Your
people;
You [b]covered all their sin. [1]Selah.
3 You [a]withdrew all Your fury;
You [b]turned away from Your burning
anger.

4 [a]Restore us, O God of our salvation,
And [b]cause Your indignation toward
us to cease.
5 Will [a]You be angry with us forever?
Will You prolong Your anger to [1]all
generations?
6 Will You not Yourself [1a]revive us again,
That Your people may [b]rejoice in You?
7 Show us Your lovingkindness, O LORD,
And [a]grant us Your salvation.

8 [1]I will hear what God the LORD will say;
For He will [a]speak peace to His
people, [2]to His godly ones;
But let them not [b]turn back to [3]folly.
9 Surely [a]His salvation is near to those
who [1]fear Him,
That [b]glory may dwell in our land.

10 [a]Lovingkindness and [1]truth have met
together;
[b]Righteousness and peace have kissed
each other.
11 [1]Truth [a]springs from the earth,
And righteousness looks down from
heaven.
12 Indeed, [a]the LORD will give what is
good,
And our [b]land will yield its produce.
13 [a]Righteousness will go before Him
And will make His footsteps into a
way.

Psalm 86

A Prayer of David.

1 [a]Incline Your ear, O LORD, *and* answer
me;
For I am [b]afflicted and needy.
2 [a]Preserve my [1]soul, for I am a [b]godly
man;

2 [1]*Selah* may mean: *Pause, Crescendo* or *Musical interlude* [a]Num 14:19; 1 Kin 8:34; Ps 78:38; 103:3; Jer 31:34 [b]Ps 32:1 **3** [a]Ps 78:38; 106:23 [b]Ex 32:12; Deut 13:17; Ps 106:23; Jon 3:9 **4** [a]Ps 80:3,7 [b]Dan 9:16 **5** [1]Lit *generation and generation* [a]Ps 74:1; 79:5; 80:4 **6** [1]Or *bring to life* [a]Ps 71:20; 80:18 [b]Ps 33:1; 90:14; 149:2 **7** [a]Ps 106:4 **8** [1]Or *Let me hear* [2]Lit *even to* [3]Or *stupidity* [a]Ps 29:11; Hag 2:9; Zech 9:10 [b]Ps 78:57; 2 Pet 2:21 **9** [1]Or *reverence* [a]Ps 34:18; Is 46:13 [b]Ps 84:11; Hag 2:7; Zech 2:5; John 1:14 **10** [1]Or *faithfulness* [a]Ps 25:10; 89:14; Prov 3:3 [b]Ps 72:3; Is 32:17 **11** [1]Or *Faithfulness* [a]Is 45:8 **12** [a]Ps 84:11; James 1:17 [b]Lev 26:4; Ps 67:6; Ezek 34:27; Zech 8:12 **13** [a]Ps 89:14 **86:1** [a]Ps 17:6; 31:2; 71:2 [b]Ps 40:17; 70:5 **2** [1]Or *life* [a]Ps 25:20 [b]Ps 4:3; 50:5

Christian liturgical usage has often employed this psalm in the Christmas season.

The psalm has two main divisions of seven (Hebrew) lines each: (1) the prayer (vv. 1–7); (2) a reassuring word (vv. 8–13). Each division contains a three-line stanza followed by a four-line stanza, with the corresponding stanzas of the second half answering to those of the first: Verses 1–3 speak of mercies granted, while vv. 8–9 speak of mercies soon to come; vv. 4–7 voice the prayer, and vv. 10–13 offer the blessed reassurance that the prayer will be heard. Each of the four stanzas contains one reference to the "LORD."

85 title *For the choir director.* See note on Ps 4 title. *of the sons of Korah.* See note on Ps 42 title.

85:1–7 Prayer for the renewal of God's favor.

85:1–3 Israel begins her prayer by appealing to the Lord's past mercies, recalling how He has forgiven and restored them before (perhaps a reference to the restoration from exile).

85:1 *restored the captivity of Jacob.* Or "restored the fortunes of Jacob" (see Jer 29:14). *Jacob.* A synonym for Israel (see Gen 32:28).

85:3 *fury . . . anger.* See v. 5; see also note on 2:5.

85:4–7 The prayer acknowledges that the present troubles are indicative of God's displeasure. No confession of sin is expressed, but in the light of v. 3 (and possibly v. 8; see below) it is probably implicit.

85:7 *lovingkindness.* See v. 10; see also note on 6:4.

85:8–13 God's reassuring answer to the prayer, conveyed through a priest or Levite, perhaps one of the Korahites (see note on 12:5–6; see also 2 Chr 20:14).

85:8–9 The assurance that God will again bless His people.

85:8 *I will hear.* The speaker awaits the word from the Lord. *speak peace.* The word from the Lord perhaps takes the form of the priestly benediction (see Num 6:22–26). *godly ones.* See note on 4:3. *But let them not turn back to folly.* And so provoke God's displeasure again. But it is also possible to translate the clause: "and to those who turn from folly." *folly.* See note on 14:1.

85:9 *glory.* Wherever God's saving power is displayed, His glory is revealed (see 57:5,11; 72:18–19; Ex 14:4,17–18; Num 14:22; Is 40:5; 44:23; 66:19; Ezek 39:21).

85:10–13 God's sure mercies to His people spring from His covenant love, to which in His faithfulness and righteousness He remains true, and that assures His people's welfare (peace).

85:10 *Lovingkindness and truth . . . Righteousness and peace.* These expressions of God's favor toward His people are here personified (see note on 23:6), and the vivid portrayal of their meeting and embracing offers one of the most beautiful images in all Scripture of God's gracious dealings with His covenant people. *righteousness.* See vv. 11,13; see also note on 5:8. *peace.* See note on Num 6:26.

85:11 *Truth springs.* As new growth springs from the earth to bless mankind with plenty. *righteousness looks down.* It shines down benevolently. From heaven and from earth, God's covenant blessings will abound till Israel's cup overflows.

85:12 *what is good.* See 31:19 and note.

85:13 *righteousness will go before.* Again the psalmist personifies. Acting either as herald or guide, righteousness leads the way and marks the course for God's engagement in His people's behalf—and righteousness is God's perfect faithfulness to all His covenant commitments (see note on 5:8).

Ps 86 A prayer for God's help when attacked by enemies, whose fierce onslaughts betray their disdain for the Lord. Whether or not David was the author (see Introduction: Authorship and Titles), the psalmist's identification of himself as God's "servant" (v. 2) suggests his royal status and thus his special relationship with the Lord (see 2 Sam 7:5,8 and note on Ps 18 title). The enemies may then be either those within the kingdom who refuse to acknowledge him as the Lord's anointed, or foreign powers that are attempting to remove him from the international scene.

The psalm has a symmetrical verse pattern (four, three, three, three, four). The author identifies himself as the Lord's servant in the first and last stanzas, which also contain the prayer for God's mercy and deliverance from the enemy threat. The center stanza (vv. 8–10) hails the Lord as the incomparable, the only God, whom all the nations will someday worship. Verse 9 is the center verse (see note on 6:6).

86 title *Prayer.* See note on Ps 17 title; see also note on 72:20. *of David.* This is the only psalm in Book 3 (Ps 73–89) that is ascribed to David. Perhaps its placement among the Korahite

O You my God, save Your servant who
[c]trusts in You.
3 Be [a]gracious to me, O Lord,
For [b]to You I cry all day long.
4 Make glad the soul of Your servant,
For to You, O Lord, [a]I lift up my soul.
5 For You, Lord, are [a]good, and [b]ready
to forgive,
And [c]abundant in lovingkindness to
all who call upon You.
6 [a]Give ear, O LORD, to my prayer;
And give heed to the voice of my
supplications!
7 In [a]the day of my trouble I shall call
upon You,
For [b]You will answer me.
8 There is [a]no one like You among the
gods, O Lord,
Nor are there any works [b]like Yours.
9 [a]All nations whom You have made
shall come and worship before You,
O Lord,
And they shall glorify Your name.
10 For You are [a]great and [b]do [1]wondrous
deeds;
You alone [c]are God.

11 [a]Teach me Your way, O LORD;
I will walk in Your truth;
[b]Unite my heart to fear Your name.
12 I will [a]give thanks to You, O Lord my
God, with all my heart,
And will glorify Your name forever.
13 For Your lovingkindness toward me is
great,
And You have [a]delivered my soul from
the [1]depths of [2]Sheol.

14 O God, arrogant men have [a]risen up
against me,
And [1]a band of violent men have
sought my [2]life,
And they have not set You before them.
15 But You, O Lord, are a God [a]merciful
and gracious,
Slow to anger and abundant in
lovingkindness and [1]truth.
16 [a]Turn to me, and be gracious to me;
Oh [b]grant Your strength to Your
servant,
And save the [c]son of Your handmaid.
17 [a]Show me a sign for good,
That those who hate me may [b]see *it*
and be ashamed,
Because You, O LORD, [c]have helped
me and comforted me.

Psalm 87

A Psalm of the sons of Korah. A Song.

1 His [a]foundation is in the holy
mountains.

2 [c]Ps 25:2; 31:14; 56:4 **3** [a]Ps 4:1; 57:1 [b]Ps 25:5; 88:9 **4** [a]Ps 25:1; 143:8 **5** [a]Ps 25:8 [b]Ps 130:4 [c]Ex 34:6; Neh 9:17; Ps 103:8; 145:8; Joel 2:13; Jon 4:2 **6** [a]Ps 55:1 **7** [a]Ps 50:15; 77:2 [b]Ps 17:6 **8** [a]Ex 15:11; 2 Sam 7:22; 1 Kin 8:23; Ps 89:6; Jer 10:6 [b]Deut 3:24 **9** [a]Ps 22:27; 66:4; Is 66:23; Rev 15:4 **10** [1]Or *miracles* [a]Ps 77:13 [b]Ex 15:11; Ps 72:18; 77:14; 136:4 [c]Deut 6:4; 32:39; Ps 83:18; Is 37:16; 44:6, 8; Mark 12:29; 1 Cor 8:4 **11** [a]Ps 25:5 [b]Jer 32:39 **12** [a]Ps 111:1

13 [1]Lit *lowest Sheol* [2]I.e. the nether world [a]Ps 30:3 **14** [1]Or *an assembly* [2]Lit *soul* [a]Ps 54:3 **15** [1]Or *faithfulness* [a]Ps 86:5 **16** [a]Ps 25:16 [b]Ps 68:35 [c]Ps 116:16 **17** [a]Judg 6:17; Ps 119:122 [b]Ps 112:10 [c]Ps 118:13 **87:1** [a]Ps 78:69; Is 28:16

psalms is because those who arranged the Psalter perceived a thematic link between v. 9 and 87:4.

86:1–4 Initial prayer for God to have mercy and protect the life of His servant.

86:1 *afflicted and needy.* See 35:10; see also 34:6 and note.

86:2 *a godly man.* The Hebrew for this phrase is *ḥasid* (see note on 4:3). *You my God.* Not that David has chosen Him, but that He has chosen David to be His servant (see 1 Sam 13:14; 15:28; 16:12; 2 Sam 7:8). David's devotion to God and God's commitment to him are deliberately juxtaposed. *Your servant.* See vv. 4,16; see also introduction.

86:4 *my soul.* See note on 6:3.

86:5–7 In his need David prays to the Lord because, out of His kindness and love, God answers prayer.

86:5 *lovingkindness.* See vv. 13,15; see also note on 6:4.

86:8–10 The God to whom David appeals is the only true God. No other "god" acts with such sovereign power (see 115:3–7; 135:13–17)—that is why David appeals to Him and why all the nations will someday worship Him.

86:9 *All nations.* See note on 46:10. This is the center verse of the psalm (see note on 6:6) and contains the psalm's most exalted confession of faith concerning God's sovereign and universal rule. *they shall glorify.* As David vows to do (v. 12). *Your name.* See vv. 11–12; see also note on 5:11.

86:10 *wondrous deeds.* See note on 9:1.

86:11–13 A prayer for godliness and a vow to praise.

86:11 *Teach me ... Unite my.* What would be the benefit if God saved him from his enemies but abandoned him to his own waywardness? David's dependence on God is complete, and so is his devotion to God—save me from the enemy outside but also from my frailty within (see 25:5; 51:7,10). Only one who is thus devoted to God may expect God's help and will truly fulfill the vow (v. 12). *Unite my heart.* See Ezek 11:19; see also 1 Chr 12:33; 1 Cor 7:35. *heart.* See note on 4:7.

86:12 Vow to praise (see note on 7:17).

86:13 David anticipates the answer to his prayer (see note on 3:8). *depths.* See note on 30:1.

86:14–17 Conclusion: the prayer renewed.

86:14 *violent.* The Hebrew for this word suggests also ferocity. *have not set You before them.* In their arrogance they dismiss the heavenly Warrior, who is David's defender (see note on 10:11; see also Jer 20:11).

86:15 Echoes v. 5, but is even more similar to Ex 34:6 (see note on Ex 34:6–7).

86:16 *grant Your strength.* Exert Your power in my behalf. *son of Your handmaid.* See 116:16.

86:17 *good.* Covenanted favors (see 27:13 and note). *may see it.* May see that You stand with me and help me (see 31:19 and note).

Ps 87 A celebration of Zion as the "city of God" (v. 3), the special object of His love and the royal city of His kingdom (see introductions to Ps 46; 48; 76). According to the ancient and consistent interpretation of Jewish and Christian scholars alike, this psalm stands in lonely isolation in the Psalter (but see 47:9) in that it foresees the ingathering of the nations into Zion as fellow citizens with Israel in the kingdom of God—after the manner of such prophetic visions as Is 2:2–4; 19:19–25; 25:6; 45:14,22–24; 56:6–8; 60:3; 66:23; Dan 7:14; Mic 4:1–3; Zech 8:23; 14:16. (Accordingly, some have assigned it to the time of Isaiah and Micah, while others have thought it to be postexilic.) So interpreted, this psalm stands in sharpest possible contrast with the other Zion songs of the Psalter (see Ps 46; 48; 76; 125; 129; 137). The key to its main thrust lies in v. 4.

87 title *of the sons of Korah.* See note on Ps 42 title. *Song.* See note on Ps 30 title.

87:1 *His foundation.* The Lord Himself has laid the foundations

2 The LORD [a]loves the gates of Zion
More than all the *other* dwelling
places of Jacob.
3 [a]Glorious things are spoken of you,
O [b]city of God. [1]Selah.
4 "I shall mention [1a]Rahab and Babylon
[2]among those who know Me;
Behold, Philistia and [b]Tyre with
[3c]Ethiopia:
'This one was born there.' "
5 But of Zion it shall be said, "This one
and that one were born in her";
And the Most High Himself will
[a]establish her.
6 The LORD will count when He
[a]registers the peoples,
"This one was born there." Selah.
7 Then those who [a]sing as well as those
who [1b]play the flutes *shall say,*
"All my [c]springs *of joy* are in you."

Psalm 88

A Song. A Psalm of the sons of Korah. For the choir director; according to Mahalath Leannoth. A †Maskil of Heman •the Ezrahite.

1 O LORD, the [a]God of my salvation,
I have [b]cried out by day and in the
night before You.

2 [a]Ps 78:67, 68
3 [1]*Selah* may mean: *Pause, Crescendo* or *Musical interlude* [a]Is 60:1 [b]Ps 46:4; 48:8
4 [1]I.e. Egypt [2]Or *as* [3]Lit *Cush* [a]Job 9:13; Ps 89:10; Is 19:23-25 [b]Ps 45:12 [c]Ps 68:31
5 [a]Ps 48:8
6 [a]Ps 69:28; Is 4:3; Ezek 13:9
7 [1]Or *dance* [a]Ps 68:25; 149:3 [b]2 Sam 6:14; Ps 30:11 [c]Ps 36:9
88:1 †Possibly, *Contemplative,* or *Didactic,* or *Skillful Psalm* •1 Kin 4:31; 1 Chr 2:6; Ps 89: title [a]Ps 24:5; 27:9 [b]Ps 22:2; 86:3; Luke 18:7
2 [a]Ps 18:6 [b]Ps 31:2; 86:1
3 [1]Or *been satisfied with* [2]I.e. the nether world [a]Ps 107:26 [b]Ps 107:18; 116:3

2 Let my prayer [a]come before You;
[b]Incline Your ear to my cry!
3 For my [a]soul has [1]had enough
troubles,
And [b]my life has drawn near to
[2]Sheol.
4 I am reckoned among those who [a]go
down to the pit;
I have become like a man [b]without
strength,
5 [1]Forsaken [a]among the dead,
Like the slain who lie in the grave,
Whom You remember no more,
And they are [b]cut off from Your hand.
6 You have put me in [a]the lowest pit,
In [b]dark places, in the [c]depths.
7 Your wrath [a]has rested upon me,
And You have afflicted me with [b]all
Your waves. [1]Selah.
8 You have removed [a]my acquaintances
far from me;
You have made me an [1b]object of
loathing to them;
I am [c]shut up and cannot go out.

4 [a]Ps 28:1; 143:7 [b]Job 29:12; Ps 22:11 **5** [1]Lit *A freed one among the dead* [a]Ps 31:12 [b]Ps 31:22; Is 53:8 **6** [a]Ps 86:13; Lam 3:55 [b]Ps 143:3 [c]Ps 69:15 **7** [1]*Selah* may mean: *Pause, Crescendo* or *Musical interlude* [a]Ps 32:4; 39:10 [b]Ps 42:7 **8** [1]Lit *abomination to them* [a]Job 19:13, 19; Ps 31:11; 142:4 [b]Job 30:10 [c]Ps 142:7; Jer 32:2; 36:5

of Zion (see Is 14:32) and of the temple as His royal house. *mountains.* Though "Zion" (v. 2) is singular, the Hebrew for this word is plural, emphasizing the majesty of the holy mountain on which God's throne has been set (see 48:2 and note).

87:2 *loves . . . More than.* As the city of His founding, His chosen seat of rule over His people, Zion is the Lord's most cherished city, even among the towns of Israel (see 9:11; 78:68; 132:12–14). *Jacob.* A synonym for Israel (see Gen 32:28).

87:4 *I shall mention. . . This one was born there.* God will list them in His royal register (see notes on 9:5; 51:1; 69:28) as those who are native (born) citizens of His royal city, having all the privileges and enjoying all the benefits and security of such citizenship. *Rahab.* Whereas elsewhere this name is applied to the mythical monster of the deep (see 89:10; see also notes on 32:6; Job 9:13), here the reference is to Egypt (Rahab was a poetic name for Egypt), as in Is 30:7 (see note there); 51:9. The nations listed are representative of all Gentile peoples. As usually interpreted, the psalm here foresees a widespread conversion to the Lord from the peoples who from time immemorial had been hostile to Him and to His kingdom (see Is 19:21; 26:18 and note).

87:5 *This one and that one.* Wherever they may be dispersed among the nations. *Most High.* See note on Gen 14:19.

87:7 *All my springs.* All that refreshes them is found in the city of God, a possible allusion to God's "river of Your delights" (36:8) "whose streams make glad the city of God" (46:4); see notes on those passages. Alternatively, "springs" may be a metaphor for sources; the sense of the line would then be: We all spring from you. *my.* Communal use of the singular pronoun (see note on Ps 30 title).

Ps 88 A cry out of the depths, the prayer of one on the edge of death, whose whole life has been lived, as it were, in the near vicinity of the grave. So troubled have been his years that he seems to have known only the back of God's hand (God's "wrath," v. 7), and even those nearest him have withdrawn themselves as from one with an infectious skin disease (see v. 8). No expressions of hopeful expectation (as in most prayers of the Psalter) burst from these lips. Ending on a desparing note, the last word says "My acquaintances are in darkness." And yet the prayer begins, "O LORD, the God of my salvation." The psalm recalls the fact that although sometimes godly persons live lives of unremitting trouble (see 73:14), they can still grasp the hope that God is Savior. In its Hebrew structure, three four-line stanzas (vv. 3–5, 6–9a, 9b–12) are framed by two two-line prayers; to this is appended an additional four-line stanza in which the psalmist complains that his present distress is but characteristic of his whole troubled life.

88 title The psalm bears a double title, perhaps representing two different traditions. *Song.* See note on Ps 30 title. *of the sons of Korah.* See note on Ps 42 title. *For the choir director.* See note on Ps 4 title. *according to.* See note on Ps 6 title. *Maskil.* See note on Ps 32 title. *Heman.* See note on Ps 39 title. *Ezrahite.* The reference appears to be to Zerah, one of Judah's sons, who is recorded as having a Heman and an Ethan (see Ps 89 title) among his sons (see 1 Chr 2:6). If so, the title here represents a confusion in the tradition, arising from the similarity between these two Judahite names and those of two famous Korahite choir leaders, Heman and Ethan (Jeduthun; see note on Ps 39 title).

88:1–2 Opening appeal to the Lord as "the God of my salvation."

88:3–5 Living on the brink of death. Whether the psalmist lies mortally ill or experiences some analogous trouble or peril cannot be known.

88:3 *my soul.* See note on 6:3.

88:4 *pit.* See note on 30:1.

88:5 *remember no more.* From the perspective of this life, death cuts off from God's care; there is no remembering by God of the needy sufferer to rescue and restore (see 25:7; 74:2; 106:4). In his dark mood the author portrays his situation in bleakest colors (see note on 6:5).

88:6–9a You, O God, have done this! The psalmist knows no reason for it (see v. 14), but he knows God's hand is in it (see

9 My [a]eye has wasted away because of
affliction;
I have [b]called upon You every day,
O LORD;
I have [c]spread out my [1]hands to You.

10 Will You perform wonders for the
dead?
Will [a]the [1]departed spirits rise *and*
praise You? Selah.
11 Will Your lovingkindness be declared
in the grave,
Your faithfulness in [1]Abaddon?
12 Will Your wonders be made known in
the [a]darkness?
And Your [1]righteousness in the land of
forgetfulness?

13 But I, O LORD, have cried out [a]to You
for help,
And [b]in the morning my prayer comes
before You.
14 O LORD, why [a]do You reject my soul?
Why do You [b]hide Your face from me?
15 I was afflicted and [a]about to die from
my youth on;
I suffer [b]Your terrors; I am [1]overcome.
16 Your [a]burning anger has passed over
me;
Your terrors have [1b]destroyed me.
17 They have [a]surrounded me [b]like water
all day long;
They have [c]encompassed me altogether.
18 You have removed [a]lover and friend
far from me;
My acquaintances are *in* darkness.

Psalm 89

A [†]Maskil of [•]Ethan [^]the Ezrahite.

1 I will [a]sing of the lovingkindness of
the LORD forever;
To all generations I will [b]make known
Your [c]faithfulness with my mouth.
2 For I have said, "[a]Lovingkindness will
be built up forever;
In the heavens You will establish Your
[b]faithfulness."
3 "I have made a covenant with [a]My
chosen;
I have [b]sworn to David My servant,
4 I will establish your [a]seed forever
And build up your [b]throne to all
generations." [1]Selah.

5 The [a]heavens will praise Your
wonders, O LORD;

9 [1]Lit *palms* [a]Ps 6:7; 31:9 [b]Ps 22:2; 86:3 [c]Job 11:13; Ps 143:6
10 [1]Or *ghosts, shades* [a]Ps 6:5; 30:9
11 [1]I.e. place of destruction
12 [1]I.e. faithfulness to His gracious promises [a]Job 10:21; Ps 88:6
13 [a]Ps 30:2 [b]Ps 5:3; 119:147
14 [a]Ps 43:2; 44:9 [b]Job 13:24; Ps 13:1; 44:24
15 [1]Or *embarrassed* [a]Prov 24:11 [b]Job 6:4; 31:23
16 [1]Or *silenced* [a]2 Chr 28:11; Is 13:13; Lam 1:12 [b]Lam 3:54; Ezek 37:11
17 [a]Ps 118:10-12 [b]Ps 124:4 [c]Ps 17:11; 22:12, 16
18 [a]Job 19:13; Ps 88:8; 31:11; 38:11
89:1 [†]Possibly, *Contemplative,* or *Didactic,* or *Skillful Psalm* [•]1 Kin 4:31 [^]Ps 88: title [a]Ps 59:16; 101:1 [b]Ps 40:10 [c]Ps 36:5; 88:11; 89:5, 8, 24, 33, 49; 92:2; 119:90; Is 25:1; Lam 3:23
2 [a]Ps 103:17 [b]Ps 36:5; 119:90
3 [a]1 Kin 8:16 [b]Ps 132:11
4 [1]*Selah* may mean: *Pause, Crescendo* or *Musical interlude* [a]2 Sam 7:16 [b]2 Sam 7:13; Is 9:7; Luke 1:33
5 [a]Ps 19:1; 97:6

Ruth 1:20–21; Amos 3:6). That his Savior-God shows him the face of wrath deepens his anguish and helplessness. But he does not try to resolve the dark enigma; he simply pleads his case—and it is to his Savior-God that he can appeal.

88:6 *lowest pit . . . dark places.* See note on 30:1.

88:7 *wrath.* See v. 16; see also note on 2:5. *all Your waves.* See note on 32:6.

88:8 *my acquaintances.* See v. 18 and note on 31:11–12.

88:9 *eye has wasted away.* See note on 6:7.

88:9b–12 Appeal to God to help before the psalmist sinks into "the land of forgetfulness" (see note on v. 5).

88:10,12 *wonders.* God's saving acts in behalf of His people (see note on 9:1).

88:10 *rise.* In the realm of the dead (not in the resurrection); see Is 14:9.

88:11 *lovingkindness . . . faithfulness.* That is, lovingkindness-and-faithfulness (see note on 36:5; see also note on 3:7). *lovingkindness.* See note on 6:4.

88:12 *righteousness.* See note on 71:24.

88:13–14 Concluding prayer.

88:14 *why . . . ?* See note on 6:3; see also Introduction: Theology. *hide Your face.* See note on 13:1.

88:15–18 The psalmist has been no stranger to trouble; all his life he has suffered the terrors of God.

88:17 *like water.* See v. 7; see also note on 32:6.

Ps 89 A prayer that mourns the downfall of the Davidic dynasty and pleads for its restoration. The bitter shock of that event (reflected partially in the sudden transition of v. 38) is almost unbearable—that God, the faithful and almighty One, has abandoned His anointed and made him the mockery of the nations, in seeming violation of His firm covenant with David—and it evokes from the psalmist a lament that borders on reproach (vv. 38–45). The event may have been the attack on Jerusalem by Nebuchadnezzar and the exile of King Jehoiachin in 597 B.C. (see 2 Kin 24:8–17).

As with Ps 44 (see introduction to that psalm), a massive foundation is laid for the prayer with which the psalm concludes. An introduction (vv. 1–4) sings of God's love and faithfulness (vv. 1–2) and His covenant with David (vv. 3–4). These two themes are then jubilantly expanded in order: vv. 5–18, God's love and faithfulness; vv. 19–37, His covenant with David. Suddenly jubilation turns to lament, and the psalmist recounts in detail how God has rejected His anointed (vv. 38–45). Thus he comes to his prayer, impatient and urgent, that God will remember once more His covenant with David (vv. 46–51). (Verse 52 concludes not the psalm but Book 3 of the Psalter.)

89 title *Maskil.* See note on Ps 32 title. *Ethan.* Jeduthun (see note on Ps 39 title). The author was no doubt a Levite (perhaps a descendant of Jeduthun) who voiced this agonizing prayer as spokesman for the nation. *Ezrahite.* See note on Ps 88 title.

89:1–2 God's love and faithfulness celebrated.

89:1 *lovingkindness . . . faithfulness.* See vv. 2,33,49; that is, lovingkindness-and-faithfulness (see v. 14); see note on 36:5. *lovingkindness.* See vv. 2,14,24,28,33,49; see also note on 6:4. It is God's love and faithfulness that appear to have failed in His rejection (see vv. 38–45) of the Davidic king. The author repeats each of these words precisely seven times.

89:2 *In the heavens.* God's love and faithfulness have been made sure in the highest seat of power and authority (see vv. 5–8).

89:3–4 God's covenant with David celebrated (see 2 Sam 7:8–16).

89:3 *servant.* See vv. 20,39,50; here an official title (see note on 78:70).

89:5–8 The Lord's faithfulness and awesome power set Him apart among all the powers in the heavenly realm, and they acknowledge Him with praise and reverence.

89:5 *The heavens.* All beings belonging to the divine realm in the heavens. *wonders.* God's mighty acts in creation and

Your faithfulness also [b]in the assembly
of the [c]holy ones.
6 For [a]who in the skies is comparable to
the LORD?
Who among the [1][b]sons of the mighty
is like the LORD,
7 A God [a]greatly feared in the council of
the [b]holy ones,
And [c]awesome above all those who
are around Him?
8 O LORD God of hosts, [a]who is like You,
O mighty [1]LORD?
Your faithfulness also surrounds You.
9 You rule the swelling of the sea;
When its waves rise, You [a]still them.
10 You Yourself crushed [1][a]Rahab like one
who is slain;
You [b]scattered Your enemies with
[2]Your mighty arm.

11 The [a]heavens are Yours, the earth also
is Yours;
The [b]world and [1]all it contains, You
have founded them.
12 The [a]north and the south, You have
created them;
[b]Tabor and [c]Hermon [d]shout for joy at
Your name.
13 You have [1]a strong arm;
Your hand is mighty, Your [a]right hand
is exalted.
14 [a]Righteousness and justice are the
foundation of Your throne;
[b]Lovingkindness and [1]truth go before
You.
15 How blessed are the people who know
the [1][a]joyful sound!
O LORD, they walk in the [b]light of Your
countenance.
16 In [a]Your name they rejoice all the day,
And by Your righteousness they are
exalted.
17 For You are the glory of [a]their strength,
And by Your favor [1]our [b]horn is
exalted.
18 For our [a]shield belongs to the LORD,
[1]And our king to the [b]Holy One of
Israel.

19 [1]Once You spoke in vision to Your
godly [2]ones,
And said, "I have [3]given help to one
who is [a]mighty;
I have exalted one [b]chosen from the
people.
20 "I have [a]found David My servant;
With My holy [b]oil I have anointed
him,
21 With whom [a]My hand will be
established;
My arm also will [b]strengthen him.
22 "The enemy will not [1]deceive him,
Nor the [2][a]son of wickedness afflict
him.
23 "But I shall [a]crush his adversaries
before him,
And strike those who hate him.
24 "My [a]faithfulness and My
lovingkindness will be with him,
And in My name his [b]horn will be
exalted.
25 "I shall also set his hand [a]on the sea
And his right hand on the rivers.
26 "He will cry to Me, 'You are [a]my Father,
My God, and the [b]rock of my
salvation.'
27 "I also shall make him *My* [a]firstborn,
The [b]highest of the kings of the
earth.

5 [b]Ps 149:1 [c]Job 5:1 **6** [1]Or *sons of gods* [a]Ps 86:8; 113:5 [b]Ps 29:1; 82:1 **7** [a]Ps 47:2; 68:35; 76:7, 11 [b]Ps 89:5 [c]Ps 96:4 **8** [1]Heb *YAH* [a]Ps 35:10; 71:19 **9** [a]Ps 65:7; 107:29 **10** [1]I.e. Egypt [2]Lit *the arm of Your might* [a]Ps 87:4; Is 30:7; 51:9 [b]Ps 18:14; 68:1; 144:6 **11** [1]Lit *its fullness* [a]Gen 1:1; 1 Chr 29:11; Ps 96:5 [b]Ps 24:1 **12** [a]Job 26:7 [b]Josh 19:22; Judg 4:6; Jer 46:18 [c]Deut 3:8; Josh 11:17; 12:1; Ps 133:3; Song 4:8 [d]Ps 98:8 **13** [1]Lit *an arm with strength* [a]Ps 98:1; 118:16 **14** [1]Or *faithfulness* [a]Ps 97:2 [b]Ps 85:13 **15** [1]Or *blast of the trumpet, shout of joy* [a]Lev 23:24; Num 10:10; Ps 98:6 [b]Ps 4:6; 44:3; 67:1; 80:3; 90:8 **16** [a]Ps 105:3

17 [1]Another reading is *You exalt our horn* [a]Ps 28:8 [b]Ps 75:10; 92:10; 148:14 **18** [1]Or *Even to the Holy One of Israel our King* [a]Ps 47:9 [b]Ps 71:22; 78:41 **19** [1]Or *At that time* [2]Some mss read *one* [3]Lit *placed help upon* [a]2 Sam 17:10 [b]1 Kin 11:34; Ps 78:70 **20** [a]1 Sam 13:14; 16:1-12; Acts 13:22 [b]1 Sam 16:13 **21** [a]Ps 18:35; 80:17 [b]Ps 18:32 **22** [1]Or *exact usury from him* [2]Or *wicked man* [a]2 Sam 7:10; Ps 125:3 **23** [a]2 Sam 7:9; Ps 18:40 **24** [a]Ps 89:1 [b]Ps 132:17 **25** [a]Ps 72:8 **26** [a]2 Sam 7:14; 1 Chr 22:10; Jer 3:19 [b]2 Sam 22:47; Ps 95:1 **27** [a]Ex 4:22; Ps 2:7; Jer 31:9; Col 1:15, 18 [b]Num 24:7; Ps 72:11; Rev 19:16

redemption (see note on 9:1). *assembly of the holy ones.* The divine council in heaven (see v. 7; see also note on 82:1).
89:6 *sons of the mighty.* Lit."sons of god(s)" (see 29:1 and note).
89:8 *LORD . . . of hosts.* See note on 1 Sam 1:3. *Your faithfulness also surrounds you.* It also surrounds this stanza (see v. 5).
89:9–13 The Lord's power as Creator—and creation's joy in Him.
89:9–10 Poetic imagery borrowed from ancient Near Eastern myths of creation, here celebrating God's power in ordering the primeval chaotic waters so that the creation order could be established (see Gen 1:6–10; see also notes on 65:6–7; 74:13–14).
89:10 *Rahab.* Mythical monster of the deep (see notes on 32:6; 87:4), probably another name for Leviathan (see 74:14; 104:26). The last half of this verse is probably echoed in Luke 1:51.
89:12 *The north and the south.* Reference may be to two mountains, here parallel to Tabor and Hermon: Mount Zaphon ("North"; see note on Is 14:13) and Mount Amana (see Song 4:8). *Tabor.* See note on Judg 4:6. *Hermon.* See note on Deut 3:8. *shout for joy.* See note on 65:13. *name.* See vv. 16,24; see also note on 5:11.
89:14–18 The Lord's righteousness and faithfulness in His rule in behalf of His people—and their joy in Him.
89:14 Righteousness and justice are the foundation stones of God's throne; love and truth are personified as angelic attendants that herald His royal movements (see note on 23:6). *Righteousness.* See v. 16; see also note on 5:8.
89:17 *horn.* King ("horn" here symbolizes "strong one"; see v. 18).
89:18 *Holy One of Israel.* See note on Is 1:4.
89:19–29 The Lord's election of David to be His regent over His people, and His everlasting covenant with him. The thought is developed by couplets: (1) introduction (v. 19); (2) I have anointed David as My servant and will sustain him (vv. 20–21); (3) I will crush all his foes (vv. 22–23); (4) I will extend his realm (vv. 24–25); (5) I will make him first among the kings (vv. 26–27); (6) I will cause his dynasty to endure forever (vv. 28–29)—a promise fulfilled in the eternal reign of Jesus Christ (see John 12:34).
89:19 *vision.* Reference is to the revelation to Samuel (see 1 Sam 16:12) and/or to Nathan (see 2 Sam 7:4–16). *godly ones.* See note on 4:3.
89:25 *sea . . . rivers.* David's rule will reach from the Mediterranean Sea to the Euphrates River (see 72:8; 80:11 and note on Ex 23:31). But the author uses imagery that underscores the fact that, as His royal "son" (see v. 26) and regent, David's rule will be a reflection of God's (see vv. 9–10 and notes; also compare v. 23 with v. 10).
89:27 *firstborn.* The royal son of highest privilege and posi-

28 "My [a]lovingkindness I will keep for
him forever,
And My [b]covenant shall be confirmed
to him.
29 "So I will establish his [1a]descendants
forever
And his [b]throne [c]as the days of heaven.

30 "If his sons [a]forsake My law
And do not walk in My judgments,
31 If they [1]violate My statutes
And do not keep My commandments,
32 Then I will punish their transgression
with the [a]rod
And their iniquity with stripes.
33 "But I will not break off [a]My
lovingkindness from him,
Nor deal falsely in My faithfulness.
34 "My [a]covenant I will not [1]violate,
Nor will I [b]alter [2]the utterance of My
lips.
35 "[1]Once I have [a]sworn by My holiness;
I will not lie to David.
36 "His [1a]descendants shall endure forever
And his [b]throne [c]as the sun before Me.
37 "It shall be established forever [a]like the
moon,
And the [b]witness in the sky is
faithful." [1]Selah.

38 But You have [a]cast off and [b]rejected,
You have been full of wrath [1]against
Your [c]anointed.
39 You have [a]spurned the covenant of
Your servant;
You have [b]profaned [c]his crown [1]in the
dust.
40 You have [a]broken down all his walls;
You have [b]brought his strongholds to
ruin.
41 [a]All who pass along the way plunder
him;
He has become a [b]reproach to his
neighbors.
42 You have [a]exalted the right hand of
his adversaries;
You have [b]made all his enemies
rejoice.

28 [a]Ps 89:33 [b]Ps 89:3, 34 **29** [1]Lit *seed* [a]Ps 18:50; 89:4, 36 [b]1 Kin 2:4; Ps 89:4; 132:12; Is 9:7; Jer 33:17 [c]Deut 11:21 **30** [a]2 Sam 7:14; Ps 119:53 **31** [1]Lit *profane* **32** [a]Job 9:34; 21:9 **33** [a]2 Sam 7:15 **34** [1]Lit *profane* [2]Lit *that which goes forth* [a]Deut 7:9; Jer 33:20, 21 [b]Num 23:19 **35** [1]Or *One thing* [a]Ps 60:6; Amos 4:2 **36** [1]Lit *seed* [a]Ps 89:29; Luke 1:33 [b]Ps 72:5 [c]Ps 72:17 **37** [1]*Selah* may mean: *Pause, Crescendo* or *Musical interlude* [a]Ps 72:5 [b]Job 16:19 **38** [1]Lit *with* [a]Ps 44:9 [b]Deut 32:19; 1 Chr 28:9 [c]Ps 20:6; 89:20, 51 **39** [1]Lit *to the ground* [a]Ps 78:59; Lam 2:7 [b]Ps 74:7 [c]Lam 5:16 **40** [a]Ps 80:12 [b]Lam 2:2, 5 **41** [a]Ps 80:12 [b]Ps 44:13; 69:9, 19; 79:4 **42** [a]Ps 13:2 [b]Ps 80:6

43 [a]Ps 44:10 **44** [1]Lit *clearness, luster* [a]Ezek 28:7 **45** [a]Ps 102:23 [b]Ps 44:15; 71:13; 109:29 **46** [a]Ps 13:1; 44:24 [b]Ps 79:5; 80:4 **47** [1]Lit *of what duration I am* [2]Or *have You...men?* [a]Job 7:7; 10:9; 14:1 [b]Ps 39:5; 62:9; Eccl 1:2; 2:11 **48** [1]Lit *hand* [2]I.e. the nether world [a]Ps 22:29; 49:9 [b]Ps 49:15

43 You also turn back the edge of his
sword
And have [a]not made him stand in
battle.
44 You have made his [1a]splendor to cease
And cast his throne to the ground.
45 You have [a]shortened the days of his
youth;
You have [b]covered him with shame.
Selah.

46 [a]How long, O LORD?
Will You hide Yourself forever?
Will Your [b]wrath burn like fire?
47 [a]Remember [1]what my span of life is;
For what [b]vanity [2]You have created all
the sons of men!
48 What man can live and not [a]see death?
Can he [b]deliver his soul from the
[1]power of [2]Sheol? Selah.

49 Where are Your former
lovingkindnesses, O Lord,
Which You [a]swore to David in Your
faithfulness?
50 Remember, O Lord, the [a]reproach of
Your servants;
[1]How I bear in my bosom *the reproach
of* all the many peoples,
51 With which [a]Your enemies have
reproached, O LORD,
With which they have reproached the
footsteps of [b]Your anointed.

52 [a]Blessed be the LORD forever!
Amen and Amen.

BOOK 4

Psalm 90

A Prayer of [†]Moses, the man of God.

1 Lord, You have been our [1a]dwelling
place in all generations.

49 [a]2 Sam 7:15; Jer 30:9; Ezek 34:23 **50** [1]Lit *My bearing in my bosom* [a]Ps 69:9; 74:18, 22 **51** [a]Ps 74:10, 18, 22 [b]Ps 89:38 **52** [a]Ps 41:13; 72:19; 106:48 **90:1** [†]Deut 33:1 [1]Or *hiding place;* some ancient mss read *place of refuge* [a]Deut 33:27; Ps 71:3; 91:1; Ezek 11:16

tion in the kingdom of God (see 2:7–12; 45:6–9; 72:8–11; 110), thus the most exalted of the kings of the earth (see Rev 1:5). So the words may speak of universal rule—ultimately fulfilled in Christ.

89:29 *as the days of heaven.* See vv. 36–37.

89:30–37 The Lord's covenant with David and his dynasty (see chart, p. 16) was everlasting (see v. 28) and unconditional—though if any of his royal descendants is unfaithful, he will individually suffer under God's rod (to the detriment of the entire nation).

89:38–45 God's present rejection of David's son, and all its fearful consequences—the undoing of all that had been promised and assured by covenant (see especially vv. 19–29).

89:46–51 The prayer, an appeal—in spite of all—to God's faithfulness to His covenant with David. In this dark hour, that remains the psalmist's hope.

89:46 *How long . . . ?* See note on 6:3; see also Introduction: Theology. *wrath.* See note on 2:5.

89:50 *Remember.* See v. 47.

89:52 A brief doxology with which the final editors concluded Book 3 of the Psalter (see note on 41:13).

Ps 90 A prayer to the everlasting God to have compassion on His servants, who live their melancholy lives under the rod of divine wrath and under His sentence of death—a plea that God will yet show them His love, give them cause for joy and bless their labors with enduring worth. No other psalm depicts so poignantly the dismal state of man before the face of God, holy and eternal. Yet there is neither defiance nor despair; honesty acknowledges guilt (God's anger is warranted), and faith knows of God's "lovingkindness" (v. 14) to which appeal can confidently be made. That Israel's 40 years of enforced sojourn in the "great and terrible wilderness" (Deut 8:15) on its pilgrimage to the

2 Before [a]the mountains were born
[1]Or You [b]gave birth to the earth and the world,
Even [c]from everlasting to everlasting, You are God.

3 You [a]turn man back into dust
And say, "Return, O children of men."
4 For [a]a thousand years in Your sight
Are like [b]yesterday when it passes by,
[1]Or *as* a [c]watch in the night.
5 You [a]have [1]swept them away like a flood, they [2b]fall asleep;
In the morning they are like [c]grass which [3]sprouts anew.
6 In the morning it [a]flourishes and [1]sprouts anew;
Toward evening it [b]fades and [c]withers away.

7 For we have been [a]consumed by Your anger
And by Your wrath we have been [1]dismayed.
8 You have [a]placed our iniquities before You,
Our [b]secret *sins* in the light of Your presence.
9 For [a]all our days have declined in Your fury;
We have finished our years like a [1]sigh.
10 As for the days of our [1]life, [2]they contain seventy years,
Or if due to strength, [a]eighty years,
Yet their pride is *but* [b]labor and sorrow;
For soon it is gone and we [c]fly away.
11 Who [1]understands the [a]power of Your anger
And Your fury, according to the [b]fear [2]that is due You?
12 So [a]teach us to number our days,
That we may [1b]present to You a heart of wisdom.

13 Do [a]return, O LORD; [b]how long *will it be?*
And [1]be [c]sorry for Your servants.
14 O [a]satisfy us in the morning with Your lovingkindness,
That we may [b]sing for joy and be glad all our days.
15 [a]Make us glad [1]according to the days You have afflicted us,
And the [b]years we have seen [2]evil.
16 Let Your [a]work appear to Your servants
And Your [b]majesty [1]to their children.
17 Let the [a]favor of the Lord our God be upon us;
And [1b]confirm for us the work of our hands;
Yes, [1]confirm the work of our hands.

2 [1]Or *And* [a]Job 15:7; Prov 8:25 [b]Gen 1:1; Ps 102:25; 104:5 [c]Ps 93:2; 102:24, 27; Jer 10:10
3 [a]Gen 3:19; Job 34:14, 15; Ps 104:29
4 [1]Or *And* [a]2 Pet 3:8 [b]Ps 39:5 [c]Ex 14:24; Judg 7:19
5 [1]Or *flooded* [2]Lit *become asleep* [3]Or *passes away* [a]Job 22:16; 27:20 [b]Job 14:12; 20:8; Ps 76:5 [c]Ps 103:15; Is 40:6
6 [1]Or *passes away* [a]Job 14:2 [b]Ps 92:7; Matt 6:30 [c]James 1:11
7 [1]Or *terrified* [a]Ps 39:11
8 [a]Ps 50:21; Jer 16:17 [b]Ps 19:12; Eccl 12:14
9 [1]Or *whisper* [a]Ps 78:33
10 [1]Lit *years* [2]Lit *in them are* [a]2 Kin 19:35
10 [b]Eccl 12:2-7; Jer 20:18 [c]Job 20:8; Ps 78:39
11 [1]Or *knows* [2]Lit *of You* [a]Ps 76:7 [b]Neh 5:9
12 [1]Or *gain, bring in* [a]Deut 32:29; Ps 39:4 [b]Prov 2:1-6
13 [1]Or *repent in regard to* [a]Ps 6:4; 80:14 [b]Ps 6:3; 74:10 [c]Ex 32:12; Deut 32:36; Ps 106:45; 135:14; Amos 7:3, 6; Jon 3:9
14 [a]Ps 36:8; 65:4; 103:5; Jer 31:14 [b]Ps 31:7; 85:6
15 [1]Or *as many days as* [2]Or *trouble* [a]Ps 86:4 [b]Deut 2:14-16; Ps 31:10
16 [1]Or *upon* [a]Deut 32:4; Ps 44:1; 77:12; 92:4; Hab 3:2 [b]1 Kin 8:11; Is 6:3
17 [1]Or *give permanence to* [a]Ps 27:4 [b]Ps 37:23; Is 26:12; 1 Cor 3:7

promised land (see Num 14:26–35) should evoke such a prayer ought not be surprising.

Two passages descriptive of the human condition under God's aggrieved anger (vv. 3–6, 7–10) are framed by two couplets (vv. 1–2, 11–12) that, by their implicit contrasts, highlight the major polarities over which the intervening stanzas brood: 1. The Lord, who has ever been our "dwelling place" (v. 1), has shown us the power of His wrath (v. 7). 2. God is the Everlasting One (v. 2), while we must come to terms with the small number of our days (v. 12). These reflections lead to the prayer with which the psalm concludes (vv. 13–17).

90 title *A Prayer.* See note on Ps 17 title. *man of God.* A phrase normally applied in the OT to prophets (see note on 1 Sam 2:27), including Moses (see, e.g., Josh 14:6).

90:1 *dwelling place.* See 91:9. The Hebrew for this phrase is translated "habitation" in 71:3.

90:3–6 Man lives under God's sentence of death—"dust . . . to dust" (Gen 3:19).

90:4–5 *For . . . You.* Perhaps better "Though . . . , You": Though for God 1,000 years are like a watch in the night, which man sleeps through with no sense of the passage of time, He cuts man's life short like new grass that shows itself at dawn's light but is withered away by the hot Canaanite sun before evening falls.

90:4 *watch in the night.* See note on Judg 7:19.

90:7–10 Even life's short span is filled with trouble, as God ferrets out man's every sin and makes him feel His righteous anger.

90:7 *anger . . . wrath.* See vv. 9,11; see also note on 2:5.

90:8 *light of Your presence.* The holy light of God that illumines the hidden corners of the heart and exposes its dark secrets.

90:10 *eighty.* Hebrew poetic convention called for 80 following 70 in parallel construction (see note on Amos 1:3). *their pride.* What people prize in their years. The thought could be: All their health, joys, riches and honor are soured by trouble and sorrow. *sorrow.* Or "emptiness."

90:11–12 *Who understands . . . ? . . . teach us.* No one has taken the measure of God's anger. But everyone ought to know the measure of his (few) days or he will play the arrogant fool, with no thought of his mortality or of his accountability to God (see Ps 49; 73:4–12).

90:11 *fear that is due You.* See note on Gen 20:11.

90:12 *present to You.* Or "harvest." *heart.* See note on 4:7.

90:13–17 Prayer for God's compassion—from Him come also joy and gladness.

90:13 *return.* Lit. "turn" (cf. v. 3). *how long . . . ?* See note on 6:3 (see also Introduction: Theology).

90:14 *in the morning.* Let there be for us a dawning of Your love to relieve this long, dark night of Your anger. Perhaps Moses (see title) pleads for the promised rest of the promised land (see Ex 33:14; Deut 12:9). The final answer to his prayer comes with the resurrection (see Rom 5:2–5; 8:18; 2 Cor 4:16–18). *lovingkindness.* See note on 6:4.

90:16 *work . . . majesty.* That is, work-of-majesty (see 111:3; see also note on 3:7). For a fuller description of such works see the whole of Ps 111. *to their children.* As to past generations (v. 1).

90:17 *favor.* Or "beauty"; see 27:4 and note. *confirm.* As You only have been our security in the world (see v. 1), so also make our labors to be effective and enduring—though we are so transient.

Psalm 91

1 He who dwells in the [a]shelter of the
Most High
Will abide in the [b]shadow of the
Almighty.
2 I will say to the LORD, "My [a]refuge
and my [b]fortress,
My God, in whom I [c]trust!"
3 For it is He who delivers you from the
[a]snare of the trapper
And from the deadly [b]pestilence.
4 He will [a]cover you with His pinions,
And [b]under His wings you may seek
refuge;
His [c]faithfulness is a [d]shield and
bulwark.

5 You [a]will not be afraid of the [b]terror
by night,
Or of the [c]arrow that flies by day;
6 Of the [a]pestilence that [1]stalks in
darkness,
Or of the [b]destruction that lays waste
at noon.
7 A thousand may fall at your side
And ten thousand at your right hand,
But [a]it shall not approach you.
8 You will only look on with your eyes
And [a]see the recompense of the
wicked.
9 [1]For you have made the LORD, [a]my
refuge,
Even the Most High, [b]your dwelling
place.
10 [a]No evil will befall you,
Nor will any plague come near your
[1]tent.

11 For He will give [a]His angels charge
concerning you,
To guard you in all your ways.
12 They will [a]bear you up in their hands,
That you do not strike your foot
against a stone.
13 You will [a]tread upon the lion and
cobra,
The young lion and the [1]serpent you
will trample down.

14 "[a]Because he has loved Me, therefore I
will deliver him;
I will [b]set him *securely* on high,
because he has [c]known My name.
15 "He will [a]call upon Me, and I will
answer him;
I will be with him in [1]trouble;
I will rescue him and [b]honor him.
16 "With [1]a [a]long life I will satisfy him
And [2b]let him see My salvation."

Psalm 92

A Psalm, a Song for the Sabbath day.

1 It is [a]good to give thanks to the LORD
And to [b]sing praises to Your name,
O Most High;

91:1 [a]Ps 27:5; 31:20; 32:7 [b]Ps 17:8; 121:5; Is 25:4; 32:2
2 [a]Ps 14:6; 91:9; 94:22; 142:5 [b]Ps 18:2; 31:3; Jer 16:19 [c]Ps 25:2; 56:4
3 [a]Ps 124:7; Prov 6:5 [b]1 Kin 8:37; 2 Chr 20:9; Ps 91:6
4 [a]Is 51:16 [b]Ps 17:8; 36:7; 57:1; 63:7 [c]Ps 40:11 [d]Ps 35:2
5 [a]Job 5:19-23; Ps 23:4; 27:1 [b]Song 3:8 [c]Ps 64:4
6 [1]Or *walks* [a]2 Kin 19:35; Ps 91:10 [b]Job 5:22
7 [a]Gen 7:23; Josh 14:10
8 [a]Ps 37:34; 58:10
9 [1]Or *For You O LORD are my Refuge; You have made the Most High your dwelling place* [a]Ps 91:2 [b]Ps 90:1
10 [1]Or *dwelling* [a]Prov 12:21
11 [a]Ps 34:7; Matt 4:6; Luke 4:10, 11; Heb 1:14
12 [a]Matt 4:6; Luke 4:11
13 [1]Or *dragon* [a]Judg 14:6; Dan 6:22; Luke 10:19
14 [a]Ps 145:20 [b]Ps 59:1 [c]Ps 9:10
15 [1]Or *distress* [a]Job 12:4; Ps 50:15 [b]1 Sam 2:30; John 12:26
16 [1]Lit *length of days* [2]Or *cause him to feast his eyes on* [a]Deut 6:2; Ps 21:4; Prov 3:1, 2 [b]Ps 50:23
92:1 [a]Ps 147:1 [b]Ps 135:3

Ps 91 A glowing testimony to the security of those who trust in God. It was probably written by one of the temple personnel (a priest or Levite) as a word of assurance to godly worshipers. Because the "you" of vv. 3–13 applies to any of the godly who make "the Most High, your dwelling place" (v. 9; see 90:1), the devil applied vv. 11–12 to Jesus (see Matt 4:6; Luke 4:10–11). Thematically, the psalm is divided into two halves. The opening couplet of the second half (vv. 9–10) echoes the theme of vv. 1–2. In the first half, the godly are assured of security from four threats (vv. 5–6)—though thousands fall (v. 7). In the second half, they are assured of triumphing over four menacing beasts (v. 13). The oracle of vv. 14–16 offers climactic assurance.

91:1 *shelter.* The temple (as in 27:5; 31:20; see also 23:6; 27:4), where the godly find safety under the protective wings of the Lord (see v. 4; 61:4). *Most High.* See v. 9; see also note on Gen 14:19. *shadow.* See note on 17:8. *Almighty.* Hebrew *Shaddai* (see note on Gen 17:1).

91:3 *snare of the trapper.* Metaphor for danger from an enemy (see 124:7). *pestilence.* These two threats are further elaborated in vv. 5–6.

91:4 *with His pinions.* See note on 17:8.

91:5 *terror.* As in 64:1 ("dread"), reference is to attack by enemies; thus it is paired with "arrow." These two references to threats from war are arrayed alongside "pestilence" and "destruction" (v. 6), two references to mortal diseases that often reached epidemic proportions. *night . . . day.* At whatever time of day or night the threat may come, you will be kept safe—the time references are not specific to their respective phrases (see also v. 6).

91:7 *ten thousand.* Hebrew poetic convention called for 10,000 following 1,000 in parallel construction (see notes on 90:10; Amos 1:3). Cf. 1 Sam 18:7.

91:9 *dwelling.* See 90:1 and note.

91:11–12 Quoted by Satan in Matt 4:6; Luke 4:10–11.

91:11 *His angels.* See note on 34:7.

91:12 *against a stone.* On the stony trails of Canaan (see Prov 3:23).

91:13 *lion . . . cobra . . . young lion . . . serpent.* These double references to lions and to poisonous snakes balance the double references of vv. 5–6, and complete the illustrative roster of mortal threats (see Amos 5:19).

91:14–16 Employing the form of a prophetic oracle, the author (see introduction) supports his testimony by assuring the godly that it is confirmed by all the promises of God to those who truly love and trust Him.

91:14 *set him securely on high.* Protect him. *My name.* See note on 5:11.

Ps 92 A joyful celebration of the righteous rule of God. Its testimony to the prosperity of the righteous, "planted in the house of the LORD" (v. 13), links it thematically with Ps 91, while its joy over God's righteous reign relates it to the cluster of psalms that follow (Ps 93–100; see especially Ps 94). In fact, celebration of God's love and faithfulness as characteristic of His reign (see v. 2; 100:5) may have served for the editors of the Psalter as a frame enclosing the collection. The psalmist here may have been the king (see vv. 10–11). Following the introduction on praise (vv. 1–3), vv. 4–5 offer the motivation for the praise ("me," "I"), which is picked up again in vv. 10–11 ("my," "I," "my," "my," "My," "me"). Verses 6–9 expound the folly and destiny of evildoers, while vv. 12–15 expound the prosperity of the righteous. Notice also the link between v. 7 and v. 13. The NASB text offers

2 To [a]declare Your lovingkindness in the morning
And Your [b]faithfulness [1]by night,
3 [1]With the [a]ten-stringed lute and [1]with the [a]harp,
[1]With resounding music [2]upon the [a]lyre.
4 For You, O LORD, have made me glad by [1]what You [a]have done,
I will [b]sing for joy at the [c]works of Your hands.

5 How [a]great are Your works, O LORD!
Your [1b]thoughts are very [c]deep.
6 A [a]senseless man has no knowledge,
Nor does a [a]stupid man understand this:
7 That when the wicked [a]sprouted up like grass
And all [b]who did iniquity flourished,
It *was only* that they might be [c]destroyed forevermore.
8 But You, O LORD, are [a]on high forever.
9 For, behold, Your enemies, O LORD,
For, behold, [a]Your enemies will perish;
All who do iniquity will be [b]scattered.

10 But You have exalted my [a]horn like *that of* the wild ox;
I have [1]been [b]anointed with fresh oil.
11 And my eye has [a]looked *exultantly* upon [1]my foes,
My ears hear of the evildoers who rise up against me.
12 The [a]righteous man will [1]flourish like the palm tree,
He will grow like a [b]cedar in Lebanon.
13 [a]Planted in the house of the LORD,
They will flourish [b]in the courts of our God.
14 They will still [1a]yield fruit in old age;
They shall be [2]full of sap and very green,
15 To [1]declare that [a]the LORD is upright;
He is my [b]rock, and there is [c]no unrighteousness in Him.

Psalm 93

1 [a]The LORD [1]reigns, He is [b]clothed with majesty;
The LORD has [c]clothed and girded Himself with strength;
Indeed, the [d]world is firmly established, it will not be moved.
2 Your [a]throne is established from of old;
You [b]are from everlasting.

3 The [a]floods have lifted up, O LORD,
The floods have lifted up their voice,
The floods lift up their pounding waves.

2 [1]Lit *nights* [a]Ps 59:16 [b]Ps 89:1 **3** [1]Lit *Upon* [2]Lit *by means of* [a]1 Sam 10:5; 1 Chr 13:8; Neh 12:27; Ps 33:2 **4** [1]Lit *Your working* [a]Ps 40:5; 90:16 [b]Ps 106:47 [c]Ps 8:6; 111:7; 143:5 **5** [1]Or *purposes* [a]Ps 40:5; 111:2; Rev 15:3 [b]Ps 33:11; 40:5; 139:17 [c]Ps 36:6; Rom 11:33 **6** [a]Ps 49:10; 73:22; 94:8 **7** [a]Job 12:6; Ps 90:5 [b]Ps 94:4 [c]Ps 37:38 **8** [a]Ps 83:18; 93:4; 113:5 **9** [a]Ps 37:20 [b]Ps 68:1; 89:10 **10** [1]Or *become moist* [a]Ps 75:10; 89:17; 112:9 [b]Ps 23:5; 45:7 **11** [1]Or *those who lie in wait for me* [a]Ps 54:7; 91:8 **12** [1]Lit *sprout* [a]Num 24:6; Ps 1:3; 52:8; 72:7; Jer 17:8; Hos 14:5, 6 [b]Ps 104:16; Ezek 31:3 **13** [a]Ps 80:15; Is 60:21 [b]Ps 100:4; 116:19 **14** [1]Or *thrive in* [2]Lit *fat and* [a]Prov 11:30; Is 37:31; John 15:2; James 3:18 **15** [1]Or *show forth* [a]Job 34:10; Ps 25:8 [b]Deut 32:4; Ps 18:2; 94:22 [c]Rom 9:14 **93:1** [1]Or *has assumed kingship* [a]Ps 96:10; 97:1; 99:1 [b]Ps 104:1 [c]Ps 65:6; Is 51:9 [d]Ps 96:10 **2** [a]Ps 45:6; Lam 5:19 [b]Ps 90:2 **3** [a]Ps 96:11; 98:7, 8

a different analysis of the psalm's structure. If the analysis presented here is followed, v. 8 should be read as concluding the thought of v. 7.

92 title *a Song.* See note on Ps 30 title. *for the Sabbath day.* In the postexilic liturgy of the temple, this psalm came to be sung at the time of the morning sacrifice on the Sabbath. (The rest of the weekly schedule was: first day, Ps 24; second day, Ps 48; third day, Ps 82; fourth day, Ps 94; fifth day, Ps 81; sixth day, Ps 93.)

92:1–3 Hymnic introduction.

92:1 *LORD . . . Most High.* That is, LORD Most High (see 7:17; see also note on 3:7). *name.* See note on 5:11. *Most High.* See note on Gen 14:19.

92:2 *lovingkindness . . . faithfulness.* That is, lovingkindness-and-faithfulness (see note on 36:5; see also note on 3:7). *love.* See note on 6:4. *morning . . . night.* Continuously.

92:3 *harp . . . lyre.* See note on 57:8. *lyre.* See note on Gen 31:27.

92:4–5 Joy over God's saving acts (see vv. 10–11).

92:5 *Your thoughts.* As shown by your deeds.

92:6–9 The fatal folly of evildoers (contrast vv. 12–15).

92:6 *senseless . . . stupid man.* See note on 14:1; see also 49:10; 94:8–11. They do not know that the Lord rules righteously. They see the wicked flourishing, but do not see the Lord or foresee the end he has appointed for them. The author thus characterizes his "evildoers" (v. 11), whom the Lord has routed.

92:7 A condensed statement of what is expounded more fully in Ps 73 (see note on 90:4–5).

92:8 *on high forever.* God's eternal exaltation assures the destruction of His enemies.

92:9 *enemies.* Here the evildoers, referred to also in v. 7.

92:10–11 Joy over God's favors (see vv. 4–5): God has made him triumphant (see 89:24) and anointed him with "the oil of joy" (45:7; see also 23:5) by giving him victory over all his enemies.

92:12–15 The secure prosperity of the righteous (contrast vv. 6–9).

92:13 *Planted in the house of the LORD.* Though the wicked may have "sprouted up like grass," their end is sure (see v. 7). But the righteous are planted in a secure place (see Ps 91) and so retain the vigor of youth into old age, rejoicing in God's just discrimination (see v. 15). *courts.* Of the temple (see 84:2,10; 2 Kin 21:5; 23:11–12).

Ps 93 A hymn to the eternal, universal and invincible reign of the Lord, a theme it shares with Ps 47; 94–100. Together they offer a majestic confession of faith in and hope for the kingdom of God on earth. These hymns were composed for the liturgy of a high religious festival in which the kingship of the Lord—over the cosmic order, over the nations and in a special sense over Israel—was annually celebrated (see introduction to Ps 47). And implicitly, where not explicitly, the Lord's kingship is hailed in contrast to the claims of all other gods; He is "a great King above all gods" (95:3). Ps 93–100 may all have been composed by temple personnel and spoken by them in the liturgy. They probably date from the preexilic era. Structurally, the psalm has two short stanzas (vv. 1–2, 3–4) and a conclusion (v. 5).

93:1–2 The Lord's reign, by which the creation order has been and will be secure throughout the ages, is from eternity (see Gen 1:1). Though Israel as a nation has come late on the scene, her God has been King since before the creation of the world.

93:1 *The LORD reigns.* The ultimate truth, and first article, in Israel's creed (see 96:10; 97:1; 99:1; see also Zech 14:9 and note).

93:3–4 Since His founding of the world, the Lord has shown

4 More than the sounds of many waters,
Than the mighty breakers of the sea,
The LORD [a]on high is mighty.
5 Your [a]testimonies are fully confirmed;
[b]Holiness befits Your house,
O LORD, [1]forevermore.

Psalm 94

1 O LORD, God of [1a]vengeance,
God of [1]vengeance, [2b]shine forth!
2 [a]Rise up, O [b]Judge of the earth,
Render recompense [c]to the proud.
3 How long shall the wicked, O LORD,
How long shall the [a]wicked exult?
4 They pour forth *words,* they [a]speak
arrogantly;
All who do wickedness [b]vaunt
themselves.
5 They [a]crush Your people, O LORD,
And [b]afflict Your heritage.
6 They [a]slay the widow and the
[1]stranger
And murder the orphans.
7 [a]They have said, "[1]The LORD does not
see,
Nor does the God of Jacob pay heed."
8 Pay heed, you [a]senseless among the
people;
And when will you understand,
[a]stupid ones?
9 He who [a]planted the ear, [1]does He not
hear?
He who formed the eye, [1]does He not
see?
10 He who [1a]chastens the nations, will
He not rebuke,
Even He who [b]teaches man
knowledge?
11 The LORD [a]knows the thoughts of
man,
[1]That they are a *mere* breath.

12 Blessed is the man whom [a]You
chasten, O [1]LORD,
And [b]whom You teach out of Your
law;
13 That You may grant him [a]relief from
the [b]days of adversity,
Until [c]a pit is dug for the wicked.
14 For [a]the LORD will not abandon His
people,
Nor will He [b]forsake His inheritance.
15 For [1a]judgment [2]will again be
righteous,
And all the upright in heart [3]will
follow it.
16 Who will [a]stand up for me against
evildoers?
Who will take his stand for me
[b]against those who do
wickedness?

17 If [a]the LORD had not been my help,
My soul would soon have dwelt in *the
abode of* silence.

4 [a]Ps 65:7; 89:6, 9; 92:8 **5** [1]Lit *for length of days* [a]Ps 19:7 [b]Ps 29:2; 96:9; 1 Cor 3:17 **94:1** [1]Or *avenging acts* [2]Or *has shone forth* [a]Deut 32:35; Is 35:4; Nah 1:2; Rom 12:19 [b]Ps 50:2; 80:1 **2** [a]Ps 7:6 [b]Gen 18:25 [c]Ps 31:23 **3** [a]Job 20:5 **4** [a]Ps 31:18; 75:5 [b]Ps 10:3; 52:1 **5** [a]Is 3:15 [b]Ps 79:1 **6** [1]Or *sojourner* [a]Is 10:2 **7** [1]Heb YAH [a]Job 22:13; Ps 10:11 **8** [a]Ps 92:6 **9** [1]Or *can* [a]Ex 4:11; Prov 20:12 **10** [1]Or *instructs* [a]Ps 44:2 [b]Job 35:11; Is 28:26 **11** [1]Or *For* [a]Job 11:11; 1 Cor 3:20 **12** [1]Heb YAH [a]Deut 8:5; Job 5:17; Ps 119:71; Prov 3:11, 12; Heb 12:5, 6 [b]Ps 119:171 **13** [a]Job 34:29; Hab 3:16 [b]Ps 49:5 [c]Ps 9:15; 55:23 **14** [a]1 Sam 12:22; Lam 3:31; Rom 11:2 [b]Ps 37:28 **15** [1]I.e. administration of justice [2]Lit *will return to righteousness* [3]Lit *will be after it* [a]Ps 97:2; Is 42:3; Mic 7:9 **16** [a]Num 10:35; Is 28:21; 33:10 [b]Ps 17:13; 59:2 **17** [a]Ps 124:1, 2

Himself to be mightier than all the forces of disorder that threaten His kingdom.

93:3 *floods.* Reference is to the primeval chaotic waters, tamed and assigned a place by the Lord's creative word (see 33:7; 104:7–9; Gen 1:6–10; Job 38:8–11). Implicitly they symbolize all that opposes the coming of the Lord's kingdom (see 65:6–7; 74:13–14 and notes).

93:4 The thunder of the chaotic waters is no match for the thunder of the Lord's ordering word (see 104:7).

93:5 *testimonies.* He whose indisputable rule has made the world secure has given His people life directives that are stable and reliable (see 19:7)—and that they must honor (see 95:8–11). *Your house.* His earthly temple—but also the heavenly. *forevermore.* Qualifies both clauses.

Ps 94 An appeal to the Lord, as "Judge of the earth" (v. 2), to redress the wrongs perpetrated against the weak by arrogant and wicked men who occupy seats of power. The psalm has links with Ps 92, but is the voice of the oppressed within Israel (thus not the king), seeking redress at God's throne for injustices done them by those smugly established in the power structures of the nation. Thus it is unique within the Ps 92–100 collection. (See introduction to Ps 93.)

94:1–3 Initial appeal to God, the Judge.

94:1 *vengeance.* Redress of wrongs (see Deut 32:35,41 and note on Deut 32:35).

94:2 *the proud.* See vv. 4–7 for a description of them.

94:3 *How long . . . ?* See note on 6:3; see also Introduction: Theology.

94:4–7 Indictment of the wicked.

94:4 *words . . . vaunt themselves.* For the arrogance of the wicked see 10:2–11 and notes.

94:5 *Your people . . . Your heritage.* Those among them who are vulnerable (see v. 6).

94:7 *They have said.* See notes on 3:2; 10:11. *Jacob.* A synonym for Israel (see Gen 32:28).

94:8–11 Warning to the wicked—those "senseless . . . stupid ones" (see 92:6–9; see also note on 14:1).

94:10 *chastens.* Keeps them in line by means of punishment (see Lev 26:18; Jer 31:18). *teaches.* Gives him some knowledge of the creation order (see Is 28:26).

94:11 *The LORD knows.* Contrary to their foolish supposition (see v. 7).

94:12–15 Those whose lives are directed by God's law are the blessed ones (see Ps 1)—contrary to the arrogant expectations of the wicked and in spite of their oppressions.

94:12 *Blessed.* See note on 1:1. *chasten . . . teach.* See v. 10. Here the author speaks of God's correcting and teaching His people in the ways of His law.

94:14 *people . . . inheritance.* See v. 5. The Lord will not abandon the powerless among His people to the injustice of their oppressors. Paul may be echoing this verse in Rom 11:1–2.

94:15 *again be righteous.* Or "restore righteousness." *heart.* See note on 4:7. *will follow it.* Or "with it." In any event, the author appears to say that God's judgment will restore justice for the upright in heart.

94:16–19 The Lord is the only sure court of appeal.

94:17 *abode of silence.* See note on 30:1. Without God's help the wicked would have silenced the psalmist in the grave, but now it is the wicked for whom the pit will be dug (see v. 13).

18 If I should say, "[a]My foot has slipped,"
Your lovingkindness, O LORD, will hold me up.
19 When my anxious thoughts [1]multiply within me,
Your [a]consolations delight my soul.
20 Can a [1a]throne of destruction be allied with You,
One [b]which devises [2]mischief by decree?
21 They [a]band themselves together against the [1]life of the righteous
And [b]condemn [2]the innocent to death.
22 But the LORD has been my [a]stronghold,
And my God the [b]rock of my refuge.
23 He has [a]brought back their wickedness upon them
And will [1b]destroy them in their evil;
The LORD our God will [1]destroy them.

Psalm 95

1 O come, let us [a]sing for joy to the LORD,
Let us shout joyfully to [b]the rock of our salvation.
2 Let us [a]come before His presence [b]with [1]thanksgiving,
Let us shout joyfully to Him [c]with [2]psalms.
3 For the LORD is a [a]great God
And a great King [b]above all gods,
4 In whose hand are the [a]depths of the earth,
The peaks of the mountains are His also.
5 [1]The sea is His, for it was He [a]who made it,
And His hands formed the dry land.

6 Come, let us [a]worship and bow down,
Let us [b]kneel before the LORD our [c]Maker.
7 For He is our God,
And [a]we are the people of His [1b]pasture and the sheep of His hand.
[c]Today, [2]if you would hear His voice,
8 Do not harden your hearts, as at [1a]Meribah,
As in the day of [2b]Massah in the wilderness,
9 "When your fathers [a]tested Me,
They tried Me, though they had seen My work.
10 "For [a]forty years I loathed *that* generation,
And said they are a people who err in their heart,
And they do not know My ways.
11 "Therefore I [a]swore in My anger,
Truly they shall not enter into My [b]rest."

18 [a]Ps 38:16; 73:2 **19** [1]Or *are many* [a]Is 57:18; 66:13 **20** [1]Or *tribunal* [2]Or *trouble, misfortune* [a]Amos 6:3 [b]Ps 50:16; 58:2 **21** [1]Or *soul* [2]Lit *innocent blood* [a]Ps 56:6; 59:3 [b]Ex 23:7; Ps 106:38; Prov 17:15; Matt 27:4 **22** [a]Ps 9:9; 59:9 [b]Ps 18:2; 71:7 **23** [1]Or *silence* [a]Ps 7:16; 140:9, 11 [b]Gen 19:15 **95:1** [a]Ps 66:1; 81:1 [b]Ps 89:26 **2** [1]Or *a song of thanksgiving* [2]Or *songs* (with instrumental accompaniment) [a]Mic 6:6 [b]Ps 100:4; 147:7; Jon 2:9 [c]Ps 81:2; Eph 5:19; James 5:13 **3** [a]Ps 48:1; 135:5; 145:3 [b]Ps 96:4; 97:9 **4** [a]Ps 135:6 **5** [1]Lit *Who has the sea* [a]Gen 1:9, 10; Ps 146:6; Jon 1:9 **6** [a]Ps 96:9; 99:5, 9 [b]2 Chr 6:13; Dan 6:10; Phil 2:10 [c]Ps 100:3; 149:2; Is 17:7; Hos 8:14

7 [1]Lit *pasturing* [2]Or *O that you would obey* [a]Ps 79:13 [b]Ps 74:1 [c]Heb 3:7-11, 15; 4:7 **8** [1]Or *place of strife* [2]Or *temptation* [a]Ex 17:2-7; Num 20:13 [b]Ex 17:7; Deut 6:16 **9** [a]Num 14:22; Ps 78:18; 1 Cor 10:9 **10** [a]Acts 7:36; 13:18; Heb 3:10, 17 **11** [a]Num 14:23, 28-30; Deut 1:35; Heb 4:3, 5 [b]Deut 12:9 **96:1** [a]1 Chr 16:23-33 [b]Ps 40:3

94:18 *If I should say.* If he feels he is about to be overwhelmed by the wicked (see note on 38:16). *lovingkindness.* See note on 6:4.

94:19 *soul.* See note on 6:3.

94:20–23 Confidence that the Lord's justice will prevail.

94:20 *throne of destruction.* A seat of authority that works mischief. The author speaks of injustice at the center of power.

94:21 *righteous.* See note on 1:5.

Ps 95 A call to worship the Lord, spoken by a priest or Levite to the assembled Israelites at the temple. (See introduction to Ps 93.) The psalm is composed of two parts: (1) a call to praise the Lord of all the earth (vv. 1–5); (2) a call to acknowledge by submissive attitude and obedient heart the Lord's kingship over His people (vv. 6–11). Each part also has two subdivisions, the latter of which forms the climax. Cf. the structure of Ps 96.

95:1–2 The call to praise.

95:1 *rock of our salvation.* See note on 18:2.

95:3–5 Why Israel is to praise the Lord—because He is above all gods, and there is no corner of the universe that is not in His hand. The ancient pagan world had different gods for different peoples, different geographical areas, different cosmic regions (heaven, earth, nether world) and different aspects of life (e.g., war, fertility, crafts).

95:4–5 *depths . . . peaks of the mountains . . . sea . . . dry land.* All the world—the extremes and all that lies between and all that is in them.

95:6–11 The exhortation to submit to the Lord with obedient hearts—a bent knee is not enough. For a NT reflection on these verses in the light of the advent of Christ see Heb 3:7–4:13.

95:6–7 The call to confess submission to the Lord by kneeling before him.

95:6 *our Maker.* Both as Creator of all things (see Gen 1) and as Israel's Redeemer, He has "made" her what she is: the people of the Lord in the earth (see Is 45:9–13; 51:12–16).

95:7 *people of His pasture.* See 100:3; Jer 23:1; Ezek 34:21. Since kings were commonly called the "shepherds" of their people (see note on 23:1), their realms could be referred to as their "pastures" (see Jer 25:36; 49:20; 50:45). *if you would hear His voice.* In the liturgy of the religious festival, possibly in some such manner as Ps 50 and/or 78.

95:8 *Meribah . . . Massah.* Meribah means "quarreling," Massah means "testing." The leader of the liturgy reminds Israel of times of her rebellion in the wilderness (see Ex 17:7; Num 20:13).

95:9 *had seen My work.* In Egypt and at the Red Sea—and His provision of food in the wilderness (see Ex 16; see also Num 14:11).

95:10 *forty years.* The climax of Israel's rebellion came when she faithlessly refused to undertake the conquest of Canaan and considered returning to Egypt (see Num 14:1–4). It was then that God condemned her to a 40-year stay in the wilderness (see Num 14:34). *that generation.* The (adult) Israelites who came out of Egypt and covenanted with God at Sinai (see Num 32:13). *they are a people . . . My ways.* A restatement of the Lord's word in Num 14:11. *heart.* See note on 4:7. *My ways.* See 25:4 and note.

95:11 *swore.* See Num 14:28. *not enter into My rest.* The language of Num 14:30 is "Surely you shall not come into the land," but since the promised land was also called the place where God will give His people "rest" (Josh 1:13,15; see Ex 33:14; Deut 12:10; 25:19), the two statements are equivalent. *rest.* Here a fertile concept indicating Israel's possession of a place with God in the earth where she is secure from all external threats and internal calamities (see 1 Kin 5:4).

Psalm 96

1 [a]Sing to the LORD a [b]new song;
Sing to the LORD, all the earth.
2 Sing to the LORD, bless His name;
[a]Proclaim good tidings of His
salvation from day to day.
3 Tell of [a]His glory among the nations,
His wonderful deeds among all the
peoples.
4 For [a]great is the LORD and [b]greatly to
be praised;
He is to be [c]feared [d]above all gods.
5 For [a]all the gods of the peoples are
[1]idols,
But [b]the LORD made the heavens.
6 [a]Splendor and majesty are before Him,
Strength and beauty are in His
sanctuary.

7 [1]Ascribe to the LORD, O [a]families of
the peoples,
[1b]Ascribe to the LORD glory and
strength.
8 [1]Ascribe to the LORD the [a]glory of His
name;
Bring an [2b]offering and come into His
courts.
9 [a]Worship the LORD in [1]holy attire;
[b]Tremble before Him, all the earth.
10 Say among the nations, "[a]The LORD
reigns;
Indeed, the [a]world is firmly
established, it will not be moved;
He will [b]judge the peoples with
[1]equity."

11 Let the [a]heavens be glad, and let the
[b]earth rejoice;
Let [c]the sea [1]roar, and [2]all it contains;
12 Let the [a]field exult, and all that is in it.
Then all the [b]trees of the forest will
sing for joy
13 Before the LORD, [a]for He is coming,
For He is coming to judge the earth.
[b]He will judge the world in
righteousness
And the peoples in His faithfulness.

Psalm 97

1 [a]The LORD [1]reigns, let the [b]earth
rejoice;
Let the many [2c]islands be glad.

2 [a]Ps 71:15 **3** [a]Ps 145:12 **4** [a]Ps 48:1; 145:3 [b]Ps 18:3 [c]Ps 89:7 [d]Ps 95:3 **5** [1]Or *non-existent things* [a]1 Chr 16:26; Jer 10:11 [b]Ps 115:15; Is 42:5 **6** [a]Ps 104:1 **7** [1]Lit *Give* [a]Ps 22:27 [b]1 Chr 16:28, 29; Ps 29:1, 2 **8** [1]Lit *Give* [2]Or *meal offering* [a]Ps 79:9; 115:1 [b]Ps 45:12; 72:10 **9** [1]Or *the splendor of holiness* [a]1 Chr 16:29; 2 Chr 20:21; Ps 29:2; 110:3 [b]Ps 33:8; 114:7 **10** [1]Or *uprightness* [a]Ps 93:1; 97:1 [b]Ps 9:8; 58:11; 67:4; 98:9 **11** [1]Or *thunder* [2]Lit *its fullness* [a]Ps 69:34; Is 49:13 [b]Ps 97:1 [c]Ps 98:7 **12** [a]Ps 65:13; Is 35:1; 55:12, 13 [b]Is 44:23 **13** [a]Ps 98:9 [b]Rev 19:11 **97:1** [1]Or *has assumed Kingship* [2]Or *coastlands* [a]Ps 96:10 [b]Ps 96:11 [c]Is 42:10, 12

Ps 96 A call to all nations to praise the Lord as the only God and to proclaim the glory of His reign throughout the world—an OT anticipation of the world mission of the NT people of God (see Matt 28:16–20). (See introductions to Ps 93; 95.) This psalm appears in slightly altered form in 1 Chr 16:23–33. The psalm is composed of two thematic parts: (1) a call to all nations to sing the praise of the Lord (vv. 1–6); (2) a call to all nations to worship the Lord and to hail throughout the world the glory of His righteous rule (vv. 7–13). Each part has two subdivisions, the last of which forms the climax to the whole psalm. Cf. the structure of Ps 95.

96:1–3 The call to all the earth to sing the praise of the Lord among the nations. Triple repetition ("Sing . . . Sing . . . Sing") was a common feature in OT liturgical calls to worship (see vv. 7–9 and note; see also 103:20–22; 118:2–4; 135:1; 136:1–3).

96:1 *new song.* See note on 33:3. *all the earth.* See v. 9; or "all the land," in which case the call is addressed to all Israel. However, the worldwide perspective of this psalm (see especially v. 7) suggests that here the psalmist has in view broader horizons (see 97:1; 100:1 and note; 117:1; see also note on 9:1).

96:2 *name.* See v. 8; see also note on 5:11. *Proclaim . . . His salvation.* Proclaim (see 40:9 and note) that deliverance comes from the Lord (see 3:8; see also 85:9).

96:3 *glory.* See note on 85:9. *wonderful deeds.* See note on 71:16–17.

96:4–6 Why "all the earth" is to praise the Lord: He alone is God (see Ps 115).

96:4 *feared.* See note on Gen 20:11.

96:5 *made the heavens.* As the Maker of the heavenly realm, in pagan eyes the abode of the gods, the Lord is greater than all the gods (see 97:7).

96:6 *Splendor and majesty . . . Strength and beauty.* Two pairs of divine attributes personified as throne attendants whose presence before the Lord heralds the exalted nature of the one, universal King. For similar personifications see 23:6 and note.

96:7–9 The call to all nations to worship the Lord (see 29:1–2 and note). The two half-sentences of 29:2 have been expanded in this psalm. The threefold "ascribe" here balances the threefold "sing" of vv. 1–2.

96:8 *courts.* Of the temple (see 84:2,10; 2 Kin 21:5; 23:11–12).

96:9 *Tremble.* In reverent awe, equivalent to "fear" (see v. 4).

96:10–13 The call to all nations to proclaim among the nations the righteous reign of the Lord.

96:10 *The Lord reigns.* See 93:1 and note. *the world . . . with equity.* In OT perspective, the world order is one, embracing both its physical and moral aspects because both have been established by God as aspects of His one kingdom and both are upheld by His one rule. Therefore God's rule over creation and over the affairs of men (also His acts of creation and redemption) is often spoken of in one breath, and "righteousness," "faithfulness" and "love" are equally ascribable to both. And since the creation order is secure in its "goodness" (see Gen 1), it often serves in OT poetry (as it does here) as a manifest assurance that God's rule over the affairs of men will also be "with equity," "in righteousness" and "in . . . faithfulness" (v. 13; see 11:3; 33:4–11; 36:5–9; 57:10; 65:6–7; 71:19; 74:13–14,16–17; 75:3; 82:5; 93:3–4; 119:89–91 and notes). *will judge.* See v. 13 and note.

96:11–12 Because God's kingdom is one (see v. 10 and note), all His creatures will rejoice when God's rule over mankind brings righteousness to full expression in His cosmic kingdom (see note on 65:13; see also 97:7–9). For the present state of the creation as it awaits the fullness of redemption see Rom 8:21–22 and notes.

96:13 *coming . . . coming . . . will judge.* Because God reigns over all things and is the Lord of history, Israel lived in hope (as the prophets announced) of the "coming" of God—His future acts by which He would decisively deal with all wickedness and establish His righteousness in the earth. *righteousness.* See note on 5:8.

Ps 97 A joyful celebration of the Lord's righteous reign over all the earth. (See introductions to Ps 93; 95.) The psalm's two main thematic divisions (vv. 1–6, 8–12) are joined by a centered verse (v. 7; see note on 6:6) that serves as a counterpoint to the main theme. The opening verses of the two main divisions are thematically linked: v. 1, "rejoice . . . be glad"; v. 8, "was glad . . . have rejoiced"—in reverse order, a frequent stylistic device in OT poetry.

97:1–6 A testimony to the nations—that they too have seen

2 [a]Clouds and thick darkness surround
Him;
[b]Righteousness and justice are the
foundation of His throne.
3 [a]Fire goes before Him
And [b]burns up His adversaries round
about.
4 His [a]lightnings lit up the world;
The earth saw and [b]trembled.
5 The mountains [a]melted like wax at
the presence of the LORD,
At the presence of the [b]Lord of the
whole earth.
6 The [a]heavens declare His righteousness,
And [b]all the peoples have seen His
glory.

7 Let all those be ashamed who serve
[a]graven images,
Who boast themselves of [b]idols;
[1c]Worship Him, all you [2]gods.
8 Zion [1]heard *this* and [a]was glad,
And the daughters of Judah have
rejoiced
Because of Your judgments, O LORD.
9 For You are the LORD [a]Most High over
all the earth;
You are exalted far [b]above all [1]gods.

10 [a]Hate evil, you who love the LORD,
Who [b]preserves the souls of His godly
ones;
He [c]delivers them from the hand of
the wicked.
11 [a]Light is sown *like seed* for the
righteous
And [b]gladness for the upright in heart.
12 Be [a]glad in the LORD, you righteous
ones,
And [b]give thanks [1]to His holy name.

Psalm 98

A Psalm.

1 O sing to the LORD a [a]new song,
For He has done [b]wonderful things,
His [c]right hand and His [d]holy arm
have [1]gained the victory for Him.
2 [a]The LORD has made known His
salvation;
He has [b]revealed His [1]righteousness in
the sight of the nations.
3 He has [a]remembered His
lovingkindness and His faithfulness
to the house of Israel;

2 [a]Ex 19:9; Deut 4:11; 1 Kin 8:12; Ps 18:11 [b]Ps 89:14 **3** [a]Ps 18:8; 50:3; Dan 7:10; Hab 3:5 [b]Mal 4:1; Heb 12:29 **4** [a]Ex 19:16; Ps 77:18 [b]Ps 96:9; 104:32 **5** [a]Ps 46:6; Amos 9:5; Mic 1:4; Nah 1:5 [b]Josh 3:11 **6** [a]Ps 19:1; 50:6 [b]Ps 98:2; Is 6:3; 40:5; 66:18 **7** [1]Or *All the gods have worshiped Him* [2]Or *supernatural powers* [a]Ps 78:58; Is 42:17; 44:9, 11; Jer 10:14 [b]Ps 106:36; Jer 50:2; Hab 2:18 [c]Heb 1:6 **8** [1]Or possibly *hears and is glad* [a]Ps 48:11; Zeph 3:14 **9** [1]Or *supernatural powers* [a]Ps 83:18 [b]Ex 18:11; Ps 95:3; 96:4; 135:5 **10** [a]Ps 34:14; Prov 8:13; Amos 5:15; Rom 12:9

10 [b]Ps 31:23; 145:20; Prov 2:8 [c]Ps 37:40; Jer 15:21; Dan 3:28 **11** [a]Job 22:28; Ps 112:4; Prov 4:18 [b]Ps 64:10 **12** [1]Lit *for the memory of His holiness* [a]Ps 32:11 [b]Ps 30:4 **98:1** [1]Or *accomplished salvation* [a]Ps 33:3 [b]Ps 40:5; 96:3 [c]Ex 15:6 [d]Is 52:10 **2** [1]I.e. faithfulness to His gracious promises [a]Is 52:10 [b]Is 62:2; Rom 3:25 **3** [a]Luke 1:54, 72

God's majesty displayed (vv. 2–6) and ought to rejoice with Israel that the Lord reigns supreme.

97:1 *The Lord reigns.* See 93:1 and note. *earth.* See 96:1; 99:1; 117:1; see also note on 9:1. *many islands.* Even distant lands reached by the far-ranging ships that sail the seas (see 1 Kin 9:26–28; 10:22; Is 60:9; Jon 1:3).

97:2–6 The Lord's majestic glory revealed in the sky's awesome displays, especially in the thunderstorm (see 18:7–15 and note; see also introduction to Ps 29).

97:2 *Clouds and thick darkness.* The dark storm clouds that hide the sun and cast a veil across the sky are dramatic visual reminders that the fierce heat and brilliance (also metaphors) of God's naked glory must be veiled from creaturely eyes (see Ex 19:9; 1 Kin 8:12). Thus also a curtain closed off the most holy place in the tabernacle and temple (see Ex 26:33; 2 Chr 3:14), veiling it in darkness. *Righteousness.* See v. 6; see also note on 5:8. *foundation of His throne.* God rules by His power (see 66:7), but His reign is founded on righteousness and justice, which also the heavens proclaim (see v. 6 and note).

97:3 *Fire.* Manifested in the storm cloud's lightning bolts (see v. 4), fire often signified God's judicial wrath (see, e.g., 21:9; 50:3; 83:14; Deut 4:24; 9:3; 32:22; 1 Kin 19:12; Is 10:17; 30:27,30).

97:4 *earth.* Here probably the physical earth personified.

97:6 *declare His righteousness.* The stable order of the heaven's vast array "speaks" (see 19:1–4); it declares that God's reign similarly upholds the moral order (see note on 96:10). *all the peoples have seen.* Verses 2–6 have spoken of general revelation (cf. 19:1–6).

97:7 The center verse (see note on 6:6) and counterpoint of the psalm: joy to all who acknowledge the Lord; shame and disgrace to those who trust in the false gods. *worship Him.* With biting irony the psalm calls on all the gods that people foolishly worship to bow in worship before the Lord (see v. 9; see also 29:1 and note).

97:8–12 A declaration of Zion's joy that the Lord reigns (vv. 8–9), and a reminder that only those who hate evil have real cause to rejoice in His righteous rule (vv. 10–12).

97:8 *Zion heard.* That "the LORD reigns" (v. 1) in "righteousness" (v. 6). *judgments.* God's righteous acts in the affairs of mankind (see 105:7; Is 26:9), especially His saving acts in Israel's behalf (see 48:11; 105:5; Deut 33:21).

97:9 *Most High.* See note on Gen 14:19.

97:10 *godly ones.* See note on 4:3.

97:11 *Light.* See 27:1 and note; see also 36:9. *righteous.* See v. 12; see also note on 1:5. *heart.* See note on 4:7.

97:12 *name.* See note on 30:4.

Ps 98 A call to celebrate with joy the righteous reign of the Lord. Its beginning and end echo Ps 96. (See introductions to Ps 93; 95.) The three stanzas progressively extend the call to ever wider circles: (1) the worshiping congregation at the temple; (2) all the peoples of the earth; (3) the whole creation. The first stanza recalls God's revelation of His righteousness (v. 2) in the past; the last stanza speaks confidently of His coming rule "with righteousness" (v. 9); the middle stanza is enclosed by the jubilant cry, "Shout joyfully" (vv. 4,6).

98:1–3 The call to celebrate in song God's saving acts in behalf of His people.

98:1 *new song.* See note on 33:3. *wonderful things.* See note on 9:1 ("wonders").

98:2 *made known . . . revealed . . . in the sight of the nations.* God's saving acts in behalf of His people are also His self-revelation to the nations; in this sense God is His own evangelist (see note on 46:10; see also Is 52:10). *salvation . . . righteousness.* God's saving acts reveal His righteousness (see notes on 5:8; 71:24).

98:3 *lovingkindness . . . faithfulness.* That is, lovingkindness-and-faithfulness (see note on 36:5; see also note on 3:7). This compound expression often sums up God's covenant commitment to His people (see note on 6:4).

[b]All the ends of the earth have seen
the salvation of our God.

4 [a]Shout joyfully to the LORD, all the
earth;
[b]Break forth and sing for joy and sing
praises.
5 Sing praises to the LORD with the [a]lyre,
With the lyre and the [1b]sound of
melody.
6 With [a]trumpets and the sound of the
horn
[b]Shout joyfully before [c]the King, the
LORD.

7 Let the [a]sea roar and [1]all it contains,
The [b]world and those who dwell in it.
8 Let the [a]rivers clap their hands,
Let the [b]mountains sing together for joy
9 Before the LORD, for He is coming to
[a]judge the earth;
He will judge the world with
righteousness
And [b]the peoples with [1]equity.

Psalm 99

1 [a]The LORD reigns, let the peoples
tremble;
He [1b]is enthroned *above* the
cherubim, let the earth shake!
2 The LORD [1]is [a]great in Zion,
And He is [b]exalted above all the
peoples.
3 Let them praise Your [a]great and
awesome name;
[b]Holy is [1]He.
4 The [1]strength of the King [a]loves
[2]justice;
You have established [3b]equity;
You have [c]executed [2]justice and
righteousness in Jacob.
5 [1a]Exalt the LORD our God
And [b]worship at His footstool;
[c]Holy is He.

6 [a]Moses and Aaron were among His
[b]priests,
And [a]Samuel was among those who
[c]called on His name;
They [d]called upon the LORD and He
answered them.
7 He [a]spoke to them in the pillar of
cloud;
They [b]kept His testimonies
And the statute that He gave
them.

3 [b]Ps 22:27 **4** [a]Ps 100:1 [b]Is 44:23 **5** [1]Or *voice of song* (accompanied by music) [a]Ps 92:3 [b]Is 51:3 **6** [a]Num 10:10; 2 Chr 15:14 [b]Ps 66:1 [c]Ps 47:7 **7** [1]Lit *its fullness* [a]Ps 96:11 [b]Ps 24:1 **8** [a]Ps 93:3; Is 55:12 [b]Ps 65:12; 89:12 **9** [1]Or *uprightness* [a]Ps 96:13 [b]Ps 96:10 **99:1** [1]Lit *sits* [a]Ps 97:1 [b]Ex 25:22; 1 Sam 4:4; Ps 80:1

2 [1]Or *in Zion is great* [a]Ps 48:1; Is 12:6 [b]Ps 97:9; 113:4 **3** [1]Or *it* [a]Deut 28:58; Ps 76:1 [b]Lev 19:2; Josh 24:19; 1 Sam 2:2; Ps 22:3; Is 6:3 **4** [1]Or *You have established in equity the strength of the King who loves justice* [2]Or *judgment* [3]Or *uprightness* [a]Ps 11:7; 33:5 [b]Ps 17:2; 98:9 [c]Ps 103:6; 146:7; Jer 23:5 **5** [1]The verb is plural [a]Ps 34:3; 107:32; 118:28 [b]Ps 132:7 [c]Ps 99:3 **6** [a]Jer 15:1 [b]Ex 24:6-8; 29:26; 40:23-27; Lev 8:1-30 [c]1 Sam 7:9; 12:18; Ps 22:4, 5 [d]Ex 15:25; 32:30-34 **7** [a]Ex 33:9; Num 12:5 [b]Ps 105:28

98:4–6 The call to all the earth to join in the celebration.
98:4 See 100:1. *all the earth.* The peoples of the earth (see 96:1 and note; see also 99:1).
98:5 *lyre.* See note on Gen 31:27.
98:6 *trumpets.* The special long, straight trumpets of the sanctuary (referred to only here in Psalms; see notes on Num 10:2–3,10). *horn.* The more common trumpet (referred to also in 47:5; 81:3; 150:3; see note on Joel 2:1).
98:7–9 The call to the whole creation to celebrate (see note on 96:11–12).
98:7 *sea . . . world.* The two great regions of creaturely life.
98:8 *rivers . . . mountains.* From the rivers to the mountains, let every feature of the whole earth clap and sing (see note on 65:13).
98:9 *coming to judge.* See 96:13 and note. Israel in faith lived between the past (see vv. 1–3) and the future righteous (saving) acts of God.
Ps 99 A hymn celebrating the Lord as the great and holy King in Zion. In developing his theme, the poet makes striking use of the symbolic significance (completeness) of the number seven: Seven times he speaks of the "LORD," and seven times he refers to Him by means of independent personal pronouns (Hebrew). (See introduction to Ps 93.) The form is symmetrical, with four stanzas of three (Hebrew) poetic lines and with each of the two main divisions concluded by the major refrain (vv. 5,9). The lesser refrain, "Holy is He" (vv. 3,5, and expanded in v. 9), probably reflects a traditional threefold liturgical rubric (see Is 6:3; Rev 4:8; see also Ps 96:1–3,7–9 and notes for further evidence of a liturgical penchant for triple repetition). The second half of the psalm develops the theme introduced in the second stanza.
99:1–3 The God enthroned in Zion is ruler over all the nations—let them acknowledge him.
99:1 *The LORD reigns.* See 93:1 and note. *tremble . . . shake!* In reverent awe before God. *cherubim.* See 80:1; see also note on Ex 25:18.
99:3 *Let them praise.* As the Great King, He ought to be shown the fear (v. 1) and honor that are His due. *name.* See v. 6; see also note on 5:11. *Holy.* See vv. 5,9; see also Introduction to Leviticus: Themes; note on Lev 11:44.
99:4–5 The Lord has shown the quality of His rule by what He has done for Israel.
99:4 See 103:6–12. *strength . . . loves justice.* Two chief characteristics of God's reign. *established equity.* As a (His) throne (see 9:7–8; 97:2; 2 Sam 7:13). *justice and righteousness.* See 97:2. Though even the heavens proclaim God's righteousness (see 97:6 and note), it is in the whole complex of His saving acts in and for Israel that the "righteousness" of God's reign is especially disclosed (see 98:2 and note). *Jacob.* A synonym for Israel (see Gen 32:28).
99:5 See also v. 9. For other refrains in the Psalms see introduction to Ps 42–43. *footstool.* God's royal footstool (see 2 Chr 9:18), here a metaphor linking the heavenly throne with the earthly; when God sits on His heavenly throne, His earthly throne is His footstool (here "His holy hill," v. 9; see 132:7; 1 Chr 28:2; Lam 2:1).
99:6–7 In Israel the Lord provided priestly intermediaries, who (1) were appointed to intercede with Him on behalf of His faltering people (v. 6), and (2) were given knowledge of His will so they could instruct Israel.
99:6 *Moses . . . Aaron . . . Samuel.* These three no doubt serve here as representatives of all those the Lord used as intermediaries with His people in times of great crises. *priests . . . who called on His name.* The priestly function of intercession is highlighted (see Ex 17:11 and note; 32:11–13,31–32; Num 14:13–19; 21:7; 1 Sam 7:5,8–9; 12:19,23; Jer 15:1). *answered them.* See v. 8; see also the Lord's responses to the intercessions referred to in note on vv. 6–7.
99:7 *spoke to them in the pillar of cloud.* Though reference may be to all Israel ("them"), more likely the hymn recalls God's speaking with Moses (see Ex 33:9) and Aaron (see Num 12:5–6).

8 O LORD our God, You [a]answered them;
You were a [b]forgiving God to them,
And *yet* an [c]avenger of their *evil* deeds.
9 Exalt the LORD our God
And worship at His holy hill,
For holy is the LORD our God.

Psalm 100

A Psalm for †Thanksgiving.

1 [a]Shout joyfully to the LORD, all the earth.
2 [a]Serve the LORD with gladness;
[b]Come before Him with joyful singing.
3 Know that [a]the LORD [1]Himself is God;
It is He who has [b]made us, and [2]not we ourselves;
We are [c]His people and the sheep of His pasture.

4 Enter His gates [a]with [1]thanksging
And His courts with praise.
Give thanks to Him, [b]bless His name.
5 For [a]the LORD is good;
[b]His lovingkindness is everlasting
And His [c]faithfulness to all generations.

8 [a]Ps 106:44 [b]Num 14:20; Ps 78:38 [c]Ex 32:28; Num 20:12; Ps 95:11; 107:12
100:1 †Or *thank offering* [a]Ps 95:1; 98:4, 6
2 [a]Deut 12:11, 12; 28:47 [b]Ps 95:2
3 [1]Or *He* [2]Some mss read *His we are* [a]Deut 4:35; 1 Kin 18:39; Ps 46:10 [b]Job 10:3, 8; Ps 95:6; 119:73 [c]Ps 74:1, 2; 95:7; Is 40:11; Ezek 34:30, 31
4 [1]Or *a thank offering* [a]Ps 95:2; 116:17
4 [b]Ps 96:2
5 [a]1 Chr 16:34; 2 Chr 5:13; 7:3; Ezra 3:11; Ps 25:8; 86:5; 106:1; 107:1; 118:1; Jer 33:11; Nah 1:7 [b]Ps 136:1 [c]Ps 119:90

Psalm 101

A Psalm of David.

1 I will [a]sing of lovingkindness and [1]justice,
To You, O LORD, I will sing praises.
2 I will [1a]give heed to the [2]blameless way.
When will You come to me?
I will walk within my house in the [3b]integrity of my heart.

101:1 [1]Or *judgment* [a]Ps 51:14; 89:1; 145:7 **2** [1]Or *behave prudently in* [2]Or *way of integrity* [3]Or *blamelessness* [a]1 Sam 18:5, 14 [b]1 Kin 9:4

But that special mode of revelation in the wilderness may also be generalized here to include God's revelations to Samuel, who was called to his prophetic ministry at the sanctuary, "where the ark of God was" (1 Sam 3:3; see also 1 Sam 12:23). *They kept.* However imperfectly, it was in Israel that God's righteous statutes and decrees were kept because only in Israel had they been made known (see 147:19–20; Deut 4:5–8).

99:8–9 The justice and righteousness of God's rule in Israel (see v. 4) have been especially shown in the manner in which He has dealt with their sins (see Ex 34:6–7; see also note on 5:8).

99:9 *holy hill.* See v. 5 and note. *holy is the LORD our God.* Climactic expansion of the secondary refrain.

Ps 100 A call to praise the Lord. Whether or not it was composed for that purpose, the final editors of the Psalter here used it to close the series that begins with Ps 93. It has special affinity with 95:1–2,6–7; see also Ps 117. (See introduction to Ps 93.) The second main division (vv. 4–5) parallels the structure of the first (vv. 1–3), namely, a call to praise followed by a declaration of why the Lord is worthy of praise—the corresponding elements of the two divisions are complementary.

100 title *Thanksgiving.* Grateful praise (see v. 4; see also note on 75:1). Perhaps it indicates that the psalm was to accompany a thank offering (see Lev 7:12).

100:1 *all the earth.* Though vv. 3,5 clearly speak of God's special relationship with Israel, the call to worship goes out to the whole world, which ought to acknowledge the Lord because of what He has done for His people (see also Ps 98–99; 117).

100:3 *Know.* Acknowledge. *made us.* See 95:6 and note. *not we ourselves.* Or "we are His" (see NASB marg.). *sheep of His pasture.* See 95:7 and note.

100:4 *His gates.* The gates of the temple (see 24:7 and note). *courts.* Of the temple (see 84:2,10; 2 Kin 21:5; 23:11–12).

100:5 *the LORD is good.* In that His lovingkindness-and-faithfulness (see note on 36:5) are unfailing through all time (see 98:3 and note). *lovingkindness.* See note on 6:4.

Ps 101 A king's pledge to reign righteously (see 2 Kin 23:3). If authored by David (see title), it may have been composed for Solomon's use at his coronation (see 1 Kin 2:2–4; see also 2 Sam 23:1–7 and introduction to Ps 72). Only Christ, the great Son of David, has perfectly fulfilled these commitments. In the final arrangement of the Psalter this psalm, together with Ps 110 (both relating to the king), frames the collection of ten psalms located between the preceding thematic group (Ps 92–100; see introduction to Ps 92) and that which follows (Ps 111–118; see introduction to Ps 111). This little psalter-within-the-Psalter is concentrically arranged: Ps 102 and 109 are individual prayers; Ps 103 and 108 praise the Lord for His "great . . . lovingkindness" (103:11; 108:4) that reaches to the heavens; Ps 104, which celebrates God's many wise and benevolent acts in creation, and Ps 107, which celebrates God's "wonders" (107:8,15,21,24,31) for man through His lordship over creation, are complements; and so also are Ps 105, which recites the history of Israel's redemption, and Ps 106, which recites the same history as a history of Israel's rebellion. As a mini-Psalter, it includes most of the forms and themes found in the rest of the Psalter. Its outer frame is devoted to royal psalms and its center pair is devoted to recitals of Israel's history with God—with its themes ranging from creation and God's eternal enthronement to the covenant with Abraham, Isaac and Jacob, the exodus from Egypt and entrance into Canaan, the exile and restoration, and finally the ultimate triumph of the Lord's anointed. The collection bears a distinctive redemption-history stamp and evokes recollection of all the salient elements of the OT message. (For the problem of the Book division at Ps 107 see introduction to that psalm.)

Composed of seven (Hebrew) couplets (the number of completeness), the psalm begins with a twofold introduction (vv. 1–3a; see notes below), followed by an elaboration (vv. 3b–8) of the theme of the second couplet. The middle one (v. 6) speaks of the king's commitment to the "faithful" and "blameless," while the other four (vv. 3b–4, 5, 7, 8) declare His repudiation of all "those who fall away" and the "wicked" in the land. (See also notes below.) The middle couplet is linked with couplets one and two also by the catchword "blameless." (For centering in the Psalms see note on 6:6.)

101:1–2a Celebration of the pattern of God's reign, which the king makes the model for his own.

101:1 *lovingkindness and justice.* Two of the chief qualities of God's rule (see 6:4; 99:4 and notes).

101:2a *blameless.* See vv. 2b,6; see also note on Gen 17:1. *When . . . ?* An urgent prayer for God to come and sustain in him his pledge (see 1 Kin 3:7–9; see also Ps 72).

101:2b–3a The essential commitment. *heart . . . eyes.* In OT understanding, a person follows the dictates of the heart—the inner man (see note on 4:7)—and/or the attractions of the

3 I will set no [a]worthless thing before
my eyes;
I hate the [1]work of those who [b]fall
away;
It shall not fasten its grip on me.
4 A [a]perverse heart shall depart from
me;
I will know no evil.
5 Whoever secretly [a]slanders his
neighbor, him I will [1]destroy;
No one who has a [b]haughty look and
an arrogant heart will I endure.

6 My eyes shall be upon the faithful of
the land, that they may dwell with
me;
He who walks in a [1][a]blameless way is
the one who will minister to me.
7 He who [a]practices deceit shall not
dwell within my house;
He who speaks falsehood [b]shall not
[1]maintain his position before me.
8 [a]Every morning I will [1][b]destroy all the
wicked of the land,
So as to [c]cut off from the [d]city of the
LORD all those who do iniquity.

3 [1]Or *practice of apostasy* [a]Deut 15:9 [b]Josh 23:6; Ps 40:4
4 [a]Prov 11:20
5 [1]Or *silence* [a]Ps 50:20; Jer 9:4 [b]Ps 10:4; 18:27; Prov 6:17
6 [1]Or *way of integrity* [a]Ps 119:1
7 [1]Lit *be established before my eyes* [a]Ps 43:1; 52:2 [b]Ps 52:4, 5
8 [1]Or *silence* [a]Jer 21:12 [b]Ps 75:10 [c]Ps 118:10-12 [d]Ps 46:4; 48:2, 8

102:1 [†]Ps 142:2 [a]Ps 39:12; 61:1 [b]Ex 2:23; 1 Sam 9:16
2 [a]Ps 69:17 [b]Ps 31:2
3 [1]Or *finished* [a]Ps 37:20; James 4:14 [b]Job 30:30; Lam 1:13
4 [1]Lit *herbage* [a]Ps 90:5, 6 [b]Ps 37:2; Is 40:7 [c]1 Sam 1:7; 2 Sam 12:17; Ezra 10:6; Job 33:20
5 [1]Lit *voice* [2]Lit *have cleaved* [a]Job 19:20; Lam 4:8
6 [1]Lit *have become similar to* [a]Is 34:11; Zeph 2:14

Psalm 102

A Prayer of the Afflicted when he is faint and
[†]pours out his complaint before the LORD.

1 [a]Hear my prayer, O LORD!
And let my cry for help [b]come to
You.
2 [a]Do not hide Your face from me in the
day of my distress;
[b]Incline Your ear to me;
In the day when I call [a]answer me
quickly.
3 For my days [a]have been [1]consumed in
smoke,
And my [b]bones have been scorched
like a hearth.
4 My heart [a]has been smitten like [1]grass
and has [b]withered away,
Indeed, I [c]forget to eat my bread.
5 Because of the [1]loudness of my
groaning
My [a]bones [2]cling to my flesh.
6 I [1]resemble a [a]pelican of the
wilderness;

eye—external influences (see 119:37; Judg 14:1–2; 2 Sam 11:2; 2 Kin 16:10; Job 31:1; Prov 4:25; 17:24). For the combination heart-eyes see v. 5; Num 15:39; Job 31:7; Prov 21:4; Eccl 2:10; Jer 22:17.

101:2b *house.* Royal administration (also in v. 7).

101:3a *worthless.* Belial (2 Cor 6:15) is derived from the Hebrew for this word (see note on Deut 13:13).

101:3b–4 A repudiation of evil deeds and those who promote them (see v. 7).

101:3b *those who fall away.* Those who rebel against what is right (see Hos 5:2, "revolters").

101:4 *perverse.* The opposite of "blameless" (see 18:26, "crooked"; see also Prov 11:20; 19:1; 28:6). A perverse heart and a deceitful tongue (see v. 7) are root and fruit (see Prov 17:20).

101:5 A pledge to remove from his presence all slanderous and all arrogant persons (see v. 8). *I will destroy.* See v. 8; 54:5; 94:23). *haughty look . . . arrogant heart.* See vv. 2b–3a and note; see also 131:1; Prov 21:4; Is 10:12. The arrogant tend to be ruthless (see Is 10:12) and are a law to themselves (see note on 31:23).

101:6 A pledge to surround himself in his reign with the faithful and blameless. *My eyes shall be upon.* I will look with favor on (see 33:18; 34:15). *the faithful.* Those who maintain moral integrity. *minister to me.* Minister as my servant (see Ex 24:13), personal servant (Gen 39:4; 1 Kin 19:21), attendant (2 Kin 4:43), commanders and officials (1 Chr 27:1; 2 Chr 17:19; Prov 29:12).

101:7 A repudiation of all those who make their way by double-dealing (see vv. 3b–4).

101:8 A pledge to remove all the wicked from the Lord's kingdom (see v. 5). *Every morning.* With diligence and persistence (see Jer 21:12; Zeph 3:5). It may have been traditional for kings to hear cases in the morning. *city of the LORD.* See Ps 46; 48; 87; see also note on 3:4.

Ps 102 The prayer of an individual in a time of great distress. It is also one of the traditional penitential psalms (see introduction to Ps 6). Some interpreters believe that the "I" of vv. 1–11,23–24 was originally communal (see note on Ps 30 title; see also note on title below). (See introduction to Ps 101.) The main body of the psalm (vv. 1–22) is developed in four themes (initial appeal for God to hear, vv. 1–2; description of distress, vv. 3–11; assurance that the Lord will surely hear, vv. 12–17; call for the Lord's certain deliverance to be recorded for His enduring praise, vv. 18–22), followed by a concluding recapitulation (vv. 23–28).

102 title Unique in the Psalter (no author named and no liturgical or historical notes), the title identifies only the life situation in which the prayer is to be used, and in accordance with vv. 1–11,23–24 it designates the prayer as that of an individual. But vv. 12–22,28 clearly indicate national involvement in the calamity. It may be that the distress suffered by the individual, while its description suggests physical illness, is the result of his sharing in a national disaster such as the exile—a suggestion supported by references to the restoration of Zion. Because of the close relationship of the fortunes of king and nation and because of the many themes shared by this and some of the royal psalms, it has been plausibly suggested that the prayer was originally that of a Davidic king, or of a member of the Davidic royal house, while in Babylonian exile. *Prayer.* See vv. 1,17. *faint.* See 61:2; 77:3; 142:3; 143:4; see also 107:5; Jon 2:7. *complaint.* See 64:1; 142:2; Job 7:13; 9:27; 10:1; 21:4.

102:1–2 Initial appeal for God to hear.

102:2 *hide Your face.* See note on 13:1.

102:3–11 The description of distress—a suffering so great that it withers body and spirit—brought on by a visitation of God's wrath (v. 10) and making him the mockery of his enemies (v. 8).

102:3 *my days.* His life wastes away—a lament that frames the whole stanza (see v. 11). *bones have been scorched.* As if a fire is consuming his physical frame (see 31:10; 32:3; 42:10).

102:4 *heart.* See note on 4:7. Here "heart" is used in combination with "bones" (v. 3) to refer to the whole man (body and spirit); see 22:14; Prov 14:30; 15:30; Is 66:14; Jer 20:9; 23:9. *smitten.* Or "scorched" (by the hot sun); see 121:6. *withered away.* See v. 11; see also note on 90:4–5.

102:6 *pelican . . . owl.* The owl was associated with wilderness areas and ruins (see Is 34:11,15; Jer 50:39; Zeph 2:14).

I have become like an owl of the
waste places.
7 I [a]lie awake,
I have become like a lonely bird on a
housetop.

8 My enemies [a]have reproached me all
day long;
Those who [1b]deride me [2]have used
my *name* as a [c]curse.
9 For I have eaten ashes like bread
And [a]mingled my drink with weeping
10 [a]Because of Your indignation and Your
wrath,
For You have [b]lifted me up and cast
me away.
11 My days are like a [1a]lengthened
shadow,
And [2]I [b]wither away like [3]grass.

12 But You, O LORD, [1a]abide forever,
And Your [2b]name to all generations.
13 You will [a]arise *and* have [b]compassion
on Zion;
For [c]it is time to be gracious to her,
For the [d]appointed time has come.
14 Surely Your servants [1]find pleasure in
her stones
And feel pity for her dust.
15 [1]So the [2a]nations will fear the name of
the LORD
And [b]all the kings of the earth Your
glory.
16 For the LORD has [a]built up Zion;
He has [b]appeared in His glory.
17 He has [a]regarded the prayer of the
[1]destitute
And has not despised their prayer.

18 [1]This will be [a]written for the
[b]generation to come,
[2]That [c]a people yet to be created [3]may
praise [4]the LORD.
19 For He [a]looked down from His holy
height;
[b]From heaven the LORD gazed [1]upon
the earth,
20 To hear the [a]groaning of the
prisoner,
To [b]set free [1]those who were doomed
to death,
21 That *men* may [a]tell of the name of the
LORD in Zion
And His praise in Jerusalem,
22 When [a]the peoples are gathered
together,
And the kingdoms, to serve the LORD.

23 He has weakened my strength in the
way;
He has [a]shortened my days.
24 I say, "O my God, [a]do not take me
away in the [1]midst of my days,
Your [b]years are throughout all
generations.
25 "Of old You [a]founded the earth,
And the [b]heavens are the work of
Your hands.
26 "[1]Even they will [a]perish, but You
endure;
And all of them will wear out like a
garment;
Like clothing You will change them
and they will be changed.
27 "But You are [1a]the same,
And Your years will not come to an
end.

7 [a]Ps 77:4
8 [1]Or *made a fool of* [2]Lit *have sworn by me* [a]Ps 31:11 [b]Acts 26:11 [c]2 Sam 16:5; Is 65:15; Jer 29:22
9 [a]Ps 42:3; 80:5
10 [a]Ps 38:3 [b]Job 27:21; 30:22
11 [1]Lit *stretched out* [2]Or *as for me, I* [3]Lit *herbage* [a]Job 14:2; Ps 109:23 [b]Ps 102:4
12 [1]Or *sit enthroned* [2]Lit *memorial* [a]Ps 9:7; 10:16; Lam 5:19 [b]Ex 3:15; Ps 135:13
13 [a]Ps 12:5; 44:26 [b]Is 60:10; Zech 1:12 [c]Ps 119:126 [d]Ps 75:2; Dan 8:19
14 [1]Or *have found*
15 [1]Or *And* [2]Or *Gentiles, heathen* [a]1 Kin 8:43; Ps 67:7 [b]Ps 138:4
16 [a]Ps 147:2 [b]Is 60:1, 2
17 [1]Or *naked* [a]Neh 1:6; Ps 22:24
18 [1]Or *Let this be written* [a]Deut 31:19; Rom 15:4; 1 Cor 10:11 [b]Ps 22:30; 48:13
18 [2]Or *And* [3]Or *will* [4]Heb YAH [c]Ps 22:31; 78:6f
19 [1]Lit *toward* [a]Deut 26:15; Ps 14:2; 53:2 [b]Ps 33:13
20 [1]Lit *the sons of death* [a]Ps 79:11 [b]Ps 146:7
21 [a]Ps 22:22
22 [a]Ps 22:27; 86:9; Is 49:22, 23; 60:3; Zech 8:20-23
23 [a]Ps 39:5
24 [1]Lit *half* [a]Ps 39:13; Is 38:10 [b]Job 36:26; Ps 90:2; 102:12; Hab 1:12
25 [a]Gen 1:1; Neh 9:6; Heb 1:10-12 [b]Ps 96:5
26 [1]Lit *They themselves* [a]Is 34:4; 51:6; Matt 24:35; 2 Pet 3:10; Rev 20:11
27 [1]Lit *He* [a]Is 41:4; 43:10; Mal 3:6; James 1:17

102:8 *enemies have reproached me.* See 109:25; see also notes on 5:9; 39:8. *used my name as a curse.* They say, "May you become like that one (the one named) is."
102:9 *drink . . . weeping.* For tears as food and drink see 42:3; 80:5.
102:10 *wrath.* See note on 2:5.
102:11 A concluding summation of vv. 3–4.
102:12–17 Assurance that the King eternal will surely hear the prayer of the destitute (v. 17) and restore Zion (see note on 3:8).
102:12 *abide forever.* A central theme of the preceding collection (Ps 92–100). Because God reigns forever and remains the same (see v. 27), His mercies to those who look to Him for salvation will not fail. *name.* Or "renown" (see NASB marg.). For elaborate celebrations of the Lord's renown see Ps 111; 135; 145.
102:13 This verse and v. 16 form an inner frame around the stanza. The two verses (see v. 14) suggest that the psalmist's distress was occasioned by the Babylonian exile. *arise.* See note on 3:7. *appointed time.* The time set by God for judgment and deliverance (see 75:2; Ex 9:5; 2 Sam 24:15; Dan 11:27,35). Perhaps the psalmist is referring to a time announced by a prophet.
102:14 *Your servants find pleasure.* If Zion, the city of God (see 46:4; 48:1–2,8; 87:3; 101:8; 132:13), is so loved by the Lord's servants (see Ps 126; 137), how much more is she cherished by the Lord!
102:15 See note on 46:10. *name.* See note on 5:11.
102:18–22 Let God's certain deliverance of His people be recorded for His continual praise (see NASB marg.).
102:18 *written.* Only here does a psalmist call for memory to be sustained by a written record of God's saving act; usually oral transmission suffices (see 22:30; 44:1; 78:1–4). *created.* Brought into being by God's sovereign act (see 51:10; 104:30; 139:13).
102:20 *prisoner . . . those who were doomed to death.* Perhaps prisoners of war, but more likely the exiles in Babylon (see 79:11 and note).
102:21 *praise.* See note on 9:1.
102:22 See note on 46:10; see also 47:9 and note; 96; 98; 100. The expectation here expressed may also be influenced by such prophecies as Is 2:2–4; Mic 4:1–3.
102:23–28 Concluding recapitulation.
102:23–24a See vv. 3–11.
102:24b–27 See v. 12 and note. For a NT application of vv. 25–27 to Christ see Heb 1:10–12 and note on Heb 1:10.
102:26 *Like clothing.* With His first creation God clothed Himself with the manifestation of His glory (see 8:1,3–4; 19:1; 29:3–9; 104:1,31; Is 6:3; see also Job 38–41, especially 40:10). But He is more enduring than what He has made—and the first creation will give way to a new creation (see Is 65:17; 66:22).
102:28 Because the Lord does not change (see v. 27), Israel's

28 "The [a]children of Your servants will
continue,
And their [1b]descendants will be
established before You."

Psalm 103

A Psalm of David.

1 [a]Bless the LORD, O my soul,
And all that is within me, *bless* His
[b]holy name.
2 Bless the LORD, O my soul,
And [a]forget none of His benefits;
3 Who [a]pardons all your iniquities,
Who [b]heals all your diseases;
4 Who [a]redeems your life from the pit,
Who [b]crowns you with lovingkindness
and compassion;
5 Who [a]satisfies your [1]years with good
things,
So that your youth is [b]renewed like
the eagle.

6 The LORD [a]performs [1]righteous deeds
And judgments for all who are
[b]oppressed.
7 He [a]made known His ways to Moses,
His [b]acts to the sons of Israel.
8 The LORD is [a]compassionate and
gracious,
[b]Slow to anger and abounding in
lovingkindness.
9 He [a]will not always strive *with us,*
Nor will He [b]keep *His anger* forever.
10 He has [a]not dealt with us according to
our sins,
Nor rewarded us according to our
iniquities.
11 For as high [a]as the heavens are above
the earth,
So great is His lovingkindness toward
those who [1]fear Him.
12 As far as the east is from the west,
So far has He [a]removed our
transgressions from us.
13 Just [a]as a father has compassion on
his children,
So the LORD has compassion on those
who [1]fear Him.
14 For [a]He Himself knows [1]our frame;
He [b]is mindful that we are *but* [c]dust.

15 As for man, his days are [a]like grass;
As a [b]flower of the field, so he
flourishes.
16 When the [a]wind has passed over it, it
is no more,
And its [b]place acknowledges it no
longer.
17 But the [a]lovingkindness of the LORD is
from everlasting to everlasting on
those who [1]fear Him,
And His [2]righteousness [b]to children's
children,
18 To [a]those who keep His covenant
And remember His precepts to do
them.

19 The LORD has established His [a]throne
in the heavens,
And His [1b]sovereignty rules over [2]all.
20 Bless the LORD, you [a]His angels,

28 [1]Lit *seed* [a]Ps 69:36 [b]Ps 89:4 **103:1** [a]Ps 104:1, 35 [b]Ps 33:21; 105:3; 145:21; Ezek 36:21; 39:7 **2** [a]Deut 6:12; 8:11 **3** [a]Ex 34:7; Ps 86:5; 130:8; Is 43:25 [b]Ex 15:26; Ps 30:2; Jer 30:17 **4** [a]Ps 49:15 [b]Ps 5:12 **5** [1]Or *desire* [a]Ps 107:9; 145:16 [b]Is 40:31 **6** [1]Or *deeds of vindication* [a]Ps 99:4; 146:7 [b]Ps 12:5 **7** [a]Ex 33:13; Ps 99:7; 147:19 [b]Ps 78:11; 106:22 **8** [a]Ex 34:6; Num 14:18; Neh 9:17; Ps 86:15; Jon 4:2; James 5:11 [b]Ps 145:8; Joel 2:13; Nah 1:3 **9** [a]Ps 30:5; Is 57:16 [b]Jer 3:5, 12; Mic 7:18 **10** [a]Ezra 9:13; Lam 3:22

11 [1]Or *revere* [a]Ps 36:5; 57:10 **12** [a]2 Sam 12:13; Is 38:17; 43:25; Zech 3:9; Heb 9:26 **13** [1]Or *revere* [a]Mal 3:17 **14** [1]I.e. what we are made of [a]Is 29:16 [b]Ps 78:39 [c]Gen 3:19; Eccl 12:7 **15** [a]Ps 90:5; Is 40:6; 1 Pet 1:24 [b]Job 14:2; James 1:10, 11

16 [a]Is 40:7 [b]Job 7:10; 8:18; 20:9 **17** [1]Or *revere* [2]I.e. faithfulness to His gracious promises [a]Ps 25:6 [b]Ex 20:6; Deut 5:10; Ps 105:8 **18** [a]Deut 7:9; Ps 25:10 **19** [1]Or *kingdom* [2]I.e. the universe [a]Ps 11:4 [b]Ps 47:2, 8; Dan 4:17, 25 **20** [a]Ps 148:2

future is secure (see Mal 3:6). *continue.* Or "dwell in the (promised) land" (see 69:36; see also 37:3,29; Is 65:9). *established before You.* See 2 Sam 7:24.

Ps 103 A hymn to God's love and compassion toward His people. (See introduction to Ps 101.) Calls to praise frame the body of the hymn (vv. 1–2, 20–22) and set its tone. The recital of praise falls into two unequal parts: (1) a three-verse celebration of personal benefits received (vv. 3–5) and (2) a 14-verse recollection of God's mercies to His people Israel (vv. 6–19). The major thematic division (vv. 6–19) is composed of six couplets framed by vv. 6 and 19, which describe the general character of God's reign. Thematic development divides the six couplets into two equal parts (vv. 7–12, 13–18), of which the first celebrates God's compassion on His people as sinners while the second sings of His compassion on them as frail mortals. The two concluding couplets proclaim the vastness of His love (vv. 11–12) and its unending perseverance (vv. 17–18). As with the hymn found in Ps 33, the length of the psalm has been determined by the number of letters in the Hebrew alphabet (see introduction to Ps 33).

103:1–2 Call to praise, directed inward (cf. vv. 20–22).

103:1–2,22 *O my soul.* A conventional Hebrew way of addressing oneself (see 104:1,35; 116:7). *soul.* See note on 6:3.

103:3–5 Recital of personal blessings received.

103:4 *redeems.* A synonym for "delivers." *pit.* A metaphor for the grave (see note on 30:1). *lovingkindness and compassion.* The key words of the hymn (see vv. 8,11,13,17). *lovingkindness.* See vv. 8,11,17; see also note on 6:4.

103:5 *like the eagle.* The vigor of youth is restored to match the proverbial unflagging strength of the eagle (see Is 40:31).

103:6–19 God's love and compassion toward His people.

103:6 Together with v. 19 (the other side of the literary frame) it characterizes the reign of God under which Israel has been so graciously blessed. *righteous.* See v. 17; see also note on 5:8.

103:7–12 God's compassion on His people as sinners.

103:7–8 See 99:7; Ex 33:13; see also note on Ex 34:6–7.

103:7 *His ways.* See 25:10 and note.

103:9 *anger.* See note on 2:5.

103:11–12 The vastness of God's love is supremely shown in His forgiving Israel's sins.

103:11 See 36:5–9. *So great is.* So prevails. *those who fear Him.* See vv. 13,17–18; see also 34:8–14 and note.

103:12 See Is 1:18; 38:17; 43:25; Jer 31:34; 50:20; Mic 7:18–19.

103:13–18 God's compassion on His people as frail mortals; perhaps echoed in Luke 1:50.

103:14 *we are but dust.* See note on 78:39.

103:17 The infinite span of God's love overarches man's little time (see v. 11). *to children's children.* See note on 109:12.

103:19 See v. 6 and note; see also 9:4,7; 11:4; 47:2,7–8; 123:1.

103:20–22 Concluding call to praise, directed to all creatures (cf. vv. 1–2). A call to praise is often the climax of praise in the Psalter (as also of the whole collection; see Ps 148–150). See note on 9:1. *Bless . . . Bless . . . Bless.* See note on 96:1–3 (the final line was probably added by the editors of the Psalter; see 104:1,35).

[b]Mighty in strength, who [c]perform His
word,
[d]Obeying the voice of His word!
21 Bless the LORD, all you [a]His hosts,
You [b]who serve Him, doing His will.
22 Bless the LORD, [a]all you works of His,
In all places of His dominion;
Bless the LORD, O my soul!

Psalm 104

1 [a]Bless the LORD, O my soul!
O LORD my God, You are very great;
You are [b]clothed with splendor and
majesty,
2 Covering Yourself with [a]light as with a
cloak,
[b]Stretching out heaven like a *tent*
curtain.
3 [1]He [a]lays the beams of His upper
chambers in the waters;
[1]He makes the [b]clouds His chariot;
[1]He walks upon the [c]wings of the
wind;
4 [1]He makes [2][a]the winds His messengers,
[3]Flaming [b]fire His ministers.

5 He [a]established the earth upon its
foundations,
So that it will not [1]totter forever and
ever.
6 You [a]covered it with the deep as with
a garment;
The waters were standing above the
mountains.
7 At Your [a]rebuke they fled,
At the [b]sound of Your thunder they
hurried away.
8 The mountains rose; the valleys sank
down
To the [a]place which You established
for them.
9 You set a [a]boundary that they may not
pass over,
So that they will not return to cover
the earth.

10 [1]He sends forth [a]springs in the
valleys;
They flow between the mountains;
11 They [a]give drink to every beast of the
field;
The [b]wild donkeys quench their thirst.
12 [1]Beside them the birds of the heavens
[a]dwell;
They [2]lift up *their* voices among the
branches.
13 [1]He [a]waters the mountains from His
upper chambers;
[b]The earth is satisfied with the fruit of
His works.

20 [b]Ps 29:1; 78:25 [c]Matt 6:10 [d]Ps 91:11; Heb 1:14
21 [a]1 Kin 22:19; Neh 9:6; Ps 148:2; Luke 2:13 [b]Ps 104:4
22 [a]Ps 145:10
104:1 [a]Ps 103:22 [b]Ps 93:1
2 [a]Dan 7:9 [b]Is 40:22
3 [1]Lit *The one who* [a]Amos 9:6 [b]Is 19:1 [c]Ps 18:10
4 [1]Lit *Who* [2]Or *His angels, spirits* [3]Or *His ministers flames of fire* [a]Ps 148:8; Heb 1:7 [b]2 Kin 2:11; 6:17
5 [1]Or *move out of place* [a]Job 38:4; Ps 24:2
6 [a]Gen 1:2
7 [a]Ps 18:15; 106:9; Is 50:2 [b]Ps 29:3; 77:18
8 [a]Ps 33:7
9 [a]Job 38:10, 11; Jer 5:22
10 [1]Lit *The one who sends* [a]Ps 107:35; Is 41:18
11 [a]Ps 104:13 [b]Job 39:5
12 [1]Or *Over, Above* [2]Lit *give forth* [a]Matt 8:20
13 [1]Lit *Who* [a]Ps 65:9; 147:8 [b]Jer 10:13

103:20 *who perform His word.* See 91:11; Heb 1:14.
103:21 *His hosts.* Uniquely here and in 148:2 the Hebrew for "hosts" is masculine, and in both places the "hosts" are associated with "angels." *You who serve Him.* Translates the participle of the Hebrew verb for "minister" in 101:6 (see note there; see also note on 104:4).
103:22 *all you works of His.* See 65:13; 96:11–12 and notes.
Ps 104 A hymn to the Creator. Obviously influenced by Gen 1, the preexilic author has adapted that account to his different purpose and has subordinated its sequence somewhat to his own design (see next paragraph). Whereas Gen 1 recounts creation as God's first work at the beginning, the poet views the creation displayed before his eyes and sings the glory of its Maker and Sustainer. Surprisingly, he only hints at the angelic world (v. 4) and mentions man only in passing (vv. 14,23); his theme is the visible creation around him, which he views as the radiant and stately robe with which the invisible Creator has clothed Himself to display His glory. (See introduction to Ps 101.)

Following his one-verse introduction, the poet designed the main body of his poem concentrically, with stanzas of three-five-nine-five-three verses. The first stanza speaks of the celestial realm (vv. 2–4) and the fifth of the nautical (vv. 24–26)—the two realms that bracket the "earth" of his experience. The second sings of the earth's solid foundations and secure boundaries (vv. 5–9) and the fourth of the orderly cycles of life on earth governed by sun and moon (vv. 19–23). At the center an eight-verse stanza celebrates the luxuriation of life in the earth (vv. 10–18). To the poem's main body he added a four-verse stanza that recites how God maintains life on earth (vv. 27–30), a two-verse conclusion (vv. 31–32—which together with v. 1 frames the whole), and a three-verse epilogue (vv. 33–35). The outer frame ("Bless the LORD, O my soul") was probably added by the editors of the Psalter when they inserted the Book division after Ps 106—thus concluding Book 4 with doxologies (see the liturgical frames added to Ps 105–106 and the similar conclusion to Book 5: Ps 146–150).
104:1 Introduction: the theme of the hymn. *clothed.* See note on 102:26.
104:2–4 The celestial realm.
104:2 *light.* Cf. the first day of creation in Gen 1. *heaven.* Cf. the second day of creation in Gen 1. *like a tent.* Over the earth and the luminaries that give it light.
104:3 *upper chambers.* Vivid imagery for the heavenly abode of God (see v. 13). In the singular, the Hebrew for this phrase usually refers to the upper-level room of a house (as in 1 Kin 17:19; 2 Kin 1:2). *waters.* The waters above the "tent" (v. 2; see Gen 1:7), from which, in the imagery of the OT, God gives the rain (see v. 13; see also 36:8 and note). *clouds His chariot.* See 18:7–15; 68:4; 77:16–19 and notes.
104:4 *winds . . . flaming fire.* The winds and lightning bolts of the thunderstorm, here personified as the agents of God's purposes (see 148:8; cf. 103:21).
104:5–9 The earth realm made secure (vv. 5,9 frame the stanza, highlighting its two main themes).
104:5 *earth.* Land in distinction from sky and seas, not the earth as a planet (see Gen 1:10). *foundations.* See 24:2 and note. *it will not totter forever.* Firmly founded (see 93:1; 96:10), it will not give way (cf. v. 9).
104:7 *rebuke.* See note on 76:6. *they fled.* Cf. the third day of creation in Gen 1.
104:9 *set a boundary.* So that the land ("earth") will never be overwhelmed by the sea (cf. v. 5; see 33:7 and note; see also Gen 9:15).
104:10–18 The earth a flourishing garden of life—the center of the psalm and the focal point of the author's contemplation of the creation (the earth, bounded by sky, vv. 2–4, and sea, vv. 24–26). Cf. the third and sixth days of creation in Gen 1.
104:10–12 The gift of water from below—watering the ravines of the Negev.

14 [1]He causes the [a]grass to grow for the
[2]cattle,
And [b]vegetation for the [3]labor of man,
So that [4]he may bring forth [5]food
[c]from the earth,
15 And [a]wine which makes man's heart
glad,
[b]So that he may make *his* face glisten
with oil,
And [1]food which [c]sustains man's
heart.
16 The trees of the LORD [1]drink their fill,
The cedars of Lebanon which He
planted,
17 Where the [a]birds build their nests,
And the [b]stork, whose home is the [1]fir
trees.

18 The high mountains are for the [a]wild
goats;
The [b]cliffs are a refuge for the
[1c]shephanim.
19 He made the moon [a]for the seasons;
The [b]sun knows the place of its
setting.
20 You [a]appoint darkness and it becomes
night,
In which all the [b]beasts of the forest
[1]prowl about.
21 The [a]young lions roar after their prey
[1]And [b]seek their food from God.
22 *When* the sun rises they withdraw
And lie down in their [a]dens.
23 Man goes forth to [a]his work
And to his labor until evening.

24 O LORD, how [a]many are Your works!
[1]In [b]wisdom You have made them all;
The [c]earth is full of Your [2]possessions.
25 [1]There is the [a]sea, great and [2]broad,
In which are swarms without number,
Animals both small and great.
26 There the [a]ships move along,
And [1b]Leviathan, which You have
formed to sport in it.

14 [1]Lit *Who* [2]Or *beasts* [3]Or *cultivation by* or *service of* [4]Or *He* [5]Lit *bread* [a]Job 38:27; Ps 147:8 [b]Gen 1:29 [c]Job 28:5
15 [1]Lit *bread* [a]Judg 9:13; Prov 31:6; Eccl 10:19 [b]Ps 23:5; 92:10; 141:5; Luke 7:46 [c]Gen 18:5; Judg 19:5, 8
16 [1]Lit *are satisfied*
17 [1]Or *cypress* [a]Ps 104:12 [b]Lev 11:19
18 [1]Small, shy, furry animals *(Hyrax syriacus)* found in the peninsula of the Sinai, northern Israel, and the region round the Dead Sea; KJV *coney,* orig NASB *rock badgers* [a]Job 39:1 [b]Prov 30:26 [c]Lev 11:5
19 [a]Gen 1:14 [b]Ps 19:6
20 [1]Lit *creep* [a]Ps 74:16; Is 45:7 [b]Ps 50:10; Is 56:9; Mic 5:8
21 [1]Lit *And to seek* [a]Job 38:39 [b]Ps 145:15; Joel 1:20
22 [a]Job 37:8
23 [a]Gen 3:19
24 [1]Or *With* [2]Or *creatures* [a]Ps 40:5 [b]Ps 136:5; Prov 3:19; Jer 10:12; 51:15 [c]Ps 65:9
25 [1]Or *This* [2]Or *broad of dimensions* (lit *hands*) [a]Ps 8:8; 69:34
26 [1]Or *a sea monster* [a]Ps 107:23; Ezek 27:9 [b]Job 41:1; Ps 74:14; Is 27:1
27 [1]Lit *its appointed time* [a]Ps 145:15 [b]Job 36:31; 38:41; Ps

27 They all [a]wait for You
To [b]give them their food in [1]due
season.
28 You give to them, they gather *it* up;
You [a]open Your hand, they are
satisfied with good.
29 You [a]hide Your face, they are dismayed;
You [b]take away their [1]spirit, they
expire
And [c]return to their dust.
30 You send forth Your [1a]Spirit, they are
created;
And You renew the face of the ground.

31 Let the [a]glory of the LORD endure
forever;
Let the LORD [b]be glad in His works;
32 [1]He [a]looks at the earth, and it
[b]trembles;
He [c]touches the mountains, and they
smoke.
33 [1]I will sing to the LORD [2a]as long as I
live;
[1]I will [b]sing praise to my God [3]while I
have my being.
34 Let my [a]meditation be pleasing to
Him;
As for me, I shall [b]be glad in the LORD.
35 Let sinners be [a]consumed from the
earth
And let the [b]wicked be no more.
[c]Bless the LORD, O my soul.
[1d]Praise [2]the LORD!

Psalm 105

1 Oh [a]give thanks to the LORD, [b]call
upon His name;

136:25; 147:9 **28** [a]Ps 145:16 **29** [1]Or *breath* [a]Deut 31:17; Ps 30:7 [b]Job 34:14, 15; Ps 146:4; Eccl 12:7 [c]Gen 3:19; Job 10:9; Ps 90:3 **30** [1]Or *breath* [a]Job 33:4; Ezek 37:9 **31** [a]Ps 86:12; 111:10 [b]Gen 1:31 **32** [1]Lit *The one who* [a]Judg 5:5; Ps 97:4, 5; 114:7 [b]Hab 3:10 [c]Ex 19:18; Ps 144:5 **33** [1]Or *Let me sing* [2]Lit *in my lifetime* [3]Lit *while I still am* [a]Ps 63:4 [b]Ps 146:2 **34** [a]Ps 19:14 [b]Ps 9:2 **35** [1]Or *Hallelujah!* [2]Heb YAH [a]Ps 59:13 [b]Ps 37:10 [c]Ps 104:1 [d]Ps 105:45; 106:48 **105:1** [a]1 Chr 16:8-22, 34; Ps 106:1; Is 12:4 [b]Ps 99:6

104:13–15 The gift of water from above—watering the uplands of Israel with their cultivated fields.
104:13 *upper chambers.* See v. 3 and note.
104:15 *heart . . . heart.* See note on 4:7. *make his face glisten.* As food (see 1 Kin 17:12), causing man's face to glow with health, and/or as cosmetic (see Esth 2:12). *oil.* Olive oil.
104:16–18 Well-watered Lebanon, with its great trees, its hordes of birds and its alpine animals, the very epitome of God's earthly parkland (see 72:16; 2 Kin 14:9; 19:23; Is 10:34; 35:2; 40:16; 60:13; Jer 22:6; Hos 14:7).
104:19–23 The orderly cycles of life on earth, governed by the moon and sun. Cf. the fourth day of creation in Gen 1.
104:21,23 *lions . . . Man.* The one (representing the animal world), lord of the night; the other, lord of the day.
104:24–26 The nautical realm. Cf. the fifth day of creation in Gen 1. The realm of the sea is structurally balanced with the celestial realm (vv. 2–4) as the other boundary to the realm of earth.
104:24 A pause to recapitulate before treating the sea.
104:25 *swarms.* See Gen 1:20–21.
104:26 *Leviathan.* That fearsome mythological monster of the deep (see Job 3:8 and note) is merely God's harmless pet playing in the ocean.
104:27–30 By God's benevolent care this zoological garden flourishes. Cf. the sixth day of creation in Gen 1.
104:29 *hide Your face.* See note on 13:1.
104:30 *created.* See note on 102:18.
104:31 *glory of the LORD.* Such as is displayed in His creation.
104:32 He is so much greater than His creation that with a look or a touch He could undo it.
104:33–35 Pious epilogue.
104:33 A vow to praise—here attached to a hymn of praise (see note on 7:17).
104:34 *my meditation.* The preceding hymn (see 19:14 and note).
104:35 May the earth be purged of that which alone mars it (cf. Rev 21:27).
Ps 105 An exhortation to Israel to worship and trust in the Lord because of all His saving acts in fulfillment of His covenant with Abraham to give his descendants the land of Canaan. It was

[c]Make known His deeds among the
peoples.
2 Sing to Him, [a]sing praises to Him;
[1b]Speak of all His [2]wonders.
3 [1]Glory in His holy name;
Let the [a]heart of those who seek the
LORD be glad.
4 Seek the LORD and [a]His strength;
[b]Seek His face continually.
5 Remember His [1a]wonders which He
has done,
His marvels and the [b]judgments
[2]uttered by His mouth,
6 O seed of [a]Abraham, His servant,
O sons of [b]Jacob, His [c]chosen ones!
7 He is the LORD our God;
His [a]judgments are in all the earth.

8 He has [a]remembered His covenant
forever,
The word which He commanded to a
[b]thousand generations,
9 *The* [a]*covenant* which He made with
Abraham,
And His [b]oath to Isaac.
10 Then He [a]confirmed it to Jacob for a
statute,
To Israel as an everlasting covenant,
11 Saying, "[a]To you I will give the land of
Canaan
As the [1b]portion of your inheritance,"
12 When they were only a [a]few men in
number,
Very few, and [b]strangers in it.
13 And they wandered about from nation
to nation,
From *one* kingdom to another people.

14 He [a]permitted no man to oppress
them,
And He [b]reproved kings for their sakes:
15 "[a]Do not touch My anointed ones,
And do My prophets no harm."

16 And He [a]called for a famine upon the
land;
He [b]broke the whole staff of bread.
17 He [a]sent a man before them,
Joseph, *who* was [b]sold as a slave.
18 They afflicted his [a]feet with fetters,
[1]He himself was laid in irons;
19 Until the time that his [a]word came to
pass,
The word of the LORD [1b]tested him.
20 The [a]king sent and released him,
The ruler of peoples, and set him free.
21 He [a]made him lord of his house
And ruler over all his possessions,
22 To [1]imprison his princes [2a]at will,
That he might teach his elders
wisdom.
23 [a]Israel also came into Egypt;
Thus Jacob [b]sojourned in the land of
Ham.
24 And He [a]caused His people to be very
fruitful,
And made them stronger than their
adversaries.

25 He [a]turned their heart to hate His
people,
To [b]deal craftily with His servants.

105:1 [c]Ps 145:12
2 [1]Or *Meditate on* [2]I.e. wonderful acts [a]Ps 96:1; 98:5 [b]Ps 77:12; 119:27; 145:5
3 [1]Or *Boast* [a]Ps 33:21
4 [a]Ps 63:2 [b]Ps 27:8
5 [1]I.e. wonderful acts [2]Lit *of His mouth* [a]Ps 40:5; 77:11 [b]Ps 119:13
6 [a]Ps 105:42 [b]Ps 135:4 [c]1 Chr 16:13; Ps 106:5; 135:4
7 [a]Is 26:9
8 [a]Ps 105:42; 106:45; Luke 1:72 [b]Deut 7:9
9 [a]Gen 12:7; 17:2, 8; 22:16-18; Gal 3:17 [b]Gen 26:3
10 [a]Gen 28:13-15
11 [1]Lit *measuring line* [a]Gen 13:15; 15:18 [b]Josh 23:4; Ps 78:55
12 [a]Gen 34:30; Deut 7:7 [b]Gen 23:4; Heb 11:9
14 [a]Gen 20:7; 35:5 [b]Gen 12:17; 20:3, 7
15 [a]Gen 26:11
16 [a]Gen 41:54 [b]Lev 26:26; Is 3:1; Ezek 4:16
17 [a]Gen 45:5 [b]Gen 37:28, 36; Acts 7:9
18 [1]Lit *His soul came into* [a]Gen 39:20; 40:15
19 [1]Or *refined* [a]Gen 40:20, 21 [b]Ps 66:10
20 [a]Gen 41:14 **21** [a]Gen 41:40-44 **22** [1]Lit *bind* [2]Lit *at his* [a]Gen 41:44 **23** [a]Gen 46:6; Acts 7:15 [b]Acts 13:17 **24** [a]Ex 1:7, 9 **25** [a]Ex 1:8; 4:21 [b]Ex 1:10; Acts 7:19

composed to be addressed to Israel by a Levite (see 1 Chr 16:7 and compare vv. 1–15 with 1 Chr 16:8–22) on one of her annual religious festivals (see chart, p. 164), possibly the Feast of Booths (see Lev 23:34) but more likely the Feast of Weeks (see Ex 23:16; Lev 23:15–21; Num 28:26; Deut 16:9–12; see also Deut 26:1–11). For other recitals of the same history (but for different purposes) see Ps 78; 106; Josh 24:2–13; Neh 9:7–25.

The introduction is composed of seven verses in two parts: (1) an exhortation (with ten imperatives) to worship the Lord (vv. 1–4); (2) a call to remember what the Lord has done (vv. 5–7). The main body that follows is framed by two four-verse groupings (vv. 8–11, 42–45) that summarize—as introduction and conclusion—its main theme: The Lord has remembered His covenant with Abraham.

105:1–4 The exhortation to worship and trust.

105:1 *give thanks.* Through praise (see note on Ps 100 title). *call upon.* In prayer (see v. 4). The first two imperatives highlight the two themes of the ten imperatives of the exhortation: praise and prayer as expressions of devotion to the Lord (celebration of His past saving acts; trust in Him for future deliverance and blessing). *His name.* See v. 3; see also note on 5:11. *Make known . . . among the peoples.* As an integral part of praise (see note on 9:1).

105:2 *wonders.* See NASB marg.; see also note on 9:1.

105:3,25 *heart.* See note on 4:7.

105:5–7 Exhortation to remember God's saving acts.

105:5 *Remember.* As a motivation for and focus of worship and the basis for trust—remember how the Lord has remembered (see vv. 8–11). *judgments.* See v. 7; see also notes on 48:11; 97:8. *uttered.* As Lord, He commands and it is done.

105:8–11 The Lord remembers His covenant with Abraham (see vv. 42–45).

105:8 *covenant.* The promissory covenant of Gen 15:9–21. This verse and v. 9 may be echoed in Luke 1:72–73. *thousand generations.* See Ex 20:6; Deut 7:9; 1 Chr 16:15.

105:10 *for a statute.* As a fixed policy governing His future actions (see note on v. 45).

105:12–41 A recital of God's saving acts in Israel's behalf from the granting of the covenant (see v. 11; Gen 15:9–20) to its fulfillment (see v. 44; Josh 21:43). Cf. the recital prescribed by Moses in conjunction with the offering of first fruits (Deut 26:1–11).

105:14–15 See Gen 20:2–7; see also note on Gen 20:7.

105:18 *fetters . . . irons.* That is, shackles of iron (see 149:8; see also note on 3:7). The poet takes the freedom to use a later conventional description of prisoners (see Job 13:27; 33:11). (Shackles are not spoken of in Gen 39:20–23, and iron came into common use for them at a later time—earlier shackles were made of bronze; see Judg 16:21.)

105:22 *imprison.* Lit. "bind," i.e., govern or control. He who was himself (v. 18; Hebrew *nephesh*) put in fetters was given authority to "bind" Pharaoh's princes "as he pleased" (Hebrew "with his *nephesh*"—here meaning his will). *elders.* Pharaoh's counselors, conventionally older men of wide experience and learning (see note on Ex 3:16).

105:23,27 *land of Ham.* See 78:51 and note.

105:25 *turned.* In OT perspective God's sovereign control over Israel's destiny is so complete that it governs—mysteriously—

26 He [a]sent Moses His servant,
And [b]Aaron, whom He had chosen.
27 They [1][a]performed His wondrous acts
among them,
And miracles in the land of Ham.
28 He [a]sent darkness and made *it* dark;
And they did not [b]rebel against His
words.
29 He [a]turned their waters into blood
And caused their fish to die.
30 Their land swarmed with [a]frogs
Even in the [b]chambers of their kings.
31 He spoke, and there came a [a]swarm of
flies
And [b]gnats in all their territory.
32 He [1]gave them [a]hail for rain,
And flaming fire in their land.
33 He [a]struck down their vines also and
their fig trees,
And shattered the trees of their territory.
34 He spoke, and [a]locusts came,
And young locusts, even without
number,
35 And ate up all vegetation in their land,
And ate up the fruit of their ground.
36 He also [a]struck down all the firstborn
in their land,
The [b]first fruits of all their vigor.

37 Then He brought them out with
[a]silver and gold,
And among His tribes there was not
one who stumbled.

26 [a]Ex 3:10; 4:12 [b]Ex 4:14; Num 16:5; 17:5-8
27 [1]Lit *set the words of His signs* [a]Ps 78:43-51; 105:27-36
28 [a]Ex 10:21, 22 [b]Ps 99:7
29 [a]Ex 7:20, 21
30 [a]Ex 8:6 [b]Ex 8:3
31 [a]Ex 8:21 [b]Ex 8:16, 17
32 [1]Or *made their rain hail* [a]Ex 9:23-25
33 [a]Ps 78:47
34 [a]Ex 10:12-15
36 [a]Ex 12:29; 13:15; Ps 135:8; 136:10 [b]Gen 49:3
37 [a]Ex 12:35, 36
38 [a]Ex 12:33 [b]Ex 15:16
39 [1]Or *curtain* [a]Ex 13:21; Neh 9:12; Ps 78:14; Is 4:5 [b]Ex 40:38
40 [1]Or *One* [2]Or *food* [a]Ex 16:12; Ps 78:18 [b]Ex 16:13; Num 11:31; Ps 78:27 [c]Ex 16:15; Neh 9:15; Ps 78:24; John 6:31
41 [1]Or *boulder* [2]Lit *They went* [a]Ex 17:6; Num 20:11; Ps 78:15; 114:8; Is 48:21; 1 Cor 10:4
42 [a]Gen 15:13, 14; Ps 105:8
43 [a]Ex 15:1; Ps 106:12
44 [1]Or *Gentiles* [a]Josh 11:16-23; 13:7; Ps 78:55 [b]Deut 6:10, 11
45 [1]Or *Hallelujah!* [2]Heb YAH [a]Deut 4:1, 40

38 Egypt was [a]glad when they departed,
For the [b]dread of them had fallen
upon them.
39 He spread a [a]cloud for a [1]covering,
And [b]fire to illumine by night.
40 [1]They [a]asked, and He brought [b]quail,
And satisfied them with the [2][c]bread of
heaven.
41 He opened the [1]rock and [a]water
flowed out;
[2]It ran in the dry places *like* a river.
42 For He [a]remembered His holy word
With Abraham His servant;
43 And He brought forth His people with
joy,
His chosen ones with a joyful [a]shout.
44 He [a]gave them also the lands of the
[1]nations,
That they [b]might take possession of
the fruit of the peoples' labor,
45 So that they might [a]keep His statutes
And observe His laws,
[1]Praise [2]the LORD!

Psalm 106

1 [1]Praise [2]the LORD!
Oh [a]give thanks to the LORD, for He
[b]is good;
For [c]His lovingkindness is everlasting.

106:1 [1]Or *Hallelujah!* [2]Heb YAH [a]Ps 105:1; 107:1; 118:1; 136:1; Jer 33:11 [b]2 Chr 5:13; 7:3; Ezra 3:11; Ps 100:5 [c]1 Chr 16:34, 41

even the evil that men commit against her; hence the bold language used here (see Ex 4:21; 7:3; Josh 11:20; 2 Sam 24:1; Is 10:5–7; 37:26–27; Jer 34:22).

105:26,42 *servant.* See 78:70 and note.

105:28–36 Recital of the plagues against Egypt. In this poetic recollection seven plagues (symbolizing completeness) represent the ten plagues of Ex 7–11. Apart from omissions (the plagues of livestock disease and boils) the poet follows the order of Exodus except that he combines the third and fourth plagues (gnats and insects)—in reverse order—to stay within the number seven. He also places the ninth plague (darkness) first in order to frame his recital with mention of the two plagues that climaxed the series.

105:39 *for a covering.* Elsewhere it is said that the cloud (symbolic of God's presence) served (1) as a guide for Israel in her wilderness journeys (see 78:14; Ex 13:21; Num 9:17; Neh 9:12,19), (2) as a shield of darkness to protect Israel from the pursuing Egyptians (see Ex 14:19–20) and (3) as a covering for the fiery manifestations of God's glorious presence (see Ex 16:10; 24:16; 34:5; 40:34–35,38; Num 11:25; 12:5; 16:42; Deut 31:15; 1 Kin 8:11). The psalmist appears to highlight yet another function: God's protective cover over His people in the wilderness, perhaps as His shading "wings" (17:8; see note there), so that the sun would not harm them by day (see 121:5–6).

105:40 *bread of heaven.* See 78:24–25 and notes.

105:41 *like a river.* Poetically heightened imagery to evoke due wonder for the event. This miracle of the wilderness wanderings concludes the recital and has been placed in climactic position as one of the most striking manifestations of God's redeeming power and benevolence (see 114:8; Is 43:19–20; cf. Is 50:2).

105:42–45 Concluding summary (balancing the introduction to the recital: vv. 8–11).

105:44 *gave them also the lands.* See v. 11.

105:45 *statutes.* God has kept His "statute" (v. 10) so that Israel might keep His "statutes"—the Hebrew word is the same (see note on v. 5: "remember"). God's redemptive working in fulfillment of His covenant promise has as its goal the creating of a people in the earth who conform their lives to His holy will. Thus the list of appropriate responses begun in v. 1—praise and prayer (trust)—is completed by the third: obedience (see Gen 18:19).

Ps 106 A confession of Israel's long history of rebellion and a prayer for God to once again save His people. In length, poetic style and shared themes it has much affinity with Ps 105 even while it contrasts with it by reciting the past as a history of rebellion (see Ps 78; Neh 9:5–37). It was most likely authored by a Levite in Jerusalem sometime after the return of some of the exiles. The first verse and the last two verses seem to have been taken over from an earlier composition (see 1 Chr 16:34–36). These may have been added, along with the "Hallelujah" (Hebrew *Hallelu Yah*, meaning "praise the Lord"), by the editors of the Psalter (borrowing from an earlier Davidic psalter) when they set the Book divisions between Ps 106 and 107. (See introduction to Ps 101.)

Apart from the fact that the psalm has an introduction (vv. 1–5) and a (composite) conclusion (vv. 44–48), the recital character of its main theme (as in Ps 105) controls its basic outline. Beginning with the events at the Red Sea (vv. 6–12), the psalm next narrates at length Israel's many rebellions during the wilderness wanderings (vv. 13–33), follows with a summary description of Israel's apostasy in the promised land (vv. 34–39) and completes its recital with a general statement of God's stern measures in the promised land (vv. 40–43).

106:1–5 Introduction.

106:1 *give thanks.* With praise (see note on Ps 100 title); a con-

2 Who can speak of the [a]mighty deeds of the LORD,
Or can show forth all His praise?
3 How blessed are those who keep [1]justice,
[2]Who [a]practice righteousness at all times!

4 Remember me, O LORD, in *Your* [a]favor [1]toward Your people;
Visit me with Your salvation,
5 That I may see the [a]prosperity of Your chosen ones,
That I may [b]rejoice in the gladness of Your nation,
That I may [c]glory with Your [1]inheritance.

6 [a]We have sinned [1b]like our fathers,
We have committed iniquity, we have behaved wickedly.
7 Our fathers in Egypt did not understand Your [1]wonders;
They [a]did not remember [2]Your abundant kindnesses,
But [b]rebelled by the sea, at the [3]Red Sea.
8 Nevertheless He saved them [a]for the sake of His name,
That He might [b]make His power known.
9 Thus He [a]rebuked the [1]Red Sea and it [b]dried up,
And He [c]led them through the deeps, as through the wilderness.
10 So He [a]saved them from the [1]hand of the one who hated *them*,
And [b]redeemed them from the [1]hand of the enemy.
11 [a]The waters covered their adversaries;
Not one of them was left.
12 Then they [a]believed His words;
They [b]sang His praise.

13 They quickly [a]forgot His works;
They [b]did not wait for His counsel,

2 [a]Ps 145:4, 12; 150:2
3 [1]Or *judgment* [2]Many Heb mss read *The one who performs* [a]Ps 15:2
4 [1]Lit *of* [a]Ps 44:3; 119:132
5 [1]I.e. people [a]Ps 1:3 [b]Ps 118:15 [c]Ps 105:3
6 [1]Lit *with* [a]1 Kin 8:47; Ezra 9:7; Neh 1:7; Jer 3:25; Dan 9:5 [b]2 Chr 30:7; Neh 9:2; Ps 78:8, 57; Zech 1:4
7 [1]I.e. wonderful acts [2]Lit *the multitude of Your lovingkindnesses* [3]Lit *Sea of Reeds* [a]Judg 3:7; Ps 78:11, 42 [b]Ex 14:11, 12; Ps 78:17
8 [a]Ezek 20:9 [b]Ex 9:16
9 [1]Lit *Sea of Reeds* [a]Ps 18:15; 78:13; Is 50:2; Nah 1:4 [b]Ex 14:21; Is 51:10 [c]Is 63:11-13
10 [1]Or *power* [a]Ex 14:30 [b]Ps 78:42; 107:2
11 [a]Ex 14:27, 28; 15:5; Ps 78:53
12 [a]Ex 14:31 [b]Ex 15:1-21; Ps 105:43
13 [a]Ex 15:24; 16:2; 17:2 [b]Ps 107:11

14 [1]Or *put God to the test* [a]Num 11:4; Ps 78:18; 1 Cor 10:6 [b]Ex 17:2; 1 Cor 10:9
15 [1]Or *leanness into their soul* [a]Num 11:31; Ps 78:29 [b]Is 10:16
16 [a]Num 16:1-3
17 [1]Or *assembly, band* [a]Num 16:32; Deut 11:6
18 [1]Or *assembly, band* [a]Num 16:35

14 But [a]craved intensely in the wilderness,
And [1b]tempted God in the desert.
15 So He [a]gave them their request,
But [b]sent a [1]wasting disease among them.

16 When they became [a]envious of Moses in the camp,
And of Aaron, the holy one of the LORD,
17 The [a]earth opened and swallowed up Dathan,
And engulfed the [1]company of Abiram.
18 And a [a]fire blazed up in their [1]company;
The flame consumed the wicked.

19 They [a]made a calf in Horeb
And worshiped a molten image.
20 Thus they [a]exchanged their glory
For the image of an ox that eats grass.
21 They [a]forgot God their Savior,
Who had done [b]great things in Egypt,
22 [1a]Wonders in the land of Ham
And awesome things by the [2]Red Sea.
23 Therefore [a]He said that He would destroy them,
Had not [b]Moses His chosen one stood in the breach before Him,
To turn away His wrath from destroying *them.*
24 Then they [a]despised the [b]pleasant land;
They [c]did not believe in His word,
25 But [a]grumbled in their tents;
They did not listen to the voice of the LORD.
26 Therefore He [1a]swore to them
That He would cast them down in the wilderness,

19 [a]Ex 32:4; Deut 9:8; Acts 7:41 **20** [a]Jer 2:11; Rom 1:23 **21** [a]Ps 78:11; 106:7, 13 [b]Deut 10:21 **22** [1]I.e. Wonderful acts [2]Lit *Sea of Reeds* [a]Ps 105:27 **23** [a]Ex 32:10; Deut 9:14; Ezek 20:8, 13 [b]Ex 32:11-14; Deut 9:25-29 **24** [a]Num 14:31 [b]Deut 8:7; Jer 3:19; Ezek 20:6 [c]Deut 1:32; 9:23; Heb 3:19 **25** [a]Num 14:2; Deut 1:27 **26** [1]Lit *lifted up His hand* [a]Num 14:28-35; Ps 95:11; Ezek 20:15; Heb 3:11

---

ventional liturgical call to praise (see 107:1; 118:1,29; 136:1–3). *lovingkindness.* See note on 6:4.

106:2 *Who can . . . ?* With integrity. *His praise.* Praise for His mighty acts (see v. 47; see also note on 9:1).

106:3 *blessed.* See note on 1:1. *justice . . . righteousness.* That is, justice-and-righteousness (see 36:6 and note; see also note on 3:7). This verse answers the question posed in v. 2.

106:4 *Remember me.* As one committed to the way of life described in v. 3. *in Your favor.* Or "with the favor You show" (see vv. 44–46). *with Your salvation.* The psalmist prays that God will include him in "the greatness of His lovingkindness" (v. 45), which He shows to His people. Thus the inner logic of the prayer seems to be completed at v. 46. The editors of the Psalter appear to have converted an individual prayer into a communal one by their additions (see introduction).

106:5 *prosperity . . . rejoice . . . glory.* A progressive sequence of cause and effect. *Your inheritance.* See v. 40.

106:6–43 Israel's history of rebellion.

106:6 A general confession of sin introducing the recital. *We.* The author identifies himself with Israel in her rebellion even as he prays for inclusion in God's mercies toward His people (see Ezra 9:6–7).

106:7,22 *wonders.* For example, the plagues against Egypt (see note on 9:1).

106:10 *redeemed.* Here, as often, a synonym for "delivered."

106:13 *His counsel.* The working out of His plan.

106:16–18 See Num 16:1–35.

106:19 *Horeb.* See note on Ex 3:1.

106:20 *glory.* Glorious One (see 1 Sam 15:29; Jer 2:11).

106:22 *land of Ham.* See 78:51 and note.

106:23 *stood in the breach.* See Ex 32:11–14,31–32. *wrath.* See note on 2:5.

106:24 *pleasant land.* So described in Jer 3:19; 12:10; Zech 7:14; see also Deut 8:7–9; Ezek 20:6.

106:26–27 *cast them down.* See note on 13:4 ("shaken").

27 And that He would [a]cast their seed
among the nations
And [b]scatter them in the lands.

28 They [a]joined themselves also to [1]Baal-peor,
And ate [b]sacrifices offered to the dead.
29 Thus they [a]provoked *Him* to anger
with their deeds,
And the plague broke out among
them.
30 Then Phinehas [a]stood up and
interposed,
And so the [b]plague was stayed.
31 And it was [a]reckoned to him for
righteousness,
To all generations forever.

32 They also [a]provoked *Him* to wrath at
the waters of [1]Meribah,
So that it [b]went hard with Moses on
their account;
33 Because they [a]were rebellious against
[1]His Spirit,
He spoke rashly with his lips.

34 They [a]did not destroy the peoples,
As [b]the LORD commanded them,
35 But [a]they mingled with the nations
And learned their [1]practices,
36 And [a]served their idols,
[b]Which became a snare to them.
37 They even [a]sacrificed their sons and
their daughters to the [b]demons,
38 And shed [a]innocent blood,
The blood of their [b]sons and their
daughters,
Whom they sacrificed to the idols of
Canaan;

27 [a]Deut 4:27 [b]Lev 26:33; Ps 44:11 **28** [1]Or *Baal of Peor* [a]Num 25:3; Deut 4:3; Hos 9:10 [b]Num 25:2 **29** [a]Num 25:4 **30** [a]Num 25:7 [b]Num 25:8 **31** [a]Gen 15:6; Num 25:11-13 **32** [1]Lit *strife* [a]Num 20:2-13; Ps 81:7; 95:9 [b]Num 20:12 **33** [1]Or *his spirit* [a]Num 20:3, 10; Ps 78:40; 107:11 **34** [a]Judg 1:21, 27-36 [b]Deut 7:2, 16 **35** [1]Lit *works* [a]Judg 3:5, 6 **36** [a]Judg 2:12 [b]Deut 7:16 **37** [a]Deut 12:31; 32:17; 2 Kin 16:3; 17:17; Ezek 16:20, 21; 1 Cor 10:20 [b]Lev 17:7 **38** [a]Ps 94:21 [b]Deut 18:10

38 [c]Num 35:33; Is 24:5; Jer 3:1, 2 **39** [1]Lit *works* [a]Lev 18:24; Ezek 20:18 [b]Lev 17:7; Num 15:39; Judg 2:17; Hos 4:12 **40** [1]I.e. people [a]Judg 2:14; Ps 78:59 [b]Lev 26:30; Deut 32:19 [c]Deut 9:29; 32:9 **41** [1]Or *Gentiles* [a]Judg 2:14; Neh 9:27 **42** [1]Lit *hand* [a]Judg 4:3; 10:12 **43** [a]Judg 2:16-18 [b]Ps 81:12 [c]Judg 6:6

And the land was [c]polluted with the
blood.
39 Thus they became [a]unclean in their
[1]practices,
And [b]played the harlot in their deeds.

40 Therefore the [a]anger of the LORD was
kindled against His people
And He [b]abhorred His [1c]inheritance.
41 Then [a]He gave them into the hand of
the [1]nations,
And those who hated them ruled over
them.
42 Their enemies also [a]oppressed them,
And they were subdued under their
[1]power.
43 Many times He would [a]deliver them;
They, however, were rebellious in
their [b]counsel,
And *so* [c]sank down in their iniquity.

44 Nevertheless He looked upon their
distress
When He [a]heard their cry;
45 And He [a]remembered His covenant
for their sake,
And [1b]relented [c]according to the
greatness of His lovingkindness.
46 He also made them [a]*objects* of
compassion
In the presence of all their captors.

47 [a]Save us, O LORD our God,
And [b]gather us from among the
nations,
To give thanks to Your holy name

44 [a]Judg 3:9; 6:7; 10:10 **45** [1]Lit *was sorry* [a]Lev 26:42; Ps 105:8 [b]Judg 2:18 [c]Ps 69:16 **46** [a]1 Kin 8:50; 2 Chr 30:9; Ezra 9:9; Neh 1:11; Jer 42:12 **47** [a]1 Chr 16:35, 36 [b]Ps 147:2

106:28–31 See Num 25.
106:31 *reckoned to him for righteousness.* When Abram "believed in the Lord, . . . He reckoned it to him as righteousness" (Gen 15:6). So, says the psalmist, was Phinehas's priestly zeal for the Lord (see Num 25:7–8). *To all generations forever.* The psalmist refers to the "covenant of a perpetual priesthood" (Num 25:13) that the Lord granted Phinehas as a gracious reward for his zealous act. It was the granting of this promissory covenant that warranted the statement about crediting righteousness, for God's granting of a promissory covenant to Abram had followed upon His crediting Abram's faith to him as righteousness (see Gen 15:9–21). Similarly, God's promissory covenants with Noah (see Gen 9:9–17) and with David (see 2 Sam 7:5–16) followed upon God's testimony to their righteousness (see Gen 7:1; 1 Sam 13:14). See chart, p. 16.
106:32 *Meribah.* See note on Ex 17:7.
106:33 *against His Spirit.* For the Spirit of God present and at work in the wilderness wanderings see Ex 31:3; Num 11:17; 24:2; Neh 9:20; Is 63:10–14.
106:34–39 A general description of the worst of rebellious Israel's sins, applicable from the time of the judges to the Babylonian exile.
106:37 *demons.* The Hebrew for this word occurs elsewhere in the OT only in Deut 32:17, where it refers to false gods. It is related to a Babylonian word referring to (pagan) protective spirits.
106:38 Cf. Jer 19:4–5. *innocent blood.* The blood of anyone not guilty of a capital crime. *polluted.* The very land itself is defiled by the slaughter of innocents (see Num 35:33; Jer 3:2,9).
106:39 *unclean.* See Lev 18:24; Jer 2:23; Ezek 20:30–31; 22:3–4. *played the harlot.* Committed prostitution by joining themselves with false gods (see Ezek 23:3,5–8; Hos 5:3; 6:10; see also note on Judg 2:17).
106:40–43 God's stern measures against His rebellious people—a general description applicable from the days of the judges to the Babylonian exile and focusing particularly on God's most severe form of covenant sanctions (see Lev 26:25–26,33,38–39; Deut 28:25,36–37,48–57,64–68).
106:40 *anger.* See note on 2:5. *abhorred.* See 5:6.
106:44–46 God's gracious remembering of His covenant—a general description applicable from the days of the judges to the Babylonian exile.
106:44 *heard their cry.* See Ex 2:23; 3:7–9; Num 20:16; Judg 3:9,15; 4:3; 6:6–7; 10:10; 1 Sam 9:16; 2 Chr 20:6–12; Neh 9:27–28.
106:45 *remembered His covenant.* See 105:8,42; Ex 2:24; Lev 26:42,45. *lovingkindness.* See note on 6:4.
106:46 *objects of compassion . . . their captors.* Makes clear that the author's recital includes the Babylonian captivity (see 1 Kin 8:50; 2 Chr 30:9; Ezra 9:9; Jer 42:12). Although there were earlier captivities of Israelite communities, no other captive group was said to have been shown pity.
106:47 A communal prayer for deliverance and restoration from dispersion (see introduction and note on v. 4). *name.* See

And [1c]glory in Your praise.
48 [a]Blessed be the LORD, the God of Israel,
From everlasting even to everlasting.
And let all the people say, "Amen."
[1]Praise [2]the LORD!

BOOK 5

Psalm 107

1 Oh [a]give thanks to the LORD, for [b]He is good,
For His lovingkindness is everlasting.
2 Let [a]the redeemed of the LORD say *so*,
Whom He has [b]redeemed from the hand of the adversary
3 And [a]gathered from the lands,
From the east and from the west,
From the north and from the [1]south.

4 They [a]wandered in the wilderness in a [1]desert region;
They did not find a way to [2]an inhabited [b]city.
5 *They were* hungry [1]and thirsty;
Their [a]soul fainted within them.
6 Then they [a]cried out to the LORD in their trouble;
He delivered them out of their distresses.
7 He led them also by a [1a]straight way,
To go to [2b]an inhabited city.
8 [a]Let them give thanks to the LORD for His lovingkindness,
And for His [1]wonders to the sons of men!
9 For He has [a]satisfied the [1]thirsty soul,
And the [b]hungry soul He has filled with what is good.

47 [1]Lit *boast* [c]Ps 47:1 **48** [1]Or *Hallelujah!* [2]Heb YAH [a]Ps 41:13; 72:18; 89:52 **107:1** [a]1 Chr 16:34; Ps 106:1; 118:1; 136:1; Jer 33:11 [b]2 Chr 5:13; 7:3; Ezra 3:11; Ps 100:5 **2** [a]Is 35:9, 10; 62:12; 63:4 [b]Ps 78:42; 106:10 **3** [1]Lit *sea* [a]Deut 30:3; Neh 1:9; Ps 106:47; Is 11:12; 43:5; 56:8; Ezek 11:17; 20:34 **4** [1]Lit *waste* [a]Num 14:33; 32:13; Deut 2:7; 32:10; Josh 5:6; 14:10 **4** [2]Or *a habitable city;* lit *a city of habitation* [b]Ps 107:7, 36 **5** [1]Lit *also* [a]Ps 77:3

6 [a]Ps 50:15; 107:13, 19, 28 **7** [1]Or *level* [2]Or *a habitable city;* lit *a city of habitation* [a]Ezra 8:21; Ps 5:8; Jer 31:9 [b]Ps 107:4, 36 **8** [1]I.e. wonderful acts [a]Ps 107:15, 21, 31 **9** [1]Or *parched* [a]Ps 22:26; 34:10; 63:5; 103:5 [b]Ps 146:7; Matt 5:6; Luke 1:53

note on 5:11. *glory in.* Triumphantly celebrate. The Hebrew for this phrase is found elsewhere only in the parallel in 1 Chr 16:35. *praise.* See note on 9:1.

106:48 The doxology for Book 4 (see 41:13 and note). *Amen.* See note on Deut 27:15.

Ps 107 An exhortation to praise the Lord for His unfailing love in that He hears the prayers of those in need and saves them (see next paragraph—on structure). It was composed for liturgical use at one of Israel's annual religious festivals. Interpretations vary widely, but the following is most likely: Having experienced anew God's mercies in her return from Babylonian exile (v. 3; see Jer 33:11), Israel is led by a Levite in celebrating God's unfailing benevolence toward those who have cried to Him in the crises of their lives. In its recitational style the psalm is closely related to Ps 104–106, and in its language to Ps 105–106. For that reason it has been seriously proposed that with these last two psalms it forms a trilogy from the same author. Whether or not this is so, its affinity with the preceding psalms strongly suggests that it was associated with them before the insertion of a Book division between Ps 106 and 107 and that it was intended to conclude the little series, Ps 104–107. Its recital of God's "wonders to the sons of men" (v. 8)—which climaxes Ps 105–106—balances the recital of His many wise works in creation (see 104:2–26) and His benevolent care over the animal world (see 104:27–30). The editors may have inserted a Book division between Ps 106 and 107 with a view to a fivefold division of the Psalter (see Introduction: Collection, Arrangement and Date). (See introduction to Ps 101.)

The introduction (vv. 1–3) and conclusion (v. 43) enclose six thematic stanzas, of which the last two (vv. 33–38, 39–42) stand apart as an instructive supplement focusing in a more general way on reversals in fortunes—which, however, end up with God restoring the "hungry" (v. 36) and the "needy" (v. 41). Of the four remaining thematic stanzas (marked by recurring refrains: vv. 6,13,19,28; vv. 8,15,21,31), the first and last refer to God's deliverance of those lost in the trackless wilderness (vv. 4–9) and those imperiled on the boisterous sea (vv. 23–32). The two central stanzas celebrate deliverance from the punishment of foreign bondage (vv. 10–16) and from the punishment of disease (vv. 17–22). Of the concluding lines to these four stanzas, the first two (vv. 9,16) and the last two (vv. 22,32) are similar. The verse pattern of these four thematic stanzas (six-seven-six-ten) makes deliberate use of the significant numbers seven and ten.

107:1–3 Introductory call to praise.

107:1 A conventional liturgical call to praise (see 106:1; 118:1,29; 136:1; Jer 33:11). *give thanks.* See vv. 8,15,21,31; see also note on Ps 100 title. *lovingkindness.* See vv. 8,15,21,31,43; see also note on 6:4.

107:2 *redeemed.* Here, as often, a synonym for "delivered."

107:3 *from the lands.* From the dispersion resulting from the Assyrian (see 2 Kin 17:6) and Babylonian captivities (see 2 Kin 24:14,16; 25:11,26; Jer 52:28–30; see also Neh 1:8; Esth 8:5,9,13; Is 11:12; 43:5–6; Ezek 11:17; 20:34). *south.* Lit. "(the) sea" (see NASB marg.), i.e., the west, as in Is 49:12. But perhaps the final letter of the Hebrew word has been lost, which if supplied yields "south."

107:4–9 Deliverance for those lost in the trackless wilderness. No reference is made to rebellion (as in the third and fourth stanzas), but since Israel had journeyed through the wilderness on her way to Canaan she had firsthand experience of the terrors of the wilderness. She was, moreover, bounded on the east by the great Arabian Desert (as on the west by the Mediterranean Sea; see vv. 23–32), across which her merchant caravans traveled.

107:4,7,36 *an inhabited city.* Where people live and where a steady supply of food and water makes human life secure.

107:6 *they cried out.* The author uses the same Hebrew verb in v. 28 to establish linkage. In vv. 13,19 he uses a different (but similar-sounding) Hebrew verb for the same reason. Just as Israel's history was a history of divine deliverance (see Ps 105) and a history of rebellion (see Ps 106), so also it was a history of crying out to the Lord in distress (see references in note on 106:44).

107:7 *straight way.* Direct route, clear of dangerous and difficult obstacles.

107:8 For other refrains see introduction to Ps 42–43. *wonders.* See vv. 15,21,24,31; see also note on 9:1.

107:9 *satisfied the thirsty . . . the hungry soul He has filled.* See v. 5; see also 105:40–41.

107:10–16 Deliverance from the punishment of foreign bondage. God even delivers those who cry to Him when their distress is a result of His discipline for their sins (see vv. 17–20,33–41).

10 There were those who [a]dwelt in darkness and in the shadow of death,
[b]Prisoners in [1]misery and [2]chains,
11 Because they had [a]rebelled against the words of God
And [b]spurned the [c]counsel of the Most High.
12 Therefore He humbled their heart with labor;
They stumbled and there was [a]none to help.
13 Then they [a]cried out to the LORD in their trouble;
He saved them out of their distresses.
14 He [a]brought them out of darkness and the shadow of death
And [b]broke their bands apart.
15 [a]Let them give thanks to the LORD for His lovingkindness,
And for His [1]wonders to the sons of men!
16 For He has [a]shattered gates of bronze
And cut bars of iron asunder.

17 Fools, because of [1]their rebellious way,
And [a]because of their iniquities, were afflicted.
18 Their [a]soul abhorred all kinds of food,
And they [b]drew near to the [c]gates of death.
19 Then they cried out to the LORD in their trouble;
He saved them out of their distresses.
20 He [a]sent His word and [b]healed them,
And [c]delivered *them* from their [1]destructions.
21 [a]Let them give thanks to the LORD for His lovingkindness,
And for His [1]wonders to the sons of men!
22 Let them also offer [a]sacrifices of thanksgiving,
And [b]tell of His works with joyful singing.

23 Those who [a]go down to the sea in ships,
Who do business on great waters;
24 They have seen the works of the LORD,
And His [1]wonders in the deep.
25 For He [a]spoke and raised up a [b]stormy wind,
Which [c]lifted up the waves [1]of the sea.
26 They rose up to the heavens, they went down to the depths;
Their soul [a]melted away in *their* misery.
27 They reeled and [a]staggered like a drunken man,
And [1]were at their wits' end.
28 Then they cried to the LORD in their trouble,
And He brought them out of their distresses.
29 He [a]caused the storm to be still,
So that the waves [1]of the sea were hushed.
30 Then they were glad because they were quiet,

10 [1]Lit *affliction* [2]Lit *irons* [a]Ps 143:3; Is 42:7; Mic 7:8; Luke 1:79 [b]Job 36:8; Ps 102:20
11 [a]Ps 78:40; 106:7; Lam 3:42 [b]Num 15:31; 2 Chr 36:16; Prov 1:25; Is 5:24 [c]Ps 73:24
12 [a]Ps 22:11; 72:12
13 [a]Ps 107:6
14 [a]Ps 86:13; 107:10 [b]Ps 116:16; Jer 2:20; 30:8; Nah 1:13; Luke 13:16; Acts 12:7
15 [1]I.e. wonderful acts [a]Ps 107:8, 21, 31
16 [a]Is 45:1, 2
17 [1]Lit *the way of their transgression* [a]Is 65:6, 7; Jer 30:14, 15; Lam 3:39; Ezek 24:23
18 [a]Job 33:20; Ps 102:4 [b]Job 33:22; Ps 88:3 [c]Job 38:17; Ps 9:13
20 [1]Or *pits* [a]Ps 147:15, 18; Matt 8:8 [b]2 Kin 20:5; Ps 30:2; 103:3; 147:3 [c]Job 33:28, 30; Ps 30:3; 49:15; 56:13; 103:4
21 [1]I.e. wonderful acts [a]Ps 107:8, 15, 31
22 [a]Lev 7:12; Ps 50:14; 116:17 [b]Ps 9:11; 73:28; 118:17
23 [a]Is 42:10; Jon 1:3
24 [1]I.e. wonderful acts
25 [1]Lit *of it* [a]Ps 105:31, 34 [b]Ps 148:8; Jon 1:4 [c]Ps 93:3, 4
26 [a]Ps 22:14; 119:28 **27** [1]Lit *all their wisdom was swallowed up* [a]Job 12:25; Is 24:20 **29** [1]Lit *of it* [a]Ps 65:7; 89:9; Matt 8:26; Luke 8:24

107:10 *dwelt in darkness . . . shadow of death.* Vivid imagery for distress (see 18:28; Is 5:30; 8:22; 59:9; see also note on 44:19). *Prisoners.* While reference is no doubt to foreign bondage, the imagery of being bound was also used by OT poets to refer to other forms of distress (see Job 36:8; Is 28:22; Lam 3:7); so the reference may be deliberately ambiguous.

107:11 *God . . . Most High.* That is, God Most High (see Gen 14:19 and note; see also note on 3:7). *counsel.* God's wise directives embodied in His words.

107:12 *humbled their heart with labor.* Lit. "brought down their heart with labor," i.e., a labor so burdensome it broke their spirit. *stumbled.* Their strength failed (see 31:10; 109:24; Neh 4:10; Is 40:30; Zech 12:8).

107:13 *cried out to.* See note on v. 6.

107:16 Either this verse is quoted from Is 45:2, or both verses quote an established saying. *gates of bronze.* City gates—normally of wood; here proverbially of bronze, the strongest gates then imaginable (see Jer 1:18). *bars of iron.* Bars that secured city gates (see Deut 3:5; Jer 51:30), usually made of wood (see Nah 3:13) but sometimes of bronze (see 1 Kin 4:13). "Can anyone smash iron . . . or bronze?" was a proverb of the time (see Jer 15:12).

107:17–22 Deliverance from the punishment of wasting disease (see note on vv. 10–16).

107:17 *Fools.* See note on 14:1; see also Jer 4:22. "Fools despise wisdom and instruction" (Prov 1:7; see v. 43). *because of their iniquities, were afflicted.* See Lev 26:16,25; Deut 28:20–22,35, 58–61.

107:18 *gates of death.* The realm of the dead was sometimes depicted as a nether world city with a series of concentric walls and gates (seven, each inside the other, according to ancient Near Eastern mythology) to keep those descending there from returning to the land of the living (see 9:13 and note on Job 38:17; see also Matt 16:18).

107:19 *cried out to.* See note on v. 6. *saved.* See v. 13; cf. vv. 6,28.

107:20 *His word.* His command, here personified as the agent of His purpose (see 147:15,18; see also note on 23:6).

107:22 *sacrifices of thanksgiving.* See Lev 7:12–15; 22:29–30. *tell of His works.* See note on 7:17. *joyful singing.* See, e.g., Ps 116.

107:23–32 Deliverance from the perils of the sea (see note on vv. 4–9). Israel's merchants also braved the sea in pursuit of trade (see Gen 49:13; Judg 5:17; 1 Kin 9:26–28; 10:22).

107:23 *great waters.* See 29:3.

107:24 *wonders in the deep.* Since the peoples of the eastern Mediterranean coastlands associated the "great waters" (v. 23) of the sea with the primeval chaotic waters (see note on 32:6), the Lord's total control of them was always for Israel a cause of wonder and of a sense of security. Therefore the terrifying storms that sometimes swept the Mediterranean (see Jon 1; Acts 27) are here included among His wonderful deeds.

So He guided them to their desired
haven.
31 [a]Let them give thanks to the LORD for
His lovingkindness,
And for His [1b]wonders to the sons of
men!
32 Let them [a]extol Him also [b]in the
congregation of the people,
And [c]praise Him at the seat of the
elders.

33 He [1a]changes rivers into a [2]wilderness
And springs of water into a thirsty
ground;
34 A [a]fruitful land into a [b]salt waste,
Because of the wickedness of those
who dwell in it.
35 He [1a]changes a [2]wilderness into a
pool of water
And a dry land into springs of water;
36 And there He makes the hungry to
dwell,
So that they may establish [1a]an
inhabited city,
37 And sow fields and [a]plant vineyards,
And [1]gather a fruitful harvest.
38 Also He blesses them and they
[a]multiply greatly,
And He [b]does not let their cattle
decrease.

39 When they are [a]diminished and
[b]bowed down
Through oppression, misery and
sorrow,
40 He [a]pours contempt upon [1]princes
And [b]makes them wander [c]in a
pathless waste.
41 But He [a]sets the needy [1]securely on
high away from affliction,
And [b]makes *his* families like a flock.
42 The [a]upright see it and are glad;
But all [b]unrighteousness shuts its
mouth.
43 Who is [a]wise? Let him give heed to
these things,
And consider the [b]lovingkindnesses of
the LORD.

Psalm 108

A Song, a Psalm of David.

1 [a]My heart is steadfast, O God;
I will sing, I will sing praises, even
with my [1]soul.
2 Awake, harp and lyre;
I will awaken the dawn!
3 I will give thanks to You, O LORD,
among the peoples,
And I will sing praises to You among
the nations.
4 For Your [a]lovingkindness is great
[b]above the heavens,
And Your truth *reaches* to the skies.
5 [a]Be exalted, O God, above the
heavens,
And Your glory above all the earth.
6 [a]That Your beloved may be delivered,
Save with Your right hand, and
answer me!

7 God has spoken in His [1]holiness:
"I will exult, I will portion out Shechem
And measure out the valley of Succoth.
8 "Gilead is Mine, Manasseh is Mine;
Ephraim also is the [1]helmet of My
head;
[a]Judah is My [2]scepter.
9 "Moab is My washbowl;
Over Edom I shall throw My shoe;
Over Philistia I will shout aloud."

31 [1]I.e. wonderful acts [a]Ps 107:8, 15, 21 [b]Ps 78:4; 111:4 **32** [a]Ps 34:3; 99:5; Is 25:1 [b]Ps 22:22, 25 [c]Ps 35:18 **33** [1]Or *turns* [2]Or *desert* [a]1 Kin 17:1, 7; Ps 74:15; Is 42:15; 50:2 **34** [a]Gen 13:10; 14:3; 19:24, 25; Deut 29:23 [b]Job 39:6; Jer 17:6 **35** [1]Or *turns* [2]Or *desert* [a]Ps 105:41; 114:8; Is 35:6, 7; 41:18 **36** [1]Or *a habitable city;* lit *a city of habitation* [a]Ps 107:4, 7 **37** [1]Lit *acquire fruits of yield* [a]2 Kin 19:29; Is 65:21; Amos 9:14 **38** [a]Gen 12:2; 17:20; Ex 1:7; Deut 1:10 [b]Deut 7:14 **39** [a]2 Kin 10:32; Ezek 5:11; 29:15 [b]Ps 38:6; 44:25; 57:6 **40** [1]Or *nobles* [a]Job 12:21 [b]Job 12:24 [c]Deut 32:10 **41** [1]Lit *in an inaccessibly high place* [a]1 Sam 2:8; Ps 59:1; 113:7, 8 [b]Job 21:11; Ps 78:52; 113:9 **42** [a]Job 22:19; Ps 52:6 **42** [b]Job 5:16; Ps 63:11; Rom 3:19 **43** [a]Ps 64:9; Jer 9:12; Hos 14:9 [b]Ps 107:1 **108:1** [1]Lit *glory* [a]Ps 57:7-11; 108:1-5

4 [a]Num 14:18; Deut 7:9; Ps 36:5; 100:5; Mic 7:18-20 [b]Ps 113:4 **5** [a]Ps 57:5 **6** [a]Ps 60:5-12; 108:6-13 **7** [1]Or *sanctuary* **8** [1]Lit *protection* [2]Or *lawgiver* [a]Gen 49:10

107:30 *haven.* Perhaps trading center.
107:32 See v. 22. *elders.* See note on Ex 3:16.
107:33–42 A twofold instructive supplement recalling how the Lord sometimes disciplined His people by turning the fruitful land (v. 34) into a virtual wilderness (see 1 Kin 17:1–7; 2 Kin 8:1) but then restored the land again (see Ruth 1:6; 1 Kin 18:44–45), so that the hungry (v. 36) could live there and prosper in the midst of plenty. But then He sent powerful armies against them (such as the Assyrians, 2 Kin 17:3–6, and the Babylonians, 2 Kin 24:10–17) that devastated the land once more and deported its people; yet afterward He restored the needy (v. 41). But the poet generalizes upon these experiences in the manner of the wisdom teachers.
107:33–35 The imagery is similar to that found in Is 35:6–7; 41:18; 42:15; 43:19–20; 50:2 and may indicate that the author has been influenced by Isaiah.
107:40 Perhaps quoted from Job 12:21,24. In their prosperity the people, led by their nobles, grow proud and turn their backs on the God who has blessed them (see Deut 31:20; 32:15), so He returns them to the wilderness (see Deut 32:10; Hos 2:3,14).
107:41 *needy.* Those in need of help (see v. 39; see also 9:18 and note).
107:42 Conclusion to the instruction (vv. 33–41); perhaps an echo of Job 5:16. *upright . . . unrighteousness.* A frequent contrast in OT wisdom literature (see Prov 2:21–22; 11:6–7; 12:6; 14:11; 15:8; 21:18,29; 29:27—but the Hebrew for "unrighteousness" here is shared more often with Job).
107:43 Conclusion to the psalm. *Who is wise?* See Deut 32:29; Hos 14:9. *these things.* The instruction in vv. 33–42. *consider the lovingkindnesses of the LORD.* The theme of vv. 4–32.
Ps 108 Praise of God's love, and prayer for His help against the enemies—a combination (with very slight modifications) of 57:7–11 and 60:5–12. For a similar composition of a new psalm by combination of portions from several psalms see 1 Chr 16:8–36. The celebration of the greatness of God's love (v. 4) links this psalm thematically with Ps 103 (see 103:11). See introduction to Ps 101.
108 title *Song.* See note on Ps 30 title. *of David.* Both sources (Ps 57; 60) were credited to him.
108:1–5 Praise of God's love, possibly intended to function here as an expression of trust in God (the God of vv. 7–9,11), to whom appeal is to be made (vv. 6,12); see 109:1 and note. For this stanza see notes on 57:7–11.
108:1 *soul.* Lit. "glory" (see note on 7:5).
108:6–13 Prayer for God's help against enemies (see notes on 60:5–12).

10 [a]Who will bring me into the besieged
city?
Who [1]will lead me to Edom?
11 Have not You Yourself, O God,
[a]rejected us?
And will You not go forth with our
armies, O God?
12 Oh give us help against the adversary,
For [a]deliverance [1]by man is in vain.
13 [1]Through God we will do valiantly,
And [a]it is He who shall tread down
our adversaries.

Psalm 109

For the choir director. A Psalm of David.

1 O [a]God of my praise,
[b]Do not be silent!
2 For they have opened the [1]wicked and
[a]deceitful mouth against me;
They have spoken [2]against me with a
[b]lying tongue.
3 They have also surrounded me with
words of hatred,
And fought against me [a]without cause.
4 In return [a]for my love they act as my
accusers;
But [b]I am *in* prayer.
5 Thus they have [1a]repaid me evil for
good
And [b]hatred for my love.

6 Appoint a wicked man over him,
And let an [1a]accuser stand at his right
hand.
7 When he is judged, let him [a]come
forth guilty,
And let his [b]prayer become sin.
8 Let [a]his days be few;
Let [b]another take his office.
9 Let his [a]children be fatherless
And his [b]wife a widow.
10 Let his [a]children wander about and
beg;
And let them [b]seek *sustenance* [1]far
from their ruined homes.
11 Let [a]the creditor [1]seize all that he has,
And let [b]strangers plunder the product
of his labor.
12 Let there be none to [1a]extend
lovingkindness to him,
Nor [b]any to be gracious to his
fatherless children.
13 Let his [a]posterity be [1]cut off;
In a following generation let their
[b]name be blotted out.

14 Let [a]the iniquity of his fathers be
remembered [1]before the LORD,
And do not let the sin of his mother
be [b]blotted out.
15 Let [a]them be before the LORD
continually,

10 [1]Or *has led* [a]Ps 60:9 **11** [a]Ps 44:9 **12** [1]Lit *of* [a]Is 30:3 **13** [1]Or *In* or *With* [a]Is 60:12; 63:1-4 **109:1** [a]Deut 10:21 [b]Ps 28:1; 83:1 **2** [1]Lit *wicked mouth and the deceitful* [2]Lit *with* [a]Ps 10:7; 52:4 [b]Ps 120:2 **3** [a]Ps 35:7; 69:4; John 15:25 **4** [a]Ps 38:20 [b]Ps 69:13; 141:5 **5** [1]Lit *laid upon me* [a]Ps 35:12; 38:20 [b]John 7:7; 10:32 **6** [1]Or *adversary, Satan* [a]Zech 3:1 **7** [a]Ps 1:5 [b]Prov 28:9 **8** [a]Ps 55:23 [b]Acts 1:20 **9** [a]Ex 22:24 [b]Jer 18:21 **10** [1]Or *out of their desolate places* [a]Gen 4:12; Job 30:5-8; Ps 59:15 [b]Ps 37:25 **11** [1]Lit *ensnare, strike at* [a]Neh 5:7; Job 5:5; 20:15 [b]Is 1:7; Lam 5:2; Ezek 7:21 **12** [1]Lit *continue* [a]Ezra 7:28; 9:9 [b]Job 5:4; Is 9:17

13 [1]Lit *for cutting off* [a]Job 18:19; Ps 21:10; 37:28 [b]Ps 9:5; Prov 10:7 **14** [1]Lit *to* [a]Ex 20:5; Num 14:18; Is 65:6, 7; Jer 32:18 [b]Neh 4:5; Jer 18:23 **15** [a]Ps 90:8; Jer 16:17

Ps 109 A prayer for God to judge a case of false accusation. The author speaks of his enemies in the singular in vv. 6–19 but in the plural elsewhere. Some therefore suppose that vv. 6–19 contain the enemies' curses pronounced against the author (if so, v. 6 would read, "They say, 'Appoint a wicked man . . .' "). But it is more likely that either (1) the author shifts here to a collective mode of speaking, or (2) the enemies are united under a leader whose personal animosity toward the psalmist has fired the antagonism of others and so is singled out for special attention. Traditional attempts to isolate a distinct class of psalms called "imprecatory" (and then identify Ps 109 as the climax of the series) are mistaken (see note on vv. 6–15). This prayer has much affinity with Ps 35. See introduction to Ps 101.

Two (Hebrew) four-line stanzas of petition frame the whole (vv. 1–5, 26–29), followed by a two-line conclusion (vv. 30–31). The remaining 20 lines fall into two main divisions of ten lines each (vv. 6–15, 16–25). Of these, the second is thematically divided into two parts of five lines each, the first of which (vv. 16–20) catalogues what "he" has done while the second (vv. 21–25) describes how "I" am suffering.

109 title See note on Ps 4 title.

109:1–5 Appeal to God to deliver him from false accusers.

109:1 *God of my praise.* The one he publicly praises as his trustworthy deliverer and defender (see 22:3 and note; see also 35:18; 74:21; 76:10; 79:13; 102:18). *silent.* (Judicially) inactive (see 28:1; 35:22; 50:3,21; 83:1).

109:2–5 The particulars of his case, which he presents before the heavenly bar of justice (see 35:11–16).

109:2 *opened the . . . mouth against me.* See note on 5:9.

109:4 *But I am in prayer.* In contrast to the enemy (see vv. 16–18). The intent may be: But I have prayed for them (as in 35:13–14).

109:6–15 Appeal for judicial redress—that the Lord will deal with them in accordance with their malicious intent against him, matching punishment with crime (see note on 5:10; see also 35:4–10 and note).

109:6 *wicked man . . . accuser.* The psalmist's enemy falsely accused him in order to bring him down; now let the enemy be confronted by an accuser.

109:7 *his prayer.* The petitions he offers in his defense.

109:8 *days be few.* The false accuser was no doubt seeking to effect David's death (see 1 Kin 21:8–15). *another take his office.* The enemy held some official position and was perhaps plotting a coup. For a NT application of these words to Judas see Acts 1:20.

109:10–11 May he also be deprived of all his property so that he has no inheritance to pass on to his children.

109:12 *none to extend lovingkindness.* See v. 16. *his . . . children.* The close identity of a man with his children and of children with their parents, resulting from the tightly bonded unity of the three- or four-generation households of that ancient society, is alien to the modern reader, whose sense of self is highly individualistic. But that deep, profoundly human bond accounts for the ancient legal principle of "visiting the iniquity of the fathers on the children, on the third and the fourth generations" (see Ex 20:5; but see also 103:17; Gen 18:19).

109:13 Since a man lived on in his children (see previous note), the focus of judgment remains on the false accuser (see 21:10; 37:28). *name be blotted out.* See note on 9:5.

109:14–15 *iniquity of his fathers . . . sin of his mother . . . them.* These verses return to the theme of vv. 7–8 (and thus form a frame around the stanza): May the indictment the accuser lodges against him include the sins of his parents (see note on v. 12).

That He may [b]cut off their memory
from the earth;
16 Because he did not remember to show
lovingkindness,
But persecuted the [a]afflicted and
needy man,
And the [b]despondent in heart, to [c]put
them to death.
17 He also loved cursing, so [a]it came to
him;
And he did not delight in blessing, so
it was far from him.
18 But he [a]clothed himself with cursing
as with his garment,
And it [b]entered into [1]his body like
water
And like oil into his bones.
19 Let it be to him as [a]a garment with
which he covers himself,
And for a belt with which he
constantly [b]girds himself.
20 [1]Let this be the [a]reward of my
accusers from the LORD,
And of those who [b]speak evil against
my soul.

21 But You, O [1]GOD, the Lord, deal *kindly*
with me [a]for Your name's sake;
Because [b]Your lovingkindness is good,
deliver me;
22 For [a]I am afflicted and needy,
And [1]my heart is [b]wounded within me.
23 I am passing [a]like a shadow when it
lengthens;
I am shaken off [b]like the locust.
24 My [a]knees [1]are weak from [b]fasting,
And my flesh has grown lean, without
fatness.
25 I also have become a [a]reproach to
them;
When they see me, they [b]wag their
head.

26 [a]Help me, O LORD my God;
Save me according to Your
lovingkindness.
27 [1]And let them [a]know that this is Your
hand;
You, LORD, have done it.
28 [a]Let them curse, but You bless;
When they arise, they shall be
ashamed,
But Your [b]servant shall be glad.
29 [1]Let [a]my accusers be clothed with
dishonor,
And [2]let them [b]cover themselves with
their own shame as with a robe.

30 With my mouth I will give thanks
abundantly to the LORD;
And in the midst of many [a]I will
praise Him.
31 For He stands [a]at the right hand of the
needy,
To save him from those who [b]judge
his soul.

Psalm 110

A Psalm of David.

1 [a]The LORD says to my Lord:
"[b]Sit at My right hand

15 [b]Job 18:17; Ps 34:16 **16** [a]Ps 37:14 [b]Ps 34:18 [c]Ps 37:32; 94:6 **17** [a]Prov 14:14; Ezek 35:9; Matt 7:2 **18** [1]Lit *his inward parts* [a]Ps 73:6; 109:29; Ezek 7:27 [b]Num 5:22 **19** [a]Ps 73:6; 109:29; Ezek 7:27 [b]2 Sam 22:40; Ps 30:11; Is 11:5 **20** [1]Lit *This is* [a]Ps 54:5; 94:23; Is 3:11; 2 Tim 4:14 [b]Ps 41:5; 71:10 **21** [1]Heb *YHWH,* usually rendered LORD [a]Ps 23:3; 25:11; 79:9; 106:8; Ezek 36:22 [b]Ps 69:16 **22** [1]Lit *one has pierced my heart within me* [a]Ps 40:17; 86:1 [b]Job 24:12; Ps 143:4; Prov 18:14 **23** [a]Ps 102:11 [b]Ex 10:19; Job 39:20 **24** [1]Or *totter* [a]Heb 12:12 [b]Ps 35:13 **25** [a]Ps 22:6 [b]Ps 22:7; Jer 18:16; Lam 2:15; Matt 27:39; Mark 15:29 **26** [a]Ps 119:86 **27** [1]Or *That they may know* [a]Job 37:7 **28** [a]2 Sam 16:11, 12 [b]Is 65:14 **29** [1]Or *My accusers will be* [2]Or *they will cover* [a]Job 8:22; Ps 132:18 [b]Job 8:22; Ps 35:26 **30** [a]Ps 22:22; 35:18; 111:1 **31** [a]Ps 16:8; 73:23; 110:5; 121:5 [b]Ps 37:33
110:1 [a]Matt 22:44; Mark 12:36; Luke 20:42, 43; Acts 2:34, 35; Heb 1:13 [b]Matt 26:64; Eph 1:20; Col 3:1; Heb 1:3; 8:1; 10:12; 12:2

109:15 *cut off their memory.* May this slanderer be the last of their family line.

109:16–20 The ruthless character of the enemy—may he be made to suffer the due consequences (see 10:2–15; 59:12–13). Accusation of the adversary is a common feature in psalms that are appeals to the heavenly Judge (see, e.g., 5:9–10; 10:2–11; 17:10–12).

109:17 *cursing.* The enemy added curses to lies (see note on 10:7).

109:18 *into his body like water, And like oil into his bones.* Cursing was his food and drink as well as his clothing; he lived by cursing (see Prov 4:17).

109:21–25 The intensity of "my" suffering—Lord, deliver me!

109:21 *for Your name's sake.* See notes on 5:11; 23:3. *lovingkindness.* See v. 26; see also note on 6:4.

109:22 The psalmist's description of his situation echoes the words of v. 16. *afflicted and needy.* Dependent on the Lord (see note on 34:6). *heart.* See note on 4:7. *is wounded.* The Hebrew for this phrase sounds like the Hebrew for "cursing" in vv. 17–18, a deliberate wordplay—while he lives by cursing, I live with deep inward pain.

109:23 *I am passing.* Apparently the psalmist suffers a life-sapping affliction, which is the occasion for his enemies to turn on him (see vv. 24–25; see also note on 5:9). *like a shadow.* See 102:11. *shaken off.* See Neh 5:13; Job 38:13.

109:26–29 Concluding petition, with many echoes of preceding themes.

109:28 *servant.* Perhaps identifies the psalmist as the Lord's anointed (see title; see also 78:70 and note).

109:30–31 A vow to praise the Lord for His deliverance (see note on 7:17).

Ps 110 Oracles concerning the Messianic King-Priest. This psalm (specifically its two brief oracles, vv. 1,4) is frequently referred to in the NT testimony to Christ. Like Ps 2, it has the marks of a coronation psalm, composed for use at the enthronement of a new Davidic king. Before the Christian era Jews already viewed it as Messianic. Because of the manner in which it has been interpreted in the NT—especially by Jesus (see Matt 22:43–45; Mark 12:36–37; Luke 20:42–44), but also by Peter (see Acts 2:34–36) and the author of Hebrews (see especially Heb 1:13; 5:6–10; 7:11–28)—Christians have generally held that this is the most directly "prophetic" of all the psalms. If so, David, speaking prophetically (see 2 Sam 23:2), composed a coronation psalm for his great future Son, of whom the prophets did not speak until later. It may be, however, that David composed the psalm for the coronation of his son Solomon, that he called him "my Lord" (v. 1) in view of his new status, which placed him above the aged David, and that in so doing he spoke a word that had far larger meaning than he knew. This would seem to be in more accord with what we know of David from Samuel, Kings and Chronicles. See introduction to Ps 101.

The psalm falls into two precisely balanced halves (vv. 1–3, 4–7). Each of the two brief oracles (vv. 1,4) is followed by thematically similar elaboration.

Until I make [c]Your enemies a footstool
for Your feet."
2 The LORD will stretch forth Your strong
[a]scepter from Zion, *saying,*
"[b]Rule in the midst of Your enemies."
3 Your [a]people [1]will volunteer freely in
the day of Your [2]power;
[b]In [3]holy array, from the womb of the
dawn,
[4]Your youth are to You *as* the [c]dew.

4 [a]The LORD has sworn and will [b]not
[1]change His mind,
"You are a [c]priest forever
According to the order of
Melchizedek."
5 The Lord is [a]at Your right hand;
He [1]will [b]shatter kings in the [c]day of
His wrath.
6 He will [a]judge among the nations,
He [1]will fill *them* with [b]corpses,
He [2]will [c]shatter the [3]chief men over a
broad country.
7 He will [a]drink from the brook by the
wayside;
Therefore He will [b]lift up *His* head.

Psalm 111

1 [1]Praise [2]the LORD!
I [a]will give thanks to the LORD with all
my heart,

110:1 [c]1 Cor 15:25; Eph 1:22 **2** [a]Ps 45:6; Jer 48:17; Ezek 19:14 [b]Ps 2:9; 72:8; Dan 7:13, 14 **3** [1]Lit *will be freewill offerings* [2]Or *army* [3]Or *the splendor of holiness* [4]Or *The dew of Your youth is Yours* [a]Judg 5:2; Neh 11:2 [b]1 Chr 16:29; Ps 96:9 [c]2 Sam 17:12; Mic 5:7 **4** [1]Lit *be sorry* [a]Heb 7:21 [b]Num 23:19 [c]Zech 6:13; Heb 5:6, 10; 6:20; 7:17, 21 **5** [a]Ps 16:8; 109:31

5 [1]Or *has shattered* [b]Ps 68:14; 76:12 [c]Ps 2:5, 12; Rom 2:5; Rev 6:17 **6** [1]Or *has filled* [2]Or *has shattered* [3]Lit *head over* [a]Is 2:4; Joel 3:12; Mic 4:3 [b]Is 66:24 [c]Ps 68:21 **7** [a]Judg 7:5, 6 [b]Ps 27:6 **111:1** [1]Or *Hallelujah! I will* [2]Heb YAH [a]Ps 35:18; 138:1

110:1–3 The Lord's decree, establishing His anointed as His regent in the face of all opposition (see 2:7–12).

110:1 The first oracle (see note on v. 4). *my Lord.* My sovereign, therefore superior to David (see Matt 22:44–45; Mark 12:36–37; Luke 20:42–44; Acts 2:34–35; Heb 1:13 and their contexts). *Sit.* Sit enthroned. *right hand.* The place of honor beside a king (see 45:9; 1 Kin 2:19); thus he is made second in authority to God Himself. NT references to Jesus' exaltation to this position are many (see Matt 26:64; Mark 14:62; 16:19; Luke 22:69; Acts 2:33; 5:31; 7:55–56; Rom 8:34; Eph 1:20; Col 3:1; Heb 1:3; 8:1; 10:12; 12:2). *enemies.* See note on 2:1–3. *footstool for Your feet.* See Heb 10:12–13. Ancient kings often had themselves portrayed as placing their feet on vanquished enemies (see Josh 10:24). For a royal footstool as part of the throne see 2 Chr 9:18. For the thought here see 1 Kin 5:3. Paul applies this word to Christ in 1 Cor 15:25; Eph 1:22.

110:2 *stretch forth Your strong scepter.* Expand Your reign in ever widening circles until no foe remains to oppose Your rule. *Zion.* David's royal city (see 2 Sam 5:7,9), but also God's (see 9:11 and note), where He rules as the Great King (see Ps 46; 48; 132:13–18). The Lord's anointed is His regent over His emerging kingdom in the world.

110:3 *volunteer freely.* Lit."freewill offerings," i.e., they will offer themselves as dedicated warriors to support You on the battlefield (see Judg 5:2)—as the Israelites offered of their treasures for the building of the tabernacle in the wilderness (see Ex 35:29; 36:3; see also Ezra 1:4; 2:68). Accordingly, Paul speaks of Christ's followers offering their bodies as "a living and holy sacrifice" (Rom 12:1) and of himself as a "drink offering" (Phil 2:17); see also 2 Cor 8:5. *holy array . . . dew.* See NASB marg. If the text is descriptive of the Lord's anointed, as seems likely, it depicts Him as clothed in royal majesty and glory and perpetually preserving the bloom of youth even as the "womb of the dawn" gives birth each morning to the dew (for a different use of this imagery see Is 26:19). If it speaks of the young warriors who flock to Him, it apparently describes them as dressed in priestly garb, ready for participation in a holy war (see 1 Sam 21:4–5; 25:28; 2 Chr 13:8,12; 20:15,21; Is 13:3–4; Jer 6:4; 51:27), and pouring into His camp morning by morning as copious as the dew (see 2 Sam 17:11–12). *holy array.* See note on 29:2.

110:4–7 The Lord's oath establishing His anointed as king-priest in Zion and assuring Him victory over all powers that oppose Him.

110:4 The second oracle (see note on v. 1). *has sworn.* In accordance also with His sworn covenant to maintain David's royal line forever (see 89:35–37). The force of this oath is elaborated by the author of Hebrews (Heb 6:16–18; 7:20–22). *priest . . . order of Melchizedek.* David and his royal sons, as chief representatives of the rule of God, performed many worship-focused activities, such as overseeing the ark of the covenant (see 2 Sam 6:1–15, especially v. 14; 1 Kin 8:1), building and overseeing the temple (see 1 Kin 5–7; 2 Kin 12:4–7; 22:3–7; 23:4–7; 2 Chr 15:8; 24:4–12; 29:3–11; 34:8) and overseeing the work of the priests and Levites and the temple liturgy (see 1 Chr 6:31; 15:11–16; 16:4–42; 23:3–31; 25:1; 2 Chr 17:7–9; 19:8–11; 29:25,30; 31:2; 35:15–16; Ezra 3:10; 8:20; Neh 12:24,36,45). In all these duties they exercised authority over even the high priest. But they could not engage in those specifically priestly functions that had been assigned to the Aaronic priesthood (see 2 Chr 26:16–18). In the present oracle the son of David is installed by God as king-priest in Zion after the manner of Melchizedek, the king-priest of God Most High at Jerusalem in the days of Abraham (see Gen 14:18). As such a king-priest, He was appointed to a higher order of priesthood than that of Aaron and his sons. (For the union of king and priest in one person see Zech 6:13.) What this means for Christ's priesthood is the main theme of Heb 7. *forever.* Permanently and irrevocably; perhaps alluded to in John 12:34.

110:5 *The Lord is at Your right hand.* God is near to assist you in your warfare (see v. 2; 109:31). Some take these words as an address to God: The Lord (David's superior son) is at your (God's) right hand (as in v. 1). *in the day of His wrath.* See 2:5 and note.

110:6 *He.* The Lord's anointed. *fill them with corpses.* Battlefield imagery (borrowed from David's victories) that depicts the victory of the Lord's anointed over all powers that oppose the kingdom of God (see 2:9; Rev 19:11–21).

110:7 *drink from the brook.* Even in the heat of battle He will find refreshment and lift up His head with undiminished vigor (see note on v. 3).

Ps 111 Praise of God for His unfailing righteousness. The psalm combines hymnic praise with wisdom instruction, as its first and last verses indicate. Close comparison with Ps 112 shows that these two psalms are twins, probably written by the same author and intended to be kept together. The two psalms are most likely postexilic. They introduce a series of Hallelujah psalms (Ps 111–118), but stand apart from them in traditional Jewish liturgical use (see introduction to Ps 113). Structurally, both Ps 111 and Ps 112 are alphabetic acrostics, but unique in that each (Hebrew) half-line advances the alphabet. Both psalms are framed by first and last verses that highlight their primary themes, and in both psalms the main body develops the theme introduced by the first verse, while the closing verse adds a counterpart. In both psalms the main body of eight verses falls thematically into two halves of four verses each, with the corresponding verses of each half containing certain thematic links (compare, e.g., 111:2 and 111:6; also vv. 5 and 9).

In the [b]company of the upright and in
the assembly.
2 [a]Great are the works of the LORD;
They are [1b]studied by all who delight
in them.
3 [1a]Splendid and majestic is His
work,
And [b]His righteousness endures
forever.
4 He has made His [1]wonders [2]to be
remembered;
The LORD is [a]gracious and
compassionate.
5 He has [a]given [1]food to those who
[2]fear Him;
He will [b]remember His covenant
forever.
6 He has made known to His people the
power of His works,
In giving them the heritage of the
nations.

7 The works of His hands are [1a]truth
and justice;
All His precepts [b]are [2]sure.
8 They are [a]upheld forever and ever;
They are performed in [1b]truth and
uprightness.
9 He has sent [a]redemption to His
people;
He has [1]ordained His covenant
forever;
[b]Holy and [2]awesome is His name.
10 The [1a]fear of the LORD is the beginning
of wisdom;
A [b]good understanding have all those
who [2]do *His commandments;*
His [c]praise endures forever.

Psalm 112

1 [1]Praise [2]the LORD!
How [a]blessed is the man who [3]fears
the LORD,
Who greatly [b]delights in His
commandments.
2 His [1a]descendants will be mighty [2]on
earth;
The generation of the [b]upright will be
blessed.
3 [a]Wealth and riches are in his house,
And his righteousness endures forever.
4 Light arises in the darkness [a]for the
upright;
He is [b]gracious and compassionate
and righteous.
5 It is well with the man who [a]is
gracious and lends;
He will [1]maintain his cause in
judgment.
6 For he will [a]never be shaken;
The [b]righteous will be [1]remembered
forever.

7 He will not fear [a]evil tidings;
His [b]heart is steadfast, [c]trusting in the
LORD.

111:1 [b]Ps 89:7; 149:1 **2** [1]Lit *sought out* [a]Ps 92:5 [b]Ps 143:5 **3** [1]Lit *Splendor and majesty* [a]Ps 96:6; 145:5 [b]Ps 112:3, 9; 119:142 **4** [1]I.e. wonderful acts [2]Lit *a memorial* [a]Ps 86:5, 15; 103:8; 145:8 **5** [1]Lit *prey* [2]Or *revere* [a]Matt 6:31-33 [b]Ps 105:8 **7** [1]Or *faithfulness* [2]Or *trustworthy* [a]Rev 15:3 [b]Ps 19:7; 93:5 **8** [1]Or *faithfulness* [a]Ps 119:160; Is 40:8; Matt 5:18 [b]Ps 19:9 **9** [1]Lit *commanded* [2]I.e. inspiring reverence [a]Luke 1:68 [b]Ps 99:3; Luke 1:49 **10** [1]Or *reverence for* [a]Job 28:28; Prov 1:7; 9:10; Eccl 12:13

10 [2]Lit *do them* [b]Ps 119:98; Prov 3:4 [c]Ps 145:2 **112:1** [1]Or *Hallelujah!* *Blessed* [2]Heb YAH [3]Or *reveres* [a]Ps 128:1 [b]Ps 1:2; 119:14, 16 **2** [1]Lit *seed* [2]Or *in the land* [a]Ps 102:28; 127:4 [b]Ps 128:4 **3** [a]Prov 3:16; 8:18; Matt 6:33 **4** [a]Job 11:17; Ps 97:11 [b]Ps 37:26 **5** [1]Or *conduct his affairs with justice* [a]Ps 37:21 **6** [1]Lit *for an eternal remembrance* [a]Ps 15:5; 55:22 [b]Prov 10:7 **7** [a]Prov 1:33 [b]Ps 57:7; 108:1 [c]Ps 56:4

Corresponding verses of the two psalms also tend to share common themes (compare, e.g., 111:3–5 with 112:3–5).
111:1 *I will give thanks.* Introductory to the praise that follows in vv. 2–9. *company of the upright.* Probably a more intimate circle than the assembly (see 107:32 for a similar distinction) and referring to those who are truly godly—such as the "upright" of 112:2,4 (see 11:7; 33:1; 49:14; 97:11; 107:42; 140:13). *in the assembly.* See note on 9:1.
111:2 *works of the LORD.* The hymn focuses especially on what God has done for His people. Verses 2,9 sum it up. *studied.* Reflectively examined (see Ezra 10:16, "investigate"; Eccl 1:13, "seek").
111:3 *righteousness.* As embodied in His deeds (see note on 4:1).
111:4 *wonders.* See note on 9:1. *gracious and compassionate.* See Ex 34:6–7 and note.
111:5 *given food.* Illustrative of His bountiful provisions for the daily needs of His people (as in the Lord's prayer: "Give us this day our daily bread," Matt 6:11). *fear.* See v. 10 and note. *His covenant.* See v. 9; see also 105:8–11.
111:6 Cf. v. 2.
111:7 *truth and justice.* Cf. "Splendid and majestic" (v. 3). *precepts are sure.* See note on 93:5.
111:8 *They.* "The works of His hands" (v. 7). *truth and uprightness.* Cf. "gracious and compassionate" (v. 4).
111:9 *sent redemption.* The other great benefit of God's deeds in behalf of His people (cf. "has given food," v. 5). *Holy and awesome.* As shown by His works. *name.* See note on 5:11.
111:10 Concluding word of godly wisdom. *The fear of the LORD is the beginning of wisdom.* The classic OT statement concerning the religious basis of what it means to be wise (see Job 28:28; Prov 1:7; 9:10; see also note on Gen 20:11). *who do His commandments.* Lit. "who do them." The plural Hebrew pronoun refers back to "precepts" in v. 7 (see 19:7–9, where "The fear of the LORD" stands parallel to "testimony," "precepts," "commandment," "judgments"; see also 112:1).
Ps 112 A eulogy to the godly man—in the spirit of Ps 1 but formed after the pattern of Ps 111 and likely intended as its complement (see introduction to Ps 111).
112:1 The basic theme, developed more fully in vv. 2–9. Verse 10 states its converse. See 1:1–2; 128:1. *blessed.* See note on 1:1. *fears the LORD.* See 34:8–14 and note.
112:2 *decendants.* The godly man brings blessing to his children and is himself blessed through them (cf. v. 6; see 37:26; 127:3–5; 128:3; see also note on 109:12). *will be mighty.* Will be persons of influence and reputation.
112:3 *Wealth and riches.* See 1:3; 128:2. *righteousness.* See v. 9; see also note on 1:5. *endures.* It is not an occasional characteristic of his actions (see "steadfast," v. 7).
112:4 *Light.* See note on 27:1. *darkness.* A metaphor for calamitous times (see 107:10 and note). *gracious and compassionate.* See Ex 34:6–7 and note.
112:5 *It is well with.* Well-being and prosperity (see 34:8–14 and note). *gracious and lends.* See v. 9; see also 111:5.
112:6 *shaken.* See note on 10:6. *remembered forever.* His righteousness will have erected an enduring memorial of honor in the memory of both God and man (see v. 2 and note).
112:7 *heart.* See v. 8; see also note on 4:7. *trusting.* His trust in God will be as steadfast as His righteousness is enduring (see v. 3). For trust and obedience to God's righteous will as the

8 His [a]heart is upheld, he [b]will not fear,
Until he [c]looks *with satisfaction* on his adversaries.
9 [1]He [a]has given freely to the poor,
His righteousness endures forever;
His [b]horn will be exalted in honor.

10 The [a]wicked will see it and be [1]vexed,
He will [b]gnash his teeth and [c]melt away;
The [d]desire of the wicked will perish.

Psalm 113

1 [1]Praise [2]the LORD!
[a]Praise, O [b]servants of the LORD,
Praise the name of the LORD.
2 [a]Blessed be the name of the LORD
From this time forth and forever.
3 [a]From the rising of the sun to its setting
The [b]name of the LORD is to be praised.
4 The LORD is [a]high above all nations;
His [b]glory is above the heavens.

5 [a]Who is like the LORD our God,
Who [b]is enthroned on high,
6 Who [1][a]humbles Himself to behold
The things that are in heaven and in the earth?
7 He [a]raises the poor from the dust
And lifts the needy from the ash heap,
8 To make *them* [a]sit with [1]princes,
With the [1]princes of His people.
9 He [a]makes the barren woman abide in the house
As a joyful mother of children.
[1]Praise [2]the LORD!

Psalm 114

1 When Israel went forth [a]from Egypt,
The house of Jacob from a people of [b]strange language,
2 Judah became [a]His sanctuary,
Israel, [b]His dominion.

8 [a]Heb 13:9 [b]Ps 27:1; 56:11; Prov 1:33; 3:24; Is 12:2 [c]Ps 54:7; 59:10 **9** [1]Lit *He has scattered, he has given to...* [a]2 Cor 9:9 [b]Ps 75:10; 89:17; 92:10; 148:14 **10** [1]Or *angry* [a]Ps 86:17 [b]Ps 35:16; 37:12; Matt 8:12; 25:30; Luke 13:28 [c]Ps 58:7 [d]Job 8:13; Prov 10:28; 11:7 **113:1** [1]Or *Hallelujah! Praise* [2]Heb YAH [a]Ps 135:1 [b]Ps 34:22; 69:36; 79:10; 90:13 **2** [a]Ps 145:21; Dan 2:20 **3** [a]Ps 50:1; Is 59:19; Mal 1:11 [b]Ps 18:3; 48:1, 10 **4** [a]Ps 97:9; 99:2 [b]Ps 8:1; 57:11; 148:13 **5** [a]Ex 15:11; Ps 35:10; 89:6

5 [b]Ps 103:19 **6** [1]Or *looks far below in the heavens and on the earth?* [a]Ps 11:4; 138:6; Is 57:15 **7** [a]1 Sam 2:8; Ps 107:41 **8** [1]Or *nobles* [a]Job 36:7 **9** [1]Or *Hallelujah!* [2]Heb YAH [a]1 Sam 2:5; Ps 68:6; Is 54:1 **114:1** [a]Ex 12:51; 13:3 [b]Ps 81:5 **2** [a]Ex 15:17; 29:45, 46; Ps 78:68, 69 [b]Ex 19:6

sum of true godliness see 34:8–14 and note.

112:8 *looks with satisfaction.* "Light arises in the darkness" (v. 4).

112:9 *given freely to the poor.* See v. 5. *exalted in honor.* As God's name is held in holy awe (see 111:9), so the godly man will be held in honor.

112:10 The counterpart. *see it and be vexed.* That godliness is the way to blessedness is the reverse of the expectations of the wicked (see 10:2–11; 107:42). *will perish.* See 1:4–6; see also Ps 37; cf. 111:10.

Ps 113 A hymn to the Lord celebrating His high majesty and His mercies to the lowly (see 138:6). It was probably composed originally for the temple liturgy. This psalm begins the "Egyptian Hallel" (Ps 113–118), which came to be used in Jewish liturgy at the great religious festivals (Passover, Weeks, Booths, Dedication, New Moon; see Lev 23; Num 10:10; John 10:22; see also chart, pp. 164–165). At Passover, Ps 113 and 114 were sung before the meal and Ps 115–118 after the meal. (See introduction to Ps 111.)

Three precisely balanced thematic stanzas (each having three verses) give the psalm a pleasing symmetry. With seven (the number of completeness) verbs the author celebrates God's praise in stanzas two and three ("is high," "is enthroned on high," "humbles Himself," "raises," "lifts," "make them sit," "makes abide")—and note the fourfold praise in the first stanza. At the center (v. 5; see note on 6:6) a rhetorical question focuses and heightens the hymnic theme.

113:1b–3 The fourfold call to praise.

113:1 *name of the LORD.* See vv. 2–3. Triple repetition was a common liturgical convention (see note on 96:1–3). *name.* See note on 5:11.

113:2 *this time forth and forever.* The praise of those who truly praise the Lord cannot rest content until it fills all time—and space (v. 3).

113:4–6 The Lord is enthroned on high, exalted over all creation.

113:4 See the refrain in 57:5,11. *above all nations.* And implicitly over all their gods (see 95:3; 96:4–5; 97:9; see also 47:2,7–8). *above the heavens.* Above even the most exalted aspect of the creation (see v. 6).

113:5 The rhetorical center (see note on 6:6). *our God.* What grace, that He has covenanted to be "our" God (see Gen 17:7; Ex 19:5–6; 20:2)!

113:7–9 The Lord exalts the lowly—the God of highest majesty does not ally Himself with the high and mighty of the earth but stands with and raises up the poor and needy (see 1 Sam 2:3–8; Luke 1:46–55).

113:7–8 Repeated almost verbatim from 1 Sam 2:8.

113:7 *poor . . . needy.* See 9:18; 34:6 and notes. *dust . . . ash heap.* Symbolic of a humble status (see Gen 18:27; 1 Kin 16:2), but here probably also of extreme distress and need (see Job 30:19; 42:6; Is 47:1; Jer 25:34).

113:9 *barren woman.* In that ancient society barrenness was for a woman the greatest disgrace and the deepest tragedy (see Gen 30:1; 1 Sam 1:6–7,10); in her old age she would be as desolate as Naomi because she would have no one to sustain her (see Ruth 1:11–13; see also 2 Kin 4:14). *house.* Family circle. *joyful mother.* Because of God's gracious provision, as in the case of Sarah (see Gen 21:2), Rebekah (see Gen 25:21), Rachel (see Gen 30:23), Hannah (see 1 Sam 1:20), the Shunammite (see 2 Kin 4:17) and others. *Praise the LORD!* Probably once stood at the beginning of Ps 114, which now lacks a Hallelujah.

Ps 114 A hymnic celebration of the exodus—one of the most exquisitely fashioned songs of the Psalter. It probably dates from the period of the monarchy sometime after the division of the kingdom (see v. 2). No doubt it was composed for liturgical use at the temple during one of the annual religious festivals (see introduction to Ps 113). The theme is progressively developed through four balanced thematic stanzas, reaching its climax in the fourth. The first two stanzas (vv. 1–4) recall the great events of the exodus; the last two (vv. 5–8) celebrate their continuing significance.

114:1–2 The great OT redemptive event.

114:1 *Israel . . . house of Jacob.* Synonyms (see Ex 19:3). *went forth from Egypt.* Recalls the exodus and all the great events of the wilderness journey.

114:2 *Judah . . . Israel.* The southern and northern kingdoms, viewed here as the one people of God. *became.* The crucial event was the establishment of the covenant at Sinai, where Israel became bound to the Lord as a "kingdom of priests and a holy nation" (Ex 19:3–6). *His.* The "antecedent" is not expressed until the climax (v. 7). *sanctuary.* His temple in which He took up His residence in the world—symbolized by the tabernacle, later the temple. In Ex 15:17 the promised land is similarly called God's sanctuary. *dominion.* The special realm over

3 The [a]sea looked and fled;
The [b]Jordan turned back.
4 The mountains [a]skipped like rams,
The hills, like lambs.
5 What [a]ails you, O sea, that you flee?
O Jordan, that you turn back?
6 O mountains, that you skip like rams?
O hills, like lambs?

7 [a]Tremble, O earth, before the Lord,
Before the God of Jacob,
8 Who [a]turned the rock into a [b]pool of water,
The [c]flint into a fountain of water.

Psalm 115

1 [a]Not to us, O LORD, not to us,
But [b]to Your name give glory
Because of Your lovingkindness,
because of Your [1]truth.
2 [a]Why should the nations say,
"[b]Where, now, is their God?"
3 But our [a]God is in the heavens;
He [b]does whatever He pleases.
4 Their [a]idols are silver and gold,
The [b]work of man's hands.
5 They have mouths, but they [a]cannot speak;
They have eyes, but they cannot see;
6 They have ears, but they cannot hear;
They have noses, but they cannot smell;
7 [1]They have hands, but they cannot feel;
[2]They have feet, but they cannot walk;
They cannot make a sound with their throat.
8 [a]Those who make them [1]will become like them,
Everyone who trusts in them.

9 O [a]Israel, [b]trust in the LORD;
He is their [c]help and their shield.
10 O house of [a]Aaron, trust in the LORD;
He is their help and their shield.
11 You who [1a]fear the LORD, trust in the LORD;
He is their help and their shield.
12 The LORD [a]has been mindful of us; He will bless *us;*
He will bless the house of Israel;
He will bless the house of Aaron.
13 He will [a]bless those who [1]fear the LORD,
[b]The small together with the great.
14 May the LORD [a]give you increase,
You and your children.
15 May you be blessed of the LORD,
[a]Maker of heaven and earth.

16 The heavens are [a]the heavens of the LORD,

3 [a]Ex 14:21; Ps 77:16 [b]Josh 3:13, 16
4 [a]Ex 19:18; Judg 5:5; Ps 18:7; 29:6; Hab 3:6
5 [a]Hab 3:8
7 [a]Ps 96:9
8 [a]Ex 17:6; Num 20:11; Ps 78:15; 105:41 [b]Ps 107:35 [c]Deut 8:15
115:1 [1]Or *faithfulness* [a]Is 48:11; Ezek 36:22 [b]Ps 29:2; 96:8
2 [a]Ps 79:10 [b]Ps 42:3, 10
3 [a]Ps 103:19 [b]Ps 135:6; Dan 4:35
4 [a]Ps 115:4-8; 135:15-18; Jer 10:4 [b]Deut 4:28; 2 Kin 19:18; Is 37:19; 44:10, 20; Jer 10:3
5 [a]Jer 10:5
7 [1]Lit *Their hands* [2]Lit *Their feet*
8 [1]Or *are like them* [a]Ps 135:18; Is 44:9-11
9 [a]Ps 118:2; 135:19 [b]Ps 37:3; 62:8 [c]Ps 33:20
10 [a]Ps 118:3; 135:19
11 [1]Or *revere* [a]Ps 22:23; 103:11; 135:20
12 [a]Ps 98:3
13 [1]Or *revere* [a]Ps 103:11; 112:1; 128:1 [b]Rev 11:18; 19:5
14 [a]Deut 1:11 **15** [a]Gen 1:1; Neh 9:6; Ps 96:5; 102:25; 121:2; 124:8; 134:3; 146:6; Acts 14:15; Rev 14:7 **16** [a]Ps 89:11

which He ruled as King. This, rather than the exodus itself, was the great wonder of God's grace.

114:3–4 The author evokes a fearsome scene such as that portrayed by other poets (see 18:7–15; 68:7–8; 77:16–19; Judg 5:4–5; Hab 3:3–10).

114:3 *sea . . . Jordan.* The Red Sea and the Jordan River, through which the Lord brought His people—here they are personified. *looked and fled.* Saw the mighty God approach in His awesome pillar of cloud and fled.

114:4 *skipped.* Or "leaped"; the mountains and hills quaked at God's approach (see 29:6).

114:7–8 The Lord of yesterday (vv. 5–6)—the God of Jacob—is still with us.

114:7 *Tremble.* In awesome recognition. *earth.* All creation. *Jacob.* A synonym for Israel (see Gen 32:28).

114:8 *turned the rock into a pool.* Thus sustaining and refreshing life (see Ex 17:6; Num 20:11).

Ps 115 Praise of the Lord, the one true God, for His love and faithfulness toward His people. It was composed as a liturgy of praise for the temple worship. It may have been written for use at the dedication of the second temple (see Ezra 6:16) when Israel was beginning to revive after the disruption of the exile. See introduction to Ps 113. Structurally, the song advances in five movements involving a liturgical exchange between the people and temple personnel: (1) vv. 1–8: the people; (2) vv. 9–11: Levitical choir leader (the refrain perhaps spoken by the Levitical choir); (3) vv. 12–13: the people; (4) vv. 14–15: the priests; (5) vv. 16–18: the people.

115:1–8 Praise of God's love and faithfulness toward His people, which silences the taunts of the nations.

115:1 *Not to us . . . not to us.* Israel's existence, and now her revival, is not her own achievement. *name.* See note on 5:11. *lovingkindness . . . truth.* The most common OT expression for God's covenant benefits (see note on 26:3; see also NASB marg.). *lovingkindness.* See note on 6:4.

115:2 *Where . . . is their God?* The taunt of the nations when Israel is decimated by natural disasters (see Joel 2:17) or crushed by enemies, especially when Judah is destroyed and the temple of God razed (see 79:10; Mic 7:10).

115:3 *is in the heavens.* Sits enthroned (see 113:5) in the "heavens of the LORD" (v. 16). *whatever He pleases.* If Israel is decimated or destroyed, it is God's doing; it is not His failure or inability to act, nor is it the achievement of the idols the nations worship. And when Israel is revived, that is also God's doing, and no other god can oppose Him.

115:4–7 Whatever glory and power the false gods are thought to have (as symbolized in the images made to represent them), they are mere figments of human imagination and utterly worthless (see 135:15–18; Is 46:1–7).

115:8 *Those who make them.* The taunting nations (cf. v. 2). *like them.* Powerless and ineffectual. For a graphic elaboration of this truth see Is 44:9–20.

115:9–11 The call to trust in the Lord, not in idols (see v. 8). For triple repetition as a liturgical convention see note on 96:1–3. For the same groupings see 118:2–4; see also 135:19–20.

115:11 *You who fear the LORD.* Perhaps proselytes (see 1 Kin 8:41–43; Ezra 6:21; Neh 10:28).

115:12–13 The people's confession of trust.

115:14–15 The priestly blessing.

115:14 *give you increase.* In numbers, wealth and strength (cf. Eccl 2:9: "became great and increased more than").

115:16–18 The people's concluding doxology.

115:16 *heavens . . . earth.* The one the exclusive realm of the exalted, all-sovereign God; the other the divinely appointed

But [b]the earth He has given to the
sons of men.
17 The [a]dead do not praise [1]the LORD,
Nor *do* any who go down into
[b]silence;
18 But as for us, we will [a]bless [1]the LORD
From this time forth and forever.
[2]Praise [1]the LORD!

Psalm 116

1 [a]I love the LORD, because He [b]hears
My voice *and* my supplications.
2 Because He has [a]inclined His ear to
me,
Therefore I shall call *upon Him* as
long as I live.
3 The [a]cords of death encompassed me
And the [1]terrors of [2]Sheol [3]came upon
me;
I found distress and sorrow.
4 Then [a]I called upon the name of the
LORD:
"O LORD, I beseech You, [1b]save my life!"

5 [a]Gracious is the LORD, and [b]righteous;
Yes, our God is [c]compassionate.
6 The LORD preserves [a]the simple;
I was [b]brought low, and He saved me.
7 Return to your [a]rest, O my soul,
For the LORD has [b]dealt bountifully
with you.
8 For You have [a]rescued my soul from
death,
My eyes from tears,
My feet from stumbling.
9 I shall walk before the LORD
In the [1a]land of the living.
10 I [a]believed when I said,
"I am [b]greatly afflicted."
11 I [a]said in my alarm,
"[b]All men are liars."

12 What shall I [a]render to the LORD
For all His [b]benefits [1]toward me?
13 I shall lift up the [a]cup of salvation
And [b]call upon the name of the LORD.
14 I shall [a]pay my vows to the LORD,
Oh *may it be* [b]in the presence of all
His people.
15 [a]Precious in the sight of the LORD
Is the death of His godly ones.
16 O LORD, [1]surely I am [a]Your servant,
I am Your servant, the [b]son of Your
handmaid,

16 [b]Ps 8:6 **17** [1]Heb YAH [a]Ps 6:5; 88:10-12; Is 38:18 [b]Ps 31:17 **18** [1]Heb YAH [2]Or *Hallelujah!* [a]Ps 113:2; Dan 2:20 **116:1** [a]Ps 18:1 [b]Ps 6:8; 66:19; Is 37:17; Dan 9:18 **2** [a]Ps 17:6; 31:2; 40:1 **3** [1]Lit *straits* [2]I.e. the nether world [3]Lit *found me* [a]Ps 18:4, 5 **4** [1]Or *deliver my soul* [a]Ps 18:6; 118:5 [b]Ps 17:13; 22:20 **5** [a]Ps 86:15; 103:8 [b]Ezra 9:15; Neh 9:8; Ps 119:137; 145:17; Jer 12:1; Dan 9:14 [c]Ex 34:6 **6** [a]Ps 19:7; Prov 1:4 [b]Ps 79:8; 142:6 **7** [a]Jer 6:16; Matt 11:29 [b]Ps 13:6; 142:7 **8** [a]Ps 49:15; 56:13; 86:13 **9** [1]Lit *lands* [a]Ps 27:13 **10** [a]2 Cor 4:13 [b]Ps 88:7

11 [a]Ps 31:22 [b]Ps 62:9; Rom 3:4 **12** [1]Lit *upon* [a]2 Chr 32:25; 1 Thess 3:9 [b]Ps 103:2 **13** [a]Ps 16:5 [b]Ps 80:18; 105:1 **14** [a]Ps 50:14; 116:18 [b]Ps 22:25 **15** [a]Ps 72:14 **16** [1]Or *because* [a]Ps 86:16; 119:125; 143:12 [b]Ps 86:16

place for man, where he lives under God's rule and care, enjoys His abundant blessings (vv. 12–13) and celebrates His praise (v. 18).

115:17 *dead do not.* The dead no longer live in "the earth" (v. 16) but have descended to the silent realm below, where blessings are no longer enjoyed and hence praise is absent (see notes on 6:5; 30:1).

Ps 116 Praise of the Lord for deliverance from death. It may have been written by a king (see v. 16 and note; cf. also Hezekiah's thanksgiving, Is 38:10–20); its language echoes many of the psalms of David. As used in Jewish liturgy (see introduction to Ps 113), the singular personal pronoun must have been used corporately (see note on Ps 30 title), and the references to "death" may have been understood as alluding to the Egyptian bondage and/or the exile. This thanksgiving song falls into three main divisions (vv. 1–6, 7–14, 15–19), each of which contains a unified thematic development.

116:1–6 I love the Lord because He has heard and saved me.

116:2 *I shall call upon Him.* In Him I will trust and my prayers will ever be to Him—a declaration repeated in each of the main divisions (see vv. 13,17).

116:3–4 See 18:4–6.

116:3 *cords of death.* See note on 18:5.

116:5 *our God.* The author is conscious of those about him; he is praising the Lord "in the presence of all His people" (vv. 14,18).

116:6 *simple.* The person who is childlike in his sense of dependence on and trust in the Lord (see note on 19:7).

116:7–14 The Lord's goodness to me and how I will repay Him.

116:7 *rest.* A state of unthreatened well-being (cf. Jer 6:16; see 1 Kin 5:4; see also note on 23:2, "quiet waters"). *O my soul.* See note on 103:1–2,22. *has dealt bountifully.* The Hebrew underlying this phrase is the same as that underlying "benefits" in v. 12 (see note there) and so marks v. 7 as introductory to vv. 7–14.

116:8 *my soul.* Me (see note on 6:3).

116:10 *I believed.* The author speaks of his faith that moved him to call on the Lord when he was threatened. *I am greatly afflicted.* This and the quotation in v. 11 should perhaps be taken, together with the one in v. 4, as a brief recollection of the prayer offered when the psalmist was in distress. The threat of death from which he had been delivered was brought on by the false accusations of enemies, as in Ps 109 (see notes on 5:9; 10:7). (For another interpretation see following note.)

116:11 *All men are liars.* The heart of the accusation he had lodged against his false accusers (for examples of similar accusations see 5:9–10; 35:11,15; 109:2–4). Others interpret these words as a declaration that all men offer but a false hope for deliverance (see 60:11; 118:8–9)—therefore the psalmist called on the Lord.

116:12 *What shall I render . . . ?* Expressions of devotion He desires (compare vv. 13–14,17–18 with 50:14–15,23). *benefits.* The Hebrew for this word occurs only here in the OT, but represents the same basic root as "has dealt bountifully" in v. 7 (see note there).

116:13 *cup of salvation.* Often thought to be related to the cup of the Passover meal referred to in Matt 26:27 and parallels, but far more likely the cup of wine drunk at the festal meal that climaxed a thank offering (cf. 22:26,29; Lev 7:11–21)—called the "cup of salvation" because the thank offering and its meal celebrated deliverance by the Lord. See the parallel with "sacrifice of thanksgiving" in the corresponding series in vv. 17–18.

116:14 *vows.* To praise the Lord (see note on 7:17).

116:15–19 Because God has counted my life precious, I offer Him the expressions of my devotion.

116:15 *Precious . . . Is the death.* Not in the sense of highly valued but of that which is carefully watched over; cf. the analogous expression, "their blood will be precious in His sight" (72:14). *godly ones.* See note on 4:3.

116:16 *Your servant.* This may identify the psalmist as the Lord's anointed (see 78:70), but in any event as one devoted to the Lord (see 19:11,13). *son of Your handmaid.* See 86:16.

You have [c]loosed my bonds.
17 To You I shall offer [a]a sacrifice of
thanksgiving,
And [b]call upon the name of the LORD.
18 I shall [a]pay my vows to the LORD,
Oh *may it be* in the presence of all His
people,
19 In the [a]courts of the LORD's house,
In the midst of you, O [b]Jerusalem.
[1]Praise [2]the LORD!

Psalm 117

1 [a]Praise the LORD, all nations;
Laud Him, all peoples!
2 For His [a]lovingkindness [1]is great
toward us,
And the [2b]truth of the LORD is
everlasting.
[3]Praise [4]the LORD!

Psalm 118

1 [a]Give thanks to the LORD, for [b]He is
good;
For His lovingkindness is everlasting.
2 Oh let [a]Israel say,
"His lovingkindness is everlasting."
3 Oh let the [a]house of Aaron say,
"His lovingkindness is everlasting."
4 Oh let those [a]who [1]fear the LORD say,
"His lovingkindness is everlasting."
5 From *my* [a]distress I called upon [1]the
LORD;
[1]The LORD answered me *and* [b]*set me*
in a large place.
6 The LORD is [a]for me; I will [b]not fear;
[c]What can man do to me?
7 The LORD is for me [a]among those who
help me;
Therefore I will [b]look *with satisfaction*
on those who hate me.
8 It is [a]better to take refuge in the LORD
Than to trust in man.
9 It is [a]better to take refuge in the LORD
Than to trust in princes.

10 All nations [a]surrounded me;
In the name of the LORD I will surely
[b]cut them off.
11 They [a]surrounded me, yes, they
surrounded me;
In the name of the LORD I will surely
cut them off.
12 They surrounded me [a]like bees;
They were extinguished as a [b]fire of
thorns;
In the name of the LORD I will surely
cut them off.
13 You [a]pushed me violently so that I
[1]was falling,

16 [c]Ps 107:14 **17** [a]Lev 7:12; Ps 50:14 [b]Ps 116:13 **18** [a]Ps 116:14 **19** [1]Or *Hallelujah!* [2]Heb YAH [a]Ps 92:13; 96:8; 135:2 [b]Ps 102:21
117:1 [a]Rom 15:11 **2** [1]Lit *prevails over us* [2]Or *faithfulness* [3]Or *Hallelujah!* [4]Heb YAH [a]Ps 103:11 [b]Ps 100:5; 146:6
118:1 [a]1 Chr 16:8, 34; Ps 106:1; 107:1; Jer 33:11 [b]2 Chr 5:13; 7:3; Ezra 3:11; Ps 100:5; 136:1-26 **2** [a]Ps 115:9 **3** [a]Ps 115:10 **4** [1]Or *revere* [a]Ps 115:11
5 [1]Heb YAH [a]Ps 18:6; 86:7; 120:1 [b]Ps 18:19 **6** [a]Job 19:27; Ps 56:9; Heb 13:6 [b]Ps 23:4; 27:1 [c]Ps 56:4, 11 **7** [a]Ps 54:4 [b]Ps 54:7; 59:10 **8** [a]2 Chr 32:7, 8; Ps 40:4; 108:12; Is 31:1, 3; 57:13; Jer 17:5 **9** [a]Ps 146:3 **10** [a]Ps 3:6; 88:17 [b]Ps 18:40
11 [a]Ps 88:17 **12** [a]Deut 1:44 [b]Ps 58:9; Nah 1:10 **13** [1]Or *fell* [a]Ps 140:4

116:19 *courts.* Of the temple (see 84:2,10; 2 Kin 21:5; 23:11–12).

Ps 117 The shortest psalm in the Psalter—and the shortest chapter in the Bible—Ps 117 is an expanded Hallelujah (sometimes joined with Ps 118). It may originally have served as the conclusion to the preceding collection of Hallelujah psalms (Ps 111–116)—of which it is the seventh. All nations and peoples are called on to praise the Lord (as in 47:1; 67:3–5; 96:7; 98:4; 100:1; see note on 9:1) for His great love and enduring faithfulness toward Israel (see Is 12:4–6). Thus the Hallelujahs of the OT Psalter, when fully expounded, express that great truth, so often emphasized in the OT, that the destiny of all peoples is involved in what God was doing in and for His people Israel (see, e.g., 2:8–12; 47:9; 67:2; 72:17; 102:15; 110; Gen 12:3; Deut 32:43; 1 Kin 8:41–43; Is 2:2–4; 11:10; 14:2; 25:6–7; 52:15; 56:7; 60:3; 66:18–24; Jer 3:17; 16:19–21; 33:9; Amos 9:11–12; Mic 5:7–9; Zeph 3:8–9; Hag 2:7; Zech 2:10–11; 8:20–23; 9:9–10; 14:2–3; Mal 3:12). See introduction to Ps 113.

117:1 Quoted in Rom 15:11 as proof that the salvation of Gentiles and the glorifying of God by Gentiles was not a divine afterthought.

117:2 The reason for the praise. *lovingkindness . . . truth.* That is, lovingkindness-and-truth (see NASB marg.; 36:5 and note; also note on 3:7). *lovingkindness.* See note on 6:4.

Ps 118 A hymn of thanksgiving for deliverance from enemies. Of the many interpretations of this psalm, three have gained the most adherents (but with much variation in detail): 1. A Davidic king leads the nation in a liturgy of thanksgiving for deliverance and victory after a hard-fought battle with a powerful confederacy of nations (cf. 2 Chr 20:27–28; see note on v. 19). 2. Israel celebrates—probably at the Feast of Booths—her deliverance from Egypt and victory over the Canaanites. 3. The postexilic Jews celebrate deliverance from their enemies, either at the dedication of the second temple (see Ezra 6:16) or at the dedication of the rebuilt walls of Jerusalem (see Neh 12:37–43). According to the first interpretation, the speaker in vv. 5–21 is the king; according to the second and third, the speaker is the Levitical (or priestly) leader of the liturgy, speaking (representatively) on behalf of the people. The notes that follow assume the first interpretation. In the postexilic liturgy developed for the annual festivals (see introduction to Ps 113), the song was used as a thanksgiving for national deliverance. As the last song of that liturgy, it may have been the hymn sung by Jesus and His disciples at the conclusion of the Last Supper (see Matt 26:30).

Following a liturgical call to praise (vv. 1–4), the king offers a song of thanksgiving for deliverance and victory in battle (vv. 5–21). In vv. 22–27 the people rejoice over what the Lord has done. Thereafter, the king speaks his final word of praise (v. 28), and a liturgical conclusion (v. 29) repeats the opening call to praise, thus framing the whole service.

118:1–4 The liturgical call to praise.

118:1 A conventional call to praise (shared in whole or in part with Ps 105–107; 136; 1 Chr 16:8,34; 2 Chr 20:21). *Give thanks.* See note on Ps 100 title. This, together with vv. 2–4 (except for the refrain) and 29, may have been by the same voice that speaks in vv. 5–21. *lovingkindness.* See vv. 2–4,29; see also note on 6:4.

118:2–4 *Israel . . . house of Aaron . . . those who fear the LORD.* See 115:9–11 and note. Triple repetition is a common feature in this psalm (see note on 96:1–3).

118:5–21 The king's song of thanksgiving for deliverance and victory.

118:5 *in a large place.* See 18:19 and note ("broad place").

118:7 *I will look.* Or "I look."

118:8–9 See 33:16–19; see also Ps 62; 146.

118:10 *In the name of the LORD.* See 1 Sam 17:45. *name.* See vv. 11–12,26; see also note on 5:11.

118:12 *as a fire of thorns.* See 58:9 and note.

But the LORD [b]helped me.
14 [1a]The LORD is my strength and song,
And He has become [b]my salvation.

15 The sound of [a]joyful shouting and salvation is in the tents of the righteous;
The [b]right hand of the LORD does valiantly.
16 The [a]right hand of the LORD is exalted;
The right hand of the LORD does valiantly.
17 I [a]will not die, but live,
And [b]tell of the works of [1]the LORD.
18 [1]The LORD has [a]disciplined me severely,
But He has [b]not given me over to death.

19 [a]Open to me the gates of righteousness;
I shall enter through them, I shall give thanks to [1]the LORD.
20 This is the gate of the LORD;
The [a]righteous will enter through it.
21 I shall give thanks to You, for You have [a]answered me,
And You have [b]become my salvation.

22 The [a]stone which the builders rejected
Has become the chief corner *stone*.
23 This is [1]the LORD's doing;
It is marvelous in our eyes.
24 This is the day which the LORD has made;
Let us [a]rejoice and be glad in it.
25 O LORD, [a]do save, we beseech You;
O LORD, we beseech You, do send [b]prosperity!
26 [a]Blessed is the one who comes in the name of the LORD;
We have [b]blessed you from the house of the LORD.
27 [a]The LORD is God, and He has given us [b]light;
Bind the festival sacrifice with cords [1]to the [c]horns of the altar.
28 [a]You are my God, and I give thanks to You;
You are my God, [b]I extol You.
29 [a]Give thanks to the LORD, for He is good;
For His lovingkindness is everlasting.

Psalm 119

א Aleph.

1 How blessed are those whose way is [1a]blameless,

13 [b]Ps 86:17
14 [1]Heb *YAH* [a]Ex 15:2; Is 12:2 [b]Ps 27:1
15 [a]Ps 68:3 [b]Ex 15:6; Ps 89:13; Luke 1:51
16 [a]Ex 15:6; Ps 89:13
17 [1]Heb *YAH* [a]Ps 6:5; 116:8, 9; Hab 1:12 [b]Ps 73:28; 107:22
18 [1]Heb *YAH* [a]Ps 73:14; Jer 31:18; 1 Cor 11:32; 2 Cor 6:9 [b]Ps 86:13
19 [1]Heb *YAH* [a]Is 26:2
20 [a]Ps 15:1, 2; 24:3-6; 140:13; Is 35:8; Rev 22:14
21 [a]Ps 116:1; 118:5 [b]Ps 118:14
22 [a]Matt 21:42; Mark 12:10, 11; Luke 20:17; Acts 4:11; Eph 2:20; 1 Pet 2:7
23 [1]Lit *from the* LORD
24 [a]Ps 31:7
25 [a]Ps 106:47 [b]Ps 122:6, 7
26 [a]Matt 21:9; 23:39; Mark 11:9; Luke 13:35; 19:38; John 12:13 [b]Ps 129:8
27 [1]Lit *unto* [a]1 Kin 18:39 [b]Esth 8:16; Ps 18:28; 27:1; 1 Pet 2:9 [c]Ex 27:2
28 [a]Ps 63:1; 140:6 [b]Ex 15:2; Is 25:1
29 [a]Ps 118:1
119:1 [1]Lit *complete;* or *having integrity* [a]Ps 101:2, 6; Prov 11:20; 13:6

118:13 *was falling.* About to be killed (see vv. 17–18; see also note on 13:4).
118:14 Perhaps recalls the triumph song of Ex 15, but more likely the verse had become a widely used testimony of praise (see Is 12:2).
118:15 *tents.* Dwellings. *righteous.* Israel as the people (ideally) committed in heart and life to the Lord (see v. 20; see also 68:3 and note). Cf. "the tents of wickedness" (84:10).
118:17 *live, And tell.* See 115:17–18; see also note on 6:5.
118:18 *disciplined me.* The king acknowledges that the grave threat through which he has passed has also served God's purpose—to discipline him and teach him humble godliness (see 6:1; 38:1; 94:12; Deut 4:36; 8:5).
118:19 *Open to me.* This line suggests a liturgical procession (see v. 27) in which the king approaches the inner court of the temple at the head of the jubilant worshipers (see Ps 24; 68). *gates.* Those leading to the inner temple court. *of righteousness.* Often thought to be the name of a particular gateway, but more likely only descriptive here of the gate through which "the righteous will enter" (v. 20). It is possible that the procession began outside the city and that "the gates of righteousness" are the gates of Jerusalem, the city of God (see note on 24:7; see also Is 26:2).
118:21 This closing verse of the thanksgiving song echoes the "Give thanks" of v. 1, the "answered . . . me" of v. 5 and the testimony of v. 14.
118:22–27 The people's exultation.
118:22 *The stone . . . the builders rejected.* Most likely a reference to the king (whose deliverance and victory are being celebrated), who had been looked on with disdain by the kings invading his realm—the builders of worldly empires. Others suppose that the stone refers to Israel, a nation held in contempt by the world powers. *chief corner stone.* Lit. "head of the corner"—either a capstone over a door (a large stone used as a lintel), or a large stone used to anchor and align the corner of a wall, or the keystone of an arch (see Zech 4:7; 10:4). By a wordplay (pun) the author hints at "chief ruler" (the Hebrew word for "corner" is sometimes used as a metaphor for leader/ruler; see Is 19:13; see also Judg 20:2; 1 Sam 14:38). This stone, disdained by the worldly powers, has become the most important stone in the structure of the new world order that God is bringing about through Israel. Jesus applied this verse (and v. 23) to Himself (see Matt 21:42; Mark 12:10–11; Luke 20:17; see also Acts 4:11; Eph 2:20; 1 Pet 2:7).
118:24 *day which the LORD has made . . . rejoice.* This day of rejoicing was made possible by God's deliverance in the victory being celebrated. Others suppose a reference to Passover or the Feast of Booths. *has made.* Or "has done it" (see vv. 15–17, 23)—has made the "stone" the "corner stone" (v. 22).
118:25 Prayer for the Lord to continue to save and sustain His people.
118:26 *who comes in the name of the LORD.* The one who with God's help had defeated the enemies "in the name of the LORD" (see vv. 10–12). *from the house of the LORD.* From God's very presence (see 134:3). *you.* The plural ("you" is plural in the Hebrew) may have been used to exalt the king (the plural was often used with reference to God), whom God had so singularly blessed (as in 1 Kin 9:6). Alternatively, it may refer to those who have come with the king victoriously from the battle. The crowds who greeted Jesus at His Triumphal Entry into Jerusalem used the words of vv. 25–26 (see John 12:13).
118:27 *He has given us light.* An echo of the priestly benediction (see Num 6:25). *Bind . . . with cords.* Apparently a call to complete the climax of the liturgy of a thank offering (see Lev 7:11–21), though others suggest the liturgy of the Feast of Booths.
118:28–29 See introduction.
Ps 119 A devotional on the word of God. The author was an

Who [b]walk in the law of the LORD.
2 How blessed are those who [a]observe
His testimonies,
Who [b]seek Him [c]with all *their* heart.
3 They also [a]do no unrighteousness;
They walk in His ways.
4 You have [1a]ordained Your precepts,
[2]That we should keep *them* diligently.
5 Oh that my [a]ways may be established
To [b]keep Your statutes!
6 Then I [a]shall not be ashamed
When I look [1]upon all Your
commandments.

119:1 [b]Ps 128:1; Ezek 11:20; 18:17; Mic 4:2 **2** [a]Ps 25:10; 99:7; 119:22, 168 [b]Deut 4:29; Ps 119:10 [c]Deut 6:5; 10:12; 11:13; 13:3; 30:2 **3** [a]1 John 3:9; 5:18 **4** [1]Lit *commanded* [2]Lit *To keep* [a]Deut 4:13; Neh 9:13 **5** [a]Ps 40:2; Prov 4:26 [b]Deut 12:1; 2 Chr 7:17 **6** [1]Lit *to* [a]Job 22:26; Ps 119:80

7 I shall [a]give thanks to You with
uprightness of heart,
When I learn Your righteous judgments.
8 I shall keep Your statutes;
Do not [a]forsake me utterly!

ב Beth.

9 How can a young man keep his way
pure?
By [a]keeping *it* according to Your word.
10 With [a]all my heart I have sought You;

7 [a]Ps 119:62 **8** [a]Ps 38:21; 71:9, 18 **9** [a]1 Kin 2:4; 8:25; 2 Chr 6:16 **10** [a]2 Chr 15:15; Ps 119:2, 145

Israelite of exemplary piety (probably postexilic) who (1) was passionately devoted to the word of God as the word of life; (2) humbly acknowledged, nevertheless, the errant ways of his heart and life; (3) knew the pain—but also the fruits—of God's corrective discipline; and (4) had suffered much at the hands of those who arrogantly disregarded God's word and made him the target of their hostility, ridicule and slander. It is possible that he was a priest (see notes on vv. 23,57)—and the psalm might well be a vehicle for priestly instruction in godliness. He elaborated on the themes of 19:7–13 and interwove with them many prayers for deliverance, composing a massive alphabetic acrostic (the psalm is an acrostic poem; the verses of each stanza begin with the same letter of the Hebrew alphabet) that demands patient, meditative reading. In regard to length, form and type it stands alone in the Psalter. And of all the psalms, this one is the most likely to have been composed originally in writing and intended to be read rather than sung or recited. Most of its lines are addressed to God, mingling prayers with professions of devotion to God's law. Yet, as the opening verses (and perhaps also its elaborate acrostic form) make clear, it was intended for godly instruction (in the manner of Ps 1; see v. 9 and note). It was included in the Psalter no doubt as a model of piety.

Whereas elsewhere in the Psalter the focus falls primarily on God's mighty acts of creation and redemption and His rule over all the world, here devotion to the word of God (and the God of the word) is the dominant theme. The author highlights two aspects of that word: (1) God's directives for life and (2) God's promises—the one calling for obedience, the other for faith (the two elements of true godliness; see 34:8–14 and note). In referring to these, he makes use of eight Hebrew terms supplied him by OT traditions: *torah,* "law"; *'edot,* "statutes"; *piqqudim,* "precepts"; *miṣwot,* "commands, commandments"; *mishpaṭim,* "laws" (all shared with 19:7–9; *mishpaṭim* is translated "judgments" in 19:9); *ḥuqqim,* "decrees"; *dabar,* "word" (sometimes in the sense of "law," sometimes in the sense of "promise"); *'imrah,* "word," but more often "promise." These terms he distributes throughout the 22 stanzas (using all eight in *He, Waw, Heth, Yodh, Kaph, Pe*—never using less than six), employing a different order in each stanza. It may be that the availability of these eight terms determined (in large part) for the author the decision to devote eight verses to each letter of the alphabet. The alphabetic acrostic form, especially one as elaborate as this, may appear arbitrary and artificial to a modern reader (as if the author merely selected a traditional form from the poet's workshop and then labored to fill it with pious sentences), but a sympathetic and reflective reading of this devotional will compel a more favorable judgment. The author had a theme that filled his soul, a theme as big as life, that ranged the length and breadth and height and depth of a person's walk with God. Nothing less than the use of the full power of language would suffice, and of that the alphabet was a most apt symbol.

Apart from the obvious formal structure dictated by the chosen acrostic form, little need (or can) be said. It must be noted, however, that the first three and the last three verses were designed as introduction and conclusion to the whole. The former sets the tone of instruction in godly wisdom; the latter succinctly restates and summarizes the main themes. It may also be observed that the middle of the psalm has been marked by a similar three-verse introduction to the second half (see note on vv. 89–91). For the rest, the thought meanders, turns back upon itself and repeats (with varied nuances). The following notes point out continuities of thought and possible structure within stanzas.

119:1–3 General introduction.

119:1–2 *blessed.* See note on 1:1.

119:1 *whose way is blameless.* This opening general description is further elaborated in the rest of the introduction, which concludes with an equally general statement: "They walk in His ways" (v. 3). See Gen 17:1; cf. Gen 26:5. *law.* Hebrew *torah,* a collective term for God's covenant directives for His people (see Deut 4:44). "Law" often came, especially later, to have a broader reference—the whole Pentateuch (see Luke 24:44) or even the whole OT (see John 15:25; 1 Cor 14:21)—but here it is limited by the synonyms with which it is used interchangeably.

119:2 *testimonies.* Hebrew *'edot,* a specifically covenantal term referring to stipulations laid down by the covenant Lord (see 25:10; Deut 4:45). *heart.* See v. 7; see also note on 4:7.

119:3 *ways.* The Hebrew for this word occurs only rarely in this psalm, but is common in Deuteronomy and elsewhere as a general reference to God's covenant requirements (see note on 25:4)—used here to balance "way" in v. 1.

119:4–8 Those who obey God's law (see vv. 4–5,8) can hope for God's help (see vv. 6–8).

119:4 *precepts.* Hebrew *piqqudim,* covenant regulations laid down by the Lord (see 19:8; 111:7).

119:5 *statutes.* Hebrew *ḥuqqim,* covenant directives (see Deut 6:2; 28:15,45; 30:10,16; 1 Kin 11:11), emphasizing their fixed character.

119:6 *not be ashamed.* The psalmist would not suffer poverty or sickness, or humiliation at the hands of his enemies, and so become the object of sneers (see vv. 31,46,80; 25:2–3,20), but he would have reason to praise the Lord (see v. 7) for blessings received and deliverances granted because the Lord does not forsake him (see v. 8). *look upon.* Respect, have regard for (see v. 15; 74:20). *commandments.* Hebrew *miṣwot,* covenant directives (see Ex 20:6; 24:12; Deut 4:2), designated specifically as that which God has commanded.

119:7 *righteous.* One of the author's favorite characterizations of God's law (see vv. 62,75,106,123,144,160,164; see also 19:9). *judgments.* Hebrew *mishpaṭim,* covenant directives (see Ex 21:1; 24:3; Deut 4:1), as the laws laid down by a ruler (king).

119:8 *not forsake me.* Not abandon me to poverty, sickness or my enemies.

Do not let me [b]wander from Your
commandments.
11 Your word I have [a]treasured in my
heart,
That I may not sin against You.
12 Blessed are You, O LORD;
[a]Teach me Your statutes.
13 With my lips I have [a]told of
All the [b]ordinances of Your mouth.
14 I have [a]rejoiced in the way of Your
testimonies,
[1]As much as in all riches.
15 I will [a]meditate on Your precepts
And [1]regard [b]Your ways.
16 I shall [1a]delight in Your statutes;
I shall [b]not forget Your word.

ג Gimel.

17 [a]Deal bountifully with Your servant,
That I may live and keep Your word.
18 Open my eyes, that I may behold
Wonderful things from Your law.
19 I am a [a]stranger in the earth;
Do not hide Your commandments
from me.
20 My soul is crushed [1a]with longing
After Your ordinances at all times.
21 You [a]rebuke the arrogant, [1]the
[b]cursed,
Who [c]wander from Your
commandments.
22 [a]Take away reproach and contempt
from me,
For I [b]observe Your testimonies.
23 Even though [a]princes sit *and* talk
against me,
Your servant [b]meditates on Your
statutes.
24 Your testimonies also are my [a]delight;
They are [1]my counselors.

ד Daleth.

25 My [a]soul cleaves to the dust;
[b]Revive me [c]according to Your word.
26 I have told of my ways, and You have
answered me;
[a]Teach me Your statutes.
27 Make me understand the way of Your
precepts,
So I will [a]meditate on Your wonders.
28 My [a]soul [1]weeps because of grief;
[b]Strengthen me according to Your
word.
29 Remove the false way from me,
And graciously grant me Your law.
30 I have chosen the faithful way;
I have [1]placed Your ordinances *before*
me.
31 I [a]cling to Your testimonies;

10 [b]Ps 119:21, 118 **11** [a]Ps 37:31; 40:8; Luke 2:19, 51 **12** [a]Ps 119:26, 64, 108, 124, 135, 171 **13** [a]Ps 40:9 [b]Ps 119:72 **14** [1]Lit *As over all* [a]Ps 119:111, 162 **15** [1]Or *look upon* [a]Ps 1:2; 119:23, 48, 78, 97; 148 [b]Ps 25:4; 27:11; Is 58:2 **16** [1]Lit *delight myself* [a]Ps 1:2; 119:24, 35, 47, 70, 77, 92, 143, 174 [b]Ps 119:93 **17** [a]Ps 13:6; 116:7 **19** [a]Gen 47:9; Lev 25:23; 1 Chr 29:15; Ps 39:12; 119:54; Heb 11:13 **20** [1]Lit *for* [a]Ps 42:1, 2; 63:1; 84:2; 119:40, 131 **21** [1]Or *Cursed are those who wander...* [a]Ps 68:30 [b]Deut 27:26; Ps 37:22 [c]Ps 119:10, 118 **22** [a]Ps 39:8; 119:39 [b]Ps 119:2 **23** [a]Ps 119:161 [b]Ps 119:15 **24** [1]Lit *the men of my counsel* [a]Ps 119:16 **25** [a]Ps 44:25 [b]Ps 119:37, 40, 88, 93, 107, 149, 154, 156, 159; 143:11 [c]Ps 119:65 **26** [a]Ps 25:4; 27:11; 86:11; 119:12 **27** [a]Ps 105:2; 145:5 **28** [1]Lit *drops* [a]Ps 22:14; 107:26 [b]Ps 20:2; 1 Pet 5:10 **30** [1]Or *accounted Your ordinances worthy* **31** [a]Deut 11:22

119:9 *young man.* Some have thought this a characterization of the author, but more likely it indicates instruction addressed to the young after the manner of the wisdom teachers (see 34:11; Prov 1:4; Eccl 11:9; 12:1). *pure.* Free from all moral taint (see 73:13). *word.* Hebrew *dabar,* a general designation for God's (word) revelation, but here used with special reference to His law (sometimes promises).
119:10 *heart.* See v. 11; see also note on 4:7. *I have sought You.* The author's devotion is first of all to the God of the law and the promises; they have meaning for him only because they are God's word of life for him.
119:11 *word.* Hebrew *'imrah,* a synonym of *dabar* ("word"; see note on v. 9; see also Deut 33:9; Prov 30:5).
119:13 *have told.* Either in meditation or in liturgies of covenant commitment to the Lord (see 50:16).
119:14 *As much as in all riches.* See vv. 72,111,162.
119:15 *ways.* The Hebrew for this word is a synonym of the Hebrew for "way" in v. 3 (the two Hebrew words parallel each other in 25:4).
119:17–24 Devotion to God's law marks the Lord's servant, but alienates him from the arrogant (v. 21) of the world.
119:17 *I may . . . keep.* Out of gratitude for God's care and blessing.
119:18 *Wonderful things.* Usually ascribed to God's redeeming acts (see 9:1 and note)—but God's law contains matters just as wonderful (see v. 27).
119:19 *stranger in the earth.* As a servant of the Lord, i.e., a citizen of His kingdom, he is not at home in any of the kingdoms of the world (see 39:12 and note; see also note on v. 54).
119:20 *My soul is.* I am (see vv. 28,81; see also note on 6:3).
119:21 *the arrogant.* Those who are a law to themselves, most fully described in 10:2–11 (see vv. 51,69,78,85,122; see also note on 31:23). The author has suffered much from their hostility because of his zeal for God and His law, as the next two verses and many others indicate. *cursed.* Ripe for God's judgment.
119:22 *reproach and contempt.* Of the arrogant.
119:23 *princes.* Because the author mentions also speaking "before kings" (v. 46) and being persecuted by "princes" (v. 161), it may be that he held some official position, such as priest (one of whose functions it would have been to teach God's law; see Lev 10:11; Ezra 7:6; Neh 8:2–8; Jer 2:8; 18:18; Mal 2:7; see also note on v. 57). (These kings and rulers are probably either Israelite from the time of the monarchy or Persian in the postexilic period.) *sit.* As those securely settled in the world—not as strangers (cf. v. 19). *talk against me.* As they share their worldly counsels, they speak derisively of the one who stands apart because he delights in God's statutes and makes them his "counselors" (v. 24).
119:25–32 Regardless of his circumstances, he is determined to "cling to" (v. 31) God's word.
119:25 *cleaves to the dust.* The author speaks much of his sorrow, suffering and affliction (see vv. 28,50,67,71,75,83,92, 107,143,153). It is likely that the ridicule, slander and persecution from his adversaries are usually occasioned by this suffering of God's devoted servant, who makes God's word (His law and promises) the hope of his life (see vv. 42,51,65,69,78,85,95, 110,134,141,150,154,157,161; see also notes on v. 6; 5:9; 31:11–12). See 44:25 and note. *word.* Especially its promises, as also in vv. 28,37,42,49,65,74,81,107,114,147.
119:27 *wonders.* See note on v. 18.
119:29 *false way.* The way that seems right but leads to death (see Prov 14:12)—in contrast to the way prescribed by God's law, which is trustworthy (see vv. 86,138) and true (see vv. 142,151,160). *grant me Your law.* By keeping me true to Your law, let me enjoy Your blessings.
119:30 *faithful way.* See note on v. 29.

O LORD, do not put me to shame!
32 I shall run the way of Your
commandments,
For You will [a]enlarge my heart.

ה He.

33 [a]Teach me, O LORD, the way of Your
statutes,
And I shall observe it to the end.
34 [a]Give me understanding, that I may
[b]observe Your law
And keep it [c]with all *my* heart.
35 Make me walk in the [a]path of Your
commandments,
For I [b]delight in it.
36 [a]Incline my heart to Your testimonies
And not to [b]*dishonest* gain.
37 Turn away my [a]eyes from looking at
vanity,
And [b]revive me in Your ways.
38 [a]Establish Your [1]word to Your servant,
[2]As that which produces reverence for
You.
39 [a]Turn away my reproach which I
dread,
For Your ordinances are good.
40 Behold, I [a]long for Your precepts;
Revive me through Your
righteousness.

ו Vav.

41 May Your [a]lovingkindnesses also
come to me, O LORD,
Your salvation [b]according to Your
[1]word;
42 So I will have an [a]answer for him who
[b]reproaches me,
For I trust in Your word.
43 And do not take the word of truth
utterly out of my mouth,

32 [a]1 Kin 4:29; Is 60:5; 2 Cor 6:11, 13
33 [a]Ps 119:5, 12
34 [a]Ps 119:27, 73, 125, 144, 169 [b]1 Chr 22:12; Ezek 44:24 [c]Ps 119:2, 69
35 [a]Ps 25:4; Is 40:14 [b]Ps 112:1; 119:16
36 [a]1 Kin 8:58 [b]Ezek 33:31; Mark 7:21, 22; Luke 12:15; Heb 13:5
37 [a]Is 33:15 [b]Ps 71:20; 119:25
38 [1]Or *promise* [2]Lit *Which is for the fear of You* [a]2 Sam 7:25
39 [a]Ps 119:22
40 [a]Ps 119:20
41 [1]Or *promise* [a]Ps 119:77 [b]Ps 119:58, 76, 116, 170
42 [a]Prov 27:11 [b]Ps 102:8; 119:39
43 [1]Or *hope in* [a]Ps 119:49, 74, 81, 114, 147
44 [a]Ps 119:33
45 [1]Lit *in a wide place* [a]Prov 4:12 [b]Ps 119:94, 155
46 [a]Matt 10:18; Acts 26:1, 2
47 [1]Lit *delight myself* [a]Ps 119:16 [b]Ps 119:97, 127, 159
48 [a]Ps 119:97, 127, 159 [b]Ps 119:15
49 [1]Lit *On*
50 [1]Or *preserved me alive* [a]Job 6:10; Rom 15:4
51 [a]Job 30:1; Jer 20:7 [b]Job 23:11; Ps 44:18; 119:157

For I [1][a]wait for Your ordinances.
44 So I will [a]keep Your law continually,
Forever and ever.
45 And I will [a]walk [1]at liberty,
For I [b]seek Your precepts.
46 I will also speak of Your testimonies
[a]before kings
And shall not be ashamed.
47 I shall [1][a]delight in Your
commandments,
Which I [b]love.
48 And I shall lift up my hands to Your
commandments,
Which I [a]love;
And I will [b]meditate on Your statutes.

ז Zayin.

49 Remember the word to Your servant,
[1]In which You have made me hope.
50 This is my [a]comfort in my affliction,
That Your word has [1]revived me.
51 The arrogant [a]utterly deride me,
Yet I do not [b]turn aside from Your
law.
52 I have [a]remembered Your ordinances
from [1]of old, O LORD,
And comfort myself.
53 Burning [a]indignation has seized me
because of the wicked,
Who [b]forsake Your law.
54 Your statutes are my songs
In the house of my [a]pilgrimage.
55 O LORD, I [a]remember Your name [b]in
the night,
And keep Your law.
56 This has become mine,
[1]That I [a]observe Your precepts.

52 [1]Or *everlasting* [a]Ps 103:18 **53** [a]Ex 32:19; Ezra 9:3; Neh 13:25; Ps 119:158 [b]Ps 89:30 **54** [a]Gen 47:9; Ps 119:19
55 [a]Ps 63:6 [b]Ps 42:8; 92:2; 119:62; Is 26:9; Acts 16:25
56 [1]Or *Because* [a]Ps 119:22, 69, 100

119:31 *put me to shame.* See note on v. 6.
119:32 *enlarge my heart.* Expand my heart with joy (see Is 60:5). Others translate it "increase my understanding" (see 1 Kin 4:29, "breadth of mind"). *heart.* See note on 4:7.
119:33–40 Prayer for instruction in God's will as he longs for His precepts.
119:34 *heart.* See v. 36; see also note on 4:7.
119:36–37 *heart . . . eyes.* See 101:2b–3a and note.
119:38 *produces reverence for You.* The Lord's saving acts in fulfillment of His promises contribute to the recognition that He is the true God (see 130:4; 2 Sam 7:25–26; 1 Kin 8:39–40; Jer 33:8–9).
119:39 *reproach which I dread.* See notes on vv. 6,25.
119:40 *righteousness.* See note on 4:1.
119:41–48 May the Lord deliver me and not take His truth from my mouth; then I will honor His law in my life and speak of it before kings, for I love His commands.
119:41 *lovingkindnesses.* See vv. 64,76,88,124,149,159; see also note on 6:4.
119:42 *him who reproaches me.* See note on v. 25 ("cleaves to the dust"). *word.* See note on v. 25.
119:43 *word of truth . . . out of my mouth.* See v. 13 and note; see also v. 46.
119:45 *liberty.* Lit. "a wide space," i.e., unconfined by affliction or oppression (see 18:19 and note).
119:46 *before kings.* Such will be his boldness (see note on v. 23).
119:48 *I shall lift up my hands to.* An act accompanying praise (as in 63:4; 134:2); so the sense may be: I praise.
119:49–56 God's word is my comfort and my guide whatever my circumstances.
119:49 *word.* See note on v. 25.
119:50–51 *in my affliction . . . The arrogant utterly deride.* See note on v. 25 ("cleaves to the dust").
119:51 *arrogant.* See note on v. 21.
119:52 *of old.* God's law is not fickle, but it is grounded firmly in His unchanging moral character. This is a major source of the author's comfort and one of the main reasons he cherishes the law so highly (see vv. 89,144,152,160).
119:53 *indignation has seized me.* Zeal for God's law (see vv. 136,139) awakens righteous anger against those who reject it (see vv. 113,115,158), and it brings abhorrence of all that is contrary to it (see vv. 104,128,163); but it draws together those who honor it (see v. 63).
119:54 *In the house of my pilgrimage.* Lit. "in my temporary house." The sense may be that of v. 19 (see note there).
119:55 *name.* See note on 5:11.

ח Heth.

57 The LORD is my [a]portion;
I have [1]promised to [b]keep Your words.
58 I [a]sought Your favor [b]with all *my* heart;
[c]Be gracious to me [d]according to Your [1]word.
59 I [a]considered my ways
And turned my feet to Your testimonies.
60 I hastened and did not delay
To keep Your commandments.
61 The [a]cords of the wicked have encircled me,
But I have [b]not forgotten Your law.
62 At [a]midnight I shall rise to give thanks to You
Because of Your [b]righteous ordinances.
63 I am a [a]companion of all those who [1]fear You,
And of those who keep Your precepts.
64 [a]The earth is full of Your lovingkindness, O LORD;
[b]Teach me Your statutes.

ט Teth.

65 You have dealt well with Your servant,
O LORD, according to Your word.
66 Teach me good [1a]discernment and knowledge,
For I believe in Your commandments.
67 [a]Before I was afflicted I went astray,
But now I keep Your word.
68 You are [a]good and [b]do good;
[c]Teach me Your statutes.
69 The arrogant [1]have [a]forged a lie against me;
With all *my* heart I will [b]observe Your precepts.
70 Their heart is [1a]covered with fat,
But I [b]delight in Your law.
71 It is [a]good for me that I was afflicted,
That I may learn Your statutes.
72 The [a]law of Your mouth is better to me
Than thousands of gold and silver *pieces.*

י Yodh.

73 [a]Your hands made me and [1]fashioned me;
[b]Give me understanding, that I may learn Your commandments.
74 May those who [1]fear You [a]see me and be glad,
Because I [2b]wait for Your word.
75 I know, O LORD, that Your judgments are [a]righteous,
And that [b]in faithfulness You have afflicted me.
76 O may Your lovingkindness [1]comfort me,
According to Your [2]word to Your servant.
77 May [a]Your compassion come to me that I may live,
For Your law is my [b]delight.
78 May [a]the arrogant be ashamed, for they subvert me [b]with a lie;
But I shall [c]meditate on Your precepts.
79 May those who [1]fear You turn to me,
Even those who know Your testimonies.
80 May my heart be [1a]blameless in Your statutes,
So that I will not [b]be ashamed.

57 [1]Lit *said that I would keep* [a]Ps 16:5; Lam 3:24 [b]Deut 33:9
58 [1]Or *promise* [a]1 Kin 13:6 [b]Ps 119:2 [c]Ps 41:4; 56:1; 57:1 [d]Ps 119:41
59 [a]Mark 14:72; Luke 15:17
61 [a]Job 36:8; Ps 140:5 [b]Ps 119:83, 141, 153, 176
62 [a]Ps 119:55 [b]Ps 119:7
63 [1]Or *revere* [a]Ps 101:6
64 [a]Ps 33:5 [b]Ps 119:12
66 [1]Or *judgment* [a]Phil 1:9
67 [a]Ps 119:71, 75; Jer 31:18, 19; Heb 12:5-11
68 [a]Ps 86:5; 100:5; 106:1; 107:1; Matt 19:17 [b]Deut 8:16; 28:63; 30:5; Ps 125:4 [c]Ps 119:12
69 [1]Lit *besmear me with lies* [a]Job 13:4; Ps 109:2 [b]Ps 119:56
70 [1]Lit *gross like fat* [a]Deut 32:15; Job 15:27; Ps 17:10; Is 6:10; Jer 5:28; Acts 28:27 [b]Ps 119:16
71 [a]Ps 119:67, 75
72 [a]Ps 19:10; 119:127; Prov 8:10, 11, 19
73 [1]Lit *established* [a]Job 10:8; 31:15; Ps 100:3; 138:8; 139:15, 16 [b]Ps 119:34
74 [1]Or *revere* [2]Or *hope in* [a]Ps 34:2; 35:27; 107:42 [b]Ps 119:43
75 [a]Ps 119:138 [b]Heb 12:10
76 [1]Lit *be for my comfort* [2]Or *promise*
77 [a]Ps 119:41 [b]Ps 119:16
78 [a]Jer 50:32 [b]Ps 119:86 [c]Ps 119:15
79 [1]Or *revere*
80 [1]Lit *complete;* or *having integrity* [a]Ps 119:1 [b]Ps 119:46

119:57–64 The Lord is the psalmist's true homestead because it is God's law that fills the earth with all that makes life secure and joyous. So God's promises are his hope, and God's righteous laws his delight.
119:57 *portion.* May identify the author as a priest or Levite (see 73:26 and note).
119:58 *heart.* See note on 4:7.
119:61 *The cords of the wicked have encircled me.* The wicked have oppressed me.
119:62 *give thanks to You.* See note on Ps 100 title. *righteous.* See note on v. 7.
119:63 *companion.* See note on v. 53.
119:65–72 Do good to me in accordance with Your goodness, even if that means affliction, because Your affliction is good for me; it teaches me knowledge and good judgment from Your law.
119:65 *dealt well.* Cf. v. 68; see 31:19; 86:17 and notes. *word.* See note on v. 25.
119:66 *believe in.* Have confidence in; God's commands are not deceitful (see note on v. 29) or fickle (see note on v. 52).
119:67 *afflicted.* At the hands of God (see v. 71; see also note on v. 25, "cleaves to the dust"). *word.* See note on v. 11.
119:69 *arrogant.* See note on v. 21.
119:70 *covered with fat.* Lit. "fat as grease." Similar expressions occur also in Is 6:10; Jer 5:28 (see also 17:10).
119:72 *Than thousands of gold and silver.* See vv. 14,57,111, 162.
119:73–80 Complete Your forming of me by helping me to conform to Your righteous laws so that the arrogant may be put to shame and those who fear You may rejoice with me. (The stanza has a concentric structure; compare vv. 73 and 80, 74 and 79, 75 and 78, 76 and 77.)
119:73 *Give me understanding.* What I need to perfect the work You began when You formed me.
119:74 *fear You.* See v. 79; see also note on 34:8–14. *see me and be glad.* When I am perfectly formed and enjoying the blessings of the godly. *word.* See note on v. 25.
119:75 *judgments.* Here the Hebrew for this word (*mishpaṭim*) may refer to God's just decisions in dealing with His servant, as the rest of the verse implies (see v. 84 and note). *You have afflicted me.* See vv. 67,71.
119:76 *lovingkindness.* See note on 6:4. *comfort me.* In my affliction.
119:77 *that I may live.* And not perish in my affliction.
119:78 *the arrogant.* See note on v. 21. *be ashamed.* As they have subjected me to shame (see note on 5:10). *for they subvert me.* See note on v. 25 ("cleaves to the dust").
119:79 *turn to me.* See v. 63 and note on v. 53.
119:80 *heart.* See note on 4:7. *will not be ashamed.* See note on v. 6.

כ Kaph.

81 My [a]soul languishes for Your salvation;
I [1b]wait for Your word.
82 My [a]eyes fail *with longing* for Your
[1]word,
[2]While I say, "When will You comfort
me?"
83 Though I have [a]become like a
wineskin in the smoke,
I do [b]not forget Your statutes.
84 How many are the [a]days of Your
servant?
When will You [b]execute judgment on
those who persecute me?
85 The arrogant have [a]dug pits for me,
Men who are not [1]in accord with Your
law.
86 All Your commandments are [a]faithful;
They have [b]persecuted me with a lie;
[c]help me!
87 They almost destroyed me [1]on earth,
But as for me, I [a]did not forsake Your
precepts.
88 Revive me according to Your
lovingkindness,
So that I may keep the testimony of
Your mouth.

ל Lamedh.

89 [a]Forever, O LORD,
Your word [1]is settled in heaven.
90 Your [a]faithfulness *continues*
[1]throughout all generations;
You [b]established the earth, and it
[c]stands.
91 They stand this day according to Your
[a]ordinances,
For [b]all things are Your servants.
92 If Your law had not been my [a]delight,
Then I would have perished [b]in my
affliction.
93 I will [a]never forget Your precepts,
For by them You have [1b]revived me.
94 I am Yours, [a]save me;
For I have [b]sought Your precepts.
95 The wicked [a]wait for me to destroy me;
I shall diligently consider Your
testimonies.
96 I have seen [1]a limit to all perfection;
Your commandment is exceedingly
broad.

מ Mem.

97 O how I [a]love Your law!
It is my [b]meditation all the day.
98 Your [a]commandments make me wiser
than my enemies,
For they are ever [1]mine.
99 I have more insight than all my
teachers,
For Your testimonies are my
[a]meditation.
100 I understand [a]more than the aged,
Because I have [b]observed Your
precepts.
101 I have [a]restrained my feet from every
evil way,
That I may keep Your word.
102 I have not [a]turned aside from Your
ordinances,
For You Yourself have taught me.
103 How [a]sweet are Your [1]words to my
[2]taste!
Yes, sweeter than honey to my mouth!

81 [1]Or *hope in* [a]Ps 84:2 [b]Ps 119:43 **82** [1]Or *promise* [2]Lit *Saying* [a]Ps 69:3; 119:123; Is 38:14; Lam 2:11 **83** [a]Job 30:30 [b]Ps 119:61 **84** [a]Ps 39:4 [b]Rev 6:10 **85** [1]Lit *according to Your law* [a]Ps 7:15; 35:7; 57:6; Jer 18:22 **86** [a]Ps 119:138 [b]Ps 35:19; 119:78, 161 [c]Ps 109:26 **87** [1]Lit *in the earth* [a]Is 58:2 **89** [1]Lit *stands firm* [a]Ps 89:2; 119:160; Is 40:8; Matt 24:35; 1 Pet 1:25 **90** [1]Lit *to* [a]Ps 36:5; 89:1, 2 [b]Ps 148:6 [c]Eccl 1:4 **91** [a]Jer 31:35; 33:25 [b]Ps 104:2-4 **92** [a]Ps 119:16 [b]Ps 119:50 **93** [1]Or *kept me alive* [a]Ps 119:16, 83 [b]Ps 119:25 **94** [a]Ps 119:146 [b]Ps 119:45 **95** [a]Ps 40:14; Is 32:7 **96** [1]Lit *an end of* **97** [a]Ps 119:47, 48, 127, 163, 165 [b]Ps 1:2; 119:15 **98** [1]Or *with me* [a]Deut 4:6; Ps 119:130 **99** [a]Ps 119:15 **100** [a]Job 32:7-9 [b]Ps 119:22, 56 **101** [a]Prov 1:15 **102** [a]Deut 17:20; Josh 23:6; 1 Kin 15:5 **103** [1]Or *promises* [2]Lit *palate* [a]Ps 19:10; Prov 8:11; 24:13, 14

119:81–88 Save me from my affliction and my persecutors, according to Your promises, and I will obey Your statutes. This last stanza of the first half of the psalm, like the closing stanza, is dominated by prayer for God's help (see note on v. 25).
119:81 *soul.* See note on 6:3.
119:82 *My eyes fail.* See note on 6:7.
119:83 *like a wineskin in the smoke.* As a wineskin hanging in the smoke and heat above a fire becomes smudged and shriveled, so the psalmist bears the marks of his affliction.
119:84 *How many . . . days?* That is, do not delay the punishment of my persecutors, because my life is short. *execute judgment.* Lit. "effect justice upon" (the Hebrew for "justice" is *mishpat*; see note on v. 7, "judgments"; see also note on 5:10).
119:85 *The arrogant.* See note on v. 21. *dug pits.* Probably referring to slander—public accusations that the psalmist must be guilty of vile sins or he would not be suffering such affliction. *not in accord with Your law.* See Ex 20:16.
119:86 *faithful.* See note on v. 29 ("false way").
119:88 *lovingkindness.* See note on 6:4.
119:89–91 God's sovereign and unchanging word governs and maintains all creation. (These first three verses of the second half of the psalm teach a general truth; cf. vv. 1–3.)
119:89 *Your word.* Here God's word by which He created, maintains and governs all things (see 33:4,6; 107:20; 147:15,18). *settled in heaven.* The secure order of the heavens and the earth (v. 90) declares (19:1–4) the reassuring truth that God's word (His "ordinances," v. 91), by which He upholds and governs all things, is enduring (eternal) and trustworthy ("Your faithfulness," v. 90). And that is the larger truth that confirms the godly man's confidence in the trustworthiness of God's word (His laws and promises) of special revelation (see notes on 93:5; 96:10; see also note on v. 29, "false way").
119:90 *Your faithfulness.* An indirect reference to God's word (see v. 89 and note).
119:92 *would have perished in my affliction.* Would not have learned the way of life (see v. 93) from your law (see vv. 67,71 and note on vv. 65–72).
119:95 *The wicked.* See note on v. 21 ("the arrogant"). *wait for me to destroy me.* See note on v. 25 ("cleaves to the dust").
119:96 *perfection.* Probably that which has been perfected in the sense of completed, given fixed bounds so that it is no longer open-ended. *exceedingly broad.* An inexhaustible source of wise counsel for life (see vv. 97–100).
119:97–104 Meditation on God's law yields the highest wisdom.
119:98 *my enemies.* Those arrogant ones (see note on v. 21) who place confidence in worldly wisdom. *they.* Your commands.
119:99 *teachers.* Merely human teachers.
119:100 *aged.* Old men, taught by experience (see note on Ex 3:16).
119:102 *You . . . have taught me.* Through Your laws.
119:103 *words.* Perhaps better understood here as "laws" (see

104 From Your precepts I [a]get
understanding;
Therefore I [b]hate every false way.

נ Nun.

105 Your word is a [a]lamp to my feet
And a light to my path.
106 I have [a]sworn and I will confirm it,
That I will keep Your righteous
ordinances.
107 I am exceedingly [a]afflicted;
[1b]Revive me, O LORD, according to
Your word.
108 O accept the [a]freewill offerings of my
mouth, O LORD,
And [b]teach me Your ordinances.
109 My [1a]life is continually [2]in my hand,
Yet I do not [b]forget Your law.
110 The wicked have [a]laid a snare for me,
Yet I have not [b]gone astray from Your
precepts.
111 I have [a]inherited Your testimonies
forever,
For they are the [b]joy of my heart.
112 I have [a]inclined my heart to perform
Your statutes
Forever, *even* [b]to the end.

ס Samekh.

113 I hate those who are [a]double-minded,
But I love Your [b]law.
114 You are my [a]hiding place and my
[b]shield;
I [1c]wait for Your word.
115 [a]Depart from me, evildoers,
That I may [b]observe the
commandments of my God.
116 [a]Sustain me according to Your [1]word,
that I may live;
And [b]do not let me be [2]ashamed of
my hope.
117 Uphold me that I may be [a]safe,

104 [a]Ps 119:130 [b]Ps 119:128 **105** [a]Prov 6:23 **106** [a]Neh 10:29 **107** [1]Or *Keep me alive* [a]Ps 119:25, 50 [b]Ps 119:25 **108** [a]Hos 14:2; Heb 13:15 [b]Ps 119:12 **109** [1]Lit *soul* [2]I.e. in danger [a]Judg 12:3; Job 13:14 [b]Ps 119:16 **110** [a]Ps 91:3; 140:5; 141:9 [b]Ps 119:10 **111** [a]Deut 33:4 [b]Ps 119:14, 162 **112** [a]Ps 119:36 [b]Ps 119:33 **113** [a]1 Kin 18:21; James 1:8; 4:8 [b]Ps 119:47 **114** [1]Or *hope in* [a]Ps 31:20; 32:7; 61:4; 91:1 [b]Ps 84:9 [c]Ps 119:74 **115** [a]Ps 6:8; 139:19; Matt 7:23 [b]Ps 119:22 **116** [1]Or *promise* [2]Lit *put to shame because of* [a]Ps 37:17, 24; 54:4 [b]Ps 25:2, 20; 31:1, 17; Rom 5:5; 9:33; Phil 1:20 **117** [a]Ps 12:5; Prov 29:25

117 [b]Ps 119:6, 15 **118** [1]Lit *made light of* [2]Lit *falsehood* [a]Ps 119:10, 21 **119** [1]Lit *caused to cease* [a]Is 1:22, 25; Ezek 22:18, 19 [b]Ps 119:47 **120** [1]Lit *bristles up from* [a]Job 4:14; Hab 3:16 [b]Ps 119:161 **121** [a]2 Sam 8:15; Job 29:14

That I may [b]have regard for Your
statutes continually.
118 You have [1]rejected all those [a]who
wander from Your statutes,
For their deceitfulness is [2]useless.
119 You have [1]removed all the wicked of
the earth *like* [a]dross;
Therefore I [b]love Your testimonies.
120 My flesh [1a]trembles for fear of You,
And I am [b]afraid of Your judgments.

ע Ayin.

121 I have [a]done justice and
righteousness;
Do not leave me to my oppressors.
122 Be [a]surety for Your servant for good;
Do not let the arrogant [b]oppress me.
123 My [a]eyes fail *with longing* for Your
salvation
And for Your righteous [1]word.
124 Deal with Your servant [a]according to
Your lovingkindness
And [b]teach me Your statutes.
125 [a]I am Your servant; [b]give me
understanding,
That I may know Your testimonies.
126 It is time for the LORD to [a]act,
For they have broken Your law.
127 Therefore I [a]love Your
commandments
Above gold, yes, above fine gold.
128 Therefore I esteem right all *Your*
[a]precepts concerning everything,
I [b]hate every false way.

פ Pe.

129 Your testimonies are [a]wonderful;
Therefore my soul [b]observes them.

122 [a]Job 17:3; Heb 7:22 [b]Ps 119:134 **123** [1]Or *promise* [a]Ps 119:82 **124** [a]Ps 51:1; 106:45; 109:26; 119:88, 149, 159 [b]Ps 119:12 **125** [a]Ps 116:16 [b]Ps 119:27 **126** [a]Jer 18:23; Ezek 31:11 **127** [a]Ps 19:10; 119:47 **128** [a]Ps 19:8 [b]Ps 119:104 **129** [a]Ps 119:18 [b]Ps 119:22

vv. 67,133,158,172 and note on v. 11).

119:104 *hate every false way.* See note on v. 53.

119:105 *lamp . . . light.* Apart from which I could only grope about in the darkness.

119:106 *have sworn . . . will confirm.* Have covenanted (see Neh 10:29).

119:107 See v. 25 and note.

119:109 *My life is continually in my hand.* By publicly honoring God's law even in the face of threats and hostility (see especially vv. 23,46,161; see also NASB marg.).

119:110 *laid a snare.* See v. 85 and note.

119:111–112 *heart.* See note on 4:7.

119:111 *inherited Your testimonies.* The possession I have received from God as my homestead and that from which I draw the provisions for my life (see note on vv. 57–64).

119:113 *hate those who are double-minded.* See v. 115; see also note on v. 53. A double-minded man is "unstable in all his ways" (James 1:8).

119:114 *word.* See note on v. 25.

119:118 *rejected.* Or "shaken off" or "made light of." *their deceitfulness.* Probably their ways, which are deceitful (see note on v. 29).

119:119 *dross.* Scum removed from molten ore or metal. The Hebrew for this word is a pun on the word for "wander" in v. 118: Those who wander are treated like dross.

119:120 *My flesh trembles.* He quivers out of his deep reverence for God.

119:121–128 As Your faithful servant I pray for deliverance from my oppressors—another stanza in which prayer for deliverance is dominant (see vv. 81–88 and note; see also note on v. 25, "cleaves to the dust").

119:121 *justice and righteousness.* God's law.

119:122 The only verse in this psalm that does not have either a direct or an indirect (as in vv. 90,121,132; see note on v. 75) reference to God's word. *the arrogant.* See note on v. 21.

119:123 *My eyes fail.* See note on 6:7.

119:124 *lovingkindness.* See note on 6:4.

119:126 *act.* Either in defense of His servant, or in judgment on the lawbreakers, or both.

119:127 *Above gold.* See vv. 14,57,72,111.

119:128 *I hate every false way.* See note on v. 53.

119:129 *wonderful.* See v. 18 and note.

130 The [a]unfolding of Your words gives
light;
It gives [b]understanding to the
simple.
131 I [a]opened my mouth wide and
[b]panted,
For I [c]longed for Your commandments.
132 [a]Turn to me and be gracious to me,
After Your manner [1]with those who
love Your name.
133 Establish my [a]footsteps in Your [1]word,
And do not let any iniquity [b]have
dominion over me.
134 [a]Redeem me from the oppression of
man,
That I may keep Your precepts.
135 [a]Make Your face shine upon Your
servant,
And [b]teach me Your statutes.
136 My eyes [1]shed [a]streams of water,
Because they [b]do not keep Your law.

צ Tsadhe.

137 [a]Righteous are You, O LORD,
And upright are Your judgments.
138 You have commanded Your
testimonies in [a]righteousness
And exceeding [b]faithfulness.
139 My [a]zeal has [1]consumed me,
Because my adversaries have forgotten
Your words.
140 Your [1a]word is very [2]pure,
Therefore Your servant [b]loves it.
141 I am small and [a]despised,
Yet I do not [b]forget Your precepts.
142 Your righteousness is an everlasting
righteousness,
And [a]Your law is truth.
143 Trouble and anguish have [1]come upon
me,
Yet Your commandments are my
[a]delight.
144 Your [a]testimonies are righteous
forever;
[b]Give me understanding that I may
live.

130 [a]Prov 6:23 [b]Ps 19:7 **131** [a]Job 29:23; Ps 81:10 [b]Ps 42:1 [c]Ps 119:20 **132** [1]Lit *to* [a]Ps 25:16; 106:4 **133** [1]Or *promise* [a]Ps 17:5 [b]Ps 19:13; Rom 6:12 **134** [a]Ps 119:84; 142:6; Luke 1:74 **135** [a]Num 6:25; Ps 4:6; 31:16; 67:1; 80:3, 7, 19 [b]Ps 119:12 **136** [1]Lit *run down* [a]Jer 9:1, 18; 14:17; Lam 3:48 [b]Ps 119:158 **137** [a]Ezra 9:15; Neh 9:33; Ps 116:5; 129:4; 145:17; Jer 12:1; Lam 1:18; Dan 9:7, 14 **138** [a]Ps 19:7-9; 119:144, 172 [b]Ps 119:86, 90 **139** [1]Lit *put an end to* [a]Ps 69:9; John 2:17 **140** [1]Or *promise* [2]Lit *refined* [a]Ps 12:6; 19:8 [b]Ps 119:47 **141** [a]Ps 22:6 [b]Ps 119:61 **142** [a]Ps 19:9; 119:151, 160 **143** [1]Lit *found me* [a]Ps 119:24 **144** [a]Ps 19:9 [b]Ps 119:27

145 [a]Ps 119:10 [b]Ps 119:22, 55 **146** [a]Ps 3:7 **147** [1]Lit *anticipate the dawn* [2]Or *hope in* [a]Ps 5:3; 57:8; 108:2 **148** [1]Or *promise* [a]Ps 63:6 [b]Ps 119:15 **149** [a]Ps 119:124 [b]Ps 119:25 **151** [a]Ps 34:18; 145:18; Is 50:8 [b]Ps 119:142 **152** [a]Ps 119:125 [b]Ps 119:89; Luke 21:33 **153** [a]Lam 5:1 [b]Ps 119:50 [c]Ps 119:16; Prov 3:1; Hos 4:6

ק Qoph.

145 I cried [a]with all my heart; answer me,
O LORD!
I will [b]observe Your statutes.
146 I cried to You; [a]save me
And I shall keep Your testimonies.
147 I [1a]rise before dawn and cry for help;
I [2]wait for Your words.
148 My eyes anticipate the [a]night watches,
That I may [b]meditate on Your [1]word.
149 Hear my voice [a]according to Your
lovingkindness;
[b]Revive me, O LORD, according to Your
ordinances.
150 Those who follow after wickedness
draw near;
They are far from Your law.
151 You are [a]near, O LORD,
And all Your commandments are
[b]truth.
152 Of old I have [a]known from Your
testimonies
That You have founded them [b]forever.

ר Resh.

153 [a]Look upon my [b]affliction and rescue
me,
For I do not [c]forget Your law.
154 [a]Plead my cause and [b]redeem me;
Revive me according to Your [1]word.
155 Salvation is [a]far from the wicked,
For they [b]do not seek Your statutes.
156 [1a]Great are Your mercies, O LORD;
Revive me according to Your
ordinances.
157 Many are my [a]persecutors and my
adversaries,
Yet I do not [b]turn aside from Your
testimonies.
158 I behold the [a]treacherous and [b]loathe
them,
Because they do not keep Your [1]word.

154 [1]Or *promise* [a]1 Sam 24:15; Ps 35:1; Mic 7:9 [b]Ps 119:134 **155** [a]Job 5:4 [b]Ps 119:45, 94 **156** [1]Or *Many* [a]2 Sam 24:14 **157** [a]Ps 7:1; 119:86, 161 [b]Ps 119:51 **158** [1]Or *promise* [a]Is 21:2; 24:16 [b]Ps 139:21

119:130 *unfolding.* Lit. "opening," here meaning (1) the revelation of Your words, (2) the interpretation (see "express," 49:4) of Your words, or (3) the entering of Your words into the heart. *the simple.* See 19:7 and note.
119:132 *After Your manner.* The Hebrew for "manner" is *mishpaṭ*; hence an indirect reference (see note on v. 122) to God's law (see note on v. 7).
119:134,154 *Redeem.* Here, as often, a synonym for "deliver."
119:134 *oppression.* See note on v. 25 ("cleaves to the dust").
119:135 *Your face shine.* See note on 13:1 ("hide Your face").
119:136 See v. 53 and note.
119:137–144 The Lord and His laws are righteous.
119:137 *Righteous.* See note on 4:1.
119:138 *faithfulness.* See v. 142; see also note on v. 29 ("false way").
119:139 *My zeal.* See note on v. 53.
119:140 *pure.* Lit. "refined," i.e., God's word contains nothing worthless or useless.
119:141 *small and despised.* Cf. v. 143; see also note on v. 25.
119:145–152 Save me, O Lord, and I will keep Your law. As the psalm draws to a close, prayer for deliverance becomes more dominant (see note on v. 25, "cleaves to the dust").
119:148 *the night watches.* See note on Judg 7:19; see also Lam 2:19.
119:149 *lovingkindness.* See note on 6:4. *Your ordinances.* Or "Your justice" (complementing "Your lovingkindness"); Hebrew *mishpaṭ* (see note on v. 75).
119:150 *far from Your law.* See vv. 21,53,85,118,126,139, 155,158.
119:151 *are truth.* See note on v. 29 ("false way").
119:152 *forever.* See note on v. 52.
119:153–160 See note on vv. 145–152.
119:155 *the wicked.* See note on v. 21 ("the arrogant").
119:156 *Your ordinances.* See v. 149 and note.
119:158 *word.* Hebrew *'imrah* (see note on v. 11).

159 Consider how I [a]love Your precepts;
[b]Revive me, O LORD, according to Your lovingkindness.
160 The [a]sum of Your word is [b]truth,
And every one of Your righteous ordinances [c]is everlasting.

ש Shin.

161 [a]Princes persecute me without cause,
But my heart [b]stands in awe of Your words.
162 I [a]rejoice at Your [1]word,
As one who [b]finds great spoil.
163 I [a]hate and despise falsehood,
But I [b]love Your law.
164 Seven times a day I praise You,
Because of Your [a]righteous ordinances.
165 Those who love Your law have [a]great peace,
And [1][b]nothing causes them to stumble.
166 I [a]hope for Your salvation, O LORD,
And do Your commandments.
167 My [a]soul keeps Your testimonies,
And I [b]love them exceedingly.
168 I [a]keep Your precepts and Your testimonies,
For all my [b]ways are before You.

ת Tav.

169 Let my [a]cry [1]come before You, O LORD;
[b]Give me understanding [c]according to Your word.
170 Let my [a]supplication come before You;
[b]Deliver me according to Your [1]word.
171 Let my [a]lips utter praise,
For You [b]teach me Your statutes.
172 Let my [a]tongue sing of Your [1]word,
For all Your [b]commandments are righteousness.
173 Let Your [a]hand be [1]ready to help me,
For I have [b]chosen Your precepts.
174 I [a]long for Your salvation, O LORD,
And Your law is my [b]delight.
175 Let my [a]soul live that it may praise You,
And let Your ordinances help me.
176 I have [a]gone astray like a lost sheep; seek Your servant,
For I do [b]not forget Your commandments.

Psalm 120

A Song of [†]Ascents.

1 [a]In my trouble I cried to the LORD,
And He answered me.
2 Deliver my soul, O LORD, from [a]lying lips,
From a [b]deceitful tongue.
3 What shall be given to you, and what more shall be done to you,
You [a]deceitful tongue?
4 [a]Sharp arrows of the warrior,

159 [a]Ps 119:47 [b]Ps 119:25 **160** [a]Ps 139:17 [b]Ps 119:142 [c]Ps 119:89, 152 **161** [a]1 Sam 24:11; 26:18; Ps 119:23 [b]Ps 119:120 **162** [1]Or *promise* [a]Ps 119:14, 111 [b]1 Sam 30:16; Is 9:3 **163** [a]Ps 31:6; 119:104, 128; Prov 13:5 [b]Ps 119:47 **164** [a]Ps 119:7, 160 **165** [1]Lit *they have no stumbling block* [a]Ps 37:11; Prov 3:2; Is 26:3; 32:17 [b]Prov 3:23; Is 63:13; 1 John 2:10 **166** [a]Gen 49:18; Ps 119:81, 174 **167** [a]Ps 119:129 [b]Ps 119:47 **168** [a]Ps 119:22 [b]Job 24:23; Ps 139:3; Prov 5:21 **169** [1]Lit *come near before* [a]Job 16:18; Ps 18:6; 102:1 [b]Ps 119:27, 144 [c]Ps 119:65, 154

170 [1]Or *promise* [a]Ps 28:2; 130:2; 140:6; 143:1 [b]Ps 22:20; 31:2; 59:1 **171** [a]Ps 51:15; 63:3 [b]Ps 94:12; 119:12; Is 2:3; Mic 4:2 **172** [1]Or *promise* [a]Ps 51:14 [b]Ps 119:138 **173** [1]Lit *to help me* [a]Ps 37:24; 73:23 [b]Josh 24:22; Luke 10:42 **174** [a]Ps 119:166 [b]Ps 119:16, 24 **175** [a]Is 55:3 **176** [a]Is 53:6; Jer 50:6; Matt 18:12; Luke 15:4 [b]Ps 119:16 **120:1** [†]Ex 34:24; 1 Kin 12:27 [a]Ps 18:6; 66:14; 102:2; Jon 2:2 **2** [a]Ps 109:2; Prov 12:22 [b]Ps 52:4; Zeph 3:13 **3** [a]Ps 52:4; Zeph 3:13 **4** [a]Ps 45:5; Prov 25:18; Is 5:28

119:160 *The sum of.* See 139:17. *truth.* See note on v. 29 ("false way"). *everlasting.* See note on v. 52.
119:161–168 See note on vv. 145–152.
119:161 *Princes.* See note on v. 23. *heart.* See note on 4:7.
119:162 *great spoil.* See vv. 14,72,111.
119:163 *I hate.* See note on v. 53. *falsehood.* Or "that which is (ways that are) deceitful" (see v. 29 and note).
119:164 *Seven.* A number signifying completeness—he praises God throughout the day.
119:165 *great peace.* Complete security and well-being.
119:169–176 See note on vv. 145–152.
119:171 *utter praise.* Because You have delivered me.
119:172 *righteousness.* See note on v. 7.
119:174–176 The conclusion to the psalm.
119:176 *I have gone astray.* See Is 53:6; the clearest expression of the author's acknowledgment that, for all his devotion to God's law, he has again and again wandered into other (deceitful) ways and, like a lost sheep, must be brought back by his heavenly Shepherd. For one who has made God's law the guide and dearest treasure of his life, the last word can only be such a confession—and such a prayer.
Ps 120 A prayer for deliverance from false accusers. Verse 7 suggests that the speaker is a king, in which case the accusers seek either to discredit him before his people or, more likely, to awaken suspicion concerning him in foreign courts. But if "war" is understood metaphorically, the psalm could be used also by a private individual beset by slanderers.
120 title *Ascents.* Some have thought that the Hebrew for this word refers to stairs leading to the temple, hence "a song of the stairs," to be used in the temple liturgy (probably at the Feast of Booths). Most believe it refers to the annual religious pilgrimages to Jerusalem (see 84:5–7; Ex 23:14–17; Deut 16:16; Mic 4:2; Zech 14:16), which brought the worshipers singing to Mount Zion (Is 30:29)—a view that does not exclude the psalm's use also in the temple liturgy. This title, found also at the head of Ps 121–134, no doubt reflects postexilic usage rather than the original purpose of composition and also marks Ps 120–134 as a collection that was taken up as a unit into the final postexilic arrangement of the Psalter. Together with Ps 135–136, it came to be known in Jewish liturgy as the "Great Hallel" (in distinction from the "Egyptian Hallel"; see introduction to Ps 113). The spirit of Ps 84 pervades it (see also Ps 42–43). Whether a thematic (or some other) scheme controls the arrangement of Ps 120–134 is unclear, though it is probably not coincidental that they begin with a prayer that evokes the experience of one far from home and beset by barbarians and end with a call to praise in the sanctuary. See introduction to Ps 122.
120:2 *lying lips . . . deceitful tongue.* See note on 5:9.
120:3–4 Assurance that God will act (see 6:8–10 and note on 3:8).
120:3 *what more.* An echo of a common oath formula (see 1 Sam 3:17 and note), thus suggesting the certainty of God's judgment on the enemies.
120:4 *Sharp arrows . . . burning coals.* As a weapon, the tongue is a sharp arrow (see Prov 25:18; Jer 9:8; see also 57:4; 64:3) and a searing fire (see Prov 16:27; James 3:6), and God's judgment will answer in kind (see 7:11–13; 11:6; 64:7). For judgment in

With the *burning* [b]coals of the broom
tree.

5 Woe is me, for I sojourn in [a]Meshech,
For I dwell among the [b]tents of
[c]Kedar!
6 Too long has my soul had its dwelling
With those who [a]hate peace.
7 I [a]am *for* peace, but when I speak,
They are [b]for war.

Psalm 121

A Song of Ascents.

1 I will [a]lift up my eyes to [b]the
mountains;
From where shall my help come?
2 My [a]help *comes* from the LORD,
Who [b]made heaven and earth.
3 He will not [a]allow your foot to slip;
He who [b]keeps you will not slumber.
4 Behold, He who keeps Israel
Will neither slumber nor sleep.

5 The LORD is your [a]keeper;
The LORD is your [b]shade on your right
hand.
6 The [a]sun will not smite you by day,
Nor the moon by night.
7 The LORD will [1a]protect you from all
evil;
He will keep your soul.
8 The LORD will [1a]guard your going out
and your coming in
[b]From this time forth and forever.

Psalm 122

A Song of Ascents, of David.

1 I was glad when they said to me,
"Let us [a]go to the house of the LORD."
2 Our feet are standing
Within your [a]gates, O Jerusalem,
3 Jerusalem, that is [a]built
As a city that is [b]compact together;
4 To which the tribes [a]go up, even the
tribes of [1]the LORD—
[2]An ordinance for Israel—
To give thanks to the name of the LORD.
5 For there [a]thrones were set for
judgment,
The thrones of the house of David.

4 [b]Ps 140:10 **5** [a]Gen 10:2; 1 Chr 1:5; Ezek 27:13; 38:2, 3; 39:1 [b]Song 1:5 [c]Gen 25:13; Is 21:16; 60:7; Jer 2:10; 49:28; Ezek 27:21 **6** [a]Ps 35:20 **7** [a]Ps 109:4 [b]Ps 55:21 **121:1** [a]Ps 123:1; Is 40:26 [b]Ps 87:1 **2** [a]Ps 124:8 [b]Ps 115:15 **3** [a]1 Sam 2:9; Ps 66:9 [b]Ps 41:2; 127:1; Is 27:3 **5** [a]Ps 91:4 [b]Ps 16:8; 91:1; Is 25:4 **6** [a]Ps 91:5; Is 49:10; Jon 4:8; Rev 7:16 **7** [1]Or *keep* [a]Ps 41:2; 91:10-12 **8** [1]Or *keep* [a]Deut 28:6 [b]Ps 113:2; 115:18 **122:1** [a]Ps 42:4; Is 2:3; Mic 4:2; Zech 8:21 **2** [a]Ps 9:14; 87:2; 116:19; Jer 7:2 **3** [a]Ps 48:13; 147:2 [b]2 Sam 5:9; Neh 4:6

4 [1]Heb YAH [2]Or *A testimony* [a]Ex 23:17; Deut 16:16; Ps 84:5
5 [a]Deut 17:8; 2 Chr 19:8; Ps 89:29

kind see 63:9–10; 64:7–8 and notes. *broom tree.* A desert shrub, sometimes large enough to provide shade.
120:5–7 Complaint over prolonged harassment.
120:5 *Meshech . . . Kedar.* The former was in central Asia Minor (see note on Gen 10:2), the latter in Arabia (see note on Is 21:16). Besieged by slanderers, the psalmist feels as if far from home, surrounded by barbarians.
Ps 121 A dialogue (perhaps liturgical) of confession and assurance. Its use as a pilgrimage song provides the key to its understanding. Whether the dialogue takes place in a single heart (cf. the refrain in Ps 42–43) or between individuals in the caravan is of no great consequence since all would share the same convictions. The comforting assurance expressed (see Ps 33) is equally appropriate for the pilgrimage to Jerusalem and for the pilgrimage of life to the "glory" into which the faithful will be received (see notes on 49:15; 73:24). The psalm is composed of four (Hebrew) couplets, each having an introductory line, which the rest of the couplet develops. Key terms are "the LORD" and "keep" ("guard" in v. 8), each occurring five times.
121 title See note on Ps 120 title.
121:1–2 Confession of trust in the Lord.
121:1 *mountains.* Those in the vicinity of Jerusalem, of which Mount Zion is one (125:2), or, if the plural indicates majesty (as in the Hebrew in 87:1; 133:3), Mount Zion itself.
121:2 *Who made heaven and earth.* The one true God, the King of all creation (see 124:8; 134:3; see also 33:6; 89:11–13; 96:4–5; 104:2–9; 136:4–9).
121:3–4 Assurance concerning the unsleeping guardian over Israel.
121:3 *not allow your foot to slip.* Not even where the way is treacherous. *not slumber.* Like the pagan god Baal (see 1 Kin 18:27).
121:4 *He who keeps Israel.* The Lord of all creation and the guardian over Israel—the One in whom the faithful may put unfaltering trust.
121:5–6 Assurance concerning unfailing protection.
121:5 *shade.* See 91:1 ("shadow") and note on 17:8. *on your right hand.* See 16:8 and note.
121:6 *sun . . . moon.* Here, in agreement with the "shade" metaphor, these serve as figures for all that distresses or threatens, day or night (see Is 4:6; 25:4–5; 49:10; Jon 4:8).
121:7–8 Assurance concerning all of life.
121:8 *your going out and your coming in.* See 1 Sam 29:6 and 2 Sam 3:25 for the use of the phrase in military contexts. See Deut 28:6 for a context perhaps more like v.8.
Ps 122 A hymn of joy over Jerusalem (see Ps 42–43; 46; 48; 84; 87; 137 and the introductions to those psalms). Sung by a pilgrim in Jerusalem (very likely at one of the three annual festivals, Deut 16:16), it expresses his deep joy over the city and his prayer for its welfare. As the third of the pilgrimage psalms (see introduction to Ps 120), it shares many dominant themes with Ps 132, the third from the end of this collection—possibly a deliberate arrangement. Structurally, a two-verse introduction locates the worshiper with the festival throng in the city of his joy, and the major themes are developed in two stanzas of four (Hebrew) lines each. References to "the house of the LORD" (vv. 1,9) frame the song.
122 title *Ascents.* See note on Ps 120 title. *of David.* This element is not present in all ancient witnesses to the text, and the content suggests a later date (see note on v. 1).
122:1–2 Joy for having joined the pilgrimage to Jerusalem.
122:1 *the house of the LORD.* The temple (2 Sam 7:5,13; 1 Kin 5:3,5; 8:10). That Jerusalem became the city of pilgrimage before the dedication of the temple is doubtful in light of 1 Kin 3:4; 8:1–11.
122:2 *gates.* Gateways.
122:3–5 Jerusalem's significance for the faithful.
122:3 *compact together.* Perhaps refers to the city's well-knit construction (see Ps 48) and probably recalls the construction of the tabernacle (cf. Ex 26:11, "join . . . so that it will be a unit"). If so, Jerusalem is being celebrated as the earthly residence of God (see note on 9:11; see also Is 4:5).
122:4 *An ordinance for Israel.* See 81:3–5; Deut 16:1–17. *To give thanks.* For God's saving acts in behalf of Israel and His blessings on the nation. *name.* See note on 5:11.
122:5 *there . . . The thrones of the house of David.* Jerusalem is

6 Pray for the [a]peace of Jerusalem:
"May they prosper who [b]love you.
7 "May peace be within your [a]walls,
And prosperity within your
[b]palaces."
8 For the sake of my [a]brothers and my
friends,
I will now say, "[b]May peace be within
you."
9 For the sake of the house of the LORD
our God,
I will [a]seek your good.

Psalm 123

A Song of Ascents.

1 To You I [a]lift up my eyes,
O You who [b]are enthroned in the
heavens!
2 Behold, as the eyes of [a]servants *look*
to the hand of their master,
As the eyes of a maid to the hand of
her mistress,
So our [b]eyes *look* to the LORD our
God,
Until He is gracious to us.

3 [a]Be gracious to us, O LORD, be
gracious to us,
For we are greatly filled [b]with
contempt.
4 Our soul is greatly filled
With the [a]scoffing of [b]those who are
at ease,
And with the [c]contempt of the
proud.

Psalm 124

A Song of Ascents, of David.

1 "[a]Had it not been the LORD who was
on our side,"
[b]Let Israel now say,
2 "Had it not been the LORD who was on
our side
When men rose up against us,
3 Then they would have [a]swallowed us
alive,
When their [b]anger was kindled
against us;
4 Then the [a]waters would have engulfed
us,
The stream would have [1]swept over
our soul;
5 Then the [a]raging waters would have
[1]swept over our soul."

6 Blessed be the LORD,
Who has not given us [1]to be [a]torn by
their teeth.
7 Our soul has [a]escaped [b]as a bird out
of the [c]snare of the trapper;
The snare is broken and we have
escaped.
8 Our [a]help is in the name of the LORD,
Who [b]made heaven and earth.

Psalm 125

A Song of Ascents.

1 Those who trust in the LORD
Are as Mount Zion, which [a]cannot be
moved but [b]abides forever.

6 [a]Ps 29:11; Jer 29:7 [b]Ps 102:14 **7** [a]Ps 51:18; Is 62:6 [b]Ps 48:3, 13; Jer 17:27 **8** [a]Ps 133:1 [b]1 Sam 25:6; John 20:19 **9** [a]Neh 2:10; Esth 10:3 **123:1** [a]Ps 121:1; 141:8 [b]Ps 2:4; 11:4 **2** [a]Prov 27:18; Mal 1:6 [b]Ps 25:15 **3** [a]Ps 4:1; 51:1 [b]Neh 4:4; Ps 119:22 **4** [a]Neh 2:19; Ps 79:4 [b]Job 12:5; Is 32:9, 11; Amos 6:1 [c]Neh 4:4; Ps 119:22

124:1 [a]Ps 94:17 [b]Ps 129:1 **3** [a]Num 16:30; Ps 35:25; 56:1; 57:3; Prov 1:12 [b]Gen 39:19; Ps 138:7 **4** [1]Or *passed over* [a]Job 22:11; Ps 18:16; 32:6; 69:2; 144:7 **5** [1]Or *passed over* [a]Job 38:11 **6** [1]Lit *as a prey to* [a]Ps 27:2; Prov 30:14 **7** [a]Ps 141:10; 2 Cor 11:33; Heb 11:34 [b]Prov 6:5 [c]Ps 91:3; Hos 9:8 **8** [a]Ps 121:2 [b]Gen 1:1; Ps 134:3 **125:1** [a]Ps 46:5 [b]Ps 61:7; Eccl 1:4

both the city of the Lord and the royal city of His chosen dynasty, through which He (ideally) protects and governs the nation (see 2:2,6–7; 89:3–4,19–37; 110; 2 Sam 7:8–16 and notes). In postexilic times it remained, though now in Messianic hope, the city of David.

122:6–9 Prayers for Jerusalem's peace.

122:6 In Hebrew a beautiful wordplay tightly binds together "pray," "peace," "Jerusalem" and "prosper." *peace.* See vv. 7–8; includes both security and prosperity. *who love you.* The psalmist, those referred to in vv. 1,8 and all who love Jerusalem because they are devoted to the Lord and His chosen king. These constitute a loving brotherhood, who worship together, pray together and seek each other's welfare as the people of God (see Ps 133).

122:7 *walls . . . palaces.* See 48:13 ("ramparts . . . palaces").

122:8–9 *For the sake of . . . For the sake of.* Because Jerusalem is the place supreme where God and His people meet together in fruitful union, the psalmist vows to seek the city's peace.

Ps 123 A prayer of God's humble people for Him to show mercy and so foil the contempt of the proud. See introduction to Ps 124. As to its structure, a one-verse introduction is followed by two couplets, each developing its own theme.

123 title See note on Ps 120 title.

123:1 *who are enthroned in the heavens.* The same God whose earthly throne is in the temple on Mount Zion (see 122:5 and note; see also 2:4; 9:11; 11:4; 80:1; 99:1; 113:5; 132:14).

123:2 *servants . . . maid.* Similes by which the faithful (men and women alike) present themselves as humbly dependent on God.

123:4 *those. . . at ease, And . . . the proud.* Those who live by their own wits and strength (see notes on 10:2–11; 31:23) pour contempt on those who humbly rely on God, especially when those who rely on God suffer or do not prosper.

Ps 124 Israel's praise of the Lord for deliverance from powerful enemies—an appropriate sequel to Ps 123. Very likely a Levite speaks in vv. 1–5, while the worshipers answer in vv. 6–8. Like Ps 129 it divides into two well-balanced stanzas.

124 title *Ascents.* See note on Ps 120 title. *of David.* Not all ancient witnesses to the text contain this element, and both language and theme suggest a postexilic date (see note on Ps 122 title). It may have been assigned to David because of supposed echoes of Ps 18; 69.

124:1–5 Let Israel acknowledge that the Lord alone has saved her from extinction (see 20:7; 94:17).

124:2 *men rose up against us.* Proud and arrogant men (123:4) may attack, but the Lord is Israel's help (v. 8).

124:3 *swallowed us.* Like death (see note on 49:14). But see 69:15.

124:4–5 *waters . . . stream . . . raging waters.* See 18:16; see also 32:6; 69:1–2 and notes.

124:6–8 Response of praise for deliverance—with a vivid enrichment of the imagery.

124:6 *torn by their teeth.* As by wild beasts (see note on 7:2).

124:7 *escaped as a bird out of the snare of the trapper.* A most apt figure for Israel's release from Babylonian captivity.

124:8 In climax, the great confession (see 121:2 and note).

Ps 125 Israel's peace: in testimony, prayer and benediction. The

2 As the mountains surround Jerusalem,
So [a]the LORD surrounds His people
[b]From this time forth and forever.
3 For the [a]scepter of wickedness shall not rest upon the [1]land of the righteous,
So that the righteous [b]will not put forth their hands to do wrong.

4 [a]Do good, O LORD, to those who are good
And to those who are [b]upright in their hearts.
5 But as for those who [a]turn aside to their [b]crooked ways,
The LORD will lead them away with the [c]doers of iniquity.
[d]Peace be upon Israel.

Psalm 126

A Song of Ascents.

1 When the LORD [a]brought back [1]the captive ones of Zion,
We were [b]like those who dream.
2 Then our [a]mouth was filled with laughter
And our [b]tongue with joyful shouting;
Then they said among the nations,
"The LORD has [c]done great things for them."
3 The LORD has done great things for us;
We are [a]glad.

4 Restore our captivity, O LORD,
As the [1][a]streams in the [2]South.
5 Those who sow in [a]tears shall reap with [b]joyful shouting.
6 He who goes to and fro weeping, carrying *his* bag of seed,
Shall indeed come again with a shout of joy, bringing his sheaves *with him.*

Psalm 127

A Song of Ascents, of Solomon.

1 Unless the LORD [a]builds the house,
They labor in vain who build it;
Unless the LORD [b]guards the city,
The watchman keeps awake in vain.
2 It is vain for you to rise up early,
To [1]retire late,
To [a]eat the bread of [2]painful labors;
For He gives to His [b]beloved [c]*even in his* sleep.

2 [a]Zech 2:5 [b]Ps 121:8
3 [1]Lit *lot* [a]Ps 89:22; Prov 22:8; Is 14:5 [b]1 Sam 24:10; Ps 55:20; Acts 12:1
4 [a]Ps 119:68 [b]Ps 7:10; 11:2; 32:11; 36:10; 94:15
5 [a]Job 23:11; Ps 40:4; 101:3 [b]Prov 2:15; Is 59:8 [c]Ps 92:7; 94:4 [d]Ps 128:6; Gal 6:16
126:1 [1]Or *those who returned to* [a]Ps 85:1; Jer 29:14; Hos 6:11 [b]Acts 12:9
2 [a]Job 8:21 [b]Ps 51:14; Is 35:6
2 [c]1 Sam 12:24; Ps 71:19; Luke 1:49
3 [a]Is 25:9; Zeph 3:14
4 [1]Lit *streambeds* [2]Heb *Negev* [a]Is 35:6; 43:19
5 [a]Ps 80:5; Jer 31:9, 16; Lam 1:2 [b]Is 35:10; 51:11; 61:7; Gal 6:9
127:1 [a]Ps 78:69 [b]Ps 121:4
2 [1]Lit *delay sitting* [2]Lit *toils* [a]Gen 3:17, 19 [b]Ps 60:5 [c]Job 11:18, 19; Prov 3:24; Eccl 5:12

psalm is most likely postexilic and was probably spoken in the temple liturgy by a Levite.
125 title See note on Ps 120 title.
125:1–2 The solid security of God's people.
125:1 *Those who trust in the LORD.* God's "people" (v. 2) are also characterized as "the righteous" (v. 3) and "those who are good," "who are upright in their hearts" (v. 4). For a similar description of the "righteous" see 34:8–14 and note. *as Mount Zion.* In their security (see Ps 46; 48).
125:2 *mountains surround Jerusalem.* Though Jerusalem is not surrounded by a ring of peaks, the city is located in what OT writers called a mountainous region. *so the LORD surrounds His people.* As surely, as substantially and as immovably (see 2 Kin 6:17; Zech 2:5).
125:3 Wicked rulers, whether by example or by oppression, tend to corrupt even the righteous, but the Lord will preserve His people also from this corrosive threat. *scepter of wickedness.* Probably referring to Persian rule (see Neh 9:36–37) and its invidious underlings, such as those Nehemiah had to contend with (see Neh 2:19; 4:1–3,7–8; 6:1–14,17–19; 13:7–8,28). *land of the righteous.* The promised land (see 78:55).
125:4–5 To each according as he is and does—that is God's way (see 18:25–27); thus the confident prayer (v. 4) and the equally confident assertion (v. 5).
125:4 *hearts.* See note on 4:7.
125:5 *Peace be upon Israel.* Perhaps a concise form of the priestly benediction (Num 6:24–26).
Ps 126 A song of joy for restoration to Zion. If not composed for those who returned from Babylonian exile (see Ezra and Nehemiah)—the place of exile is not named—it surely served to voice the joy of that restored community (cf. Ps 42–43; 84; 137). The psalm divides into two stanzas of four (Hebrew) lines each, with their initial lines sharing a common theme. Thematic unity is further served by repetition (cf. vv. 2–3) and other key words ("the LORD," "joyful shouting," "carrying . . . bringing"). References to God's action (vv. 1,3) frame the first stanza, while v. 2 offers exposition.
126 title See note on Ps 120 title.
126:1–3 Joy over restoration experienced.
126:1 *dream.* The wonder and joy of the reality were so marvelous that they hardly dared believe it. It seemed more like the dreams with which they had so long been tantalized.
126:2 The twofold effect: joy for those who returned and honor for God among the nations (see note on 46:10).
126:4–6 Prayer for restoration to be completed.
126:4 *Restore our captivity.* Either complete the repatriation of exiles or fully restore the security and prosperity of former times. *As the streams in the South.* Which are bone-dry in summer, until the winter rains renew their flow.
126:5–6 An apt metaphorical portrayal of the joy already experienced and the joy anticipated. *in tears . . . weeping.* Even when sowing is accompanied by trouble or sorrow, harvest brings joy. For a related figure see 20:5.
Ps 127 Godly wisdom concerning home and hearth. Its theme is timeless; it reminded the pilgrims on their way to Jerusalem that all of life's securities and blessings are gifts from God rather than their own achievements (see Deut 28:1–14). Two balanced stanzas develop, respectively, two distinct but related themes.
127 title *Ascents.* See note on Ps 120 title. *of Solomon.* If Solomon was not the author (not all witnesses to the text ascribe it to him), it is easy to see why some thought him so.
127:1–2 It is the Lord who provides shelter, security and food.
127:1 *house.* Domestic shelter. *They . . . who build it.* The Hebrew here is a pun on that for "Sons" in v. 3. *guards.* See 121:3–8. *city.* The center of power, the refuge when enemies invade the land. *watchman.* See 2 Sam 13:34; 18:24–27; Song 3:3; 5:7.
127:2 *He gives . . . in his sleep.* A good harvest is not the achievement of endless toil, but it is the result of God's blessing (see Prov 10:22; Matt 6:25–34; 1 Pet 5:7). *His beloved.* See especially Deut 33:12; Jer 11:15.

3 Behold, [a]children are a [1]gift of the
LORD,
The [b]fruit of the womb is a reward.
4 Like arrows in the hand of a [a]warrior,
So are the children of one's youth.
5 How [a]blessed is the man whose
quiver is full of them;
[b]They will not be ashamed
When they [c]speak with their enemies
[d]in the gate.

Psalm 128

A Song of Ascents.

1 [a]How blessed is everyone who fears
the LORD,
Who [b]walks in His ways.
2 When you shall [a]eat of the [1b]fruit of
your hands,
You will be happy and [c]it will be well
with you.
3 Your wife shall be like a [a]fruitful vine
[1]Within your house,
Your children like [b]olive plants
Around your table.
4 Behold, for thus shall the man be
blessed
Who fears the LORD.

5 [a]The LORD bless you [b]from Zion,
And may you see the prosperity of
Jerusalem all the days of your life.
6 Indeed, may you see your [a]children's
children.
[b]Peace be upon Israel!

Psalm 129

A Song of Ascents.

1 "[1]Many times they have [2a]persecuted
me from my [b]youth up,"
[c]Let Israel now say,
2 "[1]Many times they have [2]persecuted
me from my youth up;
Yet they have [a]not prevailed against
me.
3 "The plowers plowed upon my back;
They lengthened their furrows."
4 The LORD [a]is righteous;
He has cut in two the [b]cords of the
wicked.

5 May all who [a]hate Zion
Be [b]put to shame and turned
backward;
6 Let them be like [a]grass upon the
housetops,
Which withers before it [1]grows up;
7 With which the reaper does not fill his
[1]hand,
Or the binder of sheaves his [a]bosom;

3 [1]Or *heritage* [a]Gen 33:5; 48:4; Josh 24:3, 4; Ps 113:9 [b]Deut 7:13; 28:4; Is 13:18
4 [a]Ps 112:2; 120:4
5 [a]Ps 128:2, 3 [b]Prov 27:11 [c]Is 29:21; Amos 5:12 [d]Gen 34:20
128:1 [a]Ps 112:1; 119:1 [b]Ps 119:3
2 [1]Lit *labor* [a]Is 3:10 [b]Ps 109:11; Hag 2:17 [c]Eccl 8:12; Eph 6:3
3 [1]Lit *In the innermost parts of* [a]Ezek 19:10 [b]Ps 52:8; 144:12
5 [a]Ps 134:3 [b]Ps 20:2; 135:21
6 [a]Gen 48:11; 50:23; Job 42:16; Ps 103:17; Prov 17:6 [b]Ps 125:5
129:1 [1]Lit *Much* [2]Lit *showed hostility toward* [a]Ex 1:11; Judg 3:8; Ps 88:15 [b]Is 47:12; Jer 2:2; 22:21; Ezek 16:22; Hos 2:15; 11:1 [c]Ps 124:1
2 [1]Lit *Much* [2]Lit *showed hostility toward* [a]Jer 1:19; 15:20; 20:11; Matt 16:18; 2 Cor 4:8, 9
4 [a]Ps 119:137 [b]Ps 140:5 **5** [a]Mic 4:11 [b]Ps 70:3; 71:13
6 [1]Lit *draws out* [a]2 Kin 19:26; Ps 37:2; Is 37:27 **7** [1]Lit *palm* [a]Ps 79:12

127:3–5 Children are God's gift and a sign of His favor.
127:3 *children.* See note on v. 1. Children too are a gift—not the mere product of virility and fertility (see 113:9 and note; Gen 30:2). *gift.* Emphasis here is on gift rather than possession. But perhaps more is implied. In the OT economy, an Israelite's "inheritance" from the Lord was first of all property in the promised land (Num 26:53; Josh 11:23; Judg 2:6), which provided a sure place in the life and "rest" (Josh 1:13) of the Lord's kingdom. But without children the inheritance in the land would be lost (Num 27:8–11), so that offspring were a heritage in a double sense. *reward.* Bestowed by God on one who stands in His favor because he has been faithful.
127:5 *When they speak with their enemies.* Fathers with many sons have many defenders when falsely accused in court. Moreover, the very fact that they have many sons as God's "reward" (v. 3) testifies to God's favor toward them (in effect, they are God-provided character witnesses; see 128:3–4). *in the gate.* For the use of "gate" and "gates" as a judicial site see Deut 17:5; 21:19; 22:15,24; 25:7; Ruth 4:1; Is 29:21; Amos 5:12.
Ps 128 The blessedness of the godly man; another word of wisdom concerning hearth and home (see Ps 127). The concluding benediction suggests that the psalm originally served as a Levitical (or priestly) word of instruction to those assembled from their homes to worship in Jerusalem. Its date may well be pre-exilic. Structurally, the frame ("who fears the LORD") around vv. 1–4 sets off those verses as the main body of the psalm.
128 title See note on Ps 120 title.
128:1–4 Blessedness affirmed.
128:1 *blessed.* See note on 1:1. *fears the LORD.* See note on 34:8–14. *His ways.* See note on 25:4.
128:2 Blessings upon labor.
128:3 A faithful and fruitful wife. *vine.* Symbol of fruitfulness (Gen 49:22)—and perhaps also of sexual charms (Song 7:8–12) and festivity (Judg 9:13). *Within your house.* She is not like the faithless wife whose "feet do not remain at home" (Prov 7:11). *olive plants.* Ever green and with the promises of both long life and productivity (of staples: wood, fruit, oil). The vine and the olive tree are frequently paired in the OT (as, e.g., in Ex 23:11). Both were especially long-lived, and they produced the wine and the oil that played such a central role in the lives of the people. *Around your table.* Converting each family meal into a banquet of domestic joys.
128:5–6 The benediction pronounced—completing the scope of true blessedness: unbroken prosperity, secure relationship with God and secure national existence (the prosperity of Jerusalem entailed both), and long life.
128:5 *from Zion.* See 9:11 and note; 20:2; 135:21.
128:6 *Peace be upon Israel!* See 125:5 and note.
Ps 129 Israel's prayer for the continued withering of all her powerful enemies. The rescue celebrated (v. 4) is probably from Babylonian exile. Against the background of Ps 124–128, this prayer for the withholding of God's blessing is set in sharp relief. Like Ps 124 (with which Ps 129 shares other affinities), the psalm is composed of two nicely balanced stanzas.
129 title See note on Ps 120 title.
129:1–4 The wicked oppressors have not prevailed.
129:1 *from my youth.* From the time Israel was enslaved in Egypt, she has suffered much at the hands of hostile powers.
129:2 *have not prevailed.* Have not succeeded in their efforts to destroy Israel totally or to hold her permanently in bondage.
129:4 *righteous.* See note on 4:1.
129:5–8 May all who hate Zion wither.
129:5 See note on 5:10.
129:6 *like grass upon the housetops.* May those who would "plow" the backs of Israel (see v. 3) wither like grass that sprouts on the flat, sunbaked housetops, where no plow can prepare a

8 Nor do those who pass by say,
"The [a]blessing of the LORD be upon
you;
We bless you in the name of the
LORD."

Psalm 130

A Song of Ascents.

1 Out of the [a]depths I have cried to You,
O LORD.
2 Lord, [a]hear my voice!
Let [b]Your ears be attentive
To the [c]voice of my supplications.
3 If You, [1]LORD, should mark iniquities,
O Lord, who could [a]stand?
4 But there is [a]forgiveness with You,
That You may be [b]feared.

5 I wait for the LORD, my [a]soul does
wait,
And [1][b]in His word do I hope.
6 My soul *waits* for the Lord
More than the watchmen [a]for the
morning;
Indeed, more than the watchmen for
the morning.
7 O Israel, [a]hope in the LORD;
For with the LORD there is
[b]lovingkindness,
And with Him is [c]abundant
redemption.
8 And He will [a]redeem Israel
From all his iniquities.

Psalm 131

A Song of Ascents, of David.

1 O LORD, my heart is not [a]proud, nor
my eyes [1][b]haughty;
Nor do I [2]involve myself in [c]great
matters,
Or in things [d]too [3]difficult for me.
2 Surely I have [a]composed and quieted
my soul;
Like a weaned [b]child *rests* [1]against his
mother,
My soul is like a weaned child [1]within
me.
3 O Israel, [a]hope in the LORD
[b]From this time forth and forever.

Psalm 132

A Song of Ascents.

1 Remember, O LORD, on David's behalf,
All [a]his affliction;
2 How he swore to the LORD

8 [a]Ruth 2:4; Ps 118:26 **130:1** [a]Ps 42:7; 69:2; Lam 3:55 **2** [a]Ps 64:1; 119:149 [b]2 Chr 6:40; Neh 1:6, 11 [c]Ps 28:2; 140:6 **3** [1]Heb *YAH* [a]Ps 76:7; 143:2; Nah 1:6; Mal 3:2; Rev 6:17 **4** [a]Ex 34:7; Neh 9:17; Ps 86:5; Is 55:7; Dan 9:9 [b]1 Kin 8:39, 40; Jer 33:8, 9 **5** [1]Lit *for* [a]Ps 27:14; 33:20; 40:1; 62:1, 5; Is 8:17; 26:8 [b]Ps 119:74, 81 **6** [a]Ps 63:6; 119:147 **7** [a]Ps 131:3 [b]Ps 86:5; 103:4

7 [c]Ps 111:9; Rom 3:24; Eph 1:7 **8** [a]Ps 103:3, 4; Luke 1:68; Titus 2:14 **131:1** [1]Or *lofty* [2]Lit *go after, walk* [3]Or *marvelous* [a]2 Sam 22:28; Ps 101:5; Is 2:12; Zeph 3:11 [b]Prov 30:13; Is 5:15 [c]Jer 45:5; Rom 12:16 [d]Job 42:3; Ps 139:6

2 [1]Or *upon* [a]Ps 62:1 [b]Matt 18:3; 1 Cor 14:20 **3** [a]Ps 130:7 [b]Ps 113:2 **132:1** [a]Gen 49:24; 2 Sam 16:12

nurturing soil to sustain the young shoots—and so there is no harvest (v. 7).

129:8 *those who pass by.* Whoever may pass by the harvesters in the fields will exchange no joyful greetings (Ruth 2:4) because the hands of the harvesters will be empty.

Ps 130 A testimony of trust in the Lord—by one who knows that even though he is a sinner, the Lord hears his cry out of the depths. The language of the psalm suggests a postexilic date. This is the sixth of seven penitential psalms (see introduction to Ps 6). Composed of four thematic couplets, the psalm further divides into two halves of two couplets each.

130 title See note on Ps 120 title.

130:1–4 A prayer for mercy, and grounds for assurance.

130:1 *the depths.* As in 69:2 (see notes on 30:1; 32:6).

130:4 *there is forgiveness.* No doubt recalling such reassuring words as Ex 34:6–7. *feared.* Honored, worshiped, trusted and served as the one true God. If God were not forgiving, people could only flee from Him in terror.

130:5–8 Trust in the Lord: a personal testimony, expanding into a reassuring invitation (see 131:3).

130:5 *I wait.* In hopeful expectation. *my soul.* See note on 6:3. *His word.* Especially His covenant promises (see 119:25,28,37,42,49,65,74,81,107,114,147).

130:6 *watchmen.* See 127:1; 2 Sam 13:34; 18:24–27; Song 3:3; 5:7. *the morning.* See introduction to Ps 57; see also note on 59:9.

130:7 *lovingkindness.* See note on 6:4.

130:8 *From all his iniquities.* From the root of trouble—but also from all its consequences. This greatest of all hopes has been fulfilled in Christ.

Ps 131 A confession of humble trust in the Lord—appropriately placed next to Ps 130.

131 title *Ascents.* See note on Ps 120 title.

131:1 *heart.* See note on 4:7. *proud . . . haughty.* More than all else, it is human pride that pits man against God (see note on 31:23; cf. 2 Sam 6:21–22). *involve myself in.* (Presume to) walk among, live among, be party to. *great matters . . . too difficult for me.* Heroic exploits or achievements to rival, if not substitute for, the mighty works of God. The focus seems to be on not claiming Godlike powers (thus trusting in God for deliverance and blessing) rather than on seeking (or claiming) Godlike understanding.

131:2 *soul.* See note on 6:3. *weaned child.* A child of four or five who walks trustingly beside his mother.

131:3 As he has done, so ought all Israel—for all time.

Ps 132 A prayer for God's favor on the son of David who reigns on David's throne—as the structure makes clear (and see note on v. 10). Its language suggests a date early in the monarchy. The venerable belief that it was composed for the dedication of the temple may be correct (compare vv. 8–10 with 2 Chr 6:41–42), but the possibility cannot be ruled out that it was used in the coronation ritual (cf. Ps 2; 72; 110). The author of Chronicles places the prayer (or a portion of it) on the lips of the king himself. In the postexilic liturgy it had Messianic implications.

Two verses of petition (vv. 1,10) are each followed (in Hebrew) by two four-line stanzas, all having an identical form: an introductory line followed by a three-line quotation (see the structure of these quotations). A final couplet brings the prayer to its climactic conclusion. The four thematic stanzas, together with the final couplet, ground the prayer made in vv. 1,10. Verses 2–9 appeal to David's oath to the Lord to find a "place" for the Lord and to his bringing the ark to its "resting place," while vv. 11–18 appeal to the Lord's oath to David and to His election of Zion as His "resting place" (but see note on v. 10).

132 title See note on Ps 120 title.

132:1 *Remember.* See 20:3; see also 1 Kin 11:12–13; 15:4–5. *affliction.* The affliction he took on himself in his vow (vv. 2–5; see Num 30:13, where the same technical term for a self-denying oath is used).

And vowed to [a]the Mighty One of
Jacob,
3 "Surely I will not [1]enter [a]my house,
Nor [2]lie on my bed;
4 I will not [a]give sleep to my eyes
Or slumber to my eyelids,
5 Until I find a [a]place for the LORD,
[1]A dwelling place for [b]the Mighty One
of Jacob."

6 Behold, we heard of it in [a]Ephrathah,
We found it in the [b]field of [1]Jaar.
7 Let us go into His [1a]dwelling place;
Let us [b]worship at His [c]footstool.
8 [a]Arise, O LORD, to Your [b]resting
place,
You and the ark of Your [c]strength.
9 Let Your priests be [a]clothed with
righteousness,
And let Your [b]godly ones sing for joy.

10 For the sake of David Your servant,
Do not turn away the face of Your
[a]anointed.
11 The LORD has [a]sworn to David
A truth from which He will not turn
back:
"[b]Of the fruit of your body I will set
upon your throne.

2 [a]Gen 49:24; Is 49:26; 60:16
3 [1]Lit *come into the tabernacle of* [2]Lit *go up into the couch of* [a]Job 21:28
4 [a]Prov 6:4
5 [1]Lit *Dwelling places* [a]1 Kin 8:17; 1 Chr 22:7; Ps 26:8; Acts 7:46 [b]Ps 132:2
6 [1]Or *the wood* [a]Gen 35:19; 1 Sam 17:12 [b]1 Sam 7:1
7 [1]Lit *dwelling places* [a]Ps 43:3 [b]Ps 5:7; 99:5 [c]1 Chr 28:2
8 [a]Num 10:35; 2 Chr 6:41; Ps 68:1 [b]Ps 132:14 [c]Ps 78:61
9 [a]Job 29:14 [b]Ps 30:4; 132:16; 149:5
10 [a]Ps 2:2; 132:17
11 [a]Ps 89:3, 35 [b]2 Sam 7:12-16; 1 Chr 17:11-14; 2 Chr 6:16; Ps 89:4; Acts 2:30
12 [a]Luke 1:32; Acts 2:30
13 [a]Ps 48:1, 2; 78:68 [b]Ps 68:16
14 [a]Ps 132:8 [b]Ps 68:16; Matt 23:21

12 "If your sons will keep My covenant
And My testimony which I will teach
them,
Their sons also shall [a]sit upon your
throne forever."

13 For the LORD has [a]chosen Zion;
He has [b]desired it for His habitation.
14 "This is My [a]resting place forever;
Here I will [b]dwell, for I have desired
it.
15 "I will abundantly [a]bless her
provision;
I will [b]satisfy her needy with bread.
16 "Her [a]priests also I will clothe with
salvation,
And her [a]godly ones will sing aloud
for joy.
17 "There I will cause the [a]horn of David
to spring forth;
I have prepared a [b]lamp for Mine
anointed.
18 "His enemies I will [a]clothe with
shame,
But upon himself his [b]crown shall
shine."

15 [a]Ps 147:14 [b]Ps 107:9 **16** [a]2 Chr 6:41; Ps 132:9
17 [a]Ezek 29:21; Luke 1:69 [b]1 Kin 11:36; 15:4; 2 Kin 8:19; 2 Chr 21:7; Ps 18:28 **18** [a]Job 8:22; Ps 35:26; 109:29 [b]Ps 21:3

132:2 *he swore.* This prayer for David's son is grounded in the special relationship between David and the Lord, as epitomized in their mutual oaths (see vv. 11–12). In 2 Sam 6–7, which narrates the events here recalled, David's oath is not mentioned. *LORD . . . Mighty One of Jacob.* See v. 5; Is 1:24; see also note on 3:7. *Jacob.* A synonym for Israel (see Gen 32:28).

132:6 *it . . . it.* Often thought to refer to the ark, but more likely it refers to the call to worship that follows (in Hebrew the pronoun is feminine, but the Hebrew for "ark" is masculine). *Ephrathah.* The region around Bethlehem, David's hometown (see Ruth 4:11; Mic 5:2). *field of Jaar.* Kiriath-jearim; called "Baale-judah" in 2 Sam 6:2. The call to worship is depicted as emanating from David's city and the city where the ark had been since the days of Samuel (see 1 Sam 7:1). The call appears to come from a time after the temple had been built—thus involving a poetic compression of events.

132:7 *footstool.* See 99:5 and note.

132:8 *Arise.* Although the Hebrew omits (a common feature in Hebrew poetry) an introductory word, such as "saying," vv. 8–9 are probably words on the lips of the worshipers. See introduction to Ps 24. *resting place.* As the promised land was Israel's place of rest at the end of her wanderings (see Num 10:33; Josh 1:13; Mic 2:10), so the temple was the Lord's resting place after He had been moving about in a tent (see 2 Sam 7:6; see also 1 Chr 28:2). The expression may suggest that the temple was the place of God's throne (v. 14). *ark of Your strength.* See note on 78:61.

132:9 *clothed with.* Beyond their normal priestly garb—may their ministry bear the character of (see Job 29:14; Prov 31:25), i.e., result in. *righteousness.* Since the corresponding word in v. 16 is "salvation," the same word used by the author of Chronicles when quoting this verse (2 Chr 6:41), and since "righteousness" and "salvation" are often paralleled (40:10; 51:14; 71:15; 98:2; Is 45:8; 46:13; 51:5–6; 56:1; 59:17; 60:17–18; 61:10; 62:1), the reference is clearly to God's righteousness that effects the salvation of His people (see note on 5:8). *godly ones.* See note on 4:3.

132:10 See v. 1. *Your servant.* See note on Ps 18 title. *Do not turn away.* Do not refuse his petitions (as in 1 Kin 2:16–17,20; see 1 Kin 8:59; 2 Chr 6:41–42). If, as some have proposed, the petitions in vv. 1,10 form a frame around the first half of the psalm, the second half offers assurance that the prayer will be heard (perhaps spoken by a priest or Levite). In any event, David's vow to provide the Lord a dwelling place, which would be for His royal sons and for Israel a house of prayer (see 1 Kin 8:27–53; 9:3; 2 Chr 7:15–16; Is 56:7), is made the basis for the appeal that God will hear His anointed's prayer. *Your anointed.* See note on 2:2.

132:11–12 The Lord's covenant with David is recalled, as grounds for the prayer. These and vv. 13–18 are a poetic recollection of 1 Kin 9:1–5 (see 2 Chr 7:11–18).

132:11 *has sworn.* See v. 2 and note. 2 Sam 7 does not mention an oath, but elsewhere God's promise to David is called a covenant (89:3,28,34,39; 2 Sam 23:5; Is 55:3), and covenants were made on oath. *will not turn back.* See 110:4.

132:12 *covenant . . . testimony.* The stipulations of the Sinai covenant, which all Israelites were to keep (see 1 Sam 10:25 and note; see also 1 Kin 2:3–4).

132:13–16 The Lord's election of Zion recalled, as grounds for the prayer.

132:13 *desired it for His habitation.* David's and the Lord's desires harmonize (see Deut 12:5–14).

132:15 The Lord enthroned in His resting place (see vv. 8,14) will bless the land, making it a place of rest for His people (see Deut 12:9; Josh 1:13; 1 Kin 5:4).

132:16 See note on v. 9.

132:17–18 Concluding word of assurance, which addresses the petition (vv. 1,10) directly and climactically.

132:17 *horn.* The Lord's anointed. *spring forth.* Like a plant or branch. *prepared a lamp for.* See note on 1 Kin 11:36.

132:18 *clothe with shame.* In contrast with v. 16. *shall shine.* Lit. "blossom"—subtly evoking the imagery: spring forth (v. 17) and blossom.

Psalm 133

A Song of Ascents, of David.

1 Behold, how good and how pleasant it is
For [a]brothers to dwell together in unity!
2 It is like the precious [a]oil upon the head,
Coming down upon the beard,
Even Aaron's beard,
Coming down upon the [b]edge of his robes.
3 It is like the [a]dew of [b]Hermon
Coming down upon the [c]mountains of Zion;
For there the LORD [d]commanded the blessing—[e]life forever.

Psalm 134

A Song of Ascents.

1 Behold, [a]bless the LORD, all [b]servants of the LORD,
Who [1c]serve [d]by night in the house of the LORD!
2 [a]Lift up your hands to the [b]sanctuary
And bless the LORD.
3 May the LORD [a]bless you from Zion,
He who [b]made heaven and earth.

133:1 [a]Gen 13:8; Heb 13:1 **2** [a]Ex 29:7; 30:25, 30; Lev 8:12 [b]Ex 28:33; 39:24 **3** [a]Prov 19:12; Hos 14:5; Mic 5:7 [b]Deut 3:9; 4:48 [c]Ps 48:2; 74:2; 78:68 [d]Lev 25:21; Deut 28:8; Ps 42:8 [e]Ps 21:4
134:1 [1]Lit *stand* [a]Ps 103:21 [b]Ps 135:1, 2 [c]Deut 10:8; 1 Chr 23:30; 2 Chr 29:11 [d]1 Chr 9:33 **2** [a]Ps 28:2; 1 Tim 2:8 [b]Ps 63:2 **3** [a]Ps 128:5 [b]Ps 124:8
135:1 [1]Or *Hallelujah!* [2]Heb YAH [a]Ps 113:1 [b]Ps 134:1 **2** [a]Ps 92:13; 116:19 **3** [1]Or *Hallelujah!* [2]Heb YAH [a]Ps 100:5; 119:68 [b]Ps 68:4 [c]Ps 147:1 **4** [1]Heb YAH [2]Or *special treasure* [a]Deut 7:6; 10:15; Ps 105:6 [b]Ex 19:5; Mal 3:17; Titus 2:14; 1 Pet 2:9

Psalm 135

1 [1a]Praise [2]the LORD!
Praise the name of the LORD;
Praise *Him*, O [b]servants of the LORD,
2 You who stand in the house of the LORD,
In the [a]courts of the house of our God!
3 [1]Praise [2]the LORD, for [a]the LORD is good;
[b]Sing praises to His name, [c]for it is lovely.
4 For [1]the LORD has [a]chosen Jacob for Himself,
Israel for His [2b]own possession.

5 For I know that [a]the LORD is great
And that our Lord is [b]above all gods.
6 [a]Whatever the LORD pleases, He does,
In heaven and in earth, in the seas and in all deeps.
7 [1]He [a]causes the [2]vapors to ascend from the ends of the earth;
Who [b]makes lightnings for the rain,
Who [a]brings forth the wind from His treasuries.

5 [a]Ps 48:1; 95:3; 145:3 [b]Ps 97:9 **6** [a]Ps 115:3 **7** [1]Lit *The one who* [2]I.e. clouds [a]Jer 10:13; 51:16 [b]Job 28:25, 26; 38:25, 26; Zech 10:1

Ps 133 A song in praise of brotherly unity among the people of God. If David was the author (see title), he may have been moved to write it by some such occasion as when, after many years of conflict, all Israel came to Hebron to make him king (2 Sam 5:1–3). The first and last (Hebrew) lines (vv. 1,3b) frame the whole with the song's main theme. Next to these an inner frame (lines 2,4) elaborates with two striking complementary similes (vv. 2a,3a). The center line (v. 2b) extends the first simile.
133 title *Ascents.* See note on Ps 120 title. *of David.* Not all textual sources ascribe the psalm to him.
133:1 *how good and how pleasant.* See 135:3; 147:1.
133:2 *like the precious oil . . . Aaron's beard . . . upon the edge of his robes.* The oil of Aaron's anointing (Ex 29:7; Lev 21:10) saturated all the hair of his beard and ran down on his priestly robes, signifying his total consecration to holy service. Similarly, brotherly harmony sanctifies God's people.
133:3 *dew of Hermon . . . upon the mountains of Zion.* A dew as profuse as that of Mount Hermon would make the mountains of Zion (or Mount Zion) richly fruitful (see Gen 27:28; Hag 1:10; Zech 8:12). So would brotherly unity make Israel richly fruitful. The two similes (vv. 2–3) are well chosen: God's blessings flowed to Israel through the priestly ministrations at the sanctuary (Ex 29:44–46; Lev 9:22–24; Num 6:24–26)—epitomizing God's redemptive mercies—and through heaven's dew that sustained life in the fields—epitomizing God's providential mercies in the creation order. *life.* The great covenant blessing (see Deut 30:15,19–20; 32:47).
Ps 134 A liturgy of praise—a brief exchange between the worshipers, as they are about to leave the temple after the evening service, and the Levites, who kept the temple watch through the night. In the Psalter it concludes the "songs of Ascents," as Ps 117 concludes a collection of Hallelujah psalms (Ps 111–117). Its date is probably postexilic.
134 title See note on Ps 120 title.
134:1–2 The departing worshipers call on the Levites to continue the praise of the Lord through the night (see 1 Chr 9:33).
134:2 *Lift up your hands.* See 63:4.
134:3 One of the Levites responds with a benediction on the worshipers (see note on 121:2; see also 124:8; 128:5).
Ps 135 A call to praise the Lord—the one true God: Lord of all creation, Lord over all the nations, Israel's Redeemer. No doubt postexilic, it echoes many lines found elsewhere in the OT. It was clearly composed for the temple liturgy. For its place in the Great Hallel see note on Ps 120 title. Framed with "Hallelujahs" (as are also Ps 146–150), its first and last stanzas are also calls to praise. Recital of God's saving acts for Israel in Egypt and Canaan (vv. 8–12) makes up the middle of seven stanzas, while the remaining four constitute two pairs related to each other by theme and language (vv. 3–4, 13–14; vv. 5–7, 15–18).
135:1–2 Initial call to praise, addressed to priests and Levites (see 134:1–2).
135:1,3,13 *name.* See note on 5:11.
135:3–4 A central reason for Israel to praise the Lord (see vv. 13–14).
135:3 *it is lovely.* See 133:1. Or "He (the Lord) is beautiful" (see 27:4 and note).
135:4 *Jacob.* A synonym for Israel (see Gen 32:28). *His own possession.* See Ex 19:5 and note.
135:5–7 The Lord is great as well as good (v. 3); He is the absolute Lord in all creation (cf. the word about idols in vv. 15–18; see Jer 10:11–16; see also 115:3 and 96:5; 97:7 and notes).
135:6 *Whatever the Lord pleases, He does.* The idols can do nothing (vv. 16–17); they are themselves "done" (made) by their worshipers (v. 18). *heaven . . . earth . . . seas.* The three great domains of the visible creation, as the ancients viewed it (see Gen 1:8–10 and introduction to Ps 104).
135:7 *He causes the vapors to ascend.* See NASB marg. The Lord, not Baal or any other god, causes clouds to bring the life-giving rains (see Ps 29). *wind.* See 104:4; 148:8. The idols do not even

8 [1]He [a]smote the firstborn of Egypt,
[2]Both of man and beast.
9 [1]He sent [a]signs and wonders into your
midst, O Egypt,
Upon [b]Pharaoh and all his servants.
10 [1][a]He [b]smote many nations
And slew mighty kings,
11 [a]Sihon, king of the Amorites,
And [b]Og, king of Bashan,
And [c]all the kingdoms of Canaan;
12 And He [a]gave their land as a heritage,
A heritage to Israel His people.
13 Your [a]name, O LORD, is everlasting,
Your [1]remembrance, O LORD,
[2]throughout all generations.
14 For the LORD will [a]judge His people
And [b]will have compassion on His
servants.
15 The [a]idols of the nations are *but* silver
and gold,
The work of man's hands.
16 They have mouths, but they do not
speak;
They have eyes, but they do not see;
17 They have ears, but they do not hear,
Nor is there any breath at all in their
mouths.
18 Those who make them will be like
them,
Yes, everyone who trusts in them.

19 O house of [a]Israel, bless the LORD;
O house of Aaron, bless the LORD;
20 O house of Levi, bless the LORD;
You [a]who [1]revere the LORD, bless the
LORD.
21 Blessed be the LORD [a]from Zion,
Who [b]dwells in Jerusalem.
[1]Praise [2]the LORD!

Psalm 136

1 [a]Give thanks to the LORD, for [b]He is
good,
For [c]His lovingkindness is everlasting.
2 Give thanks to the [a]God of gods,
For His lovingkindness is everlasting.
3 Give thanks to the [a]Lord of lords,
For His lovingkindness is everlasting.
4 To Him who [a]alone does great
[1]wonders,
For His lovingkindness is everlasting;
5 To Him who [a]made the heavens
[1][b]with skill,
For His lovingkindness is everlasting;
6 To Him who [a]spread out the earth
above the waters,
For His lovingkindness is everlasting;
7 To Him who [a]made *the* great lights,
For His lovingkindness is everlasting:
8 The [a]sun to rule [1]by day,
For His lovingkindness is everlasting,
9 The [a]moon and stars to rule [1]by night,
For His lovingkindness is everlasting.

10 To Him who [a]smote [1]the Egyptians in
their firstborn,
For His lovingkindness is everlasting,
11 And [a]brought Israel out from their
midst,
For His lovingkindness is everlasting,
12 With a [a]strong hand and an
[b]outstretched arm,
For His lovingkindness is everlasting.
13 To Him who [a]divided the [1]Red Sea
[2]asunder,
For His lovingkindness is everlasting,
14 And [a]made Israel pass through the
midst of it,
For His lovingkindness is everlasting;
15 But [a]He [1]overthrew Pharaoh and his
army in the [2]Red Sea,
For His lovingkindness is everlasting.
16 To Him who [a]led His people through
the wilderness,
For His lovingkindness is everlasting;
17 To Him who [a]smote great kings,
For His lovingkindness is everlasting,
18 And [a]slew [1]mighty kings,

8 [1]Lit *The one who* [2]Lit *From man to beast* [a]Ex 12:12; Ps 78:51; 105:36 **9** [1]Lit *The one who* [a]Ex 7:10; Deut 6:22; Ps 78:43 [b]Ps 136:15 **10** [1]Lit *The one who* [a]Num 21:24; Ps 135:10-12; 136:17-21 [b]Ps 44:2 **11** [a]Num 21:21-26; Deut 29:7 [b]Num 21:33-35 [c]Josh 12:7-24 **12** [a]Deut 29:8; Ps 78:55; 136:21, 22 **13** [1]Or *memorial* [2]Lit *to* [a]Ex 3:15; Ps 102:12 **14** [a]Deut 32:36; Ps 50:4 [b]Ps 90:13; 106:46 **15** [a]Ps 115:4-8; 135:15-18 **19** [a]Ps 115:9 **20** [1]Lit *fear* [a]Ps 118:4 **21** [1]Or *Hallelujah!* [2]Heb YAH [a]Ps 128:5; 134:3 [b]Ps 132:14 **136:1** [a]1 Chr 16:34; Ps 106:1; 107:1; 118:1; Jer 33:11 [b]2 Chr 5:13; 7:3; Ezra 3:11; Ps 100:5 [c]1 Chr 16:41; 2 Chr 20:21; Ps 118:1-4 **2** [a]Deut 10:17 **3** [a]Deut 10:17

4 [1]I.e. wonderful acts [a]Deut 6:22; Job 9:10; Ps 72:18 **5** [1]Lit *with understanding* [a]Gen 1:1 [b]Ps 104:24; Prov 3:19; Jer 10:12; 51:15 **6** [a]Gen 1:2, 6, 9; Ps 24:2; Is 42:5; 44:24; Jer 10:12 **7** [a]Gen 1:14-18; Ps 74:16 **8** [1]Or *over the* [a]Gen 1:16 **9** [1]Or *over the* [a]Gen 1:16

10 [1]Lit *Egypt* [a]Ex 12:29; Ps 78:51; 135:8 **11** [a]Ex 12:51; 13:3; Ps 105:43 **12** [a]Ex 6:1; 13:9; 1 Kin 8:42; Neh 1:10; Ps 44:3; Jer 32:21 [b]Ex 6:6; Deut 4:34; 5:15; 7:19; 9:29; 11:2; 2 Kin 17:36; 2 Chr 6:32; Jer 32:17 **13** [1]Lit *Sea of Reeds* [2]Lit *in parts* [a]Ex 14:21; Ps 66:6; 78:13 **14** [a]Ex 14:22; Ps 106:9 **15** [1]Lit *shook off* [2]Lit *Sea of Reeds* [a]Ex 14:27; Ps 78:53; 106:11 **16** [a]Ex 13:18; 15:22; Deut 8:15; Ps 78:52 **17** [a]Ps 135:10-12; 136:17-22 **18** [1]Lit *majestic* [a]Deut 29:7

have any "wind" (breath) in their mouths (v. 17). *treasuries.* See 33:7 and note; Job 38:22.

135:8–12 The Lord's triumph over Egypt and over the kings whose lands became Israel's inheritance, a concise recollection of Ex 7–14; Num 21:21–35; Joshua.

135:13–14 See vv. 3–4 and note.

135:14 *judge.* Uphold against all attacks by the world powers both Israel's cause and her claim that the Lord is the only true God. *have compassion on.* See Ex 34:6–7. *His servants.* His covenant people.

135:15–18 The powerlessness of the false gods and of those who trust in them (see vv. 5–7 and note; see also 115:4–8 and notes).

135:19–21 Concluding call to praise, addressed to all who are assembled at the temple (see 115:9–11; 118:2–4).

Ps 136 A liturgy of praise to the Lord as Creator and as Israel's Redeemer. Its theme and many of its verses parallel much of Ps 135. Most likely a Levitical song leader led the recital, while the Levitical choir (1 Chr 16:41; 2 Chr 5:13; Ezra 3:11) or the worshipers (2 Chr 7:3,6; 20:21) responded with the refrain (see 106:1; 107:1; 118:1–4,29). This liturgy concludes the Great Hallel (see note on Ps 120 title). Following the initial call to praise (vv. 1–3), the recital devotes six verses to God's creation acts (vv. 4–9), six to His deliverance of Israel out of Egypt (vv. 10–15), one to the wilderness journey (v. 16) and six to the conquest (vv. 17–22). The four concluding verses return to the same basic themes in reverse order: God's action in history in behalf of His people (vv. 23–24), God's action in the creation order (v. 25) and a closing call to praise (v. 26).

136:1–3,26 *Give thanks to.* Or "Praise" (see 7:17 and note).

136:2 *the God of gods.* See Deut 10:17; see also 135:5.

136:5 *with skill.* See Prov 3:19; Jer 10:12.

136:6 *above the waters.* See 24:2 and note.

136:7–9 Direct echoes of Gen 1:16.

For His lovingkindness is everlasting:
19 [a]Sihon, king of the Amorites,
For His lovingkindness is everlasting,
20 And [a]Og, king of Bashan,
For His lovingkindness is everlasting,
21 And [a]gave their land as a heritage,
For His lovingkindness is everlasting,
22 Even a heritage to Israel His [a]servant,
For His lovingkindness is everlasting.

23 Who [a]remembered us in our low estate,
For His lovingkindness is everlasting,
24 And has [a]rescued us from our adversaries,
For His lovingkindness is everlasting;
25 Who [a]gives food to all flesh,
For His lovingkindness is everlasting.
26 Give thanks to the [a]God of heaven,
For His lovingkindness is everlasting.

Psalm 137

1 By the [a]rivers of Babylon,
There we sat down and [b]wept,
When we remembered Zion.
2 Upon the [1a]willows in the midst of it
We [b]hung our [2]harps.
3 For there our captors [1a]demanded of us [2]songs,
And [b]our tormentors mirth, *saying,*
"Sing us one of the songs of Zion."

4 How can we sing [a]the LORD's song
In a foreign land?
5 If I [a]forget you, O Jerusalem,
May my right hand [1]forget *her skill.*
6 May my [a]tongue cling to the roof of my mouth
If I do not remember you,
If I do not [1b]exalt Jerusalem
Above my chief joy.

7 Remember, O LORD, against the sons of [a]Edom
The day of Jerusalem,
Who said, "Raze it, raze it
[b]To its very foundation."
8 O daughter of Babylon, you [1a]devastated one,
How blessed will be the one who [b]repays you
With [2]the recompense with which you have repaid us.
9 How blessed will be the one who seizes and [a]dashes your little ones
Against the rock.

Psalm 138

A Psalm of David.

1 [a]I will give You thanks with all my heart;
I will sing praises to You before the [b]gods.

19 [a]Num 21:21-24
20 [a]Num 21:33-35
21 [a]Josh 12:1
22 [a]Ps 105:6; Is 41:8; 44:1; 45:4
23 [a]Ps 9:12; 103:14; 106:45
24 [a]Judg 6:9; Neh 9:28; Ps 107:2
25 [a]Ps 104:27; 145:15
26 [a]Gen 24:3, 7; 2 Chr 36:23; Ezra 1:2; 5:11; Neh 1:4
137:1 [a]Ezek 1:1, 3 [b]Neh 1:4
2 [1]Or *poplars* [2]Lit *lyres* [a]Lev 23:40; Is 44:4 [b]Job 30:31; Is 24:8; Ezek 26:13
3 [1]Lit *asked* [2]Lit *words of song* [a]Ps 80:6 [b]Is 49:17
4 [a]2 Chr 29:27; Neh 12:46
5 [1]I.e. become lame [a]Is 65:11
6 [1]Lit *cause to ascend* [a]Job 29:10; Ps 22:15; Ezek 3:26 [b]Neh 2:3
7 [a]Ps 83:4-8; Is 34:5, 6; Jer 49:7-22; Lam 4:21; Ezek 25:12-14; 35:2; Amos 1:11; Obad 10-14 [b]Ps 74:7; Hab 3:13
8 [1]Or *devastator* [2]Lit *your recompense* [a]Is 13:1-22; 47:1-15; Jer 25:12; 50:1-46; 51:1-64 [b]Jer 50:15; 51:24, 35, 36, 49; Rev 18:6
9 [a]2 Kin 8:12; Is 13:16; Hos 13:16; Nah 3:10
138:1 [a]Ps 111:1 [b]Ps 95:3; 96:4; 97:7

136:23–24 Probably a concluding summary of the deliverance recalled above, but may allude also to the deliverances experienced during the period of the judges and the reign of David.
136:26 *the God of heaven.* A Persian title for God (see note on Ezra 1:2) found frequently in Ezra, Nehemiah and Daniel. Its intent is similar to that of the language of vv. 2–3.
Ps 137 A plaintive song of the exile—of one who has recently returned from Babylon but in whose soul there lingers the bitter memory of the years in a foreign land and of the cruel events that led to that enforced stay. Here speaks the same deep love of Zion as that found in Ps 42–43; 46; 48; 84; 122; 126. The 12 poetic lines of the Hebrew song divide symmetrically into three stanzas of four lines each: the remembered sorrow and torment (vv. 1–3), an oath of total commitment to Jerusalem (vv. 4–6), a call for retribution on Edom and Babylon (vv. 7–9).
137:1 *rivers.* The Tigris and Euphrates and the many canals associated with them. *we sat.* Again and again the thought of their forced separation from Zion brought them down to the posture of mourning (see Job 2:8,13; Lam 2:10).
137:2 *We hung our harps.* "The gaiety of the harp ceases" (Is 24:8) because the callous Babylonians demanded exotic entertainment with the joyful songs of distant Zion, while the exiles' instruments were only "turned to mourning" (Job 30:31).
137:4–6 Only he whose heart had disowned the Lord and His holy city Jerusalem could play the puppet on a Babylonian stage. But may I never play the harp again or sing another syllable if I am untrue to that beloved city!
137:7–9 Lord, remember Edom; and as for you, Babylon, I bless whoever does to you what you did to Jerusalem: a passionate call for redress from a loyal son of the ravaged city (see note on 5:10).
137:7 *sons of Edom.* The agelong animosity of Edom—descendants of Esau, Jacob's brother—showed its most dastardly face in Jerusalem's darkest hour. No doubt the author knew the Lord's judgments against that nation announced by the prophets (Is 63:1–4; Jer 49:7–22; Ezek 25:8,12–14; 35; Obadiah). *Raze it.* Lit. "Strip her"—cities were conventionally portrayed as women. Lam 4:21 anticipates that Edom will be punished by suffering the same humiliation.
137:8 *daughter.* A personification of Babylon and its inhabitants. *devastated one.* The author may have known the Lord's announced judgments on this cruel destroyer (Is 13; 21:1–10; 47; Jer 50–51; Hab 2:4–20).
137:9 *your little ones.* War was as cruel then as now; women and children were not spared (see 2 Kin 8:12; 15:16; Is 13:16,18; Hos 10:14; 13:16; Amos 1:13; Nah 3:10). For the final announcement of the destruction of the "Babylon" that persists in its warfare against the City of God, and the joy with which that announcement is greeted, see Rev 18:1–19:4.
Ps 138 A royal song of praise for God's saving help against threatening foes. In many respects it is like Ps 18, though it is more concise and direct. Two (Hebrew) four-line stanzas (vv. 1–3, 6–8) develop the main theme; at the center a two-line stanza (vv. 4–5) expands the praise of the Lord to a universal company of earth's royalty.
138 title This begins a collection of eight "Davidic" psalms (Ps 138–145): six prayers framed by two psalms of praise.
138:1–3 Praise for God's faithful love shown in answer to prayers for help.
138:1 *heart.* See note on 4:7. *gods.* Either pagan kings (see vv. 4–5) or the gods they claimed to represent (see introduction to Ps 82; see also note on 82:1).

2 I will bow down [a]toward Your holy
temple
And [b]give thanks to Your name for
Your lovingkindness and Your
[1]truth;
For You have [c]magnified Your [2]word
[3]according to all Your name.
3 On the day I [a]called, You answered
me;
You made me bold with [b]strength in
my soul.

4 [a]All the kings of the earth will give
thanks to You, O LORD,
When they have heard the words of
Your mouth.
5 And they will [a]sing of the ways of the
LORD,
For [b]great is the glory of the LORD.
6 For [a]though the LORD is exalted,
Yet He [b]regards the lowly,
But the [c]haughty He knows from afar.

7 Though I [a]walk in the midst of
trouble, You will [1b]revive me;
You will [c]stretch forth Your hand
against the wrath of my enemies,
And Your right hand will [d]save me.
8 The LORD will [a]accomplish what
concerns me;
Your [b]lovingkindness, O LORD, is
everlasting;
[c]Do not forsake the [d]works of Your
hands.

2 [1]Or *faithfulness* [2]Or *promise* [3]Or *together with* [a]1 Kin 8:29; Ps 5:7; 28:2 [b]Ps 140:13 [c]Is 42:21
3 [a]Ps 118:5 [b]Ps 28:7; 46:1
4 [a]Ps 72:11; 102:15
5 [a]Ps 145:7 [b]Ps 21:5
6 [a]Ps 113:4-7 [b]Prov 3:34; Is 57:15; Luke 1:48; James 4:6; 1 Pet 5:5 [c]Ps 40:4; 101:5
7 [1]Or *keep me alive* [a]Ps 23:4; 143:11 [b]Ezra 9:8, 9; Ps 71:20; Is 57:15 [c]Ex 7:5; 15:12; Is 5:25; Jer 51:25; Ezek 6:14; 25:13 [d]Ps 20:6; 60:5
8 [a]Ps 57:2; Phil 1:6 [b]Ps 136:1 [c]Job 10:8; Ps 27:9; 71:9; 119:8 [d]Job 10:3; 14:15; Ps 100:3

139:1 [a]Ps 17:3; 44:21; Jer 12:3
2 [1]Lit *my sitting* [2]Lit *my rising* [a]2 Kin 19:27 [b]Ps 94:11; Is 66:18; Matt 9:4
3 [1]Lit *winnow* [2]Or *journeying* [a]Job 14:16; 31:4
4 [1]Lit *For there is not* [a]Heb 4:13
5 [a]Ps 34:7; 125:2 [b]Job 9:33
6 [a]Rom 11:33 [b]Job 42:3

Psalm 139

For the choir director. A Psalm of David.

1 O LORD, You have [a]searched me and
known *me*.
2 You [a]know [1]when I sit down and
[2]when I rise up;
You [b]understand my thought from
afar.
3 You [1a]scrutinize my [2]path and my
lying down,
And are intimately acquainted with all
my ways.
4 [1]Even before there is a word on my
tongue,
Behold, O LORD, You [a]know it all.
5 You have [a]enclosed me behind and
before,
And [b]laid Your hand upon me.
6 *Such* [a]knowledge is [b]too wonderful for
me;
It is *too* high, I cannot attain to it.

7 [a]Where can I go from Your Spirit?
Or where can I flee from Your
presence?
8 [a]If I ascend to heaven, You are there;
If I make my bed in [1]Sheol, behold,
[b]You are there.
9 If I take the wings of the dawn,
If I dwell in the remotest part of the
sea,

7 [a]Jer 23:24 **8** [1]I.e. the nether world [a]Amos 9:2-4 [b]Job 26:6; Prov 15:11

138:2 *Your holy temple.* If David is in fact the author, reference is to the tent he set up for the ark (2 Sam 6:17)—many psalms ascribed to David refer to the "temple" (see, e.g., 5:7; 11:4; 18:6; 27:4; see also Ps 30 title). *name.* See note on 5:11. *loving-kindness and . . . truth.* See note on 36:5. *lovingkindness.* See v. 8; see also note on 6:4. *Your word.* Especially God's promises. God's display of His love and faithfulness in His answers to prayer (v. 3) has made His name and promises more precious than all else that even a king may possess.
138:4–5 The center of the poem (see note on 6:6): a wish and hope that all the kings of earth may come to join him in his praise of the Lord (see note on 9:1).
138:4 *words of Your mouth.* God's grand commitments to His people.
138:5 *ways of the LORD.* See 25:10 and note. God's words and His ways are in harmony, and together they display His great glory (see Ps 145).
138:6–8 A testimony to God's condescending and faithful love, concluded with a prayer.
138:6 See 113:4–9 and notes. *regards.* With favor. *the haughty.* See notes on 31:23; 101:5; 131:1. *knows from afar.* Already from a great distance recognizes them for what they are and so does not let them "behold His face" (see note on 11:7).
138:8 *will accomplish what concerns me.* See note on 57:2. *works of Your hands.* The king himself, whom the Lord had made. The Hebrew often uses plurals to refer to God or the king.
Ps 139 A prayer for God to examine the heart and see its true devotion. Like Job, the author firmly claims his loyalty to the Lord. Nowhere (outside Job) does one find expressed such profound awareness of how awesome it is to ask God to examine not only one's life but also his soul—God, who knows every thought, word and deed, from whom there is no hiding, who has been privy even to one's formation in the dark concealment of the womb. The thought progresses steadily in four poetic paragraphs of six verses each (vv. 1–6, 7–12, 13–18, 19–24), and each paragraph is concluded with a couplet that elaborates on the unit's central theme. References to God's searching and knowing begin and end the prayer.
139 title *For the choir director.* See note on Ps 4 title. *of David.* See note on Ps 138 title.
139:1–6 God, You know me perfectly, far beyond my knowledge of myself: my every action (v. 2a), my every undertaking (v. 3a) and the manner in which I pursue it (v. 3b), even my thoughts before they are fully crystallized (v. 2b) and my words before they are uttered (v. 4).
139:5 *You have enclosed me.* To keep me under scrutiny. *laid Your hand upon me.* So that I do not escape You. The figures are different in Job 13:27, but the thought is much the same. *hand.* Or "hands."
139:6 *too wonderful for me.* Yours is a "wonder" knowledge, beyond my human capacity—the Hebrew term regularly applies to God's wondrous acts (see 77:11,14; Ex 15:11).
139:7–12 There is no hiding from You—here no abstract doctrine of divine omnipresence but an awed confession that God cannot be escaped (see Jer 23:23–24).
139:7 *Your Spirit . . . Your presence.* See 51:11; Is 63:9–10; Ezek 39:29 ("face . . . Spirit").
139:8 *to heaven . . . in Sheol.* The two vertical extremes.
139:9 *wings of the dawn . . . remotest part of the sea.* The two horizontal extremes: east and west (the sea is the Mediterranean). Using a literary figure in which the totality is denoted

10 Even there Your hand will [a]lead me,
And Your right hand will lay hold of
me.
11 If I say, "Surely the [a]darkness will
[1]overwhelm me,
And the light around me will be night,"
12 Even the [a]darkness is not dark [1]to You,
And the night is as bright as the day.
[b]Darkness and light are alike *to You.*

13 For You [a]formed my [1]inward parts;
You [b]wove me in my mother's womb.
14 I will give thanks to You, for [1]I am
fearfully and wonderfully made;
[a]Wonderful are Your works,
And my soul knows it very well.
15 My [1a]frame was not hidden from You,
When I was made in secret,
And skillfully wrought in the [b]depths
of the earth;
16 Your [a]eyes have seen my unformed
substance;
And in [b]Your book were all written
The [c]days that were ordained *for me,*
When as yet there was not one of
them.

17 How precious also are Your [a]thoughts
to me, O God!
How vast is the sum of them!
18 If I should count them, they would
[a]outnumber the sand.
When [b]I awake, I am still with You.

19 O that You would [a]slay the wicked,
O God;
[b]Depart from me, therefore, [c]men of
bloodshed.
20 For they [a]speak [1]against You wickedly,
And Your enemies [2b]take *Your name*
in vain.
21 Do I not [a]hate those who hate You,
O LORD?
And do I not [b]loathe those who rise
up against You?
22 I hate them with the utmost hatred;
They have become my enemies.

23 [a]Search me, O God, and know my
heart;
[b]Try me and know my anxious
thoughts;
24 And see if there be any [1a]hurtful way
in me,
And [b]lead me in the [c]everlasting way.

Psalm 140

For the choir director. A Psalm of David.

1 [a]Rescue me, O LORD, from evil men;
Preserve me from [b]violent men
2 Who [a]devise evil things in *their*
hearts;
They [b]continually stir up wars.

10 [a]Ps 23:2, 3 **11** [1]Lit *bruise;* some commentators read *cover* [a]Job 22:13 **12** [1]Lit *from* [a]Job 34:22; Dan 2:22 [b]1 John 1:5 **13** [1]Lit *kidneys* [a]Ps 119:73; Is 44:24 [b]Job 10:11 **14** [1]Some ancient versions read *You are fearfully wonderful* [a]Ps 40:5 **15** [1]Lit *bones were* [a]Job 10:8-10; Eccl 11:5 [b]Ps 63:9 **16** [a]Job 10:8-10; Eccl 11:5 [b]Ps 56:8 [c]Job 14:5 **17** [a]Ps 40:5; 92:5 **18** [a]Ps 40:5 [b]Ps 3:5

19 [a]Is 11:4 [b]Ps 6:8; 119:115 [c]Ps 5:6; 26:9 **20** [1]Or *of* [2]Some mss read *lift themselves up against You* [a]Jude 15 [b]Ex 20:7; Deut 5:11 **21** [a]2 Chr 19:2; Ps 26:5; 31:6 [b]Ps 119:158 **23** [a]Job 31:6; Ps 26:2 [b]Ps 7:9; Prov 17:3; Jer 11:20; 1 Thess 2:4 **24** [1]Lit *way of pain* [a]Ps 146:9; Prov 15:9; 28:10; Jer 25:5; 36:3 [b]Ps 5:8; 143:10 [c]Ps 16:11

140:1 [a]Ps 17:13; 59:2; 71:4 [b]Ps 18:48; 86:14; 140:11 **2** [a]Ps 7:14; 36;4; 52:2; Prov 6:14; Is 59:4; Hos 7:15 [b]Ps 56:6

by referring to its two extremes (merism), vv. 8–9 specify all spatial reality, the whole creation.

139:10 *lead me . . . lay hold of me.* Though this language occurs in 73:23–24 to indicate God's solicitous care, it here denotes God's inescapable supervision, not unlike the thought of v. 5.

139:11–12 Just as the whole creation offers no hiding place (vv. 8–9), neither does even the darkness.

139:13–16 You Yourself put me together in the womb and ordained the span of my life before I was born.

139:13 *inward parts.* Lit. "kidneys"—in Hebrew idiom, the innermost center of emotions and of moral sensitivity—that which God tests and examines when He "tries" a person (see note on 7:9).

139:14 *fearfully . . . wonderfully . . . Wonderful.* You know me as the One who formed me (see vv. 15–16), but I cannot begin to comprehend this creature You have fashioned. I can only look upon him with awe and wonder (see note on v. 6)—and praise You (see Eccl 11:5).

139:15 *in secret . . . depths of the earth.* Reference is to the womb: called a "secret" place because it normally conceals (see 2 Sam 12:12), and it shares with "the depths of the earth" (see note on 30:1) associations with darkness, dampness and separation from the visible realm of life. Moreover, both phrases refer to the place of the dead (63:9; Job 14:13; Is 44:23; 45:19), with which on one level the womb appears to have been associated: Man comes from the dust and returns to the dust (90:3; Gen 3:19; Eccl 3:20; 12:7), and the womb is the "depth"-like place where he is formed (see Is 44:2,24; 49:5; Jer 1:5).

139:16 *days that were ordained.* The span of life sovereignly determined. *Your book.* The heavenly royal register of God's decisions (see note on 56:8).

139:17 *Your thoughts.* As expressed in His works—and in contrast with "my thought" (v. 2).

139:18 *When I awake.* The sleep of exhaustion overcomes every attempt to count God's thoughts/works (see 63:6; 119:148), and waking only floods my soul once more with the sense of the presence of this God.

139:19–22 My zeal for You sets me against all Your adversaries.

139:19 *O that You would.* Jealous impatience with God's patience toward the wicked—whose end will come (Is 11:4). But the psalmist leaves it to God.

139:20 *take Your name in vain.* Perhaps by calling down curses on those trying to be the faithful servants of God.

139:21–22 A declaration of loyalty that echoes the pledge required by ancient Near Eastern kings of their vassals (e.g., "With my friend you shall be friend, and with my enemy you shall be enemy," from a treaty between Mursilis II, a Hittite king, and Tette of Nuhassi, 14th century B.C.).

139:23–24 Examine me, see the integrity of my devotion and keep me true (see 17:3–5 and note).

139:23 *heart.* See note on 4:7. *anxious thoughts.* See 94:19. It is no light matter to be examined by God.

139:24 *the everlasting way.* See note on 16:9–11.

Ps 140 A prayer for deliverance from the plots and slander of unscrupulous enemies. It recalls Ps 58; 64 but employs a number of words found nowhere else in the OT. The prayer is strikingly rich in physiological allusions: heart, head, tongue, lips, hands, feet—also ears ("Give ear, O Lord, to," v. 6) and teeth (by a wordplay on the Hebrew for "sharpen," v. 3). See Ps 141.

140 title *For the choir director.* See note on Ps 4 title. *of David.* See note on Ps 138 title.

140:1–3 Rescue me from those "vipers."

140:2 *hearts.* See note on 4:7.

3 They [a]sharpen their tongues as a serpent;
[b]Poison of a viper is under their lips. [1]Selah.

4 [a]Keep me, O LORD, from the hands of the wicked;
[b]Preserve me from violent men
Who have [1]purposed to [2c]trip up my feet.
5 The proud have [a]hidden a trap for me, and cords;
They have spread a [b]net by the [1]wayside;
They have set [c]snares for me. Selah.

6 I [a]said to the LORD, "You are my God;
[b]Give ear, O LORD, to the [c]voice of my supplications.
7 "O [1]GOD the Lord, [a]the strength of my salvation,
You have [b]covered my head in the day of [2]battle.
8 "Do not grant, O LORD, the [a]desires of the wicked;
Do not promote [b]his *evil* device, *that* they *not* be exalted. Selah.

9 "As for the head of those who surround me,
May the [a]mischief of their lips cover them.
10 "May [a]burning coals fall upon them;
May they be [b]cast into the fire,
Into [1]deep pits from which they [c]cannot rise.
11 "May a [1]slanderer not be established in the earth;
[a]May evil hunt the violent man [2]speedily."

12 I know that the LORD will [a]maintain the cause of the afflicted
And [b]justice for the poor.
13 Surely the [a]righteous will give thanks to Your name;
The [b]upright will dwell in Your presence.

Psalm 141

A Psalm of David.

1 O LORD, I call upon You; [a]hasten to me!
[b]Give ear to my voice when I call to You!
2 May my prayer be [1]counted as [a]incense before You;
The [b]lifting up of my hands as the [c]evening offering.
3 Set a [a]guard, O LORD, [1]over my mouth;
Keep watch over the [b]door of my lips.
4 [a]Do not incline my heart to any evil thing,
To practice deeds [1]of wickedness
With men who [b]do iniquity;
And [c]do not let me eat of their delicacies.

5 Let the [a]righteous smite me [1]in kindness and reprove me;
It is [b]oil upon the head;
Do not let my head refuse it,
[2]For still my prayer [c]is [3]against their wicked deeds.
6 Their judges are [a]thrown down by the sides of the rock,

3 [1]*Selah* may mean: *Pause, Crescendo* or *Musical interlude* [a]Ps 57:4; 64:3 [b]Ps 58:4; Rom 3:13; James 3:8
4 [1]Or *devised* [2]Lit *push violently* [a]Ps 71:4 [b]Ps 140:1 [c]Ps 36:11
5 [1]Lit *track* [a]Job 18:9; Ps 35:7; 141:9; 142:3 [b]Ps 31:4; 57:6; Lam 1:13 [c]Ps 141:9; Is 8:14; Amos 3:5
6 [a]Ps 16:2; 31:14 [b]Ps 143:1 [c]Ps 116:1; 130:2
7 [1]Heb *YHWH,* usually rendered LORD [2]Lit *weapons* [a]Ps 28:8; 118:14 [b]Ps 144:10
8 [a]Ps 112:10 [b]Esth 9:25; Ps 10:2, 3
9 [a]Ps 7:16; Prov 18:7
10 [1]Lit *watery* [a]Ps 11:6 [b]Ps 21:9; Matt 3:10 [c]Ps 36:12
11 [1]Lit *man of tongue* [2]Lit *thrust upon thrust* [a]Ps 34:21
12 [a]1 Kin 8:45, 49; Ps 9:4; 18:27; 82:3 [b]Ps 12:5; 35:10
13 [a]Ps 97:12 [b]Ps 11:7; 16:11; 17:15
141:1 [a]Ps 22:19; 38:22; 70:5 [b]Ps 5:1; 143:1
2 [1]Lit *fixed* [a]Ex 30:8; Luke 1:10; Rev 5:8; 8:3, 4 [b]1 Tim 2:8 [c]Ex 29:39, 41; 1 Kin 18:29, 36; Dan 9:21

3 [1]Lit *to* [a]Ps 34:13; 39:1; Prov 13:3; 21:23 [b]Mic 7:5 **4** [1]Lit *in* [a]Ps 119:36 [b]Is 32:6; Hos 6:8; Mal 3:15 [c]Prov 23:6 **5** [1]Or *lovingly* [2]Lit *And my prayer* [3]Or *in spite of their calamities* [a]Prov 9:8; 19:25; 25:12; 27:6; Eccl 7:5; Gal 6:1 [b]Ps 23:5; 133:2 [c]Ps 35:14
6 [a]2 Chr 25:12

140:3 *tongues.* See note on 5:9. *Poison of a viper.* See 58:4 and note.

140:4–5 Protect me from those proud and wicked hunters (see 10:2–11 and notes).

140:5 *The proud.* See note on 31:23.

140:6–8 Do not let these wicked men attain their evil designs against me.

140:9–11 Let the harm they plot against me recoil on their heads (see note on 5:10).

140:10 *burning coals.* See note on 11:6. *fire . . . deep pits.* This combination, together with the conjunction of fire and darkness in Job 15:30; 20:26, suggests the idea that the fire of God's judgment (see, e.g., 21:9; 97:3; Is 1:31; 26:11; 33:14) reaches even into the realm of the dead (see Job 31:12 and note on Ps 30:1). *from which they cannot arise.* See 36:12; Is 26:14.

140:11 *hunt.* May these hunters (vv. 4–5) themselves be hunted by the ruin they intended to bring on me.

140:12–13 Confidence in God's just judgment (see note on 3:8).

140:12 *afflicted . . . poor.* See notes on 9:18; 34:6.

140:13 *the righteous.* See note on 1:5. *will give thanks.* Having experienced God's help (see notes on 7:17; 9:1). *will dwell in Your presence.* In contrast to the wicked (v. 10; see notes on 11:7; 16:9–11).

Ps 141 A prayer for deliverance from the wicked and their evil ways. The structure of the first half (two Hebrew lines plus three lines) is repeated in the second half, while at the center a couplet develops a complementary theme (see note on v. 5). Like Ps 140, the prayer is profuse in its physiological allusions: hands, mouth, lips, heart, head, bones, eyes.

141 title See note on Ps 138 title.

141:1–2 Initial appeal for God to hear.

141:3–4 A plea that God will keep him from speaking, desiring or doing what is evil.

141:4 *Do not incline my heart.* Keep me from yielding to the example and urgings of the wicked (see Prov 1:10–16). *heart.* See note on 4:7. *their delicacies.* The luxuriant tables the wicked set from their unjust gains—keep me from acquiring an appetite for such unholy dainties.

141:5 The center of the poem (see note on 6:6). *Let the righteous smite me.* The disciplining blows and rebukes of the righteous are the true "kindness" (Hebrew *ḥesed,* meaning "faithful love"—normally translated as "lovingkindness" in the NASB—or "acts of authentic friendship"; see Prov 27:6; see also note on 6:4). *oil upon the head.* See note on 23:5.

141:6–7 The destiny of the wicked.

And they hear my words, for they are
pleasant.
7 As when one [a]plows and breaks open
the earth,
Our [b]bones have been scattered at the
[c]mouth of [1]Sheol.

8 For my [a]eyes are toward You, O [1]GOD, the Lord;
In You I [b]take refuge; [c]do not [2]leave
me defenseless.
9 Keep me from the [1a]jaws of the trap
which they have set for me,
And from the [b]snares of those who do
iniquity.
10 Let the wicked [a]fall into their own
nets,
While I pass by [1b]safely.

Psalm 142

[†]Maskil of David, when he was [•]in the cave.
A Prayer.

1 I [a]cry aloud with my voice to the LORD;
I [b]make supplication with my voice to
the LORD.
2 I [a]pour out my complaint before Him;
I declare my [b]trouble before Him.
3 When [a]my spirit [1]was overwhelmed
within me,
You knew my path.
In the way where I walk
They have [b]hidden a trap for me.
4 Look to the right and see;
For there is [a]no one who regards me;

7 [1]I.e. the nether world [a]Ps 129:3 [b]Ps 53:5 [c]Num 16:32, 33; Ps 88:3-5
8 [1]Heb *YHWH,* usually rendered LORD [2]Lit *pour out my soul* [a]Ps 25:15; 123:2 [b]Ps 2:12; 11:1 [c]Ps 27:9
9 [1]Lit *hands of the trap* [a]Ps 38:12; 64:5; 91:3; 119:110 [b]Ps 140:5
10 [1]Lit *altogether* [a]Ps 7:15; 35:8; 57:6 [b]Ps 124:7
142:1 [†]Possibly *Contemplative,* or *Didactic,* or *Skillful Psalm* [•]1 Sam 22:1; 24:3 [a]Ps 77:1 [b]Ps 30:8
2 [a]Ps 102: title [b]Ps 77:2
3 [1]Lit *fainted* [a]Ps 77:3; 143:4 [b]Ps 140:5
4 [a]Ps 31:11; 88:8, 18

4 [1]Lit *Escape has perished from me* [b]Job 11:20; Jer 25:35 [c]Jer 30:17
5 [a]Ps 91:2, 9 [b]Ps 16:5; 73:26 [c]Ps 27:13
6 [a]Ps 17:1 [b]Ps 79:8; 116:6 [c]Ps 18:17
7 [a]Ps 143:11; 146:7 [b]Ps 13:6
143:1 [a]Ps 140:6 [b]Ps 89:1, 2 [c]Ps 71:2

[1]There is no [b]escape for me;
[c]No one cares for my soul.
5 I cried out to You, O LORD;
I said, "You are [a]my refuge,
My [b]portion in the [c]land of the living.
6 "[a]Give heed to my cry,
For I am [b]brought very low;
Deliver me from my persecutors,
For they are too [c]strong for me.
7 "[a]Bring my soul out of prison,
So that I may give thanks to Your
name;
The righteous will surround me,
For You will [b]deal bountifully with
me."

Psalm 143

A Psalm of David.

1 Hear my prayer, O LORD,
[a]Give ear to my supplications!
Answer me in Your [b]faithfulness, in
Your [c]righteousness!
2 And [a]do not enter into judgment with
Your servant,
For in Your sight [b]no man living is
righteous.
3 For the enemy has persecuted my soul;
He has crushed my life [a]to the ground;
He [b]has made me dwell in dark
places, like those who have long
been dead.

2 [a]Job 14:3; 22:4 [b]1 Kin 8:46; Job 4:17; 9:2; 25:4; Ps 130:3; Eccl 7:20; Rom 3:10, 20; Gal 2:16 **3** [a]Ps 44:25 [b]Ps 88:6; Lam 3:6

141:6 *my words.* Of commitment to righteousness, as in vv. 3–5. *pleasant.* Good and right.
141:8–10 A plea that God will deliver from the designs of the wicked.
141:8 *do not leave me defenseless.* As you do the wicked (see v. 7; see also 73:18–20,23–26 and notes).
141:9 *trap . . . snares.* Perhaps, as usual, the plots of men to bring him down (as in 38:12; 64:5; 91:3; 140:5; 142:3)—but here reference may be to the enticements to evil that the wicked lay before him (see Ex 23:33; Deut 7:16; Josh 23:13; Judg 2:3).
141:10 *Let the wicked fall.* See note on 5:10.
Ps 142 A plaintive prayer for deliverance from powerful enemies—when powerless, alone and without refuge. Apart from the introduction (vv. 1–2) and conclusion (v. 7b), the prayer (in Hebrew) is composed of two four-line stanzas (vv. 3–7a).
142 title *Maskil.* See note on Ps 32 title. *of David.* See note on Ps 138 title. *when . . . cave.* See note on Ps 57 title. *A Prayer.* See note on Ps 17 title.
142:1–2 Initial appeal—using the formal third person (as was often done when addressing kings), equivalent to: "I cry aloud to You, O LORD."
142:3–4 Description of when he had been "brought very low" (v. 6).
142:3 *When my spirit was overwhelmed.* Because he is overwhelmed by his situation (see 22:14–15). *You knew.* And were concerned about (cf. v. 4).
142:4 *to the right.* To my right hand, where one's helper or defender stands (see 16:8 and note). *regards me.* In Hebrew a less common synonym of "know" (v. 3); see Ruth 2:10,19 ("notice").
142:5–7 Prayer for rescue.
142:5 *portion.* The sustainer and preserver of his life (see 73:26 and note).
142:7 *prison.* Metaphor for the sense of being fettered by affliction (see note on 18:19; see also Job 36:8). *that I may give thanks.* In celebration of God's saving help (see note on 7:17). *name.* See note on 5:11. *righteous.* See note on 1:5. *will surround me.* He will no longer be alone. The conclusion expresses an expectant word of confidence (see note on 3:8).
Ps 143 A prayer for deliverance from enemies and for divine leading. This is the seventh and final penitential psalm (see introduction to Ps 6). In the first half (vv. 1–6) the psalmist makes his appeal and describes his situation; in the second half (vv. 7–12) he presents his prayer. Appeal to God's righteousness (vv. 1,11) and the author's self-identification as "Your servant" (vv. 2,12) enclose the prayer. See also his appeal to God's faithfulness (v. 1) and lovingkindness(v. 12), which together form a frequent pair (see note on 36:5). For another enclosure see note on v. 7.
143 title See note on Ps 138 title.
143:1–2 Initial appeal.
143:1 *righteousness.* See note on 4:1.
143:2 As he begins his prayer, he pleads that God not sit in judgment over His servant (he knows his own failings) but that He focus His judicial attention on the enemy's harsh and unwarranted attacks.
143:3–4 The distress he suffers.
143:3 The last half of this verse appears almost verbatim in Lam 3:6. *in dark places.* As one cut off from the enjoyments of life (see v. 7; see also notes on 27:1; 30:1).

4 Therefore [a]my spirit [1]is overwhelmed
within me;
My heart is [2][b]appalled within me.

5 I [a]remember the days of old;
I [b]meditate on all Your doings;
I [c]muse on the work of Your hands.
6 I [a]stretch out my hands to You;
My [b]soul *longs* for You, as a [1]parched
land. [2]Selah.

7 [a]Answer me quickly, O LORD, my
[b]spirit fails;
[c]Do not hide Your face from me,
Or I will become like [d]those who go
down to the pit.
8 Let me hear Your [a]lovingkindness [b]in
the morning;
For I trust [c]in You;
Teach me the [d]way in which I should
walk;
For to You I [e]lift up my soul.
9 [a]Deliver me, O LORD, from my enemies;
[1]I take refuge in You.
10 [a]Teach me to do Your will,
For You are my God;
Let [b]Your good Spirit [c]lead me on level
[1]ground.
11 [a]For the sake of Your name, O LORD,
[b]revive me.
[c]In Your righteousness bring my soul
out of trouble.
12 And in Your lovingkindness, [1][a]cut off
my enemies
And [b]destroy all those who afflict my
soul,
For [c]I am Your servant.

4 [1]Lit *faints* [2]Or *desolate* [a]Ps 77:3; 142:3 [b]Lam 3:11
5 [a]Ps 77:5, 10, 11 [b]Ps 77:12 [c]Ps 105:2
6 [1]Lit *weary* [2]*Selah* may mean: *Pause, Crescendo* or *Musical interlude* [a]Job 11:13; Ps 88:9 [b]Ps 42:2; 63:1
7 [a]Ps 69:17 [b]Ps 73:26; 84:2; Jer 8:18; Lam 1:22 [c]Ps 27:9; 69:17; 102:2 [d]Ps 28:1; 88:4
8 [a]Ps 90:14 [b]Ps 46:5 [c]Ps 25:2 [d]Ps 27:11; 32:8; 86:11 [e]Ps 25:1; 86:4
9 [1]Lit *To You have I hidden* [a]Ps 31:15; 59:1
10 [1]Lit *land* [a]Ps 25:4, 5; 119:12 [b]Neh 9:20 [c]Ps 23:3
11 [a]Ps 25:11 [b]Ps 119:25 [c]Ps 31:1; 71:2
12 [1]Or *silence* [a]Ps 54:5 [b]Ps 52:5 [c]Ps 116:16

144:1 [a]Ps 18:2 [b]2 Sam 22:35; Ps 18:34
2 [1]Another reading is *peoples* [a]Ps 18:2; 91:2 [b]Ps 59:9 [c]Ps 3:3; 28:7; 84:9 [d]Ps 18:39
3 [a]Job 7:17; Ps 8:4; Heb 2:6
4 [a]Ps 39:11 [b]Job 8:9; 14:2; Ps 102:11; 109:23

Psalm 144

A Psalm of David.

1 Blessed be the LORD, [a]my rock,
Who [b]trains my hands for war,
And my fingers for battle;
2 My lovingkindness and [a]my fortress,
My [b]stronghold and my deliverer,
My [c]shield and He in whom I take
refuge,
Who [d]subdues [1]my people under me.
3 O LORD, [a]what is man, that You take
knowledge of him?
Or the son of man, that You think of
him?
4 [a]Man is like a mere breath;
His [b]days are like a passing shadow.

5 [a]Bow Your heavens, O LORD, and
[b]come down;
[c]Touch the mountains, that they may
smoke.
6 Flash forth [a]lightning and scatter
them;
Send out Your [b]arrows and confuse
them.
7 Stretch forth Your hand [a]from on
high;
Rescue me and [b]deliver me out of
great waters,
Out of the hand of [c]aliens
8 Whose mouths [a]speak deceit,
And whose [b]right hand is a right hand
of falsehood.

5 [a]Ps 18:9 [b]Is 64:1 [c]Ps 104:32 **6** [a]Ps 18:14 [b]Ps 7:13; 58:7; Hab 3:11; Zech 9:14 **7** [a]Ps 18:16 [b]Ps 69:1, 14 [c]Ps 18:44; 54:3
8 [a]Ps 12:2; 41:6 [b]Gen 14:22; Deut 32:40; Ps 106:26; Is 44:20

143:4 *my spirit is overwhelmed.* See note on 142:3. *heart.* See note on 4:7.
143:5–6 Remembrance of God's past acts of deliverance encourages him in his appeal.
143:6 *stretch out my hands.* In prayer (see 44:20; 88:9; Ex 9:29). *soul.* See v. 8; see also note on 6:3. *longs for You.* See note on 63:1.
143:7–10 The prayer.
143:7 *my spirit fails.* Or perhaps: "my spirit faints with longing," which parallels that in 119:81; in view of the next line the thought appears closer to that of 104:29. Ultimately, the failing of "my spirit" will be healed by the leading of "Your good Spirit" (v. 10)—the two references enclose the prayer. *hide Your face.* See note on 13:1. *the pit.* See v. 3 and note on 30:1.
143:8 *the morning.* Of salvation from the present "dark places" (v. 3; see introduction to Ps 57). *lovingkindness.* See v. 12; see also note on 6:4. *Teach me the way.* See v. 10. Deliverance from the enemy is not enough—either for God's "servant" (vv. 2,12) or for entrance into life.
143:10 *level ground.* See note on 26:12.
143:11–12 Concluding summary of the prayer (see introduction).
143:11 *For the sake of Your name.* See note on 23:3.
143:12 *destroy all those who afflict my soul.* See note on 5:10.
Ps 144 A royal prayer for victory over treacherous enemies (but see note on vv. 12–15). Verses 1–10 show much affinity with Ps 18; this section begins and ends like that psalm, and vv. 5–7 all appear to be variations on corresponding lines found there (see notes below). The remaining lines of this section contain similar echoes of other psalms, and the author may have drawn directly on them. The main body (vv. 1–10) is fairly typical of the prayers of the Psalter, but the conclusion (vv. 12–15) is unique. Verse 11 appears to be transitional.
144 title See note on Ps 138 title.
144:1–2 Praise of the Lord. As the opening words of a prayer, it seems to function both as an initial appeal (see 143:1–2) and as a confession of confidence that the prayer will be heard. Notice the unusual piling up of epithets for God—all having their counterparts in Ps 18.
144:2 *My lovingkindness.* See note on 6:4. God is here called "my lovingkindness" because He is the source of benevolent acts of love that David can count on—just as God can be called "my salvation" because He is the source of salvation (see 27:1; 35:3; 62:2).
144:3–4 Confession of man's insignificance and of his dependence on God's help.
144:3 A variation of 8:4.
144:4 See 39:4–6 and notes.
144:5–8 Prayer for deliverance.
144:5 See 18:9 and note on 18:7–15.
144:6 See 18:14 and note.
144:7 See 18:16–17 and note on 32:6. *aliens.* Bordering kingdoms.
144:8 *mouths.* See note on 5:9. *right hand.* Hand raised to

9 I will sing a [a]new song to You, O God;
Upon a [b]harp of ten strings I will sing
praises to You,
10 Who [a]gives salvation to kings,
Who [b]rescues David His servant from
the evil sword.
11 Rescue me and deliver me out of the
hand of [a]aliens,
Whose mouth [b]speaks deceit
And whose [c]right hand is a right hand
of falsehood.

12 Let our sons in their youth be as
[a]grown-up plants,
And our daughters as [b]corner pillars
[1]fashioned as for a palace;
13 Let our [a]garners be full, furnishing
every kind of produce,
And our flocks bring forth thousands
and ten thousands in our [1]fields;
14 Let our [a]cattle [1]bear
Without [2b]mishap and without [3c]loss,
Let there be no [d]outcry in our streets!
15 How blessed are the people who are
so situated;
How [a]blessed are the people whose
God is the LORD!

Psalm 145

A Psalm of Praise, of David.

1 I will [a]extol You, [b]my God, O King,
And I will [c]bless Your name forever
and ever.
2 Every day I will bless You,
And I will [a]praise Your name forever
and ever.
3 [a]Great is the LORD, and highly to be
praised,
And His [b]greatness is unsearchable.
4 One [a]generation shall praise Your
works to another,
And shall declare Your mighty acts.
5 On the [a]glorious [1]splendor of Your
majesty
And [b]on Your wonderful works, I will
meditate.
6 Men shall speak of the [1]power of Your
[a]awesome acts,
And I will [b]tell of Your greatness.
7 They shall [1]eagerly utter the memory
of Your [a]abundant goodness
And will [b]shout joyfully of Your
righteousness.

8 The LORD is [a]gracious and merciful;
Slow to anger and great in
lovingkindness.
9 The LORD is [a]good to all,
And His [b]mercies are over all His
works.
10 [a]All Your works shall give thanks to
You, O LORD,
And Your [b]godly ones shall bless You.
11 They shall speak of the [a]glory of Your
kingdom
And talk of Your power;
12 To [a]make known to the sons of men
[1]Your mighty acts
And the [b]glory of the majesty of [1]Your
kingdom.
13 Your kingdom is [1]an [a]everlasting
kingdom,
And Your dominion *endures*
throughout all generations.

14 The LORD [a]sustains all who fall
And [b]raises up all who are bowed
down.
15 The eyes of all [1]look to You,
And You [a]give them their food in due
time.
16 You [a]open Your hand
And satisfy the desire of every living
thing.

9 [a]Ps 33:3; 40:3 [b]Ps 33:2
10 [a]Ps 18:50 [b]2 Sam 18:7; Ps 140:7
11 [a]Ps 18:44; 54:3 [b]Ps 12:2; 41:6 [c]Gen 14:22; Deut 32:40; Ps 106:26; Is 44:20
12 [1]Lit *cut after the pattern of* [a]Ps 92:12-14; 128:3 [b]Song 4:4; 7:4
13 [1]Lit *outside* [a]Prov 3:9, 10
14 [1]Lit *be laden* [2]Lit *bursting forth* [3]Lit *going out* [a]Prov 14:4 [b]2 Kin 25:10, 11 [c]Amos 5:3 [d]Is 24:11; Jer 14:2
15 [a]Ps 33:12
145:1 [a]Ps 30:1; 66:17 [b]Ps 5:2 [c]Ps 34:1
2 [a]Ps 71:6
3 [a]Ps 48:1; 86:10; 147:5 [b]Job 5:9; 9:10; 11:7; Is 40:28; Rom 11:33
4 [a]Ps 22:30, 31; Is 38:19
5 [1]Or *majesty of Your splendor* [a]Ps 145:12 [b]Ps 119:27
6 [1]Or *strength* [a]Deut 10:21; Ps 66:3; 106:22 [b]Deut 32:3
7 [1]Or *bubble over with* [a]Ps 31:19; Is 63:7 [b]Ps 51:14
8 [a]Ex 34:6; Num 14:18; Ps 86:5, 15; 103:8
9 [a]Ps 100:5; 136:1; Jer 33:11; Nah 1:7; Matt 19:17; Mark 10:18 [b]Ps 145:15
10 [a]Ps 19:1; 103:22 [b]Ps 68:26
11 [a]Jer 14:21
12 [1]Lit *His* [a]Ps 105:1 [b]Ps 145:5; Is 2:10, 19, 21
13 [1]Lit *a kingdom of all ages* [a]Ps 10:16; 29:10; 1 Tim 1:17; 2 Pet 1:11
14 [a]Ps 37:24 [b]Ps 146:8
15 [1]Lit *wait; or hope for* [a]Ps 104:27; 136:25
16 [a]Ps 104:28

swear a covenant oath of allegiance or submission (see 106:26; Ex 6:8; Deut 32:40).

144:9–10 Vow to praise (see note on 7:17).

144:9 *new song.* See note on 33:3.

144:10 *David His servant.* See note on Ps 18 title.

144:11 Repetition of the prayer in vv. 7–8, apparently to serve as transition to what follows: If God will deliver His servant David, the realm will prosper and be secure.

144:12 *daughters as . . . pillars fashioned.* Temple columns in the shape of women were not uncommon (e.g., on the Acropolis in Athens).

144:14 *Let our cattle bear.* Or "Let our cattle be heavy with flesh" or "Let our cattle be heavy with young."

144:15 *blessed.* See note on 1:1.

Ps 145 A hymn to the Lord, the Great King, for His mighty acts and benevolent virtues, which are the glory of His kingly rule. It exploits to the full the traditional language of praise and, as an alphabetic acrostic, reflects the care of studied composition. Between the two-line introduction (vv. 1–2) and one-line conclusion (v. 21), four poetic paragraphs develop as many themes, each introduced with a thematic line (see vv. 3,8,13b,17).

145 title *Praise.* Hebrew *tehillah,* occurring only here in the psalm titles, but from a plural form (*tehillim*) has come the traditional Hebrew name of the Psalter. *of David.* See note on Ps 138 title.

145:1–2 Initial commitment to praise. *name.* See v. 21, thus framing the psalm (see note on 5:11).

145:3–7 Praise of God's mighty acts, which display His greatness (v. 3) and His goodness (v. 7)—as the author underscores by enclosing the paragraph with these two references. For the same combination see 86:10,17; 135:3,5.

145:4 *shall praise . . . shall declare.* See vv. 5–7,10–12,21; see also note on 9:1. *Your works.* In creation, providence and redemption.

145:7 *righteousness.* See v. 17; see also note on 4:1.

145:8–13a Praise of God's benevolent virtues, which move all creatures to celebrate the glory of His kingdom.

145:8 See Ex 34:6–7 and note.

145:10 *All Your works shall give thanks to You.* See v. 21; see also note on 65:13. *godly ones.* See note on 4:3.

145:14–16 Praise God's faithfulness.

17 The LORD is [a]righteous in all His ways
And kind in all His deeds.
18 The LORD is [a]near to all who call upon Him,
To all who call upon Him [b]in truth.
19 He will [a]fulfill the desire of those who fear Him;
He will also [b]hear their cry and will save them.
20 The LORD [a]keeps all who love Him,
But all the [b]wicked He will destroy.
21 My [a]mouth will speak the praise of the LORD,
And [b]all flesh will [c]bless His holy name forever and ever.

Psalm 146

1 [1]Praise [2]the LORD!
[a]Praise the LORD, O my soul!
2 I will praise the LORD [a]while I live;
I will [b]sing praises to my God while I have my being.
3 [a]Do not trust in princes,
In [1]mortal [b]man, in whom there is [c]no salvation.
4 His [a]spirit departs, he [b]returns to [1]the earth;
In that very day his [c]thoughts perish.
5 How [a]blessed is he whose help is the God of Jacob,
Whose [b]hope is in the LORD his God,
6 Who [a]made heaven and earth,
The [b]sea and all that is in them;
Who [c]keeps [1]faith forever;
7 Who [a]executes justice for the oppressed;
Who [b]gives food to the hungry.
The LORD [c]sets the prisoners free.
8 The LORD [a]opens *the eyes of* the blind;
The LORD [b]raises up those who are bowed down;
The LORD [c]loves the righteous;
9 The LORD [1][a]protects the [2]strangers;
He [3][b]supports the fatherless and the widow,
But He [4]thwarts [c]the way of the wicked.
10 The LORD will [a]reign forever,
Your God, O Zion, to all generations.
[1]Praise [2]the LORD!

Psalm 147

1 [1]Praise [2]the LORD!
For [a]it is good to sing praises to our God;
For [3]it is pleasant *and* praise is [b]becoming.
2 The LORD [a]builds up Jerusalem;
He [b]gathers the outcasts of Israel.
3 He heals the [a]brokenhearted
And [b]binds up their [1]wounds.
4 He [a]counts the number of the stars;
He [1][b]gives names to all of them.
5 [a]Great is our Lord and abundant in strength;
His [b]understanding is [1]infinite.
6 The LORD [1][a]supports the afflicted;
He brings down the wicked to the ground.

7 [a]Sing to the LORD with thanksgiving;
Sing praises to our God on the lyre,

17 [a]Ps 116:5 **18** [a]Deut 4:7; Ps 34:18; 119:151 [b]John 4:24 **19** [a]Ps 21:2; 37:4 [b]Ps 10:17; Prov 15:29; 1 John 5:14 **20** [a]Ps 31:23; 91:14; 97:10 [b]Ps 9:5; 37:38 **21** [a]Ps 71:8 [b]Ps 65:2; 150:6 [c]Ps 145:1, 2
146:1 [1]Or *Hallelujah!* [2]Heb YAH [a]Ps 103:1 **2** [a]Ps 63:4 [b]Ps 104:33 **3** [1]Lit *a son of a man* [a]Ps 118:9 [b]Ps 118:8; Is 2:22 [c]Ps 60:11; 108:12 **4** [1]Lit *his earth* [a]Ps 104:29 [b]Eccl 12:7 [c]Ps 33:10; 1 Cor 2:6 **5** [a]Ps 144:15; Jer 17:7 [b]Ps 71:5 **6** [1]Or *truth* [a]Ps 115:15; Rev 14:7 [b]Acts 14:15 [c]Ps 117:2 **7** [a]Ps 103:6 [b]Ps 107:9; 145:15 [c]Ps 68:6; Is 61:1
8 [a]Matt 9:30; John 9:7 [b]Ps 145:14 [c]Ps 11:7 **9** [1]Or *keeps* [2]Or *sojourners* [3]Or *relieves* [4]Lit *makes crooked* [a]Ex 22:21; Lev 19:34 [b]Deut 10:18; Ps 68:5 [c]Ps 147:6 **10** [1]Or *Hallelujah!* [2]Heb YAH [a]Ex 15:18; Ps 10:16
147:1 [1]Or *Hallelujah!* [2]Heb YAH [3]Or *He is gracious* [a]Ps 92:1; 135:3 [b]Ps 33:1 **2** [a]Ps 51:18; 102:16 [b]Deut 30:3; Ps 106:47; Is 11:12; 56:8; Ezek 39:28 **3** [1]Lit *sorrows* [a]Ps 34:18; 51:17; Is 61:1 [b]Job 5:18; Is 30:26; Ezek 34:16 **4** [1]Or *calls them all by* their *names* [a]Gen 15:5 [b]Is 40:26 **5** [1]Lit *innumerable* [a]Ps 48:1; 145:3 [b]Is 40:28 **6** [1]Or *relieves* [a]Ps 37:24; 146:8, 9 **7** [a]Ps 33:2; 95:1, 2

145:17–20 Praise of God's righteousness.
145:17 *kind.* See note on 6:4.
145:18 *in truth.* With godly integrity.
145:21 The praise of God must continue, and every creature take it up—forever. *all flesh.* Or perhaps "every human" (see 65:2, "all men"; but see also 150:6).
Ps 146 An exhortation to trust in the Lord, Zion's King. The first of five Hallelujah psalms with which the Psalter closes, its date is probably postexilic. This and the remaining four psalms are all framed with Hallelujahs, which may have been added by the final editors (see Ps 105–106; 111–117).
146:1–2 Initial vow to praise—as long as life continues (see 145:21).
146:1 *Praise the LORD, O my soul!* See the frames around Ps 103–104. *soul.* See note on 6:3.
146:3–4 The call to trust in the Lord (see vv. 5–9) is heightened by contrast.
146:5–9 Exhortation to trust in the covenant God of Jacob (see note on 14:7), who as Creator is Lord over all, as the Faithful One defends the defenseless and provides for the needy, and as the Righteous One shows favor to the righteous but checks the wicked in their pursuits.
146:6 *Who made heaven and earth.* See note on 121:2.
146:8 *righteous.* See note on 1:5.
146:10 Concluding exultant testimony to the citizens of God's royal city. *Zion.* See note on 9:11.
Ps 147 Praise of God, the Creator, for His special mercies to Israel—possibly composed for the Levitical choirs on the joyous occasion of the dedication of the rebuilt walls of Jerusalem (see Neh 12:27–43). The Septuagint (the Greek translation of the OT) divides the work into two separate psalms (vv. 1–11, 12–20), but it is actually a three-part song (vv. 1–6, 7–11, 12–20), bound together by the frame (vv. 2–3, 19–20), in which the Lord's unique favors to Israel are celebrated. See introduction to Ps 146.
147:1 See note on 135:3.
147:2 *builds up . . . gathers.* Refers to the postexilic restoration of Jerusalem and Israel.
147:3 *brokenhearted.* Such as the exiles (see Ps 137; cf. Ps 126) and those who struggled in the face of great opposition to rebuild Jerusalem's walls (Neh 2:17–20; 4:1–23).
147:4–6 He whose power and understanding are such that He fixes the number of (or counts) the stars and names them is able to sustain His humble ones and bring the wicked down (see 20:8; 146:9; see also Is 40:26–29).
147:6 *afflicted.* Those who acknowledge that they are without resources (see 149:4). *ground.* Probably the grave (see note on 61:2).
147:7–11 The God who governs the rain and thus provides food for beast and bird is not pleased by man's reliance on his own capabilities or those of the animals he has domesticated (or the technologies he has developed); He is pleased when people serve Him and trust His loving care.

8 Who [a]covers the heavens with clouds,
Who [b]provides rain for the earth,
Who [c]makes grass to [1]grow on the
mountains.
9 He [a]gives to the beast its food,
And to the [b]young ravens which cry.
10 He does not delight in the strength of
the [a]horse;
He [b]does not take pleasure in the legs
of a man.
11 The LORD [a]favors those who fear Him,
[b]Those who wait for His
lovingkindness.

12 Praise the LORD, O Jerusalem!
Praise your God, O Zion!
13 For He has strengthened the [a]bars of
your gates;
He has [b]blessed your sons within you.
14 He [a]makes [1]peace in your borders;
He [b]satisfies you with [c]the [2]finest of
the wheat.
15 He sends forth His [a]command to the
earth;
His [b]word runs very swiftly.
16 He gives [a]snow like wool;
He scatters the [b]frost like ashes.
17 He casts forth His [a]ice as fragments;
Who can stand before His [b]cold?
18 He [a]sends forth His word and melts
them;
He [b]causes His wind to blow and the
waters to flow.
19 He [a]declares His words to Jacob,
His [b]statutes and His ordinances to
Israel.
20 He [a]has not dealt thus with any
nation;
And as for His ordinances, they have
[b]not known them.
[1]Praise [2]the LORD!

8 [1]Lit *spring forth* [a]Job 26:8 [b]Job 5:10; 38:26; Ps 104:13 [c]Job 38:27; Ps 104:14 **9** [a]Ps 104:27, 28; 145:15 [b]Job 38:41; Matt 6:26 **10** [a]Ps 33:17 [b]1 Sam 16:7 **11** [a]Ps 149:4 [b]Ps 33:18 **13** [a]Neh 3:3; 7:3 [b]Ps 37:26 **14** [1]Lit *your borders peace* [2]Lit *fat* [a]Ps 29:11; Is 54:13; 60:17, 18 [b]Ps 132:15 [c]Deut 32:14; Ps 81:16 **15** [a]Job 37:12; Ps 148:5 [b]Ps 104:4 **16** [a]Job 37:6; Ps 148:8 [b]Job 38:29 **17** [a]Job 37:10 [b]Job 37:9 **18** [a]Ps 33:9; 107:20; 147:15 [b]Ps 107:25 **19** [a]Deut 33:3, 4 [b]Mal 4:4 **20** [1]Or *Hallelujah!* [2]Heb YAH [a]Deut 4:7, 8, 32-34; Rom 3:1, 2 [b]Ps 79:6; Jer 10:25

148:1 [1]Or *Hallelujah!* [2]Heb YAH [a]Ps 69:34 [b]Job 16:19; Ps 102:19; Matt 21:9 **2** [a]Ps 103:20 [b]Ps 103:21 **4** [1]Lit *heavens of heavens* [a]Deut 10:14; 1 Kin 8:27; Neh 9:6; Ps 68:33 [b]Gen 1:7 **5** [a]Gen 1:1; Ps 33:6, 9 **6** [a]Ps 89:37; Jer 31:35, 36; 33:20, 25 [b]Job 38:33 **7** [a]Gen 1:21; Ps 74:13 [b]Gen 1:2; Deut 33:13; Hab 3:10 **8** [a]Ps 18:12 [b]Ps 147:16 [c]Ps 135:7 [d]Ps 107:25 [e]Job 37:12; Ps 103:20 **9** [a]Is 44:23; 49:13 [b]Is 55:12 **10** [a]Is 43:20 [b]Hos 2:18 **11** [a]Ps 102:15 **13** [a]Is 12:4 [b]Ps 8:1; 113:4 **14** [a]1 Sam 2:1; Ps 75:10

Psalm 148

1 [1]Praise [2]the LORD!
Praise the LORD [a]from the heavens;
Praise Him [b]in the heights!
2 Praise Him, [a]all His angels;
Praise Him, [b]all His hosts!
3 Praise Him, sun and moon;
Praise Him, all stars of light!
4 Praise Him, [1a]highest heavens,
And the [b]waters that are above the
heavens!
5 Let them praise the name of the LORD,
For [a]He commanded and they were
created.
6 He has also [a]established them forever
and ever;
He has made a [b]decree which will not
pass away.

7 Praise the LORD from the earth,
[a]Sea monsters and all [b]deeps;
8 [a]Fire and hail, [b]snow and [c]clouds;
[d]Stormy wind, [e]fulfilling His word;
9 [a]Mountains and all hills;
Fruit [b]trees and all cedars;
10 [a]Beasts and all cattle;
[b]Creeping things and winged fowl;
11 [a]Kings of the earth and all peoples;
Princes and all judges of the earth;
12 Both young men and virgins;
Old men and children.

13 Let them praise the name of the LORD,
For His [a]name alone is exalted;
His [b]glory is above earth and heaven.
14 And He has [a]lifted up a horn for His
people,

147:11 *fear.* See note on 34:8–14. *lovingkindness.* See note on 6:4.

147:12–18 The Lord of all creation, Zion's God, secures His people's defenses and prosperity, their peace and abundant provision. The verses mention clouds and rain (v. 8); snow, frost and hail (vv. 16–17); icy winds and warm breezes (vv. 17–18)—the whole range of weather.

147:15 *His command . . . His word.* Personified as messengers commissioned to carry out a divine order (see notes on 23:6; 33:4; 104:4).

147:19–20 God's most unique gift to Israel: His other word, His redemptive word, by which He makes known His program of salvation and His holy will.

Ps 148 A call to all things in all creation to praise the Lord. Whatever its original liturgical purpose, its placement here serves to complete the scope of the calls to praise with which the Psalter concludes. Two balanced stanzas of six verses each are followed by a two-verse conclusion. In the first stanza (vv. 1–6) the call goes to all creatures in the heavens, in the second (vv. 7–12) to all beneath the heavens (see 103:20–22). The conclusion (vv. 13–14) focuses on motivation for praise. See introduction to Ps 146.

148:1–6 Let all creatures in the heavens praise the Lord.

148:3 *sun and moon . . . stars of light.* See note on 65:13.

148:4 *waters . . . above the heavens.* The "deep" above (see Gen 1:7; cf. "all deeps" in v. 7; see also note on 42:7).

148:5 *name of the LORD.* See v. 13; see also note on 5:11. They are to praise the Lord because He has created them and made their existence secure.

148:7–12 Let all creatures of earth praise the Lord. ("Heaven and earth" are the sum of all creation; see v. 13; see also 89:11; 113:6; 136:5–6; Gen 2:1,4.)

148:7 *Sea monsters and all deeps.* Likely with Gen 1 in mind (see Gen 1:7,10,21), the call begins with these and moves toward the human components. This and the pairs that follow employ a figure of speech (merism) that refers to all reality pertaining to the sphere to which they belong—here, all creatures great and small that belong to the realm of lakes and seas.

148:8 *His word.* See 147:15 and note.

148:13–14 Conclusion, with focus on motivation for praise.

148:13 *His name . . . His glory.* As shown in the glory of His creation. *is above.* The glory of the Creator is greater than the glory of the creation.

148:14 *horn.* The Lord's anointed ("horn" here symbolizes strong one, that is, the king; see notes on 2:2; Ps 18 title). It may be, however, that "horn" here represents the strength and vig-

[b]Praise for all His godly ones;
Even for the sons of Israel, a people
[c]near to Him.
[1]Praise [2]the LORD!

Psalm 149

1 [1]Praise [2]the LORD!
Sing to the LORD a [a]new song,
And His praise [b]in the congregation of
the godly ones.
2 Let Israel be glad in [a]his Maker;
Let the sons of Zion rejoice in their
[b]King.
3 Let them praise His name with
[a]dancing;
Let them sing praises to Him with
[b]timbrel and lyre.
4 For the LORD [a]takes pleasure in His
people;
He will [b]beautify the afflicted ones
with salvation.

5 Let the [a]godly ones exult in glory;
Let them [b]sing for joy on their beds.
6 *Let* the [a]high praises of God *be* in their
[1]mouth,
And a [b]two-edged [c]sword in their
hand,
7 To [a]execute vengeance on the nations
And punishment on the peoples,

14 [1]Or *Hallelujah!* [2]Heb YAH [b]Deut 10:21; Ps 109:1; Jer 17:14 [c]Lev 10:3; Eph 2:17
149:1 [1]Or *Hallelujah!* [2]Heb YAH [a]Ps 33:3 [b]Ps 35:18; 89:5
2 [a]Ps 95:6 [b]Judg 8:23; Ps 47:6; Zech 9:9
3 [a]2 Sam 6:14; Ps 150:4 [b]Ex 15:20; Ps 81:2
4 [a]Job 36:11; Ps 16:11; 35:27; 147:11 [b]Ps 132:16; Is 61:3
5 [a]Ps 132:16 [b]Job 35:10; Ps 42:8
6 [1]Lit *throat* [a]Ps 66:17 [b]Heb 4:12 [c]Neh 4:17
7 [a]Ezek 25:17; Mic 5:15
8 [a]Job 36:8 [b]Nah 3:10
9 [1]Or *Hallelujah!* [2]Heb YAH [a]Deut 7:12; Ezek 28:26 [b]Ps 112:9; 148:14
150:1 [1]Or *Hallelujah!* [2]Heb YAH [3]Or *firmament* [a]Ps 73:17; 102:19 [b]Ps 19:1
2 [a]Ps 145:12 [b]Deut 3:24; Ps 145:3

8 To bind their kings [a]with chains
And their [b]nobles with fetters of iron,
9 To [a]execute on them the judgment
written;
This is an [b]honor for all His godly
ones.
[1]Praise [2]the LORD!

Psalm 150

1 [1]Praise [2]the LORD!
Praise God in His [a]sanctuary;
Praise Him in His mighty [3][b]expanse.
2 Praise Him for His [a]mighty deeds;
Praise Him according to His excellent
[b]greatness.

3 Praise Him with [a]trumpet sound;
Praise Him with [b]harp and lyre.
4 Praise Him with [a]timbrel and
dancing;
Praise Him with [b]stringed instruments
and [c]pipe.
5 Praise Him with loud [a]cymbals;
Praise Him with resounding cymbals.
6 Let [a]everything that has breath praise
[1]the LORD.
[2]Praise [1]the LORD!

3 [a]Ps 98:6 [b]Ps 33:2 **4** [a]Ps 149:3 [b]Ps 45:8; Is 38:20 [c]Gen 4:21; Job 21:12 **5** [a]2 Sam 6:5; 1 Chr 13:8; 15:16; Ezra 3:10; Neh 12:27 **6** [1]Heb YAH [2]Or *Hallelujah!* [a]Ps 103:22; 145:21

or of God's people (see 92:10; 1 Sam 2:1; Jer 48:25; Lam 2:17). In any event, reference is to God's saving acts for Israel—God is to be praised for His works in creation and redemption (see note on 65:6–7). *Praise.* See 22:3 and note.

Ps 149 Praise of God for the high honor bestowed on His people. It is no doubt postexilic. Israel's unique honor has two sides: She has been granted salvation (in fact and in promise), and she has been armed to execute God's sentence of judgment on the world powers that have launched their attacks against the kingdom of God—she is the earthly contingent of the armies of the King of heaven (see 68:17 and note; see also Josh 5:14; 2 Sam 5:23–24; 2 Chr 20:15–17,22; Hab 3:3–15). This next-to-last psalm clearly marks the Psalter as the prayer book (liturgical book of prayer and praise) of OT Israel.

Following an introductory verse, the two main themes are developed in two balanced stanzas of four verses each. References to God's "godly ones" enclose the song (see also v. 5). The common pair of synonyms, "glory" (v. 5) and "honor" (v. 9), effectively link the two stanzas (see 8:5; 21:5, "glory . . . majesty"; 104:1,31, "majesty . . . glory"; 145:5, "glorious splendor"; Is 35:2, "glory . . . majesty").

149:1 *new song.* See note on 33:3. *in the congregation.* See note on 9:1. *godly ones.* See vv. 5,9; see also note on 4:3.

149:2–5 Let Israel rejoice in their King, who has crowned them with the honor of salvation.

149:3 *His name.* See note on 5:11.

149:4 *Beautify.* Endow with splendor (see Is 55:5; 60:9; 61:3). *afflicted ones.* Those who acknowledge that they are without resources (see 147:6).

149:5 *on their beds.* The salvation (v. 4) so tangible in the daytime evokes songs in the night (see 42:8; 63:6; 77:6).

149:6–9 Let Israel praise their God, who has given them the glory of bearing the sword as His army in service.

149:7 *vengeance.* God's just retribution on those who have attacked His kingdom. Of this divine retribution the OT speaks often: 58:10; 79:10; 94:1; Num 31:2; Deut 32:35,41,43; 2 Kin 9:7; Is 34:8; 35:4; 47:3; 59:17; 61:2; 63:4; Jer 46:10; 50:15,28; 51:6,11,36; Ezek 25:14,17; Mic 5:15; Nah 1:2. In the NT age, however, God's people are armed with the "sword of the Spirit" for overcoming the powers arrayed against God's kingdom (see 2 Cor 6:7; 10:4; Eph 6:12,17; Heb 4:12); their participation in God's retribution on the world awaits the final judgment (see 1 Cor 6:2–3).

149:9 *judgment written.* God's firmly determined judgment (see 139:16 and note).

Ps 150 The final great Hallelujah—perhaps composed specifically to close the Psalter. See the conclusions to the first four Books: 41:13; 72:18–19; 89:52; 106:48. This final call to praise moves powerfully by stages from place to themes to orchestra to choir, framed with Hallelujahs. See introduction to Ps 146.

150:1 Where God should be praised. *His sanctuary.* At Jerusalem. *His mighty expanse.* Lit. "the expanse of his power" (see 19:1; Gen 1:6), i.e., the expanse that displays or symbolizes His power or in which His power resides. Usually thought to refer to God's heavenly temple (see 11:4), it may signify the vaulted ceiling of the visible universe viewed as a cosmic temple.

150:2 Why God should be praised. *His mighty deeds.* In creation and redemption.

150:3–5 How God should be praised—with the whole orchestra (eight instruments: wind, string, percussion), with dancing aptly placed at the middle.

150:6 Who should praise God. Finally the choir, with articulate expression, celebrates God's mighty acts and surpassing greatness.

Proverbs

INTRODUCTION

Authors

Although the book begins with a title ascribing the proverbs to Solomon, it is clear from later chapters that he was not the only author of the book. Prov 22:17 refers to the "words of the wise," and 24:23 mentions additional "sayings of the wise." The presence of an introduction in 22:17 – 21 further indicates that these sections stem from a circle of wise men, not from Solomon himself. Ch. 30 is attributed to Agur son of Jakeh and 31:1 – 9 to King Lemuel, neither of whom is mentioned elsewhere. Lemuel's sayings contain several Aramaic spellings that point to a non-Israelite background.

Most of the book, however, is closely linked with Solomon. The headings in 10:1 and 25:1 again include his name, though 25:1 states that these proverbs were transcribed by the men of Hezekiah. This indicates that a group of wise men or scribes compiled these proverbs as editors and added chs. 25 — 29 to the earlier collections. Solomon's ability to produce proverbs is specified in 1 Kin 4:32, where 3,000 proverbs are attributed to him. Coupled with the statements about his unparalleled wisdom (1 Kin 4:29 – 31), it is quite likely that he was the source of most of Proverbs. The book contains a short prologue (1:1 – 7) and a longer epilogue (31:10 – 31), which may have been added to the other materials. It is possible that the discourses in the large opening section (1:8 — 9:18) were the work of a compiler or editor, but the similarities of this section with other chapters (compare 6:1 with 11:15; 17:18; 20:16; 27:13; compare 6:19 with 14:5,25; 19:5) fit a Solomonic origin equally well. The emphasis on the "fear of the LORD" (1:7) throughout the book ties the various segments together.

Date

If Solomon is granted a prominent role in the book, most of Proverbs would stem from the tenth century B.C. during the time of Israel's united kingdom. The peace and prosperity that characterized that era accord well with the development of reflective wisdom and the production of literary works. Moreover, several scholars have noted that the 30 sayings of the wise in 22:17 — 24:22 contain similarities to the 30 sections of the Egyptian "Wisdom of Amenemope," an instructional piece that is roughly contemporary with the time of Solomon (see chart, p. xix). Likewise, the personification of wisdom so prominent in chs. 1 — 9 (see 1:20 and note; 3:15 – 18; 8:1 – 36) can be compared with the personification of abstract ideas in both Mesopotamian and Egyptian writings of the second millennium B.C.

The role of Hezekiah's men (see 25:1) indicates that important sections of Proverbs were compiled and edited from 715 to 686 B.C. This was a time of spiritual renewal led by the king, who also showed great interest in the writings of David and Asaph (see 2 Chr 29:30). Perhaps it was also at this time that the sayings of Agur (ch. 30) and Lemuel (31:1 – 9) and the other "words of the wise" (22:17 — 24:22; 24:23 – 34) were added to the Solomonic collections, though it is possible that the task of compilation was not completed until after the reign of Hezekiah.

The Nature of a Proverb

The Hebrew word translated "proverb" is also translated "taunt" (Is 14:4), "discourse" (Num 23:7,18) and "parable" (Ezek 17:2); so its meaning is considerably broader than the English term. This may help explain the presence of the longer discourse sections in chs. 1 — 9. Most proverbs are short, compact statements that express truths about human behavior. Often there is some repetition of a word or sound that aids memorization. In 30:33, e.g., the same Hebrew verb is translated "churning" and "pressing."

In the largest section of the book (10:1 — 22:16) most of the proverbs are two lines long, and those in chs. 10 — 15 almost always express a contrast. Sometimes the writer simply makes a general observation,

such as "a bribe is a charm in the sight of its owner" (17:8; cf. 14:20), but usually he evaluates conduct: "But he who hates bribes will live" (15:27). Many proverbs, in fact, describe the consequences of a particular action or character trait: "A wise son makes a father glad" (10:1). Since the proverbs were written primarily for instruction, often they are given in the form of commands: "Do not love sleep, or you will become poor" (20:13). Even where the imperative form is not used, the desired action is quite clear (see 14:5).

A common feature of the proverbs is the use of figurative language: "Like cold water to a weary soul / So is good news from a distant land" (25:25). In ch. 25 alone there are 11 verses that begin with "like" or "as." These similes make the proverbs more vivid and powerful. Occasionally the simile is used in a humorous or sarcastic way: "As a ring of gold in a swine's snout / So is a beautiful woman who lacks discretion" (11:22; cf. 26:9), or, "As the door turns on its hinges, / So does the sluggard on his bed" (26:14). Equally effective is the use of metaphors: "The teaching of the wise is a fountain of life" (13:14), and "A soothing tongue is a tree of life" (15:4). According to 16:24, "Pleasant words are a honeycomb." The figure of sowing and reaping is used in both a positive and a negative way (cf. 11:18; 22:8).

In order to develop a proper set of values, a number of proverbs use direct comparisons: "Better is the poor who walks in his integrity / Than he who is crooked though he be rich" (28:6). This "better . . . than" pattern can be seen also in 15:16–17; 16:19,32; 17:1,12; a modified form occurs in 22:1. Another pattern found in the book is the so-called numerical proverb. Used for the first time in 6:16 (see note there), this type of saying normally has the number three in the first line and four in the second (cf. 30:15,18,21,29).

The repetition of entire proverbs (compare 6:10–11 with 24:33–34; 14:12 with 16:25; 20:16 with 27:13) or parts of proverbs may serve a poetic purpose. A slight variation allows the writer(s) to use the same image to make a related point (as in 17:3; 27:21) or to substitute a word to achieve greater clarity or a different emphasis (cf. 19:1; 28:6). In 26:4–5 the same line is repeated in a seemingly contradictory way, but this was designed to make two different points (see notes there).

At times the book of Proverbs is very direct and earthy (cf. 6:6; 21:9; 25:16; 26:3,11). This is the nature of wisdom literature as it seeks to drive home truth and to turn sinners from their wicked ways (see essay, p. 689).

Purpose and Teaching

According to the prologue, Proverbs was written to give "prudence to the naive, to the youth knowledge and discretion" (1:4), and to make wise men wiser (1:5). The frequent references to "my son" (1:8,10; 2:1; 3:1; 4:1; 5:1) emphasize instructing the young and guiding them into a happy and prosperous life. Acquiring wisdom and knowing how to avoid the pitfalls of folly will lead to health and success. Although Proverbs is a practical book dealing with the art of living, it bases wisdom solidly on the fear of the Lord (1:7). Throughout the book this reverence for God is set forth as the path to life and security (cf. 3:5; 9:10; 22:4). People must trust in the Lord (3:5) and not in themselves (28:26). The references to the "tree of life" (3:18; 11:30; 13:12) recall the joyful bliss of the Garden of Eden and figuratively say that the one who finds wisdom will be greatly blessed.

In chs. 1—9 the writer contrasts the way of wisdom with the path of violence (1:11–18) and immorality (2:16–18). The adulteress with her seductive words tries to lure a young man to her house and ultimately to death (cf. ch. 5; 6:24–35; 7; 9:13–18). Sexual immorality is thus an example of and a symbol for the antithesis of wisdom (cf. 22:14; 23:27; 30:20).

At the same time, Proverbs condemns the quarrelsome wife and her unbearable ways (19:13; 21:9,19). The home is supposed to be a place of love, not dissension (cf. 15:17; 17:1). Quarrelsome, quick-tempered men are also denounced (cf. 14:29; 26:21), and gossiping is viewed as a source of great trouble (11:13; 18:8; 26:22). If anyone is able to control his tongue, he is a man of knowledge (cf. 10:19; 17:27). At the same time, the tongue must be used to instruct one's children (cf. 1:8; 22:6; 31:26), and discipline is necessary for their well-being (see 13:24 and note).

Proverbs strongly encourages diligence and hard work (see 10:4 and note; 31:17–19) and holds the sluggard up to contempt for his laziness (see 6:6 and note). A son "who sleeps in harvest is a son who acts shamefully" (10:5), and those who love sleep are sure to grow poor (cf. 20:13). Generally, wealth is connected to righteousness (cf. 3:16) and poverty to wickedness (cf. 22:16), but some verses link riches with the wicked (15:16;

28:6). Honesty and justice are praised repeatedly, and it is expected that a king will defend the rights of the poor and needy (cf. 31:5). Those who are kind to the needy will be richly blessed (see 14:21 and note), but there are several warnings against putting up security for a neighbor (see 6:1 and note).

The proud and the arrogant are sure to be destroyed (cf. 11:2; 16:18), especially the mocker with his "insolent pride" (see 21:24 and note on 1:22). Drunkards are depicted as the epitome of the fool (cf. 20:1), and their woes and miseries are described in graphic terms in 23:29–35.

Although Proverbs is more practical than theological, God's work as Creator is especially highlighted. The role of wisdom in creation is the subject of 8:22–31 (see notes there), where wisdom as an attribute of God is personified. Twice God is called the Maker of the poor (14:31; 17:5). He also directs the steps of a man (cf. 16:9; 20:24), and his eyes observe all his actions (cf. 5:21; 15:3). God is sovereign over the kings of the earth (21:1), and all history moves forward under his control (see notes on 16:4,33).

Literary Structure

A short prologue (stating the purpose and theme, 1:1–7) opens the book, and a longer epilogue (identifiable by its subject matter and its alphabetic form, 31:10–31) closes it. The first nine chapters contain a series of discourses that contrast the way and benefits of wisdom with the way of the fool. Except for the sections where personified wisdom speaks (1:20; 8:1,22; 9:1), each discourse begins with "my son" or "my sons." These units are similar to the discourses found in Job and Ecclesiastes, which also contain speeches given in poetic form.

A key feature in the introductory discourses of Proverbs is the personification of both wisdom and folly (as women), each of whom (by appeals and warnings on the part of Lady Wisdom, by enticements on the part of Lady Folly) seeks to persuade "naive" youths to follow her ways. These discourses are strikingly organized. Beginning (1:8–33) and ending (chs. 8—9) with direct enticements and appeals, the main body of the discourses is made up of two nicely balanced sections, one devoted to the commendation of wisdom (chs. 2—4) and the other to warnings against folly (chs. 5—7). In these discourses the young man is depicted as being enticed to folly by men who try to get ahead in the world by exploiting others (1:10–19) and by women who seek sexual pleasure outside the bond of marriage (ch. 5; 6:20–25; 7). In the social structures of that day, these were the two great temptations for young men. The second especially functions here as illustrative and emblematic of the appeal of Lady Folly.

The main collection of Solomon's proverbs in 10:1—22:16 consists of individual couplets, many of which express a contrast. On the surface, there does not seem to be any discernible arrangement, though occasionally two or three proverbs deal with the same subject. For example, 11:24–25 deals with generosity, 16:12–15 mentions a king, and 19:4,6–7 talks about friendship. However, there is growing evidence that arrangements of larger units were deliberate. Further study of this possibility is necessary. The second Solomonic collection (chs. 25—29) continues the pattern of two-line verses, but there are also examples of proverbs with three (25:13; 27:10,22) or four (25:4–5,21–22; 26:18–19) lines. The last five verses of ch. 27 (vv. 23–27) present a short discourse on the benefits of raising flocks and herds.

In the "words of the wise" (22:17—24:22) and the "sayings of the wise" of 24:23–34, there is a prevalence of two- or three-verse units and something of a return to the style of chs. 1—9 (see 23:29–35 especially). These sections function as an appendix to 10:1—22:16 and contain some similar proverbs (compare 24:6 with 11:14; 24:16 with 11:5). Even stronger are the links with chs. 1—9 (compare 23:27 with 2:16; 24:33–34 with 6:10–11).

The last two chapters serve as an appendix to chs. 25 — 29. The words of Agur are dominated by the numerical proverb (30:15,18,21,24,29) and include a close parallel to Ps 18:30 in 30:5 (also compare 30:6 with Deut 4:2). After the nine verses attributed to King Lemuel (31:1 – 9), Proverbs concludes with an epilogue, an impressive acrostic poem honoring a worthy woman. She demonstrates, and thus epitomizes, many of the qualities and values identified with wisdom throughout the book. In view of the fact that Proverbs is primarily addressed to young men on the threshold of mature life, this focus on a worthy woman appears surprising. But its purpose may be twofold: (1) to offer counsel on the kind of wife a young man ought to seek, and (2) in a subtle way to advise the young man (again) to marry Lady Wisdom, thus returning to the theme of chs. 1 — 9 (as climaxed in ch. 9; compare the description of Lady Wisdom in 9:1 – 2 with the virtues of the

wife of noble character). In any event, the concluding epitomizing of wisdom in the wife of noble character forms a literary frame with the opening discourses, where wisdom is personified as a woman.

Outline

I. Prologue: Purpose and Theme (1:1–7)
II. The Superiority of the Way of Wisdom (1:8—9:18)
  A. Appeals and Warnings Confronting Youth (1:8–33)
    1. Enticements to secure happiness by violence (1:8–19)
    2. Warnings against rejecting wisdom (1:20–33)
  B. Commendation of Wisdom (chs. 2—4)
    1. Benefits of accepting wisdom's instructions (ch. 2)
    2. Wisdom's instructions and benefits (3:1–20)
    3. Wisdom's instructions and benefits (3:21–35)
    4. Challenge to hold on to wisdom (ch. 4)
  C. Warnings against Folly (chs. 5—7)
    1. Warning against adultery (ch. 5)
    2. Warning against perverse ways (6:1–19)
    3. Cost of committing adultery (6:20–35)
    4. Warning against the enticements of an adulteress (ch. 7)
  D. Appeals Addressed to Youth (chs. 8—9)
    1. Wisdom's appeal (ch. 8)
    2. Invitations of wisdom and folly (ch. 9)
III. The Main Collection of Solomon's Proverbs (10:1—22:16)
IV. The Thirty Sayings of the Wise (22:17—24:22)
V. Additional Sayings of the Wise (24:23–34)
VI. Hezekiah's Collection of Solomon's Proverbs (chs. 25—29)
VII. The Words of Agur (ch. 30)
VIII. The Words of King Lemuel (31:1–9)
IX. Epilogue: The Worthy Woman (31:10–31)

The Usefulness of Proverbs

1 The [a]proverbs of Solomon [b]the son of David, king of Israel:
2 To know [a]wisdom and instruction,
To discern the sayings of
[b]understanding,
3 To [a]receive instruction in wise
behavior,
[b]Righteousness, justice and equity;
4 To give [a]prudence to the [1]naive,
To the youth [b]knowledge and
discretion,
5 A wise man will hear and [a]increase in
learning,
And a [b]man of understanding will
acquire wise counsel,
6 To understand a proverb and a figure,
The words of the wise and their
[a]riddles.

7 [a]The fear of the LORD is the beginning
of knowledge;
Fools despise wisdom and instruction.

The Enticement of Sinners

8 [a]Hear, my son, your father's instruction
And [b]do not forsake your mother's
teaching;
9 Indeed, they are a [a]graceful wreath to
your head
And [1b]ornaments about your neck.
10 My son, if sinners [a]entice you,
[b]Do not consent.
11 If they say, "Come with us,
Let us [a]lie in wait for blood,
Let us [b]ambush the innocent without
cause;
12 Let us [a]swallow them alive like Sheol,
Even whole, as those who [b]go down
to the pit;
13 We will find all *kinds* of precious
wealth,
We will fill our houses with spoil;
14 Throw in your lot [1]with us,
We shall all have one purse,"
15 My son, [a]do not walk in the way with
them.
[b]Keep your feet from their path,
16 For [a]their feet run to evil
And they hasten to shed blood.
17 Indeed, it is [1]useless to spread the
baited net
In the sight of any [2]bird;
18 But they [a]lie in wait for their own
blood;
They ambush their own lives.
19 So are the ways of everyone who
[a]gains by violence;
It takes away the life of its possessors.

Wisdom Warns

20 [a]Wisdom shouts in the street,
She [1]lifts her voice in the square;

1:1 [a]1 Kin 4:32; Prov 10:1; 25:1; Eccl 12:9 [b]Eccl 1:1
2 [a]Prov 15:33 [b]Prov 4:1
3 [a]Prov 2:1; 19:20 [b]Prov 2:9
4 [1]Lit *simple ones* [a]Prov 8:5, 12 [b]Prov 2:10, 11; 3:21
5 [a]Prov 9:9 [b]Prov 14:6; Eccl 9:11
6 [a]Num 12:8; Ps 49:4; 78:2; Dan 8:23
7 [a]Job 28:28; Ps 111:10; Prov 9:10; 15:33; Eccl 12:13
8 [a]Prov 4:1 [b]Prov 6:20
9 [1]Lit *necklaces* [a]Prov 4:9 [b]Gen 41:42; Dan 5:29
10 [a]Prov 16:29
10 [b]Gen 39:7-10; Deut 13:8; Ps 50:18; Eph 5:11
11 [a]Prov 12:6; Jer 5:26 [b]Ps 10:8; Prov 1:18
12 [a]Ps 124:3 [b]Ps 28:1
14 [1]Lit *in the midst of us*
15 [a]Ps 1:1; Prov 4:14 [b]Ps 119:101
16 [a]Prov 6:17, 18; Is 59:7
17 [1]Lit *in vain* [2]Lit *possessor of wing*
18 [a]Prov 11:19
19 [a]Prov 15:27
20 [1]Lit *gives* [a]Prov 8:1-3; 9:3

1:1 *Solomon.* His wisdom and prolific production of proverbs and songs are mentioned in 1 Kin 4:32. His name occurs again in the headings of 10:1 and 25:1. Cf. Eccl 1:1; Song 1:1.
1:2–4 Verses 2–3 apply to the son (or student); v. 4 refers to the father (or teacher).
1:2 *wisdom.* This key term occurs over 40 times in the book. It includes skill in living—following God's design and thus avoiding moral pitfalls. A craftsman can be called a wise (skillful) man (Ex 31:3). Proverbs urges people to get wisdom (4:5), for it is worth more than silver or gold (3:13–14). The NT refers to Christ as "wisdom from God" (1 Cor 1:30; cf. Col 2:3).
1:3 *Righteousness, justice and equity.* See 2:9.
1:4 *prudence.* Good judgment or good sense (see 15:5; 19:25). Outside Proverbs the Hebrew word is used in the negative sense of "crafty" or "shrewd" (Gen 3:1; Job 5:13). *naive.* Another key word in Proverbs, occurring some 15 times. It denotes those who are easily persuaded and who "lack understanding" (9:4,16), who are immature, inexperienced and simple (cf. Ps 19:7). Generally speaking, the Hebrew term for "naive" denotes one without moral direction and inclined to evil; see 1:22.
1:6 *riddles.* The Hebrew for this word can sometimes refer to allegories (cf. Ezek 17:2).
1:7 The theme of the book (see 9:10; 31:30; cf. Job 28:28; Ps 111:10). *fear of the* L*ORD*. A loving reverence for God that includes submission to His lordship and to the commands of His word (Eccl 12:13). God is our king (Mal 1:14), but even as we stand in awe of Him we can rejoice (see Ps 2:11; Is 12:6). *Fools.* Those who hate knowledge (v. 22) and correction of any kind (12:1), who are ready to "quarrel" (20:3) and make no effort to restrain their anger (29:11), who are complacent (1:32) and who trust in themselves (28:26) rather than in God (Ps 14:1). *despise wisdom and instruction.* See 5:12 and note.
1:8 A typical introduction to an instruction speech in Proverbs, evoking a domestic situation of a father preparing his son for life in the world. Here and in 6:20 the mother is also depicted as teacher.
1:9 *graceful . . . ornaments.* Those who follow wisdom add beauty and honor to their lives.
1:11 *lie in wait for blood.* Their goal is personal enrichment by theft or oppression (vv. 13,19), even if they have to commit murder. The author uses two major enticements that confronted the young man (in that culture) as examples of the way of folly: (1) to get rich by exploiting others (here) and (2) to be drawn into illicit sexual pleasure by immoral women who fail to honor their marriage vows (5:1–6; 6:24; 7:5; cf. 2:12–19).
1:12 *swallow . . . like Sheol.* Vivid poetic imagery for shamelessly victimizing others (see note on Ps 49:14).
1:13 *precious wealth.* By contrast, the book of Proverbs teaches that wisdom brings the greatest riches man could ever gain (3:14–16; 16:16; see also Job 28:12–19).
1:15 *path.* Cf. the destructive paths of the adulteress in 2:18; 7:25.
1:16 The same as the first two lines of Is 59:7 and partially quoted in Rom 3:15. Cf. Prov 6:17–18.
1:17 *net.* Nets were used to catch birds and animals (see 6:5; 7:23; Eccl 9:12; Is 51:20; Jer 5:26).
1:18 *ambush their own lives.* The wicked unintentionally spread a net for their own feet (29:6; Ps 35:8), so they are less intelligent than birds (see 7:22–23). According to Is 17:14, the lot of those who plunder God's people is destruction.
1:19 Cf. Is 17:14. Contrast the long life enjoyed by the one who hates ill-gotten gain (28:16).
1:20 *Wisdom shouts in the street.* Here and in 3:15–18; 8; 9:1–12 wisdom is personified. This is a poetic device common also in Isaiah (cf. 55:12; 59:14). *square.* An open area inside the gate of a fortified city.

21 At the head of the noisy *streets* she
cries out;
At the entrance of the gates in the city
she utters her sayings:
22 "How long, O [1][a]naive ones, will you
love [2]being simple-minded?
And [b]scoffers delight themselves in
scoffing
And fools [c]hate knowledge?
23 "Turn to my reproof,
Behold, I will [a]pour out my spirit on
you;
I will make my words known to you.
24 "Because [a]I called and you [b]refused,
I [c]stretched out my hand and no one
paid attention;
25 And you [a]neglected all my counsel
And did not [b]want my reproof;
26 I will also [a]laugh at your [b]calamity;
I will mock when your [c]dread comes,
27 When your dread comes like a storm
And your calamity comes like a
[a]whirlwind,
When distress and anguish come
upon you.
28 "Then they will [a]call on me, but I will
not answer;
They will [b]seek me diligently but they
will not find me,
29 Because they [a]hated knowledge
And did not choose the fear of the
LORD.

22 [1]Lit *simple ones* [2]Or *naivete* [a]Prov 1:4, 32; 8:5; 9:4; 22:3 [b]Ps 1:1 [c]Prov 1:29; 5:12
23 [a]Is 32:15; Joel 2:28; John 7:39
24 [a]Is 65:12; 66:4; Jer 7:13 [b]Zech 7:11 [c]Is 65:2; Rom 10:21
25 [a]Ps 107:11; Luke 7:30 [b]Prov 15:10
26 [a]Ps 2:4 [b]Prov 6:15 [c]Prov 10:24
27 [a]Prov 10:25
28 [a]1 Sam 8:18; Job 27:9; 35:12; Ps 18:41; Is 1:15; Jer 11:11; 14:12; Ezek 8:18; Mic 3:4; Zech 7:13; James 4:3 [b]Prov 8:17
29 [a]Job 21:14; Prov 1:22
30 [a]Ps 81:11; Prov 1:25
31 [a]Job 4:8; Prov 5:22, 23; 22:8; Is 3:11; Jer 6:19 [b]Prov 14:14
32 [1]Lit *simple ones* [a]Jer 2:19
33 [1]Lit *dwell* [a]Ps 25:12, 13; Prov 3:24-26
2:1 [a]Prov 4:10 [b]Prov 3:1
2 [a]Prov 22:17
3 [1]Lit *Give*

30 "They [a]would not accept my counsel,
They spurned all my reproof.
31 "So they shall [a]eat of the fruit of their
own way
And be [b]satiated with their own
devices.
32 "For the [a]waywardness of the [1]naive
will kill them,
And the complacency of fools will
destroy them.
33 "But [a]he who listens to me shall [1]live
securely
And will be at ease from the dread of
evil."

The Pursuit of Wisdom Brings Security

2 My son, if you will [a]receive my words
And [b]treasure my commandments
within you,
2 [a]Make your ear attentive to wisdom,
Incline your heart to understanding;
3 For if you cry for discernment,
[1]Lift your voice for understanding;
4 If you seek her as [a]silver
And search for her as for [b]hidden
treasures;
5 Then you will discern the [a]fear of the
LORD
And discover the knowledge of God.
6 For [a]the LORD gives wisdom;

4 [a]Prov 3:14 [b]Job 3:21; Matt 13:44 **5** [a]Prov 1:7
6 [a]1 Kin 3:12; Job 32:8; James 1:5

1:21 *gates.* Where the leaders of the city met to hold court (see 31:23; Ruth 4:11; Job 29:7) and where the marketplace was located (2 Kin 7:1). As a young man confronts life in its social context, two voices lure him, appeal for his allegiance, and seek to shape his life: (1) the voice of wisdom (as exemplified in the instructions of the teachers of wisdom) and (2) the voice of folly (as exemplified in the sinners of vv. 10–14 and in the adulteress of 5:3; 6:24; 7:5). Thus in the midst of life the youth must learn to exercise discretion. Here and in chs. 8–9 wisdom makes her appeal. She speaks neither out of heaven (by special revelation, as do the prophets) nor out of the earth (through voices from the dead—necromancy; see Lev 19:31; Deut 18:11; 1 Sam 28:7–19), but out of the center of the life of the city, where man's communal experience of the creation order (established by God's wisdom, 8:22–31) is concentrated (see, e.g., 11:10 and note). And it is there also that the godly, the truly wise, test human experience in the crucible of faith and afterward give divine wisdom a human voice in their wise instructions—as in Proverbs.

1:22 *scoffers.* Those who are proud and arrogant (21:24), who are full of insults, hatred and strife (9:7–8; 22:10; 29:8), who resist correction (13:1; 15:12) even though they deserve flogging (19:25; 21:11).

1:23 *pour out my spirit.* Wisdom is like a fountain. Her words would constantly refresh and strengthen (see 18:4).

1:24 *refused.* As God was refused by Israel (see Is 1:4; 5:24) and Jesus by the people of Jerusalem (Matt 23:37). *stretched out my hand.* Cf. Is 65:2, where God held out His hands all day long to a stubborn people.

1:25 *neglected . . . counsel.* Cf. 8:33.

1:26 *laugh at your calamity.* Not an expression of heartlessness but a reaction to the absurdity of fools, who laugh at wisdom, choose folly and bring disaster on themselves. Cf. the Lord's response to kings who think they can rebel against Him (Ps 2:4). *dread comes.* Also the fate of "a worthless person, a wicked man" (6:12–15).

1:27 *like a storm.* See 10:25. *like a whirlwind.* When Job's family was killed by a mighty wind (Job 1:19), his comforters concluded that his wickedness was the cause of the disaster (Job 18:5,12). *distress and anguish.* See Is 8:22.

1:28 *I will not answer.* Just as God refused to listen to Israel when the people sinned (Deut 1:45; Is 1:15). *find me.* Those who find wisdom find life and blessing (see v. 33; 3:13; 8:17,35).

1:29 *fear of the LORD.* See note on v. 7.

1:31 *eat . . . be satiated.* The consequences depend on their actions (18:20; 31:31; Is 3:10). "Whatever a man sows, this he will also reap" (Gal 6:7).

1:32 *complacency.* A false sense of security (see Is 32:9; Amos 6:1; Zeph 1:12).

1:33 *securely . . . at ease.* Words used of places that enjoy God's protection (see Is 32:18; Ezek 34:27).

2:1 *treasure . . . within you.* Just as the psalmist urged young men to avoid sin by hiding God's word in their hearts (Ps 119:11).

2:2 *Make your ear attentive.* Listening implies attentiveness and obedience (Is 55:3; Jer 13:15). *heart.* The Hebrew word translated "heart" here (and in 4:21; 1 Kin 3:9) can sometimes be translated "mind" or "intelligence" (see Job 12:3).

2:4 *silver . . . hidden treasures.* Job 28:1–11 describes ancient mining techniques, comparing mining with the search for wisdom (see Job 28:12).

2:5 *fear of the LORD.* See note on 1:7. *knowledge of God.* Involves knowing God as a person (Phil 3:10) and knowing what He is teaching us (v. 6). *God.* Hebrew *Elohim* (see note on Gen 2:4); occurs elsewhere in Proverbs only in v. 17; 3:4; 25:2; 30:9.

From His mouth *come* knowledge and
understanding.
7 He stores up sound wisdom for the
upright;
He is a [a]shield to those who walk in
integrity,
8 Guarding the paths of justice,
And He [a]preserves the way of His
godly ones.
9 Then you will discern [a]righteousness
and justice
And equity *and* every [b]good course.
10 For [a]wisdom will enter your heart
And [b]knowledge will be pleasant to
your soul;
11 Discretion will [a]guard you,
Understanding will watch over you,
12 To [a]deliver you from the way of evil,
From the man who speaks [b]perverse
things;
13 From those who [a]leave the paths of
uprightness
To walk in the [b]ways of darkness;
14 Who [a]delight in doing evil
And rejoice in the perversity of evil;
15 Whose paths are [a]crooked,
And who are devious in their ways;
16 To [a]deliver you from the strange
woman,
From the [1b]adulteress who flatters
with her words;
17 That leaves the [a]companion of her
youth
And forgets the [b]covenant of her God;
18 For [a]her house [1]sinks down to death
And her tracks *lead* to the [2]dead;
19 None [a]who go to her return again,
Nor do they reach the [b]paths of life.
20 So you will [a]walk in the way of good
men
And keep to the [b]paths of the
righteous.
21 For [a]the upright will [1]live in the land
And [b]the blameless will remain in it;
22 But [a]the wicked will be cut off from
the land
And [b]the treacherous will be
[c]uprooted from it.

The Rewards of Wisdom

3 My son, [a]do not forget my [1]teaching,
But let your heart [b]keep my
commandments;
2 For [a]length of days and years of life
And peace they will add to you.
3 Do not let [a]kindness and truth leave
you;
[b]Bind them around your neck,
[c]Write them on the tablet of your heart.
4 So you will [a]find favor and [b]good
[1]repute
In the sight of God and man.
5 [a]Trust in the LORD with all your heart
And [b]do not lean on your own
understanding.

7 [a]Ps 84:11; Prov 30:5 **8** [a]1 Sam 2:9; Ps 66:9 **9** [a]Prov 8:20 [b]Prov 4:18 **10** [a]Prov 14:33 [b]Prov 22:18 **11** [a]Prov 4:6; 6:22 **12** [a]Prov 28:26 [b]Prov 6:12 **13** [a]Prov 21:16 [b]Ps 82:5; Prov 4:19; John 3:19, 20 **14** [a]Prov 10:23; Jer 11:15 **15** [a]Ps 125:5; Prov 21:8 **16** [1]Lit *strange woman* [a]Prov 6:24; 7:5 [b]Prov 23:27 **17** [a]Mal 2:14, 15 [b]Gen 2:24 **18** [1]Lit *bows down* [2]Lit *departed spirits* [a]Prov 7:27 **19** [a]Eccl 7:26 [b]Ps 16:11; Prov 5:6 **20** [a]Heb 6:12 [b]Prov 4:18 **21** [1]Or *dwell* [a]Ps 37:9, 29; Prov 10:30 [b]Prov 28:10 **22** [a]Ps 37:38; Prov 10:30 [b]Prov 11:3 [c]Deut 28:63; Ps 52:5 **3:1** [1]Or *law* [a]Ps 119:61; Prov 4:5 [b]Ex 20:6; Deut 30:16 **2** [a]Ps 91:16; Prov 3:16; 4:10; 9:11; 10:27

3 [a]2 Sam 15:20; Prov 14:22 [b]Deut 6:8; 11:18; Prov 1:9; 6:21 [c]Prov 7:3; Jer 17:1; 2 Cor 3:3 **4** [1]Lit *understanding* [a]1 Sam 2:26; Prov 8:35; Luke 2:52 [b]Ps 111:10 **5** [a]Ps 37:3, 5; Prov 22:19 [b]Prov 23:4; Jer 9:23

2:7 *stores up.* For those who "store up" ("treasure") His commands (v. 1). *shield.* Associated with victory also in Ps 18:2,35; cf. Prov 30:5. *in integrity.* See 19:1.
2:8 *Guarding . . . preserves.* See Ps 91:3–7,11–12.
2:9–11 Those who know the Lord and the wisdom He gives will know what course of action to follow (cf. Heb 5:11–14).
2:9 *righteousness and justice And equity.* See 1:3; Phil 4:8. *good course.* See "the paths of righteousness" of Ps 23:3.
2:10 *pleasant to your soul.* Just as the words of a wise man are "sweet to the soul" of another (16:24; cf. 3:17).
2:11 *guard . . . watch over.* As God guards the faithful (v. 8).
2:12–19 Wisdom will save from the enticements of men to follow perverse ways (vv. 12–15) and from the enticements of the adulteress (vv. 16–19). See note on 1:11.
2:12 *speaks perverse things.* Cf. v. 14. The deceitfulness of men's speech is also mentioned in 8:13; 10:31–32; 17:20.
2:13 *paths of uprightness.* See 3:6; 9:15–16. *ways of darkness.* Men love darkness instead of light (see John 3:19–21; see also Job 24:15–16; Is 29:15; Rom 13:12).
2:14 *delight . . . rejoice in . . . evil.* Like the sinners of 1:10–16.
2:15 *paths are crooked.* See Is 59:7–8.
2:16 *strange woman . . . adulteress.* The Hebrew for these terms occurs again in 5:20 and 7:5. The terms mean lit. "stranger" and "foreigner" (cf. 5:10) because anyone other than one's own wife was to be considered off limits, like a foreigner who worshiped another god (cf. 1 Kin 11:1). "Adulteress" is parallel to "evil woman" in 6:24 and "harlot" in 23:27. *words.* Equal to the "flattering lips" of 6:24 and the "smooth talk" of 7:21. Cf. 5:3.
2:17 *companion of her youth.* Her husband, whom she married when she was a young woman (cf. Is 54:6). *covenant of her God.* Perhaps the marriage covenant, spoken in God's presence (see Ezek 16:8; Mal 2:14). Here, however, the "covenant of her God" more likely refers to the breaking of the seventh commandment (Ex 20:14).
2:18 *sinks down to death.* According to 7:27, "her house is the way to Sheol." A life of immorality leads to the destruction and death of all who are involved (cf. 5:5; 9:18). *the dead.* See Job 26:5 and note. The deceased are in the grave (or Sheol), "the chambers of death" (7:27).
2:21 *live in the land.* Israel had been promised the land of Canaan (Gen 17:8; Deut 4:1), and Ps 37:29 says that "The righteous will inherit the land" (see Ps 37:9,11; Matt 5:5).
2:22 *cut off from the land . . . uprooted from it.* In Deut 28:63 God warned that if the people refuse to obey Him, they "will be torn from the land." Evil men and their offspring will be cut off (Ps 37:9,28).
3:2 *days and years . . . they will add to you.* Fear of the Lord (10:27; 19:23) brings health to the body (v. 8) and "prolongs life" (10:27; see also 9:10–11). *peace.* Or "prosperity." When Solomon prayed for wisdom, God promised him riches as well as long life if he obeyed God's commands (1 Kin 3:13–14). Normally the righteous are prosperous and happy (12:21), but sometimes it is the wicked who are strong and prosperous (Ps 73:3,12), temporary though that may be (Ps 73:17–19). Job 1–2 also shows how disaster and death can strike a godly person.
3:3 *Bind . . . neck.* Like a beautiful necklace (cf. 1:9; 3:22). *Write them on the tablet of your heart.* See Jer 31:33.
3:4 *favor.* See 8:35; Gen 6:8. *God and man.* See Luke 2:52; Rom 12:17; 2 Cor 8:21.
3:5 *Trust in the LORD.* Commit your way to the Lord (Ps 37:5), like Israel's forefathers, who trusted in God and were rescued

6 In all your ways [a]acknowledge Him,
And He will [b]make your paths straight.
7 [a]Do not be wise in your own eyes;
[b]Fear the LORD and turn away from evil.
8 It will be [a]healing to your [1]body
And [b]refreshment to your bones.
9 [a]Honor the LORD from your wealth
And from the [b]first of all your produce;
10 So your [a]barns will be filled with plenty
And your [b]vats will overflow with new wine.
11 [a]My son, do not reject the [1]discipline of the LORD
Or loathe His reproof,
12 For [a]whom the LORD loves He reproves,
Even [b]as a father *corrects* the son in whom he delights.

13 [a]How blessed is the man who finds wisdom
And the man who gains understanding.
14 For her [a]profit is better than the profit of silver
And her gain better than fine gold.
15 She is [a]more precious than [1]jewels;
And nothing you desire compares with her.
16 [1][a]Long life is in her right hand;
In her left hand are [b]riches and honor.
17 Her [a]ways are pleasant ways
And all her paths are [b]peace.
18 She is a [a]tree of life to those who take hold of her,
And happy are all who hold her fast.
19 The LORD [a]by wisdom founded the earth,
By understanding He [b]established the heavens.
20 By His knowledge the [a]deeps were broken up
And the [b]skies drip with dew.
21 My son, [a]let them not [1]vanish from your sight;
Keep sound wisdom and discretion,
22 So they will be [a]life to your soul
And [b]adornment to your neck.
23 Then you will [a]walk in your way securely
And your foot will not [b]stumble.
24 When you [a]lie down, you will not be afraid;
When you lie down, your sleep will be sweet.
25 [a]Do not be afraid of sudden fear
Nor of the [1][b]onslaught of the wicked when it comes;

6 [a]1 Chr 28:9; Prov 16:3; Phil 4:6; James 1:5 [b]Is 45:13; Jer 10:23 **7** [a]Rom 12:16 [b]Job 1:1; 28:28; Prov 8:13; 16:6 **8** [1]Lit *navel* [a]Prov 4:22 [b]Job 21:24 **9** [a]Is 43:23 [b]Ex 23:19; Deut 26:2; Mal 3:10 **10** [a]Deut 28:8 [b]Joel 2:24 **11** [1]Or *instruction* [a]Job 5:17; Heb 12:5, 6 **12** [a]Rev 3:19 [b]Deut 8:5; Prov 13:24 **13** [a]Prov 8:32, 34 **14** [a]Job 28:15-19; Prov 8:10, 19; 16:16 **15** [1]Lit *corals* [a]Job 28:18; Prov 8:11 **16** [1]Lit *Length of days* [a]Prov 3:2 [b]Prov 8:18; 22:4 **17** [a]Matt 11:29 [b]Ps 119:165; Prov 16:7 **18** [a]Gen 2:9; Prov 11:30; 13:12; 15:4; Rev 2:7 **19** [a]Ps 104:24; Prov 8:27 [b]Prov 8:27, 28 **20** [a]Gen 7:11 [b]Deut 33:28; Job 36:28 **21** [1]Lit *depart* [a]Prov 4:21 **22** [a]Deut 32:47; Prov 4:22; 8:35; 16:22; 21:21 [b]Prov 1:9 **23** [a]Prov 4:12; 10:9 [b]Ps 91:12; Is 5:27; 63:13 **24** [a]Job 11:19; Ps 3:5; Prov 1:33; 6:22 **25** [1]Lit *storm* [a]Ps 91:5; 1 Pet 3:14 [b]Job 5:21

(Ps 22:4–5). *with all your heart.* Like Caleb (Num 14:24; Deut 1:36) or the godly King Hezekiah (Is 38:3). David challenged Solomon to serve God with wholehearted devotion (1 Chr 28:9).

3:6 *acknowledge Him.* Be ever mindful of God and serve Him with a willing and faithful heart (see 1 Chr 28:9; Hos 4:1; 6:6). *make your paths straight.* He will remove the obstacles from your pathway and bring you to your appointed goal (see 11:5; Is 45:13).

3:7 *Fear the LORD and turn away from evil.* Cf. Job, who was a "blameless, upright" man (Job 1:1). See note on 1:7.

3:8 *bones.* The whole body. Elsewhere, good news and pleasant words bring health to the bones (15:30; 16:24; cf. 17:22).

3:9 *first of . . . your produce.* The Israelites were required to give to the priests the first part of the olive oil, wine and grain produced each year (see Lev 23:10; Num 18:12–13).

3:10 *filled with plenty.* For those who bring to the Lord His tithes and offerings, God promises to pour out more blessing than they have room for (see Mal 3:10; see also Deut 28:8,12; 2 Cor 9:8).

3:11–12 A warning that the righteous are not always prosperous (see v. 2 and note). Through times of testing and affliction, God is teaching them (see 12:1; Job 5:17; 36:22; Ps 119:71). Heb 12:5–6 quotes both of these verses to encourage believers to endure hardship (Heb 12:7). "He disciplines us for our good" (Heb 12:10).

3:12 *as a father.* God disciplined His son Israel by testing the nation in the wilderness 40 years (Deut 8:2–5).

3:13–18 A poem praising wisdom , the first and last verse of which suggest that blessedness (v.13) and happiness (v.18) attend those who find it. The same Hebrew word underlies both.

3:14 *her profit is better than . . . silver And . . . gold.* The psalmist makes the same claim for the commands and precepts of the Lord (Ps 19:10; 119:72,127).

3:15–18 Wisdom is personified.

3:15 *jewels.* See Job 28:18, where wisdom is more valuable than pearls, and Prov 31:10, where an "excellent wife" is worth more than jewels.

3:16 *Long life.* See note on v. 2. *riches and honor.* See 8:18; 22:4.

3:17 *peace.* Hebrew *shalom* (see v. 2; 16:7; Ps 119:165).

3:18 *tree of life.* Source of life. This figure of speech may allude to the tree in the Garden of Eden (see Gen 2:9 and note; cf. Prov 11:30; 13:12; 15:4).

3:19–20 The role of wisdom in creation is described more fully in 8:22–31. Divine wisdom guided the Creator and now permeates the whole creation. To live by wisdom is to imitate the Lord and conform to the divinely appointed creation order.

3:19 *founded the earth.* God's work in creation is compared to the construction of a building (see 1 Kin 5:17; 6:37; see also 8:29; Job 38:4–6; Ps 104:5; Zech 12:1). *established the heavens.* See Is 42:5; 51:16.

3:20 *broken up.* God opened up springs and streams (see Gen 7:11; 49:25; Ps 74:15). Alternatively, though perhaps less likely, reference is to the dividing of the waters above from the waters below (see Gen 1:7; Ps 42:7 and note). *dew.* Probably also includes rain (see Deut 33:13; 2 Sam 1:21).

3:22 *adornment to your neck.* Like a beautiful necklace (see v. 3).

3:23 *securely And your foot will not stumble.* Cf. 10:9.

3:24 *When you lie down, you will not be afraid.* Also listed among the covenant blessings (see Lev 26:6; Job 11:18–19; Mic 4:4; Zeph 3:13; see also Prov 1:33). *your sleep will be sweet.* See 6:22; Ps 4:8.

3:25 *fear . . . onslaught.* The Lord shields the godly from deadly arrows and plagues (see 10:25; Ps 91:3–8; Job 5:21).

26 For the LORD will be [1]your confidence
And will [a]keep your foot from being
caught.

27 [a]Do not withhold good from [1]those to
whom it is due,
When it is in your power to do *it*.
28 [a]Do not say to your neighbor, "Go,
and come back,
And tomorrow I will give *it*,"
When you have it with you.
29 [a]Do not devise harm against your
neighbor,
While he lives securely beside you.
30 [a]Do not contend with a man without
cause,
If he has done you no harm.
31 [a]Do not envy a man of violence
And do not choose any of his ways.
32 For the [a]devious are an abomination
to the LORD;
But [1]He is [b]intimate with the upright.
33 The [a]curse of the LORD is on the house
of the wicked,
But He [b]blesses the dwelling of the
righteous.
34 Though [a]He scoffs at the scoffers,
Yet [b]He gives grace to the afflicted.
35 [a]The wise will inherit honor,
But fools [1]display dishonor.

A Father's Instruction

4 Hear, *O* sons, the [a]instruction of a father,
And [b]give attention that you may [1]gain
understanding,
2 For I give you [1]sound [a]teaching;
[b]Do not abandon my [2]instruction.
3 When I was a son to my father,
[a]Tender and [b]the only son in the sight
of my mother,
4 Then he [a]taught me and said to me,
"Let your heart [b]hold fast my words;
[c]Keep my commandments and live;

26 [1]Or *at your side* [a]1 Sam 2:9
27 [1]Lit *its owners* [a]Rom 13:7; Gal 6:10
28 [a]Lev 19:13; Deut 24:15
29 [a]Prov 6:14; 14:22
30 [a]Prov 26:17; Rom 12:18
31 [a]Ps 37:1; Prov 24:1
32 [1]Lit *His private counsel is* [a]Prov 11:20 [b]Job 29:4; Ps 25:14
33 [a]Lev 26:14, 16; Deut 11:28; Zech 5:3, 4; Mal 2:2 [b]Job 8:6; Ps 1:3
34 [a]James 4:6 [b]1 Pet 5:5
35 [1]Lit *raise high* [a]Dan 12:3
4:1 [1]Lit *know* [a]Ps 34:11; Prov 1:8 [b]Prov 1:2; 2:2
2 [1]Lit *good* [2]Or *law* [a]Deut 32:2; Job 11:4 [b]Ps 89:30; 119:87; Prov 3:1
3 [a]1 Chr 22:5; 29:1 [b]Zech 12:10
4 [a]Eph 6:4 [b]Ps 119:168 [c]Prov 7:2

5 [a]Prov 4:7 [b]Prov 16:16
6 [a]2 Thess 2:10
7 [1]Or *the primary thing is wisdom* [a]Prov 8:23 [b]Prov 23:23
8 [a]1 Sam 2:30
9 [a]Prov 1:9
10 [a]Prov 2:1 [b]Prov 3:2
11 [a]1 Sam 12:23
12 [a]Job 18:7; Ps 18:36 [b]Ps 91:11; Prov 3:23
13 [a]Prov 3:18 [b]Prov 3:22; John 6:63
14 [a]Ps 1:1; Prov 1:15

5 [a]Acquire wisdom! [b]Acquire
understanding!
Do not forget nor turn away from the
words of my mouth.
6 "Do not forsake her, and she will guard
you;
[a]Love her, and she will watch over
you.
7 "[a]The [1]beginning of wisdom *is*:
[b]Acquire wisdom;
And with all your acquiring, get
understanding.
8 "[a]Prize her, and she will exalt you;
She will honor you if you embrace
her.
9 "She will place [a]on your head a
garland of grace;
She will present you with a crown of
beauty."

10 Hear, my son, and [a]accept my sayings
And the [b]years of your life will be
many.
11 I have [a]directed you in the way of
wisdom;
I have led you in upright paths.
12 When you walk, your [a]steps will not
be impeded;
And if you run, you [b]will not stumble.
13 [a]Take hold of instruction; do not let
go.
Guard her, for she is your [b]life.
14 [a]Do not enter the path of the wicked
And do not proceed in the way of evil
men.
15 Avoid it, do not pass by it;
Turn away from it and pass on.
16 For they [a]cannot sleep unless they do
evil;
And [1]they are robbed of sleep unless
they make *someone* stumble.

16 [1]Lit *their sleep is robbed* [a]Ps 36:4; Mic 2:1

3:26 *will keep your foot from being caught.* Contrast the fate of the fool in 1:18; 7:22–23.
3:27 *withhold good.* See Acts 9:36; Gal 6:10; 1 John 3:17–18. *those to whom it is due.* Especially the poor and needy.
3:28 See Luke 11:5–8; James 2:15–16.
3:30 *Do not contend . . . without cause.* See Job 2:3.
3:31 *Do not envy.* See 24:19; Ps 37:1,7. *man of violence.* Like the sinners of 1:10–16 (cf. 16:29).
3:32 *abomination.* A word that elsewhere expresses abhorrence of pagan practices (see Deut 18:9,12) and moral abuses. It is common in Proverbs (e.g., 6:16; 8:7; 11:20). *He is intimate with the upright.* See Gen 18:17–19; Job 29:4; Ps 25:14; John 15:15.
3:33 This contrast is seen also in Deut 11:26–28. *The curse of the LORD is on the house of the wicked.* See Josh 7:24–25; Zech 5:3–4. *blesses the dwelling of the righteous.* See Job 42:12–14.
3:34 *scoffs at the scoffers.* See note on 1:26. *gives grace.* Shows favor (see v. 4).
4:3 *Tender.* Cf. David's words about Solomon, who was "young and inexperienced" (1 Chr 22:5; 29:1). This is part of an autobiographical statement, such as was sometimes used by the wisdom teachers (see 24:30–34; see also the book of Ecclesiastes). *only son.* Therefore deeply loved (cf. Gen 37:3; Zech 12:10).
4:4 *Let your heart hold fast.* See note on 3:5.
4:6 *guard . . . watch over.* The Hebrew for these two verbs is used together also in 2:8,11. *Love her.* To love wisdom is to prosper (8:21); to hate wisdom is to "love death" (8:36).
4:7 *The beginning of wisdom is: Acquire.* Or "Wisdom ranks first, so acquire" (see NASB marg.; see also 1:7). *with all your acquiring.* Make acquiring wisdom the top priority. Cf. the merchant who sold everything to buy a pearl of great value (Matt 13:45–46).
4:9 *crown of beauty.* Wreaths or crowns were worn at joyous occasions, such as weddings or feasts (see Ezek 16:12; 23:42).
4:10 *years . . . will be many.* See note on 3:2.
4:11 *upright paths.* Right paths (see notes on 3:6; Ps 23:3).
4:12 *you will not stumble.* Because of some obstacle or lack of light (see v. 19; 3:23; 10:9; Ps 18:36; Is 40:30–31).
4:14 *path of the wicked.* Cf. the destructive paths of the adulteress in 2:18; 7:25; see Ps 1:1; 17:4–5.
4:16 *cannot sleep unless they do evil.* See Ps 36:4; Mic 2:1. Contrast the attitude of David, who would not sleep until he found a permanent place for God's house (Ps 132:3–5).

17 For they [a]eat the bread of wickedness
And drink the wine of violence.
18 But the [a]path of the righteous is like
the [b]light of dawn,
That [c]shines brighter and brighter
until the [d]full day.
19 The [a]way of the wicked is like
darkness;
They do not know over what they
[1b]stumble.

20 My son, [a]give attention to my words;
[b]Incline your ear to my sayings.
21 [a]Do not let them depart from your
sight;
[b]Keep them in the midst of your heart.
22 For they are [a]life to those who find
them
And [b]health to all [1]their body.
23 Watch over your heart with all
diligence,
For [a]from it *flow* the springs of life.
24 Put away from you a [a]deceitful mouth
And [b]put devious [1]speech far from
you.
25 Let your eyes look directly ahead
And let your [1]gaze be fixed straight in
front of you.
26 [a]Watch the path of your feet
And all your [b]ways will be
established.
27 [a]Do not turn to the right nor to the left;
[b]Turn your foot from evil.

Pitfalls of Immorality

5 My son, [a]give attention to my wisdom,
[b]Incline your ear to my understanding;
2 That you may [a]observe discretion
And your [b]lips may reserve knowledge.
3 For the lips of an [1a]adulteress [b]drip
honey
And [c]smoother than oil is her [2]speech;
4 But in the end she is [a]bitter as
wormwood,
[b]Sharp as a two-edged sword.
5 Her feet [a]go down to death,
Her steps take hold of Sheol.
6 [1]She does not ponder the [a]path of life;
Her ways are [b]unstable, she [c]does not
know *it*.

7 [a]Now then, *my* sons, listen to me
And [b]do not depart from the words of
my mouth.
8 [a]Keep your way far from her
And do not go near the [b]door of her
house,
9 Or you will give your vigor to others
And your years to the cruel one;
10 And strangers will be filled with your
strength
And your hard-earned goods *will go* to
the house of an alien;
11 And you groan at your [1]final end,
When your flesh and your body are
consumed;
12 And you say, "How I have [a]hated
instruction!
And my heart [b]spurned reproof!
13 "I have not listened to the voice of my
[a]teachers,
Nor inclined my ear to my instructors!
14 "I was almost in utter ruin
In the midst of the assembly and
congregation."

17 [a]Prov 13:2 **18** [a]Is 26:7; Matt 5:14; Phil 2:15 [b]2 Sam 23:4 [c]Dan 12:3 [d]Job 11:17 **19** [1]Or *may stumble* [a]Job 18:5, 6; Prov 2:13; Is 59:9, 10; Jer 23:12; John 12:35 [b]John 11:10 **20** [a]Prov 5:1 [b]Prov 2:2 **21** [a]Prov 3:21 [b]Prov 7:1, 2 **22** [1]Lit *his* [a]Prov 3:22 [b]Prov 3:8; 12:18 **23** [a]Matt 12:34; 15:18, 19; Mark 7:21; Luke 6:45 **24** [1]Or *lips* [a]Prov 6:12; 10:32 [b]Prov 19:1 **25** [1]Or *eyelids* **26** [a]Prov 5:21; Heb 12:13 [b]Ps 119:5 **27** [a]Deut 5:32; 28:14 [b]Prov 1:15; Is 1:16 **5:1** [a]Prov 4:20 [b]Prov 22:17 **2** [a]Prov 3:21

2 [b]Mal 2:7 **3** [1]Lit *strange woman* [2]Lit *palate* [a]Prov 2:16; 5:20; 7:5; 22:14 [b]Song 4:11 [c]Ps 55:21 **4** [a]Eccl 7:26 [b]Ps 57:4; Heb 4:12 **5** [a]Prov 7:27 **6** [1]Lit *That she not watch* [a]Prov 4:26; 5:21 [b]2 Pet 2:14 [c]Prov 30:20 **7** [a]Prov 7:24 [b]Ps 119:102 **8** [a]Prov 7:25 [b]Prov 9:14 **11** [1]Or *latter*

12 [a]Prov 1:7, 22, 29 [b]Prov 1:25; 12:1 **13** [a]Prov 1:8

4:17 *eat the bread . . . drink the wine.* They thrive on wickedness and violence (see 13:2; Job 15:16).
4:18 *path of the righteous is . . . brighter and brighter.* The godly have all the guidance and protection they need (see vv. 11–12) and are able to lead others to righteousness (Dan 12:3).
4:19 *darkness.* A dangerous path that leads to destruction (see note on 2:13; see also Is 59:9–10; Jer 23:12; John 11:10; 12:35).
4:21 *heart.* See 3:1,3.
4:22 *health.* Physical, psychological and spiritual (see 3:8 and note).
4:23 *springs of life.* If we store up good things (2:1) in our hearts, our words and actions will be good. "The mouth speaks out of that which fills the heart" (Matt 12:34; cf. Mark 7:21).
4:24 *Put away from you a deceitful mouth.* See note on 2:12; see also 19:1. *devious speech.* See 6:12; 19:28; Eph 4:29; James 3:6.
4:25 *look directly ahead.* Not at worthless things (Ps 119:37).
4:26 *Watch the path.* Remove every moral hindrance (see vv. 11–12; Is 26:7).
4:27 *Do not turn to the right nor to the left.* A warning found also in Deut 5:32–33; 28:14; Josh 1:7. *foot from evil.* See 1:15.
5:2 *lips may reserve knowledge.* Applied to a priest in Mal 2:7.
5:3 *lips . . . drip honey.* Probably a reference to the pleasant-sounding talk (cf. 16:24) of the adulteress, though some explain it as kisses (cf. Song 4:11; 5:13; 7:9). *adulteress.* See note on 2:16. *smoother than oil.* See 2:16. Her words are soothing (see Ps 55:21) but full of flattery (Prov 29:5) and hypocrisy (Ps 5:9).
5:4 *wormwood.* A bitter herb (see Deut 29:18; Lam 3:15,19; Amos 6:12). *two-edged sword.* A lethal weapon (see Judg 3:16; see also Ps 55:21; 149:6; Heb 4:12; Rev 1:16).
5:5 *down to death.* Her immorality hastens her end (see note on 2:18).
5:6 *ways are unstable.* See 2:15; 10:9. *does not know it.* Or "does not acknowledge it."
5:7–14 The father (teacher) warns the son (student) about the price of immorality.
5:8 *far from her.* See Gen 39:12; 2 Tim 2:22. *door of her house.* Cf. 7:25; 9:14.
5:9 *the cruel one.* Possibly the vengeful husband (see 6:34–35).
5:10 *strangers will be filled with your strength.* Contrast the riches and honor that come to the man who embraces wisdom (3:16–18). Immorality eventually reduces one "to a loaf of bread" (6:26).
5:11 *flesh and . . . body are consumed.* Possibly because of the debilitating effects of immorality (see 1 Cor 6:18; cf. Prov 3:8; 4:22), but more likely referring to the loss of vigor that accompanies old age.
5:12 *hated instruction . . . spurned reproof.* In old age he will look back and sadly acknowledge that he has played the fool (see 1:7,22,29–30).
5:13 *have not listened.* In spite of the repeated urging to "listen" or "pay attention" to their instruction (1:8; 3:1; 4:1; 5:1).
5:14 *utter ruin.* Physical, financial and social. *In the midst of the assembly.* The offender was subject to "wounds and disgrace" (6:33) or even death (see Deut 22:22).

15 Drink water from your own cistern
And [1]fresh water from your own well.
16 Should your [a]springs be dispersed abroad,
Streams of water in the streets?
17 Let them be yours alone
And not for strangers with you.
18 Let your [a]fountain be blessed,
And [b]rejoice in the [c]wife of your youth.
19 *As* a loving [a]hind and a graceful doe,
Let her breasts satisfy you at all times;
Be [1]exhilarated always with her love.
20 For why should you, my son, be exhilarated with an [1a]adulteress
And embrace the bosom of a [b]foreigner?
21 For the [a]ways of a man are before the eyes of the LORD,
And He [b]watches all his paths.
22 His [a]own iniquities will capture the wicked,
And he will be held with the cords of his sin.
23 He will [a]die for lack of instruction,
And in the greatness of his folly he will go astray.

Parental Counsel

6 My son, if you have become [a]surety for your neighbor,
Have [1]given a pledge for a stranger,
2 *If* you have been snared with the words of your mouth,
Have been caught with the words of your mouth,

15 [1]Lit *flowing* **16** [a]Prov 5:18; 9:17; Song 4:12, 15 **18** [a]Prov 9:17; Song 4:12, 15 [b]Eccl 9:9 [c]Mal 2:14 **19** [1]Lit *intoxicated* [a]Song 2:9, 17; 4:5; 7:3 **20** [1]Lit *strange woman* [a]Prov 5:3 [b]Prov 2:16; 6:24; 7:5; 23:27 **21** [a]Job 14:16; 31:4; 34:21; Ps 119:168; Prov 15:3; Jer 16:17; 32:19; Hos 7:2; Heb 4:13 [b]Prov 4:26 **22** [a]Num 32:23; Ps 7:15; 9:15; 40:12; Prov 1:31,32 **23** [a]Job 4:21; 36:12 **6:1** [1]Lit *clapped your palms* [a]Prov 11:15; 17:18; 20:16; 22:26; 27:13

3 [1]Lit *palm* **4** [a]Ps 132:4 **5** [a]Ps 91:3; 124:7 **6** [a]Prov 30:24, 25 [b]Prov 6:9; 10:26; 13:4; 20:4; 26:16 **7** [a]Prov 30:27 **8** [a]Prov 10:5 **10** [1]Lit *lie down* [a]Prov 24:33 **11** [1]Lit *one who walks* [2]Lit *a man with a shield* [a]Prov 24:34

3 Do this then, my son, and deliver yourself;
Since you have come into the [1]hand of your neighbor,
Go, humble yourself, and importune your neighbor.
4 Give no [a]sleep to your eyes,
Nor slumber to your eyelids;
5 Deliver yourself like a gazelle from *the hunter's* hand
And like a [a]bird from the hand of the fowler.

6 Go to the [a]ant, O [b]sluggard,
Observe her ways and be wise,
7 Which, having [a]no chief,
Officer or ruler,
8 Prepares her food [a]in the summer
And gathers her provision in the harvest.
9 How long will you lie down, O sluggard?
When will you arise from your sleep?
10 "[a]A little sleep, a little slumber,
A little folding of the hands to [1]rest"—
11 [a]Your poverty will come in like a [1]vagabond
And your need like [2]an armed man.

12 A [a]worthless person, a wicked man,
Is the one who walks with a [b]perverse mouth,

12 [a]Prov 16:27 [b]Prov 4:24; 10:32

5:15 *your own cistern . . . your own well.* Your own wife (see Song 4:12,15). Let your own wife be your source of pleasure, as water refreshes a thirsty man. Wells and cisterns were privately owned and of great value (2 Kin 18:31; Jer 38:6).
5:16 *springs . . . Streams of water.* Like "cistern" and "well" in v. 15 and "fountain" in v. 18, these also refer to the wife (see Song 4:12,15). *in the streets.* The wife may become promiscuous if the husband is unfaithful.
5:18 *wife of your youth.* Chosen by you when you were young.
5:19 *hind . . . doe.* Descriptive of the wife, perhaps because of the delicate beauty of the doe's limbs (see Song 2:9). *Let her breasts satisfy you at all times.* See Song 7:7–8. *exhilarated.* Or "intoxicated," "captivated." Marital love is portrayed as better than wine in Song 4:10 (cf. Song 7:9).
5:20 *why . . . ?* In light of the sheer joy found within the bonds of marriage and the "utter ruin" (v. 14) outside it, why commit adultery? *adulteress.* See v. 3; 2:16 and note.
5:21 *before the eyes of the LORD.* See 15:3; Job 31:4; 34:21; Jer 16:17. *watches all his paths.* See Job 7:18; 34:23; Ps 11:4; 26:2; 139:23; Jer 17:10.
5:22 *capture the wicked.* See 1:18 and note; Deut 7:25; 12:30. In Eccl 7:26 the sinner is captured by a woman "whose heart is snares and nets." *cords of his sin.* See Job 36:8; Eccl 4:12; Is 5:18.
5:23 The death of the fool is described in similar terms in 1:29–32; 7:21–25; cf. Job 36:12. *instruction.* See v. 12.
6:1 *become surety . . . given a pledge.* Refers to responsibility for someone else's debt (cf. 22:26) or for some other obligation. It can end in abject poverty (cf. 22:27) or even slavery if you cannot pay. For example, Judah volunteered to personally guarantee the safe return of Benjamin to Jacob (Gen 43:9), and when this seemed impossible, he had to offer himself to Joseph as a slave (Gen 44:32–33). Such an arrangement was sealed by "striking hands," equivalent to our handshake (see 11:15; 17:18; 20:16; 22:26; cf. Job 17:3).
6:2 *snared . . . caught.* Cf. v. 5; 5:22.
6:3 *deliver yourself.* To gain release from the obligation. *come into the hand of your neighbor.* Assumed responsibility for his obligation. *importune your neighbor.* Be as persistent as the man in Luke 11:8.
6:4 *no sleep . . . Nor slumber.* Like David in Ps 132:4.
6:5 *hand of the fowler.* See Ps 124:7.
6:6 *sluggard.* A lazy individual who refuses to work and whose desires are not met (see 10:26; 13:4; 15:19; 19:24; 22:13; 24:30; 26:13–16).
6:7 *no chief.* Cf. the locust in 30:27.
6:9 *How long will you lie down, O sluggard?* His love for sleep is described also in 26:14.
6:10–11 Repeated in 24:33–34.
6:11 *poverty . . . need.* Connected with too much sleep also in 10:5; 19:15; 20:13. Hard work is an antidote to poverty (see 12:11; 14:23; 28:19). *like a vagabond . . . an armed man.* Poverty will come when it is too late to do anything about it (cf. Matt 24:43).
6:12–14 A vivid description of one who uses mouth, eyes, feet and fingers (all a person's means of communication) in devious ways to achieve the deceitful plots of his heart—here especially to spread slander about someone to destroy him.
6:12 *worthless person.* See Judg 19:22; 1 Sam 25:25; Job 34:18; see also note on Deut 13:13. *perverse mouth.* See 19:28; 2:12 and note.

13 Who [a]winks with his eyes, who
[1]signals with his feet,
Who [2]points with his fingers;
14 Who *with* [a]perversity in his heart
continually [b]devises evil,
Who [1c]spreads strife.
15 Therefore [a]his calamity will come
suddenly;
[b]Instantly he will be broken and there
will be [c]no healing.

16 There are six things which the LORD
hates,
Yes, seven which are an abomination
[1]to Him:
17 [a]Haughty eyes, a [b]lying tongue,
And hands that [c]shed innocent blood,
18 A heart that devises [a]wicked plans,
[b]Feet that run rapidly to evil,
19 A [a]false witness *who* utters lies,
And one who [1b]spreads strife among
brothers.

20 [a]My son, observe the commandment
of your father
And do not forsake the [1]teaching of
your mother;
21 [a]Bind them continually on your heart;
Tie them around your neck.
22 When you [a]walk about, [1]they will
guide you;
When you sleep, [1]they will watch over
you;
And when you awake, [1]they will talk
to you.
23 For [a]the commandment is a lamp and
the [1]teaching is light;
And reproofs for discipline are the
way of life
24 To [a]keep you from the evil woman,
From the smooth tongue of the
[1]adulteress.
25 [a]Do not desire her beauty in your heart,
Nor let her capture you with her
[b]eyelids.
26 For [a]on account of a harlot *one is*
reduced to a loaf of bread,
And [1]an adulteress [b]hunts for the
precious life.
27 Can a man [1]take fire in his bosom
And his clothes not be burned?
28 Or can a man walk on hot coals
And his feet not be scorched?
29 So is the one who [a]goes in to his
neighbor's wife;
Whoever touches her [b]will not [1]go
unpunished.
30 [1]Men do not despise a thief if he steals
To [a]satisfy [2]himself when he is
hungry;
31 But when he is found, he must [a]repay
sevenfold;
He must give all the [1]substance of his
house.
32 The one who commits adultery with a
woman is [a]lacking [1]sense;
He who would [b]destroy [2]himself does
it.
33 Wounds and disgrace he will find,
And his reproach will not be blotted
out.
34 For [a]jealousy [1]enrages a man,
And he will not spare in the [b]day of
vengeance.
35 He will not [1]accept any ransom,

13 [1]Lit *scrapes* [2]Lit *instructs with* [a]Job 15:12; Ps 35:19; Prov 10:10
14 [1]Lit *sends out* [a]Prov 17:20 [b]Prov 3:29; Mic 2:1 [c]Prov 6:19; 16:28
15 [a]Prov 24:22 [b]Is 30:13, 14; Jer 19:11 [c]2 Chr 36:16
16 [1]Lit *of His soul*
17 [a]Ps 18:27; 101:5; Prov 21:4; 30:13 [b]Ps 31:18; 120:2; Prov 12:22; 17:7 [c]Deut 19:10; Prov 28:17; Is 1:15; 59:7
18 [a]Gen 6:5; Prov 24:2 [b]Prov 1:16; Is 59:7; Rom 3:15
19 [1]Lit *sends out* [a]Ps 27:12; Prov 12:17; 19:5, 9; 21:28 [b]Prov 6:14
20 [1]Or *law* [a]Eph 6:1
21 [a]Prov 3:3
22 [1]Lit *she* [a]Prov 3:23
23 [1]Or *law* [a]Ps 19:8; 119:105
24 [a]Prov 5:3; 7:5, 21

24 [1]Lit *foreign woman*
25 [a]Matt 5:28 [b]2 Kin 9:30; Jer 4:30; Ezek 23:40
26 [1]Lit *a man's wife* [a]Prov 5:9, 10; 29:3 [b]Prov 7:23; Ezek 13:18
27 [1]Lit *snatch up*
29 [1]Lit *be innocent* [a]Ezek 18:6; 33:26 [b]Prov 16:5

30 [1]Lit *They do not;* or *Do not men...?* [2]Lit *his soul* [a]Job 38:39 **31** [1]Or *wealth* [a]Ex 22:1-4 **32** [1]Lit *heart* [2]Lit *his soul* [a]Prov 7:7; 9:4, 16; 10:13, 21; 11:12; 12:11 [b]Prov 7:22, 23 **34** [1]Lit *is the rage of* [a]Prov 27:4; Song 8:6 [b]Prov 11:4 **35** [1]Lit *lift up the face of any*

6:13 *winks with his eyes.* To make insinuations (see 10:10; 16:30).
6:14 *devises evil.* See v. 18; 3:29; Mic 2:1. *spreads strife.* Through slander he creates distrust that culminates in alienation and conflict.
6:15 *calamity will come suddenly.* Usually a sign of God's judgment (see 1:26; 24:22; Job 34:20). *Instantly . . . be broken and there will be no healing.* He will suffer the same fate he thought to bring upon another—his punishment will fit his crime.
6:16–19 A further elaboration on the theme of vv. 12–15, explaining why "calamity will come suddenly" (v. 15) on the scoundrel described here.
6:16 *six . . . seven.* A way of handling numbers in synonymous parallelism in Hebrew poetry (see Introduction: The Nature of a Proverb). Such catalogues of items are frequent in the wisdom literature of the OT (see 30:15,18,21,29; see also Job 5:19). *abomination.* See 3:32 and note.
6:17 *Haughty eyes.* They reflect a proud heart, and God will judge them (see 21:4; 30:13; Ps 18:27; 101:5). *lying tongue.* See 2:12 and note; 12:19; 17:7; 21:6. *hands that shed innocent blood.* See 1:11,16 and notes; 28:17.
6:18 *heart that devises wicked plans.* See 1:31; 24:2; Gen 6:5. *Feet that run rapidly to evil.* See 1:16 and note.
6:19 *false witness.* Proverbs emphasizes the damage done by the false witness (12:17–18; 25:18; see note on Ps 5:9) and the punishment he receives (see note on v. 15; see also 19:5,9; 21:28). *utters lies.* See 14:5,25. *spreads strife.* See note on v. 14.
6:20 See 1:8.
6:21 Those who follow wisdom add beauty and honor to their lives.
6:22 *walk.* Cf. 4:11. *When you sleep.* See note on 3:24. *watch over you.* See 4:6.
6:23 *lamp . . . light.* Just as the word of God "is a lamp to my feet And a light to my path" (Ps 119:105; cf. Ps 19:8). *way of life.* See 3:22; 4:22. Contrast the way to death for the one who hates discipline (5:23).
6:24 See notes on 2:16; 5:3.
6:25 *Do not desire.* Jesus shows the close connection between lust and adultery (Matt 5:28; cf. Ex 20:17). *capture you.* See 5:20.
6:26 *reduced to a loaf of bread.* Both the prostitute (29:3) and the adulteress (5:10) reduce a man to poverty (see 1 Sam 2:36).
6:29 *Whoever . . . will not go unpunished.* See vv. 33–34; see also note on 5:14.
6:31 *sevenfold.* Hebrew law demanded no more than fivefold payment as a penalty for any theft (Ex 22:1–9). The number seven is here symbolic—he will pay in full.
6:32 *destroy himself.* See 5:14 and note; 7:22–23.
6:33 *disgrace.* Disgrace followed Amnon's raping of Tamar (2 Sam 13:13,22).
6:34 *jealousy.* Its strength is also illustrated in 27:4; Song 8:6.

Nor will he be [2]satisfied though you
give many [3]gifts.

The Wiles of the Harlot

7 My son, [a]keep my words
And treasure my commandments
within you.
2 [a]Keep my commandments and live,
And my [1]teaching [b]as the [2]apple of
your eye.
3 [a]Bind them on your fingers;
[b]Write them on the tablet of your
heart.
4 Say to wisdom, "You are my sister,"
And call understanding *your* intimate
friend;
5 That they may keep you from an
[1]adulteress,
From the foreigner who [2]flatters with
her words.

6 For [a]at the window of my house
I looked out [b]through my lattice,
7 And I saw among the [1a]naive,
And discerned among the [2]youths
A young man [b]lacking [3]sense,
8 Passing through the street near [a]her
corner;
And he [1]takes the way to [b]her house,
9 In the [a]twilight, in the [1]evening,
In the [2]middle of the night and *in* the
darkness.
10 And behold, a woman *comes* to meet
him,
[a]Dressed as a harlot and cunning of
heart.
11 She is [a]boisterous and rebellious,
Her [b]feet do not remain at home;
12 *She is* now in the streets, now [a]in the
squares,
And [b]lurks by every corner.
13 So she seizes him and kisses him
[1]And with a [a]brazen face she says to
him:
14 "[1]I was due to offer [a]peace offerings;
Today I have [b]paid my vows.
15 "Therefore I have come out to meet
you,
To seek your presence earnestly, and I
have found you.
16 "I have spread my couch with
[a]coverings,
With colored [b]linens of Egypt.
17 "I have sprinkled my bed
With [a]myrrh, aloes and [b]cinnamon.
18 "Come, let us drink our fill of love until
morning;
Let us delight ourselves with caresses.
19 "For [1]my husband is not at home,
He has gone on a long journey;
20 He has taken a [a]bag of money [1]with
him,
At the full moon he will come home."
21 With her many persuasions she
entices him;
With her [1a]flattering lips she seduces
him.
22 Suddenly he follows her
As an ox goes to the slaughter,
Or as [1]*one in* fetters to the discipline
of a fool,
23 Until an arrow pierces through his
liver;
As a [a]bird hastens to the snare,
So he does not know that it *will cost
him* his life.

24 Now therefore, *my* sons, [a]listen to me,
And pay attention to the words of my
mouth.

35 [2]Lit *willing* [3]Or *bribes* **7:1** [a]Prov 2:1; 6:20 **2** [1]Or *law* [2]Lit *pupil* [a]Prov 4:4 [b]Deut 32:10; Ps 17:8; Zech 2:8 **3** [a]Deut 6:8; 11:18; Prov 6:21 [b]Prov 3:3 **5** [1]Lit *strange woman* [2]Lit *is smooth* **6** [a]Judg 5:28 [b]Song 2:9 **7** [1]Lit *simple ones* [2]Lit *sons* [3]Lit *heart* [a]Prov 1:22 [b]Prov 6:32; 9:4 **8** [1]Lit *steps* [a]Prov 7:12 [b]Prov 7:27 **9** [1]Lit *evening of the day* [2]Lit *pupil* (of the eye) [a]Job 24:15 **10** [a]Gen 38:14, 15; 1 Tim 2:9 **11** [a]Prov 9:13 [b]1 Tim 5:13; Titus 2:5 **12** [a]Prov 9:14 [b]Prov 23:28 **13** [1]Lit *She makes bold her face and says* [a]Prov 21:29 **14** [1]Lit *Sacrifices of peace offerings are with me* [a]Lev 7:11 [b]Lev 7:16 **16** [a]Prov 31:22 [b]Is 19:9; Ezek 27:7 **17** [a]Ps 45:8 [b]Ex 30:23 **19** [1]Lit *the man* **20** [1]Lit *in his hand* [a]Gen 42:35 **21** [1]Lit *smooth* [a]Prov 5:3; 6:24 **22** [1]Or *as a stag goes into a trap;* so some ancient versions **23** [a]Eccl 9:12 **24** [a]Prov 5:7

7:1 See Ps. 119:11.
7:2 *the apple of your eye.* The pupil, which is cared for and protected because of its great value (see Deut 32:10 and note).
7:3 *Bind them on your fingers.* As a reminder (see 6:21; Deut 6:8). *tablet of your heart.* See Jer 31:33.
7:4 *wisdom.* As embodied in the instructions of the wisdom teacher (vv. 1–3). *my sister . . . intimate friend.* Make wisdom your most intimate companion. "Sister" may be used here in the sense of "bride" (see Song 4:9–10,12; 5:1–2).
7:5 See note on 2:16.
7:7 *naive.* See note on 1:4. *lacking sense.* See 6:32; 9:4,16.
7:8 *the way to her house.* See 5:8.
7:9 *middle of the night and . . . darkness.* He was hoping no one would see him (see 2:13 and note).
7:10 *Dressed as a harlot.* Perhaps in a gaudy manner (see Ezek 16:16) and heavily veiled (see Gen 38:14–15).
7:11 *boisterous.* Applied to the "woman of folly" in 9:13.
7:12 *She . . . lurks.* Ready to catch her prey (see v. 22).
7:13 *kisses him.* A bold greeting (see Gen 29:11).
7:14 *peace offerings.* Part of the meat could be eaten by the one who brought the offering and by his (or her) family (Lev 7:12–15). *Today I have paid my vows.* An offering made as the result of a vow was one of the peace offerings, and the meat had to be eaten on the first or second day (see Lev 7:15–16). So the young man had an opportunity to enjoy a real feast, one that ironically had a religious significance (cf. Amos 5:21–22).
7:16 *colored linens of Egypt.* Linen is associated with the wealthy in 31:22. Egyptian linen was of great value (see Is 19:9; Ezek 27:7).
7:17 *myrrh, aloes and cinnamon.* Fragrant perfumes that are linked with making love also in Ps 45:8; Song 4:14; 5:5.
7:18 *drink our fill of love.* Making love is compared to eating and drinking also in 9:17; 30:20; Song 4:16; 5:1. *delight ourselves.* See Song 4:10.
7:19 *not at home.* So he will never know (cf. 6:34–35). *long journey.* Perhaps he was a wealthy merchant.
7:20 *money.* Pieces of silver of various weights were a common medium of exchange, but not in the form of coins until a later period.
7:21 *persuasions . . . flattering lips.* See notes on 2:16; 5:3; see also 6:24; 7:5. *entices him.* Cf. 5:23.
7:22 *As an ox goes to the slaughter.* Totally oblivious of the fate that awaits him.
7:23 *pierces through his liver.* The terrible fate of the wicked is similarly described in Job 20:24–25. *hastens to the snare.* See notes on 1:17–18; 5:22.
7:24 See 5:7.

25 Do not let your heart [a]turn aside to
her ways,
Do not stray into her paths.
26 For many are the [1]victims she has cast
down,
And [a]numerous are all her slain.
27 Her [a]house is the way to Sheol,
Descending to the chambers of death.

The Commendation of Wisdom

8 Does not [a]wisdom call,
And understanding [1]lift up her voice?
2 On top of [a]the heights beside the way,
Where the paths meet, she takes her
stand;
3 Beside the [a]gates, at the opening to
the city,
At the entrance of the doors, she cries
out:
4 "To you, O men, I call,
And my voice is to the sons of men.
5 "O [1][a]naive ones, understand prudence;
And, O [b]fools, understand [2]wisdom.
6 "Listen, for I will speak [a]noble things;
And the opening of my lips *will reveal*
[b]right things.
7 "For my [a]mouth will utter truth;
And wickedness is an abomination to
my lips.
8 "All the utterances of my mouth are in
righteousness;
There is nothing [a]crooked or
perverted in them.
9 "They are all [a]straightforward to him
who understands,
And right to those who [b]find
knowledge.
10 "Take my [a]instruction and not silver,
And knowledge rather than choicest
gold.
11 "For wisdom is [a]better than [1]jewels;
And [b]all desirable things cannot
compare with her.

12 "I, wisdom, [a]dwell with prudence,
And I find [b]knowledge *and* discretion.
13 "The [a]fear of the LORD is to hate evil;
[b]Pride and arrogance and [c]the evil way
And the [d]perverted mouth, I hate.
14 "[a]Counsel is mine and [b]sound wisdom;
I am understanding, [c]power is mine.
15 "By me [a]kings reign,
And rulers decree justice.
16 "By me princes rule, and nobles,
All who judge rightly.
17 "I [a]love those who love me;
And [b]those who diligently seek me
will find me.
18 "[a]Riches and honor are with me,
Enduring [b]wealth and righteousness.
19 "My fruit is [a]better than gold, even
pure gold,
And my yield *better* than [b]choicest
silver.
20 "I walk in the way of righteousness,
In the midst of the paths of justice,
21 To endow those who love me with
wealth,
That I may [a]fill their treasuries.

22 "The LORD possessed me [a]at the
beginning of His way,
Before His works [1]of old.

25 [a]Prov 5:8
26 [1]Lit *mortally wounded* [a]Prov 9:18
27 [a]Prov 2:18; 5:5; 9:18; 1 Cor 6:9, 10; Rev 22:15
8:1 [1]Lit *give* [a]Prov 1:20, 21; 8:1-3; 9:3; 1 Cor 1:24
2 [a]Prov 9:3, 14
3 [a]Job 29:7
5 [1]Lit *simple* [2]Lit *heart* [a]Prov 1:4 [b]Prov 1:22, 32; 3:35
6 [a]Prov 22:20 [b]Prov 23:16
7 [a]Ps 37:30; John 8:14; Rom 15:8
8 [a]Deut 32:5; Prov 2:15; Phil 2:15
9 [a]Prov 14:6 [b]Prov 3:13
10 [a]Prov 3:14, 15; 8:19
11 [1]Lit *corals* [a]Job 28:15, 18; Ps 19:10 [b]Prov 3:15
12 [a]Prov 8:5 [b]Prov 1:4
13 [a]Prov 3:7; 16:6 [b]1 Sam 2:3; Prov 16:18; Is 13:11 [c]Prov 15:9 [d]Prov 6:12
14 [a]Prov 1:25; 19:20; Is 28:29; Jer 32:19 [b]Prov 2:7; 3:21; 18:1 [c]Eccl 7:19; 9:16
15 [a]2 Chr 1:10; Prov 29:4; Dan 2:21; Matt 28:18; Rom 13:1
17 [a]1 Sam 2:30; Prov 4:6; John 14:21 [b]Prov 2:4, 5; John 7:37; James 1:5
18 [a]Prov 3:16 [b]Ps 112:3; Matt 6:33
19 [a]Job 28:15; Prov 3:14 [b]Prov 10:20
21 [a]Prov 24:4
22 [1]Lit *from then* [a]Job 28:26-28; Ps 104:24; Prov 3:19

7:25 *her paths.* See 1:15.
7:26 *many are the victims.* See 9:18; Is 5:14.
7:27 *way to Sheol.* See notes on 2:18; 5:5; see also 14:12; 16:25; Matt 7:13; cf. 1 Cor 6:9–10.
8:1–36 Wisdom is personified (see note on 1:20) as she addresses mankind in preparation for the final plea from both "Wisdom" and "Folly" in ch. 9.
8:1 *call . . . lift up her voice.* See 1:20.
8:2–3 See notes on 1:20–21.
8:4 *sons of men.* See v. 31.
8:5 *naive ones . . . fools.* Both are addressed in wisdom's speech in 1:22,32. *naive ones, understand prudence.* See note on 1:4.
8:6 *noble things . . . right things.* See Phil 4:8.
8:7 *wickedness is an abomination to my lips .* See 3:32; 12:22.
8:8 *crooked or perverted.* See Phil 2:15; cf. Prov 2:15.
8:9 *to him who understands.* The wiser a person is, the more he appreciates words of wisdom. *who find knowledge.* Especially the knowledge of God (see note on 2:5).
8:10 *silver . . . gold.* See v. 19; 2:4; 3:14 and note.
8:11 Almost identical with 3:15 (see note there).
8:12 *dwell with prudence.* Cf. Job 28:20. *prudence . . . knowledge and discretion.* See 1:4 and note.
8:13 *The fear of the LORD is to hate evil.* See 1:7; 3:7 and notes; see also 9:10; 16:6. *Pride and arrogance . . . I hate.* See 16:18; 1 Sam 2:3; Is 13:11; see also Ps 10:2–11 and note. *evil way And the perverted mouth.* See note on 2:12; see also 6:12,16–19.
8:14 *Counsel . . . and sound wisdom . . . understanding, power.* These characterize the Lord (2:6–7; Job 12:13,16; Is 40:13–14; Rom 16:27) and the Spirit of the Lord (Is 11:2). *Counsel.* See 1:25; 19:20. *power.* Cf. Eccl 9:16.
8:15 *By me kings reign.* See 29:4. Solomon prayed for wisdom to govern Israel (see 1 Kin 3:9; 2 Chr 1:10).
8:17 *I love.* I pour out my benefits on (see 4:6 and note; see also John 14:21). *those who diligently seek me will find me.* See 2:4–5; Is 55:6; James 1:5.
8:18 *Riches and honor.* See 3:16; 22:4.
8:19 *My fruit.* Wisdom is called a "tree of life" in 3:18 (see note there). *pure gold . . . choicest silver.* See v. 10; Job 28:15; see also 3:14 and note.
8:20 *way . . . paths.* See 3:17. *justice.* See v. 15.
8:21 *endow . . . with wealth.* See v. 18; Zech 8:12. *fill their treasuries.* See note on 3:10; see also 24:4.
8:22–31 A hymn describing wisdom's role in creation. Wisdom is here personified, as in 1:20–33; 3:15–18; 9:1–12. Therefore these verses should not be interpreted as a direct description of Christ. Yet they provide part of the background for the NT portrayal of Christ as the divine Word (John 1:1–3) and as the wisdom of God (1 Cor 1:24,30; Col 2:3). Here, wisdom is an attribute of God involved with Him in creation.
8:22 *possessed me.* The Hebrew for this verb is also used in Gen 4:1; 14:19,22. *me.* Wisdom (see 3:19; Ps 104:24). *at the beginning of His way.* Cf. Job's statement about the Behemoth (Job 40:19).

23 "From everlasting I was [1][a]established,
From the beginning, [b]from the earliest
times of the earth.
24 "When there were no [a]depths I was
[1]brought forth,
When there were no springs
abounding with water.
25 "[a]Before the mountains were settled,
Before the hills I was [1]brought forth;
26 While He had not yet made the earth
and the [1]fields,
Nor the first dust of the world.
27 "When He [a]established the heavens, I
was there,
When [b]He inscribed a circle on the
face of the deep,
28 When He made firm the skies above,
When the springs of the deep became
[1]fixed,
29 When [a]He set for the sea its boundary
So that the water would not transgress
His [1]command,
When He marked out [b]the
foundations of the earth;
30 Then [a]I was beside Him, *as* a master
workman;
And I was daily *His* delight,
[1]Rejoicing always before Him,
31 [1]Rejoicing in the world, His earth,
And *having* [a]my delight in the sons of
men.

32 "Now therefore, *O* sons, [a]listen to me,
For [b]blessed are they who keep my
ways.
33 "[a]Heed instruction and be wise,
And do not neglect *it*.
34 "[a]Blessed is the man who listens to me,
Watching daily at my gates,
Waiting at my doorposts.
35 "For [a]he who finds me finds life
And [b]obtains favor from the LORD.
36 "But he who [1]sins against me [a]injures
himself;
All those who [b]hate me [c]love
death."

Wisdom's Invitation

9 Wisdom has [a]built her house,
She has hewn out her seven pillars;
2 She has [1][a]prepared her food, she has
[b]mixed her wine;
She has also [c]set her table;
3 She has [a]sent out her maidens, she
[b]calls
From the [c]tops of the heights of the
city:
4 "[a]Whoever is [1]naive, let him turn in
here!"
To him who [b]lacks [2]understanding she
says,
5 "Come, [a]eat of my food
And drink of the wine I have mixed.
6 "[1]Forsake *your* folly and [a]live,
And [b]proceed in the way of
understanding."

7 He who [a]corrects a scoffer gets
dishonor for himself,
And he who reproves a wicked man
gets [1]insults for himself.
8 [a]Do not reprove a scoffer, or he will
hate you,
[b]Reprove a wise man and he will love
you.

23 [1]Or *consecrated* [a]John 1:1-3 [b]John 17:5 **24** [1]Or *born* [a]Gen 1:2; Ex 15:5; Job 38:16; Prov 3:20 **25** [1]Or *born* [a]Job 15:7; Ps 90:2 **26** [1]Lit *outside places* **27** [a]Prov 3:19 [b]Job 26:10 **28** [1]Lit *strong* **29** [1]Lit *mouth* [a]Job 38:10; Ps 104:9 [b]Job 38:6; Ps 104:5 **30** [1]Or *Playing* [a]John 1:2, 3 **31** [1]Or *Playing* [a]Ps 16:3; John 13:1 **32** [a]Prov 5:7; 7:24 [b]Ps 119:1, 2; 128:1; Prov 29:18; Luke 11:28 **33** [a]Prov 4:1 **34** [a]Prov 3:13, 18 **35** [a]Prov 4:22; John 17:3 [b]Prov 3:4; 12:2 **36** [1]Or *misses me* [a]Prov 1:31, 32; 15:32 [b]Prov 5:12; 12:1 [c]Prov 21:6 **9:1** [a]1 Cor 3:9, 10; Eph 2:20-22; 1 Pet 2:5 **2** [1]Lit *slaughtered her slaughter* [a]Matt 22:4 [b]Song 8:2 [c]Luke 14:16, 17 **3** [a]Ps 68:11; Matt 22:3 [b]Prov 8:1, 2 [c]Prov 9:14 **4** [1]Lit *simple* [2]Lit *heart* [a]Prov 8:5; 9:16 [b]Prov 6:32

5 [a]Song 5:1; Is 55:1; John 6:27 **6** [1]Or *Forsake the simple ones* [a]Prov 8:35; 9:11 [b]Ezek 11:20; 37:24 **7** [1]Lit *a blemish* [a]Prov 23:9 **8** [a]Prov 15:12; Matt 7:6 [b]Ps 141:5; Prov 10:8

8:23 *From everlasting.* Descriptive also of Christ (see John 1:1; cf. Mic 5:2). *from the earliest times of the earth.* Wisdom was already there before God began to create the world (cf. Christ's statement in John 17:5).
8:24 *I was brought forth.* Elsewhere the sea came "bursting forth" (Job 38:8–9), the mountains "were born" (Ps 90:2) and the hills were "brought forth" (Job 15:7). *springs abounding with water.* See Ps 104:10.
8:25 *mountains.* See Ps 90:2.
8:27 *established the heavens.* See 3:19. *When He inscribed a circle on the face of the deep.* See Job 26:10.
8:28 *springs of the deep.* Earth's springs and streams (see note on 3:20; cf. Gen 7:11).
8:29 *the sea its boundary.* See Gen 1:9; Job 38:10–11; Ps 104:9. *foundations of the earth.* See note on 3:19.
8:30 *master workman.* A craftsman was sometimes called a wise man. See, e.g., Bezalel, who designed and built the tabernacle (Ex 31:3). Here the term stresses the skill demonstrated in creation. *His delight, Rejoicing always.* Cf. the joyful shouts of the angels at the time of creation (Job 38:7).
8:31 *delight in the sons of men.* Cf. v. 4. Man, made in the image of God, represented the climax of creation (see Gen 1:26–28).
8:32 *blessed.* The blessings associated with gaining wisdom are also given in 3:13–18; see also Ps 119:1–2; 128:1.
8:34 *Watching daily at my gates.* Contrast the warning not to go near the door of the adulteress's house (5:8).
8:35 *finds life.* See 3:2; 4:22 and notes. *favor.* See 3:4; 12:2; 18:22.
8:36 *All those who hate me love death.* See 1:28–33; 5:12,23; 7:27 and notes.
9:1 *has built her house.* Both wisdom and folly have a house to which mankind is invited (see v. 14; 7:8; 8:34), but wisdom has built her house (see note on 14:1)—for her there is no "sitting" (v. 14). Cf. the virtues of the wife of noble character (31:10–27). *seven pillars.* Indicating a large house. Perhaps "seven" refers to seven major aspects of wisdom.
9:2 See v. 17 and note. The banquet prepared by wisdom contrasts with the perfumed bed made ready by the adulteress in 7:17. *mixed her wine.* With spices, to make it tastier (see Song 8:2).
9:3 *she calls From the tops of the heights of the city.* See the description of folly in v. 14; see also 8:1–3.
9:4 The same invitation is given by folly in v. 16. *naive.* See 1:4 and note on 8:5. *lacks understanding.* See v. 16; 7:7.
9:5 As in v. 2, wisdom's gifts to mankind are described symbolically as a great banquet (see Is 55:1–2; cf. John 6:27,35).
9:6 *Forsake your folly.* See 1:22. *live.* See v. 11; 8:35; see also note on 3:2.
9:7 *He who corrects a scoffer gets dishonor.* See 1:22 and note; cf. 1:30. *gets insults.* Cf. 1 Pet 4:4.
9:8 *he will hate you.* See 15:12,32. *Reprove a wise man and he will love you.* See 10:8; 17:10.

9 Give *instruction* to a wise man and he will be still wiser,
Teach a righteous man and he will [a]increase *his* learning.
10 The [a]fear of the LORD is the beginning of wisdom,
And the knowledge of the Holy One is understanding.
11 For [a]by me your days will be multiplied,
And years of life will be added to you.
12 If you are wise, you are wise [a]for yourself,
And if you [b]scoff, you alone will bear it.

13 The [1]woman of folly is [a]boisterous,
She is [2]naive and [b]knows nothing.
14 She sits at the doorway of her house,
On a seat by [a]the high places of the city,
15 Calling to those who pass by,
Who are making their paths straight:
16 "[a]Whoever is [1]naive, let him turn in here,"
And to him who lacks [2]understanding she says,
17 "Stolen water is sweet;
And [a]bread *eaten* in secret is pleasant."
18 But he does not know that the [1]dead are there,
That her guests are in the [a]depths of Sheol.

9 [a]Prov 1:5
10 [a]Job 28:28; Ps 111:10; Prov 1:7
11 [a]Prov 3:16; 10:27
12 [a]Job 22:2; Prov 14:14 [b]Prov 19:29
13 [1]Or *foolish woman* [2]Lit *simple* [a]Prov 7:11 [b]Prov 5:6
14 [a]Prov 9:3
16 [1]Lit *simple* [2]Lit *heart* [a]Prov 9:4
17 [a]Prov 20:17
18 [1]Lit *departed spirits* [a]Prov 7:27

10:1 [a]Prov 1:1 [b]Prov 15:20; 29:3 [c]Prov 17:25; 29:15
2 [1]Lit *Treasures of wickedness* [a]Ps 49:7; Prov 11:4; 21:6; Ezek 7:19; Luke 12:19, 20
3 [1]Lit *soul of the righteous* [2]Lit *thrust away* [a]Ps 34:9, 10; 37:25; Prov 28:25; Matt 6:33 [b]Ps 112:10; Prov 28:9
4 [a]Prov 13:4; 21:5
6 [a]Prov 28:20 [b]Prov 10:11; Obad 10
7 [a]Ps 112:6 [b]Ps 9:5, 6; 109:13; Eccl 8:10
8 [1]Lit *the foolish of lips* [2]Lit *thrust down*

Contrast of the Righteous and the Wicked

10 The [a]proverbs of Solomon.
[b]A wise son makes a father glad,
But [c]a foolish son is a grief to his mother.
2 [1][a]Ill-gotten gains do not profit,
But righteousness delivers from death.
3 The LORD [a]will not allow the [1]righteous to hunger,
But He [b]will [2]reject the craving of the wicked.
4 Poor is he who works with a negligent hand,
But the [a]hand of the diligent makes rich.
5 He who gathers in summer is a son who acts wisely,
But he who sleeps in harvest is a son who acts shamefully.
6 [a]Blessings are on the head of the righteous,
But [b]the mouth of the wicked conceals violence.
7 The [a]memory of the righteous is blessed,
But [b]the name of the wicked will rot.
8 The [a]wise of heart will receive commands,
But [1]a babbling fool will be [2]ruined.
9 He [a]who walks in integrity walks securely,

[a]Prov 9:8; Matt 7:24 **9** [a]Ps 23:4; Prov 3:23; 28:18; Is 33:15, 16

9:9 *he will be still wiser.* See 18:15; 21:11.
9:10–12 Wisdom's final words summarize the heart of the message in chs. 1–9.
9:10 *The fear of the LORD is the beginning of wisdom.* See 1:7 and note. *knowledge of the Holy One.* See note on 2:5. "Holy One" occurs elsewhere in Proverbs only in 30:3.
9:11 *years of life will be added to you.* See note on 3:2; see also 3:16; 10:27; 14:27; 19:23.
9:12 *you are wise for yourself.* Some of wisdom's rewards are given in 3:16–18; 4:22; 8:35; 14:14. *scoff.* See v. 7; see note on 1:22. *will bear it.* See 1:26; 19:29.
9:13 *The woman of folly is boisterous.* "Boisterous" links the personified "folly" with the adulteress, the wayward wife of 2:16 and 7:11. *naive and knows nothing.* She lacks good judgment, prudence and the fear of the Lord (see 1:3–4,22,29; 5:6).
9:14 *sits.* Cf. wisdom's building her house (v. 1). *at the doorway of her house.* See 5:8; 8:34. *by the high places of the city.* Cf. the position of wisdom in v. 3; 8:2.
9:15 *Calling.* Cf. the appeal of wisdom in v. 3; 8:1,4.
9:16 Her invitation is identical to wisdom's (v. 4; see note on 1:21).
9:17 *Stolen water . . . bread eaten in secret.* The "banquet" prepared by "folly" seems poorer than the wine and meat of wisdom (v. 2). And it was stolen at that! This "meal" refers to stolen pleasures, exemplified by the illicit sex offered by the adulteress (see 7:18 and note; cf. 5:15–16). *sweet.* But see Job 20:12–14.
9:18 *the dead are there . . . her guests are in the depths of Sheol.* Similar to 2:18; 5:5; 7:27 (see notes).
10:1 *The proverbs of Solomon.* The title of a collection of individual proverbs that extends through 22:16. The numerical values of the consonants in the Hebrew word for "Solomon" total 375—the exact number of verses in 10:1–22:16; 375 of Solomon's proverbs were selected from a much larger number (cf. 1 Kin 4:32). *wise son.* See v. 5; 15:20; 17:21,25; 29:3,15. In later collections he is described as "righteous" (23:24–25) and as one "who keeps the law" (28:7).
10:2 *Ill-gotten gains do not profit.* They are fleeting (21:6) and result in God's judgment (see 1:19 and note; 10:16; Ezek 7:19). *righteousness delivers from death.* See 2:16–18; 3:2; 13:21.
10:3 *not allow the righteous to hunger.* See 13:25; 28:25; Ps 34:9–10; 37:19,25. But see note on Prov 3:2. *reject the craving of the wicked.* See Num 11:34; Ps 112:10.
10:4 Many proverbs praise diligence and the profit it brings, and they condemn laziness as a cause of hunger and poverty (see 6:6–11 and notes; 12:11,24,27; 13:4; 14:23; 18:9; 27:23–27; 28:19).
10:5 *sleeps in harvest.* Sleeping when there is work to be done is condemned also in 6:9–11; 19:15; 20:13. *son who acts shamefully.* See 17:2; 19:26; 28:7; 29:15.
10:6 *Blessings.* God's gifts and favors (see 3:13–18; 28:20; Gen 49:26; Deut 33:16). *are on the head.* See 11:26. *mouth of the wicked conceals violence.* The trouble caused by their lips will eventually ruin them (see Ps 140:9; Hab 2:17; but cf. Prov 2:11).
10:7 *memory of the righteous.* Remembering the righteous (see 22:1).
10:8 *The wise . . . receive commands.* See 9:8–9. *babbling fool will be ruined.* See vv. 10,14,18,19.
10:9 *He who walks in integrity walks securely.* See 2:7; 3:23; 13:6; Ps 23:4; Is 33:15–16. *he who perverts his ways will be found out.* See 26:26; Luke 8:17; 1 Tim 5:24–25; 2 Tim 3:9.

But [b]he who perverts his ways will be
found out.
10 He [a]who winks the eye causes trouble,
And [1b]a babbling fool will be [2]ruined.
11 The [a]mouth of the righteous is a
fountain of life,
But [b]the mouth of the wicked conceals
violence.
12 Hatred stirs up strife,
But [a]love covers all transgressions.
13 On [a]the lips of the discerning, wisdom
is found,
But [b]a rod is for the back of him who
lacks [1]understanding.
14 Wise men [a]store up knowledge,
But with [b]the mouth of the foolish,
ruin is at hand.
15 The [a]rich man's wealth is his [1]fortress,
The [b]ruin of the poor is their poverty.
16 The [1a]wages of the righteous is life,
The income of the wicked,
punishment.
17 He [a]is *on* the path of life who heeds
instruction,
But he who ignores reproof goes astray.
18 He [a]who conceals hatred *has* lying lips,
And he who spreads slander is a fool.
19 When there are [a]many words,
transgression is unavoidable,
But [b]he who restrains his lips is wise.
20 The tongue of the righteous is *as*
[a]choice silver,
The heart of the wicked is *worth* little.
21 The [a]lips of the righteous feed many,
But fools [b]die for lack of
[1]understanding.

9 [b]Prov 26:26; Matt 10:26; 1 Tim 5:25 **10** [1]Lit *the foolish of lips* [2]Lit *thrust down* [a]Ps 35:19; Prov 6:13 [b]Prov 10:8 **11** [a]Ps 37:30; Prov 13:14; 18:4 [b]Prov 10:6 **12** [a]Prov 17:9; 1 Cor 13:4-7; James 5:20; 1 Pet 4:8 **13** [1]Lit *heart* [a]Prov 10:31 [b]Prov 19:29; 26:3 **14** [a]Prov 9:9 [b]Prov 10:8, 10; 13:3; 18:7 **15** [1]Lit *strong city* [a]Job 31:24; Ps 52:7; Prov 18:11 [b]Prov 19:7 **16** [1]Or *work* [a]Prov 11:18, 19 **17** [a]Prov 6:23 **18** [a]Prov 26:24 **19** [a]Job 11:2; Prov 18:21; Eccl 5:3 [b]Prov 17:27; James 1:19; 3:2 **20** [a]Prov 8:19 **21** [1]Lit *heart* [a]Prov 10:11 [b]Prov 5:23; Hos 4:6

22 [a]Gen 24:35; 26:12; Deut 8:18; Prov 8:21 **23** [a]Prov 2:14; 15:21 **24** [a]Job 15:21; Prov 1:27; Is 66:4 [b]Ps 145:19; Prov 15:8; Matt 5:6; 1 John 5:14, 15 **25** [a]Job 21:18; Ps 58:9; Prov 12:7 [b]Ps 15:5;

22 It is the [a]blessing of the LORD that
makes rich,
And He adds no sorrow to it.
23 Doing wickedness is like [a]sport to a
fool,
And *so is* wisdom to a man of
understanding.
24 What [a]the wicked fears will come
upon him,
But the [b]desire of the righteous will be
granted.
25 When the [a]whirlwind passes, the
wicked is no more,
But the [b]righteous *has* an everlasting
foundation.
26 Like vinegar to the teeth and smoke to
the eyes,
So is the [a]lazy one to those who send
him.
27 The [a]fear of the LORD prolongs [1]life,
But the [b]years of the wicked will be
shortened.
28 The [a]hope of the righteous is
gladness,
But the [b]expectation of the wicked
perishes.
29 The [a]way of the LORD is a stronghold
to the upright,
But [b]ruin to the workers of iniquity.
30 The [a]righteous will never be shaken,
But [b]the wicked will not dwell in the
land.

Prov 12:3; Matt 7:24, 25 **26** [a]Prov 26:6 **27** [1]Lit *days* [a]Prov 3:2; 9:11; 14:27 [b]Job 15:32, 33; 22:16; Ps 55:23 **28** [a]Prov 11:23 [b]Job 8:13; 11:20; Prov 11:7 **29** [a]Prov 13:6 [b]Prov 21:15 **30** [a]Ps 37:29; 125:1; Prov 2:21 [b]Prov 2:22

10:10 *winks the eye.* See note on 6:13. *babbling fool.* See v. 8.
10:11 *fountain of life.* A source of life-giving wisdom (see 13:14; 14:27; 16:22; see also Ps 37:30). *conceals violence.* The wicked may disguise their ill intent by their words (see v. 6 and note.
10:12 *stirs up strife.* See note on 6:14. *covers all transgressions.* Promotes forgiveness (see 17:9). This line is quoted in James 5:20; 1 Pet 4:8.
10:13 *rod is for the back.* See 14:3; 19:29.
10:14 *store up knowledge.* Rather than babbling folly—and so the wise prosper. See 2:1 and note. *ruin is at hand.* Quick with his mouth, the fool only brings ruin on himself (see vv. 8,10; 13:3).
10:15 An observation about wealth and poverty. *wealth is his fortress.* Wealth brings friends (14:20; 19:4) and power (18:23; 22:7)—but ultimate security is found only in God (Ps 52:7). *The ruin of the poor is their poverty.* Poverty has no influence (18:23), no friends (19:4,7), no security. See v. 4 and note.
10:16 *wages of the righteous is life.* Not wealth (v. 15) but righteousness assures life (see note on 3:2; see also 3:16; 4:22). *income of the wicked, punishment.* See 1:13,31 and notes. "The wages of sin is death" (Rom 6:23).
10:17 *path of life.* See note on 6:23. *he who ignores reproof.* See 5:12; 15:10.
10:18 *conceals hatred.* By pretending friendliness (see 26:24,26,28).
10:20 *choice silver.* What the righteous say has great value (see 3:14; 8:10; 25:11). *heart of the wicked.* Their thoughts and schemes (see 6:14,18).
10:21 *feed many.* See v. 11 and note. *die for lack of understanding.* See 5:23 and note; see also 7:7; 9:16.
10:22 *blessing of the LORD that makes rich.* Wealth is a gift from God, not a product of human attainment (see notes on v. 6; 3:10; see also 8:21; Gen 24:35; 26:12). *adds no sorrow to it.* Unlike the "ill-gotten gains" of v. 2 (see note); cf. 15:6.
10:23 *wickedness is like sport.* See 2:14; 15:21; 26:19.
10:24 *What the wicked fears.* Calamity and distress (see 1:26–27; 3:25; Job 15:21; Is 66:4). *the desire of the righteous.* See Ps 37:4; 145:19; Matt 5:6; 1John 5:14–15.
10:25 Cf. the wise man who built his house on a rock, and the foolish man who built his on the sand (Matt 7:24–27). *the wicked is no more.* See Ps 37:10; Is 28:18. *the righteous . . . foundation.* Unshakable, unmovable (see 3:25 and note; see also 12:3,7; 14:11; Ps 15:5; 1 Cor 15:58).
10:26 *vinegar.* See 25:20; Ps 69:21. *lazy one.* See note on 6:6. *who send him.* As a messenger (cf. 25:13; 26:6) or worker.
10:27 *fear of the LORD.* See note on 1:7. *prolongs life.* See note on 3:2. *years . . . will be shortened.* See Job 22:16; Ps 37:36; 55:23.
10:28 *hope of the righteous.* See v. 24 and note; Ps 9:18. *gladness.* Of fulfillment (cf. 11:23). *expectation of the wicked perishes.* See 11:7,23.
10:29 *way of the LORD.* The way He prescribes, the life of wisdom (see Ps 27:11; 143:8; Matt 22:16; Acts 18:25). *ruin to the workers of iniquity.* Since judgment comes to those who refuse God's way (see 21:15; 2 Cor 2:15–16; 2 Pet 2:21).
10:30 *never be shaken.* See 2:21 and note; 10:25; 12:3; Ps 125:1. *not dwell in the land.* See note on 2:22.

31 The [a]mouth of the righteous flows with wisdom,
But the [b]perverted tongue will be cut out.
32 The lips of the righteous bring forth [a]what is acceptable,
But the [b]mouth of the wicked what is perverted.

Contrast the Upright and the Wicked

11 A [a]false balance is an abomination to the LORD,
But a [b]just weight is His delight.
2 When [a]pride comes, then comes dishonor,
But with the humble is wisdom.
3 The [a]integrity of the upright will guide them,
But the [b]crookedness of the treacherous will destroy them.
4 [a]Riches do not profit in the day of wrath,
But [b]righteousness delivers from death.
5 The [a]righteousness of the blameless will smooth his way,
But [b]the wicked will fall by his own wickedness.
6 The righteousness of the upright will deliver them,
But the treacherous will [a]be caught by *their own* greed.
7 When a wicked man dies, *his* [a]expectation will perish,
And the [b]hope of strong men perishes.
8 The righteous is delivered from trouble,
But the wicked [1]takes his place.
9 With *his* [a]mouth the godless man destroys his neighbor,
But through knowledge the [b]righteous will be delivered.
10 When it [a]goes well with the righteous, the city rejoices,
And when the wicked perish, there is joyful shouting.
11 By the blessing of the upright a city is exalted,
But by the mouth of the wicked it is torn down.
12 He who despises his neighbor lacks [1]sense,
But a man of understanding keeps silent.
13 He [a]who goes about as a talebearer reveals secrets,
But he who is [1]trustworthy [b]conceals a matter.
14 Where there is no [a]guidance the people fall,
But in abundance of counselors there is [1]victory.
15 He who is [a]guarantor for a stranger will surely suffer for it,
But he who hates [1]being a guarantor is secure.
16 A [a]gracious woman attains honor,
And ruthless men attain riches.
17 The [a]merciful man does [1]himself good,
But the cruel man [2]does himself harm.
18 The wicked earns deceptive wages,
But he who [a]sows righteousness *gets* a true reward.
19 He who is steadfast in [a]righteousness *will attain* to life,
And [b]he who pursues evil *will bring about* his own death.
20 The perverse in heart are an abomination to the LORD,

31 [a]Ps 37:30; Prov 10:13 [b]Prov 17:20
32 [a]Eccl 12:10 [b]Prov 2:12; 6:12
11:1 [a]Lev 19:35, 36; Deut 25:13-16; Prov 20:10, 23; Mic 6:11 [b]Prov 16:11
2 [a]Prov 16:18; 18:12; 29:23
3 [a]Prov 13:6 [b]Prov 19:3; 22:12
4 [a]Prov 10:2; Ezek 7:19; Zeph 1:18 [b]Gen 7:1
5 [a]Prov 3:6 [b]Prov 5:22
6 [a]Ps 7:15, 16; 9:15; Eccl 10:8
7 [a]Prov 10:28 [b]Job 8:13, 14
8 [1]Lit *enters*
9 [a]Prov 16:29
9 [b]Prov 11:6
10 [a]Prov 28:12
12 [1]Lit *heart*
13 [1]Lit *faithful of spirit* [a]Lev 19:16; Prov 20:19; 1 Tim 5:13 [b]Prov 19:11
14 [1]Lit *deliverance* [a]Prov 15:22; 20:18; 24:6
15 [1]Lit *those who strike hands* [a]Prov 6:1; 27:13
16 [a]Prov 31:28, 30
17 [1]Lit *good to his own soul* [2]Lit *troubles his flesh* [a]Matt 5:7; 25:34-36
18 [a]Hos 10:12; Gal 6:8, 9; James 3:18
19 [a]Prov 10:16; 12:28; 19:23 [b]Prov 21:16; Rom 6:23; James 1:15

10:31 *perverted tongue.* See note on 2:12. *cut out.* See Ps 12:3; cf. Matt 5:30.
11:1 *false balance is an abomination.* Similar denunciation is found in the law (see Lev 19:35 and note) and the prophets (Amos 8:5; Mic 6:11). See also 16:11; 20:10,23. *just weight.* Silver was weighed on scales balanced against a stone weight. Weights with dishonest labels were used for cheating.
11:2 *When pride comes, then comes dishonor.* Along with destruction (see 16:18; cf. the humbling of proud Assyria in Is 10:12; cf. also Is 14:13–15). *with the humble is wisdom.* Along with honor (see note on 15:33).
11:3 *integrity . . . will guide them.* Cf. the actions of Joseph in Gen 39:6–12. *crookedness . . . will destroy them.* See 2:22 and note; see also 19:3. *crookedness.* Cf. Luke 20:23.
11:4 *day of wrath.* The day of judgment (see Is 10:3; Zeph 1:18). *righteousness delivers from death.* See 2:16–18; 3:2; 10:2; 13:21.
11:5 *blameless.* See 2:21. *will smooth his way.* Will enable him to reach his goals (see note on 3:6; see also v. 3; 10:9).
11:6 *righteousness . . . will deliver them.* See vv. 3–4. *caught.* See 5:22 and note.
11:7 *his expectation will perish.* See v. 23; 10:28.
11:8 Cf. the rescue of Mordecai and the execution of Haman in Esth 5:14; 7:10.
11:9 *destroys his neighbor.* By spreading slander (cf. 10:18). *through knowledge.* Perhaps the knowledge of the schemes and distortions of the godless (cf. John 2:25).
11:10 *city rejoices.* See 28:12; 29:2. Thus life in the city is itself a teacher of wisdom (see note on 1:21). *joyful shouting.* Cf. the joy at the fall of Assyria (Is 30:32; Nah 3:19; cf. 2 Chr 21:20).
11:11 *blessing of the upright.* Their good influence and desire for justice as well as their prosperity (v. 10) bring honor to the city. *mouth of the wicked.* Their deceit, dishonesty and sowing of discord (see v. 9; 6:12–14).
11:12 *despises his neighbor.* Shows his contempt openly (see 10:18; 14:21). *keeps silent.* See 10:19.
11:14 See the close parallels in 15:22; 20:18; 24:6. *counselors.* See 2 Sam 16:23; Is 1:26.
11:15 See note on 6:1.
11:16 Assumes that "A good name is to be more desired than great wealth" (22:1) and insightfully observes that a woman, if she is kindhearted, will be accorded more respect than wealthy men if they are ruthless. *gracious woman.* See 31:28,30.
11:17 *does himself good.* See Matt 5:7. *does himself harm.* See Gen 34:25–30; 49:7.
11:18 *deceptive wages.* Because they do not last (see notes on 10:2,16; see also Hag 1:6). *gets a true reward.* See 10:24; Gal 6:8–9; James 3:18.
11:19 *will attain to life.* See 10:16; see also 12:28; 19:23. *will bring about his own death.* See 5:23; 21:16; Rom 6:23; James 1:15.
11:20 *perverse in heart are an abomination.* See 3:32 and note;

But the [a]blameless in *their* [1]walk are
His [b]delight.
21 [1]Assuredly, the evil man will not go
unpunished,
But the [2]descendants of the righteous
will be delivered.
22 *As* a [a]ring of gold in a swine's snout
So is a beautiful woman who lacks
[1]discretion.
23 The desire of the righteous is only
good,
But the [a]expectation of the wicked is
wrath.
24 There is one who scatters, and *yet*
increases all the more,
And there is one who withholds what
is justly due, *and yet it results* only
in want.
25 The [1a]generous man will be
[2]prosperous,
And he who [b]waters will himself be
watered.
26 He who withholds grain, the [a]people
will curse him,
But [b]blessing will be on the head of
him who [c]sells *it*.
27 He who diligently seeks good seeks
favor,
But [a]he who seeks evil, evil will come
to him.
28 He who [a]trusts in his riches will fall,
But [b]the righteous will flourish like
the *green* leaf.
29 He who [a]troubles his own house will
[b]inherit wind,
And [c]the foolish will be servant to the
wisehearted.

20 [1]Lit *way* [a]Ps 119:1; Prov 13:6 [b]1 Chr 29:17
21 [1]Lit *Hand to hand* [2]Lit *seed*
22 [1]Lit *taste* [a]Gen 24:47
23 [a]Prov 10:28; Rom 2:8, 9
25 [1]Lit *soul of blessing* [2]Lit *made fat* [a]Prov 3:9, 10; 2 Cor 9:6, 7 [b]Matt 5:7
26 [a]Prov 24:24 [b]Job 29:13 [c]Gen 42:6
27 [a]Esth 7:10; Ps 7:15, 16; 57:6
28 [a]Ps 49:6; Mark 10:25; 1 Tim 6:17 [b]Ps 1:3; 92:12; Jer 17:8
29 [a]Prov 15:27 [b]Eccl 5:16 [c]Prov 14:19
30 [1]Lit *takes* [a]Prov 3:18 [b]Prov 14:25; Dan 12:3; 1 Cor 9:19-22; James 5:20
31 [a]2 Sam 22:21, 25; Prov 13:21; 1 Pet 4:18
12:1 [1]Or *instruction*
2 [1]Lit *of evil devices* [a]Prov 3:4; 8:35
3 [a]Prov 11:5 [b]Prov 10:25
4 [1]Or *virtuous* [a]Prov 31:11; 1 Cor 11:7 [b]Prov 14:30; Hab 3:16
6 [a]Prov 1:11, 16 [b]Prov 14:3
7 [a]Job 34:25; Prov 10:25 [b]Matt 7:24-27

30 The fruit of the righteous is [a]a tree of
life,
And [b]he who is wise [1]wins souls.
31 If [a]the righteous will be rewarded in
the earth,
How much more the wicked and the
sinner!

Contrast the Upright and the Wicked

12 Whoever loves [1]discipline loves
knowledge,
But he who hates reproof is stupid.
2 A [a]good man will obtain favor from
the LORD,
But He will condemn a man [1]who
devises evil.
3 A man will [a]not be established by
wickedness,
But the root of the [b]righteous will not
be moved.
4 An [1a]excellent wife is the crown of her
husband,
But she who shames *him* is like
[b]rottenness in his bones.
5 The thoughts of the righteous are just,
But the counsels of the wicked are
deceitful.
6 The [a]words of the wicked lie in wait
for blood,
But the [b]mouth of the upright will
deliver them.
7 The [a]wicked are overthrown and are
no more,
But the [b]house of the righteous will
stand.
8 A man will be praised according to his
insight,

16:5. *blameless.* See note on 2:7.
11:21 *will not go unpunished.* See 6:29. *will be delivered.* See Ps 118:5.
11:22 *ring of gold.* Commonly worn by women on their noses (see Gen 24:47; Ezek 16:12). *lacks discretion.* Abigail was praised by David for her display of "discernment" (1 Sam 25:33).
11:23 See 10:24,28. *wrath.* Judgment (see v. 4; Is 10:3; Zeph 1:18; Rom 2:8–9).
11:24 Generosity is the path to blessing and further prosperity (see 3:9–10 and notes; Eccl 11:1–2 and notes; Ps 112:9; 2 Cor 9:6–9). By contrast, the stingy person does not make any friends and hurts himself in the long run (21:13).
11:25 *generous man will be prosperous.* "For he gives some of his food to the poor" (22:9). "He who sows bountifully will also reap bountifully" (2 Cor 9:6; cf. Luke 6:38). *be watered.* See Rom 15:32.
11:26 *withholds grain.* Probably in times of scarcity to raise the price. *blessing will be on the head.* See 10:6. *him who sells.* Like Joseph during the famine in Egypt (Gen 41:53–57).
11:27 *He who diligently seeks good seeks favor.* Like the man in v. 25 (cf. Matt 7:12). *he who seeks evil, evil will come to him.* His wicked schemes will backfire (see v. 8 and note; 1:18).
11:28 *He who trusts in his riches.* Usually said of the wicked (Ps 49:6; 62:10; but see Mark 10:25; 1 Tim 6:17). *like the green leaf.* See Ps 1:3.
11:29 *He who troubles his own house will inherit wind.* The inheritance of Levi and Simeon was affected because of their cruelty against Shechem (Gen 34:25–30; 49:7). See 15:27 and note. *servant to the wisehearted.* As the evil man serves the good (14:19; cf. 17:2).
11:30 *fruit of the righteous.* What a wise man produces (8:18–19). *tree of life.* See note on 3:18. *wins souls.* Wins people over to wisdom and righteousness (see Dan 12:3; 1 Cor 9:19–22; James 5:20). However, the Hebrew for this expression is unusual so that its translation is somewhat uncertain.
11:31 *the righteous will be rewarded.* Even Moses and David were punished for their sins (see Num 20:11–12; 2 Sam 12:10). *How much more the wicked and the sinner!* See 1:18,31 and notes; Ps 11:6; 73:18–19.
12:1 *loves discipline loves knowledge.* See 1:7; 10:17; see also 6:23 and note. *hates reproof is stupid.* See 1:22; 5:12 and note.
12:2 *obtain favor.* See 3:4; 8:35. *condemn a man who devises evil.* Cf. Job 5:12–13; 1 Cor 3:19.
12:3 *will not be established.* See 11:5. *root of the righteous will not be moved.* See 2:21; see also notes on 10:25,30.
12:4 *excellent wife.* Someone like Ruth (Ruth 3:11). Such a woman is fully described in 31:10–31. *crown of her husband.* She brings him honor and joy (see 4:9 and note). *rottenness.* See Hab 3:16. *his bones.* See note on 3:8.
12:5 *counsels of the wicked are deceitful.* See Ps 1:1.
12:6 *lie in wait for blood.* See note on 1:11; see also 1:16. *mouth of the upright will deliver them.* See 11:3–4,6,9.
12:7 See 10:25 and note.
12:8 *praised according to his insight.* See 3:4 and note. *one of perverse mind will be despised.* See Deut 32:5; Titus 3:11.

But one of perverse [1]mind will be
despised.
9 Better is he who is lightly esteemed
and has a servant
Than he who honors himself and
lacks bread.
10 A [a]righteous man has regard for the
life of his animal,
But *even* the compassion of the
wicked is cruel.
11 He [a]who tills his land will have plenty
of bread,
But he who pursues worthless *things*
lacks [1]sense.
12 The [a]wicked man desires the [1]booty
of evil men,
But the root of the righteous [b]yields
fruit.
13 [1]An evil man is ensnared by the
transgression of his lips,
But the [a]righteous will escape from
trouble.
14 A man will be [a]satisfied with good by
the fruit of his [1]words,
And the [b]deeds of a man's hands will
return to him.
15 The [a]way of a fool is right in his own
eyes,
But a wise man is he who listens to
counsel.
16 A [a]fool's anger is known at once,
But a prudent man conceals
dishonor.
17 He who [1]speaks truth tells what is
right,
But a false witness, deceit.
18 There is one who [a]speaks rashly like
the thrusts of a sword,
But the [b]tongue of the wise brings
healing.

8 [1]Lit *heart*
10 [a]Deut 25:4
11 [1]Lit *heart* [a]Prov 28:19
12 [1]Lit *net* [a]Prov 21:10 [b]Prov 11:30
13 [1]Lit *In the transgression of the lips is an evil snare* [a]Prov 11:8; 21:23; 2 Pet 2:9
14 [1]Lit *mouth* [a]Prov 13:2; 15:23; 18:20 [b]Job 34:11; Prov 1:31; 24:12; Is 3:10, 11; Hos 4:9
15 [a]Prov 14:12; 16:2; 21:2
16 [a]Prov 14:33; 27:3; 29:11
17 [1]Lit *breathes*
18 [a]Ps 57:4 [b]Prov 4:22; 15:4
19 [a]Ps 52:4, 5; Prov 19:9
21 [a]Ps 91:10; 121:7; Prov 1:33; 1 Pet 3:13
22 [a]Rev 22:15
23 [a]Prov 10:14; 11:13; 13:16; 15:2; 29:11
24 [1]Lit *slackness* [a]Gen 49:15; Judg 1:28; 1 Kin 9:21
25 [a]Prov 15:13 [b]Is 50:4
27 [1]Lit *slackness* [2]Or *catch* [a]Prov 10:4; 13:4
28 [a]Deut 30:15f; 32:46f; Jer 21:8
13:1 [a]Prov 10:1; 15:20 [b]Prov 9:7, 8; 15:12
2 [1]Lit *eats* [2]Lit *soul* [a]Prov 12:14 [b]Prov 1:31; Hos 10:13

19 Truthful lips will be established
forever,
But a [a]lying tongue is only for a
moment.
20 Deceit is in the heart of those who
devise evil,
But counselors of peace have joy.
21 [a]No harm befalls the righteous,
But the wicked are filled with trouble.
22 [a]Lying lips are an abomination to the
LORD,
But those who deal faithfully are His
delight.
23 A [a]prudent man conceals knowledge,
But the heart of fools proclaims folly.
24 The hand of the diligent will rule,
But the [1]slack *hand* will be [a]put to
forced labor.
25 [a]Anxiety in a man's heart weighs it
down,
But a [b]good word makes it glad.
26 The righteous is a guide to his
neighbor,
But the way of the wicked leads them
astray.
27 A [1]lazy man does not [2]roast his prey,
But the [a]precious possession of a man
is diligence.
28 [a]In the way of righteousness is life,
And in *its* pathway there is no death.

Contrast the Upright and the Wicked

13 A [a]wise son *accepts his* father's
discipline,
But a [b]scoffer does not listen to
rebuke.
2 From the fruit of a man's mouth he
[1a]enjoys good,
But the [2]desire of the treacherous is
[b]violence.

12:9 *has a servant.* Even people of moderate means had servants (see Judg 6:15,27). *honors himself.* Cf. 13:7.
12:10 *has regard for the life of his animal.* See 27:23; Deut 25:4; see also chart, p. 255. *compassion of the wicked is cruel.* Probably to both man and beast.
12:11 Repeated with slight variation in 28:19. *pursues worthless things.* Schemes for making easy money.
12:12 *desires the booty of evil men.* See 1:13 and note; 21:10. *root of the righteous yields fruit.* Like firmly rooted trees (see vv. 3,7; 11:30; Ps 1:3; see also 10:25 and note).
12:13 *ensnared by the transgression of his lips.* See 1:18 and note; 29:6. *righteous will escape from trouble.* See 11:8–9 and notes; 21:23; 2 Pet 2:9.
12:14 A man who speaks with wisdom will reap a harvest from his words, just as a farmer enjoys the crops he planted (see 1:31 and note; Job 34:11).
12:15 *is right.* But ends in death (see 1:25,30; 14:12; 16:25).
12:16 *conceals dishonor.* Has good self-control (see 29:11; 2 Sam 16:11–12).
12:17 *false witness, deceit.* See note on 6:19.
12:18 *speaks rashly.* Cf. Ps 106:33. *like the thrusts of a sword.* See note on Ps 5:9. *tongue of the wise brings healing.* By soothing, comforting words (see 4:22; 15:4).
12:19 *is only for a moment.* The lies will be refuted and the liar punished (see 19:9; Ps 52:4–5).
12:20 *Deceit is in the heart.* See 6:14 and note; see also 1:31; 24:2; Gen 6:5. *counselors of peace have joy.* "Blessed are the peacemakers" (Matt 5:9).
12:21 *No harm.* See 1:33 and note; 2:8; Ps 91:10–12; 121:7. *filled with trouble.* See 1:31 and note; 11:5,8; 22:8; Job 4:8.
12:22 Compare the structure of this verse with that of 11:1,20. *abomination.* See note on 3:32. *those who deal faithfully.* See 16:13.
12:23 *conceals knowledge.* Stores up knowledge (see 10:14). *proclaims folly.* See v. 16; 13:16; 15:2; 29:11.
12:24 *hand of the diligent . . . slack hand.* Contrasted also in 10:4 (see note there). *will rule.* Cf. 17:2. *forced labor.* See Judg 1:28; see also note on 2 Sam 20:24.
12:25 *Anxiety in . . . heart.* See Ps 94:19. *good word makes it glad.* See 15:23.
12:26 *leads them astray.* See 5:23; 14:22.
12:27 *does not roast his prey.* And is too lazy to lift the food from the dish to his mouth (19:24).
12:28 *is life.* Cf. 3:2; 11:4. *no death.* The way or path of righteousness does not lead to death. Cf. the identification of wisdom with the "tree of life" (3:18 and note; cf. 14:32).
13:1 *accepts his father's discipline.* See 1:8; 4:1. *scoffer does not listen to rebuke.* See 1:22; 9:7–8 and notes.
13:2 See 12:14 and note. *desire . . . is violence.* See 4:17 and note.

3 The one who [a]guards his mouth
preserves his life;
The one who [b]opens wide his lips
[1]comes to ruin.
4 The soul of the sluggard craves and
gets nothing,
But the soul of the diligent is made
fat.
5 A righteous man [a]hates falsehood,
But a wicked man [1b]acts disgustingly
and shamefully.
6 Righteousness [a]guards the [1]one whose
way is blameless,
But wickedness subverts the [2]sinner.
7 There is one who [a]pretends to be rich,
but has nothing;
Another [1]pretends to be [b]poor, but has
great wealth.
8 The ransom of a man's life is his
wealth,
But the poor hears no rebuke.
9 The [a]light of the righteous [1]rejoices,
But the [b]lamp of the wicked goes out.
10 Through insolence [1]comes nothing but
strife,
But wisdom is with those who receive
counsel.
11 Wealth *obtained* by [1]fraud dwindles,
But the one who gathers [2]by labor
increases *it*.
12 Hope deferred makes the heart sick,
But desire [1]fulfilled is a tree of life.
13 The one who [a]despises the word will
be [1]in debt to it,
But the one who fears the
commandment will be [b]rewarded.
14 The [1]teaching of the wise is a
[a]fountain of life,
To turn aside from the [b]snares of death.
15 [a]Good understanding produces favor,
But the way of the treacherous is
hard.
16 Every [a]prudent man acts with
knowledge,
But a fool [1]displays folly.
17 A wicked messenger falls into adversity,
But [a]a faithful envoy *brings* healing.
18 Poverty and shame *will come* to him
who [a]neglects [1]discipline,
But he who regards reproof will be
honored.
19 Desire realized is sweet to the soul,
But it is an abomination to fools to
turn away from evil.
20 [a]He who walks with wise men will be
wise,
But the companion of fools will suffer
harm.
21 [a]Adversity pursues sinners,
But the [b]righteous will be rewarded
with prosperity.
22 A good man [a]leaves an inheritance to
his [1]children's children,
And the [b]wealth of the sinner is stored
up for the righteous.
23 [a]Abundant food *is in* the fallow
ground of the poor,
But [1]it is swept away by injustice.
24 He who [a]withholds his [1]rod hates his
son,

3 [1]Lit *ruin is his* [a]Prov 18:21; 21:23; James 3:2 [b]Prov 18:7; 20:19
5 [1]Lit *causes a bad odor and causes shame* [a]Col 3:9 [b]Prov 3:35
6 [1]Lit *blamelessness of way* [2]Lit *sin* [a]Prov 11:3
7 [1]Lit *impoverishes himself* [a]Prov 11:24; Luke 12:20, 21 [b]Luke 12:33; 2 Cor 6:10; James 2:5
9 [1]I.e. shines brightly [a]Job 29:3; Prov 4:18 [b]Job 18:5; Prov 24:20
10 [1]Lit *gives*
11 [1]Lit *vanity* [2]Or *gradually;* lit *on the hand*
12 [1]Lit *coming*
13 [1]Lit *pledged to it* [a]Num 15:31; 2 Chr 36:16 [b]Prov 13:21
14 [1]Or *law* [a]Prov 10:11; 14:27 [b]Ps 18:5
15 [a]Ps 111:10; Prov 3:4
16 [1]Lit *spreads out* [a]Prov 12:23
17 [a]Prov 25:13
18 [1]Or *instruction* [a]Prov 15:5, 32
20 [a]Prov 2:20; 15:31
21 [a]Ps 32:10; 54:5; Is 47:11 [b]Prov 11:31; 13:13; Is 3:10
22 [1]Lit *sons'* *sons* [a]Ezra 9:12; Ps 37:25 [b]Job 27:16, 17; Prov 28:8; Eccl 2:26
23 [1]Lit *there is what is swept* [a]Prov 12:11 **24** [1]I.e. correction or discipline [a]Prov 19:18; 22:15; 23:13, 14; 29:15, 17

13:3 *guards his mouth preserves his life.* The ability to control the tongue is one of the clearest marks of wisdom. "Death and life are in the power of the tongue" (18:21; see 10:19; 21:23; James 3:2). *one who opens wide his lips comes to ruin.* See 12:18 and note; see also 10:14; 18:7; 2 Tim 3:3–4.
13:4 *sluggard.* See 6:6 and note. *craves and gets nothing.* Is never satisfied, yet refuses to work (see 21:25–26). *soul of the diligent is made fat.* Diligence yields a profit (see 6:6; see also notes on 10:4,24).
13:5 *acts disgustingly and shamefully.* Like a lazy or ungrateful son (10:5; 19:26).
13:6 This contrast repeats the thought of 2:21–22; 10:9; 11:3,5 (see notes); cf. 21:12; Ps 25:21.
13:7 Both pretenses are folly and lead to folly (see 14:8 and note; see also 11:24; 12:9).
13:8 *ransom of a man's life.* He has the means to pay off robbers or enemies (see 10:15 and note; Jer 41:8). *poor hears no rebuke.* Even poverty has its advantages.
13:9 *light . . . lamp.* Symbols of life (cf. Job 3:20). *rejoices.* There is joy and prosperity (see note on 4:18). *lamp of the wicked goes out.* His life will end (see 20:20; 24:20; Job 18:5; 21:17).
13:10 *insolence.* See 11:2 and note.
13:11 *Wealth . . . by fraud dwindles.* Such as wealth gained by extortion (Ps 62:10) or deceit (Prov 21:6). See note on 10:2; see also Jer 17:11. *increases it.* See note on 10:4.
13:12 *Hope deferred makes the heart sick.* Cf. Gen 30:1. *desire fulfilled is a tree of life.* It revives and strengthens (see note on 3:18; see also 10:28; 13:19).
13:13 *who despises the word will be in debt to it.* See 1:29–31; see also 5:12 and note. *who fears the commandment will be rewarded.* With the benefits wisdom gives (see 3:2 and note; 3:16–18; 13:21).
13:14 *fountain of life.* See note on 10:11. *from the snares of death.* See notes on 1:17; 5:22; see also 7:23; 22:5.
13:15 *produces favor.* See 3:4; 8:35. *is hard.* See v. 13 and note.
13:16 See 12:23 and note.
13:17 *falls into adversity.* Perhaps by misrepresenting those who sent him. *brings healing.* His tactful, honest approach benefits both parties (see 25:13; cf. 12:18; 15:4).
13:18 *Poverty and shame.* See 5:10–12 and notes. *who regards reproof will be honored.* See v. 1; 3:16–18; 8:35; 10:17.
13:19 *Desire realized.* See v. 12. *an abomination . . . to turn away from evil.* Cf. their hatred of correction in 5:12.
13:20 *who walks with wise men will be wise.* Choose your friends with care (see 2:20; 12:26). *companion of fools will suffer harm.* See 1:10,18; 2:12; 16:29; 22:24–25.
13:21 See v. 13 and note.
13:22 *is stored up for the righteous.* Job agrees that this is often what happens to a wicked man's possessions (Job 27:16–17; cf. Prov 28:8).
13:23 *it is swept away by injustice.* Probably a case of the rich and powerful oppressing the poor (cf. Ps 35:10).
13:24 *who withholds his rod hates his son.* Parents are encouraged to apply the rod of punishment to drive out folly (22:15) so that the child will not follow a path of destruction (19:18; 23:13–14). "The rod and reproof give wisdom" (29:15) and pro-

But he who loves him [2b]disciplines
him diligently.
25 The [a]righteous [1]has enough to satisfy
his appetite,
But the stomach of the [b]wicked is in
need.

Contrast the Upright and the Wicked

14 The [a]wise woman builds her house,
But the foolish tears it down with her
own hands.
2 He who [a]walks in his uprightness
fears the LORD,
But he who is [b]devious in his ways
despises Him.
3 In the mouth of the foolish is a rod
[1]for *his* back,
But [a]the lips of the wise will protect
them.
4 Where no oxen are, the manger is
clean,
But much revenue *comes* by the
strength of the ox.
5 A [a]trustworthy witness will not lie,
But a [b]false witness [1c]utters lies.
6 A scoffer seeks wisdom and *finds* none,
But knowledge is easy to one who has
understanding.
7 Leave the [a]presence of a fool,
Or you will not [1]discern [2]words of
knowledge.
8 The wisdom of the sensible is to
understand his way,
But [a]the foolishness of fools is deceit.
9 Fools mock at [1]sin,
But [a]among the upright there is [2]good
will.
10 The heart knows its own [a]bitterness,
And a stranger does not share its joy.

24 [2]Lit *seeks him diligently with discipline* [b]Deut 8:5; Prov 3:12; Heb 12:7
25 [1]Lit *eats to the satisfaction of his soul* [a]Ps 34:10; 103:5; 132:15; Prov 10:3 [b]Prov 13:18; Luke 15:14
14:1 [a]Ruth 4:11; Prov 31:10-27
2 [a]Prov 19:1; 28:6 [b]Prov 2:15
3 [1]Lit *of pride* [a]Prov 12:6
5 [1]Lit *breathes out* [a]Rev 1:5; 3:14 [b]Ex 23:1; Deut 19:16; Prov 6:19; 12:17 [c]Prov 19:5
7 [1]Lit *know* [2]Lit *lips* [a]Prov 23:9
8 [a]1 Cor 3:19
9 [1]Lit *guilt* [2]Or the *favor* of God [a]Prov 3:34; 11:20
10 [a]1 Sam 1:10; Job 21:25

11 [a]Job 8:15
12 [a]Prov 12:15; 16:25 [b]Rom 6:21
13 [a]Eccl 2:1, 2
14 [1]Lit *from himself* [a]Prov 1:31; 12:21 [b]Prov 12:14; 18:20
15 [1]Lit *simple*
16 [1]Lit *fears* [a]Job 28:28; Ps 34:14; Prov 3:7; 22:3
18 [1]Lit *simple*
19 [a]1 Sam 2:36; Prov 11:29
20 [a]Prov 19:7
21 [1]Or *afflicted* [a]Prov 11:12 [b]Ps 41:1; Prov 19:17; 28:8

11 The [a]house of the wicked will be
destroyed,
But the tent of the upright will
flourish.
12 There [a]is a way *which seems* right to a
man,
But its [b]end is the way of death.
13 Even in laughter the heart may be in
pain,
And the [a]end of joy may be grief.
14 The backslider in heart will have his
[a]fill of his own ways,
But a good man will [b]*be satisfied*
[1]with his.
15 The [1]naive believes everything,
But the sensible man considers his
steps.
16 A wise man [1]is cautious and [a]turns
away from evil,
But a fool is arrogant and careless.
17 A quick-tempered man acts foolishly,
And a man of evil devices is hated.
18 The [1]naive inherit foolishness,
But the sensible are crowned with
knowledge.
19 The [a]evil will bow down before the
good,
And the wicked at the gates of the
righteous.
20 The [a]poor is hated even by his
neighbor,
But those who love the rich are many.
21 He who [a]despises his neighbor sins,
But [b]happy is he who is gracious to
the [1]poor.
22 Will they not go astray who [a]devise
evil?

22 [a]Ps 36:4; Prov 3:29; 12:2; Mic 2:1

mote a healthy and happy family (29:17). Discipline is rooted in love (see 3:11–12 and note). *rod.* Probably a figure of speech for discipline of any kind.

13:25 States more specifically the teaching of vv. 13,18,21; see 10:3 and note.

14:1 *wise woman builds her house.* She is a source of strength and an example of diligence for her family (see 31:10–31). Cf. the house built by wisdom in 9:1.

14:2 *fears the LORD.* See note on 1:7.

14:3 *rod for his back.* See 10:13; 19:29; 26:3.

14:4 Perhaps the thought is that men need to take good care of their oxen (the means of production) if they expect an abundant harvest (see 12:10).

14:5 See note on 6:19.

14:6 *scoffer.* See 1:22 and note. *seeks wisdom and finds none.* Because he refuses to fear the Lord or accept any correction.

14:8 *foolishness of fools is deceit.* What a fool believes to be prudent (but is really folly) does not bring success; instead, it tends toward his ruin.

14:9 *among the upright . . . good will.* See 11:27.

14:10 *knows its own bitterness.* See 1 Kin 8:38. Cf. the experience of Hannah (1 Sam 1:10) and Peter (Matt 26:75). *share its joy.* Cf. Matt 13:44; 1 Pet 1:8.

14:11 See 10:25 and note.

14:12 *its end is the way of death.* See 5:4,23; 7:21–27; Matt 7:13–14.

14:13 *in laughter the heart may be in pain.* Cf. Ezra 3:11–12. *end of joy may be grief.* As the death of Rachel in childbirth (Gen 35:17–18).

14:14 See 1:31; 12:14 and notes; see also 11:5,8; 18:20; 22:8; Job 4:8.

14:15 *naive.* See note on 1:4. *considers his steps.* See 4:26 and note; 21:29.

14:16 *cautious and turns away from evil.* See NASB marg.; see also notes on 1:7; 3:7. *arrogant.* Cf. 21:24. *careless.* In words (12:18; 13:3) and actions (Judg 9:4).

14:17 *quick-tempered.* See Titus 1:7. *evil devices.* Cf. 12:2; Job 5:12–13; 1 Cor 3:19.

14:18 *crowned with knowledge.* Adorned and blessed with knowledge (see note on 4:9; see also v. 24; 12:4; Ps 103:4).

14:19 *evil will bow down.* Cf. 17:2. *at the gates of the righteous.* Perhaps to beg for some favor (cf. 1 Sam 2:36).

14:20 *hated even by his neighbor.* And sometimes by his relatives (see 19:7).

14:21 *happy is he who is gracious to the poor.* Sharing food (22:9), lending money (28:8) and defending rights (31:9) are ways one can show kindness. Such a person honors God (v. 31; cf. 17:5) and will lack nothing (28:27). Cf. 21:13; Ps 41:1.

14:22 *go astray.* See 5:23; 12:26. *devise evil.* See 3:29; 6:14,18; Mic 2:1. *kindness and truth . . . to those.* They receive the support and care of faithful friends (cf. 3:3; 16:6; 20:28)—perhaps God's support and care are also implied here.

But kindness and truth *will be to* those
who devise good.
23 In all labor there is profit,
But [1]mere talk *leads* only to poverty.
24 The [a]crown of the wise is their riches,
But the folly of fools is foolishness.
25 A truthful witness saves lives,
But he who [1a]utters lies is
[2]treacherous.
26 In the [1a]fear of the LORD there is
strong confidence,
And [2]his children will have refuge.
27 The [1]fear of the LORD is a fountain of
life,
That one may avoid the snares of
death.
28 In a multitude of people is a king's
glory,
But in the dearth of people is a
prince's ruin.
29 He who is [a]slow to anger has great
understanding,
But he who is [1]quick-tempered exalts
folly.
30 A [a]tranquil heart is life to the body,
But passion is [b]rottenness to the bones.
31 He [a]who oppresses the poor taunts
[b]his Maker,
But he who is gracious to the needy
honors Him.
32 The wicked is [a]thrust down by his
[1]wrongdoing,
But the [b]righteous has a refuge when
he dies.
33 Wisdom rests in the heart of one who
has understanding,
But in the [1]hearts of fools it is made
known.
34 Righteousness exalts a nation,
But sin is a disgrace to *any* people.
35 The king's favor is toward a [a]servant
who acts wisely,
But his anger is toward him who acts
shamefully.

Contrast the Upright and the Wicked

15 A [a]gentle answer turns away wrath,
But a [1b]harsh word stirs up anger.
2 The [a]tongue of the wise makes
knowledge [1]acceptable,
But the [b]mouth of fools spouts folly.
3 The [a]eyes of the LORD are in every
place,
Watching the evil and the good.
4 A [1]soothing tongue is a tree of life,
But perversion in it [2]crushes the spirit.
5 A fool [1]rejects his father's discipline,
But he who regards reproof is sensible.
6 Great wealth is *in* the house of the
[a]righteous,
But trouble is in the income of the
wicked.
7 The lips of the wise spread knowledge,
But the hearts of fools are not so.
8 The [a]sacrifice of the wicked is an
abomination to the LORD,
But [b]the prayer of the upright is His
delight.
9 The way of the wicked is an
abomination to the LORD,
But He loves one who [a]pursues
righteousness.
10 Grievous punishment is for him who
forsakes the way;
He who hates reproof will die.

23 [1]Lit *word of lips*
24 [a]Prov 10:22; 13:8; 21:20
25 [1]Lit *breathes out* [2]Lit *treachery* [a]Prov 14:5
26 [1]Or *reverence* [2]Or *His* [a]Prov 18:10; 19:23; Is 33:6
27 [1]Or *reverence*
29 [1]Lit *short of spirit* [a]Prov 16:32; 19:11; Eccl 7:9; James 1:19
30 [a]Prov 15:13 [b]Prov 12:4; Hab 3:16
31 [a]Prov 17:5; Matt 25:40; 1 John 3:17 [b]Job 31:15; Prov 22:2
32 [1]Or *calamity* [a]Prov 6:15; 24:16 [b]Gen 49:18; Ps 16:11; 17:15; 37:37; 73:24; 2 Cor 1:9; 5:8; 2 Tim 4:18
33 [1]Lit *inward part*
35 [a]Matt 24:45, 47; 25:21, 23
15:1 [1]Lit *painful* [a]Judg 8:1-3; Prov 15:18; 25:15 [b]1 Sam 25:10-13
2 [1]Lit *good* [a]Prov 15:7 [b]Prov 12:23; 13:16; 15:28
3 [a]2 Chr 16:9; Job 31:4; Jer 16:17; Zech 4:10; Heb 4:13
4 [1]Lit *healing* [2]Lit *is the crushing of the spirit*
5 [1]Or *despises*
6 [a]Prov 8:21
8 [a]Prov 21:27; Eccl 5:1; Is 1:11; Jer 6:20; Mic 6:7 [b]Prov 15:29 **9** [a]1 Tim 6:11

14:23 *in all labor there is profit.* See note on 10:4; see also 21:5.
14:24 *crown of the wise is . . . riches.* The wise obtain wealth, and it adorns them like a crown (see 10:22).
14:25 See v. 5; 12:17; see also note on 6:19.
14:26 *fear of the LORD.* See 1:7; 3:7 and notes. *strong confidence . . . refuge.* Means either that the father's godliness will result in blessing for himself and his children (see 20:7) or that the "fear of the LORD" will be a strong tower where the children also can find refuge (see 18:10; Ps 71:7; Is 33:6).
14:27 See note on 10:11; see also 13:14.
14:29 *He who is slow to anger.* See 15:18; 16:32; 19:11; James 1:19.
14:30 *life to the body.* Cf. the healthy effects of fearing the Lord and walking in wisdom in 3:7–8,16–18. *passion is rottenness to the bones.* See note on 3:8; see also 12:4; Ps 37:7–8.
14:31 *taunts his Maker.* Because God created both the rich and the poor in His image (see 22:2; Job 31:15; James 3:9). *gracious to the needy.* See note on v. 21. *honors Him.* Does God's will, and in a sense gives to God Himself (see 19:17; Matt 25:40).
14:32 *wicked is thrust down.* See 1:26–27 and note; 11:5; 24:16. *righteous has a refuge when he dies.* His faith in God gives him hope beyond the grave (see note on 12:28; see also Ps 49:14–15; 73:24).
14:33 *in the hearts of fools it is made known.* Perhaps means that even fools occasionally display a bit of wisdom (cf. Acts 17:27–28; Rom 1:19–20).
14:34 *Righteousness exalts a nation.* See note on 11:11. Israel was promised prosperity and prestige if she obeyed God's laws (see Deut 28:1–14). *sin is a disgrace to any people.* The Canaanites were driven out because of their terrible sin (Lev 18:24–25), and Israel later received the same curse (Deut 28:15–68; cf. 2 Sam 12:10).
14:35 *his anger is toward him.* See 16:14; 19:12; Dan 2:12.
15:1 *gentle answer turns away wrath.* Cf. the way Gideon calmed the anger of the men of Ephraim in Judg 8:1–3 (cf. also Prov 15:18; Eccl 10:4). *harsh word stirs up anger.* Nabal's sarcastic response put David in a fighting mood (1 Sam 25:10–13).
15:2 *spouts folly.* See vv. 7, 28; 12:23; 13:16.
15:3 *eyes of the LORD are in every place.* See 5:21; Job 31:4; 34:21; Jer 16:17.
15:4 *soothing tongue.* See note on 12:18. *tree of life.* See note on 3:18. *perversion in it crushes the spirit.* Especially false testimony in court (see 6:19; 22:22), or slander in the community.
15:6 See 10:2,16,22 and notes. *Great wealth.* See 8:18,21; 24:4; Zech 8:12; see also note on 3:10.
15:8 *sacrifice of the wicked is an abomination.* Those whose hearts are not right with God gain nothing by offering sacrifices (see 21:3,27; Eccl 5:1; Is 1:11–15; Jer 6:20). *prayer of the upright.* See 3:32.
15:9 *who pursues righteousness.* See 21:21; 1 Tim 6:11.
15:10 *the way.* The right path (see 2:13). *who hates reproof will die.* See 5:12,23 and notes.

11 [1][a]Sheol and [2]Abaddon *lie open* before
the LORD,
How much more the [b]hearts of [3]men!
12 A [a]scoffer does not love one who
reproves him,
He will not go to the wise.
13 A [a]joyful heart makes a [1]cheerful face,
But [2]when the heart is [b]sad, the [c]spirit
is broken.
14 The [a]mind of the intelligent seeks
knowledge,
But the mouth of fools feeds on folly.
15 All the days of the afflicted are bad,
But a [1]cheerful heart *has* a continual
feast.
16 [a]Better is a little with the [1]fear of the
LORD
Than great treasure and turmoil with it.
17 [a]Better is a [1]dish of [2]vegetables where
love is
Than a [b]fattened ox *served* with
hatred.
18 A [a]hot-tempered man stirs up strife,
But the [b]slow to anger [c]calms a
dispute.
19 The way of the lazy is as a hedge of
thorns,
But the path of the upright is a
highway.
20 A [a]wise son makes a father glad,
But a foolish man [b]despises his
mother.
21 Folly is joy to him who lacks [1]sense,
But a man of understanding [a]walks
straight.
22 Without consultation, plans are
frustrated,
But with many counselors they
[1]succeed.
23 A [a]man has joy in an [1]apt answer,
And how delightful is a timely [b]word!
24 The [a]path of life *leads* upward for the
wise
That he may keep away from [1]Sheol
below.
25 The LORD will [a]tear down the house of
the proud,
But He will [b]establish the boundary of
the [c]widow.
26 Evil plans are an abomination to the
LORD,
But pleasant words are pure.
27 He who [a]profits illicitly troubles his
own house,
But he who [b]hates bribes will live.
28 The heart of the righteous [a]ponders
how to answer,
But the [b]mouth of the wicked pours
out evil things.
29 The LORD is [a]far from the wicked,
But He [b]hears the prayer of the
righteous.
30 [1]Bright eyes gladden the heart;
Good news puts fat on the bones.
31 He whose ear listens to the life-giving
reproof
Will dwell among the wise.
32 He who [a]neglects discipline [b]despises
himself,
But he who [c]listens to reproof
acquires [1]understanding.
33 The [1]fear of the LORD is the instruction
for wisdom,
And before honor *comes* humility.

11 [1]I.e. the nether world [2]I.e. place of destruction [3]Lit *sons of Adam* [a]Job 26:6; Ps 139:8 [b]1 Sam 16:7; 2 Chr 6:30; Ps 44:21; Acts 1:24
12 [a]Prov 13:1; Amos 5:10
13 [1]Lit *good* [2]Lit *in sadness of heart* [a]Prov 17:22 [b]Prov 12:25 [c]Prov 17:22; 18:14
14 [a]Prov 18:15
15 [1]Lit *good*
16 [1]Or *reverence* [a]Ps 37:16; Prov 16:8; Eccl 4:6; 1 Tim 6:6
17 [1]Or *portion* [2]Or *herbs* [a]Prov 17:1 [b]Matt 22:4; Luke 15:23
18 [a]Prov 16:28; 26:21; 29:22 [b]Prov 14:29 [c]Gen 13:8; Prov 16:14; Eccl 10:4
20 [a]Prov 10:1; 29:3 [b]Prov 30:17
21 [1]Lit *heart* [a]Prov 14:8; Eph 5:15
22 [1]Or *are established*
23 [1]Lit *answer of his mouth* [a]Prov 12:14 [b]Prov 25:11; Is 50:4
24 [1]I.e. the nether world [a]Prov 4:18
25 [a]Prov 12:7; 14:11 [b]Deut 19:14; Prov 23:10 [c]Ps 68:5; 146:9
27 [a]Prov 1:19; 28:25; 1 Tim 6:10 [b]Ex 23:8; Deut 16:19; 1 Sam 12:3; Is 33:15
28 [a]1 Pet 3:15 [b]Prov 10:32; 15:2
29 [a]Ps 18:41; Prov 1:28 [b]Ps 145:18, 19
30 [1]Lit *The light of the eyes gladdens*
32 [1]Lit *heart* [a]Prov 1:7; 8:33 [b]Prov 8:36 [c]Prov 15:5
33 [1]Or *reverence*

15:11 *Sheol and Abaddon lie open before the LORD.* Not even the grave, the nether world, is inaccessible to God (see Job 26:6; Ps 139:8). Therefore He knows the secrets of man's innermost being (cf. 1 Sam 16:7).
15:12 See 1:30; 10:8; 13:1; 17:10. *scoffer.* See note on 1:22.
15:13 *joyful heart makes a cheerful face.* Cf. 14:30. *heart is sad . . . spirit is broken.* Cf. the great sorrow of Job (Job 3) and David (Ps 51:8,10).
15:15 *cheerful heart has a continual feast.* Life is as joyful and satisfying as the days of a festival (see v. 13; 14:30; cf. Lev 23:39–41).
15:16 *great treasure and turmoil.* The "ill-gotten gains" of 10:2.
15:17 *fattened ox.* Such meat was something of a luxury, reserved for special occasions (cf. 7:14; Matt 22:4; Luke 15:23).
15:18 *stirs up strife.* See note on 6:14. *slow to anger.* See 14:29; 16:32; 19:11; James 1:19.
15:19 *lazy.* See note on 6:6. *as a hedge of thorns.* Mainly because he was too lazy to remove them (see 24:30–31; Hos 2:6). *highway.* The upright can make progress and reach their goals (see note on 3:6).
15:20 See 10:1 and note.
15:21 A variation of 10:23.
15:22 See the close parallel in 11:14; 20:18; 24:6.
15:23 *apt answer.* Cf. Is 50:4. *how delightful is a timely word!* Cf. 24:26.
15:24 *leads upward.* Along the highway (v. 19), the straight course (v. 21) that leads to life. *he may keep away from Sheol below.* See note on 2:18.
15:25 *tear down the house of the proud.* See 2:22; 14:11; see also 10:25 and note. *establish the boundary of the widow.* In ancient times boundary stones marked a person's property. Anyone who moved such a stone was, in effect, stealing land (see 22:28; Job 24:2; Ps 68:5; see also Deut 19:14 and note).
15:26 *Evil plans are an abomination.* Cf. vv. 8–9. *pleasant words are pure.* See 22:11; Ps 24:4.
15:27 *who profits illicitly troubles his own house.* See 1:19; 11:29; 28:25. Achan's whole family perished because of his greed at Jericho (Josh 7:24–26). *he who hates bribes will live.* See 17:8; 28:16; Deut 16:19; 1 Sam 12:3; Eccl 7:7; 1 Tim 6:10.
15:28 *ponders how to answer.* Cf. 10:32; 1 Pet 3:15. *pours out evil things.* See v. 2; see also v. 7; 12:23.
15:29 *far from the wicked.* See 1:28 and note.
15:30 *Bright eyes gladden the heart.* Cf. v. 13; 16:15; Job 29:24. *Good news puts fat on the bones.* See 3:8 and note; see also Phil 2:19.
15:31 *whose ear listens to the life-giving reproof.* See 1:23; 6:23 and note.
15:32 *who neglects discipline despises himself.* See note on 5:12; see also 1:7; 5:23; 8:36. *who listens to reproof.* Cf. vv. 5,31.
15:33 *fear of the LORD.* See note on 1:7. *before honor comes humility.* See 22:24; 25:6–7; Matt 23:12; Luke 14:11; 18:14; 1 Pet 5:6. Wisdom also comes with humility (11:2; 13:10).

Contrast the Upright and the Wicked

16 The [a]plans of the heart belong to man,
But the answer of the tongue is from
the LORD.
2 All the ways of a man are clean in his
own sight,
But the [a]LORD weighs the [1]motives.
3 [1a]Commit your works to the LORD
And your plans will be established.
4 The LORD [a]has made everything for
[1]its own purpose,
Even the [b]wicked for the day of evil.
5 Everyone who is proud in heart is an
abomination to the LORD;
Assuredly, he will not be unpunished.
6 By [a]lovingkindness and truth iniquity
is atoned for,
And by the [1b]fear of the LORD one
keeps away from evil.
7 When a man's ways are pleasing to
the LORD,
He [a]makes even his enemies to be at
peace with him.
8 Better is a little with righteousness
Than great income with injustice.
9 The mind of [a]man plans his way,
But [b]the LORD directs his steps.
10 A divine [a]decision is in the lips of the
king;
His mouth should not [1]err in judgment.
11 A [a]just balance and scales belong to
the LORD;
All the [1]weights of the bag are His
[2]concern.
12 It is an abomination for kings to
commit wicked acts,
For a [a]throne is established on
righteousness.
13 Righteous lips are the delight of kings,
And he who speaks right is loved.
14 The fury of a king is *like* messengers
of death,
But a wise man will appease it.
15 In the light of a king's face is life,
And his favor is like a cloud with the
[1a]spring rain.
16 How much [a]better it is to get wisdom
than gold!
And to get understanding is to be
chosen above silver.
17 The [a]highway of the upright is to
depart from evil;
He who watches his way preserves his
[1]life.
18 [a]Pride *goes* before destruction,
And a haughty spirit before stumbling.
19 It is better to be [a]humble in spirit with
the lowly
Than to [b]divide the spoil with the
proud.
20 He who gives attention to the word
will [a]find good,
And [b]blessed is he who trusts in the
LORD.
21 The [a]wise in heart will be called
understanding,
And sweetness of [1]speech [b]increases
[2]persuasiveness.

16:1 [a]Prov 16:9; 19:21
2 [1]Lit *spirits* [a]1 Sam 16:7; Dan 5:27
3 [1]Lit *Roll* [a]Ps 37:5; 55:22; Prov 3:6; 1 Pet 5:7
4 [1]Or *His* [a]Gen 1:31; Eccl 3:11 [b]Rom 9:22
6 [1]Or *reverence* [a]Dan 4:27; Luke 11:41 [b]Prov 8:13; 14:16
7 [a]Gen 33:4; 2 Chr 17:10
9 [a]Prov 16:1; 19:21 [b]Ps 37:23; Prov 20:24; Jer 10:23
10 [1]Lit *be unfaithful* [a]1 Kin 3:28
11 [1]Lit *stones* [2]Lit *work* [a]Prov 11:1
12 [a]Prov 25:5
15 [1]Lit *latter* [a]Job 29:23
16 [a]Prov 8:10, 19
17 [1]Lit *soul* [a]Is 35:8
18 [a]Prov 11:2; 18:12; Jer 49:16; Obad 3, 4
19 [a]Prov 3:34; 29:23; Is 57:15 [b]Ex 15:9; Judg 5:30; Prov 1:13, 14
20 [a]Prov 19:8 [b]Ps 2:12; 34:8; Jer 17:7
21 [1]Lit *lips* [2]Or *learning* [a]Hos 14:9 [b]Prov 16:23

16:1 *the answer of the tongue is from the LORD.* God must give the ability to articulate and accomplish those plans (cf. 19:21).
16:2 *are clean.* See 14:12. *the LORD weighs the motives.* See 24:12; Ps 139:23; 1 Cor 4:4–5; Heb 4:12.
16:3 *Commit.* See 1 Pet 5:7. *plans will be established.* Goals will be reached (see 3:5–6 and notes; Ps 1:3; 55:22; 90:17).
16:4 *made everything for its own purpose.* God is sovereign in every life and in all of history (see Eccl 7:14; Rom 8:28). *the wicked for the day of evil.* Even through wicked men God displays His power (cf. Ex 9:16), and all evil will be judged (cf. Ezek 38:22–23; Rom 2:5–11).
16:5 See 11:20–21 and notes.
16:6 *By lovingkindness and truth iniquity is atoned for.* The moral quality of conduct that God desires is sometimes summed up by two Hebrew terms often translated as "lovingkindness and truth" (3:3; Hos 4:1). When His people repent of sin and bring their lives into accord with His will, God forgives and withdraws His judgment (see Is 1:18–19; 55:7; Jer 3:22; Ezek 18:23,30–32; 33:11–12,14–16; Hos 14:1–2,4). Thus it can be said that lovingkindness and truth, in a manner of speaking, "atone for" sin, i.e., they turn away God's wrath against it. *fear of the LORD.* See note on 1:7.
16:7 *makes even his enemies to be at peace with him.* As in the reigns of godly Asa and Jehoshaphat (2 Chr 14:6–7; 17:10). *peace.* See 3:17 and note; Rom 12:18; Heb 12:14.
16:8 See 10:2 and note.
16:9 *the LORD directs his steps.* Verses 1,3–4 (see notes) also emphasize God's control of men's lives (see 19:21; 20:24; Ps 37:23; Jer 10:23).
16:10 *divine decision . . . lips of the king.* In judging cases brought before him, a king functioned as God's representative (see Deut 1:17). Therefore he needed the divine gift of wisdom to discern between right and wrong in order to render God's judgment (see 1 Kin 3:9). When he did so, his judgment was tantamount to a divine oracle for the people (see 1 Kin 3:28; see also 2 Sam 14:17,20; 19:27).
16:11 See note on 11:1. *just balance . . . to the LORD.* Cf. 21:2; 24:12; Job 6:2; 31:6. *All the weights of the bag.* Merchants carried stones of different sizes with them to weigh and measure quantities of silver for payment (cf. Mic 6:11).
16:12 *throne is established on righteousness.* When the king "judges the poor with truth" (29:14), refuses to take bribes (29:4) and removes any wicked advisers (25:5). See 14:34; Deut 17:19–20; Is 16:5; Rom 13:3.
16:13 *Righteous lips.* Rather than flattering lips (cf. 20:28).
16:14 *messengers of death.* Any angry king can pronounce death quickly and effectively (see 19:12; Esth 7:7–10; Matt 22:7; Luke 19:27). *wise man will appease it.* Cf. Daniel's response to the rage of Nebuchadnezzar (Dan 2:12–16).
16:15 *light of a king's face.* Cf. Num 6:25. *his favor is like a cloud with spring rain.* The spring rain was essential for the full development of barley and wheat; it was therefore a sign of good things to come. Cf. the "dew" of 19:12; see Ps 72:6.
16:16 See 3:14 and note; 8:10,19.
16:17 *highway of the upright.* See note on 15:19. *depart from evil.* Cf. the thorns and snares in the paths of the wicked (22:5).
16:18 See 11:2 and note.
16:19 *better to be humble in spirit.* See 3:34; Is 57:15; Matt 5:3. *divide the spoil with the proud.* See 1:13–14; Judg 5:30.
16:20 *find good.* See 13:13 and note. *blessed is he who trusts in the LORD.* See v. 3; 3:5–6; 28:25; Ps 34:8; 37:4–5.
16:21 *sweetness of speech increases persuasiveness.* Cf. the last

22 Understanding is a fountain of life to
one who has it,
But the discipline of fools is folly.
23 The [a]heart of the wise instructs his
mouth
And adds [1]persuasiveness to his
lips.
24 [a]Pleasant words are a honeycomb,
Sweet to the soul and [b]healing to the
bones.
25 [a]There is a way *which seems* right to a
man,
But its end is the way of death.
26 A worker's appetite works for him,
For his [1]hunger urges him *on.*
27 A [a]worthless man digs up evil,
While [1]his words are like [b]scorching
fire.
28 A perverse man spreads strife,
And a slanderer separates intimate
friends.
29 A man of violence [a]entices his
neighbor
And leads him in a way that is not
good.
30 He who winks his eyes *does so* to
devise perverse things;
He who compresses his lips brings evil
to pass.
31 A [a]gray head is a crown of glory;
It [b]is found in the way of
righteousness.
32 He who is slow to anger is better than
the mighty,
And he who rules his spirit, than he
who captures a city.
33 The [a]lot is cast into the lap,
But its every [b]decision is from the
LORD.

Contrast the Upright and the Wicked

17 [a]Better is a dry morsel and quietness
with it
Than a house full of [1]feasting with
strife.
2 A servant who acts wisely will rule
over a son who acts shamefully,
And will share in the inheritance
among brothers.
3 The [a]refining pot is for silver and the
furnace for gold,
But [b]the LORD tests hearts.
4 An [a]evildoer listens to wicked lips;
A [1]liar pays attention to a destructive
tongue.
5 He who mocks the [a]poor taunts his
Maker;
He who [b]rejoices at calamity will not
go unpunished.
6 [a]Grandchildren are the crown of old
men,
And the [b]glory of sons is their fathers.
7 [1a]Excellent speech is not fitting for a
fool,
Much less are [b]lying lips to a prince.
8 A [a]bribe is a [1]charm in the sight of its
owner;
Wherever he turns, he prospers.
9 He who [a]conceals a transgression
seeks love,
But he who repeats a matter
[b]separates intimate friends.

23 [1]Or *learning* [a]Ps 37:30; Prov 15:28; Matt 12:34 **24** [a]Ps 19:10; Prov 15:26; 24:13, 14 [b]Prov 4:22; 17:22 **25** [a]Prov 12:15; 14:12 **26** [1]Lit *mouth* **27** [1]Lit *on his lips* [a]Prov 6:12, 14, 18 [b]James 3:6 **29** [a]Prov 1:10; 12:26 **31** [a]Prov 20:29 [b]Prov 3:1, 2

33 [a]Prov 18:18 [b]Prov 29:26 **17:1** [1]Lit *sacrifices of strife* [a]Prov 15:17 **3** [a]Prov 27:21 [b]1 Chr 29:17; Ps 26:2; Prov 15:11; Jer 17:10; Mal 3:3 **4** [1]Lit *falsehood* [a]Prov 14:15 **5** [a]Prov 14:31 [b]Job 31:29; Prov 24:17; Obad 12 **6** [a]Gen 48:11; Prov 13:22 [b]Ex 20:12; Mal 1:6 **7** [1]Lit *A lip of abundance* [a]Prov 24:7 [b]Ps 31:18; Prov 12:22 **8** [1]Lit *stone of favor* [a]Prov 21:14; Is 1:23; Amos 5:12 **9** [a]Prov 10:12; James 5:20; 1 Pet 4:8 [b]Prov 16:28

line of v. 23. "Sweetness" is expanded in v. 24. Cf. the persuasive but destructive words of the adulteress in 7:21.

16:22 *fountain of life.* See note on 10:11. *discipline of fools.* See 13:13 and note; see also 7:22; 13:15; 15:10.

16:23 *instructs his mouth.* See 22:17–18.

16:24 *Pleasant words are a honeycomb.* They are good for you (see 24:13–14), and they taste good (cf. 2:10; Ps 19:10). *healing to the bones.* See notes on 4:22; 12:18; 15:30. *bones.* See note on 3:8.

16:25 *its end is the way of death.* See 5:4,23; 7:21–27; Matt 7:13–14.

16:26 Cf. 2 Thess 3:10: "If anyone is not willing to work, then he is not to eat, either"; see also Eccl 6:7; Eph 4:28.

16:27 *worthless man.* See 6:12 and note; see also note on Deut 13:13. *digs up evil.* See 3:29; 6:14; Mic 2:1. *scorching fire.* His speech is inflammatory and destructive (see James 3:6).

16:28 *spreads strife.* See note on 6:14. *slanderer.* See 11:13.

16:30 *winks his eyes.* See note on 6:13. *compresses his lips.* Thereby making insinuations (see note on 6:12–14).

16:31 *gray head is a crown of glory.* The elderly were to receive deep respect (see Lev 19:32). *in the way of righteousness.* See 3:1–2,16.

16:32 *who is slow to anger is . . . mighty.* See 14:29; 15:18; 19:11; James 1:19. "Wisdom is better than weapons of war" (Eccl 9:18). *he who rules his spirit, than he who captures a city.* Although one who practices patience and self-control receives far less attention and acclaim than a warrior who takes a city, he accomplishes better things.

16:33 *The lot is cast into the lap.* Here the lot may have been several pebbles held in the fold of a garment and then drawn out or shaken to the ground. It was commonly used to make decisions (see notes on Ex 28:30; Num 26:53; Neh 11:1; Jon 1:7; Acts 1:26; see also Ps 22:18). *every decision is from the LORD.* God, not chance, is in control (see vv. 1,3–4,9).

17:2 *A servant . . . will rule over a son.* See 11:29 and note. *son who acts shamefully.* See 10:5; 19:26; 28:7; 29:15.

17:3 *The refining pot . . . the furnace.* Silver and gold were refined to remove their impurities (cf. Is 1:25; Mal 3:3). *tests hearts.* See 15:11; 16:2 and notes; Jer 17:10.

17:5 *who mocks the poor taunts his Maker.* See 14:31 and note. *who rejoices at calamity will not go unpunished.* The people of Edom in particular were condemned for gloating over the collapse of "brother" Israel ("Jacob," Obad 10; see Ezek 35:12,15; see also Prov 24:17).

17:6 *crown of old men.* Cf. the "gray head" of 16:31. To live to see one's grandchildren was considered a great blessing (see Gen 48:11; Ps 128:5–6). *the glory of sons is their fathers.* See Gen 47:7.

17:7 For the structure of this verse cf. 19:10; 26:1. *lying lips to a prince.* His right to rule depends on honesty and justice (see 12:22; 16:12–13).

17:8 *A bribe is a charm.* A sad commentary on human behavior (see 18:16; 21:14; Eccl 10:19). Elsewhere, bribes are condemned (see v. 23; 15:27; 28:16; Deut 16:19; 1 Sam 12:3; Eccl 7:7; Is 1:23; Amos 5:12; 1 Tim 6:10).

17:9 *He who conceals a transgression seeks love.* See 10:12 and note.

10 A rebuke goes deeper into one who
has understanding
Than a hundred blows into a fool.
11 A rebellious man seeks only evil,
So a cruel messenger will be sent
against him.
12 Let a [a]man meet a [b]bear robbed of her
cubs,
Rather than a fool in his folly.
13 He who [a]returns evil for good,
[b]Evil will not depart from his
house.
14 The beginning of strife is *like* letting
out water,
So [a]abandon the quarrel before it
breaks out.
15 He who [a]justifies the wicked and he
who condemns the righteous,
Both of them alike are an abomination
to the LORD.
16 Why is there a price in the hand of a
fool to [a]buy wisdom,
When [1]he has no sense?
17 A [a]friend loves at all times,
And a brother is born for adversity.
18 A man lacking in [1]sense [2a]pledges
And becomes guarantor in the
presence of his neighbor.
19 He who [a]loves transgression loves
strife;
He who [b]raises his door seeks
destruction.
20 He who has a crooked [1]mind [a]finds
no good,
And he who is [b]perverted in his
language falls into evil.
21 He who [a]sires a fool *does so* to his
sorrow,
And the father of a fool has no joy.

12 [a]Prov 29:9 [b]2 Sam 17:8; Hos 13:8
13 [a]Ps 35:12; 109:5; Jer 18:20 [b]2 Sam 12:10; 1 Kin 21:22; Prov 13:21
14 [a]Prov 20:3; 25:8; 1 Thess 4:11
15 [a]Ex 23:7; Prov 18:5; 24:24; Is 5:23
16 [1]Lit *there is no heart* [a]Prov 23:23
17 [a]Ruth 1:16; Prov 18:24
18 [1]Lit *heart* [2]Lit *shakes hands* [a]Prov 6:1; 11:15; 22:26
19 [a]Prov 29:22 [b]Prov 16:18; 29:23
20 [1]Lit *heart* [a]Prov 24:20 [b]James 3:8
21 [a]Prov 10:1; 17:25; 19:13
22 [1]Lit *causes good healing* [a]Prov 15:13 [b]Ps 22:15
23 [a]Prov 17:8 [b]Ex 23:8; Mic 3:11; 7:3
24 [a]Eccl 2:14
25 [a]Prov 19:13 [b]Prov 10:1
26 [a]Prov 17:15; 18:5
27 [1]Lit *knows* [a]Prov 10:19; James 1:19 [b]Prov 14:29
28 [a]Job 13:5
18:1 [1]Lit *breaks out* [a]Prov 3:21; 8:14
2 [1]Lit *heart* [a]Prov 12:23; 13:16; Eccl 10:3
4 [1]Or *A bubbling brook, a fountain of wisdom* [a]Prov 20:5

22 A [a]joyful heart [1]is good medicine,
But a broken spirit [b]dries up the bones.
23 A wicked man receives a [a]bribe from
the bosom
To [b]pervert the ways of justice.
24 Wisdom is in the presence of the one
who has understanding,
But the [a]eyes of a fool are on the ends
of the earth.
25 A [a]foolish son is a grief to his father
And [b]bitterness to her who bore him.
26 It is also not good to [a]fine the
righteous,
Nor to strike the noble for *their*
uprightness.
27 He who [a]restrains his words [1]has
knowledge,
And he who has a [b]cool spirit is a
man of understanding.
28 Even a fool, when he [a]keeps silent, is
considered wise;
When he closes his lips, he is
considered prudent.

Contrast the Upright and the Wicked

18 He who separates himself seeks *his
own* desire,
He [1a]quarrels against all sound
wisdom.
2 A fool does not delight in
understanding,
But only [a]in revealing his own [1]mind.
3 When a wicked man comes, contempt
also comes,
And with dishonor *comes* scorn.
4 The words of a man's mouth are
[a]deep waters;
[1]The fountain of wisdom is a bubbling
brook.

17:10 *rebuke goes deeper into one who has understanding.* See 9:8–9. *a hundred blows into a fool.* Fools deserved and received flogging (cf. 10:13; 19:25,29; 26:3; Deut 25:3).
17:11 *cruel messenger.* Cf. the dispatching of Abishai and Joab to end Sheba's rebellion against David (2 Sam 20:1–22; see 1 Kin 2:25,29,46; Prov 16:14).
17:12 *bear robbed of her cubs.* Sure to attack you and rip you open (see 2 Sam 17:8; Hos 13:8; cf. the raging of the fool in 29:9).
17:13 *returns evil for good.* Like Nabal, who refused to pay David's men (1 Sam 25:21; see Ps 109:5; Rom 12:17–21). *Evil will not depart from his house.* The fate of David's family after his affair with Bathsheba and the murder of Uriah (2 Sam 12:10; cf. Jer 18:20–23).
17:15 *justifies the wicked.* Perhaps because of a bribe (see v. 8; 24:24).
17:16 *price in the hand of a fool.* Perhaps to pay the fee for his schooling.
17:17 *friend loves at all times.* Cf. David's friendship with Jonathan (2 Sam 1:26; see 18:24; Ruth 1:16; 1 Cor 13:4–7).
17:18 See 6:1 and note.
17:19 *who loves transgression loves strife.* A hot-tempered man commits many sins (29:22). *raises his door.* Out of pride (cf. 16:18; 29:23). Or "door" (lit. "opening") in this context may be a figure for the mouth ("he who opens his mouth wide"), meaning "he brags too much" and so "invites destruction," including his own.
17:20 *finds no good.* Contrast 16:20. *perverted in his language.* See note on 2:12.
17:21 *sorrow . . . no joy.* See v. 25; 19:13.
17:22 *joyful heart.* See 14:30; 15:13,30; 16:15; Job 29:24. *broken spirit dries up the bones.* See note on 3:8; see also 12:4; 14:30; Ps 32:3; 37:7–8.
17:23 *receives a bribe.* See note on v. 8.
17:24 *are on the ends of the earth.* He chases fantasies and is interested in everything except wisdom (see 12:11; cf. Deut 30:11–14).
17:25 See v. 21. *bitterness.* See 14:10 and note.
17:26 *fine the righteous.* See v. 15 and note. *strike the noble.* Cf. the beating and disgrace endured by Jeremiah (Jer 20:2; see v. 10 and note).
17:27 *restrains his words.* See 10:19. *cool spirit.* See 16:32.
17:28 *a fool, when . . . silent, is considered wise.* Cf. Job's sarcastic comment in Job 13:5.
18:1 *seeks his own desire.* He is quarrelsome and hot-tempered (cf. 17:14; Gal 5:20).
18:2 *revealing his own mind.* Cf. Eccl 10:3.
18:3 *contempt . . . dishonor . . . scorn.* Cf. 3:35; 6:33; 10:5; 11:2; Ps 31:17; Is 22:18.
18:4 *deep waters.* Profound or obscure (cf. 20:5). *fountain of wisdom is a bubbling brook.* A wise man's words are refreshing and a source of life (see 1:23; 13:14; see also 10:11 and note).

5 To [a]show partiality to the wicked is not good,
Nor to [b]thrust aside the righteous in judgment.
6 A fool's lips [1]bring strife,
And his mouth calls for [a]blows.
7 A [a]fool's mouth is his ruin,
And his lips are the snare of his soul.
8 The words of a whisperer are like dainty morsels,
And they go down into the [1]innermost parts of the body.
9 He also who is [a]slack in his work
[b]Is brother to him who destroys.
10 The [a]name of the LORD is a [b]strong tower;
The righteous runs into it and [c]is [1]safe.
11 A [a]rich man's wealth is his strong city,
And like a high wall in his own imagination.
12 [a]Before destruction the heart of man is haughty,
But [b]humility *goes* before honor.
13 He who [a]gives an answer before he hears,
It is folly and shame to him.
14 The [a]spirit of a man can endure his sickness,
But *as for* a [b]broken spirit who can bear it?
15 The [1a]mind of the prudent acquires knowledge,
And the [b]ear of the wise seeks knowledge.
16 A man's [a]gift makes room for him
And brings him before great men.
17 The first [1]to plead his case *seems* right,
Until [2]another comes and examines him.
18 The *cast* [a]lot puts an end to strife
And [1]decides between the mighty ones.

5 [a]Lev 19:15; Deut 1:17; 16:19; Ps 82:2; Prov 17:15; 24:23; 28:21 [b]Ex 23:2, 6; Prov 17:26; 31:5; Mic 3:9
6 [1]Lit *come with* [a]Prov 19:29
7 [a]Ps 64:8; 140:9; Prov 10:14; 12:13; 13:3; Eccl 10:12
8 [1]Lit *chambers of the belly*
9 [a]Prov 10:4 [b]Prov 28:24
10 [1]Lit *set on high* [a]Ex 3:15 [b]2 Sam 22:2, 3, 33; Ps 18:2; 61:3; 91:2; 144:2 [c]Prov 29:25
11 [a]Prov 10:15
12 [a]Prov 11:2; 16:18; 29:23 [b]Prov 15:33
13 [a]Prov 20:25; John 7:51
14 [a]Prov 17:22 [b]Prov 15:13
15 [1]Lit *heart* [a]Prov 15:14; Eph 1:17 [b]Prov 15:31
16 [a]Gen 32:20; 1 Sam 25:27
17 [1]Lit *in his plea* [2]Lit *his neighbor*
18 [1]Lit *makes a division* [a]Prov 16:33
20 [1]I.e. speech [a]Prov 12:14 [b]Prov 14:14
21 [1]Lit *hand* [a]Prov 12:13; 13:3; Matt 12:37 [b]Prov 13:2; Is 3:10; Hos 10:13
22 [a]Gen 2:18; Prov 12:4; 19:14; 31:10-31 [b]Prov 8:35
23 [a]Prov 19:7 [b]James 2:3, 6 [c]1 Kin 12:13; 2 Chr 10:13
24 [1]Lit *be broken in pieces*

19 A brother offended *is harder to be won* than a strong city,
And contentions are like the bars of a citadel.
20 With the [1a]fruit of a man's mouth his stomach will be satisfied;
[b]He will be satisfied *with* the product of his lips.
21 [a]Death and life are in the [1]power of the tongue,
And those who love it will eat its [b]fruit.
22 He who finds a [a]wife finds a good thing
And [b]obtains favor from the LORD.
23 The [a]poor man utters supplications,
But the [b]rich man [c]answers roughly.
24 A man of *too many* friends *comes* to [1]ruin,
But there is [a]a [2]friend who sticks closer than a brother.

On Life and Conduct

19 [a]Better is a poor man who [b]walks in his integrity
Than he who is perverse in [1]speech and is a fool.
2 Also it is not good for a person to be without knowledge,
And he who hurries [1a]his footsteps [2]errs.
3 The [a]foolishness of man ruins his way,
And his heart [b]rages against the LORD.
4 [a]Wealth adds many friends,
But a poor man is separated from his friend.

[2]Or *lover* [a]Prov 17:17; John 15:14, 15 **19:1** [1]Lit *his lips* [a]Prov 28:6 [b]Ps 26:11; Prov 14:2; 20:7 **2** [1]Lit *with his feet* [2]Lit *sins* [a]Prov 21:5; 28:20; 29:20 **3** [a]Prov 11:3 [b]Is 8:21 **4** [a]Prov 14:20

18:5 *partiality to the wicked.* See 17:15 and note. Favoritism of any kind was condemned in the law (see Lev 19:15; Deut 1:17; 16:19). *to thrust aside the righteous in judgment.* See 17:26; 31:5; Mal 3:5.
18:6 *bring strife.* A fool is quick to quarrel (see 17:14,19; 20:3). *calls for blows.* By a rod on his back (see 10:13; 19:29).
18:7 See 10:14 and note.
18:8 *words of a whisperer are like dainty morsels.* They are as pleasant as a wise man's words (cf. 16:21,23), but they promote dissension (see 11:13; 26:20,22). *they go down into the innermost parts of the body.* Where they are thoroughly digested and so are carried about and live on and on.
18:9 *who is slack in his work.* See 10:4 and note.
18:10 *name of the LORD.* The "name" equals the person, since it expresses his nature and qualities (see Ex 3:14–15 and notes). *strong tower.* See Ps 18:2; 91:2; 144:2. *safe.* See 29:25; Ps 27:5.
18:11 *wealth is his strong city.* Identical to 10:15 (see note there). *high wall.* But God can bring it down (see Is 25:12).
18:12 See 15:33 and note.
18:14 See 15:13; 17:22 and notes.
18:16 *A man's gift makes room for him.* A reference to the effectiveness of a bribe (see note on 17:8).
18:17 A warning to judges to hear both sides of a case (cf. Deut 1:16), but applicable to many situations.
18:18 *The cast lot puts an end to strife.* See note on 16:33. Cf. Matt 27:35.
18:19 *A brother offended.* Cf. Esau's anger because of the blessing Jacob received from Isaac (Gen 27:41).
18:20 See 12:14 and note.
18:21 *Death and life are in the power of the tongue.* See note on 13:3. *its fruit.* See v. 20.
18:22 *who finds a wife finds a good thing.* See 12:4 and note; 19:14. *obtains favor from the LORD.* Identical to 8:35, where finding wisdom brought such favor.
18:24 *man of too many friends comes to ruin.* One must choose friends carefully (see 12:26 and note; 17:17).
19:1 *in his integrity.* See note on 2:7. *Than he who is . . . a fool.* Even if he becomes rich (see 28:6).
19:2 *be without knowledge.* Cf. Rom 10:2. *hurries.* Haste can lead to poverty (21:5) or folly (29:20). *errs.* The Hebrew for this expression often refers to sin.
19:3 *his heart rages against the LORD.* He blames God for his troubles (see Gen 4:5; Is 8:21; cf. Lam 3:39).
19:4 See v. 7; 14:20.

5 A [a]false witness will not go unpunished,
And he who [1b]tells lies will not escape.
6 [a]Many will seek the favor of a [1]generous man,
And every man is a friend to him who [b]gives gifts.
7 All the brothers of a poor man hate him;
How much more do his [a]friends abandon him!
He [b]pursues *them with* words, *but* they are [1]gone.
8 He who gets [1]wisdom loves his own soul;
He who keeps understanding will [a]find good.
9 A [a]false witness will not go unpunished,
And he who [1]tells lies will perish.
10 Luxury is [a]not fitting for a fool;
Much less for a [b]slave to rule over princes.
11 A man's [a]discretion makes him slow to anger,
And it is his glory [b]to overlook a transgression.
12 The [a]king's wrath is like the roaring of a lion,
But his favor is like [b]dew on the grass.
13 A [a]foolish son is destruction to his father,
And the [b]contentions of a wife are a constant dripping.
14 House and wealth are an [a]inheritance from fathers,
But a prudent wife is from the LORD.
15 [a]Laziness casts into a deep sleep,
And an idle [1]man will suffer hunger.
16 He who [a]keeps the commandment keeps his soul,
But he who [1]is careless of [2]conduct will die.
17 One who [a]is gracious to a poor man lends to the LORD,
And He will repay him for his [1b]good deed.
18 [a]Discipline your son while there is hope,
And do not desire [1]his death.
19 *A man of* great anger will bear the penalty,
For if you rescue *him,* you will only have to do it again.
20 [a]Listen to counsel and accept discipline,
That you may be wise [1]the rest of your days.
21 Many [a]plans are in a man's heart,
But the [b]counsel of the LORD will stand.
22 What is desirable in a man is his [1]kindness,
And *it is* better to be a poor man than a liar.
23 The [1a]fear of the LORD *leads* to life,
So that one may sleep [b]satisfied, [2c]untouched by evil.
24 The [a]sluggard buries his hand [b]in the dish,
But will not even bring it back to his mouth.
25 [a]Strike a scoffer and the [1]naive may become shrewd,
But [b]reprove one who has understanding and he will [2]gain knowledge.
26 He [a]who assaults *his* father *and* drives *his* mother away
Is a shameful and disgraceful son.
27 Cease listening, my son, to discipline,
And you will stray from the words of knowledge.

5 [1]Lit *breathes* [a]Ex 23:1; Deut 19:16-19; Prov 19:9; 21:28 [b]Prov 6:19
6 [1]Or *noble* [a]Prov 29:26 [b]Prov 18:16; 21:14
7 [1]Lit *not* [a]Ps 38:11 [b]Prov 18:23
8 [1]Lit *heart* [a]Prov 16:20
9 [1]Lit *breathes* [a]Prov 19:5; Dan 6:24
10 [a]Prov 17:7; 26:1; Eccl 10:6, 7 [b]Prov 30:22
11 [a]Prov 14:29; 16:32 [b]Matt 5:44; Eph 4:32; Col 3:13
12 [a]Prov 16:14 [b]Gen 27:28; Deut 33:28; Ps 133:3; Hos 14:5; Mic 5:7
13 [a]Prov 17:25 [b]Prov 21:9, 19; 27:15
14 [a]2 Cor 12:14
15 [1]Lit *soul* [a]Prov 6:9, 10; 24:33
16 [1]Lit *despises* [2]Lit *ways* [a]Prov 13:13; 16:17; Luke 10:28; 11:28
17 [1]Or *benefits* [a]Deut 15:7, 8; Prov 14:31; 28:27; Eccl 11:1, 2; Matt 10:42; 25:40; 2 Cor 9:6-8; Heb 6:10 [b]Prov 12:14; Luke 6:38
18 [1]Lit *causing him to die* [a]Prov 13:24; 23:13; 29:15, 17
20 [1]Lit *in your latter end* [a]Prov 4:1; 8:33; 12:15
21 [a]Prov 16:1, 9 [b]Ps 33:10, 11; Is 14:26, 27
22 [1]Or *loyalty*
23 [1]Or *reverence* [2]Lit *not visited* [a]Prov 14:27; 1 Tim 4:8 [b]Ps 25:13 [c]Ps 91:10; Prov 12:21 **24** [a]Prov 26:15 [b]Matt 26:23; Mark 14:20 **25** [1]Lit *simple* [2]Lit *discern* [a]Prov 21:11 [b]Prov 9:8
26 [a]Prov 28:24

19:5 See 6:19 and note.
19:6 *seek the favor.* Cf. Job 11:19. *friend to him who gives gifts.* Generosity (v. 4) or bribery (18:16) could be in view.
19:7 *brothers of a poor man hate him.* See v. 4; 14:20; Job 19:19; Ps 38:11.
19:8 *loves his own soul.* Cf. 8:35–36. *will find good.* See 13:13 and note.
19:10 *Luxury is not fitting for a fool.* Nor is honor (26:1). *for a slave to rule over princes.* Because of his lack of wisdom and tendency to become a tyrant (see 17:2; 29:2; Is 3:4).
19:11 *slow to anger.* See 14:29; 15:18; 16:32; Eccl 7:9; James 1:19. *overlook a transgression.* He has good self-control (see 12:16; 29:11; 2 Sam 16:11–12).
19:12 *A king's wrath is like the roaring of a lion.* See 16:14 and note. *his favor is like dew.* See 16:15 and note.
19:13 *foolish son.* See 17:21,25. *contentions of a wife.* Also denounced in 21:9,19; 25:24; 27:15. Stirring up dissension is condemned throughout Proverbs (see 6:14 and note).
19:14 *prudent wife.* See 12:4 and note; see also 18:22.
19:15 See 6:11; 10:4 and notes.
19:16 See 13:13; 15:10; 16:17 and notes.
19:17 *who is gracious to a poor man.* See note on 14:21; see also 14:31. *lends to the LORD.* The Lord regards it as a gift to Him (cf. Matt 25:40).
19:18 *Discipline your son . . . not desire his death.* See note on 13:24.
19:19 *man of great anger.* Cf. 14:16–17,29; 15:18.
19:21 See 16:1,9 and notes.
19:22 *desirable . . . is his kindness.* But such goodness is difficult to find (cf. 3:3; 14:22). *better to be a poor man than a liar.* See vv. 1,28; 6:12.
19:23 *fear of the LORD.* See note on 1:7. *leads to life.* See note on 10:11. *untouched by evil.* See 3:2; 14:26 and notes.
19:24 *sluggard.* See note on 6:6.
19:25 *Strike a scoffer.* See v. 29; 14:3; see also notes on 1:22; 17:10. *naive.* Not to be confused with the mocker (see note on 1:4).
19:26 *assaults his father and drives his mother away.* Children were expected to take care of their parents when they were sick or elderly (cf. Is 51:18). Robbing them (cf. Judg 17:1–2) and attacking them (Ex 21:15,17) were serious crimes. *shameful and disgraceful.* See 10:5; 13:5.
19:27 See 5:1–2.

28 A rascally witness makes a mockery of
justice,
And the mouth of the wicked
[1a]spreads iniquity.
29 [1]Judgments are prepared for [a]scoffers,
And [b]blows for the back of fools.

On Life and Conduct

20 [a]Wine is a mocker, [b]strong drink a
brawler,
And whoever [1]is intoxicated by it is
not wise.
2 The terror of a king is like the
growling of a lion;
He who provokes him to anger
[1a]forfeits his own life.
3 [1a]Keeping away from strife is an
honor for a man,
But any fool will [2]quarrel.
4 The [a]sluggard does not plow after the
autumn,
So he [1]begs during the harvest and
has nothing.
5 A plan in the heart of a man is *like*
deep water,
But a man of understanding draws it
out.
6 Many a man [a]proclaims his own
loyalty,
But who can find a [b]trustworthy man?
7 A righteous man who [a]walks in his
integrity—
[b]How blessed are his sons after him.
8 [a]A king who sits on the throne of
justice
[1]Disperses all evil with his eyes.
9 [a]Who can say, "I have cleansed my
heart,
I am pure from my sin"?
10 [1a]Differing weights and differing
measures,
Both of them are abominable to the
LORD.
11 It is by his deeds that a lad
[1a]distinguishes himself
If his conduct is pure and right.
12 The hearing [a]ear and the seeing eye,
The LORD has made both of them.
13 [a]Do not love sleep, or you will
become poor;
Open your eyes, *and* you will be
satisfied with [1]food.
14 "Bad, bad," says the buyer,
But when he goes his way, then he
boasts.
15 There is gold, and an abundance of
[1]jewels;
But the lips of knowledge are a more
precious thing.
16 Take his garment when he becomes
surety for a stranger;
And for foreigners, hold him in
pledge.
17 [a]Bread obtained by falsehood is sweet
to a man,
But afterward his mouth will be filled
with gravel.
18 Prepare [a]plans by consultation,
And [b]make war by wise guidance.
19 He who [a]goes about as a slanderer
reveals secrets,
Therefore do not associate with [1b]a
gossip.
20 He who [a]curses his father or his
mother,
His [b]lamp will go out in [1]time of
darkness.
21 An inheritance gained hurriedly at the
beginning
Will not be blessed in the end.

28 [1]Or *swallows* [a]Job 15:16; 20:12, 13; 34:7 **29** [1]Gr *Rods* [a]Ps 1:1; Prov 9:12 [b]Prov 10:13; 18:6; 26:3 **20:1** [1]Lit *errs* [a]Gen 9:21; Prov 23:29, 30; Is 28:7; Hos 4:11 [b]Prov 31:4; Is 5:22; 56:12 **2** [1]Lit *sins against* [a]Num 16:38; 1 Kin 2:23; Prov 8:36; Hab 2:10 **3** [1]Lit *Ceasing* [2]Lit *burst out* [a]Gen 13:7f; Prov 17:14 **4** [1]Lit *asks* [a]Prov 13:4; 21:25 **6** [a]Prov 25:14; Matt 6:2; Luke 18:11 [b]Ps 12:1; Luke 18:8 **7** [a]Prov 19:1 [b]Ps 37:26; 112:2 **8** [1]Or *Sifts* [a]Prov 20:26; 25:5 **9** [a]1 Kin 8:46; 2 Chr 6:36; Job 14:4; Eccl 7:20; Rom 3:9; 1 John 1:8 **10** [1]Lit *A stone and a stone, an ephah and an ephah* [a]Prov 11:1; 20:23 **11** [1]Or *makes himself known* [a]Matt 7:16 **12** [a]Ex 4:11; Ps 94:9 **13** [1]Lit *bread* [a]Prov 6:9, 10; 19:15; 24:33 **15** [1]Or *corals* **17** [a]Prov 9:17 **18** [a]Prov 11:14; 15:22 [b]Prov 24:6; Luke 14:31 **19** [1]Lit *one who opens his lips* [a]Prov 11:13 [b]Prov 13:3 **20** [1]Lit *pupil* (of eye) [a]Ex 21:17; Lev 20:9; Prov 30:11; Matt 15:4 [b]Job 18:5; Prov 13:9; 24:20

19:28 *rascally witness.* See v. 5; see also note on 6:19. *spreads iniquity.* Cf. the description of man as one "who drinks iniquity like water" (Job 15:16; see Job 34:7).

19:29 *Judgments . . . for scoffers.* See v. 25. *blows for the back of fools.* See 10:13; 14:3; 26:3.

20:1 *Wine is a mocker, strong drink a brawler.* Those who overindulge become mockers and brawlers (see Hos 7:5). Proverbs associates drunkenness with poverty (23:20–21), strife (23:29–30) and injustice (31:4–5). *intoxicated.* See Gen 9:21; Is 28:7.

20:2 See 16:14 and note.

20:3 *will quarrel.* See 6:14; 17:14,19; 18:6.

20:4 *sluggard.* See note on 6:6. *and has nothing.* See 13:4; 21:25–26.

20:5 *plan.* Or "motive" (cf. 16:1–2). *deep water.* Cf. 18:4. *draws it out.* As if from a well.

20:6 *loyalty.* See note on 19:22. *who can find a trustworthy man?* Cf. Eccl 7:28–29.

20:7 *walks in . . . integrity.* See note on 2:7. *blessed are his sons.* See 13:22; see also note on 14:26.

20:8 *Disperses all evil.* See 16:10; Ps 11:4.

20:9 *cleansed . . . pure from my sin.* No one is without sin (cf. Job 14:4; Rom 3:23)—but those whose sins have been forgiven have "clean hands and a pure heart" (Ps 24:4; see also 51:1–2, 9–10).

20:10 See note on 11:1; cf. 16:11.

20:13 *sleep . . . become poor.* See 24:33–34.

20:14 *Bad, bad.* Prices were often agreed upon by bargaining, so the buyer is questioning the quality of the article in order to buy it more cheaply.

20:15 *gold . . . jewels.* Earlier, wisdom itself was valued more highly than gold or jewels (3:14–15; 8:10–11).

20:16 See note on 6:1. *Take his garment.* A garment could be taken as security for a debt (Deut 24:10–13). Anyone who foolishly assumes responsibility for the debt of a stranger, whose reliability is unknown, or of a wayward woman, whose unreliability is known, ought to be held accountable, even to the degree of taking his garment as a pledge.

20:17 *is sweet to a man.* Cf. the sweet "bread" prepared by the adulteress in 9:17. Zophar observes that evil is sweet in the mouth of a wicked man, but it turns sour in his stomach (Job 20:12–18). See note on 10:2.

20:18 *consultation . . . guidance.* See 15:22; Luke 14:31.

20:20 *curses his father or his mother.* Punishable by death (see Lev 20:9; cf. Prov 30:11,17). *lamp will go out.* He will die (see note on 13:9).

20:21 *inheritance gained hurriedly . . . Will not be blessed.* Cf.

22 [a]Do not say, "I will repay evil";
[b]Wait for the LORD, and He will save you.
23 [1a]Differing weights are an abomination to the LORD,
And a [2b]false scale is not good.
24 [a]Man's steps are *ordained* by the LORD,
How then can man understand his way?
25 It is a trap for a man to say rashly, "It is holy!"
And [a]after the vows to make inquiry.
26 A [a]wise king winnows the wicked,
And [1]drives the [b]*threshing* wheel over them.
27 The [1a]spirit of man is the lamp of the LORD,
Searching all the [2]innermost parts of his being.
28 [1]Loyalty and [a]truth preserve the king,
And he upholds his throne by [1]righteousness.
29 The glory of young men is their strength,
And the [1a]honor of old men is their gray hair.
30 [a]Stripes that wound scour away evil,
And strokes *reach* the [1]innermost parts.

On Life and Conduct

21 The king's heart is *like* channels of water in the hand of the LORD;
He [a]turns it wherever He wishes.
2 [a]Every man's way is right in his own eyes,
But the LORD [b]weighs the hearts.
3 To do [a]righteousness and justice
Is desired by the LORD more than sacrifice.
4 Haughty eyes and a proud heart,
The [a]lamp of the wicked, is sin.
5 The plans of the [a]diligent *lead* surely to advantage,
But everyone [b]who is hasty *comes* surely to poverty.
6 The [a]acquisition of treasures by a lying tongue
Is a fleeting vapor, the [1]pursuit of [b]death.
7 The violence of the wicked will drag them away,
Because they [a]refuse to act with justice.
8 The way of a guilty man is [a]crooked,
But as for the pure, his conduct is upright.
9 It is better to live in a corner of a roof
Than [1]in a house shared with a contentious woman.
10 The soul of the wicked desires evil;
His [a]neighbor finds no favor in his eyes.
11 When the [a]scoffer is punished, the [1]naive becomes wise;
But when the wise is instructed, he receives knowledge.
12 The righteous one considers the house of the wicked,
Turning the [a]wicked to ruin.
13 He who [a]shuts his ear to the cry of the poor
Will also cry himself and not be [b]answered.

22 [a]Prov 24:29; Matt 5:39; Rom 12:17, 19; 1 Thess 5:15; 1 Pet 3:9 [b]Ps 27:14 **23** [1]Lit *A stone and a stone* [2]Lit *balance of deceit* [a]Prov 20:10 [b]Prov 11:1 **24** [a]Prov 16:9 **25** [a]Eccl 5:4, 5 **26** [1]Lit *turns* [a]Prov 20:8 [b]Is 28:27 **27** [1]Lit *breath* [2]Lit *chambers of the body* [a]1 Cor 2:11 **28** [1]Lit *Covenant loyalty* [a]Prov 29:14 **29** [1]Or *splendor* [a]Prov 16:31 **30** [1]Lit *chambers of the body* [a]Ps 89:32; Prov 22:15; Is 53:5; 1 Pet 2:24 **21:1** [a]Ezra 6:22 **2** [a]Prov 16:2 [b]Prov 16:2; 24:12; Luke 16:15 **3** [a]1 Sam 15:22; Prov 15:8; Is 1:11, 16, 17; Hos 6:6; Mic 6:7, 8 **4** [a]Prov 24:20; Luke 11:34 **5** [a]Prov 10:4; 13:4 [b]Prov 28:22 **6** [1]Lit *seekers* [a]Prov 13:11; 20:21 [b]Prov 8:36 **7** [a]Amos 5:7; Mic 3:9 **8** [a]Prov 2:15 **9** [1]Lit *with a woman of contentions and a house of association* **10** [a]Ps 52:3; Prov 2:14; 14:21 **11** [1]Lit *simple* [a]Prov 19:25 **12** [a]Prov 14:11 **13** [a]Matt 18:30-34; 1 John 3:17 [b]James 2:13

19:26; cf. also the sad experience of the son who "squandered his estate with loose living" (Luke 15:12–13).

20:22 *I will repay evil.* Vengeance was God's prerogative. He would repay the wicked for their actions (see Deut 32:35; Ps 94:1). *Wait for the LORD.* See Ps 27:14; 37:34.

20:23 See v. 10; see also note on 11:1.

20:24 See notes on 3:5–6; 16:9.

20:25 *say rashly.* Promise to make a special gift to the Lord if He answers an earnest request (see Lev 27:1–25; Deut 23:21; Judg 11:30–31,34–35; 1 Sam 1:11). Sometimes such a vow was made hastily and was not carried out (cf. Eccl 5:4–6).

20:26 *threshing wheel.* The wheel of the threshing cart that separated the grain from the husk (cf. Is 28:27–28). The wicked will be separated from the righteous and duly punished.

20:27 *Searching all the innermost parts of his being.* See note on 15:11.

20:28 *Loyalty and truth preserve the king . . . righteousness.* Kindness and moral uprightness endear a king to his people and encourage them to be loyal subjects (cf. 3:3; 14:22; 16:12; 29:14).

20:29 *their strength.* Cf. Jer 9:23. *honor of old men is their gray hair.* See note on 16:31.

20:30 *Stripes that wound scour away evil.* Stern punishment is necessary to restrain evil. Several verses refer to fools whose backs are beaten (10:13; 14:3; 19:29), but even then, because they are fools, they may not change their ways (cf. 17:10; 27:22).

21:1 *king's heart is . . . in the hand of the LORD.* God controls the lives and actions even of kings, such as Nebuchadnezzar (Dan 4:31–32,35) and Cyrus (Is 45:1–3; cf. Ezra 6:22). *turns it wherever He wishes.* See 16:9; see also 16:1; 19:21; 20:24.

21:2 *is right.* See 14:12; 16:2. *weighs the hearts.* See 24:12; Job 31:6; Ps 139:23; 1 Cor 4:4–5; Heb 4:12.

21:3 *desired . . . more than sacrifice.* A theme also found in the prophets (Hos 6:6; Mic 6:7–8). See v. 27; see also note on 15:8.

21:4 *Haughty eyes.* See note on 6:17; see also 16:5,18.

21:5 *The plans of the diligent lead . . . to advantage.* See note on 10:4. *hasty.* Either rash actions (19:2) or a desire to get rich quick (see 13:11 and note; 20:21; 28:20).

21:6 *treasures by a lying tongue.* See note on 10:2; cf. 19:1. *fleeting vapor.* See 13:11 and note; Eccl 1:14. *pursuit of death.* Cf. 5:22; 7:23.

21:7 *violence of the wicked will drag them away.* See 1:18–19 and notes.

21:9 *corner of a roof.* Roofs were flat, and small rooms could be built there (see Deut 22:8; 2 Kin 4:10). *contentious woman.* See note on 19:13.

21:10 *desires evil.* See 4:16; 10:23. *His neighbor finds no favor.* Cf. 14:21.

21:11 See 19:25 and note.

21:12 *house of the wicked . . . to ruin.* See 10:25 and note; 14:11.

21:13 *cry of the poor.* See note on 14:21; see also 28:27. *Will also cry himself and not be answered.* See note on 1:28. Cf. the fate of the rich man (Luke 16:19–31) and the unmerciful servant (Matt 18:23–34).

14 A [a]gift in secret subdues anger,
And a bribe in the bosom, strong wrath.
15 The exercise of justice is joy for the righteous,
But is [a]terror to the workers of iniquity.
16 A man who wanders from the way of understanding
Will [a]rest in the assembly of the [1]dead.
17 He who [a]loves pleasure *will become* a poor man;
He who loves wine and oil will not become rich.
18 The wicked is a [a]ransom for the righteous,
And the [b]treacherous is in the place of the upright.
19 [a]It is better to live in a desert land
Than with a contentious and vexing woman.
20 There is precious [a]treasure and oil in the dwelling of the wise,
But a foolish man [b]swallows it up.
21 He who [a]pursues righteousness and loyalty
Finds life, righteousness and honor.
22 A [a]wise man scales the city of the mighty
And brings down the [1]stronghold in which they trust.
23 He who [a]guards his mouth and his tongue,
Guards his soul from troubles.
24 "Proud," "Haughty," "[a]Scoffer," are his names,
Who acts with [b]insolent pride.

25 The [a]desire of the sluggard puts him to death,
For his hands refuse to work;
26 All day long he [1]is craving,
While the righteous [a]gives and does not hold back.
27 The [a]sacrifice of the wicked is an abomination,
How much more when he brings it with evil intent!
28 A [a]false witness will perish,
But the man who listens *to the truth* will speak forever.
29 A wicked man [1a]displays a bold face,
But as for the [b]upright, he makes his way sure.
30 There is [a]no wisdom and no understanding
And no counsel against the LORD.
31 The [a]horse is prepared for the day of battle,
But [b]victory belongs to the LORD.

On Life and Conduct

22 A [a]*good* name is to be more desired than great wealth,
Favor is better than silver and gold.
2 The rich and the poor [1]have a common bond,
The LORD is the [a]maker of them all.
3 The [a]prudent sees the evil and hides himself,
But the [1]naive go on, and are punished for it.
4 The reward of humility *and* the [1]fear of the LORD

14 [a]Prov 18:16; 19:6
15 [a]Prov 10:29
16 [1]Lit *departed spirits* [a]Ps 49:14
17 [a]Prov 23:21
18 [a]Is 43:3 [b]Prov 11:8
19 [a]Prov 21:9
20 [a]Ps 112:3; Prov 8:21; 22:4 [b]Job 20:15, 18
21 [a]Prov 15:9; Matt 5:6; 1 Cor 15:58
22 [1]Lit *strength of trust* [a]2 Sam 5:6-9; Prov 24:5; Eccl 7:19; 9:15, 16
23 [a]Prov 12:13; 13:3; 18:21; James 3:2
24 [a]Ps 1:1; Prov 1:22; 3:34; 24:9; Is 29:20 [b]Is 16:6; Jer 48:29
25 [a]Prov 13:4
26 [1]Lit *desires desire* [a]Ps 37:26; 112:5, 9; Matt 5:42; Eph 4:28
27 [a]Prov 15:8; Is 66:3; Jer 6:20; Amos 5:22
28 [a]Prov 19:5, 9
29 [1]Lit *makes firm with his face* [a]Eccl 8:1 [b]Ps 119:5; Prov 11:5
30 [a]Jer 9:23; Acts 5:38, 39; 1 Cor 3:19, 20
31 [a]Ps 20:7; 33:17; Is 31:1 [b]Ps 3:8; Jer 3:23; 1 Cor 15:57
22:1 [a]Prov 10:7; Eccl 7:1
2 [1]Lit *meet together* [a]Job 31:15; Prov 14:31
3 [1]Lit *simple* [a]Prov 14:16; 27:12; Is 26:20
4 [1]Or *reverence*

21:14 *gift . . . bribe.* See note on 17:8; see also 18:16; 19:6. *subdues anger . . . wrath.* Perhaps that of an offended party (see 6:34–35).

21:15 *joy for the righteous.* See 11:10 and note. *terror to the workers of iniquity.* See 10:29 and note; Rom 13:3.

21:16 Graphically illustrated by the man who succumbed to the adulteress (see 2:18; 5:23; 7:22–23; 9:18).

21:17 *wine and oil.* Both were associated with lavish feasting (see 23:20–21; Amos 6:6). Oil was used in various lotions or perfumes, some of which were very expensive (John 12:5).

21:18 *The wicked is a ransom for the righteous.* Close to the thought of 11:8. In Is 43:3–4 God gave three nations to Persia in exchange for Persia's willingness to release the exiles of Judah (see note on Is 43:4).

21:19 See 19:13 and note.

21:20 *treasure and oil . . . dwelling of the wise.* See 3:10 and note; 8:21. *oil.* Olive oil (see note on v. 17; see also Deut 7:13).

21:21 *pursues righteousness.* See 15:9. *life, righteousness and honor.* Benefits for those who seek wisdom (see note on 3:2; see also 3:16; 8:18; cf. 22:4).

21:22 *wise man . . . brings down the stronghold.* Probably another way of saying, "Wisdom is better than strength" (Eccl 9:16). Cf. 24:5; 2 Cor 10:4, where spiritual weapons are "divinely powerful for the destruction of fortresses."

21:23 See 13:3 and note; 18:21.

21:24 *"Proud," . . . "Scoffer," are his names.* See note on 1:22. God mocks and punishes him for his "insolent pride" (cf. 3:34; 19:25,29; 21:11).

21:25 *desire of the sluggard.* See notes on 6:6; 13:4.

21:26 *gives and does not hold back.* The righteous are prosperous, so they can share with those in need (see Ps 37:26; 112:9; cf. Eph 4:28).

21:27 *The sacrifice of the wicked is an abomination.* See notes on v. 3; 15:8.

21:28 *false witness will perish.* See 19:5,9; see also note on 6:19.

21:29 *bold face.* Cf. the behavior of the adulteress in 7:13.

21:30 *no counsel against the LORD.* Because He is sovereign and controls people and nations (see 16:4,9 and notes; 19:21; 21:1; 1 Cor 3:19–20).

21:31 *horse.* Many times God cautions against trusting in horses and chariots for victory (e.g., Ps 20:7; Hos 1:7; cf. Deut 17:16). *victory belongs to the LORD.* See 1 Sam 17:47; Ps 3:8.

22:1 *good name.* Its value is recognized also in 3:4; 10:7; Eccl 7:1. *better than silver and gold.* Like the possession of wisdom (see 3:14; 16:16).

22:2 *maker of them all.* See 14:31 and note.

22:3 *prudent . . . hides himself.* Cf. 14:8. *the naive.* See note on 1:4; see also 9:16.

22:4 See 18:12. *humility and the fear of the LORD.* Associated also in 15:33 (see note on 1:7). *riches, honor and life.* Benefits for those who seek wisdom (see note on 3:2; see also 3:16; 8:18; cf. 21:21).

Are riches, honor and life.
5 [a]Thorns *and* snares are in the way of
the perverse;
He who guards himself will be far
from them.
6 [a]Train up a child [1]in the way he
should go,
Even when he is old he will not depart
from it.
7 The [a]rich rules over the poor,
And the borrower *becomes* the
lender's slave.
8 He who [a]sows iniquity will reap
vanity,
And the [b]rod of his fury will perish.
9 He who [1]is [a]generous will be blessed,
For he [b]gives some of his food to the
poor.
10 [a]Drive out the scoffer, and contention
will go out,
Even strife and dishonor will cease.
11 He who loves [a]purity of heart
And [1]whose speech is [b]gracious, the
king is his friend.
12 The eyes of the LORD preserve
knowledge,
But He overthrows the words of the
treacherous man.
13 The [a]sluggard says, "There is a lion
outside;
I will be killed in the streets!"
14 The mouth of [1][a]an adulteress is a
deep pit;
He who is [b]cursed of the LORD will fall
[2]into it.
15 Foolishness is bound up in the heart
of a child;
The [a]rod of discipline will remove it
far from him.
16 He [a]who oppresses the poor to make
[1]more for himself
Or who gives to the rich, [b]*will* only
come to poverty.

17 [a]Incline your ear and hear the words
of the wise,
And apply your mind to my knowledge;
18 For it will be [a]pleasant if you keep
them within you,
[1]That they may be ready on your lips.
19 So that your [a]trust may be in the LORD,
I have [1]taught you today, even you.
20 Have I not written to you [1][a]excellent
things
Of counsels and knowledge,
21 To make you [a]know the [1]certainty of
the words of truth
That you may [2][b]correctly answer him
who sent you?

22 [a]Do not rob the poor because he is
poor,
Or [b]crush the afflicted at the gate;
23 For the LORD will [a]plead their case
And [1]take the life of those who rob
them.

24 Do not associate with a man *given* to
anger;
Or go with a [a]hot-tempered man,
25 Or you will [a]learn his ways
And [1]find a snare for yourself.

5 [a]Prov 15:19
6 [1]Lit *according to his way* [a]Eph 6:4
7 [a]Prov 18:23; James 2:6
8 [a]Job 4:8 [b]Ps 125:3
9 [1]Lit *has a good eye* [a]Prov 19:17; 2 Cor 9:6 [b]Luke 14:13
10 [a]Gen 21:9, 10; Prov 18:6; 26:20
11 [1]Lit *has grace on his lips* [a]Ps 24:4; Matt 5:8 [b]Prov 14:35; 16:13
13 [a]Prov 26:13
14 [1]Lit *strange woman* [2]Lit *there* [a]Prov 2:16; 5:3; 7:5; 23:27 [b]Eccl 7:26
15 [a]Prov 13:24; 23:14
16 [1]Lit *much* [a]Eccl 5:8; James 2:13 [b]Prov 28:22
17 [a]Prov 5:1
18 [1]Lit *They together* [a]Prov 2:10
19 [1]Lit *made you know* [a]Prov 3:5
20 [1]Or *previous* [a]Prov 8:6
21 [1]Lit *truth* [2]Lit *return to words of truth* [a]Luke 1:3, 4 [b]Prov 25:13; 1 Pet 3:15
22 [a]Ex 23:6; Job 31:16; Prov 22:16 [b]Zech 7:10; Mal 3:5
23 [1]Lit *rob the soul* [a]1 Sam 25:39; Ps 12:5; 35:10; 140:12; Prov 23:11; Jer 51:36
24 [a]Prov 29:22
25 [1]Lit *take* [a]1 Cor 15:33

22:5 *Thorns and snares.* Evil (cf. 15:19). *will be far from them.* By taking the "highway of the upright" (16:17).
22:6 *Train.* Or "Dedicate," as in 1 Kin 8:63; or "Start." Instruction (1:8) and discipline (22:15) are primarily involved. *way he should go.* The right way, the way of wisdom (see 4:11 and note). *old.* Or "grown."
22:7 *The rich.* See note on 10:15. *the borrower becomes the lender's slave.* One of the reasons why putting up security for someone else (v. 26) was frowned upon (cf. Neh 5:4–5).
22:8 *sows iniquity will reap vanity.* See 12:21. *rod of his fury.* His ability to oppress others (see Ps 125:3; Is 14:5–6).
22:9 *He who is generous will be blessed.* See note on 11:25. *gives some of his food.* See note on 14:21; see also Deut 15:8–11.
22:10 *Drive out the scoffer.* See note on 1:22; cf. Gen 21:9–10. *contention will go out.* Cf. 17:14; 18:3; 20:3.
22:11 *purity of heart.* Cf. Ps 24:4. *whose speech is gracious.* Characteristic of the wise man in Eccl 10:12. *king is his friend.* Cf. v. 29.
22:12 *The eyes of the LORD preserve.* See 5:21; 15:3; Job 31:4; 34:21; Jer 16:17; Heb 4:13. *knowledge.* God protects those who have knowledge (cf. Ps 1:6; 34:15). *overthrows . . . the treacherous man.* Overrules their plans and desires (see 16:9; see also note on 21:30).
22:13 The sluggard (see note on 6:6) creates excuses to avoid work.
22:14 *mouth of an adulteress.* Her seductive words (see note on 5:3; see also 2:16; 7:5). *deep pit.* Perhaps a well or a hunter's trap (see 5:22 and note; 7:22).
22:15 *rod of discipline.* See note on 13:24.
22:16 *who oppresses the poor.* Condemned also in 14:31; 28:3. *gives to the rich.* Perhaps bribes (see 17:8; 18:16; 19:6). *poverty.* See 21:5; 28:22.
22:17–24:22 A new section that returns more to the style of chs. 1–9. Verses 17–21 form the introduction to these 30 sayings (see Introduction: Date). The 30 sayings are (1) 22:22–23; (2) 22:24–25; (3) 22:26–27; (4) 22:28; (5) 22:29; (6) 23:1–3; (7) 23:4–5; (8) 23:6–8; (9) 23:9; (10) 23:10–11; (11) 23:12; (12) 23:13–14; (13) 23:15–16; (14) 23:17–18; (15) 23:19–21; (16) 23:22–25; (17) 23:26–28; (18) 23:29–35; (19) 24:1–2; (20) 24:3–4; (21) 24:5–6; (22) 24:7; (23) 24:8–9; (24) 24:10; (25) 24:11–12; (26) 24:13–14; (27) 24:15–16; (28) 24:17–18; (29) 24:19–20; (30) 24:21–22.
22:17 *Incline your ear and hear.* See 4:20; 5:1. *words of the wise.* A title, like "proverbs of Solomon" in 10:1.
22:18 *it will be pleasant.* See 2:10; 16:24.
22:19 *that your trust may be in the LORD.* See note on 3:5.
22:21 *correctly answer.* See 1 Pet 3:15. *him who sent you.* Possibly a parent or guardian.
22:22 *Do not rob the poor.* See v. 16; 14:31. *Or crush the afflicted at the gate.* See Is 1:17.
22:23 *the LORD will plead their case.* See 23:11; Ps 12:5; 140:12; Is 3:13–15; Mal 3:5. *take the life of those who rob them.* See Ex 22:22–24.
22:24 *Do not associate with.* Cf. 12:26. *hot-tempered man.* His characteristics are given in 14:16–17; 15:18; 29:22.
22:25 *will learn his ways.* "Bad company corrupts good morals"

26 Do not be among those who [a]give
[1]pledges,
Among those who become guarantors
for debts.
27 If you have nothing with which to pay,
Why should he [a]take your bed from
under you?

28 [a]Do not move the ancient boundary
Which your fathers have set.

29 Do you see a man skilled in his work?
He will [a]stand before kings;
He will not stand before obscure men.

On Life and Conduct

23 When you sit down to dine with a
ruler,
Consider carefully [1]what is before you,
2 And put a knife to your throat
If you are a [a]man of *great* appetite.
3 Do not [a]desire his delicacies,
For it is deceptive food.

4 [a]Do not weary yourself to gain wealth,
[b]Cease from your [1]consideration *of it*.
5 [1]When you set your eyes on it, it is
gone.
For [a]*wealth* certainly makes itself
wings
Like an eagle that flies *toward* the
heavens.

6 [a]Do not eat the bread of [1]a [b]selfish
man,
Or desire his delicacies;
7 For as he [1]thinks within himself, so he
is.
He says to you, "Eat and drink!"
But [a]his heart is not with you.

26 [1]Lit *strike hands* [a]Prov 17:18
27 [a]Ex 22:26; Prov 20:16
28 [a]Deut 19:14; 27:17; Job 24:2; Prov 23:10
29 [a]Gen 41:46; 1 Kin 10:8
23:1 [1]Or *who*
2 [a]Prov 23:20
3 [a]Ps 141:4; Prov 23:6; Dan 1:5, 8, 13, 15, 16
4 [1]Or *understanding* [a]Prov 15:27; 28:20; Matt 6:19; 1 Tim 6:9; Heb 13:5 [b]Prov 3:5, 7
5 [1]Lit *Will your eyes fly upon it and it is not?* [a]Prov 27:24; 1 Tim 6:17
6 [1]Lit *an evil eye* [a]Ps 141:4 [b]Deut 15:9; Prov 28:22
7 [1]Lit *reckons in his soul* [a]Prov 26:24, 25
8 [1]Lit *your* [2]Lit *pleasant words* [a]Prov 25:16
9 [1]Lit *ears* [a]Matt 7:6 [b]Prov 1:7
10 [a]Jer 22:3; Zech 7:10
11 [a]Job 19:25; Jer 50:34 [b]Prov 22:23
13 [1]Lit *smite* [a]Prov 13:24; 19:18
14 [1]Lit *smite* [a]1 Cor 5:5
15 [a]Prov 23:24f; 27:11; 29:3
16 [1]Lit *kidneys* [a]Prov 8:6
17 [1]Or *reverence* [2]Lit *all the day* [a]Ps 37:1; Prov 24:1, 19 [b]Prov 28:14

8 You will [a]vomit up [1]the morsel you
have eaten,
And waste your [2]compliments.

9 [a]Do not speak in the [1]hearing of a fool,
For he will [b]despise the wisdom of
your words.

10 Do not move the ancient boundary
Or [a]go into the fields of the fatherless,
11 For their [a]Redeemer is strong;
[b]He will plead their case against you.
12 Apply your heart to discipline
And your ears to words of knowledge.

13 [a]Do not hold back discipline from the
child,
Although you [1]strike him with the
rod, he will not die.
14 You shall [1]strike him with the rod
And [a]rescue his soul from Sheol.

15 My son, if your heart is [a]wise,
My own heart also will be glad;
16 And my [1]inmost being will rejoice
When your lips speak [a]what is right.

17 [a]Do not let your heart envy sinners,
But *live* in the [1][b]fear of the LORD
[2]always.
18 Surely there is a [1][a]future,
And your [b]hope will not be cut off.
19 Listen, my son, and [a]be wise,
And [b]direct your heart in the way.
20 Do not be with [a]heavy drinkers of
wine,
Or with [b]gluttonous eaters of meat;

18 [1]Lit *latter end* [a]Ps 19:11; 58:11; Prov 24:14 [b]Ps 9:18 **19** [a]Prov 6:6 [b]Prov 4:23; 9:6 **20** [a]Prov 20:1; 23:29, 30; Is 5:22; Matt 24:49; Luke 21:34; Rom 13:13; Eph 5:18 [b]Deut 21:20; Prov 28:7

(1 Cor 15:33). *find a snare.* See note on 5:22; see also 12:13; 13:14; 29:6.
22:26 See note on 6:1.
22:27 *take your bed from under you.* You will be reduced to poverty.
22:28 *ancient boundary.* See note on 15:25; see also 23:10.
22:29 *skilled in his work.* Craftsmen were considered to be wise (see note on 8:30; see also Ex 35:30–35). *stand before kings.* Like Joseph, an administrator (Gen 41:46); David, a musician (1 Sam 16:21–23); and Hiram, a worker in bronze (1 Kin 7:13–14).
23:2 *great appetite.* Cf. the similar warning in vv. 20–21.
23:3 *Do not desire his delicacies.* Repeated in a different context in v. 6. *deceptive.* Perhaps the meaning is that the ruler wants to obligate you in some way, even to influence you to support a wicked scheme (cf. Ps 141:4).
23:4 *Do not weary yourself to gain wealth.* The desire to get rich can ruin a person physically and spiritually. "For the love of money is a root of all sorts of evil" (1 Tim 6:10; cf. 15:27; 28:20; Heb 13:5).
23:5 *it is gone.* Our trust must be in God, not in riches (see Jer 17:11; Luke 12:21; 1 Tim 6:17).
23:6 *selfish man.* One eager to get rich (see 28:22).
23:7 *his heart is not with you.* Cf. 26:24–25.
23:8 *vomit.* Out of disgust at the attitude of the host.
23:9 *despise the wisdom of your words.* Fools despise wisdom (1:7) and hate knowledge and correction (1:22; 12:1). They heap abuse on one who rebukes them (9:7).
23:10 *ancient boundary.* See note on 15:25; see also 22:28. *fatherless.* Oppressing the widow and the fatherless is strongly denounced (see Is 10:2; Jer 22:3; Zech 7:10).
23:11 *Redeemer.* Kinsman-Redeemer, someone who helped a close relative regain land (see Lev 25:25 and note) or who avenged his death (Num 35:12,19). God is a "father of the fatherless and a judge for the widows" (Ps 68:5). See notes on Ruth 2:20; Jer 31:11; see also Jer 50:34. *will plead their case.* See Ps 12:5; 140:12; Is 3:13–15; Mal 3:5.
23:13–14 See 13:24 and note.
23:15 See 10:1 and note; see also v. 24; 27:11; 29:3. *My son.* See 1:8,10.
23:17 *Do not . . . envy sinners.* See 3:31; 24:1,19. *fear of the LORD.* See notes on 1:7; 3:7.
23:18 *future.* See Ps 37:37; Jer 29:11.
23:19 *the way.* Cf. 4:25–26.
23:20 *Do not be with.* See 1:15; 12:26. *heavy drinkers of wine.* Drunkenness is also condemned in vv. 29–35; 20:1 (see note there); cf. Deut 21:20; Matt 24:49; Luke 21:34; Rom 13:13; Eph 5:18; 1 Tim 3:3.

21 For the [a]heavy drinker and the glutton
will come to poverty,
And [b]drowsiness will clothe *one* with
rags.

22 [a]Listen to your father who begot you,
And [b]do not despise your mother
when she is old.
23 [a]Buy truth, and do not sell *it,*
Get wisdom and instruction and
understanding.

24 The father of the righteous will greatly
rejoice,
And [a]he who sires a wise son will be
glad in him.
25 Let your [a]father and your mother be
glad,
And let her rejoice who gave birth to
you.

26 [a]Give me your heart, my son,
And let your eyes [1b]delight in my
ways.
27 For a harlot is a [a]deep pit
And an [1b]adulterous woman is a
narrow well.
28 Surely she [a]lurks as a robber,
And increases the [1]faithless among
men.

29 Who has [a]woe? Who has sorrow?
Who has contentions? Who has
complaining?
Who has wounds without cause?
Who has redness of eyes?
30 Those who [a]linger long over wine,
Those who go to [1]taste [b]mixed wine.
31 Do not look on the wine when it is
red,
When it [1]sparkles in the cup,
When it [a]goes down smoothly;
32 At the last it [a]bites like a serpent
And stings like a [b]viper.
33 Your eyes will see strange things
And your [1]mind will [a]utter perverse
things.
34 And you will be like one who lies
down in the [1]middle of the sea,
Or like one who lies down on the top
of a [2]mast.
35 "They [a]struck me, *but* I did not become
[1]ill;
They beat me, *but* I did not know *it.*
When shall I awake?
I will [b]seek [2]another drink."

Precepts and Warnings

24 Do not be [a]envious of evil men,
Nor desire to [b]be with them;
2 For their [1]minds devise [a]violence,
And their lips [b]talk of trouble.

3 [a]By wisdom a house is built,
And by understanding it is
established;
4 And by knowledge the rooms are
[a]filled
With all precious and pleasant riches.

5 A [a]wise man is [1]strong,
And a man of knowledge [2]increases
power.
6 For [a]by wise guidance you will [1]wage
war,
And [b]in abundance of counselors
there is victory.

7 Wisdom is [a]*too* exalted for a fool,
He does not open his mouth [b]in the
gate.

8 One who [a]plans to do evil,
Men will call a [1]schemer.
9 The [a]devising of folly is sin,

21 [a]Prov 21:17 [b]Prov 6:10, 11 **22** [a]Prov 1:8; Eph 6:1 [b]Prov 15:20; 30:17 **23** [a]Prov 4:7; 18:15; Matt 13:44 **24** [a]Prov 10:1; 15:20; 29:3 **25** [a]Prov 27:11 **26** [1]Another reading is *observe* [a]Prov 3:1; 4:4 [b]Ps 1:2; 119:24 **27** [1]Lit *strange* [a]Prov 22:14 [b]Prov 5:20 **28** [1]Lit *treacherous* [a]Prov 6:26; 7:12; Eccl 7:26 **29** [a]Is 5:11, 22 **30** [1]Or *search out* [a]1 Sam 25:36; Prov 20:1; Is 5:11; 28:7; Eph 5:18 [b]Ps 75:8 **31** [1]Lit *gives its eye* [a]Song 7:9 **32** [a]Job 20:16; Prov 20:1; Eph 5:18 [b]Ps 91:13; Is 11:8

33 [1]Lit *heart* [a]Prov 2:12 **34** [1]Lit *heart* [2]Or *lookout* **35** [1]I.e. from the effect of wounds [2]Lit *it yet again* [a]Prov 27:22; Jer 5:3 [b]Prov 26:11; Is 56:12 **24:1** [a]Ps 37:1; Prov 3:31; 23:17; 24:19 [b]Ps 1:1; Prov 1:15 **2** [1]Lit *hearts* [a]Is 30:12; Jer 22:17 [b]Job 15:35; Ps 10:7; 38:12 **3** [a]Prov 9:1; 14:1 **4** [a]Prov 8:21 **5** [1]Lit *in strength* [2]Lit *strengthens power* [a]Prov 21:22 **6** [1]Lit *make battle for yourself* [a]Prov 20:18 [b]Prov 11:14 **7** [a]Ps 10:5; Prov 14:6; 17:16 [b]Job 5:4; Ps 127:5 **8** [1]Or *deviser of evil* [a]Prov 6:14; 14:22; Rom 1:30 **9** [a]Matt 15:19; Acts 8:22

23:21 *glutton.* See v. 2; 28:7; cf. Matt 11:19. *come to poverty.* See 21:17. *drowsiness.* Cf. the poverty that overtakes the sluggard in 6:9–11.
23:22 *do not despise your mother.* Cf. 15:20; 30:17.
23:23 *Buy truth . . . Get wisdom . . . understanding.* See 4:5; see also 4:7 and note.
23:24–25 See v. 15; 27:11; see also 10:1 and note.
23:27 *deep pit.* See note on 22:14. *adulterous woman.* See note on 2:16; see also 5:20; 7:17–23.
23:28 *lurks.* See 6:26; 7:12; Eccl 7:26. *increases the faithless.* Cf. 7:26.
23:29–35 A vivid description of the physical and psychological effects of drunkenness.
23:29 *Who has woe?* Cf. the woes pronounced on drunkards in Is 5:11,22. *contentions.* See 20:1. *wounds.* Cf. the "blows for the back of fools" in 19:29.
23:30 *linger long over wine.* See 1 Sam 25:36. *mixed wine.* Probably with spices (see 9:2; Ps 75:8).
23:32 *bites like a serpent.* Death will be the result (cf. Num 21:6).
23:33 *see strange things.* Perhaps a reference to the delirium that afflicts the alcoholic.
23:34 *you will be like one who lies down in the middle of the sea.* Your head will be spinning.
23:35 *They beat me, but I did not know it.* Cf. the condition of Israel in Jer 5:3. *I will seek another drink.* The woe and misery do not prevent him from repeating his folly (cf. 26:11; 27:22; Is 56:12).
24:1 *Do not be envious.* See v. 19; Ps 37:1. *Nor desire to be with them.* See 1:15; 12:26; 23:20.
24:2 *devise violence.* See 1:10–11; 6:14; Job 15:35; Ps 38:12.
24:3 *house.* Symbolic of the life of an individual or a family. *is built.* Cf. the similar expression in 9:1.
24:4 *precious and pleasant riches.* Wisdom promises to bestow wealth on those who love her (8:21).
24:5 *is strong.* See note on 21:22.
24:7 *in the gate.* The normal meeting place for official business (see note on 1:21).
24:8 *plans to do evil.* See v. 2; see also 1:10–11; 6:14; Job 15:35; Ps 38:12. *schemer.* Called a "man who devises evil" in 12:2, a "man of evil devices" in 14:17.
24:9 *devising of folly is sin.* Cf. 1:11–16; 9:13–18. *scoffer is an*

And the scoffer is an abomination to
men.

10 If you [a]are slack in the day of distress,
Your strength is limited.

11 [a]Deliver those who are being taken
away to death,
And those who are staggering to
slaughter, Oh hold *them* back.
12 If you say, "See, we did not know this,"
Does He not [a]consider *it* [b]who weighs
the hearts?
And [c]does He not know *it* who [d]keeps
your soul?
And will He not [1e]render to man
according to his work?

13 My son, eat [a]honey, for it is good,
Yes, the [b]honey from the comb is
sweet to your taste;
14 Know *that* [a]wisdom is thus for your
soul;
If you find *it*, then there will be a
[1b]future,
And your hope will not be cut off.

15 [a]Do not lie in wait, O wicked man,
against the dwelling of the
righteous;
Do not destroy his resting place;
16 For a [a]righteous man falls seven
times, and rises again,
But the [b]wicked stumble in *time of*
calamity.

17 [a]Do not rejoice when your enemy falls,
And do not let your heart be glad
when he stumbles;
18 Or the LORD will see *it* and [1]be
displeased,
And turn His anger away from him.

19 [a]Do not fret because of evildoers
Or be [b]envious of the wicked;
20 For [a]there will be no [1b]future for the
evil man;
The [c]lamp of the wicked will be put
out.

21 My son, [1a]fear the LORD and the king;
Do not associate with those who are
given to change,
22 For their [a]calamity will rise suddenly,
And who knows the ruin *that comes*
from both of them?

23 These also are [a]sayings of the wise.
To [1b]show partiality in judgment is not
good.
24 He [a]who says to the wicked, "You are
righteous,"
[b]Peoples will curse him, nations will
abhor him;
25 But [a]to those who rebuke the *wicked*
will be delight,
And a good blessing will come upon
them.
26 He kisses the lips
Who gives [1]a right answer.

27 Prepare your work outside
And [a]make it ready for yourself in the
field;
Afterwards, then, build your house.

28 Do not be a [a]witness against your
neighbor without cause,
And [b]do not deceive with your lips.
29 [a]Do not say, "Thus I shall do to him
as he has done to me;
I will [1]render to the man according to
his work."

10 [a]Deut 20:8; Job 4:5; Jer 51:46; Heb 12:3
11 [a]Ps 82:4; Is 58:6, 7
12 [1]Lit *bring back* [a]Eccl 5:8 [b]1 Sam 16:7; Prov 21:2 [c]Ps 94:9-11 [d]Ps 121:3-8 [e]Job 34:11; Prov 12:14
13 [a]Ps 19:10; 119:103; Prov 25:16; Song 5:1 [b]Prov 16:24; 27:7; Song 4:11
14 [1]Lit *latter end* [a]Prov 2:10 [b]Prov 23:18
15 [a]Ps 10:9, 10
16 [a]Job 5:19; Ps 37:24; Mic 7:8 [b]Prov 6:15; 14:32; 24:22; Jer 18:17
17 [a]Job 31:29; Ps 35:15, 19; Prov 17:5; Obad 12
18 [1]Lit it *is evil in His eyes*
19 [a]Ps 37:1 [b]Prov 23:17; 24:1
20 [1]Lit *latter end* [a]Job 15:31 [b]Prov 23:18 [c]Job 18:5, 6; 21:17; Prov 13:9; 20:20
21 [1]Or *reverence* [a]Rom 13:1-7; 1 Pet 2:17
22 [a]Prov 24:16
23 [1]Lit *regard the face* [a]Prov 1:6; 22:17 [b]Prov 18:5; 28:21
24 [a]Prov 17:15; Is 5:23 [b]Prov 11:26
25 [a]Prov 28:23
26 [1]Or *an honest*
27 [a]Prov 27:23-27
28 [a]Prov 25:18 [b]Lev 6:2, 3; 19:11; Eph 4:25
29 [1]Lit *bring back* [a]Prov 20:22; Matt 5:39; Rom 12:17

abomination to men. Because he is proud, dishonoring (9:7) and contentious (22:10). See note on 1:22.
24:10 Cf. Jer 12:5; Gal 6:9.
24:11 *those . . . being taken away to death.* Perhaps innocent men condemned to die (cf. 17:15; Is 58:6–7).
24:12 *Does He not consider it who weighs the hearts?* God knows even our thoughts and motives (see 16:2; 21:2; Ps 94:9–11).
24:14 *wisdom is thus for your soul.* It nourishes and brings healing (see 16:24 and note). *future.* See Ps 9:18; 37:37; Jer 29:11.
24:15 *lie in wait.* Cf. 1:11; 12:6; Ps 10:9–10.
24:16 *seven times.* Many times (see 6:16; Job 5:19 and note). *rises again.* God promises to uphold and rescue the righteous (cf. Ps 34:19; 37:24; Mic 7:8). *wicked stumble.* See v. 22; 4:19; 6:15; 11:3,5.
24:17 *Do not rejoice.* See 17:5 and note.
24:18 *turn His anger away from him.* Edom was made desolate because she rejoiced over Israel's destruction (see Ezek 35:15).
24:19 Almost identical to Ps 37:1; see v. 1; 23:17.
24:20 *no future.* For himself or his posterity (see Ps 37:2,28,38; contrast v. 14; 23:18). *lamp . . . will be put out.* See note on 13:9.
24:21 *Fear the LORD and the king.* Submission to civil authority is also commanded in Eccl 8:2–5. 1 Pet 2:17 says, "fear God, honor the king," and Rom 13:1–7 urges the same obedience. These passages all view the king as a terror to the wicked (cf. 20:8,26).
24:22 *calamity will rise suddenly, And . . . ruin.* God's judgment is more common (see 6:15; 11:3,5), but the power of the king is seen in 20:26. *both of them.* God and the king.
24:23–34 An appendix to 22:17–24:22, giving a few additional sayings of the wise.
24:23 *partiality in judgment is not good.* See 18:5 and note.
24:24 *You are righteous.* See 17:15. *Peoples will curse him.* Just as they curse the man who "withholds grain" (11:26).
24:25 *good blessing.* See 10:6; Deut 16:20.
24:26 *kisses the lips.* Cf. the "pleasant words" that are "sweet to the soul" in 16:24. *right answer.* Cf. 16:13.
24:27 *make it ready . . . in the field.* Plan carefully and acquire the means as you build your house. *house.* See note on v. 3.
24:28 *witness . . . without cause.* See 3:30. *deceive with your lips.* See 6:19 and note; 12:17; 25:18.
24:29 *I will render to the man.* A spirit of revenge is discouraged also in 20:22 (see note there); cf. 25:21–22; Matt 5:43–45; Rom 12:17.

30 I passed by the field of the sluggard
And by the vineyard of the man
[a]lacking [1]sense,
31 And behold, it was completely
[a]overgrown with thistles;
Its surface was covered with [1b]nettles,
And its stone [c]wall was broken down.
32 When I saw, I [1]reflected upon it;
I looked, *and* received instruction.
33 "[a]A little sleep, a little slumber,
A little folding of the hands to rest,"
34 Then your poverty will come *as* [1]a
robber
And your want like [2]an armed man.

Similitudes, Instructions

25 These also are [a]proverbs of Solomon
which the men of Hezekiah, king of
Judah, transcribed.
2 It is the glory of God to [a]conceal a
matter,
But the glory of [b]kings is to search out
a matter.
3 *As* the heavens for height and the
earth for depth,
So the heart of kings is unsearchable.
4 Take away the [a]dross from the silver,
And there comes out a vessel for the
[b]smith;
5 Take away the [a]wicked before the
king,
And his [b]throne will be established in
righteousness.
6 Do not claim honor in the presence of
the king,
And do not stand in the place of great
men;
7 For [a]it is better that it be said to you,
"Come up here,"
Than for you to be placed lower in the
presence of the prince,
Whom your eyes have seen.

8 Do not go out [a]hastily to [1]argue *your*
case;
[2]Otherwise, what will you do in [3]the
end,
When your neighbor humiliates you?
9 [1a]Argue your case with your
neighbor,
And [b]do not reveal the secret of
another,
10 Or he who hears *it* will reproach you,
And the evil report about you will not
[1]pass away.

11 *Like* apples of gold in settings of silver
Is a [a]word spoken in [1]right
circumstances.
12 *Like* [1]an [a]earring of gold and an
[b]ornament of [c]fine gold
Is a wise reprover to a [d]listening ear.
13 Like the cold of snow in the [1]time of
harvest
Is a [a]faithful messenger to those who
send him,
For he refreshes the soul of his
masters.
14 *Like* [a]clouds and [b]wind without rain
Is a man who boasts [1]of his gifts
falsely.
15 By [1a]forbearance a ruler may be
persuaded,
And a soft tongue breaks the bone.
16 Have you [a]found honey? Eat *only*
[1]what you need,
That you not have it in excess and
vomit it.

30 [1]Lit *heart* [a]Prov 6:32
31 [1]I.e. a kind of weed [a]Gen 3:18 [b]Job 30:7 [c]Is 5:5
32 [1]Lit *set my heart*
33 [a]Prov 6:10
34 [1]Or *a vagabond;* lit *one who walks* [2]Lit *a man with a shield*
25:1 [a]Prov 1:1
2 [a]Deut 29:29; Rom 11:33 [b]Ezra 6:1
4 [a]Prov 26:23; Ezek 22:18 [b]Mal 3:2, 3
5 [a]Prov 20:8 [b]Prov 16:12
7 [a]Luke 14:7-11
8 [1]Lit *contend* [2]Lit *Lest* [3]Lit *its* [a]Prov 17:14; Matt 5:25
9 [1]Lit *Contend* [a]Matt 18:15 [b]Prov 11:13
10 [1]Lit *return*
11 [1]Lit *its* [a]Prov 15:23
12 [1]Or *a nose ring* [a]Ex 32:2; 35:22; Ezek 16:12 [b]2 Sam 1:24 [c]Job 28:17 [d]Prov 15:31; 20:12
13 [1]Lit *day* [a]Prov 13:17
14 [1]Lit *in a gift of falsehood* [a]Jude 12 [b]Jer 5:13; Mic 2:11
15 [1]Lit *length of anger* [a]Gen 32:4; 1 Sam 25:24; Eccl 10:4
16 [1]Lit *your sufficiency* [a]Judg 14:8; 1 Sam 14:25

24:30 *sluggard.* See note on 6:6; see also 20:4.
24:31 *thistles . . . nettles.* Cf. 15:19; Is 34:13.
24:33–34 See 6:10–11 and note on 6:11.
25:1–29:27 Another collection of Solomon's proverbs similar to 10:1–22:16.
25:1 *proverbs of Solomon.* See notes on 1:1; 10:1. *men of Hezekiah . . . transcribed.* There was a great revival in the reign of Hezekiah (c. 715–686 B.C.), and the king restored the singing of hymns to its proper place (2 Chr 29:30). His interest in the words of David corresponds to his support of a compilation of Solomon's proverbs. Solomon was the last king to rule over all Israel during the united monarchy; Hezekiah was the first king to rule over all Israel (now restricted to the southern kingdom) after the destruction of the divided monarchy's northern kingdom.
25:2 *to conceal a matter.* God gets glory because man cannot understand His universe or the way He rules it (see Deut 29:29; Job 26:14 and note; Is 40:12–24; Rom 11:33–36). *to search out a matter.* A king gets glory if he can uncover the truth and administer justice (see 1 Kin 3:9; 4:34).
25:3 *is unsearchable.* Cannot be understood; like the four things in 30:18–19. Yet God controls the hearts of kings (see note on 21:1).
25:4 *Take away the dross from the silver.* A process compared to the purification of society in general and rulers in particular in Is 1:22–25; Ezek 22:18; Mal 3:2–3.
25:5 *his throne will be established in righteousness.* See note on 16:12; see also 20:26.
25:6 *in the presence of the king.* Probably at a feast (cf. 23:1). Jesus spoke about the place of honor at a wedding feast (Luke 14:7–11).
25:7 *Come up here.* Cf. "Friend, move up higher" (Luke 14:10); contrast Is 22:15–19.
25:8 *Do not go out hastily to argue your case.* A warning about the seriousness of disputes (see 17:14) and the need to exercise caution (see 24:28).
25:9 *do not reveal the secret of another.* If you do, you are a gossip (see 11:13; 20:19).
25:10 *evil report about you.* A good name is one of life's most valuable possessions (see 22:1 and note).
25:11 *gold . . . silver.* Cf. the fruit of wisdom in 8:19.
25:12 *earring of gold.* Comparable to the beautiful wreath and necklace that represent the adornment of wisdom and sound teaching (see 1:9; 3:22; 4:9). *wise reprover.* Cf. the "life-giving reproof" of 15:31.
25:13 *cold of snow.* Probably a drink cooled by snow from the mountains; it did not snow at harvest time. See 26:1; contrast 10:26. *faithful messenger.* See 13:17 and note.
25:14 *Like clouds . . . without rain.* An image applied to unproductive men in Jude 12.
25:15 *By forbearance a ruler may be persuaded.* Cf. 14:29. *soft tongue.* See note on 15:1.

17 Let your foot rarely be in your
neighbor's house,
Or he will become [1]weary of you and
hate you.
18 *Like* a club and a [a]sword and a sharp
[b]arrow
Is a man who bears [c]false witness
against his neighbor.
19 *Like* a bad tooth and [1]an unsteady foot
Is confidence in a [a]faithless man in
time of trouble.
20 *Like* one who takes off a garment on a
cold day, *or like* vinegar on [1]soda,
Is he who sings songs to [2]a troubled
heart.
21 [a]If [1]your enemy is hungry, give him
food to eat;
And if he is thirsty, give him water to
drink;
22 For you will [1]heap burning coals on
his head,
And [a]the LORD will reward you.
23 The north wind brings forth rain,
And a [1a]backbiting tongue, an angry
countenance.
24 It is [a]better to live in a corner of the
roof
Than [1]in a house shared with a
contentious woman.
25 *Like* cold water to a weary soul,
So is [a]good news from a distant land.
26 *Like* a [a]trampled spring and a
[1]polluted well
Is a righteous man who gives way
before the wicked.
27 It is not good to eat much honey,
Nor is it glory to [a]search out [1]one's
own glory.

17 [1]Lit *surfeited with* **18** [a]Ps 57:4; Prov 12:18 [b]Jer 9:8 [c]Ex 20:16; Prov 24:28 **19** [1]Lit *a slipping foot* [a]Job 6:15; Is 36:6 **20** [1]I.e. natron [2]Lit *an evil* **21** [1]Lit *one who hates you* [a]Ex 23:4, 5; 2 Kin 6:22; 2 Chr 28:15; Matt 5:44; Rom 12:20 **22** [1]Lit *snatch up* [a]2 Sam 16:12; Matt 6:4, 6 **23** [1]Lit *tongue of secrecy* [a]Ps 101:5 **24** [1]Lit *with a woman of contentions and a house of association* [a]Prov 21:9 **25** [a]Prov 15:30 **26** [1]Lit *ruined* [a]Ezek 32:2; 34:18, 19 **27** [1]Lit *their* [a]Prov 27:2; Luke 14:11

28 [a]Prov 16:32 [b]2 Chr 32:5; Neh 1:3 **26:1** [a]1 Sam 12:17 [b]Prov 17:7 **2** [1]Lit *wandering* [2]Lit *come* [a]Prov 27:8; Is 16:2 [b]Num 23:8; Deut 23:5; 2 Sam 16:12 **3** [a]Ps 32:9 [b]Prov 10:13; 19:29 **4** [a]Prov 23:9; 29:9; Is 36:21; Matt 7:6

28 *Like* a [a]city that is broken into *and*
without walls
Is a man [b]who has no control over his
spirit.

Similitudes, Instructions

26 Like snow in summer and like [a]rain in
harvest,
So honor is not [b]fitting for a fool.
2 Like a [a]sparrow in *its* [1]flitting, like a
swallow in *its* flying,
So a [b]curse without cause does not
[2]alight.
3 A [a]whip is for the horse, a bridle for
the donkey,
And a [b]rod for the back of fools.
4 [a]Do not answer a fool according to his
folly,
Or you will also be like him.
5 [a]Answer a fool as his folly *deserves,*
That he not be [b]wise in his own eyes.
6 He cuts off *his own* feet *and* drinks
violence
Who sends a message by the hand of
a fool.
7 *Like* the legs *which* [1]are useless to the
lame,
So is a proverb in the mouth of
fools.
8 Like [1]one who binds a stone in a
sling,
So is he who gives honor to a fool.
9 *Like* a thorn *which* [1]falls into the hand
of a drunkard,
So is a proverb in the mouth of
fools.

5 [a]Matt 16:1-4; 21:24-27 [b]Prov 3:7; 28:11; Rom 12:16 **7** [1]Lit *hang down from* **8** [1]Lit *the binding of* **9** [1]Lit *goes up*

25:18 *club . . . sword . . . arrow.* Cf. Ps 57:4; Jer 9:8. *false witness.* See note on 6:19; see also 24:28; Ex 20:16.
25:19 *bad tooth . . . unsteady foot.* Relying on Egypt was like leaning on a crushed reed (Is 36:6).
25:20 *soda.* Probably sodium carbonate, natron (see Jer 2:22). There is a vigorous reaction when vinegar is poured on it. *sings songs to a troubled heart.* The exiles were reluctant to sing the songs of Zion (Ps 137:3–4).
25:21–22 Quoted in Rom 12:20 as a way to overcome evil with good.
25:21 Kindness to one's enemy is encouraged in 20:22; Ex 23:4–5. *give him food . . . water.* At Elisha's request, a trapped Aramean army was given a great feast and then sent home (2 Kin 6:21–23; cf. 2 Chr 28:15).
25:22 *heap burning coals on his head.* Horrible punishment reserved for the wicked (see Ps 140:10). Here, however, it is kindness that will hurt the enemy (cf. the broken bone of v. 15) but perhaps win him over. Alternatively, the expression may reflect an Egyptian expiation ritual, in which a guilty person, as a sign of his repentance, carried a basin of glowing coals on his head. The meaning here, then, would be that in returning good for evil and so being kind to your enemy, you may cause him to repent or change. *LORD will reward you.* Even if the enemy remains hostile (cf. 11:18; 19:17).
25:23 *north.* Perhaps northwest (cf. Luke 12:54). *backbiting tongue.* One that spreads slander (cf. 10:18).
25:25 *good news from a distant land.* See Gen 45:25–28.
25:26 *trampled spring.* Cf. Ezek 34:18–19. *righteous man who gives way.* Perhaps through bribery (cf. 17:8; 29:4; Is 1:21–23).
25:27 *to search out one's own glory.* See vv. 6–7 and notes.
25:28 *city that is . . . without walls.* Defenseless and disgraced (cf. Neh 1:3). *man who has no control over his spirit.* See 16:32 and note.
26:1 *rain in harvest.* It rarely rains in the Holy Land from June through September, but see 1 Sam 12:17–18. *honor is not fitting for a fool.* See v. 8; 30:22.
26:2 *curse without cause does not alight.* When David was cursed by Shimei, he realized that the curse would not take effect because he was innocent of the charge of murdering members of Saul's family (2 Sam 16:8,12).
26:3 *rod for the back of fools.* See 14:3; 19:29.
26:4 *Do not answer a fool according to his folly.* Do not stoop to his level (see 23:9; Matt 7:6).
26:5 *Answer a fool as his folly deserves.* Sometimes folly must be plainly exposed and denounced.
26:6 *drinks violence.* See 4:17; Job 34:7. *sends a message by the hand of a fool.* He will likely misrepresent the one who sends him, or in some other manner frustrate the sender's purpose (see 13:17).
26:8 *Like one who binds a stone in a sling.* A fool with authority wields a formidable weapon, but it is useless in his hands—as useless as a stone that is tied, not placed, in the sling.
26:9 A fool reciting a proverb will do as much damage to himself and others as a drunkard wielding a thorn bush.

10 [1]*Like* an archer who wounds everyone,
So is he who hires a fool or who hires
those who pass by.
11 Like [a]a dog that returns to its vomit
Is a fool who [b]repeats [1]his folly.
12 Do you see a man [a]wise in his own
eyes?
[b]There is more hope for a fool than for
him.
13 The [a]sluggard says, "There is a lion in
the road!
A lion is [1]in the open square!"
14 *As* the door turns on its hinges,
So *does* the [a]sluggard on his bed.
15 The [a]sluggard buries his hand in the
dish;
He is weary of bringing it to his
mouth again.
16 The sluggard is [a]wiser in his own eyes
Than seven men who can [1]give a
discreet answer.
17 *Like* one who takes a dog by the ears
Is he who passes by *and* [1]meddles
with [a]strife not belonging to him.
18 Like a madman who throws
[a]Firebrands, arrows and death,
19 So is the man who [a]deceives his
neighbor,
And says, "[b]Was I not joking?"
20 For lack of wood the fire goes out,
And where there is no [a]whisperer,
[b]contention quiets down.
21 *Like* charcoal to hot embers and wood
to fire,
So is a [a]contentious man to kindle
strife.
22 The [a]words of a whisperer are like
dainty morsels,
And they go down into the [1]innermost
parts of the body.
23 *Like* an earthen [a]vessel overlaid with
silver [b]dross
Are burning lips and a wicked heart.
24 He who [a]hates disguises *it* with his
lips,
But he lays up [b]deceit in his [1]heart.
25 When [1]he [a]speaks graciously, do not
believe him,
For there are seven abominations in
his heart.
26 *Though his* hatred [a]covers itself with
guile,
His wickedness will be [b]revealed
before the assembly.
27 He who [a]digs a pit will fall into it,
And he who rolls a stone, it will come
back on him.
28 A lying tongue hates [1]those it crushes,
And a [a]flattering mouth works ruin.

Warnings and Instructions

27 [a]Do not boast about tomorrow,
For you [b]do not know what a day may
bring forth.
2 Let [a]another praise you, and not your
own mouth;
A stranger, and not your own lips.
3 A stone is heavy and the sand weighty,
But the provocation of a fool is
heavier than both of them.
4 Wrath is fierce and anger is a flood,
But [a]who can stand before jealousy?
5 Better is [a]open rebuke
Than love that is concealed.
6 Faithful are the [a]wounds of a friend,
But [1]deceitful are the [b]kisses of an
enemy.
7 A sated [1]man [2]loathes honey,
But to a famished [1]man any bitter
thing is sweet.
8 Like a [a]bird that wanders from her
nest,
So is a man who [b]wanders from his
[1]home.

10 [1]Or *A master workman produces all things, But he who hires a fool is like one who hires those who pass by* **11** [1]Lit *with his* [a]2 Pet 2:22 [b]Ex 8:15 **12** [a]Prov 3:7; 26:5 [b]Prov 29:20 **13** [1]Lit *within* [a]Prov 22:13 **14** [a]Prov 6:9 **15** [a]Prov 19:24 **16** [1]Lit *return discreetly* [a]Prov 27:11 **17** [1]Lit *infuriates himself* [a]Prov 3:30 **18** [a]Is 50:11 **19** [a]Prov 24:28 [b]Eph 5:4 **20** [a]Prov 16:28 [b]Prov 22:10 **21** [a]Prov 15:18; 29:22 **22** [1]Lit *chambers of the belly* [a]Prov 18:8 **23** [a]Matt 23:27; Luke 11:39 [b]Prov 25:4

24 [1]Lit *inward part* [a]Ps 41:6; Prov 10:18 [b]Prov 12:20 **25** [1]Lit *his voice is gracious* [a]Ps 28:3; Prov 26:23; Jer 9:8 **26** [a]Matt 23:28 [b]Luke 8:17 **27** [a]Esth 7:10; Prov 28:10 **28** [1]Lit *its crushed ones* [a]Prov 29:5 **27:1** [a]James 4:13-16 [b]Luke 12:19, 20; James 4:14 **2** [a]Prov 25:27; 2 Cor 10:12, 18; 12:11 **4** [a]Prov 6:34; 1 John 3:12 **5** [a]Prov 28:23; Gal 2:14

6 [1]Or *excessive* [a]Ps 141:5; Prov 20:30 [b]Matt 26:49 **7** [1]Lit *soul* [2]Lit *tramples on* **8** [1]Lit *place* [a]Prov 26:2; Is 16:2 [b]Gen 21:14

26:10 *he who hires a fool or who hires those who pass by.* Abimelech hired "worthless and reckless fellows" to help him murder his half brothers and set up a brief and ill-fated rule (Judg 9:4–6).
26:11 *Like a dog that returns to its vomit.* Quoted in 2 Pet 2:22 with reference to false teachers. *fool who repeats his folly.* The drunkard returns to his drink (23:35).
26:12 *wise in his own eyes.* This conceit is applied to the sluggard in v. 16 and the rich in 28:11; cf. 26:5.
26:13 See 22:13 and note.
26:14 The sluggard loves to sleep and seems to be attached to his bed as a door to its hinges.
26:16 *wiser in his own eyes.* See v. 12 and note.
26:17 *takes a dog by the ears.* To do so is to immediately create a disturbance.
26:18 *Like a madman who throws.* Cf. the archer in v. 10. *Firebrands.* Could easily ignite sheaves of grain (cf. Zech 12:6).
26:19 *Was I not joking?* Explaining it as a prank is a poor excuse.
26:21 *kindle strife.* See 6:14 and note.
26:22 See 18:8 and note.
26:23 *silver dross.* Or "glaze." Cf. the clean outside of the cup and dish (Luke 11:39; cf. Matt 23:27). *burning lips and a wicked heart.* The speech of the adulteress is seductive (2:16; 5:3).
26:24 *lays up deceit in his heart.* See 12:20.
26:25 *he speaks graciously.* See Jer 9:8. *seven.* Many (see note on Job 5:19). For seven things the Lord detests see 6:16–19.
26:26 *will be revealed before the assembly.* See 5:14; Luke 8:17.
26:27 *He who digs a pit will fall into it.* "His mischief will return upon his own head" (Ps 7:16). See 1:18 and note; 28:10; 29:6; Esth 7:10; Ps 7:15; Eccl 10:8–9.
26:28 *lying tongue hates those it crushes.* See 10:18. *flattering mouth works ruin.* See 29:5; cf. 16:13.
27:1 Cf. the words of the rich fool in Luke 12:19–20; see Prov 16:9; Is 56:12.
27:2 *Let another praise you.* See 2 Cor 10:12,18.
27:4 *who can stand before jealousy?* See 6:34; Song 8:6.
27:5 *open rebuke.* Called "life-giving reproof" in 15:31; cf. Gal 2:14.
27:6 *Faithful are the wounds of a friend.* Called a sign of kindness in Ps 141:5. *kisses of an enemy.* See 5:3–4; Matt 26:49.
27:7 *loathes honey.* Cf. 25:16,27.
27:8 *man who wanders from his home.* He has lost his security and may be vulnerable to temptation (cf. 7:21–23).

9 [a]Oil and perfume make the heart
glad,
So a [1]man's counsel is sweet to his
friend.
10 Do not forsake your own [a]friend or
[b]your father's friend,
And do not go to your brother's house
in the day of your calamity;
Better is a neighbor who is near than
a brother far away.
11 [a]Be wise, my son, and make my heart
glad,
That I may [b]reply to him who
reproaches me.
12 A prudent man sees evil *and* hides
himself,
The [1]naive proceed *and* pay the
penalty.
13 [a]Take his garment when he becomes
surety for a stranger;
And for an [1]adulterous woman hold
him in pledge.
14 [a]He who blesses his friend with a loud
voice early in the morning,
It will be reckoned a curse to him.
15 A [a]constant dripping on a day of
steady rain
And a contentious woman are alike;
16 He who would [1]restrain her [1]restrains
the wind,
And [2]grasps oil with his right hand.
17 Iron sharpens iron,
So one man sharpens another.
18 He who tends the [a]fig tree will eat its
fruit,
And he who [b]cares for his master will
be honored.
19 As in water face *reflects* face,
So the heart of man *reflects* man.
20 [1][a]Sheol and [2]Abaddon are [b]never
satisfied,
Nor are the [c]eyes of man ever satisfied.
21 The [a]crucible is for silver and the
furnace for gold,
And each [b]*is tested* by the praise
accorded him.
22 Though you [a]pound a fool in a mortar
with a pestle along with crushed
grain,
Yet his foolishness will not depart
from him.

23 [a]Know well the [1]condition of your
flocks,
And pay attention to your herds;
24 For riches are not forever,
Nor does a [a]crown *endure* to all
generations.
25 *When* the grass disappears, the new
growth is seen,
And the herbs of the mountains are
[a]gathered in,
26 The lambs *will be* for your clothing,
And the goats *will bring* the price of a
field,
27 And *there will be* goats' milk enough
for your food,
For the food of your household,
And sustenance for your maidens.

Warnings and Instructions

28 The wicked [a]flee when no one is
pursuing,
But the righteous are [1]bold as a lion.
2 By the transgression of a land [a]many
are its princes,
But [b]by a man of understanding *and*
knowledge, so it endures.

9 [1]Lit *soul's* [a]Ps 23:5; 141:5
10 [a]Prov 18:24 [b]1 Kin 12:6-8; 2 Chr 10:6-8
11 [a]Prov 10:1; 23:15; 29:3 [b]Ps 119:42
12 [1]Lit *simple*
13 [1]Lit *strange* [a]Prov 20:16
14 [a]Ps 12:2
15 [a]Prov 19:13
16 [1]Lit *hide(s)* [2]Lit *encounters*
18 [a]2 Kin 18:31; Song 8:12; Is 36:16; 1 Cor 3:8; 9:7; 2 Tim 2:6 [b]Luke 12:42-44; 19:17
20 [1]I.e. The nether world [2]I.e. the place of destruction [a]Job 26:6; Prov 15:11 [b]Prov 30:15, 16; Hab 2:5 [c]Eccl 1:8; 4:8
21 [a]Prov 17:3 [b]Luke 6:26
22 [a]Prov 23:35; 26:11; Jer 5:3
23 [1]Lit *face* [a]Jer 31:10; Ezek 34:12; John 10:3
24 [a]Job 19:9; Ps 89:39; Jer 13:18; Lam 5:16; Ezek 21:26
25 [a]Is 17:5; Jer 40:10, 12
28:1 [1]Lit *confident* [a]Lev 26:17, 36; Ps 53:5
2 [a]1 Kin 16:8-28; 2 Kin 15:8-15 [b]Prov 11:11

27:9 *Oil.* See note on 21:17. *perfume.* Cf. the one "perfumed with myrrh and frankincense" (Song 3:6). *sweet to his friend.* Cf. 16:21,24.
27:10 Do not fail a friend in need; when in need rely on friendship rather than on mere family relationships. *brother far away.* Either physically or emotionally.
27:11 *Be wise, my son.* See 10:1 and note. *That I may reply to him who reproaches me.* A wise son (or student) serves as a powerful testimony that the father (or teacher) who has shaped him has shown himself to be a man of worth.
27:12 *The naive.* See note on 1:4. *proceed and pay the penalty.* See 7:22–23; 9:16–18.
27:13 A repetition of 20:16 (see note there).
27:14 *blesses his friend.* Perhaps to win his favor (cf. Ps 12:2).
27:15 See 19:13 and note.
27:17 *sharpens another.* Develops and molds his character.
27:18 *will eat its fruit.* Cf. 2 Tim 2:6. *will be honored.* Cf. Gen 39:4; see also Matt 25:21; Luke 12:42–44; John 12:26.
27:19 *heart of man reflects man.* The condition of a man's heart indicates his true character (see Matt 5:8).
27:20 *Sheol and Abaddon.* See note on Job 26:6; see also 15:11. *are never satisfied.* Their appetite is insatiable (see Is 5:14). *Nor are the eyes of man.* See Eccl 4:8.
27:21 *crucible . . . gold.* Silver and gold were refined to remove their impurities (cf. Is 1:25; Mal 3:3). *each is tested by the praise accorded him.* He must not become proud, and he must be wary of flattery (cf. 12:8; Luke 6:26).
27:22 *mortar.* A bowl (see Num 11:8). *pestle.* A club-like tool for pounding grain in a mortar. *his foolishness will not depart from him.* In spite of severe punishment, fools refuse to change (see note on 20:30; see also 26:11; Jer 5:3).
27:23–27 A section praising the basic security afforded by agricultural pursuits—reflecting the agricultural base of the ancient economy.
27:23 *pay attention to your herds.* Like Jacob, with Laban's flocks (Gen 31:38–40).
27:24 *riches are not forever.* See note on 23:5. *Nor does a crown endure.* Even kings may lose their wealth and power (see Job 19:9; Lam 5:16).
27:25 *grass disappears.* This began in March or April.
27:26 *price of a field.* See 31:16. Sheep and goats sometimes also served as tribute payments (see 2 Kin 3:4).
27:27 *goats' milk.* Commonly drunk along with cows' milk (see Deut 32:13–14; Is 7:21–22). *maidens.* See 31:15.
28:1 *wicked flee.* See Lev 26:17,36; Ps 53:5. *bold as a lion.* Like David in 1 Sam 17:46; cf. Ps 18:33–38.
28:2 *many are its princes.* Israel's rebellion often brought rapid change in leadership (see 1 Kin 16:8–28; 2 Kin 15:8–15). *by a man of understanding . . . it endures.* A wise ruler will be successful (see 8:15–16; 24:5; 29:4).

3 A [a]poor man who oppresses the lowly
Is *like* a driving rain [1]which leaves no
food.
4 Those who forsake the law [a]praise the
wicked,
But those who keep the law [b]strive
with them.
5 Evil men [a]do not understand justice,
But those who seek the LORD
[b]understand all things.
6 [a]Better is the poor who walks in his
integrity
Than he who is [1]crooked though he
be rich.
7 He who keeps the law is a discerning
son,
But he who is a companion of
[a]gluttons humiliates his father.
8 He who increases his wealth by
[a]interest and usury
Gathers it [b]for him who is gracious to
the poor.
9 He who turns away his ear from
listening to the law,
Even his [a]prayer is an abomination.
10 He who leads the upright astray in an
evil way
Will [a]himself fall into his own pit,
But the [b]blameless will inherit good.
11 The rich man is [a]wise in his own
eyes,
But the poor who has understanding
[1]sees through him.
12 When the [a]righteous triumph, there is
great glory,
But [b]when the wicked rise, men [1]hide
themselves.
13 He who [a]conceals his transgressions
will not prosper,
But he who [b]confesses and forsakes
them will find compassion.
14 How blessed is the man who [a]fears
always,
But he who [b]hardens his heart will fall
into calamity.
15 *Like* a [a]roaring lion and a rushing bear
Is a [b]wicked ruler over a poor people.
16 A [a]leader who is a great oppressor
lacks understanding,
But he who hates unjust gain will
prolong *his* days.
17 A man who is [a]laden with the guilt of
human blood
Will [1]be a fugitive until death; let no
one support him.
18 He who walks blamelessly will be
delivered,
But he who is [1a]crooked will fall all at
once.
19 [a]He who tills his land will [b]have
plenty of food,
But he who follows empty *pursuits*
will have poverty in plenty.
20 A [a]faithful man will abound with
blessings,
But he who [b]makes haste to be rich
will not go unpunished.
21 To [1a]show partiality is not good,
[b]Because for a piece of bread a man
will transgress.
22 A man with an [a]evil eye [b]hastens after
wealth

3 [1]Lit *and there is no bread* [a]Matt 18:28
4 [a]Ps 49:18; Rom 1:32 [b]1 Kin 18:18; Neh 13:11, 15; Matt 3:7; 14:4; Eph 5:11
5 [a]Ps 92:6; Is 6:9; 44:18 [b]Ps 119:100; Prov 2:9; John 7:17; 1 Cor 2:15; 1 John 2:20, 27
6 [1]Lit *perverse of two ways* [a]Prov 19:1
7 [a]Prov 23:20
8 [a]Ex 22:25; Lev 25:36 [b]Job 27:17; Prov 13:22; 14:31
9 [a]Ps 66:18; 109:7; Prov 15:8; 21:27
10 [a]Ps 7:15; Prov 26:27 [b]Matt 6:33; Heb 6:12; 1 Pet 3:9
11 [1]Lit *examines him* [a]Prov 3:7; 26:5, 12
12 [1]Lit *will be searched for* [a]Prov 11:10; 29:2 [b]Prov 28:28; Eccl 10:5, 6
13 [a]Job 31:33; Ps 32:3 [b]Ps 32:5; 1 John 1:9
14 [a]Prov 23:17 [b]Ps 95:8; Rom 2:5
15 [a]Prov 19:12; 1 Pet 5:8 [b]Ex 1:14; Prov 29:2; Matt 2:16
16 [a]Eccl 10:16; Is 3:12
17 [1]Lit *flee to the pit* [a]Gen 9:6; Ex 21:14
18 [1]Lit *perverse of two ways* [a]Prov 10:27 **19** [a]Prov 12:11 [b]Prov 20:13 **20** [a]Prov 10:6; Matt 24:45; 25:21 [b]Prov 20:21; 28:22; 1 Tim 6:9 **21** [1]Lit *regard the face* [a]Prov 24:23 [b]Ezek 13:19 **22** [a]Prov 23:6 [b]Prov 21:5

28:3 *who oppresses the lowly.* See 14:31. *driving rain.* Describes the destructive power of Assyria's army in Is 28:2. The gentle rain is compared to a righteous king in Ps 72:6–7.
28:4 *law.* Either the teachings of wisdom (3:1; 7:2) or the law of Moses (Ps 119:53). *praise the wicked.* Cf. Rom 1:32. *who keep the law.* See v. 7; 29:18; cf. v. 9. *strive with them.* See Eph 5:11; cf. Rom 1:32.
28:5 *who seek the LORD.* Who fear Him (see note on 1:7). *understand all things.* They know "righteousness and justice And equity" (2:9).
28:6 *walks in his integrity.* See 2:7 and note.
28:7 *who keeps the law.* See note on v. 4. *companion of gluttons.* See notes on 23:20–21.
28:8 *interest and usury.* Prohibited in Ex 22:25; Lev 25:35–37; Deut 23:19–20; Ezek 22:12. *Gathers it for him.* See 13:22 and note. *gracious to the poor.* See 14:31; see also note on 14:21.
28:9 *law.* See note on v. 4. *his prayer is an abomination.* Like the sacrifice of the wicked in 15:8 (see note on 3:32; see also Ps 66:18; Is 1:15; 59:1–2).
28:10 *into his own pit.* See note on 26:27. *blameless.* See note on 2:7. *inherit good.* See 3:35; Heb 6:12; 1 Pet 3:9.
28:11 *rich man is wise in his own eyes.* Like the fool (26:5) or the sluggard (26:16).
28:12 *there is great glory.* See 11:10 and note. *men hide themselves.* Obadiah hid 100 prophets during the reign of Ahab (1 Kin 18:13), and Joash was hidden for six years while the wicked Athaliah ruled (2 Kin 11:2–3).
28:13 *He who conceals his transgressions will not prosper.* Note the physical and psychological pain referred to in 3:7–8; Ps 32:3. *he who confesses and forsakes them will find compassion.* Note the joy of forgiveness in Ps 32:5,10–11.
28:14 *fears always.* See note on 1:7; see also 23:17. *who hardens his heart.* Like Pharaoh (Ex 7:13), and the Israelites who tested the Lord at Horeb (Ex 17:7; cf. Ps 95:8; Rom 2:5).
28:15 *roaring lion.* Full of rage and murderous intent (cf. 19:12; Matt 2:16; 1 Pet 5:8). *rushing bear.* See 17:12 and note. *wicked ruler.* See v. 12.
28:16 *he who hates unjust gain will prolong his days.* Unlike those who love such gain (see 1:19).
28:17 *Will be a fugitive until death.* Cain was a "vagrant and a wanderer" in fear of his life (Gen 4:14). Murder was punishable by death (see Gen 9:6; Ex 21:14).
28:18 *blamelessly . . . crooked.* Contrasted also in v. 6; 19:1. *will fall all at once.* Cf. 11:5.
28:19 *follows empty pursuits.* Schemes for making easy money.
28:20 *abound with blessings.* With God's gifts and favors (see 3:13–18; 10:6; Gen 49:26; Deut 33:16). *he who makes haste to be rich will not go unpunished.* Cf. similar warnings in 20:21; 23:4 (see notes).
28:21 *To show partiality is not good.* See 18:5 and note; 24:23. *for a piece of bread a man will transgress.* Perhaps a reference to a bribe, however small (cf. Ezek 13:19).
28:22 *man with an evil eye.* See 23:6. *hastens after wealth.* A warning to him is given in v. 20 (cf. similar warnings in 20:21;

And does not know that want will
come upon him.
23 He who [a]rebukes a man will afterward
find *more* favor
Than he who [b]flatters with the
tongue.
24 He who [a]robs his father or his mother
And says, "It is not a transgression,"
Is the [b]companion of a man who
destroys.
25 An [1]arrogant man [a]stirs up strife,
But he who [b]trusts in the LORD [c]will
[2]prosper.
26 He who [a]trusts in his own heart is a
fool,
But he who walks wisely will be
delivered.
27 He who [a]gives to the poor will never
want,
But he who [1]shuts his eyes will have
many curses.
28 When the wicked rise, men hide
themselves;
But when they perish, the righteous
increase.

Warnings and Instructions

29 A man who hardens *his* neck after
[a]much reproof
Will [b]suddenly be broken [1]beyond
remedy.
2 When the [a]righteous [1]increase, the
people rejoice,
But when a wicked man rules, people
groan.
3 A man who [a]loves wisdom makes his
father glad,
But he who [b]keeps company with
harlots wastes *his* wealth.
4 The [a]king gives stability to the land by
justice,
But a man who takes bribes
overthrows it.
5 A man who [a]flatters his neighbor
Is spreading a net for his steps.
6 By transgression an evil man is
[a]ensnared,
But the righteous [b]sings and rejoices.
7 The [a]righteous [1]is concerned for the
rights of the poor,
The wicked does not understand *such*
[2]concern.
8 Scorners [a]set a city aflame,
But [b]wise men turn away anger.
9 When a wise man has a controversy
with a foolish man,
[1]The foolish man either rages or
laughs, and there is no rest.
10 Men of [a]bloodshed hate the blameless,
But the upright [1]are concerned for his
life.
11 A [a]fool [1]always loses his temper,
But a [b]wise man holds it back.
12 If a [a]ruler pays attention to falsehood,
All his ministers *become* wicked.
13 The [a]poor man and the oppressor
[1]have this in common:
The LORD gives [b]light to the eyes of
both.
14 If a [a]king judges the poor with truth,
His [b]throne will be established forever.
15 The [a]rod and reproof give wisdom,
But a child [1]who gets his own way
[b]brings shame to his mother.
16 When the wicked [1]increase,
transgression increases;
But the [a]righteous will see their fall.
17 [a]Correct your son, and he will give
you comfort;

23 [a]Prov 27:5, 6 [b]Prov 29:5
24 [a]Prov 19:26 [b]Prov 18:9
25 [1]Lit *broad soul* [2]Lit *be made fat* [a]Prov 15:18 [b]Prov 29:25; 1 Tim 6:6 [c]Prov 11:25
26 [a]Prov 3:5
27 [1]Lit *hides* [a]Prov 11:24; 19:17
29:1 [1]Lit *and there is no remedy* [a]1 Sam 2:25; 2 Chr 36:16; Prov 1:24-31 [b]Prov 6:15
2 [1]Or *become great* [a]Esth 8:15; Prov 11:10; 28:12
3 [a]Prov 10:1; 15:20; 27:11; 28:7 [b]Prov 5:10; 6:26; Luke 15:30
4 [a]2 Chr 9:8; Prov 8:15; 29:14
5 [a]Ps 5:9
6 [a]Prov 22:5; Eccl 9:12 [b]Ex 15:1
7 [1]Lit *knows the cause* [2]Lit *knowledge* [a]Job 29:16; Ps 41:1; Prov 31:8, 9
8 [a]Prov 11:11 [b]Prov 16:14
9 [1]Lit *He*
10 [1]Lit *seek his soul* [a]Gen 4:5-8; 1 John 3:12
11 [1]Lit *sends forth all his spirit* [a]Prov 12:16; 14:33 [b]Prov 19:11
12 [a]1 Kin 12:14
13 [1]Lit *meet together* [a]Prov 22:2 [b]Ezra 9:8; Ps 13:3
14 [a]Ps 72:4; Is 11:4 [b]Prov 16:12; 25:5
15 [1]Lit *left to himself* [a]Prov 13:24; 22:15 [b]Prov 10:1; 17:25
16 [1]Or *become great* [a]Ps 37:34, 36; 58:10; 91:8; 92:11; Prov 21:12
17 [a]Prov 13:24; 29:15

23:4). *want will come upon him.* Because it is the generous man who prospers (see note on 11:25).

28:23 *He who rebukes a man.* See Gal 2:14; cf. 15:31; 25:12. *who flatters with the tongue.* Cf. 16:13; 26:28; 29:5.

28:24 *who robs his father or his mother.* See note on 19:26; cf. Matt 15:4–6; Mark 7:10–12.

28:25 *stirs up strife.* See note on 6:14. *will prosper.* As does also the generous person (11:25) and the one who is diligent (13:4, "the soul of the diligent is made fat").

28:26 *who walks wisely.* Equals "who trusts in the LORD" in 29:25; cf. 3:5.

28:27 *gives to the poor.* See note on 14:21. *will never want.* Generosity is the path to blessing (see 11:24 and note; 14:21; 19:17). *shuts his eyes.* See 21:13.

28:28 *men hide themselves.* See v. 12 and note. *righteous increase.* See 11:10; 29:2.

29:1 *hardens his neck after much reproof.* Eli's sons died because of their stubbornness (see 1 Sam 2:25; cf. Deut 9:6,13). *Will suddenly be broken beyond remedy.* Identical to 6:15. Cf. the fate of the mockers in 1:22–27.

29:2 *When the righteous increase, the people rejoice.* See 11:10 and note. *when a wicked man rules, people groan.* See 28:12 and note; see also Judg 2:18. The Israelites groaned in Egypt (Ex 2:23–24).

29:3 *man who loves wisdom makes his father glad.* See 10:1 and note. *he who keeps company with harlots wastes his wealth.* See 5:10; 6:26 and notes.

29:4 *The king gives stability to the land by justice.* See 16:12 and note. *bribes.* See 17:8 and note.

29:6 *By transgression . . . ensnared.* See 1:18 and note; 22:5.

29:7 *The righteous is concerned for . . . the poor.* Like Job (Job 29:16); cf. v. 14; 19:17; 22:22.

29:8 *Scorners set a city aflame.* See notes on 6:14; 11:11; see also 26:21. *Scorners.* See 1:22 and note. *wise men turn away anger.* See James 3:17–18.

29:9 *The foolish man . . . rages.* Like an angry bear (17:12) or the tossing sea (Is 57:20–21).

29:10 *Men of bloodshed hate the blameless.* Their schemes are described in 1:11–16; cf. Ps 5:6.

29:11 *always loses his temper.* See v. 9; 14:16–17. *holds it back.* See 16:32 and note.

29:12 *All his ministers become wicked.* Cf. Is 1:23.

29:14 See note on 16:12; see also v. 4; Is 9:7.

29:15 *rod.* See note on 13:24.

29:16 *When the wicked increase.* See v. 2; 11:11; 28:12,28. *righteous will see their fall.* See 10:25 and note; 14:11; 21:12.

29:17 *Correct your son.* Teach him and train him (see 13:24 and note; 22:6).

He will also [1][b]delight your soul.
18 Where there is [a]no [1]vision, the people
[b]are unrestrained,
But [c]happy is he who keeps the law.
19 A slave will not be instructed by
words *alone;*
For though he understands, there will
be no response.
20 Do you see a man who is [a]hasty in his
words?
There is [b]more hope for a fool than for
him.
21 He who pampers his slave from
childhood
Will in the end find him to be a son.
22 An [a]angry man stirs up strife,
And a hot-tempered man abounds in
transgression.
23 A man's [a]pride will bring him low,
But a [b]humble spirit will obtain honor.
24 He who is a partner with a thief hates
his own life;
He [a]hears the oath but tells nothing.
25 The [a]fear of man [1]brings a snare,
But he who [b]trusts in the LORD will be
exalted.
26 [a]Many seek the ruler's [1]favor,
But [b]justice for man *comes* from the
LORD.
27 An [a]unjust man is abominable to the
righteous,
And he who is [b]upright in the way is
abominable to the wicked.

The Words of Agur

30 The words of Agur the son of Jakeh,
the [1]oracle.
The man declares to Ithiel, to Ithiel and
Ucal:
2 Surely I am more [a]stupid than any
man,
And I do not have the understanding
of a man.
3 Neither have I learned wisdom,
Nor do I have the [a]knowledge of the
Holy One.
4 Who has [a]ascended into heaven and
descended?
Who has gathered the [b]wind in His
fists?
Who has [c]wrapped the waters in [1]His
garment?
Who has [d]established all the ends of
the earth?
What is His [e]name or His son's name?
Surely you know!

5 Every [a]word of God is tested;
He is a [b]shield to those who take
refuge in Him.
6 [a]Do not add to His words
Or He will reprove you, and you will
be proved a liar.

7 Two things I asked of You,
Do not refuse me before I die:
8 Keep deception and [1]lies far from me,
Give me neither poverty nor riches;
Feed me with the [a]food that is my
portion,
9 That I not be [a]full and deny [b]*You* and
say, "Who is the LORD?"
Or that I not be [c]in want and steal,
And [d]profane the name of my God.

17 [1]Lit *give delight to* [b]Prov 10:1
18 [1]Or *revelation* [a]1 Sam 3:1; Ps 74:9; Amos 8:11, 12 [b]Ex 32:25 [c]Ps 1:1, 2; 106:3; 119:2; Prov 8:32; John 13:17
20 [a]James 1:19 [b]Prov 26:12
22 [a]Prov 15:18; 26:21
23 [a]Prov 11:2; 16:18; Dan 4:30, 31; Matt 23:12; James 4:6 [b]Prov 15:33; 18:12; 22:4; Is 66:2; Luke 14:11; 18:14; James 4:10
24 [a]Lev 5:1
25 [1]Lit *gives* [a]Gen 12:12; 20:2; Luke 12:4; John 12:42, 43 [b]Ps 91:1-16; Prov 18:10; 28:25
26 [1]Lit *face* [a]Prov 19:6 [b]Is 49:4; 1 Cor 4:4
27 [a]Ps 6:8; 139:21, 22; Prov 12:8 [b]Ps 69:4; Prov 29:10; Matt 10:22; 24:9; John 15:18; 17:14; 1 John 3:13
30:1 [1]Or *burden*
2 [a]Ps 49:10; 73:22; Prov 12:1
3 [a]Prov 9:10
4 [1]Lit *the* [a]Ps 68:18; John 3:13; Eph 4:8 [b]Ex 15:10; Ps 135:7 [c]Job 26:8; 38:8, 9 [d]Ps 24:2; Is 45:18 [e]Rev 19:12
5 [a]Ps 12:6; 18:30 [b]Ps 3:3; 84:11; Prov 2:7 **6** [a]Deut 4:2; 12:32; Rev 22:18 **8** [1]Lit *words of falsehood* [a]Job 23:12; Matt 6:11 **9** [a]Deut 8:12; 31:20; Neh 9:25; Hos 13:6 [b]Josh 24:27; Job 31:28 [c]Prov 6:30 [d]Ex 20:7

29:18 *vision.* A message from God given through a prophet; a prophetic vision (see 1 Sam 3:1; Is 1:1; Amos 8:11–12). *people are unrestrained.* Possibly an allusion to the sinful actions of the Israelites while Moses was on Mount Sinai (see Ex 32:25 and note). *happy is he who keeps the law.* See 28:4 and note; see also 8:32; 28:14.
29:19 *will not be instructed by words alone.* Servants, like sons (vv. 15,17), must be disciplined (see note on 22:6).
29:20 *hasty in his words.* See 10:19; 17:27–28; James 1:19. *There is more hope for a fool than for him.* Identical to 26:12.
29:21 *pampers his slave.* See v. 19.
29:22 *angry man stirs up strife.* See note on 6:14; see also 15:18.
29:23 See 15:33 and note; see also 18:12.
29:24 *He hears the oath.* He will be held responsible for failing to testify (cf. Lev 5:1).
29:25 *fear of man.* Cf. 1 Sam 15:24; Is 51:12; John 12:42–43. *he who trusts in the LORD will be exalted.* See 18:10 and note; cf. 3:5–6.
29:26 *Many seek the ruler's favor.* See 2 Sam 14:22; 16:4; Esth 4:8; 5:2; 7:3; 8:5. *justice for man comes from the LORD.* God controls a king's actions (see note on 21:1) and defends the cause of the poor and the just (cf. Job 36:6).
30:1–33 The first of two chapters that serve as an appendix to Proverbs.
30:1 *Agur the son of Jakeh.* Probably a wise man like Ethan and Heman (1 Kin 4:31). *oracle.* Usually the message of a prophet (see note on Is 13:1). If "oracle" is taken as the place name "Massa" (that is, "Jakeh of Massa"), Agur would then be associated with an Ishmaelite people (cf. Gen 25:13–14). *Ithiel . . . Ucal.* Perhaps students of Agur.
30:2 *I am more stupid than any man.* Paul described himself as "the foremost of sinners" (1 Tim 1:16).
30:3 *knowledge of the Holy One.* See note on 2:5. "Holy One" occurs elsewhere in Proverbs only in 9:10.
30:4 The use of rhetorical questions to express God's greatness as Creator occurs also in Job 38:4–11; Is 40:12. *gathered the wind.* Cf. Ps 135:7. *wrapped up the waters in His garment.* See Job 26:8; 38:8–9. *Surely you know!* God similarly challenged Job (Job 38:4).
30:5 Almost identical to Ps 18:30. *shield.* See note on 2:7. *to those who take refuge in Him.* See 14:32; 18:10.
30:6 *Do not add to His words.* Cf. Moses' warning to the Israelites in Deut 4:2.
30:7 *Two things.* The use of lists characterizes Agur's sayings (see vv. 15,18,21,24,29).
30:8 *food that is my portion.* Cf. Job 23:12 and the Lord's Prayer (Matt 6:11).
30:9 *I not be full and deny You.* Moses predicted that Israel would forget God when their food was plentiful and their herds large (Deut 8:12–17; 31:20). *Who is the LORD?* Or, Why should I serve Him (see Job 21:14–16)? *not be in want and steal.* Cf. 6:30.

10 Do not slander a slave to his master,
Or he will [a]curse you and you will be
found guilty.

11 There is a [1]kind of *man* who [a]curses
his father
And does not bless his mother.
12 There is a [1]kind who is [a]pure in his
own eyes,
Yet is not washed from his filthiness.
13 There is a [1]kind—oh how [a]lofty are
his eyes!
And his eyelids are raised *in*
arrogance.
14 There is a [1]kind of *man* whose [a]teeth
are *like* swords
And his [b]jaw teeth *like* knives,
To [c]devour the afflicted from the earth
And the needy from among men.

15 The leech has two daughters,
"Give," "Give."
There are three things that will not be
satisfied,
Four that will not say, "Enough":
16 [1a]Sheol, and the [b]barren womb,
Earth that is never satisfied with
water,
And fire that never says, "Enough."
17 The eye that [a]mocks a father
And [1b]scorns a mother,
The [c]ravens of the valley will pick it
out,
And the young [c]eagles will eat it.

18 There are three things which are too
wonderful for me,
Four which I do not understand:
19 The way of an [a]eagle in the sky,
The way of a serpent on a rock,
The way of a ship in the middle of the
sea,
And the way of a man with a maid.
20 This is the way of an [a]adulterous
woman:
She eats and wipes her mouth,
And says, "I have done no wrong."

21 Under three things the earth quakes,
And under four, it cannot bear up:
22 Under a [a]slave when he becomes
king,
And a fool when he is satisfied with
food,
23 Under an unloved woman when she
gets a husband,
And a maidservant when she
supplants her mistress.

24 Four things are small on the earth,
But they are exceedingly wise:
25 The [a]ants are not a strong people,
But they prepare their food in the
summer;
26 The [1a]shephanim are not mighty
people,
Yet they make their houses in the
rocks;
27 The locusts have no king,
Yet all of them go out in [a]ranks;
28 The lizard you may grasp with the
hands,
Yet it is in kings' palaces.

29 There are three things which are
stately in *their* march,
Even four which are stately when they
walk:
30 The lion *which* is [a]mighty among
beasts
And does not [1b]retreat before any,
31 The [1]strutting rooster, the male goat
also,
And a king *when his* army is with him.

10 [a]Eccl 7:21
11 [1]Or *generation* [a]Ex 21:17; Prov 20:20
12 [1]Or *generation* [a]Prov 16:2; Is 65:5; Luke 18:11; Titus 1:15, 16
13 [1]Or *generation* [a]Prov 6:17; Is 2:11; 5:15
14 [1]Or *generation* [a]Ps 57:4 [b]Job 29:17 [c]Ps 14:4; Amos 8:4
16 [1]I.e. The nether world [a]Prov 27:20 [b]Gen 30:1
17 [1]Lit *despises to obey* [a]Gen 9:22 [b]Prov 15:20 [c]Deut 28:26
19 [a]Deut 28:49; Jer 48:40; 49:22
20 [a]Prov 5:6
22 [a]Prov 19:10; Eccl 10:7
25 [a]Prov 6:6
26 [1]Small, shy, furry animals *(Hyrax syriacus)* found in the peninsula of the Sinai, northern Israel, and the region round the Dead Sea; KJV *coney*, orig NASB *badgers* [a]Lev 11:5; Ps 104:18
27 [a]Joel 2:7
30 [1]Lit *turn back* [a]Judg 14:18; 2 Sam 1:23 [b]Mic 5:8
31 [1]Lit *girt in the loins*

30:10 *you will be found guilty.* Since the accusation is false, the servant's curse will be effective (cf. 26:2)—so do not suppose you can take advantage of a servant's lowly position.
30:11 *curses his father.* Punishable by death (see Ex 21:17; Lev 20:9; cf. v. 17).
30:12 *who is pure in his own eyes.* Like the Pharisee (Luke 18:11; cf. Is 65:5).
30:13 *how lofty are his eyes!* See note on 6:17; see also Is 3:16.
30:14 *whose teeth are like swords . . . like knives.* The wicked are like ravenous beasts that devour the prey (see Job 29:17). *To devour the afflicted . . . the needy.* Cf. Ps 14:4; Mic 3:2–3.
30:15,18,21,29 *three . . . four.* See note on 6:16.
30:16 *Sheol.* Its appetite is never satisfied (Is 5:14; Hab 2:5). *barren womb.* In ancient Israel, a wife without children was desolate, even desperate (cf. Gen 16:2; 30:1; Ruth 1:11–13,20–21; 1 Sam 1:6,10–11; 2 Kin 4:14).
30:17 *The eye.* Haughty and disdainful (see v. 13). *mocks a father And scorns a mother.* See v. 11 and note; 15:20. *The ravens . . . will pick it out, And the young eagles.* The loss of an eye was a terrible curse (see the story of Samson in Judg 16:21). Since vultures normally devoured the dead (see Jer 16:4; Matt 24:28), the meaning may be that the body of a disgraceful son will lie unburied and exposed.
30:18–19 It is difficult to understand the four "ways" because there are no tracks that can be readily followed.
30:19 *way of an eagle.* Soaring and swooping majestically (cf. Job 39:27; Jer 48:40; 49:22). *way of a man with a maid.* Probably a reference to the mystery of courting and how it leads to consummation.
30:20 *adulterous.* See 2:16 and note. *She eats and wipes her mouth.* Making love is compared to eating food also in 9:17 (see note there; see also 7:18 and note).
30:22 *slave when he becomes king.* See 19:10 and note.
30:23 *unloved woman when she gets a husband.* Probably one of several wives, who is miserable because her husband does not love her (cf. Leah in Gen 29:31–32). *maidservant when she supplants her mistress.* Perhaps because she was able to bear a child, whereas the wife was barren (cf. Hagar and Sarah in Gen 16:1–6).
30:26 *in the rocks.* Which provide a refuge for them (see Ps 104:18).
30:27 *locusts have no king.* Cf. 6:7. *all . . . go out in ranks.* Locusts are portrayed as a mighty army in Joel 2:3–9.
30:28 *in kings' palaces.* Lizards climb stone walls easily.
30:30 *lion . . . mighty among beasts.* See 2 Sam 1:23; Mic 5:8.
30:31 *male goat.* Goats were used to lead flocks of sheep (see Jer 50:8; Dan 8:5).

32 If you have been foolish in exalting
yourself
Or if you have plotted *evil*, [a]*put your*
hand on your mouth.
33 For the [1]churning of milk produces
butter,
And pressing the nose brings forth
blood;
So the [1]churning of [a]anger produces
strife.

The Words of Lemuel

31 The words of King Lemuel, the [1]oracle
which his mother taught him:
2 What, O my son?
And what, O [a]son of my womb?
And what, O son of my [b]vows?
3 [a]Do not give your strength to women,
Or your ways to that which [b]destroys
kings.
4 It is not for [a]kings, O Lemuel,
It is not for kings to [b]drink wine,
Or for rulers to desire strong drink,
5 For they will drink and forget what is
decreed,
And [a]pervert the [1]rights of all the
[2]afflicted.
6 Give strong drink to him who is
[a]perishing,
And wine to him [1b]whose life is
bitter.
7 Let him drink and forget his poverty
And remember his trouble no more.
8 [a]Open your mouth for the mute,
For the [1]rights of all the [2]unfortunate.
9 Open your mouth, [a]judge righteously,
And [1]defend the [b]rights of the afflicted
and needy.

32 [a]Job 21:5; 40:4; Mic 7:16
33 [1]Lit *pressing* [a]Prov 10:12; 29:22
31:1 [1]Or *burden*
2 [a]Is 49:15 [b]1 Sam 1:11
3 [a]Prov 5:9 [b]Deut 17:17; 1 Kin 11:1; Neh 13:26
4 [a]Eccl 10:17 [b]Prov 20:1; Is 5:22; Hos 4:11
5 [1]Lit *judgment* [2]Lit *sons of affliction* [a]Ex 23:6; Deut 16:19; Prov 17:15
6 [1]Lit *bitter of soul* [a]Job 29:13 [b]Job 3:20; Is 38:15
8 [1]Lit *judgment* [2]Lit *sons of passing away* [a]Job 29:12-17; Ps 82
9 [1]Lit *judge the afflicted* [a]Lev 19:15; Deut 1:16 [b]Is 1:17; Jer 22:16

10 [a]Ruth 3:11; Prov 12:4; 19:14 [b]Job 28:18; Prov 8:11
13 [1]Lit *palms* [2]Or *willingly*
14 [a]Ezek 27:25
15 [1]Or *prescribed tasks* [a]Prov 20:13; Rom 12:11 [b]Luke 12:42
16 [1]Lit *the fruit of her palms*
17 [1]Lit *her loins* [a]1 Kin 18:46; 2 Kin 4:29; Job 38:3
19 [1]Lit *palms*
20 [1]Lit *spreads out her palm* [a]Deut 15:11; Job 31:16-20; Prov 22:9; Rom 12:13; Eph 4:28
21 [a]2 Sam 1:24 **22** [a]Prov 7:16 [b]Gen 41:42; Rev 19:8, 14 [c]Judg 8:26; Luke 16:19 **23** [a]Deut 16:18; Ruth 4:1, 11

Description of a Worthy Woman

10 An [a]excellent wife, who can find?
For her worth is far [b]above jewels.
11 The heart of her husband trusts in her,
And he will have no lack of gain.
12 She does him good and not evil
All the days of her life.
13 She looks for wool and flax
And works with her [1]hands [2]in
delight.
14 She is like [a]merchant ships;
She brings her food from afar.
15 She [a]rises also while it is still night
And [b]gives food to her household
And [1]portions to her maidens.
16 She considers a field and buys it;
From [1]her earnings she plants a
vineyard.
17 She [a]girds [1]herself with strength
And makes her arms strong.
18 She senses that her gain is good;
Her lamp does not go out at night.
19 She stretches out her hands to the
distaff,
And her [1]hands grasp the spindle.
20 She [1a]extends her hand to the poor,
And she stretches out her hands to the
needy.
21 She is not afraid of the snow for her
household,
For all her household are [a]clothed
with scarlet.
22 She makes [a]coverings for herself;
Her clothing is [b]fine linen and [c]purple.
23 Her husband is known [a]in the gates,

30:32 *exalting yourself.* Pride is condemned in 8:13; 11:2; 16:18. *plotted evil.* Cf. 6:14; 16:27. *put your hand on your mouth.* Stop your plotting immediately (cf. Job 21:5; 40:4).

30:33 *churning of anger produces strife.* See notes on 6:14; 15:1; see also 29:22.

31:1–9 This brief section is also of non-Israelite origin. King Lemuel is otherwise unknown.

31:1 *oracle.* See note on 30:1. *his mother.* This entire chapter emphasizes the role and significance of wise women. The queen mother was an influential figure (see 1 Kin 1:11–13; 15:13).

31:2 *son of my vows.* Hannah made a vow as she prayed for a son (1 Sam 1:11). *vows.* See 20:25 and note.

31:3 *strength to women.* A warning against a large harem and sexual immorality (see 5:9–11 and notes; 1 Kin 11:1; Neh 13:26).

31:4 *It is not for kings . . . to drink wine.* Woe to the land whose rulers are drunkards (Eccl 10:16–17; see 20:1 and note; Hos 7:5).

31:5 *pervert the rights of all the afflicted.* See 30:14 and note; see also 17:15; Is 5:23; 10:2.

31:8–9 The king represents God as the defender of the poor and needy (see 16:10; Ps 82:3; cf. Lev 19:15; Job 29:12–17; Is 1:17).

31:10–31 The epilogue: an acrostic poem (each verse begins with a successive letter of the Hebrew alphabet) praising the "excellent wife" (v. 10). It corresponds to 1:1–7 (the prologue) as it describes a "woman who fears the LORD" (v. 30; see note on 1:7). Such a wife is almost a personification of wisdom. Like wisdom, "her worth is far above jewels" (v. 10; 3:15; 8:11), and he who finds her "obtains favor from the LORD" (8:35; 18:22). See Introduction: Literary Structure.

31:10 *excellent wife.* Like Ruth (Ruth 3:11). She is "the crown of her husband" (12:4).

31:12 *She does him good.* See 18:22; 19:14.

31:13 *flax.* Its fibers were made into linen (see vv. 19,22,24; cf. Is 19:9).

31:14 *like merchant ships.* She is an enterprising person (see v. 18).

31:15 *She rises also while it is still night.* She is the opposite of the sluggard (see 6:9–10; 20:13). *portions to her maidens.* See 27:27; Luke 12:42.

31:16 *considers a field . . . plants a vineyard.* She shows good judgment—unlike the sluggard, whose vineyard is overgrown with thorns and weeds (24:30–31).

31:17 *girds herself with strength.* See 10:4 and note.

31:18 *her gain is good.* Like wisdom, "her worth is far above jewels" (v. 10; 3:15; 8:11). The profit of wisdom "is better than the profit of silver" (3:14).

31:19 *distaff . . . spindle.* Spinning thread was women's work.

31:20 *extends her hand to the poor.* See note on 14:21; see also 22:9; Job 31:16–20.

31:21 *clothed with scarlet.* Of high quality, probably made of wool (cf. 2 Sam 1:24; Rev 18:16).

31:22 *fine linen.* Associated with nobility (see note on 7:16; see also Gen 41:42). *purple.* Linked with kings (Judg 8:26; Song 3:10) or the rich (Luke 16:19; Rev 18:16).

31:23 *in the gates.* The court (see note on 1:21).

When he sits among the elders of the
land.
24 She makes [a]linen garments and sells
them,
And [1]supplies belts to the [2]tradesmen.
25 Strength and [a]dignity are her
clothing,
And she smiles at the [1]future.
26 She [a]opens her mouth in wisdom,
And the [1]teaching of kindness is on
her tongue.
27 She looks well to the ways of her
household,
And does not eat the [a]bread of
idleness.
28 Her children rise up and bless her;
Her husband *also,* and he praises her,
saying:
29 "Many daughters have done nobly,
But you excel them all."
30 Charm is deceitful and beauty is vain,
But a woman who [1a]fears the LORD,
she shall be praised.
31 Give her the [1]product of her hands,
And let her works praise her in the
gates.

24 [1]Lit *gives* [2]Lit *Canaanite* [a]Judg 14:12
25 [1]Lit *latter days* [a]1 Tim 2:9, 10
26 [1]Or *law* [a]Prov 10:31
27 [a]Prov 19:15
30 [1]Or *reverences* [a]Ps 112:1; Prov 22:4
31 [1]Lit *fruit*

31:24 *linen garments.* See Judg 14:12–13; Is 3:23. *tradesmen.* Cf. v. 18.
31:25 *Strength and dignity are her clothing.* See Is 52:1; 1 Tim 2:9–10. The opposite is to be "clothed with shame and dishonor" (Ps 35:26). *she smiles at the future.* She is free of anxiety and worry (cf. Job 39:7).
31:26 *teaching of kindness.* Given to her children and friends. She is a wise and loving counselor (see 1:8; 6:20).
31:28 *bless her.* Because of the happy environment she creates and the joy she radiates to others. See Gen 30:13; Ps 72:17; Song 6:9; Mal 3:12; cf. Ruth 4:14–15.
31:29 *done nobly.* See Is 32:8.
31:30 *Charm is deceitful.* Cf. 5:3. *beauty is vain.* Cf. Job 14:2; 1 Pet 3:3–5. *who fears the LORD.* See note on 1:7.
31:31 *product of her hands.* See 12:14 and note. *praise her.* Honor comes through "humility and the fear of the LORD" (22:4). *in the gates.* See v. 23; see also note on 1:21.

Ecclesiastes

INTRODUCTION

Author and Date

No time period or writer's name is mentioned in the book, but several passages strongly suggest that King Solomon is the author (1:1,12,16; 2:4 – 9; 7:26 – 29; 12:9; cf. 1 Kin 2:9; 3:12; 4:29 – 34; 5:12; 10:1 – 8). On the other hand, the writer's title ("Preacher," Hebrew *qoheleth;* see note on 1:1), his unique style of Hebrew and his attitude toward rulers (suggesting that of a subject rather than a monarch — see, e.g., 4:1 – 2; 5:8 – 9; 8:2 – 4; 10:20) may point to another person and a later period.

Purpose and Method

With his life largely behind him, the author takes stock of the world as he has experienced it between the horizons of birth and death — the latter a horizon beyond which man cannot see. The world is seen as being full of enigmas, the greatest of which is man himself.

From the perspective of his own understanding, the Preacher takes measure of man, examining his capabilities. He discovers that human wisdom, even that of a godly person, has limits (1:13,16 – 18; 7:24; 8:16 – 17). It cannot find out the larger purposes of God or the ultimate meaning of man's existence.

As the author looks about at the human enterprise, he sees man in mad pursuit of one thing and then another — laboring as if he could master the world, lay bare its secrets, change its fundamental structures, break through the bounds of human limitations and master his own destiny. He sees man vainly pursuing hopes and expectations that in reality are "vanity and striving after wind" (1:14; 2:11,17,26; 4:4,16; 6:9; cf. 1:17; 4:6).

But faith teaches him that God has ordered all things according to His own purposes (3:1 – 15; 5:19; 6:1 – 2; 9:1) and that man's role is to accept these, including his own limitations, as God's appointments. Man, therefore, should be patient and enjoy life as God gives it. He should know his own limitations and not vex himself with unrealistic expectations. He should be prudent in everything, living carefully before God and the king and, above all, fearing God and keeping His commandments (12:13).

Teaching

Life not centered on God is purposeless and meaningless (see notes on 1:2; 2:24–25). Without Him, nothing else can satisfy (2:25). With Him, all of life and His other good gifts are to be gratefully received (see James 1:17) and used and enjoyed to the full (2:26; 11:8). The book contains the philosophical and theological reflections of an old man (12:1 – 7), most of whose life was meaningless because he had not himself relied on God as he should have.

Outline

I. Author (1:1)
II. Theme: The vanity of man's efforts on earth apart from God (1:2)
III. Introduction: The profitlessness of working to accumulate things to achieve happiness (1:3 – 11)
IV. Discourse, Part 1: In spite of life's apparent enigmas and vanity, it is to be enjoyed as a gift from God (1:12 — 11:6)
V. Discourse, Part 2: Since old age and death will soon come, man should enjoy life in his youth, remembering that God will judge (11:7 — 12:7)
VI. Theme Repeated (12:8)
VII. Conclusion: Reverently trust in and obey God (12:9 – 14)

The Futility of All Endeavor

1 The words of the [a]Preacher, the son of
David, king in Jerusalem.
2 "[1a]Vanity of vanities," says the Preacher,
"[1]Vanity of vanities! All is [2]vanity."

3 [a]What advantage does man have in all
his work
Which he does under the sun?
4 A generation goes and a generation
comes,
But the [a]earth [1]remains forever.
5 Also, [a]the sun rises and the sun sets;
And [1]hastening to its place it rises
there *again*.
6 [1a]Blowing toward the south,
Then turning toward the north,
The wind continues [2]swirling along;
And on its circular courses the wind
returns.
7 All the rivers [1]flow into the sea,
Yet the sea is not full.
To the place where the rivers [1]flow,
There they [1]flow again.
8 All things are wearisome;
Man is not able to tell *it*.
[a]The eye is not satisfied with seeing,
Nor is the ear filled with hearing.
9 [a]That which has been is that which
will be,
And that which has been done is that
which will be done.
So there is nothing new under the sun.
10 Is there anything of which one might
say,
"See this, it is new"?
Already it has existed for ages
Which were before us.
11 There is [a]no remembrance of [1]earlier
things;
And also of the [2]later things which
will occur,
There will be for them no
remembrance
Among those who will come [2]later
still.

The Futility of Wisdom

12 I, the [a]Preacher, have been king over
Israel in Jerusalem.
13 And I [a]set my [1]mind to seek and
[b]explore by wisdom concerning all that has
been done under heaven. *It* is [2]a grievous
[c]task *which* God has given to the sons of
men to be afflicted with.
14 I have seen all the works which have
been done under the sun, and behold, all is
[1a]vanity and striving after wind.
15 What is [a]crooked cannot be straightened and what is lacking cannot be counted.
16 I [1]said to myself, "Behold, I have magnified and increased [a]wisdom more than all
who were over Jerusalem before me; and my
[2]mind has observed [3]a wealth of wisdom
and knowledge."
17 And I [a]set my [1]mind to know wisdom
and to [b]know madness and folly; I realized
that this also is [c]striving after wind.

1:1 [a]Eccl 1:12; 7:27; 12:8-10
2 [1]Or *Futility of futilities* [2]Or *futile* [a]Ps 39:5, 6; 62:9; 144:4; Eccl 12:8; Rom 8:20
3 [a]Eccl 2:11; 3:9; 5:16
4 [1]Lit *stands* [a]Ps 104:5; 119:90
5 [1]Lit *panting* [a]Ps 19:6
6 [1]Lit *Going* [2]Lit *turning* [a]Eccl 11:5; John 3:8
7 [1]Lit *go*
8 [a]Prov 27:20; Eccl 4:8
9 [a]Eccl 1:10; 2:12; 3:15; 6:10
11 [1]Lit *first* or *former* [2]Lit *latter* or *after* [a]Eccl 2:16; 9:5
12 [a]Eccl 1:1; 7:27; 12:8-10
13 [1]Lit *heart* [2]Lit *an evil* [a]Eccl 1:17 [b]Eccl 3:10, 11; 7:25; 8:17 [c]Eccl 2:23, 26; 3:10; 4:8
14 [1]Or *futility* [a]Eccl 2:11, 17; 4:4; 6:9
15 [a]Eccl 7:13
16 [1]Lit *spoke with my heart, saying* [2]Lit *heart* [3]Lit *an abundance* [a]1 Kin 3:12; 4:30; 10:23; Eccl 2:9
17 [1]Lit *heart* [a]Eccl 1:13; 7:25 [b]Eccl 2:12; 7:25 [c]Eccl 1:14; 2:11, 17; 4:4, 6, 16; 6:9

1:1 *Preacher.* The preacher of wisdom (12:9). The Hebrew term for "Preacher" (*qoheleth*) is related to that for "assembly" (possibly meaning "leader of the assembly"; also in vv. 2,12; Ex 16:3; Num 16:3). Perhaps the Preacher, whose work is described in 12:9–10, also held an office in the assembly. The Septuagint (the Greek translation of the OT) word for "Preacher" is *ekklesiastes*, from which most English titles of the book are taken, and from which such English words as "ecclesiastical" are derived. *son of David.* Suggests Solomon, though his name occurs nowhere in the book. The Hebrew word for "son" can refer to a descendant (even many generations removed)—or even to someone who follows in the footsteps of another (see Gen 4:21; see also Introduction: Author and Date).

1:2 Briefly states the author's theme (see 12:8). *Vanity.* This key term is translated "vanity" or "vanities" about 22 times in Ecclesiastes and only a few other places in the OT (see 2 Kin 17:15; Ps 62;9; Is 49:4). The Hebrew for it originally meant "breath" (see Ps 39:5,11; 62:9; 144:4). The basic thrust of Ecclesiastes is that all of life is meaningless, useless, hollow, futile and vain if it is not rightly related to God. Only when based on God and His word is life worthwhile. *All.* See v. 8; whatever man undertakes apart from God.

1:3–11 In this section the author elaborates his theme that human effort appears to be without benefit or purpose.

1:3 Jesus expands on this question in Mark 8:36–38. *under the sun.* Another key expression (used 29 times), which refers to this present world and the limits of what it offers. "Under heaven," though it occurs less frequently (v. 13; 2:3; 3:1), is used synonymously.

1:4 *earth remains forever.* By contrast, man's life is fleeting.

1:8 *All things.* Everything mentioned in vv. 4–7 (see note on v. 2).

1:10 *new.* Many things seem to be new simply because the past is easily and quickly forgotten. The old ways reappear in new guises.

1:12–18 Having set forth his theme that all human striving seems futile (see especially vv. 3,11, which frame the section), the Preacher shows that both human endeavor (vv. 12–15; cf. 2:1–11) and the pursuit of human wisdom (vv. 16–18; cf. 2:12–17) are futile and meaningless.

1:12 *I.* The author shifts to the first person, returning to the third person only in the conclusion (12:9–14).

1:13 *God.* The only Hebrew word the writer uses for God is *Elohim* (used almost 30 times), which emphasizes His absolute sovereignty. He does not use the covenant name, *Yahweh* (translated "LORD"; see note on Ex 3:15).

1:14 *striving after wind.* A graphic illustration of futility and meaninglessness (see Introduction: Purpose and Method). These words are used nine times in the first half of the discourse (here; v. 17; 2:11,17,26; 4:4,6,16; 6:9; see also 5:16).

1:15 See 7:13 and note. Because of the unalterableness of events, human effort is meaningless and hopeless. We should therefore learn to happily accept things the way they are and to accept our divinely appointed lot in life, as the Preacher later counsels.

1:16 *all who were over Jerusalem before me.* See 2:7,9. This does not necessarily exclude Solomon as the Preacher. The reference could include kings prior to David, such as Melchizedek (Gen 14:18), Adoni-zedek (Josh 10:1) and Abdi-khepa (mentioned in the Amarna letters from Egypt; see chart, p. xix).

18 Because [a]in much wisdom there is
much grief, and increasing knowledge *results*
in increasing pain.

The Futility of Pleasure and Possessions

2 I said [1]to myself, "Come now, I will test
you with [a]pleasure. So [2]enjoy yourself."
And behold, it too was futility.
2 [a]I said of laughter, "It is madness," and
of pleasure, "What does it accomplish?"
3 I explored with my [1]mind *how* to [a]stim-
ulate my body with wine while my [1]mind
was guiding *me* wisely, and how to take hold
of [b]folly, until I could see [c]what good there is
for the sons of men [2]to do under heaven the
few [3]years of their lives.
4 I enlarged my works: I [a]built houses for
myself, I planted [b]vineyards for myself;
5 I made [a]gardens and [b]parks for myself
and I planted in them all kinds of fruit trees;
6 I made [a]ponds of water for myself from
which to irrigate a forest of growing trees.
7 I bought male and female slaves and I
had [1a]homeborn slaves. Also I possessed
flocks and [b]herds larger than all who preceded me in Jerusalem.
8 Also, I collected for myself silver and
[a]gold and the treasure of kings and provinces. I provided for myself [b]male and female
singers and the pleasures of men—many
concubines.
9 Then I became [a]great and increased
more than all who preceded me in Jerusalem. My wisdom also stood by me.
10 [a]All that my eyes desired I did not
refuse them. I did not withhold my heart
from any pleasure, for my heart was pleased
because of all my labor and this was my
[b]reward for all my labor.
11 Thus I considered all my activities
which my hands had done and the labor
which I had [1]exerted, and behold all was
[2a]vanity and striving after wind and there
was [b]no profit under the sun.

Wisdom Excels Folly

12 So I turned to [a]consider wisdom, madness and folly; for what *will* the man *do* who
will come after the king *except* [b]what has
already been done?
13 And I saw that [a]wisdom excels folly as
light excels darkness.
14 The wise man's eyes are in his head,
but the [a]fool walks in darkness. And yet I
know that [b]one fate befalls them both.
15 Then I said [1]to myself, "[a]As is the fate
of the fool, it will also befall me. [b]Why then
have I been extremely wise?" So [2]I said to
myself, "This too is vanity."
16 For there is [a]no [1]lasting remembrance
of the wise man *as* with the fool, inasmuch
as *in* the coming days all will be forgotten.
And [b]how the wise man and the fool alike
die!
17 So I [a]hated life, for the work which had
been done under the sun was [1]grievous to
me; because everything is futility and striving after wind.

The Futility of Labor

18 Thus I hated [a]all the fruit of my labor
for which I had labored under the sun, for I
must [b]leave it to the man who will come
after me.
19 And who knows whether he will be a
wise man or [a]a fool? Yet he will have [1]con-
trol over all the fruit of my labor for which I
have labored by acting wisely under the sun.
This too is [b]vanity.
20 Therefore I [1]completely despaired of all
the fruit of my labor for which I had labored
under the sun.
21 When there is a man who has labored
with wisdom, knowledge and [a]skill, then he
[b]gives his [1]legacy to one who has not
labored with them. This too is vanity and a
great evil.
22 For what does a man get in [a]all his
labor and in [1]his striving with which he
labors under the sun?
23 Because all his days his task is painful
and [a]grievous; even at night his [1]mind [b]does
not rest. This too is vanity.

18 [a]Eccl 2:23; 12:12
2:1 [1]Lit *in my heart* [2]Lit *consider with goodness* [a]Eccl 7:4; 8:15
2 [a]Prov 14:13; Eccl 7:3, 6
3 [1]Lit *heart* [2]Lit *which they do* [3]Lit *days* [a]Judg 9:13; Ps 104:15; Eccl 10:19 [b]Eccl 7:25 [c]Eccl 2:24; 3:12, 13; 5:18; 6:12; 8:15; 12:13
4 [a]1 Kin 7:1-12 [b]Song 8:11
5 [a]Song 4:16; 5:1 [b]Neh 2:8
6 [a]Neh 2:14; 3:15, 16
7 [1]Lit *sons of the house* [a]Gen 14:14; 15:3 [b]1 Kin 4:23
8 [a]1 Kin 9:28; 10:10, 14, 21 [b]2 Sam 19:35
9 [a]1 Chr 29:25; Eccl 1:16
10 [a]Eccl 6:2 [b]Eccl 3:22; 5:18; 9:9
11 [1]Lit *labored to do* [2]Or *futility,* and so throughout the ch [a]Eccl 1:14; 2:22, 23 [b]Eccl 1:3; 3:9; 5:16
12 [a]Eccl 1:17
12 [b]Eccl 1:9, 10; 3:15
13 [a]Eccl 7:11, 12, 19; 9:18; 10:10
14 [a]1 John 2:11 [b]Ps 49:10; Eccl 3:19; 6:6; 7:2; 9:2, 3
15 [1]Lit *in my heart* [2]Lit *I spoke in my heart* [a]Eccl 2:16 [b]Eccl 6:8, 11
16 [1]Lit *forever* [a]Eccl 1:11; 9:5 [b]Eccl 2:14
17 [1]Lit *evil* [a]Eccl 4:2, 3
18 [a]Eccl 1:3; 2:11 [b]Ps 39:6; 49:10
19 [1]Lit *dominion* [a]1 Kin 12:13 [b]1 Tim 6:10

20 [1]Lit *turned aside my heart to despair* **21** [1]Lit *share* [a]Eccl 4:4 [b]Eccl 2:18 **22** [1]Lit *the striving of his heart* [a]Eccl 1:3; 2:11 **23** [1]Lit *heart* [a]Job 5:7; 14:1; Eccl 1:18; 5:17 [b]Ps 127:2

1:18 Humanistic wisdom—wisdom without God—leads to grief and sorrow.
2:1–11 The Preacher now shows that mere pleasure cannot give meaning or satisfaction (see 1:12–15; see also note on 1:12–18).
2:1 *I said to myself.* See v. 15; 1:16.
2:3 *my mind was guiding me wisely.* From first to last (v. 9) the author used wisdom to discover the good (v. 1) and the worthwhile (v. 3).
2:4–9 See 1 Kin 4–11, which tells of Solomon's splendor and of his wives.
2:8 *concubines.* The Hebrew for this word occurs only here in Scripture, and its meaning is uncertain. The meaning seems to be indicated in an early Egyptian letter that uses a similar Canaanite term for concubines. It fits the situation of Solomon, who had 300 concubines in addition to 700 wives (1 Kin 11:3).
2:10 *labor . . . labor.* A key thought in Ecclesiastes is the vanity (v. 11), apart from God, of toil, labor, work—words that occur more than 25 times.
2:12–17 The Preacher returns to the folly of trying to find satisfaction in merely human wisdom (see 1:16–18; see also note on 1:12–18).
2:13 *wisdom excels folly.* Even secular wisdom is better than folly, but in the end it is of no value, since "one fate befalls them both" (i.e., befalls both the wise believer and the foolish unbeliever, v. 14; see Ps 49:10).
2:14 *eyes.* Understanding.
2:16 People tend to soon forget even the greatest leaders and heroes (see 1:11).
2:18 *leave it to the man who will come after me.* See v. 21; Ps 39:6; Luke 12:20.
2:19 *who knows . . . ?* For a more searching "Who knows . . . ?" for secular man see 3:21.

24 There is [a]nothing better for a man *than*
to eat and drink and [1]tell himself that his
labor is good. This also I have seen that it is
[b]from the hand of God.
25 For who can eat and who can have
enjoyment without [1]Him?
26 For to a person who is good in His sight
[a]He has given wisdom and knowledge and
joy, while to the sinner He has given the task
of gathering and collecting so that he may
[b]give to one who is good in God's sight. This
too is [c]vanity and striving after wind.

A Time for Everything

3 There is an appointed time for everything.
And there is a [a]time for every [1]event
under heaven—
2 A time to give birth and a [a]time to die;
A time to plant and a time to uproot
what is planted.
3 A [a]time to kill and a time to heal;
A time to tear down and a time to
build up.
4 A time to [a]weep and a time to [b]laugh;
A time to mourn and a time to [c]dance.
5 A time to throw stones and a time to
gather stones;
A time to embrace and a time to shun
embracing.
6 A time to search and a time to give up
as lost;
A time to keep and a time to throw
away.
7 A time to tear apart and a time to sew
together;
A time to [a]be silent and a time to
speak.
8 A time to love and a time to [a]hate;
A time for war and a time for peace.
9 [a]What profit is there to the worker
from that in which he toils?
10 I have seen the [a]task which God has
given the sons of men with which to occupy
themselves.

God Set Eternity in the Heart of Man

11 He has [a]made everything [1]appropriate
in its time. He has also set eternity in their
heart, [2]yet so that man [b]will not find out the
work which God has done from the beginning even to the end.
12 I know that there is [a]nothing better for
them than to rejoice and to do good in one's
lifetime;
13 moreover, that every man who eats and
drinks sees good in all his labor—it is the
[a]gift of God.
14 I know that everything God does will
remain forever; there is nothing to add to it
and there is nothing to take from it, for God
has *so* worked that men should [1a]fear Him.
15 That [a]which is has been already and
that which will be has already been, for God
seeks what has passed by.
16 Furthermore, I have seen under the sun
that in the place of justice there is [a]wicked-
ness and in the place of righteousness there
is wickedness.
17 I said [1]to myself, "[a]God will judge both
the righteous man and the wicked man," for
a [b]time for every [2]matter and for every deed
is there.
18 I said [1]to myself concerning the sons of
men, "God has surely tested them in order
for them to see that they are but [a]beasts."
19 [a]For the fate of the sons of men and the
fate of beasts [1]is the same. As one dies so
dies the other; indeed, they all have the same
breath and there is no advantage for man
over beast, for all is [2]vanity.
20 All go to the same place. All came from
the [a]dust and all return to the dust.
21 Who knows that the [a]breath of man
ascends upward and the breath of the beast
descends downward to the earth?

24 [1]Lit *cause his soul to see good in his labor* [a]Eccl 2:3; 3:12, 13, 22; 5:18; 6:12; 8:15; 9:7; Is 56:12; Luke 12:19; 1 Cor 15:32; 1 Tim 6:17 [b]Eccl 3:13 **25** [1]So Gr; Heb *me* **26** [a]Job 32:8; Prov 2:6 [b]Job 27:16, 17; Prov 13:22 [c]Eccl 1:14 **3:1** [1]Lit *delight* [a]Eccl 3:17; 8:6 **2** [a]Job 14:5; Heb 9:27 **3** [a]Gen 9:6; 1 Sam 2:6; Hos 6:1, 2 **4** [a]Rom 12:15 [b]Ps 126:2 [c]Ex 15:20 **7** [a]Amos 5:13 **8** [a]Ps 101:3; Prov 13:5 **9** [a]Eccl 1:3; 2:11; 5:16 **10** [a]Eccl 1:13; 2:26

11 [1]Lit *beautiful* [2]Or *without which man* [a]Gen 1:31 [b]Job 5:9; Eccl 7:23; 8:17; Rom 11:33 **12** [a]Eccl 2:24 **13** [a]Eccl 2:24; 5:19 **14** [1]Or *be in awe before Him* [a]Eccl 5:7; 7:18; 8:12, 13; 12:13 **15** [a]Eccl 1:9; 6:10 **16** [a]Eccl 4:1; 5:8; 8:9 **17** [1]Lit *in my heart* [2]Or *delight* [a]Gen 18:25; Ps 96:13; 98:9; Eccl 11:9; Matt 16:27; Rom 2:6-10; 2 Thess 1:6-9 [b]Eccl 3:1; 8:6 **18** [1]Lit *in my heart* [a]Ps 49:12, 20; 73:22 **19** [1]Lit *and they have one fate* [2]Or *futility* [a]Ps 49:12; Eccl 9:12 **20** [a]Gen 3:19; Ps 103:14; Eccl 12:7 **21** [a]Eccl 12:7

2:24–25 The heart of Ecclesiastes, a theme repeated in 3:12–13,22; 5:18–20; 8:15; 9:7 and climaxed in 12:13. Only in God does life have meaning and true pleasure. Without Him nothing satisfies, but with Him we find satisfaction and enjoyment. True pleasure comes only when we acknowledge and revere God (12:13).
2:26 *while to the sinner.* For exceptions to this general principle see 8:14; Ps 73:1–12.
3:1–22 The Preacher shows that we are subject to times and changes over which we have little or no control, and contrasts this state with God's eternity and sovereignty. God sovereignly predetermines all of life's activities (e.g., the 14 opposites of vv. 2–8).
3:1 Cf. 8:6. *under heaven.* See note on 1:3.
3:2 *A time.* Divinely appointed (see Ps 31:15; Prov 16:1–9).
3:11 The chapter summarized: God's beautiful but tantalizing world is too big for us, yet its satisfactions are too small. Since we were made for eternity, the things of time cannot fully and permanently satisfy.
3:12–13 A pointer to the book's conclusion. God's people find meaning in life when they cheerfully accept it from the hand of God.
3:14 *forever.* In this word the "eternity" of v. 11 becomes clearer. *fear.* Sums up the message of the book (cf. 12:13).
3:15 See 1:9.
3:17 *judge.* God's true judgments are the answer to human cynicism about man's injustices. "What has passed by" (v. 15) is not meaningless (as people dismiss it as being, 1:11), and God will override the perverse judgments (v. 16) of men (see 12:14).
3:18 *but beasts.* Man "under the sun" (man on his own) is as mortal as any animal; but, unlike them, he must be made to see this condition and, through his dim awareness of eternity (v. 11), be distressed.
3:19 *same breath.* See Ps 104:27–30.
3:20 *to the same place.* Not heaven or hell but man's observable destination, which is a return to dust, just like the animals. Death is the great leveler of all living things (see Gen 3:19; Ps 103:14).
3:21 *Who knows . . . ?* See 2:19 and note; cf. 12:7. Man on his own cannot know; he can only guess. The answer, revealed at first in glimpses (e.g., Ps 16:9–11; 49:15; 73:23–26; Is 26:19; Dan

22 I have seen that [a]nothing is better than
that man should be happy in his activities,
for that is his lot. For who will bring him to
see [b]what will occur after him?

The Evils of Oppression

4 Then I looked again at all the acts of
[a]oppression which were being done
under the sun. And behold *I saw* the tears of
the oppressed and *that* they had [b]no one to
comfort *them;* and on the side of their
oppressors was power, but they had no one
to comfort *them.*
2 So [a]I congratulated the dead who are
already dead more than the living who are
still living.
3 But [a]better *off* than both of them is the
one who has never existed, who has never
seen the evil activity that is done under the
sun.
4 I have seen that every labor and every
[a]skill which is done is *the result of* rivalry
between a man and his neighbor. This too is
[1b]vanity and striving after wind.
5 The fool [a]folds his hands and [b]con-
sumes his own flesh.
6 One hand full of rest is [a]better than two
fists full of labor and striving after wind.
7 Then I looked again at vanity under the
sun.
8 There was a certain man without a
[1]dependent, having neither a son nor a
brother, yet there was no end to all his labor.
Indeed, [a]his eyes were not satisfied with
riches *and he never asked,* "And [b]for whom
am I laboring and depriving myself of pleasure?" This too is vanity and it is a [c]grievous
task.
9 Two are better than one because they
have a good return for their labor.
10 For if [1]either of them falls, the one will
lift up his companion. But woe to the one
who falls when there is not [2]another to lift
him up.
11 Furthermore, if two lie down together
they [1]keep warm, but [a]how can one be
warm *alone?*
12 And if [1]one can overpower him who is
alone, two can resist him. A cord of three
strands is not quickly torn apart.
13 A [a]poor yet wise lad is better than an
old and foolish king who no longer knows
how to receive [1]instruction.
14 For he has come [a]out of prison to
become king, even though he was born poor
in his kingdom.
15 I have seen all the living under the sun
throng to the side of the second lad who
[1]replaces him.
16 There is no end to all the people, to all
who were before them, and even the ones
who will come later will not be happy with
him, for this too is [a]vanity and striving after
wind.

Your Attitude Toward God

5 [1a]Guard your steps as you go to the house
of God and draw near to listen rather than
to offer the [b]sacrifice of fools; for they do not
know they are doing evil.
2 [1]Do not be [a]hasty [2]in word or [3]impul-
sive in thought to bring up a matter in the
presence of God. For God is in heaven and
you are on the earth; therefore let your
[b]words be few.
3 For the dream comes through much
[1]effort and the voice of a [a]fool through many
words.
4 When you [a]make a vow to God, do not
be late in paying it; for *He takes* no delight in
fools. [b]Pay what you vow!
5 It is [a]better that you should not vow
than that you should vow and not pay.
6 Do not let your [1]speech cause [2]you to
sin and do not say in the presence of the messenger *of God* that it was a [a]mistake. Why
should God be angry on account of your
voice and destroy the work of your hands?

22 [a]Eccl 2:24 [b]Eccl 2:18; 6:12; 8:7; 10:14
4:1 [a]Job 35:9; Ps 12:5; Eccl 3:16; 5:8; Is 5:7 [b]Jer 16:7; Lam 1:9
2 [a]Job 3:11-26; Eccl 2:17; 7:1
3 [a]Job 3:11-22; Eccl 6:3; Luke 23:29
4 [1]Or *futility,* and so throughout the ch [a]Eccl 2:21 [b]Eccl 1:14
5 [a]Prov 6:10; 24:33 [b]Is 9:20
6 [a]Prov 15:16, 17; 16:8
8 [1]Lit *second* [a]Prov 27:20; Eccl 1:8; 5:10 [b]Eccl 2:21 [c]Eccl 1:13
10 [1]Lit *they fall* [2]Lit *a second*
11 [1]Lit *have warmth* [a]1 Kin 1:1-4
12 [1]Lit *he*
13 [1]Or *warning* [a]Eccl 7:19; 9:15
14 [a]Gen 41:14, 41-43
15 [1]Lit *stands in his stead*
16 [a]Eccl 1:14
5:1 [1]Ch 4:17 in Heb [a]Ex 3:5; 30:18-20; Is 1:12 [b]1 Sam 15:22; Prov 15:8; 21:27
2 [1]Ch 5:1 in Heb [2]Lit *with your mouth* [3]Lit *hurry your heart* [a]Prov 20:25 [b]Prov 10:19; Matt 6:7
3 [1]Lit *task* [a]Job 11:2; Prov 15:2; Eccl 10:14
4 [a]Num 30:2; Ps 50:14; 76:11 [b]Ps 66:13, 14
5 [a]Prov 20:25; Acts 5:4
6 [1]Lit *mouth* [2]Lit *your body* [a]Lev 4:2, 22; Num 15:25

12:2–3), was brought fully "to light through the gospel" (2 Tim 1:10).

3:22 *nothing is better.* As an end in itself, work too is meaningless (see 4:4; 9:9). Only receiving it as a gift from God (v. 13) gives it enduring worth (v. 14).

4:1 *oppression.* A theme already touched on (3:16) and another ingredient in the human tragedy. To find life meaningless is sad enough, but to taste its cruelty is bitter beyond words.

4:2 *more than the living.* See Job 3; Jer 20:14–18. For faith that sees a bigger picture see Rom 8:35–39.

4:4–6 Neither hard work (motivated by envy) nor idleness brings happiness, meaning or fulfillment.

4:4 *every labor and every skill.* This too is meaningless unless done with God's blessing (see 3:13; cf. the selfless success of Joseph, Gen 39).

4:5 The ruin of the idle person is vividly pictured in 10:18; Prov 6:6–11; 24:30–34.

4:6 *rest.* See Prov 30:7–9. Paul says the last word on this subject (Phil 4:11–13).

4:7–12 The loner, too, has a meaningless and difficult life if he is an unbeliever.

4:12 *two . . . three.* A climactic construction.

4:13–16 Advancement without God is another example of the vanity of secularism.

5:1–7 The theme of this section is the vanity of superficial religion, as reflected in making rash vows.

5:1 *Guard your steps.* Think about what you ought to say and do. *listen.* Obey. 1 Sam 15:22 uses the same Hebrew verb and makes the same contrast between real and superficial worship. *sacrifice.* Probably connected with the vow of vv. 4–6.

5:2 *hasty in word.* As in a rash vow.

5:3 A proverb. In the context it suggests that in the midst of cares a person dreams of bliss (as a starving man dreams of a banquet), and in anticipation may offer rash vows ("many words") to God (see v. 7).

5:4 *vow.* See Deut 23:21–23; 1 Sam 1:11, 24–28. *no delight in fools.* In Scripture the fool is not one who cannot learn, but one who refuses to learn due to moral deficiency (see Prov 1:7,20–27).

5:6 *messenger.* See Mal 2:7.

7 For in many dreams and in many words there is [1]emptiness. Rather, [2][a]fear God.

8 If you see [a]oppression of the poor and [b]denial of justice and righteousness in the province, do not be [c]shocked at the [1]sight; for one [2]official watches over another [2]official, and there are higher [3]officials over them.

9 After all, a king who cultivates the field is an advantage to the land.

The Folly of Riches

10 [a]He who loves money will not be satisfied with money, nor he who loves abundance *with its* income. This too is [1]vanity.

11 [a]When good things increase, those who consume them increase. So what is the advantage to their owners except to [1]look on?

12 The sleep of the working man is [a]pleasant, whether he eats little or much; but the [1]full stomach of the rich man does not allow him to sleep.

13 There is a grievous evil *which* I have seen under the sun: [a]riches being [1]hoarded by their owner to his hurt.

14 When those riches were lost through [1]a bad investment and he had fathered a son, then there was nothing [2]to support him.

15 [a]As he had come naked from his mother's womb, so will he return as he came. He will [b]take nothing from the fruit of his labor that he can carry in his hand.

16 This also is a grievous evil—exactly as a man [1]is born, thus will he [2]die. So [a]what is the advantage to him who [b]toils for the wind?

17 Throughout his life [a]*he* also eats in darkness with [b]great vexation, sickness and anger.

18 Here is what I have seen to be [a]good and [1]fitting: to eat, to drink and [2]enjoy oneself in all one's labor in which he toils under the sun *during* the few [3]years of his life which God has given him; for this is his [4][b]reward.

19 Furthermore, as for every man to whom [a]God has given riches and wealth, He has also [b]empowered him to eat from them and to receive his [1]reward and rejoice in his labor; this is the [c]gift of God.

20 For he will not often [1]consider the [2]years of his life, because [a]God keeps [3]him occupied with the gladness of his heart.

The Futility of Life

6 There is an [a]evil which I have seen under the sun and it is prevalent [1]among men—

2 a man to whom God has [a]given riches and wealth and honor so that his soul [b]lacks nothing of all that he desires; yet God has not empowered him to eat from them, for a foreigner [1]enjoys them. This is [2]vanity and a severe affliction.

3 If a man fathers a hundred *children* and lives many years, however many [1]they be, but his soul is not satisfied with good things and he does not even have a *proper* [a]burial, *then* I say, "Better [b]the miscarriage than he,

4 for it comes in futility and goes into obscurity; and its name is covered in obscurity.

5 "It never sees the sun and it never knows *anything;* [1]it is better off than he.

6 "Even if the *other* man lives a thousand years twice and does not [1]enjoy good things—[a]do not all go to one place?"

7 [a]All a man's labor is for his mouth and yet the [1]appetite is not [2]satisfied.

8 For [a]what advantage does the wise man have over the fool? What *advantage* does the poor man have, knowing *how* to walk before the living?

9 What the eyes [a]see is better than what the soul [1]desires. This too is [b]futility and a striving after wind.

10 Whatever [a]exists has already been named, and it is known what man is; for he [b]cannot dispute with him who is stronger than he is.

11 For there are many words which increase futility. What *then* is the advantage to a man?

12 For who knows what is good for a man during *his* lifetime, *during* the few [1]years of his futile life? He will [2]spend them like a shadow. For who can tell a man [a]what will be after him under the sun?

7 [1]Lit *vanity* [2]Or *revere* [a]Eccl 3:14; 7:18; 8:12, 13; 12:13
8 [1]Lit *delight* [2]Lit *high one* [3]Lit *ones* [a]Eccl 4:1 [b]Ezek 18:18 [c]1 Pet 4:12
10 [1]Or *futility* [a]Eccl 1:8; 2:10, 11; 4:8
11 [1]Lit *see with their eyes* [a]Eccl 2:9
12 [1]Lit *satiety* [a]Prov 3:24
13 [1]Lit *guarded* [a]Eccl 6:2
14 [1]Lit *an evil task* [2]Lit *in his hand*
15 [a]Job 1:21 [b]Ps 49:17; 1 Tim 6:7
16 [1]Lit *comes* [2]Lit *go* [a]Eccl 1:3; 2:11; 3:9 [b]Prov 11:29
17 [a]Ps 127:2 [b]Eccl 2:23
18 [1]Lit *beautiful* [2]Lit *see good* [3]Or *days* [4]Or *share* [a]Eccl 2:24 [b]Eccl 2:10
19 [1]Or *share* [a]2 Chr 1:12; Eccl 6:2 [b]Eccl 6:2 [c]Eccl 3:13
20 [1]Lit *remember* [2]Or *days* [3]So with Gr [a]Ex 23:25
6:1 [1]Lit *upon* [a]Eccl 5:13
2 [1]Lit *eats from them* [2]Or *futility* [a]1 Kin 3:13 [b]Ps 17:14; 73:7; Eccl 2:10
3 [1]Lit *the days of his years* [a]Is 14:20; Jer 8:2; 22:19 [b]Job 3:16; Eccl 4:3
5 [1]Lit *more rest has this one than that*
6 [1]Lit *see* [a]Eccl 2:14
7 [1]Lit *soul* [2]Lit *filled* [a]Prov 16:26
8 [a]Eccl 2:15
9 [1]Lit *goes after* [a]Eccl 11:9 [b]Eccl 1:14
10 [a]Eccl 1:9; 3:15 [b]Job 9:32; 40:2; Prov 21:30; Is 45:9
12 [1]Lit *days* [2]Lit *do* [a]Eccl 3:22

5:8 *do not be shocked.* For other frank appraisals of human society see 4:1–3. This teacher, like Jesus, who "knew what was in man" (John 2:25), had no illusions or utopian schemes.
5:10 Greater wealth does not bring satisfaction (see 1 Tim 6:9–10).
5:11–12 Greater wealth brings greater anxiety.
5:13 *hurt.* Including worry about his possessions.
5:15 *He will take nothing.* See Luke 12:14–21.
5:18–20 See note on 2:24–25.
6:2 *enjoys.* Comparing v. 2 with 5:19 demonstrates that the ability to enjoy God's blessings is a bonus—a gift of God, not a right or guarantee (see also vv.3,6). God calls the person who forgets this truth a fool (Luke 12:20).
6:3 *does not even have a proper burial.* Dies unlamented or dishonored, like King Jehoiakim (Jer 22:18–19). *miscarriage.* For the secularist, life is a pointless journey to extinction, to which miscarriage is the quickest and easiest route (cf. Job 3:16; Ps 58:8).
6:6 *to one place.* Still talking in terms of what we can observe (that all men die), not of what lies beyond death (see v. 12; 3:21).
6:7–12 In confronting complacency, the Preacher gives several causes for concern: the short-lived (v. 7), debatable (v. 8) and elusive (v. 9) rewards of life; the limits of our creativity, power and wisdom (vv. 10–11); and the unreliability of merely human values and predictions (v. 12).
6:10 *named.* Predetermined by God. *known.* Foreknown by God. *him who is stronger than he is.* Especially if the "stronger" one is God.
6:12 *like a shadow.* See 1 Chr 29:15.

Wisdom and Folly Contrasted

7 A [a]good name is better than a good ointment,
And the [b]day of *one's* death is better than the day of one's birth.
2 It is better to go to a house of mourning
Than to go to a house of feasting,
Because [1]that is the [a]end of every man,
And the living [2b]takes *it* to [3]heart.
3 [a]Sorrow is better than laughter,
For [b]when a face is sad a heart may be happy.
4 The [1]mind of the wise is in the house of mourning,
While the [1]mind of fools is in the house of pleasure.
5 It is better to [a]listen to the rebuke of a wise man
Than for one to listen to the song of fools.
6 For as the [1]crackling of [a]thorn bushes under a pot,
So is the [b]laughter of the fool;
And this too is futility.
7 For [a]oppression makes a wise man mad,
And a [b]bribe [1]corrupts the heart.
8 The [a]end of a matter is better than its beginning;
[b]Patience of spirit is better than haughtiness of spirit.
9 Do not be [1a]eager in your heart to be angry,
For anger resides in the bosom of fools.
10 Do not say, "Why is it that the former days were better than these?"
For it is not from wisdom that you ask about this.
11 Wisdom along with an inheritance is good
And an [a]advantage to those who see the sun.
12 For [a]wisdom is [1]protection *just as* money is [1]protection,
But the advantage of knowledge is that [b]wisdom preserves the lives of its possessors.

7:1 [a]Prov 22:1 [b]Eccl 4:2; 7:8 **2** [1]I.e. death [2]Lit *gives* [3]Lit *his heart* [a]Eccl 2:14, 16; 3:19, 20; 6:6; 9:2, 3 [b]Ps 90:12 **3** [a]Eccl 2:2 [b]2 Cor 7:10 **4** [1]Lit *heart* **5** [a]Ps 141:5; Prov 6:23; 13:18; 15:31, 32; 25:12; Eccl 9:17 **6** [1]Lit *voice* [a]Ps 58:9; 118:12 [b]Eccl 2:2 **7** [1]Lit *destroys* [a]Eccl 4:1; 5:8 [b]Ex 23:8; Deut 16:19; Prov 17:8, 23 **8** [a]Eccl 7:1 [b]Prov 14:29; 16:32; Gal 5:22; Eph 4:2 **9** [1]Lit *hasty in your spirit* [a]Prov 14:17; James 1:19 **11** [a]Prov 8:10, 11; Eccl 2:13 **12** [1]Lit *in a shadow* [a]Eccl 7:19; 9:18 [b]Prov 3:18; 8:35

13 [a]Eccl 3:11; 8:17 [b]Eccl 1:15 **14** [a]Deut 26:11; Eccl 3:22; 9:7; 11:9 [b]Deut 8:5; Job 2:10 [c]Eccl 3:22 **15** [1]Lit *days* [a]Eccl 6:12; 9:9 [b]Eccl 8:14 [c]Eccl 8:12, 13 **16** [a]Prov 25:16; Phil 3:6 [b]Rom 12:3 **17** [a]Job 22:16; Ps 55:23; Prov 10:27 **18** [1]Lit *rest your hand* [2]Lit *all* [a]Eccl 3:14; 5:7; 8:12, 13; 12:13 **19** [a]Eccl 7:12; 9:13-18 **20** [a]1 Kin 8:46; 2 Chr 6:36; Ps 143:2; Prov 20:9; Rom 3:23 **21** [1]Lit *give your heart to* [a]Prov 30:10 **22** [1]Lit *your heart knows also* **23** [a]Eccl 3:11; 8:17

13 Consider the [a]work of God,
For who is [b]able to straighten what He has bent?
14 [a]In the day of prosperity be happy,
But [b]in the day of adversity consider—
God has made the one as well as the other
So that man will [c]not discover anything *that will be* after him.
15 I have seen everything during my
[1a]lifetime of futility; there is [b]a righteous
man who perishes in his righteousness and
there is [c]a wicked man who prolongs *his life*
in his wickedness.
16 Do not be excessively [a]righteous and
do not [b]be overly wise. Why should you ruin
yourself?
17 Do not be excessively wicked and do
not be a fool. Why should you [a]die before
your time?
18 It is good that you grasp one thing and
also not [1]let go of the other; for the one who
[a]fears God comes forth with [2]both of them.
19 [a]Wisdom strengthens a wise man more
than ten rulers who are in a city.
20 Indeed, [a]there is not a righteous man
on earth who *continually* does good and
who never sins.
21 Also, do not [1]take seriously all words
which are spoken, so that you will not hear
your servant [a]cursing you.
22 For [1]you also have realized that you
likewise have many times cursed others.
23 I tested all this with wisdom, *and* I
said, "I will be wise," [a]but it was far from
me.
24 What has been is remote and [a]exceed-
ingly [1]mysterious. [b]Who can discover it?
25 I [1a]directed my [2]mind to know, to
investigate and to seek wisdom and an
explanation, and to know the evil of folly
and the foolishness of madness.
26 And I discovered more [a]bitter than
death the woman whose heart is [b]snares and
nets, whose hands are chains. [c]One who is
pleasing to God will escape from her, but
[d]the sinner will be captured by her.

24 [1]Lit *deep* [a]Rom 11:33 [b]Job 11:7; 37:23; Eccl 8:17 **25** [1]Lit *turned about* [2]Lit *heart* [a]Eccl 1:15, 17; 10:13 **26** [a]Prov 5:4 [b]Prov 7:23 [c]Prov 6:23, 24 [d]Prov 22:14

7:1 *day of one's death is better.* Omit "one's." The Christian has ample reason to say this (2 Cor 5:1–10; Phil 1:21–23). But the Preacher's point is valid, as explained in vv. 2–6, namely, that happy times generally teach us less than hard times.
7:7 *bribe.* See Matt 28:11–15; Luke 22:4–6.
7:9 *anger.* See, e.g., Prov 16:32; 17:14; 1 Cor 13:4–5.
7:12 *preserves the lives.* The Hebrew for this expression can also mean "gives life" or "renews life" (see Prov 3:13–18; 13:14).
7:13 *who is able to straighten . . . ?* Not fatalism, but a reminder of who is God. Man cannot change what God determines (see note on 1:15).
7:14 *God has made the one* [bad times] *as well as the other* [good times]. Cf. Rom 8:28–29.
7:15 *righteous man who perishes.* Righteousness is no sure protection against hard times or an early death.
7:16 *not . . . excessively righteous . . . overly wise.* If true righteousness and wisdom do not necessarily prevent ruin, then extreme, legalistic righteousness and wisdom will surely not help.
7:17 *not . . . excessively wicked.* Extreme wickedness is even more foolhardy.
7:18 *one thing . . . the other.* The God-fearing person will avoid both extremes (legalism and libertinism) and lead a balanced—truly righteous and wise—life.
7:20 *not a righteous man on earth.* A sober Biblical truth (see Rom 3:10–20).
7:24 See Job 28:12–28; 1 Cor 2:9–16.
7:26 See Prov 7:6–27.

27 "Behold, I have discovered this," says
the Preacher, "*adding* one thing to another to
find an explanation,
28 which [1]I am still seeking but have not
found. I have found one man among a thousand, but I have not found a [a]woman among
all these.
29 "Behold, I have found only this, that
[a]God made men upright, but they have
sought out many devices."

Obey Rulers

8 Who is like the wise man and who knows
the interpretation of a matter? A man's
wisdom [a]illumines [1]him and causes his
[b]stern face to [2]beam.
2 I say, "Keep the [1]command of the king
because of the [a]oath [2]before God.
3 "Do not be in a hurry [1a]to leave him. Do
not join in an evil matter, for he will do
whatever he pleases."
4 Since the word of the king is authoritative, [a]who will say to him, "What are you
doing?"
5 He who [a]keeps a *royal* command
[b]experiences no [1]trouble, for a wise heart
knows the proper time and procedure.
6 For [a]there is a proper time and procedure for every delight, though a man's trouble is heavy upon him.
7 If no one [a]knows what will happen,
who can tell him when it will happen?
8 [a]No man has authority to restrain the
wind with the wind, or authority over the
day of death; and there is no discharge in the
time of war, and [b]evil will not deliver [1]those
who practice it.
9 All this I have seen and applied my
[1]mind to every deed that has been done
under the sun wherein a man has exercised
[a]authority over *another* man to his hurt.
10 So then, I have seen the wicked buried,
those who used to go in and out from the
holy place, and they are [a]*soon* forgotten in
the city where they did thus. This too is futility.
11 Because the [a]sentence against an evil
deed is not executed quickly, therefore [b]the
hearts of the sons of men among them are
given fully to do evil.
12 Although a sinner does evil a hundred
times and may [a]lengthen his *life,* still I know
that it will be [b]well for those who fear God,
who fear [1]Him openly.
13 But it will [a]not be well for the evil man
and he will not lengthen his days like a
[b]shadow, because he does not fear God.
14 There is futility which is done on the
earth, that is, there are [a]righteous men to
whom it [1]happens according to the deeds of
the wicked. On the other hand, there are
[b]evil men to whom it [1]happens according to
the deeds of the righteous. I say that this too
is futility.
15 So I commended pleasure, for there is
nothing good for [a]a man under the sun
except to eat and to drink and to be merry,
and this will stand by him in his [1]toils
throughout the days of his life which God has
given him under the sun.
16 When I [a]gave my heart to know wisdom and to see the task which has been
done on the earth (even though one should
[1b]never sleep day or night),
17 and I saw every work of God, *I concluded* that [a]man cannot discover the work
which has been done under the sun. Even
though man should seek laboriously, he will
not discover; and [b]though the wise man
should say, "I know," he cannot discover.

Men Are in the Hand of God

9 For I have taken all this to my heart and
explain [1]it that righteous men, wise men,
and their deeds are [a]in the hand of God.
[b]Man does not know whether *it will be* [c]love
or hatred; anything [2]awaits him.
2 [a]It is the same for all. There is [b]one fate
for the righteous and for the wicked; for the
good, for the clean and for the unclean; for
the man who offers a sacrifice and for the
one who does not sacrifice. As the good man
is, so is the sinner; as the swearer is, so is the
one who [1]is afraid to swear.

28 [1]Lit *my soul still seeks* [a]1 Kin 11:3
29 [a]Gen 1:27
8:1 [1]Lit *his face* [2]Or *change* [a]Ex 34:29, 30 [b]Deut 28:50
2 [1]Lit *mouth* [2]Lit *of* [a]Ex 22:11; 2 Sam 21:7; Ezek 17:18
3 [1]Lit *to go out from his presence* [a]Eccl 10:4
4 [a]Job 9:12; Dan 4:35
5 [1]Lit *evil thing* [a]Eccl 12:13 [b]Prov 12:21
6 [a]Eccl 3:1, 17
7 [a]Eccl 3:22; 6:12; 7:14; 9:12
8 [1]Lit *its possessors* [a]Ps 49:7 [b]Eccl 8:13
9 [1]Lit *heart* [a]Eccl 4:1; 5:8; 7:7
10 [a]Eccl 1:11; 2:16; 9:5, 15
11 [a]Ex 34:6; Ps 86:15; Rom 2:4; 2 Pet 3:9
11 [b]Eccl 9:3
12 [1]Lit *before Him* [a]Eccl 7:15 [b]Deut 4:40; 12:25; Ps 37:11; Prov 1:33; Is 3:10
13 [a]Eccl 8:8; Is 3:11 [b]Job 14:2; Eccl 6:12
14 [1]Lit *strikes* [a]Ps 73:14; Eccl 7:15 [b]Job 21:7; Ps 73:3, 12; Jer 12:1; Mal 3:15
15 [1]Lit *labor* [a]Eccl 2:24; 3:12, 13; 5:18; 9:7
16 [1]Lit *see no sleep in his eyes* [a]Eccl 1:13, 14 [b]Eccl 2:23
17 [a]Eccl 3:11 [b]Ps 73:16; Eccl 7:23; Rom 11:33
9:1 [1]Lit *all this* [2]Lit *is before them* [a]Deut 33:3; Job 12:10; Ps 119:109 [b]Eccl 10:14 [c]Eccl 9:6
2 [1]Lit *fears an oath* [a]Job 9:22; Eccl 9:11 [b]Eccl 2:14; 3:19; 6:6; 7:2

7:27 *Preacher.* See note on 1:1. *adding one thing to another to find an explanation.* This inductive method can never be complete, nor can we reliably interpret all that we manage to observe (3:11b). Human wisdom and understanding must always yield to revealed truth.

7:29 *God made men upright, but.* See Gen 3:1–6; Rom 5:12.

8:2 *command of the king.* Both principle (v. 2) and prudence (vv. 3–6) set limits on our freedom. *the oath.* Of loyalty to the king (as seen, e.g., in 1 Chr 29:24).

8:4 *who will say . . . , "What are you doing?"* Cf. Is 45:9; Rom 9:20.

8:6 *a man's trouble.* One should put the king's command above his own misery.

8:7–8 *no one knows . . . . No man has authority.* See Ps 31:15; 2Cor 5:1–10; James 4:13–16.

8:10 *the wicked buried.* In this context it implies undeserved respect (see note on 6:3; cf. Job 21:28–33; Luke 16:22).

8:11 Delayed punishment tends to induce more wrongdoing.

8:12 *I know.* Here the Preacher speaks from mature faith, not as one "still seeking" but not finding (7:28). For similar declarations see 3:17; 11:9; 12:14.

8:14 Job 21–24 enlarges on this; Ps 73 draws the sting of it; and John 5:28–29 gives the final explanation.

8:15 *eat . . . drink . . . be merry.* Spoken gratefully (see 5:19; 9:7; Deut 8). For such words spoken arrogantly see Luke 12:19–20; 1 Cor 15:32.

8:17 *man cannot discover.* Deut 29:29 sums up what we are allowed and not allowed to know.

9:1 *whether . . . love or hatred.* The future is under God's control, and no one knows whether that future will be good or bad.

9:2 *the same for all.* Not only the wise and foolish (2:14), but also the good and the bad are seen leveled, in the sense noted at 3:20. For the Preacher's conviction (beyond mere observation) that God ultimately will see justice done see note on 8:12.

3 This is an evil in all that is done under
the sun, that there is [a]one fate for all men.
Furthermore, [b]the hearts of the sons of men
are full of evil and [c]insanity is in their hearts
throughout their lives. Afterwards they *go* to
the dead.
4 For whoever is joined with all the living, there is hope; surely a live dog is better
than a dead lion.
5 For the living know they will die; but
the dead [a]do not know anything, nor have
they any longer a reward, for their [b]memory
is forgotten.
6 Indeed their love, their hate and their
zeal have already perished, and they will no
longer have a [a]share in all that is done under
the sun.
7 Go *then,* [a]eat your bread in happiness
and drink your wine with a cheerful heart;
for God has already approved your works.
8 Let your [a]clothes be white all the time,
and let not [b]oil be lacking on your head.
9 Enjoy life with the woman whom you
love all the days of your [1a]fleeting life which
He has given to you under the sun[2]; for this
is your [b]reward in life and in your toil in
which you have labored under the sun.

Whatever Your Hand Finds to Do

10 Whatever your hand finds to do, [a]do *it*
with *all* your might; for there is no [b]activity
or planning or knowledge or wisdom in
[c]Sheol where you are going.
11 I again saw under the sun that the
[a]race is not to the swift and the [b]battle is not
to the warriors, and neither is bread to the
wise nor [c]wealth to the discerning nor favor
to men of ability; for time and [d]chance overtake them all.
12 Moreover, man does not [a]know his
time: like fish caught in a treacherous net
and [b]birds trapped in a snare, so the sons of
men are [c]ensnared at an evil time when it
[d]suddenly falls on them.
13 Also this I came to see as wisdom
under the sun, and [1]it impressed me.
14 There [a]was a small city with few men
in it and a great king came to it, surrounded
it and constructed large siegeworks against
it.

3 [a]Eccl 9:2; Jer 17:10 [b]Eccl 8:11 [c]Eccl 1:17
5 [a]Job 14:21 [b]Ps 88:12; Eccl 1:11; 2:16; 8:10; Is 26:14
6 [a]Eccl 2:10; 3:22
7 [a]Eccl 2:24; 8:15
8 [a]Rev 3:4 [b]Ps 23:5
9 [1]Lit *life of vanity* [2]Heb adds *all the days of your vanity* [a]Eccl 6:12; 7:15 [b]Eccl 2:10
10 [a]Eccl 11:6; Rom 12:11; Col 3:23 [b]Eccl 9:5 [c]Gen 37:35; Job 21:13; Is 38:10
11 [a]Amos 2:14, 15 [b]2 Chr 20:15; Ps 76:5; Zech 4:6 [c]Deut 8:17, 18 [d]1 Sam 6:9
12 [a]Eccl 8:7 [b]Prov 7:23 [c]Prov 29:6; Is 24:18; Hos 9:8 [d]Luke 21:34, 35
13 [1]Lit *great it was to me*
14 [a]2 Sam 20:16-22
15 [1]Or *might have delivered* [a]Eccl 4:13 [b]2 Sam 20:22 [c]Eccl 2:16; 8:10
16 [a]Prov 21:22; Eccl 7:12, 19
17 [a]Eccl 7:5; 10:12
18 [a]Eccl 9:16 [b]Josh 7:1-26; 2 Kin 21:2-17
10:1 [a]Ex 30:25
2 [a]Matt 6:33; Col 3:1
3 [1]Lit *heart* [2]Lit *says* [a]Prov 13:16; 18:2
4 [1]Lit *spirit* [a]Eccl 8:3 [b]1 Sam 25:24-33; Prov 25:15
6 [a]Esth 3:1, 5f; Prov 28:12; 29:2
7 [a]Prov 19:10 [b]Esth 6:8-10
8 [a]Ps 7:15; Prov 26:27 [b]Amos 5:19
10 [1]Lit *iron* [2]Lit *strengthen*
11 [1]Lit *without enchantment* [a]Ps 58:4, 5; Jer 8:17

15 But there was found in it a [a]poor wise
man and he [1]delivered the city [b]by his wisdom. Yet [c]no one remembered that poor
man.
16 So I said, "[a]Wisdom is better than
strength." But the wisdom of the poor man is
despised and his words are not heeded.
17 The [a]words of the wise heard in quietness are *better* than the shouting of a ruler
among fools.
18 [a]Wisdom is better than weapons of
war, but [b]one sinner destroys much good.

A Little Foolishness

10 Dead flies make a [a]perfumer's oil stink,
so a little foolishness is weightier than
wisdom *and* honor.
2 A wise man's heart *directs him* toward
the right, but the foolish [a]man's heart *directs*
him toward the left.
3 Even when the fool walks along the
road, his [1]sense is lacking and he [2a]demon-
strates to everyone *that* he is a fool.
4 If the ruler's [1]temper rises against you,
[a]do not abandon your position, because
[b]composure allays great offenses.
5 There is an evil I have seen under the
sun, like an error which goes forth from the
ruler—
6 [a]folly is set in many exalted places
while rich men sit in humble places.
7 I have seen [a]slaves *riding* [b]on horses
and princes walking like slaves on the land.
8 [a]He who digs a pit may fall into it, and
a [b]serpent may bite him who breaks through
a wall.
9 He who quarries stones may be hurt by
them, and he who splits logs may be endangered by them.
10 If the [1]axe is dull and he does not
sharpen *its* edge, then he must [2]exert more
strength. Wisdom has the advantage of giving success.
11 If the serpent bites [1a]before being
charmed, there is no profit for the charmer.
12 [a]Words from the mouth of a wise man
are gracious, while the lips of a [b]fool consume him;

12 [a]Prov 10:32; 22:11; Luke 4:22 [b]Prov 10:14; 18:7; Eccl 4:5

9:3 *evil . . . evil.* The apparently common destiny (both the righteous and the wicked die) encourages some people to sin.
9:5 *nor . . . any longer a reward.* The dead have lost all opportunity in this life for enjoyment and reward from labor (see v. 6).
9:7–9 The Babylonian *Epic of Gilgamesh* contains a section (10.3.6–14) remarkably similar to this passage, illustrating the international flavor of ancient wisdom literature (see chart, p. xix).
9:7 See note on 8:15.
9:10 Cf. Col 3:23.
9:11 *time and chance.* Success is uncertain—more evidence that man does not ultimately control events.
9:12 *time.* Of disaster. *men are ensnared.* Success is unpredictable, because man is not wise enough to know when misfortune may overtake him.
9:15 *Yet no one remembered.* Further warning against placing too high hopes on one's wisdom. Its reputation fades, its good is soon undone (v. 18b), and it has no answer to death (2:15–16).
10:1 *a little foolishness is weightier.* 2 Kin 20:12–19 presents a striking example.
10:2 *toward the right . . . toward the left.* These can stand for the greater and the lesser good (cf. Gen 48:13–20); or perhaps here, as in some later Jewish writings, for good and evil.
10:5 *error . . . from the ruler.* For the Preacher's observations on human regimes see vv. 4,6–7,16–17,20; 3:16; 4:1–3,13–16; 5:8–9; 8:2–6,10–11; 9:17.
10:12 *Words.* A favorite topic in wisdom literature (see, e.g., Prov 15).

13 the beginning of [1]his talking is folly
and the end of [2]it is wicked [a]madness.
14 Yet the [a]fool multiplies words. No man
knows what will happen, and who can tell
him [b]what will come after him?
15 The toil of [1]a fool *so* wearies him that
he does not *even* know how to go to a city.
16 Woe to you, O land, whose [a]king is a
lad and whose princes [1]feast in the morning.
17 Blessed are you, O land, whose king is
of nobility and whose princes eat at the
appropriate time—for strength and not for
[a]drunkenness.
18 Through [a]indolence the rafters sag, and
through slackness the house leaks.
19 *Men* prepare a meal for enjoyment, and
[a]wine makes life merry, and [b]money [1]is the
answer to everything.
20 Furthermore, [a]in your bedchamber do
not [b]curse a king, and in your sleeping
rooms do not curse a rich man, for a bird of
the heavens will carry the sound and the
winged creature will make the matter
known.

Cast Your Bread on the Waters

11 [a]Cast your bread on the surface of the
waters, for you [a]will find it [1]after many
days.
2 [a]Divide your portion to seven, or even
to eight, for you do not know what [b]misfor-
tune may occur on the earth.
3 If the clouds are full, they pour out rain
upon the earth; and whether a tree falls
toward the south or toward the north, wherever the tree falls, there it [1]lies.
4 He who watches the wind will not sow
and he who looks at the clouds will not reap.
5 Just as you do not [a]know [1]the path of
the wind and [b]how bones *are formed* in the
womb of the [2]pregnant woman, so you do
not [c]know the activity of God who makes all
things.
6 Sow your seed [a]in the morning and do
not [1]be idle in the evening, for you do not
know whether [2]morning or evening sowing
will succeed, or whether both of them alike
will be good.
7 The light is pleasant, and *it is* good for
the eyes to [a]see the sun.
8 Indeed, if a man should live many
years, let him [a]rejoice in them all, and let
him remember the [b]days of darkness, for
they will be many. Everything that is to come
will be futility.
9 Rejoice, young man, during your childhood, and let your heart be pleasant during
the days of young manhood. And follow the
[1]impulses of your heart and the [2a]desires of
your eyes. Yet know that [b]God will bring you
to judgment for all these things.
10 So, remove grief and anger from your
heart and put away [1a]pain from your body,
because childhood and the prime of life are
fleeting.

Remember God in Your Youth

12 [a]Remember also your Creator in the
days of your youth, before the [b]evil
days come and the years draw near when
you will say, "I have no delight in them";
2 before the [a]sun and the light, the moon
and the stars are darkened, and clouds
return after the rain;
3 in the day that the watchmen of the
house tremble, and mighty men [a]stoop, the
grinding ones stand idle because they are
few, and [b]those who look through [1]windows
grow dim;
4 and the doors on the street are shut as
the [a]sound of the grinding mill is low, and
one will arise at the sound of the bird, and
all the [b]daughters of song will [1]sing softly.

13 [1]Lit *the words of his mouth* [2]Lit *his mouth* [a]Eccl 7:25
14 [a]Prov 15:2; Eccl 5:3 [b]Eccl 3:22; 6:12; 7:14; 8:7
15 [1]Lit *fools*
16 [1]Lit *eat* [a]Is 3:4, 12
17 [a]Prov 31:4; Is 5:11
18 [a]Prov 24:30-34
19 [1]Lit *answers all* [a]Judg 9:13; Ps 104:15; Eccl 2:3 [b]Eccl 7:12
20 [a]2 Kin 6:12; Luke 12:3 [b]Ex 22:28; Acts 23:5
11:1 [1]Lit *in, within* [a]Deut 15:10; Prov 19:17; Matt 10:42; Gal 6:9; Heb 6:10
2 [a]Ps 112:9; Matt 5:42; Luke 6:30; 1 Tim 6:18, 19 [b]Eccl 11:8; 12:1
3 [1]Lit *is*
5 [1]Or with many mss *how the spirit* enters *the bones in the womb* [2]Lit *full* [a]John 3:8 [b]Ps 139:13-16 [c]Eccl 1:13; 3:10, 11; 8:17
6 [1]Lit *let down your hand* [2]Lit *this or that* [a]Eccl 9:10
7 [a]Eccl 6:5; 7:11
8 [a]Eccl 9:7 [b]Eccl 12:1
9 [1]Lit *ways* [2]Lit *sights* [a]Num 15:39; Job 31:7; Eccl 2:10 [b]Eccl 3:17; 12:14; Rom 14:10
10 [1]Lit *evil* [a]2 Cor 7:1; 2 Tim 2:22
12:1 [a]Deut 8:18; Neh 4:14; Ps 63:6; 119:55 [b]Eccl 11:8
2 [a]Is 5:30; 13:10; Ezek 32:7, 8; Joel 3:15; Matt 24:29
3 [1]Or *holes* [a]Ps 35:14; 38:6 [b]Gen 27:1; 48:10; 1 Sam 3:2
4 [1]Lit *be brought low* [a]Jer 25:10; Rev 18:22 [b]2 Sam 19:35

10:15 *does not even know how to go to a city.* Since in Scripture a fool is one who refuses God's teaching (see note on 5:4), this caustic saying (probably proverbial) refers to more than mere stupidity.

10:16 *whose king is a lad.* A small-minded upstart, not a "poor yet wise lad" as in 4:13. See 2 Kin 15:8–25; Hos 7:3–7, which portray some of the short-lived usurpers and vicious courtiers who hastened the downfall of Israel.

10:18 *indolence . . . slackness.* See note on 4:5.

10:19 *money is the answer to everything.* Can be read at various levels—as a wry comment on human values, as sober advice to earn a good living rather than have a good time (see the first two lines) or as stating the great versatility of money (cf. Luke 16:9).

11:1 *Cast your bread on the . . . waters.* Be adventurous, like those who accept the risks and reap the benefits of seaborne trade. Do not always play it safe (see Prov 11:24).

11:2 *Divide your portion to seven.* Be generous while you have plenty; unforeseen disasters may make you dependent on the generosity of others.

11:3–6 *clouds . . . tree . . . wind . . . seed.* Do not toy with maybes and might-have-beens. Start where you can, and recognize how limited your role (or knowledge) is.

11:5 *wind.* See NASB marg.; cf. John 3:8 ("wind" and "spirit" translate the same word in the original in both verses).

11:7–10 Live life to the fullest.

11:8,10 *futility . . . fleeting.* Warns against letting the wonderful gifts mentioned in vv. 7–10 dazzle and distract us. Verse 9 sets us on the true course.

11:9 *judgment.* See 12:14 and note. The prospect of divine praise or blame makes every detail of life significant rather than meaningless. To know this gives direction to our heart and discrimination to our eyes. The stage is set for ch. 12.

12:2–5 A graphic description of man's progressive deterioration; an allegory of aging.

12:3 *watchmen of the house.* This and the other metaphors may refer to parts of the body (hands, legs, etc.). But the imagery should not be pressed to the extent that it destroys the poetry, which moves freely between figures such as darkness, storm, a house in decline and a deserted well, and such literal descriptions as in v. 5a.

5 Furthermore, [1]men are afraid of a high place and of terrors on the road; the almond tree blossoms, the grasshopper drags himself along, and the caperberry is ineffective. For man goes to his eternal [a]home while [b]mourners go about in the street.

6 *Remember Him* before the silver cord is [1]broken and the [a]golden bowl is crushed, the pitcher by the well is shattered and the wheel at the cistern is crushed;

7 then the [a]dust will return to the earth as it was, and the [1][b]spirit will return to [c]God who gave it.

8 "[a]Vanity of vanities," says the Preacher, "all is vanity!"

Purpose of the Preacher

9 In addition to being a wise man, the Preacher also taught the people knowledge; and he pondered, searched out and arranged [a]many proverbs.

10 The Preacher sought to find [a]delightful words and to write [b]words of truth correctly.

11 The [a]words of wise men are like [b]goads, and masters of *these* collections are like [1]well-driven [c]nails; they are given by one Shepherd.

12 But beyond this, my son, be warned: the [1]writing of [a]many books is endless, and excessive [b]devotion *to books* is wearying to the body.

13 The conclusion, when all has been heard, *is:* [a]fear God and [b]keep His commandments, because this *applies to* [c]every person.

14 For [a]God will bring every act to judgment, everything which is hidden, whether it is good or evil.

5 [1]Lit *they* [a]Job 17:13; 30:23 [b]Gen 50:10; Jer 9:17
6 [1]So with Gr; Heb *removed* [a]Zech 4:2, 3
7 [1]Or *breath* [a]Gen 3:19; Job 34:15; Ps 104:29; Eccl 3:20 [b]Job 34:14; Eccl 3:21; Luke 23:46; Acts 7:59 [c]Num 16:22; 27:16; Is 57:16; Zech 12:1
8 [a]Eccl 1:2
9 [a]1 Kin 4:32
10 [a]Prov 10:32 [b]Prov 22:20, 21
11 [1]Lit *planted* [a]Prov 1:6; 22:17; Eccl 7:5; 10:12 [b]Acts 2:37 [c]Ezra 9:8; Is 22:23
12 [1]Lit *making* [a]1 Kin 4:32 [b]Eccl 1:18
13 [a]Eccl 3:14; 5:7; 7:18; 8:12 [b]Deut 4:2; Eccl 8:5 [c]Deut 10:12; Mic 6:8
14 [a]Eccl 3:17; 11:9; Matt 10:26; Rom 2:16; 1 Cor 4:5

12:5 *almond tree.* Its pale blossom possibly suggests the white hair of age. *grasshopper.* Normally agile, its slow movements on a cold morning (cf. Nah 3:17) recall the stiffness of old age. *eternal home.* In context, probably points simply to the grave, not beyond it (cf. Job 10:21; 17:13).

12:6 *silver cord . . . golden bowl.* A hanging lamp suspended by a silver chain. If only one link snaps, this light and beauty will perish, suggesting how fragile life is.

12:8 *Vanity.* Such is life "under the sun" (on earth, apart from God), ending in brokenness. But with a relationship to our Creator already demanded (v. 1), and with the fact of His judgment affirmed (11:9), vanity is not the last word. *Preacher.* See note on 1:1.

12:9 *pondered, searched.* The rigorous process on man's side, with no pains spared in seeking truth and comprehension.

12:11 *given by one Shepherd.* The other side of the matter, recognizing that Scripture is in a class of its own, as v. 12 insists.

12:13–14 The chief end of man.

12:13 *fear God.* Loving reverence is the foundation of wisdom (Ps 111:10; Prov 1:7; 9:10), as well as its content (Job 28:28) and its goal and conclusion. *this applies to every person.* To "fear God" is our fulfillment, our all—a far cry from "vanity."

12:14 *every act to judgment.* Glimpses of this truth are given at intervals in the book: 3:17; 8:12–13; 11:9 and note; see Matt 12:36; 1 Cor 3:12–15; 2 Cor 5:9–10; Heb 4:12–13. *everything which is hidden.* See Rom 2:16.

Song of Solomon

INTRODUCTION

Title

The title in the Hebrew text is "Solomon's Song of Songs," meaning a song by, for, or about Solomon. The phrase "Song of Songs" means the greatest of songs (cf. Deut 10:17, "God of gods and the Lord of lords"; 1 Tim 6:15, "King of kings").

Author and Date

Verse 1 appears to ascribe authorship to Solomon (see note on 1:1; but see also Title above). Solomon is referred to seven times (1:1,5; 3:7,9,11; 8:11–12), and several verses speak of the "king" (1:4,12; 7:5), but whether he was the author remains an open question.

To date the Song in the tenth century B.C. during Solomon's reign is not impossible. In fact, mention of Tirzah and Jerusalem in one breath (6:4) has been used to prove a date prior to King Omri (885–874 B.C.; see 1 Kin 16:23–24), though the reason for Tirzah's mention is not clear. On the other hand, many have appealed to the language of the Song as proof of a much later date, but on present evidence the linguistic data are ambiguous.

Consistency of language, style, tone, perspective and recurring refrains seems to argue for a single author. However, many who have doubted that the Song came from one pen, or even from one time or place, explain this consistency by ascribing all the Song's parts to a single literary tradition, since Near Eastern traditions were very careful to maintain stylistic uniformity.

Interpretation

To find the key for unlocking the Song, interpreters have looked to prophetic, wisdom and apocalyptic passages of Scripture, as well as to ancient Egyptian and Babylonian love songs, traditional Semitic wedding songs and songs related to ancient Mesopotamian fertility cults. The closest parallels appear to be those found in Proverbs (see Prov 5:15–20; 6:24–29; 7:6–23). The description of love in 8:6–7 (cf. the descriptions of wisdom found in Prov 1—9 and Job 28) seems to confirm that the Song belongs to Biblical wisdom literature and that it is wisdom's description of an amorous relationship. The Bible speaks of both wisdom and love as gifts of God, to be received with gratitude and celebration.

This understanding of the Song contrasts with the long-held view that the Song is an allegory of the love relationship between God and Israel, or between Christ and the church, or between Christ and the soul (the NT nowhere quotes from or even alludes to the Song). It is also distinct from more modern interpretations of the Song, such as that which sees it as a poetic drama celebrating the triumph of a maiden's pure, spontaneous love for her rustic shepherd lover over the courtly blandishments of Solomon, who sought to win her for his royal harem. Rather, it views the Song as a linked chain of lyrics depicting love in all its spontaneity, beauty, power and exclusiveness—experienced in its varied moments of separation and intimacy, anguish and ecstasy, tension and contentment. The Song shares with the love poetry of many cultures its extensive use of highly sensuous and suggestive imagery drawn from nature.

Theme and Theology

In ancient Israel everything human came to expression in words: reverence, gratitude, anger, sorrow, suffering, trust, friendship, commitment, loyalty, hope, wisdom, moral outrage, repentance. In the Song, it is love that finds words—inspired words that disclose its exquisite charm and beauty as one of God's choicest gifts. The voice of love in the Song, like that of wisdom in Prov 8:1—9:12, is a woman's voice, suggesting that love and wisdom draw men powerfully with the subtlety and mystery of a woman's allurements.

This feminine voice speaks profoundly of love. She portrays its beauty and delights. She claims its exclusiveness ("My beloved is mine, and I am his," 2:16) and insists on the necessity of its pure spontaneity ("Do not arouse or awaken my love until she pleases," 2:7; see NASB marg.). She also proclaims its overwhelming power — it rivals that of the fearsome enemy, death; it burns with the intensity of a blazing fire; it is unquenchable even by the ocean depths (8:6 – 7a). She affirms its preciousness: All a man's possessions cannot purchase it, nor (alternatively) should they be exchanged for it (8:7b). She hints, without saying so explicitly (see 8:6), that it is a gift of the Lord to man.

God intends that such love — grossly distorted and abused by both ancient and modern people — be a normal part of marital life in His good creation (see Gen 1:26 – 31; 2:24).

Literary Features

No one who reads the Song with care can question the artistry of the poet. The subtle delicacy with which he evokes intense sensuous awareness while avoiding crude titillation is one of the chief marks of his achievement. This he accomplishes largely by indirection, by analogy and by bringing to the foreground the sensuous in the world of nature (or in food, drink, cosmetics and jewelry). To liken a lover's enjoyment of his beloved to one who "pastures his flock among the lilies" (2:16), or her breasts to "two fawns, twins of a gazelle which feed among the lilies" (4:5), or the beloved herself to a garden filled with choice fruits inviting the lover to feast (4:12 – 16) — these combine exquisite artistry and fine sensitivity.

Whether the Song has the unity of a single dramatic line linking all the subunits into a continuing story is a matter of ongoing debate among interpreters. There do appear to be connected scenes in the love relationship (see Outline).

Virtually all agree that the literary climax of the Song is found in 8:6 – 7, where the unsurpassed power and value of love — the love that draws man and woman together — are finally expressly asserted. Literary relaxation follows the intenseness of that declaration. A final expression of mutual desire between the lovers brings the Song to an end, suggesting that love goes on. This last segment (8:8 – 14) is in some sense also a return to the beginning, as references to the beloved's brothers, to her vineyard and to Solomon (the king) link 8:8 – 12 with 1:2 – 6.

In this song of love the voice of the beloved is dominant. It is her experience of love, both as the one who loves and as the one who is loved, that is most clearly expressed. The Song begins with her wish for the lover's kiss and ends with her urgent invitation to him for love's intimacy.

Outline

I. Title (1:1)
II. The First Meeting (1:2 — 2:7)
III. The Second Meeting (2:8 — 3:5)
IV. The Third Meeting (3:6 — 5:1)
V. The Fourth Meeting (5:2 — 6:3)
VI. The Fifth Meeting (6:4 — 8:4)
VII. The Literary Climax (8:5 – 7)
VIII. The Conclusion (8:8 – 14)

The Young Shulammite Bride and Jerusalem's Daughters

1 The [1]Song of [a]Songs, which is Solomon's.
2 “[1]May he kiss me with the kisses of
his mouth!
For your [a]love is better than wine.
3 “Your [a]oils have a pleasing fragrance,
Your [b]name is *like* [1]purified oil;
Therefore the [2][c]maidens love you.
4 “Draw me after you *and* let us run
together!
The [a]king has brought me into his
chambers.”

“[1]**W**e will rejoice in you and be glad;
We will [2]extol your [b]love more than
wine.
Rightly do they love you.”

5 “[1]I am black but [a]lovely,
O [b]daughters of Jerusalem,
Like the [c]tents of [d]Kedar,
Like the curtains of Solomon.
6 “Do not stare at me because I am
[1]swarthy,
For the sun has burned me.
My [a]mother's sons were angry with
me;
They made me [b]caretaker of the
vineyards,
But I have not taken care of my own
vineyard.
7 “Tell me, O you [a]whom my soul loves,
Where do you [b]pasture *your flock*,
Where do you make *it* [c]lie down at
noon?
For why should I be like one who
[1]veils herself
Beside the flocks of your
[d]companions?”

Solomon, the Lover, Speaks

8 “[1]If you yourself do not know,
[a]Most beautiful among women,
Go forth on the trail of the flock
And pasture your young goats
By the tents of the shepherds.

9 “[1]To me, [a]my darling, you are like
My [b]mare among the chariots of
Pharaoh.
10 “Your [a]cheeks are lovely with
ornaments,
Your neck with strings of [b]beads.”

11 “[1]We will make for you ornaments of
gold
With beads of silver.”

12 “[1]While the king was at his [2]table,
My [3][a]perfume gave forth its fragrance.
13 “My beloved is to me a pouch of
[a]myrrh
Which lies all night between my
breasts.
14 “My beloved is to me a cluster of
[a]henna blossoms
In the vineyards of [b]Engedi.”

1:1 [1]Or *Best of the Songs* [a]1 Kin 4:32
2 [1]BRIDE [a]Song 1:4; 4:10
3 [1]Lit *oil which is emptied* (from one vessel to another) [2]Or *virgins* [a]Song 4:10; John 12:3 [b]Eccl 7:1 [c]Ps 45:14
4 [1]CHORUS [2]Lit *mention with praise* [a]Ps 45:14, 15 [b]Song 1:4; 4:10
5 [1]BRIDE [a]Song 2:14; 4:3; 6:4 [b]Song 2:7; 3:5, 10; 5:8, 16; 8:4 [c]Ps 120:5 [d]Is 60:7
6 [1]Or *black* [a]Ps 69:8 [b]Song 8:11
7 [a]Song 3:1-4 [b]Song 2:16; 6:3
7 [1]Some versions read *wanders* [c]Is 13:20; Jer 33:12 [d]Song 8:13
8 [1]BRIDEGROOM [a]Song 5:9; 6:1
9 [1]Lit *I have compared you to* [a]Song 1:15; 2:2, 10, 13 [b]2 Chr 1:16, 17
10 [a]Song 5:13 [b]Gen 24:53; Is 61:10
11 [1]CHORUS
12 [1]BRIDE [2]Or *couch* [3]Lit *nard* [a]Song 4:14; Mark 14:3; John 12:3
13 [a]Ps 45:8; John 19:39 **14** [a]Song 4:13 [b]1 Sam 23:29

1:1 *Song of Songs.* Greatest of songs (see Introduction: Title). 1 Kin 4:32 says that Solomon wrote 1,005 songs. *Solomon's.* See Introduction: Title; Author and Date.
1:2–3 *kisses . . . your love . . . Your oils.* Cf. 4:10–11, "your love . . . your oils . . . Your lips."
1:2 *he . . . his . . . your.* These pronouns all refer to the same person, the lover (Solomon). *love.* Expressions of love—caresses, embraces and consummation (see v. 4; 4:10; 7:12; see also Prov 7:18; Ezek 16:8; 23:17). *better than wine.* See v. 4. In 4:10 the lover speaks similarly of the beloved's love.
1:3 *oils . . . fragrance.* Aromatic spices and gums blended in cosmetic oil. *Your name.* The very mention of the lover's name fills the air as with a pleasant aroma. The Hebrew words for "name" and "fragrance" sound alike. *maidens.* Probably young women of the court or of the royal city (see 6:8–9).
1:4 *king.* Solomon. *his chambers.* The king's private quarters. *We.* Probably the maidens of v. 3. *extol your love more than wine.* For the reason given in v. 2.
1:5 *black.* Deeply browned by the sun (see v. 6); not considered desirable. *daughters of Jerusalem.* Probably the maidens of v. 3. *tents . . . curtains.* Handwoven from black goat hair. *Kedar.* See note on Is 21:16.
1:6 *my own vineyard.* Her body, as in 8:12 (see 2:15). Vineyard is an apt metaphor since it yields wine, and the excitements of love are compared with those produced by wine (see note on v. 2). The beloved is also compared to a garden, yielding precious fruits for the lover (see note on 4:12).
1:7 *whom my soul loves.* See 3:1. *Where do you pasture your flock . . . ?* The lover is portrayed as a shepherd. In v. 8 the beloved is depicted as a shepherdess. *noon.* A time of rest in warm climates. *one who veils herself.* Prostitute (see Gen 38:14–15). The beloved does not wish to look for her lover among the shepherds, appearing as though she were a prostitute.
1:8 *beautiful.* The beloved; also in v. 15; 2:10,13; 4:1,7; 5:9; 6:1,4,10. The lover is called "handsome" in v. 16 (in Hebrew the same word as that for "beautiful"). *your young goats.* The beloved is pictured as a shepherdess (see v. 7). *By the tents of the shepherds.* The beloved is instructed to learn where the lover is by joining the shepherds in the fields.
1:9 *my darling.* Used only of the beloved (see note on v. 13). *mare.* A flattering comparison, similar to Theocritus's praise of the beautiful Helen of Troy (*Idyl*, 18.30–31). *among the chariots of Pharaoh.* Her beauty attracts attention the way a mare would among the Egyptian chariot stallions. According to 1 Kin 10:28, Solomon imported horses from Egypt.
1:11 *We.* Perhaps the "daughters of Jerusalem" (v. 5).
1:12 *king.* Solomon. *at his table.* Reclining on his couch at the table. *My perfume.* Nard, an aromatic oil extracted from the roots of a perennial herb that grows in India (see 4:13–14; Mark 14:3; John 12:3).
1:13 *My beloved.* Used only of the lover (see note on v. 9). *myrrh.* An aromatic gum exuding from the bark of a balsam tree that grows in Arabia, Ethiopia and India. It was commonly used as an alluring feminine perfume (Esth 2:12; Prov 7:17). It was also used to perfume royal nuptial robes (Ps 45:8). The Magi brought myrrh to the young Jesus as a gift fit for a king (Matt 2:2,11). Myrrh was an ingredient in the holy anointing oil (Ex 30:23).
1:14 *henna.* A shrub of the Holy Land (perhaps the cypress) with tightly clustered, aromatic blossoms. *Engedi.* An oasis

15 "[1,2][a]How beautiful you are, my darling,
[2]How beautiful you are!
Your [b]eyes are *like* doves."

16 "[1,2]How handsome you are, [a]my beloved,
And so pleasant!
Indeed, our couch is luxuriant!
17 "The beams of our houses are [a]cedars,
Our rafters, [1b]cypresses.

The Bride's Admiration

2 "[1]I am the [2a]rose of [b]Sharon,
The [c]lily of the valleys."

2 "[1]Like a lily among the thorns,
So is [a]my darling among the [2]maidens."

3 "[1]Like an [2a]apple tree among the trees of the forest,
So is my beloved among the [3]young men.
In his shade I took great delight and sat down,
And his [b]fruit was sweet to my [4]taste.
4 "He has [a]brought me to *his* [1]banquet hall,
And his [b]banner over me is love.
5 "Sustain me with [a]raisin cakes,
Refresh me with [1b]apples,
Because [c]I am lovesick.
6 "Let [a]his left hand be under my head
And [a]his right hand [b]embrace me."

7 "[1]I [a]adjure you, O [b]daughters of Jerusalem,
By the [c]gazelles or by the [d]hinds of the field,
[a]That you do not arouse or awaken *my* love
Until [2]she pleases."

8 "[1]Listen! My beloved!
Behold, he is coming,
Climbing [a]on the mountains,
Leaping on the hills!
9 "My beloved is like a [a]gazelle or a [b]young [1]stag.
Behold, he is standing behind our wall,
He is looking through the windows,
He is peering [c]through the lattice.

10 "My beloved responded and said to me,
'[a]Arise, my darling, my beautiful one,
And come along.
11 'For behold, the winter is past,
The rain is over *and* gone.
12 'The flowers have *already* appeared in the land;
The time has arrived for [1]pruning *the vines,*
And the voice of the [a]turtledove has been heard in our land.
13 'The [a]fig tree has ripened its figs,
And the [b]vines in blossom have given forth *their* fragrance.
Arise, my darling, my beautiful one,
And come along!' "

14 "[1]O [a]my dove, [b]in the clefts of the [2]rock,
In the secret place of the steep [3]pathway,
Let me see your [4]form,
[c]Let me hear your voice;
For your voice is sweet,
And your [4]form is [d]lovely."

15 "[1a]Catch the foxes for us,
The [2]little foxes that are ruining the vineyards,
While our [b]vineyards are in blossom."

15 [1]BRIDEGROOM [2]Lit *Behold* [a]Song 1:16; 2:10, 13; 4:1, 7; 6:4, 10 [b]Song 4:1; 5:12
16 [1]BRIDE [2]Lit *Behold* [a]Song 2:3, 9, 17; 5:2, 5, 6, 8
17 [1]Or *junipers* [a]1 Kin 6:9, 10; Jer 22:14 [b]2 Chr 3:5
2:1 [1]BRIDE [2]Lit *crocus* [a]Is 35:1 [b]Is 33:9; 35:2 [c]Song 5:13; 7:2; Hos 14:5
2 [1]BRIDEGROOM [2]Lit *daughters* [a]Song 1:9
3 [1]BRIDE [2]Or *apricot* [3]Lit *sons* [4]Lit *palate* [a]Song 8:5 [b]Song 4:13, 16; 8:11, 12
4 [1]Lit *house of wine* [a]Song 1:4 [b]Ps 20:5
5 [1]Or *apricots* [a]2 Sam 6:19; 1 Chr 16:3; Hos 3:1 [b]Song 7:8 [c]Song 5:8
6 [a]Song 8:3 [b]Prov 4:8
7 [1]BRIDEGROOM [2]Or *it* [a]Song 3:5; 5:8, 9; 8:4 [b]Song 1:5 [c]Prov 6:5; Song 2:9, 17; 3:5; 8:14 [d]Gen 49:21; Ps 18:33; Hab 3:19
8 [1]BRIDE
8 [a]Song 2:17; Is 52:7
9 [1]Lit *of the stags* [a]Prov 6:5; Song 2:17; 3:5; 8:14 [b]Song 2:17; 8:14 [c]Judg 5:28
10 [a]Song 2:13
12 [1]Or *singing* [a]Gen 15:9; Ps 74:19; Jer 8:7
13 [a]Matt 24:32 [b]Song 7:12
14 [1]BRIDEGROOM [2]Or *crag* [3]Or *cliff* [4]Lit *appearance* [a]Song 5:2; 6:9 [b]Jer 48:28 [c]Song 8:13 [d]Song 1:5
15 [1]CHORUS [2]Or *young* [a]Ezek 13:4; Luke 13:32 [b]Song 2:13

watered by a spring, located on the west side of the Dead Sea. David sought refuge there from King Saul (1 Sam 24:1).
1:15 *How beautiful . . . darling.* See 4:1; 6:4; cf. v. 16. *my darling.* See note on v. 9. *doves.* See 4:1.
1:16 *handsome.* See note on v. 8 ("beautiful"). *luxuriant.* The lovers lie together in the field under the trees.
2:1 *rose.* Possibly a member of the crocus family (see NASB marg.; see also Is 35:1–2). *Sharon.* The fertile coastal plain south of Mount Carmel (see map No. 2 at the end of the study Bible). *lily.* Probably either lotus or anemone.
2:2 *my darling.* See note on 1:9. *maidens.* See note on 1:3.
2:3 *apple tree.* The precise nature of this fruit tree is uncertain.
2:4 *banner.* See 6:4; Num 2:2; Ps 20:5. The king's love for her is displayed for all to see, like a large military banner.
2:5 *raisin cakes . . . apples.* Probably metaphors for love's caresses and embraces.
2:7 A recurring refrain in the Song (see 3:5; 8:4; cf. 5:8). It is always spoken by the beloved and always in a context of physical intimacy with her lover. *adjure.* Place under oath. *daughters of Jerusalem.* See note on 1:5. *gazelles . . . hinds.* Perhaps in the imaginative language of love the gazelles and hinds are portrayed as witnesses to the oath. This would be in harmony with the author's frequent reference to nature. *Until she pleases.* Out of the beloved's experience of love comes wise admonition that love is not to be artificially stimulated; utter spontaneity is essential to its genuine truth and beauty.
2:9 *gazelle.* Celebrated for its form and beauty. *young stag.* An apt simile for youthful vigor (cf. Is 35:6). *looking . . . lattice.* The eager lover tries to catch sight of the beloved while she is still preparing herself for their meeting.
2:10 *Arise . . . come along.* See v. 13; cf. 7:11–13. *my beautiful one.* See note on 1:8.
2:11–13 The first signs of spring appear (see 6:11; 7:12)—the time of love.
2:14 *dove . . . of the steep pathway.* Cf. Ps 55:6–8; Jer 48:28.
2:15 Perhaps spoken by the beloved. *vineyards.* As in 1:6 ("my own vineyard"), probably a metaphor for the lovers' physical beauty. Thus the desire is expressed that the lovers be kept safe from whatever ("foxes") might mar their mutual attractiveness. *in blossom.* Their attractiveness is in its prime.

16 "[1][a]My beloved is mine, and I am his;
He [b]pastures *his flock* among the
lilies.
17 "[a]Until [1]the cool of the day when the
shadows flee away,
Turn, my beloved, and be like a
[b]gazelle
Or a young stag [c]on the mountains of
[2]Bether."

The Bride's Troubled Dream

3 "[1]On my bed night after night I sought
him
[a]Whom my soul loves;
I [b]sought him but did not find him.
2 '[1]I must arise now and [1]go about the
city;
In the [a]streets and in the squares
[2]I must seek him whom my soul
loves.'
I sought him but did not find him.
3 "[a]The watchmen who make the rounds
in the city found me,
And I said, 'Have you seen him whom
my soul loves?'
4 "[a]Scarcely had I [1]left them
When I found him whom my soul
loves;
I [b]held on to him and would not let
him go
Until I had [c]brought him to my
mother's house,
And into the room of her who
conceived me."

5 "[1]I [a]adjure you, O daughters of
Jerusalem,
By the [b]gazelles or by the hinds of the
field,
That you will not arouse or awaken
my love
Until [2]she pleases."

16 [1]BRIDE [a]Song 6:3; 7:10 [b]Song 4:5; 6:2, 3 **17** [1]Lit *the day blows* [2]Or *cleavage* or *a kind of spice* [a]Song 4:6 [b]Song 2:9 [c]Song 2:8 **3:1** [1]BRIDE [a]Song 1:7 [b]Song 5:6 **2** [1]Or *Let me arise* [2]Or *Let me seek* [a]Jer 5:1 **3** [a]Song 5:7; Is 21:6-8, 11, 12 **4** [1]Lit *passed* [a]Prov 8:17 [b]Prov 4:13; Rom 8:35, 39 [c]Song 8:2 **5** [1]BRIDEGROOM [2]Or *it* [a]Song 2:7; 5:8; 8:4 [b]Song 2:7

6 [1]CHORUS [2]Lit *Who* [a]Song 8:5 [b]Ex 13:21; Joel 2:30 [c]Song 1:13; 4:6, 14; Matt 2:11 [d]Ex 30:34; Rev 18:13 **8** [1]Lit *terror in the nights* [a]Jer 50:9 [b]Ps 45:3 [c]Ps 91:5 **10** [1]Or *support* [a]Song 1:5 **11** [1]Or *wreath* [a]Is 3:16, 17; 4:4 [b]Is 62:5 **4:1** [1]BRIDEGROOM [2]Lit *Behold* [a]Song 1:15 [b]Song 1:15; 5:12 [c]Song 6:7 [d]Song 6:5 [e]Mic 7:14

Solomon's Wedding Day

6 "[1,2][a]What is this coming up from the
wilderness
Like [b]columns of smoke,
Perfumed with [c]myrrh and
[d]frankincense,
With all scented powders of the
merchant?
7 "Behold, it is the *traveling* couch of
Solomon;
Sixty mighty men around it,
Of the mighty men of Israel.
8 "All of them are wielders of the sword,
[a]Expert in war;
Each man has his [b]sword at his side,
Guarding against the [1][c]terrors of the
night.
9 "King Solomon has made for himself a
sedan chair
From the timber of Lebanon.
10 "He made its posts of silver,
Its [1]back of gold
And its seat of purple fabric,
With its interior lovingly fitted out
By the [a]daughters of Jerusalem.
11 "Go forth, O [a]daughters of Zion,
And gaze on King Solomon with the
[1]crown
With which his mother has crowned
him
On the [b]day of his wedding,
And on the day of his gladness of
heart."

Solomon's Love Expressed

4 "[1,2]How beautiful [a]you are, my darling,
[2]How beautiful you are!
Your [b]eyes are *like* doves [c]behind your
veil;
Your [d]hair is like a flock of goats
That have descended from Mount
[e]Gilead.

2:16 *My beloved is mine, and I am his.* See 6:3; 7:10. They belong to each other exclusively in a relationship that allows no intrusion. *pastures . . . among the lilies.* The lover is compared to a gazelle (see v. 17). The pasturing is a metaphor for the lover's intimate enjoyment of her charms (see 6:2–3).
3:1 This verse begins a new moment in love's experience. *night after night.* Night, with its freedom from the distractions of the day, allows the heart to be filled with its own preoccupations.
3:3 *watchmen.* Were stationed at the city gates (see Neh 3:29; 11:19; 13:22) and on the walls (see 5:7; 2 Sam 13:34; 18:24–27; 2 Kin 9:17–20; Ps 127:1; Is 52:8; 62:6). Apparently they also patrolled the streets at night (see 5:7).
3:4 *mother's.* Mothers are referred to frequently in the Song; fathers are never mentioned.
3:5 See note on 2:7. Once again the charge occurs at the moment of intimacy.
3:6–11 Perhaps spoken by friends (see 8:5). If so, this section probably portrays the wedding procession of Solomon and his bride approaching the city.
3:6 This verse begins a new moment in the relationship. *What . . . wilderness.* See 8:5, where the reference is to the beloved. *wilderness.* Uncultivated seasonal grasslands. *smoke.* Incense (see note on Ex 30:34). *of the merchant.* Imported.
3:7 *couch.* A richly adorned royal conveyance, a palanquin (see vv. 9–10).
3:8 *terrors of the night.* See Ps 91:5.
3:10 *posts.* Supporting the canopy. *silver . . . gold.* Probably metals that overlay the Lebanon wood. *purple.* See notes on 7:5; Ex 25:4.
3:11 *daughters of Zion.* Elsewhere "daughters of Jerusalem" (see note on 1:5). *crown.* A wedding wreath (see Is 61:10). *mother.* See note on v. 4. Here the reference is to Bathsheba.
4:1–7 For other exuberant descriptions of the beloved's beauty see 6:4–9; 7:1–7.
4:1b–2 See 6:5b–6.
4:1 *How beautiful . . . darling.* See 1:15 and note. *eyes . . . behind your veil.* With the rest of her face concealed, the lover's attention is focused on the beloved's eyes. *doves.* See 1:15 and note. *flock of goats.* The goats of Canaan were usually black (see note on 1:5). The lover's hair was also black (5:11). *descended from Mount Gilead.* The beloved's black tresses flowing from her head remind the lover of a flock of sleek black goats streaming down one of the hills of Gilead (noted for its good pasturage).

2 "Your [a]teeth are like a flock of *newly*
shorn ewes
Which have come up from *their*
washing,
All of which bear twins,
And not one among them has [1]lost
her young.
3 "Your lips are like a [a]scarlet thread,
And your [b]mouth is lovely.
Your [c]temples are like a slice of a
pomegranate
Behind your veil.
4 "Your [a]neck is like the tower of David,
Built [1]with rows of stones
On which are [b]hung a thousand
shields,
All the round [c]shields of the mighty
men.
5 "Your [a]two breasts are like two fawns,
Twins of a gazelle
Which [b]feed among the lilies.
6 "[a]Until [1]the cool of the day
When the shadows flee away,
I will go my way to the mountain of
[b]myrrh
And to the hill of [b]frankincense.

7 "[a]You are altogether beautiful, my
darling,
And there is no blemish in you.
8 "*Come* with me from [a]Lebanon, *my*
[b]bride,
May you come with me from
Lebanon.
[1]Journey down from the summit of
[c]Amana,
From the summit of [d]Senir and
Hermon,
From the dens of lions,
From the mountains of leopards.
9 "You have made my heart beat faster,
[a]my sister, *my* bride;
You have made my heart beat faster
with a single *glance* of your eyes,
With a single strand of your [b]necklace.
10 "[a]How beautiful is your love, my sister,
my bride!
How much [b]better is your love than
wine,
And the [c]fragrance of your oils
Than all *kinds* of [1]spices!
11 "Your lips, *my* bride, [a]drip [b]honey;
Honey and milk are under your tongue,
And the fragrance of your garments is
like the [c]fragrance of Lebanon.
12 "A garden locked is my sister, *my* bride,
A [1]rock garden locked, a [a]spring
[b]sealed up.
13 "Your shoots are an [1a]orchard of
[b]pomegranates
With [c]choice fruits, [d]henna with nard
plants,
14 [a]Nard and saffron, calamus and
[b]cinnamon,
With all the trees of [c]frankincense,
[d]Myrrh and aloes, along with all the
finest [1]spices.
15 "*You are* a garden spring,
A well of [1a]fresh water,
And streams *flowing* from Lebanon."

2 [1]Or *miscarried* [a]Song 6:6
3 [a]Josh 2:18 [b]Song 5:16 [c]Song 6:7
4 [1]Or *for an arsenal* [a]Song 7:4 [b]Ezek 27:10, 11 [c]2 Sam 1:21
5 [a]Song 7:3 [b]Song 2:16; 6:2, 3
6 [1]Lit *the day blows* [a]Song 2:17 [b]Song 4:14
7 [a]Song 1:15; Eph 5:27
8 [1]Or *Look* [a]1 Kin 4:33; Ps 72:16 [b]Song 5:1; Is 62:5 [c]2 Kin 5:12
8 [d]Deut 3:9; 1 Chr 5:23; Ezek 27:5
9 [a]Song 4:10, 12; 5:1, 2 [b]Gen 41:42; Prov 1:9; Ezek 16:11; Dan 5:7
10 [1]Or *balsam odors* [a]Song 7:6 [b]Song 1:2, 4 [c]Song 1:3
11 [a]Prov 5:3 [b]Ps 19:10; Prov 24:13 [c]Gen 27:27; Hos 14:6
12 [1]Lit *stone heap* [a]Prov 5:15-18 [b]Gen 29:3
13 [1]Or *park* or *paradise* [a]Eccl 2:5 [b]Song 6:11; 7:12 [c]Song 2:3; 4:16; 7:13 [d]Song 1:14
14 [1]Or *balsam odors* [a]Song 1:12 [b]Ex 30:23 [c]Song 4:6 [d]Ps 45:8; Song 3:6; John 19:39
15 [1]Lit *living* [a]Zech 14:8; John 4:10

4:2 *newly shorn.* Clean and white. *come up from their washing.* Still wet, like moistened teeth.
4:3 *Your lips . . . scarlet.* Perhaps the beloved painted her lips, like Egyptian women. *temples . . . Behind your veil.* See note on v. 1. *slice of a pomegranate.* Round and blushed with red.
4:4 The beloved's erect, bespangled neck is like a tower on the city wall adorned with warriors' shields (cf. 7:4).
4:5 See 7:3. *fawns.* Representing tender, delicate beauty, and promise rather than full growth (cf. 8:8). *gazelle.* See note on 2:9. Elsewhere the simile is used of the lover. *feed among the lilies.* For a different use of this phrase see 2:16 and note.
4:6 *Until . . . shadows flee.* See 2:17. *mountain of myrrh . . . hill of frankincense.* Metaphors for lovers' intimacy.
4:8 To the lover the beloved seems to have withdrawn as if to a remote mountain. *Lebanon . . . Amana . . . Hermon.* Mountain peaks on the northern horizon. *Senir.* Amorite name for Mount Hermon (Deut 3:9).
4:9 *my sister.* For lovers to address each other as "brother" and "sister" was common in the love poetry of the ancient Near East (see vv. 10,12; 5:1). *single glance of your eyes.* See 6:5 and note.
4:10 *better . . . than wine.* See note on 1:2. *fragrance of your oils.* See 1:3. *spices.* See v. 14; 5:1,13; 6:2; 8:14. Spice was an imported luxury item (see 1 Kin 10:2,10,25; Ezek 27:22). Spices were used for fragrance in the holy anointing oil (Ex 25:6; 30:23–25; 35:8) and for fragrant incense (Ex 25:6; 35:8) as well as for perfume.
4:11 *Your lips . . . drip honey.* The beloved speaks to him of love (cf. Prov 5:3; 16:24). People in the ancient Near East associated sweetness with the delights of love. *Honey and milk.* Perhaps reminiscent of the description of the promised land (see note on Ex 3:8). *under your tongue.* See Job 20:12; Ps 10:7.
4:12 *garden.* A place of sensual delights (see v. 16; 5:1; 6:2; see also note on 1:6). *locked . . . locked . . . sealed up.* Metaphors for the beloved's virginity—or perhaps for the fact that she keeps herself exclusively for her husband. *rock garden . . . spring.* Sources of refreshment; metaphors for the beloved as a sexual partner, as in Prov 5:15–20.
4:13–15 Verses 13–14 elaborate on the garden metaphor of v. 12a, and v. 15 on the fountain metaphor of v. 12b. The trees and spices in vv. 13–14 are mostly exotic, referring to the beloved's charms.
4:13 *Your shoots.* All the beloved's features that delight the lover. *orchard.* Hebrew *pardes* (from which the English word "paradise" comes), a loanword from Old Persian meaning "enclosure" or "park." In Neh 2:8 and Eccl 2:5 it refers to royal parks and forests. *henna.* See note on 1:14. *nard.* See note on 1:12.
4:14 *saffron.* A plant of the crocus family bearing purple or white flowers, parts of which, when dried, were used as a cooking spice. *calamus.* An imported (see Jer 6:20), aromatic spice cane, used also in the holy anointing oil and incense ("cane" in Ex 30:23,25; Is 43:23–24). *cinnamon.* Used in the holy anointing oil (Ex 30:23,25). *Myrrh.* See note on 1:13. *aloes.* Aromatic aloes, used to perfume royal nuptial robes (Ps 45:8). Prov 7:17 says that the adulteress perfumed her bed "with myrrh, aloes and cinnamon."
4:15 *fresh.* Not stagnant. *streams . . . from Lebanon.* Fresh, cool, sparkling water from the snowfields on the Lebanon mountains.

16 "[1]Awake, O north *wind*,
And come, *wind of* the south;
Make my [a]garden breathe out *fragrance*,
Let its [2]spices [3]be wafted abroad.
May [b]my beloved come into his garden
And eat its [c]choice fruits!"

The Torment of Separation

5 "[1]I have [a]come into my garden, [b]my sister, *my* bride;
I have gathered my [c]myrrh along with my balsam.
I have eaten my honeycomb [2]and my [d]honey;
I have [e]drunk my wine [2]and my milk.
Eat, [f]friends;
Drink and [3]imbibe deeply, O lovers."

2 "[1]I was asleep but my heart was awake.
A voice! My beloved was knocking:
'Open to me, [a]my sister, my darling,
[b]My dove, my perfect one!
For my head is [2]drenched with dew,
My [c]locks with the [3]damp of the night.'
3 "I have [a]taken off my dress,
How can I put it on *again?*
I have [b]washed my feet,
How can I dirty them *again?*
4 "My beloved extended his hand through the opening,
And my [1a]feelings were aroused for him.
5 "I arose to open to my beloved;
And my hands [a]dripped with myrrh,
And my fingers with [1]liquid myrrh,
On the handles of the bolt.
6 "I opened to my beloved,
But my beloved had [a]turned away *and* had gone!
My [1]heart went out *to him* as he [b]spoke.
I [c]searched for him but I did not find him;
I [d]called him but he did not answer me.
7 "The [a]watchmen who make the rounds in the city found me,
They struck me *and* wounded me;
The guardsmen of the walls took away my shawl from me.
8 "I [a]adjure you, O daughters of Jerusalem,
If you find my beloved,
As to what you will tell him:
For [b]I am lovesick."

9 "[1,2]What kind of beloved is your beloved,
O [a]most beautiful among women?
[2]What kind of beloved is your beloved,
That thus you adjure us?"

Admiration by the Bride

10 "[1]My beloved is dazzling and [a]ruddy,
[2b]Outstanding among ten thousand.
11 "His head is *like* gold, pure gold;
His [a]locks are *like* clusters of dates
And black as a raven.
12 "His [a]eyes are like doves
Beside streams of water,
Bathed in milk,
And [1]reposed in *their* [b]setting.
13 "His cheeks are like a [a]bed of balsam,
Banks of sweet-scented herbs;
His lips are [b]lilies
[c]Dripping with liquid myrrh.
14 "His hands are rods of gold
Set with [a]beryl;
His abdomen is carved ivory
Inlaid with [1b]sapphires.
15 "His legs are pillars of alabaster
Set on pedestals of pure gold;
His appearance is like [a]Lebanon
Choice as the [b]cedars.
16 "His [1a]mouth is *full of* sweetness.
And he is wholly [b]desirable.
This is my beloved and this is my friend,
O daughters of Jerusalem."

16 [1]BRIDE [2]Or *balsam odors* [3]Lit *flow forth* [a]Song 5:1; 6:2 [b]Song 1:13; 2:3, 8; 6:2 [c]Song 4:13
5:1 [1]BRIDEGROOM [2]Lit *with* [3]Or *become drunk* [a]Song 6:2 [b]Song 4:9 [c]Song 1:13; 4:14 [d]Song 4:11 [e]Prov 9:5; Is 55:1 [f]Judg 14:11, 20; John 3:29
2 [1]BRIDE [2]Lit *filled* [3]Lit *drops* [a]Song 4:9 [b]Song 2:14; 6:9 [c]Song 5:11
3 [a]Luke 11:7 [b]Gen 19:2
4 [1]Lit *bowels* [a]Jer 31:20
5 [1]Lit *passing* [a]Song 5:13
6 [1]Lit *soul* [a]Song 6:1 [b]Song 5:2 [c]Song 3:1
6 [d]Prov 1:28
7 [a]Song 3:3
8 [a]Song 2:7; 3:5 [b]Song 2:5
9 [1]CHORUS [2]Or *What is your beloved more than another beloved* [a]Song 1:8; 6:1
10 [1]BRIDE [2]Lit *Lifted up banner* [a]1 Sam 16:12 [b]Ps 45:2
11 [a]Song 5:2
12 [1]Lit *sitting upon* [a]Song 1:15; 4:1 [b]Ex 25:7
13 [a]Song 6:2 [b]Song 2:1 [c]Song 5:5
14 [1]Lit *lapis lazuli* [a]Ex 28:20; 39:13; Ezek 1:16; Dan 10:6 [b]Ex 24:10; 28:18; Job 28:16; Is 54:11
15 [a]Song 7:4 [b]1 Kin 4:33; Ps 80:10; Ezek 17:23; 31:8
16 [1]Lit *palate* [a]Song 7:9 [b]2 Sam 1:23

4:16 May the fragrance of my charms be wafted about to draw my lover to me so that we may enjoy love's intimacies. *his garden.* She belongs to him and she yields herself to her lover (see 6:2).
5:1 The lover claims the beloved as his garden and enjoys all her delights. *my sister.* See note on 4:9. *Eat . . . O lovers.* The friends of the lovers applaud their enjoyment of love.
5:2–8 See 3:1–5 and note on 3:1.
5:2 *I was asleep . . . was awake.* Love holds sway even in sleep—just as a new mother sleeps with an ear open to her baby's slightest whimper.
5:3 Instinctive reaction raises a foolish complaint before the language of love takes over.
5:5 *my hands . . . liquid myrrh.* Love's eager imagination extravagantly lotioned the beloved's hands with perfume.
5:9 The friends' question provides an opportunity for the beloved to describe the beauty of her lover—which she does only here.
5:10 *ruddy.* See 1 Sam 16:12.
5:11 *black.* The beloved's hair was also black (see note on 4:1).
5:12 *doves.* See note on 1:15. *Beside streams of water.* The lover's eyes sparkle. *Bathed in milk.* Describing the white of the eye.
5:13 *balsam . . . lilies.* These similes probably compare sensuous effects rather than appearances, as do the following similes and metaphors, at least in part. *lilies.* See note on 2:1. *Dripping with . . . myrrh.* Love's pleasant excitements are aroused by the lover's lips.
5:14 *beryl.* See note on Ezek 1:16. *sapphires.* Hebrew *sappir* (from which the English word "sapphire" comes).
5:15 *appearance is like Lebanon.* Awesome and majestic. *Choice as the cedars.* The cedars of Lebanon were renowned throughout the ancient Near East, and their wood was desired for adorning temples and palaces.
5:16 *mouth.* The lover's kisses and loving speech. *daughters of Jerusalem.* See note on 1:5.

Mutual Delight in Each Other

6 "[1][a]Where has your beloved gone,
O [b]most beautiful among women?
Where has your beloved turned,
That we may seek him with you?"

2 "[1]My beloved has gone down to his
[a]garden,
To the [b]beds of balsam,
To [c]pasture *his flock* in the gardens
And gather [d]lilies.
3 "[a]I am my beloved's and my beloved is
mine,
He who [b]pastures *his flock* among the
lilies."

4 "[1][a]You are as beautiful as [b]Tirzah, my
darling,
As [c]lovely as [d]Jerusalem,
As [e]awesome as [2]an army with
banners.
5 "Turn your eyes away from me,
For they have confused me;
[a]Your hair is like a flock of goats
That have descended from Gilead.
6 "[a]Your teeth are like a flock of ewes
Which have come up from *their*
washing,
All of which bear twins,
And not one among them has [1]lost
her young.
7 "[a]Your temples are like a slice of a
pomegranate
Behind your veil.
8 "There are sixty [a]queens and eighty
concubines,
And [1][b]maidens without number;
9 *But* [a]my dove, my perfect one, is
[1]unique:
She is her mother's [1]only *daughter;*

6:1 [1]CHORUS [a]Song 5:6 [b]Song 1:8
2 [1]BRIDE [a]Song 4:16; 5:1 [b]Song 5:13 [c]Song 1:7 [d]Song 2:1; 5:13
3 [a]Song 2:16; 7:10 [b]Song 2:16; 4:5
4 [1]BRIDEGROOM [2]Lit *bannered ones* [a]Song 1:15 [b]1 Kin 14:17 [c]Song 1:5 [d]Ps 48:2; 50:2 [e]Song 6:10
5 [a]Song 4:1
6 [1]Or *miscarried* [a]Song 4:2
7 [a]Song 4:3
8 [1]Or *virgins* [a]1 Kin 11:3 [b]Song 1:3
9 [1]Lit *one* [a]Song 2:14; 5:2

9 [2]Lit *daughters* [b]Gen 30:13 [c]1 Kin 11:3
10 [1]Lit *looks down* [2]Lit *bannered ones* [a]Job 31:26 [b]Matt 17:2; Rev 1:16 [c]Song 6:4
11 [a]Song 7:12 [b]Song 4:13
12 [1]Another reading is *Ammi-nadib*
13 [1]CHORUS [2]Ch 7:1 in Heb [3]BRIDEGROOM [4]Or *Mahanaim* [a]Judg 21:21 [b]Gen 32:2; 2 Sam 17:24
7:1 [1]Ch 7:2 in Heb [2]Lit *footsteps* [3]Or *nobleman's* [4]Or *ornaments* [a]Ps 45:13

She is the pure *child* of the one who
bore her.
The [2][b]maidens saw her and called her
blessed,
The [c]queens and the concubines *also,*
and they praised her, *saying,*

10 'Who is this that [1]grows like the dawn,
As beautiful as the full [a]moon,
As pure [b]as the sun,
As [c]awesome as [2]an army with
banners?'
11 "I went down to the orchard of nut
trees
To see the blossoms of the valley,
To see whether [a]the vine had budded
Or the [b]pomegranates had bloomed.
12 "Before I was aware, my soul set me
Over the chariots of [1]my noble
people."

13 "[1,2]Come back, come back,
O Shulammite;
Come back, come back, that we may
gaze at you!"
"[3]**Why** should you gaze at the
Shulammite,
As at the [a]dance of [4][b]the two
companies?

Admiration by the Bridegroom

7 "[1]How beautiful are your [2]feet in
sandals,
O [3][a]prince's daughter!
The curves of your hips are like
[4]jewels,
The work of the hands of an artist.
2 "Your navel is *like* a round goblet
Which never lacks mixed wine;

6:1 The question asked by the friends forms a transition from the beloved's description of the lover to her delighted acknowledgment of his intimacy with her and the exclusiveness of their relationship.
6:2 *his garden.* The beloved. *beds of balsam.* Her sensuous attractions (cf. 5:13). *gather lilies.* See note on 2:1. The lover, enjoying intimacies with the beloved, is compared to a graceful gazelle (see notes on 2:7,9) nibbling from lily to lily in undisturbed enjoyment of exotic delicacies.
6:3 *I . . . mine.* See note on 2:16. Notice the reversal; here her yielding to her lover is emphasized.
6:4 *Tirzah.* An old Canaanite city in the middle of the land (see Josh 12:24). It was chosen by Jeroboam I (930–909 B.C.) as the first royal city of the northern kingdom (see 1 Kin 14:17; see also 1 Kin 15:21; 16:23–24). The meaning of its name ("pleasure, beauty") suggests that it was a beautiful site, perhaps explaining why the author here sets it alongside Jerusalem (though what constituted the beauty of Tirzah is not known). Comparison of the beloved's beauty to that of cities was perhaps not so unusual in the ancient Near East, since cities were regularly depicted as women (see note on 2 Kin 19:21). *awesome.* See v. 10. *as an army with banners.* The beloved's noble beauty evoked in the lover emotions like those aroused by a troop marching under its banners.
6:5–7 See 4:1–3 and notes.
6:5 *your eyes . . . have confused me.* The beloved's eyes awaken in the lover such intensity of love that he is held captive (see 4:9).
6:8 *queens . . . concubines . . . maidens.* The reference is either to Solomon's harem or to all the beautiful women of the realm.
6:9 *perfect one.* See 5:2. *only daughter.* Not literally, but the one uniquely loved (cf. Gen 22:2; Judg 11:34; Prov 4:3). *maidens . . . praised her.* All the other women praised her beauty (see 1:8; 5:9; 6:1).
6:10 See 5:9; 6:1.
6:11 *nut.* Perhaps walnut. *see . . . the valley.* For the first signs of spring (see note on 2:11–13).
6:12 See NASB marg. *chariots.* Solomon was famous for his chariots (1 Kin 10:26).
6:13 *Shulammite.* The beloved. It is either a variant of "Shunammite" (see 1 Kin 1:3), i.e., a young woman from Shunem (see Josh 19:18), or a feminine form of the word "Solomon," meaning "Solomon's girl." In ancient Semitic languages the letters *l* and *n* were sometimes interchanged.
7:1–7 Here the description moves up from the feet rather than down from the head (cf. 5:11–15).
7:1 Cf. v. 6. *prince's daughter.* Alludes to the nobility of her beauty (see Ps 45:13).
7:2 *goblet.* A large, two-handled, ring-based bowl (see Ex 24:6; Is 22:24; see also Amos 6:6). *Fenced about with lilies.* The

Your belly is like a heap of wheat
Fenced about with lilies.
3 "Your [a]two breasts are like two fawns,
Twins of a gazelle.
4 "Your [a]neck is like a tower of ivory,
Your eyes *like* the pools in [b]Heshbon
By the gate of Bath-rabbim;
Your nose is like the tower of Lebanon,
Which faces toward Damascus.
5 "Your head [1]crowns you like [a]Carmel,
And the flowing locks of your head
are like purple threads;
The king is captivated by *your* tresses.
6 "How [a]beautiful and how delightful
you are,
[1]*My* love, with *all* your charms!
7 "[1]Your stature is like a palm tree,
And your breasts are *like its* clusters.
8 "I said, 'I will climb the palm tree,
I will take hold of its fruit stalks.'
Oh, may your breasts be like clusters
of the vine,
And the fragrance of your [1]breath like
[2a]apples,
9 And your [1a]mouth like the best wine!"

"[2]It [b]goes *down* smoothly for my
beloved,
Flowing gently *through* the lips of
those who fall asleep.

The Union of Love

10 "[a]I am my beloved's,
And his [b]desire is for me.
11 "Come, my beloved, let us go out into
the [1]country,
Let us spend the night in the villages.
12 "Let us rise early *and go* to the
vineyards;
Let us [a]see whether the vine has
budded
And its blossoms have opened,
And whether the pomegranates have
bloomed.
There I will give you my love.
13 "The [a]mandrakes have given forth
fragrance;
And over our doors are all [b]choice
fruits,
Both new and old,
Which I have saved up for you, my
beloved.

The Lovers Speak

8 "Oh that you were like a brother to me
Who nursed at my mother's breasts.
If I found you outdoors, I would kiss
you;
No one would despise me, either.
2 "I would lead you *and* [a]bring you
Into the house of my mother, who
used to instruct me;
I would give you spiced wine to drink
from the juice of my pomegranates.
3 "Let [a]his left hand be under my head
And his right hand embrace me."

4 "[1a]I want you to swear, O daughters of
Jerusalem,
[2]Do not arouse or awaken *my* love
Until [3]she pleases."

5 "[1a]Who is this coming up from the
wilderness
Leaning on her beloved?"

"[2]Beneath the [3b]apple tree I awakened
you;
There your mother was in labor with
you,
There she was in labor *and* gave you
birth.
6 "Put me like a [1]seal over your heart,
Like a [a]seal on your arm.

3 [a]Song 4:5
4 [a]Song 4:4 [b]Num 21:26
5 [1]Lit *is upon* [a]Is 35:2
6 [1]Or With *love among your delights* [a]Song 1:15, 16; 4:10
7 [1]Lit *This stature of yours*
8 [1]Lit *nose* [2]Or *apricots* [a]Song 2:5
9 [1]Lit *palate* [2]BRIDE [a]Song 5:16 [b]Prov 23:31
10 [a]Song 2:16; 6:3 [b]Ps 45:11; Gal 2:20
11 [1]Lit *field*
12 [a]Song 6:11
13 [a]Gen 30:14 [b]Song 2:3; 4:13, 16; Matt 13:52
8:2 [a]Song 3:4
3 [a]Song 2:6
4 [1]BRIDEGROOM [2]Or *Why should you arouse* [3]Or *it* [a]Song 2:7; 3:5
5 [1]CHORUS [2]BRIDE [3]Or *apricot* [a]Song 3:6 [b]Song 2:3
6 [1]Or *signet* [a]Is 49:16; Jer 22:24; Hag 2:23

beloved perhaps wore a loose garland of flowers around her waist.
7:3 See note on 4:5.
7:4 *tower of ivory.* Mixed imagery, referring to shape as well as to color and texture. *pools.* The beloved's eyes reflect like the surface of a pool; or the imagery may depict serenity and gentleness. *Heshbon.* Once the royal city of King Sihon (Num 21:26), it was blessed with an abundant supply of spring water. *Bath-rabbim.* Means "daughter of many"; perhaps a popular name for Heshbon. *tower of Lebanon.* Perhaps a military tower on the northern frontier of Solomon's kingdom, but more likely the beautiful, towering Lebanon mountain range.
7:5 *Carmel.* A promontory midway along the western coast of the kingdom, with a wooded top and known for its beauty. *purple threads.* A reference to purple, royal cloth, as in 3:10 (see note on Ex 25:4). *king.* Solomon. *tresses.* The Hebrew for this word suggests a similarity to flowing water (cf. 4:1; 6:5).
7:7 *palm.* The stately date palm.
7:8 *I said.* To myself. *I will climb.* The beloved's beauty draws him irresistibly. *vine.* Grape. *apples.* Perhaps the fragrance of apple blossoms (but see note on 2:3).
7:9 *It goes down smoothly for my beloved.* The beloved offers the wine (see 5:1) of her love to her lover.
7:10 *I am my beloved's.* See notes on 2:16; 6:3. *desire.* Cf. Gen 3:16.
7:11–12 In 2:10–13 the beloved reports a similar invitation from her lover.
7:12 *I will give you my love.* She offers herself completely to her lover.
7:13 *mandrakes.* Short-stemmed herbs associated with fertility (see note on Gen 30:14). The odor of its blossom is pungent. *over our doors.* The doors where the lovers meet. *choice fruits.* Metaphor for the delights the beloved has for her lover from her "garden" (cf. 4:13–14). *Both new and old.* Those already shared and those still to be enjoyed.
8:1 *No one would despise me.* The beloved could openly show affection without any public disgrace.
8:2 *I would give you.* She would offer her lover the delights of her love. *juice.* The Hebrew for this word refers to intoxicating juices.
8:4 See 2:7 and note.
8:5 *Who . . . wilderness.* See 3:6. *Beneath the apple tree.* In the ancient world, sexual union and birth were often associated with fruit trees.

For love is as strong as death,
[2b]Jealousy is as severe as Sheol;
Its flashes are flashes of fire,
[3]The *very* flame of the LORD.
7 "Many waters cannot quench love,
Nor will rivers overflow it;
[a]If a man were to give all the riches of his house for love,
It would be utterly despised."

8 "[1]We have a little sister,
And she [a]has no breasts;
What shall we do for our sister
On the day when she is spoken for?
9 "If she is a wall,
We will build on her a battlement of silver;
But if she is a door,
We will barricade her with [a]planks of cedar."

10 "[1]I was a wall, and [a]my breasts were like towers;
Then I became in his eyes as one who finds peace.
11 "Solomon had a [a]vineyard at Baal-hamon;
He [b]entrusted the vineyard to [c]caretakers.
Each one was to bring a [d]thousand *shekels* of silver for its [e]fruit.
12 "My very own vineyard is [1]at my disposal;
The thousand *shekels* are for you, Solomon,
And two hundred are for those who take care of its fruit."

13 "[1]O you who sit in the gardens,
My [a]companions are listening for your voice—
[b]Let me hear it!"

14 "[1,2]Hurry, my beloved,
And be [a]like a gazelle or a young [3]stag
On the [b]mountains of spices."

6 [2]Or Its *ardor is as inflexible* [3]Another reading is *A vehement flame* [b]Prov 6:34
7 [a]Prov 6:35
8 [1]CHORUS [a]Ezek 16:7
9 [a]1 Kin 6:15
10 [1]BRIDE [a]Ezek 16:7
11 [a]Eccl 2:4 [b]Matt 21:33 [c]Song 1:6 [d]Is 7:23 [e]Song 2:3; 8:12
12 [1]Lit *before me*
13 [1]BRIDEGROOM [a]Song 1:7 [b]Song 2:14
14 [1]BRIDE [2]Lit *Flee* [3]Lit *of the stags* [a]Song 2:7, 9, 17 [b]Song 4:6

8:6–7 *love is . . . Sheol. Its flashes . . . flame. Many waters . . . overflow it.* These three wisdom statements (see essay, p. 689) characterize marital love as the strongest, most unyielding and invincible force in human experience. With these statements the Song reaches its literary climax and discloses its purpose.
8:6 *seal.* Seals were precious to their owners, as personal as their names (see note on Gen 38:18). *arm.* Probably a poetic synonym for "hand." *as severe as Sheol.* As the grave will not give up the dead, so love will not surrender the loved one. *flame of the Lord.* The Hebrew expression conveys the idea of a most intense flame.
8:7 *Many waters.* Words that suggest not only the ocean depths (see Ps 107:23) but also the primeval waters that the people of the ancient Near East regarded as a permanent threat to the world (see note on Ps 32:6). The waters were also associated with the realm of the dead (see note on Ps 30:1). *If a man . . . despised.* A fourth wisdom statement (see note on vv. 6–7), declaring love's unsurpassed worth.
8:8–14 In the closing lines of the Song, the words of the brothers (vv. 8–9), the beloved's reference to her own vineyard (v. 12) and her final reference to Solomon (vv. 11–12) suggest a return to the beginning of the Song (see 1:2–7). The lines may recall the beloved's development into the age for love and marriage and the blossoming of her relationship with her lover.
8:8 In the ancient Near East, brothers often were guardians of their sisters, especially in matters pertaining to marriage (see Gen 24:50–60; 34:13–27). *On the day when she is spoken for.* Marriage was often contracted at an early age.
8:9 This imaginative verse probably expresses the brothers' determination to defend their young sister (the beloved) until her proper time for love and marriage has come. Or it may mean that the brothers are concerned to see that she is properly adorned for marriage before she is spoken for.
8:10 *I . . . like towers.* In contrast to the time when she was watched over by her brothers, the beloved rejoices in her maturity (see Ezek 16:7–8). *his.* The lover's.
8:11–12 *thousand shekels . . . two hundred.* Whether these figures are to be taken literally (see Is 7:23) is uncertain.
8:11 *Baal-hamon.* Location unknown. The Hebrew *hamon* sometimes means "wealth" or "abundance"; hence Baal (i.e., "lord") Hamon could mean "lord of abundance," bringing to mind Solomon's great wealth.
8:12 *My very own vineyard.* Her body (see note on 1:6). *at my disposal.* As Solomon is master of his vineyard, so the beloved is mistress of her attractions to dispense them as she will. She offers Solomon the owner's portion of her vineyard.
8:13 *in the gardens.* In 7:11–12 the beloved invites her lover to accompany her to the countryside and the vineyards. Here the imagery places her appropriately in a garden. *companions.* Male; perhaps the companions of the lover (see 1:7). *Let me hear it!* See 2:14.
8:14 *be like a gazelle or . . . stag.* Display your virile strength and agility for my delight (see note on 2:9). *On the mountains of spices.* Cf. 2:17.

Isaiah

INTRODUCTION

Author

Isaiah son of Amoz is often thought of as the greatest of the writing prophets. His name means "The LORD saves." He was a contemporary of Amos, Hosea and Micah, beginning his ministry in 740 B.C., the year King Uzziah died (see note on 6:1). According to an unsubstantiated Jewish tradition (*The Ascension of Isaiah*), he was sawed in half during the reign of Manasseh (cf. Heb 11:37). Isaiah was married and had at least two sons, Shear-jashub (7:3) and Maher-shalal-hash-baz (8:3). He probably spent most of his life in Jerusalem, enjoying his greatest influence under King Hezekiah (see 37:1–2). Isaiah is also credited with writing a history of the reign of King Uzziah (2 Chr 26:22).

Many scholars today challenge the claim that Isaiah wrote the entire book that bears his name. Yet his is the only name attached to it (see 1:1; 2:1; 13:1). The strongest argument for the unity of Isaiah is the expression "the Holy One of Israel," a title for God that occurs 12 times in chs. 1—39 and 14 times in chs. 40—66. Outside Isaiah it appears in the OT only 6 times. There are other striking verbal parallels between chs. 1—39 and chs. 40—66. Compare the following verses:

1:2	66:24
1:5–6	53:4–5
5:27	40:30
6:1	52:13; 57:15
6:11–12	62:4
11:1	53:2
11:6–9	65:25
11:12	49:22
35:10	51:11

Altogether, there are at least 25 Hebrew words or forms found in Isaiah (i.e., in both major divisions of the book) that occur in no other prophetic writing.

Isaiah's use of fire as a figure of punishment (see 1:31; 10:17; 26:11; 33:11–14; 34:9–10; 66:24), his references to the "holy mountain" of Jerusalem (see note on 2:2–4) and his mention of the highway to Jerusalem (see note on 11:16) are themes that recur throughout the book.

The structure of Isaiah also argues for its unity. Chs. 36—39 constitute a historical interlude, which concludes chs. 1—35 and introduces chs. 40—66 (see note on 36:1).

Several NT verses refer to the prophet Isaiah in connection with various parts of the book: Matt 12:17–21 (Is 42:1–4); Matt 3:3 and Luke 3:4 (Is 40:3); Rom 10:16,20 (Is 53:1; 65:1); see especially John 12:38–41 (Is 53:1; 6:10).

Date

Most of the events discussed in chs. 1—39 occurred during Isaiah's ministry (see 6:1; 14:28; 36:1), so it is likely that these chapters were completed not long after 701 B.C., the year the Assyrian army was destroyed (see note on 10:16). The prophet lived until at least 681 (see note on 37:38) and may have written chs. 40—66 during his later years. In his message to the exiles of the sixth century B.C., Isaiah was projected into the future, just as the apostle John was in Rev 4—22.

Background

Isaiah wrote during the stormy period marking the expansion of the Assyrian empire and the decline of Israel. Under King Tiglath-pileser III (745–727 B.C.) the Assyrians swept westward into Aram (Syria) and Canaan.

About 733 the kings of Aram and Israel tried to pressure Ahaz king of Judah into joining a coalition against Assyria. Ahaz chose instead to ask Tiglath-pileser for help, a decision condemned by Isaiah (see note on 7:1). Assyria did assist Judah and conquered the northern kingdom in 722–721. This made Judah even more vulnerable, and in 701 King Sennacherib of Assyria threatened Jerusalem itself (see 36:1 and note). The godly King Hezekiah prayed earnestly, and Isaiah predicted that God would force the Assyrians to withdraw from the city (37:6–7).

Nevertheless Isaiah warned Judah that her sin would bring captivity at the hands of Babylon. The visit of the Babylonian king's envoys to Hezekiah set the stage for this prediction (see 39:1,6 and notes). Although the fall of Jerusalem would not take place until 586 B.C., Isaiah assumes the demise of Judah and proceeds to predict the restoration of the people from captivity (see 40:2–3 and notes). God would redeem His people from Babylon just as He rescued them from Egypt (see notes on 35:9; 41:14). Isaiah predicts the rise of Cyrus the Persian, who would unite the Medes and Persians and conquer Babylon in 539 (see 41:2 and note). The decree of Cyrus would allow the Jews to return home in 538, a deliverance that prefigured the greater salvation from sin through Christ (see 52:7 and note).

Themes and Theology

Isaiah is a book that unveils the full dimensions of God's judgment and salvation. God is "the Holy One of Israel" (see 1:4; 6:1 and notes) who must punish His rebellious people (1:2) but will afterward redeem them (41:14,16). Israel is a nation blind and deaf (6:9–10; 42:7), a vineyard that will be trampled (5:1–7), a people devoid of justice or righteousness (5:7; 10:1–2). The awful judgment that will be unleashed upon Israel and all the nations that defy God is called "the day of the LORD." Although Israel has a foretaste of that day (5:30; 42:25), the nations bear its full power (see 2:11,17,20 and note). It is a day associated in the NT with Christ's second coming and the accompanying judgment (see 24:1,21; 34:1–2 and notes). Throughout the book, God's judgment is referred to as "fire" (see 1:31; 30:33 and notes). He is the "Lord GOD" (see note on 25:8), far above all nations and rulers (40:15–24).

Yet God will have compassion on His people (14:1–2) and will rescue them from both political and spiritual oppression. Their restoration is like a new exodus (43:2,16–19; 52:10–12) as God redeems them (see 35:9; 41:14 and notes) and saves them (see 43:3; 49:8 and notes). Israel's mighty Creator (40:21–22; 48:13) will make streams spring up in the desert (32:2) as He graciously leads them home. The theme of a highway for the return of exiles is a prominent one (see 11:16; 40:3 and notes) in both major parts of the book. The Lord raises a banner to summon the nations to bring Israel home (see 5:26 and note).

Peace and safety mark this new Messianic age (11:6–9). A king descended from David will reign in righteousness (9:7; 32:1), and all nations will stream to the holy mountain of Jerusalem (see 2:2–4 and note). God's people will no longer be oppressed by wicked rulers (11:14; 45:14), and Jerusalem will truly be the "city of the LORD" (60:14).

The Lord calls the Messianic King "My Servant" in chs. 42—53, a term also applied to Israel as a nation (see 41:8–9; 42:1 and notes). It is through the suffering of the servant that salvation in its fullest sense is achieved. Cyrus was God's instrument to deliver Israel from Babylon (41:2), but Christ delivered mankind from the prison of sin (52:13—53:12). He became a "light to the Gentiles" (42:6), so that those nations that faced judgment (chs. 13—23) could find salvation (55:4–5). These Gentiles also became "servants of the LORD" (see 54:17 and note).

The Lord's kingdom on earth, with its righteous Ruler and His righteous subjects, is the goal toward which the book of Isaiah steadily moves. The restored earth and the restored people will then conform to the divine ideal, and all will result in the praise and glory of the Holy One of Israel for what He has accomplished.

Literary Features

Isaiah contains both prose and poetry; the beauty of its poetry is unsurpassed in the OT. The main prose material is found in chs. 36—39, the historical interlude that unites the two parts of the book (see Author). The poetic material includes a series of oracles in chs. 13—23. A taunting song against the king of Babylon is found in 14:4–23. Chs. 24—27 comprise an apocalyptic section stressing the last days (see note on 24:1—27:13). A wisdom poem is found in 28:23–29 (also cf. 32:5–8). The song of the vineyard (5:1–7) begins as a love

song as Isaiah describes God's relationship with Israel. Hymns of praise are given in 12:1–6 and 38:10–20, and a national lament occurs in 63:7—64:12. The poetry is indeed rich and varied, as is the prophet's vocabulary (e.g., he uses nearly 2,200 different Hebrew words—more than any other OT writer).

One of Isaiah's favorite techniques is personification. The sun and moon are ashamed (24:23), while the desert and parched land rejoice (see 35:1 and note) and the mountains and forests burst into song (44:23). The trees "clap their hands" (55:12). A favorite figure is the vineyard, which represents Israel (5:7). Treading the wine press is a picture of judgment (see 63:3 and note), and to drink God's "cup of anger" is to stagger under His punishment (see 51:17 and note). Isaiah uses the name "rock" to describe God (17:10), and animals such as Leviathan and Rahab represent nations (see 27:1; 30:7; 51:9).

The power of Isaiah's imagery is seen in 30:27–33, and he makes full use of sarcasm in his denunciation of idols in 44:9–20. A forceful example of wordplay appears in 5:7 (see note there), and one finds chiasm (inversion) in 6:10 (see note there; see also note on 16:7) and alliteration and assonance in 24:17 (see note there). The "overwhelming scourge" of 28:15,18 is an illustration of mixed metaphor.

Isaiah often alludes to earlier events in Israel's history, especially the exodus from Egypt. The crossing of the Red Sea forms the background for 11:15 and 43:2,16–17, and other allusions occur in 4:5–6; 31:5; 37:36 (see notes on these verses). The overthrow of Sodom and Gomorrah is referred to in 1:9, and Gideon's victory over Midian is mentioned in 9:4; 10:26 (see also 28:21). Several times Isaiah draws upon the song of Moses in Deut 32 (cf. 1:2 and Deut 32:1; 30:17 and Deut 32:30; 43:11,13 and Deut 32:39). Isaiah, like Moses, called the nation to repentance and to faith in a holy, all-powerful God. See also note on 49:8.

Outline

Part 1: The Book of Judgment (chs. 1—39)

I. Messages of Rebuke and Promise (chs. 1—6)
- A. Introduction: Charges against Judah for Breaking the Covenant (ch. 1)
- B. The Future Discipline and Glory of Judah and Jerusalem (chs. 2—4)
  1. Jerusalem's future blessings (2:1–5)
  2. The Lord's discipline of Judah (2:6—4:1)
  3. The restoration of Zion (4:2–6)
- C. The Nation's Judgment and Exile (ch. 5)
- D. Isaiah's Unique Commission (ch. 6)

II. Prophecies Occasioned by the Aramean and Israelite Threat against Judah (chs. 7—12)
- A. Ahaz Warned Not to Fear the Aramean and Israelite Alliance (ch. 7)
- B. Isaiah's Son and David's Son (8:1—9:7)
- C. Judgment against Israel (9:8—10:4)
- D. The Assyrian Empire and the Davidic Kingdom (10:5—12:6)
  1. The destruction of Assyria (10:5–34)
  2. The establishment of the Davidic king and his kingdom (ch. 11)
  3. Songs of joy for deliverance (ch. 12)

III. Judgment against the Nations (chs. 13—23)
- A. Against Assyria and Its Ruler (13:1—14:27)
- B. Against Philistia (14:28–32)
- C. Against Moab (chs. 15—16)
- D. Against Aram and Israel (ch. 17)
- E. Against Cush (Ethiopia) (ch. 18)
- F. Against Egypt and Cush (Ethiopia) (chs. 19—20)
- G. Against Babylon (21:1–10)
- H. Against Dumah (Edom) (21:11–12)
- I. Against Arabia (21:13–17)
- J. Against the Valley of Vision (Jerusalem) (ch. 22)
- K. Against Tyre (ch. 23)

IV. Judgment and Promise (the Lord's Kingdom) (chs. 24—27)

A. Universal Judgments for Universal Sin (ch. 24)
B. Deliverance and Blessing (ch. 25)
C. Praise for the Lord's Sovereign Care (ch. 26)
D. Israel's Enemies Punished but Israel's Remnant Restored (ch. 27)

V. Six Woes: Five on the Unfaithful in Israel and One on Assyria (chs. 28—33)
A. Woe to Ephraim (Samaria)—and to Judah (ch. 28)
B. Woe to David's City, Jerusalem (29:1–14)
C. Woe to Those Who Rely on Foreign Alliances (29:15–24)
D. Woe to the Obstinate Nation (ch. 30)
E. Woe to Those Who Rely on Egypt (chs. 31—32)
F. Woe to Assyria—but Blessing for God's People (ch. 33)

VI. More Prophecies of Judgment and Promise (chs. 34—35)
A. The Destruction of the Nations and the Avenging of God's People (ch. 34)
B. The Future Blessings of Restored Zion (ch. 35)

VII. A Historical Transition from the Assyrian Threat to the Babylonian Exile (chs. 36—39)
A. Jerusalem Preserved from the Assyrian Threat (chs. 36—37)
1. The siege of Jerusalem by Sennacherib and the Assyrian army (ch. 36)
2. The Lord's deliverance of Jerusalem (ch. 37)
B. The Lord's Extension of Hezekiah's Life (ch. 38)
C. The Babylonian Exile Predicted (ch. 39)

Part 2: The Book of Comfort (chs. 40—66)

VIII. The Deliverance and Restoration of Israel (chs. 40—48)
A. The Coming of the Victorious God (40:1–26)
B. Unfailing Strength for the Weary Exiles (40:27–31)
C. The Lord of History (41:1—42:9)
D. Praise and Exhortation (42:10–25)
E. The Regathering and Renewal of Israel (43:1—44:5)
F. The Only God (44:6—45:25)
G. The Lord's Superiority over Babylon's Gods (ch. 46)
H. The Fall of Babylon (ch. 47)
I. The Lord's Exhortations to His People (ch. 48)

IX. The Servant's Ministry and Israel's Restoration (chs. 49—57)
A. The Call and Mission of the Servant (49:1–13)
B. The Repopulation of Zion (49:14–26)
C. Israel's Sin and the Servant's Obedience (ch. 50)
D. The Remnant Comforted Because of Their Glorious Prospect (51:1—52:12)
E. The Sufferings and Glories of the Lord's Righteous Servant (52:13—53:12)
F. The Future Glory of Zion (ch. 54)
G. The Lord's Call to Salvation and Covenant Blessings (55:1—56:8)
H. The Condemnation of the Wicked in Israel (56:9—57:21)

X. Everlasting Deliverance and Everlasting Judgment (chs. 58—66)
A. False and True Worship (ch. 58)
B. Zion's Confession and Redemption (ch. 59)
C. Zion's Peace and Prosperity (ch. 60)
D. The Lord's Favor (ch. 61)
E. Zion's Restoration and Glory (62:1—63:6)
F. Prayer for Divine Deliverance (63:7—64:12)
G. The Lord's Answer: Mercy and Judgment (ch. 65)
H. Judgment for False Worshipers and Blessing for True Worshipers (ch. 66)

Rebellion of God's People

1 The vision of Isaiah the son of Amoz concerning [a]Judah and Jerusalem, which he
saw during the [1]reigns of [b]Uzziah, [c]Jotham,
[d]Ahaz *and* [e]Hezekiah, kings of Judah.

2 [a]Listen, O heavens, and hear, O [b]earth;
For the LORD speaks,
"[c]Sons I have reared and brought up,
But they have [d]revolted against Me.
3 "An ox knows its owner,
And a donkey its master's manger,
But Israel [a]does not know,
My people [b]do not understand."

4 Alas, sinful nation,
People weighed down with iniquity,
[1a]Offspring of evildoers,
Sons who [b]act corruptly!
They have [c]abandoned the LORD,
They have [d]despised the Holy One of
Israel,
They have turned away [2]from Him.

5 Where will you be stricken again,
As you [a]continue in *your* rebellion?
The whole head is [b]sick
And the whole heart is faint.
6 [a]From the sole of the foot even to the
head
There is [b]nothing sound in it,
Only bruises, welts and raw wounds,
[c]Not pressed out or bandaged,
Nor softened with oil.

7 Your [a]land is desolate,
Your cities are burned with fire,
Your fields—strangers are devouring
them in your presence;
It is desolation, as overthrown by
strangers.
8 The daughter of Zion is left like a
shelter in a vineyard,
Like a watchman's hut in a cucumber
field, like a besieged city.
9 [a]Unless the LORD of hosts
Had left us a few [b]survivors,
We would be like [c]Sodom,
We would be like Gomorrah.

God Has Had Enough

10 Hear [a]the word of the LORD,
You rulers of [b]Sodom;
Give ear to the instruction of our God,
You people of Gomorrah.
11 "[a]What are your multiplied sacrifices to
Me?"
Says the LORD.
"I [1]have had enough of burnt offerings
of rams
And the fat of fed cattle;
And I take no pleasure in the blood of
bulls, lambs or goats.
12 "When you come [a]to appear before Me,
Who requires [1]of you this trampling of
My courts?
13 "Bring your worthless offerings no
longer,
[a]Incense is an abomination to Me.
[b]New moon and sabbath, the [c]calling
of assemblies—
I cannot [d]endure iniquity and the
solemn assembly.
14 "I hate your new moon *festivals* and
your [a]appointed feasts,
They have become a burden to Me;
I am [b]weary of bearing *them*.

1:1 [1]Lit *days* [a]Is 2:1; 40:9 [b]2 Kin 15:1-7, 13; 2 Chr 26:1-23 [c]2 Kin 15:32-38; 2 Chr 27:1-9 [d]2 Kin 16:1-20; 2 Chr 28:1-27; Is 7:1 [e]2 Kin 18:1-20:21; 2 Chr 29:1-32:33
2 [a]Deut 32:1 [b]Mic 1:2 [c]Jer 3:22 [d]Is 30:1, 9; 65:2
3 [a]Jer 9:3, 6 [b]Is 44:18
4 [1]Lit *Seed* [2]Lit *backward* [a]Is 14:20 [b]Neh 1:7 [c]Is 1:28 [d]Is 5:24
5 [a]Is 31:6 [b]Is 33:24; Ezek 34:4, 16
6 [a]Job 2:7 [b]Ps 38:3 [c]Jer 8:22
7 [a]Lev 26:33; Jer 44:6
9 [a]Rom 9:29 [b]Is 10:20-22; 11:11, 16; 37:4, 31, 32; 46:3 [c]Gen 19:24
10 [a]Is 8:20; 28:14 [b]Is 3:9; Ezek 16:49; Rom 9:29; Rev 11:8
11 [1]Or *am sated with* [a]Ps 50:8; Jer 6:20; Amos 5:21, 22; Mal 1:10
12 [1]Lit *of your hand* [a]Ex 23:17
13 [a]Is 66:3 [b]1 Chr 23:31 [c]Ex 12:16 [d]Jer 7:9, 10
14 [a]Is 29:1, 2 [b]Is 7:13; 43:24

1:1–31 Compare the indictment of ch. 1 with that of ch. 5; the two enclose the first series of oracles. Ch. 1 also serves as an introduction to the whole book.

1:1 The title of the book. Other headings occur in 2:1; 13:1; 14:28; 15:1; 17:1; 19:1; 21:1,11,13; 22:1; 23:1. *vision.* In the sense of "revelation" or "prophecy" (see 1 Sam 3:1; Prov 29:18; Obad 1). *Amoz.* Not to be confused with the prophet Amos. *Uzziah, Jotham, Ahaz and Hezekiah.* These kings reigned from 792 to 686 B.C. None of the kings of Israel is mentioned since Isaiah ministered primarily to the southern kingdom (Judah).

1:2 Isaiah begins and ends (66:24) with a condemnation of those who rebel against God. The prophet calls on heaven and earth to testify to the truth of God's accusation against Israel and the rightness of His judgment—since they were witnesses of His covenant (see Deut 30:19; 31:28; 32:1).

1:3 *manger.* Feeding trough. *does not know.* Refusal to know and understand God later resulted in Judah's exile from her land (5:13).

1:4 *Holy One of Israel.* Occurs 25 times in Isaiah (see especially 5:24) and only 6 times elsewhere in the OT (see Introduction: Author).

1:5–6 The pitiable moral and spiritual condition of Israel is transferred to the suffering servant in 53:4–5. The Hebrew words for "stricken," "sick" and "welts" correspond to those for "smitten," "griefs" and "scourging."

1:6 The disease ravages the entire body, as with Job (2:7). *oil.* Commonly used for treating wounds (see Luke 10:34).

1:7–9 The desolation of the land of Judah is the result of foreign invasion: e.g., by Aram, the northern kingdom of Israel, Edom and Philistia (2 Chr 28:5–18); later (701 B.C.), by King Sennacherib and the Assyrian army (36:1–2); still later (605–586), by King Nebuchadnezzar and the Neo-Babylonian army.

1:8 *Daughter of Zion.* A personification of Jerusalem and its inhabitants. *shelter . . . hut.* Temporary structures used by watchmen (Job 27:18), who were on the lookout for thieves and intruders. Thus Jerusalem was not very defensible.

1:9–10 *Sodom . . . Gomorrah.* Classic examples of sinful cities that were completely destroyed (see 3:9; Gen 13:13; 18:20–21; 19:5,24–25). Just as Jesus addressed Peter as though he were Satan (Matt 16:23), so Isaiah addresses his countrymen as though they were the rulers of Sodom and the people of Gomorrah.

1:9 Quoted in Rom 9:29, where it is linked with Is 10:22–23. Isaiah often refers to the remnant that will survive God's judgment on the nation and take possession of the land (see 4:3; 10:20–23; 11:11,16; 46:3).

1:11–15 The sincerity of the worshiper, not the number of his religious activities, is most important (see 66:3; Jer 7:21–26; Hos 6:6; Amos 5:21–24; Mic 6:6–8).

1:11 *fed cattle.* Those kept in confinement for special feeding.

1:14 *new moon festivals.* Celebrated on the first day of each Hebrew month. Special sacrifices and feasts were part of the observance (see Num 28:11–15). *appointed feasts.* Included the annual feasts, such as Passover, Weeks (Pentecost) and Booths (Ex 23:14–17; 34:18–25; Lev 23; Deut 16:1–17).

15 "So when you [a]spread out your hands
in prayer,
[b]I will hide My eyes from you;
Yes, even though you [c]multiply prayers,
I will not listen.
[d]Your hands are [1]covered with blood.

16 "[a]Wash yourselves, [b]make yourselves
clean;
[c]Remove the evil of your deeds from
My sight.
[d]Cease to do evil,
17 Learn to do good;
[a]Seek justice,
Reprove the ruthless,
[1b]Defend the orphan,
Plead for the widow.

"Let Us Reason"

18 "Come now, and [a]let us reason
together,"
Says the LORD,
"[b]Though your sins are as scarlet,
They will be as white as snow;
Though they are red like crimson,
They will be like wool.
19 "[a]If you consent and obey,
You will [b]eat the best of the land;
20 "But if you refuse and rebel,
You will be [a]devoured by the sword."
Truly, [b]the mouth of the LORD has
spoken.

Zion Corrupted, to be Redeemed

21 How the faithful city has become a
[a]harlot,
She *who* was full of justice!
Righteousness once lodged in her,
But now murderers.
22 Your silver has become dross,
Your drink diluted with water.
23 Your [a]rulers are rebels
And companions of thieves;
Everyone [b]loves a bribe
And chases after rewards.
They [c]do not [1]defend the [2]orphan,
Nor does the widow's plea come
before them.

24 Therefore the Lord [1]GOD of hosts,
The [a]Mighty One of Israel, declares,
"Ah, I will be relieved of My
adversaries
And [b]avenge Myself on My foes.
25 "I will also turn My hand against you,
And will [a]smelt away your dross as
with lye
And will remove all your alloy.
26 "Then I will restore your [a]judges as at
the first,
And your counselors as at the
beginning;
After that you will be called the [b]city
of righteousness,
A faithful city."

27 Zion will be [a]redeemed with justice
And her [1]repentant ones with
righteousness.
28 But [1]transgressors and sinners will be
[a]crushed together,
And those who forsake the LORD will
come to an end.
29 Surely [1]you will be ashamed of the
[2a]oaks which you have desired,
And you will be embarrassed at the
[b]gardens which you have chosen.
30 For you will be like an [1]oak whose
[a]leaf fades away
Or as a garden that has no water.
31 The strong man will become tinder,
His work also a spark.
Thus they shall both [a]burn together
And there will be [b]none to quench
them.

God's Universal Reign

2 The word which [a]Isaiah the son of Amoz
saw concerning Judah and Jerusalem.
2 Now it will come about that
[a]In the last days

15 [1]Lit *full of* [a]1 Kin 8:22; Lam 1:17 [b]Is 8:17; 59:2 [c]Mic 3:4 [d]Is 59:3
16 [a]Ps 26:6 [b]Is 52:11 [c]Is 55:7 [d]Jer 25:5
17 [1]Or *Vindicate the fatherless* [a]Jer 22:3; Zeph 2:3 [b]Ps 82:3
18 [a]Is 41:1, 21; 43:26; Mic 6:2 [b]Ps 51:7; Is 43:25; 44:22; Rev 7:14
19 [a]Deut 28:1; 30:15, 16 [b]Is 55:2
20 [a]Is 3:25; 65:12 [b]Is 40:5; 58:14; Mic 4:4; Titus 1:2
21 [a]Is 57:3-9; Jer 2:20
23 [1]Or *vindicate* [2]Or *fatherless* [a]Hos 5:10; Mic 7:3 [b]Ex 23:8; Mic 7:3 [c]Is 10:2; Jer 5:28; Ezek 22:7; Zech 7:10
24 [1]Heb *YHWH,* usually rendered *LORD* [a]Ps 132:2; Is 49:26; 60:16 [b]Deut 28:63; Is 35:4; 59:18; 61:2; 63:4
25 [a]Ezek 22:19-22; Mal 3:3
26 [a]Is 60:17 [b]Is 33:5; 60:14; 62:1, 2; Zech 8:3
27 [1]Or *returnees* [a]Is 35:9f; 62:12; 63:4
28 [1]Lit *crushing of transgressors and sinners shall be together* [a]Ps 9:5; Is 66:24; 2 Thess 1:8, 9
29 [1]So with some mss; M.T. *they* [2]Or *terebinths* [a]Is 57:5 [b]Is 65:3; 66:17
30 [1]Or *terebinth* [a]Is 64:6
31 [a]Is 5:24; 9:19; 26:11; 33:11-14 [b]Is 66:24; Matt 3:12; Mark 9:43
2:1 [a]Is 1:1 **2** [a]Mic 4:1-3

1:15 *hide My eyes.* In 8:17; 59:2 God hides His face from Israel (see also Mic 3:4).
1:17 See Jer 22:16; James 1:27. *orphan . . . widow.* Represented the weak and often oppressed part of society. Rulers were warned not to take advantage of them (see v. 23; 10:2; Jer 22:3).
1:18 *scarlet . . . crimson.* Refers to the blood that has stained the hands of murderers (see vv. 15,21). *white as snow.* A powerful figurative description of the result of forgiveness (see Ps 51:7). This offer of forgiveness is conditioned on the reformation of life called for in v. 19.
1:19–20 *eat . . . be devoured.* The vivid contrast is stressed by the use of the same Hebrew verb.
1:21 Jerusalem (representing all Judah) has been an unfaithful wife to the Lord. By following idols and foreign gods she has become a harlot in a spiritual sense (see v. 4; Jer 3:6–14; Ezek 16:25–26).
1:24 *the Lord GOD of hosts, The Mighty One of Israel.* Stressing God's authority as Judge.
1:25–26 *turn . . . restore.* The use of the same Hebrew verb emphasizes the contrast (see note on vv. 19–20).
1:25 *smelt away your dross.* Purifying fire is also mentioned in 4:4; 48:10.
1:26 *faithful city.* See v. 21. Using a related Hebrew noun, Zech 8:3 similarly refers to the future Jerusalem as the "City of Truth."
1:27–28 This contrast between the redemption of Zion (Jerusalem) as a whole and the perishing of individuals who refuse to repent is developed in 65:8–16.
1:29 *oaks . . . gardens.* Pagan sacrifices were offered and sexual immorality occurred at such places (see 65:3; 66:17).
1:31 *burn.* Fire is often a figure of punishment (see 33:11–14; 34:9–10).
2:1 A second introduction, probably relating to chs. 2–4 or to chs. 2–12 (see 13:1).
2:2–5 See note on 4:2–6.
2:2–4 Almost identical to Mic 4:1–3. The theme of the "mountain of the LORD" (Mount Zion) is common in Isaiah; it occurs in

The [b]mountain of the house of the LORD
Will be established [1]as the chief of the mountains,
And will be raised above the hills;
And [c]all the nations will stream to it.
3 And many peoples will come and say,
"Come, let us go up to the mountain of the LORD,
To the house of the God of Jacob;
That He may teach us [1]concerning His ways
And that we may walk in His paths."
For the [2]law will go forth [a]from Zion
And the word of the LORD from Jerusalem.
4 And He will judge between the nations,
And will [1]render decisions for many peoples;
And [a]they will hammer their swords into plowshares and their spears into pruning hooks.
[b]Nation will not lift up sword against nation,
And never again will they learn war.

5 Come, [a]house of Jacob, and let us walk in the [b]light of the LORD.
6 For You have [a]abandoned Your people, the house of Jacob,
Because they are filled *with influences* from the east,
And *they are* soothsayers [b]like the Philistines,
And they [c]strike *bargains* with the children of foreigners.
7 Their land has also been filled with silver and gold
And there is no end to their treasures;
Their land has also been filled with [a]horses
And there is no end to their chariots.
8 Their land has also been [a]filled with idols;
They worship the [b]work of their hands,
That which their fingers have made.
9 So [a]the *common* man has been humbled
And the man *of importance* has been abased,
But [b]do not forgive them.
10 [a]Enter the rock and hide in the dust
[b]From the terror of the LORD and from the splendor of His majesty.
11 The [1a]proud look of man will be abased
And the [b]loftiness of man will be humbled,
And the LORD alone will be exalted in that day.

A Day of Reckoning Coming

12 For the LORD of hosts will have a day *of reckoning*
Against [a]everyone who is proud and lofty
And against everyone who is lifted up,
That he may be abased.
13 And *it will be* against all the cedars of Lebanon that are lofty and lifted up,
Against all the [a]oaks of Bashan,
14 Against all the [a]lofty mountains,
Against all the hills that are lifted up,
15 Against every [a]high tower,
Against every fortified wall,
16 Against all the [a]ships of Tarshish
And against all the beautiful craft.
17 The pride of man will be humbled
And the loftiness of men will be abased;
And the LORD alone will be exalted in that day,

2 [1]Lit *on* [b]Is 27:13; 66:20 [c]Is 56:7
3 [1]Or *some of* [2]Or *instruction* [a]Is 51:4, 5; Luke 24:47
4 [1]Or *reprove many* [a]Is 32:17, 18; Joel 3:10 [b]Is 9:5, 7; 11:6-9; Hos 2:18; Zech 9:10
5 [a]Is 58:1 [b]Is 60:1, 2, 19, 20; 1 John 1:5
6 [a]Deut 31:17 [b]2 Kin 1:2 [c]2 Kin 16:7, 8; Prov 6:1
7 [a]Deut 17:16; Is 30:16; 31:1; Mic 5:10
8 [a]Is 10:11 [b]Ps 115:4-8; Is 17:8; 37:19; 40:19; 44:17
9 [a]Ps 49:2; 62:9; Is 5:15 [b]Neh 4:5
10 [a]Is 2:19, 21; Rev 6:15, 16 [b]2 Thess 1:9
11 [1]Lit *eyes of the loftiness of men* [a]Is 5:15; 37:23 [b]Ps 18:27; Is 13:11; 23:9; 2 Cor 10:5
12 [a]Job 40:11, 12; Is 24:4, 21; Mal 4:1
13 [a]Zech 11:2
14 [a]Is 40:4
15 [a]Is 25:12
16 [a]1 Kin 10:22; Is 23:1, 14; 60:9

passages that depict the coming of both Jews and Gentiles to Jerusalem (Zion) in the last days (see 11:9; 27:13; 56:7; 57:13; 65:25; 66:20; see also 60:3–5; Zech 14:16). Some believe that the peace described in this passage has been inaugurated through the coming of Christ and the preaching of the gospel, and will be consummated at the return of Christ. Others maintain that it is a prophecy of conditions during a future reign of Christ on the earth.

2:2 *the last days.* Can refer to the future generally (see Gen 49:1), but usually it seems to have in view the Messianic era. In a real sense the last days began with the first coming of Christ (see Acts 2:17; Heb 1:2) and will be fulfilled at His second coming.

2:4 *swords into plowshares.* The reverse process occurs in Joel 3:10. What is here called a plowshare was actually an iron point mounted on a wooden beam. Ancient plows did not have a plowshare proper.

2:6 *east.* Probably means Aram (Syria) and Mesopotamia. *soothsayers like the Philistines.* See 1 Sam 6:2; see also Deut 18:10–11 for a description of such practices.

2:7 *silver and gold . . . horses.* Accumulating large quantities of these was forbidden to the king (Deut 17:16–17). They usually led to a failure to trust in God (see 31:1).

2:10,19,21 These verses form a refrain that builds to a climax in v. 21. Lines 3–4 of each verse are identical.

2:10 *rock . . . dust.* During times of severe oppression the Israelites took refuge in caves and holes in the ground (see Judg 6:1–2; 1 Sam 13:6). *majesty.* The Hebrew for this word is translated "pride" when used of man. Pride is an attempt by man to be his own god (see 14:13–14).

2:11,17,20 *in that day.* The phrase occurs seven times in chs. 2–4 (see 3:7, "on that day," 18; 4:1–2). The day of the Lord (see also v. 12) is a time of judgment and/or blessing as God intervenes decisively in the affairs of the nations (see Zeph 1:14–2:3). Assyria and Babylon would bring the terror of judgment upon Judah in Isaiah's day (5:30).

2:13 *cedars of Lebanon.* Even inanimate things that people stand in awe of will be humbled so that "the LORD alone will be exalted" (v. 11). *Bashan.* A region east of the Jordan River and north of Gilead. It was famous for its oaks (Ezek 27:6) and its animals (Ezek 39:18).

2:16 *ships of Tarshish.* Large vessels such as those used by Solomon (1 Kin 10:22) and the Phoenicians (Is 23:1,14) to ply the sea in far-flung commercial ventures. For the location of Tarshish see notes on 23:6; Ezek 27:12.

18 But the [a]idols will completely vanish.
19 *Men* will [a]go into caves of the rocks
And into holes of the [1]ground
Before the terror of the LORD
And the splendor of His majesty,
When He arises [b]to make the earth tremble.
20 In that day men will [a]cast away to the moles and the [b]bats
Their idols of silver and their idols of gold,
Which they made for themselves to worship,
21 In order to [a]go into the caverns of the rocks and the clefts of the cliffs
Before the terror of the LORD and the splendor of His majesty,
When He arises to make the earth tremble.
22 [1a]Stop regarding man, whose breath *of life* is in his nostrils;
For [2b]why should he be esteemed?

God Will Remove the Leaders

3 For behold, the Lord [1]GOD of hosts [a]is going to remove from Jerusalem and Judah
Both [2]supply and support, the whole [2]supply of bread
And the whole [2]supply of water;
2 [a]The mighty man and the warrior,
The judge and the prophet,
The diviner and the elder,
3 The captain of fifty and the honorable man,
The counselor and the expert artisan,
And the skillful enchanter.
4 And I will make mere [a]lads their princes,
And [1]capricious children will rule over them,
5 And the people will be [a]oppressed,
Each one by another, and each one by his [b]neighbor;
The youth will storm against the elder
And the inferior against the honorable.
6 When a man [a]lays hold of his brother in his father's house, *saying,*
"You have a cloak, you shall be our ruler,
And these ruins will be under your [1]charge,"
7 He will [1]protest on that day, saying,
"I will not be *your* [2a]healer,
For in my house there is neither bread nor cloak;
You should not appoint me ruler of the people."
8 For [a]Jerusalem has stumbled and Judah has fallen,
Because their [1b]speech and their actions are against the LORD,
To [c]rebel against [2]His glorious presence.
9 [1]The expression of their faces bears witness against them,
And they display their sin like [a]Sodom;
They do not *even* conceal *it.*
Woe to [2]them!
For they have [b]brought evil on themselves.
10 Say to the [a]righteous that *it will go* well *with them,*
For they will eat the fruit of their actions.
11 Woe to the wicked! *It will go* badly *with him,*
For [1a]what he deserves will be done to him.
12 O My people! Their oppressors [1]are [a]children,
And women rule over them.
O My people! [b]Those who guide you lead *you* astray
And confuse the direction of your paths.

God Will Judge

13 [a]The LORD arises to contend,
And stands to judge the people.
14 The LORD [a]enters into judgment with the elders and princes of His people,
"It is you who have [b]devoured the vineyard;
The [c]plunder of the poor is in your houses.

18 [a]Is 21:9; Mic 1:7
19 [1]Lit *dust* [a]Is 2:10 [b]Ps 18:7; Is 2:21; 13:13; 24:1, 19, 20; Hag 2:6, 7; Heb 12:26
20 [a]Is 30:22; 31:7 [b]Lev 11:19
21 [a]Is 2:19
22 [1]Lit *Cease from man* [2]Lit *in what* [a]Ps 146:3; Jer 17:5 [b]Ps 8:4; 144:3, 4; Is 40:15, 17; James 4:14
3:1 [1]Heb *YHWH,* usually rendered *LORD* [2]Lit *staff* [a]Lev 26:26; Is 5:13; 9:20; Ezek 4:16
2 [a]2 Kin 24:14; Is 9:14, 15; Ezek 17:12, 13
4 [1]Lit *arbitrary power will rule* [a]Eccl 10:16
5 [a]Mic 7:3-6 [b]Is 9:19; Jer 9:3-8
6 [a]Is 4:1
6 [1]Lit *hand*
7 [1]Lit *lift up his voice* [2]Lit *binder of wounds* [a]Ezek 34:4; Hos 5:13
8 [1]Lit *tongue* [2]Lit *the eyes of His glory* [a]Is 1:7; 6:11 [b]Ps 73:9-11; Is 9:17; 59:3 [c]Is 65:3
9 [1]Or *Their partiality bears* [2]Lit *their soul* [a]Gen 13:13; Is 1:10-15 [b]Prov 8:36; 15:32; Rom 6:23
10 [a]Deut 28:1-14; Eccl 8:12; Is 54:17
11 [1]Lit *the dealing of his hands* [a]Deut 28:15-68; Is 65:6, 7
12 [1]Or *deal severely* [a]Is 3:4 [b]Is 9:16; 28:14, 15
13 [a]Is 66:16; Hos 4:1; Mic 6:2
14 [a]Job 22:4; Ps 143:2; Ezek 20:35, 36 [b]Ps 14:4; Mic 3:3 [c]Job 24:9, 14; Ps 10:9; Prov 30:14; Is 10:1, 2; Ezek 18:12; James 2:6

2:20 The futility of worshiping idols is repeatedly noted by Isaiah (see, e.g., 30:22; 31:7; 40:19–20; 44:9–20). See also note on 40:18–20.
2:22 *Stop regarding man.* Lit. "Cease from man" or "Give up on man." The term describes the rejection of the Messiah in 53:3. Ironically, the one Man who should have been trusted and "esteemed" (equals "why should he be esteemed?" here) was "forsaken," "given up on" by men. He alone was worthy of the esteem wrongly given to frail leaders.
3:1–3 Leaders would be taken away by either death or deportation (see 2 Kin 24:14; 25:18–21).
3:2–3 *diviner . . . enchanter.* Occult practitioners and snake charmers (see Deut 18:10; Jer 8:17), whose activities were condemned. Both legitimate and illegitimate kinds of assistance would be removed or deported (see 2 Kin 24:14–16; Hos 3:4).
3:3 *captain of fifty.* A company of 50 was a common military unit (see 2 Kin 1:9). It was also used for civil groupings (Ex 18:25).
3:6 Normally it was unnecessary to force anyone to be a leader. In 4:1 the same social upheaval is seen as seven women "take hold of" one man. *You have a cloak.* Perhaps the one brother was not as poor as the others. *ruins.* Probably Jerusalem (v. 8).
3:7,18 *that day.* See note on 2:11,17,20.
3:8 *Judah has fallen.* A prophecy not completely fulfilled until almost 150 years later.
3:9 *Sodom.* See note on 1:9–10.
3:12 In the Near East, neither the rule of the young nor that of women was looked on with favor.
3:14 *vineyard.* Represents Israel (see 5:1).

15 "What do you mean by [a]crushing My people
And grinding the face of the poor?"
Declares the Lord [1]GOD of hosts.

Judah's Women Denounced

16 Moreover, the LORD said, "Because the [a]daughters of Zion are proud
And walk with [1]heads held high and seductive eyes,
And go along with mincing steps
And tinkle the bangles on their feet,
17 Therefore the Lord will afflict the scalp of the daughters of Zion with scabs,
And the LORD will make their foreheads bare."
18 In that day the Lord will take away the
beauty of *their* anklets, headbands, [a]crescent
ornaments,
19 dangling earrings, bracelets, veils,
20 [a]headdresses, ankle chains, sashes,
perfume boxes, amulets,
21 [1]finger rings, [a]nose rings,
22 festal robes, outer tunics, cloaks, money purses,
23 hand mirrors, undergarments, turbans
and veils.
24 Now it will come about that instead of [1]sweet [a]perfume there will be putrefaction;
Instead of a belt, a rope;
Instead of [b]well-set hair, a [c]plucked-out scalp;
Instead of fine clothes, a [d]donning of sackcloth;
And branding instead of beauty.
25 Your men will [a]fall by the sword
And your [1]mighty ones in battle.
26 And her [1a]gates will lament and mourn,
And deserted she will [b]sit on the ground.

15 [1]Heb *YHWH,* usually rendered LORD [a]Ps 94:5
16 [1]Lit *outstretched necks* [a]Song 3:11; Is 3:16-4:1, 4; 32:9-15
18 [a]Judg 8:21, 26
20 [a]Ex 39:28
21 [1]Or *signet rings* [a]Gen 24:47; Ezek 16:12
24 [1]Or *balsam oil* [a]Esth 2:12 [b]1 Pet 3:3 [c]Is 22:12; Ezek 27:31; Amos 8:10 [d]Is 15:3; Lam 2:10
25 [1]Lit *strength* [a]Is 1:20; 65:12
26 [1]Lit *entrances* [a]Jer 14:2; Lam 1:4 [b]Lam 2:10
4:1 [a]Is 13:12 [b]Gen 30:23; Is 54:4
2 [a]Is 11:1; 53:2; Jer 23:5; 33:15; Zech 3:8; 6:12 [b]Ps 72:16 [c]Is 10:20; 37:31, 32; Joel 2:32; Obad 17
3 [a]Is 28:5; 46:3; Rom 11:4, 5 [b]Is 52:1; 62:12 [c]Ex 32:32; Ps 69:28; Luke 10:20
4 [1]Lit *rinsed away* [a]Is 3:16 [b]Is 1:15 [c]Is 28:6 [d]Is 1:31; 9:19; Matt 3:11
5 [a]Ex 13:21, 22; 24:16; Num 9:15-23 [b]Is 60:1, 2
6 [1]Lit *a hiding place* [a]Ps 27:5; Is 25:4; 32:1, 2

A Remnant Prepared

4 For seven women will take hold of [a]one
man in that day, saying, "We will eat our
own bread and wear our own clothes, only
let us be called by your name; [b]take away
our reproach!"
2 In that day the [a]Branch of the LORD will
be beautiful and glorious, and the [b]fruit of
the earth *will be* the pride and the adornment of the [c]survivors of Israel.
3 It will come about that he who is [a]left
in Zion and remains in Jerusalem will be
called [b]holy—everyone who is [c]recorded for
life in Jerusalem.
4 When the Lord has washed away the
filth of the [a]daughters of Zion and [1]purged
the [b]bloodshed of Jerusalem from her midst,
by the [c]spirit of judgment and the [d]spirit of
burning,
5 then the LORD will create over the
whole area of Mount Zion and over her
assemblies [a]a cloud by day, even smoke, and
the brightness of a flaming fire by night; for
over all the [b]glory will be a canopy.
6 There will be a [a]shelter to *give* shade
from the heat by day, and refuge and [1]pro-
tection from the storm and the rain.

Parable of the Vineyard

5 Let me sing now for my well-beloved
A song of my beloved concerning His vineyard.

3:15 The leaders were grinding the poor, as men grind grain between two millstones.
3:16–24 For a NT warning against overemphasis on outward adornment see 1 Pet 3:3–4.
3:16 *walk with . . . mincing steps.* In the Near East the way one walked communicated specific attitudes. Ornaments on ankles made short steps necessary.
3:17 *bare.* Baldness was associated with mourning over catastrophe (see v. 24; 15:2).
3:18 *crescent ornaments.* Probably moon-shaped; they implied veneration of the popular moon-god.
3:20 *headdresses.* Perhaps a kind of turban (see Ezek 24:17,23).
3:21 *finger rings.* Contained a seal and were a mark of authority (see Gen 41:42 and note). *nose rings.* Sometimes made of gold and worn by brides.
3:24 *rope . . . branding.* Captives were treated like cattle. They were led away by ropes and sometimes branded.
3:26 *her gates.* The gates are personified, as in Ps 24:7,9. They will lament because the crowds that used to assemble there are gone.
4:1–2 *in that day.* See notes on 2:2 and 2:11,17,20. After judgment comes salvation.
4:1 See note on 3:6. War will decimate the male population (3:25; see 13:12), leaving many women with the double disgrace of being widows and childless. See 54:4.
4:2–6 An oracle of redemption just before the long message of indictment and judgment in ch. 5. It balances that found in 2:2–5, which immediately follows the long message of indictment and judgment in ch. 1 (see note on 1:1–31). These two oracles of redemption were intended to complement each other.
4:2–3 *survivors . . . left.* See note on 1:9.
4:2 *Branch.* A Messianic title related to the "shoot" and "branch" (11:1; 53:2) descended from David—but some believe that here "branch" refers to Judah. *pride.* A legitimate pride in the fruitfulness of the land that will characterize the Messiah's reign (see Ps 72:3,6,16). Contrast the pride of 2:11,17. *adornment.* Here the fruitfulness of the land will be Israel's glory; in 46:13 God's salvation will be her glory; in 60:19 God Himself will be her glory.
4:3 *holy.* Means "set apart" to God. See 1:26; 6:13; see also Zech 14:20.
4:4 *judgment . . . burning.* Purifying fire is also mentioned in 1:25; 48:10.
4:5–6 *cloud . . . fire . . . shelter.* These words recall Israel's wilderness wanderings, when the pillar of cloud and fire guided and protected the people (Ex 13:21–22; 14:21–22). Isaiah often refers to the time of the exodus (see 11:15–16; 31:5; 51:10).
4:5 *the glory.* The manifestation of God's presence represented by a glow of flaming fire (see Ex 16:10; 24:17; 40:34–35). *canopy.* The cloud of smoke.
4:6 God's presence in cloud and fire will protect and preserve redeemed Zion (cf. Ps 121:5–6).
5:1–30 See note on 1:1–31.
5:1 *well-beloved.* God. *vineyard.* Israel (see v. 7; 3:14; Ps

My well-beloved had a [a]vineyard on
[1]a fertile hill.
2 He dug it all around, removed its
stones,
And planted it with [1]the [a]choicest vine.
And He built a tower in the middle of it
And also hewed out a [2]wine vat in it;
Then He [b]expected *it* to produce *good*
grapes,
But it produced *only* [3]worthless ones.

3 "And now, O inhabitants of Jerusalem
and men of Judah,
[a]Judge between Me and My vineyard.
4 "[a]What more was there to do for My
vineyard [1]that I have not done in it?
Why, when I expected *it* to produce
good grapes did it produce
[2]worthless ones?
5 "So now let Me tell you what I am
going to do to My vineyard:
I will [a]remove its hedge and it will be
consumed;
I will [b]break down its wall and it will
become [c]trampled ground.
6 "I will [a]lay it waste;
It will not be pruned or hoed,
But briars and thorns will come up.
I will also charge the clouds to [b]rain
no rain on it."

7 For the [a]vineyard of the LORD of hosts
is the house of Israel
And the men of Judah His delightful
plant.
Thus He looked for justice, but
behold, [b]bloodshed;
For righteousness, but behold, a cry of
distress.

Woes for the Wicked

8 Woe to those who [a]add house to
house *and* join field to field,
Until there is no more room,
So that you have to live alone in the
midst of the land!
9 In my ears the LORD of hosts *has
sworn*, "Surely, [a]many houses shall
become [b]desolate,

5:1 [1]Lit *a horn, the son of fatness* [a]Ps 80:8; Jer 12:10; Matt 21:33; Mark 12:1; Luke 20:9 **2** [1]Lit *a bright red grape* [2]Or *wine press* [3]Or *wild grapes* [a]Jer 2:21 [b]Matt 21:19; Mark 11:13; Luke 13:6 **3** [a]Matt 21:40 **4** [1]Lit *and I have not done* [2]Or *wild grapes* [a]2 Chr 36:16; Jer 2:5; 7:25, 26; Mic 6:3; Matt 23:37 **5** [a]Ps 89:40 [b]Ps 80:12 [c]Is 10:6; 28:18; Lam 1:15; Luke 21:24; Rev 11:2 **6** [a]2 Chr 36:19-21; Is 7:19-25; 24:1, 3; Jer 25:11 [b]1 Kin 8:35; 17:1; Jer 14:1-22 **7** [a]Ps 80:8-11 [b]Is 3:14, 15; 30:12; 59:13 **8** [a]Jer 22:13-17; Mic 2:2; Hab 2:9-12 **9** [a]Is 6:11, 12 [b]Matt 23:38 **10** [1]I.e. Approx 10 1/2 gal. [2]I.e. Approx one bu [a]Lev 26:26; Is 7:23; Hag 1:6; 2:16 [b]Ezek 45:11 **11** [a]Prov 23:29, 30; Eccl 10:16, 17; Is 5:22; 22:13; 28:1, 3, 7, 8 **12** [a]Amos 6:5, 6 [b]Job 34:27; Ps 28:5 **13** [1]Lit *their glory are men of famine* [a]Is 1:3; 27:11; Hos 4:6 [b]Is 3:3 **14** [1]Or *appetite* [2]Lit *her* [a]Prov 30:16; Hab 2:5 **15** [a]Is 2:11; 10:33 **16** [a]Is 28:17; 30:18; 61:8 [b]Is 2:11, 17; 33:5, 10 [c]Is 8:13; 29:23; 1 Pet 3:15

Even great and fine ones, without
occupants.
10 "For [a]ten acres of vineyard will yield
only one [1]bath *of wine*,
And a [b]homer of seed will yield *but* an
[2]ephah of grain."
11 Woe to those who rise early in the
morning that they may pursue
[a]strong drink,
Who stay up late in the evening that
wine may inflame them!
12 Their banquets are *accompanied* by
lyre and [a]harp, by tambourine and
flute, and by wine;
But they [b]do not pay attention to the
deeds of the LORD,
Nor do they consider the work of His
hands.

13 Therefore My people go into exile for
their [a]lack of knowledge;
And [1]their [b]honorable men are
famished,
And their multitude is parched with
thirst.
14 Therefore [a]Sheol has enlarged its
[1]throat and opened its mouth
without measure;
And [2]Jerusalem's splendor, her
multitude, her din *of revelry* and the
jubilant within her, descend *into it*.
15 So the *common* man will be humbled
and the man of *importance* abased,
[a]The eyes of the proud also will be
abased.
16 But the [a]LORD of hosts will be [b]exalted
in judgment,
And the holy God will show Himself
[c]holy in righteousness.
17 [a]Then the lambs will graze as in their
pasture,
And strangers will eat in the waste
places of the [1]wealthy.

18 Woe to those who drag [a]iniquity with
the cords of [1]falsehood,
And sin as if with cart ropes;

17 [1]Lit *the fat* [a]Is 7:25; Mic 2:12; Zeph 2:6 **18** [1]Or *worthlessness* [a]Is 59:4-8; Jer 23:10-14

80:8–16). Jesus' parable of the tenants (Matt 21:33–44; Mark 12:1–11; Luke 20:9–18) is probably based on this song. See John 15:1–17.

5:2 *tower.* Contrast the more modest "shelter" of 1:8. God's vineyard had every advantage (see Matt 21:33). *wine vat.* A trough into which the grape juice flowed (see 16:10). *He expected . . . But.* The interpretation (v. 7) uses the same expression ("He looked for . . . but").

5:6 *briers and thorns.* This pair occurs five more times (7:23–25; 9:18; 27:4). *to rain no rain.* The withholding of rain constituted a curse on the land. See Deut 28:23–24; 2 Sam 1:21; 1 Kin 17:1.

5:7 The song of the vineyard (vv. 1–6) is now interpreted. A powerful play on words makes the point: The words for "justice" and "bloodshed" (*mishpaṭ* and *mispaḥ*) sound alike, as do those for "righteousness" (*ṣedaqah*) and "distress" (*ṣeʻaqah*).

5:8–23 A series of six woes are pronounced (vv. 8, 11–12, 18–19, 20, 21, 22–23), followed by three judgment sections (vv. 9–10, 13–15, 24–25).

5:8 *house to house . . . field to field.* Land in Israel could only be leased, never sold, because parcels had been permanently assigned to individual families (see Num 27:7–11; 1 Kin 21:1–3).

5:10 *ephah.* A tenth of a homer. Meager crops often accompanied national sin (Deut 28:38–39; Hag 2:16–17). The amount of wine and grain is only a tiny fraction of what a ten-acre vineyard and a homer of seed would normally produce.

5:11–13 See Amos 4:1–3; 6:6–7, where a style of life characterized by drunkenness and revelry is likewise condemned.

5:14 *Sheol.* See note on Gen 37:35. The grave has an insatiable appetite (see Ps 49:14 and note; Hab 2:5).

5:18 Contrast Hos 11:4, where God leads His people with "cords of . . . love."

19 [a]Who say, "Let Him make speed, let
Him hasten His work, that we may
see *it;*
And let the purpose of the Holy One
of Israel draw near
And come to pass, that we may know
it!"
20 Woe to those who [a]call evil good, and
good evil;
Who [1b]substitute darkness for light
and light for darkness;
Who [1]substitute bitter for sweet and
sweet for bitter!
21 Woe to those who are [a]wise in their
own eyes
And clever in their own sight!
22 [a]Woe to those who are heroes in
drinking wine
And valiant men in mixing strong
drink,
23 [a]Who justify the wicked for a bribe,
And [b]take away the [1]rights of the ones
who are in the right!

24 Therefore, [a]as a tongue of fire
consumes stubble
And dry grass collapses into the flame,
So their [b]root will become [c]like rot and
their blossom [1]blow away as dust;
For they have [d]rejected the law of the
LORD of hosts
And despised the word of the Holy
One of Israel.
25 On this account the [a]anger of the LORD
has burned against His people,
And He has stretched out His hand
against them and struck them down.
And the [b]mountains quaked, and their
[c]corpses [1]lay like refuse in the
middle of the streets.

19 [a]Ezek 12:22; 2 Pet 3:4
20 [1]Lit *set* [a]Prov 17:15; Amos 5:7 [b]Job 17:12; Matt 6:22, 23; Luke 11:34, 35
21 [a]Prov 3:7; Rom 12:16; 1 Cor 3:18-20
22 [a]Prov 23:20; Is 5:11; 56:12; Hab 2:15
23 [1]Lit *righteousness* [a]Ex 23:8; Is 1:23; 10:1, 2; Mic 3:11; 7:3 [b]Ps 94:21; James 5:6
24 [1]Lit *ascend* [a]Is 9:18, 19; Joel 2:5 [b]Job 18:16 [c]Hos 5:12 [d]Is 8:6; 30:9, 12; Acts 13:41
25 [1]Lit *were* [a]2 Kin 22:13, 17; Is 66:15 [b]Ps 18:7; Is 64:3; Jer 4:24; Nah 1:5 [c]2 Kin 9:37; Is 14:19; Jer 16:4
25 [2]Lit *has not turned away* [d]Is 9:12, 17, 19, 21; 10:4; Jer 4:8; Dan 9:16 [e]Ex 7:19; Is 23:11
26 [1]Lit *nations;* probably Assyria [a]Is 13:2, 3 [b]Is 7:18; Zech 10:8 [c]Deut 28:49 [d]Is 13:4, 5
27 [a]Joel 2:7, 8 [b]Job 12:18
28 [1]Lit *Which, its arrows* [2]Lit *are regarded as* [a]Ps 7:12, 13; 45:5; Is 13:18 [b]Is 21:1; Jer 4:13

[d]For all this His anger [2]is not spent,
But His [e]hand is still stretched out.

26 He will also lift up a [a]standard to the
[1]distant nation,
And will [b]whistle for it [c]from the ends
of the earth;
And behold, it will [d]come with speed
swiftly.
27 [a]No one in it is weary or stumbles,
None slumbers or sleeps;
Nor is the [b]belt at its waist undone,
Nor its sandal strap broken.
28 [1a]Its arrows are sharp and all its bows
are bent;
The hoofs of its horses [2]seem like flint
and its *chariot* [b]wheels like a
whirlwind.
29 Its [a]roaring is like a lioness, and it
roars like young lions;
It growls as it [b]seizes the prey
And carries *it* off with [c]no one to
deliver *it.*
30 And it will [a]growl over it in that day
like the roaring of the sea.
If one [b]looks to the land, behold, there
is darkness *and* distress;
Even the light is darkened by its
clouds.

Isaiah's Vision

6 In the year of [a]King Uzziah's death [b]I saw the Lord sitting on a throne, lofty and exalted, with the train of His robe filling the temple.
2 Seraphim stood above Him, [a]each hav-

29 [a]Jer 51:38; Zeph 3:3; Zech 11:3 [b]Is 10:6; 49:24, 25; Mic 5:8 [c]Is 42:22 **30** [a]Is 17:12; Jer 6:23; Luke 21:25 [b]Is 8:22; Jer 4:23-28; Joel 2:10; Luke 21:25, 26 **6:1** [a]2 Kin 15:7; 2 Chr 26:23; Is 1:1 [b]John 12:41; Rev 4:2, 3; 20:11 **2** [a]Rev 4:8

5:19 The Hebrew for the words "make speed" and "hasten" corresponds to that of the first and third elements of the name "Maher-shalal-hash-baz" (meaning, "Swift is the booty, speedy is the prey"; see 8:1,3). When Isaiah named his son (8:3), he may have been responding to the sarcastic taunts of these sinners. God did bring swift judgment, according to v. 26. *Holy One of Israel.* See 1:4 and note.
5:22 *mixing strong drink.* Spices were added to beer and wine (see Prov 23:30).
5:23 See 1:23; 10:1–2.
5:24 *despised . . . the Holy One of Israel.* See v. 19; see also 1:4 and note.
5:25 *the mountains quaked.* When God takes action, even the mountains tremble (see 64:3; Jer 4:24–26). This is the language of theophany (a manifestation or appearance of God). *For . . . stretched out.* A refrain repeated in 9:12,17,21; 10:4.
5:26 *lift up a standard.* A pole with a banner was often placed on a hill as a signal for gathering troops (13:2) or for summoning the nations to bring Israel back home (11:10,12; 49:22; 62:10). *distant nation.* Such as Assyria, whose armies struck Israel and Judah in 722 and 701 B.C., and Babylon, which began its invasions in 605. *from the ends of the earth.* Nations like Egypt and Assyria.
5:27 *No one . . . is weary or stumbles.* Cf. the use of these terms in 40:29–31.
5:30 *in that day.* See note on 2:11,17,20. *darkness and distress.* Similar words describe the horrors of war in 8:22.
6:1 *the year of King Uzziah's death.* 740 B.C. Isaiah's commission probably preceded his preaching ministry; the account was postponed to serve as a climax to the opening series of oracles and to provide warrant for the shocking announcements of judgment they contain. The people had mocked the "Holy One of Israel" (5:19), and now He has commissioned Isaiah to call them to account. Uzziah reigned from 792 to 740 and was a godly and powerful king. When he insisted on burning incense in the temple, however, he was struck with leprosy and remained leprous until his death (2 Chr 26:16–21). He was also called Azariah (2 Kin 14:21; 2 Chr 26:1). *I saw.* Probably in a vision in the temple. *the Lord.* The true King (see v. 5). *lofty and exalted.* The same Hebrew words are applied to God in 57:15, and similar terms are used of the suffering servant in 52:13. *train of His robe.* A long, flowing garment. Cf. the robe of the "son of man" in Rev 1:13. *temple.* Probably the heavenly temple, with which the earthly temple was closely associated. John's vision of God on His throne is similar (Rev 4:1–8).
6:2 *Seraphim.* See v. 6; angelic beings not mentioned elsewhere. The Hebrew root underlying this word means "burn," perhaps to indicate their purity as God's ministers. (It refers to venomous snakes in 14:29; 30:6; see Num 21:6.) They correspond to the "living creatures" of Rev 4:6–9, each of whom also

ing six wings: with two he covered his face,
and with two he covered his feet, and with
two he flew.
3 And one called out to another and said,
"[a] Holy, Holy, Holy, is the LORD of hosts,
The [1b] whole earth is full of His glory."
4 And the [1] foundations of the thresholds
trembled at the voice of him who called out,
while the [2a] temple was filling with smoke.
5 Then I said,
"[a] Woe is me, for I am ruined!
Because I am a man of [b] unclean lips,
And I live among a [c] people of unclean
lips;
For my eyes have seen the [d] King, the
LORD of hosts."
6 Then one of the seraphim flew to me
with a burning coal in his hand, which he
had taken from the [a] altar with tongs.
7 He [a] touched my mouth *with it* and
said, "Behold, this has touched your lips;
and [b] your iniquity is taken away and your
sin is [1] forgiven."

Isaiah's Commission

8 Then I heard the [a] voice of the Lord,
saying, "Whom shall I send, and who will go
for Us?" Then [b] I said, "Here am I. Send me!"
9 He said, "Go, and tell this people:
'Keep on [a] listening, but do not
perceive;
Keep on looking, but do not
understand.'
10 "[a] Render the hearts of this people
[1b] insensitive,
Their ears [2] dull,
And their eyes [3] dim,
[c] Otherwise they might see with their
eyes,
Hear with their ears,
Understand with their hearts,
And return and be healed."
11 Then I said, "Lord, [a] how long?" And
He answered,
"Until [b] cities are devastated *and*
without inhabitant,
Houses are without people
And the land is utterly desolate,
12 "The LORD has [a] removed men far away,
And the [1b] forsaken places are many in
the midst of the land.
13 "Yet there will be a tenth portion in it,
And it will again be *subject* to burning,
Like a terebinth or an [a] oak
Whose stump remains when it is
felled.
The [b] holy seed is its stump."

War against Jerusalem

7 Now it came about in the days of [a] Ahaz,
the son of Jotham, the son of Uzziah,
king of Judah, that [b] Rezin the king of Aram
and [c] Pekah the son of Remaliah, king of Israel, went up to Jerusalem to *wage* war against
it, but [d] could not [1] conquer it.
2 When it was reported to the [a] house of
David, saying, "The Arameans [1b] have
camped in [c] Ephraim," his heart and the
hearts of his people shook as the trees of the
forest shake [2] with the wind.
3 Then the LORD said to Isaiah, "Go out
now to meet Ahaz, you and your son [1] Shear-

3 [1] Lit *fullness of the whole earth is His glory* [a] Rev 4:8 [b] Num 14:21; Ps 72:19
4 [1] Lit *door sockets* [2] Lit *house* [a] Rev 15:8
5 [a] Ex 33:20; Luke 5:8 [b] Ex 6:12, 30 [c] Is 59:3; Jer 9:3-8 [d] Jer 51:57
6 [a] Rev 8:3
7 [1] Lit *atoned for* [a] Jer 1:9; Dan 10:16 [b] Is 40:2; 53:5, 6, 11; 1 John 1:7
8 [a] Ezek 10:5; Acts 9:4 [b] Acts 26:19
9 [a] Is 43:8; Matt 13:14; Mark 4:12; Luke 8:10; John 12:40; Acts 28:26; Rom 11:8
10 [1] Lit *fat* [2] Lit *heavy* [3] Lit *besmeared* [a] Matt 13:15 [b] Deut 31:20; 32:15
10 [c] Jer 5:21
11 [a] Ps 79:5 [b] Lev 26:31; Is 1:7; 3:8, 26
12 [1] Or *forsakenness will be great* [a] Deut 28:64 [b] Jer 4:29
13 [a] Job 14:7 [b] Deut 7:6; Ezra 9:2
7:1 [1] Lit *fight against* [a] 2 Kin 16:1; Is 1:1 [b] 2 Kin 15:37 [c] 2 Kin 15:25; 2 Chr 28:6 [d] Is 7:6, 7
2 [1] Lit *has settled down on* [2] Lit *from before* [a] Is 7:13; 22:22 [b] Is 8:12 [c] Is 9:9 **3** [1] I.e. *a remnant shall return*

had six wings. *covered his face.* Apparently the Seraphim could not gaze directly at the glory of God.

6:3 *Holy, Holy, Holy.* The repetition underscores God's infinite holiness. Note the triple use of "the temple of the LORD" in Jer 7:4 to stress the people's confidence in the security of Jerusalem because of the presence of that sanctuary. *full of His glory.* In Num 14:21–22; Ps 72:18–19 the worldwide glory of God is linked with His miraculous signs.

6:4 *foundations . . . trembled . . . filling with smoke.* Similarly the power of God's voice terrified the Israelites at Mount Sinai, and the mountain was covered with smoke (see Ex 19:18–19; 20:18–19).

6:5 *eyes have seen the King.* Isaiah was dismayed because anyone who saw God expected to die immediately (see Gen 16:13; 32:30 and notes; Ex 33:20).

6:6 *burning coal.* Coals of fire were taken inside the most holy place on the day of atonement (Lev 16:12), when sacrifice was made to atone for sin. See note on 1:25.

6:7 *touched my mouth.* When God commissioned Jeremiah, His hand touched the prophet's mouth (Jer 1:9).

6:8–10 Isaiah's prophetic commission will have the ironic but justly deserved effect of hardening the callous hearts of rebellious Israel—and so rendering the warnings of judgment sure (see vv. 11–13). See also Jer 1:8,19; Ezek 2:3–4.

6:8 *for Us.* The heavenly King speaks in the divine council. As a true prophet, Isaiah is made privy to that council, as were Micaiah (1 Kin 22:19–20) and Jeremiah (23:18,22). Cf. Gen 1:26; 11:7; Amos 3:7. *Here am I.* See note on Gen 22:1.

6:9–10 Quoted by Jesus in the parable of the sower (Matt 13:14–15; Mark 4:12; Luke 8:10). See also Rom 11:7–10,25.

6:10 *hearts . . . ears . . . eyes . . . eyes . . . ears . . . hearts.* The *a-b-c/c-b-a* inversion is called a "chiastic" arrangement, a common literary device in the OT. *ears dull . . . eyes dim.* Israel's deafness and blindness are also mentioned in 29:9; 42:18; 43:8. One day, however, the nation will be able to see and hear (29:18; 35:5).

6:12 *far away.* See 5:13.

6:13 *a tenth.* A remnant—even it will be laid waste. *holy seed.* The few who are faithful in Israel (cf. 1 Kin 19:18; see note on 1:9). *stump.* Out of which the nation will grow again. For a similar use of this imagery see 11:1.

7:1–12:6 The second section of Isaiah's prophecies, climaxing in the songs of praise found in ch. 12.

7:1 The invasion of Rezin and Pekah (probably in 735/734 B.C.) is known as the Syro-Ephraimite War. Aram (Syria) and Israel (Ephraim; see note on v. 2) were trying unsuccessfully to persuade Ahaz to join a coalition against Assyria, which had strong designs on lands to the west. Isaiah was trying to keep Ahaz from forming a counteralliance with Assyria (see 2 Kin 16:5–18; 2 Chr 28:16–21). *Pekah.* Ruled 752–732 B.C. (see 2 Kin 15:27–31).

7:2 *house of David.* A reference to Ahaz, who belonged to David's dynasty (see 2 Sam 7:8–11). *Ephraim.* Another name for Israel, the northern kingdom. *hearts . . . shook.* Ahaz had been defeated by Aram and Israel earlier (2 Chr 28:5–8).

7:3 *Shear-jashub.* See NASB marg.; see also 10:21–22. Isaiah gave each of his sons symbolic names (see 8:1,3,18). *conduit*

jashub, at the end of the [a]conduit of the upper pool, on the highway to the [2]fuller's field,

4 and say to him, 'Take care and be [a]calm, have no [b]fear and [c]do not be fainthearted because of these two stubs of smoldering [d]firebrands, on account of the fierce anger of Rezin and Aram and the [e]son of Remaliah.

5 'Because [a]Aram, *with* Ephraim and the son of Remaliah, has planned evil against you, saying,

6 "Let us go up against Judah and [1]terrorize it, and make for ourselves a breach in [2]its walls and set up the son of Tabeel as king in the midst of it,"

7 thus says the Lord [1]GOD: "[a]It shall not stand nor shall it come to pass.

8 "For the head of Aram is [a]Damascus and the head of Damascus is Rezin (now within another 65 years Ephraim will be shattered, *so that it is* no longer a people),

9 and the head of Ephraim is Samaria and the head of Samaria is the son of Remaliah. [a]If you will not believe, you surely shall not [1]last." ' "

The Child Immanuel

10 Then the LORD spoke again to Ahaz, saying,

11 "Ask a [a]sign for yourself from the LORD your God; [1]make *it* deep as Sheol or high as [2]heaven."

12 But Ahaz said, "I will not ask, nor will I test the LORD!"

13 Then he said, "Listen now, O [a]house of David! Is it too slight a thing for you to try the patience of men, that you will [b]try the patience of [c]my God as well?

14 "Therefore the Lord Himself will give you a sign: Behold, [a]a [1]virgin will be with child and bear a son, and she will call His name [2b]Immanuel.

15 "He will eat [a]curds and honey [1]at the time He knows *enough* to refuse evil and choose good.

16 "[a]For before the boy will know *enough* to refuse evil and choose good, [b]the land whose two kings you dread will be forsaken.

Trials to Come for Judah

17 "The LORD will bring on you, on your people, and on your father's house such days as have never come since the day that [a]Ephraim separated from Judah, the [b]king of Assyria."

18 In that day the LORD will [a]whistle for the fly that is in the [1b]remotest part of the rivers of Egypt and for the bee that is in the land of Assyria.

19 They will all come and settle on the steep [1]ravines, on the [a]ledges of the cliffs, [b]on all the thorn bushes and on all the [2]watering places.

3 [2]I.e. *laundryman's* [a]2 Kin 18:17; Is 36:2
4 [a]Ex 14:13; Is 30:15; Lam 3:26 [b]Is 10:24; Matt 24:6 [c]Deut 20:3; 1 Sam 17:32; Is 35:4 [d]Amos 4:11; Zech 3:2 [e]Is 7:1, 9
5 [a]Is 7:2
6 [1]Lit *cause it a sickening dread* [2]Lit *it*
7 [1]Heb *YHWH,* usually rendered *LORD* [a]Is 8:10; 28:18; Acts 4:25, 26
8 [a]Gen 14:15; Is 17:1-3
9 [1]Or *be established* [a]2 Chr 20:20; Is 5:24; 8:6-8; 30:12-14
11 [1]So with the versions; M.T. *make the request deep or high* [2]Lit *heights* [a]2 Kin 19:29; Is 37:30; 38:7, 8; 55:13
13 [a]Is 7:2 [b]Is 1:14; 43:24 [c]Is 25:1
14 [1]Or *maiden* [2]I.e. God is with us [a]Matt 1:23 [b]Is 8:8, 10
15 [1]Lit *with respect to his knowing* [a]Is 7:22
16 [a]Is 8:4 [b]Is 8:14; 17:3; Jer 7:15; Hos 5:3, 9, 14; Amos 1:3-5
17 [a]1 Kin 12:16 [b]2 Chr 28:20; Is 8:7, 8; 10:5, 6
18 [1]Or *mouth of the rivers;* i.e. the Nile Delta [a]Is 5:26 [b]Is 13:5
19 [1]Or *wadis* [2]Or *pastures* [a]Is 2:19; Jer 16:16 [b]Is 7:24, 25

of the upper pool. Location unknown. Ahaz was probably inspecting the city's water supply. *fuller's field.* Clothes were cleaned by trampling on them in cold water and using a kind of soap (soda) or bleach (see Mal 3:2; Mark 9:3).

7:4 *two stubs . . . smoldering.* Damascus (Aram's capital; see v. 8) was crushed by Tiglath-pileser III in 732 B.C., and Israel was soundly defeated the same year.

7:6 *Tabeel.* An Aramaic name sometimes associated with the "land of Tob" east of the Jordan River (see Judg 11:3).

7:8 *within another 65 years.* By c. 670 B.C. Esarhaddon (and, shortly after him, Ashurbanipal) king of Assyria settled foreign colonists in Israel. Their intermarriage with the few Israelites who had not been deported resulted in the "Samaritans" (see 2 Kin 17:24–34 and note on 2 Kin 17:29) and marked the end of Ephraim as a separate nation.

7:9 *son of Remaliah.* Pekah was a usurper and hardly worthy to challenge Ahaz, a son of David. Aram (v. 8) and Israel (v. 9) had human heads. Judah had a divine head; God was with them (v. 14; 8:8,10). *believe . . . last.* The use of the same Hebrew verb emphasizes the seriousness of the Lord's warning (see 1:19–20,25–26 and notes).

7:11 *a sign.* God was willing to strengthen the faith of Ahaz through a sign (see Ex 3:12).

7:13 *house of David.* See note on v. 2.

7:14 *sign.* A sign was normally fulfilled within a few years (see 20:3; 37:30; cf. 8:18). *virgin.* May refer to a young woman betrothed to Isaiah (8:3), who was to become his second wife (his first wife presumably having died after Shear-jashub was born). In Gen 24:43 the same Hebrew word *('almah)* refers to a woman about to be married (see also Prov 30:19). Matt 1:23 apparently understood the woman mentioned here to be a type (a foreshadowing) of the Virgin Mary. *Immanuel.* The name "God is with us" was meant to convince Ahaz that God could rescue him from his enemies. See Num 14:9; 2 Chr 13:12; Ps 46:7. The Hebrew for "Immanuel" is used again in 8:8,10, and it may be another name for Maher-shalal-hash-baz (8:3). If so, the boy's names had complementary significance (see note on 8:3). Jesus was the final fulfillment of this prophecy, for He was "God with us" in the fullest sense (Matt 1:23; cf. Is 9:6–7).

7:15 *curds and honey.* Curds (a kind of yogurt) and honey meant a return to the simple diet of those who lived off the land. The Assyrian invasion would devastate the countryside and make farming impossible. (See vv. 22–25 for the significance of the expression.) *at the time He knows . . . evil . . . good.* Suggests the age of moral determination and responsibility under the law—most likely 12 or 13 years of age. Thus, "at the time" this boy is 12 or 13 (722/721 B.C.), he will be eating curds and honey instead of agricultural products—due to the devastation of Israel by Assyria. Some believe that this expression involves a shorter period of time, identical to that in v. 16 and 8:4.

7:16 *before the boy will know . . . land . . . forsaken.* See note on v. 4; cf. 8:4. "Before" the boy is 12 or 13 years old, Aram and Israel will be plundered. This happened in 732 B.C., when the boy was about two years old.

7:17 *Ephraim separated from Judah.* Almost two centuries earlier (see 1 Kin 12:19–20). *king of Assyria.* Ahaz's appeal to Assyria would bring temporary relief (2 Kin 16:8–9), but eventually Assyria would attack Judah (see 8:7–8; 36:1).

7:18,20,23 *In that day.* Their difficulties will be a foretaste of the "day of the LORD." See note on 2:11,17,20.

7:18 *fly . . . bee.* See Ex 23:28 and note.

7:19 *ledges of the cliffs.* See note on 2:10. It will be impossible to escape from the invaders.

20 In that day the Lord will [a]shave with a [b]razor, [c]hired from regions beyond [d]the [1]Euphrates (*that is,* with the king of Assyria), the head and the hair of the legs; and it will also remove the beard.

21 Now in that day a man may keep alive a [a]heifer and a pair of sheep;

22 and because of the abundance of the milk produced he will eat curds, for everyone that is left within the land will eat [a]curds and honey.

23 And it will come about in that day, [a]that every place where there used to be a thousand vines, *valued* at a thousand *shekels* of silver, will become [b]briars and thorns.

24 *People* will come there with bows and arrows because all the land will be briars and thorns.

25 As for all the hills which used to be cultivated with the hoe, you will not go there for fear of briars and thorns; but they will become a place for [1][a]pasturing oxen and for sheep to trample.

Damascus and Samaria Fall

8 Then the LORD said to me, "Take for yourself a large tablet and [a]write on it [1]in ordinary letters: [2][b]Swift is the booty, speedy is the prey.

2 "And [1]I will take to Myself faithful witnesses for testimony, [a]Uriah the priest and Zechariah the son of Jeberechiah."

3 So I approached the prophetess, and she conceived and gave birth to a son. Then the LORD said to me, "Name him [1][a]Maher-shalal-hash-baz;

4 for [a]before the boy knows how to cry out 'My father' or 'My mother,' the wealth of [b]Damascus and the spoil of Samaria will be carried away before the king of Assyria."

5 Again the LORD spoke to me further, saying,

6 "Inasmuch as these people have
[a]rejected the gently flowing waters
of Shiloah
And rejoice in [b]Rezin and the son of
Remaliah;
7 "Now therefore, behold, the Lord is
about to bring on them the [a]strong
and abundant waters of the
[1][b]Euphrates,
Even the [c]king of Assyria and all his
glory;
And it will [d]rise up over all its
channels and go over all its banks.
8 "Then [a]it will sweep on into Judah, it
will overflow and pass through,
It will [b]reach even to the neck;
And the spread of its wings will [1]fill
the breadth of [2]your land,
O [c]Immanuel.

A Believing Remnant

9 "[a]Be broken, O peoples, and be
[1][b]shattered;
And give ear, all remote places of the
earth.
Gird yourselves, yet be [1]shattered;
Gird yourselves, yet be [1]shattered.
10 "[a]Devise a plan, but it will be thwarted;
State a [1]proposal, but [b]it will not
stand,
For [2][c]God is with us."

11 For thus the LORD spoke to me [1]with [a]mighty power and instructed me [b]not to walk in the way of this people, saying,

12 "You are not to say, '*It is* a
[a]conspiracy!'
In regard to all that this people call a
conspiracy,

20 [1]Lit *River* [a]2 Kin 18:13-16; Is 24:1 [b]Ezek 5:1-4 [c]Is 10:5, 15 [d]Is 8:7; 11:15; Jer 2:18
21 [a]Is 14:30; 27:10; Jer 39:10
22 [a]Is 8:15
23 [a]Is 5:10; 32:13, 14 [b]Is 5:6
25 [1]Lit *sending* [a]Is 5:17
8:1 [1]Lit *with the stylus of man* [2]Heb *Maher-shalal-hash-baz* [a]Is 30:8; Hab 2:2 [b]Is 8:3
2 [1]Another reading is *take for me* [a]2 Kin 16:10, 11, 15, 16
3 [1]I.e. swift is the booty, speedy is the prey [a]Is 8:1
4 [a]Is 7:16 [b]Is 7:8, 9
6 [a]Is 1:20; 5:24; 7:9; 30:12 [b]Is 7:1
7 [1]Lit *River* [a]Is 17:12, 13 [b]Is 7:20; 11:15 [c]Is 7:17; 10:5 [d]Amos 8:8; 9:5
8 [1]Lit *be the fullness of* [2]Or *Your* [a]Is 10:6 [b]Is 30:28 [c]Is 7:14
9 [1]Or *dismayed* [a]Is 17:12-14 [b]Dan 2:34, 35
10 [1]Lit *word* [2]Heb *Immanu-el* [a]Job 5:12; Is 28:18 [b]Is 7:7 [c]Is 8:8; Rom 8:31
11 [1]Lit *with strength of the hand* [a]Ezek 3:14 [b]Ezek 2:8
12 [a]Is 7:2; 30:1

7:20 *shave . . . head . . . beard.* The forcible shaving of the beard was considered a great insult (2 Sam 10:4–5). In times of mourning, a man would shave his own head and beard (see 15:2; see also note on 3:17).
7:23 *briers and thorns.* See note on 5:6. The destruction of the vineyards and the farmlands would fulfill 5:5–6.
8:1–2 *tablet . . . witnesses.* The witnesses would attest to a legal transaction, either the marriage of Isaiah (see note on 7:14) or a symbolic deed connected with Maher-shalal-hash-baz. The Hebrew word for "tablet" is related to the word for "open copy" in Jer 32:11.
8:2 *Uriah the priest.* Served under King Ahaz (see 2 Kin 16:10–11).
8:3–10 See 7:14–17.
8:3 *prophetess . . . son.* Probably the initial fulfillment of 7:14. This is the only known case of a prophetess (see note on Ex 15:20) marrying a prophet. But the young woman may be called a prophetess here because she had become the wife of a prophet. *Maher-shalal-hash-baz.* This symbolic name ("Swift is the booty, speedy is the prey"; see v. 1) meant that Ahaz's enemies would be plundered (see v. 4 and note on 7:4), but it also implied that Judah would suffer (see vv. 7–8).
8:4 *knows how to cry out.* At about age two. The time period is identical to that in 7:16 (see notes on 7:4,16). *spoil of Samaria will be carried away.* The first stage of the destruction of the northern kingdom (see note on 7:4), which was not completed until 722–721 B.C. (see note on 7:15).
8:6 *waters of Shiloah.* The waters in Jerusalem that flow from the Gihon spring (see 2 Chr 32:30) to the Pool of Siloam (see John 9:7) may be intended (see Neh 3:15). Here they symbolize the sustaining power of the Lord. *Rezin and the son of Remaliah.* Rezin and Pekah both died in 732 B.C. (see 2 Kin 16:9; see note on Is 7:1).
8:7–8 *strong . . . waters . . . sweep on.* Mighty rivers were often used to symbolize a powerful invading army (see 28:17–19).
8:8 *even to the neck.* Sennacherib's invasion in 701 B.C. overwhelmed all the cities of Judah except Jerusalem (see 1:7–9). *spread of its wings.* The figure changes to a bird of prey, perhaps the eagle, renowned for its speed. *Immanuel.* All seems lost, but "God is with us" (v. 10) and defeats the enemy (see note on 7:14).
8:9 *peoples . . . be shattered.* Just as Aram and Israel would be shattered (7:7–9), so Assyria and Babylon would eventually fall.
8:10 *it will not stand.* Only God's plans and purposes will last.
8:11 *with mighty power.* See Ezek 1:3; 37:1; 40:1. The prophets were conscious of God's presence in and control over their lives.
8:12 *conspiracy.* Isaiah's warning against relying on Assyria was considered treason (see note on 7:1; cf. Jer 37:13–14).

And [b]you are not to fear [1]what they
fear or be in dread of *it*.
13 "It is the [a]LORD of hosts [b]whom you
should regard as holy.
And He shall be your fear,
And He shall be your dread.
14 "Then He shall become a [a]sanctuary;
But to both the houses of Israel, a
[b]stone to strike and a rock to
stumble over,
And a snare and a [c]trap for the
inhabitants of Jerusalem.
15 "Many [a]will stumble over them,
Then they will fall and be broken;
They will even be snared and caught."
16 [a]Bind up the testimony, [b]seal the [1]law
among [c]my disciples.
17 And I will [a]wait for the LORD [b]who is
hiding His face from the house of Jacob; I
will even look eagerly for Him.
18 [a]Behold, I and the children whom the
LORD has given me are for [b]signs and wonders in Israel from the LORD of hosts, who
[c]dwells on Mount Zion.
19 When they say to you, "[a]Consult the
mediums and the spiritists who whisper and
mutter," should not a people [b]consult their
God? *Should they* [c]*consult* the dead on behalf
of the living?
20 To the [1a]law and to the testimony! If
they do not speak according to this word, it
is because [b]they have no dawn.
21 They will pass through [1]the land [a]hard-
pressed and famished, and it will turn out
that when they are hungry, they will be
enraged and curse [2]their king and their God
as they face upward.
22 Then they will [a]look to the earth, and
behold, distress and darkness, the gloom of
anguish; and *they will be* [b]driven away into
darkness.

12 [1]Lit *their fear* [b]1 Pet 3:14, 15
13 [a]Is 5:16; 29:23 [b]Num 20:12
14 [a]Is 4:6; 25:4; Ezek 11:16 [b]Luke 2:34; Rom 9:33; 1 Pet 2:8 [c]Is 24:17, 18
15 [a]Is 28:13; 59:10; Luke 20:18; Rom 9:32
16 [1]Or *teaching* [a]Is 8:1, 2; 29:11, 12 [b]Dan 12:4 [c]Is 50:4
17 [a]Is 25:9; 30:18; Hab 2:3 [b]Deut 31:17; Is 1:15; 45:15; 54:8
18 [a]Heb 2:13 [b]Luke 2:34 [c]Ps 9:11; Zech 8:3
19 [a]Lev 20:6; 2 Kin 21:6; 23:24; Is 19:3; 29:4; 47:12, 13 [b]Is 30:2; 45:11 [c]1 Sam 28:8-11
20 [1]Or *teaching* [a]Is 1:10; 8:16; Luke 16:29 [b]Is 8:22; Mic 3:6
21 [1]Lit *it* [2]Or *by their king* [a]Is 9:20, 21
22 [a]Is 5:30; 59:9; Jer 13:16; Amos 5:18, 20; Zeph 1:14, 15 [b]Is 8:20

9:1 [1]Ch 8:23 in Heb [2]Or *nations* [a]Is 8:22 [b]2 Kin 15:29; 2 Chr 16:4 [c]Matt 4:15, 16
2 [1]Ch 9:1 in Heb [a]Matt 4:16; Luke 1:79; Eph 5:8
3 [1]Another reading is *not increase* [2]Lit *the* [3]Lit *in* [4]Lit *they*

Birth and Reign of the Prince of Peace

9 [1]But there will be no *more* [a]gloom for her
who was in anguish; in earlier times He
[b]treated the [c]land of Zebulun and the land of
Naphtali with contempt, but later on He
shall make *it* glorious, by the way of the sea,
on the other side of Jordan, Galilee of the
[2]Gentiles.
2 [1a]The people who walk in darkness
Will see a great light;
Those who live in a dark land,
The light will shine on them.
3 [a]You shall multiply the nation,
You [b]shall [1]increase [2]their gladness;
They will be glad in Your presence
As with the gladness [3]of harvest,
As [4c]men rejoice when they divide the
spoil.
4 For [a]You shall break the yoke of their
burden and the staff on their
shoulders,
The rod of their [b]oppressor, as [1]at the
battle of [c]Midian.
5 For every boot of the booted warrior
in the *battle* tumult,
And cloak rolled in blood, will be for
burning, fuel for the fire.
6 For a [a]child will be born to us, a [b]son
will be given to us;
And the [c]government will [1]rest [d]on
His shoulders;
And His name will be called
[e]Wonderful Counselor, [f]Mighty
God,
Eternal [g]Father, Prince of [h]Peace.

[a]Is 26:15 [b]Is 35:10; 65:14, 18, 19; 66:10 [c]1 Sam 30:16 **4** [1]Lit *in the day of Midian* [a]Is 10:27; 14:25 [b]Is 14:4; 49:26; 51:13; 54:14 [c]Judg 7:25; Is 10:26 **6** [1]Lit *be* [a]Is 7:14; 11:1, 2; 53:2; Luke 2:11 [b]John 3:16 [c]Matt 28:18; 1 Cor 15:25 [d]Is 22:22 [e]Is 28:29 [f]Deut 10:17; Neh 9:32; Is 10:21 [g]Is 63:16; 64:8 [h]Is 26:3, 12; 54:10; 66:12

8:13 *shall be your fear.* See 7:2; Prov 1:7.
8:14 *sanctuary . . . stone . . . stumble.* Either the Lord is the cornerstone of our lives (see 28:16) or He is a rock over which we fall. See Rom 9:33; 1 Pet 2:6–8 for an application to Christ. *both the houses.* The northern and southern kingdoms, Israel and Judah.
8:16 Perhaps a reference to the legal transaction connected with vv. 1–2 (see note there). *testimony.* See v. 20. By preserving Isaiah's teaching ("the law"), his disciples could later prove that his predictions had come true. This term occurs elsewhere only in Ruth 4:7 ("manner of attestation in Israel"). *law.* The Hebrew for this word can also mean "teaching" or "instruction." The legal document containing Isaiah's teaching about Assyria's invasion was tied and sealed and then given to the prophet's followers, who were to preserve it until the time of its fulfillment, when God would authenticate it by the events of history (see Jer 32:12–14,44).
8:17–18 In Heb 2:13 these verses are applied to Christ.
8:17 *hiding His face.* See 1:15; 59:2; Mic 3:4.
8:18 *signs and wonders.* See notes on 7:3,14; cf. 20:3.
8:19 *mediums . . . spiritists.* In the present crisis, people were turning to the spirits of the dead (necromancy), as King Saul did when he went to a medium to contact the spirit of Samuel (1 Sam 28:8–11) and learn about the future. See note on 3:2–3.
8:20 *the law . . . the testimony.* See v. 16 and note. Only by heeding the Lord's word through Isaiah—reinforced by the "signs and wonders" (v. 18) that Isaiah and his sons represented—would the light dawn for Israel.
8:21–22 The Assyrian invasion would bring deep distress on all Israel.
8:21 *curse . . . king and . . . God.* Because of their terrible suffering (cf. Prov 19:3)—but severe punishment awaited anyone who cursed God or a ruler (Ex 22:28; Lev 24:15–16).
9:1 *Naphtali.* This tribe in northern Israel suffered greatly when the Assyrian Tiglath-pileser III attacked in 734 and 732 B.C. (2 Kin 15:29). *shall make it glorious . . . Galilee.* Fulfilled when Jesus ministered in Capernaum—near the major highway from Egypt to Damascus, called the "way of the sea" (Matt 4:13–15).
9:2 *great light.* Jesus and His salvation would be a "light to the nations" (42:6; "light of the nations," 49:6).
9:4 *battle of Midian.* Gideon defeated the hordes of Midian and broke their domination over Israel (Judg 7:22–25). *yoke . . . staff.* In 10:26–27 Isaiah predicts that God will destroy the Assyrian army and their oppressive yoke. This was fulfilled in 701 B.C. (see 37:36–38).
9:5 *boot . . . cloak.* Military equipment will no longer be needed. See notes on 2:2–4.
9:6 *son.* A royal son, a son of David (see v. 7; see also 2 Sam

7 There will be [a]no end to the increase
of *His* government or of peace,
On the [b]throne of David and over his
kingdom,
To establish it and to uphold it with
[c]justice and righteousness
From then on and forevermore.
[d]The zeal of the LORD of hosts will
accomplish this.

God's Anger with Israel's Arrogance

8 The Lord sends a [1]message against
Jacob,
And it falls on Israel.
9 And all the people know *it,*
That is, [a]Ephraim and the inhabitants
of Samaria,
Asserting in pride and in [b]arrogance of
heart:
10 "The bricks have fallen down,
But we will [a]rebuild with smooth
stones;
The sycamores have been cut down,
But we will replace *them* with
cedars."
11 Therefore the LORD raises against them
adversaries from [a]Rezin
And spurs their enemies on,
12 The Arameans on the east and the
[a]Philistines on the west;
And they [b]devour Israel with [1]gaping
jaws.
[c]In *spite of* all this, His anger does not
turn away
And His hand is still stretched out.

13 Yet the people [a]do not turn back to
Him who struck them,
Nor do they [b]seek the LORD of hosts.
14 So the LORD cuts off [a]head and tail
from Israel,
Both palm branch and bulrush [b]in a
single day.

7 [a]Dan 2:44; Luke 1:32, 33 [b]Is 16:5 [c]Is 11:4, 5; 32:1; 42:3, 4; 63:1 [d]Is 37:32; 59:17
8 [1]Lit *word*
9 [a]Is 7:8, 9; 28:1, 3 [b]Is 46:12
10 [a]Mal 1:4
11 [a]Is 7:1, 8
12 [1]Lit *the whole mouth* [a]2 Chr 28:18 [b]Ps 79:7; Jer 10:25 [c]Is 5:25
13 [a]Jer 5:3; Hos 7:10 [b]Is 31:1; Hos 3:5
14 [a]Is 19:15 [b]Rev 18:8
15 [a]Is 3:2, 3 [b]Is 28:15; 59:3, 4; Jer 23:14, 32; Matt 24:24
16 [1]Or *swallowed up* [a]Is 3:12; Matt 15:14; 23:16, 24
17 [1]Or *fatherless* [a]Jer 18:21; Amos 4:10; 8:13 [b]Is 27:11 [c]Is 10:6; 32:6 [d]Is 1:4; 14:20; 31:2 [e]Matt 12:34 [f]Is 5:25
18 [a]Ps 83:14; Is 1:7; Nah 1:10; Mal 4:1
19 [a]Is 10:6; 13:9, 13; 42:25 [b]Joel 2:3 [c]Is 1:31; 24:6 [d]Mic 7:2, 6
20 [1]Lit *he slices* [2]Lit *he eats* [a]Is 8:21, 22 [b]Is 49:26
21 [a]2 Chr 28:6, 8; Is 11:13 [b]Is 5:25

15 The head is [a]the elder and honorable
man,
And the prophet who teaches
[b]falsehood is the tail.
16 [a]For those who guide this people are
leading *them* astray;
And those who are guided by them
are [1]brought to confusion.
17 Therefore the Lord does [a]not take
pleasure in their young men,
[b]Nor does He have pity on their
[1]orphans or their widows;
For every one of them is [c]godless and
an [d]evildoer,
And every [e]mouth is speaking
foolishness.
[f]In *spite of* all this, His anger does not
turn away
And His hand is still stretched out.

18 [a]For wickedness burns like a fire;
It consumes briars and thorns;
It even sets the thickets of the forest
aflame
And they roll upward in a column of
smoke.
19 By the [a]fury of the LORD of hosts the
[b]land is burned up,
And the [c]people are like fuel for the
fire;
No [d]man spares his brother.
20 [1]They slice off *what is* on the right
hand but *still* are [a]hungry,
And [2]they eat *what is* on the left hand
but they are not satisfied;
Each of them eats the [b]flesh of his
own arm.
21 Manasseh *devours* Ephraim, and
Ephraim Manasseh,
[a]*And* together they are against Judah.
[b]In *spite of* all this, His anger does not
turn away
And His hand is still stretched out.

7:14; Ps 2:7; Matt 1:1; 3:17; Luke 1:32). *Wonderful Counselor.* Each of the four throne names of the Messiah consists of two elements. Unlike Immanuel (see note on 7:14), these titles were not like normal OT personal names. "Counselor" points to the Messiah as a king (see Mic 4:9) who determines upon and carries out a program of action (see 14:27,"planned"; Ps 20:4,"counsel"). As Wonderful Counselor, the coming Son of David will carry out a royal program that will cause all the world to marvel. What that program will be is spelled out in ch. 11, and more fully in chs. 24–27 (see 25:1—"worked wonders, Plans formed [counseled] long ago"). *Mighty God.* See 10:21. His divine power as a warrior is stressed. *Eternal Father.* He will be an enduring, compassionate provider and protector (cf. 40:9–11). *Prince of Peace.* His rule will bring wholeness and well-being to individuals and to society (see 11:6–9).

9:7 *throne of David . . . righteousness . . . forevermore.* In spite of the sins of kings like Ahaz, Christ will be a descendant of David who will rule in righteousness forever (see 11:3–5; 2 Sam 7:12–13,16; Jer 33:15,20–22). *The zeal . . . this.* God is like a jealous lover who will not abandon His people.

9:9 *Ephraim.* See note on 7:2.

9:10 *bricks have fallen down.* Bricks made of clay and dried by the sun crumbled easily. *smooth stone.* Amos denounces the stone mansions of the wicked (Amos 5:11). *cedars.* The cedars of Lebanon provided the most valuable wood in the ancient Near East (see 1 Kin 7:2–3).

9:12,17,21 *In spite of . . . still stretched out.* See 5:25. This refrain is repeated in 10:4, where the anger of the Lord reaches a climax in the captivity of His people.

9:14 *head and tail . . . palm branch and bulrush.* The leaders of Israel (see also 3:1–3). These two pairs refer to Egyptian leaders in 19:15.

9:17 *orphans or . . . widows.* They often suffered at the hands of the powerful (see note on 1:17), but now even they are wicked.

9:18 *briars and thorns.* See note on 5:6.

9:19 *fuel for the fire.* Contrast v. 5.

9:21 *Manasseh . . . Ephraim.* These two prominent tribes in the northern kingdom were descended from the two sons of Joseph (see Gen 46:20; see also Gen 48:5–6 and notes). They had fought each other centuries earlier (Judg 12:4).

Assyria Is God's Instrument

10 Woe to those who [a]enact evil statutes
And to those who constantly record
[1]unjust decisions,
2 So as [a]to [1]deprive the needy of justice
And rob the poor of My people of *their* rights,
So [b]that widows may be their spoil
And that they may plunder the [2]orphans.
3 Now [a]what will you do in the [b]day of punishment,
And in the devastation which will come [c]from afar?
[d]To whom will you flee for help?
And where will you leave your [1]wealth?
4 Nothing *remains* but to crouch
[1]among the [a]captives
Or fall [1]among the [b]slain.
[c]In *spite of* all this, His anger does not turn away
And His hand is still stretched out.

5 Woe to [a]Assyria, the [b]rod of My anger
And the staff in whose hands is [c]My indignation,
6 I send it against a [a]godless nation
And commission it against the [b]people of My fury
To capture booty and [c]to seize plunder,
And to [1]trample them down like [d]mud in the streets.
7 Yet it [a]does not so intend,
Nor does [1]it plan so in its heart,
But rather it is [2]its purpose to destroy
And to cut off [3]many nations.
8 For it says, "Are not my princes [1]all kings?
9 "Is not [a]Calno like [b]Carchemish,
Or [c]Hamath like Arpad,
Or [d]Samaria like [e]Damascus?
10 "As my hand has reached to the [a]kingdoms of the idols,
Whose graven images *were* greater than those of Jerusalem and Samaria,
11 Shall I not [1]do to Jerusalem and her images
Just as I have done to Samaria and [a]her idols?"

12 So it will be that when the Lord has
completed all His [a]work on Mount Zion and
on Jerusalem, *He will say,* "I will [1]punish the
fruit of the arrogant heart of the king of
Assyria and [b]the pomp of [2]his haughtiness."
13 For [a]he has said,
"By the power of my hand and by my wisdom I did *this,*
For I have understanding;
And I [b]removed the boundaries of the peoples
And plundered their treasures,
And like a mighty man I brought down [1]*their* inhabitants,
14 And my hand reached to the riches of the peoples like a [a]nest,
And as one gathers abandoned eggs, I gathered all the earth;
And there was not one that flapped its wing or opened *its* beak or chirped."

15 Is the [a]axe to [b]boast itself over the one who chops with it?
Is the saw to exalt itself over the one who wields it?
That would be like [c]a [1]club wielding those who lift it,
Or like [c]a rod lifting *him who* is not wood.
16 Therefore the Lord, the [1]GOD of hosts, will send a [a]wasting disease among his [b]stout warriors;
And under his [c]glory a fire will be kindled like a burning flame.
17 And the [a]light of Israel will become a fire and his [b]Holy One a flame,
And it will [c]burn and devour his thorns and his briars in a single day.

10:1 [1]Lit *mischief* or *misfortune* [a]Ps 94:20; Is 29:21; 59:4, 13 **2** [1]Lit *turn aside from* [2]Or *fatherless* [a]Is 5:23 [b]Is 1:23; 3:14, 15 **3** [1]Lit *glory* [a]Job 31:14 [b]Is 13:6; 26:14, 21; 29:6; Jer 9:9; Hos 9:7; Luke 19:44 [c]Is 5:26 [d]Is 20:6; 30:5, 7; 31:3 **4** [1]Lit *under* [a]Is 24:22 [b]Is 22:2; 34:3; 66:16 [c]Is 5:25 **5** [a]Is 7:17; 8:7; 14:24-27; Zeph 2:13-15 [b]Jer 51:20 [c]Is 13:5; 30:30; 34:2; 66:14 **6** [1]Lit *make them a trampled place* [a]Is 9:17 [b]Is 9:19 [c]Is 5:29 [d]Is 5:25 **7** [1]Lit *its heart so plan* [2]Lit *in its heart* [3]Lit *not a few* [a]Gen 50:20; Mic 4:11, 12; Acts 2:23, 24 **8** [1]Lit *altogether* **9** [a]Gen 10:10; Amos 6:2 [b]2 Chr 35:20 [c]Num 34:8 [d]2 Kin 17:6 [e]2 Kin 16:9 **10** [a]2 Kin 19:17, 18

11 [1]Lit *do thus* [a]Is 2:8 **12** [1]Lit *visit* [2]Lit *haughtiness of his eyes* [a]2 Kin 19:31; Is 28:21, 22; 29:14; 65:7 [b]Is 37:23 **13** [1]Or *those who sit on thrones* [a]2 Kin 19:22-24; Is 37:24-27; Ezek 28:4; Dan 4:30 [b]Hab 2:6-11 **14** [a]Jer 49:16; Obad 4 **15** [1]Lit *staff* [a]Jer 51:20 [b]Is 29:16; 45:9; Rom 9:20, 21 [c]Is 10:5

16 [1]Heb *YHWH,* usually rendered LORD [a]Ps 106:15 [b]Is 17:4 [c]Is 8:7; 10:18 **17** [a]Is 30:33; 31:9 [b]Is 37:23 [c]Num 11:1-3; Is 27:4; 33:12; Jer 4:4; 7:20

10:1 *Woe.* Cf. the series of woes in 5:8–23.
10:2 *widows . . . orphans.* See notes on 1:17; 9:17.
10:4 *captives . . . slain.* Jer 39:6–7 similarly describes the plight of Judah's rulers when Nebuchadnezzar captured Jerusalem in 586 B.C. *In spite of . . . still stretched out.* See note on 9:12,17,21.
10:5 *rod . . . staff.* See 9:4 and note. Babylon also was a hammer or club used by God to punish other nations (Jer 50:23; 51:20; Hab 1:6).
10:6 *godless nation.* Judah (see v. 10). *booty . . . plunder.* The last part of the fulfillment symbolized by Maher-shalal-hash-baz ("booty" here is the translation of Hebrew *shalal,* and "plunder" is the translation of *baz*). See 8:1–4 and note on 8:3.
10:9 *Calno.* A region in northern Aram (Syria). See Calneh in Amos 6:2. *Carchemish.* The great fortress on the Euphrates River east of Calno (see Jer 46:2). *Hamath.* A city on the Orontes River that marked the northern extent of Solomon's rule (2 Chr 8:4). See note on 2 Kin 17:24. *Arpad.* A city near Hamath and just south of Calno. All these areas submitted to Assyria by c. 717 B.C. (see 36:19).
10:10 *images . . . of Jerusalem and Samaria.* No Israelite was supposed to worship idols, but the land was full of them (2:8). Samaria fell to Shalmaneser V (2 Kin 17:3–6) and Sargon II in 722–721 B.C.
10:12 *arrogant heart.* Judgment against the proud was announced in 2:11,17.
10:13–14 *my . . . I.* The king of Assyria boastfully refers to himself eight times. Cf. 14:13–14; Ezek 28:2–5.
10:15 *axe . . . saw . . . club . . . rod.* See v. 5; 9:4 and notes.
10:16 *the Lord, the GOD of hosts.* See 1:24 and note. *wasting disease.* When the angel put to death 185,000 soldiers of the Assyrian king Sennacherib in 701 B.C., he may have used a rapidly spreading plague (see note on 37:36; see also 2 Sam 24:15–16; 1 Chr 21:22,27).
10:17,20 *Holy One.* See note on 1:4.

18 And He will [a]destroy the glory of his
forest and of his fruitful garden,
both soul and body,
And it will be as when a sick man
wastes away.
19 And the [a]rest of the trees of his forest
will be so small in number
That a child could write them down.

A Remnant Will Return

20 Now in that day the [a]remnant of Israel,
and those of the house of Jacob [b]who have
escaped, will never again rely on the one
who struck them, but will truly [c]rely on the
LORD, the Holy One of Israel.
21 A [a]remnant will return, the remnant
of Jacob, to the [b]mighty God.
22 For [a]though your people, O Israel,
may be like the sand of the sea,
Only a remnant within them will
return;
A [b]destruction is determined,
overflowing with righteousness.
23 For a complete destruction, one that is
decreed, [a]the Lord [1]GOD of hosts will execute
in the midst of the whole land.
24 Therefore thus says the Lord [1]GOD of
hosts, "O My people who dwell in [a]Zion, [b]do
not fear the Assyrian [2]who [c]strikes you with
the rod and lifts up his staff against you, the
way Egypt *did.*
25 "For in a very [a]little while [b]My indignation *against you* will be spent and My anger
will be directed to their destruction."
26 The LORD of hosts will [a]arouse a
scourge against him like the slaughter of
[b]Midian at the rock of Oreb; and His [c]staff
will be over the sea and He will lift it up [d]the
way *He did* in Egypt.
27 So it will be in that day, that [1]his [a]bur-
den will be removed from your shoulders
and his yoke from your neck, and the yoke
will be broken because [b]of fatness.

28 He has come against Aiath,
He has passed through [a]Migron;
At [b]Michmash he deposited his
[c]baggage.
29 They have gone through [a]the pass,
saying,
"[b]Geba will be our lodging place."
[c]Ramah is terrified, and [d]Gibeah of
Saul has fled away.
30 Cry aloud with your voice, O daughter
of [a]Gallim!
Pay attention, Laishah *and* [1]wretched
[b]Anathoth!
31 Madmenah has fled.
The inhabitants of Gebim have sought
refuge.
32 Yet today he will halt at [a]Nob;
He [b]shakes his fist at the mountain of
the [1c]daughter of Zion, the hill of
Jerusalem.

33 Behold, the Lord, the [1]GOD of hosts,
will lop off the boughs with a
terrible crash;
Those also who are [a]tall in stature will
be cut down
And those who are lofty will be
abased.
34 He will cut down the thickets of the
forest with an iron *axe,*
And [a]Lebanon will fall [1]by the Mighty
One.

Righteous Reign of the Branch

11 Then a [a]shoot will spring from the
[b]stem of Jesse,

18 [a]Is 10:33, 34 **19** [a]Is 21:17 **20** [a]Is 1:9; 11:11, 16; 46:3 [b]Is 4:2; 37:31, 32 [c]2 Chr 14:11; Is 17:7, 8; 50:10 **21** [a]Is 7:3 [b]Is 9:6 **22** [a]Rom 9:27, 28 [b]Is 28:22; Dan 9:27; Rom 9:28 **23** [1]Heb *YHWH,* usually rendered *LORD* [a]Is 28:22; Dan 9:27; Rom 9:28 **24** [1]Heb *YHWH,* usually rendered *LORD* [2]Lit *he* [a]Ps 87:5, 6 [b]Is 7:4; 12:2; 37:6 [c]Ex 5:14-16 **25** [a]Is 17:14; Hag 2:6 [b]Is 10:5; 26:20; Dan 11:36 **26** [a]Is 37:36-38 [b]Judg 7:25; Is 9:4 [c]Ex 14:16 [d]Ex 14:27 **27** [1]I.e. the Assyrian [a]Is 9:4; 14:25

27 [b]Is 30:23; 55:2 **28** [a]1 Sam 14:2 [b]1 Sam 13:2, 5 [c]Judg 18:21; 1 Sam 17:22 **29** [a]1 Sam 13:23 [b]Josh 21:17; 1 Sam 13:16 [c]Josh 18:25; 1 Sam 7:17 [d]1 Sam 10:26 **30** [1]An ancient version reads *Answer her, O Anathoth* [a]1 Sam 25:44 [b]Josh 21:18; Jer 1:1 **32** [1]Another reading is *house of* [a]1 Sam 21:1; 22:9 [b]Is 19:16; Zech 2:9 [c]Is 1:8; Jer 6:23

33 [1]Heb *YHWH,* usually rendered *LORD* [a]Is 37:24, 36-38; Ezek 31:3; Amos 2:9 **34** [1]Or *as a mighty one* [a]Is 2:13; 33:9; 37:24
11:1 [a]Is 4:2; 53:2 [b]Is 9:7; 11:10; Acts 13:23

10:18–19 *forest.* A reference to the Assyrian army. See vv. 33–34.

10:19 Probably fulfilled between 612 B.C. (fall of Nineveh) and 605 (battle of Carchemish).

10:20,27 *in that day.* The day of victory and joy, the positive aspect of the "day of the LORD" (see notes on 2:11,17,20; 9:4). Israel is restored and the people praise God. Ch. 11 connects this "day" with the Messianic age (see 11:10–11; see also 12:1,4).

10:20–22 *remnant.* See note on 1:9. "A remnant shall return" was the name of Isaiah's first son (see NASB marg. on 7:3). A faithful remnant led by Hezekiah survived the Assyrian invasion of 701 B.C. (see 37:4). Later, a remnant returned from Babylonian exile.

10:20 *the one who struck them.* The king of Assyria (see note on 7:17).

10:21 *mighty God.* See note on 9:6.

10:22 *the sand of the sea.* See notes on Gen 13:16; 22:17. *destruction is determined.* Because of Israel's sin, God would punish the nation through foreign invaders.

10:23–24 *the Lord GOD of hosts.* See 1:24 and note.

10:24 *rod . . . staff.* See v. 5; 9:4 and notes.

10:26–27 *Midian . . . burden . . . yoke.* See note on 9:4.

10:26 *Oreb.* One of the Midianite leaders (Judg 7:25). *the sea . . . in Egypt.* When Moses stretched out his hand over the Red Sea, the waters engulfed the chariots of Pharaoh (see Ex 14:26–28).

10:27 *fatness.* Like a sturdy animal, Israel is able to break the yoke.

10:28–32 As if seeing a vision, Isaiah describes the approach of the Assyrian army to Jerusalem from about ten miles north of the city.

10:28 *Michmash.* Located about seven miles north of Jerusalem.

10:29 *Ramah.* The home of Samuel. It was about five miles from Jerusalem (1 Sam 7:17). *Gibeah of Saul.* About three miles from Jerusalem. It had been the capital of Israel's first king (see 1 Sam 10:26).

10:30 *wretched Anathoth.* Jeremiah's hometown (see Jer 1:1). The Hebrew for "wretched" sounds like the word "Anathoth," thus a wordplay.

10:32 *Nob.* Perhaps on present-day Mount Scopus, on the outskirts of Jerusalem. *daughter of Zion.* A personification of Jerusalem and its inhabitants.

10:33 *the Lord, the GOD of hosts.* See 1:24 and note. *boughs . . . tall in stature.* Sennacherib and his armies will fall (see vv. 16–19 and notes).

10:34 *Lebanon.* Refers to the famed cedars of Lebanon (see note on 2:13).

And a [c]branch from [d]his roots will bear fruit.
2 The [a]Spirit of the LORD will rest on Him,
The spirit of [b]wisdom and understanding,
The spirit of counsel and [c]strength,
The spirit of knowledge and the fear of the LORD.
3 And He will delight in the fear of the LORD,
And He will not judge by what His eyes [a]see,
Nor make a decision by what His ears hear;
4 But with [a]righteousness He will judge the [b]poor,
And decide with fairness for the [c]afflicted of the earth;
And He will strike the earth with the [d]rod of His mouth,
And with the [e]breath of His lips He will slay the wicked.
5 Also [a]righteousness will be the belt about His loins,
And [b]faithfulness the belt about His waist.

6 And the [a]wolf will dwell with the lamb,
And the leopard will lie down with the young goat,
And the calf and the young lion [1]and the fatling together;
And a little boy will lead them.
7 Also the cow and the bear will graze,
Their young will lie down together,
And the [a]lion will eat straw like the ox.
8 The nursing child will play by the hole of the cobra,
And the weaned child will put his hand on the viper's den.
9 They will [a]not hurt or destroy in all My holy mountain,
For the [b]earth will be full of the knowledge of the LORD
As the waters cover the sea.

10 Then in that day
The [a]nations will resort to the [b]root of Jesse,
Who will stand as a [1c]signal for the peoples;
And His [d]resting place will be [2]glorious.

The Restored Remnant

11 Then it will happen on that day that the Lord
Will again recover the second time with His hand
The [a]remnant of His people, who will remain,
From [b]Assyria, [c]Egypt, Pathros, Cush, [d]Elam, Shinar, Hamath,
And from the [1e]islands of the sea.
12 And He will lift up a [a]standard for the nations
And [b]assemble the banished ones of Israel,
And will gather the dispersed of Judah
From the four corners of the earth.
13 Then the [a]jealousy of Ephraim will depart,
And those who harass Judah will be cut off;
Ephraim will not be jealous of Judah,
And Judah will not harass Ephraim.

11:1 [c]Is 6:13; Jer 23:5; Zech 3:8 [d]Rev 5:5; 22:16
2 [a]Is 42:1; 48:16; 61:1; Matt 3:16; John 1:32 [b]John 16:13; 1 Cor 1:30; Eph 1:17, 18 [c]2 Tim 1:7
3 [a]John 2:25; 7:24
4 [a]Is 9:7; 16:5; 32:1 [b]Ps 72:2, 13, 14; Is 3:14 [c]Is 29:19; 32:7; 61:1 [d]Ps 2:9; Is 49:2; Mal 4:6 [e]Job 4:9; Is 30:28, 33; 2 Thess 2:8
5 [a]Eph 6:14 [b]Is 25:1
6 [1]Some versions read *will feed together* [a]Is 65:25
7 [a]Is 65:25
9 [a]Job 5:23; Is 65:25; Ezek 34:25; Hos 2:18 [b]Ps 98:2, 3; Is 45:6; 52:10; 66:18-23; Hab 2:14
10 [1]Or *standard* [2]Lit *glory* [a]Luke 2:32; Acts 11:18 [b]Is 11:1; Rom 15:12 [c]Is 11:12; 49:22; 62:10; John 3:14, 15; 12:32 [d]Is 14:3; 28:12; 32:17, 18
11 [1]Or *coastlands* [a]Is 10:20-22; 37:4, 31, 32; 46:3 [b]Is 19:23-25; Hos 11:11; Zech 10:10 [c]Is 19:21, 22; Mic 7:12 [d]Gen 10:22; 14:1 [e]Is 24:15; 42:4, 10, 12; 49:1; 51:5; 60:9; 66:19
12 [a]Is 11:10 [b]Is 56:8; Zeph 3:10; Zech 10:6 **13** [a]Is 9:21; Jer 3:18; Ezek 37:16, 17, 22; Hos 1:11

11:1 *shoot . . . stem.* The Assyrians all but destroyed Judah, but it was the Babylonian exile that brought the kingdom of Judah to an end in 586 B.C. The Messiah will grow as a shoot from that stump of David's dynasty. See 6:13 and note. *Jesse.* David's father (see 1 Sam 16:10–13). *branch.* See notes on 4:2; Matt 2:23.
11:2 *The Spirit . . . will rest on Him.* The Messiah, like David (1 Sam 16:13), will be empowered by the Holy Spirit. *counsel and strength.* The Spirit will endow Him with the wisdom to undertake wise purposes and with the power to carry them out (see note on 9:6). *fear of the LORD.* See Prov 1:7.
11:3 *delight in the fear of the LORD.* See John 8:29.
11:4 *righteousness . . . fairness.* The rulers of Isaiah's day lacked these qualities (see 1:17; 5:7; see also note on 9:7). *rod of his mouth.* Assyria was God's rod in 10:5,24, but the Messiah will rule the nations with an iron scepter (Ps 2:9; Rev 19:15).
11:5 *belt.* When a man prepared for vigorous action, he tied up his loose, flowing garments with a belt (see 5:27).
11:6–9 The peace and safety of the Messianic age are reflected in the fact that little children will be unharmed as they play with formerly ferocious animals. Such conditions are a description of the future consummation of the Messianic kingdom. See 2:2–4 and notes; 35:9; 65:20–25; Ezek 34:25–29.
11:9 *My holy mountain.* See 2:2–4 and note. *full of the knowledge.* See 2:3, where the word of the Lord is taught in Jerusalem. Cf. Hab 2:14.
11:10 *in that day.* See note on 10:20,27. *root of Jesse.* A Messianic title closely connected with v. 1 (see also 53:2; Rom 15:12; Rev 5:5; 22:16). *signal.* See 5:26 and note.
11:11 *second time.* The first time was the exodus from Egypt (see v. 16). The second is probably the return from Assyrian and Babylonian exile, though some interpreters, who believe that the passage refers to the dispersion after the destruction of Jerusalem in A.D. 70, place the regathering at Christ's second coming. *remnant.* See notes on 1:9; 10:20–22. *Egypt.* The delta region of the Nile, in the north. *Pathros.* Southern Egypt, upstream from the delta. *Elam.* The land northeast of the lower Tigris Valley (see 21:2; Jer 49:34–39; Dan 8:2). *Hamath.* See note on 10:9. *islands of the sea.* The coastlands and islands of the Mediterranean are probably intended (see 41:1,5; 42:4; Gen 10:5).
11:12 *assemble the banished ones.* See 27:13; 49:22; 56:8; 62:10; 66:20. *four corners.* Lit. "four wings." "Four corners of the earth" is equivalent to "ends of the earth" (see 24:16; Job 37:3).
11:13 *jealousy of Ephraim.* See note on 7:2. Prior to the exile, Ephraim and Judah were frequently fighting each other (see 9:21).

14 They will [a]swoop down on the slopes
of the Philistines on the [b]west;
Together they will [c]plunder the sons of
the east;
[1]They will possess [d]Edom and [e]Moab,
And the sons of Ammon will be
[2]subject to them.
15 And the LORD will [1a]utterly destroy
The tongue of the [2]Sea of Egypt;
And He will [b]wave His hand over the
[3c]River
With His scorching wind;
And He will strike it into seven streams
And make *men* walk over [4]dry-shod.
16 And there will be a [a]highway from
Assyria
For the [b]remnant of His people who
will be left,
Just as there was for Israel
In [c]the day that they came up out of
the land of Egypt.

Thanksgiving Expressed

12 Then you will say on that day,
"[a]I will give thanks to You, O LORD;
For [b]although You were angry with me,
Your anger is turned away,
And You comfort me.
2 "Behold, [a]God is my salvation,
I will [b]trust and not be afraid;
For [c]the LORD GOD is my strength and
song,
And He has become my salvation."
3 Therefore you will joyously [a]draw
water
From the [b]springs of salvation.
4 And in that day you will [a]say,
"[b]Give thanks to the LORD, call on His
name.
[c]Make known His deeds among the
peoples;
[1]Make *them* remember that His name
is exalted."
5 [a]Praise the LORD in song, for He has
done [1]excellent things;
Let this be known throughout the earth.
6 [a]Cry aloud and shout for joy,
O inhabitant of Zion,
For [b]great in your midst is the Holy
One of Israel.

Prophecies about Babylon

13 The [1a]oracle concerning [b]Babylon
which [c]Isaiah the son of Amoz saw.
2 [a]Lift up a standard on the [1b]bare hill,
Raise your voice to them,
[c]Wave the hand that they may [d]enter
the doors of the nobles.
3 I have commanded My consecrated
ones,

14 [1]Lit *Edom and Moab will be the outstretching of their hand* [2]Lit *their obedience* [a]Jer 48:40; 49:22; Hab 1:8 [b]Is 9:12 [c]Jer 49:28 [d]Is 63:1; Dan 11:41; Joel 3:19; Amos 9:12 [e]Is 16:14; 25:10 **15** [1]Another reading is *dry up the tongue* [2]Perhaps the Red Sea [3]I.e. Euphrates [4]Lit *in sandals* [a]Is 43:16; 44:27; 50:2; 51:10, 11 [b]Is 19:16 [c]Is 7:20; 8:7; Rev 16:12 **16** [a]Is 19:23; 35:8; 40:3; 62:10 [b]Is 11:11 [c]Ex 14:26-29 **12:1** [a]Ps 9:1; Is 25:1 [b]Ps 30:5; Is 40:1, 2; 54:7-10 **2** [a]Is 32:2; 45:17; 62:11 [b]Is 26:3 [c]Ex 15:2; Ps 118:14 **3** [a]John 4:10; 7:37, 38 [b]Is 41:18; Jer 2:13 **4** [1]Or *Proclaim to them that* [a]Is 24:15; 42:12; 48:20 [b]Ps 105:1 [c]Ps 145:4 **5** [1]Or *gloriously* [a]Ex 15:1; Ps 98:1; Is 24:14; 42:10, 11; 44:23 **6** [a]Is 52:9; 54:1; Zeph 3:14 [b]Is 1:24; 49:26; 60:16; Zeph 3:15-17; Zech 2:5, 10, 11 **13:1** [1]Or *burden of* [a]Is 14:28; 15:1 [b]Is 13:19; 14:4; 47:1-15; Jer 24:1; 50:1-51:64; Matt 1:11; Rev 14:8 [c]Is 1:1 **2** [1]Or *wind-swept mountain* [a]Is 5:26; Jer 50:2 [b]Jer 51:25 [c]Is 10:32; 19:16 [d]Is 45:1-3; Jer 51:58

11:14 *sons of the east.* Perhaps the Midianites, who plundered Israel, along with other eastern peoples (see 9:4). *Edom . . . Moab . . . sons of Ammon.* After the exodus, Israel did not attack these nations (see Judg 11:14–18). Israel's future political domination is also referred to in 14:2; 49:23; 60:12 (see also 25:10; 34:5).

11:15 *destroy . . . the Sea of Egypt.* An allusion to the drying up of the Red Sea during the exodus (see Ex 14:21–22). *tongue.* See "bay" in Josh 15:2,5. *the River.* Rev 16:12 refers to the drying up of the Euphrates, perhaps symbolizing the removal of barriers preventing the coming of "the kings from the east."

11:16 *highway.* The removal of obstacles and the building of a highway leading to Jerusalem are also described in 57:14; 62:10 (cf. 40:3–4).

12:1–6 Two short psalms of praise for deliverance (vv. 1–3, 4–6) climax chs. 7–11 (see note on 7:1–12:6; see also note on 6:1).

12:1 *on that day.* Also "in that day," v. 4. For both see note on 10:20,27. *I will give thanks to You.* The "I" is probably the nation, praising the Lord for the deliverance He is sure to bring. *Your anger is turned away.* See note on 9:12,17,21. After God punishes Israel, His anger will be directed against nations like Assyria and Babylon.

12:2 *the LORD GOD.* Two Hebrew forms for the personal name of God are given: The first is "Yah"; the second was probably pronounced "Yahweh." See note on Ex 3:15. *the LORD . . . salvation.* These lines quote Ex 15:2, a verse commemorating the defeat of the Egyptians at the Red Sea. See also Ps 118:14.

12:3 *springs.* Perhaps an allusion to God's abundant provision of water for Israel during the wilderness wanderings (cf. Ex 15:25,27). But here God's future saving act is itself the "spring" from which Israel will draw life-giving water (see Ps 36:9; Jer 2:13; John 4:10).

12:6 *Cry aloud and shout for joy.* These two imperatives occur again in 54:1, where Zion rejoices over the restoration of her people. *Holy One of Israel.* See notes on 1:4; 6:1.

13:1–23:18 A series of prophecies against the nations (see also Jer 46–51; Ezek 25–32; Amos 1–2; Zeph 2:4–15). They begin with Babylon (13:1–14:23) and Assyria (14:24–27) before moving on to smaller nations. God's judgment on His people does not mean that the pagan nations will be spared (see Jer 25:29). In fact, God's judgments on the nations are often a part of His salvation of His people (see, e.g., 10:12).

13:1–14:27 This prophecy concerns Babylon during the Assyrian empire rather than during the Neo-Babylonian empire. Thus the prophecy is actually against the Assyrian empire, Babylon being its most important city. From 729 B.C. on, the kings of Assyria also assumed the title "king of Babylon." Note that there is no new "oracle" heading at 14:24, even though 14:24–27 clearly pertains to Assyria; so 13:1–14:27 forms a unit.

13:1 See note on 1:1. *oracle.* The Hebrew for this word is related to a Hebrew verb meaning "to lift up, carry" and is possibly to be understood as either lifting up one's voice or carrying a burden. Such an "oracle" often contains a message of doom. *Babylon.* See 21:1–9; 46:1–2; 47:1–15; Jer 50–51. Its judgment is announced first because of the present Assyrian threat and because Babylon would later bring about the downfall of Judah and Jerusalem between 605 and 586 B.C. Babylon was conquered by Cyrus the Persian (see 45:1; 47:1) in 539. Subsequently it came to symbolize the world powers arrayed against God's kingdom (cf. 1 Pet 5:13), and its final destruction is announced in Rev 14:8; 16:19; 17–18. Here, however, Babylon is still part of the Assyrian empire (see 14:24–27; see also note on 13:1–14:27).

13:2 *Lift up a standard.* See note on 5:26.

13:3 *My consecrated ones.* Those set apart to carry out God's will. Cf. 10:5, where the Lord calls Assyria "the rod of My anger";

I have even called My [a]mighty warriors,
My proudly exulting ones,
To *execute* My anger.
4 A [a]sound of tumult on the mountains,
Like that of many people!
A sound of the uproar of kingdoms,
Of nations gathered together!
The LORD of hosts is mustering the army for battle.
5 They are coming from a far country,
From the [1][a]farthest horizons,
The LORD and His instruments of [b]indignation,
To [c]destroy the whole land.

Judgment on the Day of the LORD

6 Wail, for the [a]day of the LORD is near!
It will come as [b]destruction from [1]the Almighty.
7 Therefore [a]all hands will fall limp,
And every man's [b]heart will melt.
8 They will be [a]terrified,
Pains and anguish will take hold of *them;*
They will [b]writhe like a woman in labor,
They will look at one another in astonishment,
Their faces aflame.
9 Behold, [a]the day of the LORD is coming,
Cruel, with fury and burning anger,
To make the land a desolation;
And He will exterminate its sinners from it.
10 For the [a]stars of heaven and their constellations
Will not flash forth their light;
The [b]sun will be dark when it rises
And the moon will not shed its light.

3 [a]Joel 3:11
4 [a]Is 5:30; 17:12; Joel 3:14
5 [1]Lit *end of heaven* [a]Is 5:26; 7:18 [b]Is 10:5 [c]Is 24:1
6 [1]Heb *Shaddai* [a]Is 2:12; 10:3; 13:9; 34:2, 8; 61:2; Ezek 30:3; Amos 5:18; Zeph 1:7 [b]Is 10:25; 14:23; Joel 1:15
7 [a]Ezek 7:17 [b]Is 19:1; Ezek 21:7; Nah 2:10
8 [a]2 Kin 19:26; Is 21:3; Jer 46:5 [b]Is 26:17; Jer 4:31; John 16:21
9 [a]Is 13:6
10 [a]Is 5:30; Ezek 32:7; Joel 2:10; Matt 24:29; Mark 13:24; Luke 21:25; Rev 6:13; 8:12 [b]Is 24:23; 50:3; Ezek 32:7; Acts 2:20; Rev 6:12
11 [1]Or *tyrants, despots* [a]Is 26:21 [b]Is 3:11; 11:4; 14:5 [c]Is 2:11; 23:9; Dan 5:22, 23 [d]Jer 48:29 [e]Is 25:3; 29:5, 20
12 [1]Lit *more precious* [a]Is 4:1; 6:11, 12 [b]1 Kin 9:28; Job 28:16; Ps 45:9
13 [a]Is 34:4; 51:6 [b]Ps 18:7; Is 2:19; 24:1, 19, 20; Hag 2:6 [c]Lam 1:12
14 [a]1 Kin 22:17; Matt 9:36; Mark 6:34; 1 Pet 2:25
15 [a]Is 14:19; Jer 50:25; 51:3, 4
16 [a]Ps 137:8, 9; Is 13:18; 14:21; Hos 10:14; Nah 3:10

11 Thus I will [a]punish the world for its evil
And the [b]wicked for their iniquity;
I will also put an end to the [c]arrogance of the proud
And abase the [d]haughtiness of the [1][e]ruthless.
12 I will make mortal man [1][a]scarcer than pure gold
And mankind than the [b]gold of Ophir.
13 Therefore I will make the [a]heavens tremble,
And [b]the earth will be shaken from its place
At the fury of the LORD of hosts
In [c]the day of His burning anger.
14 And it will be that like a hunted gazelle,
Or like [a]sheep with none to gather *them,*
They will each turn to his own people,
And each one flee to his own land.
15 Anyone who is found will be [a]thrust through,
And anyone who is captured will fall by the sword.
16 Their [a]little ones also will be dashed to pieces
Before their eyes;
Their houses will be plundered
And their wives ravished.

Babylon Will Fall to the Medes

17 Behold, I am going to [a]stir up the Medes against them,
Who will not value silver or [b]take pleasure in gold.
18 And *their* bows will [1]mow down the [a]young men,

17 [a]Jer 51:11; Dan 5:28 [b]Prov 6:34, 35 **18** [1]Lit *dash in pieces* [a]2 Kin 8:12; 2 Chr 36:17

see also 45:1. *anger.* God's anger is no longer turned against Israel (see 5:25; 9:12,17,21; 10:4) but against her enemies (see vv. 5,9,13; cf. 30:27). God must punish sin, particularly arrogance (see v. 11).

13:4 *The LORD of hosts is mustering the army.* The Hebrew for "army" is the singular form of the word for "Almighty." God is the head of the armies of Israel (1 Sam 17:45), of angelic powers (1 Kin 22:19; Luke 2:13) and, here, of the armies that will destroy Babylon. See note on 1 Sam 1:3.

13:5 *instruments of indignation.* Assyria was the club in God's hand during Isaiah's day, and Babylon itself would later serve as God's weapon (see 10:5 and note).

13:6,9 *day of the LORD.* See note on 2:11,17,20.

13:6 *destruction.* Hebrew *shod,* forming a wordplay on "Almighty" (Hebrew *Shaddai*)—as also in Joel 1:15. See note on 5:7. For *Shaddai* see note on Gen 17:1.

13:7 *hands will fall limp.* Courage will fail. See Jer 6:24.

13:8 *terrified.* Holy war usually brings panic to the enemy (see Ex 15:14–16; Judg 7:21–22). *Pains . . . labor.* The prophets often compare the suffering of judgment and war with the pain and anguish that frequently accompany childbirth (see 26:17; Jer 4:31; 6:24).

13:10 *stars . . . sun . . . moon.* Cosmic darkness is associated with the day of the Lord also in Joel 2:10,31; Rev 6:12–13. Cf. Judg 5:20.

13:11 *arrogance . . . haughtiness.* Cf. 2:9,11,17; 5:15.

13:12 *scarcer . . . than.* War will reduce the male population drastically (see 4:1 and note). *gold of Ophir.* Solomon imported large quantities of gold from this place (see 1 Kin 9:28; 10:11 and notes).

13:13 *heavens tremble . . . earth . . . be shaken.* Thunderstorms and earthquakes often accompany the powerful presence of the Lord (see notes on v. 10; 34:4; Ex 19:16). Hail may also be involved (cf. 30:30; Josh 10:11).

13:14 *flee.* From parts of the Assyrian empire.

13:16 *little ones . . . dashed to pieces.* Invading armies often slaughtered infants and children; thus there would be no future warriors, nor would there be a remnant through which the city (or country or people) might be revived (see Ps 137:8–9; Hos 10:14; Nah 3:10). *wives ravished.* Women also suffered greatly in war. With their husbands killed, they were often used as prostitutes (see note on Amos 7:17).

13:17 *the Medes.* Located in what is today northwestern Iran. There was conflict between Assyria and Media during the eighth century B.C. Some, however, relate the fulfillment of this verse to the period when the Medes joined the Babylonians in defeating Assyria in 612–609 but later united with Cyrus to conquer Babylon in 539. See Jer 51:11,28; Dan 5:31; 6:28.

They will not even have compassion
on the fruit of the womb,
Nor will their [b]eye pity [2]children.
19 And [a]Babylon, the [b]beauty of
kingdoms, the glory of the
Chaldeans' pride,
Will be as when God [c]overthrew
Sodom and Gomorrah.
20 It will [a]never be inhabited or lived in
from generation to generation;
Nor will the [b]Arab pitch *his* tent there,
Nor will shepherds make *their flocks*
lie down there.
21 But [a]desert creatures will lie down
there,
And their houses will be full of [1]owls;
Ostriches also will live there, and
[2]shaggy goats will frolic there.
22 [1]Hyenas will howl in their fortified
towers
And jackals in their luxurious [a]palaces.
Her *fateful* time also [2]will soon come
And her days will not be prolonged.

Israel's Taunt

14 When the LORD will [a]have compassion
on Jacob and again [b]choose Israel, and
settle them in their own land, then [c]strangers
will join them and attach themselves to the
house of Jacob.
2 The peoples will take them along and
bring them to their place, and the [a]house of
Israel will possess them as an inheritance in
the land of the LORD [b]as male servants and
female servants; and [1]they will take their captors captive and will rule over their oppressors.
3 And it will be in the day when the LORD
gives you [a]rest from your pain and turmoil
and harsh service in which you have been
enslaved,

4 that you will [a]take up this [1]taunt
against the king of Babylon, and say,
"How [b]the oppressor has ceased,
And how [2]fury has ceased!
5 "The LORD has broken the staff of the
wicked,
The scepter of rulers
6 [a]Which used to strike the peoples in
fury with unceasing strokes,
Which [1]subdued the nations in anger
with unrestrained persecution.
7 "The whole earth is at rest *and* is quiet;
They [a]break forth into shouts of joy.
8 "Even the [a]cypress trees rejoice over
you, *and* the cedars of Lebanon,
saying,
'Since you were laid low, no *tree* cutter
comes up against us.'
9 "[a]Sheol from beneath is excited over
you to meet you when you come;
It arouses for you the [1]spirits of the
dead, all the [2]leaders of the earth;
It raises all the kings of the nations
from their thrones.
10 "[a]They will all respond and say to you,
'Even you have been made weak as we,
You have become like us.
11 'Your [a]pomp *and* the music of your
harps
Have been brought down to Sheol;
Maggots are spread out *as your bed*
beneath you
And worms are your covering.'
12 "How you have [a]fallen from heaven,
O [1b]star of the morning, son of the
dawn!
You have been cut down to the earth,
You who have weakened the nations!

18 [2]Lit *sons* [b]Ezek 9:5, 10
19 [a]Is 21:9; 48:14 [b]Dan 4:30; Rev 18:11-16, 19, 21 [c]Gen 19:24; Deut 29:23; Jer 49:18; Amos 4:11
20 [a]Is 14:23; 34:10-15; Jer 51:37-43 [b]2 Chr 17:11
21 [1]Or *howling creatures* [2]Or *goat demons* [a]Is 34:11-15; Zeph 2:14; Rev 18:2
22 [1]Or *howling creatures* [2]Lit *is near to come* [a]Is 25:2; 32:14; 34:13
14:1 [a]Ps 102:13; Is 49:13, 15; 54:7, 8 [b]Is 41:8, 9; 44:1; 49:7; Zech 1:17; 2:12 [c]Is 56:3, 6; Eph 2:12-19
2 [1]Lit *the captors will become their captives* [a]Is 45:14; 49:23; 54:3 [b]Is 60:10; 61:5; Dan 7:18, 27
3 [a]Ezra 9:8, 9; Is 11:10; 40:2; Jer 30:10; 46:27

4 [1]Or *proverb* [2]Amended from the meaningless *medhebah* to *marhebah* [a]Hab 2:6 [b]Is 9:4; 16:4; 49:26; 51:13; 54:14
6 [1]Or *ruled* [a]Is 10:14; 47:6
7 [a]Ps 47:1-3; 98:1-9; 126:1-3
8 [a]Is 55:12; Ezek 31:16
9 [1]Or *shades* (Heb *Repha'im*) [2]Lit *male goats* [a]Is 5:14
10 [a]Ezek 32:21
11 [a]Is 5:14 **12** [1]Heb *Helel;* i.e. shining one [a]Is 34:4; Luke 10:18; Rev 8:10; 9:1 [b]2 Pet 1:19; Rev 2:28; 22:16

13:19 *glory . . . pride.* Babylon with its temples and palaces became a very beautiful city (see Dan 4:29–30). The hanging gardens of Nebuchadnezzar were one of the seven wonders of the ancient world. In 4:2 the Hebrew words for "adornment" and "pride" were used to describe the "Branch of the LORD." *Chaldeans.* The Neo-Babylonian empire of 612–539 B.C. was led by the Chaldean people of southern Babylonia. Nabopolassar welded the tribes together c. 626, and his son Nebuchadnezzar became their most powerful ruler (605–562). *Sodom and Gomorrah.* Previously Isaiah compared Judah to these cities (see 1:9–10 and note).
13:20–22 See the similar description of the desolation of Edom in 34:10–15. Cf. Rev 18:2.
13:20 *never be inhabited.* Babylon was completely deserted by the seventh century A.D.
13:21 *shaggy goats.* This term is connected with demons in Lev 17:7 ("goat idols") and 2 Chr 11:15 ("satyrs"). In Rev 18:2 fallen Babylon is described as a home for demons and evil spirits.
14:1 *will have compassion . . . and settle them.* Babylon's fall will be linked with Israel's restoration. God's compassion on His people is the theme of chs. 40–66 (see 40:1–2). *in their own land.* See 2:2–4; 11:10–12 and notes. *strangers will join them.* See 11:10; 56:6–7; 60:3.
14:2 *peoples . . . place.* See note on 5:26. *will possess them.* See note on 11:14.
14:3–21 However exalted (and almost divine) the king of Babylon may have thought himself (see vv. 12–14), he will go the way of all world rulers—down to the grave.
14:3 *pain . . . enslaved.* The Babylonian captivity was much like Israel's experience in Egypt (cf. Ex 1:14).
14:4 *taunt.* Cf. the taunts against Babylon in Rev 18. *king of Babylon.* Another title used by the king of Assyria at this time.
14:5 *staff . . . scepter.* See 10:5 and note; see also 10:24.
14:7 *break forth into shouts of joy.* See 12:6 and note.
14:8 *cypress trees . . . cedars.* Isaiah often personified nature. The trees along with the mountains burst into song in 44:23 (cf. 55:12). *cedars of Lebanon.* These highly prized timbers were hauled away by the kings of Assyria and Babylon for centuries.
14:9 *leaders.* Lit. "goats"; a goat often led a flock of sheep (see Jer 50:8). In Zech 10:3 the term is parallel to "shepherds." *raises . . . from their thrones.* Conditions among the dead are described in terms of their roles on earth.
14:11 *pomp . . . Sheol.* Cf. 5:14. *music of your harps.* Music is sometimes a sign of luxury and pleasure (see Amos 6:5–6).
14:12–15 Some believe that Isaiah is giving a description of the fall of Satan (cf. Luke 10:18—where, however, Jesus seems to be referring to an event contemporary with Himself). But the passage clearly applies to the king of Babylon, who is later used

13 "But you said in your heart,
'I will [a]ascend to heaven;
I will [b]raise my throne above the stars
of God,
And I will sit on the mount of assembly
In the recesses of the north.
14 'I will ascend above the heights of the
clouds;
[a]I will make myself like the Most High.'
15 "Nevertheless you [a]will be thrust down
to Sheol,
To the recesses of the pit.
16 "Those who see you will gaze at you,
They will [1]ponder over you, *saying,*
'Is this the man who made the earth
tremble,
Who shook kingdoms,
17 Who made the world like a [a]wilderness
And overthrew its cities,
Who [b]did not [1]allow his prisoners to
go home?'
18 "All the kings of the nations lie in glory,
Each in his own [1]tomb.
19 "But you have been [a]cast out of your
tomb
Like [1]a rejected branch,
[2]Clothed with the slain who are
pierced with a sword,
Who go down to the stones of the [b]pit
Like a [c]trampled corpse.
20 "You will not be united with them in
burial,
Because you have ruined your country,
You have slain your people.
May the [a]offspring of evildoers not be
mentioned forever.
21 "Prepare for his sons a place of
slaughter
Because of the [a]iniquity of their
fathers.

13 [a]Ezek 28:2 [b]Dan 5:22, 23; 8:10; 2 Thess 2:4
14 [a]Is 47:8; 2 Thess 2:4
15 [a]Ezek 28:8; Matt 11:23; Luke 10:15
16 [1]Lit *show themselves attentive to*
17 [1]Lit *open* [a]Joel 2:3 [b]Is 45:13
18 [1]Lit *house*
19 [1]Lit *an abhorred branch* [2]Or *As the clothing of those who are slain* [a]Is 22:16-18 [b]Jer 41:7, 9 [c]Is 5:25
20 [a]Job 18:16, 19; Ps 21:10; 37:28; Is 1:4; 31:2
21 [a]Ex 20:5; Lev 26:39; Is 13:16; Matt 23:35
22 [a]Prov 10:7 [b]Job 18:19; Is 47:9
23 [a]Is 34:11; Zeph 2:14 [b]1 Kin 14:10; Is 13:6
24 [a]Job 23:13; Is 46:11; 55:8, 9; Acts 4:28
25 [a]Is 10:12; 30:31; 31:8 [b]Is 9:4; 10:27; Nah 1:13
26 [1]Lit *planned* [a]Is 23:9; Zeph 3:6, 8 [b]Ex 15:12
27 [a]2 Chr 20:6; Is 43:13; Dan 4:31, 35
28 [1]Or *burden* [a]2 Kin 16:20; 2 Chr 28:27 [b]Is 13:1

They must not arise and take
possession of the earth
And fill the face of the world with
cities."
22 "I will rise up against them," declares
the LORD of hosts, "and will cut off from Babylon [a]name and survivors, [b]offspring and
posterity," declares the LORD.
23 "I will also make it a possession for the
[a]hedgehog and swamps of water, and I will
sweep it with the broom of [b]destruction,"
declares the LORD of hosts.

Judgment on Assyria

24 The LORD of hosts has sworn saying,
"Surely, [a]just as I have intended so it has
happened, and just as I have planned so it
will stand,
25 to [a]break Assyria in My land, and I will
trample him on My mountains. Then his
[b]yoke will be removed from them and his
burden removed from their shoulder.
26 "This is the [a]plan [1]devised against the
whole earth; and this is the [b]hand that is
stretched out against all the nations.
27 "For [a]the LORD of hosts has planned, and
who can frustrate *it?* And as for His
stretched-out hand, who can turn it back?"
28 In the [a]year that King Ahaz died this
[1b]oracle came:

Judgment on Philistia

29 "Do not rejoice, O [a]Philistia, all of you,
Because the rod that [b]struck you is
broken;
For from the serpent's root a [c]viper
will come out,
And its fruit will be a [d]flying serpent.

29 [a]Is 2:6; 11:14; Jer 47:1-7; Ezek 25:15-17; Joel 3:4-8; Amos 1:6-8; Zeph 2:4-7; Zech 9:5-7 [b]2 Chr 26:6 [c]Is 11:8 [d]Is 30:6

as a type (prefiguration) of the "beast" who will lead the Babylon of the last days (see Rev 13:4; 17:3). Cf. the description of the ruler of Tyre in Ezek 28.

14:12 *star of the morning.* The Hebrew for this expression is translated "Lucifer" in the Latin Vulgate.

14:13 *of the north.* Most likely referring to Mount Zaphon (see Ps 48:1–2), also called Mount Casius, which was about 25 miles northeast of Ugarit in Syria. The Canaanites considered it the home and meeting place of the gods, much like Mount Olympus for the Greeks (see Ps 48:2 and note). Cf. Ps 82:1.

14:16–20a These verses seem to take place on earth, not in the realm of the dead (Sheol)—probably also vv. 9–10.

14:17 *prisoners to go home.* Babylon, like Assyria, deported large segments of defeated populations to subdue the rebellious among them (see 2 Kin 24:14–16).

14:19 *cast out of your tomb.* A proper burial was considered important for an ordinary individual, and especially so for a king. To have one's body simply discarded was a terrible fate. *trampled corpse.* See 5:25.

14:21 *sons a place of slaughter.* A man's children, as well as his tombstone, were his memorial (cf. 2 Sam 18:18). The king of Babylon would have neither (cf. 47:9).

14:22–23 The taunt is extended to include Babylon itself (see note on vv. 3–21); fulfilled, at least partially, through Sennacherib's destruction of Babylon in 689 B.C.—ultimately by the Medes and Persians after they took Babylon in 539.

14:22 *survivors.* A remnant; Israel will survive through a remnant (see 10:20–22; 11:11,16), but Babylon will not.

14:23 See 13:20–22 and notes. *swamps.* Southern Babylonia, where the Chaldean tribes once lived, was a region of marshlands.

14:24–27 See Zeph 2:13–15; see also note on 13:1–14:27.

14:24 *it will stand.* See 8:10 and note. God's sovereign purposes regarding Assyria and Babylon will be carried out.

14:25 *yoke . . . burden.* See 9:4 and note.

14:26 *hand . . . stretched out.* See 9:12; 12:1 and notes. God's hand was stretched out against Egypt at the Red Sea (see Ex 15:12).

14:28–32 See Jer 47; Ezek 25:15–17; Amos 1:6–8; Zeph 2:4–7.

14:28 *the year.* Perhaps 715 B.C. The occasion appears to be the Philistine revolt against Assyria while King Sargon (see 20:1) was too preoccupied with serious revolts elsewhere to give much attention to Canaan. *oracle.* See note on 13:1.

14:29 *Philistia.* See note on Gen 10:14. Philistine territory was vulnerable to attack by the great empires (Egypt and Assyria) since it lay along the main route from Egypt to Mesopotamia. *the rod.* Probably Sargon of Assyria. *is broken.* If the rod was Sargon, reference is to the threats to his empire by a series of

30 "[1]Those who are most [a]helpless will
eat,
And the needy will lie down in
security;
I will [2]destroy your root with [b]famine,
And it will kill off your survivors.
31 "Wail, O [a]gate; cry, O city;
[1]Melt away, O [b]Philistia, all of you;
For smoke comes from the [c]north,
And [d]there is no straggler in his
ranks.
32 "How then will one answer the
[a]messengers of the nation?
That [b]the LORD has founded Zion,
And [c]the afflicted of His people will
seek refuge in it."

Judgment on Moab

15 The [1]oracle concerning [a]Moab.
Surely in a night [b]Ar of Moab is
devastated *and* ruined;
Surely in a night Kir of Moab is
devastated *and* ruined.
2 They have gone up to the [1]temple and
to [a]Dibon, *even* to the high places
to weep.
Moab wails over Nebo and Medeba;
Everyone's head is [b]bald *and* every
beard is cut off.
3 In their streets they have girded
themselves with [a]sackcloth;
[b]On their housetops and in their
squares
Everyone is wailing, [1c]dissolved in
tears.
4 [a]Heshbon and Elealeh also cry out,
Their voice is heard all the way to
Jahaz;
Therefore the [1]armed men of Moab
cry aloud;
His soul trembles within him.
5 My heart cries out for Moab;
His fugitives are as far as [a]Zoar *and*
Eglath-shelishiyah,
For they go up the [b]ascent of Luhith
weeping;
Surely on the road to Horonaim they
raise a cry of distress [c]over *their*
ruin.
6 For the [a]waters of Nimrim are
[1]desolate.
Surely the grass is withered, the
tender grass [2]died out,
There is [b]no green thing.
7 Therefore the [a]abundance *which* they
have acquired and stored up
They carry off over the brook of
[1]Arabim.
8 For the cry of distress has gone
around the territory of Moab,
Its wail *goes* as far as Eglaim and its
wailing even to Beer-elim.
9 For the waters of Dimon are full of
[1]blood;
Surely I will bring added *woes* upon
Dimon,
A [a]lion upon the fugitives of Moab
and upon the remnant of the land.

30 [1]Lit *the firstborn of the helpless* [2]Lit *put to death* [a]Is 3:14, 15; 7:21, 22; 11:4 [b]Is 8:21; 9:20; 51:19 **31** [1]Or *Become demoralized* [a]Is 3:26; 24:12; 45:2 [b]Is 14:29 [c]Jer 1:14 [d]Is 34:16 **32** [a]Is 37:9 [b]Ps 87:1, 5; 102:16; Is 28:16; 44:28; 54:11 [c]Is 4:6; 25:4; 57:13; Zeph 3:12; Heb 11:10; James 2:5 **15:1** [1]Or *burden of* [a]Is 11:14; 25:10; Jer 48:1; Ezek 25:8-11; Amos 2:1-3; Zeph 2:8-11 [b]Num 21:28 **2** [1]Lit *house* [a]Jer 48:18, 22 [b]Lev 21:5; Jer 48:37 **3** [1]Lit *going down in weeping* [a]Jon 3:6-8 [b]Jer 48:38 [c]Is 22:4

4 [1]Another reading is *the loins of* [a]Num 21:28; 32:3; Jer 48:34 **5** [a]Jer 48:34 [b]Jer 48:5 [c]Is 59:7; Jer 4:20 **6** [1]Lit *desolations* [2]Lit *come to an end* [a]Is 19:5-7; Jer 48:34 [b]Joel 1:10-12; 2:3 **7** [1]Or *the poplars* [a]Is 30:6; Jer 48:36

9 [1]Heb *dam* (a wordplay) [a]2 Kin 17:25; Jer 50:17

revolts in Babylonia and Asia Minor. *root . . . fruit.* A figure of speech that refers to the whole (tree) by speaking of its two extremes. After Sargon will come other Assyrian kings: Sennacherib, Esarhaddon, Ashurbanipal.

14:30 *helpless . . . needy.* Israelites (see v. 32).

14:31 *Wail.* Cf. the similar reaction in 13:6; 15:2; 16:7; 23:1. *smoke.* The dust raised by the marching feet and the chariots of the Assyrians—who always invaded Canaan from the north. *no straggler.* A longer description is found in 5:26–29.

14:32 *has founded Zion.* God will protect Jerusalem from the Assyrians (compare 31:4–5 with 2:2).

15:1–16:14 See Jer 48; Ezek 25:8–11; Amos 2:1–3; Zeph 2:8–11.

15:1 *oracle.* See note on 13:1. *Moab.* A country east of the Dead Sea that was a perpetual enemy of Israel (see 25:10; 2 Kin 13:20). *Ar.* The location of this city is unknown. *devastated.* The same Hebrew word describes Isaiah's feelings about himself in 6:5. The destruction of Moab was probably connected with an invasion by Sargon of Assyria in 715/713 B.C. Cf. Jer 48:1–17. *Kir.* Probably Kir Hareseth, 15 miles south of the Arnon River and perhaps the capital of Moab at this time. Kir means "city."

15:2 *Dibon.* Located four miles north of the Arnon River and given to the tribe of Gad at one time (see Num 32:34). *high places.* Shrines originally built on hilltops and usually associated with pagan worship. *Nebo.* North of the Arnon River, perhaps near Mount Nebo (Deut 34:1). *Medeba.* About six miles south of Heshbon (see v. 4) and once captured by Israel from Sihon (see Num 21:26,30). *head is bald . . . beard is cut off.* Characteristic of intense mourning (Jer 48:37).

15:3 *sackcloth.* The coarse garb of mourners (see Job 16:15; Jer 48:37; Lam 2:10), made of goat hair. *housetops.* Perhaps chosen because incense was sometimes offered there (see Jer 19:13).

15:4 *Heshbon.* Located about 18 miles east of the northern tip of the Dead Sea. See also Jer 48:34. It was King Sihon's capital before Israel captured it (see Num 21:23–26). *Elealeh.* About a mile north of Heshbon and always mentioned with it. *Jahaz.* Just north of the Arnon River and about 20 miles from Heshbon (Num 21:23; Jer 48:34).

15:5 *Zoar.* Probably located near the southern end of the Dead Sea. Lot fled there from Sodom (see Gen 14:2; 19:23,30). *Eglath-shelishiyah.* Location unknown (see also Jer 48:34). The words may mean "a three-year-old heifer" (cf. 1 Sam 1:24). *Luhith.* Location unknown (see also Jer 48:5). *Horonaim.* Location unknown (see also Jer 48:3,5,34).

15:6 *waters of Nimrim.* Perhaps to be identified with the Wadi en-Numeirah, ten miles from the southern end of the Dead Sea (cf. Jer 48:34). *grass is withered.* The advancing enemy may have stopped up the major springs of Moab.

15:7 *brook of Arabim.* Probably at the border between Moab and Edom (see v. 8).

15:8 *Eglaim.* Perhaps near the northern border of Moab. *Beer-elim.* Beer means "well" (cf. Num 21:16). This site may have been close to the southern border.

15:9 *waters of Dimon . . . blood.* The Hebrew for "blood" (*dam*) sounds like "Dimon." This is probably also a wordplay on the name "Dibon" (v. 2), close to the Arnon River. Many Moabites will die in the conflict. *A lion.* A reference to either the Assyrian army (cf. 5:29; Jer 50:17) or actual lions (cf. 13:21–22).

Prophecy of Moab's Devastation

16 [a]Send the *tribute* lamb to the ruler of
the land,
From [1][b]Sela by way of the wilderness
to the [c]mountain of the daughter of
Zion.
2 Then, like [1][a]fleeing birds *or* scattered
[2]nestlings,
The daughters of [b]Moab will be at the
fords of the [c]Arnon.
3 "[1]Give *us* advice, make a decision;
[2]Cast your [a]shadow like night [3]at high
noon;
[b]Hide the outcasts, do not betray the
fugitive.
4 "Let the [1]outcasts of Moab stay with
you;
Be a hiding place to them from the
destroyer."
For the extortioner has come to an
end, destruction has ceased,
[a]Oppressors have completely
disappeared from the land.
5 A [a]throne will even be established in
lovingkindness,
And a judge will sit on it in
faithfulness in the tent of [b]David;
Moreover, he will seek justice
And be prompt in righteousness.

6 [a]We have heard of the pride of Moab,
an excessive pride;
Even of his arrogance, pride, and
fury;
[b]His idle boasts are [1]false.
7 Therefore Moab will wail; everyone of
Moab will wail.
You will moan for the [a]raisin cakes of
[b]Kir-hareseth
As those who are utterly stricken.

16:1 [1]I.e. Petra in Edom [a]2 Kin 3:4; Ezra 7:17 [b]2 Kin 14:7; Is 42:11 [c]Is 10:32
2 [1]Or *fluttering* [2]Lit *nest* [a]Prov 27:8 [b]Jer 48:20, 46 [c]Num 21:13, 14
3 [1]Lit *Bring* [2]Lit *Set* [3]Lit *in the midst of the noon* [a]Is 25:4; 32:2 [b]1 Kin 18:4
4 [1]So the versions; M.T. *My outcasts, as for Moab* [a]Is 9:4; 14:4; 49:26; 51:13; 54:14
5 [a]Is 9:6, 7; 32:1; 55:4; Dan 7:14; Mic 4:7; Luke 1:33 [b]Is 9:7
6 [1]Lit *not so* [a]Jer 48:29; Amos 2:1; Obad 3, 4; Zeph 2:8, 10 [b]Jer 48:30
7 [a]1 Chr 16:3 [b]2 Kin 3:25; Jer 48:31
8 [1]Or *languished* [a]Is 15:4 [b]Num 32:38 [c]Jer 48:32
9 [a]Jer 48:32 [b]Is 15:4 [c]Jer 40:10, 12; 48:32
10 [a]Is 24:8; Jer 48:33 [b]Judg 9:27; Is 24:7; Amos 5:11, 17 [c]Job 24:11; Amos 9:13
11 [1]Lit *entrails murmur* [2]Lit *inward part* [a]Is 15:5; 63:15; Jer 48:36; Hos 11:8; Phil 2:1
12 [a]Num 22:39-41; Jer 48:35 [b]1 Kin 18:29 [c]Is 15:2
14 [1]Lit *the years of a hireling*

8 For the fields of [a]Heshbon have
[1]withered, the vines of [b]Sibmah *as
well;*
The lords of the nations have trampled
down its choice clusters
Which reached as far as Jazer *and*
wandered to the deserts;
[c]Its tendrils spread themselves out
and passed over the sea.
9 Therefore I will [a]weep bitterly for
Jazer, for the vine of Sibmah;
I will drench you with my tears,
O [b]Heshbon and Elealeh;
For the shouting over your [c]summer
fruits and your harvest has fallen
away.
10 [a]Gladness and joy are taken away
from the fruitful field;
In the [b]vineyards also there will be no
cries of joy or jubilant shouting,
No [c]treader treads out wine in the
presses,
For I have made the shouting to cease.
11 Therefore my [1][a]heart intones like a
harp for Moab
And my [2]inward feelings for
Kir-hareseth.
12 So it will come about when Moab
[a]presents himself,
When he [b]wearies himself upon *his*
[c]high place
And comes to his sanctuary to pray,
That he will not prevail.
13 This is the word which the LORD spoke
earlier concerning Moab.
14 But now the LORD speaks, saying,
"Within three years, as [1][a]a hired man would
count them, the glory of [b]Moab will be
degraded along with all *his* great population,

[a]Job 7:1; 14:6; Is 21:16 [b]Is 25:10; Jer 48:42

16:1 *tribute lamb.* As King Mesha sent 100,000 lambs to King Ahab of Israel each year (see 2 Kin 3:4), so now proud Moab, which has often oppressed Israel, is advised in her crisis to submit to the king in Jerusalem. *Sela.* The naturally fortified capital of the Edomites south of the Dead Sea, situated on a rocky plateau that towers 1,000 feet above the nearby Petra (cf. 42:11). The name means "cliff." The tribute would be sent around the southern end of the Dead Sea. *daughter of Zion.* A personification of Jerusalem and its inhabitants.
16:2 *fords of the Arnon.* The women were fleeing south, away from the northern invader.
16:3 *Hide the outcasts.* The Moabites are asking Judah for refuge (contrast Ruth 1:1; 1 Sam 22:3–4).
16:4 *destroyer.* Probably Assyria (see notes on 15:1; 33:1). *extortioner.* Moab.
16:5 *tent of David.* See 9:7; Amos 9:11 and notes. "Tent" equals "dynasty" (see note on 7:2). *judge . . . will seek justice.* See 11:2–4 and notes. The Messiah is again in view.
16:6 *pride of Moab.* Though a small nation, Moab is proud and defiant like Assyria and Babylon. Cf. 10:12; 14:13; 25:11; Jer 48:42.
16:7 *raisin cakes.* Or "men," a wordplay. *Kir-hareseth.* See note on 15:1. The four cities in vv. 7–8 appear in inverted (chiastic) order in vv. 9–11.
16:8 *Heshbon.* See note on 15:4. *Sibmah.* Perhaps three miles west of Heshbon. See Jer 48:32. *choice clusters.* The poet shifts to a metaphor, comparing Moab to a vineyard (see 5:1–7). He returns to a literal description again in v. 10. *Jazer.* Possibly located about 15 miles north of the Dead Sea. *deserts.* On the eastern edge of Moab. *tendrils spread themselves.* This is hyperbole, as in Ps 80:11, where Israel is the vineyard. *sea.* Probably the Dead Sea.
16:9–11 *I . . . I . . . I . . . my . . . my.* The Lord (and/or Isaiah) weeps and laments over the destruction brought on proud Moab to humble her.
16:9 *Elealeh.* See note on 15:4.
16:10 *treads out wine.* The grapes were trampled on, and the juice flowed into the wine vat (see note on 5:2; cf. Jer 48:33; Amos 9:13).
16:11 Cf. Jer 48:36.
16:12 *high place.* See 15:2 and note. *pray . . . not prevail.* Moab's god, Chemosh, was a mere idol (see 44:17–20; 1 Kin 11:7).
16:13–14 An epilogue to 15:1–16:12.
16:14 *Within three years.* Other signs that have a three-year limit are given in 20:3; 37:30; see also notes on 7:14,16. Moab's three years were over by c. 715 B.C. (see note on 15:1). *hired man.* Cf. 21:16–17, where the prophecy against Kedar follows the pattern of this verse.

and *his* remnant will be very small *and*
[2]impotent."

Prophecy about Damascus

17 The [1][a]oracle concerning [b]Damascus.
"Behold, Damascus is about to be
[c]removed from being a city
And will become a [d]fallen ruin.
2 "The cities [1]of [a]Aroer are forsaken;
They will be for [b]flocks [2]to lie down
in,
And there will be [c]no one to frighten
them.
3 "The [1][a]fortified city will disappear from
Ephraim,
And [2]sovereignty from Damascus
And the remnant of Aram;
They will be like the [b]glory of the sons
of Israel,"
Declares the LORD of hosts.

4 Now in that day the [a]glory of Jacob
will [1]fade,
And [b]the fatness of his flesh will
become lean.
5 It will be [a]even like the [1]reaper
gathering the standing grain,
As his arm harvests the ears,
Or it will be like one gleaning ears of
grain
In the [b]valley of Rephaim.
6 Yet [a]gleanings will be left in it like the
[1]shaking of an olive tree,
Two *or* three olives on the topmost
bough,
Four *or* five on the branches of a
fruitful tree,
Declares the LORD, the God of Israel.
7 In that day man will [a]have regard for
his Maker
And his eyes will look to the Holy One
of Israel.
8 He will not have regard for the [a]altars,
the work of his hands,
Nor will he look to that which his
[b]fingers have made,
Even the [1][c]Asherim and [2]incense
stands.
9 In that day [1]their strong cities will be
like [2]forsaken places in the forest,
Or like [3]branches which they
abandoned before the sons of Israel;
And [4]the land will be a desolation.
10 For [a]you have forgotten the [b]God of
your salvation
And have not remembered the [c]rock
of your refuge.
Therefore you plant delightful plants
And set them with vine slips of a
strange *god.*
11 In the day that you plant *it* you
carefully fence *it* in,
And in the [a]morning you bring your
seed to blossom;
But the harvest will [b]*be* a heap
In a day of sickliness and incurable
pain.

12 Alas, the uproar of many peoples
[a]Who roar like the roaring of the seas,
And the rumbling of nations
Who rush on like the [b]rumbling of
mighty waters!
13 The [a]nations rumble on like the
rumbling of many waters,
But He will [b]rebuke them and they
will flee far away,
And be chased [c]like chaff in the
mountains before the wind,
Or like whirling dust before a gale.

14 [2]Lit *not mighty*
17:1 [1]Or *burden of* [a]Is 13:1 [b]Gen 14:15; 15:2; 2 Kin 16:9; Jer 49:23; Amos 1:3-5; Zech 9:1; Acts 9:2 [c]Is 7:16; 8:4; 10:9 [d]Is 25:2; Jer 49:2; Mic 1:6
2 [1]Gr reads *forever and ever* [2]Lit *and they will lie down* [a]Num 32:34 [b]Is 7:21, 22; Ezek 25:5; Zeph 2:6 [c]Mic 4:4
3 [1]Or *fortification* [2]Or *royal power, kingdom* [a]Is 7:8, 16; 8:4 [b]Is 17:4; Hos 9:11
4 [1]Lit *become thin* [a]Is 10:3 [b]Is 10:16
5 [1]Lit *gathering of the harvest, the standing grain* [a]Is 17:11; Jer 51:33; Joel 3:13; Matt 13:30 [b]2 Sam 5:18, 22
6 [1]Lit *striking* [a]Deut 4:27; Is 24:13; 27:12; Obad 5
7 [a]Is 10:20; Hos 3:5; 6:1; Mic 7:7
8 [1]I.e. wooden symbols of a female deity [2]Or *sun pillars* [a]2 Chr 34:7; Is 27:9 [b]Is 2:8, 20; 30:22; 31:7 [c]Ex 34:13; Deut 7:5; Mic 5:14
9 [1]I.e. man's [2]Gr reads *the deserted places of the Amorites and the Hivites which they abandoned* [3]Or *the treetop* [4]Lit *it*
10 [a]Is 51:13 [b]Ps 68:19; Is 12:2; 33:2; 61:10; 62:11 [c]Deut 32:4, 18, 31; Is 26:4; 30:29; 44:8
11 [a]Ps 90:6 [b]Job 4:8; Hos 8:7; 10:13 **12** [a]Is 5:30; Jer 6:23; Ezek 43:2; Luke 21:25 [b]Ps 18:4 **13** [a]Is 33:3 [b]Ps 9:5; Is 41:11 [c]Job 21:18; Ps 1:4; 83:13; Is 29:5; 41:15, 16

17:1–14 See Jer 49:23–27; Amos 1:3–5.
17:1 *oracle.* See note on 13:1. *Damascus.* The capital of Aram (Syria), located northeast of Mount Hermon on strategic trade routes between Mesopotamia, Egypt and Arabia. Since the time of David, the Arameans of Damascus were frequent enemies of Israel (see 2 Sam 8:5; 1 Kin 22:31).
17:2 *Aroer.* About 14 miles east of the Dead Sea on the Arnon River. It marked the southern boundary of Aram's sphere of control (see 2 Kin 10:32–33).
17:3 *Ephraim.* The northern kingdom (see note on 7:2) is mentioned here because of its alliance with Damascus against Assyria (see note on 7:1). *sovereignty.* In 732 B.C. Tiglath-pileser III captured Damascus and made it an Assyrian province. Many of the cities of Israel were also captured (see note on 9:1).
17:4–11 The prophet shifts from Damascus to Israel (likely the northern kingdom)—a shift prepared for at the end of v. 3. This association of judgment on Damascus and Israel reflects the same linkage as that in ch. 7.
17:4,7,9 *in that day.* See notes on 2:11,17,20; 10:20,27.
17:5 *harvests the ears.* Harvest can signify a time of judgment (see Joel 3:13). *valley of Rephaim.* A fertile area west of Jerusalem (Josh 15:8) and the scene of Philistine raids (1 Chr 14:9).
17:7–8 Cf. 2:20; 10:20.
17:7 *Holy One of Israel.* See note on 1:4.
17:8 *altars.* Probably altars for Baal (cf. 1 Kin 16:32). *Asherim.* Wooden symbols of the goddess Asherah; see notes on Ex 34:13; Judg 2:13. *incense stands.* Associated with high places in Lev 26:30 and with altars for Baal in 2 Chr 34:4.
17:9 *forest . . . branches.* Cf. 7:23–25. *they.* Perhaps the Canaanites, whose religious practices are referred to in v. 8.
17:10 *the rock.* See 26:4; 30:29; 44:8; Deut 32:4,15,18; Ps 19:14. *vine slips.* Probably representing the people of Israel (see 5:7; 18:5; 37:30–31).
17:11 *sickliness and incurable pain.* Brought by the Assyrian invasions.
17:12–14 The same sequence of a powerful invader that is quickly cut down occurs in 10:28–34. Both passages may refer to Sennacherib's invasion of 701 B.C. (see 37:36–37). But it is more likely that the prophet here speaks more generally of Israel's experience of the world of nations as a perpetual threat to her existence.
17:12 *roaring of the seas.* Assyria is called "strong and abundant waters" in 8:7.
17:13 *chaff . . . whirling dust.* Symbolic of the enemy also in 29:5; 41:15–16; Ps 83:13.

14 At evening time, behold, *there is* terror!
Before morning [a]they are no more.
[1]Such *will be* the portion of those who plunder us
And the lot of those who pillage us.

Message to Ethiopia

18 Alas, oh land of whirring wings
Which lies beyond the rivers of [1a]Cush,
2 Which sends envoys by the sea,
Even in [a]papyrus vessels on the surface of the waters.
Go, swift messengers, to a nation
[1b]tall and smooth,
To a people [c]feared [2]far and wide,
A powerful and oppressive nation
Whose land the rivers divide.
3 [a]All you inhabitants of the world and dwellers on earth,
As soon as a standard is raised on the mountains, [b]you will see *it*,
And as soon as the trumpet is blown, you will hear *it*.
4 For thus the LORD has told me,
"I will look [1]from My [a]dwelling place quietly
Like dazzling heat in the [2b]sunshine,
Like a cloud of [c]dew in the heat of harvest."
5 For [a]before the harvest, as soon as the bud [1]blossoms
And the flower becomes a ripening grape,
Then He will cut off the sprigs with pruning knives
And remove *and* cut away the spreading branches.
6 They will be left together for mountain birds [a]of prey,
And for the beasts of the earth;
And the birds of prey will spend the summer *feeding* on them,
And all the beasts of the earth will spend harvest time on them.

7 At that time a gift of homage will be brought to the LORD of hosts
[1]From a [a]people [2]tall and smooth,
Even from a people feared [3]far and wide,
A powerful and oppressive nation,
Whose land the rivers divide—
To the [b]place of the name of the LORD of hosts, *even* Mount Zion.

Message to Egypt

19 The [1a]oracle concerning [b]Egypt.
Behold, the LORD is [c]riding on a swift cloud and is about to come to Egypt;
The [d]idols of Egypt will tremble at His presence,
And the [e]heart of the Egyptians will melt within them.
2 "So I will incite Egyptians against Egyptians;
And they will [a]each fight against his brother and each against his neighbor,
City against city *and* kingdom against kingdom.
3 "Then the spirit of the Egyptians will be demoralized within them;
And I will confound their strategy,
So that [a]they will resort to idols and ghosts of the dead
And to [1]mediums and spiritists.
4 "Moreover, I will deliver the Egyptians into the hand of a [a]cruel master,
And a [1]mighty king will rule over them," declares the Lord [2]GOD of hosts.

5 [a]The waters from the sea will dry up,
And the river will be parched and dry.
6 The [1a]canals will emit a stench,

14 [1]Lit *This* [a]2 Kin 19:35; Is 41:12
18:1 [1]Or *Ethiopia* [a]2 Kin 19:9; Is 20:3-5; Ezek 30:4, 5, 9; Zeph 2:12; 3:10
2 [1]Lit *drawn out* [2]Lit *from it and beyond* [a]Ex 2:3 [b]Is 18:7 [c]Gen 10:8, 9; 2 Chr 12:2-4; 14:9; 16:8
3 [a]Ps 49:1; Mic 1:2 [b]Is 26:11
4 [1]Lit *in* [2]Lit *light* [a]Is 26:21; Hos 5:15 [b]2 Sam 23:4 [c]Prov 19:12; Is 26:19; Hos 14:5
5 [1]Lit *is finished* [a]Is 17:10, 11; Ezek 17:6-10
6 [a]Is 46:11; 56:9; Jer 7:33; Ezek 32:4-6; 39:17-20
7 [1]So with some ancient versions and DSS; M.T. implies *Consisting of a people* [2]Lit *drawn out* [3]Lit *from it and beyond* [a]Ps 68:31; Is 45:14; Zeph 3:10; Acts 8:27-38 [b]Zech 14:16, 17
19:1 [1]Or *burden of* [a]Is 13:1 [b]Joel 3:19 [c]Ps 18:9, 10; 104:3; Matt 26:64; Rev 1:7 [d]Ex 12:12; Jer 43:12; 44:8 [e]Josh 2:11; Is 13:7
2 [a]Judg 7:22; 1 Sam 14:20; 2 Chr 20:23; Matt 10:21, 36
3 [1]Or *ghosts and spirits* [a]1 Chr 10:13; Is 8:19; Dan 2:2
4 [1]Or *fierce* [2]Heb *YHWH,* usually rendered LORD [a]Is 20:4; Jer 46:26; Ezek 29:19 **5** [a]Is 50:2; Jer 51:36; Ezek 30:12
6 [1]Lit *rivers* [a]Ex 7:18

18:1–7 See Zeph 2:12.
18:1 *whirring wings.* Either a reference to insects (perhaps locusts) or a figurative description of the armies of Cush (see 7:18–19). *Cush.* Nubia or ancient Ethiopia (not to be confused with modern Ethiopia, which is located farther to the southeast), south of Egypt. In 715 B.C. a Cushite named Shabako gained control of Egypt and founded the 25th dynasty.
18:2 *sea.* Perhaps the Nile River (cf. 19:5; Nah 3:8). *papyrus vessels.* See note on Ex 2:3. *Go, swift messengers.* With the message contained in vv. 3–6. *nation tall and smooth.* Probably the peoples of Cush and Egypt. Unlike Semites, they were clean-shaven (see note on Gen 41:14). *rivers.* The Nile and its tributaries.
18:3 *All you inhabitants of the world.* All the nations arrayed against God's people Israel (see 17:12–14 and note). *standard.* See 5:26 and note. *trumpet.* Used to summon troops.
18:4 *look . . . quietly.* In the face of the hostility of the nations, the Lord will not act immediately; but when they are in the full growth of summer (v. 5), He will cut them down.
18:6 *birds of prey . . . beasts of the earth.* Cf. 56:9; Jer 7:33; Ezek 32:4; 39:17–20.
18:7 See v. 2. *gift.* According to 2 Chr 32:23 gifts were brought to Hezekiah after Sennacherib's death. The Moabites were asked to send tribute to Mount Zion in 16:1 (cf. 45:14; Zeph 3:10). *place of the name.* See Deut 12:5 and note.
19:1–20:6 See Jer 46; Ezek 29–32.
19:1 *oracle.* See note on 13:1. *riding on a swift cloud.* A metaphor used also in Ps 68:4; 104:3; cf. Matt 26:64. *idols . . . tremble.* See Jer 50:2. God had also previously judged Egypt's idols during the ten plagues (see Ex 12:12 and note). *heart . . . melt.* See 13:7.
19:2 *Egyptians against Egyptians.* Cf. 9:21. The Libyan dynasty clashed with the "Ethiopians" (Cushites; see note on 18:1) and with the Saites of Dynasty 24.
19:3 *resort to . . . spiritists.* Israel also did so in desperate times (see 8:19 and note).
19:4 *cruel master.* The king of Assyria (see 20:4). Esarhaddon conquered Egypt in 670 B.C.
19:5 *sea will dry up.* The Nile was the lifeline of Egypt; its annual flooding provided essential water and produced the only fertile soil there.
19:6 *canals.* For irrigation.

The [2b]streams of Egypt will thin out
and dry up;
[c]The reeds and rushes will rot away.
7 The bulrushes by the [a]Nile, by the
[1]edge of the Nile
And all the sown fields by the Nile
Will become dry, be driven away, and
be no more.
8 And the [a]fishermen will lament,
And all those who cast a [1]line into the
Nile will mourn,
And those who spread nets on the
waters will [2]pine away.
9 Moreover, the manufacturers of linen
made from combed flax
And the weavers of white [a]cloth will
be [1]utterly dejected.
10 And [1]the [a]pillars *of Egypt* will be
crushed;
All the hired laborers will be grieved
in soul.

11 The princes of [1a]Zoan are mere fools;
The advice of Pharaoh's wisest
advisers has become [2]stupid.
How can you *men* say to Pharaoh,
"I am a son of the [b]wise, a son of
ancient kings"?
12 Well then, where are your wise men?
Please let them tell you,
And let them [1]understand what the
LORD of hosts
Has [a]purposed against Egypt.
13 The princes of [1]Zoan have acted
foolishly,
The princes of [a]Memphis are deluded;

6 [2]Or *Nile branches;* i.e. the delta [b]Is 37:25 [c]Ex 2:3; Job 8:11; Is 15:6 **7** [1]Or *mouth* [a]Is 23:3, 10 **8** [1]Lit *hook* [2]Or *languish* [a]Ezek 47:10; Hab 1:15 **9** [1]Lit *ashamed* [a]Prov 7:16; Ezek 27:7 **10** [1]Lit *her pillars* or, *her weavers* [a]Ps 11:3 **11** [1]Or *Tanis* [2]Or *brutish* [a]Num 13:22; Ps 78:12, 43; Is 30:4 [b]Gen 41:38, 39; 1 Kin 4:30; Acts 7:22 **12** [1]Or *know* [a]Is 14:24; Rom 9:17 **13** [1]Or *Tanis* [a]Jer 2:16; 46:14, 19; Ezek 30:13

13 [2]Or *have caused Egypt to stagger* [b]Zech 10:4 **14** [1]Lit *its work* [2]Or *goes astray* [a]Prov 12:8; Matt 17:17 [b]Is 3:12; 9:16 [c]Is 28:7 **15** [a]Is 9:14, 15 **16** [a]2 Cor 5:11; Heb 10:31 [b]Is 11:15 **17** [1]Or *cause of shame* [2]Lit *who mentions it will be in dread to it* [a]Is 14:24; Dan 4:35 **18** [1]Some ancient mss and versions read *the Sun* [a]Is 45:23; 65:16 **19** [a]Is 56:7;

Those who are the [b]cornerstone of her
tribes
Have [2]led Egypt astray.
14 The LORD has mixed within her a spirit
of [a]distortion;
[b]They have led Egypt astray in all
[1]that it does,
As a [c]drunken man [2]staggers in his
vomit.
15 There will be no work for Egypt
[a]Which *its* head or tail, *its* palm
branch or bulrush, may do.

16 In that day the Egyptians will become
like women, and they will tremble and be in
[a]dread because of the [b]waving of the hand of
the LORD of hosts, which He is going to wave
over them.
17 The land of Judah will become a [1]terror
to Egypt; everyone [2]to whom it is mentioned
will be in dread of it, because of the [a]pur-
pose of the LORD of hosts which He is pur-
posing against them.
18 In that day five cities in the land of Egypt
will be speaking the language of Canaan and
[a]swearing *allegiance* to the LORD of hosts; one
will be called the City of [1]Destruction.
19 In that day there will be an [a]altar to the
LORD in the midst of the land of Egypt, and a
[b]pillar to the LORD near its border.
20 It will become a sign and a witness to
the LORD of hosts in the land of Egypt; for
they will cry to the LORD because of oppressors, and He will send them a [a]Savior and a
[1b]Champion, and He will deliver them.

60:7 [b]Gen 28:18; Ex 24:4; Josh 22:10, 26, 27 **20** [1]Lit *Mighty One* [a]Is 43:3, 11; 45:15, 21; 49:26; 60:16; 63:8 [b]Is 49:25

19:7 *sown fields.* Egypt's crops were normally abundant, and some were exported.
19:8 *fishermen.* Fish were usually plentiful (see Num 11:5).
19:9 *manufacturers of linen.* Large amounts of water were needed to process flax. *white cloth.* Another well-known Egyptian export.
19:11 *Zoan.* A city (possibly Tanis) in the northeastern part of the Nile delta. It would have been familiar to the Israelites enslaved in Egypt (see Num 13:22; Ps 78:12,43). It was the northern capital for the 25th dynasty (see note on 18:1). *son of the wise.* See v. 12. Egypt was famous for its wise men (see 1 Kin 4:30).
19:13 *Memphis.* An important city 15 miles south of the delta that was the capital during the Old Kingdom (c. 2686–2160 B.C.). *cornerstone.* Prophets and priests, as well as political leaders (see 9:15–16).
19:14 *drunken man staggers.* Israel's leaders stagger in 28:7–8.
19:15 *head or tail . . . palm branch or bulrush.* Egypt's leaders. The same two pairs are used of Israel's leaders in 9:14–15.
19:16–25 A chain of four announcements of coming events associated with "that day": 1. An act of divine judgment will cause Egypt to "tremble and be in dread" (v. 16) and be in terror of Judah (vv. 16–17). 2. "Five cities" in Egypt will be "swearing allegiance" to the Lord (v. 18). 3. Because of a divine act of deliverance and healing in Egypt, an altar will be erected in Egypt where Egyptians will offer sacrifices to the Lord (vv. 19–22). 4. Egypt, Assyria and Israel will be linked into one people of the Lord (vv. 23–25). The prophet looks well beyond the present realities in which the world powers do not acknowledge the true God and proudly pursue their own destinies, running roughshod over the people of the Lord. He foresees a series of divine acts that will bring about the conversion of the nations.
19:16,18–19,23–24 *In that day.* The coming day of the Lord (see 10:20,27 and note; cf. 11:10–11).
19:16 *tremble and be in dread.* Like the people of Jericho (Josh 2:9,11). *hand of the LORD . . . wave over them.* See 14:26–27 and note.
19:17 *land of Judah.* The Egyptians will somehow recognize (perhaps through court contacts with Hezekiah) that it is the God of Judah who has brought judgment upon them.
19:18 *five.* Perhaps in the sense of "many." *speaking the language of Canaan.* Either a symbolic reference to Egypt's allegiance to the Lord (see vv. 21–22,25) or a literal reference to Jews living in Egypt. After the fall of Jerusalem in 586 B.C., many Jews fled to Egypt (Jer 44:1). *City of Destruction.* Probably a reference to Heliopolis, city of the sun-god; it was destroyed by Nebuchadnezzar (see Jer 43:12–13). The Hebrew for "destruction" is almost identical to the Hebrew for "sun."
19:19 *altar.* Some relate this to the temple built in Egypt by the Jewish high priest Onias IV, who fled to Egypt in the second century B.C., but the reference appears to be to a conversion to the Lord of a significant number of Egyptians.
19:20 *sign and a witness.* Cf. the purpose of the altar built near the Jordan River by the Transjordan tribes in Josh 22:26–27. *oppressors . . . Savior.* The language of the book of Judges (see Judg 2:18). The "Savior" is the promised Son of the house of David (see 11:1–10).

21 Thus the LORD will make Himself
known to Egypt, and the Egyptians will
know the LORD in that day. They will even
worship with [a]sacrifice and offering, and will
make a vow to the LORD and perform it.
22 The LORD will strike Egypt, striking but
[a]healing; so they will [b]return to the LORD,
and He will respond to them and will heal
them.
23 In that day there will be a [a]highway
from Egypt to Assyria, and the Assyrians will
come into Egypt and the Egyptians into
Assyria, and the Egyptians will [b]worship
with the Assyrians.
24 In that day Israel will be the third *party*
with Egypt and Assyria, a blessing in the
midst of the earth,
25 whom the LORD of hosts has blessed,
saying, "Blessed is [a]Egypt My people, and
Assyria [b]the work of My hands, and Israel
My inheritance."

Prophecy about Egypt and Ethiopia

20 In the year that the [1a]commander came
to [b]Ashdod, when Sargon the king of
Assyria sent him and he fought against Ashdod and captured it,
2 at that time the LORD spoke through
[a]Isaiah the son of Amoz, saying, "Go and
loosen the [b]sackcloth from your hips and
take your [c]shoes off your feet." And he did
so, going [d]naked and barefoot.
3 And the LORD said, "Even as My servant Isaiah has gone naked and barefoot
three years as a [1a]sign and token against
Egypt and [2b]Cush,
4 so the [a]king of Assyria will lead away
the captives of Egypt and the exiles of Cush,
[b]young and old, naked and barefoot with
buttocks uncovered, to the [1]shame of Egypt.
5 "Then they will be [a]dismayed and
ashamed because of Cush their hope and
Egypt their [b]boast.
6 "So the inhabitants of this coastland will
say in that day, 'Behold, such is our hope,
where we fled [a]for help to be delivered from
the king of Assyria; and we, [b]how shall we
escape?' "

God Commands That Babylon Be Taken

21 The [1a]oracle concerning the [2b]wilder-
ness of the sea.
As [c]windstorms in the [3]Negev sweep
on,
It comes from the wilderness, from a
terrifying land.
2 A [a]harsh vision has been shown to
me;
The [b]treacherous one *still* deals
treacherously, and the destroyer
still destroys.
Go up, [c]Elam, lay siege, Media;
I have made an end of all [1]the
groaning she has caused.
3 For this reason my [a]loins are full of
anguish;
Pains have seized me like the pains of
a [b]woman in labor.
I am so bewildered I cannot hear, so
terrified I cannot see.

21 [a]Is 56:7; 60:7; Zech 14:16-18
22 [a]Deut 32:39; Is 30:26; 57:18; Heb 12:11 [b]Is 27:13; 45:14; Hos 14:1
23 [a]Is 11:16; 35:8; 49:11; 62:10 [b]Is 27:13
25 [a]Is 45:14 [b]Ps 100:3; Is 29:23; 45:11; 60:21; 64:8; Eph 2:10
20:1 [1]Heb *Tartan* [a]2 Kin 18:17 [b]1 Sam 5:1
2 [a]Is 1:1; 13:1 [b]Zech 13:4; Matt 3:4 [c]Ezek 24:17, 23 [d]1 Sam 19:24; Mic 1:8
3 [1]Or *wonder* [2]Or *Ethiopia,* so in vv 4, 5 [a]Is 8:18 [b]Is 37:9; 43:3
4 [1]Lit *nakedness* [a]Is 19:4 [b]Is 47:2, 3
5 [a]2 Kin 18:21; Is 30:3-5; 31:1; Ezek 29:6, 7 [b]Jer 9:23, 24; 17:5; 1 Cor 3:21
6 [a]Is 10:3; 30:7; 31:3; Jer 30:1, 7, 15-17; 31:1-3 [b]Matt 23:33; 1 Thess 5:3; Heb 2:3
21:1 [1]Or *burden of* [2]Or *sandy wastes, sea country* [3]I.e. South country [a]Is 13:1 [b]Is 13:20-22; 14:23; Jer 51:42 [c]Zech 9:14
2 [1]Lit *her groaning* [a]Ps 60:3 [b]Is 24:16; 33:1 [c]Is 22:6; Jer 49:34
3 [a]Is 13:8; 16:11 [b]Ps 48:6; Is 13:8; 26:17; 1 Thess 5:3

19:21 *make Himself known.* Cf. Ex 7:5. *worship with sacrifice.* Offerings of foreigners are also mentioned in 56:7; 60:7 (cf. Zech 14:16–19).

19:22 *strike Egypt.* Oppression (see v. 20) and plague were two common forms of divine affliction. Contrast the results of the plague on the firstborn in Ex 12:23. *respond . . . heal.* Cf. 6:10; here parallel to sending Egypt a "Savior and Champion" (v. 20). Earlier a hardhearted pharaoh had not turned to the Lord (Ex 9:34–35).

19:23 *highway.* Cf. the highway to Jerusalem in 11:16 (see note there). For centuries Egyptians and Assyrians had fought each other (see 20:4), but in the future they would be linked in a bond of friendship sealed by their common allegiance to the Lord (cf. 25:3). *worship with.* This description of peace and of unity in worship is similar to 2:2–4 (see note there; see also note on v. 21).

19:25 *has blessed.* A fulfillment of Gen 12:3. *Egypt My people.* Such a universal vision seems possible for Isaiah only in the light of what has been said about the "shoot . . . from the stem of Jesse" (11:1; see 11:1–10). Cf. 45:14; Eph 2:11–13.

20:1–6 An epilogue to chs. 18–19, as 16:13–14 is to 15:1–16:12.

20:1 *the year.* Probably 712 B.C. *Sargon.* Sargon II, who reigned 721–705 B.C. He is mentioned by name only here in the OT. *Ashdod.* One of the five Philistine cities (see map, p. 312), Ashdod was located near the Mediterranean Sea about 18 miles northeast of Gaza. The city had rebelled against Assyria in 713 under King Azuri. In 1963 three fragments of an Assyrian monument commemorating Sargon's victory and mentioning Sargon by name were discovered at Ashdod.

20:2 *sackcloth.* Normally the garment of mourners (see note on 15:3), but perhaps also the usual garb of prophets (see 2 Kin 1:8; Zech 13:4).

20:3 *My servant.* A title for prophets and others used by God in a special way. *three years.* See 16:14 and note. *sign and token.* See 8:18; see also 7:3,14 and notes. The prophet Ezekiel's behavior also had symbolic significance (Ezek 24:24,27; cf. Zech 3:8). *Egypt and Cush.* See 18:1; 19:1.

20:4 *naked and barefoot.* Cf. 2 Chr 28:15; Mic 1:8.

20:5 *Cush their hope . . . Egypt their boast.* After Assyria conquered the northern kingdom of Israel in 722–721 B.C., King Hezekiah of Judah was under great pressure to make an alliance with Egypt. Isaiah urgently warned against such a policy (cf. 30:1–2; 31:1).

21:1 *oracle.* See note on 13:1. *wilderness.* The coming judgment would eventually turn Babylon (see v. 9) into a wasteland (cf. 13:20–22). *the sea.* Refers either to the Persian Gulf, which was just south of Babylon, or to the alluvial plain deposited by the Euphrates and Tigris rivers and their tributaries. *windstorms . . . wilderness.* The wilderness sometimes spawns powerful winds (see Hos 13:15). *it.* It is not clear whether "comes from the wilderness, from a terrifying land" is ascribed to an invader or continues the description of the whirlwinds.

21:2 *Elam.* See note on 11:11. The Elamites were a perpetual enemy of Assyria and Babylon. Much later, they were part of the Persian army that conquered Babylon under Cyrus in 539 B.C. *Media.* See note on 13:17. *she.* Babylon.

21:3 *full of anguish; Pains have seized me.* See Daniel's reaction to visions in Dan 8:27; 10:16–17; but see also notes on 29:9–11.

4 My [1]mind reels, [2]horror overwhelms
me;
The twilight I longed for has been
[a]turned for me into trembling.
5 They [a]set the table, they [1]spread out
the cloth, they eat, they drink;
"Rise up, captains, oil the shields,"
6 For thus the Lord says to me,
"Go, station the lookout, let him
[a]report what he sees.
7 "When he sees [a]riders, horsemen in
pairs,
A train of donkeys, a train of camels,
Let him pay close attention, very close
attention."
8 Then [1]the lookout called,
"[a]O Lord, I stand continually by day on
the watchtower,
And I am stationed every night at my
guard post.
9 "Now behold, here comes a troop of
riders, horsemen in pairs."
And one said, "[a]Fallen, fallen is
Babylon;
And all the [b]images of her gods [1]are
shattered on the ground."
10 O my [a]threshed *people*, and my
[1]afflicted of the threshing floor!
What I have heard from the LORD of
hosts,
The God of Israel, I make known to
you.

Oracles about Edom and Arabia

11 The [1]oracle concerning [2][a]Edom.
One keeps calling to me from [b]Seir,
"Watchman, [3]how far gone is the night?
Watchman, [3]how far gone is the
night?"
12 The watchman says,
"Morning comes but also night.
If you would inquire, inquire;
Come back again."

13 The [1]oracle about [a]Arabia.
In the thickets of Arabia you [2]must
spend the night,
O caravans of [b]Dedanites.
14 Bring water [1]for the thirsty,
O inhabitants of the land of [a]Tema,
Meet the fugitive with bread.
15 For they have [a]fled from the swords,
From the drawn sword, and from the
bent bow
And from the press of battle.
16 For thus the Lord said to me, "In a
[a]year, as [1]a hired man would count it, all the
splendor of [b]Kedar will terminate;
17 and the [a]remainder of the number of
bowmen, the mighty men of the sons of
Kedar, will be few; for the LORD God of Israel
[b]has spoken."

The Valley of Vision

22 The [1]oracle concerning the [a]valley of
vision.
What is the matter with you now, that
you have all gone up to the
[b]housetops?
2 You who were full of noise,
You boisterous town, you [a]exultant
city;

4 [1]Lit *heart has wandered* [2]Lit *shuddering* [a]Deut 28:67
5 [1]Or *spread out the rugs* or possibly *they arranged the seating* [a]Jer 51:39, 57; Dan 5:1-4
6 [a]2 Kin 9:17-20
7 [a]Is 21:9
8 [1]So DSS; M.T. *he called* like *a lion* [a]Hab 2:1
9 [1]Lit *he has shattered to the earth* [a]Is 13:19; 47:5, 9; 48:14; Jer 51:8; Rev 14:8; 18:2 [b]Is 46:1; Jer 50:2; 51:44
10 [1]Lit *son* [a]Jer 51:33; Mic 4:13
11 [1]Or *burden* [2]So the Gr; Heb *Dumah, silence* [3]Lit *what* is the time *of the night?* [a]Gen 25:14 [b]Gen 32:3
11 [3]Lit *what* is the time *of the night?*
13 [1]Or *burden* [2]Or *will spend* [a]Jer 25:23, 24; 49:28 [b]Gen 10:7; Ezek 27:15
14 [1]Lit *to meet* [a]Gen 25:15; Job 6:19
15 [a]Is 13:14, 15; 17:13
16 [1]Lit *the years of a hireling* [a]Is 16:14 [b]Ps 120:5; Song 1:5; Is 42:11; 60:7; Ezek 27:21
17 [a]Is 10:19 [b]Num 23:19; Zech 1:6 **22:1** [1]Or *burden of* [a]Ps 125:2; Jer 21:13; Joel 3:12, 14 [b]Is 15:3 **2** [a]Is 23:7; 32:13

21:4 *twilight.* Perhaps the end of the Babylonian empire (see note on v. 12). *turned for me into trembling.* The devastation is beyond even what he had desired.
21:5 *eat . . . drink.* With the kind of confident assurance reflected in Belshazzar's feast (see Dan 5:1). *Rise up.* Rhetorically the prophet, who has seen in a vision the coming attack on Babylon, calls on the officers of Babylon to prepare. *oil the shields.* See note on 2 Sam 1:21.
21:6 *Go, station the lookout.* Probably on the walls of Jerusalem.
21:7 *riders . . . donkeys . . . camels.* Bearing messengers from afar.
21:9 *Fallen . . . is Babylon.* See 13:19. Babylon fell in 689 B.C. and again in 539. These words were adapted by John in Rev 14:8; 18:2. *images . . . are shattered.* The fall of a kingdom meant the disgrace of its gods (cf. 46:1–2).
21:10 *afflicted.* Judah would be punished by the Babylonians and taken into captivity (see 39:5–7). *of the threshing floor.* Threshing was a common metaphor for judgment or destruction from war (see Amos 1:3).
21:11–12 See Jer 49:7–22; Ezek 25:12–14; Amos 1:11–12.
21:11 *oracle.* See note on 13:1. *Seir.* A synonym for Edom (Gen 32:3), homeland of Esau's descendants, south of the Dead Sea. Edom is dealt with more extensively in 34:5–15 (cf. 63:1).
21:12 *Morning . . . but also night.* Perhaps meaning that the long night of Assyrian oppression is almost over, but only a short "morning" will precede Babylonian domination.
21:13–17 See Jer 49:28–33.
21:13 *oracle.* See note on 13:1. *thickets.* The caravans had to hide from the invader (cf. Judg 5:6). The Assyrians began to attack the Arabs in 732 B.C., and the Babylonians did the same under Nebuchadnezzar (see Jer 25:17,23–24). *Dedanites.* An Arabian tribe whose merchant activities are mentioned also in Ezek 27:20; 38:13.
21:14 *Tema.* An oasis in northern Arabia about 400 miles southwest of Babylon (cf. Job 6:19; Jer 25:23).
21:15 *sword . . . bow.* The simple bows of the Arabs were ineffective against the swords and composite bows of Assyria.
21:16 *hired man.* See 16:14 and note. *splendor.* See 14:11; 16:14. *Kedar.* The home of Bedouin tribes in the Arabian Desert. Kedar was known for its flocks (60:7; Ezek 27:21). Nebuchadnezzar defeated the people of Kedar (Jer 49:28–29; cf. Jer 2:10).
21:17 *remainder . . . will be few.* Cf. 10:19; 16:14; 17:6.
22:1–13 The notes on this prophecy assume that it refers primarily to the final Babylonian siege of Jerusalem in 588–586 B.C. But it is also possible that the primary reference is to the siege by the Assyrian king Sennacherib in 701.
22:1 *oracle.* See note on 13:1. *valley of vision.* A valley where God revealed Himself in visions, probably one of the valleys near Jerusalem (see note on v. 7). See also v. 5. *housetops.* See 15:3 and note.
22:2 *boisterous . . . exultant.* See v. 13; 5:11–12; 32:13. Jerusalem is behaving just like Babylon (see 21:5; cf. 23:7). *not*

Your slain were [b]not slain with the
sword,
Nor [1]did they die in battle.
3 [a]All your rulers have fled together,
And have been captured [1]without the
bow;
All of you who were found were taken
captive together,
[2]Though they had fled far away.
4 Therefore I say, "Turn your eyes away
from me,
Let me [a]weep bitterly,
Do not [1]try to comfort me concerning
the destruction of the daughter of
my people."
5 [a]For the Lord [1]GOD of hosts has a [b]day
of panic, [c]subjugation and
confusion
[d]In the valley of vision,
A breaking down of walls
And a crying [2]to the mountain.
6 [a]Elam took up the quiver
With the chariots, [1]infantry *and*
horsemen;
And [b]Kir uncovered the shield.
7 Then your choicest valleys were full of
chariots,
And the horsemen took up fixed
positions at the gate.
8 And He removed the [1]defense of
Judah.
In that day you [2]depended on the
weapons of the [a]house of the forest,
9 And you saw that the breaches
In the *wall* of the city of David were
many;
And you [a]collected the waters of the
lower pool.
10 Then you counted the houses of
Jerusalem
And tore down houses to fortify the
wall.
11 And you made a reservoir [a]between
the two walls
For the waters of the [b]old pool.
But you did not [1]depend on Him who
made it,
Nor did you [2]take into consideration
Him who planned it long ago.

12 Therefore in that day the Lord [1]GOD of
hosts called *you* to [a]weeping, to
wailing,
To [b]shaving the head and to wearing
sackcloth.
13 Instead, there is [a]gaiety and gladness,
Killing of cattle and slaughtering of
sheep,
Eating of meat and drinking of wine:
"[b]Let us eat and drink, for tomorrow
we may die."
14 But the LORD of hosts revealed Himself
[1]to me,
"Surely this [a]iniquity [b]shall not be
[2]forgiven you
[c]Until you die," says the Lord [3]GOD of
hosts.

15 Thus says the Lord [1]GOD of hosts,
"Come, go to this steward,
To [a]Shebna, who is in charge of the
royal household,
16 'What right do you have here,
And whom do you have here,
That you have [a]hewn a tomb for
yourself here,
You who hew a tomb on the height,
You who carve a resting place for
[1]yourself in the rock?
17 'Behold, the LORD is about to hurl you
headlong, O man.
And He is about to grasp you firmly
18 *And* roll you tightly like a ball,
To be [a]*cast* into a vast country;
There you will die
And there your splendid chariots will
be,

2 [1]Lit *dead in battle* [b]Jer 14:18; Lam 2:20
3 [1]Lit *from a bow* [2]So with ancient versions; Heb *They fled far away* [a]Is 21:15
4 [1]Lit *insist* [a]Is 15:3; Jer 9:1; Luke 19:41
5 [1]Heb *YHWH,* usually rendered LORD [2]Or *against* [a]Lam 1:5; 2:2 [b]Is 37:3 [c]Is 10:6; 63:3 [d]Is 22:1
6 [1]Lit *man* [a]Is 21:2; Jer 49:35 [b]2 Kin 16:9; Amos 1:5; 9:7
8 [1]Lit *screen, covering* [2]Or *looked to, considered* [a]1 Kin 7:2; 10:17
9 [a]2 Kin 20:20; Neh 3:16
11 [a]2 Kin 25:4; Jer 39:4
11 [1]Or *look to, consider* [2]Lit *see...Him* [b]2 Kin 20:20; 2 Chr 32:3, 4
12 [1]Heb *YHWH,* usually rendered LORD [a]Is 32:11; Joel 1:13; 2:17 [b]Mic 1:16
13 [a]Is 5:11, 22; 28:7, 8; Luke 17:26-29 [b]Is 56:12; 1 Cor 15:32
14 [1]Lit *in my ears* [2]Lit *atoned for* [3]Heb *YHWH,* usually rendered LORD [a]Is 13:11; 26:21; 30:13; 65:7 [b]1 Sam 3:14; Ezek 24:13 [c]Is 65:20
15 [1]Heb *YHWH,* usually rendered LORD [a]2 Kin 18:18, 26, 37; Is 36:3, 11, 22; 37:2
16 [1]Lit *himself* [a]2 Sam 18:18; 2 Chr 16:14; Matt 27:60
18 [a]Job 18:18; Is 17:13

slain with the sword. Perhaps a reference to death from disease and famine when the Babylonians besieged Jerusalem in 586 B.C.
22:3 *rulers have fled.* King Zedekiah and his army fled Jerusalem but were captured near Jericho (see 2 Kin 25:4–6).
22:5 *has a day.* See 2:12 and note on 2:11,17,20. Also cf. "in that day" in vv. 8,12. *panic.* A fulfillment of the curse of Deut 28:20.
22:6 *Elam.* See note on 11:11. Elamites probably fought in the Babylonian army. *Kir.* Perhaps another name for Media (see 21:2).
22:7 *choicest valleys.* The Kidron Valley lay east of Jerusalem (see John 18:1), the Hinnom Valley to the south and west (see Josh 15:8).
22:8 *house of the forest.* Built by King Solomon out of cedars from Lebanon (see 1 Kin 7:2–6; 10:17,21).
22:9 *city of David.* See 2 Sam 5:6–7,9. *lower pool.* Probably the same as the "old pool" of v. 11. Hezekiah made a pool and a tunnel as a precaution against Sennacherib's invasion (see 2 Kin 20:20). The "upper pool" is mentioned in 7:3; 36:2.
22:10 *fortify the wall.* Cf. Hezekiah's preparations in 2 Chr 32:5.
22:11 *did not depend on Him.* In 31:1 those who look to horses and chariots rather than to God are similarly condemned.
22:12 *shaving the head.* The hair was either torn out or shaved off (cf. Jer 16:6; Ezek 27:31).
22:13 *gaiety and gladness.* The same Hebrew phrase is translated "gladness and joy" in 35:10; 51:11, passages depicting great hope in connection with restoration. But this was a time to mourn (Eccl 3:4). See note on v. 2.
22:15 *Shebna.* Apparently a foreigner, possibly Egyptian; a contemporary of King Hezekiah. *in charge of the royal household.* A position second only to the king (see note on v. 21; cf. 36:3; 1 Kin 4:6; 2 Kin 15:5).
22:16 *hewn a tomb.* One's place of burial was considered very important, and Shebna coveted a tomb worthy of a king (cf. 2 Chr 16:14).
22:17 *hurl you headlong.* Cf. Jer 22:24–26.
22:18 *There you will die.* Apparently without an honorable burial (see note on 14:19). *chariots.* A sign of luxury and high office (see 2:7; Gen 41:43).

You shame of your master's house.'
19 "I will [a]depose you from your office,
And [1]I will pull you down from your station.
20 "Then it will come about in that day,
That I will summon My servant
[a]Eliakim the son of Hilkiah,
21 And I will clothe him with your tunic
And tie your sash securely about him.
I will entrust him with your [1]authority,
And he will become a [a]father to the inhabitants of Jerusalem and to the house of Judah.
22 "Then I will set [a]the key of the [b]house of David on his shoulder,
When he opens no one will shut,
When he shuts no one will [c]open.
23 "I will drive him *like* a [a]peg in a firm place,
And he will become a [b]throne of glory to his father's house.
24 "So they will hang on him all the glory
of his father's house, offspring and [1]issue, all
the least of vessels, from bowls to all the jars.
25 "In that day," declares the LORD of hosts,
"the [a]peg driven in a firm place will give
way; it will even [b]break off and fall, and the
load hanging on it will be cut off, for the
[c]LORD has spoken."

The Fall of Tyre

23 The [1]oracle concerning [a]Tyre.
Wail, O [b]ships of [c]Tarshish,
For *Tyre* is destroyed, without house *or* [2d]harbor;
It is reported to them from the land of [3e]Cyprus.
2 [a]Be silent, you inhabitants of the coastland,
You merchants of Sidon;
[1]Your messengers crossed the sea
3 And *were* on many waters.
[a]The grain of the [1b]Nile, the harvest of the River was her revenue;
And she was the [c]market of nations.
4 Be ashamed, O [a]Sidon;
For the sea speaks, the stronghold of the sea, saying,
"I have neither travailed nor given birth,
I have neither brought up young men *nor* reared virgins."
5 When the report *reaches* Egypt,
They will be in [a]anguish at the report of Tyre.
6 Pass over to [a]Tarshish;
Wail, O inhabitants of the coastland.
7 Is this your [a]jubilant *city,*
Whose origin is from antiquity,
Whose feet used to carry her to [1]colonize distant places?

8 Who has planned this against Tyre,
[a]the bestower of crowns,
Whose merchants were princes, whose traders were the honored of the earth?
9 [a]The LORD of hosts has planned it, to [b]defile the pride of all beauty,
To despise all the [c]honored of the earth.
10 [1]Overflow your land like the Nile, O daughter of Tarshish,
There is no more [2]restraint.

19 [1]So with many ancient versions; Heb *He* [a]Job 40:11, 12; Ezek 17:24
20 [a]2 Kin 18:18; Is 36:3, 22; 37:2
21 [1]Lit *rule* [a]Gen 45:8; Job 29:16
22 [a]Rev 3:7 [b]Is 7:2, 13 [c]Job 12:14
23 [a]Ezra 9:8; Zech 10:4 [b]1 Sam 2:8; Job 36:7
24 [1]Or perhaps, *leaf*
25 [a]Is 22:23 [b]Esth 9:24, 25 [c]Is 46:11; Mic 4:4
23:1 [1]Or *burden of* [2]Lit *entering* [3]Heb *Kittim* [a]Josh 19:29; 1 Kin 5:1; Jer 25:22; 47:4; Ezek 26:1-27:36; Joel 3:4-8; Amos 1:9; Zech 9:2-4 [b]Is 2:16 [c]Gen 10:4; 1 Kin 10:22 [d]Is 24:10 [e]Gen 10:4; Is 23:12; Ezek 27:6
2 [a]Is 47:5
2 [1]So DSS; M.T. *Who passed over the sea, they replenished you*
3 [1]Heb *Shihor* [a]Is 19:7-9 [b]Josh 13:3; 1 Chr 13:5; Jer 2:18 [c]Ezek 27:3-23
4 [a]Gen 10:15, 19; Josh 11:8; Judg 10:6; Jer 25:22; 27:3; 47:4; Ezek 28:21, 22
5 [a]Ex 15:14-16; Josh 2:9-11
6 [a]Is 23:1
7 [1]Lit *sojourn afar off* [a]Is 22:2; 32:13 **8** [a]Ezek 28:2
9 [a]Is 2:11; 13:11 [b]Job 40:11, 12; Dan 4:37 [c]Is 5:13; 9:15
10 [1]Lit *Pass over* [2]Perhaps *girdle* or *shipyard*

22:20 *in that day.* When the Lord acts in judgment (see vv. 17–19). *My servant.* See note on 20:3. *Eliakim.* See 36:3,11,22; 37:2.

22:21 *entrust him with your authority.* By 701 B.C. (see 36:3) Eliakim had replaced Shebna, who was demoted to "scribe."

22:22 Quoted in part in Rev 3:7. The mention of "father" (v. 21) and of the responsibility "on his shoulder" recalls the words about the Messiah in 9:6. *key of the house of David.* The authority delegated to him by the king, who belongs to David's dynasty—perhaps controlling entrance into the royal palace. Cf. the "keys of the kingdom" given to Peter (Matt 16:19).

22:23 *peg.* Normally the Hebrew for this word refers to a tent peg, but here to a peg driven into wood (see Ezek 15:3). *throne of glory.* Cf. 1 Sam 2:8.

22:25 *In that day.* Another (unspecified) day when the Lord will come in judgment. *peg . . . will give way.* Eliakim, like Shebna, will eventually fall from power.

23:1–18 See Ezek 26:1–28:19; Amos 1:9–10.

23:1 *oracle.* See note on 13:1. *Tyre.* The main seaport along the Phoenician coast, about 35 miles north of Mount Carmel. Part of the city was built on two rocky islands about half a mile from the shore. King Hiram of Tyre supplied cedars and craftsmen for the temple (see 1 Kin 5:8–9) and sailors for Solomon's commercial fleet (1 Kin 9:27). *Wail, O ships.* See v. 14. *ships of Tarshish.* Trading ships (see note on 2:16). *destroyed.* Fulfilled through Assyria, Nebuchadnezzar and Alexander. Nebuchadnezzar captured the mainland city in 572 B.C. (see Ezek 26:7–11), but the island fortress was not taken until Alexander the Great destroyed it in 332 (cf. Ezek 26:3–5). *Cyprus.* An island that had close ties with Tyre (see Ezek 27:6).

23:2,4,12 *Sidon.* See Ezek 28:20–26, the other prominent Phoenician city, about 25 miles north of Tyre.

23:2 *merchants . . . messengers.* Tyre's commercial ventures affected the entire Mediterranean world (see vv. 3,8).

23:3 *Nile.* Probably the easternmost branch of the Nile. *harvest of the River.* See 19:7 and note.

23:4 *stronghold of the sea.* Tyre (see note on v. 1). *travailed . . . birth.* Contrast 54:1.

23:6 *Tarshish.* Perhaps Tartessus in Spain (see Jon 1:3 and note), or an island in the western Mediterranean, or a site on the coast of North Africa.

23:7 *jubilant.* See note on 22:2. *from antiquity.* Tyre was founded before 2000 B.C. *colonize distant places.* Carthage in North Africa was a colony of Tyre. Tarshish may have been another.

23:8–9 *planned.* See 14:24,26–27; 25:1.

23:8 *bestower of crowns.* Tyre crowned kings in her colonies. *traders were . . . honored.* See Ezek 28:4–5.

23:9 *pride of all beauty.* See Ezek 27:3–4.

23:10 *daughter of Tarshish.* A personification of Tarshish and its inhabitants.

11 He has [a]stretched His hand out [b]over
the sea,
He has [c]made the kingdoms
tremble;
The LORD has given a command
concerning Canaan to [d]demolish its
strongholds.

12 He has said, "[a]You shall exult no
more, O crushed virgin daughter of
Sidon.
Arise, pass over to [1b]Cyprus; even
there you will find no rest."

13 Behold, the land of the Chaldeans—
this is the people *which* was not; [a]Assyria
appointed it for [b]desert creatures—they
erected their siege towers, they stripped its
palaces, [c]they made it a ruin.

14 Wail, O [a]ships of Tarshish,
For your stronghold is destroyed.

15 Now in that day Tyre will be forgotten
for [a]seventy years like the days of one king.
At the end of seventy years it will happen to
Tyre as *in* the song of the harlot:

16 Take *your* harp, walk about the
city,
O forgotten harlot;
Pluck the strings skillfully, sing many
songs,
That you may be remembered.

17 It will come about at [a]the end of seventy years that the LORD will visit Tyre. Then
she will go back to her harlot's wages and
will [b]play the harlot with all the kingdoms
[1]on the face of the earth.

18 Her [a]gain and her harlot's wages will
be [b]set apart to the LORD; it will not be stored
up or hoarded, but her gain will become sufficient food and choice attire for those who
dwell in the presence of the LORD.

11 [a]Ex 14:21; Is 14:26 [b]Is 19:5; 50:2 [c]Is 13:13 [d]Is 25:2; Zech 9:3, 4
12 [1]Heb *Kittim* [a]Ezek 26:13, 14; Rev 18:22 [b]Is 23:1
13 [a]Is 10:5 [b]Is 13:21; 18:6 [c]Is 10:7
14 [a]Is 2:16; Ezek 27:25, 26
15 [a]Jer 25:11, 22
17 [1]Lit *of the earth on the face of the land* [a]Is 23:15 [b]Ezek 16:25-29; Nah 3:4
18 [a]Ps 72:10, 11; Is 60:5-9; Mic 4:13 [b]Ex 28:36; Zech 14:20

24:1 [a]Is 2:19; 13:13; 24:19, 20; 30:32; 33:9
2 [a]Lev 25:36, 37; Deut 23:19, 20
4 [a]Is 33:9 [b]Is 2:12; 24:21
5 [1]Lit *under* [a]Gen 3:17; Num 35:33; Is 9:17; 10:6 [b]Is 33:8
6 [a]Josh 23:15; Is 34:5; 43:28; Zech 5:3, 4 [b]Is 1:31; 5:24; 9:19
7 [a]Is 16:10; Joel 1:10, 12
8 [a]Is 5:12, 14; Ezek 26:13; Hos 2:11; Rev 18:22
9 [a]Is 5:11, 22 [b]Is 5:20
10 [a]Is 34:11 [b]Is 23:1
11 [1]Lit *is darkened* [a]Jer 14:2; 46:12 [b]Is 16:10; 32:13
12 [a]Is 14:31; 45:2

Judgment on the Earth

24 Behold, the LORD [a]lays the earth waste,
devastates it, distorts its surface and
scatters its inhabitants.
2 And the people will be like the priest,
the servant like his master, the maid like her
mistress, the buyer like the seller, the lender
like the borrower, the [a]creditor like the
debtor.
3 The earth will be completely laid waste
and completely despoiled, for the LORD has
spoken this word.
4 The [a]earth mourns *and* withers, the
world fades *and* withers, the [b]exalted of the
people of the earth fade away.
5 The earth is also [a]polluted [1]by its
inhabitants, for they transgressed laws, violated statutes, [b]broke the everlasting covenant.
6 Therefore, a [a]curse devours the earth,
and those who live in it are held guilty.
Therefore, the [b]inhabitants of the earth are
burned, and few men are left.

7 The [a]new wine mourns,
The vine decays,
All the merry-hearted sigh.
8 The [a]gaiety of tambourines ceases,
The noise of revelers stops,
The gaiety of the harp ceases.
9 They do not drink wine with song;
[a]Strong drink is [b]bitter to those who
drink it.
10 The [a]city of chaos is broken down;
[b]Every house is shut up so that none
may enter.
11 There is an [a]outcry in the streets
concerning the wine;
[b]All joy [1]turns to gloom.
The gaiety of the earth is banished.
12 Desolation is left in the city
And the [a]gate is battered to ruins.

23:11 *stretched His hand out.* See note on 14:26–27. *Canaan.* Here roughly the same as modern Lebanon.
23:12 *crushed.* Sidon was captured by Esarhaddon in the seventh century B.C. and later by Nebuchadnezzar c. 587 (cf. Jer 25:22). *virgin daughter of Sidon.* See note on v. 10.
23:13 *Assyria.* Sennacherib destroyed the city of Babylon in 689 B.C. Phoenicia would look like the Babylon of that time. *desert creatures.* Cf. 13:21. *siege towers.* See note on 2 Kin 25:1.
23:14 See v. 1 and note.
23:15 *seventy years.* Also the length of the Babylonian captivity (see Jer 25:11; 29:10), and the length of time Sennacherib decreed that Babylon should remain devastated.
23:16 Cf. Prov 7:10–15.
23:17 *her harlot's wages.* A "harlot" nation was one that sought to make the highest profits, regardless of the means. Self-gratification was the key (cf. Rev 17:5).
23:18 *set apart to the LORD.* The earnings of a prostitute could not be given to the Lord (Deut 23:18), but the silver and gold of a city devoted to destruction (see note on Deut 2:34) were placed in the Lord's treasury (see Josh 6:17,19; cf. Mic 4:13). *for those.* Israel will one day receive the wealth of the nations (see note on 18:7; cf. 60:5–11; 61:6).
24:1–27:13 Chs. 24–27 deal with judgment and blessing in the last days, the time of God's final victory over the forces of evil. These chapters form a conclusion to chs. 13–23 just as chs. 34–35 form a conclusion to chs. 28–33.
24:1 *lays the earth waste.* Cf. 2:10,19,21; see also 13:13 and note. *scatters its inhabitants.* See Gen 11:9.
24:2 Social distinctions will provide no escape from the judgment (cf. 3:1–3).
24:4 *mourns and withers.* Words applied to Moab in 15:6; 16:8. Cf. 34:4.
24:5 *broke the everlasting covenant.* Reference is probably to the covenant of Gen 9:8–17 (see Gen 9:11 and note). See also v. 18 and note. Although everlasting from the divine viewpoint, God's covenants can be broken by sinful mankind.
24:6 *curse.* Because of the intensification of evil in the world, God's devastating curse will burn up the earth's inhabitants (cf. Gen 8:21–22; cf. also the covenant of Gen 9:8–17).
24:7 *vine decays.* See v. 4 and note.
24:8 *gaiety . . . ceases.* Cf. 22:2,13; 23:7.
24:9 *wine with song.* Characteristic of Judah in 5:11–13 (see note there).
24:10 *city of chaos.* The same idea appears in 25:2; 26:5 (cf. 17:1; 19:18). It is probably a composite of all the cities opposed to God—such as Babylon, Tyre, Jerusalem and Rome.

13 For [a]thus it will be in the midst of the
earth among the peoples,
As the [1]shaking of an olive tree,
As the gleanings when the grape
harvest is over.
14 [a]They raise their voices, they shout for
joy;
They cry out from the [1]west
concerning the majesty of the LORD.
15 Therefore [a]glorify the LORD in the
[1]east,
The [b]name of the LORD, the God of
Israel,
In the [2c]coastlands of the sea.
16 From the [a]ends of the earth we hear
songs, "[b]Glory to the Righteous
One,"
But I say, "[1c]Woe to me! [1]Woe to me!
Alas for me!
The [d]treacherous deal treacherously,
And the treacherous deal very
treacherously."
17 [a]Terror and pit and snare
[1]Confront you, O inhabitant of the
earth.
18 Then it will be that he who flees the
[1]report of disaster will fall into the
pit,
And he who [2]climbs out of the pit will
be caught in the snare;
For the [a]windows [3]above are opened,
and the [b]foundations of the earth
shake.
19 [a]The earth is broken asunder,
The earth is [b]split through,
The earth is shaken violently.
20 The earth [a]reels to and fro like a
drunkard
And it totters like a [1]shack,
For its [b]transgression is heavy upon it,
And it will fall, [c]never to rise again.
21 So it will happen in that day,
That the LORD will [a]punish the host of
[1]heaven on high,
And the [b]kings of the earth on earth.
22 They will be gathered together
Like [a]prisoners in the [1]dungeon,
And will be confined in prison;
And after many days they *will* [b]*be*
punished.
23 Then the [a]moon will be abashed and
the sun ashamed,
For the [b]LORD of hosts will reign on
[c]Mount Zion and in Jerusalem,
And *His* glory will be before His
elders.

Song of Praise for God's Favor

25 O LORD, You are [a]my God;
I will exalt You, I will give thanks to
Your name;
For You have [b]worked wonders,
[c]Plans *formed* long ago, with perfect
faithfulness.
2 For You have made a city into a [a]heap,
A [b]fortified city into a ruin;
A [c]palace of strangers is a city no
more,
It will never be rebuilt.
3 Therefore a strong people will [a]glorify
You;
[b]Cities of ruthless nations will revere
You.
4 For You have been a [a]defense for the
helpless,
A defense for the needy in his
distress,
A [b]refuge from the storm, a shade
from the heat;
For the breath of the [c]ruthless
Is like a *rain* storm *against* a wall.
5 Like heat in drought, You subdue the
[a]uproar of aliens;
Like heat by the shadow of a cloud,
the song of the ruthless is
[1]silenced.

13 [1]Lit *striking* [a]Is 17:6; 27:12
14 [1]Lit *sea* [a]Is 12:6; 48:20; 52:8; 54:1
15 [1]Lit *region of light* [2]Or *islands* [a]Is 25:3 [b]Mal 1:11 [c]Is 11:11; 42:4, 10, 12; 49:1; 51:5; 60:9; 66:19
16 [1]Lit *Wasting to me!* [a]Is 11:12; 42:10 [b]Is 28:5; 60:21 [c]Lev 26:39 [d]Is 21:2; 33:1; Jer 3:20; 5:11
17 [1]Lit *Are upon you* [a]Jer 48:43; Amos 5:19
18 [1]Lit *sound of terror* [2]Lit *goes up from the midst of* [3]Lit *from the height;* i.e. heaven [a]Gen 7:11 [b]Ps 18:7; 46:2; Is 2:19, 21; 13:13
19 [a]Is 24:1 [b]Num 16:31, 32; Deut 11:6
20 [1]Or *hut* [a]Is 19:14; 24:1; 28:7 [b]Is 1:28; 43:27; 66:24 [c]Dan 11:19; Amos 8:14
21 [1]Lit *the height in the height* [a]Is 10:12; 13:11
21 [b]Ps 76:12
22 [1]Lit *pit* [a]Is 10:4; 42:22 [b]Ezek 38:8; Zech 9:11, 12
23 [a]Is 13:10 [b]Is 60:19, 20; Zech 14:6, 7; Rev 21:23; 22:5 [c]Mic 4:7; Heb 12:22
25:1 [a]Ex 15:2; Ps 118:28; Is 7:13; 49:4, 5; 61:10 [b]Ps 40:5; 98:1 [c]Eph 1:11
2 [a]Is 17:1; 26:5; 27:10; 32:19 [b]Is 17:3; 25:12 [c]Is 13:22; 32:14; 34:13
3 [a]Is 24:15 [b]Is 13:11
4 [a]Is 14:32; 17:10; 27:5; 33:16 [b]Is 4:6; 32:2 [c]Is 29:5, 20; 49:25
5 [1]Lit *humbled* [a]Jer 51:54-56

24:13 Only a few olives and grapes will be left (see v. 6; 17:6,11).
24:14 *They.* The godly remnant that survives the judgment.
24:15 *coastlands.* See note on 11:11.
24:16 *ends of the earth.* See note on 11:12. *I.* Probably collective for the godly community that wastes away because of the villainy of the treacherous nations that seek to crush the people of God. *Woe to me . . . treacherously.* In the Hebrew text these last four lines of the verse (*Razi li, razi li! 'Oy li! Bogedim bagadu! Ubeged bogedim bagadu!*) contain a powerful example of alliteration and assonance. *Woe to me!* Isaiah had the same reaction in 6:5 ("Woe is me"). *the treacherous.* The enemies of God's people.
24:17–18 Cf. Amos 5:19.
24:17 *Terror and pit and snare.* Another example (see note on v. 16) of alliteration and assonance (see note on Jer 48:43). The Hebrew words are *paḥad, paḥat* and *paḥ.*
24:18 *windows above.* An echo of Noah's flood (Gen 7:11; 8:2). *foundations . . . shake.* Earthquakes and thunder (see note on 13:13; cf. Joel 3:16).
24:20 *like a drunkard.* Cf. 19:14. *like a shack.* See 1:8 and note.
24:21 *in that day.* The day of the Lord (see notes on 2:11,17,20; 10:20,27; cf. 25:9; 26:1; 27:1–2,12–13). *host of heaven.* Satan and the fallen angels (see Eph 6:11–12).
24:22 *confined in prison.* Cf. Rev 20:2. *punished.* Or "released"; cf. Rev 20:7–10.
24:23 *moon . . . abashed and the sun ashamed.* The sun and moon do not shine during judgment (see note on 13:10) or when the Lord is the "everlasting light" (60:19–20; cf. Rev 21:23; 22:5). *reign on Mount Zion.* See 2:2–4 and note.
25:1–5 A song of praise celebrating the deliverance brought about by the judgments of ch. 24 (see 24:14–16; see also ch. 12).
25:1 *Plans formed long ago.* See 14:24,26–27; 23:8–9.
25:2 *a city . . . a ruin.* See 24:10 and note. *never be rebuilt.* Cf. 24:20.
25:3 *strong people . . . ruthless nations.* Such as Egypt and Assyria (see 19:18–25 and notes). *glorify You . . . revere You.* See 24:15.
25:4–5 *defense . . . refuge . . . shade . . . cloud.* See 4:5–6 and note; cf. 32:2.

6 [a]The LORD of hosts will prepare a
[1]lavish banquet for [b]all peoples on
this mountain;
A banquet of [2]aged wine, [3]choice
pieces with marrow,
And [4]refined, aged wine.
7 And on this mountain He will swallow
up the [1a]covering which is over all
peoples,
Even the veil which is [2]stretched over
all nations.
8 He will [a]swallow up death for all
time,
And the Lord [1]GOD will [b]wipe tears
away from all faces,
And He will remove the [c]reproach of
His people from all the earth;
For the LORD has spoken.
9 And it will be said in that day,
"Behold, [a]this is our God for whom we
have [b]waited that [c]He might save
us.
This is the LORD for whom we have
waited;
[d]Let us rejoice and be glad in His
salvation."
10 For the hand of the LORD will rest on
this mountain,
And [a]Moab will be trodden down in
his place
As straw is trodden down in the water
of a manure pile.
11 And he will [a]spread out his hands in
the middle of it
As a swimmer spreads out *his hands*
to swim,
But *the Lord* will [b]lay low his pride
together with the trickery of his
hands.
12 The [a]unassailable fortifications of
your walls He will bring down,
Lay low *and* cast to the ground, even
to the dust.

6 [1]Lit *feast of fat things;* i.e. abundance [2]Lit *wine on the lees* [3]Lit *fat pieces* [4]Lit *wine refined on the lees* [a]Is 1:19 [b]Is 2:2-4; 56:7
7 [1]Lit *face of the covering* [2]Lit *woven* [a]2 Cor 3:15, 16; Eph 4:18
8 [1]Heb *YHWH,* usually rendered LORD [a]Hos 13:14; 1 Cor 15:54 [b]Is 30:19; 35:10; 51:11; 65:19; Rev 7:17; 21:4 [c]Ps 69:9; 89:50, 51; Is 51:7; 54:4; Matt 5:11; 1 Pet 4:14
9 [a]Is 35:2; 40:9; 52:10 [b]Is 8:17; 30:18; 33:2 [c]Is 33:22; 35:4; 49:25, 26; 60:16 [d]Ps 20:5; Is 35:1, 2, 10; 65:18; 66:10
10 [a]Is 16:14; Jer 48:1-47; Ezek 25:8-11; Amos 2:1-3; Zeph 2:9
11 [a]Is 5:25; 14:26 [b]Job 40:11; Is 2:10-12, 15-17; 16:6, 14
12 [a]Is 15:1; 25:2; 26:5

26:1 [1]Or *salvation* [a]Is 4:2; 12:1 [b]Is 14:31; 31:5, 9; 33:5, 6, 20-24 [c]Is 60:18
2 [1]Lit *keeps faithfulness* [a]Is 60:11, 18; 62:10 [b]Is 45:25; 54:14, 17; 58:8; 60:21; 61:3; 62:1, 2
3 [a]Is 26:12; 27:5; 57:19; 66:12
4 [1]Heb *YAH,* usually rendered LORD [a]Is 12:2; 50:10; 51:5 [b]Is 17:10; 30:29; 44:8

Song of Trust in God's Protection

26 [a]In that day this song will be sung in
the land of Judah:
"We have a [b]strong city;
He sets up walls and ramparts for
[1c]security.
2 "Open the [a]gates, that the [b]righteous
nation may enter,
The one that [1]remains faithful.
3 "The steadfast of mind You will keep in
perfect [a]peace,
Because he trusts in You.
4 "[a]Trust in the LORD forever,
For in [1]GOD the LORD, *we have* an
everlasting [b]Rock.
5 "For He has brought low those who
dwell on high, the [a]unassailable
city;
[b]He lays it low, He lays it low to the
ground, He casts it to the dust.
6 "[a]The foot will trample it,
The feet of the [b]afflicted, the steps of
the helpless."

7 The [a]way of the righteous is smooth;
O Upright One, [b]make the path of the
righteous level.
8 Indeed, *while following* the way of
[a]Your judgments, O LORD,
We have waited for You eagerly;
[b]Your name, even Your [c]memory, is
the desire of *our* souls.
9 [a]At night [1]my soul longs for You,
Indeed, [2]my spirit within me [b]seeks
You diligently;
For when the earth [3]experiences Your
judgments
The inhabitants of the world [c]learn
righteousness.
10 *Though* the wicked is shown favor,

5 [a]Is 25:12 [b]Job 40:11-13 **6** [a]Is 28:3 [b]Is 3:14, 15; 11:4; 29:19
7 [a]Is 57:2 [b]Ps 25:4, 5; 27:11; Is 42:16; 52:12 **8** [a]Is 51:4; 56:1 [b]Is 12:4; 24:15; 25:1; 26:13 [c]Ex 3:15 **9** [1]Lit with *my soul I long* [2]Lit with *my spirit...I seek* [3]Lit *has* [a]Ps 63:5, 6; 77:2; 119:62; Is 50:10; Luke 6:12 [b]Ps 63:1; 78:34; Matt 6:33 [c]Is 55:6; Hos 5:15

25:6–8 The eschatological feast of God.
25:6–7,10 *this mountain.* Mount Zion. See 2:2–4 and note; cf. 24:23.
25:6 *lavish.* Rich food is symbolic of great spiritual blessings (see 55:2). *banquet.* Associated with a coronation (1 Kin 1:25) or wedding (Judg 14:10); cf. the "marriage supper of the Lamb" (Rev 19:9). *aged wine.* The best wine—aged by being left on its dregs (see Jer 48:11; Zeph 1:12).
25:7 *covering . . . veil.* Used to cover faces in mourning—in any event, the associations are with death.
25:8 Quoted in part in 1 Cor 15:54. *swallow up death.* Death, the great swallower (see Ps 49:14 and note), will be swallowed up. *Lord GOD.* See 7:7; 28:16; 30:15; 40:10; 49:22; 52:4; 61:11; 65:13. *remove the reproach.* See 54:4.
25:9 Another brief song of praise. *in that day.* See 12:1,4; 24:21; see also 10:20,27 and note. *we have waited that He might save.* Cf. Ps 22:4–5. *rejoice and be glad.* Cf. 35:10; 51:11; 66:10.
25:10–12 An elaboration on the theme of judgment.
25:10 *Moab.* Symbolic of all the enemies of God, like Edom in 34:5–17. See note on 15:1.
25:11 *pride.* See note on 16:6.
25:12 *unassailable . . . walls.* See v. 2; 2:15; 2 Kin 3:27; Jer 51:58.
26:1–15 Another song of praise for God's deliverance.
26:1 *In that day.* See 12:1,4; 24:21; 25:9; see also note on 10:20,27. *ramparts.* Sloping fortifications of earth or stone (cf. 2 Sam 20:15).
26:3 See 30:15. *steadfast of mind.* Cf. Ps 112:6–8. *trusts.* Cf. 25:9.
26:4 *Rock.* See 17:10 and note.
26:5 *unassailable city.* See note on 24:10. *lays it low . . . to the dust.* Cf. 25:2,12.
26:6 *feet of the afflicted.* The oppressors are humiliated also in 49:24–26; 51:22–23 (contrast 3:14–15).
26:7 *way . . . smooth; . . . path . . . level.* A theme found also in 40:3–4; 42:16; 45:13.
26:8 A desire for God to reveal His power in their behalf (see Hos 12:5–6). *name . . . memory.* See v. 13; 24:15; 25:1.
26:9 *judgments.* Punishment (cf. 4:4).
26:10 *favor.* Such as the blessings of harvest and general prosperity (cf. Mt. 5:45).

He does not [a]learn righteousness;
He [b]deals unjustly in the land of uprightness,
And does not perceive the majesty of the LORD.

11 O LORD, Your hand is lifted up *yet* they [a]do not see it.
[1]They see [b]*Your* zeal for the people and are put to shame;
Indeed, [2c]fire will devour Your enemies.
12 LORD, You will establish [a]peace for us,
Since You have also performed for us all our works.
13 O LORD our God, [a]other masters besides You have ruled us;
But through You alone we [1b]confess Your name.
14 [a]The dead will not live, the [1]departed spirits will not rise;
Therefore You have [b]punished and destroyed them,
And You have wiped out all remembrance of them.
15 [a]You have increased the nation, O LORD,
You have increased the nation, You are glorified;
You have [b]extended all the borders of the land.
16 O LORD, they sought You [a]in distress;
They [1]could only whisper a prayer,
Your chastening was upon them.
17 [a]As the pregnant woman approaches *the time* to give birth,
She writhes *and* cries out in her labor pains,
Thus were we before You, O LORD.
18 We were pregnant, we writhed *in labor,*
We [a]gave birth, as it seems, *only* to wind.
We could not accomplish deliverance for the earth,
Nor were [b]inhabitants of the world [1]born.
19 Your [a]dead will live;
[1]Their corpses will rise.
You who lie in the dust, [b]awake and shout for joy,
For your dew *is as* the dew of the [2]dawn,
And the earth will [3]give birth to the [4]departed spirits.

20 Come, my people, [a]enter into your rooms
And close your doors behind you;
Hide for a little [1b]while
Until [c]indignation [2]runs *its* course.
21 For behold, the LORD is about to [a]come out from His place
To [b]punish the inhabitants of the earth for their iniquity;
And the earth will [c]reveal her bloodshed
And will no longer cover her slain.

The Deliverance of Israel

27 In that day [a]the LORD will punish
[1b]Leviathan the fleeing serpent,
With His fierce and great and mighty sword,
Even [1]Leviathan the twisted serpent;
And [c]He will kill the dragon who *lives* in the sea.

2 In that day,
"A [1a]vineyard of wine, sing of it!

10 [a]Is 22:12, 13; 32:6, 7 [b]Hos 11:7; John 5:37, 38
11 [1]Or *Let them see...and be* [2]Or *let the fire for Your adversaries devour them* [a]Is 44:9, 18 [b]Is 9:7; 37:32; 59:17 [c]Is 5:24; 9:18, 19; 10:17; 66:15, 24; Heb 10:27
12 [a]Is 26:3
13 [1]Or *cause to be remembered* [a]Is 2:8; 10:11 [b]Is 63:7
14 [1]Or *shades* [a]Deut 4:28; Ps 135:17; Is 8:19; Hab 2:19 [b]Is 10:3
15 [a]Is 9:3 [b]Is 33:17; 54:2, 3
16 [1]Lit *sound forth a whisper* [a]Is 37:3; Hos 5:15
17 [a]Is 13:8; 21:3; John 16:21
18 [1]Lit *fallen* [a]Is 33:11; 59:4 [b]Ps 17:14
19 [1]So with some ancient versions; Heb *My* [2]Lit *lights* [3]Lit *cause to fall* [4]Or *shades* [a]Is 25:8; Ezek 37:1-14; Dan 12:2; Hos 13:14 [b]Eph 5:14
20 [1]Lit *moment* [2]Lit *passes over* [a]Ex 12:22, 23; Ps 91:1, 4 [b]Ps 30:5; Is 54:7, 8; 2 Cor 4:17 [c]Is 10:5, 25; 13:5; 34:2; 66:14
21 [a]Mic 1:3; Jude 14 [b]Is 13:11; 30:12-14; 65:6, 7 [c]Job 16:18; Luke 11:50
27:1 [1]Or *sea monster*

[a]Is 66:16 [b]Job 3:8; 41:1; Ps 74:14; 104:26 [c]Is 51:9 **2** [1]Some mss read *a vineyard of delight* [a]Ps 80:8; Is 5:7; Jer 2:21

26:11 *hand is lifted up.* A sign of power. See 9:12,17,21 and note; Ps 89:13. *zeal.* See 9:7 and note; cf. 37:32; 63:15. *fire.* See note on 1:31.

26:12 *peace.* See v. 3.

26:13 *other masters.* Foreign rulers, such as those of Egypt or Assyria.

26:14 *dead . . . departed spirits.* Cf. the fate of the king of Babylon in 14:9–10.

26:15 *increased the nation.* Applied to the return from Babylonian exile in 54:2–3; also cf. 9:3.

26:16–18 The prophet speaks to the Lord on behalf of God's people.

26:16 *distress.* Perhaps the Assyrian oppression, described in 5:30; 8:21–22. The period of the judges is also possible (see Judg 6:2,6).

26:17–18 *give birth . . . writhes . . . in labor.* See 13:8 and note (cf. 37:3).

26:18 *deliverance for the earth.* Israel was designed to be "a light to the nations" (42:6—see note there; see also 9:2; 49:6 and notes).

26:19–21 The prophet speaks a word of reassurance to God's people.

26:19 *dead will live . . . corpses will rise.* A reference to the restoration of Israel (see Ezek 37:11–12)—perhaps including the resurrection of the body (Dan 12:2). Cf. 25:8; contrast 26:14. *dew.* A symbol of fruitfulness (see 2 Sam 1:21; Hos 14:5).

26:20–21 See 24:21–22 and note on 2:11,17,20.

26:20 *a little while . . . indignation.* Cf. 10:25; 54:7–8. Assyrian tyranny and Babylonian exile, as well as all other oppressions, will end.

26:21 *punish.* See 66:14–16. *will reveal . . . will no longer cover.* The blood and bodies of the innocent/righteous who have been slaughtered by the oppressive powers will no longer be hidden in the ground, but will be brought forth to testify against their murderers, so that God may in judgment avenge their deaths (see Gen 4:10).

27:1–2,12–13 *In that day.* See 10:20,27 and note; see also 12:1,4; 24:21; 25:9; 26:1.

27:1 The climactic word of judgment. *Leviathan . . . dragon.* A symbol (drawn from Canaanite myths) of wicked nations, such as Egypt (see 30:7 and note; 51:9; Ezek 29:3; 32:2). *fleeing . . . twisted serpent.* Cf. Job 3:8; 41:1; Ps 74:14. Such descriptions of Leviathan occur outside the Bible as well.

27:2–6 A second vineyard song (see 5:1–7 and notes).

27:2 *vineyard.* Israel.

3 "I, the LORD, am its keeper;
[a]I water it every moment.
So that no one will [1]damage it,
I [b]guard it night and day.
4 "I have no wrath.
Should [1]someone give Me [a]briars *and*
thorns in battle,
Then I would step on them, [b]I would
burn them [2]completely.
5 "Or let him [1][a]rely on My protection,
Let him make peace with Me,
Let him [b]make peace with Me."
6 [1]In the days to come Jacob [a]will take
root,
Israel will [b]blossom and sprout,
And they will fill the [2]whole world
with [c]fruit.

7 Like the striking of Him who has
struck them, has [a]He struck them?
Or like the slaughter of His slain,
[1]have they been slain?
8 You contended with them [1]by
banishing them, by [a]driving them
away.
With His fierce wind He has expelled
them on the day of the [b]east wind.
9 Therefore through this Jacob's iniquity
will be [a]forgiven;
And this will be [1]the full price of the
[2][b]pardoning of his sin:
When he makes all the [c]altar stones
like pulverized chalk stones;
When [3]Asherim and incense altars
will not stand.
10 For the fortified city is [a]isolated,
A [1]homestead forlorn and forsaken
like the desert;
[b]There the calf will graze,
And there it will lie down and [2]feed
on its branches.
11 When its [a]limbs are dry, they are
broken off;
Women come *and* make a fire with
them,
For they are not a people of
[b]discernment,
Therefore [c]their Maker [d]will not have
compassion on them.
And their Creator will not be gracious
to them.
12 In that day the LORD [a]will start *His*
threshing from the flowing stream of the [b]Eu-
phrates to the brook of Egypt, and you will be
[c]gathered up one by one, O sons of Israel.
13 It will come about also in that day that
a great [a]trumpet will be blown, and those
who were perishing in the land of [b]Assyria
and who were scattered in the land of Egypt
will come and [c]worship the LORD in the holy
mountain at Jerusalem.

Ephraim's Captivity Predicted

28 Woe to the proud crown of the
[a]drunkards of [b]Ephraim,
And to the fading flower of its glorious
beauty,
Which is at the head of the [1]fertile
valley
Of those who are [2]overcome with
wine!
2 Behold, the Lord has a strong and
[a]mighty *agent;*
As a storm of [b]hail, a tempest of
destruction,
Like a storm of [c]mighty overflowing
waters,
He has cast *it* down to the earth with
His hand.
3 The proud crown of the drunkards of
Ephraim is [a]trodden under foot.
4 And the fading flower of its glorious
beauty,

3 [1]Lit *punish* [a]Is 58:11 [b]1 Sam 2:9; Is 31:5; John 10:28
4 [1]Lit *who* [2]Lit *altogether* [a]2 Sam 23:6; Is 10:17 [b]Is 33:12; Matt 3:12; Heb 6:8
5 [1]Lit *take hold of* [a]Is 12:2; 25:4 [b]Job 22:21; Is 26:3, 12; Rom 5:1; 2 Cor 5:20
6 [1]Lit *Those coming* [2]Lit *face of* [a]Is 37:31 [b]Is 35:1, 2; Hos 14:5, 6 [c]Is 4:2
7 [1]Lit *he was slain* [a]Is 10:12, 17; 30:31-33; 31:8, 9; 37:36-38
8 [1]Some ancient versions read *by exact measure* [a]Is 50:1; 54:7 [b]Jer 4:11; Ezek 19:12; Hos 13:15
9 [1]Lit *all the fruit* [2]Lit *removing* [3]I.e. wooden symbols of a female deity [a]Is 1:25; 48:10; Dan 11:35 [b]Rom 11:27 [c]Ex 34:13; Deut 12:3; 2 Kin 10:26; Is 17:8
10 [1]Lit *pasture* [2]Lit *consume* [a]Is 32:13, 14 [b]Is 17:2
11 [a]Is 18:5
11 [b]Deut 32:28; Is 1:3; 5:13; Jer 8:7 [c]Deut 32:18; Is 43:1, 7; 44:2, 21, 24 [d]Is 9:17
12 [a]Is 11:11; 17:6; 24:13; 56:8 [b]Gen 15:18 [c]Deut 30:3, 4; Neh 1:9
13 [a]Lev 25:9; 1 Chr 15:24; Matt 24:31; Rev 11:15 [b]Is 19:24, 25 [c]Is 19:21, 23; 49:7; 66:23; Zech 14:16; Heb 12:22

28:1 [1]Lit *valley of fatness* [2]Lit *smitten* [a]Is 28:7; Hos 7:5 [b]Is 9:9
2 [a]Is 8:7; 40:10 [b]Is 28:17; 30:30; 32:19; Ezek 13:11 [c]Is 8:6, 7; 30:28; Nah 1:8 **3** [a]Is 26:6; 28:18

27:4–5 A picture of Israel's lukewarmness toward the Lord—not "briars and thorns" (v. 4) like the other nations, but not fully trusting in the Lord either (see 29:13).
27:4 *briars and thorns.* See 5:6 and note.
27:6 *take root.* See 11:1,10 and notes. *blossom and sprout.* See 4:2 and note. The Messianic age is in view. *fill the whole world.* Contrast 26:18.
27:7–11 What the Lord is going to do with Israel in the judgments that are about to overtake her in Isaiah's day.
27:7 *struck them.* Cf. 10:24–26.
27:8 *banishing them.* Probably the Babylonian captivity. *east wind.* A hot wind from the desert (see Jer 4:11; Ezek 19:12).
27:9 *forgiven.* Israel (Jacob) will have to atone for her guilt through the coming judgment. *altar . . . Asherim . . . incense altars.* See 17:8 and note. *pulverized.* See Ex 34:13.
27:10 *fortified city.* Jerusalem. *isolated . . . forsaken.* Cf. 6:11–12. *calf will graze.* Cf. 5:5; 7:25.
27:12–13 The redemption that lies beyond the coming judgment.
27:12 *start His threshing.* Judgment on the nations into which Israel has been dispersed (see note on 21:10). The threshing will separate Israelites from Gentiles. *brook of Egypt.* Probably the Wadi el-Arish, the southern border of the promised land (the Euphrates is the northern border). See Gen 15:18 and note; 1 Kin 4:21; 8:65.
27:13 *great trumpet.* Used especially to summon troops (see 1 Sam 13:3). *Assyria . . . Egypt.* See 11:11–12 and notes. *holy mountain.* Mount Zion (see 2:2–4 and note; see also 24:23; 25:6–7,10 and note).
28:1–35:10 A series of six woes (28:1; 29:1; 29:15; 30:1; 31:1; 33:1), concluded with an announcement of judgment on the nations (ch. 34) and a song celebrating the joy of the redeemed (ch. 35). Cf. the six woes in ch. 5 (see note on 5:8–23).
28:1 *proud.* See v. 3 and note on 16:6. *crown.* Samaria, the capital of the northern kingdom, was a beautiful city on a prominent hill (see note on 1 Kin 16:24). *drunkards.* In the eighth century B.C. Samaria was a city of luxury and indulgence. See 5:11–13 and note; Amos 6:4–7. *Ephraim.* See note on 7:2. *fertile valley.* Cf. 5:1.
28:2 *strong . . . agent.* The king of Assyria. *storm of hail . . . overflowing waters.* See v. 17; 8:7–8 and note; 17:12 and note. Cf. 30:30; 32:19.

Which is at the head of the [1]fertile valley,
Will be like the [a]first-ripe fig prior to summer,
Which [2]one sees,
And [3]as soon as it is in his [4]hand,
He swallows it.
5 In that day the [a]LORD of hosts will become a beautiful [b]crown
And a glorious diadem to the remnant of His people;
6 A [a]spirit of justice for him who sits in judgment,
A [b]strength to those who repel the [1]onslaught at the gate.
7 And these also [a]reel with wine and stagger from strong drink:
[b]The priest and [c]the prophet reel with strong drink,
They are confused by wine, they stagger from [d]strong drink;
They reel while [1]having [e]visions,
They totter *when rendering* judgment.
8 For all the tables are full of filthy [a]vomit, without a *single clean* place.

9 "To [a]whom would He teach knowledge,
And to whom would He interpret the message?
Those *just* [b]weaned from milk?
Those *just* taken from the breast?
10 "For *He says,*
'[1a]Order on order, order on order,
Line on line, line on line,
A little here, a little there.' "
11 Indeed, He will speak to this people
Through [a]stammering lips and a foreign tongue,
12 He who said to them, "Here is [a]rest, give rest to the weary,"
And, "Here is repose," but they would not listen.
13 So the word of the LORD to them will be,
"[1]Order on order, order on order,
Line on line, line on line,
A little here, a little there,"
That they may go and [a]stumble backward, be broken, snared and taken captive.

Judah Is Warned

14 Therefore, [a]hear the word of the LORD,
O [b]scoffers,
Who rule this people who are in Jerusalem,
15 Because you have said, "We have made a [a]covenant with death,
And with [1]Sheol we have made a [2]pact.
[b]The overwhelming [3]scourge will not reach us when it passes by,
For we have made [c]falsehood our refuge and we have [d]concealed ourselves with deception."
16 Therefore thus says the Lord [1]GOD,
"[a]Behold, I am laying in Zion a stone, a tested [b]stone,
A costly cornerstone *for* the foundation, [2]firmly placed.
He who believes *in it* will not be [3]disturbed.
17 "I will make [a]justice the measuring line
And righteousness the level;
Then [b]hail will sweep away the refuge of lies
And the waters will overflow the secret place.
18 "Your [a]covenant with death will be [1b]canceled,
And your pact with Sheol will not stand;
When the [a]overwhelming scourge passes through,
Then you become its [c]trampling *place.*
19 "As [a]often as it passes through, it will [1]seize you;

4 [1]Lit *valley of fatness* [2]Lit *the one seeing sees* [3]Lit *while it is yet* [4]Lit *palm* [a]Hos 9:10; Mic 7:1; Nah 3:12
5 [a]Is 41:16; 45:25; 60:1, 19 [b]Is 62:3
6 [1]Lit *battle* [a]1 Kin 3:28; Is 11:2; 32:15, 16; John 5:30 [b]2 Chr 32:6-8; Is 25:4
7 [1]Lit *seeing* [a]Is 5:11, 22; 22:13; 56:12; Hos 4:11 [b]Is 24:2 [c]Is 9:15 [d]Hab 2:15, 16 [e]Is 29:11
8 [a]Jer 48:26
9 [a]Is 2:3; 28:26; 30:20; 48:17; 50:4; 54:13 [b]Ps 131:2
10 [1]Heb *Sav lasav, sav lasav, Kav lakav, kav lakav, Ze' er sham, ze' er sham* These Hebrew monosyllables, imitating the babbling of a child, mock the prophet's preaching [a]2 Chr 36:15; Neh 9:30
11 [a]Is 33:19; 1 Cor 14:21
12 [a]Is 11:10; 30:15; 32:17, 18; Jer 6:16; Matt 11:28, 29
13 [1]V 10, note 1 The LORD responds to their scoffing by imitating their mockery, to represent the unintelligible language of a conqueror
13 [a]Is 8:15; Matt 21:44
14 [a]Is 1:10; 28:22 [b]Is 29:20
15 [1]I.e. the nether world [2]So some ancient versions; Heb *seer* [3]Or *flood* [a]Is 28:18 [b]Is 8:8; 28:2; 30:28; Dan 11:22 [c]Is 9:15; 30:9; 44:20; 59:3, 4; Ezek 13:22 [d]Is 29:15
16 [1]Heb *YHWH,* usually rendered LORD [2]Lit *well-laid* [3]Lit *in a hurry* [a]Rom 9:33; 10:11; 1 Pet 2:6 [b]Ps 118:22; Is 8:14, 15; Matt 21:42; Mark 12:10; Luke 20:17; Acts 4:11; Eph 2:20
17 [a]2 Kin 21:13; Is 5:16; 30:18; 61:8; Amos 7:7-9 [b]Is 28:2
18 [1]Lit *covered over* [a]Is 28:15 [b]Is 7:7; 8:10 [c]Is 28:3; Dan 8:13
19 [1]Lit *take* [a]2 Kin 24:2

28:5 *In that day.* See 4:1–2; 10:20,27 and note; 12:1,4; 24:21; 25:9; 26:1; 27:1–2,12–13. *beautiful . . . glorious.* See 4:2. *remnant.* See note on 1:9.

28:6 *spirit of justice.* See 11:2–4 and notes. *gate.* The most vulnerable part of a city.

28:7 *wine . . . strong drink.* The religious leaders should have been filled with the Spirit, not with wine. See Lev 10:9; Num 11:29; Eph 5:18.

28:8 *vomit.* Cf. Jer 25:16,27.

28:9–10 The mocking response of Isaiah's hearers (see NASB marg.). Cf. the mocking tones of 5:19.

28:11–12 Quoted in part in 1 Cor 14:21.

28:11 *stammering lips.* The language of the Assyrians.

28:12 *rest.* The land given to them by the Lord, in whom they were to trust (see 26:3; 30:15; 40:31; Josh 1:13). *would not listen.* Cf. Jer 6:16.

28:13 *will be.* They say the prophet is speaking nonsense, so the word of the Lord that he speaks will remain nonsense to them (see 6:9–10 and notes).

28:15,18 *covenant with death.* Possibly an allusion to necromancy and worship of idols (see 8:19). By using a vivid figure of speech, Isaiah mocks their sense of assurance against national calamity, placing on their lips a claim to have a covenant with death that it will not harm them (see Hos 2:18). *overwhelming scourge.* A mixed metaphor referring to the armies of Assyria and Babylonia. "Overwhelming" pictures an army as a flooding river (see 8:7); a "scourge" is a whip (10:26).

28:16 *stone.* The Lord (see 8:14; 17:10 and notes). *cornerstone.* Cf. the "chief corner stone" of Ps 118:22. *foundation.* See 1 Cor 3:11; cf. 1 Pet 2:4–7.

28:17 *measuring line . . . level.* The standards and tests the Lord will apply are His justice and righteousness. *hail.* See v. 2; 30:30; 32:19.

For [b]morning after morning it will
pass through, *anytime* during the
day or night,
And it will be [2]sheer [c]terror to
understand [3]what it means."
20 The bed is too short on which to
stretch out,
And the [a]blanket is too [1]small to wrap
oneself in.
21 For the LORD will rise up as *at* Mount
[a]Perazim,
He will be stirred up as in the valley
of [b]Gibeon,
To do His [c]task, His [1d]unusual task,
And to work His work, His
[2]extraordinary work.
22 And now do not carry on as [a]scoffers,
Or your fetters will be made stronger;
For I have heard from the Lord [1]GOD
of hosts
Of decisive [b]destruction on all the
earth.

23 Give ear and hear my voice,
Listen and hear my words.
24 Does the [1]farmer plow [2]continually to
plant seed?
Does he *continually* [3]turn and harrow
the ground?
25 Does he not level its surface
And sow dill and scatter [a]cummin
And [1]plant [b]wheat in rows,
Barley in its place and rye within its
[2]area?
26 For his God instructs and teaches him
properly.
27 For dill is not threshed with a
[a]threshing sledge,
Nor is the cartwheel [1]driven over
cummin;
But dill is beaten out with a rod, and
cummin with a club.
28 *Grain for* bread is crushed,
Indeed, he does not continue to thresh
it forever.
Because the wheel of *his* cart and his
horses *eventually* [1]damage *it,*
He does not thresh it longer.
29 This also comes from the LORD of
hosts,
Who has made *His* counsel
[a]wonderful and *His* wisdom [b]great.

Jerusalem Is Warned

29 Woe, O [1]Ariel, [1]Ariel the city *where*
David *once* [a]camped!
Add year to year, [2b]observe *your* feasts
on schedule.
2 I will bring distress to Ariel,
And she will be *a city of* lamenting
and [a]mourning;
And she will be like an Ariel to me.
3 I will [a]camp against you [1]encircling
you,
And I will set siegeworks against you,
And I will raise up battle towers
against you.
4 Then you will [a]be brought low;
From the earth you will speak,
And from the dust *where* you are
prostrate
Your words *will come.*
Your voice will also be like that of a
[1]spirit from the ground,
And your speech will whisper from
the dust.

5 But the multitude of your [1]enemies
will become like fine [a]dust,
And the multitude of the [b]ruthless
ones like the chaff which [2]blows
away;
And it will happen [c]instantly,
suddenly.
6 From the LORD of hosts you will be
[a]punished with [b]thunder and
earthquake and loud noise,
With whirlwind and tempest and the
flame of a consuming fire.

19 [2]Lit *only* [3]Lit *the report,* or, *the message* [b]Is 50:4 [c]Job 6:4; 18:11; 24:17; Ps 55:4; 88:15; Lam 2:22
20 [1]Lit *narrow* [a]Is 59:6
21 [1]Lit *task is strange* [2]Lit *work is alien* [a]2 Sam 5:20; 1 Chr 14:11 [b]Josh 10:10, 12; 2 Sam 5:25; 1 Chr 14:16 [c]Is 10:12; 29:14; 65:7 [d]Lam 2:15; 3:33; Luke 19:41-44
22 [1]Heb *YHWH,* usually rendered LORD [a]Is 28:14 [b]Is 10:22, 23
24 [1]Lit *plowman* [2]Lit *all day* [3]Lit *open*
25 [1]Lit *put* [2]Lit *region* [a]Matt 23:23 [b]Ex 9:32
27 [1]Lit *rolled* [a]Amos 1:3
28 [1]Lit *discomfit*
29 [a]Is 9:6 [b]Is 31:2; Rom 11:33
29:1 [1]I.e. Lion of God, or Jerusalem [2]Lit *let your feasts run their round* [a]2 Sam 5:9 [b]Is 1:14; 5:12; 22:12, 13; 29:9, 13
2 [a]Is 3:26; Lam 2:5
3 [1]Lit *like a circle* [a]Luke 19:43, 44
4 [1]Or *ghost* [a]Is 8:19
5 [1]Lit *strangers* [2]Lit *passes away* [a]Is 17:13; 41:15, 16 [b]Is 13:11; 25:3; 29:20 [c]Is 17:14; 30:13; 47:11; 1 Thess 5:3
6 [a]Is 10:3; 26:14, 21 [b]1 Sam 2:10; Matt 24:7; Mark 13:8; Luke 21:11; Rev 11:13, 19; 16:18

28:20 *too short . . . too small.* Israel was unprepared both militarily and spiritually.
28:21 *Mount Perazim.* Where God "broke through" against the Philistines (2 Sam 5:20). *valley of Gibeon.* Where God sent hail to demolish the Amorites (Josh 10:10–12). *unusual task . . . extraordinary work.* This time God would fight against Israel.
28:22 *decisive destruction.* See 10:22–23 and note on 10:22.
28:23–29 A wisdom poem (a poetic parable) in two stanzas, each ending in a verse that praises the wisdom of God. In the context, and since "threshing" is emphasized (vv. 27–28), the point may be that though God must punish Israel, His actions will be as measured and as well-timed as a farmer's. See 27:12 and note.
28:25 *cummin.* An herb for seasoning. *rye.* A kind of wheat (see note on Ex 9:32).
28:27 *rod.* See 10:5 and note.
28:29 *counsel wonderful.* See 9:6 and note.
29:1–2,7 *Ariel.* Jerusalem. Fighting and bloodshed will turn Jerusalem into a virtual "altar hearth" (Hebrew *'ari'el*; the Hebrew for "altar and hearth" and Ariel sound the same). Similar Hebrew words for the same term are used in Ezek 43:15–16 (see note there).
29:1 *Woe.* See note on 28:1. *city where David . . . camped.* See 2 Sam 5:6–9. *feasts on schedule.* See 1:13–14 and note on 1:14.
29:3 *towers.* Pushed up to the city wall by attackers so they could fight the defenders on the same level.
29:4 *whisper.* Used of mediums and spiritists in 8:19. Judah speaks as from the realm of the dead—so much for their covenant with death (see 28:15,18).
29:5–8 In God's time, those nations that devastate Jerusalem will be devastated (see 10:5–19; 27:1). The sudden destruction of the enemy resembles that of Assyria's army in 701 B.C. (see 10:16 and note).
29:5 *chaff.* See 17:13; Ps 1:4 and notes.
29:6 *thunder and earthquake . . . whirlwind and tempest.* As in Judg 5:4–5; Ps 18:7–15; Hab 3:3–7; see also 28:2; Ps 83:13–15 and notes.

7 And the [a]multitude of all the nations
who wage war against [1]Ariel,
Even all who wage war against her
and her stronghold, and who
distress her,
Will be like a dream, a [b]vision of the
night.
8 It will be as when a hungry man
dreams—
And behold, he is eating;
But when he awakens, his [1]hunger is
not satisfied,
Or as when a thirsty man dreams—
And behold, he is drinking,
But when he awakens, behold, he is
faint
And his [1]thirst is not quenched.
[a]Thus the multitude of all the nations
will be
Who wage war against Mount Zion.

9 [a]Be delayed and wait,
Blind yourselves and be blind;
They [b]become drunk, but not with
wine,
They stagger, but not with strong drink.
10 For the LORD has poured over you a
spirit of deep [a]sleep,
He has [b]shut your eyes, the prophets;
And He has covered your heads, the
seers.

11 The entire vision will be to you like the
words of a sealed [1][a]book, which when they
give it to the one who [2]is literate, saying,
"Please read this," he will say, "I cannot, for
it is sealed."
12 Then the [1]book will be given to the one
who [2]is illiterate, saying, "Please read this."
And he will say, "I [3]cannot read."
13 Then the Lord said,
"Because [a]this people draw near with
their [1]words
And honor Me with their [2]lip service,
But they remove their hearts far from
Me,
And their [3]reverence for Me [4]consists
of [5]tradition learned *by rote*,
14 Therefore behold, I will once again
deal [a]marvelously with this people,
wondrously marvelous;
And [b]the wisdom of their wise men
will perish,
And the discernment of their
discerning men will be
concealed."

15 Woe to those who deeply [a]hide their
[1]plans from the LORD,
And whose [b]deeds are *done* in a dark
place,
And they say, "[c]Who sees us?" or
"Who knows us?"
16 You turn *things* around!
Shall the potter be considered [1]as
equal with the clay,
That [a]what is made would say to its
maker, "He did not make me";
Or what is formed say to him who
formed it, "He has no
understanding"?

Blessing after Discipline

17 Is it not yet just a little while
[1]Before Lebanon will be turned into a
[a]fertile field,
And the fertile field will be considered
as a forest?
18 On that day the [a]deaf will hear [b]words
of a book,
And out of *their* gloom and darkness
the [c]eyes of the blind will see.
19 The [a]afflicted also will increase their
gladness in the LORD,
And the [b]needy of mankind will
rejoice in the Holy One of Israel.
20 For the [a]ruthless will come to an end
and the [b]scorner will be finished,
Indeed [c]all who [1]are intent on doing
evil will be cut off;
21 Who [1]cause a person to be indicted by
a word,
And [a]ensnare him who adjudicates at
the gate,

7 [1]V 1, note 1 [a]Mic 4:11, 12; Zech 12:9 [b]Job 20:8; Ps 73:20; Is 17:14
8 [1]Lit *soul* [a]Is 54:17
9 [a]Is 29:1 [b]Is 51:17, 21, 22; 63:6
10 [a]Ps 69:23; Is 6:9, 10; Mic 3:6; Rom 11:8 [b]Is 44:18; 2 Thess 2:9-12
11 [1]Or *scroll* [2]Lit *knows books* [a]Is 8:16; Dan 12:4, 9; Matt 13:11
12 [1]Or *scroll* [2]Lit *does not know books* [3]Lit *do not know books*
13 [1]Lit *mouth* [2]Lit *lips* [3]Lit *fear of Me* [4]Lit *is* [5]Lit *commandment of rulers* [a]Ezek 33:31; Matt 15:8, 9; Mark 7:6, 7
14 [a]Is 6:9, 10; 28:21; 65:7; Hab 1:5 [b]Is 44:25; Jer 8:9; 49:7; 1 Cor 1:19
15 [1]Lit *counsel* [a]Ps 10:11, 13; Is 28:15; 30:1 [b]Job 22:13; Is 57:12; Ezek 8:12 [c]Ps 94:7; Is 47:10; Mal 2:17
16 [1]Lit *like* [a]Is 45:9; 64:8; Jer 18:1-6; Rom 9:19-21
17 [1]Lit *And* [a]Ps 84:6; 107:33, 35; Is 32:15
18 [a]Is 35:5; 42:18, 19; 43:8; Matt 11:5; Mark 7:37 [b]Is 29:11 [c]Ps 119:18; Prov 20:12; Is 32:3
19 [a]Ps 25:9; 37:11; Is 11:4; 61:1; Matt 5:5; 11:29 [b]Is 3:14, 15; 11:4; 14:30, 32; 25:4; 26:6; Matt 11:5; James 1:9; 2:5
20 [1]Lit *watch evil* [a]Is 29:5 [b]Is 28:14 [c]Is 59:4; Mic 2:1
21 [1]Lit *bring a person under condemnation* [a]Amos 5:10

29:9–14 Isaiah speaks again of Israel's spiritual state and warns of the Lord's impending judgment.
29:9 *Blind yourselves . . . become drunk.* Refers to spiritual stupor (see 6:10 and note; cf. 28:1,7).
29:10 Quoted in part in Rom 11:8. *seers.* See 1 Sam 9:9 and note; 2 Kin 17:13.
29:11 *vision.* See 1:1 and note. *I cannot.* God's word is a closed book even to the educated.
29:13 Quoted in part by Jesus to show the hypocrisy of the Pharisees (Matt 15:8–9). *this people.* Not "my people" (cf. 8:6,11–12; Jer 14:10–11; Hag 1:2).
29:14 Quoted in part in 1 Cor 1:19. *wondrously marvelous.* He who showed them wonders in the exodus (see Ex 15:11; Ps 78:12) will now show them wonders in judgment. *wisdom . . . will perish.* Cf. 44:25; Jer 8:9.
29:15 *Woe.* A new woe begins (see note on 28:1–35:10). *their plans.* Perhaps the alliance between Ahaz and Assyria or between Hezekiah and Egypt (see 30:1–2). *Who sees us?* See note on Ps 10:11.
29:16 Quoted in part in Rom 9:20. Cf. the creation of Adam in Gen 2:7; also cf. Is 10:15.
29:17–24 Another sudden shift to the theme of redemption, as in 28:5–8.
29:17 *Lebanon.* Perhaps symbolic of Assyria (see 10:34). The forests of Lebanon were unequaled (see 2:13), so "fertile field" represents a lesser status (see 32:15).
29:18 *On that day.* See notes on 10:20,27; 26:1. Beyond the day of Assyria's destruction lies the day of Israel's restoration. *deaf will hear . . . blind will see.* Linked with the Messianic age in 35:5.
29:19 *needy.* See 11:4. *Holy One of Israel.* See note on 1:4.
29:20 *ruthless.* See v. 21. *scorner.* Cf. 28:14,22.
29:21 *defraud.* See 1:17; 9:17 and notes; see also 10:2; Amos 5:10,12.

And [2b]defraud the one in the right
with [3]meaningless arguments.
22 Therefore thus says the LORD, who
redeemed [a]Abraham, concerning the house
of Jacob:
"Jacob [b]shall not now be ashamed, nor
shall his face now turn pale;
23 But when [1]he sees his [a]children, the
[b]work of My hands, in his midst,
They will sanctify My name;
Indeed, they will [c]sanctify the Holy
One of Jacob
And will stand in awe of the God of
Israel.
24 "Those who [a]err in [1]mind will [b]know
[2]the truth,
And those who [3]criticize will [4c]accept
instruction.

Judah Warned against Egyptian Alliance

30 "Woe to the [a]rebellious children,"
declares the LORD,
"Who [b]execute a plan, but not Mine,
And [1c]make an alliance, but not of My
Spirit,
In order to add sin to sin;
2 Who [a]proceed down to Egypt
Without [b]consulting [1]Me,
[c]To take refuge in the safety of
Pharaoh
And to seek shelter in the shadow of
Egypt!
3 "Therefore the safety of Pharaoh will
be [a]your shame
And the shelter in the shadow of
Egypt, your humiliation.
4 "For [a]their princes are at Zoan
And their ambassadors arrive at
Hanes.
5 "Everyone will be [a]ashamed because of
a people who cannot profit them,
Who are [b]not for help or profit, but for
shame and also for reproach."

6 The [1]oracle concerning the [a]beasts of
the [b]Negev.
Through a land of [c]distress and
anguish,
From [2]where *come* lioness and lion,
viper and [d]flying serpent,
They [e]carry their riches on the [3]backs
of young donkeys
And their treasures on [f]camels'
humps,
To a people who cannot profit *them;*
7 Even Egypt, whose [a]help is vain and
empty.
Therefore, I have called [1]her
"[2b]Rahab who has been exterminated."
8 Now go, [a]write it on a tablet before
them
And inscribe it on a scroll,
That it may [1]serve in the time to
come
[2]As a witness forever.
9 For this is a [a]rebellious people, [b]false
sons,
Sons who [1]refuse to [c]listen
To the [2]instruction of the LORD;
10 Who say to the [a]seers, "You must not
see *visions*";
And to the prophets, "You must not
[b]prophesy to us what is right,
[c]Speak to us [1]pleasant words,
Prophesy illusions.
11 "Get out of the way, [a]turn aside from
the path,
[1b]Let us hear no more about the Holy
One of Israel."
12 Therefore thus says the Holy One of
Israel,
"[a]Since you have rejected this word

21 [2]Lit *turn aside* [3]Lit *confusion* [b]Is 32:7; Amos 5:12 **22** [a]Is 41:8; 51:2; 63:16 [b]Is 45:17; 49:23; 50:7; 54:4 **23** [1]Or *his children see* [a]Is 49:20-26 [b]Is 26:12; 45:11; Eph 2:10 [c]Is 5:16; 8:13 **24** [1]Lit *spirit* [2]Lit *understanding* [3]Lit *murmur* [4]Lit *learn* [a]Is 30:21; Heb 5:2 [b]Is 41:20; 60:16 [c]Is 54:13 **30:1** [1]Lit *pour out a drink offering* [a]Is 1:2, 23; 30:9; 65:2 [b]Is 29:15 [c]Is 8:11, 12 **2** [1]Lit *My mouth* [a]Is 31:1; Jer 43:7 [b]Is 8:19 [c]Is 36:9 **3** [a]Is 20:5, 6; 36:6; Jer 42:18, 22 **4** [a]Is 19:11 **5** [a]Jer 2:36 [b]Is 10:3; 30:7; 31:3

6 [1]Or *burden of* [2]Lit *them* [3]Lit *shoulders* [a]Is 46:1, 2 [b]Gen 12:9 [c]Ex 5:10, 21; Deut 4:20; 8:15; Is 5:30; 8:22; Jer 11:4 [d]Deut 8:15; Is 14:29 [e]Is 15:7; 46:1, 2 [f]1 Kin 10:2 **7** [1]Lit *this* one [2]M.T. reads *They are Rahab* (or *arrogance*), *to remain* [a]Is 30:5 [b]Job 9:13; Ps 87:4; 89:10; Is 51:9 **8** [1]Lit *be* [2]So the versions; Heb *Forever and ever*

[a]Is 8:1 **9** [1]Lit *are not willing* [2]Or *law* [a]Is 30:1 [b]Is 28:15; 59:3, 4 [c]Is 1:10; 5:24; 24:5 **10** [1]Lit *smooth things* [a]Is 29:10 [b]Is 5:20; Jer 11:21; Amos 2:12; 7:13 [c]1 Kin 22:8, 13; Jer 6:14; 23:17, 26; Ezek 13:7; Rom 16:18; 2 Tim 4:3, 4 **11** [1]Lit *Cause to cease from our presence* the [a]Acts 13:8 [b]Job 21:14 **12** [a]Is 5:24; 7:9; 8:6

29:22 *redeemed.* Normally used of the deliverance of Israel from Egypt (see Ex 6:6; 15:13). Cf. 43:1,3,14. But Abraham also had an "exodus" out of a pagan world (see Gen 12:1; Josh 24:2–3,14–15). *be ashamed.* Cf. 45:17; 50:7; 54:4. *turn pale.* From fear of the enemy.
29:23 *sees his children.* Cf. 49:20–21; 54:1–2. Restoration from exile may be in view. See also 53:10. *children, the work of My hands.* See 45:11 (cf. Eph 2:10). *sanctify . . . stand in awe.* See 8:13. Isaiah's contemporaries showed little respect for the Lord. *Holy One of Jacob.* Cf. v. 19; see note on 1:4.
29:24 *err in mind.* See 19:14. *know the truth.* Contrast 1:3.
30:1 *Woe.* See note on 28:1–35:10. *rebellious children.* See 1:2 and note. *plan . . . not Mine.* See 29:15 and note. *alliance.* After Shabako became pharaoh in 715 B.C., the smaller nations in Aram (Syria) and Canaan sought his help against Assyria. Judah apparently joined them (see 20:5 and note). *My Spirit.* Who spoke through His prophet.
30:2 Hezekiah did this (see 2 Kin 18:21). *shadow.* A metaphor for a king as one who provides protection (see Judg 9:15; Lam 4:20). The Lord should have been Israel's "shadow" (cf. 49:2; 51:16; see Ps 91:1; 121:5).
30:3 *shame . . . humiliation.* See also "shame . . . reproach" in v. 5. Cf. 20:4–5; see Judg 9:14–15 and notes.
30:4 *Zoan.* Ironically, where the Israelites once served as slaves; see 19:11 and note. *Hanes.* Possibly Heracleopolis Magna, about 50 miles south of Cairo, or perhaps a city in the Nile delta, close to Zoan.
30:6 *oracle.* See 13:1 and note. *Negev.* The dry region in the southern part of the Holy Land (see Gen 12:9 and note; cf. Judg 1:9). *distress and anguish.* Perhaps it was necessary to use back roads because the Assyrians had control of the main coastal road (see Deut 8:15; Judg 5:6). *flying serpent.* See 14:29.
30:7 *Rahab.* A mythical sea monster, here symbolic of Egypt. The name itself means "storm," and also "arrogance." See 27:1 and note.
30:8 *write it.* Probably the name "Rahab who has been exterminated."
30:9 *rebellious people.* See v. 1; see also 1:2 and note.
30:10 *seers.* See 1 Sam 9:9 and note; 2 Kin 17:13. *You must not see visions.* Cf. Amos 2:12. *Speak to us pleasant words.* As false prophets do (1 Kin 22:13; Jer 6:14; 8:11; 23:17,26).
30:11–12,15 *Holy One of Israel.* See 1:4 and note.

And have put your trust in
[b]oppression and guile, and have
relied on them,
13 Therefore this [a]iniquity will be to you
Like a [b]breach about to fall,
A bulge in a high wall,
Whose collapse comes [c]suddenly in
an instant,
14 Whose collapse is like the smashing of
a [a]potter's jar,
[1]So ruthlessly shattered
That a sherd will not be found among
its pieces
To [2]take fire from a hearth
Or to scoop water from a cistern."
15 For thus the Lord [1]GOD, the Holy One
of Israel, has said,
"In [2]repentance and [a]rest you will be
saved,
In [b]quietness and trust is your
strength."
But you were not willing,
16 And you said, "No, for we will flee on
[a]horses,"
Therefore you shall flee!
"And we will ride on swift *horses*,"
Therefore those who pursue you shall
be swift.
17 [a]One thousand *will flee* at the threat
of one *man*;
You will flee at the threat of five,
Until you are left as a [1]flag on a
mountain top
And as a signal on a hill.

God Is Gracious and Just

18 Therefore the LORD [1][a]longs to be
gracious to you,
And therefore He [2]waits on [b]high to
have compassion on you.
For the LORD is a [c]God of justice;
How blessed are all those who [3][d]long
for Him.
19 [1]O people in Zion, [a]inhabitant in Jerusalem, you will [b]weep no longer. He will
surely be gracious to you at the sound of your
cry; when He hears it, He will [c]answer you.
20 Although the Lord has given you
[a]bread of privation and water of oppression,
He, your Teacher will no longer [b]hide Himself, but your eyes will behold your Teacher.
21 Your ears will hear a word behind you,
"[1]This is the [a]way, walk in it," whenever you
[b]turn to the right or to the left.
22 And you will defile your graven
[a]images overlaid with silver, and your
molten [a]images plated with gold. You will
scatter them as an impure thing, *and* say to
[1]them, "[b]Be gone!"
23 Then He will [a]give *you* rain for [1]the
seed which you will sow in the ground, and
bread *from* the yield of the ground, and it will
be [2]rich and [3]plenteous; on that day [b]your
livestock will graze in a roomy pasture.
24 Also the oxen and the donkeys which
work the ground will eat salted fodder, which
[1]has been [a]winnowed with shovel and fork.
25 On every lofty mountain and on [a]every
high hill there will be [1]streams running with
water on the day of the great [b]slaughter,
when the towers fall.
26 [a]The light of the moon will be as the
light of the sun, and the light of the sun will
be seven times *brighter,* like the light of sev-
en days, on the day [b]the LORD binds up the
[c]fracture of His people and [d]heals the bruise
[1]He has inflicted.
27 Behold, [a]the name of the LORD comes
from a [1]remote place;
[b]Burning is His anger and [2]dense is
His [3]smoke;
His lips are filled with [c]indignation
And His tongue is like a [d]consuming
fire;

12 [b]Is 3:14, 15; 5:7; 59:13 **13** [a]Is 26:21 [b]1 Kin 20:30; Ps 62:4; Is 58:12 [c]Is 29:5; 47:11 **14** [1]Lit *Crushed, it will not be spared* [2]Lit *snatch up* [a]Ps 2:9; Jer 19:10, 11 **15** [1]Heb *YHWH,* usually rendered *LORD* [2]Lit *returning* [a]Ps 116:7; Is 28:12 [b]Is 7:4; 32:17 **16** [a]Is 2:7; 31:1, 3 **17** [1]Lit *pole* [a]Lev 26:36; Deut 28:25; 32:30; Josh 23:10; Prov 28:1 **18** [1]Lit *waits* [2]Lit *is on high* [3]Lit *wait* [a]Is 42:14, 16; 48:9; Jon 3:4, 10; 2 Pet 3:9, 15 [b]Is 2:11, 17; 33:5 [c]Is 5:16; 28:17; 61:8 [d]Is 8:17; 25:9; 26:8; 33:2 **19** [1]M.T. reads *A people will inhabit Zion, Jerusalem* [a]Is 65:9; Ezek 37:25, 28

19 [b]Is 25:8; 60:20; 61:1-3 [c]Ps 50:15; Is 58:9; 65:24; Matt 7:7-11 **20** [a]1 Kin 22:27; Ps 80:5 [b]Ps 74:9; Amos 8:11 **21** [1]Lit *saying, "This* [a]Ps 25:8, 9; Prov 3:6; Is 35:8, 9; 42:16 [b]Is 29:24 **22** [1]Lit *it "Go out"* [a]Ex 32:2, 4; Judg 17:3, 4; Is 46:6 [b]Matt 4:10 **23** [1]Lit *your* [2]Lit *fatness* [3]Lit *fat* [a]Ps 65:9-13; 104:13, 14 [b]Ps 144:13; Is 32:20; Hos 4:16 **24** [1]Lit *one winnows* [a]Matt 3:12; Luke 3:17

25 [1]Lit *canals, streams of water* [a]Is 35:6, 7; 41:18; 43:19, 20 [b]Is 34:2 **26** [1]Lit *of His blow* [a]Is 24:23; 60:19, 20; Rev 21:23; 22:5 [b]Is 61:1 [c]Is 1:6; 30:13, 14 [d]Deut 32:39; Job 5:18; Is 33:24; Jer 33:6; Hos 6:1, 2 **27** [1]Lit *distance* [2]Lit *heaviness* [3]Lit *uplifting* [a]Is 59:19 [b]Is 10:17 [c]Is 10:5; 13:5; 66:14 [d]Is 66:15

30:12 *oppression.* Especially in their domestic policy (see 1:15–17,23; 5:7; 29:21; 58:3–4; 59:3,6–8,13). *guile.* Especially in their foreign policy (see vv. 1–2; 29:15).

30:13 *Like a breach . . . bulge in a high wall.* Oppression and deceit (v. 12) had been the "wall" they built to assure their safety and prosperity, but it will be shattered to pieces.

30:15 See 26:3. *repentance and rest.* The true way to salvation and security.

30:16 *horses.* See Ps 33:17.

30:17 *One thousand will flee.* A fulfillment of the curse of Deut 32:30. *flag . . . signal.* See 5:26 and note (see also 1:8 and note).

30:18 *longs to be gracious.* After punishing Israel, God will once again bless them (cf. 40:2).

30:19 *weep no longer.* See 25:8 and note. God's response is similar to His zeal for the vineyard (Israel) in 27:2–6.

30:20 *bread of privation . . . water of oppression.* Prisoners' food (see 1 Kin 22:27). *Teacher.* God Himself.

30:21 *This is the way.* Contrast the attitude shown in vv. 10–11 (cf. 29:24).

30:22 *defile your . . . images.* In repentance, not in despair as in 2:20 (see note there).

30:23 *rain . . . bread . . . rich and plenteous.* Part of the covenant blessings promised in Deut 28:11–12. See 5:6 and note. *on that day.* Cf. 29:18; see notes on 10:20,27; 26:1. *livestock will graze.* Cf. 32:20.

30:24 *salted fodder.* Seasoned and tasty.

30:25 *on every high hill . . . streams.* Paradise-like conditions will return to the land (see 41:18; Ps 104:13–15). *day of the great slaughter.* Cf. 24:1; 34:2,6. Assyria's fall (v. 31) is one illustration.

30:26 *moon . . . brighter.* The darkness will be past: Night will be like the day, and day will be illumined with sevenfold light. *binds up the fracture . . . heals the bruise.* Israel was bruised politically because of the sins of the people (see 1:6; 61:1; Jer 33:6).

30:27 *the name.* The revelation of God, especially His power and glory. *anger . . . His smoke.* The language of theophany (a manifestation or appearance of God). God is portrayed as coming in a storm (see v. 30; see also 28:2; 29:6; Ps 18:7–15 and notes). *consuming fire.* Perhaps lightning.

28 His [a]breath is like an overflowing
torrent,
Which [b]reaches to the neck,
To [c]shake the nations back and forth
in a [1]sieve,
And to *put* in the jaws of the peoples
[d]the bridle which [2]leads to ruin.
29 You will have [1]songs as in the night
when you keep the festival,
And gladness of heart as when one
marches to *the sound of* the flute,
To go to the mountain of the LORD, to
the Rock of Israel.
30 And the LORD will cause [1]His voice of
authority to be heard,
And the [2]descending of His arm to be
seen in fierce anger,
And *in* the flame of a consuming fire
In cloudburst, downpour and
hailstones.
31 For [a]at the voice of the LORD [b]Assyria
will be terrified,
When He strikes with the [c]rod.
32 And every [1]blow of the [2a]rod of
punishment,
Which the LORD will lay on him,
Will be with *the music of*
[b]tambourines and lyres;
And in battles, [c]brandishing weapons,
He will fight them.
33 For [1a]Topheth has long been ready,
Indeed, it has been prepared for the
king.
He has made it deep and large,
[2]A pyre of fire with plenty of wood;
The [b]breath of the LORD, like a torrent
of [c]brimstone, sets it afire.

Help Not in Egypt but in God

31 Woe to those who go down to [a]Egypt
for help
And [b]rely on horses,
And trust in chariots because they are
many
And in horsemen because they are
very strong,
But they do not [c]look to the [d]Holy
One of Israel, nor seek the LORD!
2 Yet He also is [a]wise and will [b]bring
disaster
And does [c]not retract His words,
But will arise against the house of
[d]evildoers
And against the help of the [e]workers
of iniquity.
3 Now the Egyptians are [a]men and not
God,
And their [b]horses are flesh and not
spirit;
So the LORD will [c]stretch out His hand,
And [d]he who helps will stumble
And he who is helped will fall,
And all of them will come to an end
together.

4 For thus says the LORD to me,
"As the [a]lion or the young lion growls
over his prey,
Against which a band of shepherds is
called out,
And he will not be terrified at their
voice nor disturbed at their noise,
So will the LORD of hosts come down
to wage [b]war on Mount Zion and
on its hill."
5 Like [1]flying [a]birds so the LORD of hosts
will protect Jerusalem.
He will [b]protect and deliver *it;*
He will pass over and rescue *it.*
6 [a]Return to Him from whom [1]you have
[b]deeply defected, O sons of Israel.
7 For in that day every man will [a]cast
away his silver idols and his gold idols,
which your [b]sinful hands have made for you
as [b]a sin.
8 And the [a]Assyrian will fall by a sword
not of man,
And a [b]sword not of man will devour
him.
So he will [1c]not escape the sword,

28 [1]Lit *sifting of the worthless* [2]Lit *misleads* [a]Is 11:4; 30:33; 2 Thess 2:8 [b]Is 8:8 [c]Amos 9:9 [d]2 Kin 19:28; Is 37:29
29 [1]Lit *the song*
30 [1]Lit *the majesty of His voice* [2]Lit *descent*
31 [a]Is 11:4 [b]Is 10:12; 14:25; 31:8 [c]Is 10:26; 11:4
32 [1]Lit *passing* [2]Lit *staff of foundation* [a]Is 10:24 [b]1 Sam 18:6; Jer 31:4 [c]Ezek 32:10
33 [1]I.e. the place of human sacrifice to Molech [2]Lit *Its pile* [a]2 Kin 23:10; Jer 7:31; 19:6 [b]Is 11:4; 30:28 [c]Gen 19:24; Is 34:9
31:1 [a]Is 30:2, 7; 36:6 [b]Deut 17:16; Ps 20:7; 33:17; Is 2:7; 30:16

31:1 [c]Is 9:13; Dan 9:13; Amos 5:4-8 [d]Is 10:17; 43:15; Hos 11:9; Hab 1:12; 3:3
2 [a]Is 28:29; Rom 16:27 [b]Is 45:7 [c]Num 23:19; Jer 44:29 [d]Is 1:4; 9:17; 14:20 [e]Is 22:14; 32:6
3 [a]Ezek 28:9; 2 Thess 2:4 [b]Is 36:9 [c]Is 9:17; Jer 15:6; Ezek 20:33, 34 [d]Is 30:5, 7; Matt 15:14
4 [a]Num 24:9; Hos 11:10; Amos 3:8 [b]Is 42:13; Zech 12:8
5 [1]Or *hovering* [a]Deut 32:11; Ps 91:4 [b]Is 37:35; 38:6
6 [1]Lit *they* [a]Is 44:22; 55:7; Jer 3:10, 14, 22; Ezek 18:31, 32 [b]Is 1:2, 5
7 [a]Is 2:20; 30:22 [b]1 Kin 12:30
8 [1]Lit *flee* [a]Is 10:12; 14:25; 30:31-33; 37:7, 36-38 [b]Is 66:16 [c]Is 21:15

30:28 *reaches to the neck.* The army of Assyria was similarly described in 8:8 (see note there). *bridle.* Cf. 37:29.
30:29 *songs . . . festival.* Perhaps the Passover, alluded to in 31:5 (cf. Matt 26:30). *mountain of the LORD.* Zion, where the temple was (see 2:2–4 and note). *Rock.* God Himself (see 17:10 and note).
30:30–31 *voice.* Associated with thunder in Ex 20:18–19; Ps 29:3–4.
30:30 *descending . . . arm.* See 9:12,17,21; 51:9 and notes. *cloudburst . . . hailstones.* See 28:2.
30:31 *voice of the LORD . . . terrified.* Cf. Ps 29:5–9.
30:32 *rod of punishment.* See 11:4 and note. *music of tambourines.* After a great victory the women rejoiced with singing and dancing (see Ex 15:20–21; 1 Sam 18:6).
30:33 *Topheth.* A region outside Jerusalem where children were sacrificed to Molech (see 2 Kin 23:10; Jer 7:31–32; 19:6, 11–14), the god of the Ammonites (see 1 Kin 11:7). Thus it was a place of burning. *king.* Of Assyria. *brimstone.* See 1:31; Gen 19:24 and notes.
31:1 See 30:1 and note. Ch. 31 recapitulates ch. 30. *go down to Egypt.* See Gen 26:2. *horses . . . chariots.* Egypt had large numbers of horses and chariots (see 1 Kin 10:28–29). *Holy One of Israel.* See 1:4 and note.
31:2 *He also is wise.* People had questioned God's wisdom in 29:14–16.
31:3 *stretch out His hand.* Cf. the refrain in 5:25; 9:12,17,21; 10:4. *helps will stumble.* Cf. 30:3,5.
31:4 *lion.* A simile, but perhaps also an allusion to the Assyrian king (see note on 15:9). *shepherds.* Perhaps an allusion to the rulers of the nations (see Nah 3:18 and note).
31:5 *birds . . . will protect.* Cf. Deut 32:10–11. *pass over.* The technical word used of the destroying angel who "passed over" every house in Egypt that had blood on the doorposts (see Ex 12:13,23). Cf. Is 37:35.
31:6 *deeply defected.* See 1:2 and note.
31:7 *cast away his . . . idols.* See 2:20 and note.
31:8 *sword not of man.* The angel of the Lord struck down

And his young men will become
[d]forced laborers.
9 "His [a]rock will pass away because of
panic,
And his princes will be terrified at the
[b]standard,"
Declares the LORD, whose [c]fire is in
Zion and whose furnace is in
Jerusalem.

The Glorious Future

32 Behold, a [a]king will reign righteously
And princes will rule justly.
2 Each will be like a [a]refuge from the
wind
And a shelter from the storm,
Like [1b]streams of water in a dry
country,
Like the [a]shade of a [2]huge rock in [3]a
parched land.
3 Then [a]the eyes of those who see will
not be [1]blinded,
And the ears of those who hear will
listen.
4 The [1]mind of the [a]hasty will discern
the [2]truth,
And the tongue of the stammerers will
hasten to speak clearly.
5 No longer will the [a]fool be called
noble,
Or the rogue be spoken of *as* generous.
6 For a fool speaks nonsense,
And his heart [1a]inclines toward
wickedness:
To practice [b]ungodliness and to speak
error against the LORD,
To [2c]keep the hungry person
unsatisfied
And [3]to withhold drink from the
thirsty.
7 As for a rogue, his weapons are evil;
He [a]devises wicked schemes
To [b]destroy *the* afflicted with [1]slander,
[c]Even though *the* needy one speaks
[2]what is right.
8 But [a]the noble man devises noble
plans;
And by noble plans he stands.
9 Rise up, you [a]women who are at ease,
And hear my voice;
[b]Give ear to my word,
You complacent daughters.
10 Within a year and *a few* days
You will be troubled, O complacent
daughters;
[a]For the vintage is ended,
And the *fruit* gathering will not come.
11 Tremble, you *women* who are at ease;
[a]Be troubled, you complacent
daughters;
[b]Strip, undress and put *sackcloth* on
your waist,
12 [a]Beat your breasts for the pleasant
fields, for the fruitful vine,
13 [a]For the land of my people *in which*
thorns *and* briars shall come up;
Yea, for all the joyful houses *and for*
the [b]jubilant city.
14 Because [a]the palace has been
abandoned, the [1]populated [b]city
forsaken.
[2]Hill and watch-tower have become
[c]caves forever,
A delight for [d]wild donkeys, a pasture
for flocks;
15 Until the [a]Spirit is poured out upon us
from on high,
And the wilderness becomes a [b]fertile
field,
And the fertile field is considered as a
forest.
16 Then [a]justice will dwell in the
wilderness

8 [d]Gen 49:15; Is 14:2
9 [a]Deut 32:31, 37 [b]Is 5:26; 13:2; 18:3 [c]Is 10:16, 17; 30:33; Zech 2:5
32:1 [a]Ps 72:1-4; Is 9:6, 7; 11:4, 5; Jer 23:5; 33:15; Ezek 37:24; Zech 9:9
2 [1]Lit *canals* [2]Lit *heavy* [3]Lit *an exhausted* [a]Is 4:6; 25:4 [b]Is 35:6; 41:18; 43:19, 20
3 [1]Or *turned away* [a]Is 29:18
4 [1]Lit *heart* [2]Lit *knowledge* [a]Is 29:24
5 [a]1 Sam 25:25
6 [1]Or *does* [2]Lit *make empty the hungry soul* [3]Lit *he causes to lack* [a]Prov 19:3; 24:7-9; Is 59:7, 13 [b]Is 9:17; 10:6 [c]Is 3:15; 10:2
7 [1]Lit *words of falsehood* [a]Jer 5:26-28; Mic 7:3 [b]Is 11:4; 61:1
7 [2]Lit *justly* [c]Is 5:23
8 [a]Prov 11:25
9 [a]Is 47:8; Amos 6:1; Zeph 2:15 [b]Is 28:23
10 [a]Is 5:5, 6; 7:23; 24:7
11 [a]Is 22:12 [b]Is 47:2
12 [a]Nah 2:7
13 [a]Is 5:6, 10, 17; 27:10 [b]Is 22:2; 23:9
14 [1]Lit *multitude of the* [2]Or *Ophel* [a]Is 13:22; 25:2; 34:13 [b]Is 6:11; 22:2; 24:10, 12 [c]Is 13:21; 34:13 [d]Ps 104:11; Jer 14:6
15 [a]Is 11:2; 44:3; 59:21; Ezek 39:29; Joel 2:28 [b]Ps 107:35; Is 29:17; 35:1, 2
16 [a]Is 33:5; Zech 8:3

185,000 soldiers (see 37:36). *become forced laborers.* As prisoners of war.

31:9 *rock.* Nineveh was destroyed by the Medes and Babylonians in 612 B.C. (see Nah 3:7). *princes will be terrified.* Cf. Nah 2:10. *fire . . . furnace.* The Lord's glory resides in Zion, and from that center of His people His fire of judgment breaks out upon the wicked (see 10:17; 30:33; cf. Lev 10:2; Joel 3:16; Amos 1:2).

32:1 *king . . . reign righteously.* The Messianic age is again in view (see 9:7; 11:4; 16:5 and notes). Cf. vv. 16–17; 33:17.

32:2 *Each.* The Lord's redeemed, as sources of protection and blessing, will reflect Him (see the rest of this note; see also vv. 3–8). *refuge . . . shelter . . . shade.* Similar terms are applied to the Lord in 25:4 (see 4:5–6 and note). *streams . . . in a dry country.* See 35:6–7; 41:18; 49:10.

32:3 *eyes . . . not be blinded . . . ears . . . will listen.* See 35:5 and note (contrast 6:9–10).

32:5–8 The redeemed will no longer be among the fools. The contrast between the fool and the wise or noble man is characteristic of wisdom literature (compare Prov 9:1–6 with Prov 9:13–18).

32:6 *fool speaks nonsense.* Cf. 9:16–17; Ps 14:1; 53:1.

32:7 *the needy one speaks.* See 1:17 and note.

32:8 *plans . . . stands.* See 8:10 and note.

32:9 *women.* Cf. 3:16–4:1. *at ease . . . complacent.* See v. 11; Amos 6:1. These words are used in a good sense in v. 18 (the Hebrew for "undisturbed" is the same as that for "complacent").

32:10 *a year.* Perhaps the invasion of Sennacherib (701 B.C.) is in view. *the vintage is ended.* Cf. 37:30. The armies of Assyria would bring widespread destruction, ruining the summer fruit.

32:11 *Strip.* Cf. 47:2–3. *sackcloth.* Cf. 3:24; 22:12; see note on Gen 37:34.

32:12 *Beat your breasts.* Like the slave girls of Nineveh (Nah 2:7). *for the fruitful vine.* Cf. the Lord's weeping in 16:9.

32:13 *thorns and briars.* See 5:6; 7:23 and notes. *joyful . . . jubilant.* See 22:2 and note; cf. Jer 16:8–9.

32:14 *palace . . . populated city.* Assyria's invasion is a warning that Jerusalem (see 24:10 and note) will one day be destroyed. *donkeys . . . flocks.* Cf. 7:25; 13:21–22; 34:13.

32:15 *Until the Spirit.* The outpouring of the Spirit is linked with abundance also in 44:3 (see v. 2; 11:2 and notes; see also Joel 2:28–32). *fertile field . . . forest.* The forest probably stands for Lebanon (see 29:17 and note; cf. 35:1–2).

And righteousnes
fertile field.
17 And the [a]work
be peace,
And the se
[b]quiet
18 Then m
[a]pe
And

abide in the
iteousness will
ghteousness,
onfidence forever.
l live in a
tion,
llings and in
sting places;
when the [b]forest
l be utterly laid low.
19 ill you be, you who
ll waters,
eely the ox and the

O destroyer,
ere not destroyed;
o is treacherous, while
d not deal treacherously
h.
as you finish destroying, [c]you
l be destroyed;
soon as you cease to deal
treacherously, *others* will [d]deal
treacherously with you.
2 O LORD, [a]be gracious to us; we have
[b]waited for You.
Be [1]their [2c]strength every morning,
Our salvation also in the [d]time of
distress.
3 At the sound of the tumult [a]peoples
flee;
At the [b]lifting up of Yourself nations
disperse.
4 Your spoil is gathered *as* the
caterpillar gathers;
As locusts rushing about men rush
about on it.
5 The LORD is [a]exalted, for He dwells on
high;
He has [b]filled Zion with justice and
righteousness.
6 And He will be the [1a]stability of your
times,
A [b]wealth of salvation, wisdom and
[c]knowledge;
The [d]fear of the LORD is his treasure.
7 Behold, their brave men cry in [1]the
streets,
The [2a]ambassadors of peace weep
bitterly.
8 The highways are desolate, [1]the
[a]traveler has ceased,
He has [b]broken the covenant, he has
despised the cities,
He has no regard for man.
9 [a]The land mourns *and* pines away,
[b]Lebanon is shamed *and* withers;
[c]Sharon is like a desert plain,
And Bashan and Carmel [1]lose *their*
foliage.
10 "Now [a]I will arise," says the LORD,
"Now I will be exalted, now I will be
lifted up.
11 "You have [a]conceived [1]chaff, you will
give birth to stubble;
[2]My [b]breath will consume you like a
fire.
12 "The peoples will be burned to lime,
[a]Like cut thorns which are burned in
the fire.

13 "You who are far away, [a]hear what I
have done;
And you who are near, [1]acknowledge
My might."

17 [1]Or *security* [a]Ps 72:2, 3; 85:8; 119:165; Is 2:4; Rom 14:17; James 3:18 [b]Is 30:15
18 [a]Is 26:3, 12 [b]Is 11:10; 14:3; 30:15; Hos 2:18-23; Zech 2:5; 3:10
19 [a]Is 28:2, 17; 30:30 [b]Is 10:18, 19, 34 [c]Is 24:10, 12; 26:5; 27:10; 29:4
20 [1]Lit *send out the foot of the ox* [a]Eccl 11:1; Is 30:23, 24
33:1 [a]Is 10:6; 21:2 [b]Is 24:16; 48:8 [c]Is 10:12; 14:25; 31:8; Hab 2:8 [d]Jer 25:12-14; Matt 7:2
2 [1]Some versions read *our* [2]Lit *arm* [a]Is 30:18, 19 [b]Is 25:9 [c]Is 40:10; 51:5; 59:16 [d]Is 37:3
3 [a]Is 17:13; 21:15 [b]Is 10:33; 17:13; 59:16-18; Jer 25:30, 31
5 [a]Ps 97:9 [b]Is 1:26; 28:6; 32:16
6 [1]Or *faithfulness* [a]Is 33:20 [b]Is 45:17; 51:6 [c]Is 11:9 [d]2 Kin 18:7; Ps 112:1-3; Is 11:3; Matt 6:33
7 [1]Lit *the outside* [2]Lit *messengers* [a]2 Kin 18:18, 37
8 [1]Lit *he who passes along the way* [a]Is 35:8 [b]Is 24:5
9 [1]Lit *shake off* [a]Is 3:26; 24:4; 29:2 [b]Is 2:13; 10:34 [c]Is 35:2; 65:10
10 [a]Ps 12:5; Is 2:19, 21
11 [1]Lit *dry grass* [2]So one ancient version; M.T. reads *Your breath will* [a]Ps 7:14; Is 26:18; 59:4; James 1:15 [b]Is 1:31
12 [a]2 Sam 23:6, 7; Is 10:17; 27:4
13 [1]Lit *know* [a]Ps 48:10; Is 49:1

32:16 *justice . . . righteousness.* See v. 1 and note.
32:17 *peace.* Cf. 9:7; 11:6–9. *quietness and confidence.* Contrast 30:15.
32:18 *secure . . . undisturbed.* See note on v. 9. *resting places.* See 28:12 and note.
32:19 *hail.* Cf. 28:2. *forest.* Probably Assyria. See 10:33–34 and notes. *city.* See 24:10 and note.
32:20 The abundance of the day of the Lord is described (see 30:23–24 and notes).
33:1 *Woe.* See note on 28:1–35:10. *destroyer . . . who is treacherous.* Probably Assyria—depicted as deceitful (see 10:5–6; 16:4; 21:2; 24:16 and notes).
33:2–9 A prayer asking the Lord to bring about the promised destruction of Assyria.
33:2 *be gracious.* See 30:18 and note. *strength . . . salvation.* See 12:2 and note; cf. 59:16. *distress.* See 37:3.
33:3 *sound of the tumult.* See 30:30–31 and note. *lifting up . . . disperse.* An allusion to Num 10:35; cf. Ps 68:1.
33:5 *filled . . . righteousness.* See 1:26; 32:1 and note.
33:6 *wisdom . . . knowledge . . . fear of the LORD.* Terms linked with the Messiah in 11:2. See 9:6; Prov 1:7 and notes.
33:7 *their brave men.* The men of Judah, during Sennacherib's invasion of 701 B.C. (see 10:28–34). *ambassadors of peace.* Perhaps the three officials who conferred with the Assyrian field commander (see 36:3,22).
33:8 *highways are desolate.* Travel and trade were impossible, creating economic hardship (see Judg 5:6). *covenant.* Perhaps the agreement made when Hezekiah paid large sums to Sennacherib (2 Kin 18:14).
33:9 *land . . . pines away.* Farmland and pastures were ruined by the invaders. See 24:4 and note. *Lebanon.* Renowned for its cedars (2:13) and animals (40:16). *Sharon.* A plain along the Mediterranean coast north of Joppa, known for its beautiful foliage and superb grazing land (see 35:2; 65:10; 1 Chr 27:29). *desert plain.* Desert land associated with the Jordan River and the Dead Sea (see Deut 1:1; 2:8). *Bashan.* See 2:13 and note. *Carmel.* See note on 1 Kin 18:19; means "fertile field" (as in 29:17; 32:15) or "fruitful field" (as in 16:10) and is also associated with lush pasturelands (see 35:2; Mic 7:14; Nah 1:4).
33:10 *be exalted.* Through the judgment He brings on His rebellious people (see v. 14 and note).
33:11 *conceived . . . give birth.* Cf. 26:18. *breath . . . like a fire.* They only produce what results in their destruction.
33:12 *to lime.* The burning will be complete (see Amos 2:1). *thorns.* They burn very quickly (see 27:4; 2 Sam 23:6–7).
33:13 *hear . . . acknowledge.* Cf. 34:1.

14 [a]Sinners in Zion are terrified;
[b]Trembling has seized the godless.
"Who among us can live with [c]the
consuming fire?
Who among us can live with
[1]continual [d]burning?"
15 He who [a]walks righteously and speaks
with sincerity,
He who rejects [1]unjust gain
And shakes his hands so that they
hold no bribe;
He who stops his ears from hearing
about bloodshed
And [b]shuts his eyes from looking
upon evil;
16 He will dwell on the heights,
[a]His refuge will be the [1]impregnable
rock;
[b]His bread will be given *him*,
His water will be sure.

17 Your eyes will see [a]the King in His
beauty;
They will behold [b]a far-distant land.
18 Your heart will meditate on [a]terror:
"Where is [b]he who counts?
Where is he who weighs?
Where is he who counts the towers?"
19 You will no longer see a fierce people,
A people of [1][a]unintelligible speech
[2]which no one comprehends,
Of a stammering tongue [3]which no
one understands.
20 [a]Look upon Zion, the city of our
appointed feasts;
Your eyes will see Jerusalem, an
[b]undisturbed habitation,
[c]A tent which will not be folded;
Its stakes will never be pulled up,
Nor any of its cords be torn apart.
21 But there the majestic *One*, the LORD,
will be for us

A place of [a]r...
On which no ... nd wide canals
And on which ... h oars will go,
pass— ... ship will
22 For the LORD is ou...
The LORD is [b]our l...
The LORD is [c]our ki...
[d]He will save us—
23 Your tackle hangs sla...
It cannot hold the base...
firmly,
Nor spread out the sail.
Then the [a]prey of an abu...
will be divided;
[b]The lame will take the plu...
24 And no resident will say, "I a...
The people who dwell [1]there ...
[b]forgiven *their* iniquity.

God's Wrath against Nations

34 Draw near, [a]O nations, to hear; an...
listen, O peoples!
[b]Let the earth and [1]all it contains he...
and the world and all that springs
from it.
2 For the LORD's [a]indignation is against
all the nations,
And *His* wrath against all their armies;
He has [1][b]utterly destroyed them,
He has given them over to [c]slaughter.
3 So their slain will be [a]thrown out,
And their corpses [1]will give off their
[b]stench,
And the mountains will [2]be drenched
with their [c]blood.
4 And [a]all the host of heaven will [1]wear
away,

14 [1]Lit *everlasting* [a]Is 1:28 [b]Is 32:11 [c]Is 30:27, 30; Heb 12:29 [d]Is 9:18, 19; 10:16; 47:14 **15** [1]Lit *gain of extortioners* [a]Ps 15:2; 24:4; Is 58:6-11 [b]Ps 119:37 **16** [1]Lit *stronghold of rock* [a]Is 25:4 [b]Is 49:10 **17** [a]Is 6:5; 24:23; 33:21, 22 [b]Is 26:15 **18** [a]Is 17:14 [b]1 Cor 1:20 **19** [1]Lit *deepness of lip* [2]Lit *from hearing* [3]Lit *there is no understanding* [a]Deut 28:49, 50; Is 28:11; Jer 5:15 **20** [a]Ps 48:12 [b]Ps 46:5; 125:1, 2; Is 32:18 [c]Is 54:2 **21** [a]Is 41:18; 43:19, 20; 48:18; 66:12 **22** [a]Is 2:4; 11:4; 16:5; 51:5 [b]Is 1:10; 51:4, 7; James 4:12 [c]Ps 89:18; Is 33:17; Zech 9:9 [d]Is 25:9; 35:4; 49:25, 26; 60:16 **23** [a]2 Kin 7:16 [b]2 Kin 7:8; Is 35:6 **24** [1]Lit *in it* [a]Is 30:26; 58:8; Jer 30:17 [b]Is 40:2; 44:22; Jer 50:20; Mic 7:18, 19; 1 John 1:7-9 **34:1** [1]Lit *its fullness* [a]Ps 49:1; Is 41:1; 43:9 [b]Deut 32:1; Is 1:2 **2** [1]Lit *put under the ban* [a]Is 26:20 [b]Is 13:5; 24:1 [c]Is 30:25; 63:6; 65:12 **3** [1]Lit *their stench will go up* [2]Lit *dissolve* [a]Is 14:19 [b]Joel 2:20; Amos 4:10 [c]Ezek 14:19; 35:6; 38:22 **4** [1]Lit *rot* [a]Is 13:13; 51:6; Ezek 32:7, 8; Joel 2:31; Matt 24:29; 2 Pet 3:10

33:14 *Sinners in Zion.* See 1:27–28; 4:4. *consuming fire.* The presence of the God of judgment (see 29:6; 30:27,30; Ex 24:17; Deut 4:24; 9:3; 2 Sam 22:9; Ps 18:8; Heb 12:29).
33:15 Similar requirements are found in Ps 15:2–5; 24:4. *bribe.* See 1:23.
33:16 *heights . . . rock.* Symbolic of the security found in God (cf. Ps 18:1–3). *bread . . . water.* Cf. 49:10.
33:17 *King.* See 32:1 and note; cf. 6:5. *in His beauty.* Reflecting on the splendor and majesty of a Davidic king; probably a foreshadowing of the Messianic kingdom (cf. 4:2; Ps 45:3–4; contrast Is 53:2). *far-distant land.* See 26:15 and note.
33:18 *terror.* The Assyrian invasion (see 17:12–14 and note). *he who weighs.* Forced tribute (see note on v. 8). *towers.* Judah's fortifications were probably under strict Assyrian control (see 2:15).
33:19 *fierce.* Cf. 10:12. *unintelligible speech.* The Assyrian language was related to Hebrew but was different enough to sound strange to Israelite ears. See 28:11; Deut 28:49.
33:20 *Look upon Zion.* The redeemed city, in contrast to the city described in vv. 7–9. *feasts.* See 1:14 and note. *undisturbed habitation.* See 32:17–18 and notes. *tent . . . not . . . folded.* Her exile will be over. *stakes . . . cords.* Cf. the similar description of Jerusalem in 54:2.
33:21 *majestic One.* See 10:34 (cf. Ps 93:4). *wide canals.* To prevent easy access to her borders—thus like Tyre (23:1) or Thebes (see Nah 3:8).
33:22 *our judge.* See 2:4; 11:4 and note. *our lawgiver.* See 2:3; 51:4; Gen 49:10. *our king.* See v. 17; 32:1 and note; see also Ps 46; 48. *save.* See Judg 2:16.
33:23 *tackle.* Jerusalem is pictured as a ship, unprepared to sail into battle against Assyria. *Then.* When God strikes down the Assyrian army (see 10:33–34; 37:36). *plunder.* See v. 4.
33:24 Looking beyond Isaiah's own day to the physically and spiritually whole Jerusalem of vv. 17,20–22.
34:1–35:10 Chs. 34–35 conclude chs. 28–33 and comprise an eschatological section corresponding to chs. 24–27, which conclude chs. 13–23 (see note on 24:1–27:13).
34:2 *indignation . . . wrath.* In the day of the Lord (see 2:11,17,20; 26:20–21 and notes). See also 13:3 and note; 13:13. *utterly destroyed.* The kind of destruction the Canaanites had deserved. The Hebrew term refers to the irrevocable giving over of things or persons to the LORD, often by totally destroying them (see v. 5; see also Josh 6:17). *slaughter.* See 30:25 and note.
34:3 *thrown out.* Not to have a proper burial was considered a disgrace (see 14:19 and note).
34:4 *host of heaven . . . wear away.* Disturbances in the heav-

And the [b]sky will be rolled up like a scroll;
All their hosts will also wither away
As a leaf withers from the vine,
Or as *one* withers from the fig tree.
5 For [a]My sword is satiated in heaven,
Behold it shall descend for judgment upon [b]Edom
And upon the people whom I have [c]devoted to destruction.
6 The sword of the LORD is filled with blood,
It is [1]sated with fat, with the blood of lambs and goats,
With the fat of the kidneys of rams.
For the LORD has a sacrifice in [a]Bozrah
And a great slaughter in the land of [b]Edom.
7 [a]Wild oxen will also [1]fall with them
And [b]young bulls with strong ones;
Thus their land will be [c]soaked with blood,
And their dust [2]become greasy with fat.
8 For the LORD has a day of [a]vengeance,
A year of recompense for the [1]cause of Zion.
9 [1]Its streams will be turned into pitch,
And its loose earth into [a]brimstone,
And its land will become burning pitch.
10 It will [a]not be quenched night or day;
Its [b]smoke will go up forever.
From [c]generation to generation it will be desolate;
[d]None will pass through it forever and ever.
11 But [1a]pelican and hedgehog will possess it,
And [2]owl and raven will dwell in it;
And He will stretch over it the [b]line of [3]desolation
And the [4]plumb line of emptiness.

4 [b]Rev 6:12-14
5 [a]Deut 32:41, 42; Jer 46:10; Ezek 21:3-5 [b]Is 63:1; Jer 49:7, 8, 20; Ezek 25:12-14; 35:1-15; Amos 1:11, 12; Obad 1-14; Mal 1:4 [c]Is 24:6; 43:28
6 [1]Lit *made fat* [a]Is 63:1; Jer 49:13 [b]Is 63:1
7 [1]Lit *go down* [2]Lit *made fat* [a]Num 23:22; Ps 22:21 [b]Ps 68:30; Jer 50:27 [c]Is 63:6
8 [1]Or *controversy* [a]Is 13:6; 35:4; 47:3; 61:2; 63:4
9 [1]I.e. Edom's [a]Deut 29:23; Ps 11:6; Is 30:33
10 [a]Is 1:31; 66:24 [b]Rev 14:11; 19:3 [c]Is 13:20-22; 24:1; 34:10-15; Mal 1:3, 4 [d]Ezek 29:11
11 [1]Or *owl* or *jackdaw* [2]Or *great horned owl* [3]Or *formlessness* [4]Lit *stones of void* [a]Zeph 2:14 [b]2 Kin 21:13; Is 24:10; Lam 2:8
12 [a]Jer 27:20; 39:6 [b]Is 41:11, 12
13 [a]Is 13:22; 25:2; 32:13 [b]Ps 44:19; Jer 9:11; 10:22
14 [1]Or *howling creatures* [2]Or *demon* [3]Heb *Lilith* [a]Is 13:21
15 [1]Lit *shade* [2]Or *kites* [a]Deut 14:13
16 [1]So DSS; M.T. *My* [a]Is 30:8 [b]Is 1:20; 40:5; 58:14

12 Its nobles—there is [a]no one there
Whom they may proclaim king—
And all its princes will be [b]nothing.
13 Thorns will come up in its [a]fortified towers,
Nettles and thistles in its fortified cities;
It will also be a haunt of [b]jackals
And an abode of ostriches.
14 The desert [a]creatures will meet with the [1]wolves,
The [2a]hairy goat also will cry to its kind;
Yes, the [3]night monster will settle there
And will find herself a resting place.
15 The tree snake will make its nest and lay *eggs* there,
And it will hatch and gather *them* under its [1]protection.
Yes, [a]the [2]hawks will be gathered there,
Every one with its kind.

16 Seek from the [a]book of the LORD, and read:
Not one of these will be missing;
None will lack its mate.
For [1b]His mouth has commanded,
And His Spirit has gathered them.
17 He has cast the [a]lot for them,
And His hand has divided it to them by [b]line.
They shall possess it forever;
From [c]generation to generation they will dwell in it.

Zion's Happy Future

35 The [a]wilderness and the desert will be glad,

17 [a]Is 17:13, 14; Jer 13:25 [b]Is 34:11 [c]Is 34:10 **35:1** [a]Is 6:11; 7:21-25; 27:10; 41:18; 55:12, 13

ens characterize the day of the Lord (see 13:10,13 and notes; cf. Ezek 32:7–8). *sky . . . scroll . . . hosts will also wither away.* Referred to in Matt 24:29; Rev 6:13–14 in connection with the "great tribulation" (Matt 24:21) and the second coming of Christ. *As a leaf withers.* Cf. 24:4; 40:7–8.

34:5 *satiated.* Cf. Ezek 39:18–20. *Edom.* Symbolic of all the enemies of God and His people, like Moab in 25:10–12. See note on 21:11. The Edomites were driven from their homeland by the Nabatean Arabs, perhaps as early as 500 B.C.

34:6 *fat.* Considered the best part of the meat, and therefore offered to the Lord in the sacrifices (see Lev 3:9–11). *lambs and goats.* Symbolizing the people. *sacrifice.* Battles are often compared to sacrifices (see Jer 46:10; 50:27; Ezek 39:17–19). *Bozrah.* An important city of Edom and a sheepherding center, it was located about 25 miles southeast of the southern end of the Dead Sea. The name means "grape-gathering" (cf. 63:1–3).

34:7 *Wild oxen . . . strong ones.* Symbolizing the troops and/or leaders of the nations. *soaked with blood.* See v. 3.

34:8 *day of vengeance.* See 35:4; 61:2. The Edomites opposed Israel at every opportunity (see 2 Sam 8:13–14) and rejoiced when Jerusalem was destroyed (Lam 4:21; Ps 137:7). But Edom's day would come (see 63:4).

34:9 *brimstone.* Edom's destruction is compared with the overthrow of Sodom and Gomorrah (see Jer 49:17–18). See also 1:31 and note; Gen 19:24 and note.

34:10 *smoke . . . forever.* Applied to Babylon in Rev 19:3 (see also Rev 14:10–11). *be desolate.* See 13:20–22 and note; Mal 1:3–4.

34:11 *pelican . . . owl . . . raven.* "Unclean" birds (see Deut 14:14–17). Such birds would also live in the ruins of Babylon (13:21) and Nineveh (Zeph 2:14). *line . . . plumb line.* See 28:17 and note. *desolation . . . emptiness.* The Hebrew for these words is used in Gen 1:2 (see note there) to describe the earth in its "formless" and "void" state (see also Jer 4:23 and note).

34:13 *Thorns . . . Nettles.* Cf. 7:24–25.

34:14 *desert creatures . . . wolves.* See 13:21–22. *hairy goat.* Sometimes connected with demons (see note on 13:21). *night monster.* Outside the Bible a related Semitic word refers to a "night demon."

34:15 *hawks.* Ceremonially unclean (see v. 11 and note; Deut 14:13,15–17).

34:16 *book.* After the destruction of Edom, people will read this prophecy given by Isaiah. *these.* The creatures just listed.

34:17 *cast the lot for them.* God will give the creatures of vv. 11,13–15 clear title to the land of Edom.

35:1 *desert will be glad.* The personification of nature is com-

And the [1][b]Arabah will rejoice and blossom;
Like the crocus
2 It will [a]blossom profusely
And [b]rejoice with rejoicing and shout of joy.
The [c]glory of Lebanon will be given to it,
The majesty of [d]Carmel and Sharon.
They will see the [e]glory of the LORD,
The majesty of our God.
3 [a]Encourage the [1]exhausted, and strengthen the [2]feeble.
4 Say to those with [a]anxious heart,
"Take courage, fear not.
Behold, your God will come *with* [b]vengeance;
The [c]recompense of God will come,
But He will [d]save you."
5 Then the [a]eyes of the blind will be opened
And the ears of the deaf will be unstopped.
6 Then the [a]lame will leap like a deer,
And the [b]tongue of the mute will shout for joy.
For waters will break forth in the [c]wilderness
And streams in the [1]Arabah.
7 The [1]scorched land will become a pool
And the thirsty ground [a]springs of water;
In the [b]haunt of jackals, its resting place,
Grass *becomes* reeds and rushes.
8 [a]A highway will be there, [b]a roadway,
And it will be called the Highway of [c]Holiness.
The unclean will not travel on it,
But it *will* be for him who walks *that* way,
And [d]fools will not wander *on it.*
9 No [a]lion will be there,
Nor will any vicious beast go up on it;
[1]These will not be found there.
But [b]the redeemed will walk *there,*
10 And [a]the ransomed of the LORD will return
And come with joyful shouting to Zion,
With everlasting joy upon their heads.
They will [1]find gladness and joy,
And [b]sorrow and sighing will flee away.

Sennacherib Invades Judah

36 [a]Now in the fourteenth year of King
Hezekiah, [b]Sennacherib king of Assyria
came up against all the fortified cities of
Judah and seized them.
2 And the [a]king of Assyria sent Rabshakeh from Lachish to Jerusalem to King
Hezekiah with a large army. And he stood by
the [b]conduit of the upper pool on the highway of the [1]fuller's field.
3 Then [a]Eliakim the son of Hilkiah, who
was over the household, and [b]Shebna the
scribe, and Joah the son of Asaph, the
recorder, came out to him.

35:1 [1]Or *desert* [b]Is 41:19; 51:3 **2** [a]Is 27:6; 32:15 [b]Is 25:9; 35:10; 55:12, 13; 66:10, 14 [c]Is 60:13 [d]Song 7:5 [e]Is 25:9 **3** [1]Lit *slack hands* [2]Lit *tottering knees* [a]Job 4:3, 4; Heb 12:12 **4** [a]Is 32:4 [b]Is 1:24; 47:3; 61:2; 63:4 [c]Is 34:8; 59:18 [d]Ps 145:19; Is 33:22; 35:4 **5** [a]Is 29:18; 32:3, 4; 42:7, 16; 50:4; Matt 11:5; John 9:6, 7 **6** [1]Or *desert* [a]Matt 15:30; John 5:8, 9; Acts 3:8 [b]Matt 9:32; Luke 11:14 [c]Is 35:1; 41:18; 43:19; 49:10; 51:3; John 7:38 **7** [1]Or *mirage* [a]Is 49:10 [b]Is 13:22; 34:13 **8** [a]Is 11:16; 19:23; 40:3; 49:11; 62:10 [b]Is 30:21; 51:10 [c]Is 4:3; 52:1; Matt 7:13, 14; 1 Pet 1:15, 16 [d]Is 33:8 **9** [1]Lit *It* [a]Is 5:29; 30:6 [b]Is 51:10; 62:12; 63:4 **10** [1]Lit *overtake* [a]Is 1:27; 51:11 [b]Is 25:8; 30:19; 65:19; Rev 7:17; 21:4 **36:1** [a]2 Kin 18:13 [b]2 Chr 32:1

2 [1]I.e. launderer's [a]2 Kin 18:17-20:11; 2 Chr 32:9-24; Is 36:2-38:8 [b]Is 7:3 **3** [a]Is 22:20 [b]Is 22:15

mon in Isaiah (see 33:9; 44:23; 55:12). *Arabah.* The wilderness (see note on 33:9). *crocus.* See Song 2:1 and note.
35:2 *rejoice . . . shout of joy.* See 54:1. *Lebanon . . . Carmel . . . Sharon.* Fertile areas renowned for their beautiful trees and foliage (see note on 33:9). *glory of the LORD.* In the great transformation just announced. See 6:3 and note.
35:4 *Take courage, fear not.* Cf. God's words of encouragement to Joshua in Josh 1:6–7,9,18. *God will come.* Similar language is used of the coming of the Messiah (see 62:11; cf. Rev 22:12). *vengeance . . . recompense.* See note on 34:8.
35:5 *eyes . . . ears.* See 29:18; 32:3; 42:7 and notes. Spiritual and physical healing are also linked together in Christ's ministry (see Matt 11:5).
35:6 *lame will leap . . . tongue of the mute will shout.* Signs of the Messianic age (see Matt 12:22; Acts 3:7–8). *waters . . . streams.* See 32:2 and note. Cf. God's provision of water in Ex 17:6; 2 Kin 3:15–20.
35:7 *springs.* Cf. 41:18. *reeds and rushes.* Plants that grow in marshes and lakes (cf. 19:6–7).
35:8 *highway.* A road built up to make travel easier (see 11:16; 40:3 and notes). *Highway of Holiness.* The way set apart for those who are holy; only the redeemed (v. 9) could use it. In ancient times, certain roads between temples were open only to those who were ceremonially pure.
35:9 *lion . . . beast.* Sometimes wild animals made travel dangerous (see Deut 8:15; Judg 14:5). *redeemed.* Those the Lord has delivered from bondage (cf. 1:27; 51:10; 62:12; Lev 25:47–48; Deut 7:8).
35:10 Repeated verbatim in 51:11. *come with joyful shouting to Zion.* As the Israelites did when they returned from Babylonian exile (see Ps 126). *They will find.* They will encounter not wild animals, (v. 9) but gladness and joy (cf. Ps 23:6). *sorrow . . . will flee.* Cf. 25:8; 65:19.

36:1–39:8 Much of chs. 36–39 is paralleled, sometimes verbatim, in 2 Kin 18:13–20:19. The compiler of 2 Kings may have used Is 36–39 as one of his sources, or both may have drawn on a common source. Chs. 36–37 describe the fulfillment of many predictions about Assyria's collapse, while chs. 38–39 point toward the Babylonian context of chs. 40–66.
36:1 *fourteenth year of King Hezekiah.* 701 B.C., the 14th year of his sole reign. Hezekiah ruled as sole king from 715 to 686 but was a co-regent from c. 729 (see note on 2 Kin 18:1). *Sennacherib.* Reigned over Assyria from 705 to 681. *all the . . . cities.* In his annals Sennacherib lists 46 such cities (see note on 2 Kin 18:13).
36:2 *Lachish.* An important city about 30 miles southwest of Jerusalem that guarded the main approach to Judah's capital from that quarter (see Jer 34:7). *large army.* Cf. 37:36. *conduit . . . field.* See 7:3 and note; see also note on 2 Kin 18:17.
36:3 *Eliakim.* See 22:20–21 and notes. *over the household.* In charge of the palace (see 22:15 and note). *Shebna.* See 22:15 and note. *scribe.* Perhaps equivalent to secretary of state (see Jer 36:12; see also note on 2 Sam 8:17). *recorder.* An official position also associated elsewhere with "secretary" (see 1 Kin 4:3). See also note on 2 Sam 8:16.

4 Then [a]Rabshakeh said to them, "Say
now to Hezekiah, 'Thus says the great king,
the king of Assyria, "What is this confidence
that you [1]have?
5 "I say, 'Your counsel and strength for the
war are only [1]empty words.' Now on whom
do you rely, that [a]you have rebelled against
me?
6 "Behold, you rely on the [a]staff of this
crushed reed, *even* on Egypt, on which if a
man leans, it will go into his [1]hand and
pierce it. [b]So is Pharaoh king of Egypt to all
who rely on him.
7 "But if you say to me, 'We trust in the
LORD our God,' is it not He [a]whose high
places and whose altars Hezekiah has taken
away and has said to Judah and to Jerusalem, 'You shall worship before this altar'?
8 "Now therefore, [1]come make a bargain
with my master the king of Assyria, and I
will give you two thousand horses, if you are
able on your part to set riders on them.
9 "How then can you [1]repulse one [2]offi-
cial of the least of my master's servants and
[3a]rely on Egypt for chariots and for horsemen?
10 "Have I now come up [1]without the
LORD's approval against this land to destroy
it? [a]The LORD said to me, 'Go up against this
land and destroy it.' " ' "
11 Then Eliakim and Shebna and Joah
said to Rabshakeh, "Speak now to your servants in [a]Aramaic, for we [1]understand *it;*
and do not speak with us in [2b]Judean in the
hearing of the people who are on the wall."
12 But Rabshakeh said, "Has my master
sent me only to your master and to you to
speak these words, *and* not to the men who
sit on the wall, *doomed* to eat their own
dung and drink their own urine with you?"
13 Then Rabshakeh stood and [a]cried with
a loud voice in Judean and said, "Hear the
words of the great king, the king of Assyria.
14 "Thus says the king, 'Do not let Hezekiah [a]deceive you, for he will not be able to
deliver you;
15 nor let Hezekiah make you [a]trust in the
LORD, saying, "The LORD will surely deliver
us, this city will not be given into the hand of
the king of Assyria."
16 'Do not listen to Hezekiah,' for thus says
the king of Assyria, '[1]Make your peace with
me and come out to me, and eat each of his
[a]vine and each of his fig tree and drink each
of the [b]waters of his own cistern,
17 until I come and take you away to a
land like your own land, a land of grain and
new wine, a land of bread and vineyards.
18 '*Beware* that Hezekiah does not mislead
you, saying, "[a]The LORD will deliver us." Has
any one of the gods of the nations delivered
his land from the hand of the king of Assyria?
19 'Where are the gods of [a]Hamath and
Arpad? Where are the gods of [a]Sepharvaim?
And when have they [b]delivered Samaria
from my hand?
20 'Who among all the [a]gods of these
lands have delivered their land from my
hand, that the [b]LORD would deliver Jerusalem from my hand?' "
21 But they were silent and [a]answered
him not a word; for the king's commandment was, "Do not answer him."
22 Then [a]Eliakim the son of Hilkiah, who
was over the household, and [b]Shebna the
scribe and Joah the son of Asaph, the
recorder, came to Hezekiah with their clothes
torn and told him the words of Rabshakeh.

Hezekiah Seeks Isaiah's Help

37 And [a]when King Hezekiah heard *it,* he
tore his clothes, covered himself with
sackcloth and entered the house of the LORD.

4 [1]Lit *trust* [a]2 Kin 18:19 **5** [1]Lit *words of lips* [a]2 Kin 18:7 **6** [1]Lit *palm* [a]Ezek 29:6, 7 [b]Ps 146:3; Is 30:3, 5, 7 **7** [a]Deut 12:2-5; 2 Kin 18:4, 5 **8** [1]Lit *please exchange pledges* **9** [1]Lit *turn away the face of* [2]Or *governor* [3]Lit *rely on for yourself* [a]Is 20:5; 30:2-5, 7; 31:3 **10** [1]Lit *without the LORD* [a]1 Kin 13:18; 22:6, 12 **11** [1]Lit *hear* [2]I.e. Hebrew [a]Ezra 4:7; Dan 2:4 [b]Is 36:13 **13** [a]2 Chr 32:18

14 [a]Is 37:10 **15** [a]Is 36:18, 20; 37:10, 11 **16** [1]Lit *Make with me a blessing* [a]1 Kin 4:25; Mic 4:4; Zech 3:10 [b]Prov 5:15 **18** [a]Is 36:15 **19** [a]Is 10:9-11; 37:11-13; Jer 49:23 [b]2 Kin 17:6 **20** [a]1 Kin 20:23, 28 [b]Is 36:15 **21** [a]Prov 9:7, 8; 26:4 **22** [a]Is 22:20; 36:3 [b]Is 22:15 **37:1** [a]2 Kin 19:1-37; Is 37:1-38

36:4,13 *great king.* See note on 2 Kin 18:19.
36:5 *rebelled.* By refusing to pay the expected tribute (see 2 Kin 17:4; 18:7).
36:6 *crushed reed.* Egypt is compared to a reed again in Ezek 29:6–7. *Egypt.* Hezekiah had been under pressure to make an alliance with Egypt since 715 B.C. or earlier (see 20:5; 30:1 and notes). *So is Pharaoh.* Cf. 30:3,7.
36:7 *high places and . . . altars.* Hezekiah had destroyed these popular shrines often dedicated to Baal worship (see note on 2 Kin 18:4; see also 2 Chr 31:1). *this altar.* In Solomon's temple.
36:8 *two thousand horses.* A sizable number for any army. Horses and chariots were highly prized (see note on 30:16). *if you are able . . . to set riders on them.* See note on 2 Kin 18:23. *riders.* Probably charioteers, since cavalry was not employed by these nations this early (see v. 9).
36:10 *The LORD said to me.* The Lord had used Assyria to punish Israel (see 10:5–6), but now it was Assyria's turn to be judged. Pharaoh Neco claimed God's approval on his mission according to 2 Chr 35:21.
36:11 *Eliakim . . . Joah.* See v. 3 and note. *Aramaic.* The diplomatic language of that day (see note on 2 Kin 18:26). *do not speak . . . in Judean.* The officials feared that the commander's speech might damage the people's morale.
36:12 *eat . . . dung . . . drink . . . urine.* A crude way of describing the horrors of famine if Jerusalem was to be besieged (cf. 2 Kin 6:25). Contrast v. 16.
36:14 *deceive you.* Cf. 37:10.
36:16 *his vine . . . his fig tree.* Symbols of security and prosperity in the best of times (see 1 Kin 4:25; Mic 4:4).
36:17 *come and take you.* The Assyrians deported rebellious peoples to reduce their will to revolt (see 2 Kin 15:29; 17:6). *grain and new wine.* Two of the staples of Israel (cf. Deut 28:51; Hag 1:11).
36:18–20 The commander's words echo the boasts of the proud Assyrians in 10:8–11. See note on 2 Kin 18:33–35.
36:19 *Hamath and Arpad.* See 10:9 and note. *Sepharvaim.* Probably located in northern Aram (Syria) not far from Hamath. Residents of Sepharvaim were deported to Samaria, though they still worshiped the gods Adrammelech and Anammelech. See 2 Kin 17:24,31. *Samaria.* The Assyrians assumed that each people had its own gods and so did not associate the God of Judah with that of Samaria.
36:21 *they were silent.* The Assyrians had hoped that the masterful psychology of vv. 4–20 would produce panic.
36:22 See v. 3 and note. *clothes torn.* See note on 2 Kin 18:37.
37:1 *clothes . . . sackcloth.* See Gen 37:34 and note; see also

2 Then he sent [a]Eliakim who was over
the household with [b]Shebna the scribe and
the elders of the priests, covered with sackcloth, to [c]Isaiah the prophet, the son of Amoz.
3 They said to him, "Thus says Hezeki-
ah, 'This day is a [a]day of distress, rebuke
and rejection; for [b]children have come to
birth, and there is no strength to [1]deliver.
4 'Perhaps the LORD your God will hear
the words of Rabshakeh, whom his master
the king of Assyria has sent to [a]reproach the
living God, and will rebuke the words which
the LORD your God has heard. Therefore,
offer a prayer for [b]the remnant that is left.' "
5 So the servants of King Hezekiah came
to Isaiah.
6 Isaiah said to them, "Thus you shall
say to your master, 'Thus says the LORD,
"[a]Do not be afraid because of the words that
you have heard, with which the servants of
the king of Assyria have blasphemed Me.
7 "Behold, I will put a spirit in him so that
he will [a]hear a rumor and [b]return to his own
land. And I will make him fall by the sword
in his own land." ' "
8 Then Rabshakeh returned and found
the king of Assyria fighting against [a]Libnah,
for he had heard that [1]the king had left
[b]Lachish.
9 When he [a]heard *them* say concerning
Tirhakah king of [1b]Cush, "He has come out
to fight against you," and when he heard *it*
he sent messengers to Hezekiah, saying,
10 "Thus you shall say to Hezekiah king of
[1]Judah, '[a]Do not let your God in whom you
trust deceive you, saying, "Jerusalem will
not be given into the hand of the king of
Assyria."
11 '[a]Behold, you have heard what the
kings of Assyria have done to all the lands,

2 [a]Is 22:20 [b]Is 22:15 [c]Is 1:1; 20:2
3 [1]Lit *give birth* [a]Is 22:5; 26:16; 33:2 [b]Is 26:17, 18; 66:9; Hos 13:13
4 [a]Is 36:13-15, 18, 20 [b]Is 1:9; 10:20-22; 37:31, 32; 46:3
6 [a]Is 7:4; 35:4
7 [a]Is 37:9 [b]Is 37:37, 38
8 [1]Lit *he* [a]Num 33:20; Josh 10:29 [b]Josh 10:31, 32
9 [1]Or *Ethiopia* [a]Is 37:7 [b]Is 18:1; 20:5
10 [1]Lit *Judah, saying* [a]Is 36:15
11 [a]Is 10:9-11; 36:18-20

11 [1]Lit *delivered*
12 [1]Lit *the* [a]2 Kin 17:6; 18:11 [b]Gen 11:31; 12:1-4; Acts 7:2
14 [1]Lit *letters* [2]Lit *Hezekiah spread*
16 [a]Ex 25:22; 1 Sam 4:4; Ps 80:1; 99:1 [b]Deut 10:17; Ps 86:10; 136:2, 3 [c]Is 42:5; 45:12; Jer 10:12
17 [a]2 Chr 6:40; Ps 17:6; Dan 9:18 [b]Ps 74:22 [c]Is 37:4
18 [a]2 Kin 15:29; 16:9; 17:6, 24; 1 Chr 5:26
19 [a]Is 2:8; 17:8; 41:24, 29 [b]Is 26:14
20 [1]So DSS and 2 Kin 19:19; M.T. omits *God* [a]Is 25:9; 33:22; 35:4 [b]1 Kin 18:36, 37; Ps 46:10; Is 37:16; Ezek 36:23
21 [a]Is 37:2

destroying them completely. So will you be
[1]spared?
12 'Did the gods of [1]those nations which
my fathers have destroyed deliver them, *even*
[a]Gozan and [b]Haran and Rezeph and the sons
of Eden who *were* in Telassar?
13 'Where is the king of Hamath, the king
of Arpad, the king of the city of Sepharvaim,
and of Hena and Ivvah?' "

Hezekiah's Prayer in the Temple

14 Then Hezekiah took the [1]letter from
the hand of the messengers and read it, and
he went up to the house of the LORD and
[2]spread it out before the LORD.
15 Hezekiah prayed to the LORD saying,
16 "O LORD of hosts, the God of Israel,
[a]who is enthroned *above* the cherubim, You
are the [b]God, You alone, of all the kingdoms
of the earth. [c]You have made heaven and
earth.
17 "[a]Incline Your ear, O LORD, and hear;
open Your eyes, O LORD, and see; and [b]listen
to all the words of Sennacherib, who sent
them to [c]reproach the living God.
18 "Truly, O LORD, the [a]kings of Assyria
have devastated all the countries and their
lands,
19 and have cast their gods into the fire,
for they were not gods but the [a]work of
men's hands, wood and stone. So they have
[b]destroyed them.
20 "Now, O LORD our God, [a]deliver us from
his hand that [b]all the kingdoms of the earth
may know that You alone, LORD, [1]are God."

God Answers through Isaiah

21 Then [a]Isaiah the son of Amoz sent
word to Hezekiah, saying, "Thus says the
LORD, the God of Israel, 'Because you have

note on 2 Kin 18:37. *house of the LORD.* Designated as a place of prayer by Solomon (see 1 Kin 8:33). The Assyrian references to Hezekiah's dependence on the Lord (36:7,15,18) were true.
37:2 *Eliakim . . . Shebna.* See note on 36:3. *elders of the priests.* See note on 2 Kin 19:2. *Isaiah . . . son of Amoz.* See note on 1:1. Prophet, priests and king join in supplication.
37:3 *day of distress.* See 5:30; 26:16; 33:2 and notes. *come to birth.* An even more vivid description than that of the pains of childbirth (see 13:8 and note).
37:4 *reproach.* See vv. 17,23–24. *offer a prayer.* See note on 2 Kin 19:4. *remnant.* Jerusalem was left almost alone (see 36:1 and notes on 1:9; 2 Kin 19:4; see also 10:20–22).
37:6 *Do not be afraid.* Cf. 7:4; see 35:4 and note.
37:7 *spirit.* Perhaps a compulsion or a disposition (cf. 1 Chr 5:26). *rumor.* See note on 2 Kin 19:7. *return . . . fall by the sword.* See vv. 37–38.
37:8 *Libnah.* See note on 2 Kin 8:22; see also Josh 10:31. *Lachish.* See note on 36:2.
37:9 *Tirhakah, king of Cush.* In 701 B.C. he was actually a prince (the brother of the new pharaoh Shebitku, who sent him with an army to help Hezekiah withstand the Assyrian invasion); he did not become king until 690. But this part of Isaiah was not written before 681 (see note on v. 38), so it was natural to speak of Tirhakah as king. See 18:1 and note.
37:10 *God . . . deceive.* See 36:14–15,18. The message of vv. 10–13 is similar to that of 36:18–20 (see note there).
37:12 *Gozan.* A city in northern Mesopotamia to which some of the Israelites had been deported by the Assyrians (see 2 Kin 17:6). *Haran.* A city west of Gozan where Abraham lived for a number of years (see Gen 11:31 and note). *Rezeph.* A city between Haran and the Euphrates River. *Eden.* The state of Bit Adini, located between the Euphrates and Balikh rivers (see note on 2 Kin 19:12).
37:13 *Hamath . . . Arpad.* See 10:9 and note. *Sepharvaim.* See 36:19 and note.
37:14 *house of the LORD.* See v. 1 and note. *spread it out.* Contrast the hypocritical spreading out of hands to pray in 1:15.
37:16 *LORD of hosts.* See 13:4 and note. *enthroned . . . cherubim.* See note on 1 Sam 4:4. *all the kingdoms.* Cf. 40:17. *made heaven and earth.* The role of God as Creator is emphasized also in 40:26,28; 42:5; 45:12.
37:17 *Incline Your ear . . . open Your eyes.* Cf. Solomon's prayer in 1 Kin 8:52; 2 Chr 6:40. *reproach the living God.* See v. 4 and note.
37:19 *not gods.* See 36:19 and note. *wood and stone.* Cf. 2:8; 44:9–20.
37:20 *You alone . . . are God.* Cf. 43:11; 45:18,21–22.

prayed to Me about Sennacherib king of Assyria,
22 this is the word that the LORD has spoken against him:
"She has despised you and mocked you,
The [a]virgin [b]daughter of Zion;
She has [c]shaken *her* head behind you,
The daughter of Jerusalem!
23 "Whom have you [a]reproached and blasphemed?
And against whom have you raised *your* voice
And [1]haughtily [b]lifted up your eyes?
Against the [c]Holy One of Israel!
24 "Through your servants you have reproached the Lord,
And you have said, 'With my many chariots I came up to the heights of the mountains,
To the remotest parts of [a]Lebanon;
And I cut down its tall [b]cedars *and* its choice cypresses.
And I will go to its [1]highest peak, its thickest [c]forest.
25 'I dug *wells* and drank waters,
And [a]with the sole of my feet I dried up
All the rivers of [1]Egypt.'
26 "[a]Have you not heard?
Long ago I did it,
From ancient times I [b]planned it.
Now [c]I have brought it to pass,
That [d]you should turn fortified cities into [e]ruinous heaps.
27 "Therefore their inhabitants were short of strength,
They were dismayed and put to shame;
They were *as* the [a]vegetation of the field and *as* the green herb,
As [b]grass on the housetops [1]is scorched before it is grown up.
28 "But I [a]know your sitting down
And your going out and your coming in
And your raging against Me.
29 "Because of your raging against Me
And because your [1a]arrogance has come up to My ears,
Therefore I will put My [b]hook in your nose
And My [c]bridle in your lips,
And I will turn you back [d]by the way which you came.

30 "Then this shall be the sign for you:
[1]you will eat this year what [a]grows of itself,
in the second year what springs from the
same, and in the third year sow, reap, plant
vineyards and eat their fruit.
31 "The [a]surviving [b]remnant of the house
of Judah will again [c]take root downward and
bear fruit upward.
32 "For out of Jerusalem will go forth a
[a]remnant and out of Mount Zion [1]survivors.
The [b]zeal of the LORD of hosts will perform
this."
33 "Therefore, thus says the LORD concerning the king of Assyria, 'He will not come to
this city or shoot an arrow there; and he will
not come before it with a shield, or throw up
a [a]siege ramp against it.
34 '[a]By the way that he came, by the same
he will return, and he will not come to this
city,' declares the LORD.
35 'For I will [a]defend this city to save it
[b]for My own sake and for My servant
David's sake.' "

Assyrians Destroyed

36 Then the [a]angel of the LORD went out
and struck 185,000 in the camp of the Assyrians; and when [1]men arose early in the
morning, behold, all of these were [2]dead.
37 So Sennacherib king of Assyria departed and [1]returned *home* and lived at [a]Nineveh.

22 [a]Jer 14:17; Lam 2:13 [b]Ps 9:14; Zeph 3:14; Zech 2:10 [c]Job 16:4
23 [1]Lit *on high* [a]Is 37:4 [b]Is 2:11; 5:15, 21 [c]Ezek 39:7; Hab 1:12
24 [1]Lit *farthest height* [a]Is 10:33, 34 [b]Is 14:8 [c]Is 10:18
25 [1]Or *the besieged place* [a]Deut 11:10; 1 Kin 20:10
26 [a]Is 40:21, 28 [b]Acts 2:23; 4:27, 28; 1 Pet 2:8 [c]Is 46:11 [d]Is 10:6 [e]Is 17:1; 25:2
27 [1]So DSS and 2 Kin 19:26; M.T. as *a plowed field* [a]Is 40:7 [b]Ps 129:6
28 [a]Ps 139:1
29 [1]Lit *complacency* [a]Is 10:12 [b]Ezek 29:4; 38:4 [c]Is 30:28 [d]Is 37:34
30 [1]Lit *eating* [a]Lev 25:5, 11
31 [a]Is 4:2; 10:20 [b]Is 37:4 [c]Is 27:6
32 [1]Lit *those who escape* [a]Is 37:4 [b]2 Kin 19:31; Is 9:7; 59:17; Joel 2:18; Zech 1:14
33 [a]Jer 6:6; 32:24
34 [a]Is 37:29
35 [a]2 Kin 20:6; Is 31:5; 38:6 [b]Is 43:25; 48:9, 11
36 [1]Lit *they* [2]Lit *dead bodies* [a]2 Kin 19:35; Is 10:12, 33, 34
37 [1]Lit *went and returned* [a]Gen 10:11; Jon 1:2; 3:3; 4:11; Zeph 2:13

37:22 *virgin daughter of Zion.* A personification of Jerusalem and its inhabitants. *shaken her head.* A gesture of mocking (see Ps 22:7; 44:14).

37:23 *haughtily lifted.* Assyria's great pride had been condemned earlier (see 10:12 and note). *Holy One of Israel.* A designation of the God of Israel characteristic of Isaiah (see 1:4 and note).

37:24 *many chariots.* See 36:8 and note. *came up to the heights.* Cf. the words of the king of Babylon in 14:13–14. *Lebanon.* See 33:9; 35:2 and notes. *cut down . . . cedars.* For many centuries the kings of Mesopotamia had used the cedars of Lebanon in their royal buildings (cf. 1 Kin 5:8–10).

37:25 *dug wells.* Desert lands could not stop him. *dried up All the rivers.* The branches of the Nile were no obstacle either. This boast was almost a claim to deity. See 11:15; 44:27 and notes.

37:26 Cf. 40:21. *fortified cities into ruinous heaps.* Assyria had been God's tool of judgment against the nations (see 10:5–6).

37:27 See 40:6–8; Ps 37:1–2. *grass on the housetops.* Roofs in the Near East were flat.

37:29 *hook in your nose.* The Assyrians often led away captives by tying ropes to rings placed in their noses (see note on 2 Kin 19:28). *bridle.* Cf. 30:28.

37:30 *sign.* See 7:11,14 and notes. *what grows of itself.* See note on 2 Kin 19:29. *second . . . third year.* See note on 2 Kin 19:29. Probably the second year was to begin shortly, so the total time was less than 36 months. Another three-year sign was given in 20:3. *plant vineyards and eat.* The response to Assyria's proposal in 36:16 (see note there).

37:31–32 *remnant.* See notes on v. 4; 1:9; 2 Kin 19:4,30–31.

37:31 *take root . . . bear fruit.* See 4:2; 11:1,10; 27:6 and notes.

37:32 *The zeal . . . this.* See 9:7 and note.

37:33 *siege ramp.* To help the invaders bring up battering rams and scale the walls (see 2 Sam 20:15).

37:35 *David's sake.* God had promised David an enduring throne in Jerusalem (see 9:7; 55:3; 2 Sam 7:16).

37:36 *angel of the LORD . . . struck.* Cf. the striking down of the firstborn in Egypt (Ex 12:12) and the angel's sword poised against Jerusalem (2 Sam 24:16). The Greek historian Herodotus attributed this destruction to a bubonic plague. The death of these soldiers fulfills the prophecies of 10:33–34; 30:31; 31:8.

37:37 *Nineveh.* The capital of Assyria. See Jon 1:2.

38 It came about as he was worshiping in
the house of Nisroch his god, that Adrammelech and Sharezer his sons killed him
with the sword; and they escaped into the
land of [a]Ararat. And [b]Esarhaddon his son
became king in his place.

Hezekiah Healed

38 [a]In those days Hezekiah became [1]mor-
tally ill. And [b]Isaiah the prophet the
son of Amoz came to him and said to him,
"Thus says the LORD, '[c]Set your house in
order, for you shall die and not live.' "
2 Then Hezekiah turned his face to the
wall and prayed to the LORD,
3 and said, "[a]Remember now, O LORD, I
beseech You, how I have [b]walked before You
in truth and with a [c]whole heart, and [d]have
done what is good in Your sight." And Hezekiah [e]wept [1]bitterly.
4 Then the word of the LORD came to Isaiah, saying,
5 "Go and say to Hezekiah, 'Thus says the
LORD, the God of your father David, "I have
heard your prayer, I have seen your tears;
behold, I will add [a]fifteen years to your [1]life.
6 "I will [a]deliver you and this city from
the hand of the king of Assyria; and I will
defend this city." '
7 "This shall be the [a]sign to you from the
LORD, that the LORD will do this thing that He
has spoken:
8 "Behold, I will [a]cause the shadow on
the stairway, which has gone down with the
sun on the stairway of Ahaz, to go back ten
steps." So the [b]sun's *shadow* went back ten
steps on the stairway on which it had gone
down.
9 A writing of Hezekiah king of Judah
after his illness and [1]recovery:

10 I said, "[a]In the middle of my [1]life
I am to enter the [b]gates of Sheol;
I am to be [c]deprived of the rest of my
years."
11 I said, "I will not see the LORD,
The LORD [a]in the land of the living;
I will look on man no more among the
inhabitants of the world.
12 "Like a shepherd's [a]tent my dwelling is
pulled up and removed from me;
As a [b]weaver I [c]rolled up my life.
He [d]cuts me off from the loom;
From [e]day until night You make an
end of me.
13 "I composed *my soul* until morning.
[a]Like a lion—so He [b]breaks all my
bones,
From [c]day until night You make an
end of me.
14 "[a]Like a swallow, *like* a crane, so I
twitter;
I [b]moan like a dove;
My [c]eyes look wistfully to the heights;
O Lord, I am oppressed, be my
[d]security.

15 "[a]What shall I say?
[1]For He has spoken to me, and He
Himself has done it;
I will [b]wander about all my years
because of the [c]bitterness of my
soul.
16 "O Lord, [a]by *these* things *men* live,
And in all these is the life of my spirit;
[1][b]O restore me to health and [c]let me
live!
17 "Lo, for *my own* welfare I had great
bitterness;
It is You who has [1][a]kept my soul from
the pit of [2]nothingness,
For You have [b]cast all my sins behind
Your back.
18 "For [a]Sheol cannot thank You,
Death cannot praise You;
Those who go down [b]to the pit cannot
hope for Your faithfulness.

38 [a]Gen 8:4; Jer 51:27 [b]Ezra 4:2
38:1 [1]Lit *sick to the point of death* [a]2 Kin 20:1-6, 9-11; 2 Chr 32:24; Is 38:1-8 [b]Is 1:1; 37:2 [c]2 Sam 17:23
3 [1]Lit *great weeping* [a]Neh 13:14 [b]2 Kin 18:5, 6; Ps 26:3 [c]1 Chr 28:9; 29:19 [d]Deut 6:18 [e]Ps 6:6-8
5 [1]Lit *days* [a]2 Kin 18:2, 13
6 [a]Is 31:5; 37:35
7 [a]Judg 6:17, 21, 36-40; Is 7:11, 14; 37:30
8 [a]2 Kin 20:9-11 [b]Josh 10:12-14
9 [1]Lit *he lived after his illness*
10 [1]Lit *days* [a]Ps 102:24 [b]Ps 107:18 [c]Job 17:11, 15; 2 Cor 1:9
11 [a]Ps 27:13; 116:9
12 [a]2 Cor 5:1, 4; 2 Pet 1:13, 14 [b]Job 7:6 [c]Heb 1:12 [d]Job 6:9 [e]Job 4:20; Ps 73:14
13 [a]Job 10:16 [b]Ps 51:8; Dan 6:24 [c]Ps 32:4
14 [a]Job 30:29; Ps 102:6 [b]Is 59:11; Ezek 7:16; Nah 2:7 [c]Ps 119:123 [d]Job 17:3; Ps 119:122
15 [1]Targum and DSS read *And what shall I say for He* [a]Ps 39:9 [b]1 Kin 21:27 [c]Job 7:11; 10:1; Is 38:17
16 [1]Lit *You will* [a]Ps 119:71, 75 [b]Ps 39:13 [c]Ps 119:25
17 [1]So some versions; Heb *loved* [2]Or *destruction* [a]Ps 30:3; 86:13; Jon 2:6 [b]Is 43:25; Jer 31:34; Mic 7:19
18 [a]Ps 6:5; 30:9; 88:11; Eccl 9:10 [b]Num 16:33; Ps 28:1

37:38 *in the house.* Hezekiah had gone to the Lord's temple and gained strength (vv. 1,14). Twenty years later (681 B.C.) Sennacherib went to the temple of his god and was killed. *Ararat.* Urartu, north of Assyria in Armenia (see note on Gen 8:4). *Esarhaddon.* Reigned 681–669. See Ezra 4:2.
38:1 *In those days.* Sometime before Sennacherib's invasion of 701 B.C. (see v. 6). *Isaiah.* He is prominent in this historical interlude (chs. 36–39). *Set your house in order.* See note on 2 Kin 20:1. *you shall die.* Elisha similarly predicted the death of Ben-Hadad (2 Kin 8:9–10). See note on 2 Kin 20:1.
38:2 *wall.* Perhaps of the nearby temple. *prayed.* Hezekiah apparently had no son and successor to the throne yet (cf. 39:7; 2 Kin 21:1).
38:3 *whole heart.* Like David (1 Kin 11:4), Hezekiah was truly faithful (see 36:7; 2 Kin 18:3–5).
38:6 *deliver . . . this city.* See 31:5; 37:35.
38:7 *sign.* See 7:11,14 and notes.
38:8 *sun's shadow went back.* Perhaps the miracle involved the refraction of light. See 2 Kin 20:9–11; Josh 10:12–14.
38:10–20 A hymn of thanksgiving in two stanzas, similar to many of the psalms. Hezekiah was deeply interested in the psalms of David and Asaph (see 2 Chr 29:30).
38:10–14 Hezekiah voices his complaint.
38:11 *the LORD, The LORD.* See 26:4. *land of the living.* Cf. Ps 27:13.
38:12 *rolled up my life.* Cf. the rolling up of the sky like a scroll in 34:4 (see also Heb 1:12).
38:13 *breaks all my bones.* Physical or spiritual distress is often described in terms of aching or broken bones (see Ps 6:2; 32:3).
38:15–20 Hezekiah offers praise for God's healing.
38:15 *What shall I say?* See 2 Sam 7:20. Hezekiah wonders how he can praise God.
38:16 *by these things.* Perhaps referring to God's promises and gracious acts, though His gracious acts can include such experiences as sickness and peril.
38:17 *pit of nothingness.* The grave (see Ps 55:23). *all my sins.* Physical and spiritual healing are sometimes linked together (see 53:4–5). *sins behind Your back.* God not only puts our sins out of sight; He also puts them out of reach (Mic 7:19; Ps 103:12), out of mind (Jer 31:34) and out of existence (Is 43:25; 44:22; Ps 51:1,9; Acts 3:19).
38:18 *cannot hope.* Knowledge about the afterlife was limit-

19 "It is the [a]living who give thanks to
You, as I do today;
A [b]father tells his sons about Your
faithfulness.
20 "The LORD will surely save me;
So we will [a]play my songs on stringed
instruments
[b]All *the* days of our life [c]at the house
of the LORD."

21 Now [a]Isaiah had said, "Let them take a
cake of figs and apply it to the boil, that he
may recover."
22 Then Hezekiah had said, "What is the
[a]sign that I shall go up to the house of the
LORD?"

Hezekiah Shows His Treasures

39 [a]At that time Merodach-baladan son of
Baladan, king of Babylon, sent letters
and a present to Hezekiah, for he heard that
he had been sick and had recovered.
2 Hezekiah [1]was [a]pleased, and showed
them *all* his treasure house, the [b]silver and
the gold and the spices and the precious oil
and his whole armory and all that was found
in his treasuries. There was nothing in his
house nor in all his dominion that Hezekiah
did not show them.
3 Then Isaiah the [a]prophet came to King
Hezekiah and said to him, "What did these
men say, and from where have they come to
you?" And Hezekiah said, "They have come
to me from a far [b]country, from Babylon."
4 He said, "What have they seen in your
house?" So Hezekiah [1]answered, "They have
seen all that is in my house; there is nothing
among my treasures that I have not shown
them."
5 Then Isaiah said to Hezekiah, "Hear
the [a]word of the LORD of hosts,
6 'Behold, the days are coming when [a]all
that is in your house and all that your fathers
have laid up in store to this day will be carried to Babylon; nothing will be left,' says the
LORD.
7 'And *some* of your sons who will issue
from you, whom you will beget, [a]will be tak-
en away, and [b]they will become officials in
the palace of the king of Babylon.'"
8 [a]Then Hezekiah said to Isaiah, "The
word of the LORD which you have spoken is
good." For he [1]thought, "For there will be
peace and truth [b]in my days."

The Greatness of God

40 "[a]Comfort, O comfort My people,"
says your God.
2 "[a]Speak [1]kindly to Jerusalem;
And call out to her, that her [2b]warfare
has ended,
That her [3c]iniquity has been removed,
That she has received of the LORD's
hand
[d]Double for all her sins."

3 [a]A voice [1]is calling,
"[b]Clear the way for the LORD in the
wilderness;

19 [a]Ps 118:17; 119:175 [b]Deut 6:7; 11:19; Ps 78:5-7
20 [a]Ps 33:1-3; 68:24-26 [b]Ps 104:33; 116:2; 146:2 [c]Ps 116:17-19
21 [a]2 Kin 20:7, 8
22 [a]Is 38:7
39:1 [a]2 Kin 20:12-19; 2 Chr 32:31; Is 39:1-8
2 [1]Lit *rejoiced over them* [a]2 Chr 32:25, 31; Job 31:25 [b]2 Kin 18:15, 16
3 [a]2 Sam 12:1; 2 Chr 16:7 [b]Deut 28:49; Jer 5:15
4 [1]Lit *said*
5 [a]1 Sam 13:13, 14; 15:16
6 [a]2 Kin 24:13; 25:13-15; Jer 20:5
7 [a]2 Kin 24:10-16; 2 Chr 36:10 [b]Dan 1:1-7
8 [1]Lit *said* [a]2 Chr 32:26 [b]2 Chr 34:28
40:1 [a]Is 12:1; 49:13; 51:3, 12; 52:9; 61:2; 66:13; Jer 31:10-14; Zeph 3:14-17; 2 Cor 1:4
2 [1]Lit *to the heart of* [2]Or *hard service* [3]Or *penalty of iniquity accepted as paid off* [a]Is 35:4; Zech 1:13 [b]Is 41:11-13; 49:25; 54:15, 17 [c]Is 33:24; 53:5, 6, 11 [d]Jer 16:18; Zech 9:12; Rev 18:6
3 [1]Or *of one calling out* [a]Matt 3:3; Mark 1:3; Luke 3:4-6; John 1:23 [b]Mal 3:1; 4:5, 6

ed in the OT period, but the gospel of Christ has "brought . . . immortality to light" (2 Tim 1:10).

38:20 *play . . . on stringed instruments.* Instrumental music and hymns of praise were closely linked in worship (cf. Ps 33:1–3). *All . . . our life at the house of the LORD.* Hezekiah, like David (Ps 23:6), loved God's house.

38:21 *take . . . apply.* The verbs are plural (probably addressed to the court physicians). *cake of figs.* Figs were used for medicinal purposes in ancient Ugarit. *he may recover.* Contrast v. 1. God answered Hezekiah's prayer for healing (see v. 5).

38:22 *sign.* Perhaps the healing of the boil (see v. 21).

39:1 *Merodach-baladan.* Reigned 721–710 B.C. and again later (see note on 2 Kin 20:12). *Babylon.* See note on 13:1. *sent letters and a present.* Merodach-baladan probably wanted Hezekiah's support in a campaign against Assyria. During his career, he organized several revolts against his hated neighbors. See note on 2 Kin 20:12.

39:2 *silver . . . gold . . . treasuries.* See 2 Chr 32:27–29,31. Probably Hezekiah was seeking help from the Babylonians against the Assyrian threat (see note on 2 Kin 20:13). But the information gained during this ill-advised tour escorted by Hezekiah would be valuable to Merodach-Baladan's powerful successors (vv. 5–7).

39:3 *Isaiah the prophet.* Earlier God had sent Isaiah to confront Ahaz (7:3); cf. also Nathan's rebuke of David (2 Sam 12:1,7).

39:5 *word of the LORD.* Contrast the word of hope in 38:4–6.

39:6 *carried to Babylon.* The first mention of Babylon as Jerusalem's conqueror, though 14:3–4 implied the Babylonian captivity. The wickedness of Hezekiah's son Manasseh was a major cause of the captivity (see 2 Kin 21:11–15). See also note on 2 Kin 20:17.

39:7 *your sons.* Such as King Jehoiachin (2 Kin 24:15). *officials.* The Hebrew word can be translated "eunuch" (see 56:3; see also Esth 2:3, 14–15; Jer 38:7). *king of Babylon.* Nebuchadnezzar.

39:8 *word . . . is good.* See note on 2 Kin 20:19. *peace . . . in my days.* See 2 Kin 22:20. "Peace" recurs in a refrain in 48:22; 57:21, dividing the last 27 chapters into 3 sections of 9 chapters each (40–48; 49–57; 58–66).

40:1–66:24 In chs. 1–35 Isaiah prophesied against the backdrop of the Assyrian threat against Judah and Jerusalem, in chs. 36–39 he recorded Assyria's failure and warned about the future rise of Babylon, and in chs. 40–66 he wrote as if the Babylonian exile of Judah was almost over.

40:1 *Comfort, O comfort.* Repeated for emphasis ("Comfort greatly"). The double imperative is found also in 51:9,17; 52:1,11; 57:14; 62:10.

40:2 *Speak kindly.* The Hebrew for this phrase is used also in 2 Chr 32:6, where Hezekiah "spoke encouragingly" to Judah that she might trust in God in spite of the Assyrian invasion. *warfare.* The exile in Babylon (cf. Ps 137:1–6; Lam 1:1–2,9,16–17,21). *iniquity . . . removed.* By enduring the punishment of captivity (see Lev 26:41). *Double.* Full (or enough) punishment. Cf. the "two things" of 51:19.

40:3 *voice.* Three voices are mentioned (vv. 3,6,9), each showing how the comfort of v. 1 will come about. The NT links the voice of v. 3 with John the Baptist in Matt 3:3; Mark 1:3; Luke 3:4; John 1:23. *Clear the way.* Clear obstacles out of the road (cf. 57:14; 62:10). The language of vv. 3–4 has in view the ancient Near Eastern custom of sending representatives ahead to prepare the way for the visit of a monarch. The picture is that of

Make smooth in the desert a highway
for our God.
4 "Let every valley be lifted up,
And every mountain and hill be made
low;
And let the rough ground become a
plain,
And the rugged terrain a broad valley;
5 [1]Then the [a]glory of the LORD will be
revealed,
And [b]all flesh will see *it* together;
For the [c]mouth of the LORD has
spoken."
6 A voice says, "Call out."
Then [1]he answered, "What shall I call
out?"
[a]All flesh is grass, and all its
[2]loveliness is like the flower of the
field.
7 The [a]grass withers, the flower fades,
[1]When the [b]breath of the LORD blows
upon it;
Surely the people are grass.
8 The grass withers, the flower fades,
But [a]the word of our God stands
forever.

9 Get yourself up on a [a]high mountain,
O Zion, bearer of [b]good news,
Lift up your voice mightily,
O Jerusalem, bearer of good news;
Lift *it* up, do not fear.
Say to the [c]cities of Judah,
"[d]Here is your God!"
10 Behold, the Lord [1]GOD will come
[a]with might,
With His [b]arm ruling for Him.
Behold, His [c]reward is with Him
And His recompense before Him.
11 Like a shepherd He will [a]tend His
flock,
In His arm He will gather the lambs
And carry *them* in His bosom;
He will gently lead the nursing *ewes*.

12 Who has [a]measured the [1]waters in the
hollow of His hand,
And marked off the heavens by the
[2]span,
And [3]calculated the dust of the earth
by the measure,
And weighed the mountains in a
balance
And the hills in a pair of scales?
13 [a]Who has [1]directed the Spirit of the
LORD,
Or as His [b]counselor has informed
Him?
14 [a]With whom did He consult and *who*
[b]gave Him understanding?
And *who* taught Him in the path of
justice and taught Him knowledge
And informed Him of the way of
understanding?
15 Behold, the [a]nations are like a drop
from a bucket,
And are regarded as a speck of [b]dust
on the scales;
Behold, He lifts up the [1]islands like
fine dust.
16 Even Lebanon is not enough to burn,
Nor its [a]beasts enough for a burnt
offering.
17 [a]All the nations are as nothing before
Him,
They are regarded by Him as less than
nothing and [1]meaningless.

18 [a]To whom then will you liken God?

5 [1]Or *In order that the* [a]Is 6:3; Hab 2:14 [b]Is 52:10; Joel 2:28 [c]Is 1:20; 34:16; 58:14
6 [1]Another reading is *I said* [2]Or *constancy* [a]Job 14:2; Ps 102:11; 103:15; 1 Pet 1:24, 25
7 [1]Or *Because* [a]Ps 90:5, 6; James 1:10, 11 [b]Job 4:9; 41:21; Is 11:4; 40:24
8 [a]Is 55:11; 59:21; Matt 5:18
9 [a]Is 52:7 [b]Is 61:1 [c]Is 44:26 [d]Is 25:9; 35:2
10 [1]Heb *YHWH*, usually rendered LORD [a]Is 9:6, 7 [b]Is 59:16, 18 [c]Is 62:11; Rev 22:12
11 [a]Jer 31:10; Ezek 34:12-14, 23, 31; Mic 5:4; John 10:11, 14-16
12 [1]DSS reads *waters of the sea* [2]Or *half cubit;* i.e. 9 in. [3]Lit *contained* or *comprehended* [a]Job 38:8-11; Ps 102:25, 26; Is 48:13; Heb 1:10-12
13 [1]Or *measured, marked off* [a]Rom 11:34; 1 Cor 2:16 [b]Is 41:28
14 [a]Job 38:4 [b]Job 21:22; Col 2:3
15 [1]Or *coastlands* [a]Jer 10:10 [b]Is 17:13; 29:5
16 [a]Ps 50:9-11; Mic 6:6, 7; Heb 10:5-9
17 [1]Or *void* [a]Is 29:7
18 [a]Ex 8:10; 15:11; 1 Sam 2:2; Is 40:25; 46:5; Mic 7:18; Acts 17:29

preparing a processional highway for the Lord's coming to Jerusalem. In Matt 3:1–8 John declares that repentance is necessary to prepare the way for Christ. *Make smooth . . . a highway.* See 11:16; 35:8 and notes.
40:4 *rough ground . . . plain.* See 26:7 and note.
40:5 *glory . . . revealed.* God would redeem Israel from Babylon (see 35:2 and note; 44:23), and all the nations would see the deliverance (52:10; cf. Luke 3:6). Ultimately the glory of the redeeming God would be seen in Jesus Christ (John 1:14; 11:4,40; 17:4; Heb 1:3), especially at His return (Matt 16:27; 24:30; 25:31; Rev 1:7)—but also in the redeemed (see 1 Cor 10:31; 2 Cor 3:18; Eph 3:21). See also Is 6:3 and note.
40:6,8 Quoted in part in 1 Pet 1:24–25.
40:6 *is grass.* See 37:27 and note; 51:12. *all its loveliness . . . field.* Even the power of Assyria and Babylon would soon vanish.
40:8 *word of our God stands.* The plans and purposes of the nations will not prevail (see 8:10 and note).
40:9 *good news.* The news that God is leading His people back to Judah (vv. 10–11). He cares for His people and will redeem them (52:7–10; 61:1). The NT expands this "good news" or "gospel" to refer to the salvation that Christ brings to all people (1 Cor 15:1–4). *Here is your God!* The Lord is returning to Jerusalem. These words apply to the return from exile (52:7–9), the first coming of Christ (Matt 21:5) and the second coming of Christ (62:11; Rev 22:12). See 35:4 and note.
40:10 *arm ruling.* Cf. 51:9; 59:16. He is characterized by both strength and gentleness (v. 11). *reward . . . recompense.* His delivered people, the flock of v. 11 (see 62:11–12).
40:11 *tend His flock.* Cf. Jer 31:10; Ezek 34:11–16.
40:12–31 Rhetorical questions are used to persuade the people to trust in the Lord, who has the ability to deliver, strengthen and restore His people.
40:12 *measured the waters.* See Job 28:25; 38:8. In Job 38–41 the Lord overwhelms Job with a description of His greatness. *marked off the heavens.* See 48:13.
40:13 Quoted in Rom 11:34; 1 Cor 2:16. *counselor.* See 9:6 and note.
40:15 *nations . . . a drop from a bucket.* See note on v. 6. *dust.* See 17:13 and note; 29:5.
40:16 *Lebanon.* The wood of its cedar trees. *its beasts.* Cf. Ps 104:16–18. Sacrifices, however numerous, could never do justice to the greatness of God.
40:17 *nothing . . . meaningless.* In spite of the temporary splendor they might possess (see 13:19 and note).
40:18–20 More than any other prophet, Isaiah shows the folly of worshiping idols. His sarcastic caricature, satire and denunciation of these false gods reach a peak in 44:9–20 (see 41:7,22–24; 42:17; 46:5–7; 48:5).

Or what likeness will you compare
with Him?
19 *As for* the [1][a]idol, a craftsman casts it,
A goldsmith [b]plates it with gold,
And a silversmith *fashions* chains of
silver.
20 He who is too impoverished for *such*
an offering
Selects a [a]tree that does not rot;
He seeks out for himself a skillful
craftsman
To [1]prepare [2]an idol that [b]will not
totter.

21 [a]Do you not know? Have you not
heard?
Has it not been declared to you from
the beginning?
Have you not understood [b]from the
foundations of the earth?
22 It is He who [1]sits above the [2][a]circle of
the earth,
And its inhabitants are like
[b]grasshoppers,
Who [c]stretches out the heavens like a
[d]curtain
And spreads them out like a [e]tent to
dwell in.
23 He *it is* who reduces [a]rulers to nothing,
Who [b]makes the judges of the earth
[1]meaningless.
24 [1]Scarcely have they been planted,
[1]Scarcely have they been sown,
[1]Scarcely has their stock taken root in
the earth,
But He merely blows on them, and
they wither,
And the [a]storm carries them away like
stubble.
25 "[a]To whom then will you liken Me
That I would be *his* equal?" says the
Holy One.

26 [a]Lift up your eyes on high
And see [b]who has created these *stars*,
The [c]One who leads forth their host
by number,
He calls them all by name;
Because of the [d]greatness of His might
and the [1]strength of *His* power,
[e]Not one *of them* is missing.

27 [a]Why do you say, O Jacob, and assert,
O Israel,
"My way is [b]hidden from the LORD,
And the [c]justice due me [1]escapes the
notice of [d]my God"?
28 [a]Do you not know? Have you not
heard?
The [b]Everlasting God, the LORD, the
Creator of the ends of the earth
Does not become weary or tired.
His understanding is [c]inscrutable.
29 He gives strength to the [a]weary,
And to *him who* lacks might He
[b]increases power.
30 Though [a]youths grow weary and tired,
And vigorous [b]young men stumble
badly,
31 Yet those who [1]wait for the LORD
Will [a]gain new strength;
They will [2][b]mount up *with* [3]wings like
eagles,
They will run and not get tired,
They will walk and not become weary.

Israel Encouraged

41 "[a]Coastlands, listen to Me [b]in silence,
And let the peoples [c]gain new strength;
[d]Let them come forward, then let
them speak;
[e]Let us come together for judgment.

19 [1]Or *graven image* [a]Ps 115:4-8; Is 41:7; 44:10; Hab 2:18, 19 [b]Is 2:20; 30:22
20 [1]Or *set up* [2]Or a *graven image* [a]Is 44:14 [b]1 Sam 5:3, 4; Is 41:7; 46:7
21 [a]Ps 19:1; 50:6; Is 37:26; Acts 14:17; Rom 1:19 [b]Is 48:13; 51:13
22 [1]Or *is enthroned* [2]Or *vault* [a]Job 22:14; Prov 8:27 [b]Num 13:33 [c]Job 9:8; Is 37:16; 42:5; 44:24 [d]Ps 104:2 [e]Job 36:29; Ps 18:11; 19:4
23 [1]Or *void* [a]Job 12:21; Ps 107:40; Is 34:12 [b]Is 5:21; Jer 25:18-27
24 [1]Or *Not even* [a]Is 17:13; 41:16
25 [a]Is 40:18
26 [1]So DSS and ancient versions; M.T. *strong* [a]Is 51:6 [b]Is 42:5; 48:12, 13 [c]Ps 147:4 [d]Ps 89:11-13 [e]Is 34:16; 48:13
27 [1]Lit *passes by my God* [a]Is 49:4, 14 [b]Is 54:8 [c]Job 27:2; 34:5; Luke 18:7, 8 [d]Is 25:1
28 [a]Is 40:21 [b]Gen 21:33; Ps 90:2 [c]Ps 147:5; Rom 11:33
29 [a]Is 50:4; Jer 31:25 [b]Is 41:10
30 [a]Jer 6:11; 9:21 [b]Is 9:17
31 [1]Or *hope in* [2]Or *sprout wings* [3]Or *pinions* [a]Job 17:9; Ps 103:5; 2 Cor 4:8-10, 16 [b]Ex 19:4; Deut 32:11; Luke 18:1; 2 Cor 4:1, 16; Gal 6:9; Heb 12:3
41:1 [a]Is 11:11 [b]Hab 2:20; Zech 2:13 [c]Is 40:31 [d]Is 34:1; 48:16 [e]Is 1:18; 43:26; 50:8

40:18 *To whom . . . liken God?* See v. 25; 46:5.
40:19 *craftsman . . . goldsmith.* See 41:7; 44:10–12. *gold . . . silver.* See 2:20; Hab 2:18–19 and notes.
40:20 *tree.* See 44:14–16,19. *that will not totter.* See 41:7; 46:7.
40:21 *from the beginning.* God's work as Creator is emphasized in the rest of the chapter (cf. 37:26; 41:4,26).
40:22 *sits above.* Cf. 66:1; see 37:16 and note. *circle.* Or "horizon." See Job 22:14; Prov 8:27. *stretches out the heavens . . . like a tent.* See 42:5; 44:24; 51:13; Ps 19:4; 104:2.
40:23 *rulers . . . judges . . . meaningless.* See v. 17; 2:22 and notes; cf. Jer 25:17–26; Dan 2:21.
40:24 *storm . . . like stubble.* See 17:13 and note; 41:15–16.
40:25 See v. 18. Apparently some Israelite doubters were comparing their God with the gods of their captors, and they believed that the Lord was failing the test. *Holy One.* See 1:4 and note.
40:26 *created.* See vv. 21–22 and notes. *leads forth.* The Hebrew for this expression is used for bringing forth the constellations in Job 38:32. *their host.* The stars were worshiped by the people (see 47:13; Jer 19:13). *all by name.* See Ps 147:4. *Not one . . . missing.* See 34:16 and note.
40:27–31 As in many psalms of praise, Isaiah now stresses the goodness of God after describing His majesty (vv. 12–26). Such a God is able to deliver and restore His distressed people if they will wait in faith for Him to act. They are to trust in Him and draw strength from Him.
40:27 *way.* Condition. *hidden . . . escapes the notice.* Cf. 49:14; 54:8.
40:28 *Everlasting God.* See 9:6. *Creator.* See vv. 21–22 and notes. *ends of the earth.* See 11:12 and note; cf. 5:26; 41:9; 43:6. *not become weary.* Contrast 44:12.
40:30 *grow weary . . . stumble.* See note on 5:27.
40:31 *wait for.* Trust in or look expectantly to (see 5:2; 49:23). *gain.* Lit. "exchange." Their weakness will give way to God's strength (v. 29). The Hebrew for this verb is used of changes of clothes (Gen 35:2; Judg 14:12), which can symbolize strength and beauty (Is 52:1). Paul tells believers to clothe themselves with Christ (Rom 13:14; cf. Eph 4:24; Col 3:10). *eagles.* Known for their vigor (Ps 103:5) and speed (Jer 4:13; 48:40).
41:1,5 *Coastlands.* See 11:11 and note).
41:1 *gain new strength.* See 40:31. The nations and their gods are challenged to display the same power and wisdom as Israel's God (see vv. 21–24).

2 "[a]Who has aroused one from the east
Whom He [b]calls in righteousness to
His [1]feet?
He [c]delivers up nations before him
And subdues kings.
He makes them like [d]dust with his
sword,
As the wind-driven [e]chaff with his
bow.
3 "He pursues them, passing on in safety,
By a way he had not been [1]traversing
with his feet.
4 "[a]Who has performed and
accomplished *it*,
Calling forth the generations from the
beginning?
'[b]I, the LORD, am the first, and with the
last. [c]I am He.' "

5 The [a]coastlands have seen and are
afraid;
The [b]ends of the earth tremble;
They have drawn near and have come.
6 Each one helps his neighbor
And says to his brother, "Be strong!"
7 So the [a]craftsman encourages the
[b]smelter,
And he who smooths *metal* with the
hammer *encourages* him who beats
the anvil,
Saying of the soldering, "It is good";
And he fastens it with nails,
[c]*So that* it will not totter.
8 "But you, Israel, [a]My servant,
Jacob whom I have chosen,
Descendant of [b]Abraham My [c]friend,
9 You whom I have [1][a]taken from the
ends of the earth,
And called from its [b]remotest parts
And said to you, 'You are [c]My
servant,
I have [d]chosen you and not rejected
you.
10 'Do not [a]fear, for I am with you;
Do not anxiously look about you, for I
am your God.
I will strengthen you, surely [b]I will
help you,
Surely I will uphold you with My
righteous [c]right hand.'
11 "Behold, [a]all those who are angered at
you will be shamed and
dishonored;
[b]Those who contend with you will be
as nothing and will perish.
12 "[a]You will seek those who quarrel with
you, but will not find them,
Those who war with you will be as
nothing and non-existent.
13 "For I am the LORD your God, [a]who
upholds your right hand,
Who says to you, '[b]Do not fear, I will
help you.'
14 "Do not fear, you [a]worm Jacob, you
men of Israel;
I will help you," declares the LORD,
"[1]and [b]your Redeemer is the Holy
One of Israel.

14 [1]Or *even your Redeemer, the Holy One* [a]Job 25:6; Ps 22:6 [b]Is 35:10; 43:14; 44:6, 22-24

2 [1]Lit *foot* [a]Is 41:25; 45:1-3; 46:11 [b]Is 42:6 [c]2 Chr 36:23; Ezra 1:2 [d]2 Sam 22:43 [e]Is 40:24
3 [1]Lit *going*
4 [a]Is 41:26; 44:7; 46:10 [b]Is 43:10; 44:6; Rev 1:8, 17; 22:13 [c]Is 43:13; 46:4; 48:12
5 [a]Is 41:1; Ezek 26:15, 16 [b]Josh 5:1; Ps 67:7
7 [a]Is 44:12, 13 [b]Is 40:19 [c]Is 40:20; 46:7
8 [a]Is 42:19; 43:10; 44:1, 2, 21
8 [b]Is 29:22; 51:2; 63:16 [c]2 Chr 20:7; James 2:23
9 [1]Or *taken hold of* [a]Is 11:11 [b]Is 43:5-7 [c]Is 42:1; 44:1 [d]Deut 7:6; 14:2; Ps 135:4
10 [a]Deut 20:1; 31:6; Josh 1:9; Ps 27:1; Is 41:13, 14; 43:2, 5; Rom 8:31 [b]Is 41:14; 44:2; 49:8 [c]Ps 89:13, 14
11 [a]Is 45:24 [b]Is 17:13; 29:5, 7, 8
12 [a]Job 20:7-9; Ps 37:35, 36; Is 17:14
13 [a]Is 42:6; 45:1 [b]Is 41:10

41:2 *one from the east.* Cyrus the Great, king of Persia (559–530 B.C.), who conquered Babylon in 539 (see 13:17 and note) and issued the decree allowing the Jews to return to Jerusalem (see Ezra 1:1–4; 6:3–5). Cyrus is referred to also in v. 25; 44:28–45:5,13; 46:11. *calls in righteousness.* Like the servant of the Lord in 42:6, Cyrus was chosen to carry out God's righteous purposes. *subdues kings.* Such as Croesus king of Lydia in Asia Minor. *wind-driven chaff.* See 17:13 and note. *his bow.* The Persians were renowned for their ability as archers.
41:4 *from the beginning.* See 40:21 and note. *am the first . . . with the last.* Since the Lord was present when the first generations were called and will still be there with the last of them, He is the eternal Lord of history and nations (see Heb 13:8; Rev 1:8,17; 2:8; 21:6; 22:13).
41:5–7 By 546 B.C. Cyrus had fought his way victoriously to the west coast of Asia Minor, where his leading opponent was Croesus king of Lydia. Sarcasm and satire are used in the description of the frantic efforts in vv. 6–7—all of them futile (cf. 40:19–20).
41:5 *ends of the earth.* See 11:12 and note.
41:6 *Be strong!* See 35:4 and note.
41:7 *hammer.* Cf. 44:12. *So that it will not totter.* See 40:18–20 and notes.
41:8–9 *My servant.* A significant term in chs. 41–53, referring sometimes to the nation of Israel and other times to an individual. In these passages the title refers to one who occupies a special position in God's royal administration of His kingdom, as in "His servant Moses" (Ex 14:31; Num 12:7), "My servant David" (2 Sam 3:18; 7:5,8), "My servants the prophets" (2 Kin 17:13; Jer 7:25). See note on 42:1; see also 20:3; 22:20; 42:1,19; 43:10; 44:1–2,21; 45:4; 49:3,5–7; 50:10; 52:13; 53:11.
41:8 *But.* In contrast to the nations of vv. 5–7, Israel does not need to be afraid (v. 10). *My friend.* See Gen 18; 2 Chr 20:7; James 2:23. Some believe, however, that here "My friend" refers to "descendants" (Israel), thus paralleling "My servant" and "whom I have chosen."
41:9 *ends of the earth.* See v. 5; probably a reference to Mesopotamia and Egypt (see Gen 11:31; 12:1; 15:7; Ps 114:1–2; Jer 31:32).
41:10 *Do not fear . . . anxiously look about.* See vv. 13–14; 43:1,5; see also 35:4 and note. *strengthen . . . help you.* As one called to God's service (see vv. 9,15–16). See also v. 14; 40:29; 44:2; 49:8. *right hand.* A hand of power and salvation (see Ex 15:6,12; Ps 20:6; 48:10; 89:13; 98:1).
41:11 *be ashamed and dishonored.* Cf. 45:17; 50:7; 54:4. *will be as nothing.* See vv. 15–16 and notes.
41:13 *upholds your right hand.* To strengthen them and keep them from stumbling. *Do not fear.* See v. 10 and note.
41:14 *worm.* A reference to their feeble and despised condition in exile (cf. Job 25:6). *Redeemer.* Deliverer from Babylonian exile (in a new exodus). The Hebrew for this word refers to an obligated family protector and thus portrays the Lord as the Family Protector of Israel. He is related to Israel as Father (63:16; 64:8) and Husband (54:5). As Redeemer (or Family Protector), He redeems their property (for He regathers them to their land, 54:1–8), guarantees their freedom (35:9; 43:1–4; 48:20; 52:11–12), avenges them against their tormentors (47:3; 49:25–26; 64:4) and secures their posterity for the future (61:8–9). See note on Ruth 2:20. *Holy One of Israel.* See vv. 16,20; see also 1:4 and note. The title occurs with "Redeemer" also in 43:14; 47:4; 48:17; 49:7; 54:5.

15 "Behold, I have made you a new, sharp
threshing sledge with double edges;
[a]You will thresh the [b]mountains and
pulverize *them,*
And will make the hills like chaff.
16 "You will [a]winnow them, and the wind
will carry them away,
And the storm will scatter them;
But you will [b]rejoice in the LORD,
You will glory in the Holy One of
Israel.

17 "The [1]afflicted and needy are seeking
[a]water, but there is none,
And their tongue is parched with
thirst;
I, the LORD, [b]will answer them Myself,
As the God of Israel I [c]will not forsake
them.
18 "I will open [a]rivers on the bare heights
And springs in the midst of the
valleys;
I will make [b]the wilderness a pool of
water
And the dry land fountains of water.
19 "I will put the cedar in the wilderness,
The acacia and the [a]myrtle and the
[1]olive tree;
I will place the [a]juniper in the desert
Together with the box tree and the
cypress,
20 That [a]they may see and recognize,
And consider and gain insight as well,
That the [b]hand of the LORD has done
this,
And the Holy One of Israel has created
it.

21 "[1]Present your case," the LORD says.
"Bring forward your strong *arguments,*"
The [a]King of Jacob says.
22 [a]Let them bring forth and declare to
us what is going to take place;
As for the [b]former *events,* declare
what they *were,*
That we may consider them and know
their outcome.
Or announce to us what is coming;
23 [a]Declare the things that are going to
come afterward,
That we may know that you are
gods;
Indeed, [b]do good or evil, that we may
anxiously look about us and fear
together.
24 Behold, [a]you are of [1]no account,
And [b]your work amounts to
nothing;
He who chooses you is an
[c]abomination.

25 "I have aroused [a]one from the north,
and he has come;
From the rising of the sun he will call
on My name;
And he will come upon rulers as *upon*
[b]mortar,
Even as the potter treads clay."
26 Who has [a]declared *this* from the
beginning, that we might know?
Or from former times, that we may
say, "*He is* right!"?
Surely there was [b]no one who
declared,
Surely there was no one who
proclaimed,
Surely there was no one who heard
your words.
27 "[a]Formerly *I said* to Zion, 'Behold, here
they are.'
And to Jerusalem, 'I will give a
[b]messenger of good news.'
28 "But [a]when I look, there is no one,
And there is no [b]counselor [1]among
them
Who, if I ask, can [c]give an answer.
29 "Behold, all of them are [1]false;
Their [a]works are [b]worthless,
Their molten images are [c]wind and
emptiness.

15 [a]Mic 4:13; Hab 3:12 [b]Is 42:15; 64:1; Jer 9:10; Ezek 33:28
16 [a]Jer 51:2 [b]Is 25:9; 35:10; 51:3; 61:10
17 [1]Or *poor* [a]Is 43:20; 44:3; 49:10; 55:1 [b]Is 30:19; 65:24 [c]Is 42:16; 62:12
18 [a]Is 30:25; 43:19 [b]Ps 107:35; Is 35:6, 7
19 [1]Or *oleaster* [a]Is 35:1; 55:13; 60:13
20 [a]Is 40:5; 43:10 [b]Job 12:9; Is 66:14
21 [1]Lit *Bring near* [a]Is 44:6
22 [a]Is 44:7; 45:21; 46:10 [b]Is 43:9
23 [a]Is 42:9; 44:7, 8; 45:3; John 13:19 [b]Jer 10:5
24 [1]Lit *nothing* [a]Ps 115:8; Is 44:9; 1 Cor 8:4 [b]Is 37:19; 41:29 [c]Prov 3:32; 28:9
25 [a]Is 41:2; Jer 50:3 [b]2 Sam 22:43; Is 10:6; Mic 7:10; Zech 10:5
26 [a]Is 41:22; 44:7; 45:21 [b]Hab 2:18, 19
27 [a]Is 48:3-8 [b]Is 40:9; 44:28; 52:7; Nah 1:15
28 [1]Lit *out of those* [a]Is 50:2; 59:16; 63:5 [b]Is 40:13, 14 [c]Is 46:7
29 [1]Another reading is *nothing* [a]Is 2:8; 17:8; 41:24 [b]Is 44:9 [c]Jer 5:13

41:15 *threshing sledge.* Cf. 28:27; Mic 4:13; Hab 3:12. *mountains . . . hills.* Probably represents the nations. See 2:14. *make . . . like chaff.* See v. 2; 17:13 and note; 29:5–6.
41:16 *winnow.* A figure of judgment used also in Jer 51:2. *rejoice.* Cf. 25:9; 35:10; 51:11.
41:17 *afflicted and needy.* Israel in exile or on the way home (cf. v. 14; 32:7). *will answer.* See 30:19 and note.
41:18 *rivers on the bare heights.* See 30:25 and note. *wilderness a pool . . . fountains.* See 32:2; 35:6–7 and notes.
41:19 These trees will beautify the wilderness (cf. 35:1–2). Several are named in 60:13 in connection with adorning the place of God's sanctuary. Acacia wood was used for the tabernacle (Ex 25:5,10,13). The pine tree and myrtle replace thorns and briers in 55:13.
41:20 *created it.* These fruitful conditions are part of God's new creation in behalf of His people (see 48:7; 57:19; 65:17–18).
41:21–22 God takes the nations and their idols to court (see v. 1 and note).
41:22 *former events.* Earlier predictions or accomplishments (see 42:9; 43:9,18; 46:9; 48:3).
41:23 *do good or evil.* See note on 40:18–20.
41:24 *no account . . . nothing.* Like the nations that worship them. See 40:17; 44:9; Hos 9:10. *abomination.* Like those who marry idolaters (see Mal 2:11).
41:25 *aroused.* See v. 2 and note. *from the north.* Cyrus came from the east (v. 2) but conquered a number of kingdoms north of Babylon early in his reign. From the perspective of a writer in Jerusalem, invasions came primarily from the north (see 14:31; Jer 1:14; 6:1,22; 10:22; 46:20; 50:3,9,41; 51:48). *call on My name.* Cyrus used the Lord's name in his decree (Ezra 1:2) but did not acknowledge Him (see 45:4–5). *come upon . . . mortar . . . clay.* Similar to Assyria in 10:6. Cf. Mic 7:10; Nah 3:14.
41:26 *from the beginning.* Before these events began to unfold (cf. v. 4). *your.* Referring to idols or their worshipers.
41:27 *here they are.* Words about the deliverance from Babylon. *messenger of good news.* Isaiah. See 40:9; 52:7 and notes.
41:28 *no counselor . . . can give an answer.* See 46:7.
41:29 *worthless.* See v. 24.

God's Promise concerning His Servant

42 "[a]Behold, My [b]Servant, whom I
[1]uphold;
My [c]chosen one *in whom* My [d]soul
delights.
I have put My [e]Spirit upon Him;
He will bring forth [f]justice to the
[2]nations.
2 "He will not cry out or raise *His voice,*
Nor make His voice heard in the street.
3 "A bruised reed He will not break
And a dimly burning wick He will not
extinguish;
He will faithfully bring forth [a]justice.
4 "He will not be [a]disheartened or
crushed
Until He has established justice in the
earth;
And the [b]coastlands will wait
expectantly for His [1]law."

5 Thus says God the LORD,
Who [a]created the heavens and
[b]stretched them out,
Who spread out the [c]earth and its
[1]offspring,
Who [d]gives breath to the people on it
And spirit to those who walk in it,
6 "I am the LORD, I have [a]called you in
righteousness,
I will also [b]hold you by the hand and
[c]watch over you,
And I will appoint you as a [d]covenant
to the people,
As a [e]light to the nations,
7 To [a]open blind eyes,
To [b]bring out prisoners from the
dungeon
And those who dwell in darkness
from the prison.

42:1 [1]Or *hold fast* [2]Or *Gentiles* [a]Matt 12:18-21 [b]Is 41:8; 43:10; 49:3-6; 52:13; 53:11; Matt 12:18-21; Phil 2:7 [c]Luke 9:35; 1 Pet 2:4, 6 [d]Matt 3:17; 17:5; Mark 1:11; Luke 3:22 [e]Is 11:2; 59:21; 61:1; Matt 3:16; Luke 4:18, 19, 21 [f]Is 2:4
3 [a]Ps 72:2, 4; 96:13
4 [1]Or *instruction* [a]Is 40:28 [b]Is 11:11; 24:15; 42:10, 12; 49:1; 51:5; 60:9; 66:19
5 [1]Or *vegetation* [a]Ps 102:25, 26; Is 45:18 [b]Ps 104:2; Is 40:22 [c]Ps 24:1, 2; 136:6 [d]Job 12:10; 33:4; Is 57:16; Dan 5:23; Acts 17:25
6 [a]Is 41:2; Jer 23:5, 6 [b]Is 41:13; 45:1 [c]Is 26:3; 27:3 [d]Is 49:8 [e]Is 49:6; 51:4; 60:1, 3; Luke 2:32; Acts 13:47; 26:23
7 [a]Is 29:18; 35:5 [b]Is 49:9; 61:1
8 [1]Or *idols* [a]Is 43:3, 11, 15 [b]Ex 3:15; Ps 83:18 [c]Ex 20:3-5; Is 48:11
9 [a]Is 48:3 [b]Is 43:19; 48:6
10 [a]Ps 33:3; 40:3; 98:1 [b]Is 49:6; 62:11 [c]Ps 65:5; 107:23 [d]Ex 20:11; 1 Chr 16:32; Ps 96:11 [e]Is 42:4

8 "[a]I am the LORD, that is [b]My name;
I will not give My [c]glory to another,
Nor My praise to [1]graven images.
9 "Behold, the [a]former things have come
to pass,
Now I declare [b]new things;
Before they spring forth I proclaim
them to you."

10 Sing to the LORD a [a]new song,
Sing His praise from the [b]end of the
earth!
[c]You who go down to the sea, and [d]all
that is in it.
You [e]islands, and those who dwell on
them.
11 Let the [a]wilderness and its cities lift
up *their voices,*
The settlements where [b]Kedar inhabits.
Let the inhabitants of [c]Sela sing aloud,
Let them shout for joy from the tops
of the [d]mountains.
12 Let them [a]give glory to the LORD
And declare His praise in the
[b]coastlands.
13 [a]The LORD will go forth like a warrior,
He will arouse *His* [b]zeal like a man of
war.
He will utter a shout, yes, He will
raise a war cry.
He will [c]prevail against His enemies.

The Blindness of the People

14 "[a]I have kept silent for a long time,
I have kept still and restrained Myself.
Now like a woman in labor I will
groan,
I will both gasp and pant.

11 [a]Is 32:16; 35:1, 6 [b]Is 21:16; 60:7 [c]Is 16:1 [d]Is 52:7; Nah 1:15
12 [a]Is 24:15 [b]Is 42:4 **13** [a]Ex 15:3 [b]Is 9:7; 26:11; 37:32; 59:17 [c]Is 66:14-16 **14** [a]Ps 50:21; Is 57:11

42:1–4 Quoted in part in Matt 12:18–21 with reference to Christ. There are four "servant songs" in which the servant is the Messiah: 42:1–4 (or 42:1–7 or 42:1–9); 49:1–6 (or 49:1–7 or 49:1–13); 50:4–9 (or 50:4–11); 52:13–53:12. He is "Israel" in its ideal form (49:3). The nation was to be a kingdom of priests (Ex 19:6), but the Messiah would be the high priest who would atone for the sins of the world (53:4–12). Cyrus was introduced in ch. 41 as a deliverer from Babylon, but the servant would deliver the world from the prison of sin (see v. 7).
42:1 *My servant.* See 41:8–9 and note; Zech 3:8. In the royal terminology of the ancient Near East "servant" meant something like "trusted envoy" or "confidential representative." *chosen one.* See 41:8–9 and note. *delights.* Cf. Luke 3:22. *My Spirit upon Him.* Like the "branch" of 11:1–2 (see note on 11:2); cf. 61:1. *justice.* A righteous world order (see v. 4); see also 9:7 and note; 11:4 and note.
42:2 *not cry out . . . raise His voice.* He will bring peace (see 9:6).
42:3 *bruised reed.* Someone who is weak (see Ps 72:2,4). The servant will mend broken lives.
42:4 *disheartened.* Cf. 40:28. *justice.* Perfect order (see v. 1 and note). *wait . . . for His law.* As do the nations in 2:2–4. The servant will be a new Moses (see Deut 18:15–18; Acts 3:21–23,26). *coastlands.* See note on 11:11.
42:5 *created the heavens . . . stretched.* See 40:22 and note. *gives breath . . . spirit.* Cf. 57:15.
42:6 *called . . . righteousness.* Similar to the call of Cyrus (see 41:2 and note). *hold you by the hand.* See 41:13 and note. *covenant.* See 49:8. The Messiah will fulfill the Davidic covenant as king (9:7) and will institute the new covenant by His death (Jer 31:31–34; Heb 8:6–13; 9:15). *people.* Probably the Israelites (see 49:8; Acts 26:17–18). *light.* Parallel to "salvation" in 49:6 (cf. 51:4).
42:7 *open blind eyes.* See 29:18; 32:3; 35:5 and notes. *bring out . . . dungeon.* From the prison of Babylon and also from spiritual and moral bondage (compare 61:1 with Luke 4:18).
42:8 *My glory.* See 40:5 and note.
42:9 *former things.* See 41:22 and note. *new things.* The restoration of Israel (43:19). Cf. 48:6.
42:10 *new song.* To celebrate the "new things" of v. 9. *end of the earth.* See 11:12 and note; 41:5. *islands.* See v. 12; 11:11 and note.
42:11 *wilderness.* See 35:1 and note. *Kedar.* See note on 21:16. *Sela.* See note on 16:1.
42:12 *give glory . . . praise.* See 24:14–16.
42:13 *warrior.* God will fight as He did at the Red Sea (Ex 15:3); see 9:6 and note. *zeal.* Cf. 9:7; 37:32; 59:17; 63:15. *raise a war cry.* To cause panic among the enemy (see 1 Sam 4:5–8).
42:14 *for a long time.* During Israel's humiliation and exile.

15 "I will [a]lay waste the mountains and hills
And wither all their vegetation;
I will [b]make the rivers into coastlands
And dry up the ponds.
16 "I will [a]lead the blind by a way they do not know,
In paths they do not know I will guide them.
I will [b]make darkness into light before them
And [c]rugged places into plains.
These are the things I will do,
And I will [d]not leave them undone."
17 They will be turned back *and* be [a]utterly put to shame,
Who trust in [1]idols,
Who say to molten images,
"You are our gods."

18 [a]Hear, you deaf!
And look, you blind, that you may see.
19 Who is blind but My [a]servant,
Or so deaf as My [b]messenger whom I send?
Who is so blind as he that is [1c]at peace *with Me*,
Or so blind as the servant of the LORD?
20 [a]You have seen many things, but you do not observe *them;*
Your ears are open, but none hears.
21 The LORD was pleased for His righteousness' sake
To make the law [a]great and glorious.
22 But this is a people plundered and despoiled;
All of them are [a]trapped in [1]caves,
Or are [b]hidden away in prisons;
They have become a prey with none to deliver *them,*
And a spoil, with none to say, "Give *them* back!"

15 [a]Is 2:12-16; Ezek 38:19, 20 [b]Is 44:27; 50:2; Nah 1:4-6
16 [a]Is 29:18; 30:21; 32:3; Jer 31:8, 9; Luke 1:78, 79 [b]Is 29:18; Eph 5:8 [c]Is 40:4; Luke 3:5 [d]Josh 1:5; Ps 94:14; Is 41:17; Heb 13:5
17 [1]Or *graven images* [a]Ps 97:7; Is 1:29; 44:9, 11; 45:16
18 [a]Is 29:18; 35:5
19 [1]Or *the devoted one* [a]Is 41:8 [b]Is 44:26 [c]Is 26:3; 27:5
20 [a]Rom 2:21
21 [a]Is 42:4; 51:4
22 [1]Or *holes* [a]Is 24:18 [b]Is 24:22
24 [a]Is 30:15 [b]Is 48:18; 57:17
25 [1]Lit *did not lay it to heart* [a]Is 5:25; 9:19 [b]Is 29:13; 47:7; 57:1; Hos 7:9
43:1 [a]Is 43:15 [b]Is 43:7, 21; 44:2, 21, 24 [c]Is 43:5 [d]Is 44:22, 23; 48:20 [e]Gen 32:28; Is 43:7; 45:3, 4 [f]Is 43:21
2 [a]Ps 66:12; Is 8:7, 8 [b]Deut 31:6, 8 [c]Is 29:6; 30:27-29; Dan 3:25, 27
3 [1]Or *Ethiopia* [a]Ex 20:2 [b]Is 19:20; 43:11; 45:15, 21; 49:26; 60:16; 63:8 [c]Is 20:3-5
4 [a]Ex 19:5, 6 [b]Is 49:5 [c]Is 63:9

23 Who among you will give ear to this?
Who will give heed and listen hereafter?
24 Who gave Jacob up for spoil, and Israel to plunderers?
Was it not the LORD, against whom we have sinned,
And in whose ways they [a]were not willing to walk,
And whose law they did not [b]obey?
25 So He poured out on him the heat of His anger
And the [a]fierceness of battle;
And it set him aflame all around,
Yet he did not recognize *it;*
And it burned him, but he [1b]paid no attention.

Israel Redeemed

43 But now, thus says the LORD, your [a]Creator, O Jacob,
And He who [b]formed you, O Israel,
"Do not [c]fear, for I have [d]redeemed you;
I have [e]called you by name; you are [f]Mine!
2 "When you [a]pass through the waters, [b]I will be with you;
And through the rivers, they will not overflow you.
When you [c]walk through the fire, you will not be scorched,
Nor will the flame burn you.
3 "For [a]I am the LORD your God,
The Holy One of Israel, your [b]Savior;
I have given Egypt as your ransom,
[1c]Cush and Seba in your place.
4 "Since you are [a]precious in My sight,
Since you are [b]honored and I [c]love you,
I will give *other* men in your place and *other* peoples in exchange for your life.

---

restrained Myself. See 63:15; 64:12. The Hebrew verb is also used of Joseph, who controlled his emotions while he tested his brothers (Gen 43:31; 45:1). See 30:18 and note.
42:15 *lay waste . . . wither.* The opposite of 35:1–2; 41:18. *rivers into coastlands.* Perhaps to make travel easier. See 37:25; 44:27.
42:16 *blind.* Israel (vv. 19–20). *rugged places into plains.* See 40:4. *not leave them.* Cf. 40:27; 49:14; 54:8.
42:18 *deaf . . . blind.* See 6:10 and note.
42:19 *My servant.* Israel. See note on 41:8–9. *messenger whom I send.* A term associated with prophets (see Hag 1:13; cf. Is 44:26; Mal 3:1).
42:21 *law great and glorious.* Especially the law of Moses, given in the awesome setting of Mount Sinai (see Ex 34:29).
42:22 *plundered and despoiled.* By the Assyrians (see 10:6 and note) and the Babylonians (see 39:6). *trapped in caves . . . prisons.* See v. 7 and note. Cf. Judg 6:2–4.
42:24 *Who gave Jacob up . . . ?* Babylon conquered Israel, not because their gods were stronger than the Lord (see 40:17–18; 1 Kin 20:23), but because the Lord was punishing His people.
42:25 *poured out . . . anger.* Israel had a foretaste of the day of the Lord (see 5:25; 9:12,17,21; 13:3; 34:2 and notes; cf. Jer 10:25).
43:1 *Creator . . . who formed.* God made the nation Israel as surely as He made the first man (see Gen 1:27; see also Is 43:7,15,21; 44:2,24). *Do not fear.* See 41:10 and note. *redeemed you.* See notes on 35:9; 41:14. The verb is also used in 29:22; 44:22–23; 48:20 (cf. Ex 15:13). *called . . . by name.* God chose Israel to serve Him in a special way. See 45:3–4 (Cyrus).
43:2 *waters . . . rivers.* Probably an allusion to crossing the Red Sea (Ex 14:21–22) and the Jordan River (Josh 3:14–17). Cf. Ps 66:6,12. *walk through the fire.* Fulfilled literally in the experience of Shadrach, Meshach and Abednego (Dan 3:25–27). Contrast 42:25.
43:3 *Holy One of Israel.* See notes on 1:4; 41:14. *Savior.* Who delivers from the oppression of Egypt or Babylon and from the spiritual oppression of sin (see 19:20 and note; 25:9 and note; 33:22; 35:4 and note; 43:11–12; 45:15,21–22; 49:25; 60:16; 63:8–9). The name "Isaiah" means "The LORD saves." *ransom.* The Persians conquered Egypt, Cush and Seba, and perhaps this was a reward or ransom for Persia's kindness to Israel (see note on 41:2; cf. Ezek 29:19–20). *Cush.* See note on 18:1. *Seba.* A land near Cush (cf. 45:14) or Sheba (Ps 72:10). It was probably either in south Arabia (see Gen 10:7 and note; see also Ezek 27:21–22) or across the Red Sea in Africa.

5 "Do not fear, for [a]I am with you;
I will bring [b]your offspring from the east,
And [c]gather you from the west.
6 "I will say to the [a]north, 'Give *them* up!'
And to the south, 'Do not hold *them* back.'
Bring My [b]sons from afar
And My daughters from the [c]ends of the earth,
7 Everyone who is [a]called by My name,
And whom I have [b]created for My [c]glory,
[d]Whom I have formed, even whom I have made."

Israel Is God's Witness

8 Bring out the people who are [a]blind, even though they have eyes,
And the deaf, even though they have ears.
9 All the nations have [a]gathered together
So that the peoples may be assembled.
Who among them can [b]declare this
And proclaim to us the former things?
Let them present [c]their witnesses
[d]that they may be justified,
Or let them hear and say, "It is true."
10 "You are [a]My witnesses," declares the LORD,
"And [b]My servant whom I have chosen,
So that you may know and believe Me
And understand that [c]I am He.
[d]Before Me there was no God formed,
And there will be none after Me.
11 "I, even I, am the LORD,
And there is no [a]savior [b]besides Me.
12 "It is I who have declared and saved and proclaimed,
And there was no [a]strange *god* among you;
So you are My witnesses," declares the LORD,
"And I am God.
13 "Even [1a]from eternity [b]I am He,
And there is [c]none who can deliver out of My hand;
[d]I act and who can reverse it?"

Babylon to Be Destroyed

14 Thus says the LORD your [a]Redeemer, the Holy One of Israel,
"For your sake I have sent to Babylon,
And will bring them all down as fugitives,
[1]Even the [b]Chaldeans, into the [c]ships [2]in which they rejoice.
15 "I am the LORD, your Holy One,
[a]The Creator of Israel, your [b]King."
16 Thus says the LORD,
Who [a]makes a way through the sea
And a path through the mighty waters,
17 Who brings forth the [a]chariot and the horse,
The army and the mighty man
(They will lie down together *and* not rise again;
They have been [b]quenched *and* extinguished like a wick):
18 "[a]Do not call to mind the former things,
Or ponder things of the past.
19 "Behold, I will do something [a]new,
Now it will spring forth;
Will you not be aware of it?
I will even [b]make a roadway in the wilderness,
Rivers in the desert.
20 "The beasts of the field will glorify Me,
The [a]jackals and the ostriches,
Because I have [b]given waters in the wilderness
And rivers in the desert,
To give drink to My chosen people.

5 [a]Is 8:10; 43:2 [b]Is 41:8; 49:12; 61:9 [c]Is 49:12
6 [a]Ps 107:3 [b]2 Cor 6:18 [c]Is 45:22
7 [a]Is 56:5; 62:2; James 2:7 [b]Ps 100:3; Is 29:23; Eph 2:10 [c]Is 44:23; 46:13 [d]Is 43:1
8 [a]Is 6:9; 42:19; Ezek 12:2
9 [a]Is 34:1; 41:1 [b]Is 41:22, 23, 26 [c]Is 44:9 [d]Is 43:26
10 [a]Is 44:8 [b]Is 41:8 [c]Is 41:4 [d]Is 45:5, 6
11 [a]Is 43:3; 45:21; Hos 13:4 [b]Is 44:6, 8
12 [a]Deut 32:16; Ps 81:9
13 [1]So with Gr; Heb *from the day* [a]Ps 90:2; Is 48:16 [b]Is 41:4 [c]Ps 50:22 [d]Job 9:12; Is 14:27
14 [1]Another reading is *As for the Chaldeans, their rejoicing* is turned *into lamentations* [2]Lit *of their rejoicing* [a]Is 41:14 [b]Is 23:13 [c]Jer 51:13
15 [a]Is 43:1 [b]Is 41:20; 44:6
16 [a]Ex 14:21, 22; Ps 77:19; Is 11:15; 44:27; 50:2; 51:10; 63:11, 12
17 [a]Ex 15:19 [b]Ps 118:12; Is 1:31
18 [a]Is 65:17; Jer 23:7
19 [a]Is 42:9; 48:6; 2 Cor 5:17 [b]Ex 17:6; Num 20:11; Deut 8:15; Ps 78:16; Is 35:1, 6; 41:18, 19; 49:10; 51:3
20 [a]Is 13:22; 35:7 [b]Is 41:17, 18; 48:21

43:5 *Do not fear.* See 41:10 and note. *east.* Especially Assyria and Babylonia. See 11:11–12 and notes; cf. Ps 107:3. *west.* For example, the "islands" of 11:11 (see also 24:14–15; 49:12).
43:6 *north.* For example, Hamath (see 10:9 and note; 11:11). *south.* Egypt. *ends of the earth.* See note on 11:12 (cf. 41:5; 42:10).
43:7 *called by My name.* People belonging to God. *created . . . formed.* See v. 1 and note.
43:8 *blind . . . deaf.* Probably referring to Israel (see 6:10 and note; 42:18–20).
43:9–13 A court scene; see also 41:21–22.
43:9 *nations . . . peoples may be assembled.* See 41:1 and note. *former things.* See 41:22 and note. *witnesses.* To verify the accuracy of earlier predictions by idols or their worshipers (see 41:26).
43:10 *You are My witnesses.* See also v. 12; 44:8. God's work in behalf of Israel is proof of His saving power. *My servant.* See 41:8–9 and note.
43:11 The main thrust is repeated in 44:6,8; 45:5–6,18,21–22; 46:9 (see also Deut 32:39). *savior.* See v. 3 and note.
43:12 *strange god.* Cf. Deut 32:12,16. Israel repeatedly worshiped other gods (see Judg 2:12–13). *witnesses.* See v. 10 and note.
43:13 See v. 11. *none who can deliver . . . hand.* Quoted verbatim from Deut 32:39.
43:14 *Redeemer.* See 41:14 and note. *Holy One of Israel.* See 1:4; 41:14 and notes. *Babylon.* See note on 13:1. *fugitives . . . into the ships.* The Babylonians used the Persian Gulf, as well as the Tigris and Euphrates rivers, for trading purposes. But their splendid ships (cf. 2:16) would one day become their means of flight (cf. Jer 51:13).
43:15 *Creator.* See v. 1 and note. *King.* God was called "king in Jeshurun" (Israel) in Deut 33:5 (contrast 1 Sam 8:7).
43:16–17 A reference to crossing the Red Sea (see v. 2 and note). Pharaoh's chariots and horsemen were destroyed as Israel's God fought against them (see 51:10; Ex 14:28; 15:4).
43:17 *extinguished like a wick.* Contrast 42:3.
43:19 *something new.* See 42:9 and note. *roadway in the wilderness.* See 35:8; 40:3 and notes. *Rivers in the desert.* See v. 20; 32:2 and note. Contrast 42:15 and note.
43:20 *jackals . . . ostriches.* Creatures of the desert (see 13:21–22; 34:13–15; 35:7).

21 "The people whom [a]I formed for Myself
[b]Will declare My praise.

The Shortcomings of Israel

22 "Yet you have not called on Me, O Jacob;
But you have become [a]weary of Me, O Israel.
23 "You have [a]not brought to Me the sheep of your burnt offerings,
Nor have you [b]honored Me with your sacrifices.
I have not [c]burdened you with [1]offerings,
Nor wearied you with [d]incense.
24 "You have bought Me not [1][a]sweet cane with money,
Nor have you [2]filled Me with the fat of your sacrifices;
Rather you have burdened Me with your sins,
You have [b]wearied Me with your iniquities.

25 "I, even I, am the one who [a]wipes out your transgressions [b]for My own sake,
And I will [c]not remember your sins.
26 "[1]Put Me in remembrance, [a]let us argue our case together;
State your *cause,* [b]that you may be proved right.
27 "Your [a]first [1]forefather sinned,
And your [2][b]spokesmen have [3]transgressed against Me.
28 "So I will [1]pollute the [2]princes of the sanctuary,
And I will consign Jacob to the [a]ban and Israel to [b]revilement.

The Blessings of Israel

44 "But now listen, O Jacob, My [a]servant,
And Israel, whom I have chosen:
2 Thus says the LORD who made you
And [a]formed you from the womb, who [b]will help you,
'[c]Do not fear, O Jacob My servant;
And you [d]Jeshurun whom I have chosen.
3 'For [a]I will pour out water on [1]the thirsty *land*
And streams on the dry ground;
I will [b]pour out My Spirit on your [c]offspring
And My blessing on your descendants;
4 And they will spring up [1]among the grass
Like [a]poplars by streams of water.'
5 "This one will say, 'I am the LORD's';
And that one [1]will call on the name of Jacob;
And another will [a]write [2]*on* his hand, 'Belonging to the LORD,'
And will name Israel's name with honor.

6 "Thus says the LORD, the [a]King of Isra-
el and his [b]Redeemer, the LORD of hosts:
'I am the [c]first and I am the last,
And there is no God [d]besides Me.
7 'Who is like Me? [a]Let him proclaim and declare it;
Yes, let him recount it to Me in order,
[1]From the time that I established the ancient [2]nation.
And let them declare to them the things that are coming
And the events that are going to take place.
8 'Do not tremble and do not be afraid;
[a]Have I not long since announced *it* to you and declared *it?*
And [b]you are My witnesses.

21 [a]Is 43:1 [b]Ps 102:18; Is 42:12; Luke 1:74, 75; 1 Pet 2:9 **22** [a]Mic 6:3; Mal 1:13; 3:14 **23** [1]Or *a meal offering* [a]Amos 5:25 [b]Zech 7:5, 6; Mal 1:6-8 [c]Jer 7:21-26 [d]Ex 30:34; Lev 2:1; 24:7 **24** [1]Or *calamus* [2]Or *saturated* [a]Ex 30:23; Jer 6:20 [b]Ps 95:10; Is 1:14; 7:13; Ezek 6:9; Mal 2:17 **25** [a]Is 44:22; 55:7; Jer 50:20 [b]Is 37:35; 48:9, 11; Ezek 36:22 [c]Is 38:17; Jer 31:34 **26** [1]Or *Report to Me* [a]Is 1:18; 41:1; 50:8 [b]Is 43:9 **27** [1]Lit *father* [2]Or *interpreters* [3]Or *rebelled* [a]Is 51:2; Ezek 16:3 [b]Is 9:15; 28:7; 29:10; Jer 5:31 **28** [1]Or *pierce through* [2]Or *holy princes* [a]Is 24:6; 34:5; Jer 24:9; Dan 9:11; Zech 8:13 [b]Ps 79:4; Ezek 5:15 **44:1** [a]Is 41:8; Jer 30:10; 46:27, 28

2 [a]Is 44:21, 24 [b]Is 41:10 [c]Is 43:5 [d]Deut 32:15; 33:5, 26 **3** [1]Or *him who is thirsty* [a]Is 41:17; Ezek 34:26; Joel 3:18 [b]Is 32:15; Joel 2:28 [c]Is 61:9; 65:23 **4** [1]Another reading is *like grass among the waters* [a]Lev 23:40; Job 40:22 **5** [1]Another reading is *will be called by the name of Jacob* [2]Or *with* [a]Ex 13:9; Neh 9:38 **6** [a]Is 41:21; 43:15 [b]Is 41:14; 43:1, 14 [c]Is 41:4; 43:10; 48:12; Rev 1:8, 17; 22:13 [d]Is 43:11; 44:8; 45:5, 6, 21 **7** [1]Lit *From My establishing of* [2]Or *people* [a]Is 41:22, 26 **8** [a]Is 42:9; 48:5 [b]Is 43:10

43:21 *people . . . declare My praise.* Cf. 42:12.
43:22–24 The Israelites may have brought sacrifices (see 1:11–15 and note), but their hearts were not right with God.
43:22 *not called . . . become weary.* Apparently their prayers were halfhearted (contrast Ps 69:3).
43:23 *not burdened . . . Nor wearied.* God did not make excessive demands on His people.
43:24 *cane.* Linked with incense (see v. 23) also in Song 4:14; Jer 6:20. *fat.* See note on 34:6. *burdened . . . wearied.* See 1:14.
43:25 *wipes out . . . transgressions.* In spite of the punishment Israel must suffer (v. 28), God is eager to forgive His people (see 1:18; 44:22; see also 40:2 and note).
43:26 *State your cause.* The Lord takes Israel to court, as He did the nations in 41:21–22.
43:27 *first forefather.* See 51:2. Even Abraham was a sinner (see Gen 12:18; 20:9). *spokesmen.* Probably the priests and prophets.
43:28 *consign . . . to the ban.* See note on 34:2. Any town of Israel that harbored idolatry was to receive this fate (Deut 13:12–15). Jerusalem suffered destruction at the hands of the Babylonians (2 Kin 25:8–9) because of idolatry (see Ezek 7:15–22).
44:1–2 *My servant.* See 41:8–9 and note.
44:2 *formed you.* See 43:1 and note. *from the womb.* See v. 24. The tenderness of the Creator is shown (see also 49:5; Jer 1:5). *Do not fear.* See v. 8; 41:10 and note. *Jeshurun.* Israel (see v. 1), meaning "the upright one"; found elsewhere only in Deut 32:15; 33:5,26.
44:3 *pour out water . . . streams.* See 30:25; 32:2; 35:6–7 and notes; see also 41:18. *pour out My Spirit.* Associated with the Messianic age in 32:15 (see note there) and Joel 2:28.
44:4 *grass.* A symbol of luxuriant growth also in 35:7 (contrast 37:27; 40:6–8).
44:5 *call on the name.* A willingness to identify with Jacob, the Lord's people. See 43:7 and note. *write on his hand.* Perhaps a mark of ownership (cf. 49:16; Rev 13:16) or a reminder of one's allegiance (cf. Ex 13:9,16).
44:6 *King.* See 43:15 and note. *Redeemer.* See v. 24; 41:14 and note. *first . . . last.* See 41:4 and note. *there is . . . Me.* See 43:11 and note.
44:8 *You are My witnesses.* See 43:10 and note. *Rock.* See 17:10 and note. As in v. 2; 43:11–13, Isaiah may be drawing on the song of Moses, which describes God as "the Rock" (Deut

Is there any God [c]besides Me,
Or is there any *other* [d]Rock?
I know of none.' "

The Folly of Idolatry

9 Those who fashion [1]a graven image are
all of them futile, and their precious things
are of no profit; even their own witnesses fail
to see or know, so that they will be [a]put to
shame.
10 Who has fashioned a god or cast [1]an
idol to [a]no profit?
11 Behold, all his companions will be [a]put
to shame, for the craftsmen themselves are
mere men. Let them all assemble themselves, let them stand up, let them tremble,
let them together be put to shame.
12 The [a]man shapes iron into a cutting
tool and does his work over the coals, [1]fash-
ioning it with hammers and working it with
his strong arm. He also gets hungry and [2]his
strength fails; he drinks no water and
becomes weary.
13 [a]*Another* shapes wood, he extends a
measuring line; he outlines it with red chalk.
He works it with planes and outlines it with
a compass, and makes it like the form of a
man, like the beauty of [b]man, so that it may
sit in a [c]house.
14 Surely he cuts cedars for himself, and
takes a [1]cypress or an oak and [2]raises *it* for
himself among the trees of the forest. He
plants a fir, and the rain makes it grow.
15 Then it becomes *something* for a man
to burn, so he takes one of them and warms
himself; he also makes a fire to bake bread.
He also [a]makes a god and worships it; he
makes it a graven image and [b]falls down
before it.
16 Half of it he burns in the fire; over *this*
half he eats meat as he roasts a roast and is
satisfied. He also warms himself and says,
"Aha! I am warm, I have seen the fire."

8 [c]Deut 4:35, 39; 1 Sam 2:2; Is 45:5; Joel 2:27 [d]Is 17:10; 26:4; 30:29
9 [1]Or *an idol* [a]Ps 97:7; Is 42:17; 44:11; 45:16
10 [1]Or *a graven image* [a]Is 41:29; Jer 10:5; Hab 2:18; Acts 19:26
11 [a]Ps 97:7; Is 42:17; 44:9; 45:16
12 [1]Lit *and fashions* [2]Lit *there is no strength* [a]Is 40:19, 20; 41:6, 7; 46:6, 7; Jer 10:3-5; Hab 2:18
13 [a]Is 41:7 [b]Ps 115:5-7 [c]Judg 17:4, 5; Ezek 8:10, 11
14 [1]Or *holm-oak* [2]Lit *makes strong*
15 [a]Is 44:17 [b]2 Chr 25:14
17 [a]Is 44:15 [b]1 Kin 18:26, 28; Is 45:20
18 [a]Is 1:3; Jer 10:8, 14 [b]Ps 81:12; Is 6:9, 10; 29:10
19 [1]Lit *returns to his heart* [2]Or *shall I make?* [3]Or *shall I fall...?* [a]Is 5:13; 44:18, 19; 45:20 [b]Deut 27:15; 1 Kin 11:5, 7; 2 Kin 23:13, 14
20 [1]Or *is a companion of ashes* [2]Lit *his soul* [a]Ps 102:9 [b]Job 15:31; Hos 4:12; Rom 1:21, 22; 2 Thess 2:11; 2 Tim 3:13 [c]Is 57:11; 59:3, 4, 13; Rom 1:25
21 [a]Is 46:8; Zech 10:9 [b]Is 44:1, 2 [c]Is 49:15
22 [1]Or *cloud* [a]Ps 51:1, 9;

17 But the rest of it he [a]makes into a god,
his graven image. He falls down before it and
worships; he also [b]prays to it and says,
"Deliver me, for you are my god."
18 They do not [a]know, nor do they understand, for He has [b]smeared over their eyes
so that they cannot see and their hearts so
that they cannot comprehend.
19 No one [1]recalls, nor is there [a]knowl-
edge or understanding to say, "I have
burned half of it in the fire and also have
baked bread over its coals. I roast meat and
eat *it*. Then [2]I make the rest of it into an
[b]abomination, [3]I fall down before a block of
wood!"
20 He [1a]feeds on ashes; a [b]deceived heart
has turned him aside. And he cannot deliver
[2]himself, nor say, "[c]Is there not a lie in my
right hand?"

God Forgives and Redeems

21 "[a]Remember these things, O Jacob,
And Israel, for you are [b]My servant;
I have formed you, you are My
servant,
O Israel, you will [c]not be forgotten by
Me.
22 "I have [a]wiped out your transgressions
like a thick cloud
And your sins like a [1]heavy mist.
[b]Return to Me, for I have [c]redeemed
you."
23 [a]Shout for joy, O heavens, for the
LORD has done *it!*
Shout joyfully, you lower parts of the
earth;
[b]Break forth into a shout of joy, you
mountains,
O forest, and every tree in it;
For [c]the LORD has redeemed Jacob

Is 43:25; Acts 3:19 [b]Is 31:6; 55:7 [c]Is 43:1; 48:20; 1 Cor 6:20; 1 Pet 1:18, 19 **23** [a]Ps 69:34; 96:11, 12; Is 42:10; 49:13 [b]Ps 98:7, 8; 148:7, 9; Is 55:12 [c]Is 43:1

32:4,15,30–31), but the metaphor is also common in the Psalms (see note on Ps 18:2).

44:9–20 A satire on the folly of idolatry (see 40:18–20 and note).

44:9 *futile . . . no profit.* Like the nations and their idols (see 40:17; 41:24 and notes). *shame.* Cf. v. 11; 42:17; 45:16.

44:11 *craftsmen.* See 40:19 and note.

44:12–20 Two idols are described: a metal one in v. 12 and a wooden one in vv. 13–20. The latter was more common (see 40:20).

44:12 *becomes weary.* But God never gets tired (40:28).

44:13 *like the form of man.* Man was made in the image of God (see Gen 1:26–27 and notes), but an idol is made in the image of man (Deut 4:16; Rom 1:23).

44:14 *cedars . . . cypress . . . oak.* The most valuable kinds of wood then known. See 9:10; 41:19 and notes.

44:15 *worships . . . falls down.* Repeated in vv. 17,19; see 2:8,20.

44:16 *roasts a roast . . . warms himself.* Although wood serves common purposes, it is also made into an idol (see v. 19).

44:17 *Deliver me.* King Amaziah was condemned for worshiping the gods of Seir, a nation he had defeated in battle (2 Chr 25:14–15). Isaiah denounces such idolatry as totally irrational (see 45:20). Whereas those who worshiped idols associated the god with the idol, for Isaiah there was no god for the idol to represent, so he depicts idolatry as worship of a mere "block of wood" (v. 19).

44:18 *smeared over their eyes . . . and their hearts.* Israel's condition in 6:9–10 (see note there). The description ironically characterizes both the idols and those who worship them. See also Ps 82:5.

44:19 *an abomination.* The Lord detests idols (see Deut 27:15). In 1 Kin 11:5,7; 2 Kin 23:13 Molech and Chemosh are called detestable gods and an abomination. Those who worship idols are also called an abomination (see 41:24 and note).

44:20 *feeds on ashes.* Even devoted worship does not benefit the idolater. Cf. Hos 12:1. *lie.* Or "fraud." See 2 Thess 2:11.

44:21 *My servant.* See vv. 1–2; 41:8–9 and note.

44:22 *wiped out your transgressions.* As in 40:2 (see note there), the suffering of Israel has paved the way for forgiveness and the restoration of the nation (see 43:25 and note). *Return to Me.* Cf. Jer 31:18. *redeemed.* Cf. v. 23; see notes on 35:9; 41:14; 43:1.

44:23 *Shout for joy . . . Shout joyfully.* Nature is called on to join in praise (see also 35:1; 49:13). *Break forth . . . you mountains.*

And in Israel He [d]shows forth His
glory.

24 Thus says the LORD, your [a]Redeemer,
and the one who [b]formed you from the
womb,
"I, the LORD, am the maker of all things,
[c]Stretching out the heavens by Myself
And spreading out the earth [1]all alone,
25 [a]Causing the [1]omens of boasters to
fail,
[2]Making fools out of diviners,
[b]Causing wise men to draw back
And [3]turning their knowledge into
foolishness,
26 [a]Confirming the word of His servant
And [1]performing the purpose of His
messengers.
It is I who says of Jerusalem, 'She
shall be inhabited!'
And of the [b]cities of Judah, '[c]They
shall be built.'
And I will raise up her ruins *again*.
27 "*It is I* who says to the depth of the sea,
'Be dried up!'
And I will make your rivers [a]dry.
28 "*It is I* who says of [a]Cyrus, '*He is* My
shepherd!
And he will perform all My desire.'
And [1]he declares of Jerusalem, '[b]She
will be built,'
And of the temple, '[2]Your foundation
will be laid.'"

God Uses Cyrus

45 Thus says the LORD to [a]Cyrus His
anointed,
Whom I have taken by the right
[b]hand,
To [c]subdue nations before him
And [1]to [d]loose the loins of kings;
To open doors before him so that gates
will not be shut:
2 "I will go before you and [a]make the
[1]rough places smooth;
I will [b]shatter the doors of bronze and
cut through their iron [c]bars.
3 "I will give you the [1a]treasures of
darkness
And hidden wealth of secret places,
So that you may know that it is I,
The LORD, the God of Israel, who
[b]calls you by your name.
4 "For the sake of [a]Jacob My servant,
And Israel My chosen *one*,
I have also [b]called you by your name;
I have given you a title of honor
Though you have [c]not known Me.
5 "I am the LORD, and [a]there is no other;
[b]Besides Me there is no God.
I will [1c]gird you, though you have not
known Me;
6 That [1a]men may know from the rising
to the setting of the sun
That there is [b]no one besides Me.
I am the LORD, and there is no other,
7 The One [a]forming light and [b]creating
darkness,
Causing [1]well-being and [c]creating
calamity;
I am the LORD who does all these.

God's Supreme Power

8 "[a]Drip down, O heavens, from above,
And let the clouds pour down
righteousness;
Let the [b]earth open up and salvation
bear fruit,
[c]And righteousness spring up with it.
I, the LORD, have created it.

[a]Is 42:16 [b]Ps 104:20; 105:28 [c]Is 31:2; 47:11; Amos 3:6 **8** [a]Ps 72:6; Hos 10:12; 14:5; Joel 3:18 [b]Ps 85:11 [c]Is 60:21; 61:11

23 [d]Is 49:3; 61:3
24 [1]Or *who was with Me?* [a]Is 41:14; 43:14 [b]Is 44:2 [c]Is 40:22; 42:5; 45:12, 18; 51:13
25 [1]Lit *signs* [2]Lit *He makes* [3]Lit *He turns* [a]Is 47:13 [b]2 Sam 15:31; Job 5:12-14; Ps 33:10; Is 29:14; Jer 51:57; 1 Cor 1:20, 27
26 [1]Lit *He performs* [a]Zech 1:6; Matt 5:18 [b]Is 40:9 [c]Jer 32:15, 44
27 [a]Is 42:15; 50:2; Jer 50:38; 51:36
28 [1]Lit *to say* [2]Lit *You will be founded* [a]Is 45:1 [b]2 Chr 36:22, 23; Ezra 1:1; Is 14:32; 45:13; 54:11
45:1 [1]Lit *I will loose* [a]Is 44:28 [b]Ps 73:23; Is 41:13; 42:6 [c]Is 41:2, 25; Jer 50:3, 35; 51:11, 20, 24 [d]Job 12:21; Is 45:5

2 [1]Another reading is *mountains* [a]Is 40:4 [b]Ps 107:16 [c]Jer 51:30
3 [1]Or *hoarded treasures* [a]Jer 41:8; 50:37 [b]Ex 33:12, 17; Is 43:1; 49:1
4 [a]Is 41:8, 9; 44:1 [b]Is 43:1 [c]Acts 17:23
5 [1]Or *arm* [a]Is 45:6, 14, 18, 21; 46:9 [b]Is 44:6, 8 [c]Ps 18:39
6 [1]Lit *they* [a]Ps 102:15; Mal 1:11 [b]Is 45:5
7 [1]Or *peace*

See 49:13; 55:12. *shows forth His glory.* See 35:2 and note; 40:5 and note.

44:24 *Redeemer.* See 41:14 and note. *Stretching out . . . spreading out.* See 40:22 and note; cf. 51:13.

44:25 *omens of boasters . . . fail.* See Deut 13:1–3. *diviners.* The Hebrew for this word is used of Balaam (Josh 13:22), the witch of Endor (1 Sam 28:8) and false prophets (Jer 27:9). It is linked with soothsaying and sorcery (see 3:2–3 and note; Deut 18:10–11). *wise men . . . draw back.* See 29:14 and note.

44:26 *servant . . . messengers.* The true prophets (see 42:19 and note; Jer 7:25). *inhabited . . . built.* See Jer 32:15; cf. Is 58:12; 61:4. *raise up . . . ruins.* Contrast 6:11.

44:27 *Be dried up!* A reference to the crossing of the Red Sea (see 11:15; 37:25; 43:16–17 and notes; cf. 50:2; 51:10).

44:28 *Cyrus.* See 41:2 and note. *shepherd.* Often applied to rulers (see 2 Sam 5:2; Jer 23:2). *Jerusalem . . . temple.* The decree of Cyrus (Ezra 1:2–4; 6:3–5) authorized the rebuilding of the temple, which would lead to a restored Jerusalem (see 45:13).

45:1 *anointed.* "Messiah" comes from the Hebrew for this word. Cyrus, a foreign emperor, is called "his anointed" just as he is called "my shepherd" (44:28), because God has appointed him to carry out a divine commission in his role as king. Nebuchadnezzar is similarly called "my servant" (Jer 25:9; 27:6; 43:10). The servant—Christ (see note on 42:1–4)—is called "the Messiah" ("the Anointed One") in Dan 9:25–26 (*Christ* in Greek means "the Anointed One," just as *Messiah* does in Hebrew). See also Ps 2:2 and note. *taken by the right hand.* See 41:13 and note.

45:2 *doors of bronze . . . iron bars.* Normally the doors of city gates were made of wood, and the bars were metal (see Judg 16:3 and note).

45:3 *that you may know.* God's actions reveal His power (cf. Ezek 6:7; 7:27). *calls you by your name.* To indicate God's control of Cyrus's activities. See v. 4; see also note on 43:1.

45:4 *My servant.* See 41:8–9 and note. *title of honor.* Perhaps "anointed" (v. 1). *Though . . . not known Me.* See v. 5. Cyrus apparently worshiped the chief Babylonian deity, Marduk, whom he praised in his inscriptions.

45:5 *I . . . there is no other.* See vv. 6,14,18,21–22; 43:11 and note.

45:6 *rising to . . . setting.* The whole earth (see Mal 1:11 and note).

45:7 *darkness . . . calamity.* Such as the darkness that plagued the Egyptians (see Ex 10:21–23; Ps 105:28; cf. Is 47:11; Amos 3:6).

45:8 *Drip down . . . pour down.* A picture of abundance (see Hos 10:12). *righteousness.* In v. 13; 41:2 Cyrus is mentioned in connection with God's righteousness. God is "making things right" through the Persian king. *salvation bear fruit.* God will

9 "Woe to *the one* who [a]quarrels with his
[1]Maker—
An earthenware vessel [2]among the
vessels of earth!
Will the [b]clay say to the [1]potter, 'What
are you doing?'
Or the thing you are making *say,* 'He
has no hands'?
10 "Woe to him who says to a father,
'What are you begetting?'
Or to a woman, 'To what are you
[1]giving birth?' "

11 Thus says the [a]LORD, the Holy One of
Israel, and his [1][b]Maker:
"[2][c]Ask Me about the things to come
[3]concerning My [d]sons,
And you shall commit to Me [e]the
work of My hands.
12 "It is I who [a]made the earth, and
created man upon it.
I [b]stretched out the heavens with My
hands
And I [1]ordained [c]all their host.
13 "I have aroused him in [a]righteousness
And I will [b]make all his ways smooth;
He will [c]build My city and will let My
exiles go [d]free,
Without any payment or reward," says
the LORD of hosts.

14 Thus says the LORD,
"The [1]products of [a]Egypt and the
merchandise of [2][b]Cush
And the Sabeans, men of stature,
Will [c]come over to you and will be
yours;
They will walk behind you, they will
come over in [d]chains
And will [e]bow down to you;
They will make supplication to you:
'[3]Surely, [f]God is [4]with you, and [g]there
is none else,
No other God.' "
15 Truly, You are a God who [a]hides
Himself,
O God of Israel, [b]Savior!

9 [1]Lit *Fashioner* [2]Lit *with* [a]Job 15:25; 40:8, 9; Ps 2:2, 3; Prov 21:30; Jer 50:24 [b]Is 29:16; 64:8; Jer 18:6; Rom 9:20, 21
10 [1]Lit *in labor pains with*
11 [1]Lit *Fashioner* [2]Or *Will you ask* [3]Or *upon* [a]Is 43:15; 48:17; Ezek 39:7 [b]Is 44:2; 54:5 [c]Is 8:19 [d]Jer 31:9 [e]Is 19:25; 29:23; 60:21; 64:8
12 [1]Or *commanded* [a]Is 42:5; 45:18; Jer 27:5 [b]Ps 104:2; Is 42:5; 44:24 [c]Gen 2:1; Neh 9:6
13 [a]Is 41:2 [b]Is 45:2 [c]2 Chr 36:22, 23; Is 44:28 [d]Is 52:3
14 [1]Lit *labor* [2]Or *Ethiopia* [3]Or *God is with you alone* [4]Or *in* [a]Ps 68:31; Is 19:21 [b]Is 18:1; 43:3 [c]Is 14:1, 2; 49:23; 54:3 [d]Ps 149:8 [e]Is 49:23; 60:14 [f]Jer 16:19; Zech 8:20-23; 1 Cor 14:25 [g]Is 45:5
15 [a]Ps 44:24; Is 1:15; 8:17; 57:17 [b]Is 43:3
16 [a]Is 42:17; 44:9 [b]Is 44:11
17 [a]Is 26:4; 51:6; Rom 11:26 [b]Is 49:23; 50:7; 54:4
18 [1]Or *in vain* [a]Is 42:5 [b]Is 45:12 [c]Gen 1:2 [d]Gen 1:26; Ps 115:16 [e]Is 45:5
19 [1]Lit *a place of a land of darkness* [2]Lit *seed* [3]Or *vain* [a]Is 48:16 [b]Is 45:25; 65:9 [c]2 Chr 15:2; Ps 78:34; Jer 29:13, 14 [d]Ps 19:8; Is 45:23; 63:1 [e]Is 43:12; 44:8

16 They will be [a]put to shame and even
humiliated, all of them;
The [b]manufacturers of idols will go
away together in humiliation.
17 Israel has been saved by the LORD
With an [a]everlasting salvation;
You [b]will not be put to shame or
humiliated
To all eternity.

18 For thus says the LORD, who [a]created
the heavens (He is the God who [b]formed the
earth and made it, He established it *and* did
not create it [1]a [c]waste place, *but* formed it to
be [d]inhabited),
"I am the LORD, and [e]there is none else.
19 "[a]I have not spoken in secret,
In [1]some dark land;
I did not say to the [2][b]offspring of
Jacob,
'[c]Seek Me in [3]a waste place';
I, the LORD, [d]speak righteousness,
[e]Declaring things that are upright.
20 "[a]Gather yourselves and come;
Draw near together, you fugitives of
the nations;
[b]They have no knowledge,
Who [c]carry about [1]their wooden idol
And [d]pray to a god who cannot save.
21 "[a]Declare and set forth *your case;*
Indeed, let them consult together.
[b]Who has announced this from of old?
Who has long since declared it?
Is it not I, the LORD?
And there is [c]no other God besides Me,
A righteous God and a [d]Savior;
There is none except Me.
22 "[a]Turn to Me and [b]be saved, all the
ends of the earth;
For I am God, and there is no other.
23 "[a]I have sworn by Myself,

20 [1]Lit *the wood of their graven image* [a]Is 43:9 [b]Is 44:18, 19; 48:5-7 [c]Is 46:1, 7; Jer 10:5 [d]Is 44:17; 46:6, 7 **21** [a]Is 41:23; 43:9 [b]Is 41:26; 44:7; 48:14 [c]Is 45:5 [d]Is 43:3, 11 **22** [a]Num 21:8, 9; 2 Chr 20:12; Mic 7:7; Zech 12:10 [b]Is 30:15; 49:6, 12; 52:10
23 [a]Gen 22:16; Is 62:8; Heb 6:13

---

deliver His people. *righteousness spring up.* Peace and justice will prevail (see 11:4 and note).

45:9 *clay say to the potter.* See 29:16 and note; cf. 64:8; Jer 18:6.

45:11 *Holy One of Israel.* See 1:4 and note. *sons . . . work of My hands.* See 29:23 and note.

45:12 *stretched . . . heavens.* See 40:22 and note. *ordained . . . their host.* See 40:26 and note.

45:13 *him in righteousness.* See note on 41:2. *make . . . ways smooth.* Enabling him to reach his goals (see v. 2; see also 40:3 and note; cf. Prov 3:6). *build My city.* See note on 44:28. *Without . . . payment.* Since God had not received a payment when He sold them (see 52:3 and note; contrast note on 43:3).

45:14 *products . . . merchandise.* See 18:7 and note. *Egypt . . . Cush . . . Sabeans.* See notes on 18:1; 43:3. *come over to you . . . bow down.* See Ps 68:31. Israel's future domination over her former enemies has been mentioned in 11:14; 14:1–2 (see note on 14:1); it is also the theme of 49:23; 54:3; 60:11–14. *Surely God is with you.* One day the nations will acknowledge Israel's God (see v. 23; 19:23–25; Zech 8:20–23).

45:15 *hides Himself.* God's plans and actions are a mystery to man (cf. 54:8; 55:8–9). *Savior.* See v. 21 and note on 43:3.

45:16 *put to shame.* See 42:17; 44:9.

45:17 *everlasting salvation.* Cf. the "everlasting lovingkindness" of 54:8. *not be put to shame.* See 29:22 and note.

45:18 *created . . . formed.* See 40:21–22 and notes. *waste place.* Or "formless" or "chaotic" (see Gen 1:2 and note). *to be inhabited.* The Holy Land was now empty (see 6:11; Jer 4:23–26) and chaotic but would soon have inhabitants (see 44:26,28) and be orderly again.

45:19 *in secret . . . dark land.* Probably an allusion to the clandestine ways of mediums and spiritists (see 8:19; 29:4). *Seek me in a waste place.* Cf. Jer 29:13–14.

45:20 *no knowledge . . . save.* See 44:17–18 and notes.

45:21 *Declare . . . set forth.* See 41:21–22 and note. *announced . . . long since declared.* See 41:26 and note.

45:22 *Turn . . . be saved.* Cf. 49:6 and the invitation of 55:7. *ends of the earth.* See 11:12 and note; 42:10.

45:23 *I have sworn by Myself.* Explained in Heb 6:13. See also

The [b]word has gone forth from My
mouth in righteousness
And will not turn back,
That to Me [c]every knee will bow,
every tongue will [d]swear *allegiance.*
24 "They will say of Me, 'Only [a]in the LORD
are righteousness and strength.'
Men will come to Him,
And [b]all who were angry at Him will
be put to shame.
25 "In the LORD all the offspring of Israel
Will be [a]justified and will [b]glory."

Babylon's Idols and the True God

46 [a]Bel has bowed down, Nebo stoops
over;
Their images are *consigned* to the
beasts and the cattle.
The things [1]that you carry are
burdensome,
A load for the weary *beast.*
2 They stooped over, they have bowed
down together;
They could not rescue the burden,
But [1]have themselves [a]gone into
captivity.

3 "[a]Listen to Me, O house of Jacob,
And all [b]the remnant of the house of
Israel,
You who have been [c]borne by Me
from [1]birth
And have been carried from the
womb;
4 Even to *your* old age [a]I [1]will be the
same,
And even to *your* [2][b]graying years I will
bear *you!*
I have [3]done *it,* and I will carry *you;*
And I will bear *you* and I will deliver
you.

5 "[a]To whom would you liken Me
And make Me equal and compare Me,
That we would be alike?

23 [b]Is 55:11 [c]Rom 14:11; Phil 2:10 [d]Deut 6:13; Ps 63:11; Is 19:18; 65:16
24 [a]Jer 33:16 [b]Is 41:11
25 [a]1 Kin 8:32; Is 53:11 [b]Is 41:16; 60:19
46:1 [1]Lit *carried by you* [a]Is 2:18; 21:9; Jer 50:2-4; 51:44
2 [1]Or *their soul has* [a]Judg 18:17, 18, 24; 2 Sam 5:21; Jer 43:12, 13; 48:7; Hos 10:5, 6
3 [1]Lit *the belly* [a]Is 46:12 [b]Is 10:21, 22 [c]Ps 71:6; Is 49:1
4 [1]Lit *I am He* [2]Lit *gray hairs* [3]Or *made* you [a]Is 41:4; 43:13; 48:12 [b]Ps 71:18
5 [a]Is 40:18, 25
6 [a]Is 40:19; 41:7; 44:12-17; Jer 10:4 [b]Is 44:15, 17
7 [a]Is 45:20; 46:1; Jer 10:5 [b]Is 40:20; 41:7 [c]Is 41:28 [d]Is 45:20
8 [1]Lit *firm* [2]Lit *heart* [a]Is 44:21 [b]Is 44:19 [c]Is 50:1
9 [a]Deut 32:7; Is 42:9; 65:17 [b]Is 45:5, 21 [c]Is 41:26, 27
10 [a]Ps 33:11; Prov 19:21; Is 14:24; 25:1; 40:8; Acts 5:39
11 [1]Lit *His* [a]Is 18:6 [b]Is 41:2 [c]Num 23:19; Is 14:24; 37:26
12 [a]Is 46:3 [b]Ps 76:5; Is 48:4; Zech 7:11, 12; Mal 3:13 [c]Ps 119:150; Is 48:1; Jer 2:5
13 [a]Is 51:5; 61:11; Rom 3:21 [b]Is 61:3; 62:11; Joel 3:17; 1 Pet 2:6 [c]Is 43:7; 44:23

6 "Those who [a]lavish gold from the
purse
And weigh silver on the scale
Hire a goldsmith, and he makes it *into*
a god;
They [b]bow down, indeed they
worship it.
7 "They [a]lift it upon the shoulder *and*
carry it;
They set it in its place and it stands
there.
[b]It does not move from its place.
Though one may cry to it, it [c]cannot
answer;
It [d]cannot deliver him from his
distress.

8 "[a]Remember this, and be [1]assured;
[b]Recall it to [2]mind, you [c]transgressors.
9 "Remember the [a]former things long
past,
For I am God, and there is [b]no other;
I am God, and there is [c]no one like
Me,
10 Declaring the end from the beginning,
And from ancient times things which
have not been done,
Saying, '[a]My purpose will be
established,
And I will accomplish all My good
pleasure';
11 Calling a [a]bird of prey from the [b]east,
The man of [1]My purpose from a far
country.
Truly I have [c]spoken; truly I will bring
it to pass.
I have planned *it,* *surely* I will do it.

12 "[a]Listen to Me, you [b]stubborn-minded,
Who are [c]far from righteousness.
13 "I [a]bring near My righteousness, it is
not far off;
And My salvation will not delay.
And I will grant [b]salvation in Zion,
And My [c]glory for Israel.

62:8. *word . . . not turn back.* See 55:10–11. *every knee . . . every tongue.* See v. 14 and note. Paul quotes this portion of Isaiah in Rom 14:11 and Phil 2:10–11 to describe Christ's exalted position.
45:24 *Only in the LORD . . . strength.* See v. 5 and note. This is the climax of the refrain that runs through the chapter. *all . . . put to shame.* Very similar to 41:11 except for "at you" (Israel).
45:25 *glory.* See 41:16.
46:1 *Bel.* Another name for Marduk, the chief deity of Babylon. The name "Bel" is equivalent to Canaanite "Baal" and means "lord." *bowed down . . . stoops.* In disgrace (see v. 2; 21:9 and note). *Nebo.* Nabu, the god of learning and writing who was the son of Marduk.
46:2 *have . . . gone into captivity.* The idols join their worshipers in exile (see Jer 48:7; 49:3; Hos 10:5; Amos 1:15).
46:3 *all . . . the house.* The remnant (see 1:9 and note). *from birth . . . from the womb.* See 44:2 and note.
46:4 *old age . . . graying years.* Cf. Ps 37:25. *bear . . . done . . . deliver.* Unlike the helpless idols of vv. 1–2. See 41:10,13; 43:1–2 and notes.
46:5–7 See 40:18–20 and note.
46:6 *bow down . . . worship.* See 44:15,17,19.
46:7 *carry.* See v. 1. *cannot deliver.* See 44:17 and note.
46:8 *transgressors.* Israel. See 1:2 and note; cf. 1:20,23,28; 30:1; 57:4.
46:9 *former things.* See 41:22 and note. *there is no other.* See 43:11 and note.
46:10–11 *My purpose.* Especially God's purposes and plans regarding Babylon and Israel (see 8:9–10; 14:24; 48:14 and notes). Cf. Ps 33:11.
46:10 *from the beginning.* See 41:26 and note.
46:11 *bird of prey . . . east.* Cyrus king of Persia (see 41:2 and note). The swiftness and power of a bird of prey are in view (see 8:8 and note; Jer 49:22; cf. Dan 8:4).
46:12 *stubborn-minded.* See v. 8; 48:4; Ezek 2:4.
46:13 *righteousness.* Here equivalent to salvation. See 41:2 and note; 45:8 and note. *salvation.* See note on 43:3. *glory.* See 35:2 and note; 40:5 and note; see also 44:23; 49:3.

Lament for Babylon

47 "[a]Come down and sit in the dust,
O [b]virgin [c]daughter of Babylon;
Sit on the ground without a throne,
O daughter of the Chaldeans!
For you shall no longer be called
[d]tender and delicate.
2 "Take the [a]millstones and [b]grind meal.
Remove your [c]veil, [d]strip off the skirt,
Uncover the leg, cross the rivers.
3 "Your [a]nakedness will be uncovered,
Your shame also will be exposed;
I will [b]take vengeance and will not
[1]spare a man."
4 Our [a]Redeemer, the LORD of hosts is
His name,
The Holy One of Israel.
5 "[a]Sit silently, and go into [b]darkness,
O daughter of the Chaldeans,
For you will no longer be called
The [c]queen of [d]kingdoms.
6 "I was angry with My people,
I profaned My heritage
And gave them into your hand.
You did not show mercy to them,
On the [a]aged you made your yoke
very heavy.
7 "Yet you said, 'I will be a [a]queen
forever.'
These things you did not [b]consider
Nor remember the [c]outcome of [1]them.

8 "Now, then, hear this, you [a]sensual
one,
Who [b]dwells securely,
Who says in [1]your heart,
'[c]I am, and there is no one besides me.
I will [d]not sit as a widow,
Nor know loss of children.'
9 "But these [a]two things will come on
you [b]suddenly in one day:
Loss of children and widowhood.
They will come on you in full measure
In spite of your many [c]sorceries,
In spite of the great power of your
spells.
10 "You felt [a]secure in your wickedness
and said,
'[b]No one sees me,'
Your [c]wisdom and your knowledge,
[1]they have deluded you;
For you have said in your heart,
'[d]I am, and there is no one besides me.'
11 "But [a]evil will come on you
Which you will not know how to
charm away;
And disaster will fall on you
For which you cannot atone;
And [b]destruction about which you do
not know
Will come on you [c]suddenly.

12 "Stand *fast* now in your [a]spells
And in your many sorceries
With which you have labored from
your youth;
Perhaps you will be able to profit,
Perhaps you may cause trembling.
13 "You are [a]wearied with your many
counsels;
Let now the [b]astrologers,
Those who prophesy by the stars,
Those who predict by the new moons,
Stand up and [c]save you from what
will come upon you.
14 "Behold, they have become [a]like
stubble,
[b]Fire burns them;
They cannot deliver themselves from
the power of the flame;
There will be [c]no coal to warm by
Nor a fire to sit before!
15 "So have those become to you with
whom you have labored,
Who have [a]trafficked with you from
your youth;
Each has wandered in his own [1]way;
There is [b]none to save you.

47:1 [a]Is 3:26; Jer 48:18 [b]Is 23:12; 37:22; Jer 46:11 [c]Ps 137:8; Jer 50:42; 51:33; Zech 2:7 [d]Deut 28:56
2 [a]Ex 11:5; Jer 25:10 [b]Job 31:10; Eccl 12:4; Matt 24:41 [c]Gen 24:65; Is 3:23; 1 Cor 11:5 [d]Is 32:11
3 [1]Lit *meet* [a]Ezek 16:37; Nah 3:5 [b]Is 34:8; 63:4
4 [a]Is 41:14
5 [a]Is 23:2; Jer 8:14; Lam 2:10 [b]Is 13:10 [c]Is 47:7 [d]Is 13:19; Dan 2:37
6 [a]Deut 28:50
7 [1]Lit *it* [a]Is 47:5 [b]Is 42:25; 57:11 [c]Deut 32:29; Jer 5:31; Ezek 7:2, 3
8 [1]Lit *her* [a]Is 22:13; 32:9; Jer 50:11 [b]Is 32:9, 11; Zeph 2:15 [c]Is 45:5, 6, 18; 47:10; Zeph 2:15 [d]Rev 18:7
9 [a]Is 13:16, 18; 14:22 [b]Ps 73:19; 1 Thess 5:3; Rev 18:8, 10 [c]Is 47:13; Nah 3:4; Rev 18:23
10 [1]Lit *it has* [a]Ps 52:7; 62:10; Is 59:4 [b]Is 29:15; Ezek 8:12; 9:9 [c]Is 5:21; 44:20 [d]Is 47:8
11 [a]Is 57:1 [b]Is 13:6; Jer 51:8, 43; Luke 17:27; 1 Thess 5:3 [c]Is 47:9
12 [a]Is 47:9
13 [a]Jer 51:58, 64 [b]Is 8:19; 44:25; 47:9; Dan 2:2, 10 [c]Is 47:15
14 [a]Is 5:24; Nah 1:10; Mal 4:1 [b]Is 10:17; Jer 51:30, 32, 58 [c]Is 44:16
15 [1]Lit *side, region* [a]Rev 18:11 [b]Is 5:29; 43:13; 46:7

47:1 *sit in the dust . . . on the ground.* A sign of mourning (see 3:26). *virgin daughter of Babylon.* A personification of Babylon and its inhabitants.
47:2 *millstones and grind.* A menial task performed by women (see Ex 11:5 and note; Judg 9:53 and note). *cross the rivers.* Probably on the way to exile.
47:3 *nakedness will be uncovered.* See Ezek 16:36. Babylon is no longer a queen (see vv. 5,7); she is reduced to a servant girl or a prostitute (see v. 8). *take vengeance.* See 34:8 and note. *will not spare.* See 13:18–20.
47:4 *Redeemer.* See note on 41:14. *LORD of hosts.* See 13:4 and note. *Holy One of Israel.* See 1:4; 41:14 and notes.
47:5 *queen of kingdoms.* Babylon was a very beautiful city (see 13:19 and note).
47:6 *angry . . . profaned My heritage.* See 10:5–6 (where Assyria is God's tool); 42:24 and note; 43:28 and note; Lam 2:2. *On the aged.* Their suffering fulfilled Moses' curse for covenant disobedience (Deut 28:49–50).
47:7 *I will be a queen forever.* Cf. the arrogant words of Nebuchadnezzar in Dan 4:30.
47:8,10 *I am . . . no one besides me.* Almost a claim of deity (cf. the Lord's words in 43:11; 45:5–6,18,22). See also 14:12–15 and note.
47:8 *dwells securely.* Similar language is used of the complacent women of Jerusalem in 32:9,11. *widow.* Deserted and distressed. *loss of children.* See v. 9; 13:16,18; 14:22.
47:9,12 *sorceries . . . spells.* Magical practices to avoid danger and to inflict harm on the enemy (see 3:2–3 and note).
47:10 *No one sees me.* See 29:15 and note.
47:11 *cannot atone.* The Medes and Persians would not accept any settlement short of surrender (see 13:17).
47:13 *astrologers . . . who prophesy by the stars.* Babylon probably utilized their services more than any other nation (see Dan 2:2,10).
47:14 *stubble.* This will be a rapid, powerful fire. See note on 1:31; cf. Mal 4:1. *cannot . . . deliver themselves.* In contrast to the mighty Savior of Israel (see 43:3 and note), astrologers and sorcerers are as helpless as idols (see 44:17 and note). *no coal to warm by.* A subtle reference to firewood, a material from which pagans sometimes made idols (see 44:15).

Israel's Obstinacy

48 "[a]Hear this, O house of Jacob, who
are named Israel
And who came forth from the [1b]loins
of Judah,
Who [c]swear by the name of the LORD
And invoke the God of Israel,
But not in truth nor in [d]righteousness.
2 "For they call themselves after the
[a]holy city
And [b]lean on the God of Israel;
The LORD of hosts is His name.
3 "I [a]declared the former things long ago
And they went forth from My mouth,
and I proclaimed them.
[b]Suddenly I acted, and they [c]came to
pass.
4 "Because I know that you are
[1a]obstinate,
And your [b]neck is an iron sinew
And your [c]forehead bronze,
5 Therefore I declared *them* to you long
ago,
Before [1]they took place I proclaimed
them to you,
So that you would not say, 'My [a]idol
has done them,
And my graven image and my molten
image have commanded them.'
6 "You have heard; look at all this.
And you, will you not declare it?
I proclaim to you [a]new things from
this time,
Even hidden things which you have
not known.
7 "They are created now and not long ago;
And before today you have not heard
them,
So that you will not say, 'Behold, I
knew them.'
8 "You have not [a]heard, you have not
known.
Even from long ago your ear has not
been open,
Because I knew that you would deal
very treacherously;
And you have been called a [1b]rebel
from [2]birth.
9 "[a]For the sake of My name I [b]delay My
wrath,
And *for* My praise I restrain *it* for you,
In order not to cut you off.
10 "Behold, I have refined you, but [a]not
as silver;
I have tested you in the [b]furnace of
affliction.
11 "[a]For My own sake, for My own sake, I
will act;
For how can *My name* be profaned?
And My [b]glory I will not give to
another.

Deliverance Promised

12 "Listen to Me, O Jacob, even Israel
[1]whom I called;
[a]I am He, [b]I am the first, I am also the
last.
13 "Surely My hand [a]founded the earth,
And My right hand spread out the
heavens;
When I [b]call to them, they stand
together.
14 "[a]Assemble, all of you, and listen!
[b]Who among them has declared these
things?
The LORD loves him; he will [c]carry out
His good pleasure on [d]Babylon,
And His arm *will be against* the
Chaldeans.
15 "I, even I, have spoken; indeed I have
[a]called him,

48:1 [1]Lit *waters* [a]Is 46:12 [b]Num 24:7; Deut 33:28; Ps 68:26 [c]Deut 6:13; Is 45:23; 65:16 [d]Is 58:2; Jer 4:2
2 [a]Is 52:1; 64:10 [b]Is 10:20; Jer 7:4; 21:2; Mic 3:11; Rom 2:17
3 [a]Is 41:22; 42:9; 43:9; 44:7, 8; 45:21; 46:10 [b]Is 29:5; 30:13 [c]Josh 21:45; Is 42:9
4 [1]Or *harsh* [a]Ex 32:9; Deut 31:27; Ezek 2:4; 3:7 [b]2 Chr 36:13; Prov 29:1; Acts 7:51 [c]Ezek 3:7-9
5 [1]Lit *it* [a]Jer 44:15-18
6 [a]Is 42:9; 43:19
8 [a]Is 42:25; 47:11; Hos 7:9
8 [1]Or *transgressor* [2]Lit *the belly* [b]Deut 9:7, 24; Ps 58:3; Is 46:8
9 [a]Is 48:11 [b]Neh 9:30, 31; Ps 78:38; 103:8-10; Is 30:18; 65:8
10 [a]Jer 9:7; Ezek 22:18-22 [b]Deut 4:20; 1 Kin 8:51; Jer 11:4
11 [a]1 Sam 12:22; Ps 25:11; 106:8; Is 37:35; 43:25; Jer 14:7; Ezek 20:9, 14, 22, 44; Dan 9:17-19 [b]Deut 32:26, 27; Is 42:8
12 [1]Lit *My called one* [a]Is 41:4; 43:10-13; 46:4 [b]Is 44:6; Rev 1:17; 22:13
13 [a]Ex 20:11; Ps 102:25; Is 42:5; 45:12, 18; Heb 1:10-12 [b]Is 40:26 **14** [a]Is 43:9; 45:20 [b]Is 45:21 [c]Is 46:10, 11 [d]Is 13:4, 5, 17-19; Jer 50:21-29; 51:24 **15** [a]Is 41:2; 45:1, 2

48:1 *named.* They belong to Israel (see 43:7 and note). *Israel.* See Gen 32:28 and note. *Judah.* The main tribe of the southern kingdom. See Gen 49:8 and note. *not in truth.* Contrast the oaths of 65:16.
48:2 *holy city.* Jerusalem, where the temple was located (see 2:2–4 and note; 52:1; 56:7; 57:13; 64:10–11; 65:11). See also 1:26 and note; 4:3 and note; Dan 9:24. *lean on . . . God.* Theoretically at least (10:20). Contrast 31:1; 36:6,9; Ezek 29:6–7. *LORD of hosts.* See 13:4 and note.
48:3 *former things.* See 41:22 and note. *they came to pass.* See 42:9.
48:4 *obstinate . . . bronze.* See Jer 6:28; cf. Ezek 3:7.
48:5 *My idol has done them.* See Isaiah's harsh words about idolatry in 44:17–20 (see also notes there). *graven image and . . . molten image.* See note on 44:12–20.
48:6 *new things.* For example, Israel's restoration (see 42:9 and note). The Messianic age and the new heavens and new earth may also be in view (cf. 65:17). *hidden things.* Cf. Rom 16:25–26.
48:7 *created now.* Now given substance in the prophetic announcement of their coming.
48:8 *not heard . . . not known.* See 1:3. *ear . . . not . . . open.* See 6:10 and note. *rebel.* See 1:2; 46:8 and notes.
48:9 *delay My wrath.* Cf. Ps 78:38. *My praise.* The praise God is worthy of.
48:10 *refined . . . tested.* Images of judgment (see Jer 9:7; Ezek 22:18–22). Purifying fire is also mentioned in 1:25; 4:4. *furnace of affliction.* For Israel, Egypt had been an "iron furnace" (Deut 4:20; 1 Kin 8:51; Jer 11:4). The fall of Jerusalem and the Babylonian exile were a similar furnace.
48:11 *For . . . profaned.* Jerusalem's fall and God's scattered people had brought dishonor to God's name (see Ezek 36:20–23). *My glory.* See 40:5 and note.
48:12 *called.* To be God's servant, His chosen people. See 42:6; see also 41:2; 43:1 and notes. *first . . . last.* See 41:4 and note.
48:13 *founded the earth, And . . . the heavens.* Isaiah often refers to God as Creator (see 40:21–22; 42:5; 51:13 and notes). Cf. Ps 102:25. *When I call . . . they stand.* All creation does God's bidding (see 40:26 and note; Ps 103:22).
48:14 *Who . . . has declared.* See 41:21–23,26; 43:9 and notes. *loves him.* Cyrus the Great (see 41:2 and note). *His good pleasure.* See 46:10–11 and note. *Babylon.* See 13:1 and note.
48:15 *called him.* Cyrus (see 41:2 and note). *ways successful.* See 44:28; 45:1–4 and notes.

I have brought him, and He will make
his ways successful.
16 "[a]Come near to Me, listen to this:
From the first I have [b]not spoken in
secret,
[c]From the time it took place, I was
there.
And now [d]the Lord [1]GOD has sent Me,
and His Spirit."

17 Thus says the LORD, your [a]Redeemer,
the Holy One of Israel,
"I am the LORD your God, who teaches
you to profit,
Who [b]leads you in the way you
should go.
18 "If only you had [a]paid attention to My
commandments!
Then your [1b]well-being would have
been like a river,
And your [c]righteousness like the
waves of the sea.
19 "Your [1a]descendants would have been
like the sand,
And [2]your offspring like its grains;
[b]Their name would never be cut off or
destroyed from My presence."

20 [a]Go forth from Babylon! Flee from the
Chaldeans!
Declare with the sound of [b]joyful
shouting, proclaim this,
[c]Send it out to the end of the earth;
Say, "[d]The LORD has redeemed His
servant Jacob."

21 They did not [a]thirst when He led them
through the deserts.
He [b]made the water flow out of the
rock for them;
He split the rock and [c]the water
gushed forth.
22 "[a]There is no peace for the wicked,"
says the LORD.

Salvation Reaches to the End of the Earth

49 Listen to Me, O [a]islands,
And pay attention, you peoples from
afar.
[b]The LORD called Me from the womb;
From the [1]body of My mother He
named Me.
2 He has made My [a]mouth like a sharp
sword,
In the [b]shadow of His hand He has
concealed Me;
And He has also made Me a [1]select
[c]arrow,
He has hidden Me in His quiver.
3 He said to Me, "[a]You are My Servant,
Israel,
[b]In Whom I will [1]show My glory."
4 But I said, "I have [a]toiled in vain,
I have spent My strength for nothing
and vanity;
Yet surely the justice *due* to Me is with
the LORD,
And My [b]reward with My God."

16 [1]Heb *YHWH,* usually rendered *LORD* [a]Is 34:1; 41:1; 57:3 [b]Is 45:19 [c]Is 43:13 [d]Zech 2:9, 11
17 [a]Is 41:14; 43:14; 49:7, 26; 54:5, 8 [b]Ps 32:8; Is 30:21; 49:9, 10
18 [1]Or *peace* [a]Deut 5:29; 32:29; Ps 81:13-16 [b]Ps 119:165; Is 32:16-18; 66:12 [c]Is 45:8; 61:10, 11; 62:1; Hos 10:12; Amos 5:24
19 [1]Lit *seed* [2]Lit *the offspring of your inward parts* [a]Gen 22:17; Is 10:22; 44:3, 4; 54:3; Jer 33:22 [b]Is 56:5; 66:22
20 [a]Jer 50:8; 51:6, 45; Zech 2:6, 7; Rev 18:4 [b]Is 42:10; 49:13; 52:9 [c]Is 62:11; Jer 31:10; 50:2 [d]Is 43:1; 52:9; 63:9
21 [a]Is 30:25; 35:6, 7; 41:17, 18; 43:19, 20; 49:10 [b]Ex 17:6; Ps 78:15, 16 [c]Ps 78:20; 105:41
22 [a]Is 57:21
49:1 [1]Lit *inward parts* [a]Is 42:4 [b]Is 44:2, 24; 46:3; Jer 1:5
2 [1]Or *sharpened* [a]Is 11:4; Heb 4:12; Rev 1:16; 2:12, 16 [b]Is 51:16 [c]Hab 3:11 **3** [1]Or *glorify Myself* [a]Zech 3:8 [b]Is 44:23
4 [a]Is 65:23 [b]Is 35:4; 59:18

48:16 *the first.* The prediction about Cyrus and his mission (see 41:25–27 and notes). *not spoken in secret.* See 45:19 and note. *has sent Me, and His Spirit.* A reference to either Isaiah or the servant of the Lord. The Spirit of the Lord comes upon the servant in 42:1 (see note there) and upon the Messianic prophet of 61:1 (see note there).
48:17 *Redeemer, the Holy One of Israel.* See 41:14 and note. *teaches you . . . the way you should go.* Through the prophets (see 30:20–21 and notes; Ps 32:8).
48:18 *well being . . . like a river . . . righteousness like the waves.* Abundant and overflowing peace and righteousness (see 45:8 and note; Amos 5:24 and note). Peace (or "well-being") and righteousness are also linked in 9:7; 32:17; 54:13–14; 60:17; Ps 85:10; Heb 7:2.
48:19 *descendants . . . like the sand.* See 10:22; see also Gen 13:16 and note; Gen 22:17; Jer 33:22 and note. *name . . . never be cut off.* Israel's name would not be completely obliterated (see v. 9; 54:3).
48:20 *Go forth from Babylon! Flee . . . !* Although the Jews did not have to flee (see 52:12), they were encouraged to depart quickly because of the judgment coming on Babylon (cf. Rev 18:4). This is the last mention of Babylon by name in Isaiah. *joyful shouting.* See 44:23; 49:13; 52:9 and notes. *end of the earth.* See 11:12; 42:10 and notes. *redeemed.* See 43:1 and note. *His servant.* See 41:8–9 and note.
48:21 *did not thirst . . . water . . . out of the rock.* A reference to God's provision after the exodus (see Ex 17:6 and note; Num 20:11; see also Is 32:2; 35:6; 43:19; 49:10 and notes). God's people would have water on the way home from Babylonian exile also.
48:22 Repeated almost verbatim in 57:21. *peace.* See 39:8 and note. *wicked.* Those who rebel against the Lord (see note on 1:2).
49:1–6 (or 1–7 or 1–13) The second of the four servant songs (see note on 42:1–4).
49:1 *islands.* Or "coastlands." In 42:4 the islands "wait expectantly" for the servant's law. *called Me from the womb.* Cf. v. 5. The language is similar to that of the call of the prophet Jeremiah (Jer 1:5) and of the apostle Paul (Gal 1:15). Cf. 41:9. *He named Me.* See 43:1 and note.
49:2 *My mouth . . . sharp sword.* See Eph 6:17; Heb 4:12; Rev 1:16; 2:12,16. In 11:4 a powerful rod comes from the mouth of the Messiah. *shadow of His hand.* Descriptive of protection (see 30:2–3; 51:16). *select arrow.* Arrows are used of God's judgment in Deut 32:23,42, of the deadly words of the wicked in Ps 64:3–4 and of Satan's schemes and temptations in Eph 6:11,16.
49:3 *My Servant, Israel.* See notes on 41:8–9; 42:1–4; 42:1. "Servant" here cannot mean literally national Israel, since in v. 5 this servant has a mission to Israel. Rather, the Messianic servant is the ideal Israel through whom the Lord will be glorified. He will succeed where national Israel failed. *show My glory.* Through the redemption He will accomplish (see notes on 35:2; 40:5).
49:4 *toiled in vain.* Just as the nation Israel had toiled in vain (see 65:23), so Christ would encounter strong opposition during His ministry and would temporarily suffer apparent failure. The "suffering servant" theme is developed in the third and fourth of the four servant songs (50:4–9 or 50:4–11; 52:13–53:12). *due to Me . . . My reward.* Perhaps referring to the spiritual offspring of the servant (see 53:10)—Jews and Gentiles alike who believe in Him (vv. 5–6); see 40:10 and note. In

5 And now says [a]the LORD, who formed
Me from the womb to be His
Servant,
To bring Jacob back to Him, so that
[b]Israel might be gathered to Him
(For I am [c]honored in the sight of the
LORD,
And My God is My [d]strength),
6 He says, "It is too [1]small a thing that
You should be My Servant
To raise up the tribes of Jacob and to
restore the [a]preserved ones of
Israel;
I will also make You a [b]light [2]of the
nations
So that My salvation may [3]reach to
the [c]end of the earth."
7 Thus says the LORD, the [a]Redeemer of
Israel *and* its Holy One,
To the [b]despised One,
To the One abhorred by the nation,
To the Servant of rulers,
"[c]Kings will see and arise,
Princes will also [d]bow down,
Because of the LORD who is faithful,
the Holy One of Israel who has
chosen You."

8 Thus says the LORD,
"In a [a]favorable time I have answered
You,
And in a day of salvation I have
helped You;
And I will [b]keep You and [c]give You for
a covenant of the people,
To [1][d]restore the land, to make *them*
inherit the desolate heritages;
9 Saying to those who are [a]bound, 'Go
forth,'
To those who are in darkness, 'Show
yourselves.'
Along the roads they will feed,
And their pasture *will be* on all [b]bare
heights.
10 "They will [a]not hunger or thirst,
Nor will the scorching [b]heat or sun
strike them down;
For [c]He who has compassion on them
will [d]lead them
And will guide them to [e]springs of
water.
11 "I will make all [a]My mountains a road,
And My [b]highways will be raised up.
12 "Behold, these will come [a]from afar;
And lo, these *will come* from the
[b]north and from the west,
And these from the land of Sinim."
13 [a]Shout for joy, O heavens! And
rejoice, O earth!
Break forth into joyful shouting,
O mountains!
For the [b]LORD has comforted His
people
And will [c]have compassion on His
afflicted.

Promise to Zion

14 But Zion said, "The LORD has forsaken
me,
And the Lord has forgotten me."
15 "Can a woman forget her nursing child
And have no compassion on the son
of her womb?
Even these may forget, but [a]I will not
forget you.
16 "Behold, I have [a]inscribed you on the
palms *of My hands;*
Your [b]walls are continually before Me.

5 [a]Is 44:2 [b]Is 11:12; 27:12 [c]Is 43:4 [d]Is 12:2
6 [1]Lit *light* [2]Or *to* [3]Lit *be* [a]Ps 37:28; 97:10 [b]Is 42:6; 51:4; Luke 2:32; Acts 13:47; 26:23 [c]Is 48:20
7 [a]Is 48:17 [b]Ps 22:6-8; 69:7-9; Is 53:3 [c]Is 52:15 [d]Is 19:21, 23; 27:13; 66:23
8 [1]Lit *establish* [a]Ps 69:13; 2 Cor 6:2 [b]Is 26:3; 27:3; 42:6 [c]Is 42:6 [d]Is 44:26
9 [a]Is 42:7; 61:1; Luke 4:18
9 [b]Is 41:18
10 [a]Is 33:16; 48:21; Rev 7:16 [b]Ps 121:6 [c]Is 14:1 [d]Ps 23:2; Is 40:11 [e]Is 35:7; 41:17
11 [a]Is 40:4 [b]Is 11:16; 19:23; 35:8; 62:10
12 [a]Is 49:1; 60:4 [b]Is 43:5, 6
13 [a]Is 44:23 [b]Is 40:1; 51:3, 12 [c]Is 54:7, 8, 10
15 [a]Is 44:21
16 [a]Song 8:6; Hag 2:23 [b]Ps 48:12, 13; Is 62:6, 7

any case, He will be vindicated and rewarded (50:8; 53:10–12; 1 Tim 3:16).

49:5 *formed Me from the womb.* See v. 1; 44:2 and notes. *bring Jacob back . . . Israel might be gathered.* A prophecy of release from captivity in Babylon (see vv. 9–12,22; 41:2 and note) and from the greater captivity of sin (see 42:7 and note). *My strength.* See 12:2.

49:6 Together with Gen 12:1–3; Ex 19:5–6, this verse is sometimes called the "great commission of the OT" and is quoted in part by Paul and Barnabas in Acts 13:47. *preserved ones.* Probably referring to the remnant (see 1:9 and note). *light of the nations.* See 42:6 and note; Acts 26:23. Christ is the light of the world (Luke 2:30–32; John 8:12; 9:5), and Christians reflect His light (Matt 5:14). *end of the earth.* See 11:12 and note; see also 41:5; 42:10; 48:20.

49:7 *Redeemer of Israel . . . Holy One.* See 41:14 and note. *despised.* Applied twice to the suffering servant in 53:3. In 60:14 Zion is despised by her enemies. *nation.* Refers to either Israel (1:4) or Gentiles. *Kings will see . . . bow down.* See v. 23. This reaction to the servant is similar to that of 52:15. Former oppressors bow before a restored Jerusalem in 60:14 (cf. 45:14; 60:11–12; 66:23). *chosen You.* See 41:8–9; 42:1 and notes.

49:8 Quoted in part in 2 Cor 6:2. *favorable time . . . day of salvation.* The background of this verse is probably the year of jubilee (see 61:1–2; Lev 25:10). The return from exile will bring the same restoration of land for the people as that year of liberty did. *keep You . . . for a covenant.* See 42:6 and note. *make . . . the desolate heritages.* See 44:26. It was under Joshua that the land had been divided among individual tribes and families (Josh 14:1–5). The Messianic servant will be a new Joshua—as well as a new Moses (see vv. 9–10, which echo Israel's deliverance from Egypt and her wilderness experiences under Moses during the period of the exodus).

49:9 *those . . . bound.* The exiles. See 42:7 and note. *bare heights.* See 41:18 and note.

49:10 *not hunger or thirst.* See 48:21 and note. *has compassion.* See 14:1 and note. *will lead them.* As a shepherd (see 40:11 and note). This whole verse is also a picture of heaven according to Rev 7:16–17.

49:11 *mountains a road.* See 26:7 and note. *highways . . . raised up.* See 11:16; 35:8; 40:3; 62:10 and notes.

49:12 *come from afar.* See 11:11 and note; 60:4. *north . . . west.* See 43:5–6 and notes. *Sinim.* See Ezek 29:10; 30:6; located in the most southern part of Egypt (Aswan).

49:13 *Shout for joy . . . mountains.* Nature is personified often in Isaiah. See 44:23 and note. *comforted His people.* As He redeemed and saved them. Cf. 2 Cor 1:3–4. *will have compassion.* See v. 10 and note; 54:7–10.

49:14 *forsaken . . . forgotten.* See 40:27; 54:7; Lam 5:20–22.

49:15 *Can a woman forget . . . ?* Cf. Ps 27:10.

49:16 *inscribed you on . . . My hands.* As the names of the tribes of Israel were engraved on stones and fastened to the ephod

17 "Your [1]builders hurry;
Your [a]destroyers and devastators
Will depart from you.
18 "[a]Lift up your eyes and look around;
[b]All of them gather together, [c]they
come to you.
[d]As I live," declares the LORD,
"You will surely [e]put on all of them as
[1]jewels and bind them on as a bride.
19 "For [a]your waste and desolate places
and your destroyed land—
Surely now you will be [b]too cramped
for the inhabitants,
And those who [c]swallowed you will
be far away.
20 "The [a]children of [1]whom you were
bereaved will yet say in your ears,
'The place is too cramped for me;
Make room for me that I may live
here.'
21 "Then you will [a]say in your heart,
'Who has begotten these for me,
Since I have been bereaved of my
children
And am [b]barren, an [c]exile and a
wanderer?
And who has reared these?
Behold, I was [d]left alone;
[1][e]From where did these come?' "

22 Thus says the Lord [1]GOD,
"Behold, I will lift up My hand to the
nations
And set up My [a]standard to the
peoples;
And they will [b]bring your sons in *their*
bosom,
And your daughters will be carried on
their shoulders.
23 "[a]Kings will be your guardians,
And their princesses your nurses.
They will [b]bow down to you with
their faces to the earth
And [c]lick the dust of your feet;
And *you* will [d]know that I am the
LORD;
Those who hopefully [e]wait for Me will
[f]not be put to shame.
24 "[a]Can the prey be taken from the
mighty man,
Or the captives of [1]a tyrant be
rescued?"
25 Surely, thus says the LORD,
"Even the [a]captives of the mighty man
will be taken away,
And the prey of the tyrant will be
rescued;
For I will contend with the one who
contends with you,
And I will [b]save your sons.
26 "I will feed your [a]oppressors with their
[b]own flesh,
And they will become drunk with
their own blood as with sweet
wine;
And [c]all flesh will know that I, the
LORD, am your [d]Savior
And your [e]Redeemer, the Mighty One
of Jacob."

God Helps His Servant

50 Thus says the LORD,
"Where is the [a]certificate of divorce
By which I have [b]sent your mother
away?
Or to whom of My creditors did I [c]sell
you?
Behold, you were sold for your
[d]iniquities,
And for your [e]transgressions your
mother [f]was sent away.
2 "Why was there [a]no man when I came?
When I called, *why* was there none to
answer?

17 [1]So ancient versions and DSS; M.T. reads *sons* [a]Is 10:6; 37:18
18 [1]Lit *an ornament* [a]Is 60:4; John 4:35 [b]Is 43:5; 54:7; 60:4 [c]Is 49:12 [d]Is 45:23; 54:9 [e]Is 52:1; 61:10
19 [a]Is 1:7; 3:8; 5:6; 51:3 [b]Is 54:1, 2; Zech 10:10 [c]Ps 56:1, 2
20 [1]Lit *your bereavement* [a]Is 54:1-3
21 [1]Lit *These, where are they?* [a]Is 29:23; 54:6, 7 [b]Is 27:10; Lam 1:1 [c]Is 5:13 [d]Is 1:8 [e]Is 60:8
22 [1]Heb *YHWH,* usually rendered *LORD* [a]Is 11:10, 12; 18:3; 62:10 [b]Is 14:2; 43:6; 60:4
23 [a]Is 14:1, 2; 60:3, 10, 11 [b]Is 45:14; 60:14
23 [c]Ps 72:9; Mic 7:17 [d]Is 41:20; 43:10; 60:16 [e]Ps 37:9; Is 25:9; 26:8 [f]Ps 25:3; Is 45:17; Joel 2:27
24 [1]So ancient versions and DSS; M.T. reads *the righteous,* cf v 25 [a]Matt 12:29; Luke 11:21
25 [a]Is 10:6; 14:1, 2; Jer 50:33, 34 [b]Is 25:9; 33:22; 35:4
26 [a]Is 9:4; 14:4; 16:4; 51:13; 54:14 [b]Is 9:20 [c]Is 45:6; Ezek 39:7 [d]Is 43:3 [e]Is 49:7
50:1 [a]Deut 24:1, 3; Jer 3:8 [b]Is 54:6, 7 [c]Deut 32:30; 2 Kin 4:1; Neh 5:5 [d]Is 52:3; 59:2 [e]Is 1:28; 43:27 [f]Jer 3:8
2 [a]Is 41:28; 59:16; 66:4

of the high priest as a memorial before the Lord (Ex 28:9–12; cf. Song 8:6). *continually before Me.* Cf. Ps 137:5–6.

49:17 *builders.* Or "sons," following the reading of the Masoretic Text (see note on 62:5; see also NASB marg. here).

49:18 *All . . . gather.* See vv. 5,12 and notes. *jewels.* Beautiful clothes and jewels symbolize strength and joy.

49:19–20 *too cramped.* The restoration of Israel will be astonishing and complete. The prophecy was partially fulfilled in the return from Babylon (see note on 11:11) and may include spiritual offspring among both Jews and Gentiles (see 54:17 and note).

49:19 *waste . . . desolate.* Cf. v. 8; see 44:26 and note.

49:21 *bereaved . . . barren.* The concept of Israel as a barren woman is stressed in 54:1.

49:22 *set up My standard.* See 5:26 and note; 13:2. *bring your sons . . . daughters.* See 11:12 and note. The nations bring Israel back also in 14:2; 43:6; 60:9. *in their bosom.* Cf. 60:4; see 40:11 and note.

49:23 *Kings . . . will bow down.* See v. 7; 11:14 and notes. *know that I am the LORD.* See v. 26; 60:16; Ezek 12:20; 13:9; 36:38. *hopefully wait for Me.* See 40:31 and note. *be put to shame.* See 29:22 and note.

49:24 *mighty man . . . tyrant.* The Babylonians (see 51:13).

49:25 *captives . . . will be taken.* See Ezra 2:1,64–65; Jer 50:33–34; 52:27–30. *I will contend.* God takes up the case of His people. He will "plead their case" (Jer 50:34). *I will save.* See 35:4 and note.

49:26 *oppressors.* See 14:4; 16:4; 51:13. *with their own flesh.* During the siege of Jerusalem its people were reduced to cannibalism (Lam 4:10). *drunk with their own blood.* Cf. 51:22–23. *all flesh will know.* See v. 23 and note. *Savior.* See 43:3 and note; 60:16. *Redeemer.* See 41:14 and note. *Mighty One of Jacob.* See 1:24 and note; 60:16.

50:1 *certificate of divorce.* A husband was required to give this to a wife he wished to divorce (see Deut 24:1,3; Matt 19:7; Mark 10:4). According to Jer 3:8 God gave the northern kingdom of Israel her certificate of divorce, and Is 54:6–7 indicates that God had left Judah (see 62:4). Perhaps Isaiah's point is that God did not initiate the divorce; Judah broke her relationship with Him. The exile, then, was actually a temporary period of separation (see 54:7) rather than a divorce. *My creditors.* If a man's debts were not paid, his children could be sold into slavery (see 2 Kin 4:1). But God has no creditors. *you were sold.* Cf. 45:13; 52:3.

50:2 *I came . . . called.* Through His servants the prophets (see

Is My [b]hand so short that it cannot
ransom?
Or have I no power to deliver?
Behold, I [c]dry up the sea with My
rebuke,
I [d]make the rivers a wilderness;
Their fish stink for lack of water
And die of thirst.
3 "I [a]clothe the heavens with blackness
And make sackcloth their covering."

4 The Lord [1]GOD has given Me the
tongue of [a]disciples,
That I may know how to [b]sustain the
weary one with a word.
He awakens *Me* [c]morning by morning,
He awakens My ear to listen as a
disciple.
5 The Lord GOD has [a]opened My ear;
And I was [b]not disobedient
Nor did I turn back.
6 I [a]gave My back to those who strike
Me,
And My cheeks to those who pluck
out the beard;
I did not cover My face from
humiliation and spitting.
7 For the Lord GOD [a]helps Me,
Therefore, I am [b]not disgraced;
Therefore, I have set My face like
[c]flint,
And I know that I will not be
ashamed.
8 He who [a]vindicates Me is near;
Who will contend with Me?
Let us [b]stand up to each other;
Who has a case against Me?
Let him draw near to Me.
9 Behold, [a]the Lord GOD helps Me;
[b]Who is he who condemns Me?
Behold, [c]they will all wear out like a
garment;
The moth will eat them.
10 Who is among you that fears the LORD,
That obeys the voice of His [a]servant,
That [b]walks in darkness and has no
light?
Let him [c]trust in the name of the LORD
and rely on his God.
11 Behold, all you who [a]kindle a fire,
Who [1]encircle yourselves with
firebrands,
Walk in the light of your fire
And among the brands you have set
ablaze.
This you will have from My hand:
You will [b]lie down in torment.

Israel Exhorted

51 "[a]Listen to me, you who [b]pursue
righteousness,
Who seek the LORD:
Look to the [c]rock from which you
were hewn
And to the [1]quarry from which you
were dug.
2 "Look to [a]Abraham your father
And to Sarah who gave birth to you in
pain;
When *he* [b]*was but* one I called him,
Then I blessed him and multiplied
him."
3 Indeed, [a]the LORD will comfort Zion;
He will comfort all her [b]waste places.

2 [b]Gen 18:14; Num 11:23; Is 59:1 [c]Ex 14:21; Is 19:5; 43:16; 44:27 [d]Josh 3:16; Is 42:15
3 [a]Is 13:10; Rev 6:12
4 [1]Heb *YHWH,* usually rendered LORD, and so throughout the ch [a]Is 8:16; 54:13 [b]Is 57:19; Jer 31:25 [c]Ps 5:3; 88:13; 119:147; 143:8
5 [a]Ps 40:6; Is 35:5 [b]Matt 26:39; John 8:29; 14:31; 15:10; Acts 26:19; Phil 2:8; Heb 5:8; 10:7
6 [a]Matt 26:67; 27:30; Mark 14:65; 15:19; Luke 22:63
7 [a]Is 42:1; 49:8 [b]Is 45:17; 54:4 [c]Ezek 3:8, 9
8 [a]Is 45:25; Rom 8:33, 34 [b]Is 1:18; 41:1; 43:26
9 [a]Is 41:10 [b]Is 54:17 [c]Job 13:28; Is 51:8
10 [a]Is 49:2, 3; 50:4 [b]Is 9:2; 26:9; Eph 5:8 [c]Is 12:2; 26:4
11 [1]Lit *gird* [a]Prov 26:18; Is 9:18; James 3:6 [b]Is 8:22; 65:13-15; Amos 4:9, 10
51:1 [1]Lit *excavation of a pit* [a]Is 46:3; 48:12; 51:7 [b]Ps 94:15; Prov 15:9 [c]Gen 17:15-17
2 [a]Is 29:22; 41:8; 63:16 [b]Gen 12:1; 15:5; Deut 1:10; Ezek 33:24
3 [a]Is 40:1; 49:13 [b]Is 52:9

Jer 25:4). *none to answer.* Israel was deaf toward God (see 6:10 and note; 66:4). *hand so short.* The hand represented power. *dry up the sea.* A reference to crossing the Red Sea (see 43:16–17 and notes; Ps 106:9). *rivers a wilderness.* See 42:15 and note. *fish stink.* Perhaps a reference to one of the plagues in Egypt (see 19:5–6,8; Ex 7:18).

50:3 *heavens with blackness.* Perhaps an allusion to the plague of darkness (Ex 10:21); but see 13:10 and note.

50:4–9 (or 4–11) The third of the four servant songs (see note on 42:1–4).

50:4–5,7,9 *Lord GOD.* The only uses of this title in the servant songs.

50:4 *sustain the weary one with a word.* In 42:3 the servant assisted the weak (contrast 49:2). Cf. Jer 31:25. *awakens My ear.* Unlike Israel (see v. 2), the servant was responsive to God.

50:5 *opened My ear.* A sign of obedience (see 1:19; Ps 40:6 and note). *was not disobedient.* Unlike Israel (see 1:2 and note; 1:20).

50:6 *My back to those who strike Me.* Beatings were for criminals or fools (see Prov 10:13; 19:29; 26:3; Matt 27:26; John 19:1). *pluck out the beard.* A sign of disrespect and contempt (see 2 Sam 10:4–5; Neh 13:25). *humiliation and spitting.* To show hatred (Job 30:10) or to insult or disgrace (Deut 25:9; Job 17:6; Matt 27:30). This treatment of the servant anticipates His ultimate suffering in 52:13–53:12.

50:7 *helps Me.* See v. 9; 49:8. *not disgraced . . . not be ashamed.* See 29:22 and note. Ultimately the servant will be honored (see 49:7; 52:13; 53:10–12). *My face like flint.* Like the prophets, the servant will endure with great determination. Cf. Luke 9:51, where Jesus "determined to go to Jerusalem" (lit. "resolutely set His face to go to Jerusalem").

50:8 *vindicates Me.* The Lord will find Him righteous (see 45:25; for its ultimate fulfillment see 1 Tim 3:16). *contend with.* See 49:25 and note. Because Christ was sinless, He also nullifies the charges brought against any who believe in Him (see Rom 8:31–34). *Who . . . against Me?* Cf. 54:17.

50:9 *wear out like a garment; The moth.* Those who falsely accuse the righteous succumb to moths in 51:8 (i.e., they will be destroyed).

50:10 *fears the LORD.* See Gen 20:11; Prov 1:7 and notes. Cf. 25:3; 59:19. *in darkness.* Perhaps trouble or distress, similar to the experience of the servant (cf. 8:22). *trust . . . rely.* The Lord encouraged such trust in 12:2; 31:1.

50:11 *kindle a fire . . . firebrands.* Perhaps a reference to wicked practices that will ultimately destroy those who engage in them. Fire is a frequent figure of punishment (see 1:31 and note; cf. 9:18; 47:14; Ps 7:13). *torment.* Cf. 66:24.

51:1 *who pursue righteousness.* Cf. v. 7; Deut 16:20; Prov 15:9. *rock.* Abraham (v. 2). Elsewhere God is called "the rock" (see 17:10 and note).

51:2 *was but one.* See Gen 12:1; Ezek 33:24. *blessed him and multiplied him.* See Gen 12:2–3; 13:16; 15:5; 17:5; 22:17.

51:3 *comfort . . . comfort.* See 49:13 and note. *wilderness . . . like Eden.* See 35:1–2. The contrast between the lush splendor of

And her [c]wilderness He will make like
[d]Eden,
And her desert like the [e]garden of the
LORD;
[f]Joy and gladness will be found in her,
Thanksgiving and sound of a melody.

4 "[a]Pay attention to Me, O My people,
And give ear to Me, O My [1]nation;
For a [b]law will go forth from Me,
And I will [2]set My [c]justice for a [d]light
of the peoples.
5 "My [a]righteousness is near, My
salvation has gone forth,
And My [b]arms will judge the peoples;
The [c]coastlands will wait for Me,
And for My [d]arm they will wait
expectantly.
6 "[a]Lift up your eyes to the sky,
Then look to the earth beneath;
For the [b]sky will vanish like smoke,
And the [b]earth will wear out like a
garment
And its inhabitants will die [1]in like
manner;
But My [c]salvation will be forever,
And My righteousness will not [2]wane.
7 "[a]Listen to Me, you who know
righteousness,
A people in whose [b]heart is My law;
Do not fear the [c]reproach of man,
Nor be dismayed at their revilings.
8 "For the [a]moth will eat them like a
garment,
And the [b]grub will eat them like wool.
But My [c]righteousness will be forever,
And My salvation to all generations."

9 [a]Awake, awake, put on strength,
O arm of the LORD;
Awake as in the [b]days of old, the
generations of long ago.
[c]Was it not You who cut Rahab in
pieces,
Who pierced the [d]dragon?
10 Was it not You who [a]dried up the sea,
The waters of the great deep;
Who made the depths of the sea a
pathway
For the [b]redeemed to cross over?
11 So the [a]ransomed of the LORD will
return
And come with joyful shouting to
Zion,
And [b]everlasting joy *will be* on their
heads.
They will obtain gladness and joy,
And [c]sorrow and sighing will flee
away.

12 "I, even I, am He who [a]comforts you.
Who are you that you are afraid of
[b]man who dies
And of the son of man who is made
[c]like grass,
13 That you have [a]forgotten the LORD
your Maker,
Who [b]stretched out the heavens
And laid the foundations of the earth,
That you [c]fear continually all day long
because of the fury of the
oppressor,
As he makes ready to destroy?
But where is the fury of the
[d]oppressor?
14 "The [1a]exile will soon be set free, and
will not die in the dungeon, [b]nor will his
bread be lacking.
15 "For I am the LORD your God, who [a]stirs
up the sea and its waves roar (the LORD of
hosts is His name).
16 "I have [a]put My words in your mouth
and have [b]covered you with the shadow of
My hand, to [1c]establish the heavens, to
found the earth, and to say to Zion, 'You are
My people.' "

3 [c]Is 35:1; 41:19 [d]Gen 2:8; Joel 2:3 [e]Gen 13:10 [f]Is 25:9; 41:16; 65:18; 66:10
4 [1]Or *people* [2]Lit *cause to rest* [a]Ps 50:7; 78:1 [b]Deut 18:18; Is 2:3; Mic 4:2 [c]Is 1:27; 42:4 [d]Is 42:6; 49:6
5 [a]Is 46:13; 54:17 [b]Is 40:10 [c]Is 42:4; 60:9 [d]Is 59:16; 63:5
6 [1]Or *like gnats* [2]Lit *be broken* [a]Is 40:26 [b]Ps 102:25, 26; Is 13:13; 34:4; Matt 24:35; Heb 1:10-12; 2 Pet 3:10 [c]Is 45:17; 51:8
7 [a]Is 51:1 [b]Ps 37:31 [c]Is 25:8; 54:4; Matt 5:11; Acts 5:41
8 [a]Is 50:9 [b]Is 14:11; 66:24 [c]Is 51:6
9 [a]Is 51:17; 52:1 [b]Ex 6:6; Deut 4:34 [c]Job 26:12; Ps 89:10; Is 30:7
9 [d]Ps 74:13; Is 27:1
10 [a]Is 11:15, 16; 50:2; 63:11, 12 [b]Ex 15:13; Ps 106:10; Is 63:9
11 [a]Is 35:10; Jer 31:11, 12 [b]Is 60:19; 61:7 [c]Is 25:8; 60:20; 65:19; Rev 7:17; 21:1, 4; 22:3
12 [a]Is 51:3 [b]Ps 118:6; Is 2:22 [c]Is 40:6, 7; 1 Pet 1:24
13 [a]Deut 6:12; 8:11; Is 17:10 [b]Job 9:8; Ps 104:2; Is 40:22; 45:12, 18; 48:13 [c]Is 7:4; 10:24 [d]Is 49:26; 54:14
14 [1]Lit *one in chains* [a]Is 48:20; 52:2 [b]Is 33:6; 49:10
15 [a]Ps 107:25; Jer 31:35 [b]Ex 33:22; Is 49:2 [c]Is 66:22
16 [1]Lit *plant* [a]Deut 18:18; Is 59:21

Eden and the barrenness of the wilderness is found also in Joel 2:3. Cf. Gen 2:8,10. *Joy and gladness.* See v. 11; 25:9 and note.
51:4 *law . . . My justice.* The rule of the servant would bring justice also (see 2:2–4; 42:4 and notes). *light of the peoples.* The servant is the light in 42:6; 49:6.
51:5 *righteousness is near.* In the deliverance from exile. Ultimately, salvation through Christ will come to all nations. See 46:13 and note. *arms.* Symbolic of power. *coastlands.* See 11:11 and note. *wait for Me . . . expectantly.* See 40:31 and note; 42:4 and note.
51:6 *Lift . . . to the sky.* See 40:26. *sky will vanish.* See 34:4 and note. *earth will wear out like a garment.* See 24:4; Heb 1:10–11; cf. Is 50:9. *be forever.* See v. 8; 45:17. The word of God will also endure forever (see 40:8 and note; Matt 24:35; Luke 21:33).
51:7 *who know righteousness.* See v. 1 and note. *in whose heart is My law.* See Ps 37:31; Jer 31:33. *reproach . . . revilings.* Such as those borne by the servant in 50:6–7.
51:8 *moth . . . like a garment.* See 50:9 and note; cf. 51:6.
51:9 *Awake, awake.* See 51:17 ("Rouse yourself"); 52:1 for the same double command (see also 40:1 and note).
51:9 *put on strength.* Cf. 50:2; see note on 40:31. *arm of the LORD.* Symbol of God's power (cf. v. 5). See 30:30; 50:2 and notes; 52:10; 53:1; 63:12. *Rahab . . . the dragon.* Egypt. See 27:1 and note; 30:7 and note.
51:10 *sea.* The Red Sea (see 50:2 and note). *the redeemed.* See 35:9 and note.
51:11 This verse is the same as 35:10 (see note there).
51:12 *who comforts.* See v. 3; 49:13 and note. *grass.* See 37:27; 40:6 and notes.
51:13 *stretched out the heavens And . . . earth.* See v. 16; 48:13 and note. *fury of the oppressor.* See 49:26 and note. Babylon's wrath was insignificant beside the mighty wrath of God (cf. 13:3,5; 30:27).
51:14 *exile . . . set free.* The exiles in Babylon (see 42:7 and note; 49:9). *in the dungeon.* Cf. 42:7; Jer 37:16.
51:15 *stirs up the sea.* Cf. Job 26:12; Ps 107:25; Jer 31:35. *LORD of hosts.* See 13:4 and note.
51:16 *My words.* Primarily the law of Moses, mentioned in v. 7. Like the servant of 49:2, the people are responding to God's word (cf. 59:21; Josh 1:8). *shadow of My hand.* See 49:2 and

17 [a]Rouse yourself! Rouse yourself!
Arise, O Jerusalem,
You who have [b]drunk from the LORD's
hand the cup of His anger;
The [1]chalice of reeling you have
[2]drained to the dregs.
18 There is [a]none to guide her among all
the sons she has borne,
Nor is there one to take her by the
hand among all the sons she has
reared.
19 These two things have befallen you;
Who will mourn for you?
The [a]devastation and destruction,
famine and sword;
How shall I comfort you?
20 Your sons have fainted,
They [a]lie *helpless* at the head of every
street,
Like an [b]antelope in a net,
Full of the wrath of the LORD,
The [c]rebuke of your God.

21 Therefore, please hear this, you
[a]afflicted,
Who are [b]drunk, but not with wine:
22 Thus says your Lord, the LORD, even
your God
Who [a]contends for His people,
"Behold, I have taken out of your hand
the [b]cup of reeling,
The [1]chalice of My anger;
You will never drink it again.
23 "I will [a]put it into the hand of your
tormentors,
Who have said to [1]you, '[b]Lie down
that we may walk over *you*.'
You have even made your back like
the ground
And like the street for those who walk
over *it*."

17 [1]Lit *bowl of the cup of reeling* [2]Lit *drunk* [a]Is 51:9; 52:1 [b]Job 21:20; Is 29:9; 63:6; Jer 25:15; Rev 14:10; 16:19
18 [a]Ps 88:18; 142:4; Is 49:21
19 [a]Is 8:21; 9:20; 14:30
20 [a]Is 5:25; Jer 14:16 [b]Deut 14:5 [c]Is 66:15
21 [a]Is 54:11 [b]Is 29:9; 51:17; 63:6
22 [1]Lit *bowl of the cup of* [a]Is 3:12, 13; 49:25; Jer 50:34 [b]Is 51:17
23 [1]Lit *your soul* [a]Is 49:26; Jer 25:15-17, 26, 28; Zech 12:2 [b]Josh 10:24

52:1 [a]Is 51:9, 17 [b]Ex 28:2, 40; 1 Chr 16:29; Ps 110:3; Is 49:18; 61:3, 10; Zech 3:4 [c]Neh 11:1; Is 48:2; 64:10; Zech 14:20, 21; Matt 4:5; Rev 21:2-27 [d]Is 35:8
2 [a]Is 29:4 [b]Is 60:1 [c]Is 9:4; 10:27; 14:25; Zech 2:7
3 [a]Ps 44:12; Jer 15:13 [b]Is 1:27; 62:12; 63:4 [c]Is 45:13
4 [1]Heb *YHWH*, usually rendered LORD [a]Gen 46:6
5 [a]Ezek 36:20, 23; Rom 2:24
6 [a]Is 49:23
7 [1]Or *well-being* [2]Lit *good* [3]Or *is King* [a]Is 40:9; 61:1; Nah 1:15; Rom 10:15; Eph 6:15 [b]Ps 93:1; Is 24:23
8 [a]Is 62:6

Cheer for Prostrate Zion

52 [a]Awake, awake,
Clothe yourself in your strength,
O Zion;
Clothe yourself in your [b]beautiful
garments,
O Jerusalem, the [c]holy city;
For the uncircumcised and the
[d]unclean
Will no longer come into you.
2 Shake yourself [a]from the dust, [b]rise up,
O captive Jerusalem;
[c]Loose yourself from the chains
around your neck,
O captive daughter of Zion.
3 For thus says the LORD, "You were [a]sold
for nothing and you will be [b]redeemed
[c]without money."
4 For thus says the Lord [1]GOD, "My people [a]went down at the first into Egypt to
reside there; then the Assyrian oppressed
them without cause.
5 "Now therefore, what do I have here,"
declares the LORD, "seeing that My people
have been taken away without cause?"
Again the LORD declares, "Those who rule
over them howl, and My [a]name is continually blasphemed all day long.
6 "Therefore My people shall [a]know My
name; therefore in that day I am the one who
is speaking, 'Here I am.'"
7 How lovely on the mountains
Are the feet of him who brings [a]good
news,
Who announces [1]peace
And brings good news of [2]happiness,
Who announces salvation,
And says to Zion, "Your [b]God [3]reigns!"
8 Listen! Your watchmen lift up *their*
[a]voices,

note. *establish the heavens . . . earth.* See v. 13 and note.
51:17 *cup of His anger.* See vv. 20–22; 13:3 and note. Experiencing God's judgment is often compared to becoming drunk on strong wine. It is the fate of wicked nations in particular. See 29:9; 63:6; Ps 60:3; 75:8; Jer 25:15–16; Lam 4:21; Ezek 23:32–34; Hab 2:16; Zech 12:2; cf. John 18:11.
51:18 Children were expected to take care of parents who were sick or unsteady.
51:19 *Who will mourn for you?* A question also asked in Jer 15:5. Contrast v. 3.
51:20 *in a net.* Cf. Prov 7:22. *rebuke.* See 17:13; 54:9; 66:15.
51:21 *you afflicted.* Jerusalem (see 54:11). *Who are drunk.* On God's wrath (see v. 17 and note).
51:22 *contends for His people.* See 49:25 and note. *chalice of My anger.* See v. 17 and note.
51:23 *your tormentors.* The Babylonians. See vv. 13–14; 14:4. *your back like the ground.* Perhaps figurative, but cf. Josh 10:24.
52:1 *Awake, awake, Clothe . . . in your strength.* See 51:9,17 and notes. *beautiful garments.* Perhaps the robes of the priests, which belong to Jerusalem as a "holy city." See 49:18 and note. *holy city.* See 48:2 and note. *uncircumcised . . . unclean.* Foreign invaders. See 35:8 and note; Judg 14:3 and note.
52:2 *Shake yourself from the dust.* Contrast the fate of Babylon in 47:1 (see note there). *Loose yourself.* See 42:7 and note; 49:9; 51:14. *daughter of Zion.* A personification of Jerusalem and its inhabitants.
52:3 *sold for nothing.* The enemy paid the Lord nothing for acquiring Jerusalem. See 45:13; 50:1 and notes. *redeemed without money.* See 41:14 and note; 43:1; 45:13.
52:4 *Assyrian oppressed them.* See 9:4 and note.
52:5 Quoted in part in Rom 2:24. *without cause.* See v. 3 and note. *My name is . . . blasphemed.* The captivity brought disrespect to the God of helpless Jerusalem (see Ezek 36:20–23). Cf. Assyria's blasphemy in 37:23–24.
52:6 *know My name.* See 49:26 and note. *in that day.* The day of deliverance from Babylon. See 10:20,27 and note.
52:7 *feet of him who brings good news.* A reference to a messenger who ran from the scene of a battle to bring news of the outcome to a waiting king and people (see 2 Sam 18:26). Here the news refers to the return from exile (vv. 11–12; see 40:9 and note; 41:27), a deliverance that prefigures Christ's deliverance from sin. See Rom 10:15; Eph 6:15. *salvation.* See 49:8 and note. *Your God reigns!* See Ps 96:10. The return of God's people to Jerusalem emphasizes His sovereign rule over the world (see 40:9 and note). God's kingdom will come more fully at the second coming of Christ (see Rev 19:6).
52:8 *watchmen.* Those in Jerusalem watching for the arrival of the messengers (cf. 62:6–7; 2 Sam 18:24–27).

They shout joyfully together;
For they will see [1]with their own eyes
When the LORD restores Zion.
9 [a]Break forth, shout joyfully together,
You [b]waste places of Jerusalem;
For the LORD has comforted His people,
He has [c]redeemed Jerusalem.
10 The LORD has bared His holy [a]arm
In the sight of all the nations,
[1]That [b]all the ends of the earth may
see
The salvation of our God.

11 [a]Depart, depart, go out from there,
[b]Touch nothing unclean;
Go out of the midst of her, [c]purify
yourselves,
You who carry the vessels of the LORD.
12 But you will not go out in [a]haste,
Nor will you go [1]as fugitives;
For the [b]LORD will go before you,
And [c]the God of Israel *will be* your
rear guard.

The Exalted Servant

13 Behold, My [a]servant will prosper,
He will be high and lifted up and
[1]greatly [b]exalted.
14 Just as many were astonished at you,
My people,
So His [a]appearance was marred more
than any man
And His form more than the sons of
men.

8 [1]Lit *eye to eye*
9 [a]Ps 98:4; Is 44:23 [b]Is 44:26; 51:3; 61:4 [c]Is 43:1; 48:20
10 [1]Lit *And...earth will see* [a]Ps 98:1-3; Is 51:9; 66:18, 19 [b]Is 45:22; 48:20
11 [a]Is 48:20; Jer 50:8; Zech 2:6, 7; 2 Cor 6:17 [b]Num 19:11, 16 [c]Lev 22:2; Is 1:16
12 [1]Lit *in flight* [a]Ex 12:11, 33; Deut 16:3 [b]Is 26:7; 42:16; 49:10, 11 [c]Ex 14:19, 20; Is 58:8
13 [1]Or *very high* [a]Is 42:1; 49:1-7; 53:11 [b]Is 57:15; Phil 2:9
14 [a]Is 53:2, 3
15 [a]Num 19:18-21; Ezek 36:25 [b]Job 21:5 [c]Rom 15:21; Eph 3:5
53:1 [a]John 12:38; Rom 10:16
2 [1]Lit *suckling* [2]Lit *desire* [a]Is 11:1 [b]Is 52:14
3 [1]Or *pains* [2]Or *sickness* [a]Ps 22:6; Is 49:7; Luke 18:31-33 [b]Is 53:10 [c]Mark 10:33, 34 [d]John 1:10, 11
4 [1]Or *sickness* [2]Or *pains* [3]Or *Struck down by* [a]Matt 8:17 [b]John 19:7

15 Thus He will [a]sprinkle many nations,
Kings will [b]shut their mouths on
account of Him;
For [c]what had not been told them they
will see,
And what they had not heard they will
understand.

The Suffering Servant

53 [a]Who has believed our message?
And to whom has the arm of the LORD
been revealed?
2 For He grew up before Him like a
[a]tender [1]shoot,
And like a root out of parched
ground;
He has [b]no *stately* form or majesty
That we should look upon Him,
Nor appearance that we should [2]be
attracted to Him.
3 He was [a]despised and forsaken of
men,
A man of [1]sorrows and [b]acquainted
with [2]grief;
And like one from whom men hide
their face
He was [c]despised, and we did not
[d]esteem Him.

4 Surely our [1]griefs He Himself [a]bore,
And our [2]sorrows He carried;
Yet we ourselves esteemed Him
stricken,
[3]Smitten of [b]God, and afflicted.

52:9 *Break forth.* See 44:23 and note. *comforted.* See 49:13 and note. *redeemed.* See v. 3 and note.
52:10 *holy arm.* See 51:9 and note. God's arm is often associated with redemption and salvation (see Ex 6:6). *all the ends of the earth.* Equivalent to "all flesh" in 40:5 (see note there). Cf. 45:22.
52:11 *Depart, depart.* See note on 40:1. *unclean.* Perhaps referring to pagan religious objects (cf. Gen 31:19; 35:2). *You who carry the vessels.* Cyrus allowed the people to take back the articles of the temple seized by Nebuchadnezzar (Ezra 1:7–11). The priests and Levites were responsible for them (see Num 3:6–8; 2 Chr 5:4–7).
52:12 *not go out in haste.* See 48:20 and note. *go before you . . . be your rear guard.* As He did for the Israelites when they were freed from Egypt (see Ex 13:21; 14:19–20; cf. Is 42:16; 49:10; 58:8).
52:13–53:12 The fourth and longest of the four servant songs (see note on 42:1–4). It constitutes the central and most important unit in chs. 40–66 as well as in chs. 49–57 (see note on 39:8). The song contains five stanzas of three numbered verses each. It is quoted more frequently in the NT than any other OT passage and is often referred to as the "gospel in the OT."
52:13 *My servant.* See note on 42:1. *will prosper.* A mark of God's blessing (see 1 Sam 18:14) and of obedience to God's word (see Josh 1:8). *high and lifted up.* Words that describe the Lord in Isaiah's vision (see 6:1 and note; 57:15). Christ's exaltation is referred to in Acts 2:33; 3:13; Eph 1:20–23; Phil 2:9–11 (see also 1 Pet 1:10–11).
52:14 *astonished at you.* When they saw Christ's suffering on the cross. Cf. the reaction to the ruined city of Tyre (Ezek 27:35). *marred.* A term used of a "blemished animal," which should not be offered to the Lord (Mal 1:14). Cf. the disgraceful treatment of the servant (see 50:6 and note). *more than any man.* Cf. Ps 22:6. His treatment was inhuman.
52:15 *sprinkle many nations.* With the sprinkling of cleansing (see Lev 14:7; Num 8:7; 19:18–19) and/or of consecration (see Ex 29:21; Lev 8:11,30). *Kings will shut their mouths.* In astonishment at the suffering and exaltation of the servant (see 49:6–7 and notes). Cf. Job 21:5. *For what . . . understand.* Quoted in Rom 15:21. Even though they have not heard the prophetic word, kings will understand the mission of the servant when they see His humiliation and exaltation (contrast 6:9–10).
53:1 Quoted in whole or in part in John 12:38; Rom 10:16. *our message.* The good news about salvation, given by the prophets to Israel and the nations (see 52:7,10). *arm of the LORD.* See 51:9 and note.
53:2 *tender shoot.* The Messiah would grow from the "stem of Jesse." See 4:2; 11:1 and notes. His beginnings would be humble. *root.* See 11:10 and note. *stately form.* The Hebrew for this word is used of David in 1 Sam 16:18, where it is translated "handsome." Christ had nothing of the bearing or trappings of royalty.
53:3 *despised.* See 49:7 and note; Ps 22:6. *despised . . . forsaken.* The Hebrew words used here occur together also in 2:22 (see note there). Cf. John 1:10–11. *sorrows.* The Hebrew for this word is used of both physical and mental pain (see v. 4; Ex 3:7). *hide their face.* See 1:15 and note; 8:17.
53:4 Quoted in part in Matt 8:17 with reference to Jesus' healing ministry. *griefs.* Diseases often result from sinful living and are ultimately the consequences of original (Adamic) sin. See 1:5–6 and note. *stricken.* With a terrible disease (see Gen 12:17; 2 Kin 15:5). People (Israel in particular) thought the servant

5 But He was [1]pierced through for [a]our
transgressions,
He was crushed for [b]our iniquities;
The [c]chastening for our [2]well-being
fell upon Him,
And by [d]His scourging we are healed.
6 All of us like sheep have gone astray,
Each of us has turned to his own way;
But the LORD has caused the iniquity
of us all
To [1]fall on Him.

7 He was oppressed and He was
afflicted,
Yet He did not [a]open His mouth;
[b]Like a lamb that is led to slaughter,
And like a sheep that is silent before
its shearers,
So He did not open His mouth.
8 By oppression and judgment He was
taken away;
And as for His generation, who
considered
That He was cut off out of the land of
the [1]living
[a]For the transgression of my people, to
whom the stroke *was due?*
9 His grave was assigned with wicked
men,
Yet He was with a [a]rich man in His
death,
[b]Because He had [c]done no violence,
Nor was there any deceit in His mouth.

10 But the LORD was pleased
To [a]crush Him, [1b]putting *Him* to grief;
If [2]He would render Himself *as* a guilt
[c]offering,
He will see [d]*His* [3]offspring,
He will prolong *His* days,
And the [4]good [e]pleasure of the LORD
will prosper in His hand.
11 As a result of the [1]anguish of His soul,
He will [a]see [2]*it and* be satisfied;
By His [b]knowledge the Righteous One,
My Servant, will justify the many,
As He will [c]bear their iniquities.
12 Therefore, I will allot Him a [a]portion
with the great,
And He will divide the booty with the
strong;
Because He poured out [1b]Himself to
death,
And was [c]numbered with the
transgressors;
Yet He Himself [d]bore the sin of many,
And interceded for the transgressors.

The Fertility of Zion

54 "[a]Shout for joy, O barren one, you
who have borne no *child;*
Break forth into joyful shouting and cry
aloud, you who have not travailed;
For the sons of the [b]desolate one *will
be* [c]more numerous
Than the sons of the married
woman," says the LORD.

5 [1]Or *wounded* [2]Or *peace* [a]Is 53:8; Heb 9:28 [b]Is 53:10; Rom 4:25; 1 Cor 15:3 [c]Deut 11:2; Heb 5:8 [d]1 Pet 2:24, 25
6 [1]Lit *encounter Him*
7 [a]Matt 26:63; 27:12-14; Mark 14:61; 15:5; Luke 23:9; John 19:9 [b]Acts 8:32, 33; Rev 5:6
8 [1]Or *life* [a]Is 53:5, 12
9 [a]Matt 27:57-60 [b]Is 42:1-3 [c]1 Pet 2:22
10 [1]Lit *He made Him sick* [2]Lit *His soul* [3]Lit *seed* [4]Or *will of* [a]Is 53:5 [b]Is 53:3, 4 [c]Is 53:6, 12; John 1:29 [d]Ps 22:30; Is 54:3; 61:9; 66:22 [e]Is 46:10
11 [1]Or *toilsome labor* [2]Another reading is *light* [a]John 10:14-18 [b]Is 45:25; Rom 5:18, 19 [c]Is 53:5, 6
12 [1]Lit *His soul* [a]Is 52:13; Phil 2:9-11 [b]Matt 26:38, 39, 42 [c]Mark 15:28; Luke 22:37 [d]Is 53:6, 11; 2 Cor 5:21
54:1 [a]Gal 4:27 [b]Is 62:4 [c]1 Sam 2:5; Is 49:20

was suffering for His own sins. *afflicted.* Or "humbled," or "oppressed" (see v. 7; 58:10).

53:5 *pierced.* See Ps 22:16; Zech 12:10; John 19:34. *crushed.* In spirit (see Ps 34:18; cf. Is 57:15). The sins of the world weighed heavily upon Him. *healed.* Here probably equivalent to "forgiven" (see 6:10; Jer 30:17; see also note on 1 Pet 2:24).

53:6 *have gone astray.* Cf. Ps 119:176; Jer 50:6; Ezek 34:4–6,16; 1 Pet 2:25. *caused the iniquity of us all To fall on Him.* Just as the priest laid his hands on the scapegoat and symbolically put Israel's sins on it (Lev 16:21). See 1 Pet 2:24.

53:7–8 Verses read by the Ethiopian eunuch in the presence of Philip (Acts 8:32–33).

53:7 *oppressed.* Like Israel. See 49:26 and note. The Hebrew for this word is translated "taskmasters" in Ex 5:6. *lamb . . . to slaughter.* Cf. Ps 44:22; Rev 5:6. John the Baptist called Jesus "the Lamb of God" (John 1:29,36). *did not open His mouth.* Jesus remained silent before the chief priests and Pilate (Matt 27:12–14; Mark 14:60–61; 15:4–5; John 19:8–9) and before Herod (Luke 23:8–9).

53:8 *By oppression and judgment.* Jesus was given an unfair trial. *His generation.* Cf. v. 10.

53:9 *wicked men.* The manner of His death would indicate that, as far as those who condemned Him were concerned, He was to be buried with executed criminals. *a rich man.* Not as a burial with honor. The parallelism (with its effective wordplay in Hebrew) makes clear that Isaiah here associates the rich with the wicked, as do many OT writers—because they acquired their wealth by wicked means and/or trusted in their wealth rather than in God (see, e.g., Ps 37:16,35; Prov 18:23; 28:20; Jer 5:26–27; Mic 6:10,12). According to the Gospels (Matt 27:57–60 and parallels), the wealthy Joseph of Arimathea gave Jesus an honorable burial by placing His body in his own tomb. But this was undoubtedly an act of love growing out of his awareness that he had been forgiven much (see Luke 7:47). Thus the fulfillment fitted but also transcended the prophecy. *He had done no violence, Nor . . . deceit in His mouth.* Peter quotes these lines as he encourages believers to endure unjust suffering (1 Pet 2:22).

53:10 *crush Him.* See v. 5 and note. *guilt offering.* An offering where restitution was usually required (Lev 5:16; 6:5) and the offender sacrificed a ram (Lev 5:15). *His offspring.* Spiritual descendants. *prolong His days.* Christ would live forever (see 9:7 and note). *prosper.* See 52:13.

53:11 *be satisfied.* In 1:11, where the same Hebrew word appears, God had "enough" of innumerable sacrifices that accomplished nothing. Here the one sacrifice of Christ brings perfect satisfaction. *His knowledge.* His true knowledge of the true God (see 1:3; 6:9; 43:10; 45:4–5; 52:6; 56:10). The Spirit of knowledge (11:2) rested on the Messiah. Cf. 52:13. *My servant.* See 41:8–9; 42:1 and notes. *justify.* Cause many to be declared righteous. See 5:23; Rom 5:19 and note. *many.* See 52:15; Dan 12:3.

53:12 *with the great . . . with the strong.* God will reward His servant as if he was a king sharing in the spoils of a great victory (see 52:15). *divide the booty.* God's gift to His suffering servant (cf. 9:3). *poured out Himself.* As a sacrifice (see v. 10). *to death.* See Phil 2:8. *And was numbered with the transgressors.* Quoted in Luke 22:37 with reference to Jesus. *interceded.* See Jer 7:16 ("pray"); 27:18 ("entreat"). Cf. 59:16; Heb 7:25.

54:1 This verse is applied by Paul to Sarah and the covenant of promise, representing "the Jerusalem above" (Gal 4:26–27). *Shout . . . Break forth.* See 12:6; 44:23; 52:9 and notes. *barren one.* Jerusalem (representing Israel), especially during the exile (see 49:21). In the Near East, barrenness was considered a disgrace (see 4:1 and note). *sons of the desolate one will be more numerous.* See 49:19–20 and note. Israel will be restored both

2 "[a]Enlarge the place of your tent;
[1]Stretch out the curtains of your dwellings, spare not;
Lengthen your [b]cords
And strengthen your [b]pegs.
3 "For you will [a]spread abroad to the right and to the left.
And your [1]descendants will [b]possess nations
And will [c]resettle the desolate cities.

4 "Fear not, for you will [a]not be put to shame;
And do not feel humiliated, for you will not be disgraced;
But you will forget the [b]shame of your youth,
And the [c]reproach of your widowhood you will remember no more.
5 "For your [a]husband is your Maker,
Whose name is the LORD of hosts;
And your [b]Redeemer is the Holy One of Israel,
Who is called the [c]God of all the earth.
6 "For the LORD has called you,
Like a wife [a]forsaken and grieved in spirit,
Even like a wife of *one's* youth when she is rejected,"
Says your God.
7 "[1]For a [a]brief moment I forsook you,
But with great compassion I will [b]gather you.
8 "In an [1a]outburst of anger
I hid My face from you for a moment,
But with everlasting [b]lovingkindness I will [c]have compassion on you,"
Says the LORD your [d]Redeemer.

9 "For [1]this is like the days of Noah to Me,
When I swore that the waters of Noah
Would [a]not [2]flood the earth again;
So I have sworn that I will [b]not be angry with you
Nor will I rebuke you.
10 "For the [a]mountains may be removed and the hills may shake,
But My lovingkindness will not be removed from you,
And My [b]covenant of peace will not be shaken,"
Says [c]the LORD who has compassion on you.

11 "O [a]afflicted one, storm-tossed, *and* [b]not comforted,
Behold, I will set your stones in antimony,
And your foundations I will [c]lay in [1d]sapphires.
12 "Moreover, I will make your battlements of [1]rubies,
And your gates of [2]crystal,
And your entire [3]wall of precious stones.
13 "[a]All your sons will be [1]taught of the LORD;
And the well-being of your sons will be [b]great.
14 "In [a]righteousness you will be established;
You will be far from [b]oppression, for you will [c]not fear;
And from [d]terror, for it will not come near you.
15 "If anyone fiercely assails *you* it will not be from Me.
[a]Whoever assails you will fall because of you.
16 "Behold, I Myself have created the smith who blows the fire of coals
And brings out a weapon for its work;
And I have created the destroyer to ruin.

2 [1]Lit *Let them stretch out* [a]Is 33:20; 49:19, 20 [b]Ex 35:18; 39:40
3 [1]Lit *seed* [a]Gen 28:14; Is 43:5, 6; 60:3 [b]Is 14:1, 2 [c]Is 49:19
4 [a]Is 45:17 [b]Jer 31:19 [c]Is 4:1; 25:8; 51:7
5 [a]Jer 3:14; Hos 2:19 [b]Is 43:14; 48:17 [c]Is 6:3; 11:9; 65:16
6 [a]Is 49:14-21; 50:1, 2; 62:4
7 [1]Lit *In* [a]Is 26:20 [b]Is 11:12; 43:5; 49:18
8 [1]Lit *overflowing* [a]Is 60:10 [b]Is 54:10; 63:7 [c]Is 49:10, 13 [d]Is 54:5
9 [1]Some mss read *the waters of Noah this is to Me* [2]Lit *cross over* [a]Gen 9:11
9 [b]Is 12:1; Ezek 39:29
10 [a]Ps 102:26; Is 51:6 [b]2 Sam 23:5; Ps 89:34; Is 55:3; 59:21; 61:8 [c]Is 54:8
11 [1]Or *lapis lazuli* [a]Is 51:21 [b]Is 51:18, 19 [c]Is 14:32; 28:16; 44:28 [d]Job 28:16; Rev 21:19
12 [1]I.e. bright red [2]Or *carbuncles* [3]Lit *border, boundary*
13 [1]Or *disciples* [a]John 6:45 [b]Is 48:18; 66:12
14 [a]Is 1:26, 27; 9:7; 62:1 [b]Is 9:4; 14:4 [c]Is 54:4 [d]Is 33:18
15 [a]Is 41:11-16

physically and spiritually (cf. 62:4). *married woman.* See 50:1 and note.
54:2 See 26:15; 33:20 and notes. *your tent.* Jerusalem is viewed as a woman living in her own tent.
54:3 *spread abroad.* See 49:19–20 and note; cf. Gen 28:14. *possess nations.* See 11:14; 49:7 and notes.
54:4 *not be put to shame . . . humiliated.* See 29:22 and note; 45:17. *shame of your youth.* Probably the period of slavery in Egypt. Cf. Jer 31:19; Ezek 16:60. *reproach of your widowhood.* Probably referring to the exile, when Israel was alone, like a widow (vv. 6–7).
54:5 *husband.* See 62:4–5. *Redeemer . . . Holy One of Israel.* See 1:4, 41:14 and notes.
54:6–7 *wife forsaken . . . forsook.* Israel's experience in exile (see 49:14; 50:1 and note; 62:4).
54:7–8,10 *compassion.* See 14:1; 49:10,13; 51:3.
54:7 *brief moment.* The Babylonian exile was relatively brief (see 26:20; 50:1 and notes).
54:8 *outburst of anger.* See 9:12,17,21 and note; 60:10. *hid My face.* See 1:15 and note. *everlasting lovingkindness.* See v. 10; 55:3 and note. Cf. 45:17. *Redeemer.* See v. 5.
54:9 *not flood the earth again.* See Gen 9:11 and note. *not be angry.* See 12:1 and note.
54:10 *mountains . . . may shake.* Cf. 51:6; Ps 46:2; 102:26–27. *lovingkindness . . . covenant of peace.* A reference to either the covenant with Israel or the Davidic covenant, described in similar terms in 55:3 (see note there). Cf. Jer 33:20–21; for the language see Num 25:11–13.
54:11–12 A figurative description of restored Jerusalem, echoed in the description of the new Jerusalem in Rev 21:10,18–21.
54:11 *afflicted one.* Jerusalem. See 51:21. *storm-tossed.* See 28:2 and note. *antimony.* Perhaps a bluish-green stone. It was used in Solomon's temple (1 Chr 29:2). *sapphires.* Cf. the "pavement of sapphire" (a blue stone) in Ex 24:10 (see also Ezek 1:26; 10:1).
54:12 *battlements.* Parapets on the top of walls. *wall.* Cf. 26:1.
54:13–14 *well-being . . . righteousness.* See 48:18 and note.
54:13 *taught of the LORD.* Like the servant of the Lord in 50:4. Cf. Jer 31:34.
54:14 *oppression . . . terror.* Cf. 14:4; 33:18–19.
54:15 *fall because of you.* See v. 3.
54:16 *created the destroyer.* God raised up nations such as Assyria and Babylonia to punish Israel (see 10:5 and note; 33:1 and note).

17 "[a]No weapon that is formed against
you will prosper;
And [b]every tongue that [1]accuses you
in judgment you will condemn.
This is the heritage of the servants of
the LORD,
And their [c]vindication is from Me,"
declares the LORD.

The Free Offer of Mercy

55 "Ho! Every one who [a]thirsts, come to
the waters;
And you who have [b]no [1]money come,
buy and eat.
Come, buy [c]wine and milk
[d]Without money and without cost.
2 "Why do you [1]spend money for what is
[a]not bread,
And your wages for what does not
satisfy?
Listen carefully to Me, and [b]eat what
is good,
And [c]delight yourself in abundance.
3 "[a]Incline your ear and come to Me.
Listen, that [1]you may [b]live;
And I will make [c]an everlasting
covenant with you,
According to the [d]faithful mercies
[2]shown to David.
4 "Behold, I have made [a]him a witness to
the peoples,
A [b]leader and commander for the
peoples.
5 "Behold, you will call a [a]nation you do
not know,
And a nation which knows you not
will [b]run to you,
Because of the LORD your God, even
the Holy One of Israel;
For He has [c]glorified you."
6 [a]Seek the LORD while He may be
found;
[b]Call upon Him while He is near.
7 [a]Let the wicked forsake his way
And the unrighteous man his
[b]thoughts;
And let him [c]return to the LORD,
And He will have [d]compassion on him,
And to our God,
For He will [e]abundantly pardon.
8 "For My thoughts are not [a]your
thoughts,
Nor are [b]your ways My ways,"
declares the LORD.
9 "For [a]*as* the heavens are higher than
the earth,
So are My ways higher than your ways
And My thoughts than your thoughts.
10 "For as the [a]rain and the snow come
down from heaven,
And do not return there without
watering the earth
And making it bear and sprout,
And furnishing [b]seed to the sower and
bread to the eater;
11 So will My [a]word be which goes forth
from My mouth;
It will [b]not return to Me empty,
Without [c]accomplishing what I desire,
And without succeeding *in the matter*
for which I sent it.
12 "For you will go out with [a]joy
And be led forth with [b]peace;
The [c]mountains and the hills will
break forth into shouts of joy before
you,
And all the [d]trees of the field will clap
their hands.

17 [1]Lit *rises against* [a]Is 17:12-14; 29:8 [b]Is 50:8, 9 [c]Is 45:24; 46:13
55:1 [1]Lit *silver* [a]Ps 42:1, 2; 63:1; 143:6; Is 41:17; 44:3; John 4:14; 7:37; Rev 21:6 [b]Lam 5:4 [c]Song 5:1; Joel 3:18 [d]Hos 14:4; Matt 10:8
2 [1]Lit *weigh out silver* [a]Eccl 6:2; Hos 8:7 [b]Ps 22:26; Is 1:19; 62:8, 9 [c]Is 25:6; Jer 31:14
3 [1]Lit *your soul* [2]Lit *of David* [a]Is 51:4 [b]Lev 18:5; Rom 10:5 [c]Is 61:8 [d]Acts 13:34
4 [a]Ps 18:43; Jer 30:9; Hos 3:5 [b]Ezek 34:24; 37:24, 25; Dan 9:25; Mic 5:2
5 [a]Is 45:14, 22-24; 49:6, 12, 23 [b]Zech 8:22 [c]Is 60:9
6 [a]Ps 32:6; Is 45:19, 22; 49:8; Amos 5:6 [b]Is 58:9; 65:24
7 [a]Is 1:16, 19; 58:6 [b]Is 32:7; 59:7 [c]Is 31:6; 44:22 [d]Is 14:1; 54:8, 10 [e]Is 1:18; 40:2; 43:25; 44:22
8 [a]Is 65:2; 66:18 [b]Is 53:6
9 [a]Ps 103:11
10 [a]Is 30:23 [b]2 Cor 9:10
11 [a]Is 45:23; Matt 24:35 [b]Is 44:26; 59:21 [c]Is 46:10; 53:10
12 [a]Ps 105:43; Is 51:11; 52:9 [b]Is 54:10, 13; Jer 29:11 [c]Is 44:23; 49:13 [d]1 Chr 16:33

54:17 *every tongue . . . you will condemn.* Just as no legitimate charges could be brought against the servant of 50:8–9. *servants of the LORD.* After ch. 53 the singular "servant" no longer occurs in Isaiah. The "servants" (see 63:17; 65:8–9,13–15; 66:14) are true believers—both Jew and Gentile (see 56:6–8)—who are faithful to the Lord. They are in a sense the "offspring" of the servant (53:10). See 49:19–20 and note.
55:1 The exiles are summoned to return and be restored. *thirsts.* Spiritual thirst is primary (see 41:17; 44:3; Ps 42:1–2; 63:1). *waters.* Figurative for spiritual refreshment. Cf. Wisdom's invitation in Prov 9:5. Christ similarly invited people to drink the water of life (John 4:14; 7:37). *no money.* In hard times even water had to be purchased (see Lam 5:4). *wine and milk.* Symbols of abundance, enjoyment and nourishment. *Without money.* The death of the servant (53:5–9) paid for the free gift of life (see Rom 6:23).
55:2 *what is not bread.* Perhaps the husks of pagan religious practices. Cf. Deut 8:3. *in abundance.* Great spiritual blessings are compared to a banquet (see 25:6 and note; Ps 22:26; 34:8; Jer 31:14).
55:3 *everlasting covenant.* David had been promised an unending dynasty, one that would culminate in the Messiah (see 9:7; 54:10; 61:8; 2 Sam 7:14–16 and notes). *faithful mercies.* Assuring the continuation of the nation. See 54:8 and note. Christ's resurrection was further proof of God's faithfulness to David (see Acts 13:34, which quotes from this verse).
55:4 *witness to the peoples.* A reference either to David, who exalted the Lord among the nations (Ps 18:43,49–50), or to David's Son, the Messiah, who was a light to the nations (see 42:6; 49:6 and notes). *leader . . . for the peoples.* Similar titles are used of David (1 Sam 13:14; 25:30) and the Messiah (Dan 9:25).
55:5 *you will call a nation.* The attraction of nations to Zion and to the God of Israel is a major Biblical theme (see, e.g., 2:2–4; 45:14; Zech 8:22 and notes). *which knows you not.* The reverse of the exile, when Israel was sent to a nation unknown to them (see Deut 28:36). Ruth left Moab to live with a people she "did not previously know" (Ruth 2:11). *Holy One of Israel.* See 1:4; 41:14 and notes. *glorified.* See 4:2; 60:9. The nation will be restored physically and spiritually.
55:6 *Seek the LORD.* See Jer 29:13–14; Hos 3:5; Amos 5:4,6,14 (contrast the hypocritical seeking of 58:2).
55:7 *wicked forsake.* See 1:16. *return to the LORD . . . abundantly pardon.* See 43:25 and note; 44:22 and note.
55:9 *My ways higher.* See Ps 145:3.
55:11 *My word.* Especially the promises of vv. 3,5,12. The word is viewed as a messenger also in 9:8; Ps 107:20. Cf. John 1:1. *succeeding.* See 46:10–11 and note; cf. 40:8; Heb 4:12.
55:12 *go out with joy.* The departure from Babylon provides the background (see 35:10 and note; 52:9–12 and notes). *mountains . . . will break forth into shouts.* See 44:23 and note.

13 "Instead of the [a]thorn bush the
[b]cypress will come up,
And instead of the [c]nettle the myrtle
will come up,
And [1]it will be a [2d]memorial to the
LORD,
For an everlasting [e]sign which [f]will
not be cut off."

Rewards for Obedience to God

56 Thus says the LORD,
"[a]Preserve justice and do
righteousness,
For My [b]salvation is about to come
And My righteousness to be revealed.
2 "How [a]blessed is the man who does
this,
And the son of man who [b]takes hold
of it;
Who [c]keeps from profaning the
sabbath,
And keeps his hand from doing any
evil."
3 Let not the [a]foreigner who has joined
himself to the LORD say,
"The LORD will surely separate me from
His people."
Nor let the [b]eunuch say, "Behold, I am
a dry tree."
4 For thus says the LORD,
"To the eunuchs who [a]keep My
sabbaths,
And choose what pleases Me,
And [b]hold fast My covenant,
5 To them I will give in My [a]house and
within My [b]walls a memorial,
And a name better than that of sons
and daughters;
I will give [1]them an everlasting [c]name
which [d]will not be cut off.

13 [1]I.e. the transformation of the desert [2]Lit *name* [a]Is 7:19 [b]Is 60:13 [c]Is 5:6; 7:24; 32:13 [d]Is 63:12, 14; Jer 33:9 [e]Is 19:20 [f]Is 56:5
56:1 [a]Is 1:17; 33:5; 61:8 [b]Ps 85:9; Is 46:13; 51:5
2 [a]Ps 112:1; 119:1, 2 [b]Is 56:4, 6 [c]Ex 20:8-11; 31:13-17; Is 56:6; 58:13; Jer 17:21, 22; Ezek 20:12, 20
3 [a]Is 14:1; 56:6 [b]Deut 23:1; Jer 38:7; Acts 8:27
4 [a]Is 56:2, 6 [b]Is 56:6
5 [1]So DSS; M.T. reads *him* [a]Is 2:2, 3; 56:7; 66:20 [b]Is 26:1; 60:18 [c]Is 62:2 [d]Is 48:19; 55:13
6 [a]Is 56:3; 60:10; 61:5 [b]Is 56:2, 4
7 [a]Is 2:2, 3; 60:11; Mic 4:1, 2 [b]Is 11:9; 65:25 [c]Is 61:10 [d]Is 60:7 [e]Matt 21:13; Mark 11:17; Luke 19:46
8 [1]Heb *YHWH*, usually rendered LORD [2]Lit *him* [a]Is 11:12 [b]Is 60:3-11; 66:18-21; John 10:16
9 [a]Is 18:6; 46:11
10 [1]So DSS; M.T. *Ravers* [a]Ezek 3:17 [b]Is 29:9-14; Jer 14:13, 14
11 [1]Lit *strong of soul/appetite*

6 "Also the [a]foreigners who join
themselves to the LORD,
To minister to Him, and to love the
name of the LORD,
To be His servants, every one who
[b]keeps from profaning the sabbath
And holds fast My covenant;
7 Even [a]those I will bring to My [b]holy
mountain
And [c]make them joyful in My house
of prayer.
Their burnt offerings and their
sacrifices will be acceptable on [d]My
altar;
For [e]My house will be called a house
of prayer for all the peoples."
8 The Lord [1]GOD, who [a]gathers the
dispersed of Israel, declares,
"Yet [b]*others* I will gather to [2]them, to
those *already* gathered."

9 All you [a]beasts of the field,
All you beasts in the forest,
Come to eat.
10 His [a]watchmen are [b]blind,
All of them know nothing.
All of them are mute dogs unable to
bark,
[1]Dreamers lying down, who love to
slumber;
11 And the dogs are [1a]greedy, they [2]are
not satisfied.
And they are shepherds who have [b]no
understanding;
They have all [c]turned to their own
way,
Each one to his unjust gain, to the last
one.

[2]Lit *do not know satisfaction* [a]Is 28:7; Ezek 13:19; Mic 3:5, 11 [b]Is 1:3 [c]Is 57:17; Jer 22:17

hands. Branches. The language is figurative (cf. 1 Chr 16:33; Ps 98:8; 114:3–6).

55:13 *thorn bush . . . cypress . . . nettle . . . myrtle.* The reverse of the desolation Isaiah had prophesied about earlier (5:6; 32:13). For the significance of trees see 35:2; see also 41:19 and note. *memorial to the LORD.* Similar to God's fame in the exodus (see 63:12,14). *everlasting sign.* God's deliverance would never be forgotten. Cf. 19:20; 56:5.

56:1 *salvation . . . righteousness.* See 45:8; 46:13; 51:5 and notes.

56:2 *keeps . . . the sabbath.* See vv. 4,6. Just as the sabbath had been instituted after the exodus from Egypt (see Ex 20:8–11) as a sign of the Mosaic covenant (see Ex 31:13–17), so God's new deliverance (55:12) afforded an opportunity to obey Him fully, an obedience summed up in "keeping the sabbath" (see 58:13; 66:23; Jer 17:21–27; Ezek 20:20–21).

56:3 *foreigner.* See v. 6. Members of certain nations who came to live among the Israelites had been excluded from worship, at least for several generations (see Ex 12:43; Deut 23:3,7–8). But the work of the servant of the Lord would change this (see 49:19–20; 54:17; 60:10 and notes). Cf. 14:1. *eunuch.* See v. 4. Eunuchs were also excluded from the assembly of the Lord (Deut 23:1), but they could still be part of God's offspring (see Acts 8:27,38–40).

56:4 *hold fast My covenant.* Keeping the sabbath was a sign of the covenant (see Ex 31:13–17; Ezek 20:12,20), as was circumcision (see Gen 17:11). See also v. 6.

56:5 *memorial.* Absalom built a "Monument" (same Hebrew word) as a memorial since he had no surviving sons (2 Sam 18:18). *name.* The Hebrew for "a memorial and a name" (*yad vashem*) was chosen from v. 5 as the name of the main Holocaust monument in Jerusalem in modern Israel. *which will not be cut off.* An idiom sometimes referring to the preserving of a name through one's descendants.

56:6 *minister.* Cf. 60:7,10.

56:7 *My holy mountain.* See 2:2–4 and note. *offerings . . . acceptable on My altar.* Cf. 60:7; contrast 1:11–13. *house of prayer for all the peoples.* Solomon may have anticipated this in his prayer of dedication for the temple (1 Kin 8:41–43).

56:8 *gathers the dispersed.* See 11:11–12 and notes. *others I will gather.* Including Gentiles (see v. 3 and note; cf. John 10:16).

56:9–59:15 Many verses in these sections could apply to conditions before or during the Babylonian exile.

56:9 *beasts.* Foreign invaders (see 18:6 and note).

56:10 *watchmen.* The prophets (see Hab 2:1). *blind . . . love to slumber.* Cf. 29:9–10. *mute dogs.* Watchdogs who guarded the sheep (cf. Job 30:1).

56:11 *greedy.* They devour the sheep. See Ezek 34:3. *shepherds.* Rulers may be included. See Ezek 34:1–6.

12 "Come," *they say,* "let [1]us get [a]wine,
and let us drink heavily of strong drink;
And [b]tomorrow will be like today,
only more so."

Evil Leaders Rebuked

57 The righteous man perishes, and no
man [a]takes it to heart;
And devout men are taken away,
while no one understands.
For the righteous man is taken away
from [b]evil,
2 He enters into peace;
They rest in their [1]beds,
Each one who [a]walked in his upright
way.
3 "But come here, you sons of a
[a]sorceress,
[b]Offspring of an adulterer and [1]a
[c]prostitute.
4 "Against whom do you jest?
Against whom do you open wide your
mouth
And stick out your tongue?
Are you not children of [a]rebellion,
Offspring of deceit,
5 *Who* inflame yourselves among the
[1][a]oaks,
[b]Under every luxuriant tree,
Who [c]slaughter the children in the
[2]ravines,
Under the clefts of the crags?
6 "Among the [1][a]smooth *stones* of the
[2]ravine
Is your portion, [3]they are your lot;
Even to them you have [b]poured out a
drink offering,
You have made a grain offering.
Shall I [4][c]relent concerning these
things?
7 "Upon a [a]high and lofty mountain
You have [b]made your bed.
You also went up there to offer
sacrifice.
8 "Behind the door and the doorpost
You have set up your sign;
Indeed, far removed from Me, you
have [a]uncovered yourself,
And have gone up and made your bed
wide.
And you have made an agreement for
yourself with them,
You have loved their [1]bed,
You have looked on *their* [2]manhood.
9 "You have journeyed to the king with
oil
And increased your perfumes;
You have [a]sent your envoys a great
distance
And made *them* go down to [1]Sheol.
10 "You were tired out by the length of
your road,
Yet you did not say, '[a]It is hopeless.'
You found [1]renewed strength,
Therefore you did not [2]faint.

11 "Of [a]whom were you worried and
fearful
When you lied, and did [b]not
remember Me
[1]Nor [c]give *Me* a thought?
Was I not silent even for a long time
So you do not fear Me?
12 "I will [a]declare your righteousness and
your [b]deeds,
But they will not profit you.
13 "When you cry out, [a]let your collection
of idols deliver you.
But the wind will carry all of them
up,
And a breath will take *them away.*
But he who [b]takes refuge in Me will
[c]inherit the land
And will [d]possess My holy mountain."

14 And it will be said,
"[a]Build up, build up, prepare the way,
Remove *every* obstacle out of the way
of My people."

12 [1]So DSS and many versions; M.T. *me* [a]Is 5:11, 12, 22 [b]Ps 10:6; Luke 12:19, 20
57:1 [a]Is 42:25; 47:7 [b]2 Kin 22:20; Is 47:11; Jer 18:11
2 [1]I.e. graves [a]Is 26:7
3 [1]So ancient versions; Heb *she prostitutes herself* [a]Mal 3:5 [b]Is 1:4; Matt 16:4 [c]Is 1:21; 57:7-9
4 [a]Is 48:8
5 [1]Or *terebinths* [2]Or *wadis* [a]Is 1:29 [b]2 Kin 16:4; Jer 2:20; 3:13 [c]2 Kin 23:10; Ps 106:37, 38; Jer 7:31
6 [1]I.e. symbols of fertility gods [2]Or *wadi* [3]Lit *they, they* [4]Or *repent* [a]Jer 3:9; Hab 2:19 [b]Jer 7:18 [c]Jer 5:9, 29; 9:9
7 [a]Jer 3:6; Ezek 16:16 [b]Ezek 23:41
8 [1]Or *lying down* [2]Lit *hand* [a]Ezek 23:18
9 [1]I.e. the nether world [a]Ezek 23:16, 40
10 [1]Lit *the life of your hand* [2]Or *become sick* [a]Jer 2:25; 18:12
11 [1]Lit *You did not set it upon your heart* [a]Prov 29:25; Is 51:12, 13 [b]Jer 2:32; 3:21 [c]Ps 50:21; Is 42:14
12 [a]Is 58:1, 2 [b]Is 29:15; 59:6; 65:7; 66:18; Mic 3:2-4
13 [a]Jer 22:20; 30:14 [b]Ps 37:3, 9; Is 25:4 [c]Is 49:8; 60:21 [d]Is 65:9
14 [a]Is 62:10; Jer 18:15

56:12 *wine . . . strong drink.* Cf. the behavior of priests and prophets in 28:7. *tomorrow will be . . . more so.* Cf. the words of the rich fool in Luke 12:19.
57:1 *taken away from evil.* Huldah explained that righteous King Josiah would die before disaster struck (2 Kin 22:19–20).
57:2 *peace.* Contrast v. 21. *rest.* Cf. Paul's words in Phil 1:21,23.
57:3 *sorceress.* One who practices soothsaying or magic (see 3:2; 47:12; Deut 18:10). *adulterer and a prostitute.* Spiritual adultery (idolatry) is in view (see vv. 5–8).
57:4 *jest . . . open wide your mouth.* The people mocked Isaiah in 28:9,14. *children of rebellion.* See 1:4; 46:8 and note.
57:5 *oaks.* Sacred trees (see 1:29 and note). *luxuriant tree.* Associated with high places of pagan worship in 1 Kin 14:23. Cf. Jer 2:20; 3:13. *slaughter the children.* Often associated with the worship of Molech (cf. v. 9; see note on 30:33, "Topheth") or Baal (Jer 19:5). Ps 106:37–38 says that children were sacrificed to idols and demons.
57:6 *ravine.* Possibly the Hinnom Valley, southwest of Jerusalem, where Molech was worshiped. *drink offering.* This pagan libation was especially popular.
57:7 *high and lofty mountain.* "High places" or "mountain shrines" (see Jer 3:6; Ezek 16:16; 22:9).
57:8 *them.* Pagan deities or idols.
57:9 *oil.* Used as an ointment for perfume (see Song 4:10). *to Sheol.* Cf. 8:19.
57:10 *It is hopeless.* Ironically, the people said that turning away from their own plans or from foreign gods was hopeless. *renewed strength.* Contrast 40:30–31.
57:11 *Of whom . . . worried and fearful.* They feared men (see 51:12). *did not remember Me.* See 51:13. *silent . . . for a long time.* God had not acted in judgment (see 42:14 and note).
57:12 *righteousness.* See 58:2–3; 64:6.
57:13 *idols deliver you.* See 44:17 and note. *wind will carry . . . breath will take.* Idols are no stronger than men. *refuge in Me.* See 25:4. *inherit the land.* See 49:8 and note. *My holy mountain.* See 2:2–4 and note.
57:14 *Build up, build up.* See note on 40:1. *prepare the way.* See 40:3 and note.

15 For thus says the [a]high and exalted
One
Who [1][b]lives forever, whose name is
Holy,
"I [c]dwell *on* a high and holy place,
And *also* with the [d]contrite and lowly
of spirit
In order to [e]revive the spirit of the
lowly
And to revive the heart of the contrite.
16 "For I will [a]not contend forever,
[b]Nor will I always be angry;
For the spirit would grow faint before
Me,
And the [c]breath *of those whom* I have
made.
17 "Because of the iniquity of his [a]unjust
gain I was angry and struck him;
I hid *My face* and was angry,
And he went on [b]turning away, in the
way of his heart.
18 "I have seen his ways, but I will [a]heal
him;
I will [b]lead him and [c]restore comfort
to him and to his mourners,
19 Creating the [1][a]praise of the lips.
[b]Peace, peace to him who is [c]far and
to him who is near,"
Says the LORD, "and I will heal him."
20 But the [a]wicked are like the tossing
sea,
For it cannot be quiet,
And its waters toss up refuse and
mud.
21 "[a]There is no peace," says [b]my God,
"for the wicked."

Observances of Fasts

58 "[a]Cry loudly, do not hold back;
Raise your voice like a trumpet,
And declare to My people their
[b]transgression
And to the house of Jacob their sins.
2 "Yet they [a]seek Me day by day and
delight to know My ways,
As a nation that has done
[b]righteousness
And [c]has not forsaken the ordinance
of their God.
They ask Me *for* just decisions,
They delight [d]in the nearness of God.
3 'Why have we [a]fasted and You do not
see?
Why have we humbled ourselves and
You do not [1]notice?'
Behold, on the [b]day of your fast you
find *your* desire,
And drive hard all your workers.
4 "Behold, you fast for contention and
[a]strife and to strike with a wicked
fist.
You do not fast like *you do* today to
[b]make your voice heard on high.
5 "Is it a fast like this which I choose, a
day for a man to humble himself?
Is it for bowing [1]one's head like a
reed
And for spreading out [a]sackcloth and
ashes as a bed?
Will you call this a fast, even an
[b]acceptable day to the LORD?
6 "Is this not the fast which I choose,
To [a]loosen the bonds of wickedness,
To undo the bands of the yoke,
And to [b]let the oppressed go free
And [c]break every yoke?
7 "Is it not to [a]divide your bread [1]with
the hungry
And [b]bring the homeless poor into the
house;
When you see the [c]naked, to cover
him;
And not to [d]hide yourself from your
own flesh?

15 [1]Or *dwells in eternity* [a]Is 52:13 [b]Deut 33:27; Is 40:28 [c]Is 33:5; 66:1 [d]Ps 34:18; 51:17; Is 66:2 [e]Ps 147:3; Is 61:1-3 **16** [a]Gen 6:3 [b]Ps 85:5; 103:9; Mic 7:18 [c]Is 42:5 **17** [a]Is 2:7; 56:11; Jer 6:13 [b]Is 1:4; Jer 3:14, 22 **18** [a]Is 19:22; 30:26; 53:5 [b]Is 52:12 [c]Is 61:1-3 **19** [1]Lit *fruit of the lips* [a]Is 6:7; 51:16; 59:21; Heb 13:15 [b]Is 26:12; 32:17 [c]Acts 2:39; Eph 2:17 **20** [a]Job 18:5-14; Is 3:9, 11 **21** [a]Is 48:22; 59:8 [b]Is 49:4 **58:1** [a]Is 40:6 [b]Is 43:27; 50:1; 59:12

2 [a]Is 1:11; Titus 1:16 [b]Is 48:1; Jer 7:9, 10 [c]Is 1:4, 28; 59:13 [d]Ps 119:151; Is 29:13; 57:3; James 4:8 **3** [1]Lit *know* [a]Mal 3:14; Luke 18:12 [b]Is 22:12, 13; Zech 7:5, 6 **4** [a]Is 3:14, 15; 59:6 [b]Is 1:15; 59:2; Joel 2:12-14 **5** [1]Lit *his* [a]1 Kin 21:27 [b]Is 49:8; 61:2 **6** [a]Neh 5:10-12; Jer 34:8 [b]Is 1:17 [c]Is 58:9 **7** [1]Lit *for* [a]Job 31:19, 20; Is 58:10; Ezek 18:7, 16 [b]Is 16:3, 4; Heb 13:2 [c]Matt 25:35, 36; Luke 3:11 [d]Deut 22:1-4; Luke 10:31, 32

57:15 *high and exalted One.* See 6:1; 52:13 and notes; cf. 33:5. *contrite.* Or "crushed" (see 53:5).

57:16 *not contend forever.* He had taken Israel to court repeatedly (see 3:13–14). *Nor . . . be angry.* See 54:9 and note; Jer 3:12.

57:17 *hid My face and was angry.* See 54:8; see also 1:15 and note.

57:18 *heal him.* See v. 19; 6:10; 30:26; Jer 3:22. God will forgive and restore His people. *lead.* Cf. 40:11; 42:16; 49:10. *restore comfort.* See 49:13 and note.

57:19 *lips.* Of those mourning the judgment on Jerusalem (see 66:10). *Peace, peace.* Contrast Jer 6:13–14; 8:10–11. *him who is far.* Either Gentiles or exiled Jews. Paul probably had this verse in mind in Eph 2:17.

57:20 *like the tossing sea.* See Jer 49:23. *cannot be quiet.* Contrast v. 2.

57:21 See 39:8; 48:22 and notes.

58:1 *voice like a trumpet.* God's powerful voice is compared to a trumpet blast at Mount Sinai (see Ex 19:19; 20:18–19). *transgression.* See 1:2 and note. *sins.* See 1:4; 59:12–13.

58:2 *seek Me.* See 55:6 and note. Cf. the frequent sacrifices of 1:11. *delight in the nearness of God.* The same hypocrisy is mentioned in 29:13 (see note there).

58:3 *fasted . . . fast.* See v. 6; a time of self-denial and repentance for sin. After the fall of Jerusalem, the number of fast days increased (see Lev 16:29; see also Zech 7:5). *humbled ourselves.* Cf. 2 Chr 7:14; 1 Kin 21:29. *You do not notice.* Note the same attitude in Mal 3:14; cf. Luke 18:12. *drive hard all your workers.* See 3:14–15; 10:2.

58:4 *voice heard on high.* Hypocritical religious activity is a hindrance to prayer (see 1:15; 59:2).

58:5 *like a reed.* A sign of weakness and humility (see 42:3 and note). *sackcloth and ashes.* Cf. 1 Kin 21:27; Jon 3:5–8. *acceptable.* A term often applied to sacrifices (see 56:7; 60:7; Lev 1:3).

58:6 *bonds of wickedness.* During the siege of Jerusalem, Hebrew slaves were rightly released—only to be reclaimed by their masters (see Jer 34:8–11). *yoke.* See v. 9; 9:4; 10:27, where the yoke imposed by Assyria is mentioned. *oppressed.* See 1:17.

58:7 *divide your bread . . . bring . . . house . . . cover.* The outward evidence of genuine righteousness. See Job 31:17–20; Ezek 18:7,16 and Jesus' identification with the hungry and naked in Matt 25:35–36. *flesh.* Probably refers to close relatives (Gen 37:27), but see 2 Sam 5:1.

8 "Then your [a]light will break out like
the dawn,
And your [b]recovery will speedily
spring forth;
And your [c]righteousness will go
before you;
The glory of the [d]LORD will be your
rear guard.
9 "Then you will [a]call, and the LORD will
answer;
You will cry, and He will say, 'Here I
am.'
If you [b]remove the yoke from your
midst,
The [1c]pointing of the finger and
[d]speaking wickedness,
10 And if you [1a]give yourself to the
hungry
And satisfy the [2]desire of the afflicted,
Then your [b]light will rise in darkness
And your gloom *will become* like
midday.
11 "And the [a]LORD will continually guide
you,
And [b]satisfy your [1]desire in scorched
places,
And [c]give strength to your bones;
And you will be like a [d]watered
garden,
And like a [e]spring of water whose
waters do not [2]fail.
12 "Those from among you will [a]rebuild
the ancient ruins;
You will [b]raise up the age-old
foundations;
And you will be called the repairer of
the [c]breach,
The restorer of the [1]streets in which to
dwell.

Keeping the Sabbath

13 "If because of the sabbath, you [a]turn
your foot
From doing your *own* pleasure on My
holy day,
And call the sabbath a [b]delight, the
holy *day* of the LORD honorable,
And honor it, desisting from your
[c]*own* ways,
From seeking your *own* pleasure
And [d]speaking *your own* word,
14 Then you will take [a]delight in the
LORD,
And I will make you ride [b]on the
heights of the earth;
And I will feed you *with* the heritage
of Jacob your father,
For the [c]mouth of the LORD has
spoken."

Separation from God

59 Behold, [a]the LORD's hand is not so
short
That it cannot save;
[b]Nor is His ear so dull
That it cannot hear.
2 But your [a]iniquities have made a
separation between you and your
God,
And your sins have hidden *His* [1]face
from you so that He does [b]not hear.
3 For your [a]hands are defiled with blood
And your fingers with iniquity;
Your lips have spoken [b]falsehood,
Your tongue mutters wickedness.
4 [a]No one sues righteously and [b]no one
pleads [1]honestly.
They [c]trust in confusion and speak lies;
They [d]conceive mischief and bring
forth iniquity.
5 They hatch adders' eggs and [a]weave
the spider's web;
He who eats of their eggs dies,
And *from* that which is crushed a
snake breaks forth.
6 Their webs will not become clothing,
Nor will they [a]cover themselves with
their works;
Their [b]works are works of iniquity,

8 [a]Is 58:10 [b]Is 30:26; 33:24; Jer 30:17; 33:6 [c]Ps 85:13; Is 62:1 [d]Ex 14:19; Is 52:12
9 [1]Lit *sending out* [a]Ps 50:15; Is 55:6; 65:24 [b]Is 58:6 [c]Prov 6:13 [d]Ps 12:2; Is 59:13
10 [1]Lit *furnish* [2]Or *soul* [a]Deut 15:7; Is 58:7 [b]Job 11:17; Ps 37:6; Is 42:16; 58:8
11 [1]Or *soul* [2]Or *deceive* [a]Is 49:10; 57:18 [b]Ps 107:9; Is 41:17 [c]Is 66:14 [d]Song 4:15; Is 27:3; Jer 31:12 [e]John 4:14; 7:38
12 [1]Lit *paths* [a]Is 49:8; 61:4; Ezek 36:10 [b]Is 44:28 [c]Is 30:13; Amos 9:11
13 [a]Ex 31:16, 17; 35:2, 3; Is 56:2, 4, 6; Jer 17:21-27
13 [b]Ps 27:4; 42:4; 84:2, 10 [c]Is 55:8 [d]Is 59:13
14 [a]Job 22:26; Is 61:10 [b]Deut 32:13; 33:29; Is 33:16; Hab 3:19 [c]Is 1:20; 40:5
59:1 [a]Num 11:23; Is 50:2; Jer 32:17 [b]Is 58:9; 65:24; Ezek 8:18
2 [1]So versions; M.T. *faces* [a]Is 1:15; 50:1 [b]Is 58:4
3 [a]Is 1:15, 21; Jer 2:30, 34; Ezek 7:23; Hos 4:2 [b]Is 28:15; 30:9; 59:13
4 [1]Lit *in truth* [a]Is 5:7; 59:14 [b]Is 59:14, 15 [c]Is 30:12; Jer 7:4, 8 [d]Job 15:35; Ps 7:14; Is 33:11
5 [a]Job 8:14
6 [a]Is 28:20 [b]Is 57:12; Jer 6:7

58:8 *light.* The joy, prosperity and salvation brought by the Lord (see 9:2; 60:1–3). *recovery.* See 57:18 and note. *go before you . . . be your rear guard.* See 52:12 and note. The Lord will protect them and guide them. *glory of the LORD.* Probably a reference to the pillar of cloud and fire in the wilderness (see 4:5–6; Ex 13:21; 14:20 and notes).
58:9 *LORD will answer.* See 30:19 and note. *Here I am.* See 65:1. *pointing of the finger.* A gesture of either contempt (see Prov 6:13) or accusation. *speaking wickedness.* See Prov 6:12–14.
58:10 *hungry . . . afflicted.* See vv. 6–7 and notes. *light.* See v. 8 and note.
58:11 *guide you.* See 57:18 and note. *desire.* Both material and spiritual (see note on 32:2). *scorched places.* See 35:7; 49:10. *watered garden.* In 1:30 Jerusalem was a garden without water. *spring . . . not fail.* Cf. the "living water" Jesus gives in John 4:10,14.
58:12 *ancient ruins . . . age-old foundations.* See 44:26,28 and notes; 61:4; Ezek 36:10; Amos 9:11,14. *repairer of the breach.* Cf. the work of Nehemiah in Neh 2:17.
58:13 *sabbath.* See 56:2 and note. *My holy day.* A day set apart to God (see Ex 3:5 and note). *delight.* They were also to delight themselves in the Lord (Ps 37:4) and in His law (Ps 1:2). *your own ways.* Perhaps to engage in business (see Amos 8:5).
58:14 *delight in the LORD.* See 61:10. *ride on the heights.* Thus controlling the land. See 33:16 and note; see also Hab 3:19. *feed you with the heritage.* Enjoying plentiful food in the promised land (see Deut 32:13–14). *mouth . . . has spoken.* See 40:5 and note.
59:1 *hand . . . so short.* See 51:9 and note. *so dull . . . hear.* See 30:19 and note.
59:2 *hidden His face . . . He does not hear.* See 1:15 and note.
59:3–4 *falsehood.* See v. 13; 28:15; Hos 4:2.
59:3 *defiled with blood.* See v. 7; 1:15,21; Ezek 7:23.
59:4 *sues righteously . . . pleads.* The poor and helpless could not receive fair trials (see v. 14; 1:17–23; 5:7,23). *They conceive . . . iniquity.* This statement appears verbatim in Job 15:35. Cf. Is 33:11; Ps 7:14.
59:5 *spider's web.* Verse 6 and Job 8:14–15 stress how fragile it is.

And an [c]act of violence is in their
[1]hands.
7 [a]Their feet run to evil,
And they hasten to shed innocent
blood;
[b]Their thoughts are thoughts of
iniquity,
Devastation and destruction are in
their highways.
8 They do not know the [a]way of peace,
And there is [b]no justice in their tracks;
They have made their paths crooked,
[c]Whoever treads on [1]them does not
know peace.

A Confession of Wickedness

9 Therefore [a]justice is far from us,
And righteousness does not overtake
us;
We [b]hope for light, but behold,
darkness,
For brightness, but we walk in gloom.
10 We [a]grope along the wall like blind
men,
We grope like those who have no eyes;
We [b]stumble at midday as in the
twilight,
Among those who are vigorous *we are*
[c]like dead men.
11 All of us growl like bears,
And [a]moan sadly like doves;
We hope for [b]justice, but there is
none,
For salvation, *but* it is far from us.
12 For our [a]transgressions are multiplied
before You,
And our [b]sins [1]testify against us;
For our transgressions are with us,
And [2]we know our iniquities:

6 [1]Lit *palms* [c]Is 58:4; Ezek 7:11
7 [a]Prov 1:16; 6:17; Rom 3:15-17 [b]Is 65:2; 66:18; Mark 7:21, 22
8 [1]Lit *it* [a]Luke 1:79 [b]Is 59:9, 11; Hos 4:1 [c]Is 57:20, 21
9 [a]Is 59:14 [b]Is 5:30; 8:21, 22
10 [a]Deut 28:29; Job 5:14 [b]Is 8:14, 15; 28:13 [c]Lam 3:6
11 [a]Is 38:14; Ezek 7:16 [b]Is 59:9, 14
12 [1]Lit *answer* [2]Lit *our iniquities we know them* [a]Ezra 9:6; Is 58:1 [b]Is 3:9; Jer 14:7; Hos 5:5
13 [a]Josh 24:27; Prov 30:9; Matt 10:33; Titus 1:16 [b]Is 5:7; 30:12; Jer 9:3, 4 [c]Is 59:3, 4; Mark 7:21, 22
14 [a]Is 1:21; 5:7 [b]Is 46:12; Hab 1:4
15 [1]Or *evil* [a]Is 5:23; 10:2; 29:21; 32:7 [b]Is 1:21-23
16 [a]Is 41:28; 63:5; Ezek 22:30 [b]Ps 98:1; Is 52:10; 63:5
17 [a]Eph 6:14 [b]Eph 6:17; 1 Thess 5:8 [c]Is 63:2, 3 [d]Is 9:7; 37:32; Zech 1:14
18 [1]Lit *recompense* [2]Lit *accordingly* [3]Lit *repay* [a]Job 34:11; Is 65:6, 7; 66:6; Jer 17:10
19 [a]Is 49:12 [b]Ps 113:3

13 Transgressing and [a]denying the LORD,
And turning away from our God,
Speaking [b]oppression and revolt,
Conceiving *in* and [c]uttering from the
heart lying words.
14 [a]Justice is turned back,
And [b]righteousness stands far away;
For truth has stumbled in the street,
And uprightness cannot enter.
15 Yes, truth is lacking;
And he who turns aside from evil
[a]makes himself a prey.

Now the LORD saw,
And it was [1]displeasing in His sight
[b]that there was no justice.
16 And He saw that there was [a]no man,
And was astonished that there was no
one to intercede;
Then His [b]own arm brought salvation
to Him,
And His righteousness upheld Him.
17 He put on [a]righteousness like a
breastplate,
And a [b]helmet of salvation on His head;
And He put on [c]garments of
vengeance for clothing
And wrapped Himself with [d]zeal as a
mantle.
18 [a]According to *their* [1]deeds, [2]so He will
repay,
Wrath to His adversaries, recompense
to His enemies;
To the coastlands He will [3]make
recompense.
19 So they will fear the name of the LORD
from the [a]west
And His glory from the [b]rising of the
sun,

59:6 *act of violence.* See v. 3; Jer 6:7; Ezek 7:11.
59:7–8 Quoted in part in Rom 3:15–17 by Paul to show the universality of sin.
59:7 *Their feet run . . . to shed innocent blood.* This sentence appears in Prov 1:16. *thoughts of iniquity.* God's thoughts are different (see 55:7–9). *Devastation and destruction.* Contrast 60:18.
59:8 *way of peace.* Cf. 26:3,12; 57:20–21; Luke 1:79. *paths crooked.* Unsafe (see Judg 5:6 and note).
59:9 *us . . . We.* The prophet includes himself with the people. *justice . . . righteousness.* Personified here and in v. 14. See v. 4 and note; 1:21. *darkness . . . gloom.* Similar language describes conditions when Assyria invaded Israel (see 5:30; 8:21–22; 9:1–2). Contrast 58:8.
59:10 *We grope . . . like blind men . . . at midday.* The fulfillment of the curse for disobedience in Deut 28:29. Cf. Job 5:14. *vigorous.* Perhaps enemies or oppressors.
59:11 *growl like bears.* Impatient and frustrated.
59:12 *transgressions are multiplied.* See 58:1. *we know our iniquities.* Like Ezra (9:6–7), Isaiah confesses the sins of the nation. In this verse he uses the three most common Hebrew words for evil thoughts and deeds.
59:13 *Transgressing and denying.* See 46:8; 48:8 and notes. *turning away from.* See 1:4. *oppression.* See 30:12. *lying words.* See vv. 3–4.
59:14 *Justice . . . truth.* Cf. the personification of wisdom in Prov 8:1–9:12. *righteousness stands far away.* Cf. v. 9; contrast 46:13 and note.
59:15 *truth.* Restored Jerusalem is called the "City of Truth" in Zech 8:3 (see 1:21 and note). *makes himself a prey.* See 32:7.
59:16 *there was no man.* To help (see 63:5, a parallel to the whole verse). Cf. Ezek 22:30. *astonished.* Cf. the reaction to the servant in 52:14. *intercede.* Cf. the intercession of the servant in 53:12 (see note there). *His own arm brought salvation.* See 51:9; 52:10. For the meaning of salvation see 43:3; 49:8; 52:7 and notes. *righteousness.* For the relationship between righteousness and salvation see 45:8; 46:13 and notes.
59:17 *righteousness like a breastplate.* The Lord's armor is compared to the believer's armor in the battle against Satan in Eph 6:14. *garments of vengeance.* Cf. the blood-spattered garments of 63:1–3. God's vengeance is described also in 34:8 (see note there); 63:4. It is part of the day of the Lord (see 34:2 and note). *zeal.* God's jealous love (see 9:7 and note; 37:32; 42:13).
59:18 *adversaries . . . enemies.* God will judge the nations, but He must also punish wicked Israelites (see 65:6–7; 66:6; Jer 25:29). Only the remnant will be blessed (see v. 20; see also 1:9 and note). *coastlands.* See note on 11:11.
59:19 *name.* See 30:27 and note. *from the west . . . rising of the sun.* All nations will see God's saving work in behalf of His people (see 40:5; 45:6; 52:10 and notes). *rushing stream.* The

For He will [c]come like a [1]rushing
stream
Which the wind of the LORD drives.
20 "A [a]Redeemer will come to Zion,
And to those who [b]turn from
transgression in Jacob," declares
the LORD.

21 "As for Me, this is My [a]covenant with
them," says the LORD: "My [b]Spirit which is
upon you, and My [c]words which I have put
in your mouth shall not depart from your
mouth, nor from the mouth of your [1]off-
spring, nor from the mouth of your [1]off-
spring's offspring," says the LORD, "from
now and forever."

A Glorified Zion

60 "[a]Arise, shine; for your [b]light has
come,
And the [c]glory of the LORD has risen
upon you.
2 "For behold, [a]darkness will cover the
earth
And deep darkness the peoples;
But the LORD will rise upon you
And His [b]glory will appear upon you.
3 "[a]Nations will come to your light,
And kings to the brightness of your
rising.

4 "[a]Lift up your eyes round about and
see;
They all gather together, they [b]come
to you.
Your sons will come from afar,
And your [c]daughters will be [1]carried
in the arms.

5 "Then you will see and be [a]radiant,
And your heart will [1]thrill and rejoice;
Because the [b]abundance of the sea
will be turned to you,
The [c]wealth of the nations will come
to you.
6 "A multitude of camels will cover you,
The young camels of Midian and
[a]Ephah;
All those from [b]Sheba will come;
They will bring [c]gold and
frankincense,
And will [d]bear good news of the
praises of the LORD.
7 "All the flocks of [a]Kedar will be
gathered together to you,
The rams of Nebaioth will minister to
you;
They will go up with acceptance on
My [b]altar,
And I shall [1c]glorify My [2]glorious
house.
8 "[a]Who are these who fly like a cloud
And like the doves to their [1]lattices?
9 "Surely the [a]coastlands will wait for
Me;
And the [b]ships of Tarshish *will come*
first,
To [c]bring your sons from afar,
Their silver and their gold with them,
For the name of the LORD your God,
And for the Holy One of Israel because
He has [1d]glorified you.

10 "[a]Foreigners will build up your walls,
And their [b]kings will minister to you;
For in My [c]wrath I struck you,

19 [1]Lit *narrow* [c]Is 30:28; 66:12 **20** [a]Rom 11:26 [b]Ezek 18:30, 31; Acts 2:38, 39 **21** [1]Lit *seed* [a]Jer 31:31-34; Rom 11:27 [b]Is 11:2; 32:15; 44:3 [c]Is 55:11 **60:1** [a]Is 52:2 [b]Is 60:19, 20 [c]Is 24:23; 35:2; 58:8 **2** [a]Is 58:10; Jer 13:16; Col 1:13 [b]Is 4:5 **3** [a]Is 2:3; 45:14, 22-25; 49:23 **4** [1]Lit *nursed upon the side* [a]Is 11:12; 49:18 [b]Is 49:20-22 [c]Is 43:6; 49:22

5 [1]Lit *tremble and be enlarged* [a]Ps 34:5 [b]Is 23:18; 24:14 [c]Is 61:6 **6** [a]Gen 25:4 [b]Gen 25:3; Ps 72:10 [c]Is 60:9; Matt 2:11 [d]Is 42:10 **7** [1]Or *beautify* [2]Or *beautiful* [a]Gen 25:13 [b]Is 19:19; 56:7 [c]Is 60:13; Hag 2:7, 9 **8** [1]Or *dovecotes, windows* [a]Is 49:21 **9** [1]Lit *beautified* [a]Is 11:11; 24:15; 42:4, 10, 12; 49:1; 51:5; 66:19 [b]Ps 48:7; Is 2:16 [c]Is 14:2; 43:6; 49:22 [d]Is 55:5 **10** [a]Is 14:1, 2; 61:5; Zech 6:15 [b]Is 49:23; Rev 21:24 [c]Is 54:8

---

coming of the Lord will be irresistible, like a "overflowing torrent" that overwhelms the enemy (see 30:28).

59:20 *Redeemer.* See 41:14 and note. *come to Zion.* In the return from exile, but more fully in the person of Christ. See 35:4; 40:9; 52:7 and notes. Cf. Zech 8:3. *those . . . who turn.* See 1:27–28 and note; 30:15; 31:6; Ezek 18:30–32.

59:21 *covenant.* The description fits the "new covenant" best (see 42:6 and note; Jer 31:31–34). *My Spirit.* See 11:2 and note; 32:15; Ezek 36:27; John 16:13. *you . . . your . . . your . . . your. . . your.* In Hebrew the pronouns are singular but are probably intended in a collective sense—the citizens of Zion. *My words . . . in your mouth.* Then Israel will truly be God's people (see 51:16 and note; Jer 31:33). *not depart from your mouth.* See Josh 1:8.

60:1–2 *glory.* Probably an allusion to the pillar of cloud, but announcing a new manifestation of God's redeeming glory (see 58:8 and note). See also 35:2 and note.

60:1 *light.* See 58:8 and note. Here the Lord Himself is viewed as the light (see vv. 19–20).

60:2 *darkness.* A symbol of gloom, oppression and sin (see 8:22; 9:2; 59:9).

60:3 *Nations will come.* See vv. 5,10–12 and notes. This theme was first mentioned in 2:2–4 (see note there). *light.* See 42:6; 49:6 and notes.

60:4 The first two lines are almost identical to the beginning of 49:18, the last two to the end of 49:22 (see note there). The setting there was the return from exile, but here much broader implications are involved. *afar.* See v. 9; 49:12 and note.

60:5 *abundance of the sea.* Jerusalem will be enriched by the nations (see v. 11; 61:6; 66:12; see also 18:7; 23:18; 45:14 and notes). The contribution of King Darius to Zerubbabel's temple may be a partial fulfillment (Ezra 6:8–9). Some interpret this verse as referring to conditions during the future phase of the Messianic kingdom, while others apply it to the influx of Gentiles into the church (see note on 2:2–4). See Rev 21:26 (the new Jerusalem); see also Hag 2:7; Zech 14:14 and notes.

60:6 *camels will cover you.* As caravans bringing goods. Ironically it was on camels that the Midianites once devastated Israel (see 9:4; Judg 6:1–6). *Midian.* Abraham's son through Keturah (Gen 25:2). The Midianites roamed the deserts of Transjordan. *Ephah.* A son of Midian (Gen 25:4). *Sheba.* A wealthy land in southern Arabia, perhaps roughly equal to modern Yemen (see Gen 25:3; 1 Kin 10:1–2). *gold and frankincense.* The queen of Sheba brought gold and spices to Solomon (1 Kin 10:2). Jer 6:20 mentions the incense of Sheba. Cf. Ps 72:10; Matt 2:11. *bear . . . the praises.* Cf. the queen's words in 1 Kin 10:9.

60:7 *flocks of Kedar.* See note on 21:16. *Nebaioth.* The firstborn son of Ishmael (Gen 25:13). The name is probably preserved in that of the later Nabatean kingdom. *minister.* See v. 10; 56:6. *go up with acceptance.* See 56:7; 58:5 and notes.

60:9 *coastlands will wait for Me.* See 11:11 and note. *ships of Tarshish.* See note on 2:16. *bring your sons.* See 49:22 and note. *silver and . . . gold.* Ships of Tarshish had brought these to Solomon every three years (1 Kin 10:22). *Holy One of Israel.* See v. 14; 1:4 and note. *glorified you.* See 55:5 and note.

60:10 *Foreigners . . . kings.* See vv. 12,14; 49:7,23; 61:5. *will build up your walls.* In 445 B.C. King Artaxerxes issued the decree

And in My favor I have had
compassion on you.
11 "Your [a]gates will be open continually;
They will not be closed day or night,
So that *men* may [b]bring to you the
wealth of the nations,
With [c]their kings led in procession.
12 "For the [a]nation and the kingdom
which will not serve you will perish,
And the nations will be utterly ruined.
13 "The [a]glory of Lebanon will come to
you,
The [b]juniper, the box tree and the
cypress together,
To beautify the place of My sanctuary;
And I shall make the [c]place of My feet
glorious.
14 "The [a]sons of those who afflicted you
will come bowing to you,
And all those who despised you will
bow themselves at the soles of your
feet;
And they will call you the [b]city of the
LORD,
The [c]Zion of the Holy One of Israel.

15 "Whereas you have been [a]forsaken and
[b]hated
With no one passing through,
I will make you an everlasting [c]pride,
A joy from generation to generation.
16 "You will also [a]suck the milk of nations
And suck the breast of kings;
Then you will know that I, the LORD,
am your [b]Savior
And your [c]Redeemer, the Mighty One
of Jacob.
17 "Instead of bronze I will bring gold,
And instead of iron I will bring silver,
And instead of wood, bronze,
And instead of stones, iron.
And I will make peace your
administrators
And righteousness your overseers.
18 "[a]Violence will not be heard again in
your land,
Nor [b]devastation or destruction within
your borders;
But you will call your [c]walls salvation,
and your [d]gates praise.
19 "No longer will you have the [a]sun for
light by day,
Nor for brightness will the moon give
you light;
But you will have the [b]LORD for an
everlasting light,
And your [c]God for your [1]glory.
20 "Your [a]sun will no longer set,
Nor will your moon wane;
For you will have the LORD for an
everlasting light,
And the days of your [b]mourning will
be over.
21 "Then all your [a]people *will be* righteous;
They will [b]possess the land forever,
The branch of [1]My planting,
The [c]work of My hands,
That I may be [d]glorified.
22 "The [a]smallest one will become a
[1]clan,
And the least one a mighty nation.
I, the LORD, will hasten it in its time."

Exaltation of the Afflicted

61 The [a]Spirit of the Lord [1]GOD is upon
me,
Because the LORD has anointed me

11 [a]Is 26:2; 60:18; 62:10; Rev 21:25, 26 [b]Is 60:5 [c]Ps 149:8; Is 24:21 **12** [a]Is 14:2; Zech 14:17 **13** [a]Is 35:2 [b]Is 41:19 [c]1 Chr 28:2; Ps 99:5; 132:7 **14** [a]Is 14:1, 2; 45:14, 23; 49:23; Rev 3:9 [b]Is 1:26 [c]Heb 12:22 **15** [a]Is 1:7-9; 6:11-13; Jer 30:17 [b]Is 66:5 [c]Is 4:2; 65:18 **16** [a]Is 66:11 [b]Is 19:20; 43:3, 11; 45:15, 21; 63:8 [c]Is 59:20; 63:16

18 [a]Is 54:14 [b]Is 51:19 [c]Is 26:1 [d]Is 60:11 **19** [1]Or *beauty* [a]Rev 21:23; 22:5 [b]Is 2:5; 9:2 [c]Is 41:16; 45:25; Zech 2:5 **20** [a]Is 30:26 [b]Is 35:10; 65:19; Rev 21:4 **21** [1]Lit *His* [a]Is 45:24, 25; 52:1 [b]Ps 37:11, 22; Is 57:13; 61:7 [c]Is 19:25; 29:23; 45:11; 64:8 [d]Is 61:3 **22** [1]Or *thousand* [a]Is 10:22; 51:2 **61:1** [1]Heb *YHWH,* usually rendered LORD [a]Is 11:2; 48:16; Luke 4:18

allowing Nehemiah to rebuild the walls of Jerusalem (Neh 2:8). Some also apply the rebuilt walls to the building up of the church through Gentile believers (Acts 15:14–16). *in My wrath I . . . had compassion.* See 54:7–8 and notes.

60:11 *gates will be open continually.* As are the gates of the new Jerusalem (Rev 21:25). *wealth.* See v. 5.

60:12 *nation . . . will perish.* Israel's future political domination is referred to also in 11:14; 14:2; 49:23 (cf. vv. 10,14).

60:13 *glory of Lebanon.* Its magnificent cedar trees, which were used in the construction of Solomon's temple, along with pine trees (1 Kin 5:10,18). See also 35:2. The glory of Solomon's era would return. *juniper . . . box . . . cypress.* See 41:19 and note. Perhaps the trees would be ornamental rather than building material. *beautify . . . sanctuary.* See v. 7. *place of My feet.* The temple, and especially the ark of the covenant, God's "footstool."

60:14 *afflicted . . . come bowing.* See 49:7,23 and notes. Cf. vv. 10,12. *the city of the LORD.* Cf. the names for the future Jerusalem in 1:26; 62:4; Ezek 48:35; Zech 8:3; Heb 12:22.

60:15 *forsaken and hated.* See 6:11–12; 62:4; Jer 30:17. *pride . . . joy.* See 4:2 and note.

60:16 *suck the breast of kings.* Jerusalem will receive the very best nourishment, the "wealth of the nations" (v. 5). *Then . . . Jacob.* For this sentence see 49:26 and note.

60:17 *gold . . . silver.* As in Solomon's day gold and silver were plentiful (1 Kin 10:21,27), so the future Jerusalem will have the most valuable metals as well as the strongest (iron). Cf. 9:10. *peace . . . righteousness.* Both are also present in the rule of the Messianic king in 9:7. See note on 48:18.

60:18 *Violence will not be heard.* Cf. 54:14. *devastation or destruction.* See 51:19 and note. *walls salvation.* See 26:1.

60:19 *sun . . . moon.* According to Rev 21:23; 22:5 their light will no longer be needed in the new Jerusalem, since God and the Lamb will be the "everlasting light." *glory.* See vv. 1–2 and note; Zech 2:5.

60:20 *sun will no longer set.* There will be no night there (cf. Rev 22:5) but only the light of joy and salvation (see 58:8 and note). *mourning will be over.* See 25:8; 35:10; 51:11; 65:19; Rev 21:4.

60:21 *people will be righteous.* Only the redeemed will be there (see 4:3; 35:8; Rev 21:27). *possess the land forever.* Enter into full blessing (see 49:8 and note; see also 57:13; 61:7; Ps 37:11,22). *branch of My planting.* Cf. the vineyard of 5:2,7 (see also 11:1). *work of My hands.* God made them as a potter forms clay (see 64:8; see also 29:23; 45:11). *I may be glorified.* They are the evidence of God's redemptive work. See 49:3; 61:3; see also notes on 35:2; 40:5.

60:22 *smallest one will become a clan.* See 51:2; 54:3 and notes. The blessing of Lev 26:8 is similar.

61:1–2 Jesus applied these verses to Himself in the synagogue at Nazareth (see Luke 4:16–21; cf. Matt 11:5).

61:1 *Spirit . . . is upon me.* The statement may refer to Isaiah in

To [b]bring good news to the [2c]afflicted;
He has sent me to [d]bind up the brokenhearted,
To [e]proclaim liberty to captives
And [3]freedom to prisoners;
2 To [a]proclaim the favorable year of the LORD
And the [b]day of vengeance of our God;
To [c]comfort all who mourn,
3 To [a]grant those who mourn *in* Zion,
Giving them a garland instead of ashes,
The [b]oil of gladness instead of mourning,
The mantle of praise instead of a spirit of fainting.
So they will be called [1c]oaks of righteousness,
The planting of the LORD, that He may be glorified.

4 Then they will [a]rebuild the ancient ruins,
They will raise up the former devastations;
And they will repair the ruined cities,
The desolations of many generations.
5 [a]Strangers will stand and pasture your flocks,
And [1]foreigners will be your farmers and your vinedressers.
6 But you will be called the [a]priests of the LORD;
You will be spoken of *as* [b]ministers of our God.
You will eat the [c]wealth of nations,
And in their [1]riches you will boast.
7 Instead of your [a]shame *you will have* a [b]double *portion*,
And *instead of* humiliation they will shout for joy over their portion.

61:1 [2]Or *humble* [3]Lit *opening to those who are bound* [b]Matt 11:5; Luke 7:22 [c]Is 11:4; 29:19; 32:7 [d]Is 57:15 [e]Is 42:7; 49:9
2 [a]Is 49:8; 60:10 [b]Is 2:12; 13:6; 34:2, 8 [c]Is 57:18; Jer 31:13; Matt 5:4
3 [1]Or *terebinths* [a]Is 60:20 [b]Ps 23:5; 45:7; 104:15 [c]Is 60:21; Jer 17:7, 8
4 [a]Is 49:8; 58:12; Ezek 36:33; Amos 9:14
5 [1]Lit *sons of the foreigner* [a]Is 14:2; 60:10
6 [1]Or *glory* [a]Is 66:21 [b]Is 56:6 [c]Is 60:5, 11
7 [a]Is 54:4 [b]Is 40:2; Zech 9:12
7 [c]Ps 16:11
8 [1]Or *with iniquity* [a]Is 5:16; 28:17; 30:18 [b]Gen 17:7; Ps 105:10; Is 55:3; Jer 32:40
9 [a]Is 44:3
10 [a]Is 12:1, 2; 25:9; 41:16; 51:3 [b]Is 49:4 [c]Is 49:18; 52:1 [d]Rev 21:2
11 [1]Heb *YHWH,* usually rendered LORD [a]Is 4:2; 55:10 [b]Is 45:23, 24; 60:18, 21 [c]Ps 72:3; 85:11

Therefore they will possess a double *portion* in their land,
[c]Everlasting joy will be theirs.
8 For I, the LORD, [a]love justice,
I hate robbery [1]in the burnt offering;
And I will faithfully give them their recompense
And make an [b]everlasting covenant with them.
9 Then their offspring will be known among the nations,
And their descendants in the midst of the peoples.
All who see them will recognize them
Because they are the [a]offspring *whom* the LORD has blessed.

10 I will [a]rejoice greatly in the LORD,
My soul will exult in [b]my God;
For He has [c]clothed me with garments of salvation,
He has wrapped me with a robe of righteousness,
As a bridegroom decks himself with a garland,
And [d]as a bride adorns herself with her jewels.
11 For as the [a]earth brings forth its sprouts,
And as a garden causes the things sown in it to spring up,
So the Lord [1]GOD will [b]cause [c]righteousness and praise
To spring up before all the nations.

Zion's Glory and New Name

62 For Zion's sake I will not keep silent,
And for Jerusalem's sake I will not keep quiet,

a limited sense, but the Messianic servant is the main figure intended (cf. what is said of Him in 42:1; see 11:2; 48:16 and notes). *Lord GOD.* See 50:4–5,7,9 and note. *anointed me.* See 45:1 and note. *good news.* See 40:9 and note. *afflicted.* Cf. 11:4; 29:19. *bind up the brokenhearted.* See 30:26 and note. *liberty to captives.* Freedom is used of the year of jubilee in Lev 25:10 (see 49:8 and note). Release from sin has as its background release from Babylon (see 42:7 and note).

61:2 *favorable year of the LORD.* Corresponds to the "day of salvation" in 49:8 (see note there) and the "My year of redemption" in 63:4. Christ ended His quotation at this point (Luke 4:19–20), probably because the "day of vengeance" will not occur until His second coming. *day of vengeance.* See 34:2,8 and notes. *comfort all who mourn.* See 49:13; 57:19 and notes; 66:10; Jer 31:13; Matt 5:4.

61:3 *garland.* A "turban" (as the Hebrew for this phrase is translated in Ezek 24:17) or headdress. In 3:20 the women of Jerusalem were to lose their beautiful headdresses. *oil of gladness.* Anointing with olive oil was common on joyous occasions (see Ps 23:5; 45:7; 104:15; 133:1–2; cf. 2 Sam 14:2). See also 1:6 and note. *mantle of praise.* Contrast the "garments of vengeance" in 59:17. *oaks of righteousness.* Contrast the oaks of 1:30. *planting . . . that He may be glorified.* See 60:21 and note.

61:4 *rebuild the ancient ruins . . . ruined cities.* See 58:12 and note.

61:5 *Strangers . . . foreigners.* See 14:1–2; 56:3; 60:10 and notes.

61:6 *priests of the LORD.* See 66:21. True Israel will be a "kingdom of priests" among the Gentiles (see Ex 19:6 and note). *ministers.* Priests. *wealth of nations.* See 60:5 and note.

61:7 *shame . . . humiliation.* See 45:17; 54:4. *double portion.* The firstborn son received a double share of the inheritance (see Deut 21:17; Zech 9:12). Contrast the "double" punishment Israel received (40:2). *Everlasting joy.* See 35:10; 51:11; cf. Ps 16:11.

61:8 *love justice.* Cf. 30:18; 59:15. *robbery in the burnt offering.* See NASB marg. Israel had been mistreated by her conquerors. Cf. 42:24; 59:18. *everlasting covenant.* Probably the new covenant (see 55:3; 59:21 and notes; cf. Jer 31:35–37; 32:40).

61:9 *offspring whom the LORD has blessed.* See 44:3; 65:23 and the promises to Abraham in Gen 12:1–3.

61:10 Zion is probably the speaker. *garments of salvation.* See v. 3; 52:1 and note. *decks himself with a garland.* Putting on a turban or headband (see note on v. 3). *bride . . . with her jewels.* See 49:18 and note.

61:11 *sprouts . . . spring up.* Cf. 55:10. *righteousness and praise To spring up.* See 45:8 and note.

62:1,6 *I.* The Lord.

62:1 *not keep silent . . . quiet.* See v. 6; 42:14; 57:11 and note;

Until her [a]righteousness goes forth
like brightness,
And her [b]salvation like a torch that is
burning.
2 The [a]nations will see your
righteousness,
And all kings your glory;
And you will be called by a new [b]name
Which the mouth of the LORD will
designate.
3 You will also be a [a]crown of beauty in
the hand of the LORD,
And a royal [1]diadem in the hand of
your God.
4 It will no longer be said to you,
"[1][a]Forsaken,"
Nor to your land will it any longer be
said, "[2]Desolate";
But you will be called, "[3]My delight is
in her,"
And your land, "[4][b]Married";
For the [c]LORD delights in you,
And *to Him* your land will be married.
5 For *as* a young man marries a virgin,
So your sons will marry you;
And *as* the [1]bridegroom rejoices over
the bride,
So your [a]God will rejoice over you.

6 On your walls, O Jerusalem, I have
appointed [a]watchmen;
All day and all night they will never
keep silent.
You who [b]remind the LORD, take no
rest for yourselves;
7 And [a]give Him no rest until He
establishes
And makes [b]Jerusalem a praise in the
earth.
8 [a]The LORD has sworn by His right
hand and by His strong arm,
"I will [b]never again give your grain *as*
food for your enemies;
Nor will [1]foreigners drink your new
wine for which you have labored."
9 But those who [a]garner it will eat it
and praise the LORD;
And those who gather it will drink it
in the courts of My sanctuary.

10 Go through, [a]go through the gates,
Clear the way [1]for the people;
[b]Build up, build up the [c]highway,
Remove the stones, lift up a [d]standard
over the peoples.
11 Behold, the LORD has proclaimed to
the [a]end of the earth,
[b]Say to the daughter of Zion, "Lo,
your [c]salvation comes;
[d]Behold His reward is with Him, and
His recompense before Him."
12 And they will call them, "[a]The holy
people,
The [b]redeemed of the LORD";
And you will be called, "Sought out, a
city [c]not forsaken."

God's Vengeance on the Nations

63 Who is this who comes from [a]Edom,
With [b]garments of [1]glowing colors
from [c]Bozrah,
This One who is majestic in His
apparel,
[2]Marching in the greatness of His
strength?
"It is I who speak in righteousness,
[d]mighty to save."
2 Why is Your apparel red,
And Your garments like the one who
[a]treads in the wine press?

62:1 [a]Is 1:26; 58:8; 61:11 [b]Is 46:13; 52:10
2 [a]Is 60:3 [b]Is 56:5; 62:4, 12; 65:15
3 [1]Lit *turban* [a]Is 28:5; Zech 9:16; 1 Thess 2:19
4 [1]I.e. Azubah [2]I.e. Shemamah [3]I.e. Hephzibah [4]I.e. Beulah [a]Is 54:6, 7; 60:15, 18 [b]Hos 2:19, 20 [c]Jer 32:41; Zeph 3:17
5 [1]Lit *exultation of the bridegroom* [a]Is 65:19
6 [a]Is 52:8; Jer 6:17; Ezek 3:17; 33:7 [b]Ps 74:2; Jer 14:21; Lam 5:1, 20
7 [a]Luke 18:1-8 [b]Is 60:18; Jer 33:9; Zeph 3:19, 20
8 [a]Is 45:23; 54:9
8 [1]Lit *sons of foreigners* [b]Lev 26:16; Deut 28:31, 33; Judg 6:3-6; Is 1:7; Jer 5:17
9 [a]Is 65:13, 21-23
10 [1]Lit *of* [a]Is 26:1; 60:11, 18 [b]Is 57:14 [c]Is 11:16; 19:23; 35:8; 49:11 [d]Is 11:10, 12; 49:22
11 [a]Is 42:10; 49:6 [b]Matt 21:5; Zech 9:9 [c]Is 51:5 [d]Is 40:10; Rev 22:12
12 [a]Deut 7:6; Is 4:3; 1 Pet 2:9 [b]Is 35:9; 51:10 [c]Is 41:17; 42:16; 62:4
63:1 [1]Or *crimson* [2]Lit *Inclining* [a]Ps 137:7; Is 34:5, 6; Ezek 25:12-14; 35:1-15; Obad 1-14; Mal 1:2-5 [b]Is 63:2 [c]Is 34:6; Jer 49:13; Amos 1:12 [d]Zeph 3:17 **2** [a]Rev 19:13, 15

64:12; 65:6; see also Ps 28:1. *righteousness . . . salvation.* See 46:13 and note. *dawn.* Cf. 58:8.
62:2 *nations will see . . . glory.* See 52:10; see also 40:5; 60:3 and notes. *your.* Jerusalem's (see vv. 1,6). *new name.* To reflect a new status (see vv. 4,12; see also 1:26; 60:14; Gen 32:28 and notes).
62:3 *crown of beauty.* In 28:5 the Lord is a "beautiful crown" for His people (cf. Zech 9:16).
62:4 *Forsaken . . . Desolate.* See 54:6–7; 60:15 and note. *My delight is in her.* Also the name of Hezekiah's wife (2 Kin 21:1; Hephzibah means "My delight is in her"). *married.* Israel's relationship with the Lord will be restored. See 50:1 and note.
62:5 *sons will marry you.* The Israelites will again possess the land once deserted. Cf. 54:1. Or the Hebrew for "sons" could be read as "Builder," referring to God (see note on 49:17).
62:6 *watchmen.* Probably those (the prophets especially; see 56:10) waiting for the messenger with good news (see 52:8 and note). *never keep silent.* They will be praying that God will not be silent (see v. 1) but will restore Jerusalem. *take no rest for yourselves.* Cf. David's intense prayer as he searched for a home for the ark (Ps 132:1–5).
62:7 *praise in the earth.* Cf. Jer 33:9; Zeph 3:19–20; see 60:3 and note.
62:8 *has sworn.* Cf. 45:23; 54:9. *strong arm.* See 51:9 and note. *grain . . . for your enemies . . . foreigners drink your new wine.* Punishment Moses warned about in Lev 26:16; Deut 28:33. See also 52:1 and note; Jer 5:17.
62:9 *eat it . . . drink it.* See 65:13,21–23. *in the courts of My sanctuary.* During a festival, or when they brought the tithe to the Lord (Lev 23:39–40; Deut 14:22–26).
62:10 *Go through, go through.* See note on 40:1. *gates.* Probably of Babylon (cf. 48:20; Mic 2:12–13). *Clear the way . . . build up the highway.* See 40:3; 49:11 and notes. *Remove the stones.* See 57:14. *standard.* See 5:26 and note.
62:11 *end of the earth.* See 11:12; 49:6 and notes. *daughter of Zion.* A personification of Jerusalem and its inhabitants. *your salvation comes.* See 40:9 and note; Zech 9:9; Matt 21:5; see also 43:3 and note. *reward . . . recompense.* See 40:10 and note.
62:12 *holy people.* See 4:3; Ex 19:6 and notes. *redeemed.* See 35:9 and note. *Sought out, a city not forsaken.* See v. 4.
63:1 *Edom.* See 21:11; 34:5 and notes. Edom here symbolizes a world that hates God's people. *Bozrah.* See 34:6 and note. *glowing colors.* Cf. Christ's robe "dipped in blood" (Rev 19:13) as He wages war at His second coming. *righteousness, mighty to save.* See 45:8; 46:13; 59:16 and notes.
63:2 *Why . . . ?* Isaiah responds with a question. *treads in the wine press.* See 16:10 and note.

3 "[a]I have trodden the wine trough alone,
And from the peoples there was no
man with Me.
I also [b]trod them in My anger
And [c]trampled them in My wrath;
And [d]their [1]lifeblood is sprinkled on
My garments,
And I [2]stained all My raiment.
4 "For the [a]day of vengeance was in My
heart,
And My year of redemption has come.
5 "I looked, and there was [a]no one to
help,
And I was astonished and there was
no one to uphold;
So My [b]own arm brought salvation to
Me,
And My wrath upheld Me.
6 "I [a]trod down the peoples in My anger
And made them [b]drunk in My wrath,
And I [1]poured out their lifeblood on
the earth."

God's Ancient Mercies Recalled

7 I shall make mention of the
[a]lovingkindnesses of the LORD, the
praises of the LORD,
According to all that the LORD has
granted us,
And the great [b]goodness toward the
house of Israel,
Which He has granted them according
to His [c]compassion
And according to the abundance of
His lovingkindnesses.
8 For He said, "Surely, they are [a]My
people,
Sons who will not deal falsely."
So He became their [b]Savior.
9 In all their affliction [1a]He was afflicted,
And the [b]angel of His presence saved
them;
In His [c]love and in His mercy He
[d]redeemed them,
And He [e]lifted them and carried them
all the days of old.
10 But they [a]rebelled
And grieved His [b]Holy Spirit;
Therefore He turned Himself to
become their enemy,
He fought against them.
11 Then [a]His people remembered the
days of old, of Moses.
Where is [b]He who brought them up
out of the sea with the [1]shepherds
of His flock?
Where is He who [c]put His Holy Spirit
in the midst of [2]them,
12 Who caused His [a]glorious arm to go at
the right hand of Moses,
Who [b]divided the waters before them
to make for Himself an everlasting
name,
13 Who led them through the depths?
Like the horse in the wilderness, they
did not [a]stumble;
14 As the cattle which go down into the
valley,
The Spirit of the [a]LORD gave [1]them
rest.
So You [b]led Your people,
To make for Yourself a glorious name.

"You Are Our Father"

15 [a]Look down from heaven and see
from Your holy and glorious
[b]habitation;
Where are Your [c]zeal and Your mighty
deeds?
The [d]stirrings of Your heart and Your
compassion are restrained toward
me.

3 [1]Lit *juice* [2]Lit *defiled* [a]Rev 14:20; 19:15 [b]Is 22:5; 28:3 [c]Mic 7:10 [d]Rev 19:13
4 [a]Is 34:8; 35:4; 61:2; Jer 51:6
5 [a]Is 59:16 [b]Ps 44:3; Is 40:10; 52:10
6 [1]Lit *brought down their juice to the earth* [a]Is 22:5; 34:2; 65:12 [b]Is 29:9; 51:17, 21
7 [a]Ps 25:6; 92:2; Is 54:8, 10 [b]1 Kin 8:66; Neh 9:25, 35 [c]Ps 51:1; 86:5, 15; Is 54:7, 8; Eph 2:4
8 [a]Ex 6:7; Is 3:15; 51:4 [b]Is 60:16
9 [1]Another reading is *He was not an adversary* [a]Judg 10:16 [b]Ex 23:20-23; 33:14, 15
9 [c]Deut 7:7, 8 [d]Is 43:1; 52:9 [e]Deut 1:31; 32:10-12; Is 46:3
10 [a]Ps 78:40; 106:33; Acts 7:51; Eph 4:30 [b]Ps 51:11; Is 63:11
11 [1]Some mss read *shepherd* [2]Lit *him* [a]Ps 106:44, 45 [b]Is 51:10 [c]Num 11:17, 25, 29; Hag 2:5
12 [a]Ex 6:6; 15:16 [b]Ex 14:21, 22; Is 11:15; 51:10
13 [a]Jer 31:9
14 [1]Lit *him* [a]Josh 21:44; 23:1 [b]Deut 32:12
15 [a]Deut 26:15; Ps 80:14 [b]Ps 68:5; 123:1 [c]Is 9:7; 26:11; 37:32; 42:13; 59:17 [d]Jer 31:20; Hos 11:8

63:3 *trodden the wine trough.* A figure of judgment also in Lam 1:15; Joel 3:13; Rev 14:17–20; 19:15. *in My anger . . . wrath.* The day of the Lord. See v. 6; 13:3; 34:2 and notes.
63:4 *day of vengeance . . . My year of redemption.* See 61:2 and note. The day of judging the enemy meant at the same time redemption for God's people. See 35:9; 41:14 and notes.
63:5 See 59:16 (a parallel to the whole verse) and note. *wrath.* In 59:16 "righteousness" is used. God's righteousness and holiness resulted in His wrath.
63:6 *made them drunk.* They drank the "cup of His anger" (see 51:17 and note). *poured out their lifeblood.* Here the battle is compared to a sacrifice, as in 34:6.
63:7–64:12 A prayer of Isaiah, asking the Lord to bring about the redemption He has promised—as one of the "watchmen" the Lord has posted on the walls of Jerusalem (see 62:6 and note). It is similar to a national lament (see, e.g., Ps 44).
63:7 *lovingkindnesses.* A demonstration of God's unfailing love as He stood true to His covenant with Israel. *great goodness.* Cf. Josh 21:45; 1 Kin 8:66. *compassion.* See 54:7–8,10 and note.
63:8 *My people, Sons who will not deal falsely.* But see 1:2–4. *Savior.* See 43:3 and note.
63:9 *In all their affliction He was afflicted.* The suffering in Egypt and during the period of the judges is probably in view (see Judg 10:16). *angel of His presence.* See Ex 23:20–23; 33:14–15. *redeemed.* See 41:14; 43:1 and notes. *lifted . . . carried.* Like a father (see Deut 1:31; 32:10–12).
63:10 *rebelled.* In the wilderness (see 1:2 and note; 30:1; Num 20:10; Ps 78:40). *grieved His Holy Spirit.* See Ps 106:33; cf. Is 11:1–2; 42:1. *become their enemy.* See 43:28 and note.
63:11 *sea.* The Red Sea (see 50:2 and note; 51:10). *shepherds.* Moses and Aaron (Ps 77:20). *Holy Spirit.* See note on Ps 51:11. The Spirit rested on Moses and 70 elders (Num 11:17,25). See also v. 14.
63:12 *arm.* See 51:9 and note; Ex 15:16. *divided the waters.* See Ex 14:21; cf. 11:15; 51:10. *everlasting name.* See 55:13 and note.
63:13 *depths.* Of the Red Sea (see Ex 15:5,8; Ps 106:9). But the crossing of the Jordan may be intended as well (see v. 14 and note).
63:14 *into the valley.* To find pasture and water. *gave them rest.* They found a home in Canaan, the promised land (see Deut 12:9; Josh 1:13; 21:44).
63:15 *zeal.* See 9:7; 42:13 and notes. *stirrings of . . . heart and . . . compassion.* Cf. Hos 11:8. *restrained.* See 42:14 and note.

16 For You are our [a]Father, though
[b]Abraham does not know us
And Israel does not recognize us.
You, O LORD, are our Father,
Our [c]Redeemer from of old is Your
name.
17 Why, O LORD, do You [a]cause us to
stray from Your ways
And [b]harden our heart from fearing
You?
[c]Return for the sake of Your servants,
the tribes of Your heritage.
18 Your holy people possessed Your
sanctuary for a little while,
Our adversaries have [a]trodden *it*
down.
19 We have become *like* those over
whom You have never ruled,
Like those who were not called by
Your name.

Prayer for Mercy and Help

64 [1]Oh, that You would rend the heavens
and [a]come down,
That the mountains might [b]quake at
Your presence—
2 [1]As fire kindles the brushwood, *as* fire
causes water to boil—
To make Your name known to Your
adversaries,
That the [a]nations may tremble at Your
presence!
3 When You did [a]awesome things which
we did not expect,
You came down, the mountains
quaked at Your presence.
4 For from days of old [a]they have not
heard or perceived by ear,
Nor has the eye seen a God besides
You,
Who acts in behalf of the one who
[b]waits for Him.
5 You [a]meet him who rejoices in [b]doing
righteousness,
Who [c]remembers You in Your ways.
Behold, [d]You were angry, for we
sinned,
We continued in them a long time;
And shall we be saved?
6 For all of us have become like one
who is [a]unclean,
And all our [b]righteous deeds are like a
filthy garment;
And all of us [c]wither like a leaf,
And our [d]iniquities, like the wind,
take us away.
7 There is [a]no one who calls on Your
name,
Who arouses himself to take hold of
You;
For You have [b]hidden Your face from
us
And have [1]delivered us into the power
of our iniquities.

8 But now, O LORD, [a]You are our
Father,
We are the [b]clay, and You our potter;
And all of us are the [c]work of Your
hand.
9 Do not be [a]angry beyond measure,
O LORD,
[b]Nor remember iniquity forever;
Behold, look now, all of us are [c]Your
people.
10 Your [a]holy cities have become a
[b]wilderness,
Zion has become a wilderness,
Jerusalem a desolation.
11 Our holy and beautiful [a]house,
Where our fathers praised You,
Has been burned *by* fire;
And [b]all our precious things have
become a ruin.

16 [a]Is 1:2; 64:8 [b]Is 29:22; 41:8; 51:2 [c]Is 41:14; 44:6; 60:16
17 [a]Is 30:28; Ezek 14:7-9 [b]Is 29:13, 14 [c]Num 10:36
18 [a]Ps 74:3-7; Is 64:11
64:1 [1]Ch 63:19b in Heb [a]Ex 19:18; Ps 18:9; 144:5; Mic 1:3, 4; Hab 3:13 [b]Judg 5:5; Ps 68:8; Nah 1:5
2 [1]Ch 64:1 in Heb [a]Ps 99:1; Jer 5:22; 33:9
3 [a]Ps 65:5; 66:3, 5; 106:22
4 [a]1 Cor 2:9 [b]Is 25:9; 30:18; 40:31
5 [a]Ex 20:24 [b]Is 56:1 [c]Is 26:13; 63:7 [d]Is 12:1
6 [a]Is 6:5 [b]Is 46:12; 48:1 [c]Ps 90:5, 6; Is 1:30 [d]Is 50:1
7 [1]Reading with the DSS and versions; M.T. *melted* [a]Is 59:4; Ezek 22:30 [b]Deut 31:18; Is 1:15; 54:8
8 [a]Is 63:16 [b]Is 29:16; 45:9 [c]Ps 100:3; Is 60:21
9 [a]Is 57:17; 60:10 [b]Is 43:25; Mic 7:18 [c]Ps 79:13; Is 63:8
10 [a]Is 48:2; 52:1 [b]Is 1:7; 6:11
11 [a]2 Kin 25:9; Ps 74:5-7; Is 63:18 [b]Lam 1:7, 10, 11

63:16 *Father.* See 64:8; Deut 32:6. *Abraham does not know.* Even if their human fathers abandon them, God will not (see 49:14–15 and notes). *Redeemer.* See 41:14 and note.
63:17 *cause us to stray.* When Israel went astray (see 53:6), God let them wander. *harden our heart.* The people's hearts were hard (see 6:10; Ps 95:8), and the Lord confirmed that condition (see 6:10; Ex 4:21 and notes). *servants.* True believers (see 54:17 and note).
63:18 *adversaries.* The Babylonians. *trodden it down.* The temple, graphically described in Ps 74:3–7; cf. Is 64:11. Since it was God's sanctuary, His honor was at stake (cf. 48:11).
63:19 *called by Your name.* See 43:7 and note.
64:1 *rend the heavens.* The sky is compared to a tent curtain. For this and the further description of the cosmic effects of God's coming in judgment and redemption see Judg 5:4–5; Ps 18:7–15; 144:5; Nah 1:5; Hab 3:3–7.
64:2 *make Your name known.* See 30:27 and note.
64:3 *awesome things.* See Ps 66:3,5–6.
64:4 *Nor . . . a God besides You.* See 43:11 and note. *waits for Him.* See 30:18; see also 40:31 and note.
64:5 *doing righteousness.* See 56:1. *You were angry.* See 9:12,17,21 and note. God's anger culminated in the exile. *saved.* Or "delivered" (see 43:3 and note).
64:6 *unclean.* Ceremonially unclean, like a person with a terrible disease (see 6:5; Lev 5:2; 13:45). *righteous deeds.* See 57:12 and note. *filthy garment.* The cloths a woman uses during her period, a time when she is "unclean" (see Lev 15:19–24; Ezek 36:17). *wither like a leaf.* A figure used also in 1:30. *like the wind.* Which blows away the chaff (see 17:13; 40:24 and note).
64:7 *no one who calls on Your name.* The Lord urges earnest prayer in times of distress (see, e.g., 2 Chr 7:14). *hidden Your face.* See 1:15 and note.
64:8 *Father.* See 63:16 and note. *clay . . . potter.* See 45:9 and note. *work of Your hand.* See 60:21 and note.
64:9 *Do not be angry.* Cf. the promise to end that anger in 54:7–8 (see notes there). *Nor remember iniquity.* See 43:25 and note; Jer 31:34; Mic 7:18. *Your people.* See 63:17–19; Ps 79:13.
64:10 *holy cities.* Sacred because Israel was the "holy land" (Ps 78:54). Jerusalem is often called the "holy city" (see 48:2 and note). *Zion has become a wilderness . . . desolation.* See 1:7–9 and note; 6:11; Jer 12:11.
64:11 *holy and beautiful house.* See 60:7; 63:15. *burned by fire.* Isaiah here reaches the climax of his lament. See 63:18 and note.

12 Will You [a]restrain Yourself at these
things, O LORD?
Will You keep silent and afflict us
beyond measure?

A Rebellious People

65 "I permitted Myself to be sought by
[a]those who did not ask *for Me;*
I permitted Myself to be found by
those who did not seek Me.
I said, 'Here am I, here am I,'
To a nation which [b]did not call on My
name.
2 "[a]I have spread out My hands all day
long to a [b]rebellious people,
Who walk *in* the way which is not
good, [1]following their own
[c]thoughts,
3 A people who continually [a]provoke
Me to My face,
Offering sacrifices in [b]gardens and
[c]burning incense on bricks;
4 Who sit among graves and spend the
night in secret places;
Who [a]eat swine's flesh,
And the broth of unclean meat is *in*
their pots.
5 "Who say, '[a]Keep to yourself, do not
come near me,
For I am holier than you!'
These are smoke in My [1]nostrils,
A fire that burns all the day.
6 "Behold, it is written before Me,
I will [a]not keep silent, but [b]I will
repay;
I will even repay into their bosom,
7 Both [1]their own [a]iniquities and the
iniquities of their fathers together,"
says the LORD.
"Because they have [b]burned incense on
the mountains
And [c]scorned Me on the hills,
Therefore I will [d]measure their former
work into their bosom."

8 Thus says the LORD,
"As the new wine is found in the
cluster,
And one says, 'Do not destroy it, for
there is [1]benefit in it,'
So I will act on behalf of My
servants
In order [a]not to destroy [2]all of them.
9 "I will bring forth [a]offspring from
Jacob,
And an [b]heir of My mountains from
Judah;
Even [c]My chosen ones shall inherit it,
And [d]My servants will dwell there.
10 "[a]Sharon will be a pasture land for
flocks,
And the [b]valley of Achor a resting
place for herds,
For My people who [c]seek Me.
11 "But you who [a]forsake the LORD,
Who forget My [b]holy mountain,
Who set a table for [1]Fortune,
And who fill *cups* with mixed wine for
[2]Destiny,
12 I will destine you for the [a]sword,
And all of you will bow down to the
[b]slaughter.
Because I called, but you [c]did not
answer;
I spoke, but you did not hear.
And you did evil in My sight
And chose that in which I did not
delight."

12 [a]Ps 74:10, 11, 18, 19; Is 42:14; 63:15
65:1 [a]Rom 9:24-26; 10:20 [b]Is 63:19; Hos 1:10
2 [1]Lit *after* [a]Rom 10:21 [b]Is 1:2, 23; 30:1, 9 [c]Ps 81:11, 12; Is 59:7; 66:18
3 [a]Job 1:11; 2:5; Is 3:8 [b]Is 1:29; 66:17 [c]Is 66:3
4 [a]Lev 11:7; Is 66:3, 17
5 [1]Lit *nose* [a]Matt 9:11; Luke 7:39; 18:9-12
6 [a]Ps 50:3, 21; Is 42:14; 64:12 [b]Jer 16:18
7 [1]Lit *your* [a]Is 13:11; 22:14; 26:21; 30:13, 14
7 [b]Is 57:7; Hos 2:13 [c]Ezek 20:27, 28 [d]Jer 5:29; 13:25
8 [1]Lit *blessing* [2]Lit *the whole* [a]Is 1:9; 10:21, 22; 48:9
9 [a]Is 45:19, 25; Jer 31:36, 37 [b]Is 49:8; 60:21; Amos 9:11-15 [c]Is 57:13 [d]Is 32:18
10 [a]Is 33:9; 35:2 [b]Josh 7:24, 26; Hos 2:15 [c]Is 51:1; 55:6
11 [1]Heb *Gad* [2]Heb *Meni* [a]Deut 29:24, 25; Is 1:4, 28 [b]Is 2:2, 3; 66:20
12 [a]Is 27:1; 34:5, 6; 66:16 [b]Is 63:6 [c]2 Chr 36:15, 16; Prov 1:24; Is 41:28; 50:2; 66:4; Jer 7:13

64:12 *restrain Yourself . . . keep silent.* See 42:14; 57:11; 62:1,6–7 and notes.
65:1–66:24 The grand conclusion to chs. 58–66, as well as to chs. 40–66 and to the whole book.
65:1 *did not ask . . . did not seek.* The Lord now proceeds to answer Isaiah's prayer. Israel failed to stay close to the Lord, though they sought Him in a superficial way (see 55:6; 58:2 and notes). *Here am I.* See 58:9. *did not call on My name.* See 64:7.
65:2 *rebellious people.* See 1:2; 30:1,9 and notes. *their own thoughts.* See 59:7 and note.
65:3 *provoke Me.* By worshiping idols (see Judg 2:12–13). *to My face.* Defiantly (cf. 3:8–9). *gardens.* See 1:29 and note. *burning incense.* As when worshiping the queen of Heaven (see Jer 44:17–19).
65:4 *sit among graves.* Perhaps to consult the dead (see 8:19 and note; 57:9; Deut 18:11). *swine's flesh.* Considered ceremonially unclean (see 66:3,17; Lev 11:7–8).
65:5 *I am holier than you.* Those who engage in pagan rituals believe they are superior to others (cf. the attitude of the Pharisees in Matt 9:11; Luke 7:39; 18:9–12).
65:6 *not keep silent.* The answer to 64:12. *repay.* See 59:18 and note.
65:7 *burned incense on the mountains.* Offered to Baal on the high places (see 57:7; Hos 2:13). *scorned Me.* See Ezek 20:27–28.
65:8 *the cluster.* Israel was a vineyard that had produced bad grapes (5:2,4,7). *servants.* See vv. 9,13–15; 54:17 and note. Here the Lord's servants are equivalent to the remnant (see 1:9 and note).
65:9 *offspring.* See Jer 31:36. *Jacob . . . Judah.* The northern and southern kingdoms respectively. *heir of My mountains.* See 49:8; 60:21 and notes. "Mountains" refers to the whole land, since so much of it was hilly (see Judg 1:9; Ezek 6:2–3). *chosen ones.* See 41:8–9 and note. *inherit.* See 57:13 and note.
65:10 *Sharon.* See 33:9 and note. *valley of Achor.* A valley near Jericho (see Josh 7:24,26; Hos 2:15). Since Sharon and Achor are on the western and eastern edges of the land respectively, they probably represent the whole country. *seek Me.* See v. 1; 51:1 and notes.
65:11 *forsake the LORD.* See 1:4. *holy mountain.* See 2:2–4 and note. *set a table . . . mixed wine.* A meal and drink offering presented to deities. See note on 5:22; cf. v. 3; Jer 7:18. *Fortune . . . Destiny.* The pagan gods of good fortune and fate. See Josh 11:17, where "Gad" may mean "Fortune."
65:12 *sword.* Designed for God's enemies, such as Edom (34:5–6), but the wicked of Israel would also suffer (see 1:20; 59:18 and note; 66:16). *called . . . not answer.* See 50:2 and note; 2 Chr 36:15–16. *chose . . . I did not delight.* Contrast the faithfulness of the eunuchs in 56:4. The last four lines of v. 12 are almost identical to those of 66:4.

13 Therefore, thus says the Lord [1]GOD,
"Behold, My servants will [a]eat, but you will be [b]hungry.
Behold, My servants will [c]drink, but you will be [d]thirsty.
Behold, My servants will [e]rejoice, but you will be [f]put to shame.
14 "Behold, My servants will [a]shout joyfully with a glad heart,
But you will [b]cry out with a [1]heavy heart,
And you will wail with a broken spirit.
15 "You will leave your name for a [a]curse to My chosen ones,
And the Lord [1]GOD will slay you.
But [2]My servants will be called by [b]another name.
16 "Because he who [1]is blessed in the earth
Will [1]be blessed by the [a]God of truth;
And he who swears in the earth
Will [b]swear by the God of truth;
Because the former troubles are forgotten,
And because they are hidden from My sight!

New Heavens and a New Earth

17 "For behold, I create [a]new heavens and a new earth;
And the [b]former things will not be remembered or come to [1]mind.
18 "But be [a]glad and rejoice forever in what I create;
For behold, I create Jerusalem *for* rejoicing
And her people *for* gladness.
19 "I will also [a]rejoice in Jerusalem and be glad in My people;
And there will no longer be heard in her
The voice of [b]weeping and the sound of crying.
20 "No longer will there be [1]in it an infant *who lives but a few* days,
Or an old man who does [a]not [2]live out his days;
For the youth will die at the age of one hundred
And the [3b]one who does not reach the age of one hundred
Will be *thought* accursed.
21 "They will [a]build houses and inhabit *them;*
They will also [b]plant vineyards and eat their fruit.
22 "They will not build and [a]another inhabit,
They will not plant and another eat;
For [b]as the [1]lifetime of a tree, *so will be* the days of My people,
And My chosen ones will [c]wear out the work of their hands.
23 "They will [a]not labor in vain,
Or bear *children* for calamity;
For they are the [1b]offspring of those blessed by the LORD,
And their descendants with them.
24 "It will also come to pass that before
they call, I will [a]answer; and while they are
still speaking, I will hear.
25 "The [a]wolf and the lamb will graze
together, and the [b]lion will eat straw like the
ox; and [c]dust will be the serpent's food.
They will [d]do no evil or harm in all My [e]holy
mountain," says the LORD.

Heaven Is God's Throne

66 Thus says the LORD,
"[a]Heaven is My throne and the earth is My footstool.
Where then is a [b]house you could build for Me?

13 [1]Heb *YHWH*, usually rendered LORD [a]Is 1:19 [b]Is 8:21 [c]Is 41:17, 18; 49:10 [d]Is 5:13 [e]Is 61:7; 66:14 [f]Is 42:17; 44:9, 11; 66:5 **14** [1]Lit *pain of* [a]Ps 66:4; Is 51:11; James 5:13 [b]Is 13:6; Matt 8:12 **15** [1]Heb *YHWH*, usually rendered LORD [2]So with Gr; Heb *He will call His servants* [a]Jer 24:9; 25:18; Zech 8:13 [b]Is 62:2 **16** [1]Or *bless(es) himself* [a]Ex 34:6; Ps 31:5 [b]Is 19:18; 45:23 **17** [1]Lit *heart* [a]Is 66:22; 2 Pet 3:13; Rev 21:1 [b]Is 43:18; Jer 3:16 **18** [a]Ps 98; Is 12:1, 2; 25:9; 35:10; 41:16; 51:3; 61:10 **19** [a]Is 62:4, 5; Jer 32:41 [b]Is 25:8; 30:19; 35:10; 51:11; Rev 7:17; 21:4

20 [1]Lit *from there* [2]Lit *fill out* [3]Lit *one who misses the mark* [a]Deut 4:40; Job 5:26; Ps 34:12 [b]Eccl 8:12, 13; Is 3:11; 22:14 **21** [a]Is 32:18; Amos 9:14 [b]Is 30:23; 37:30; Jer 31:5 **22** [1]Lit *days* [a]Is 62:8, 9 [b]Ps 92:12-14 [c]Ps 21:4; 91:16 **23** [1]Lit *seed* [a]Deut 28:3-12; Is 55:2 [b]Is 61:9; Jer 32:38, 39; Acts 2:39

24 [a]Ps 91:15; Is 55:6; 58:9; Dan 9:20-23; 10:12 **25** [a]Is 11:6 [b]Is 11:7 [c]Gen 3:14; Mic 7:17 [d]Is 11:9; Mic 4:3 [e]Is 65:11
66:1 [a]1 Kin 8:27; Ps 11:4; Matt 5:34, 35; 23:22 [b]2 Sam 7:5-7; Jer 7:4; John 4:20, 21; Acts 7:48-50

65:13 *eat . . . drink.* See 41:17–18; 49:10. *be hungry . . . thirsty.* See 5:13; 8:21. *rejoice.* See 61:7 and note; 66:14. *put to shame.* See 42:17; 44:9,11.
65:14 *shout joyfully.* See 35:10; 54:1 and notes. *broken spirit.* They had refused God's healing. See 61:1 and note.
65:15 *chosen ones.* See v. 9 and note. *for a curse.* The rebellious Israelites will be used as an example when curses are uttered (see Jer 29:22). *another name.* Perhaps the "new name" of 62:2 (see note there).
65:16 *God of truth.* God is true to His promises. The Hebrew word for "truth" here is *amen* (see 2 Cor 1:20; cf. Rev 3:14). *swear by.* See 45:23. Perhaps a contrast is intended with those who took oaths in the name of Baal (see Jer 12:16).
65:17 *new heavens and a new earth.* The climax of the "new things" Isaiah has been promising (see 42:9; 48:6 and notes). *former things.* The "first things" (Rev 21:4), including pain and sorrow.
65:18 *be glad and rejoice.* See 66:10; see also 51:3 and note. *create Jerusalem.* John links the notion of a new heaven and a new earth with the "new Jerusalem" (Rev 21:1–2). A restored Jerusalem after the exile and in the Messianic kingdom pointed toward this greater Jerusalem. See note on 54:11–12.
65:19 *rejoice . . . be glad.* See 62:4–5 and notes. *weeping . . . crying.* See 25:8 and note; 35:10.
65:20–25 See 11:6–9 and note.
65:20 *youth . . . one hundred.* Comparable to the longevity of Adam and his early descendants. See the genealogy of Gen 5 (but see note on Gen 5:5).
65:21–22 Contrast Moses' curse for disobedience in Deut 28:30.
65:21 *plant vineyards.* See 62:8–9.
65:22 *lifetime of a tree.* Compared to the righteous also in Ps 1:3; 92:12–14. *chosen ones.* See 41:8–9 and note. *wear out.* Cf. Ps 91:16.
65:23 *labor in vain.* See 49:4 and note. *calamity.* Such as death or captivity. *those blessed by the LORD.* See 61:9 and note.
65:24 *before they call, I will answer.* See 30:19; 58:9; Matt 6:8.
65:25 *wolf . . . lamb . . . lion.* See 11:6–9 and notes. *dust . . . serpent's food.* See Gen 3:14 and note. The serpent will be harmless (see 11:8). *They . . . mountain.* Identical to the first two lines of 11:9.
66:1 *throne . . . footstool.* See 40:22 and note. *Where then is*

And where is a place that [1]I may rest?
2 "For [a]My hand made all these things,
Thus all these things came into
being," declares the LORD.
"But to this one I will look,
To him who is humble and [b]contrite of
spirit, and who [c]trembles at My
word.

Hypocrisy Rebuked

3 "*But* he who kills an ox is *like* one who
slays a man;
He who sacrifices a lamb is *like* the
one who breaks a dog's neck;
He who offers a grain offering *is like
one who offers* [a]swine's blood;
He who [1b]burns incense is *like* the
one who blesses an idol.
As they have chosen their [c]*own* ways,
And their soul delights in their
[d]abominations,
4 So I will [a]choose their [1]punishments
And will [b]bring on them what they
dread.
Because I called, but [c]no one
answered;
I spoke, but they did not listen.
And they did [d]evil in My sight
And chose that in which I did not
delight."
5 Hear the word of the LORD, you who
[a]tremble at His word:
"Your brothers who [b]hate you, who
[c]exclude you for My name's sake,
Have said, 'Let the LORD be glorified,
that we may see your joy.'
But [d]they will be put to shame.
6 "A voice of uproar from the city, a
voice from the temple,
The voice of the LORD who is
[a]rendering recompense to His
enemies.

7 "Before she travailed, [a]she brought
forth;
Before her pain came, [b]she gave birth
to a boy.
8 "[a]Who has heard such a thing? Who
has seen such things?
Can a land be [1]born in one day?
Can a nation be brought forth all at
once?
As soon as Zion travailed, she also
brought forth her sons.
9 "Shall I bring to the point of birth and
[a]not give delivery?" says the LORD.
"Or shall I who gives delivery shut *the
womb?*" says your God.

Joy in Jerusalem's Future

10 "Be [a]joyful with Jerusalem and rejoice
for her, all you who [b]love her;
Be exceedingly [c]glad with her, all you
who mourn over her,
11 That you may nurse and [a]be satisfied
with her comforting breasts,
That you may suck and be delighted
with her [b]bountiful bosom."
12 For thus says the LORD, "Behold, I
extend [a]peace to her like a river,
And the [b]glory of the nations like an
overflowing stream;
And you will [1]be nursed, you will be
[c]carried on the [2]hip and fondled on
the knees.
13 "As one whom his mother comforts, so
I will [a]comfort you;
And you will be comforted in
Jerusalem."
14 Then you will [a]see *this,* and your
[b]heart will be glad,
And your [c]bones will flourish like the
new grass;
And the [d]hand of the LORD will be
made known to His servants,
But He will be [e]indignant toward His
enemies.
15 For behold, the LORD will come in [a]fire
And His [b]chariots like the whirlwind,

66:1 [1]Lit *is My resting place?*
2 [a]Is 40:26 [b]Ps 34:18; Is 57:15; Matt 5:3, 4; Luke 18:13, 14 [c]Ps 119:120; Is 66:5
3 [1]Lit *offers a memorial of incense* [a]Is 65:4 [b]Lev 2:2; Is 1:13 [c]Is 57:17; 65:2 [d]Is 44:19
4 [1]Lit *ill treatments* [a]Prov 1:31, 32; Is 65:7 [b]Prov 10:24 [c]Prov 1:24; Is 65:12; Jer 7:13 [d]2 Kin 21:2, 6; Is 59:7; 65:12; Jer 7:30
5 [a]Is 66:2 [b]Ps 38:20; Is 60:15 [c]Matt 5:10-12; 10:22; John 9:34; 15:18-20 [d]Luke 13:17
6 [a]Is 59:18; 65:6; Joel 3:7
7 [a]Is 37:3; 54:1
7 [b]Rev 12:5
8 [1]Lit *travailed with* [a]Is 64:4
9 [a]Is 37:3
10 [a]Deut 32:43; Is 65:18; Rom 15:10 [b]Ps 26:8; 122:6 [c]Ps 137:6
11 [a]Is 49:23; 60:16; Joel 3:18 [b]Is 60:1, 2; 62:2
12 [1]Lit *nurse* [2]Lit *side* [a]Ps 72:3, 7; Is 48:18 [b]Is 60:5; 61:6 [c]Is 60:4
13 [a]Is 12:1; 40:1, 2; 49:13; 51:3; 2 Cor 1:3, 4
14 [a]Is 33:20 [b]Zech 10:7 [c]Prov 3:8; Is 58:11 [d]Ezra 7:9; 8:31 [e]Is 10:5; 13:5; 34:2
15 [a]Is 10:17; 30:27, 33; 31:9 [b]Ps 68:17; Is 5:28; Hab 3:8

a house . . . ? Solomon realized that God could not be localized in a man-made temple, magnificent though it may be (1 Kin 8:27).
66:2 *made all these things.* See 40:26 and note. *humble and contrite.* See 57:15 and note.
66:3 Cf. Isaiah's harsh words about ineffective sacrifices in 1:11–14. *breaks a dog's neck.* The dog was "unclean" and not used in offerings. Cf. the law about breaking a donkey's neck in Ex 13:13. *swine's blood.* See 65:4 and note. The dog and pig are mentioned together also in Matt 7:6; 2 Pet 2:22. *blesses an idol.* See 44:19 and note. *abominations.* Probably idols (see Jer 4:1).
66:4 *choose their punishments.* Cf. 65:7. *Because . . . I did not delight.* For these last four lines see 65:12 and note.
66:5 *tremble.* See v. 2. *Your brothers.* Fellow Israelites (see Acts 22:1). *Let . . . joy.* Apparently spoken sarcastically, much like 5:19; Ps 22:8.
66:6 *city.* Probably Jerusalem. *rendering recompense to His enemies.* See 59:18 and note; 65:6–7.
66:7 *Before she travailed.* See 54:1 (and note), where Zion was barren.
66:8 *land . . . born in one day.* See 49:19–20 and note.
66:9 *point of birth.* See 37:3 and note.
66:10 *Be joyful . . . rejoice.* See 65:18 and note. *all . . . who love her.* Cf. Ps 137:6. *who mourn.* See 57:19; 61:2 and notes.
66:11 *nurse and be satisfied.* In 60:16 (see note there) Jerusalem was drinking the milk of nations. Here she is the mother (cf. v. 12; 49:23).
66:12 *peace . . . like a river.* See 48:18 and note. *glory of the nations.* See 60:5 and note. *overflowing stream.* Contrast the destructive flood of 8:7–8 (see note there). *on the hip.* See 40:11.
66:13 *comforted in Jerusalem.* See 49:13 and note. Cf. 2 Cor 1:3–4.
66:14 *heart will be glad.* See 60:5. *grass.* Usually a symbol of weakness. See 37:27 and note; 51:12; but contrast 44:4. *hand of the LORD.* Cf. Ezra 7:9; 8:31. *servants.* See 54:17 and note. *indignant.* See v. 15; 13:3 and note.
66:15–16 *fire.* A figure of judgment (see 1:31 and note; 30:27).
66:15 *chariots like the whirlwind.* See 5:28; 2 Kin 2:11; 6:17; Ps

To render His anger with fury,
And His rebuke with flames of fire.
16 For the LORD will execute judgment by [a]fire
And by His [b]sword on all flesh,
And those slain by the LORD will be many.
17 "Those who sanctify and purify themselves *to go* to the [a]gardens,
[1]Following one in the center,
Who eat [b]swine's flesh, detestable things and mice,
Will [c]come to an end altogether,"
declares the LORD.

18 "For I [1]know their works and their
[a]thoughts; [2]the time is coming to [b]gather all
nations and tongues. And they shall come
and see My glory.
19 "I will set a [a]sign among them and will
send survivors from them to the nations:
[b]Tarshish, [1]Put, [c]Lud, [2]Meshech, Rosh,
[d]Tubal and [3]Javan, to the distant [e]coastlands
that have neither heard My fame nor seen
My glory. And they will [f]declare My glory
among the nations.
20 "Then they shall [a]bring all your brethren
from all the nations as a grain offering to the
LORD, on horses, in chariots, in litters, on
mules and on camels, to My [b]holy mountain
Jerusalem," says the LORD, "just as the sons
of Israel bring their grain offering in a [c]clean
vessel to the house of the LORD.
21 "I will also take some of them for
[a]priests *and* for Levites," says the LORD.

22 "For just as the [a]new heavens and the new earth
Which I make will endure before Me,"
declares the LORD,
"So your [b]offspring and your [c]name will endure.
23 "And it shall be from [a]new moon to new moon
And from sabbath to sabbath,
All [1]mankind will come to [b]bow down before Me," says the LORD.
24 "Then they will go forth and look
On the [a]corpses of the men
Who have [1][b]transgressed against Me.
For their [c]worm will not die
[d]And their fire will not be quenched;
And they will be an [e]abhorrence to all [2]mankind."

16 [a]Is 30:30; Ezek 38:22 [b]Is 65:12; Ezek 38:21
17 [1]Lit *After* [a]Is 1:29; 65:3 [b]Lev 11:7; Is 65:4 [c]Is 1:28, 31
18 [1]So with Gr; Heb omits *know* [2]Lit *it is coming* [a]Is 59:7; 65:2 [b]Is 45:22-25; Jer 3:17
19 [1]So with Gr; Heb *Pul* [2]So with Gr; Heb *those who draw the bow* [3]I.e. Greece [a]Is 11:10, 12; 49:22; 62:10 [b]Is 2:16; 60:9 [c]Ezek 27:10 [d]Gen 10:2 [e]Is 11:11; 24:15; 60:9 [f]1 Chr 16:24; Is 42:12
20 [a]Is 43:6; 49:22; 60:4
20 [b]Is 2:2, 3; 11:9; 56:7; 65:11, 25 [c]Is 52:11
21 [a]Ex 19:6; Is 61:6; 1 Pet 2:5, 9
22 [a]Is 65:17; Heb 12:26, 27; 2 Pet 3:13; Rev 21:1 [b]Is 61:8, 9; 65:22, 23; John 10:27-29; 1 Pet 1:4, 5 [c]Is 56:5
23 [1]Lit *flesh* [a]Is 1:13, 14; Ezek 46:1, 6 [b]Is 19:21, 23; 27:13; 49:7
24 [1]Or *rebelled* [2]Lit *flesh* [a]Is 5:25; 34:3 [b]Is 1:28; 24:20 [c]Is 14:11; Mark 9:48 [d]Is 1:31; Matt 3:12 [e]Dan 12:2

68:17. *anger.* See 34:2; 42:25 and notes. *rebuke.* See 51:20 and note.

66:16 *execute judgment.* The day of the Lord (see note on 2:11,17,20; cf. Ezek 38:21–22). *sword.* See 27:1; 34:6 and note.

66:17 *sanctify and purify themselves.* By special rituals required by their pagan religion. Cf. 2 Chr 30:17. *gardens.* See 1:29 and note. *swine's flesh.* See 65:4 and note.

66:18 *their thoughts.* See 65:2 and note. Wicked Israelites may be the antecedent. *gather all nations.* Cf. Joel 3:2; Zeph 3:8; Zech 14:2. *see My glory.* Usually linked with God's deliverance of His people (see 35:2–4; 40:5 and notes).

66:19 *sign.* Possibly the banner of 11:10,12 (see note on 5:26; cf. Ps 74:4). Cf. the "sign of the Son of Man" (Matt 24:30) at the second coming. *survivors.* After the judgment of v. 16. Cf. Zech 14:16. *Tarshish.* See 23:6 and note. *Put.* People who lived west of Egypt (in Lybia). See Nah 3:9. *Lud.* People from either west-central Asia Minor (see Gen 10:13 and note) or Africa. *Tubal.* Usually mentioned with Meshech (see Gen 10:2 and note; Ezek 27:13; 38:2–3; 39:1). It was probably a region southeast of the Black Sea. *coastlands.* See 11:11 and note. *declare My glory.* See 42:12; 1 Chr 16:24.

66:20 *bring all your brethren.* Gentiles will bring back the remnant (see 11:11–12; 49:22; 60:4 and notes). *holy mountain.* See 2:2–4 and note. *grain offering . . . to the house of the LORD.* As the Israelites were to bring their tithes and offerings (see Deut 12:5–7).

66:21 *some of them.* A reference either to believing Jews (see 61:6 and note) or to Gentiles as part of the church or Messianic kingdom (see 1 Pet 2:5,9 and notes).

66:22 *new heavens . . . new earth.* See 65:17 and note. *offspring . . . name will endure.* See 48:19 and note.

66:23 *new moon.* See 1:14 and note. *All mankind . . . bow down.* See 19:21; Zech 14:16 and notes.

66:24 Quoted in part in Mark 9:48. *go forth and look.* The Valley of Hinnom (Hebrew *ge' hinnom,* from which the word "Gehenna" comes) was located southwest of Jerusalem and became a picture of hell. See Neh 11:30; Jer 7:32. *corpses.* See 5:25; 34:3. *transgressed.* See 1:2 and note; 24:20. *worm will not die.* There will be everlasting torment. See 14:11; 48:22; 50:11; 57:21. *fire . . . quenched.* See 1:31 and note; Matt 3:12. *abhorrence.* The Hebrew for this word is translated "contempt" in Dan 12:2.

Jeremiah

INTRODUCTION

Author and Date

The book preserves an account of the prophetic ministry of Jeremiah, whose personal life and struggles are known to us in greater depth and detail than those of any other OT prophet. The meaning of his name is uncertain. Suggestions include "The LORD exalts" and "The LORD establishes," but a more likely proposal is "The LORD throws," either in the sense of "hurling" the prophet into a hostile world or of "throwing down" the nations in divine judgment for their sins. Jeremiah's prophetic ministry began in 626 B.C. and ended sometime after 586 (see notes on 1:2 – 3). His ministry was immediately preceded by that of Zephaniah. Habakkuk was a contemporary, and Obadiah may have been also. Since Ezekiel began his ministry in Babylon in 593 he too was a late contemporary of the great prophet in Jerusalem. How and when Jeremiah died is not known; Jewish tradition, however, asserts that while living in Egypt he was put to death by being stoned (cf. Heb 11:37).

Jeremiah was a priest, a member of the household of Hilkiah. His hometown was Anathoth (1:1), so he may have been a descendant of Abiathar (1 Kin 2:26), a priest during the days of King Solomon. The Lord commanded Jeremiah not to marry and raise children because the impending divine judgment on Judah would sweep away the next generation (16:1 – 4). Primarily a prophet of doom, he attracted only a few friends, among whom were Ahikam (26:24), Gedaliah (Ahikam's son, 39:14) and Ebed-melech (38:7 – 13; cf. 39:15 – 18). Jeremiah's closest companion was his faithful secretary, Baruch, who wrote down Jeremiah's words as the prophet dictated them (36:4 – 32). He was advised by Jeremiah not to succumb to the temptations of ambition but to be content with his lot (ch. 45). He also received from Jeremiah and deposited for safekeeping a deed of purchase (32:11 – 16), and accompanied the prophet on the long road to exile in Egypt (43:6 – 7). It is possible that Baruch was also responsible for the final compilation of the book of Jeremiah itself, since no event recorded in chs. 1 — 51 occurred after 580 B.C. (ch. 52 is an appendix added by a later hand).

Given to self-analysis and self-criticism (10:24), Jeremiah has revealed a great deal about his character and personality. Although timid by nature (1:6), he received the Lord's assurance that he would become strong and courageous (1:18; 6:27; 15:20). In his "confessions" (11:18 – 23; 12:1 – 4; 15:10 – 21; 17:12 – 18; 18:18 – 23; 20:7 – 18) he laid bare the deep struggles of his inmost being, sometimes making startlingly honest statements about his feelings toward God (12:1; 15:18). On occasion, he engaged in calling for redress against his personal enemies (12:1 – 3; 15:15; 17:18; 18:19 – 23) — a practice that explains the origin of the English word "jeremiad," referring to a denunciatory tirade or complaint. Jeremiah, so often characterized by anguish of spirit (4:19; 9:1; 10:19 – 20; 23:9), has justly been called the "weeping prophet." But it is also true that the memory of his divine call (1:17) and the Lord's frequent reaffirmations of his commissioning as a prophet (see, e.g., 3:12; 7:2,27 – 28; 11:2,6; 13:12 – 13; 17:19 – 20) made Jeremiah fearless in the service of his God (cf. 15:20).

Background

Jeremiah began prophesying in Judah halfway through the reign of Josiah (640 – 609 B.C.) and continued throughout the reigns of Jehoahaz (609), Jehoiakim (609 – 598), Jehoiachin (598 – 597) and Zedekiah (597 – 586). It was a period of storm and stress when the doom of entire nations — including Judah itself — was being sealed. The smaller states of western Asia were often pawns in the power plays of such imperial giants as Egypt, Assyria and Babylon, and the time of Jeremiah's ministry was no exception. Ashurbanipal, last of the great Assyrian rulers, died in 627. His successors were no match for Nabopolassar, the founder of the Neo-Babylonian empire, who began his rule in 626 (the year of Jeremiah's call to prophesy). Soon after Assyria's capital city Nineveh fell under the onslaught of a coalition of Babylonians and Medes in 612, Egypt (no friend of Babylon) marched northward in an attempt to rescue Assyria, which was near destruction. King Josiah of Judah made the mistake of trying to stop the Egyptian advance, and his untimely death near Megiddo

in 609 at the hands of Pharaoh Neco II was the sad result (2 Chr 35:20–24). Jeremiah, who had found a kindred spirit in the godly Josiah and had perhaps proclaimed the messages recorded in 11:1–8; 17:19–27 during the king's reformation movement, lamented Josiah's death (2 Chr 35:25).

Josiah's son Jehoahaz (his throne name; note on 22:11), also known as Shallum, is mentioned only briefly in the book of Jeremiah (22:10b-12), and then in an unfavorable way. Neco put Jehoahaz in chains and made Eliakim, another of Josiah's sons, king in his place, renaming him Jehoiakim. Jehoahaz had ruled for a scant three months (2 Chr 36:2), and his reign marks the turning point in the court's attitude toward Jeremiah. Once the king's friend and confidant, the prophet now entered a dreary round of persecution and imprisonment, alternating with only brief periods of freedom (20:1–2; 26:8–9; 32:2–3; 33:1; 36:26; 37:12–21; 38:6–13,28).

Jehoiakim was relentlessly hostile toward Jeremiah. On one occasion, when an early draft of the prophet's writings was being read to Jehoiakim (36:21), the king used a scribe's knife to cut the scroll apart, three or four columns at a time, and threw it piece by piece into the firepot in his winter apartment (vv. 22–23). At the Lord's command, however, Jeremiah simply dictated his prophecies to Baruch a second time, adding "many similar words" to them (v. 32).

Just prior to this episode in Jeremiah's life, an event of extraordinary importance took place that changed the course of history: In 605 B.C., the Egyptians were crushed at Carchemish on the Euphrates by Nebuchadnezzar (46:2), the gifted general who succeeded his father Nabopolassar as ruler of Babylon that same year. Neco returned to Egypt with heavy losses, and Babylon was given a virtually free hand in western Asia for the next 70 years. Nebuchadnezzar besieged Jerusalem in 605, humiliating Jehoiakim (Dan 1:1–2) and carrying off Daniel and his three companions to Babylon (Dan 1:3–6). Later, in 598–597, Nebuchadnezzar attacked Jerusalem again, and the rebellious Jehoiakim was heard of no more. His son Jehoiachin ruled Judah for only three months (2 Chr 36:9). Jeremiah foretold the captivity of Jehoiachin and his followers (22:24–30), a prediction that was later fulfilled (24:1; 29:1–2).

Mattaniah, Jehoiachin's uncle and a son of Josiah, was renamed Zedekiah and placed on Judah's throne by Nebuchadnezzar in 597 B.C. (37:1; 2 Chr 36:9–14). Zedekiah, a weak and vacillating ruler, sometimes befriended Jeremiah and sought his advice but at other times allowed the prophet's enemies to mistreat and imprison him. Near the end of Zedekiah's reign, Jeremiah entered into an agreement with him to reveal God's will to him in exchange for his own personal safety (38:15–27). Even then the prophet was under virtual house arrest until Jerusalem was captured in 586 (38:28).

While trying to flee the city, Zedekiah was overtaken by the pursuing Babylonians. In his presence his sons were executed, after which he himself was blinded by Nebuchadnezzar (39:1–7). Nebuzaradan, commander of the imperial guard, advised Jeremiah to live with Gedaliah, whom Nebuchadnezzar had made governor over Judah (40:1–6). After a brief reign, Gedaliah was murdered by his opponents (ch. 41). Others in Judah feared Babylonian reprisal and fled to Egypt, taking Jeremiah and Baruch with them (43:4–7). By that time the prophet was probably over 70 years old. His last recorded words are found in 44:24–30, the last verse of which is the only explicit reference in the Bible to Pharaoh Hophra, who ruled Egypt from 589 to 570 B.C.

Themes and Message

Referred to frequently as "Jeremiah the prophet" in the book that bears his name (20:2; 25:2; 28:5,10–12,15; 29:1,29; 32:2; 34:6; 36:8,26; 37:2,3,6; 38:9–10,14; 42:2,4; 43:6; 45:1; 46:1,13; 47:1; 49:34; 50:1) and elsewhere (2 Chr 36:12; Dan 9:2; Matt 2:17; 27:9; see Matt 16:14), Jeremiah was ever conscious of his call from the Lord (1:5; 15:19) to be a prophet. As such, he proclaimed words that were spoken first by God Himself (19:2) and were therefore certain of fulfillment (28:9; 32:24). Jeremiah had only contempt for false prophets (14:13–18; 23:13–40; 27:14–18) like Hananiah (ch. 28) and Shemaiah (29:24–32). Many of his own predictions were fulfilled in the short term (e.g., 16:15; 20:4; 25:11–14; 27:19–22; 29:10; 34:4–5; 43:10–11; 44:30; 46:13), and others were—or will yet be—fulfilled in the long term (e.g., 23:5–6; 30:8–9; 31:31–34; 33:15–16).

As hinted earlier, an aura of conflict surrounded Jeremiah almost from the beginning. He lashed out against the sins of his countrymen (44:23), scoring them severely for their idolatry (16:10–13,20; 22:9; 32:29; 44:2–3,8,17–19,25)—which sometimes even involved sacrificing their children to foreign gods (7:30–34). But Jeremiah loved the people of Judah in spite of their sins, and he prayed for them (14:7,20) even when the Lord told him not to (7:16; 11:14; 14:11).

Judgment is one of the all-pervasive themes in Jeremiah's writings, though he was careful to point out that repentance, if sincere, would postpone the inevitable. His counsel of submission to Babylon and his message of "life as usual" for the exiles of the early deportations branded him as a traitor in the eyes of many. Actually, of course, his advice against rebellion marked him as a true patriot, a man who loved his countrymen too much to stand by silently and watch them destroy themselves. By warning them to submit and not rebel, Jeremiah was revealing God's will to them — always the most sensible prospect under any circumstances.

For Jeremiah, God was ultimate. The prophet's theology conceived of the Lord as the Creator of all that exists (10:12 – 16; 51:15 – 19), as all-powerful (32:27; 48:15; 51:57), as everywhere present (23:24). Jeremiah ascribed the most elevated attributes to the God whom he served (32:17 – 25), viewing Him as the Lord not only of Judah but also of the nations (5:15; 18:7 – 10; 25:17 – 28; chs. 46 — 51).

At the same time, God is very much concerned about individual people and their accountability to Him. Jeremiah's emphasis in this regard (see, e.g., 31:29 – 30) is similar to that of Ezekiel (see Ezek 18:2 – 4), and the two men have become known as the "prophets of individual responsibility." The undeniable relationship between sin and its consequences, so visible to Jeremiah as he watched his beloved Judah in her death throes, made him — in the pursuit of his divine vocation — a fiery preacher (5:14; 20:9; 23:29) of righteousness, and his oracles have lost none of their power with the passing of the centuries.

Called to the unhappy task of announcing the destruction of the kingdom of Judah (thoroughly corrupted by the long and evil reign of Manasseh and only superficially affected by Josiah's efforts at reform), it was Jeremiah's commission to lodge God's indictment against His people and proclaim the end of an era. At long last, the Lord was about to inflict on the remnant of His people the ultimate covenant curse (see Lev 26:31 – 33; Deut 28:49 – 68). He would undo all that He had done for them since the day He brought them out of Egypt. It would then seem that the end had come, that Israel's stubborn and uncircumcised (unconsecrated) heart had sealed her final destiny, that God's chosen people had been cast off, that all the ancient promises and covenants had come to nothing.

But God's judgment of His people (and the nations), though terrible, was not to be the last word, the final work of God in history. Mercy and covenant faithfulness would triumph over wrath. Beyond the judgment would come restoration and renewal. Israel would be restored, the nations that crushed her would be crushed, and the old covenants (with Israel, David and the Levites) would be honored. God would make a new covenant with His people in which He would write His law on their hearts (31:31 – 34) and thus consecrate them to His service. The house of David would rule them in righteousness, and faithful priests would serve. God's commitment to Israel's redemption was as unfailing as the secure order of creation (ch. 33).

Jeremiah's message illumined the distant as well as the near horizon. It was false prophets who proclaimed peace to a rebellious nation, as though the God of Israel's peace was indifferent to her unfaithfulness. But the very God who compelled Jeremiah to denounce sin and pronounce judgment was the God who authorized him to announce that the divine wrath had its bounds, its 70 years. Afterward forgiveness and cleansing would come — and a new day, in which all the old expectations, aroused by God's past acts and His promises and covenants, would yet be fulfilled in a manner transcending all God's mercies of old.

Literary Features

Jeremiah is the longest book in the Bible, containing more words than any other book. Although a number of chapters were written mainly in prose (chs. 7; 11; 16; 19; 21; 24 — 29; 32 — 45), including the appendix (ch. 52), most sections are predominantly poetic in form. Jeremiah's poetry is as lofty and lyrical as any found elsewhere in Scripture. A creator of beautiful phrases, he has given us an abundance of memorable passages (e.g., 2:13,26 – 28; 7:4,11,34; 8:20,22; 9:23 – 24; 10:6 – 7,10,12 – 13; 13:23; 15:20; 17:5 – 9; 20:13; 29:13; 30:7,22; 31:3,15,29 – 30,31 – 34; 33:3; 51:10).

Poetic repetition was used by Jeremiah with particular skill (see, e.g., 4:23 – 26; 51:20 – 23). He understood the effectiveness of repeating a striking phrase over and over. An example is "sword, famine and pestilence," found in 15 separate verses (14:12; 21:7,9; 24:10; 27:8,13; 29:17 – 18; 32:24,36; 34:17; 38:2; 42:17,22; 44:13). He made use of cryptograms (see NASB marg. notes on 25:26; 51:1,41) on appropriate occasions. Alliteration and

assonance were also a part of his literary style, examples being *zarim wezeruha* ("foreigners ... winnow her," 51:2) and *paḥad wapaḥat wapaḥ* ("Terror, pit and snare," 48:43; see note on Is 24:17).

Like Ezekiel, Jeremiah was often instructed to use symbolism to highlight his message: a ruined and useless belt (13:1–11), a smashed clay jar (19:1–12), a yoke of straps and crossbars (ch. 27), large stones in a brick pavement (43:8–13). Symbolic value is also seen in the Lord's commands to Jeremiah not to marry and raise children (16:1–4), not to enter a house where there is a funeral meal or where there is feasting (16:5–9), and to buy a field in his hometown, Anathoth (32:6–15). Similarly, the Lord used visual aids in conveying his message to Jeremiah: potter's clay (18:1–10), two baskets of figs (ch. 24).

Outline

Unlike Ezekiel, the oracles in Jeremiah are not arranged in chronological order. Had they been so arranged, the sequence of sections within the book would have been approximately as follows: 1:1—7:15; ch. 26; 7:16—20:18; ch. 25; chs. 46—51; 36:1–8; ch. 45; 36:9–32; ch. 35; chs. 21—24; chs. 27—31; 34:1–7; 37:1–10; 34:8–22; 37:11—38:13; 39:15–18; chs. 32–33; 38:14—39:14; 52:1–30; chs. 40—44; 52:31–34. The outline below represents an analysis of the book of Jeremiah in its present canonical order.

- I. Call of the Prophet (ch. 1)
- II. Warnings and Exhortations to Judah (chs. 2—35)
  - A. Earliest Discourses (chs. 2—6)
  - B. Temple Message (chs. 7—10)
  - C. Covenant and Conspiracy (chs. 11—13)
  - D. Messages concerning the Drought (chs. 14—15)
  - E. Disaster and Comfort (16:1—17:18)
  - F. Command to Keep the Sabbath Holy (17:19–27)
  - G. Lessons from the Potter (chs. 18—20)
  - H. Condemnation of Kings, Prophets and People (chs. 21—24)
  - I. Foretelling the Babylonian Exile (chs. 25—29)
  - J. Promises of Restoration (chs. 30—33)
  - K. Historical Appendix (chs. 34—35)
- III. Sufferings and Persecutions of the Prophet (chs. 36—38)
  - A. Burning Jeremiah's Scroll (ch. 36)
  - B. Imprisoning Jeremiah (chs. 37—38)
- IV. The Fall of Jerusalem and Its Aftermath (chs. 39—45)
  - A. The Fall Itself (ch. 39)
  - B. Accession and Assassination of Gedaliah (40:1—41:15)
  - C. Migration to Egypt (41:16—43:13)
  - D. Prophecy against Those in Egypt (ch. 44)
  - E. Historical Appendix: Promise to Baruch (ch. 45)
- V. Judgment against the Nations (chs. 46—51)
  - A. Against Egypt (ch. 46)
  - B. Against Philistia (ch. 47)
  - C. Against Moab (ch. 48)
  - D. Against Ammon (49:1–6)
  - E. Against Edom (49:7–22)
  - F. Against Damascus (49:23–27)
  - G. Against Kedar and Hazor (Arabia) (49:28–33)
  - H. Against Elam (49:34–39)
  - I. Against Babylon (chs. 50—51)
- VI. Historical Appendix (ch. 52)

Jeremiah's Call and Commission

1 The words of [a]Jeremiah the son of Hilkiah, of the priests who were in [b]Anathoth in the land of Benjamin,

2 to whom the word of the LORD came in the days of [a]Josiah the son of [b]Amon, king of Judah, in the [c]thirteenth year of his reign.

3 It came also in the days of [a]Jehoiakim the son of Josiah, king of Judah, until the end of the eleventh year of [b]Zedekiah the son of Josiah, king of Judah, until the exile of Jerusalem in the fifth month.

4 Now the word of the LORD came to me saying,

5 "Before I [a]formed you in the womb I
knew you,
And [b]before you were born I
consecrated you;
I have [c]appointed you a prophet to the
nations."

6 Then [a]I said, "Alas, Lord [1]GOD!
Behold, I do not know how to speak,
Because [b]I am a youth."

7 But the LORD said to me,
"Do not say, 'I am a youth,'
[a]Because everywhere I send you, you
shall go,
And [b]all that I command you, you
shall speak.

8 "[a]Do not be afraid of them,
For [b]I am with you to deliver you,"
declares the LORD.

9 Then the LORD stretched out His hand and [a]touched my mouth, and the LORD said to me,
"Behold, I have [b]put My words in your
mouth.

10 "See, [a]I have appointed you this day
over the nations and over the
kingdoms,
[b]To pluck up and to break down,
To destroy and to overthrow,
[c]To build and to plant."

1:1 [a]2 Chr 35:25; 36:12, 21, 22; Ezra 1:1; Dan 9:2; Matt 2:17; 16:14; 27:9 [b]Josh 21:18; 1 Kin 2:26; 1 Chr 6:60; Is 10:30; Jer 11:21; 32:7
2 [a]1 Kin 13:2; 2 Kin 21:24; 22:3; 2 Chr 34:1; Jer 3:6; 36:2 [b]2 Kin 21:18, 24 [c]Jer 25:3
3 [a]2 Kin 23:34; 1 Chr 3:15; 2 Chr 36:5-8; Jer 25:1 [b]2 Kin 24:17; 1 Chr 3:15; 2 Chr 36:11-13; Jer 39:2
5 [a]Ps 139:15, 16 [b]Is 49:1, 5; Luke 1:15 [c]Jer 1:10; 25:15-26
6 [1]Heb *YHWH,* usually rendered *LORD* [a]Ex 4:10 [b]1 Kin 3:7
7 [a]Ezek 2:3, 4 [b]Num 22:20; Jer 1:17
8 [a]Ex 3:12; Deut 31:6; Josh 1:5; Jer 15:20 [b]Ezek 2:6
9 [a]Is 6:7; Mark 7:33-35 [b]Ex 4:11-16; Deut 18:18; Is 51:16
10 [a]Rev 11:3-6 [b]Jer 18:7-10; Ezek 32:18; 2 Cor 10:4 [c]Is 44:26-28; Jer 24:6; 31:28, 40

1:1–3 The background and setting of Jeremiah's call are stated concisely but comprehensively.

1:1 *The words of.* See 36:10; see also Neh 1:1; Eccl 1:1; Amos 1:1; cf. Deut 1:1. *Jeremiah.* For the meaning of the name see Introduction: Author and Date. Nine other OT men had the same name (see 1 Chr 5:24; 12:4,10,13; Neh 10:2; 12:1,34), two of whom were the prophet's contemporaries (Jer 35:3; 52:1). *Hilkiah.* Means "The LORD is my portion." For Hilkiah's possible relationship to a priestly house dating back to King Solomon see Introduction: Author and Date. Two other men named Hilkiah (a common OT name) were also Jeremiah's contemporaries (see 29:3; Ezra 7:1 and note). *priests.* Like Ezekiel (Ezek 1:3) and Zechariah (see Introduction to Zechariah: Author), Jeremiah was both prophet and priest. *Anathoth.* See 11:21–23; 32:6–9. The Hebrew word is the plural form of the name of the Canaanite deity Anat(h), goddess of war. Anathoth had had priestly connections in Israel as early as the times of Joshua (Josh 21:18) and Solomon (1 Kin 2:26), and its pagan origins had presumably been almost forgotten by Jeremiah's time. Present-day Anata, three miles northeast of Jerusalem, preserves the ancient name, though the ancient site was about half a mile southwest of Anata. *Benjamin.* Anathoth was one of the four Levitical towns in the tribal territory of Benjamin (Josh 21:17–18), and after the exile Benjamites settled there again (Neh 11:31–32).

1:2 *to whom.* Beginning in v. 4, Jeremiah speaks in the first person (see, e.g., vv. 11,13; 2:1). *the word of the LORD came.* The most common way of introducing a divine oracle at the beginning of a prophetic book (see Ezek 1:3; Jon 1:1; Hag 1:1; Zech 1:1; cf. Hos 1:1; Joel 1:1; Mic 1:1; Zeph 1:1). *Josiah.* See 3:6; 36:2. He was the last good and godly king of Judah. Jeremiah sympathized with and supported his attempts at spiritual reformation and renewal (see 22:15b–16), which began in earnest in 621 (see 2 Kin 22:3–23:25; 2 Chr 34:8–35:19; cf. 2 Chr 34:3–7). *thirteenth year.* 626 B.C. (see 25:3).

1:3 *Jehoiakim.* His predecessor (Jehoahaz) and successor (Jehoiachin) are not mentioned, since they each reigned only three months. In contrast to his father Josiah, Jehoiakim was a wicked ruler (see 2 Kin 23:36–37; 2 Chr 36:5)—as Jeremiah discovered almost immediately (see Introduction: Background; see also 22:13–15a,17–19; 26:20–23). *eleventh year . . . in the fifth month.* Ab (July-August), 586 B.C. (see 52:12). *Zedekiah.* The last king of Judah (see Introduction: Background), as wicked in his own way as Jehoiakim (see 52:1–2; 2 Chr 36:11–14; see also Jer 24:8; 37:1–2). *exile.* The main captivity of Judah's people coincided with the destruction of Jerusalem and Solomon's temple by Nebuchadnezzar in 586 (see 2 Kin 25:8–11).

1:4–19 The account of Jeremiah's call includes two prophetic visions (vv. 10–16) and some closing words of exhortation and encouragement (vv. 17–19).

1:4 See note on v. 2.

1:5 See Judg 13:5; Gal 1:15. *I formed you.* See Is 49:5. God's creative act (see Gen 2:7; Ps 119:73) is the basis of His sovereign right (see 18:4–6; Is 43:21) to call Jeremiah into His service. *I knew you.* In the sense of making Jeremiah the object of His choice. The Hebrew verb used here can be translated "chose" (Gen 18:19); in Amos 3:2 it is rendered "chosen." *I have appointed you.* The Hebrew for this verb is not the same as that in v. 10, but both refer to the commissioning of the prophet. *prophet.* Lit. "one who has been called" to be God's spokesman (see Ex 7:1–2; 1 Sam 9:9 and notes). *nations.* Although Judah's neighbors are probably the primary focus (see 25:8–38; chs. 46–51), Judah herself is not excluded.

1:6 *not know how to speak.* Like Moses (Ex 4:10), Jeremiah claimed inability to be a prophet; God nevertheless made him His spokesman (15:19). *a youth.* See 1 Kin 3:7. Jeremiah's objection is denied immediately by the Lord (v. 7).

1:7 Youth and inexperience do not disqualify when God calls (see 1 Tim 4:12); He equips and sustains those He commissions.

1:8 *Do not be afraid.* See 10:5; 30:10; 40:9; 42:11; 46:27–28; 51:46; see also Is 35:4 and note; 41:10. *I am with you.* See v. 19; 15:20. God's promise of His continuing presence should calm the fears of the most reluctant of prophets (see Ex 3:12; see also note on Gen 26:3). *deliver.* See v. 19; 15:20; 39:17. The Lord does not promise that Jeremiah will not be persecuted or imprisoned, but that no serious physical harm will come to him.

1:9 *touched my mouth.* Either in prophetic vision (see note on v. 11) or figuratively—or both (cf. Is 6:7). *I have put My words in your mouth.* Continues the figure of speech begun earlier in the verse and provides a classic description of the relationship between the Lord and His prophet (see 5:14; Ex 4:15; Num 22:38; 23:5,12,16; Deut 18:18; Is 51:16; cf. 2 Pet 1:21).

1:10 *appointed.* See note on v. 5. *pluck up . . . break down . . . destroy . . . overthrow . . . build . . . plant.* See 12:14–15,17; 18:7–10; 24:6; 31:28; 42:10; 45:4. The first two pairs of verbs are

The Almond Rod and Boiling Pot

11 The word of the LORD came to me saying, "What do you see, [a]Jeremiah?" And I
said, "I see a rod of an [1]almond tree."
12 Then the LORD said to me, "You have
seen well, for [a]I am [1]watching over My word
to perform it."
13 The word of the LORD came to me a
second time saying, "[a]What do you see?"
And I said, "I see a boiling [b]pot, facing away
from the north."
14 Then the LORD said to me, "[a]Out of the
north the evil [1]will break forth on all the
inhabitants of the land.
15 "For, behold, I am calling [a]all the families of the kingdoms of the north," declares
the LORD; "and they will come and they will
[b]set each one his throne at the entrance of
the gates of Jerusalem, and against all its
walls round about and against all the [c]cities
of Judah.
16 "I will [1]pronounce My judgments on
them concerning all their wickedness,
whereby they have [a]forsaken Me and have
[2b]offered sacrifices to other gods, and worshiped the [c]works of their own hands.
17 "Now, [a]gird up your loins and arise, and
speak to them all which I command you.
[b]Do not be dismayed before them, or I will
dismay you before them.
18 "Now behold, I have made you today as
a fortified city and as a pillar of iron and as
walls of bronze against the whole land, to
the kings of Judah, to its princes, to its
priests and to the people of the land.
19 "They will fight against you, but they
will not overcome you, for [a]I am with you to
deliver you," declares the LORD.

Judah's Apostasy

2 Now the word of the LORD came to me
saying,
2 "Go and [a]proclaim in the ears of Jerusalem, saying, 'Thus says the LORD,
"I remember concerning you the
[1b]devotion of your youth,
The love of your betrothals,
[c]Your following after Me in the
wilderness,
Through a land not sown.
3 "Israel was [a]holy to the LORD,
The [b]first of His harvest.
[c]All who ate of it became guilty;
Evil came upon them," declares the
LORD.' "
4 Hear the word of the LORD, O house of

11 [1]Heb *shaqed* [a]Jer 24:3; Amos 7:8
12 [1]Heb *shoqed* [a]Jer 31:28
13 [a]Zech 4:2 [b]Ezek 11:3, 7
14 [1]Lit *will be opened* [a]Is 41:25; Jer 4:6; 10:22
15 [a]Jer 25:9 [b]Is 22:7; Jer 39:3 [c]Jer 4:16; 9:11
16 [1]Lit *speak* [2]Or *burned incense* [a]Deut 28:20 [b]Jer 7:9; 19:4; 44:17 [c]Is 2:8; 37:19; Jer 10:3-5
17 [a]1 Kin 18:46; Job 38:3
17 [b]Ezek 2:6; 3:16-18
19 [a]Num 14:9; Jer 1:8; 20:11
2:2 [1]Or *lovingkindness* [a]Is 58:1; Jer 7:2; 11:6 [b]Ezek 16:8; Hos 2:15 [c]Deut 2:7; Jer 2:6
3 [a]Ex 19:5, 6; Deut 7:6; 14:2 [b]James 1:18; Rev 14:4 [c]Is 41:11; Jer 30:16; 50:7

negative, stressing the fact that Jeremiah is to be primarily a prophet of doom, while the last pair is positive, indicating that he is also to be a prophet of restoration—even if only secondarily. The first verb ("pluck up") is the opposite of the last ("plant"), and fully half of the verbs ("break down," "destroy," "overthrow") are the opposite of "build."

1:11 *What do you see . . . ?* Often spoken by the Lord (or His representative) to introduce a prophetic vision (see v. 13; Amos 7:8; 8:2; Zech 4:2; 5:2).

1:12 *watching.* The Hebrew for "watching" sounds like the Hebrew for "almond tree." Just as the almond tree blooms first in the year (and therefore "wakes up" early—the Hebrew word for "watching" means to be wakeful), so the Lord is ever watchful to make sure that His word is fulfilled.

1:13 *pot.* The Hebrew for "pot" stresses its large size (see Job 41:31; Ezek 24:3–5).

1:14 *Out of the north the evil.* See note on Is 41:25. *will break forth.* The Hebrew for this word has a similar sound to that for "boiling" in v. 13. *land.* Judah (see v. 15).

1:15 *kingdoms of the north.* Since Assyria posed a minimal threat to Judah after the death of Ashurbanipal in 627 B.C., reference is most likely to Babylon and her allies. *set each one his throne at . . . the gates of Jerusalem.* For the fulfillment see 39:3. Since the gateway of a city was the place where its ruling council sat (see notes on Gen 19:1; Ruth 4:1), the Babylonians replaced Judah's royal authority with their own (cf. 43:10; 49:38).

1:16 *My judgments on them.* God, sovereign over His own, judges His own for their sins, using the Babylonians as His agents of judgment. *offered sacrifices to other gods.* A common feature of pagan worship (e.g., 7:9; 11:12–13,17; 18:15; 19:13; 32:29; 44:17). *the works of their own hands.* Idols (see 16:19–20; 25:6; 2 Kin 22:17; 2 Chr 33:22; Is 46:6).

1:17 *gird up your loins.* Lit. "Tighten your belt around your waist!" For related expressions see Ex 12:11; 1 Kin 18:46; 2 Kin 4:29; 9:1; Job 38:3; 40:7.

1:18 *fortified city.* A symbol of security and impregnability (see 5:17; Prov 18:11,19). *pillar of iron.* Unique in the OT, the expression signifies dignity and strength. *walls of bronze.* See 15:20. Jeremiah would be able to withstand the abuse and persecution that his divine commission would evoke, even though his enemies themselves would be "bronze and iron" (6:28). *kings . . . princes . . . priests . . . people.* The whole nation would defy the prophet and his God (see, e.g., 2:26; 23:8; 32:32).

1:19 See note on v. 8; see also 15:20.

2:1–6:30 It is generally agreed that these chapters are among Jeremiah's earliest discourses, delivered during the reign of Josiah (3:6). The basic theme is the virtually total apostasy of Judah (chs. 2–5), leading inevitably to divine retribution through foreign invasion (ch. 6).

2:1–3:5 The wickedness and backsliding of God's people are vividly portrayed in numerous colorful figures of speech.

2:1 See note on 1:2.

2:2 *devotion.* The Hebrew for this word refers to the most intimate degree of loyalty, love and faithfulness that can exist between two people or between an individual and the Lord. *youth . . . your betrothals.* Early in her history, Israel had enjoyed a close and cordial relationship with the Lord, who is often described figuratively as Israel's husband (3:14; 31:32; Is 54:5; Hos 2:16). *love.* But later God's people forsook Him and loved "strangers" (foreign gods, v. 25), tragically abandoning their first love (cf. Rev 2:4). *following after Me.* But later they followed "emptiness" (v. 5), "things that did not profit" (v. 8), "the Baals" (v. 23). *wilderness.* Sinai (see v. 6).

2:3 *holy to the LORD.* Set apart to Him and His service (see notes on Ex 3:5; Lev 11:44; Deut 7:6). *The first.* Just as the "choice first fruits" of Israel's crops were to be brought to the Lord (Ex 23:19; see Num 18:12; 2 Chr 31:5; Ezek 44:30), so also the people themselves were His first and choicest treasure (cf. James 1:18; Rev 14:4). *Evil came upon them.* See, e.g., Ex 17:8–16.

2:4 *Hear.* A common divine imperative in prophetic writings, summoning God's people—as well as the nations—into His courts to remind them of their legal obligations to Him and,

Jacob, and all the families of the house of Israel.

5 Thus says the LORD,
"[a]What injustice did your fathers find in Me,
That they went far from Me
And walked after [b]emptiness and became empty?
6 "They did not say, 'Where is the LORD
Who [a]brought us up out of the land of Egypt,
Who [b]led us through the wilderness,
Through a land of deserts and of pits,
Through a land of drought and of [1]deep darkness,
Through a land that no one crossed
And where no man dwelt?'
7 "I brought you into the [a]fruitful land
To eat its fruit and its good things.
But you came and [b]defiled My land,
And My inheritance you made an abomination.
8 "The [a]priests did not say, 'Where is the LORD?'
And those who handle the law [b]did not know Me;
The [1]rulers also transgressed against Me,
And the [c]prophets prophesied by Baal
And walked after [d]things that did not profit.

5 [a]Is 5:4; Mic 6:3 [b]2 Kin 17:15; Jer 8:19; Rom 1:21
6 [1]Or *the shadow of death* [a]Ex 20:2; Is 63:11 [b]Deut 8:15; 32:10
7 [a]Deut 8:7-9; 11:10-12 [b]Ps 106:38; Jer 3:2; 16:18
8 [1]Lit *shepherds* [a]Jer 10:21 [b]Jer 4:22; Mal 2:7, 8 [c]Jer 23:13 [d]Jer 16:19; Hab 2:18
9 [a]Jer 2:35; Ezek 20:35, 36
10 [1]I.e. Cyprus and other islands [a]Is 23:12 [b]Ps 120:5; Is 21:16; Jer 49:28
11 [a]Is 37:19; Jer 5:7; 16:20 [b]Ps 106:20; Rom 1:23
12 [a]Is 1:2; Jer 4:23
13 [a]Ps 36:9; Jer 17:13; John 4:14 [b]Jer 14:3
14 [a]Jer 5:19; 17:4
15 [1]Lit *given their voice* [a]Jer 50:17 [b]Jer 4:7

9 "Therefore I will yet [a]contend with you," declares the LORD,
"And with your sons' sons I will contend.
10 "For [a]cross to the coastlands of [1]Kittim and see,
And send to [b]Kedar and observe closely
And see if there has been such *a thing* as this!
11 "Has a nation changed gods
When [a]they were not gods?
But My people have [b]changed their glory
For that which does not profit.
12 "Be appalled, [a]O heavens, at this,
And shudder, be very desolate,"
declares the LORD.
13 "For My people have committed two evils:
They have forsaken Me,
The [a]fountain of living waters,
To hew for themselves [b]cisterns,
Broken cisterns
That can hold no water.

14 "Is Israel [a]a slave? Or is he a homeborn servant?
Why has he become a prey?
15 "The young [a]lions have roared at him,
They have [1]roared loudly.
And they have [b]made his land a waste;

when necessary, to pass judgment on them (see, e.g., 7:2; 17:20; 19:3; 21:11; 22:2,29; 31:10; 42:15; 44:24,26; Is 1:10; Ezek 13:2; Hos 4:1; Amos 7:16).

2:5 *Thus says the LORD.* The so-called messenger formula, introducing God's word through the prophet. Though frequent in overall occurrence, its use is restricted to Jeremiah, Isaiah (e.g., 7:7), Ezekiel (e.g., 2:4), Amos (e.g., 1:3), Obadiah (1), Micah (3:5), Nahum (1:12), Haggai (e.g., 1:2), Zechariah (e.g., 1:3) and Malachi (1:4). *went far.* See 4:1; 23:13,32; 31:19; 50:6; Is 53:6; Ezek 34:4–6,16; 1 Pet 2:25. *walked after emptiness.* See vv. 8,23; see also note on v. 2. Jeremiah describes the objects of Israel's idolatry in a variety of ways (8:19; 10:8,15; 14:22; 16:19; 51:18). *became empty.* See 2 Kin 17:15. Idolaters are no better than the idols they worship (see Ps 115:8).

2:6 *LORD . . . brought us up out of . . . Egypt.* The Lord, Israel's Redeemer (see notes on Gen 2:4; Ex 3:15), freed His people from Egyptian bondage so that they might serve Him alone (Ex 20:2–6). *led us.* As a shepherd leads his sheep (see v. 17; Deut 8:15; Ps 23:2–3). *land of deserts . . . land of . . . darkness.* The desert often symbolized darkness with its attendant dangers, including death (v. 31; 9:10; 12:12; 17:6; 23:10; Ps 44:19).

2:7 *fruitful.* The Hebrew for this word is *karmel,* translated "fruitful field" in 48:33 and also used as the name of a place (see Is 33:9 and note). Rendered "fruitful land" in 4:26, it is the opposite of a desert. *defiled My land.* Made it ceremonially unclean (see 3:1–2,9; 16:18; see also note on Lev 4:12). *inheritance.* The promised land, given by God to Israel as a legacy and often intimately associated with the people themselves (see especially 12:7–9,14–15). *abomination.* See note on Lev 7:21.

2:8 No one consulted the Lord (see v. 6). *priests . . . rulers . . . prophets.* See note on 1:18. *those who handle the law.* Priests (see Deut 31:11 and note). *rulers.* Lit. "shepherds," a term used elsewhere to denote rulers (23:1–4; 49:19; 50:44; see especially Ezek 34:1–10,23–24). *by Baal.* In the name of Baal (cf. 11:21; 14:15; 23:25; 26:9). *that did not profit.* Lit. "unprofitable" (see v. 11; the Hebrew for this word is not the same as that in v. 5, though the meaning is similar).

2:9 *contend with.* See note on v. 4; see also 25:31; Hos 4:1; 12:2; Mic 6:2.

2:10 *Kittim.* Represents the western nations and regions. *Kedar.* Represents the eastern nations and regions (see 49:28; Is 21:16 and note).

2:11 *Has . . . gods?* A rhetorical question, clearly expecting a negative answer and emphasizing how incredible is Judah's practice of substituting idolatry for the worship of the Lord. *their Glory.* God (see Ps 106:20; Hos 4:7; see also 1 Sam 15:29). *that which does not profit.* See note on v. 8.

2:12 *Be appalled, O heavens.* See note on Is 1:2; see also Mic 6:1–2 and note. The Hebrew for these phrases offers a striking play on words: *shommu shamayim.*

2:13 See 1:16. *Me, The fountain of living waters.* See 17:13. God Himself provides life-giving power to His people (see Ps 36:9; see also note on John 4:10; Is 55:1 and note; Rev 21:6). *Broken cisterns.* Watertight plaster was used to keep cisterns from losing water. Idols, like broken cisterns, will always fail their worshipers; by contrast, God provides life abundant and unfailing.

2:14 *Is . . . servant?* Another rhetorical question (see note on v. 11), again expecting a negative answer in the light of God's redemptive acts during the period of the exodus (see Ex 6:6; 20:2). *prey.* To Assyria and Egypt (see vv. 15–16).

2:15 *lions.* Possibly literal (see 2 Kin 17:25–26), though probably here symbolizing Assyria (see v. 18; 50:17; see also notes on 4:7; Is 15:9). *roared . . . roared.* See Amos 3:4. *made his land a waste.* See 4:7; 18:16; 50:3. *cities have been destroyed.* The Hebrew for this phrase is very similar to that in 4:7, rendered there "cities will be ruins Without inhabitant" (cf. 22:6).

His cities have been destroyed,
without inhabitant.
16 "Also the [1]men of [a]Memphis and
Tahpanhes
Have [2]shaved the [b]crown of your head.
17 "Have you not [a]done this to yourself
By your forsaking the LORD your God
When He [a]led you in the way?
18 "But now what are you doing [a]on the
road to Egypt,
To drink the waters of the [1][b]Nile?
Or what are you doing on the road to
Assyria,
To drink the waters of the [2]Euphrates?
19 "[a]Your own wickedness will correct
you,
And your [b]apostasies will reprove you;
Know therefore and see that it is evil
and [c]bitter
For you to forsake the LORD your God,
And [d]the dread of Me is not in you,"
declares the Lord [1]GOD of hosts.

20 "For long ago [1][a]I broke your yoke
And tore off your bonds;
But you said, 'I will not serve!'
For on every [b]high hill
And under every green tree
You have lain down as a harlot.
21 "Yet I [a]planted you a choice vine,
A completely faithful seed.
How then have you turned yourself
before Me
Into the [b]degenerate shoots of a
foreign vine?
22 "Although you [a]wash yourself with lye
And [1]use much soap,
The [b]stain of your iniquity is before
Me," declares the Lord [2]GOD.
23 "[a]How can you say, 'I am not defiled,
I have not gone after the [b]Baals'?
Look at your way in the [c]valley!
Know what you have done!
You are a swift young camel
[d]entangling her ways,
24 A [a]wild donkey accustomed to the
wilderness,
That sniffs the wind in her passion.
In *the time of* her [1]heat who can turn
her away?
All who seek her will not become
weary;
In her month they will find her.
25 "Keep your feet from being unshod
And your throat from thirst;
But you said, '[a]It is [1]hopeless!
No! For I have [b]loved strangers,
And after them I will walk.'

26 "As the [a]thief is shamed when he is
discovered,
So the house of Israel is shamed;
They, their kings, their princes
And their priests and their prophets,
27 Who say to a tree, 'You are my
father,'
And to a stone, 'You gave me birth.'
For they have turned *their* [a]back to
Me,
And not *their* face;

16 [1]Or *sons* [2]Lit *grazed* [a]Is 19:13; Jer 44:1; Hos 9:6 [b]Deut 33:20; Jer 48:45
17 [a]Deut 32:10; Jer 4:18
18 [1]Heb *Shihor* [2]Lit *River* [a]Is 30:2 [b]Josh 13:3
19 [1]Heb *YHWH,* usually rendered LORD [a]Is 3:9; Jer 4:18; Hos 5:5 [b]Jer 3:6, 8, 11, 14; Hos 11:7 [c]Job 20:12-16; Amos 8:10 [d]Ps 36:1; Jer 5:24
20 [1]Or *you* [a]Lev 26:13 [b]Deut 12:2; Is 57:5, 7; Jer 3:2, 6; 17:2
21 [a]Ex 15:17; Ps 44:2; 80:8; Is 5:2 [b]Is 5:4
22 [1]Lit *cause to be great to you* [2]Heb *YHWH,* usually rendered LORD [a]Jer 4:14 [b]Job 14:17; Hos 13:12
23 [a]Prov 30:12 [b]Jer 9:14 [c]Jer 7:31 [d]Jer 2:33, 36; 31:22
24 [1]Lit *occasion* [a]Jer 14:6
25 [1]Or *desperate* [a]Jer 18:12 [b]Deut 32:16; Jer 14:10
26 [a]Jer 48:27
27 [a]Jer 18:17; 32:33

2:16 *Memphis.* See 44:1; 46:14,19; see also note on Is 19:13. *Tahpanhes.* Probably the city later called Daphnai by the Greeks, located just south of Lake Menzaleh in the eastern delta region of Egypt and known today as Tell Defneh (see 43:7–9; 44:1; 46:14; Ezek 30:18). *shaved the crown of your head.* Figurative for bringing disgrace and devastation (see 47:5; 48:37; see also notes on Is 3:17; 7:20).
2:17 *He led you.* See note on v. 6. *the way.* See Ex 18:8; 23:20; Deut 1:33.
2:18 See v. 36. The tendency of Israel or Judah to seek help alternately from Egypt and Assyria was not restricted to Jeremiah's time (see, e.g., Hos 7:11; 12:2). *drink the waters.* Provided by enemies, whether national or spiritual, rather than by God (see v. 13; Is 8:6–8 and notes).
2:19 *apostasies.* See 3:22; 5:6; 14:7. The word implies repeated apostasy.
2:20–3:6 The rebellion of Judah against God is vividly portrayed by Jeremiah with the use of numerous figures of speech.
2:20 Like a stubborn draft animal (see Hos 4:16), Judah refuses to obey the Lord's commands. *broke your yoke And tore off your bonds.* See 5:5; see also 31:18; cf. Ps 2:3. Judah has broken God's law and violated His covenant. *on every high hill And under every green tree.* Locales of pagan worship (see 1 Kin 14:23; 2 Kin 17:10; Ezek 6:13). *as a harlot.* Ritual prostitution was a particularly detestable practice (see, e.g., Hos 4:10–14).
2:21 See Is 5:1–7; see also Ps 80:8–16; Ezek 17:1–10; Hos 10:1–2; cf. John 15:1–8. *choice vine.* See Is 5:2. The Hebrew for this word refers to a grape of exceptional quality. *foreign vine.* A vine symbolizing Israel should not be like a vine symbolizing Israel's enemies (see Deut 32:32).
2:22 *lye . . . soap.* Mineral alkali and vegetable alkali respectively. Sins can be removed and forgiven (see Ps 51:2,7; Is 1:18), but only when the sinner repents and confesses (see Prov 28:13; cf. 1John 1:7,9).
2:23 *defiled.* Ceremonially unclean (see 19:13; see also note on Lev 4:12). *gone after.* See note on v. 2; see also v. 25. *Baals.* See 9:14; see also note on Judg 2:11. *the valley.* Probably the Hinnom Valley (see note on Josh 15:5), known also as the Valley of Ben-hinnom (7:31–32; 19:2,6; 32:35). *entangling her ways.* Instead, the people of Judah should have been obeying the Lord, not turning aside either "to the right or to the left" (Deut 28:14).
2:24 *wild donkey.* An unruly (see Gen 16:12) and intractable (see Job 39:5–8) animal. *accustomed to the wilderness.* See 14:6; Job 24:5. *sniffs the wind.* The picture is one of active searching, not passive waiting (see Hos 2:7,13).
2:25 *feet . . . unshod.* You wear out your sandals. *It is hopeless!* See 18:12; see also note on Is 57:10. *I have loved strangers.* As opposed to the love Judah was expected to express toward God under the terms of their covenant relationship (see, e.g., Deut 6:6; 7:7–13; Hos 2:14–3:1). *after them.* See v. 23; see also note on v. 2.
2:26 *shamed when he is discovered.* See, e.g., Ex 22:3–4. The Hebrew word underlying "shame" is often used as a pejorative synonym for the name of Baal, the chief god of Canaan (see 11:13 and note; Hos 9:10; see also note on Judg 6:32). *kings . . . princes . . . priests . . . prophets.* See note on 1:18.
2:27 See Is 44:13–17; contrast Deut 32:6,18; Is 64:8; Mal 2:10. *Arise . . . save.* See v. 28.

But in the [b]time of their [1]trouble they
will say,
'Arise and save us.'
28 "But where are your [a]gods
Which you made for yourself?
Let them arise, if they can [b]save you
In the time of your [1]trouble;
For [c]*according to* the number of your
cities
Are your gods, O Judah.

29 "Why do you contend with Me?
You have [a]all transgressed against
Me," declares the LORD.
30 "[a]In vain I have struck your sons;
They accepted no chastening.
Your [b]sword has devoured your
prophets
Like a destroying lion.
31 "O generation, heed the word of the
LORD.
Have I been a wilderness to Israel,
Or a [a]land of thick darkness?
Why do My people say, '[b]We *are free*
to roam;
We will no longer come to You'?
32 "Can a virgin forget her ornaments,
Or a bride her attire?
Yet My people have [a]forgotten Me
Days without number.
33 "How well you prepare your way
To seek love!
Therefore even [1]the wicked women
You have taught your ways.
34 "Also on your skirts is found
The [a]lifeblood of the innocent poor;
You did not find them [b]breaking in.
But in spite of all these things,
35 Yet you said, 'I am innocent;
Surely His anger is turned away from
me.'

27 [1]Or *evil* [b]Judg 10:10; Is 26:16
28 [1]Or *evil* [a]Deut 32:37; Judg 10:14; Is 45:20; Jer 1:16 [b]Jer 11:12 [c]2 Kin 17:30, 31; Jer 11:13
29 [a]Jer 5:1; 6:13; Dan 9:11
30 [a]Is 1:5; Jer 5:3; 7:28 [b]Neh 9:26; Jer 26:20-24; Acts 7:52; 1 Thess 2:15
31 [a]Is 45:19 [b]Deut 32:15; Jer 2:20, 25
32 [a]Ps 106:21; Is 17:10; Jer 3:21; 13:25; Hos 8:14
33 [1]Or *in wickedness*
34 [a]2 Kin 21:16; 24:4; Ps 106:38; Jer 7:6; 19:4 [b]Ex 22:2
35 [a]Jer 25:31 [b]Prov 28:13; 1 John 1:8, 10
36 [a]Jer 2:23; 31:22; Hos 12:1 [b]Is 30:3 [c]2 Chr 28:16, 20, 21
37 [a]2 Sam 13:19; Jer 14:3, 4 [b]Jer 37:7-10
3:1 [1]Lit *saying* [2]Or *alienated* [3]Lit *companions* [a]Deut 24:1-4 [b]Jer 2:20; Ezek 16:26, 28, 29 [c]Jer 4:1; Zech 1:3
2 [a]Deut 12:2; Jer 2:20; 3:21; 7:29 [b]Gen 38:14; Ezek 16:25 [c]Jer 2:7
3 [a]Lev 26:19; Jer 14:3-6 [b]Jer 6:15; 8:12
4 [1]Lit *leader* [a]Jer 3:19; 31:9 [b]Ps 71:17; Prov 2:17 [c]Jer 2:2; Hos 2:15

Behold, I will [a]enter into judgment
with you
Because you [b]say, 'I have not sinned.'
36 "Why do you [a]go around so much
Changing your way?
Also, [b]you will be put to shame by
Egypt
As you were put to shame by [c]Assyria.
37 "From this *place* also you will go out
With [a]your hands on your head;
For the LORD has rejected [b]those in
whom you trust,
And you will not prosper with them."

The Polluted Land

3 God [1]says, "[a]If a husband divorces his
wife
And she goes from him
And belongs to another man,
Will he still return to her?
Will not that land be completely
[2]polluted?
But you [b]are a harlot *with* many
[3]lovers;
Yet you [c]turn to Me," declares the LORD.
2 "Lift up your eyes to the [a]bare heights
and see;
Where have you not been violated?
By the roads you have [b]sat for them
Like an Arab in the desert,
And you have [c]polluted a land
With your harlotry and with your
wickedness.
3 "Therefore the [a]showers have been
withheld,
And there has been no spring rain.
Yet you had a [b]harlot's forehead;
You refused to be ashamed.
4 "Have you not just now called to Me,
'[a]My Father, You are the [1b]friend of my
[c]youth?

2:28 *according to . . . your cities Are your gods.* See 11:13; cf. 1 Cor 8:5. Every ancient Near Eastern town of any importance had its own patron deity (cf. Acts 19:28,34–35), and many towns were named after deities (see, e.g., note on 1:1).
2:29 *content with.* Cf. v. 9; see 12:1; Job 33:13.
2:30 *I have struck your sons.* Cf. Heb 12:6. *accepted no chastening.* See 5:3. *sword has devoured your prophets.* See, e.g., 26:20–23; 2 Kin 21:16; 24:4; see also Neh 9:26.
2:31 *generation.* Often has negative connotations (see, e.g., Deut 32:5). *Have I been a wilderness . . . a land of thick darkness?* On the contrary, the Lord led His people through the wilderness and its darkness (v. 6). The phrase "thick darkness" translates the Hebrew for "darkness of the LORD" (i.e., darkness sent by the Lord; cf. 1 Sam 26:12 and "The very flame of the LORD" in Song 8:6).
2:32 See Is 49:15,18 and notes. *bride.* Cf. v. 2. *My people have forgotten Me.* See 18:15; see also 3:21; 13:25; Is 17:10; Ezek 22:12; 23:35; Hos 8:14. Israel was always to "remember" the Lord and all that He had done for her (Deut 7:18; 8:18) and so trust and worship Him alone, but she often "forgot" Him—put Him out of mind (see Judg 2:10; Hos 2:13).
2:33 *love.* Here, worship of pagan gods (see note on v. 20).
2:34 See Amos 2:6–8; 4:1; 5:11–12. *find them breaking in.* See Ex 22:2 and note.
2:36 *put to shame by Egypt . . . by Assyria.* See vv. 15–18 and notes. The days of Ahaz (see 2 Chr 28:21), and perhaps the days of Zedekiah (see 37:7), are in view here.
2:37 *With your hands on your head.* Ancient reliefs depict captives with wrists tied together above their heads. *those . . . you trust.* Egypt and Assyria.
3:1 *If . . . polluted?* Cf. Deut 24:1–4. Divorce and remarriage on a widespread scale defiles not only the participants but also the land in which they live (cf. v. 2; Lev 18:25–28). *are a harlot.* See note on 2:20. *many.* See note on 2:28. *turn to Me.* Repent of your sins against me (see vv. 12–14,22; 4:1).
3:2 *bare heights.* Places where pagan gods were consulted and worshiped (see v. 21; 12:12; Num 23:3). *violated.* Cf. Deut 28:30. *By the roads you have sat.* See Gen 38:14 and note; Prov 7:10,12. The connection of this imagery with ritual prostitution is made explicit in Ezek 16:25. *Like an Arab in the desert.* Waiting in ambush to waylay a traveler (see Luke 10:30). *polluted a land.* See v. 9.
3:3 *showers have been withheld.* See 14:1–6; Amos 4:7–8. This is the reverse of God's gracious response to His people in Hos 2:21; 6:3. *spring rain.* See note on Deut 11:14. *harlot's forehead.* A shameless, brazen countenance (see Prov 7:13).
3:4 *My Father.* See v. 19; contrast 2:27 and see note there. Com-

5 '[a]Will He be angry forever?
Will He [1]be indignant to the end?'
Behold, you have spoken
And have done evil things,
And you have [2]had your way."

Faithless Israel

6 Then the LORD said to me in the days of
Josiah the king, "Have you seen what faithless Israel did? She [a]went up on every high
hill and under every green tree, and she was
a harlot there.
7 "[a]I [1]thought, 'After she has done all
these things she will return to Me'; but she
did not return, and her [b]treacherous sister
Judah saw it.
8 "And I saw that for all the adulteries of
faithless Israel, I had sent her away and [a]giv-
en her a writ of divorce, yet her [b]treacherous
sister Judah did not fear; but she went and
was a harlot also.
9 "Because of the lightness of her harlotry,
she [a]polluted the land and committed adultery with [b]stones and trees.
10 "Yet in spite of all this her treacherous
sister Judah did not return to Me with all her
heart, but rather in [a]deception," declares the
LORD.

God Invites Repentance

11 And the LORD said to me, "[a]Faithless
Israel has proved herself more righteous than
treacherous Judah.
12 "Go and proclaim these words toward
the north and say,

'[a]Return, faithless Israel,' declares the
LORD;
'[b]I will not [1]look upon you in anger.
For I am [c]gracious,' declares the LORD;
'I will not be angry forever.
13 'Only [1a]acknowledge your iniquity,
That you have transgressed against
the LORD your God
And have [b]scattered your [2]favors to
the strangers [c]under every green
tree,
And you have not obeyed My voice,'
declares the LORD.
14 'Return, O faithless sons,' declares the
LORD;
'For I am a [a]master to you,
And I will take you one from a city
and two from a family,
And [b]I will bring you to Zion.'
15 "Then I will give you [a]shepherds after
My own heart, who will [b]feed you on knowledge and understanding.
16 "It shall be in those days when you are
multiplied and increased in the land,"
declares the LORD, "they will [a]no longer say,
'The ark of the covenant of the LORD.' And it
will not come to mind, nor will they remember it, nor will they miss *it*, nor will it be
made again.
17 "At that time they will call Jerusalem
'The [a]Throne of the LORD,' and [b]all the
nations will be gathered to it, to Jerusalem,
for the [c]name of the LORD; nor will they
[d]walk anymore after the stubbornness of
their evil heart.
18 "[a]In those days the house of Judah will

5 [1]Lit *keep it* [2]Lit *been able* [a]Ps 103:9; Is 57:16; Jer 3:12
6 [a]Jer 17:2; Ezek 23:4-10
7 [1]Lit *said* [a]2 Kin 17:13 [b]Jer 3:11; Ezek 16:47
8 [a]Deut 24:1, 3; Is 50:1 [b]Ezek 16:46, 47; 23:11
9 [a]Jer 2:7; 3:2 [b]Is 57:6; Jer 2:27; 10:8
10 [a]Jer 12:2; Hos 7:14
11 [a]Ezek 16:51, 52; 23:11
12 [1]Lit *cause My countenance to fall* [a]Jer 3:14, 22; Ezek 33:11 [b]Jer 3:5 [c]Ps 86:15; Jer 12:15; 31:20; 33:26
13 [1]Lit *know* [2]Lit *ways* [a]Deut 30:1-3; Jer 3:25; 14:20; 1 John 1:9 [b]Jer 2:20, 25; 3:2, 6 [c]Deut 12:2
14 [a]Jer 31:32; Hos 2:19 [b]Jer 31:6, 12
15 [a]Jer 23:4; 31:10; Ezek 34:23; Eph 4:11 [b]Acts 20:28
16 [a]Is 65:17
17 [a]Jer 17:12; Ezek 43:7 [b]Jer 3:19; 4:2; 12:15, 16; 16:19 [c]Is 60:9 [d]Jer 11:8
18 [a]Is 11:13; Jer 50:4, 5; Hos 1:11

pared to the NT, the title "Father" for God is relatively rare in the OT. However, it often occurs in personal names—compound names that begin with Abi- (e.g., Abinadab and Abiram) refer to God as "(my) Father." *friend.* Claiming intimate association (see Ps 55:13; Prov 16:28; 17:9; Mic 7:5); perhaps even claiming to be the Lord's faithful wife (cf. Prov 2:17). *of my youth.* See note on 2:2.

3:5 *Will He be indignant to the end?* Not if God's people repent (vv. 12–13).

3:6–6:30 The unfaithfulness of Judah (3:6–5:31) will ultimately bring the Babylonians as God's instrument of judgment (ch. 6).

3:6 *Josiah the king.* See Introduction: Background; see also note on 1:2. *faithless Israel.* The northern kingdom, destroyed in 722–721 B.C. (see vv. 8,11–12). *on every high hill and under every green tree . . . she was a harlot.* See note on 2:20.

3:7 *her treacherous sister Judah.* The southern kingdom (see vv. 8,10–11). Samaria (Israel's capital) and Jerusalem (Judah's capital) are similarly compared as adulterous sisters in Ezek 23. *it.* Israel's adultery.

3:8 *sent her away.* Into exile in 721 B.C. *writ of divorce.* See v. 1 and note; see also Deut 24:1–14; Is 50:1 and notes. *Judah did not fear.* She refused to learn from Israel's tragic experience.

3:9 *committed adultery with stones and trees.* Worshiped pagan deities (see 2:27).

3:10 *in deception.* Judah's response to Josiah's reform measures (see note on 1:2) was superficial and hypocritical.

3:11 *Israel . . . more righteous than . . . Judah.* See note on v. 8; see also Ezek 16:51–52; 23:11.

3:12 *Go and proclaim.* See 2:2. *north.* Assyria's northern provinces, to which many Israelites had been exiled. *Return.* Repent (see v. 13). *gracious.* The Hebrew for this word is used of God elsewhere only in Ps 145:17, where it is translated "kind." *not be angry forever.* See note on v. 5.

3:13 *scattered your favors.* See Ezek 16:15,33–34. *strangers.* See note on 2:25. *under every green tree.* See note on 2:20.

3:14 *master.* See 31:32; Hos 2:16–17. The Hebrew root underlying this word is *ba'al.* Instead of allowing God to be their husband, His people followed "the Baals" (2:23; see note on Judg 2:11). *one . . . two.* A remnant will return (see note on Is 10:20–22). *Zion.* Jerusalem.

3:15 See 23:4. *shepherds.* Rulers (see note on 2:8). *after My own heart.* Like David (see 1 Sam 13:14; see also Ezek 34:23; Hos 3:5).

3:16 *in those days.* The Messianic age (see v. 18; 31:29). *you are multiplied.* See 23:3; Ezek 36:11. For the fuller meaning of the Hebrew underlying this phrase see note on Gen 1:28. *nor will it be made again.* The ark of the covenant, formerly symbolizing God's royal presence (see 1 Sam 4:3 and NASB marg.), will be irrelevant when the Messiah comes.

3:17 *Throne.* The Lord had been sits enthroned "above the cherubim" above the ark (see 1 Sam 4:4 and note), but Jerusalem itself would someday be His throne. *all the nations will be gathered.* See Zech 2:11; see also note on Is 2:2–4. *they.* Israel. *walk anymore after the stubbornness of their evil heart.* A stock phrase referring to Israel's disobedience and often involving the worship of pagan gods (see 9:14; 11:8; 13:10; 16:12; 18:12; 23:17).

3:18 *Judah will walk with . . . Israel.* In the Messianic age God's divided people will again be united (see, e.g., Is 11:12; Ezek

walk with the house of Israel, and they will
come together [b]from the land of the north to
the [c]land that I gave your fathers as an inheritance.

19 "Then I said,
'How I would set you among [1]My sons
And give you a pleasant land,
The most [a]beautiful inheritance of the nations!'
And I said, 'You shall call Me, [b]My Father,
And not turn away from following Me.'
20 "Surely, as a woman treacherously departs from her [1]lover,
So you have [a]dealt treacherously with Me,
O house of Israel," declares the LORD.

21 A voice is heard on the [a]bare heights,
The weeping *and* the supplications of the sons of Israel;
Because they have perverted their way,
They have [b]forgotten the LORD their God.
22 "Return, O faithless sons,
[a]I will heal your faithlessness."
"Behold, we come to You;
For You are the LORD our God.
23 "Surely, [a]the hills are a deception,
A tumult *on* the mountains.
Surely in the [b]LORD our God
Is the salvation of Israel.

24 "But [a]the shameful thing has consumed
the labor of our fathers since our youth, their
flocks and their herds, their sons and their
daughters.
25 "Let us lie down in our [a]shame, and let
our humiliation cover us; for we have sinned
against the LORD our God, we and our
fathers, [b]from our youth even to this day.
And we have not obeyed the voice of the
LORD our God."

18 [b]Jer 16:15; 31:8 [c]Amos 9:15
19 [1]Lit *the* [a]Ps 16:6 [b]Is 63:16; Jer 3:4
20 [1]Or *companion* [a]Is 48:8
21 [a]Is 15:2; Jer 3:2; 7:29 [b]Is 17:10; Jer 2:32; 13:25
22 [a]Jer 30:17; 33:6; Hos 6:1; 14:4
23 [a]Jer 17:2 [b]Ps 3:8; Jer 17:14; 31:7
24 [a]Hos 9:10
25 [a]Ezra 9:6, 7
25 [b]Jer 22:21
4:1 [a]Jer 3:22; 15:19; Joel 2:12 [b]Jer 7:3, 7; 35:15
2 [a]Deut 10:20; Is 45:23; 65:16; Jer 12:16 [b]Is 48:1 [c]Gen 22:18; Jer 3:17; 12:15, 16; Gal 3:8 [d]Is 45:25; Jer 9:24; 1 Cor 1:31
3 [1]Lit *Plow for yourselves plowed ground* [a]Hos 10:12 [b]Matt 13:7
4 [a]Deut 10:16; 30:6; Jer 9:25, 26; Rom 2:28, 29; Col 2:11 [b]Is 30:27, 33; Jer 21:12; Zeph 2:2 [c]Amos 5:6; Mark 9:43, 48
5 [a]Jer 6:1; Hos 8:1 [b]Josh 10:20; Jer 8:14

Judah Threatened with Invasion

4 "If you will [a]return, O Israel," declares the LORD,
"*Then* you should return to Me.
And [b]if you will put away your detested things from My presence,
And will not waver,
2 And you will [a]swear, 'As the LORD lives,'
[b]In truth, in justice and in righteousness;
Then the [c]nations will bless themselves in Him,
And [d]in Him they will glory."

3 For thus says the LORD to the men of
Judah and to Jerusalem,
"[1][a]Break up your fallow ground,
And [b]do not sow among thorns.
4 "[a]Circumcise yourselves to the LORD
And remove the foreskins of your heart,
Men of Judah and inhabitants of Jerusalem,
Or else My [b]wrath will go forth like fire
And burn with [c]none to quench it,
Because of the evil of your deeds."

5 Declare in Judah and proclaim in Jerusalem, and say,
"[a]Blow the trumpet in the land;
Cry aloud and say,
'[b]Assemble yourselves, and let us go
Into the fortified cities.'

37:15–23; Hos 1:11). *land of the north.* Where they had been exiles (see note on v. 12; see also 31:8). *land that I gave . . . as an inheritance.* See note on 2:7.

3:19 *sons.* Israel was the Lord's firstborn (see Ex 4:22; cf. Hos 11:1). *pleasant land.* See Ps 106:24; Zech 7:14. *beautiful inheritance.* Judah, Jerusalem, the people themselves—ideally, all were beautiful in God's eyes (see 6:2; 11:16). *Father.* See note on v. 4.

3:20 A concise summary of the story told in Hos 1–3.

3:21 *bare heights.* See note on v. 2. *weeping and . . . supplications.* A description of repentance, verbalized in vv. 22b–25. *forgotten.* See note on 2:32.

3:22 See v. 14. *Return . . . faithless . . . faithlessness.* Each of these three words is derived from the same Hebrew root, producing a striking series of puns. *I will heal your faithlessness.* See 30:17; 33:6; Hos 6:1; 14:1,4. *Behold.* The people's repentance begins.

3:23 *tumult.* See, e.g., 1 Kin 18:25–29. *in the LORD . . . Is . . . salvation.* See Gen 49:18; Ps 3:8; Jon 2:9 and note.

3:24 *shameful thing.* See notes on 2:26; 11:13. *consumed the labor.* False worship is costly, both financially and spiritually. *our youth.* The period of the judges. *sons and . . . daughters.* Often sacrificed to pagan gods (see note on 7:31).

3:25 *shame.* The Hebrew for this word is translated "shameful thing" in v. 24.

4:1 *waver.* The Hebrew for this word implies wandering, as in Gen 4:12,14 (see Gen 4:16 and note).

4:2 *truth . . . justice . . . righteousness.* The piling up of qualifying words underscores the need for repentance that is sincere and not perfunctory. *As the LORD lives.* See note on Gen 42:15. *nations will bless themselves in Him.* Reflects the language of the seventh of God's great promises to Abram (see Gen 12:2–3 and note). Israel's repentance is a necessary precondition for the ultimate blessing of the nations.

4:3 *Break up your fallow ground.* Probably quoted from Hos 10:12. *do not sow among thorns.* See Matt 13:7,22. Openness to the Lord's overtures is necessary, as is total commitment to Him (see Ezek 18:31).

4:4 *remove the foreskins of your heart.* Consecrate your hearts (see 6:10, where "closed" means "uncircumcised"; 9:26; see also Gen 17:10 and note; Deut 10:16; 30:6). *wrath will . . . burn with none to quench.* See 21:12; see also Is 1:31; Amos 5:6. *Because of the evil of your deeds.* Probably quoted from Deut 28:20.

4:5–31 The invaders from the north will bring God's judgment against His unrepentant people (see ch. 6).

4:5 *Blow the trumpet.* To warn of impending doom (see 6:1; see also note on Joel 2:1). *go Into the fortified cities.* See v. 6. To avoid capture by hostile troops, people living in the countryside would take refuge in the nearest walled town (see 5:17; 8:14; 34:7; 48:18).

6 "Lift up a [a]standard toward Zion!
Seek refuge, do not stand *still*,
For I am bringing [b]evil from the north,
And great destruction.
7 "A [a]lion has gone up from his thicket,
And a [b]destroyer of nations has set out;
He has gone out from his place
To [c]make your land a waste.
Your cities will be ruins
Without inhabitant.
8 "For this, [a]put on sackcloth,
Lament and wail;
For the [b]fierce anger of the LORD
Has not turned back from us."

9 "It shall come about in that day,"
declares the LORD, "that the [a]heart of the
king and the heart of the princes will fail;
and the priests will be appalled and the
[b]prophets will be astounded."
10 Then I said, "Ah, Lord [1]GOD! Surely You
have utterly [a]deceived this people and
Jerusalem, saying, '[b]You will have peace';
whereas a sword touches the [2]throat."
11 In that time it will be said to this people
and to Jerusalem, "A [a]scorching wind from
the bare heights in the wilderness in the
direction of the daughter of My people—not
to winnow and not to cleanse,
12 a wind too strong for [1]this—will come
[2]at My command; now I will also pronounce
judgments against them.

13 "Behold, he [a]goes up like clouds,
And his [b]chariots like the whirlwind;
His horses are [c]swifter than eagles.
Woe to us, for [d]we are ruined!"

14 Wash your heart from evil,
O Jerusalem,
That you may be saved.
How long will your [a]wicked thoughts
Lodge within you?
15 For a voice declares from [a]Dan,
And proclaims wickedness from
Mount Ephraim.
16 "Report *it* to the nations, now!
Proclaim over Jerusalem,
'Besiegers come from a [a]far country,
And [b]lift their voices against the cities
of Judah.
17 'Like watchmen of a field they are
[a]against her round about,
Because she has [b]rebelled against Me,'
declares the LORD.
18 "Your [a]ways and your deeds
Have [1]brought these things to you.
This is your evil. How [b]bitter!
How it has touched your heart!"

Lament over Judah's Devastation

19 [a]My [1]soul, my [1]soul! I am in anguish!
[2]Oh, my heart!
My [b]heart is pounding in me;
I cannot be silent,
Because [3]you have heard, O my soul,
The [c]sound of the trumpet,
The alarm of war.
20 [a]Disaster on disaster is proclaimed,
For the [b]whole land is devastated;
Suddenly my [c]tents are devastated,
My curtains in an instant.
21 How long must I see the standard
And hear the sound of the trumpet?
22 "[a]For My people are foolish,
They know Me not;

6 [a]Is 62:10; Jer 4:21; 50:2 [b]Jer 1:14, 15; 6:1, 22 **7** [a]Jer 5:6; 25:38; 50:17 [b]Jer 25:9; Ezek 26:7-10 [c]Is 1:7; 6:11; Jer 2:15 **8** [a]Is 22:12; Jer 6:26 [b]Is 5:25; 10:4; Jer 30:24 **9** [a]Is 22:3-5; Jer 48:41 [b]Is 29:9, 10; Ezek 13:9-16 **10** [1]Heb *YHWH*, usually rendered LORD [2]Or *life* [a]Ezek 14:9; 2 Thess 2:11 [b]Jer 5:12; 14:13 **11** [a]Jer 13:24; 51:1; Ezek 17:10; Hos 13:15 **12** [1]Lit *these* [2]Lit *for Me* **13** [a]Is 19:1; Nah 1:3 [b]Is 5:28; 66:15 [c]Lam 4:19; Hab 1:8 [d]Is 3:8 **14** [a]Prov 1:22; Jer 6:19; 13:27; James 4:8 **15** [a]Jer 8:16 **16** [a]Is 39:3; Jer 5:15 [b]Ezek 21:22 **17** [a]2 Kin 25:1, 4 [b]Is 1:20, 23; Jer 5:23 **18** [1]Lit *done* [a]Ps 107:17; Is 50:1; Jer 2:17, 19 [b]Jer 2:19 **19** [1]Lit *inward parts* [2]Lit *The walls of my heart* [3]Or *I, my soul, heard* [a]Is 15:5; 16:11; 21:3; 22:4; Jer 9:1, 10; 20:9 [b]Hab 3:16 [c]Num 10:9 **20** [a]Ps 42:7; Ezek 7:26 [b]Jer 4:27 [c]Jer 10:20 **22** [a]Jer 5:4, 21; 10:8; Rom 1:22

4:6 See 6:1. *Lift up a standard.* See note on Is 5:26. *evil from the north.* The Babylonians (see 1:14; see also note on Is 41:25). *great destruction.* See 6:1; cf. 48:3; 50:22; 51:54.
4:7 *lion.* A symbol of Babylon (see note on 2:15). *destroyer.* Usually refers to Babylon (6:26; 15:8; 48:8,32), but in 51:1,56 it refers to Persia and her allies (see 51:48,53). *cities . . . Without inhabitant.* See note on 2:15; see also v. 25; 46:19.
4:8 *sackcloth.* See note on Gen 37:34. *anger . . . Has not turned back.* Contrast 2:35.
4:9 *in that day.* See note on Is 2:11,17,20. *king . . . princes . . . priests . . . prophets.* See note on 1:18.
4:10 *You have utterly deceived.* Not directly, but through false prophets (see, e.g., 1 Kin 22:20–23 and note on 1 Kin 22:23). *You will have peace.* Here the words of false prophets, not of God (see 14:13; 23:17; see also 6:13–14; 8:10–11). *throat.* The Hebrew for this word is usually translated "soul" or "life," but originally it had the meaning "throat, neck" (see, e.g., Ps 69:1).
4:11 *scorching wind.* The sirocco or khamsin, a hot, dry wind that brings sand and dust (see Ps 11:6; Is 11:15; Jon 4:8). *winnow.* See note on Ruth 1:22.
4:12 *too strong for this.* Neither winnowing (separating grain from chaff) nor cleansing (blowing dust from the grain), God's judgments will sweep away good and bad alike.
4:13 *goes up like clouds.* Cf. Ezek 38:16. *chariots like the whirlwind.* See 2 Kin 2:11; 6:17; Ps 68:17; Is 66:15. *horses are swifter than eagles.* See Hab 1:8, where the Babylonians (Hab 1:6) use horses that are "swifter than leopards" and employ cavalry that "fly like an eagle" (the Hebrew word for "vulture" is translated "eagle" in 4:13; see Deut 28:49). *ruined.* See v. 20; 9:19; 48:1.
4:14 *Wash.* See 2:22 and note. *wicked thoughts.* Against other people (see Prov 6:18; Is 59:7).
4:15 *Dan.* Far away, close to the northern border of Israel (see 8:16). *Ephraim.* A few miles north of Jerusalem. The enemy, in the mind's eye of the prophet, is making fearfully rapid progress toward the holy city.
4:16 *Besiegers.* See Is 1:8. *far country.* Babylon. *lift their voices.* The Hebrew underlying this phrase is translated "roared" in 2:15.
4:17 *against her round about.* See 1:15.
4:19–26 A brief personal interlude, broken only by the divine complaint in v. 22. Jeremiah voices his agony at the approaching destruction of his beloved land and its people.
4:19 See 10:19–20. *anguish.* Often associated with labor pangs, as here (see 6:24; 49:24; 50:43). *heart is pounding.* See Job 37:1; Ps 38:10; Hab 3:16. *sound of the trumpet.* See note on v. 5.
4:20 *is devastated.* See v. 13; 9:19; 48:1. *curtains.* Tent curtains (see Is 54:2) were usually made of goat hair (see Ex 26:7) and therefore strong enough to protect from cold and rain (see 10:20).
4:21 *standard . . . sound of the trumpet.* See notes on vv. 5–6.
4:22 The Lord speaks. *foolish.* The Hebrew word refers to one who is morally deficient. *know Me not.* See 2:8. Leaders and people alike had committed the ultimate sin (see Is 1:3; Hos

They are stupid children
And have no understanding.
They are shrewd to [b]do evil,
But to do good they do not know."

23 I looked on the earth, and behold, *it was* [1a]formless and void;
And to the heavens, and they had no light.
24 I looked on the mountains, and behold, they were [a]quaking,
And all the hills [1]moved to and fro.
25 I looked, and behold, there was no man,
And all the [a]birds of the heavens had fled.
26 I looked, and behold, [1]the [a]fruitful land was a wilderness,
And all its cities were pulled down
Before the LORD, before His fierce anger.

27 For thus says the LORD,
"The [a]whole land shall be a desolation,
Yet I will [b]not execute a complete destruction.
28 "For this the [a]earth shall mourn
And the [b]heavens above be dark,
Because I have [c]spoken, I have purposed,
And I will not [1]change My mind, nor will I turn from it."
29 At the sound of the horseman and bowman [a]every city flees;
They [b]go into the thickets and climb among the rocks;
[c]Every city is forsaken,
And no man dwells in them.
30 And you, O desolate one, [a]what will you do?
Although you dress in scarlet,

22 [b]Jer 9:3; 13:23; Rom 16:19; 1 Cor 14:20
23 [1]Or *a waste and emptiness* [a]Gen 1:2; Is 24:19
24 [1]Lit *moved lightly* [a]Is 5:25; Jer 10:10; Ezek 38:20
25 [a]Jer 9:10; 12:4; Zeph 1:3
26 [1]Or *Carmel* [a]Jer 9:10
27 [a]Jer 12:11, 12; 25:11 [b]Jer 5:10, 18; 30:11; 46:28
28 [1]Lit *be sorry* [a]Jer 12:4, 11; 14:2; Hos 4:3 [b]Is 5:30; 50:3; Joel 2:30, 31 [c]Num 23:19; Jer 23:20; 30:24
29 [a]2 Kin 25:4 [b]Is 2:19-21; Jer 16:16 [c]Jer 4:7
30 [a]Is 10:3; 20:6; Jer 13:21
30 [1]Lit *paramours* [b]2 Kin 9:30; Ezek 23:40 [c]Jer 22:20, 22; Lam 1:2, 19; Ezek 23:9, 10, 22
31 [1]Lit *sound* [2]Lit *palms* [3]Lit *my soul faints* [a]Is 42:14 [b]Is 1:15; Lam 1:17
5:1 [1]Lit *faithfulness* [a]2 Chr 16:9; Dan 12:4 [b]Ezek 22:30 [c]Gen 18:26, 32
2 [a]Is 48:1; Titus 1:16
3 [1]Lit *faithfulness* [2]Or *become sick* [a]2 Chr 16:9 [b]Is 1:5; 9:13; Jer 2:30 [c]Jer 7:28; 8:5; Zeph 3:2 [d]Jer 7:26; 19:15; Ezek 3:8

Although you decorate *yourself with* ornaments of gold,
Although you [b]enlarge your eyes with paint,
In vain you make yourself beautiful.
Your [1c]lovers despise you;
They seek your life.
31 For I heard a [1]cry as of a woman in labor,
The anguish as of one giving birth to her first child,
The [1]cry of the daughter of Zion
[a]gasping for breath,
[b]Stretching out her [2]hands, *saying,*
"Ah, woe is me, for [3]I faint before murderers."

Jerusalem's Godlessness

5 "[a]Roam to and fro through the streets of Jerusalem,
And look now and take note.
And seek in her open squares,
If you can [b]find a man,
[c]If there is one who does justice, who seeks [1]truth,
Then I will pardon her.
2 "And [a]although they say, 'As the LORD lives,'
Surely they swear falsely."
3 O LORD, do not [a]Your eyes *look* for [1]truth?
You have [b]smitten them,
But they did not [2]weaken;
You have consumed them,
But they [c]refused to take correction.
They have [d]made their faces harder than rock;
They have refused to repent.

4 Then I said, "They are only the poor,
They are foolish;

4:1). *stupid.* See 5:21; 10:8,14,21; 51:17. *shrewd to do evil.* See Mic 7:3.
4:23–26 The striking repetition of "I looked" at the beginning of each verse ties this poem together and underscores its visionary character, as the prophet sees his beloved land in ruins after the Babylonian onslaught. Creation, as it were, has been reversed.
4:23 *formless and void.* The phrase occurs elsewhere only in Gen 1:2 (see note there). In Jeremiah's vision, the primeval chaos has returned. *had no light.* Contrast Gen 1:3.
4:24 See Nah 1:5.
4:25 *there was no man.* The Hebrew underlying this phrase occurs elsewhere only in Gen 2:5. Again, uncreation has replaced creation.
4:26 *fruitful land.* See note on 2:7. *fierce anger.* See v. 8; Is 13:13; Nah 1:6.
4:27 *not execute a complete destruction.* See 5:10,18; 30:11; 46:28. God's mercy tempers the total judgment envisioned by Jeremiah in vv. 23–26.
4:28 *will not change My mind.* Unless His people repent (see 18:7–8).
4:29 *bowman.* Babylon's evil deeds against Judah will someday recoil on her (see 50:29). *They go.* See Judg 6:2; 1 Sam 13:6; Is 2:19,21. Even people living in fortified towns feel unsafe. *forsaken.* Contrast Is 62:4.
4:30 *paint.* Antimony, a black powder used to enlarge the eyes and make them more attractive (see 2 Kin 9:30; Ezek 23:40). *lovers.* The Hebrew root underlying this word is found elsewhere only in Ezek 23:5,7,9,12,16,20, where it is used of Samaria and Jerusalem, the adulterous sisters (see notes on 2:20; 3:7) who "lusted" after foreign nations and their gods. *seek your life.* They are intent only on murdering you (see v. 31).
4:31 *daughter of Zion.* A personification of Jerusalem and its inhabitants (see 6:2,23). *Stretching out her hands.* In prayer for help (see Job 11:13).
5:1–31 Jeremiah resumes his vivid description of the wickedness of the people of Judah and Jerusalem.
5:1 See Zeph 1:12. The Lord challenges anyone to find just one righteous person in Israel—a rhetorical way of charging that corruption pervaded the city (see Ps 14:1–3; Is 64:6–7; Hos 4:1–2; Mic 7:2). *If you can find . . . I will pardon.* See Gen 18:26–32.
5:2 *As the LORD lives.* See 4:2; see also Gen 42:15 and note. *they swear falsely.* In violation of Lev 19:12 (see note on Ex 20:7). The Hebrew could be translated "swear by false gods."
5:3 *refused . . . correction.* See 2:30. *made their faces harder than rock.* A striking portrayal of rebellion (see Ezek 3:7–9).
5:4 *poor.* Concerned about basic physical needs (cf. 39:10; 40:7), they are uninformed of God's word and way. *foolish.* See

For they [a]do not know the way of the
LORD
Or the ordinance of their God.
5 "I will go to the great
And will speak to them,
For [a]they know the way of the LORD
And the ordinance of their God."
But they too, with one accord, have
[b]broken the yoke
And burst the bonds.
6 Therefore [a]a lion from the forest will
slay them,
A [b]wolf of the deserts will destroy
them,
A [c]leopard is watching their cities.
Everyone who goes out of them will
be torn in pieces,
Because their [d]transgressions are many,
Their apostasies are numerous.

7 "Why should I pardon you?
Your sons have forsaken Me
And [a]sworn by those who are [b]not
gods.
When I had fed them to the full,
They [c]committed adultery
And trooped to the harlot's house.
8 "They were well-fed lusty horses,
Each one neighing after his
[a]neighbor's wife.
9 "Shall I not punish [1]these *people,*"
declares the LORD,
"And on a nation such as this
[a]Shall I not avenge Myself?

10 "Go up through her vine rows and
destroy,
But do not execute a complete
destruction;
Strip away her branches,
For they are not the LORD's.
11 "For the [a]house of Israel and the house
of Judah

4 [a]Is 27:11; Jer 8:7; Hos 4:6
5 [a]Mic 3:1 [b]Ex 32:25; Ps 2:3; Jer 2:20
6 [a]Jer 4:7 [b]Ezek 22:27; Hab 1:8; Zeph 3:3 [c]Hos 13:7 [d]Jer 30:14, 15
7 [a]Josh 23:7; Jer 12:16; Zeph 1:5 [b]Deut 32:21; Jer 2:11; Gal 4:8 [c]Jer 7:9
8 [a]Jer 13:27; 29:23; Ezek 22:11
9 [1]Or *for these things* [a]Jer 9:9
11 [a]Jer 3:6, 7, 20
12 [1]Lit *He is not* [a]2 Chr 36:16 [b]Prov 30:9; Jer 14:22; 43:1-4 [c]Jer 23:17 [d]Jer 14:13
13 [a]Job 8:2; Jer 14:13, 15; 22:22
14 [a]Is 24:6; Jer 1:9; 23:29; Hos 6:5; Zech 1:6
15 [a]Deut 28:49; Is 5:26; Jer 4:16 [b]Is 28:11
16 [a]Is 5:28; 13:18 [b]Ps 5:9
17 [a]Lev 26:16; Deut 28:31, 33; Jer 8:16; 50:7; 17 [b]Jer 8:13 [c]Hos 8:14

Have dealt very treacherously with
Me," declares the LORD.
12 They have [a]lied about the LORD
And said, "[1][b]Not He;
Misfortune will [c]not come on us,
And we [d]will not see sword or famine.
13 "The [a]prophets are *as* wind,
And the word is not in them.
Thus it will be done to them!"

Judgment Proclaimed

14 Therefore, thus says the LORD, the God
of hosts,
"Because you have spoken this word,
Behold, I am [a]making My words in
your mouth fire
And this people wood, and it will
consume them.
15 "Behold, I am [a]bringing a nation
against you from afar, O house of
Israel," declares the LORD.
"It is an enduring nation,
It is an ancient nation,
A nation whose [b]language you do not
know,
Nor can you understand what they
say.
16 "Their [a]quiver is like an [b]open grave,
All of them are mighty men.
17 "They will [a]devour your harvest and
your food;
They will devour your sons and your
daughters;
They will devour your flocks and your
herds;
They will devour your [b]vines and your
fig trees;
They will demolish with the sword
your [c]fortified cities in which you
trust.
18 "Yet even in those days," declares the
LORD, "I will not make you a complete
destruction.

4:22 and note; see also Num 12:11. *do not know . . . ordinance of their God.* They are more ignorant than the birds of the heavens (see 8:7).
5:5 *the great.* Although possessing every advantage, they were no more righteous than the poorest of the common people. *broken . . . bonds.* See note on 2:20.
5:6 *lion . . . wolf . . . leopard.* See Lev 26:22; Ezek 14:15; cf. 2 Kin 17:25–26. *apostasies.* See 2:19; 3:22; 14:7. The word implies repeated apostasy.
5:7 *Why should I pardon you?* See v. 1. *those who are not gods.* Idols (see 2:11). *When I had fed . . . They.* See Deut 32:15–16; Hos 2:8. *committed adultery.* See note on 2:20.
5:8 Religious prostitution (v. 7; see Amos 2:7) leads quite naturally to literal adultery, the breaking of God's law (see Ex 20:14,17). *lusty horses.* See 13:27; 50:11; Ezek 23:20.
5:10 *Go.* Addressed to Israel's enemies (see v. 15). *vine rows.* Vines and vineyards are often symbolic of Israel (see notes on 2:21; Is 5:1). *not . . . a complete destruction.* See v. 18; see also note on 4:27. *Strip away her branches.* See Is 18:5; John 15:2,6. *are not the LORD's.* See Hos 1:9.
5:11 See note on 3:7.
5:12 *Not He.* The Lord will do nothing, either good or bad (see Zeph 1:12). *sword or famine.* Jeremiah introduces us to the first two elements of his characteristic triad: "sword, famine and pestilence" (see note on 14:12).
5:13 *prophets are as wind.* Like images of false gods (see Is 41:29). *Thus it will be done to them!* See note on 4:29; see also Ps 7:16; 54:5.
5:14 *My words in your mouth fire.* In contrast to the total lack of God's word in the mouths of false prophets (v. 13). *consume.* See note on Is 1:31.
5:15 *nation . . . from afar.* See note on 4:16. *enduring . . . ancient nation.* Babylon's history reached back 2,000 years and more. *whose language you do not know.* See Deut 28:49 and note.
5:16 *open grave.* Symbolizing insatiability, destruction and death (see Ps 5:9; Prov 30:15–16).
5:17 *devour your sons and your daughters.* Either as sacrifices to pagan gods (see note on 3:24), or as casualties of war (see 10:25). *fortified cities in which you trust.* See note on 4:5; see also Deut 28:52.
5:18 See v. 10; see also note on 4:27.

19 "It shall come about [a]when [1]they say,
'Why has the LORD our God done all these
things to us?' then you shall say to them, 'As
you have forsaken Me and served foreign
gods in your land, so you will [b]serve
strangers in a land that is not yours.'

20 "Declare this in the house of Jacob
And proclaim it in Judah, saying,
21 'Now hear this, O foolish and
[1]senseless people,
Who have [a]eyes but do not see;
Who have ears but do not hear.
22 'Do you not [a]fear Me?' declares the
LORD.
'Do you not tremble in My presence?
For I have [b]placed the sand as a
boundary for the sea,
An eternal decree, so it cannot cross
over it.
Though the waves toss, yet they
cannot prevail;
Though they roar, yet they cannot
cross over it.
23 'But this people has a [a]stubborn and
rebellious heart;
They have turned aside and departed.
24 'They do not say in their heart,
"Let us now fear the LORD our God,
Who [a]gives rain in its season,
Both [b]the autumn rain and the spring
rain,
Who keeps for us
The [c]appointed weeks of the harvest."
25 'Your [a]iniquities have turned these
away,
And your sins have withheld good
from you.
26 'For wicked men are found among My
people,
They [a]watch like fowlers [1]lying in wait;
They set a trap,
They catch men.
27 'Like a cage full of birds,
So their houses are full of [a]deceit;
Therefore they have become great and
rich.
28 'They are [a]fat, they are sleek,
They also [1]excel in deeds of
wickedness;
They do not plead the cause,
The cause of the [2b]orphan, that they
may prosper;
And they do not [3]defend the rights of
the poor.
29 '[a]Shall I not punish [1]these *people?*'
declares the LORD,
'On a nation such as this
Shall I not avenge Myself?'

30 "An appalling and [a]horrible thing
Has happened in the land:
31 The [a]prophets prophesy falsely,
And the priests rule [1]on their *own*
authority;
And My people [b]love it so!
But what will you do at the end of it?

Destruction of Jerusalem Impending

6 "Flee for safety, O sons of [a]Benjamin,
From the midst of Jerusalem!
Now blow a trumpet in Tekoa
And raise a signal over [1b]Beth-
haccerem;
For evil looks down from the [c]north,
And a great destruction.
2 "The comely and [a]dainty one, [b]the
daughter of Zion, I will cut off.
3 "[a]Shepherds and their flocks will come
to her,

19 [1]Or *you* [a]Deut 29:24-26; 1 Kin 9:8, 9; Jer 13:22; 16:10-13 [b]Deut 28:48; Jer 16:13
21 [1]Lit *without heart* [a]Is 6:9; 43:8; Ezek 12:2; Matt 13:14; Mark 8:18; John 12:40; Acts 28:26; Rom 11:8
22 [a]Deut 28:58; Ps 119:120; Jer 2:19; 10:7; Rev 15:4 [b]Job 38:8-11; Ps 104:9; Prov 8:29
23 [a]Deut 21:18; Ps 78:8; Jer 4:17; 6:28
24 [a]Ps 147:8; Jer 3:3; Matt 5:45; Acts 14:17 [b]Joel 2:23 [c]Gen 8:22
25 [a]Jer 2:17; 4:18
26 [1]Perhaps, *crouching down* [a]Ps 10:9; Prov 1:11; Jer 18:22; Hab 1:15
27 [a]Jer 9:6
28 [1]Lit *pass over,* or, *overlook deeds* [2]Or *fatherless* [3]Lit *judge* [a]Deut 32:15 [b]Is 1:23; Jer 7:6; 22:3; Zech 7:10
29 [1]Or *for these things* [a]Jer 5:9; Mal 3:5
30 [a]Jer 23:14; Hos 6:10
31 [1]Lit *over their own hands* [a]Ezek 13:6 [b]Mic 2:11
6:1 [1]I.e. house of the vineyard [a]Josh 18:28 [b]Neh 3:14 [c]Jer 1:14; 4:6; 6:22
2 [a]Deut 28:56 [b]Is 1:8; Jer 4:31 **3** [a]Jer 12:10

5:21 *hear this.* See note on 2:4. *foolish and senseless.* See 4:22 and note. *Who have eyes . . . do not hear.* See note on Is 6:10; see also Deut 29:4; Ps 115:4–8; 135:15–18.
5:22 *fear Me.* See note on Gen 20:11. *boundary for the sea.* See Job 38:8–11; Ps 104:6–9.
5:23 Though the sea never crosses its divinely appointed boundaries, God's people have violated the limits He has set for them.
5:24 *God, Who gives.* See v. 7 and note. *autumn . . . spring rain.* See 3:3; see also note on Deut 11:14. *appointed weeks of the harvest.* Perhaps the seven weeks between Passover and the Feast of Weeks (see Lev 23:15–16).
5:26 *trap.* Lit. "destroyer" (see, e.g., Ex 12:23) or "destruction" (see, e.g., Ezek 21:31). *men.* Innocent (see Is 29:21), godly, upright people (see Mic 7:2).
5:27 *cage.* A trap woven of wicker; the Hebrew for this word is translated "basket" in Amos 8:1–2. *deceit.* Riches gained through extortion and deception (see Hab 2:6).
5:28 *fat . . . sleek.* Symbolic of prosperity (see Deut 32:15). *excel in deeds of wickedness.* See Ps 73:7. *They do not plead the cause.* What the wicked will not do, God must do (see Deut 10:18)—and so must those who truly know and serve Him (see 22:16; James 1:27).
5:29 Repeated from v. 9.
5:31 See 1:18 and note. *prophesy falsely.* See 20:6 (often, and arrogantly, in God's name; see 23:25; 27:15; 29:9). *people love it so.* See note on Amos 4:5.
6:1–30 The prophet envisions the future Babylonian attack on Jerusalem.
6:1 The Lord speaks in vv. 1–3. Verse 1 is strongly reminiscent of 4:6 (see note there). But whereas in 4:6 the command was to seek protection in Jerusalem, in 6:1 the people are to flee from Jerusalem, because no place—not even the holy city itself—will be safe from the invader. *Benjamin.* The tribal territory bordering Judah north of Jerusalem. Jeremiah himself was from Benjamite territory (see 1:1). *blow . . . Tekoa.* In the Hebrew there is a play on these words. Tekoa was the hometown of Amos (see Introduction to Amos: Author). *raise . . . signal.* In the Hebrew there is a play on words, made possible by using a different Hebrew word (found also in Lachish Letter 4:10) for "signal" (caused by the smoke of a fire; see Judg 20:38,40) than the one used in 4:6. *Beth-haccerem.* Mentioned elsewhere only in Neh 3:14 (see note there). *evil . . . from the north.* See 1:14 and note.
6:2 *dainty.* The Hebrew word is used to describe the city of Babylon in Is 47:1 ("delicate"). *daughter of Zion.* See v. 23; see also note on 4:31.
6:3 See 1:15. *Shepherds and their flocks.* Rulers (see note on

They will [b]pitch *their* tents [1]around
her,
They will pasture each in his [2]place.
4 "[1a]Prepare war against her;
Arise, and let us [2]attack at [b]noon.
Woe to us, for the day declines,
For the shadows of the evening
lengthen!
5 "Arise, and let us [1]attack by night
And [a]destroy her [2]palaces!"
6 For thus says the LORD of hosts,
"[a]Cut down her trees
And cast up a [b]siege against Jerusalem.
This is the city to be punished,
In whose midst there is only
[c]oppression.
7 "[a]As a well [1]keeps its waters fresh,
So she [1]keeps fresh her wickedness.
[b]Violence and destruction are heard in
her;
[c]Sickness and wounds are ever before
Me.
8 "[a]Be warned, O Jerusalem,
Or [1b]I shall be alienated from you,
And make you a desolation,
A land not inhabited."

9 Thus says the LORD of hosts,
"They will [a]thoroughly glean as the
vine the [b]remnant of Israel;
Pass your hand again like a grape
gatherer
Over the branches."
10 To whom shall I speak and give
warning
That they may hear?
Behold, their [a]ears are [1]closed
And they cannot listen.
Behold, [b]the word of the LORD has
become a reproach to them;
They have no delight in it.
11 But I am [a]full of the wrath of the LORD;
I am [b]weary with holding *it* in.
"[c]Pour *it* out on the children in the
street
And on the [1]gathering of young men
together;
For both husband and wife shall be
taken,
The aged [2]and the very old.
12 "Their [a]houses shall be turned over to
others,
Their fields and their wives together;
For I will [b]stretch out My hand
Against the inhabitants of the land,"
declares the LORD.
13 "For [a]from the least of them even to the
greatest of them,
Everyone is [b]greedy for gain,
And from the prophet even to the
priest
Everyone [1]deals falsely.
14 "They have [a]healed the brokenness of
My people superficially,
Saying, 'Peace, peace,'
But there is no peace.
15 "Were they [a]ashamed because of the
abomination they have done?
They were not even ashamed at all;
They did not even know how to blush.
Therefore they shall fall among those
who fall;
At the time that I punish them,
They shall be cast down," says the
LORD.

16 Thus says the LORD,
"Stand by the ways and see and ask for
the [a]ancient paths,
Where the good way is, and walk in it;

3 [1]Lit *against her round about* [2]Lit *hand* [b]2 Kin 25:1; Jer 4:17; Luke 19:43
4 [1]Lit *Sanctify* [2]Lit *go up* [a]Jer 6:23; Joel 3:9 [b]Jer 15:8; Zeph 2:4
5 [1]Lit *go up* [2]Or *fortified towers* [a]Is 32:14; Jer 52:13
6 [a]Deut 20:19, 20 [b]Jer 32:24; 33:4 [c]Jer 22:17
7 [1]Lit *keeps cold* [a]James 3:11f [b]Jer 20:8; Ezek 7:11, 23 [c]Jer 30:12, 13
8 [1]Lit *my soul* [a]Jer 7:28; 17:23 [b]Ezek 23:18; Hos 9:12
9 [a]Jer 16:16; 49:9; Obad 5, 6 [b]Jer 8:3; 11:23
10 [1]Lit *uncircumcised* [a]Jer 5:21; 7:26; Acts 7:51 [b]Jer 20:8
11 [1]Lit *council* [2]Lit *with fullness of days* [a]Job 32:18, 19; Mic 3:8 [b]Jer 15:6; 20:9 [c]Jer 7:20; 9:21
12 [a]Deut 28:30; Jer 8:10; 38:22, 23 [b]Jer 15:6
13 [1]Or *makes lies* [a]Jer 8:10 [b]Is 56:11; 57:17; Jer 8:10; 22:17
14 [a]Jer 8:11; Ezek 13:10
15 [a]Jer 3:3; 8:12
16 [a]Is 8:20; Jer 12:16; 18:15; 31:21; Mal 4:4; Luke 16:29

2:8) with their troops. *pitch.* The Hebrew for this verb continues the pun on "Tekoa" in v. 1 (see note on v. 8). *pasture.* Graze or depasture, and thus destroy. *each in his place.* The Hebrew for this phrase is used similarly ("every man in his place") in Num 2:17.

6:4 The invaders speak in vv. 4–5. *Prepare.* Lit. "Consecrate" (also in Joel 3:9; Mic 3:5). Since ancient battles had religious connotations, soldiers had to prepare themselves ritually as well as militarily (see Deut 20:2–4; 1 Sam 25:28). *at noon.* To take advantage of the element of surprise, since the usual time of attack was early in the morning.

6:5 *by night.* Since attacking soldiers normally retired for the night and resumed siege the following morning, the phrase underscores their eagerness and determination.

6:6 The Lord addresses the Babylonian troops. *siege.* That is, siege ramps, to help them bring up battering rams and scale Jerusalem's walls (see 33:4). *oppression.* Against its own people (see note on Is 30:12).

6:7 *Sickness and wounds.* Jerusalem suffers from spiritual decay and disease (see v. 14), and is not aware of it.

6:8 *Be warned.* The better part of wisdom (see v. 10; Ps 2:10). *be alienated.* In sorrow, but also in disgust. The Hebrew for this phrase continues the pun on "Tekoa" in v. 1 (see note on v. 3). *desolation, A land not inhabited.* See 22:6.

6:9 *thoroughly.* Stopping just short of complete destruction (see 4:27; 5:10,18; 30:11; 46:28). *glean.* See notes on Ruth 2:2; Is 17:5. *vine.* Symbolic of Israel (see 2:21 and note; 5:10). *remnant.* See 11:23; 23:3; 31:7; 40:11,15; 42:2,15,19; 43:5; 44:7,12,14, 28; 50:20; see also note on Is 10:20–22.

6:10 Jeremiah speaks. *give warning.* See note on v. 8. *closed.* Uncircumcised (see also 4:4 and note). The imagery of uncircumcised ears is found elsewhere only in Acts 7:51.

6:11 The prophet speaks, then the Lord resumes His speech (through v. 23). *full of the wrath.* See 25:15. *children . . . young men . . . husband and wife . . . old.* All will be judged, from youngest to oldest (see v. 13). *in the street.* Where children play (see 9:21; Zech 8:5).

6:12–15 Repeated almost verbatim in 8:10–12.

6:12 *houses . . . fields . . . wives.* See Ex 20:17; Deut 5:21. *turned over to others.* As Deut 28:30 warned—one of the covenant curses. *stretch out My hand Against.* To destroy (see 15:6).

6:13 See 1:18 and note.

6:14 *brokenness.* See note on v. 7. *Peace . . . no peace.* A common message of false and greedy prophets (see Ezek 13:10; Mic 3:5). The wicked, in any case, cannot expect to enjoy peace (Is 48:22; 57:21).

6:16 *ancient paths.* The tried and true ways of Judah's godly ancestors (see 18:15; Deut 32:7). *walk in it.* See Is 30:21. *you will find rest for your souls.* Quoted by Jesus in Matt 11:29 (see Is 28:12; cf. Ps 119:165).

And [b]you will find rest for your souls.
But they said, 'We will not walk *in it.*'
17 "And I set [a]watchmen over you, *saying,*
'Listen to the sound of the trumpet!'
But they said, 'We will not listen.'
18 "Therefore hear, O nations,
And know, O congregation, what is among them.
19 "[a]Hear, O earth: behold, I am bringing disaster on this people,
The [b]fruit of their [1]plans,
Because they have not listened to My words,
And as for My law, they have [c]rejected it also.
20 "[a]For what purpose does [b]frankincense come to Me from Sheba
And the [1c]sweet cane from a distant land?
[d]Your burnt offerings are not acceptable
And your sacrifices are not pleasing to Me."
21 Therefore, thus says the LORD,
"Behold, [a]I am [1]laying stumbling blocks before this people.
And they will stumble against them,
[b]Fathers and sons together;
Neighbor and [2]friend will perish."

The Enemy from the North

22 Thus says the LORD,
"Behold, [a]a people is coming from the north land,
And a great nation will be aroused from the [b]remote parts of the earth.
23 "They seize [a]bow and spear;
They are [b]cruel and have no mercy;
Their voice [c]roars like the sea,
And they ride on horses,
Arrayed as a man for the battle
Against you, O daughter of Zion!"
24 We have [a]heard the report of it;
Our hands are limp.
[b]Anguish has seized us,
Pain as of a woman in childbirth.
25 [a]Do not go out into the field
And [b]do not walk on the road,
For the enemy has a sword,
[c]Terror is on every side.
26 O daughter of my people, [a]put on sackcloth
And [b]roll in ashes;
[1c]Mourn as for an only son,
A lamentation most bitter.
For suddenly the destroyer
Will come upon us.

27 "I have [a]made you an assayer *and* a tester among My people,
That you may know and assay their way."
28 All of them are stubbornly rebellious,
[a]Going about as a talebearer.
They are [b]bronze and iron;
They, all of them, are corrupt.
29 The bellows blow fiercely,
The lead is consumed by the fire;
In vain the refining goes on,
But the [a]wicked are not [1]separated.
30 [a]They call them rejected silver,
Because the [b]LORD has rejected them.

Message at the Temple Gate

7 The word that came to Jeremiah from the LORD, saying,
2 "[a]Stand in the gate of the LORD's house

16 [b]Matt 11:29 **17** [a]Is 21:11; 58:1; Jer 25:4; Ezek 3:17; Hab 2:1 **19** [1]Or *devices* [a]Is 1:2; Jer 19:3, 15; 22:29 [b]Prov 1:31 [c]Jer 8:9 **20** [1]Lit *good* [a]Ps 50:7-9; Is 1:11; 66:3; Mic 6:6 [b]Is 60:6 [c]Ex 30:23 [d]Ps 40:6; Amos 5:22 **21** [1]Lit *giving* [2]Lit *his friend* [a]Is 8:14; Jer 13:16 [b]Is 9:14-17; Jer 9:21, 22 **22** [a]Jer 1:15; 10:22; 50:41-43 [b]Neh 1:9 **23** [a]Is 13:18; Jer 4:29 [b]Jer 50:42

23 [c]Is 5:30 **24** [a]Is 28:19; Jer 4:19-21 [b]Is 21:3; Jer 4:31; 13:21; 30:6; 49:24; 50:43 **25** [a]Jer 14:18 [b]Judg 5:6 [c]Jer 20:10; 46:5; 49:29 **26** [1]Lit *Make for yourself mourning* [a]Jer 4:8 [b]Jer 25:34; Mic 1:10 [c]Amos 8:10; Zech 12:10 **27** [a]Jer 1:18; 15:20 **28** [a]Jer 9:4 [b]Ezek 22:18 **29** [1]Or *drawn off* [a]Jer 15:19 **30** [a]Ps 119:119; Is 1:22 [b]Jer 7:29; Hos 9:17; Zech 11:8 **7:2** [a]Jer 17:19; 26:2

6:17 *watchmen.* True prophets (see Ezek 3:17; 33:7; Hab 2:1). *sound of the trumpet.* To warn of approaching danger (see v. 1; see also note on Joel 2:1).
6:18 *hear, O nations.* See Mic 1:2.
6:19 *My law, they have rejected.* Disobeyed the law of Moses (see 8:8–9).
6:20 *Sheba.* Located in southwestern Arabia, it was the center of the spice trade (see Is 60:6 and note). *sweet cane.* See Ex 20:23; Song 4:14 "calamus"; Is 43:24. Cane, which probably came from India, was an ingredient in the sacred anointing oil (Ex 30:25). *burnt offerings are not acceptable.* The attitude of one's heart and the manner of one's life are far more important than the ritual of sacrifice (see note on Is 1:11–15).
6:21 *stumbling blocks.* The Babylonian invaders (see v. 22).
6:22–24 Repeated almost verbatim in 50:41–43.
6:22 *the north land.* Babylonia (see 4:6; Is 41:25 and notes). *from the remote parts of the earth.* See 25:32; 31:8.
6:23 *spear.* The Hebrew for this word is translated "javelin" in 1 Sam 17:6. Another possibility is "sword," as attested in *The War of the Sons of Light against the Sons of Darkness,* one of the Dead Sea Scrolls (see essay, p. 1356). *roars like the sea.* See Is 5:30; see also Is 17:12 and note. *horses.* See note on 4:13; see also 8:16. *daughter of Zion.* A personification of Jerusalem and its inhabitants (see v. 2; 4:31).
6:24–26 The prophet speaks to, and on behalf of, the people of Judah.
6:24 *hands are limp.* Courage will fail (see Is 13:7). *Anguish.* See note on 4:19.
6:25 *Terror is on every side.* A favorite expression of Jeremiah (20:10; 46:5; 49:29). The Hebrew for this phrase is used once as a proper name, "Magor-missabib" (20:3; see note there).
6:26 *put on sackcloth.* See 4:8; see also note on Gen 37:34. *roll in ashes; Mourn.* See Ezek 27:30–31; cf. Mic 1:10. *only son.* A father's most precious possession (see Gen 22:12,16; Amos 8:10; Zech 12:10; Rom 8:32). *destroyer.* Babylon (see note on 4:7).
6:27–30 The Lord speaks to Jeremiah and appoints him to test the people of Judah as a refiner tests metals (see 9:7; Is 1:25; Mal 3:2–3).
6:27 *assayer and . . . tester.* See Job 23:10.
6:28 *Going . . . as a talebearer.* Contrary to Lev 19:16. *bronze and iron.* Base metals when compared to gold and silver. *are corrupt.* See Deut 31:29; Is 1:4.
6:29 In ancient times, lead was added to silver ore in the refining process. When the crucible was heated, the lead oxidized and acted as a flux to remove the alloys. Here the process fails because the ore is not pure enough (cf. Ezek 24:11–13).
6:30 *call them rejected.* The "stubbornly rebellious" (v. 28), the "wicked" (v. 29), have failed to pass the Lord's test. Nothing worthwhile can be made of them.
7:1–10:25 A series of temple messages delivered by Jeremiah, perhaps over a period of several years. Since 26:2–6,12–15 is very similar in content to ch. 7, it is possible that chs. 7–10

and proclaim there this word and say, 'Hear
the word of the LORD, all you of Judah, who
enter by these gates to worship the LORD!' "
3 Thus says the LORD of hosts, the God of
Israel, "[a]Amend your ways and your deeds,
and I will let you dwell in this place.
4 "[a]Do not trust in deceptive words, saying, '[1]This is the temple of the LORD, the temple of the LORD, the temple of the LORD.'
5 "For [a]if you truly amend your ways and
your deeds, if you truly [b]practice justice
between a man and his neighbor,
6 *if* you do not oppress the alien, the
[1a]orphan, or the widow, and do not shed
[b]innocent blood in this place, nor [c]walk after
other gods to your own ruin,
7 then I will let you [a]dwell in this place,
in the [b]land that I gave to your fathers forever and ever.
8 "Behold, you are trusting in [a]deceptive
words to no avail.
9 "Will you steal, murder, and commit
adultery and swear falsely, and [1a]offer sacrifices to Baal and walk after [b]other gods that
you have not known,
10 then [a]come and stand before Me in
[b]this house, which is called by My name,
and say, 'We are delivered!'—that you may
do all these abominations?
11 "Has [a]this house, which is called by My
name, become a [b]den of robbers in your
sight? Behold, [c]I, even I, have seen *it*,"
declares the LORD.
12 "But go now to My place which was in
[a]Shiloh, where I [b]made My name dwell at
the first, and [c]see what I did to it because of
the wickedness of My people Israel.
13 "And now, because you have done all
these things," declares the LORD, "and I
spoke to you, [a]rising up early and [b]speaking,
but you did not hear, and I [c]called you but
you did not answer,
14 therefore, I will do to the [a]house which
is called by My name, [b]in which you trust,
and to the place which I gave you and your
fathers, as I [c]did to Shiloh.
15 "I will [a]cast you out of My sight, as I
have cast out all your brothers, all the [1]off-
spring of [b]Ephraim.

3 [a]Jer 4:1; 7:5; 18:11; 26:13 **4** [1]Lit *They are* [a]Jer 7:8; Mic 3:11 **5** [a]Is 1:19; Jer 4:1, 2 [b]1 Kin 6:12; Jer 21:12; 22:3 **6** [1]Or *fatherless* [a]Ex 22:21-24; Jer 5:28 [b]Jer 2:34; 19:4 [c]Deut 6:14, 15; 8:19; 11:28; Jer 13:10 **7** [a]Deut 4:40 [b]Jer 3:18 **8** [a]Jer 7:4; 28:15 **9** [1]Or *burn incense* [a]Jer 11:13, 17 [b]Ex 20:3; Jer 7:6; 19:4 **10** [a]Ezek 23:39

10 [b]Jer 7:11, 14, 30; 32:34 **11** [a]Is 56:7 [b]Matt 21:13; Mark 11:17; Luke 19:46 [c]Jer 29:23 **12** [a]Judg 18:31; Jer 26:6 [b]Josh 18:1, 10 [c]1 Sam 4:10, 11, 22; Ps 78:60-64

13 [a]Jer 7:25 [b]Jer 35:17 [c]Prov 1:24; Is 65:12; 66:4 **14** [a]Deut 12:5; 1 Kin 9:7 [b]Jer 7:4 [c]Jer 7:12 **15** [1]Lit *seed* [a]Jer 15:1; 52:3 [b]Ps 78:67; Hos 7:13; 9:13; 12:1

(or at least ch. 7) date to the reign of Jehoiakim (see 26:1). On the other hand, Jeremiah may have repeated various themes on several occasions during his lengthy ministry. In any event, nothing in chs. 7–10 is inappropriate to the time of King Josiah.

7:1–8:3 The straightforward narrative of this section asserts that Solomon's temple in Jerusalem will not escape the fate of the earlier sanctuary at Shiloh if the people of Judah persist in worshiping false gods.

7:1 *The word that came.* See 1:2 and note; 1:4,11,13; 2:1.

7:2 *gate.* In the wall between the inner and outer courts of the temple, perhaps the so-called New Gate (26:10; 36:10). *Hear.* See note on 2:4. *all you . . . who enter . . . to worship.* Perhaps during one of the three annual pilgrimage festivals (see Deut 16:16 and note). *gates.* Leading into the outer court.

7:3 *this place.* The land God had given them (see v. 7; 14:13,15; 24:5–6).

7:4 *deceptive words.* Spoken by false prophets. The idea that God would not destroy Jerusalem simply because His dwelling, the temple, was located there was a delusion, fostered in part by the miraculous deliverance of the city during the reign of Hezekiah (see 2 Kin 19:32–36; cf. 2 Sam 7:11b–13; Ps 132:13–14). In the light of Judah's sinful rebellion against the Lord such an idea was of "no avail" (v. 8; see Mic 3:11). *This is.* Lit. "They are," referring to the buildings that constituted the entire temple complex. *temple . . . temple . . . temple.* Vain and repetitious babbling (cf. Matt 6:7). Often such a threefold repeating of a word or phrase is for emphasis (see 22:29; see also note on Is 6:3).

7:6 Rulers and people alike needed to hear and act on these prophetic words (see 22:2–3). *alien . . . orphan . . . widow.* See Deut 16:11,14; 24:19–21; 26:12–13; 27:19. *innocent blood.* See 19:4; 22:17; 26:15; see also the frightening example of King Manasseh (2 Kin 21:16).

7:7 *land . . . forever and ever.* See Gen 17:8 and note.

7:8 *deceptive words.* See note on v. 4.

7:9 This one verse mentions the violation of fully half of the Ten Commandments (cf. Hos 4:2). *offer sacrifices to Baal.* See note on 1:16. *walk after other gods that you have not known.* See 19:4. Tragically, such sins would be the cause of their exile to lands they had not known (see 9:14,16; 16:11,13).

7:10 *house, which is called by My name.* See vv. 11,14,30; 25:29; 32:34; 34:15; 1 Kin 8:43; 2 Chr 6:33; 20:9; Dan 9:18. The "name" of God is equivalent to His gracious presence in such passages (see vv. 12,15). *We are delivered!* See 12:12. *abominations.* See 2:7; see also note on Lev 7:21.

7:11 Together with the last half of Is 56:7, part of this verse is quoted by Jesus in Matt 21:13; Mark 11:17; Luke 19:46. *den of robbers.* As thieves hide in caves and think they are safe, so the people of Judah falsely trust in the temple to protect them in spite of their sins.

7:12 See note on 7:1–8:3. *place . . . in Shiloh . . . see what I did to it.* See v. 14; 26:6,9; Ps 78:60–61. The tabernacle had been set up in Shiloh after the conquest of Canaan (Josh 18:1) and was still there at the end of the period of the judges (see 1 Sam 1:9 and note). Modern Seilun, near a main highway about 18 miles north of Jerusalem, preserves the name of the ancient site. Archaeological excavations there indicate that it was destroyed by the Philistines c. 1050 B.C. The tabernacle itself was not included in that destruction, since it was still in existence at Gibeon during David's reign (see 1 Chr 21:29). One or more auxiliary buildings had apparently been erected at Shiloh near the tabernacle in connection with various aspects of public worship there (cf. the reference to the "doors of the house of the LORD" in 1 Sam 3:15). Such structures would have been destroyed with the city itself, perhaps sometime after the events of 1 Sam 4.

7:13 *rising . . . speaking.* The Hebrew idiom underlying this phrase, suggesting repetition or intensity of action, is found frequently in Jeremiah (v. 25; 11:7; 25:3–4; 26:5; 29:19; 32:33; 35:14–15; 44:4), but appears nowhere else in the OT.

7:15 *cast you out of My sight.* Into exile (see Deut 29:28). *as I have . . . all your brothers.* God sent Israel, the northern kingdom, into captivity in 721 B.C. (see 2 Kin 17:20). *Ephraim.* Another name for Israel (see, e.g., 31:9)—and, ironically, the tribal territory in which Shiloh was located.

16 "As for you, [a]do not pray for this people, and do not lift up cry or prayer for them, and do not intercede with Me; for I do not hear you.

17 "Do you not see what they are doing in the cities of Judah and in the streets of Jerusalem?

18 "The [1]children gather wood, and the fathers kindle the fire, and the women knead dough to make cakes for the queen of heaven; and *they* [a]pour out drink offerings to other gods in order to [b]spite Me.

19 "[a]Do they spite Me?" declares the LORD. "Is it not themselves *they spite,* to [1]their own [b]shame?"

20 Therefore thus says the Lord [1]GOD, "Behold, My [a]anger and My wrath will be poured out on this place, on man and on beast and on the [b]trees of the field and on the fruit of the ground; and it will burn and not be quenched."

21 Thus says the LORD of hosts, the God of Israel, "Add your [a]burnt offerings to your sacrifices and [b]eat flesh.

22 "For I did not [a]speak to your fathers, or command them in the day that I brought them out of the land of Egypt, concerning burnt offerings and sacrifices.

23 "But this is [1]what I commanded them, saying, '[a]Obey My voice, and [b]I will be your God, and you will be My people; and you will walk in all the way which I command you, that it may [c]be well with you.'

24 "Yet they [a]did not obey or incline their ear, but walked in *their own* counsels *and* in the stubbornness of their evil heart, and [1][b]went backward and not forward.

16 [a]Ex 32:10; Deut 9:14; Jer 11:14
18 [1]Lit *sons* [a]Jer 19:13 [b]Deut 32:16, 21; 1 Kin 14:9; 16:2; Jer 11:17; Ezek 8:17
19 [1]Lit *their faces'* [a]Job 35:6; 1 Cor 10:22 [b]Jer 9:19; 15:9; 22:22
20 [1]Heb *YHWH,* usually rendered *LORD* [a]Is 42:25; Jer 6:11, 12; 42:18; Lam 2:3-5; 4:11 [b]Jer 8:13; 11:16
21 [a]Is 1:11; Jer 6:20; 14:12; Amos 5:22 [b]Ezek 33:25; Hos 8:13
22 [a]1 Sam 15:22; Ps 51:16; Hos 6:6
23 [1]Lit *the word which* [a]Ex 15:26; 16:32; Deut 6:3 [b]Ex 19:5, 6; Lev 26:12; Jer 11:4; 13:11 [c]Is 3:10; Jer 38:20; 42:6
24 [1]Lit *they were* [a]Deut 29:19; Ps 81:11; Jer 11:8; Ezek 20:8, 13, 16, 21 [b]Jer 15:6
25 [a]2 Chr 36:15; Jer 25:4; 29:19; Luke 11:49
26 [a]Neh 9:16; Jer 17:23; 19:15 [b]Jer 16:12; Matt 23:32
27 [a]Jer 1:7; 26:2; Ezek 2:7 [b]Is 50:2; 65:12; Zech 7:13
28 [1]Lit *faithfulness* [a]Jer 6:17; 11:10 [b]Is 59:14, 15; Jer 9:5
29 [1]Lit *your crown* [a]Job 1:20; Is 15:2; 22:12; Jer 16:6; Mic 1:16 [b]Jer 3:21; 9:17, 18 [c]Jer 6:30; 14:19
30 [a]2 Kin 21:3f; 2 Chr 33:3-5, 7; Jer 32:34, 35; Ezek 7:20; Dan 9:27; 11:31
31 [1]Lit *heart* [a]2 Kin 23:10; Jer 19:5; 32:35 [b]Lev 18:21; 2 Kin 17:17; Ps 106:38 [c]Deut 17:3
32 [a]Jer 19:6, 11

25 "Since the day that your fathers came out of the land of Egypt until this day, I have [a]sent you all My servants the prophets, daily rising early and sending *them.*

26 "Yet they did not listen to Me or incline their ear, but [a]stiffened their neck; they [b]did more evil than their fathers.

27 "You shall [a]speak all these words to them, but they will not listen to you; and you shall call to them, but they will [b]not answer you.

28 "You shall say to them, 'This is the nation that [a]did not obey the voice of the LORD their God or accept correction; [1][b]truth has perished and has been cut off from their mouth.

29 '[a]Cut off [1]your hair and cast *it* away,
And [b]take up a lamentation on the bare heights;
For the LORD has [c]rejected and forsaken
The generation of His wrath.'

30 "For the sons of Judah have done that which is evil in My sight," declares the LORD, "they have [a]set their detestable things in the house which is called by My name, to defile it.

31 "They have [a]built the high places of Topheth, which is in the valley of the son of Hinnom, to [b]burn their sons and their daughters in the fire, which I [c]did not command, and it did not come into My [1]mind.

32 "[a]Therefore, behold, days are coming,"

7:16 Perhaps the events of ch. 26 belong chronologically between vv. 15 and 16 (see Introduction: Outline). *do not pray for this people.* As a true prophet would (see 27:18; Ex 32:31–32; 1 Sam 12:23). See 11:14; 14:11. There is virtually no hope for them. On various occasions, however, Jeremiah prayed for his countrymen (see, e.g., 18:20).

7:18 *children . . . fathers . . . women.* Entire families participate in idolatrous worship. *cakes.* See 44:19. *queen of heaven.* A Babylonian title for Ishtar, an important goddess in the Babylonian pantheon (see 44:17–19,25). *drink offerings to other gods.* And sometimes to the queen of heaven herself (see 44:19,25). *to spite Me.* See Deut 31:29.

7:19 *their own shame.* See 3:25.

7:20 All nature suffers when God judges sinners (see 5:17; Rom 8:20–22). *burn and not be quenched.* See 4:4; 21:12; see also Is 1:31; Amos 5:6.

7:21 Because of your sinful deeds your sacrifices are worthless, so you might as well eat them yourselves.

7:22–23 Sacrifices are valid only when accompanied by sincere repentance and joyful obedience (see 6:20; Is 1:11–15 and note).

7:23 *your God . . . My people.* The most basic summary of the relationship between God and Israel implied in the covenant at Sinai (see Ex 6:7; Lev 26:12 and notes; Deut 26:17–18).

7:24 *walked in . . . evil heart.* See note on 3:17; see also Gen 6:5 and note.

7:25 *sent . . . sending.* See note on v. 13. *My servants the prophets.* See 25:4; 26:5; 29:19; 35:15; 44:4; see also Zech 1:6 and note. God had promised that Moses would be the first in a long line of prophets who would speak in the Lord's name and serve Him faithfully (see Deut 18:15–22 and notes).

7:26 *stiffened their neck.* See 17:23; 19:15; see also notes on Ex 32:9; Neh 3:5.

7:28 *not . . . accept correction.* See 2:30; 5:3. *truth . . . has been cut off from their mouth.* No one seeks the truth (see 5:1 and note).

7:29 Addressed to Jerusalem. *Cut off your hair.* A sign of mourning (see Job 1:20; Mic 1:16). The Hebrew for the word "hair" is related to the word "Nazirite" (see Num 6:2) and referred originally to the diadem worn by the high priest (see Ex 29:6). The Nazirite's hair was the symbol of his separation or consecration (Num 6:7). As the Nazirite was commanded to cut off his hair when he became ceremonially unclean (Num 6:9), so also Jerusalem must cut off her hair because of her sins. *lamentation on the bare heights.* See 3:21; see also note on 3:2.

7:30 *set their detestable things in the house.* Manasseh had put a carved Asherah pole (a wooden symbol of the goddess Asherah; see 2 Kin 13:6 and note) in the temple (2 Kin 21:7). Jeremiah's contemporary, the good King Josiah, removed the pole and other accessories to idol worship (2 Kin 23:4–7). But less than 20 years after Josiah's death, Ezekiel reported that there were numerous idols in the temple courts (see Ezek 8:3,5–6,10,12). *defile it.* See note on 2:7.

7:31 *high places.* Pagan cult centers, usually (but not here) located on natural heights (see 1 Sam 9:13–14; 10:5; 1 Kin 11:7). *Topheth.* See v. 32; 19:6,11–14; see also note on Is 30:33. The

declares the LORD, "when it will no longer be called Topheth, or the valley of the son of Hinnom, but the valley of the Slaughter; for they will [b]bury in Topheth [1]because there is no *other* place.

33 "The [a]dead bodies of this people will be food for the birds of the sky and for the beasts of the earth; and no one will frighten *them away.*

34 "Then I will make to [a]cease from the cities of Judah and from the streets of Jerusalem the voice of joy and the voice of gladness, the voice of the bridegroom and the voice of the bride; for the [b]land will become a ruin.

The Sin and Treachery of Judah

8 "At that time," declares the LORD, "they will [a]bring out the bones of the kings of Judah and the bones of its princes, and the bones of the priests and the bones of the prophets, and the bones of the inhabitants of Jerusalem from their graves.

2 "They will spread them out to the sun, the moon and to all the [a]host of heaven, which they have loved and which they have served, and which they have gone after and which they have sought, and which they have worshiped. They will not be gathered [b]or buried; [c]they will be as dung on the face of the ground.

3 "And [a]death will be chosen rather than life by all the remnant that remains of this evil family, that remains in all the [b]places to which I have driven them," declares the LORD of hosts.

4 "You shall say to them, 'Thus says the LORD,

"Do *men* [a]fall and not get up again?
Does one turn away and not [1]repent?
5 "Why then has this people, Jerusalem,
[a]Turned away in continual apostasy?
They [b]hold fast to deceit,
They [c]refuse to return.
6 "I [a]have listened and heard,
They have spoken what is not right;
[b]No man repented of his wickedness,
Saying, 'What have I done?'
Everyone turned to his course,
Like a [c]horse charging into the battle.
7 "Even the stork in the sky
[a]Knows her seasons;
And the [b]turtledove and the swift and the thrush
Observe the time of their [1]migration;
But [c]My people do not know
The ordinance of the LORD.

8 "[a]How can you say, 'We are wise,
And the law of the LORD is with us'?
But behold, the lying pen of the scribes
Has made *it* into a lie.
9 "The wise men are [a]put to shame,

32 [1]Or *until there is no place left* [a]Jer 19:6, 11 [b]2 Kin 23:10
33 [a]Deut 28:26; Ps 79:2; Jer 12:9; 19:7
34 [a]Is 24:7, 8; Jer 16:9; 25:10; Ezek 26:13; Hos 2:11; Rev 18:23 [b]Lev 26:33; Is 1:7; Jer 4:27
8:1 [a]Ezek 6:5
2 [a]2 Kin 23:5; Jer 19:13; Zeph 1:5; Acts 7:42 [b]Jer 22:19; 36:30 [c]2 Kin 9:37; Ps 83:10; Jer 9:22
3 [a]Job 3:21, 22; 7:15, 16; Jon 4:3; Rev 9:6
3 [b]Deut 30:1, 4; Jer 23:3, 8; 29:14
4 [1]Lit *turn back* [a]Prov 24:16; Amos 5:2; Mic 7:8
5 [a]Jer 5:6; 7:24 [b]Jer 5:27; 9:6 [c]Jer 5:3
6 [a]Ps 14:2; Mal 3:16 [b]Ezek 22:30; Mic 7:2; Rev 9:20 [c]Job 39:21-25
7 [1]Lit *coming* [a]Prov 6:6-8; Is 1:3 [b]Song 2:12 [c]Jer 5:4
8 [a]Job 5:12, 13; Jer 4:22; Rom 1:22
9 [a]Is 19:11; Jer 6:15; 1 Cor 1:27

---

word may be of Aramaic origin with the meaning "fireplace," though in cultures outside Israel it was used as a common noun meaning "place of child sacrifice." Its vocalization was perhaps intentionally conformed to that of Hebrew *bosheth,* "shameful thing" (see note on Judg 6:32), often used in connection with idol worship (see notes on 2:26; 3:25). The OT Topheth had a fire pit (see Is 30:33), into which the hapless children were apparently thrown. *valley of the son of Hinnom.* See v. 32; 19:2,6; 32:35; see also note on Josh 15:5. It was used as a trash dump and also as a place for sacrificing children to pagan gods. From the abbreviated name "valley of Hinnom" (see Neh 11:30 and note), Hebrew *ge'hinnom,* came "Gehenna" (Greek *geenna*), consistently translated in the NT as "hell," the place of eternal, fiery punishment for all who die without having trusted Christ as Savior (see, e.g., Matt 18:9; Mark 9:47–48). *burn their sons and their daughters in the fire.* A horrible ritual, prohibited in the law of Moses (see Lev 18:21 and note; Deut 18:10) but practiced by Ahaz (see 2 Kin 16:2–3) and Manasseh (2 Kin 21:1,6).

7:32 *behold . . . valley of the Slaughter.* Repeated almost verbatim in 19:6. Their place of sacrifice would become their cemetery when the people of Judah were slaughtered by the Babylonian invaders.

7:33 The punishment announced here is one of the curses for covenant disobedience (see Deut 28:26). *food for the birds . . . of the earth.* See 16:4; 19:7; see also 34:20, where the same judgment is the result of violating God's covenant (34:18–19). To remain unburied was an unspeakable abomination in ancient times.

7:34 See 16:9; 25:10; contrast 33:10–11. *land will become a ruin.* Another covenant curse (Lev 26:31,33).

8:1 *bring out the bones . . . from their graves.* A gross indignity and sacrilege (see 2 Kin 23:16,18; Amos 2:1 and note). *kings . . . princes . . . priests . . . prophets.* See 2:26; see also note on 1:18.

8:2 *spread them out to the sun . . . moon . . . host of heaven.* To hasten their disintegration, and perhaps also to demonstrate that the heavenly bodies, which had been worshiped by some of Judah's kings (see 2 Kin 21:3,5; 23:11), among others, were powerless to help. *loved . . . served . . . gone after . . . sought . . . worshiped.* Acts of homage and adoration that should have been given to God alone. *They.* The bones. *not be gathered or buried.* Contrast 2 Sam 21:13–14. *dung.* See 9:22; 16:4; 25:33.

8:3 *remnant that remains.* See note on 6:9.

8:4–9:26 In contrast to 7:1–8:3, this section is almost completely in poetic form. Jeremiah resumes his extended commentary on the inevitability of divine judgment against sinners.

8:4 *say to them.* Connects this section with the previous (see 7:28). *turn away . . . repent.* The Hebrew for these two verbs is identical, forming a play on words.

8:5 The general truths stated in v. 4 are routinely and perversely violated by the people of Jerusalem. *Turned away . . . continual . . . return.* Continuing the wordplay of v. 4.

8:6 *I.* The Lord. *turned.* The Hebrew for this word continues the wordplay of vv. 4–5. *his course.* And therefore evil (see 23:10).

8:7 See Is 1:3. Although migratory birds obey their God-given instincts, God's rebellious people refuse to obey His laws. *do not know The ordinance of the LORD.* See note on 5:4.

8:8–9 *law of the LORD . . . word of the LORD.* Misinterpreting and manipulating the first (the written law of Moses) leads to rejection of the second (God's truth as found in the law and proclaimed by His servants the prophets).

8:8 *lying pen.* Symbolizes mistreatment of the written law. *scribes.* The earliest mention of them as a recognizable group. They were apparently organized on the basis of families (see 1 Chr 2:55; 2 Chr 34:13). *made it into a lie.* Contrast 2 Tim 2:15.

They are dismayed and caught;
Behold, they have [b]rejected the word
of the LORD,
And what kind of wisdom do they
have?
10 "Therefore I will [a]give their wives to
others,
Their fields to [1]new owners;
Because from the least even to the
greatest
Everyone is [b]greedy for gain;
From the prophet even to the priest
Everyone practices deceit.
11 "They [a]heal the brokenness of the
daughter of My people superficially,
Saying, 'Peace, peace,'
But there is no peace.
12 "Were they [a]ashamed because of the
abomination they had done?
They certainly were not ashamed,
And they did not know how to blush;
Therefore they shall [b]fall among those
who fall;
At the [c]time of their punishment they
shall be brought down,"
Says the LORD.

13 "I will [a]surely snatch them away,"
declares the LORD;
"There will be [b]no grapes on the vine
And [c]no figs on the fig tree,
And the leaf will wither;
And what I have given them will pass
away." ' "
14 Why are we sitting still?
[a]Assemble yourselves, and let us [b]go
into the fortified cities
And let us perish there,
Because the LORD our God has
doomed us
And given us [c]poisoned water to drink,
For [d]we have sinned against the LORD.

9 [b]Jer 6:19
10 [1]Lit *possessing ones* [a]Deut 28:30; Jer 6:12, 13; 38:22f [b]Is 56:11; 57:17; Jer 6:13
11 [a]Jer 6:14; 14:13, 14; Lam 2:14; Ezek 13:10
12 [a]Ps 52:1, 7; Is 3:9; Jer 3:3; 6:15; Zeph 3:5 [b]Is 9:14; Jer 6:21; Hos 4:5 [c]Deut 32:35; Jer 10:15
13 [a]Jer 14:12; Ezek 22:20, 21 [b]Jer 5:17; 7:20; Joel 1:7 [c]Matt 21:19; Luke 13:6
14 [a]Jer 4:5 [b]2 Sam 20:6; Jer 35:11 [c]Deut 29:18; Ps 69:21; Jer 9:15; 23:15; Lam 3:19; Matt 27:34 [d]Jer 3:25; 14:20
15 [a]Jer 8:11; 14:19
16 [a]Judg 18:29; Jer 4:15 [b]Judg 5:22 [c]Jer 3:24; 10:25
17 [a]Num 21:6; Deut 32:24 [b]Ps 58:4, 5
18 [1]So Gr and versions [a]Is 22:4; Lam 1:16, 17 [b]Jer 23:9; Lam 5:17
19 [1]Lit *vanities* [a]Is 13:5; 39:3; Jer 4:16; 9:16 [b]Deut 32:21; Jer 7:19 [c]Ps 31:6
21 [a]Jer 4:19; 9:1; 14:17 [b]Jer 14:2; Joel 2:6; Nah 2:10
22 [1]Or *healing* [2]Lit *gone up* [a]Gen 37:25; Jer 46:11 [b]Jer 14:19; 30:13
9:1 [1]Ch 8:23 in Heb [a]Is 22:4; Jer 8:18; 13:17; Lam 2:18

15 *We* [a]waited for peace, but no good
came;
For a time of healing, but behold,
terror!
16 From [a]Dan is heard the snorting of his
horses;
At the sound of the neighing of his
[b]stallions
The whole land quakes;
For they come and [c]devour the land
and its fullness,
The city and its inhabitants.
17 "For behold, I am [a]sending serpents
against you,
Adders, for which there is [b]no charm,
And they will bite you," declares the
LORD.

18 [1]My [a]sorrow is beyond healing,
My [b]heart is faint *within me!*
19 Behold, listen! The cry of the daughter
of my people from a [a]distant land:
"Is the LORD not in Zion? Is her King
not within her?"
"Why have they [b]provoked Me with
their graven images, with foreign
[1][c]idols?"
20 "Harvest is past, summer is ended,
And we are not saved."
21 For the [a]brokenness of the daughter of
my people I am broken;
I [b]mourn, dismay has taken hold of
me.
22 Is there no [a]balm in Gilead?
Is there no physician there?
[b]Why then has not the [1]health of the
daughter of my people [2]been
restored?

A Lament over Zion

9 [1][a]Oh that my head were waters
And my eyes a fountain of tears,

8:9 *rejected . . . wisdom.* Contrast Deut 4:5–6.
8:10–12 See 6:12–15 and notes.
8:13–9:24 This section is read aloud in synagogues every year on the ninth of Ab (see chart, p. 92), the day the temple in Jerusalem was destroyed by the Babylonians in 586 B.C. and by the Romans in A.D. 70.
8:13 *grapes . . . figs.* Symbolic of individual people also in Mic 7:1; see ch. 24. *vine.* Israel (see 2:21 and note). *leaf will wither.* Contrast 17:8; Ps 1:3.
8:14–16 On behalf of the people the prophet speaks, envisioning the Babylonian invasion.
8:14 *Assemble yourselves.* See 4:5. The Hebrew for this phrase forms a wordplay with the Hebrew for "snatch them away" in v. 13. *go into to the fortified cities.* See note on 4:5. *poisoned water.* The phrase is unique to the prophet Jeremiah (see 9:15; 23:15; cf. 25:15).
8:15 Repeated almost verbatim in 14:19. *peace.* Under the circumstances, a false hope (see notes on 4:10; 6:14). *healing.* See note on 6:7.
8:16 *Dan.* Far away, close to the northern border of Israel. *his horses.* See note on 4:13. *stallions.* Lit. "mighty ones"; see 47:3; 50:11.
8:17 *serpents . . . for which there is no charm.* Such are the wicked always (see Ps 58:4–5).
8:18 The prophet speaks. *My heart is faint.* See Lam 1:22; 5:17.
8:19 The prophet speaks in the first part of the verse, the Lord in the last part. *my people from a distant land.* Judah in Babylonian exile (see Ps 137:1–4) as Jeremiah envisions the future. *Is the LORD not in Zion?* Cf. Mic 3:11. The people are perplexed at their fate, still wondering how God could have permitted the destruction of His land and temple (see note on 7:4). *King.* God (see Is 33:22). *provoked Me.* See 7:18; Deut 31:29. *graven . . . idols.* See note on 2:5.
8:20 The people speak from the hopelessness of their exile. *we are not saved.* We have been captured by the enemy.
8:21 Jeremiah identifies himself with his exiled countrymen. *taken hold of me.* See 6:24.
8:22 *balm in Gilead.* See 46:11; 51:8. The territory of Gilead was an important source of spices and medicinal herbs (see note on Gen 37:25). *not the health . . . been restored.* Contrast 30:17.
9:1–2 The prophet's frustration is highlighted as he speaks of his countrymen with tender sympathy in v. 1 and with indignant disgust in v. 2.
9:1 Jeremiah is often called the "weeping prophet"—a well-

That I might weep day and night
For the slain of the [b]daughter of my people!
2 [1][a]Oh that I had in the desert
A wayfarers' lodging place;
That I might leave my people
And go from them!
For all of them are [b]adulterers,
An assembly of [c]treacherous men.
3 "They [a]bend their tongue *like* their bow;
Lies and not truth prevail in the land;
For they [b]proceed from evil to evil,
And they [c]do not know Me," declares the LORD.
4 "Let everyone [a]be on guard against his neighbor,
And [b]do not trust any brother;
Because every [c]brother deals [1]craftily,
And every neighbor [d]goes about as a slanderer.
5 "Everyone [a]deceives his neighbor
And does not speak the truth,
They have taught their tongue to speak lies;
They [b]weary themselves committing iniquity.
6 "Your [a]dwelling is in the midst of deceit;
Through deceit they [b]refuse to know Me," declares the LORD.

7 Therefore thus says the LORD of hosts,
"Behold, I will refine them and [a]assay them;
For [b]what *else* can I do, because of the daughter of My people?
8 "Their [a]tongue is a deadly arrow;
It speaks deceit;
With his mouth one [b]speaks peace to his neighbor,
But inwardly he [c]sets an ambush for him.
9 "[a]Shall I not punish them for these things?" declares the LORD.
"On a nation such as this
Shall I not avenge Myself?

10 "For the [a]mountains I will take up a weeping and wailing,
And for the pastures of the [b]wilderness a dirge,
Because they are [c]laid waste so that no one passes through,
And the lowing of the cattle is not heard;
Both the [d]birds of the sky and the beasts have fled; they are gone.
11 "I will make Jerusalem a [a]heap of ruins,
A haunt of [b]jackals;
And I will make the cities of Judah a [c]desolation, without inhabitant."

12 Who is the [a]wise man that may understand this? And *who is* he to whom [b]the
mouth of the LORD has spoken, that he may
declare it? [c]Why is the land ruined, laid waste
like a desert, so that no one passes through?
13 The LORD said, "Because they have
[a]forsaken My law which I set before them,
and have not obeyed My voice nor walked
according to it,
14 but have [a]walked after the stubbornness of their heart and after the [b]Baals, as
their [c]fathers taught them,"
15 therefore thus says the LORD of hosts,
the God of Israel, "behold, [a]I will feed them,
this people, with wormwood and give them
[b]poisoned water to drink.
16 "I will [a]scatter them among the nations,
whom neither they nor their fathers have
known; and I will send the [b]sword after
them until I have annihilated them."

9:1 [b]Jer 6:26; 8:21, 22
2 [1]Ch 9:1 in Heb [a]Ps 55:6, 7; 120:5, 6 [b]Jer 5:7, 8; 23:10; Hos 4:2 [c]Jer 5:11; 12:1, 6
3 [a]Ps 64:3; Is 59:4; Jer 9:8 [b]Jer 4:22 [c]Judg 2:10; 1 Sam 2:12; Jer 4:22; 5:4, 5; Hos 4:1; 1 Cor 15:34
4 [1]I.e. like Jacob (a play on words) [a]Ps 12:2; Prov 26:24, 25; Jer 9:8; Mic 7:5, 6 [b]Jer 12:6 [c]Gen 27:35 [d]Ps 15:3; Prov 10:18; Jer 6:28
5 [a]Mic 6:12 [b]Jer 12:13; 51:58, 64
6 [a]Ps 120:5, 6; Jer 5:27; 8:5 [b]Job 21:14, 15; Prov 1:24; Jer 11:10; 13:10; John 3:19, 20
7 [a]Is 1:25; Jer 6:27; Mal 3:3 [b]Hos 11:8
8 [a]Jer 9:3 [b]Ps 28:3 [c]Jer 5:26
9 [a]Is 1:24; Jer 5:9, 29
10 [a]Jer 4:24; 7:29 [b]Jer 4:26; Hos 4:3 [c]Jer 12:4, 10; Ezek 14:15; 29:11; 33:28 [d]Jer 4:25; 12:4; Hos 4:3
11 [a]Is 25:2; Jer 51:37 [b]Is 13:22; 34:13 [c]Jer 4:27; 26:9
12 [a]Ps 107:43; Is 42:23; Hos 14:9 [b]Jer 9:20; 23:16 [c]Ps 107:34; Jer 23:10
13 [a]2 Chr 7:19; Ps 89:30; Jer 5:19; 22:9
14 [a]Jer 7:24; 11:8; Rom 1:21-24 [b]Jer 2:8, 23; 23:27 [c]Gal 1:14; 1 Pet 1:18
15 [a]Ps 80:5 [b]Deut 29:18; Jer 8:14; 23:15; Lam 3:15
16 [a]Lev 26:33; Deut 28:64; Jer 13:24 [b]Jer 44:27; Ezek 5:2, 12

deserved title (see v. 10; the book of Lamentations; cf. 2 Sam 18:33; Matt 23:37; Rom 9:2–4; 10:1).

9:2 The prophet wants to get as far away from his wicked countrymen as possible (cf. Ps 55:6–8). *adulterers.* See note on 2:20. *assembly.* The Hebrew for this word is always used elsewhere in the OT in the sense of a solemn religious assembly (see, e.g., Deut 16:8), sometimes perverted by the worshipers and therefore falling under divine judgment (see Is 1:13; Amos 5:21). *treacherous.* Toward God (see note on 3:7).

9:3–9 The Lord speaks.

9:3 *tongue like their bow.* See vv. 5,8; see also Ps 64:3–4; James 3:5–12. *do not know Me.* See v. 6; Judg 2:10; 1 Sam 2:12; Job 18:21; Hos 4:1; Rom 1:28; contrast Hos 6:3.

9:4 *deals craftily.* A deceiving Jacob (see Gen 25:26 and note; 27:36; Hos 12:2–3).

9:6 *refuse to know Me.* The situation has deteriorated even further (v. 3 says simply "do not know Me").

9:7 *refine . . . and assay.* See 6:27–30 and notes. The Lord will test His people "in the furnace of affliction" (see Is 48:10 and note).

9:8 *tongue . . . deceit.* See v. 3 and note. *With his mouth . . . But inwardly.* See Ps 55:21. *peace.* See 6:14 and note.

9:9 Repeated from 5:9,29.

9:10 The prophet speaks. See 4:23–26 and notes. *weeping and wailing.* See v. 18; see also note on v. 1. *pastures of the wilderness.* Good for poor grazing at best (see 1 Sam 17:28; cf. Ex 3:1). *laid waste.* Lit. "burned"; here parched by the blazing sun. *no one passes through.* See v. 12; Ezek 33:28.

9:11 The Lord speaks. *haunt of jackals.* See 10:22; 49:33; 51:37; Ps 44:19; Is 13:21–22; Lam 5:18; Ezek 13:4; Mal 1:3; contrast Is 35:7. *without inhabitant.* See 2:15; 4:7 and notes.

9:12 The prophet asks a series of questions. *Who is the wise man . . . ?* See Hos 14:9.

9:13 The Lord answers the prophet and then continues to speak through v. 19. *law which I set before them.* In the days of Moses (see Deut 4:8).

9:14 *stubbornness.* See note on 3:17. *Baals.* See 2:23; see also note on Judg 2:11.

9:15 *feed them . . . with wormwood and . . . poisoned water.* Repeated in 23:15; see note on 8:14. Centuries earlier, Moses had warned the Israelites concerning just such a fate (see Deut 29:18).

9:16 *I will scatter them.* See 13:24; 18:17; 30:11; 46:28. This warning was given in Deut 28:64 as one of the covenant curses. *send the sword after them.* See 42:16. *annihilated them.* But not to the last man (see note on 4:27; see especially 44:27–28).

17 Thus says the LORD of hosts,
"Consider and call for the [a]mourning
women, that they may come;
And send for the [1b]wailing women,
that they may come!
18 "Let them make haste and take up a
wailing for us,
That our [a]eyes may shed tears
And our eyelids flow with water.
19 "For a voice of [a]wailing is heard from
Zion,
'[b]How are we ruined!
We are put to great shame,
For we have [c]left the land,
Because they have cast down our
dwellings.' "
20 Now hear the word of the LORD, O you
[a]women,
And let your ear receive the word of
His mouth;
Teach your daughters wailing,
And everyone her neighbor a dirge.
21 For [a]death has come up through our
windows;
It has entered our palaces
To cut off the [b]children from the
streets,
The young men from the town squares.
22 Speak, "Thus says the LORD,
'The corpses of men will fall [a]like dung
on the open field,
And like the sheaf after the reaper,
But no one will gather *them.*' "
23 Thus says the LORD, "[a]Let not a wise
man boast of his wisdom, and let not the
[b]mighty man boast of his might, let not a
[c]rich man boast of his riches;
24 but let him who boasts [a]boast of this,
that he understands and knows Me, that I
am the LORD who [b]exercises lovingkindness,
justice and righteousness on earth; for I
[c]delight in these things," declares the LORD.
25 "Behold, the days are coming," declares
the LORD, "that I will punish all who are circumcised and yet [a]uncircumcised—
26 Egypt and Judah, and Edom and the
sons of Ammon, and Moab and [a]all those
inhabiting the desert who clip the hair on
their temples; for all the nations are uncircumcised, and all the house of Israel are
[b]uncircumcised of heart."

A Satire on Idolatry

10 Hear the word which the LORD speaks
to you, O house of Israel.
2 Thus says the LORD,
"[a]Do not learn the way of the nations,
And do not be terrified by the signs of
the heavens
Although the nations are terrified by
them;
3 For the customs of the peoples are
[1a]delusion;
Because [b]it is wood cut from the forest,
The work of the hands of a craftsman
with a cutting tool.
4 "They [a]decorate *it* with silver and with
gold;
They [b]fasten it with nails and with
hammers

17 [1]Lit *skilled* [a]2 Chr 35:25; Eccl 12:5 [b]Amos 5:16
18 [a]Is 22:4; Jer 9:1; 14:17
19 [a]Jer 7:29; Ezek 7:16-18 [b]Deut 28:29; Jer 4:13 [c]Jer 7:15; 15:1
20 [a]Is 32:9
21 [a]2 Chr 36:17; Jer 15:7; 18:21; Ezek 9:5, 6; Amos 6:9, 10 [b]Jer 6:11
22 [a]Ps 83:10; Is 5:25; Jer 8:2; 16:4; 25:33
23 [a]Eccl 9:11; Is 47:10; Ezek 28:3-7
23 [b]1 Kin 20:10, 11; Is 10:8-12 [c]Job 31:24, 25; Ps 49:6-9
24 [a]Ps 20:7; 44:8; Is 41:16; Jer 4:2; 1 Cor 1:31; 2 Cor 10:17; Gal 6:14 [b]Ex 34:6, 7; Ps 36:5, 7; 51:1 [c]Is 61:8; Mic 7:18
25 [a]Jer 4:4; Rom 2:28, 29
26 [a]Jer 25:23 [b]Lev 26:41; Jer 4:4; 6:10; Ezek 44:7; Rom 2:28
10:2 [a]Lev 18:3; 20:23; Deut 12:30
3 [1]Lit *vanity* [a]Jer 14:22 [b]Is 44:9-20
4 [a]Is 40:19 [b]Is 40:20; 41:7

9:17 *mourning women.* Professionals, paid to mourn at funerals and other sorrowful occasions (see 2 Chr 35:25; Eccl 12:5; Amos 5:16).
9:18 The purpose of the professional mourners was to arouse the bereaved to weep and lament. *wailing.* See v. 10. *eyes may shed tears.* See v. 1.
9:19 *How are we ruined!* See 4:13,20; 48:1.
9:20–21 The prophet speaks.
9:20 The wailing women will have to teach their daughters how to lament, so great will be the need for their services.
9:21 *death.* Personified here (as in Hab 2:5). Canaanite mythology included a deity named Mot (a word related to the Hebrew word for "death"), the god of infertility and the netherworld. *come up through our windows.* Said of enemy soldiers in Joel 2:9. *children . . . young men.* See 6:11.
9:22 *corpses.* See 7:33 and note. *like dung.* See note on 8:2. *reaper.* The concept of death as the "grim reaper" comes largely from this verse.
9:23 *Let not . . . a rich man boast of his riches.* An almost exact parallel occurs in the Aramaic *Words of Ahiqar,* written about a century after Jeremiah's time: "Let not the rich man say, 'In my riches I am glorious.' "
9:24 1 Cor 1:31 summarizes: "Let him who boasts, boast in the Lord." *this . . . these.* Ultimately, only God and our knowledge of and love for Him are worthwhile. *understands and knows.* See 3:15; see also note on 4:22. *I am the LORD.* Ex 6:2–8, a key passage on the doctrine of redemption, begins and ends with this statement of divine self-disclosure. *lovingkindness.* The Hebrew for this word is translated "devotion" in 2:2 (see note there). *I delight in these things.* See Ps 11:7; 33:5; 99:4; 103:6; Mic 6:8; 7:18.
9:25–26 See Rom 2:25–29; see also note on Gen 17:10.
9:26 *inhabiting . . . on their temples.* Arab tribes (see 25:23; 49:32), later to be attacked by the Babylonians under Nebuchadnezzar (see 49:28–33). Cf. Lev 19:27. *uncircumcised of heart.* See 4:4 and note.
10:1–25 Jeremiah concludes his series of temple messages with a poetic section that focuses primarily on the vast difference between idols and the Lord (vv. 2–16). Idols and their worshipers are condemned in vv. 2–5,8–9,11,14–15, while the one true God is praised in the alternate passages (vv. 6–7,10,12–13,16). See Is 40:18–20; 41:7; 44:9–20; 46:5–7.
10:1 *Hear.* See note on 2:4.
10:2 *Do not . . . be terrified.* See 1:17. *way.* Refers to the religious practices of the nations. The early Christians often called their distinctive beliefs "the Way" (see Acts 9:2; 19:9,23; 22:4; 24:14,22). *signs of the heavens.* The heavenly bodies were created by the Lord for purposes other than idolatrous worship (see Gen 1:14–18 and notes). *nations are terrified.* Not only by the heavenly bodies themselves but also by unusual phenomena associated with them (such as comets, meteors and eclipses).
10:3 *delusion.* A term that Jeremiah often applies to idols (see vv. 8,15; see also note on 2:5). *wood . . . forest.* See Is 44:14–15. *craftsman.* The word is often used of idol-makers who work usually—but not always (see Is 40:19)—with wood (see Is 41:7). *cutting tool.* Cf. Is 44:13.
10:4 *with silver and . . . gold.* Wooden idols were plated with precious metals to beautify them (see Is 30:22; 40:19). *fasten it . . . So that it will not totter.* See Is 40:20; 41:7; cf. 46:7; contrast 1 Sam 5:2–4.

So that it will not totter.
5 "Like a scarecrow in a cucumber field
are they,
And they [a]cannot speak;
They must be [b]carried,
Because they cannot walk!
Do not fear them,
For they [c]can do no harm,
Nor can they do any good."

6 [a]There is none like You, O LORD;
You are [b]great, and great is Your name
in might.
7 [a]Who would not fear You, O [b]King of
the nations?
Indeed it is Your due!
For among all the [c]wise men of the
nations
And in all their kingdoms,
There is none like You.
8 But they are altogether [a]stupid and
foolish
In their discipline of [1]delusion—[2]their
idol is wood!
9 Beaten [a]silver is brought from
[b]Tarshish,
And [c]gold from Uphaz,
The work of a craftsman and of the
hands of a goldsmith;
Violet and purple are their clothing;
They are all the [d]work of skilled men.
10 But the LORD is the [a]true God;
He is the [b]living God and the
[c]everlasting King.
At His wrath the [d]earth quakes,
And the nations cannot [e]endure His
indignation.

11 [1]Thus you shall say to them, "The
[a]gods that did not make the heavens and the
earth will [b]perish from the earth and from
under the [2]heavens."

12 *It is* [a]He who made the earth by His
power,
Who [b]established the world by His
wisdom;
And by His understanding He has
[c]stretched out the heavens.
13 When He utters His [a]voice, *there is* a
tumult of waters in the heavens,
And He causes the [b]clouds to ascend
from the end of the earth;
He makes lightning for the rain,
And brings out the [c]wind from His
storehouses.
14 Every man is [a]stupid, devoid of
knowledge;
Every goldsmith is put to shame by
his [1]idols;
For his molten images are deceitful,
And there is no breath in them.
15 They are [a]worthless, a work of
mockery;
In the [b]time of their punishment they
will perish.
16 The [a]portion of Jacob is not like these;
For the [1][b]Maker of all is He,
And [c]Israel is the tribe of His
inheritance;
The [d]LORD of hosts is His name.

17 [a]Pick up your bundle from the ground,
You who dwell under siege!
18 For thus says the LORD,
"Behold, I am [a]slinging out the
inhabitants of the land
At this time,
And will cause them distress,
That they may [1]be found."

19 [a]Woe is me, because of my [1]injury!
My [b]wound is incurable.

5 [a]Ps 115:5; Is 46:7; Jer 10:14; 1 Cor 12:2 [b]Ps 115:7; Is 46:1, 7 [c]Is 41:23, 24
6 [a]Ex 15:11; Deut 33:26; Ps 86:8, 10; Jer 10:16 [b]Ps 48:1; 96:4; Is 12:6; Jer 32:18
7 [a]Rev 15:4 [b]Ps 22:28 [c]Dan 2:27, 28; 1 Cor 1:19, 20
8 [1]Lit *vanities,* or *idols* [2]Lit *it is* [a]Jer 4:22; 5:4; 10:14
9 [a]Is 40:19 [b]Ps 72:10; Is 23:6 [c]Dan 10:5 [d]Ps 115:4
10 [a]Is 65:16 [b]Jer 4:2 [c]Ps 10:16; 29:10 [d]Jer 4:24; 50:46 [e]Ps 76:7
11 [1]This verse is in Aram [2]Or *these heavens* [a]Ps 96:5 [b]Is 2:18; Zeph 2:11
12 [a]Gen 1:1, 6; Job 38:4-7; Ps 136:5; 148:4, 5; Jer 51:15, 19 [b]Ps 78:69; Is 45:18 [c]Job 9:8; Is 40:22
13 [a]Ps 29:3-9 [b]Job 36:27-29 [c]Ps 135:7
14 [1]Or *graven image* [a]Jer 10:8; 51:17, 18
15 [a]Is 41:24; Jer 8:19; 14:22 [b]Jer 8:12; 51:18
16 [1]Lit *Fashioner* [a]Ps 16:5; 73:26; 119:57; Jer 51:19; Lam 3:24 [b]Is 45:7; Jer 10:12 [c]Deut 32:9; Ps 74:2 [d]Jer 31:35; 32:18
17 [a]Ezek 12:3-12
18 [1]Lit *find* [a]1 Sam 25:29
19 [1]Lit *breaking* [a]Jer 4:31 [b]Jer 14:17

10:5 The impotence of idols is described in classic form in Ps 115:4–7; 135:15–18. *scarecrow.* Verse 70 in the Apocryphal *Letter of Jeremiah* uses the same imagery. *must be carried.* Usually on the backs of animals. See Is 46:1. *harm, Nor . . . good.* Idols can do nothing at all (see Is 41:23).

10:6 *none.* Among the gods (see Ps 86:8). *great is Your name in might.* See 16:21.

10:7 *King of the nations.* See Ps 47:8–9; 96:10. Unlike the tribal deities, limited to their own territories, the Lord is King over all. *it.* Fear, respect. *among all the wise men . . . none like You.* See Is 19:12; 29:14; 1 Cor 1:20.

10:8 *stupid and foolish.* See vv. 14,21; 5:21; see also 4:22 and note. *discipline of delusion.* Contrast Deut 11:2; Job 5:17; Prov 3:11.

10:9 *silver . . . from Tarshish.* See Ezek 27:12; see also notes on Is 23:6; Jon 1:3. *Uphaz.* Mentioned only here; location unknown. *craftsman and . . . goldsmith.* See Is 40:19; 41:7. *Violet and purple . . . clothing.* To make the idols look regal. *all.* The idols.

10:10 Everything that idols are not, the Lord is. *true.* See 1 Thess 1:9. *living.* See Deut 5:26. *everlasting.* See Ex 15:18; Ps 10:16; 29:10. *At His . . . indignation.* See Ps 97:5; Nah 1:5.

10:11 The text of this verse is in Aramaic. The other major Aramaic passages in the OT are Ezra 4:8–6:18; 7:12–26; Dan 2:4–7:28. This verse is in prose. *them.* Pagan idolaters, who would have been more likely to understand Aramaic (the language of diplomacy during this period) than Hebrew.

10:12–16 Repeated almost verbatim in 51:15–19.

10:12 *It is He.* In contrast to the false gods of v. 11. *stretched out the heavens.* Like a tent or canopy (see Ps 104:2; Is 40:22 and note).

10:13 *He causes the clouds . . . from His storehouses.* Repeated in Ps 135:7, where the one true God is contrasted to false gods (see Ps 135:5,15–17); cf. Job 38:22.

10:14 *stupid.* See vv. 8,21; see also note on 4:22. *images.* Cast in metal; the Hebrew for this word is translated "molten image" in Is 48:5 and "metal images" in Dan 11:8. *no breath.* See Ps 135:17.

10:15 *worthless.* See note on v. 3.

10:16 *portion of Jacob.* A title for God, used again only in 51:19 (see Ps 73:26; 119:57; 142:5; Lam 3:24). *tribe of His inheritance.* See Is 63:17. *The LORD of hosts is His name.* See Is 54:5; Amos 4:13.

10:17–22 Destruction and exile are imminent.

10:19–20 On behalf of his countrymen, the prophet bemoans their fate and his own (see 4:19–21).

But I said, "Truly this is a sickness,
And I [c]must bear it."
20 My [a]tent is destroyed,
And all my ropes are broken;
My [b]sons have gone from me and are no more.
There is [c]no one to stretch out my tent again
Or to set up my curtains.
21 For the shepherds have become stupid
And [a]have not sought the LORD;
Therefore they have not prospered,
And [b]all their flock is scattered.
22 The sound of a [a]report! Behold, it comes—
A great commotion [b]out of the land of the north—
To [c]make the cities of Judah
A desolation, a haunt of jackals.

23 I know, O LORD, that [a]a man's way is not in himself,
[b]Nor is it in a man who walks to direct his steps.
24 [a]Correct me, O LORD, but with justice;
Not with Your anger, or You will [1]bring me to nothing.
25 [a]Pour out Your wrath on the nations that [b]do not know You
And on the families that [c]do not call Your name;
For they have devoured Jacob;
They have [d]devoured him and consumed him
And have laid waste his [1]habitation.

The Broken Covenant

11 The word which came to Jeremiah from the LORD, saying,
2 "[a]Hear the words of this [b]covenant, and
speak to the men of Judah and to the inhabitants of Jerusalem;
3 and say to them, 'Thus says the LORD,
the God of Israel, "[a]Cursed is the man who
does not heed the words of this covenant
4 which I commanded your forefathers in
the [a]day that I brought them out of the land
of Egypt, from the [b]iron furnace, saying,
'[c]Listen to My voice, and [1]do according to all
which I command you; so you shall be [d]My
people, and I will be your God,'
5 in order to confirm the [a]oath which I
swore to your forefathers, to give them a
land flowing with milk and honey, as *it is*
this day." ' " Then I said, "[b]Amen, O LORD."
6 And the LORD said to me, "[a]Proclaim all
these words in the cities of Judah and in the
streets of Jerusalem, saying, '[b]Hear the
words of this covenant and [c]do them.
7 'For I solemnly [a]warned your fathers in
the [b]day that I brought them up from the
land of Egypt, even to this day, [1c]warning
persistently, saying, "[d]Listen to My voice."
8 'Yet they [a]did not obey or incline their
ear, but walked, each one, in the stubbornness of his evil heart; therefore I brought on
them all the [b]words of this covenant, which
I commanded *them* to do, but they did not.' "
9 Then the LORD said to me, "A [a]conspir-
acy has been found among the men of Judah
and among the inhabitants of Jerusalem.
10 "They have [a]turned back to the iniquities of their [1]ancestors who [b]refused to hear
My words, and they [c]have gone after other
gods to serve them; the house of Israel and

19 [c]Mic 7:9 **20** [a]Jer 4:20; Lam 2:4 [b]Jer 31:15; Lam 1:5 [c]Is 51:18 **21** [a]Jer 2:8 [b]Jer 23:2 **22** [a]Jer 4:15 [b]Jer 1:14; 25:9 [c]Jer 9:11; 49:33 **23** [a]Prov 16:1; 20:24 [b]Is 26:7 **24** [1]Lit *diminish me* [a]Ps 6:1; 38:1 **25** [1]Or *pasture* [a]Ps 79:6, 7; Zeph 3:8 [b]Job 18:21; 1 Thess 4:5; 2 Thess 1:8 [c]Zeph 1:6 [d]Jer 8:16; 50:7, 17

11:2 [a]Jer 11:6 [b]Ex 19:5 **3** [a]Deut 27:26; Jer 17:5; Gal 3:10 **4** [1]Lit *do them* [a]Ex 24:3-8; Jer 31:32 [b]Deut 4:20; 1 Kin 8:51 [c]Lev 26:3; Deut 11:27; Jer 7:23; 26:13 [d]Jer 24:7; Zech 8:8 **5** [a]Ex 13:5; Deut 7:12; Ps 105:9; Jer 32:22 [b]Jer 28:6 **6** [a]Jer 3:12; 7:2 [b]Jer 11:2 [c]John 13:17; Rom 2:13; James 1:22 **7** [1]Lit *rising early and warning* [a]1 Sam 8:9 [b]Jer 11:4 [c]Ex 15:26; 2 Chr 36:15; Jer 7:25 [d]Jer 11:7 **8** [a]Jer 7:24; 9:14; 35:15; Ezek 20:8 [b]Lev 26:14-43 **9** [a]Ezek 22:25; Hos 6:9 **10** [1]Lit *former fathers* [a]1 Sam 15:11; Jer 3:10, 11; Ezek 20:18 [b]Deut 9:7; Ps 78:8-10; Jer 13:10 [c]Judg 2:11-13

10:20 *sons.* The people of Judah and Jerusalem (Jeremiah never married or had children; see 16:2). *curtains.* See note on 4:20.
10:21 *shepherds . . . flock.* Rulers and people (see note on 2:8). *stupid.* See vv. 8,14; see also note on 4:22. *have not sought the LORD.* Instead, they consult the heavenly bodies (see 8:2). *scattered.* See note on 9:16.
10:22 *great commotion.* The sound of the invaders (see 6:23; 8:16). *land of the north.* Babylonia (see 4:6; 6:22; see also note on Is 41:25). *haunt of jackals.* See 9:11 and note.
10:23–25 On the people's behalf, the prophet prays for divine justice.
10:23 Only the Lord can direct people's steps (see Ps 37:23; Prov 16:9).
10:25 Repeated almost verbatim in Ps 79:6–7, where the context (see Ps 79:1–5) shows that the prayer is not vengeful but is an appeal for God's justice. The verse is recited annually by Jews during their Passover service.
11:1–13:27 Because of Judah's violations of its covenant obligations, the people will be exiled to Babylonia. The section is perhaps to be dated to the reign of Josiah (but see note on 13:18).
11:1–17 God's people have broken His covenant with them.
11:2 *Hear.* See note on 2:4. *words.* A technical term for covenant stipulations (see vv. 3–4,6; 34:18; see also note on Ex 20:1). *this covenant.* See vv. 3,6,8,10; Deut 29:9. Reference is to the covenant established by God with Israel through Moses at Mount Sinai (see v. 4; Ex 19–24). *speak to.* Periodic public reading of covenants was a common and necessary practice (see Deut 31:10–13; Josh 8:34–35).
11:3 *Cursed is the man.* The phrase ("Cursed is he") appears at the beginning of every verse in Deut 27:15–26 (and "Amen" appears at the end; see note on v. 5). Blessings resulted from obedience to the covenant (see Deut 28:1–14); curses resulted from disobedience (see Deut 28:15–68; see also Deut 11:26–28; 29:20–21).
11:4 *out of . . . Egypt, from the iron furnace.* See note on Deut 4:20. *Listen to My voice.* See v. 7; 7:23; Ex 19:5. *you shall be My people . . . your God.* See note on 7:23.
11:5 *confirm the oath . . . I swore.* See Gen 15:17–18 and notes; Deut 7:8. *land flowing with milk and honey.* See 32:22; see also note on Ex 3:8. *Amen.* Appears at the end of every verse in Deut 27:15–26 (and "Cursed is he" appears at the beginning; see note on v. 3).
11:6 *Proclaim.* See 2:2; 3:12.
11:7 *persistently.* See note on 7:13.
11:8 See 7:24. *stubbornness of his evil heart.* See note on 3:17. *therefore I brought on them.* See 2 Kin 17:18–23.
11:9 *conspiracy.* Against the intended reforms of Josiah (see Introduction: Background; see also note on 1:2).
11:10 *refused.* Their sin was deliberate (see note on 9:6).

the house of Judah have [d]broken My covenant which I made with their fathers."
11 Therefore thus says the LORD, "Behold I
am [a]bringing disaster on them which they
will [b]not be able to escape; though they will
[c]cry to Me, yet I will not listen to them.
12 "Then the cities of Judah and the inhabitants of Jerusalem will [a]go and cry to the
gods to whom they burn incense, but they
surely will not save them in the time of their
disaster.
13 "For your gods are [1][a]as many as your
cities, O Judah; and [1]as many as the streets
of Jerusalem are the altars you have set up to
the [b]shameful thing, altars to [c]burn incense
to Baal.
14 "Therefore [a]do not pray for this people,
nor lift up a cry or prayer for them; for I will
[b]not listen when they call to Me because of
their disaster.

15 "What right has My [a]beloved in My house
When [b]she has done many vile deeds?
Can the sacrificial flesh take away from you your disaster,
[1]So *that* you can rejoice?"
16 The LORD called your name,
"A [a]green olive tree, beautiful in fruit and form";
With the [b]noise of a great tumult
He has [c]kindled fire on it,
And its branches are worthless.

17 The LORD of hosts, who [a]planted you,
has [b]pronounced evil against you because of
the evil of the house of Israel and of the
house of Judah, which they have [1]done to
provoke Me by [2][c]offering up sacrifices to
Baal.

Plots against Jeremiah

18 Moreover, the LORD [a]made it known to me and I knew it;
Then You showed me their deeds.
19 But I was like a gentle [a]lamb led to the slaughter;
And I did not know that they had [b]devised plots against me, *saying,*
"Let us destroy the tree with its [1]fruit,
And [c]let us cut him off from the [d]land of the living,
That his [e]name be remembered no more."
20 But, O LORD of hosts, who [a]judges righteously,
Who [b]tries the [1]feelings and the heart,
Let me see Your vengeance on them,
For to You have I [2]committed my cause.

21 Therefore thus says the LORD concerning
the men of [a]Anathoth, who [b]seek your life,
saying, "[c]Do not prophesy in the name of the
LORD, so that you will not [d]die at our hand";
22 therefore, thus says the LORD of hosts,
"Behold, I am about to [a]punish them! The
[b]young men will die by the sword, their sons
and daughters will die by famine;
23 and a remnant [a]will not be left to them,
for I will [b]bring disaster on the men of Anathoth—[c]the year of their punishment."

Jeremiah's Prayer

12 [a]Righteous are You, O LORD, that I would plead *my* case with You;
Indeed I would [b]discuss matters of justice with You:

10 [d]Jer 3:6-11; Ezek 16:59 **11** [a]2 Kin 22:16; Jer 6:19; 11:17 [b]Is 24:17; Jer 25:35 [c]Ps 18:41; Prov 1:28; Is 1:15; Jer 11:14; 14:12; Ezek 8:18; Mic 3:4; Zech 7:13 **12** [a]Deut 32:37; Jer 44:17 **13** [1]Lit *the number of* [a]2 Kin 23:13; Jer 2:28 [b]Jer 3:24 [c]Jer 7:9 **14** [a]Ex 32:10; Jer 7:16; 14:11; 1 John 5:16 [b]Ps 66:18; Jer 11:11; Hos 5:6 **15** [1]Lit *Then* [a]Jer 13:27 [b]Ezek 16:25 **16** [a]Ps 52:8; Rom 11:17 [b]Ps 83:2 [c]Ps 80:16; Is 27:11; Jer 21:14 **17** [1]Or *done for themselves* [2]Or *burning incense* [a]Is 5:2; Jer 2:21; 12:2 [b]Jer 1:14; 16:10; 19:15 [c]Jer 7:9; 11:13; 32:29

18 [a]1 Sam 23:11, 12; 2 Kin 6:9, 10; Ezek 8:6 **19** [1]Lit *bread* [a]Is 53:7 [b]Jer 18:18; 20:10 [c]Ps 83:4; Is 53:8 [d]Job 28:13; Ps 52:5 [e]Ps 109:13 **20** [1]Lit *kidneys* [2]Lit *revealed* [a]Gen 18:25; Ps 7:8; Jer 20:12 [b]1 Sam 16:7; Ps 7:9; Jer 17:10 **21** [a]Jer 1:1 [b]Jer 12:5, 6; 20:10 [c]Amos 2:12 [d]Jer 26:8; 38:4

22 [a]Jer 21:14 [b]2 Chr 36:17; Jer 18:21 **23** [a]Jer 6:9 [b]Jer 23:12; Hos 9:7; Mic 7:4 [c]Luke 19:44 **12:1** [a]Ezra 9:15; Ps 51:4; 129:4; Jer 11:20 [b]Job 13:3

My covenant. Emphasizing its origin in God Himself.

11:11 *I am bringing . . . on them.* Judah will be judged, just as Israel had been judged earlier (see v. 10; see also 2 Kin 17:18–23).

11:12 *burn incense.* See vv. 13,17; see also note on 1:16.

11:13 *gods are as many as . . . cities.* See note on 2:28. *as many as the streets . . . are the altars.* See 2 Chr 28:24. *to the shameful thing . . . Baal.* Lit. "to the shame(ful god) . . . to Baal." See 3:24; see also notes on 2:26; Judg 6:32.

11:14 *do not pray for this people.* See note on 7:16; cf. 1 John 5:16.

11:15 See 7:10–11,21–24. *My beloved.* Judah (see 12:7; cf. Deut 33:12, where Benjamin is called the "beloved of the LORD").

11:16 *called your name . . . olive tree.* See Ps 52:8; 128:3. *tumult.* The Hebrew for this word appears elsewhere only in Ezek 1:24, where it refers to the noise made by an army (see Is 13:4). *branches are worthless.* See Ezek 31:12.

11:17 Fulfilled when Judah was destroyed in 586 B.C. (see 44:2–3). *provoke Me.* See 8:19; Deut 31:29.

11:18–23 The first of Jeremiah's "confessions" (see Introduction: Author and Date).

11:18 *their.* Jeremiah's personal enemies, the "men of Anathoth" (vv. 21,23), his hometown.

11:19 *lamb led to the slaughter.* See 51:40; see also Is 53:7 and note. *destroy the tree with its fruit.* Contrast 12:2. *cut him off from the land of the living.* See Is 53:8; contrast Ps 27:13. *name.* Since Jeremiah had no children (see 16:2), his name would die with him. *be remembered no more.* As though he were evil (see Job 24:20; Ezek 21:32).

11:20 Repeated almost verbatim in 20:12; see also 17:10. *O LORD . . . who judges righteously.* See note on Gen 18:25.

11:21 *men of Anathoth, who seek your life.* See 12:6. "A man's enemies are the men of his own household" (Mic 7:6, quoted by Jesus in Matt 10:36).

11:22 *sword . . . famine.* See note on 5:12.

11:23 *remnant.* See 6:9; Is 10:20–22 and notes. *them.* The conspirators in Anathoth, not its entire population, since 128 men of Anathoth returned to their hometown after the exile (see Ezra 2:23).

12:1–6 The second of Jeremiah's "confessions," continuing (and closely related to) the first (11:18–23). Jeremiah speaks in vv. 1–4, and God responds in vv. 5–6.

12:1 *Righteous are You.* See note on Gen 18:25; see also 11:20; Ps 51:4; Rom 3:4. Because God is righteous, He is a dependable arbiter and judge. *Indeed.* He is ready to listen to our questions and complaints. *Why has . . . the wicked prospered?* The question is not unique to Jeremiah (see, e.g., Job 21:7–15; Mal 3:15). The Lord replies that ultimately the wicked in Judah will perish (vv. 7–13) and that the wicked invaders who destroy them will themselves be destroyed (vv. 14–17).

Why has the [c]way of the wicked
prospered?
Why are all those who [d]deal in
treachery at ease?
2 You have [a]planted them, they have
also taken root;
They grow, they have even produced
fruit.
You are [b]near [1]to their lips
But far from their [2]mind.
3 But You [a]know me, O LORD;
You see me;
And You [b]examine my heart's *attitude*
toward You.
Drag them off like sheep for the
slaughter
And [1]set them apart for a [c]day of
carnage!
4 How long is the [a]land to mourn
And the [b]vegetation of the countryside
to wither?
For the [c]wickedness of those who
dwell in it,
[d]Animals and birds have been
snatched away,
Because *men* have said, "He will not
see our latter [e]ending."

5 "If you have run with footmen and they
have tired you out,
Then how can you compete with
horses?
If you fall down in a land of peace,
How will you do in the [1a]thicket of
the Jordan?
6 "For even your [a]brothers and the
household of your father,
Even they have dealt treacherously
with you,
Even they have cried aloud after you.

12:1 [c]Job 12:6; Jer 5:27, 28; Hab 1:4; Mal 3:15 [d]Jer 3:7, 20; 5:11
2 [1]Lit *in their mouth* [2]Lit *kidneys* [a]Jer 11:17; 45:4; Ezek 17:5-10 [b]Is 29:13; Jer 3:10; Ezek 33:31; Titus 1:16
3 [1]Lit *sanctify them* [a]Ps 139:1-4 [b]Ps 7:9; 11:5; Jer 11:20 [c]Jer 17:18; 50:27; James 5:5
4 [a]Jer 4:28; 9:10; 23:10 [b]Joel 1:10-17 [c]Ps 107:34 [d]Jer 4:25; 7:20; 9:10; Hos 4:3; Hab 3:17 [e]Jer 5:31; Ezek 7:2
5 [1]Lit *pride* [a]Jer 49:19; 50:44
6 [a]Gen 37:4-11; Job 6:15; Ps 69:8; Jer 9:4, 5
6 [b]Ps 12:2; Prov 26:25
7 [a]Is 2:6; Jer 7:29; 23:39 [b]Jer 11:15; Hos 11:1-8
8 [1]Lit *raised her voice* [a]Is 59:13 [b]Hos 9:15; Amos 6:8
9 [a]2 Kin 24:2; Ezek 23:22-25 [b]Is 56:9; Jer 7:33; 15:3; 34:20
10 [a]Jer 6:3; 23:1 [b]Ps 80:8-16; Is 5:1-7 [c]Is 63:18 [d]Jer 3:19
11 [1]Lit *One has made it* [2]Or *upon* [a]Jer 12:4; 14:2; 23:10 [b]Jer 4:20, 27; 25:11 [c]Is 42:25

Do not believe them, although they
may say [b]nice things to you."

God's Answer

7 "I have [a]forsaken My house,
I have abandoned My inheritance;
I have given the [b]beloved of My soul
Into the hand of her enemies.
8 "My inheritance has become to Me
Like a lion in the forest;
She has [1a]roared against Me;
Therefore I have come to [b]hate her.
9 "Is My inheritance like a speckled bird
of prey to Me?
Are the [a]birds of prey against her on
every side?
Go, gather all the [b]beasts of the field,
Bring them to devour!
10 "Many [a]shepherds have ruined My
[b]vineyard,
They have [c]trampled down My field;
They have made My [d]pleasant field
A desolate wilderness.
11 "[1]It has been made a desolation,
Desolate, it [a]mourns [2]before Me;
The [b]whole land has been made
desolate,
Because no man [c]lays it to heart.
12 "On all the [1a]bare heights in the
wilderness
Destroyers have come,
For a [b]sword of the LORD is devouring
From one end of the land even to the
[2]other;
There is [c]no peace for [3]anyone.
13 "They have [a]sown wheat and have
reaped thorns,

12 [1]Or *caravan trails* [2]Lit *other end of the land* [3]Lit *all flesh* [a]Jer 3:2, 21 [b]Is 34:6; Jer 47:6; Amos 9:4 [c]Jer 16:5; 30:5 **13** [a]Lev 26:16; Deut 28:38; Mic 6:15; Hag 1:6

12:2 *You have planted them.* But a sovereign God can always reconsider His intentions if conditions warrant a change (see 18:9–10). *produced fruit.* The wicked flourish, while Jeremiah's fellow citizens plot to destroy his own "fruit" (see 11:19). *near to their lips . . . far from their mind.* Quoted in part by Jesus in Matt 15:8–9.

12:3 *examine my heart's attitude.* See 11:20. *like sheep for the slaughter.* Jeremiah asks that his wicked countrymen receive the fate mentioned for himself in 11:19. His request arises not so much out of a desire for revenge as for the vindication of God's righteousness.

12:4 *mourn . . . wither.* See 23:10; see also 3:3; 14:1. Apparently there was a series of droughts in Judah during Jeremiah's ministry. *He will not see.* The prophet's enemies do not believe that his predictions will be fulfilled.

12:5 The Lord warns Jeremiah that in the future his troubles will increase (see, e.g., 38:4–6). *fall down.* The Hebrew for this word, which usually means "trust" ("If you put your trust in a land of peace"), has a negative meaning in a few passages (see, e.g., Prov 14:16, where it is translated "careless"). *thicket.* Providing cover for lions (see 49:19; 50:44; Zech 11:3). If the Hebrew for this word means "flooding" ("the flooding of the Jordan") here, an ancient example is described in Josh 3:15.

12:6 *household.* Linking this verse verbally with the following context (see v. 7). Apparently, members of Jeremiah's own family were included in the "men of Anathoth" (11:21,23) who wanted to kill him.

12:7–17 The Lord will judge Judah (vv. 7–13) as well as the wicked neighboring nations (vv. 14–17).

12:7 *house.* Judah (see, e.g., 11:17). *inheritance.* God's land and people (see vv. 8–9,14–15; see also Ex 15:17 and note; Deut 4:20; Is 19:25; 47:6). *the beloved of My soul.* See note on 11:15.

12:8 *I . . . hate her.* I will withdraw my love from her by giving her "Into the hand of her enemies" (v. 7; see Mal 1:3).

12:9 *birds of prey . . . beasts of the field.* Judah's enemies (see Is 56:9 and note).

12:10 *shepherds.* Rulers (see note on 2:8). *My vineyard.* Judah (see 2:21 and note). *pleasant field.* See 3:19 and note.

12:11 *it mourns.* See v. 4 and note. A total of seven *s*-sounds and seven *m*-sounds in the Hebrew of this brief verse provides a striking example of Jeremiah's literary gifts.

12:12 *bare heights.* Places of idolatrous worship (see 3:2; Num 23:3). *Destroyers.* The Babylonians (see note on 4:7). *sword of the LORD.* Symbolizing God's instruments of judgment (see 25:29; 47:6). *From one end . . . to the other.* See 25:33. *no peace for anyone.* See 6:14 and note).

12:13 See 14:2–4.

They have [b]strained themselves [1]to no
profit.
But be ashamed of your [2c]harvest
Because of the [d]fierce anger of the
LORD."

14 Thus says the LORD concerning all My
[a]wicked neighbors who [b]strike at the inheritance with which I have endowed My people
Israel, "Behold I am about to uproot them
from their land and will [c]uproot the house of
Judah from among them.
15 "And it will come about that after I have
uprooted them, I will [a]again have compassion on them; and I will [b]bring them back,
each one to his inheritance and each one to
his land.
16 "Then if they will really [a]learn the ways
of My people, to [b]swear by My name, 'As the
LORD lives,' even as they taught My people to
[c]swear by Baal, they will be [d]built up in the
midst of My people.
17 "But if they will not listen, then I will
[a]uproot that nation, uproot and destroy it,"
declares the LORD.

The Ruined Waistband

13 Thus the LORD said to me, "Go and
[a]buy yourself a linen waistband and
put it around your waist, but do not put it in
water."
2 So I bought the waistband in accordance with the [a]word of the LORD and put it
around my waist.
3 Then the word of the LORD came to me
a second time, saying,
4 "Take the waistband that you have
bought, which is around your waist, and
arise, go to [1]the [a]Euphrates and hide it there
in a crevice of the rock."
5 So I went and hid it by the Euphrates,
[a]as the LORD had commanded me.
6 After many days the LORD said to me,
"Arise, go to the Euphrates and take from
there the waistband which I commanded
you to hide there."
7 Then I went to the Euphrates and dug,
and I took the waistband from the place
where I had hidden it; and lo, the waistband
was ruined, it was totally worthless.
8 Then the word of the LORD came to me,
saying,
9 "Thus says the LORD, 'Just so will I
destroy the [a]pride of Judah and the great
pride of Jerusalem.
10 'This wicked people, who [a]refuse to listen to My words, who [b]walk in the stubbornness of their hearts and have gone after
other gods to serve them and to bow down
to them, let them be just like this waistband
which is totally worthless.
11 'For as the waistband clings to the waist
of a man, so I made the whole household of
Israel and the whole household of Judah
[a]cling to Me,' declares the LORD, 'that they
might be for Me a people, for [1b]renown, for
[c]praise and for glory; but they [d]did not listen.'

Captivity Threatened

12 "Therefore you are to speak this word to
them, 'Thus says the LORD, the God of Israel,
"Every jug is to be filled with wine."' And
when they say to you, 'Do we not very well
know that every jug is to be filled with wine?'
13 then say to them, 'Thus says the LORD,
"Behold I am about to fill all the inhabitants
of this land—the kings that sit for David on
his throne, the priests, the prophets and all

13 [1]Lit *they do not profit* [2]Lit *products* [b]Is 55:2; Jer 9:5 [c]Jer 17:10 [d]Jer 4:26; 25:37, 38
14 [a]Jer 49:1, 7; Zeph 2:8-10 [b]Jer 2:3; 50:11, 12; Zech 2:8 [c]Deut 30:3; Ps 106:47; Is 11:11-16
15 [a]Jer 48:47; 49:6, 39 [b]Amos 9:14
16 [a]Is 42:6; 49:6 [b]Jer 4:2; Zeph 1:5 [c]Josh 23:7; Jer 5:7 [d]Jer 3:17; 4:2; 16:19
17 [a]Ps 2:8-12; Is 60:12
13:1 [a]Jer 13:11
2 [a]Is 20:2; Ezek 2:8
4 [1]Or *Parah*, cf Josh 18:23; so through v 7 [a]Jer 51:63
5 [a]Ex 39:42, 43; 40:16
9 [a]Lev 26:19; Is 2:10-17; 23:9; Jer 13:15-17; Zeph 3:11
10 [a]Num 14:11; 2 Chr 36:15, 16; Jer 11:10 [b]Jer 9:14; 11:8; 16:12
11 [1]Lit *a name* [a]Ex 19:5, 6; Deut 32:10, 11 [b]Jer 32:20 [c]Is 43:21; Jer 33:9 [d]Ps 81:11; Jer 7:13, 24, 26

12:14 *wicked neighbors.* See, e.g., 2 Kin 24:2. *strike.* Lit. "touch," used in the context of attack and plunder in Zech 2:8. *uproot.* Carry off into exile (see, e.g., 1 Kin 14:15).

12:15 The exiles from Judah, and those from the neighboring nations, will eventually be brought back to their respective lands (see v. 16; 32:37,44; 33:26; 48:47; 49:6).

12:16 See Is 56:6–7. The Messianic age is in view (see Is 2:2–4). *ways.* See note on 10:2.

13:1–27 A series of five warnings, the first two (vv. 1–11, 12–14) written in prose and the last three (vv. 15–17, 18–19, 20–27) in poetry.

13:1–11 The story of the ruined, useless belt is the first major example of the Lord's commanding Jeremiah to perform symbolic acts to illustrate his message (see Introduction: Literary Features).

13:1–2,4–7 *Go and buy . . . So I bought . . . Take the waistband . . . and hide it . . . So I went and hid it . . . go to the Euphrates and take . . . the waistband . . . Then I went to the Euphrates and dug, and I took the waistband.* Like his spiritual ancestor Abraham (see note on Gen 12:4), Jeremiah was characterized by prompt obedience.

13:1 *linen.* The material of which the priests' garments were made (see Ezek 44:17–18), symbolic of Israel's holiness as a "kingdom of priests" (see Ex 19:6 and note). The linen belt is a symbol of the formerly intimate relationship between God and Judah (see v. 11). *do not put it in water.* Do not wash it—symbolic of Judah's sinful pride (see v. 9).

13:3 *Then.* Some time later.

13:4 *Euphrates.* The Euphrates serves as an appropriate symbol of the corrupting Assyrian and Babylonian influence on Judah that began during the reign of Ahaz (see 2 Kin 16).

13:6 *After many days.* Perhaps a reference to the lengthy Babylonian exile.

13:7 *dug.* The belt had either been buried by the prophet or silted over by the water of the river. *the waistband was ruined.* As foreseen in Lev 26:39, God's people in exile would waste away because of their sins and the sins of their ancestors.

13:9 *pride . . . great pride.* Contrast 9:23–24. Judah's vaunted pride would be a cause of her downfall and exile (see vv. 15,17), as foreshadowed in Lev 26:19.

13:10 *refuse to listen.* See note on 9:6. *stubbornness of their hearts.* See note on 3:17. *totally worthless.* See 24:8.

13:11 *but they did not listen.* And therefore the promise of Deut 26:19 can no longer be fulfilled in them.

13:12–14 The Lord uses the imagery of filled wineskins to point toward the eventual destruction of Judah's leaders and people.

13:13 *kings . . . priests . . . prophets . . . all the inhabitants of Jerusalem.* See 26:16; see also note on 1:18. *drunkenness.* In a literal sense (see, e.g., Is 28:7), but also symbolizing the effects

the inhabitants of Jerusalem—with [a]drunk-
enness!
14 "I will [a]dash them against each other,
both the [b]fathers and the sons together,"
declares the LORD. "I will [c]not show pity nor
be sorry nor have compassion so as not to
destroy them." ' "

15 Listen and give heed, do not be
[a]haughty,
For the LORD has spoken.
16 [a]Give glory to the LORD your God,
Before He brings [b]darkness
And before your [c]feet stumble
On the dusky mountains,
And while you are hoping for light
He makes it into [d]deep darkness,
And turns *it* into gloom.
17 But [a]if you will not listen to it,
My soul will [b]sob in secret for *such*
pride;
And my eyes will bitterly weep
And flow down with tears,
Because the [c]flock of the LORD has
been taken captive.
18 Say to the [a]king and the queen mother,
"[b]Take a lowly seat,
For your beautiful [c]crown
Has come down from your head."
19 The [a]cities of the Negev have been
locked up,
And there is no one to open *them;*
All [b]Judah has been carried into exile,
Wholly carried into exile.

20 "Lift up your eyes and see
Those coming [a]from the north.
Where is the [b]flock that was given you,
Your beautiful sheep?
21 "What will you say when He appoints
over you—
And you yourself had taught them—
Former [1][a]companions to be head over
you?
Will not [b]pangs take hold of you
Like a woman in childbirth?
22 "If you [a]say in your heart,
'[b]Why have these things happened to
me?'
Because of the [c]magnitude of your
iniquity
[d]Your skirts have been removed
And your heels have [1]been exposed.
23 "[a]Can the Ethiopian change his skin
Or the leopard his spots?
Then you also can [b]do good
Who are accustomed to doing evil.
24 "Therefore I will [a]scatter them like
drifting straw
To the desert [b]wind.
25 "This is your [a]lot, the portion
measured to you
From Me," declares the LORD,
"Because you have [b]forgotten Me
And trusted in falsehood.
26 "So I Myself have also [a]stripped your
skirts off over your face,
That your shame may be seen.
27 "As for your [a]adulteries and your
lustful neighings,
The [b]lewdness of your prostitution
On the [c]hills in the field,
I have seen your abominations.
Woe to you, O Jerusalem!
[d]How long will you remain unclean?"

Drought and a Prayer for Mercy

14 That which came as the word of the LORD to Jeremiah in regard to the [a]drought:

13 [a]Ps 60:3; 75:8; Is 51:17; 63:6; Jer 25:27; 51:7, 57
14 [a]Is 9:20, 21; Jer 19:9-11 [b]Jer 6:21; Ezek 5:10 [c]Deut 29:20; Is 27:11; Jer 16:5; 21:7
15 [a]Prov 16:5; Is 28:14-22
16 [a]Josh 7:19; Ps 96:8 [b]Is 5:30; 8:22; 59:9; Amos 5:18; 8:9 [c]Prov 4:19; Jer 23:12 [d]Ps 44:19; 107:10, 14; Jer 2:6
17 [a]Mal 2:2 [b]Ps 119:136; Jer 9:1; 14:17; Luke 19:41, 42 [c]Ps 80:1; Jer 23:1, 2
18 [a]2 Kin 24:12, 15; Jer 22:26 [b]2 Chr 33:12, 19 [c]Ex 39:28; Is 3:20; Ezek 24:17, 23; 44:18
19 [a]Jer 32:44 [b]Jer 20:4; 52:27-30
20 [a]Jer 1:15; 6:22; Hab 1:6 [b]Jer 13:17; 23:2

21 [1]Or *chieftains* [a]Jer 2:25; 38:22 [b]Is 13:8; Jer 4:31
22 [1]Or *suffered violence* [a]Deut 7:17 [b]Jer 5:19; 16:10 [c]Jer 2:17-19; 9:2-9 [d]Is 47:2; Ezek 16:37; Nah 3:5
23 [a]Prov 27:22; Is 1:5 [b]Jer 4:22; 9:5
24 [a]Lev 26:33; Jer 9:16; Ezek 5:2, 12 [b]Jer 4:11; 18:17
25 [a]Job 20:29; Ps 11:6; Matt 24:51 [b]Ps 9:17; Jer 2:32; 3:21
26 [a]Lam 1:8; Ezek 23:29; Hos 2:10 **27** [a]Jer 5:7, 8 [b]Jer 11:15 [c]Is 65:7; Jer 2:20; Ezek 6:13 [d]Prov 1:22; Hos 8:5 **14:1** [a]Jer 17:8

of the wine of God's wrath (see 25:15–29; Ps 60:3; Is 51:17–20; Ezek 23:32–34).
13:14 *dash them against each other.* The various factions in Judah produced only confusion and chaos in the face of determined outside enemies. *not show pity . . . sorry . . . compassion.* See 21:7; see also Ezek 5:11.
13:15–17 Sinful pride carries the seeds of its own destruction, says the prophet.
13:15 *Listen.* See note on 2:4. *do not be haughty.* See v. 17; see also note on v. 9.
13:16 *Give glory to . . . God.* An exhortation to speak the truth and confess one's sins (see Josh 7:19 and note; John 9:24). *while you are hoping for light.* Cf. the description of the day of the Lord in Amos 5:18–20; 8:9.
13:17 *My soul will sob.* See note on 9:1. *pride.* See v. 15; see also note on v. 9. *flock.* People (see v. 20; Zech 10:3; see also notes on 2:8; 10:21). *taken captive.* Into exile (see v. 19).
13:18–19 The prophet speaks: Exile is imminent.
13:18 *king and . . . queen mother.* Probably Jehoiachin and Nehushta (2 Kin 24:8). If so, the date is 597 B.C., about 12 years after Josiah's death (see note on 11:1–13:27). *crown Has come down.* See 22:24–26; 29:2; 2 Kin 24:15.
13:19 *Negev.* The dry southland (see note on Gen 12:9). *locked up.* Blocked by debris (see Is 24:10). *Wholly carried into exile.* See Amos 1:6,9.
13:20–27 First the prophet speaks (vv. 20–23), then the Lord (vv. 24–27). Judah's willful rebellion has made exile inevitable.
13:20 *your . . . you, Your.* Jerusalem, personified as a woman (see vv. 21–22,26–27), is being addressed. *the north.* Babylonia (see 4:6; see also note on Is 41:25). *flock . . . sheep.* See note on v. 17.
13:21 *Former companions.* Perhaps Egypt and Babylon, who alternated in dominating Judah (see Introduction: Background). *Like a woman in childbirth.* See 6:24; 49:24; 50:43.
13:22 *skirts . . . removed.* Disgraced publicly, like a common prostitute (see vv. 26–27; Is 47:3; Hos 2:3,10).
13:23 A rhetorical question, expecting a negative answer (see 17:9).
13:24 *like drifting straw.* The fate of the wicked (see, e.g., Ps 1:4). *desert wind.* See note on 4:11.
13:25 *forgotten Me.* See note on 2:32.
13:26 See v. 22 and note.
13:27 *adulteries and . . . lustful neighings.* See note on 5:8. *lewdness of . . . prostitution.* See Ezek 16:27. *How long . . . ?* There is yet hope, however slender, to postpone the divine wrath (cf., e.g., 12:14–16).
14:1–15:21 Messages delivered by Jeremiah during an especially severe drought, the date of which is unknown.
14:1–15:9 After an initial vivid description of the drought

2 "Judah mourns
And [a]her gates languish;
They sit on the ground [b]in mourning,
And the [c]cry of Jerusalem has ascended.
3 "Their nobles have [a]sent their [1]servants for water;
They have come to the [b]cisterns and found no water.
They have returned with their vessels empty;
They have been [c]put to shame and humiliated,
And they [d]cover their heads.
4 "Because the [a]ground is [1]cracked,
For there has been [b]no rain on the land;
The [c]farmers have been put to shame,
They have covered their heads.
5 "For even the doe in the field has given birth only to abandon *her young,*
Because there is [a]no grass.
6 "The [a]wild donkeys stand on the bare heights;
They pant for air like jackals,
Their eyes fail
For there is [b]no vegetation.
7 "Although our [a]iniquities testify against us,
O LORD, act [b]for Your name's sake!
Truly our [c]apostasies have been many,
We have [d]sinned against You.
8 "O [a]Hope of Israel,
Its [b]Savior in [c]time of distress,
Why are You like a stranger in the land
Or like a traveler who has pitched his *tent* for the night?
9 "Why are You like a man dismayed,
Like a mighty man who [a]cannot save?
Yet [b]You are in our midst, O LORD,
And we are [c]called by Your name;
Do not forsake us!"

10 Thus says the LORD to this people,
"Even so they have [a]loved to wander; they
have not [b]kept their feet in check. Therefore
the LORD does [c]not accept them; now He will
[d]remember their iniquity and call their sins
to account."
11 So the LORD said to me, "[a]Do not pray
for the welfare of this people.
12 "When they fast, I am [a]not going to listen to their cry; and when they offer [b]burnt
offering and grain offering, I am not going to
accept them. Rather I am going to [c]make an
end of them by the [d]sword, famine and pestilence."

False Prophets

13 But, "Ah, Lord [1]GOD!" I said, "Look,
the prophets are telling them, 'You [a]will not
see the sword nor will you have famine, but
I will give you [2]lasting [b]peace in this place.' "
14 Then the LORD said to me, "The [a]proph-
ets are prophesying falsehood in My name. [b]I
have neither sent them nor commanded them
nor spoken to them; they are prophesying to
you a [c]false vision, divination, futility and the
deception of their own [1]minds.
15 "Therefore thus says the LORD concerning the prophets who are prophesying in My
name, although it was not I who sent them—
yet they keep saying, 'There will be no sword
or famine in this land'—[a]by sword and
famine those prophets shall [1]meet their end!
16 "The people also to whom they are
prophesying will be [a]thrown out into the
streets of Jerusalem because of the famine
and the sword; and there will be no one to
[b]bury them—*neither* them, *nor* their wives,

2 [a]Is 3:26 [b]Jer 8:21 [c]1 Sam 5:12; Jer 11:11; 46:12; Zech 7:13 **3** [1]Lit *little ones* [a]1 Kin 18:5 [b]2 Kin 18:31; Jer 2:13 [c]Job 6:20; Ps 40:14 [d]2 Sam 15:30 **4** [1]Lit *shattered* [a]Joel 1:19, 20 [b]Jer 3:3 [c]Joel 1:11 **5** [a]Is 15:6 **6** [a]Job 39:5, 6; Jer 2:24 [b]Joel 1:18 **7** [a]Is 59:12; Hos 5:5 [b]Ps 25:11; Jer 14:21 [c]Jer 5:6; 8:5 [d]Jer 3:25; 8:14; 14:20 **8** [a]Jer 17:13 [b]Is 43:3; 63:8 [c]Ps 9:9; 50:15 **9** [a]Num 11:23; Is 50:2; 59:1 [b]Ex 29:45; Ps 46:5; Jer 8:19

9 [c]Is 63:19; Jer 15:16 **10** [a]Jer 2:25; 3:13 [b]Ps 119:101 [c]Jer 6:20; Amos 5:22 [d]Jer 44:21-23; Hos 8:13; 9:9 **11** [a]Ex 32:10; Jer 7:16; 11:14 **12** [a]Prov 1:28; Is 1:15; Jer 11:11; Ezek 8:18; Mic 3:4; Zech 7:13 [b]Jer 6:20; 7:21 [c]Jer 8:13 [d]Jer 21:9 **13** [1]Heb *YHWH,* usually rendered *LORD* [2]Lit *peace of truth* [a]Jer 5:12; 23:17 [b]Jer 6:14; 8:11 **14** [1]Lit *hearts* [a]Jer 5:31; 23:25 [b]Jer 23:21 [c]Jer 23:16, 26; 27:9, 10; Ezek 12:24

15 [1]Lit *be finished* [a]Jer 23:15; Ezek 14:10 **16** [a]Ps 79:2, 3; Jer 7:33; 15:2, 3 [b]Jer 8:1, 2

(14:2–6), Jeremiah alternately prays (14:7–9,13,19–22) and God responds (14:10–12,14–18; 15:1–9).
14:1 *drought.* See 17:8. Unlike that in 3:3; 12:4, the suffering is increased because an enemy has invaded the land (see v. 18). Drought was one of the curses threatened (see 23:10) for disobedience to the covenant (see Lev 26:19–20; Deut 28:22–24).
14:2 *gates.* See 15:7; see also note on Gen 22:17.
14:3 *nobles.* A drought is no respecter of class distinctions. *cover their heads.* In mourning (see v. 4; 2 Sam 15:30; cf. 2 Sam 19:4).
14:4 *For there has been no rain.* See 1 Kin 17:7. Unlike Egypt, where the mighty Nile waters the ground, the Holy Land depends on adequate rainfall.
14:6 *pant.* The Hebrew underlying this word is translated "sniff the wind" in 2:24. There a female wild donkey (Jerusalem) was in the heat of desire, while here the male wild donkeys are panting because of a drought brought on by Judah's sin.
14:7–9 The prophet prays on behalf of the people (see v. 11).
14:7 *for Your name's sake.* See v. 21; Josh 7:9; Is 48:9–11. *apostasies.* See 2:19; 3:22; 5:6.
14:8 *O Hope of Israel.* See v. 22; 17:13; 50:7; Acts 28:20.
14:9 *we are called by Your name.* We belong to you, our ever-present Savior (see note on 7:10).
14:10–12 The Lord responds.
14:10–11 *this people.* God does not acknowledge them as His own (see Is 6:9–10; 8:6,11–12).
14:10 *wander.* After false gods (see 2:23,31). *the LORD does not . . . account.* The Hebrew for these three lines is quoted verbatim from Hos 8:13 (cf. Hos 9:9).
14:11 *Do not pray.* See note on 7:16; cf. 1 Sam 7:8; 12:19.
14:12 *not . . . accept them.* See v. 10. Sacrifice is to no avail when unaccompanied by repentance (see note on 6:20). *sword, famine and pestilence.* Curses for violating God's covenant (see Lev 26:25–26); the first occurrence of this triad, which occurs 15 times in Jeremiah (see Introduction: Literary Features).
14:13 Jeremiah reminds the Lord of what the false prophets are saying. *not . . . sword nor . . . famine.* See 5:12. *lasting peace.* Jeremiah's elaboration of the false prophets' "Peace, peace" (see 6:14; 8:11).
14:14–18 The Lord responds.
14:14 *falsehood.* See 5:12. *in My name.* See Deut 18:20,22. *deception of their own minds.* See 23:26.
14:15 *those prophets shall meet their end.* See 28:15–17; Deut 18:20.
14:16 *no one to bury them.* See note on 7:33. *wives . . . sons . . . daughters.* All would perish, because all had worshiped false gods (see note on 7:18).

nor their sons, nor their daughters—for I will
[c]pour out their *own* wickedness on them.
17 " You will say this word to them,
'[a]Let my eyes flow down with tears
night and day,
And let them not cease;
For the virgin [b]daughter of my people
has been crushed with a mighty
blow,
With a sorely [c]infected wound.
18 'If I [a]go out to the country,
Behold, those [1]slain with the sword!
Or if I enter the city,
Behold, diseases of famine!
For [b]both prophet and priest
Have [2]gone roving about in the land
that they do not know.' "

19 Have You completely [a]rejected
Judah?
Or have [1]You loathed Zion?
Why have You stricken us so that we
[b]are beyond healing?
We [c]waited for peace, but nothing
good *came;*
And for a time of healing, but behold,
terror!
20 We [a]know our wickedness, O LORD,
The iniquity of our fathers, for [b]we
have sinned against You.
21 Do not despise *us,* [a]for Your own
name's sake;
Do not disgrace the [b]throne of Your
glory;
Remember *and* do not annul Your
covenant with us.
22 Are there any among the [1a]idols of the
nations who [b]give rain?
Or can the heavens grant showers?
Is it not You, O LORD our God?
Therefore we [2c]hope in You,
For You are the one who has done all
these things.

16 [c]Prov 1:31; Jer 13:22-25 **17** [a]Jer 9:1; 13:17; Lam 1:16 [b]Is 37:22; Jer 8:21; Lam 1:15; 2:13 [c]Jer 10:19; 30:14 **18** [1]Lit *pierced* [2]Or *gone around trading* [a]Jer 6:25; Lam 1:20; Ezek 7:15 [b]Jer 6:13; 8:10 **19** [1]Lit *Your soul* [a]Jer 6:30; 7:29; 12:7; Lam 5:22 [b]Jer 30:13 [c]Job 30:26; Jer 8:15; 1 Thess 5:3 **20** [a]Neh 9:2; Ps 32:5; Jer 3:25 [b]Jer 8:14; 14:7; Dan 9:8 **21** [a]Ps 25:11; Jer 14:7 [b]Jer 3:17; 17:12 **22** [1]Lit *vanities* [2]Or *wait for* [a]Is 41:29; Jer 10:3 [b]1 Kin 17:1; Jer 5:24 [c]Lam 3:26

15:1 [1]Lit *soul* [2]Lit *toward* [a]Ps 99:6; Ezek 14:14, 20 [b]Ex 32:11-14; Num 14:13-20; Ps 99:6; 106:23 [c]1 Sam 7:9; 12:23 [d]Jer 15:19; 18:20; 35:19 [e]2 Kin 17:20; Jer 7:15; 10:18; 52:3 **2** [a]Jer 14:12; 24:10; 43:11; Ezek 5:2, 12; Zech 11:9; Rev 13:10 **3** [a]Lev 26:16, 22, 25; Ezek 14:21 [b]1 Kin 21:23, 24 [c]Deut 28:26; Is 18:6; Jer 7:33 **4** [a]Lev 26:33; Jer 24:9; 29:18; Ezek 23:46 [b]2 Kin 21:1-18; 23:26, 27; 24:3, 4; 2 Chr 33:1-9 **5** [a]Ps 69:20; Is 51:19; Jer 13:14; 21:7 [b]Nah 3:7 **6** [a]Jer 6:19; 8:9 [b]Is 1:4; Jer 7:24 [c]Jer 6:12; Zeph 1:4 [d]Jer 6:11; 7:16

Judgment Must Come

15 Then the LORD said to me, "Even
[a]though [b]Moses and [c]Samuel were to
[d]stand before Me, My [1]heart would not be
[2]with this people; [e]send them away from My
presence and let them go!
2 " And it shall be that when they say to
you, 'Where should we go?' then you are to
tell them, 'Thus says the LORD:
"Those *destined* [a]for death, to death;
And those *destined* for the sword, to
the sword;
And those *destined* for famine, to
famine;
And those *destined* for captivity, to
captivity." '
3 " I will [a]appoint over them four kinds *of*
doom," declares the LORD: "the sword to slay,
the [b]dogs to drag off, and the [c]birds of the
sky and the beasts of the earth to devour and
destroy.
4 " I will [a]make them an object of horror
among all the kingdoms of the earth because
of [b]Manasseh, the son of Hezekiah, the king
of Judah, for what he did in Jerusalem.
5 " Indeed, who will have [a]pity on you, O
Jerusalem,
Or who will [b]mourn for you,
Or who will turn aside to ask about
your welfare?
6 " You who have [a]forsaken Me," declares
the LORD,
"You keep [b]going backward.
So I will [c]stretch out My hand against
you and destroy you;
I am [d]tired of relenting!

14:17 *my eyes flow down with tears.* See 9:18; 13:17. *virgin daughter.* Used of Jerusalem in Is 37:22 (see note there; see also Is 23:12 and note); see 18:13.

14:19–22 The prophet prays on behalf of the people.

14:20 *iniquity of our fathers.* See 2:5–6; 7:25–26. *we have sinned.* Repentance brings restoration (see Deut 30:2–3).

14:21 *throne of Your glory.* The Jerusalem temple (see 17:12; 2 Kin 19:14–15; Ps 99:1–2). *Remember and do not annul Your covenant.* Jeremiah pleads the ancient promise of God in Lev 26:44–45.

14:22 See Hos 2:8,21–22. *idols.* See note on 2:5. *Is it not You . . . ?* Only the Lord (not Baal) can send the showers to end the drought (see v. 1). *we hope in You.* See note on v. 8.

15:1–9 The Lord responds, concluding this section (see note on 14:1–15:9).

15:1 *Moses and Samuel.* Famed for their intercession for sinful Israel (see Ex 32:11–14,30–34; Num 14:13–23; Deut 9:18–20, 25–29; 1 Sam 7:5–9; 12:19–25; Ps 99:6–8). *stand before Me.* The posture of God's servants as they are about to pray to Him (see Gen 18:22). *send them away.* The people are so wicked that God refuses to hear prayers offered on their behalf. They are beyond divine help (see notes on 7:16; 14:11–12).

15:2 See Ezek 14:21; 33:27. *death.* Probably by plague; see 14:12 (and note), where "sword, famine and pestilence" are God's three agents of destruction, paralleling the first three here.

15:3–4 Foreseen in Deut 28:25–26.

15:3 *four kinds.* Not the same four as in v. 2, but an elaboration of three of the fates awaiting the corpses of those killed by the sword. The seventh-century B.C. vassal treaties of Esarhaddon present similar curses: "May Ninurta, leader of the gods, fell you with his fierce arrow, fill the plain with your corpses, and give your flesh to the eagles and vultures to feed on . . . May dogs and pigs eat your flesh." *dogs.* See 1 Kin 21:23. *beasts of the earth.* See Rev 6:8.

15:4 *an object of horror.* The Hebrew for this phrase is translated "an example of terror" in the parallel in Deut 28:25. *Manasseh . . . what he did in Jerusalem.* Manasseh, good King Josiah's grandfather, was the most wicked king in Judah's long history (see 2 Kin 21:1–11,16). His sins were a primary cause of Judah's eventual destruction (see 2 Kin 21:12–15; 23:26–27; 24:3–4).

15:5–9 A poem concerning the forthcoming destruction of Jerusalem in 586 B.C (see Lam 1:1,12,21; 2:13,20).

15:5 Cf. Matt 23:37.

15:6 *You keep going backward.* Cf. 7:24; see note on 2:19).

7 "I will [a]winnow them with a winnowing fork
At the gates of the land;
I will [b]bereave *them* of children, I will destroy My people;
[c]They did not [1]repent of their ways.
8 "Their [a]widows will be more numerous before Me
Than the sand of the seas;
I will bring against them, against the mother of a young man,
A [b]destroyer at noonday;
I will suddenly bring down on her
Anguish and dismay.
9 "She who [a]bore seven *sons* pines away;
[1]Her breathing is labored.
Her [b]sun has set while it was yet day;
She has been [c]shamed and humiliated.
So I will [d]give over their survivors to the sword
Before their enemies," declares the LORD.

10 [a]Woe to me, my mother, that you have borne me
As a [b]man of strife and a man of contention to all the land!
I have not [c]lent, nor have men lent money to me,
Yet everyone curses me.
11 The LORD said, "Surely I will [a]set you free for *purposes of* good;
Surely I will cause the [b]enemy to make supplication to you
In a time of disaster and a time of distress.
12 "Can anyone smash iron,
[a]Iron from the north, or bronze?
13 "Your [a]wealth and your treasures
I will give for booty [b]without cost,
Even for all your sins
And within all your borders.
14 "Then I will cause your enemies to bring [1]*it*
Into a [a]land you do not know;
For a [b]fire has been kindled in My anger,
It will burn upon you."

Jeremiah's Prayer and God's Answer

15 [a]You who know, O LORD,
Remember me, take notice of me,
And [b]take vengeance for me on my persecutors.
Do not, in view of Your patience, take me away;
Know that [c]for Your sake I endure reproach.
16 Your words were found and I [a]ate them,
And Your [b]words became for me a joy and the delight of my heart;
For I have been [c]called by Your name,
O LORD God of hosts.
17 I [a]did not sit in the circle of merrymakers,
Nor did I exult.
Because of Your hand *upon me* I sat [b]alone,
For You [c]filled me with indignation.
18 Why has my pain been perpetual
And my [a]wound incurable, refusing to be healed?

7 [1]Lit *turn back from* [a]Ps 1:4; Jer 51:2 [b]Jer 18:21; Hos 9:12-16 [c]Is 9:13
8 [a]Is 3:25, 26; 4:1 [b]Jer 22:7
9 [1]Or *She has breathed out her soul* [a]1 Sam 2:5; Is 47:9 [b]Jer 6:4; Amos 8:9 [c]Jer 50:12 [d]Jer 21:7
10 [a]Job 3:1, 3; Jer 20:14 [b]Jer 1:18, 19; 15:20; 20:7, 8 [c]Ex 22:25; Lev 25:36, 37; Deut 23:19
11 [a]Ps 138:3; Is 41:10 [b]Jer 21:2; 37:3; 38:14; 42:2
12 [a]Jer 28:14
13 [a]Jer 17:3; 20:5 [b]Ps 44:12; Is 52:3
14 [1]I.e. your possessions [a]Deut 28:36, 64; Jer 16:13 [b]Deut 32:22; Ps 21:9; Jer 17:4
15 [a]Jer 12:3 [b]Jer 11:20 [c]Ps 44:22; 69:7-9; Jer 20:8
16 [a]Ezek 3:3 [b]Job 23:12; Ps 119:103 [c]Jer 14:9
17 [a]Ps 1:1; Jer 16:8; 2 Cor 6:17 [b]Ps 102:7; Jer 13:17; Lam 3:28; Ezek 3:24, 25 [c]Jer 6:11
18 [a]Job 34:6; Jer 30:12, 15; Mic 1:9

15:7 *winnow.* See note on Ruth 1:22. Winnowing as a figure of judgment is found also in 51:2; Prov 20:8,26; Is 41:16. *gates of the land.* The approaches to the land. *bereave . . . My people.* The young men will fall in battle, and Judah and Jerusalem will be left childless (see Ezek 5:17). *did not repent.* Reminiscent of the refrain in Amos 4:6,8–11: "Yet you have not returned to Me," where the same Hebrew verb is used (see note on 3:1).

15:8 *widows . . . more numerous . . . Than the sand of the seas.* A tragic reversal of the covenant promise of innumerable offspring (see Gen 22:17 and note). *destroyer.* Babylon (see note on 4:7). *at noonday . . . suddenly.* Military attacks at noon were unexpected (see note on 6:4). *Anguish.* See note on 4:19.

15:9 *seven.* The complete, ideal number of sons (see Ruth 4:15 and note)—soon to be destroyed. *sun has set while it was yet day.* See Amos 8:9; cf. Matt 27:45. *survivors.* Lit. "remnant" (see note on 6:9). Even they will be put to the sword (see Mic 6:14).

15:10–21 The third of Jeremiah's "confessions" (see Introduction: Author and Date), including in this case two responses by the Lord (vv. 11–14, 19–21).

15:10 See 20:14–15; Job 3:3–10. *mother.* See v. 8. In the OT, adjacent paragraphs are often linked by key words. *have not lent, nor have men lent.* Have not become involved in matters likely to evoke dispute or difference of opinion.

15:11–14 The Lord speaks, first to Jeremiah (v. 11), then to the people of Judah (vv. 12–14).

15:11 God encourages Jeremiah. *I will cause the enemy to make supplication to you.* Fulfilled, e.g., in 21:1–2; 37:3; 38:14–26; 42:1–3.

15:12 A rhetorical question assuming a negative answer. *iron.* Symbolic of great strength (see 28:13). *from the north.* From Babylonia (see note on Is 41:25).

15:13–14 Repeated in large part in 17:3–4.

15:13 Fulfilled in 52:17–23. *without cost.* Cf. Is 55:1. People and plunder alike would be free for the taking (see note on Is 52:3).

15:14 *a fire has been kindled in My anger.* Quoted verbatim from Deut 32:22, where the Hebrew is translated "For a fire is kindled in My anger."

15:15 *You who know.* The Lord is aware of what Jeremiah has suffered (see v. 10). *Remember.* Express concern for (see note on Gen 8:1).

15:16 *Your words . . . I ate them.* I digested them, I assimilated them, I made them a part of me (see Ezek 2:8–3:3; Rev 10:9–10). *were found.* Perhaps referring to the discovery of the Book of the Law in the temple during the reign of Josiah in 621 B.C. (see 2 Kin 22:13; 23:2; see also note on 1:2). *became . . . the delight of my heart.* See Ps 1:2. *I have been called by Your name.* See 14:9. I belong to You (see note on 7:10).

15:17 *Your hand.* Divine constraint (see 2 Kin 3:15; Is 8:11 and note; Ezek 1:3; 3:14,22; 37:1; 40:1). *sat alone.* Jeremiah never married (see 16:1), and he attracted only a few friends (see Introduction: Author and Date). *indignation.* At the sins of Judah (see 6:11).

15:18 Two rhetorical questions used by Jeremiah to express his nagging doubts about himself, his mission and God's faithfulness. *pain been perpetual . . . wound incurable.* Jerusalem is

Will You indeed be to me [b]like a
deceptive *stream*
With water that is unreliable?

19 Therefore, thus says the LORD,
"[a]If you return, then I will restore you—
[b]Before Me you will stand;
And [c]if you extract the precious from
the worthless,
You will become [1]My spokesman.
They for their part may turn to you,
But as for you, you must not turn to
them.
20 "Then I will [a]make you to this people
A fortified wall of bronze;
And though they fight against you,
They will not prevail over you;
For [b]I am with you to save you
And deliver you," declares the LORD.
21 "So I will [a]deliver you from the hand of
the wicked,
And I will [b]redeem you from the
[1]grasp of the violent."

Distresses Foretold

16 The word of the LORD also came to me
saying,
2 "You shall not take a wife for yourself
nor have sons or daughters in this place."
3 For thus says the LORD concerning the
sons and daughters born in this place, and
concerning their [a]mothers who bear them,
and their [b]fathers who beget them in this
land:
4 "They will [a]die of deadly diseases, they
[b]will not be lamented or buried; they will be
as [c]dung on the surface of the ground and
come to an end by sword and famine, and
their carcasses will become food for the [d]birds
of the sky and for the beasts of the earth."
5 For thus says the LORD, "Do not enter a
house of [1a]mourning, or go to lament or to
console them; for I have [b]withdrawn My
peace from this people," declares the LORD,
"*My* [c]lovingkindness and compassion.
6 "Both [a]great men and small will die in
this land; they will not be buried, they will
not be lamented, nor will anyone [b]gash himself or [c]shave his head for them.
7 "Men will not [a]break *bread* in mourning
for them, to comfort anyone for the dead,
nor give them a cup of consolation to drink
for anyone's father or mother.
8 "Moreover you shall [a]not go into a
house of feasting to sit with them to eat and
drink."
9 For thus says the LORD of hosts, the God
of Israel: "Behold, I am going to [1a]eliminate
from this place, before your eyes and in your
time, the voice of rejoicing and the voice of
gladness, the voice of the groom and the
voice of the bride.
10 "Now when you tell this people all these
words, they will say to you, '[a]For what reason has the LORD declared all this great
calamity against us? And what is our iniquity, or what is our sin which we have committed against the LORD our God?'
11 "Then you are to say to them, '*It is*
[a]because your forefathers have forsaken Me,'
declares the LORD, 'and have followed [b]other
gods and served them and bowed down to
them; but Me they have forsaken and have
not kept My law.
12 'You too have done evil, *even* [a]more
than your forefathers; for behold, you are
each one walking according to the [b]stub-
bornness of his own [c]evil heart, without listening to Me.

18 [b]Job 6:15, 20; Jer 14:3 **19** [1]Lit *as My mouth* [a]Jer 4:1; Zech 3:7 [b]1 Kin 17:1; Jer 15:1; 35:19 [c]Jer 6:29; Ezek 22:26; 44:23 **20** [a]Jer 1:18, 19; Ezek 3:9 [b]Ps 46:7; Is 41:10; Jer 1:8, 19; 15:15; 20:11 **21** [1]Lit *palm* [a]Ps 37:40; Is 49:25; Jer 20:13; 39:11, 12 [b]Gen 48:16; Is 49:26; 60:16; Jer 31:11; 50:34 **16:3** [a]Jer 15:8 [b]Jer 6:21 **4** [a]Jer 15:2 [b]Jer 25:33 [c]Ps 83:10; Jer 9:22; 25:33 [d]Ps 79:2; Is 18:6; Jer 15:3; 34:20

5 [1]Or *banqueting* [a]Ezek 24:16-23 [b]Jer 12:12; 15:1-4 [c]Ps 25:6; Is 27:11; Jer 13:14 **6** [a]2 Chr 36:17; Ezek 9:6 [b]Deut 14:1; Jer 41:5; 47:5 [c]Is 22:12 **7** [a]Deut 26:14; Ezek 24:17; Hos 9:4 **8** [a]Eccl 7:2-4; Is 22:12-14; Jer 15:17; Amos 6:4-6 **9** [1]Lit *cause to cease* [a]Jer 7:34; 25:10; Ezek 26:13; Hos 2:11; Rev 18:23 **10** [a]Deut 29:24; 1 Kin 9:8; Jer 5:19; 13:22; 22:8 **11** [a]Deut 29:25; 1 Kin 9:9; 2 Chr 7:22; Neh 9:26-29; Jer 22:9 [b]Deut 29:26; 1 Kin 9:9; Ps 106:35-41; Jer 5:7-9; 8:2; Ezek 11:21; 1 Pet 4:3 **12** [a]Jer 7:26 [b]1 Sam 15:23; Jer 7:24; 9:14; 13:10 [c]Eccl 9:3; Mark 7:21

similarly described in 30:12–15, together with God's promise of healing in 30:17. *Will You indeed be to me . . . ?* See Ps 22:1; Matt 27:46. *deceptive stream.* See Mic 1:14, where also "deception" probably refers to the kind of intermittent streams described in Job 6:15–20. Jeremiah here accuses God of being undependable, in contrast to the Lord's own earlier description of Himself as a "fountain of living waters" (see 2:13 and note).

15:19–21 The Lord commands Jeremiah to repent, then encourages him and renews his call.

15:19 *return . . . restore . . . turn . . . turn.* The Hebrew root is the same for all four words (see notes on 3:1; Is 1:25–26). *Before Me you will stand.* The appropriate posture for the obedient servant (see Num 16:9; Deut 10:8). *spokesman.* Lit. "mouth" (see 1:9 and note; Ex 4:15–16; see also note on Ex 7:1–2).

15:20 See 1:8,18–19 and notes.

15:21 *deliver you from the . . . wicked.* See, e.g., 36:26; 38:6–13.

16:1–17:18 Messages of disaster and comfort, with the note of disaster predominating (16:1–13,16–18; 16:21–17:6; 17:9–13,18). The first half of the section is prose (16:1–18), the second half poetry (16:19–17:18).

16:2 Jeremiah's ministry was such that he had to face life alone (see note on 15:17), without the comfort and support a family can provide. *You shall not.* The Hebrew underlying this phrase is used for the most forceful of negative commands, as, e.g., in the Ten Commandments (see Ex 20:3–4,7,13–17). *this place.* Judah and Jerusalem, especially the latter (see, e.g., Zeph 1:4).

16:4 *diseases.* Cf. 14:18. *not be lamented or buried.* See v. 6; 7:33 and note; 8:2; 14:16; 25:33. *dung.* See 8:2; 9:22; 25:33. *end by sword and famine.* See 14:15–16; see also note on 5:12. *food for the birds . . . for the beasts.* See note on 7:33.

16:5 *Do not . . . go to lament.* See the similar command of God in Ezek 24:16–17,22–23.

16:6 *gash himself or shave his head.* Actions forbidden in the law (see Lev 19:28; 21:5 and note; Deut 14:1 and note), but sometimes practiced by Israelites (see 41:5; Ezek 7:18; Mic 1:16).

16:7 Food was customarily offered to mourners (see 2 Sam 3:35; 12:16–17; Ezek 24:17,22; Hos 9:4). *cup of consolation.* In later Judaism a special cup of wine given to the chief mourner.

16:8 *not go into a house of.* The present crisis is a time for neither feasting nor mourning (see v. 5).

16:9 See 7:34; 25:10; contrast 33:10–11.

16:10–13 The same question but a more elaborate answer than in 5:19 (see 9:12–16; 22:8–9; Deut 29:24–28; 1 Kin 9:8–9).

16:10 Cf. the similar questions in Mal 1:6–7; 2:17; 3:7–8,13.

16:11 See 11:10, where committing sins like those mentioned here is called breaking the Lord's covenant.

16:12 *done evil . . . more than your forefathers.* See 1 Kin 14:9. The coming judgment cannot be blamed on the sins of previ-

13 'So I will [a]hurl you out of this land into the [b]land which you have not known, neither you nor your fathers; and there you will [c]serve other gods day and night, for I will grant you no favor.'

God Will Restore Them

14 "[a]Therefore behold, days are coming," declares the LORD, "when it will no longer be said, 'As the LORD lives, who [b]brought up the sons of Israel out of the land of Egypt,'

15 but, 'As the LORD lives, who brought up the sons of Israel from the [a]land of the north and from all the countries where He had banished them.' For I will restore them to their own land which I gave to their fathers.

16 "Behold, I am going to send for many [a]fishermen," declares the LORD, "and they will fish for them; and afterwards I will send for many hunters, and they will [b]hunt them [c]from every mountain and every hill and from the clefts of the rocks.

17 "[a]For My eyes are on all their ways; they are not hidden from My face, [b]nor is their iniquity concealed from My eyes.

18 "I will first [a]doubly repay their iniquity and their sin, because they have [b]polluted My land; they have filled My inheritance with the carcasses of their [c]detestable idols and with their abominations."

19 O LORD, my [a]strength and my
stronghold,
And my [b]refuge in the day of distress,
To You the [c]nations will come
From the ends of the earth and say,
"Our fathers have inherited nothing but
[d]falsehood,
Futility and [1e]things of no profit."
20 Can man make gods for himself?
Yet they are [a]not gods!

21 "Therefore behold, I am going to make
them know—
This time I will [a]make them know
My [1]power and My might;
And they shall [b]know that My name is
the LORD."

13 [a]Deut 4:26, 27; 2 Chr 7:20; Jer 15:1 [b]Jer 15:14; 17:4 [c]Deut 4:28; 28:36; Jer 5:19 **14** [a]Is 43:18; Jer 23:7 [b]Ex 20:2; Deut 15:15 **15** [a]Ps 106:47; Is 11:11-16; 14:1; Jer 3:18; 23:8; 24:6 **16** [a]Amos 4:2; Hab 1:14, 15 [b]1 Sam 26:20; Mic 7:2 [c]Is 2:21; Amos 9:3 **17** [a]2 Chr 16:9; Job 34:21; Ps 90:8; Prov 5:21; 15:3; Jer 23:24; 32:19; Zech 4:10; Luke 12:2; 1 Cor 4:5; Heb 4:13 [b]Jer 2:22 **18** [a]Jer 17:18; Rev 18:6 [b]Num 35:33, 34; Jer 2:7; 3:9 [c]Jer 7:30; Ezek 11:18, 21 **19** [a]Ps 18:1, 2; Is 25:4 [b]Nah 1:7 [c]Ps 22:27; Is 2:2; Jer 3:17; 4:2

19 [1]Lit *there is nothing profitable in them* [d]Is 44:20; Hab 2:18 [e]Is 44:10 **20** [a]Ps 115:4-8; Is 37:19; Jer 2:11; 5:7; Hos 8:4-6; Gal 4:8 **21** [1]Lit *hand* [a]Ps 9:16 [b]Ps 83:18; Is 43:3; Jer 33:2; Amos 5:8

The Deceitful Heart

17 The [a]sin of Judah is written down
with an [b]iron stylus;
With a diamond point it is [c]engraved
upon the tablet of their heart
And on the horns of [1]their altars,
2 As they remember their [a]children,
So they *remember* their altars and
their [1b]Asherim
By [c]green trees on the high hills.
3 O [a]mountain of Mine in the
countryside,
I will [b]give over your wealth and all
your treasures for booty,
Your high places for sin throughout
your borders.
4 And you will, even of yourself, [a]let go
of your inheritance

17:1 [1]So ancient versions; M.T. *your* [a]Jer 2:22; 4:14 [b]Job 19:24 [c]Prov 3:3; 7:3; Is 49:16; 2 Cor 3:3 **2** [1]I.e. wooden symbols of a female deity [a]Jer 7:18 [b]Ex 34:13; 2 Chr 24:18; 33:3; Is 17:8 [c]Jer 3:6 **3** [a]Jer 26:18; Mic 3:12 [b]2 Kin 24:13; Is 39:4-6; Jer 15:13; 20:5 **4** [a]Jer 12:7; Lam 5:2

ous generations (see 31:29–30; Ezek 18:2–4). *according to the stubbornness of his own evil heart.* See note on 3:17; see also 7:24.

16:13 See Deut 28:36,64. *I will hurl you out.* Into exile (see 7:15; 22:26; Deut 29:28). *land . . . you have not known . . . nor your fathers.* Babylonia (see 9:16).

16:14–15 Repeated almost verbatim in 23:7–8, the passage outlines nearly 1,000 years of Israelite history: exodus (c. 1446 B.C.), exile (586), restoration (537). See Is 43:16–21; 48:20–21; 51:9–11. *As the LORD lives.* See note on Gen 42:15.

16:15 *land of the north.* Babylonia (see note on Is 41:25).

16:16 *fishermen . . . hunters.* Symbolic of conquerors (see Ezek 12:13; 29:4; Amos 4:2 and note). *mountain and . . . hill.* To which the people would flee in vain (see 4:29 and note). *clefts of the rocks.* The phrase occurs outside Jeremiah only in Is 7:19. The Lord may be recalling here the episode of the ruined linen belt, hidden in a "crevice of the rock" (13:4).

16:17 *My eyes are on all their ways.* See 32:19. *they are not hidden from My face.* See 23:24.

16:18 *doubly repay.* See 17:18; Is 40:2 and note. *polluted My land.* Made it ceremonially unclean (see 2:7; 3:1–2; see also note on Lev 4:12). *My inheritance.* God's land (see 17:4; see also note on 2:7). *carcasses of their detestable idols.* See Lev 26:30. Idols have no life in them (see Ps 115:4–7; 135:15–17). *abominations.* Detestable in the Lord's eyes (see 2:7; see also note on Lev 7:21).

16:19–20 The prophet interjects a few brief words of hope.

16:19 *strength . . . stronghold . . . refuge in the day of distress.* Such descriptions of God's dependability and protecting power are common in the Psalms (see, e.g., Ps 18:1–2; 28:7–8; 59:9,16–17). *To You the nations will come.* See 4:2 and note; see also Is 2:2–4; 42:4; 45:14; 49:6; Zech 8:20–23; 14:16. *Futility.* See note on 2:5. *things of no profit.* See note on 2:8.

16:20 *not gods.* See 5:7.

16:21–17:4 The Lord responds to Jeremiah and continues His solemn warnings that began in v. 1.

16:21 *make them know . . . make them know . . . shall know.* The same Hebrew root underlies each of these words. God would "cause them to know," and then they would surely "know." *them . . . they.* Probably includes Judah as well as the nations (see Ezek 36:23; 37:14). *know that My name is the LORD.* "Name" often means "person" or "being" in the OT (see note on Ps 5:11). Ezekiel's equivalent of Jeremiah's phrase is "know that I am the LORD," found in his prophecy about 65 times (see Introduction to Ezekiel: Theological Themes).

17:1 *written . . . with an iron stylus.* The method used to inscribe the most permanent of records (see Job 19:24). *diamond.* Or "flint," which was one of the hardest of stones known to ancient man (see Ezek 3:9; Zech 7:12). *tablet of their heart.* For the same imagery see Prov 3:3; 7:3. *horns of their altars.* The people of Judah have backslid so badly that their sins are engraved not only on their hearts but also on their altars—to be remembered by God rather than to be atoned for (see Lev 16:18).

17:2 *altars and their Asherim.* See notes on Ex 34:13; Deut 7:5. *green trees . . . high hills.* See note on 2:20.

17:3–4 Repeated in large part from 15:13–14 (see notes there).

17:3 *mountain of Mine.* Mount Zion, the location of the temple in Jerusalem (see Ps 24:3; Is 2:3; Zech 8:3). *high places.* Locales of idolatrous worship.

17:4 *inheritance.* The land of Canaan (see 16:18; see also note on 2:7).

That I gave you;
And I will make you serve your
[b]enemies
In the [c]land which you do not know;
For you have [d]kindled a fire in My
anger
Which will burn forever.

5 Thus says the LORD,
"[a]Cursed is the man who trusts in
mankind
And makes [b]flesh his [1]strength,
And whose heart turns away from the
LORD.
6 "For he will be like a [a]bush in the
desert
And will not see when prosperity
comes,
But will live in stony wastes in the
wilderness,
A [b]land of salt [1]without inhabitant.
7 "[a]Blessed is the man who trusts in the
LORD
And whose [b]trust is the LORD.
8 "For he will be like a [a]tree planted by
the water,
That extends its roots by a stream
And will not fear when the heat comes;
But its leaves will be green,
And it will not be anxious in a year of
[b]drought
Nor cease to yield fruit.

9 "The [a]heart is more [b]deceitful than all
else
And is desperately [c]sick;
Who can understand it?
10 "I, the LORD, [a]search the heart,
I test the [1]mind,
Even [b]to give to each man according
to his ways,
According to the [2]results of his deeds.
11 "As a partridge that hatches eggs which
it has not laid,
So is he who [a]makes a fortune, but
unjustly;
In the midst of his days it will forsake
him,
And in [1]the end he will be a [b]fool."

12 [a]A glorious throne on high from the
beginning
Is the place of our sanctuary.
13 O LORD, the [a]hope of Israel,
All who [b]forsake You will be put to
shame.
Those who turn [1]away on earth will
be [c]written down,
Because they have forsaken the
fountain of living water, even the
LORD.
14 [a]Heal me, O LORD, and I will be
healed;
[b]Save me and I will be saved,
For You are my [c]praise.
15 Look, they keep [a]saying to me,
"Where is the word of the LORD?
Let it come now!"
16 But as for me, I have not hurried away
from *being* a shepherd after You,
Nor have I longed for the woeful day;
[a]You Yourself know that the utterance
of my lips
Was in Your presence.
17 Do not be a [a]terror to me;
You are my [b]refuge in the day of
disaster.

4 [b]Deut 28:48; Is 14:3; Jer 15:14; 27:12, 13 [c]Jer 16:13 [d]Is 5:25; Jer 7:20; 15:14
5 [1]Lit *arm* [a]Ps 146:3; Is 2:22; 30:1; Ezek 29:7 [b]2 Chr 32:8; Is 31:3
6 [1]Lit *and is not inhabited* [a]Jer 48:6 [b]Deut 29:23; Job 39:6
7 [a]Ps 2:12; 34:8; 84:12; Prov 16:20 [b]Ps 40:4
8 [a]Ps 1:3; 92:12-14; Ezek 31:3-9 [b]Jer 14:1-6
9 [a]Eccl 9:3; Mark 7:21, 22 [b]Rom 7:11; Eph 4:22 [c]Is 1:5, 6; 6:10; Matt 13:15; Mark 2:17; Rom 1:21
10 [1]Lit *kidneys* [a]1 Sam 16:7; 1 Chr 28:9; Ps 139:23; Prov 17:3; Jer 11:20; 20:12; Rom 8:27; Rev 2:23
10 [2]Lit *fruit* [b]Ps 62:12; Jer 32:19; Rom 2:6
11 [1]Lit *his* [a]Jer 6:13; 8:10; 22:13, 17 [b]Luke 12:20
12 [a]Jer 3:17; 14:21
13 [1]Lit *away from Me* [a]Jer 14:8; 50:7 [b]Is 1:28 [c]Luke 10:20
14 [a]Jer 30:17; 33:6 [b]Ps 54:1; 60:5 [c]Deut 10:21; Ps 109:1
15 [a]Is 5:19; 2 Pet 3:4
16 [a]Jer 12:3
17 [a]Ps 88:15 [b]Jer 16:19; Nah 1:7

17:5–8 See Ps 1 and notes.

17:5 *Cursed.* See note on 11:3. *flesh.* The opposite of "spirit" (see Is 31:3; see also Job 10:4).

17:6 *bush.* See 48:6. Apart from these two places in Jeremiah, the Hebrew for this word appears elsewhere in the OT only in Ps 102:17, where it is translated "destitute." *prosperity.* Lit. "good," as in Deut 28:12, where it refers to rain. *land of salt.* An evidence of God's curse also in Deut 29:23.

17:8 *planted.* Or "transplanted." *stream.* See Is 44:4, where the same Hebrew root is used again to illustrate the source of the righteous man's strength. *drought.* See note on 14:1. *yield fruit.* The Lord's answer to Jeremiah's complaint in 12:1–2 (see notes there).

17:9 The prophet makes an observation, then asks a rhetorical question. *The heart.* The source of the "springs of life," in which wickedness must not be allowed to take root (Prov 4:23). *deceitful.* The Hebrew root for this word is the basis of the name Jacob (see note on Gen 27:36).

17:10 The Lord responds to Jeremiah's question. *search . . . test.* See 11:20; 12:3. *mind.* Lit. "kidneys" (see 11:20). *According to . . . his deeds.* Lit. "the fruit of his deeds" (cf. 6:19).

17:11 The prophet uses a proverb to make his point (as in v. 9); see especially Prov 23:5. *partridge.* Mentioned elsewhere in the OT only in 1 Sam 26:20. *hatches eggs.* The Hebrew root underlying this phrase is found again only in Is 34:15. Its Aramaic cognate, however, is used to explain Job 39:14 in the Targum (ancient Aramaic paraphrase). *In the midst of his days.* See Ps 102:24. *fool.* Morally and spiritually reprobate (see note on Prov 1:7).

17:12–18 The fourth of Jeremiah's "confessions" (see Introduction: Author and Date).

17:12 *glorious throne.* See note on 14:21; see also Is 6:1. The Lord is often represented as sitting on a throne between the cherubim on the ark of the covenant in the temple (see, e.g., Ps 80:1; 99:1). *on high.* Mount Zion is the "high mountain of Israel" (Ezek 20:40). *from the beginning.* From time immemorial, Zion had been chosen by God as the place of His sanctuary (see Ex 15:17).

17:13 *forsaken . . . fountain of living water.* Contrast 15:18; see note on 2:13.

17:14 *Heal me.* See 15:18; Ps 6:2. *You are my praise.* Equals "you are the One I praise" (likewise in Deut 10:21).

17:15 See 20:8. Jeremiah's enemies accuse him of being a false prophet (see Deut 18:21–22). The accusation must have been voiced before the first invasion of Judah by the Babylonians in 605 B.C. after the battle of Carchemish (see 46:2; see also Introduction: Background).

17:16 *shepherd.* Symbolic of leadership (see note on 2:8), and therefore of Jeremiah's role as a prophet.

17:17 *my refuge.* See note on 16:19. *day of disaster.* See v. 18; 15:11.

18 Let those who persecute me be [a]put to shame, but as for me, [b]let me not be put to shame;
Let them be dismayed, but let me not be dismayed.
[c]Bring on them a day of disaster,
And crush them with twofold destruction!

The Sabbath Must Be Kept

19 Thus the LORD said to me, "Go and
stand in the [1]public gate, through which the
kings of Judah come in and go out, as well as
in all the gates of Jerusalem;
20 and say to them, '[a]Listen to the word of
the LORD, [b]kings of Judah, and all Judah and
all inhabitants of Jerusalem who come in
through these gates:
21 'Thus says the LORD, "[a]Take heed for
yourselves, and [b]do not carry any load on
the sabbath day or bring anything in through
the gates of Jerusalem.
22 "You shall not bring a load out of your
houses on the sabbath day [a]nor do any
work, but keep the sabbath day holy, as I
[b]commanded your [1]forefathers.
23 "Yet they [a]did not listen or incline their
ears, but [b]stiffened their necks in order not
to listen or take correction.
24 "But it will come about, if you [a]listen
attentively to Me," declares the LORD, "to
[b]bring no load in through the gates of this
city on the sabbath day, [c]but to keep the sabbath day holy by doing no work on it,
25 [a]then there will come in through the
gates of this city kings and princes [b]sitting
on the throne of David, riding in chariots and
on horses, they and their princes, the men of
Judah and the inhabitants of Jerusalem, and
this [c]city will be inhabited forever.
26 "They will come in from the [a]cities of
Judah and from the environs of Jerusalem,
from the land of Benjamin, from the [b]low-
land, from the hill country and from the
[c]Negev, bringing burnt offerings, sacrifices,
grain offerings and incense, and bringing
sacrifices of thanksgiving to the house of the
LORD.
27 "But [a]if you do not listen to Me to keep
the sabbath day holy by not carrying a load
and coming in through the gates of Jerusalem
on the sabbath day, then [b]I will kindle a fire
in its gates and it will [c]devour the palaces of
Jerusalem and [d]not be quenched." ' "

The Potter and the Clay

18 The word which came to Jeremiah
from the LORD saying,
2 "Arise and [a]go down to the potter's
house, and there I will announce My words
to you."
3 Then I went down to the potter's
house, and there he was, making something
on the [1]wheel.
4 But the vessel that he was making of
clay was spoiled in the hand of the potter; so

18 [a]Ps 35:4, 26; Jer 17:13; 20:11 [b]Jer 1:17 [c]Ps 35:8
19 [1]Lit *gate of the sons of the people*
20 [a]Ezek 2:7 [b]Ps 49:1, 2; Jer 19:3, 4
21 [a]Deut 4:9, 15, 23; Mark 4:24 [b]Num 15:32-36; Neh 13:15-21; John 5:9-12
22 [1]Lit *fathers* [a]Ex 16:23-29; 20:8-10; Deut 5:12-14; Is 56:2-6; 58:13 [b]Ex 31:13-17; Ezek 20:12; Zech 1:4
23 [a]Jer 7:24, 28; 11:10 [b]Prov 29:1; Jer 7:26; 19:15
24 [a]Ex 15:26; Deut 11:13; Is 21:7; 55:2 [b]Jer 17:21, 22 [c]Ex 20:8-11; Ezek 20:20
25 [a]Jer 22:4 [b]2 Sam 7:16; Is 9:7; Jer 33:15, 17, 21; Luke 1:32 [c]Ps 132:13, 14; Heb 12:22
26 [a]Jer 32:44; 33:13 [b]Zech 7:7 [c]Ps 107:22; Jer 33:11
27 [a]Is 1:20; Jer 22:5; 26:4; Zech 7:11-14 [b]Lam 4:11 [c]2 Kin 25:9; Jer 39:8; Amos 2:5 [d]Jer 7:20; Ezek 20:47
18:2 [a]Jer 19:1, 2
3 [1]Lit *pair of stone discs*

17:18 *those who persecute me.* See 15:15. *twofold.* see 16:18; Is 40:2 and note.

17:19–27 An extended commentary on the sabbath-day commandment (the covenant sign of God's relationship with Israel; see Ex 31:13–17; Ezek 20:12), probably the version recorded in Deut 5:12–15 (see especially note on v. 22).

17:19 *public.* Lit. "sons of the people." The Hebrew for this word is translated "common people" in 26:23; 2 Kin 23:6 and "lay people" in 2 Chr 35:5,7. The latter meaning seems intended here, and therefore the "public gate" is most likely the east gate of the temple, where the people assembled in large numbers and which the kings would be expected to use frequently.

17:20 *kings of Judah.* The current king and all subsequent ruling members of David's dynasty (see, e.g., v. 25; 1:18; 2:26; 13:13; 19:3).

17:21 *Take heed.* See Josh 23:11. The Hebrew underlying this phrase is translated "watch yourselves carefully" in Deut 4:15, and a similar expression is translated "Take heed then to your spirit" in Mal 2:15, stressing the urgency and solemnity of the Lord's command.

17:22 *You shall not.* See note on 16:2. The Hebrew for this negative expression is stronger than that in v. 21. *not . . . do any work . . . keep the sabbath day holy.* Specific references to the sabbath-day commandment of Ex 20:8,10; Deut 5:12,14. *as I commanded.* The Hebrew underlying this phrase is unique to the Ten Commandments as recorded in Deuteronomy (see Deut 5:12,15–16; see note on vv. 19–27).

17:23 *did not listen . . . stiffened their necks.* Repeated from 7:26 (see note there; see also 11:10). *not . . . take correction.* See 2:30; 5:3.

17:25 Repeated in part in 22:4. King David's dynasty will last forever (see 23:5–6; 30:9; 33:15; 2 Sam 7:12–17), and Jerusalem will be inhabited for all time (Zech 2:2–12; 8:3; 14:11), if the people of Judah obey the Lord (see v. 27)—and they will, according to 31:33–34.

17:26 *land of Benjamin.* Jeremiah's hometown was located there (see 1:1). *lowland . . . hill country.* See note on Deut 1:7. *Negev.* See note on Gen 12:9. *sacrifices of thanksgiving.* The repetition here of "bringing" from earlier in the verse separates the thank offerings from the other specific sacrifices mentioned and gives them the more general designation of offerings of thanksgiving (as intended also in 33:11).

17:27 Disobedience will bring disaster and will negate—at least temporarily—the promises of vv. 24–26. *gates of Jerusalem.* The symbols of sabbath violation would be the first structures destroyed. *kindle a fire . . . devour the palaces.* Common prophetic language for divine judgment against rebellious cities (see 49:27; 50:32; Amos 1:4,7,10,12,14; 2:2,5; cf. Jer 21:14).

18:1–20:18 Three chapters focusing on lessons the Lord taught Jeremiah at the potter's workshop, probably before 605 B.C. (see note on 17:15).

18:1–17 As the potter controls what he does with the clay, so the Lord is sovereign over the people of Judah.

18:2 *go down.* The potter's workshop was probably located on the slopes of the Valley of Ben-hinnom near the potsherd gate (see 19:2 and note).

18:3 *wheel.* Lit. "two stones." Both wheels were attached to a single upright shaft, one end of which was sunk permanently in the ground. The potter would spin the lower wheel with his foot and would work the clay on the upper wheel; the process is described in the Apocryphal book of Ecclesiasticus (38:29–30).

18:4 *spoiled.* The Hebrew for this word is translated "ruined"

he remade it into another vessel, as it
pleased the potter to make.
5 Then the word of the LORD came to me
saying,
6 "Can I not, O house of Israel, deal with
you as this potter *does?*" declares the LORD.
"Behold, like the [a]clay in the potter's hand,
so are you in My hand, O house of Israel.
7 "At one moment I might speak concerning a nation or concerning a kingdom to
[a]uproot, to pull down, or to destroy *it;*
8 [a]if that nation against which I have
spoken turns from its evil, I will [1b]relent
concerning the calamity I planned to bring
on it.
9 "Or at another moment I might speak
concerning a nation or concerning a kingdom to [a]build up or to plant *it;*
10 if it does [a]evil in My sight by not obeying My voice, then I will [1b]think better of the
good with which I had promised to [2]bless it.
11 "So now then, speak to the men of
Judah and against the inhabitants of Jerusalem saying, 'Thus says the LORD, "Behold,
I am [a]fashioning calamity against you and
devising a plan against you. Oh [b]turn back,
each of you from his evil way, and [1]reform
your ways and your deeds." '
12 "But [a]they will say, 'It's hopeless! For
we are going to follow our own plans, and
each of us will act according to the [b]stub-
bornness of his evil heart.'
13 "Therefore thus says the LORD,
'[a]Ask now among the nations,
Who ever heard the like of [1]this?
The [b]virgin of Israel
Has done a most [c]appalling thing.

6 [a]Is 45:9; 64:8; Matt 20:15; Rom 9:21
7 [a]Jer 1:10
8 [1]Lit *repent of* [a]Jer 7:3-7; 12:16; Ezek 18:21 [b]Ps 106:45; Jer 26:3, 13, 19; Hos 11:8; Joel 2:13, 14; Jon 3:10
9 [a]Jer 1:10; 31:28; Amos 9:11-15
10 [1]Lit *repent* [2]Lit *do it good* [a]Ps 125:5; Jer 7:24-28; Ezek 33:18 [b]1 Sam 2:30; 13:13
11 [1]Lit *make good* [a]Is 5:5; Jer 4:6; 11:11 [b]2 Kin 17:13; Is 1:16-19; Jer 4:1; Acts 26:20
12 [a]Is 57:10; Jer 2:25 [b]Deut 29:19; Jer 7:24; 16:12
13 [1]Lit *these* [a]Is 66:8; Jer 2:10, 11 [b]Jer 14:17; 31:4 [c]Jer 5:30; 23:14; Hos 6:10
15 [1]Lit *to worthlessness* [2]So ancient versions; Heb *caused them to* [3]Or *in* [a]Jer 2:32; 3:21 [b]Is 65:7; Jer 7:9; 10:15; 44:17 [c]Jer 6:16 [d]Is 57:14; 62:10
16 [a]Jer 25:9; 49:13; 50:13; Ezek 33:28, 29 [b]1 Kin 9:8; Lam 2:15; Mic 6:16

14 'Does the snow of Lebanon forsake the
rock of the open country?
Or is the cold flowing water *from* a
foreign *land* ever snatched away?
15 'For [a]My people have forgotten Me,
[b]They burn incense [1]to worthless gods
And they [2]have stumbled [3]from their
ways,
[3]From the [c]ancient paths,
To walk in bypaths,
Not on a [d]highway,
16 To make their land a [a]desolation,
An object of perpetual [b]hissing;
Everyone who passes by it will be
astonished
And [c]shake his head.
17 'Like an [a]east wind I will [b]scatter them
Before the enemy;
I will [1]show them [c]My back and not
My face
[d]In the day of their calamity.' "
18 Then they said, "Come and let us
[a]devise plans against Jeremiah. Surely the
[b]law is not going to be lost to the priest, nor
[c]counsel to the sage, nor the *divine* [d]word to
the prophet! Come on and let us [e]strike at
him with *our* tongue, and let us [f]give no
heed to any of his words."
19 Do give heed to me, O LORD,
And listen to [1]what my opponents are
saying!
20 [a]Should good be repaid with evil?

[c]Ps 22:7; Is 37:22; Jer 48:27 **17** [1]So ancient versions; M.T. reads *look them in the back and not in the face* [a]Ps 48:7 [b]Job 27:21; Jer 13:24 [c]Jer 2:27; 32:33 [d]Jer 46:21 **18** [a]Jer 11:19; 18:11 [b]Jer 2:8; Mal 2:7 [c]Job 5:13; Jer 8:8 [d]Jer 5:13 [e]Ps 52:2; Jer 20:10 [f]Jer 43:2 **19** [1]Lit *the voice of my opponents*
20 [a]Ps 109:4

in 13:7 with respect to the linen belt that Jeremiah had hidden (see note there). *as it pleased the potter.* The flaw was in the clay itself, not in the potter's skill.

18:6 *like the clay . . . so are you.* Biblical imagery often pictures mankind as made of clay by a potter (see Job 4:19 and note). *potter's.* The Hebrew for this word is translated "Maker" in 10:16 with reference to God.

18:7–10 The Lord retains the right of limiting His own absolute sovereignty on the basis of human response to His offers of pardon and restoration and His threats of judgment and destruction. *At . . . if . . . at . . . if.* God's promises and threats are conditioned on man's actions. God, who Himself does not change (see Num 23:19; Mal 3:6; James 1:17), nevertheless will change His preannounced response to man, depending on what the latter does (see note on 4:28; see also Joel 2:13; Jon 3:9 and note; Jon 3:8–4:2; 4:11).

18:7 *uproot . . . pull down . . . destroy.* See 1:10 and note.

18:8 See 26:3. *evil . . . calamity.* The Hebrew is the same for both words (also in v. 11).

18:9 *built up . . . plant it.* See 1:10 and note.

18:11 *devising a plan.* See Esth 8:3; 9:25; Ezek 38:10.

18:12 *It's hopeless!* See 2:25; see also note on Is 57:10. *act according to . . . his evil heart.* See note on 3:17.

18:13–17 See 2:10–13.

18:13 *virgin of Israel.* See 14:17 and note. *appalling thing.* See 5:30; 23:14; Hos 6:10.

18:14–15 Although nature is reliable (v. 14), Judah is fickle and unfaithful (v. 15).

18:14 *Lebanon.* One of the highest of the northern mountains (see 22:6), reaching an altitude of over 10,000 feet.

18:15 *My people have forgotten Me.* Repeated from 2:32 (see note there). *burn incense.* See note on 1:16. *worthless gods.* Lit. "nothing" (see Ps 31:6). The Hebrew for this phrase is different from that in either 2:5 or 2:8 (see note on 2:8). *they have stumbled.* See 2 Chr 28:23. *ancient paths.* See note on 6:16. *Not on a highway.* See note on Is 35:8.

18:16 *desolation . . . astonished.* The same Hebrew root underlies both words. *object of . . . hissing.* See 19:8; 25:9,18; 29:18; 51:37. The phrase implies hissing or whistling to express shock, ridicule and contempt. *Everyone . . . astonished.* See 19:8; 1 Kin 9:8. *shake his head.* See 48:27; Job 16:4 and note; see also Ps 44:14; 109:25.

18:17 *east wind.* See note on 4:11; see also Ps 48:7. *show them My back and not My face.* As the people themselves had done to God (see 2:27). His face symbolizes His gracious blessing and favor (see Num 6:24–26).

18:18–23 The fifth of Jeremiah's "confessions" (see Introduction: Author and Date).

18:18 *they.* Jeremiah's enemies (see note on 17:15). *plans against Jeremiah.* See v. 12; 11:18–23; 12:6; 15:10–11,15–21. *the law.* Delegated to the priests (see note on Deut 31:11). *priest . . . sage . . . prophet.* See 8:8–10; see also Ezek 7:26, where the wise are replaced by the elders. *strike at him with our tongue.* See note on 9:3.

18:20 *good . . . repaid with evil.* See Ps 35:12. *dug a pit.* Symbolic of his enemies' plots against him (see v. 22; Ps 57:6 and

For they have [b]dug a pit for [1]me.
Remember how I [c]stood before You
To speak good on their behalf,
So as to turn away Your wrath from
them.
21 Therefore, [a]give their children over to
famine
And deliver them up to the [1]power of
the sword;
And let their wives become [b]childless
and [c]widowed.
Let their men also be smitten to death,
Their [d]young men struck down by the
sword in battle.
22 May an [a]outcry be heard from their
houses,
When You suddenly bring raiders
upon them;
[b]For they have dug a pit to capture me
And [c]hidden snares for my feet.
23 Yet You, O LORD, know
All their [1]deadly designs against me;
[a]Do not [2]forgive their iniquity
Or blot out their sin from Your sight.
But may they be [3][b]overthrown before
You;
Deal with them in the [c]time of Your
anger!

The Broken Jar

19 Thus says the LORD, "Go and buy a [a]potter's earthenware [b]jar, and *take* some of the [c]elders of the people and some of the [1][d]senior priests.

2 "Then go out to the [a]valley of Ben-hinnom, which is by the entrance of the potsherd gate, and [b]proclaim there the words that I tell you,

3 and say, 'Hear the word of the LORD, O [a]kings of Judah and inhabitants of Jerusalem: thus says the LORD of hosts, the God of Israel, "Behold I am about to bring a [b]calamity upon this place, at which the [c]ears of everyone that hears of it will tingle.

4 "Because they have [a]forsaken Me and have [b]made this an alien place and have burned [1]sacrifices in it to [c]other gods, that neither they nor their forefathers nor the kings of Judah had *ever* known, and *because* they have filled this place with the [d]blood of the innocent

5 and have built the [a]high places of Baal to burn their [b]sons in the fire as burnt offerings to Baal, a thing which I never commanded or spoke of, nor did it *ever* enter My [1]mind;

6 therefore, behold, [a]days are coming," declares the LORD, "when this place will no longer be called [b]Topheth or [c]the valley of Ben-hinnom, but rather the valley of Slaughter.

7 "I will [a]make void the counsel of Judah and Jerusalem in this place, and [b]I will cause them to fall by the sword before their enemies and by the hand of those who seek their life; and I will give over their [c]carcasses as food for the birds of the sky and the beasts of the earth.

8 "I will also make this city a [a]desolation and an *object of* hissing; [b]everyone who

20 [1]Lit *my soul* [b]Ps 35:7; 57:6; Jer 5:26; 18:22 [c]Ps 106:23
21 [1]Lit *hands of* [a]Ps 109:9-20; Jer 11:22; 14:16 [b]1 Sam 15:33; Is 13:18 [c]Jer 15:8; Ezek 22:25 [d]Jer 9:21; 11:22
22 [a]Jer 6:26; 25:34, 36 [b]Jer 18:20 [c]Ps 140:5
23 [1]Lit *unto death* [2]Lit *cover over, atone for* [3]Lit *ones made to stumble* [a]Neh 4:5; Ps 109:14; Is 2:9 [b]Jer 6:15, 21 [c]Jer 7:20; 17:4
19:1 [1]Or *elders of* [a]Jer 18:2 [b]Jer 19:10 [c]Num 11:16 [d]2 Kin 19:2; Ezek 8:11
2 [a]Josh 15:8; 2 Kin 23:10; Jer 7:31, 32; 32:35
2 [b]Prov 1:20
3 [a]Jer 17:20 [b]Jer 6:19; 19:15 [c]1 Sam 3:11
4 [1]Or *incense* [a]Deut 28:20; Is 65:11; Jer 2:13, 17, 19; 17:13 [b]Ezek 7:22; Dan 11:31 [c]Jer 7:9; 11:13 [d]2 Kin 21:6, 16; Jer 2:34; 7:6
5 [1]Lit *heart* [a]Num 22:41; Jer 32:35 [b]Lev 18:21; 2 Kin 17:17; Ps 106:37, 38
6 [a]Jer 7:32 [b]Is 30:33 [c]Josh 15:8
7 [a]Ps 33:10, 11; Is 28:17, 18; Jer 8:8, 9 [b]Lev 26:17; Deut 28:25; Jer 15:2, 9 [c]Ps 79:2; Jer 16:4
8 [a]Jer 18:16; 49:13; 50:13 [b]1 Kin 9:8; 2 Chr 7:21

---

note; Prov 22:14; 23:27). *stood before You.* See note on 15:1. *speak good on their behalf.* See 14:7–9,21.

18:21 *deliver them up to the power of the sword.* The Hebrew underlying this phrase occurs also in Ps 63:10; Ezek 35:5. *be smitten to death.* Lit. "be slain by death," probably referring to plague, as in 15:2 (see note there).

18:22–23 See Ps 141:8–10.

18:22 *hidden snares.* See Ps 140:5; 142:3.

18:23 *You, O LORD, know.* See 12:3; 15:15. *Do not forgive their iniquity . . . may they be overthrown before You.* A prayer not for human vengeance but for divine vindication. *blot out.* The Phoenician cognate of the Hebrew for this phrase appears in a ninth-century B.C. inscription on a gateway: "If . . . a man . . . blots out the name of Azitawadda from this gate . . . may (the gods) wipe out . . . that man!"

19:1–15 A jar deliberately broken by Jeremiah (vv. 1–10) symbolizes the forthcoming destruction of Judah and Jerusalem (vv. 11–15). In ch. 18, the potter's clay was still moist and pliable, making it possible to reshape and rework it (see 18:1–11). In ch. 19, however, the clay jar is hard and, if unsuitable for the owner's use, can only be destroyed (see v. 11).

19:1 *jar.* The Hebrew for this word implies a vessel with a narrow neck, perhaps the water decanter frequently found in excavations and ranging from 5 to 12 inches high. *elders.* See note on Ex 3:16. *of the people.* See 1 Kin 8:1–3. *of the senior priests.* See 2 Kin 19:2, "elders of the priests." Elders in Israel were of two kinds, one performing primarily civil functions and the other primarily religious functions.

19:2 *valley of Ben-hinnom.* See note on 7:31. *potsherd gate.* The Hebrew underlying the word "potsherd" is the same as that translated "clay" in v. 1. The Jerusalem Targum identified the potsherd gate (so called because it overlooked the main dump for broken pottery) with the Rubbish Gate of Neh 2:13 (see note there); 3:13–14; 12:31.

19:3 *kings.* See note on 17:20. *calamity . . . ears . . . will tingle.* Echoed from 2 Kin 21:12 (see 1 Sam 3:11). The phrase refers to the shock of hearing an announcement of threatened punishment.

19:4 *they.* All who tried to combine the worship of idols with the worship of the one true God. *this . . . place.* Jerusalem. *burned sacrifices.* The Hebrew for this phrase is mostly translated this same way elsewhere in Jeremiah (see note on 1:16). *filled this place with the blood of the innocent.* The blood of godly people (see 2:34; 7:6; 22:3,17; 26:15), specifically as shed by wicked King Manasseh (see 15:4 and note; see also especially 2 Kin 21:16).

19:5–6 Repeated in large part from 7:31–32 (see notes there).

19:7 *make void.* Lit. "pour out." The Hebrew for "make void" ("pour out") sounds like the Hebrew for "jar" (see note on v. 1). As Jeremiah was saying this, he may have been pouring water from the jar to the ground (cf. 2 Sam 14:14). *fall by the sword before their enemies.* The Babylonians are the instruments of the divine threat (see 20:6). *carcasses as food . . . beasts of the earth.* See 7:33 and note.

19:8 Echoes the language of 18:16 (see note there; see also Ezek 27:35; Zeph 2:15). *desolation . . . astonished.* The same Hebrew root underlies both words. *hissing . . . hiss.* The same Hebrew root underlies both words.

passes by it will be astonished and hiss because of all its [1]disasters.

9 "I will make them [a]eat the flesh of their sons and the flesh of their daughters, and they will eat one another's flesh in the siege and in the distress with which their enemies and those who seek their life will distress them." '

10 "Then you are to break the [a]jar in the sight of the men who accompany you

11 and say to them, 'Thus says the LORD of hosts, "Just so will I [a]break this people and this city, even as one breaks a potter's vessel, which cannot again be repaired; and they will [b]bury in Topheth [1]because there is no *other* place for burial.

12 "This is how I will treat this place and its inhabitants," declares the LORD, "so as to make this city like Topheth.

13 "The [a]houses of Jerusalem and the houses of the kings of Judah will be [b]defiled like the place Topheth, because of all the [c]houses on whose rooftops they burned [1]sacrifices to [d]all the heavenly host and [e]poured out drink offerings to other gods." ' "

14 Then Jeremiah came from Topheth, where the LORD had sent him to prophesy; and he stood in the [a]court of the LORD's house and said to all the people:

15 "Thus says the LORD of hosts, the God of Israel, 'Behold, I am about to bring on this city and all its towns the entire calamity that I have declared against it, because they have [a]stiffened their necks so [b]as not to heed My words.' "

Pashhur Persecutes Jeremiah

20 When Pashhur the priest, the son of [a]Immer, who was [b]chief officer in the house of the LORD, heard Jeremiah prophesying these things,

2 Pashhur had Jeremiah the prophet [a]beaten and put him in the [b]stocks that were at the upper [c]Benjamin Gate, which was by the house of the LORD.

3 On the next day, when Pashhur released Jeremiah from the stocks, Jeremiah said to him, "Pashhur is not the name the LORD has [a]called you, but rather [1b]Magor-missabib.

4 "For thus says the LORD, 'Behold, I am going to make you a [a]terror to yourself and to all your friends; and while [b]your eyes look on, they will fall by the sword of their enemies. So I will [c]give over all Judah to the hand of the king of Babylon, and he will carry them away as [d]exiles to Babylon and will slay them with the sword.

5 'I will also give over all the [a]wealth of this city, all its produce and all its costly things; even all the treasures of the kings of Judah I will give over to the [b]hand of their

8 [1]Lit *blows*
9 [a]Lev 26:29; Deut 28:53, 55; Is 9:20; Lam 4:10; Ezek 5:10
10 [a]Jer 19:1
11 [1]Or *until there is no place* left *to bury* [a]Ps 2:9; Is 30:14; Lam 4:2; Rev 2:27 [b]Jer 7:32
13 [1]Or *incense* [a]Jer 52:13 [b]2 Kin 23:10; Ps 74:7; 79:1; Ezek 7:21, 22 [c]Jer 32:29; Zeph 1:5 [d]Deut 4:19; 2 Kin 17:16; Jer 8:2 [e]Jer 7:18; 44:18; Ezek 20:28
14 [a]2 Chr 20:5; Jer 26:2
15 [a]Neh 9:17, 29; Jer 7:26; 17:23 [b]Ps 58:4
20:1 [a]1 Chr 24:14; Ezra 2:37, 38 [b]2 Kin 25:18
2 [a]1 Kin 22:27; 2 Chr 16:10; 24:21; Jer 1:19; Amos 7:10-13 [b]Job 13:27; 33:11 [c]Jer 37:13; 38:7; Zech 14:10
3 [1]I.e. terror on every side [a]Is 8:3; Hos 1:4, 9 [b]Jer 6:25; 20:10
4 [a]Job 18:11-21; Jer 6:25; 46:5; Ezek 26:21 [b]Jer 29:21; 39:6, 7 [c]Jer 21:4-10; 25:9 [d]Jer 13:10; 52:27
5 [a]Jer 15:13; 17:3 [b]2 Kin 20:17, 18; 2 Chr 36:10; Jer 27:21, 22

19:9 One of the covenant curses (see Lev 26:29; Deut 28:53–57). *eat the flesh of their sons and . . . daughters . . . eat one another's flesh.* When Jerusalem's food supply ran out during the Babylonian siege in 586 B.C., cannibalism resulted (see Lam 2:20; 4:10; Ezek 5:10). Such shocking activity was not unprecedented in Israel (see 2 Kin 6:28–29), and it would occur again in A.D. 70 during the Roman siege of Jerusalem (see Zech 11:9 and note): "A woman . . . who . . . had fled to Jerusalem . . . killed her son, roasted him, and ate one half, concealing and saving the rest" (Josephus, *Jewish War,* 6.3.4).

19:11 *break this people . . . as one breaks a potter's vessel.* Egyptians of the 12th Dynasty (1991–1786 B.C.) inscribed the names of their enemies on pottery bowls and then smashed them, hoping to break the power of their enemies by so doing. *cannot again be repaired.* See note on vv. 1–15.

19:13 *will be defiled like . . . Topheth.* King Josiah had earlier "defiled Topheth" (2 Kin 23:10). *burned sacrifices.* See note on 1:16. *rooftops.* See 32:29; see also note on Is 15:3. The kings of Judah had built pagan altars on the roof of the palace in Jerusalem (see 2 Kin 23:12). The Ugaritic Keret epic of the 14th century B.C. (see chart, p. xix) describes a similar practice: "Go to the top of a tower, bestride the top of the wall . . . Honor Baal with your sacrifice . . . Then descend . . . from the housetops." *heavenly host.* Worship of the sun, moon and stars was common in Judah throughout much of the later history of the monarchy (see, e.g., 2 Kin 17:16; 21:3,5; 23:4–5; Zeph 1:5). *drink offerings to other gods.* See note on 7:18.

19:14 *all the people.* A much larger audience than the elders of v. 1.

19:15 *all its towns.* The towns of Judah that were dependent on Jerusalem (see 1:15; 9:11). *stiffened their necks . . . not to heed My words.* Repeated from 7:26 (see note there; see also 11:10).

20:1–6 Pashhur's response to Jeremiah's symbolic act (vv. 1–2), and Jeremiah's rejoinder (vv. 3–6).

20:1 *Pashhur.* One or more different men with the same name appear in 21:1; 38:1. *Immer.* Perhaps a descendant of the head of the 16th division of priests in the Jerusalem temple (see 1 Chr 24:14). *chief officer.* The priest in charge of punishing troublemakers, real or imagined, in the temple courts (see v. 2; 29:26). The position was second only to that of the chief priest himself (compare 29:25–26 with 52:24).

20:2 The first of many recorded acts of physical violence against Jeremiah. *the prophet.* The first time Jeremiah is so called in the book (see Introduction: Themes and Message), here to stress the enormity of Pashhur's actions. *beaten.* Probably in accordance with the Mosaic law of Deut 25:2–3 (see note on Deut 25:3). *stocks.* Lit. "restraint, confinement" (the Hebrew for this word is translated "prison" in 2 Chr 16:10). *upper Benjamin Gate.* Probably the same as the "north gate of the inner court" (Ezek 8:3; see 2 Kin 15:35; see also Ezek 9:2). *by the house of the LORD.* This qualifying phrase distinguishes the temple's Gate of Benjamin from the "Benjamin Gate" in the city wall (37:13; 38:7). Both gates were in the northern part of the city, facing the territory of Benjamin.

20:3 *Magor-missabib.* Means "terror on every side." (See note on 6:25). The phrase "terror on every side" (see v. 10) is found in the plural in Lam 2:22.

20:4 Pashhur's new name symbolizes terror to all Judah, whose people will be exiled to Babylonia or put to death. *friends.* Associates and allies in the sense of covenant partners (see v. 6). *king of Babylon.* Nebuchadnezzar, who acceded to the Babylonian throne in 605 B.C. (see notes on 17:15; 18:1–20:18).

20:5 Fulfilled in 597 B.C. (see 2 Kin 24:13) and in 586 (see 52:17–23; 2 Kin 25:13–17).

enemies, and they will plunder them, take them away and bring them to Babylon.
6 'And you, [a]Pashhur, and all who live in your house will go into captivity; and you will enter Babylon, and there you will die and there you will be buried, you and all your [b]friends to whom you have [c]falsely prophesied.'"

Jeremiah's Complaint

7 O LORD, You have deceived me and I
was deceived;
You have [a]overcome me and prevailed.
I have become a [b]laughingstock all
day long;
Everyone [c]mocks me.
8 For each time I speak, I cry aloud;
I [a]proclaim violence and destruction,
Because for me the [b]word of the LORD
has [1]resulted
In reproach and derision all day long.
9 But if I say, "I will not [a]remember
Him
Or speak anymore in His name,"
Then in [b]my heart it becomes like a
burning fire
Shut up in my bones;
And I am weary of holding *it* in,
And [c]I cannot endure *it.*
10 For [a]I have heard the whispering of
many,
"[b]Terror on every side!
[c]Denounce *him;* yes, let us denounce
him!"
[1]All my [d]trusted friends,
Watching for my fall, say:
"Perhaps he will be [2]deceived, so that
we may [e]prevail against him
And take our revenge on him."
11 But the [a]LORD is with me like a dread
champion;
Therefore my [b]persecutors will
stumble and not prevail.
They will be utterly ashamed, because
they have [1]failed,
With an [c]everlasting disgrace that will
not be forgotten.
12 Yet, O LORD of hosts, You who [a]test
the righteous,
Who see the [1]mind and the heart;
Let me [b]see Your vengeance on them;
For [c]to You I have set forth my cause.
13 [a]Sing to the LORD, praise the LORD!
For He has [b]delivered the soul of the
needy one
From the hand of evildoers.

14 Cursed be the [a]day when I was born;
Let the day not be blessed when my
mother bore me!
15 Cursed be the man who brought the
news
To my father, saying,
"A [1][a]baby boy has been born to you!"
And made him very happy.
16 But let that man be like the cities
Which the LORD [a]overthrew without
[1]relenting,

6 [a]Jer 20:1 [b]Jer 20:4; 29:21 [c]Jer 14:14, 15; Lam 2:14
7 [a]Ezek 3:14 [b]Job 12:4; Lam 3:14 [c]Ps 22:7; Jer 38:19
8 [1]Lit *become* [a]Jer 6:7 [b]2 Chr 36:16; Jer 6:10
9 [a]1 Kin 19:3, 4; Jon 1:2, 3 [b]Job 32:18-20; Ps 39:3; Jer 4:19; 23:9; Ezek 3:14; Acts 4:20 [c]Job 32:18-20
10 [1]Lit *Every man of my peace* [a]Ps 31:13 [b]Jer 6:25 [c]Neh 6:6-13; Is 29:21; Jer 18:18 [d]Ps 41:9
10 [2]Or *persuaded* [e]1 Kin 19:2
11 [1]Lit *not succeeded;* or *not acted wisely* [a]Jer 1:8; 15:20; Rom 8:31 [b]Deut 32:35, 36; Jer 15:15, 20; 17:18 [c]Jer 23:40
12 [1]Lit *kidneys* [a]Ps 7:9; 11:5; 17:3; 139:23; Jer 11:20; 17:10 [b]Ps 54:7; 59:10; Jer 11:20 [c]Ps 62:8
13 [a]Jer 31:7 [b]Ps 34:6; 69:33; Jer 15:21
14 [a]Job 3:3-6; Jer 15:10
15 [1]Lit *male child* [a]Gen 21:6, 7 **16** [1]Lit *being sorry* [a]Gen 19:25

20:6 *you, Pashhur, . . . will go into captivity.* Probably in 597 B.C., because shortly after that year (see 29:2) two other men in succession had replaced Pashhur as chief officer in the temple (see 29:25–26). *you have falsely prophesied.* The priest Pashhur had pretended to be a prophet.
20:7–18 The sixth, last and longest of Jeremiah's "confessions" (see Introduction: Author and Date). In some respects, it is the most daring and bitter of them all.
20:7 Cf. 15:18. *deceived.* Lit. "seduced" (Ex 22:16) or "enticed" (1 Kin 22:20–22); see v. 10. Jeremiah feels that when the Lord originally called him to be a prophet, He had overly persuaded him (see 1:7–8,17–19; cf. Ezek 14:9).
20:8 Jeremiah attributes his suffering to the Lord's demands on his life. *violence and destruction.* The prophet's message echoes the Lord's word (see 6:7). *reproach.* See Ps 44:13; 79:4.
20:9 A classic description of prophetic reluctance overcome by divine compulsion (see 1:6–8; Amos 3:8; Acts 4:20; 1 Cor 9:16). *in my heart . . . like a burning fire.* See 5:14; 23:29. The figure is unique to the prophet Jeremiah (see also Lam 1:13).
20:10 The Hebrew of the first two lines is identical with that of the first two lines of Ps 31:13. *Terror on every side!* See note on 6:25. The phrase is here used as a nickname for Jeremiah in the light of his doleful message. *friends.* Lit. "men of my peace/welfare" (a similar Hebrew phrase appears in Ps 41:9, where it is translated "close friend"). *Watching for my fall.* See Ps 35:15; 38:16. *deceived.* See v. 7 and note. *we may prevail against him.* Or so they think (see v. 11). *take our revenge on him.* His enemies will not give up, no matter what it takes (see 11:19; 12:6; 26:11; cf. Ps 56:5–6; 71:10).
20:11 *the LORD is with me.* See 1:8 and note. *dread.* The Lord's strength produces dread in His opponents. The Hebrew for this word is translated "violent" in 15:21, where it describes Jeremiah's enemies. Here it has a different nuance and is applied to God, whose "dread" overcomes all "violence." *champion.* See notes on Ex 14:14; 15:3.
20:12 Repeated almost verbatim from 11:20.
20:13 *Sing . . . praise.* See 31:7; see also introduction to Ps 9. *delivered . . . From the hand of evildoers.* See 15:21; 21:12. *needy.* See 22:16. By Jeremiah's time, "poor/needy" had become virtually synonymous with "righteous" (see Amos 2:6; see also notes on Ps 9:18; 34:6).
20:14–18 See Job 3:3–19. From the heights of exultation (v. 13), Jeremiah now sinks to the depths of despair. The irreversibility of his divine call (v. 9), the betrayal of his friends (v. 10), the relentless pursuit of his enemies (vv. 7,11), the negative and condemnatory nature of his message (v. 8)—all have combined to bring to his lips a startling expression of despondency and hopelessness. The passage serves also as a transition to the next major section of the book. Judah and Jerusalem, Jeremiah will soon say, are now irrevocably doomed (see 21:1–10).
20:14 *Cursed be the day when I was born.* See note on Job 3:3. The prophet questions the very basis of his divine commission (see 1:5).
20:15 News of the birth of a son, normally a blessing in ancient times (see, e.g., Gen 29:31–35), Jeremiah sees as a curse in his own case. *Cursed be the man.* A rhetorical curse, not directed against the man personally.
20:16 *cities . . . the LORD overthrew.* Sodom and Gomorrah (see Gen 19:24–25,29). By Jeremiah's time, their wickedness had long

And let him hear an [b]outcry in the
morning
And a [2]shout of alarm at noon;
17 Because he did not [a]kill me [1]before
birth,
So that my mother would have been
my grave,
And her womb ever pregnant.
18 Why did I ever come forth from the
womb
To [a]look on trouble and sorrow,
So that my [b]days have been spent in
[c]shame?

Jeremiah's Message for Zedekiah

21 The word which came to Jeremiah
from the LORD when [a]King Zedekiah
sent to him [b]Pashhur the son of Malchijah,
and [c]Zephaniah the priest, the son of Maaseiah, saying,
2 "Please [a]inquire of the LORD on our
behalf, for [b]Nebuchadnezzar king of [c]Bab-
ylon is warring against us; perhaps the LORD
will deal with us [d]according to all His [1]won-
derful acts, so that *the enemy* will withdraw
from us."
3 Then Jeremiah said to them, "You shall
say to Zedekiah as follows:
4 'Thus says the LORD God of Israel,
"Behold, I am about to [a]turn back the
weapons of war which are in your hands,
with which you are warring against the king
of Babylon and the Chaldeans who are
besieging you outside the wall; and I will
[b]gather them into the center of this city.
5 "I [a]Myself will war against you with an
[b]outstretched hand and a mighty arm, even
in [c]anger and wrath and great indignation.
6 "I will also strike down the inhabitants
of this city, both man and beast; they will die
of a great [a]pestilence.
7 "Then afterwards," declares the LORD,
"[a]I will give over Zedekiah king of Judah
and his servants and the people, even those
who survive in this city from the pestilence,
the sword and the famine, into the hand of
Nebuchadnezzar king of Babylon, and into
the hand of their foes and into the hand of
those who seek their lives; and he will strike
them down with the edge of the sword. He
[b]will not spare them nor have pity nor compassion." '
8 "You shall also say to this people, 'Thus
says the LORD, "Behold, I [a]set before you the
way of life and the way of death.
9 "He who [a]dwells in this city will die by
the [b]sword and by famine and by pestilence;
but he who goes out and falls away to the
Chaldeans who are besieging you will live,
and he will have his own life as booty.
10 "For I have [a]set My face against this city

16 [2]Or *trumpet blast* [b]Jer 18:22; 48:3, 4
17 [1]Lit *from the womb* [a]Job 3:10, 11, 16; 10:18, 19
18 [a]Job 3:20; 5:7; 14:1; Jer 15:10; Lam 3:1 [b]Ps 90:9; 102:3 [c]Ps 69:19; Jer 3:25; 1 Cor 4:9-13
21:1 [a]2 Kin 24:17, 18; Jer 32:1-3; 37:1; 52:1-3 [b]1 Chr 9:12; Jer 38:1 [c]2 Kin 25:18; Jer 29:25, 29; 37:3; 52:24
2 [1]Or *miracles* [a]Ex 9:28; Jer 37:3, 17; Ezek 14:7; 20:1-3 [b]2 Kin 25:1 [c]Gen 10:10; 2 Kin 17:24 [d]Ps 44:1-3; Jer 32:17
4 [a]Jer 32:5; 33:5; 37:8-10; 38:2, 3, 17, 18
4 [b]Is 5:5; 13:4; Jer 39:3; Lam 2:5, 7; Zech 14:2
5 [a]Is 63:10 [b]Ex 6:6; Deut 4:34; Jer 6:12 [c]Is 5:25; Jer 32:37
6 [a]Jer 14:12; 32:24
7 [a]2 Kin 25:5-7, 18-21; Jer 37:17; 39:5-9; 52:9 [b]2 Chr 36:17; Jer 13:14; Ezek 7:9; Hab 1:6-10
8 [a]Deut 30:15, 19; Is 1:19, 20
9 [a]Jer 38:2, 17-23; 39:18; 45:5 [b]Jer 14:12; 24:10
10 [a]Lev 17:10; Jer 44:11, 27; Amos 9:4

been proverbial (see 23:14; Deut 29:23; see also note on Is 1:9–10). *shout of alarm.* See 4:19. *at noon.* See note on 6:4.

20:17 *pregnant.* In his anguish, Jeremiah wishes that his mother's womb, which gave him birth, had been instead his eternal tomb.

21:1–24:10 The prophet denounces Judah's rulers (21:1–23:7), false prophets (23:8–40) and sinful people (ch. 24). Although for the most part chs. 1–20 relate events in chronological order, chs. 21–52 are arranged on the basis of subject matter rather than chronology (see 24:1; 25:1; 26:1; 27:1; 29:2; 32:1; 35:1; 36:1; 37:1; 45:1; 49:34; 51:59; 52:4).

21:1–23:7 The rulers of Judah, who bear the primary responsibility for the nation's economic, social and spiritual ills, are the first to be denounced by Jeremiah.

21:1 *The word which came.* The phrase does not appear again until 25:1, suggesting that chs. 21–24 constitute an integral section in the book. *Zedekiah.* Means "The LORD is my righteousness." See Introduction: Background. *Pashhur the son of Malchijah.* Not the same as the Pashhur of 20:1–6 (see 38:1). *Zephaniah the priest . . . son of Maaseiah.* Not the same as the prophet Zephaniah (see 29:25,29; 37:3; 52:24; see also Zeph 1:1).

21:2 *inquire of the LORD.* A request for knowledge or information (see Gen 25:22; 2 Kin 22:13), not necessarily for help. *Nebuchadnezzar.* The name means "O Nabu [a god], protect my son/boundary!" He was the most famous ruler (605–562 B.C.) of the Neo-Babylonian empire (612–539). *is warring.* About 588, because the brash Zedekiah had rebelled against Babylon (see 52:3). *us.* Jerusalem. *wonderful acts.* For example, in the days of Hezekiah (see Is 37:36). *the enemy will withdraw.* See Is 37:37.

21:4 *turn back the weapons.* Your defense of Jerusalem will fail. *Chaldeans.* See note on Job 1:17. *gather them into . . . this city.* Either (1) the weapons, meaning that Judah's troops would be totally unable to defend the approaches to the city, or (2) the Babylonians, meaning that Jerusalem's defeat is imminent and inevitable.

21:5 *I Myself will war against you.* The Lord, usually His people's defender, will now destroy them and seal their doom. *with an outstretched hand and a mighty arm.* See 27:5; 32:17. A similar phrase is used to describe God's powerful redemption of Israel at the exodus (see 32:21; Deut 4:34; 5:15; 7:19; 26:8), but here God turns His wrath against His own people. *in anger and wrath and great indignation.* Probably quoted from Deut 29:28, where the Hebrew for this phrase is translated "in anger and in fury and in great wrath."

21:7 *I will give over Zedekiah . . . his servants and the people.* Fulfilled in 52:8–11,24–27 (see Ezek 12:13–14). *pestilence, the sword and the famine.* See v. 9. For this triad see note on 14:12. *not spare them nor have pity nor compassion.* For this triad see 13:14; see also Ezek 5:11. The three triads here heighten the literary effect of the passage.

21:8–10 See 27:12–13. Similar advice is offered in 38:2–3, 17–18 (see Deut 30:15–20).

21:8 *Behold, I set before you.* See Deut 11:26. The people are offered a choice, but few of them will make the right decision. *the way of life and the way of death.* See Deut 30:15,19; see also Prov 6:23.

21:9 Repeated almost verbatim in 38:2. Jeremiah's counsel of surrender branded him as a traitor in the eyes of many (see 37:13), but he was in fact a true patriot who wanted to stay in Judah even after Jerusalem was destroyed (see 37:14; 40:6; 42:7–22). *he who . . . falls away to the Chaldeans . . . will live.* Fulfilled in 39:9; 52:15. *he will have his own life.* Lit. "his life will be his (only) booty." The victorious in battle can expect to share plunder; the defeated are fortunate indeed if their lives are spared.

21:10 *set My face.* See 44:11. *harm and not for good.* See

for [1]harm and not for good," declares the
LORD. "It will be [b]given into the hand of the
king of Babylon and he will [c]burn it with
fire." '
11 "Then *say* to the household of the [a]king
of Judah, 'Hear the word of the LORD,
12 O [a]house of David, thus says the LORD:
"[b]Administer justice [1]every [c]morning;
And deliver the *person* who has been
robbed from the [2]power of *his*
oppressor,
[d]That My wrath may not go forth like
fire
And [e]burn with none to extinguish *it*,
Because of the evil of their deeds.
13 "Behold, [a]I am against you, O [b]valley
dweller,
O [1]rocky plain," declares the LORD,
"You men who say, '[c]Who will come
down against us?
Or who will enter into our
habitations?'
14 "But I will punish you [a]according to
the [1]results of your deeds," declares
the LORD,
"And I will [b]kindle a fire in its forest
That it may devour all its environs." ' "

Warning of Jerusalem's Fall

22 Thus says the LORD, "Go down to the
house of the king of Judah, and there
speak this word
2 and say, 'Hear the word of the LORD, O
king of Judah, who [a]sits on David's throne,
you and your servants and your people who
enter these gates.
3 'Thus says the LORD, "[a]Do justice and
righteousness, and deliver the one who has
been robbed from the power of *his* [b]oppres-
sor. Also [c]do not mistreat *or* do violence to
the stranger, the orphan, or the widow; and
do not [d]shed innocent blood in this place.
4 "For if you men will indeed perform this
thing, then [a]kings will enter the gates of this
house, sitting [1]in David's place on his
throne, riding in chariots and on horses, *even
the king* himself and his servants and his
people.
5 "[a]But if you will not obey these words, I
[b]swear by Myself," declares the LORD, "that
this house will become a desolation." ' "
6 For thus says the LORD concerning the
house of the king of Judah:
"You are *like* [a]Gilead to Me,
Like the summit of Lebanon;
Yet most assuredly I will make you
like a [b]wilderness,
Like cities which are not inhabited.
7 "For I will set apart [a]destroyers against
you,
Each with his weapons;
And they will [b]cut down your choicest
cedars
And [c]throw *them* on the fire.
8 "Many nations will pass by this city; and
they will [a]say to one another, 'Why has the
LORD done thus to this great city?'
9 "Then they will [1]answer, 'Because they
[a]forsook the covenant of the LORD their God
and bowed down to other gods and served
them.' "

10 [1]Lit *evil* [b]Jer 32:28, 29; 38:3 [c]2 Chr 36:19; Jer 34:2; 37:10; 38:18; 39:8; 52:13
11 [a]Jer 17:20
12 [1]Or *in the* [2]Lit *hand* [a]Is 7:2, 13 [b]Ps 72:1; Is 1:17; Jer 7:5; 22:3; Zech 7:9, 10 [c]Ps 101:8; Zeph 3:5 [d]Jer 4:4; 17:4; Ezek 20:47, 48; Nah 1:6 [e]Is 1:31; Jer 7:20
13 [1]Lit *rock of the level place* [a]Jer 23:30-32; Ezek 13:8 [b]Ps 125:2; Is 22:1 [c]2 Sam 5:6, 7; Jer 49:4; Lam 4:12; Obad 3, 4
14 [1]Lit *fruit* [a]Is 3:10, 11; Jer 17:10; 32:19 [b]2 Chr 36:19; Is 10:16, 18; Jer 11:16; 17:27; 52:13; Ezek 20:47, 48
22:2 [a]Is 9:7; Jer 17:25; 22:4, 30; Luke 1:32
3 [a]Is 58:6, 7; Jer 7:5, 23; 21:12; Mic 6:8; Zech 7:9; 8:16; Matt 23:23 [b]Ps 72:4 [c]Ex 22:21-24 [d]Jer 7:6; 19:4; 22:17
4 [1]Lit *for David* [a]Jer 17:25
5 [a]Jer 17:27; 26:4 [b]Gen 22:16; Amos 6:8; Heb 6:13
6 [a]Gen 37:25; Num 32:1; Song 4:1 [b]Ps 107:34; Is 6:11; Jer 7:34; Mic 3:12
7 [a]Is 10:3-6; Jer 4:6, 7 [b]Is 10:33, 34; 37:24 [c]Jer 21:14
8 [a]Deut 29:24-26; 1 Kin 9:8, 9; 2 Chr 7:20-22; Jer 16:10
9 [1]Lit *say* [a]2 Kin 22:17; 2 Chr 34:25; Jer 11:3

Amos 9:4; contrast 24:6. *It will be given . . . burn it with fire.* See 34:2.

21:12 *Administer justice.* See 5:28; 22:16; 1 Kin 3:28; Lam 3:59. The king was obliged and expected to do so, as was the future Messiah (see 23:5; 33:15). *every morning.* When the mind is clear and the day is cool (court sessions were held outside, at the city gate; see notes on Gen 19:1; Ruth 4:1). *deliver . . . robbed.* Repeated in 22:3. *That My wrath . . . none to extinguish it.* The Hebrew is repeated verbatim from 4:4 (see Amos 5:6). *wrath may . . . burn.* See 15:14; 17:4,27.

21:13 *valley.* Jerusalem, surrounded on three sides by valleys (see note on Is 22:7), is called the "Valley of vision" in Is 22:1,5. *rocky plain.* Mount Zion. *You . . . who say.* The pronouns are plural in the second half of the verse (referring to Jerusalem's inhabitants), singular in the first half (referring to Jerusalem personified). *Who will come . . . against us?* The people think that no one can successfully besiege them (see notes on 7:4; 8:19).

21:14 *according to . . . your deeds.* See note on 17:10. *kindle a fire . . . devour.* See note on 17:27. *forests.* Perhaps refers figuratively to Jerusalem's royal palace, called the "house of the forest of Lebanon" (1 Kin 7:2; 10:17,21; see Is 22:8) because of the cedar (see 22:7,14,15,23) used in its construction. The palace (see 22:1) is compared to the "summit of Lebanon" in 22:6 (see 22:23 and note).

22:1 *Go down.* The palace was at a lower elevation than the temple (see 26:10; 36:10–12).

22:2 *king of Judah.* Probably Zedekiah (see 21:3,7; compare v. 3 with 21:12), whose predecessors are mentioned in sequence later in the chapter (Josiah, vv. 10a,15b–16; Jehoahaz/Shallum, vv. 10b–12; Jehoiakim, vv. 13–15a,17–19; Jehoiachin/Coniah, vv. 24–30). *David's throne.* Though all the kings of the Davidic dynasty failed to a greater or lesser degree, the victorious Messiah would someday appear as the culmination of David's royal line (see 23:5 and note; 33:15; Ezek 34:23–24; Matt 1:1). *who enter these gates.* See 17:25 and note.

22:3 Contrast Is 11:3–5 with Ezek 22:6–7.

22:4 Repeated in part from 17:25.

22:5 See 17:27 and note. *swear by Myself.* See notes on Gen 22:16; Is 45:23; see also 49:13; 51:14; cf. 44:26. *become a desolation.* Fulfilled in 52:13 (see 27:17).

22:6 *Gilead . . . Lebanon.* Renowned for their forests. Lebanon in particular supplied cedar for the royal palace (see note on 21:14; see also 1 Kin 5:6,8–10; 7:2–3; 10:27).

22:7 *set apart.* Lit. "consecrate" (see note on 6:4). *destroyers.* The Babylonians (see note on 4:7; see also 12:12). *Each with his weapons.* See Ezek 9:2. *cut down your . . . cedars.* Cf. Is 10:33–34; cf. especially the vivid description of the Babylonian troops smashing the carved paneling of the Jerusalem temple with their axes and hatchets (Ps 74:3–6).

22:8–9 Echoed in 1 Kin 9:8–9; see Deut 29:24–26.

22:9 *forsook the covenant . . . bowed down to other gods . . . served them.* A gross violation of the first and second stipulations of the Mosaic covenant (see Ex 20:3–5 and notes).

10 [a]Do not weep for the dead or mourn
for him,
But weep continually for the one who
goes away;
For [b]he will never return
Or see his native land.

11 For thus says the LORD in regard to
[1a]Shallum the son of Josiah, king of Judah,
who became king in the place of Josiah his
father, who went forth from this place, "He
will never return there;
12 but in the place where they led him
captive, there he will [a]die and not see this
land again.

Messages about the Kings

13 "Woe to him who builds his house
[a]without righteousness
And his [1]upper rooms without
justice,
Who uses his neighbor's services
without pay
And [b]does not give him his wages,
14 Who says, 'I will [a]build myself a
roomy house
With spacious [1]upper rooms,
And cut out its windows,
[2]Paneling *it* with [b]cedar and painting
it [3]bright red.'
15 "Do you become a king because you
are competing in cedar?
Did not your father eat and drink
And [a]do justice and righteousness?
Then it was [b]well with him.
16 "He pled the cause of the [a]afflicted and
needy;
Then it was well.
[b]Is not that what it means to know
Me?"
Declares the LORD.
17 "But your eyes and your heart
Are *intent* only upon your own
[a]dishonest gain,
And on [b]shedding innocent blood
And on practicing oppression and
extortion."

18 Therefore thus says the LORD in regard to
[a]Jehoiakim the son of Josiah, king of Judah,
"They will not [b]lament for him:
'[c]Alas, my brother!' or, 'Alas, sister!'
They will not lament for him:
'Alas for the master!' or, 'Alas for his
splendor!'
19 "He will be [a]buried with a donkey's
burial,
Dragged off and thrown out beyond
the gates of Jerusalem.
20 "Go up to Lebanon and cry out,
And lift up your voice in Bashan;
Cry out also from [a]Abarim,
For all your [b]lovers have been crushed.
21 "I spoke to you in your prosperity;
But [a]you said, 'I will not listen!'
[b]This has been your practice [c]from
your youth,
That you have not obeyed My voice.
22 "The wind will sweep away all your
[a]shepherds,

10 [a]Eccl 4:2; Is 57:1; Jer 16:7; 22:18 [b]Jer 25:27; 44:14
11 [1]I.e. Jehoahaz [a]2 Kin 23:30-34; 1 Chr 3:15; 2 Chr 36:1-4
12 [a]2 Kin 23:34; Jer 22:18
13 [1]Or *roof chambers* [a]Jer 17:11; Mic 3:10; Hab 2:9 [b]Lev 19:13; James 5:4
14 [1]Or *roof chambers* [2]Or *Paneled* [3]Or *vermilion* [a]Is 5:8 [b]2 Sam 7:2; Hag 1:4
15 [a]2 Kin 23:25; Jer 7:5; 21:12 [b]Ps 128:2; Is 3:10; Jer 42:6
16 [a]Ps 72:1-4, 12, 13 [b]1 Chr 28:9; Jer 9:24
17 [a]Jer 6:13; 8:10; Luke 12:15-20 [b]2 Kin 24:4; Jer 22:3
18 [a]2 Kin 23:36-24:6; 2 Chr 36:5 [b]Jer 22:10; 34:5 [c]1 Kin 13:30
19 [a]1 Kin 21:23, 24; Jer 36:30
20 [a]Num 27:12; Deut 32:49 [b]Jer 2:25; 3:1
21 [a]Jer 13:10; 19:15 [b]Jer 3:25 [c]Jer 3:24; 32:30
22 [a]Jer 23:1

22:10 *weep for the dead.* Josiah, who was mourned long after his death (see 2 Chr 35:24–25). *one who goes away.* Jehoahaz/Shallum. In 609 B.C., Pharaoh Neco "brought him to Egypt, and he died there" (2 Kin 23:34).
22:11 *Shallum.* See 1 Chr 3:15. "Shallum" was his personal name, "Jehoahaz" his throne name (the latter means "The LORD seizes").
22:12 *the place where they led him captive.* Egypt (see note on v. 10).
22:13–19 A scathing denunciation of King Jehoiakim, who is described in the third person (vv. 13–14), then rhetorically addressed in the second person (vv. 15,17), then identified by name (v. 18), meaning "The LORD raises up." Good King Josiah is referred to in vv. 15b–16 by way of contrast.
22:13 *Woe to him who builds.* See Hab 2:9,12. *without righteousness . . . without justice.* Contrast v. 3; 21:12. *upper rooms.* See note on Judg 3:20. *uses his neighbor's services without pay.* Contrary to the law (see Lev 25:39; Deut 24:14–15). Jehoiakim's refusal to pay them may have been due partly to inability, since Judah was under heavy tribute to Egypt during the early part of his reign (see 2 Kin 23:35).
22:14 *windows.* The windows described here may well be the same as those found in the ruins of Beth-hakkerem (see 6:1; see also note on Neh 3:14) by archaeologists in the early 1960s. *Paneling.* Haggai similarly deplores the use of paneling as an extravagant and unneeded luxury in certain situations (see Hag 1:4).
22:15 *your father.* Josiah. *eat and drink.* Enjoy life (see Eccl 2:24–25; 3:12–13). *do justice and righteousness.* Like his ancestor David (see 2 Sam 8:15); contrast v. 13 (see note there).
22:16 James defines a proper relationship to God in similar terms (see James 1:27); contrast 5:28 (see note there). *afflicted and needy.* See note on 20:13. *to know Me.* To love God fully, which results in living a pious life and serving those in need (see Deut 10:12–13; Hos 6:6; Mic 6:8).
22:17 *your.* Jehoiakim's (see v. 18). *dishonest gain.* See 6:13; 8:10. *shedding innocent blood.* See note on 19:4; for an illustration of Jehoiakim's cruelty in this regard see 26:20–23. *oppression.* See v. 3; 6:6; 21:12.
22:18 Contrast 2 Chr 35:24–25. *They will not lament for him: "Alas, my brother!"* Contrast 1 Kin 13:30.
22:19 *a donkey's burial.* Tantamount to no burial at all (see 36:30); fulfilled in 2 Kin 24:6, where no burial is described and where it says that Jehoiakim "slept with his fathers," a euphemism for dying (see notes on Gen 25:8; 1 Kin 1:21). *Dragged off.* See 15:3.
22:20–23 The Lord speaks to Jerusalem, which is personified as a woman (see v. 23).
22:20 *Lebanon . . . Bashan . . . Abarim.* Mountainous regions (see v. 6; Num 27:12; 33:47–48; Deut 32:49; Judg 3:3; Ps 68:15), the first two in the north and the third in the south, suitable heights from which the whole land of Israel could be rhetorically addressed. *lovers.* See 4:30 and note. "Lovers" here refers to nations joined together by treaty. Judah's onetime allies included Egypt, Assyria (see 2:36), Edom, Moab, Ammon and Phoenicia (see 27:3), all of whom had been—or soon would be—conquered by Babylonia (see 27:6–7; 28:14). *crushed.* See 14:17.
22:21 *not listen . . . not obeyed My voice.* See 7:22–26; 11:7–8. *your youth.* The days of Israel's early history in Egypt (see 2:2 and note; Hos 2:15).
22:22 *sweep . . . shepherds . . . wickedness.* The Hebrew root is the same for the first two words, and that of the third is very

And your [b]lovers will go into captivity;
Then you will surely be [c]ashamed and
humiliated
Because of all your wickedness.
23 "You who dwell in Lebanon,
Nested in the cedars,
How you will groan when pangs come
upon you,
[a]Pain like a woman in childbirth!
24 "As I live," declares the LORD, "even
though [1a]Coniah the son of Jehoiakim king
of Judah were a [b]signet *ring* on My right
hand, yet I would pull [1]you [2]off;
25 and I will [a]give you over into the hand
of those who are seeking your life, yes, into
the hand of those whom you dread, even
into the hand of Nebuchadnezzar king of
Babylon and into the hand of the Chaldeans.
26 "I will [a]hurl you and your [b]mother who
bore you into another country where you
were not born, and there you will die.
27 "But as for the land to which they desire
to return, they will not return to it.
28 "Is this man Coniah a despised,
shattered jar?
Or is he an [a]undesirable vessel?
Why have he and his descendants
been [b]hurled out
And cast into a [c]land that they had
not known?
29 "[a]O land, land, land,
Hear the word of the LORD!
30 "Thus says the LORD,
'Write this man down [a]childless,
A man who will [b]not prosper in his
days;
For no man of his [c]descendants will
prosper
Sitting on the throne of David
Or ruling again in Judah.' "

The Coming Messiah: the Righteous Branch

23 "[a]Woe to the shepherds who are
[b]destroying and scattering the [c]sheep of
My pasture!" declares the LORD.
2 Therefore thus says the LORD God of
Israel concerning the shepherds who are
[1]tending My people: "You have scattered My
flock and driven them away, and have not
attended to them; behold, I am about to
[a]attend to you for the [b]evil of your deeds,"
declares the LORD.
3 "Then I Myself will [a]gather the remnant
of My flock out of all the countries where I
have driven them and bring them back to
their pasture, and they will be fruitful and
multiply.
4 "I will also raise up [a]shepherds over
them and they will [1]tend them; and they will
[b]not be afraid any longer, nor be terrified,
[c]nor will any be missing," declares the LORD.
5 "Behold, *the* [a]days are coming,"
declares the LORD,
"When I will raise up for David a
righteous [1b]Branch;

22 [b]Jer 30:14 [c]Is 65:13; Jer 20:11
23 [a]Jer 4:31; 6:24
24 [1]I.e. Jehoiachin [2]Lit *off from there* [a]2 Kin 24:6; 1 Chr 3:16; 2 Chr 36:9; Jer 37:1 [b]Song 8:6; Is 49:16; Hag 2:23
25 [a]2 Kin 24:15, 16; Jer 21:7; 34:20, 21
26 [a]2 Kin 24:15; Jer 10:18; 16:13 [b]2 Kin 24:8
28 [a]Ps 31:12; Jer 48:38; Hos 8:8 [b]Jer 15:1 [c]Jer 17:4
29 [a]Deut 4:26; Jer 6:19; Mic 1:2
30 [a]1 Chr 3:17; Matt 1:12
30 [b]Jer 2:37; 10:21 [c]Ps 94:20; Jer 36:30
23:1 [a]Ezek 13:3; 34:2; Zech 11:17 [b]Is 56:9-12; Jer 10:21; 50:6 [c]Ezek 34:31
2 [1]Lit *shepherding* [a]Ex 32:34 [b]Jer 21:12; 44:22
3 [a]Is 11:11, 12, 16; Jer 31:7, 8; 32:37
4 [1]Or *shepherd* [a]Jer 3:15; 31:10; Ezek 34:23 [b]Jer 30:10; 46:27, 28 [c]John 6:39; 10:28; 1 Pet 1:5
5 [1]Lit *Sprout* [a]Jer 33:14 [b]Is 4:2; 11:1-5; 53:2; Jer 30:9; 33:15, 16; Zech 3:8; 6:12, 13

similar. For "shepherds" see 2:8 and note; 10:21; 23:1–4. The initial fulfillment of this verse took place in 597 B.C. (see 2 Kin 24:12–16). *wind will sweep away.* See 13:24; Job 27:21; Is 27:8.

22:23 *Lebanon . . . cedars.* The palace in Jerusalem (see 1 Kin 7:2; see also 21:14 and note; Ezek 17:3–4,12. *Pain like a woman in childbirth!* See 4:31; 6:24; 13:21; see also note on 4:19.

22:24–30 A prophecy against King Jehoiachin (fulfilled in 24:1; 29:2), who was also known as Coniah (vv. 24, 28), a shortened form of Jeconiah (24:1); see Introduction: Background. Jehoiachin (52:31), Coniah (22:24) and Jeconiah (24:1) were the same person. All three forms of the name mean "The LORD establishes."

22:24 *As I live.* See note on Gen 42:15. *even though Coniah . . . were a signet ring.* The curse on Coniah is apparently reversed in Hag 2:23 (see note there).

22:25 *give you over into . . . those whom you dread.* Contrast 39:17.

22:26 Fulfilled in 597 B.C. (see 29:2; 2 Kin 24:15). *hurl . . . into another country.* Send into exile in Babylonia (see 7:15; 16:13; Deut 29:28). *you and your mother who bore you.* Coniah and Nehushta (see note on 13:18).

22:28 A rhetorical question, answered in v. 30. *shattered jar . . . hurled out.* Coniah and his descendants, like Judah itself (see 19:10–11), are under God's judgment. *he and his descendants.* Though Coniah was only 18 years old at the time of his exile (see 2 Kin 24:8), he already had more than one wife (see 2 Kin 24:15) and therefore probably one or more children.

22:29 *land, land, land.* The repetition implies the strongest possible emphasis and intensity (see 7:4; 23:30–32; Ezek 21:27; see also note on Is 6:3).

22:30 *childless.* Not in the sense of Coniah's having no children at all (he had at least seven; see 1 Chr 3:17–18), but of having none to sit on the throne of David in Judah. Coniah's grandson Zerubbabel (1 Chr 3:17–19; Matt 1:12) became governor of Judah (see Hag 1:1), but not king. Zedekiah was a son of Josiah (see 37:1), not of Coniah, and he and his sons died before the latter (see 52:10–11). Coniah therefore was Judah's last surviving Davidic king—until Christ.

23:1–8 A summary statement (probably dating to Zedekiah's reign; see note on v. 6) that includes God's intention to judge the wicked rulers and leaders of Judah (vv. 1–2), to ultimately bring His people back from exile (vv. 3–4,7–8), and to raise up an ideal Davidic King (vv. 5–6).

23:1 See 10:21 and note. *sheep.* The people of Judah (see v. 2).

23:2 *attended to . . . attend to.* The same Hebrew root underlies both phrases (see v. 4 and note). What Judah's rulers had failed to do is summarized in Ezek 34:4.

23:3 *remnant.* See notes on 6:9; Is 10:20–22. *I have driven.* Although Judah's sins and the sins of their leaders had caused them to be "driven . . . away" (v. 2) into exile, the Lord Himself ultimately carried out the results of His people's repeated violations of their covenant commitments. *be fruitful and multiply.* See note on Gen 1:28.

23:4 *be afraid . . . terrified.* The absence of a concerned shepherd invites attacks by wild animals (see Ezek 34:8). *be missing.* See Num 31:49. The Hebrew root underlying this phrase is the same as that for "attended to" and "attend to" in v. 2 (see note there).

23:5–6 One of the most important Messianic passages in Jeremiah, echoed in 33:15–16.

23:5 *raise up.* See 2 Sam 7:12; see also 30:9; Ezek 34:23–24; 37:24. *for David.* See Matt 1:1; 1:17 and note. The Messiah,

And He will [c]reign as king and [2]act
wisely
And [d]do justice and righteousness in
the land.
6 "In His days Judah will be saved,
And [a]Israel will dwell securely;
And this is His [b]name by which He
will be called,
'The [c]LORD our righteousness.'
7 "[a]Therefore behold, *the* days are coming," declares the LORD, "when they will no
longer say, 'As the LORD lives, who brought
up the sons of Israel from the land of Egypt,'
8 [a]but, 'As the LORD lives, who [b]brought
up and led back the descendants of the
household of Israel from *the* north land and
from all the countries where I had driven
them.' Then they will live on their own soil."

False Prophets Denounced

9 As for the prophets:
My [a]heart is broken within me,
All my bones tremble;
I have become like a drunken man,
Even like a man overcome with wine,
Because of the LORD
And because of His holy words.
10 For the land is full of [a]adulterers;
For the land [b]mourns because of the
curse.
The [c]pastures of the wilderness have
dried up.
Their course also is evil
And their might is not right.
11 "For [a]both prophet and priest are
polluted;
Even in My house I have found their
wickedness," declares the LORD.
12 "Therefore their way will be like
[a]slippery paths to them,
They will be driven away into the
[b]gloom and fall down in it;
For I will bring [c]calamity upon
them,
The year of their punishment,"
declares the LORD.
13 "Moreover, among the prophets of
Samaria I saw an [a]offensive thing:
They [b]prophesied by Baal and [c]led My
people Israel astray.
14 "Also among the prophets of Jerusalem
I have seen a [a]horrible thing:
The committing of [b]adultery and
walking in falsehood;
And they strengthen the hands of
[c]evildoers,
So that no one has turned back from
his wickedness.
All of them have become to Me like
[d]Sodom,
And her inhabitants like Gomorrah.
15 "Therefore thus says the LORD of hosts
concerning the prophets,
'Behold, I am going to [a]feed them
wormwood
And make them drink poisonous
water,
For from the prophets of Jerusalem
Pollution has gone forth into all the
land.' "

16 Thus says the LORD of hosts,
"[a]Do not listen to the words of the
prophets who are prophesying to
you.
They are [b]leading you into futility;
They speak a [c]vision of their own
[1]imagination,
Not [d]from the mouth of the LORD.

5 [2]Or *succeed* [c]Is 9:7; 52:13; Luke 1:32, 33 [d]Ps 72:2; Is 9:7; 32:1; Dan 9:24
6 [a]Deut 33:28; Jer 30:10; Zech 14:11 [b]Is 7:14; 9:6; Matt 1:21-23 [c]Is 45:24; Jer 33:16; Dan 9:24; Rom 3:22; 1 Cor 1:30
7 [a]Is 43:18, 19; Jer 16:14, 15
8 [a]Jer 16:15 [b]Is 43:5, 6; Ezek 34:13; Amos 9:14, 15
9 [a]Jer 8:18; Hab 3:16
10 [a]Jer 9:2; Hos 4:2, 3; Mal 3:5 [b]Jer 12:4 [c]Ps 107:34; Jer 9:10
11 [a]Jer 6:13; Zeph 3:4
12 [a]Ps 35:6; Prov 4:19; Jer 13:16
12 [b]Is 8:22; John 12:35 [c]Jer 11:23
13 [a]Hos 9:7, 8 [b]1 Kin 18:18-21; Jer 2:8; 23:32 [c]Is 9:16
14 [a]Jer 5:30 [b]Jer 29:23 [c]Jer 23:22; Ezek 13:22, 23 [d]Gen 18:20; Deut 32:32; Is 1:9, 10; Jer 20:16; 49:18; Matt 11:24
15 [a]Deut 29:18; Jer 8:14; 9:15
16 [1]Lit *heart* [a]Jer 27:9, 10, 14-17; 1 John 4:1 [b]Matt 7:15; 2 Cor 11:13-15; Gal 1:8, 9 [c]Jer 14:14; Ezek 13:3, 6 [d]Jer 9:12, 20

unlike any previous descendant of David, would be the ideal King. He would sum up in Himself all the finest qualities of the best rulers, and infinitely more. *Branch.* A Messianic title (see note on Is 4:2). The Targum (ancient Aramaic paraphrase) reads "Messiah" here. *reign . . . wisely.* See note on Is 52:13. *do justice and righteousness.* See 22:3,15; said also of King David (see 2 Sam 8:15).

23:6 *Judah . . . And Israel.* God's reunited people will be restored (see Ezek 37:15–22). *be saved . . . dwell securely.* The deliverance will be both spiritual and physical (see Deut 33:28–29). *The LORD our righteousness.* Although Zedekiah did not live up to the meaning of his name, "The LORD is my righteousness," Jesus the Messiah would bestow on His people the abundant blessings (see Ezek 34:25–31) that come from the hands of a King who does "justice and righteousness" (v. 5).

23:7–8 Repeated almost verbatim from 16:14–15 (see notes there).

23:9–40 False prophets denounced (see 2:8; 4:9; 5:30–31; 6:13–15; 8:10–12; 14:13–15; 18:18–23; 26:8,11,16; 27–28; Is 28:7–13; Ezek 13; Mic 3:5–12).

23:9 *As for.* The Hebrew for "as for" introduces headings also in 46:2; 48:1; 49:1,7,23,28. *His holy words.* Contrast the unholy words of the false prophets (see vv. 16–18).

23:10 See Is 24:4–6. *adulterers.* See 5:7–8; 9:2; see also note on 2:20. *mourns . . . dried up.* See 12:4 and note. To worship other gods is to deny to the land the fertility that only the Lord can bring (see Hos 2:5–8,21–22; Amos 4:4–9). *curse.* Brought on by violating the Lord's covenant (see 11:3 and note; 11:8). *pastures of the wilderness.* See note on 9:10. *course . . . is evil.* Evil because it is their own and not God's (see 8:6).

23:11 *Even in My house . . . wickedness.* For examples see 32:34; 2 Kin 16:10–14; 21:5; Ezek 8:5,10,14,16.

23:12 *their way . . . into the gloom.* See Ps 35:5–6; see also Ps 73:18.

23:13 *prophesied by Baal.* See 2:8 and note; see also 1 Kin 18:19–40.

23:14 *walking in falsehood.* See 14:13. *strengthen the hands of.* The Hebrew underlying this phrase is translated "encouraged" in Ezek 13:22. *no one has turned back from his wickedness.* See Ezek 13:22. *like Sodom . . . like Gomorrah.* See note on 20:16.

23:15 *I am going . . . poisonous water.* Repeated almost verbatim from 9:15 (see note there). *Pollution.* See v. 11.

23:16 *vision.* "Revelation" or "prophecy" (see 1 Sam 3:1; Prov 29:18; Is 1:1; Obad 1). *of their own imagination.* See v. 26; 14:14. False prophets are like preachers of a "different gospel" (Gal 1:6–9).

17 "They keep saying to those who
[a]despise Me,
'The LORD has said, "[b]You will have
peace" ';
And as for everyone who walks in the
[c]stubbornness of his own heart,
They say, '[d]Calamity will not come
upon you.'
18 "But [a]who has stood in the council of
the LORD,
That he should see and hear His word?
Who has given [b]heed to [1]His word
and listened?
19 "Behold, the [a]storm of the LORD has
gone forth in wrath,
Even a whirling tempest;
It will swirl down on the head of the
wicked.
20 "The [a]anger of the LORD will not turn
back
Until He has [b]performed and carried
out the purposes of His heart;
[c]In the last days you will clearly
understand it.
21 "[a]I did not send *these* prophets,
But they ran.
I did not speak to them,
But they prophesied.
22 "But if they had [a]stood in My council,
Then they would have [b]announced
My words to My people,
And would have turned them back
from their evil way
And from the evil of their deeds.

23 "Am I a God who is [a]near," declares
the LORD,
"And not a God far off?
24 "Can a man [a]hide himself in hiding
places
So I do not see him?" declares the LORD.
"[b]Do I not fill the heavens and the
earth?" declares the LORD.

25 "I have [a]heard what the prophets have said who [b]prophesy falsely in My name, saying, 'I had a [c]dream, I had a dream!'

26 "How long? Is there *anything* in the hearts of the prophets who prophesy falsehood, even *these* prophets of the [a]deception of their own heart,

27 who intend to [a]make My people forget My name by their dreams which they relate to one another, just as their fathers [b]forgot My name because of Baal?

28 "The prophet who has a dream may relate *his* dream, but let him who has [a]My word speak My word in truth. [b]What does straw have *in common* with grain?" declares the LORD.

29 "Is not My word like [a]fire?" declares the LORD, "and like a [b]hammer which shatters a rock?

30 "Therefore behold, [a]I am against the prophets," declares the LORD, "who steal My words from each other.

31 "Behold, I am against the prophets," declares the LORD, "who use their tongues and declare, '*The Lord* declares.'

32 "Behold, I am against those who have prophesied [a]false dreams," declares the LORD, "and related them and led My people astray by their falsehoods and [b]reckless boasting; yet [c]I did not send them or command them, nor do they [d]furnish this people the slightest benefit," declares the LORD.

33 "Now when this people or the prophet or a priest asks you saying, 'What is the [1][a]oracle of the LORD?' then you shall say to

17 [a]Mic 2:11 [b]Jer 8:11; Ezek 13:10 [c]Jer 13:10; 18:12 [d]Jer 5:12; Amos 9:10; Mic 3:11
18 [1]Another reading is *My* [a]Job 15:8, 9; Jer 23:22; 1 Cor 2:16 [b]Job 33:31
19 [a]Jer 25:32; 30:23; Amos 1:14
20 [a]2 Kin 23:26, 27; Jer 30:24 [b]Is 55:11; Zech 1:6 [c]Gen 49:1
21 [a]Jer 14:14; 23:32; 27:15
22 [a]Jer 9:12; 23:18 [b]Jer 35:15; Zech 1:4
23 [a]Ps 139:1-10
24 [a]Job 22:13, 14; 34:21, 22; Ps 139:7-12; Is 29:15; Jer 49:10; Heb 4:13
24 [b]1 Kin 8:27; 2 Chr 2:6; Is 66:1
25 [a]Jer 8:6; 1 Cor 4:5 [b]Jer 14:14 [c]Num 12:6; Jer 23:28, 32; 29:8; Joel 2:28
26 [a]1 Tim 4:1, 2
27 [a]Deut 13:1-3; Jer 29:8 [b]Judg 3:7; 8:33, 34
28 [a]Jer 9:12, 20 [b]1 Cor 3:12, 13
29 [a]Jer 5:14; 20:9 [b]2 Cor 10:4, 5
30 [a]Deut 18:20; Ps 34:16; Jer 14:14, 15; Ezek 13:8
32 [a]Deut 13:1, 2; Jer 23:25 [b]Zeph 3:4 [c]Jer 23:21; Lam 3:37 [d]Jer 7:8; Lam 2:14

33 [1]Or *burden*, and so throughout the ch [a]Is 13:1; Nah 1:1; Hab 1:1; Zech 9:1; Mal 1:1

23:17 *You will have peace.* The essential message of the false prophets (see 6:14 and note; 8:11; 14:13 and note; cf. 28:8–9). *stubbornness of his own heart.* See note on 3:17.
23:18 *council of the LORD.* God's heavenly confidants (see v. 22; Job 15:7–10 and note; see also 1 Kin 22:19–22; Job 1:6; 2:1; 29:4 and note; Ps 89:7). In Amos 3:7 the Hebrew for "council" is translated "counsel," the purposes that God has promised to reveal to His chosen servants (see v. 20).
23:19–20 Repeated almost verbatim in 30:23–24.
23:19 *storm . . . whirling tempest.* A vivid image of God's wrath.
23:20 *you will clearly understand it.* Unlike the false prophets, who continued to mislead their hearers even in Babylonia after the exile of 597 B.C. (see 29:20–23).
23:21 *I did not send.* See v. 32; 29:9; contrast 1:7; Is 6:8; Ezek 3:5. *did not speak to them.* See 29:23.
23:22 *My council.* See note on v. 18.
23:23 *God who is near . . . God far off.* God is both transcendent and immanent; He lives "on a high and holy place, And also with the . . . lowly of spirit" (Is 57:15).
23:24 *hide . . . So I do not see him.* See Job 26:6; Ps 139:7–12; Amos 9:2–4. *fill the heavens and the earth.* See Is 66:1.
23:25 *prophesy falsely.* See 5:12. *in My name.* See Deut 18:20,22. *dream.* Usually not a means of divine revelation to a true prophet (see 27:9; Deut 13:1–3; 1 Sam 28:6; Zech 10:2; but cf. Num 12:6; Joel 2:28).
23:26 *their own heart.* See note on v. 16.
23:27 *My name.* To forget the Lord's name is tantamount to forgetting Him. *forgot . . . because of Baal.* When Judah's ancestors forgot God, they began to serve Baal (see Judg 3:7; 1 Sam 12:9–10).
23:28–29 The true word of God is symbolized in three figures of speech (grain, fire, hammer).
23:28 *straw . . . grain.* Of the two, only grain can feed and nourish (see note on 15:16).
23:29 *like fire.* See note on 20:9. The fire of the divine word ultimately tests "the quality of each man's work" (1 Cor 3:13). *like a hammer.* Similarly, the divine word works relentlessly, like a sword or hammer, to judge "the thoughts and intentions of the heart" (Heb 4:12).
23:30–32 *I am against.* The threefold statement is for emphasis (see note on 22:29).
23:31 *prophets . . . who . . . declare.* False prophets are claiming that their own prophecies are the oracles of God. The Hebrew for this verb is used only here with someone other than God as the subject. The phrase "declares the LORD" or its equivalent occurs hundreds of times in the OT, more frequently in Jeremiah (over 175 times) than in any other book.
23:32 *did not send.* See v. 21 and note.
23:33 *oracle.* The Hebrew for this word can also mean "burden" (see NASB marg.), a term that may refer to a burdensome

them, 'What [1]oracle?' The LORD declares, 'I will [b]abandon you.'

34 "Then as for the prophet or the priest or the people who say, 'The [a]oracle of the LORD,' I will bring punishment upon that man and his household.

35 "Thus will each of you say to his neighbor and to his brother, '[a]What has the LORD answered?' or, 'What has the LORD spoken?'

36 "For you will no longer remember the oracle of the LORD, because every man's own word will become the oracle, and you have [a]perverted the words of the [b]living God, the LORD of hosts, our God.

37 "Thus you will say to *that* prophet, 'What has the LORD answered you?' and, 'What has the LORD spoken?'

38 "For if you say, 'The oracle of the LORD!' surely thus says the LORD, 'Because you said this word, "The oracle of the LORD!" I have also sent to you, saying, "You shall not say, 'The oracle of the LORD!'"'

39 "Therefore behold, [a]I will surely forget you and cast you away from My presence, along with the city which I gave you and your fathers.

40 "I will put an everlasting [a]reproach on you and an everlasting humiliation which will not be forgotten."

Baskets of Figs and the Returnees

24 After [a]Nebuchadnezzar king of Babylon had carried away captive Jeconiah the son of Jehoiakim, king of Judah, and the officials of Judah with the craftsmen and smiths from Jerusalem and had brought them to Babylon, the LORD showed me: behold, two [b]baskets of figs set before the temple of the LORD!

2 One basket had very good figs, like [a]first-ripe figs, and the other basket had [b]very bad figs which could not be eaten due to rottenness.

3 Then the LORD said to me, "[a]What do you see, Jeremiah?" And I said, "Figs, the good figs, very good; and the bad *figs,* very bad, which cannot be eaten due to rottenness."

4 Then the word of the LORD came to me, saying,

5 "Thus says the LORD God of Israel, 'Like these good figs, so I will regard [a]as good the captives of Judah, whom I have sent out of this place *into* the land of the Chaldeans.

6 'For I will set My eyes on them for good, and I will [a]bring them again to this land; and I will [b]build them up and not overthrow them, and I will [c]plant them and not pluck them up.

7 'I will give them a [a]heart to know Me, for I am the LORD; and they will be [b]My people, and I will be their God, for they will [c]return to Me with their whole heart.

8 'But like the [a]bad figs which cannot be eaten due to rottenness—indeed, thus says the LORD—so I will [1]abandon [b]Zedekiah king of Judah and his officials, and the [c]remnant of Jerusalem who remain in this land and the ones who dwell in the land of [d]Egypt.

9 'I will [a]make them a terror *and an* evil for all the kingdoms of the earth, as a [b]reproach and a proverb, a taunt and a [c]curse in all places where I will scatter them.

10 'I will send the [a]sword, the famine and the pestilence upon them until they are destroyed from the land which I gave to them and their forefathers.'"

Prophecy of the Captivity

25 The word that came to Jeremiah concerning all the people of Judah, in the

33 [1]Or *burden,* and so throughout the ch [b]Jer 12:7; 23:39
34 [a]Lam 2:14; Zech 13:3
35 [a]Jer 33:3; 42:4
36 [a]Gal 1:7, 8; 2 Pet 3:16 [b]2 Kin 19:4; Jer 10:10
39 [a]Jer 7:14, 15; 23:33; Ezek 8:18
40 [a]Jer 20:11; 42:18; Ezek 5:14, 15
24:1 [a]2 Kin 24:10-16; 2 Chr 36:10; Jer 27:20; 29:1, 2 [b]Amos 8:1
2 [a]Mic 7:1; Nah 3:12
2 [b]Is 5:4, 7; Jer 29:17
3 [a]Jer 1:11, 13; Amos 8:2; Zech 4:2
5 [a]Nah 1:7; Zech 13:9
6 [a]Jer 12:15; 29:10; 32:37; Ezek 11:17 [b]Jer 31:4; 32:41; 33:7; 42:10 [c]Jer 32:41
7 [a]Deut 30:6; Jer 31:33; 32:40; Ezek 11:19; 36:26 [b]Is 51:16; Jer 7:23; 30:22; 31:33; 32:38; Ezek 14:11; Zech 8:8; Heb 8:10 [c]1 Sam 7:3; Ps 119:2; Jer 29:13
8 [1]Lit *give up* [a]Jer 29:17 [b]Jer 39:5; Ezek 12:12, 13 [c]Jer 39:9 [d]Jer 44:1, 26-30
9 [a]Jer 15:4; 29:18; 34:17 [b]1 Kin 9:7; Ps 44:13, 14 [c]Is 65:15
10 [a]Is 51:19; Jer 21:9; 27:8; Ezek 5:12-17

message from the Lord (see, e.g., Nah 1:1).
23:36 The three divine titles at the end of the verse enhance the solemnity of what is being said. *living God.* See 10:10; Deut 5:26.
23:39 *forget.* The Hebrew for this word is a pun on the Hebrew for the word "oracle" in vv. 33–34,36,38. *the city.* Jerusalem.
23:40 Echoed from 20:11.
24:1–10 See Amos 8:1–3. Having denounced Judah's leaders (21:1–23:8) and false prophets (23:9–40), Jeremiah now describes the division of Judah's people into good and bad (24:1–3) and summarizes the Lord's determination to restore the good (vv. 4–7) but destroy the bad (vv. 8–10).
24:1 *Jeconiah . . . and the officials . . . to Babylon.* In 597 B.C. *craftsmen and smiths.* See 29:2; 2 Kin 24:14,16. Only the poorest and weakest people were left behind in Judah (see 2 Kin 24:14). *the LORD showed me.* A common way of introducing prophetic visions (see Amos 7:1,4,7). *figs.* See note on 8:13. *set.* The Hebrew root underlying this word is translated "meet" in Ex 29:42–43. As the Lord desired to "meet" with the Israelites at the entrance to the tabernacle, so the figs (symbolizing the people of Judah) would be "met" by him in front of the Jerusalem temple.
24:2 *very good figs, like first-ripe figs.* The first figs in June are especially juicy and delicious (see Is 28:4; Hos 9:10; Mic 7:1; Nah 3:12).
24:3 *What do you see . . . ?* See note on 1:11.
24:5–6 Just as good figs should be protected and preserved by their owner, so also the exiles of 597 B.C., who were the best of Judah's leaders and craftsmen (see 2 Kin 24:14–16), would be watched over and cared for by the Lord (see 29:4–14).
24:6 *I will set My eyes on them for good.* Contrast Amos 9:4. *bring them again.* In 538 B.C. *build them up . . . overthrow . . . plant . . . pluck.* See 1:10 and note.
24:7 *a heart to know Me.* For a more comprehensive prediction including the same promise see 31:31–34. *My people . . . their God.* The classic statement of covenant relationship (see 31:33; 32:38; see also notes on Gen 17:7; Zech 8:8). *with their whole heart.* See 29:13.
24:8 *dwell in . . . Egypt.* Perhaps those deported with Jehoahaz in 609 B.C. (see 22:10b–12 and notes; 2 Kin 23:31–34) and/or those who fled to Egypt after the Babylonians defeated the Egyptians in the battle of Carchemish in 605 (see 46:2).
24:9 *terror . . . for all the kingdoms.* See 34:17. *reproach . . . taunt.* See Deut 28:37. *proverb.* See notes on 1 Kin 9:7; Job 17:6.
24:10 *sword, the famine and the pestilence.* See note on 14:12. *destroyed from the land.* In 586 B.C. (see 52:4–27).
25:1–29:32 The dominant theme in chs. 25–29 is the forthcoming destruction of Jerusalem and exile to Babylonia in 586 B.C. (hinted at briefly in 24:10).

[a]fourth year of [b]Jehoiakim the son of Josiah, king of Judah (that was the [c]first year of Nebuchadnezzar king of Babylon),

2 which Jeremiah the prophet spoke to all the [a]people of Judah and to all the inhabitants of Jerusalem, saying,

3 "From the [a]thirteenth year of [b]Josiah the son of Amon, king of Judah, even to this day, [1]these [c]twenty-three years the word of the LORD has come to me, and I have spoken to you [2][d]again and again, but you have not listened.

4 "And the LORD has sent to you all His [a]servants the prophets [1]again and again, but you have not listened nor inclined your ear to hear,

5 saying, '[a]Turn now everyone from his evil way and from the evil of your deeds, and dwell on the land which the LORD has given to you and your forefathers [b]forever and ever;

6 and [a]do not go after other gods to [1]serve them and to [2]worship them, and do not provoke Me to anger with the work of your hands, and I will do you no harm.'

7 "Yet you have not listened to Me," declares the LORD, "in order that you might [a]provoke Me to anger with the work of your hands to your own harm.

8 "Therefore thus says the LORD of hosts, 'Because you have not obeyed My words,

9 behold, I will [a]send and take all the families of the north,' declares the LORD, 'and *I will send* to Nebuchadnezzar king of Babylon, [b]My servant, and will bring them against this land and against its inhabitants and against all these nations round about; and I will [1]utterly destroy them and [c]make them a horror and a hissing, and an everlasting desolation.

10 'Moreover, I will [1][a]take from them the voice of joy and the voice of gladness, the voice of the bridegroom and the voice of the bride, the [b]sound of the millstones and the light of the lamp.

11 '[a]This whole land will be a desolation and a horror, and these nations will serve the king of Babylon [b]seventy years.

Babylon Will Be Judged

12 'Then it will be [a]when seventy years are completed I will [b]punish the king of Babylon and that nation,' declares the LORD, 'for their iniquity, and the land of the Chaldeans; and [c]I will make it an everlasting desolation.

13 'I will bring upon that land all My words which I have pronounced against it, all that is written in [a]this book which Jeremiah has prophesied against [b]all the nations.

14 '([1]For [a]many nations and great kings will make slaves of them, even them; and I will [b]recompense them according to their deeds and according to the work of their hands.)' "

15 For thus the LORD, the God of Israel, says to me, "Take this [a]cup of the wine of wrath from My hand and cause all the nations to whom I send you to drink it.

16 "They will [a]drink and stagger and go

25:1 [a]Jer 36:1; 46:2 [b]2 Kin 24:1, 2; 2 Chr 36:4-6; Dan 1:1, 2 [c]Jer 32:1
2 [a]Jer 18:11
3 [1]Lit *this* [2]Lit *rising early and speaking* [a]Jer 1:2 [b]2 Chr 34:1-3, 8 [c]Jer 36:2 [d]Jer 7:25; 11:7; 26:5
4 [1]Lit *rising early and sending* [a]2 Chr 36:15; Jer 26:5
5 [a]2 Kin 17:13; Is 55:6, 7; Jer 4:1; 35:15; Ezek 18:30; Jon 3:8-10 [b]Gen 17:8; Jer 7:7; 17:25
6 [1]Or *worship* [2]Or *bow down to* [a]Deut 6:14; 8:19; 2 Kin 17:35; Jer 35:15
7 [a]2 Kin 17:17; 21:15; Jer 7:19; 32:30-33
9 [a]Jer 1:15; 6:22, 23 [b]Is 13:3; Jer 27:6; 43:10
9 [1]Or *put them under the ban* [c]1 Kin 9:7, 8; Jer 18:16; 25:18
10 [1]Lit *cause to perish* [a]Is 24:8-11; Jer 7:34; 16:9; Ezek 26:13; Rev 18:23 [b]Eccl 12:4; Is 47:2
11 [a]Jer 4:27; 12:11, 12 [b]2 Chr 36:21; Jer 29:10; Dan 9:2; Zech 7:5
12 [a]Ezra 1:1; Jer 29:10; Dan 9:2 [b]Is 13:14; Jer ch 50, 51 [c]Is 13:19 **13** [a]Jer 36:4, 29, 32 [b]Jer 1:5, 10; 36:2 **14** [1]Or *For they have served many nations and great kings* [a]Jer 27:7; 50:9, 41; 51:27, 28 [b]Jer 51:6, 24, 56 **15** [a]Job 21:20; Ps 75:8; Is 51:17, 22; Jer 51:7 **16** [a]Nah 3:11

25:1–38 Divine judgment will descend not only on Judah but on "all . . . nations round about" (v. 9) as well.
25:1 *fourth year of Jehoiakim . . . first year of Nebuchadnezzar.* The synchronism yields the date 605 B.C. (see note on Dan 1:1).
25:3 *thirteenth year of Josiah.* 626 B.C. (or possibly as early as 627); see 1:2. *twenty-three years.* Nineteen under Josiah and four under Jehoiakim (see v. 1). *again and again.* See v. 4; see also note on 7:13. *you have not listened.* Jeremiah, now halfway through his prophetic ministry, had been warned at the time of his call that the people of Judah would oppose him (see 1:17–19).
25:4 Echoed from 7:25–26; see also 35:15. *His servants the prophets.* See note on 7:25.
25:5 *dwell on the land . . . LORD has given . . . your forefathers forever.* Echoed from 7:7; see Gen 17:8 and note.
25:6 *provoke Me to anger.* See 7:18; Deut 31:29. *the work of your hands.* Idols (see note on 1:16).
25:7 *to your own harm.* See 7:6.
25:9 *families of the north.* Babylonia and her allies (see 1:15 and note). *Nebuchadnezzar . . . My servant.* See 27:6; 43:10. "Servant" is used here not in the sense of "worshiper" but of "vassal" or "agent of judgment," just as the pagan ruler Cyrus is called the Lord's "shepherd" in Is 44:28 and His "anointed" in Is 45:1. *this land.* Judah. *nations round about.* Named in vv. 19–26. *utterly destroy.* The Hebrew term refers to the irrevocable giving over of things to the LORD, often by totally destroying them. See 50:21,26; 51:3; see also note on Deut 2:34. *a horror and a hissing.* See note on 18:16. *everlasting desolation.* See 49:13; Ps 74:3; Is 58:12 and note.
25:11–12 *seventy years.* See 29:10. This round number (as in Ps 90:10; Is 23:15) probably represents the period from 605 (see notes on v. 1; Dan 1:1) to 538 B.C., which marked the beginning of Judah's return from exile (see 2 Chr 36:20–23; see also notes on Dan 9:1–2). The 70 years of Zech 1:12 are not necessarily the same as those here and in 29:10. They probably represent the period from 586 (when Solomon's temple was destroyed) to 516 (when Zerubbabel's temple was completed). See note on Zech 7:5.
25:11 *This . . . land . . . and these nations.* Judah and the nations named in vv. 19–26.
25:12 *punish the king . . . and that nation.* See 50:18. The city of Babylon was captured by the Medes and Persians in 539 B.C. (near the end of Jeremiah's 70 years; see note on vv. 11–12). *for their iniquity.* See 50:11,31–32; 51:6,49,53,56; Is 13:19. *an everlasting desolation.* See 50:12–13; 51:26; see also note on Is 13:20.
25:13 *book.* After this word, the Septuagint (the Greek translation of the OT) inserts the material found in chs. 46–51, though rearranged.
25:14 *many nations.* Media, Persia and their allies. *great kings.* Cyrus and his associates. *recompense them according to their deeds.* See 50:29; 51:24.
25:15 *cup of the wine of wrath.* Symbolic of divine judgment, especially against wicked nations (see Is 51:17 and note; see also 51:7; Rev 18:6). *nations to whom I send you.* See 1:5 and note.
25:16 *stagger and go mad.* See 13:12–14 and notes; Rev 14:8. *because of the sword.* As the sting of wine causes people to

mad because of the sword that I will send
among them."
17 Then I took the cup from the LORD's
hand and [a]made all the nations to whom the
LORD sent me drink it:
18 [a]Jerusalem and the cities of Judah and
its kings *and* its princes, to make them a
ruin, a horror, a hissing and a curse, as it is
this day;
19 [a]Pharaoh king of Egypt, his servants,
his princes and all his people;
20 and all the [1a]foreign people, all the
kings of the [b]land of Uz, all the kings of the
land of the [c]Philistines (even Ashkelon,
Gaza, Ekron and the remnant of [d]Ashdod);
21 [a]Edom, [b]Moab and the sons of
[c]Ammon;
22 and all the kings of [a]Tyre, all the kings
of Sidon and the kings of [b]the coastlands
which are beyond the sea;
23 and [a]Dedan, Tema, [b]Buz and all who
[c]cut the corners *of their hair;*
24 and all the kings of [a]Arabia and all the
kings of the [1b]foreign people who dwell in
the desert;
25 and all the kings of Zimri, all the kings
of [a]Elam and all the kings of [b]Media;
26 and all the kings of the north, near and
far, one with another; and [a]all the kingdoms
of the earth which are upon the face of the
ground, and the king of [1b]Sheshach shall
drink after them.
27 "You shall say to them, 'Thus says the
LORD of hosts, the God of Israel, "[a]Drink, be
drunk, vomit, fall and rise no more because of
the [b]sword which I will send among you." '
28 "And it will be, if they [a]refuse to take
the cup from your hand to drink, then you
will say to them, 'Thus says the LORD of
hosts: "[b]You shall surely drink!
29 "For behold, I am [a]beginning to work
calamity in *this* city which is [b]called by My
name, and shall you be completely free from
punishment? You will not be free from punishment; for [c]I am summoning a sword
against all the inhabitants of the earth,"
declares the LORD of hosts.'
30 "Therefore you shall prophesy against
them all these words, and you shall say to
them,

'The [a]LORD will [b]roar from on high
And utter His voice from His holy
habitation;
He will roar mightily against His [1]fold.
He will shout like those who tread *the*
grapes,
Against all the inhabitants of the
earth.
31 'A clamor has come to the end of the
earth,
Because the LORD has [a]a controversy
with the nations.
He is entering into [b]judgment with all
flesh;
As for the wicked, He has given them
to the sword,' declares the LORD."

17 [a]Jer 1:10; 25:28
18 [a]Ps 60:3; Is 51:17
19 [a]Jer 46:2-28; Nah 3:8-10
20 [1]Or *mixed multitude* [a]Jer 25:24; 50:37; Ezek 30:5 [b]Job 1:1; Lam 4:21 [c]Jer 47:1-7 [d]Is 20:1
21 [a]Ps 137:7; Jer 49:7-22 [b]Jer 48:1-47; Amos 2:1-3 [c]Jer 49:1-6; Amos 1:13-15
22 [a]Jer 47:4; Zech 9:2-4 [b]Jer 31:10
23 [a]Is 21:13; Jer 49:7, 8 [b]Gen 22:21 [c]Jer 9:26; 49:32
24 [1]Or *mixed multitude* [a]2 Chr 9:14 [b]Jer 25:20; 50:37; Ezek 30:5
25 [a]Gen 10:22; Is 11:11; Jer 49:34 [b]Is 13:17; Jer 51:11, 28
26 [1]Cryptic name for Babylon [a]Jer 25:9; 50:9 [b]Jer 51:41
27 [a]Jer 25:16; Hab 2:16
27 [b]Ezek 21:4, 5
28 [a]Job 34:33 [b]Jer 49:12
29 [a]Prov 11:31; Is 10:12; Jer 13:13; Ezek 9:6; 1 Pet 4:17 [b]1 Kin 8:43 [c]Ezek 38:21

30 [1]Or *pasture* [a]Is 42:13; Jer 25:38 [b]Joel 2:11; 3:16; Amos 1:2
31 [a]Hos 4:1; Mic 6:2 [b]Is 66:16; Ezek 20:35, 36; Joel 3:2

stagger, so the stroke of the sword causes them to fall, never to rise again (see v. 27).

25:17 A symbolic description of Jeremiah's announcement of divine judgment against the nations.

25:18 *Jerusalem and . . . Judah.* God's own people are to be judged first (see v. 29; see also Ezek 9:6; 1 Pet 4:17). *its kings.* See note on 17:20. *ruin . . . horror . . . hissing . . . curse.* See vv. 9,11; 18:16; 19:8.

25:19–26 The roster of nations begins with Egypt and ends with Babylon, as in chs. 46–51; but Damascus (see 49:23–27) is omitted, and a few other regions are added.

25:19 *Egypt.* See 46:2–28.

25:20 *foreign people.* See v. 24; Neh 13:3. *Uz.* See note on Job 1:1. *Philistines.* See ch. 47; see also note on Gen 10:14. *Ashkelon, Gaza, Ekron.* See note on Judg 1:18. *remnant of Ashdod.* According to the Greek historian Herodotus (2.157), the Egyptian pharaoh Psammetichus I (664–610 B.C.) destroyed Ashdod after a long siege. By Nehemiah's time, it was inhabited again (see note on Neh 4:7). The fifth main Philistine city, Gath (see Josh 13:3), though important earlier (see, e.g., 1 Sam 21:10–12), was destroyed and apparently not rebuilt (in later centuries it is not mentioned with the other four cities; see Amos 1:6–8; Zeph 2:4; Zech 9:5–6).

25:21–22 See 27:3–5.

25:21 *Edom.* See 49:7–22; see also note on Gen 36:1. *Moab and . . . Ammon.* See 48:1–49:6; see also note on Gen 19:36–38.

25:22 *Tyre . . . Sidon.* See 47:4; see also notes on Is 23:1–2,4,12. *coastlands . . . beyond the sea.* Island and maritime regions, some of them Phoenician colonies, located to the west and northwest of Tyre and Sidon (see notes on Ezek 27:15; Dan 11:18).

25:23 *Dedan.* See 49:8; see also notes on Is 21:13; Ezek 25:13. *Tema.* See note on Is 21:14. *Buz.* A desert region in the east. *who cut the corners of their hair.* See 9:26 and note. Cutting the forelocks of the hair (Lev 19:27) was something only a non-Israelite would do.

25:24 *Arabia.* See 49:28–33; see also 3:2. *foreign people.* See v. 20; Neh 13:3. The same Hebrew root underlies "Arabia" and "foreign people."

25:25 *Zimri.* Not to be confused with the Israelite king of that name, Zimri is perhaps the same as Zimran, whom Keturah bore to Abraham (see Gen 25:1–2). The region known as Zimri (location unknown) would then have been named after him. *Elam.* See 49:34–39; see also note on Gen 10:22. *Media.* Later to join the Persians in conquering Babylon (see 51:11,28; see also note on Is 13:17).

25:26 *Sheshach.* A cryptogram for Babylon. The cryptogram is formed by substituting the first consonant of the Hebrew alphabet for the last, the second for the next-to-last, etc. Its purpose is not fully understood, though in some cases the cryptogram itself bears a suitable meaning (see note on 51:1). *shall drink after them.* The Lord's agents of judgment are not themselves exempt from His judgment (see 51:48–49).

25:27 *fall . . . because of the sword.* See note on v. 16.

25:29 *beginning.* See note on v. 18. *city . . . called by My name.* Jerusalem (see note on 7:10).

25:30 *The LORD will roar . . . And utter His voice.* An echo of Joel 3:16; Amos 1:2 (see note there; see also Hos 11:10; Amos 3:8). *His fold.* Judah. *shout like those who tread the grapes.* See Is 9:3; 16:9–10; 63:3 and note; see also Is 16:10 and note.

25:31 *clamor.* The sounds of war (see Amos 2:2). *controversy . . . judgment.* See note on 2:9; see also 2:35; 12:1.

32 Thus says the LORD of hosts,
"Behold, evil is going forth
From [a]nation to nation,
And a great [b]storm is being stirred up
From the remotest parts of the earth.
33 "Those [a]slain by the LORD on that day
will be from one end of the earth to the [1]oth-
er. They will [b]not be lamented, gathered or
buried; they will be like [c]dung on the face of
the ground.
34 "Wail, you shepherds, and cry;
And [a]wallow *in ashes,* you masters of
the flock;
For the days of your [b]slaughter and
your dispersions [1]have come,
And you will fall like a choice vessel.
35 "[a]Flight will perish from the shepherds,
And escape from the masters of the
flock.
36 "*Hear* the sound of the cry of the
shepherds,
And the wailing of the masters of the
flock!
For the LORD is destroying their
pasture,
37 "And the peaceful [1][a]folds are made
silent
Because of the [b]fierce anger of the
LORD.
38 "He has left His hiding place [a]like the
lion;
For their land has become a horror
Because of the fierceness of the
[1]oppressing *sword*
And because of His fierce anger."

Cities of Judah Warned

26 In the beginning of the reign of
[a]Jehoiakim the son of Josiah, king of
Judah, this word came from the LORD, saying,
2 "Thus says the LORD, '[a]Stand in the
court of the LORD'S house, and speak to all
the cities of Judah who have [b]come to worship *in* the LORD'S house [c]all the words that I
have commanded you to speak to them. [d]Do
not omit a word!
3 '[a]Perhaps they will listen and everyone
will turn from his evil way, that [b]I may
repent of the calamity which I am planning
to do to them because of the evil of their
deeds.'
4 "And you will say to them, 'Thus says
the LORD, "[a]If you will not listen to Me, to
[b]walk in My law which I have set before you,
5 to listen to the words of [a]My servants
the prophets, whom I have been sending to
you [1]again and again, but you have not listened;
6 then I will make this house like [a]Shi-
loh, and this city I will make a [b]curse to all
the nations of the earth." ' "

A Plot to Murder Jeremiah

7 The [a]priests and the prophets and all
the people heard Jeremiah speaking these
words in the house of the LORD.
8 When Jeremiah finished speaking all
that the LORD had commanded *him* to speak
to all the people, the priests and the prophets
and all the people seized him, saying, "[a]You
must die!
9 "Why have you prophesied in the name
of the LORD saying, 'This house will be like
Shiloh and this city will be [a]desolate, without inhabitant'?" And [b]all the people gathered about Jeremiah in the house of the
LORD.
10 When the [a]officials of Judah heard
these things, they came up from the king's
house to the house of the LORD and sat in the
[b]entrance of the New Gate of the LORD'S
house.

32 [a]2 Chr 15:6; Is 34:2 [b]Is 30:30; Jer 23:19
33 [1]Lit *other end of the earth* [a]Is 34:2, 3; 66:16 [b]Ps 79:3; Jer 16:4; Ezek 39:4, 17 [c]Is 5:25
34 [1]Lit *are full* [a]Jer 6:26; Ezek 27:30 [b]Is 34:6, 7; Jer 50:27
35 [a]Job 11:20; Jer 11:11; Amos 2:14
37 [1]Or *pastures* [a]Is 27:10, 11; Jer 5:17; 13:20 [b]Ps 97:1-3; Is 66:15; Heb 12:29
38 [1]Or *oppressor* [a]Jer 4:7; 5:6; Hos 5:14; 13:7, 8
26:1 [a]2 Kin 23:36; 2 Chr 36:4, 5
2 [a]2 Chr 24:20, 21; Jer 7:2; 19:14
2 [b]Deut 12:5 [c]Jer 1:17; 42:4; Matt 28:20; Acts 20:20, 27 [d]Deut 4:2
3 [a]Is 1:16-19; Jer 36:3-7 [b]Jer 18:8; Jon 3:8
4 [a]Lev 26:14; 1 Kin 9:6; Is 1:20; Jer 17:27; 22:5 [b]Jer 32:23; 44:10, 23
5 [1]Lit *rising early and sending* [a]2 Kin 9:7; Ezra 9:11; Jer 7:13; 25:3, 4
6 [a]Josh 18:1; 1 Sam 4:12; Ps 78:60, 61; Jer 7:12, 14 [b]2 Kin 22:19; Is 65:15; Jer 24:9; 25:18
7 [a]Jer 5:31; Mic 3:11
8 [a]Jer 11:19; 18:23; Lam 4:13, 14; Matt 21:35, 36; 23:34, 35; 27:20
9 [a]Jer 9:11; 33:10 [b]Acts 3:11; 5:12 **10** [a]Jer 26:21 [b]Jer 36:10

25:32 *great storm . . . From the remotest parts of the earth.* The wrath of God (see 23:19), mediated through the coming invasion of the Babylonians (see note on Is 41:25).
25:33 *not be lamented . . . like dung on . . . the ground.* Repeated from 8:2 (see note there); 16:4.
25:34–36 *shepherds . . . masters of the flock.* See 10:21; 22:22.
25:34 *wallow in ashes.* See 6:26. *the days . . . have come.* See Lam 4:18. *fall like a choice vessel.* Cf. the description of Jehoiachin (Coniah) in 22:28.
26:1–24 A summary (vv. 2–6)—and its results (vv. 7–24)—of one of Jeremiah's temple messages in ch. 7 (see note on 7:1–10:25).
26:1 *beginning of the reign.* See 27:1. The Babylonian equivalent of the Hebrew for this phrase implies that the first year of King Jehoiakim (609–608 B.C.) is probably meant.
26:2 *court of the LORD'S house.* Perhaps near the New Gate (see v. 10; see also note on 7:2). *who have come to worship.* See 7:2 and note. *Do not omit a word!* See Deut 4:2 and note.
26:3 See 7:3,5–7. *repent.* See vv. 13,19; see also notes on 4:28; 18:7–10.
26:4 *If you will not listen.* See v. 5; 7:13. *My law.* See 7:6,9 and notes.
26:5 See 7:13,25–26. *My servants the prophets.* See note on 7:25. *again and again.* See note on 7:13.
26:6 *make this house like Shiloh.* See v. 9; see also note on 7:12. *this city.* Jerusalem. *a curse.* See 24:9; 25:18; see also note on Zech 8:13.
26:8 *You must die!* The Hebrew for this phrase is translated "you will surely die" in Gen 2:17. A similar phrase describes the ultimate penalty for gross violations of the law of Moses (see, e.g., Ex 21:15–17; Lev 24:16–17,21; Deut 18:20; cf. 1 Kin 21:13).
26:9 *gathered about.* With hostile intent (see Num 16:3).
26:10 *officials of Judah.* Those responsible for making legal decisions concerning disputes taking place in the temple precincts. The priests and (false) prophets, who had a vested interest in Jerusalem and its temple, felt that Jeremiah should be sentenced to death because he was predicting the destruction of both the city and the Lord's house (see vv. 8–9,11). After hearing Jeremiah's defense (vv. 12–15), the officials decided in his favor (v. 16). The people, fickle and easily swayed, first opposed Jeremiah (vv. 8–9), then supported him (v. 16). *New Gate.* See 36:10; possibly the same as the "upper Benjamin Gate" (see 20:2 and note).

11 Then the priests and the prophets
[a]spoke to the officials and to all the people,
saying, "A [b]death sentence for this man! For
he has prophesied [c]against this city as you
have heard in your hearing."
12 Then Jeremiah spoke to all the officials
and to all the people, saying, "[a]The LORD
sent me to prophesy against this house and
against this city all the words that you have
heard.
13 "Now therefore [a]amend your ways and
your deeds and obey the voice of the LORD
your God; and the LORD will [1]change His
mind about the misfortune which He has
pronounced against you.
14 "But as for me, behold, [a]I am in your
hands; do with me as is good and right in
your sight.
15 "Only know for certain that if you put me
to death, you will bring [a]innocent blood on
yourselves, and on this city and on its inhabitants; for truly the LORD has sent me to you to
speak all these words in your hearing."

Jeremiah Is Spared

16 Then the officials and all the people
[a]said to the priests and to the prophets, "No
[b]death sentence for this man! For he has spoken to us in the name of the LORD our God."
17 Then [a]some of the elders of the land
rose up and spoke to all the assembly of the
people, saying,
18 "[1][a]Micah of Moresheth prophesied in
the days of Hezekiah king of Judah; and he
spoke to all the people of Judah, saying,
'Thus the LORD of hosts has said,

"[b]Zion will be plowed *as* a field,
And Jerusalem will become ruins,
And the [c]mountain of the house as the
[2]high places of a forest." '
19 "Did Hezekiah king of Judah and all
Judah put him to death? Did he not [a]fear the
LORD and entreat the favor of the LORD, and
[b]the LORD [1]changed His mind about the misfortune which He had pronounced against
them? But we are [c]committing a great evil
against ourselves."
20 Indeed, there was also a man who
prophesied in the name of the LORD, Uriah
the son of Shemaiah from [a]Kiriath-jearim;
and he prophesied against this city and
against this land words similar to all those of
Jeremiah.
21 When King Jehoiakim and all his
mighty men and all the officials heard his
words, then the [a]king sought to put him to
death; but Uriah heard *it,* and he was afraid
and [b]fled and went to Egypt.
22 Then King Jehoiakim sent men to
Egypt: [a]Elnathan the son of Achbor and *certain* men with him *went* into Egypt.
23 And they brought Uriah from Egypt
and led him to King Jehoiakim, who [a]slew
him with a sword and cast his dead body
into the [1]burial place of the [2]common people.
24 But the hand of [a]Ahikam the son of
Shaphan was with Jeremiah, so that he was
[b]not given into the hands of the people to
put him to death.

11 [a]Jer 18:23 [b]Deut 18:20; Matt 26:66 [c]Jer 38:4; Acts 6:11-14
12 [a]Jer 1:17, 18; 26:15; Amos 7:15; Acts 4:19; 5:29
13 [1]Lit *be sorry for* [a]Jer 7:3, 5; 18:8, 11; 26:3; 35:15; Joel 2:14; Jon 3:9; 4:2
14 [a]Jer 38:5
15 [a]Num 35:33; Prov 6:16, 17; Jer 7:6
16 [a]Jer 26:11; 36:19, 25; 38:7, 13 [b]Acts 5:34-39; 23:9, 29; 25:25; 26:31
17 [a]Acts 5:34
18 [1]Lit *Micaiah the Morasthite* [a]Mic 1:1
18 [2]Or *a wooded height* [a]Mic 1:1
19 [1]Lit *was sorry for* [a]2 Chr 29:6-11; 32:26; Is 37:1, 4, 15-20 [b]Ex 32:14; 2 Sam 24:16 [c]Jer 44:7; Hab 2:10
20 [a]Josh 9:17; 1 Sam 6:21; 7:2
21 [a]2 Chr 16:10; 24:21; Jer 36:26; Matt 14:5 [b]1 Kin 19:2-4; Matt 10:23
22 [a]Jer 36:12
23 [1]Lit *graves* [2]Lit *sons of the people* [a]Jer 2:30
24 [a]2 Kin 22:12-14; Jer 39:14; 40:5-7 [b]1 Kin 18:4; Jer 1:18, 19

26:11 Jeremiah's enemies judge him before he has a chance to defend himself (see Deut 19:6).
26:12 *The LORD sent me.* Contrast 23:21.
26:13 *amend your ways and your deeds.* Repeated from 7:3 (see also 18:11; 35:15). *change His mind.* See vv. 3,19; see also notes on 4:28; 18:7–10.
26:15 *innocent blood.* See 7:6 and note; see also Matt 27:24–25; Acts 5:28.
26:16 Contrast v. 11; see note on v. 10.
26:17 *elders.* See 19:1; see also note on Ex 3:16.
26:18–19 The elders cite the precedent of Micah, who lived a century earlier and who (together with Isaiah) convinced King Hezekiah to pray for forgiveness on behalf of his people. The Lord answered the prayers of the king and the prophets, and in 701 B.C. Jerusalem and the temple were spared (see Is 37:33–37).
26:18 *Micah of Moresheth.* See Introduction to Micah: Author. *Zion will be plowed . . . as the high places of a forest.* The Hebrew is quoted verbatim from Mic 3:12—the only place in the OT where one prophet quotes another and identifies his source.
26:19 *entreat the favor of the LORD.* Cf. Ex 32:11; 1 Sam 13:12; 2 Kin 13:4; Ps 119:58). *changed His mind.* See vv. 3,13; see also notes on 4:28; 18:7–10.
26:20–23 A parenthesis, cited as an example of the contrast between how a good king, Hezekiah, treated the Lord's prophets and how a wicked king, Jehoiakim, was known to have treated them.
26:20 *Uriah.* Not mentioned elsewhere in the OT, though it has been claimed (but not substantiated) that he appears in one of the Lachish letters (see note on 34:7; see also chart, p. xix).
26:21 *mighty men.* Perhaps the royal bodyguard. *Uriah . . . fled . . . to Egypt.* A fatal mistake, for now he could be accused of treason and sedition.
26:22 *Elnathan the son of Achbor.* One of King Jehoiakim's highest officials (see 36:12), he was impressed on another occasion by Jeremiah's prophecies (see 36:16), "pleaded with the king not to burn" Jeremiah's scroll (36:25), and warned the prophet to hide (see 36:19). An Elnathan (perhaps the same man) was Jehoiakim's father-in-law (see 2 Kin 24:6,8). An Achbor (perhaps the father of this Elnathan) was one of King Josiah's officials (see 2 Kin 22:12,14; see also note on v. 24).
26:23 *brought Uriah from Egypt.* Mutual rights of extradition were a part of the treaty imposed on Judah by Egypt when Jehoiakim became the vassal of Pharaoh Neco II (see 2 Kin 23:34–35). *Jehoiakim . . . slew him.* Apart from divine intervention, Jeremiah probably would have fallen victim to the same fate (see 36:26). *burial place of the common people.* See note on 17:19. Commoners were buried in the Kidron Valley east of Jerusalem (see 2 Kin 23:6).
26:24 *Ahikam the son of Shaphan.* One of King Josiah's officials (see 2 Kin 22:12,14), along with an Achbor who may have been the father of the Elnathan in v. 22 (see note there). Ahikam was also the father of Gedaliah, who would become governor of Judah after Jerusalem was destroyed in 586 B.C. (see 40:5) and who also befriended Jeremiah (see 39:14). *was with Jeremiah.* Ahikam's high position in Jehoiakim's court was doubtless instrumental in saving the prophet's life.

The Nations to Submit to Nebuchadnezzar

27 In the beginning of the reign of [1][a]Zede-
kiah the son of Josiah, king of Judah,
this word came to Jeremiah from the LORD,
saying—
2 thus says the LORD to me—"Make for
yourself [a]bonds and [b]yokes and put them on
your neck,
3 and send [1]word to the king of [a]Edom,
to the king of [a]Moab, to the king of the sons
of [a]Ammon, to the king of [a]Tyre and to the
king of [a]Sidon [2]by the messengers who come
to Jerusalem to Zedekiah king of Judah.
4 "Command them *to go* to their masters,
saying, 'Thus says the LORD of hosts, the
God of Israel, thus you shall say to your
masters,
5 "[a]I have made the earth, the men and
the beasts which are on the face of the earth
[b]by My great power and by My outstretched
arm, and I will [c]give it to the one who is
[1]pleasing in My sight.
6 "Now I [a]have given all these lands into
the hand of Nebuchadnezzar king of Babylon, [b]My servant, and I have given him also
the [c]wild animals of the field to serve him.
7 "[a]All the nations shall serve him and his
son and his grandson [b]until the time of his
own land comes; then [c]many nations and
great kings will [1]make him their servant.
8 "It will be, *that* the nation or the kingdom which [a]will not serve him, Nebuchadnezzar king of Babylon, and which will not
put its neck under the yoke of the king of
Babylon, I will punish that nation with the
[b]sword, with famine and with pestilence,"
declares the LORD, "until I have destroyed [1]it
by his hand.
9 "But as for you, [a]do not listen to your
prophets, your diviners, your [1]dreamers,
your soothsayers or your sorcerers who
speak to you, saying, 'You will not serve the
king of Babylon.'
10 "For they prophesy a [a]lie to you in order
to [b]remove you far from your land; and I will
drive you out and you will perish.
11 "But the nation which will [a]bring its
neck under the yoke of the king of Babylon
and serve him, I will [b]let remain on its land,"
declares the LORD, "and they will till it and
dwell in it." ' "
12 I spoke words like all these to [a]Zedeki-
ah king of Judah, saying, "Bring your necks
under the yoke of the king of Babylon and
serve him and his people, and live!
13 "Why will you [a]die, you and your people, by the sword, famine and pestilence, as
the LORD has spoken to that nation which
will not serve the king of Babylon?
14 "So [a]do not listen to the words of the
prophets who speak to you, saying, 'You will
not serve the king of Babylon,' for they
prophesy a [b]lie to you;
15 for [a]I have not sent them," declares the
LORD, "but they [b]prophesy falsely in My
name, in order that I may [c]drive you out and
that you may perish, [d]you and the prophets
who prophesy to you."
16 *Then* I spoke to the priests and to all
this people, saying, "Thus says the LORD: Do

27:1 [1]Many mss read *Jehoiakim* [a]2 Kin 24:18-20; 2 Chr 36:11-13
2 [a]Jer 30:8 [b]Jer 28:10, 13
3 [1]Lit *them* [2]Lit *by the hand of* [a]Jer 25:21, 22
5 [1]Or *upright* [a]Ps 96:5; 146:5, 6; Is 42:5; 45:12; Jer 10:12; 51:15 [b]Deut 9:29; Jer 32:17; Dan 4:17 [c]Ps 115:15, 16; Acts 17:26
6 [a]Jer 21:7; 22:25; Ezek 29:18-20 [b]Is 44:28; Jer 25:9; 43:10 [c]Jer 28:14; Dan 2:38
7 [1]Or *enslave him* [a]2 Chr 36:20; Jer 44:30; 46:13 [b]Dan 5:26; Zech 2:8, 9 [c]Is 14:4-6; Jer 25:12
8 [a]Jer 38:17-19; 42:15, 16; Ezek 17:19-21 [b]Jer 24:10; 27:13; 29:17, 18; Ezek 14:21
8 [1]Lit *them*
9 [1]Lit *dreams* [a]Ex 22:18; Deut 18:10; Prov 19:27; Is 8:19; Mal 3:5; Eph 5:6
10 [a]Jer 23:25 [b]Jer 8:19; 32:31
11 [a]Jer 27:2, 8, 12 [b]Jer 21:9; 38:2; 40:9-12; 42:10, 11
12 [a]Jer 27:3; 28:1; 38:17
13 [a]Prov 8:36; Jer 27:8; 38:23; Ezek 18:31
14 [a]Jer 27:9; 2 Cor 11:13-15 [b]Jer 14:14; 23:21; 27:10; 29:8, 9; Ezek 13:22
15 [a]Jer 23:21; 29:9 [b]Jer 23:25 [c]2 Chr 25:16; Jer 27:10 [d]Jer 6:13-15; 14:15, 16

27:1–29:32 Further attempts by Jeremiah to counteract the teachings of false prophets, who were claiming that Babylon's doom was near and that rebellion against Nebuchadnezzar was therefore warranted and desirable.

27:1–22 Jeremiah tells the nations (see vv. 3–11), King Zedekiah (see vv. 12–15), and the priests and people of Judah (see vv. 16–22) to submit to the Babylonian yoke.

27:1 *In the beginning of the reign.* See note on 26:1. In this case, however, the phrase has been extended in meaning to include Zedekiah's fourth year (593 B.C.; see 28:1).

27:2 *yokes.* The kind worn by oxen. The yoke was a symbol of political submission (see vv. 8,11–12; Lev 26:13). That Jeremiah actually wore such a yoke for a time is clear from 28:10,12.

27:3 *send word.* In his role as a "prophet to the nations" (1:5). *Edom, Moab, Ammon.* Lands east and south of Judah (see 25:21 and note). *Tyre . . . Sidon.* Prominent cities in Phoenicia, north of Judah (see 25:22 and note). *messengers who come . . . to Zedekiah.* Perhaps to discuss rebellion against Babylonia. They may have counted on support from Egypt, where Psammetichus II had become pharaoh a year earlier (594 B.C.). Zedekiah went to Babylon in 593 (see 51:59), perhaps to be interrogated by Nebuchadnezzar. In any case, Zedekiah rebelled against him (see 52:3).

27:5 *great power and . . . outstretched arm.* See note on 21:5.

27:6 *Nebuchadnezzar . . . My servant.* See note on 25:9. *given him . . . wild animals . . . to serve him.* Nothing would be beyond the reach of Nebuchadnezzar's dominion (see 28:14; Dan 2:38).

27:7 *him . . . his son . . . his grandson.* Three generations of rulers, not necessarily in direct father-son relationships (cf. Deut 6:2). The words "son" and "father" are often used figuratively in the OT. "Son" may mean "descendants" or "successors" or "nations," while "father" may mean "ancestor" or "predecessor" or "founder." See notes on Gen 10:2,8; Dan 5:1. *time of his own land comes.* Babylonia will be judged (see note on 25:26). *many nations and great kings.* See note on 25:14.

27:8 *yoke.* See note on v. 2. *sword, with famine and with pestilence.* See note on 14:12. *until I have destroyed.* See 9:16; 24:10.

27:9 See 29:8. *your prophets.* False prophets. *diviners . . . soothsayers . . . sorcerers.* Forbidden in Israel (see Lev 19:26; Deut 18:10–11). The Hebrew for "soothsayers" is a loanword from Akkadian (the language of Assyria and Babylonia). *dreamers.* Including prophets and diviners (see 23:25–28; 29:8).

27:10 *prophesy a lie.* See note on 5:31; cf. 2 Tim 4:3–4.

27:11 *yoke.* See note on v. 2. *serve . . . till.* The Hebrew underlying both words is the same ("work" is the common denominator in serving and tilling).

27:12 *your necks . . . serve . . . live.* The Hebrew for all these words is plural, since Jeremiah is speaking to the people of Judah as well as to Zedekiah (see v. 13). *yoke.* See note on v. 2.

27:13 See v. 8. *sword, famine and pestilence.* See note on 14:12.

27:14 See v. 10.

27:15 See 14:14; 23:21 and note.

27:16 *prophets . . . saying, ' . . . shortly . . . '* As the prophet Hananiah was saying (see 28:1–3). *vessels of the LORD's house.* Some were carried off to Babylon by Nebuchadnezzar in 605 B.C. (see

not listen to the words of your prophets who
prophesy to you, saying, 'Behold, the [a]ves-
sels of the LORD's house will now shortly be
brought again from Babylon'; for they are
prophesying a [b]lie to you.
17 "Do not listen to them; serve the king of
Babylon, and live! Why should this city
[a]become a ruin?
18 "But [a]if they are prophets, and if the
word of the LORD is with them, let them now
[b]entreat the LORD of hosts that the vessels
which are left in the house of the LORD, in
the house of the king of Judah and in
Jerusalem may not go to Babylon.
19 "For thus says the LORD of hosts concerning the [a]pillars, concerning the sea, concerning the stands and concerning the rest of
the vessels that are left in this city,
20 which Nebuchadnezzar king of Babylon did not take when he [a]carried into exile
Jeconiah the son of Jehoiakim, king of
Judah, from Jerusalem to Babylon, and all
the nobles of Judah and Jerusalem.
21 "Yes, thus says the LORD of hosts, the
God of Israel, concerning the vessels that are
left in the house of the LORD and in the house
of the king of Judah and in Jerusalem,
22 'They will be [a]carried to Babylon and
they will be there until the [b]day I visit them,'
declares the LORD. 'Then I will [c]bring them
[1]back and restore them to this place.' "

Hananiah's False Prophecy

28 Now in the same year, [a]in the beginning of the reign of [b]Zedekiah king of
Judah, in the fourth year, in the fifth month,
[c]Hananiah the son of Azzur, the prophet,
who was from [d]Gibeon, spoke to me in the
house of the LORD in the presence of the
priests and all the people, saying,
2 "[a]Thus says the LORD of hosts, the God
of Israel, 'I have broken the yoke of the king
of Babylon.
3 'Within two years I am going to bring
back to this place [a]all the vessels of the
LORD's house, which Nebuchadnezzar king
of Babylon took away from this place and
carried to Babylon.
4 'I am [a]also going to bring back to this
place [b]Jeconiah the son of Jehoiakim, king of
Judah, and all the [c]exiles of Judah who went
to Babylon,' declares the LORD, 'for I will
break the [d]yoke of the king of Babylon.' "
5 Then the prophet Jeremiah spoke to
the prophet Hananiah in the presence of the
priests and in the presence of all the people
who were standing in the [a]house of the
LORD,
6 and the prophet Jeremiah said,
"[a]Amen! May the LORD do so; may the LORD
[1]confirm your words which you have prophesied to bring back the vessels of the LORD's
house and all the exiles, from Babylon to this
place.
7 "Yet [a]hear now this word which I am
about to speak in your hearing and in the
hearing of all the people!
8 "The prophets who were before me and
before you from ancient times [a]prophesied
against many lands and against great kingdoms, of war and of calamity and of pestilence.
9 "The prophet who prophesies of peace,
[a]when the word of the prophet comes to
pass, then that prophet will be known *as* one
whom the LORD has truly sent."
10 Then Hananiah the prophet took the
[a]yoke from the neck of Jeremiah the prophet
and broke it.
11 Hananiah spoke in the presence of all
the people, saying, "[a]Thus says the LORD,
'Even so will I break within two full years
the yoke of Nebuchadnezzar king of Babylon
from the neck of all the nations.' " Then the
prophet Jeremiah went his way.

16 [a]2 Kin 24:13; 2 Chr 36:7, 10; Jer 28:3; Dan 1:2 [b]Jer 27:10
17 [a]Jer 7:34
18 [a]1 Kin 18:24 [b]1 Sam 7:8; 12:19, 23; Jer 18:20
19 [a]1 Kin 7:15; 2 Kin 25:13, 17; Jer 52:17-23
20 [a]2 Kin 24:12, 14-16; 2 Chr 36:10, 18; Jer 22:28; 24:1
22 [1]Lit *up* [a]Jer 34:2, 3 [b]Jer 25:11, 12; 27:7; 29:10; 32:5 [c]Ezra 1:7-11; 5:13-15; 7:19
28:1 [a]Jer 27:1; 49:34 [b]2 Kin 24:18-20; 2 Chr 36:11-13; Jer 27:3, 12 [c]Jer 28:17 [d]Josh 9:3; 10:12; 1 Kin 3:4
2 [a]Jer 27:12; 28:11
3 [a]2 Kin 24:13; 2 Chr 36:10; Jer 27:16; Dan 1:2
4 [a]Jer 22:26, 27 [b]2 Kin 25:27; Jer 22:24; 24:1 [c]Jer 22:10 [d]Jer 27:8
5 [a]Jer 28:1
6 [1]Or *fulfill* [a]1 Kin 1:36; Ps 41:13; Jer 11:5
7 [a]1 Kin 22:28
8 [a]Lev 26:14-39; 1 Kin 14:15; 17:1; 22:17; Is 5:5-7; Joel 1:20; Amos 1:2; Nah 1:2
9 [a]Deut 18:22
10 [a]Jer 27:2
11 [a]Jer 14:14; 27:10; 28:15

Dan 1:1–2), others in 597 (see 2 Kin 24:13). Still others would be carried off in 586 (see vv. 21–22; 52:17–23).

27:18 *if they are prophets . . . let them now entreat.* If they are true prophets and in communion with the Lord, let them intercede for Judah, because the Lord has announced His intention to judge the nation.

27:19 *the pillars . . . the sea . . . the stands.* See 52:17; see also 1 Kin 7:15–37 and notes.

27:22 *They will be carried to Babylon.* In 586 B.C. (see 52:17–23). *I will bring them back.* In 538 and shortly afterward (see Ezra 1:7–11).

28:1–17 The true prophet Jeremiah confronts the false prophet Hananiah.

28:1 *in the beginning of the reign.* See notes on 26:1; 27:1. *the reign of Zedekiah . . . the fourth year.* 593 B.C. *Hananiah.* Means "The LORD is gracious," an appropriate name for a prophet who believed strongly (though mistakenly) that the Lord would soon bring back the exiles of Judah and the temple articles (see vv. 3–4,11). *prophet.* The word is used for all prophets, whether true (vv. 5,10–12,15) or false (vv. 1,5,10,12,15,17). *Gibeon.* See 41:12,16; see also note on Josh 9:3.

28:2 *Thus says the LORD.* See v. 11. Though a false prophet, Hananiah claims to have the same authority as Jeremiah (see vv. 13–14,16; see also 23:31). *yoke.* See note on 27:2.

28:3 Hananiah's prediction directly contradicts the words of Jeremiah (see 27:16–22 and notes). *two years.* See v. 11. Contrast Jeremiah's 70 years (25:11–12; 29:10).

28:4 *bring back.* Contradicting Jeremiah's prophecy (see 22:24–27), which was fulfilled (see 52:34). *Jeconiah . . . went to Babylon.* In 597 B.C. *yoke.* See note on 27:2.

28:6 See 1 Kin 1:36. *Amen.* See 11:5 and note. *May the LORD do so.* Fulfillment is one of the signs of a true prophecy (see v. 9).

28:7 *Yet.* Though in sympathy with what Hananiah is predicting, Jeremiah reminds him that their true predecessors were basically prophets of doom (see v. 8).

28:8 *war . . . calamity . . . pestilence.* An appropriate modification of Jeremiah's usual triad (see note on 14:12).

28:9 *peace.* Ordinarily the message of false prophets (see 6:14 and note).

28:10 *yoke from the neck of . . . the prophet.* See note on 27:2. *broke it.* Perhaps symbolically to break the power of Jeremiah's earlier prophecies (see 25:11–12; 27:7), which contradicted his own.

28:11 *two full years.* See note on v. 3.

12 The [a]word of the LORD came to Jeremiah after Hananiah the prophet had broken the yoke from off the neck of the prophet Jeremiah, saying,

13 "Go and speak to Hananiah, saying, 'Thus says the LORD, "You have broken the yokes of wood, but you have made instead of them [a]yokes of iron."

14 'For thus says the LORD of hosts, the God of Israel, "I have put a [a]yoke of iron on the neck of all these nations, that they may serve Nebuchadnezzar king of Babylon; and they will [b]serve him. And [c]I have also given him the beasts of the field." ' "

15 Then Jeremiah the prophet said to Hananiah the prophet, "Listen now, Hananiah, the LORD has not sent you, and [a]you have made this people trust in a lie.

16 "Therefore thus says the LORD, '[a]Behold, I am about to [1]remove you from the face of the earth. This year you are going to [b]die, because you have [2c]counseled rebellion against the LORD.' "

17 So Hananiah the prophet died in the same year in the seventh month.

Message to the Exiles

29 Now these are the words of the [a]letter which Jeremiah the prophet sent from Jerusalem to the rest of the elders of the exile, the priests, the prophets and all the people whom Nebuchadnezzar had taken into exile from Jerusalem to Babylon.

2 (This was after King [a]Jeconiah and the [b]queen mother, the court officials, the princes of Judah and Jerusalem, the craftsmen and the smiths had departed from Jerusalem.)

3 *The letter was sent* by the hand of Elasah the son of Shaphan, and Gemariah the son of [a]Hilkiah, whom Zedekiah king of Judah sent to Babylon to Nebuchadnezzar king of Babylon, saying,

4 "Thus says the LORD of hosts, the God of Israel, to all the exiles whom I have [a]sent into exile from Jerusalem to Babylon,

5 '[a]Build houses and live *in them;* and plant gardens and eat their [1]produce.

6 'Take [a]wives and [1]become the fathers of sons and daughters, and take wives for your sons and give your daughters to husbands, that they may bear sons and daughters; and multiply there and do not decrease.

7 '[a]Seek the [1]welfare of the city where I have sent you into exile, and [b]pray to the LORD on its behalf; for in its [1]welfare you will have [1]welfare.'

8 "For thus says the LORD of hosts, the God of Israel, 'Do not let your [a]prophets who are in your midst and your diviners [b]deceive you, and do not listen to [1c]the dreams which [2]they dream.

9 'For they [a]prophesy falsely to you in My name; [b]I have not sent them,' declares the LORD.

10 "For thus says the LORD, 'When [a]seventy years have been completed for Babylon, I will visit you and fulfill My [b]good word to you, to bring you back to this place.

11 'For I know the [a]plans that I [1]have for you,' declares the LORD, 'plans for [b]welfare and not for calamity to give you a future and a [c]hope.

12 [a]Jer 1:2
13 [a]Ps 107:16; Is 45:2
14 [a]Deut 28:48; Jer 27:8 [b]Jer 25:11 [c]Jer 27:6
15 [a]Jer 20:6; 29:31; Lam 2:14; Ezek 13:2, 3, 22; 22:28; Zech 13:3
16 [1]Lit *send you away* [2]Lit *spoken* [a]Gen 7:4; Ex 32:12; Deut 6:15; 1 Kin 13:34 [b]Jer 20:6 [c]Deut 13:5; Jer 29:32
29:1 [a]2 Chr 30:1, 6; Esth 9:20; Jer 29:25, 29
2 [a]2 Kin 24:12-16; 2 Chr 36:9, 10; Jer 22:24-28; 24:1; 27:20 [b]2 Kin 24:12, 15; Jer 13:18; 22:26
3 [a]1 Chr 6:13
4 [a]Jer 24:5
5 [1]Lit *fruit* [a]Jer 29:28
6 [1]Lit *beget* [a]Jer 16:2-4
7 [1]Or *peace* [a]Dan 4:27; 6:4, 5 [b]Ezra 6:10; 7:23; Dan 4:19; 1 Tim 2:1, 2
8 [1]Lit *your* [2]Lit *you* [a]Jer 27:9; 29:1 [b]Jer 14:14; 23:21; 27:14, 15; 28:15; Eph 5:6 [c]Jer 23:25, 27
9 [a]Jer 27:15; 29:21 [b]Jer 29:31
10 [a]2 Chr 36:21-23; Jer 25:12; 27:22; Dan 9:2; Zech 7:5 [b]Jer 24:6, 7; Zeph 2:7
11 [1]Lit *am planning* [a]Ps 40:5; Jer 23:5, 6; 30:9, 10 [b]Is 40:9-11; Jer 30:18-22 [c]Jer 31:17; Hos 2:15

28:13 *yokes of iron.* The wooden yoke of submission (see note on 27:2) would be exchanged for the iron yoke of servitude (see v. 14; 38:17–23).

28:14 *all these nations . . . will serve him.* See 27:7. *given him the beasts of the field.* See 27:6 and note.

28:15 *the LORD has not sent you.* A mark of the false prophet (see 23:21 and note).

28:16 *remove.* The Hebrew root underlying this word is the same as that underlying "sent" in v. 15. The Lord had not "sent" Hananiah to prophesy, and therefore he would soon be "sent away" to his death. *counseled rebellion.* Such activity on the part of false prophets was punishable by death (see Deut 13:5; see also Deut 18:20; cf. Ezek 11:13; Acts 5:1–11).

28:17 *Hananiah . . . died . . . in the seventh month.* He who had falsely prophesied restoration "within two years" (vv. 3,11) himself died within two months (see v. 1).

29:1–32 Jeremiah's letter to the exiles of 597 B.C. (vv. 4–23) is followed by God's message of judgment against the false prophet Shemaiah (vv. 24–32).

29:2 *queen mother.* Nehushta (2 Kin 24:8). *craftsmen and . . . smiths.* See 24:1 and note.

29:3 *letter was sent by the hand of.* It was placed it in the ancient equivalent of the diplomatic pouch to ensure its safe arrival. *Shaphan.* Perhaps the father also of Ahikam (see 26:24 and note) and/or Gemariah (see 36:10), both of whom were sympathetic to Jeremiah and his mission. *Hilkiah.* Perhaps the Hilkiah who was high priest under Josiah (see 2 Kin 22:12, where Hilkiah and one or more Shaphans are mentioned together). *Zedekiah . . . sent to . . . Nebuchadnezzar.* Possibly at or about the same time (593 B.C.) that Zedekiah himself went to Babylon for a brief period (see 51:59). The purpose of the journey(s) is unknown.

29:4 *I.* The Lord (see v. 7). Since it is God who has exiled His people, they are to submit to their captors and not rebel against them.

29:5 *Build . . . plant.* Reminiscent of Jeremiah's call (see 1:10), but here used in a literal sense. *live in them.* Ezekiel, e.g., lived in his own house in Babylonia (see Ezek 8:1).

29:6 *Take wives.* But among the exiles themselves, not among the women of Babylonia (cf. Deut 7:3–4; Ezra 9:1–2).

29:7 An unprecedented and unique concept in the ancient world: working toward and praying for the prosperity of one's captors. *welfare . . . welfare . . . welfare.* The Hebrew word is *shalom* in all three cases. *city.* Every place in which the exiles settle down. *pray . . . on its behalf.* See Ezra 6:10 and note; Matt 5:44; in the Apocrypha cf. 1 Maccabees 7:33.

29:8 *prophets . . . diviners . . . dreams.* See 27:9 and notes. *in your midst.* The exiles in Babylon had their share of false prophets (see vv. 21,31), who had doubtless accompanied them when they were deported in 597 B.C.

29:9 See v. 31; see also notes on 23:16,21.

29:10 *seventy years.* See note on 25:11–12. *bring you back.* See note on 27:22.

29:11 *I know.* See v. 23. Appearances to the contrary notwithstanding, the Lord has not forgotten His people. *welfare.* See note on v. 7. *and not . . . calamity.* God is the ultimate source

12 'Then you will [a]call upon Me and come and pray to Me, and I will [b]listen to you.

13 'You will [a]seek Me and find *Me* when you [b]search for Me with all your heart.

14 'I will be [a]found by you,' declares the LORD, 'and I will [b]restore your [1]fortunes and will [c]gather you from all the nations and from all the places where I have driven you,' declares the LORD, 'and I will [d]bring you back to the place from where I sent you into exile.'

15 "Because you have said, 'The LORD has raised up [a]prophets for us in Babylon'—

16 for thus says the LORD concerning the king who sits on the throne of David, and concerning all the people who dwell in this city, your brothers who did [a]not go with you into exile—

17 thus says the LORD of hosts, 'Behold, I am sending upon them the [a]sword, famine and pestilence, and I will make them like [b]split-open figs that cannot be eaten due to rottenness.

18 'I will pursue them with the sword, with famine and with pestilence; and I will [a]make them a terror to all the kingdoms of the earth, to be a [b]curse and a horror and a [c]hissing, and a reproach among all the nations where I have driven them,

19 because they have [a]not listened to My words,' declares the LORD, 'which I sent to them again and again by [b]My servants the prophets; but you did not listen,' declares the LORD.

20 "You, therefore, hear the word of the LORD, all you exiles, whom I have [a]sent away from Jerusalem to Babylon.

21 "Thus says the LORD of hosts, the God of Israel, concerning Ahab the son of Kolaiah and concerning Zedekiah the son of Maaseiah, who are [a]prophesying to you falsely in My name, 'Behold, I will deliver them into the hand of Nebuchadnezzar king of Babylon, and he will slay them before your eyes.

22 'Because of them a [a]curse will be [1]used by all the exiles from Judah who are in Babylon, saying, "May the LORD make you like Zedekiah and like Ahab, whom the king of Babylon [b]roasted in the fire,

23 because they have [a]acted foolishly in Israel, and [b]have committed adultery with their neighbors' wives and have [c]spoken words in My name falsely, which I did not command them; and I am He who [d]knows and am a witness," declares the LORD.' "

24 To [a]Shemaiah the Nehelamite you shall speak, saying,

25 "Thus says the LORD of hosts, the God of Israel, 'Because you have sent [a]letters in your own name to all the people who are in Jerusalem, and to [b]Zephaniah the son of Maaseiah, the priest, and to all the priests, saying,

26 "The LORD has made you priest instead of Jehoiada the priest, to be the [1a]overseer in the house of the LORD over every [b]madman who [c]prophesies, to [d]put him in the stocks and in the iron collar,

27 now then, why have you not rebuked Jeremiah of [a]Anathoth who prophesies to you?

28 "For he has [a]sent to us in Babylon, saying, '*The exile* will be [b]long; [c]build houses and live *in them* and plant gardens and eat their [1]produce.' " ' "

29 [a]Zephaniah the priest read this letter [1]to Jeremiah the prophet.

30 Then came the word of the LORD to Jeremiah, saying,

31 "Send to [a]all the exiles, saying, 'Thus

12 [a]Ps 50:15; Jer 33:3; Dan 9:3 [b]Ps 145:19 **13** [a]Deut 4:29; Ps 32:6; Matt 7:7 [b]1 Chr 22:19; 2 Chr 22:9; Jer 24:7 **14** [1]Or *captivity* [a]Deut 30:1-10; Ps 32:6; Is 55:6 [b]Jer 30:3; 32:37-41 [c]Is 43:5, 6; Jer 23:8; 32:37 [d]Jer 3:14; 12:15; 16:15 **15** [a]Jer 29:21, 24 **16** [a]Jer 38:2, 3, 17-23 **17** [a]Jer 27:8; 29:18; 32:24 [b]Jer 24:3, 8-10 **18** [a]Deut 28:25; 2 Chr 29:8; Jer 15:4; 24:9; 34:17; Ezek 12:15 [b]Is 65:15; Jer 42:18 [c]Jer 25:9; Lam 2:15, 16 **19** [a]Jer 6:19 [b]Jer 25:4; 26:5; 35:15 **20** [a]Jer 24:5; Ezek 11:9; Mic 4:10 **21** [a]Jer 14:14, 15; 29:8, 9; Lam 2:14; 2 Pet 2:1 **22** [1]Lit *taken* [a]Is 65:15 [b]Dan 3:6, 21 **23** [a]Gen 34:7; 2 Sam 13:12 [b]Jer 5:8; 23:14 [c]Jer 29:8, 9, 21 [d]Prov 5:21; Jer 7:11; 16:17; Mal 3:5; Heb 4:13 **24** [a]Jer 29:31, 32 **25** [a]Jer 29:1 [b]2 Kin 25:18; Jer 21:1; 29:29; 37:3; 52:24 **26** [1]Lit *overseers* [a]Jer 20:1 [b]2 Kin 9:11; Hos 9:7; Mark 3:21; John 10:20; Acts 26:24, 25; 2 Cor 5:13 [c]Deut 13:1-5; Zech 13:1-5 [d]Jer 20:1, 2; Acts 16:24 **27** [a]Jer 1:1 **28** [1]Lit *fruit* [a]Jer 29:1 [b]Jer 29:10 [c]Jer 29:5 **29** [1]Lit *in the ears of* [a]Jer 29:25 **31** [a]Jer 29:20

of both prosperity and disaster (see Is 45:7).

29:12–13 Echoed from Deut 4:29–30. The Lord's gracious gift of prosperity is contingent on His people's willingness to repent.

29:14 A summary of Deut 30:3–5. *restore your fortunes.* See 30:3,18; 31:23; 32:44; 33:7,11,26; 48:47; 49:6,39; and note on Ps 126:4. The Hebrew for "restore" sounds very similar to that for "fortunes."

29:15 *prophets . . . in Babylon.* See note on v. 8.

29:16 *the king . . . on the throne of David.* Zedekiah. *sits . . . dwell.* The Hebrew for both words is identical. King and people alike are guilty.

29:17 *sword, famine and pestilence.* See v. 18; see also note on 14:12. *split-open figs that cannot be eaten.* See 24:8.

29:18 See 24:9 and note.

29:19 *again and again.* See note on 7:13. *My servants the prophets.* See note on 7:25. *you did not listen.* See Ezek 2:5,7; 3:7,11.

29:21 *Ahab . . . and . . . Zedekiah.* Not the well-known kings (of Israel and Judah respectively); rather, they were false prophets (see note on v. 8).

29:22 *curse . . . roasted.* The Hebrew underlying each of these words sounds like Kolaiah, the name of Ahab's father (v. 21). *fire.* Used in Babylonia as a method of execution (see Dan 3:6,24; this is also evident in the Code of Hammurapi, sections 25; 110; 157).

29:23 *acted foolishly in Israel.* See Gen 34:7 and note. *committed adultery . . . and . . . spoken . . . falsely.* See note on 23:10. *I am He who knows.* See v. 11.

29:24 *Shemaiah.* A false prophet (see v. 31). *Nehelamite.* The Hebrew root underlying this word is the same as that for "dreams" in v. 8 (see 27:9 and note).

29:25 *Zephaniah.* Not the prophet of that name (see note on 21:1).

29:26 *Jehoiada.* Not the same as the priest during the days of King Joash (see 2 Kin 12:7). *overseer in the house of the LORD.* See note on 20:1. *madman.* Prophetic behavior sometimes appeared deranged to the casual observer (see 2 Kin 9:11). *stocks.* See note on 20:2.

29:27 *Anathoth.* See note on 1:1.

29:28 See v. 5 and note. *long.* Here 70 years (see 25:11–12 and note; see also 2 Sam 3:1).

29:29 *Zephaniah . . . read.* He was apparently sympathetic toward Jeremiah (see 21:1–2; 37:3).

29:31–32 The Lord's threat against Shemaiah is similar to that against Hananiah (see 28:15–16).

says the LORD concerning [b]Shemaiah the
Nehelamite, "Because Shemaiah has [c]proph-
esied to you, although I did not send him,
and he has [d]made you trust in a lie,"
32 therefore thus says the LORD, "Behold, I
am about to [a]punish Shemaiah the Nehelamite and his [1]descendants; he will [b]not have
anyone living among this people, [c]and he will
not see the good that I am about to do to My
people," declares the LORD, "because he has
[2d]preached rebellion against the LORD." ' "

Deliverance from Captivity Promised

30 The word which came to Jeremiah
from the LORD, saying,
2 "Thus says the LORD, the God of Israel,
'[a]Write all the words which I have spoken to
you in a book.
3 'For behold, [a]days are coming,' declares
the LORD, 'when I will [b]restore the [1]fortunes
of My people [c]Israel and Judah.' The LORD
says, 'I will also [d]bring them back to the land
that I gave to their forefathers and they shall
possess it.' "
4 Now these are the words which the
LORD spoke concerning Israel and concerning
Judah:
5 "For thus says the LORD,
'[1]I have heard a sound of [a]terror,
Of dread, and there is no peace.
6 'Ask now, and see
If a male can give birth.
Why do I see every man
With his hands on his loins, [a]as a
woman in childbirth?
And *why* have all faces turned pale?

31 [b]Jer 29:24 [c]Jer 14:14, 15; 29:9, 23; Ezek 13:8-16, 22, 23 [d]Jer 28:15
32 [1]Lit *seed* [2]Lit *spoken* [a]Jer 36:31 [b]1 Sam 2:30-34; Jer 22:30 [c]2 Kin 7:2, 19, 20; Jer 17:6; 29:10 [d]Deut 13:5; Jer 28:16
30:2 [a]Is 30:8; Jer 25:13; 36:4, 28, 32; Hab 2:2
3 [1]Or *captivity* [a]Jer 29:10 [b]Ps 53:6; Jer 29:14; 30:18; 32:44; Ezek 39:25; Amos 9:14; Zeph 3:20 [c]Jer 3:18 [d]Jer 16:15; 23:7, 8; Ezek 20:42; 36:24
5 [1]Lit *We* [a]Is 5:30; Jer 6:25; 8:16; Amos 5:16-18
6 [a]Jer 4:31; 6:24; 22:23
7 [a]Is 2:12; Hos 1:11; Joel 2:11; Amos 5:18; Zeph 1:14 [b]Lam 1:12; Dan 9:12; 12:1 [c]Jer 2:27, 28; 14:8 [d]Jer 30:10; 50:19
8 [1]So Gr; Heb *your* [2]Lit *him their slave* [a]Is 9:4; Jer 2:20; Ezek 34:27 [b]Jer 27:2 [c]Ezek 34:27
9 [a]Is 55:3-5; Ezek 34:23, 24; 37:24, 25; Hos 3:5; Luke 1:69; Acts 2:30; 13:23, 34

7 'Alas! for that [a]day is great,
There is [b]none like it;
And it is the time of Jacob's [c]distress,
But he will be [d]saved from it.
8 'It shall come about on that day,'
declares the LORD of hosts, 'that I will [a]break
his yoke from off [1]their neck and will tear off
[1]their [b]bonds; and strangers will no longer
[c]make [2]them their slaves.
9 'But they shall serve the LORD their God
and [a]David their king, whom I will raise up
for them.
10 '[a]Fear not, O Jacob My servant,'
declares the LORD,
'And do not be dismayed, O Israel;
For behold, I will save you [b]from afar
And your [1]offspring from the land of
their captivity.
And Jacob will return and will be
[c]quiet and at ease,
And [d]no one will make him afraid.
11 'For [a]I am with you,' declares the LORD,
'to save you;
For I will [b]destroy completely all the
nations where I have scattered you,
Only I will [c]not destroy you
completely.
But I will [d]chasten you justly
And will by no means leave you
unpunished.'

12 "For thus says the LORD,
'Your wound is incurable

10 [1]Lit *seed* [a]Is 41:13; 43:5; 44:2; Jer 46:27, 28 [b]Is 60:4; Jer 23:3, 8; 29:14 [c]Is 35:9; Jer 33:16; Hos 2:18 [d]Mic 4:4 **11** [a]Jer 1:8, 19 [b]Jer 46:28; Amos 9:8 [c]Jer 4:27; 5:10, 18 [d]Ps 6:1; Jer 10:24

29:31 *made you trust in a lie.* See 28:15.
29:32 *preached rebellion against.* See 28:16 and note.
30:1–33:26 Often called Jeremiah's "book of consolation," the section depicts the ultimate restoration of both Israel (the northern kingdom) and Judah (the southern kingdom) and is the longest sustained passage in Jeremiah concerned with the future hope of the people of God (for other and briefer passages on restoration see 3:14–18; 16:14–15; 23:3–8; 24:4–7). The information in 32:1 may be used to date the entire section to 587 B.C., the year before Jerusalem was destroyed by Nebuchadnezzar and its people exiled to Babylon.
30:1–31:40 Written almost entirely in poetry, these two chapters are filled with optimism as the prophet looks forward to the time when God would redeem His people.
30:1 The heading for chs. 30–31 (and perhaps chs. 32–33 as well).
30:2 *Write.* In order to preserve for future generations the predictions of restoration. *book.* In scroll form (see, e.g., 36:2,4; 45:1; see also note on Ex 17:14). *all the words which I have spoken to you.* Concerning the future redemption of God's people. The phrase is less comprehensive here than in 36:2.
30:3 *restore the fortunes.* See note on 29:14. *Israel and Judah.* The northern and southern kingdoms, the first of which was exiled in 721 B.C. and the second of which would be entering the final stage of its exile in about a year (see note on 30:1–33:26).
30:5 *sound of terror.* The sound of battle and destruction.
30:6 *woman in childbirth.* A symbol of anguish and distress (see note on 4:19).
30:7 A description of the day of the Lord (see notes on Is 2:11,17,20; Amos 5:18; 8:9). Jeremiah's immediate reference is to the foreseeable future (see vv. 8,18), but a more remote time in the Messianic age is also in view. *great.* See Joel 2:11; Zeph 1:14; cf. Joel 1:15. *There is none like it.* See Dan 12:1; Joel 2:2; Matt 24:21. *time of . . . distress.* See Dan 12:1; Matt 24:21 and note; Rev 16:18). *Jacob's.* Israel's (see v. 10).
30:8 *on that day.* See note on Is 2:11,17,20. *yoke.* See note on 27:2. *tear off their bonds.* The Hebrew underlying this phrase is translated "tear their fetters apart" in Ps 2:3, where the nations plot to free themselves from the Lord and His anointed ruler. Here the Lord promises to free His people from enslavement to the nations. *strangers.* Including, but not limited to, Babylonia.
30:9 *David their king.* The Messiah (see note on 23:5). The Targum (ancient Aramaic paraphrase) here reads "Messiah, the son of David, their king." *raise up.* See note on 23:5.
30:10–11 Repeated almost verbatim in 46:27–28.
30:10 *Jacob My servant.* See Is 41:8–9 and note; 44:1–2,21; 45:4; 48:20. *no one will make him afraid.* Contrast v. 5; see Lev 26:6; Job 11:19; Is 17:2; Ezek 34:28; 39:26; Mic 4:4 and note; Zeph 3:13.
30:11 *I am with you . . . to save you.* Words spoken originally to Jeremiah alone (see 1:8,19; 15:20) are now spoken to all God's people. *scattered.* See 9:16 and note; 23:1–2. *not destroy you completely.* See 4:27 and note. *by no means leave you unpunished.* See 25:29; 49:12.
30:12–13 See 8:22; Hos 5:13; 6:1; 7:1; 11:3.
30:12 *Your.* Judah's. *wound is incurable.* See 15:18 and note. *injury is serious.* See 14:17.

And your [a]injury is serious.
13 ‘There is no one to plead your cause;
No healing for *your* sore,
[a]No recovery for you.
14 ‘All your [a]lovers have forgotten you,
They do not seek you;
For I have [b]wounded you with the
wound of an enemy,
With the [c]punishment of a [d]cruel one,
Because your [e]iniquity is great
And your [f]sins are numerous.
15 ‘Why do you cry out over your injury?
Your pain is incurable.
Because your iniquity is great
And your sins are numerous,
I have done these things to you.
16 ‘Therefore all who [a]devour you will be
devoured;
And all your adversaries, every one of
them, [b]will go into captivity;
And those who plunder you will be
for plunder,
And all who prey upon you I will give
for prey.
17 ‘For I will [1]restore you to [2][a]health
And I will heal you of your wounds,’
declares the LORD,
‘Because they have called you an
[b]outcast, saying:
“It is Zion; no one [3]cares for her.” ’

Restoration of Jacob

18 “Thus says the LORD,
‘Behold, I will [a]restore the [1]fortunes of
the tents of Jacob
And [b]have compassion on his
dwelling places;
And the [c]city will be rebuilt on its
ruin,
And the [d]palace will stand on its
rightful place.
19 ‘From them will proceed [a]thanksgiving
And the voice of those who
[1][b]celebrate;
And I will [c]multiply them and they
will not be diminished;
I will also [d]honor them and they will
not be insignificant.
20 ‘[1]Their children also will be as
formerly,
And [2]their congregation shall be
[a]established before Me;
And I will punish all [2]their
oppressors.
21 ‘[1]Their [a]leader shall be one of them,
And [1]their ruler shall come forth from
[1]their midst;
And I will [b]bring him near and he
shall approach Me;
For [2]who would dare to risk his life to
[c]approach Me?’ declares the LORD.
22 ‘You shall be [a]My people,
And I will be your God.’ ”

23 Behold, the [a]tempest of the LORD!
Wrath has gone forth,
A [1]sweeping tempest;
It will burst on the head of the
wicked.
24 The [a]fierce anger of the LORD will not
turn back
Until He has performed and until He
has accomplished
The intent of His heart;
In the [b]latter days you will understand
this.

Israel’s Mourning Turned to Joy

31 “At that time,” declares the LORD, “I will
be the [a]God of all the [b]families of Israel, and they shall be My people.”
2 Thus says the LORD,

12 [a]2 Chr 36:16; Jer 15:18; 30:15
13 [a]Jer 14:19; 46:11
14 [a]Jer 22:20, 22; Lam 1:2 [b]Lam 2:4, 5 [c]Job 30:21 [d]Jer 6:23; 50:42 [e]Jer 32:30-35; 44:22 [f]Jer 5:6
16 [a]Jer 2:3; 8:16; 10:25 [b]Is 14:2; Joel 3:8
17 [1]Lit *cause to go up* [2]Or *healing* [3]Lit *is seeking* [a]Ex 15:26; Ps 107:20; Is 30:26; Jer 8:22; 33:6 [b]Is 11:12; 56:8; Jer 33:24
18 [1]Or *captivity* [a]Jer 30:3; 31:23 [b]Ps 102:13 [c]Jer 31:4, 38-40 [d]1 Chr 29:1, 19; Ps 48:3, 13; 122:7
19 [1]Or *dance* [a]Is 12:1; 35:10; 51:3; Jer 17:26; 33:11 [b]Ps 126:1, 2; Is 51:11; Jer 31:4; Zeph 3:14 [c]Jer 33:22 [d]Is 55:5; 60:9
20 [1]Lit *His* [2]Lit *his* [a]Is 54:14
21 [1]Lit *his* [2]Lit *who is he that gives his heart in pledge* [a]Jer 30:9; Ezek 34:23, 24; 37:24 [b]Num 16:5; Ps 65:4 [c]Ex 3:5; Jer 50:44
22 [a]Ex 6:7; Jer 32:38; Ezek 36:28; Hos 2:23; Zech 13:9
23 [1]Or *raging* [a]Jer 23:19
24 [a]Jer 4:8 [b]Jer 23:20
31:1 [a]Jer 30:22 [b]Gen 17:7, 8; Is 41:10; Rom 11:26-28

30:13 *plead your cause.* Against your enemies. *No healing for your sore.* See Hos 5:13.
30:14 *lovers.* See note on 22:20. Egypt, e.g., often supported Judah against the Babylonians (see 37:5–7). *Because your . . . sins are numerous.* See 5:6; 13:22. The Hebrew for this clause is repeated verbatim in v. 15.
30:16 *all who devour you.* See 3:24; 5:17; 8:16; 10:25. *will be devoured.* See note on 25:26; see also 51:48–49. *will be for plunder.* See Is 17:14.
30:17 *restore you to health.* Contrast 8:22; see 33:6; Is 58:8.
30:18 *restore the fortunes.* See note on 29:14. *the city . . . the palace.* Lit. “a city . . . a palace,” perhaps referring to Judah’s cities and palaces in general (see Amos 9:14). It is possible, however, that only Jerusalem and its palace are intended (see 31:38). *ruin.* The Hebrew for this word is *tel(l)*, referring to a mound of ruins resulting from the accumulation of the debris of many years or centuries of occupation and on which successive series of towns were often built (see, e.g., Josh 11:13).
30:19 *thanksgiving.* See 33:11. *celebrate.* See 31:4 and note; contrast 15:17. *multiply . . . not be diminished.* See 29:6; Ezek 36:37–38. *honor . . . not be insignificant.* See Is 9:1.
30:20 *formerly.* Probably the early days of the united kingdom, especially the reign of David. *congregation.* In 1 Kin 12:20 the Hebrew for this word is translated “assembly,” the political and religious governing body of the people. *shall be established before Me.* See Ps 102:28; 2 Sam 7:24.
30:21 *leader . . . ruler.* Although the Targum renders “Messiah” here, the terms probably refer in the first place to the rulers of Judah immediately after the exile. But Jesus Christ ultimately fulfills the promise. *one of them . . . from their midst.* Not foreigners (cf. Deut 18:15,18). *bring him near . . . approach.* See Num 16:5; contrast Ex 24:2. Unauthorized approaches into God’s presence were punishable by death (see Ex 19:21; Num 8:19).
30:22 See 31:1; see also note on 7:23.
30:23–24 Repeated almost verbatim from 23:19–20 (see notes there).
31:1–40 Continuing the theme of restoration begun in 30:1, Jeremiah records the words of the Lord to (1) all the people of God, v. 1; (2) the restored northern kingdom of Israel, vv. 2–22; (3) the restored southern kingdom of Judah, vv. 23–26; and (4) Israel and Judah together, vv. 27–40 (prologue, vv. 27–30; body, vv. 31–37; epilogue, vv. 38–40—each section beginning with the words “Behold, days are coming”).
31:1 See 30:22; see also note on 7:23. *all the families of Israel.* All 12 tribes.

"The people who survived the sword
[a]Found grace in the wilderness—
Israel, when it went to [b]find its rest."
3 The LORD appeared to [1]him from afar, *saying,*
"I have [a]loved you with an everlasting love;
Therefore I have drawn you with [b]lovingkindness.
4 "[a]Again I will build you and you will be rebuilt,
O virgin of Israel!
Again you will [1]take up your [b]tambourines,
And go forth to the dances of the [c]merrymakers.
5 "Again you will [a]plant vineyards
On the [1]hills of Samaria;
The planters will plant
And will [2]enjoy *them.*
6 "For there will be a day when watchmen
On the hills of Ephraim call out,
'Arise, and [a]let us go up *to* Zion,
To the LORD our God.' "

7 For thus says the LORD,
"[a]Sing aloud with gladness for Jacob,
And shout among the [1][b]chief of the nations;
Proclaim, give praise and say,
'O LORD, [c]save Your people,
The [d]remnant of Israel.'
8 "Behold, I am [a]bringing them from the north country,
And I will [b]gather them from the remote parts of the earth,
Among them the [c]blind and the [d]lame,
The woman with child and she who is in labor with child, together;
A great [1]company, they will return here.
9 "[a]With weeping they will come,
And by supplication I will lead them;
I will make them walk by [b]streams of waters,
On a straight path in which they will [c]not stumble;
For I am a [d]father to Israel,
And Ephraim is [e]My firstborn."

10 Hear the word of the LORD,
O nations,
And declare in the [a]coastlands afar off,
And say, "He who scattered Israel will [b]gather him
And keep him as a [c]shepherd keeps his flock."
11 For the LORD has [a]ransomed Jacob
And redeemed him from the hand of him who was [b]stronger than he.
12 "They will [a]come and shout for joy on the [b]height of Zion,

2 [a]Num 14:20 [b]Ex 33:14; Num 10:33; Deut 1:33; Josh 1:13
3 [1]Lit *me* [a]Deut 4:37; 7:8; Mal 1:2 [b]Ps 25:6
4 [1]Or *be adorned with* [a]Jer 24:6; 33:7 [b]Is 30:32 [c]Jer 30:19
5 [1]Or *mountains* [2]Lit *defile* [a]Ps 107:37; Is 65:21; Ezek 28:26; Amos 9:14
6 [a]Is 2:3; Jer 31:12; 50:4, 5; Mic 4:2
7 [1]Lit *heads* [a]Ps 14:7; Jer 20:13 [b]Deut 28:13; Is 61:9 [c]Ps 28:9
7 [d]Is 37:31; Jer 23:3
8 [1]Or *assembly* [a]Jer 3:18; 23:8 [b]Deut 30:4; Is 43:6; Ezek 34:13 [c]Is 42:16 [d]Is 40:11; Ezek 34:16; Mic 4:6
9 [a]Ps 126:5; Jer 50:4 [b]Is 43:20; 49:10 [c]Is 63:13 [d]Is 64:8; Jer 3:4, 19 [e]Ex 4:22
10 [a]Is 66:19; Jer 25:22 [b]Jer 50:19 [c]Is 40:11; Ezek 34:12
11 [a]Is 44:23; 48:20; Jer 15:21; 50:34 [b]Ps 142:6
12 [a]Jer 31:6, 7 [b]Ezek 17:23

31:2 *people who survived the sword.* The righteous remnant (see v. 7; see also note on 6:9), who will return from captivity. *wilderness.* The Arabian Desert, the antitype of the Sinai wilderness through which Israel's ancestors marched after the exodus. Return from exile is often pictured as or compared to release from Egyptian slavery at the time of the exodus (see 16:14–15 and note; see also Is 35:1–11 and notes; 40:3–4; 42:14–16; 43:18–21; 48:20–21; 51:9–11; cf. Hos 2:14–15). *Israel.* The northern kingdom (see also vv. 4,7,9–10,21). Other names for it are Samaria (v. 5), Ephraim (vv. 6,9,18,20), Jacob (vv. 7,11) and Rachel (v. 15). *rest.* See 6:16; contrast Deut 28:65. See notes on Deut 3:20; Josh 1:13.
31:3 *drawn . . . with lovingkindness.* The Hebrew underlying this phrase is translated "continue Your lovingkindness" in Ps 36:10 (see note on Ps 6:4).
31:4 *build.* See 1:10 and note. *virgin of Israel.* See v. 21; 18:13; see also 14:17 and note. *tambourines.* Used on joyful occasions (see Ps 68:25), especially following a military victory (see Ex 15:20 and note; Judg 11:34)—in contrast to Judah's experience during the exile (see Ps 137:1–3). *dances.* See v. 13; often a religious activity in ancient times (see 2 Sam 6:14). *merrymakers.* The Hebrew for this word is translated "celebrate" in 30:19.
31:5 *plant.* See 1:10 and note. *Samaria.* Conquered in 722–721 B.C. (see 2 Kin 17:24), it would someday be resettled by God's people. *plant And will enjoy them.* See Deut 28:30; Is 62:8–9; 65:21–22. Since the law stipulated that the fruit of a tree could not be eaten until the fifth year after planting it (see Lev 19:23–25), a return to normalcy is envisioned here.
31:6 *watchmen On the hills.* For example, in later times watchmen were stationed in appropriate locations to observe and give notice of the appearance of various phases of the moon to fix the times of the most important feasts (see Deut 16:16). *Ephraim . . . to Zion.* In the days of Jeroboam I, the people of the northern kingdom had been required to worship at northern shrines (see 1 Kin 12:26–30). In the future, however, they would worship the Lord only in Jerusalem (cf. John 4:20). *go up.* The verb is often used of journeys to Jerusalem (see, e.g., Ezra 1:3; 7:7; Is 2:3), whose elevation is above the surrounding countryside.
31:7 *chief of the nations.* See Deut 26:19; Amos 6:1. Israel was the greatest nation not because of intrinsic merit but because of divine grace and appointment (see Deut 7:6–8; 2 Sam 7:23–24). *save.* The Hebrew for this word is the basis of "Hosanna," the cry of the people of Jerusalem on Palm Sunday (see Matt 21:9 and note; see also Ps 20:9; 28:9; 86:2; and especially 118:25). *remnant.* See note on 6:9.
31:8 *the north country.* See 3:18 and note; 4:6 and note; 6:22; 16:15. *remote parts of the earth.* See 6:22; 25:32. *blind . . . lame.* See Is 35:5–6 and notes; 42:16.
31:9 *With weeping.* Contrast Ps 126:5–6; Is 55:12. *make them walk.* See Is 40:11; 48:21; contrast Is 20:4. *by streams of waters.* See Is 49:10; see also 41:18. *straight path.* See Is 40:3–4 and notes; 43:16,19. *I am a father to Israel.* See 3:4 and note; see also Deut 32:6; Is 63:16; 64:8. *firstborn.* Cf. v. 20; see Ex 4:22 and note; Hos 11:1–4.
31:10 *coastlands.* Remote areas to the west of Israel (see 2:10; 25:22 and note; 47:4; Ps 72:10; Is 41:1,5; 42:10,12; 49:1). *scattered Israel . . . keep him as a shepherd keeps his flock.* See 23:1–3 and notes.
31:11 *redeemed.* See note on Ruth 2:20. As the Lord had redeemed His people from Egyptian slavery (see Ex 6:6; 15:13; Deut 7:8; 9:26), so now He would redeem their descendants from Babylonian exile (see Is 41:14 and note; 43:1 and note; 52:9). *from . . . him who was stronger than he.* See Ps 35:10.
31:12 *height of Zion.* See note on 17:12. *bounty of the LORD.* Primarily material blessings (see v. 14; Hos 3:5). *grain . . . new*

And they will be [c]radiant over the
[1]bounty of the LORD—
Over the [d]grain and the new wine and
the oil,
And over the young of the [e]flock and
the herd;
And their life will be like a [f]watered
garden,
And they will [g]never languish again.
13 "Then the virgin will rejoice in the
[a]dance,
And the young men and the old,
together,
For I will [b]turn their mourning into joy
And will comfort them and give them
[c]joy for their sorrow.
14 "I will [1]fill the soul of the priests with
[2]abundance,
And My people will be [a]satisfied with
My goodness," declares the LORD.

15 Thus says the LORD,
"[a]A voice is heard in [b]Ramah,
Lamentation *and* bitter weeping.
Rachel is weeping for her children;
She [c]refuses to be comforted for her
children,
Because [d]they are no more."
16 Thus says the LORD,
"[a]Restrain your voice from weeping
And your eyes from tears;
For your [b]work will be rewarded,"
declares the LORD,
"And they will [c]return from the land of
the enemy.
17 "There is [a]hope for your future,"
declares the LORD,
"And *your* children will return to their
own territory.

12 [1]Lit *goodness* [c]Is 2:2; Mic 4:1 [d]Hos 2:22; Joel 3:18 [e]Jer 31:24; 33:12, 13 [f]Is 58:11 [g]Is 35:10; 60:20; 65:19; John 16:22; Rev 21:4
13 [a]Judg 21:21; Ps 30:11; Zech 8:4, 5 [b]Is 61:3 [c]Is 51:11
14 [1]Lit *saturate* [2]Lit *fatness* [a]Jer 50:19
15 [a]Matt 2:18 [b]Josh 18:25; Judg 4:5; Is 10:29; Jer 40:1 [c]Gen 37:35; Ps 77:2 [d]Gen 5:24; 42:13, 36; Jer 10:20
16 [a]Is 25:8; 30:19 [b]Ruth 2:12; Heb 6:10 [c]Jer 30:3; Ezek 11:17
17 [a]Jer 29:11
18 [a]Jer 3:21 [b]Job 5:17; Ps 94:12 [c]Hos 4:16 [d]Ps 80:3, 7, 19; Jer 17:14; Lam 5:21; Acts 3:26
19 [a]Ezek 36:31; Zech 12:10 [b]Ezek 21:12; Luke 18:13 [c]Jer 3:25
20 [1]Lit *inward parts* [a]Hos 11:8 [b]Gen 43:30; Judg 10:16; Is 63:15; Hos 11:8 [c]Is 55:7; 57:18; Hos 14:4; Mic 7:18
21 [1]Lit *heart* [a]Jer 50:5 [b]Is 48:20; 52:11
22 [a]Jer 3:6; 49:4
23 [1]Or *captivity* [a]Jer 30:18; 32:44 [b]Is 1:26; Jer 50:7 [c]Ps 48:1; 87:1; Zech 8:3

18 "I have surely heard Ephraim [a]grieving,
'You have [b]chastised me, and I was
chastised,
Like an untrained [c]calf;
[d]Bring me back that I may be restored,
For You are the LORD my God.
19 'For after I turned back, I [a]repented;
And after I was instructed, I [b]smote
on *my* thigh;
I was [c]ashamed and also humiliated
Because I bore the reproach of my
youth.'
20 "Is [a]Ephraim My dear son?
Is he a delightful child?
Indeed, as often as I have spoken
against him,
I certainly *still* remember him;
Therefore My [1b]heart yearns for him;
I will surely [c]have mercy on him,"
declares the LORD.

21 "Set up for yourself roadmarks,
Place for yourself guideposts;
[a]Direct your [1]mind to the highway,
The way by which you went.
[b]Return, O virgin of Israel,
Return to these your cities.
22 "How long will you go here and there,
O [a]faithless daughter?
For the LORD has created a new thing
in the earth—
A woman will encompass a man."
23 Thus says the LORD of hosts, the God of
Israel, "Once again they will speak this word
in the land of Judah and in its cities when I
[a]restore their [1]fortunes,
'The LORD bless you, O [b]abode of
righteousness,
O [c]holy hill!'

wine . . . oil. See note on Deut 7:13; see also Hos 2:8. *like a watered garden.* See Is 58:11 and note. *never languish again.* See note on Is 25:8.

31:14 *abundance.* Either (1) a synonym for God's bounty (see Ps 36:8; 63:5; Is 55:2) or (2) a reference to the special portions of the sacrificial animal reserved for the priests (see Lev 7:31–36).

31:15 Quoted in Matt 2:18, where Herod's orders to kill all the male infants "in Bethlehem and all its vicinity" (Matt 2:16) are stated to be a fulfillment of this passage. *Ramah.* Located about five miles north of Jerusalem, it was one of the towns through which Jerusalem's people passed on their way to exile in Babylonia (see 40:1; cf. Is 10:29; Hos 5:8). *Rachel.* Jacob's favorite wife (see Gen 29:30) and the grandmother of Ephraim and Manasseh (see Gen 30:22–24; 48:1–2), the two most prominent and powerful tribes in the northern kingdom. The name is used here to personify that kingdom (see note on v. 2).

31:16 *For your work will be rewarded.* Echoed in 2 Chr 15:7. Here the work is the bearing and raising of children.

31:17 *hope for your future.* See 29:11. *children will return.* Cf. Hos 11:10–11.

31:18–19 *Bring me back . . . be restored . . . turned back.* The same Hebrew root underlies all three phrases (see 8:4–5 and notes).

31:18 *Like an untrained calf.* The same figure of speech is used in Hos 4:16; 10:11.

31:19 *smote on my thigh.* A gesture of mourning and grief (see Ezek 21:12). Similar expressions are found in other ancient literature, such as the Babylonian *Descent of Ishtar,* verse 21; Homer, *Iliad,* 15.397–398; 16.125; *Odyssey,* 13.198–199. *ashamed and . . . humiliated.* See Is 45:16. *youth.* Early history (see 2:2; 3:24–25; 22:21; 32:30; Is 54:4; Ezek 16:22).

31:20 *delightful child.* Cf. Is 5:7. *Therefore . . . I will surely have mercy on him.* See Hos 11:1–4,8–9. *My heart yearns.* See Is 16:11.

31:21 The departing exiles are advised to set up markers along their path to exile so that in due time they will be able to find their way back to Judah. *roadmarks.* Tombstone-shaped markers (see 2 Kin 23:17; Ezek 39:15). *virgin of Israel.* See v. 4; see also 14:17 and note.

31:22 *faithless daughter.* The people of Judah are apostate (see 3:14,22). *created a new thing.* See Is 42:9 and note. *encompass.* Embrace with tender and unfailing love (see Ps 32:7,10; see also Ps 26:6). Judah would someday return to the Lord and love Him without reservation.

31:23 *restore their fortunes.* See note on 29:14. *The LORD bless you.* See Ps 128:5; 134:3. *abode of righteousness.* Jerusalem (cf. Is 1:21,26). *holy hill.* The temple hill (see Ps 2:6; 48:1–2; Is 2:2–3; 11:9; 27:13; 66:20).

24 "Judah and all its cities will [a]dwell
together in it, the farmer and they who go
about with flocks.
25 "[a]For I satisfy the weary ones and
[1]refresh everyone who languishes."
26 At this I [a]awoke and looked, and my
[b]sleep was pleasant to me.

A New Covenant

27 "Behold, days are coming," declares the
LORD, "when I will [a]sow the house of Israel
and the house of Judah with the seed of man
and with the seed of beast.
28 "As I have [a]watched over them to
[b]pluck up, to break down, to overthrow, to
destroy and to bring disaster, so I will watch
over them to [c]build and to plant," declares
the LORD.
29 "In those days they will not say again,
'[a]The fathers have eaten sour grapes,
And the children's teeth are [1]set on
edge.'
30 "But [a]everyone will die for his own iniquity; each man who eats the sour grapes, his
teeth will be [1]set on edge.
31 "[a]Behold, days are coming," declares
the LORD, "when I will make a [b]new covenant with the house of Israel and with the
house of Judah,
32 not like the [a]covenant which I made
with their fathers in the day I [b]took them by
the hand to bring them out of the land of
Egypt, My [c]covenant which they broke,
although I was a husband to them," declares
the LORD.
33 "But [a]this is the covenant which I will
make with the house of Israel after those
days," declares the LORD, "[b]I will put My law
within them and on their heart I will write it;
and [c]I will be their God, and they shall be
My people.
34 "They will [a]not teach again, each man
his neighbor and each man his brother, saying, 'Know the LORD,' for they will all [b]know
Me, from the least of them to the greatest of
them," declares the LORD, "for I will [c]forgive
their iniquity, and their [d]sin I will remember
no more."
35 Thus says the LORD,
Who [a]gives the sun for light by day
And the [1]fixed order of the moon and
the stars for light by night,
Who [b]stirs up the sea so that its waves
roar;
[c]The LORD of hosts is His name:
36 "[a]If [1]this fixed order departs

24 [a]Jer 31:12; Ezek 36:10; Zech 8:4-8 **25** [1]Lit *fill* [a]Ps 107:9; Jer 31:12, 14; Matt 5:6; John 4:14 **26** [a]Zech 4:1 [b]Prov 3:24 **27** [a]Ezek 36:9, 11; Hos 2:23 **28** [a]Jer 44:27; Dan 9:14 [b]Jer 1:10; 18:7 [c]Jer 24:6 **29** [1]Or *dull* [a]Lam 5:7; Ezek 18:2 **30** [1]Or *dull* [a]Deut 24:16; Is 3:11; Ezek 18:4, 20 **31** [a]Jer 31:31-34; Heb 8:8-12 [b]Jer 32:40; 33:14; Ezek 37:26; Luke 22:20; 1 Cor 11:25; 2 Cor 3:6; Heb 8:8-12; 10:16, 17 **32** [a]Ex 19:5; 24:6-8; Deut 5:2, 3

32 [b]Deut 1:31; Is 63:12 [c]Jer 11:7, 8 **33** [a]Jer 32:40; Heb 10:16 [b]Ps 40:8; 2 Cor 3:3 [c]Jer 24:7; 30:22; 32:38 **34** [a]1 Thess 4:9; 1 John 2:27 [b]Is 11:9; 54:13; Jer 24:7; Hab 2:14; John 6:45; 1 John 2:20 [c]Jer 33:8; 50:20; Mic 7:18; Rom 11:27 [d]Is 43:25; Heb 10:17 **35** [1]Lit *statutes* [a]Gen 1:14-18; Deut 4:19; Ps 19:1-6; 136:7-9 [b]Is 51:15 [c]Jer 10:16; 32:18; 50:34 **36** [1]Lit *these statutes* [a]Ps 89:36, 37; 148:6; Is 54:9, 10; Jer 33:20-26

31:26 *I awoke.* Jeremiah had evidently received the previous divine revelation (beginning in 30:3) in a dream (for similar examples see Dan 10:9; Zech 4:1). *sleep . . . pleasant.* See Prov 3:24.

31:27 *sow . . . seed.* See Ezek 36:8–11. The same Hebrew root underlies both words. *Israel and . . . Judah.* North and south would again be united (see 3:18 and note.)

31:28 *watched . . . watch.* See note on 1:12. *pluck up . . . break down . . . overthrow, to destroy . . . build . . . plant.* See note on 1:10.

31:29 *The fathers . . . set on edge.* Repeated in Ezek 18:2. This was apparently a popular proverb that originated in a misunderstanding of such passages as Ex 20:5 and Num 14:18, which teach that a man's sins can have a negative effect on his descendants. In the time of Jeremiah and Ezekiel, many people felt that God's hand of judgment against them was due not to their own sins, but to the sins of their ancestors.

31:30 *everyone will die for his own iniquity.* See Deut 24:16; Ezek 18:3,20; 33:7–18. Although group or collective responsibility is an important concept, Jeremiah and Ezekiel emphasize individual responsibility as both preparation and explanation for the imminent destruction of Jerusalem, which the people might have been tempted to blame on the sins of their forefathers.

31:31–34 The high point of Jeremiah's prophecies, this passage is the longest sequence of OT verses to be quoted in its entirety in the NT (see note on Heb 8:8–12; see also Heb 10:16–17). Verse 31 contains the only OT use of the phrase "new covenant," which (together with its NT echoes) has come down to us (via Latin) as "new testament," the name that would later be applied to the distinctively Christian part of the Biblical canon.

31:31 *days are coming.* See vv. 27,38. The phrase often refers to the Messianic era. *make.* Lit. "cut" (see notes on 34:18; Gen 15:18). *new covenant.* See note on vv. 31–34; see also 1 Cor 11:25; 2 Cor 3:6; Heb 9:15; 12:24; and note on Mark 14:24). As the old covenant was solemnized by the blood of sacrificial animals, so the new would be solemnized by the blood of Christ. *house of Israel . . . house of Judah.* The reunited people of God (see 3:18 and note).

31:32 *covenant which I made with their fathers.* See 7:23; 11:1–8; Ex 19:5; 20:22–23:19 and notes. The covenant at Sinai eventually became known as the "old covenant" (2 Cor 3:14) or "first covenant" (Heb 8:7; 9:15,18). *took them by the hand.* See Hos 11:3–4. *My covenant which they broke.* See 11:10. The people, not God, were responsible for violating His covenant (see note on Is 24:5). *I was a husband.* See 3:14 and note.

31:33 *house of Israel.* Here includes both Israel and Judah (see v. 31 and note on 3:18). *put My law within them.* Internally (see Deut 6:6; 11:18; 30:14; Ezek 11:19; 18:31; 36:26–27), in contrast to setting it before them externally (see 9:13; Deut 4:8; 11:32). *on their heart I will write it.* So that it effectively governs their lives, in contrast to the ineffectiveness of merely presenting it in writing, though inscribed on durable stone (see Ex 24:4; 31:18; 32:15–16; 34:28–29; Deut 4:13; 5:22; 9:9,11; 10:4). *I will be . . . My people.* See note on 7:23. The "new" covenant does not abolish the "old" but supersedes it in the sense that through the new covenant the old is fulfilled and its purpose achieved.

31:34 *not teach . . . his neighbor.* When the Lord has done His new work, there will no longer be among His people those who are ignorant of Him and His will for human lives. True knowledge of the Lord will be shared by all—young and old, the peasant and the powerful (see 5:4–5 and notes; see also 32:38–40; Is 54:13 and note; Ezek 11:19–20; 36:25–27; Eph 3:12; Heb 4:16; 10:19–22). *Know.* In the experiential, not the academic, sense (see Ex 6:3 and note). *I will forgive . . . their sin.* The glorious basis of the new covenant (see Heb 10:14–17).

31:35 *gives the sun . . . moon . . . stars.* See Gen 1:16–18 and notes. *Who stirs up . . . is His name.* The same line is found in Is 51:15 (see Ps 46:3; Is 17:12).

From before Me," declares the LORD,
"Then the offspring of Israel also will
[b]cease
From being a nation before Me
[2]forever."
37 Thus says the LORD,
"[a]If the heavens above can be
measured
And the foundations of the earth
searched out below,
Then I will also [b]cast off all the
offspring of Israel
For all that they have done," declares
the LORD.
38 "Behold, days are coming," declares the
LORD, "when the [a]city will be rebuilt for the
LORD from the [b]Tower of Hananel to the [c]Cor-
ner Gate.
39 "The [a]measuring line will go out farther
straight ahead to the hill Gareb; then it will
turn to Goah.
40 "And [a]the whole valley of the dead bodies and of the ashes, and all the fields as far
as the brook [b]Kidron, to the corner of the
[c]Horse Gate toward the east, shall be [d]holy
to the LORD; it will not be plucked up or overthrown anymore forever."

Jeremiah Imprisoned

32 The word that came to Jeremiah from
the LORD in the [a]tenth year of Zedekiah
king of Judah, which was the eighteenth
year of Nebuchadnezzar.
2 Now at that time the army of the king
of Babylon was besieging Jerusalem, and
Jeremiah the prophet was shut up in the
[a]court of the guard, which *was in* the house
of the king of Judah,
3 because Zedekiah king of Judah had
[a]shut him up, saying, "Why do you [b]proph-
esy, saying, '[c]Thus says the LORD, "Behold, I
am about to [d]give this city into the hand of
the king of Babylon, and he will take it;
4 and Zedekiah king of Judah will [a]not
escape out of the hand of the Chaldeans, but
he will surely be given into the hand of the
king of Babylon, and he will [b]speak with him
[1]face to face and see him eye to eye;
5 and he will [a]take Zedekiah to Babylon,
and he will be there until I visit him,"
declares the LORD. "If you fight against the
Chaldeans, you will [b]not succeed" '?"
6 And Jeremiah said, "The word of the
LORD came to me, saying,
7 'Behold, Hanamel the son of Shallum
your uncle is coming to you, saying, "Buy for
yourself my field which is at [a]Anathoth, for
you have the [b]right of redemption to buy
it." '
8 "Then Hanamel my uncle's son came to
me in the [a]court of the guard according to
the word of the LORD and said to me, 'Buy
my field, please, that is at [b]Anathoth, which
is in the land of Benjamin; for you have the
right of possession and the redemption is
yours; buy *it* for yourself.' Then I knew that
this was the [c]word of the LORD.
9 "I bought the field which was at Anathoth from Hanamel my uncle's son, and I
[a]weighed out the silver for him, seventeen
[b]shekels of silver.
10 "I [1a]signed and [b]sealed the deed, and
[c]called in witnesses, and weighed out the silver on the scales.

36 [2]Lit *all the days* [b]Amos 9:8, 9 **37** [a]Is 40:12; Jer 33:22 [b]Jer 33:24-26; Rom 11:2-5, 26, 27 **38** [a]Jer 30:18; 31:4 [b]Neh 3:1; 12:39; Zech 14:10 [c]2 Kin 14:13; 2 Chr 26:9 **39** [a]Zech 2:1 **40** [a]Jer 7:32; 8:2 [b]2 Sam 15:23; 2 Kin 23:6, 12; John 18:1 [c]2 Kin 11:16; 2 Chr 23:15; Neh 3:28 [d]Joel 3:17; Zech 14:20 **32:1** [a]2 Kin 25:1, 2; Jer 39:1, 2 **2** [a]Neh 3:25; Jer 33:1; 37:21; 38:6; 39:14

3 [a]2 Kin 6:32 [b]Jer 26:8, 9 [c]Jer 21:3-7; 34:2, 3 [d]Jer 21:4-7; 32:28, 29; 34:2, 3 **4** [1]Lit *mouth to mouth* [a]2 Kin 25:4-7; Jer 37:17; 38:18, 23; 39:4-7 [b]Jer 39:5 **5** [a]Jer 27:22; 39:7; Ezek 12:12, 13 [b]Ezek 17:9, 10, 15 **7** [a]Jer 1:1; 11:21 [b]Lev 25:25; Ruth 4:3, 4 **8** [a]Jer 32:2; 33:1 [b]Jer 1:1; 32:7 [c]1 Sam 9:16, 17; 10:3-7; 1 Kin 22:25; Jer 32:25

9 [a]Gen 23:16; Zech 11:12 [b]Gen 24:22; Ex 21:32; Neh 5:15; Ezek 4:10 **10** [1]Or *wrote...on the document* [a]Is 44:5; Jer 32:44 [b]Deut 32:34; Job 14:17 [c]Ruth 4:1, 9; Is 8:2

31:36 See 33:20–21,25–26. Just as God's creation order is established and secure, so also Israel will always have descendants.
31:37 *cast off all.* Israel will continue to exist, even though a terrible judgment is about to sweep the kingdom of Judah away.
31:38–40 See Zech 14:10–11.
31:38 *the city.* Jerusalem. *Tower of Hananel . . . Corner Gate.* The eastern and western ends of the northern wall (see note on Zech 14:10).
31:39 *measuring line.* Mentioned in connection with restored Jerusalem also in Ezek 40:3; Zech 1:16; 2:1. *Gareb . . . Goah.* Exact locations unknown, but probably to the west of Jerusalem.
31:40 *valley.* Probably the Hinnom Valley (see 2:23 and note). *Horse Gate.* See note on Neh 3:28. *holy to the LORD.* See Zech 14:20 and note. *plucked up . . . overthrown.* See note on 1:10.
32:1–44 Though with some reluctance (see v. 25), Jeremiah obeys the Lord's command to buy a field in Anathoth from his cousin (see vv. 8–9) even as the Babylonians are besieging Jerusalem (see vv. 2,24).
32:1 *tenth year of Zedekiah . . . eighteenth year of Nebuchadnezzar.* 587 B.C., the year before Jerusalem was destroyed by the Babylonians (see 52:12–13). The siege began in 588 (see 39:1; 52:4).
32:2 *shut up in the court of the guard.* See Neh 3:25 and note. Jeremiah was imprisoned by King Zedekiah (see 37:21) and remained in the courtyard of the guard until Jerusalem fell (see 38:13,28; 39:14).
32:3–5 See 21:3–7; 34:2–5; 37:17. The fulfillment is recorded in 52:7–14.
32:5 *until I visit him.* After his capture by the Babylonians, Zedekiah was taken to Babylon, where he eventually died (see 52:11). *you will not succeed.* See note on 29:4.
32:7 *Anathoth.* Jeremiah's hometown (see note on 1:1). *you have the right . . . to buy it.* In accordance with the ancient law of redemption (see Lev 25:23–25; see also notes on Ruth 2:20; 4:3).
32:8 *came to me in the court.* Though imprisoned, Jeremiah was allowed to have visitors. *in the land of Benjamin.* Some time earlier, Jeremiah had been on his way home "to take possession of some property . . . among the people" in Benjamin (37:12), but he was arrested, falsely accused of treason, and thrown into prison (see 37:13–16).
32:9 *I bought.* In obedience to the Lord's command (see v. 7). *weighed out.* Coinage had not yet been invented. *seventeen shekels of silver.* About 7 ounces of silver. The size of the field is unknown, but the price was probably not exorbitant (contrast Gen 23:15; see note there).
32:10 *sealed.* Not to attest his signature (as, e.g., in Esth 3:12; see note on Gen 38:18) but to guarantee the contents of the deed and keep it from being tampered with (see Is 8:16; 29:11; Dan 12:4,9; Rev 15:1–5).

11 "Then I took the deeds of purchase, both the sealed *copy containing* the [a]terms and conditions and the open *copy;*

12 and I gave the deed of purchase to [a]Baruch the son of [b]Neriah, the son of Mahseiah, in the sight of Hanamel my uncle's *son* and in the sight of the witnesses who signed the deed of purchase, before all the Jews who were sitting in the court of the guard.

13 "And I commanded Baruch in their presence, saying,

14 'Thus says the LORD of hosts, the God of Israel, "Take these deeds, this sealed deed of purchase and this open deed, and put them in an earthenware jar, that they may [1]last a long time."

15 'For thus says the LORD of hosts, the God of Israel, "[a]Houses and fields and vineyards will again be bought in this land." '

Jeremiah Prays and God Explains

16 "After I had given the deed of purchase to Baruch the son of Neriah, then I [a]prayed to the LORD, saying,

17 '[a]Ah Lord [1]GOD! Behold, You have [b]made the heavens and the earth by Your great power and by Your outstretched arm! [c]Nothing is too difficult for You,

18 who [a]shows lovingkindness to thousands, but [b]repays the iniquity of fathers into the bosom of their children after them, O [c]great and [d]mighty God. The [e]LORD of hosts is His name;

19 [a]great in counsel and mighty in deed, whose [b]eyes are open to all the ways of the sons of men, [c]giving to everyone according to his ways and according to the fruit of his deeds;

20 who has [a]set signs and wonders in the land of Egypt, *and* even to this day both in Israel and among mankind; and You have [b]made a name for Yourself, as at this day.

21 'You [a]brought Your people Israel out of the land of Egypt with signs and with wonders, and with a strong hand and with an outstretched arm and with great terror;

22 and gave them this land, which You [a]swore to their forefathers to give them, a land flowing with milk and honey.

23 'They [a]came in and took possession of it, but they [b]did not obey Your voice or [c]walk in Your law; they have done nothing of all that You commanded them to do; therefore You have made [d]all this calamity come upon them.

24 'Behold, the [a]siege ramps have reached the city to take it; and the city is [b]given into the hand of the Chaldeans who fight against it, because of the [c]sword, the famine and the pestilence; and what You have spoken has [d]come to pass; and behold, You see *it.*

25 'You have said to me, O Lord [1]GOD, "Buy for yourself the field with money and call in witnesses"—although the city is given into the hand of the Chaldeans.' "

26 Then the word of the LORD came to Jeremiah, saying,

27 "Behold, I am the LORD, the [a]God of all flesh; is anything [b]too difficult for Me?"

28 Therefore thus says the LORD, "Behold, I am about to [a]give this city into the hand of the Chaldeans and into the hand of Nebuchadnezzar king of Babylon, and he will take it.

11 [a]Luke 2:27 **12** [a]Jer 32:16; 36:4, 5, 32; 43:3; 45:1 [b]Jer 51:59 **14** [1]Lit *stand many days* **15** [a]Jer 30:18; 31:5, 12, 24; 32:37, 43, 44; 33:12, 13; Amos 9:14, 15; Zech 3:10 **16** [a]Gen 32:9-12; Jer 12:1; Phil 4:6, 7 **17** [1]Heb *YHWH,* usually rendered *LORD* [a]Jer 1:6; 4:10 [b]2 Kin 19:15; Ps 102:25; Is 40:26-29; Jer 27:5 [c]Gen 18:14; Jer 32:27; Zech 8:6; Matt 19:26; Mark 10:27; Luke 1:37; 18:27 **18** [a]Ex 20:6; 34:6, 7; Deut 5:9, 10; 7:9, 10 [b]1 Kin 14:9, 10; 16:1-3; Matt 23:32-36 [c]Ps 145:3 [d]Ps 50:1; Is 9:6; Jer 20:11 [e]Jer 10:16; 31:35 **19** [a]Is 9:6; 28:29 [b]Job 34:21; Jer 23:24 [c]Ps 62:12; Jer 17:10; 21:14; Matt 16:27; John 5:29 **20** [a]Ps 78:43; 105:27

20 [b]Ex 9:16; Is 63:12, 14; Dan 9:15 **21** [a]Ex 6:6; Deut 4:34; 7:19; 26:8; 2 Sam 7:23; 1 Chr 17:21; Ps 136:11 **22** [a]Ex 3:8, 17; 13:5; Deut 1:8; Ps 105:9-11; Jer 11:5 **23** [a]Ps 44:2, 3; 78:54, 55; Jer 32:7 [b]Neh 9:26; Jer 11:8; Dan 9:10-14 [c]Ezra 9:7; Jer 26:4; 44:10 [d]Lam 1:18; Dan 9:11, 12 **24** [a]Jer 33:4; Ezek 21:22 [b]Jer 20:5; 21:4-7; 32:5 [c]Jer 14:12; 29:17, 18; 32:36; 34:17; Ezek 14:21 [d]Deut 4:26; Josh 23:15, 16; Zech 1:6 **25** [1]Heb *YHWH,* usually rendered *LORD* **27** [a]Num 16:22; 27:16 [b]Jer 32:17; Matt 19:26 **28** [a]2 Kin 25:11; 2 Chr 36:17-21; Jer 19:7-12; 32:3, 24, 36; 34:2, 3

32:11 *open copy.* For ready reference, the authenticity of which would then be guaranteed by the sealed copy if the unsealed deed should be lost, damaged or changed (deliberately or otherwise). Examples of tied and sealed papyrus documents of the fifth and subsequent centuries B.C. have been found at Elephantine in southern Egypt, in the desert of Judah west of the Dead Sea, and elsewhere (see chart, p. xix).
32:12 *Baruch.* Means "blessed (by the Lord)." He was Jeremiah's faithful secretary and friend (see Introduction: Author and Date).
32:14 *put them in an earthenware jar, that they may last a long time.* Documents found in clay jars at Elephantine (see note on v. 11) and Qumran (west of the Dead Sea) were preserved almost intact for more than 2,000 years (see essay, p. 1356).
32:15 Jeremiah's deed of purchase would enable him (or his heirs) to reclaim the field as soon as normal economic activity resumed after the exile.
32:17 See 27:5. *great power and by Your outstretched arm.* See v. 21; see also note on 21:5. *Nothing is too difficult for you.* See note on Gen 18:14. The Lord's reply to Jeremiah echoes these words (see v. 27).
32:18 *shows lovingkindness to thousands . . . repays the iniquity of fathers.* See Ex 20:5–6; 34:7; see also note on Ex 20:6. *repays . . . into the bosom.* A symbol of retribution (see Ps 79:12; Is 65:6–7; cf. Luke 6:38). *great and mighty God.* See Deut 10:17. *LORD of hosts is His name.* See 31:35; Is 54:5; Amos 4:13.
32:19 *great in counsel and mighty in deed.* See Ps 66:5; Is 9:6; 28:29. *giving to everyone according to . . . his deeds.* The Hebrew is repeated verbatim from 17:10 (see note there; see also 1 Cor 3:8; Eph 6:8).
32:20 *signs and wonders.* See v. 21; Ex 7:3; see also notes on Ex 3:12; 4:8. *to this day.* See 11:7.
32:21 Repeated almost verbatim from Deut 26:8 (see Deut 4:34). *strong hand . . . outstretched arm.* See v. 17 and note on 21:5. *great terror.* See Ex 15:14–16.
32:22 *land flowing with milk and honey.* See 11:5; see also note on Ex 3:8.
32:24 *siege ramps.* See 6:6; 33:4; see also note on Is 37:33. *sword . . . famine . . . pestilence.* See note on 14:12.
32:25 Jeremiah expresses his doubts concerning what must seem to him to be an unwise investment. Nevertheless, he remains the obedient servant (see vv. 8–9).
32:27 *the LORD, the God of all flesh.* Echoes Num 16:22; 27:16, emphasizing God's universal dominion. *is anything too difficult for Me?* Responds to the description in Jeremiah's prayer (see v. 17 and note on Gen 18:14), stressing God's omnipotence. God is worthy of obedience because He is always faithful in fulfilling His promises.

29 "The Chaldeans who are fighting against
this city will enter and [a]set this city on fire
and burn it, with the [b]houses where *people*
have offered incense to Baal on their roofs
and poured out drink offerings to other gods
to provoke Me to anger.
30 "Indeed the sons of Israel and the sons
of Judah have been doing only [a]evil in My
sight from their youth; for the sons of Israel
have been only [b]provoking Me to anger by
the work of their hands," declares the LORD.
31 "Indeed this city has been to Me *a*
[a]*provocation of* My anger and My wrath from
the day that they built it, even to this day, so
that it should be [b]removed from before My
face,
32 because of all the evil of the sons of
Israel and the sons of Judah which they have
done to provoke Me to anger—they, their
[a]kings, their leaders, their priests, their
prophets, the men of Judah and the inhabitants of Jerusalem.
33 "They have turned *their* back to Me and
not *their* face; though *I* taught them, [1a]teach-
ing again and again, they would not listen
[2]and receive instruction.
34 "But they [a]put their detestable things in
the house which is called by My name, to
defile it.
35 "They built the [a]high places of Baal that
are in the valley of Ben-hinnom to cause
their sons and their daughters to pass
through *the fire* to [b]Molech, which I had not
commanded them nor had it [1]entered My
mind that they should do this abomination,
to cause Judah to sin.
36 "Now therefore thus says the LORD God
of Israel concerning this city of which you
say, 'It is [a]given into the hand of the king of
Babylon by sword, by famine and by pestilence.'
37 "Behold, I will [a]gather them out of all
the lands to which I have driven them in My
anger, in My wrath and in great indignation;
and I will bring them back to this place and
[b]make them dwell in safety.
38 "They shall be [a]My people, and I will be
their God;
39 and I will [a]give them one heart and one
way, that they may fear Me always, for their
own [b]good and for *the good of* their children
after them.
40 "I will make an [a]everlasting covenant
with them that I will [b]not turn away from
them, to do them good; and I will [c]put the
fear of Me in their hearts so that they will
not turn away from Me.
41 "I will [a]rejoice over them to do them
good and will [1]faithfully [b]plant them in this
land with [c]all My heart and with all My soul.
42 "For thus says the LORD, '[a]Just as I
brought all this great disaster on this people,
so I am going to [b]bring on them all the good
that I am promising them.
43 '[a]Fields will be bought in this land of
which you say, "[b]It is a desolation, without
man or beast; it is given into the hand of the
Chaldeans."
44 'Men will buy fields for money, [1a]sign
and seal deeds, and call in witnesses in the
[b]land of Benjamin, in the environs of
Jerusalem, in the cities of Judah, in the cities
of the hill country, in the cities of the lowland and in the cities of the [2]Negev; for I will
[c]restore their [3]fortunes,' declares the LORD."

Restoration Promised

33 Then the word of the LORD came to Jeremiah the second time, while he was

29 [a]2 Chr 36:19; Jer 21:10; 37:8, 10; 39:8 [b]Jer 19:13; 44:17-19, 25; 52:13 **30** [a]Deut 9:7-12; Is 63:10; Jer 2:7; 7:22-26 [b]Jer 8:19; 11:17; 25:7 **31** [a]1 Kin 11:7, 8; 2 Kin 21:4-7, 16; Jer 5:9-11; 6:6, 7; Matt 23:37 [b]2 Kin 23:27; 24:3, 4; Jer 27:10 **32** [a]Ezra 9:7; Is 1:4-6, 23; Jer 2:26; 44:17, 21; Dan 9:8 **33** [1]Lit *rising up early and teaching* [2]Lit *to* [a]2 Chr 36:15, 16; Jer 7:13; 25:3; 26:5; 35:15; John 8:2 **34** [a]2 Kin 21:1-7; Jer 7:30; 19:4-6; Ezek 8:5 **35** [1]Lit *come up into My heart* [a]2 Chr 28:2, 3; 33:6; Jer 7:31; 19:5 [b]Lev 18:21; 20:2-5; 1 Kin 11:7; 2 Kin 23:10; Acts 7:43 **36** [a]Jer 32:24 **37** [a]Deut 30:3; Ps 106:47; Is 11:11-16; Jer 16:14, 15; 23:3, 8; Ezek 11:17; Hos 1:11; Amos 9:14, 15

37 [b]Jer 23:6; Ezek 34:25, 28; Zech 14:11 **38** [a]Jer 24:7 **39** [a]2 Chr 30:12; Jer 31:33; Ezek 11:19; John 17:21; Acts 4:32 [b]Deut 11:18-21; Ezek 37:25 **40** [a]Is 55:3; Jer 31:33, 34; 50:5; Ezek 37:26 [b]Deut 31:6, 8; Ezek 39:29 [c]Jer 24:7; 31:33 **41** [1]Or *truly* [a]Deut 30:9; Is 62:5; 65:19 [b]Jer 24:6; 31:28; Amos 9:15 [c]Hos 2:19, 20 **42** [a]Jer 31:28; Zech 8:14, 15 [b]Jer 33:14 **43** [a]Jer 32:15, 25; Ezek 37:11-14 [b]Jer 33:10 **44** [1]Or *write...on the document* [2]I.e. South country [3]Or *captivity* [a]Jer 32:10 [b]Jer 17:26; 33:13 [c]Jer 31:23; 33:7, 11, 26

32:29 *burn it.* See 21:10; 34:2; 37:8. *offered incense to Baal.* See 1:16 and note. *on their roofs.* See note on 19:13. *drink offerings to other gods.* See 7:18 and note; 19:13. *provoke Me to anger.* See 7:18; Deut 31:29.

32:30 Echoes Deut 31:29. *youth.* See note on 31:19. *the work of their hands.* A reference to idols.

32:31 *removed from before My face.* See 52:3; 2 Kin 24:3.

32:32 *kings . . . leaders . . . priests . . . prophets.* See 1:18 and note.

32:33 *again and again.* See note on 7:13. *not . . . receive instruction.* See 2:30; 5:3; 7:28; 17:23.

32:34–35 Repeated from 7:30–31 (see notes there).

32:35 *Molech.* The god of the Ammonites (see 49:1,3; see also note on Lev 18:21).

32:36 *Now therefore.* After judgment on the wicked comes restoration for the righteous. *you.* The pronoun is plural, referring to the people of Judah as a whole. *sword . . . famine . . . pestilence.* See note on 14:12.

32:37 See Deut 30:1–5. *My anger . . . wrath . . . great indignation.* See note on 21:5. *bring them back . . . make them dwell.* See Ezek 36:11,33; Hos 11:11. The Hebrew underlying the first phrase sounds like that underlying the second.

32:38 See 31:33; see also note on 7:23.

32:39 *one heart.* See 24:7; 31:32 and note; Ezek 11:19. *their children after them.* See Deut 4:9–10.

32:40 *everlasting covenant.* See Is 55:3 and note; Ezek 16:60; 37:26. Unlike the old covenant (see 31:32; Is 24:5), the new covenant would never be broken. *put the fear of Me in their hearts.* See Deut 6:24; see also note on Gen 20:11. *not turn away from Me.* See 26:3; Is 53:6.

32:41 *rejoice . . . to do them good.* See Deut 30:9; Is 62:5; 65:19.

32:43–44 *Fields will be bought.* The field purchased by Jeremiah (see v. 9) is symbolic of the many fields that will be purchased in Judah after the Babylonian exile, when economic conditions return to normal (see note on v. 15).

32:43 *you.* See note on v. 36. *desolation, without man or beast.* See 4:23–26 and notes.

32:44 *land of Benjamin.* See 1:1. Here Benjamin is mentioned first because it was the region in which Jeremiah's hometown was located (see vv. 7–8 and notes). *hill country . . . lowland.* See note on Deut 1:7. *Negev.* See note on Gen 12:9. *restore their fortunes.* See note on 29:14.

33:1–26 Concluding Jeremiah's "book of consolation" (see note on 30:1–33:26), the section is divided into two roughly equal parts: (1) vv. 1–13, which continues and builds on ch. 32, and (2) vv. 14–26, which summarizes a wider range of earlier pas-

still [1][a]confined in the court of the guard, saying,

2 "Thus says [a]the LORD who made [1]*the earth,* the LORD who formed it to establish it, the [b]LORD is His name,

3 '[a]Call to Me and I will answer you, and I will tell you [b]great and mighty things, [c]which you do not know.'

4 "For thus says the LORD God of Israel concerning the [a]houses of this city, and concerning the houses of the kings of Judah which are broken down *to make a defense* against the [b]siege ramps and against the sword,

5 'While *they* are coming to [a]fight with the Chaldeans and to fill them with the corpses of men whom I have slain in My anger and in My wrath, and I have [b]hidden My face from this city because of all their wickedness:

6 'Behold, I will bring to it [a]health and healing, and I will heal them; and I will reveal to them an [b]abundance of peace and truth.

7 'I will [a]restore the [1]fortunes of Judah and the fortunes of Israel and will [b]rebuild them as they were at first.

8 'I will [a]cleanse them from all their iniquity by which they have sinned against Me, and I will pardon all their iniquities by which they have sinned against Me and by which they have transgressed against Me.

9 '[1]It will be to Me a [a]name of joy, praise and glory before [b]all the nations of the earth which will hear of all the [c]good that I do for them, and they will [d]fear and tremble because of all the good and all the peace that I make for it.'

10 "Thus says the LORD, 'Yet again there will be heard in this place, of which you say, "It is a [a]waste, without man and without beast," *that is,* in the cities of Judah and in the streets of Jerusalem that are [b]desolate, without man and without inhabitant and without beast,

11 the voice of [a]joy and the voice of gladness, the voice of the bridegroom and the voice of the bride, the voice of those who say,

"[b]Give thanks to the LORD of hosts,
For the LORD is good,
For His lovingkindness is everlasting";

and of those who bring a [c]thank offering into the house of the LORD. For I will restore the [1]fortunes of the land as they were at first,' says the LORD.

12 "Thus says the LORD of hosts, 'There will again be in this place which is waste, [a]without man or beast, and in all its cities, a [1]habitation of shepherds who rest their [b]flocks.

13 'In the [a]cities of the hill country, in the cities of the lowland, in the cities of the Negev, in the land of Benjamin, in the environs of Jerusalem and in the cities of Judah, the flocks will again [b]pass under the hands of the one who numbers them,' says the LORD.

The Davidic Kingdom

14 'Behold, [a]days are coming,' declares the LORD, 'when I will [b]fulfill the good word which I have spoken concerning the house of Israel and the house of Judah.

15 'In those days and at that time I will cause a [a]righteous Branch of David to spring forth; and He shall execute [b]justice and righteousness on the earth.

16 'In those days [a]Judah will be saved and Jerusalem will dwell in safety; and this is *the name* by which she will be called: the [b]LORD is our righteousness.'

17 "For thus says the LORD, '[1]David shall

33:1 [1]Lit *shut up* [a]Jer 32:2, 8; 37:21; 38:28 **2** [1]Lit *it* [a]Jer 51:19 [b]Ex 3:15; 6:3; 15:3; Jer 10:16 **3** [a]Ps 50:15; 91:15; Is 55:6, 7; Jer 29:12 [b]Jer 32:17, 27 [c]Is 48:6 **4** [a]Is 32:13, 14 [b]Jer 32:24; Ezek 4:2; 21:22; Hab 1:10 **5** [a]Jer 21:4-7; 32:5 [b]Is 8:17; Jer 21:10; Mic 3:4 **6** [a]Jer 17:14; 30:17; Hos 6:1 [b]Is 66:12; Gal 5:22, 23 **7** [1]Or *captivity* [a]Ps 85:1; Jer 30:18; 32:44; 33:26; Amos 9:14 [b]Is 1:26; Jer 30:18; 31:4, 38; Amos 9:14, 15 **8** [a]Ps 51:2; Is 44:22; Jer 50:20; Ezek 36:25, 33; Mic 7:18, 19; Zech 13:1; Heb 9:11-14 **9** [1]I.e. This city [a]Is 62:2, 4, 7; Jer 13:11 [b]Jer 3:17, 19; 4:2; 16:19 [c]Jer 24:6; 32:42 [d]Neh 6:16; Ps 40:3; Is 60:5; Hos 3:5 **10** [a]Jer 32:43 [b]Jer 26:9; 34:22 **11** [1]Or *captivity* [a]Is 35:10; 51:3, 11 [b]1 Chr 16:8, 34; 2 Chr 5:13; 7:3; Ezra 3:11; Ps 100:4, 5; 106:1; 107:1; 118:1; 136:1 [c]Lev 7:12, 13; Ps 107:22; 116:17; Jer 17:26; Heb 13:15 **12** [1]Or *pasture* [a]Jer 32:43; 36:29; 51:62 [b]Is 65:10; Jer 31:12; Ezek 34:12-15; Zeph 2:6, 7 **13** [a]Jer 17:26; 32:44 [b]Lev 27:32; Luke 15:4 **14** [a]Jer 23:5 [b]Is 32:1, 2; Jer 29:10; 32:42; 33:9; Ezek 34:23-25; Hag 2:6-9 **15** [a]Is 4:2; 11:1-5; Jer 23:5, 6; 30:9; Zech 3:8; 6:12, 13 [b]Ps 72:1-5 **16** [a]Is 45:17, 22; Jer 23:6 [b]Is 45:24, 25; Jer 23:6; 1 Cor 1:30; 2 Cor 5:21; Phil 3:9 **17** [1]Lit *There shall not be cut off for David*

---

sages in Jeremiah and elsewhere—it is not found in the Septuagint (the Greek translation of the OT).

33:1 *the second time.* Ch. 32 comprises the first time. *still confined.* In 587 B.C. (see note on 32:1). *court of the guard.* See 32:2 and note.

33:2 See 10:12; 32:17; 51:15; see also 31:35 and note.

33:3 *Call . . . and I will answer.* Man's prayer invites—and assures—God's response (see Ps 3:4; 4:3; 18:6; 27:7; 28:1–2; 30:8; 55:17; Matt 7:7; contrast 11:14). *great and mighty.* The Hebrew for this phrase usually refers to the formidable cities of Canaan and is translated "large and fortified to heaven" (Deut 1:28; see Num 13:28; Deut 9:1; Josh 14:12). *mighty things, which you do not know.* The Hebrew (with the change of one letter) for this phrase echoes Is 48:6: "hidden things which you have not known." As the rest of ch. 33 demonstrates, the Lord will first judge His people (vv. 4–5) and then restore them in ways that will be nothing short of incredible (vv. 6–26).

33:4 Jerusalem's houses—including those of the king—were torn down so that their stones could be used to repair the city's battered walls (see Is 22:10 and note). *siege ramps.* To help the invaders bring up battering rams and scale Jerusalem's walls (see 6:6).

33:5 *fight with the Chaldeans.* See 32:5. *corpses.* Of Jerusalem's defenders.

33:6 *health and healing.* See 30:17; contrast 8:22.

33:7 *restore the fortunes.* See vv. 11,26; see also note on 29:14. *Judah and . . . Israel.* See note on 3:18.

33:8 *pardon all their iniquities.* The basis of the institution of the new covenant (see 31:34 and note; see also 50:20; Ezek 36:25–26).

33:9 *tremble because of all the good.* See Hos 3:5.

33:10 See 32:43 and note.

33:11 *voice of joy . . . voice of the bride.* The glorious reversal of the judgment proclaimed in 7:34; 16:9; 25:10. *those who say, "Give thanks . . ."* See note on 17:26. *restore the fortunes.* See note on 29:14.

33:13 *hill country . . . cities of Judah.* See 17:26 and note; 32:44. *flocks . . . pass under the hands . . . numbers them.* See Ezek 20:37.

33:15–16 Repeated from 23:5–6 (see notes there).

33:16 *she will be called.* Because of Jerusalem's intimate relationship to the Messiah, it is given the same name by which He is called in 23:6 (for other examples see Judg 6:24; Ezek 48:35).

33:17–26 In the face of the impending judgment in which the nation will be swept away and the promised land reduced to a

[a]never lack a man to sit on the throne of the
house of Israel;
18 [1]and the [a]Levitical priests shall never
lack a man before Me to offer burnt offerings, to burn grain offerings and to [b]prepare
sacrifices [2]continually.' "
19 The word of the LORD came to Jeremiah, saying,
20 "Thus says the LORD, 'If you can [a]break
My covenant for the day and My covenant
for the night, so that day and night will not
be at their appointed time,
21 then [a]My covenant may also be broken
with David My servant so that he will not
have a son to reign on his throne, and with
the Levitical priests, My ministers.
22 'As the [a]host of heaven cannot be
counted and the [b]sand of the sea cannot be
measured, so I will [c]multiply the [1]descen-
dants of David My servant and the [d]Levites
who minister to Me.' "
23 And the word of the LORD came to Jeremiah, saying,
24 "Have you not observed what this people have spoken, saying, 'The [a]two families
which the LORD chose, He has [b]rejected
them'? Thus they [c]despise My people, no
longer are they as a nation [1]in their sight.
25 "Thus says the LORD, 'If My [a]covenant
for day and night *stand* not, *and* the [1]fixed
patterns of heaven and earth I have [b]not
established,
26 then I would [a]reject the [1]descendants
of Jacob and David My servant, [2]not taking
from his [1]descendants [b]rulers over the
[1]descendants of Abraham, Isaac and Jacob.
But I will [c]restore their [3]fortunes and will
have [d]mercy on them.' "

A Prophecy against Zedekiah

34 The word which came to Jeremiah
from the LORD, when [a]Nebuchadnezzar
king of Babylon and all his army, with [b]all
the kingdoms of the earth that were under
his dominion and all the peoples, were fighting against Jerusalem and against all its cities, saying,
2 "Thus says the LORD God of Israel, '[a]Go
and speak to Zedekiah king of Judah and say
to him: "Thus says the LORD, 'Behold, [b]I am
giving this city into the hand of the king of
Babylon, and [c]he will burn it with fire.
3 '[a]You will not escape from his hand, for
you will surely be captured and delivered into
his hand; and you will [b]see the king of Babylon eye to eye, and he will speak with you
[1]face to face, and you will go to Babylon.' " '

17 [a]2 Sam 7:16; 1 Kin 2:4; 8:25; 1 Chr 17:11-14; Ps 89:29-37 **18** [1]Lit *there shall not be cut off for the Levitical priests* [2]Lit *all the days* [a]Num 3:5-10; Deut 18:1; 24:8; Josh 3:3; Ezek 44:15 [b]Ezra 3:5; Heb 13:15 **20** [a]Ps 89:37; 104:19-23; Is 54:9, 10; Jer 31:35-37; 33:25 **21** [a]2 Sam 23:5; 2 Chr 7:18; 21:7 **22** [1]Lit *seed* [a]Gen 15:5; Jer 31:37 [b]Gen 22:17 [c]Ezek 37:24-27 [d]Is 66:21; Jer 33:18 **24** [1]Lit *to their faces* [a]Is 7:17; 11:13; Jer 3:7, 8, 10, 18; 33:26; Ezek 37:22 [b]Jer 30:17 [c]Neh 4:2-4; Esth 3:6, 8, 9; Ps 44:13, 14; 83:4 **25** [1]Lit *statutes* [a]Gen 8:22; Jer 31:35, 36; 33:20 **25** [b]Ps 74:16, 17 **26** [1]Lit *seed* [2]Lit *from taking* [3]Or *captivity* [a]Jer 31:37 [b]Gen 49:10 [c]Jer 33:7 [d]Is 14:1; 54:8; Jer 31:20; Ezek 39:25; Hos 1:7; 2:23
34:1 [a]2 Kin 25:1; Jer 32:2; 39:1; 52:4 [b]Jer 1:15; 27:7; Dan 2:37, 38 **2** [a]2 Chr 36:11, 12; Jer 22:1, 2; 37:1, 2 [b]Jer 21:10; 32:3; 34:22; 37:8-10 [c]Jer 32:29 **3** [1]Lit *mouth to mouth* [a]2 Kin 25:4, 5; Jer 21:7; 32:4; 34:21 [b]2 Kin 25:6, 7; Jer 39:6, 7

desolate wasteland, all God's past covenants with His people appear to be rendered of no effect—His covenants with Israel, with David and with Phinehas (see chart, p. 16). This series of oracles, however, gives reassurance that the ancient covenants are not being repudiated, that they are as secure as God's covenant concerning the creation order, and that in the future restoration they will all yet be fulfilled.

33:17 See 2 Sam 7:12–16; 1 Kin 2:4; 8:25; 9:5; 2 Chr 6:16; 7:18. This passage is fulfilled ultimately in Jesus (see Luke 1:32–33).

33:18 See Num 25:13. The priestly covenant with the Levites, like the royal covenant with David, was not a private grant to the priestly family involving only that family and the Lord. It was rather an integral part of the Lord's dealings with His people in which Israel was assured of the ministry of a priesthood that was acceptable to the Lord and through whose mediation they could enjoy communion with Him. That ministry was and is being fulfilled by Jesus, who administers a higher and better priesthood (see Ps 110:4; Heb 5:6–10; 6:19–20; 7:11–25). *Levitical priests.* See Deut 17:9,18.

33:20 *covenant for the day and . . . the night.* See v. 25; 31:35–36. Although reference may be to God's sovereign establishment of the creation order in the beginning, more likely the covenant of Gen 9:8–17 (see Gen 8:22) is in view.

33:21 *covenant . . . with the Levitical priests.* See Mal 2:4.

33:22 In words that echo the covenant promises to the patriarchs (Abraham, Gen 22:17; Isaac, Gen 26:4; Jacob, Gen 32:12), the Lord assures the flourishing of the two mediatorial (royal and priestly) families and thus the continuation of this ministry in the spiritual commonwealth He has established with His people. This promise of a numerous progeny to both the royal and priestly families is no doubt fulfilled in that great throng who (will) reign with Christ (see Rom 5:17; 8:17; 1 Cor 6:3; 2 Tim 2:12; Rev 3:21; 5:10; 20:5–6; 22:5; see also Matt 19:28; Luke 22:30) and who in Christ have been consecrated to be priests (see 1 Pet 2:5,9; Rev 1:6; 5:10; 20:6; see also Is 66:21; Rom 6:13; 12:1; 15:16; Eph 5:2; Phil 4:18; Heb 13:15–16).

33:24 *two families.* Israel and Judah. But because of the use of the word "families" instead of "kingdoms," the reference may be to the two mediatorial (royal and priestly) families, or to the families of Jacob and David (see v. 26). *the LORD chose.* See Amos 3:2 and note.

33:25–26 See v. 20 and note.

33:26 *restore their fortunes and . . . have mercy.* Echoes Deut 30:3; see note on 29:14.

34:1–35:19 The first major division of the book (chs. 2–35) now draws to a close. Jeremiah's warnings and exhortations to Judah are concluded with a historical appendix (chs. 34–35), a technique used to conclude the third major division of the book (chs. 39–45) as well (see note on 45:1–5). Ch. 52, written by someone other than Jeremiah, serves as a fitting historical appendix to the entire book.

34:1–22 The chapter divides naturally into two parts (vv. 1–7 and 8–22), each of which dates to 588 B.C. (see notes on vv. 7,21–22).

34:1–7 Jeremiah's warning to King Zedekiah parallels the prophet's similar admonition in 21:1–10 (see notes there).

34:1 *kingdoms . . . under his dominion and all the peoples.* Nebuchadnezzar's empire was vast (see Ezek 26:7; Dan 3:2–4; 4:1; cf. the similar description of the Medes in 51:28). *fighting against Jerusalem.* Subject nations were expected to supply troops to fight alongside those of their overlord (see 2 Kin 24:2). In a 14th-century B.C. treaty between the Hittite ruler Mursilis II and Duppi-tessub king of the Amorites, Mursilis says, "If you do not send your son or brother with your foot soldiers and charioteers to help the Hittite king, you act in disregard of the gods of the oath." *all its cities.* See 19:15 and note.

34:2–3 See 32:3–5 and note; see also 39:4–7; Ezek 12:12–13; 17:11–20.

4 "Yet hear the word of the LORD, O Zedekiah king of Judah! Thus says the LORD concerning you, 'You will not die by the sword.

5 'You will die in peace; and as *spices* were burned for your fathers, the former kings who were before you, so they will [a]burn *spices* for you; and [b]they will lament for you, "Alas, lord!" ' For I have spoken the word," declares the LORD.

6 Then Jeremiah the prophet spoke [a]all these words to Zedekiah king of Judah in Jerusalem

7 when the army of the king of Babylon was fighting against Jerusalem and against all the remaining cities of Judah, *that is,* [a]Lachish and [b]Azekah, for they *alone* remained as [c]fortified cities among the cities of Judah.

8 The word which came to Jeremiah from the LORD after King Zedekiah had [a]made a covenant with all the people who were in Jerusalem to [b]proclaim [1]release to them:

9 that each man should set free his male servant and each man his female servant, a [a]Hebrew man or a Hebrew woman; so that [b]no one should keep them, a Jew his brother, in bondage.

10 And all the [a]officials and all the people obeyed who had entered into the covenant that each man should set free his male servant and each man his female servant, so that no one should keep them any longer in bondage; they obeyed, and set *them free.*

11 But afterward they turned around and took back the male servants and the female servants whom they had set free, and brought them into subjection for male servants and for female servants.

5 [a]2 Chr 16:14; 21:19 [b]Jer 22:18
6 [a]1 Sam 3:18; 15:16-24
7 [a]Josh 10:3, 5; 2 Kin 14:19; 18:14; Is 36:2 [b]Josh 10:10; 2 Chr 11:9 [c]2 Chr 11:5-10
8 [1]Or *liberty* [a]2 Kin 11:17; 23:2, 3 [b]Ex 21:2; Lev 25:10, 39-46; Neh 5:1-13; Is 58:6; Jer 34:14, 17
9 [a]Gen 14:13; Ex 2:6 [b]Lev 25:39
10 [a]Jer 26:10, 16
13 [a]Ex 24:3, 7, 8; Deut 5:2, 3, 27; Jer 31:32 [b]Ex 20:2
14 [1]Or *has sold himself* [a]Ex 21:2; Deut 15:12; 1 Kin 9:22 [b]1 Sam 8:7, 8; 2 Kin 17:13, 14
15 [1]Or *liberty* [a]Jer 34:8 [b]2 Kin 23:3; Neh 10:29 [c]Jer 7:10f; 32:34
16 [1]Lit *caused them to return* [a]1 Sam 15:11; Jer 34:11; Ezek 3:20; 18:24 [b]Ex 20:7; Lev 19:12
17 [1]Or *liberty* [a]Lev 26:34, 35; Esth 7:10; Dan 6:24; Matt 7:2 [b]Jer 32:24; 38:2 [c]Deut 28:25; Jer 29:18
18 [a]Deut 17:2; Hos 6:7; 8:1; Rom 2:8 [b]Gen 15:10
19 [a]Jer 34:10; Ezek 22:27; Zeph 3:3, 4

12 Then the word of the LORD came to Jeremiah from the LORD, saying,

13 "Thus says the LORD God of Israel, 'I [a]made a covenant with your forefathers in the day that I [b]brought them out of the land of Egypt, from the house of bondage, saying,

14 "[a]At the end of seven years each of you shall set free his Hebrew brother who [1]has been sold to you and has served you six years, you shall send him out free from you; but your forefathers [b]did not obey Me or incline their ear to Me.

15 "Although recently you *had* turned and [a]done what is right in My sight, each man proclaiming [1]release to his neighbor, and you had [b]made a covenant before Me [c]in the house which is called by My name.

16 "Yet you [a]turned and [b]profaned My name, and each man [1]took back his male servant and each man his female servant whom you had set free according to their desire, and you brought them into subjection to be your male servants and female servants." '

17 "Therefore thus says the LORD, 'You have not obeyed Me in proclaiming [1]release each man to his brother and each man to his neighbor. Behold, I am [a]proclaiming a [1]release to you,' declares the LORD, 'to the [b]sword, to the pestilence and to the famine; and I will make you a [c]terror to all the kingdoms of the earth.

18 'I will give the men who have [a]transgressed My covenant, who have not fulfilled the words of the covenant which they made before Me, *when* they [b]cut the calf in two and passed between its parts—

19 the [a]officials of Judah and the officials of Jerusalem, the court officers and the

34:4 *not die by the sword.* See 32:5; 38:17,20; 52:11; Ezek 17:16.
34:5 *spices were burned for . . . the former kings.* Not cremation (see 2 Chr 16:14; 21:19; see also note on Amos 6:10). *Alas, lord!* Words of mourning at the death of a king (see 22:18; cf. 1 Kin 13:30).
34:7 *Lachish and Azekah.* Solomon's son Rehoboam had fortified them (see 2 Chr 11:5,9), but Lachish was later besieged (701 B.C.) during Hezekiah's reign by the Assyrian king Sennacherib (see 2 Chr 32:9). A contemporary relief depicting Sennacherib's conquest states that he "sat on a throne and passed in review the plunder taken from Lachish." In 1935, 18 ostraca (broken pottery fragments used as writing material) were discovered at Lachish, nearly all of them in the ruins of the latest occupation level (588 B.C.) of the Israelite gate-tower. Ostracon 4, written to the commander at Lachish shortly after the events described here, ends as follows: "We are watching for the fire-signals of Lachish . . . for we cannot see Azekah." See note on 6:1.
34:8–22 Contemporary with the events of 37:4–12 (see note on vv. 21–22).
34:8 *proclaim release.* See Lev 25:10 and note. *release to them.* In accordance with the general provisions of the law of Moses (see Ex 21:2–11 and notes; Lev 25:39–55; Deut 15:12–18).
34:9 *Hebrew.* See Ex 21:2; see also note on Gen 14:13. *no one should keep . . . a Jew . . . in bondage.* See Lev 25:39,42.
34:10 *they . . . set them free.* To gain God's blessing, and/or in the hope that the freed slaves would be more willing to help defend Jerusalem.
34:11 *afterward.* When the Babylonian siege was temporarily lifted due to Egyptian intervention (see vv. 21–22; 37:5,11). *took back the . . . servants . . . they had set free.* In violation of Deut 15:12. *brought them into subjection.* Cf. 2 Chr 28:10.
34:13 *house of bondage.* Lit. "house of slaves" (see Ex 13:3,14; 20:2; Deut 5:6; 6:12; 8:14; 13:5; Josh 24:17; Judg 6:8). The Israelites were to free their slaves because God had earlier freed the Israelites (see Deut 15:15).
34:14 *end of seven years . . . send him out free.* A loose quotation of Deut 15:12.
34:15–16 *you had turned . . . Yet you turned.* The Hebrew for the two phrases is identical, providing an ironic play on words (see note on v. 18).
34:16 *you . . . profaned My name.* By breaking the Lord's covenant. Zedekiah was a man whose word could not be trusted (see Ezek 17:15,18). *free according to their desire.* See Deut 21:14.
34:17 *sword . . . pestilence . . . famine.* See note on 14:12. *a terror to all the kingdoms of the earth.* See 15:4 and note.
34:18 *transgressed . . . passed.* The Hebrew root underlying both words is the same, again providing an ironic play on words (see note on vv. 15–16). *made . . . cut.* The Hebrew for the two words is identical. In ancient times, making a covenant involved a self-maledictory oath ("May thus and so be done to me if I do not keep this covenant"), which was often symbolized by cutting an animal in two and walking between the two halves (see Gen 15:18 and note). *between its parts.* See note on Gen 15:17.

priests and all the people of the land who
passed between the parts of the calf—
20 I will give them into the hand of their
enemies and into the hand of those who
[a]seek their life. And their [b]dead bodies will
be food for the birds of the sky and the
beasts of the earth.
21 '[a]Zedekiah king of Judah and his officials I will give into the hand of their enemies
and into the hand of those who seek their
life, and into the hand of the army of the king
of Babylon which has [b]gone away from you.
22 'Behold, I am going to command,'
declares the LORD, 'and I will bring them
back to this city; and they will fight against it
and [a]take it and burn it with fire; and I will
make the cities of Judah a [b]desolation [c]with-
out inhabitant.' "

The Rechabites' Obedience

35 The word which came to Jeremiah
from the LORD in the days of [a]Jehoia-
kim the son of Josiah, king of Judah, saying,
2 "Go to the house of the [a]Rechabites and
speak to them, and bring them into the
house of the LORD, into one of the [b]cham-
bers, and give them wine to drink."
3 Then I took Jaazaniah the son of Jeremiah, son of Habazziniah, and his brothers
and all his sons and the whole house of the
Rechabites,
4 and I brought them into the house of
the LORD, into the chamber of the sons of
Hanan the son of Igdaliah, the [a]man of God,
which was near the chamber of the officials,
which was above the chamber of Maaseiah
the son of Shallum, [b]the doorkeeper.

20 [a]Jer 11:21; 21:7; 22:25 [b]Deut 28:26; 1 Sam 17:44, 46; 1 Kin 14:11; 16:4; Ps 79:2; Jer 7:33; 16:4; 19:7 **21** [a]2 Kin 25:18-21; Jer 32:3, 4; 39:6; 52:10, 24-27; Ezek 17:16 [b]Jer 37:5-11 **22** [a]Jer 34:2; 39:1, 2, 8; 52:7, 13 [b]Jer 4:7; 9:11 [c]Jer 33:10; 44:22 **35:1** [a]2 Kin 23:34-36; 24:1; 2 Chr 36:5-7; Jer 1:3; 27:20; Dan 1:1 **2** [a]2 Kin 10:15; 1 Chr 2:55 [b]1 Kin 6:5, 8; 1 Chr 9:26, 33 **4** [a]Deut 33:1; Josh 14:6; 1 Kin 12:22; 2 Kin 1:9-13 [b]1 Chr 9:18f

5 [1]Lit *sons* [a]Amos 2:12 **6** [a]2 Kin 10:15, 23 [b]1 Chr 2:55 [c]Lev 10:9; Num 6:2-4; Judg 13:7, 14; Luke 1:15 **7** [a]Gen 25:27; Heb 11:9 [b]Ex 20:12; Eph 6:2, 3 [c]Gen 36:7 **8** [a]Prov 1:8, 9; 4:1, 2, 10; 6:20; Eph 6:1; Col 3:20 **9** [a]Ps 37:16; Jer 35:7; 1 Tim 6:6 **10** [a]Jer 35:7 [b]Jer 35:6 **11** [a]2 Kin 24:1, 2; Dan 1:1, 2 [b]Jer 4:5-7; 8:14 **13** [a]Is 28:9-12; Jer 5:3; 6:8-10; 32:33

5 Then I set before the [1]men of the house
of the Rechabites pitchers full of wine and
cups; and I said to them, "[a]Drink wine!"
6 But they said, "We will not drink wine,
for [a]Jonadab the son of [b]Rechab, our father,
commanded us, saying, 'You shall [c]not drink
wine, you or your sons, forever.
7 'You shall not build a house, and you
shall not sow seed and you shall not plant a
vineyard or own one; but in [a]tents you shall
dwell all your days, that you may live [b]many
days in the land where you [c]sojourn.'
8 "We have [a]obeyed the voice of Jonadab
the son of Rechab, our father, in all that he
commanded us, not to drink wine all our days,
we, our wives, our sons or our daughters,
9 nor to build ourselves houses to dwell
in; and we [a]do not have vineyard or field or
seed.
10 "We have only [a]dwelt in tents, and have
obeyed and have done according to all that
[b]Jonadab our father commanded us.
11 "But when [a]Nebuchadnezzar king of
Babylon came up against the land, we said,
'Come and let us [b]go to Jerusalem before the
army of the Chaldeans and before the army
of the Arameans.' So we have dwelt in Jerusalem."

Judah Rebuked

12 Then the word of the LORD came to Jeremiah, saying,
13 "Thus says the LORD of hosts, the God of
Israel, 'Go and say to the men of Judah and
the inhabitants of Jerusalem, "[a]Will you not
receive instruction by listening to My
words?" declares the LORD.

34:20 *food for the birds . . . of the earth.* See 7:33 and note.
34:21–22 Because of the arrival of the Egyptians on the scene, the Babylonians in 588 B.C. temporarily lifted the siege of Jerusalem (see note on v. 11).
34:21 *gone away from you.* See the hope expressed in 21:2.
34:22 *I will bring them back.* See 37:8.
35:1–19 The family of the Recabites, who obeyed their forefather's command, are an example and rebuke to the people of Judah, who have disobeyed the Lord (see v. 16). The mention of "the army of the Chaldeans and . . . Arameans" (v. 11) dates the chapter to no earlier than the eighth year of King Jehoiakim, who began his reign in 609 B.C., whose capital city of Jerusalem was besieged in 605 (see Dan 1:1 and note) by Nebuchadnezzar, and who rebelled against Nebuchadnezzar three or four years later—an unwise act that led to raids on his territory by Babylonians, Arameans and others (see 2 Kin 24:1–2). (The raids are perhaps reflected in 12:7–13.)
35:1 *in the days of Jehoiakim.* Chs. 35–36 (see 36:1) are a flashback to the reign of Jehoiakim (609–598 B.C.; see Introduction: Outline).
35:2 *Rechabites.* A nomadic tribal group related to the Kenites (see 1 Chr 2:55), some of whom lived among or near the Israelites (see Judg 1:16; 4:11; 1 Sam 27:10) and were on friendly terms with them (see 1 Sam 15:6; 30:26,29). *the house of the LORD . . . the chambers.* Used for storage and/or as living quarters (see 1 Kin 6:5; 1 Chr 28:12; 2 Chr 31:11; Neh 13:4–5).
35:3 *Jaazaniah.* Means "The LORD hears." It was a common name in Jeremiah's time (see 40:8; Ezek 8:11; 11:1) and appears on a stamp seal (discovered at Tell en-Nasbeh north of Jerusalem and dating c. 600 B.C.) as well as on one of the Lachish ostraca (see note on 34:7). *Jeremiah.* Not the prophet.
35:4 *sons.* Perhaps here in the sense of "disciples" (see Amos 7:14 and note). *man of God.* A synonym for "prophet" (see 1 Kin 12:22; see also note on 1 Sam 9:9), emphasizing his relationship to the One who has called him. *Maaseiah.* Perhaps the man of the same name mentioned in 21:1; 29:25; 37:3. *doorkeeper.* One of three supervisors (see 52:24) over those who guarded the entrances to the temple (see 2 Kin 12:9).
35:5 *pitchers.* Large vessels, from which smaller cups would be filled.
35:6 *We will not drink wine.* A permanent vow taken by the Recabites; cf. the Nazirites' temporary vow (see Num 6:2–3,20; Judg 13:4–7). Malkijah son of Recab may have been a later renegade exception to the Recabite vow, since he was "official of the district of Beth-haccherem" (Neh 3:14), which means "house of the vineyard." *Jonadab.* Spelled "Jehonadab" in 2 Kin 10:15,23. Nearly 250 years before the days of Jeremiah, he helped King Jehu destroy Baal worship (at least temporarily) in the northern kingdom.
35:7 *in tents you shall dwell.* Except during times of national emergency (see v. 11). *you may live many days in the land.* An echo of Ex 20:12, where honoring one's parents is commanded.
35:8 *We have obeyed . . . Jonadab.* Contrast Judah's disobedience toward God (see v. 16).
35:11 See note on vv. 1–19.
35:13 *receive instruction.* The Hebrew underlying this phrase

14 "The [a]words of Jonadab the son of
Rechab, which he commanded his sons not
to drink wine, are observed. So they do not
drink *wine* to this day, for they have obeyed
their father's command. But I have spoken
to you [1b]again and again; yet you have [c]not
listened to Me.
15 "Also I have sent to you all My [a]servants
the prophets, sending *them* [1]again and again,
saying: '[b]Turn now every man from his evil
way and amend your deeds, and [c]do not go
after other gods to worship them. Then you
will [d]dwell in the land which I have given to
you and to your forefathers; but you have
not [e]inclined your ear or listened to Me.
16 'Indeed, the sons of Jonadab the son of
Rechab have [a]observed the command of
their father which he commanded them, but
this people has not listened to Me.' " '
17 "Therefore thus says the LORD, the God
of hosts, the God of Israel, 'Behold, [a]I am
bringing on Judah and on all the inhabitants
of Jerusalem all the disaster that I have pronounced against them; because I [b]spoke to
them but they did not listen, and I have
called them but they did not answer.' "
18 Then Jeremiah said to the house of the
Rechabites, "Thus says the LORD of hosts, the
God of Israel, 'Because you have [a]obeyed
the command of Jonadab your father, kept
all his commands and done according to all
that he commanded you;
19 therefore thus says the LORD of hosts,
the God of Israel, "Jonadab the son of
Rechab [a]shall not lack a man to [b]stand
before Me [1]always." ' "

Jeremiah's Scroll Read in the Temple

36 In the [a]fourth year of Jehoiakim the
son of Josiah, king of Judah, this word
came to Jeremiah from the LORD, saying,
2 "Take a [1a]scroll and write on it all the
[b]words which I have spoken to you concerning [c]Israel and concerning Judah, and concerning all the [d]nations, from the [e]day I *first*
spoke to you, from the days of Josiah, even
to this day.
3 "[a]Perhaps the house of Judah will hear
all the calamity which I plan to bring on
them, in order that every man will [b]turn
from his evil way; then I will [c]forgive their
iniquity and their sin."
4 Then Jeremiah called [a]Baruch the son
of Neriah, and Baruch wrote on a [1b]scroll [2]at
the dictation of Jeremiah all the words of the
LORD which He had spoken to him.
5 Jeremiah commanded Baruch, saying,
"I am [1a]restricted; I cannot go into the house
of the LORD.
6 "So you go and [a]read from the scroll
which you have [b]written [1]at my dictation the
words of the LORD [2]to the people in the
LORD's house on a [c]fast day. And also you
shall read them [2]to all *the people of* Judah
who come from their cities.
7 "[a]Perhaps their supplication will [1]come
before the LORD, and everyone will turn from
his evil way, for [b]great is the anger and the
wrath that the LORD has pronounced against
this people."
8 Baruch the son of Neriah did according
to all that Jeremiah the prophet commanded
him, [a]reading from the book the words of
the LORD in the LORD's house.
9 Now in the [a]fifth year of Jehoiakim the
son of Josiah, king of Judah, in the [b]ninth
month, all the people in Jerusalem and all
the people who [c]came from the cities of
Judah to Jerusalem proclaimed a [d]fast before
the LORD.
10 Then Baruch read from the book the
words of Jeremiah in the house of the LORD
in the [a]chamber of [b]Gemariah the son of

14 [1]Lit *rising early and speaking* [a]Jer 35:6-10 [b]2 Chr 36:15; Jer 7:13, 25; 11:7; 25:3, 4 [c]Is 30:9; 50:2 **15** [1]Lit *rising early and speaking* [a]Jer 7:25; 25:4; 26:5; 29:19; 32:33 [b]Is 1:16, 17; Jer 4:1; 18:11; 25:5f; Ezek 18:30-32; Acts 26:20 [c]Deut 6:14; Jer 7:6; 13:10; 25:6 [d]Jer 7:7; 25:5, 6 [e]Jer 7:24, 26; 11:8; 17:23; 34:14 **16** [a]Jer 35:14; Mal 1:6 **17** [a]Josh 23:15; Jer 19:3, 15; 21:4-10; Mic 3:12 [b]Prov 1:24, 25; Is 65:12; 66:4; Jer 7:13, 26, 27; 26:5; Luke 13:34, 35; Rom 10:21 **18** [a]Ex 20:12; Eph 6:1-3 **19** [1]Lit *all the days* [a]1 Chr 2:55; Jer 33:17 [b]Jer 15:19; Luke 21:36 **36:1** [a]2 Kin 24:1; 2 Chr 36:5-7; Jer 25:1, 3; 45:1; 46:2; Dan 1:1 **2** [1]Lit *scroll of a book* [a]Ex 17:14; Is 8:1; Jer 36:6, 23, 28; Zech 5:1, 2 [b]Jer 1:9, 10; 30:2; Hab 2:2 [c]Jer 3:3-10; 23:13, 14; 32:30-32 [d]Jer 1:5, 10; 25:9-29; chs 47-51 [e]Jer 1:2, 3; 25:3

3 [a]Jer 26:3; 36:7; Ezek 12:3 [b]Deut 30:2, 8; 1 Sam 7:3; Is 55:7; Jer 18:8, 11; 35:15; Jon 3:8 [c]Jon 3:10; Mark 4:12; Acts 3:19 **4** [1]Lit *scroll of a book* [2]Lit *from the mouth of* [a]Jer 32:12; 36:18; 43:3; 45:1 [b]Jer 36:14; Ezek 2:9 **5** [1]Lit *shut up* [a]Jer 32:2; 33:1; 2 Cor 11:23 **6** [1]Lit *from my mouth* [2]Lit *in the ears of,* and so throughout this context [a]Jer 36:8 [b]Jer 36:4 [c]Jer 36:9; Zech 8:19 **7** [1]Lit *fall* [a]1 Kin 8:33; 2 Chr 33:12, 13; Jer 26:3; 36:3 [b]Deut 28:15; 31:16, 17; 2 Kin 22:13, 17; Jer 4:4; 21:5; Lam 4:11 **8** [a]Jer 1:17; 36:6 **9** [a]Jer 36:1 [b]Jer 36:22 [c]Jer 36:6 [d]Judg 20:26; 1 Sam 7:6; 2 Chr 20:3; Esth 4:16; Joel 1:14; 2:15; Jon 3:5 **10** [a]Jer 35:4 [b]Jer 36:11, 25

---

is translated "accepted . . . chastening" in 2:30 and "accept correction" 7:28 (see 5:3; 17:23 and note).

35:14–15 *again and again.* See note on 7:13.

35:15 See 25:4–5 and notes.

35:17 See 11:11.

35:19 *not lack a man to stand before Me.* See 33:18. Various traditions in the Jewish Mishnah claim that the Recabites were later given special duties to perform in connection with the Jerusalem temple built after the return from Babylonian exile.

36:1–38:28 Three chapters united by the common theme of Jeremiah's suffering and persecution.

36:1–32 An account of King Jehoiakim's attempt to destroy Jeremiah's written prophecies.

36:1 *fourth year of Jehoiakim.* 605 B.C.—a critical year in Judah's history (see notes on 25:1; 46:2).

36:2 *scroll.* See notes on 30:2; Ex 17:14. *write on it.* To preserve Jeremiah's messages for future generations. *all the words which I have spoken to you.* This "earliest edition" of Jeremiah's prophecies may have included all or most of chs. 1–26; 46–51. *first spoke to you, from the days of Josiah.* See note on 1:2.

36:3 *Perhaps . . . then.* If the people repent, the Lord will relent (see 18:7–10 and note; 26:3).

36:4 *Baruch.* See note on 32:12.

36:5 *I am restricted.* Perhaps because of his unpopular temple message(s) (see 7:2–15; 26:2–6), or perhaps because of the events recorded in 19:1–20:6.

36:6 *fast day.* Proclaimed because of a national emergency (cf. Joel 2:15), perhaps in this case the Babylonian attack of 605 B.C. (see Dan 1:1 and note).

36:7 See v. 3 and note.

36:8 If the book were in chronological order, ch. 45 would appear after this verse (see Introduction: Outline).

36:9 *fifth year . . . in the ninth month.* December, 604 B.C., during a time of cold weather (see v. 22).

36:10 Cf. 2 Kin 23:2. *chamber.* See note on 35:2. *Gemariah.* A common name in Jeremiah's time (see 29:3), found on one of the Lachish ostraca (see note on 34:7) as well as in at least two of the Elephantine papyri (see note on 32:11) a century later.

Shaphan the [c]scribe, in the upper court, at the [d]entry of the New Gate of the LORD's house, to all the people.

11 Now when [a]Micaiah the son of Gemariah, the son of Shaphan, had heard all the words of the LORD from the book,

12 he went down to the king's house, into the scribe's chamber. And behold, all the officials were sitting there—[a]Elishama the scribe, and [b]Delaiah the son of Shemaiah, and [c]Elnathan the son of Achbor, and Gemariah the son of Shaphan, and Zedekiah the son of Hananiah, and all the *other* officials.

13 Micaiah [a]declared to them all the words that he had heard when Baruch read from the book to the people.

14 Then all the officials sent [a]Jehudi the son of Nethaniah, the son of Shelemiah, the son of Cushi, to Baruch, saying, "Take in your hand the scroll from which you have read to the people and come." So Baruch the son of Neriah [b]took the scroll in his hand and went to them.

15 They said to him, "Sit down, please, and read it to us." So Baruch [a]read it to them.

16 When they had heard all the words, they turned in [a]fear one to another and said to Baruch, "We will surely [b]report all these words to the king."

17 And they asked Baruch, saying, "Tell us, please, [a]how did you write all these words? *Was it* [1]at his dictation?"

18 Then Baruch said to them, "He [a]dictated all these words to me, and I wrote them with ink on the book."

19 Then the officials said to Baruch, "Go, [a]hide yourself, you and Jeremiah, and do not let anyone know where you are."

The Scroll Is Burned

20 So they went to the [a]king in the court, but they had deposited the scroll in the chamber of [a]Elishama the scribe, and they reported all the words to the king.

21 Then the king sent Jehudi to get the scroll, and he took it out of the chamber of Elishama the scribe. And Jehudi [a]read it to the king as well as to all the officials who stood beside the king.

22 Now the king was sitting in the [a]winter house in the [b]ninth month, with *a fire* burning in the brazier before him.

23 When Jehudi had read three or four columns, *the king* cut it with a scribe's knife and [a]threw *it* into the fire that was in the brazier, until all the scroll was consumed in the fire that was in the brazier.

24 Yet the king and all his servants who heard all these words were [a]not afraid, nor did they [b]rend their garments.

25 Even though Elnathan and Delaiah and Gemariah [a]pleaded with the king not to burn the scroll, he would not listen to them.

26 And the king commanded Jerahmeel the king's son, Seraiah the son of Azriel, and Shelemiah the son of Abdeel to [a]seize Baruch the scribe and Jeremiah the prophet, but the [b]LORD hid them.

The Scroll Is Replaced

27 Then the word of the LORD came to Jeremiah after the king had [a]burned the scroll and the words which [b]Baruch had written at the dictation of Jeremiah, saying,

28 "[a]Take again another scroll and write on it all the former words that were [b]on the first scroll which Jehoiakim the king of Judah burned.

29 "And concerning Jehoiakim king of Judah you shall say, 'Thus says the LORD, "You have [a]burned this scroll, saying, '[b]Why have you written on it [1]that the [c]king of Babylon will certainly come and destroy this land, and will make man and beast to cease from it?'"

30 'Therefore thus says the LORD concerning Jehoiakim king of Judah, "He shall have [a]no one to sit on the throne of David, and his [b]dead body shall be cast out to the heat of the day and the frost of the night.

31 "I will also [a]punish him and his [1]descendants and his servants for their iniq-

10 [c]2 Sam 8:17; Jer 52:25 [d]Jer 26:10
11 [a]Jer 36:13
12 [a]Jer 36:20 [b]Jer 36:25 [c]Jer 26:22
13 [a]2 Kin 22:10
14 [a]Jer 36:21 [b]Jer 36:2; Ezek 2:7-10
15 [a]Jer 36:21
16 [a]Jer 36:24; Acts 24:25 [b]Jer 13:18; Amos 7:10, 11
17 [1]Lit *from his mouth,* and so throughout this context [a]John 9:10, 15, 26
18 [a]Jer 36:4
19 [a]1 Kin 17:3; 18:4, 10; Jer 26:20-24; 36:26
20 [a]Jer 36:12
21 [a]2 Kin 22:10; 2 Chr 34:18; Ezek 2:4, 5
22 [a]Judg 3:20; Amos 3:15 [b]Jer 36:9
23 [a]1 Kin 22:8, 27; Prov 1:30; Is 5:18, 19; 28:14, 22; Jer 36:29
24 [a]Ps 36:1; 64:5; Jer 36:16 [b]Gen 37:29, 34; 2 Sam 1:11; 1 Kin 21:27; 2 Kin 19:1, 2; 22:11, 19; Is 36:22; 37:1; Jon 3:6
25 [a]Gen 37:22, 26, 27; Acts 5:34-39
26 [a]1 Kin 19:1-3, 10, 14; Matt 23:34, 37 [b]Ps 91:1
27 [a]Jer 36:23 [b]Jer 36:4, 18
28 [a]Zech 1:5, 6 [b]Jer 36:4, 23
29 [1]Lit *saying* [a]Deut 29:19; Job 15:24, 25; Is 45:9 [b]Is 29:21; 30:10; Jer 26:9; 32:3 [c]Jer 25:9-11
30 [a]2 Kin 24:12-15; Jer 22:30 [b]Jer 22:19
31 [1]Lit *seed* [a]Jer 23:34

Shaphan. Secretary of state under King Josiah (see 2 Kin 22:3; see also notes on 26:24; 29:3). *entry of the New Gate.* See 26:10 and note.
36:12 *Elnathan the son of Achbor.* See note on 26:22.
36:18 *ink.* Mentioned only here in the OT (but see also 2 Cor 3:3; 2 John 12; 3 John 13). In ancient times, ink was made from soot or lampblack mixed with gum arabic, oil, or a metallic substance (as in the case of the Lachish ostraca; see note on 34:7).
36:19 The officials were understandably concerned about the safety of Jeremiah and Baruch (cf. 26:20–23).
36:20 *deposited.* For safekeeping (see Is 10:28).
36:22 *winter house.* See Amos 3:15; here probably a large room in the king's palace. *ninth month.* See note on v. 9. *brazier.* A depression or container in the middle of the floor where coals were kept burning to warm the room.
36:23 Contrast King Josiah's desire to know the word of God and obey it (see 2 Kin 22:11–23:3; 23:21–24). *columns.* Lit. "doors," so called because of their rectangular shape. *cut.* Lit. "tore." Instead of tearing his clothes (see note on v. 24), the king tore the prophet's scroll.
36:24 *servants . . . were not afraid.* See v. 31. Contrast the response of the "officials" (v. 12; see vv. 16,25). *nor did they rend their garments.* Contrast the response of Jehoiakim's father Josiah (see 2 Kin 22:11; cf. 1 Kin 21:27).
36:26 *the king's son.* Since Jehoiakim was only about 30 years old (see 2 Kin 23:36), the phrase probably is not to be understood literally but means "member of the royal court" (as also in 38:6; 1 Kin 22:26; Zeph 1:8).
36:30 *Jehoiakim . . . shall have no one to sit on the throne.* His son Jehoiachin (see 2 Kin 24:6) "ruled" only 3 months (see 2 Kin 24:8) and then was captured and carried off to exile in Babylonia (see 2 Kin 24:15), where he eventually died (see 52:33–34). *his dead body shall be cast out.* As punishment for the fact that he "threw" (v. 23) the prophet's scroll into the fire (see 22:18–19 and notes).
36:31 See 11:11; 19:15; 35:17. *servants.* See note on v. 24.

uity, and I will [b]bring on them and the
inhabitants of Jerusalem and the men of
Judah all the calamity that I have declared to
them—but they did not listen."' "

32 Then Jeremiah took another scroll and
gave it to Baruch the son of Neriah, the
scribe, and he [a]wrote on it at the dictation of
Jeremiah all the words of the book which
Jehoiakim king of Judah had burned in the
fire; and many [1]similar words were added to
them.

Jeremiah Warns against Trust in Pharaoh

37 Now [a]Zedekiah the son of Josiah
whom Nebuchadnezzar king of Babylon had [b]made king in the land of Judah,
reigned as king in place of [c]Coniah the son of
Jehoiakim.

2 But [a]neither he nor his servants nor the
people of the land listened to the words of
the LORD which He spoke through Jeremiah
the prophet.

3 Yet [a]King Zedekiah sent Jehucal the
son of Shelemiah, and [b]Zephaniah the son
of Maaseiah, the priest, to Jeremiah the
prophet, saying, "[c]Please pray to the LORD
our God on our behalf."

4 Now Jeremiah was *still* coming in and
going out among the people, for they had not
yet [a]put him in the prison.

5 Meanwhile, [a]Pharaoh's army had set
out from Egypt; and when the Chaldeans
who had been besieging Jerusalem heard the
report about them, they [b]lifted the *siege* from
Jerusalem.

6 Then the word of the LORD came to Jeremiah the prophet, saying,

7 "Thus says the LORD God of Israel,
'[a]Thus you are to say to the king of Judah,
who sent you to Me to inquire of Me:
"Behold, [b]Pharaoh's army which has come
out for your assistance is going to return to
its own land of Egypt.

8 "The Chaldeans will also [a]return and
fight against this city, and they will capture it
and burn it with fire." '

9 "Thus says the LORD, 'Do not [a]deceive
yourselves, saying, "The Chaldeans will
surely go away from us," for they will not go.

10 'For [a]even if you had defeated the entire
army of Chaldeans who were fighting against
you, and there were *only* wounded men left
among them, each man in his tent, they
would rise up and [b]burn this city with fire.' "

Jeremiah Imprisoned

11 Now it happened when the army of the
Chaldeans had lifted *the siege* from Jerusalem because of Pharaoh's army,

12 that Jeremiah went out from Jerusalem
to go to the land of Benjamin in order to
[a]take [1]possession of *some* property there
among the people.

13 While he was at the [a]Gate of Benjamin,
a captain of the guard whose name was Irijah, the son of Shelemiah the son of Hananiah was there; and he [b]arrested Jeremiah the
prophet, saying, "You are [1]going over to the
Chaldeans!"

14 But Jeremiah said, "[a]A lie! I am not
[1]going over to the Chaldeans"; yet he would
not listen to him. So Irijah arrested Jeremiah
and brought him to the officials.

15 Then the officials were [a]angry at Jeremiah and beat him, and they [b]put him in jail
in the house of Jonathan the scribe, which
they had made into the prison.

16 For Jeremiah had come into the [1a]dungeon, that is, the vaulted cell; and Jeremiah
stayed there many days.

17 Now King Zedekiah sent and took him
out; and in his palace the king [a]secretly
asked him and said, "Is there a [b]word from

31 [b]Deut 28:15; Prov 29:1; Jer 19:15; 35:17
32 [1]Lit *like those* [a]Ex 4:15, 16; 34:1; Jer 36:4, 18, 23
37:1 [a]2 Kin 24:17; 1 Chr 3:15; 2 Chr 36:10 [b]Ezek 17:12-21 [c]2 Kin 24:12; 1 Chr 3:16; 2 Chr 36:9, 10; Jer 22:24, 28; 24:1; 52:31
2 [a]2 Kin 24:19, 20; 2 Chr 36:12-16; Prov 29:12
3 [a]Jer 21:1, 2 [b]Jer 29:25; 52:24 [c]1 Kin 13:6; Jer 2:27; 15:11; 21:1, 2; 42:1-4, 20; Acts 8:24
4 [a]Jer 32:2, 3; 37:15
5 [a]2 Kin 24:7; Jer 37:7; Ezek 17:15 [b]Jer 37:11
7 [a]2 Kin 22:18; Jer 21:1, 2; 37:3 [b]Is 30:1-3; 31:1-3; Jer 2:18, 36; Lam 4:17; Ezek 17:17
8 [a]Jer 34:22; 38:23; 39:2-8
9 [a]Jer 29:8; Obad 3; Matt 24:4, 5; Eph 5:6
10 [a]Lev 26:36-38; Is 30:17; Jer 21:4, 5 [b]Jer 37:8
12 [1]Or *part in a dividing* [a]Jer 32:8
13 [1]Lit *falling* [a]Jer 38:7; Zech 14:10 [b]Jer 18:18; 20:10; Luke 23:2; Acts 6:11; 24:5-9, 13
14 [1]Lit *falling* [a]Ps 27:12; 52:1, 2; Jer 40:4-6; Matt 5:11, 12
15 [a]Jer 18:23; 20:1-3; 26:16; Matt 21:35 [b]Gen 39:20; 2 Chr 16:10; 18:26; Jer 38:26; Acts 5:18
16 [1]Lit *house of the cistern-pit* [a]Jer 38:6
17 [a]1 Kin 14:1-4; Jer 38:5, 14-16, 24-27 [b]1 Kin 22:15, 16; 2 Kin 3:11, 12; Jer 15:11; 21:1, 2; 37:3

36:32 *another scroll.* Cf. similarly Ex 34:1.
37:1–38:28 During the last two years of Zedekiah's reign (588–586 B.C.), Jeremiah is imprisoned by the authorities (see 20:2 and note).
37:1 See 2 Kin 24:15,17–18. *Zedekiah.* Means "The LORD is my righteousness." See Introduction: Background. *reigned . . . in place of Coniah.* In 597 B.C. This fulfills the prophecy concerning Jehoiakim in 36:30.
37:3 *Zedekiah sent . . . to Jeremiah.* See 21:1. *Jehucal the son of Shelemiah.* Later became Jeremiah's enemy (see 38:1,4). *Zephaniah the son of Maaseiah, the priest.* "Priest" here refers to Zephaniah (see 21:1 and note). *pray . . . on our behalf.* See 21:2 and note; perhaps to ask the Lord to make the temporary withdrawal of the Babylonians in 588 B.C. (see note on 34:21–22) permanent.
37:5 *Pharaoh's army.* The troops of Hophra (see 44:30), called Apries by Greek historians. *set out from Egypt.* Probably to help Zedekiah at his request; Lachish ostracon 3 (see note on 34:7) mentions a visit to Egypt made by the commander of Judah's army. All such ploys by Zedekiah would fail, however (see Ezek 17:15,17). *Chaldeans . . . lifted the siege.* To deal with the Egyptian threat (see 34:21 and note).
37:7 *Pharaoh's army . . . return to . . . Egypt.* Hophra would soon be defeated by Nebuchadnezzar (see note on Ezek 30:21).
37:10 *wounded.* Lit. "pierced through," "mortally wounded." Though seriously handicapped, the Babylonians would still destroy Jerusalem.
37:12 *land of Benjamin.* Where Jeremiah's hometown, Anathoth, was located (see note on 1:1). *take possession of some property.* See 1 Sam 30:24. While there was a brief lull in the Babylonian invasion, Jeremiah wanted to settle matters of estate with the other members of his family.
37:13 *Gate of Benjamin.* See 38:7; see also note on Zech 14:10. *You are going over to the Chaldeans.* Irijah's fear was understandable, since Jeremiah recommended surrendering to the Babylonians (see 21:9; 38:2) and since many Judahites in fact defected (see 38:19; 39:9; 52:15).
37:14 *A lie!* See 2 Kin 9:12).
37:15 *beat him.* See 20:2 and note. *house of Jonathan.* Jeremiah would later look back on this prison as a place of great danger for him (see v. 20; 38:26).
37:16 *dungeon.* Lit. "house of the cistern," probably underground (see Ex 12:29).
37:17 *Zedekiah . . . secretly asked him.* Not wanting to do so in

the LORD?" And Jeremiah said, "There is!"
Then he said, "You will be [c]given into the
hand of the king of Babylon!"
18 Moreover Jeremiah said to King Zedekiah, "[a]*In* what *way* have I sinned against
you, or against your servants, or against this
people, that you have put me in prison?
19 "[a]Where then are your prophets who
prophesied to you, saying, 'The [b]king of Babylon will not come against you or against
this land'?
20 "But now, please listen, O my lord the
king; please let my [a]petition [1]come before you
and do not make me return to the house of
Jonathan the scribe, that I may not die there."
21 Then King Zedekiah gave commandment, and they committed Jeremiah to the
[a]court of the guardhouse and gave him a loaf
of [b]bread daily from the bakers' street, until
all the bread in the city was [c]gone. So Jeremiah remained in the court of the guardhouse.

Jeremiah Thrown into the Cistern

38 Now Shephatiah the son of Mattan, and
Gedaliah the son of Pashhur, and Jucal
the [a]son of Shelemiah, and [b]Pashhur the son
of Malchijah heard the words that Jeremiah
was speaking to all the people, saying,
2 "Thus says the LORD, 'He who [a]stays in
this city will die by the [b]sword and by
famine and by pestilence, but he who goes
out to the Chaldeans will live and have his
own [c]life as booty and stay alive.'
3 "Thus says the LORD, 'This city will certainly be [a]given into the hand of the army of
the king of Babylon and he will capture it.'"
4 Then the [a]officials said to the king,
"Now let this man be put to death, inasmuch
as he is [1][b]discouraging the men of war who
are left in this city and [2]all the people, by
speaking such words to them; for this man
[c]is not seeking the well-being of this people
but rather their harm."
5 So King Zedekiah said, "Behold, he is
in your [1]hands; for the king [a]can *do* nothing
against you."
6 Then they took Jeremiah and cast him
into the [a]cistern *of* Malchijah the king's son,
which was in the court of the guardhouse;
and they let Jeremiah down with ropes. Now
in the cistern there was no water but only
[b]mud, and Jeremiah sank into the mud.
7 But [a]Ebed-melech the Ethiopian, [1]a
[b]eunuch, while he was in the king's palace,
heard that they had put Jeremiah into the
cistern. Now the king was sitting in the [c]Gate
of Benjamin;
8 and Ebed-melech went out from the
king's palace and spoke to the king, saying,
9 "My lord the king, these men have acted
wickedly in all that they have done to Jeremiah the prophet whom they have cast into
the cistern; and he [1]will die right where he is
because of the famine, for there is [a]no more
bread in the city."
10 Then the king commanded Ebed-
melech the Ethiopian, saying, "Take thirty
men from here [1]under your authority and
bring up Jeremiah the prophet from the cistern before he dies."
11 So Ebed-melech took the men under
his [1]authority and went into the king's
palace to *a place* beneath the storeroom and
took from there worn-out clothes and worn-
out rags and let them down by ropes into the
cistern to Jeremiah.
12 Then Ebed-melech the Ethiopian said to
Jeremiah, "Now put these worn-out clothes
and rags under your armpits under the
ropes"; and Jeremiah did so.

17 [c]Jer 21:7; 24:8; Ezek 12:12, 13; 17:19, 20
18 [a]1 Sam 24:9; 26:18; Dan 6:22; John 10:32; Acts 25:8, 11, 25
19 [a]Deut 32:37, 38; 2 Kin 3:13; Jer 2:28 [b]Jer 27:14; 28:1-4, 10-17
20 [1]Lit *fall* [a]Jer 36:7; 38:26
21 [a]Jer 32:2; 38:13, 28 [b]1 Kin 17:6; Job 5:20; Ps 33:18, 19; Is 33:16 [c]2 Kin 25:3; Jer 38:9; 52:6
38:1 [a]Jer 37:3 [b]Jer 21:1
2 [a]Jer 21:9 [b]Jer 34:17; 42:17 [c]Jer 21:9; 39:18; 45:5
3 [a]Jer 21:10; 32:3-5
4 [1]Lit *weakening the hands of* [2]Lit *the hands of all* [a]Jer 18:23; 26:11, 21; 36:12 [b]Ex 5:4; 1 Kin 18:17, 18; 21:20; Neh 6:9; Amos 7:10; Acts 16:20
4 [c]Jer 29:7
5 [1]Lit *hand* [a]2 Sam 3:39
6 [a]Jer 37:16, 21; Acts 16:24 [b]Ps 40:2; 69:2, 14, 15; Jer 38:22; Zech 9:11
7 [1]Or *an official* [a]Jer 39:16 [b]Jer 29:2; Acts 8:27 [c]Deut 21:19; Job 29:7; Jer 37:13; Amos 5:10
9 [1]M.T. reads *has died* [a]Jer 37:21; 52:6
10 [1]Lit *in your hand*
11 [1]Lit *hand*

the presence of his officials, whom he apparently feared. *You will be given into the hand of the king of Babylon.* See 32:4; 34:3.

37:19 *your prophets.* False prophets (see Deut 18:22).

37:20 *let my petition come before you.* See 36:7.

37:21 *court of the guardhouse.* A less objectionable prison than the dungeon of v. 16 (see note on 32:2). *bakers' street.* Perhaps near the Tower of the Ovens (see note on Neh 3:11). *until all the bread . . . was gone.* The Hebrew word for "bread" is translated "food" in 52:6.

38:1 *Pashhur.* See note on 20:1. *Jucal the son of Shelemiah.* See note on 37:3. *Pashhur the son of Malchijah.* See note on 21:1. *Jeremiah was speaking to all the people.* Though he was confined in the courtyard of the guard (see 37:21), he was allowed to have visitors and to speak freely to them (see 32:8,12).

38:2 Echoes 21:9 (see note there).

38:3 Echoes 32:28 (see 34:2; 37:8).

38:4 *officials.* Those named in v. 1. *discouraging.* See Ezra 4:4; lit. "weakening the hands of," as in a similar situation in Lachish ostracon 6 (see note on 34:7): "The words of the officials are not good; they serve only to weaken our hands." Contrast Is 35:3. *seeking the well-being.* The Hebrew underlying this phrase is translated "Seek the welfare" in 29:7 (see note there). *well-being . . . harm.* The Hebrew for these words is translated "prosperity . . . calamity" in Is 45:7.

38:5 *the king can do nothing.* Not because of inability or lack of authority but through failure of nerve. He feared his own officials (see vv. 25–26; see also 37:17 and note).

38:6 *cistern.* Shaped like a bell, with the narrow end at the top (see 37:16 and note). *king's son.* See note on 36:26. *in the cistern there was no water.* Zedekiah's officials wanted to kill Jeremiah (see v. 4), but not by taking his life with their own hands (cf. Gen 37:20–24).

38:7 *Ebed-melech.* Means "king's servant." *king was sitting in the Gate of Benjamin.* See 37:13; see also note on Zech 14:10. Since a city gateway was often used as a courtroom or town hall (see notes on Gen 19:1; Ruth 4:1), Zedekiah may have been settling various legal complaints on this occasion (see 2 Sam 15:2–4) and would therefore be in a position to help Ebed-melech.

38:9 *no more bread in the city.* See 37:21 and note.

38:10 *thirty men.* The large number was probably to keep the officials (see v. 4) and their friends from trying to prevent Jeremiah's rescue.

38:11 *place beneath the storeroom.* Perhaps a wardrobe storeroom (see 2 Kin 10:22).

38:12 *put these worn-out clothes . . . under the ropes.* Ebed-melech's kindnesses to Jeremiah were evidence that he trusted in the Lord, and the Lord rewarded him (see 39:15–18).

13 So they pulled Jeremiah up with the ropes and lifted him out of the cistern, and Jeremiah stayed in the [a]court of the guardhouse.

14 Then King Zedekiah [a]sent and [1]had Jeremiah the prophet brought to him at the third entrance that is in the house of the LORD; and the king said to Jeremiah, "I am going to [b]ask you something; do not hide anything from me."

15 Then Jeremiah said to Zedekiah, "[a]If I tell you, will you not certainly put me to death? Besides, if I give you advice, you will not listen to me."

16 But King Zedekiah swore to Jeremiah in [a]secret saying, "As the LORD lives, who made this [1][b]life for us, surely I will not put you to death nor will I give you over to the hand of [c]these men who are seeking your [1]life."

Interview with Zedekiah

17 Then Jeremiah said to Zedekiah, "Thus says the LORD [a]God of hosts, the [b]God of Israel, 'If you will indeed [c]go out to the officers of the king of Babylon, then [1]you will live, this city will not be burned with fire, and you and your household will [2]survive.

18 'But if you will [a]not go out to the officers of the king of Babylon, then this city [b]will be given over to the hand of the Chaldeans; and they will burn it with fire, and [c]you yourself will not escape from their hand.' "

19 Then King Zedekiah said to Jeremiah, "I [a]dread the Jews who have [1][b]gone over to the Chaldeans, for they may give me over into their hand and they will [c]abuse me."

20 But Jeremiah said, "They will not give you over. Please [1][a]obey the LORD in what I am saying to you, that it may go [b]well with you and [2][c]you may live.

21 "But if you keep refusing to go out, this is the word which the LORD has shown me:

22 'Then behold, all of the [a]women who have been left in the palace of the king of Judah are going to be brought out to the [1]officers of the king of Babylon; and those women will say,

"[2]Your close friends
Have misled and overpowered you;
While your feet were sunk in the mire,
They turned back."

23 'They will also bring out all your wives and your [a]sons to the Chaldeans, and [b]you yourself will not escape from their hand, but will be seized by the hand of the king of Babylon, and [b]this city will be burned with fire.' "

24 Then Zedekiah said to Jeremiah, "Let no man know about these words and you will not die.

25 "But if the [a]officials hear that I have talked with you and come to you and say to you, 'Tell us now what you said to the king and what the king said to you; do not hide *it* from us and we will not put you to death,'

26 then you are to say to them, 'I was [a]presenting my petition before the king, not to make me return to the house of Jonathan to die there.' "

27 Then all the officials came to Jeremiah and questioned him. So he reported to them in accordance with all these words which the king had commanded; and they ceased speaking with him, since the [1]conversation had not been overheard.

28 So Jeremiah [a]stayed in the court of the guardhouse until the day that Jerusalem was captured.

Jerusalem Captured

39 [1]Now when Jerusalem was captured
[2][a]in the ninth year of Zedekiah king of Judah, in the tenth month, Nebuchadnezzar king of Babylon and all his army came to Jerusalem and laid siege to it;

2 in the eleventh year of Zedekiah, in the fourth month, in the ninth *day* of the month, the city *wall* was [a]breached.

13 [a]Neh 3:25; Jer 32:2; 37:21; 38:6; 39:14, 15; Acts 23:35; 24:27; 28:16, 30
14 [1]Lit *took Jeremiah the prophet to him* [a]Jer 21:1, 2; 37:17 [b]1 Sam 3:17, 18; 1 Kin 22:16; Jer 15:11; 42:2-5, 20
15 [a]Luke 22:67, 68
16 [1]Lit *soul* [a]Jer 37:17; John 3:2 [b]Num 16:22; 27:16; Is 42:5; 57:16; Zech 12:1; Acts 17:25, 28 [c]Jer 34:20; 38:4-6
17 [1]Lit *your soul* [2]Lit *live* [a]Ps 80:7, 14; Amos 5:27 [b]1 Chr 17:24; Ezek 8:4 [c]2 Kin 24:12; 25:27-30; Jer 21:8-10; 27:12, 17; 38:2; 39:3
18 [a]Jer 27:8 [b]2 Kin 25:4-10; Jer 24:8-10; 32:3-5; 37:8; 38:3 [c]Jer 32:4; 34:3
19 [1]Lit *fallen* [a]Is 51:12, 13; 57:11; John 12:42; 19:12, 13 [b]Jer 39:9 [c]2 Chr 30:10; Neh 4:1; Jer 38:22
20 [1]Lit *listen to the voice of* [2]Lit *your soul* [a]2 Chr 20:20; Jer 11:4, 8; 26:13; Dan 4:27; Acts 26:29 [b]Jer 7:23 [c]Gen 19:20; Is 55:3
22 [a]Jer 6:12; 8:10; 43:6
22 [1]Or *princes* [2]Lit *The men of your peace*
23 [a]2 Kin 25:7; Jer 39:6; 41:10 [b]Jer 38:18
25 [a]Jer 38:4-6, 27
26 [a]Jer 37:20 **27** [1]Lit *word* **28** [a]Ps 23:4; Jer 15:20, 21; 37:20, 21; 38:13; 39:13, 14 **39:1** [1]Ch 38:28-b in Heb [2]Ch 39:1 in Heb [a]2 Kin 25:1-12; Jer 52:4; Ezek 24:1, 2 **2** [a]2 Kin 25:4; Jer 52:7

38:13 *stayed in the court of the guardhouse.* See note on 32:2.
38:14 *something . . . anything.* Lit. "a word . . . a word," probably referring to a "word from the LORD" (37:17).
38:16 *As the LORD lives.* See note on Gen 42:15. *these men who are seeking your life.* Zedekiah's officials (see v. 4 and note).
38:17–18 See vv. 2–3; 21:9–10; 32:3–4; 34:2–5. *go out to.* See 2 Kin 18:31; 24:12. *officers of the king of Babylon.* Those in charge of the siege of Jerusalem (see 39:3,13).
38:19 *I dread.* See v. 5 and note. If Zedekiah had trusted in the Lord, he would not have had to fear either officials or deserters (see Prov 29:25). *gone over to the Chaldeans.* See 37:13 and note. *abuse me.* See Judg 19:25; 1 Chr 10:4.
38:22 *women . . . in the palace . . . brought out to the officers.* Women in a conquered king's harem became the property of the conquerors (cf. 2 Sam 16:21–22). *Your close friends Have misled and overpowered you.* Repeated almost verbatim in Obad 7 (see 20:10 and note). Zedekiah's so-called friends were his officials (see v. 4) and false prophets (see 37:19). *feet were sunk in the mire.* Symbolic of great distress (see Ps 69:14).
38:26 See 37:20. *house of Jonathan.* See 37:15 and note.
38:27 *reported to them . . . all . . . which the king had commanded.* Jeremiah was not obliged to give the officials the other information, which had been shared in confidence.
38:28 *stayed in the court of the guardhouse.* See v. 13; see also note on 32:2.
39:1–45:5 The most detailed account in the OT of the Babylonian conquest of Jerusalem and its aftermath. The section concludes with a brief appendix (ch. 45).
39:1–10 A vivid summary of the siege and fall of Jerusalem and of the exile of its inhabitants (see 52:4–27).
39:1–2 Summarizes 52:4–7a.
39:1 *ninth year of Zedekiah . . . tenth month.* The final Babylonian siege of Jerusalem began on the tenth day of the month (see 52:4; 2 Kin 25:1; Ezek 24:1–2), or Jan. 15, 588 B.C.
39:2 *eleventh year . . . fourth month . . . ninth day.* July 18, 586 B.C. (see 52:5–6; 2 Kin 25:2–3). The siege lasted just over two

3 Then all the [a]officials of the king of
Babylon came in and sat down at the [b]Mid-
dle Gate: Nergal-sar-ezer, Samgar-nebu, Sar-
sekim the [1]Rab-saris, Nergal-sar-ezer *the*
[2]Rab-mag, and all the rest of the officials of
the king of Babylon.
4 When Zedekiah the king of Judah and
all the men of war saw them, they [a]fled and
went out of the city at night by way of the
king's garden through the gate [b]between the
two walls; and he went out toward the [1]Ara-
bah.
5 But the army of the [a]Chaldeans pursued them and overtook Zedekiah in the
[b]plains of Jericho; and they seized him and
brought him up to Nebuchadnezzar king of
Babylon at [c]Riblah in the land of Hamath,
and he passed sentence on him.
6 Then the [a]king of Babylon slew the
sons of Zedekiah [b]before his eyes at Riblah;
the king of Babylon also slew all the [c]nobles
of Judah.
7 He then [a]blinded Zedekiah's eyes and
bound him in [b]fetters of bronze to bring him
to [c]Babylon.
8 The Chaldeans also [a]burned with fire
the king's palace and the houses of the people, and they [b]broke down the walls of
Jerusalem.
9 As for the rest of the people who were
left in the city, the [1a]deserters who had gone
over to him and [b]the rest of the people who
remained, [c]Nebuzaradan the [d]captain of the
bodyguard carried *them* into exile in Babylon.
10 But some of the [a]poorest people who
had nothing, [a]Nebuzaradan the captain of
the bodyguard left behind in the land of
Judah, and gave them vineyards and fields
[1]at that time.

Jeremiah Spared

11 Now Nebuchadnezzar king of Babylon
gave orders about [a]Jeremiah through Nebuzaradan the captain of the bodyguard, saying,
12 "Take him and [1]look after him, and [a]do
nothing harmful to him, but rather deal with
him just as he tells you."
13 So Nebuzaradan the captain of the
bodyguard sent *word,* along with Nebu-
shazban the [1]Rab-saris, and Nergal-sar-ezer
the [2]Rab-mag, and all the leading officers of
the king of Babylon;
14 they even sent and [a]took Jeremiah out
of the court of the guardhouse and entrusted
him to [b]Gedaliah, the son of [c]Ahikam, the
son of Shaphan, to take him home. So he
stayed among the people.
15 Now the word of the LORD had come to
Jeremiah while he was [a]confined in the
court of the guardhouse, saying,
16 "Go and speak to [a]Ebed-melech the
Ethiopian, saying, 'Thus says the LORD of
hosts, the God of Israel, "Behold, I am about
to bring My words on this city [b]for disaster
and not for [1]prosperity; and they will [c]take
place before you on that day.
17 "But I will [a]deliver you on that day,"
declares the LORD, "and you will not be giv-
en into the hand of the men whom you
dread.
18 "For I will certainly rescue you, and you
will not fall by the sword; but you will have
your *own* [a]life as booty, because you have
[b]trusted in Me," declares the LORD.' "

Jeremiah Remains in Judah

40 The word which came to Jeremiah from
the LORD after [a]Nebuzaradan captain of
the bodyguard had released him from
[b]Ramah, when he had taken him bound in
[c]chains among all the exiles of Jerusalem and
Judah who were being exiled to Babylon.

3 [1]I.e. chief official [2]I.e. title of a high official [a]Jer 38:17 [b]Jer 21:4
4 [1]I.e. Jordan valley [a]2 Kin 25:4; Is 30:16; Jer 52:7; Amos 2:14 [b]2 Chr 32:5
5 [a]Jer 32:4, 5; 38:18, 23; 52:8 [b]Josh 4:13; 5:10 [c]2 Kin 23:33; Jer 52:9, 26, 27
6 [a]2 Kin 25:7; Jer 52:10 [b]Deut 28:34 [c]Jer 21:7; 24:8-10; 34:19-21
7 [a]2 Kin 25:7; Jer 52:11; Ezek 12:13 [b]Judg 16:21 [c]Jer 32:5
8 [a]2 Kin 25:9; Jer 21:10; 38:18; 52:13 [b]2 Kin 25:10; Neh 1:3; Jer 52:14
9 [1]Lit *fallers who had fallen* [a]Jer 38:19; 52:15 [b]Jer 24:8 [c]2 Kin 25:11, 20; Jer 39:13; 40:1; 52:12-16, 26 [d]Gen 37:36
10 [1]Lit *on that day* [a]2 Kin 25:12; Jer 52:16
11 [a]Job 5:15, 16; Jer 1:8; 15:20, 21; Acts 24:23
12 [1]Lit *set your eyes on* [a]Ps 105:14, 15; Prov 16:7; 21:1; 1 Pet 3:13
13 [1]I.e. chief official [2]I.e. title of a high official
14 [a]Jer 38:28; 40:1-6 [b]Jer 40:5 [c]2 Kin 22:12, 14; 2 Chr 34:20; Jer 26:24
15 [a]Jer 38:28
16 [1]Lit *good* [a]Jer 38:7 [b]Jer 21:10; Dan 9:12; Zech 1:6 [c]Ps 91:8
17 [a]Ps 41:1, 2; 50:15 **18** [a]Jer 21:9; 38:2; 45:5 [b]Ps 34:22; Jer 17:7, 8 **40:1** [a]Jer 39:9, 11 [b]Jer 31:15 [c]Acts 12:6, 7; 21:13; 28:20; Eph 6:20

and a half years.

39:3 *sat down at the Middle Gate.* In fulfillment of 1:15. The Middle Gate may have been located in the wall separating the citadel of Mount Zion from the lower city, therefore serving as a strategic vantage point for the invaders. *Nergal-sar-ezer.* Means "Nergal [a god; see 2 Kin 17:30], protect the king." One of the two men so named here (see v. 13) is probably Neriglissar, who later became a successor of Nebuchadnezzar as ruler of Babylonia (560–556 B.C.). *Rab-saris.* See v. 13; see also note on 2 Kin 18:17. *Rab-mag.* See v. 13. The Hebrew for this phrase is cognate to Babylonian *rab mu(n)gi,* a high military official who sometimes served as an envoy to foreign rulers.
39:4–7 See 52:7–11; see also 2 Kin 25:4–7 and notes.
39:5 *plains.* The Hebrew for this word is the plural of the word for "Arabah" (v. 4).
39:8–10 See 52:12–16; see also 2 Kin 25:8–12 and notes.
39:12 *look after him.* See note on 40:4.
39:13 *Nergal-sar-ezer.* See note on v. 3.
39:14 *took Jeremiah out.* Either (1) a summary statement of Jeremiah's release from prison, the specific details of which are given in 40:1–6; or (2) a brief description of the first of two releases, the second of which (made necessary because Jeremiah had been arrested again by mistake in the confusion surrounding the capture and transporting of thousands of exiles) is detailed in 40:1–6. *court of the guardhouse.* See note on 32:2. *Gedaliah, the son of Ahikam, the son of Shaphan.* See note on 26:24. *home.* The governor's residence. An early sixth-century seal impression found at Lachish reads: "Belonging to Gedaliah [probably the man named in this verse], who is over the house."
39:15–18 See note on 38:12.
39:16 *Go and speak.* Though confined in prison, Jeremiah was permitted to have visitors (see note on 38:1). *I am about to bring My words on this city.* See 19:15.
39:17 *the men . . . you dread.* The court officials (see 38:1) who, in Ebed-melech's judgment, had "acted wickedly" (38:9).
39:18 *your own life as booty.* See note on 21:9. *you have trusted in Me.* Ebed-melech had expressed his faith in God by securing Jeremiah's release from the cistern (see 38:7–13; see also note on 38:12).
40:1–44:30 A lively narrative of the aftermath of the fall of Jerusalem. Chronologically, the chapters are the latest in the book (although 52:31–34 is later, it is part of the appendix and not of the book proper).
40:1 *The word which came.* A heading introducing the prophe-

2 Now the captain of the bodyguard had
taken Jeremiah and said to him, "The [a]LORD
your God promised this calamity against this
place;
3 and the LORD has brought *it* on and
done just as He promised. Because you *people* [a]sinned against the LORD and did not listen to His voice, therefore this thing has happened to you.
4 "But now, behold, I am [a]freeing you
today from the chains which are on your
hands. If [1]you would prefer to come with me
to Babylon, come *along*, and I will [2]look after
you; but if [3]you would prefer not to come
with me to Babylon, [4]never mind. Look, the
[b]whole land is before you; go wherever it
seems good and right for you to go."
5 As [1]Jeremiah was still not going back,
[2]*he said,* "Go on back then to [a]Gedaliah the
son of Ahikam, the son of Shaphan, whom
the king of Babylon has [b]appointed over the
cities of Judah, and stay with him among the
people; or else go anywhere it seems right for
you to go." So the captain of the bodyguard
gave him a [c]ration and a [d]gift and let him go.
6 Then Jeremiah went to [a]Mizpah to
[b]Gedaliah the son of Ahikam and stayed
with him among the people who were left in
the land.
7 [a]Now all the [1]commanders of the
forces that were in the field, they and their
men, heard that the king of Babylon had
appointed Gedaliah the son of Ahikam over
the land and that he had put him in charge of
the men, women and [2]children, those of the
[b]poorest of the land who had not been exiled
to Babylon.
8 So they came to Gedaliah at Mizpah,
along with [a]Ishmael the son of Nethaniah,
and [b]Johanan and Jonathan the sons of
Kareah, and Seraiah the son of Tanhumeth,
and the sons of Ephai the [c]Netophathite, and
[d]Jezaniah the son of the [e]Maacathite, *both*
they and their men.
9 Then Gedaliah the son of Ahikam, the
son of Shaphan, [a]swore to them and to their
men, saying, "[b]Do not be afraid of serving
the Chaldeans; stay in the land and serve the
king of Babylon, that it may go well with you.
10 "Now as for me, behold, I am going to
stay at Mizpah to [a]stand *for you* before the
Chaldeans who come to us; but as for you,
[b]gather in wine and [c]summer fruit and oil
and put *them* in your *storage* vessels, and
live in your cities that you have taken over."
11 Likewise, also all the Jews who were in
[a]Moab and among the sons of [b]Ammon and
in [c]Edom and who were in all the *other*
countries, heard that the king of Babylon had
left a remnant for Judah, and that he had
appointed over them Gedaliah the son of
Ahikam, the son of Shaphan.
12 Then all the Jews [a]returned from all
the places to which they had been driven
away and came to the land of Judah, to Gedaliah at Mizpah, and gathered in wine and
summer fruit in great abundance.
13 Now Johanan the son of Kareah and all
the commanders of the forces that were in
the field came to Gedaliah at Mizpah
14 and said to him, "Are you well aware
that Baalis the king of the sons of [a]Ammon
has sent Ishmael the son of Nethaniah to
take your life?" But Gedaliah the son of Ahikam did not believe them.
15 Then Johanan the son of Kareah spoke
secretly to Gedaliah in Mizpah, saying, "[a]Let
me go and kill Ishmael the son of Nethaniah,
and not a man will know! Why should he
[b]take your life, so that all the Jews who are
gathered to you would be scattered and the
[c]remnant of Judah would perish?"
16 But Gedaliah the son of Ahikam said to
Johanan the son of Kareah, "[a]Do not do this
thing, for you are telling a lie about Ishmael."

Gedaliah Is Murdered

41 [a]In the seventh month [b]Ishmael the
son of Nethaniah, the son of Elishama,
of the royal [1]family and *one* of the chief officers of the king, along with ten men, came to
Mizpah to [c]Gedaliah the son of Ahikam.
While they [d]were eating bread together there
in Mizpah,

2 [a]Lev 26:14-38; Deut 28:15-68; 29:24-28; 31:17; 32:19-25; Jer 22:8, 9
3 [a]Jer 50:7; Dan 9:11; Rom 2:5
4 [1]Lit *it is good in your eyes* [2]Lit *set my eyes on* [3]Lit *it is evil in your eyes* [4]Lit *refrain!* [a]Jer 39:11, 12 [b]Gen 13:9; 20:15; 47:6
5 [1]Lit *he* [2]I.e. Nebuzaradan [a]Jer 39:14 [b]2 Kin 25:23 [c]Jer 52:34 [d]2 Kin 8:7-9
6 [a]Judg 20:1; 21:1; 1 Sam 7:5; 2 Chr 16:6 [b]Jer 39:14
7 [1]Or *princes* [2]Lit *infants* [a]2 Kin 25:23 [b]Jer 39:10; 52:16
8 [a]Jer 40:14; 41:2 [b]Jer 40:13, 15; 42:1; 43:2 [c]2 Sam 23:28, 29; Ezra 2:22; Neh 7:26 [d]Jer 42:1 [e]Deut 3:14; Josh 12:5; 2 Sam 10:6, 8
9 [a]1 Sam 20:16, 17; 2 Kin 25:24 [b]Jer 27:11; 38:17-20
10 [a]Deut 1:38; 1 Kin 10:8; Jer 35:19 [b]Deut 16:13; Jer 39:10 [c]Is 16:9; Jer 40:12; 48:32
11 [a]Num 22:1; 25:1, 2; Is 16:4; Jer 9:26 [b]1 Sam 11:1; 12:12 [c]Gen 36:8; Is 11:14
12 [a]Jer 43:5
14 [a]1 Sam 11:1-3; 2 Sam 10:1-6; Jer 25:21; 41:10
15 [a]1 Sam 26:8 [b]2 Sam 21:17 [c]Jer 42:2
16 [a]Matt 10:16; 1 Cor 13:5
41:1 [1]Lit *seed* [a]2 Kin 25:25 [b]Jer 40:8, 14 [c]Jer 39:14; 40:5, 6 [d]Ps 41:9; Jer 40:13, 14

cies of Jeremiah after the exile, just as "the word . . . came" (1:2) introduces his prophecies from the time of his call up to the exile (see 1:3). *Nebuzaradan . . . released him.* See note on 39:14. *Ramah.* See note on 31:15. *chains.* Manacles that were fastened to the wrists (see v. 4; see also Job 36:8; Is 45:14).

40:2–3 Nebuzaradan doubtless knew the basic content of Jeremiah's prophetic message against Jerusalem, and he here repeats it to the prophet in summary fashion.

40:4 *I will look after you.* Nebuzaradan promises to carry out Nebuchadnezzar's wishes concerning Jeremiah (see 39:12). *the whole land is before you.* Cf. Abram's offer to Lot in Gen 13:9.

40:5–9 See 2 Kin 25:22–24 and notes.

40:5 *Gedaliah the son of Ahikam.* See note on 26:24. *ration.* The Hebrew for this word is translated "allowance" in 52:34.

40:8 *Jezaniah.* See note on 2 Kin 25:23.

40:10 *gather in wine and summer fruit and oil.* Nebuzaradan (see 39:9) had arrived in Jerusalem in August of 586 B.C. (see note on 52:12). Grapes, figs and olives are harvested in the Holy Land during August and September.

40:14 *Baalis.* Either (1) "King Ba'lay," as his name is written on an early sixth-century B.C. bottle discovered in Jordan, or (2) Ba'al-Yasha', an Ammonite king whose name appears on a stamp seal found at Tell el-'Umeiri in Jordan in 1984. *sons of Ammon.* Ammon was among the nations that earlier had been allies against Babylonia (see 27:3 and note; see also Ezek 21:18–32).

40:15 *secretly.* See note on 38:16. *remnant.* See note on 6:9.

40:16 *telling a lie.* See 37:14 and note. Gedaliah's naive faith in Ishmael's integrity would cost him his life.

41:1–3 See 2 Kin 25:25 and note.

41:1 *one of the chief officers of the king.* Ishmael's loyalty to Zedekiah might explain his assassination of Gedaliah, whom he considered to be a Babylonian puppet ruler. *they were eating bread together.* Ancient custom with respect to hospitality

2 Ishmael the son of Nethaniah and the ten men who were with him arose and [a]struck down Gedaliah the son of Ahikam, the son of Shaphan, with the sword and [b]put to death the one [c]whom the king of Babylon had appointed over the land.

3 Ishmael also struck down all the Jews who were with him, *that is* with Gedaliah at Mizpah, and the Chaldeans who were found there, the men of war.

4 Now it happened on the [1]next day after the killing of Gedaliah, when no one knew about *it,*

5 that eighty men [a]came from [b]Shechem, from [c]Shiloh, and from [d]Samaria with [e]their beards shaved off and their clothes torn and [1]their bodies [f]gashed, having grain offerings and incense in their hands to bring to the [g]house of the LORD.

6 Then Ishmael the son of Nethaniah went out from Mizpah to meet them, [a]weeping as he went; and as he met them, he said to them, "Come to Gedaliah the son of Ahikam!"

7 Yet it turned out that as soon as they came inside the city, Ishmael the son of Nethaniah and the men that were with him [a]slaughtered them *and cast them* into the cistern.

8 But ten men who were found among them said to Ishmael, "Do not put us to death; for we have [a]stores of wheat, barley, oil and honey hidden in the field." So he refrained and did not put them to death along with their companions.

9 Now as for the cistern where Ishmael had cast all the corpses of the men whom he had struck down [1]because of Gedaliah, it was the [a]one that King Asa had made on [b]account of Baasha, king of Israel; Ishmael the son of Nethaniah filled it with the slain.

10 Then Ishmael took captive all the [a]remnant of the people who were in Mizpah, the [b]king's daughters and all the people who were left in Mizpah, whom Nebuzaradan the captain of the bodyguard had put under the charge of Gedaliah the son of Ahikam; thus Ishmael the son of Nethaniah took them captive and proceeded to cross over to the sons of [c]Ammon.

Johanan Rescues the People

11 But Johanan the son of Kareah and all the [a]commanders of the forces that were with him heard of all the evil that Ishmael the son of Nethaniah had done.

12 So they took all the men and went to [a]fight with Ishmael the son of Nethaniah and they found him by the [b]great [1]pool that is in Gibeon.

13 Now as soon as all the people who were with Ishmael saw Johanan the son of Kareah and the commanders of the forces that were with him, they were glad.

14 So all the people whom Ishmael had taken captive from Mizpah turned around and came back, and went to Johanan the son of Kareah.

15 But Ishmael the son of Nethaniah [a]escaped from Johanan with eight men and went to the sons of Ammon.

16 Then Johanan the son of Kareah and all the commanders of the forces that were with him took from Mizpah [a]all the remnant of the people whom he had [1]recovered from Ishmael the son of Nethaniah, after he had struck down Gedaliah the son of Ahikam, *that is,* the men who were [2]soldiers, *the* women, *the* [3]children, and *the* eunuchs, whom he had brought back from Gibeon.

17 And they went and stayed in [1a]Geruth Chimham, which is beside Bethlehem, in order to [b]proceed into Egypt

18 because of the Chaldeans; for they were [a]afraid of them, since Ishmael the son of Nethaniah had struck down Gedaliah the son of Ahikam, whom [b]the king of Babylon had appointed over the land.

2 [a]2 Sam 3:27; 20:9, 10; 2 Kin 25:25; Ps 41:9; 109:5; John 13:18 [b]2 Kin 25:25 [c]Jer 40:5
4 [1]Or *second*
5 [1]Lit *having cut themselves* [a]2 Kin 10:13, 14 [b]Gen 33:18; 37:12; Judg 9:1; 1 Kin 12:1, 25 [c]Josh 18:1; Judg 18:31; 1 Sam 3:21; Ps 78:60 [d]1 Kin 16:24, 29 [e]Lev 19:27; Deut 14:1 [f]Deut 14:1; Jer 16:6 [g]1 Sam 1:7; 2 Kin 25:9
6 [a]2 Sam 3:16; Jer 50:4
7 [a]Ps 55:23; Is 59:7; Ezek 22:27; 33:24, 26
8 [a]Is 45:3
9 [1]Or *by the side of* [a]1 Kin 15:17-22; 2 Chr 16:1-6 [b]Judg 6:2; 1 Sam 13:6; 2 Sam 17:9; Heb 11:38
10 [a]Jer 40:11, 12 [b]Jer 43:6
10 [c]Neh 2:10, 19; 4:7; Jer 40:14
11 [a]Jer 40:7, 8, 13-16
12 [1]Lit *waters* [a]Gen 14:14-16; 1 Sam 30:1-8, 18, 20 [b]2 Sam 2:13
15 [a]1 Sam 30:17; 1 Kin 20:20; Job 21:30; Prov 28:17
16 [1]Lit *brought back* [2]Lit *men of war* [3]Lit *infants* [a]Jer 42:8; 43:4-7
17 [1]Or *the lodging place of Chimham* [a]2 Sam 19:37, 38, 40 [b]Jer 42:14
18 [a]Is 51:12, 13; 57:11; Jer 42:11, 16; 43:2, 3; Luke 12:4, 5 [b]Jer 40:5

---

probably made Gedaliah assume that his guests would not harm him, much less kill him (see note on Judg 4:21).

41:5 *came.* In the "seventh month" (v. 1) to celebrate the Feast of Booths (see note on Ex 23:16). *beards shaved . . . clothes torn . . . bodies gashed.* Signs of mourning (see 16:6 and note; see also note on Ezra 9:3), probably over the destruction of Jerusalem. *Shechem . . . Shiloh . . . Samaria.* Formerly worship centers in the north (see notes on 7:12; Gen 12:6; see also Josh 24:25–26). After the northern kingdom was destroyed in 722–721 B.C., many Israelites made periodic pilgrimages to Jerusalem, especially during the reform movements of Hezekiah (see 2 Chr 30:11) and Josiah (see 2 Chr 34:9). *grain offerings and incense.* Bloodless offerings, since the altar of the Jerusalem temple had been destroyed. *house of the LORD.* Though the temple itself was in ruins, the site was still considered holy.

41:6 *weeping.* Pretending to share the sorrow of the mourners from the north.

41:7 *the city.* Mizpah. *cistern.* A favorite place to dispose of victims, whether living or dead (see 37:16 and note; 38:6).

41:8 *wheat, barley, oil and honey.* Supplies that Ishmael perhaps would have taken with him when he fled to Ammon (see v. 15).

41:9 *the cistern . . . was the one King Asa had made.* Probably as part of the fortifications Asa had built at Mizpah (see 1 Kin 15:22), since cisterns were essential for storing water during times of siege. Archaeologists have discovered numerous cisterns in the ruins of ancient Mizpah (modern Tell en-Nasbeh, seven and a half miles north of Jerusalem).

41:10 *king's daughters.* Women who had been members of King Zedekiah's court, not necessarily daughters of the king himself (see note on 36:26). *sons of Ammon.* See 40:14 and note.

41:12 *great pool . . . in Gibeon.* Perhaps the same as the one mentioned in 2 Sam 2:13.

41:15 *escaped . . . with eight men.* Ishmael lost only two of his men (see v. 2) in the fight with Johanan.

41:17 *Geruth Chimham.* Location unknown; perhaps means "lodging place of Chimham," a friend of David who returned with him to Jerusalem after Absalom's death (see 2 Sam 19:37–40).

Warning against Going to Egypt

42 Then all the [1]commanders of the forces, [a]Johanan the son of Kareah, Jezaniah the son of Hoshaiah, and all the people [b]both small and great approached

2 and said to Jeremiah the prophet, "Please let our [a]petition [1]come before you, and [b]pray for us to the LORD your God, *that is* for all this remnant; because we are left *but* a [c]few out of many, as your own eyes *now* see us,

3 that the LORD your God may tell us the [a]way in which we should walk and the thing that we should do."

4 Then Jeremiah the prophet said to them, "I have heard *you.* Behold, I am going to [a]pray to the LORD your God in accordance with your words; and I will tell you the whole [1]message which the [b]LORD will answer you. I will [c]not keep back a word from you."

5 Then they said to Jeremiah, "May the [a]LORD be a true and faithful witness against us if we do not act in accordance with the whole [1]message with which the LORD your God will send you to us.

6 "Whether *it* is [1]pleasant or [2]unpleasant, we will [a]listen to the voice of the LORD our God to whom we are sending you, so that it may go [b]well with us when we listen to the voice of the LORD our God."

7 Now at the [a]end of ten days the word of the LORD came to Jeremiah.

8 Then he called for Johanan the son of Kareah and all the [1]commanders of the forces that were with him, and for all the people both small and great,

9 and said to them, "Thus [a]says the LORD the God of Israel, to whom you sent me to present your petition before Him:

10 'If you will indeed stay in this land, then I will [a]build you up and not tear you down, and I will plant you and not uproot you; for I [1]will [b]relent concerning the calamity that I have inflicted on you.

11 '[a]Do not be afraid of the king of Babylon, whom you are *now* fearing; do not be afraid of him,' declares the LORD, 'for [b]I am with you to save you and deliver you from his hand.

12 'I will also show you compassion, so that [a]he will have compassion on you and restore you to your own soil.

13 'But if you are going to say, "We will [a]not stay in this land," so as not to listen to the voice of the LORD your God,

14 saying, "No, but we will [a]go to the land of Egypt, where we will not see war or [b]hear the sound of a trumpet or hunger for bread, and we will stay there";

15 then [1]in that case listen to the word of the LORD, O remnant of Judah. Thus says the LORD of hosts, the God of Israel, "If you really set your [2]mind to enter [a]Egypt and go in to reside there,

16 then the [a]sword, which you are afraid of, will overtake you there in the land of Egypt; and the famine, about which you are anxious, will follow closely after you there *in* Egypt, and you will die there.

17 "So all the men who set their [1]mind to go to Egypt to reside there will die by the [a]sword, by famine and by pestilence; and they will [b]have no survivors or refugees from the calamity that I am going to bring on them." '"

18 For thus says the LORD of hosts, the God of Israel, "As My [a]anger and wrath have been poured out on the inhabitants of Jerusalem, so My wrath will be poured out on you when you enter Egypt. And you will become a [b]curse, an object of horror, an imprecation and a reproach; and [c]you will see this place no more."

19 The LORD has spoken to you, O remnant of Judah, "Do not [a]go into Egypt!" You should clearly [b]understand that today I have [c]testified against you.

20 For you have *only* [1a]deceived yourselves; for it is you who sent me to the LORD your God, saying, "Pray for us to the LORD our God; and whatever the LORD our God says, tell us so, and we will do it."

21 So I have [a]told you today, but you have [b]not [1]obeyed the LORD your God, even in whatever He has sent me to *tell* you.

42:1 [1]Or *princes* [a]Jer 40:8, 13; 41:11, 18 [b]Jer 6:13; 8:10; 42:8; 44:12; Acts 8:10 **2** [1]Lit *fall* [a]Jer 36:7; 37:20 [b]Ex 8:28; 1 Sam 7:8; 12:19; 1 Kin 13:6; Is 37:4; Jer 37:3; 42:20; Acts 8:24; James 5:16 [c]Lev 26:22; Deut 28:62; Is 1:9; Lam 1:1 **3** [a]Ps 86:11; Prov 3:6; Jer 6:16; Mic 4:2 **4** [1]Lit *word* [a]Ex 8:29; 1 Sam 12:23 [b]1 Kin 22:14; Jer 23:28 [c]1 Sam 3:17, 18; Ps 40:10; Acts 20:20 **5** [1]Lit *word* [a]Gen 31:50; Judg 11:10; Jer 43:2; Mic 1:2; Mal 2:14; 3:5 **6** [1]Lit *good* [2]Lit *evil* [a]Ex 24:7; Deut 5:27; Josh 24:24 [b]Deut 5:29, 33; 6:3; Jer 7:23 **7** [a]Ps 27:14; Is 30:18 **8** [1]Or *princes* **9** [a]2 Kin 19:4, 6, 20; 22:15 **10** [1]Or *shall have changed my mind about* [a]Jer 24:6; 31:28; 33:7; Ezek 36:36 [b]Jer 18:7, 8; Hos 11:8; Joel 2:13; Amos 7:3, 6; Jon 3:10; 4:2 **11** [a]Jer 1:8; 27:12, 17; 41:18 [b]Num 14:9; 2 Chr 32:7, 8; Ps 46:7, 11; 118:6; Is 8:9, 10; 43:2, 5; Jer 1:19; 15:20; Rom 8:31 **12** [a]Neh 1:11; Ps 106:46; Prov 16:7 **13** [a]Ex 5:2; Jer 44:16 **14** [a]Is 31:1; Jer 41:17 [b]Ex 16:3; Num 11:4; Jer 4:19, 21 **15** [1]Lit *now therefore* [2]Lit *face* [a]Deut 17:16; Jer 42:17; 44:12-14 **16** [a]Jer 44:13, 27; Ezek 11:8; Amos 9:1-4 **17** [1]Lit *face* [a]Jer 24:10; 38:2; 42:22; 44:13 [b]Jer 44:14, 28 **18** [a]2 Chr 36:16-19; Jer 7:20; 33:5; 39:1-9 [b]Deut 29:21; Is 65:15; Jer 18:16; 24:9; 29:18; 44:12 [c]Jer 22:10, 27 **19** [a]Deut 17:16; Is 30:1-7 [b]Ezek 2:5 [c]Neh 9:26, 29, 30 **20** [1]Or *acted errantly in your souls* [a]Jer 43:2; Ezek 14:3 **21** [1]Lit *listened to the voice of* [a]Deut 11:26; Jer 43:1; Ezek 2:7; Zech 7:11; Acts 20:26, 27 [b]Jer 43:4

42:1 *Jezaniah the son of Hoshaiah.* Possibly the same as "Jezaniah the son of the Maacathite" (40:8). Apparently, Jezaniah was also known as Jaazaniah (2 Kin 25:23) and Azariah (as found in the Septuagint of this verse; see also 43:2), as was King Uzziah (see notes on 2 Kin 14:21; 2 Chr 26:1).

42:2 *Jeremiah.* Had probably been among the "remnant" from Mizpah (41:16). *let our petition come before you.* See v. 9; 37:20.

42:3 The people may be asking the Lord to confirm what they sincerely believe to be their only option: flight to Egypt (see v. 17; 41:17).

42:6 *we will listen to . . . the LORD our God.* Though they twice declare here their desire to do God's will, they soon demonstrate that they have already decided to follow their own inclinations (see 43:2).

42:7 *end of ten days.* Jeremiah does not bring God's word to the people until he is sure of it himself (see 28:10–12).

42:10 *build you up . . . tear you down . . . plant . . . uproot.* See 1:10 and note; see also 31:4,28; 33:7.

42:12 *he will have compassion on you.* For similar examples see Gen 43:14; 1 Kin 8:50.

42:16 *the sword, which you are afraid of, will overtake you.* See 43:11 and note.

42:17–18 See 44:11–14.

42:17 *sword . . . famine . . . pestilence.* See note on 14:12.

42:18 *My anger and wrath have been poured out.* See 7:20; 44:6. *a curse . . . and a reproach.* See notes on 24:9; 25:18; see also 29:18. *this place.* Jerusalem.

42:19 *I have testified.* See 11:7.

22 Therefore you should now clearly
understand that you will [a]die by the sword,
by famine and by pestilence, in the [b]place
where you wish to go to reside.

In Egypt Jeremiah Warns of Judgment

43 But as soon as Jeremiah, whom the
LORD their God had sent, had [a]finished
telling all the people all the words of the
LORD their God—that is, all these words—
2 Azariah the [a]son of Hoshaiah, and
Johanan the son of Kareah, and all the arrogant men said to Jeremiah, "You are [b]telling
a lie! The LORD our God has not sent you to
say, 'You are not to enter Egypt to reside
there';
3 but [a]Baruch the son of Neriah is inciting you against us to give us over into the
hand of the Chaldeans, so they will put us to
death or exile us to Babylon."
4 So [a]Johanan the son of Kareah and all
the [1]commanders of the forces, and all the
people, [b]did not obey the voice of the LORD to
[c]stay in the land of Judah.
5 But Johanan the son of Kareah and all
the [1]commanders of the forces took the
[a]entire remnant of Judah who had returned
from all the nations to which they had been
driven away, in order to reside in the land of
Judah—
6 the men, the women, the [1]children, the
[a]king's daughters and [b]every person that
Nebuzaradan the captain of the bodyguard
had left with Gedaliah the son of Ahikam
[2]and grandson of Shaphan, together with
[c]Jeremiah the prophet and Baruch the son of
Neriah—
7 and they entered the land of Egypt (for
they did not obey the voice of the LORD) and
went in as far as [a]Tahpanhes.
8 Then the word of the LORD came to Jeremiah in [a]Tahpanhes, saying,
9 "Take *some* large stones in your [1]hands
and hide them in the mortar in the [2]brick *ter-
race* which is at the entrance of Pharaoh's

22 [a]Jer 43:11; Ezek 6:11 [b]Hos 9:6
43:1 [a]Jer 26:8; 51:63
2 [a]Jer 42:1 [b]2 Chr 36:13; Is 7:9; Jer 5:12, 13; 42:5
3 [a]Jer 36:4, 10, 26, 32; 43:6; 45:1-3
4 [1]Or *princes* [a]Jer 42:8 [b]2 Chr 25:16; Jer 42:5, 6; 44:5 [c]Ps 37:3; Jer 42:10-12
5 [1]Or *princes* [a]Jer 40:11
6 [1]Lit *infants* [2]Lit *the son* [a]Jer 41:10 [b]Jer 39:10; 40:7 [c]Eccl 9:1, 2; Lam 3:1
7 [a]Jer 2:16; 44:1
8 [a]Jer 2:16; 44:1; 46:14; Ezek 30:18
9 [1]Lit *hand* [2]Or *brickwork*
9 [3]Lit *house* [4]Lit *men*
10 [a]Jer 25:9, 11 [b]Is 44:28; 45:1; Jer 25:9; 27:6 [c]Ps 18:11; 27:5; 31:20
11 [a]Is 19:1-25; Jer 25:15-19; 44:13; 46:1, 2, 13-26; Ezek 29:19, 20 [b]Jer 15:2
12 [1]Some ancient versions read *He will set* [a]Ex 12:12; Is 19:1; Jer 46:25; Ezek 30:13 [b]Ps 104:2; 109:18, 19; Is 49:18
13 [1]Or *stone pillars* [2]Heb *Beth-shemesh;* i.e. the house of the sun-god
44:1 [a]Ex 14:2; Jer 46:14 [b]Jer 43:7; Ezek 30:18 [c]Is 19:13; Jer 2:16; 46:14; Ezek 30:13, 16; Hos 9:6 [d]Is 11:11; Ezek 29:14; 30:14

[3]palace in Tahpanhes, in the sight of [4]some
of the Jews;
10 and say to them, 'Thus says the LORD of
hosts, the God of Israel, "Behold, I am going
to send and get [a]Nebuchadnezzar the king of
Babylon, [b]My servant, and I am going to set
his throne *right* over these stones that I have
hidden; and he will spread his [c]canopy over
them.
11 "He will also come and [a]strike the land
of Egypt; those who are *meant* for death *will
be given over* to death, and those for captivity to captivity, and [b]those for the sword to
the sword.
12 "And [1]I shall set fire to the temples of
the [a]gods of Egypt, and he will burn them
and take them captive. So he will [b]wrap himself with the land of Egypt as a shepherd
wraps himself with his garment, and he will
depart from there safely.
13 "He will also shatter the [1]obelisks of
[2]Heliopolis, which is in the land of Egypt;
and the temples of the gods of Egypt he will
burn with fire." ' "

Conquest of Egypt Predicted

44 The word that came to Jeremiah for all
the Jews living in the land of Egypt,
those who were living in [a]Migdol, [b]Tahpan-
hes, [c]Memphis, and the land of [d]Pathros,
saying,
2 "Thus says the LORD of hosts, the God of
Israel, 'You yourselves have seen all the
calamity that I have brought on Jerusalem
and all the cities of Judah; and behold, this
day they are in [a]ruins and no one lives in
them,
3 [a]because of their wickedness which
they committed so as to [b]provoke Me to
anger by continuing to [c]burn [1]sacrifices *and*
to [d]serve other gods whom they had not
known, *neither* they, you, nor your fathers.

2 [a]Is 6:11; Jer 4:7; 9:11; 34:22; Mic 3:12 **3** [1]Or *incense* [a]Neh 9:33; Jer 2:17-19; 44:23; Ezek 8:17, 18; Dan 9:5 [b]Is 3:8; Jer 7:19; 32:30-32; 44:8 [c]Jer 19:4 [d]Deut 13:6; 29:26; 32:17

43:2 *Azariah.* See note on 42:1. *arrogant men.* They demonstrate themselves to be such by their words.
43:3 *Baruch.* See note on 32:12. Jeremiah's opponents decide to put the blame on someone they consider less spiritually formidable than the prophet himself.
43:6 *king's daughters.* See note on 41:10. *Jeremiah . . . and Baruch.* No doubt they went to Egypt unwillingly, in the light of 32:6–15; 40:1–6; 42:13–22.
43:7 *Tahpanhes.* See note on 2:16.
43:9 *Pharaoh's palace.* Not necessarily his main residence. One of the Elephantine papyri, e.g., mentions the "king's house," apparently a more modest dwelling for Pharaoh's use when he visited Elephantine in southern Egypt.
43:10 *Nebuchadnezzar . . . My servant.* See note on 25:9. *his throne.* Symbolizing his authority.
43:11 See 15:2 and note. *He will . . . strike . . . Egypt.* A fragmentary text now owned by the British Museum in London states that Nebuchadnezzar carried out a punitive expedition against Egypt in his 37th year (568–567 B.C.) during the reign of Pharaoh Amasis (see Ezek 29:17–20 and notes).
43:12 *he will wrap . . . as a shepherd wraps.* Routinely and confidently.
43:13 *obelisks of Heliopolis . . . in the land of Egypt.* Lit. "Beth-shemesh in Egypt," with the qualifying phrase being used to distinguish the site from "Beth-shemesh, which belongs to Judah" (2 Kin 14:11). The Egyptian city is probably to be identified with Heliopolis (Greek for "city of the sun"), called *On* in Hebrew (see note on Gen 41:45). *obelisks.* Sacred pillars, for which ancient Heliopolis was famous.
44:1–30 The last of Jeremiah's recorded prophecies (see note on 40:1–44:30).
44:1 *Jews living in . . . Egypt.* As a result of previous deportations (see, e.g., 2 Kin 23:34) and/or the Jews mentioned in 43:5–7. In either case, some time must have elapsed between chs. 43 and 44 to bring about the gathering mentioned in v. 15. *land of Egypt . . . land of Pathros.* See note on Is 11:11. *Migdol.* Location uncertain; probably in northern Egypt (see 46:14). The name means "watchtower." *Tahpanhes, Memphis.* See notes on 2:16; Is 19:13.
44:3 See note on 1:16; see also 11:17; 19:4; 32:32.

4 'Yet I [a]sent you all My servants the prophets, [1]again and again, saying, "Oh, do not do this [b]abominable thing which I hate."

5 'But [a]they did not listen or incline their ears to turn from their wickedness, so as not to burn [1]sacrifices to other gods.

6 'Therefore My [a]wrath and My anger were poured out and burned in the [b]cities of Judah and in the streets of Jerusalem, so they have become a ruin and a [c]desolation as it is this day.

7 'Now then thus says the LORD God of hosts, the God of Israel, "Why are you [a]doing great harm to yourselves, so as to [b]cut off from you man and woman, child and infant, from among Judah, leaving yourselves without remnant,

8 [a]provoking Me to anger with the works of your hands, [b]burning [1]sacrifices to other gods in the land of Egypt, where you are entering to reside, so that you might be cut off and become a [c]curse and a reproach among all the nations of the earth?

9 "Have you forgotten the [a]wickedness of your fathers, the wickedness of the kings of Judah, and the wickedness of their wives, your own wickedness, and the wickedness of your wives, which they committed in the land of Judah and in the streets of Jerusalem?

10 "But they [a]have not become [1]contrite even to this day, nor have they feared nor [b]walked in My law or My statutes, which I have set before you and before your fathers." '

11 "Therefore thus says the LORD of hosts, the God of Israel, 'Behold, I am going to [a]set My face against you for [1]woe, even to cut off all Judah.

12 'And I will [a]take away the remnant of Judah who have set their [1]mind on entering the land of Egypt to reside there, and they will all [2b]meet their end in the land of Egypt; they will fall by the sword *and* meet their end by famine. Both small and great will die by the sword and famine; and they will become a [c]curse, an object of horror, an imprecation and a reproach.

13 'And I will [a]punish those who live in the land of Egypt, as I have punished Jerusalem, with the sword, with famine and with pestilence.

14 'So there will be [a]no refugees or survivors for the remnant of Judah who have entered the land of Egypt to reside there and then to return to the land of Judah, to which they are [1b]longing to return and live; for none will [c]return except *a few* refugees.' "

15 Then [a]all the men who were aware that their wives were burning [1]sacrifices to other gods, along with all the women who were standing by, *as* a large assembly, [2]including all the people who were living in Pathros in the land of Egypt, responded to Jeremiah, saying,

16 "As for the [1a]message that you have spoken to us in the name of the LORD, [b]we are not going to listen to you!

17 "But rather we will certainly [a]carry out every word that has proceeded from our mouths, [1]by burning [2]sacrifices to the [b]queen of heaven and pouring out drink offerings to her, just as [c]we ourselves, our forefathers, our kings and our princes did in the cities of Judah and in the streets of Jerusalem; for *then* we had [d]plenty of [3]food and were well off and saw no [4]misfortune.

18 "But since we stopped burning [1]sacrifices to the queen of heaven and pouring out drink offerings to her, we have [a]lacked everything and have [2]met our end by the sword and by famine."

19 "And," *said the women,* "when we were [a]burning [1]sacrifices to the queen of heaven and [2]were pouring out drink offerings to her, was it [b]without our husbands that we made for her *sacrificial* cakes [3]in her image and poured out drink offerings to her?"

Calamity for the Jews

20 Then Jeremiah said to all the people, to the men and women—even to all the people who were giving him *such* an answer—saying,

4 [1]Lit *rising early and sending* [a]Jer 7:13, 25; 25:4; 26:5; 29:19; 35:15; Zech 7:7 [b]Jer 16:18; 32:34, 35; Ezek 8:10
5 [1]Or *incense* [a]Jer 11:8, 10; 13:10
6 [a]Is 51:17-20; Jer 42:18; Ezek 8:18 [b]Jer 7:17, 34 [c]Jer 4:27; 34:22
7 [a]Num 16:38; Jer 26:19; Ezek 33:11; Hab 2:10 [b]Jer 3:24; 9:21; 51:22
8 [1]Or *incense* [a]2 Kin 17:15-17; Jer 25:6, 7; 44:3; 1 Cor 10:21, 22 [b]Jer 7:9; 11:12, 17; 44:3; Hos 4:13; Hab 1:16 [c]1 Kin 9:7, 8; 2 Chr 7:20; Jer 42:18
9 [a]Jer 7:9, 10, 17, 18; 44:17, 21
10 [1]Lit *crushed* [a]Jer 6:15; 8:12 [b]Jer 26:4; 32:23; 44:23
11 [1]Lit *evil* [a]Lev 17:10; 20:5, 6; 26:17; Jer 21:10; Amos 9:4
12 [1]Lit *face* [2]Lit *be finished* [a]Jer 42:15-18, 22 [b]Is 1:28; Jer 16:4; 44:7 [c]Is 65:15; Jer 18:16; 24:9; 26:6; 29:18; 42:18; Zech 8:13
13 [a]Jer 11:22; 44:27, 28
14 [1]Lit *lifting up their soul* [a]Jer 22:10; 44:27 [b]Jer 22:26, 27 [c]Is 4:2; 10:20; Jer 44:28; Rom 9:27
15 [1]Or *incense* [2]Lit *and* [a]Prov 11:21; Is 1:5; Jer 5:1-5
16 [1]Lit *word* [a]Jer 43:2 [b]Prov 1:24-27; Jer 11:8, 10; 13:10
17 [1]Or *so as to burn* [2]Or *incense* [3]Lit *bread* [4]Lit *evil* [a]Num 30:12; Deut 23:23 [b]2 Kin 17:16; Jer 7:18 [c]Neh 9:34; Jer 32:32; 44:21 [d]Ex 16:3; Hos 2:5-9; Phil 3:19
18 [1]Or *incense* [2]Lit *been finished* [a]Num 11:5, 6; Jer 40:12; Mal 3:13-15
19 [1]Or *incense* [2]Lit *to pour* [3]Lit *to make an image of her* [a]Jer 7:18 [b]Num 30:6, 7; Jer 44:15

44:4 See note on 7:25. *do not do this abominable thing.* See Judg 19:24.
44:6 *My wrath and My anger were poured out.* See 7:20; 42:18.
44:7 *doing great harm to yourselves.* See 26:19. *man and woman, child and infant.* A stock phrase meaning "everyone" (see 1 Sam 15:3; 22:19).
44:8 *works of your hands.* Idols (see 1:16 and note). *a curse and a reproach.* See 42:18; see also notes on 24:9; 25:18.
44:9 *wickedness of . . . kings . . . their wives . . . your wives.* The women joined their husbands in worshiping the "queen of heaven" (v. 19; see v. 15).
44:10 *nor walked in My law.* See 9:13; 26:4; see also 7:9 and note.
44:11–14 See 42:17–18 and notes.
44:11 *set My face.* See 21:10).
44:15 *wives . . . women.* See v. 19; see also note on v. 9. *Pathros in the land of Egypt.* See v. 1; see also note on Is 11:11.
44:17 *queen of heaven.* See note on 7:18. *then we . . . were well off.* Judah had been relatively prosperous during King Manasseh's lengthy reign.
44:18 *since we stopped.* As a result of King Josiah's reform movement, which began in 621 B.C. *we have lacked everything.* Beginning with Josiah's death in 609, a series of disasters, including invasion and exile, had struck Judah. The people understandably (though mistakenly) attributed their misfortune to their failure to worship the queen of heaven.
44:19 *women.* Since Ishtar (the "queen of heaven") was a Babylonian goddess of fertility, women played a major role in her worship. *was it without our husbands . . . ?* To have validity, a religious vow made by a married woman (see v. 25) had to be confirmed by her husband (see Num 30:10–15). *we made for her . . . cakes in her image.* See 7:18 and note.

21 "As for the [1][a]smoking sacrifices that you burned in the cities of Judah and in the [b]streets of Jerusalem, you and your forefathers, your kings and your princes, and the people of the land, did not the LORD [c]remember them and did not *all this* come into His [2]mind?

22 "So the LORD was [a]no longer able to endure *it,* [b]because of the evil of your deeds, because of the abominations which you have committed; thus your land has become a [c]ruin, an object of horror and a curse, without an inhabitant, as *it is* this day.

23 "Because you have burned [1]sacrifices and have sinned against the LORD and [a]not obeyed the voice of the LORD or [b]walked in His law, His statutes or His testimonies, therefore this [c]calamity has befallen you, as *it has* this day."

24 Then Jeremiah said to all the people, including all the women, "[a]Hear the word of the LORD, all Judah who are [b]in the land of Egypt,

25 thus says the LORD of hosts, the God of Israel, as follows: 'As for you and your wives, you have spoken with your mouths and fulfilled *it* with your hands, saying, "We will [a]certainly perform our vows that we have vowed, to burn [1]sacrifices to the queen of heaven and pour out drink offerings to her." [2][b]Go ahead and confirm your vows, and certainly perform your vows!'

26 "[1]Nevertheless hear the word of the LORD, all Judah who are living in the land of Egypt, 'Behold, I have [a]sworn by My great name,' says the LORD, '[b]never shall My name be invoked again by the mouth of any man of Judah in all the land of Egypt, saying, "[c]As the Lord [2]GOD lives."

27 'Behold, I am watching over them [a]for harm and not for good, and [b]all the men of Judah who are in the land of Egypt will [1]meet their end by the sword and by famine until they [2]are completely gone.

21 [1]Or *incense* [2]Lit *heart* [a]Ezek 8:10, 11 [b]Jer 11:13; 44:9, 17 [c]Ps 79:8; Is 64:9; Jer 14:10; Hos 7:2; Amos 8:7
22 [a]Is 7:13; 43:24; Mal 2:17 [b]Jer 4:4; 21:12; 30:14 [c]Gen 19:13; Ps 107:33, 34; Jer 25:11, 18, 38; 29:18; 42:18; 44:12
23 [1]Or *incense* [a]Jer 7:13-15; 40:3 [b]Jer 44:10; Ps 119:136, 150 [c]1 Kin 9:9; Neh 13:18; Jer 44:2; Dan 9:11, 12
24 [a]Jer 42:15; 44:16 [b]Jer 43:7; 44:15, 26
25 [1]Or *incense* [2]Lit *Surely cause to stand* [a]Jer 44:17; Matt 14:9; Acts 23:12 [b]Ezek 20:39
26 [1]Lit *Therefore* [2]Heb *YHWH,* usually rendered LORD [a]Gen 22:16; Deut 32:40, 41; Jer 22:5; Amos 6:8; Heb 6:13 [b]Ps 50:16; Ezek 20:39 [c]Is 48:1, 2; Jer 5:2
27 [1]Lit *be finished* [2]Lit *come to an end* [a]Jer 1:10; 31:28; 39:16 [b]2 Kin 21:14; Jer 44:14
28 [1]Lit *men of number* [a]Jer 44:14 [b]Is 10:19; 27:12, 13 [c]Ps 33:11; Is 14:27; 46:10, 11; Zech 1:6
29 [a]Is 7:11, 14; 8:18; Jer 44:30; Matt 24:15, 16, 32 [b]Prov 19:21; Is 40:8
30 [a]Jer 43:9-13; 46:25; Ezek 29:3; 30:21

28 '[a]Those who escape the sword will return out of the land of Egypt to the land of Judah [1][b]few in number. Then all the remnant of Judah who have gone to the land of Egypt to reside there will know [c]whose word will stand, Mine or theirs.

29 'This will be the [a]sign to you,' declares the LORD, 'that I am going to punish you in this place, so that you may know that [b]My words will surely stand against you for harm.'

30 "Thus says the LORD, 'Behold, I am going to give over [a]Pharaoh Hophra king of Egypt to the hand of his enemies, to the hand of those who seek his life, just as I gave over [b]Zedekiah king of Judah to the hand of Nebuchadnezzar king of Babylon, *who was* his enemy and was seeking his life.' "

Message to Baruch

45 *This is* the message which Jeremiah the prophet spoke to [a]Baruch the son of Neriah, when he had [b]written down these words in a book [1]at Jeremiah's dictation, in the [c]fourth year of Jehoiakim the son of Josiah, king of Judah, saying:

2 "Thus says the LORD the God of Israel to you, O Baruch:

3 'You said, "Ah, woe is me! For the LORD has added sorrow to my pain; I am [a]weary with my groaning and have found no rest." '

4 "Thus you are to say to him, 'Thus says the LORD, "Behold, [a]what I have built I am about to tear down, and what I have planted I am about to uproot, that is, the whole land."

5 'But you, are you [a]seeking great things for yourself? Do not seek *them;* for behold, I am going to [b]bring disaster on all flesh,' declares the LORD, 'but I will [c]give your life to you as booty in all the places where you may go.' "

[b]2 Kin 25:4-7; Jer 34:21; 39:5-7 **45:1** [1]Lit *from the mouth of Jeremiah* [a]Jer 32:12, 16; 43:3, 6 [b]Jer 36:4, 18, 32 [c]2 Kin 24:1; 2 Chr 36:5-7; Jer 25:1; 36:1; 46:2; Dan 1:1 **3** [a]Ps 6:6; 69:3; 2 Cor 4:1, 16; Gal 6:9 **4** [a]Is 5:5; Jer 1:10; 11:17; 18:7-10; 31:28 **5** [a]1 Kin 3:9, 11; 2 Kin 5:26; Matt 6:25, 32; Rom 12:16 [b]Is 66:16; Jer 25:31 [c]Jer 21:9; 38:2; 39:18

44:22 *ruin.* See v. 6. *a curse.* See v. 12.

44:23 *testimonies.* Of the Lord's covenant with His people (see Deut 4:45; 6:17,20).

44:25 *Go ahead.* Spoken in irony (see 7:21 and note).

44:26 *I have sworn by My great name.* See notes on 22:5; Gen 22:16. *As the LORD God lives.* See note on Gen 42:15.

44:27 *watching.* See note on 1:12; see also 31:28.

44:28 *few in number.* See v. 14.

44:30 *Hophra.* Ruled Egypt 589–570 B.C. (see 37:5 and note). *his enemies . . . who seek his life.* Hophra was killed by his Egyptian rivals during a power struggle. *I gave over Zedekiah . . . to . . . Nebuchadnezzar.* See 39:5–7.

45:1–5 A brief message of encouragement to Baruch, Jeremiah's faithful secretary (see note on 32:12). Though out of chronological order, the section provides a suitable historical appendix to chs. 39–44 as well as a smooth transition to chs. 46–51 (see notes on v. 1; 46:2).

45:1 *had written . . . in a book.* See 36:4; see also 36:2 and note. *fourth year of Jehoiakim.* 605 B.C. Ch. 45 fits chronologically between 36:8 and 36:9 (see note on 36:8).

45:3 To some extent Baruch shared Jeremiah's anguish, the result of Jeremiah's prophetic call and ministry (see, e.g., 8:18–9:2; 20:7–18). *weary with my groaning.* See Ps 6:6. *found no rest.* See Lam 5:5.

45:4 *built . . . tear down . . . planted . . . uproot.* See note on 1:10; see also 2:21; 31:4–5,28,40; 32:41; 33:7. *land.* Or "earth" (see "all flesh" in v. 5; see also 25:15,31; 46–51).

45:5 *great things . . . Do not seek them.* See Ps 131:1. Baruch's brother Seraiah would occupy an important position under King Zedekiah (see 32:12; 51:59), but Baruch himself was not to be ambitious or self-seeking. *give your life to you as booty.* See note on 21:9.

46:1–51:64 See notes on 25:1–38; 25:13; 25:19–26. Chs. 46–51 consist of a series of prophecies against the nations (see Is 13–23; Ezek 25–32; Amos 1–2; Zeph 2:4–15). They begin with Egypt (ch. 46) and end with Babylonia (chs. 50–51), the two powers that vied for control of Judah during Jeremiah's ministry. The arrangement of the prophecies is in a generally west-to-east direction.

Defeat of Pharaoh Foretold

46 That which came as the word of the LORD to Jeremiah the prophet [a]concerning the nations.

2 To [a]Egypt, concerning the army of [b]Pharaoh Neco king of Egypt, which was by the Euphrates River at [c]Carchemish, which Nebuchadnezzar king of Babylon defeated in the [d]fourth year of Jehoiakim the son of Josiah, king of Judah:

3 "[a]Line up the shield and [1]buckler,
And draw near for the battle!
4 "Harness the horses,
And [1]mount the steeds,
And take your stand with helmets *on!*
[a]Polish the spears,
Put on the [b]scale-armor!
5 "Why have I seen *it?*
They are terrified,
They are [a]drawing back,
And their [b]mighty men are defeated
And have taken refuge in flight,
Without facing back;
[1c]Terror is on every side!"
Declares the LORD.
6 Let not the [a]swift man flee,
Nor the mighty man escape;
In the north beside the river
Euphrates
They have [b]stumbled and fallen.
7 Who is this that [a]rises like the Nile,
Like the rivers whose waters surge
about?
8 Egypt rises like the Nile,
Even like the rivers whose waters
surge about;
And He has said, "I will [a]rise and
cover *that* land;
I will surely [b]destroy the city and its
inhabitants."
9 Go up, you horses, and [1a]drive madly,
you chariots,
That the mighty men may [2]march
forward:
Ethiopia and [3b]Put, that handle the
shield,
And the [4c]Lydians, that handle *and*
bend the bow.
10 For [a]that day belongs to the Lord [1]GOD
of hosts,
A day of [b]vengeance, so as to avenge
Himself on His foes;
And the [c]sword will devour and be
satiated
And [2]drink its fill of their blood;
For there will be a [d]slaughter for the
Lord [1]GOD of hosts,
In the land of the north by the river
Euphrates.
11 Go [a]up to Gilead and obtain balm,
[b]O virgin daughter of Egypt!
In vain have you multiplied [1]remedies;
There is [c]no healing for you.
12 The nations have heard of your [a]shame,
And the earth is full of your [b]cry *of
distress;*
For one [c]warrior has stumbled over
[1]another,
And both of them have fallen down
together.

13 *This is* the [1]message which the LORD spoke to Jeremiah the prophet about the [a]coming of Nebuchadnezzar king of Babylon to [b]smite the land of Egypt:

14 "Declare in Egypt and proclaim in
[a]Migdol,
Proclaim also in Memphis and
[b]Tahpanhes;

46:1 [a]Jer 1:10; 25:15-38
2 [a]Jer 46:14; Ezek chs 29-32 [b]2 Kin 18:21; 23:29, 33-35; Jer 25:19 [c]2 Chr 35:20; Is 10:9 [d]Jer 45:1
3 [1]I.e. small shield [a]Is 21:5; Jer 51:11; Joel 3:9; Nah 2:1; 3:14
4 [1]Or *go up, you horsemen* [a]Ezek 21:9-11 [b]1 Sam 17:5, 38; 2 Chr 26:14; Neh 4:16; Jer 51:3
5 [1]Heb *Magor-missabib;* i.e. Terror is on every side [a]Is 42:17; Jer 46:21 [b]Is 5:25; Ezek 39:18 [c]Jer 6:25; 20:3; 49:29
6 [a]Is 30:16 [b]Jer 46:12, 16; Dan 11:19
7 [a]Jer 47:2
8 [a]Is 37:24 [b]Is 10:13
9 [1]Lit *act like madmen* [2]Lit *go forth* [3]I.e. Libya (or Somaliland) [4]Heb *Ludim* [a]Jer 47:3; Nah 2:4 [b]Nah 3:9 [c]Is 66:19
10 [1]Heb *YHWH,* usually rendered LORD [2]Lit *be saturated with* [a]Joel 1:15 [b]Jer 50:15, 18 [c]Deut 32:42; Is 31:8; Jer 12:12 [d]Is 34:6; Zeph 1:7
11 [1]Lit *healings* [a]Jer 8:22 [b]Is 47:1; Jer 31:4, 21 [c]Jer 30:13; Mic 1:9; Nah 3:19
12 [1]Lit *warrior* [a]Jer 2:36; Nah 3:8-10 [b]Jer 14:2 [c]Is 19:2
13 [1]Lit *word* [a]Jer 43:10-13 [b]Is 19:1
14 [a]Jer 44:1 [b]Jer 43:8

46:1 *the word of the LORD . . . concerning.* See 14:1; 47:1; 49:34; 50:1. *nations.* To whom Jeremiah was called to prophesy (see 1:5 and note).

46:2 *concerning . . . Egypt.* See Is 19–20; Ezek 29–32. *Neco.* Ruled Egypt 610–595 B.C. *Carchemish.* See 2 Chr 35:20; Is 10:9. The name means "fortress of Chemosh" (chief god of Moab; see 2 Kin 23:13), as clarified by the Ebla tablets (see Introduction to Genesis: Background; see also chart, p. xix). *which Nebuchadnezzar.* Egypt's defeat by Babylonia at Carchemish was one of the most decisive battles in the ancient world, ending Egypt's age-long claims and pretensions to power in Syro-Palestine. *fourth year of Jehoiakim.* 605 B.C., the first year of Nebuchadnezzar's reign (see 25:1).

46:3 *Line up.* Spoken to the Egyptians in sarcasm (see, e.g., Nah 2:1; 3:14).

46:4 *horses.* Egypt was a prime source for the finest horses (see 1 Kin 10:28). *Put on the scale-armor!* See 51:3.

46:5 *Terror is on every side!* The phrase is used in 6:25 (see note there) with reference to the Babylonian army (see 6:22 and note).

46:7–8 *rivers whose waters surge about.* In the northern Egyptian delta, where the Nile branches out into numerous streams.

46:8 *rise and cover that land.* The same metaphor is used of Assyria in Is 8:7–8 (see note there). *city.* The Hebrew for this word is in the singular but should be interpreted as a generic plural ("city" is generic also in 8:16).

46:9 *Go up.* See note on v. 3; see also 8:6; Nah 3:3. *drive madly, you chariots.* See Nah 2:4. *Put.* See note on Gen 10:6. *Lydians.* See note on Is 66:19. Men from Cush, Put and Lydia were mercenaries in the Egyptian army.

46:10 *day of vengeance.* See Is 34:8 and note. The Lord will avenge Egypt's cruelties toward Judah (see, e.g., 2 Kin 23:29,33–35). *sword will devour.* See v. 14. *drink its fill of their blood . . . a slaughter.* The imagery of "blood" and "slaughter" found in the Israelite sacrificial ritual was often used to describe battles (see Is 34:5–7 and notes; Zeph 1:7–8).

46:11 *Gilead . . . balm.* See 8:22 and note. *virgin daughter of Egypt.* See v. 19; Is 23:12 and note; Is 47:1; see also 14:17 and note; 18:13; 31:4,21. *In vain . . . remedies. . . no healing for you.* The statement is ironic in the light of Egypt's reputation for expertise in the healing arts.

46:12 *stumbled . . . fallen.* See vv. 6,16.

46:13 *Nebuchadnezzar . . . to smite . . . Egypt.* In 568–567 B.C. (see note on 43:11), long after the battle of Carchemish (see note on v. 2).

46:14 *Migdol.* See note on 44:1. *Memphis and Tahpanhes.* See 44:1; see also notes on 2:16; Is 19:13. *Take your stand.* See v. 4. *sword has devoured.* See v. 10.

Say, 'Take your stand and get yourself
ready,
For the [c]sword has devoured those
around you.'
15 "Why have your [a]mighty ones become
prostrate?
They do not stand because the LORD
has [b]thrust them down.
16 "They have repeatedly [a]stumbled;
Indeed, they have fallen one against
another.
Then they said, 'Get up! And [b]let us
go back
To our own people and our native land
Away from the [1c]sword of the
oppressor.'
17 "[1]They cried there, 'Pharaoh king of
Egypt *is but* [a]a big noise;
He has let the appointed time pass by!'
18 "As I live," declares the [a]King
Whose name is the LORD of hosts,
"Surely one shall come *who looms up*
like [b]Tabor among the mountains,
Or like [c]Carmel by the sea.
19 "Make your baggage ready for [a]exile,
O [b]daughter dwelling in Egypt,
For [c]Memphis will become a
desolation;
It will even be burned down *and*
[1]bereft of inhabitants.
20 "Egypt is a pretty [a]heifer,
But a [1]horsefly is coming [b]from the
north—it is coming!
21 "Also her [a]mercenaries in her midst
Are like [1]fattened [b]calves,
For even they too have turned back
and have fled away together;
They did not stand *their ground.*
For the day of their calamity has come
upon them,
The time of their [c]punishment.
22 "Its sound moves along like a
serpent;
For they move on [1]like an army
And come to her as woodcutters with
axes.
23 "They have cut down her [a]forest,"
declares the LORD;
"Surely it will no *more* be found,
Even though [1]they are *now* more
numerous than [b]locusts
And are without number.
24 "The daughter of Egypt has been put to
shame,
Given over to the [1]power of the
[a]people of the north."
25 The LORD of hosts, the God of Israel,
says, "Behold, I am going to punish Amon of
[a]Thebes, and [b]Pharaoh, and Egypt along
with her [c]gods and her kings, even Pharaoh
and those who [d]trust in him.
26 "I shall give them over to the [1]power of
those who are [a]seeking their lives, even into
the hand of Nebuchadnezzar king of Babylon and into the hand of his [2]officers.
[b]Afterwards, however, it will be inhabited as
in the days of old," declares the LORD.
27 "But as for you, O Jacob My servant,
[a]do not fear,
Nor be dismayed, O Israel!
For, see, I am going to [b]save you from
afar,
And your descendants from the land
of their captivity;
And Jacob will return and be
[c]undisturbed
And secure, with no one making *him*
tremble.

14 [c]Is 1:20; Jer 2:30; 46:10; Nah 2:13
15 [a]Is 66:15, 16; Jer 46:5 [b]Ps 18:14, 39; 68:1, 2
16 [1]Lit *oppressing sword* [a]Lev 26:36, 37; Jer 46:6 [b]Jer 51:9 [c]Jer 50:16
17 [1]Some ancient versions read *Call the name of Pharaoh a big noise* [a]Ex 15:9, 10; 1 Kin 20:10, 11; Is 19:11-16
18 [a]Jer 48:15; Mal 1:14 [b]Josh 19:22; Judg 4:6; Ps 89:12 [c]Josh 12:22; 1 Kin 18:42
19 [1]Lit *without* [a]Is 20:4 [b]Jer 48:18 [c]Jer 46:14; Ezek 30:13
20 [1]Or possibly *mosquito* [a]Hos 10:11 [b]Jer 1:14; 47:2
21 [1]Lit *of the stall* [a]2 Sam 10:6; 2 Kin 7:6; Jer 46:5 [b]Is 34:7
21 [c]Jer 48:44; Hos 9:7; Obad 13; Mic 7:4
22 [1]Or *in force*
23 [1]I.e. trees of the forest, the Egyptians [a]Jer 21:14 [b]Judg 6:5; 7:12; Joel 2:25
24 [1]Lit *hand* [a]Jer 1:15
25 [a]Ezek 30:14-16; Nah 3:8 [b]Jer 44:30 [c]Ex 12:12; Jer 43:12, 13; Ezek 30:13; Zeph 2:11 [d]Is 20:5
26 [1]Lit *hand* [2]Lit *servants* [a]Jer 44:30; Ezek 32:11 [b]Ezek 29:8-14
27 [a]Is 41:13, 14; Jer 30:10, 11 [b]Is 11:11; Jer 23:3, 4; 29:14; Mic 7:12 [c]Jer 23:6; 50:19

46:15 *mighty ones.* The Hebrew for this word is not the same as that for "mighty men" (vv. 5,9) or "warrior" (v. 12). It is lit. "strong ones," often referring to powerful animals ("stallions" in 8:16; 47:3; 50:11; "steeds" in Judg 5:22). In Ps 22:12; 50:13; 68:30; Is 34:7 the Hebrew word is translated "bulls" (see note on Ps 68:30). *became prostrate.* The Hebrew for this phrase is translated "Apis has fled" in the Septuagint (the Greek translation of the OT). Apis was a bull-god worshiped in Egypt, especially at Memphis (see v. 14). An alternative translation of v. 15 would then read as follows: "Why did Apis flee? Why did your bull [many manuscripts have the singular form] not stand? Because the LORD pushed him down."
46:16 *They have repeatedly stumbled.* See vv. 6,12; lit. "He will make many stumble." *they said, '. . . let us go . . .'* The mercenaries in Pharaoh's army (see v. 9 and note) will decide to return to their homelands. *sword of the oppressor.* See 25:38; 50:16.
46:17 *a big noise.* In Is 30:7, Egypt is called the one "who has been exterminated." *let the appointed time pass by.* After the battle of Carchemish (see v. 2), Nebuchadnezzar returned to Babylonia on learning of his father's death. Egypt failed to press its advantage at that time.
46:18 *As I live.* See notes on Gen 22:16; 42:15. *King.* God is called "King" also in 8:19; 10:7,10; 48:15; 51:57. *one.* Nebuchadnezzar. *Tabor . . . Carmel.* Two prominent mountains in Israel (see notes on Judg 4:6; Song 7:5; Is 33:9).
46:19 *Make your baggage ready for exile.* Echoed in Ezek 12:3. *Egypt.* Lit. "Daughter of Egypt" (see v. 11 and note). *become a desolation.* Judah is so described in 2:15; 9:12.
46:20 *heifer.* Perhaps an ironic reference to Egyptian bull-worship (see note on v. 15). *horsefly.* Nebuchadnezzar. Insects are often used to symbolize an attacking enemy (see note on Ex 23:28).
46:21 *mercenaries.* See note on v. 9. *calves.* See note on v. 20. *day of their calamity.* See 18:17. *time of their punishment.* See 11:23; 23:12; 50:27.
46:22 *serpent.* Often used by Egyptian pharaohs as a symbol of their sovereignty (see note on Ex 4:3). *woodcutters with axes.* See 21:14; see also Is 10:18–19,33–34 and notes.
46:23 *more numerous than locusts.* Here an invading army is compared to locusts. In Joel 2:11,25 locusts are compared to an invading army.
46:24 *daughter of Egypt.* See note on v. 11.
46:25 *Amon.* The chief god of Egypt during much of its history. Wicked King Manasseh may have named his son after the Egyptian deity (see 2 Kin 21:18; 2 Chr 33:22). *Thebes.* The capital of Upper (southern) Egypt (see Ezek 30:14–16).
46:26 *it will be inhabited as in the days of old.* Cf. 48:47; 49:6,39. Egypt would be restored in the Messianic age (see Is 19:23–25).
46:27–28 Repeated almost verbatim from 30:10–11 (see notes there).

28 "O Jacob My servant, do not fear,"
declares the LORD,
"For [a]I am with you.
For I will make a full end of all the nations
Where I have driven you,
Yet I will [b]not make a full end of you;
But I will [c]correct you properly
And by no means leave you unpunished."

Prophecy against Philistia

47 That which came as the word of the
LORD to Jeremiah the prophet concern-
ing the [a]Philistines, before Pharaoh [1]con-
quered [b]Gaza.
2 Thus says the LORD:
"Behold, waters are going to rise from [a]the north
And become an overflowing torrent,
And [b]overflow the land and all its fullness,
The city and those who live in it;
And the men will [c]cry out,
And every inhabitant of the land will wail.
3 "Because of the noise of the [1][a]galloping hoofs of his [2]stallions,
The tumult of his chariots, *and* the rumbling of his wheels,
The fathers have not turned back for *their* children,
Because of the limpness of *their* hands,
4 On account of the day that is coming
To [a]destroy all the Philistines,
To cut off from [b]Tyre and Sidon
Every ally that is left;
For the LORD is going to destroy the Philistines,
The remnant of the coastland of [c]Caphtor.
5 "[a]Baldness has come upon Gaza;
[b]Ashkelon has been ruined.
O remnant of their valley,
How long will you [c]gash yourself?
6 "Ah, [a]sword of the LORD,
How long will you not be quiet?
Withdraw into your sheath;
Be at rest and stay still.
7 "How can [1]it be quiet,
When the LORD has [a]given it an order?
Against Ashkelon and against the seacoast—
There He has [b]assigned it."

Prophecy against Moab

48 Concerning [a]Moab. Thus says the LORD of hosts, the God of Israel,
"Woe to [b]Nebo, for it has been destroyed;
[c]Kiriathaim has been put to shame, it has been captured;
The lofty stronghold has been put to shame and [1]shattered.
2 "There is praise for Moab no longer;
In [a]Heshbon they have devised calamity against her:
'Come and let us cut her off from *being* a nation!'
You too, [1]Madmen, will be silenced;
The sword will follow after you.
3 "The sound of an outcry from [a]Horonaim,
'Devastation and great destruction!'
4 "Moab is broken,
Her little ones have sounded out a cry *of distress.*
5 "For by the ascent of [a]Luhith

28 [a]Ps 46:7, 11; Is 8:10; 43:2; Jer 1:19 [b]Jer 4:27; Amos 9:8, 9 [c]Jer 10:24; Hab 3:2
47:1 [1]Lit *smote* [a]Jer 25:20; Zech 9:6 [b]Gen 10:19; 1 Kin 4:24; Jer 25:20; Amos 1:6; Zeph 2:4
2 [a]Is 14:31; Jer 1:14; 6:22; 46:20, 24 [b]Is 8:7, 8 [c]Is 15:2-5; Jer 46:12
3 [1]Lit *stamping of the* [2]Lit *mighty ones* [a]Judg 5:22; Jer 8:16; Nah 3:2
4 [a]Is 14:31 [b]Is 23:5; Jer 25:22; Joel 3:4; Amos 1:9, 10; Zech 9:2-4
4 [c]Gen 10:14; Deut 2:23; Amos 9:7
5 [a]Jer 48:37; Mic 1:16 [b]Judg 1:18; Jer 25:20; Amos 1:7, 8; Zeph 2:4, 7; Zech 9:5 [c]Jer 16:6; 41:5
6 [a]Judg 7:20; Jer 12:12; Ezek 21:3-5
7 [1]Lit *you* [a]Is 10:6; Ezek 14:17 [b]Mic 6:9
48:1 [1]Or *dismayed* [a]Is 15:1; Ezek 25:9 [b]Num 32:3, 38; Jer 48:22 [c]Num 32:37; Jer 48:23; Ezek 25:9
2 [1]I.e. a city of Moab [a]Num 21:25; Jer 48:34, 45; 49:3
3 [a]Is 15:5; Jer 48:5, 34
5 [a]Is 15:5

47:1 *concerning the Philistines.* See Is 14:28–32; Ezek 25:15–17; Amos 1:6–8; Zeph 2:4–7. *Pharaoh.* It is uncertain whether Neco II (see 46:2; see also note on 2 Kin 23:29) or Hophra (see notes on 37:5; 44:30) is intended. *Gaza.* See v. 5; 25:20; see also note on Judg 1:18.
47:2 *waters are going to rise.* See notes on 46:7–8. *the north.* Babylonia, as in 1:13–14; 46:20. *the land . . . live in it.* The Hebrew for this phrase is repeated verbatim from 8:16. *land.* Phoenicia and Philistia. *city.* A generic singular used as a plural (see note on 46:8); includes Tyre and Sidon (see v. 4) as well as Gaza, Ashkelon (see v. 5) and other Philistine cities.
47:3 *stallions.* Lit. "strong ones" (see note on 46:15). *limpness of their hands.* Paralyzed by terror (see 6:24; Is 13:7).
47:4 *Tyre and Sidon.* See notes on v. 2; 25:22; 27:3. *remnant.* See v. 5. *Caphtor.* Crete (the Kerethites of Zeph 2:5 and elsewhere were probably Cretans), one of many islands in the Mediterranean believed to be the original homeland of the Philistines (see Gen 10:14 and note; see also Deut 2:23).
47:5 *Baldness has come.* See note on 16:6; see also 48:37. *Gaza.* See v. 1; 25:20; see also note on Judg 1:18. *Ashkelon.* See v. 7; 25:20; see also note on Judg 1:18. *remnant.* See note on v. 4. *valley.* Roughly equivalent to the modern Gaza Strip, it lay west of the foothills that separated Philistia from Judah. *gash yourself.* See note on 16:6; see also 48:37.
47:6 *you.* The Philistines.
47:7 *Against Ashkelon.* The immediate fulfillment took place under Nebuchadnezzar in 604 B.C. *seacoast.* See Ezek 25:16; the Philistine plain (see note on v. 5).
48:1 *Concerning Moab.* See Is 15–16; Ezek 25:8–11; Amos 2:1–3; Zeph 2:8–11. Josephus (*Antiquities,* 10.9.7) implies that Jeremiah's prophecy concerning the future destruction of Moab was fulfilled in the "twenty-third year of Nebuchadnezzar's reign" (582 B.C.; see 52:30). *Nebo.* See v. 22; a town originally allotted to the tribe of Reuben (see Num 32:3,37–38; see also Is 15:2 and note). *Kiriathaim.* See v. 23. An ancient town (see Gen 14:5), it too was allotted to Reuben (see Josh 13:19 and note). Nebo, Kiriathaim and several other towns referred to in this chapter are mentioned also in an important Moabite inscription written by Mesha king of Moab (see 2 Kin 3:4) and discovered in 1868 (see chart, p. xix).
48:2 *Heshbon.* See vv. 34,45; 49:3; Num 21:25. Originally allotted to Reuben (see Num 32:37; Josh 13:17), it was later reassigned to Gad as a Levitical town (see Josh 21:39). *have devised.* The Hebrew for this phrase is a pun on "Heshbon." *Madmen.* Location unknown; perhaps a longer spelling of "Dimon" (Is 15:9—but see note there). In Is 25:10, the feminine form of the Hebrew word *madmen* is translated "manure pile." *sword will follow after you.* See 9:16; 42:16.
48:3 *Horonaim.* See vv. 5,34; location unknown.
48:4 *broken.* Like a clay jar (see 19:11).
48:5 *Luhith.* Location unknown (see Is 15:5).

They will ascend with continual
weeping;
For at the descent of Horonaim
They have heard the [1]anguished cry of
destruction.
6 "[a]Flee, save your lives,
That you may be like a juniper in the
wilderness.
7 "For because of your [a]trust in your own
achievements and treasures,
Even you yourself will be captured;
And [b]Chemosh will go off into exile
Together with his priests and his
princes.
8 "A destroyer will come to every city,
So that no city will escape;
The valley also will be ruined
And the [a]plateau will be destroyed,
As the LORD has said.
9 "Give [1a]wings to Moab,
For she will [2]flee away;
And her cities will become a
[b]desolation,
Without inhabitants in them.
10 "[a]Cursed be the one who does the
LORD's work [b]negligently,
And cursed be the one who restrains
his [c]sword from blood.

11 "Moab has been [a]at ease since his
youth;
He has also been [b]undisturbed, *like*
wine on [1]its dregs,
And he has not been [c]emptied from
vessel to vessel,
Nor has he gone into exile.
Therefore [2]he retains his flavor,
And his aroma has not changed.
12 "Therefore behold, the days are coming," declares the LORD, "when I will send to
him those who tip *vessels,* and they will tip
him over, and they will empty his vessels
and shatter [1]his jars.
13 "And Moab will be [a]ashamed of [b]Che-
mosh, as the house of Israel was ashamed of
[c]Bethel, their confidence.
14 "How can you say, 'We are [a]mighty
warriors,
And men valiant for battle'?
15 "Moab has been destroyed and [1]men
have gone up to [2]his cities;
His choicest [3a]young men have also
gone down to the slaughter,"
Declares the [b]King, whose name is the
LORD of hosts.
16 "The disaster of Moab will [a]soon come,
And his calamity has swiftly hastened.
17 "Mourn for him, all you who *live*
around him,
Even all of you who know his name;
Say, 'How has the mighty [1a]scepter
been broken,
A staff of splendor!'
18 "[a]Come down from your glory
And sit [1]on the parched ground,
O [b]daughter dwelling in [c]Dibon,
For the destroyer of Moab has come
up against you,
He has ruined your strongholds.
19 "Stand by the road and keep watch,
O inhabitant of [a]Aroer;
[b]Ask him who flees and her who
escapes
And say, 'What has happened?'
20 "Moab has been put to shame, for it
has been [1]shattered.
Wail and cry out;
Declare by the [a]Arnon
That Moab has been destroyed.

5 [1]Lit *distresses of outcry*
6 [a]Jer 51:6
7 [a]Ps 52:7; Is 59:4; Jer 9:23 [b]Num 21:29; 1 Kin 11:33; Jer 48:13, 46
8 [a]Josh 13:9, 17, 21
9 [1]Or *salt* [2]Or *fall in ruins* [a]Ps 11:1; Is 16:2; Jer 48:28 [b]Jer 44:22
10 [a]Jer 11:3 [b]1 Kin 20:39, 40, 42; 2 Kin 13:19 [c]Jer 47:6, 7
11 [1]Lit *his* [2]Lit *his flavor has stayed in him* [a]Jer 22:21; Ezek 16:49; Zech 1:15 [b]Zeph 1:12 [c]Nah 2:2
12 [1]Lit *their*
13 [a]Is 45:16; Jer 48:39 [b]Judg 11:24 [c]1 Kin 12:29; Hos 8:5, 6
14 [a]Ps 33:16; Is 10:13-16
15 [1]Lit *one has* [2]Lit *her* [3]I.e. warriors [a]Is 40:30, 31; Jer 50:27 [b]Jer 46:18; 51:57; Mal 1:14
16 [a]Is 13:22
17 [1]Or *rod* [a]Is 9:4; 14:5
18 [1]Lit *in thirst* [a]Is 47:1 [b]Jer 46:19 [c]Num 21:30; Josh 13:9, 17; Is 15:2; Jer 48:22
19 [a]Deut 2:36; Josh 12:2 [b]1 Sam 4:13, 14, 16
20 [1]Or *dismayed* [a]Num 21:13

48:6 *Flee, save your lives.* See 51:6. *like a juniper.* See note on 17:6.
48:7 *Chemosh.* See vv. 13,46; the national god of Moab (see 1 Kin 11:7,33; 2 Kin 23:13). The Hebrew text here implies the alternate spelling Chemish, as in "Carchemish" (see note on 46:2). *will go off into exile . . . and his princes.* A stock phrase (see 49:3; Amos 1:15). Images of pagan deities were often carried about from place to place (see 43:12; Amos 5:26).
48:8 *destroyer.* See v. 32; probably Nebuchadnezzar. *valley . . . plateau.* Much of western Moab overlooks the Jordan Valley.
48:9 See 17:6. *Give wings to Moab.* Or "put salt on Moab"—to make its farmland unproductive and barren (see note on Judg 9:45).
48:10 *negligently.* Or "slack" (as in Prov 12:24). Those whom the Lord designates to destroy Moab are urged on in their appointed task.
48:11 A copy of the Hebrew text of this verse has been found inscribed on a large clay seal, dating to the early Christian era and apparently used for stamping the bitumen with which the mouths of wine jars were sealed. *since his youth.* From her early history. *like wine.* An apt figure, since Moab was noted for her vineyards (see vv. 32–33; Is 16:8–10). *on its dregs.* In order to improve with age (see Is 25:6). *Nor has he gone into exile.* Unlike Israel.
48:12 *days are coming.* Moab will be destroyed (see note on v. 1). *tip vessels.* Gently, in order to leave the unwanted sediment in the bottom. But these men will be the agents of divine judgment and will "shatter" Moab (see v. 4 and note).
48:13 *Chemosh.* See note on v. 7. *house of Israel.* The northern kingdom, destroyed and exiled in 722–721 B.C. *Bethel.* Either (1) the well-known town where one of Jeroboam's golden calves was placed (see 1 Kin 12:28–30) or, (2) in parallelism with Chemosh, the West Semitic deity known from contemporary Babylonian inscriptions as well as from the Elephantine papyri a century later.
48:14 *How can you say . . . ?* See 2:23; 8:8.
48:15 *gone down to the slaughter.* See 50:27; for war depicted as the slaughter of sacrificial animals see Is 34:6 and note. *King.* See note on 46:18. The true King is the Lord, not Chemosh.
48:16 See Deut 32:35.
48:17 *who live around him . . . who know his name.* Nations near and far respectively. *mighty.* At one time Moab had been powerful and feared (see 27:3; 2 Kin 1:1; 3:5; 24:2). *scepter . . . staff.* Symbols of authority and dominion (see Gen 49:10; Ps 2:9; Ezek 19:11,14).
48:18 *Come down . . . sit.* See Is 47:1 and note. *daughter.* See note on Is 23:10. *Dibon.* See v. 22; Num 21:30; see also note on Is 15:2.
48:19 *Aroer.* See Num 32:34; Deut 2:36.
48:20 *Arnon.* Moab's most important river.

21 "Judgment has also come upon the plain,
upon Holon, [a]Jahzah and against [b]Mephaath,
22 against Dibon, Nebo and Beth-diblathaim,
23 against Kiriathaim, Beth-gamul and
[a]Beth-meon,
24 against [a]Kerioth, Bozrah and all the cities of the land of Moab, far and near.
25 "The [a]horn of Moab has been cut off
and his [b]arm broken," declares the LORD.
26 "[a]Make him drunk, for he has [1]become
[b]arrogant toward the LORD; so Moab will
[2]wallow in his vomit, and he also will
become a laughingstock.
27 "Now was not Israel a [a]laughingstock to
you? Or was he [1][b]caught among thieves? For
each time you speak about him you [c]shake
your head in scorn.
28 "Leave the cities and dwell among the
[a]crags,
O inhabitants of Moab,
And be like a [b]dove that nests
Beyond the mouth of the chasm.
29 "[a]We have heard of the pride of
Moab—he *is* very proud—
Of his haughtiness, his [b]pride, his
arrogance and [1]his self-exaltation.
30 "I know his [a]fury," declares the LORD,
"But it is futile;
His idle boasts have accomplished
nothing.
31 "Therefore I will [a]wail for Moab,
Even for all Moab will I cry out;
[1]I will moan for the men of [b]Kir-heres.
32 "More than the [a]weeping for [b]Jazer
I will weep for you, O vine of Sibmah!
Your tendrils stretched across the sea,
They reached to the sea of Jazer;
Upon your summer fruits and your
grape harvest
The destroyer has fallen.
33 "So [a]gladness and joy are taken away
From the fruitful field, even from the
land of Moab.
And I have made the wine to [b]cease
from the wine presses;
No one will tread *them* with shouting,
The shouting will not be shouts *of*
joy.
34 "[a]From the outcry at Heshbon even to
[b]Elealeh, even to Jahaz they have [1]raised
their voice, from [c]Zoar even to Horonaim
and to Eglath-shelishiyah; for even the
waters of Nimrim will become desolate.
35 "I will make an end of Moab," declares
the LORD, "the one who offers *sacrifice* on the
[a]high place and the one who [1][b]burns incense to his gods.
36 "Therefore My [a]heart [1]wails for Moab
like flutes; My heart also [1]wails like flutes for
the men of Kir-heres. Therefore they have
[b]lost the abundance it produced.
37 "For [a]every head is bald and every beard
cut short; there are gashes on all the hands
and [b]sackcloth on the loins.
38 "On all the [a]housetops of Moab and in
its streets [1]there is lamentation everywhere;
for I have broken Moab like an undesirable
[b]vessel," declares the LORD.
39 "How [1]shattered it is! *How* they have
wailed! How Moab has turned his back—he
is ashamed! So Moab will become a laughingstock and an [a]object of terror to all around
him."
40 For thus says the LORD:
"Behold, one will [a]fly swiftly like an
eagle

21 [a]Num 21:23; Is 15:4; Jer 48:34 [b]Josh 13:18 **23** [a]Josh 13:17 **24** [a]Jer 48:41; Amos 2:2 **25** [a]Ps 75:10; Zech 1:19-21 [b]Job 22:9; Ps 10:15 **26** [1]Or *magnified himself against* [2]Or *splash into* [a]Jer 25:15 [b]Ex 5:2; Jer 48:42; Dan 5:23 **27** [1]Or *found* [a]Lam 2:15-17; Mic 7:8-10 [b]Jer 2:26 [c]Job 16:4; Jer 18:16 **28** [a]Judg 6:2; Is 2:19; Jer 49:16; Obad 3 [b]Ps 55:6; Song 2:14 **29** [1]Lit *elevation of his heart* [a]Is 16:6; Zeph 2:8 [b]Job 40:11, 12; Ps 138:6 **30** [a]Is 37:28 **31** [1]Another reading is *He* [a]Is 15:5; 16:7, 11 [b]2 Kin 3:25; Is 16:7, 11; Jer 48:36 **32** [a]Is 16:8, 9 [b]Num 21:32 **33** [a]Is 16:10; Jer 25:10; Joel 1:12 [b]Is 5:10; Hag 2:16 **34** [1]Lit *given forth* [a]Is 15:4-6 [b]Num 32:3, 37 [c]Gen 13:10; 14:2; Is 15:5, 6 **35** [1]Or *offers up in smoke* [a]Is 15:2; 16:12 [b]Jer 7:9; 11:13 **36** [1]Lit *sounds* [a]Is 15:5; 16:11 [b]Is 15:7 **37** [a]Is 15:2; Jer 16:6; 41:5; 47:5 [b]Gen 37:34; Is 15:3; 20:2 **38** [1]Lit *all of it is lamentation* [a]Is 22:1 [b]Jer 19:10, 11; 22:28; 25:34 **39** [1]Or *dismayed* [a]Ezek 26:16 **40** [a]Deut 28:49; Jer 49:22; Hos 8:1; Hab 1:8

48:21 *plain.* See note on v. 8. *Holon.* Not the same as the town mentioned in Josh 15:51; 21:15. Its location is unknown. *Jahzah.* See 1 Chr 6:78; elsewhere called Jahaz (see v. 34; see also Is 15:4 and note).

48:22 *Dibon.* See v. 18. *Nebo.* See note on v. 1. *Beth-diblathaim.* Perhaps the same as, or near, Almon-diblathaim (see Num 33:46).

48:23 *Kiriathaim.* See note on v. 1. *Beth-gamul.* Modern Khirbet Jumeil, five miles east of Aroer. *Beth-meon.* The same as Baal-meon (see Num 32:38) and Beth-baal-meon (see Josh 13:17).

48:24 *Kerioth.* See note on Amos 2:2. Its location is unknown. *Bozrah.* Not the same as Bozrah in Edom (see 49:13,22), but another name for Bezer in Moab (see note on Deut 4:43).

48:26 The Lord speaks to the Babylonian invaders. *Make him drunk.* By drinking down the cup of God's wrath (see 13:13; 25:15–17,28). *wallow in his vomit.* See 25:27; Is 19:14. *he also will become a laughingstock.* As she had once ridiculed others (see v. 27; Zeph 2:8,10).

48:27 *shake your head in scorn.* See 18:16 and note; see also Ps 64:8.

48:28 *like a dove . . . mouth of the chasm.* See Ps 55:6–8; Song 2:14.

48:29–30 An expanded version of the description of Moab found in Is 16:6.

48:29 *pride of Moab.* It had long since become proverbial (see Is 25:10–11; Zeph 2:8–10).

48:31–33 See Is 16:7–10.

48:31–32 *I.* The prophet (as in Is 16:9; cf. Is 15:5).

48:31 *moan.* Like a mourning dove (see Is 38:14; 59:11). *Kir-heres.* See Is 16:7,11; see also note on Is 15:1.

48:32 *More than . . . for Jazer.* See Is 16:9. *Jazer . . . Sibmah . . . sea.* See note on Is 16:8. *vine.* See note on v. 11. *destroyer.* See v. 8; probably Nebuchadnezzar.

48:33 *tread.* See note on Is 16:10. *not be shouts of joy.* Instead, shouts of judgment (see 25:30; 51:14).

48:34 See Is 15:4–6 and notes.

48:36 See Is 16:11. *flutes.* Played by mourners at funerals (see Matt 9:23–24).

48:37 Signs of mourning (see Is 15:2–3 and notes). *gashes.* See note on 16:6.

48:38 *broken . . . like an undesirable vessel.* See v. 4 and note on v. 12; cf. the description of King Jehoiachin in 22:28 (see note there).

48:39 *laughingstock.* See v. 26 and note.

48:40–41 Echoed in 49:22 with respect to Edom.

48:40 *eagle.* Nebuchadnezzar (as in Ezek 17:3); see Deut 28:49 and note.

And [b]spread out his wings against
Moab.
41 "Kerioth has been captured
And the strongholds have been seized,
So the [a]hearts of the mighty men of
Moab in that day
Will be like the heart of a [b]woman in
labor.
42 "Moab will be [a]destroyed from *being* a
people
Because he has [1]become [b]arrogant
toward the LORD.
43 "[a]Terror, pit and snare are *coming* upon
you,
O inhabitant of Moab," declares the
LORD.
44 "The one who [a]flees from the terror
Will fall into the pit,
And the one who climbs up out of the
pit
Will be caught in the snare;
For I shall bring upon her, *even* upon
Moab,
The year of their [b]punishment,"
declares the LORD.

45 "In the shadow of Heshbon
The fugitives stand without strength;
For a fire has gone forth from
Heshbon
And a [a]flame from the midst of [b]Sihon,
And it has devoured the [c]forehead of
Moab
And the scalps of the [1]riotous revelers.
46 "[a]Woe to you, Moab!
The people of [b]Chemosh have
perished;
For your sons have been taken away
captive
And your daughters into captivity.
47 "Yet I will [a]restore the [1]fortunes of
Moab
In the [2]latter days," declares the LORD.
Thus far the judgment on Moab.

40 [b]Is 8:8 **41** [a]Jer 49:22 [b]Is 13:8; 21:3; Jer 30:6; Mic 4:9, 10 **42** [1]Or *magnified himself against* [a]Ps 83:4; Jer 48:2 [b]Is 37:23; Jer 48:26 **43** [a]Is 24:17, 18; Lam 3:47 **44** [a]1 Kin 19:17; Is 24:18; Amos 5:19 [b]Jer 46:21 **45** [1]Lit *sons of tumult* [a]Num 21:28, 29 [b]Num 21:21, 26; Ps 135:11 [c]Num 24:17 **46** [a]Num 21:29 [b]Judg 11:24; 1 Kin 11:7; Jer 48:7 **47** [1]Or *captivity* [2]Lit *end of the days* [a]Jer 12:14-17; 49:6, 39

49:1 [1]In 1 Kin 11:5, 33 and Zeph 1:5, *Milcom* [a]Deut 23:3, 4; 2 Chr 20:1; Ezek 21:28-32; 25:2-10; Amos 1:13-15; Zeph 2:8-11 **2** [1]Or *shout of* [a]Num 10:9; Jer 4:19 [b]Deut 3:11; 2 Sam 11:1; Ezek 21:20 [c]Josh 17:11, 16 [d]Is 14:2 **3** [1]Cf v 1 [a]Jer 48:2 [b]Josh 7:2-5; 8:1-29; Ezra 2:28 [c]Is 32:11; Jer 48:37 [d]Jer 46:25; 48:7 **4** [a]Jer 9:23 [b]Jer 31:22 [c]Ps 62:10; Ezek 28:4, 5; 1 Tim 6:17 [d]Jer 21:13 **5** [1]Heb *YHWH,* usually rendered LORD [2]Lit *before him* [a]Jer 48:43f; 49:29 [b]Jer 16:16; 46:5 [c]Lam 4:15

Prophecy against Ammon

49 Concerning the sons of [a]Ammon. Thus
says the LORD:
"Does Israel have no sons?
Or has he no heirs?
Why then has [1]Malcam taken
possession of Gad
And his people settled in its cities?
2 "Therefore behold, the days are
coming," declares the LORD,
"That I will cause a [1a]trumpet blast of
war to be heard
Against [b]Rabbah of the sons of
Ammon;
And it will become a desolate heap,
And her [c]towns will be set on fire.
Then Israel will take [d]possession of
his possessors,"
Says the LORD.
3 "Wail, O [a]Heshbon, for [b]Ai has been
destroyed!
Cry out, O daughters of Rabbah,
[c]Gird yourselves with sackcloth and
lament,
And rush back and forth inside the
walls;
For [1]Malcam will [d]go into exile
Together with his priests and his
princes.
4 "How [a]boastful you are about the
valleys!
Your valley is flowing *away*,
O [b]backsliding daughter
Who trusts in her [c]treasures, *saying*,
'[d]Who will come against me?'
5 "Behold, I am going to bring [a]terror
upon you,"
Declares the Lord [1]GOD of hosts,
"From all *directions* around you;
And each of you will be [b]driven out
[2]headlong,
With no one to gather the [c]fugitives
together.

48:41 *Kerioth.* Location uncertain (see v. 24; see also note on Amos 2:2).
48:43 *Terror, pit and snare.* The Hebrew original illustrates Jeremiah's fondness for the well-turned phrase (see Introduction: Literary Features)—though in this case Jeremiah was not its creator (see note on Is 24:17).
48:44 *one who flees . . . Will fall . . . one who climbs . . . Will be caught.* Divine judgment, once determined, is unavoidable (see Amos 5:19).
48:45–46 Echoed from Num 21:28–29; 24:17. Balaam's oracles against Moab are about to be fulfilled.
48:45 *Heshbon.* See note on v. 2. Apparently at this time it was controlled by the Ammonites (see 49:3). *Sihon.* Refers to the associates of Sihon king of the Amorites, whose chief city was Heshbon (see Num 21:27) during the time of the exodus. *revelers.* See note on v. 29.
48:46 *Chemosh.* See note on v. 7.
48:47 See 46:26. *restore the fortunes.* See note on 29:14. *In the latter days.* During the Messianic era. *Thus far.* A note by the final compiler of the book of Jeremiah (see 51:64).
49:1 *Concerning the sons of Ammon.* See Ezek 25:1–7; Amos 1:13–15; Zeph 2:8–11. Ammon was east of the Jordan and north of Moab (see note on Gen 19:36–38). *Malcam.* The chief god of the Ammonites (see 1 Kin 11:5,7,33), also known as Milcom (see 1 Kin 11:5). Both titles are related to the West Semitic word for "king" (Hebrew *melek*). *taken possession of Gad.* Probably refers to the aftermath of Tiglath-pileser III's conquest of Transjordan in 734–732 B.C. The Ammonites later apparently recovered from their defeat and overran some of the territory owned by the Israelite tribe of Gad. *his.* Molech's.
49:2 *trumpet blast of war.* See Amos 1:14. *Rabbah of the sons of Ammon.* See note on Deut 3:11. *heap.* See note on 30:18.
49:3 *Heshbon.* See note on 48:45; see also Judg 11:26–27. *Ai.* Not the Ai of Josh 8. Its location is unknown. *walls.* The Hebrew for this word refers not to city walls but to walls separating vineyards from each other (see Num 21:24). *Malcam.* See note on v. 1. *will go into exile . . . and his princes.* See note on 48:7.
49:4 *backsliding daughter.* Applied to the people of Judah in 31:22. *Who trusts in her treasures.* Spoken to Moab in 48:7. *Who will come against me?* According to Josephus (*Antiquities*, 10.9.7) Nebuchadnezzar destroyed Ammon in the 23rd year of his reign (582 B.C.).

6 "But afterward I will [a]restore
The [1]fortunes of the sons of Ammon,"
Declares the LORD.

Prophecy against Edom

7 Concerning [a]Edom.
Thus says the LORD of hosts,
"Is there no longer any [b]wisdom in
[c]Teman?
Has good counsel been lost to the
prudent?
Has their wisdom decayed?
8 "Flee away, turn back, dwell in the
depths,
O inhabitants of [a]Dedan,
For I [1]will bring the [b]disaster of Esau
upon him
At the time I [2]punish him.
9 "[a]If grape gatherers came to you,
Would they not leave gleanings?
If thieves *came* by night,
They would destroy *only* [1]until they
had enough.
10 "But I have [a]stripped Esau bare,
I have uncovered his hiding places
So that he will not be able to conceal
himself;
His [1]offspring has been destroyed
along with his [2]relatives
And his neighbors, and [b]he is no more.
11 "Leave your [1a]orphans behind, I will
keep *them* alive;
And let your [b]widows trust in Me."
12 For thus says the LORD, "Behold, those
[1]who were not sentenced to drink the [a]cup
will certainly drink *it*, and are you the one
who will be [b]completely acquitted? You will
not be acquitted, but you will certainly
drink *it*.
13 "For I have [a]sworn by Myself," declares
the LORD, "that [b]Bozrah will become an
[c]object of horror, a reproach, a ruin and a
curse; and all its cities will become perpetual ruins."
14 I have [a]heard a message from the LORD,
And an [b]envoy is sent among the
nations, *saying*,
"[c]Gather yourselves together and come
against her,
And rise up for battle!"
15 "For behold, I have made you small
among the nations,
Despised among men.
16 "As for the terror of you,
The arrogance of your heart has
deceived you,
O you who live in the clefts of [1]the
[a]rock,
Who occupy the height of the hill.
Though you make your nest as [b]high
as an eagle's,
I will [c]bring you down from there,"
declares the LORD.
17 "Edom will become an [a]object of horror;
everyone who passes by it will be horrified
and will [b]hiss at all its wounds.
18 "Like the [a]overthrow of Sodom and
Gomorrah with its neighbors," says the LORD,
"[b]no one will live there, nor will a son of
man reside in it.
19 "[a]Behold, one will come up like a lion
from the [1b]thickets of the Jordan against [2]a
perennially watered pasture; for in an instant
I will make him run away from it, and whoever is [c]chosen I shall appoint over it. For
who is [d]like Me, and who will summon Me
into court? And who then is the shepherd
[e]who can stand against Me?"
20 Therefore hear the [a]plan of the LORD
which He has planned against Edom, and

6 [1]Or *captivity* [a]Jer 48:47; 49:39 **7** [a]Gen 25:30; 32:3; Is 34:5, 6; Jer 25:21; Ezek 25:12; Amos 1:11; Obad 1-21 [b]Job 2:11; Jer 8:9 [c]Gen 36:11, 15, 34; Jer 49:20 **8** [1]Or *brought* [2]Or *punished* [a]Is 21:13; Jer 25:23 [b]Jer 46:21; Mal 1:3, 4 **9** [1]Lit *their sufficiency* [a]Obad 5 **10** [1]Lit *seed* [2]Lit *brothers* [a]Jer 13:26 [b]Is 17:14 **11** [1]Or *fatherless* [a]Ps 68:5; Hos 14:3 [b]Ps 68:5; Zech 7:10 **12** [1]Lit *whose judgment was not to* [a]Jer 25:15 [b]Jer 25:28, 29; 1 Pet 4:17 **13** [a]Gen 22:16; Is 45:23; Jer 44:26; Amos 6:8 [b]Gen 36:33; 1 Chr 1:44; Is 34:6; 63:1; Amos 1:12

13 [c]Is 34:9-15; Jer 18:16 **14** [a]Obad 1-4 [b]Is 18:2; 30:4 [c]Jer 50:14 **16** [1]Or *Sela* [a]2 Kin 14:7; Jer 48:28 [b]Job 39:27; Is 14:13-15 [c]Amos 9:2 **17** [a]Jer 18:16; 49:13; 50:13; Ezek 35:7 [b]1 Kin 9:8; Jer 51:37 **18** [a]Gen 19:24, 25; Deut 29:23; Jer 50:40; Amos 4:11; Zeph 2:9 [b]Job 18:15-18; Jer 49:33 **19** [1]Lit *pride* [2]Or *an enduring habitation* [a]Jer 50:44 [b]Josh 3:15; Jer 12:5 [c]Num 16:5 [d]Ex 15:11; Is 46:9 [e]Job 41:10 **20** [a]Is 14:24, 27; Jer 50:45

49:6 See 48:47; see also note on 29:14.
49:7–22 Shares many memorable phrases and concepts with the book of Obadiah.
49:7 *Concerning Edom.* See Is 21:11–12; Ezek 25:12–14; Amos 1:11–12; Obad 1–16. *wisdom.* For which Edom was justly famed (see notes on Job 1:1; 2:11). *Teman.* An important Edomite town located south of the Dead Sea (see note on Job 2:11). In v. 20 it is used in parallelism with Edom itself.
49:8 *Flee away, turn back.* See v. 24; 46:21. *Dedan.* See 25:23; see also notes on Is 21:13; Ezek 25:13. *Esau.* The patriarch Jacob's brother, and another name for Edom (see Gen 25:29–30; 36:1), just as Israel was another name for Jacob (see Gen 32:28). The fact that Esau was Jacob's brother made Edom's enmity toward Israel all the more reprehensible (see Amos 1:11; Obad 10).
49:9–10 Paralleled in Obad 5–6.
49:9 *grape gatherers.* See note on v. 13. *leave gleanings.* For the poor to glean (see note on Ruth 2:2).
49:10 *stripped . . . bare.* See note on 13:22. *is no more.* See 31:15; Is 19:7.
49:12 Echoed from 25:28–29. *those . . . not sentenced to drink . . . will certainly drink.* Though they are God's chosen ones, the people of Judah will be punished because of their sin (see Amos 3:2).
49:13 *sworn by Myself.* See notes on Gen 22:16; Is 45:23; see also 22:5; 51:14. *Bozrah.* Not the Bozrah of 48:24 (see note there); the Edomite Bozrah was probably the capital of Edom in the days of Jeremiah (see v. 22; Gen 36:33; see also notes on Is 34:6; Amos 1:12). The Hebrew root underlying Bozrah is the same as that for "grape gatherers" in v. 9. *ruin . . . curse.* See 25:18. *perpetual ruins.* See 25:9; Ps 74:3; Is 58:12 and note.
49:14–16 Paralleled in Obad 1–4.
49:16 *arrogance.* Edom's besetting sin (see v. 4; Obad 11–13; cf. 48:29–30). *rock.* Perhaps a reference to Petra (see note on 2 Kin 14:7), the most spectacular of the mountain strongholds for which Edom was noted.
49:17 Echoed from 19:8.
49:18 Repeated almost verbatim in 50:40, and echoed in part in v. 33. *overthrow of Sodom and Gomorrah.* See Gen 19:24–25. Later calamities were often compared with the one that befell Sodom and Gomorrah (see note on Amos 4:11). *its neighbors.* Primarily Admah and Zeboiim (see Gen 14:2,8; Deut 29:23; Hos 11:8).
49:19–21 Repeated almost verbatim in the oracle against Babylon (see 50:44–46).
49:19 *thickets of the Jordan.* See 12:5 and note. *shepherd.* Ruler (see note on 2:8).

His purposes which He has purposed against the inhabitants of Teman: surely they will drag them off, *even* the little ones of the flock; surely He will make their [1]pasture [b]desolate because of them.

21 The [a]earth has quaked at the noise of their downfall. There is an outcry! The noise of it has been heard at the [1]Red Sea.

22 Behold, [1]He will mount up and [a]swoop like an eagle and spread out His wings [2]against Bozrah; and the [b]hearts of the mighty men of Edom in that day will be like the heart of a woman in labor.

Prophecy against Damascus

23 Concerning [a]Damascus.
"[b]Hamath and [c]Arpad are put to shame,
For they have heard bad news;
They are [d]disheartened.
There is anxiety by the sea,
It [e]cannot be calmed.
24 "Damascus has become helpless;
She has turned away to flee,
And panic has gripped her;
[a]Distress and pangs have taken hold of her
Like a woman in childbirth.
25 "How [1]the [a]city of praise has not been deserted,
The town of My joy!
26 "Therefore, her [a]young men will fall in her streets,
And all the men of war will be [1]silenced in that day," declares the LORD of hosts.
27 "I will [a]set fire to the wall of Damascus,
And it will devour the [1]fortified towers of [b]Ben-hadad."

Prophecy against Kedar and Hazor

28 Concerning [a]Kedar and the kingdoms of Hazor, which Nebuchadnezzar king of Babylon defeated. Thus says the LORD,
"Arise, go up to Kedar
And devastate the [1b]men of the east.
29 "They will take away their tents and their flocks;
They will carry off for themselves
Their tent [a]curtains, all their goods and their [b]camels,
And they will call out to one another,
'[c]Terror on every side!'
30 "Run away, flee! Dwell in the depths,
O inhabitants of Hazor," declares the LORD;
"For [a]Nebuchadnezzar king of Babylon has formed a plan against you
And devised a scheme against you.
31 "Arise, go up against a nation which is [a]at ease,
Which lives securely," declares the LORD.
"It has [b]no gates or bars;
They [c]dwell alone.
32 "Their camels will become plunder,
And their many cattle for booty,
And I will [a]scatter to all the winds those who [b]cut the corners *of their hair;*
And I will bring their disaster from every side," declares the LORD.
33 "Hazor will become a [a]haunt of jackals,
A desolation forever;
No one will live there,
Nor will a son of man reside in it."

Prophecy against Elam

34 That which came as the word of the LORD to Jeremiah the prophet concerning [a]Elam, [b]at the beginning of the reign of Zedekiah king of Judah, saying:
35 "Thus says the LORD of hosts,
'Behold, I am going to [a]break the bow of Elam,
The [1]finest of their might.
36 'I will bring upon Elam the [a]four winds
From the four ends of heaven,

20 [1]Or *habitation* [b]Mal 1:3, 4
21 [1]Lit *Sea of Reeds* [a]Jer 50:46; Ezek 26:15, 18
22 [1]Or *one* [2]Or *over* [a]Jer 4:13; 48:40; Hos 8:1 [b]Is 13:8; Jer 30:6; 48:41
23 [a]Gen 14:15; 15:2; 2 Kin 5:12; 2 Chr 16:2; Is 7:8; 17:1; Amos 1:3; Acts 9:2 [b]Num 13:21; Is 10:9; Jer 39:5; Amos 6:2 [c]2 Kin 18:34; 19:13; Is 10:9 [d]Ex 15:15; Nah 2:10 [e]Is 57:20
24 [a]Is 13:8
25 [1]Or *deserted is the city of praise* [a]Jer 33:9; 51:41
26 [1]Or *destroyed* [a]Jer 11:22; 50:30; Amos 4:10
27 [1]Or *palaces* [a]Jer 43:12; Amos 1:3-5 [b]1 Kin 15:18-20; 2 Kin 13:3
28 [1]Lit *sons* [a]Gen 25:13; Ps 120:5; Is 21:16, 17; Jer 2:10; Ezek 27:21 [b]Job 1:3; Is 11:14
29 [a]Hab 3:7 [b]1 Chr 5:21 [c]Jer 46:5
30 [a]Jer 25:9; 27:6
31 [a]Judg 18:7; Is 47:8 [b]Is 42:11 [c]Num 23:9; Deut 33:28; Mic 7:14
32 [a]Ezek 5:10; 12:14, 15 [b]Jer 9:26; 25:23
33 [a]Is 13:20-22; Jer 9:11; 10:22; 51:37; Zeph 2:9, 13-15; Mal 1:3
34 [a]Gen 10:22; 14:1, 9; Is 11:11; Jer 25:25; Ezek 32:24; Dan 8:2 [b]2 Kin 24:17, 18; Jer 28:1

35 [1]Lit *first* [a]Ps 46:9; Is 22:6; Jer 51:56 **36** [a]Dan 7:2; 8:8; Rev 7:1

49:20 *Teman.* See note on v. 7. *flock.* The people of Edom.
49:22 Echoed from 48:40–41. *eagle.* Represents Nebuchadnezzar in 48:40 (see note there), and probably here also. A more complete subjugation of the Edomites, however, was accomplished by Nabatean Arabs (perhaps the "jackals of the wilderness" of Mal 1:3) beginning c. 550 B.C. *Bozrah.* See note on v. 13.
49:23 *Concerning Damascus.* See Is 17; Amos 1:3–5 (see also note on Is 17:1). *Hamath.* An important city in the kingdom of Aram (see Is 10:9 and note). *Arpad.* See note on Is 10:9. *anxiety by the sea.* See Is 57:20.
49:24 *Distress.* See note on 4:19.
49:26 Repeated almost verbatim in 50:30.
49:27 A conventional word of judgment (see note on Amos 1:4).
49:28 *Concerning Kedar.* See Is 21:13–17; see also 2:10 and note. *kingdoms of Hazor.* See vv. 30,33; not the Hazor north of the Sea of Galilee (see Josh 11:1). These kingdoms may have included Dedan, Tema, Buz and other Arab regions (see 25:23–24 and notes), since the Hebrew root of the proper name Hazor often serves as a common noun meaning "settlement" (see especially Is 42:11; see also Gen 25:16). *Nebuchadnezzar . . . defeated.* In 599–598 B.C. *men of the east.* See Job 1:3; Ezek 25:4. The Hebrew for this phrase is translated "sons of the east" in Judg 6:3 (see note there).
49:29 *Terror on every side!* See note on 6:25.
49:30 *Dwell in the depths.* See v. 8.
49:31 *at ease.* Completely secure (see Job 21:23). *securely.* In safety, unsuspecting (see Judg 18:7; Ezek 38:11). *has no gates or bars.* Lives in unwalled villages (see Deut 3:5; cf. 1 Sam 23:7). *alone.* A condition that elsewhere characterizes Israel (see Num 23:9; Deut 33:28).
49:32 *scatter to all the winds.* See Ezek 5:12; 12:4. *who cut the corners of their hair.* See note on 9:26. *disaster from every side.* Contrast the description of Solomon's realm in 1 Kin 5:4.
49:33 *haunt of jackals.* See note on 9:11. *No one . . . reside in it.* Repeated verbatim from v. 18.
49:34 *the word of the LORD . . . concerning.* See note on 46:1. *Elam.* See note on Is 11:11. *Zedekiah.* Ruled 597–586 B.C.
49:35 *bow.* The Elamites were skilled archers (see Is 22:6).
49:36 Contrast Is 11:12. *to all these winds.* In every direction

And will [b]scatter them to all these
winds;
And there will be no nation
To which the outcasts of Elam will not
go.
37 'So I will [1]shatter Elam before their
enemies
And before those who seek their lives;
And I will [a]bring calamity upon them,
Even My [b]fierce anger,' declares the
LORD,
'And I will [c]send out the sword after
them
Until I have consumed them.
38 'Then I will set My throne in Elam
And destroy [1]out of it king and
princes,'
Declares the LORD.
39 'But it will come about in the last days
That I will [a]restore the [1]fortunes of
Elam,'"
Declares the LORD.

Prophecy against Babylon

50 The word which the LORD spoke concerning [a]Babylon, the land of the Chaldeans, through Jeremiah the prophet:

2 "[a]Declare and proclaim among the
nations.
Proclaim it and [b]lift up a standard.
Do not conceal *it but* say,
'[c]Babylon has been captured,
[d]Bel has been put to shame, [1]Marduk
has been [2]shattered;
Her [e]images have been put to shame,
her idols have been shattered.'

3 "For a nation has come up against her
out of the [a]north; it will make her land [b]an
object of horror, and there will be [c]no inhabitant in it. Both man and beast have wandered off, they have gone away!
4 "In those days and at that time," declares the LORD, "the sons of Israel will come,
both they and the sons of Judah [a]as well;
they will go along [b]weeping as they go, and
it will be [c]the LORD their God they will seek.
5 "They will [a]ask for the way to Zion,
turning their faces [1]in its direction; [2]they
[3]will come that they may join themselves to
the LORD *in* an [b]everlasting covenant that
will not be forgotten.

6 "My people have become [a]lost sheep;
[b]Their shepherds have led them astray.
They have made them turn aside *on*
the [c]mountains;
They have gone along from mountain
to hill
And have forgotten their [d]resting place.
7 "All who came upon them have
devoured them;
And their adversaries have said, '[a]We
are not guilty,
Inasmuch as they have sinned against
the LORD *who is* the [b]habitation of
righteousness,
Even the LORD, the [c]hope of their
fathers.'
8 "Wander away from the [a]midst of
Babylon
And [1]go forth from the land of the
Chaldeans;
Be also like male goats [2]at the head of
the flock.
9 "For behold, I am going to [a]arouse and
bring up against Babylon
A horde of great nations from the land
of the north,
And they will draw up *their* battle
lines against her;
From there she will be taken captive.
Their arrows will be like [1]an expert
warrior
Who does not return empty-handed.

36 [b]Jer 49:32; Ezek 5:10; Amos 9:9
37 [1]Or *dismay* [a]Jer 6:19 [b]Jer 30:24 [c]Jer 9:16; 48:2
38 [1]Or *from there*
39 [1]Or *captivity* [a]Jer 48:47
50:1 [a]Gen 10:10; 11:9; 2 Kin 17:24; Is 13:1; 47:1; Dan 1:1; Rev 14:8
2 [1]Heb *Merodach* [2]Or *dismayed* [a]Jer 4:16 [b]Jer 51:27 [c]Jer 51:31 [d]Is 46:1 [e]Jer 51:47
3 [a]Is 13:17; Jer 50:9; 51:11, 27 [b]Is 14:22, 23; Jer 50:13 [c]Jer 9:10, 11; Zeph 1:3
4 [a]Is 11:12, 13; Jer 3:18; 31:31; 33:7; Hos 1:11 [b]Ezra 3:12, 13; Ps 126:5; Jer 31:9 [c]Hos 3:5
5 [1]Lit *hither* [2]M.T. reads *come ye!* [3]Or *will have come* [a]Is 35:8; Jer 6:16 [b]Is 55:3; Jer 32:40; Heb 8:6-10
6 [a]Is 53:6; Ezek 34:15, 16; Matt 9:36; 10:6 [b]Jer 23:11-14 [c]Jer 13:16; Ezek 34:6 [d]Jer 33:12; 50:19
7 [a]Jer 2:3; Zech 11:5 [b]Jer 31:23; 40:2, 3 [c]Ps 22:4; Jer 14:8; 17:13
8 [1]Another reading is *let them go forth* [2]Or *in front of* [a]Is 48:20; Jer 51:6; Rev 18:4
9 [1]So some mss and versions; M.T. reads *a warrior who makes childless* [a]Jer 51:1

(see Ezek 37:9; Dan 7:2; 8:8; see also Zech 6:5, where "spirits" could be translated "winds".

49:37 *I will send out . . . have consumed them.* The Hebrew for this sentence is repeated verbatim from 9:16.

49:38 *set My throne in.* See 1:15 and note.

49:39 See note on 29:14.

50:1–51:64 See Is 13:1–14:23; 21:1–9. Jeremiah's prophecy concerning Babylon is by far the longest of his oracles against foreign nations (chs. 46–51) and expands on his earlier and briefer statements (see 25:12–14,26). Its date, in whole or in part, is 593 B.C. (see 51:59 and note). The two chapters divide into three main sections (50:2–28; 50:29–51:26; 51:27–58), each of which begins with a summons concerning war against Babylon, Judah's mortal enemy (see 50:2–3; 50:29–32; 51:27–32).

50:1 *word.* Or "message" (as in 46:13), comprising chs. 50–51. *through.* See 37:2. The message would eventually be sent by the prophet to Babylon itself (see 51:59–61).

50:2 *Declare and proclaim.* See 4:5; 46:14. *lift up a standard.* See note on Is 5:26. See 4:6. *Babylon has been captured.* Fulfilled in 539 B.C. *Bel.* See 51:44; Is 46:1 and note. *put to shame . . . shattered.* The repetition of each of these phrases emphasizes that the chief god of Babylon and his images and idols are alike doomed. *Her . . . her.* Babylon's. *idols.* Lit. "little pellets of dung." Derogatory references concerning idols and idolatry are common in the OT (see, e.g., Is 44:9–20).

50:3 *nation . . . out of the north.* In Jeremiah, the foe from the north is almost always Babylon (see, e.g., 1:14–15). Here, however, the reference is probably to Persia. Babylon's nemesis is expanded to "A horde of great nations" in v. 9, specified by name in 51:27–28. *man and beast have wandered off.* See 33:12.

50:4 *Israel . . . Judah as well.* See note on 3:18. *weeping.* Tears of repentance (see 3:21–22; 31:9).

50:5 *everlasting covenant.* See 32:40 and note; see also 31:31–34; 33:20–21.

50:6 *lost sheep.* See Jesus' parable in Luke 15:3–7. *shepherds.* Rulers (see note on 2:8). *mountain to hill.* Places where pagan gods were worshiped (see note on 2:20). *their resting place.* The Lord (see v. 7).

50:7 *hope of their fathers.* See 14:8,22; Acts 28:20.

50:8 *like male goats at the head of the flock.* Judah would be among the first of the captive peoples to be released from exile in Babylon.

50:9 *horde of great nations.* See Is 13:4. They are named in 51:27–28 (see note on v. 3). *not return empty-handed.* See Is 55:11.

10 "[1][a]Chaldea will become plunder;
All who plunder her will have
enough," declares the LORD.

11 "Because you are glad, because you are
jubilant,
O you who [a]pillage My heritage,
Because you skip about [1]like a
threshing [b]heifer
And neigh like [2]stallions,
12 Your [a]mother [1]will be greatly ashamed,
She who gave you birth [1]will be
humiliated.
Behold, *she will be* the least of the
nations,
A [b]wilderness, a parched land and a
desert.
13 "Because of the indignation of the LORD
she will [a]not be inhabited,
But she will be [b]completely desolate;
Everyone who passes by Babylon [c]will
be horrified
And will hiss because of all her
wounds.
14 "Draw up your battle lines against
Babylon on every side,
All you who [1]bend the bow;
Shoot at her, do not be sparing with
your arrows,
For she has [a]sinned against the LORD.
15 "Raise your battle cry against her on
every side!
She has [a]given [1]herself up, her pillars
have fallen,
Her [b]walls have been torn down.
For this is the [c]vengeance of the LORD:
Take vengeance on her;
[d]As she has done *to others, so* do to
her.
16 "Cut off the [a]sower from Babylon
And the one who wields the sickle at
the time of harvest;

10 [1]Or *the Chaldeans* [a]Jer 51:24, 35; Ezek 11:24
11 [1]Another reading is *in the grass* [2]Lit *mighty ones* [a]Jer 12:14 [b]Jer 46:20
12 [1]Or *has become* [a]Jer 15:9 [b]Jer 22:6; 51:43
13 [a]Jer 34:22 [b]Jer 51:26 [c]Jer 18:16; 49:17
14 [1]Lit *tread* (in order to string) [a]Hab 2:8, 17
15 [1]Lit *her hand* [a]1 Chr 29:24; 2 Chr 30:8; Lam 5:6 [b]Jer 50:44; 51:58 [c]Jer 46:10 [d]Ps 137:8; Rev 18:6
16 [a]Joel 1:11
16 [1]Or *the oppressing sword* [b]Jer 25:38; 46:16 [c]Is 13:14
17 [1]Lit *sheep* [a]Joel 3:2 [b]Jer 2:15; 4:7 [c]2 Kin 15:19; 17:6; 18:9-13 [d]2 Kin 24:1, 10-12; 25:1-7
18 [a]Is 10:12; Ezek 31:3, 11, 12; Nah 3:7, 18, 19
19 [1]Lit *soul* [a]Is 65:10; Jer 31:10; 33:12; Ezek 34:13 [b]Jer 31:6
20 [a]Is 43:25; Jer 31:34; Mic 7:19 [b]Is 1:9
21 [1]Or *Double Rebellion* [2]Or *Punishment* [3]Lit *put under the ban* [a]Ezek 23:23
22 [a]Jer 4:19-21; 51:54-56
23 [a]Jer 51:20-24
24 [a]Jer 48:43, 44 [b]Jer 51:31; Dan 5:30, 31

From before [1]the [b]sword of the
oppressor
[c]They will each turn back to his own
people
And they will each flee to his own
land.

17 "Israel is a [a]scattered [1]flock, the [b]lions
have driven *them* away. The first one *who*
devoured him was the [c]king of Assyria, and
this last one *who* has broken his bones is
[d]Nebuchadnezzar king of Babylon.
18 "Therefore thus says the LORD of hosts,
the God of Israel: 'Behold, I am going to punish the king of Babylon and his land, just as
I [a]punished the king of Assyria.
19 'And I will [a]bring Israel back to his pasture and he will graze on Carmel and
Bashan, and his [1]desire will be satisfied in
the [b]hill country of Ephraim and Gilead.
20 'In those days and at that time,' declares
the LORD, 'search will be made for the iniquity of Israel, but [a]there will be none; and for
the sins of Judah, but they will not be found;
for I will pardon those [b]whom I leave as a
remnant.'

21 "Against the land of [1]Merathaim, go up
against it,
And against the inhabitants of [2][a]Pekod.
Slay and [3]utterly destroy them,"
declares the LORD,
"And do according to all that I have
commanded you.
22 "The [a]noise of battle is in the land,
And great destruction.
23 "How the [a]hammer of the whole earth
Has been cut off and broken!
How Babylon has become
An object of horror among the
nations!
24 "I [a]set a snare for you and you were
also [b]caught, O Babylon,
While you yourself were not aware;

50:11 *you.* Babylon. *My heritage.* God's land and people (see 2:7; 12:7 and notes). *skip about like a threshing heifer.* See Mal 4:2. *stallions.* See note on 8:16.
50:12 *mother.* Either (1) the city or, more likely, (2) the land (see Is 50:1; Hos 2:5). *least.* Lit. "last." As Amalek, "first of the nations" (Num 24:20) to attack Israel, was destroyed, so Babylon, the last to attack Israel (up to Jeremiah's time), would be destroyed.
50:13 *not be inhabited.* See Is 13:20 and note. *Everyone who passes . . . because of all her wounds.* Said of Jerusalem in 19:8 and of Edom in 49:17.
50:14 *you who bend the bow.* Including the Medes (see Is 13:17–18).
50:15 *Raise your battle cry.* See Josh 6:16. *vengeance of the LORD.* See v. 28; 51:11. Though originating in His sovereign holiness, it was often carried out by His people (see Num 31:3).
50:16 *sword of the oppressor.* See 46:16. *They will each . . . to his own land.* The Hebrew for this passage has a parallel in Is 13:14. The captive peoples are warned to flee Babylon in order to avoid being cut down by her invaders.
50:17 *scattered flock.* See Joel 3:2. *lions.* Symbolic of Assyria and Babylon (see 4:7; Is 15:9 and notes). *The first . . . was the king of Assyria.* The Assyrians destroyed Israel (the northern kingdom) in 722–721 B.C. *this last . . . is Nebuchadnezzar.* The Babylonians destroyed Judah (the southern kingdom) in 586 B.C.
50:18 *I punished the king of Assyria.* Nineveh, the proud Assyrian capital, fell in 612 B.C., and Assyria herself was conquered by a coalition of Medes and Babylonians in 609.
50:19 *Carmel.* See Is 33:9 and note. *Bashan.* See note on Is 2:13. *hill country of Ephraim.* The lush mountainsides of central Israel (see Ezek 34:13–14). *Gilead.* See Num 32:1; Mic 7:14.
50:20 See 33:8 and note; see also 36:3; Mic 7:18–19.
50:21 *Merathaim.* Means "double rebellion [against the Lord]," perhaps referring to vv. 24,29 (see Judg 3:8; Is 40:2 and notes). It is probably a pun on the Babylonian word *marratu,* which sometimes referred to a region in southern Babylonia that was characterized by briny waters. *Pekod.* See Ezek 23:23; means "punishment [from the Lord]," a pun on *Puqudu,* the Babylonian name for an Aramean tribe living on the eastern bank of the lower Tigris River. *utterly destroy.* See v. 26; 25:9 and note; 51:3; see also note on Deut 2:34.
50:22 *great destruction.* See 4:6; 6:1; cf. 48:3; 51:54.
50:23 *hammer of the whole earth.* See note on Is 10:5. *object of horror among the nations.* The Hebrew for this sentence is repeated verbatim in 51:41.
50:24 *caught . . . not aware.* The Persian attack in 539 B.C.

You have been found and also seized
Because you have engaged in [c]conflict
with the LORD."
25 The LORD has opened His armory
And has brought forth the [a]weapons
of His indignation,
For it is a [b]work of the Lord [1]GOD of
hosts
In the land of the Chaldeans.
26 Come to her from the [1]farthest border;
[a]Open up her barns,
Pile her up like heaps
And [2b]utterly destroy her,
Let nothing be left to her.
27 [a]Put all her young bulls to the sword;
Let them [b]go down to the slaughter!
Woe be upon them, for their [c]day has
come,
The time of their punishment.
28 There is a [a]sound of fugitives and
refugees from the land of Babylon,
To declare in Zion the [b]vengeance of
the LORD our God,
Vengeance for His [c]temple.

29 "Summon [1]many against Babylon,
All those who [2]bend the bow:
Encamp against her on every side,
Let there be no escape[3].
Repay her according to her work;
[a]According to all that she has done, *so*
do to her;
For she has become [b]arrogant against
the LORD,
Against the Holy One of Israel.
30 "Therefore her [a]young men will fall in
her streets,
And all her men of war will be
[1b]silenced in that day," declares the
LORD.
31 "Behold, [a]I am against you,
O [1]arrogant one,"
Declares the Lord [2]GOD of hosts,
"For your day has come,
The time [3]when I will punish you.
32 "The [1a]arrogant one will stumble and
fall
With no one to raise him up;
And I will [b]set fire to his cities
And it will devour all his environs."

33 Thus says the LORD of hosts,
"The sons of Israel are oppressed,
And the sons of Judah as well;
And [a]all who took them captive have
held them fast,
They have refused to let them go.
34 "Their [a]Redeemer is strong, [b]the LORD
of hosts is His name;
He will vigorously [c]plead their case
So that He may [d]bring rest to [1]the
earth,
But turmoil to the inhabitants of
Babylon.
35 "A [a]sword against the Chaldeans,"
declares the LORD,
"And against the inhabitants of
Babylon
And against her [b]officials and her
[c]wise men!
36 "A sword against the [a]oracle priests,
and they will become fools!
A sword against her [b]mighty men, and
they will be [1c]shattered!
37 "A sword against [1]their [a]horses and
against [1]their chariots
And against all the [2b]foreigners who
are in the midst of her,
And they will become [c]women!
A sword against her treasures, and
they will be plundered!
38 "A [1a]drought on her waters, and they
will be dried up!
For it is a land of [b]idols,
And they are mad over fearsome
idols.

24 [c]Job 9:4; 40:2, 9
25 [1]Heb *YHWH,* usually rendered *LORD* [a]Is 13:5 [b]Jer 50:15; 51:12, 25, 55
26 [1]Lit *end* [2]Lit *put under the ban* [a]Is 45:3; Jer 50:10 [b]Is 14:23
27 [a]Is 34:7 [b]Jer 48:10 [c]Ps 37:13; Jer 46:21; 48:44; Ezek 7:7
28 [a]Is 48:20 [b]Ps 149:6-9; Jer 50:15; 51:10 [c]Lam 1:10; 2:6, 7
29 [1]Another reading is *archers* [2]Lit *tread* (in order to string) [3]Some mss add *to her* [a]Ps 137:8; Jer 50:15; 51:56; 2 Thess 1:6 [b]Ex 10:3; Jer 49:16; Dan 4:37
30 [1]Or *made lifeless* or *destroyed* [a]Is 13:17, 18; Jer 9:21; 18:21; 49:26; 51:4 [b]Jer 51:57
31 [1]Lit *arrogance* [2]Heb *YHWH,* usually rendered *LORD* [3]Another reading is *of your punishment* [a]Jer 21:13; Nah 2:13
32 [1]Lit *arrogance* [a]Is 10:12-15 [b]Jer 21:14; 49:27
33 [a]Is 14:17; 58:6
34 [1]Or their *land* [a]Prov 23:11; Is 43:14; Jer 15:21; 31:11; Rev 18:8 [b]Is 47:4; Jer 32:18; 51:19 [c]Jer 51:36; Mic 7:9 [d]Is 14:3-7
35 [a]Jer 47:6; Hos 11:6 [b]Dan 5:1, 2 [c]Dan 5:7, 8
36 [1]Or *dismayed* [a]Is 44:25 [b]Jer 49:22 [c]Nah 3:13 **37** [1]Lit *his* [2]Lit *mixed multitude* [a]Ps 20:7, 8; Jer 51:21, 22 [b]Jer 25:20; Ezek 30:5 [c]Jer 48:41; 51:30; Nah 3:13 **38** [1]Another reading is *sword* [a]Is 44:27; Jer 51:32, 36; Rev 16:12 [b]Is 46:1, 6, 7

would catch the city of Babylon completely by surprise (see 51:8; Is 47:11).

50:25 *weapons of His indignation.* The nations (see 51:27–28) that the Lord would use to conquer Babylon (see Is 13:5 and note). *a work of the Lord.* See 48:10.

50:26 *heaps.* The Hebrew for this expression is used in Neh 4:2 to describe heaps of rubble that had been burned. *utterly destroy her.* By burning (see note on v. 21; see also Josh 11:11–13).

50:27 *young bulls.* The people of Babylon, including especially her fighting men (see Is 34:6–7 and notes). *go down to the slaughter.* See note on 48:15. *time of their punishment.* See 11:23; 23:12; 46:21.

50:28 *fugitives and refugees.* Jewish exiles who had fled the destruction overtaking Babylon. *vengeance . . . Vengeance for His temple.* See v. 15 and note; 46:10; 51:6. The conquest of Babylon was the Lord's response to Babylon's burning of the Jerusalem temple.

50:29 *Repay her according to her work.* Echoed from 25:14 (see 51:24). *According to all that she has done.* See v. 15. *Holy One of Israel.* A title of God found frequently in Isaiah (see note on Is 1:4), it occurs in Jeremiah only here and in 51:5.

50:30 Repeated almost verbatim from 49:26.

50:31–32 A distant echo of 21:13–14, spoken there to Jerusalem but here to Babylon.

50:33 *all who took them captive.* See Is 14:2. *refused to let them go.* Reminiscent of Pharaoh's repeated refusals before the exodus (see, e.g., Ex 7:14; 8:2,32; 9:2,7).

50:34 *Redeemer.* See 31:11 and note. *plead their case.* See 51:36. *bring rest.* See 31:2 and note; see also Is 14:3,7 and notes on Deut 3:20; Josh 1:13.

50:35–38 Cf. Ezek 21.

50:36 *oracle priests . . . will become fools.* The Hebrew words rendered "fool" in the OT usually denote one who is morally deficient. See Is 44:25; see also Num 12:11.

50:37 *against their horses and . . . chariots.* See Is 43:17; see also Ps 20:7. *foreigners.* See 25:20,24; Neh 13:3. *will become women.* See Nah 3:13.

50:38 *idols.* See 51:52; see also note on Is 21:9. *are mad.* See 25:16 and note.

39 "Therefore the [a]desert creatures will
live *there* along with the jackals;
The ostriches also will live in it,
And it will [b]never again be
inhabited
Or dwelt in from generation to
generation.
40 "As when God overthrew [a]Sodom
And Gomorrah with its neighbors,"
declares the LORD,
"No man will live there,
Nor will *any* son of man reside in it.

41 "Behold, a people is coming [a]from the
north,
And a great nation and many kings
Will be aroused from the remote parts
of the earth.
42 "They [a]seize *their* bow and javelin;
They are [b]cruel and have no mercy.
Their [c]voice roars like the sea;
And they ride on [d]horses,
[e]Marshalled like a man for the battle
Against you, O daughter of
Babylon.
43 "The [a]king of Babylon has heard the
report about them,
And his hands hang limp;
[b]Distress has gripped him,
Agony like a woman in
childbirth.

44 "[a]Behold, one will come up like a lion
from the [1]thicket of the Jordan to [2]a perennially watered pasture; for in an instant I will
make them run away from it, and whoever is
[b]chosen I will appoint over it. For who is
[c]like Me, and who will summon Me *into*
court? And who then is the shepherd who
can [d]stand before Me?"
45 Therefore hear the [a]plan of the LORD
which He has planned against Babylon, and
His purposes which He has purposed against
the land of the Chaldeans: [b]surely they will
drag them off, *even* the little ones of the
flock; surely He will make their [1]pasture
desolate because of them.
46 At the [1]shout, "Babylon has been
seized!" the [a]earth is shaken, and an [b]outcry
is heard among the nations.

39 [a]Is 13:21; 34:14; Rev 18:2 [b]Is 13:20; Jer 25:12 **40** [a]Gen 19:24, 25; Is 13:19; Jer 49:18; Luke 17:28-30; 2 Pet 2:6; Jude 7 **41** [a]Is 13:2-5; Jer 6:22; 50:3, 9; 51:27, 28 **42** [a]Jer 6:23 [b]Is 13:17, 18; 47:6 [c]Is 5:30 [d]Jer 8:16; 47:3; Hab 1:8 [e]Jer 50:9, 14; Joel 2:5 **43** [a]Jer 51:31 [b]Jer 30:6; 49:24 **44** [1]Lit *pride* [2]Or *an enduring habitation* [a]Jer 49:19-21 [b]Num 16:5 [c]Is 46:9 [d]Job 41:10; Jer 30:21 **45** [1]Or *habitation* [a]Ps 33:11; Is 14:24; Jer 51:10, 11 [b]Jer 49:20 **46** [1]Lit *voice* [a]Jer 10:10; 49:21; Ezek 26:18; 31:16 [b]Is 5:7; 15:5; Jer 46:12; 51:54; Ezek 27:28

51:1 [1]Cryptic name for Chaldea; or *the heart of those who rise up against Me* [2]Or *a destroying wind* [a]Jer 4:11, 12; 23:19; Hos 13:15 **2** [1]Some versions read *winnowers* [a]Is 41:16; Jer 15:7; Matt 3:12 **3** [1]M.T. reads *Against him who* [2]I.e. the Chaldean defender [3]Lit *tread(s)* (in order to string) [a]Jer 50:14, 29 [b]Jer 46:4 **4** [1]Or *wounded* [a]Is 13:15; 14:19; Jer 49:26; 50:30, 37 **5** [1]Lit *widowed* [2]Lit *From* [a]Is 54:7, 8; Jer 33:24-26 [b]Hos 4:1, 2

Babylon Judged for Sins against Israel

51 Thus says the LORD:
"Behold, I am going to arouse against
Babylon
And against the inhabitants of
[1]Leb-kamai
[2]The [a]spirit of a destroyer.
2 "I will dispatch [1]foreigners to Babylon
that they may [a]winnow her
And may devastate her land;
For on every side they will be opposed
to her
In the day of *her* calamity.
3 "[1]Let not [2]him who [3a]bends his bow
[3]bend *it*,
[1]Nor let him rise up in his [b]scale-armor;
So do not spare her young men;
Devote all her army to destruction.
4 "They will fall down [1]slain in the land
of the Chaldeans,
And [a]pierced through in their streets."

5 For [a]neither Israel nor Judah has been
[1]forsaken
By his God, the LORD of hosts,
Although their land is [b]full of guilt
[2]Before the Holy One of Israel.
6 [a]Flee from the midst of Babylon,
And each of you save his life!
Do not be [1b]destroyed in her
[2]punishment,
For this is the [c]LORD's time of
vengeance;
He is going to [d]render recompense to
her.
7 Babylon has been a golden [a]cup in the
hand of the LORD,
Intoxicating all the earth.
The [b]nations have drunk of her wine;
Therefore the nations are [c]going mad.
8 Suddenly [a]Babylon has fallen and
been broken;
[b]Wail over her!
[c]Bring [1]balm for her pain;
Perhaps she may be healed.

6 [1]Or *silenced* or *made lifeless* [2]Or *penalty for iniquity* [a]Jer 50:8, 28; Rev 18:4 [b]Num 16:26 [c]Jer 50:15 [d]Jer 25:14 **7** [a]Jer 25:15; Hab 2:16; Rev 14:8; 17:4 [b]Rev 14:8; 18:3 [c]Jer 25:16 **8** [1]Or *balsam resin* [a]Is 21:9; Jer 50:2; Rev 14:8; 18:2 [b]Is 13:6; Rev 18:9 [c]Jer 46:11

50:39 See Is 13:20–22 and notes.
50:40 Repeated almost verbatim from 49:18 (see note there).
50:41–43 Repeated almost verbatim from 6:22–24 (see notes there). The earlier oracle, referring to Jerusalem, is here applied to Babylon.
50:44–46 Repeated almost verbatim from 49:19–21 (see notes there). The oracle against Edom is here applied to Babylon.
51:1 *arouse . . . The spirit.* See 1 Chr 5:26; Hag 1:14. The Hebrew underlying this phrase is translated "stirred up . . . the spirit of" in 2 Chr 21:16. *Leb-kamai.* Lit. "the heart of my attackers" (cf. Rev 17:5, where Babylon is called "the mother of harlots and of the abominations of the earth"). For Leb-kamai as a cryptogram for Chaldea (Babylon), see note on 25:26. *destroyer.* See note on 4:7; here including the "kings of the Medes" (v. 11).
51:2 *foreigners . . . may winnow her.* The Hebrew for this phrase is an excellent example of alliteration and assonance (see Introduction: Literary Features).
51:3 *Devote . . . to destruction.* See note on 25:9. See also note on Deut 2:34.
51:4 *fall . . . in their streets.* See 49:26; 50:30.
51:5 *forsaken.* Lit. "widowed"; contrast Is 54:4,6–7 and notes. *Holy One of Israel.* See note on 50:29.
51:6 *Flee . . . each of you save his life!* See v. 45; 48:6. This was spoken to the people of Judah (as in 50:8). *the LORD's time of vengeance.* See note on 50:15. *render recompense to her.* See Is 59:18; 66:6.
51:7 See 25:15–16 and notes. *Babylon . . . a golden cup.* See note on Dan 2:32–43.
51:8 *Babylon has fallen.* See Is 21:9 and note. *balm.* See note on 8:22.

9 We applied healing to Babylon, but
she was not healed;
Forsake her and [a]let us each go to his
own country,
For her judgment has [b]reached to
heaven
And [1]towers up to the very skies.
10 The LORD has [a]brought [1]about our
vindication;
Come and let us [b]recount in Zion
The work of the LORD our God!

11 [a]Sharpen the arrows, fill the quivers!
The LORD has aroused the spirit of the
kings of the Medes,
Because His purpose is against
Babylon to destroy it;
For it is the [b]vengeance of the LORD,
vengeance for His temple.
12 [a]Lift up a [1]signal against the walls of
Babylon;
Post a strong guard,
Station [2]sentries,
Place men in ambush!
For the LORD has both [b]purposed and
performed
What He spoke concerning the
inhabitants of Babylon.
13 O you who [a]dwell by many waters,
Abundant in [b]treasures,
Your end has come,
The [1]measure of your [2c]end.
14 The [a]LORD of hosts has sworn by
Himself:
"Surely I will fill you with a
[1]population like [b]locusts,
And they will cry out with [2]shouts of
victory over you."

15 *It is* [a]He who made the earth by His
power,
Who established the world by His
wisdom,
And by His understanding He
[b]stretched out the heavens.
16 When He utters His [a]voice, *there is* a
tumult of waters in the heavens,
And He causes the [b]clouds to ascend
from the end of the earth;
He makes lightning for the rain
And brings forth the [c]wind from His
storehouses.
17 [a]All mankind is stupid, devoid of
knowledge;
Every goldsmith is put to shame by
his [1]idols,
For his molten images are [b]deceitful,
And there is no breath in them.
18 They are [a]worthless, a work of
mockery;
In the time of their punishment they
will perish.
19 The [a]portion of Jacob is not like
these;
For the [1]Maker of all is He,
And of the [2]tribe of His inheritance;
The [b]LORD of hosts is His name.
20 *He says,* "You are My [1a]war-club, *My*
weapon of war;
And with you I [b]shatter nations,
And with you I destroy kingdoms.
21 "With you I [a]shatter the horse and his
rider,
And with you I shatter the [b]chariot
and its rider,
22 And with you I shatter [a]man and
woman,
And with you I shatter old man and
[b]youth,
And with you I shatter young man
and virgin,
23 And with you I shatter the shepherd
and his flock,
And with you I shatter the farmer and
his team,
And with you I shatter governors and
prefects.
24 "But I will repay Babylon and all the
inhabitants of [a]Chaldea for [b]all their evil that
they have done in Zion before your eyes,"
declares the LORD.
25 "Behold, [a]I am against you,
[b]O destroying mountain,

9 [1]Lit *is lifted* [a]Is 13:14; Jer 46:16; 50:16 [b]Ezra 9:6; Rev 18:5
10 [1]Lit *forth* [a]Ps 37:6; Mic 7:9 [b]Is 40:2; Jer 50:28
11 [a]Jer 46:4, 9; Joel 3:9, 10 [b]Jer 50:28
12 [1]Or *standard* [2]Or *watchmen* [a]Is 13:2; Jer 50:2; 51:27 [b]Jer 4:28; 23:20; 51:29
13 [1]Lit *cubit* [2]Lit *being cut off* [a]Rev 17:1 [b]Is 45:3 [c]Is 57:17; Hab 2:9-11
14 [1]Or *mankind* [2]I.e. like the song of grape treaders [a]Jer 49:13 [b]Jer 51:27; Nah 3:15
15 [a]Gen 1:1; Jer 10:12-16; 51:15-19 [b]Job 9:8; Ps 146:5, 6; Jer 32:17; Acts 14:15; Rom 1:20
16 [a]Job 37:2-6; Ps 18:13
16 [b]Ps 135:7; Jer 10:13 [c]Jon 1:4
17 [1]Or *graven images* [a]Is 44:18-20; Jer 10:14 [b]Hab 2:18, 19
18 [a]Jer 18:15
19 [1]Lit *Fashioner* [2]Or *Scepter;* cf Num 24:17 [a]Ps 73:26; Jer 10:16 [b]Jer 50:34
20 [1]Lit *shatterer* [a]Is 10:5; 41:15, 16; Jer 50:23 [b]Is 8:9; 41:15, 16; Mic 4:12, 13
21 [a]Ex 15:1
22 [a]Ex 15:4; Is 43:17 [b]2 Chr 36:17; Is 13:15, 16 [c]Is 13:18
24 [a]Jer 50:10 [b]Jer 50:15, 29
25 [a]Jer 50:31 [b]Is 13:2; Zech 4:7

51:9 The speakers are the nations conquered by Babylon. *each go to his own country.* See 50:16 and note. *her judgment.* Her sin, deserving of judgment. *reached to heaven . . . up to the very skies.* Poetic exaggeration (see Deut 1:28; Ps 57:10; 108:4).
51:10 Judah speaks (see 50:28). *The LORD has brought . . . vindication.* See Ps 37:6.
51:11 *aroused.* Lit. "stirred up the spirit of" (see note on v. 1). *Medes.* See v. 28; Is 13:17 and note; Is 21:2; Dan 5:28,31; 6:8,12,15; 8:20. *vengeance . . . vengeance for His temple.* See note on 50:28.
51:12 *Place men in ambush!* To keep defenders from retreating to the safety of their fortifications (see Josh 8:14–22; Judg 20:29–39).
51:13 *many waters.* The "rivers of Babylon" (Ps 137:1), including the mighty Euphrates along with a magnificent system of irrigation canals, were proverbial. *measure of your end.* Like a thread from the loom (see Is 38:12).
51:14 *sworn by Himself.* See note on Gen 22:16. *like locusts.* See 46:23. *cry out with . . . victory.* See note on 48:33.
51:15–19 Repeated almost verbatim from 10:12–16 (see notes there).
51:20–23 Illustrates Jeremiah's fondness for the effective use of repetition (see 4:23–26; see also Introduction: Literary Features).
51:20 *You are My war-club.* Cf. Prov 25:18; either (1) Cyrus of Persia, soon to conquer Babylon, or, more likely, (2) Babylon, destroyer of nations (see 50:23; see also note on Is 10:5). *shatter.* See vv. 21–23. The Hebrew root for this verb is the same as that for "war-club." See also Ex 15:6. The Hebrew verb is translated "dash (to pieces)" in Ps 137:9; Hos 10:14; 13:16.
51:24 *repay . . . for all their evil that they have done.* See v. 6; 50:15,29. *your.* Judah's.
51:25 *destroying mountain.* Symbolizes a powerful kingdom (see Dan 2:35,44–45), here Babylon. *burnt out mountain.* After being judged by the Lord, Babylon will be like an extinct volcano.

Who destroys the whole earth,"
declares the LORD,
"And I will stretch out My hand against
you,
And roll you down from the crags,
And I will make you a [c]burnt out
mountain.
26 "They will not take from you *even* a
stone for a corner
Nor a stone for foundations,
But you will be [a]desolate forever,"
declares the LORD.

27 [a]Lift up a [1]signal in the land,
Blow a trumpet among the nations!
Consecrate the nations against her,
Summon against her the [b]kingdoms of
[c]Ararat, Minni and [d]Ashkenaz;
Appoint a marshal against her,
Bring up the [e]horses like bristly
locusts.
28 Consecrate the nations against her,
The kings of the Medes,
[1]Their governors and all [1]their
[2]prefects,
And every land of [3]their dominion.
29 So the [a]land quakes and writhes,
For the purposes of the LORD against
Babylon stand,
To make the land of Babylon
[1]A [b]desolation without inhabitants.
30 The [a]mighty men of Babylon have
ceased fighting,
They stay in the strongholds;
[b]Their strength is [1]exhausted,
They are becoming [b]*like* women;
Their dwelling places are set on fire,
The [c]bars of her *gates* are broken.
31 One [1a]courier runs to meet [1]another,
And one [2b]messenger to meet
[2]another,
To tell the king of Babylon
That his city has been captured from
end *to end;*
32 The fords also have been seized,
And they have burned the marshes
with fire,
And the men of war are terrified.
33 For thus says the LORD of hosts, the God
of Israel:
"The daughter of Babylon is like a
[a]threshing floor
At the time [1]it is stamped firm;
Yet in a little while the time of
[b]harvest will come for her."

34 "Nebuchadnezzar king of Babylon has
[a]devoured me *and* crushed me,
He has set me down *like* an [b]empty
vessel;
He has [c]swallowed me like a monster,
He has filled his stomach with my
delicacies;
He has washed me away.
35 "May the [a]violence *done* to me and to
my flesh be upon Babylon,"
The [1]inhabitant of Zion will say;
And, "May my blood be upon the
inhabitants of Chaldea,"
Jerusalem will say.
36 Therefore thus says the LORD,
"Behold, I am going to [a]plead your
case
And [b]exact full vengeance for you;
And [c]I will dry up her [1]sea
And make her fountain dry.
37 "[a]Babylon will become a heap *of ruins,*
a haunt of jackals,
An [b]object of horror and hissing,
without inhabitants.
38 "They will roar together like [a]young
lions,
They will growl like lions' cubs.
39 "When they become heated up, I will
serve *them* their banquet
And [a]make them drunk, that they may
become jubilant
And may [b]sleep a perpetual sleep
And not wake up," declares the LORD.
40 "I will bring them down like [1]lambs [a]to
the slaughter,
Like rams together with male goats.

25 [c]Rev 8:8
26 [a]Is 13:19-22; Jer 50:13; 51:29
27 [1]Or *standard* [a]Is 13:2-5; 18:3; Jer 50:2; 51:12 [b]Jer 50:3, 9 [c]Gen 8:4; 2 Kin 19:37; Is 37:38 [d]Gen 10:3 [e]Jer 50:42
28 [1]Lit *Her* [2]I.e. lieutenant governors [3]Lit *his*
29 [1]Or *An object of horror* [a]Jer 8:16; 10:10; 50:46; Amos 8:8 [b]Is 13:19, 20; 47:11; Jer 50:13; 51:26, 43
30 [1]Lit *dried up* [a]Ps 76:5; Jer 50:15, 36, 37 [b]Is 13:7, 8; Nah 3:13 [c]Is 45:1, 2; Lam 2:9; Amos 1:5; Nah 3:13
31 [1]Lit *runner* [2]Lit *announcer* [a]2 Chr 30:6 [b]2 Sam 18:19-31
33 [1]Lit *of treading it* [a]Is 21:10; 41:15, 16; Mic 4:13 [b]Is 17:5; Hos 6:11; Joel 3:13; Rev 14:15
34 [a]Jer 50:17 [b]Is 24:1-3 [c]Job 20:15; Jer 51:44
35 [1]Lit *inhabitress* [a]Ps 137:8
36 [1]Or *broad river* [a]Ps 140:12 [b]Jer 51:6, 11; Rom 12:19 [c]Jer 50:38
37 [a]Rev 18:2 [b]Jer 25:9
38 [a]Jer 2:15
39 [a]Jer 25:27; 48:26; 51:57 [b]Ps 76:5
40 [1]Or *young rams* [a]Jer 48:15; 50:27

51:26 *desolate forever.* See 25:12; 50:12–13; see also note on Is 13:20.
51:27 See 50:29. *Lift up a signal . . . Blow a trumpet . . . !* See 4:5–6; 6:1 and notes. *Consecrate . . . against her.* See note on 6:4. *the kingdoms.* Allies of the Medes (see v. 11 and note). *Ararat.* See note on Gen 8:4. *Minni.* A region mentioned in Assyrian inscriptions, it was located somewhere in Armenia. *Ashkenaz.* See note on Gen 10:3. *marshal.* The Hebrew for this word appears again in the OT only in Nah 3:17. It is a Babylonian loanword meaning lit. "scribe." *like . . . locusts.* See note on 46:23.
51:28 *Medes.* See note on v. 11. *every land of their dominion.* See note on 34:1; see also 1 Kin 9:19.
51:29 *land quakes and writhes.* At the fearful prospect of war.
51:30 *exhausted . . . women.* In the Hebrew there is a play on words. *becoming like women.* See 50:37; Nah 3:13.
51:31 *One courier runs to meet another.* They run to the palace from all parts of the city.
51:32 *fords.* Ferries (and perhaps bridges). *burned the marshes with fire.* To destroy the reeds and prevent fugitives from hiding among them.
51:33 *daughter of Babylon.* See 50:42; see also note on Is 47:1. *threshing floor.* The destruction of a city or nation is often depicted as a harvest (see Is 27:12; Joel 3:13; Mic 4:12–13).
51:34 *monster.* The Hebrew for this word is translated "dragon" in Is 51:9, where it symbolizes Egypt (see note on Gen 1:21). *delicacies.* See Gen 49:20.
51:35 *flesh.* See Mic 3:2–3.
51:36 *exact full vengeance for you.* See vv. 6,11; see also note on 50:15. *sea . . . fountain.* See note on v. 13. Babylonia is called the "wilderness of the sea" in Is 21:1 (see note there).
51:37 See 9:11; 18:16 and notes.
51:38 *roar . . . like young lions.* See 2:15 and note.
51:39 *heated up.* For a similar image see Hos 7:4–7. *drunk.* See v. 57; see also notes on 25:15–16,26.
51:40 *lambs . . . rams . . . goats.* Symbolic of the people (see Is 34:6; Ezek 39:18) of Babylon. *slaughter.* See Is 53:7 and note.

41 "How [1][a]Sheshak has been captured,
And [b]the praise of the whole earth been seized!
How Babylon has become an object of horror among the nations!
42 "The [1][a]sea has come up over Babylon;
She has been engulfed with its tumultuous waves.
43 "Her cities have become an [a]object of horror,
A parched land and a desert,
A land in which [b]no man lives
And through which no son of man passes.
44 "[a]I will punish Bel in Babylon,
And I will make what he has swallowed [b]come out of his mouth;
And the nations will no longer [c]stream to him.
Even the [d]wall of Babylon has fallen down!

45 "[a]Come forth from her midst, My people,
And each of you [b]save yourselves
From the fierce anger of the LORD.
46 "Now [a]so that your heart does not grow faint,
And you are not afraid at the [b]report that *will be* heard in the land—
For the report will come [1]one year,
And after that [2]another report in [2]another year,
And violence *will be* in the land
With [c]ruler against ruler—
47 Therefore behold, days are coming
When I will punish the [a]idols of Babylon;
And her whole land will be [b]put to shame
And all her slain will fall in her midst.
48 "Then [a]heaven and earth and all that is in them
Will shout for joy over Babylon,
For [b]the destroyers will come to her from the north,"
Declares the LORD.

49 [a]Indeed Babylon is to fall *for* the slain of Israel,
As also for Babylon [b]the slain of all the earth have fallen.
50 You [a]who have escaped the sword,
Depart! Do not stay!
[b]Remember the LORD from afar,
And let Jerusalem [1]come to your mind.
51 [a]We are ashamed because we have heard reproach;
Disgrace has covered our faces,
For [b]aliens have entered
The holy places of the LORD's house.

52 "Therefore behold, the days are coming," declares the LORD,
"When I will punish her [a]idols,
And the mortally wounded will groan throughout her land.
53 "Though Babylon should [a]ascend to the heavens,
And though she should fortify [1]her lofty stronghold,
From [b]Me destroyers will come to her," declares the LORD.

54 The [a]sound of an outcry from Babylon,
And of great destruction from the land of the Chaldeans!
55 For the LORD is going to destroy Babylon,
And He will make *her* loud [1]noise vanish from her.
And their [a]waves will roar like many waters;
The tumult of their voices [2]sounds forth.
56 For the [a]destroyer is coming against her, against Babylon,
And her mighty men will be captured,
Their [b]bows are shattered;
For the LORD is a God of [c]recompense,
He will fully repay.
57 "I will [a]make her princes and her wise men drunk,
Her governors, her prefects and her mighty men,

---

41 [1]Cryptic name for Babylon [a]Jer 25:26 [b]Jer 49:25
42 [1]Or *broad river* [a]Is 8:7, 8; Jer 51:55; Dan 9:26
43 [a]Jer 50:12 [b]Is 13:20; Jer 2:6
44 [a]Is 46:1; Jer 50:2 [b]Ezra 1:7, 8 [c]Is 2:2 [d]Jer 50:15; 51:58
45 [a]Is 48:20; Jer 50:8, 28; 51:6; Rev 18:4 [b]Gen 19:12-16; Acts 2:40
46 [1]Lit *in the* [2]Lit *the* [a]Is 43:5; Jer 46:27, 28 [b]2 Kin 19:7; Is 13:3-5 [c]Is 19:2
47 [a]Is 21:9; 46:1, 2; Jer 50:2; 51:52 [b]Jer 50:12, 35-37
48 [a]Is 44:23; 48:20; 49:13; Rev 18:20 [b]Jer 50:3
49 [a]Ps 137:8; Jer 50:29 [b]Rev 18:24
50 [1]Lit *come upon your heart* [a]Jer 44:28 [b]Deut 4:29-31; Ps 137:6
51 [a]Ps 44:15 [b]Ps 74:3-8; Lam 1:10
52 [a]Jer 50:38
53 [1]Lit *the height of her strength* [a]Gen 11:4; Job 20:6; Ps 139:8-10; Is 14:12-14; Jer 49:16; Amos 9:2; Obad 4 [b]Is 13:3
54 [a]Jer 48:3-5; 50:22, 46
55 [1]Or *voice* [2]Lit *is given* [a]Ps 18:4; 69:2; 124:2, 4, 5; Jer 51:42
56 [a]Jer 51:48, 53; Hab 2:8 [b]Ps 46:9; 76:3 [c]Deut 32:35; Ps 94:1, 2; Jer 51:6, 24
57 [a]Jer 25:27

51:41 *Sheshak.* See note on 25:26.
51:42 *sea . . . tumultuous waves.* See Is 17:12 and note; here and in v. 55, Babylon's enemies (see 46:7 and note).
51:43 See 48:9; 49:18,33; 50:12–13.
51:44 *Bel.* See 50:2; Is 46:1 and note. *what he has swallowed.* Captive peoples (including Judah) and plundered goods (including vessels from the temple in Jerusalem; see Dan 5:2–3). *wall of Babylon.* A wall of double construction, the outer wall (12 feet thick) being separated from the inner wall (21 feet thick) by a dry moat 23 feet wide.
51:45 *save yourselves.* See note on v. 6. *fierce anger.* See 4:8,26; Is 13:13; Nah 1:6.
51:46 *not afraid at the report . . . heard in the land.* While giving His Olivet discourse, Jesus may have had this passage in mind (see Matt 24:6; Mark 13:7; Luke 21:9).
51:47 *punish the idols of Babylon.* See v. 52; see also note on 50:2.
51:48 *heaven and earth . . . Will shout for joy.* See Is 44:23; Rev 18:20; 19:1–3. *from the north.* See note on 50:3.
51:49 See note on 25:26.
51:50 *Depart!* See note on v. 6.
51:51 *aliens have entered The holy places.* Refers to Nebuchadnezzar's defiling the Jerusalem temple in 586 B.C. The same sacrilege would occur under Antiochus Epiphanes in 168 B.C. and under the Romans in A.D. 70.
51:52 *punish her idols.* See note on 50:2.
51:53 *ascend to the heavens.* Cf. Job 20:6; see Gen 11:4 and note; see also Is 14:13–15. *destroyers.* See vv. 48,56.
51:54 See 50:46. *great destruction.* See note on 4:6.
51:55 *waves.* See note on v. 42. *like many waters.* See note on Ps 32:6.
51:56 *God of recompense.* See note on v. 24.
51:57 *princes and . . . wise men.* See 50:35. *drunk.* See v. 39; see also notes on 25:15–16,26. *King.* See note on 46:18. The

That they may sleep ...erpetual
sleep and not w...,"
ᶜDeclares the King ...e name is the
LORD of hosts. ...osts,
58 Thus says the L...lon will be
"The broad ᵃw... ...ll be set on fire;
complete... ...l for nothing,
And her hi... ...e ᵈexhausted
So the pe...
And then ...h Jeremiah the
onl... ...aiah the son of
...ahseiah, when he
59 The ... king of Judah to
prophet ... of his reign. (Now
ᵃNeriah ... r.)
went ... in a single ¹scroll
Baby... would come upon
Sera... e words which have
...Babylon.
Nebu... ...id to Seraiah, "As
...n; ...bylon, then see that
...ebuchad- ...s aloud,
...n of the ...ORD, have ¹promised
...people; to ᵃcut it off, so that
...ing dwelling in it,
...y-sev- ...st, but it will be a per-
...ng of
...nty- ...s you finish reading this
...ing ...a stone to it and ᵃthrow it
...n ...of the Euphrates,
...h ...'Just so shall Babylon sink
...not rise again because of the
...at I am going to bring upon her;
...will become ᵇexhausted.' " ᶜThus
the words of Jeremiah.

Fall of Jerusalem

52 ᵃZedekiah was twenty-one years old
when he became king, and he reigned
eleven years in Jerusalem; and his mother's
name was ¹ᵇHamutal the daughter of Jeremiah of ᶜLibnah.
2 He did ᵃevil in the sight of the LORD like
all that ᵇJehoiakim had done.
3 For through the ᵃanger of the LORD *this*
came about in Jerusalem and Judah until He
cast them out from His presence. And Zedekiah ᵇrebelled against the king of Babylon.
4 ᵃNow it came about in the ninth year
of his reign, on the tenth *day* of the tenth
month, that Nebuchadnezzar king of Babylon came, he and all his army, against Jerusalem, camped against it and built a ᵇsiege
wall all around ¹it.
5 ᵃSo the city was under siege until the
eleventh year of King Zedekiah.
6 On the ninth *day* of the ᵃfourth month
the ᵇfamine was so severe in the city that
there was no food for the people of the land.
7 Then the city was ᵃbroken into, and all
the ᵇmen of war fled and went forth from the
city at night by way of the gate between the
two walls which *was* by the king's garden,
though the Chaldeans were ¹ᶜall around the
city. And they went by way of the Arabah.
8 But the army of the Chaldeans pursued
the king and ᵃovertook Zedekiah in the
¹plains of Jericho, and all his army was scattered from him.
9 Then they captured the king and
ᵃbrought him up to the king of Babylon at
ᵇRiblah in the land of ᶜHamath, and he
¹passed sentence on him.
10 The king of Babylon ᵃslaughtered the
sons of Zedekiah before his eyes, and he also
slaughtered all the ¹princes of Judah in Riblah.
11 Then he ᵃblinded the eyes of Zedekiah;
and the king of Babylon bound him with
bronze fetters and brought him to Babylon and
put him in prison until the day of his death.
12 ᵃNow on the tenth *day* of the fifth
month, which was the ᵇnineteenth year of
King Nebuchadnezzar, king of Babylon,
ᶜNebuzaradan the captain of the bodyguard,
¹who was in the service of the king of Babylon, came to Jerusalem.

57 ᵇPs 76:5, 6 ᶜJer 46:18; 48:15 **58** ᵃJer 50:15 ᵇIs 45:1, 2 ᶜHab 2:13 ᵈJer 9:5; 51:64; Lam 5:5 **59** ¹Lit *word* ᵃJer 32:12; 36:4; 45:1 ᵇJer 28:1; 52:1 **60** ¹Or *book* ᵃIs 30:8; Jer 30:2, 3; 36:2, 4, 32 **62** ¹Lit *spoken* ²Lit *from man even to beast* ᵃIs 13:19-22; 14:22, 23; Jer 50:3, 13, 39, 40 ᵇJer 51:43; Ezek 35:9 **63** ¹Or *book* ᵃJer 19:10, 11; Rev 18:21 **64** ᵃNah 1:8, 9 ᵇJer 51:58 ᶜJob 31:40; Ps 72:20 **52:1** ¹Another reading is *Hamital* ᵃ2 Kin 24:18; 2 Chr 36:11 ᵇ2 Kin 23:31; 24:18 ᶜJosh 10:29; 2 Kin 8:22; Is 37:8 **2** ᵃ1 Kin 14:22; 2 Kin 24:19; 2 Chr 36:12 ᵇJer 36:30, 31

3 ᵃ2 Kin 24:20; Is 3:1, 4, 5 ᵇ2 Chr 36:13; Ezek 17:12-16 **4** ¹Lit *against it* ᵃ2 Kin 25:1; Jer 39:1; Ezek 24:1, 2; Zech 8:19 ᵇJer 32:24 **5** ᵃ2 Kin 25:2 **6** ᵃJer 39:2 ᵇ2 Kin 25:3; Is 3:1; Jer 38:9; Ezek 4:16; 5:16; 14:13 **7** ¹Lit *against the city on every side* ᵃ2 Kin 25:4; Jer 39:2 ᵇJer 39:4-7; 51:32 ᶜEzek 33:21 **8** ¹Lit *Arabah* ᵃJer 21:7; 32:4; 34:21; 37:17; 38:23 **9** ¹Lit *spoke judgments with* ᵃ2 Kin 25:6; Jer 32:4; 39:5 ᵇNum 34:11; Jer 39:5 ᶜNum 13:21; Josh 13:5 **10** ¹Or *commanders* ᵃ2 Kin 25:7; Jer 22:30; 39:6 **11** ᵃJer 39:7; Ezek 12:13 **12** ¹Lit *stood before the king* ᵃ2 Kin 25:8-21; Zech 7:5; 8:19 ᵇ2 Kin 24:12; 25:8; Jer 52:29 ᶜJer 39:9

true King is the Lord, not Bel/Marduk (see 50:2 and note).
51:58 *broad wall.* See note on v. 44. *high gates.* The famous Ishtar Gate was almost 40 feet high. *the peoples . . . only for fire.* Very similar to Hab 2:13.
51:59–64 A prose conclusion to the book in general and to the oracle against Babylon in particular.
51:59 *Seraiah the son of Neriah.* An ancient seal has been found that bears the inscription "Belonging to Seraiah son of Neriah," and it no doubt refers to the man mentioned here. He was a brother of Jeremiah's secretary, Baruch (see 32:12). *he.* Seraiah. *Zedekiah . . . fourth year.* 593 B.C. Zedekiah may have been summoned to Babylon by Nebuchadnezzar to be interrogated by him (see note on 27:3). *quartermaster.* Lit. "resting-place officer" (see Num 10:33), the official responsible for determining when and where his men on the march should stay overnight.
51:60 *scroll.* See note on Ex 17:14. *all . . . which have been written concerning Babylon.* Probably the oracle of 50:2–51:58 (see note on 50:1).
51:62 *You . . . have promised.* See v. 26.
51:64 *Thus far are the words of Jeremiah.* A note by the final compiler of the book of Jeremiah (see 48:47).
52:1–27,31–34 Paralleled almost verbatim in 2 Kin 24:18–25:21,27–30 (see notes there). (52:4–27 is summarized in 39:1–10; see notes there.) The writer(s) of Kings and the writer of the appendix to Jeremiah (perhaps Baruch) doubtless had access to the same sources. It is unlikely that either of the two accounts copied from the other, since each has peculiarities characteristic of the larger work that it concludes. In a few passages, Jeremiah is fuller than Kings (compare especially vv. 10–11 with 2 Kin 25:7; v. 15 with 2 Kin 25:11; vv. 19–23 with 2 Kin 25:15–17; v. 31 with 2 Kin 25:27; v. 34 with 2 Kin 25:30).
52:1 *Jeremiah.* Not the prophet.
52:12 *tenth day.* The parallel in 2 Kin 25:8 reads "seventh day"; one of the numbers is a copyist's error, but we cannot tell which (see vv. 22,25,31).

13 He [a]burned the house of the LORD, the
[b]king's house and all the houses of Jerusalem; even every large house he burned
with fire.
14 So all the army of the Chaldeans who
were with the captain of the guard [a]broke
down all the walls around Jerusalem.
15 Then Nebuzaradan the captain of the
guard [a]carried away into exile some of the
poorest of the people, the rest of the people
who were left in the city, the [1b]deserters who
had deserted to the king of Babylon and the
rest of the artisans.
16 But [a]Nebuzaradan the captain of the
guard left some of the poorest of the land to
be vinedressers and [1]plowmen.
17 Now the bronze [a]pillars which
belonged to the house of the LORD and the
[b]stands and the bronze [c]sea, which were in
the house of the LORD, the Chaldeans broke in
pieces and carried all their bronze to Babylon.
18 They also took away the [a]pots, the
shovels, the snuffers, the basins, the [1]pans
and all the bronze vessels which were used
in *temple* service.
19 The captain of the guard also took
away the [a]bowls, the firepans, the basins,
the pots, the lampstands, the [1]pans and the
drink offering bowls, what was fine gold and
what was fine silver.
20 The two pillars, the one sea, and the
twelve bronze bulls that were under [1]the sea,
and the stands, which King Solomon had
made for the house of the LORD—the bronze
of all these vessels was [a]beyond weight.
21 As for the pillars, the [a]height of each
pillar *was* eighteen [1]cubits, and [2]it *was*
twelve cubits in [a]circumference and four fingers in thickness, *and* hollow.
22 Now a [a]capital of bronze was on it; and
the height of each capital was five cubits,
with network and [b]pomegranates upon the
capital all around, all of bronze. And the second pillar was like these, including pomegranates.
23 There were ninety-six [1]exposed pomegranates; all [a]the pomegranates *numbered* a
hundred on the network all around.
24 Then the captain of the guard took

[a]Seraiah the chi
second priest, w
temple.
25 He also took
who was overseer
seven [1]of the [a]kin
found in the city, an
mander of the army
ple of the land, and si
of the land who were
the city.

est and [b]Zephaniah the
three [1c]officers of the
city one official
of war, and
who were
f the com-
the peo-
people
t of

26 Nebuzaradan the c
took them and [a]brought t
Babylon at Riblah.
27 Then the king of Baby
down and put them to death
land of Hamath. So Judah
into exile from its land.
28 These are the people w
chadnezzar carried away into
[1]seventh year 3,023 Jews;
29 in the eighteenth year of
nezzar 832 persons from Jerusale
30 in the twenty-third year of N
nezzar, [a]Nebuzaradan the captai
guard carried into exile 745 Jewish
there were 4,600 persons in all.
31 [a]Now it came about in the thirt
enth year of the exile of Jehoiachin ki
Judah, in the twelfth month, on the twe
fifth of the month, that [1]Evil-merodach
of Babylon, in the *first* year of his reig
[2b]showed favor to Jehoiachin king of Juda
and brought him out of prison.
32 [a]Then he spoke kindly to him and se
his throne above the thrones of the kings
who *were* with him in Babylon.
33 So [1]Jehoiachin [a]changed his prison
clothes, and [2b]had his meals in [3]the king's
presence regularly all the days of his life.
34 For his allowance, a [a]regular allowance
was given him by the king of Babylon, a daily portion all the days of his life until the day
of his death.

13 [a]1 Kin 9:8; 2 Kin 25:9; 2 Chr 36:19; Ps 74:6-8; 79:1; Is 64:10, 11; Lam 2:7; Mic 3:12 [b]Jer 39:8 **14** [a]2 Kin 25:10; Neh 1:3 **15** [1]Lit *fallers who had fallen* [a]2 Kin 25:11 [b]Jer 39:9 **16** [1]Or *unpaid laborers* [a]2 Kin 25:12; Jer 39:10; 40:2-6 **17** [a]1 Kin 7:15-22; 2 Kin 25:13; Jer 27:19-22; 52:20-23 [b]1 Kin 7:27-37 [c]1 Kin 7:23-26 **18** [1]Or *spoons for incense* [a]Ex 27:3; 1 Kin 7:40, 45; 2 Kin 25:14 **19** [1]Or *spoons for incense* [a]1 Kin 7:49, 50; 2 Kin 25:15 **20** [1]So Gr and Syriac; Heb omits *the sea* [a]1 Kin 7:47; 2 Kin 25:16 **21** [1]I.e. One cubit equals approx 18 in. [2]Lit *a line of 12 cubits would encircle it* [a]1 Kin 7:15; 2 Kin 25:17; 2 Chr 3:15 **22** [a]1 Kin 7:16; 2 Kin 25:17 [b]1 Kin 7:20, 42 **23** [1]Lit *windward* [a]1 Kin 7:20 **24** [1]Lit *keepers of the door* [a]2 Kin 25:18; 1 Chr 6:14; Ezra 7:1 [b]2 Kin 25:18; Jer 21:1; 29:25, 29; 37:3 [c]1 Chr 9:19; Jer 35:4 **25** [1]Lit *men of those seeing the king's face* [a]2 Kin 25:19; Esth 1:14 **26** [a]2 Kin 25:20 **27** [a]2 Kin 25:21; Ezek 8:11-18 [b]Is 6:11, 12; 27:10; 32:13, 14; Jer 13:19; 20:4; 25:9-11; 39:9; Ezek 33:28; Mic 4:10

28 [1]Or possibly *seventeenth* [a]2 Kin 24:2, 3, 12-16; 2 Chr 36:20; Ezra 2:1; Neh 7:6; Dan 1:1-3 **30** [a]2 Kin 25:11; Jer 39:9 **31** [1]Or *Awil-Marduk* ("Man of Marduk") [2]Lit *lifted up the head of* [a]2 Kin 25:27 [b]Gen 40:13, 20; Ps 3:3; 27:6 **32** [a]2 Kin 25:28 **33** [1]Lit *he* [2]Lit *ate* [3]Lit *his presence* [a]Gen 41:14, 42; 2 Kin 25:29 [b]2 Sam 9:7, 13; 1 Kin 2:7 **34** [a]2 Sam 9:10; 2 Kin 25:30

52:18–19 See notes on 1 Kin 7:40,45,50.

52:20 *twelve bronze bulls.* See note on 2 Chr 4:4.

52:21–23 See notes on 1 Kin 7:15–22.

52:22 *five cubits.* About 7 1/2 feet. The parallel in 2 Kin 25:17 reads "three cubits" (about 4 1/2 feet; see note there), probably a copyist's error.

52:25 *seven.* The parallel in 2 Kin 25:19 reads "five"; see note on v. 12.

52:28 *seventh year.* Of Nebuchadnezzar's reign (see vv. 29–30), which was 597 B.C. *3,023.* Probably includes only adult males, since the corresponding figure(s) in 2 Kin 24:14,16 are significantly higher.

52:29 *eighteenth year.* 586 B.C. In v. 12 the same year is called the "nineteenth year"; the difference is due to alternate ways of computing regnal years (for a similar case see note on Dan 1:1).

52:30 *twenty-third year.* 581 B.C. *Nebuzaradan . . . carried into exile.* Either (1) to quell further rebellion (see v. 3), or (2) in belated reprisal for Gedaliah's assassination (see 41:1–3).

52:31–34 Paralleled almost verbatim in 2 Kin 25:27–30 (see notes there). Jeremiah and Kings thus conclude with the same happy ending.

52:31 *twenty-fifth.* The parallel in 2 Kin 25:27 reads "twenty-seventh"; see note on v. 12.

52:34 *until the day of his death.* See v. 11. Since the phrase does not appear in the parallel verses in 2 Kings in either case, its intention is probably to highlight the contrast between Zedekiah, who remained in prison till the day he died (see v. 11), and Jehoiachin, who was released from prison and treated well by the Babylonian kings till the day he died.

Lamentations

INTRODUCTION

Title

The Hebrew title of the book is *'ekah* ("How . . . !"), the first word not only in 1:1 but also in 2:1; 4:1. Because of its subject matter, the book is also referred to in Jewish tradition as *qinot*, "Lamentations" (the title given to it in the Greek Septuagint and Latin Vulgate).

Author and Date

Although Lamentations is anonymous and we cannot be certain who wrote it, ancient Jewish and Christian tradition ascribes it to Jeremiah. This is partly on the basis of 2 Chr 35:25 (though the "Lamentations" are not to be identified with the OT book of Lamentations); partly on the basis of such texts as Jer 7:29; 8:21; 9:1,10,20; and partly because of the similarity of vocabulary and style between the books of Jeremiah and Lamentations. Also, since the prophet Jeremiah was an eyewitness to the divine judgment on Jerusalem in 586 B.C., it is reasonable to assume that he was the author of the book that so vividly portrays the event. Lamentations poignantly shares the overwhelming sense of loss that accompanied the destruction of the city, temple and ritual as well as the exile of Judah's inhabitants.

The earliest possible date for the book is 586 B.C., and the latest is 516 (when the rebuilt Jerusalem temple was dedicated). The graphic immediacy of Lamentations argues for an earlier date, probably before 575.

Literary Features

The entire book is poetic. Each of its five laments contains 22 verses (except the third, which has 66 verses—3 times 22), reflecting the number of letters in the Hebrew alphabet. Moreover, the first four are alphabetic acrostics (beginning in 1:1; 2:1; 3:1; 4:1). The first three laments are equal in length; in the first and second each verse (except 1:7) has three Hebrew lines, while in the third each of the 66 verses has one Hebrew line. The fourth is shorter (each of its 22 verses has two Hebrew lines), and the fifth is shorter still (each verse has one Hebrew line). Use of the alphabet as a formal structure indicates that, however passionate these laments, they were composed with studied care.

Themes and Theology

Lamentations is not the only OT book that contains individual or community laments. (A large number of the Psalms are lament poems, and every prophetic book except Haggai includes one or more examples of the lament genre.) However, it is the only book that consists solely of laments.

As a series of laments over the destruction of Jerusalem in 586 B.C., it stands in a tradition with such ancient non-Biblical writings as the Sumerian "Lamentation over the Destruction of Ur," "Lamentation over the Destruction of Sumer and Ur," and "Lamentation over the Destruction of Nippur." Orthodox Jews customarily read it aloud in its entirety on the ninth day of Ab, the traditional date of the destruction of Solomon's temple in 586 as well as the date of the destruction of Herod's temple in A.D. 70. Many also read it each week at the Western Wall (known also as the "Wailing Wall") in the Old City of Jerusalem. In addition the book is important in traditional Roman Catholic liturgy, where it is read during the last three days of Holy Week.

This latter tradition reminds us that the book of Lamentations describes Jerusalem's destruction not only for its own sake but also for the profound theological lessons to be learned from it. The horrors of 586 B.C. are not overlooked, of course:

1. Wholesale devastation and slaughter engulf kings (2:6,9; 4:20), princes (1:6; 2:2,9; 4:7–8; 5:12), elders (1:19; 2:10; 4:16; 5:12), priests (1:4,19; 2:6,20; 4:16), prophets (2:9,20) and commoners (2:10–12; 3:48; 4:6) alike.
2. Starving mothers are reduced to cannibalism (2:20; 4:10).
3. The flower of Judah's citizenry is dragged off into ignominious exile (1:3,18).
4. An elaborate system of ceremony and worship comes to an end (1:4,10).

But other matters, ultimately of far greater significance, are probed as well.

The author of Lamentations understands clearly that the Babylonians were merely the human agents of divine retribution and that God Himself has destroyed His city and temple (1:12–15; 2:1–8,17,22; 4:11). Nor was the Lord's action arbitrary; blatant, God-defying sin and covenant-breaking rebellion were the root causes of his people's woes (1:5,8–9; 4:13; 5:7,16). Although weeping (1:16; 2:11,18; 3:48–51) is to be expected and cries for redress against the enemy (1:22; 3:59–66) are understandable, the proper response in the wake of judgment is sincere, heartfelt contrition (3:40–42). The book that begins with lament (1:1–2) rightly ends in repentance (5:21–22).

In the middle of the book, the theology of Lamentations reaches its apex as it focuses on the goodness of God. He is the Lord of hope (3:21,24–25), of love (3:22), of faithfulness (3:23), of salvation (3:26). In spite of all evidence to the contrary, "His compassions never fail. They are new every morning; Great is Your faithfulness" (3:22–23).

Outline

I. Jerusalem's Misery and Desolation (ch. 1)
II. The Lord's Anger against His People (ch. 2)
III. Judah's Complaint—and Basis for Consolation (ch. 3)
IV. The Contrast between Zion's Past and Present (ch. 4)
V. Judah's Appeal for God's Forgiveness (ch. 5)

The Sorrows of Zion

1 How [a]lonely sits the city
That was [b]full of people!
She has become like a [c]widow
Who was *once* [d]great among the
nations!
She who was a princess among the
[1]provinces
Has become a [e]forced laborer!
2 She [a]weeps bitterly in the night
And her tears are on her cheeks;
She has none to comfort her
Among all her [b]lovers.
All her friends have [c]dealt
treacherously with her;
They have become her enemies.
3 [a]Judah has gone into exile [1]under
affliction
And [1]under [2]harsh servitude;
She dwells [b]among the nations,
But she has found no rest;
All [c]her pursuers have overtaken her
In the midst of [3]distress.
4 The roads [1]of Zion are in mourning
Because [a]no one comes to the
appointed feasts.
All her gates are [b]desolate;
Her priests are groaning,
Her [c]virgins are afflicted,
And she herself [2]is [d]bitter.
5 Her adversaries have become [1]her
masters,
Her enemies [2]prosper;
For the LORD has [a]caused her grief
Because of the multitude of her
transgressions;
Her little ones have gone away
As captives before the adversary.
6 All her [a]majesty
Has departed from the daughter of
Zion;
Her princes have become like deer
That have found no pasture;
And they have [1][b]fled without strength
Before the pursuer.
7 In the days of her affliction and
homelessness
[a]Jerusalem remembers all her
precious things
That were from the days of old,
When her people fell into the hand of
the adversary
And [b]no one helped her.
The adversaries saw her,
They [c]mocked at her [1]ruin.
8 Jerusalem sinned [a]greatly,
Therefore [b]she has become an unclean
thing.
All who honored her despise her
Because they have seen her
nakedness;
Even [c]she herself groans and turns
away.
9 Her [a]uncleanness was in her skirts;
She [1]did not consider her [b]future.
Therefore she has [2][c]fallen
astonishingly;
[d]She has no comforter.
"[e]See, O LORD, my affliction,
For the enemy has [f]magnified himself!"
10 The adversary has stretched out his
hand
Over all her precious things,
For she has seen the [a]nations enter
her sanctuary,
The ones whom You commanded
That they should [b]not enter into Your
congregation.
11 All her people groan [a]seeking bread;
They have given their precious things
for food
To [b]restore their [1]lives themselves.
"See, O LORD, and look,
For I am [c]despised."

1:1 [1]Or *districts* [a]Is 3:26 [b]Is 22:2 [c]Is 54:4 [d]1 Kin 4:21; Ezra 4:20; Jer 31:7 [e]2 Kin 23:35; Jer 40:9
2 [a]Ps 6:6; 77:2-6; Lam 1:16 [b]Jer 2:25; 3:1; 22:20-22 [c]Job 19:13, 14; Ps 31:11; Mic 7:5
3 [1]Or *by reason of* [2]Lit *great* [3]Or *narrow places* [a]Jer 13:19 [b]Lev 26:39; Deut 28:64-67 [c]2 Kin 25:4, 5
4 [1]Or *to* [2]Or *suffers bitterly* [a]Is 24:4-6; Lam 2:6, 7 [b]Jer 9:11; 10:22 [c]Lam 2:10, 21 [d]Joel 1:8-13
5 [1]Lit *head* [2]Or *are at ease* [a]Ps 90:7, 8; Ezek 8:17, 18; 9:9, 10
6 [a]Jer 13:18
6 [1]Lit *gone* [b]2 Kin 25:4, 5
7 [1]Lit *cessation* [a]Ps 42:4; 77:5-9 [b]Jer 37:7; Lam 4:17 [c]Ps 79:4; Jer 48:27
8 [a]Is 59:2-13; Lam 1:5, 20 [b]Lam 1:17 [c]Lam 1:11, 21, 22
9 [1]Lit *did not remember her latter end* [2]Lit *come down* [a]Jer 2:34; Ezek 24:13 [b]Deut 32:29; Is 47:7 [c]Is 3:8; Jer 13:17, 18 [d]Eccl 4:1; Jer 16:7 [e]Ps 25:18; 119:153 [f]Ps 74:23; Zeph 2:10
10 [a]Ps 74:4-8; Is 64:10, 11; Jer 51:51 [b]Deut 23:3
11 [1]Lit *soul* [a]Jer 38:9; 52:6 [b]1 Sam 30:12 [c]Jer 15:19

1:1 *How . . . !* Expresses a mixture of shock and despair (see 2:1; 4:1–2; Is 1:21; Jer 48:17). *lonely sits.* The Hebrew underlying this phrase is translated "sat alone" in Jer 15:17. There the prophet sat alone; here his beloved city does the same. *city.* Jerusalem. *was full of people.* See Is 1:21. *full . . . great.* The Hebrew is the same for both words. *great among the nations.* Contrast Jer 49:15. *forced laborer.* See Ex 1:11; 1 Kin 4:6.
1:2 *She weeps bitterly.* As did Jeremiah, and for much the same reason (see Jer 13:17). *in the night.* See 2:18–19. *none to comfort her.* See vv. 9,16–17,21. *lovers . . . friends.* Political allies (see, e.g., Jer 2:36–37; 27:3). *All . . . have dealt treacherously with her.* See v. 19; like Edom (see 4:21–22; Ps 137:7) and Ammon (see Jer 40:14; Ezek 25:2–3,6). *become her enemies.* See v. 17.
1:3 *among the nations . . . found no rest.* As Moses warned in Deut 28:65.
1:4 *in mourning.* Deserted and desolate (see Judg 5:6; Is 33:8 and notes). *appointed feasts.* See Ex 23:14–17 and notes; Lev 23:2. *virgins are afflicted.* A sign of utter defeat (contrast Ex 15:20 and note; Judg 21:19,21; Ps 68:25; Jer 31:13).
1:5 *masters.* Lit. "head"—in accordance with Deut 28:44 (contrast Deut 28:13). *prosper.* See Jer 12:1.
1:6 *daughter of Zion.* A personification of Jerusalem and its inhabitants. *Her princes . . . have fled . . . Before the pursuer.* See Jer 52:7–8.
1:7 *affliction and homelessness.* See 3:19. *precious things.* See vv. 10–11. *days of old.* For example, the days of David and Solomon. *fell into the hand of the adversary.* See 2 Sam 24:14. *ruin.* Lit. "cessation." The Hebrew root for this word is the same as that for "sabbath"—and may be intended as an ironic pun (see Lev 26:34–35).
1:8 *unclean.* See v. 17 and note. It refers to the ceremonial uncleanness of a woman during her monthly period (see Lev 12:2,5; 15:19); Jerusalem is here personified as a woman (see v. 6).
1:9 *uncleanness.* Ceremonial uncleanness (see note on Lev 4:12), here caused by willful sin. *did not consider her future.* See Is 47:7. *See, O LORD.* See vv. 11,20. *enemy has magnified himself.* See v. 16.
1:10 *commanded . . . not enter into Your congregation.* See Ezek 44:7,9.
1:11 *seeking bread.* Food shortages were an ever-present problem during and after the siege of Jerusalem. *restore their lives.* See v. 19; 1 Sam 30:12.

12 "Is [a]it nothing to all you who pass this
way?
Look and see if there is any [1]pain like
my [1]pain
Which was severely dealt out to me,
Which the [b]LORD inflicted on the day
of His [c]fierce anger.
13 "From on high He sent fire into my
[a]bones,
And it [1]prevailed *over them.*
He has spread a [b]net for my feet;
He has turned me back;
He has made me [c]desolate,
[2]Faint all day long.
14 "The [a]yoke of my transgressions is
bound;
By His hand they are knit together.
They have [b]come upon my neck;
He has made my strength [1]fail.
The Lord [c]has given me into the hands
Of *those against whom* I am not able
to stand.
15 "The [a]Lord has rejected all my strong
men
In my midst;
He has called an appointed [1]time
against me
To crush my [b]young men;
The Lord has [c]trodden *as in* a wine
press
The virgin daughter of Judah.
16 "For these things I [a]weep;
[1]My eyes run down with water;
Because far from me is a [b]comforter,
One who restores my soul.
My children are desolate
Because the enemy has prevailed."
17 Zion [a]stretches out her hands;
There is no one to comfort her;
The LORD has [b]commanded
concerning Jacob
That the ones round about him should
be his adversaries;
[c]Jerusalem has become an unclean
thing among them.
18 "The LORD is [a]righteous;
For I have [b]rebelled against His
[1]command;
Hear now, all peoples,
And [c]behold my [2]pain;
[d]My virgins and my young men
Have gone into captivity.
19 "I [a]called to my lovers, *but* they
deceived me;
My [b]priests and my elders perished in
the city
While they sought food to [c]restore
[1]their strength themselves.
20 "See, O LORD, for I am in distress;
My [1][a]spirit is greatly troubled;
My heart is overturned within me,
For I have been very [b]rebellious.
In the street the sword [2]slays;
In the house it is like death.
21 "They have heard that I [a]groan;
There is no one to comfort me;
All my enemies have heard of my
[1]calamity;
They are [b]glad that You have done *it.*
Oh, that You would bring the day
which You have proclaimed,
That they may become [c]like me.
22 "Let all their wickedness come before
You;
And [a]deal with them as You have
dealt with me
For all my transgressions;
For my groans are many and my heart
is faint."

12 [1]Or *sorrow* [a]Jer 18:16; 48:27 [b]Jer 30:23, 24 [c]Is 13:13; Jer 4:8
13 [1]Or *descended, overthrew* [2]Or *Sick* [a]Job 30:30; Ps 22:14; Hab 3:16 [b]Job 19:6; Ps 66:11 [c]Jer 44:6
14 [1]Lit *stumble* [a]Prov 5:22; Is 47:6 [b]Jer 28:13, 14 [c]Jer 32:3, 5; Ezek 25:4, 7
15 [1]Or *feast* [a]Is 41:2; Jer 13:24; 37:10 [b]Jer 6:11; 18:21 [c]Mal 4:3
16 [1]Lit *My eye, my eye* [a]Jer 14:17; Lam 2:11, 18; 3:48, 49 [b]Ps 69:20; Eccl 4:1; Lam 1:2
17 [a]Is 1:15; Jer 4:31 [b]2 Kin 24:2-4; Jer 12:9
17 [c]Lam 1:8
18 [1]Lit *mouth* [2]Or *sorrow* [a]Ps 119:75; Jer 12:1 [b]1 Sam 12:14, 15; Jer 4:17 [c]Lam 1:12 [d]Deut 28:32, 41
19 [1]Lit *their soul* [a]Job 19:13-19; Lam 1:2 [b]Jer 14:15; Lam 2:20 [c]Lam 1:11
20 [1]Lit *inward parts are in ferment* [2]Lit *bereaves* [a]Is 16:11; Lam 2:11 [b]Jer 14:20
21 [1]Lit *evil* [a]Lam 1:4, 8, 22 [b]Ps 35:15; Jer 50:11; Lam 2:15 [c]Is 14:5, 6; 47:6, 11; Jer 30:16
22 [a]Neh 4:4, 5; Ps 137:7, 8
2:1 [a]Ezek 30:18 [b]Is 14:12-15; Ezek 28:14-16 [c]Is 64:11

God's Anger over Israel

2 How the Lord has [a]covered the
daughter of Zion
With a cloud in His anger!
He has [b]cast from heaven to earth
The [c]glory of Israel,

1:12 See v. 18. Up to this point, the author has been the main speaker. Now, at the halfway mark of ch. 1, the main speaker changes to Jerusalem personified. *fierce anger.* See 2:3,6; 4:11. The Hebrew for this expression is common in Jeremiah (see Jer 4:8,26; 12:13; 25:37–38; 44:6; 49:37; 51:45).

1:13 *From on high He sent fire.* See 1 Kin 18:38; 2 Kin 1:10,12,14; 2 Chr 7:1. *my bones.* The bones of Jerusalem (personified as a woman; see note on v. 8). In a strikingly similar image, the word of the Lord was like fire in the bones of the prophet (see Jer 20:9 and note). *spread a net for my feet.* See Ps 57:6; Prov 29:5. *desolate.* Like Absalom's sister Tamar (see 2 Sam 13:20).

1:15 *trodden as in a wine press.* A common metaphor of divine judgment (see Is 63:2–3; Joel 3:13; Rev 14:19–20; 19:15). *virgin daughter of Judah.* See 2:13; see also notes on 2 Kin 19:21; Jer 14:17.

1:16 *eyes run down with water.* See 3:48; Jer 9:18; 13:17; 14:17; see also Jer 9:1. *enemy has prevailed.* See v. 9.

1:17 *be his adversaries.* See v. 2. *unclean thing.* See note on v. 8; for the same imagery elsewhere see Ezra 9:11; Is 30:22; 64:6; Ezek 7:19–20; 36:17.

1:18 *The LORD is righteous.* See Deut 32:4; 2 Chr 12:6; Ps 119:137; Jer 12:1; see also note on Ps 4:1. *rebelled against His command.* See Num 20:24. *Hear now, all peoples.* See 1 Kin 22:28; Ps 49:1; Mic 1:2.

1:19 *lovers . . . deceived me.* See v. 2 and note. *restore their strength themselves.* See note on v. 11.

1:20 *My spirit is greatly troubled.* Repeated in 2:11. *In the street . . . In the house.* See Jer 14:18. The Sumerian "Lamentation over the Destruction of Ur" contains a striking parallel: "Inside it we die of famine, outside we are killed by weapons" (lines 403–404).

1:21 *day which You have proclaimed.* Day of God's judgment on the nations (see Jer 25:15–38).

1:22 *wickedness . . . before You.* See Ps 109:14–15. *my heart is faint.* The same expression is found in Jer 8:18; see Lam 5:17; Is 1:5.

2:1 *How . . . !* See note on 1:1. *daughter of Zion.* See 1:6 and note. *cast from . . . The glory of Israel.* The imagery is that of a falling star (as in Is 14:12). *footstool.* Either (1) the ark of the covenant (see 1 Chr 28:2) or, more likely, (2) Mount Zion (see Ps 99:5,9).

And has not remembered His [d]footstool
In the day of His anger.
2 The Lord has [a]swallowed up; He has not spared
All the habitations of Jacob.
In His wrath He has [b]thrown down
The strongholds of the daughter of Judah;
He has [c]brought *them* down to the ground;
He has [d]profaned the kingdom and its princes.
3 In fierce anger He has cut off
[1]All the [a]strength of Israel;
He has [b]drawn back His right hand
From before the enemy.
And He has [c]burned in Jacob like a flaming fire
Consuming round about.
4 He has bent His [a]bow like an enemy;
He has set His right hand like an adversary
And slain all that were [b]pleasant to the eye;
In the tent of the daughter of Zion
He has [c]poured out His wrath like fire.
5 The Lord has become like an [a]enemy.
He has [b]swallowed up Israel;
He has swallowed up all its [c]palaces,
He has destroyed its strongholds
And [d]multiplied in the daughter of Judah
Mourning and moaning.
6 And He has violently treated His
[1]tabernacle like a garden *booth;*
He has [a]destroyed His appointed
[2]meeting place.
The LORD has [b]caused to be forgotten
The appointed feast and sabbath in Zion,
And He has [c]despised king and priest
In the indignation of His anger.
7 The Lord has [a]rejected His altar,
He has abandoned His sanctuary;
He [b]has delivered into the hand of the enemy
The walls of her palaces.
They have made a [c]noise in the house of the LORD
As in the day of an appointed feast.
8 The LORD [1]determined to destroy
The wall of the daughter of Zion.
He has [a]stretched out a line,
He has not restrained His hand from
[2]destroying,
And He has [b]caused rampart and wall to lament;
They have languished together.
9 Her [a]gates have sunk into the ground,
He has destroyed and broken her bars.
Her king and her princes are among the nations;
The [b]law is no more.
Also, her prophets find
[c]No vision from the LORD.
10 The elders of the daughter of Zion
[a]Sit on the ground, they [b]are silent.
They have thrown [c]dust on their heads;
They have girded themselves with
[d]sackcloth.
The [e]virgins of Jerusalem
Have bowed their heads to the ground.
11 My [a]eyes fail because of tears,
My [1][b]spirit is greatly troubled;
My [2][c]heart is poured out on the earth
[d]Because of the [3]destruction of the daughter of my people,
When [e]little ones and infants faint
In the streets of the city.
12 They say to their mothers,
"[a]Where is grain and wine?"
As they faint like a wounded man
In the streets of the city,
As their [b]life is poured out
On their mothers' bosom.
13 How shall I admonish you?
To what [a]shall I compare you,
O daughter of Jerusalem?

2:1 [d]Ps 99:5; 132:7
2 [a]Ps 21:9; Lam 3:43 [b]Lam 2:5; Mic 5:11, 14 [c]Is 25:12; 26:5 [d]Ps 89:39, 40; Is 43:28
3 [1]Lit *Every horn* [a]Ps 75:5, 10; Jer 48:25 [b]Ps 74:11; Jer 21:4, 5 [c]Is 42:25; Jer 21:14
4 [a]Job 6:4; 16:13; Lam 3:12, 13 [b]Ezek 24:25 [c]Is 42:25; Jer 7:20
5 [a]Jer 30:14 [b]Lam 2:2 [c]Jer 52:13; Lam 2:2 [d]Jer 9:17-20
6 [1]Lit *booth* [2]Or *feast* [a]Jer 52:13 [b]Jer 17:27; Lam 1:4; Zeph 3:18 [c]Lam 4:16
7 [a]Ps 78:59-61; Is 64:11; Ezek 7:20-22
7 [b]Jer 33:4, 5; 52:13 [c]Ps 74:3-8
8 [1]Lit *thought* [2]Lit *swallowing up* [a]2 Kin 21:13; Is 34:11; Amos 7:7-9 [b]Is 3:26; Jer 14:2
9 [a]Neh 1:3 [b]Hos 3:4 [c]Jer 14:14; 23:16; Ezek 7:26
10 [a]Job 2:13; Is 3:26; 47:1 [b]Amos 8:3 [c]Job 2:12; Ezek 27:30 [d]Is 15:3; Jon 3:6-8 [e]Lam 1:4
11 [1]Lit *inward parts are in ferment* [2]Lit *liver* [3]Lit *breaking* [a]Lam 1:16; 3:48, 51 [b]Jer 4:19 [c]Job 16:13 [d]Is 22:4; Lam 4:10 [e]Jer 44:7; Lam 2:19
12 [a]Jer 5:17 [b]Job 30:16; Ps 42:4; 62:8
13 [a]Lam 1:12

2:2 *swallowed up . . . All the inhabitants.* See v. 5. *daughter of Judah.* See note on 1:15.
2:3 *flaming fire Consuming.* See Num 11:3; Job 1:16; Ps 106:18.
2:4 *bent His bow.* See Deut 32:42; Ps 7:12–13; Zech 9:13–14. *poured out His wrath.* See Ps 69:24; 79:6; Jer 6:11; 7:20; 10:25; 42:18; 44:6; Hos 5:10; Zeph 3:8.
2:5 *palaces . . . strongholds.* See Hos 8:14. *multiplied . . . moaning.* The Sumerian "Lamentation over the Destruction of Sumer and Ur" offers this parallel: "In the desolate city there was uttered nothing but laments and dirges" (lines 361–362, 486–487). *daughter of Judah.* See note on 1:15.
2:6 *His tabernacle.* The Hebrew word can refer to either the tabernacle or the temple, as here (see Ps 27:4–5). *like a garden.* Cf. Is 5:5–6; Jer 5:10; 12:10. *His appointed meeting place.* The tabernacle/temple, where God met with His people (see Ex 25:22; 29:42–43; Ps 74:4).
2:7 *rejected . . . abandoned.* These two verbs are found in Ps 89:38–39 ("cast off . . . spurned") in connection with the Lord's forsaking of the king from the dynasty of David. *made a noise in the house of the LORD.* See Ps 74:4. *As in the day of an appointed feast.* See Hos 12:9.
2:8 *determined to destroy.* See Jer 32:31. *daughter of Zion.* A personification of Jerusalem and its inhabitants. *stretched out a line.* To destroy with the same standards of precision and propriety used in building (see Is 28:17 and note; Amos 7:7–8 and notes). *rampart . . . wall.* See Is 26:1. The ramparts were the outer fortifications (see 2 Sam 20:15).
2:9 *prophets find No vision.* The Lord was no longer communicating to His people through prophets (see Ps 74:9; Amos 8:11 and note; Mic 3:7).
2:10 *elders.* See note on Ex 3:16. *Sit on the ground . . . throw dust on their heads . . . girded themselves with sackcloth . . . bowed their heads.* Signs of mourning (see Job 2:12–13; Ps 35:13–14). *virgins of Jerusalem.* See 1:4 and note.
2:11 *My eyes fail.* See note on Ps 6:7. *tears.* See note on 1:16. *My spirit is greatly troubled.* Repeated from 1:20. *my people.* See 3:48; 4:10; see also note on Jer 14:17.
2:12 *life is poured out.* See Job 30:16; Ps 107:5; Jon 2:7.
2:13 *admonish you.* See Job 29:11. *daughter of Jerusalem . . . virgin daughter of Zion.* See notes on 1:6; Jer 14:17.

To what shall I liken you as I comfort
you,
O [b]virgin daughter of Zion?
For your [1]ruin is as vast as the sea;
Who can [c]heal you?
14 Your [a]prophets have seen for you
False and foolish *visions;*
And they have not [b]exposed your
iniquity
So as to restore you from captivity,
But they have [c]seen for you false and
misleading [1]oracles.
15 All who pass along the way
[a]Clap their hands *in derision* at you;
They [b]hiss and shake their heads
At the daughter of Jerusalem,
"Is this the city of which they said,
'[c]The perfection of beauty,
[d]A joy to all the earth'?"
16 All [a]your enemies
Have opened their mouths wide
against you;
They hiss and [b]gnash *their* teeth.
They say, "We have [c]swallowed *her* up!
Surely this is the [d]day for which we
waited;
We have reached *it,* we have seen *it.*"
17 The LORD has [a]done what He purposed;
He has accomplished His word
Which He commanded from days of
old.
He has thrown down [b]without sparing,
And He has caused the enemy to
[c]rejoice over you;
He has [d]exalted the [1]might of your
adversaries.
18 Their [a]heart cried out to the Lord,
"O [b]wall of the daughter of Zion,
Let *your* [c]tears run down like a river
day and night;
Give yourself no relief,
Let [1]your eyes have no rest.
19 "Arise, cry aloud in the [a]night
At the beginning of the night
watches;
[b]Pour out your heart like water
Before the presence of the Lord;
Lift up your hands to Him
For the [c]life of your little ones
Who are [d]faint because of hunger
At the head of every street."
20 See, O LORD, and look!
With [a]whom have You dealt thus?
Should women [b]eat their [1]offspring,
The little ones who were [2]born
healthy?
Should [c]priest and prophet be slain
In the sanctuary of the Lord?
21 On the ground in the streets
Lie [a]young and old;
My [b]virgins and my young men
Have fallen by the sword.
You have slain *them* in the day of Your
anger,
You have slaughtered, [c]not sparing.
22 You called as in the day of an
appointed feast
My [a]terrors on every side;
And there was [b]no one who escaped
or survived
In the day of the LORD's anger.
Those [c]whom I [1]bore and reared,
My enemy annihilated them.

13 [1]Lit *breaking* [b]Is 37:22 [c]Jer 8:22; 30:12-15
14 [1]Lit *burdens* [a]Jer 23:25-29; 29:8, 9 [b]Is 58:1; Ezek 23:36; Mic 3:8 [c]Jer 23:36; Ezek 22:25, 28
15 [a]Job 27:23; Ezek 25:6 [b]Ps 22:7; Is 37:22; Jer 18:16; 19:8; Zeph 2:15 [c]Ps 50:2 [d]Ps 48:2
16 [a]Job 16:10; Ps 22:13; Lam 3:46 [b]Job 16:9; Ps 35:16; 37:12 [c]Ps 56:2; 124:3; Jer 51:34 [d]Obad 12-15
17 [1]Lit *horn* [a]Jer 4:28 [b]Lam 2:1, 2; Ezek 5:11; 7:8, 9; 8:18 [c]Ps 35:24, 26; 89:42; Is 14:29 [d]Deut 28:43, 44; Lam 1:5
18 [1]Lit *the daughter of your eye* [a]Ps 119:145; Hos 7:14 [b]Lam 2:8; Hab 2:11 [c]Ps 119:136; Jer 9:1; Lam 1:2, 16; 3:48, 49
19 [a]Ps 42:3; Is 26:9 [b]1 Sam 1:15; Ps 42:4; 62:8 [c]Lam 2:11 [d]Is 51:20
20 [1]Lit *fruit* [2]Or *tenderly cared for* [a]Ex 32:11; Deut 9:26 [b]Jer 19:9; Lam 4:10 [c]Ps 78:64; Jer 14:15; 23:11, 12
21 [a]2 Chr 36:17; Jer 6:11 [b]Ps 78:62, 63 [c]Jer 13:14; Zech 11:6
22 [1]Lit *bore healthy* or, *tenderly cared for* [a]Ps 31:13; Is 24:17; Jer 6:25 [b]Jer 11:11 [c]Jer 16:2-4; 44:7

Jeremiah Shares Israel's Affliction

3 I am the man who has [a]seen affliction
Because of the rod of His wrath.
2 He has driven me and made me walk
In [a]darkness and not in light.
3 Surely against me He has [a]turned His
hand
Repeatedly all the day.

3:1 [a]Ps 88:7, 15, 16 **2** [a]Job 30:26; Is 59:9; Jer 4:23 **3** [a]Ps 38:2; Is 5:25

2:14 *prophets . . . False.* Jeremiah often denounced false prophets (see Jer 5:12–13; 6:13–15; 8:10–12; 14:13–15; 23:9–40; 27:9–28:17). *foolish.* Or "whitewash(ed)"; for an explanation of this image see Ezek 13:10–16; 22:28. *misleading.* The unusual Hebrew word underlying this word comes from the same root as that underlying "drive you out" in Jer 27:10,15: The lies of false prophets "mislead" the people and thus lead to "banishment" by the Lord—so they are "banishing" in their effect.
2:15 *who pass along the way.* See 1:12. *Clap their hands.* See Job 27:23. *hiss.* See v. 16; see also note on Jer 19:8. *shake their heads.* See note on Job 16:4; see also Ps 44:14; 109:25; Jer 18:16. *daughter of Jerusalem.* See notes on 1:6; Jer 14:17. *they said, 'The perfection of beauty.'* As in Ps 50:2 (see note there). *they said . . . '. . . A joy to all the earth.'* As in Ps 48:2 (see note there; cf. Jer 51:41).
2:16 *swallowed her up.* See vv. 2,5; Jer 51:34.
2:17 *accomplished His word.* See Is 55:11 and note. *from days of old.* The days of Moses (see, e.g., the threats of Lev 26:23–39; Deut 28:15–68). *exalted the might.* Increased the strength (see 1 Sam 2:1; Ps 75:4).
2:18 See Jer 14:17. *O wall.* A city gate is similarly addressed in Is 14:31. *daughter of Zion.* A personification of Jerusalem and its inhabitants.
2:19 *beginning of the night watches.* See note on Judg 7:19; see also Ps 63:6. *Pour out your heart.* In earnest prayer (see Ps 62:8). *like water.* A common simile with "pour out" (see Deut 12:16,24; 15:23; Ps 79:3; Hos 5:10). *Lift up your hands.* In prayer and praise (see Ps 28:2; 63:4; 1 Tim 2:8). *little ones . . . faint because of hunger.* See vv. 11–12.
2:20–22 The prayer called for in v. 19.
2:20 *women eat their offspring.* See note on Jer 19:9.
2:21 See Jer 6:11 and note.
2:22 *called . . . My.* See 1:15. *terrors on every side.* See note on Jer 6:25. *no one who escaped or survived.* See Jer 42:17; 44:14. *day of the LORD's anger.* The chapter ends as it began (see v. 1).
3:1–2 *I . . . me.* Whether the author is Jeremiah or an anonymous mourner, he speaks not only for himself but also for the suffering community of which he is a part (see "we" and "us" in vv. 40–47). The Hebrew text of v. 1 is at the exact center of the book.
3:1 *affliction.* See v. 19. *rod of His wrath.* See Job 9:34; 21:9. The reference is to Babylon (see Is 10:5 and note).
3:2 *darkness and not in light.* See Job 12:25; characteristic of the "day of the LORD" (Amos 5:18).

4 He has caused my [a]flesh and my skin
to waste away,
He has [b]broken my bones.
5 He has [a]besieged and encompassed
me with [b]bitterness and hardship.
6 In [a]dark places He has made me
dwell,
Like those who have long been dead.
7 He has [a]walled me in so that I cannot
go out;
He has made my [1b]chain heavy.
8 Even when I cry out and call for help,
He [a]shuts out my prayer.
9 He has [a]blocked my ways with hewn
stone;
He has made my paths crooked.
10 He is to me like a bear lying in wait,
Like a lion in secret places.
11 He has turned aside my ways and
[a]torn me to pieces;
He has made me desolate.
12 He [a]bent His bow
And [b]set me as a target for the arrow.
13 He made the [1]arrows of His [a]quiver
To enter into my [2]inward parts.
14 I have become a [a]laughingstock to all
my people,
Their *mocking* [b]song all the day.
15 He has [a]filled me with bitterness,
He has made me drunk with
wormwood.
16 He has [a]broken my teeth with [b]gravel;
He has made me cower in the [c]dust.
17 My soul has been rejected [a]from peace;
I have forgotten [1]happiness.
18 So I say, "My strength has perished,
And *so has* my [a]hope from the LORD."

Hope of Relief in God's Mercy

19 Remember my affliction and my
[1]wandering, the [a]wormwood and
bitterness.
20 Surely [a]my soul remembers
And is [b]bowed down within me.
21 This I recall to my mind,
Therefore I have [a]hope.
22 The LORD's [a]lovingkindnesses [1]indeed
never cease,
[b]For His compassions never fail.
23 *They* are new [a]every morning;
Great is [b]Your faithfulness.
24 "The LORD is my [a]portion," says my
soul,
"Therefore I [b]have hope in Him."
25 The LORD is good to those who [a]wait
for Him,
To the [1]person who [b]seeks Him.
26 *It is* good that he [a]waits silently
For the salvation of the LORD.
27 *It is* good for a man that he should
bear
The yoke in his youth.
28 Let him [a]sit alone and be silent
Since He has laid *it* on him.
29 Let him [1]put his mouth in the [a]dust,
Perhaps there is [b]hope.
30 Let him give his [a]cheek to [1]the smiter,
Let him be filled with reproach.
31 For the Lord will [a]not reject forever,
32 For if He causes grief,
Then He will have [a]compassion

4 [a]Ps 31:9, 10; 38:2-8; 102:3-5 [b]Ps 51:8; Is 38:13 **5** [a]Job 19:8 [b]Jer 23:15; Lam 3:19 **6** [a]Ps 88:5, 6; 143:3 **7** [1]Lit *bronze piece* [a]Job 3:23; 19:8 [b]Jer 40:4 **8** [a]Job 30:20; Ps 22:2 **9** [a]Is 63:17; Hos 2:6 **11** [a]Job 16:12, 13; Jer 15:3; Hos 6:1 **12** [a]Ps 7:12; Lam 2:4 [b]Job 6:4; 7:20; Ps 38:2 **13** [1]Lit *sons* [2]Lit *kidneys* [a]Jer 5:16 **14** [a]Ps 22:6, 7; 123:4; Jer 20:7 [b]Job 30:9; Lam 3:63 **15** [a]Jer 9:15 **16** [a]Ps 3:7; 58:6 [b]Prov 20:17 [c]Jer 6:26 **17** [1]Lit *good* [a]Is 59:11; Jer 12:12 **18** [a]Job 17:15; Ezek 37:11

19 [1]Or *bitterness* [a]Jer 9:15; Lam 3:5, 15 **20** [a]Job 21:6 [b]Ps 42:5, 6, 11; 43:5; 44:25 **21** [a]Ps 130:7 **22** [1]Or *that we are not consumed* [a]Ps 78:38; Jer 3:12; 30:11 [b]Mal 3:6 **23** [a]Is 33:2; Zeph 3:5 [b]Heb 10:23 **24** [a]Ps 16:5; 73:26 [b]Ps 33:18 **25** [1]Lit *soul* [a]Ps 27:14; Is 25:9 [b]Is 26:9 **26** [a]Ps 37:7 **28** [a]Jer 15:17 **29** [1]Lit *give* [a]Job 16:15; 40:4 [b]Jer 31:17 **30** [1]Lit *his* [a]Job 16:10; Is 50:6 **31** [a]Ps 77:7; 94:14; Is 54:7-10 **32** [a]Ps 78:38; 106:43-45; Hos 11:8

3:4 *waste away.* See Job 13:28 ("decaying"); Ps 49:14 ("consume"). *broken my bones.* See Is 38:13 and note.
3:5 *bitterness.* Lit. "poison" (see Jer 8:14 and note).
3:6 Reminiscent of Ps 143:3.
3:7 *walled.* The Hebrew for this word is the same as that for "blocked" in v. 9 (see Job 19:8; Hos 2:6). *cannot go out.* See Ps 88:8.
3:8 *shuts out my prayer.* See v. 44; Ps 18:41; Prov 1:28; Jer 7:16 and note.
3:9 *hewn stone.* Of enormous size, like those used in the foundation of Solomon's temple (see 1 Kin 5:17). *made . . . crooked.* Or "distorted/destroyed" (as in Is 24:1); for the imagery see Job 30:13.
3:10 *like a bear . . . Like a lion.* See Ps 10:9; 17:12; Jer 4:7; 5:6; 49:19; 50:44.
3:11 See 1:2.
3:12 *bent His bow.* See note on 2:4. *set me as a target.* See note on Job 6:4.
3:13 *inward parts.* Lit. "kidneys" (as in Job 16:13).
3:14 See Jeremiah's complaint in Jer 20:7. *mocking song.* See v. 63; Ps 69:12.
3:15 *filled me with bitterness.* The Hebrew underlying this phrase is translated "saturates me with bitterness" in Job 9:18 (see note on Jer 9:15). For the significance of the bitter herbs eaten during the Passover meal see note on Ex 12:8.
3:18 *the LORD.* The first mention of God in ch. 3.
3:19 The poet remembers all these experiences and verbalizes them once again. *affliction and . . . wandering.* See 1:7.
3:21–26 The theological high point of the book of Lamentations (see Introduction: Themes and Theology).
3:22 *lovingkindness.* See v. 32. The Hebrew for this phrase is plural (as also in Ps 107:43) and denotes the Lord's loving faithfulness to His covenant promises (see Ps 89:1). See note on Ps 6:4.
3:23 *They.* The "lovingkindnesses" and "compassions" (v. 22) of the Lord. *every morning.* See Is 33:2. *Great is Your faithfulness.* It is beyond measure (see note on v. 32; see also Ps 36:5).
3:24 *The LORD is my portion.* See Ps 73:26; 142:5. He was the inheritance share of the priests and Levites (see Num 18:20; see also note on Gen 15:1). *Therefore I have hope.* This phrase serves as a refrain (see v. 21).
3:25 *The LORD is good.* See Ps 34:8; 86:5. *who wait for Him.* See Ps 25:3; 69:7.
3:26 See Is 26:3; 30:15.
3:27 *a man . . . should bear The yoke.* Echoes the thought of v. 1: "the man who has seen affliction."
3:28 *sit alone.* See note on 1:1. *it.* The yoke (see v. 27).
3:29 *Perhaps there is hope.* See Job 11:18.
3:30 *give his cheek.* See Matt 5:39. *filled with reproach.* See Ps 123:3–4.
3:31 See Jer 3:5 and note.
3:32 The same God who judges also restores (see Job 5:18; Ps 30:5; Is 54:8). *His abundant lovingkindness.* See note on v. 22; see also "great is Your faithfulness" (v. 23)—faithfulness and unfailing love are often used together to sum up God's covenant mercies toward His people.

According to His abundant
lovingkindness.
33 For He [a]does not afflict [1]willingly
Or grieve the sons of men.
34 To crush under His feet
All the prisoners of the [1]land,
35 To [1]deprive a man of [a]justice
In the presence of the Most High,
36 To [1a]defraud a man in his lawsuit—
Of these things the Lord does not
[2]approve.
37 Who is [1]there who speaks and it
[a]comes to pass,
Unless the Lord has commanded *it?*
38 *Is it* not from the mouth of the Most
High
That [1a]both good and ill go forth?

39 Why should *any* living [1]mortal, or *any*
man,
Offer [a]complaint [2]in view of his sins?
40 Let us [a]examine and probe our ways,
And let us return to the LORD.
41 We [a]lift up our heart [1]and hands
Toward God in heaven;
42 We have [a]transgressed and rebelled,
You have [b]not pardoned.
43 You have covered *Yourself* with [a]anger
And [b]pursued us;
You have slain *and* [c]have not spared.
44 You have [a]covered Yourself with a
cloud
So that [b]no prayer can pass through.
45 *You have made us mere* [a]offscouring
and refuse
In the midst of the peoples.
46 All our enemies have [a]opened their
mouths against us.
47 [a]Panic and pitfall have befallen us,
Devastation and destruction;
48 My [1a]eyes run down with streams of
water
Because of the destruction of the
daughter of my people.

33 [1]Lit *from His heart* [a]Ps 119:67, 71, 75; Ezek 33:11; Heb 12:10
34 [1]Or *earth*
35 [1]Or *turn aside a man's case* [a]Ps 140:12; Prov 17:15
36 [1]Lit *make crooked* [2]Lit *see* [a]Jer 22:3; Hab 1:13
37 [1]Lit *this* [a]Ps 33:9-11
38 [1]Lit *the evil* things *and the good* [a]Job 2:10; Is 45:7; Jer 32:42
39 [1]Or *human being* [2]Or *on the basis of* [a]Jer 30:15; Mic 7:9; Heb 12:5, 6
40 [a]Ps 119:59; 139:23, 24; 2 Cor 13:5
41 [1]Lit *toward* our [a]Ps 25:1; 28:2; 141:2
42 [a]Neh 9:26; Jer 14:20; Dan 9:5 [b]2 Kin 24:4; Jer 5:7, 9
43 [a]Lam 2:21 [b]Ps 83:15; Lam 3:66 [c]Lam 2:2, 17, 21
44 [a]Ps 97:2 [b]Lam 3:8; Zech 7:13
45 [a]1 Cor 4:13
46 [a]Job 30:9, 10; Ps 22:6-8; Lam 2:16
47 [a]Is 24:17, 18; Jer 48:43, 44
48 [1]Lit *eye brings* [a]Ps 119:136; Jer 9:1, 18; Lam 1:16; 2:11, 18

49 [a]Ps 77:2; Jer 14:17
50 [a]Ps 80:14; Is 63:15; Lam 5:1
52 [a]Ps 35:7, 19 [b]1 Sam 26:20; Ps 11:1; 124:7
53 [1]Lit *my life* [2]Or *cast stones* [a]Jer 37:16; 38:6,

49 My eyes pour down [a]unceasingly,
Without stopping,
50 Until the LORD [a]looks down
And sees from heaven.
51 My eyes bring pain to my soul
Because of all the daughters of my city.
52 My enemies [a]without cause
Hunted me down [b]like a bird;
53 They have silenced [1]me [a]in the pit
And have [2b]placed a stone on me.
54 Waters flowed [a]over my head;
I said, "I am cut off!"
55 I [a]called on Your name, O LORD,
Out of the lowest pit.
56 You have [a]heard my voice,
"[b]Do not hide Your ear from my *prayer
for* relief,
From my cry for help."
57 You [a]drew near when I called on You;
You said, "[b]Do not fear!"
58 O Lord, You [a]have pleaded my soul's
cause;
You have [b]redeemed my life.
59 O LORD, You have [a]seen my oppression;
[b]Judge my case.
60 You have seen all their vengeance,
All their [a]schemes against me.
61 You have heard their [a]reproach,
O LORD,
All their schemes against me.
62 The [a]lips of my assailants and their
whispering
Are against me all day long.
63 Look on their [a]sitting and their rising;
[b]I am their mocking song.
64 You will [a]recompense them, O LORD,
According to the work of their hands.
65 You will give them [1a]hardness of heart,

9 [b]Dan 6:17 **54** [a]Ps 69:2; Jon 2:3-5 **55** [a]Ps 130:1; Jon 2:2
56 [a]Job 34:28 [b]Ps 55:1 **57** [a]Ps 145:18 [b]Is 41:10, 14
58 [a]Jer 50:34 [b]Ps 34:22 **59** [a]Jer 18:19, 20 [b]Ps 26:1; 43:1
60 [a]Jer 11:19 **61** [a]Ps 74:18; 89:50; Lam 5:1; Zeph 2:8
62 [a]Ps 59:7, 12; 140:3; Ezek 36:3 **63** [a]Ps 139:2 [b]Job 30:9; Lam 3:14 **64** [a]Ps 28:4; Jer 51:6, 24, 56 **65** [1]Or *insolence* [a]Ex 14:8; Deut 2:30; Is 6:10

3:33 *does not afflict willingly.* See Ezek 18:23,32; Hos 11:8; 2 Pet 3:9.
3:34 *crush under His feet.* As the Babylonians had done in 586 B.C.
3:35 *deprive . . . justice.* As the leaders of Judah had done, in direct violation of the law (see Ex 23:6). *In the presence of the Most High.* In the presence of those whom the Most High designates to dispense justice (see Ex 22:8–9 and NASB marg.; see also introduction to Ps 82). *Most High.* See note on Gen 14:19.
3:36 *defraud . . . in his lawsuit.* Men might act unjustly, but God never does (see Job 8:3; 34:12).
3:37 *speaks . . . comes to pass.* See note on Gen 1:3.
3:38 See Amos 3:6.
3:39 *Offer complaint.* As the Israelites did in the wilderness (see Num 11:1).
3:40 *us.* See note on vv. 1–2. *examine . . . our ways.* See 1 Cor 11:28.
3:41 *lift up . . . hands.* See note on 2:19. *heaven.* Where God is enthroned (see Ps 2:4).
3:42 *We have transgressed and rebelled.* For similar confessions see Ps 106:6; Dan 9:5.
3:43 *with anger . . . pursued us.* See v. 66; Jer 29:18. *slain . . . not spared.* See 2:21.
3:46 See note on 2:16.
3:48 *eyes run down with . . . water.* See note on 1:16. *my people.* See note on 2:11.
3:51 *daughters of my city.* See 1:4,18; 2:20–21; 5:11.
3:52 *enemies without cause.* See note on Ps 35:19. *like a bird.* See Ps 11:1.
3:53 *placed a stone on.* See Lev 20:2,27; 1 Kin 12:18.
3:54 *Waters flowed over my head.* See note on Ps 42:7. *cut off.* See Ps 31:22; Is 53:8.
3:55 *lowest pit.* See note on Ps 30:1.
3:56 *cry for help.* See Job 32:20; Ps 118:5.
3:57 *near when I called.* See Ps 145:18. *Do not fear!* Reminiscent of Jeremiah's call to prophesy (see Jer 1:8 and note).
3:58 *redeemed my life.* See Ps 103:4; see also note on Ps 25:22.
3:63 *sitting and . . . rising.* Engaging in any kind of activity (see Deut 6:7; 11:19; Ps 139:2; Is 37:28). *I am their mocking song.* See note on v. 14.
3:64 Paralleled in Ps 28:4; see note on Ps 5:10.

Your curse will be on them.
66 You will [a]pursue them in anger and
destroy them
From under the [b]heavens of the LORD!

Distress of the Siege Described

4 How [a]dark the gold has become,
How the pure gold has changed!
The sacred stones are poured out
At the [1]corner of every street.
2 The precious sons of Zion,
Weighed against fine gold,
How they are regarded as [a]earthen jars,
The work of a potter's hands!
3 Even [a]jackals offer the breast,
They nurse their young;
But the daughter of my people has
become [b]cruel
Like [c]ostriches in the wilderness.
4 The [a]tongue of the infant cleaves
To the roof of its mouth because of
[b]thirst;
The little ones [c]ask for bread,
But no one breaks *it* for them.
5 Those who ate [a]delicacies
Are desolate in the streets;
Those [1]reared in purple
Embrace ash pits.
6 For the [1]iniquity of the daughter of my
people
Is greater than the [2a]sin of Sodom,
Which was [b]overthrown as in a
moment,
And no hands were [3]turned toward
her.
7 Her [1]consecrated ones were [a]purer
than snow,
They were whiter than milk;
They were more ruddy *in* [2]body than
corals,
Their polishing *was like* [3b]lapis lazuli.
8 Their appearance is [a]blacker than
soot,
They are not recognized in the streets;
Their [b]skin is shriveled on their bones,
It is withered, it has become like wood.
9 Better are those [1a]slain with the sword
Than those [1]slain with hunger;
For they [2b]pine away, being stricken
For lack of the fruits of [3]the field.
10 The hands of compassionate women
[a]Boiled their own children;
They became [b]food for them
Because of the destruction of the
daughter of my people.
11 The LORD has [a]accomplished His
wrath,
He has poured out His fierce anger;
And He has [b]kindled a fire in Zion
Which has consumed its foundations.
12 The kings of the earth did not believe,
Nor *did* any of [a]the inhabitants of the
world,
That the adversary and the enemy
Could [b]enter the gates of Jerusalem.
13 Because of the sins of her [a]prophets
And the iniquities of her priests,
Who have shed in her midst
The [b]blood of the righteous;
14 They wandered, [a]blind, in the streets;
They were defiled with [b]blood
So that no one could touch their
[c]garments.
15 "Depart! [a]Unclean!" [1]they cried of
themselves.
"Depart, depart, do not touch!"
So they [b]fled and wandered;
Men among the nations said,
"They shall not continue to dwell *with*
us."
16 The presence of the LORD has scattered
them,
He will not continue to regard them;
They did not [1a]honor the priests,
They did not favor the elders.
17 Yet our eyes failed,
Looking for [1]help was [a]useless;
In our watching we have watched
For a [b]nation that could not save.

66 [a]Lam 3:43 [b]Ps 8:3
4:1 [1]Lit *head* [a]Ezek 7:19-22
2 [a]Is 30:14; Jer 19:1, 11
3 [a]Is 13:22; 34:13 [b]Is 49:15; Ezek 5:10 [c]Job 39:14-17
4 [a]Ps 22:15 [b]Jer 14:3 [c]Lam 2:12
5 [1]Lit *established in crimson* [a]Jer 6:2; Amos 6:3-7
6 [1]Or *punishment for iniquity* [2]Or *punishment for sin* [3]Or *wrung over her* [a]Gen 19:24 [b]Gen 19:25; Jer 20:16
7 [1]Or *Nazirites* [2]Lit *bones* [3]Heb *sappir* [a]Ps 51:7 [b]Ex 24:10; Job 28:16
8 [a]Job 30:30; Lam 5:10 [b]Job 19:20; Ps 102:3-5
9 [1]Lit *pierced* [2]Lit *flow away* [3]Lit *my fields* [a]Jer 16:4 [b]Lev 26:39; Ezek 24:23
10 [a]Lev 26:29; Deut 28:57; 2 Kin 6:29; Jer 19:9; Lam 2:20; Ezek 5:10 [b]Deut 28:53-55
11 [a]Jer 7:20; Lam 2:17; Ezek 22:31 [b]Deut 32:22; Jer 17:27
12 [a]Deut 29:24 [b]Jer 21:13
13 [a]Jer 5:31; 6:13; Lam 2:14; Ezek 22:26-28 [b]Jer 2:30; 26:8, 9; Matt 23:31
14 [a]Deut 28:28, 29; Is 29:10; 56:10; 59:9, 10 [b]Is 1:15 [c]Jer 2:34
15 [1]Or *they* (men) *cried to them* [a]Lev 13:45, 46 [b]Jer 49:5
16 [1]Lit *lift up the faces of* [a]Is 9:14-16; Jer 52:24-27 **17** [1]Lit *our help* [a]Jer 37:7; Lam 1:7 [b]Ezek 29:6, 7, 16

3:65 *Your curse will be on them.* Contrast Ps 3:8.
4:1 *How . . . !* See note on 1:1. *gold . . . sacred stones.* Symbolic of God's chosen people (see v. 2). For the imagery see Song 5:11–12,14–15; Zech 9:16; see also "The Babylonian Theodicy": "O . . . my precious brother, . . . jewel of gold" (lines 56–57). *has changed.* Contrast Mal 3:6. *at the corner of every street.* See 2:19; Is 51:20.
4:2 *Weighed against fine gold.* See Job 28:15–19. *earthen jars . . . potter's hands.* See Is 45:9; 60:21 and notes.
4:3 *my people.* See vv. 6,10; see also note on 2:11.
4:5 *delicacies . . . purple.* See Gen 49:20. Purple was the color of royalty (see, e.g., Judg 8:26; see also note on Song 7:5); cf. the expressions "born to the purple" and "royal blue." *desolate.* See note on 1:13.
4:6 *my people.* See note on 2:11. *Sodom.* See note on Jer 20:16. *overthrown as in a moment.* And therefore spared the suffering of a lengthy siege (like that of Jerusalem).
4:7 *whiter . . . ruddy.* The Hebrew underlying these two words is translated "dazzling . . . ruddy" in Song 5:10. *than corals.* See Job 28:18. *lapis lazuli.* See Song 5:14 and note; Is 54:11 and note.
4:8 *skin is shriveled on their bones.* See Job 19:20.
4:10 See note on Jer 19:9. *my people.* See note on 2:11.
4:11 *fierce anger.* See note on 1:12. *kindled a fire . . . consumed.* See note on Jer 17:27.
4:13 *Because of the sins of her prophets And . . . priests.* See Jer 26:7–11,16; see also Jer 6:13–15; 23:11–12; Ezek 22:26,28.
4:14 *wandered, blind, in the streets.* See Deut 28:28–29; Is 29:9 and note; 59:10 and note; Zeph 1:17. *defiled with blood.* See Is 59:3.
4:15 *Unclean!* The cry of the person with a skin disease (see Lev 13:45). *Men . . . not continue to dwell.* Threatened in Deut 28:65–66.
4:16 Threatened in Deut 28:49–50.
4:17 *our eyes failed.* See Deut 28:28; Ps 69:3. *nation that could not save.* For example, Egypt (see Ezek 29:16).

18 They [a]hunted our steps
So that we could not walk in our
streets;
Our [b]end drew near,
Our days were [1]finished
For our end had come.
19 Our pursuers were [a]swifter
Than the eagles of the sky;
They chased us on the mountains,
They waited in ambush for us in the
wilderness.
20 The [a]breath of our nostrils, the
[b]LORD's anointed,
Was [c]captured in their pits,
Of whom we had said, "Under his
[d]shadow
We shall live among the nations."
21 Rejoice and be glad, O daughter of
[a]Edom,
Who dwells in the land of Uz;
But the [b]cup will come around to you
as well,
You will become drunk and make
yourself naked.
22 *The punishment* of your iniquity has
been [a]completed, O daughter of
Zion;
He will exile you no longer.
But He [b]will punish your iniquity,
O daughter of Edom;
He will expose your sins!

A Prayer for Mercy

5 Remember, O LORD, what has befallen
us;
Look, and see our [a]reproach!
2 Our inheritance has been turned over
to [a]strangers,
Our [b]houses to aliens.
3 We have become orphans [a]without a
father,
Our mothers are like widows.
4 [1]We have to pay for our drinking
[a]water,
Our wood comes *to us* at a price.
5 [1]Our pursuers are at our necks;
We are worn out, there is [a]no rest for
us.
6 We have [1]submitted to [a]Egypt *and*
Assyria [2]to get enough bread.
7 Our [a]fathers sinned, *and* are no
more;
It is we who have borne their
iniquities.
8 [a]Slaves rule over us;
There is [b]no one to deliver us from
their hand.
9 We get our bread [1]at the [a]risk of our
lives
[2]Because of the sword in the
wilderness.
10 Our skin has become as [a]hot as an
oven,
Because of [1]the burning heat of
famine.
11 They ravished the [a]women in Zion,
The virgins in the cities of Judah.
12 Princes were hung by their hands;
[1a]Elders were not respected.
13 Young men [1a]worked at the grinding
mill,
And youths [b]stumbled under *loads* of
wood.
14 Elders [1]are gone from the gate,
Young men from their [a]music.
15 The joy of our hearts has [a]ceased;
Our dancing has been turned into
mourning.
16 The [a]crown has fallen from our head;
[b]Woe to us, for we have sinned!
17 Because of this our [a]heart is faint,
Because of these things our [b]eyes are
dim;
18 Because of [a]Mount Zion which lies
desolate,
[b]Foxes prowl in it.

18 [1]Lit *full* [a]Jer 16:16 [b]Jer 5:31; Ezek 7:2-12; Amos 8:2 **19** [a]Is 5:26-28; 30:16, 17; Jer 4:13; Hab 1:8 **20** [a]Gen 2:7 [b]2 Sam 1:14; 19:21 [c]Jer 39:5; 52:9 [d]Dan 4:12 **21** [a]Ps 137:7; Jer 25:21 [b]Obad 16 **22** [a]Is 40:2; Jer 33:7, 8 [b]Jer 49:10; Mal 1:3, 4 **5:1** [a]Ps 44:13-16 **2** [a]Is 1:7; Hos 8:7, 8 [b]Zeph 1:13 **3** [a]Ex 22:24; Jer 15:8; 18:21 **4** [1]Lit *We drink our water for silver* [a]Is 3:1

5 [1]Lit *We have been pursued upon* [a]Neh 9:36, 37 **6** [1]Lit *given the hand to* [2]Lit *to be satisfied with* [a]Hos 9:3; 12:1 **7** [a]Jer 14:20; 16:12 **8** [a]Neh 5:15 [b]Ps 7:2; Zech 11:6 **9** [1]Lit *with our soul* [2]Or *In the face of* [a]Jer 40:9-12 **10** [1]Or *the ravages of hunger* [a]Job 30:30; Lam 4:8 **11** [a]Is 13:16; Zech 14:2 **12** [1]Lit *The faces of elders* [a]Is 47:6; Lam 4:16 **13** [1]Lit *carry* [a]Judg 16:21 [b]Jer 7:18 **14** [1]Lit *have ceased* [a]Is 24:8; Jer 7:34 **15** [a]Jer 25:10; Amos 8:10

16 [a]Job 19:9; Ps 89:39; Jer 13:18 [b]Is 3:9-11 **17** [a]Is 1:5 [b]Job 17:7; Lam 2:11 **18** [a]Mic 3:12 [b]Neh 4:3

4:19 *eagles.* See Jer 4:13; 48:40 and notes. *wilderness.* The "plains of Jericho" (Jer 39:5; 52:8).
4:20 *The breath of our nostrils.* A title used also of Pharaoh Rameses II in an inscription found at Abydos in Egypt. *the LORD's anointed.* King Zedekiah. *Was captured.* See Jer 39:4–7; 52:7–11. *shadow.* Protection (see note on Judg 9:15).
4:21 *Edom.* See note on Jer 49:8. *land of Uz.* See Jer 25:20; see also note on Job 1:1. *cup.* See note on Jer 25:15. *make yourself naked.* See 1:8; see also Jer 49:10; Nah 3:5.
4:22 *daughter of Zion.* A personification of Jerusalem and its inhabitants. *expose your sins.* Contrast Ps 32:1; 85:2.
5:2 *Our inheritance.* The land of Judah (see Jer 2:7 and note; 3:18).
5:4 *We have to pay for . . . water . . . wood.* Contrast Deut 29:11; Josh 9:21,23,27. *wood.* Firewood.
5:6 *submitted.* See 1 Chr 29:24; 2 Chr 30:8; Jer 50:15; lit. "gave the hand" (as in 2 Kin 10:15). *Assyria.* Either (1) Assyria literally (see Jer 2:18), or (2) territory formerly occupied by Assyrians (see note on Ezra 6:22).
5:7 Fathers and sons alike are responsible for the calamity that has befallen Jerusalem (see v. 16; Jer 16:11–12; 31:29–30; Ezek 18:2–4; cf. Is 65:7).
5:8 *Slaves.* An ironic reference to the Babylonians, who now rule over Jerusalem (formerly "princess among the provinces," 1:1); see Prov 30:21–22.
5:9 *sword in the wilderness.* Marauding bandits.
5:12 *hung.* An added indignity following execution (see notes on Deut 21:22–23).
5:13 *worked at the grinding mill.* Humiliating work (see note on Judg 9:53; see also Is 47:2).
5:14 *gate.* The municipal court (see Josh 20:4), but also a gathering place for conversation and entertainment (cf. 1:4).
5:15 See Jer 7:34; 16:9; 25:10; contrast Ps 30:11; Jer 31:13.
5:16 *crown.* Symbolizes the glory and honor embodied in the city of Jerusalem (see 1:1; 2:15; cf. Is 28:1,3).
5:17 *heart is faint.* See note on 1:22. *eyes are dim.* See 2:11; see also note on Ps 6:7.
5:18 *Foxes.* The Hebrew for this word, different from that used in 4:3, can also mean "jackals" (see note on Judg 15:4).

19 [a]You, O LORD, [1]rule forever;
Your [b]throne is from generation to
generation.
20 Why do You [a]forget us forever?
Why do You forsake us [1]so long?
21 [a]Restore us to You, O LORD, that we
may be restored;
Renew [b]our days as of old,
22 Unless [a]You have utterly rejected
us
And are exceedingly [b]angry with
us.

19 [1]Lit *sit* [a]Ps 102:12, 25-27 [b]Ps 45:6
20 [1]Lit *to length of days* [a]Ps 13:1; 44:24
21 [a]Ps 80:3; Jer 31:18
21 [b]Is 60:20-22
22 [a]Ps 60:1, 2; Jer 7:29 [b]Is 64:9

5:19 Paralleled in Ps 102:12 (see note there).
5:21 *Restore . . . be restored.* See Jer 31:18; see also note on Jer 31:18–19.
5:22 See Jer 14:19. *Unless.* Or "but." A similarly somber ending characterizes not only other laments (e.g., Ps 88) but also other OT books (e.g., Isaiah and Malachi).

Ezekiel

INTRODUCTION

Background

Ezekiel lived during a time of international upheaval. The Assyrian empire that had once conquered the Syro-Palestinian area and destroyed the northern kingdom of Israel (which fell to the Assyrians in 722–721 B.C.) began to crumble under the blows of a resurgent Babylon. In 612 the great Assyrian city of Nineveh fell to a combined force of Babylonians and Medes. Three years later, Pharaoh Neco II of Egypt marched north to assist the Assyrians and to try to reassert Egypt's age-old influence over Palestine and Aram (Syria). At Megiddo, King Josiah of Judah, who may have been an ally of Babylon as King Hezekiah had been, attempted to intercept the Egyptian forces but was crushed, losing his life in the battle (see 2 Kin 23:29–30; 2 Chr 35:20–24).

Jehoahaz, a son of Josiah, ruled Judah for only three months, after which Neco installed Jehoiakim, another son of Josiah, as his royal vassal in Jerusalem (609 B.C.). In 605 the Babylonians overwhelmed the Egyptian army at Carchemish (see Jer 46:2), then pressed south as far as the Philistine plain. In the same year, Nebuchadnezzar was elevated to the Babylonian throne and Jehoiakim shifted allegiance to him. When a few years later the Egyptian and Babylonian forces met in a standoff battle in southwestern Palestine, Jehoiakim rebelled against his new overlord.

Nebuchadnezzar soon responded by sending a force against Jerusalem, subduing it in 597 B.C. Jehoiakim's son Jehoiachin and about 10,000 Jews (see 2 Kin 24:14), including Ezekiel, were exiled to Babylon, where they joined those who had been exiled in Jehoiakim's "third year" (see Dan 1:1 and note). Nebuchadnezzar placed Jehoiachin's uncle, Zedekiah, on the throne in Jerusalem, but within five or six years he too rebelled. The Babylonians laid siege to Jerusalem in 588, and in July, 586, the walls were breached and the city plundered. On Aug. 14, 586, the city and temple were burned.

Under Nebuchadnezzar and his successors, Babylon dominated the international scene until it was crushed by Cyrus the Persian in 539 B.C. Israel's monarchy was ended; the City of David and the Lord's temple no longer existed.

Author

What is known of Ezekiel is derived solely from the book that bears his name. He was among the Jews exiled to Babylon by Nebuchadnezzar in 597 B.C., and there among the exiles he received his call to become a prophet (see 1:1–3). He was married (see 24:15–18), lived in a house of his own (see 3:24; 8:1) and, along with his fellow exiles, had a relatively free existence.

He was of a priestly family (see note on 1:3) and therefore was eligible to serve as a priest. As a priest-prophet called to minister to the exiles (cut off from the temple of the Lord with its symbolism, sacrifices, priestly ministrations and worship rituals), his message had much to do with the temple (see especially chs. 8—11; 40—48) and its ceremonies.

Ezekiel was obviously a man of broad knowledge, not only of his own national traditions but also of international affairs and history. His acquaintance with general matters of culture, from shipbuilding to literature, is equally amazing. He was gifted with a powerful intellect and was capable of grasping large issues and of dealing with them in grand and compelling images. His style is often detached, but in places it is passionate and earthy (see chs. 16; 23).

More than any other prophet he was directed to involve himself personally in the divine word by acting it out in prophetic symbolism.

Occasion, Purpose and Summary of Contents

Though Ezekiel lived with his fellow exiles in Babylon, his divine call forced him to suppress any natural expectations he may have had of an early return to an undamaged Jerusalem. For the first seven years of his ministry (593 – 586 B.C.) he faithfully relayed to his fellow Jews the harsh, heart-rending, hope-crushing word of divine judgment: Jerusalem would fall (see chs. 1—24). Their being God's covenant people and Jerusalem's being the city of His temple would not bring their early release from exile or prevent Jerusalem from being destroyed (see Jer 29—30). The only hope the prophet was authorized to extend to his hearers was that of living at peace with themselves and with God during their exile.

After being informed by the Lord that Jerusalem was under siege and would surely fall (24:1 – 14), Ezekiel was told that his beloved wife would soon die. The delight of his eyes would be taken from him just as the temple, the delight of Israel's eyes, would be taken from her. He was not to mourn openly for his wife, as a sign to his people not to mourn openly for Jerusalem (24:15 – 27). He was then directed to pronounce a series of judgments on the seven nations of Ammon, Moab, Edom, Philistia, Tyre, Sidon and Egypt (chs. 25—32). The day of God's wrath was soon to come, but not on Israel alone.

Once news was received that Jerusalem had fallen, Ezekiel's message turned to the Lord's consoling word of hope for His people—they would experience revival, restoration and a glorious future as the redeemed and perfected kingdom of God in the world (chs. 33—48).

Date

Since the book of Ezekiel contains more dates (see chart below) than any other OT prophetic book, its prophecies can be dated with considerable precision. In addition, modern scholarship, using archaeology (Babylonian annals on cuneiform tablets) and astronomy (accurate dating of eclipses referred to in ancient archives), provides precise modern calendar equivalents.

Twelve of the 13 dates specify times when Ezekiel received a divine message. The other is the date of the arrival of the messenger who reported the fall of Jerusalem (33:21).

Having received his call in July, 593 B.C., Ezekiel was active for 22 years, his last dated oracle being received in April, 571 (see 29:17). If the "thirtieth year" of 1:1 refers to Ezekiel's age at the time of his call, his prophetic career exceeded a normal priestly term of service by two years (see Num 4:3). His period of activity coincides with Jerusalem's darkest hour, preceding the 586 destruction by 7 years and following it by 15.

Themes

The OT in general and the prophets in particular presuppose and teach God's sovereignty over all creation, over people and nations and the course of history. And nowhere in the Bible are God's initiative and control expressed more clearly and pervasively than in the book of Ezekiel. From the first chapter, which graphically describes the overwhelming invasion of the divine presence into Ezekiel's world, to the last phrase of Ezekiel's vision ("The LORD is there") the book sounds and echoes God's sovereignty.

This sovereign God resolved that He would be known and acknowledged. No less than 65 occurrences of the clause (or variations) "Then they will know that I am the LORD" testify to that divine desire and intention. Chs. 1—24 teach that God will be revealed in the fall of Jerusalem and the destruction of the temple; chs. 25—32 teach that the nations likewise will know God through His judgments; and chs. 33—48 promise that God will be known through the restoration and spiritual renewal of Israel.

God's total sovereignty is also evident in His mobility. He is not limited to the temple in Jerusalem. He can respond to His people's sin by leaving His sanctuary in Israel, and He can graciously condescend to visit His exiled children in Babylon.

God is free to judge, and He is equally free to be gracious. His stern judgments on Israel ultimately reflect His grace. He allows the total dismemberment of Israel's political and religious life so that her renewed life and His presence with her will be clearly seen as a gift from the Lord of the universe.

Furthermore, as God's spokesman, Ezekiel's "son of man" status (see note on 2:1) testifies to the sovereign God he was commissioned to serve.

Literary Features

The three major prophets (Isaiah, Jeremiah, Ezekiel) and Zephaniah all have the same basic sequence of messages: (1) oracles against Israel, (2) oracles against the nations, (3) consolation for Israel. In no other book is this pattern as clear as in Ezekiel (see Outline).

Besides clarity of structure, the book of Ezekiel reveals symmetry. The vision of the desecrated temple fit for destruction (chs. 8—11) is balanced by the vision of the restored and purified temple (chs. 40—48). The God presented in agitated wrath (ch. 1) is also shown to be a God of comfort ("The LORD is there," 48:35). Ezekiel's call to be a watchman of divine judgment (ch. 3) is balanced by his call to be a watchman of the new age (ch. 33). In one place (ch. 6) the mountains of Israel receive a prophetic rebuke, but in another (ch. 36) they are consoled.

Prophetic books are usually largely poetic, the prophets apparently having spoken in imaginative and rhythmic styles. Most of Ezekiel, however, is prose, perhaps due to his priestly background. His repetitions have an unforgettable hammering effect, and his priestly orientation is also reflected in a case-law type of sentence (compare 3:19, "If you have warned the wicked . . . ," with Ex 21:2, "If you buy a Hebrew slave . . .").

The book contains four visions (chs. 1—3; 8—11; 37:1–14; 40—48) and 12 symbolic acts (3:22–26; 4:1–3; 4:4–8; 4:9–11; 4:12–14; 5:1–3; 12:1–16; 12:17–20; 21:6–7; 21:18–24; 24:15–24; 37:15–28). Five messages are in the form of parables (chs. 15; 16; 17; 19; 23).

Theological Significance

Other prophets deal largely with Israel's idolatry, with her moral corruption in public and private affairs, and with her international intrigues and alliances on which she relied instead of the Lord. They announce God's impending judgment on His rebellious nation but speak also of a future redemption: a new exodus, a new covenant, a restored Jerusalem, a revived Davidic dynasty, a worldwide recognition of the Lord and His Messiah and a paradise-like peace.

Dates in Ezekiel

REFERENCE	YEAR	MONTH	DAY	MODERN RECKONING	EVENT
1. 1:1	30	4	5	July 31, 593 B.C.	Inaugural vision
1:2	5	—	5		
3:16	"At the end of seven days"				
2. 8:1	6	6	5	Sept. 17, 592	Transport to Jerusalem
3. 20:1-2	7	5	10	Aug. 14, 591	Negative view of Israel's history
4. 24:1	9	10	10	Jan. 15, 588	Beginning of siege (see also 2 Kin 25:1)
5. 26:1	11	—	1	Apr. 23, 587 to Apr. 13, 586	Oracle against Tyre
6. 29:1	10	10	12	Jan. 7, 587	Oracle against Egypt
7. 29:17	27	1	1	Apr. 26, 571	Egypt in exchange for Tyre
8. 30:20	11	1	7	Apr. 29, 587	Oracle against Pharaoh
9. 31:1	11	3	1	June 21, 587	Oracle against Pharaoh
10. 32:1	12	12	1	Mar. 3, 585	Lament over Pharaoh
11. 32:17	12	—	15	Apr. 13, 586 to Apr. 1, 585	Egypt dead
12. 33:21	12	10	5	Jan. 8, 585	Arrival of first fugitive
13. 40:1	25	1	10	Apr. 28, 573	Vision of the future
40:1	"fourteenth year after the the city was taken"				

The contours and sweep of Ezekiel's message are similar, but he focuses uniquely on Israel as the holy people of the holy temple, the holy city and the holy land. By defiling her worship, Israel had rendered herself unclean and had defiled temple, city and land. From such defilement God could only withdraw and judge His people with national destruction.

But God's faithfulness to His covenant and His desire to save were so great that He would revive His people once more, shepherd them with compassion, cleanse them of all their defilement, reconstitute them as a perfect expression of His kingdom in the promised land under the hand of David, overwhelm all the forces and powers arrayed against them, display His glory among the nations and restore the glory of His presence to the holy city.

Ezekiel powerfully depicts the grandeur and glory of God's sovereign rule (see Themes) and His holiness, which He jealously safeguards. The book's theological center is the unfolding of God's saving purposes in the history of the world — from the time in which He must withdraw from the defilement of His covenant people to the culmination of His grand design of redemption. The message of Ezekiel, which is ultimately eschatological, anticipates — even demands — God's future works in history proclaimed by the NT.

Outline

I. Oracles of Judgment against Israel (chs. 1—24)
  A. Ezekiel's Inaugural Vision (chs. 1—3)
    1. The divine overwhelming (ch. 1)
    2. The equipping and commissioning (2:1—3:15)
    3. The watchman (3:16–21)
    4. Further stipulations (3:22–27)
  B. Symbolic Acts Portraying the Siege of Jerusalem (chs. 4—5)
    1. The city of Jerusalem on a brick (4:1–3)
    2. Prophetic immobility (4:4–8)
    3. Diet for the siege and exile (4:9–17)
    4. The divine razor and its consequences (ch. 5)
  C. Oracles Explaining Divine Judgment (chs. 6—7)
    1. Doom for the mountains of Israel (ch. 6)
    2. The end (ch. 7)
  D. Vision of the Corrupted Temple (chs. 8—11)
    1. Four abominations (ch. 8)
    2. Destruction of the city (ch. 9)
    3. God's glory leaves Jerusalem (ch. 10)
    4. Conclusion of the vision (ch. 11)
  E. Symbolic Acts Portraying Jerusalem's Exile (ch. 12)
    1. An exile's baggage (12:1–16)
    2. Anxious eating (12:17–20)
    3. The nearness of judgment (12:21–28)
  F. Oracles Explaining Divine Judgment (chs. 13—24)
    1. False prophets and magic charms (ch. 13)
    2. The penalty for idolatry (14:1–11)
    3. Noah, Daniel and Job (14:12–23)
    4. Jerusalem as a burnt vine branch (ch. 15)
    5. Jerusalem as a wayward foundling (16:1–43)
    6. Jerusalem compared to other cities (16:44–63)
    7. Jerusalem's kings allegorized (17:1–21)
    8. The new tree (17:22–24)
    9. The lesson of three generations (ch. 18)
    10. The twofold lament (ch. 19)
    11. Israel as a hardened repeater (ch. 20)

12. The sword of the Lord (ch. 21)
13. Jerusalem the city of blood (ch. 22)
14. Oholah and Oholibah (ch. 23)
15. The final fire: Jerusalem's end (24:1–14)
16. The death of Ezekiel's wife and the destruction of the temple (24:15–27)

II. Oracles of Judgment against the Nations (chs. 25—32)
- A. Against Ammon (25:1–7)
- B. Against Moab (25:8–11)
- C. Against Edom (25:12–14)
- D. Against Philistia (25:15–17)
- E. Against Tyre (26:1—28:19)
  1. The end of the city (ch. 26)
  2. A lament for Tyre (ch. 27)
  3. Against the king of Tyre (28:1–19)
- F. Against Sidon (28:20–24)
- G. A Note of Promise for Israel (28:25–26)
- H. Against Egypt (chs. 29—32)
  1. As a doomed monster (29:1–16)
  2. As payment to Nebuchadnezzar (29:17–21)
  3. The approaching day (30:1–19)
  4. Pharaoh's arms are broken (30:20–26)
  5. As a felled cedar (ch. 31)
  6. A lament over Pharaoh (32:1–16)
  7. As consigned to the pit among the uncircumcised (32:17–32)

III. Oracles of Consolation for Israel (chs. 33—48)
- A. The Watchman (33:1–20)
- B. Jerusalem's Fall Reported and Explained (33:21–33)
- C. The Lord as the Good Shepherd (ch. 34)
- D. Oracles against Edom (ch. 35)
- E. Consolations for the Mountains of Israel (36:1–15)
- F. Summary of Ezekiel's Theology (36:16–38)
- G. Vision of National Restoration (ch. 37)
  1. National resurrection (37:1–14)
  2. National reunification (37:15–28)
- H. The Final Battle (chs. 38—39)
- I. Vision of Renewed Worship (chs. 40—48)
  1. Wall around the temple (40:1–47)
  2. Temple exterior (40:48—41:26)
  3. Temple interior (ch. 42)
  4. The return of God's glory (ch. 43)
  5. The priesthood (ch. 44)
  6. Land allotment (ch. 45)
  7. The duties of the prince (ch. 46)
  8. Life-giving water (47:1–12)
  9. Land allotment (47:13—48:35)

The Vision of Four Figures

1 Now it came about in the thirtieth year,
on the fifth *day* of the fourth month,
while I was by the [a]river Chebar among the
exiles, the [b]heavens were opened and I saw
[1c]visions of God.
2 (On the fifth of the month [1]in the [a]fifth
year of King Jehoiachin's exile,
3 the [a]word of the LORD came expressly
to Ezekiel the priest, son of Buzi, in the [b]land
of the Chaldeans by the river Chebar; and
there [c]the hand of the LORD came upon him.)
4 As I looked, behold, a [a]storm wind was
coming from the north, a great cloud with
fire flashing forth continually and a bright
light around it, and in its midst something
like [b]glowing metal in the midst of the fire.
5 Within it there were figures resembling
[a]four living beings. And this was their
appearance: they had human [b]form.
6 Each of them had [a]four faces and [b]four
wings.
7 Their legs were straight and [1]their feet
were like a calf's hoof, and they gleamed like
[a]burnished bronze.
8 Under their wings on their [a]four sides
were human [b]hands. As for the faces and
wings of the four of them,
9 their wings touched one another; *their
faces* did [a]not turn when they moved, each
[b]went straight forward.
10 As for the [a]form of their faces, *each*
had the [b]face of a man; [1]all four had the face
of a lion on the right and the face of a bull on
the left, and [1]all four had the face of an
eagle.
11 Such were their faces. Their wings
were spread out above; each had two touching another *being*, and [a]two covering their
bodies.
12 And [a]each went straight forward;
[b]wherever the spirit was about to go, they
would go, without turning as they went.
13 [1]In the midst of the living beings there
was something that looked like burning coals
of [a]fire, [2]like torches darting back and forth
among the living beings. The fire was bright,
and lightning was [3]flashing from the fire.
14 And the living beings [a]ran to and fro
like bolts of [b]lightning.
15 Now as I looked at the living beings,
behold, there was one [a]wheel on the earth
beside the living beings, [1]for *each of* the four
of them.
16 The [a]appearance of the wheels and
their workmanship *was* like [1]sparkling
[b]beryl, and all four of them had the same
form, their appearance and workmanship
being as if [2]one wheel were within another.
17 Whenever they [1]moved, they [1]moved
in any of their four [2]directions without [a]turn-
ing as they [1]moved.
18 As for their rims they were lofty and
awesome, and the rims of all four of them
were [a]full of eyes round about.
19 [a]Whenever the living beings [1]moved,
the wheels [1]moved with them. And whenever the living beings [b]rose from the earth, the
wheels rose *also*.
20 [a]Wherever the spirit was about to go,
they would go in that direction[1]. And the
wheels rose close beside them; for the spirit
of the living [2]beings *was* in the wheels.
21 [a]Whenever those went, these went; and
whenever those stood still, these stood still.

1:1 [1]Some ancient mss and versions read *a vision* [a]Ezek 3:23; 10:15, 20 [b]Matt 3:16; Mark 1:10; Luke 3:21; Acts 7:56; 10:11; Rev 4:1; 19:11 [c]Ex 24:10; Num 12:6; Is 1:1; 6:1; Ezek 8:3; 11:24; 40:2; Dan 8:1, 2
2 [1]Lit *it was* [a]2 Kin 24:12-15; Ezek 8:1; 20:1
3 [a]2 Pet 1:21 [b]Ezek 12:13 [c]1 Kin 18:46; 2 Kin 3:15; Ezek 3:14, 22
4 [a]Is 21:1; Jer 23:19; Ezek 13:11, 13 [b]Ezek 1:27; 8:2
5 [a]Ezek 10:15, 17, 20; Rev 4:6-8 [b]Ezek 1:26
6 [a]Ezek 1:10; 10:14, 21 [b]Ezek 1:23
7 [1]Lit *the soles of their feet* [a]Dan 10:6; Rev 1:15
8 [a]Ezek 1:17; 10:11 [b]Ezek 10:8, 21
9 [a]Ezek 1:17 [b]Ezek 1:12; 10:22
10 [1]Lit *the four of them* [a]Rev 4:7 [b]Ezek 10:14
11 [a]Is 6:2; Ezek 1:23
12 [a]Ezek 1:9 [b]Ezek 1:20
13 [1]So with some ancient versions; Heb *as the likeness of the living beings* [2]Lit *like the appearance of* [3]Lit *coming out* [a]Ps 104:4; Rev 4:5
14 [a]Zech 4:10 [b]Matt 24:27; Luke 17:24 **15** [1]Lit *for his four faces* [a]Ezek 1:19-21; 10:9 **16** [1]Lit *the look of beryl* [2]Lit *the wheel in the midst of the wheel* [a]Ezek 10:9-11 [b]Ezek 10:9; Dan 10:6 **17** [1]Lit *went* [2]Lit *sides* [a]Ezek 1:9, 12; 10:11 **18** [a]Ezek 10:12; Rev 4:6, 8 **19** [1]Lit *went* [a]Ezek 10:16 [b]Ezek 10:19 **20** [1]M.T. adds *the spirit to go* [2]M.T. reads *being* [a]Ezek 1:12 **21** [a]Ezek 10:17

1:1 *the thirtieth year.* Or "my thirtieth year," probably Ezekiel's age. According to Num 4:3, a person entered the Levitical priesthood in his 30th year. Denied the priesthood in exile, Ezekiel received another commission—that of prophet. *River Chebar.* A canal of the Euphrates near the city of Nippur, south of Babylon, and possibly a place of prayer for the exiles (see Ps 137:1; cf. Acts 16:13). *visions of God.* A special term, always in the plural and always with the word "God" (not with the more personal "LORD"). The expression precedes this and the two other major visions of the prophet (8:3; 40:2).

1:2 *fifth year of King Jehoiachin's exile.* Verses 2–3, written in the third person (the only third-person narrative in the book), clarify the date in v. 1. *King Jehoiachin's.* Led an early group of exiles to Babylon in 597 B.C. (see Introduction: Historical Background). Ezekiel was among them and received his prophetic call in 593.

1:3 *Ezekiel.* See 24:24. Means "God is strong" (cf. 3:14), "God strengthens" (cf. 30:25; 34:16) or "God makes hard" (cf. 3:8). Jehezkel (1 Chr 24:16) is the same name in Hebrew but does not refer to the same person. *priest.* Member of a priestly family (the text could be translated "Ezekiel the son of Buzi the priest"). *hand of the LORD.* A phrase repeated six times in the book (3:14,22; 8:1; 33:22; 37:1; 40:1), indicating an overpowering experience of divine revelation.

1:4 *I looked.* Introduces the first part of the vision: storm and living creatures (vv. 4–14). The "I looked" of v. 15 introduces the second part: wheels and the glory of the Lord. *storm wind.* See Ps 18:10–12.

1:5 *four living beings.* "Four," which stands for completeness (cf. the four directions in Gen 13:14 and the four quarters of the earth in Is 11:12), is used often in this chapter—and over 40 times in the book. The living creatures, called "cherubim" in ch. 10, are throne attendants, here (see v. 10) representing God's creation: "man," God's ordained ruler of creation (see Gen 1:26–28; Ps 8); "lion," the strongest of the wild beasts; "bull," the most powerful of the domesticated animals; "eagle," the mightiest of the birds. These four creatures appear again in Rev 4:7 and often are seen in the paintings and sculpture of the Middle Ages, where they represent the four Gospels.

1:7 *like a calf's.* Perhaps indicates agility (cf. Ps 29:6; Mal 4:2).

1:12 *the spirit.* See v. 20.

1:16 *beryl.* The precise identification of this stone is uncertain. See Ex 28:20, where the stone appears in the priestly breastplate. *as if one wheel were within another.* Probably two wheels intersecting at right angles in order to move in all four directions (see v. 17). The imagery symbolizes the omnipresence of God.

1:18 *full of eyes.* Symbolizes God's all-seeing nature.

And whenever those rose from the earth, the wheels rose close beside them; for the spirit of the living [1]beings *was* in the wheels.

Vision of Divine Glory

22 Now [a]over the heads of the living [1]beings *there was* something like an expanse, like the awesome gleam of [2]crystal, spread out over their heads.

23 Under the expanse their wings *were stretched out* straight, one toward the other; each one also had [a]two wings covering its body on the one side and on the other.

24 I also heard the sound of their wings like the [a]sound of abundant waters as they went, like the [b]voice of [1]the Almighty, a sound of tumult like the [c]sound of an army camp; whenever they stood still, they dropped their wings.

25 And there came a voice from above the [a]expanse that was over their heads; whenever they stood still, they dropped their wings.

26 Now [a]above the expanse that was over their heads there was something [b]resembling a throne, like [1c]lapis lazuli in appearance; and on that which resembled a throne, high up, *was* a figure with the appearance of a [d]man.

27 Then I [1]noticed from the appearance of His loins and upward something [a]like [2]glowing metal that looked like fire all around within it, and from the appearance of His loins and downward I saw something like fire; and *there was* a radiance around Him.

28 As the appearance of the [a]rainbow [1]in the clouds on a rainy day, so *was* the appearance of the surrounding radiance. Such *was* the appearance of the likeness of the [b]glory of the LORD. And when I saw *it*, I [c]fell on my face and heard a voice speaking.

The Prophet's Call

2 Then He said to me, "Son of man, [a]stand on your feet that I may speak with you!"

2 As He spoke to me the [a]Spirit entered me and set me on my feet; and I heard *Him* speaking to me.

3 Then He said to me, "Son of man, I am sending you to the sons of Israel, to a rebellious people who have [a]rebelled against Me; [b]they and their fathers have transgressed against Me to this very day.

4 "I am sending you to them who are [1a]stubborn and obstinate children, and you shall say to them, 'Thus says the Lord [2]GOD.'

5 "As for them, [a]whether they listen or [1]not—for they are a rebellious house—they will [b]know that a prophet has been among them.

6 "And you, son of man, [a]neither fear them nor fear their words, though [b]thistles and thorns are with you and you sit on scorpions; neither fear their words nor be dismayed at their presence, for they are a rebellious house.

7 "But you shall [a]speak My words to them [b]whether they listen or [1]not, for they are rebellious.

8 "Now you, son of man, listen to what I am speaking to you; do not be rebellious like that rebellious house. Open your mouth and [a]eat what I am giving you."

9 Then I looked, and behold, a [a]hand was extended to me; and lo, a [1b]scroll *was* in it.

10 When He spread it out before me, it was written on the front and back, and written on it were lamentations, mourning and [a]woe.

Ezekiel's Commission

3 Then He said to me, "Son of man, eat what you find; [a]eat this scroll, and go, speak to the house of Israel."

2 So I [a]opened my mouth, and He fed me this scroll.

3 He said to me, "Son of man, feed your

21 [1]M.T. reads *being* **22** [1]So some ancient mss and versions; M.T. reads *being* [2]Or *ice* [a]Ezek 10:1 **23** [a]Ezek 1:6, 11 **24** [1]Heb *Shaddai* [a]Ezek 43:2; Rev 1:15; 19:6 [b]Ezek 10:5 [c]2 Kin 7:6; Dan 10:6 **25** [a]Ezek 1:22; 10:1 **26** [1]Heb *eben-sappir* [a]Ezek 1:22; 10:1 [b]Is 6:1; Ezek 10:1; Dan 7:9 [c]Ex 24:10; Is 54:11 [d]Ezek 43:6, 7; Rev 1:13 **27** [1]Lit *saw* [2]Or *electrum* [a]Ezek 1:4; 8:2 **28** [1]Lit *which occurs in* [a]Gen 9:13; Rev 4:3; 10:1 [b]Ex 24:16; Ezek 8:4; 11:22, 23; 43:4, 5 [c]Gen 17:3; Ezek 3:23; Dan 8:17; Rev 1:17 **2:1** [a]Dan 10:11; Acts 9:6 **2** [a]Ezek 3:24; Dan 8:18

3 [a]1 Sam 8:7, 8; Jer 3:25 [b]Ezek 20:18, 30 **4** [1]Lit *the sons, stiff-faced and hard-hearted* [2]Heb *YHWH*, usually rendered LORD [a]Ps 95:8; Is 48:4; Jer 5:3; 6:15; Ezek 3:7 **5** [1]Lit *forbear* [a]Ezek 2:7; 3:11, 27; Matt 10:12-15; Acts 13:46 [b]Ezek 33:33; Luke 10:10, 11; John 15:22 **6** [a]Is 51:12; Jer 1:8, 17; Ezek 3:9 [b]2 Sam 23:6, 7; Ezek 28:24; Mic 7:4

7 [1]Lit *forbear* [a]Jer 1:7, 17; Ezek 3:10, 17 [b]Ezek 2:5 **8** [a]Jer 15:16; Ezek 3:3; Rev 10:9 **9** [1]Lit *scroll of a book* [a]Ezek 8:3 [b]Jer 36:2; Ezek 3:1; Rev 5:1-5; 10:8-11 **10** [a]Is 3:11; Rev 8:13 **3:1** [a]Ezek 2:9 **2** [a]Jer 25:17

1:22 *expanse.* The same word occurs in Gen 1:6–8, where its function is to separate the waters above from the waters below. Here it separates the creatures from the glory of the Lord.

1:26 *a figure with the appearance of a man.* Ezekiel is reporting his vision of God, but he carefully avoids saying he saw God directly (see Gen 16:13; Ex 3:6; Judg 13:22).

1:28 *likeness.* See note on v. 26. *glory of the LORD.* When God's glory was symbolically revealed, it took the form of brilliant light (see Ex 40:34; Is 6:3). What is remarkable about Ezekiel's experience is that God's glory had for centuries been associated with the temple in Jerusalem (see 1 Kin 8:11; Ps 26:8; 63:2; 96:6; 102:16). Now God had left His temple and was appearing to His exiled people in Babylon—a major theme in the first half of Ezekiel's message (see 10:4; 11:23). In his vision of the restored Jerusalem the prophet saw the glory of the Lord returning (43:2).

2:1 *Son of man.* A term used 93 times in Ezekiel, emphasizing the prophet's humanity as he was addressed by the transcendent God (see note on Ps 8:4). Dan 7:13 and 8:17 are the only other places where the phrase is used as a title in the OT. Jesus' frequent use of the phrase in referring to Himself showed that He was the eschatological figure spoken of in Dan 7:13 (see, e.g., Mark 8:31 and note).

2:2 *the Spirit entered me and set me on my feet.* The Spirit of God, who empowered the chariot wheels (1:12,19; 10:16–17) and the creatures (1:20), now entered Ezekiel—symbolizing the Lord's empowering of the prophet's entire ministry.

2:3 *rebellious people.* A keynote of Ezekiel's preaching: The entire nation throughout its history had been rebellious against God.

2:6 *thistles and thorns . . . scorpions.* Vivid images of those who would make life difficult for the prophet.

2:10 *on the front and back.* Normally, ancient scrolls were written on one side only. The implication here is that the scroll was thoroughly saturated with words of divine judgment. See Zech 5:3 and Rev 5:1 for the same figure. *lamentations, mourning and woe.* Although Ezekiel was later commanded to preach hope (see note on 33:1–48:35), his initial commission (until the fall of Jerusalem) was to declare God's displeasure and the certainty of His judgment on Jerusalem and all of Judah.

stomach and [a]fill your [1]body with this scroll which I am giving you." Then I [b]ate it, and it was sweet as [c]honey in my mouth.

4 Then He said to me, "Son of man, [1]go to the house of Israel and speak with My words to them.

5 "For [a]you are not being sent to a people of [1][b]unintelligible speech or difficult language, *but* to the house of Israel,

6 nor to many peoples of [1]unintelligible speech or difficult language, whose words you cannot understand. [2]But I have sent you to them [3]who should listen to you;

7 yet the house of Israel will not be willing to listen to you, since they are [a]not willing to listen to Me. Surely the whole house of Israel is [1]stubborn and obstinate.

8 "Behold, I have made your face as hard as their faces and your forehead as hard as their foreheads.

9 "Like [1]emery harder than flint I have made your forehead. Do not be afraid of them or be dismayed before them, though they are a rebellious house."

10 Moreover, He said to me, "Son of man, take into your heart all My [a]words which I will speak to you and listen [1]closely.

11 "[1]Go to the exiles, to the sons of your people, and speak to them and tell them, whether they listen or [2]not, 'Thus says the Lord [3]GOD.' "

12 Then the [a]Spirit lifted me up, and I heard a great [b]rumbling sound behind me, "Blessed be the glory of the LORD [1]in His place."

13 And I *heard* the sound of the wings of the living beings touching one another and the sound of the [a]wheels beside them, even a great rumbling sound.

14 So the Spirit lifted me up and took me away; and I went embittered in the rage of my spirit, and [a]the hand of the LORD was strong on me.

15 Then I came to the exiles who lived beside the river Chebar at Tel-abib, and I sat there [a]seven days where they were living, causing consternation among them.

16 [a]At the end of seven days the word of the LORD came to me, saying,

17 "Son of man, I have appointed you a [a]watchman to the house of Israel; whenever you hear a word from My mouth, [b]warn them from Me.

18 "When I say to the wicked, 'You will surely die,' and you do not warn him or speak out to warn the wicked from his wicked way that he may live, that wicked man shall die in his iniquity, but his [a]blood I will require at your hand.

19 "Yet if you have [a]warned the wicked and he does not turn from his wickedness or from his wicked way, he shall die in his iniquity; but you have [b]delivered yourself.

20 "Again, [a]when a righteous man turns away from his righteousness and commits iniquity, and I place an [b]obstacle before him, he will die; since you have not warned him, he shall die in his sin, and his righteous deeds which he has done shall not be remembered; but his blood I will require at your hand.

21 "However, if you have [a]warned [1]the righteous man that the righteous should not sin and he does not sin, he shall surely live because he took warning; and you have delivered yourself."

22 The hand of the LORD was on me there, and He said to me, "Get up, go out to the plain, and there I will [a]speak to you."

23 So I got up and went out to the plain; and behold, the [a]glory of the LORD was standing there, like the glory which [b]I saw by the river Chebar, and I fell on my face.

24 The [a]Spirit then entered me and made

3 [1]Lit *inward parts* [a]Jer 6:11; 20:9 [b]Jer 15:16 [c]Ps 19:10; 119:103; Rev 10:9, 10
4 [1]Lit *go, come*
5 [1]Lit *deepness of lip and heaviness of tongue* [a]Jon 1:2; Acts 14:11; 26:17 [b]Is 28:11; 33:19
6 [1]Lit *deepness of lip and heaviness of tongue* [2]Or *If I had sent you to them, they would listen to you* [3]Lit *they*
7 [1]Lit *of a hard forehead and a stiff heart* [a]1 Sam 8:7
9 [1]Lit *corundum*
10 [1]Lit *with your ears* [a]Job 22:22; Ezek 2:8; 3:1-3
11 [1]Lit *Go, come* [2]Lit *forbear* [3]Heb *YHWH*, usually rendered LORD
12 [1]Or *from* [a]Ezek 3:14; 8:3; Acts 8:39 [b]Acts 2:2
13 [a]Ezek 1:15; 10:16, 17
14 [a]2 Kin 3:15
15 [a]Job 2:13
16 [a]Jer 42:7
17 [a]Is 52:8; 56:10; 62:6; Jer 6:17; Ezek 33:7-9 [b]2 Chr 19:10; Is 58:1; Hab 2:1
18 [a]Ezek 3:20; 33:6, 8
19 [a]2 Kin 17:13, 14; Ezek 33:3, 9 [b]Ezek 14:14, 20; Acts 18:6; 1 Tim 4:16
20 [a]Ps 125:5; Ezek 18:24; 33:18; Zeph 1:6 [b]Is 8:14; Jer 6:21; Ezek 14:3, 7-9
21 [1]Lit *him, the righteous* [a]Acts 20:31
22 [a]Acts 9:6
23 [a]Ezek 1:28; Acts 7:55 [b]Ezek 1:1
24 [a]Ezek 2:2

3:3 *sweet as honey in my mouth.* What Jeremiah experienced emotionally (Jer 15:16) was experienced by Ezekiel in a more sensory way: Words from God are sweet to the taste (see Ps 19:10; 119:103)—even when their content is bitter (see Rev 10:9–10).
3:6 *I have sent you to them who should listen.* Jesus spoke similar words to Israel (see Matt 11:21).
3:9 *harder than flint I have made your forehead.* Strength and courage were necessary equipment for a prophet, especially when preaching judgment. Jeremiah was similarly equipped (see Jer 1:18).
3:10 *take into your heart . . . listen closely.* The prophet is to stand in marked contrast to the people, who do not listen.
3:11 *Go to the exiles . . . the sons of your people.* Ezekiel's ministry was to the exilic community, most of whom refused to believe that God would abandon Jerusalem and the temple. After the fall of Jerusalem, therefore, they were strongly inclined to despair.
3:14 *embittered in the rage of my spirit.* The prophet, knowing the righteousness of God's anger, personally identified with the divine emotions. *hand of the LORD was strong on me.* See note on 1:3.
3:15 *Tel-abib.* The only mention of the specific place where the exiles lived. In Babylonian the name meant "mound of the flood [i.e., destruction]," apparently referring to the ruined condition of the site. When used of the modern Israeli city, Tel Aviv, this name (Abib and Aviv are the same word in Hebrew) is understood to mean "hill of grain." *seven days.* Considering Ezekiel's priestly background (see note on 1:3), the seven-day period may have been a parallel to the time required for a priest's ordination (see Lev 8:1–33).
3:17 *I have appointed you a watchman.* In ancient Israel, watchmen were stationed on the highest parts of the city wall to inform its inhabitants of the progress of a battle (1 Sam 14:16) or of approaching messengers (2 Sam 18:24–27; 2 Kin 9:17–20). The prophets were spiritual watchmen, relaying God's word to the people (see Jer 6:17; Hos 9:8; Hab 2:1). Ezekiel's function as a watchman was not so much to warn the exiles of the impending doom of Jerusalem as to teach that God holds each one responsible for his own behavior. This commission, repeated in 33:7–9, is spelled out in ch. 18.
3:22 *hand of the LORD.* See note on 1:3.

me stand on my feet, and He spoke with me and said to me, "Go, shut yourself up in your house.

25 "As for you, son of man, they will [a]put ropes on you and bind you with them so that you cannot go out among them.

26 "Moreover, [a]I will make your tongue stick to [1]the roof of your mouth so that you will be mute and cannot be a man who rebukes them, for they are a rebellious house.

27 "But [a]when I speak to you, I will open your mouth and you will say to them, 'Thus says the Lord [1]GOD.' He who hears, let him hear; and he who refuses, let him refuse; [b]for they are a rebellious house.

Siege of Jerusalem Predicted

4 "Now you son of man, [a]get yourself a brick, place it before you and inscribe a city on it, Jerusalem.

2 "Then [a]lay siege against it, build a siege wall, [1]raise up a ramp, pitch camps and place battering rams against it all around.

3 "Then get yourself an iron plate and set it up as an iron wall between you and the city, and set your face toward it so that [a]it is under siege, and besiege it. This is a [b]sign to the house of Israel.

4 "As for you, lie down on your left side and lay the iniquity of the house of Israel on it; you shall [a]bear their iniquity for the number of days that you lie on it.

5 "For I have assigned you a number of days corresponding to the years of their iniquity, three hundred and ninety days; thus [a]you shall bear the iniquity of the house of Israel.

6 "When you have completed these, you shall lie down a second time, *but* on your right side and bear the iniquity of the house of Judah; I have assigned it to you for forty days, a day for [a]each year.

7 "Then you shall set your face toward the siege of Jerusalem with your arm bared and [a]prophesy against it.

8 "Now behold, I will [a]put ropes on you so that you cannot turn from one side to the other until you have completed the days of your siege.

Defiled Bread

9 "But as for you, take wheat, barley, beans, lentils, millet and [a]spelt, put them in one vessel and make them into bread for yourself; you shall eat it according to the number of the days that you lie on your side, three hundred and ninety days.

10 "Your food which you eat *shall be* [a]twenty shekels a day by weight; you shall eat it from time to time.

11 "The water you drink shall be the sixth part of a hin by measure; you shall drink it from time to time.

12 "You shall eat it as a barley cake, having baked *it* in their sight over human [a]dung."

13 Then the LORD said, "Thus will the sons of Israel eat their bread [a]unclean among the nations where I will banish them."

14 But I said, "[a]Ah, Lord [1]GOD! Behold, I have [b]never been defiled; for from my youth until now I have never eaten what [c]died of itself or was torn by beasts, nor has any [d]unclean meat ever entered my mouth."

15 Then He said to me, "See, I will give you cow's dung in place of human dung over which you will prepare your bread."

16 Moreover, He said to me, "Son of man, behold, I am going to [a]break the staff of bread in Jerusalem, and they will eat bread by [b]weight and with anxiety, and drink water by [c]measure and in horror,

17 because bread and water will be scarce; and they will be appalled with one another and [a]waste away in their iniquity.

Jerusalem's Desolation Foretold

5 "As for you, son of man, take a [a]sharp sword; take and [1]use it *as* a barber's razor on your head and beard. Then take [b]scales for weighing and divide [2]the hair.

25 [a]Ezek 4:8
26 [1]Lit *your palate* [a]Luke 1:20, 22
27 [1]Heb *YHWH,* usually rendered LORD [a]Ezek 24:27; 33:22 [b]Ezek 12:2, 3
4:1 [a]Is 20:2; Jer 13:1; 18:2; 19:1
2 [1]Lit *cast* [a]Jer 6:6; Ezek 21:22
3 [a]Jer 39:1, 2; Ezek 5:2 [b]Is 8:18; 20:3; Ezek 12:6, 11; 24:24-27
4 [a]Lev 10:17; 16:22; Num 18:1
5 [a]Num 14:34
6 [a]Num 14:34; Dan 9:24-26; 12:11, 12; Rev 11:2, 3
7 [a]Ezek 21:2
8 [a]Ezek 3:25
9 [a]Ex 9:32; Is 28:25
10 [a]Ezek 45:12
12 [a]Is 36:12
13 [a]Dan 1:8; Hos 9:3
14 [1]Heb *YHWH,* usually rendered LORD [a]Jer 1:6; Ezek 9:8; 20:49 [b]Acts 10:14 [c]Lev 17:15; 22:8; Ezek 44:31 [d]Deut 14:3; Is 65:4; 66:17
16 [a]Lev 26:26; Is 3:1; Ezek 5:16; 14:13 [b]Ezek 4:10, 11; 12:19 [c]Lam 5:4; Ezek 12:18, 19
17 [a]Lev 26:39; Ezek 24:23; 33:10
5:1 [1]Lit *make it pass over your head* [2]Lit *them* [a]Lev 21:5; Is 7:20; Ezek 44:20 [b]Dan 5:27

3:26 *you will be mute.* Verses 26–27 indicate that the prophet would be unable to speak except when he had a direct word from the Lord. His enforced silence underscored Israel's stubborn refusal to take God's word seriously. This condition was relieved only after the fall of Jerusalem (24:27; 33:22). From that time on, Ezekiel was given messages of hope, which he continually shared with his fellow exiles.

4:1 *get . . . a brick.* The first of several symbolic acts to be performed by the prophet. After inscribing a likeness of the city of Jerusalem on a moist clay brick, such as those commonly used in Babylonia, Ezekiel was to place around it models of siege works to represent the city under attack (v. 2). He was then to place an iron plate (perhaps a baking griddle) between himself and the symbolized city (v. 3) to indicate the unbreakable strength of the siege.

4:3 *besiege it.* Ezekiel's own presence in the scene signified that the siege would actually be laid by the Lord Himself.

4:4 *you shall bear their iniquity.* A representative rather than a substitutionary bearing of sin. The prophet's action symbolized Israel's sins; it did not remove them.

4:5 *three hundred and ninety days.* The 390 years (see v. 6) may represent the period from the time of Solomon's unfaithfulness to the fall of Jerusalem. Correspondingly, the 40 years of v. 6 may represent the long reign of wicked Manasseh before his repentance (see 2 Kin 21:11–15; 23:26–27; 24:3–4; 2 Chr 33:12–13).

4:6 *on your right side.* Lying on his left side (see v. 5) placed Ezekiel to the north of the symbolic city; lying on his right side placed him to the south—signifying the northern and southern kingdoms respectively.

4:9 *take wheat, barley, beans, lentils, millet and spelt.* A scant, vegetarian diet representing the meager provisions of a besieged city.

4:15 *cow's dung.* Commonly used in the Near East as a fuel for baking, even today. Ezekiel again showed his sensitivity to things ceremonially unclean (see note on 1:3), and God graciously responded to the prophet's objection by allowing this substitute for human excrement.

5:1 *take a sharp sword.* What Isaiah had expressed in a metaphor (Is 7:20) Ezekiel acted out in prophetic symbolism.

2 "One third you shall burn in the fire at the center of the city, when the [a]days of the siege are completed. Then you shall take one third and strike *it* with the sword all around [1]the city, and one third you shall scatter to the wind; and I will [b]unsheathe a sword behind them.

3 "Take also a few in number from [1]them and bind them in the edges of your *robes.*

4 "Take again some of them and throw them into the fire and burn them in the fire; from it a fire will [1]spread to all the house of Israel.

5 "Thus says the Lord [1]GOD, 'This is [a]Jerusalem; I have set her at the [b]center of the nations, with lands around her.

6 'But she has rebelled against My ordinances more wickedly than the nations and against My statutes [a]more than the lands which surround her; for they have [b]rejected My ordinances and have not walked [1]in My statutes.'

7 "Therefore, thus says the Lord GOD, 'Because you have [a]more turmoil than the nations which surround you *and* have not walked in My statutes, nor observed My ordinances, nor observed the ordinances of the nations which surround you,'

8 therefore, thus says the Lord GOD, 'Behold, I, even I, am [a]against you, and I will [b]execute judgments among you in the sight of the nations.

9 'And because of all your abominations, I will do among you what I have [a]not done, and the like of which I will never do again.

10 'Therefore, [a]fathers will eat *their* sons among you, and sons will eat their fathers; for I will execute judgments on you and [b]scatter all your remnant to every wind.

11 'So as I live,' declares the Lord GOD, 'surely, because you have [a]defiled My sanctuary with all your [b]detestable idols and with all your abominations, therefore I will also withdraw, and My eye will have no pity and I will not spare.

12 'One third of you will die by [a]plague or be consumed by famine among you, one third will fall by the sword around you, and one third I will [b]scatter to every wind, and I will [c]unsheathe a sword behind them.

2 [1]Lit *it* [a]Jer 39:1, 2; Ezek 4:2-8 [b]Lev 26:33
3 [1]Lit *there*
4 [1]Lit *go out*
5 [1]Heb *YHWH,* usually rendered *LORD,* and so throughout the ch [a]Jer 6:6; Ezek 4:1 [b]Deut 4:6; Lam 1:1; Ezek 16:14
6 [1]Lit *in them, My statutes* [a]2 Kin 17:8-20; Ezek 16:47, 48, 51 [b]Neh 9:16, 17; Ps 78:10; Jer 11:10; Zech 7:11
7 [a]2 Kin 21:9-11; 2 Chr 33:9; Jer 2:10, 11
8 [a]Jer 21:5, 13; Ezek 15:7; 21:3; Zech 14:2 [b]Jer 24:9; Ezek 5:15; 11:9
9 [a]Dan 9:12; Amos 3:2; Matt 24:21
10 [a]Lev 26:29; Jer 19:9; Lam 4:10 [b]Ps 44:11; Ezek 5:2, 12; 6:8; 12:14; Amos 9:9; Zech 2:6; 7:14
11 [a]Jer 7:9-11; Ezek 8:5, 6, 16 [b]Jer 16:18; Ezek 7:20
12 [a]Jer 15:2; 21:9; Ezek 5:17; 6:11, 12 [b]Ezek 5:2, 10; Amos 9:9; Zech 2:6 [c]Jer 43:10, 11; 44:27; Ezek 5:2; 12:14

13 [1]Lit *cause to rest* [2]Lit *comforted* [a]Is 1:24 [b]Is 59:17; Ezek 36:5, 6; 38:19
14 [a]Ps 74:3-10; 79:1-4; Ezek 22:4
15 [1]Ancient versions read *you* [a]Is 26:9; Jer 22:8, 9; 1 Cor 10:11 [b]Is 66:15, 16; Ezek 5:8; 25:17
16 [1]Lit *evil* [2]Or *are for destruction, which I will send*
17 [a]Lev 26:22; Rev 6:8 [b]Ezek 38:22
6:2 [a]Ezek 36:1

13 'Thus My anger will be spent and I will [1]satisfy My wrath on them, and I will be [2][a]appeased; then they will know that I, the LORD, have [b]spoken in My zeal when I have spent My wrath upon them.

14 'Moreover, I will make you a desolation and a [a]reproach among the nations which surround you, in the sight of all who pass by.

15 'So [1]it will be a reproach, a reviling, a [a]warning and an object of horror to the nations who surround you when I [b]execute judgments against you in anger, wrath and raging rebukes. I, the LORD, have spoken.

16 'When I send against them the [1]deadly arrows of famine which [2]were for the destruction of those whom I will send to destroy you, then I will also intensify the famine upon you and break the staff of bread.

17 'Moreover, [a]I will send on you famine and wild beasts, and they will bereave you of children; [b]plague and bloodshed also will pass through you, and I will bring the sword on you. I, the LORD, have spoken.' "

Idolatrous Worship Denounced

6 And the word of the LORD came to me saying,

2 "Son of man, set your face toward the [a]mountains of Israel, and prophesy against them

3 and say, 'Mountains of Israel, listen to the word of the Lord [1]GOD! Thus says the Lord [1]GOD to the mountains, the hills, the ravines and the valleys: "Behold, I Myself am going to bring a sword on you, and [a]I will destroy your high places.

4 "So your [a]altars will become desolate and your incense altars will be smashed; and I will make your slain fall in front of your idols.

5 "I will also lay the dead bodies of the sons of Israel in front of their idols; and I will scatter your [a]bones around your altars.

6 "In all your dwellings, [a]cities will become waste and the high places will be desolate, that your altars may become waste and [1]desolate, your [b]idols may be broken

3 [1]Heb *YHWH,* usually rendered *LORD* [a]Lev 26:30 4 [a]Lev 26:30; 2 Chr 14:5; Is 27:9; Ezek 6:6 5 [a]2 Kin 23:14, 16, 20; Jer 8:1, 2 6 [1]So some ancient versions; Heb *bear their guilt* [a]Lev 26:31; Is 6:11; Ezek 5:14 [b]Ezek 6:4; Mic 1:7; Zech 13:2

5:5 *This is Jerusalem.* After wordlessly acting out the symbols (beginning in 4:1), Ezekiel received and probably related the divine explanations. *center of the nations.* A privileged position, which made Israel's responsibility and judgment all the more severe (see note on 38:12).

5:8 *I, even I, am against you.* A short and effective phrase of judgment used often by Ezekiel (see 13:8; 21:3; 26:3; 28:22; 29:3,10; 30:22; 34:10; 35:3; 38:3; 39:1; see also Jer 23:30–32; 50:31; 51:25; Nah 2:13; 3:5).

5:10 *fathers will eat their sons.* Cannibalism, the most gruesome extremity of life under siege, was threatened as a consequence of breaking the covenant (Deut 28:53; see Jer 19:9; Lam 2:20; Zech 11:9).

5:11 *So as I live.* See note on 18:3.

5:13 *they will know that I, the LORD, have spoken.* The first of 65 occurrences in Ezekiel of this or similar declarations. God's acts of judgment and salvation reveal who He is. Since the people would not listen to God's words, they would be taught by His actions. *spent My wrath upon.* An expression frequently used by the Lord in this book (see 6:12; 7:8; 13:15; 20:8,21).

5:15 *a reproach, a reviling, a warning and an object of horror.* A fourfold list (see note on 1:5).

6:3 *high places.* Open-air sanctuaries of Canaanite origin, condemned throughout the OT. The high places, together with the "altars," "incense altars" and "idols" (v. 4), make up a list of four objects (see note on 1:5).

6:4 *incense altars.* Made of burnt clay, about two feet high, usually inscribed with animal figures and idols of Canaanite

and brought to an end, your incense altars
may be cut down, and your works may be
blotted out.
7 "The slain will fall among you, and you
will know that I am the LORD.
8 "However, I will leave a [a]remnant, for
you will have those who [b]escaped the sword
among the nations when you are scattered
among the countries.
9 "Then those of you who escape will
[a]remember Me among the nations to which
they will be carried captive, how I have
[1][b]been hurt by their adulterous hearts which
turned away from Me, and by their eyes
which played the harlot after their idols; and
they will [c]loathe themselves in their own
sight for the evils which they have committed, for all their abominations.
10 "Then they will know that I am the
LORD; I have not said in vain [1]that I would
inflict this disaster on them."'
11 "Thus says the Lord [1]GOD, 'Clap your
hand, [a]stamp your foot and say, "[b]Alas,
because of all the evil abominations of the
house of Israel, which will fall by [c]sword,
famine and plague!
12 "He who is [a]far off will die by the
plague, and he who is near will fall by the
sword, and he who remains and is besieged
will die by the famine. Thus will I [b]spend My
wrath on them.
13 "Then you will know that I am the LORD,
when their [a]slain are among their idols
around their altars, on [b]every high hill, on
all the tops of the mountains, under every
green tree and under every leafy oak—the
places where they offered soothing aroma to
all their idols.
14 "So throughout all their habitations I
will [a]stretch out My hand against them and
make the land more desolate and waste than
the wilderness toward Diblah; thus they will
know that I am the LORD."'"

Punishment for Wickedness Foretold

7 Moreover, the word of the LORD came to
me saying,
2 "And you, son of man, thus says the
Lord [1]GOD to the land of Israel, 'An [a]end! The
end is coming on the four corners of the land.
3 'Now the end is upon you, and I will
send My anger against you; I will judge you
according to your ways and bring all your
abominations upon you.
4 'For My eye will have no pity on you,
nor will I spare *you*, but I will [a]bring your
ways upon you, and your abominations will
be among you; then you will [b]know that I
am the LORD!'
5 "Thus says the Lord [1]GOD, 'A [a]disaster,
unique disaster, behold it is coming!
6 'An end is coming; the end has come! It
has [a]awakened against you; behold, it has
come!
7 'Your doom has come to you, O inhabitant of the land. The [a]time has come, the
[b]day is near—tumult rather than joyful
shouting on the mountains.
8 'Now I will shortly [a]pour out My wrath
on you and spend My anger against you;
[b]judge you according to your ways and bring
on you all your abominations.
9 'My eye will show no pity nor will I
spare. I will [1]repay you according to your
ways, while your abominations are in your
midst; then you will know that I, the LORD,
do the smiting.
10 'Behold, the day! Behold, it is coming!
Your doom has gone forth; the [a]rod has budded, arrogance has blossomed.
11 'Violence [1]has grown into a rod of
[a]wickedness. None of them *shall remain*,
none of their people, none of their [b]wealth,
nor anything eminent among them.
12 'The [a]time has come, the day has
arrived. Let not the [b]buyer rejoice nor the
seller mourn; for [c]wrath is against all their
multitude.
13 'Indeed, the seller will not [1][a]regain
[2]what he sold as long as [3]they *both* live; for
the vision regarding all their multitude will
not [4]be averted, nor will any of them maintain his life by his iniquity.
14 'They have [a]blown the trumpet and
made everything ready, but no one is going
to the battle, for My wrath is against all
[1]their multitude.

8 [a]Is 6:13; Jer 30:11 [b]Jer 44:14, 28; Ezek 7:16; 14:22
9 [1]Lit *been broken*, or, *broken for Myself their* [a]Deut 4:29; 30:2; Jer 51:50 [b]Ps 78:40; Is 7:13; 43:24; Hos 11:8 [c]Job 42:6; Ezek 20:43; 36:31
10 [1]Lit *to do this evil to*
11 [1]Heb *YHWH*, usually rendered *LORD* [a]Ezek 25:6 [b]Ezek 9:4 [c]Ezek 5:12; 7:15
12 [a]Dan 9:7 [b]Lam 4:11, 22; Ezek 5:13
13 [a]Ezek 6:4-7 [b]1 Kin 14:23; 2 Kin 16:4; Is 57:5-7; Ezek 20:28; Hos 4:13
14 [a]Is 5:25; 9:12; Ezek 14:13; 20:33, 34
7:2 [1]Heb *YHWH*, usually rendered *LORD* [a]Ezek 7:3, 5, 6; 11:13; Amos 8:2, 10
4 [a]Ezek 11:21; 22:31; Hos 9:7 [b]Ezek 6:7, 14; 7:27
5 [1]Heb *YHWH*, usually rendered *LORD* [a]2 Kin 21:12, 13; Nah 1:9
6 [a]Zech 13:7
7 [a]Ezek 7:12; 12:23-25, 28 [b]Is 22:5
8 [a]Is 42:25; Ezek 9:8; 14:19; Nah 1:6 [b]Ezek 7:3; 33:20; 36:19
9 [1]Lit *give*
10 [a]Ps 89:32; Is 10:5
11 [1]Lit *has risen* [a]Ps 73:8; 125:3; Is 59:6-8 [b]Zeph 1:18
12 [a]Ezek 7:5-7, 10; 1 Cor 7:29-31; James 5:8, 9 [b]Prov 20:14; 1 Cor 7:30 [c]Is 5:13, 14; Ezek 6:11, 12; 7:14

13 [1]Lit *return to* [2]Lit *thing sold*, i.e. his inherited land [3]Lit *their life among the living ones* [4]Lit *return* [a]Lev 25:24-28, 31
14 [1]Lit *her* [a]Num 10:9; Jer 4:5

gods. *idols.* The Hebrew for this word is a derisive term (lit. "dung pellets"), used especially by Ezekiel (38 times, as opposed to only 9 times elsewhere in the OT).

6:7 *know that I am the LORD.* See Introduction: Themes.

6:9 *those of you who escape will remember Me.* The corrective outcome God intends from the severe judgment to come (see v. 10).

6:11 *Clap your hand.* A command to Ezekiel, calling for his personal involvement in the tragedy—though Israel's enemies were condemned for the same practice (see 25:6).

6:14 *I will stretch out My hand against.* A common expression in Ezekiel (see 14:9,13; 16:27; 25:7; 35:3). *Diblah.* Perhaps the Beth-diblathaim of Jer 48:22, a city in Moab; or Riblah, a city north of Damascus on the Orontes River (a few Hebrew manuscripts read "Riblah").

7:2 *four corners of the land.* The whole world would be affected by God's judgment on the land of Israel (see note on 1:5).

7:7 *the day.* The day of the Lord. Beginning with Amos (Amos 5:18–20), that day is seen by all the prophets as a day of great judgment—and often (though not here) as a judgment that sweeps away all the enemies that threaten God's people, thereby bringing peace. *tumult rather than joyful shouting.* Cf. Amos 5:20 ("darkness instead of light").

7:8 *pour out My wrath.* A common expression in Ezekiel (see 9:8; 14:19; 20:8,13,21; 22:31; 30:15; 36:18).

7:12 *Let not the buyer rejoice.* End-time advice similar to that of Jesus (see Matt 24:17–18).

15 'The [a]sword is outside and the plague and the famine are within. He who is in the field will die by the sword; famine and the plague will also consume those in the city.

16 'Even when their survivors [a]escape, they will be on the mountains like [b]doves of the valleys, all of them [1][c]mourning, each over his own iniquity.

17 'All [a]hands will hang limp and all knees will [1]become *like* water.

18 'They will [a]gird themselves with sackcloth and [b]shuddering will overwhelm them; and shame *will be* on all faces and [c]baldness on all their heads.

19 'They will [a]fling their silver into the streets and their gold will become an abhorrent thing; their [b]silver and their gold will not be able to deliver them in the day of the wrath of the LORD. They cannot satisfy their [1]appetite nor can they fill their stomachs, for their iniquity has become an occasion of stumbling.

The Temple Profaned

20 'They transformed the beauty of His ornaments into pride, and [a]they made the images of their abominations *and* their detestable things with it; therefore I will make it an abhorrent thing to them.

21 'I will give it into the hands of the [a]foreigners as plunder and to the wicked of the earth as spoil, and they will profane it.

22 'I will also turn My [a]face from them, and they will profane My secret place; then robbers will enter and profane it.

23 '[a]Make the chain, for the land is full of [1][b]bloody crimes and the city is [c]full of violence.

24 'Therefore, I will bring the worst of the [a]nations, and they will possess their houses. I will also make the [b]pride of the strong ones cease, and their [c]holy places will be profaned.

25 'When anguish comes, they will seek [a]peace, but there will be none.

26 '[a]Disaster will come upon disaster and [b]rumor will be *added* to rumor; then they will seek a [c]vision from a prophet, but the [d]law will be lost from the priest and [e]counsel from the elders.

27 'The king will mourn, the prince will be [a]clothed with horror, and the hands of the people of the land will [1]tremble. According to their conduct I will deal with them, and by their judgments I will judge them. And they will know that I am the LORD.'"

Vision of Abominations in Jerusalem

8 It came about in the sixth year, on the fifth *day* of the sixth month, as I was sitting in my house with the elders of Judah sitting before me, that the hand of the Lord [1]GOD fell on me there.

2 Then I looked, and behold, a likeness as the appearance of [1]a man; from His loins and downward *there was* the [a]appearance of fire, and from His loins and upward the appearance of brightness, like the appearance [b]of [2]glowing metal.

3 He stretched out the form of a hand and caught me by a lock of my head; and the [a]Spirit lifted me up between earth and heaven and brought me in the visions of God to Jerusalem, to the entrance of the [1]north gate of the inner *court*, where the seat of the idol of jealousy, which [b]provokes to jealousy, was *located*.

4 And behold, the [a]glory of the God of Israel *was* there, like the appearance which I saw in the plain.

5 Then He said to me, "Son of man, [a]raise your eyes now toward the north." So I raised my eyes toward the north, and behold, to the north of the altar gate *was* this [b]idol of jealousy at the entrance.

6 And He said to me, "Son of man, do you see what they are doing, the great [a]abominations which the house of Israel are committing here, so that I would be far from

15 [a]Jer 14:18; Ezek 5:12; 6:11, 12; 12:16
16 [1]Lit *moaning* [a]Ezra 9:15; Is 37:31; Ezek 6:8; 14:22 [b]Is 38:14 [c]Is 59:11; Nah 2:7
17 [1]Lit *run with water* [a]Is 13:7; Ezek 21:7; 22:14; Heb 12:12
18 [a]Is 15:3; Ezek 27:31; Amos 8:10 [b]Job 21:6; Ps 55:5 [c]Ezek 27:31
19 [1]Lit *soul* [a]Is 2:20; 30:22 [b]Prov 11:4; Zeph 1:18
20 [a]Jer 7:30
21 [a]2 Kin 24:13; Ps 74:2-8; Jer 52:13
22 [a]Jer 18:17; Ezek 39:23, 24
23 [1]Lit *judgment of blood* [a]Jer 27:2 [b]Ezek 9:9; Hos 4:2 [c]Ezek 8:17
24 [a]Ezek 21:31; 28:7 [b]Ezek 33:28 [c]2 Chr 7:20; Ezek 24:21
25 [a]Ezek 13:10, 16
26 [a]Is 47:11; Jer 4:20
26 [b]Ezek 21:7 [c]Jer 21:2; 37:17 [d]Ps 74:9; Ezek 22:26; Mic 3:6 [e]Jer 18:18; Ezek 11:2
27 [1]Lit *be terrified* [a]Job 8:22; Ps 35:26; 109:18, 29; Ezek 26:16
8:1 [1]Heb *YHWH,* usually rendered *LORD*
2 [1]Lit *fire* [2]Or *electrum* [a]Ezek 1:27 [b]Ezek 1:4, 27
3 [1]Lit *facing north* [a]Ezek 3:12; 11:1 [b]Ex 20:4; Deut 32:16
4 [a]Ezek 1:28; 3:22, 23
5 [a]Jer 3:2; Zech 5:5 [b]Ps 78:58; Jer 7:30; 32:34; Ezek 8:3
6 [a]2 Kin 23:4, 5; Ezek 5:11; 8:9, 17

7:19 *They will fling their silver.* See Is 2:20.
7:20 *beauty of His ornaments.* See Ex 32:2–4.
7:22 *My secret place.* The Jerusalem temple.
7:24 *pride of the strong ones.* The Jerusalem temple, described by the word "pride" (as in 24:21; 33:28).
7:26 *prophet . . . priest . . . elders.* There would be no guidance from God and no direction from the elders (see 1 Sam 28:6; Amos 8:11–12; Mic 3:6–7).
7:27 *king . . . prince.* Here both nouns describe the same person. Ezekiel considered Jehoiachin to be the true king (1:2) and Zedekiah a mere prince (12:12). *people of the land.* Full citizens of Judah who owned land and served in the army (cf. 12:19; 45:16,22; 46:3).
8:1–11:25 The vision contained in these four chapters vividly depicts the departure of the divine glory from the corrupted temple (see 8:4; 9:3; 10:18–19; 11:23).
8:1 *in the sixth year, on the fifth day of the sixth month.* Sept. 17, 592 B.C.—the second of 13 dates in Ezekiel. This one, like those in 1:2 and 40:1, introduces a vision. *sitting in my house.* The exiles were free to build houses (see Jer 29:5). *elders of Judah sitting before me.* They also had freedom of movement, assembly and worship. A year and two months after his inaugural vision and preaching, the prophet commanded a hearing. Some have seen in such meetings the beginnings of the synagogue form of worship. *hand of the Lord GOD.* See note on 1:3.
8:2 *likeness as the appearance of a man.* An angel, similar in appearance to God in 1:26–27. *the appearance of fire . . . like . . . glowing metal.* A way of describing the blinding brightness of the divine messenger (see Matt 28:3; cf. Acts 9:3).
8:3 *brought me . . . to Jerusalem.* Ezekiel had been directed to prophesy stern judgments on Jerusalem (chs. 1–7). Now he was transported to Jerusalem in visions of God (see 11:24) and shown the reason for the judgments. *idol . . . which provokes to jealousy.* Any idol in the temple provoked the Lord to jealousy, but this one seems to be a statue of Asherah, the Canaanite goddess of fertility, which Josiah had removed some 30 years previously (see 2 Kin 23:6).
8:5 *idol of jealousy.* See note on v. 3.

My sanctuary? But yet you will see still greater abominations."

7 Then He brought me to the entrance of the court, and when I looked, behold, a hole in the wall.

8 He said to me, "Son of man, now [a]dig through the wall." So I dug through the wall, and behold, an entrance.

9 And He said to me, "Go in and see the wicked abominations that they are committing here."

10 So I entered and looked, and behold, every form of creeping things and beasts *and* detestable things, with all the idols of the house of Israel, were carved on the wall all around.

11 Standing in front of them were [a]seventy [b]elders of the house of Israel, with Jaazaniah the son of Shaphan standing among them, each man with his [c]censer in his hand and the fragrance of the cloud of incense rising.

12 Then He said to me, "Son of man, do you see what the elders of the house of Israel are committing in the dark, each man in the room of his carved images? For they say, '[a]The LORD does not see us; the LORD has [b]forsaken the land.' "

13 And He said to me, "Yet you will see still greater abominations which they are committing."

14 Then He brought me to the entrance of the [a]gate of the LORD's house which *was* toward the north; and behold, women were sitting there weeping for Tammuz.

15 He said to me, "Do you see *this*, son of man? Yet you will see still greater abominations than these."

16 Then He brought me into the inner court of the LORD's house. And behold, at the entrance to the temple of the LORD, between the porch and the altar, *were* about twenty-five men with their [a]backs to the temple of the LORD and their faces toward the east; and [b]they were [1]prostrating themselves eastward toward the sun.

17 He said to me, "Do you see *this*, son of man? Is it too light a thing for the house of Judah to commit the abominations which they have committed here, that they have [a]filled the land with violence and [b]provoked Me repeatedly? For behold, they are putting the twig to their nose.

18 "Therefore, I indeed will deal in wrath. My eye will have no pity nor will I spare; and [a]though they cry in My ears with a loud voice, yet I will not listen to them."

The Vision of Slaughter

9 Then He cried out in my hearing with a loud [a]voice saying, "Draw near, [1]O executioners of the city, each with his destroying weapon in his hand."

2 Behold, six men came from the direction of the upper gate which faces north, each with his shattering weapon in his hand; and among them was [a]a certain man clothed in linen with a [1]writing case at his loins. And they went in and stood beside the bronze altar.

3 Then the [a]glory of the God of Israel went up from the cherub on which it had been, to the threshold of the [1]temple. And He called to the man clothed in linen at whose loins was the writing case.

4 The LORD said to him, "Go through the midst of the city, *even* through the midst of Jerusalem, and put a [a]mark on the foreheads of the men who [b]sigh and groan over all the abominations which are being committed in its midst."

5 But to the others He said in my hearing, "Go through the city after him and strike; do not let your eye have pity and do not spare.

6 "[1]Utterly [a]slay old men, young men, maidens, little children, and women, but do not [b]touch any man on whom is the mark; and you shall [c]start from My sanctuary." So they started with the [2]elders who *were* before the [3]temple.

7 And He said to them, "[a]Defile the [1]temple and fill the courts with the slain. Go out!" Thus they went out and struck down *the people* in the city.

8 As they were striking *the people* and I *alone* was left, I [a]fell on my face and cried out [1]saying, "[b]Alas, Lord [2]GOD! Are You

8 [a]Is 29:15
11 [a]Num 11:16, 25; Luke 10:1 [b]Jer 19:1 [c]Num 16:17, 35
12 [a]Ps 14:1; Is 29:15; Ezek 9:9 [b]Ps 10:11
14 [a]Ezek 44:4; 46:9
16 [1]I.e. worshiping [a]2 Chr 29:6; Jer 2:27; Ezek 23:39 [b]Deut 4:19; 17:3; Job 31:26-28; Jer 44:17
17 [a]Ezek 7:11, 23; 9:9; Amos 3:10; Mic 2:2 [b]Jer 7:18, 19; Ezek 16:26
18 [a]Is 1:15; Jer 11:11; Mic 3:4; Zech 7:13
9:1 [1]Lit *you who punish* [a]Is 6:8
2 [1]Or *scribal inkhorn* [a]Lev 16:4
3 [1]Lit *house* [a]Ezek 10:4; 11:22, 23
4 [a]Ex 12:7, 13; Ezek 9:6; 2 Cor 1:22; 2 Tim 2:19; Rev 7:2, 3; 9:4; 14:1 [b]Ps 119:53, 136; Jer 13:17; Ezek 6:11; 21:6
6 [1]Lit To *destruction* [2]Or *old men* [3]Lit *house* [a]2 Chr 36:17 [b]Ex 12:23; Rev 9:4 [c]Jer 25:29; Amos 3:2; Luke 12:47
7 [1]Lit *house* [a]2 Chr 36:17; Ezek 7:20-22
8 [1]Lit *and said* [2]Heb *YHWH*, usually rendered *LORD* [a]1 Chr 21:16 [b]Ezek 11:13; Amos 7:2-6

8:10 *every form of creeping things . . . detestable things.* Probably reflecting Egyptian influence (see 2 Kin 23:31–35).
8:11 *Jaazaniah.* Not the same person as in 11:1. Ironically, the name means "The LORD hears," and the irony is sharpened by the quotation in v. 12.
8:14 *Tammuz.* The only Biblical reference to this Babylonian fertility god. The women of Jerusalem were bewailing his dying, which they felt caused the annual wilting of vegetation. According to some interpreters, he is alluded to in Dan 11:37 ("the desire of women"—see note there).
8:16 *with their backs to the temple.* Almost all ancient temples were oriented toward the east. Worshiping the sun as it rose required one to turn his back to the temple.
8:17 *putting the twig to their nose.* A ceremonial gesture in nature worship, not documented elsewhere in the Bible.
9:1 *loud voice.* The thunderous voice of God (see Ex 19:19 and NASB marg.; see also Ps 29).
9:2 *six men came from the direction of the upper gate.* These six guardian angels of the city, plus the seventh clothed in linen (cf. the seven angels of the judgment in Rev 8:2,6), came from the place where the idol that provoked to jealousy stood (see 8:3 and note). *shattering weapon.* Probably a war club or a battle-ax.
9:3 *the glory . . . went up.* God began to vacate the temple, His glory moving to the door (see note on 8:1–11:25).
9:4 *mark.* A *taw*, the last letter of the Hebrew alphabet, which originally looked like an "x" (cf. Rev 7:2–4; 13:16; 14:9,11; 20:4; 22:4). *the men who sigh and groan.* The remnant (see Ex 12:23; 1 Kin 19:18).
9:6 *start from My sanctuary.* Judgment begins with God's people (see 1 Pet 4:17).
9:8 *Are You . . . Jerusalem?* One of the few times Ezekiel questioned the Lord (see 11:13).

destroying the whole remnant of Israel [3]by
pouring out Your wrath on Jerusalem?"
9 Then He said to me, "The iniquity of
the house of Israel and Judah is very, very
great, and the land is [a]filled with blood and
the city is [b]full of perversion; for [c]they say,
'The LORD has forsaken the land, and the
LORD does not see!'
10 "But as for Me, [a]My eye will have no
pity nor will I spare, but [b]I will bring their
conduct upon their heads."
11 Then behold, the man clothed in linen
at whose loins was the [1]writing case [2]report-
ed, saying, "I have done just as You have
commanded me."

Vision of God's Glory Departing from the Temple

10 Then I looked, and behold, in the
[1a]expanse that was over the heads of
the cherubim something like a [b]sapphire
stone, in appearance resembling a [c]throne,
appeared above them.
2 And He spoke to the man clothed in
linen and said, "Enter between the [a]whirling
wheels under the [1]cherubim and fill your
hands with [b]coals of fire from between the
cherubim and scatter *them* over the city."
And he entered in my sight.
3 Now the cherubim were standing on
the right side of the [1]temple when the man
entered, and the cloud filled the [a]inner court.
4 Then the [a]glory of the LORD went up
from the cherub to the threshold of the temple, and the [b]temple was filled with the
cloud and the court was filled with the
[c]brightness of the glory of the LORD.
5 Moreover, the sound of the wings of
the cherubim was heard as far as the outer
court, like the [a]voice of [1]God Almighty when
He speaks.
6 It came about when He commanded
the man clothed in linen, saying, "Take fire
from between the whirling wheels, from
between the cherubim," he entered and
stood beside a wheel.
7 Then the cherub stretched out his hand
from between the cherubim to the fire which
was between the cherubim, took *some* and
put *it* into the hands of the one clothed in
linen, who took *it* and went out.
8 The cherubim appeared to have the
form of a man's hand under their wings.
9 Then I looked, and behold, [a]four wheels
beside the cherubim, one wheel beside each
cherub; and the appearance of the wheels *was*
like the gleam of a [1b]Tarshish stone.
10 As for their appearance, all four of
them had the same likeness, as if one wheel
were within another wheel.
11 When they moved, they went [a]in *any of*
their four [1]directions without turning as they
went; but they followed in the direction which
[2]they faced, without turning as they went.
12 Their [a]whole body, their backs, their
hands, their wings and the [b]wheels were full
of eyes all around, the wheels belonging to
all four of them.
13 The wheels were called in my hearing,
the whirling wheels.
14 And [a]each one had four faces. The first
face *was* the face of a cherub, the second
face *was* the face of a man, the third the face
of a lion, and the fourth the face of an eagle.
15 Then the cherubim rose up. They are
the [a]living beings that I saw by the river
Chebar.
16 Now when the cherubim moved, the
wheels would go beside them; also when the
cherubim lifted up their wings to rise from
the ground, the wheels would not turn from
beside them.
17 When [1]the cherubim [a]stood still, [1]the
wheels would stand still; and when they rose
up, [1]the wheels would rise with them, for
the spirit of the living beings *was* in them.
18 Then the glory of the LORD departed
from the threshold of the temple and stood
[a]over the cherubim.
19 When [a]the cherubim departed, they
lifted their wings and rose up from the earth
in my sight with the wheels beside them;
and they stood still at the entrance of the
east gate of the LORD's house, and the glory
of the God of Israel [1]hovered over them.
20 These are the [a]living beings that I saw
beneath the God of Israel by [b]the river
Chebar; so I knew that they *were* cherubim.
21 [a]Each one had four faces and each one
four wings, and beneath their wings *was* the
form of human hands.
22 As for the likeness of their faces, they
were the same faces whose appearance I had
seen by the river Chebar. Each one went
straight ahead.

Evil Rulers to Be Judged

11 Moreover, the [a]Spirit lifted me up and
brought me to the east gate of the

8 [3]Lit *by Your pouring* **9** [a]2 Kin 21:16; Jer 2:34; Ezek 7:23; 22:2, 3 [b]Ezek 22:29; Mic 3:1-3; 7:3 [c]Job 22:13; Ps 10:11; 94:7; Is 29:15; Ezek 8:12 **10** [a]Is 65:6; Ezek 8:18; 24:14 [b]Ezek 7:4; 11:21; Hos 9:7 **11** [1]Or *inkhorn* [2]Lit *brought back word* **10:1** [1]Or *firmament* [a]Ezek 1:22, 26 [b]Ex 24:10 [c]Rev 4:2, 3 **2** [1]So with Gr; Heb *cherub* [a]Ezek 1:15-21; 10:13 [b]Ps 18:10-13; Is 6:6; Ezek 1:13; Rev 8:5 **3** [1]Lit *house*, and so throughout the ch [a]Ezek 8:3, 16 **4** [a]Ezek 9:3; 11:22, 23 [b]Ex 40:34, 35; Is 6:1-4 [c]Ezek 1:28 **5** [1]Heb *El Shaddai* [a]Job 40:9; Ezek 1:24; Rev 10:3 **9** [a]Ezek 1:15-17

9 [1]Perhaps, *beryl* [b]Dan 10:6; Rev 21:20 **11** [1]Lit *sides* [2]Lit *the head turned* [a]Ezek 1:17 **12** [a]Rev 4:6, 8 [b]Ezek 1:18 **14** [a]1 Kin 7:29, 36; Ezek 1:6, 10; 10:21; Rev 4:7 **15** [a]Ezek 1:3, 5 **17** [1]Lit *they* [a]Ezek 1:21 **18** [a]Ps 18:10 **19** [1]Lit *over them from above* [a]Ezek 11:22 **20** [a]Ezek 1:5, 22, 26; 10:15 [b]Ezek 1:1 **21** [a]Ezek 1:6, 8; 10:14; 41:18, 19 **11:1** [a]Ezek 3:12, 14; 8:3; 11:24; 43:5

10:1 *I looked.* Ch. 10 echoes ch. 1, underscoring the identity of what Ezekiel saw at the River Chebar with what he now sees in his vision (see 8:4). The creatures in ch. 1 are here called cherubim (see note on 1:5).

10:2 *coals of fire.* While in 1:13 the living creatures looked like burning coals, here there are real coals. *scatter them over the city.* A judgment by fire (see Gen 19:24; Amos 7:4).

10:7 *the cherub stretched out his hand.* Though the "man clothed in linen" was initially commanded to get the coals himself (v. 2), he received them from the hand of one of the creatures (see 1:8). *who took it and went out.* No further report is given, but the destructive spreading of the coals over Jerusalem is assumed.

10:14 *The first face was the face of a cherub.* While the faces of the man, lion and eagle are identical with those in 1:10, the ox is here called a cherub (see note on Gen 3:24).

10:19 *of the east gate . . . and the glory of the God of Israel hovered over them.* A second movement of the glory, again in an easterly direction (see 9:3; 10:4; see also note on 8:1–11:25).

LORD's house which faced eastward. And behold, *there were* twenty-five men at the entrance of the gate, and among them I saw Jaazaniah son of Azzur and [b]Pelatiah son of Benaiah, leaders of the people.

2 He said to me, "Son of man, these are the men who devise iniquity and [a]give evil advice in this city,

3 who say, '[1]Is not *the time* near to build houses? [2]This [a]*city* is the pot and we are the flesh.'

4 "Therefore, [a]prophesy against them, son of man, prophesy!"

5 Then the Spirit of the LORD fell upon me, and He said to me, "Say, 'Thus says the LORD, "So you think, house of Israel, for [a]I know [1]your [b]thoughts.

6 "You have [a]multiplied your slain in this city, filling its streets with [1]them."

7 'Therefore, thus says the Lord [1]GOD, "Your [a]slain whom you have laid in the midst of [2]the city are the flesh and this *city* is the pot; but [3]I will [b]bring you out of it.

8 "You have [a]feared a sword; so I will [b]bring a sword upon you," the Lord GOD declares.

9 "And I will bring you out of the midst of [1]the city and deliver you into the hands of [a]strangers and [b]execute judgments against you.

10 "You will [a]fall by the sword. I will judge you to the [b]border of Israel; so you shall know that I am the LORD.

11 "This *city* will [a]not be a pot for you, nor will you be flesh in the midst of it, *but* I will judge you to the border of Israel.

12 "Thus you will know that I am the LORD; for you have not walked in My statutes nor have you [a]executed My ordinances, but have acted according to the ordinances of the [b]nations around you." ' "

13 Now it came about as I prophesied, that [a]Pelatiah son of Benaiah died. Then I fell on my face and cried out with a loud voice and said, "[b]Alas, Lord GOD! Will You bring the remnant of Israel to a complete end?"

Promise of Restoration

14 Then the word of the LORD came to me, saying,

15 "Son of man, your brothers, your [1]relatives, [2]your fellow exiles and the whole house of Israel, all of them, *are those* to whom the inhabitants of Jerusalem have said, 'Go far from the LORD; this land has been given [a]us as a possession.'

16 "Therefore say, 'Thus says the Lord GOD, "Though I had removed them far away among the nations and though I had scattered them among the countries, yet I was a [a]sanctuary for them a little while in the countries where they had gone." '

17 "Therefore say, 'Thus says the Lord GOD, "I will [a]gather you from the peoples and assemble you out of the countries among which you have been scattered, and I will give you the land of Israel." '

18 "When they come there, they will [a]remove all its [b]detestable things and all its abominations from it.

19 "And I will [a]give them one heart, and put a new spirit within [1]them. And I will take the [b]heart of stone out of their flesh and give them a [c]heart of flesh,

20 that they may [a]walk in My statutes and keep My ordinances and do them. Then they will be [b]My people, and I shall be their God.

21 "[1]But as for those whose hearts go after their [a]detestable things and abominations, I will [b]bring their conduct down on their heads," declares the Lord GOD.

22 Then the cherubim [a]lifted up their wings with the wheels beside them, and [b]the glory of the God of Israel [1]hovered over them.

23 The [a]glory of the LORD went up from the midst of the city and [b]stood over the mountain which is east of the city.

24 And the [a]Spirit lifted me up and brought me in a vision by the Spirit of God to the exiles [1]in Chaldea. So the vision that I had seen [2b]left me.

25 Then I [a]told the exiles all the things that the LORD had shown me.

11:1 [b]Ezek 11:13
2 [a]Ps 2:1, 2; 52:2; Is 30:1; Jer 5:5; Mic 2:1
3 [1]Or The time *is not near* [2]Or *This is* [a]Jer 1:13; Ezek 11:7, 11; 24:3, 6
4 [a]Ezek 3:4, 17
5 [1]Lit *what comes up in your spirit* [a]Jer 11:20; 17:10 [b]Ezek 38:10
6 [1]Lit *the slain* [a]Is 1:15; Ezek 7:23; 22:2-6, 9, 12, 27
7 [1]Heb *YHWH*, usually rendered *LORD*, and so throughout the ch [2]Lit *it* [3]So with Gr; Heb *he will bring you out* [a]Ezek 24:3-13; Mic 3:2, 3 [b]2 Kin 25:18-22; Jer 52:24-27; Ezek 11:9
8 [a]Prov 10:24; Is 66:4 [b]Job 3:25; Is 24:17, 18
9 [1]Lit *it* [a]Deut 28:36, 49, 50; Ps 106:41 [b]Ezek 5:8; 16:41
10 [a]Jer 52:9, 10 [b]2 Kin 14:25
11 [a]Ezek 11:3, 7; 24:3, 6
12 [a]Ezek 18:8, 9 [b]Ezek 8:10, 14, 16
13 [a]Ezek 11:1 [b]Ezek 9:8

15 [1]Lit *brothers* [2]So with Gr and some ancient versions; Heb *the men of your redemption* [a]Ezek 33:24
16 [a]Ps 31:20; 90:1; 91:9; Is 8:14; Jer 29:7, 11
17 [a]Is 11:11-16; Jer 3:12, 18; 24:5; Ezek 20:41, 42; 28:25
18 [a]Ezek 37:23 [b]Ezek 5:11; 7:20
19 [1]So with Gr and many mss; Heb *you* [a]Jer 24:7; 32:39; Ezek 18:31; 36:26 [b]Zech 7:12; Rom 2:4, 5 [c]2 Cor 3:3
20 [a]Ps 105:45; Ezek 36:27 [b]Ezek 14:11
21 [1]Lit *And to the heart of their detestable things and their abomination their heart goes* [a]Jer 16:18; Ezek 11:18 [b]Ezek 9:10; 16:43
22 [1]Lit *over them from above* [a]Ezek 10:19 [b]Ezek 43:2
23 [a]Ezek 8:4 [b]Zech 14:4
24 [1]I.e. Babylonia [2]Lit *went up from* [a]Ezek 8:3; 11:1; 37:1; 2 Cor 12:2-4 [b]Acts 10:16
25 [a]Ezek 2:7; 3:4, 17, 27

11:1 *Jaazaniah.* See note on 8:11. *Pelatiah.* Means "The LORD delivers."

11:3 *time near to build houses?* The residents of Jerusalem who were not exiled in 597 B.C. felt smugly secure, thinking that nothing worse would befall them. *pot.* As in ch. 24, Jerusalem is compared to a cooking pot. Those left behind boasted that they were the "meat," the choice portions—the inference being that the exiles in Babylon were the discarded bones (see v. 15).

11:7 *Your slain whom you have laid . . . are the flesh.* The meat, redefined by the prophet, is not those in power in Jerusalem (who will be driven out) but the innocent people they killed.

11:11 *to the border of Israel.* At Riblah (see 2 Kin 25:20–21).

11:13 *Will You . . . end?* See note on 9:8.

11:16 *I was a sanctuary for them.* A key verse in Ezekiel. Although the exiles had been driven from Jerusalem and its sanctuary (the symbol of God's presence among His people), God Himself became their sanctuary, i.e., He was present among them. Later Christ also became a substitute for the temple (see John 2:19–21).

11:19 *one heart . . . new spirit.* Inner spiritual and moral transformation that results in single-minded commitment to the Lord and to His will (see 36:26).

11:20 *they will be My people, and I shall be their God.* The heart of God's covenant promise (see Ex 6:7).

11:23 *The glory of the LORD went up.* The final eastward movement of the glory (as the Lord left His temple), which stopped above the Mount of Olives (see 9:3; 10:4,19; see also note on 8:1–11:25).

11:24 See note on 8:3.

Ezekiel Prepares for Exile

12 Then the word of the LORD came to me, saying,

2 "Son of man, you live in the [a]midst of the [b]rebellious house, who [c]have eyes to see but do not see, ears to hear but do not hear; for they are a rebellious house.

3 "Therefore, son of man, prepare for yourself baggage for exile and go into exile by day in their sight; even go into exile from your place to another place in their sight. [a]Perhaps they will [1]understand though they are a rebellious house.

4 "Bring your baggage out by day in their sight, as baggage for exile. Then you will go out [a]at evening in their sight, as those going into exile.

5 "Dig a hole through the wall in their sight and [1]go out through it.

6 "Load *the baggage* on *your* shoulder in their sight *and* carry *it* out in the dark. You shall [a]cover your face so that you cannot see the land, for I have set you as a [b]sign to the house of Israel."

7 I [a]did so, as I had been commanded. By day I [b]brought out my baggage like the baggage of an exile. Then in the evening I dug through the wall with my hands; I went out in the dark *and* carried *the baggage* on *my* shoulder in their sight.

8 In the morning the word of the LORD came to me, saying,

9 "Son of man, has not the house of Israel, the [a]rebellious house, said to you, '[b]What are you doing?'

10 "Say to them, 'Thus says the Lord [1]GOD, "This [2a]burden *concerns* the prince in Jerusalem as well as all the house of Israel who are [3]in it." '

11 "Say, 'I am [1]a [a]sign to you. As I have done, so it will be done to them; they will [b]go into exile, into captivity.'

12 "The [a]prince who is among them will load *his baggage* on *his* shoulder in the dark and go out. [1]They will dig a hole through the wall to bring *it* out. He will cover his face so that he can not see the land with *his* eyes.

13 "I will also spread My [a]net over him, and he will be caught in My snare. And I will bring him to Babylon in the land of the Chaldeans; yet he will [b]not see it, though he will die there.

14 "I will [a]scatter to every wind all who are around him, his helpers and all his troops; and I will draw out a sword after them.

15 "So they will [a]know that I am the LORD when I scatter them among the nations and spread them among the countries.

16 "But I will [1]spare a few of them from the [a]sword, the famine and the pestilence that they may tell all their abominations among the nations where they go, and [2]may [b]know that I am the LORD."

17 Moreover, the word of the LORD came to me saying,

18 "Son of man, [a]eat your bread with trembling and drink your water with quivering and anxiety.

19 "Then say to the people of the land, 'Thus says the Lord GOD concerning the inhabitants of Jerusalem in the land of Israel, "They will eat their bread with anxiety and drink their water with horror, because [1]their land will be [2a]stripped of its fullness on account of the violence of all who live in it.

20 "The inhabited [a]cities will be laid waste and the [b]land will be a desolation. So you will know that I am the LORD." ' "

21 Then the word of the LORD came to me, saying,

22 "Son of man, what is this [a]proverb you *people* have concerning the land of Israel, saying, 'The [b]days are long and every [c]vision fails'?

23 "Therefore say to them, 'Thus says the Lord GOD, "I will make this proverb cease so that they will no longer use it as a proverb in Israel." But tell them, "[a]The days draw near as well as the [1]fulfillment of every vision.

24 "For there will no longer be any [1a]false vision or flattering divination within the house of Israel.

12:2 [a]Is 6:5 [b]Ps 78:40; Is 1:23; Ezek 2:7, 8 [c]Is 6:9f; 43:8; Jer 5:21; Matt 13:13, 14; Mark 4:12; 8:18; Luke 8:10; John 9:39-41; 12:40; Acts 28:26f; Rom 11:8
3 [1]Or *see that they are* [a]Jer 26:3; 36:3, 7; Luke 20:13; 2 Tim 2:25
4 [a]2 Kin 25:4; Jer 39:4; Ezek 12:12
5 [1]Lit *bring it out*
6 [a]1 Sam 28:8; Ezek 12:12, 13 [b]Is 8:18; 20:3; Ezek 4:3; 12:11; 24:24
7 [a]Ezek 24:18; 37:7, 10 [b]Ezek 12:3-6
9 [a]Ezek 2:5-8; 12:1-3 [b]Ezek 17:12; 20:49; 24:19
10 [1]Heb *YHWH,* usually rendered *LORD,* and so throughout the ch [2]Or *oracle* [3]Lit *in their midst* [a]2 Kin 9:25; Is 13:1; Ezek 12:3-8
11 [1]Lit *your sign* [a]Ezek 12:6 [b]Jer 15:2; 52:15, 28-30; Ezek 12:3
12 [1]I.e. the king's attendants [a]2 Kin 25:4; Jer 39:4; 52:7; Ezek 12:6
13 [a]Is 24:17, 18; Ezek 17:20; 19:8; Hos 7:12
13 [b]Jer 39:7; 52:11
14 [a]2 Kin 25:4, 5; Ezek 5:2; 17:21
15 [a]Ezek 6:7, 14; 12:16, 20
16 [1]Lit *leave over* [2]Or *they will know* [a]Ezek 7:15; 14:21 [b]Jer 22:8, 9
18 [a]Lam 5:9; Ezek 4:16
19 [1]Lit *her* [2]Lit *desolate* [a]Jer 10:22; Ezek 6:6, 7, 14; Mic 7:13; Zech 7:14
20 [a]Is 3:26; Jer 4:7; Ezek 5:14 [b]Is 7:23, 24; Jer 25:9; Ezek 36:3
22 [a]Ezek 16:44; 18:2, 3 [b]Jer 5:12; Ezek 11:3; 12:27; Amos 6:3; 2 Pet 3:4 [c]Ezek 7:26
23 [1]Lit *word* [a]Ps 37:13; Joel 2:1; Zeph 1:14
24 [1]Lit *vain* [a]Jer 14:13-16; Ezek 13:6, 23; Zech 13:2-4

12:2 *eyes to see but do not see.* The hardening about which the Lord had spoken to Isaiah (Is 6:9–10).

12:3 *prepare for yourself baggage.* Another symbolic act, which, like those in chs. 4–5, follows a vision. *Perhaps they will understand.* Some hope remained that they would change.

12:5 *Dig . . . through the wall.* Not the city wall, which was made of stone and was many feet thick, but the sun-dried brick wall of his house.

12:6 *sign.* Prophets were often instructed to perform symbolic acts (see, e.g., v. 11; 24:24,27).

12:8 *In the morning.* After Ezekiel "did . . . as . . . commanded" (v. 7). Again the divine explanation follows the prophet's unquestioning obedience (see note on 8:3).

12:9 *What are you doing?* The book's first indication of the people's response to the prophet's symbolic acts.

12:10 *prince in Jerusalem.* Zedekiah (see note on 7:27).

12:13 *he will not see it.* Nebuchadnezzar's men would put out Zedekiah's eyes (see 2 Kin 25:7).

12:18 *eat . . . with trembling.* Another prophetic symbol. Ezekiel's trembling must have been particularly violent, because the Hebrew word for "tremble" is used elsewhere to describe an earthquake (see 1 Kin 19:11; Amos 1:1).

12:19 *people of the land.* See note on 7:27.

12:22 *proverb.* A mocking proverb (probably coined by false prophets; see ch. 13; Jer 23:9–40; 28), which had become a popular saying. *vision.* The Hebrew for this word is not the same as that used in 1:1 but is the one used in 7:26, referring to a message that could be written down (see Hab 2:2)—specifically Ezekiel's oracles of judgment.

12:23 *fulfillment of every vision.* Divine affirmation of the true prophetic word (cf. Is 55:11).

25 "For I the LORD will speak, and whatever [a]word I speak will be performed. It will no longer be delayed, for in [b]your days, O [c]rebellious house, I will speak the word and perform it," declares the Lord GOD.' "

26 Furthermore, the word of the LORD came to me, saying,

27 "Son of man, behold, the house of Israel is saying, 'The vision that he sees is for [a]many [1]years *from now,* and he prophesies of times far off.'

28 "Therefore say to them, 'Thus says the Lord GOD, "None of My words will be delayed any longer. Whatever word I speak will be performed," ' " declares the Lord GOD.

False Prophets Condemned

13 Then the word of the LORD came to me saying,

2 "Son of man, prophesy against the [a]prophets of Israel who prophesy, and say to those who prophesy from their own [1]inspiration, '[b]Listen to the word of the LORD!

3 'Thus says the Lord [1]GOD, "Woe to the [a]foolish prophets who are following their own spirit and have [b]seen nothing.

4 "O Israel, your prophets have been like foxes among ruins.

5 "You have not [a]gone up into the [b]breaches, nor did you build the wall around the house of Israel to stand in the battle on the [c]day of the LORD.

6 "They see [1a]falsehood and lying divination who are saying, 'The LORD declares,' when the LORD has not sent them; [b]yet they hope for the fulfillment of *their* word.

7 "[a]Did you not see a false vision and speak a lying divination when you said, 'The LORD declares,' but it is not I who have spoken?" ' "

8 Therefore, thus says the Lord GOD, "Because you have spoken [1]falsehood and seen a lie, therefore behold, [a]I am against you," declares the Lord GOD.

9 "So My hand will be against the [a]prophets who see false visions and utter lying divinations. They will [1]have no place in the council of My people, [b]nor will they be written down in the register of the house of Israel, nor will they enter the land of Israel, [2]that you may know that I am the Lord GOD.

10 "It is definitely because they have [a]misled My people by saying, '[b]Peace!' when there is [c]no peace. And when anyone builds a wall, behold, they plaster it over with whitewash;

11 *so* tell those who plaster *it* over with whitewash, that it will fall. A [a]flooding rain will come, and you, O hailstones, will fall; and a violent wind will break out.

12 "Behold, when the wall has fallen, will you not be asked, 'Where is the plaster with which you plastered *it?*' "

13 Therefore, thus says the Lord GOD, "I will make a violent wind break out in My wrath. There will also be in My anger a flooding rain and [a]hailstones to consume *it* in wrath.

14 "So I will tear down the wall which you plastered over with whitewash and bring it down to the ground, so that its [a]foundation is laid bare; and when it falls, you will be [b]consumed in its midst. And you will [c]know that I am the LORD.

15 "Thus I will spend My wrath on the wall and on those who have plastered it over with whitewash; and I will say to you, 'The wall [1]is gone and its plasterers are gone,

16 *along with* the prophets of Israel who prophesy to Jerusalem, and who [a]see visions of peace for her when there is [b]no peace,' declares the Lord GOD.

17 "Now you, son of man, set your face against the daughters of your people who are [a]prophesying [b]from their own [1]inspiration. Prophesy against them

18 and say, 'Thus says the Lord GOD, "Woe to the women who sew *magic* bands on [1]all wrists and make veils for the heads of *persons* of every stature to [a]hunt down [2]lives! Will you hunt down the [2]lives of My people, but preserve the [2]lives *of others* for yourselves?

19 "[a]For handfuls of barley and fragments of bread, you have profaned Me to My people to put to death [1]some who should not die

[2]Or *souls* [a]2 Pet 2:14 **19** [1]Or *souls* [a]Prov 28:21; Mic 3:5

25 [a]Num 14:28-34; Is 14:24; Ezek 6:10; 12:28 [b]Jer 16:9; Hab 1:5 [c]Ezek 12:2
27 [1]Lit *days* [a]Ezek 12:22; Dan 10:14
13:2 [1]Lit *heart* [a]Is 9:15; Jer 37:19; Ezek 22:25, 28 [b]Is 1:10; Amos 7:16
3 [1]Heb *YHWH,* usually rendered *LORD,* and so throughout the ch [a]Lam 2:14; Hos 9:7; Zech 11:15 [b]Jer 23:28-32
5 [a]Ps 106:23; Jer 23:22; Ezek 22:30 [b]Is 58:12 [c]Is 13:6, 9; Ezek 7:19
6 [1]Lit *vanity* [a]Jer 29:8; Ezek 22:28 [b]Jer 28:15; 37:19
7 [a]Ezek 22:28
8 [1]Lit *vanity* [a]Ezek 5:8; 21:3; Nah 2:13
9 [1]Lit *not be in* [a]Jer 20:3-6; 28:15-17 [b]Ps 69:28; 87:6; Jer 17:13; Dan 12:1
9 [2]Or *and you will know*
10 [a]Jer 23:32; 50:6 [b]Jer 6:14; 8:11; 14:13 [c]Ezek 7:25; 13:16
11 [a]Ezek 38:22
13 [a]Ex 9:24, 25; Ps 18:12, 13; Is 30:30; Rev 11:19; 16:21
14 [a]Mic 1:6; Hab 3:13 [b]Jer 6:15; 14:15 [c]Ezek 13:9
15 [1]Lit *is not...are not*
16 [a]Jer 6:14; 8:11; Ezek 13:10 [b]Is 57:21
17 [1]Lit *heart* [a]Judg 4:4; 2 Kin 22:14; Luke 2:36; Acts 21:9 [b]Ezek 13:2; Rev 2:20
18 [1]Lit *all joints of the hand;* M.T. reads *of my hands*

12:27 *many years from now.* Whereas the first proverb denies that Ezekiel's words would ever be fulfilled, this one allows that they might be fulfilled in the distant future, beyond the concern of the present generation.
13:2 *from their own inspiration.* Cf. Jer 23:21–22.
13:3 *have seen nothing.* No revelation from God was received.
13:4 *foxes.* Animals that travel in packs and feed on dead flesh—a powerfully negative image (see Ps 63:10; Lam 5:18).
13:5 *You have not gone up.* The function of true prophets is described (cf. 22:30; Ps 106:23). *day of the LORD.* See note on 7:7.
13:6 *They see falsehood.* Whether the false prophets had actual visions is unknown, but they claimed to have received revelations from God when in reality their messages only proclaimed what their hearers wanted to hear (see Is 30:10; Jer 23:9–17; 2 Tim 4:3).
13:8 *I am against you.* See 5:8 and note.
13:9 *They will have no place.* Part of a threefold punishment, resulting in total exclusion from the community.
13:10 *'Peace!' when there is no peace.* See v. 16; Jer 6:14; 8:11. *whitewash.* The Hebrew for this word is used only by Ezekiel (see 22:28). A similar-sounding Hebrew word means "unsatisfying things," and Ezekiel may have chosen the word he did because of its similarity to the other one.
13:11 *flooding rain will come.* The violent thunderstorm of God's judgment (imagery frequently used in the OT) was about to sweep them away (see, e.g., Ps 18:7–15; 77:17–18; 83:15; Is 28:17; 30:30; Jer 23:19; 30:23).
13:18 *magic bands.* Exactly what the women were doing is not known, but that it was some kind of black magic or voodoo is clear. The Bible consistently avoids explicit description of occult practices.
13:19 *For handfuls of barley.* Involvement in religious matters

and to [b]keep [1]others alive who should not live, by your lying to My people who listen to lies." ' "

20 Therefore, thus says the Lord GOD, "Behold, I am against your *magic* bands by which you hunt [1]lives there as [2]birds and I will tear them from your arms; and I will let [1]them go, even those [1]lives whom you hunt as [2]birds.

21 "I will also tear off your veils and [a]deliver My people from your hands, and they will no longer be in your hands to be hunted; and you will know that I am the LORD.

22 "Because you [a]disheartened the righteous with falsehood when I did not cause him grief, but have [1b]encouraged the wicked not to [c]turn from his wicked way *and* preserve his life,

23 therefore, you women will no longer see [1a]false visions or practice divination, and I will [b]deliver My people out of your hand. Thus you will [c]know that I am the LORD."

Idolatrous Elders Condemned

14 Then some [a]elders of Israel came to me and [b]sat down before me.

2 And the word of the LORD came to me, saying,

3 "Son of man, these men have [a]set up their idols in their hearts and have [b]put right before their faces the stumbling block of their iniquity. Should I be [c]consulted by them at all?

4 "Therefore speak to them and tell them, 'Thus says the Lord [1]GOD, "Any man of the house of Israel who sets up his idols in his heart, puts right before his face the stumbling block of his iniquity, and *then* comes to the prophet, I the LORD will be brought to give him an answer in [2]the matter in view of the [a]multitude of his idols,

5 in order to lay hold of [1a]the hearts of the house of Israel who are [2b]estranged from Me through all their idols." '

6 "Therefore say to the house of Israel, 'Thus says the Lord GOD, "[a]Repent and turn away from your idols and turn your faces away from all your [b]abominations.

7 "For anyone of the house of Israel or of the [a]immigrants who stay in Israel who separates himself from Me, sets up his idols in his heart, puts right before his face the stumbling block of his iniquity, and *then* comes to the prophet to inquire of Me for himself, [b]I the LORD will be brought to answer him in My own person.

8 "I will [a]set My face against that man and make him a [b]sign and [1]a proverb, and I will cut him off from among My people. So you will know that I am the LORD.

9 "But if the prophet is [1]prevailed upon to speak a word, it is I, the LORD, who have [1]prevailed upon that prophet, and I will stretch out My hand against him and [a]destroy him from among My people Israel.

10 "They will bear *the punishment of* their iniquity; as the iniquity of the inquirer is, so the iniquity of the prophet will be,

11 in order that the house of Israel may no longer [a]stray from Me and no longer [b]defile themselves with all their transgressions. Thus they will be [c]My people, and I shall be their God," ' declares the Lord GOD."

The City Will Not Be Spared

12 Then the word of the LORD came to me saying,

13 "Son of man, if a country sins against Me by [a]committing unfaithfulness, and I stretch out My hand against it, [1]destroy its [b]supply of bread, send famine against it and cut off from it both man and beast,

14 even [a]*though* these three men, [b]Noah, [c]Daniel and [d]Job were in its midst, by their *own* righteousness they could *only* deliver [e]themselves," declares the Lord GOD.

15 "If I were to cause [a]wild beasts to pass through the land and they [1]depopulated it, and it became desolate so that no one would pass through it because of the beasts,

16 *though* these three men were in its midst, as I live," declares the Lord GOD, "they could not deliver either *their* sons or *their* daughters. [a]They alone would be delivered, but the country would be desolate.

17 "Or *if* I should [a]bring a sword on that country and say, 'Let the sword pass through

19 [1]Or *souls* [b]Jer 23:14, 17
20 [1]Lit *souls* [2]Or *flying ones*
21 [a]Ps 91:3; 124:7
22 [1]Lit *strengthen the hands of* [a]Amos 5:12 [b]Jer 23:14; 34:16, 22 [c]Ezek 18:21, 27, 30-32; 33:14-16
23 [1]Lit *vanity* [a]Ezek 12:24; 13:6; Mic 3:6; Zech 13:3 [b]Ezek 13:21; 34:10 [c]Ezek 13:9, 21
14:1 [a]2 Kin 6:32; Ezek 8:1; 20:1 [b]Is 29:13; Ezek 33:31, 32
3 [a]Ezek 20:16 [b]Ezek 7:19; 14:4, 7; Zeph 1:3 [c]Is 1:15; Jer 11:11; Ezek 20:3, 31
4 [1]Heb *YHWH*, usually rendered LORD, and so throughout the ch [2]Lit *it* [a]1 Kin 21:20-24; 2 Kin 1:16; Is 66:4
5 [1]Lit *their* [2]Or *all estranged from Me through their idols* [a]Jer 17:10; Zech 7:12 [b]Is 1:4; Jer 2:11; Zech 11:8
6 [a]1 Sam 7:3; Neh 1:9; Is 2:20; 30:22; 55:6, 7; Ezek 18:30 [b]Ezek 8:6; 14:4
7 [a]Ex 12:48; 20:10
7 [b]Ezek 14:4
8 [1]Lit *proverbs* [a]Jer 44:11; Ezek 15:7 [b]Is 65:15; Ezek 5:15
9 [1]Or *enticed* [a]Jer 6:14, 15; 14:15
11 [a]Ezek 44:10, 15; 48:11 [b]Ezek 11:18; 37:23 [c]Ezek 11:20; 34:30; 36:28
13 [1]Lit *break the staff* [a]Ezek 15:8; 20:27 [b]Lev 26:26; Is 3:1; Ezek 4:16
14 [a]Jer 15:1 [b]Gen 6:8; 7:1; Heb 11:7 [c]Ezek 28:3; Dan 1:6; 9:21; 10:11 [d]Job 1:1, 5; 42:8, 9 [e]Ezek 16:18, 20; 18:20
15 [1]Lit *bereave of children* [a]Lev 26:22; Num 21:6; Ezek 5:17; 14:21
16 [a]Gen 19:29; Ezek 18:20
17 [a]Lev 26:25; Ezek 5:12; 21:3, 4

of any kind for mere gain is consistently condemned in the Bible (see, e.g., Jer 6:13; 8:10; Mic 3:5,11; Acts 8:9–24; Titus 1:11). For the proper attitude and motivation see 2 Cor 11:7; 2 Thess 3:8; 1 Tim 3:3. *you have . . . put to death.* The women had used their evil powers to unjust ends, involving even matters of life and death.

14:1 *elders of Israel.* Apparently interchangeable with "elders of Judah" (see note on 8:1).

14:3 *idols.* See note on 6:4. *be consulted.* A technical term for seeking an oracle from a prophet (see 2 Kin 1:16; 3:11; 8:8).

14:4 *I the LORD will . . . give him an answer.* The punishment for idolatry was death (Deut 13:6–18).

14:6 *Repent.* First of three calls for repentance from Ezekiel, who elsewhere proclaims inescapable judgment (see 18:30; 33:11, "turn back").

14:9 *prevailed upon.* Related to the divine hardening (3:20; cf. 1 Kin 22:19–23).

14:14,20 *Noah, Daniel and Job.* Three ancient men of renown, selected because of their proverbial righteousness. Because the Hebrew here spells "Danel" instead of "Daniel," another Daniel may be referred to (Ugaritic literature speaks of an honored "Danel"; see chart, p. xix), since the Biblical Daniel's righteousness probably had not become proverbial so soon (Daniel and Ezekiel were contemporaries; see Dan 1:1). If the Biblical Daniel is meant, what he shared in common with Noah and Job was not only righteousness but also deliverance (part of Ezekiel's emphasis).

the country and [b]cut off man and beast from
it,'
18 even *though* these three men were in
its midst, as I live," declares the Lord GOD,
"they could not deliver either *their* sons or
their daughters, but they alone would be
delivered.
19 "Or *if* I should send a [a]plague against
that country and pour out My wrath in blood
on it to cut off man and beast from it,
20 even *though* Noah, Daniel and Job
were in its midst, as I live," declares the Lord
GOD, "they could not deliver either *their* son
or *their* daughter. They would deliver only
themselves by their righteousness."
21 For thus says the Lord GOD, "How
much more when [a]I send My four [1]severe
judgments against Jerusalem: sword, famine,
wild beasts and plague to cut off man and
beast from it!
22 "Yet, behold, [1]survivors will be left in it
who will be brought out, *both* sons and
daughters. Behold, they are going to come
forth to you and you will [a]see their conduct
and actions; then you will be [b]comforted for
the calamity which I have brought against
Jerusalem for everything which I have
brought upon it.
23 "Then they will comfort you when you
see their conduct and actions, for you will
know that I have not done [a]in vain whatever I did [1]to it," declares the Lord GOD.

Jerusalem like a Useless Vine

15 Then the word of the LORD came to me,
saying,
2 "Son of man, how is the wood of the
[a]vine *better* than any wood of a branch
which is among the trees of the forest?
3 "Can wood be taken from it to make
[1]anything, or can *men* take a peg from it on
which to hang any vessel?
4 "[1]If it has been put into the [a]fire for fuel,
and the fire has consumed both of its ends
and its middle part has been charred, is it
then useful for [2]anything?
5 "Behold, while it is intact, it is not made
into [1]anything. How much less, when the
fire has consumed it and it is charred, can it
still be made into [1]anything!
6 "Therefore, thus says the Lord [1]GOD, 'As
the wood of the vine among the trees of the
forest, which I have given to the fire for fuel,
so have I given up the inhabitants of Jerusalem;
7 and I [a]set My face against them.
Though they have [b]come out of the fire, yet
the fire will consume them. Then you will
know that I am the LORD, when I set My face
against them.
8 'Thus I will make the land desolate,
because they have [a]acted unfaithfully,'"
declares the Lord GOD.

God's Grace to Unfaithful Jerusalem

16 Then the word of the LORD came to me,
saying,
2 "Son of man, [a]make known to Jerusalem her abominations
3 and say, 'Thus says the Lord [1]GOD to
Jerusalem, "Your origin and your birth are
from the land of the Canaanite, your father
was an Amorite and your mother a Hittite.
4 "As for your birth, [a]on the day you were
born your navel cord was not cut, nor were
you washed with water for cleansing; you
were not rubbed with salt or even wrapped
in cloths.
5 "No eye looked with pity on you to do
any of these things for you, to have compassion on you. Rather you were thrown out
into the [1a]open field, [2]for you were abhorred
on the day you were born.
6 "When I passed by you and saw you

17 [b]Ezek 25:13; Zeph 1:3
19 [a]Jer 14:12; Ezek 5:12; 14:21
21 [1]Lit *evil* [a]Ezek 5:17; 33:27; Amos 4:6-10; Rev 6:8
22 [1]Lit *escaped ones* [a]Ezek 12:16; 36:20 [b]Ezek 16:54; 31:16; 32:31
23 [1]Or *in* [a]Jer 22:8, 9
15:2 [a]Ps 80:8-16; Is 5:1-7; Hos 10:1
3 [1]Lit *a work*
4 [1]Or *Behold* [2]Lit *a work* [a]Is 27:11; Ezek 15:6; 19:14
5 [1]Lit *a work*
6 [1]Heb *YHWH*, usually rendered LORD, and so throughout the ch
7 [a]Lev 26:17; Ps 34:16; Jer 21:10; Ezek 14:8 [b]1 Kin 19:17; Is 24:18; Amos 9:1-4
8 [a]Ezek 14:13; 17:20
16:2 [a]Is 58:1; Ezek 20:4; 22:2
3 [1]Heb *YHWH*, usually rendered LORD, and so throughout the ch
4 [a]Hos 2:3
5 [1]Lit *surface* [2]Lit *in the loathing of your soul* [a]Deut 32:10

14:20 *not . . . their son or their daughter.* When God comes in judgment against a nation or people, no one can count on another's righteousness—not even that of his parents—to deliver him.

14:21 *My four severe judgments.* See note on 1:5. *sword, famine, wild beasts and plague.* Cf. the "four horsemen of the Apocalypse" (see Rev 6:1–8, and especially Rev 6:8).

14:23 *will comfort you.* When the exiles see the wickedness of those brought to Babylon from Jerusalem, they will know that God's judgment on the city was just. *you.* Plural; i.e., the exiles in Babylon.

15:2 *vine.* For Israel as a vine see Ps 80:8–13; cf. Luke 20:9–19; John 15:1–17.

15:3 *can men take a peg . . . to hang any vessel?* See Is 22:23–25.

15:4 *is it then useful for anything?* Whereas Isaiah (5:1–7) and Jeremiah (2:21) express divine disappointment over Israel's failure to produce good fruit, Ezekiel typically laments her total uselessness.

15:7 *Though they have come out of the fire.* A reference to the siege of Jerusalem in 597 B.C., which resulted in the exile of which Ezekiel was a part (see 1:2; 2 Kin 24:10–16). *fire will consume them.* Prophecy threatening another and more devastating siege—Ezekiel's main message before 586 (see 5:2,4; 10:2,7).

16:3 Cf. Deut 26:5. *Your origin and your birth.* Jerusalem had a centuries-old, pre-Israelite history (Gen 14:18), and the city long resisted Israelite conquest (Josh 15:63). It became fully Israelite only after David's conquest (2 Sam 5:6–9). *father . . . mother.* A reference to Jerusalem's non-Israelite origin generally, not to any specific individuals. *Amorite.* Cf. v. 45. Like the Canaanites, the Amorites were pre-Israelite, Semitic inhabitants of Canaan (Gen 48:22; Josh 5:1; 10:5; Judg 1:34–36). *Hittite.* The Hittites were non-Semitic residents of Canaan, who earlier had flourished in Asia Minor during the second millennium B.C. (see Gen 23:10–20; 26:34; 1 Sam 26:6; 2 Sam 11:2–27; 1 Kin 11:1).

16:4 *rubbed with salt.* This practice has been observed among Arab peasants in the Holy Land as late as A.D. 1918. *wrapped in cloths.* Cf. Luke 2:7.

16:5 *thrown out into the open field.* Abandoned to die. Exposure of infants, common in ancient pagan societies, was abhorrent to Israel.

squirming in your blood, I said to you *while*
you were in your blood, 'Live!' Yes, I said to
you *while you were* in your blood, 'Live!'
7 "I [a]made you [1]numerous like plants of
the field. Then you grew up, became tall and
reached the age for fine ornaments; *your*
breasts were formed and your hair had
grown. Yet you were naked and bare.
8 "Then I passed by you and saw you, and
behold, [1]you were at the time for love; so I
[a]spread My skirt over you and covered your
nakedness. I also [b]swore to you and [c]entered
into a covenant with you so that you
[d]became Mine," declares the Lord GOD.
9 "Then I bathed you with water, washed
off your blood from you and [a]anointed you
with oil.
10 "I also clothed you with [a]embroidered
cloth and put sandals of porpoise skin on
your feet; and I wrapped you with fine linen
and covered you with silk.
11 "I adorned you with ornaments, put
[a]bracelets on your hands and a [b]necklace
around your neck.
12 "I also put a [a]ring in your nostril, earrings in your ears and a [b]beautiful crown on
your head.
13 "Thus you were adorned with [a]gold and
silver, and your dress was of fine linen, silk
and embroidered cloth. You ate fine flour,
honey and oil; so you were exceedingly
beautiful and advanced to [b]royalty.
14 "Then your [a]fame went forth among the
nations on account of your beauty, for it was
[b]perfect because of My splendor which I
bestowed on you," declares the Lord GOD.
15 "But you [a]trusted in your beauty and
[b]played the harlot because of your fame, and
you poured out your harlotries on every
passer-by [1]who might be *willing*.
16 "You took some of your clothes, made
for yourself high places of various colors and
played the harlot on them, [1]which should
never come about nor happen.
17 "You also took your beautiful [1a]jewels
made of My gold and of My silver, which I
had given you, and made for yourself male
images that you might play the harlot with
them.
18 "Then you took your embroidered cloth
and covered them, and offered My oil and
My incense before them.
19 "Also [a]My bread which I gave you, fine
flour, oil and honey with which I fed you, [1]you
would offer before them for a soothing aroma;
so it happened," declares the Lord GOD.
20 "Moreover, you took your sons and
daughters whom you had borne to [a]Me and
[b]sacrificed them to [1]idols to be devoured.
Were your harlotries so small a matter?
21 "You slaughtered [a]My children and
offered them up to [1]idols by [b]causing them
to pass through *the fire*.
22 "Besides all your abominations and harlotries you did not remember the days of
[a]your youth, when you were naked and bare
and squirming in your blood.
23 "Then it came about after all your
wickedness ('Woe, woe to you!' declares the
Lord GOD),
24 that you built yourself a [a]shrine and
made yourself a [b]high place in every square.
25 "You built yourself a high place at the
top of [a]every street and made your beauty
abominable, and you spread your legs to
every passer-by to multiply your harlotry.
26 "You also played the harlot with the
Egyptians, your [1]lustful neighbors, and multiplied your harlotry to [a]make Me angry.

7 [1]Lit *a myriad* [a]Ex 1:7; Deut 1:10
8 [1]Lit *your time was* [a]Ruth 3:9; Jer 2:2 [b]Gen 22:16-18 [c]Ex 24:7, 8 [d]Ex 19:5; Ezek 20:5; Hos 2:19, 20
9 [a]Ruth 3:3
10 [a]Ex 26:36; Ezek 16:13, 18; 26:16; 27:7, 16
11 [a]Gen 24:22, 47; Is 3:19; Ezek 23:42 [b]Gen 41:42; Prov 1:9
12 [a]Gen 24:47; Is 3:21 [b]Is 28:5; Jer 13:18; Ezek 16:14
13 [a]Ps 45:13, 14; Ezek 16:17 [b]1 Sam 10:1; 1 Kin 4:21
14 [a]1 Kin 10:1, 24 [b]Ps 50:2; Lam 2:15
15 [1]Lit *to whom it might be* [a]Ezek 16:25; 27:3 [b]Is 57:8; Jer 2:20
16 [1]Lit *things which had not happened nor will it be*
17 [1]Lit *articles of beauty* [a]Ezek 16:11, 12
19 [1]Lit *and you...offer it* [a]Hos 2:8
20 [1]Lit *them* [a]Ex 13:2, 12; Deut 29:11, 12 [b]Ps 106:37, 38; Jer 7:31; Ezek 20:31; 23:37
21 [1]Lit *them* [a]Ex 13:2 [b]2 Kin 17:17; Jer 19:5
22 [a]Jer 2:2
24 [a]Jer 11:13; Ezek 16:31, 39; 20:28, 29 [b]Ps 78:58; Is 57:7
25 [a]Prov 9:14
26 [1]Lit *great of flesh* [a]Jer 7:18, 19; Ezek 8:17

16:6 *blood.* Of childbirth. *Live!* God's basic desire for all people, summed up in one word (see 18:23,32; 1 Tim 2:4; 2 Pet 3:9).
16:7 *hair.* Pubic hair (see Is 7:20).
16:8 *spread My skirt.* Symbolic of entering a marriage relationship (see notes on Deut 22:30; Ruth 3:9). *covenant.* Since the maiden symbolizes Jerusalem, this does not refer to the Sinai covenant but to marriage as a covenant (see Mal 2:14).
16:9 *blood.* Menstrual blood, indicating sexual maturity.
16:10 *embroidered cloth . . . sandals of porpoise skin . . . fine linen.* Representative of the very best garments. *embroidered cloth.* See 27:16,24; colored, variegated material fit for a queen (see Ps 45:14). *sandals of porpoise skin.* The same kind of leather was used to cover the tabernacle ("porpoise skins," Ex 25:5; 26:14).
16:11 *bracelets on your hands.* See Gen 24:22.
16:12 *ring.* Not piercing the nose but worn on the outer part of the nose (see Gen 24:47). *earrings.* Circular ear ornaments, worn by men (Num 31:50). The Hebrew for this word is not the same as that used in Gen 35:4; Ex 32:2–3. *crown.* The wedding crown (see Song 3:11, where the groom wears it).
16:13 *gold and silver.* Cf. Hos 2:8. *fine flour.* Used in offerings, therefore of high quality (see v. 19; 46:14). *oil.* Cf. Hos 2:8. For the combination of honey and oil see Deut 32:13. *you were exceedingly beautiful.* Cf. Eph 5:27.
16:14 *your fame went forth.* Especially in the time of David and Solomon.
16:15 *harlot.* The accusation of prostitution referred both to spiritual turning away from the Lord and to physical involvement with the fertility rites of Canaanite paganism (cf. Jer 3:1–5; Hos 4:13–14; 9:1). *harlotries.* Sexual favors. Verb and noun forms of the Hebrew for this word occur 23 times in this chapter. *every passer-by.* Cf. Gen 38:14–16.
16:16 *clothes.* All of the Lord's previous gifts were used by Jerusalem in prostituting herself. Cloths of some kind were needed in the Asherah cult practices (see 2 Kin 23:7). They may have been used as curtains or as bedding (see Amos 2:7–8).
16:17 *male images.* Phallic symbols or pictures of naked men (see 23:14).
16:20 *sons and daughters . . . sacrificed.* See 20:26,31; 23:37; 2 Kin 21:6; 23:10; Jer 7:31; 19:5; 32:35. Laws against child sacrifice are recorded in Lev 18:21; 20:2; Deut 12:31; 18:10.
16:24 *shrine . . . high place.* Cultic prostitution was moved from the high places (v. 15), which were outside the towns, into Jerusalem.
16:26 *lustful.* The Hebrew is more graphic: "having oversized organs." The language reflects both God's and Ezekiel's disgust with Jerusalem's apostasy. *neighbors.* Nowhere else in the OT are the Egyptians called "neighbors."

27 "Behold now, I have stretched out My hand against you and diminished your rations. And I delivered you up to the desire of those who hate you, the [a]daughters of the Philistines, who are ashamed of your lewd conduct.

28 "Moreover, you played the harlot with the [a]Assyrians because you were not satisfied; you played the harlot with them and still were not satisfied.

29 "You also multiplied your harlotry with the land of merchants, Chaldea, yet even with this you were not satisfied." ' "

30 "How [a]languishing is your heart," declares the Lord GOD, "while you do all these things, the actions of a [1][b]bold-faced harlot.

31 "When you built your shrine at the beginning of every street and made your high place in every square, in [a]disdaining money, you were not like a harlot.

32 "You adulteress wife, who takes strangers instead of her husband!

33 "[1]Men give gifts to all harlots, but you [a]give your gifts to all your lovers to bribe them to come to you from every direction for your harlotries.

34 "Thus you are different from those women in your harlotries, in that no one plays the harlot [1]as you do, because you give money and no money is given you; thus you are different."

35 Therefore, O harlot, hear the word of the LORD.

36 Thus says the Lord GOD, "Because your lewdness was poured out and your nakedness uncovered through your harlotries with your lovers and with all your detestable [a]idols, and because of the blood of your sons which you gave to [1]idols,

37 therefore, behold, I will [a]gather all your lovers with whom you took pleasure, even all those whom you loved *and* all those whom you [b]hated. So I will gather them against you from every direction and [c]expose your nakedness to them that they may see all your nakedness.

38 "Thus I will [a]judge you like women who commit adultery or shed blood are judged; and I will bring on you the blood of [b]wrath and jealousy.

39 "I will also give you into [1]the hands of your lovers, and they will tear down your shrines, demolish your high places, [a]strip you of your clothing, take away your [2]jewels, and will leave you naked and bare.

40 "They will [1]incite a [a]crowd against you and they will stone you and cut you to pieces with their swords.

41 "They will [a]burn your houses with fire and execute judgments on you in the sight of many women. Then I will [b]stop you from playing the harlot, and you will also no longer pay [1]your lovers.

42 "So I [a]will calm My fury against you and My jealousy will depart from you, and I will be pacified and angry [b]no more.

43 "Because you have [a]not remembered the days of your youth but [1]have [b]enraged Me by all these things, behold, I in turn will [c]bring your conduct down on your own head," declares the Lord GOD, "so that you will not commit this lewdness on top of all your *other* abominations.

44 "Behold, everyone who quotes [a]proverbs will quote *this* proverb concerning you, saying, '[1]Like mother, [1]like daughter.'

45 "You are the daughter of your mother, who loathed her husband and children. You are also the [a]sister of your sisters, who [b]loathed their husbands and children. Your mother was a Hittite and your father an Amorite.

46 "Now your [a]older sister is Samaria, who lives [1]north of you with her [2]daughters; and your younger sister, who lives [3]south of you, is [b]Sodom with her [2]daughters.

47 "Yet you have not merely walked in their ways or done according to their abominations; but, as if that were [a]too little, you acted [b]more corruptly in all your conduct than they.

48 "As I live," declares the Lord GOD, "Sodom, your sister and her daughters have [a]not done as you and your daughters have done.

49 "Behold, this was the guilt of your sister Sodom: she and her daughters had [a]arrogance, [b]abundant food and [c]careless ease, but she did not [1]help the [d]poor and needy.

50 "Thus they were haughty and committed [a]abominations before Me. Therefore I [b]removed them [1]when I saw *it*.

27 [a]Is 9:12; Ezek 16:57 **28** [a]2 Kin 16:7, 10-18; 2 Chr 28:16, 20-23; Jer 2:18, 36; Ezek 23:12; Hos 10:6 **30** [1]Lit *domineering* [a]Prov 9:13; Is 1:3; Jer 4:22 [b]Is 3:9; Jer 3:3 **31** [a]Is 52:3 **33** [1]Lit *They* [a]Is 57:9; Ezek 16:41; Hos 8:9, 10 **34** [1]Lit *after you* **36** [1]Lit *them* [a]Jer 19:5; Ezek 20:31; 23:37 **37** [a]Jer 13:22, 26; Ezek 23:9, 22; Hos 2:3, 10; Nah 3:5, 6 [b]Ezek 23:17, 28 [c]Is 47:3 **38** [a]Ezek 23:45 [b]Ps 79:3, 5; Jer 18:21; Ezek 23:25; Zeph 1:17 **39** [1]Lit *their hands, and they* [a]Ezek 23:26; Hos 2:3

39 [2]Lit *articles of beauty* **40** [1]Lit *bring up an assembly* [a]Ezek 23:47; Hab 1:6-10 **41** [1]Lit *a harlot's hire* [a]2 Kin 25:9; Jer 39:8; 52:13 [b]Ezek 23:48 **42** [a]2 Sam 24:25; Ezek 5:13; 21:17; Zech 6:8 [b]Is 40:1, 2; 54:9, 10; Ezek 39:29 **43** [1]So with ancient versions; Heb *are angry against* [a]Ps 78:42; 106:13; Ezek 16:22 [b]Is 63:10; Ezek 6:9 [c]Ezek 11:21; 22:31 **44** [1]Lit *Her* [a]1 Sam 24:13; Ezek 12:22, 23; 18:2, 3 **45** [a]Ezek 23:2 [b]Is 1:4; Ezek 23:37-39; Zech 11:8 **46** [1]Lit *on your left* [2]I.e. environs; so through v 55 [3]Lit *from your right* [a]Jer 3:8-11; Ezek 23:4 [b]Gen 13:10-13; 18:20; Ezek 16:48, 49, 53-56, 61 **47** [a]1 Kin 16:31 [b]2 Kin 21:9; Ezek 5:6; 16:48, 51 **48** [a]Matt 10:15; 11:23, 24 **49** [1]Lit *grasp the hand of* [a]Gen 19:9; Ps 138:6; Is 3:9; Ezek 28:2, 9, 17 [b]Gen 13:10; Is 22:13; Amos 6:4-6 [c]Luke 12:16-20; 16:19 [d]Ezek 18:7, 12, 16 **50** [1]Many ancient mss and versions read *as you have seen* [a]Gen 13:13; 18:20; 19:5 [b]Gen 19:24, 25

16:33 *you give your gifts to all your lovers.* Jerusalem's perversity is here pictured as worse than adultery and ordinary prostitution (see also v. 34).

16:37 *expose your nakedness.* A reversal of the marriage covering (v. 8) and a return to the state described in v. 7.

16:38 *judge you.* The punishment was death (see Lev 20:10; Deut 22:22) by stoning (see v. 40; Deut 22:21–24; John 8:5–7) or burning (Gen 38:24).

16:39 *your shrines . . . your high places.* The cultic centers within the city (see v. 24).

16:40 *crowd . . . will stone you.* Cf. 23:47.

16:41 *burn your houses.* A common form of punishment (see Judg 12:1; 15:6). *no longer pay your lovers.* See v. 33.

16:44 *Like mother, like daughter.* Referring to Jerusalem's continual and seemingly hereditary tendency toward evil (cf. vv. 3,45).

16:46 *daughters.* Suburbs or satellite cities.

16:47 *more corruptly . . . than they.* The Bible frequently compares a city or people to Sodom (see v. 46) as the epitome of evil and degradation (see Deut 29:23; 32:32; Is 1:9–10; 3:9; Jer 23:14; Lam 4:6; Matt 10:15; 11:23–24; Jude 7).

16:49 *guilt of your sister Sodom.* Here social injustice rather than sexual perversion (Gen 19) is highlighted.

51 "Furthermore, Samaria did not commit
half of your sins, for you have multiplied
your abominations more than they. Thus you
have made your sisters appear [a]righteous by
all your abominations which you have committed.
52 "Also bear your disgrace in that you
have [1]made judgment favorable for your sisters. Because of your sins in which you acted [a]more abominably than they, they are
more in the right than you. Yes, be also
ashamed and bear your disgrace, in that you
made your sisters appear righteous.
53 "Nevertheless, I will restore their captivity, the captivity of Sodom and her daughters, the captivity of Samaria and her daughters, and [1]along with them [2]your own
captivity,
54 in order that you may bear your humiliation and feel [a]ashamed for all that you
have done when you become [b]a consolation
to them.
55 "Your sisters, Sodom with her daughters
and Samaria with her daughters, [1]will return
to their former state, and you with your
daughters will *also* return to your former
state.
56 "As *the name of* your sister Sodom was
not heard from your lips in your day of pride,
57 before your [a]wickedness was uncovered, [1]so now you have become the
[b]reproach of the daughters of [2]Edom and of
all who are around her, of the daughters of
the Philistines—those surrounding *you* who
despise you.
58 "You have [a]borne *the penalty of* your
lewdness and abominations," the LORD
declares.
59 For thus says the Lord GOD, "I will also
do with you as you have done, you who have
[a]despised the oath by breaking the covenant.

The Covenant Remembered

60 "Nevertheless, I will remember My covenant with you in the days of your youth,
and I will establish an [a]everlasting covenant
with you.
61 "Then you will [a]remember your ways
and be ashamed when you receive your sisters, *both* your older and your younger; and
I will give them to you as daughters, but not
because of your covenant.
62 "Thus I will [a]establish My covenant
with you, and you shall [b]know that I am the
LORD,
63 so that you may [a]remember and be
ashamed and [b]never open your mouth anymore because of your humiliation, when I
have [c]forgiven you for all that you have
done," the Lord GOD declares.

Parable of Two Eagles and a Vine

17 Now the word of the LORD came to me
saying,
2 "Son of man, propound a riddle and
speak a [a]parable to the house of Israel,
3 [1]saying, 'Thus says the Lord [2]GOD, "A
great [a]eagle with [b]great wings, long pinions
and a full plumage of many colors came to
[c]Lebanon and took away the top of the
cedar.
4 "He plucked off the topmost of its young
twigs and brought it to a land of merchants;
he set it in a city of traders.
5 "He also took some of the seed of the
land and planted it in [1][a]fertile soil. He
[2]placed *it* beside abundant waters; he set it
like a [b]willow.
6 "Then it sprouted and became a low,
spreading vine with its branches turned
toward him, but its roots remained under it.
So it became a vine and yielded shoots and
sent out branches.
7 "But there was [1]another great eagle with
great wings and much plumage; and behold,
this vine bent its roots toward him and sent
out its branches toward him from the beds
where it was [a]planted, that he might water
it.
8 "It was planted in good [1]soil beside
abundant waters, that it might yield
branches and bear fruit *and* become a splendid vine." '
9 "Say, 'Thus says the Lord GOD, "Will it
thrive? Will he not pull up its roots and cut
off its fruit, so that it withers—so that all its
sprouting leaves wither? And neither by
great [1]strength nor by many people can it be
raised from its roots *again*.
10 "Behold, though it is planted, will it

51 [a]Jer 3:8-11 **52** [1]Lit *mediated for* [a]Ezek 16:47, 48, 51 **53** [1]Lit *in their midst* [2]Lit *the captivity of your captivity* **54** [a]Jer 2:26 [b]Ezek 14:22, 23 **55** [1]Heb includes *will return...state* after Sodom also **57** [1]Lit *as at the time of* [2]So with many mss and one version; M.T. *Aram* [a]Ezek 16:36, 37 [b]2 Kin 16:5-7; 2 Chr 28:5, 6, 18-23; Ezek 5:14, 15; 22:4 **58** [a]Ezek 23:49 **59** [a]Is 24:5; Ezek 17:19 **60** [a]Is 55:3; Jer 32:38-41; Ezek 37:26 **61** [a]Jer 50:4, 5; Ezek 6:9

62 [a]Ezek 20:37; 34:25; 37:26 [b]Jer 24:7; Ezek 20:43, 44 **63** [a]Ezek 36:31, 32; Dan 9:7, 8 [b]Ps 39:9; Rom 3:19 [c]Ps 65:3; 78:38; 79:9 **17:2** [a]Ezek 20:49; 24:3 **3** [1]Lit *and you shall say* [2]Heb *YHWH*, usually rendered *LORD*, and so throughout the ch [a]Jer 48:40; Ezek 17:12; Hos 8:1 [b]Dan 4:22 [c]Jer 22:23 **5** [1]Lit *a field of seed* [2]Lit *took* [a]Deut 8:7-9 [b]Is 44:4 **7** [1]So with several ancient versions; M.T. *one* [a]Ezek 31:4 **8** [1]Lit *field* **9** [1]Lit *arm*

16:56 *your day of pride.* Referring to a time long before Ezekiel, when Jerusalem (as an Israelite city) was still relatively uncorrupted—as in the days of David and the early years of Solomon.
16:57 *reproach of the daughters of Edom.* The OT frequently condemns Edom for this (see 25:12–14; 35; Is 63:1; Obadiah).
16:59 *covenant.* See v. 8 and note.
16:60 *everlasting covenant.* See 37:26; Is 55:3; Jer 32:40.
17:2 *riddle . . . parable.* The riddle/parable is in vv. 3–10, the explanation in vv. 11–21.
17:3 *great eagle.* Nebuchadnezzar (see v. 12). *Lebanon.* Jerusalem (see v. 12). *cedar.* David's dynasty; his royal family.
17:4 *topmost of its young twigs.* Jehoiachin. *land of merchants.* The country of Babylonia (see v. 12; 16:29). *city of traders.* Babylon.
17:5 *seed.* Zedekiah son of Josiah; he was the brother of Jehoahaz and Jehoiakim and uncle of Jehoiachin (see 2 Kin 23–24). *planted it.* Made him king (2 Kin 24:17).
17:6 *low, spreading vine.* No longer a tall cedar, because thousands of Judah's leading citizens had been deported (see 2 Kin 24:15–16; see also Jer 52:28). But see note on 15:2.
17:7 *another great eagle.* An Egyptian pharaoh, either Psammetichus II (595–589 B.C.) or Hophra (589–570). Hophra, mentioned in Jer 44:30, is probably the pharaoh who offered help to Jerusalem in 586 (see Jer 37:5). If the fact that ch. 17 is located between ch. 8 (dated 592) and ch. 20 (dated 591) is chronologically meaningful, Psammetichus is meant. *bent its roots toward him.* Zedekiah appealed to Egypt for military aid (v. 15), an act of rebellion against Nebuchadnezzar (see 2 Kin 24:20).

thrive? Will it not [a]completely wither as soon
as the east wind strikes it—wither on the
beds where it grew?" ' "

Zedekiah's Rebellion

11 Moreover, the word of the LORD came
to me, saying,
12 "Say now to the [a]rebellious house, 'Do
you not [b]know what these things *mean?*'
Say, 'Behold, the [c]king of Babylon came to
Jerusalem, took its king and princes and
brought them to him in Babylon.
13 'He took one of the royal [1a]family and
made a covenant with him, [2]putting him
under [b]oath. He also took away the [c]mighty
of the land,
14 that the kingdom might [a]be [1]in subjection, not exalting itself, *but* keeping his covenant that it might continue.
15 'But he [a]rebelled against him by sending
his envoys to Egypt that they might give him
horses and many [1]troops. Will he succeed?
Will he who does such things [b]escape? Can
he indeed break the covenant and escape?
16 'As I live,' declares the Lord GOD, 'Surely in the [1]country of the king who [2]put him
on the throne, whose oath he [a]despised and
whose covenant he broke, [3b]in Babylon he
shall die.
17 '[a]Pharaoh with *his* mighty army and
great company will not [1]help him in the war,
when they cast up ramps and build siege
walls to cut off many lives.
18 'Now he despised the oath by breaking
the covenant, and behold, he [1a]pledged his
allegiance, yet did all these things; he shall
not escape.' "
19 Therefore, thus says the Lord GOD, "As
I live, surely My oath which he despised and
My covenant which he broke, I will [1]inflict
on his head.
20 "I will spread My [a]net over him, and he
will be [b]caught in My snare. Then I will
bring him to Babylon and [c]enter into judgment with him there *regarding* the unfaithful
act which he has committed against Me.
21 "All the [1a]choice men in all his troops
will fall by the sword, and the survivors will
be scattered to every wind; and you will
know that I, the LORD, have spoken."
22 Thus says the Lord GOD, "I will also
take *a sprig* from the lofty top of the cedar
and set *it* out; I will pluck from the topmost
of its young twigs a tender one and I will
plant *it* on a [a]high and lofty mountain.
23 "On the high mountain of Israel I will
plant it, that it may bring forth boughs and
bear fruit and become a stately [a]cedar. And
birds of every [1]kind will [2]nest under it; they
will [2]nest in the shade of its branches.
24 "All the [a]trees of the field will know that
I am the LORD; I bring down the high tree,
exalt the low tree, dry up the green tree and
make the dry tree [b]flourish. I am the LORD; I
have spoken, and I will perform *it.*"

God Deals Justly with Individuals

18 Then the word of the LORD came to me,
saying,
2 "[a]What do you mean by using this proverb concerning the land of Israel, saying,

> '[b]The fathers eat the sour grapes,
> But the children's teeth [1]are set on
> edge'?

3 "As I live," declares the Lord [1]GOD, "you
are surely not going to use this proverb in
Israel anymore.
4 "Behold, [a]all [1]souls are Mine; the [2]soul
of the father as well as the [2]soul of the son is
Mine. The [3]soul who [b]sins will die.
5 "But if a man is righteous and practices
justice and righteousness,
6 and does not [a]eat at the mountain
shrines or [b]lift up his eyes to the idols of the

10 [a]Ezek 19:14; Hos 13:15 **12** [a]Ezek 2:3-5 [b]Ezek 12:9-11; 24:19 [c]2 Kin 24:11, 12, 15; Ezek 1:2; 17:3 **13** [1]Lit *seed* [2]Lit *and caused him to enter into an oath* [a]2 Kin 24:17; Ezek 17:5 [b]2 Chr 36:13 [c]2 Kin 24:15, 16 **14** [1]Lit *low* [a]Ezek 29:14 **15** [1]Lit *people* [a]2 Kin 24:20; 2 Chr 36:13; Jer 52:3; Ezek 17:7 [b]Jer 34:3; 38:18, 23; Ezek 17:18 **16** [1]Lit *place* [2]Lit *made him king* [3]Lit *with him in Babylon* [a]2 Kin 24:17, 20; Ezek 16:59; 17:13, 18, 19 [b]Jer 52:11; Ezek 12:13 **17** [1]Lit *act with* [a]Is 36:6; Jer 37:5, 7; Ezek 29:6, 7 **18** [1]Lit *gave his hand* [a]1 Chr 29:24 **19** [1]Lit *give it* **20** [a]Ezek 12:13; 32:3 [b]Jer 39:5-7 [c]Jer 2:35; Ezek 20:35, 36

21 [1]So many ancient mss and versions; M.T. *fugitives* [a]2 Kin 25:5, 11; Ezek 5:2, 10, 12-14 **22** [a]Ps 72:16; Ezek 20:40; 37:22 **23** [1]Lit *wing* [2]Lit *dwell* [a]Ps 92:12 **24** [a]Ps 96:12; Is 55:12 [b]Amos 9:11 **18:2** [1]Lit *become dull* [a]Is 3:15 [b]Jer 31:29; Lam 5:7

3 [1]Heb *YHWH*, usually rendered LORD, and so throughout the ch **4** [1]Or *lives* [2]Or *life* [3]Or *person* [a]Num 16:22; 27:16; Is 42:5; 57:16 [b]Ezek 18:20; Rom 6:23 **6** [a]Ezek 6:13; 18:15; 22:9 [b]Deut 4:19; Ezek 18:12, 15; 20:24; 33:25

17:10 *east wind.* The hot, dry wind known as the khamsin, which withers vegetation (see 19:12). Here it stands for Nebuchadnezzar and his Babylonian forces.
17:12 *the rebellious house.* See 2:3 and note.
17:15 *Can he indeed break the covenant and escape?* The point of the chapter (see vv. 16,18).
17:16 *in Babylon he shall die.* See 2 Kin 25:7.
17:19 *My oath . . . My covenant.* The king of Judah would have sworn faithfulness to the treaty in the name of the Lord. To swear such an oath and then violate it was to despise God.
17:22 *I will.* A beautiful Messianic promise follows, using the previous imagery in a totally new and unexpected way. *sprig.* A member of David's family (cf. Is 11:1; Zech 3:8; 6:12). *cedar.* See note on v. 3. *plant it.* Make him king (see v. 5). *high and lofty mountain.* Jerusalem.
17:23 *birds . . . will nest under it.* See Mark 4:32.
18:2 *this proverb.* Cf. Jer 31:29, which indicates that the proverb arose first in Jerusalem. Jeremiah predicted the cessation of the proverb, and Ezekiel said its end had come. *concerning the land of Israel.* And about the fate of those who have suffered loss. *The fathers . . . on edge.* The proverb, though it expresses self-pity, fatalism and despair, and though it mocks the justice of God, had its origin in Israelite belief in corporate solidarity (see Ex 20:5; 34:7 and Ezekiel's own words in chs. 16; 23). In Lam 5:7 the thought appears as a sincere confession. *set on edge.* The Hebrew for this phrase perhaps means "blunted" or "worn" (cf. Eccl 10:10), but it may refer to the sensation in the mouth when eating something bitter or sour.
18:3 *As I live.* A divine oath, revealing God's unalterable intention. It is used often in Ezekiel (5:11; 14:16,18,20; 16:48; 17:16,19; 20:3,31,33; 33:11,27; 34:8; 35:6,11).
18:4 *The soul who sins will die.* Or "Only the soul . . ." Ezekiel spoke out against a false use the people were making of a doctrine of inherited guilt (perhaps based on a false understanding of Ex 20:5; 34:7). What follows is his description of three men, standing for three generations, who break the three/four-generation pattern. *soul.* "Life" or "person," not used here to distinguish spirit from body.
18:5 *man is righteous.* The first generation that keeps the law. The following 15 commandments are partly ceremonial but are mostly moral injunctions. See the Ten Commandments in Ex 20 and Deut 5; cf. Ps 15:2–5; 24:3–6; Is 33:15.

house of Israel, or [c]defile his neighbor's wife
or approach a woman during her menstrual
period—
7 if a man does not oppress anyone, but
[a]restores to the debtor his pledge, [b]does not
commit robbery, *but* [c]gives his bread to the
hungry and covers the naked with clothing,
8 if he does not lend *money* on [a]interest
or take [b]increase, *if* he keeps his hand from
iniquity *and* [c]executes true justice between
man and man,
9 *if* he walks in [a]My statutes and My
ordinances so as to deal faithfully—[b]he is
righteous *and* will surely [c]live," declares the
Lord GOD.
10 "Then he may [1]have a violent son who
sheds blood and who does any of these
things to a brother
11 (though he himself did not do any of
these things), that is, he even eats at the
mountain *shrines*, and [a]defiles his neighbor's
wife,
12 oppresses the [a]poor and needy, [b]com-
mits robbery, does not restore a pledge, but
lifts up his eyes to the idols *and* [c]commits
abomination,
13 he [a]lends *money* on interest and takes
increase; will he live? He will not live! He
has committed all these abominations, he
will surely be put to death; his [b]blood will be
[1]on his own head.
14 "Now behold, he [1]has a son who has
observed all his father's sins which he committed, and [a]observing does not do likewise.
15 "He does not eat at the mountain *shrines*
or lift up his eyes to the idols of the house of
Israel, or defile his neighbor's wife,
16 or oppress anyone, or retain a pledge, or
commit robbery, *but* he [a]gives his bread to the
hungry and covers the naked with clothing,
17 he keeps his hand from [1]the poor, does
not take interest or increase, *but* executes My
ordinances, and walks in My statutes; [a]he
will not die for his father's iniquity, he will
surely live.

6 [c]Ezek 18:15; 22:11
7 [a]Deut 24:13; Ezek 33:15; Amos 2:8 [b]Lev 19:13; Amos 3:10 [c]Deut 15:11; Ezek 18:16; Matt 25:35-40; Luke 3:11
8 [a]Ex 22:25; Deut 23:19, 20 [b]Lev 25:36 [c]Zech 7:9; 8:16
9 [a]Lev 18:5 [b]Rom 8:1 [c]Amos 5:4; Hab 2:4; Rom 1:17
10 [1]Lit *beget*
11 [a]1 Cor 6:9
12 [a]Amos 4:1; Zech 7:10 [b]Is 59:6, 7; Jer 22:3, 17; Ezek 7:23; 18:7, 16, 18 [c]2 Kin 21:11; Ezek 8:6, 17
13 [1]Lit *on him* [a]Ex 22:25 [b]Ezek 33:4, 5
14 [1]Lit *begets* [a]2 Chr 29:6-10; 34:21
16 [a]Job 31:16, 20; Ps 41:1; Is 58:7, 10; Ezek 18:7
17 [1]So M.T.; Gr reads *iniquity* as in v 8 [a]Rom 2:7
19 [a]Ex 20:5; Jer 15:4; Ezek 18:2 [b]Ezek 18:9; 20:18-20; Zech 1:3-6
20 [a]2 Kin 14:6; 22:18-20; Ezek 18:4 [b]Deut 24:16; Jer 31:30 [c]1 Kin 8:32; Is 3:10, 11; Matt 16:27; Rom 2:6-9
21 [a]Ezek 18:27, 28; 33:12, 19
22 [a]Is 43:25; Jer 50:20; Ezek 18:24; 33:16; Mic 7:19 [b]Ps 18:20-24
23 [1]Lit *is it not* [a]Ezek 18:32; 33:11 [b]Ps 147:11; Mic 7:18

18 "As for his father, because he practiced
extortion, robbed *his* brother and did what
was not good among his people, behold, he
will die for his iniquity.
19 "Yet you say, '[a]Why should the son not
bear the punishment for the father's iniquity?' When the son has practiced [b]justice and
righteousness and has observed all My statutes and done them, he shall surely live.
20 "The person who [a]sins will die. The
[b]son will not bear the punishment for the
father's iniquity, nor will the father bear
the punishment for the son's iniquity; the
[c]righteousness of the righteous will be upon
himself, and the wickedness of the wicked
will be upon himself.
21 "But if the [a]wicked man turns from all
his sins which he has committed and
observes all My statutes and practices justice
and righteousness, he shall surely live; he
shall not die.
22 "[a]All his transgressions which he has
committed will not be remembered against
him; because of his [b]righteousness which he
has practiced, he will live.
23 "[a]Do I have any pleasure in the death of
the wicked," declares the Lord GOD, "[1]rather
than that he should [b]turn from his ways and
live?
24 "But when a righteous man [a]turns away
from his righteousness, commits iniquity and
does according to all the abominations that a
wicked man does, will he live? [b]All his righteous deeds which he has done will not be
remembered for his [c]treachery which he has
committed and his sin which he has committed; for them he will die.
25 "Yet you say, '[a]The way of the Lord is
not right.' Hear now, O house of Israel! Is
[b]My way not right? Is it not your ways that
are not right?
26 "When a righteous man turns away

24 [a]1 Sam 15:11; 2 Chr 24:2, 17-22; Ezek 3:20; 18:26; 33:18 [b]Ezek 18:22; Gal 3:3, 4 [c]Prov 21:16; Ezek 17:20; 20:27
25 [a]Ezek 18:29; 33:17, 20; Mal 2:17; 3:13-15 [b]Gen 18:25; Jer 12:1; Zeph 3:5

18:6 *eat at the mountain shrines.* Eating meat sacrificed to idols on the high places (see 6:3; Hos 4:13). *lift up his eyes to.* Seek help from (see 23:27; 33:25; Ps 121:1). *idols.* See note on 6:4. *defile.* Adultery (condemned in Ex 20:14; Deut 22:22; Lev 18:20; 20:10) is here associated with a menstrual prohibition (see Lev 15:19–24; 18:19; 20:18), which is absent from the two listings that follow (cf. vv. 11,15).

18:7 *oppress.* The rich taking advantage of the poor. *restores to the debtor his pledge.* See Ex 22:26; Deut 24:12–13; Amos 2:8. *robbery.* See the commandment against stealing in Ex 20:15; Deut 5:19. This is violent ("armed") robbery rather than secret theft or burglary (see Lev 19:13). *bread to the hungry.* See Deut 15:7–11; Matt 25:31–46.

18:8 *lend . . . on interest.* See 22:12; Ps 15:5; Prov 28:8. What is forbidden in Ex 22:25; Lev 25:35–37; Deut 23:19 is interest on loans to the needy. Deut 23:20 allows an Israelite to "charge interest to a foreigner"; Ezekiel condemns usury. (Interest on modern commercial loans is a different matter.)

18:9 *he is righteous and will surely live.* After the checklist of commandments has been gone over, the verdict is rendered (cf. Ps 15:5; 24:5). *live.* See note on 16:6. This is life as more than mere existence; it includes communion with God (see Ps 63:3; 73:27–28).

18:10 *violent son.* Evil, second generation. About half (eight) of the previous commandments follow, but in a different order.

18:13 *his blood will be on his own head.* He is held responsible for his own sin (see Lev 20:9,11–12,16,27).

18:14 *a son.* Righteous, third generation. Twelve commandments follow.

18:21 *But if the wicked man turns . . . and observes . . . he shall surely live.* Verses 1–20 indicate that the chain of inherited guilt can be broken, and vv. 21–29 teach that the power of guilt accumulated within a person's life can be overcome.

18:24 *But when a righteous man turns.* See Heb 2:3; 2 Pet 2:20–22 for warnings against those who knowingly and willfully turn from righteousness.

18:26 *When a righteous man.* Verses 26–29 repeat the argument developed in vv. 21–25.

from his righteousness, commits iniquity and dies because of it, for his iniquity which he has committed he will die.

27 "Again, when a wicked man turns away [a]from his wickedness which he has committed and practices justice and righteousness, he will save his life.

28 "Because he considered and turned away from all his transgressions which he had committed, he shall surely live; he shall not die.

29 "But the house of Israel says, 'The way of the Lord is not right.' Are My ways not right, O house of Israel? Is it not your ways that are not right?

30 "Therefore I will judge you, O house of Israel, each according to his conduct," declares the Lord GOD. "[a]Repent and turn away from all your transgressions, so that iniquity may not become a stumbling block to you.

31 "[a]Cast away from you all your transgressions which you have committed and make yourselves a [b]new heart and a new spirit! For why will you die, O house of Israel?

32 "For I have [a]no pleasure in the death of anyone who dies," declares the Lord GOD. "Therefore, repent and live."

Lament for the Princes of Israel

19 "As for you, take up a [a]lamentation for the [b]princes of Israel
2 and say,
[1]What was your mother?
A lioness among lions!
She lay down among young lions,
She reared her cubs.
3 'When she brought up one of her cubs,
He became a lion,
And he learned to tear *his* prey;
He devoured men.
4 'Then nations heard about him;
He was captured in their pit,
And they [a]brought him with hooks
To the land of Egypt.
5 'When she saw, as she waited,
That her hope was lost,
She took [1]another of her cubs
And made him a young lion.
6 'And he [a]walked about among the lions;
He became a young lion,
He learned to tear *his* prey;
He devoured men.
7 'He [1]destroyed their [2]fortified towers
And laid waste their cities;
And the land and its fullness were appalled
Because of the sound of his roaring.
8 'Then [a]nations set against him
On every side from *their* provinces,
And they spread their net over him;
He was captured in their pit.
9 '[a]They put him in a cage with hooks
And [b]brought him to the king of Babylon;
They brought him in hunting nets
So that his voice would be heard no more
On the mountains of Israel.
10 'Your mother was [a]like a vine in your [1]vineyard,
Planted by the waters;
It was fruitful and full of branches
Because of abundant waters.
11 'And it had [1a]strong branches *fit* for scepters of rulers,
And its [b]height was raised above the clouds
So that it was seen in its height with the mass of its branches.
12 'But it was [a]plucked up in fury;
It was [b]cast down to the ground;
And the [c]east wind dried up its fruit.
Its [1d]strong branch [2]was torn off
So that [3]it withered;
The fire consumed it.
13 'And now it is planted in the [a]wilderness,
In a dry and thirsty land.
14 'And [a]fire has gone out from *its* branch;

27 [a]Is 1:18; 55:7 **30** [a]Ezek 14:6; 33:11; Hos 12:6 **31** [a]Is 1:16, 17; 55:7 [b]Ps 51:10; Ezek 11:19; 36:26 **32** [a]Ezek 18:23; 33:11 **19:1** [a]Ezek 2:10; 19:14 [b]2 Kin 23:29, 30, 34; 24:6, 12; 25:5-7 **2** [1]Or *Why did your mother, a lioness, lie down among lions; among young lions rear her cubs?* **4** [a]2 Kin 23:34; 2 Chr 36:4, 6

5 [1]Lit *one* **6** [a]2 Kin 24:9; 2 Chr 36:9 **7** [1]So Targum; M.T. *knew* [2]Or *widows* **8** [a]2 Kin 24:11 **9** [a]2 Chr 36:6 [b]2 Kin 24:15 **10** [1]So with some ancient mss; M.T. *blood* [a]Ps 80:8-11 **11** [1]Lit *rods of strength* [a]Ps 80:15 [b]Ezek 31:3 **12** [1]Lit *rods of her strength* [2]So Gr; M.T. *they were* [3]So Gr; M.T. *they* [a]Jer 31:28 [b]Lam 2:1; Ezek 28:17 [c]Ezek 17:10; Hos 13:15 [d]Is 27:11; Ezek 19:11 **13** [a]2 Kin 24:12-16; Ezek 19:10; 20:35; Hos 2:3 **14** [a]Ezek 15:4; 20:47, 48

18:30 *Therefore.* Concluding, summary oracle. *each.* While the house of Israel as a whole was guilty, God's judgment would be just and individual. *Repent.* Second call to repentance (see 14:6).
18:31 *make . . . a new heart.* What had been promised unconditionally (11:19; 36:26) is here portrayed as attainable but not inevitable (cf. the same tension between Phil 2:12 and 2:13).
18:32 *I have no pleasure.* Verse 23 is echoed in this final, grand summary, called by some the most important message in the whole book of Ezekiel (see note on 16:6).
19:1 *lamentation.* A metered (three beats plus two beats) chant usually composed for funerals of fallen leaders (as in 2 Sam 1:17–27), but often used sarcastically by the OT prophets to lament or to ironically predict the death of a nation (see Is 14:4–21; Amos 5:1–3). See also 2:10. *princes.* Kings.
19:2 *lioness.* Although a lament, this chapter is an allegory like that in ch. 17 (to which it is related in content). Ch. 17 gives an interpretation, but this one does not. The lioness may be a personification of Israel (see v. 1), Judah (see 4:6; 8:1,17; 9:9) or Jerusalem (see 5:5), all of which may be considered to be mother to the kings (see vv. 10–14).
19:3 *one of her cubs.* Jehoahaz (see 2 Kin 23:31–34; Jer 22:10–12), who reigned only three months. *devoured men.* A reference to his oppressive policies (see Jer 22:13).
19:5 *another of her cubs.* Perhaps Jehoiachin (who reigned only three months, 2 Kin 24:8), but probably Zedekiah (of whom v. 7 appears a more likely description). Both were taken to Babylon (v. 9). If the reference is to Jehoiachin (2 Kin 24:15), this was a true lament; if to Zedekiah, it was a prediction (2 Kin 25:7).
19:10 *Your mother was like a vine.* The one previously pictured as a lioness (v. 2) is here a vine (see 15:2 and note; 17:7).
19:12 *east wind.* Nebuchadnezzar and his army (see note on 17:10).
19:13 *wilderness.* Babylonia—which to Israel seemed like a wilderness (see 20:35).
19:14 *fire.* Rebellion (see 2 Kin 24:20). *its branch.* Zedekiah.

It has consumed its shoots *and* fruit,
So that there is not in it a [1]strong branch,
A scepter to rule.' "
This is a lamentation, and has become a lamentation.

God's Dealings with Israel Rehearsed

20 Now in the seventh year, in the fifth *month,* on the tenth of the month, [1]certain of the [a]elders of Israel came to inquire of the LORD, and sat before me.

2 And the word of the LORD came to me saying,

3 "Son of man, speak to the elders of Israel and say to them, 'Thus says the Lord [1]GOD, "Do you come to inquire of Me? As I live," declares the Lord GOD, "[a]I will not be inquired of by you." '

4 "Will you judge them, will you judge them, son of man? [a]Make them know the abominations of their fathers;

5 and say to them, 'Thus says the Lord GOD, "On the day when I [a]chose Israel and [1]swore to the [2]descendants of the house of Jacob and made Myself known to them in the land of Egypt, when I [1]swore to them, saying, [b]I am the LORD your God,

6 on that day I swore to them, [a]to bring them out from the land of Egypt into a land that I had [1]selected for them, [b]flowing with milk and honey, which is [c]the glory of all lands.

7 "I said to them, '[a]Cast away, each of you, the detestable things of his eyes, and [b]do not defile yourselves with the idols of Egypt; [c]I am the LORD your God.'

8 "But they [a]rebelled against Me and were not willing to listen to Me; [1]they did not cast away the detestable things of their eyes, nor did they forsake the [b]idols of Egypt.

Then I [2]resolved to [c]pour out My wrath on them, to accomplish My anger against them in the midst of the land of Egypt.

9 "But I acted [a]for the sake of My name, that it should [b]not be profaned in the sight of the nations among whom they *lived,* in whose sight I made Myself known to them by bringing them out of the land of Egypt.

10 "So I took them out of the land of Egypt and brought them into the [a]wilderness.

11 "I gave them My [a]statutes and informed them of My ordinances, by [b]which, if a man [1]observes them, he will live.

12 "Also I gave them My sabbaths to be a [a]sign between Me and them, that they might know that I am the LORD who sanctifies them.

13 "But the house of Israel [a]rebelled against Me in the wilderness. They did not walk in My statutes and they rejected My ordinances, [b]by which, if a man [1]observes them, he will live; and My [c]sabbaths they greatly profaned. Then I [2]resolved to [d]pour out My wrath on them in the wilderness, to annihilate them.

14 "But I acted for the sake of My name, that it should not be profaned in the sight of the nations, before whose sight I had brought them out.

15 "Also [a]I swore to them in the wilderness that I would not bring them into the land which I had given them, flowing with milk and honey, which is the glory of all lands,

16 because they rejected My ordinances, and as for My statutes, they did not walk in them; they even profaned My sabbaths, for their [a]heart continually went after their idols.

17 "Yet My eye spared them rather than destroying them, and I did not cause their [a]annihilation in the wilderness.

18 "I said to their [1a]children in the wilderness, '[b]Do not walk in the statutes of your fathers or keep their ordinances or defile yourselves with their idols.

14 [1]Lit *rod of strength*
20:1 [1]Lit *men* [a]Ezek 8:1, 11, 12
3 [1]Heb *YHWH,* usually rendered LORD, and so throughout the ch [a]Ezek 14:3
4 [a]Ezek 16:2; 22:2; Matt 23:32
5 [1]Lit *lifted up My hand,* and so throughout the ch [2]Lit *seed* [a]Ex 6:6-8 [b]Ex 6:2, 3
6 [1]Lit *spied out* [a]Jer 32:22 [b]Ex 13:5; 33:3 [c]Ps 48:2
7 [a]Ex 20:4, 5; 22:20 [b]Lev 18:3; Deut 29:16-18 [c]Ex 20:2
8 [1]Lit *each one* [2]Lit *said* [a]Deut 9:7; Is 63:10 [b]Ex 32:1-9 [c]Ezek 5:13; 7:8; 20:13, 21
9 [a]Ex 32:11-14; Ezek 20:14, 22; 36:21, 22 [b]Ezek 39:7
10 [a]Ex 19:1
11 [1]Lit *does* [a]Ex 20:1-23:33 [b]Lev 18:5; Ezek 20:13
12 [a]Ex 31:13, 17; Ezek 20:20
13 [1]Lit *does* [2]Lit *said* [a]Num 14:11, 12, 22; Ezek 20:8 [b]Lev 18:5 [c]Is 56:6; Ezek 20:21 [d]Ex 32:10; Deut 9:8; Ezek 20:8, 21
15 [a]Num 14:30; Ps 95:11; 106:26
16 [a]Ezek 11:21; 14:3-7; 20:8
17 [a]Jer 4:27; 5:18; Ezek 11:13
18 [1]Lit *sons* [a]Num 14:31; Deut 4:3-6 [b]Zech 1:4

has become a lamentation. Indicates repeated use (see Ps 137:1).
20:1 *seventh year . . . fifth month . . . tenth of the month.* Aug. 14, 591 B.C., the third date (see 1:2; 8:1). Since Ezekiel had received many revelations before this (see opening verses of chs. 12–18), the date must emphasize the importance of this chapter. Like chs. 16 and 23, it presents a negative view of Israel's history; unlike them, it does not employ allegory. *elders of Israel.* See notes on 8:1; 14:1. *inquire.* See v. 3 and note on 14:3.
20:3 *As I live.* See note on 18:3. *inquired of.* See note on 14:3.
20:5 *I chose.* The only occurrence of the word "choose" in Ezekiel. Verses 5–26 present Israel's history in three acts (vv. 5–9, Egypt; vv. 10–17, Wilderness, Part 1; vv. 18–26, Wilderness, Part 2); but see note on v. 28. Each act has four scenes: (1) revelation, (2) rebellion, (3) wrath, (4) reconsideration. *I swore.* See vv. 15,23,42. *I am the LORD your God.* See Ex 3:6,14–15 and notes.
20:6 *land . . . flowing with milk and honey.* See note on Ex 3:8. *the glory of all lands.* Cf. Deut 8:7–10; Jer 3:19 for the land's natural beauty. Its real beauty lay in being selected as God's dwelling place (Deut 12:5,11).
20:7 *idols.* See note on 6:4.
20:8 *But they rebelled.* See vv. 13,21; see also Josh 24:14. *Then I resolved to pour out My wrath on them.* An internal refrain (see vv. 13,21); see also note on 7:8. *accomplish My anger against.* See note on 5:13.
20:9 *for the sake of My name.* See vv. 14,22,44. Name and person are closely connected in the Bible. God's name is His identity and reputation—that by which He is known. The phrase used here is equivalent to "for My own sake" (cf. Is 37:35; 43:25). God's acts of deliverance—past and future—identify Him, revealing His true nature (see 36:22; Ps 23:3; Is 48:9). *profaned.* By ridicule (see Num 14:15–16).
20:10 *wilderness.* Act Two (see note on v. 5).
20:11 *will live.* See vv. 13,21; contrast v. 25. See notes on 16:6; 18:9; see also Lev 18:5 and note.
20:12 *sabbaths to be a sign.* Israel's observance of the sabbath was to serve as a sign that she was the Lord's holy people (see Ex 31:13–17). Ezekiel highlights the sabbath (see 22:8,26; 23:38; 44:24; 45:17; 46:3), as did Jeremiah (Jer 17:19–27; cf. Neh 13:17–18). Jewish legalism later corrupted the sabbath law (see Matt 12:1–14).
20:13 *profaned.* By not observing the sabbath-rest (see Jer 17:21–23) or by not observing it in the manner and spirit God intended (see Amos 8:5).
20:18 *I said to their children.* Act Three (see note on v. 5). God

19 '[a]I am the LORD your God; [b]walk in My statutes and keep My ordinances and [1]observe them.

20 '[a]Sanctify My sabbaths; and they shall be a sign between Me and you, that you may know that I am the LORD your God.'

21 "But the [a]children rebelled against Me; they did not walk in My statutes, nor were they careful to observe My ordinances, by which, *if* a man observes them, he will live; they profaned My sabbaths. So I [1]resolved to pour out My wrath on them, to accomplish My anger against them in the wilderness.

22 "But I [a]withdrew My hand and acted [b]for the sake of My name, that it should not be profaned in the sight of the nations in whose sight I had brought them out.

23 "Also I swore to them in the wilderness that I would [a]scatter them among the nations and disperse them among the lands,

24 because they had not observed My ordinances, but had rejected My statutes and had profaned My sabbaths, and [a]their eyes were [1]on the idols of their fathers.

25 "I also gave them statutes that were [a]not good and ordinances by which they could not live;

26 and I pronounced them [a]unclean because of their gifts, in that they [b]caused all [1]their firstborn to pass through *the fire* so that I might make them desolate, in order that they might [c]know that I am the LORD." '

27 "Therefore, son of man, [a]speak to the house of Israel and say to them, 'Thus says the Lord GOD, "Yet in this your fathers have [b]blasphemed Me by [c]acting treacherously against Me.

28 "When I had [a]brought them into the land which I swore to give to them, then they saw every [b]high hill and every leafy tree, and they offered there their sacrifices and there they presented the provocation of their offering. There also they made their soothing aroma and there they poured out their drink offerings.

29 "Then I said to them, 'What is the high place to which you go?' So its name is called [1]Bamah to this day." '

30 "Therefore, say to the house of Israel, 'Thus says the Lord GOD, "Will you defile yourselves [1]after the manner of your [a]fathers and play the harlot after their detestable things?

31 "[1]When you offer your gifts, when you [a]cause your sons to pass through the fire, you are defiling yourselves with all your idols to this day. And shall I be inquired of by you, O house of Israel? As I live," declares the Lord GOD, "I will not be inquired of by you.

32 "What [a]comes [1]into your mind will not come about, when you say: 'We will be like the nations, like the tribes of the lands, [b]serving wood and stone.'

God Will Restore Israel to Her Land

33 "As I live," declares the Lord GOD, "surely with a mighty hand and with an [a]outstretched arm and with wrath poured out, I shall be [b]king over you.

34 "I will [a]bring you out from the peoples and gather you from the lands where you are scattered, with a mighty hand and with an outstretched arm and with [b]wrath poured out;

35 and I will bring you into the [a]wilderness of the peoples, and there I will enter into judgment with you face to face.

36 "As I [a]entered into judgment with your fathers in the [b]wilderness of the land of Egypt, so I will enter into judgment with you," declares the Lord GOD.

37 "I will make you [a]pass under the rod, and I will bring you into the bond of the covenant;

38 and I will [a]purge from you the rebels and those who transgress against Me; I will bring them out of the land where they sojourn, but they will [b]not enter the [1]land of Israel. Thus you will know that I am the LORD.

39 "As for you, O house of Israel," thus says the Lord GOD, "[a]Go, serve everyone his idols; [1]but later you will surely listen to Me, and My holy name you will [b]profane no longer with your gifts and with your idols.

19 [1]Lit *do* [a]Ex 6:7; 20:2 [b]Deut 5:32, 33; 6:1, 2; 8:1, 2; 11:1; 12:1
20 [a]Jer 17:22
21 [1]Lit *said* [a]Num 21:5; 25:1-3
22 [a]Job 13:21; Ps 78:38; Ezek 20:17 [b]Is 48:9-11; Jer 14:7, 21; Ezek 20:9, 14
23 [a]Lev 26:33; Deut 4:27; 28:64
24 [1]Lit *after* [a]Ezek 6:9
25 [a]Ps 81:12; Is 66:4; Rom 1:21-25, 28
26 [1]Lit *that which opens the womb* [a]Lev 18:21; 20:2-5; Is 63:17; Ezek 20:30; Rom 11:8 [b]Jer 7:31; 19:4-9 [c]Ezek 6:7; 20:12, 20
27 [a]Ezek 2:7; 3:4, 11, 27 [b]Num 15:30; Rom 2:24 [c]Ezek 18:24; 39:23, 26
28 [a]Josh 23:3, 14; Neh 9:22-26; Ps 78:55; Jer 2:7 [b]1 Kin 14:23; Ps 78:58; Is 57:5-7; Jer 3:6; Ezek 6:13
29 [1]Or *High Place*
30 [1]Lit *in the way of* [a]Judg 2:19; Jer 7:26; 16:12
31 [1]Lit *In your lifting up* [a]Ps 106:37-39; Jer 7:31; Ezek 16:20; 20:26
32 [1]Lit *upon your spirit* [a]Ezek 11:5 [b]Jer 2:25; 44:17
33 [a]Jer 21:5 [b]Jer 51:57
34 [a]Is 27:12, 13; Ezek 20:38; 34:16 [b]Jer 42:18; 44:6; Lam 2:4
35 [a]Ezek 19:13; 20:36; Hos 2:14
36 [a]Num 11:1-35; Ps 106:15; Ezek 20:13, 21; 1 Cor 10:5-10 [b]Deut 32:10
37 [a]Lev 27:32; Jer 33:13
38 [1]Lit *ground* or *soil* [a]Ezek 34:17-22; Amos 9:9, 10; Zech 13:8, 9; Mal 3:3; 4:1-3 [b]Num 14:29, 30; Ps 95:11; Ezek 13:9; 20:15, 16; Heb 4:3
39 [1]Or *and afterwards, if you will not listen to Me, but* [a]Jer 44:25, 26 [b]Is 1:13-15; Ezek 23:38, 39; 43:7

began anew with the second generation in the wilderness (see Num 14:26–35).

20:25–26 Cf. the principle of divine working in Rom 1:24–32.

20:26 *caused all their firstborn . . . through the fire.* See v. 31 and note on 16:20. *that they might know that I am the LORD.* God will go to any lengths to get His people to acknowledge Him (see Introduction: Themes, also see note on 5:13).

20:28 *When I had brought them into the land.* Apparently Act Four in Ezekiel's history (see note on v. 5), but it is not carried through with the same schematic consistency.

20:30 *Will you . . . ?* The point of the chapter: "How will you act?"

20:31 *inquired of.* See note on 14:3.

20:32 *will not come about.* As happened to those who were exiled to Egypt (see Jer 44:15–19). *like the nations.* The temptation to lose its uniqueness was always present for Israel (see 1 Sam 8:5).

20:33 *mighty hand . . . outstretched arm.* Terminology of the exodus (cf. Deut 4:34; 5:15; 7:19; 11:2; 26:8).

20:35 *wilderness of the peoples.* Exile among the nations would be for Israel like a return to the wilderness through which she journeyed on the way to the promised land (see Hos 2:14).

20:37 *pass under the rod.* The way a shepherd counts or separates his flock (see Jer 33:13; Matt 25:32–33). *I will bring you into the bond of the covenant.* As He had in the Sinai wilderness (see 16:60,62).

20:38 *purge.* As in the first wilderness experience, many were not allowed to enter the land (see Num 14:26–35).

20:39 *Go, serve everyone his idols.* Irony; the opposite is meant (cf. 1 Kin 22:15; Amos 4:4).

40 "For on My holy mountain, on the high mountain of Israel," declares the Lord GOD, "there the whole house of Israel, [a]all of them, will serve Me in the land; there I will [b]accept them and there I will [1]seek your contributions and the choicest of your gifts, with all your holy things.

41 "[1]As a soothing aroma I will accept you when I [a]bring you out from the peoples and gather you from the lands where you are scattered; and I will prove Myself [b]holy among you in the sight of the nations.

42 "And [a]you will know that I am the LORD, [b]when I bring you into the land of Israel, into the [c]land which I swore to give to your forefathers.

43 "There you will [a]remember your ways and all your deeds with which you have defiled yourselves; and you will [b]loathe yourselves in your own [1]sight for all the things that you have done.

44 "Then [a]you will know that I am the LORD when I have dealt with you [b]for My name's sake, not according to your evil ways or according to your corrupt deeds, O house of Israel," declares the Lord GOD.' "

45 [1]Now the word of the LORD came to me, saying,

46 "Son of man, set your face toward [1]Teman, and speak out against the [a]south and [b]prophesy against the [c]forest [2]land of the Negev,

47 and say to the forest of the Negev, 'Hear the word of the LORD: thus says the Lord GOD, "Behold, I am about to [a]kindle a fire in you, and it will consume every [1]green tree in you, as well as every dry tree; the blazing flame will not be quenched and [2b]the whole surface from south to north will be burned by it.

48 "All flesh will see that I, the LORD, have kindled it; it shall [a]not be quenched." ' "

49 Then I said, "Ah Lord GOD! They are saying of me, 'Is he not *just* speaking [a]parables?' "

40 [1]Or *require* [a]Is 66:23; Ezek 37:22, 24 [b]Is 56:7; 60:7; Ezek 43:12, 27
41 [1]Lit *With* [a]Is 27:12, 13; Ezek 11:17; 28:25 [b]Is 5:16; Ezek 28:25; 36:23
42 [a]Ezek 36:23; 38:23 [b]Ezek 11:17; 34:13; 36:24 [c]Ezek 20:6, 15
43 [1]Lit *faces* [a]Ezek 6:9; 16:61, 63; Hos 5:15 [b]Jer 31:18; Ezek 36:31; Zech 12:10
44 [a]Ezek 24:24 [b]Ezek 36:22
45 [1]Ch 21:1 in Heb
46 [1]Or *the South* [2]Lit *of the field* [a]Jer 13:19; Ezek 21:4 [b]Ezek 21:2; Amos 7:16 [c]Is 30:6-11
47 [1]Lit *moist* [2]Or *all the faces* [a]Is 9:18, 19; Jer 21:14 [b]Is 13:8
48 [a]Jer 7:20; 17:27
49 [a]Ezek 17:2; Matt 13:13; John 16:25
21:1 [1]Ch 21:6 in Heb
2 [1]Lit *flow* [a]Ezek 20:46; 25:2; 28:21 [b]Job 29:22; Ezek 20:46
3 [a]Jer 21:13; Ezek 5:8; Nah 2:13; 3:5 [b]Is 57:1
4 [a]Jer 12:12; Ezek 7:2; 20:47
5 [a]1 Sam 3:12; Jer 23:20; Ezek 21:30; Nah 1:9
6 [1]Lit *loins*

Parable of the Sword of the LORD

21 [1]And the word of the LORD came to me saying,

2 "Son of man, [a]set your face toward Jerusalem, and [1b]speak against the sanctuaries and prophesy against the land of Israel;

3 and say to the land of Israel, 'Thus says the LORD, "Behold, [a]I am against you; and I will draw My sword out of its sheath and cut off from you the [b]righteous and the wicked.

4 "Because I will cut off from you the righteous and the wicked, therefore My sword will go forth from its sheath against [a]all flesh from south *to* north.

5 "Thus all flesh will know that I, the LORD, have drawn My sword out of its sheath. It will [a]not return *to its sheath* again." '

6 "As for you, son of man, groan with breaking [1]heart and bitter grief, groan in their sight.

7 "And when they say to you, 'Why do you groan?' you shall say, 'Because of the [a]news that is coming; and [b]every heart will melt, all hands will be feeble, every spirit will [1]faint and all knees will [2]be weak as water. Behold, it comes and it will happen,' declares the Lord [3]GOD."

8 Again the word of the LORD came to me, saying,

9 "Son of man, prophesy and say, 'Thus says the LORD.' Say,

7 [1]Lit *be dim* [2]Lit *flow* [3]Heb *YHWH,* usually rendered LORD, and so throughout the ch [a]Ezek 7:26 [b]Is 13:7; Nah 2:10

20:40 *My holy mountain.* Mentioned only here in Ezekiel, it refers to Jerusalem or Zion (see Ps 2:6; 3:4; 15:1; see also Is 11:9; 56:7; 57:13; 65:11; Obad 16; Zeph 3:11). *whole house of Israel.* Includes the northern kingdom, which fell in 722–721 B.C. (see 11:15; 36:10). *I will seek.* See Deut 23:21 ("require"); Mic 6:8. *contributions.* Possibly refers to a prescribed contribution. The other 19 occurrences in Ezekiel of the Hebrew for this word are confined to chs. 44–48, where the reference is to the land set aside for the temple and priests (see 45:1; 48:8–10, "allotment") or to the special gifts for the priests (see 44:30). *choicest . . . gifts.* Voluntary contributions (but possibly including first fruits).

20:41 *As a soothing aroma.* Either in a metaphorical sense (as in Eph 5:2) or in a literal sense (as in 6:13). *bring you out.* Cf. v. 34.

20:43 *you will remember . . . and . . . loathe yourselves.* A thorough repentance (see 6:9; 16:63; 36:31; Luke 15:17–19).

20:44 *for My name's sake.* Summarizes and concludes the oracle (see note on v. 9).

20:46 *set your face.* A posture required eight times of Ezekiel (here; 13:17; 21:2; 25:2; 28:21; 29:2; 35:2; 38:2). *toward Teman.* Or "toward the south," i.e., toward Judah and Jerusalem, the object of all of Ezekiel's prophesying in these chapters. Any Babylonian invasion would traverse the Holy Land from north to south (see 26:7).

20:47 *kindle a fire.* Common figurative language for invading forces (see Is 10:16–19; Jer 15:14; 17:4,27; 21:14; see also note on 15:7). *green . . . as well as . . . dry tree.* All trees (cf. 17:24; Luke 23:31). *from south to north.* Expresses totality, not direction; equivalent to saying, "from the border on the right to that on the left."

20:49 *parables.* See note on 17:2; for other ridiculing of the prophet see 12:21–28; 33:32.

21:2 *set your face.* See note on 20:46. *against the sanctuaries.* See 9:6 and note.

21:3 *I am against you.* See note on 5:8. *My sword.* For the sword of the Lord's judgment see Is 31:8; 34:6; 66:16. This is the first of five sword oracles (see vv. 8–17, 18–24, 25–27, 28–32). Here the sword refers to Babylon and Nebuchadnezzar (v. 19). *the righteous and the wicked.* Indicates the completeness of the judgment that is about to come on Israel. No one will escape its devastating effects, not even the righteous in the land. Contrast God's deliverance of Noah (Gen 6:7–8) and Lot (Gen 18:23; 19:12–13).

21:4 *from south to north.* See note on 20:47.

21:6 *groan with breaking heart and bitter grief.* Ezekiel's display of intense grief is to serve as another prophetic sign and as an occasion for a new message of impending judgment.

21:7 *when they say to you.* Cf. 12:9 for the people's response to Ezekiel's behavior. This is Ezekiel's seventh symbolic act (see Introduction: Literary Features).

'[a]A sword, a sword sharpened
And also polished!
10 'Sharpened to make a [a]slaughter,
Polished [1]to flash like lightning!'
Or shall we rejoice, the [2]rod of My son
[b]despising every tree?
11 "It is given to be polished, that it may be
handled; the sword is sharpened and polished, to give it into the hand of the slayer.
12 "[a]Cry out and wail, son of man; for it is
against My people, it is against all the [b]offi-
cials of Israel. They are delivered over to the
sword with My people, therefore strike *your*
thigh.
13 "For *there is* a testing; and what if even
the [1]rod which despises will be no more?"
declares the Lord GOD.
14 "You therefore, son of man, prophesy
and clap *your* hands together; and let the
sword be [a]doubled the third time, the sword
for the slain. It is the sword for the great one
slain, which surrounds them,
15 that *their* [a]hearts may melt, and many
[b]fall at all their [c]gates. I have given the glittering sword. Ah! It is made *for striking* like
lightning, it is wrapped up *in readiness* for
slaughter.
16 "[1]Show yourself sharp, go to the right;
set yourself; go to the left, wherever your
[2]edge is appointed.
17 "I will also clap My hands together, and
I will [1a]appease My wrath; I, the LORD, have
spoken."

The Instrument of God's Judgment

18 The word of the LORD came to me saying,
19 "As for you, son of man, [1a]make two
ways for the sword of the king of Babylon to
come; both of them will go out of one land.
And [2]make a signpost; [3]make it at the head
of the way to the city.
20 "You shall [1]mark a way for the sword to
come to [a]Rabbah of the sons of Ammon, and
to Judah into [b]fortified Jerusalem.
21 "For the king of Babylon stands at the
[1]parting of the way, at the head of the two
ways, to use [a]divination; he [b]shakes the
arrows, he consults the [2c]household idols, he
looks at the liver.
22 "Into his right hand came the divination, 'Jerusalem,' to [a]set battering rams, to
open the mouth [1]for slaughter, to lift up the
voice with a battle cry, to set battering rams
against the gates, to cast up ramps, to build
a siege wall.
23 "And it will be to them like a false divination in their eyes; [a]they have *sworn*
solemn oaths. But he [b]brings iniquity to
remembrance, that they may be seized.
24 "Therefore, thus says the Lord GOD,
'Because you have made your iniquity to be
remembered, in that your transgressions are
uncovered, so that in all your deeds your sins
appear—because you have come to remembrance, you will be seized with the hand.
25 'And you, O slain, wicked one, the
prince of Israel, whose [a]day has come, in the
time of the [1]punishment of the end,'
26 thus says the Lord GOD, 'Remove the
turban and take off the [a]crown; this *will* [1]no
longer *be* the same. [b]Exalt that which is low
and abase that which is high.
27 '[a]A ruin, a ruin, a ruin, I will make it.
This also will be no more until [b]He comes
whose right it is, and I will give it *to Him*.'

9 [a]Deut 32:41
10 [1]Lit *lightning to be to her* [2]Or *scepter* [a]Is 34:5, 6 [b]Ps 110:5, 6; Ezek 20:47
12 [a]Ezek 21:6; Joel 1:13 [b]Ezek 21:25; 22:6
13 [1]Or *scepter*
14 [a]Lev 26:21, 24; 2 Kin 24:1, 10-16; 25:1
15 [a]Josh 2:11; 2 Sam 17:10; Ps 22:14; Ezek 21:7 [b]Is 59:10; Jer 13:16; 18:15 [c]Jer 17:27; Ezek 21:19
16 [1]Or *Unite yourself* [2]Lit *face*
17 [1]Lit *cause to rest* [a]Ezek 5:13
19 [1]Or *set for yourself* [a]Jer 1:10; Ezek 4:1-3
19 [2]Lit *cut out a hand* [3]Lit *cut it*
20 [1]Lit *set* [a]Deut 3:11; Jer 49:2; Ezek 25:5; Amos 1:14 [b]Ps 48:12, 13; 125:1, 2
21 [1]Lit *mother* [2]Heb *teraphim* [a]Num 22:7; 23:23 [b]Prov 16:33 [c]Gen 31:19, 30; Judg 17:5; 18:17, 20
22 [1]Lit *in* [a]Ezek 4:2; 26:9
23 [a]Ezek 17:16, 18 [b]Num 5:15; Ezek 21:24; 29:16
25 [1]Or *iniquity* [a]Ps 37:13; Ezek 7:2, 3, 7
26 [1]Lit *not this* [a]Jer 13:18; Ezek 16:12 [b]Ps 75:7; Ezek 17:24
27 [a]Hag 2:21, 22 [b]Ps 2:6; 72:7, 10; Jer 23:5, 6; Ezek 34:24; 37:24

21:9 *A sword, a sword.* A sword song (see note on v. 3), possibly accompanied by dancing or symbolic actions. Such songs may have been sung by warriors about to go into battle (see note on 2 Sam 1:18).
21:10 To think that the Babylonians would conquer every other country except Judah was a false hope. *rod.* Represents rule, government or kingdom. *My son.* Corresponds to "My people" in v. 12 (see Gen 49:9).
21:11 *slayer.* Nebuchadnezzar (v. 19).
21:12 *Cry out and wail . . . strike your thigh.* Eighth symbolic act (see Introduction: Literary Features).
21:13 *there is a testing.* Of Judah. *what if even the rod . . . will be no more?* See note on v. 10. The question anticipates the final interruption of Davidic kingship, which came in 586 B.C. (see vv. 25–27).
21:14 *clap your hands.* See 6:11 and note. *let the sword be doubled.* Cf. 2 Kin 13:18–19.
21:17 *clap My hands.* In scorn and in harmony with God's command to Ezekiel in v. 14.
21:19 *king of Babylon.* Nebuchadnezzar. *one land.* Babylon, or possibly Aram (Syria)—Nebuchadnezzar headquartered at Riblah in northern Aram (see 2 Kin 25:6).
21:20 *Rabbah.* Capital of Ammon (Jer 49:2); modern Amman (capital of Jordan).
21:21 *to use divination . . . the arrows.* For the purpose of seeking good omens for the coming campaign—a practice not elsewhere mentioned in the Bible. Apparently arrows were labeled (e.g., "Rabbah," "Jerusalem"), placed into a quiver and drawn out, one with each hand. Right-hand selection was seen as a good omen (see v. 22). *idols.* Miniature representations of the gods worshiped by the family or clan (see Gen 31:19). Consulting them is referred to in Hos 3:4; Zech 10:2. The household idols of Gen 31:19–35 were small enough to hide in a saddle, but others were life-size (1 Sam 19:13–16). *looks at the liver.* Looking at the color and configurations of sheep livers to foretell the future was common in ancient Babylonia and Rome, but the practice is not mentioned elsewhere in the Bible.
21:23 *false divination.* The leaders of Jerusalem, once submissive to Nebuchadnezzar but now in rebellion (2 Kin 24:20), hoped that the result of the omen-seeking (vv. 21–22) was misleading.
21:25 *prince of Israel.* Zedekiah (see note on 7:27).
21:26 *turban.* Only here is it mentioned as royal headwear. Elsewhere it is worn by priests (Ex 28:4,37,39; 29:6; 39:28,31; Lev 8:9; 16:4), as a setting for the crown (Ex 28:36–37; 29:6; 39:31; Lev 8:9). It was made of fine linen (Ex 28:39; 39:28). *Exalt . . . low . . . abase . . . high.* A common Biblical expression for the reversal of human conditions because of the intervention of the Lord (see 17:24; 1 Sam 2:7–8; Luke 1:52–53).
21:27 *A ruin, a ruin, a ruin.* Threefold repetition for emphasis (see Is 6:3; Jer 7:4). *until He comes whose right it is.* The Messiah; apparently an allusion to Gen 49:10 (see note there). Or

28 "And you, son of man, prophesy and
say, 'Thus says the Lord GOD concerning the
sons of Ammon and concerning their
[a]reproach,' and say: 'A sword, a sword is
drawn, polished for the slaughter, to cause it
[1]to [b]consume, that it may be like lightning—
29 while they see for you [a]false visions,
while they divine lies for you—to place you
on the necks of the wicked who are slain,
whose day has come, in the [b]time of the
[1]punishment of the end.
30 '[a]Return *it* to its sheath. In the [b]place
where you were created, in the land of your
origin, I will judge you.
31 'I will [a]pour out My indignation on you;
I will [b]blow on you with the fire of My
wrath, and I will give you into the hand of
brutal men, [1c]skilled in destruction.
32 'You will be [1a]fuel for the fire; your
blood will be in the midst of the land. You
will [b]not be remembered, for I, the LORD,
have spoken.' "

The Sins of Israel

22 Then the word of the LORD came to me,
saying,
2 "And you, son of man, will you judge,
will you judge the bloody city? Then cause
her to know all her abominations.
3 "You shall say, 'Thus says the Lord
[1]GOD, "A city [a]shedding blood in her midst,
so that her time will come, and that makes
idols, contrary to her *interest,* for defilement!
4 "You have become [a]guilty by [1]the blood
which you have shed, and defiled by your
idols which you have made. Thus you have
brought your [2]day near and have come to
your years; therefore I have made you a
[b]reproach to the nations and a mocking to
all the lands.
5 "Those who are near and those who are
far from you will mock you, you of ill repute,
full of [a]turmoil.
6 "Behold, the [a]rulers of Israel, each
according to his [1]power, have been in you for
the purpose of shedding blood.
7 "They have [a]treated father and mother
lightly within you. The [b]alien they have
oppressed in your midst; the [c]fatherless and
the widow they have wronged in you.
8 "You have [a]despised My holy things and
[b]profaned My sabbaths.
9 "Slanderous men have been in you for
the purpose of shedding blood, and in you
they have eaten at the mountain *shrines.* In
your midst they have [a]committed acts of
lewdness.
10 "In you [1]they have [a]uncovered *their*
fathers' nakedness; in you they have humbled her who was [b]unclean in her menstrual
impurity.
11 "One has committed abomination with
his [a]neighbor's wife and another has lewdly
defiled his [b]daughter-in-law. And another in
you has [c]humbled his sister, his father's
daughter.
12 "In you they have [a]taken bribes to shed
blood; you have taken [b]interest and profits,
and you have injured your neighbors for gain
by [c]oppression, and you have [d]forgotten
Me," declares the Lord GOD.
13 "Behold, then, I smite My hand at your
[a]dishonest gain which you have acquired
and at [1]the bloodshed which is among you.
14 "Can [a]your heart endure, or can your
hands be strong in the days that I will deal
with you? [b]I, the LORD, have spoken and will
act.
15 "I will [a]scatter you among the nations
and I will disperse you through the lands,
and I will [b]consume your uncleanness from
you.
16 "You will profane yourself in the sight of
the nations, and you will [a]know that I am
the LORD." ' "
17 And the word of the LORD came to me,
saying,
18 "Son of man, the house of Israel has
become [a]dross to Me; all of them are [b]bronze
and tin and iron and lead in the [c]furnace;
they are the dross of silver.

28 [1]Lit *to finish* [a]Ezek 36:15; Zeph 2:8-10 [b]Is 31:8; Jer 12:12; 46:10, 14 **29** [1]Or *iniquity* [a]Jer 27:9; Ezek 13:6-9; 22:28 [b]Ezek 21:25; 35:5 **30** [a]Jer 47:6, 7 [b]Ezek 25:5 **31** [1]Or *artisans of* [a]Ezek 14:19; 25:7; Nah 1:6 [b]Ps 18:15; Is 30:33; Ezek 22:20, 21; Hag 1:9 [c]Jer 4:7; 6:22, 23; 51:20-23; Hab 1:6, 10 **32** [1]Lit *food* [a]Ezek 20:47, 48; Mal 4:1 [b]Ezek 25:10 **22:3** [1]Heb *YHWH,* usually rendered LORD, and so throughout the ch [a]Ezek 22:6, 27; 23:37, 45 **4** [1]Lit *your* [2]Lit *days* [a]2 Kin 21:16; Ezek 24:7, 8 [b]Ps 44:13, 14; Ezek 5:14, 15; 16:57 **5** [a]Is 22:2 **6** [1]Lit *arm* [a]Is 1:23; Ezek 22:27 **7** [a]Ex 20:12; Lev 20:9; Deut 5:16; 27:16

7 [b]Ex 22:21f; 23:9; Deut 24:17; Jer 7:6; Zech 7:10 [c]Ex 22:22; Ezek 22:25; Mal 3:5 **8** [a]Ezek 22:26 [b]Ezek 20:13, 21, 24; 23:38, 39 **9** [a]Ezek 23:29; Hos 4:2, 10, 14 **10** [1]Lit *he has* [a]Lev 18:8 [b]Lev 18:19; Ezek 18:6 **11** [a]Ezek 18:11; 33:26 [b]Lev 18:15 [c]2 Sam 13:11-14 **12** [a]Ex 23:8; Deut 16:19; 27:25; Mic 7:2, 3 [b]Lev 25:36; Deut 23:19 [c]Lev 19:13 [d]Ps 106:21; Ezek 23:35

13 [1]Lit *your* [a]Is 33:15; Amos 2:6-8; Mic 2:2 **14** [a]Ezek 21:7 [b]Ezek 17:24 **15** [a]Deut 4:27; Neh 1:8; Ezek 20:23; Zech 7:14 [b]Ezek 23:27, 48 **16** [a]Ps 83:18; Ezek 6:7 **18** [a]Ps 119:119; Is 1:22; Lam 4:1 [b]Jer 6:28-30 [c]Prov 17:3; Is 48:10

possibly the reference is to Nebuchadnezzar, translating "... whose is the judgment" or "... who pronounces sentence" (see 2 Kin 25:6).

21:28 *sons of Ammon.* See v. 20. After judgment on Jerusalem, the foreigners would be dealt with (cf. Is 10:5). *their reproach.* See 25:3,6; also cf. 36:15. *A sword, a sword.* Nebuchadnezzar's (see vv. 9,19 and notes).

21:29 *false visions ... divine lies.* Apparently Ammon also had false prophets of peace (see v. 10 and note; 13:10; Jer 6:14; 8:11–12). *you.* Nebuchadnezzar's sword.

21:30 *Return it.* Addressing Nebuchadnezzar.

21:31 *brutal men.* The people of the East, as in 25:4.

22:2 *will you judge ... ?* Cf. 20:4. *the bloody city.* Jerusalem, the usual focal point of Ezekiel's prophecy (see 5:5).

22:3 *shedding blood ... makes idols.* Two categories of sins are developed: social injustices and idol worship. *idols.* See note on 6:4.

22:6 *rulers of Israel.* Leaders generally, not kings; contrast 21:12 with 19:1.

22:7 *fatherless ... widow they have wronged.* Cf. Is 1:17.

22:8 *sabbaths.* A major concern in Ezekiel (see note on 20:12).

22:9 *eaten at the mountain shrines ... acts of lewdness.* See notes on 6:3; 16:15; 18:6.

22:10 *humbled her who was unclean.* Cf. 18:6.

22:11 *abomination.* All the sins mentioned in this verse were specifically forbidden in the law (Lev 18:7–20; 20:10–21; Deut 22:22–23,30; 27:22).

22:12 *interest and profits.* See note on 18:8.

22:13 *smite My hand.* In anger (see 21:14,17).

22:18 *dross.* For references to Jerusalem as a furnace see Is 1:21–26; Jer 6:27–30. Typically, imagery used by others to represent purifying was used by Ezekiel to picture total destruction (see note on 15:4).

19 "Therefore, thus says the Lord GOD, 'Because all of you have become dross, therefore, behold, I am going to gather you into the midst of Jerusalem.

20 'As they gather silver and bronze and iron and lead and tin into the [a]furnace to blow fire on it in order to melt *it,* so I will gather *you* in My anger and in My wrath and I will lay you *there* and melt you.

21 'I will gather you and blow on you with the fire of My wrath, and you will be melted in the midst of it.

22 'As silver is melted in the furnace, so you will be melted in the midst of it; and you will know that I, the LORD, have [a]poured out My wrath on you.' "

23 And the word of the LORD came to me, saying,

24 "Son of man, say to her, 'You are a land that is [a]not cleansed or rained on in the day of indignation.'

25 "There is a [a]conspiracy of her prophets in her midst like a roaring lion tearing the prey. They have [b]devoured lives; they have taken treasure and precious things; they have made many [c]widows in the midst of her.

26 "Her [a]priests have done violence to My law and have [b]profaned My holy things; they have made no [c]distinction between the holy and the profane, and they have not taught the difference between the [d]unclean and the clean; and they hide their eyes from My sabbaths, and I am profaned among them.

27 "Her princes within her are like wolves tearing the prey, by shedding blood *and* [a]destroying lives in order to get [b]dishonest gain.

28 "Her prophets have smeared whitewash for them, seeing [a]false visions and divining lies for them, saying, 'Thus says the Lord GOD,' when the LORD has not spoken.

29 "The people of the land have practiced [a]oppression and committed robbery, and they have wronged the poor and needy and have [b]oppressed the sojourner without justice.

30 "I [a]searched for a man among them who would [b]build up the wall and [c]stand in the gap before Me for the land, so that I would not destroy it; but I found [1]no one.

31 "Thus I have poured out My [a]indignation on them; I have consumed them with the fire of My wrath; [b]their way I have brought upon their heads," declares the Lord GOD.

Oholah and Oholibah's Sin and Its Consequences

23 The word of the LORD came to me again, saying,

2 "Son of man, there were [a]two women, the daughters of one mother;

3 and they played the harlot in Egypt. They [a]played the harlot in their youth; there their breasts were pressed and there their virgin bosom was handled.

4 "Their names were Oholah the elder and Oholibah her sister. And they became Mine, and they bore sons and daughters. And *as for* their names, Samaria is Oholah and Jerusalem is Oholibah.

5 "Oholah played the harlot [1]while she was Mine; and she lusted after her lovers, after the [a]Assyrians, *her* neighbors,

6 who were clothed in purple, [a]governors and officials, all of them desirable young men, horsemen riding on horses.

7 "She bestowed her harlotries on them, all of whom *were* the choicest [1]men of Assyria; and with all whom she lusted after, with all their idols she [a]defiled herself.

8 "She did not forsake her harlotries [a]from *the time in* Egypt; for in her youth [1]men had lain with her, and they handled her virgin bosom and poured out their [2]lust on her.

9 "Therefore, I gave her into the hand of her [a]lovers, into the hand of the [1]Assyrians, after whom she lusted.

10 "They [a]uncovered her nakedness; they took her sons and her daughters, but they slew her with the sword. Thus she became a [1]byword among women, and they executed judgments on her.

11 "Now her sister Oholibah saw *this,* yet she was [a]more corrupt in her lust than she, and her harlotries were more than the harlotries of her sister.

20 [a]Is 1:25
22 [a]Ezek 20:8, 33; Hos 5:10
24 [a]Is 9:13; Jer 2:30; Ezek 24:13; Zeph 3:2
25 [a]Jer 11:9; Hos 6:9 [b]Jer 2:34; Ezek 13:19; 22:27 [c]Jer 15:8; Ezek 22:7
26 [a]Jer 2:8, 26; Ezek 7:26 [b]1 Sam 2:12-17, 22; Ezek 22:8 [c]Lev 10:10; Ezek 44:23 [d]Hag 2:11-14
27 [a]Ezek 22:25 [b]Ezek 22:13
28 [a]Jer 23:25-32; Ezek 13:6
29 [a]Is 5:7; Ezek 9:9; 22:7; Amos 3:10 [b]Ex 23:9
30 [a]Is 59:16; 63:5; Jer 5:1 [b]Ezek 13:5 [c]Ps 106:23; Jer 15:1

30 [1]Lit *not*
31 [a]Is 10:5; 13:5; 30:27; Ezek 22:20 [b]Ezek 7:3, 8, 9; 9:10; 16:43; Rom 2:8, 9
23:2 [a]Ezek 16:46
3 [a]Lev 17:7; Jer 3:9
5 [1]Lit *under Me* [a]2 Kin 15:19; 16:7; 17:3; Ezek 16:28; Hos 5:13; 8:9, 10
6 [a]Ezek 23:12, 13
7 [1]Lit *sons of Asshur* [a]Ezek 20:7; 22:3, 4; Hos 5:3; 6:10
8 [1]Lit *they* [2]Lit *harlotry* [a]Ex 32:4; 1 Kin 12:28; 2 Kin 10:29; 17:16; Ezek 23:3, 19
9 [1]Lit *sons of Asshur* [a]Ezek 16:37; 23:22
10 [1]Lit *name* [a]Ezek 16:37, 41
11 [a]Jer 3:8-11; Ezek 16:51

22:25 *prophets.* Ezekiel begins to speak plainly concerning the "dross" of vv. 18–22. All of Jerusalem's leaders and people were included: prophets (here and v. 28), priests (v. 26), princes (v. 27), people (v. 29). *like a roaring lion.* Cf. v. 27; 13:4; Zeph 3:3.

22:26 *distinction between the holy and the profane.* The main duty of priests (see 44:23). *sabbaths.* See note on v. 8.

22:28 *whitewash.* See 13:10 and note.

22:29 *people of the land.* See 7:27 and note.

22:30 *I searched for a man.* Cf. Is 51:18; 59:16; 63:5. *stand in the gap before Me.* See note on 13:5. To intercede with God in behalf of the people was part of a prophet's task (Gen 20:7; 1 Sam 12:23; Jer 37:3; 42:2). Some interpret the task here as teaching, particularly calling the people to repentance. Cf. the task of the prophetic "watchman" (3:17–21; 33:1–6).

23:4 *Oholah.* Means "her tent." *Oholibah.* Means "My tent is in her." Cf. the two sisters of Jer 3:6–12. "Tent" could stand for Canaanite high places, for the Lord's tabernacle (except that Ezekiel never uses the word elsewhere for the legitimate shrine) or for Israel's tent-dwelling origin.

23:5 *played the harlot.* Here represents political alliances with pagan powers—not idolatry as in ch. 16 (see note on 16:15). The graphic language of the chapter underscores God's and Ezekiel's disgust with Israel for playing the worldly game of international politics rather than relying on the Lord for her security—as clear a case of religious prostitution as idolatry. *Assyrians.* See 2 Kin 15:19.

23:8 *in Egypt.* Cf. 20:5–8. Israel's entire history was marked by unfaithfulness. For her attachment to Egypt see Ex 17:3; Num 11:5,18,20; 14:2–4; 21:5.

23:10 *uncovered her nakedness.* A reference to the fall of Samaria to the Assyrians in 722–721 B.C.

12 "She lusted after the [1][a]Assyrians, governors and officials, the ones near, magnificently dressed, horsemen riding on horses, all of them desirable young men.

13 "I saw that she had defiled herself; they both took [1]the same way.

14 "So she increased her harlotries. And she saw men [a]portrayed on the wall, images of the [b]Chaldeans portrayed with vermilion,

15 girded with belts on their loins, with flowing turbans on their heads, all of them looking like officers, [1]like the [2]Babylonians *in* Chaldea, the land of their birth.

16 "[1]When she saw them she [a]lusted after them and sent messengers to them in Chaldea.

17 "The [1][a]Babylonians came to her to the bed of love and defiled her with their harlotry. And when she had been defiled by them, [2]she became disgusted with them.

18 "She [a]uncovered her harlotries and uncovered her nakedness; then [1]I became [b]disgusted with her, as [1]I had become disgusted with her [c]sister.

19 "Yet she multiplied her harlotries, remembering the days of her youth, when she played the harlot in the land of Egypt.

20 "She [a]lusted after their paramours, whose flesh is *like* the flesh of donkeys and whose issue is *like* the issue of horses.

21 "Thus you longed for the [a]lewdness of your youth, when [1]the Egyptians handled your bosom because of the breasts of your youth.

22 "Therefore, O Oholibah, thus says the Lord [1]GOD, 'Behold I will arouse your lovers against you, from whom [2]you were alienated, and I will bring them against you from every side:

23 the [1][a]Babylonians and all the [b]Chaldeans, [c]Pekod and Shoa and Koa, *and* all the [2][d]Assyrians with them; desirable young men, governors and officials all of them, officers and [3]men of renown, all of them riding on horses.

24 'They will come against you with weapons, [a]chariots and [1]wagons, and with a company of peoples. They will set themselves against you on every side with buckler and shield and helmet; and I will commit the [b]judgment to them, and they will judge you according to their customs.

25 'I will set My [a]jealousy against you, that they may deal with you in wrath. They will remove your nose and your ears; and your [1]survivors will fall by the sword. They will take your [b]sons and your daughters; and your [1]survivors will be consumed by the fire.

26 'They will also [a]strip you of your clothes and take away your [b]beautiful jewels.

27 'Thus [a]I will make your lewdness and your harlotry *brought* from the land of Egypt to cease from you, so that you will not lift up your eyes to them or remember Egypt anymore.'

28 "For thus says the Lord GOD, 'Behold, I will give you into the hand of those whom you [a]hate, into the hand of those from whom [1]you were alienated.

29 'They will [a]deal with you in hatred, take all your property, and leave you naked and bare. And the nakedness of your harlotries will be uncovered, both your lewdness and your harlotries.

30 'These things will be done to you because you have [a]played the harlot with the nations, because you have defiled yourself with their idols.

31 'You have walked in the way of your sister; therefore I will give [a]her cup into your hand.'

32 "Thus says the Lord GOD,

'You will [a]drink your sister's cup,
Which is deep and wide.
[1]You will be [b]laughed at and held in derision;
It contains much.

33 'You will be filled with [a]drunkenness and sorrow,
The cup of horror and desolation,
The cup of your sister Samaria.

34 'You will [a]drink it and drain it.
Then you will gnaw its fragments
And tear your breasts;
for I have spoken,' declares the Lord GOD.

35 "Therefore, thus says the Lord GOD, 'Because you have [a]forgotten Me and [b]cast Me behind your back, bear now the *punishment* of your lewdness and your harlotries.'"

36 Moreover, the LORD said to me, "Son of man, will you [a]judge Oholah and Oholibah? Then [b]declare to them their abominations.

37 "For they have committed adultery, and blood is on their hands. Thus they have

12 [1]Lit *sons of Asshur* [a]2 Kin 16:7
13 [1]Lit *one*
14 [a]Ezek 8:10 [b]Ezek 16:29
15 [1]Lit *the likeness of* [2]Lit *sons of Babel*
16 [1]Lit *At the sight of her eyes* [a]Ezek 23:20; Matt 5:28
17 [1]Lit *sons of Babel* [2]Lit *her soul* [a]2 Kin 24:17
18 [1]Lit *My soul* [a]Jer 8:12; Ezek 21:24; 23:10 [b]Ps 78:59; 106:40; Jer 12:8 [c]Ezek 23:9; Amos 5:21
20 [a]Ezek 16:26; 17:15
21 [1]So two mss; M.T. *from Egypt* [a]Jer 3:9; Ezek 23:3
22 [1]Heb *YHWH*, usually rendered *LORD*, and so throughout the ch [2]Lit *your soul was alienated*
23 [1]Lit *sons of Babylon* [2]Lit *sons of Assyria* [3]Lit *the called ones* [a]2 Kin 20:14-17; Ezek 21:19; 23:14-17 [b]2 Kin 24:2; Job 1:17; Is 23:13 [c]Jer 50:21 [d]Gen 2:14; 25:18; Ezra 6:22
24 [1]Lit *wheels* [a]Jer 47:3; Ezek 26:10; Nah 2:3, 4 [b]Jer 39:5, 6; Ezek 16:38; 23:45
25 [a]Ex 34:14; Ezek 5:13; 8:17, 18; Zeph 1:18

25 [1]Lit *remainder* [b]Ezek 23:47; Hos 2:4
26 [a]Jer 13:22; Ezek 16:39; 23:29 [b]Is 3:18-23
27 [a]Ezek 16:41
28 [1]Lit *your soul was alienated* [a]Jer 21:7-10; 34:20; Ezek 16:37; 23:17, 22
29 [a]Deut 28:48; Ezek 23:25, 26, 45-47
30 [a]Ezek 6:9
31 [a]2 Kin 21:13; Jer 7:14, 15; Ezek 23:33
32 [1]Or *It will be for jesting and deriding because of its great size* [a]Ps 60:3; Is 51:17; Jer 25:15 [b]Ezek 5:14, 15; 16:57; 22:4, 5 **33** [a]Jer 25:15, 16, 27; Hab 2:16 **34** [a]Ps 75:8; Is 51:17 **35** [a]Is 17:10; Jer 3:21; Ezek 22:12; Hos 8:14; 13:6 [b]1 Kin 14:9; Jer 2:27; 32:33 **36** [a]Jer 1:10; Ezek 20:4; 22:2 [b]Is 58:1; Ezek 16:2; Mic 3:8

23:14 *men portrayed on the wall.* Arousal through pictures was even more perverted (see 16:17 and note). *portrayed with vermilion.* Jeremiah, too, noted red interior decorations with disfavor (Jer 22:14).

23:15 *belts.* Cf. Is 5:27 for similar Assyrian military equipment.

23:20 *flesh.* Probably referring to genitals (see note on 16:26).

23:23 *Babylonians . . . Chaldeans.* Often identified with one another (see 12:13), here distinguished (as in v. 15), probably because the Chaldeans were relative newcomers. *Pekod.* Aramaic people located east of Babylon. *Shoa and Koa.* Babylonian allies of uncertain origin and location.

23:24 *their customs.* Which were cruel and gruesome (see v. 25).

23:25 *fire.* See notes on 15:7; 20:47.

23:27 *of Egypt.* See note on v. 8.

23:31 *cup.* Filled with the anger of the Lord. To drink it was to die. For a development of the imagery cf. Ps 75:8; Is 51:17,22; Jer 25:15–29; 49:12; Lam 4:21; Obad 16; Hab 2:16; Matt 20:22; 26:39; Rev 14:10.

committed adultery with their idols and even caused their sons, [a]whom they bore to Me, to pass through *the fire* to [1]them as food.

38 "Again, they have done this to Me: they have [a]defiled My sanctuary on the same day and have [b]profaned My sabbaths.

39 "For when they had slaughtered their children for their idols, they entered My [a]sanctuary on the same day to profane it; and lo, thus they did within My house.

40 "Furthermore, [1]they have even sent for men who come from afar, to whom a messenger was sent; and lo, they came—for whom you bathed, [a]painted your eyes and [b]decorated yourselves with ornaments;

41 and you sat on a splendid [a]couch with a [b]table arranged before it on which you had set My [c]incense and My [c]oil.

42 "The sound of a [1a]carefree multitude was with her; and [b]drunkards were brought from the wilderness with men of the [2]common sort. And they put [c]bracelets on [3]the hands of the women and beautiful crowns on their heads.

43 "Then I said concerning her who was [a]worn out by adulteries, '[1]Will they now commit adultery with her when she is *thus?*'

44 "[1]But they went in to her as they would go in to a harlot. Thus they went in to Oholah and to Oholibah, the lewd women.

45 "But they, righteous men, will [a]judge them with the judgment of adulteresses and with the judgment of women who shed blood, because they are adulteresses and blood is on their hands.

46 "For thus says the Lord GOD, 'Bring up a company against them and give them over to [a]terror and plunder.

47 'The company will [a]stone them with stones and cut them down with their swords; they will slay their sons and their daughters and [b]burn their houses with fire.

48 'Thus I will make lewdness cease from the land, that all women may be admonished and not commit [1]lewdness as you have done.

49 'Your lewdness [1]will be [a]requited upon you, and you will bear the penalty of *worshiping* your idols; thus you will know that I am the Lord GOD.' "

37 [1]I.e. idols [a]Ezek 16:20; 20:26
38 [a]2 Kin 21:4, 7; Ezek 5:11; 7:20 [b]Jer 17:27; Ezek 20:13, 24
39 [a]Jer 7:9-11
40 [1]Or *you (women)* [a]2 Kin 9:30; Jer 4:30 [b]Is 3:18-23; Ezek 16:13-16
41 [a]Esth 1:6; Is 57:7; Amos 6:4 [b]Is 65:11; Ezek 44:16 [c]Jer 44:17; Hos 2:8
42 [1]Lit *at ease* [2]Lit *multitude of mankind* [3]Lit *their hands* [a]Ezek 16:49; Amos 6:3-6 [b]Jer 51:7 [c]Gen 24:30; Ezek 16:11, 12
43 [1]Or *Now they will commit adultery with her, and she with them* [a]Ezek 23:3
44 [1]Or *And*
45 [a]Ezek 16:38
46 [a]Jer 15:4; 24:9; 29:18
47 [a]Lev 20:10; Ezek 16:40 [b]Jer 39:8
48 [1]Lit *according to your lewdness*
49 [1]Lit *they will give* [a]Is 59:18; Ezek 7:4, 9; 9:10; 23:35

Parable of the Boiling Pot

24 And the word of the LORD came to me in the ninth year, in the tenth month, on the tenth of the month, saying,

2 "Son of man, write the name of the day, this very day. The king of Babylon [1]has [a]laid siege to Jerusalem this very day.

3 "Speak a [a]parable to the [b]rebellious house and say to them, 'Thus says the Lord [1]GOD,

"Put on the [c]pot, put *it* on and also
pour water in it;
4 [1a]Put in it the pieces,
Every good piece, the thigh and the
shoulder;
Fill *it* with choice bones.
5 "Take the [a]choicest of the flock,
And also pile [1]wood under [2]the pot.
Make it boil vigorously.
Also seethe its bones in it."

6 'Therefore, thus says the Lord GOD,
"Woe to the [a]bloody city,
To the pot in which there is rust
And whose rust has not gone out of it!
Take out of it piece after piece,
[1]Without making a choice.
7 "For her blood is in her midst;
She placed it on the bare rock;
She did not [a]pour it on the ground
To cover it with dust.
8 "That it may [a]cause wrath to come up
to take vengeance,
I have put her blood on the bare rock,
That it may not be covered."
9 'Therefore, thus says the Lord GOD,
"[a]Woe to the bloody city!
I also will make the pile great.
10 "Heap on the wood, kindle the fire,
[1]Boil the flesh well
And mix in the spices,
And let the bones be burned.

24:2 [1]Lit *leaned on* [a]2 Kin 25:1; Jer 39:1; 52:4
3 [1]Heb *YHWH,* usually rendered LORD, and so throughout the ch [a]Ps 78:2; Ezek 17:2; 20:49 [b]Is 1:2; 30:1, 9; Ezek 2:3, 6, 8 [c]Jer 1:13, 14; Ezek 11:3, 7, 11; 24:6
4 [1]Lit *Gather her pieces* [a]Mic 3:2, 3
5 [1]Lit *bones* [2]Lit *it* [a]Jer 39:6; 52:10, 24-27
6 [1]Lit *No lot has fallen on it* [a]2 Kin 24:3, 4; Ezek 22:2, 3, 27; Mic 7:2; Nah 3:1
7 [a]Lev 17:13; Deut 12:16
8 [a]Is 26:21
9 [a]Ezek 24:6; Hab 2:12
10 [1]Lit *Complete*

23:37 *sons . . . to pass through the fire.* See note on 16:20.
23:38 *defiled My sanctuary.* See ch. 8. *sabbaths.* See note on 22:8.
23:40 *they have even sent for men.* Possibly a reference to the Jerusalem summit meeting in Zedekiah's time (Jer 27). *you.* Jerusalem. *painted your eyes.* By daubing them with kohl, a soot-like compound, to draw attention to the eyes.
23:41 *couch with a table arranged before it.* Ready for a banquet (see Is 21:5; also Prov 9:2).
24:1 *ninth year . . . tenth month . . . tenth of the month.* Jan. 15, 588 B.C.; Ezekiel's fourth date (see 1:2; 8:1; 20:1).
24:2 *write . . . this very day. The king . . . this very day.* God revealed to Ezekiel what was happening in Jerusalem.
24:3 *parable.* Cf. 17:2; 20:49. *rebellious house.* The last occurrence of this condemning phrase in Ezekiel (see 2:5,6,8; 3:9,26–27; 12:2–3,9,25; 17:12). Jerusalem's rebellion would soon be crushed. *pot.* The image of 11:3–12, a discussion of the remnant, here pictures total destruction. The cooking pot is Jerusalem (cf. 11:3).
24:4 *Every good piece.* The people of Jerusalem who thought they were spared the exile in 597 B.C. because of their goodness (see 11:3 and note).
24:5 *wood.* Nebuchadnezzar's siege equipment.
24:6 *bloody city.* Cf. 22:3. *there is rust.* Representing Jerusalem's irredeemable situation. *Without making a choice.* After the siege of Jerusalem in 597, perhaps the Babylonians had cast lots to see whom they would take away into exile. Now everyone would go.
24:7 *blood . . . on the bare rock.* Jerusalem had brazenly left on display the blood she unjustly shed (cf. Is 3:9). For uncovered blood see Gen 4:10; Job 16:18; Is 26:21.
24:8 *wrath.* God's wrath. What Jerusalem had begun (v. 7), God would complete through judgment. Compare Ex 8:32 with Ex 9:12.

11 "Then [a]set it empty on its coals
So that it may be hot
And its bronze may [1]glow
And its [b]filthiness may be melted in it,
Its rust consumed.
12 "She has [a]wearied *Me* with toil,
Yet her great rust has not gone from
her;
Let her rust *be* in the fire!
13 "In your filthiness is lewdness.
Because I *would* have cleansed you,
Yet you are [a]not clean,
You will not be cleansed from your
filthiness again
Until I have [1b]spent My wrath on you.
14 "I, the LORD, have spoken; it is [a]coming
and I will act. I will not relent, and I will not
[b]pity and I will not be sorry; [c]according to
your ways and according to your deeds [1]I
will judge you," declares the Lord GOD.' "

Death of Ezekiel's Wife Is a Sign

15 And the word of the LORD came to me
saying,
16 "Son of man, behold, I am about to take
from you the [a]desire of your eyes with a
[b]blow; but you shall not [c]mourn and you
shall not weep, and your [d]tears shall not
come.
17 "Groan silently; make [a]no mourning for
the dead. Bind on your turban and put your
shoes on your feet, and do not cover *your*
mustache and [b]do not eat the bread of men."
18 So I spoke to the people in the morning, and in the evening my wife died. And in
the morning I did as I was commanded.
19 The people said to me, "Will you not
tell us what these things that you are doing
mean for us?"
20 Then I said to them, "The word of the
LORD came to me saying,
21 'Speak to the house of Israel, "Thus
says the Lord GOD, 'Behold, I am about to
profane My sanctuary, the pride of your
power, the [a]desire of your eyes and the
delight of your soul; and your [b]sons and
your daughters whom you have left behind
will fall by the sword.
22 'You will do as I have done; you will not
cover *your* mustache and you will not eat the
bread of men.
23 'Your turbans will be on your heads and
your shoes on your feet. You [a]will not mourn
and you will not weep, but [b]you will rot
away in your iniquities and you will groan
[1]to one another.
24 'Thus Ezekiel will be a [a]sign to you;
according to all that he has done you will do;
when it comes, then you will know that I am
the Lord GOD.' "
25 'As for you, son of man, will *it* not be
on the day when I take from them their
[a]stronghold, the joy of their [1]pride, the
desire of their eyes and [2]their heart's delight,
their sons and their daughters,
26 that on that day he who [a]escapes will
come to you with information for *your* ears?
27 'On that day your [a]mouth will be
opened to him who escaped, and you will
speak and be mute no longer. Thus you will
be a sign to them, and they will know that I
am the LORD.' "

Judgment on Gentile Nations—Ammon

25 And the word of the LORD came to me
saying,
2 "Son of man, set your face toward the
[a]sons of Ammon and prophesy against them,
3 and say to the sons of Ammon, 'Hear
the word of the Lord [1]GOD! Thus says the
Lord GOD, "Because you said, '[a]Aha!' against
My sanctuary when it was profaned, and
against the land of Israel when it was made
desolate, and against the house of Judah
when they went into exile,
4 therefore, behold, I am going to give
you to the [a]sons of the east for a possession,
and they will set their encampments among

11 [1]Lit *become hot* [a]Jer 21:10; Mal 4:1 [b]Ezek 22:15; 23:27
12 [a]Jer 9:5
13 [1]Lit *caused to rest* [a]Jer 6:28-30; Ezek 22:24 [b]Ezek 5:13; 8:18
14 [1]So with several ancient mss and versions; M.T. *they* [a]Ps 33:9; Is 55:11 [b]Jer 13:14; Ezek 9:10 [c]Is 3:11; Ezek 18:30; 36:19
16 [a]Song 7:10; Ezek 24:18 [b]Job 23:2 [c]Jer 16:5; 22:10 [d]Jer 13:17
17 [a]Lev 21:10-12 [b]Jer 16:7; Hos 9:4
21 [a]Ps 27:4; 84:1; Ezek 24:16 [b]Jer 6:11; 16:3, 4; Ezek 23:25, 47
23 [1]Lit *a man to his brother* [a]Job 27:15; Ps 78:64 [b]Lev 26:39; Ezek 33:10
24 [a]Ezek 4:3; Luke 11:29, 30
25 [1]Or *beauty* [2]Lit *the lifting up of their soul* [a]Ps 48:2; 50:2; Ezek 24:21
26 [a]1 Sam 4:12; Job 1:15-19
27 [a]Ezek 3:26; 33:22
25:2 [a]Jer 49:1-6; Amos 1:13-15; Zeph 2:9
3 [1]Heb *YHWH,* usually rendered LORD, and so throughout the ch [a]Ps 70:2, 3; Ezek 21:28; 25:6; 26:2; 36:2
4 [a]Judg 6:3, 33; 1 Kin 4:30

24:11 *it empty.* Jerusalem, emptied of inhabitants, would be set to the torch, in a vain final effort at purification.
24:13 *lewdness.* See 16:27; 22:9.
24:16 *desire of your eyes.* The object of loving attention (see vv. 21,25)—apparently a conventional way of referring to a man's wife. *blow.* Some swiftly fatal disease, one that often reached plague proportions (see Ex 9:14; Num 14:37).
24:17 *Bind on your turban.* The mourner normally removed it and put dust on his head (see Josh 7:6; 1 Sam 4:12). *shoes on your feet.* To remove them showed grief (see 2 Sam 15:30). *cover your mustache.* A gesture of shame (Mic 3:7) or uncleanness (Lev 13:45). *bread of men.* The funeral meal (see Jer 16:7).
24:19 *The people said to me.* The third time that the people responded to Ezekiel's behavior (see 12:9; 21:7).
24:21 *profane.* By letting Nebuchadnezzar burn it down.
24:24 *Ezekiel.* The prophet speaks of himself in the third person. Elsewhere his name occurs only in 1:3. *sign.* See note on 12:6.
24:26 *he who escapes.* The first of the exiles of 586 B.C. *information.* About the siege—its beginning (verifying the accuracy of vv. 1–2) and its ending (see note on 33:21).
24:27 *be mute no longer.* Ezekiel's wife died the same day the temple was burned (Aug. 14, 586 B.C.; see 2 Kin 25:8–9). See notes on 3:26; 33:21. *sign.* See note on 12:6.
25:1–32:32 Oracles against the nations. Frequently in the prophets, God's word of judgment on Israel is accompanied by oracles of judgment on the nations. These make clear that, while judgment begins "with the household of God" (1 Pet 4:17), the pagan nations would not escape God's wrath. Often these judgments are implicit messages of salvation for Israel (see 28:25–26) since the Lord's victories over hostile powers remove an enemy of His people or punish them for their cruel attacks on His people. In the case of Ezekiel there are seven oracles (the seventh of which has seven parts, each introduced by the phrase "The word of the LORD came to me"; see Introduction: Outline).
25:2 *set your face.* See note on 20:46. *sons of Ammon.* Ammon (part of modern Jordan) was immediately east of Israel (see 21:20; see also Jer 9:26; 49:1–6; Amos 1:13–15; Zeph 2:8–11). For hostile Ammonite action during this time and later see 2 Kin 24:2; Neh 4:7.
25:3 *Aha!* A cry of malicious joy (cf. 26:2; 36:2; Ps 35:21–25).
25:4 *sons of the east.* Probably nomadic tribes of the desert

you and make their dwellings among you;
they will [b]eat your fruit and drink your milk.
5 "I will make [a]Rabbah a pasture for
camels and the sons of Ammon a resting
place for flocks. Thus you will know that I
am the LORD."
6 'For thus says the Lord GOD, "Because
you have [a]clapped your hands and stamped
your feet and [b]rejoiced with all the scorn of
your soul against the land of Israel,
7 therefore, behold, I have [a]stretched out
My hand against you and I will give you for
[b]spoil to the nations. And I will [c]cut you off
from the peoples and [d]make you perish from
the lands; I will destroy you. Thus you will
[e]know that I am the LORD."

Moab

8 'Thus says the Lord GOD, "Because
[a]Moab and Seir say, 'Behold, the house of
Judah is like all the nations,'
9 therefore, behold, I am going to
[1]deprive the flank of Moab of *its* cities, of its
cities which are on its [2]frontiers, the glory of
the land, [a]Beth-jeshimoth, [b]Baal-meon and
[c]Kiriathaim,
10 and I will give it for a possession along
with the sons of Ammon to the [a]sons of the
east, so that the sons of Ammon will not be
remembered among the nations.
11 "Thus I will execute judgments on
Moab, and they will know that I am the
LORD."

Edom

12 'Thus says the Lord GOD, "Because
[a]Edom has acted against the house of Judah
by taking vengeance, and has incurred
grievous guilt, and avenged themselves
upon them,"
13 therefore thus says the Lord GOD, "I
will also [a]stretch out My hand against Edom
and [b]cut off man and beast from it. And I
will lay it waste; from [c]Teman even to
[d]Dedan they will fall by the sword.
14 "[a]I will lay My vengeance on Edom by
the hand of My people Israel. Therefore, they
will act in Edom [b]according to My anger and
according to My wrath; thus they will know
My vengeance," declares the Lord GOD.

Philistia

15 'Thus says the Lord GOD, "Because the
Philistines have acted in [a]revenge and have
taken vengeance with scorn of soul to
destroy with everlasting enmity,"
16 therefore thus says the Lord GOD,
"Behold, I will [a]stretch out My hand against
the Philistines, even cut off the [b]Cherethites
and destroy the remnant of the seacoast.
17 "I will execute great vengeance on them
with wrathful rebukes; and they will [a]know
that I am the LORD when I lay My vengeance
on them." ' "

Judgment on Tyre

26 Now in the eleventh year, on the first of
the month, the word of the LORD came
to me saying,
2 "Son of man, because [a]Tyre has said
concerning Jerusalem, 'Aha, the [b]gateway of
the peoples is broken; it has [1c]opened to me.
I shall be filled, *now that* she is laid waste,'
3 therefore thus says the Lord [1]GOD,
'Behold, I am against you, O Tyre, and I will

4 [b]Deut 28:33, 51; Is 1:7
5 [a]Deut 3:11; 2 Sam 12:26; Jer 49:2; Ezek 21:20
6 [a]Job 27:23; Nah 3:19 [b]Obad 12; Zeph 2:8, 10
7 [a]Ezek 25:13, 16; Zeph 1:4 [b]Is 33:4; Ezek 26:5 [c]Ezek 21:32 [d]Amos 1:14, 15 [e]Ezek 6:14
8 [a]Is 15:1; Jer 48:1; Amos 2:1, 2
9 [1]Lit *open* [2]Lit *end* [a]Num 33:49; Josh 12:3; 13:20 [b]Num 32:3, 38; Josh 13:17; 1 Chr 5:8; Jer 48:23 [c]Num 32:37; Josh 13:19; Jer 48:1, 23
10 [a]Ezek 25:4
12 [a]2 Chr 28:17; Ps 137:7; Jer 49:7-22
13 [a]Jer 49:8, 13 [b]Ezek 29:8; Mal 1:3, 4 [c]Gen 36:34; Jer 49:7; Amos 1:12 [d]Jer 25:23; 49:8
14 [a]Is 11:14 [b]Ezek 35:11
15 [a]Is 14:29-31; Ezek 25:6, 12; Joel 3:4
16 [a]Jer 25:20; 47:1-7 [b]1 Sam 30:14; Zeph 2:5
17 [a]Ps 9:16
26:2 [1]Lit *turned* [a]2 Sam 5:11; Is 23:1; Jer 25:22 [b]Is 62:10 [c]Ezek 25:8; 35:10

3 [1]Heb *YHWH*, usually rendered *LORD*, and so throughout the ch

east of Ammon, though this could be a reference to Nebuchadnezzar and his army (see 21:31).

25:5 *Rabbah.* See note on 21:20. *pasture . . . resting place.* A common OT description for destroyed cities (see Is 34:13–15; Zeph 2:13–15). The sites were returned to the conditions they were in before the cities were built, representing the undoing of human efforts.

25:6 *clapped your hands.* See 6:11 and note.

25:7 *I have stretched out My hand against.* See note on 6:14. *spoil to the nations.* Cf. 26:5; 34:28. *cut you off.* Cf. v. 16.

25:8 *Moab.* Immediately to the south of Ammon, east of the Dead Sea (see Is 15–16; Jer 48; Amos 2:1–3; Zeph 2:8–11). *Seir.* Edom, a country south of Moab and south of the Dead Sea (see ch. 35, especially v. 15; 36:5; Is 34:5–17; 63:1–6; Jer 49:7–11; Amos 1:11–12). *like all the nations.* Israel wanted to be like the nations (see 20:32 and note), but when the nations saw Judah in her apparent vulnerability and lost their awe of her, they failed to take her God seriously (cf. Lam 4:12).

25:9 *flank of Moab.* Lower hills rising from the Dead Sea, visible from Jerusalem. *Beth-jeshimoth.* A town in the plains of Moab. *Baal-meon.* A major Moabite town mentioned in an inscribed monument of Mesha, king of Moab (see chart, p. xix). *Kiriathaim.* A city also mentioned in the Mesha inscription (cf. 2 Kin 3:4–5).

25:12 *Edom.* See note on v. 8 ("Sier"). *taking vengeance.* By not harboring Judah's refugees after 586 B.C. (see Obad 11–14).

25:13 *Teman.* A district near Petra in central Edom (see Jer 49:7,20; Amos 1:12; Obad 9; Hab 3:3). *Dedan.* A tribe and territory in southern Edom (see 27:20; 38:13; Is 21:13; Jer 49:8).

25:15 *Philistines.* Inhabitants of the coastal plain along the Mediterranean west of Judah (1 Sam 6:17), who strove for control of Canaan until subdued by David. Their hostility to Israel continued, however (see Is 14:29–31; Jer 47; Amos 1:6–8; Zeph 2:4–7), until Nebuchadnezzar deported them.

25:16 *Cherethites.* Related to, if not identical with, the Philistines (see 1 Sam 30:14 and note; 2 Sam 8:18; 15:18; 20:7). *seacoast.* Of the Mediterranean.

26:1 *eleventh year . . . first of the month.* The number of the month is missing. The entire year dates from Apr. 23, 587, to Apr. 13, 586 B.C. The oracle must date from the end of that year, in the 11th (Feb. 13, 586) or the 12th month (Mar. 15, 586). See note on 33:21. This is the fifth date in the book (see 1:2; 8:1; 20:1; 24:1).

26:2 *Tyre.* The island capital of Phoenicia, present-day Lebanon. It was involved in an anti-Assyrian coalition in 594 B.C. (see Jer 27:3). Ezekiel, more than any other prophet, prophesied against Tyre (see chs. 27–28; but see Is 23; Jer 25:22; 47:4; Joel 3:4–5; Amos 1:9–10; Zech 9:2–4). *Aha.* See note on 25:3. *gateway of the peoples.* Because of its geographical location, its political importance and the central role it played in international trade. The anti-Assyrian summit meeting was held there (see Jer 27).

26:3 *I am against you.* See note on 5:8. *as the sea brings up its waves.* For invading armies likened to waves of the sea cf. Is

bring up [a]many nations against you, as the
[b]sea brings up its waves.
4 'They will [a]destroy the walls of Tyre and
break down her towers; and I will scrape her
debris from her and make her a bare rock.
5 'She will be a place for the spreading of
nets in the midst of the sea, for I have spoken,' declares the Lord GOD, 'and she will
become [a]spoil for the nations.
6 'Also her [a]daughters who are [1]on the
mainland will be slain by the sword, and
they will know that I am the LORD.' "
7 For thus says the Lord GOD, "Behold, I
will bring upon Tyre from the north Nebuchadnezzar king of Babylon, [a]king of kings,
with horses, [b]chariots, cavalry and [1]a great
army.
8 "He will slay your daughters [1]on the
mainland with the sword; and he will make
[a]siege walls against you, cast up a [b]ramp
against you and raise up a large shield
against you.
9 "The blow of his battering rams he will
direct against your walls, and with his [1]axes
he will break down your towers.
10 "Because of the multitude of his
[a]horses, the dust *raised by* them will cover
you; your walls will [b]shake at the noise of
cavalry and [1]wagons and chariots when he
[c]enters your gates as men enter a city that is
breached.
11 "With the hoofs of his [a]horses he will
trample all your streets. He will slay your
people with the sword; and your strong pillars will [b]come down to the ground.
12 "Also they will make a spoil of your
riches and a prey of your [a]merchandise,
[b]break down your walls and destroy your
[c]pleasant houses, and [1]throw your stones and
your timbers and your debris [d]into the water.
13 "So I will [1]silence the sound of your
[a]songs, and the sound of your [b]harps will be
heard no more.
14 "I will make you a bare rock; you will be
a place for the spreading of nets. You will be
[a]built no more, for I the [b]LORD have spoken,"
declares the Lord GOD.
15 Thus says the Lord GOD to Tyre, "Shall
not the [a]coastlands [b]shake at the sound of
your fall when the wounded groan, when the
slaughter occurs in your midst?
16 "Then all the princes of the sea will [a]go
down from their thrones, remove their robes
and strip off their embroidered garments.
They will [b]clothe themselves with [1]trem-
bling; they will sit on the ground, [c]tremble
every moment and be appalled at you.
17 "They will take up a [a]lamentation over
you and say to you,

'[b]How you have perished, O inhabited
one,
From the seas, O renowned city,
Which was [c]mighty on the sea,
She and her inhabitants,
Who [1]imposed [2]her terror
On all her inhabitants!
18 'Now the [a]coastlands will tremble
On the day of your fall;
Yes, the coastlands which are by the
sea
Will be terrified at your [b]passing.' "

19 For thus says the Lord GOD, "When I
make you a desolate city, like the cities
which are not inhabited, when I [a]bring up
the deep over you and the great waters cover you,
20 then I will bring you down with those
who [a]go down to the pit, to the people of
old, and I will make you dwell in the [b]lower
parts of the earth, like the ancient waste
places, with those who go down to the pit,
so that you will not [1]be inhabited; but I will
set [c]glory in the land of the living.
21 "I will [1]bring [a]terrors on you and you
will be no more; though you will be sought,
[b]you will never be found again," declares the
Lord GOD.

Lament over Tyre

27 Moreover, the word of the LORD came
to me saying,
2 "And you, son of man, [a]take up a
lamentation over Tyre;

3 [a]Mic 4:11 [b]Is 5:30; Jer 50:42; 51:42 **4** [a]Is 23:11; Ezek 26:9; Amos 1:10 **5** [a]Ezek 25:7; 29:19 **6** [1]Lit *in the field* [a]Ezek 16:46, 53; 26:8 **7** [1]Lit *an assembly, even many people* [a]Ezra 7:12; Is 10:8; Jer 52:32; Dan 2:37, 47 [b]Ezek 23:24; Nah 2:3, 4 **8** [1]Lit *in the field* [a]Jer 52:4; Ezek 21:22 [b]Jer 32:24 **9** [1]Lit *swords* **10** [1]Lit *wheels* [a]Jer 4:13; 47:3 [b]Ezek 26:15; 27:28 [c]Jer 39:3 **11** [a]Is 5:28; Hab 1:8 [b]Is 26:5; Jer 43:13 **12** [1]Lit *put* [a]Is 23:8, 18; Ezek 27:3-27; Zech 9:3 [b]Jer 52:14 [c]2 Chr 32:27; Amos 5:11 [d]Ezek 27:27, 32, 34; 28:8 **13** [1]Lit *cause to cease* [a]Is 23:16; 24:8, 9; Amos 6:5 [b]Is 5:12; Rev 18:22 **14** [a]Deut 13:16; Job 12:14; Mal 1:4 [b]Is 14:27 **15** [a]Ezek 26:18; 27:35 [b]Jer 49:21; Ezek 31:16 **16** [1]Lit *tremblings* [a]Jon 3:6 [b]Job 8:22; Ps 35:26; Ezek 7:27; 1 Pet 5:5 [c]Ezek 32:10; Hos 11:10 **17** [1]Lit *put* [2]Lit *their* [a]Ezek 19:1, 14; 27:2, 32; 32:2, 16 [b]Is 14:12; Jer 48:39; 50:23 [c]Ezek 27:3, 10, 11; 28:2 **18** [a]Is 41:5; Ezek 26:15; 27:35 [b]Is 23:5-7, 10, 11 **19** [a]Is 8:7, 8; Ezek 26:3

20 [1]Or *return* [a]Is 14:9, 10; Ezek 32:30 [b]Ps 88:6; Amos 9:2; Jon 2:2, 6 [c]Jer 33:9; Zech 2:8 **21** [1]Lit *give you terrors* [a]Ezek 26:15, 16; 27:36 [b]Rev 18:21 **27:2** [a]Jer 9:10, 17-20; Ezek 28:12

17:12–13. Since Tyre was an island, the metaphor is especially appropriate here.

26:5 *spoil for the nations.* Cf. 25:7; 34:28.

26:7 *I will bring.* A clear indication of God's sovereignty over the nations (cf. 28:7; 29:8). *north.* The direction from which Nebuchadnezzar would descend on Tyre after first marching his army up the Euphrates River valley rather than across the Arabian Desert (cf. Jer 1:13). *Nebuchadnezzar.* The first of four references to him in Ezekiel (see 29:18–19; 30:10). He ruled from 605 to 562 B.C., and his name means "O (god) Nabu, protect my son" or "O (god) Nabu, protect my boundary." Jeremiah and Ezekiel both proclaimed that this pagan king would be used by God to do His work (see Jer 25:9; 27:6).

26:8 *siege.* Nebuchadnezzar's 15-year siege of Tyre began shortly after the fall of Jerusalem. There is no record that Tyre fell at this time (see note on 29:18).

26:14 *be built no more.* Eventually fulfilled by Alexander's devastating siege in 332 B.C. (see note on Is 23:1).

26:16 *princes of the sea.* Called kings in 27:35, they were probably trading partners with Tyre. *remove their robes.* Usually mourners tore their clothes (Job 2:12) and put on sackcloth, but cf. the king of Nineveh (Jon 3:6). *clothe themselves with trembling.* Because of political shock waves from the fall of such a powerful city (cf. 7:27; Ps 35:26; 109:29).

26:17 *lamentation.* See note on 19:1.

26:19 *the deep.* The primeval, chaotic mass (as in Gen 1:2). Tyre's collapse into the sea is described in almost cosmic terms.

26:20 *pit.* The grave, "the earth below" (cf. Ps 69:15). *people of old.* Those long dead (Ps 143:3; Lam 3:6).

26:21 See 27:36; 28:19.

27:2 *lamentation.* See note on 19:1.

3 and say to Tyre, [a]who dwells at the
[1]entrance to the sea, [b]merchant of the peoples to many coastlands, 'Thus says the Lord
[2]GOD,

"O Tyre, you have said, 'I am perfect in beauty.'
4 "Your borders are in the heart of the seas;
Your builders have perfected your beauty.
5 "They have [1]made all *your* planks of fir trees from [a]Senir;
They have taken a cedar from Lebanon to make a mast for you.
6 "Of [a]oaks from [b]Bashan they have made your oars;
With ivory they have [1]inlaid your deck of boxwood from the coastlands of [c]Cyprus.
7 "Your sail was of fine embroidered linen from Egypt
So that it became your [1]distinguishing mark;
Your [2]awning was [3][a]blue and purple from the coastlands of [b]Elishah.
8 "The inhabitants of Sidon and [a]Arvad were your rowers;
Your [b]wise men, O Tyre, were [1]aboard; they were your pilots.
9 "The elders of [a]Gebal and her wise men were with you repairing your seams;
All the ships of the sea and their sailors were with you in order to deal in your merchandise.

10 "[a]Persia and [a]Lud and [a]Put were in
your army, your men of war. They hung
shield and helmet in you; they set forth your
splendor.
11 "The sons of Arvad and your army were
on your walls, *all* around, and the [1]Gammadim were in your towers. They hung their
shields on your walls *all* around; they perfected your beauty.
12 "Tarshish was your customer because of
the abundance of all *kinds* of wealth; with
silver, iron, tin and lead they paid for your
wares.
13 "[a]Javan, [a]Tubal and [b]Meshech, they
were your traders; with the [c]lives of men and
vessels of bronze they paid for your merchandise.
14 "Those from [a]Beth-togarmah gave
horses and war horses and mules for your
wares.
15 "The sons of [a]Dedan were your traders.
Many coastlands were [1]your market; [b]ivory
tusks and ebony they brought as your payment.
16 "[a]Aram was your customer because of
the abundance of your [1]goods; they paid for
your wares with [b]emeralds, purple, [c]embroidered work, fine linen, coral and rubies.
17 "Judah and the land of Israel, they were
your traders; with the wheat of [a]Minnith,
[1]cakes, honey, oil and balm they paid for
your merchandise.
18 "[a]Damascus was your customer because
of the abundance of your [1]goods, because of
the abundance of all *kinds* of wealth,
because of the wine of Helbon and white
wool.
19 "Vedan and Javan paid for your wares
[1]from Uzal; wrought iron, cassia and [2]sweet
cane were among your merchandise.

3 [1]Lit *entrances* [2]Heb *YHWH*, usually rendered LORD, and so throughout the ch [a]Ezek 28:2 [b]Is 23:3
5 [1]Lit *built* [a]Deut 3:9; 1 Chr 5:23; Song 4:8
6 [1]Lit *made* [a]Is 2:13; Zech 11:2 [b]Num 21:33; Is 2:13; Jer 22:20 [c]Gen 10:4; Is 23:1, 12; Jer 2:10
7 [1]Or *standard* [2]Lit *covering* [3]Or *violet* [a]Ex 25:4; Jer 10:9 [b]Gen 10:4
8 [1]Lit *in you* [a]Gen 10:18; 1 Chr 1:16; Ezek 27:11 [b]1 Kin 9:27
9 [a]Josh 13:5; 1 Kin 5:18
10 [a]Ezek 30:5; 38:5
11 [1]Or *valorous ones*
13 [a]Gen 10:2; Is 66:19; Ezek 27:19 [b]Gen 10:2; Ezek 38:2; 39:1 [c]Joel 3:3; Rev 18:13
14 [a]Gen 10:3; Ezek 38:6
15 [1]Lit *the market of your hand* [a]Jer 25:23; Ezek 25:13; 27:20 [b]1 Kin 10:22; Rev 18:12
16 [1]Lit *works* [a]Judg 10:6; Is 7:1-8; Ezek 16:57 [b]Ezek 28:13 [c]Ezek 16:13, 18
17 [1]Heb *pannag* [a]Judg 11:33
18 [1]Lit *works* [a]Gen 14:15; Is 7:8; Jer 49:23; Ezek 47:16-18
19 [1]Or *with yarn* [2]Or *calamus*

27:3 *I am perfect in beauty.* See 28:12; cf. 28:2 for a similar prideful statement. Since Tyre is described as a stately ship in the following verses, some translate, "You are a ship, perfect in beauty."
27:4 *perfected your beauty.* See v. 11.
27:5 *Senir.* Amorite name for Hermon, the Anti-Lebanon mountain (or range) famed for cedar.
27:6 *Bashan.* See note on 39:18. *Cyprus.* Hebrew *Kittim*, which was originally the name of a town in southern Cyprus colonized by Phoenicia.
27:7 *Elishah.* A city on the east side of Cyprus; also the oldest name for Cyprus (but see note on Gen 10:4).
27:8 *Sidon.* A harbor city 25 miles north of Tyre, which sometimes rivaled her in political and commercial importance (see note on 28:21). *Arvad.* Another Phoenician island-city, off the Mediterranean coast and north of Sidon.
27:9 *Gebal.* Byblos, an important ancient city on the coast between Sidon and Arvad (see 1 Kin 5:18).
27:10 *Lud.* In Asia Minor (Lydia). *Put.* Libya, in North Africa, west of Egypt. *men of war.* The ship image is abandoned, and Tyre is now described literally—as a city (see "walls" and "towers" in v. 11), complete with a mercenary army gathered from the whole world.
27:11 *Arvad.* See note on v. 8. *Gammadim.* Men of Gammad, which was either (1) northern Asia Minor, or (2) a coastal town near Arvad. It is not mentioned elsewhere in the Bible.
27:12 *Tarshish.* Traditionally located on the coast of southern Spain, but the island of Sardinia has also been suggested. Passages such as 1 Kin 10:22; Jon 1:3 imply that it was a long distance from the Canaanite coast. The list of places in vv. 12–23 generally follows a west-to-east direction.
27:13 *Tubal and Meshech.* Both in Asia Minor.
27:14 *Beth-togarmah.* In eastern Asia Minor, present-day Armenia (see 38:6). *horses.* Asia Minor was known for its horses (see 1 Kin 10:28).
27:15 *Dedan.* See note on 25:13.
27:16 *Aram.* Syria. Since Damascus, the capital of Aram, is mentioned in v. 18, perhaps Edom is meant here (some manuscripts read "Edom" instead of "Aram"; see also 25:12 and note).
27:17 *Israel . . . your traders.* In the past. Since 722–721 B.C. Israel had ceased to exist as a political state. *Minnith.* An Ammonite town, apparently famous for its wheat; "wheat from Minnith" possibly denoted a superior quality of wheat. *balm.* Gum or oil from one of several plants; a product of Gilead (see Gen 37:25; Jer 8:22; 46:11).
27:18 *Damascus.* Capital of Aram (see note on v. 16; see also Is 7:8). *Helbon.* A town north of Damascus, still in existence and still a wine-making center. The name occurs only here in the Bible.
27:19 *Vedan.* Or, if "Ve" in "Vedan" is read as a conjunction, "And Dan." Dan was a term that Homer used for Greeks. Some read (as does the Septuagint) "and wine from" for "Vedan and Javan . . ." *Uzal.* See Gen 10:27; 1 Chr 1:21; perhaps Yemen or the area between Haran and the Tigris. *cassia.* Similar to the

20 "[a]Dedan traded with you in saddlecloths for riding.

21 "[a]Arabia and all the princes of Kedar, they were [1]your customers for [b]lambs, rams and goats; for these they were your customers.

22 "The traders of [a]Sheba and Raamah, they traded with you; they paid for your wares with the best of all *kinds* of [b]spices, and with all *kinds* of precious stones and gold.

23 "Haran, Canneh, [a]Eden, the traders of Sheba, Asshur *and* Chilmad traded with you.

24 "They traded with you in choice garments, in clothes of [1]blue and embroidered work, and in carpets of many colors *and* tightly wound cords, *which were* among your merchandise.

25 "The [a]ships of Tarshish were [1]the carriers for your merchandise.
And you were filled and were very
[2]glorious
In the heart of the seas.

26 "Your rowers have brought you
Into [a]great waters;
The [b]east wind has broken you
In the heart of the seas.

27 "Your wealth, your wares, your
merchandise,
Your sailors and your pilots,
Your repairers of seams, your dealers
in merchandise
And all your men of war who are in
you,
With all your company that is in your
midst,
Will fall into the heart of the seas
On the day of your overthrow.

28 "At the sound of the cry of your pilots
The pasture lands will [a]shake.

29 "All who handle the oar,
The [a]sailors *and* all the pilots of the
sea
Will come down from their ships;
They will stand on the land,

30 And they will [a]make their voice heard
over you
And will cry bitterly.
They will [b]cast dust on their heads,
They will [c]wallow in ashes.

31 "Also they will make themselves [a]bald
for you
And [b]gird themselves with sackcloth;
And they will [c]weep for you in
bitterness of soul
With bitter mourning.

32 "Moreover, in their wailing they will
take up a [a]lamentation for you
And lament over you:
'Who is like Tyre,
Like her who is silent in the midst of
the sea?

33 'When your wares went out from the
seas,
You satisfied many peoples;
With the [a]abundance of your wealth
and your merchandise
You enriched the kings of earth.

34 '[1]Now that you are [a]broken by the seas
In the depths of the waters,
Your [b]merchandise and all your
company
Have fallen in the midst of you.

35 'All the [a]inhabitants of the coastlands
Are appalled at you,
And their kings are horribly afraid;
They are troubled in countenance.

36 'The merchants among the peoples
[a]hiss at you;
You have become [1]terrified
And you [b]will cease to be forever.' " ' "

Tyre's King Overthrown

28 The word of the LORD came again to me, saying,

2 "Son of man, say to the [1]leader of Tyre,
'Thus says the Lord [2]GOD,
"Because your heart is lifted up
And you have said, '[a]I am a god,
I sit in the seat of [3]gods
In the heart of the seas';
Yet you are a [b]man and not God,
Although you make your heart like the
heart of God—

20 [a]Gen 25:3
21 [1]Lit *customers of your hand* [a]Is 21:13 [b]Is 60:7
22 [a]Gen 10:7; Is 60:6; Ezek 38:13 [b]Gen 43:11; 1 Kin 10:2
23 [a]2 Kin 19:12; Is 37:12; Amos 1:5
24 [1]Or *violet*
25 [1]Lit *your travelers* [2]Lit *honored* [a]Is 2:16
26 [a]Ezek 26:19 [b]Ps 48:7; Jer 18:17; Acts 27:14
28 [a]Ezek 26:10, 15, 18
29 [a]Rev 18:17-19
30 [a]Is 23:1-6; Ezek 26:17
30 [b]1 Sam 4:12; 2 Sam 1:2; Lam 2:10; Rev 18:19 [c]Jer 6:26; Jon 3:6
31 [a]Is 15:2; Ezek 29:18 [b]Is 22:12; Ezek 7:18 [c]Is 16:9; 22:4
32 [a]Ezek 26:17; 27:2; 28:12
33 [a]Ezek 27:12, 18; 28:4, 5
34 [1]Lit *The time* [a]Ezek 26:12; 27:26, 27 [b]Zech 9:3, 4
35 [a]Is 23:6; Ezek 26:16
36 [1]Lit *terrors* [a]Jer 18:16; 19:8; 49:17; 50:13; Zeph 2:15 [b]Ps 37:10, 36
28:2 [1]Or *ruler, prince* [2]Heb *YHWH*, usually rendered *LORD*, and so throughout the ch [3]Or *God* [a]Is 14:14; 47:8; Ezek 28:9; 2 Thess 2:4 [b]Ps 9:20; 82:6, 7; Is 31:3; Ezek 28:9

---

cinnamon tree. The only other Biblical mention of it is in Ex 30:24, where it appears in a list of aromatic plants. *sweet cane.* An aromatic reed.

27:20 *Dedan.* See note on 25:13.

27:21 *Arabia and . . . Kedar.* A general expression for the Bedouin tribes from Aram to the Arabian Desert. For Kedar see Is 42:11; 60:7; Jer 49:28.

27:22 *Sheba.* See note on 23:42. *Raamah.* A city in southern Arabia.

27:23 *Haran.* A city east of Carchemish, in present-day eastern Turkey. It was well-known in ancient times as a center both for trade and for the worship of the moon-god Sin. From here Abraham moved to Canaan (see Gen 11:31; 12:4). *Canneh.* Of uncertain location, presumably in Mesopotamia. It is often identified with Calneh (Is 10:9, "Calno"; Amos 6:2). *Eden.* A district south of Haran, mentioned in connection with Haran in 2 Kin 19:12. See Beth-eden in Amos 1:5. *Sheba.* See note on 23:42. *Asshur.* Can mean the city, the country (Assyria) or the people (Assyrians). Here it is probably the city south of Nineveh that gave its name to the country. *Chilmad.* If a town, it is yet unidentified; presumably in Mesopotamia. Some read "all Media."

27:25 *Tarshish.* See note on v. 12. The ship image is resumed (see notes on vv. 3,10).

27:26 *east wind.* Disastrous at sea (Ps 48:7) as well as on land (Jer 18:17). It possibly symbolizes Nebuchadnezzar (as in 17:10; 19:12).

27:30 *dust on their heads.* See 26:16 for a similar scene. *wallow in ashes.* Cf. Mic 1:10.

27:31 *make themselves bald.* Cf. 7:18; Is 15:2; 22:12.

28:2 *leader of Tyre.* May refer to the city of Tyre as ruler, or to Ethbaal II, the king then ruling Tyre (see v. 12). His namesake Ethbaal I was the father of Jezebel (1 Kin 16:31). *lifted up.* In pride; cf. 27:3; Prov 16:18; Acts 12:21–23.

3 Behold, you are wiser than [a]Daniel;
There is no secret that is a match for
you.
4 "By your wisdom and understanding
You have acquired [a]riches for yourself
And have acquired gold and silver for
your treasuries.
5 "By your great wisdom, by your [a]trade
You have increased your riches
And your [b]heart is lifted up because of
your riches—
6 Therefore thus says the Lord GOD,
'Because you have [a]made your heart
Like the heart of God,
7 Therefore, behold, I will bring
[a]strangers upon you,
The [b]most ruthless of the nations.
And they will draw their swords
Against the beauty of your wisdom
And defile your splendor.
8 'They will bring you down to the pit,
And you will die the [a]death of those
who are slain
In the heart of the seas.
9 'Will you still say, "I am a god,"
In the presence of your slayer,
Though you are a man and not God,
In the hands of those who wound
you?
10 'You will die the death of the
[a]uncircumcised
By the hand of strangers,
For I have spoken!' declares the Lord
GOD!" ' "

11 Again the word of the LORD came to me
saying,
12 "Son of man, [a]take up a lamentation
over the king of Tyre and say to him, 'Thus
says the Lord GOD,
"You [1]had the seal of perfection,
Full of wisdom and perfect in beauty.
13 "You were in [a]Eden, the garden of God;
[b]Every precious stone was your
covering:
The [c]ruby, the topaz and the diamond;
The beryl, the onyx and the jasper;
The lapis lazuli, the turquoise and the
emerald;
And the gold, the workmanship of
your [1][d]settings and [2]sockets,
Was in you.
On the day that you were created
They were prepared.
14 "You were the [a]anointed cherub who
[1]covers,
And I placed you *there.*
You were on the holy [b]mountain of
God;
You walked in the midst of the [c]stones
of fire.
15 "You were [a]blameless in your ways
From the day you were created
Until [b]unrighteousness was found in
you.
16 "By the [a]abundance of your trade
[1]You were internally [b]filled with
violence,
And you sinned;
Therefore I have cast you as profane
From the mountain of God.
And I have destroyed you, O [2]covering
cherub,
From the midst of the stones of fire.
17 "Your heart was lifted up because of
your [a]beauty;
You [b]corrupted your wisdom by
reason of your splendor.
I cast you to the ground;
I put you before [c]kings,
That they may see you.
18 "By the multitude of your iniquities,
In the unrighteousness of your
trade
You profaned your sanctuaries.
Therefore I have brought [a]fire from
the midst of you;
It has consumed you,
And I have turned you to [b]ashes on
the earth
In the eyes of all who see you.
19 "All who know you among the
peoples
Are appalled at you;
You have become [1][a]terrified
And you will cease to be
[b]forever." ' "

3 [a]Dan 1:20; 2:20-23, 28; 5:11, 12
4 [a]Ezek 27:33; Zech 9:2, 3
5 [a]Ezek 27:12; Hos 12:7, 8 [b]Job 31:24, 25; Ps 52:7; Ezek 28:2; Hos 13:6
6 [a]Ex 9:17; Ezek 28:2
7 [a]Ezek 26:7 [b]Ezek 30:11; 31:12; 32:12; Hab 1:6-8
8 [a]Ezek 27:26, 27, 34
10 [a]1 Sam 17:26, 36; Ezek 31:18; 32:30
12 [1]Lit *were the one sealing a pattern* [a]Ezek 19:1; 26:17; 27:2
13 [a]Gen 2:8; Is 51:3; Ezek 31:8, 9, 16; 36:35 [b]Ezek 27:16, 22 [c]Ex 28:17-20
13 [1]Or *tambourines* [2]Or *flutes* [d]Is 24:8; 30:32
14 [1]Or *guards* [a]Ex 25:17-20; 30:26; 40:9; Ezek 28:16 [b]Ezek 20:40; 28:16 [c]Ezek 28:13, 16; Rev 18:16
15 [a]Ezek 27:3, 4; 28:3-6, 12 [b]Ezek 28:17, 18
16 [1]Lit *They filled your midst* [2]Or *guardian* [a]Ezek 27:12 [b]Ezek 8:17; Hab 2:8, 17
17 [a]Ezek 27:3, 4; 28:7 [b]Is 19:11 [c]Ezek 26:16
18 [a]Amos 1:9, 10 [b]Mal 4:3
19 [1]Lit *terrors* [a]Ezek 26:21; 27:36 [b]Jer 51:64

28:3 *Daniel.* See note on 14:14.
28:7 *strangers.* The Babylonians; see next phrase.
28:8 *pit.* Cf. Job 33:22,24; see note on 26:20.
28:10 *uncircumcised.* Used here in the sense of barbarian or uncouth. The Phoenicians, like the Israelites and the Egyptians, practiced circumcision (see 31:18; 32:19).
28:12 *lamentation.* See note on 19:1. *king of Tyre.* Cf. v. 2, but see note on Is 14:12–15. *seal of perfection.* See Hag 2:23, where Zerubbabel is called God's "signet ring." With cutting irony Ezekiel depicts the proud king of Tyre as the first man created, radiant with wisdom and beauty.
28:13 *You were in Eden.* Like Adam (Gen 2:15). Ezekiel continues to use imagery of the creation and the fall to picture the career of the king of Tyre (see 31:9,16,18). *Every precious stone.* Unlike Adam, who was naked (Gen 2:25), the king is pictured as a fully clothed priest, ordained (v. 14) to guard God's holy place. The 9 stones are among the 12 worn by the priest (Ex 28:17–20). (The Septuagint lists all 12.) *settings and sockets.* For the precious stones. *On the day that you were created.* Cf. v. 15; Gen 5:2.
28:14 *cherub who covers.* Cf. v. 16. The Genesis account has cherubim (plural) stationed at the border of the garden after the expulsion of Adam and Eve (Gen 3:24). *holy mountain of God.* Cf. v. 16. This does not reflect the Genesis story. See Is 14:13 for the figure of God dwelling on a mountain. *stones of fire.* The precious stones (v. 13; cf. Rev 4:1–6; 21:15–21).
28:15 *You were blameless . . . Until.* The parallel to Gen 2–3 is clear (see Gen 6:9; 17:1).
28:16 *abundance of your trade . . . filled with violence.* Tyre's major crime.
28:17 *cast you to the ground.* Expulsion from the heavenly garden.

Judgment of Sidon

20 And the word of the LORD came to me
saying,
21 "Son of man, [a]set your face toward
[b]Sidon, prophesy against her
22 and say, 'Thus says the Lord GOD,
"Behold, I am against you, O Sidon,
And I will [1]be glorified in your midst.
Then they will know that I am the
LORD when I [a]execute judgments in
her,
And I will manifest My holiness in her.
23 "For [a]I will send pestilence to her
And blood to her streets,
And the [b]wounded will [1]fall in her
midst
By the sword upon her on every side;
Then they will know that I am the
LORD.
24 "And there will be no more for the
house of Israel a [a]prickling brier or a painful
thorn from any round about them who
scorned them; then they will know that I am
the Lord GOD."

Israel Regathered

25 'Thus says the Lord GOD, "When I
[a]gather the house of Israel from the peoples
among whom they are scattered, and will
manifest My holiness in them in the sight of
the nations, then they will [b]live in their [1]land
which I gave to My servant Jacob.
26 "They will [a]live in it securely; and they
will [b]build houses, plant vineyards and live
securely when I [c]execute judgments upon all
who scorn them round about them. Then
they will know that I am the LORD their
God."' "

Judgment of Egypt

29 In the [a]tenth year, in the tenth *month*,
on the twelfth of the month, the word
of the LORD came to me saying,
2 "Son of man, set your face against
[a]Pharaoh king of Egypt and prophesy against
him and against all [b]Egypt.
3 "Speak and say, 'Thus says the Lord
[1]GOD,
"Behold, I am against you, Pharaoh
king of Egypt,
The great [2a]monster that lies in the
midst of his [3]rivers,
That [b]has said, 'My Nile is mine, and I
myself have made *it*.'
4 "I will put [a]hooks in your jaws
And make the fish of your [1]rivers cling
to your scales.
And I will bring you up out of the
midst of your [1]rivers,
And all the fish of your [1]rivers will
cling to your scales.
5 "I will [a]abandon you to the wilderness,
you and all the fish of your [1]rivers;
You will fall on the [2]open field; you
will not be brought together or
[3b]gathered.
I have given you for [c]food to the
beasts of the earth and to the birds
of the sky.
6 "Then all the inhabitants of Egypt will
know that I am the LORD,
Because they have been *only* a [a]staff
made of reed to the house of Israel.
7 "When they took hold of you with the
hand,
You [a]broke and tore all their [1]hands;
And when they leaned on you,
You broke and made all their loins
[2]quake."
8 'Therefore thus says the Lord GOD,
"Behold, I will [a]bring upon you a sword and
I will cut off from you man and beast.
9 "The [a]land of Egypt will become a desolation and waste. Then they will know that I
am the LORD.

21 [a]Ezek 6:2; 25:2 [b]Gen 10:15, 19; Is 23:2, 4; Ezek 27:8
22 [1]Or *glorify Myself* [a]Ezek 28:26; 30:19
23 [1]Or *be judged* [a]Ezek 38:22 [b]Jer 51:52
24 [a]Num 33:55; Josh 23:13; Is 55:13; Ezek 2:6
25 [1]Lit *ground* [a]Ps 106:47; Is 11:12, 13; Jer 32:37; Ezek 20:41; 34:13, 27 [b]Jer 23:8; 27:11
26 [a]Jer 23:6; Ezek 34:25-28; 38:8 [b]Jer 32:15, 43, 44; Amos 9:13, 14 [c]Ezek 25:11; 28:22
29:1 [a]Ezek 26:1; 29:17; 30:20
2 [a]Jer 44:30 [b]Is 19:1-17; Jer 46:2-26; Ezek 30:1-32:32
3 [1]Heb *YHWH*, usually rendered LORD, and so throughout the ch [2]Lit *tannim* [3]Or *Nile* [a]Is 27:1; Ezek 32:2 [b]Ezek 29:9; 30:12
4 [1]Or *Nile* [a]2 Kin 19:28; Ezek 38:4
5 [1]Or *Nile* [2]Lit *faces of the field* [3]Or with several mss and Targum, *buried* [a]Ezek 32:4-6 [b]Jer 8:2; 25:33 [c]Jer 7:33; 34:20; Ezek 39:4
6 [a]2 Kin 18:21; Is 36:6
7 [1]So with some ancient versions; M.T. *shoulders* [2]Lit *stand* [a]2 Kin 18:21; Is 36:6; Ezek 17:15-17
8 [a]Jer 46:13; Ezek 14:17
9 [a]Ezek 29:10-12; 30:7, 8, 13-19

28:21 *set your face.* See note on 20:46. *Sidon.* See 27:8 and note. This is the only time in the OT that Sidon is mentioned apart from Tyre (cf. Is 23:1–4; Jer 47:4; Joel 3:4; Zech 9:2).
28:22 *I am against you.* Possibly because of Sidon's involvement in the Jerusalem summit conference (Jer 27:3; see note on 5:8). *I will be glorified in your midst.* The Lord's glory would be recognized in Sidon's punishment.
28:24 *prickling brier.* For references to Israel's enemies as briers see Num 33:55; Josh 23:13.
28:25 *When I gather . . . Israel.* A frequent promise in Ezekiel and later (see 11:17; 20:34,41–42; 29:13; 34:13; 36:24; 37:21; 38:8; 39:27; Neh 1:9; Zech 10:8,10). *My servant Jacob.* Cf. 37:25. For the promise see Gen 28:13; 35:12; Ps 105:10–11.
28:26 *live in it securely.* A perennial ideal that had become an especially meaningful promise (cf. 34:28; 38:8,11,14; 39:26; Lev 25:18–19; Jer 23:6; 32:37; 33:16). *houses . . . vineyards.* Basic necessities of the good life (cf. Is 65:21; Jer 29:5,28; Amos 9:14).
29:1 *tenth year . . . tenth month . . . twelfth of the month.* Jan. 7, 587 B.C.; the sixth date in Ezekiel (see 1:2; 8:1; 20:1; 24:1; 26:1). This is the first of seven oracles against Egypt, all of which are dated, except one (30:1). They represent divine and prophetic anger at Egypt's actions (or nonactions) at this time.
29:2 *set your face.* See note on 20:46. *Pharaoh.* Hophra, 589–570 B.C. (see Jer 44:30).
29:3 *I am against you.* See note on 5:8. *great monster.* Or "crocodile"; pictured as being in the Nile. See note on Ex 4:3; see also Job 41:1 and note; Is 27:1 ("dragon"). *his rivers.* Nile delta and canals (cf. Is 7:18; 19:6; 37:25). *That has said.* Boasts inscribed on Egyptian monuments (such as in Shelley's "Ozymandias") had become proverbial.
29:4 *hooks.* Cf. 19:4. *fish of your rivers.* Egypt's conquered territories or mercenaries.
29:5 *food to the beasts.* Particularly frustrating to the pharaoh's great hopes for an afterlife, as symbolized by the pyramids and expressed in the Egyptian "Book of the Dead."
29:6 *they have been . . . a staff . . . of reed.* A comparison made earlier (see Is 36:6). Hophra briefly but unsuccessfully diverted the Babylonians from laying siege to Jerusalem (see Jer 37:1–10).
29:8 *sword.* Nebuchadnezzar's (see note on 21:3). For the entire expression, which is not found in other prophetic books, see 6:3; 11:8; 14:17; 33:2; see also Lev 26:25.

Because [1]you [b]said, 'The Nile is mine,
and I have made *it*,'
10 therefore, behold, I am [a]against you
and against your [1]rivers, and I will make the
land of Egypt an utter waste and desolation,
from Migdol *to* Syene and even to the border
of [2]Ethiopia.
11 "A man's foot will [a]not pass through it,
and the foot of a beast will not pass through
it, and it will not be inhabited for forty years.
12 "So I will make the land of Egypt a desolation in the [a]midst of desolated lands. And
her cities, in the midst of cities that are laid
waste, will be desolate forty years; and I will
[b]scatter the Egyptians among the nations
and disperse them among the lands."
13 'For thus says the Lord GOD, "At the end
of forty years I will [a]gather the Egyptians
from the peoples [1]among whom they were
scattered.
14 "I will turn the fortunes of Egypt and
make them return to the land of [a]Pathros, to
the land of their origin, and there they will
be a lowly kingdom.
15 "It will be the [a]lowest of the kingdoms,
and it will never again lift itself up above the
nations. And I will make them so small that
they will not [b]rule over the nations.
16 "And it will never again be the [a]confi-
dence of the house of Israel, [1b]bringing to
mind the iniquity of their having turned [2]to
Egypt. Then they will know that I am the
Lord GOD." ' "
17 Now in the [a]twenty-seventh year, in
the first *month*, on the first of the month, the
word of the LORD came to me saying,
18 "Son of man, [a]Nebuchadnezzar king of
Babylon made his army labor [1]hard against
Tyre; every head was made [b]bald and every
shoulder was rubbed bare. But he and his
army had no wages from Tyre for the labor
that he had [2]performed against it."
19 Therefore thus says the Lord GOD,

9 [1]Lit *he* [b]Prov 16:18; 18:12; Ezek 29:3
10 [1]Or *Nile* [2]Lit *Cush* [a]Ezek 13:8; 21:3; 26:3; 29:3
11 [a]Jer 43:11, 12; 46:19; Ezek 32:13
12 [a]Jer 25:15-19; 27:6-11; Ezek 30:7 [b]Jer 46:19; Ezek 30:23, 26
13 [1]Lit *where* [a]Is 19:22; Jer 46:26
14 [a]Is 11:11; Jer 44:1, 15; Ezek 30:14
15 [a]Ezek 17:6, 14; 30:13; Zech 10:11 [b]Ezek 31:2; 32:2; Nah 3:8-10
16 [1]Lit *causing to remember* [2]Lit *after them* [a]Is 20:5; 30:1-3; 31:1; 36:6; Ezek 17:15; 29:6, 7 [b]Is 64:9; Jer 14:10; Ezek 21:23; Hos 8:13
17 [a]Ezek 24:1; 26:1; 29:1; 30:20;40:1
18 [1]Lit *a great labor* [2]Lit *labored* [a]Jer 25:9; 27:6; Ezek 26:7-12 [b]Jer 48:37; Ezek 27:31
19 [1]Or *multitude* [a]Ezek 30:10, 24, 25; 32:11 [b]Jer 43:10-13; Ezek 30:14
20 [1]Lit *labored* [a]Is 10:6, 7; 45:1-3; Jer 25:9
21 [1]Lit *give you an opening of the mouth* [a]1 Sam 2:10; Ps 92:10; 132:17 [b]Ezek 3:27; 24:27; 33:22; Amos 3:7, 8; Luke 21:15
30:2 [1]Heb *YHWH*, usually rendered LORD, and so throughout the ch [a]Is 13:6; 15:2; Ezek 21:12; Joel 1:5, 11, 13 **3** [a]Ezek 7:19; 13:5; Joel 1:15; 2:1; Obad 15 [b]Ezek 30:18; 32:7; 34:12 **4** [1]Lit *Cush* [2]Or *multitude* [a]Ezek 29:19 **5** [1]Lit *Cush* [2]Or *the mixed people* [3]Or *Cub* [4]Lit *sons* [5]Lit *of the covenant* [a]Jer 25:20, 24 **6** [a]Is 20:3-6

"Behold, I [a]will give the land of Egypt to
Nebuchadnezzar king of Babylon. And he
will carry off her [1b]wealth and capture her
spoil and seize her plunder; and it will be
wages for his army.
20 "I have given him the land of Egypt *for*
his labor which he [1a]performed, because
they acted for Me," declares the Lord GOD.
21 "On that day I will make a [a]horn sprout
for the house of Israel, and I will [1b]open your
mouth in their midst. Then they will know
that I am the LORD."

Lament over Egypt

30 The word of the LORD came again to me
saying,
2 "Son of man, prophesy and say, 'Thus
says the Lord [1]GOD,
"[a]Wail, 'Alas for the day!'
3 "For the day is near,
Even [a]the day of the LORD is near;
It will be a day of [b]clouds,
A time *of doom* for the nations.
4 "A sword will come upon Egypt,
And anguish will be in [1]Ethiopia;
When the slain fall in Egypt,
They [a]take away her [2]wealth,
And her foundations are torn down.
5 "[1]Ethiopia, Put, Lud, all [2a]Arabia, [3]Lib-
ya and the [4]people of the land [5]that is in
league will fall with them by the sword."
6 'Thus says the LORD,
"Indeed, those who support [a]Egypt will
fall
And the pride of her power will come
down;
From Migdol *to* Syene
They will fall within her by the sword,"
Declares the Lord GOD.

29:10 *Migdol.* Location unknown; probably in northern Egypt (see Jer 44:1; 46:14). *Syene.* A town in southern Egypt. "From Migdol to Syene" (see 30:6) probably indicated all Egypt, just as "from Dan to Beersheba" meant all Israel (see, e.g., Judg 20:1; 1 Sam 3:20).

29:11 *forty years.* Sometimes used to signify a long and difficult period (cf. 4:6).

29:14 *Pathros.* Southern Egypt (see 30:14; Jer 44:1,15).

29:17 The second oracle against Egypt (see note on v. 1). *twenty-seventh year . . . first month . . . first of the month.* Apr. 26, 571 B.C.; the seventh date in Ezekiel (see v. 1; 1:2; 8:1; 20:1; 24:1; 26:1) and the latest date given in the book. Since the remaining dated oracles are in more or less chronological order, the date is mentioned here probably because of the subject matter (Egypt).

29:18 *made his army labor hard.* Nebuchadnezzar besieged Tyre for 15 years, from 586 to 571 B.C. (see 26:7–14). *every head was made bald.* Probably from the leather helmets.

29:19 *I will give.* God's sovereignty over the nations is again proclaimed.

29:21 *make a horn sprout for.* Revive the strength of. The passage is not a Messianic prophecy. *open your mouth.* Ezekiel's muteness (3:26; 24:27) would be removed, and this word anticipates that of 33:22.

30:1 The third oracle against Egypt (see note on 29:1). No date is given, but it was probably between January and April of 587 B.C. Compare 29:1 with 30:20. Jerusalem was under siege at this time.

30:2–3 *the day . . . the day of the LORD.* The day of God's coming in judgment (see 7:7 and note). Egypt's judgment is announced.

30:3 *the day is near.* Cf. Is 13:6. *day of clouds.* Cf. Joel 2:2; Zeph 1:15.

30:4 *sword.* Nebuchadnezzar's (see v. 10; see also note on 21:3).

30:5 *Put.* Libya, in Africa (see note on 27:10). *Lud.* Not in Asia Minor (see note on 27:10) but somewhere in northern Africa. *Libya.* Hebrew *Cub* (see NASB marg.), probably best understood as an unidentified place. *people of the land . . . in league.* Apparently Jews living in Egypt (see Jer 44).

30:6 *From Migdol to Syene.* See note on 29:10.

7 "They will be desolate
In the [a]midst of the desolated lands;
And her cities will be
In the midst of the devastated cities.
8 "And they will [a]know that I am the
LORD,
When I set a [b]fire in Egypt
And all her helpers are broken.
9 "On that day [a]messengers will go forth
from Me in ships to frighten [b]secure [1]Ethi-
opia; and [c]anguish will be on them as on the
day of Egypt; for behold, it comes!"
10 'Thus says the Lord GOD,
"[a]I will also make the [1]hordes of Egypt
cease
By the hand of Nebuchadnezzar king
of Babylon.
11 "He and his people with him,
[a]The most ruthless of the nations,
Will be brought in to destroy the land;
And they will draw their swords
against Egypt
And fill the land with the slain.
12 "Moreover, I will make the [a]Nile canals
dry
And [b]sell the land into the hands of
evil men.
And I will make the land desolate
And [1]all that is in it,
By the hand of strangers; I the LORD
have spoken."

13 'Thus says the Lord GOD,
"I will also [a]destroy the idols
And make the [1]images cease from
[2b]Memphis.
And there will no longer be a prince
in the land of Egypt;
And I will put fear in the land of Egypt.
14 "I will make [a]Pathros desolate,
Set a fire in [b]Zoan
And execute judgments on [1c]Thebes.
15 "I will pour out My wrath on [1]Sin,
The stronghold of Egypt;
I will also cut off the hordes of
[2]Thebes.
16 "I will set a fire in Egypt;

7 [a]Jer 25:18-26; Ezek 29:12 **8** [a]Ps 58:11; Ezek 29:6, 9, 16 [b]Ezek 22:31; 30:14, 16; Amos 1:4, 7, 10, 12, 14 **9** [1]Lit *Cush* [a]Is 18:1, 2 [b]Is 47:8; Ezek 38:11; 39:6 [c]Is 19:17; 23:5; Ezek 32:9, 10 **10** [1]Or *people;* lit *crowd,* and so throughout the ch [a]Ezek 29:19 **11** [a]Ezek 28:7 **12** [1]Lit *her fullness* [a]Ezek 29:3, 9 [b]Is 19:4 **13** [1]Or *futile ones* [2]Or *Noph* [a]Is 2:18 [b]Is 19:13; Jer 2:16; 44:1; 46:14; Ezek 30:16 **14** [1]Or *No* [a]Is 11:11; Jer 44:1, 15; Ezek 29:14 [b]Ps 78:12, 43; Is 19:11, 13 [c]Jer 46:25; Ezek 30:15, 16; Nah 3:8 **15** [1]Or *Pelusium* [2]Or *No*

16 [1]Or *Pelusium* [2]Or *No* [3]Or *Noph* [4]Or *adversaries* **17** [1]Or *Aven* [2]Lit *they* [a]Gen 41:45; 46:20 **18** [1]So with many mss and ancient versions; M.T. *restrain* [a]Jer 43:8-13 [b]Ezek 30:3 [c]Lev 26:13; Is 10:27; Jer 27:2; 28:10, 13; 30:8; Ezek 34:27 **19** [a]Ps 9:16; Ezek 5:8, 15; 25:11; 30:14 **20** [a]Ezek 26:1; 29:1, 17; 31:1 **21** [1]Lit *to give healing* [2]Lit *to put a bandage, to wrap it* [a]Ps 10:15; 37:17; Ezek 30:24 [b]Jer 30:13; 46:11 **22** [a]Jer 46:25; Ezek 29:3 [b]2 Kin 24:7; Jer 37:7 [c]Jer 46:21

[1]Sin will writhe in anguish,
[2]Thebes will be breached
And [3]Memphis *will have* [4]distresses
daily.
17 "The young men of [1a]On and of
Pi-beseth
Will fall by the sword,
And [2]the women will go into captivity.
18 "In [a]Tehaphnehes the day will [1]be
[b]dark
When I [c]break there the yoke bars of
Egypt.
Then the pride of her power will cease
in her;
A cloud will cover her,
And her daughters will go into
captivity.
19 "Thus I will [a]execute judgments on
Egypt,
And they will know that I am the
LORD." ' "

Victory for Babylon

20 In the [a]eleventh year, in the first
month, on the seventh of the month, the
word of the LORD came to me saying,
21 "Son of man, I have [a]broken the arm of
Pharaoh king of Egypt; and, behold, it has
not been [b]bound up [1]for healing [2]or
wrapped with a bandage, that it may be
strong to hold the sword.
22 "Therefore thus says the Lord GOD,
'Behold, I am [a]against Pharaoh king of Egypt
and will break his arms, both the strong and
the [b]broken; and I will make the sword [c]fall
from his hand.
23 'I will [a]scatter the Egyptians among the
nations and disperse them among the lands.
24 'For I will [a]strengthen the arms of the
king of Babylon and put [b]My sword in his
hand; and I will break the arms of Pharaoh,
so that he will groan before him with the
groanings of a wounded man.
25 'Thus I will strengthen the arms of the
king of Babylon, but the arms of Pharaoh

23 [a]Ezek 29:12; 30:17, 18, 26 **24** [a]Neh 6:9; Is 45:1, 5; Ezek 30:10, 25; Zech 10:12 [b]Ezek 30:11, 25; Zeph 2:12

30:8 *set a fire in.* Make war on.
30:9 *messengers . . . in ships.* See Is 18 for a similar oracle on Cush, involving ships on the Nile.
30:11 *most ruthless of the nations.* A common phrase for the Babylonians, who were known for their cruelty (see 2 Kin 25:7).
30:13 *idols.* See note on 6:4. *Memphis.* Located 15 miles south of Cairo, Memphis was a former capital of Egypt and one of her largest cities. The list of towns reveals no discernible pattern but is a literary device used to underscore the scope of the destruction (cf. Is 10:9–11,27–32; Mic 1:10–15; Zeph 2:4). *prince.* King.
30:14 *Pathros.* See 29:14 and note. *Zoan.* A city in northeast Egypt in the delta region; also called Raamses (see Ex 1:11), Avaris and Tanis (see Is 19:11,13;30:4). *Thebes.* Capital of Upper Egypt; present-day Luxor and Karnak (see NASB marg.).
30:15 *Sin.* A fortress in the eastern delta region of the Nile (see NASB marg.).
30:17 *On.* Heliopolis ("city of the sun"), the Greek name for On (see NASB marg.); located six miles northeast of Cairo. *Pi-beseth.* Bubastis, at one time the capital of Lower (northern) Egypt; located 40 miles northeast of Cairo.
30:18 *Tehaphnehes.* Tahpanhes, in extreme northeast Egypt. Johanan son of Kareah and his men fled there after the murder of Gedaliah (see Jer 43:4–7). *dark.* A common Biblical metaphor describing ruin, destruction or death. *cloud will cover her.* See v. 3 and note; 32:7.
30:20 The fourth oracle against Egypt (see note on 29:1). *eleventh year . . . first month . . . seventh of the month.* Apr. 29, 587 B.C.; the eighth date in Ezekiel (see 1:2; 8:1; 20:1; 24:1; 26:1; 29:1,17).
30:21 *broken the arm.* Refers to Pharaoh Hophra's defeat by Nebuchadnezzar the previous year (see notes on 29:6; Jer 37:10).
30:24 *put My sword in his hand.* See note on 21:3.

will fall. Then they will know that I am the
LORD, when I put My sword into the hand of
the king of Babylon and he [a]stretches it out
against the land of Egypt.
26 'When I scatter the Egyptians among the
nations and disperse them among the lands,
then they will know that I am the LORD.' "

Pharaoh Warned of Assyria's Fate

31 In the [a]eleventh year, in the third
month, on the first of the month, the
word of the LORD came to me saying,
2 "Son of man, say to Pharaoh king of
Egypt and to his [a]hordes,

'Whom are you like in your greatness?
3 'Behold, Assyria *was* a [a]cedar in
Lebanon
With beautiful branches and forest
shade,
And [1][b]very high,
And its top was among the [2]clouds.
4 'The [a]waters made it grow, the [1]deep
made it high.
With its rivers it continually [2]extended
all around its planting place,
And sent out its channels to all the
trees of the field.
5 'Therefore [a]its height was loftier than
all the trees of the field
And its boughs became many and its
branches long
Because of [b]many waters [1]as it spread
them out.
6 'All the [a]birds of the heavens nested in
its boughs,
And under its branches all the beasts
of the field gave birth,
And all great nations lived under its
shade.
7 'So it was beautiful in its greatness, in
the length of its branches;
For its [1]roots extended to many
waters.
8 'The [a]cedars in [b]God's garden [1]could
not match it;
The [2]cypresses [1]could not compare
with its boughs,
And the plane trees [3]could not match
its branches.
No tree in [b]God's garden [1]could
compare with it in its beauty.

25 [a]Josh 8:18; 1 Chr 21:16; Is 5:25
31:1 [a]Jer 52:5, 6; Ezek 30:20; 32:1
2 [a]Ezek 29:19; 30:10; Nah 3:9
3 [1]Lit *high of stature* [2]So Gr; M.T. *thick boughs* [a]Is 10:33, 34; Ezek 17:3, 4, 22; 31:16; Dan 4:10, 20-23 [b]Is 10:33; Ezek 31:5, 10
4 [1]I.e. subterranean waters [2]Lit *was going* [a]Ezek 17:5, 8; Rev 17:1, 15
5 [1]Lit *in its sending forth* [a]Dan 4:11 [b]Ps 1:3; Ezek 17:5
6 [a]Ezek 17:23; 31:13; Dan 4:12, 21; Matt 13:32
7 [1]Lit *root was*
8 [1]Lit *did* [2]Or *Phoenician junipers* [3]Lit *were not like* [a]Ps 80:10; Ezek 31:3 [b]Gen 2:8, 9; 13:10; Is 51:3; Ezek 28:13; 31:16, 18
9 [a]Gen 2:8, 9; 13:10; Is 51:3; Ezek 28:13; 31:16, 18
10 [1]Heb *YHWH,* usually rendered LORD, and so throughout the ch [2]Lit *you are* [3]Or *thick boughs* [a]2 Chr 32:25; Is 10:12; 14:13, 14; Ezek 28:17; Dan 5:20
11 [1]Or *mighty one* [a]Ezek 30:10, 11; 32:11, 12; Dan 5:18, 19 [b]Deut 18:12; Nah 3:18
12 [a]Ezek 7:21; 28:7; 30:12; Hab 1:6 [b]Ezek 28:7; 30:11; 32:12 [c]Ezek 32:5; 35:8 [d]Ezek 31:17; Dan 4:14; Nah 3:17, 18
13 [a]Is 18:6; Ezek 29:5; 31:6; 32:4
14 [1]Or *thick boughs* [2]Lit *drinkers of water*

9 'I made it beautiful with the multitude
of its branches,
And all the trees of [a]Eden, which were
in the [a]garden of God, were jealous
of it.

10 'Therefore thus says the Lord [1]GOD,
"Because [2]it is high in stature and has set its
top among the [3]clouds, and its [a]heart is
haughty in its loftiness,
11 therefore I will give it into the hand of
a [1][a]despot of the nations; he will thoroughly
deal with it. According to its wickedness I
have [b]driven it away.
12 "[a]Alien [b]tyrants of the nations have cut
it down and left it; on the [c]mountains and in
all the valleys its branches have fallen and its
boughs have been broken in all the ravines of
the land. And all the peoples of the earth
have [d]gone down from its shade and left it.
13 "On its ruin all the [a]birds of the heavens
will dwell, and all the beasts of the field will
be on its *fallen* branches
14 so that all the trees by the waters may
not be exalted in their stature, nor set their
top among the [1]clouds, nor their [2]well-
watered mighty ones stand *erect* in their
height. For they have all been given over to
death, to the [a]earth beneath, among the sons
of men, with those who go down to the pit."
15 'Thus says the Lord GOD, "On the day
when it went down to Sheol I [a]caused
lamentations; I closed the [1]deep over it and
held back its rivers. And *its* many waters
were stopped up, and I made Lebanon
[2]mourn for it, and all the trees of the field
wilted away on account of it.
16 "I made the nations [a]quake at the sound
of its fall when I made it [b]go down to Sheol
with those who go down to the pit; and all
the [1]well-watered trees of Eden, the choicest
and best of [c]Lebanon, were [d]comforted in
the earth beneath.
17 "They also [a]went down with it to Sheol
to those who were [b]slain by the sword; and
those who were its [1]strength lived [c]under its
shade among the nations.

[a]Num 16:30, 33; Ps 63:9; Ezek 26:20; 31:18; 32:24; Amos 9:2; Jon 2:2, 6; Eph 4:9 **15** [1]I.e. subterranean waters [2]Lit *be darkened* [a]Ezek 32:7; Nah 2:10 **16** [1]Lit *drinkers of water* [a]Ezek 26:15; 27:28; Hag 2:7 [b]Is 14:15; Ezek 32:18 [c]Is 14:8; Hab 2:17 [d]Ezek 14:22, 23; 32:31 **17** [1]Lit *arm* [a]Ps 9:17 [b]Ezek 32:20f [c]Ezek 31:3, 6; Dan 4:12

31:1 The fifth oracle against Egypt (see note on 29:1). *eleventh year . . . third month . . . first of the month.* June 21, 587 B.C.; the ninth date in Ezekiel (see 1:2; 8:1; 20:1; 24:1; 26:1; 29:1, 17; 30:20).

31:3 *Behold, Assyria.* A great nation that had fallen. In 609 B.C. Pharaoh Neco went to Carchemish to help the Assyrian empire, which was reeling from Babylonian attacks. The effort failed and Assyria passed from history. *was a cedar.* The beginning of another allegory (see Ezekiel's allegorical use of the cedar in ch. 17). *Lebanon.* Known for its cedars (see vv. 15–18; Judg 9:15; 1 Kin 4:33; 5:6; 2 Kin 14:9; Ezra 3:7; Ps 29:5; 92:12; 104:16).

31:4 *waters.* The Tigris and Euphrates. *the deep.* See note on 26:19.

31:6 *birds of the heavens.* See 17:23 and note; see also Dan 4:12.

31:8 *God's garden.* The note of pride is introduced (see v. 10; cf. 28:13).

31:11 *despot of the nations.* Probably Nabopolassar; or possibly Nebuchadnezzar. *its wickedness.* Pride (see v. 10; Gen 11:1–8).

31:12 *Alien tyrants.* Babylon (see note on 30:11).

31:15 *the deep.* See v. 4; see also note on 26:19.

31:16 *nations quake.* As at Tyre's fall (see 27:35; 28:19). *were comforted.* Because the mightiest of trees had joined them in the "grave" (Sheol).

31:17 *those . . . slain by the sword.* Those who met a premature death.

18 "To which among the trees of Eden are you thus [1]equal in glory and greatness? Yet you will be brought down with the trees of Eden to the earth beneath; you will lie in the midst of the [a]uncircumcised, with those who were slain by the sword. [b]So is Pharaoh and all his hordes!" ' declares the Lord GOD."

Lament over Pharaoh and Egypt

32 In the [a]twelfth year, in the twelfth *month,* on the first of the month, the word of the LORD came to me saying,

2 "Son of man, take up a [a]lamentation over Pharaoh king of Egypt and say to him,

'You [1]compared yourself to a young
[b]lion of the nations,
Yet you are like the [c]monster in the
seas;
And you [d]burst forth in your rivers
And muddied the waters with your feet
And [2]fouled their rivers.' "

3 Thus says the Lord [1]GOD,
"Now I will [a]spread My net over you
With a company of many peoples,
And they shall lift you up in My net.
4 "I will leave you on the land;
I will cast you on the [1]open field.
And I will cause all the [a]birds of the
heavens to dwell on you,
And I will satisfy the beasts of the
whole earth [2]with you.
5 "I will lay your flesh [a]on the mountains
And fill the valleys with your refuse.
6 "I will also make the land drink the
discharge of your [a]blood
As far as the mountains,
And the ravines will be full of you.
7 "And when *I* [a]extinguish you,
I will [b]cover the heavens and darken
their [c]stars;
I will cover the [d]sun with a cloud
And the moon will not give its light.
8 "All the shining [a]lights in the heavens
I will darken over you
And will set darkness on your land,"
Declares the Lord GOD.

18 [1]Lit *like* [a]Jer 9:25, 26; Ezek 28:10; 32:19, 21 [b]Ps 52:7; Matt 13:19
32:1 [a]Ezek 30:20; 31:1; 32:17; 33:21
2 [1]Or *were like* [2]Lit *fouled by stamping* [a]Ezek 19:1; 27:2; 28:12; 32:16 [b]Jer 4:7; Ezek 19:2-6; Nah 2:11-13 [c]Is 27:1; Ezek 29:3 [d]Jer 46:7, 8
3 [1]Heb *YHWH,* usually rendered *LORD,* and so throughout the ch [a]Ezek 12:13
4 [1]Lit *surface of the field* [2]Lit *from* [a]Is 18:6
5 [a]Ezek 31:12
6 [a]Ex 7:17; Is 34:3, 7; Ezek 35:6; Rev 14:20
7 [a]Job 18:5, 6; Prov 13:9 [b]Ex 10:21-23; Is 34:4; Ezek 30:3, 18; 34:12 [c]Is 13:10 [d]Joel 2:2, 31; 3:15; Amos 8:9; Matt 24:29; Mark 13:24f; Luke 21:25; Rev 6:12; 8:12
8 [a]Gen 1:14

9 [a]Ezek 27:29-32; 28:19; Rev 18:10-15 [b]Ex 15:14-16
10 [a]Ezek 27:35 [b]Ezek 26:16
11 [a]Jer 46:26
12 [a]Ezek 28:7 [b]Ezek 28:19
13 [a]Ezek 29:11
15 [a]Ps 107:33, 34; Ezek 29:12, 19, 20 [b]Ex 7:5; 14:4, 18; Ps 9:16; 83:17, 18; Ezek 6:7; 30:19, 26
16 [1]Or *lament* [a]2 Sam 1:17; 3:33, 34; 2 Chr 35:25; Jer 9:17; Ezek 26:17; 32:2

9 "I will also [a]trouble the hearts of many peoples when I [b]bring your destruction among the nations, into lands which you have not known.

10 "I will make many peoples [a]appalled at you, and their kings will be horribly afraid of you when I brandish My sword before them; and [b]they will tremble every moment, every man for his own life, on the day of your fall."

11 For [a]thus says the Lord GOD, "The sword of the king of Babylon will come upon you.

12 "By the swords of the mighty ones I will cause your hordes to fall; all of them are [a]tyrants of the nations,
And they will [b]devastate the pride of
Egypt,
And all its hordes will be destroyed.
13 "I will also destroy all its cattle from
beside many waters;
And [a]the foot of man will not muddy
them anymore
And the hoofs of beasts will not
muddy them.
14 "Then I will make their waters settle
And will cause their rivers to run like
oil,"
Declares the Lord GOD.
15 "When I make the land of Egypt a
[a]desolation,
And the land is destitute of that which
filled it,
When I smite all those who live in it,
Then they shall [b]know that I am the
LORD.

16 "This is a [a]lamentation and they shall [1]chant it. The daughters of the nations shall [1]chant it. Over Egypt and over all her hordes they shall [1]chant it," declares the Lord GOD.

17 In the [a]twelfth year, on the [a]fifteenth of the month, the word of the LORD came to me saying,

18 "Son of man, [a]wail for the hordes of

17 [a]Ezek 31:1; 32:1; 33:21 **18** [a]Is 16:9; Ezek 21:6; 32:2, 16; Mic 1:8

31:18 *you.* The Egyptian pharaoh. *Yet you.* It would happen to Pharaoh as it had happened to Assyria. *uncircumcised.* See note on 28:10.

32:1 The sixth oracle against Egypt (see note on 29:1). *twelfth year . . . twelfth month . . . first of the month.* Mar. 3, 585 B.C.; the tenth date in Ezekiel (see 1:2; 8:1; 20:1; 24:1; 26:1; 29:1,17; 30:20; 31:1). If the Septuagint and Syriac are followed ("eleventh year"), then the chronological order of the Egypt oracles is preserved (and the date would be Mar. 13, 586). Cf. 29:1; 30:20; 31:1; see v. 17 and note.

32:2 *lamentation.* See note on 19:1. *lion of the nations.* A figure for royalty and grandeur (see 19:1–9). *monster.* See 29:3 and note. *seas . . . rivers.* Canals of the Nile (see note on 29:3).

32:3 *spread My net.* Earlier it was Zedekiah over whom God's net was thrown (see 12:13; 17:20; 19:8).

32:4 *I will leave.* God's actions here are very similar to those described in 29:3–5.

32:7 *I will cover the heavens.* The first of seven clauses threatening the darkness associated with the day of the Lord (see Joel 2:2,10,31; 3:15; Amos 5:18–20; Zeph 1:15).

32:9 *trouble the hearts.* This and the next verse reflect the fear brought about whenever great world powers fall, reminding lesser nations that they are even more vulnerable. Cf. similar feelings aroused by Tyre's fall (26:16–18; 27:35; 28:19).

32:10 *My sword.* See note on 21:3.

32:11 *king of Babylon.* Nebuchadnezzar (cf. 21:19).

32:12 *tyrants of the nations.* Babylon (see note on 30:11).

32:14 *rivers to run like oil.* Their surface undisturbed by any form of life. This is the only place in the Bible where this eerie metaphor is used to describe desolation.

32:16 *daughters of the nations.* A world chorus of professional wailers (see Jer 9:17–18).

32:17 The seventh and last oracle against Egypt (see note on 29:1). *twelfth year . . . fifteenth of the month.* No month is given (as in 26:1; 40:1). The whole year dates from Apr. 13, 586, to Apr. 1, 585 B.C. The Septuagint suggests the first month, the 15th day of which would be Apr. 27, 586.

Egypt and [b]bring it down, her and the daughters of the powerful nations, to the [c]nether world, with those who go down to the pit;

19 'Whom do you surpass in beauty?
Go down and make your bed with the [a]uncircumcised.'

20 "They shall fall in the midst of those who are slain by the sword. [1]She is given over to the sword; they have [a]drawn her and all her hordes away.

21 "The [a]strong among the mighty ones shall speak of him *and* his helpers from the midst of Sheol, 'They have gone down, they lie still, the uncircumcised, slain by the sword.'

22 "[a]Assyria is there and all her company; [1]her graves are round about [2]her. All of them are slain, fallen by the sword,

23 whose [a]graves are set in the remotest parts of the pit and her company is round about her grave. All of them are slain, fallen by the sword, who [1]spread terror in the land of the living.

24 "[a]Elam is there and all her hordes around her grave; all of them slain, fallen by the sword, who went down uncircumcised to the [b]lower parts of the earth, who instilled their terror in the [c]land of the living and [d]bore their disgrace with those who went down to the pit.

25 "They have made a [a]bed for her among the slain with all her hordes. Her graves are around it, they are all uncircumcised, slain by the sword (although their terror was [1]instilled in the land of the living), and they bore their disgrace with those who go down to the pit; [2]they were put in the midst of the slain.

26 "[a]Meshech, [b]Tubal and all their hordes are there; their graves [1]surround them. All of them were slain by the sword [c]uncircumcised, though they instilled their terror in the land of the living.

27 "[a]Nor do they lie beside the fallen [1b]heroes of the uncircumcised, who went down to Sheol with their weapons of war and whose swords were laid under their heads; but the punishment for their [c]iniquity rested on their bones, though the terror of *these* [1]heroes *was once* in the land of the living.

28 "But in the midst of the uncircumcised you will be broken and lie with those slain by the sword.

29 "There also is [a]Edom, its kings and all its [1]princes, who [2]for *all* their might are laid with those slain by the sword; they will lie with the uncircumcised and with those who go down to the pit.

30 "There also are the [1]chiefs of the [a]north, all of them, and all the [b]Sidonians, who in spite of the terror resulting from their might, in shame went down with the slain. So they lay down uncircumcised with those slain by the sword and bore their disgrace with those who go down to the pit.

31 "These Pharaoh will see, and he will be [a]comforted for all his hordes slain by the sword, *even* Pharaoh and all his army," declares the Lord GOD.

32 "Though I instilled a terror of him in the land of the living, yet he will be made to lie down among *the* uncircumcised *along* with those slain by the sword, *even* Pharaoh and all his hordes," declares the Lord GOD.

The Watchman's Duty

33 And the word of the LORD came to me, saying,

2 "Son of man, speak to the [a]sons of your people and say to them, 'If I bring a sword upon a land, and the people of the land take one man from among them and make him their watchman,

3 and he sees the sword coming upon the land and [a]blows on the trumpet and warns the people,

4 then he who hears the sound of the trumpet and [a]does not take warning, and a sword comes and takes him away, his [b]blood will be on his *own* head.

5 'He heard the sound of the trumpet but did not take warning; his blood will be on himself. But had he taken warning, he would have [a]delivered his life.

6 'But if the watchman sees the sword coming and does not blow the trumpet and the people are not warned, and a sword comes and takes a person from them, he is [a]taken away [1]in his iniquity; but his [b]blood I will require from the watchman's hand.'

18 [b]Jer 1:10; Ezek 43:3; Hos 6:5 [c]Ezek 31:14, 16, 18; 32:24
19 [a]Jer 9:25, 26; Ezek 31:18; 32:21, 24, 29, 30
20 [1]Or *The sword is given* [a]Ps 28:3
21 [a]Is 14:9-12; Ezek 32:27
22 [1]Lit *his* [2]Lit *him* [a]Ezek 27:23; 31:3, 16
23 [1]Lit *gave*, and so throughout the ch [a]Is 14:15
24 [a]Gen 10:22; 14:1; Is 11:11; Jer 25:25; 49:34-39 [b]Ezek 26:20; 31:14, 18; 32:18 [c]Job 28:13; Ps 27:13; 52:5; 142:5; Is 38:11; Jer 11:19 [d]Ezek 16:52, 54; 32:25, 30
25 [1]Lit *given* [2]So with ancient versions; M.T. reads *he was* [a]Ps 139:8
26 [1]Lit *are around him* [a]Gen 10:2; Ezek 27:13; 38:2, 3; 39:1 [b]Gen 10:2; Is 66:19; Ezek 27:13; 38:2, 3; 39:1 [c]Ezek 32:19
27 [1]Or *mighty ones* [a]Is 14:18, 19 [b]Job 3:13-15; Ezek 32:21 [c]Job 20:11; Ps 109:18
29 [1]Or *leaders* [2]Or *in* [a]Is 34:5-15; Jer 49:7-22; Ezek 25:13; 35:9, 15
30 [1]Or *princes* [a]Jer 1:15; 25:26; Ezek 38:6, 15; 39:2 [b]Jer 25:22; Ezek 28:21-23
31 [a]Ezek 14:22; 31:16
33:2 [a]Ezek 3:11; 33:12, 17, 30; 37:18
3 [a]Neh 4:18-20; Is 58:1; Ezek 33:9; Hos 8:1; Joel 2:1
4 [a]2 Chr 25:16; Jer 6:17; Zech 1:4 [b]Ezek 18:13; 33:5, 9; Acts 18:6
5 [a]Ex 9:19-21; Heb 11:7
6 [1]Or *for*, and so throughout the ch [a]Ezek 18:20, 24; 33:8, 9 [b]Ezek 3:18, 20

32:18 *daughters of the powerful nations.* See note on v. 16. *nether world.* Same as "Sheol" (grave) in 31:15.

32:19 *uncircumcised.* See note on 28:10.

32:24 *Elam.* A country east of Assyria; in present-day Iran.

32:26 *Meshech, Tubal.* Peoples and territories in Asia Minor.

32:30 *Sidonians.* See note on 28:21.

33:1–48:35 A section depicting consolation for Israel (see Introduction: Outline).

33:1–37:28 Sermons and oracles of comfort following the fall of Jerusalem. Interspersed are words of warning and judgment (e.g., 33:23–29; 34:1–19; 35; 36:1–7), some of which may have been intended to comfort a downtrodden people.

33:2 *sons of your people.* Fellow Israelites in exile with Ezekiel. *sword.* The invading army. *people of the land.* Full citizens who owned land and served in the army (see 7:27; 12:19; 45:16,22; 46:3). *watchman.* A figure introduced in ch. 3 and expanded in ch. 18 (see note on 3:16).

33:3 *trumpet.* An instrument made from a ram's horn (Josh 6:4,6,13), used to warn of approaching danger (Neh 4:18–20; Jer 4:19; Amos 3:6) and to announce the beginnings of religious periods (e.g., day of atonement, Lev 25:9; new moon festival, Ps 81:3).

33:4 *his blood will be on his own head.* See note on 18:13.

33:6 *his blood.* His life, blood being the life principle (see Gen 9:5; 42:22).

7 "Now as for you, son of man, I have [1][a]appointed you a watchman for the house of Israel; so you will hear a [2]message from My mouth and give them [b]warning from Me.

8 "When I say to the wicked, 'O wicked man, you will [a]surely die,' and you do not speak to warn the wicked from his way, that wicked man shall die in his iniquity, but his blood I will require from your hand.

9 "But if you on your part warn a wicked man to turn from his way and he [a]does not turn from his way, he will die in his iniquity, but you have [b]delivered your life.

10 "Now as for you, son of man, say to the house of Israel, 'Thus you have spoken, saying, "Surely our transgressions and our sins are upon us, and we are [a]rotting away in them; [b]how then can we [1]survive?"'

11 "Say to them, '[a]As I live!' declares the Lord [1]GOD, 'I take [b]no pleasure in the death of the wicked, but rather that the wicked [c]turn from his way and live. [d]Turn back, turn back from your evil ways! Why then will you die, O house of Israel?'

12 "And you, son of man, say to [1]your fellow citizens, 'The [a]righteousness of a righteous man will not deliver him in the day of his transgression, and as for the wickedness of the wicked, he will [b]not stumble because of it in the day when he turns from his wickedness; whereas a righteous man will not be able to live [2]by his righteousness on the day when he commits sin.'

13 "When I say to the righteous he will surely live, and he *so* trusts in his righteousness that he [a]commits iniquity, none of his righteous deeds will be remembered; but in that same iniquity of his which he has committed he will die.

14 "But when I say to the wicked, 'You will surely die,' and he [a]turns from his sin and practices [b]justice and righteousness,

15 *if a* wicked man restores a pledge, [a]pays back what he has taken by robbery, walks by the [b]statutes [1]which ensure life without committing iniquity, he shall surely live; he shall not die.

16 "[a]None of his sins that he has committed will be remembered against him. He has practiced justice and righteousness; he shall surely live.

17 "Yet [1]your fellow citizens say, 'The way of the Lord is not right,' when it is their own way that is not right.

18 "When the righteous turns from his righteousness and [a]commits iniquity, then he shall die in [1]it.

19 "But when the wicked turns from his wickedness and practices justice and righteousness, he will live by them.

20 "Yet you say, '[a]The way of the Lord is not right.' O house of Israel, I will judge each of you according to his ways."

Word of Jerusalem's Capture

21 Now [a]in the [b]twelfth year of our exile, on the fifth of the tenth month, the [1]refugees from Jerusalem came to me, saying, "[c]The city has been [2]taken."

22 Now the [a]hand of the LORD had been upon me in the evening, before the [1]refugees came. And He [b]opened my mouth [2]at the time *they* came to me in the morning; so my mouth was [c]opened and I was no longer [3]speechless.

23 Then the word of the LORD came to me saying,

24 "Son of man, they who [a]live in these waste places in the land of Israel are saying, '[b]Abraham was *only* one, yet he possessed the land; so to [c]us who are many the land has been given as a possession.'

25 "Therefore say to them, 'Thus says the Lord GOD, "You eat *meat* with the [a]blood *in it*, lift up your eyes to your idols as you shed blood. [b]Should you then possess the land?

7 [1]Or *given* [2]Lit *word* [a]Is 62:6; Ezek 3:17-21 [b]Jer 1:17; 26:2; Ezek 2:7, 8; Acts 5:20
8 [a]Is 3:11; Ezek 18:4, 13, 18, 20; 33:14
9 [a]Acts 13:40, 41, 46 [b]Ezek 3:19, 21; Acts 20:26
10 [1]Lit *live* [a]Lev 26:39; Ezek 4:17; 24:23 [b]Is 49:14; Ezek 37:11
11 [1]Heb *YHWH*, usually rendered *LORD*, and so throughout the ch [a]Is 49:18; Ezek 5:11 [b]Ezek 18:23, 32; Hos 11:8 [c]Jer 31:20; 1 Tim 2:4; 2 Pet 3:9 [d]Is 55:6, 7; Jer 3:22; Ezek 18:30, 31; Hos 14:1; Acts 3:19
12 [1]Lit *the sons of your people* [2]Lit *by it* [a]Ezek 3:18; 18:24; 33:20 [b]2 Chr 7:14; Ezek 18:21; 33:19
13 [a]Ezek 18:26; Heb 10:38; 2 Pet 2:20, 21
14 [a]Is 55:7; Jer 18:7, 8; Ezek 18:27; 33:8, 19; Hos 14:1, 4 [b]Mic 6:8
15 [1]Lit *of life* [a]Ex 22:1-4; Lev 6:4, 5; Luke 19:8 [b]Ps 119:59; 143:8; Ezek 20:11
16 [a]Is 1:18; 43:25; Ezek 18:22
17 [1]Lit *the sons of your people*
18 [1]Lit *them* [a]Ezek 3:20; 18:24; 33:12, 13
20 [a]Ezek 18:25
21 [1]Or *refugee* [2]Lit *smitten* [a]Ezek 31:1; 32:1, 17 [b]Jer 39:1, 2; 40:1; 52:4-7; Ezek 24:1, 2 [c]2 Kin 25:10; Jer 39:8
22 [1]Lit *refugee* [2]Lit *until he came* [3]Or *mute* [a]Ezek 1:3; 8:1; 37:1 [b]Ezek 3:26, 27; 24:27 [c]Luke 1:64
24 [a]Jer 39:10; 40:7; Ezek 33:27 [b]Is 51:2; Luke 3:8; Acts 7:5; Rom 4:12 [c]Ezek 11:15
25 [a]Lev 17:10, 12, 14; Deut 12:16, 23; 15:23 [b]Jer 7:9, 10

33:7 *house of Israel.* Both the nation and the individuals. Compare vv. 7–9 with 3:17–19.

33:10 *our transgressions and our sins.* The first time the exiles expressed consciousness of sin. Previously they had blamed their fathers (18:2) and even God (18:19,25).

33:11 *As I live!* See note on 18:3. *I take no pleasure.* The question of 18:23 is now a statement. God's basic intention for His creation is life, not death (see note on 16:6). *Turn back.* The third call for repentance (see 14:6; 18:30).

33:12–20 Deals with the same subject as 18:21–29—namely, that the individual, whether righteous or wicked, has a choice to live righteously each day.

33:15 *restores a pledge, pays back what he has taken.* See note on 18:7. *statutes which ensure life.* The purpose of God's law was to foster and protect life (cf. 20:13,21). *he shall surely live.* The entire section is Ezekiel's answer to the despairing question of v. 10.

33:17 *The way of the Lord is not right.* Cf. 18:25,29.

33:21 *twelfth year . . . fifth of the tenth month.* Jan. 8, 585 B.C., five months after the Jerusalem temple was burned. See date in 2 Kin 25:8, which in modern reckoning is Aug. 14, 586. The journey between Jerusalem and Babylon could be made in four months (Ezra 7:9). *refugees from Jerusalem.* The first of the exiles of 586 (see 24:26, "he who escapes"). They (or "He"; see NASB marg.) had escaped alive from the disaster at Jerusalem. *The city has been taken.* With this statement all of Ezekiel's previous prophecies were fulfilled and vindicated. He was then sent with a new mission: pastoral comfort.

33:22 *no longer speechless.* The muteness that had come upon him at the beginning of his ministry was lifted (see 3:26 and note).

33:24 *they . . . in these waste places.* The residents of Jerusalem not exiled in 586 B.C. *Abraham was only one . . . us who are many.* A boast by the unrepentant, similar to that of 11:15 (cf. Luke 3:8).

33:25 *eat meat with the blood.* Forbidden in Gen 9:4; Lev 7:26–27; 17:10; Deut 12:16,23. *lift up your eyes to your idols.* See note on 18:6.

26 "You [1a]rely on your sword, you commit abominations and each of you defiles his neighbor's wife. Should you then possess the land?" '

27 "Thus you shall say to them, 'Thus says the Lord GOD, "As I live, surely those who are in the waste places will [a]fall by the sword, and whoever is in the [1]open field I will give to the beasts to be devoured, and those who are in the strongholds and in the [b]caves will die of pestilence.

28 "I will [a]make the land a desolation and a waste, and the [b]pride of her power will cease; and the mountains of Israel will be desolate so that no one will pass through.

29 "Then they will know that I am the LORD, when I make the land a desolation and a waste because of all their abominations which they have committed." '

30 "But as for you, son of man, [1]your fellow citizens who talk about you by the walls and in the doorways of the houses, speak to one another, each to his brother, saying, '[a]Come now and hear what the [2]message is which comes forth from the LORD.'

31 "They come to you as people come, and sit before you *as* My people and hear your words, but they do not do them, for they do the lustful desires *expressed* by their [a]mouth, *and* their heart goes after their [b]gain.

32 "Behold, you are to them like a sensual song by one who has a [a]beautiful voice and plays well on an instrument; for they hear your words but they do not practice them.

33 "So when it [a]comes to pass—[1]as surely it will—then they will know that a prophet has been in their midst."

Prophecy against the Shepherds of Israel

34 Then the word of the LORD came to me saying,

2 "Son of man, prophesy against the [a]shepherds of Israel. Prophesy and say to [1]those shepherds, 'Thus says the Lord [2]GOD, "Woe, shepherds of Israel who have been [3b]feeding themselves! Should not the shepherds [3c]feed the flock?

3 "You [a]eat the fat and clothe yourselves with the wool, you [b]slaughter the fat *sheep* without [1]feeding the flock.

4 "Those who are sickly you have not strengthened, the [1]diseased you have not healed, [a]the broken you have not bound up, the scattered you have not brought back, nor have you [b]sought for the lost; but with force and with severity you have dominated them.

5 "They were [a]scattered for lack of a shepherd, and they became [b]food for every beast of the field and were scattered.

6 "My flock [a]wandered through all the mountains and on every high hill; [b]My flock was scattered over all the surface of the earth, and there was [c]no one to search or seek *for them.*" ' "

7 Therefore, you shepherds, hear the word of the LORD:

8 "As I live," declares the Lord GOD, "surely because My flock has become a [a]prey, My flock has even become food for all the beasts of the field for lack of a shepherd, and My shepherds did not search for My flock, but *rather* the shepherds fed themselves and did not feed My flock;

9 therefore, you shepherds, hear the word of the LORD:

10 'Thus says the Lord GOD, "Behold, I am [a]against the shepherds, and I will demand My [1]sheep [2]from them and make them [b]cease from feeding [1]sheep. So the shepherds will not [3]feed themselves anymore, but I will [c]deliver My flock from their mouth, so that they will not be food for them." ' "

The Restoration of Israel

11 For thus says the Lord GOD, "Behold, I Myself will [a]search for My sheep and seek them out.

12 "[a]As a shepherd [1]cares for his herd in the day when he is among his scattered [2]sheep, so I will [1b]care for My [2]sheep and will deliver

26 [1]Lit *stand* [a]Mic 2:1, 2; Zeph 3:3
27 [1]Lit *surface of the field* [a]Jer 15:2, 3; 42:22; Ezek 5:12 [b]1 Sam 13:6; Is 2:19
28 [a]Ezek 5:14; 6:14; Mic 7:13 [b]Ezek 7:24; 24:21; 30:6
30 [1]Lit *the sons of your people* [2]Lit *word* [a]Is 29:13; 58:2; Ezek 14:3; 20:3, 31
31 [a]Ps 78:36, 37; Is 29:13; 1 John 3:18 [b]Ezek 22:13, 27; Luke 12:15
32 [a]Mark 6:20
33 [1]Lit *behold, it is coming* [a]Jer 28:9; Ezek 33:29
34:2 [1]Lit *them, the shepherds* [2]Heb *YHWH,* usually rendered *LORD,* and so throughout the ch [3]Lit *pasturing, pasture* [a]Jer 2:8; 3:15; 10:21; 12:10 [b]Jer 23:1; Ezek 22:25; 34:8-10; Mic 3:1-3, 11 [c]Ps 78:71, 72; Is 40:11; Ezek 34:14, 15; John 10:11; 21:15-17
3 [1]Lit *pasturing* [a]Zech 11:16 [b]Ezek 22:25, 27
4 [1]Lit *sick* [a]Zech 11:16 [b]Matt 9:36; 10:6; 18:12, 13; Luke 15:4
5 [a]Num 27:17; 2 Chr 18:16; Jer 10:21; 23:2; 50:6, 7; Matt 9:36; Mark 6:34 [b]Ezek 34:8, 28
6 [a]Jer 40:11, 12; Ezek 7:16; 1 Pet 2:25 [b]John 10:16 [c]Ps 142:4
8 [a]Acts 20:29
10 [1]Or (a) *flock* [2]Lit *from their hand* [3]Lit *pasture,* and so throughout the ch [a]Jer 21:13; Ezek 5:8; 13:8; 34:2; Zech 10:3 [b]1 Sam 2:29, 30; Jer 52:24-27 [c]Ps 72:12-14; Ezek 13:23
11 [a]Ezek 11:17; 20:41
12 [1]Or *seek(s) out* [2]Or *flock* [a]Jer 31:10 [b]Is 40:11; 56:8; Jer 23:3; 31:8; Luke 19:10; John 10:16

33:27 *As I live.* See note on 18:3. *sword . . . beasts . . . pestilence.* Cf. the threefold threat in 5:12; 7:15; 12:16 and the fourfold threat in 14:12–21.

33:30–33 Words of assurance meant for Ezekiel alone.

33:31 *sit before you.* As the elders had (8:1; 14:1). *goes after their gain.* The people were waiting for Ezekiel to tell them how they could personally profit from the situation rather than what God's larger designs were for them (cf. Matt 20:20–28).

33:32 *one who has a beautiful voice.* May indicate that Ezekiel chanted his oracles (see 2 Kin 3:15; Is 5:1), but more likely the prophet was using a metaphor. *they hear . . . but they do not practice.* See Is 29:13; Matt 21:28–32; cf. James 1:22–25.

34:2 *shepherds of Israel.* Those responsible for providing leadership, especially the kings and their officials (see 2 Sam 7:7; Jer 25:18–19), but also the prophets and priests (see Is 56:11; Jer 23:9–11). Ezekiel had earlier singled out the princes, priests and prophets for special rebuke (ch. 22). To call a king a shepherd was common throughout the ancient Near East. For David's rise from shepherd to shepherd-king see Ps 78:70–71. For condemnation of the shepherds cf. Jer 23:1–4.

34:3 *eat . . . clothe . . . slaughter.* Legitimate rewards for shepherds. Their crime was that they did not care for the flock.

34:4 *sought for the lost.* Cf. Jer 50:6; Matt 18:12–14; Luke 15:4; 19:10.

34:5 *scattered.* Often used by Ezekiel to describe Israel's exile and dispersion (11:16–17; 12:15; 20:23,34,41; 22:15; 28:25). *lack of a shepherd.* A picture used often in the Bible (e.g., Mark 6:34).

34:8 *beasts of the field.* Hostile foreign nations; but see v. 28, where they are contrasted.

34:10 *I am against the shepherds.* See note on 5:8.

34:11 *I Myself will search for My sheep.* Having dealt with the faithless shepherds (vv. 1–10), the Lord committed Himself to shepherd His flock (see Jer 23:3–4).

34:12 *from all the places.* Babylon was not the only place where the Israelites had gone (see Jer 43:1–7). *cloudy and*

them from all the places to which they were scattered on a [c]cloudy and gloomy day.

13 "I will bring them out from the peoples and gather them from the countries and bring them to their own land; and I will [a]feed them on the mountains of Israel, by the [b]streams, and in all the inhabited places of the land.

14 "I will feed them in a [a]good pasture, and their grazing ground will be on the mountain heights of Israel. There they will lie down on good grazing ground and feed in [1][b]rich pasture on the mountains of Israel.

15 "I will [a]feed My flock and I will [1]lead them to rest," declares the Lord GOD.

16 "I will seek the lost, bring back the scattered, bind up the broken and strengthen the sick; but the [a]fat and the strong I will destroy. I will [b]feed them with judgment.

17 "As for you, My flock, thus says the Lord GOD, 'Behold, I will [a]judge between one [1]sheep and another, between the rams and the male goats.

18 'Is it too [a]slight a thing for you that you should feed in the good pasture, that you must tread down with your feet the rest of your pastures? Or that you should drink of the clear waters, that you must [1]foul the rest with your feet?

19 'As for My flock, they must eat what you tread down with your feet and drink what you [1]foul with your feet!' "

20 Therefore, thus says the Lord GOD to them, "Behold, I, even I, will judge between the fat sheep and the lean sheep.

21 "Because you push with side and with shoulder, and [a]thrust at all the [1]weak with your horns until you have scattered them [2]abroad,

22 therefore, I will [a]deliver My flock, and they will no longer be a prey; and I will judge between one sheep and another.

23 "Then I will [a]set over them one [b]shepherd, My servant [c]David, and he will feed them; he will feed them himself and be their shepherd.

24 "And I, the LORD, will be their God, and My servant [a]David will be prince among them; I the LORD have spoken.

25 "I will make a [a]covenant of peace with them and [b]eliminate harmful beasts from the land so that they may [c]live securely in the wilderness and sleep in the woods.

26 "I will make them and the places around My hill a [a]blessing. And I will cause [b]showers to come down in their season; they will be showers of [c]blessing.

27 "Also the tree of the field will yield its fruit and the earth will yield its increase, and they will be [a]secure on their land. Then they will know that I am the LORD, when I have [b]broken the bars of their yoke and have delivered them from the hand of those who enslaved them.

28 "They will no longer be a prey to the nations, and the beasts of the earth will not devour them; but they will [a]live securely, and no one will make *them* afraid.

29 "I will establish for them a [a]renowned planting place, and they will [b]not again be [1]victims of famine in the land, and they will not [c]endure the insults of the nations anymore.

30 "Then they will know that [a]I, the LORD their God, am with them, and that they, the house of Israel, are My people," declares the Lord GOD.

31 "As for you, My [a]sheep, the [b]sheep of My pasture, you are men, and I am your God," declares the Lord GOD.

12 [c]Jer 13:16; Ezek 30:3; Joel 2:2
13 [a]Ezek 34:23; 36:29, 30; Mic 7:14 [b]Is 30:25
14 [1]Lit *fat* [a]Ps 23:2; Jer 31:12-14, 25; John 10:9 [b]Ezek 28:25, 26; 36:29, 30
15 [1]Lit *cause them to lie down* [a]Ps 23:1, 2; Ezek 34:23
16 [a]Is 10:16 [b]Is 49:26
17 [1]Or *lamb* [a]Ezek 20:38; 34:20-22; Mal 4:1; Matt 25:32
18 [1]Lit *foul by trampling* [a]Num 16:9, 13; 2 Sam 7:19; Is 7:13
19 [1]Lit *foul by trampling*
21 [1]Or *sick* [2]Lit *to the outside* [a]Deut 33:17; Dan 8:4; Luke 13:14-16
22 [a]Ps 72:12-14; Jer 23:3; Ezek 34:10
23 [a]Rev 7:17 [b]Is 40:11; John 10:11 [c]Jer 30:9; Ezek 37:24
24 [a]Is 55:3; Jer 30:9; Ezek 37:24, 25; Hos 3:5
25 [a]Ezek 16:60; 20:37; 37:26 [b]Job 5:22, 23; Is 11:6-9 [c]Jer 33:16; Ezek 28:26; 34:27, 28
26 [a]Gen 12:2; Ezek 34:14 [b]Deut 11:13-15; 28:12 [c]Lev 25:21; Is 44:3
27 [a]Ezek 38:8, 11 [b]Lev 26:13; Is 52:2, 3; Jer 30:8
28 [a]Jer 30:10; Ezek 39:26
29 [1]Lit *those gathered* [a]Is 4:2; 60:21; 61:3 [b]Ezek 34:26, 27; 36:29 [c]Ezek 36:6, 15
30 [a]Ps 46:7, 11; Ezek 14:11; 36:28
31 [a]Ps 78:52; 80:1; Ezek 36:38 [b]Ps 100:3; Jer 23:1

gloomy day. The day of the Lord that had come upon Israel when Jerusalem fell in August of 586 B.C. (see 7:7 and note).

34:13 *I will bring them out.* The promises of restoration—begun in 11:17 and repeated in 20:34,41–42; 28:25—find special emphasis in this part (chs. 33–39) of Ezekiel (see 36:24; 37:21; 38:8; 39:27). *mountains of Israel.* Compare the tone of 6:3–7 with judgment now past (see v. 12). The mountains perhaps represented the scene of salvation.

34:14 *I will feed them.* See Is 40:11; John 10:11.

34:16 *the fat and the strong.* Those with power who had fattened themselves by oppressing the other "sheep" (see vv. 17–22).

34:17 *rams and . . . goats.* People of power and influence who were oppressing poorer Israelites. This prophetic word shows the same concern for social justice found elsewhere in the prophets (see Is 3:13–15; 5:8; Amos 5:12; 6:1–7; Mic 2:1–5). Cf. the treatment of slaves Jeremiah observed (Jer 34:8–11).

34:23 *My servant David.* A ruler like David and from his line (see Ps 89:4,20,29; Jer 23:5–6).

34:24 *prince.* The Lord announced a theocracy, a kingdom where He would be King and the earthly king a "prince" (cf. 37:25; 44:3; 45:7,16–17,22; 46:2–18; 48:21–22).

34:25 *covenant of peace.* Cf. 37:26. All of God's covenants aim at peace (see Gen 26:28–31; Num 25:12; Is 54:10; Mal 2:5). This covenant (the "new covenant" spoken of by Jeremiah, 31:31–34) looks to the final peace, initiated by Christ (Phil 4:7) and still awaiting final fulfillment. "Peace" (Hebrew *shalom*) is more than absence of hostility; it is fullness of life enjoyed in complete security. *sleep in the woods.* Often dangerous (see Ps 104:20–21; Jer 5:6).

34:26 *showers . . . in their season.* Autumn rains, which signal the beginning of the rainy season, and spring rains, which come at the end (cf. Jer 5:24). *showers of blessing.* Blessing, the power of life promised to God's people through Abraham (Gen 12:1–3), is beautifully symbolized in the life-giving effects of rain.

34:27 *bars of their yoke.* The bars were wooden pegs inserted down through holes in the yoke and tied below the animal's neck with cords (Is 58:6) to form a collar (cf. 30:18; Lev 26:13; Jer 27:2; 28:10–13). The entire picture represents foreign domination.

34:29 *insults of the nations.* See 22:4.

34:30 *I, the LORD their God, am with them . . . they . . . are My people.* Covenant language (cf. 11:20; Ex 6:7; Hos 1:9), though the exact wording of this verse has no parallel elsewhere in Ezekiel.

Prophecy against Mount Seir

35 Moreover, the word of the LORD came
to me saying,
2 "Son of man, set your face against
[a]Mount Seir, and prophesy against it
3 and say to it, 'Thus says the Lord [1]GOD,
"Behold, I am against you, Mount Seir,
And I will [a]stretch out My hand
against you
And make you a [b]desolation and a
waste.
4 "I will [a]lay waste your cities
And you will become a desolation.
Then you will know that I am the LORD.
5 "Because you have had everlasting
[a]enmity and have [1]delivered the sons of Israel to the power of the sword at the time of
their calamity, at the time of the [2b]punish-
ment of the end,
6 therefore as I live," declares the Lord
GOD, "I will [1]give you over to [a]bloodshed,
and bloodshed will pursue you; since you
have not hated bloodshed, therefore bloodshed will pursue you.
7 "I will make Mount Seir a waste and a
desolation and I will cut off from it the one
who passes through and returns.
8 "I will [a]fill its mountains with its slain;
on your hills and in your valleys and in all
your ravines those slain by the sword will
[1]fall.
9 "I will make you an everlasting [a]desola-
tion and your cities will not be inhabited.
Then you will know that I am the LORD.
10 "Because you have [a]said, 'These two
nations and these two lands will be mine,
and we will possess [1]them,' although the
[b]LORD was there,
11 therefore as I live," declares the Lord
GOD, "I will deal *with you* [a]according to your
anger and according to your envy which you
showed because of your hatred against them;
so I will [b]make Myself known among them
when I judge you.
12 "Then you will know [1]that I, the LORD,
have heard all your revilings which you have
spoken against the mountains of Israel saying, 'They are laid desolate; they are [a]given
to us for food.'
13 "And you have [1a]spoken arrogantly
against Me and have multiplied your words
against Me; [b]I have heard *it.*"
14 'Thus says the Lord GOD, "As all the
[a]earth rejoices, I will make you a desolation.
15 "As you [a]rejoiced over the inheritance of
the house of Israel because it was desolate,
[b]so I will do to you. You will be a [c]desola-
tion, O Mount Seir, and all Edom, all of it.
Then they will know that I am the LORD."'

The Mountains of Israel to Be Blessed

36 "And you, son of man, prophesy to the
mountains of Israel and say, 'O mountains of Israel, hear the word of the LORD.
2 'Thus says the Lord [1]GOD, "Because the
enemy has spoken against you, 'Aha!' and,
'The everlasting [2a]heights have become our
possession,'
3 therefore prophesy and say, 'Thus says
the Lord GOD, "[1]For good reason they have
made you [a]desolate and crushed you from
every side, that you would become a possession of the rest of the nations and you have
been taken up in the [2b]talk and the whispering of the people."'"
4 'Therefore, O [a]mountains of Israel, hear
the word of the Lord GOD. Thus says the Lord
GOD to the mountains and to the hills, to the
ravines and to the valleys, to the desolate
wastes and to the forsaken cities which have
become a [b]prey and a derision to the rest of
the nations which are round about,
5 therefore thus says the Lord GOD,
"Surely in the fire of My [a]jealousy I have
spoken against the [b]rest of the nations, and
against all Edom, who [1]appropriated My
land for themselves as a possession with
wholehearted [c]joy *and* with scorn of soul, to
drive it out for a prey."

35:2 [a]Gen 36:8; Ezek 25:12; 36:5 **3** [1]Heb *YHWH,* usually rendered LORD, and so throughout the ch [a]Jer 6:12; 15:6; Ezek 25:13 [b]Jer 49:13, 17, 18; Ezek 35:7 **4** [a]Ezek 6:6; 35:9; Mal 1:3, 4 **5** [1]Lit *poured* [2]Or *iniquity* [a]Ps 137:7; Ezek 25:12, 15; 36:5; Amos 1:11; Obad 10 [b]Ezek 7:2; 21:25, 29 **6** [1]Lit *prepare you for* [a]Is 63:2-6; Ezek 16:38; 32:6 **8** [1]Lit *fall in them* [a]Is 34:5, 6; Ezek 31:12; 32:4, 5; 39:4, 5 **9** [a]Jer 49:13; Ezek 25:13 **10** [1]Lit *it* [a]Ps 83:4-12; Ezek 36:2, 5 [b]Ps 48:1-3; 132:13, 14; Is 12:6; Ezek 48:35; Zeph 3:15 **11** [a]Ps 137:7; Ezek 25:14; Amos 1:11 [b]Ps 9:16; 73:17, 18 **12** [1]Or *that I am the LORD: I have heard*

12 [a]Jer 50:7; Ezek 36:2 **13** [1]Lit *made great with your mouth* [a]Is 10:13, 14; 36:20; Jer 48:26, 42; Dan 11:36 [b]Jer 7:11; 29:23 **14** [a]Is 44:23; 49:13; Jer 51:48 **15** [a]Jer 50:11; Lam 4:21 [b]Obad 15 [c]Is 34:5, 6; Ezek 35:3, 4 **36:2** [1]Heb *YHWH,* usually rendered LORD, and so throughout the ch [2]Heb *Bamoth* [a]Deut 32:13; Ps 78:69; Is 58:14; Hab 3:19 **3** [1]Lit *Because;* or *By the cause* [2]Lit *lip of the tongue* [a]Jer 2:15 [b]Ps 44:13, 14; Jer 18:16; Ezek 35:13 **4** [a]Deut 11:11; Ezek 36:1, 6, 8 [b]Ezek 34:8, 28 **5** [1]Lit *gave* [a]Ezek 5:13; 36:6; 38:19 [b]Jer 25:9, 15-29; Ezek 36:3 [c]Jer 50:11; Ezek 35:15; Mic 7:8

35:2 *set your face against.* See note on 20:46. *Mount Seir.* Edom (v. 15), Israel's relative (Jacob and Esau being twins, Gen 25:21–30) and constant enemy, from whom brotherhood was sought but seldom found (cf. Amos 1:11). Edom had to be dealt with before Israel could find peace (cf. Gen 32–33). See 25:12 and note; Is 63:1–6.
35:3 *I am against you.* See note on 5:8.
35:5 *everlasting enmity.* Beginning with Jacob's deception of Isaac for Esau's blessing (Gen 27; see especially v. 41) and continuing later (Num 20:14–21; 2 Sam 8:13–14; 1 Kin 9:26–28). *time of their calamity.* Edom looted Jerusalem in 586 B.C. (see Obad 11–14).
35:6 *as I live.* See note on 18:3. *bloodshed will pursue you.* Retributive justice based on Gen 9:6.
35:9 *everlasting desolation.* To experience no restoration like Egypt's (see 29:13–16).
35:10 *These two nations.* Israel and Judah.
35:11 *as I live.* See note on 18:3.
35:13 *you have spoken arrogantly against Me.* Cf. Obad 12; Zeph 2:8,10; also Ps 35:26; Jer 48:26,42.
36:1–15 The comforting counterpart to ch. 6. Verses 1–7 announce punishment for the nations, vv. 8–15 restoration for Israel.
36:2 *the enemy has spoken against you.* See 25:3; 26:2. *Aha!* See note on 25:3. *everlasting heights.* The promised land, of which the elevated region between the Jordan Valley and the Mediterranean coast was the central core.
36:3 *rest of the nations.* All nations that in the past had conquered parts of Israel—until finally they took full possession.
36:4 *mountains . . . hills . . . ravines . . . valleys.* See 6:3 and note on 1:5.
36:5 *fire of My jealousy.* The Lord was personally offended by the ridicule of the nations because it was His special land they were mocking and plundering (see "My land" later in the verse). *Edom.* Singled out because of their long-standing hostility to Israel (see ch. 35, especially vv. 2,5 and notes).

6 'Therefore prophesy concerning the land of Israel and say to the mountains and to the hills, to the ravines and to the valleys, "Thus says the Lord GOD, 'Behold, I have spoken in My jealousy and in My wrath because you have [a]endured the insults of the nations.'

7 "Therefore thus says the Lord GOD, 'I have [1]sworn that surely the nations which are around you will themselves endure their insults.

8 'But you, O mountains of Israel, you will [a]put forth your branches and bear your fruit for My people Israel; for they will soon come.

9 'For, behold, I am for you, and I will [a]turn to you, and you will be [b]cultivated and sown.

10 'I will multiply men on you, [a]all the house of Israel, all of it; and the [b]cities will be inhabited and the waste places will be rebuilt.

11 'I will multiply on you man and beast; and they will increase and be fruitful; and I will cause you to be inhabited as you were [a]formerly and will [1]treat you [b]better than at the first. Thus you will know that I am the LORD.

12 'Yes, I will cause [a]men—My people Israel—to walk on you and possess you, so that you will become their [b]inheritance and never again [c]bereave them of children.'

13 "Thus says the Lord GOD, 'Because they say to you, "You are a [a]devourer of men and have bereaved your [1]nation of children,"

14 therefore you will no longer devour men and no longer bereave your nation of children,' declares the Lord GOD.

15 "I will not let you hear [a]insults from the nations anymore, nor will you bear [b]disgrace from the peoples any longer, nor will you cause your nation to [c]stumble any longer," declares the Lord GOD.' "

6 [a]Ps 74:10; 123:3, 4; Ezek 34:29
7 [1]Lit *lifted up My hand*
8 [a]Is 4:2; 27:6; Ezek 17:23; 34:26-29
9 [a]Lev 26:9 [b]Ezek 28:26; 34:14; 36:34
10 [a]Is 27:6; 49:17-23; Ezek 37:21, 22 [b]Jer 31:27, 28; 33:12; Ezek 36:33
11 [1]Lit *cause good* [a]Jer 30:18; Ezek 16:55; Mic 7:14 [b]Job 42:12; Is 51:3
12 [a]Ezek 34:13, 14 [b]Ezek 47:14 [c]Jer 15:7; Ezek 22:12, 27
13 [1]Or *nations,* and so throughout the ch [a]Num 13:32
15 [a]Is 60:14; Ezek 34:29; 36:7 [b]Ps 89:50; Is 54:4; Ezek 22:4 [c]Is 63:13; Jer 13:16; 18:15
17 [a]Jer 2:7 [b]Lev 15:19
18 [a]2 Chr 34:21, 25; Lam 2:4; 4:11; Ezek 22:20, 22
19 [a]Deut 28:64; Ezek 5:12; 22:15; Amos 9:9 [b]Ezek 24:14; 39:24; Rom 2:6
20 [a]Is 52:5; Ezek 12:16; Rom 2:24 [b]Jer 33:24
21 [1]Lit *compassion* [a]Ps 74:18; Is 48:9; Ezek 20:44
22 [a]Deut 7:7, 8; 9:5, 6; Ezek 36:32
23 [a]Is 5:16; Ezek 20:41; 38:23; 39:7, 25 [b]Ps 102:15; 126:2

16 Then the word of the LORD came to me saying,

17 "Son of man, when the house of Israel was living in their own land, they [a]defiled it by their ways and their deeds; their way before Me was like [b]the uncleanness of a woman in her impurity.

18 "Therefore I [a]poured out My wrath on them for the blood which they had shed on the land, because they had defiled it with their idols.

19 "Also I [a]scattered them among the nations and they were dispersed throughout the lands. [b]According to their ways and their deeds I judged them.

20 "When they came to the nations where they went, they [a]profaned My holy name, because it was said of them, 'These are the [b]people of the LORD; yet they have come out of His land.'

21 "But I had [1]concern for My [a]holy name, which the house of Israel had profaned among the nations where they went.

Israel to Be Renewed for His Name's Sake

22 "Therefore say to the house of Israel, 'Thus says the Lord GOD, "It is [a]not for your sake, O house of Israel, that I am about to act, but for My holy name, which you have profaned among the nations where you went.

23 "I will [a]vindicate the holiness of My great name which has been profaned among the nations, which you have profaned in their midst. Then the [b]nations will know that I am the LORD," declares the Lord GOD, "when I prove Myself holy among you in their sight.

24 "For I will [a]take you from the nations, gather you from all the lands and bring you into your own land.

24 [a]Is 43:5, 6; Ezek 34:13; 37:21

36:8 *branches and . . . fruit.* Signs of productivity (see 17:8,23) and the Lord's restored favor (see Lev 26:3–5); to be contrasted with Edom's desolation in 35:3,7,15. *soon.* As judgment neared (7:7; 12:23), a speedy return of the exiles was announced.

36:9 *I will turn to you.* Cf. Lev 26:9 for the identical clause in a similar context.

36:10 *all the house of Israel.* In this chapter (as in 37:15–23) Ezekiel is speaking of the restoration of all Israel.

36:11 *increase and be fruitful.* Identical terminology to the divine blessing at creation (Gen 1:22,28; see Gen 8:17; 9:1,7) and the subsequent covenant blessing (see Gen 17:6; 35:11; 48:3–4; Ex 1:7). *Thus you will know that I am the LORD.* These words of recognition, used throughout the book to express God's revelation through judgment, here point to God's self-disclosure in salvation (see note on 5:13; cf. 34:30).

36:12 *walk on you.* The mountains of Israel are still being addressed. *bereave them of children.* The mountains are poetically pictured as having contributed to the depopulation brought by the exile. This may refer to the fact that Canaan contained the Canaanites and their religious centers ("high places"), which had led Israel astray and so brought God's wrath down on His people (see 6:3 and note).

36:16–38 Summarizes all that Ezekiel prophesied concerning Israel.

36:18 *blood . . . defiled it with their idols.* A summary reference to Israel's social injustices and idolatrous religious practices (see 22:3 and note). *idols.* See note on 6:4.

36:20 *they profaned My holy name.* Because Israel had been removed from her land, it seemed to the nations that her God was unable to protect and preserve His people (cf. Num 14:15–16; 2 Kin 18:32–35; 19:10–12).

36:22 *It is not for your sake.* Not because God did not care for Israel, but because they did not deserve what He was about to do (cf. Deut 9:4–6). Statements like these make Ezekiel a preacher of pure grace. *for My holy name.* The reason given in ch. 20 for the withholding of divine punishment (see 20:9,14,22) is here given as a reason for divine restoration.

36:23 *Then the nations will know that I am the LORD.* The ultimate purpose of God's plans with Israel is that the whole world may know the true God.

36:24–30 There are four stages of restoration in this central passage of Ezekiel: (1) return of the exiles (v. 24), (2) cleansing from sin (v. 25), (3) enablement by God's Spirit to live God's way (vv. 26–27), and (4) prosperity in the land (vv. 28–30).

25 "Then I will [a]sprinkle clean water on you, and you will be clean; I will cleanse you from all your [b]filthiness and from all your [c]idols.

26 "Moreover, I will give you a [a]new heart and put a new spirit within you; and I will remove the [b]heart of stone from your flesh and give you a heart of flesh.

27 "I will [a]put My Spirit within you and cause you to walk in My statutes, and you will be careful to observe My ordinances.

28 "You will live in the land that I gave to your forefathers; so you will be [a]My people, and I will be your God.

29 "Moreover, I will save you from all your uncleanness; and I will call for the grain and multiply it, and I [a]will not [1]bring a famine on you.

30 "I will [a]multiply the fruit of the tree and the produce of the field, so that you will not receive again the disgrace of famine among the nations.

31 "Then you will [a]remember your evil ways and your deeds that were not good, and you will loathe yourselves in your own sight for your iniquities and your abominations.

32 "I am not doing *this* [a]for your sake," declares the Lord GOD, "let it be known to you. Be ashamed and confounded for your ways, O house of Israel!"

33 'Thus says the Lord GOD, "On the day that I cleanse you from all your iniquities, I will cause the [a]cities to be inhabited, and the [b]waste places will be rebuilt.

34 "The desolate land will be cultivated instead of being a desolation in the sight of everyone who passes by.

35 "They will say, 'This desolate land has become like the [a]garden of Eden; and the waste, desolate and ruined cities are fortified *and* inhabited.'

36 "Then the nations that are left round about you will know that I, the LORD, have rebuilt the ruined places *and* planted that which was desolate; I, the LORD, have spoken and [a]will do it."

37 'Thus says the Lord GOD, "This also I will let the house of Israel ask Me to do for them: I will increase their men like a flock.

38 "Like the [a]flock [1]for sacrifices, like the flock at Jerusalem during her appointed feasts, so will the waste cities be filled with [b]flocks of men. Then they will know that I am the LORD."'"

25 [a]Num 19:17-19; Ps 51:7; Titus 3:5, 6; Heb 9:13, 19; 10:22 [b]Is 4:4; Zech 13:1 [c]Is 2:18, 20; Hos 14:3, 8
26 [a]Ps 51:10; Ezek 11:19; 18:31; John 3:3, 5; 2 Cor 5:17 [b]Ezek 11:19; Zech 7:12
27 [a]Is 44:3; 59:21; Ezek 37:14; 39:29; Joel 2:28, 29
28 [a]Ezek 14:11; 37:23, 27
29 [1]Lit *put* [a]Ezek 34:27, 29; Hos 2:21-23
30 [a]Lev 26:4; Ezek 34:27
31 [a]Ezek 16:61-63; 20:43
32 [a]Deut 9:5
33 [a]Ezek 36:10; Zech 8:7, 8 [b]Is 58:12
35 [a]Is 51:3; Ezek 31:9; Joel 2:3
36 [a]Ezek 17:24; 22:14; 37:14; Hos 14:4-9
38 [1]Lit *of holy things* [a]1 Kin 8:63; 2 Chr 35:7-9; John 2:14 [b]Ps 74:1; 100:3; Jer 23:1; John 10:7, 9, 16
37:1 [1]Or *in* [a]Ezek 1:3; 33:22; 40:1 [b]Ezek 8:3; 11:24; 43:5; Acts 8:39 [c]Jer 7:32-8:2
3 [1]Heb *YHWH,* usually rendered LORD, and so throughout the ch [a]Ezek 26:19 [b]Deut 32:39; 1 Sam 2:6
4 [a]Ezek 37:9, 12 [b]Jer 22:29; Ezek 36:1
5 [1]Or *spirit,* and so throughout the ch [a]Gen 2:7; Ps 104:29, 30; Ezek 37:9, 10, 14

Vision of the Valley of Dry Bones

37 The [a]hand of the LORD was upon me, and He [b]brought me out [1]by the Spirit of the LORD and set me down in the middle of the [c]valley; and it was full of bones.

2 He caused me to pass among them round about, and behold, *there were* very many on the surface of the valley; and lo, *they were* very dry.

3 He said to me, "Son of man, [a]can these bones live?" And I answered, "O Lord [1]GOD, [b]You know."

4 Again He said to me, "[a]Prophesy over these bones and say to them, 'O dry bones, [b]hear the word of the LORD.'

5 "Thus says the Lord GOD to these bones, 'Behold, I will cause [1][a]breath to enter you that you may come to life.

36:25 *I will sprinkle clean water.* For sprinkling with water as a ritual act of cleansing see Ex 30:19–20; Lev 14:51; Num 19:18; cf. Zech 13:1; Heb 10:22. *I will cleanse.* See v. 33; 37:23; Jer 33:8. *idols.* See note on 6:4.

36:26–27 Contains "new covenant" terminology (see Jer 31:33–34).

36:26 *new heart.* See notes on 11:19; 18:31. *put a new spirit within you.* Transform your mind and heart. Here and in 11:19 God declared that He would bring about the change. In 18:31 (see note there) He called on His people to effect the change. What He requires of His people He always provides. *heart of flesh.* "Flesh" in the OT is often a symbol for weakness and frailty (Is 31:3); in the NT it often stands for the sinful nature as a God-opposing force (as in Rom 8:5–8). Here it stands (in opposition to stone) for a pliable, teachable heart.

36:27 *My Spirit.* God bestows His Spirit to enable the human spirit to do His will. Verses 25–27 are closely paralleled in Ps 51:7–11.

36:28 *My people . . . your God.* Covenant language (see 11:20 and note).

36:29 *from all your uncleanness.* From cultic and moral defilement (see v. 25; 37:23). *I will call.* As at the beginning when God called creation into being (cf. Gen 1:5,8,10).

36:30 *disgrace.* As in v. 15.

36:31 *Then you will remember.* God's undeserved grace leads to recollection and repentance (cf. 6:9; 16:63; 20:43; Ps 130:4).

36:32 *not . . . for your sake.* See note on v. 22.

36:33 *On the day.* Connects the promise of cleansing (vv. 24–32) and the promise of repopulation (vv. 33–36).

36:35 *garden of Eden.* Primeval fertility is suggested (cf. 28:13; 31:9). *fortified.* In contrast to 38:11.

36:36 *nations . . . will know.* See note on v. 23.

36:37 *let the house of Israel ask.* Allowing petitions to come to Him again, God reversed His earlier refusals to hear (cf. 14:3; 20:3,31).

36:38 *Like the flock for sacrifices.* See 1 Kin 8:63; 1 Chr 29:21; 2 Chr 35:7 for the appropriateness of the comparison.

37:1–28 One of Ezekiel's major visions. Surprisingly no date is given (as in 1:2; 8:1; 40:1), but the event must have occurred sometime after 586 B.C.

37:1 *hand of the LORD.* See note on 1:3. *Spirit of the LORD.* Used elsewhere in Ezekiel only in 11:5; usually simply "the Spirit," as in 8:3; 11:1,24. *valley.* The Hebrew for this word is the same as that translated "plain" in 3:22–23; 8:4. Ezekiel now received a message of hope, where he had previously heard God's word of judgment. *bones.* Verse 11 interprets them as symbolizing Israel's apparently hopeless condition in exile.

37:2 *there were very many.* Symbolizing the whole community of exiles. *very dry.* Long dead, far beyond the reach of resuscitation (1 Kin 17:17–24; 2 Kin 4:18–37; but see 2 Kin 13:21).

37:4 *Prophesy over these bones.* Ezekiel had previously prophesied to inanimate objects (mountains, 6:2; 36:1; forests, 20:47) and now prophesied to lifeless bones and the "breath" (v. 9).

6 ‘I will put sinews on you, make flesh
grow back on you, cover you with skin and
put breath in you that you may come alive;
and you will [a]know that I am the LORD.’ ”
7 So I prophesied [a]as I was commanded;
and as I prophesied, there was a [1]noise, and
behold, a rattling; and the bones came
together, bone to its bone.
8 And I looked, and behold, sinews were
on them, and flesh grew and skin covered
them; but there was no breath in them.
9 Then He said to me, “Prophesy to the
breath, prophesy, son of man, and say to the
breath, ‘Thus says the Lord GOD, “Come
from the four winds, O breath, and [a]breathe
on these slain, that they [b]come to life.” ’ ”
10 So I prophesied as He commanded me,
and the [a]breath came into them, and they
came to life and stood on their feet, an
[b]exceedingly great army.

The Vision Explained

11 Then He said to me, “Son of man, these
bones are the [a]whole house of Israel; behold,
they say, ‘Our [b]bones are dried up and our
hope has perished. We are [1]completely [c]cut
off.’
12 “Therefore prophesy and say to them,
‘Thus says the Lord GOD, “Behold, I will
open your graves and [a]cause you to come up
out of your graves, My people; and I will
bring you into the land of Israel.
13 “Then you will know that I am the
LORD, when I have opened your graves and
caused you to come up out of your graves,
My people.
14 “I will [a]put My [1]Spirit within you and
you will come to life, and I will place you on
your own land. Then you will know that I,
the LORD, have spoken and done it,” declares
the LORD.’ ”

6 [a]Is 49:23; Ezek 35:9; 38:23; 39:6; Joel 2:27; 3:17
7 [1]Lit *voice;* or *thunder* [a]Jer 13:5-7
9 [a]Ps 104:30 [b]Hos 13:14
10 [a]Rev 11:11 [b]Jer 30:19; 33:22
11 [1]Lit *cut off to ourselves* [a]Jer 33:24; Ezek 36:10; 39:25 [b]Ps 141:7 [c]Ps 88:5; Lam 3:54
12 [a]Deut 32:39; 1 Sam 2:6; Is 26:19; 66:14; Hos 13:14
14 [1]Or *breath* [a]Is 32:15; Ezek 11:19; 36:27; 37:6, 9; 39:29; Joel 2:28, 29; Zech 12:10
16 [a]Num 17:2, 3 [b]2 Chr 10:17; 11:11-17; 15:9 [c]1 Kin 12:16-20; 2 Chr 10:19
17 [a]Is 11:13; Jer 50:4; Ezek 37:22-24; Hos 1:11; Zeph 3:9
18 [a]Ezek 12:9; 17:12; 20:49; 24:19
21 [a]Is 43:5, 6; Jer 29:14; Ezek 36:24; 39:27; Amos 9:14, 15
22 [a]Jer 3:18; 50:4, 5; Ezek 36:10 [b]Ezek 34:23, 24; 37:24
23 [1]Another reading is *backslidings* [a]Ezek 36:25 [b]Ezek 36:28, 29

Reunion of Judah and Israel

15 The word of the LORD came again to me
saying,
16 “And you, son of man, take for yourself
[a]one stick and write on it, ‘For [b]Judah and
for the sons of Israel, his companions’; then
take another stick and write on it, ‘For
[c]Joseph, the stick of Ephraim and all the
house of Israel, his companions.’
17 “Then [a]join them for yourself one to
another into one stick, that they may become
one in your hand.
18 “When the sons of your people speak to
you saying, ‘Will you not declare to us [a]what
you mean by these?’
19 say to them, ‘Thus says the Lord GOD,
“Behold, I will take the stick of Joseph,
which is in the hand of Ephraim, and the
tribes of Israel, his companions; and I will
put them with it, with the stick of Judah, and
make them one stick, and they will be one in
My hand.” ’
20 “The sticks on which you write will be
in your hand before their eyes.
21 “Say to them, ‘Thus says the Lord GOD,
“Behold, I will [a]take the sons of Israel from
among the nations where they have gone,
and I will gather them from every side and
bring them into their own land;
22 and I will make them [a]one nation in
the land, on the mountains of Israel; and
[b]one king will be king for all of them; and
they will no longer be two nations and no
longer be divided into two kingdoms.
23 “They will [a]no longer defile themselves
with their idols, or with their detestable
things, or with any of their transgressions;
but [b]I will deliver them from all their
[1]dwelling places in which they have sinned,
and will cleanse them. And they will be My
people, and I will be their God.

37:6 *sinews . . . flesh . . . skin . . . breath.* Lists of four items are common in Ezekiel (see note on 1:5).
37:7 *a rattling.* Probably the sound of the bones coming together, but possibly recalling the sound accompanying God's presence, as in 3:12–13 ("rumbling sound").
37:8 *but there was no breath.* This visionary re-creation of God's people recalls the two-step creation of man in Gen 2:7, where man was first formed from the dust and then received the breath of life.
37:9 *breath.* The Hebrew for this word can also mean "wind" or "spirit." *four.* See note on 1:5. *slain.* What Ezekiel saw was a battlefield strewn with the bones of the fallen (see v. 10).
37:11 *Our bones . . . cut off.* A sense of utter despair, to which the vision offers hope.
37:12 *graves.* The imagery shifts from a scattering of bones on a battlefield (see note on v. 9) to a cemetery with sealed graves.
37:14 *I will place you on your own land.* These words make it clear that the Lord is not speaking here of a resurrection from the dead but of the national restoration of Israel.
37:16 *take . . . one stick.* Ezekiel's last symbolic act involving a material object (cf. 4:1,3,9; 5:1). *write on it.* Zech 11:7 seems to be based on this passage in Ezekiel.
37:17 *join them . . . one to another.* The sticks may have been miraculously joined, or Ezekiel may have joined the sticks together in his hand.
37:18 *Will you not declare to us . . . ?* The symbolic act successfully aroused the people's curiosity (see 12:9; 21:7; 24:19).
37:19 *they will be one in My hand.* God would duplicate Ezekiel's symbolic act by uniting the two kingdoms separated since Solomon's death (see 1 Kin 12). For similar prophecies of the reunion of Israel see 33:23,29; Jer 3:18; 23:5–6; Hos 1:11; Amos 9:11.
37:22 *mountains of Israel.* See 6:2–3; 34:13; 36:1. *one king.* Only here and in v. 24 is the word "king" used of the future ruler. Usually "prince" is used (see note on 34:24), as in v. 25. See 7:27 and note; see also 44:3; 45:7–9 and frequently in chs. 45–48, where the ruler in the ideal age is always referred to as "prince."
37:23 *idols.* The old and basic offense (see note on 6:4). *dwelling places.* See NASB marg. ("backslidings") and Jer 2:19; 3:22. *cleanse.* Cf. 36:25 for the same notion. *My people . . . their God.* See note on 11:20.

The Davidic Kingdom

24 "My servant [a]David will be king over
them, and they will all have [b]one shepherd;
and they will walk in My ordinances and
keep My statutes and observe them.
25 "They will live on the land that I gave to
Jacob My servant, in which your fathers lived;
and they will live on it, they, and their sons
and their sons' sons, forever; and [a]David My
servant will be their prince forever.
26 "I will make a [a]covenant of peace with
them; it will be an [b]everlasting covenant
with them. And I will [1]place them and [c]mul-
tiply them, and will set My [d]sanctuary in
their midst forever.
27 "My [a]dwelling place also will be with
them; and [b]I will be their God, and they will
be My people.
28 "And the nations will know that I am
the LORD [a]who sanctifies Israel, when My
sanctuary is in their midst forever." ' "

Prophecy about Gog and Future Invasion of Israel

38 And the word of the LORD came to me
saying,
2 "Son of man, set your face toward [a]Gog
of the land of [b]Magog, the [1]prince of [c]Rosh,
[d]Meshech and [d]Tubal, and prophesy against
him
3 and say, 'Thus says the Lord [1]GOD,
"Behold, I am against you, O Gog, [2]prince of
Rosh, Meshech and Tubal.
4 "I will turn you about and put hooks
into your jaws, and I will [a]bring you out, and
all your army, [b]horses and horsemen, all of
them [1]splendidly attired, a great company
with buckler and shield, all of them wielding
swords;
5 [a]Persia, [1][b]Ethiopia and [c]Put with them,
all of them *with* shield and helmet;
6 [a]Gomer with all its troops; [b]Beth-togar-
mah *from* the remote parts of the north with
all its troops—many peoples with you.
7 "[a]Be prepared, and prepare yourself,
you and all your companies that are assembled about you, and be a guard for them.
8 "[a]After many days you will be summoned; in the latter years you will come into
the land that is restored from the sword,
whose inhabitants have been [b]gathered from
many [1]nations to the [c]mountains of Israel
which had been a continual waste; but [2]its
people were brought out from the [1]nations,
and they are [d]living securely, all of them.
9 "You will go up, you will come [a]like a
storm; you will be like a [b]cloud covering the
land, you and all your troops, and many peoples with you."
10 'Thus says the Lord GOD, "It will come
about on that day, that [1]thoughts will come

24 [a]Jer 30:9; Ezek 34:24; 37:25; Hos 3:5 [b]Ps 78:71; Is 40:11; Ezek 34:23 **25** [a]Is 11:1; Ezek 37:24; Zech 6:12 **26** [1]Lit *give* [a]Ezek 16:62; 20:37; 34:25 [b]Ps 89:3, 4; Is 55:3; 59:21; Ezek 16:60 [c]Jer 30:19; Ezek 36:10, 11, 37 [d]Ezek 20:40; 43:7 **27** [a]John 1:14; Rev 21:3 [b]Ezek 37:23; 2 Cor 6:16 **28** [a]Ex 31:13; Ezek 20:12 **38:2** [1]Or *chief prince of Meshech* [a]Ezek 38:3, 14, 16, 18; 39:1, 11; Rev 20:8 [b]Gen 10:2; Ezek 39:6; Rev 20:8 [c]Ezek 38:3; 39:1 [d]Ezek 27:13; 38:3; 39:1 **3** [1]Heb *YHWH*, usually rendered LORD, and so throughout the ch [2]Or *chief prince of Meshech* **4** [1]Or *clothed in full armor* [a]Is 43:17 [b]Ezek 38:15; Dan 11:40 **5** [1]Lit *Cush* [a]2 Chr 36:20; Ezra 1:1; Ezek 27:10; Dan 8:20 [b]Gen 10:6-8; Ezek 30:4, 5 [c]Ezek 27:10; 30:5 **6** [a]Gen 10:2, 3 [b]Gen 10:3; Ezek 27:14 **7** [a]Is 8:9 **8** [1]Lit *peoples* [2]Lit *it was* [a]Is 24:22 [b]Is 11:11; Ezek 36:24; 37:21; 38:12; 39:27, 28 [c]Ezek 34:13; 36:1-8 [d]Ezek 38:11, 14; 39:26 **9** [a]Is 5:28; 21:1; 25:4; 28:2; Jer 4:13 [b]Ezek 30:18; 38:16; Joel 2:2 **10** [1]Lit *words*

37:24 *My servant David.* As in 34:23 (see note there) the coming Messianic ruler is called David because He would be a descendant of David and would achieve for Israel what David had—except more fully. *king.* See note on v. 22. *shepherd.* As in 34:23 the coming ruler is likened to a shepherd who cares for his flock (cf. John 10, especially v. 16).
37:25 *Jacob My servant.* See 28:25 and note.
37:26 *covenant of peace.* See 34:25 and note. *everlasting covenant.* See 16:60 and note. The phrase occurs 16 times in the OT, referring at times to the Noahic covenant (Gen 9:16), the Abrahamic (Gen 17:7,13,19), the Davidic (2 Sam 23:5) and the "new" (Jer 32:40). Cf. the covenant with Phinehas (Num 25:12–13). *set My sanctuary in their midst.* As he had done before. This word is further developed in Ezekiel's vision of the future age, in which the rebuilt sanctuary would have central position (chs. 40–48). See vv. 27–28.
38:1 This statement, repeated often for receiving God's word, stands as an introduction to chs. 38–39, which are a unit. The future restoration of Israel under the reign of the house of David (ch. 37) will bring about a massive coalition of world powers to destroy God's kingdom. But the vast host that comes against Jerusalem will end up as dead bodies strewn over the fields of the promised land. Israel will become the cemetery of the enemy hordes (cf. ch. 37).
38:2 *Son of man.* See note on 2:1. *set your face.* See note on 20:46. *Gog.* Apparently a leader or king whose name appears only here and in Rev 20:8. Several identifications have been attempted, notably Gyges, king of Lydia (c. 660 B.C.). Possibly the name is purposely vague, standing for a mysterious, as yet undisclosed, enemy of God's people. *of the land of Magog.* In Gen 10:2; 1 Chr 1:5 Magog is one of the sons of Japheth, thus the name of a people. In Ezek 39:6 it appears to refer to a people. But since the Hebrew prefix *ma-* can mean "place of," Magog may here simply mean "land of Gog." Israel had long experienced the hostility of the Hamites and other Semitic peoples; the future coalition here envisioned will include—and in fact be led by—peoples descended from Japheth (cf. Gen 10). *prince of Rosh.* "Prince of Rosh" can be translated "chief prince of," which would refer to a military commander-in-chief. *Meshech and Tubal.* These sons of Japheth (see Gen 10:2; 1 Chr 1:5) are probably located in eastern Asia Minor (cf. 27:13; 32:26). They are peoples and territories to the north of Israel (cf. vv. 6,15; 39:2). As in the days of the Assyrians and Babylonians, the major attack will come from the north.
38:3 *I am against you.* See note on 5:8.
38:4 *I will turn you about.* Emphasis is on the fact that God is completely in control of all that is to follow. *put hooks into your jaws.* As with Pharaoh in 29:4, Gog is likened to a beast led around by God.
38:5 *Ethiopia.* Hebrew *Cush*, the upper (southern) Nile region. The invading forces from the north (see v. 2 and note) are joined by armies from the south. *Put.* Libya (Africa).
38:6 *Gomer.* Another of Gog's northern allies (see note on v. 2), mentioned in Gen 10:3; 1 Chr 1:6 as one of the sons of Japheth. According to non-Biblical sources, these peoples originated north of the Black Sea. *Beth-togarmah.* See note on 27:14. According to Gen 10:3 and 1 Chr 1:6 Togarmah is one of the children of Gomer.
38:8 *After many days . . . in the latter years.* After all the events of national restoration, the immigration and settlement in Israel as described in chs. 34–37 will be completed.
38:9 *like a cloud.* Jeremiah similarly describes the invasion from the north in Jer 4:13.
38:10 *on that day.* A phrase also common to other prophetic writings; here it refers to the day of Gog's invasion of Israel. *thoughts will come into your mind.* The divine initiative (v. 4) is

into your mind and you will [a]devise an evil
plan,
11 and you will say, 'I will go up against
the land of [1a]unwalled villages. I will go
against those who are [b]at rest, that live
securely, all of them living without walls and
having no bars or gates,
12 to [a]capture spoil and to seize plunder,
to turn your hand against the waste places
which are *now* inhabited, and against the
people who are gathered from the nations,
who have acquired cattle and goods, who
live at the [1]center of the world.'
13 "[a]Sheba and [b]Dedan and the merchants
of [c]Tarshish with all its [1]villages will say to
you, 'Have you come to capture spoil? Have
you assembled your company to seize plunder, to carry away silver and gold, to take
away cattle and goods, to capture great
[d]spoil?' " '
14 "Therefore prophesy, son of man, and
say to Gog, 'Thus says the Lord GOD, "On
that day when My people Israel are [a]living
securely, will you not know *it*?
15 "[a]You will come from your place out of
the remote parts of the north, you and many
peoples with you, all of them riding on
horses, a great assembly and a mighty army;
16 and you will come up against My people Israel like a cloud to cover the land. It
shall come about in the last days that I will
bring you against My land, so that the
nations may [a]know Me when I am [b]sancti-
fied through you before their eyes, O Gog."
17 'Thus says the Lord GOD, "Are you the
one of whom I spoke in former days through
My servants the prophets of Israel, who
[a]prophesied in those days for *many* years
that I would bring you against them?
18 "It will come about on that day, when
Gog comes against the land of Israel,"
declares the Lord GOD, "that My fury will
mount up in My [a]anger.
19 "In My [a]zeal and in My blazing wrath I
declare *that* on that day there will surely be
a great [1b]earthquake in the land of Israel.
20 "[a]The fish of the sea, the birds of the
heavens, the beasts of the field, all the creeping things that creep on the earth, and all the
men who are on the face of the earth will
shake at My presence; the [b]mountains also
will be thrown down, the steep pathways
will [1]collapse and every wall will fall to the
ground.
21 "I will call for a [a]sword against [1]him on
all My mountains," declares the Lord GOD.
"[b]Every man's sword will be against his
brother.
22 "With pestilence and with blood I will
enter into [a]judgment with him; and I will
rain on him and on his troops, and on the
many peoples who are with him, [1]a torrential rain, with [b]hailstones, fire and brimstone.
23 "I will magnify Myself, sanctify Myself,
and [a]make Myself known in the sight of
many nations; and they will know that I am
the LORD." '

Prophecy against Gog—Invaders Destroyed

39 "And [a]you, son of man, prophesy
against Gog and say, 'Thus says the
Lord [1]GOD, "Behold, I am against you, O
Gog, [2]prince of Rosh, Meshech and Tubal;
2 and I will turn you around, drive you
on, take you up from the remotest parts of
the north and bring you against the mountains of Israel.
3 "I will [a]strike your bow from your left
hand and dash down your arrows from your
right hand.
4 "You will [a]fall on the mountains of Israel, you and all your troops and the peoples
who are with you; I will give you as [b]food to
every [1]kind of predatory bird and beast of
the field.

10 [a]Ps 36:4; Mic 2:1
11 [1]Or *open country* [a]Zech 2:4 [b]Jer 49:31
12 [1]Lit *navel* [a]Is 10:6; Ezek 29:19
13 [1]Or *young lions* [a]Ezek 27:22, 23 [b]Ezek 25:13; 27:15, 20 [c]Ezek 27:12 [d]Is 10:6; 33:23; Jer 15:13
14 [a]Jer 23:6; Ezek 38:8, 11; Zech 2:5, 8
15 [a]Ezek 39:2
16 [a]Ps 83:18; Ezek 36:23; 38:23 [b]Is 5:16; 8:13; 29:23; Ezek 28:22
17 [a]Is 5:26-29; 34:1-6; 63:1-6; 66:15, 16; Joel 3:9-14
18 [a]Ps 18:8, 15
19 [a]Deut 32:22; Ps 18:7, 8; Ezek 5:13; 36:5, 6; Nah 1:2; Heb 12:29
19 [1]Or *shaking* [b]Joel 3:16; Hag 2:6, 7, 21
20 [1]Lit *fall* [a]Jer 4:24, 25; Hos 4:3; Nah 1:4-6 [b]Zech 14:4
21 [1]I.e. Gog [a]Ezek 14:17 [b]Judg 7:22; 1 Sam 14:20; 2 Chr 20:23; Hag 2:22
22 [1]Lit *an overflowing* [a]Is 66:16; Jer 25:31 [b]Ps 11:6; 18:12-14; Is 28:17
23 [a]Ps 9:16; Ezek 37:28; 38:16
39:1 [1]Heb *YHWH,* usually rendered *LORD,* and so throughout the ch [2]Or *chief prince of Meshech* [a]Ezek 38:2

3 [a]Ps 76:3; Jer 21:4, 5; Ezek 30:21-24; Hos 1:5 **4** [1]Lit *wing* [a]Is 14:24, 25; Ezek 39:17-20 [b]Ezek 29:5; 32:4, 5; 33:27

paralleled, as it often is in Scripture, by human action (cf. Deut 31:3; Is 10:6–7). *evil plan.* A raiding expedition (see v. 12).

38:11 *land of unwalled villages.* Speaks of a blissfully peaceful, ideal future time when walls no longer will be needed. See Zech 2:4–5, which assumes, as does this passage, that the Lord alone is sufficient protection (cf. 36:35–36).

38:12 *center of the world.* The Hebrew for "center" also means "navel," a graphic image for the belief that Israel was the vital link between God and the world (the idea occurs also in 5:5). The word occurs elsewhere in the Bible only in Judg 9:37. Since the Hebrew for "world" can also mean "land," theologically Jerusalem is both the center of the land of Israel and the center of the earth.

38:13 *Sheba.* Southwest corner of the Arabian peninsula (modern Yemen), known for trading (Job 6:19; see 23:42; 27:22; 1 Kin 10:1–2). *Dedan.* See note on 25:13. *Tarshish.* See note on 27:12.

38:17 *Are you the one of whom I spoke . . . ?* Probably a general reference to earlier prophecies of divine judgment on the nations arrayed against God and His people.

38:19 *earthquake.* Signaling the mighty presence of God, who comes to overwhelm the great army invading His land.

38:20 The fourfold listing of the animal world indicates the totality of nature (see note on 1:5; cf. Gen 9:2; 1 Kin 4:33; Job 12:7–8 for similar listings).

38:21 *I will call for a sword.* God's sword of judgment (Is 34:5–6; Jer 25:29). *Every man's sword will be against his brother.* The coalition of Israel's enemies will turn on itself, as did the armies that attacked Judah in the time of Jehoshaphat (2 Chr 20:22–23).

38:22 The list of divine weapons suggests that God will intervene directly without the benefit of an earthly army.

39:1 *Gog, prince of Rosh, Meshech.* Or "Gog, chief prince of Meshech"; see note on 38:2. While vv. 1–16 add new details, the same basic events as those in ch. 38 are described.

39:2 *from the remotest parts of the north.* As in 38:6,15.

39:3 *bow.* Cf. Jer 6:23. The Lord will disarm Israel's enemies before they can shoot an arrow.

39:4 *food to every kind of predatory bird.* A theme expanded in vv. 17–20.

5 "You will fall on the [1]open field; for it is
I who have spoken," declares the Lord GOD.
6 "And I will send [a]fire upon Magog and
those who inhabit the [b]coastlands in safety;
and they will know that I am the LORD.
7 "My [a]holy name I will make known in
the midst of My people Israel; and I will not
let My holy name be [b]profaned anymore.
And the [c]nations will know that I am the
LORD, the [d]Holy One in Israel.
8 "Behold, it is coming and it shall be
done," declares the Lord GOD. "That is the
day of which I have spoken.
9 "Then those who inhabit the cities of
Israel will [a]go out and make [b]fires with the
weapons and burn *them*, both shields and
bucklers, bows and arrows, war clubs and
spears, and for seven years they will make
fires of them.
10 "They will not take wood from the field
or gather firewood from the forests, for they
will make fires with the weapons; and they
will take the spoil of those who despoiled
them and seize the [a]plunder of those who
plundered them," declares the Lord GOD.
11 "On that day I will give Gog a burial
ground there in Israel, the valley of those
who pass by east of the sea, and it will block
off those who would pass by. So they will
bury Gog there with all his [1]horde, and they
will call *it* the valley of [2]Hamon-gog.
12 "For seven months the house of Israel
will be burying them in order to [a]cleanse the
land.
13 "Even all the people of the land will
bury *them;* and it will be [1]to their [a]renown
on the day that I [b]glorify Myself," declares
the Lord GOD.
14 "They will set apart men who will constantly pass through the land, [a]burying those
who were passing through, even those left
on the surface of the ground, in order to
cleanse it. At the end of seven months they
will make a search.
15 "As those who pass through the land
pass through and anyone sees a man's bone,
then he will [1]set up a marker by it until the
buriers have buried it in the valley of
[2]Hamon-gog.
16 "And even *the* name of *the* city will be
Hamonah. So they will cleanse the land." '
17 "As for you, son of man, thus says the
Lord GOD, 'Speak to every [1]kind of [a]bird and
to every [a]beast of the field, "Assemble and
come, gather from every side to My sacrifice
which I am going to [b]sacrifice for you, as a
great sacrifice on the mountains of Israel,
that you may eat flesh and drink blood.
18 "You will [a]eat the flesh of mighty men
and drink the blood of the princes of the
earth, as *though they were* [b]rams, lambs,
goats and [c]bulls, all of them fatlings of
[d]Bashan.
19 "So you will eat fat until you are glutted,
and drink blood until you are drunk, from
My sacrifice which I have sacrificed for you.
20 "You will be glutted at My table with
[a]horses and charioteers, with mighty men
and all the men of war," declares the Lord
GOD.
21 "And I will set My [a]glory among the
nations; and all the nations will see My judgment which I have executed and My hand
which I have laid on them.
22 "And the house of Israel will [a]know that
I am the LORD their God from that day
onward.
23 "The nations will know that the house
of Israel went into exile for their [a]iniquity
because they acted treacherously against Me,

5 [1]Lit *face of the*
6 [a]Ezek 30:8, 16; 38:19, 22; Amos 1:4, 7, 10; Nah 1:6 [b]Ps 72:10; Is 66:19; Jer 25:22
7 [a]Ezek 36:20-22; 39:25 [b]Ex 20:7; Ezek 20:9, 14, 39 [c]Ezek 38:16, 23 [d]Is 12:6; 43:3, 14; 55:5; 60:9, 14
9 [a]Is 66:24; Mal 1:5 [b]Josh 11:6; Ps 46:9
10 [a]Is 14:2; 33:1; Mic 5:8; Hab 2:8
11 [1]Lit *crowd* [2]Or *the multitude of Gog*
12 [a]Deut 21:23; Ezek 39:14, 16
13 [1]Or *a memorial for them* [a]Jer 33:9; Zeph 3:19, 20 [b]Ezek 28:22
14 [a]Jer 14:16
15 [1]Lit *build* [2]Or *the multitude of Gog*
17 [1]Lit *wing* [a]Is 56:9; Jer 12:9; Ezek 39:4; Rev 19:17, 18 [b]Is 34:6, 7; Jer 46:10; Zeph 1:7
18 [a]Ezek 29:5; Rev 19:18 [b]Jer 51:40 [c]Jer 50:27 [d]Ps 22:12; Amos 4:1
20 [a]Ps 76:5, 6; Ezek 38:4; Hag 2:22; Rev 19:18
21 [a]Ex 9:16; Is 37:20; Ezek 36:23; 38:16, 23; 39:13
22 [a]Jer 24:7
23 [a]Jer 22:8, 9; 44:22; Ezek 36:18, 19

39:6 *I will send fire.* See 30:8 and note.
39:9 *burn them.* Cf. Ps 46:9, where God does the burning. *seven.* A symbolic number signifying the finality of this great battle against God's people, as well as indicating the size of the invading armies.
39:12 *seven.* As in v. 9, the number seven symbolizes totality, completeness and finality, and it also reveals the large number of invaders. *cleanse the land.* Ritual purity is a basic element in Ezekiel's theology (see 22:26; 24:13; 36:25,33; 37:23). Corpses were especially unclean (see Lev 5:2; 21:1,11; 22:4; Num 5:2; 6:6–12; 19:16; 31:19).
39:13 *people of the land.* See 7:27 and note, though here a special class may not be implied.
39:14 *set apart men . . . constantly pass through.* After the seven-month burial period observed by all the people, special squads will be hired full time to ensure total cleansing of the land—by marking for burial any human bones that may have been missed. Total ritual purity is the aim.
39:15 *marker.* Probably of stone, either a large one or a heap of smaller ones.
39:17 *Speak to every kind of bird . . . to My sacrifice.* Various interpretations are: 1. Since the enemies are all dead and buried, this section (vv. 17–20) is perhaps to be understood as poetic imagery. 2. However, if the passage reverts back to v. 4, a more literal interpretation is possible—the dead bodies were not all buried at once. 3. Verses 17–20 involve a restating of vv. 9–16, employing a different figure (see Is 34:6; Jer 46:10; Zeph 1:7). The metaphor of sacrifice suggests a consecration to the Lord in judgment, as with Jericho (see Josh 6:17 and note).
39:18 *You will eat the flesh of mighty men.* A gory description of what birds of prey commonly do (see previous note and Rev 19:17–21). *as though they were.* The bodies of the victims are compared to animals commonly used for sacrifices. *Bashan.* Rich pastureland east of the Sea of Galilee, known for its sleek cattle (Deut 32:14; Ps 22:12; Amos 4:1) and its oak trees (27:6; Is 2:13).
39:19 *eat fat . . . drink blood.* Further indication that this is the Lord's sacrificial feast, in that fat and blood were normally reserved for God (see 44:15; Lev 3:17).
39:20 *My table.* Sacrificial altar. See 40:38–43 and 41:22 for description of the tables in the new temple.
39:21 *My glory.* God's visible presence in the world (see note on 1:28). Here that visibility is due to divine intervention in history.
39:22–23 *the house of Israel will know . . . The nations will know.* As God had made Himself known to Israel and the nations through His saving acts in Israel's behalf (see Ex 6:7; 7:5,17; 10:2; 14:18; 16:6–7,12; Josh 3:10; 4:24; cf. Josh 2:9–11; 5:1), so now Israel and the nations will see Him again at work as He judges His people for their sin (see v. 27).

and I [b]hid My face from them; so I gave them
into the hand of their adversaries, and all of
them fell by the sword.
24 "[a]According to their uncleanness and
according to their transgressions I dealt with
them, and I hid My face from them." ' "

Israel Restored

25 Therefore thus says the Lord GOD,
"Now I will [1a]restore the fortunes of Jacob
and have mercy on the whole [b]house of Israel; and I will be [c]jealous for My holy name.
26 "They will [1a]forget their disgrace and all
their treachery which they [2]perpetrated
against Me, when they [b]live securely on their
own land with [c]no one to make *them* afraid.
27 "When I [a]bring them back from the peoples and gather them from the lands of their
enemies, then I shall be [b]sanctified [1]through
them in the sight of the many nations.
28 "Then they will know that I am the LORD
their God because I made them go into exile
among the nations, and then gathered them
again to their own land; and I will leave
none of them there any longer.
29 "I will not hide My face from them any
longer, for I will have [a]poured out My Spirit
on the house of Israel," declares the Lord GOD.

Vision of the Man with a Measuring Rod

40 In the [a]twenty-fifth year of our exile, at
the beginning of the year, on the tenth
of the month, in the fourteenth year after the
[b]city was [1]taken, on that same day the [c]hand
of the LORD was upon me and He brought me
there.
2 In the [a]visions of God He brought me
into the land of Israel and set me on a very
[b]high mountain, and on it [c]to the south *there*
was a [d]structure like a city.
3 So He brought me there; and behold,
there was a man whose appearance was like
the appearance of [a]bronze, with a [b]line of
flax and a [c]measuring [1]rod in his hand; and
he was standing in the gateway.
4 The man said to me, "[a]Son of man,
[b]see with your eyes, hear with your ears, and
give attention to all that I am going to show
you; for you have been brought here in order
to show *it* to you. [c]Declare to the house of
Israel all that you see."

Measurements Relating to the Temple

5 And behold, there was a [a]wall on the
outside of the [1]temple all around, and in the
man's hand was a measuring rod of six
cubits, *each of which was* a cubit and a
[2]handbreadth. So he measured the thickness
of the [3]wall, one rod; and the height, one
rod.
6 Then he went to the gate which faced
[a]east, went up its steps and measured the
threshold of the gate, one rod [1]in width; and
the other threshold *was* one rod [1]in width.
7 The [a]guardroom *was* one rod long and
one rod wide; and *there were* five cubits
between the guardrooms. And the threshold
of the gate by the porch of the gate [1]facing
inward *was* one rod.
8 Then he measured the porch of the
gate [1]facing inward, one rod.
9 He measured the porch of the gate,

23 [b]Is 1:15; 59:2; Ezek 39:29 **24** [a]2 Kin 17:7; Jer 2:17, 19; 4:18; Ezek 36:19 **25** [1]Or *return the captivity* [a]Is 27:12, 13; Jer 33:7; Ezek 34:13 [b]Jer 31:1; Ezek 36:10; 37:21, 22; Hos 1:11 [c]Ex 20:5; Nah 1:2 **26** [1]Another reading is *bear* [2]Lit *did treacherously* [a]Ezek 16:63; 20:43; 36:31 [b]1 Kin 4:25; Ezek 34:25-28 [c]Is 17:2; Mic 4:4 **27** [1]Lit *in* [a]Ezek 36:24; 37:21 [b]Ezek 36:23; 38:16, 23 **29** [a]Is 32:15; Ezek 36:27; 37:14; Joel 2:28 **40:1** [1]Lit *struck* [a]Ezek 32:1, 17; 33:21 [b]2 Kin 25:1-7; Jer 39:1-9; 52:4-11; Ezek 33:21 [c]Ezek 1:3; 3:14, 22; 37:1 **2** [a]Ezek 1:1; 8:3; Dan 7:1, 7

2 [b]Is 2:2, 3; Ezek 17:23; 20:40; 37:22; Mic 4:1; Rev 21:10 [c]Ps 48:2; Is 14:13 [d]1 Chr 28:12, 19 **3** [1]Lit *reed,* and so throughout the ch [a]Ezek 1:7; Dan 10:6; Rev 1:15 [b]Ezek 47:3; Zech 2:1, 2 [c]Rev 11:1; 21:15 **4** [a]Ezek 2:1, 3, 6, 8; 44:5 [b]Ezek 2:7, 8; 44:5 [c]Is 21:10; Jer 26:2; Acts 20:27 **5** [1]Lit *house* [2]I.e. 204 in. [3]Lit *building* [a]Is 26:1; Ezek 42:20 **6** [1]Or *in depth* [a]Ezek 8:16; 11:1; 40:20; 43:1 **7** [1]Lit *from the house* [a]Ezek 40:10-16, 21, 29, 33, 36 **8** [1]Lit *from the house*

39:23 *I hid My face.* Expression of divine displeasure (see Ps 30:7; Is 54:8; 57:17).
39:24 *their uncleanness and . . . their transgressions.* Spelled out especially in ch. 22, but also throughout chs. 6–24.
39:25 *Jacob.* The nation of Israel, as in 20:5. The parallelism within the verse supports this identity. *My holy name.* See note on 20:9.
39:26 *They will forget their disgrace.* The remembrance of shame previously called for (6:9; 20:43; 36:31) is here erased.
39:27 *I shall be sanctified through them.* God will reveal Himself anew in a restored, holy people (cf. 20:41; 28:25; 36:23).
39:28 *Then they will know.* See note on v. 22.
39:29 *I will have poured out My Spirit.* The gift of God's enabling Spirit (see 11:19; 36:26–27; 37:14).
40:1 *twenty-fifth year . . . beginning . . . tenth.* Apr. 28, 573 B.C. *of our exile.* All the dates in the book of Ezekiel (see chart, p. 1158) are reckoned from the 597 exile, but only here and in 33:21 is the exile specifically mentioned (see 1:2). *the beginning of the year.* Hebrew *Rosh Hashanah,* the well-known Jewish New Year festival. It has long occurred in the fall (in either September or October), but since throughout the book Ezekiel uses a different and older religious calendar, the spring date as given above is correct (see note on Lev 23:24). *hand of the LORD was upon me.* See note on 1:3.
40:2 *visions of God.* Introduces all three of Ezekiel's major visions (see 1:1; 8:3). *very high mountain.* Mount Zion, also seen as extraordinarily high in other prophetic visions (17:22; Is 2:2; Mic 4:1; Zech 14:10). Height here signifies importance, as the earthly seat of God's reign. *on it to the south.* With the city located on its southern slopes, the mountain is to the north (cf. Ps 48; see Ps 48:2 and note).
40:3 *like . . . bronze.* Indicates the man was other than human. *line of flax.* Used for longer measurements such as those in 47:3. *measuring rod.* Used for shorter measurements—about ten feet and four inches long. *in the gateway.* Presumably of the outer court (see vv. 17–19).
40:5 *wall on the outside of the temple all around.* Separating the sacred from the secular. *six cubits.* In using the long cubit (seven handbreadths, or about 21 inches), which was older than the shorter cubit (six handbreadths, or about 18 inches), Ezekiel was returning to more ancient standards for the new community (see 2 Chr 3:3).
40:6 *gate which faced east.* The gate of the outer court. The three gates (east, north, south) of the outer court were similar to the three in the inner court (v. 32), having six alcoves for the guards (three on each side) and a portico (vv. 8–9). Comparable gate plans have been discovered at Megiddo, Gezer and Hazor, all dating from the time of Solomon (see 1 Kin 9:15). The guards kept out anyone who might profane the temple area (see Ezra 2:62). *went up its steps.* The first of three sets of stairs leading to the temple. This one had seven steps (v. 22); the next one (inner court), eight (v. 31); the last (temple), ten (v. 49; based on the Septuagint reading of this verse)— possibly indicating increasing degrees of "holiness" (sacredness).

Ezekiel's Temple

A. Wall (40:5,16-20)
B. East gate (40:6-14,16)
C. Portico (40:8)
D. Outer court (40:17)
E. Pavement (40:17)
F. Inner court (40:19)
G. North gate (40:20-22)
H. Inner court (40:23)
I. South gate (40:24-26)
J. South inner court (40:27)
K. Gateway (40:28-31)
L. Gateway (40:32-34)
M. Gateway (40:35-38)
N. Priests' rooms (40:44-45)
O. Court (40:47)
P. Temple portico (40:48-49)
Q. Outer sanctuary (41:1-2)
R. Most holy place (41:3-4)
S. Temple walls (41:5-7,9,11)
T. Base (41:8)
U. Open area (41:10)
V. West building (41:12)
W. Priests' rooms (42:1-10)
X. Altar (43:13-17)
AA. Rooms for preparing sacrifices (40:39-43)
BB. Ovens (46:19-20)
CC. Kitchens (46:21-24)

Ezekiel uses a long or "royal" cubit, 20.4 inches or 51.81 cm ("cubit and a handbreadth," Ezek 40:5) as opposed to the standard Hebrew cubit of 17.6 inches or 44.7 cm.

Scripture describes a floor plan, but provides few height dimensions. This artwork shows an upward projection of the temple over the floor plan. This temple existed only in a vision of Ezekiel (Eze 40:2), and has never actually been built as were the temples of Solomon, Zerubbabel and Herod.

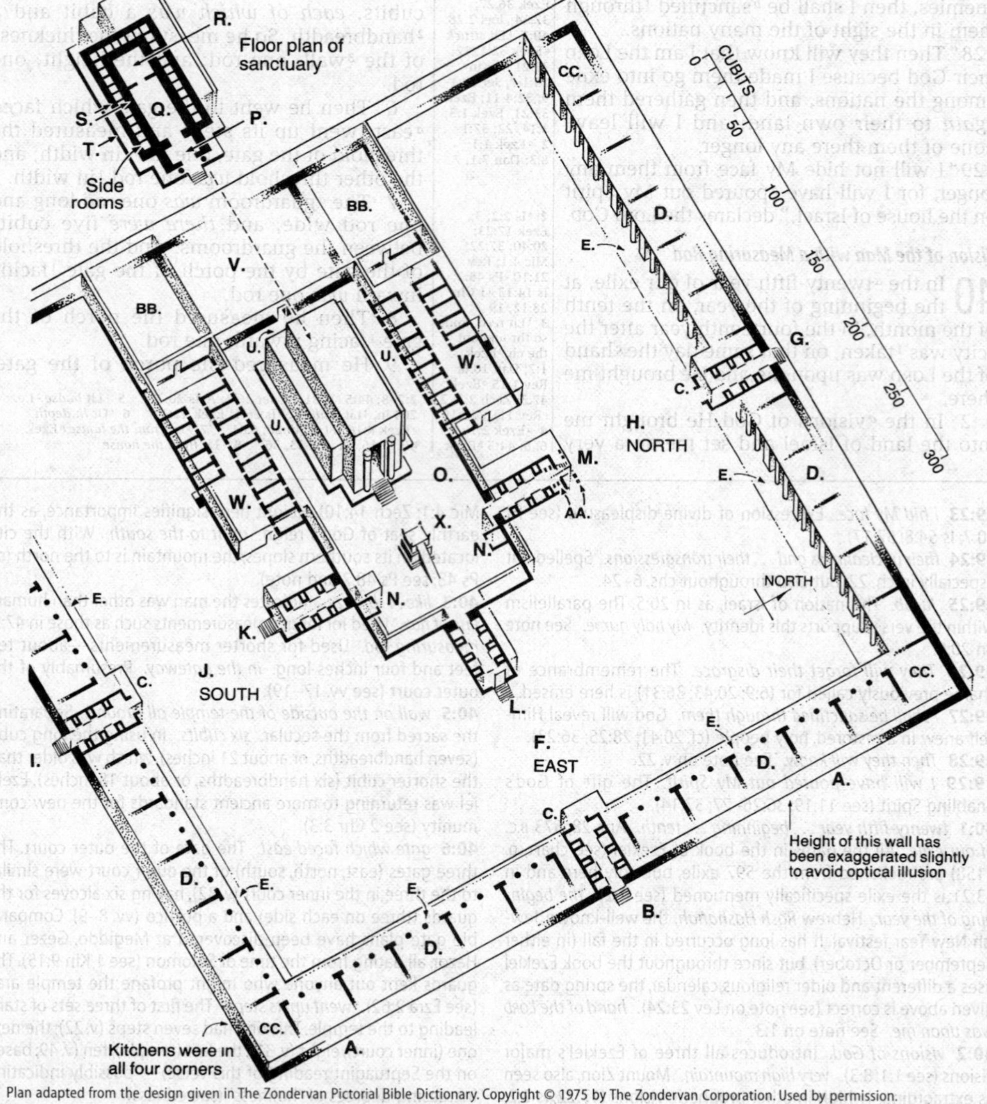

R.
Floor plan of sanctuary
S.
Q.
P.
T.
Side rooms
CC.
CUBITS
0
50
100
150
200
250
300
BB.
D.
E.
V.
BB.
G.
U.
U.
W.
C.
U.
H.
NORTH
W.
O.
M.
E.
D.
AA.
X.
N.
NORTH
E.
N.
K.
C.
J.
SOUTH
CC.
L.
E.
F.
EAST
D.
A.
I.
C.
Height of this wall has been exaggerated slightly to avoid optical illusion
D.
E.
E.
B.
D.
CC.
A.
Kitchens were in all four corners

Plan adapted from the design given in The Zondervan Pictorial Bible Dictionary. Copyright © 1975 by The Zondervan Corporation. Used by permission.

eight cubits; and its side pillars, two cubits.
And the porch of the gate was [1]faced inward.
10 The guardrooms of the gate toward the
east *numbered* three on each side; the three
of them had the same measurement. The
side pillars also had the same measurement
on each side.
11 And he measured the width of the
[1]gateway, ten cubits, and the length of the
gate, thirteen cubits.
12 *There was* a [1]barrier *wall* one cubit
wide in front of the guardrooms on each
side; and the guardrooms *were* six cubits
square on each side.
13 He measured the gate from the roof of
the one guardroom to the roof of the other, a
width of twenty-five cubits from *one* door to
the door opposite.
14 He made the side pillars sixty cubits
high; the gate *extended* round about to the
side pillar of the [a]courtyard.
15 *From* the front of the entrance gate to
the front of the inner porch of the gate *was*
fifty cubits.
16 *There were* [1a]shuttered windows *looking* toward the guardrooms, and toward their
side pillars within the gate all around, and
likewise for the porches. And *there were* windows all around inside; and on *each* side pillar *were* [b]palm tree ornaments.
17 Then he brought me into the [a]outer
court, and behold, *there were* [b]chambers and
a pavement made for the court all around;
thirty chambers [1]faced the pavement.
18 The pavement (*that is,* the lower pavement) *was* by the [1]side of the gates, corresponding to the length of the gates.
19 Then he measured the width from the
front of the [a]lower gate to the front of the
exterior of the inner court, a [b]hundred cubits
on the east and on the north.
20 *As for* the [a]gate of the outer court
which faced the north, he measured its
length and its width.
21 [1]It had three [a]guardrooms on each
side; and its [b]side pillars and its porches
[2]had the same measurement as the first gate.
Its length *was* [c]fifty cubits and the width
[d]twenty-five cubits.
22 Its [a]windows and its porches and its
palm tree ornaments *had* the same measurements as the [b]gate which faced toward the
east; and [1]it was reached by seven [c]steps,
and its [2]porch *was* in front of them.
23 The inner court had a gate opposite the

9 [1]Lit *from the house*
11 [1]Lit *entrance of the gate*
12 [1]Lit *border*
14 [a]Ex 27:9; 1 Chr 28:6; Ps 100:4; Is 62:9; Ezek 8:7; 42:1
16 [1]Or *beveled inwards* [a]1 Kin 6:4; Ezek 41:16, 26 [b]1 Kin 6:29, 32, 35; 2 Chr 3:5; Ezek 40:22, 26, 31, 34, 37; 41:18-20, 25, 26
17 [1]Lit *to* [a]Ezek 10:5; 42:1; 46:21; Rev 11:2 [b]2 Kin 23:11; 1 Chr 9:26; 23:28; 2 Chr 31:11; Ezek 40:38
18 [1]Lit *shoulder*
19 [a]Ezek 40:23, 27; 46:1, 2 [b]Ezek 40:23, 27
20 [a]Ezek 40:6
21 [1]Lit *its guardrooms were three* [2]Lit *were* [a]Ezek 40:7 [b]Ezek 40:16, 30 [c]Ezek 40:15 [d]Ezek 40:13
22 [1]Lit *they were going up into it* [2]Or *porches* [a]Ezek 40:16 [b]Ezek 40:6 [c]Ezek 40:26, 31, 34, 37, 49
23 [a]Ezek 40:19, 27
24 [1]Lit *these measurements,* and so throughout the ch [a]Ezek 40:6, 20, 35; 46:9 [b]Ezek 40:21
25 [1]Lit *It* [2]Lit *these windows* [a]Ezek 40:16, 22, 29 [b]Ezek 40:21, 33
26 [a]Ezek 40:6, 22 [b]Ezek 40:16
27 [a]Ezek 40:23, 32 [b]Ezek 40:19
28 [a]Ezek 40:32, 35
29 [1]Lit *it* [a]Ezek 40:7, 10, 21 [b]Ezek 40:16, 22, 25 [c]Ezek 40:21
30 [a]Ezek 40:16, 21
31 [a]Ezek 40:16 [b]Ezek 40:22, 26, 34, 37
32 [a]Ezek 40:28-31, 35 [b]Ezek 40:28

gate on the north as well as *the gate* on the
east; and he measured a [a]hundred cubits
from gate to gate.
24 Then he led me toward the south, and
behold, there was a [a]gate toward the south;
and he measured its [b]side pillars and its
porches according to [1]those same measurements.
25 [1]The gate and its porches had [a]win-
dows all around like [2]those other windows;
the length *was* [b]fifty cubits and the width
twenty-five cubits.
26 *There were* seven [a]steps going up to it,
and its porches *were* in front of them; and it
had [b]palm tree ornaments on its side pillars,
one on each side.
27 The inner court had a gate toward the
[a]south; and he measured from gate to gate
toward the south, a [b]hundred cubits.
28 Then he brought me to the inner court
by the south gate; and he measured the
south gate [a]according to those same measurements.
29 Its [a]guardrooms also, its side pillars and
its [b]porches *were* according to those same
measurements. And [1]the gate and its porches
had [b]windows all around; it *was* [c]fifty cubits
long and twenty-five cubits wide.
30 *There were* [a]porches all around, twenty-five cubits long and five cubits wide.
31 Its porches *were* toward the outer
court; and [a]palm tree ornaments *were* on its
side pillars, and its stairway *had* eight [b]steps.
32 He brought me into the [a]inner court
toward the east. And he measured the gate
[b]according to those same measurements.
33 Its [a]guardrooms also, its side pillars
and its porches *were* according to those same
measurements. And [1]the gate and its porches had [b]windows all around; it *was* [c]fifty
cubits long and twenty-five cubits wide.
34 Its [a]porches *were* toward the outer
court; and [a]palm tree ornaments *were* on its
side pillars, on each side, and its stairway
had eight [b]steps.
35 Then he brought me to the [a]north gate;
and he measured *it* according to those same
measurements,
36 *with* its [a]guardrooms, its side pillars
and its [b]porches. And [1]the gate had [b]win-
dows all around; the length *was* [c]fifty cubits
and the width twenty-five cubits.

33 [1]Lit *it* [a]Ezek 40:29 [b]Ezek 40:16 [c]Ezek 40:21 **34** [a]Ezek 40:16 [b]Ezek 40:22, 37 **35** [a]Ezek 40:27, 32; 44:4; 47:2
36 [1]Lit *it* [a]Ezek 40:7, 29 [b]Ezek 40:16 [c]Ezek 40:21

40:9 *porch of the gate was faced inward.* The reverse position of the porticoes of the inner court gates, which faced away from the temple (v. 34).
40:10 *guardrooms . . . numbered three.* The alcoves for the guards, mentioned in v. 7.
40:16 *palm tree.* As in Solomon's temple (see 1 Kin 6:29,32,35).
40:17 *thirty chambers.* The exact location of these rooms is not given. They were probably intended for the people's use (see Jer 35:2,4).
40:19 *hundred cubits.* Over 170 feet separated the outer wall from the inner wall and was the width of the outer court.
40:20 *gate . . . which faced the north.* Both it and the south gate (v. 24) were identical to the east gate.
40:22 *seven steps.* See note on v. 6.
40:28 *south gate.* Of the inner wall, which is not described but must be assumed. *he measured . . . according to those same measurements.* In both the outer walls (see note on v. 6).
40:34 *eight steps.* See note on v. 6.

37 Its side pillars *were* toward the outer court; and [a]palm tree ornaments *were* on its side pillars on each side, and its stairway had eight [b]steps.

38 A [a]chamber with its doorway was by the side pillars at the gates; there they [b]rinse the burnt offering.

39 In the porch of the gate *were* two [a]tables on each side, on which to slaughter the [b]burnt offering, the sin offering and the guilt offering.

40 On the outer [1]side, [2]as one went up to the [3]gateway toward the north, *were* two tables; and on the other [1]side of the porch of the gate *were* two tables.

41 Four [a]tables *were* on each side [1]next to the gate; *or,* eight tables on which they slaughter *sacrifices.*

42 For the burnt offering *there were* four [a]tables of [b]hewn stone, a cubit and a half long, a cubit and a half wide and one cubit high, on which they lay the instruments with which they slaughter the [a]burnt offering and the sacrifice.

43 The double [1]hooks, one handbreadth in length, were installed [2]in the house all around; and on the tables *was* the flesh of the offering.

44 From the outside to the [a]inner gate were [1b]chambers for the [c]singers in the inner court, *one of* which was at the [2]side of the north gate, with [3]its front toward the south, and one at the [2]side of the [4]south gate facing toward the north.

45 He said to me, "This is the [a]chamber which faces toward the south, *intended* for the priests who [b]keep charge of the [1]temple;

46 but the [a]chamber which faces toward the north is for the priests who [b]keep charge of the altar. These are the [c]sons of Zadok, who from the sons of Levi [d]come near to the LORD to minister to Him."

47 He measured the court, a *perfect* square, a [a]hundred cubits long and a hundred cubits wide; and the altar was in front of the [1]temple.

48 Then he brought me to the [a]porch of the [1]temple and measured *each* side pillar of the porch, five cubits on each side; and the width of the gate was three cubits on each side.

49 The length of the porch *was* twenty cubits and the width eleven cubits; and at the [a]stairway by which it was ascended *were* [b]columns belonging to the side pillars, one on each side.

37 [a]Ezek 40:16 [b]Ezek 40:34 **38** [a]1 Chr 28:12; Neh 13:5, 9; Jer 35:4; 36:10; Ezek 40:17; 41:10; 42:13 [b]2 Chr 4:6 **39** [a]Ezek 40:42 [b]Lev 1:3-17; Ezek 46:2 **40** [1]Lit *shoulder* [2]Lit *to the one going up* [3]Lit *entrance of the gate* **41** [1]Lit *by the shoulder of* [a]Ezek 40:39, 40 **42** [a]Ezek 40:39 [b]Ex 20:25 **43** [1]Or *ledges* [2]Or *inside* **44** [1]Gr reads *in two chambers* [2]Lit *shoulder* [3]Lit *their* [4]Gr reads *east* [a]Ezek 40:23, 27 [b]Ezek 40:17, 38 [c]1 Chr 6:31, 32; 16:41-43; 25:1-7 **45** [1]Or *house* [a]Ezek 40:17, 38 [b]1 Chr 9:23; Ps 134:1 **46** [a]Ezek 40:17, 38 [b]Lev 6:12, 13; Ezek 44:15 [c]1 Kin 2:35; Ezek 43:19; 48:11 [d]Lev 10:3; Num 16:5, 40; Ezek 42:13; 45:4 **47** [1]Lit *house* [a]Ezek 40:19, 23, 27 **48** [1]Lit *house* [a]1 Kin 6:3; 2 Chr 3:4 **49** [a]Ezek 40:31, 34, 37 [b]1 Kin 7:15-22; 2 Chr 3:17; Jer 52:17-23; Rev 3:12 **41:1** [1]I.e. the main inner hall [2]Lit *tent* [a]Ezek 40:2, 3, 17 [b]Ezek 41:21, 23 [c]Ezek 40:9; 41:3 **2** [1]Lit *shoulders* [2]Lit *its length,* [a]1 Kin 6:2, 17; 2 Chr 3:3 **3** [1]I.e. of the inner sanctuary [a]Ezek 40:16 [b]Ezek 41:1 **4** [a]1 Kin 6:20

The Inner Temple

41 Then he [a]brought me to the [1b]nave and measured the [c]side pillars; six cubits wide on each side *was* the width of the [2]side pillar.

2 The width of the entrance *was* ten cubits and the [1]sides of the entrance *were* five cubits on each side. And he measured [2]the length of the nave, [a]forty cubits, and the width, [a]twenty cubits.

3 Then he went [1a]inside and measured each [b]side pillar of the doorway, two cubits, and the doorway, six cubits *high;* and the width of the doorway, seven cubits.

4 He measured its length, [a]twenty cubits, and the width, twenty cubits, before the [b]nave; and he said to me, "This is the [c]most holy *place.*"

5 Then he measured the wall of the [1]temple, six cubits; and the width of the [a]side chambers, four cubits, all around about the house on every side.

6 [a]The side chambers were in three stories, [1]one above another, and [2]thirty in each story; and [3]the side chambers [b]extended to the wall which *stood* on [4]their inward side all around, that they might be fastened, and not be fastened into the wall of the temple *itself.*

7 The side chambers surrounding the temple were wider at each successive story. Because the [a]structure surrounding the temple went upward by stages on all sides of the temple, therefore the width of the temple *increased* as it went higher; and thus one went up from the lowest *story* to the highest by way of the [1]second *story.*

8 I saw also that the house had a raised

[b]1 Kin 6:5 [c]Ex 26:33, 34; 1 Kin 6:16; 7:50; 8:6; 2 Chr 5:7; Heb 9:3-8 **5** [1]Lit *house,* and so throughout the ch [a]1 Kin 6:5; Ezek 41:6-11 **6** [1]Lit *chamber upon chamber* [2]Lit *thirty times* [3]Lit *they were coming* [4]Lit *the inside of the side chambers* [a]1 Kin 6:5-10 [b]1 Kin 6:6, 10 **7** [1]Lit *middle* [a]1 Kin 6:8

40:38 *side pillars at the gates.* The porticoes of the inner gateways were on the side of the outer court, facing away from the temple. *rinse.* The inner parts and the legs were washed (Lev 1:9).

40:39 *burnt offering.* Probably one of the oldest kinds of sacrifice. The entire animal was burned in consecration to God (see Lev 1). *sin offerings and guilt offerings.* Discussed in Lev 4–7. The peace offerings, which were more festive, are notable by their absence from this listing (see 43:27; 45:17; 46:2,12).

40:46 *sons of Zadok.* For the distinction between the sons of Zadok and the Levites see the fuller discussion in the notes on 44:15–31.

40:47 *altar.* Described in 43:13–17.

40:48 *porch.* Similar to the portico in Solomon's temple but slightly larger (see 1 Kin 6:3).

40:49 *columns.* Called Jachin and Boaz in Solomon's temple (see 1 Kin 7:21).

41:1 *nave.* The largest of the three rooms comprising the temple (see NASB marg., the main inner hall). This outer sanctuary was identical in size to Solomon's (see 1 Kin 6:17).

41:3 *he went inside.* Only the angel, not Ezekiel, entered the most holy place. Lev 16 forbids any but the high priest to enter it, and then only once a year (see Heb 9:7). *six cubits high.* Or "six cubits wide"; note the progressive narrowness of the door openings as one approaches the inner sanctuary (40:48, 14 cubits; 41:2, 10 cubits).

41:6 *thirty in each story.* These 90 side rooms were probably storerooms for the priests, possibly for the tithes (see Mal 3:10).

[1]platform all around; the foundations of the
side chambers were a full rod of [a]six [2]long
cubits *in height.*
9 The [1]thickness of the outer wall of the
side chambers *was* five cubits. But the [a]free
space between the side chambers belonging
to the temple
10 and the *outer* [a]chambers *was* twenty
cubits in width all around the temple on
every side.
11 The [1]doorways of the [2]side chambers
toward the [a]free space *consisted of* one doorway toward the north and another doorway
toward the south; and the width of the [a]free
space *was* five cubits all around.
12 The [a]building that *was* in front of the
[b]separate area at the side toward the west
was seventy cubits wide; and the wall of the
building *was* five cubits [1]thick all around,
and its length *was* ninety cubits.
13 Then he measured the temple, a [a]hun-
dred cubits long; the [b]separate area with the
[c]building and its walls *were* also a [a]hundred
cubits long.
14 Also the width of the front of the temple and *that of* the separate [1]areas along the
east *side totaled* a hundred cubits.
15 He measured the length of the [a]build-
ing [1]along the front of the [b]separate area
behind it, with a [2c]gallery on each side, a
hundred cubits; *he* also *measured* the inner
nave and the porches of the court.
16 The [a]thresholds, the [1b]latticed windows and the [2c]galleries round about their
[d]three stories, opposite the threshold, were
[e]paneled with wood all around, and *from* the
ground to the windows (but the windows
were covered),
17 over the entrance, and to the inner
house, and on the outside, and on all the wall
all around inside and outside, by measurement.
18 It was [1]carved with [a]cherubim and
[b]palm trees; and a palm tree was between
cherub and cherub, and every cherub had
two faces,
19 a [a]man's face toward the palm tree on
one side and a young [a]lion's face toward the
palm tree on the other side; they were
[1]carved on all the house all around.
20 From the ground to above the entrance
[a]cherubim and [a]palm trees were [1]carved, as
well as *on* the wall of the nave.
21 The [a]doorposts of the [b]nave were
square; as for the front of the sanctuary, the
appearance of one doorpost was like that of
the other.
22 The [a]altar *was* of wood, three cubits
high and its length two cubits; its corners, its
[1]base and its [2]sides *were* of wood. And he
said to me, "This is the [b]table that is before
the LORD."
23 The [a]nave and the [b]sanctuary each had
a double [c]door.
24 Each of the doors had two leaves, two
[1a]swinging leaves; two *leaves* for one door
and two leaves for the other.
25 Also there were [1]carved on them, on
the doors of the nave, [a]cherubim and [a]palm
trees like those [1]carved on the walls; and
there was a [2b]threshold of wood on the front
of the porch outside.
26 *There were* [1a]latticed windows and
[b]palm trees on one side and on the other, on
the sides of the [c]porch; thus *were* the [d]side
chambers of the house and the [2]thresholds.

Chambers of the Temple

42 Then he [a]brought me out into the [b]out-
er court, the way [c]toward the north;
and he brought me to the [d]chamber which
was opposite the [e]separate area and opposite
the [f]building toward the north.
2 Along the length, *which was* a [a]hun-
dred cubits, *was* the north door; the width
was fifty cubits.
3 Opposite the [a]twenty *cubits* which
belonged to the inner court, and opposite the
[b]pavement which belonged to the outer
court, *was* [1c]gallery corresponding to [1]gal-
lery in three stories.
4 Before the [a]chambers *was* an inner
walk ten cubits wide, a way of one *hundred*
cubits; and their openings *were* on the north.
5 Now the upper chambers *were* [1]smaller
because the [2a]galleries took more *space*
away from them than from the lower and
middle ones in the building.
6 For they *were* in [a]three stories and had
no pillars like the pillars of the courts; therefore *the upper chambers* were [1]set back from
the ground upward, more than the lower and
middle ones.
7 As for the [a]outer wall by the side of the

8 [1]Lit *height* [2]Or *to the joint* [a]Ezek 40:5
9 [1]Lit *width* [a]Ezek 41:11
10 [a]Ezek 40:17
11 [1]Lit *doorway* [2]Lit *side chamber* [a]Ezek 41:9
12 [1]Lit *wide* [a]Ezek 41:13, 15; 42:1 [b]Ezek 41:14; 42:10, 13
13 [a]Ezek 40:47 [b]Ezek 41:13-15; 42:1, 10, 13 [c]Ezek 41:12
14 [1]Lit *area*
15 [1]Lit *to* [2]Or *passageway* [a]Ezek 41:12, 13; 42:1 [b]Ezek 41:14; 42:1, 10, 13 [c]Ezek 41:16; 42:3, 5
16 [1]Or *framed* [2]Or *passageways* [a]Is 6:4; Ezek 10:18; 40:6; 41:25 [b]1 Kin 6:4; Ezek 40:16, 25; 41:26 [c]Ezek 41:15 [d]Ezek 42:3 [e]1 Kin 6:15
18 [1]Lit *made* [a]1 Kin 6:29, 32, 35; 7:36; Ezek 41:20, 25 [b]2 Chr 3:5; Ezek 40:16
19 [1]Lit *made* [a]Ezek 1:10; 10:14
20 [1]Lit *made* [a]Ezek 41:18
21 [a]1 Kin 6:33; Ezek 40:9, 14, 16; 41:1 [b]Ezek 41:1
22 [1]Lit *length* [2]Lit *walls* [a]Ex 30:1-3; 1 Kin 6:20; Rev 8:3 [b]Ex 25:23, 30; Lev 24:6; Ezek 23:41; 44:16; Mal 1:7, 12
23 [a]Ezek 41:1 [b]Ezek 41:4 [c]1 Kin 6:31-35
24 [1]Or *turning* [a]1 Kin 6:34
25 [1]Lit *made* [2]Or *canopy of wood over* [a]Ezek 41:18 [b]Ezek 41:16
26 [1]Or *framed* [2]Or *canopies* [a]Ezek 41:16 [b]Ezek 40:16 [c]Ezek 40:9, 48 [d]Ezek 41:5
42:1 [a]Ezek 40:17, 28, 48; 41:1 [b]Ezek 40:17, 20 [c]Ezek 40:20 [d]Ezek 40:17; 42:4 [e]Ezek 41:12; 42:10, 13 [f]Ezek 41:12
2 [a]Ezek 41:13
3 [1]Or *passageway* [a]Ezek 41:10 [b]Ezek 40:17 [c]Ezek 41:15, 16; 42:5
4 [a]Ezek 46:19
5 [1]Lit *shorter* [2]Or *passageways* [a]Ezek 42:3
6 [1]Or *reduced* [a]Ezek 41:6
7 [a]Ezek 42:10, 12

41:13 *hundred.* The 100-cubit symmetry stood for perfection.
41:16 *paneled with wood all around.* As in Solomon's temple (1 Kin 6:15).
41:18 *cherubim.* Who served as guards (cf. Gen 3:24). These, as opposed to those mentioned in ch. 10, have only two faces—a man's and a lion's (see 1 Kin 6:29,32,35).
41:22 *altar . . . of wood.* As the great altar stood outside the temple proper (43:13–17), so a smaller altar (3′5″ square by 5′ high) stood outside the most holy place. It served as a table, no doubt to hold the bread of the Presence (Ex 25:30; Lev 24:5–9; see 1 Kin 7:48 and note). Ezekiel makes no mention of an altar of incense or of lampstands, such as were found in Solomon's temple and in the tabernacle before it. Also not included are the "sea" (1 Kin 7:23) and the ark of the covenant.
41:23 *double door.* Folding doors, so that the entry could be made still narrower.
42:1 *chamber . . . opposite the separate area.* The chambers' function is described in vv. 13–14. They have no parallel in Solomon's temple as described in 1 Kin 6.

chambers, toward the outer court facing the chambers, its length *was* fifty cubits.

8 For the length of the chambers which *were* in the outer court *was* fifty cubits; and behold, *the length of those* facing the temple *was* a [a]hundred cubits.

9 Below these chambers *was* the [a]entrance on the east side, as one enters them from the outer court.

10 In the [1]thickness of the [a]wall of the court toward the east, facing the [b]separate area and facing the building, *there were* [c]chambers.

11 The [a]way in front of them *was* like the appearance of the chambers which *were* on the north, according to their length so was their width, and all their exits *were* both according to their arrangements and openings.

12 Corresponding to the openings of the chambers which were toward the south was an opening at the head of the way, the way in front of the [a]wall toward the east, as one enters them.

13 Then he said to me, "The north chambers *and* the south chambers, which are opposite the [a]separate area, they are the [b]holy chambers where the priests who are [c]near to the LORD shall eat the [d]most holy things. There they shall lay the most holy things, the grain offering, the sin offering and the guilt offering; for the place is holy.

14 "When the priests enter, then they shall not go out into the outer court from the sanctuary [1]without [a]laying there their [b]garments in which they minister, for they are holy. They shall put on other garments; then they shall approach that which is for the people."

15 Now when he had finished measuring the inner house, he brought me out by the way of the [a]gate which faced toward the east and measured it all around.

16 He measured on the east side with the measuring reed five hundred reeds by the [a]measuring reed.

17 He measured on the north side five hundred reeds by the measuring reed.

18 On the south side he measured five hundred reeds with the measuring reed.

19 He turned to the west side *and* measured five hundred reeds with the measuring reed.

20 He measured it [1]on the four sides; it had a [a]wall all around, the [b]length five hundred and the [b]width five hundred, to [c]divide between the holy and the profane.

Vision of the Glory of God Filling the Temple

43 Then he led me to the [a]gate, the gate facing toward the east;

2 and behold, the [a]glory of the God of Israel was coming from the way of the [b]east. And His [c]voice was like the sound of many waters; and the earth [d]shone with His glory.

3 And *it was* like the appearance of the vision which I saw, like the [a]vision which I saw when [1]He came to [b]destroy the city. And the visions *were* like the vision which I saw by the [c]river Chebar; and I [d]fell on my face.

4 And the glory of the LORD came into the house by the way of the gate facing toward the [a]east.

5 And the [a]Spirit lifted me up and brought me into the inner court; and behold, the [b]glory of the LORD filled the house.

6 Then I heard one speaking to me from the house, while a [a]man was standing beside me.

7 He said to me, "Son of man, *this is* the place of My [a]throne and the place of the soles of My feet, where I will [b]dwell among the sons of Israel forever. And the house of Israel will not again defile My holy name, neither they nor their kings, by their harlotry and by the [1][c]corpses of their kings [2]when they die,

8 [a]Ezek 41:13, 14
9 [a]Ezek 44:5; 46:19
10 [1]Lit *width* [a]Ezek 42:7 [b]Ezek 42:1, 13 [c]Ezek 40:17
11 [a]Ezek 42:4
12 [a]Ezek 42:7
13 [a]Ezek 42:1, 10 [b]Ex 29:31; Lev 7:6; 10:13, 14, 17 [c]Lev 10:3; Deut 21:5; Ezek 40:46 [d]Lev 6:25, 29; 14:13; Num 18:9, 10
14 [1]Lit *but there they shall lay* [a]Ezek 44:19 [b]Ex 29:4-9; Lev 8:7, 13; Is 61:10; Zech 3:4, 5
15 [a]Ezek 40:6; 43:1
16 [a]Ezek 40:3
20 [1]Lit *toward the four winds* [a]Is 60:18; Ezek 40:5; Zech 2:5 [b]Ezek 45:2; Rev 21:16 [c]Ezek 22:26; 44:23; 48:15
43:1 [a]Ezek 10:19; 40:6; 42:15; 43:4; 44:1; 46:1
2 [a]Is 6:3; Ezek 1:28; 3:23; 10:18, 19 [b]Ezek 11:23 [c]Ezek 1:24; Rev 1:15; 14:2 [d]Ezek 1:28; 10:4; Rev 18:1
3 [1]So with some mss and some ancient versions; M.T. *I* [a]Ezek 1:4-28 [b]Jer 1:10; Ezek 9:1, 5; 32:18 [c]Ezek 1:3; 10:20 [d]Ezek 1:28; 3:23
4 [a]Ezek 10:19; 11:23; 43:2
5 [a]Ezek 3:14; 8:3; 11:1, 24; 2 Cor 12:2-4 [b]Ezek 10:4
6 [a]Ezek 1:26; 40:3

7 [1]Or *monuments* as in Ugaritic [2]Or *in their high places* [a]Ps 47:8; Ezek 1:26 [b]Ezek 37:26, 28 [c]Lev 26:30; Ezek 6:5, 13

42:13 *priests who are near to the LORD.* The sons of Zadok (see 40:6 and note on 44:15). *eat the most holy things.* The priests normally received partial maintenance by being allowed to eat certain sacrifices (see Lev 2:3; 5:13; 6:16,26,29; 7:6,10).

42:20 *length five hundred and . . . width five hundred.* Perfect symmetry in the ideal temple's total area.

43:2 *behold, the glory.* The high point of chs. 40–48. The temple had been prepared for this moment, and all that follows flows from this appearance. *coming from the . . . east.* The direction Ezekiel had seen God leave (see 11:23). In the book of Ezekiel God's glory is always active (see vv. 4–5; 3:23; 9:3; 10:4,18; 44:4). *like the sound of many waters.* Ezekiel experienced an audition as well as a vision. For the comparison see 1:24; Rev 1:15; 14:2; 19:6. *the earth shone with His glory.* God's visible glory is always described as being very bright (see 10:4; Luke 2:9; Rev 21:11,23).

43:3 *like the vision which I saw.* And yet it was different, for no creatures or wheels are mentioned here. *when He came to destroy the city.* See ch. 9. *by the River Chebar.* See ch. 1. *I fell on my face.* See 1:28; 3:23; 9:8; 11:13; 44:4.

43:4 *by the . . . gate facing . . . east.* See note on v. 2.

43:5 *And the Spirit lifted me up.* With God being nearer, the function of the guiding angel was taken over by the Spirit of God. Ezekiel was transported into the inner court but not into the temple (cf. 3:14; 8:3; 11:1,24). *filled the house.* As at the consecration of Solomon's temple (1 Kin 8:11; see Ex 40:34–35; Is 6:4).

43:6 *one.* God, but out of reverence not named here, preserving an air of awe and mystery.

43:7 *place of My throne.* See Is 6:1; Jer 3:17. *place of the soles of My feet.* See 1 Chr 28:2; Ps 99:5; 132:7; Is 60:13; Lam 2:1. *I will dwell among the sons of Israel forever.* Renewing the promise of 37:26–28 (see v. 9; 1 Kin 6:13; Zech 2:11). *harlotry.* The word can stand either for the sacred prostitution in the Canaanite religion (Baalism) or for spiritual apostasy from true worship of the Lord (see note on 16:15). *corpses.* The reference is either to idols or to monuments or graves of past kings. Fourteen kings of Judah were buried in Jerusalem, possibly near (too near for Ezekiel) the temple area (see 2 Kin 21:18,26; 23:30).

8 by setting their threshold by My threshold and their door post beside My door post, with *only* the wall between Me and them. And they have [a]defiled My holy name by their abominations which they have committed. So I have consumed them in My anger.

9 "Now let them [a]put away their harlotry and the [1]corpses of their kings far from Me; and I will [b]dwell among them forever.

10 "As for you, son of man, [1][a]describe the [2]temple to the house of Israel, that they may be [b]ashamed of their iniquities; and let them measure the [3][c]plan.

11 "If they are ashamed of all that they have done, make known to them the [1]design of the house, its structure, its [a]exits, its entrances, all its designs, all its statutes[2], and all its laws. And write *it* [b]in their sight, so that they may observe its whole [1]design and all its statutes and [c]do them.

12 "This is the [1]law of the house: its entire [2]area on the top of the [a]mountain all around *shall be* most holy. Behold, this is the [1]law of the house.

The Altar of Sacrifice

13 "And these are the measurements of the [a]altar by cubits (the [b]cubit being a cubit and a handbreadth): the [1]base *shall be* a cubit and the width a cubit, and its border on its edge round about one span; and this *shall be* the *height* of the [2]base of the altar.

14 "From the base on the ground to the lower [a]ledge *shall be* two cubits and the width one cubit; and from the smaller ledge to the larger ledge *shall be* four cubits and the width [1]one cubit.

15 "The [1]altar hearth *shall be* four cubits; and from the [1]altar hearth shall extend upwards four [a]horns.

16 "Now the [1]altar hearth *shall be* twelve *cubits* long by twelve wide, [a]square in its four sides.

17 "The ledge *shall be* fourteen *cubits* long by fourteen wide in its four sides, the border around it *shall be* half a cubit and its base *shall be* a cubit round about; and its [a]steps shall [1][b]face the east."

The Offerings

18 And He said to me, "[a]Son of man, thus says the Lord [1]GOD, 'These are the statutes for the altar on the day it is built, to offer [b]burnt offerings on it and to [c]sprinkle blood on it.

19 'You shall give to the Levitical priests who are from the offspring of [a]Zadok, who draw [b]near to Me to minister to Me,' declares the Lord GOD, 'a [c]young bull for a [d]sin offering.

20 'You shall take some of its blood and put it on its four [a]horns and on the four corners of the [b]ledge and on the border round about; thus you shall [c]cleanse it and make atonement for it.

21 'You shall also take the bull for the sin offering, and it *shall be* [a]burned in the appointed place of the house, outside the sanctuary.

22 'On the second day you shall offer a [a]male goat without blemish for a sin offering, and they shall [b]cleanse the altar as they cleansed *it* with the bull.

23 'When you have finished cleansing *it*, you shall present a [a]young bull without blemish and a [b]ram without blemish from the flock.

24 'You shall present them before the LORD, and the priests shall throw [a]salt on them, and they shall offer them up as a burnt offering to the LORD.

25 '[a]For seven days you shall prepare daily a goat for a sin offering; also a young bull and a ram from the flock, without blemish, shall be prepared.

26 'For seven days they shall make atonement for the altar and purify it; so shall they [1]consecrate it.

27 'When they have completed the days, it shall be that on the [a]eighth day and onward,

8 [a]Ezek 8:3, 16 **9** [1]Or *monuments* as in Ugaritic [a]Ezek 18:30, 31 [b]Ezek 37:26-28; 43:7 **10** [1]Lit *declare* [2]Lit *house* [3]Lit *perfection* or *pattern* [a]Ezek 40:4 [b]Ezek 16:61, 63; 43:11 [c]Ezek 28:12 **11** [1]Or *form(s)* [2]M.T. repeats *and all its designs* after *statutes* [a]Ezek 44:5 [b]Ezek 12:3 [c]Ezek 11:20; 36:27 **12** [1]Or *instruction for* [2]Lit *border* [a]Ezek 40:2 **13** [1]Lit *lap* [2]Or *back* [a]Ex 27:1-8; 2 Chr 4:1 [b]Ezek 40:5; 41:8 **14** [1]Lit *the* [a]Ezek 43:17, 20; 45:19 **15** [1]Or *ariel* shall [a]Ex 27:2; Lev 9:9; 1 Kin 1:50; Ps 118:27 **16** [1]Or *ariel* shall [a]Ex 27:1 **17** [1]Or *be on the east side* [a]Ex 20:26 [b]Ezek 40:6 **18** [1]Heb *YHWH,* usually rendered LORD, and so throughout the ch [a]Ezek 2:1 [b]Ex 40:29 [c]Lev 1:5, 11; Heb 9:21, 22 **19** [a]1 Kin 2:35; Ezek 40:46; 44:15 [b]Num 16:5, 40 [c]Lev 4:3; Ezek 43:23; 45:18 [d]Ezek 45:19; Heb 7:27 **20** [a]Lev 8:15; 9:9; Ezek 43:15 [b]Ezek 43:14, 17 [c]Lev 16:19; Ezek 43:22, 26 **21** [a]Ex 29:14; Lev 4:12; Heb 13:11 **22** [a]Ezek 43:25 [b]Ezek 43:20, 26

23 [a]Ex 29:1, 10; Ezek 45:18 [b]Ex 29:1 **24** [a]Lev 2:13; Num 18:19; Mark 9:49, 50; Col 4:6 **25** [a]Ex 29:35-37; Lev 8:33, 35 **26** [1]Lit *fill its hands* **27** [a]Lev 9:1

43:8 *their threshold by My threshold.* Solomon's temple was surrounded by many of his own private structures (see 1 Kin 7:1–12). The distinction between God's holy temple and the rest of the world is a central idea in the book of Ezekiel (see v. 12; 44:23). *So I have consumed them.* As elsewhere in Ezekiel, the unstable practices of the people and their kings brought about their destruction (see 5:11; 18:10–12; and especially 22:1–15).
43:12 *This is the law.* Refers to the contents of chs. 40–42.
43:13 *altar.* Alluded to in 40:47 and here described in detail. Although the material is not mentioned, dressed stones were probably to be used. Ex 20:24–26 allowed an altar to be made of earth, but use of dressed stones for those altars was strictly forbidden (see notes on Ex 20:24–25). Solomon's altar was bronze (1 Kin 8:64). Ezekiel's altar, much larger than Solomon's, was over 20 feet tall, made up of three slabs of decreasing size, like a pyramid or Babylonian ziggurat: the "lower ledge" (v. 14), two cubits high; the "larger ledge" (v. 14), four cubits high; and the "altar hearth" (v. 15), four cubits high.
43:15 *altar hearth.* The Hebrew for this term appears only here in the OT and may also mean "mountain of God" or "lion of God"; it is a variant of a form that appears in Is 29:1–2. *four horns.* Stone projections from each of the four corners of the altar hearth. On earlier altars they afforded a refuge of last resort for an accused person (see Ex 21:12–14; 1 Kin 1:50–51; 2:28–29).
43:17 *its steps.* Forbidden in Ex 20:26 but here required because of the size (see note on v. 13).
43:18 *burnt offerings.* See note on 40:39. *sprinkle blood.* See Ex 29:16; Lev 4:6; 5:9.
43:19 *from the offspring of Zadok.* See note on 44:15. *sin offering.* To cleanse the altar from the pollution of human sin (see note on 40:39).
43:21 *outside the sanctuary.* As prescribed in Ex 29:14; Lev 4:12,21; 8:17; 9:11; 16:27. This action foreshadows one aspect of Christ's sacrifice (see Heb 13:11–13).
43:22 *cleanse.* By the sprinkling of the blood (see v. 20).

the priests shall [1]offer your burnt offerings on the altar, and your [b]peace offerings; and I will [c]accept you,' declares the Lord GOD."

Gate for the Prince

44 Then He brought me back by the way of the [a]outer gate of the sanctuary, which faces the east; and it was shut.

2 The LORD said to me, "This gate shall be shut; it shall not be opened, and no one shall enter by it, for the [a]LORD God of Israel has entered by it; therefore it shall be shut.

3 "As for the [a]prince, he shall sit in it as prince to [b]eat bread before the LORD; he shall [c]enter by way of the [d]porch of the gate and shall go out [1]by the same way."

4 Then He brought me by way of the [a]north gate to the front of the house; and I looked, and behold, the [b]glory of the LORD filled the house of the LORD, and I [c]fell on my face.

5 The LORD said to me, "Son of man, [1a]mark well, see with your eyes and hear with your ears all that I say to you concerning all the [b]statutes of the house of the LORD and concerning all its laws; and [1]mark well the entrance of the house, with all exits of the sanctuary.

6 "You shall say to the [1a]rebellious ones, to the house of Israel, 'Thus says the Lord [2]GOD, "[b]Enough of all your abominations, O house of Israel,

7 when you brought in [a]foreigners, [b]uncircumcised in heart and uncircumcised in flesh, to be in My sanctuary to profane it, *even* My house, when you [c]offered My food, the fat and the blood; for they [d]made My covenant void—*this* in addition to all your abominations.

8 "And you have not [a]kept charge of My holy things yourselves, but you have set *foreigners* [1]to keep charge of My sanctuary."

27 [1]Lit *make* [b]Lev 3:1; 17:5 [c]Ezek 20:40
44:1 [a]Ezek 40:6, 17; 42:14
2 [a]Ezek 43:2-4
3 [1]Lit *by his way* [a]Ezek 34:24; 37:25 [b]Gen 31:54; Ex 24:9-11 [c]Ezek 46:2, 8-10 [d]Ezek 40:9
4 [a]Ezek 40:20, 40 [b]Is 6:3, 4; Ezek 1:28; 3:23; 43:4, 5; Hag 2:7 [c]Ezek 1:28; 43:3
5 [1]Lit *set your heart on* [a]Deut 32:46; Ezek 40:4 [b]Deut 12:32; Ezek 43:10, 11
6 [1]Lit *rebellion* [2]Heb *YHWH,* usually rendered LORD, and so throughout the ch [a]Ezek 2:5-7; 3:9 [b]Ezek 45:9; 1 Pet 4:3
7 [a]Ex 12:43-49 [b]Lev 26:41; Deut 10:16; Jer 4:4; 9:26 [c]Lev 22:25 [d]Gen 17:14
8 [1]Lit *as keepers of My charge in My* [a]Lev 22:2; Num 18:7
9 [a]Ezek 44:7; Joel 3:17; Zech 14:21
10 [a]2 Kin 23:8, 9; Ezek 22:26; 44:12 [b]Num 18:23
11 [a]Num 3:5-37; 4:1-33; 18:2-7 [b]1 Chr 26:1-19 [c]Ezek 40:45; 44:14 [d]2 Chr 29:34; 30:17 [e]Num 16:9
12 [1]Lit *lifted up My hand* [a]2 Kin 16:10-16 [b]Ezek 14:3, 4 [c]Ezek 20:15, 23 [d]Ezek 44:10

9 'Thus says the Lord GOD, "[a]No foreigner uncircumcised in heart and uncircumcised in flesh, of all the foreigners who are among the sons of Israel, shall enter My sanctuary.

10 "But the Levites who went far from Me when Israel went astray, who [a]went astray from Me after their idols, shall [b]bear the punishment for their iniquity.

11 "Yet they shall be [a]ministers in My sanctuary, having [b]oversight at the gates of the house and [c]ministering in the house; they shall [d]slaughter the burnt offering and the sacrifice for the people, and they shall [e]stand before them to minister to them.

12 "Because they ministered to them [a]before their idols and became a [b]stumbling block of iniquity to the house of Israel, therefore I have [1c]sworn against them," declares the Lord GOD, "that they shall [d]bear *the punishment for* their iniquity.

13 "And they shall [a]not come near to Me to serve as a priest to Me, nor come near to any of My holy things, to the things that are most holy; but they will [b]bear their shame and their abominations which they have committed.

14 "Yet I will [1]appoint them [2]to [a]keep charge of the house, of all its service and of all that shall be done in it.

Ordinances for the Levites

15 "But the [a]Levitical priests, the sons of [b]Zadok, who [c]kept charge of My sanctuary when the sons of Israel [d]went astray from Me, shall come near to Me to minister to Me; and they shall [e]stand before Me to offer Me the [f]fat and the blood," declares the Lord GOD.

13 [a]Num 18:3 [b]Ezek 16:61, 63; 39:26 **14** [1]Lit *give* [2]Lit *keepers of the charge* [a]Num 18:4; 1 Chr 23:28-32; Ezek 44:11
15 [a]Jer 33:18-22 [b]Ezek 40:46; 43:19; 48:11 [c]Num 18:7; Ezek 40:45 [d]Ezek 44:10; 48:11 [e]Zech 3:1, 7 [f]Lev 3:16, 17; 17:5, 6; Ezek 44:7

43:27 *peace offerings.* After the seven-day consecration by burnt offerings and sin offerings, the altar was ready for the celebration of the more festive peace offerings where the people partook of some of the meat (see Lev 3).
44:2 *therefore it shall be shut.* The reason given here is that God entered through the east gate (43:1–2), thus making it holy. Related reasons may be that God would never again leave as before (10:19; 11:23) and that sun worship would be made impossible (see 8:16). Today the east gate (called the Golden Gate) of the sacred Moslem area (*Haram esh-Sharif*) in Jerusalem is likewise sealed shut as a result of a later but possibly related tradition.
44:3 *prince.* The first mention of the prince in chs. 40–48 (see 34:24 and note). *to eat.* Probably his part of the peace offering (see Lev 7:15; Deut 12:7; see also Ezek 43:27 and note). While this honor is accorded the prince, it is significant that he is given no other part in the ceremonial functions, reserved now solely for the priests (see 2 Chr 26:16–20). *by way of the porch.* From the inside of the outer court.
44:7 *uncircumcised in heart.* Spiritually unfit.
44:9 *No foreigner uncircumcised . . . shall enter My sanctuary.* Nehemiah enforced this restriction when he dismissed Tobiah (Neh 13:8), an Ammonite (Neh 2:10; see Deut 23:3). Foreigners could, however, be a part of Israel (see 47:22).
44:10 *Levites.* Members of the tribe of Levi served as priests from the earliest days (see Deut 33:8–11; Judg 17:13). *when Israel went astray.* The reference is mainly to the period of the monarchy, especially to the last years, during which Ezekiel so often criticized the people's idolatry (see 6:3–6; 14:3–11; 16:18–21; 23:36–49; 36:17–18; 37:23).
44:11 *stand before them.* Cf. standing before the Lord (see v. 15); the Levites still had an honorable position.
44:15 *Zadok.* Traced his Levitical lineage to Aaron through Aaron's son Eleazar (1 Chr 6:50–53). He served as priest under David, along with Abiathar (see 2 Sam 8:17 and note; 15:24–29; 20:25). He supported Solomon (as opposed to Abiathar, who pledged himself to Adonijah) and thus secured for himself and his descendants the privilege of serving in the Jerusalem temple (see 1 Kin 1). Later the Zadokites were removed from office, but the Qumran (Dead Sea Scrolls) community remained loyal to them. *who kept charge.* A distinction Ezekiel did not make in his oracles of judgment (see 7:26; 22:26 and the thrust of all of ch. 8). In chs. 40–48, however, the Zadokites received special consideration because of their faithfulness.

16 "They shall [a]enter My sanctuary; they shall come near to My [b]table to minister to Me and keep My charge.

17 "It shall be that when they enter at the gates of the inner court, they shall be clothed with [a]linen garments; and wool shall not [1]be on them while they are ministering in the gates of the inner court and in the house.

18 "Linen [a]turbans shall be on their heads and [b]linen undergarments shall be on their loins; they shall not gird themselves with *anything which makes them* sweat.

19 "When they go out into the outer court, into the outer court to the people, they shall [a]put off their garments in which they have been ministering and lay them in the holy chambers; then they shall put on other garments so that they will [b]not transmit holiness to the people with their garments.

20 "Also they shall [a]not shave their heads, yet they shall not [b]let their locks [1]grow long; they shall only trim *the hair of* their heads.

21 "[a]Nor shall any of the priests drink wine when they enter the inner court.

22 "And they shall not [1]marry a widow or a [a]divorced woman but shall [b]take virgins from the offspring of the house of Israel, or a widow who is the widow of a priest.

23 "Moreover, they shall teach My people *the [a]difference* between the holy and the profane, and cause them to discern between the unclean and the clean.

24 "In a dispute [a]they shall take their stand to judge; they shall judge it according to My ordinances. They shall also keep My laws and My statutes in all My [b]appointed feasts and [c]sanctify My sabbaths.

25 "[1a]They shall not go to a dead person to defile *themselves;* however, for father, for mother, for son, for daughter, for brother, or for a sister who has not had a husband, they may defile themselves.

26 "After he is [a]cleansed, seven days shall [1]elapse for him.

27 "On the day that he goes into the sanctuary, into the [a]inner court to minister in the sanctuary, he shall offer his [b]sin offering," declares the Lord GOD.

28 "And it shall be with regard to an inheritance for them, *that* [a]I am their inheritance; and you shall give them no possession in Israel—I am their possession.

29 "They shall [a]eat the grain offering, the sin offering and the guilt offering; and every [1b]devoted thing in Israel shall be theirs.

30 "The first of all the [a]first fruits of every kind and every [1]contribution of every kind, from all your [1]contributions, shall be for the priests; you shall also give to the priest the [b]first of your [2]dough to cause a [c]blessing to rest on your house.

31 "The priests shall not eat any bird or beast that has [a]died a natural death or has been torn to pieces.

The LORD's Portion of the Land

45 "And when you [a]divide by lot the land for inheritance, you shall offer [1]an [b]allotment to the LORD, a [c]holy portion of the land; the length shall be the length of 25,000 [d]*cubits,* and the width shall be [2]20,000. It shall be holy within all its boundary round about.

2 "Out of this there shall be for the holy place a square round about [a]five hundred by five hundred *cubits,* and fifty cubits for its [1b]open space round about.

3 "From this [1]area you shall measure a length of 25,000 *cubits* and a width of 10,000 *cubits;* and in it shall be the sanctuary, the most holy place.

16 [a]Num 18:5, 7, 8 [b]Ezek 41:22; Mal 1:7, 12
17 [1]Lit *come upon* [a]Ex 28:42, 43; 39:27-29; Rev 19:8
18 [a]Ex 28:40; Is 3:20; Ezek 24:17, 23 [b]Ex 28:42; Lev 16:4
19 [a]Lev 6:10; 16:4, 23, 24; Ezek 42:14 [b]Lev 6:27; Ezek 46:20
20 [1]Or *hang loose* [a]Lev 21:5 [b]Num 6:5
21 [a]Lev 10:9
22 [1]Lit *take as wives for themselves* [a]Lev 21:7, 14 [b]Lev 21:13
23 [a]Lev 10:10; Ezek 22:26; Hos 4:6; Mic 3:9-11; Zeph 3:4; Hag 2:11-13; Mal 2:6-8
24 [a]Deut 17:8, 9; 19:17; 21:5; 1 Chr 23:4; 2 Chr 19:8-10 [b]Lev 23:2, 4, 44 [c]Ezek 20:12, 20
25 [1]Lit *He* [a]Lev 21:1-4
26 [1]Lit *be counted* [a]Num 19:13-19
27 [a]Ezek 44:17 [b]Lev 5:3, 6; Num 6:9-11
28 [a]Num 18:20; Deut 10:9; 18:1, 2; Josh 13:33
29 [1]Or *dedicated* [a]Num 18:9, 14; Josh 13:14 [b]Lev 27:21, 28; Num 18:14
30 [1]Or *heave offering(s)* [2]Or *coarse meal* [a]Num 18:12, 13; 2 Chr 31:4-6, 10; Neh 10:35-37

[b]Num 15:20, 21 [c]Mal 3:10 **31** [a]Lev 22:8; Deut 14:21; Ezek 4:14 **45:1** [1]Or *a contribution* [2]Or with Gr *10,000* [a]Num 34:13; Josh 13:7; 14:3; Ezek 47:21; 48:29 [b]Ezek 48:8, 9 [c]Zech 14:20, 21 [d]Ezek 42:16; 45:2 **2** [1]Or *pasture land* [a]Ezek 42:20 [b]Ezek 27:28 **3** [1]Lit *measure*

44:16 *They shall enter.* This elevation of the Zadokites and demotion of the Levites were part of the concern for ritual purity, a major theme of chs. 40–48. Only the fittest were to serve. *My table.* Either the table that held the bread (see 41:22 and note) or the large altar on which the Lord's food was presented (v. 7).
44:17 *linen.* Cooler than wool (see v. 18).
44:18 *turbans.* Ezekiel wore one (24:17).
44:19 *put off their garments.* In the interest of ritual purity.
44:20 *shall not shave their heads.* Because it was a mourning ritual (7:18) that rendered the mourner unclean (see Lev 21:1–5). *not let their locks grow long.* Because it implied the taking of a vow that might prevent the priest from serving (see Num 6:5; Acts 21:23–26).
44:23 *difference between the holy and the profane.* One of Ezekiel's central concerns. The important task of declaring God's will on matters of clean and unclean food, the fitness of sacrificial animals and ritual purity either had been done for pay (see Mic 3:11) or had been neglected altogether (see Jer 2:8; Ezek 22:26). See Hag 2:10–13 for a positive example.
44:24 *they shall . . . judge.* One of their functions from earliest days (see 1 Sam 4:18 and note; see also 2 Chr 19:8–11).
44:25 *dead person.* Contact with the dead made a person ceremonially unclean (Lev 21:1–3; Hag 2:13).
44:28 *no possession.* The statement that priests were not to own land agrees with Num 18:20,23–24; Deut 10:9; Josh 13:14,33; 18:7.
44:31 *died a natural death.* This restriction applied to all Israel according to Lev 7:24.
45:1 *when you divide by lot the land.* Envisioned a new acquisition and redistribution of the land. *offer . . . to the LORD.* The entire square area in the center of the land was to be set aside for the Lord. *20,000 cubits.* With the 5,000-cubit city area (v. 6) it was a perfect square. *holy within all its boundary.* Set apart for the Lord and owned by no tribe.
45:2 *square round about five hundred by five hundred cubits.* The temple area discussed in 42:16–20. *open space.* An unoccupied strip of land that served as a buffer between the more holy and the less holy, though the whole area was holy (see 42:20).
45:3 *you shall measure.* The middle strip of the holy square was specifically for the temple.

4 "It shall be the holy portion of the land;
it shall be for the [a]priests, the ministers of
the sanctuary, who [b]come near to minister
to the LORD, and it shall be a place for their
houses and a holy place for the sanctuary.
5 "*An area* [a]25,000 *cubits* in length and
10,000 in width shall be for the Levites, the
ministers of the house, *and* for their possession [1]cities to dwell in.
6 "You shall give the [a]city possession of
an area 5,000 *cubits* wide and 25,000 *cubits*
long, alongside the [1]allotment of the holy
portion; it shall be for the whole house of
Israel.

Portion for the Prince

7 "The [a]prince shall have *land* on either
side of the holy [1]allotment and the [2]property
of the city, adjacent to the holy [1]allotment
and the [2]property of the city, on the west
side toward the west and on the east side
toward the east, and in length comparable to
one of the portions, from the west border to
the east border.
8 "This shall be his land for a possession
in Israel; so My princes shall no longer
[a]oppress My people, but they shall give *the
rest of* the land to the house of Israel [b]accord-
ing to their tribes."
9 'Thus says the Lord [1]GOD, "[a]Enough,
you princes of Israel; put away [b]violence and
destruction, and [c]practice justice and righteousness. Stop your [d]expropriations from
My people," declares the Lord GOD.
10 "You shall have [a]just balances, a just
[b]ephah and a just [b]bath.
11 "The ephah and the bath shall be [1]the
same quantity, so that the bath will contain a
tenth of a [a]homer and the ephah a tenth of a
homer; [2]their standard shall be according to
the homer.
12 "The [a]shekel shall be twenty [a]gerahs;
twenty shekels, twenty-five shekels, *and* fifteen shekels shall be your [1]maneh.
13 "This is the offering that you shall offer:
a sixth of an ephah from a homer of wheat;
a sixth of an ephah from a homer of barley;
14 and the prescribed portion of oil
(*namely,* the bath of oil), a tenth of a bath
from *each* kor (*which is* ten baths *or* a homer,
for ten baths are a homer);
15 and one sheep from *each* flock of two
hundred from the watering places of Israel—
for a [a]grain offering, for a burnt offering and
for peace offerings, to [b]make atonement for
them," declares the Lord GOD.
16 "[a]All the people of the land shall [1]give
to this offering for the [b]prince in Israel.
17 "It shall be the [a]prince's part *to provide*
the [b]burnt offerings, the grain offerings and
the drink offerings, at the [c]feasts, on the
[d]new moons and on the sabbaths, at all the
appointed feasts of the house of Israel; he
shall provide the sin offering, the grain offering, the burnt offering and the [e]peace offerings, to make atonement for the house of
Israel."
18 'Thus says the Lord GOD, "In the [a]first
month, on the first of the month, you shall
take a young bull [b]without blemish and
[c]cleanse the sanctuary.
19 "The priest shall take some of the blood
from the sin offering and put *it* on the door
posts of the house, on the [a]four corners of
the [b]ledge of the altar and on the posts of the
gate of the inner court.
20 "Thus you shall do on the seventh *day*
of the month for everyone who goes [a]astray
or is [1]naive; so you shall make [b]atonement
for the house.
21 "In the [a]first *month,* on the fourteenth
day of the month, you shall have the
[b]Passover, a feast of seven days; unleavened
bread shall be eaten.
22 "On that day the prince shall provide for
himself and all the people of the land a [a]bull
for a sin offering.
23 "*During* the [a]seven days of the feast he

4 [a]Ezek 48:10, 11 [b]Num 16:5; Ezek 40:45; 43:19
5 [1]So with Gr; M.T. *twenty chambers* [a]Ezek 48:13
6 [1]Or *contribution* [a]Ezek 48:15-18, 30-35
7 [1]Or *contribution* [2]Lit *possession* [a]Ezek 34:24; 37:24; 46:16-18; 48:21
8 [a]Is 11:3-5; Jer 23:5; Ezek 19:7; 22:27; 46:18 [b]Josh 11:23
9 [1]Heb *YHWH,* usually rendered LORD, and so throughout the ch [a]Ezek 44:6 [b]Jer 6:7; Ezek 7:11, 23; 8:17 [c]Jer 22:3; Zech 8:16 [d]Neh 5:1-5
10 [a]Lev 19:36; Deut 25:15; Prov 16:11; Amos 8:4-6; Mic 6:10, 11 [b]Is 5:10
11 [1]Lit *one* [2]Lit *its measure* [a]Is 5:10
12 [1]Or *mina* [a]Ex 30:13; Lev 27:25; Num 3:47
15 [a]Ezek 45:17 [b]Lev 1:4; 6:30
16 [1]Lit *be* [a]Ex 30:14, 15 [b]Is 16:1
17 [a]Ezek 46:4-12 [b]1 Kin 8:64; 1 Chr 16:2; 2 Chr 31:3 [c]Lev 23:1-44; Num 28:1-29:39 [d]Is 66:23 [e]1 Kin 8:63; Ezek 43:27
18 [a]Ex 12:2 [b]Lev 22:20; Heb 9:14 [c]Lev 16:16, 33; Ezek 43:22, 26
19 [a]Lev 16:18-20; Ezek 43:20 [b]Ezek 43:14, 17, 20
20 [1]Lit *simple* [a]Lev 4:27; Ps 19:12 [b]Lev 16:20; Ezek 45:15, 18
21 [a]Num 28:16f [b]Ex 12:1-24; Lev 23:5-8
22 [a]Lev 4:14
23 [a]Lev 23:8

45:4 *land . . . for the priests.* Not to own (see 44:28) but to live on.

45:5 *area . . . for the Levites.* A section of equal size just to the north was for the Levites to dwell on, even though it was in the holy area. The Levites, as opposed to the Zadokite priests, could hold land as a possession.

45:6 *city.* The former Jerusalem contained the temple area. The new holy city would not, but would be adjacent to the temple. *5,000 cubits wide.* The southernmost section of the city completed the perfectly square area. *it shall be for the whole house of Israel.* Not to any one tribe or person as in former days.

45:7 *The prince shall have land.* A considerable portion of territory. In view of the next verse (cf. 46:18) the generous allotment should have kept the prince from greed like that of Ahab (see 1 Kin 21). The prince was also responsible for sizable offerings (v. 17).

45:9 *you princes of Israel.* The language of this verse is reminiscent of the preaching Ezekiel did before 586 B.C. (see 22:6).

45:10 *You shall have just balances.* Israel was not to repeat the economic injustices of the past. The OT often warns against cheating in weights and measures (see Lev 19:35–36; Deut 25:13–16; Mic 6:10–12).

45:11 *same quantity.* A little more than half a bushel. *homer.* About six bushels.

45:13 *offering.* Given to the prince as distinct from the gifts given to the priests (44:30). The prince is to use these gifts in part for the offerings to the Lord (see v. 16).

45:17 *drink offerings.* Usually wine is meant (see Num 15:5; Hos 9:4); but wine is not mentioned here, though oil is (vv. 14,24).

45:18–46:24 This entire section involves so many variations from Pentateuchal law that the rabbis spent a great deal of effort trying to reconcile them. For example, the provision in 45:18 for an annual purification of the temple does not seem to take into consideration the day of atonement ritual of Lev 16.

45:19 *priest.* High priest.

45:22 *sin offering.* See note on 40:39.

shall provide as a [b]burnt offering to the LORD
[c]seven bulls and seven rams without blemish
on every day of the seven days, and a male
goat daily for a sin offering.
24 "He shall provide as a [a]grain offering an
ephah [1]with a bull, an ephah [1]with a ram
and a hin of oil [1]with an ephah.
25 "In the [a]seventh *month*, on the fifteenth
day of the month, at the feast, he shall provide like this, seven days [1]for the sin offering, the burnt offering, the grain offering and
the oil."

The Prince's Offerings

46 'Thus says the Lord [1]GOD, "The [a]gate
of the [b]inner court facing east shall be
[c]shut the six [d]working days; but it shall be
opened on the [e]sabbath day and opened on
the day of the [f]new moon.
2 "The [a]prince shall enter by way of the
porch of the gate from outside and stand by
the [b]post of the gate. Then the priests shall
provide his burnt offering and his peace
offerings, and he shall worship at the threshold of the gate and then go out; but the gate
shall not be [c]shut until the evening.
3 "The [a]people of the land shall also worship at the doorway of that gate before the
LORD on the sabbaths and on the [b]new moons.
4 "The [a]burnt offering which the prince
shall offer to the LORD on the sabbath day
shall be [b]six lambs without blemish and a
ram without blemish;
5 and the [a]grain offering shall be an
ephah [1]with the ram, and the grain offering
[1]with the lambs [2]as much as he is [b]able to
give, and a hin of oil [1]with an ephah.
6 "On the day of the [a]new moon *he shall
offer* a young bull without blemish, also six
lambs and a ram, *which* shall be without
blemish.
7 "And he shall provide a [a]grain offering,
an ephah [1]with the bull and an ephah [1]with
the ram, and [1]with the lambs as [2]much as he
is [b]able, and a hin of oil [1]with an ephah.
8 "When the [a]prince enters, he shall go in
by way of the porch of the gate and go out
[1]by the same way.
9 "But when the people of the land come
[a]before the LORD at the appointed feasts, he
who enters by way of the north gate to worship shall go out by way of the south gate.
And he who enters by way of the south gate
shall go out by way of the north gate. [1]No
one shall return by way of the gate by which
he entered but shall go straight out.
10 "When they go in, the prince shall go in
[a]among them; and when they go out, [1]he
shall go out.
11 "At the [a]festivals and the appointed
feasts the [b]grain offering shall be an ephah
[1]with a bull and an ephah [1]with a ram, and
[1]with the lambs as [2]much as one is able to
give, and a hin of oil [1]with an ephah.
12 "When the prince provides a [a]freewill
offering, a burnt offering, or peace offerings
as a freewill offering to the LORD, the gate
facing east shall be [b]opened for him. And he
shall provide his burnt offering and his peace
offerings as he does on the [c]sabbath day.
Then he shall go out, and the gate shall be
shut after he goes out.
13 "And you shall provide a [a]lamb a year
old without blemish for a burnt offering to
the LORD daily; [b]morning by morning you
shall provide it.
14 "Also you shall provide a grain offering
with it morning by morning, a [a]sixth of an
ephah and a third of a hin of oil to moisten
the fine flour, a grain offering to the LORD
continually by a perpetual [1]ordinance.
15 "Thus they shall provide the lamb, the
grain offering and the oil, morning by morning, for a [a]continual burnt offering."
16 'Thus says the Lord GOD, "If the prince
gives a [a]gift *out of* his inheritance to any of
his sons, it shall belong to his sons; it is their
possession by inheritance.
17 "But if he gives a gift from his inheritance
to one of his servants, it shall be his until the
[a]year of liberty; then it shall return to the

23 [b]Num 28:16-25 [c]Num 23:1, 2; Job 42:8 **24** [1]Lit *for* [a]Num 28:12-15; Ezek 46:5-7 **25** [1]Lit *according to* [a]Lev 23:33-43; Num 29:12-38; 2 Chr 5:3; 7:8, 10 **46:1** [1]Heb *YHWH*, usually rendered LORD, and so throughout the ch [a]Ezek 45:19 [b]Ezek 8:16; 10:3 [c]Ezek 44:1, 2 [d]Ex 20:9 [e]Is 66:23; Ezek 45:17 [f]Ezek 45:18; 46:3, 6 **2** [a]Ezek 44:3; 46:8 [b]Ezek 45:19 [c]Ezek 46:12 **3** [a]Luke 1:10 [b]Ezek 46:1 **4** [a]Ezek 45:17 [b]Num 28:9 **5** [1]Lit *for* [2]Lit *a gift of his hand* [a]Num 28:12; Ezek 45:24; 46:7, 11 [b]Ezek 46:7 **6** [a]Ezek 46:1 **7** [1]Lit *for* [2]Lit *his hand can reach* [a]Ezek 46:5 [b]Lev 14:21; Deut 16:17; Ezek 46:5 **8** [a]Ezek 44:3; 46:2

8 [1]Lit *by its way* **9** [1]Lit *He shall not* [a]Ex 34:23; Ps 84:7; Mic 6:6 **10** [1]So with many mss and the ancient versions; M.T. *they* [a]2 Sam 6:14, 15; 1 Chr 29:20, 22; 2 Chr 6:3; 7:4; Ps 42:4 **11** [1]Lit *for* [2]Lit *a gift of his hand* [a]Ezek 45:17 [b]Ezek 46:5, 7 **12** [a]Lev 23:38; 2 Chr 29:31 [b]Ezek 44:3; 46:1, 2, 8 [c]Ezek 45:17 **13** [a]Num 28:3-5 [b]Is 50:4 **14** [1]Lit *statute* [a]Num 28:5

15 [a]Ex 29:42; Num 28:6 **16** [a]2 Chr 21:3 **17** [a]Lev 25:10

45:25 *seventh month . . . fifteenth day . . . at the feast.* In some respects the most important of the festivals—called the Feast of Ingathering (Ex 23:16; 34:22) and the Feast of Booths (Deut 16:16).

46:1 *gate of the inner court.* While the east gate of the outer court was permanently closed (44:2), the east gate of the inner court could be opened on festival days.

46:2 *by way of the porch of the gate.* The portico of the gate of the inner court faced the outer court. *stand by the post of the gate.* Which had been ritually cleansed (45:19). From there the prince could observe the sacrifices being performed on the great altar in the inner court, but he was not allowed into the inner court itself.

46:3 *at the doorway of that gate.* But in the outer court.

46:4 *six lambs . . . and a ram.* Another example of a difference from Pentateuchal laws (see note on 45:18–46:24). Num 28:9 calls for two lambs and no ram on the Sabbath.

46:5 *ephah.* Contrast Num 28:9.

46:6 *day of the new moon.* The first day of the month. Contrast the requirement of Num 28:11.

46:7 *a grain offering, an ephah.* Contrast Num 28:12.

46:9 *he who enters by . . . the north gate.* These appear to be crowd control measures. If so, the new era would see masses of people thronging the sanctuary on the festival day.

46:12 *freewill offering.* Above and beyond what was required of the prince.

46:13 *morning by morning.* Contrast Num 28:3–8, where the daily sacrifice consists of one lamb in the morning and one in the evening (see 1 Chr 16:40; 2 Chr 13:11; 31:3). A different custom appears in 2 Kin 16:15, where a burnt offering was offered in the mornings, a grain offering in the evenings.

46:14 *sixth of an ephah . . . third of a hin.* Contrast Num 28:5.

46:16 *his sons.* Ezekiel pictured a hereditary rulership.

46:17 *until the year of liberty.* The year of jubilee—held, theoretically, every 50th year (see Lev 25:8–15, especially v. 13).

prince. His inheritance *shall be* only his sons'; it shall belong to them.

18 "The prince shall [a]not take from the people's inheritance, [1b]thrusting them out of their possession; he shall give his sons inheritance from his own possession so that My people will not be scattered, anyone from his possession." ' "

The Boiling Places

19 Then he brought me through the [a]entrance, which *was* at the side of the gate, into the holy chambers for the priests, which faced north; and behold, there *was* a place at the extreme rear toward the west.

20 He said to me, "This is the place where the priests shall boil the [a]guilt offering and the sin offering *and* where they shall [b]bake the grain offering, in order that they may not bring *them* out into the outer court to transmit holiness to the people."

21 Then he brought me out into the outer court and led me across to the four corners of the court; and behold, in every corner of the court *there was* a *small* court.

22 In the four corners of the court *there were* enclosed courts, forty *cubits* long and thirty wide; these four in the corners *were* [1]the same size.

23 *There was* a row *of masonry* round about in them, around the four of them, and boiling places were made under the rows round about.

24 Then he said to me, "These are the boiling [1]places where the ministers of the house shall boil the sacrifices of the people."

Water from the Temple

47 Then he brought me back to the [a]door of the house; and behold, [b]water was flowing from under the threshold of the house toward the east, for the house faced east. And the water was flowing down from under, from the right side of the house, from south of the altar.

2 He brought me out by way of the north gate and led me around [1]on the outside to the outer gate by way of *the gate* that faces east. And behold, water was trickling from the south side.

3 When the man went out toward the east with a line in his hand, he measured a thousand cubits, and he led me through the water, water *reaching* the ankles.

4 Again he measured a thousand and led me through the water, water *reaching* the knees. Again he measured a thousand and led me through *the water,* water *reaching* the loins.

5 Again he measured a thousand; *and it was* a river that I could not ford, for the water had risen, *enough* water to swim in, a [a]river that could not be forded.

6 He said to me, "Son of man, have you [a]seen *this?*" Then he brought me [1]back to the bank of the river.

7 Now when I had returned, behold, on the bank of the river there *were* very many [a]trees on the one side and on the other.

8 Then he said to me, "These waters go out toward the eastern region and go down into the [a]Arabah; then they go toward the sea, being made to flow into the [b]sea, and the waters *of the sea* become [1]fresh.

9 "It will come about that every living creature which swarms in every place where the [1]river goes, will live. And there will be very many fish, for these waters go there and *the others* [2]become fresh; so [a]everything will live where the river goes.

10 "And it will come about that [a]fishermen will stand beside it; from [b]Engedi to Eneglaim there will be a place for the [c]spreading of nets. Their fish will be according to their kinds, like the fish of the [d]Great Sea, [e]very many.

11 "But its swamps and marshes will not become [1]fresh; they will be [2]left for [a]salt.

12 "[a]By the river on its bank, on one side and on the other, will grow all *kinds of* [b]trees for food. Their [c]leaves will not wither and their fruit will not fail. They will bear every

18 [1]Lit *oppressing* [a]Ezek 45:8 [b]1 Kin 21:19; Ezek 22:27; Mic 2:1, 2
19 [a]Ezek 42:9; 44:5
20 [a]2 Chr 35:13; Ezek 44:29 [b]Lev 2:4-7
22 [1]Lit *one measure*
24 [1]Lit *houses*
47:1 [a]Ezek 41:2, 23-25 [b]Ps 46:4; Is 30:25; 55:1; Jer 2:13; Joel 3:18; Zech 13:1; 14:8; Rev 22:1, 17
2 [1]Lit *by way of*
5 [a]Is 11:9; Hab 2:14
6 [1]Lit *and caused me to return* [a]Ezek 8:6; 40:4; 44:5
7 [a]Is 60:13, 21; 61:3; Ezek 47:12
8 [1]Lit *healed* [a]Deut 3:17; Is 35:6, 7; 41:17-19; 44:3 [b]Josh 3:16
9 [1]Lit *two rivers* [2]Lit *are healed* [a]Is 12:3; 55:1; John 4:14; 7:37, 38
10 [a]Matt 4:19; 13:47; Luke 5:10 [b]Gen 14:7; Josh 15:62; 1 Sam 23:29; 24:1; 2 Chr 20:2 [c]Ezek 26:5, 14 [d]Num 34:6; Ps 104:25; Ezek 47:15; 48:28 [e]Luke 5:5-9; John 21:6
11 [1]Lit *healed* [2]Lit *given* [a]Deut 29:23
12 [a]Ezek 47:7; Rev 22:2 [b]Gen 2:9 [c]Ps 1:3; Jer 17:8

46:18 *The prince shall not take.* See note on 45:7.
46:19–24 Fits well after 42:13–14, where other rooms for priests are described. The provisions here are a fitting conclusion to the sacrifice laws. The priests' area (vv. 19–20) was to be kept separate from the cooking areas of the Levites (vv. 21–24).
47:1 *he.* The angelic guide (40:3), who here appears for the last time, concluded Ezekiel's visionary tour of the new temple. *door of the house.* Ezekiel was standing in the inner court. *water.* The rest of this section (vv. 1–12) makes it clear that healing, life-nurturing water is meant (see Ps 36:8; 46:4 and notes; see also Joel 3:18; Zech 13:1; 14:8; Rev 22:1–2). In the larger background was the river flowing from the Garden of Eden (Gen 2:10).
47:2 *brought me out by way of the north gate.* Because the east gate was closed (44:2).
47:5 *measured a thousand.* For a total of four measurings (see note on 1:5). *river that could not be forded.* Amazing, in that a stream fed by no tributaries does not increase as it flows.
47:7 *very many trees.* Reminiscent of Eden (Gen 2:9).
47:8 *toward the eastern region.* Contrast Zech 14:8. *Arabah.* Here the waterless region between Jerusalem and the Dead Sea (i.e., part of the Jordan Valley). *the sea.* Usually means the Mediterranean Sea, but here obviously the Dead Sea is intended. *become fresh.* The Hebrew says, figuratively, "become healed." That this lowest (1,300 feet below sea level) and saltiest (25 percent) body of water in the world should sustain such an abundance of life indicates the wonderful renewing power of this "river of the water of life" (Rev 22:1).
47:9 *every living creature which swarms.* Overtones of Gen 1:20–21 point to a new creation.
47:10 *Engedi.* Means "spring of the goat"; a strong spring midway along the western side of the Dead Sea. *Eneglaim.* Means "spring of the two calves." It is possibly Ain Feshkha, at the northwestern corner of the Dead Sea, though some suggest a location on the east bank. *the Great Sea.* The Mediterranean.
47:11 *they will be left for salt.* Perhaps to provide the salt needed in the sacrifices (43:24).

month because their water flows from the
sanctuary, and their fruit will be for food and
their [d]leaves for healing."

Boundaries and Division of the Land

13 Thus says the Lord [1]GOD, "This *shall*
be the [a]boundary by which you shall divide
the land for an inheritance among the
twelve tribes of Israel; Joseph *shall have* two
[b]portions.
14 "You shall divide it for an inheritance,
each one [1]equally with the other; for I
[2a]swore to give it to your forefathers, and
this land shall fall to you [3]as an inheritance.
15 "This *shall be* the boundary of the land:
on the [a]north side, from the Great Sea *by* the
way of Hethlon, to the entrance of [1b]Zedad;
16 [1a]Hamath, Berothah, Sibraim, which is
between the border of [b]Damascus and the
border of Hamath; Hazer-hatticon, which is
by the border of Hauran.
17 "The boundary shall [1]extend from the
sea *to* [a]Hazar-enan *at* the border of Damascus, and on the north toward the north is the
border of Hamath. This is the north side.
18 "The [a]east side, from between Hauran,
Damascus, [b]Gilead and the land of Israel,
shall be the [c]Jordan; from the *north* border to
the eastern sea you shall measure. This is the
east side.
19 "The [a]south side toward the south *shall*
extend from [b]Tamar as far as the waters of
[c]Meribath-kadesh, to the [d]brook *of Egypt*
and to the [e]Great Sea. This is the south side
toward the south.
20 "The [a]west side *shall be* the Great Sea,
from the *south* border to a point opposite
[1b]Lebo-hamath. This is the west side.
21 "So you shall divide this land among
yourselves according to the tribes of Israel.
22 "You shall divide it by [a]lot for an inheritance among yourselves and among the
[b]aliens who stay in your midst, who bring
forth sons in your midst. And they shall be to
you as the native-born among the sons of
Israel; they shall be allotted an [c]inheritance
with you among the tribes of Israel.
23 "And in the tribe with which the alien
stays, there you shall give *him* his inheritance," declares the Lord GOD.

Division of the Land

48 "Now [a]these are the names of the
tribes: from the northern extremity,
[1]beside the way of Hethlon to [2]Lebo-hamath,
as far as Hazar-enan *at* the border of Damascus, toward the north [1]beside Hamath, [3]run-
ning from east to west, [b]Dan, one *portion.*
2 "Beside the border of Dan, from the east
side to the west side, [a]Asher, one *portion.*
3 "Beside the border of Asher, from the
east side to the west side, [a]Naphtali, one *por-*
tion.
4 "Beside the border of Naphtali, from the
east side to the west side, [a]Manasseh, one
portion.
5 "Beside the border of Manasseh, from
the east side to the west side, [a]Ephraim, one
portion.

12 [d]Rev 22:2 **13** [1]Heb *YHWH,* usually rendered LORD, and so throughout the ch [a]Num 34:2-12 [b]Gen 48:5; Ezek 48:4, 5 **14** [1]Lit *like his brother* [2]Lit *lifted up My hand* [3]Lit *in* [a]Deut 1:8; Ezek 20:6 **15** [1]Or *Hamath* [a]Num 34:7-9 [b]Num 34:8 **16** [1]Or *Zedad* [a]Num 13:21; Is 10:9; Ezek 47:17, 20; 48:1; Zech 9:2 [b]Gen 14:15; Ezek 47:17, 18; 48:1 **17** [1]Lit *be* [a]Num 34:9 **18** [a]Num 34:10-12 [b]Gen 37:25; Jer 50:19 [c]Gen 13:10, 11 **19** [a]Num 34:3-5 [b]Ezek 48:28 [c]Deut 32:51 [d]Num 34:5; 1 Kin 8:65; Is 27:12 [e]Ezek 47:10, 15 **20** [a]Num 34:6

20 [1]Or *entrance of Hamath* [b]Judg 3:3; 2 Chr 7:8; Ezek 48:1; Amos 6:14 **22** [a]Num 26:55, 56 [b]Is 14:1; 56:6, 7 [c]Acts 11:18; 15:9; Eph 2:12-14; 3:6; Col 3:11 **48:1** [1]Lit *at the hand of* [2]Or *the entrance of Hamath* [3]Lit *and there shall be to it an east and west side* [a]Ex 1:1 [b]Josh 19:40-48 **2** [a]Josh 19:24-31 **3** [a]Josh 19:32-39 **4** [a]Josh 13:29-31; 17:1-11 **5** [a]Josh 16:5-9; 17:8-10, 14-18

47:12 *They will bear every month.* A marvelous extension of the promises in 34:27; 36:30 (see Amos 9:13).
47:13 *Joseph shall have two portions.* Since the tribe of Levi received none (44:28), Ephraim and Manasseh, Joseph's two sons adopted by Jacob (Gen 48:17–20), each received an allotment (see 48:4–5).
47:14 *for I swore.* A reference to the covenant made with Abram (Gen 15:9–21; see Ezek 20:5; 36:28).
47:15 *This shall be the boundary.* Approximates Israel's borders at the time of David and Solomon, except that Transjordan is not included (see v. 18)—which, in any event, was never within the boundaries of the promised land proper. The following specified boundaries closely resemble those in Num 34:1–12. *way of Hethlon.* Probably situated on the Mediterranean coast, somewhere in present-day Lebanon. *to the entrance of Zedad.* Or "past Lebo Hamath to Zedad." Lebo, however, probably does not mean "entrance," but should be identified with modern Lebweh, about 15 miles northeast of Baalbek and 20 miles southwest of Kadesh on the Orontes River, near Riblah. At one time Lebo must have served as a fortress guarding the southern route to Hamath. Perhaps the phrase should be translated "Lebo of Hamath" (see NASB marg.). It is often referred to in Scripture as the northern limit of Israel (see v. 20; 48:1; Num 13:21; 34:8; Josh 13:5; 1 Kin 8:65; 2 Kin 14:25; Amos 6:14). *Zedad.* Mentioned in Num 34:8 but otherwise unknown.
47:16 *Berothah.* Probably to be identified with the Berothai of 2 Sam 8:8, but otherwise unknown. *Sibraim.* Location unknown; probably the Sephar-vaim of 2 Kin 17:24; 18:34. *Damascus.* Capital of Aram (Syria); according to v. 17 it was included in Israel. *Hamath.* A city about 120 miles north of Damascus on the Orontes River. *Hazer-hatticon.* Means "the middle enclosure." Its location is unknown, but it is possibly the same as Hazar-enan in v. 17.
47:18 *eastern sea.* The Dead Sea (see Joel 2:20; Zech 14:8).
47:19 *Meribath-kadesh.* A district about 50 miles south of Beersheba, identified with Kadesh-barnea in Num 34:4. *brook of Egypt.* The Wadi el-Arish, a deeply cut riverbed with seasonal flow that runs from the Sinai north-northwest until it enters the Mediterranean, 50 miles south of Gaza. It marked the southernmost extremity of Solomon's kingdom (1 Kin 8:65).
47:22 *they shall be to you as the native-born . . . of Israel.* A gracious inclusiveness that went beyond the provision of 14:7. It reflects the same universalism that is found in such prophecies as Is 56:3–8.
48:1 *Hethlon to Lebo-hamath.* See note on 47:15. *Hazar-enan.* See note on 47:16. *Dan.* Occupies its historical location as the northernmost tribe (see the phrase "from Dan to Beersheba," giving northern and southern boundaries—e.g., in Judg 20:1; 1 Sam 3:20). Dan was born to Rachel's maidservant Bilhah (Gen 35:25).
48:2 *Asher.* Born to Leah's maidservant Zilpah (Gen 35:26). The tribes descended from maidservants were placed farthest from the sanctuary (see Dan, v. 1; Naphtali, v. 3; Gad, v. 27).
48:3 *Naphtali.* Born to Rachel's maidservant Bilhah (see note on v. 2).
48:4 *Manasseh.* See note on 47:13.
48:5 *Ephraim.* See note on 47:13.

6 "Beside the border of Ephraim, from the east side to the west side, [a]Reuben, one *portion.*

7 "Beside the border of Reuben, from the east side to the west side, [a]Judah, one *portion.*

8 "And beside the border of Judah, from the east side to the west side, shall be the [1]allotment which you shall [2]set apart, 25,000 [3]*cubits* in width, and in length like one of the portions, from the east side to the west side; and the [a]sanctuary shall be in the middle of it.

9 "The allotment that you shall set apart to the LORD *shall be* 25,000 *cubits* in length and 10,000 in width.

Portion for the Priests

10 "The holy allotment shall be for these, *namely* for the [a]priests, toward the north 25,000 *cubits in length,* toward the west 10,000 in width, toward the east 10,000 in width, and toward the south 25,000 in length; and the sanctuary of the LORD shall be in its midst.

11 "*It shall be* for the priests who are sanctified of the [a]sons of Zadok, who have kept My charge, who did not go astray when the sons of Israel went astray as the [b]Levites went astray.

12 "It shall be an allotment to them from the allotment of the land, a most holy place, by the border of the Levites.

13 "Alongside the border of the priests the Levites *shall have* 25,000 *cubits* in length and 10,000 in width. The whole length *shall be* 25,000 *cubits* and the width 10,000.

14 "Moreover, they [a]shall not sell or exchange any of it, or alienate this [1]choice *portion* of land; for it is holy to the LORD.

15 "The remainder, 5,000 *cubits* in width and 25,000 [1]in length, shall be for [a]common use for the city, for dwellings and for [2]open spaces; and the city shall be in its midst.

16 "These *shall be* its measurements: the north side 4,500 *cubits,* the south side [a]4,500 *cubits,* the east side 4,500 *cubits,* and the west side 4,500 *cubits.*

17 "The city shall have [1]open spaces: on the north 250 *cubits,* on the south 250 *cubits,* on the east 250 *cubits,* and on the west 250 *cubits.*

18 "The remainder of the length alongside the holy allotment shall be 10,000 *cubits* toward the east and 10,000 toward the west; and it shall be [1]alongside the holy allotment. And its produce shall be food for the workers of the city.

19 "The workers of the city, out of all the tribes of Israel, shall cultivate it.

20 "The whole allotment *shall be* 25,000 by 25,000 *cubits;* you shall [1]set apart the holy allotment, a [2]square, with the [3]property of the city.

Portion for the Prince

21 "The [a]remainder *shall be* for the prince, on the one side and on the other of the holy allotment and of the [1]property of the city; in front of the 25,000 *cubits* of the allotment toward the east border and westward in front of the 25,000 toward the west border, alongside the portions, *it shall be* for the prince. And the holy allotment and the sanctuary of the house shall be in the middle of it.

22 "Exclusive of the [1]property of the Levites and the [1]property of the city, *which* are in the middle of that which belongs to the prince, *everything* between the border of Judah and the border of Benjamin shall be for the prince.

Portion for Other Tribes

23 "As for the rest of the tribes: from the east side to the west side, [a]Benjamin, one *portion.*

24 "Beside the border of Benjamin, from the east side to the west side, [a]Simeon, one *portion.*

25 "Beside the border of Simeon, from the east side to the west side, [a]Issachar, one *portion.*

26 "Beside the border of Issachar, from the east side to the west side, [a]Zebulun, one *portion.*

27 "Beside the border of Zebulun, from the east side to the west side, [a]Gad, one *portion.*

28 "And beside the border of Gad, at the south side toward the south, the border shall be from [a]Tamar to the waters of Meribath-kadesh, to the brook *of Egypt,* to the [b]Great Sea.

29 "This is the [a]land which you shall divide by lot to the tribes of Israel for an inheritance, and these are their *several* portions," declares the Lord [1]GOD.

6 [a]Josh 13:15-21
7 [a]Josh 15:1-63; 19:9
8 [1]Or *contribution,* and so throughout the ch [2]Lit *offer* [3]Or possibly *reeds,* and so throughout the ch [a]Is 12:6; 33:20-22; Ezek 45:3, 4
10 [a]Ezek 44:28; 45:4
11 [a]Ezek 40:46; 44:15 [b]Ezek 44:10, 12
14 [1]Lit *first* or *first fruits* [a]Lev 25:32-34; 27:10, 28, 33
15 [1]Lit *in front* [2]Or *pasture land* [a]Ezek 42:20; 45:6
16 [a]Rev 21:16
17 [1]Or *pasture land*
18 [1]Or *exactly as*
20 [1]Lit *offer* [2]Lit *fourth* [3]Or *possession*
21 [1]Or *possession* [a]Ezek 34:24; 45:7; 48:22
22 [1]Or *possession*
23 [a]Josh 18:21-28
24 [a]Josh 19:1-9
25 [a]Josh 19:17-23
26 [a]Josh 19:10-16
27 [a]Josh 13:24-28
28 [a]Gen 14:7; 2 Chr 20:2; Ezek 47:19 [b]Ezek 47:10, 15, 19, 20
29 [1]Heb *YHWH,* usually rendered LORD [a]Ezek 47:13-20

48:6 *Reuben.* Leah's firstborn (Gen 29:31).
48:7 *Judah.* Son of Leah (Gen 35:23). He had the most prestigious place, bordering the central holy portion (v. 8), because his tribe was given the Messianic promise (Gen 49:8–12).
48:8–22 An expansion of 45:1–8.
48:9 *10,000 in width.* The width of the entire sacred district was 20,000 cubits (see 45:1). This must refer to the width of either the priests' or the Levites' area. The Septuagint reads "20,000."
48:11 *sons of Zadok, who have kept My charge.* See note on 44:15.
48:14 *not sell or exchange.* Since it was the Lord's, it was not to be an object of commerce.
48:19 *out of all the tribes of Israel.* The sacred district was national property, not the prince's private domain.
48:23 *Benjamin.* Rachel's son (Gen 35:24).
48:24 *Simeon.* Leah's son (Gen 35:23).
48:25 *Issachar.* Leah's son (Gen 35:23).
48:26 *Zebulun.* Leah's son (Gen 35:23).
48:27 *Gad.* Son of Zilpah, Leah's maid (see note on v. 2).
48:28 *Tamar.* See note on 47:18. *Meribah-kadesh.* See note on 47:19. *brook of Egypt.* See note on 47:19.

The City Gates

30 "These are the exits of the city: on the
[a]north side, 4,500 *cubits* by measurement,
31 [1]shall be the gates of the city, [2a]named
for the tribes of Israel, three gates toward the
north: the gate of Reuben, one; the gate of
Judah, one; the gate of Levi, one.
32 "On the east side, 4,500 *cubits,* [1]shall be
three gates: the gate of Joseph, one; the gate
of Benjamin, one; the gate of Dan, one.
33 "On the south side, 4,500 *cubits* by
measurement, [1]shall be three gates: the gate
of Simeon, one; the gate of Issachar, one; the
gate of Zebulun, one.
34 "On the west side, 4,500 *cubits, shall be*
three gates: the gate of Gad, one; the gate of
Asher, one; the gate of Naphtali, one.
35 "*The city shall be* 18,000 *cubits* round
about; and the [a]name of the city from *that*
day *shall be,* '[1]The [b]LORD is there.' "

30 [a]Ezek 48:32-34
31 [1]Lit *and* [2]Lit *according to the names of* [a]Rev 21:12, 13
32 [1]Lit *and*
33 [1]Lit *and*
35 [1]Heb *YHWH-shammah*

[a]Jer 23:6; 33:16 [b]Is 12:6; 14:32; 24:23; Jer 3:17; 8:19; 14:9; Ezek 35:10; Joel 3:21; Zech 2:10; Rev 21:3; 22:3

48:31 *Reuben . . . Judah . . . Levi.* The three most influential tribes—Reuben, the firstborn; Judah, the Messianic tribe; Levi, the tribe of the priesthood—had gates together on the north side. Since Levi was included in this list, Joseph (v. 32) represented Ephraim and Manasseh (see note on 47:13) in order to keep the number at 12. For the gates cf. Rev 21:12–14.

48:35 *The LORD is there.* The great decisive word concerning the holy city; in Hebrew *Yahweh-Shammah,* a possible wordplay on *Yerushalayim,* the Hebrew pronunciation of Jerusalem. For other names of Jerusalem see 23:4; Is 1:26; 60:14; 62:2–4,12; Jer 3:17; 33:16; Zech 8:3.

Daniel

INTRODUCTION

Author, Date and Authenticity

The book mentions Daniel as its author in several passages, such as 9:2 and 10:2. That Jesus concurred is clear from His reference to " 'the abomination of desolation,' which was spoken of through Daniel the prophet" (Matt 24:15), quoting 9:27; 11:31; 12:11. The book was probably completed c. 530 B.C., shortly after the capture of Babylon by Cyrus in 539.

The widely held view that the book of Daniel is largely fictional rests mainly on the modern philosophical assumption that long-range predictive prophecy is impossible. Therefore all fulfilled predictions in Daniel, it is claimed, had to have been composed no earlier than the Maccabean period (second century B.C.), after the fulfillments had taken place. But objective evidence excludes this hypothesis on several counts:

1. To avoid fulfillment of long-range predictive prophecy in the book, the adherents of the late-date view usually maintain that the four empires of chs. 2 and 7 are Babylon, Media, Persia and Greece. But in the mind of the author, "the Medes and Persians" (5:28) together constituted the second in the series of four kingdoms (2:36–43). Thus it becomes clear that the four empires are the Babylonian, Medo-Persian, Greek and Roman. See chart on "Visions in Daniel," p. 1239.

2. The language itself argues for a date earlier than the second century. Linguistic evidence from the Dead Sea Scrolls (which furnish authentic samples of Hebrew and Aramaic writing from the second century B.C.; see "The Time between the Testaments," p. 1356) demonstrates that the Hebrew and Aramaic chapters of Daniel must have been composed centuries earlier. Furthermore, as recently demonstrated, the Persian and Greek words in Daniel do not require a late date. Some of the technical terms appearing in ch. 3 were already so obsolete by the second century B.C. that translators of the Septuagint (the Greek translation of the OT) translated them incorrectly.

3. Several of the fulfillments of prophecies in Daniel could not have taken place by the second century anyway, so the prophetic element cannot be dismissed. The symbolism connected with the fourth kingdom makes it unmistakably predictive of the Roman empire (see 2:33; 7:7,19), which did not take control of Syro-Palestine until 63 B.C. Also, the prophecy concerning the coming of "the Messiah, the Prince," 483 years after "the issuing of a decree to restore and rebuild Jerusalem" (9:25), works out to the time of Jesus' ministry.

Objective evidence, therefore, appears to exclude the late-date hypothesis and indicates that there is insufficient reason to deny Daniel's authorship.

Theme

The theological theme of the book is God's sovereignty: "The Most High God is ruler over the realm of mankind" (5:21). Daniel's visions always show God as triumphant (7:11,26–27; 8:25; 9:27; 11:45; 12:13). The climax of His sovereignty is described in Revelation: "The kingdom of the world has become the kingdom of our Lord and of His Christ; and He will reign forever and ever" (Rev 11:15; cf. Dan 2:44; 7:27).

Literary Form

The book is made up primarily of historical narrative (found mainly in chs. 1—6) and apocalyptic (revelatory) material (found mainly in chs. 7—12). The latter may be defined as symbolic, visionary, prophetic literature, usually composed during oppressive conditions and being chiefly eschatological in theological content. Apocalyptic literature is primarily a literature of encouragement to the people of God (see Introduction to Zechariah: Literary Form; see also Introduction to Revelation: Literary Form). For the symbolic use of numbers in apocalyptic literature see Introduction to Revelation: Distinctive Feature.

Outline

I. Prologue: The Setting (ch. 1; in Hebrew)
   - A. Historical Introduction (1:1–2)
   - B. Daniel and His Friends Are Taken Captive (1:3–7)
   - C. The Young Men Are Faithful (1:8–16)
   - D. The Young Men Are Elevated to High Positions (1:17–21)

II. The Destinies of the Nations of the World (chs. 2—7; in Aramaic, beginning at 2:4b)
   - A. Nebuchadnezzar's Dream of a Large Statue (ch. 2)
   - B. Nebuchadnezzar's Making of a Gold Image and His Decree That It Be Worshiped (ch. 3)
   - C. Nebuchadnezzar's Dream of an Enormous Tree (ch. 4)
   - D. Belshazzar's and Babylon's Downfall (ch. 5)
   - E. Daniel's Deliverance (ch. 6)
   - F. Daniel's Dream of Four Beasts (ch. 7)

III. The Destiny of the Nation of Israel (chs. 8—12; in Hebrew)
   - A. Daniel's Vision of a Ram and a Goat (ch. 8)
   - B. Daniel's Prayer and His Vision of the 70 "Sevens" (ch. 9)
   - C. Daniel's Vision of Israel's Future (chs. 10—12)
     1. Revelation of things to come (10:1–3)
     2. Revelation from the angelic messenger (10:4—11:1)
     3. Prophecies concerning Persia and Greece (11:2–4)
     4. Prophecies concerning Egypt and Syria (11:5–35)
     5. Prophecies concerning the antichrist (11:36–45)
     6. Distress and deliverance (12:1)
     7. Two resurrections (12:2–3)
     8. Instruction to Daniel (12:4)
     9. Conclusion (12:5–13)

The Choice Young Men

1 In the third year of the reign of [a]Jehoiakim king of Judah, [b]Nebuchadnezzar king of Babylon came to Jerusalem and besieged it.

2 The [a]Lord gave Jehoiakim king of Judah into his hand, along with some of the [b]vessels of the house of God; and he brought them to the land of [c]Shinar, to the house of his [1]god, and he brought the vessels into the treasury of his [1d]god.

3 Then the king [1]ordered Ashpenaz, the chief of his [2]officials, to bring in some of the sons of Israel, including some of the [3]royal [a]family and of the nobles,

4 youths in whom was [a]no defect, who were good-looking, showing [b]intelligence in every *branch of* wisdom, endowed with understanding and discerning knowledge, and who had ability for [1]serving in the king's [2]court; and *he ordered him* to teach them the [3]literature and [c]language of the [d]Chaldeans.

5 The king appointed for them a daily ration from the [a]king's choice food and from the wine which he drank, and *appointed* that they should be [1]educated three years, at the end of which they were to [2b]enter the king's personal service.

6 Now among them from the sons of Judah were [a]Daniel, Hananiah, Mishael and Azariah.

7 Then the commander of the officials assigned *new* names to them; and to Daniel he assigned *the name* [a]Belteshazzar, to Hananiah [b]Shadrach, to Mishael [b]Meshach and to Azariah [b]Abed-nego.

Daniel's Resolve

8 But Daniel [1]made up his mind that he would not [a]defile himself with the [b]king's choice food or with the [c]wine which he drank; so he sought *permission* from the commander of the officials that he might not defile himself.

9 Now God granted Daniel [1a]favor and compassion in the sight of the commander of the officials,

10 and the commander of the officials said to Daniel, "I am afraid of my lord the king, who has appointed your food and your drink; for why should he see your faces looking more haggard than the youths who are your own age? Then you would [1]make me forfeit my head to the king."

11 But Daniel said to the overseer whom the commander of the officials had appointed over Daniel, Hananiah, Mishael and Azariah,

12 "Please test your servants for ten days, and let us be [a]given some vegetables to eat and water to drink.

13 "Then let our appearance be [1]observed in your presence and the appearance of the youths who are eating the king's choice food; and deal with your servants according to what you see."

14 So he listened to them in this matter and tested them for ten days.

15 At the end of ten days their appearance seemed [a]better and [1]they were fatter than all the youths who had been eating the king's choice food.

16 So the overseer continued to [1]withhold their choice food and the wine they were to drink, and kept [a]giving them vegetables.

17 As for these four youths, [a]God gave them knowledge and intelligence in every *branch of* [1]literature and wisdom; Daniel even understood all *kinds of* [b]visions and dreams.

18 Then at the end of the days which the king had [1]specified [2]for presenting them, the

1:1 [a]2 Kin 24:1; 2 Chr 36:5, 6 [b]Jer 25:1; 52:12, 28-30
2 [1]Or *gods* [a]Is 42:24; Dan 2:37, 38 [b]2 Chr 36:7; Jer 27:19, 20; Dan 5:2 [c]Gen 10:10; 11:2; Is 11:11; Zech 5:11 [d]Jer 50:2; 51:44
3 [1]Or *said to* [2]Or *eunuchs,* and so throughout the ch [3]Lit *seed of the* [a]2 Kin 24:15; Is 39:7
4 [1]Lit *standing* [2]Lit *palace* [3]Or *writing* [a]2 Sam 14:25 [b]Dan 1:17 [c]Is 36:11; Jer 5:15; Dan 2:4 [d]Dan 2:2, 4, 5, 10; 3:8; 4:7; 5:7, 11, 30; 9:1
5 [1]Or *reared* [2]Lit *stand before the king* [a]Dan 1:8 [b]1 Sam 16:22; Dan 1:19
6 [a]Ezek 14:14, 20; 28:3; Matt 24:15
7 [a]Dan 2:26; 4:8; 5:12 [b]Dan 2:49; 3:12
8 [1]Lit *set upon his heart* [a]Lev 11:47; Ezek 4:13, 14; Hos 9:3, 4 [b]Ps 141:4; Dan 1:5 [c]Deut 32:38; Dan 5:4
9 [1]Lit *lovingkindness* [a]Gen 39:21; 1 Kin 8:50; Job 5:15, 16; Ps 106:46; Prov 16:7
10 [1]Lit *make my head guilty*
12 [a]Dan 1:16
13 [1]Lit *seen*
15 [1]Lit *fat of flesh* [a]Ex 23:25; Prov 10:22
16 [1]Lit *take away* [a]Dan 1:12
17 [1]Or *writing* [a]1 Kin 3:12, 28; Job 32:8; Dan 1:20; 2:21, 23; Acts 7:22 [b]Dan 2:19; 7:1; 8:1
18 [1]Lit *said* [2]Lit *to bring them in*

1:1 *third year.* According to the Babylonian system of computing the years of a king's reign, the third year of Jehoiakim would have been 605 B.C., since his first full year of kingship began on New Year's Day after his accession in 608. But according to the Judahite system, which counted the year of accession as the first year of reign, this was the fourth year of Jehoiakim (Jer 25:1; 46:2).

1:2 *brought them.* Judah was exiled to Babylonia because she disobeyed God's word regarding covenant-keeping, the sabbath years and idolatry (see Lev 25:1–7; 26:27–35; 2 Chr 36:14–21). The first deportation (605 B.C.) included Daniel, and the second (597) included Ezekiel. A third deportation took place in 586, when the Babylonians destroyed Jerusalem and the temple.

1:4 *literature and language of the Chaldeans.* Including the classical literature in Sumerian and Akkadian cuneiform, a complicated syllabic writing system. But the language of normal communication in multiracial Babylon was Aramaic, written in an easily learned alphabetic script (see 2:4).

1:6 *Daniel.* Means "God is (my) Judge." *Hananiah.* Means "The LORD shows grace." *Mishael.* Means "Who is what God is?" *Azariah.* Means "The LORD helps."

1:7 *Belteshazzar.* Probably means, in Babylonian, "Bel (i.e., Marduk), protect his life!" *Shadrach.* Probably means "command of Aku (Sumerian moon-god)." *Meshach.* Probably means "Who is what Aku is?" *Abed-nego.* Means "servant of Nego/Nebo (i.e., Nabu)."

1:8 *king's choice food or . . . wine.* Israelites considered food from Nebuchadnezzar's table to be contaminated because the first portion of it was offered to idols. Likewise a portion of the wine was poured out on a pagan altar. Ceremonially unclean animals were used and were neither slaughtered nor prepared according to the regulations of the law. *he sought . . . that he might not defile himself.* He demonstrated the courage of his convictions.

1:9 *God granted Daniel favor.* The careers of Joseph and Daniel were similar in many respects (see Gen 39–41).

1:12 *test your servants.* Daniel used good judgment by offering an alternative instead of rebelling. *ten.* Often had the symbolic significance of completeness.

1:17 With God's help, Daniel and his friends mastered the Babylonian literature on astrology and divination by dreams. But in the crucial tests of interpretation and prediction (see 2:3–11; 4:7), all the pagan literature proved worthless. Only by God's special revelation (2:17–28) was Daniel able to interpret correctly.

commander of the officials [3]presented them
before Nebuchadnezzar.
19 The king talked with them, and out of
them all not one was found like [a]Daniel,
Hananiah, Mishael and Azariah; so they
[1b]entered the king's personal service.
20 As for every matter of [a]wisdom [1]and
understanding about which the king consulted them, he found them [b]ten times [c]better
than all the [2d]magicians *and* conjurers who
were in all his realm.
21 And Daniel [1]continued until the [a]first
year of Cyrus the king.

The King's Forgotten Dream

2 Now in the second year of the reign of
Nebuchadnezzar, Nebuchadnezzar [1a]had
dreams; and his spirit was troubled and his
[b]sleep [2]left him.
2 Then the king [1]gave orders to call in the
[2a]magicians, the conjurers, the sorcerers and
the [3]Chaldeans to tell the king his dreams. So
they came in and stood before the king.
3 The king said to them, "I [1a]had a
dream and my spirit [2]is anxious to [3]under-
stand the dream."
4 Then the Chaldeans spoke to the king
in [1a]Aramaic: "[b]O king, live forever! [c]Tell the
dream to your servants, and we will declare
the interpretation."
5 The king replied to the Chaldeans,
"[1]The command from me is firm: if you do
not make known to me the dream and its
interpretation, you will be [2a]torn limb from
limb and your houses will be made a rubbish heap.
6 "But if you declare the dream and its
interpretation, you will receive from me
[a]gifts and a reward and great honor; therefore declare to me the dream and its interpretation."
7 They answered a second time and said,
"Let the king [a]tell the dream to his servants,
and we will declare the interpretation."
8 The king replied, "I know for certain
that you are [1]bargaining for time, inasmuch
as you have seen that [2]the command from
me is firm,
9 that if you do not make the dream
known to me, there is only [a]one [1]decree for
you. For you have agreed together to speak
lying and corrupt [2]words before me until the
[3]situation is changed; therefore tell me the
dream, that I may [b]know that you can
declare to me its interpretation."
10 The Chaldeans answered [1]the king and
said, "There is not a man on earth who could
declare the matter [2]for the king, inasmuch as
no great king or ruler has *ever* asked anything like this of any [3a]magician, conjurer or
Chaldean.
11 "Moreover, the thing which the king
demands is [1]difficult, and there is no one
else who could declare it [2]to the king except
[a]gods, whose [b]dwelling place is not with
mortal flesh."
12 Because of this the king became
[a]indignant and very furious and gave orders
to destroy all the wise men of Babylon.
13 So the [1]decree went forth that the wise
men should be slain; and they looked for
[a]Daniel and his friends to [2]kill *them.*
14 Then Daniel replied with discretion and
discernment to [a]Arioch, the captain of the
king's [1]bodyguard, who had gone forth to
slay the wise men of Babylon;
15 he said to Arioch, the king's commander, "For what reason is the [1]decree from the
king *so* [2]urgent?" Then Arioch informed
Daniel about the matter.
16 So Daniel went in and requested of the
king that he would [1]give him time, in order
that he might declare the interpretation to
the king.
17 Then Daniel went to his house and
informed his friends, [a]Hananiah, Mishael
and Azariah, about the matter,
18 so that they might [a]request compassion
from the God of heaven concerning this mystery, so that Daniel and his friends would not
be [b]destroyed with the rest of the wise men
of Babylon.

The Secret Is Revealed to Daniel

19 Then the mystery was revealed to Daniel in a night [a]vision. Then Daniel blessed
the God of heaven;
20 Daniel said,

18 [3]Lit *brought in* **19** [1]Lit *stood before the king* [a]Dan 1:6, 7 [b]Gen 41:46; Dan 1:5 **20** [1]Lit *of* [2]Or *soothsayer priests* [a]1 Kin 4:30, 31; Dan 1:17 [b]Gen 31:7; Num 14:22; Neh 4:12; Job 19:3 [c]Dan 2:27, 28, 46, 48 [d]Is 19:3; Dan 2:2; 4:18; 5:7 **21** [1]Lit *was until* [a]Dan 6:28; 10:1 **2:1** [1]Lit *dreamed dreams* [2]Lit *was gone upon him* [a]Gen 40:5-8; 41:1, 8; Job 33:15-17; Dan 2:3; 4:5 [b]Esth 6:1; Dan 6:18 **2** [1]Lit *said to call* [2]Or *soothsayer priests* [3]Or *master astrologers,* and so throughout the ch [a]Gen 41:8; Ex 7:11; Is 47:12, 13; Dan 1:20; 2:10, 27; 4:6; 5:7 **3** [1]Lit *dreamed* [2]Lit *was troubled* [3]Lit *know* [a]Gen 40:8; 41:15; Dan 4:5 **4** [1]The text is in Aramaic from here through 7:28 [a]Ezra 4:7; Is 36:11 [b]Dan 3:9; 5:10 [c]Dan 2:7 **5** [1]Another reading is *The word has gone from me* [2]Lit *made into limbs* [a]Ezra 6:11; Dan 2:12; 3:29 **6** [a]Dan 2:48; 5:7, 16, 29 **7** [a]Dan 2:4 **8** [1]Lit *buying* [2]V 5, note 1 **9** [1]Or *law* [2]Lit *word* [a]Esth 4:11; Dan 3:15

9 [3]Lit *time* [b]Is 41:23 **10** [1]Lit *before the* [2]Lit *of* [3]Or *soothsayer priest* [a]Dan 2:2, 27

11 [1]Or *rare* [2]Lit *before* [a]Gen 41:39; Dan 5:11 [b]Ex 29:45; Is 57:15 **12** [a]Ps 76:10; Dan 2:5; 3:13, 19 **13** [1]Or *law* [2]Lit *be killed* [a]Dan 1:19, 20 **14** [1]Or *executioners* [a]Dan 2:24 **15** [1]Or *law* [2]Or *harsh* **16** [1]Or *appoint a time for him* **17** [a]Dan 1:6 **18** [a]Esth 4:15, 16; Is 37:4; Jer 33:3; Ezek 36:37; Dan 2:23 [b]Gen 18:28; Mal 3:18 **19** [a]Num 12:6; Job 33:15, 16; Dan 1:17; 7:2, 7, 13

1:20 *ten.* See note on v. 12. *magicians.* See note on Gen 41:8.

1:21 *first year of Cyrus the king.* Over Babylon (539 B.C.). Daniel was still living in the year 537 (10:1), so he saw the exiles return to Judah from Babylonian captivity.

2:1 *second year of . . . Nebuchadnezzar.* 604 B.C.

2:4 *Aramaic.* Since the astrologers were of various racial backgrounds, they communicated in Aramaic, the language everyone understood. From here to the end of ch. 7 the entire narrative is in Aramaic. These six chapters deal with matters of importance to the Gentile nations of the Near East and were written in a language understandable to all. But the last five chapters (8–12) revert to Hebrew, since they deal with special concerns of the chosen people.

2:11 *whose dwelling place is not with mortal flesh.* Who are not readily accessible.

2:14 *Arioch.* Meaning uncertain. It is also the name of a Mesopotamian king who lived centuries earlier (Gen 14:1,9).

2:18 *God of heaven.* See note on Ezra 1:2. *mystery.* A key word in Daniel (2:19,27–30,47; 4:9). It also appears often in the writings (Dead Sea Scrolls) of the Qumran sect (see essay, p. 1356). The Greek equivalent is used in the NT to refer to the secret purposes of God that He reveals only to His chosen prophets and apostles (see note on Rom 11:25).

"Let the name of God be [a]blessed
forever and ever,
For [b]wisdom and power belong to Him.
21 "It is He who [a]changes the times and
the epochs;
He [b]removes kings and [1]establishes
kings;
He gives [c]wisdom to wise men
And knowledge to [2]men of
understanding.
22 "It is He who [a]reveals the profound
and hidden things;
[b]He knows what is in the darkness,
And the [c]light dwells with Him.
23 "To You, O [a]God of my fathers, I give
thanks and praise,
For You have given me [b]wisdom and
power;
Even now You have made known to
me what we [c]requested of You,
For You have made known to us the
king's matter."

24 Therefore, Daniel went in to Arioch,
whom the king had appointed to destroy the
wise men of Babylon; he went and spoke to
him as follows: "[a]Do not destroy the wise
men of Babylon! Take me [1]into the king's
presence, and I will declare the interpretation
to the king."
25 Then Arioch hurriedly [a]brought Daniel
[1]into the king's presence and spoke to him as
follows: "I have found a man among the
[2][b]exiles from Judah who can make the interpretation known to the king!"
26 The king said to Daniel, whose name
was [a]Belteshazzar, "Are you able to make
known to me the dream which I have seen
and its interpretation?"
27 Daniel answered before the king and
said, "As for the mystery about which the
king has inquired, neither [a]wise men, conjurers, [1]magicians *nor* diviners are able to
declare *it* to the king.
28 "However, there is a [a]God in heaven
who reveals mysteries, and He has made
known to King Nebuchadnezzar what will
take place in the [1][b]latter days. This was your
dream and the [c]visions [2]in your mind *while*
on your bed.
29 "As for you, O king, *while* on your bed
your thoughts [1]turned to what would take
place [2]in the future; and [a]He who reveals
mysteries has made known to you what will
take place.
30 "But as for me, this mystery has not
been revealed to me for any [a]wisdom [1]resid-
ing in me more than *in* any *other* living man,
but for the purpose of making the interpretation known to the king, and that you may
[2]understand the [b]thoughts of your [3]mind.

The King's Dream

31 "You, O king, were looking and behold,
there was a single great statue; that statue,
which was large and [1]of extraordinary splendor, was standing in front of you, and its
appearance was [a]awesome.
32 "The [a]head of that statue *was made* of
fine gold, its breast and its arms of silver, its
belly and its thighs of bronze,
33 its legs of iron, its feet partly of iron
and partly of clay.
34 "You [1]continued looking until a [a]stone
was cut out [b]without hands, and it struck the
statue on its feet of iron and clay and
[c]crushed them.
35 "Then the iron, the clay, the bronze, the
silver and the gold were crushed [1]all at the
same time and became [a]like chaff from
the summer threshing floors; and the wind
carried them away so that [b]not a trace of
them was found. But the stone that struck
the statue became a great [c]mountain and
filled the whole earth.

The Interpretation—Babylon the First Kingdom

36 "This *was* the dream; now we will tell
[a]its interpretation before the king.
37 "You, O king, are the [a]king of kings, to
whom the God of heaven has given the [1]king-
dom, the [b]power, the strength and the glory;
38 and wherever the sons of men dwell,
or the [a]beasts of the field, or the birds of the
sky, He has given *them* into your hand and
has caused you to rule over them all. You are
the head of gold.

Medo-Persia and Greece

39 "After you there will arise another kingdom inferior to you, then another third kingdom of bronze, which will rule over all the
earth.

Rome

40 "Then there will be a [a]fourth kingdom
as strong as iron; inasmuch as iron crushes

20 [a]Ps 103:1, 2; 113:1, 2; 115:18; 145:1, 2, 21 [b]1 Chr 29:11, 12; Job 12:13, 16-22; Dan 2:21-23
21 [1]Or *sets up* [2]Lit *knowers* [a]Ps 31:15; Dan 2:9; 7:25 [b]Job 12:18; Ps 75:6, 7; Dan 4:17, 32 [c]1 Kin 3:9, 10; 4:29; James 1:5
22 [a]Job 12:22; Ps 25:14; Dan 2:19, 28 [b]Job 26:6; Ps 139:12; Is 45:7; Jer 23:24; Heb 4:13 [c]Ps 36:9; Dan 5:11, 14; James 1:17; 1 John 1:5
23 [a]Gen 31:42; Ex 3:15 [b]Dan 1:17; 2:21 [c]Ps 21:2, 4; Dan 2:18, 29, 30
24 [1]Lit *in before the king* [a]Dan 2:12, 13; Acts 27:24
25 [1]Lit *in before the king* [2]Lit *sons of the exile of* [a]Gen 41:14 [b]Dan 1:6; 5:13; 6:13
26 [a]Dan 1:7; 4:8; 5:12
27 [1]Or *soothsayer priests* [a]Dan 2:2, 10, 11; 5:7, 8
28 [1]Lit *end of the days* [2]Lit *of your head* [a]Gen 40:8; 41:16; Dan 2:22, 45 [b]Gen 49:1; Is 2:2; Dan 10:14; Mic 4:1 [c]Dan 4:5
29 [1]Lit *came up* [2]Lit *after this* [a]Dan 2:23, 47
30 [1]Lit *which is* [2]Lit *know* [3]Lit *heart* [a]Gen 41:16; Dan 1:17 [b]Ps 139:2; Amos 4:13
31 [1]Lit *its splendor was surpassing* [a]Hab 1:7
32 [a]Dan 2:38
34 [1]Lit *were* [a]Dan 2:45 [b]Dan 8:25; Zech 4:6 [c]Ps 2:9; Is 60:12
35 [1]Lit *like one* [a]Ps 1:4; Is 17:13; 41:15, 16; Hos 13:3 [b]Ps 37:10, 36 [c]Is 2:2; Mic 4:1
36 [a]Dan 2:24
37 [1]Or *sovereignty* [a]Is 47:5; Jer 27:6, 7; Ezek 26:7 [b]Ps 62:11
38 [a]Ps 50:10, 11; Dan 4:21, 22
40 [a]Dan 7:23

2:22 *light dwells with Him.* See Ps 36:9.

2:32–43 See map No. 7b and map No. 13 at the end of the study Bible. The gold head represents the Neo-Babylonian empire (v. 38; see Jer 51:7); the silver chest and arms, the Medo-Persian empire established by Cyrus in 539 B.C. (the date of the fall of Babylon); the bronze belly and thighs, the Greek empire established by Alexander the Great c. 330; the iron legs and feet, the Roman empire. The toes (v. 41) are understood by some to represent a later confederation of states occupying the territory formerly controlled by the Roman empire. The diminishing value of the metals from gold to silver to bronze to iron represents the decreasing power and grandeur (v. 39) of the rulers of the successive empires, from the absolute despotism of Nebuchadnezzar to the democratic system of checks and balances that characterized the Roman senates and assemblies. The metals also symbolize a growing degree of toughness and endurance, with each successive empire lasting longer than the preceding one.

2:35 *crushed.* See Matt 21:44.

and shatters all things, so, like iron that breaks in pieces, it will crush and break all these in pieces.

41 "In that you saw the feet and toes, partly of potter's clay and partly of iron, it will be a divided kingdom; but it will have in it the toughness of iron, inasmuch as you saw the iron mixed with [1]common clay.

42 "*As* the toes of the feet *were* partly of iron and partly of pottery, *so* some of the kingdom will be strong and part of it will be brittle.

43 "And in that you saw the iron mixed with [1]common clay, they will combine with one another [2]in the seed of men; but they will not adhere to one another, even as iron does not combine with pottery.

The Divine Kingdom

44 "In the days of those kings the [a]God of heaven will [b]set up a [c]kingdom which will never be destroyed, and *that* kingdom will not be [1]left for another people; it will [d]crush and put an end to all these kingdoms, but it will itself endure forever.

45 "Inasmuch as you saw that a [a]stone was cut out of the mountain without hands and that it crushed the iron, the bronze, the clay, the silver and the gold, the [b]great God has made known to the king what [c]will take place [1]in the future; so the dream is true and its interpretation is trustworthy."

Daniel Promoted

46 Then King Nebuchadnezzar fell on his face and did [a]homage to Daniel, and gave orders to present to him an offering and [1b]fragrant incense.

47 The king answered Daniel and said, "Surely [a]your God is a [b]God of gods and a Lord of kings and a [c]revealer of mysteries, since you have been able to reveal this mystery."

48 Then the king [1a]promoted Daniel and gave him many great gifts, and he made him ruler over the whole [b]province of Babylon and chief [2]prefect over all the wise men of Babylon.

49 And Daniel made request of the king, and he [a]appointed [b]Shadrach, Meshach and Abed-nego over the administration of the province of Babylon, while Daniel *was* at the king's [1c]court.

41 [1]Lit *clay of mud*
43 [1]Lit *clay of mud* [2]Or *with*
44 [1]Or *passed on to* [a]Dan 2:28, 37 [b]Is 9:6, 7 [c]Ps 145:13; Ezek 37:25; Dan 4:3, 34; 6:26; 7:14, 27; Mic 4:7; Luke 1:32, 33 [d]Ps 2:9; Is 60:12; Dan 2:34, 35
45 [1]Lit *after this* [a]Dan 2:34 [b]Deut 10:17; 2 Sam 7:22; Ps 48:1; Jer 32:18, 19; Dan 2:29; Mal 1:11 [c]Gen 41:28, 32
46 [1]Lit *sweet odors* [a]Dan 3:5, 7; Acts 10:25; 14:13; Rev 19:10; 22:8 [b]Lev 26:31; Ezra 6:10
47 [a]Dan 3:15; 4:25 [b]Deut 10:17; Ps 136:2, 3; Dan 11:36 [c]Dan 2:22, 30; Amos 3:7
48 [1]Lit *made great* [2]Lit *of the prefects* [a]Gen 41:39-43; Dan 2:6; 5:16, 29 [b]Dan 3:1, 12, 30
49 [1]Lit *gate* [a]Dan 3:12 [b]Dan 1:7 [c]Esth 2:19, 21; Amos 5:15

3:1 [1]I.e. One cubit equals approx 18 in. [a]1 Kin 12:28; Is 46:6; Jer 16:20; Dan 2:31; Hos 2:8; 8:4; Hab 2:19 [b]Dan 2:48; 3:30
2 [a]Dan 3:3, 27; 6:1-7
4 [1]Lit *they command* [2]Lit *tongue* [a]Dan 3:7; 4:1; 6:25
5 [1]Or *zither* [2]I.e. triangular lyre [3]Or *a type of harp* [a]Dan 3:7, 10, 15
6 [1]Or *in the same hour* [a]Dan 3:11, 15, 21; 6:7 [b]Jer 29:22; Ezek 22:18-22; Matt 13:42, 50; Rev 9:2; 14:11
7 [1]V 5, notes 1, 2, 3 [2]Lit *tongue*
8 [1]Lit *ate the pieces of* [a]Dan 2:2, 10; 4:7 [b]Ezra 4:12-16; Esth 3:8, 9; Dan 6:12, 13

The King's Golden Image

3 Nebuchadnezzar the king made an [a]image of gold, the height of which *was* sixty [1]cubits *and* its width six [1]cubits; he set it up on the plain of Dura in the [b]province of Babylon.

2 Then Nebuchadnezzar the king sent *word* to assemble the [a]satraps, the prefects and the governors, the counselors, the treasurers, the judges, the magistrates and all the rulers of the provinces to come to the dedication of the image that Nebuchadnezzar the king had set up.

3 Then the satraps, the prefects and the governors, the counselors, the treasurers, the judges, the magistrates and all the rulers of the provinces were assembled for the dedication of the image that Nebuchadnezzar the king had set up; and they stood before the image that Nebuchadnezzar had set up.

4 Then the herald loudly proclaimed: "To you [1]the command is given, [a]O peoples, nations and *men of every* [2]language,

5 that at the moment you [a]hear the sound of the horn, flute, [1]lyre, [2]trigon, [3]psaltery, bagpipe and all kinds of music, you are to fall down and worship the golden image that Nebuchadnezzar the king has set up.

6 "But whoever does not fall down and worship shall [1]immediately be [a]cast into the midst of a [b]furnace of blazing fire."

7 Therefore at that time, when all the peoples heard the sound of the horn, flute, [1]lyre, trigon, psaltery, bagpipe and all kinds of music, all the peoples, nations and *men of every* [2]language fell down *and* worshiped the golden image that Nebuchadnezzar the king had set up.

Worship of the Image Refused

8 For this reason at that time certain [a]Chaldeans came forward and [1b]brought charges against the Jews.

9 They responded and said to Nebuchadnezzar the king: "[a]O king, live forever!

10 "You, O king, have [a]made a decree that every man who hears the sound of the horn, flute, [1]lyre, trigon, psaltery, and bagpipe and all kinds of music, is to [b]fall down and worship the golden image.

11 "But whoever does not fall down and

9 [a]Dan 2:4; 5:10; 6:6, 21 **10** [1]V 5, notes 1, 2, 3 [a]Esth 3:12-14; Dan 3:4-6; 6:12 [b]Dan 3:5, 7, 15

2:44 The fifth kingdom is the eternal kingdom of God, built on the ruins of the sinful empires of man. Its authority will extend over "the whole earth" (v. 35) and ultimately over "a new heaven and a new earth" (Rev 21:1).
2:48 Cf. the story of Joseph (Gen 41:41–43).
3:1 *image of gold.* Large statues of this kind were not made of solid gold but were plated with gold. *height . . . was sixty cubits.* Ninety feet, including the lofty pedestal on which it no doubt stood. *Dura.* Either the name of a place now marked by a series of mounds (located a few miles south of Babylon) or a common noun meaning "walled enclosure."
3:2 The seven classifications of government officials were to pledge full allegiance to the newly established empire as they stood before the image. The image probably represented the god Nabu, whose name formed the first element in Nebuchadnezzar's name (in Akkadian *Nabu-kudurri-uṣur,* meaning "Nabu, protect my son!" or "Nabu, protect my boundary!").
3:5 The words for "lyre," "psaltery" and "bagpipe" are the only Greek loanwords in Daniel. Greek musicians and instruments are mentioned in Assyrian inscriptions written before the time of Nebuchadnezzar.

worship shall be cast into the midst of a furnace of blazing fire.

12 "There are certain Jews whom you have [a]appointed over the administration of the province of Babylon, *namely* Shadrach, Meshach and Abed-nego. These men, O king, have disregarded you; they do not serve your gods or worship the golden image which you have set up."

13 Then Nebuchadnezzar in [a]rage and anger gave orders to bring Shadrach, Meshach and Abed-nego; then these men were brought before the king.

14 Nebuchadnezzar responded and said to them, "Is it true, Shadrach, Meshach and Abed-nego, that you do not serve [a]my gods or worship the golden image that I have set up?

15 "Now if you are ready, [a]at the moment you hear the sound of the horn, flute, [1]lyre, trigon, psaltery and bagpipe and all kinds of music, to fall down and worship the image that I have made, *very well.* But if you do not worship, you will [2]immediately be [b]cast into the midst of a furnace of blazing fire; and [c]what god is there who can deliver you out of my hands?"

16 [a]Shadrach, Meshach and Abed-nego replied to the king, "O Nebuchadnezzar, we do not need to give you an answer concerning this matter.

17 "[1]If it be *so,* our [a]God whom we serve is able to deliver us from the furnace of blazing fire; [2]and [b]He will deliver us out of your hand, O king.

18 "[a]But *even* if *He does* not, [b]let it be known to you, O king, that we are not going to serve your gods or worship the golden image that you have set up."

Daniel's Friends Protected

19 Then Nebuchadnezzar was filled with [a]wrath, and his facial expression was altered toward Shadrach, Meshach and Abed-nego. He answered [1]by giving orders to heat the furnace seven times more than it was usually heated.

20 He commanded certain valiant warriors who *were* in his army to tie up Shadrach, Meshach and Abed-nego in order to cast *them* into the furnace of blazing fire.

21 Then these men were tied up in their [1a]trousers, their [2]coats, their caps and their *other* clothes, and were cast into the midst of the furnace of blazing fire.

22 For this reason, because the king's [1]command *was* [2a]urgent and the furnace had been made extremely hot, the flame of the fire slew those men who carried up Shadrach, Meshach and Abed-nego.

23 But these three men, Shadrach, Meshach and Abed-nego, [a]fell into the midst of the furnace of blazing fire *still* tied up.

24 Then Nebuchadnezzar the king was astounded and stood up in haste; he said to his high officials, "Was it not three men we cast bound into the midst of the fire?" They replied to the king, "Certainly, O king."

25 He said, "Look! I see four men loosed *and* [a]walking *about* in the midst of the fire [1]without harm, and the appearance of the fourth is like a son of *the* [b]gods!"

26 Then Nebuchadnezzar came near to the door of the furnace of blazing fire; he responded and said, "Shadrach, Meshach and Abed-nego, come out, you servants of the [a]Most High God, and come here!" Then Shadrach, Meshach and Abed-nego [b]came out of the midst of the fire.

27 The [a]satraps, the prefects, the governors and the king's high officials gathered around *and* saw in regard to these men that the [b]fire had no [1]effect on [2]the bodies of these men nor was the hair of their head singed, nor were their [3c]trousers [4]damaged, nor had the smell of fire *even* come upon them.

28 Nebuchadnezzar responded and said, "Blessed be the [a]God of Shadrach, Meshach and Abed-nego, who has [b]sent His angel and delivered His servants who put their [c]trust in Him, [1]violating the king's command, and yielded up their bodies so as [d]not to serve or worship any god except their own God.

29 "Therefore I [a]make a decree that any people, nation or tongue that speaks anything offensive against the God of [b]Shadrach, Meshach and Abed-nego shall be torn limb from limb and their [c]houses reduced to a rubbish heap, inasmuch as there is [d]no other god who is able to deliver in this way."

30 Then the king [a]caused Shadrach, Meshach and Abed-nego to prosper in the province of Babylon.

The King Acknowledges God

4 [1]Nebuchadnezzar the king to all the peoples, nations, and *men of every* [2]language that live in all the earth: "May your [3a]peace abound!

12 [a]Dan 2:49
13 [a]Dan 2:12; 3:19
14 [a]Is 46:1; Jer 50:2; Dan 3:1; 4:8
15 [1]V 5, notes 1, 2, 3 [2]Or *in the same hour* [a]Dan 3:5 [b]Dan 3:6 [c]Ex 5:2; Is 36:18-20; Dan 2:47
16 [a]Dan 1:7; 3:12
17 [1]Or *If our God...is able* [2]Or *then* [a]Job 5:19; Ps 27:1, 2; Is 26:3, 4; Jer 1:8; 15:20, 21 [b]1 Sam 17:37; Mic 7:7; 2 Cor 1:10
18 [a]Josh 24:15; 1 Kin 19:14, 18; Is 51:12, 13; Dan 3:28 [b]Heb 11:25
19 [1]Lit *and ordered to* [a]Esth 7:7; Dan 3:13
21 [1]Or *leggings* [2]Or *cloaks* [a]Dan 3:27
22 [1]Lit *word* [2]Or *harsh* [a]Ex 12:33; Dan 2:15
23 [a]Is 43:2
25 [1]Lit *there is no injury in them* [a]Ps 91:3-9; Is 43:2 [b]Jer 1:8, 19; 15:21
26 [a]Dan 3:17; 4:2 [b]Deut 4:20; 1 Kin 8:51; Jer 11:4
27 [1]Lit *power over* [2]Lit *their* [3]Or *cloaks* [4]Lit *changed* [a]Dan 3:2, 3 [b]Is 43:2; Heb 11:34 [c]Dan 3:21
28 [1]Lit *and changed the king's word* [a]Dan 2:47; 3:15-17 [b]Ps 34:7, 8; Is 37:36; Dan 3:25; 6:22; Acts 5:19; 12:7 [c]Ps 22:4, 5; 40:4; 84:12; Is 12:2; 26:3, 4; 50:10; Jer 17:7 [d]Dan 3:16-18
29 [a]Dan 6:26 [b]Dan 1:7, 19; 2:17, 49; 3:12 [c]Ezra 6:11; Dan 2:5 [d]Dan 2:47; 3:15
30 [a]Dan 2:49; 3:12
4:1 [1]Ch 3:31 in Aram [2]Lit *tongue* [3]Or *welfare* or *prosperity* [a]Ezra 4:17; Dan 6:25

3:12 *they do not serve your gods or worship the golden image.* They obeyed the word of God (Ex 20:3–5) above the word of the king.
3:17 See Heb 11:34.
3:18 *if He does not.* Whether God decides to rescue them (v. 17) or not, their faith is fully resigned to His will.
3:19 The temperature was controlled by the number of bellows forcing air into the fire chamber. Therefore sevenfold intensification was achieved by seven bellows pumping at the same time. But the expression "seven times more than it was usually heated" may have been figurative for "as hot as possible" (seven signifies completeness).
3:25 See Ps 91:9–12. *son of the gods.* Nebuchadnezzar was speaking as a pagan polytheist and was content to conceive of the fourth figure as a lesser heavenly being (v. 28) sent by the all-powerful God of the Israelites.
3:29 See 2:5.
4:1–3 Nebuchadnezzar reached this conclusion after the expe-

2 "It has seemed good to me to declare the signs and wonders which the [a]Most High God has done for me.

3 "How great are His [a]signs
And how mighty are His wonders!
His [b]kingdom is an everlasting
kingdom
And His dominion is from generation
to generation.

The Vision of a Great Tree

4 "[1]I, Nebuchadnezzar, was at ease in my house and [a]flourishing in my palace.
5 "I saw a [a]dream and it made me fearful; and *these* fantasies *as I lay* on my bed and the [b]visions [1]in my mind kept alarming me.
6 "So I gave orders to [a]bring into my presence all the wise men of Babylon, that they might make known to me the interpretation of the dream.
7 "Then the [1a]magicians, the conjurers, the [2]Chaldeans and the diviners came in and I related the dream [3]to them, but they could not make its [b]interpretation known to me.
8 "But finally Daniel came in before me, whose name is [a]Belteshazzar according to the name of my god, and in whom is [1b]a spirit of the holy gods; and I related the dream [2]to him, *saying,*
9 'O Belteshazzar, [a]chief of the magicians, since I know that [b]a spirit of the holy gods is in you and [c]no mystery baffles you, [d]tell *me* the visions of my dream which I have seen, along with its interpretation.
10 'Now *these were* the [a]visions [1]in my mind *as I lay* on my bed: I was looking, and behold, *there was* a [b]tree in the midst of the [2]earth and its height *was* great.

11 'The tree grew large and became strong
And its height [a]reached to the sky,
And it *was* visible to the end of the
whole earth.
12 'Its foliage *was* [a]beautiful and its fruit
abundant,
And in it *was* food for all.
The [b]beasts of the field found [c]shade
under it,
And the [d]birds of the sky dwelt in its
branches,
And all [1]living creatures fed
themselves from it.

13 'I was looking in the [a]visions [1]in my mind *as I lay* on my bed, and behold, [b]an *angelic* watcher, a [c]holy one, descended from heaven.
14 'He shouted out and spoke as follows:

"[a]Chop down the tree and cut off its
branches,
Strip off its foliage and scatter its fruit;
Let the [b]beasts flee from under it
And the birds from its branches.
15 "Yet [a]leave the stump [1]with its roots in
the ground,
But with a band of iron and bronze
around it
In the new grass of the field;
And let him be drenched with the dew
of heaven,
And let [2]him share with the beasts in
the grass of the earth.
16 "Let his [1]mind be changed from *that of*
a man
And let a beast's [1]mind be given to
him,
And let [a]seven [2]periods of time pass
over him.
17 "This sentence is by the decree of the
angelic watchers
And the decision is a command of the
holy ones,
In order that the living may [a]know
That the Most High is ruler over the
realm of mankind,
And [b]bestows it on whom He wishes
And sets over it the [c]lowliest of men."

18 'This is the dream *which* I, King Nebuchadnezzar, have seen. Now you, Belteshazzar, tell *me* its interpretation, inasmuch as none of the [a]wise men of my kingdom is able to make known to me the interpretation; but you are able, for a [b]spirit of the holy gods is in you.'

Daniel Interprets the Vision

19 "Then Daniel, whose name is Belteshazzar, was appalled for a while as his [a]thoughts alarmed him. The king responded and said, 'Belteshazzar, do not [b]let the dream or its interpretation alarm you.' Belteshazzar replied, 'My lord, *if only* the dream applied to those who hate you and its interpretation to [d]your adversaries!
20 'The [a]tree that you saw, which became

2 [a]Dan 3:26; 4:17, 24, 25, 32, 34
3 [a]Ps 77:19; 105:27; Is 25:1; Dan 6:27 [b]Dan 2:44; 4:34; 6:26
4 [1]Ch 4:1 in Aram [a]Ps 30:6; Is 47:7, 8
5 [1]Lit *of my head* [a]Dan 2:3 [b]Dan 2:1, 28; 4:10, 13
6 [a]Gen 41:8; Dan 2:2
7 [1]Or *soothsayer priests,* and so throughout the ch [2]Or *master astrologers* [3]Lit *before* [a]Gen 41:8; Dan 2:10, 27; 5:7 [b]Is 44:25; Jer 27:9, 10; Dan 2:7
8 [1]Or possibly *the Spirit of the holy God,* and so throughout the ch [2]Lit *before* [a]Dan 1:7; 2:26; 5:12 [b]Dan 4:9, 18; 5:11, 14
9 [a]Dan 1:20; 2:48; 5:11 [b]Gen 41:38; Dan 4:8 [c]Ezek 28:3; Dan 2:47 [d]Gen 41:15; Dan 2:4, 5
10 [1]Lit *of my head* [2]Or *land,* and so throughout the ch [a]Dan 4:5 [b]Ezek 31:3, 6
11 [a]Deut 9:1; Dan 4:21, 22
12 [1]Lit *flesh* [a]Ezek 31:7 [b]Jer 27:6; Ezek 31:6 [c]Lam 4:20 [d]Ezek 17:23; Matt 13:32; Luke 13:19
13 [1]Lit *of my head* [a]Dan 7:1 [b]Dan 4:17, 23
13 [c]Deut 33:2; Ps 89:7; Dan 8:13
14 [a]Ezek 31:10-14; Dan 4:23; Matt 3:10; 7:19; Luke 13:7-9 [b]Ezek 31:12, 13; Dan 4:12
15 [1]Lit *of* [2]Lit *his portion be with* [a]Job 14:7-9
16 [1]Lit *heart* [2]I.e. years [a]Dan 4:23, 25, 32
17 [a]Ps 9:16; 83:18; Dan 2:21; 5:21 [b]Jer 27:5-7; Dan 4:25; 5:18, 19 [c]1 Sam 2:8; Dan 11:21
18 [a]Gen 41:8, 15; Dan 4:7; 5:8, 15 [b]Dan 4:8, 9
19 [a]Jer 4:19; Dan 7:15, 28; 8:27; 10:16, 17 [b]1 Sam 3:17; Dan 4:4, 5 [c]2 Sam 18:31; Dan 4:24; 10:16 [d]2 Sam 18:32
20 [a]Dan 4:10-12

riences of vv. 4–37. The language of his confession may reflect Daniel's influence.

4:8 *according to the name of my god.* See note on 1:7. Bel ("lord") was a title for the god Marduk.

4:10 *tree.* Interpreted in v. 22.

4:11 *grew large and . . . strong.* In one of Nebuchadnezzar's building inscriptions, Babylon is compared to a spreading tree (cf. v. 22). *its height reached to the sky.* A phrase often used of Mesopotamian temple-towers (see also note on Gen 11:4).

4:13 *angelic watcher.* Or "watchman"; also in vv. 17,23.

4:15 *leave the stump.* Implies that the tree will be revived later (see v. 26).

4:16 *seven.* Signifies completeness. *periods of time.* Or "years." The term referred to a given season of the year, and so to the year as a whole (see 7:25). For example, every recurrent spring meant that another full year had elapsed since the previous spring. Alternatively, the "periods of time" can be indefinite.

4:17 *angelic watchers.* The agents of God, who is the ultimate source (v. 24).

4:19 *Daniel . . . was appalled.* Possibly over how to state the interpretation in an appropriate way.

large and grew strong, whose height reached
to the sky and was visible to all the earth
21 and whose foliage *was* beautiful and its
fruit abundant, and in which *was* food for
all, under which the beasts of the field dwelt
and in whose branches the birds of the sky
lodged—
22 it is [a]you, O king; for you have become
great and grown strong, and your [1]majesty
has become great and reached to the sky and
your [b]dominion to the end of the earth.
23 'In that the king saw an *angelic* watcher, a holy one, descending from heaven and
saying, "[a]Chop down the tree and destroy it;
yet leave the stump [1]with its roots in the
ground, but with a band of iron and bronze
around it in the new grass of the field, and
let him be drenched with the dew of heaven,
and let [2]him share with the beasts of the
field until [b]seven [3]periods of time pass over
him,"
24 this is the interpretation, O king, and
this is the decree of the Most High, which
has [a]come upon my lord the king:

22 [1]Lit *greatness* [a]2 Sam 12:7; Dan 2:37, 38 [b]Jer 27:6, 7
23 [1]Lit *of* [2]Lit *his portion be with* [3]I.e. years [a]Dan 4:14, 15 [b]Dan 4:16
24 [a]Job 40:11, 12; Ps 107:40
25 [1]I.e. years [a]Dan 4:33; 5:21 [b]Ps 83:18; Jer 27:5; Dan 4:2, 17 [c]Dan 2:37; 4:17; 5:21
26 [1]Lit *of* [2]Lit *enduring* [a]Dan 4:15, 23 [b]Dan 2:18, 19, 28, 37, 44; 4:31
27 [1]Or *redeem now your sins* [a]Gen 41:33-37 [b]Prov 28:13; Is 55:6, 7; Ezek 18:7, 21, 22; Acts 8:22 [c]Ps 41:1-3; Is 58:6, 7, 10 [d]1 Kin 21:29; Jon 3:9
28 [a]Num 23:19; Zech 1:6
29 [a]2 Pet 3:9

25 that you be [a]driven away from mankind
and your dwelling place be with the beasts of
the field, and you be given grass to eat like
cattle and be drenched with the dew of heav-
en; and seven [1]periods of time will pass over
you, until you recognize that the [b]Most High
is ruler over the realm of mankind and
[c]bestows it on whomever He wishes.
26 'And in that it was commanded to
[a]leave the stump [1]with the roots of the tree,
your kingdom will be [2]assured to you after
you recognize that *it is* [b]Heaven *that* rules.
27 'Therefore, O king, may my [a]advice be
pleasing to you: [1b]break away now from
your sins by *doing* righteousness and from
your iniquities by [c]showing mercy to *the*
poor, in case there may be a [d]prolonging of
your prosperity.'

The Vision Fulfilled

28 "All *this* [a]happened to Nebuchadnezzar
the king.
29 "[a]Twelve months later he was walking
on the *roof of* the royal palace of Babylon.

4:25 *recognize that the Most High is ruler.* He learned the lesson (compare v. 30 with v. 37).
4:26 *Heaven.* A Jewish title for God, later reflected in the NT expression "kingdom of heaven" (compare Matt 5:3 with Luke 6:20).
4:28 *All this happened.* But only because Nebuchadnezzar

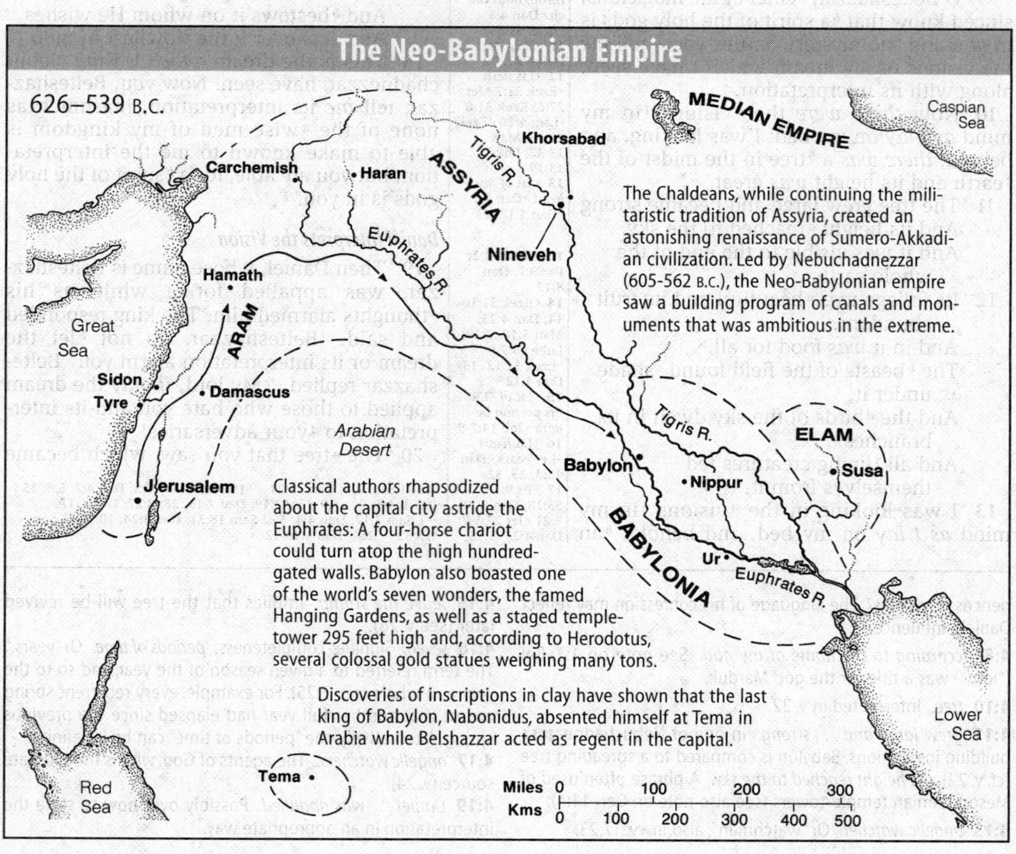

The Neo-Babylonian Empire
626–539 B.C.
MEDIAN EMPIRE
Caspian Sea
Khorsabad
Tigris R.
ASSYRIA
Carchemish
Haran
Euphrates R.
Nineveh
Hamath
ARAM
Great Sea
Sidon
Tyre
Damascus
Arabian Desert
Jerusalem
Tigris R.
ELAM
Babylon
Susa
Nippur
BABYLONIA
Ur
Euphrates R.
Lower Sea
Red Sea
Tema
Miles 0 100 200 300
Kms 0 100 200 300 400 500
The Chaldeans, while continuing the militaristic tradition of Assyria, created an astonishing renaissance of Sumero-Akkadian civilization. Led by Nebuchadnezzar (605-562 B.C.), the Neo-Babylonian empire saw a building program of canals and monuments that was ambitious in the extreme.
Classical authors rhapsodized about the capital city astride the Euphrates: A four-horse chariot could turn atop the high hundred-gated walls. Babylon also boasted one of the world's seven wonders, the famed Hanging Gardens, as well as a staged temple-tower 295 feet high and, according to Herodotus, several colossal gold statues weighing many tons.
Discoveries of inscriptions in clay have shown that the last king of Babylon, Nabonidus, absented himself at Tema in Arabia while Belshazzar acted as regent in the capital.

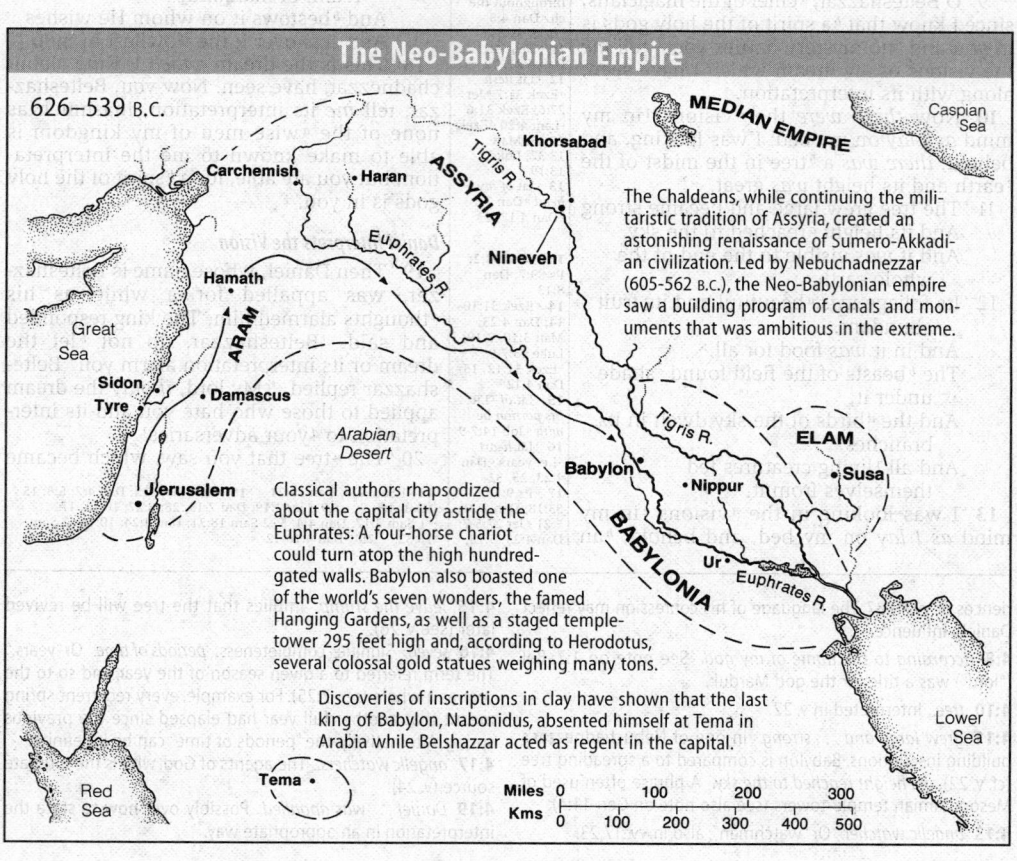

30"The king [1]reflected and said, 'Is this
not Babylon the [a]great, which I myself have
built as a royal [2]residence by the might of my
power and for the glory of my majesty?'
31"While the word *was* in the king's
mouth, a voice [1]came from heaven, *saying,*
'King Nebuchadnezzar, to you it is declared:
[2]sovereignty has been removed from you,
32 and [a]you will be driven away from
mankind, and your dwelling place *will be*
with the beasts of the field. You will be giv-
en grass to eat like cattle, and [b]seven [1]peri-
ods of time will pass over you until you recognize that the [c]Most High is ruler over the
realm of mankind and bestows it on whomever He wishes.'
33"Immediately the word concerning Nebuchadnezzar was fulfilled; and he was [a]driv-
en away from mankind and began eating
grass like cattle, and his body was drenched
with the dew of heaven until his hair had
grown like eagles' *feathers* and his nails like
birds' *claws.*
34"But at the end of [1]that period, I, Nebuchadnezzar, raised my eyes toward heaven
and my [2]reason returned to me, and I
blessed the [a]Most High and praised and honored [b]Him who lives forever;
For His dominion is an [c]everlasting
dominion,
And His kingdom *endures* from
generation to generation.
35"[a]All the inhabitants of the earth are
accounted as nothing,
But [b]He does according to His will in
the host of heaven
And *among* the inhabitants of earth;
And [c]no one can [1]ward off His hand
Or say to Him, '[d]What have You
done?'
36"At that time my [1a]reason returned to
me. And my majesty and [b]splendor were
[2]restored to me for the glory of my kingdom,
and my counselors and my nobles began
seeking me out; so I was reestablished in my
[3]sovereignty, and surpassing [c]greatness was
added to me.
37"Now I, Nebuchadnezzar, praise, exalt
and honor the King of [a]heaven, for [b]all His
works are [1]true and His ways [2]just, and He is
able to humble those who [c]walk in pride."

Belshazzar's Feast

5 Belshazzar the king [1]held a great [a]feast
for a thousand of his nobles, and he was
drinking wine in the presence of the thousand.
2 When Belshazzar tasted the wine, he
gave orders to bring the gold and silver [a]ves-
sels which Nebuchadnezzar his [1]father had
taken out of the temple which *was* in Jerusalem, so that the king and his nobles, his
wives and his concubines might drink from
them.
3 Then they brought the gold vessels that
had been taken out of the temple, the house
of God which *was* in Jerusalem; and the king
and his nobles, his wives and his concubines
drank from them.
4 They [a]drank the wine and praised the
gods of [b]gold and silver, of bronze, iron,
wood and stone.
5 Suddenly the fingers of a man's hand
emerged and began writing opposite the
lampstand on the plaster of the wall of the
king's palace, and the king saw the [1]back of
the hand that did the writing.
6 Then the king's [1a]face grew pale and
his thoughts alarmed him, and his [b]hip joints
went slack and his [c]knees began knocking
together.
7 The king called aloud to bring in the
[a]conjurers, the [1]Chaldeans and the diviners.
The king spoke and said to the wise men of
Babylon, "Any man who can read this
inscription and explain its interpretation to
me shall be [b]clothed with purple and *have* a
[c]necklace of gold around his neck, and have
authority as [2d]third *ruler* in the kingdom."
8 Then all the king's wise men came in,
but [a]they could not read the inscription or
make known its interpretation to the king.
9 Then King Belshazzar was greatly
[a]alarmed, his [1b]face grew *even* paler, and his
nobles were perplexed.
10 The queen entered the banquet [1]hall
because of the words of the king and his
nobles; the queen spoke and said, "[a]O king,
live forever! Do not let your thoughts alarm
you or your [2]face be pale.

30 [1]Lit *answered* [2]Lit *house* [a]Hab 2:4
31 [1]Lit *fell* [2]Or *kingdom*
32 [1]I.e. years [a]Dan 4:25 [b]Dan 4:16 [c]Dan 4:17
33 [a]Dan 4:25; 5:21
34 [1]Lit *the days* [2]Lit *knowledge* [a]Dan 4:2; 5:18, 21 [b]Ps 102:24-27; Dan 6:26; 12:7; Rev 4:10 [c]Ps 145:13; Jer 10:10; Dan 4:3; Mic 4:7; Luke 1:33
35 [1]Lit *strike against* [a]Ps 39:5; Is 40:15, 17 [b]Ps 33:11; 115:3; 135:6; Dan 6:27 [c]Job 42:2; Is 43:13 [d]Job 9:12; Is 45:9; Rom 9:20
36 [1]Lit *knowledge* [2]Lit *returning* [3]Or *kingdom* [a]2 Chr 33:12, 13; Dan 4:34 [b]Dan 2:31 [c]Prov 22:4; Dan 4:22
37 [1]Lit *truth* [2]Lit *justice* [a]Dan 4:26; 5:23 [b]Deut 32:4; Ps 33:4, 5; Is 5:16 [c]Ex 18:11; Job 40:11, 12; Dan 5:20

5:1 [1]Lit *made* [a]Esth 1:3; Is 22:12-14
2 [1]Or *forefather,* and so throughout the ch [a]2 Kin 24:13; 25:15; Ezra 1:7-11; Dan 1:2
4 [a]Is 42:8; Dan 5:23; Rev 9:20 [b]Ps 115:4; 135:15; Is 40:19, 20; Dan 3:1; Hab 2:19
5 [1]Or *palm*
6 [1]Lit *brightness changed for him* [a]Dan 5:9, 10; 7:28 [b]Ps 69:23 [c]Ezek 7:17; 21:7; Nah 2:10
7 [1]Or *master astrologers* [2]Or *a triumvir* [a]Is 44:25; 47:13; Dan 4:6, 7; 5:11, 15 [b]Gen 41:42-44; Dan 5:16, 29 [c]Ezek 16:11 [d]Dan 2:48; 5:16, 29; 6:2, 3

8 [a]Gen 41:8; Dan 2:27; 4:7; 5:15 **9** [1]Lit *brightness was changing upon him* [a]Job 18:11; Is 21:2-4; Jer 6:24; Dan 2:1; 5:6 [b]Is 13:6-8 **10** [1]Lit *house* [2]Lit *brightness be changed* [a]Dan 3:9; 6:6

did not follow Daniel's advice.

4:30 *Babylon the great.* Illustrated, e.g., in the city's ramparts, temples and hanging gardens (see note on Is 13:19).

4:31 *the word was in the king's mouth.* See Luke 12:19–20.

4:33 *the word . . . was fulfilled.* See Prov 16:18. *driven away.* Possibly into the palace gardens. His counselors, perhaps led by Daniel (see 2:48–49), could have administered the kingdom efficiently.

4:34 *His dominion . . . from generation to generation.* See v. 3; 6:26; 7:14.

4:36 See Job 42:10,12.

4:37 *He is able to humble those who walk in pride.* See Prov 3:34; James 4:10; 1 Pet 5:5–6.

5:1–4 The orgy of revelry and blasphemy on such occasions is confirmed by the ancient Greek historians Herodotus and Xenophon.

5:1 *king.* Belshazzar (meaning "Bel, protect the king!") was the son and viceroy of Nabonidus. He is called the "son" of Nebuchadnezzar (v. 22), but the Aramaic term could also mean "grandson" or "descendant" or even "successor." Likewise, "father" could mean "ancestor" or "predecessor" (see vv. 2,11,13,18). See also note on v. 10.

5:5 *Suddenly.* See notes on 4:31; 1 Thess 5:3.

5:7 *authority as third ruler in the kingdom.* Nabonidus was first, Belshazzar second.

5:10 *queen.* Or "queen mother." She could have been (1) the

11 "There is a [a]man in your kingdom in whom is [1]a [b]spirit of the holy gods; and in the days of your father, illumination, insight and wisdom like the wisdom of the gods were found in him. And King Nebuchadnezzar, your father, your father [2c]the king, appointed him chief of the [3]magicians, conjurers, [4]Chaldeans *and* diviners.

12 "*This was* because an [a]extraordinary spirit, knowledge and insight, interpretation of dreams, explanation of enigmas and solving of difficult problems were found in this Daniel, whom the king named [b]Belteshazzar. Let Daniel now be summoned and he will declare the interpretation."

Daniel Interprets Handwriting on the Wall

13 Then Daniel was brought in before the king. The king spoke and said to Daniel, "Are you that Daniel who is one of the [1a]exiles from Judah, whom my father the king [b]brought from Judah?

14 "Now I have heard about you that [1]a spirit of the gods is in you, and that illumination, insight and extraordinary wisdom have been found in you.

15 "Just now the [a]wise men *and* the conjurers were brought in before me that they might read this inscription and make its interpretation known to me, but they [b]could not declare the interpretation of the [1]message.

16 "But I personally have heard about you, that you are able to give interpretations and solve difficult problems. Now if you are able to read the inscription and make its [a]interpretation known to me, you will be [b]clothed with purple and *wear* a necklace of gold around your neck, and you will have authority as the [1]third *ruler* in the kingdom."

17 Then Daniel answered and said before the king, "[1]Keep your [a]gifts for yourself or give your rewards to someone else; however, I will read the inscription to the king and make the interpretation known to him.

18 "[1]O king, the [a]Most High God [b]granted [2]sovereignty, [c]grandeur, glory and majesty to Nebuchadnezzar your father.

19 "Because of the grandeur which He bestowed on him, all the peoples, nations and *men of every* [1]language feared and trembled before him; [a]whomever he wished he killed and whomever he wished he spared alive; and whomever he wished he elevated and whomever he wished he humbled.

20 "But when his heart was [a]lifted up and his spirit became so [1b]proud that he behaved arrogantly, he was [c]deposed from his royal throne and *his* glory was taken away from him.

21 "He was also [a]driven away from [1]mankind, and his heart was made like *that of* beasts, and his dwelling place *was* with the [b]wild donkeys. He was given grass to eat like cattle, and his body was drenched with the dew of heaven until he recognized that the [c]Most High God is ruler over the realm of mankind and *that* He sets over it whomever He wishes.

22 "Yet you, his [1]son, Belshazzar, have [a]not humbled your heart, [2]even though you knew all this,

23 but you have [a]exalted yourself against the [b]Lord of heaven; and they have brought the vessels of His house before you, and you and your nobles, your wives and your concubines have been drinking wine from them; and you have praised the [c]gods of silver and gold, of bronze, iron, wood and stone, which do not see, hear or understand. But the God [d]in whose hand are your life-breath and your [e]ways, you have not glorified.

24 "Then the [1a]hand was sent from Him and this inscription was written out.

25 "Now this is the inscription that was written out: '[1]MENĒ, [1]MENĒ, [2]TEKĒL, [3]UPHARSIN.'

26 "This is the interpretation of the [1]message: 'MENĒ'—God has numbered your kingdom and [a]put an end to it.

27 " 'TEKĒL'—you have been [a]weighed on the scales and found deficient.

28 " 'PERĒS'—your kingdom has been divided and given over to the [a]Medes and [1]Persians."

29 Then Belshazzar gave orders, and they [a]clothed Daniel with purple and *put* a necklace of gold around his neck, and issued a proclamation concerning him that he *now* had authority as the [1]third *ruler* in the kingdom.

11 [1]Or possibly *the Spirit of the holy God* [2]Or *O king* [3]Or *soothsayer priests* [4]Or *master astrologers* [a]Gen 41:11-15; Dan 2:47 [b]Dan 4:8, 9, 18; 5:14 [c]Dan 2:48
12 [a]Dan 5:14; 6:3 [b]Dan 1:7; 4:8
13 [1]Lit *sons of the exile* [a]Ezra 4:1; 6:16, 19, 20; Dan 2:25; 6:13 [b]Dan 1:1, 2
14 [1]Or possibly *the Spirit of God*
15 [1]Lit *word* [a]Dan 5:7 [b]Is 47:12f; Dan 5:8
16 [1]Or *triumvir* [a]Gen 40:8 [b]Dan 5:7, 29
17 [1]Lit *Let...be for* [a]2 Kin 5:16
18 [1]Lit *You, O king* [2]Or *the kingdom* [a]Dan 4:2; 5:21 [b]Dan 2:37, 38; 4:17 [c]Jer 25:9; 27:5-7
19 [1]Lit *tongue* [a]Dan 2:12, 13; 3:6; 11:3, 16, 36
20 [1]Lit *strong* [a]Ex 9:17; Job 15:25; Is 14:13-15; Dan 4:30, 31 [b]2 Kin 17:14; 2 Chr 36:13 [c]Job 40:11, 12; Jer 13:18
21 [1]Lit *the sons of man* [a]Job 30:3-7; Dan 4:32, 33 [b]Job 39:5-8 [c]Ex 9:14-16; Ps 83:17, 18; Ezek 17:24; Dan 4:17, 34, 35
22 [1]Or *descendant* [2]Lit *inasmuch as you* [a]Ex 10:3; 2 Chr 33:23; 36:12
23 [a]2 Kin 14:10; Is 2:12; 37:23; Jer 50:29; Dan 5:3, 4 [b]Dan 4:37 [c]Ps 115:4-8; Is 37:19; Hab 2:18, 19 [d]Job 12:10 [e]Job 31:4; Ps 139:3; Prov 20:24; Jer 10:23
24 [1]Lit *palm of the hand* [a]Dan 5:5
25 [1]Or *a mina* (50 shekels) from verb "to number" [2]Or *a shekel* from verb "to weigh" [3]Or *and half-shekels* (sing: *perēs*) from verb "to divide"
26 [1]Lit *word* [a]Is 13:6, 17-19; Jer 50:41-43
27 [a]Job 31:6; Ps 62:9
28 [1]Aram: *Pāras* [a]Is 13:17; 21:2; 45:1, 2; Dan 5:31; 6:8, 28; Acts 2:9
29 [1]Or *triumvir* [a]Dan 5:7, 16

wife of Nebuchadnezzar, or (2) the daughter of Nebuchadnezzar and wife of Nabonidus, or (3) the wife of Nabonidus but not the daughter of Nebuchadnezzar.

5:11 *the days of your father.* Nebuchadnezzar died in 562 B.C.; the year is now 539.

5:17 *Keep your gifts for yourself.* See Gen 14:23 and note.

5:21 *until he recognized.* See note on 4:25.

5:22–23 Three charges were brought against Belshazzar: (1) He sinned not through ignorance but through disobedience and pride (v. 22); (2) he defied God by desecrating the sacred vessels (v. 23a); and (3) he praised idols and so did not honor God (v. 23b).

5:26–28 See NASB marg. on v. 25. Three weights (mina, shekel, and half mina/shekel) may be intended, symbolizing three rulers (respectively): (1) Nebuchadnezzar, (2) either Evil-merodach (2 Kin 25:27; Jer 52:31) or Nabonidus, and (3) Belshazzar.

5:27 *weighed on the scales.* Measured in the light of God's standards (cf. Job 31:6; Ps 62:9; Prov 24:12).

5:28 *Medes and Persians.* The second kingdom of the series of four predicted in ch. 2 (see Introduction: Author, Date and Authenticity).

5:30 *That same night.* See Prov 29:1; Luke 12:20.

30 That same night [a]Belshazzar the Chaldean king was [b]slain.
31 [1]So [a]Darius the Mede received the
kingdom at about the age of sixty-two.

Daniel Serves Darius

6 [1]It seemed good to Darius to appoint 120
satraps over the kingdom, that they
would be in charge of the whole kingdom,
2 and over them three commissioners (of
whom [a]Daniel was one), that these satraps
might be accountable to them, and that the
king might not suffer [b]loss.
3 Then this Daniel began distinguishing
himself [1]among the commissioners and
satraps because [2]he possessed an [a]extraordi-
nary spirit, and the king planned to appoint
him over the [b]entire kingdom.
4 Then the commissioners and satraps
began [a]trying to find a ground of accusation
against Daniel in regard to [1]government
affairs; but they could find [b]no ground of
accusation or *evidence of* corruption, inasmuch as he was faithful, and no negligence
or corruption was *to be* found in him.
5 Then these men said, "We will not find
any ground of accusation against this Daniel
unless we find *it* against him with regard to
the [a]law of his God."
6 Then these commissioners and satraps
came [1]by agreement to the king and spoke to
him as follows: "King Darius, [a]live forever!
7 "All the [a]commissioners of the kingdom, the prefects and the satraps, the high
officials and the governors have [b]consulted
together that the king should establish a
statute and enforce an injunction that anyone who makes a petition to any god or man
besides you, O king, for thirty days, shall [c]be
cast into the lions' [1]den.
8 "Now, O king, [a]establish the injunction
and sign the document so that it may not be
changed, according to the [b]law of the Medes
and Persians, which [1]may not be revoked."
9 Therefore King Darius [a]signed the document, that is, the injunction.
10 Now when Daniel knew that the document was signed, he entered his house (now
in his roof chamber he had windows open
[a]toward Jerusalem); and he continued
[b]kneeling on his knees three times a day,
[c]praying and [d]giving thanks before his God,
[1]as he had been doing previously.
11 Then these men came [1a]by agreement
and found Daniel making petition and supplication before his God.
12 Then they approached and [a]spoke
before the king about the king's injunction,
"Did you not sign an injunction that any
man who makes a petition to any god or
man besides you, O king, for thirty days, is
to be cast into the lions' den?" The king
replied, "The statement is true, according to
the [b]law of the Medes and Persians, which
[1]may not be revoked."
13 Then they answered and spoke before
the king, "[a]Daniel, who is one of the [1]exiles
from Judah, pays [b]no attention to you, O
king, or to the injunction which you signed,
but keeps making his petition three times a
day."
14 Then, as soon as the king heard this
statement, he was deeply [a]distressed and set
his mind on delivering Daniel; and even until
sunset he kept exerting himself to rescue him.
15 Then these men came [1]by agreement to
the king and said to the king, "Recognize, O
king, that it is a [a]law of the Medes and Persians that no injunction or statute which the
king establishes may be changed."

Daniel in the Lions' Den

16 Then the king gave orders, and Daniel
was brought in and [a]cast into the lions' den.
The king spoke and said to Daniel, "[1b]Your
God whom you constantly serve will Himself
deliver you."
17 A [a]stone was brought and laid over the
mouth of the den; and the king sealed it with
his own signet ring and with the signet rings
of his nobles, so that nothing would be
changed in regard to Daniel.
18 Then the king went off to his palace
and spent the night [a]fasting, and no entertainment was brought before him; and his
[b]sleep fled from him.
19 Then the king arose at dawn, at the
break of day, and went in haste to the lions'
den.
20 When he had come near the den to
Daniel, he cried out with a troubled voice.
The king spoke and said to Daniel, "Daniel,
servant of the living God, has [a]your God,
whom you constantly serve, been [b]able to
deliver you from the lions?"
21 Then Daniel spoke [1]to the king, "[a]O
king, live forever!
22 "My God [a]sent His angel and [b]shut the

30 [a]Dan 5:1, 2 [b]Is 21:4-9; 47:9; Jer 51:11, 31, 39, 57 **31** [1]Ch 6:1 in Aram [a]Dan 6:1; 9:1 **6:1** [1]Ch 6:2 in Aram **2** [a]Dan 2:48, 49; 5:16, 29 [b]Ezra 4:22; Esth 7:4 **3** [1]Lit *above* [2]Lit *there was in him* [a]Dan 5:12, 14; 9:23 [b]Gen 41:40; Esth 10:3 **4** [1]Lit *the kingdom* [a]Gen 43:18; Judg 14:4; Jer 20:10; Dan 3:8; Luke 20:20 [b]Dan 6:22; Luke 20:26; 23:14, 15; Phil 2:15; 1 Pet 2:12; 3:16 **5** [a]Acts 24:13-16, 20, 21 **6** [1]Or *thronging* [a]Neh 2:3; Dan 2:4; 5:10; 6:21 **7** [1]Or *pit,* and so throughout the ch [a]Dan 3:2, 27 [b]Ps 59:3; 62:4; 64:2-6; 83:1-3 [c]Ps 10:9; Dan 3:6; 6:16 **8** [1]Lit *does not pass away* [a]Esth 3:12; 8:10; Is 10:1 [b]Esth 1:19; 8:8; Dan 6:12, 15 **9** [a]Ps 118:9; 146:3 **10** [1]Or *because* [a]1 Kin 8:44, 48, 49; Ps 5:7; Jon 2:4 [b]Ps 55:17; 95:6 [c]Dan 9:4-19 [d]Ps 34:1; Phil 4:6; 1 Thess 5:17, 18 **11** [1]Or *thronging* [a]Ps 37:32, 33; Dan 6:6 **12** [1]Lit *does not pass away* [a]Dan 3:8-12; Acts 16:19-21 [b]Esth 1:19; Dan 6:8, 15 **13** [1]Lit *sons of the exile* [a]Dan 2:25; 5:13 [b]Esth 3:8; Dan 3:12; Acts 5:29 **14** [a]Mark 6:26 **15** [1]Or *thronging* [a]Esth 8:8; Ps 94:20, 21; Dan 6:8, 12 **16** [1]Or *May your God...Himself deliver you* [a]2 Sam 3:39; Jer 38:5; Dan 6:7 [b]Job 5:19; Ps 37:39, 40; Is 41:10; Dan 3:17, 28; 6:20; 2 Cor 1:10 **17** [a]Lam 3:53; Matt 27:66 **18** [a]2 Sam 12:16, 17 [b]Esth 6:1; Ps 77:4; Dan 2:1 **20** [a]Dan 6:16, 27 [b]Gen 18:14; Num 11:23; Jer 32:17; Dan 3:17 **21** [1]Lit *with* [a]Dan 2:4; 6:6 **22** [a]Num 20:16; Is 63:9; Dan 3:28; Acts 12:11; Heb 1:14 [b]Ps 91:11-13; 2 Tim 4:17; Heb 11:33

5:31 *Darius the Mede.* Perhaps another name for Gubaru, referred to in Babylonian inscriptions as the governor that Cyrus put in charge of the newly conquered Babylonian territories. Or "Darius the Mede" may have been Cyrus's throne name in Babylon (see 6:28, which can be read, "in the reign of Darius, that is, the reign of Cyrus the Persian"; see also 1 Chr 5:26 for a similar phenomenon). *received the kingdom.* The head of gold is now no more, as predicted in 2:39.

6:7 The conspirators lied in stating that "all" the royal administrators supported the proposed decree, since they knew that Daniel (totally unaware of the proposal) was the foremost of the three administrators.

6:8,12 *may not be revoked.* See notes on Esth 1:19; 8:8.

6:10 *toward Jerusalem.* See 2 Chr 6:38–39. *three times a day.* See Ps 55:17.

6:16 *constantly serve.* See 1 Cor 15:58.

lions' mouths and they have not harmed me,
inasmuch as [1]I was found innocent before
Him; and also [2]toward you, O king, I have
committed no crime."
23 Then the king was very pleased and
gave orders for Daniel to be taken up out of
the den. So Daniel was taken up out of the
den and [a]no injury whatever was found on
him, because he had [b]trusted in his God.
24 The king then gave orders, and they
brought those men who had [1]maliciously
accused Daniel, and they [a]cast them, their
[b]children and their wives into the lions' den;
and they had not reached the bottom of the
den before the lions overpowered them and
crushed all their bones.
25 Then Darius the king wrote to all the
[a]peoples, nations and *men of every* [1]lan-
guage who were living in all the land: "[b]May
your [2]peace abound!
26 "[1]I [a]make a decree that in all the dominion of my kingdom men are to fear and
tremble before the God of Daniel;

For He is the [b]living God and
[c]enduring forever,
And [d]His kingdom is one which will
not be destroyed,
And His dominion *will be* [2]forever.
27 "He delivers and rescues and performs
[a]signs and wonders
In heaven and on earth,
Who has *also* delivered Daniel from
the [1]power of the lions."

28 So this [a]Daniel enjoyed success in the
reign of Darius and in the reign of [b]Cyrus the
Persian.

Vision of the Four Beasts

7 In the first year of Belshazzar king of
Babylon Daniel saw a [a]dream and visions
[1]in his mind *as he lay* on his bed; then he
[b]wrote the dream down *and* related the [2]*following* summary of [3]it.
2 Daniel [1]said, "I was [a]looking in my
vision by night, and behold, the [b]four winds
of heaven were stirring up the great sea.
3 "And four great [a]beasts were coming up
from the sea, different from one another.
4 "The first *was* [a]like a lion and had *the*
wings of an eagle. I kept looking until its
wings were plucked, and it was lifted up from
the ground and made to stand on two feet like
a man; a human [1]mind also was given to it.
5 "And behold, another beast, a second
one, resembling a bear. And it was raised up
on one side, and three ribs *were* in its mouth
between its teeth; and thus they said to it,
'Arise, devour much meat!'
6 "After this I kept looking, and behold,
another one, [a]like a leopard, which had on its
[1]back four wings of a bird; the beast also had
[b]four heads, and dominion was given to it.
7 "After this I kept looking in the night
visions, and behold, a [a]fourth beast, dreadful
and terrifying and extremely strong; and it
had large iron teeth. It devoured and crushed
and trampled down the remainder with its
feet; and it was different from all the beasts
that were before it, and it had [b]ten horns.
8 "While I was contemplating the horns,
behold, [a]another horn, a little one, came up
among them, and three of the first horns
were pulled out by the roots before it; and
behold, [1]this horn possessed eyes like the
eyes of a man and [b]a mouth uttering great
boasts.

The Ancient of Days Reigns

9 "I kept looking
Until [a]thrones were set up,
And the Ancient of Days took *His* seat;
His [b]vesture *was* like white snow
And the [c]hair of His head like pure
wool.
His [d]throne *was* [1]ablaze with flames,
Its [e]wheels *were* a burning fire.
10 "A river of [a]fire was flowing
And coming out from before Him;
[b]Thousands upon thousands were
attending Him,

22 [1]Lit *innocence was found for me* [2]Lit *before*
23 [a]Dan 3:25, 27 [b]1 Chr 5:20; 2 Chr 20:20; Ps 118:8, 9; Is 26:3; Dan 3:17, 28
24 [1]Lit *eaten the pieces of Daniel* [a]Deut 19:18, 19; Esth 7:10 [b]Deut 24:16; 2 Kin 14:6; Esth 9:10
25 [1]Lit *tongue* [2]Or *welfare* or *prosperity* [a]Ezra 1:1, 2; Esth 3:12; 8:9; Dan 4:1 [b]Ezra 4:17; 1 Pet 1:2
26 [1]Lit *From me a decree is made* [2]Lit *to the end* [a]Ezra 6:8-12; 7:13, 21; Dan 3:29 [b]Dan 4:34; 6:20; Hos 1:10; Rom 9:26 [c]Ps 93:1, 2; Mal 3:6 [d]Dan 2:44; 4:3; 7:14, 27; Luke 1:33
27 [1]Lit *hand* [a]Dan 4:2, 3
28 [a]Dan 1:21 [b]2 Chr 36:22, 23; Dan 10:1
7:1 [1]Lit *of his head* [2]Or *beginning* [3]Lit *words* [a]Job 33:14-16; Dan 1:17; 2:1, 26-28; 4:5-9; Joel 2:28 [b]Jer 36:4, 32
2 [1]Lit *spoke and said* [a]Dan 7:7, 13 [b]Rev 7:1
3 [a]Dan 7:17; Rev 13:1; 17:8
4 [1]Lit *heart* [a]Jer 4:7
6 [1]Or *sides* [a]Rev 13:2 [b]Dan 8:22
7 [a]Dan 7:19, 20, 23 [b]Rev 12:3; 13:1
8 [1]Lit *in this horn were eyes* [a]Dan 8:9 [b]Rev 13:5, 6
9 [1]Lit *flames of fire* [a]Rev 20:4 [b]Mark 9:3 [c]Rev 1:14 [d]Ezek 1:13, 26 [e]Ezek 10:2, 6
10 [a]Ps 18:8; 50:3; 97:3; Is 30:27, 33 [b]Deut 33:2; 1 Kin 22:19; Rev 5:11

6:23 *he . . . trusted in his God.* That the lions were ravenously hungry (v. 24) was no obstacle to the Lord's rewarding Daniel's faith by saving his life.

6:24 *them, their children and their wives.* In accordance with Persian custom.

7:1 *first year of Belshazzar.* Probably 553 B.C. The events of ch. 7 preceded those of ch. 5.

7:2 *the great sea.* The world of nations and peoples (see also vv. 3,17).

7:3 *beasts.* The insignia or symbols of many Gentile nations were beasts (or birds) of prey (see v. 17).

7:4–7 The lion with an eagle's wings is a cherub (see note on Gen 3:24), symbolizing the Neo-Babylonian empire. The rest of v. 4 perhaps reflects the humbling experience of Nebuchadnezzar, as recorded in ch. 4. The bear (v. 5), raised up on one of its sides, refers to the superior status of the Persians in the Medo-Persian federation. The three ribs may represent the three principal conquests: Lydia (546 B.C.), Babylon (539) and Egypt (525). The leopard with four wings (v. 6) represents the speedy conquests of Alexander the Great (334–330), and the four heads correspond to the four main divisions into which his empire fell after his untimely death in 323 (see 8:22): Macedon and Greece (under Antipater and Cassander), Thrace and Asia Minor (under Lysimachus), Syria (under Seleucus I), the Holy Land and Egypt (under Ptolemy I). The fourth, unnamed, beast (v. 7), with its irresistible power and surpassing all its predecessors, points to the Roman empire. Its ten horns correspond to the ten toes of 2:41–42.

7:7 *ten horns.* Indicative of the comprehensiveness of the beast's sphere of authority (see note on 1:12).

7:8 *another horn, a little one.* The antichrist, or a world power sharing in the characteristics of the antichrist. *mouth uttering great boasts.* See 11:36; 2 Thess 2:4; Rev 13:5–6.

7:9 *Ancient of Days.* God. *throne . . . wheels.* See Ezek 1:15–21, 26–27.

7:10 *Thousands . . . myriads.* See 1 Sam 18:7 and note.

And myriads upon myriads were
standing before Him;
The [c]court sat,
And [d]the books were opened.

11 "Then I kept looking because of the
sound of the [1]boastful words which the horn
was speaking; I kept looking until the beast
was slain, and its body was destroyed and
given to the [a]burning [2]fire.
12 "As for the rest of the beasts, their
dominion was taken away, but an extension
of life was granted to them for an appointed
period of time.

The Son of Man Presented

13 "I kept looking in the night visions,
And behold, with the clouds of
heaven
One like a [a]Son of Man was coming,
And He came up to the Ancient of
Days
And was presented before Him.
14 "And to Him was given [a]dominion,
Glory and [1b]a kingdom,
[c]That all the peoples, nations and *men
of every* [2]language
Might serve Him.
[d]His dominion is an everlasting
dominion
Which will not pass away;
[e]And His kingdom is one
Which will not be destroyed.

The Vision Interpreted

15 "As for me, Daniel, my spirit was distressed [1]within me, and the [a]visions [2]in my
mind kept [b]alarming me.
16 "I approached one of those who were
[a]standing by and began asking him the
[1]exact meaning of all this. So he [b]told me
and made known to me the interpretation of
these things:
17 'These great beasts, which are four *in
number,* are four kings *who* will arise from
the earth.

10 [c]Ps 96:11-13; Dan 7:22, 26 [d]Dan 12:1; Rev 20:11-15
11 [1]Lit *great* [2]Lit *of the fire* [a]Rev 19:20; 20:10
13 [a]Matt 24:30; 26:64; Mark 13:26; 14:62; Luke 21:27; Rev 1:7, 13; 14:14
14 [a]Dan 7:27; John 3:35; 1 Cor 15:27; Eph 1:20-22; Phil 2:9-11; Rev 1:6; 11:15
14 [1]Or *sovereignty* [2]Lit *tongue* [b]Dan 2:37 [c]Ps 72:11; 102:22 [d]Mic 4:7; Luke 1:33 [e]Heb 12:28
15 [1]Lit *in the midst of* its *sheath* [2]Lit *of my head* [a]Dan 7:1 [b]Dan 4:19; 7:28
16 [1]Lit *truth concerning* [a]Zech 1:9, 19; Rev 5:5; 7:13, 14 [b]Dan 8:16, 17; 9:22

7:13 *like a Son of Man.* See Rev 1:13. This is the first reference to the Messiah as the Son of Man, a title that Jesus applied to Himself. He will be enthroned as ruler over the whole earth (previously misruled by the four kingdoms of men), and His kingdom "will not be destroyed" (v. 14), whether on earth or in heaven. *with the clouds of heaven . . . was coming.* See Mark 14:62; Rev 1:7.
7:16 *one of those . . . standing by.* An angel.

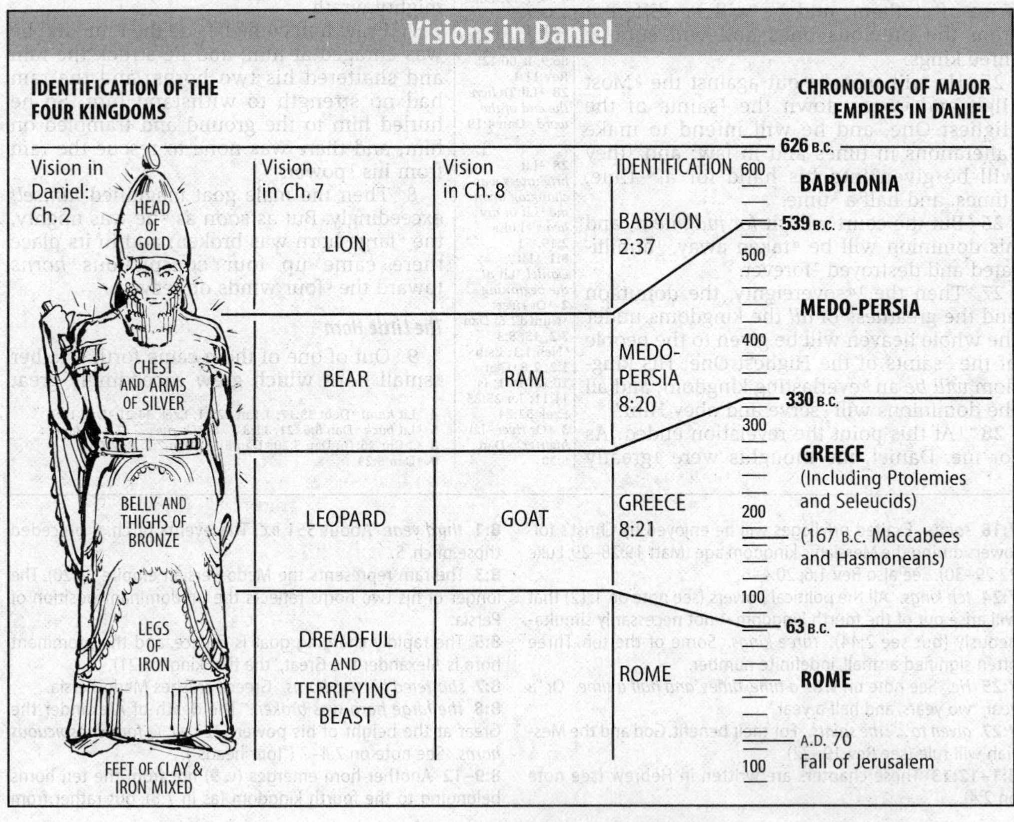

Visions in Daniel
IDENTIFICATION OF THE FOUR KINGDOMS
Vision in Daniel: Ch. 2
Vision in Ch. 7
Vision in Ch. 8
IDENTIFICATION
HEAD OF GOLD
LION
BABYLON 2:37
CHEST AND ARMS OF SILVER
BEAR
RAM
MEDO-PERSIA 8:20
BELLY AND THIGHS OF BRONZE
LEOPARD
GOAT
GREECE 8:21
LEGS OF IRON
DREADFUL AND TERRIFYING BEAST
ROME
FEET OF CLAY & IRON MIXED
CHRONOLOGY OF MAJOR EMPIRES IN DANIEL
626 B.C.
600
BABYLONIA
539 B.C.
500
MEDO-PERSIA
400
330 B.C.
300
GREECE
(Including Ptolemies and Seleucids)
200
(167 B.C. Maccabees and Hasmoneans)
100
63 B.C.
ROME
A.D. 70
100
Fall of Jerusalem

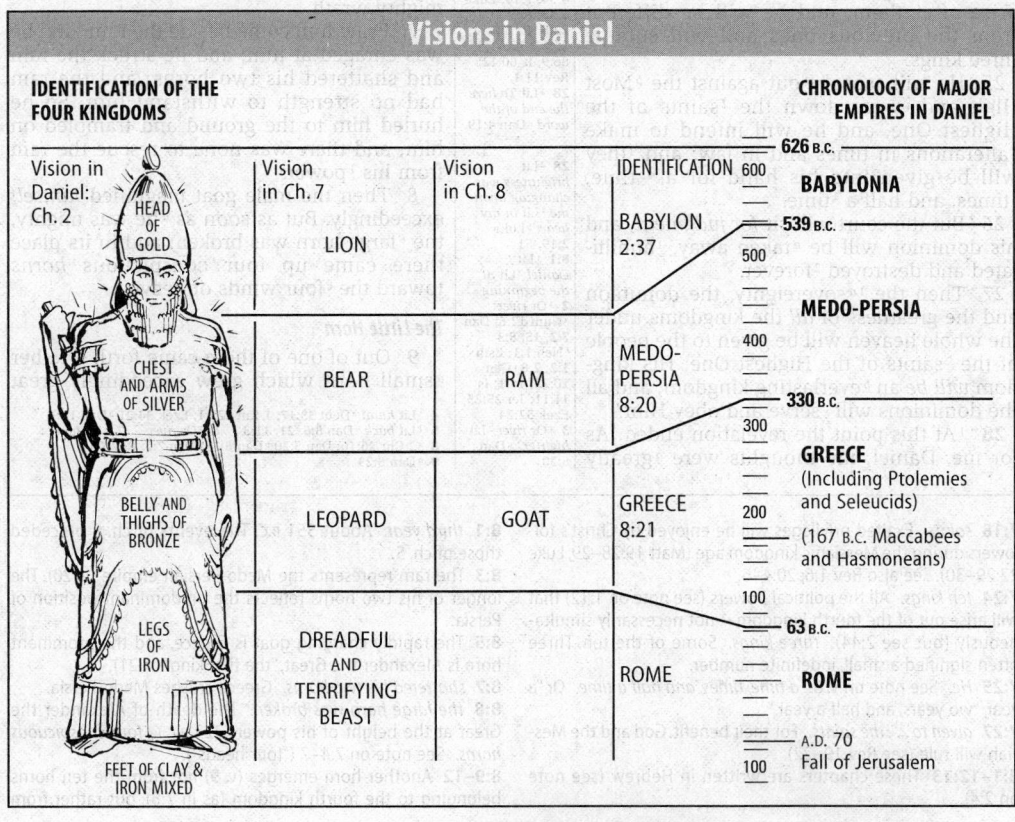

18 ‘But the [1][a]saints of the Highest One will
[b]receive the kingdom and possess the kingdom forever, [2]for all ages to come.’
19 “Then I desired to know the [1]exact
meaning of the [a]fourth beast, which was
different from all [2]the others, exceedingly
dreadful, with its teeth of iron and its claws
of bronze, *and which* devoured, crushed
and trampled down the remainder with its
feet,
20 and *the meaning* of the ten horns that
were on its head and the other *horn* which
came up, and before which three *of them*
fell, namely, that horn which had eyes and a
mouth uttering great *boasts* and [1]which was
larger in appearance than its associates.
21 “I kept looking, and that horn was [a]wag-
ing war with the [1]saints and overpowering
them
22 until the Ancient of Days came and
[a]judgment was [1]passed in favor of the
[2]saints of the Highest One, and the time
arrived when the [2]saints took possession of
the kingdom.
23 “Thus he said: ‘The fourth beast will be
a fourth kingdom on the earth, which will be
different from all the *other* kingdoms and
will devour the whole earth and tread it
down and crush it.
24 ‘As for the [a]ten horns, out of this kingdom ten kings will arise; and another will
arise after them, and he will be different
from the previous ones and will subdue
three kings.
25 ‘He will [a]speak [1]out against the [b]Most
High and [c]wear down the [2]saints of the
Highest One, and he will intend to make
[d]alterations in times and in law; and [3]they
will be given into his hand for a [4][e]time,
[4]times, and half a [4]time.
26 ‘But the court will sit *for judgment*, and
his dominion will be [a]taken away, [1]annihi-
lated and destroyed [2]forever.
27 ‘Then the [1][a]sovereignty, the dominion
and the greatness of *all* the kingdoms under
the whole heaven will be given to the people
of the [2]saints of the Highest One; His kingdom *will be* an [b]everlasting kingdom, and all
the dominions will [c]serve and obey Him.’
28 “[1]At this point the revelation ended. As
for me, Daniel, my thoughts were [a]greatly
alarming me and my [2]face grew pale, but I
[b]kept the matter [3]to myself.”

Vision of the Ram and Goat

8 In the third year of the reign of Belshazzar the king a vision appeared to me,
[1]Daniel, subsequent to the one which
appeared to me [2]previously.
2 I [a]looked in the vision, and while I was
looking I was in the citadel of [b]Susa, which
is in the province of [c]Elam; and I looked in
the vision and I myself was beside the Ulai
[1]Canal.
3 Then I lifted my eyes and looked, and
behold, a [a]ram which had two horns was
standing in front of the [1]canal. Now the two
horns *were* [2]long, but one *was* [2]longer than
the other, with the [2]longer one coming up last.
4 I saw the ram [a]butting westward,
northward, and southward, and no *other*
beasts could stand before him nor was there
anyone to rescue from his [1]power, but [b]he
did as he pleased and magnified *himself*.
5 While I was observing, behold, a male
goat was coming from the west over the surface of the whole earth without touching the
ground; and the [1]goat *had* a [a]conspicuous
horn between his eyes.
6 He came up to the ram that had the
two horns, which I had seen standing in
front of the [1]canal, and rushed at him in his
mighty wrath.
7 I saw him come beside the ram, and he
was enraged at him; and he struck the ram
and shattered his two horns, and the ram
had no strength to withstand him. So he
hurled him to the ground and trampled on
him, and there was none to rescue the ram
from his [1]power.
8 Then the male goat magnified *himself*
exceedingly. But as soon as [a]he was mighty,
the [b]large horn was broken; and in its place
there came up four conspicuous *horns*
toward the [c]four winds of heaven.

The Little Horn

9 Out of one of them came forth a rather
[a]small horn which grew exceedingly great

18 [1]Lit *holy ones* [2]Lit *and unto the age of the ages* [a]Dan 7:22, 25, 27 [b]Ps 149:5-9; Is 60:12-14; Dan 7:14; Rev 2:26, 27; 20:4; 22:5
19 [1]Lit *truth concerning* [2]Lit *of them* [a]Dan 7:7, 8
20 [1]Lit *its appearance was larger*
21 [1]Lit *holy ones* [a]Rev 11:7; 13:7
22 [1]Lit *given for* [2]Lit *holy ones* [a]Dan 7:10; 1 Cor 6:2, 3
24 [a]Dan 7:7; Rev 17:12
25 [1]Lit *words* [2]Lit *holy ones* [3]I.e. the saints [4]I.e. year(s) [a]Dan 11:36; Rev 13:6 [b]Dan 3:26; 4:2, 17, 34 [c]Rev 13:7; 18:24 [d]Dan 2:21 [e]Dan 12:7; Rev 12:14
26 [1]Lit *to annihilate and to destroy* [2]Lit *to the end* [a]Rev 17:14; 19:2
27 [1]Or *kingdom* [2]Lit *holy ones* [a]Is 54:3; Dan 7:14, 18, 22; Rev 20:4 [b]Ps 145:13; Is 9:7; Dan 2:44; 4:34; 7:14; Luke 1:33; Rev 11:15; 22:5 [c]Ps 2:6-12; 22:27; 72:11; 86:9; Is 60:12; Rev 11:1
28 [1]Lit *To here the end of the word* [a]Dan 4:19

28 [2]Lit *brightness was changing upon me* [3]Lit *in my heart* [b]Luke 2:19, 51
8:1 [1]Lit *I, Daniel* [2]Lit *at the beginning*
2 [1]Or *river* [a]Num 12:6; Dan 7:2, 15; 8:3 [b]Neh 1:1; Esth 1:2; 2:8 [c]Gen 10:22; 14:1; Is 11:11; Jer 25:25; Ezek 32:24
3 [1]Or *river* [2]Lit *high(er)* [a]Dan 8:20

4 [1]Lit *hand* [a]Deut 33:17; 1 Kin 22:11; Ezek 34:21 [b]Dan 11:3
5 [1]Lit *buck* [a]Dan 8:8, 21; 11:3 **6** [1]Or *river* **7** [1]Lit *hand*
8 [a]2 Chr 26:16; Dan 5:20 [b]Dan 8:22 [c]Dan 7:2; Rev 7:1
9 [a]Dan 8:23

7:18 *saints.* Exalted privileges will be enjoyed by Christ’s followers during the Messianic kingdom age (Matt 19:28–29; Luke 22:29–30). See also Rev 1:6; 20:4–6.

7:24 *ten kings.* All the political powers (see note on 1:12) that will arise out of the fourth kingdom—not necessarily simultaneously (but see 2:44). *three kings.* Some of the ten. Three often signified a small, indefinite number.

7:25 *He.* See note on v. 8. *a time, times, and half a time.* Or “a year, two years, and half a year.”

7:27 *given to . . . the saints.* For their benefit. God and the Messiah will rule (see Rev 19–22).

8:1–12:13 These chapters are written in Hebrew (see note on 2:4).

8:1 *third year.* About 551 B.C. The events of ch. 8 preceded those of ch. 5.

8:3 The ram represents the Medo-Persian empire (v. 20). The longer of his two horns reflects the predominant position of Persia.

8:5 The rapidly charging goat is Greece, and the prominent horn is Alexander the Great, “the first king” (v. 21).

8:7 *shattered his two horns.* Greece crushes Medo-Persia.

8:8 *the large horn was broken.* The death of Alexander the Great at the height of his power (323 B.C.). *four conspicuous horns.* See note on 7:4–7 (“four heads”).

8:9–12 Another horn emerges (v. 9) not from the ten horns belonging to the fourth kingdom (as in 7:8), but rather from

toward the south, toward the east, and toward the [1b]Beautiful *Land.*

10 It grew up to the host of heaven and caused some of the host and some of the [a]stars to fall to the earth, and it [b]trampled them down.

11 It even [a]magnified *itself* [1]to be equal with the [2]Commander of the host; and it removed the [b]regular sacrifice from Him, and the place of His sanctuary was thrown down.

12 And on account of transgression the host will be given over *to the horn* along with the regular sacrifice; and it will [a]fling truth to the ground and perform *its will* and prosper.

13 Then I heard a [a]holy one speaking, and another holy one said to that particular one who was speaking, "[b]How long will the vision *about* the regular sacrifice apply, [1]while the transgression causes horror, so as to allow both the holy place and the host [2]to be [c]trampled?"

14 He said to me, "For [a]2,300 evenings *and* mornings; then the holy place will be [1]properly restored."

Interpretation of the Vision

15 When [a]I, Daniel, had seen the vision, I sought [1]to understand it; and behold, standing before me was one [2]who looked like a [b]man.

16 And I heard the voice of a man between *the banks of* Ulai, and he called out and said, "[a]Gabriel, give this *man* an understanding of the vision."

17 So he came near to where I was standing, and when he came I was frightened and [a]fell on my face; but he said to me, "Son of man, understand that the vision pertains to the [b]time of the end."

18 Now while he was talking with me, I [a]sank into a deep sleep with my face to the ground; but he [b]touched me and made me stand [1]upright.

19 He said, "Behold, I am going to [a]let you know what will occur at the final period of the indignation, for *it* pertains to the appointed time of the end.

The Ram's Identity

20 "The [a]ram which you saw with the two horns represents the kings of Media and Persia.

The Goat

21 "The shaggy [1]goat *represents* the [2]kingdom of Greece, and the large horn that is between his eyes is the first king.

22 "The [a]broken *horn* and the four *horns that* arose in its place *represent* four kingdoms *which* will arise from *his* nation, although not with his power.

23 "In the latter period of their [1]rule,
When the transgressors have [2]run *their course,*
A king will arise,
[3]Insolent and skilled in [4]intrigue.

24 "His power will be mighty, but not by his *own* power,
And he will [1a]destroy to an extraordinary degree
And prosper and perform *his will;*
He will [1]destroy mighty men and [2]the holy people.

25 "And through his shrewdness
He will cause deceit to succeed by his [1]influence;
And he will magnify *himself* in his heart,
And he will [2]destroy many while *they are* [3]at ease.
He will even [4a]oppose the Prince of princes,
But he will be broken [b]without [1]human agency.

26 "The vision of the evenings and mornings
Which has been told is [a]true;
But [b]keep the vision secret,
For *it* pertains to many [c]days *in the future.*"

27 Then I, Daniel, was [1a]exhausted and

9 [1]I.e. Palestine [b]Ps 48:2; Dan 11:16, 41 **10** [a]Is 14:13; Jer 48:26; Rev 12:4 [b]Dan 7:7; 8:7 **11** [1]Lit *up to the* [2]Or *Prince* [a]2 Kin 19:22, 23; 2 Chr 32:15-17; Is 37:23; Dan 8:25; 11:36, 37 [b]Ezek 46:14; Dan 11:31; 12:11 **12** [a]Is 59:14 **13** [1]Or possibly *and the transgression that horrifies* [2]Lit *as a trampling* [a]Dan 4:13, 23; 1 Pet 1:12 [b]Ps 74:10; 79:5; Is 6:11; Dan 12:6, 8; Rev 6:10 [c]Is 63:18; Jer 12:10; Luke 21:24; Heb 10:29; Rev 11:2 **14** [1]Lit *vindicated* [a]Dan 7:25; 12:7, 11; Rev 11:2, 3; 12:14; 13:5 **15** [1]Lit *understanding* [2]Lit *like the appearance of a man* [a]Dan 8:1 [b]Dan 7:13; 10:16, 18 **16** [a]Dan 9:21; Luke 1:19, 26 **17** [a]Ezek 1:28; 44:4; Dan 2:46; Rev 1:17 [b]Dan 8:19; 11:35, 40 **18** [1]Lit *on my standing* [a]Dan 10:9; Luke 9:32 [b]Ezek 2:2; Dan 10:10, 16, 18 **19** [a]Dan 8:15-17

20 [a]Dan 8:3 **21** [1]Lit *buck* [2]Lit *king* **22** [a]Dan 8:8 **23** [1]Or *kingdom* [2]Lit *finished* [3]Lit *Strong of face* [4]Or *ambiguous speech* **24** [1]Or *corrupt* [2]Lit *people of the saints* [a]Dan 8:11-13; 11:36; 12:7

25 [1]Lit *hand* [2]Or *corrupt* [3]Or *secure* [4]Lit *stand against* [a]Dan 8:11 [b]Job 34:20; Dan 2:34, 45 **26** [a]Dan 10:1 [b]Ezek 12:27; Dan 12:4, 9; Rev 22:10 [c]Dan 10:14 **27** [1]Or *done in* [a]Dan 7:28; 8:17; Hab 3:16

one of the four horns belonging to the third kingdom. This "rather small horn" is Antiochus IV Epiphanes, who during the last few years of his reign (168–164 B.C.) made a determined effort to destroy the Jewish faith. He in turn served as a type of the even more ruthless beast of the last days, who is also referred to in 7:8 as "another horn, a little one." Antiochus was to extend his power over Israel, "the Beautiful Land" (v. 9; see Jer 3:19), and defeat the godly believers there (referred to as "the host of heaven," v. 10; see also v. 12), many of whom died for their faith. Then he set himself up to be the equal of God ("the Commander of the host," v. 11) and ordered the daily sacrifices to end. Eventually the army of Judas Maccabeus recaptured Jerusalem and rededicated the temple (v. 14) to the Lord (December, 165)—the origin of the Feast of Hanukkah (see John 10:22), still celebrated by Jews today (in the Apocrypha see 1 Maccabees 1–4).

8:13 *a holy one.* An angel.

8:14 There were two daily sacrifices for the continual burnt offering (9:21; Ex 29:38–42), representing the atonement required for Israel as a whole. The 2,300 evenings and mornings probably refer to the number of sacrifices consecutively offered on 1,150 days, the interval between the desecration of the Lord's altar and its reconsecration by Judas Maccabeus on Kislev 25, 165 B.C. The pagan altar set up by Antiochus on Kislev 25, 168, was apparently installed almost two months after the Lord's altar was removed, accounting for the difference between 1,095 days (an exact three years) and the 1,150 specified here.

8:17 *Son of man.* See note on Ezek 2:1.

8:23–25 A description of Antiochus IV and his rise to power by intrigue and deceit (he was not the rightful successor to the Seleucid throne).

8:25 *Prince of princes.* God. *broken without human agency.* Antiochus died in 164 B.C. at Tabae in Persia through illness or accident; God "broke" him.

sick for days. Then I got up *again* and [b]carried on the king's business; but I was astounded at the vision, and there was none to [2]explain *it.*

Daniel's Prayer for His People

9 In the first year of [a]Darius the son of Ahasuerus, of Median descent, who was made
king over the kingdom of the Chaldeans—
2 in the first year of his reign, I, Daniel,
observed in the books the number of the
years which was *revealed as* the word of the
LORD to [a]Jeremiah the prophet for the completion of the desolations of Jerusalem,
namely, [a]seventy years.
3 So I [1]gave my attention to the Lord God
to seek *Him by* prayer and supplications,
with fasting, sackcloth and ashes.
4 I prayed to the LORD my God and confessed and said, "Alas, O Lord, the [a]great and
awesome God, who [b]keeps His covenant and
lovingkindness for those who love Him and
keep His commandments,
5 [a]we have sinned, committed iniquity,
acted wickedly and [b]rebelled, even [c]turning
aside from Your commandments and ordinances.
6 "Moreover, we have not [a]listened to
Your servants the prophets, who spoke in
Your name to our kings, our princes, our
fathers and all the people of the land.
7 "[a]Righteousness belongs to You, O Lord,
but to us [1b]open shame, as it is this day—to
the men of Judah, the inhabitants of Jerusalem and all Israel, those who are nearby
and those who are far away in [c]all the countries to which You have driven them,
because of their unfaithful deeds which they
have committed against You.
8 "[1]Open shame belongs to us, O Lord, to
our kings, our princes and our fathers,
because we have sinned against You.
9 "To the Lord our God *belong* [a]compas-
sion and forgiveness, [1]for we have [b]rebelled
against Him;
10 nor have we obeyed the voice of the
LORD our God, to walk in His [1]teachings
which He [a]set before us through His servants
the prophets.
11 "Indeed [a]all Israel has transgressed Your
law and turned aside, not obeying Your
voice; so the [b]curse has been poured out on
us, along with the oath which is written in
the law of Moses the servant of God, for we
have sinned against Him.
12 "Thus He has [a]confirmed His words
which He had spoken against us and against
our [1b]rulers who ruled us, to bring on us
great calamity; for under the whole heaven
there has [c]not been done *anything* like what
was done to Jerusalem.
13 "As it is written in the [a]law of Moses, all
this calamity has come on us; yet we have
[b]not [1]sought the favor of the LORD our God
by [c]turning from our iniquity and [2]giving
attention to Your truth.
14 "Therefore the LORD has [1a]kept the
calamity in store and brought it on us; for
the LORD our God is [b]righteous with respect
to all His deeds which He has done, but we
have not obeyed His voice.
15 "And now, O Lord our God, who have
[a]brought Your people out of the land of
Egypt with a mighty hand and have [b]made a
name for Yourself, as it is this day—we have
sinned, we have been wicked.
16 "O Lord, in accordance with all Your
[1]righteous acts, let now Your [a]anger and
Your wrath turn away from Your city
Jerusalem, Your [b]holy mountain; for because
of our sins and the iniquities of our fathers,
Jerusalem and Your people *have become* a
[c]reproach to all those around us.
17 "So now, our God, listen to the prayer of
Your servant and to his supplications, and
for [1]Your sake, O Lord, [a]let Your face shine
on Your [b]desolate sanctuary.
18 "O my God, [a]incline Your ear and hear!
Open Your eyes and [b]see our desolations and
the city which is [c]called by Your name; for
we are not [1d]presenting our supplications
before You on account of [2]any merits of our
own, but on account of Your great compassion.
19 "O Lord, hear! O Lord, forgive! O Lord,
listen and take action! For Your own sake, O
my God, [a]do not delay, because Your city
and Your people are called by Your name."

Gabriel Brings an Answer

20 Now while I was [a]speaking and praying, and [b]confessing my sin and the sin of
my people Israel, and [1]presenting my supplication before the LORD my God in behalf of
the holy mountain of my God,
21 while I was still speaking in prayer,
then the man [a]Gabriel, whom I had seen in
the vision [1]previously, [2]came to me [3]in *my*
extreme weariness about the time of the
[b]evening offering.
22 He gave *me* instruction and talked with
me and said, "O Daniel, I have now come
forth to give you insight with [a]understanding.

27 [2]Lit *make me understand* [b]Dan 2:48
9:1 [a]Dan 5:31; 11:1
2 [a]2 Chr 36:21; Ezra 1:1; Jer 25:11, 12; 29:10; Zech 7:5
3 [1]Lit *set my face*
4 [a]Deut 7:21; Neh 9:32 [b]Deut 7:9
5 [a]1 Kin 8:48; Neh 9:33; Ps 106:6; Is 64:5-7; Jer 14:7 [b]Lam 1:18, 20 [c]Ps 119:176; Is 53:6; Dan 9:11
6 [a]2 Chr 36:16; Jer 44:4, 5
7 [1]Lit *the shame of face* [a]Jer 23:6; 33:16; Dan 9:18 [b]Ps 44:15; Jer 2:26, 27; 3:25 [c]Deut 4:27
8 [1]Lit *The shame of face*
9 [1]Or *though* [a]Neh 9:17; Ps 130:4 [b]Ps 106:43; Jer 14:7; Dan 9:5, 6
10 [1]Or *laws* [a]2 Kin 17:13-15; 18:12
11 [a]Is 1:3, 4; Jer 8:5-10 [b]Deut 27:15-26
12 [1]Lit *judges who judged us* [a]Is 44:26; Jer 44:2-6; Lam 2:17; Zech 1:6 [b]Job 12:17; Ps 82:2-7; 148:11
12 [c]Lam 1:12; 2:13; Ezek 5:9
13 [1]Lit *softened the face of* [2]Or *having insight into* [a]Lev 26:14-45; Deut 28:15-68; Dan 9:11 [b]Job 36:13; Is 9:13; Jer 2:30; 5:3 [c]Jer 31:18
14 [1]Lit *watched over the evil* [a]Jer 31:28; 44:27 [b]Ps 51:14; Dan 9:7
15 [a]Deut 5:15 [b]Neh 9:10; Jer 32:20
16 [1]Lit *righteousnesses* [a]Jer 32:31, 32 [b]Ps 87:1-3; Dan 9:20; Joel 3:17; Zech 8:3 [c]Ezek 5:14
17 [1]Lit *the sake of the Lord* [a]Num 6:24-26; Ps 80:3, 7, 19 [b]Lam 5:18
18 [1]Lit *causing to fall* [2]Lit *our righteousnesses* [a]Is 37:17 [b]Ps 80:14 [c]Jer 7:10-12 [d]Jer 36:7
19 [a]Ps 44:23; 74:10, 11
20 [1]Lit *causing to fall* [a]Ps 145:18; Is 58:9; Dan 9:3; 10:12 [b]Is 6:5
21 [1]Lit *at the beginning* [2]Lit *was reaching;* or *touching* [3]Lit *wearied with weariness* [a]Dan 8:16; Luke 1:19, 26 [b]Ex 29:39; 1 Kin 18:36; Ezra 9:4
22 [a]Dan 8:16; 10:21; Zech 1:9

9:1 *first year.* 539–538 B.C. *Ahasuerus.* Or "Xerxes"; not the Ahasuerus (Xerxes) of the book of Esther.
9:2 *Jeremiah . . . seventy years.* See note on Jer 25:11–12.
9:3–19 Daniel's prayer contains humility (v. 3), worship (v. 4), confession (vv. 5–15) and petition (vv. 16–19).
9:3 *sackcloth and ashes.* See note on Gen 37:34.
9:11 *curse . . . written in the law.* See Lev 26:33; Deut 28:63–67.
9:18 *on account of Your great compassion.* God answers prayer because of His grace, not because of our works.
9:20 *while I was speaking.* See Is 65:24.

23 "At the [a]beginning of your supplications
the [1]command was issued, and I have come
to tell *you,* for you are [2b]highly esteemed; so
give heed to the message and gain [c]under-
standing of the vision.

Seventy Weeks and the Messiah

24 "Seventy [1a]weeks have been decreed for
your people and your holy city, to [2]finish the
transgression, to [3]make an end of sin, to
[b]make atonement for iniquity, to bring in
[c]everlasting righteousness, to seal up vision
and [4]prophecy and to anoint the most holy
place.
25 "So you are to know and discern *that*
from the issuing of a [1a]decree to restore
and rebuild Jerusalem until [2b]Messiah the
[c]Prince *there will be* seven weeks and sixty-
two weeks; it will be built again, with [3]plaza
and moat, even in times of distress.
26 "Then after the sixty-two weeks the
[1]Messiah will be [a]cut off and have [2]nothing,
and the people of the prince who is to come
will [b]destroy the city and the sanctuary. And
[3]its end *will come* with a [c]flood; even to the
end [4]there will be war; desolations are determined.
27 "And he will make a firm covenant with
the many for one week, but in the middle of
the week he will put a stop to sacrifice and
grain offering; and on the wing of [1a]abomi-
nations *will come* one who [2]makes desolate,
even until a [b]complete destruction, one that
is decreed, is poured out on the one who
[2]makes desolate."

Daniel Is Terrified by a Vision

10 In the third year of [a]Cyrus king of Persia a [1]message was revealed to [b]Daniel,
who was named Belteshazzar; and the
[1c]message was true and *one of* great [2]con-
flict, but he understood the [1]message and
had an [d]understanding of the vision.

23 [1]Lit *word went out* [2]Lit *desirable;* or *precious* [a]Dan 10:12 [b]Dan 10:11, 19 [c]Matt 24:15
24 [1]Or *units of seven,* and so throughout the ch [2]Or *restrain* [3]Another reading is *seal up sins* [4]Lit *prophet* [a]Lev 25:8; Num 14:34; Ezek 4:5, 6 [b]2 Chr 29:24; Is 53:10; Rom 5:10 [c]Is 51:6, 8; 56:1; Jer 23:5, 6; Rom 3:21, 22
25 [1]Lit *word* [2]Or *an anointed one* [3]Or *streets* [a]Ezra 4:24; 6:1-15; Neh 2:1-8; 3:1 [b]John 1:41; 4:25 [c]Is 9:6; Dan 8:11, 25
26 [1]Or *anointed one* [2]Or *no one* [3]Or *his* [4]Or *war will be decreed for desolations* [a]Is 53:8; Mark 9:12; Luke 24:26 [b]Matt 24:2; Mark 13:2; Luke 19:43, 44 [c]Nah 1:8
27 [1]Or *detestable things* [2]Or *causes horror* [a]Dan 11:31; Matt 24:15; Mark 13:14; Luke 21:20 [b]Is 10:23; 28:22
10:1 [1]Lit *word* [2]Or *warfare* [a]Dan 1:21; 6:28 [b]Dan 1:7 [c]Dan 8:26 [d]Dan 1:17; 2:21
2 [a]Ezra 9:4, 5; Neh 1:4
3 [1]Lit *bread of desirability* [a]Dan 6:18
4 [1]Heb *Hiddekel* [a]Ezek 1:3; Dan 8:2

2 In those days, I, Daniel, had been
[a]mourning for three entire weeks.
3 I [a]did not eat any [1]tasty food, nor did
meat or wine enter my mouth, nor did I use
any ointment at all until the entire three
weeks were completed.
4 On the twenty-fourth day of the first
month, while I was by the bank of the great
[a]river, that is, the [1]Tigris,
5 I lifted my eyes and looked, and
behold, there was a certain man [a]dressed in
linen, whose waist was [b]girded with *a belt of*
pure [c]gold of Uphaz.
6 His body also *was* like [1]beryl, his face
[2]had the appearance of lightning, [a]his eyes
were like flaming torches, his arms and feet
like the gleam of polished bronze, and the
sound of his words like the sound of a
[3]tumult.
7 Now I, Daniel, [a]alone saw the vision,
while the [b]men who were with me did not
see the vision; nevertheless, a great [c]dread
fell on them, and they ran away to hide
themselves.
8 So I was [a]left alone and saw this great
vision; yet [b]no strength was left in me, for
my [1]natural color turned to [2]a deathly pallor,
and I retained no strength.
9 But I heard the sound of his words; and
as soon as I heard the sound of his words, I
[a]fell into a deep sleep on my face, with my
face to the ground.

Daniel Comforted

10 Then behold, a hand [a]touched me and
set me trembling on my [1]hands and knees.
11 He said to me, "O [a]Daniel, man of
[1]high esteem, [b]understand the words that I

5 [a]Ezek 9:2; Dan 12:6, 7 [b]Rev 1:13; 15:6 [c]Jer 10:9 **6** [1]Or *yellow serpentine* [2]Lit *like* [3]Or *roaring* [a]Rev 1:14; 2:18; 19:12 **7** [a]2 Kin 6:17-20 [b]Acts 9:7 [c]Ezek 12:18 **8** [1]Lit *splendor* [2]Lit *corruption* [a]Gen 32:24 [b]Dan 7:28; 8:27; Hab 3:16 **9** [a]Gen 15:12; Job 4:13; Dan 8:18 **10** [1]Lit *knees and the palms of my hands* [a]Jer 1:9; Dan 8:18 **11** [1]Lit *desirability;* or *preciousness* [a]Dan 10:19 [b]Dan 8:16, 17

9:24 *weeks.* Probably seven-year periods of time, making a total of 490 years, but the numbers may be symbolic. Of the six purposes mentioned (all to be fulfilled through the Messiah), some believe that the last three were not achieved by the crucifixion and resurrection of Christ but await His further action: the establishment of everlasting righteousness (on earth), the complete fulfillment of vision and prophecy, and the anointing of the "most holy" (either "most holy place" or "most holy One").
9:25–27 The time between the decree authorizing the rebuilding of Jerusalem (v. 25) and the coming of the Messiah ("the Anointed One") was to be 69 (7 plus 62) "weeks," or 483 years (see note on Ezra 7:11). The "seven weeks" may refer to the period of the complete restoration of Jerusalem (partially narrated in Ezra and Nehemiah) and the "sixty-two weeks" to the period between that restoration and the Messiah's coming to Israel. The final (70th) "week" is not mentioned specifically until v. 27, following the prophecy of the destruction of Jerusalem by "the people of the prince who is to come" (Titus in A.D. 70). Therefore, while many hold that the 70th "week" was fulfilled during Christ's earthly ministry and the years immediately following, others conclude that there is an indeterminate interval between the 69th and the 70th "week"—a period of "war" and "desolations" (v. 26). According to this latter opinion, in the 70th "week" the little horn or beast of the last days (referred to here as the one who "on the wing of abominations . . . makes desolate" and who is the antitype of the Roman Titus) will establish a covenant for seven years with the Jews (the "many") but will violate the covenant halfway through that period (but see also note on v. 27). The cutting off of the Messiah (v. 26) refers to the crucifixion of Christ.
9:27 *he will make a firm covenant . . . will put a stop to sacrifice.* According to some, a reference to the Messiah's (v. 26) instituting the new covenant and putting "a stop" to the OT sacrificial system; according to others, a reference to the antichrist's ("the [ultimate] prince who is to come," v. 26) making a treaty with the Jews in the future and then disrupting their system of worship. *abominations.* See note on 11:31.
10:1 *third year of Cyrus.* The third year after his conquest of Babylonia in 539 B.C.
10:3 See 1:8–16.
10:5–6 See Rev 1:12–16.
10:7 Cf. Acts 9:7.

am about to tell you and [c]stand [2]upright, for I have now been sent to you." And when he had spoken this word to me, I stood up [d]trembling.

12 Then he said to me, "[a]Do not be afraid, Daniel, for from the first day that you set your heart on understanding *this* and on [b]humbling yourself before your God, your words were heard, and I have come in response [c]to your words.

13 "But the prince of the kingdom of Persia was [1]withstanding me for twenty-one days; then behold, [a]Michael, one of the chief princes, came to help me, for I had been left there with the kings of Persia.

14 "Now I have come to [a]give you an understanding of what will happen to your people in the [1b]latter days, for the vision pertains to [c]the days yet *future*."

15 When he had spoken to me according to these words, I [1]turned my face toward the ground and became [a]speechless.

16 And behold, [1a]one who resembled a human being was [b]touching my lips; then I opened my mouth and spoke and said to him who was standing before me, "O my lord, as a result of the vision [2c]anguish has come upon me, and I have retained no strength.

17 "For [a]how can such a servant of my lord talk with such as my lord? As for me, there remains just now [b]no strength in me, nor has any breath been left in me."

18 Then *this* one with human appearance touched me again and [a]strengthened me.

19 He said, "O man of [1]high esteem, [a]do not be afraid. Peace [2]be with you; take [b]courage and be courageous!" Now as soon as he spoke to me, I received strength and said, "May my lord speak, for you have [c]strengthened me."

20 Then he said, "Do you [1]understand why I came to you? But I shall now return to fight against the [2]prince of Persia; so I am going forth, and behold, the [2a]prince of [3]Greece is about to come.

21 "However, I will tell you what is inscribed in the writing of [a]truth. Yet there is no one who [1]stands firmly with me against these *forces* except [b]Michael your prince.

Conflicts to Come

11 "In the [a]first year of Darius the Mede, [1]I arose to be [2]an encouragement and a protection for him.

2 "And now I will tell you the [a]truth. Behold, three more kings are going to arise [1]in Persia. Then a fourth will gain far more riches than all *of them;* as soon as he becomes strong through his riches, [2]he will arouse the whole *empire* against the realm of [3b]Greece.

3 "And a [a]mighty king will arise, and he will rule with great authority and [b]do as he pleases.

4 "But as soon as he has arisen, his kingdom will be broken up and parceled out [a]toward the [b]four [1]points of the compass, though not to his *own* descendants, nor according to his authority which he wielded, for his sovereignty will be [c]uprooted and *given* to others besides [2]them.

5 "Then the [a]king of the South will grow strong, [1]along with *one* of his princes [2]who will gain ascendancy over him and obtain dominion; his domain *will be* a great dominion *indeed*.

6 "After some years they will form an alliance, and the daughter of the king of the South will come to the [a]king of the North to carry out [1]a peaceful arrangement. But she will not retain her [2]position of power, nor will he remain with his [3]power, but she will be given up, along with those who brought her in and the one who sired her as well as he who supported her in *those* times.

7 "But one of the [1]descendants of her line will arise in his place, and he will come against *their* army and enter the [a]fortress of the king of the North, and he will deal with them and display *great* strength.

11 [2]Lit *upon your standing* [c]Ezek 2:1 [d]Job 4:14, 15
12 [a]Is 41:10, 14; Dan 10:19 [b]Dan 9:20-23; 10:2, 3 [c]Acts 10:30, 31
13 [1]Lit *standing opposite* [a]Dan 10:21; 12:1; Jude 9; Rev 12:7
14 [1]Lit *end of the days* [a]Dan 8:16; 9:22 [b]Deut 31:29; Dan 2:28 [c]Dan 8:26; 12:4, 9
15 [1]Lit *set* [a]Ezek 3:26; 24:27; Luke 1:20
16 [1]Lit *as a likeness of sons of man* [2]Lit *my pains have* [a]Dan 8:15 [b]Is 6:7; Jer 1:9 [c]Dan 7:15, 28; 8:17, 27; 10:8, 9
17 [a]Ex 24:10, 11; Is 6:1-5 [b]Dan 10:8
18 [a]Is 35:3, 4
19 [1]Lit *desirability;* or *preciousness* [2]Lit *to you* [a]Judg 6:23; Is 43:1; Dan 10:12 [b]Josh 1:6, 7, 9; Is 35:4 [c]Ps 138:3; 2 Cor 12:9
20 [1]Lit *know* [2]I.e. Satanic angel [3]Heb *Javan* [a]Dan 8:21; 11:2
21 [a]Dan 12:4

21 [1]Lit *shows himself strong* [b]Dan 10:13; Rev 12:7
11:1 [1]Lit *my standing up* was [2]Lit *for a strengthener* [a]Dan 5:31; 9:1
2 [1]Lit *for* [2]Or they *all will stir up the realm of Greece* [3]Heb *Javan* [a]Dan 8:26; 10:1, 21 [b]Dan 8:21; 10:20
3 [a]Dan 8:5, 21 [b]Dan 5:19; 8:4; 11:16, 36

4 [1]Lit *winds of the heaven* [2]I.e. his descendants [a]Dan 8:8, 22 [b]Jer 49:36; Ezek 37:9; Dan 7:2; 8:8; Zech 2:6; Rev 7:1 [c]Jer 12:15, 17; 18:7 **5** [1]Lit *and* [2]Lit *and he* [a]Dan 11:9, 11, 14, 25, 40
6 [1]Or *an equitable agreement* [2]Lit *strength of arm* [3]Lit *arm* [a]Dan 11:7, 13, 15, 40 **7** [1]Lit *branch of her roots* [a]Dan 11:19, 38, 39

10:13 *prince of the kingdom of Persia.* Apparently a demon exercising influence over the Persian realm in the interests of Satan (see also v. 20). His resistance was finally overcome by the archangel Michael, "the great prince who stands guard" over the people of God (12:1).
10:20 *prince of Greece.* See note on v. 13. This spiritual power will also have to be opposed.
10:21 *writing of truth.* See 12:1; perhaps a reference to the divine record of the destinies of all human beings (see note on Ex 32:32).
11:1 *Darius the Mede.* See note on 5:31.
11:2 *three more kings.* Cambyses (530–522 B.C.), Pseudo-Smerdis or Gaumata (522) and Darius I (522–486). *fourth.* Xerxes I (486–465), who attempted to conquer Greece in 480 (see note on Esth 1:1).
11:3 *mighty king.* Alexander the Great (336–323).
11:4 *four points.* See 7:2–3 and note on 7:4–7 (four heads).
11:5 *king of the South.* Ptolemy I Soter (323–285 B.C.) of Egypt. *one of his princes.* Seleucus I Nicator (311–280). *his domain.* Initially Babylonia, to which he then added extensive territories both east and west.
11:6 *daughter of the king of the South.* Berenice, daughter of Ptolemy II Philadelphus (285–246 B.C.) of Egypt. *king of the North.* Antiochus II Theos (261–246) of Syria. *peaceful arrangement.* A treaty cemented by the marriage of Berenice to Antiochus. *she will not retain her . . . power, nor will he remain.* Antiochus's former wife, Laodice, conspired to have Berenice and Antiochus put to death. *the one who sired her.* Berenice's father Ptolemy died at about the same time.
11:7 *one of . . . her line.* Berenice's brother, Ptolemy III Euergetes (246–221 B.C.) of Egypt, who did away with Laodice. *the fortress of.* Either (1) Seleucia (see Acts 13:4), which was the port of Antioch, or (2) Antioch itself. *king of the North.* Seleucus II Callinicus (246–226 B.C.) of Syria.

8 "Also their [a]gods with their [1]metal
images *and* their precious vessels of silver
and gold he will take into captivity to Egypt,
and he on his part will [2]refrain from *attack-*
ing the king of the North for *some* years.
9 "Then [1]the latter will enter the realm of
the king of the South, but will return to his
own land.
10 "His sons will [1]mobilize and assemble a
multitude of great forces; and one of them
will keep on coming and [a]overflow and pass
through, that he may [2]again wage war up to
his *very* fortress.
11 "The [a]king of the South will be enraged
and go forth and fight [1]with the king of the
North. Then the latter will raise a great multitude, but *that* multitude will be given into
[2]the hand of the *former.*
12 "When the multitude is carried away, his
heart will be lifted up, and he will cause tens
of thousands to fall; yet he will not prevail.
13 "For the king of the North will again raise
a greater multitude than the former, and [1]after
an [a]interval of some years he will [2]press on
with a great army and much equipment.
14 "Now in those times many will rise up
against the king of the South; the violent
ones among your people will also lift themselves up in order to fulfill the vision, but
they will [1]fall down.
15 "Then the king of the North will come,
cast up a [a]siege ramp and capture a well-fortified city; and the forces of the South will
not stand *their ground,* not even [1]their choicest troops, for there will be no strength to
make a stand.
16 "But he who comes against him will [a]do
as he pleases, and [b]no one will *be able to*
withstand him; he will also stay *for a time* in
the [1c]Beautiful Land, with destruction in his
hand.

8 [1]Lit *cast images* [2]Or *stand against the king* [a]Is 37:19; 46:1, 2; Jer 43:12, 13
9 [1]Lit *he will,* and so throughout the ch
10 [1]Or *wage war* [2]Or *return and wage* [a]Is 8:8; Jer 46:7, 8; 51:42; Dan 11:26, 40
11 [1]Lit *with him, with* [2]Lit *his hand* [a]Dan 11:5
13 [1]Lit *at the end of the times, years* [2]Or *keep on coming* [a]Dan 4:16; 12:7
14 [1]Lit *stumble,* and so throughout the ch
15 [1]Lit *the people of its choice ones* [a]Jer 6:6; Ezek 4:2; 17:17
16 [1]I.e. Palestine [a]Dan 5:19; 11:3, 36 [b]Josh 1:5 [c]Dan 8:9; 11:41
17 [1]Lit *and* [2]Lit *equitable things* [3]Lit *for him;* i.e. for her father [a]2 Kin 12:17; Ezek 4:3, 7
18 [a]Gen 10:5; Is 66:19; Jer 2:10; 31:10; Zeph 2:11 [b]Hos 12:14
19 [a]Ps 27:2; Jer 46:6 [b]Job 20:8; Ps 37:36; Ezek 26:21
20 [1]Or *exactor of tribute* [2]Lit *adornment;* i.e. probably Jerusalem and its temple [a]Is 60:17
21 [a]2 Sam 15:6

17 "He will [a]set his face to come with the
power of his whole kingdom, [1]bringing with
him [2]a proposal of peace which he will put
into effect; he will also give him the daughter of women to ruin it. But she will not take
a stand *for him* or be [3]on his side.
18 "Then he will turn his face to the [a]coast-
lands and capture many. But a commander
will put a stop to his scorn against him;
moreover, he will [b]repay him for his scorn.
19 "So he will turn his face toward the
fortresses of his own land, but he will [a]stum-
ble and fall and be [b]found no more.
20 "Then in his place one will arise who will
[a]send an [1]oppressor through the [2]Jewel of *his*
kingdom; yet within a few days he will be
shattered, though not in anger nor in battle.
21 "In his place a despicable person will
arise, on whom the honor of kingship has
not been conferred, but he will come in a
time of tranquility and [a]seize the kingdom
by intrigue.
22 "The overflowing [a]forces will be flooded
away before him and shattered, and also the
prince of the covenant.
23 "After an alliance is made with him he
will practice deception, and he will go up
and gain power with a small *force of* people.
24 "[1]In a time of tranquility he will enter
the [a]richest *parts* of the [2]realm, and he will
accomplish what his fathers never did, nor
his [3]ancestors; he will distribute plunder,
booty and possessions among them, and he
will devise his schemes against strongholds,
but *only* for a time.
25 "He will stir up his strength and
[1]courage against the [a]king of the South with
a large army; so the king of the South will

22 [a]Dan 9:26; 11:10 **24** [1]Lit *Into tranquility and the richest...he will enter* [2]Or *province* [3]Lit *fathers' fathers* [a]Num 13:20; Neh 9:25; Ezek 34:14 **25** [1]Lit *heart* [a]Dan 11:5

11:8 *their gods.* Images of Syrian deities, and also of Egyptian gods that the Persian Cambyses had carried off after conquering Egypt in 525 B.C.

11:10 *His sons.* Seleucus III Ceraunus (226–223 B.C.) and Antiochus III (the Great) (223–187), sons of Seleucus II. *his very fortress.* Ptolemy's fortress at Raphia (southwest of Gaza).

11:11 *king of the South.* Ptolemy IV Philopator (221–203 B.C.) of Egypt. *king of the North.* Antiochus III. *given into the hand of.* At Raphia in 217.

11:12 *cause . . . thousands to fall.* The historian Polybius records that Antiochus lost nearly 10,000 infantrymen at Raphia.

11:14 *king of the South.* Ptolemy V Epiphanes (203–181 B.C.) of Egypt. *violent ones among your people.* Jews who joined the forces of Antiochus. *they will fall down.* The Ptolemaic general Scopas crushed the rebellion in 200.

11:15 *well-fortified city.* The Mediterranean port of Sidon.

11:16 *he who comes.* Antiochus, who was in control of the Holy Land by 197 B.C. *Beautiful Land.* See note on 8:9–12.

11:17 *he will also give him the daughter of women.* Antiochus gave his daughter Cleopatra I in marriage to Ptolemy V in 194 B.C.

11:18 *he.* Antiochus. *coastlands.* Asia Minor and perhaps also mainland Greece. *commander.* The Roman consul Lucius Cornelius Scipio Asiaticus, who defeated Antiochus at Magnesia in Asia Minor in 190 B.C.

11:19 *stumble and fall.* Antiochus died in 187 B.C. while attempting to plunder a temple in the province of Elymais.

11:20 *in his place one will arise.* Seleucus IV Philopator (187–175 B.C.), son and successor of Antiochus the Great. *oppressor.* Seleucus's finance minister, Heliodorus. *he will be shattered.* Seleucus was the victim of a conspiracy engineered by Heliodorus.

11:21 *despicable person.* Seleucus's younger brother, Antiochus IV Epiphanes (175–164 B.C.). *honor of kingship has not been conferred.* Antiochus seized power while the rightful heir to the throne, the son of Seleucus (later to become Demetrius I), was still very young. *kingdom.* Syro-Palestine.

11:22 *prince of the covenant.* Either the high priest Onias III, who was murdered in 170 B.C., or, if the Hebrew for this phrase is translated "confederate prince," Ptolemy VI Philometor (181–146) of Egypt.

11:23 *he.* Antiochus.

11:24 *richest parts.* Either of the Holy Land or of Egypt. *strongholds.* In Egypt.

11:25 *king of the South.* Ptolemy VI.

mobilize an extremely large and mighty army for war; but he will not stand, for schemes will be devised against him.

26 "Those who eat his choice food will [1]destroy him, and his army will [2a]overflow, but many will fall down slain.

27 "As for both kings, their hearts will be *intent* on [a]evil, and they will [b]speak lies *to each other* at the same table; but it will not succeed, for the [c]end is still *to come* at the appointed time.

28 "Then he will return to his land with much [1]plunder; but his heart will be *set* against the holy covenant, and he will take action and *then* return to his *own* land.

29 "At the appointed time he will return and come into the South, but [1]this last time it will not turn out the way it did before.

30 "For ships of [1a]Kittim will come against him; therefore he will be disheartened and will return and become enraged at the holy covenant and take action; so he will come back and show regard for those who forsake the holy covenant.

31 "Forces from him will arise, [a]desecrate the sanctuary fortress, and do away with the regular sacrifice. And they will set up the [b]abomination [1]of desolation.

32 "By [a]smooth *words* he will [1]turn to godlessness those who act wickedly toward the covenant, but the people who know their God will display [b]strength and take action.

33 "[1a]Those who have insight among the people will give understanding to the many; yet they will [b]fall by sword and by flame, by captivity and by plunder for *many* days.

34 "Now when they fall they will be granted a little help, and many will [a]join with them in [b]hypocrisy.

35 "Some of [1]those who have insight will

26 [1]Lit *break* [2]Or *be swept away, and many* [a]Dan 11:10, 40 **27** [a]Ps 52:1; 64:6 [b]Ps 12:2; Jer 9:3-5; 41:1-3 [c]Dan 8:19; 11:35, 40; Hab 2:3 **28** [1]Lit *possessions* **29** [1]Lit *it will not happen as the first and as the last* **30** [1]I.e. Cyprus [a]Gen 10:4; Num 24:24; Is 23:1, 12; Jer 2:10 **31** [1]Lit *that makes desolate;* or *that causes horror* [a]Dan 8:11-13; 12:11 [b]Dan 9:27; Matt 24:15; Mark 13:14 **32** [1]Or *pollute those* [a]Dan 11:21, 34 [b]Mic 5:7-9; Zech 9:13-16; 10:3-6 **33** [1]Or *Instructors of the people* [a]Mal 2:7 [b]Matt 24:9; John 16:2; Heb 11:36-38 **34** [a]Matt 7:15; Acts 20:29, 30 [b]Dan 11:21, 32; Rom 16:18 **35** [1]Or *the instructors*

11:26 *his army.* That of Ptolemy.
11:27 *both kings.* Antiochus and Ptolemy, who was living in Antiochus's custody.
11:28 *against the holy covenant.* In 169 B.C. Antiochus plundered the temple in Jerusalem, set up a garrison there and massacred many Jews in the city.
11:30 *ships of Kittim.* Roman vessels under the command of Popilius Laenas. *those who forsake the holy covenant.* Apostate Jews (see also v. 32).
11:31 *abomination of desolation.* See 9:27; 12:11; the altar to the pagan god Zeus Olympius, set up in 168 B.C. by Antiochus Epiphanes and prefiguring a similar abomination that Jesus predicted would be erected (see note on Matt 24:15; see also Luke 21:20).
11:33 *Those who have insight.* The godly leaders of the Jewish resistance movement, also called the Hasidim. *fall by sword and by flame, by captivity and by plunder.* See Heb 11:36–38.
11:34 *a little help.* The early successes of the guerrilla uprising (168 B.C.) that originated in Modein, 17 miles northwest of Jerusalem, under the leadership of Mattathias and his son Judas Maccabeus. In December, 165, the altar of the temple was rededicated.

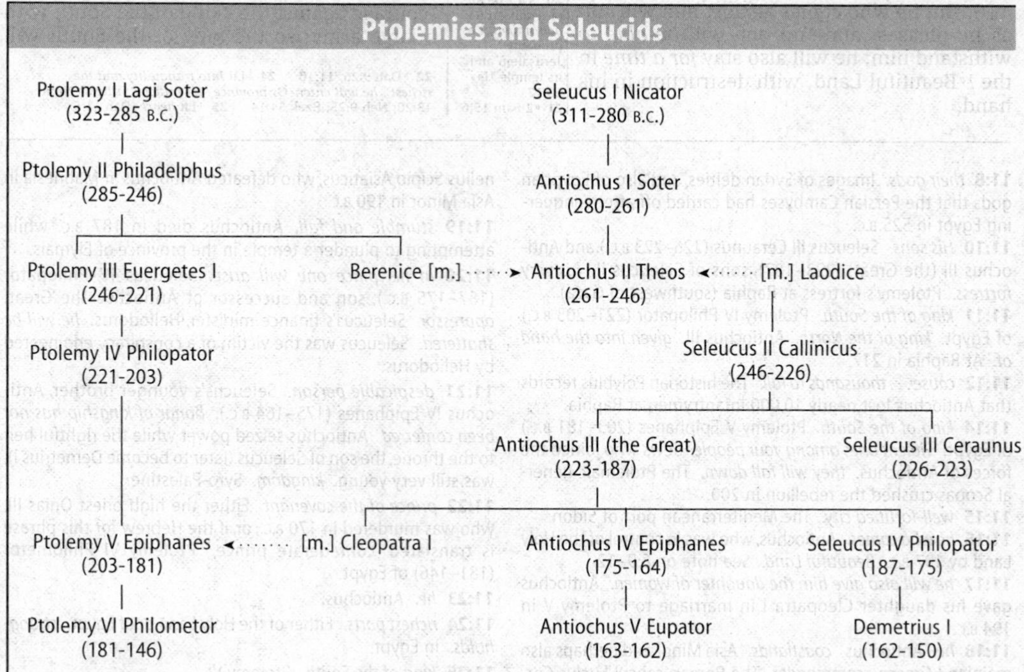
Ptolemies and Seleucids
Ptolemy I Lagi Soter
(323-285 B.C.)
Seleucus I Nicator
(311-280 B.C.)
Ptolemy II Philadelphus
(285-246)
Antiochus I Soter
(280-261)
Ptolemy III Euergetes I
(246-221)
Berenice [m.]
Antiochus II Theos
(261-246)
[m.] Laodice
Ptolemy IV Philopator
(221-203)
Seleucus II Callinicus
(246-226)
Antiochus III (the Great)
(223-187)
Seleucus III Ceraunus
(226-223)
Ptolemy V Epiphanes
(203-181)
[m.] Cleopatra I
Antiochus IV Epiphanes
(175-164)
Seleucus IV Philopator
(187-175)
Ptolemy VI Philometor
(181-146)
Antiochus V Eupator
(163-162)
Demetrius I
(162-150)

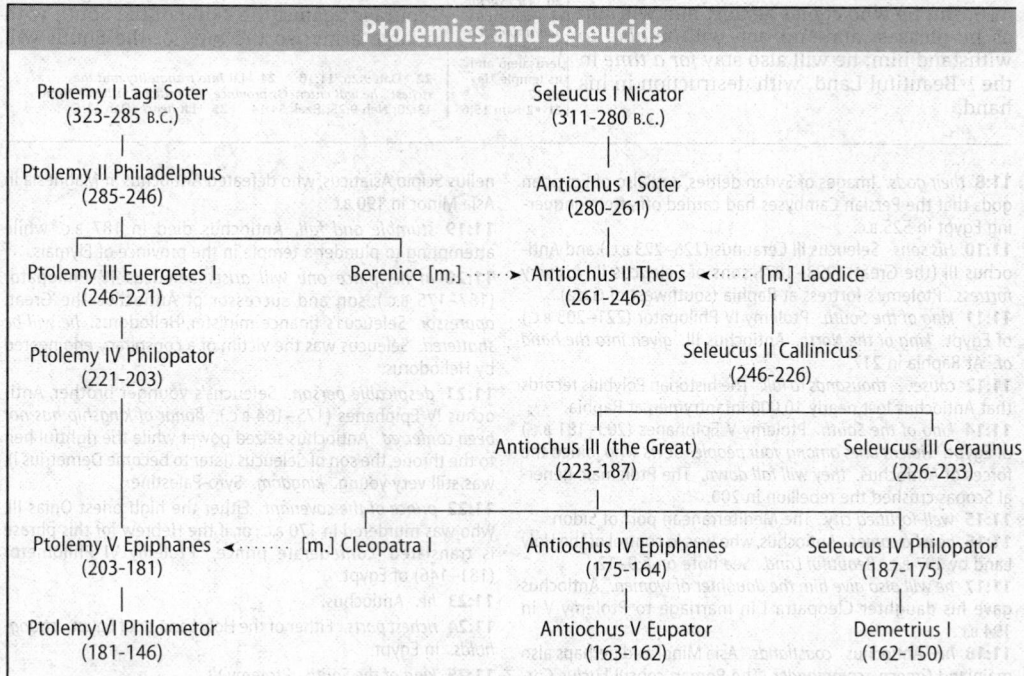

fall, in order to [a]refine, [b]purge and make them [2c]pure until the [d]end time; because *it is* still *to come* at the appointed time.

36 "Then the king will [a]do as he pleases, and he will exalt and [b]magnify himself above every god and will [c]speak [1]monstrous things against the [d]God of gods; and he will prosper until the [e]indignation is finished, for that which is [f]decreed will be done.

37 "He will show no regard for the [1]gods of his fathers or for the desire of women, nor will he show regard for any *other* god; for he will magnify himself above *them* all.

38 "But [1]instead he will honor a god of fortresses, a god whom his fathers did not know; he will honor *him* with gold, silver, costly stones and treasures.

39 "He will take action against the strongest of fortresses with *the help of* a foreign god; he will give great honor to [1]those who acknowledge *him* and will cause them to rule over the many, and will parcel out land for a price.

40 "At the [a]end time the [b]king of the South will collide with him, and the [c]king of the North will [d]storm against him with chariots, with horsemen and with many ships; and he will enter countries, [e]overflow *them* and pass through.

41 "He will also enter the [1a]Beautiful Land, and many *countries* will fall; but these will be rescued out of his hand: Edom, [b]Moab and the foremost of the sons of [c]Ammon.

42 "Then he will stretch out his hand against *other* countries, and the land of Egypt will not escape.

43 "But he will [1]gain control over the hidden treasures of gold and silver and over all the precious things of Egypt; and [a]Libyans and [b]Ethiopians *will follow* at his [2]heels.

44 "But rumors from the East and from the North will disturb him, and he will go forth with great wrath to destroy and [1]annihilate many.

45 "He will pitch the tents of his royal pavilion between the seas and the beautiful [a]Holy Mountain; yet he will come to his end, and no one will help him.

35 [2]Lit *white* [a]Deut 8:16; Prov 17:3; Dan 12:10; Zech 13:9; Mal 3:2, 3 [b]John 15:2 [c]Rev 7:14 [d]Dan 11:27
36 [1]Lit *extraordinary* [a]Dan 5:19; 11:3, 16 [b]Is 14:13; Dan 5:20; 8:11, 25; 2 Thess 2:4 [c]Rev 13:5, 6 [d]Deut 10:17; Ps 136:2; Dan 2:47 [e]Is 10:25; 26:20; Dan 8:19 [f]Dan 9:27
37 [1]Or *God*
38 [1]Lit *in his place*
39 [1]Lit *the one who acknowledges*
40 [a]Dan 11:27, 35; 12:4, 9 [b]Dan 11:11, 25 [c]Dan 11:7, 13, 15 [d]Is 5:28; Jer 4:13
40 [e]Dan 11:10, 26
41 [1]I.e. Palestine [a]Dan 8:9; 11:16 [b]Jer 48:47 [c]Jer 49:6
43 [1]Or *rule over* [2]Lit *footsteps* [a]2 Chr 12:3; Nah 3:9 [b]2 Chr 12:3; Ezek 30:4, 5; Nah 3:9 **44** [1]Lit *devote to destruction* **45** [a]Is 11:9; 27:13; 65:25; 66:20; Dan 9:16, 20

11:35 *the end time.* See v. 40; 12:4,9. Daniel concludes his predictions about Antiochus Epiphanes and begins to prophesy concerning the more distant future.

11:36 From here to the end of ch. 11 the antichrist (see notes on 7:8; 9:27) is in view. The details of this section do not fit what is known of Antiochus Epiphanes. See 2 Thess 2:4; cf. Rev 13:5–8.

11:37 *the desire of women.* Usually interpreted as either Tammuz (see note on Ezek 8:14) or the Messiah.

11:40–45 Conflicts to be waged between the antichrist and his political enemies. He will meet his end at the "beautiful Holy Mountain" (v. 45), Jerusalem's temple mount, doubtless in connection with the battle of Armageddon (Rev 16:13–16).

Soon after the death of Alexander the Great in 323 B.C., his generals divided his empire into four parts, two of which—Egypt and Syria—were under the rule of the Ptolemies and Seleucids respectively. Palestine was controlled from Egypt by the Ptolemaic dynasty from 323 to 198, and was subsequently governed by the Seleucids of Syria from 198 to 142.

The Diadochi, as the successors of Alexander were called, struggled bitterly for power over his domain. At first Ptolemy I seized his own satrapy, Egypt and North Africa, which had splendid resources and natural defense capabilities. Seleucus gained Syria and Mesopotamia, and by 301 Lysimachus held Thrace and Asia Minor and Cassander ruled Macedon. The situation changed again by 277, when only three major Hellenistic kingdoms stabilized in Egypt, in Syria, and in Macedonia under the Antigonids (277-168). Each continued until the eventual triumph of Rome.

Dan 11 treats the "king of the South" and the "king of the North," describing their conflicts, wars and alliances. Their hostility toward the people of God culminated in the "abomination of desolation" (Dan 11:31), identified historically with the reign of Antiochus IV Epiphanes (175-164). The Maccabean revolt followed, leading eventually to the founding of the Hasmonean dynasty.

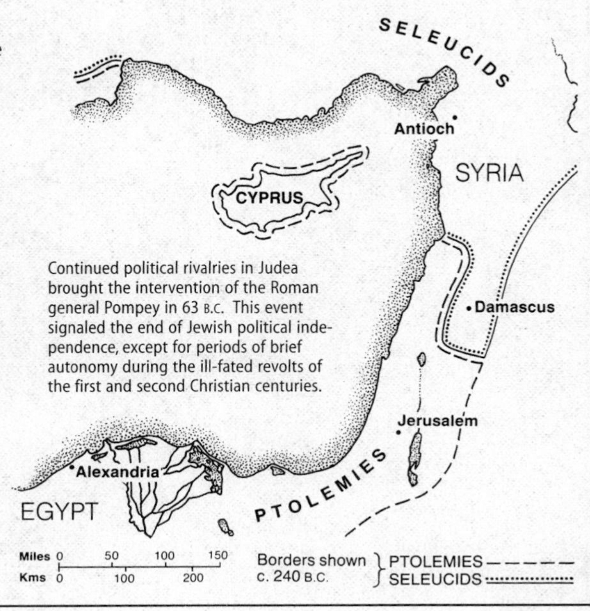

SELEUCIDS
Antioch
SYRIA
CYPRUS
Continued political rivalries in Judea brought the intervention of the Roman general Pompey in 63 B.C. This event signaled the end of Jewish political independence, except for periods of brief autonomy during the ill-fated revolts of the first and second Christian centuries.
Damascus
Jerusalem
Alexandria
EGYPT
PTOLEMIES
Miles 0 50 100 150
Kms 0 100 200
Borders shown c. 240 B.C.
PTOLEMIES
SELEUCIDS

The Time of the End

12 "Now at that time [a]Michael, the great
prince who stands *guard* over the sons
of your people, will arise. And there will be a
[b]time of distress [c]such as never occurred
since there was a nation until that time; and
at that time your people, everyone who is
found written in the [d]book, will be rescued.
2 "[a]Many of those who sleep in the dust
of the ground will awake, [b]these to everlasting life, but the others to disgrace *and* everlasting [1]contempt.
3 "[1]Those who have [a]insight will [b]shine
brightly like the brightness of the [2]expanse
of heaven, and those who [c]lead the many to
righteousness, like the stars forever and ever.
4 "But as for you, Daniel, [a]conceal these
words and [b]seal up the book until the [c]end
of time; [d]many will go back and forth, and
knowledge will increase."
5 Then I, Daniel, looked and behold, two
others were standing, one on this bank of the
river and the other on that bank of the river.
6 And [a]one said to the man [b]dressed in
linen, who was above the waters of the river,
"[c]How long *will it be* until the end of *these*
wonders?"
7 I heard the man dressed in linen, who
was above the waters of the river, [1]as he
[a]raised his right hand and his left toward
heaven, and swore by [b]Him who lives forever that it would be for a [2c]time, [2]times, and
half *a* [2]*time;* and as soon as [3]they finish
[d]shattering the [4]power of the holy people, all
these *events* will be completed.
8 As for me, I heard but could not understand; so I said, "My lord, what *will be* the
[1]outcome of these *events?*"
9 He said, "Go *your way,* Daniel, for *these*
words are concealed and [a]sealed up until the
end time.
10 "[a]Many will be purged, [1]purified and
refined, but the [b]wicked will act wickedly;
and none of the wicked will understand, but
[2]those who [c]have insight will understand.
11 "From the time that the regular sacrifice
is abolished and the [1a]abomination of desolation is set up, *there will be* 1,290 days.
12 "How [a]blessed is he who keeps waiting
and attains to the [b]1,335 days!
13 "But as for you, go *your way* to the [1]end;
then you will enter into [a]rest and rise *again* for
your [b]allotted portion at the end of the [2]age."

12:1 [a]Dan 10:13, 21; Rev 12:7 [b]Rev 7:14; 16:18 [c]Jer 30:7; Ezek 5:9; Dan 9:12; Matt 24:21; Mark 13:19 [d]Dan 7:10; 10:21
2 [1]Lit *abhorrence* [a]Is 26:19; Ezek 37:12-14 [b]Matt 25:46; John 5:28, 29
3 [1]Or *The instructors will* [2]Or *firmament* [a]Dan 11:33, 35; 12:10 [b]John 5:35 [c]Is 53:11; Dan 11:33
4 [a]Dan 8:26; 12:9 [b]Is 8:16; Dan 12:9; Rev 22:10 [c]Dan 8:17; 12:9, 13 [d]Is 11:9; 29:18, 19; Dan 11:33
6 [a]Dan 8:16; Zech 1:12, 13 [b]Ezek 9:2; Dan 10:5 [c]Dan 8:13; 12:8; Matt 24:3; Mark 13:4
7 [1]Lit *and*
7 [2]I.e. year(s) [3]Lit *to finish* [4]Lit *hand* [a]Ezek 20:5; Rev 10:5, 6 [b]Dan 4:34 [c]Dan 7:25; Rev 12:14 [d]Dan 8:24; Luke 21:24
8 [1]Or *final end*
9 [a]Dan 12:4
10 [1]Lit *made white* [2]Or *the instructors will* [a]Zech 13:9 [b]Is 32:6, 7; Rev 22:11 [c]Dan 12:3; Hos 14:9; John 7:17; 8:47
11 [1]Or *horrible abomination* [a]Dan 9:27; 11:31; Matt 24:15; Mark 13:14
12 [a]Is 30:18 [b]Dan 8:14; Rev 11:2; 12:6; 13:5
13 [1]I.e. end of your life [2]Lit *days* [a]Is 57:2; Rev 14:13 [b]Ps 16:5

12:1 *Michael.* See note on 10:13. *time of distress.* See Jer 30:7; Matt 24:21 and note; cf. Rev 16:18. *book.* See 10:21; see also notes on Ps 9:5; 51:1; 69:28.

12:2 The first clear reference to a resurrection of both the righteous and the wicked. Cf. John 5:24–30. *everlasting life.* The phrase occurs only here in the OT.

12:5 *two others.* Two was the minimum number of witnesses to an oath (see v. 7; Deut 19:15).

12:7 *time, times, and half a time.* See note on 7:25.

12:11–12 Apparently representing either (1) further calculations relating to the persecutions of Antiochus Epiphanes (see 8:14; 11:28 and notes) or (2) further end-time calculations.

12:13 *rest.* Die (see Job 3:17).

The Book of the Twelve, or the Minor Prophets

In Ecclesiasticus (an Apocryphal book written c. 190 B.C.), Jesus ben Sira spoke of "the twelve prophets" (Ecclesiasticus 49:10) as a unit parallel to Isaiah, Jeremiah and Ezekiel. He thus indicated that these 12 prophecies were at that time thought of as a unit and were probably already written together on one scroll, as is the case in later times. Josephus (*Against Apion,* 1.8.3) also was aware of this grouping. Augustine (*The City of God,* 18.25) called them the "Minor Prophets," referring to the small size of these books by comparison with the major prophetic books and not at all suggesting that they are of minor importance.

In the traditional Jewish canon these works are arranged in what was thought to be their chronological order: (1) the books that came from the period of Assyrian power (Hosea, Joel, Amos, Obadiah, Jonah, Micah), (2) those written about the time of the decline of Assyria (Nahum, Habakkuk, Zephaniah) and (3) those dating from the postexilic era (Haggai, Zechariah, Malachi). On the other hand, their order in the Septuagint (the earliest Greek translation of the OT) is: Hosea, Amos, Micah, Joel, Obadiah, Jonah, Nahum, Habakkuk, Zephaniah, Haggai, Zechariah, Malachi (the order of the first six was probably determined by length, except for Jonah, which is placed last among them because of its different character).

In any event, it appears that within a century after the composition of Malachi the Jews had brought together the 12 shorter prophecies to form a book (scroll) of prophetic writings, which was received as canonical and paralleled the three major prophetic books of Isaiah, Jeremiah and Ezekiel. The great Greek manuscripts Alexandrinus and Vaticanus place the Twelve before the major prophets, but in the traditional Jewish canon and in all modern versions they appear after them.

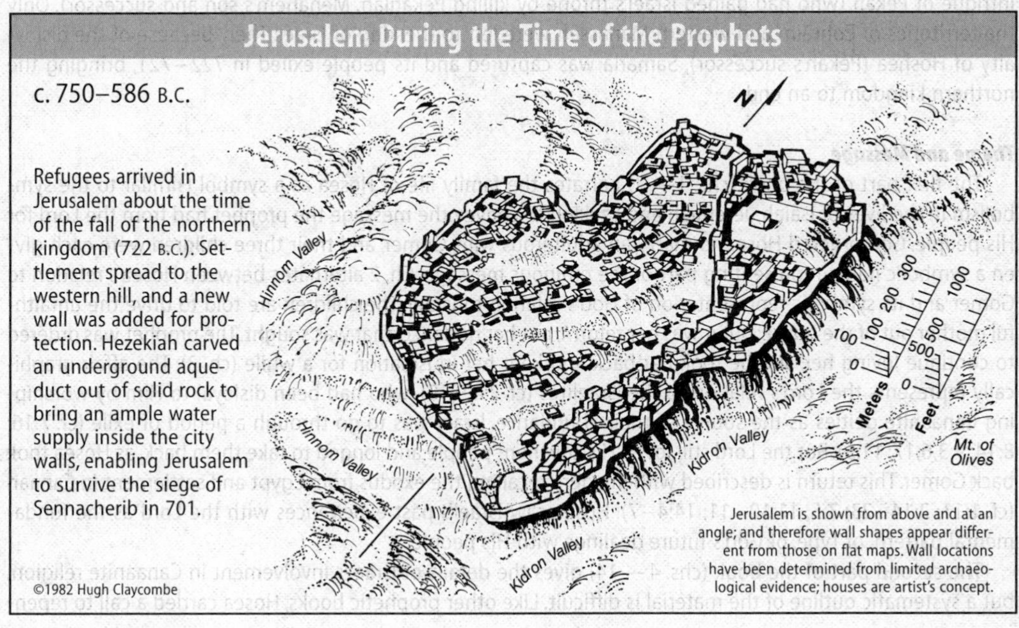

Jerusalem During the Time of the Prophets

c. 750–586 B.C.

Refugees arrived in Jerusalem about the time of the fall of the northern kingdom (722 B.C.). Settlement spread to the western hill, and a new wall was added for protection. Hezekiah carved an underground aqueduct out of solid rock to bring an ample water supply inside the city walls, enabling Jerusalem to survive the siege of Sennacherib in 701.

Jerusalem is shown from above and at an angle; and therefore wall shapes appear different from those on flat maps. Wall locations have been determined from limited archaeological evidence; houses are artist's concept.

©1982 Hugh Claycombe

Hosea

INTRODUCTION

Author and Date

Hosea son of Beeri prophesied about the middle of the eighth century B.C., his ministry beginning during or shortly after that of Amos. Amos threatened God's judgment on Israel at the hands of an unnamed enemy; Hosea identifies that enemy as Assyria (7:11; 8:9; 10:6; 11:11). Judging from the kings mentioned in 1:1, Hosea must have prophesied for at least 38 years, though almost nothing is known about him from sources outside his book. He was the only one of the writing prophets to come from the northern kingdom (Israel), and his prophecy is primarily directed to that kingdom. But since his prophetic activity is dated by reference to kings of Judah, the book was probably written in Judah after the fall of the northern capital, Samaria (722–721)—an idea suggested by references to Judah throughout the book (1:7,11; 4:15; 5:5,10,13; 6:4,11; 10:11; 11:12; 12:2). Whether Hosea himself authored the book that preserves his prophecies is not known. The book of Hosea stands first in the division of the Bible called the Book of the Twelve (in the Apocrypha; see Ecclesiasticus 49:10) or the Minor Prophets (a name referring to the brevity of these books as compared to Isaiah, Jeremiah and Ezekiel).

Background

Hosea lived in the tragic final days of the northern kingdom, during which six kings (following Jeroboam II) reigned within 25 years (2 Kin 15:8—17:41). Four (Zechariah, Shallum, Pekahiah, Pekah) were murdered by their successors while in office, and one (Hoshea) was captured in battle; only one (Menahem) was succeeded on the throne by his son. These kings, given to Israel by God "in . . . anger" and taken away "in . . . wrath" (13:11), floated away "like a stick on the surface of the water" (10:7). "Bloodshed" followed "bloodshed" (4:2). Assyria was expanding westward, and Menahem accepted that world power as overlord and paid tribute (2 Kin 15:19–20). But shortly afterward, in 733 B.C., Israel was dismembered by Assyria because of the intrigue of Pekah (who had gained Israel's throne by killing Pekahiah, Menahem's son and successor). Only the territories of Ephraim and western Manasseh were left to the king of Israel. Then, because of the disloyalty of Hoshea (Pekah's successor), Samaria was captured and its people exiled in 722–721, bringing the northern kingdom to an end.

Theme and Message

The first part of the book (chs. 1—3) narrates the family life of Hosea as a symbol (similar to the symbolism in the lives of Isaiah, Jeremiah and Ezekiel) to convey the message the prophet had from the Lord for His people. God ordered Hosea to marry an adulterous wife, Gomer, and their three children were each given a symbolic name representing part of the ominous message. Ch. 2 alternates between Hosea's relation to Gomer and its symbolic representation of God's relation to Israel. The children are told to drive the unfaithful mother out of the house; but it was her reform, not her riddance, that was sought. The prophet was ordered to continue loving her, and he took her back and kept her in isolation for a while (ch. 3). The affair graphically represents the Lord's relation to the Israelites (cf. 2:4,9,18), who had been disloyal to Him by worshiping Canaanite deities as the source of their abundance. Israel was to go through a period of exile (cf. 7:16; 8:14; 9:3,6,17; 11:5). But the Lord still loved His covenant people and longed to take them back, as Hosea took back Gomer. This return is described with imagery recalling the exodus from Egypt and settlement in Canaan (cf. 1:11; 2:14–23; 3:5; 11:10–11; 14:4–7). Hosea saw Israel's past experiences with the Lord as the fundamental pattern, or type, of God's future dealings with His people.

The second part of the book (chs. 4—14) gives the details of Israel's involvement in Canaanite religion, but a systematic outline of the material is difficult. Like other prophetic books, Hosea carried a call to repen-

tance. Israel's alternative to destruction was to forsake her idols and return to the Lord (chs. 6; 14). Information gleaned from materials discovered at Ugarit (dating from the 15th century B.C.; see chart, p. xix) and from the writings of the early Christian historian Eusebius enables us to know more clearly the religious practices against which Hosea protested.

Hosea saw the failure to acknowledge God (4:6; 13:4) as Israel's basic problem. God's relation to Israel was that of love (2:19; 4:1; 6:6; 10:12; 12:6). The intimacy of the covenant relationship between God and Israel, illustrated in the first part of the book by the husband-wife relationship, is later amplified by the father-child relationship (11:1–4). Disloyalty to God was spiritual adultery (4:13–14; 5:4; 9:1; cf. Jer 3). Israel had turned to Baal worship and had sacrificed at the pagan high places, which included associating with the sacred prostitutes at the sanctuaries (4:14) and worshiping the calf image at Samaria (8:5; 10:5–6; 13:2). There was also international intrigue (5:13; 7:8–11) and materialism. Yet despite God's condemnation and the harshness of language with which the unavoidable judgment was announced, the major purpose of the book is to proclaim God's compassion and love that cannot—finally—let Israel go.

Special Problems

The book of Hosea has at least two perplexing problems. The first concerns the nature of the story told in chs. 1—3 and the character of Gomer. While some interpreters have thought the story to be merely an allegory of the relation between God and Israel, others claim, more plausibly, that the story is to be taken literally. Among the latter, some insist that Gomer was faithful at first and later became unfaithful, others that she was unfaithful even before the marriage.

The second problem of the book is the relation of ch. 3 to ch. 1. Despite the fact that no children are mentioned in ch. 3, some interpreters claim that the two chapters are different accounts of the same episode. The traditional interpretation, however, is more likely, namely, that ch. 3 is a sequel to ch. 1—i.e., after Gomer proved unfaithful, Hosea was instructed to take her back.

Outline

- I. Superscription (1:1)
- II. The Unfaithful Wife and the Faithful Husband (1:2—3:5)
  - A. The Children as Signs (1:2—2:1)
  - B. The Unfaithful Wife (2:2–23)
    1. The Lord's judgment of Israel (2:2–13)
    2. The Lord's restoration of Israel (2:14–23)
  - C. The Faithful Husband (ch. 3)
- III. The Unfaithful Nation and the Faithful God (chs. 4—14)
  - A. Israel's Unfaithfulness (4:1—6:3)
    1. The general charge (4:1–3)
    2. The cause declared and the results described (4:4–19)
    3. A special message to the people and leaders (ch. 5)
    4. A sorrowful plea (6:1–3)
  - B. Israel's Punishment (6:4—10:15)
    1. The case stated (6:4—7:16)
    2. The judgment pronounced (chs. 8—9)
    3. Summary and appeal (ch. 10)
  - C. The Lord's Faithful Love (chs. 11—14)
    1. The Lord's fatherly love (11:1–11)
    2. Israel's punishment for unfaithfulness (11:12—13:16)
    3. Israel's restoration after repentance (ch. 14)

Hosea's Wife and Children

1 The word of the LORD which came to
[a]Hosea the son of Beeri, during the days
of [b]Uzziah, [c]Jotham, [d]Ahaz *and* [e]Hezekiah,
kings of Judah, and during the days of [f]Jero-
boam the son of Joash, king of Israel.
2 When the LORD first spoke through
Hosea, the LORD said to Hosea, "[a]Go, take to
yourself a wife of harlotry and *have* children
of harlotry; for [b]the land commits flagrant
harlotry, [1]forsaking the LORD."
3 So he went and took Gomer the daughter of Diblaim, and she conceived and [a]bore
him a son.
4 And the LORD said to him, "Name him
[a]Jezreel; for yet a little while, and [b]I will
[1]punish the house of Jehu for the bloodshed
of Jezreel, and [c]I will put an end to the kingdom of the house of Israel.
5 "On that day I will [a]break the bow of
Israel in the [b]valley of Jezreel."
6 Then she conceived again and gave
birth to a daughter. And [1]the LORD said to
him, "Name her [2]Lo-ruhamah, for I will no
longer [a]have compassion on the house of
Israel, that I would ever forgive them.
7 "But I will have [a]compassion on the
house of Judah and [b]deliver them by the
LORD their God, and will not deliver them by
[c]bow, sword, battle, horses or horsemen."
8 When she had weaned Lo-ruhamah,
she conceived and gave birth to a son.
9 And [1]the LORD said, "Name him [2]Lo-
ammi, for you are not My people and I am
not [3]your God."

10 [1]Yet the number of the sons of Israel
Will be like the [a]sand of the sea,
Which cannot be measured or
numbered;
And [b]in the place
Where it is said to them,
"You are [c]not My people,"
It will be said to them,
"*You are* the [d]sons of the living God."
11 And the [a]sons of Judah and the sons
of Israel will be [b]gathered together,
And they will appoint for themselves
[c]one leader,
And they will go up from the land,
For great will be the day of Jezreel.

Israel's Unfaithfulness Condemned

2 [1]Say to your brothers, "[2]Ammi," and to
your sisters, "[3]Ruhamah."
2 "Contend with your mother, [a]contend,
For she is [b]not my wife, and I am not
her husband;
And let her put away her [c]harlotry
from her face
And her adultery from between her
breasts,
3 Or I will strip her [a]naked
And expose her as on the [b]day when
she was born.
I will also [c]make her like a wilderness,
Make her like desert land

1:1 [a]Rom 9:25 [b]2 Chr 26:1-23; Is 1:1; Amos 1:1 [c]2 Kin 15:5, 7, 32-38; 2 Chr 27:1-9 [d]2 Kin 16:1-20; 2 Chr 28:1-27; Is 1:1; 7:1-17; Mic 1:1 [e]2 Kin 18:1-20:21; 2 Chr 29:1-32:33; Mic 1:1 [f]2 Kin 13:13; 14:23-29; Amos 1:1
2 [1]Lit *from not following after* [a]Hos 3:1 [b]Deut 31:16; Jer 3:1; Ezek 23:3-21; Hos 2:5; 5:3
3 [a]Ezek 23:4
4 [1]Lit *visit the bloodshed of Jezreel on the house of Jehu* [a]Hos 2:22 [b]2 Kin 10:11 [c]2 Kin 15:8-10
5 [a]Jer 49:35; Ezek 39:3 [b]Josh 17:16; Judg 6:33
6 [1]Lit *He* [2]I.e. she has not obtained compassion [a]Hos 2:4
7 [a]2 Kin 19:29-35; Is 30:18 [b]Jer 25:5, 6; Zech 9:9, 10 [c]Ps 44:3-7; Zech 4:6
9 [1]Lit *He* [2]I.e. not my people [3]Lit *yours*
10 [1]Ch 2:1 in Heb [a]Gen 22:17; 32:12; Jer 33:22 [b]Rom 9:26 [c]Is 65:1; Hos 1:9 [d]Is 63:16; 64:8; John 1:12; 1 Pet 2:10
11 [a]Is 11:12 [b]Jer 23:5, 6; 50:4, 5; Ezek 37:21-24 [c]Jer 30:21; Hos 3:5
2:1 [1]Ch 2:3 in Heb [2]I.e. my people [3]I.e. she has obtained compassion
2 [a]Ezek 23:45; Hos 2:5; 4:5 [b]Is 50:1 [c]Jer 3:1, 9, 13
3 [a]Jer 13:22; Ezek 16:7, 22, 39 [b]Ezek 16:4 [c]Is 32:13, 14; Hos 13:15

1:1 *word of the LORD.* A claim of authority paralleling that of Joel (1:1), Micah (1:1) and Zechariah (1:1,7). *Hosea.* Means "salvation." *Uzziah.* Reigned 792–740 B.C. *Jotham.* 750–732. *Ahaz.* 735–715. *Hezekiah.* 729–686. Some of the reigns overlapped, the co-regency of Ahaz and Hezekiah being the longest (see note on Is 36:1). *Jeroboam.* Jeroboam II, 793–753. Hosea was a contemporary of Isaiah, Amos and Micah (see the similar first verse in their prophecies).

1:2 *take . . . a wife of harlotry.* See Introduction: Special Problems. *harlotry.* Spiritual harlotry (unfaithfulness) is the one great sin of which the Lord (through Hosea) accuses Israel.

1:3 *Gomer.* Not mentioned outside this book. *him.* The omission of this word in vv. 6, 8 may indicate that Hosea was not the father of Gomer's next two children.

1:4 *Jezreel.* Means "God scatters," here used to reinforce the announcement of judgment on the reigning house (see notes on v. 11; 2:22). Jeroboam II was of the dynasty of Jehu (841–814 B.C.), which was established at Jezreel by the overthrow of Ahab's son Joram (2 Kin 9:14–37; cf. 1 Kin 19:16–17). Jehu's dynasty ended with the murder of Zechariah in 753 (2 Kin 15:8–10).

1:5 *the bow of Israel.* Israel's military power, broken in 724 B.C., though Samaria held out under siege for some two years longer (2 Kin 17:5–6).

1:6 *Lo-ruhamah.* See NASB marg. The naming represents a reversal of the love (compassion) that God had earlier shown to Israel (Ex 33:19; Deut 7:6–8) but that later was promised again (2:23).

1:7 *Judah . . . deliver them.* They were saved from Assyria by the Lord in 722–721 B.C. and again in 701 (see 2 Kin 19:32–36).

1:9 *Lo-ammi.* See NASB marg. The naming represents a break in the covenant relationship between the Lord and Israel (see Ex 6:7; Jer 7:23), which later, however, would be restored (v. 10; 2:1,23). The warnings became more severe in moving from the first to the third child.

1:10 Cited in Rom 9:26; 1 Pet 2:10 and applied to the mission to the Gentiles. *Yet.* The threatened punishment (vv. 4–9) would be for only a limited time, and a period of blessing would follow. *sand of the sea.* See the promise to Abraham and Jacob (Gen 22:17; 32:12; cf. Jer 33:22; Heb 11:12). *sons.* Contrasts with "children of harlotry" (v. 2; 2:4). *living God.* Contrasts with idols—"who were not God" (Deut 32:17).

1:11 *gathered together.* Israel and Judah would become one nation again. *up from the land.* Possibly the land of exile (cf. Ex 1:10). Another interpretation is that they would spring up from the ground as plants do. *Jezreel.* Here "God scatters" (see note on v. 4) refers to sowing or planting, indicating a reversal of the meaning of the first child's name (see 2:21–23).

2:1 *Ammi . . . Ruhamah.* See NASB marg. The negatives associated with the names of Hosea's children (see notes on 1:6,9) are dropped.

2:2 *not my wife.* The marriage was broken by unfaithfulness, but reconciliation, not divorce, was sought (cf. vv. 7–15).

2:3 *strip her.* The husband supplied the wife's clothing (see Ex 21:10; Ezek 16:10), and here her unfaithfulness was exposed (see Jer 13:26; Ezek 16:39). *expose her . . . when she was born.* As Israel was when the Lord found her in Egypt—in slavery and with nothing (cf. Ezek 16:4–8; Nah 3:5).

And slay her with [d]thirst.
4 "Also, I will have no compassion on her children,
Because they are [a]children of harlotry.
5 "For their mother has [a]played the harlot;
She who conceived them has acted shamefully.
For she said, '[a]I will go after my lovers,
Who [b]give *me* my bread and my water,
My wool and my flax, my [c]oil and my drink.'
6 "Therefore, behold, I will [a]hedge up [1]her way with [b]thorns,
And I will build [2]a wall against her so that she cannot find her [c]paths.
7 "She will [a]pursue her lovers, but she will not overtake them;
And she will seek them, but will not find *them*.
Then she will say, '[b]I will go back to my [c]first husband,
For it was [d]better for me then than now!'
8 "For she does [a]not know that it was [b]I who gave her the grain, the new wine and the oil,
And lavished on her silver and gold,
Which they [1]used for Baal.
9 "Therefore, I will [a]take back My grain at [1]harvest time
And My new wine in its season.
I will also take away My wool and My flax
Given to cover her nakedness.
10 "And then I will [a]uncover her lewdness
In the sight of her lovers,
And no one will rescue her out of My hand.
11 "I will also [a]put an end to all her gaiety,
Her [b]feasts, her [c]new moons, her sabbaths
And all her festal assemblies.
12 "I will [a]destroy her vines and fig trees,
Of which she said, 'These are my wages
Which my lovers have given me.'
And I will [b]make them a forest,
And the [c]beasts of the field will devour them.
13 "I will punish her for the [a]days of the Baals
When she used to [1b]offer sacrifices to them
And [c]adorn herself with her [2]earrings and jewelry,
And follow her lovers, so that she [d]forgot Me," declares the LORD.

Restoration of Israel

14 "Therefore, behold, I will allure her,
[a]Bring her into the wilderness
And speak [1]kindly to her.
15 "Then I will give her her [a]vineyards from there,
And [b]the valley of Achor as a door of hope.
And she will [1c]sing there as in the days of her youth,
As in the [d]day when she came up from the land of Egypt.
16 "It will come about in that day," declares the LORD,
"That you will call Me [1a]Ishi
And will no longer call Me [2]Baali.

3 [d]Jer 14:3; Amos 8:11-13 **4** [a]Jer 13:14 **5** [a]Is 1:21; Jer 2:25; 3:1, 2; Hos 3:1 [b]Jer 44:17, 18; Hos 2:12 [c]Hos 2:8 **6** [1]So with some ancient versions; Heb *your* [2]Lit *her wall so that* [a]Job 19:8; Lam 3:7, 9 [b]Hos 9:6; 10:8 [c]Jer 18:15 **7** [a]Hos 5:13 [b]Luke 15:17, 18 [c]Jer 2:2; 3:1; Ezek 16:8; 23:4 [d]Jer 14:22; Hos 13:6 **8** [1]Or *made into the* [a]Is 1:3 [b]Ezek 16:19 **9** [1]Lit *its time* [a]Hos 8:7; 9:2 **10** [a]Ezek 16:37
11 [a]Jer 7:34; 16:9 [b]Hos 3:4; Amos 5:21; 8:10 [c]Is 1:13, 14 **12** [a]Jer 5:17; 8:13 [b]Is 5:5; 7:23 [c]Hos 13:8 **13** [1]Or *burn incense* [2]Or *nose rings* [a]Hos 4:13; 11:2 [b]Jer 7:9 [c]Ezek 16:12, 17; 23:40 [d]Hos 4:6; 8:14; 13:6 **14** [1]Lit *upon her heart* [a]Ezek 20:33-38 **15** [1]Or *give answer* [a]Ezek 28:25, 26 [b]Josh 7:26 [c]Jer 2:1-3; Ezek 16:8-14 [d]Hos 11:1; 12:9, 13; 13:4 **16** [1]I.e. *my husband* [2]I.e. *my master, or my Baal* [a]Is 54:5; Hos 2:7

2:4 *children of harlotry.* See 1:2. This contrasts with being "sons" of the Lord (1:10; 11:1).
2:5 *go after.* The wife was chasing other men (see Jer 3:2; Ezek 16:33). *lovers.* See vv. 7,10. The reference is to Canaanite deities (such as Baal), whose worshipers hoped to gain agricultural fertility. *Who give me my bread . . . my drink.* Ugaritic texts attribute crops to rain given by Baal. *wool . . . flax . . . oil . . . drink.* The agricultural staples of the Holy Land. Israel does not know the true source of her blessings.
2:6 *hedge up her way.* Rather than punish Israel with death (cf. Deut 22:21; Ezek 16:39–40; Nah 3:5–7), the Lord would isolate her.
2:7 *pursue.* A cultic term in Hosea; elsewhere the Hebrew for this word is translated "press on" or "pursue" (6:3; 8:3; 12:1). *seek.* See 5:6,15. *not find.* See 5:6. *go back.* The Hebrew for this expression often means "repent." *my first husband.* The Lord.
2:8 *she does not know.* The Canaanites attributed grain, wine and oil to Baal. *silver and gold.* Used for making idols (see 8:4; 9:6; 13:2). *Baal.* The Canaanite god who was believed to control the weather and the fertility of crops, animals and man (see note on Judg 2:13).
2:9 *take back.* By withholding the fruits of field and flock, the Lord made known the true source of those blessings.
2:10 *uncover her lewdness.* The unfaithful wife was exposed to public shame (see Lam 1:8; Ezek 16:37; 23:29). *no one will rescue her.* Baal had no power.
2:11 *put an end to . . . gaiety.* In exile these joyous seasons would be only a memory. *feasts.* See Ex 23:14–17; Deut 16:16. See also chart, pp. 164–165. *new moons.* See 2 Kin 4:23; Is 1:13; Amos 8:5. *sabbaths.* See Ex 20:8–11.
2:12 *wages . . . my lovers have given.* The harlot's pay (see 9:1; Deut 23:18; Ezek 16:33; Mic 1:7). Israel attributed her agricultural products to the false gods she worshiped, rather than to the Lord (see Deut 11:13–14). *forest.* See Is 5:5–6; 7:23; 32:13; Mic 3:12.
2:13 *days.* Festival days. *Baals.* See v. 17; 11:2. Hosea used the plural here, suggesting the idols at the many local shrines (see Jer 2:23; 9:14). *follow.* See note on v. 5. *forgot.* The opposite of "know" in Hosea (cf. 13:4–6).
2:14 *into the wilderness.* For a second betrothal (see vv. 19–20). It refers back to the days of Israel's wilderness wandering, before she was tempted by the Baals in Canaan. *speak kindly to.* Reassure, encourage, comfort (cf. Gen 34:3; Ruth 2:13; Is 40:2). God continually shows love in the midst of judgment.
2:15 *valley of Achor.* Near Jericho (see Josh 7:1–26; 15:7; Is 65:10). As the prophet reversed the meaning of the names of his children, so also the meaning of Achor ("trouble")—where God first judged His people in the promised land—became a symbol of new opportunity.
2:16–17 *Ishi . . . Baali . . . Baals.* Ishi means "my husband," and

17 "For [a]I will remove the names of the
Baals from her mouth,
So that they will be [1]mentioned by
their names no more.
18 "In that day I will also make a
covenant for them
With the [a]beasts of the field,
The birds of the sky
And the creeping things of the ground.
And I will [1b]abolish the bow, the
sword and war from the land,
And will make them [c]lie down in
safety.
19 "I will [a]betroth you to Me forever;
Yes, I will betroth you to Me in
[b]righteousness and in justice,
In lovingkindness and in compassion,
20 And I will betroth you to Me in
faithfulness.
Then you will [a]know the LORD.

21 "It will come about in that day that [a]I
will respond," declares the LORD.
"I will respond to the heavens, and
they will respond to the earth,
22 And the [a]earth will respond to the
grain, to the new wine and to the
oil,
And they will respond to [1]Jezreel.
23 "I will [a]sow her for Myself in the land.
[b]I will also have compassion on [1]her
who had not obtained compassion,
And [c]I will say to [2]those who were
[d]not My people,
'You are My people!'
And [3]they will say, '*You are* my God!' "

Hosea's Second Symbolic Marriage

3 Then the LORD said to me, "Go again, love a [1]woman *who* is loved by *her* [2]husband, yet an adulteress, even [a]as the LORD loves the sons of Israel, though they turn to other gods and love raisin [b]cakes."

2 So I [a]bought her for myself for fifteen *shekels* of silver and a homer and a [1]half of barley.

3 Then I said to her, "You shall [a]stay with me for many days. You shall not play the harlot, nor shall you have a [1]man; so I will also be toward you."

4 For the sons of Israel will remain for many days [a]without king or prince, [b]without sacrifice or *sacred* [c]pillar and without [d]ephod or [1e]household idols.

5 Afterward the sons of Israel will [a]return and seek the LORD their God and [b]David their

17 [1]Or *remembered* [a]Ex 23:13; Josh 23:7; Ps 16:4
18 [1]Lit *break* [a]Job 5:23; Is 11:6-9; Ezek 34:25 [b]Is 2:4; Ezek 39:1-10 [c]Lev 26:5; Jer 23:6; Ezek 34:25
19 [a]Is 62:4, 5 [b]Is 1:27; 54:6-8
20 [a]Jer 31:33, 34; Hos 6:6; 13:4
21 [a]Is 55:10; Zech 8:12; Mal 3:10, 11
22 [1]I.e. God sows [a]Jer 31:12; Joel 2:19
23 [1]Heb *Lo-ruhamah* [2]Heb *Lo-ammi* [3]Lit *he* [a]Jer 31:27 [b]Hos 1:6 [c]Rom 9:25; 1 Pet 2:10 [d]Hos 1:9
3:1 [1]I.e. Gomer [2]Lit *companion* [a]Jer 3:20 [b]2 Sam 6:19; 1 Chr 16:3; Song 2:5
2 [1]Heb *lethech* [a]Ruth 4:10
3 [1]Or *husband* [a]Deut 21:13
4 [1]Heb *teraphim* [a]Hos 10:3; 13:10, 11 [b]Dan 9:27; 11:31; 12:11; Hos 2:11 [c]Hos 10:1, 2 [d]Ex 28:4-12; 1 Sam 23:9-12 [e]Gen 31:19, 34; Judg 17:5; 18:14, 17; 1 Sam 15:23
5 [a]Jer 50:4, 5 [b]Jer 30:9; Ezek 34:24

Baali means "my master." Of the two Hebrew words for husband, one (master) is identical with the name of the god Baal (see NASB marg. on v. 16). There will be such a vigorous reaction against Baal worship that this Hebrew word for "master" will no longer be used of the Lord.

2:18 *make a covenant.* See 6:7; 8:1. Animals, the instruments of destruction in v. 12, as well as birds and insects, would no longer threaten life. Nature and history combine in a picture of peace (see Is 11:6–9; 65:25). *bow . . . sword.* See 1:5. War is terminated. *land.* Israel (see 1:2; 4:1,3; 9:3; 10:1). *lie down in safety.* See Jer 33:16; Ezek 34:24–28.

2:19–20 Rather than money, these five traits necessary to the covenant relationship make up the bride-price (see Ex 22:16–17; Deut 22:23–29; 1 Sam 18:25; 2 Sam 3:14).

2:19 *righteousness.* See 10:12; Jer 23:6; Amos 6:12; Mic 6:5. *justice.* See Amos 5:24. *lovingkindness.* See 4:1; 6:4; 10:12; 12:6. *compassion.* A reversal of God's threatened withdrawal of compassion (see 1:6 and note). "Lo-ruhamah" means lit. "not shown compassion" (cf. Ps 51:1; 103:3–14).

2:20 *faithfulness.* Dependability (see Deut 32:4; Ps 88:11). *know.* The Hebrew for this word can refer to intimate marital relations (Gen 19:8; Num 31:17–18,35), but it also refers to active acknowledgment of a covenant partner (see 4:1,6; 5:4; 6:3,6; 8:2; 11:3; 13:4).

2:21 *respond.* The woman (Israel) responded to the Lord's overtures (see NASB marg. on v. 15); now God responded to her new behavior. The land also responded in becoming productive (vv. 21–22).

2:22 *Jezreel.* Here used in the sense "God sows" (see NASB marg. and v. 23; see also note on 1:11). The threats represented by the names of the children are turned into blessings (see 1:10). The terms of the covenant were: "I will take you for My people, and I will be your God" (Ex 6:7; see note on Zech 8:8).

2:23 *You are my God.* The people respond to God's graciousness. This verse is quoted in part in Rom 9:25; 1 Pet 2:10 and applied to Gentiles coming into the church.

3:1 *said to me.* Ch. 3 is narrated in the first person, ch. 1 in the third person. *Go . . . love a woman.* Hosea's love for unfaithful Gomer illustrated God's love for unfaithful Israel. God's love for Israel (see 11:1; 14:4) is the basic theme of the book. *other gods.* See Ex 20:3; Deut 31:20. *raisin cakes.* Offered to Baal in thanksgiving for harvest.

3:2 Gomer had evidently become a slave, and Hosea bought her back. *fifteen shekels.* Half the usual price of a slave (Ex 21:7,32) or of the redemption value of a woman's vow (Lev 27:4). *a homer and a half.* Probably about 10 bushels. Comparison with prices in 2 Kin 7:1,16,18 suggests that half was paid in money (silver) and half in produce (barley)—for a total value of 30 shekels.

3:3–5 A picture of exile and return.

3:3 *many days.* Not forever. There would be an "afterward" (v. 5), a future. *be toward.* Or "wait for"; suggests a period of isolation (see 2:6 and note), comparable to Israel's exile.

3:4 *king.* See 1:4; 5:1; 8:4,10; 10:15; 13:10–11. *prince.* See 5:10; 7:3,5; 8:4; 13:10. *without sacrifice.* See 6:6; 8:11,13. *sacred pillar.* See 10:1–2; Deut 16:22; 1 Kin 14:23; 2 Kin 17:10; Mic 5:13. *ephod.* Here an image associated with idols (see Judg 8:27; 17:5). *idols.* See Gen 31:30; 1 Sam 19:13,16.

3:5 *return.* A basic word in Hosea's vocabulary (see 2:7; 5:4; 6:1; 7:10; 11:5; 12:6; 14:1–2). *seek.* Israel's repentance is envisioned (cf. 5:15)—the reverse of her present stubborn rebellion (7:10). *LORD their God.* See 12:9; 13:4; Jer 50:4. *David their king.* The Messianic king from the dynasty of David (see Jer 30:9; Ezek 34:24). After the death of Solomon, Israel (the northern kingdom) had abandoned the Davidic kings. *His goodness.* The vineyards and olive groves that had been taken away (see 2:12–13,21) and all of God's gifts (see Jer 31:12–14). *last days.* The Hebrew for this phrase occurs 13 times in the OT, sometimes simply meaning the future ("days to come," Gen 49:1), but most of the time, as no doubt here, referring to the Messianic age ("after this," Joel 2:28; cf. Acts 2:17; Heb 1:2).

king; and [c]they will come trembling to the LORD and to His goodness in the last days.

God's Controversy with Israel

4 [a]Listen to the word of the LORD,
O sons of Israel,
For the LORD has a [b]case against the
inhabitants of the land,
Because there is [c]no [1]faithfulness or
[2]kindness
Or [d]knowledge of God in the land.
2 *There is* [a]swearing, [b]deception,
[c]murder, [d]stealing and [e]adultery.
They employ violence, so that
[f]bloodshed [1]follows bloodshed.
3 Therefore the land [a]mourns,
And everyone who lives in it
languishes
Along with the beasts of the field and
the birds of the sky,
And also the fish of the sea
[1]disappear.

4 Yet let no one [1][a]find fault, and let
none offer reproof;
For your people are like those who
[b]contend with the priest.
5 So you will [a]stumble by day,
And the prophet also will stumble
with you by night;
And I will destroy your [b]mother.
6 [a]My people are destroyed for lack of
knowledge.
Because you have [b]rejected
knowledge,
I also will [c]reject you from being My
priest.
Since you have [d]forgotten the [e]law of
your God,
I also will forget your children.
7 The more they [a]multiplied, the more
they sinned against Me;
I will [b]change their glory into shame.
8 They [a]feed on the [1]sin of My people
And [b]direct their desire toward their
iniquity.
9 And it will be, like people, [a]like
priest;
So I will [b]punish them for their ways
And repay them for their deeds.
10 [a]They will eat, but not have enough;
They will [b]play the harlot, but not
increase,
Because they have [1][c]stopped giving
heed to the LORD.

11 Harlotry, [a]wine and new wine take
away the [1]understanding.
12 My people [a]consult their wooden idol,
and their *diviner's* wand informs
them;
For a spirit of harlotry has led *them*
astray,
And they have played the harlot,
departing [1]from their God.
13 They offer sacrifices on the [a]tops of
the mountains
And [1][b]burn incense on the hills,
[c]Under oak, poplar and terebinth,
Because their shade is pleasant.

5 [c]Is 2:2, 3; Jer 31:9
4:1 [1]Or *truth* [2]Or *loyalty* [a]Hos 5:1 [b]Hos 12:2; Mic 6:2 [c]Is 59:4; Jer 7:28 [d]Jer 4:22
2 [1]Lit *touches* [a]Deut 5:11; Hos 10:4 [b]Hos 7:3; 10:13; 11:12 [c]Gen 4:8; Hos 6:9 [d]Deut 5:19; Hos 7:1 [e]Deut 5:18; Hos 7:4 [f]Hos 6:8; 12:14
3 [1]Lit *are taken away* [a]Is 24:4; 33:9; Amos 5:16; Zeph 1:3
4 [1]Lit *contend* [a]Ezek 3:26; Amos 5:10, 13 [b]Deut 17:12
5 [a]Ezek 14:3, 7; Hos 5:5 [b]Jer 15:8; Hos 2:2, 5
6 [a]Is 5:13 [b]Hos 4:14; Mal 2:7, 8 [c]Zech 11:8, 9, 15-17
6 [d]Hos 2:13; 8:14; 13:6 [e]Hos 8:1, 12
7 [a]Hos 10:1; 13:6 [b]Hab 2:16
8 [1]Or *sin offering* [a]Hos 10:13 [b]Is 56:11; Mic 3:11
9 [a]Is 24:2; Jer 5:31 [b]Hos 8:13; 9:9
10 [1]Lit *forsaken giving heed;* or *forsaken the* LORD *to practice* (v 11) *harlotry* [a]Lev 26:26; Is 65:13; Mic 6:14 [b]Hos 7:4 [c]Hos 9:17
11 [1]Lit *heart* [a]Prov 20:1; Is 5:12; 28:7 **12** [1]Lit *from under* [a]Is 44:19; Jer 2:27 **13** [1]Or *offer sacrifices* [a]Jer 3:6 [b]Hos 2:13; 11:2 [c]Is 1:29; Jer 2:20

4:1–14:9 Deals with Israel's involvement in Canaanite religion, her moral sins and her international intrigues.
4:1 *Listen to the word.* See, e.g., Is 1:10; Jer 2:4; Ezek 6:3. *case.* As the Lord's spokesman, Hosea brought charges against unfaithful, covenant-breaking Israel (cf. v. 4; Is 3:13; Jer 2:9; Mic 6:2). *faithfulness.* Loyalty to the covenant Lord (Josh 24:14) and right dealing with men (Prov 3:3). *kindness.* See 2:19; 10:12. *knowledge of God.* See 2:20 and note; 5:4; 6:6.
4:2 *swearing . . . adultery.* The sins detailed (paralleled in Jer 7:9) transgress the Ten Commandments (see Ex 20:13–16; Deut 5:17–20). *bloodshed.* Includes (1) murder (see 6:8–9), (2) the assassinations following the death of Jeroboam II when three kings reigned in one year (2 Kin 15:10–14) and (3) human sacrifice (Ps 106:38; Ezek 16:20–21; 23:37). Where God is not acknowledged (v. 1), moral uprightness disappears.
4:3 *land mourns.* God's judgment on man's sin affects all living things in man's world (see, e.g., Is 24:3–6; Jer 4:23–28). *languishes.* See Is 19:8; Jer 14:2; 15:9; Joel 1:10.
4:4–9 An indictment against the priests, whose duty it was to be guardians of God's law and to furnish religious instruction (see Deut 31:9–13; 33:10; 2 Chr 17:8–9; Ezra 7:6,10; Jer 18:18). Hosea warned the priests not to lodge charges against the people for bringing God's judgment down on the nation, for they themselves were guilty, and the people could also bring charges against them—as Hosea proceeded to do (see v. 9; Is 28:7; Jer 2:26; 4:9; 23:11).
4:5 *stumble.* See 5:5. *prophet.* See Mic 2:6,11; 3:5–7. *your mother.* The nation (see 2:2,5; Is 50:1).
4:6 *My people.* Israel (see vv. 8,12; 2:1,23; 6:11; 11:7; Mic 6:3). *destroyed for lack of knowledge.* Partly because the priests had failed to teach God's word to the people. *rejected knowledge . . . reject you.* Punishment in kind. *law of your God.* Israel's source of life (see Deut 32:47), which the priests should have been faithfully promoting.
4:7 *their Glory.* God (see Ps 106:20).
4:8 *feed on the sin.* Priests devoured the sacrifices (1 Sam 2:13–17), profiting from the continuation of the sin rather than helping to cure it (see 8:13).
4:9 *like people, like priest.* Without exception, all would be punished for their sins.
4:10 *eat, but not have enough.* The punishment fit the sin. *play the harlot.* See vv. 12,18; 2:4; 6:10; 9:1; Ps 106:39. Instead of giving themselves to the Lord, they gave themselves to prostitution.
4:11 *wine.* See 7:5; 9:10; 14:7. *new wine.* See 2:8–9,22; 7:14; 9:2.
4:12 *wooden idol.* An image of a god (see Jer 2:27; 10:8; Hab 2:19). *diviner's wand.* See Ezek 21:21 and note. *spirit of harlotry.* See 5:4. Hebrew idioms often describe inner tendencies in terms of "spirit."
4:13 *offer sacrifices.* See 8:13. *tops of the mountains.* Places commonly chosen for pagan altars (see 10:8; Deut 12:2; 1 Kin 14:23; 2 Kin 17:10; Jer 2:20; 3:6). Clay tablets from Ugarit (see chart, p. xix) tell of fertility rites carried out by the Canaanites at the high places. *oak . . . terebinth.* Trees noted for their shade. *play the harlot.* Canaanite fertility rites involved sexual activity (v. 14) that led to general erosion of morals.

Therefore your daughters play the harlot
And your [2]brides commit adultery.
14 I will not punish your daughters when they play the harlot
Or your [1]brides when they commit adultery,
For *the men* themselves go apart with harlots
And offer sacrifices with [a]temple prostitutes;
So the people without understanding are [2]ruined.

15 Though you, Israel, play the harlot,
Do not let Judah become guilty;
Also do not go to [a]Gilgal,
Or go up to Beth-aven
[b]And take the oath:
"As the LORD lives!"
16 Since Israel is [a]stubborn
Like a stubborn heifer,
[1]Can the LORD now [b]pasture them
Like a lamb in a large field?
17 Ephraim is joined to [a]idols;
[b]Let him alone.
18 Their liquor gone,
They play the harlot continually;
[a]Their [1]rulers dearly love shame.
19 [a]The wind wraps them in its wings,
And they will be ashamed because of their sacrifices.

13 [2]Or *daughters-in-law* **14** [1]Or *daughters-in-law* [2]Lit *thrust down* [a]Deut 23:17 **15** [a]Hos 9:15; 12:11 [b]Jer 5:2; 44:26; Amos 8:14 **16** [1]Or *Now the LORD will pasture...field* [a]Ps 78:8 [b]Is 5:17; 7:25 **17** [a]Hos 13:2 [b]Ps 81:12; Hos 4:4 **18** [1]Lit *shields* [a]Mic 3:11 **19** [a]Hos 12:1; 13:15

5:1 [a]Hos 9:8 **2** [1]Or *waded deep in slaughter* [a]Hos 9:15 [b]Is 29:15; Hos 4:2; 6:9 **3** [a]Amos 3:2; 5:12 **4** [a]Hos 4:12 [b]Hos 4:6, 14 **5** [a]Hos 7:10 [b]Ezek 23:31-35 **6** [a]Hos 8:13; Mic 6:6, 7 [b]Prov 1:28; Is 1:15; Jer 14:12 [c]Ezek 8:6 **7** [a]Is 48:8; Jer 3:20; Hos 6:7

The People's Apostasy Rebuked

5 Hear this, O priests!
Give heed, O house of Israel!
Listen, O house of the king!
For the judgment applies to you,
For you have been a [a]snare at Mizpah
And a net spread out on Tabor.
2 The [a]revolters have [1b]gone deep in depravity,
But I will chastise all of them.
3 I [a]know Ephraim, and Israel is not hidden from Me;
For now, O Ephraim, you have played the harlot,
Israel has defiled itself.
4 Their deeds will not allow them
To return to their God.
For a [a]spirit of harlotry is within them,
And they [b]do not know the LORD.
5 Moreover, the [a]pride of Israel testifies against him,
And Israel and Ephraim stumble in their iniquity;
[b]Judah also has stumbled with them.
6 They will [a]go with their flocks and herds
To seek the LORD, but they will [b]not find *Him;*
He has [c]withdrawn from them.
7 They have [a]dealt treacherously against the LORD,

4:14 *not punish.* The men would punish their women for immorality, but God would have no part in their hypocrisy. *harlots.* Common prostitutes (see Gen 34:31; Lev 21:14; Ezek 16:31). *temple prostitutes.* Women of the sanctuaries who served as partners for men in cultic sexual activity (cf. Gen 38:21–22; Deut 23:18). *without understanding.* Contrast 14:9.
4:15 *Judah.* An aside warning (see Introduction: Author and Date). *guilty.* See 10:2; 13:1; 14:1. *do not go.* The nation as a whole was addressed. *Gilgal.* A site near Jericho (see 9:15; 12:11; Josh 4:19–20; 1 Sam 11:13–15) where the Israelites had established a religious shrine. *Beth-aven.* A sarcastic substitute name for Bethel (Beth-aven means "house of wickedness," while Bethel means "house of God"; see also 5:8), site of one of the cult centers established by Jeroboam I (1 Kin 12:29). *As the LORD lives.* A form of solemn oath (see Judg 8:19; Ruth 3:13; 1 Sam 14:39; 26:10,16; Jer 4:2; 38:16). Though proper in itself—since it invoked the true God (see Deut 6:13; 10:20; Josh 23:7)—it was here forbidden because it was being used deceitfully, as though the Israelites were truly honoring the Lord (see Jer 5:2).
4:16 *stubborn.* See Neh 9:29; Zech 7:11. *stubborn heifer.* See 10:11; Jer 2:20; an apt figure for unruly Israel (see 11:4; Jer 31:18).
4:17 *Ephraim.* Israel, the northern kingdom. *idols.* The golden calf (8:5; 13:2; 1 Kin 12:28) and the cult of Baal (2:8,13). *Let him alone.* Nothing could be done to help (see 2 Sam 16:11; 2 Kin 23:18).
4:19 *The wind wraps them in its wings.* Probably a metaphor from the threshing floor (see 13:3; Ps 1:4) for the sudden violence that would bring the exile. Since the Hebrew for the words "wind" and "spirit" is the same, there is a possible play on words with the "spirit of harlotry" (v. 12; 5:4). *ashamed.* By means of their sacrifices they hoped to flourish, but God's punishment for their idolatry would bring them into disgrace among the nations (see 10:6).
5:1 *priests . . . house of Israel . . . house of the king.* The three groups addressed were all responsible for maintaining justice, but it miscarried at their hands. *snare . . . net.* Devices for catching animals and birds, here used as metaphors for those who by economic and legal devices took cruel advantage of innocent people (see Job 18:8–10; Ps 140:5; Prov 29:5; Lam 1:13). *Mizpah.* Either (1) Mizpah in Gilead east of the Jordan (Gen 31:43–49) or (2) Mizpah in Benjamin (1 Sam 7:5–6; 10:17). *Tabor.* A mountain at the southeastern edge of the Jezreel Valley. Reference must have been to well-known events that illustrated Israel's corruption.
5:2 *chastise.* A significant word in the prophets for God's corrective action against His people (see Is 26:16; Jer 2:30; 5:3; 7:28).
5:3 *Ephraim.* Israel, the northern kingdom. *played the harlot.* See 1:2; 4:10,18.
5:4 *Their deeds.* See 4:9; 7:2; 9:15; 12:2. Persistent sin can make repentance impossible (see Jer 13:23; John 8:34; Rom 6:6,16). *spirit of harlotry.* See 4:12. *know the LORD.* See 4:6; Is 1:2–4.
5:5 *pride.* Stubborn rebellion against the Lord (see Deut 1:43; 1 Sam 15:23; Neh 9:16; Job 35:12; Ps 10:2; Ezek 16:56–57). *testifies.* In the case God presented against His people (see 4:1 and note). *stumble.* Experience calamity (see 4:5). *Judah.* See Introduction: Author and Date.
5:6 *seek the LORD.* Go to Him with prayer and sacrifices (see 3:5; Amos 5:4–5). *not find Him.* Offering sacrifices in their situation was useless (see 2:7; cf. Is 1:10–14; Amos 5:21–25; Mic 6:6–8). The Lord would be "found" by Israel only when she turned to Him with integrity of heart (see 3:5; 5:15; Deut 4:29–31; Jer 29:13).
5:7 *dealt treacherously.* See Jer 5:11. *illegitimate children.* Chil-

For they have borne [1b]illegitimate
children.
Now the [c]new moon will devour them
with their [2]land.

8 [a]Blow the horn in [b]Gibeah,
The trumpet in Ramah.
Sound an alarm at Beth-aven:
"[c]Behind you, Benjamin!"
9 Ephraim will become a [a]desolation in
the [b]day of rebuke;
Among the tribes of Israel I [c]declare
what is sure.
10 The princes of Judah have become
like those who [a]move a boundary;
On them I will [b]pour out My wrath
[c]like water.
11 Ephraim is [a]oppressed, crushed in
judgment,
[b]Because he was determined to
[1]follow *man's* command.
12 Therefore I am like a [a]moth to Ephraim
And like rottenness to the house of
Judah.
13 When Ephraim saw his sickness,
And Judah his [1]wound,
Then Ephraim went to [a]Assyria
And sent to [2b]King Jareb.
But he is [c]unable to heal you,
Or to cure you of your [1]wound.
14 For I *will be* [a]like a lion to Ephraim
And like a young lion to the house of
Judah.
[b]I, even I, will tear to pieces and go
away,
I will carry away, and there will be
[c]none to deliver.
15 I will go away *and* return to My place
Until they [1a]acknowledge their guilt
and seek My face;
In their affliction they will earnestly
[b]seek Me.

The Response to God's Rebuke

6 "[a]Come, let us return to the LORD.
For [b]He has torn *us,* but [c]He will
heal us;
He has [1]wounded *us,* but He will
[d]bandage us.
2 "He will [a]revive us after two days;
He will [b]raise us up on the third day,
That we may live before Him.
3 "So let us [a]know, let us press on to
know the LORD.
His [b]going forth is as certain as the
dawn;
And He will come to us like the [c]rain,
Like the spring rain watering the
earth."

4 What shall I do with you,
O [a]Ephraim?
What shall I do with you, O Judah?
For your [1]loyalty is like a [b]morning
cloud
And like the dew which goes away
early.
5 Therefore I have [a]hewn *them* in pieces
by the prophets;
I have slain them by the [b]words of My
mouth;
And the judgments on you are *like* the
light that goes forth.
6 For [a]I delight in loyalty [b]rather than
sacrifice,
And in the knowledge of God rather
than burnt offerings.

7 [1]Lit *strange* [2]Lit *portions* [b]Hos 2:4 [c]Is 1:14; Hos 2:11
8 [a]Joel 2:1 [b]Hos 9:9; 10:9 [c]Judg 5:14
9 [a]Is 28:1-4; Hos 9:11-17 [b]Is 37:3 [c]Is 46:10; Zech 1:6
10 [a]Deut 19:14; 27:17 [b]Ezek 7:8 [c]Ps 32:6; 93:3, 4
11 [1]Or with some ancient versions, *follow nothingness* [a]Deut 28:33 [b]Mic 6:16
12 [a]Ps 39:11; Is 51:8
13 [1]Or *ulcer* [2]Or *the avenging king* or *the great king* [a]Hos 7:11; 8:9; 12:1 [b]Hos 10:6 [c]Jer 30:12-15
14 [a]Ps 7:2; Hos 13:7, 8; Amos 3:4 [b]Ps 50:22 [c]Mic 5:8
15 [1]Or *bear their punishment* [a]Is 64:7-9; Jer 3:13, 14
15 [b]Ps 50:15; 78:34; Jer 2:27; Hos 3:5
6:1 [1]Lit *struck* [a]Jer 50:4, 5 [b]Deut 32:39; Hos 5:14 [c]Jer 30:17; Hos 14:4 [d]Is 30:26
2 [a]Ps 30:5 [b]1 Cor 15:4
3 [a]Is 2:3; Mic 4:2 [b]Ps 19:6; Mic 5:2 [c]Job 29:23; Ps 72:6; Joel 2:23

4 [1]Or *lovingkindness* [a]Hos 7:1; 11:8 [b]Ps 78:34-37; Hos 13:3
5 [a]1 Sam 15:32, 33; Jer 1:10; 5:14 [b]Jer 23:29 **6** [a]Matt 9:13; 12:7 [b]Is 1:11

dren they had prayed to the Baals for and had credited to their fertility rites. *new moon.* Usually a festive occasion (see, e.g., 2:11; 1 Sam 20:5,18; Amos 8:5; Col 2:16), but now a time of judgment. Or the meaning may be that one month would be sufficient to accomplish their punishment.

5:8 Some interpreters suggest that the Aramean (Syrian)-Ephraimite (Israelite) war (2 Kin 16:5–9; Is 7:1–9) forms the background of this oracle. *horn.* Made of a ram's horn, which here sounds the alarm that an army is approaching (see 8:1). *Gibeah.* Two miles north of Jerusalem. *Ramah.* North of Gibeah. *Beth-aven.* See note on 4:15. *Behind you, Benjamin.* Thought to be the Benjamite war cry (see Judg 5:14).

5:9 *desolation.* See Jer 25:11,38.

5:10 *move a boundary.* Judah had seized Israelite territory (1 Kin 15:16–22; see Deut 19:14; 27:17; Prov 22:28; 23:10; Is 5:8; Mic 2:2). *My wrath.* See 13:11.

5:12 *moth . . . rottenness.* Both consume (see Job 13:28).

5:13 *sickness . . . wound.* Metaphors for the national wounds the two nations had suffered at the hands of their enemies (see Is 1:5–6; 17:4,11; Jer 30:12–13). *went to Assyria.* Assyrian records tell of the tribute paid to Tiglath-pileser III by the Israelite kings Menahem and Hoshea (cf. 2 Kin 15:19–20; 17:3). *unable to heal.* The alliances were worthless.

5:14 *lion.* See 13:7. The Lord might use human agents (Is 10:5–6), but He would be responsible for Israel's punishment, from which there was no escape (see Is 5:29; 42:22; Amos 9:1–4; Mic 5:8).

5:15 *return to My place.* God threatened to withdraw from Israel until, out of desperation, she truly repented. This idea sets the stage for the prophet's next theme.

6:1 *let us return.* A shallow (see v. 4) proposal of repentance (using phrases from 5:13–15), in which Israel acknowledged that God, not Assyria (cf. 5:13), was the true physician (cf. 7:1).

6:2 *two days . . . third day.* A brief time. Israel supposed that God's wrath would only be temporary.

6:3 *know the LORD.* A key concept in Hosea (see v. 6; 2:8,20; 4:1,6; 5:4). *like the rain . . . the spring rain.* Israel believed that, as surely as seasonal rains fell, reviving the earth, God's favor would return and restore her.

6:4 *What shall I do . . . ?* See Is 5:4. God saw through Israel's superficial repentance. *Ephraim.* Israel, the northern kingdom. *Judah.* See Introduction: Author and Date. *loyalty.* Or "lovingkindness" (see NASB marg.) See 2:19; see also note on v. 6. *morning cloud . . . dew.* Figurative for that which is temporary.

6:5 *the prophets.* God's spokesmen (see Jer 1:9; 15:19) had denounced the people's sin. *words of My mouth.* The judgments spoken by the Lord's faithful prophets. *like the light that goes forth.* See Deut 32:41.

6:6 *loyalty.* See v. 4; Hebrew *hesed,* a word that can refer to right conduct toward one's fellowman or loyalty to the Lord or

7 But [a]like [1]Adam they have
[b]transgressed the covenant;
There they have [c]dealt treacherously
against Me.
8 [a]Gilead is a city of wrongdoers,
Tracked with [b]bloody *footprints.*
9 And as [a]raiders wait for a man,
So a band of priests [b]murder on the
way to Shechem;
Surely they have committed [1c]crime.
10 In the house of Israel I have seen a
[a]horrible thing;
Ephraim's [b]harlotry is there, Israel has
defiled itself.
11 Also, O Judah, there is a [a]harvest
appointed for you,
When I [b]restore the fortunes of My
people.

Ephraim's Iniquity

7 When I [a]would heal Israel,
The iniquity of Ephraim is uncovered,
And the evil deeds of Samaria,
For they deal [b]falsely;
The thief enters in,
[c]Bandits raid outside,
2 And they do not [1]consider in their
hearts
That I [a]remember all their wickedness.
Now their [b]deeds are all around them;
They are before My face.
3 [a]With their wickedness they make the
[b]king glad,
And the princes with their [c]lies.
4 They are [a]all adulterers,
Like an oven heated by the baker
Who ceases to stir up *the fire*
From the kneading of the dough until
it is leavened.
5 On the [1]day of our king, the princes
[a]became sick with the heat of wine;
He stretched out his hand with
[b]scoffers,
6 For their hearts are like an [a]oven
As they approach their [1]plotting;
Their [2]anger [3]smolders all night,
In the morning it burns like a flaming
fire.
7 All of them are hot like an oven,
And they consume their [a]rulers;
All their kings have fallen.
[b]None of them calls on Me.

8 Ephraim [a]mixes himself with the
[1]nations;
Ephraim has become a cake not
turned.
9 [a]Strangers devour his strength,
Yet he [b]does not know *it;*
Gray hairs also are sprinkled on him,
Yet he does not know *it.*
10 Though the [a]pride of Israel testifies
against him,
Yet [b]they have not returned to the
LORD their God,
Nor have they sought Him, for all this.
11 So [a]Ephraim has become like a silly
dove, [b]without [1]sense;
They call to [c]Egypt, they go to
[d]Assyria.

7 [1]Or *men* [a]Job 31:33 [b]Hos 8:1 [c]Hos 5:7
8 [a]Hos 12:11 [b]Hos 4:2
9 [1]Or *lewdness* [a]Hos 7:1 [b]Jer 7:9, 10; Hos 4:2 [c]Ezek 22:9; 23:27; Hos 2:10
10 [a]Jer 5:30, 31; 23:14 [b]Hos 5:3
11 [a]Jer 51:33; Joel 3:13 [b]Zeph 2:7
7:1 [a]Ezek 24:13; Hos 6:4; 7:13; 11:8 [b]Hos 4:2 [c]Hos 6:9
2 [1]Lit *say to their heart* [a]Ps 25:7; Jer 14:10; 17:1; Hos 8:13; 9:9; Amos 8:7 [b]Jer 2:19; 4:18; Hos 4:9
3 [a]Rom 1:32 [b]Jer 28:1-4; Hos 7:5; Mic 7:3 [c]Hos 4:2; 11:12
4 [a]Jer 9:2; 23:10
5 [1]I.e. a festive occasion [a]Is 28:1, 7 [b]Is 28:14
6 [1]Lit *ambush* [2]So with some ancient versions; M.T. *baker* [3]Lit *sleeps* [a]Ps 21:9
7 [a]Hos 13:10 [b]Is 64:7
8 [1]Lit *peoples* [a]Ps 106:35
9 [a]Is 1:7; Hos 8:7 [b]Hos 4:6
10 [a]Hos 5:5 [b]Is 9:13
11 [1]Lit *heart* [a]Hos 11:11 [b]Hos 4:6, 11, 14; 5:4 [c]Hos 8:13; 9:3, 6 [d]Hos 5:13; 8:9; 12:1

both—the sum of what God requires of His servants. Here it perhaps refers to both. *rather than sacrifice.* Sacrifice apart from faithfulness to the Lord's will is wholly unacceptable to Him (see 1 Sam 15:22–23; Is 1:11–20; Jer 7:21–22; Amos 5:21–24; Mic 6:6–8; Matt 9:13; 12:7).

6:7 *like Adam.* The allusion is uncertain, since Scripture records no covenant with Adam. Two other possibilities exist. "Adam" could be a reference to the place named Adam (see Josh 3:16), as suggested by "There" in the verse. Or "Adam" could be a reference to mankind in general rather than the man Adam. *transgressed the covenant.* See 8:1; Josh 7:11.

6:8 *Gilead.* See 12:11; Judg 10:17; 12:7. *bloody footprints.* The allusion is unclear, but Hosea may have been referring to a more recent event than the bloodbath of Judg 12:1–6—such as Pekah's rebellion against Pekahiah (see 2 Kin 15:25).

6:9 *murder.* The specific event is unknown.

6:10 *harlotry.* See chs. 2; 4.

6:11 *harvest.* A figure for God's judgments (see 8:7; 10:12–13; Jer 51:33; Joel 3:13; Matt 13:39; Rev 14:15). *restore the fortunes.* Paralleling "heal" (7:1), the phrase refers to the restoration of the wounded national body (see Joel 3:1; Zeph 3:20).

7:1 *heal.* See 5:13; 6:1; 11:3; 14:4; Jer 51:8–9. *iniquity.* See 4:8; 5:5; 8:13. *Ephraim.* Israel, the northern kingdom. *uncovered.* God sees them. *evil deeds.* See v. 3. *Samaria.* Another name for the northern kingdom, of which Samaria was the royal city, selected by Omri to be capital of Israel (1 Kin 16:24). *deal falsely.* See Jer 6:13; 8:10; probably refers to both feigned repentance and treacherous foreign alliances. *thief.* See 4:2. *Bandits.* See 6:9; Gen 49:19; Jer 18:22.

7:2 *I remember.* All is open before the Lord (see Ps 90:8), but the wicked believe God does not see (see Ps 10:6,11; 14:1; Ezek 8:12).

7:3 *make the king glad.* Probably in conjunction with one of the palace revolts (see 2 Kin 15:8–30). *king . . . princes.* Paired also in 3:4; 8:4; 13:10. *lies.* See 11:12; Ps 59:12; Nah 3:1.

7:4 *adulterers.* See 3:1; 4:2,13; Jer 9:2; Ezek 23:37. *baker.* Perhaps the leader of the conspiracy. *fire.* A metaphor for political intrigue (see vv. 6–7). The fire was banked until ready to use; then it broke out.

7:5 *day of our king.* Probably a coronation or birthday that became a drunken party. King Elah died in drunkenness (1 Kin 16:9–10). *scoffers.* See Prov 21:24. Isaiah (28:1–8,14) condemned Israel's drunkenness and her scoffers.

7:6 The intrigue was kept secret until a suitable time.

7:7 *rulers . . . kings.* Four kings were assassinated in 20 years, Zechariah and Shallum in a seven-month period (2 Kin 15:10–15). *None of them calls on Me.* The reason for the shameful situation.

7:8 *cake not turned.* A metaphor describing unwise policies. Baked on hot stones (cf. 1 Kin 19:6), the cake was burned on the bottom and raw on the top.

7:9 *Gray hairs.* He was old before his time, but ignored the danger signals. Tribute to Tiglath-pileser (2 Kin 15:19–20,29) and to Egypt had sapped the country economically.

7:10 *returned.* See 3:5; 5:4; Amos 4:6–11. *sought.* See 2:7; 5:6.

7:11 *dove.* See 11:11 and note, where a different image is intended. See also note on Ps 68:13. *without sense.* See Jer

12 When they go, I will [a]spread My net
over them;
I will bring them down like the birds
of the sky.
I will [b]chastise them in accordance
with the [1]proclamation to their
assembly.
13 [a]Woe to them, for they have [b]strayed
from Me!
Destruction is theirs, for they have
rebelled against Me!
I [c]would redeem them, but they speak
lies against Me.
14 And [a]they do not cry to Me from their
heart
When they wail on their beds;
For the sake of grain and new wine
they [1b]assemble themselves,
They [c]turn away from Me.
15 Although I trained *and* strengthened
their arms,
Yet they [a]devise evil against Me.
16 They turn, *but* not [1]upward,
They are like a [a]deceitful bow;
Their princes will fall by the sword
Because of the [2b]insolence of their
tongue.
This *will be* their [c]derision in the land
of Egypt.

Israel Reaps the Whirlwind

8 [a]*Put* the trumpet to your [1]lips!
[b]Like an eagle *the enemy comes*
[c]against the house of the LORD,
Because they have [d]transgressed My
covenant
And rebelled against My [e]law.
2 [a]They cry out to Me,
"My God, [b]we of Israel know You!"
3 Israel has rejected the good;
The enemy will pursue him.
4 [a]They have set up kings, but not by
Me;
They have appointed princes, but I did
not know *it*.
With their [b]silver and gold they have
made idols for themselves,
That [1]they might be cut off.
5 [1]He has rejected your [a]calf,
O Samaria, *saying*,
"My anger burns against them!"
How long will they be incapable of
[b]innocence?
6 For from Israel is even this!
A [a]craftsman made it, so it is not God;
Surely the calf of Samaria will be
broken to [1]pieces.
7 For [a]they sow the wind
And they reap the [b]whirlwind.
The standing grain has no [1]heads;
It yields [c]no [2]grain.
Should it yield, strangers would
swallow it up.

8 Israel is [a]swallowed up;
They are now among the nations
Like a [b]vessel in which no one
delights.
9 For they have gone up to [a]Assyria,
Like [b]a wild donkey all alone;
Ephraim has [c]hired [1]lovers.
10 Even though they hire *allies* among
the nations,
Now I will [a]gather them up;
And they will begin [b]to [1]diminish
Because of the burden of the [c]king of
princes.

12 [1]Lit *report* [a]Ezek 12:13 [b]Lev 26:14-39; Deut 28:15 **13** [a]Hos 9:12 [b]Jer 14:10; Ezek 34:6; Hos 9:17 [c]Jer 51:9; Hos 7:1; Matt 23:37 **14** [1]Or with Gr and many ancient mss *gash themselves* [a]Job 35:9-11; Hos 8:2; Zech 7:5 [b]Judg 9:27; Amos 2:8; Mic 2:11 [c]Hos 13:16 **15** [a]Nah 1:9 **16** [1]Or possibly *to the Most High* [2]Lit *indignation;* or *cursing* [a]Ps 78:57 [b]Ps 12:3, 4; 17:10; 73:9; Dan 7:25; Mal 3:13, 14 [c]Ezek 23:32; Hos 9:3, 6 **8:1** [1]Lit *palate* [a]Jer 4:13; Hos 5:8 [b]Hab 1:8 [c]Deut 28:49 [d]Hos 6:7 [e]Hos 4:6 **2** [a]Ps 78:34; Hos 7:14 [b]Titus 1:16 **4** [1]Lit *he* [a]2 Kin 15:13, 17, 25; Hos 13:10, 11 [b]Hos 2:8; 13:1, 2 **5** [1]Or *Your calf has rejected you* [a]Hos 10:5; 13:2 [b]Ps 19:13; Jer 13:27 **6** [1]Or *splinters* [a]Hos 13:2 **7** [1]Lit *growth* [2]Or *meal* [a]Prov 22:8 [b]Is 66:15; Nah 1:3 [c]Hos 2:9 **8** [a]2 Kin 17:6; Jer 51:34 [b]Jer 22:28; 25:34 **9** [1]Lit *loves* [a]Hos 7:11 [b]Jer 2:24 [c]Ezek 16:33, 34 **10** [1]Or *suffer for awhile* [a]Ezek 16:37; 22:20 [b]Jer 42:2 [c]Is 10:8

5:21. Menahem turned to Assyria (2 Kin 15:19–20), and Pekah to Egypt. Hoshea alternated in allegiance to both (2 Kin 17:4).
7:12 *My net.* The Lord Himself was the hunter—not the nations—and Israel was certain to be caught.
7:13 *Woe.* Often used in conjunction with threats of judgment (see 9:12). *Destruction.* See 9:6; Is 13:6. *redeem.* See 13:14; also used for deliverance from Egypt (see, e.g., Ex 6:6; Mic 6:4). *lies.* Possibly of ascribing prosperity and destiny to gods other than the Lord.
7:14 *wail.* See Joel 1:13. *grain and new wine.* See 2:8,22; 9:1–2. *assemble themselves.* See NASB marg.; cf. Lev 19:28; 21:5.
7:15 *I trained.* As children (or, perhaps, as troops). *strengthened their arms.* See Ezek 30:24–25.
7:16 *deceitful bow.* See Ps 78:57. The arrow missed the mark; Israel missed her purpose for being. *derision.* Egypt would fail to assist Israel and then would belittle God's power (see Deut 9:28). *Egypt.* See 8:13; 9:6; 11:5. There is no record of a forced exile of large numbers to Egypt. Some captives were taken there (2 Kin 23:34; Jer 22:11–14), and some fugitives voluntarily went there (2 Kin 25:26; Jer 42–44). A return from Egypt is envisioned in 11:11; Is 11:11; 27:13; Zech 10:10.
8:1 *trumpet.* Of alarm (see 5:8; Joel 2:1; Amos 3:6). *your.* The prophet's. *eagle.* Or "vulture," referring to Assyria. *house of the LORD.* The land of Israel, not just the temple (see 9:15 and note; cf. Ex 15:17). *covenant.* The demands of the covenant.
8:2 *we . . . know You.* But their worship of the Lord was thoroughly corrupted by pagan notions and practices, as vv. 3–6 indicate (see Amos 2:4,7–8; 3:14; 5:26).
8:4 *set up kings.* After Jeroboam II, five kings ruled over Israel in 13 years (2 Kin 15:8–30), three of whom seized the throne by violence (see 7:7).
8:5 *calf.* Jeroboam I (930–909 B.C.) had set up golden calves in Bethel and Dan, saying, "behold your gods" (see 1 Kin 12:28–33 and note on 1 Kin 12:28).
8:6 *A craftsman made it.* For prophetic satire on idolatry see Is 40:20; 41:22–24; 44:9–20; see also Ps 115:4–8. Aaron (Ex 32:8) and Jeroboam I had said, "behold your gods"; but Hosea said, "It is not God."
8:7 *sow . . . reap.* A familiar proverb about the results of doing evil (see 10:13; Job 4:8; Ps 126:5–6; Prov 11:18; 22:8; 2 Cor 9:6; Gal 6:7). Israel sowed the wind of idolatry and reaped the whirlwind of Assyria. *standing grain . . . grain.* The prophet played on the similar sound of the Hebrew words. *strangers.* Assyria.
8:8 Israel was chosen to be God's own people (Ex 19:5; Amos 3:2), but since she had conformed to the other nations, she lost her special identity and so became worthless to God.
8:9 *Ephraim has hired lovers.* For the "prostitute's fees" of Assyrian protection. Menahem (2 Kin 15:19) and Hoshea (2 Kin 17:3), kings of Israel, paid tribute to Assyria.
8:10 Even though Israel paid tribute to Assyria, that would not

11 Since Ephraim has [a]multiplied altars
for sin,
They have become altars of sinning
for him.
12 Though [a]I wrote for him ten thousand
precepts of My [b]law,
They are regarded as a strange thing.
13 As for My [a]sacrificial gifts,
They [b]sacrifice the flesh and eat *it,*
But the LORD has taken no delight in
them.
Now He will [c]remember their iniquity,
And [d]punish *them* for their sins;
They will return to [e]Egypt.
14 For Israel has [a]forgotten his Maker
and [b]built palaces;
And Judah has multiplied fortified
cities,
But I will send a [c]fire on its cities that it
may consume its palatial dwellings.

Ephraim Punished

9 [a]Do not rejoice, O Israel, [1]with
exultation like the [2]nations!
For you have [b]played the harlot,
[3]forsaking your God.
You have loved *harlots'* earnings on
[4]every threshing floor.
2 Threshing floor and wine press will
[a]not feed them,
And the new wine will fail [1]them.
3 They will not remain in [a]the LORD's
land,
But Ephraim will return to [b]Egypt,
And in [c]Assyria they will eat [d]unclean
food.
4 They will not pour out drink offerings
of [a]wine to the LORD,
[b]Their sacrifices will not please Him.
Their bread will [1]*be* like [2]mourners'
bread;
All who eat of it will be [c]defiled,
For their bread will be for [3]themselves
alone;
It will not enter the house of the LORD.
5 [a]What will you do on the day of the
appointed festival
And on the day of the [b]feast of the
LORD?
6 For behold, they will go because of
destruction;
Egypt will gather them up, [a]Memphis
will bury them.
Weeds will take over their treasures of
silver;
[b]Thorns *will be* in their tents.
7 The days of [a]punishment have come,
The days of [b]retribution have come;
[1]Let Israel know *this!*
The prophet is a [c]fool,
The [2]inspired man is [d]demented,
Because of the grossness of your
[e]iniquity,
And *because* your hostility is *so*
great.
8 Ephraim *was* a watchman with my
God, a prophet;
Yet the snare of a bird catcher is in all
his ways,
And there is *only* hostility in the
house of his God.
9 They have gone [a]deep [1]in depravity
As in the days of [b]Gibeah;

11 [a]Hos 10:1
12 [a]Deut 4:6, 8 [b]Hos 4:6
13 [a]Hos 5:6 [b]Jer 6:20; 7:21 [c]Jer 14:10; Hos 7:2; Luke 12:2; 1 Cor 4:5 [d]Hos 4:9; 9:7 [e]Hos 9:3, 6
14 [a]Deut 32:18; Hos 2:13; 4:6; 13:6 [b]Is 9:9, 10 [c]Jer 17:27
9:1 [1]Lit *to* [2]Lit *peoples* [3]Lit *away from your God* [4]Lit *all threshing floors of grain* [a]Is 22:12, 13; Hos 10:5 [b]Hos 4:12
2 [1]Lit *her* [a]Hos 2:9
3 [a]Lev 25:23; Jer 2:7 [b]Hos 7:16; 8:13 [c]Hos 7:11 [d]Ezek 4:13
4 [a]Ex 29:40
4 [1]Lit be *to them* [2]Or *bread of misfortune* [3]Lit *their appetite* [b]Jer 6:20; Hos 8:13 [c]Hag 2:13, 14
5 [a]Is 10:3; Jer 5:31 [b]Hos 2:11; Joel 1:13
6 [a]Is 19:13; Jer 2:16; 44:1; 46:14, 19; Ezek 30:13, 16 [b]Is 5:6; 7:23; Hos 10:8
7 [1]Or *Israel will know it* [2]Lit *man of the spirit* [a]Is 10:3; Jer 10:15; Mic 7:4; Luke 21:22 [b]Is 34:8; Jer 16:18; 25:14 [c]Lam 2:14; Ezek 13:3, 10 [d]Is 44:25 [e]Ezek 14:9, 10
9 [1]Lit *they have corrupted* [a]Is 31:6 [b]Judg 19:12, 16-30; Hos 10:9

buy her security, for God would send judgment by the king of Assyria. Israel's real "enemy" was the Lord Himself (see 2:8–9,13; 7:12).

8:11 *multiplied altars.* To Baal.

8:13 *sacrificial gifts.* See v. 2 and note. *eat it.* Some of the sacrifices were partly eaten by the offerer and priests (see Lev 7:11–18; Deut 12:7; Jer 7:21). *taken no delight in them.* See note on 6:6. *Egypt.* Israel, who had trusted in Egypt and Assyria, was to go back to "Egypt," i.e., into bondage in a foreign land, primarily Assyria (see 9:3). But see note on 7:16.

8:14 *Israel has forgotten.* The cause of all their problems (cf. Judg 2:10). *built palaces . . . multiplied fortified cities.* Israel's trust was not in her Maker but in what she herself had accomplished. *Judah.* See Introduction: Author and Date. *fire.* See Amos 1:4,7,10,14; 2:5.

9:1 This verse begins a section that was probably spoken at a harvest festival, such as the Feast of Booths (Lev 23:33–43; Deut 16:13–15). *played the harlot.* See 1:2; 2:2–5. *harlots' earnings.* See 2:5,12; not to be taken literally, but in the sense of spiritual adultery. *on every threshing floor.* Since the threshing floor at threshing time was a man's world—the threshers stayed there all night to protect the grain and feasted at the end of the day's labors—prostitutes were not uncommon visitors (see Ruth 3:2–3 and notes).

9:3 *LORD's land.* The promised land, which the Lord claimed as His own (cf. Lev 25:23; Josh 22:19; Jer 2:7; Ezek 38:16; Joel 1:6). *Ephraim.* Israel, the northern kingdom. *Egypt . . . Assyria.* Israel was threatened with exile to the lands it depended on—where the temple sacrifice could not be offered (see 8:13 and note). *unclean.* A foreign country was ceremonially unclean (see Amos 7:17 and note). What grew there was likewise unclean, because it was the product of fertility credited to pagan gods (see Ezek 4:13).

9:4 *bread will be like mourners' bread.* Unclean, like bread in a house where there had been a death (see Num 19:14; Deut 26:14; Jer 16:7). All who touched it became ceremonially unclean. *not enter the house of the LORD.* In exile Israel would have no place (not even those places established by Jeroboam I; 1 Kin 12:28–33) where she could bring sacrifices to the Lord or celebrate her religious festivals (v. 5).

9:6 *Egypt.* See 7:16 and note. *Memphis.* The capital of Lower (northern) Egypt. *Weeds . . . Thorns.* Cf. a similar threat against Edom (Is 34:13).

9:7 *inspired man.* See Mic 2:11; 3:8. *demented.* See 2 Kin 9:11; Jer 29:26; cf. 1 Sam 21:15.

9:8 *watchman.* See Is 56:10; Jer 6:17; Ezek 3:17; 33:2–8. *snare . . . hostility.* Israel showed only hostility toward the watchmen (the true prophets) whom God sent to warn His people of the great dangers that threatened (see Jer 1:19; 11:19; 15:10; Amos 7:10–12).

9:9 *depravity.* The word used of the Israelites who worshiped the golden calf (Ex 32:7; Deut 9:12; 32:5). *days of Gibeah.* A reference to the corrupt events of Judg 19–21. *He will remember.* Sins unrepented of are remembered, as well as the accu-

He will [c]remember their iniquity,
He will punish their sins.

10 I found Israel like [a]grapes in the wilderness;
I saw your forefathers as the [b]earliest fruit on the fig tree in its first *season*.
But they came to [c]Baal-peor and devoted themselves to [1d]shame,
And they became as [e]detestable as that which they loved.
11 As for Ephraim, their [a]glory will fly away like a bird—
No birth, no pregnancy and no conception!
12 Though they bring up their children,
Yet I will bereave them [1]until not a man is left.
Yes, [a]woe to them indeed when I depart from them!
13 Ephraim, as I have seen,
Is planted in a pleasant meadow like [a]Tyre;
But Ephraim will bring out his children for slaughter.
14 Give them, O LORD—what will You give?
Give them a [a]miscarrying womb and dry breasts.

15 All their evil is at [a]Gilgal;
Indeed, I came to hate them there!
Because of the [b]wickedness of their deeds
I will drive them out of My house!
I will love them no more;
All their princes are [c]rebels.
16 [a]Ephraim is stricken, their root is dried up,
They will bear [b]no fruit.
Even though they bear children,
I will slay the [c]precious ones of their womb.
17 My God will cast them away
Because they have [a]not listened to Him;
And they will be [b]wanderers among the nations.

Retribution for Israel's Sin

10 Israel is a [1]luxuriant [a]vine;
He produces fruit for himself.
The more his fruit,
The more altars he [b]made;
The [2]richer his land,
The better [3]he made the *sacred* [c]pillars.
2 Their heart is [1a]faithless;
Now they must bear their [b]guilt.
[2]The LORD will [c]break down their altars
And destroy their *sacred* pillars.

3 Surely now they will say, "We have [a]no king,
For we do not revere the LORD.
As for the king, what can he do for us?"
4 They speak *mere* words,
[1]With [a]worthless oaths they make covenants;
And [b]judgment sprouts like poisonous weeds in the furrows of the field.
5 The inhabitants of Samaria will fear
For the [1a]calf of [b]Beth-aven.
Indeed, its people will mourn for it,
And its [c]idolatrous priests [2]will cry out over it,
Over its [d]glory, since it has departed from it.
6 The thing itself will be carried to [a]Assyria
As tribute to [1b]King Jareb;
Ephraim will [2]be [c]seized with shame
And Israel will be ashamed of its [d]own counsel.

9 [c]Hos 7:2; 8:13 **10** [1]I.e. Baal [a]Mic 7:1 [b]Jer 24:2 [c]Num 25:1-5; Ps 106:28, 29 [d]Jer 11:13; Hos 4:18 [e]Ps 115:8; Ezek 20:8 **11** [a]Hos 4:7; 10:5 **12** [1]Lit *without a man* [a]Deut 31:17; Hos 7:13 **13** [a]Ezek 26:1-21 **14** [a]Hos 9:11 **15** [a]Hos 4:15; 12:11 [b]Hos 4:9; 7:2; 12:2 [c]Is 1:23; Hos 5:2 **16** [a]Hos 5:11 [b]Hos 8:7 [c]Ezek 24:21
17 [a]Hos 4:10 [b]Hos 7:13 **10:1** [1]Or *degenerate* [2]Or *better* [3]Lit *they* [a]Is 5:1-7; Ezek 15:1-6 [b]Jer 2:28; Hos 8:11; 12:11 [c]1 Kin 14:23; Hos 3:4 **2** [1]Lit *smooth* [2]Lit *He* [a]1 Kin 18:21; Zeph 1:5 [b]Hos 13:16 [c]Hos 10:8; Mic 5:13 **3** [a]Ps 12:4; Is 5:19 **4** [1]Or *Swearing falsely in making a covenant* [a]Ezek 17:13-19; Hos 4:2 [b]Deut 31:16, 17; 2 Kin 17:3, 4; Amos 5:7 **5** [1]So with some ancient versions; Heb *calves* [2]Or *who used to rejoice over* [a]Hos 8:5, 6 [b]Hos 4:15; 5:8 [c]2 Kin 23:5 [d]Hos 9:11 **6** [1]Or *the avenging king* or *the great king* [2]Lit *receive shame* [a]Hos 11:5 [b]Hos 5:13 [c]Hos 4:7 [d]Is 30:3; Jer 7:24

mulated sins of generations (see 13:12).

9:10 The covenant relation is traced back to the wilderness (see 2:14–15; 13:5; Deut 32:10). *grapes . . . fig.* Refreshing delicacies (see Is 28:4; Mic 7:1). The images used here (grapes in the wilderness, early fruit of the fig tree) beautifully convey God's delight in Israel when she, out of all the nations, committed herself to Him in covenant at Sinai. *Baal-peor.* A shortened form of Beth-baal-peor. Peor was a mountain (Deut 3:29). Baal-peor refers to the god of Peor (Num 25:1–4) and was used interchangeably with Beth-peor, "the temple of Peor" (see Deut 3:29; 4:3,46; Josh 13:20). Hosea refers here to the incident in Num 25. *became . . . detestable.* See Is 5:2,4,7.

9:11 *Ephraim, their glory.* Their large population and prosperity. The punishment fit the sin. Prostitution produces no increase (see 4:10).

9:12 *to them.* To the children.

9:13 *Tyre.* Noted for its wealth, pleasant environment and security (see Ezek 27:2–26).

9:14 Hosea did not pray out of hateful vengeance against Israel, but because he shared God's holy wrath against her sins.

9:15 *Gilgal.* See note on 4:15. *drive them out of My house.* As the unfaithful wife was driven from the husband's house, so Israel was driven from God's "house"—i.e., His land (see 8:1 and note). *princes . . . rebels.* A wordplay in Hebrew.

9:17 *My God.* Hosea's words alone, for God was no longer Israel's God. *cast . . . away.* See 4:6; 2 Kin 17:20. *wanderers.* Like Cain (Gen 4:14–15).

10:1 *Israel.* The nation personified and called by the name of its ancestor. *vine.* A frequent metaphor for Israel (Deut 32:32; Ps 80:8–11; Is 5:1; Jer 2:21; cf. John 15:1). *the richer his land.* The prosperity during the period of Jeroboam II (793–753 B.C.) was probably in view.

10:2 *Their heart is faithless.* Israel formally called to God (8:2), but they dishonored Him by pagan worship.

10:3 *We have no king.* Such would soon be their condition when Assyria destroyed the nation.

10:4 *They speak mere words.* The last kings of Israel were notoriously corrupt and deceitful.

10:5 *Samaria.* The royal city of Israel (see note on 7:1). *calf of Beth-aven.* The idol that Jeroboam set up at Bethel (Beth-aven means "house of wickedness,' a name for Bethel, which means "house of God'; see also 1 Kin 12:32–33).

10:6 *Ephraim.* Israel, the northern kingdom.

7 Samaria will be [a]cut off *with* her king
Like a stick on the surface of the
water.
8 Also the [a]high places of Aven, the [b]sin
of Israel, will be destroyed;
[c]Thorn and thistle will grow on their
altars;
Then they will [d]say to the mountains,
"Cover us!" And to the hills, "Fall on
us!"
9 From the days of Gibeah you have
sinned, O Israel;
There they stand!
Will not the battle against the sons of
iniquity overtake them in Gibeah?
10 When it is My [a]desire, I will [1][b]chastise
them;
And [c]the peoples will be gathered
against them
When they are bound for their double
guilt.

11 Ephraim is a trained [a]heifer that loves
to thresh,
But I will [b]come over her fair neck
with a yoke;
I will harness Ephraim,
Judah will plow, Jacob will harrow for
himself.
12 [a]Sow with a view to righteousness,
Reap in accordance with [1]kindness;
[b]Break up your fallow ground,
For it is time to [c]seek the LORD
Until He [d]comes to [2][e]rain
righteousness on you.
13 You have [a]plowed wickedness, you
have reaped injustice,
You have eaten the fruit of [b]lies.
Because you have trusted in your way,
in your [c]numerous warriors,

7 [a]Hos 13:11 **8** [a]Hos 4:13 [b]1 Kin 12:28-30; 13:34 [c]Is 32:13; Hos 9:6; 10:2 [d]Is 2:19; Luke 23:30; Rev 6:16 **10** [1]Or *bind* [a]Ezek 5:13 [b]Hos 4:9 [c]Jer 16:16 **11** [a]Jer 50:11; Hos 4:16; Mic 4:13 [b]Jer 28:14 **12** [1]Or *loyalty* [2]Or *teach* [a]Prov 11:18 [b]Jer 4:3 [c]Hos 12:6 [d]Hos 6:3 [e]Is 44:3; 45:8 **13** [a]Job 4:8; Prov 22:8; Gal 6:7, 8 [b]Hos 4:2; 7:3; 11:12 [c]Ps 33:16

14 [a]Is 17:3 [b]Hos 13:16 **11:1** [a]Hos 2:15; 12:9, 13; 13:4 [b]Ex 4:22, 23; Matt 2:15 **2** [1]I.e. God's prophets [a]2 Kin 17:13-15 [b]Hos 2:13; 4:13 [c]Is 65:7; Jer 18:15 **3** [1]So ancient versions; Heb *He...His* [a]Deut 1:31; 32:10, 11 [b]Ps 107:20; Jer 30:17 **4** [a]Jer 31:2, 3 [b]Lev 26:13 [c]Ex 16:32; Ps 78:25 **5** [1]Lit *He* [2]Lit *his* [a]Hos 7:16 **6** [1]Lit *his* [a]Hos 13:16 [b]Lam 2:9 [c]Hos 4:16, 17

14 Therefore a tumult will arise among
your people,
And all your [a]fortresses will be
destroyed,
As Shalman destroyed Beth-arbel on
the day of battle,
When [b]mothers were dashed in pieces
with *their* children.
15 Thus it will be done to you at Bethel
because of your great wickedness.
At dawn the king of Israel will be
completely cut off.

God Yearns over His People

11 When Israel *was* a youth I loved him,
And [a]out of Egypt I [b]called My son.
2 The more [1][a]they called them,
The more they went from [1]them;
They kept [b]sacrificing to the Baals
And [c]burning incense to idols.
3 Yet it is I who taught Ephraim to
walk,
[1]I [a]took them in My arms;
But they did not know that I [b]healed
them.
4 I [a]led them with cords of a man, with
bonds of love,
And [b]I became to them as one who
lifts the yoke from their jaws;
And I bent down *and* [c]fed them.

5 [1]They will not return to the land of
Egypt;
But Assyria—he will be [2]their king
Because they [a]refused to return *to Me.*
6 The [a]sword will whirl against [1]their
cities,
And will demolish [1]their gate bars
And [b]consume *them* because of their
[c]counsels.

10:8 *high places.* See 4:13–14. *Aven.* Refers to Beth-aven ("house of wickedness"; see v. 5 and note). *Cover us! . . . Fall on us!* Cries of utter despair; quoted by Jesus (Luke 23:30) and alluded to in Rev 6:16 (see Is 2:19).
10:9 *Gibeah.* See 9:9 and note. As war came on Gibeah, so war and captivity would come on Israel.
10:11 *trained heifer.* Up to now Ephraim (Israel) had been as contented as a young cow that ate while threshing grain. But now God would cause Israel (here called both Ephraim and Jacob) and Judah to do the heavy work of plowing and harrowing under a yoke—a picture of going into the Assyrian and Babylonian captivities. *Judah.* See Introduction: Author and Date.
10:12 *Reap in accordance with kindness.* If Israel would only do what was right ("kindness" translates the Hebrew word *hesed;* see note on 6:6, "loyalty"), she would be blessed by God. *Break up your fallow ground.* Be no longer unproductive, but repentant, making a radical new beginning and becoming productive and fruitful. *righteousness.* God's covenant blessings that in righteousness He would shower on His people if they in righteousness were loyal to Him, their covenant Lord.
10:13 *lies.* Israel had been living a lie—and by lies (see 7:3; 10:4; 12:1).
10:14 *Shalman destroyed Beth-arbel.* The event is otherwise unknown, as are the names mentioned. Atrocities against civilians were common in ancient warfare (cf. 9:13; 13:16; 2 Kin 8:12–13; Ps 137:8–9; Is 13:16; Amos 1:13; Nah 3:10).
11:1 A third appeal to history (see 9:10; 10:9) traces God's choice of Israel back to Egypt, the exodus from that country (cf. 12:9; 13:4) having given birth to the nation. Israel's response to the Lord is now illustrated by the wayward son rather than by the unfaithful wife (chs. 1–3). For Israel as a son see Ex 4:22–23; Is 1:2–4; and for God as Father see Deut 32:6; Jer 2:14. Hosea saw God's love as the basis (cf. 3:1) for the election of Israel. Matthew found in the call of Israel from Egypt a typological picture of Jesus' coming from Egypt (see Matt 2:15 and note).
11:2 *idols.* See Deut 7:25; 12:3.
11:3 *Ephraim.* Israel, the northern kingdom. *walk.* This picture of a father teaching his child to walk is one of the most tender in the OT. *did not know.* See 2:5–8. *healed.* See 5:13; 6:1; 7:1.
11:4 The imagery is unclear, but the figure seems to change to a farmer tending his work animals. Another interpretation sees a continuation of the son image, with the father lifting the son to his cheek. *fed them.* God supplied miraculous food in the wilderness (see Ex 16; Deut 8:16).
11:5 *Egypt . . . Assyria.* See 8:13 and note; 9:3. The tender tone (vv. 1–4) changes to threat of exile to the two countries between which Israel had vacillated. It is ironic that the people rescued from Egypt should be returned there because of their disloyalty to the One who had rescued them.

7 So My people are bent on [a]turning
from Me.
Though [1]they call [2]them to *the One* on
high,
None at all exalts *Him.*

8 [a]How can I give you up, O Ephraim?
How can I surrender you, O Israel?
How can I [1]make you like [b]Admah?
How can I treat you like [b]Zeboiim?
My heart is turned over within Me,
[2]All My compassions are kindled.
9 I will [a]not execute My fierce anger;
I will not destroy Ephraim [b]again.
For [c]I am God and not man, the [d]Holy
One in your midst,
And I will not come in [1]wrath.
10 They will [a]walk after the LORD,
He will [b]roar like a lion;
Indeed He will roar
And *His* sons will come [c]trembling
from the west.
11 They will come trembling like birds
from [a]Egypt
And like [b]doves from the land of
[a]Assyria;
And I will [c]settle them in their houses,
declares the LORD.

12 [1]Ephraim surrounds Me with [a]lies
And the house of Israel with deceit;
Judah is also unruly against God,
Even against the Holy One who is
faithful.

Ephraim Reminded

12 [1]Ephraim feeds on [a]wind,
And pursues the [b]east wind continually;
He multiplies lies and violence.
Moreover, [2]he makes a covenant with
Assyria,
And oil is carried to Egypt.
2 The LORD also has a [a]dispute with
Judah,
And will punish Jacob [b]according to
his ways;
He will repay him according to his
deeds.
3 In the womb he [a]took his brother by
the heel,
And in his maturity he [b]contended
with God.
4 Yes, he wrestled with the angel and
prevailed;
He wept and [a]sought His favor.
He found Him at [b]Bethel
And there He spoke with us,
5 Even the LORD, the God of hosts,
The LORD is His [1a]name.
6 Therefore, [a]return to your God,
[b]Observe [1]kindness and justice,
And [c]wait for your God continually.
7 A [1]merchant, in whose hands are false
[a]balances,
He loves to oppress.
8 And Ephraim said, "Surely I have
become [a]rich,
I have found wealth for myself;
In all my labors they will find in me
[b]No iniquity, which *would be* sin."
9 But I *have been* the LORD your God
since the land of Egypt;
I will make you [a]live in tents again,
As in the days of the appointed
festival.

7 [1]I.e. God's prophets [2]Lit *him;* i.e. Israel [a]Jer 3:6, 7; 8:5
8 [1]Lit *give* [2]Lit *Together* [a]Hos 6:4; 7:1 [b]Gen 14:8; Deut 29:23
9 [1]Lit *excitement* [a]Deut 13:17 [b]Jer 26:3; 30:11 [c]Num 23:19 [d]Is 5:24; 12:6; 41:14, 16
10 [a]Hos 3:5; 6:1-3 [b]Is 31:4; Joel 3:16; Amos 1:2 [c]Is 66:2, 5
11 [a]Is 11:11 [b]Is 60:8; Hos 7:11 [c]Ezek 28:25, 26; 34:27, 28
12 [1]Ch 12:1 in Heb [a]Hos 4:2; 7:3
12:1 [1]Ch 12:2 in Heb [a]Jer 22:22 [b]Gen 41:6; Ezek 17:10

12:1 [2]Lit *they make*
2 [a]Hos 4:1; Mic 6:2 [b]Hos 4:9; 7:2
3 [a]Gen 25:26 [b]Gen 32:28
4 [a]Gen 32:26 [b]Gen 28:13-19; 35:10-15
5 [1]Lit *memorial* [a]Ex 3:15
6 [1]Or *loyalty* [a]Hos 6:1-3; 10:12 [b]Mic 6:8 [c]Mic 7:7
7 [1]Or *Canaanite* [a]Prov 11:1; Amos 8:5; Mic 6:11
8 [a]Ps 62:10; Hos 13:6; Rev 3:17 [b]Hos 4:8; 14:1
9 [a]Lev 23:42

11:7 *call . . . to the One on high.* See 7:16.
11:8 The stubborn son was subject to stoning (Deut 21:18–21), but the Lord's compassion overcame His wrath and He refused to destroy Ephraim (Israel). *Admah . . . Zeboiim.* Cities of the plain (Gen 10:19; 14:2,8), overthrown when Sodom was destroyed (Gen 19:24–25; Deut 29:23; Jer 49:18) and symbolizing total destruction.
11:9 *God and not man.* Although Israel has been as unreliable as man, God will not be untrue to the love He has shown toward Israel (see vv. 1–4; see also 1 Sam 15:29; Mal 3:6). Israel was to be punished, but not destroyed. *the Holy One in your midst.* See notes on Is 1:4; 6:1; cf. Is 12:6. God's holiness is alluded to only here in Hosea.
11:10 The return from exile. *roar like a lion.* Rather than threatening destruction (cf. 5:14; 13:7), God's roar was now a clear signal to return from exile. *the west.* The islands of the sea (as well as coastlands).
11:11 *from Egypt . . . Assyria.* See 9:3. *like birds . . . like doves.* Suggests swiftness of return (cf. Is 60:8) and is not derogatory, as was the earlier comparison to a silly dove (7:11). *declares the* LORD. See 2:13,16,21.
11:12 *lies . . . deceit.* See 7:3; 10:13 and note. *Judah.* See Introduction: Author and Date. *unruly against God.* See Jer 2:31.
12:1 *wind.* See 8:7; Eccl 1:14. *east wind.* See 13:15; Job 15:2; 27:21; Is 27:8; Jer 18:17. Pursuing the wind symbolized Israel's futile foreign policy, which vacillated between Egypt (2 Kin 17:4; Is 30:6–7) and Assyria (cf. 5:13; 7:11; 8:9; 2 Kin 17:3).
12:2 *dispute.* See 4:1. *Judah.* See Introduction: Author and Date. *Jacob.* Israel (see 10:11). The Lord indicted both kingdoms—all the descendants of Father Jacob. In their deceitfulness, Israel and Judah were living up to the name of their forefather (Jacob means "he grasps the heel"; figuratively, "he deceives").
12:3 *In the womb.* See Gen 25:26; 27:36. *took his brother by the heel.* See note on v. 2. God's covenant people here relived the experiences of Father Jacob and now had to return to God, just as Jacob was called back to Bethel (Gen 35:1–15).
12:4 *wrestled with the angel.* See Gen 32:22–28. The Hebrew for "Israel" means "he struggles with God." *Bethel.* See Gen 28:12–19; 35:1–15. In Hosea's time, Bethel was the most important royal sanctuary in the northern kingdom (cf. Amos 7:13).
12:5 *LORD, the God of hosts.* Paralleled in Amos 3:13; 6:14; 9:5.
12:6 *kindness.* Hebrew *ḥesed;* see 6:6 ("loyalty") and note. *justice.* See Amos 5:15,24; Mic 6:8.
12:7 *merchant.* As Hosea had played on the meaning of Jacob in v. 2, he here uses a wordplay on Canaan (the Hebrew for "merchant" sounds like Canaan) to charge that Israel was no better than a Canaanite.
12:8 *I have become rich.* Riches brought a sense of self-sufficiency (cf. 10:13; Deut 32:15–18). *find in me No iniquity.* Like a dishonest merchant, Ephraim (Israel) was confident that her deceitfulness (cf. 11:12) would not come to light.
12:9 *I have been the LORD your God.* See 13:4; cf. Ex 20:2. *tents.* As during the wilderness journey long ago (cf. 2:14–15).

10 I have also spoken to the [a]prophets,
And I [1]gave numerous visions,
And through the prophets I gave
[b]parables.
11 Is there iniquity *in* Gilead?
Surely they are worthless.
In Gilgal they sacrifice bulls,
Yes, [a]their altars are like the stone
heaps
Beside the furrows of the field.

12 Now [a]Jacob fled to the [1]land of Aram,
And [b]Israel worked for a wife,
And for a wife he kept *sheep.*
13 But by a [a]prophet the LORD brought
Israel from Egypt,
And by a prophet he was kept.
14 [a]Ephraim has provoked to bitter
anger;
So his Lord will leave his [b]bloodguilt
on him
And bring back his [c]reproach to him.

Ephraim's Idolatry

13 [a]When Ephraim [1]spoke, *there was*
trembling.
He [b]exalted himself in Israel,
But through [c]Baal he [2]did wrong and
died.
2 And now they sin more and more,
And make for themselves [a]molten
images,
Idols [1][b]skillfully made from their
silver,
All of them the [c]work of craftsmen.
They say of them, "Let the [2]men who
sacrifice kiss the [d]calves!"

10 [1]Lit *multiplied the vision* [a]2 Kin 17:13; Jer 7:25 [b]Ezek 17:2; 20:49
11 [a]Hos 8:11; 10:1, 2
12 [1]Lit *field* [a]Gen 28:5 [b]Gen 29:20
13 [a]Ex 14:19-22; Is 63:11-14
14 [a]2 Kin 17:7-18 [b]Ezek 18:10-13 [c]Dan 11:18; Mic 6:16
13:1 [1]Or *spoke with trembling* [2]Or *became guilty* [a]Job 29:21, 22 [b]Judg 8:1; 12:1 [c]Hos 2:8-17; 11:2
2 [1]Or *according to their own understanding* [2]Lit *sacrificers of* or, *(among) mankind* [a]Is 46:6; Jer 10:4; Hos 2:8 [b]Is 44:17-20 [c]Hos 8:6 [d]Hos 8:5, 6; 10:5

3 [1]Lit *goes away early* [2]Lit *window* [a]Hos 6:4 [b]Ps 1:4; Is 17:13; Dan 2:35 [c]Ps 68:2
4 [a]Hos 12:9 [b]Ex 20:3; 2 Kin 18:35 [c]Is 43:11; 45:21, 22
5 [1]Or *knew* [a]Deut 2:7; 32:10 [b]Deut 8:15
6 [a]Deut 8:12, 14; 32:13-15; Jer 5:7 [b]Hos 7:14 [c]Hos 2:13; 4:6; 8:14

3 Therefore they will be like the
[a]morning cloud
And like dew which [1]soon disappears,
Like [b]chaff which is blown away from
the threshing floor
And like [c]smoke from a [2]chimney.

4 Yet I *have been* the [a]LORD your God
Since the land of Egypt;
And you were not to know [b]any god
except Me,
For there is no savior [c]besides Me.
5 I [1][a]cared for you in the wilderness,
[b]In the land of drought.
6 As *they had* their pasture, they
became [a]satisfied,
And being satisfied, their [b]heart
became proud;
Therefore they [c]forgot Me.
7 So I will be [a]like a lion to them;
Like a [b]leopard I will [1]lie in wait by
the wayside.
8 I will encounter them [a]like a bear
robbed of her cubs,
And I will tear open [1]their chests;
There I will also [b]devour them like a
lioness,
As a wild beast would tear them.

9 *It is* your destruction, O Israel,
[1]That *you are* [a]against Me, against
your [b]help.
10 Where now is your [a]king

7 [1]Or *watch* [a]Lam 3:10; Hos 5:14 [b]Jer 5:6 **8** [1]Lit *the enclosure of their heart* [a]2 Sam 17:8 [b]Ps 50:22 **9** [1]Or *But in Me is your help* [a]Jer 2:17, 19; Mal 1:12, 13 [b]Deut 33:26, 29 **10** [a]2 Kin 17:4; Hos 8:4

appointed festival. Probably the Feast of Booths (Lev 23:42–44), which commemorated the wilderness journey.

12:10 *spoken to the prophets.* See 6:5; Amos 2:11; Heb 1:1. There had been ample warning. *visions.* Revelations (see Num 12:6–8; Amos 1:1). *parables.* Containing messages of warning from God (see 2 Sam 12:1–4; Ps 78:2; Is 5:1–7; Ezek 17:2; 24:3).

12:11 *iniquity in Gilead.* See 6:8–9 and notes. Gilead was overrun by Assyria in 734–732 B.C. (2 Kin 15:29). *Gilgal.* See 4:15; 9:15. The Hebrew contains a wordplay between "Gilgal" and "heaps" (Hebrew *gallim*). Rather than assuring safety, the altars themselves would be destroyed. *Beside the . . . field.* Israelite farmers gathered into piles the stones turned up by their plows.

12:12 Jacob fled from Esau to Paddan-aram (Gen 28:2,5), serving Laban seven years for each wife (Gen 29:20–28), and then continued as Laban's herdsman (Gen 30:31; 31:41).

12:13 *prophet.* Moses (cf. Num 12:6–8; Deut 18:15; 34:10). *he was kept.* As Jacob had cared for Laban's flocks, so the Lord cared for Israel during her wilderness wandering. Earlier leadership by the prophet Moses stands in contrast with Israel's present disregard for prophets (cf. 4:5; 6:5; 9:7).

12:14 *Ephraim has provoked.* Despite warnings. *bloodguilt.* Cf. 1:4; 4:2; 5:2; 6:8. This may refer either to violence against the prophets or to human sacrifice (cf. 2 Kin 17:17). In legal passages (Lev 20:11–27), "their bloodguiltiness is upon them" describes guilt. The prophet drew a contrast between past divine preservation and present divine anger that would bring punishment. *bring back.* See Is 65:7.

13:1 *When Ephraim spoke.* In accordance with Jacob's blessing (Gen 48:10–20), Ephraim became a powerful tribe (Judg 8:1–3; 12:1–7; 1 Sam 1:1–4), from which came such prominent leaders as Joshua (Josh 24:30) and Jeroboam I (1 Kin 11:26; 12:20). *Israel.* The 12 tribes. *died.* The wages of sin was death (cf. Rom 6:23), and the end of the nation was at hand.

13:2 *Idols.* See 4:12; 8:5–6; 11:2. *men . . . kiss the calves!* This phrase calls to mind the calves (and the sacrifices made to them) set up by Jeroboam to win the allegiance of the northern tribes in Israel (see 1 Kin 12:26–33). *kiss.* Show homage to (cf. 1 Kin 19:18).

13:3 "Cloud" and "dew" (see 6:4), "chaff" (see Ps 1:4; 35:5; Is 17:13; 29:5) and "smoke" (see Ps 37:20; 68:2; Is 51:6) are all figurative for Ephraim, who was soon to vanish as a nation.

13:4 *I have been the* LORD. See 12:9; Ex 20:2–3; Deut 5:6. The contrast is with Jeroboam's declaration, "behold your gods" (1 Kin 12:28). *know any god.* See 4:1; 6:3; 8:2.

13:5 *wilderness.* See 2:14; 9:10.

13:6 *satisfied.* See Deut 6:11–12; 8:10–14; 11:15–16. *forgot Me.* Cf. Deut 8:14; 31:20; 32:15,18.

13:7–8 The Lord, previously pictured as a shepherd (4:16), would attack like the wild beasts that often ravaged the flocks.

13:7 *lion.* See 5:14. *leopard.* See Jer 5:6; Rev 13:2.

13:8 *bear robbed of her cubs.* See 2 Sam 17:8; 2 Kin 2:24; Prov 17:12.

13:9 *help.* See Ps 10:14; 30:10; 54:4.

13:10 *Where now is your king . . . ?* Help is only from the Lord, not from kings. The prophet likely alludes to the royal assassinations of his day (see 3:4; 7:7; 8:4; 10:3). *Give me a king.*

That he may save you in all your
cities,
And your [b]judges of whom you
[1]requested,
"Give me a king and princes"?
11 I [a]gave you a king in My anger
And [b]took him away in My wrath.

12 The iniquity of Ephraim is bound up;
His sin is [a]stored up.
13 The pains of [a]childbirth come upon
him;
He is [b]not a wise son,
For [1]it is not the time that he should
[c]delay at the opening of the womb.
14 Shall I [a]ransom them from the [1]power
of Sheol?
Shall I redeem them from death?
[b]O Death, where are your thorns?
O Sheol, where is your sting?
[c]Compassion will be hidden from My
sight.

15 Though he [a]flourishes among the
[1]reeds,
An [b]east wind will come,
The wind of the LORD coming up from
the wilderness;
And his fountain will [c]become dry
And his spring will be dried up;
It will [d]plunder *his* treasury of every
precious article.
16 [1]Samaria will be held [a]guilty,
For she has [b]rebelled against her God.
[c]They will fall by the [d]sword,
Their little ones will be [e]dashed in
pieces,
And their pregnant [f]women will be
ripped open.

10 [1]Lit *said* [b]1 Sam 8:5, 6
11 [a]1 Sam 8:7; 10:17-24 [b]1 Sam 15:26; 1 Kin 14:7-10; Hos 10:7
12 [a]Deut 32:34, 35; Job 14:17; Rom 2:5
13 [1]Lit *it is the time that he should not tarry at the breaking forth of children* [a]Is 13:8; Mic 4:9, 10 [b]Deut 32:6; Hos 5:4 [c]Is 37:3; 66:9
14 [1]Lit *hand* [a]Ps 49:15; Ezek 37:12, 13 [b]1 Cor 15:55 [c]Jer 20:16; 31:35-37
15 [1]Or *brothers* [a]Gen 49:22; Hos 10:1 [b]Gen 41:6; Jer 4:11, 12; Ezek 17:10; 19:12 [c]Jer 51:36 [d]Jer 20:5
16 [1]Ch 14:1 in Heb [a]Hos 10:2 [b]Hos 7:14 [c]2 Kin 8:12 [d]Hos 11:6 [e]Hos 10:14 [f]2 Kin 15:16

14:1 [1]Ch 14:2 in Heb [2]Or *in* [a]Hos 6:1; 10:12; 12:6; Joel 2:13 [b]Hos 4:8; 5:5; 9:7
2 [1]Or *accept that which is good* [2]So with ancient versions; M.T. *our lips as bulls* [a]Mic 7:18, 19 [b]Ps 51:16, 17; Hos 6:6; Heb 13:15
3 [1]Or *fatherless* [a]Ps 33:17; Is 31:1 [b]Hos 8:6; 13:2 [c]Hos 4:12 [d]Ps 10:14; 68:5

Israel's Future Blessing

14 [1][a]Return, O Israel, to the LORD your
God,
For you have stumbled [2]because of
your [b]iniquity.
2 Take words with you and return to the
LORD.
Say to Him, "[a]Take away all iniquity
And [1]receive *us* graciously,
That we may [b]present [2]the fruit of our
lips.
3 "Assyria will not save us,
We will [a]not ride on horses;
Nor will we say again, '[b]Our god,'
To the [c]work of our hands;
For in [d]You the [1]orphan finds mercy."

4 I will [a]heal their apostasy,
I will [b]love them freely,
For My anger has [c]turned away from
them.
5 I will be like the [a]dew to Israel;
He will blossom like the [b]lily,
And he will [1]take root like *the cedars
of* [c]Lebanon.
6 His shoots will [1]sprout,
And his [2]beauty will be like the [a]olive
tree
And his fragrance like *the cedars of*
[b]Lebanon.
7 Those who [a]live in his shadow
Will [1]again raise [b]grain,
And they will blossom like the vine.
His renown *will be* like the wine of
Lebanon.

4 [a]Is 57:18; Hos 6:1 [b]Zeph 3:17 [c]Is 12:1 **5** [1]Lit *strike his roots* [a]Prov 19:12; Is 26:19 [b]Song 2:1; Matt 6:28 [c]Is 35:2 **6** [1]Lit *go* [2]Or *splendor* [a]Jer 11:16 [b]Song 4:11 **7** [1]Or *return, they will raise grain* [a]Ezek 17:23 [b]Hos 2:21, 22

Though all Israel asked for a king in the days of Samuel (1 Sam 8:5,20), the reference here is only to the northern monarchy. They selected Jeroboam I (1 Kin 12:26) in preference to the Davidic kings.

13:11 The monarchy is here considered a rebellion (see 1 Sam 8:7).

13:12 *iniquity . . . bound up.* See 9:9 and note; Job 14:17. *Ephraim.* Israel, the northern kingdom. *sin . . . stored up.* See 7:2; Deut 32:34–35.

13:13 *pains of childbirth.* Their helpless situation was comparable to that of a woman in childbirth (see Is 13:8; 21:3; 26:17; Jer 4:31; 13:21; Mic 4:9–10; Matt 24:8) who cannot deliver the child (see 2 Kin 19:3; Is 37:3) and consequently dies.

13:14 *death.* The personified reference is to the death of the nation (see v. 1). Paul applies this passage to resurrection (1 Cor 15:55). *Sheol.* For a description of Sheol see Job 3:13–19; Ps 18:5; 116:3; Is 14:9–10; see also notes on Gen 37:35; Jon 2:2.

13:15 *flourishes.* In Hebrew a wordplay on Ephraim (meaning "fruitful"). The drought-bringing east wind (cf. Job 1:19; Is 27:8; Jer 4:11; 13:24; 18:17) is here a figure for Assyria, an instrument of the Lord (Is 10:5,15). Assyria invaded the northern kingdom in 734 B.C., then crushed it and exiled its people in 722–721. *every precious article.* See Nah 2:9.

13:16 *Samaria.* See 7:1 and note; 8:5–6; 10:5,7; here, the northern kingdom. *rebelled against.* See Ps 5:10; Ezek 20:8,13,21. *little ones . . . women.* For atrocities against women and children see 10:14; 2 Kin 8:12; 15:16; Ps 137:8–9; Is 13:16; Amos 1:13; Nah 3:10.

14:1 *Return.* Another appeal for repentance (see 10:12; 12:6). Unlike that of ch. 6, this repentance would have to be sincere in order for the people to receive the gracious response from the Lord promised in vv. 4–8 (cf. Ps 130:7–8; Is 55:6–9).

14:2 *Take words.* None could appear empty-handed (Ex 23:15; 34:20), but animal sacrifices would not be enough. Only words of true repentance would be sufficient. *fruit of our lips.* As thank offerings to the Lord.

14:3 *orphan.* Penitent Israel (see Ps 10:14; 68:5; Lam 5:3). *finds mercy.* Cf. the name of the child Lo-ruhamah (see 1:6 and note; see also 2:1,23).

14:4 *heal.* See 11:3. *apostasy.* See 11:7. *love . . . freely.* See Is 54:6–8. *love.* See 3:1; 11:1,8–9. *anger . . . turned away.* Contrasts with the burning anger that brought destruction (see 8:5).

14:5 *dew.* Here not a symbol of transitoriness (cf. 6:4; 13:3) but of God's blessing (cf. Deut 33:13). *cedars of Lebanon.* See notes on Judg 9:15; 1 Kin 5:6; Is 9:10. *cedars.* See Ps 80:9–11. *Lebanon.* See Ps 104:16; Is 35:2; 60:13.

14:7 *shadow.* Protection (cf. Judg 9:15; Song 2:3; Lam 4:20; Ezek 31:6). *vine.* See 10:1; Is 5:1–7.

8 O Ephraim, what more have I to do
with [a]idols?
It is I who answer and look after [1]you.
I am like a luxuriant [b]cypress;
From [c]Me comes your fruit.

9 [a]Whoever is wise, let him understand
these things;
Whoever is discerning, let him know
them.
For the [b]ways of the LORD are
right,
And the [c]righteous will walk in
them,
But [d]transgressors will stumble in
them.

8 [1]Lit *him* [a]Job 34:32; Hos 14:3 [b]Is 41:19 [c]Ezek 17:23
9 [a]Ps 107:43; Jer 9:12
9 [b]Ps 111:7, 8; Prov 10:29; Zeph 3:5 [c]Is 26:7 [d]Is 1:28

14:8 *Ephraim.* Israel, the northern kingdom. *cypress.* Only here in the OT is God compared to a tree. For the point of the imagery see Ezek 31:3–7; Dan 4:12. *fruit.* Ephraim ("fruitful"; cf. Gen 41:52) received his fruitfulness from the Lord (cf. 2:8).

14:9 *ways of the LORD.* See Ps 18:21. The prophet concludes by offering each reader the alternatives of walking or stumbling (cf. 4:5; 5:5)—of obedience or rebellion.

Joel

INTRODUCTION

Author

The prophet Joel cannot be identified with any of the 12 other figures in the OT who have the same name. He is not mentioned outside the books of Joel and Acts (Acts 2:16). The non-Biblical legends about him are unconvincing. His father, Pethuel (1:1), is also unknown. Judging from his concern with Judah and Jerusalem (see 2:32; 3:1,6,8,16–20), it seems likely that Joel lived in that area.

Date

The book contains no references to datable historical events, but a good case can be made for its being written in the ninth century B.C. Many interpreters, however, date the book as late as the postexilic period (sixth century), after Haggai and Zechariah. In either case, its message is not significantly affected by its dating.

The book of Joel has striking linguistic parallels to those of Amos, Micah, Zephaniah, Jeremiah and Ezekiel. The literary relationships of these books are determined by one's view of the date of Joel. If it was written early, the other prophets borrowed his phrases; if it was later, the reverse may have taken place. Some scholars maintain that all the prophets drew more or less from the religious literary traditions that they and their readers shared in common — liturgical and otherwise.

Message

Joel sees the massive locust plague and severe drought devastating Judah as a harbinger of the "great and awesome day of the LORD" (2:31). (The locusts he mentions in 1:4; 2:25 are best understood as real, not as allegorical representations of the Babylonians, Medo-Persians, Greeks and Romans, as held by some interpreters.) Confronted with this crisis, he calls on everyone to repent: old and young (1:2–3), drunkards (1:5), farmers (1:11) and priests (1:13). He describes the locusts as the Lord's army and sees in their coming a reminder that the day of the Lord is near. He does not voice the popular notion that the day will be one of judgment on the nations but deliverance and blessing for Israel. Instead — with Isaiah (2:10–21), Jeremiah (4:6), Amos (5:18–20) and Zephaniah (1:7–18) — he describes the day as one of punishment for unfaithful Israel as well. Restoration and blessing will come only after judgment and repentance.

Outline

I. Title (1:1)
II. Judah Experiences a Foretaste of the Day of the Lord (1:2—2:17)
  A. A Call to Mourning and Prayer (1:2–14)
  B. The Announcement of the Day of the Lord (1:15—2:11)
  C. A Call to Repentance and Prayer (2:12–17)
III. Judah Is Assured of Salvation in the Day of the Lord (2:18—3:21)
  A. The Lord's Restoration of Judah (2:18–27)
  B. The Lord's Renewal of His People (2:28–32)
  C. The Coming of the Day of the Lord (ch. 3)
    1. The nations judged (3:1–16)
    2. God's people blessed (3:17–21)

The Devastation of Locusts

1 The [a]word of the LORD that came to [b]Joel, the son of Pethuel:
2 [a]Hear this, O [b]elders,
And listen, all inhabitants of the land.
[c]Has *anything like* this happened in your days
Or in your fathers' days?
3 [a]Tell your sons about it,
And *let* your sons *tell* their sons,
And their sons the next generation.

4 What the [a]gnawing locust has left, the swarming locust has eaten;
And what the [b]swarming locust has left, the creeping locust has eaten;
And what the creeping locust has left, the [c]stripping locust has eaten.
5 Awake, [a]drunkards, and weep;
And wail, all you wine drinkers,
On account of the sweet wine
That is [b]cut off from your mouth.
6 For a [a]nation has [1]invaded my land,
Mighty and without number;
[b]Its teeth are the teeth of a lion,
And it has the fangs of a lioness.
7 It has [a]made my vine a waste
And my fig tree [1]splinters.
It has stripped them bare and cast *them* away;
Their branches have become white.

8 [a]Wail like a virgin [b]girded with sackcloth
For the bridegroom of her youth.
9 The [a]grain offering and the drink offering are cut off
From the house of the LORD.
The [b]priests mourn,
The ministers of the LORD.
10 The field is [a]ruined,
[b]The land mourns;
For the grain is ruined,
The new wine dries up,
Fresh oil [1]fails.
11 [1][a]Be ashamed, O farmers,
Wail, O vinedressers,
For the wheat and the barley;
Because the [b]harvest of the field is destroyed.
12 The [a]vine dries up
And the fig tree [1]fails;
The [b]pomegranate, the [c]palm also, and the [2][d]apple tree,
All the trees of the field dry up.
Indeed, [e]rejoicing dries up
From the sons of men.

13 [a]Gird yourselves *with sackcloth*
And lament, O priests;
[b]Wail, O ministers of the altar!
Come, [c]spend the night in sackcloth
O ministers of my God,
For the grain offering and the drink offering
Are withheld from the house of your God.

Starvation and Drought

14 [a]Consecrate a fast,
Proclaim a [b]solemn assembly;
Gather the elders
And all the inhabitants of the land
To the house of the LORD your God,
And [c]cry out to the LORD.
15 [a]Alas for the day!

1:1 [a]Jer 1:2; Ezek 1:3; Hos 1:1 [b]Acts 2:16
2 [a]Hos 4:1; 5:1 [b]Job 8:8; Joel 1:14 [c]Jer 30:7; Joel 2:2
3 [a]Ex 10:2; Ps 78:4
4 [a]Deut 28:38; Joel 2:25; Amos 4:9 [b]Nah 3:15, 16 [c]Is 33:4
5 [a]Joel 3:3 [b]Is 32:10
6 [1]Lit *come up against* [a]Joel 2:2, 11, 25 [b]Rev 9:8
7 [1]Or *a stump* [a]Is 5:6; Amos 4:9
8 [a]Is 22:12 [b]Joel 1:13; Amos 8:10
9 [a]Hos 9:4; Joel 1:13; 2:14
9 [b]Joel 2:17
10 [1]Lit *wastes away* [a]Is 24:4, 7 [b]Jer 12:11
11 [1]Or *The farmers are ashamed, The vinedressers wail* [a]Jer 14:4; Amos 5:16 [b]Is 17:11; Jer 9:12
12 [1]Lit *wastes away* [2]Or *apricot* [a]Joel 1:10; Hab 3:17 [b]Hag 2:19 [c]Song 7:8 [d]Song 2:3 [e]Is 16:10; 24:11; Jer 48:33
13 [a]Jer 4:8; Ezek 7:18 [b]Jer 9:10 [c]1 Kin 21:27
14 [a]Joel 2:15, 16 [b]Lev 23:36 [c]Jon 3:8
15 [a]Is 13:9; Jer 30:7; Amos 5:16

1:1 *The word of the LORD . . . came to Joel.* Joel's claim of prophetic authority is similar to that of several other prophets (see Jer 1:2; Ezek 1:3; Hos 1:1; Jon 1:1,3; 3:1; Mic 1:1; Zeph 1:1; Hag 1:1; Zech 1:1; Mal 1:1). *Joel.* Means "The LORD is God"; cf. Elijah's name, which means "(My) God is the LORD."
1:2 *elders.* Either the older men of the community or the recognized officials (see v. 14; 2:16,28; see also note on Ex 3:16).
1:4 See 2:25.
1:5 *drunkards.* Although Joel calls for repentance, drunkenness is the only specific sin mentioned in the book. It suggests a self-indulgent life-style (cf. Is 28:7–8; Amos 4:1) pursued by those who value material things more than spiritual. *weep.* Various segments of the community (drunkards, here; general population, v. 8; farmers, v. 11; priests, v. 13) are called to mourn. The destruction of the vines by the locusts leaves the drunkards without a source of wine.
1:6 The locusts are compared here to a nation; cf. the ants and shephanim (or hyraxes or coneys) in Prov 30:25–26. Elsewhere they are called the Lord's "army" (2:11,25). The reverse comparison—that of armies to locusts in regard to numbers—is as old as Ugaritic literature (15th century B.C.) and is common in the OT (see Judg 6:5; 7:12; Jer 46:23; 51:14,27; Nah 3:15). *without number.* A phrase used to describe the locusts in the plague in Egypt (see Ps 105:34; see also Ex 10:4–6,12–15). *teeth.* Joel's comparison of the locusts' teeth to lions' teeth is reflected in Rev 9:8.
1:7 *my.* The personal pronouns here and elsewhere in Joel (vv. 6,13–14; 2:13–14,17–18,23,26–27; 3:2–5,17) offer a hint of hope, since they indicate that the people belong to the Lord (cf. Josh 22:19).
1:8 *virgin.* The community is addressed. In Israel, when a woman was pledged to be married to a man, he was called her husband and she his wife, though she was still a virgin (see Deut 22:23–24). This verse refers to such a husband who died before the marriage was consummated. *sackcloth.* See v. 13; Gen 37:34 and note.
1:9 *offering.* The locusts have left nothing that can be offered as sacrifice. The grain offering (Lev 2:1–2) and the drink offering, which was a libation of wine (Lev 23:13), were part of the daily offering (Ex 29:40; Num 28:5–8).
1:10 *mourns.* The land is thrown into "mourning" because of the locusts' devastation. *grain . . . new wine . . . oil.* An important OT triad, related to the agriculture of that day (see 2:19). *dries up.* See v. 12. The destruction caused by the locusts was intensified by drought.
1:13 *your God.* See note on v. 7. The phrase occurs eight times in Joel (here; v. 14; 2:13; 2:14; 2:23; 2:26; 2:27; 3:17).
1:14 *fast . . . assembly.* See 2:15. Fasting, required on the day of atonement (see note on Lev 16:29,31) and also practiced in times of calamity (see Judg 20:26; 2 Sam 12:16; Jer 14:12; Jon 3:4–5; Zech 7:3, "abstain"), was a sign of penitence and humility. The Bible speaks against outward signs that do not reflect a corresponding inward belief or attitude (see Matt 6:1–8; 23:1–36).

For the [b]day of the LORD is near,
And it will come as [c]destruction from
the [1]Almighty.
16 Has not [a]food been cut off before our
eyes,
Gladness and [b]joy from the house of
our God?
17 The [1][a]seeds shrivel under their [2]clods;
The storehouses are desolate,
The barns are torn down,
For the grain is dried up.
18 How [a]the beasts groan!
The herds of cattle wander aimlessly
Because there is no pasture for them;
Even the flocks of sheep [1]suffer.
19 [a]To You, O LORD, I cry;
For [b]fire has devoured the pastures of
the wilderness
And the flame has burned up all the
trees of the field.
20 Even the beasts of the field [1][a]pant for
You;
For the [b]water brooks are dried up
And fire has devoured the pastures of
the wilderness.

The Terrible Visitation

2 [a]Blow a trumpet in Zion,
And sound an alarm on My holy
mountain!
Let all the inhabitants of the land
tremble,
For the [b]day of the LORD is coming;
Surely it is near,
2 A day of [a]darkness and gloom,
A day of clouds and thick darkness.

15 [1]Heb *Shaddai* [b]Joel 2:1, 11, 31 [c]Is 13:6; Ezek 7:2-12
16 [a]Is 3:7; Amos 4:6 [b]Deut 12:7; Ps 43:4
17 [1]Or *dried figs* [2]Or *shovels* [a]Is 17:10, 11
18 [1]Lit *bear punishment* [a]1 Kin 8:5; Jer 12:4; 14:5, 6; Hos 4:3
19 [a]Ps 50:15; Mic 7:7 [b]Jer 9:10; Amos 7:4
20 [1]Lit *long for* [a]Ps 104:21; 147:9; Joel 1:18 [b]1 Kin 17:7; 18:5
2:1 [a]Jer 4:5; Joel 2:15; Zeph 1:16 [b]Joel 1:15; 2:11, 31; 3:14; Obad 15; Zeph 1:14
2 [a]Joel 2:10, 31; Amos 5:18; Zeph 1:15
2 [b]Joel 1:6; 2:11, 25 [c]Lam 1:12; Dan 9:12; 12:1; Joel 1:2
3 [a]Ps 97:3; Is 9:18, 19 [b]Is 51:3; Ezek 36:35 [c]Ex 10:5, 15; Ps 105:34, 35; Zech 7:14
4 [a]Rev 9:7
5 [1]Lit *Like the noise of chariots* [2]Lit *noise* [a]Rev 9:9 [b]Is 5:24; 30:30
6 [1]Or *become flushed* [a]Is 13:8; Nah 2:10 [b]Jer 30:6

As the dawn is spread over the
mountains,
So there is a [b]great and mighty people;
There has [c]never been *anything* like it,
Nor will there be again after it
To the years of many generations.
3 A [a]fire consumes before them
And behind them a flame burns.
The land is [b]like the garden of Eden
before them
But a [c]desolate wilderness behind
them,
And nothing at all escapes them.
4 Their [a]appearance is like the
appearance of horses;
And like war horses, so they run.
5 [1]With a [a]noise as of chariots
They leap on the tops of the
mountains,
Like the [2]crackling of a [b]flame of fire
consuming the stubble,
Like a mighty people arranged for
battle.
6 Before them the people are in
[a]anguish;
All [b]faces [1]turn pale.
7 They run like mighty men,
They climb the wall like soldiers;
And they each [a]march [1]in line,
Nor do they deviate from their paths.
8 They do not crowd each other,
They march everyone in his path;
When they [1]burst through the
[2]defenses,

7 [1]Lit *in his ways* [a]Prov 30:27 **8** [1]Lit *fall* [2]Lit *weapon,* probably *javelin*

1:15 *day of the LORD.* This phrase occurs five times in Joel and is the dominant theme (here; 2:1; 2:11; 2:31; 3:14). Six other prophets also use it: Isaiah (13:6,9), Ezekiel (13:5; 30:3), Amos (5:18,20), Obadiah (15), Zephaniah (1:7,14) and Malachi (4:5); and an equivalent expression occurs in Zech 14:1. Sometimes abbreviated as "that day," the term often refers to the decisive intervention of God in history, such as through the invasion of locusts in Joel or at the battle of Carchemish, 605 B.C. (see Jer 46:2,10). It can also refer to Christ's coming to consummate history (see Mal 4:5; Matt 11:24; 1 Cor 5:5; 2 Cor 1:14; 1 Thess 5:2; 2 Pet 3:10). When the term is not used for divine judgments in the midst of history, it refers to the final day of the Lord, which generally has two aspects: (1) God's triumph over and punishment of His enemies and (2) His granting of rest (security) and blessing to His people. *destruction . . . Almighty.* The Hebrew for each of these two words is a pun on the other (as in Is 13:6).
1:18 Cf. the description of a drought in Jer 14:5–6. *groan.* The Hebrew for this word is used for the groaning of Israel in Egypt (Ex 2:23) and of others in distress (Prov 29:2; Is 24:7; Lam 1:4,8,11,21; Ezek 9:4; 21:12). *wander aimlessly.* The Hebrew for this verb is used to describe Israel's confused movements in the desert (Ex 14:3). *Even . . . sheep.* Sheep are the last to suffer, because they can even grub the grass roots out of the soil.
1:19–20 *fire.* Although the destruction caused by the locusts is elsewhere compared to that of a fire (see 2:3), here the prophet likely is describing the effects of a drought. In both cases he evokes the fire of God's judgment (see, e.g., Jer 4:4; 15:14; 17:27; Ezek 5:4; 15:6–7; 20:47; 21:32; Hos 8:14; Amos 1:4,7,10,12,14; 2:2,5).
2:1 *trumpet.* See v. 15. Made of a ram's or bull's horn, it was used to signal approaching danger (Jer 4:5; 6:1; Ezek 33:3). Its sound brought trembling (from fear) to the people (see Amos 3:6). *Zion.* See v. 15; 3:17. Here, parallel to God's "holy mountain" (see note on Ps 2:6), it refers to Jerusalem as the capital of the nation.
2:2 *day of darkness.* Darkness is a common prophetic figure used of the day of the Lord (see Amos 5:18,20) and is generally a metaphor for distress and suffering (see Is 5:30; 8:22; 50:3; 59:9; Jer 2:6,31; 13:16; Lam 3:6; Ezek 34:12). *dawn.* Usually suggests relief from sorrow or gloom, the end of darkness (cf. Is 8:20; 58:8). Here, however, it is used as bitter irony, describing the locust infestation that spreads across the land like the light of dawn, which first lights up the eastern horizon and then spreads across the whole countryside.
2:3–11 The staccato character of the poetry is appropriate for the imagery of war.
2:3 *before them.* Joel creates a special impact by using this phrase four times (twice in v. 3, once in v. 6 and once in v. 10) and "behind them" twice (v. 3). *Eden.* See Gen 2:8,15 (the garden before the fall); Gen 13:10 (the Jordan Valley before the destruction of Sodom); and Is 51:3; Ezek 28:13; 31:8–9,16,18; 36:35 (all of which describe a desert that has become like Eden).
2:4 *horses.* Whereas Job compared the horse to a locust (Job 39:20), Joel does the opposite.
2:5 Mountains, though barriers to ordinary horses and chariots, are no deterrent to locusts.
2:6 *in anguish.* Because of the famine that the locusts will cause.

They do not break ranks.
9 They rush on the city,
They run on the wall;
They climb into the [a]houses,
They [b]enter through the windows like
a thief.
10 Before them the earth [a]quakes,
The heavens tremble,
The [b]sun and the moon grow dark
And the stars lose their brightness.
11 The LORD [a]utters His voice before [b]His
army;
Surely His camp is very great,
For [c]strong is he who carries out His
word.
The [d]day of the LORD is indeed great
and very awesome,
And [e]who can endure it?
12 "Yet even now," declares the LORD,
"[a]Return to Me with all your heart,
And with [b]fasting, weeping and
mourning;
13 And [a]rend your heart and not [b]your
garments."
Now return to the LORD your God,
For He is [c]gracious and compassionate,
Slow to anger, abounding in
lovingkindness
And [d]relenting of evil.
14 Who knows [a]whether He will *not* turn
and relent
And leave a [b]blessing behind Him,
Even [c]a grain offering and a drink
offering
For the LORD your God?
15 [a]Blow a trumpet in Zion,
[b]Consecrate a fast, proclaim a solemn
assembly,
16 Gather the people, [a]sanctify the
congregation,
Assemble the elders,
Gather the children and the nursing
infants.
Let the [b]bridegroom come out of his
room
And the bride out of her *bridal*
chamber.
17 Let the priests, the LORD's ministers,
Weep [a]between the porch and the
altar,
And let them say, "[b]Spare Your
people, O LORD,
And do not make Your inheritance a
[c]reproach,
A byword among the nations.
Why should they among the peoples
say,
'[d]Where is their God?' "

Deliverance Promised

18 Then the LORD [1]will be [a]zealous for
His land
And [2]will have [b]pity on His people.
19 The LORD [1]will answer and say to His
people,
"Behold, I am going to [a]send you grain,
new wine and oil,
And you will be satisfied *in full* with
[2]them;
And I will [b]never again make you a
reproach among the nations.
20 "But I will remove the [a]northern *army*
far from you,
And I will drive it into a parched and
desolate land,
And its vanguard into the [b]eastern sea,
And its rear guard into the [c]western
sea.

9 [a]Ex 10:6 [b]Jer 9:21; John 10:1
10 [a]Ps 18:7; Joel 3:16; Nah 1:5 [b]Is 13:10; 34:4; Jer 4:23; Ezek 32:7, 8; Joel 2:31; 3:15; Matt 24:29; Rev 8:12
11 [a]Ps 46:6; Is 13:4; Jer 25:30; Joel 3:16 [b]Joel 2:25 [c]Jer 50:34; Rev 18:8 [d]Jer 30:7; Joel 1:15; 2:1, 31; 3:14; Zeph 1:14, 15; Rev 6:17 [e]Ezek 22:14; Mal 3:2
12 [a]Deut 4:29; Jer 4:1, 2; Ezek 33:11; Hos 12:6 [b]Dan 9:3
13 [a]Ps 34:18; 51:17; Is 57:15 [b]Gen 37:34; 2 Sam 1:11; Job 1:20; Jer 41:5 [c]Ex 34:6 [d]Jer 18:8; 42:10; Amos 7:3, 6
14 [a]Jer 26:3; Jon 3:9 [b]Hag 2:19 [c]Joel 1:9, 13
15 [a]Num 10:3; 2 Kin 10:20 [b]Joel 1:14
16 [a]1 Sam 16:5; 2 Chr 29:5
16 [b]Ps 19:5
17 [a]2 Chr 8:12; Ezek 8:16 [b]Ex 32:11, 12; Is 37:20; Amos 7:2, 5 [c]Ps 44:13; 74:10 [d]Ps 42:10; 79:10; 115:2
18 [1]Or *was zealous* [2]Or *had pity* [a]Zech 1:14; 8:2 [b]Is 60:10; 63:9, 15
19 [1]Or *answered and said* [2]Lit *it* [a]Jer 31:12; Hos 2:21, 22; Joel 1:10; Mal 3:10 [b]Ezek 34:29; 36:15
20 [a]Jer 1:14, 15 [b]Zech 14:8 [c]Deut 11:24

2:9 *climb into the houses.* As in the Egyptian plague of locusts (Ex 10:6). Latticed windows with no glass would not stop them.
2:10 *earth quakes.* See Ps 68:8; 77:18; Is 24:18–20; Jer 4:23–24; Amos 8:8; Nah 1:5–6. *heavens tremble.* See 2 Sam 22:8; Is 13:13; Hag 2:21; Heb 12:26–28. *grow dark.* Joel links God's judgment through the locusts to the cosmic phenomena of the day of the Lord.
2:11 Just as Isaiah saw the Assyrians (Is 10:5–7; 13:4) and Jeremiah the Babylonians (Jer 25:9; 43:10) as the Lord's instruments, so Joel sees the locusts as the Lord's army (cf. Josh 5:14; Ps 68:7,17; Hab 3:8–9)—the army of the Lord with which He will come against His enemies in the day of the Lord (see 3:9–11). This passage parallels Zeph 1:14 (cf. v. 31; 3:14; Mal 4:1,5). *utters His voice.* See 3:16. *great . . . very awesome.* Two ideas often associated in the OT (see Deut 7:21; 10:21; Ps 106:21–22). The terms are frequently used to describe the day of the Lord (see v. 31; Mal 4:5). *who can endure it?* See Nah 1:6; Mal 3:2; Rev 6:17. There is no escape except in turning to God.
2:13 *gracious . . . abounding in lovingkindness.* Recalls the great self-characterization of God in Ex 34:6–7, which runs like a golden thread through the OT (see note on Ex 34:6–7; see also Deut 4:31; Mic 7:18).
2:15 *trumpet.* Not an alarm as in v. 1, but a call to religious assembly (see Lev 23:24; 25:9; Num 10:10; Josh 6:4–5; 2 Chr 15:14; Ps 47:5; 81:3; 98:6; 150:3). *fast . . . assembly.* See note on 1:14.
2:16 As with the call to mourning in ch. 1, no segment of the community was exempt. *congregation.* The Hebrew for this word refers to the religious community (see Num 16:3; 2 Chr 30:2,4,13,23–25; Mic 2:5). *elders.* See note on 1:2. *chamber.* The place where the marriage was consummated.
2:17 *Your inheritance.* Israel is God's special possession (see Ex 19:5 and note; see also Ex 15:17; 34:9). Judah is to plead, not her innocence, but that God's honor is at stake before the world (see Ex 32:12; Num 14:13; Deut 9:28; Josh 7:9). *byword.* See note on 1 Kin 9:7. *Where is their God?* A rhetorical question with sarcastic intent (see Ps 42:3,10; 79:10; 115:2; Mic 7:10).
2:18 Joel begins a new section by turning from the destruction caused by the locusts to the blessings God will give to a repentant people. *zealous.* See note on Ex 20:5. The Lord will respond to the prayer of v. 17 and arouse Himself to defend His honor and have pity on His people.
2:19 *grain, new wine and oil.* See note on 1:10.
2:20 *northern army.* Since enemies in ancient times did not invade from the sea or across the desert, Canaan's geographical location made her vulnerable only from the south (Egypt) and from the north (Assyria and Babylon). The hordes of locusts are pictured here as a vast army of Israel's most feared enemies. *stench.* Because the locusts are now dead.

And its [d]stench will arise and its foul
smell will come up,
For it has done great things."

21 [a]Do not fear, O land, rejoice and be
glad,
For the LORD has done [b]great things.
22 Do not fear, beasts of the field,
For the [a]pastures of the wilderness
have turned green,
For the tree has borne its fruit,
The fig tree and the vine have yielded
[1]in full.
23 So rejoice, O [a]sons of Zion,
And [b]be glad in the LORD your God;
For He has [c]given you [1]the early rain
for *your* vindication.
And He has poured down for you the
rain,
The [2]early and [3][d]latter rain [4]as before.
24 The threshing floors will be full of
grain,
And the vats will [a]overflow with the
new wine and oil.
25 "Then I will make up to you for the
years
That the swarming [a]locust has eaten,
The creeping locust, the stripping
locust and the gnawing locust,
My great army which I sent among you.
26 "You will have plenty to [a]eat and be
satisfied
And [b]praise the name of the LORD
your God,
Who has [c]dealt wondrously with you;
Then My people will [d]never be put to
shame.
27 "Thus you will [a]know that I am in the
midst of Israel,
And that I am the LORD your God,
And there is [b]no other;
And My people will never be [c]put to
shame.

The Promise of the Spirit

28 "[1][a]It will come about after this
That I will [b]pour out My Spirit on all
[2][c]mankind;
And your sons and daughters will
prophesy,
Your old men will dream dreams,
Your young men will see visions.
29 "Even on the [a]male and female servants
I will pour out My Spirit in those days.

The Day of the LORD

30 "I will [a]display wonders in the sky and
on the earth,
Blood, fire and columns of smoke.
31 "The [a]sun will be turned into darkness
And the moon into blood
Before the [b]great and awesome day of
the LORD comes.
32 "And it will come about that [a]whoever
calls on the name of the LORD
Will be delivered;
For [b]on Mount Zion and in Jerusalem
There will be those who [c]escape,
As the LORD has said,
Even among the [d]survivors whom the
LORD calls.

The Nations Will Be Judged

3 "[1]For behold, [a]in those days and at that
time,

20 [d]Is 34:3; Amos 4:10 **21** [a]Is 54:4; Jer 30:10; Zeph 3:16, 17 [b]Ps 126:3; Joel 2:26 **22** [1]Lit *their wealth* [a]Ps 65:12, 13 **23** [1]I.e. autumn; or possibly *the teacher for righteousness* [2]I.e. autumn [3]I.e. spring [4]So with ancient versions; Heb *in the first* [a]Ps 149:2 [b]Is 12:2-6 [c]Deut 11:14; Is 41:16; Jer 5:24; Hab 3:18; Zech 10:7 [d]Lev 26:4; Hos 6:3; Zech 10:1 **24** [a]Lev 26:10; Amos 9:13; Mal 3:10 **25** [a]Joel 1:4-7; 2:2-11 **26** [a]Lev 26:5; Deut 11:15; Is 62:9 [b]Deut 12:7; Ps 67:5-7 [c]Ps 126:2, 3; Is 25:1 [d]Is 45:17 **27** [a]Lev 26:11, 12; Joel 3:17, 21 **27** [b]Is 45:5, 6 [c]Is 49:23 **28** [1]Ch 3:1 in Heb [2]Lit *flesh* [a]Acts 2:17-21 [b]Is 32:15; 44:3; Ezek 39:29; Zech 12:10 [c]Is 40:5; 49:26 **29** [a]1 Cor 12:13; Gal 3:28 **30** [a]Matt 24:29; Mark 13:24, 25; Luke 21:11, 25, 26; Acts 2:19 **31** [a]Is 13:10; 34:4; Joel 2:10; 3:15; Matt 24:29; Mark 13:24; Luke 21:25; Acts 2:20; Rev 6:12, 13 [b]Is 13:9; Zeph 1:14-16; Mal 4:1, 5 **32** [a]Jer 33:3; Acts 2:21; Rom 10:13 [b]Is 46:13; Rom 11:26 [c]Is 4:2; Obad 17 [d]Is 11:11; Jer 31:7; Mic 4:7; Rom 9:27 **3:1** [1]Ch 4:1 in Heb [a]Jer 30:3; Ezek 38:14

2:21–23 As there was a threefold call to grief (1:5,8,13), so there is a threefold call to joy: The land (v. 21), the wild animals (v. 22) and the people (v. 23) are called on to rejoice in the Lord's bounty.

2:22 The wild animals now find green open pastures (cf. 1:19–20). The same land, with its trees (see 1:7,12,19) that the locusts and drought had devastated, is now productive.

2:23 *early rain for your vindication.* See NASB marg. ("the teacher for righteousness'). The religious sect at Qumran (which produced most of the Dead Sea Scrolls; see essay, p. 1356) hailed their most revered teacher of the law, whom they called the "Teacher of Righteousness," as the fulfillment of this prophecy. The immediate context, however, seems to support the translation in the NASB text.

2:24 *threshing floors.* See note on Ruth 1:22.

2:25 See 1:4.

2:26 *dealt wondrously.* God worked wonders for the people when they were in Egypt (see Ex 7:3), and now will work wonders in restoring the devastated land.

2:27 *Israel.* Probably refers to all God's people, with no distinction between the northern and southern kingdoms, as also in 3:2,16. *I am the LORD your God.* This clause recalls the covenant at Sinai (see Ex 20:2). *there is no other.* See note on Deut 4:35.

2:28–32 Quoted by Peter at Pentecost (Acts 2:16–21), but with a few variations from both the Hebrew text and the Septuagint (the Greek translation of the OT).

2:28 *after this.* In the Messianic period, beyond the restoration just spoken of. *pour out My Spirit.* See v. 29; Is 32:15; 44:3; Jer 31:33–34; Ezek 36:26–27; 39:29; Zech 12:10–13:1. *all mankind.* All will participate without regard to sex, age or rank; and then Moses' wish (Num 11:29) will be realized (cf. Gal 3:28). Peter extends the "all" of this verse and the "whoever" of v. 32 to the Gentiles ("all who are far off," Acts 2:39), who will not be excluded from the Spirit's outpouring or deliverance (cf. Rom 11:11–24). *prophesy . . . dream dreams . . . see visions.* See Num 12:6.

2:30–31 These cosmic events are often associated with the day of the Lord (see Is 13:9–10; 34:4; Matt 24:29; Rev 6:12; 8:8–9; 9:1–19; 14:14–20; 16:4,8–9).

2:30 *Blood.* From war. *fire . . . smoke.* Signs of God's presence (see Gen 15:17 and note; Ex 19:18).

2:31 *blood.* The moon will become blood-red.

2:32 *calls on the name of the LORD.* Worships God (cf. Gen 4:26; 12:8) and prays to Him (see Ps 116:4). *delivered.* From the wrath of God's judgment (see Matt 24:13). *As the LORD has said.* Perhaps Joel is recalling the Lord's covenant with David (see 2 Sam 7; Ps 132:13–18). *survivors.* See Zech 13:8–9; 14:2.

3:1 *in those days.* At the time of Israel's final redemption. *restore the fortunes of.* Or "bring back from captivity" (see vv. 6–7; see also Jer 29:14 and note).

When I [b]restore the fortunes of Judah
and Jerusalem,
2 I will [a]gather all the nations
And bring them down to the [b]valley of
[1]Jehoshaphat.
Then I will [c]enter into judgment with
them there
On behalf of My people and My
inheritance, Israel,
Whom they have [d]scattered among
the nations;
And they have [e]divided up My land.
3 "They have also [a]cast lots for My
people,
[1b]Traded a boy for a harlot
And sold a girl for wine that they may
drink.

4 "Moreover, what are you to Me, O [a]Tyre,
Sidon and all the regions of [b]Philistia? Are
you rendering Me a recompense? But if you
do recompense Me, swiftly and speedily I
will [c]return your recompense on your head.
5 "Since you have [a]taken My silver and
My gold, brought My precious [1]treasures to
your temples,
6 and sold the [a]sons of Judah and
Jerusalem to the [1]Greeks in order to remove
them far from their territory,
7 behold, I am going to [a]arouse them
from the place where you have sold them,
and return your recompense on your head.
8 "Also I will [a]sell your sons and your
daughters into the hand of the sons of Judah,
and they will sell them to the [b]Sabeans, to a
distant nation," for the LORD has spoken.
9 [a]Proclaim this among the nations:

[b]Prepare a war; [c]rouse the mighty
men!
Let all the soldiers draw near, let them
come up!
10 [a]Beat your plowshares into swords
And your pruning hooks into spears;
[b]Let the weak say, "I am a mighty
man."
11 [1a]Hasten and come, all you
surrounding nations,
And gather yourselves there.
Bring down, O LORD, Your [b]mighty
ones.
12 Let the nations be aroused
And come up to the [a]valley of
[1]Jehoshaphat,
For there I will sit to [b]judge
All the surrounding nations.
13 [a]Put in the sickle, for the [b]harvest is
ripe.
Come, [c]tread, for the [d]wine press is
full;
The vats overflow, for their
[e]wickedness is great.
14 [a]Multitudes, multitudes in the [b]valley
of [1]decision!
For the [c]day of the LORD is near in the
valley of [1]decision.
15 The [a]sun and moon grow dark
And the stars lose their brightness.
16 The LORD [a]roars from Zion
And [b]utters His voice from Jerusalem,

3:1 [b]Jer 16:15 **2** [1]I.e. YHWH judges [a]Is 66:18; Mic 4:12; Zech 14:2 [b]Joel 3:12, 14 [c]Is 66:16; Jer 25:31; Ezek 38:22 [d]Jer 50:17; Ezek 34:6 [e]Ezek 35:10; 36:1-5 **3** [1]Lit *Given* [a]Obad 11; Nah 3:10 [b]Amos 2:6 **4** [a]Is 23:1-18; Amos 1:9, 10; Zech 9:2-4; Matt 11:21, 22; Luke 10:13, 14 [b]Is 14:29-31; Jer 47:1-7; Ezek 25:15-17; Amos 1:6-8; Zech 9:5-7 [c]Is 34:8; 59:18 **5** [1]Lit *goodly things* [a]2 Kin 12:18; 2 Chr 21:16, 17 **6** [1]Lit *sons of Javan* [a]Ezek 27:13 **7** [a]Is 43:5, 6; Jer 23:8; Zech 9:13 **8** [a]Is 14:2; 60:14 [b]Job 1:15; Ps 72:10; Ezek 38:13 **9** [a]Jer 51:27

9 [b]Jer 6:4; Ezek 38:7; Mic 3:5 [c]Is 8:9, 10; Jer 46:3, 4; Zech 14:2, 3 **10** [a]Is 2:4; Mic 4:3 [b]Zech 12:8 **11** [1]Or *Lend aid* [a]Ezek 38:15, 16 [b]Is 13:3 **12** [1]I.e. YHWH judges [a]Joel 3:2, 14 [b]Ps 7:6; 96:13; 98:9; Is 2:4; 3:13

13 [a]Rev 14:14-19 [b]Jer 51:33; Hos 6:11 [c]Rev 14:19, 20; 19:15 [d]Is 63:3; Lam 1:15 [e]Gen 18:20 **14** [1]I.e. God's verdict [a]Is 34:2-8 [b]Joel 3:2, 12 [c]Joel 1:15; 2:1, 11, 31 **15** [a]Joel 2:10, 31 **16** [a]Hos 11:10; Amos 1:2 [b]Joel 2:11

3:2 *valley of Jehoshaphat.* See v. 12. Called the "valley of decision" in v. 14, it seems to be a symbolic name for a valley near Jerusalem that is here depicted as the place of God's ultimate judgment on the nations gathered against Jerusalem (see NASB marg.). There King Jehoshaphat had witnessed one of the Lord's historic victories over the nations (see 2 Chr 20:1–30). *My inheritance.* See note on 2:17. Seven times in four verses (vv. 2–5) God uses "My," emphasizing His covenant relationship with Israel. *Israel.* See note on 2:27.

3:3 *cast lots for My people.* This happened to Judah at the time of the captivity (586 B.C.) and is mentioned in Obad 11. The Israelites were treated by their enemies as mere chattel, to be traded off for the pleasures of prostitution and wine.

3:4–8 A parenthetical interlude. In vv. 1–3,9–11 God announces judgment against the nations hostile to Israel, but here He addresses the nations directly.

3:4 *Me.* The Lord. *Tyre, Sidon . . . Philistia.* Tyre had sold Israelites as slaves (see Amos 1:9), and Philistia had often plundered Israel (see Judg 13:1; 1 Sam 5:1; 2 Chr 21:16–17; Ezek 25:15–17). God punished them by allowing Sidon to be enslaved by Antiochus III in 345 B.C. and by allowing Tyre to be besieged by the Babylonians in 586 and to be captured by the Greeks (under Alexander the Great) in 332.

3:6 The Greeks were trading with the Phoenicians as early as 800 B.C.

3:8 *Sabeans.* From Sheba, whose queen visited Solomon (see 1 Kin 10:1–13). *distant.* It was located in the southern part of the Arabian peninsula (present-day Yemen).

3:9–21 In vv. 9–11 Joel is the speaker; in vv. 12–13 God speaks; in vv. 14–16, Joel; and in vv. 17–21, God. When Joel speaks, he does so as the spokesman of the Lord, who has commissioned him to be His prophet.

3:9–11 Joel commands that the nations be told to prepare for battle, for the Lord would come against them with His invincible heavenly army and bring them into judgment (cf. Ezek 38–39; Rev 19).

3:10 The first part of this verse is the reverse of Is 2:4 and Mic 4:3, where the peaceful effect of God's reign is portrayed. Here God's enemies are summoned to their last great confrontation with Him.

3:11 *gather yourselves there.* In the valley of Jehoshaphat for judgment (vv. 2,12).

3:13 As a result of the Lord's great army that had marched against Judah (2:3–11), there had been no harvest (2:3). That harvest was to be restored (2:19,22,24,26). In the final great day of the Lord, there will also be a harvest—the harvest of God's judgment on the nations. Rev 14:14–20 draws heavily on this picture of judgment.

3:14 *valley of decision.* The valley of Jehoshaphat (judgment) of vv. 2,12. "Jehoshaphat" speaks of God's role as Judge (see note on v. 2). Here "decision" (from a different Hebrew word) refers to the heavenly Judge's decision or judicial decree. The valley is now viewed as the place where that decree will be executed.

3:15 See 2:10 and note.

3:16 *roars.* Like a lion, God will destroy the nations. The first two lines occur also in Amos 1:2 (see Jer 25:30). *utters His voice.* As God at the head of His army had thundered against Jerusalem (2:11), so He will then thunder against Jerusalem's

And the [c]heavens and the earth
tremble.
But the LORD is a [d]refuge for His
people
And a [e]stronghold to the sons of
Israel.
17 Then you will [a]know that I am the
LORD your God,
Dwelling in Zion, My [b]holy mountain.
So Jerusalem will be [c]holy,
And [d]strangers will pass through it no
more.

Judah Will Be Blessed

18 And in that day
The [a]mountains will drip with [1]sweet
wine,
And the hills will [b]flow with milk,
And all the [c]brooks of Judah will flow
with water;
And a [d]spring will go out from the
house of the LORD
To water the valley of [2]Shittim.
19 Egypt will become a waste,
And Edom will become a desolate
wilderness,
Because of the [a]violence [1]done to the
sons of Judah,
In whose land they have shed
innocent blood.
20 But Judah will be [a]inhabited forever
And Jerusalem for all generations.
21 And I will [a]avenge their blood which I
have not avenged,
For the LORD dwells in Zion.

16 [c]Ezek 38:19; Joel 2:10; Hag 2:6 [d]Ps 61:3; Is 33:16; Jer 17:17 [e]Jer 16:19; Nah 1:7
17 [a]Joel 2:27 [b]Is 11:9; 56:7; Ezek 20:40 [c]Is 4:3; Obad 17 [d]Is 52:1; Nah 1:15
18 [1]Lit *freshly pressed out grape juice* [a]Amos 9:13 [b]Ex 3:8
18 [2]Or *acacias* [c]Is 30:25; 35:6 [d]Ezek 47:1-12
19 [1]Lit *of the sons* [a]Obad 10
20 [a]Ezek 37:25; Amos 9:15
21 [a]Is 4:4

enemies, and He will do so from His royal city, from which He rules His "inheritance" (see v. 17; Amos 1:2).

3:17–21 God blesses His people in a dual way: negatively, by destroying their enemies; and positively, by giving them good things.

3:17 *I . . . Dwelling in Zion.* The Lord Himself will dwell with them (see v. 21). The same picture is found in 2:27; Ps 46:4 (cf. Rev 21:3). The final blessed state of the now unholy and vulnerable city will be God's abiding presence in her (see v. 21 and note; Rev 21). Then she will be holy and impregnable.

3:18 *in that day.* The same as "In those days" of v. 1. The Edenic lushness pictured in this verse is in great contrast to the drought in 1:10 (see Amos 9:13). *a spring will go out from the house of the LORD.* Flowing from God's presence, streams of blessing will refresh His people and make their place endlessly fruitful (cf. Ps 36:8; 46:4; 87:7; Ezek 47:1–12; Rev 22:1–2). *Shittim.* See notes on Num 25:1; Josh 2:1. But see also NASB marg.

3:19 *Egypt . . . Edom.* As old enemies of Israel, they here represent all the nations hostile to God's people. *waste . . . desolate wilderness.* Figures for the removal of all life-sustaining blessings, thus setting in sharp focus the contrasting destinies of God's people and the enemies of God's kingdom. This picture of desolation also recalls the earlier description of Judah's condition (2:3).

3:20 *will be inhabited forever.* When God's judgment and redemption are consummated, His kingdom will endure and flourish eternally.

3:21 This book of judgment ends on a promising and encouraging note: "The LORD dwells in Zion," and therefore all is right with those who trust in God and live with Him.

Amos

INTRODUCTION

Author

Amos was from Tekoa (1:1), a small town about 6 miles south of Bethlehem and 11 miles from Jerusalem. He was not a man of the court like Isaiah, or a priest like Jeremiah. He earned his living from the flock and the sycamore-fig grove (1:1; 7:14–15). Whether he owned the flocks and groves or only worked as a hired hand is not known. His skill with words and the strikingly broad range of his general knowledge of history and the world preclude his being an ignorant peasant. Though his home was in Judah, he was sent to announce God's judgment on the northern kingdom (Israel). He probably ministered for the most part at Bethel (7:10–13; see note on Gen 12:8), Israel's main religious sanctuary, where the upper echelons of the northern kingdom worshiped.

The book brings his prophecies together in a carefully organized form intended to be read as a unit. It offers few, if any, clues as to the chronological order of his spoken messages — he may have repeated them on many occasions to reach everyone who came to worship. The book is addressed also to the southern kingdom (hence the references to Judah and Jerusalem).

Date and Historical Situation

According to the first verse, Amos prophesied during the reigns of Uzziah over Judah (792–740 B.C.) and Jeroboam II over the Israel (793–753). The main part of his ministry was probably carried out c. 760–750. Both kingdoms were enjoying great prosperity and had reached new political and military heights (cf. 2 Kin 14:23—15:7; 2 Chr 26). It was also a time of idolatry, extravagant indulgence in luxurious living, immorality, corruption of judicial procedures and oppression of the poor. As a consequence, God would soon bring about the Assyrian captivity of the northern kingdom (722–721).

Israel at the time was politicaly secure and spiritually smug. About 40 years earlier, at the end of his ministry, Elisha had prophesied the resurgence of Israel's power (2 Kin 13:17–19), and more recently Jonah had prophesied her restoration to a glory not known since the days of Solomon (2 Kin 14:25). The nation felt sure, therefore, that she was in God's good graces. But prosperity increased Israel's religious and moral corruption. God's past punishments for unfaithfulness were forgotten, and His patience was at an end — which He sent Amos to announce.

With Amos, the messages of the prophets began to be preserved in permanent form, being brought together in books that would accompany Israel through the coming debacle and beyond. Since Amos was a contemporary of Hosea and Jonah, see Introductions to those books.

Theme and Message

The dominant theme is clearly stated in 5:24, which calls for social justice as the indispensable expression of true piety. Amos was a vigorous spokesman for God's justice and righteousness, whereas Hosea emphasized God's love, grace, mercy and forgiveness. Amos declared that God was going to judge His unfaithful, disobedient, covenant-breaking people. Despite His special choice of Israel and His kindnesses to her during the exodus and conquest and in the days of David and Solomon, His people continually failed to honor and obey Him. The shrines at Bethel and other places of worship were often paganized, and Israel had a worldly view of even the ritual that the Lord Himself had prescribed. They thought performance of the rites was all God required, and, with that done, they could do whatever they pleased — an essentially pagan notion. Without commitment to God's law, they had no basis for standards of conduct. Amos condemns all who make themselves powerful or rich at the expense of others. Those who had acquired two splendid houses (3:15),

expensive furniture and richly furnished tables by cheating, perverting justice and crushing the poor would lose everything they had.

God's imminent judgment on Israel would not be a mere punitive blow to warn (as often before, 4:6 – 11), but an almost total destruction. The unthinkable was about to happen: Because they had not faithfully consecrated themselves to His lordship, God would uproot His chosen people by the hands of a pagan nation. Even so, if they would repent, there was hope that "the LORD God of hosts (would) be gracious to the remnant" (5:15; see 5:4 – 6,14). In fact, the Lord had a glorious future for His people, beyond the impending judgment. The house of David would again rule over Israel — even extend its rule over many nations — and Israel would once more be secure in the promised land, feasting on wine and fruit (9:11 – 15). The God of Israel, the Lord of history, would not abandon His chosen people or His chosen program of redemption.

The God for whom Amos speaks is God of more than merely Israel. He also uses one against another to carry out His purposes (6:14). He is the Great King who rules the whole universe (4:13; 5:8; 9:5 – 6). Because He is all-sovereign, the God of Israel holds the history and destiny of all peoples and of the world in His hands. Israel must know not only that He is the Lord of her future, but also that He is Lord over all, and that He has purposes and concerns that reach far beyond her borders. Israel had a unique, but not an exclusive, claim on God. She needed to remember not only His covenant commitments to her but also her covenant obligations to Him. (See further the prophecy of Jonah.)

Outline

- I. Superscription (1:1)
- II. Introduction to Amos's Message (1:2)
- III. Judgments on the Nations (1:3 — 2:16)
  - A. Judgment on Aram (1:3 – 5)
  - B. Judgment on Philistia (1:6 – 8)
  - C. Judgment on Phoenicia (1:9 – 10)
  - D. Judgment on Edom (1:11 – 12)
  - E. Judgment on Ammon (1:13 – 15)
  - F. Judgment on Moab (2:1 – 3)
  - G. Judgment on Judah (2:4 – 5)
  - H. Judgment on Israel (2:6 – 16)
    - 1. Ruthless oppression of the poor (2:6 – 7a)
    - 2. Unbridled profanation of religion (2:7b-8)
    - 3. Contrasted position of the Israelites (2:9 – 12)
    - 4. The oppressive system will perish (2:13 – 16)
- IV. Oracles against Israel (3:1 — 5:17)
  - A. Judgment on the Chosen People (ch. 3)
    - 1. God's punishment announced (3:1 – 2)
    - 2. The announcement vindicated (3:3 – 8)
    - 3. The punishment vindicated (3:9 – 15)
  - B. Judgment on a Unrepentant People (ch. 4)
    - 1. Judgment on the socialites (4:1 – 3)
    - 2. Perversion of religious life (4:4 – 5)
    - 3. Past calamities brought no repentance (4:6 – 11)
    - 4. No hope for a hardened people (4:12 – 13)
  - C. Judgment on an Unjust People (5:1 – 17)
    - 1. The death dirge (5:1 – 3)
    - 2. Exhortation to life (5:4 – 6)
    - 3. Indictment of injustices (5:7 – 13)
    - 4. Exhortation to life (5:14 – 15)
    - 5. Prosperity will turn to grief (5:16 – 17)
- V. Announcements of Exile (5:18 — 6:14)

A. A Message of Woe against Israel's Perverted Religion (5:18–27)
B. A Message of Woe against Israel's Complacent Pride (6:1–7)
C. A Sworn Judgment on the Proud and Unjust Nation (6:8–14)

VI. Visions of Divine Retribution (7:1—9:10)
  A. Judgment Relented (7:1–6)
    1. A swarm of locusts (7:1–3)
    2. A consuming fire (7:4–6)
  B. Judgment Unrelented (7:7—9:10)
    1. The plumb line (7:7–17)
      a. The vision (7:7–9)
      b. Challenged and vindicated (7:10–17)
    2. The basket of ripe fruit (ch. 8)
      a. The vision (8:1–3)
      b. The exposition (8:4–14)
    3. The Lord by the altar (9:1–10)
      a. The vision (9:1–4)
      b. The exposition (9:5–10)

VII. Restored Israel's Blessed Future (9:11–15)
  A. Revival of the House of David (9:11–12)
  B. Restoration of Israel to an Edenic Promised Land (9:13–15)

Judgment on Neighbor Nations

1 The words of Amos, who was among the
[a]sheepherders from [b]Tekoa, which he
[1]envisioned in visions concerning Israel in
the days of [c]Uzziah king of Judah, and in the
days of [d]Jeroboam son of Joash, king of Israel, two years before the [e]earthquake.

2 He said,
"The [a]LORD roars from Zion
And from Jerusalem He utters His
voice;
And the shepherds' [b]pasture grounds
mourn,
And the [1c]summit of Carmel dries
up."

3 Thus says the LORD,
"For [a]three transgressions of
[b]Damascus and for four
I will not [1]revoke its *punishment*,
Because they threshed Gilead with
implements of sharp iron.
4 "So I will send fire upon the house of
Hazael
And it will consume the citadels of
[a]Ben-hadad.
5 "I will also [a]break the *gate* bar of
Damascus,
And cut off the inhabitant from the
[1]valley of Aven,
And him who holds the scepter, from
Beth-eden;
So the people of Aram will go exiled
to [b]Kir,"
Says the LORD.

6 Thus says the LORD,
"For three transgressions of [a]Gaza and
for four
I will not revoke its *punishment*,
Because they deported an entire
population
To [b]deliver *it* up to Edom.
7 "So I will send fire upon the wall of
Gaza
And it will consume her citadels.
8 "I will also cut off the inhabitant from
[a]Ashdod,
And him who holds the scepter, from
[b]Ashkelon;
I will even [1]unleash My [2]power upon
Ekron,
And the remnant of the [c]Philistines
will perish,"
Says the Lord [3]GOD.

1:1 [1]Lit *saw concerning* [a]Amos 7:14 [b]2 Sam 14:2; Jer 6:1 [c]2 Chr 26:1-23; Is 1:1 [d]2 Kin 14:23-29; Hos 1:1; Amos 7:10, 11 [e]Zech 14:5
2 [1]Lit *head* [a]Is 42:13; Jer 25:30; Joel 3:16 [b]Jer 12:4; Joel 1:18, 19 [c]Amos 9:3
3 [1]Lit *cause it to turn back*, and so throughout the ch [a]Amos 2:1, 4, 6 [b]Is 8:4; 17:1-3; Jer 49:23-27; Zech 9:1
4 [a]1 Kin 20:1; 2 Kin 6:24
5 [a]Jer 51:30; Lam 2:9
5 [1]Possibly, *Baalbek* [b]2 Kin 16:9; Amos 9:7
6 [a]1 Sam 6:17; Jer 47:1, 5; Zeph 2:4 [b]Ezek 35:5; Obad 11
8 [1]Lit *cause to return* [2]Lit *hand* [3]Heb *YHWH*, usually rendered LORD [a]2 Chr 26:6; Amos 3:9; Zech 9:6 [b]Jer 47:5; Zeph 2:4 [c]Is 14:29-31; Jer 47:1-7; Ezek 25:16; Joel 3:4-8; Zeph 2:4-7; Zech 9:5-7

1:1 *Amos.* Apparently a shortened form of a name like Amasiah (2 Chr 17:16), meaning "The LORD carries" or "The LORD upholds." *sheepherders.* The Hebrew for this word occurs elsewhere in the OT only in reference to the king of Moab (2 Kin 3:4, where it is translated "sheep breeder"). Cf. 7:14, where a different Hebrew word is used. Amos was not a professional prophet who earned his living from his ministry; he stood outside religious institutions. *Tekoa.* See Introduction: Author. *envisioned.* Received by divine revelation. *Uzziah.* See Introduction: Date and Historical Situation; see also note on Is 6:1. *Jeroboam.* See Introduction: Date and Historical Situation. *earthquake.* Evidently a major shock, long remembered, and probably the one mentioned in Zech 14:5. Reference to the earthquake suggests that the author viewed it as a kind of divine reinforcement of the words of judgment.

1:2–2:16 A series of oracles against the nations. After pronouncing judgments on Israel's neighbors for various atrocities—judgments that Israel would naturally applaud—Amos announces God's condemnation of His own two kingdoms for despising God's laws. His listing of Israel's sins under the same form of indictment used against the other nations shockingly pictures Israel's sins alongside those of her pagan neighbors.

1:2 A thematic verse, ominously announcing the main thrust of Amos's message. *roars.* Amos, a shepherd, was sent to Israel to warn her that he had heard a lion roar and that the lion is none other than the Lord Himself, who has only wanted to be Israel's shepherd. For the use of this imagery in other contexts see Jer 25:30; Joel 3:16. *from Zion.* The Lord established His earthly throne in Jerusalem, among His special people, and from there He announces His judgments on them, as well as on the other nations. *pasture . . . summit of Carmel.* See 9:3. From the driest portion of the land to the greenest, the Lord's judgment will be felt like a severe drought that devastates the whole land.

1:3 *For three transgressions . . . four.* For their many sins, especially the one named; see also vv. 6,9,11,13; 2:1,4,6. For similar numerical expressions see Prov 6:16; 30:15,18,21,29; Mic 5:5. *Damascus.* Capital of the Aramean state directly north of Israel and a constant enemy in that day. Her crime was brutality to the conquered people of Gilead, Israel's territory east of Galilee. *threshed . . . implements of sharp iron.* Heads of grain were threshed by driving a wooden sledge fitted with sharp teeth over the cut grain (cf. Job 41:30; Is 28:27; 41:15; see 2 Kin 13:7 and note on Ruth 1:22).

1:4 *send fire . . . it will consume.* See vv. 7,10,12; 2:2,5; cf. v. 14; a common description of the threat of divine judgment, usually carried out by a devastating war that resulted in the burning of major cities and fortresses. See the judgments mentioned in Jer 17:27; 49:27; 50:32; Hos 8:14. *Hazael.* King of Damascus c. 842–796 B.C. and founder of a new line of kings (see 2 Kin 8:7–15). *citadels.* See vv. 7,10,12,14; 2:2,5; perhaps referring to the fortress-like palatial dwellings of the rich and powerful. *Ben-hadad.* Son of Hazael (2 Kin 13:24) and the second king with this name (cf. 2 Kin 8:14–15), ruling c. 796–775.

1:5 *inhabitant.* See v. 8; lit. "one who sits [enthroned]." *valley of Aven.* Possibly the Beqaa Valley between the Lebanon and Anti-Lebanon mountains, but may refer to the river valley in which Damascus is located, calling it the "valley of wickedness" ("Aven" means "wickedness"). *Beth-eden.* Probably Damascus, the garden spot of that region. *Aram.* See note on Gen 10:22. *Kir.* An unidentified place, possibly in the vicinity of Elam (2 Kin 16:9; Is 22:6), from which the Arameans of Damascus are said to have come (9:7).

1:6 *Gaza.* One of the five Philistine cities (see map, p. 312); it guarded the entry to Canaan from Egypt. *entire population.* See v. 9; not just warriors captured in battle. The reference may be to villages in south Judah on the trade route from Edom to Gaza. *to Edom.* See v. 9; trading the people like cattle to another country.

1:8 *Ashdod . . . Ashkelon . . . Ekron.* Three more cities of the Philistine group (see note on v. 6). Gath, the fifth (cf. 6:2), may already have been subdued by Uzziah (see 2 Chr 26:6). *the remnant.* There would be no remnant. Philistia was finally destroyed by Nebuchadnezzar.

9 Thus says the LORD,
"For three transgressions of [a]Tyre and for four
I will not revoke its *punishment,*
Because they delivered up an entire population to Edom
And did not remember *the* covenant of [1b]brotherhood.
10 "So I will [a]send fire upon the wall of Tyre
And it will consume her citadels."

11 Thus says the LORD,
"For three transgressions of [a]Edom and for four
I will not revoke its *punishment,*
Because he [b]pursued his brother with the sword,
While he [1]stifled his compassion;
His anger also [c]tore continually,
And he maintained his fury forever.
12 "So I will send fire upon [a]Teman
And it will consume the citadels of Bozrah."

13 Thus says the LORD,
"For three transgressions of the sons of [a]Ammon and for four
I will not revoke its *punishment,*
Because they [b]ripped open the pregnant women of Gilead
In order to [c]enlarge their borders.
14 "So I will kindle a fire on the wall of [a]Rabbah
And it will consume her citadels
Amid [1b]war cries on the day of battle,
And a [c]storm on the day of tempest.
15 "Their [a]king will go into exile,
He and his princes together," says the LORD.

Judgment on Judah and Israel

2 Thus says the LORD,
"For three transgressions of [a]Moab and for four
I will not [1]revoke its *punishment,*
Because he [b]burned the bones of the king of Edom to lime.
2 "So I will send fire upon Moab
And it will consume the citadels of [a]Kerioth;
And Moab will die amid [b]tumult,
With [1]war cries and the sound of a trumpet.
3 "I will also cut off the [1a]judge from her midst
And slay all her [b]princes with him,"
says the LORD.

4 Thus says the LORD,
"For three transgressions of [a]Judah and for four
I will not revoke its *punishment,*
Because they [b]rejected the law of the LORD
And have not kept His statutes;
Their [1c]lies also have led them astray,
Those after which their [d]fathers walked.
5 "So I will [a]send fire upon Judah
And it will consume the citadels of Jerusalem."

6 Thus says the LORD,
"For three transgressions of [a]Israel and for four
I will not revoke its *punishment,*
Because they [b]sell the righteous for money
And the needy for a pair of sandals.

9 [1]Lit *brothers* [a]Is 23:1-18; Jer 25:22; Ezek 26:2-4; Joel 3:4-8; Zech 9:1-4; Matt 11:21, 22; Luke 10:13, 14 [b]1 Kin 9:11-14
10 [a]Zech 9:4
11 [1]Lit *corrupted* [a]Is 34:5, 6; 63:1-6; Jer 49:7-22; Ezek 25:12-14; 35:1-15; Obad 1-14; Mal 1:2-5 [b]Num 20:14-21; 2 Chr 28:17; Obad 10-12 [c]Is 57:16; Mic 7:18
12 [a]Jer 49:7, 20; Obad 9
13 [a]Jer 49:1-6; Ezek 21:28-32; 25:2-7; Zeph 2:8, 9 [b]2 Kin 15:16; Hos 13:16 [c]Is 5:8; Ezek 35:10
14 [1]Or *shouts* [a]Deut 3:11; 1 Chr 20:1; Jer 49:2 [b]Ezek 21:22; Amos 2:2 [c]Is 29:6; 30:30
15 [a]Jer 49:3

2:1 [1]Lit *cause it to turn back,* and so throughout the ch [a]Is 15:1-16:14; 25:10-12; Jer 48:1-47; Ezek 25:8-11; Zeph 2:8, 9 [b]2 Kin 3:26, 27
2 [1]Or *shouts* [a]Jer 48:24, 41 [b]Jer 48:45
3 [1]Or *executive officer* [a]Ps 2:10; 141:6; Amos 5:7, 12; 6:12 [b]Job 12:21; Is 40:23
4 [1]Or *false gods* [a]2 Kin 17:19; Hos 12:2; Amos 3:2 [b]Judg 2:17-20; 2 Kin 22:11-17; Jer 6:19; 8:9 [c]Is 9:15, 16; 28:15; Jer 16:19; Hab 2:18 [d]Jer 9:14; 16:11, 12; Ezek 20:18, 24, 30
5 [a]Jer 17:27; 21:10; Hos 8:14
6 [a]2 Kin 18:11, 12 [b]Joel 3:3; Amos 5:11, 12; 8:6

1:9 *Tyre.* The senior Phoenician merchant city, allied to Israel by a "treaty of brotherhood" in the days of David (1 Kin 5:1), later in the time of Solomon (1 Kin 5:12) and later still during the reign of Ahab, whose father-in-law ruled Tyre and Sidon (1 Kin 16:30–31). *they delivered.* Their crime was like Philistia's (v. 6).

1:10 *wall.* Tyre was an almost impregnable island, boastful of her security (cf. Ezek 26:1–28:19).

1:11 *Edom.* The nation descended from Esau (Gen 36; cf. Gen 25:23–30; 27:39–40). *brother.* Israel (cf. Obad 8–10). Reference may be to treaty "brother" (see note on v. 9). Edom's crime was in violating this relationship by persistent hostility.

1:12 *Teman . . . Bozrah.* Major cities of Edom, the former thought to be near Petra, the latter now identified with Buseirah, 37 miles to the north. With their destruction, Edom would lose its capacity for continual warfare.

1:13 *Ammon.* Judgment centered on Rabbah (see note on Deut 3:11), modern Amman. Greed for land bred a brutal genocide that would be punished by a tumult of men and nature, leaving the state without leaders to continue such practices.

1:14 Fulfilled through the Assyrians.

1:15 *Their king.* See Jer 49:1,3 and notes ("Malcam" can be read as "their king").

2:1 *burned the bones of the king of Edom.* Thus depriving the king's spirit of the rest that was widely believed to result from decent burial.

2:2 *Kerioth.* Perhaps a plural noun meaning "cities" (therefore "citadels of her cities") or the name of a major town (see Jer 48:24) and shrine of Chemosh, the national god of Moab (see 1 Kin 11:7,33).

2:4 *rejected the law of the LORD.* Judah's sins differed in kind from those of the other nations. Those nations violated the generally recognized laws of humanity, but Judah disobeyed the revealed law of God. These sins may be included in the indictment against Israel that follows.

2:5 *fire . . . consume the citadels.* Judah's punishment is the same as Aram's (1:4), Gaza's (1:7), Tyre's (1:10), Edom's (1:12), Ammon's (1:14) and Moab's (2:2)—loss of the defenses and wealth in which they trusted.

2:6 Israel's sins revealed the general moral deterioration of the nation. *the righteous.* Probably those who were not in debt and whom there was no lawful reason to sell (cf. Lev 25:39–43). *the needy.* God had commanded that they be helped (Deut 15:7–11), but they were instead sold for failure to repay a (perhaps paltry) debt, for which a pair of sandals had been given in pledge (see 8:6).

7 "These who [1]pant after the *very* dust of
the earth on the head of the
[a]helpless
Also [b]turn aside the way of the
humble;
And a [c]man and his father [2]resort to
the same [3]girl
In order to profane My holy name.
8 "On garments [a]taken as pledges they
stretch out beside [b]every altar,
And in the house of their God they
[c]drink the wine of those who have
been fined.

9 "Yet it was I who destroyed the
[a]Amorite before them,
[1]Though his [b]height *was* like the
height of cedars
And he *was* strong as the oaks;
I even destroyed his [c]fruit above and
his root below.
10 "It was I who [a]brought you up from the
land of Egypt,
And I led you in the wilderness [b]forty
years
[1]That you might take possession of
the land of the [c]Amorite.
11 "Then I [a]raised up some of your sons
to be prophets
And some of your young men to be
[b]Nazirites.
Is this not so, O sons of Israel?"
declares the LORD.
12 "But you made the Nazirites drink wine,
And you commanded the prophets
saying, 'You [a]shall not prophesy!'

13 "Behold, I am [1][a]weighted down
beneath you
As a wagon [2]is weighted down when
filled with sheaves.
14 "[1][a]Flight will perish from the swift,
And the stalwart will not strengthen
his power,
Nor the [b]mighty man save his [2]life.
15 "He who [a]grasps the bow will not
stand *his ground,*
The swift of foot will not escape,
Nor will he who rides the [b]horse save
his [1]life.
16 "Even the [1]bravest among the warriors
will [a]flee naked in that day,"
declares the LORD.

All the Tribes Are Guilty

3 Hear this word which the LORD has spoken against you, sons of Israel, against
the entire [1][a]family which [2]He brought up
from the land of Egypt:

2 "[a]You only have I [1]chosen among all
the families of the earth;
Therefore I will [2][b]punish you for all
your iniquities."
3 Do two men walk together unless they
have made an [1]appointment?
4 Does a [a]lion roar in the forest when
he has no prey?
Does a young lion [1]growl from his den
unless he has captured *something?*
5 Does a bird fall into a trap on the
ground when there is no [1]bait in it?

7 [1]Or *trample or, snap at the head of the helpless on the dust* [2]Lit *go* [3]Possibly a harlot, or a temple prostitute [a]Amos 8:4; Mic 2:2, 9 [b]Amos 5:12 [c]Hos 4:14
8 [a]Ex 22:26 [b]Amos 3:14 [c]Amos 4:1; 6:6
9 [1]Lit *Whose height* [a]Num 21:23-25; Josh 10:12 [b]Num 13:32 [c]Ezek 17:9; Mal 4:1
10 [1]Lit *To possess* [a]Ex 12:51; 20:2; Amos 3:1; 9:7 [b]Deut 2:7 [c]Ex 3:8
11 [a]Deut 18:18; Jer 7:25 [b]Num 6:2, 3; Judg 13:5
12 [a]Is 30:10; Jer 11:21; Amos 7:13, 16; Mic 2:6
13 [1]Or *tottering* [2]Or *totters* [a]Is 1:14
14 [1]Or *A place of refuge* [2]Lit *soul* [a]Is 30:16, 17 [b]Ps 33:16; Jer 9:23
15 [1]Lit *soul* [a]Jer 51:56; Ezek 39:3 [b]Is 31:3
16 [1]Lit *stout of heart* [a]Judg 4:17
3:1 [1]I.e. nation [2]Lit *I* [a]Jer 8:3; 13:11
2 [1]Lit *known* [2]Lit *visit* [a]Gen 18:19; Ex 19:5, 6; Deut 4:32-37; 7:6 [b]Jer 14:10; Ezek 20:36; Dan 9:12; Rom 2:9
3 [1]Or *agreement*
4 [1]Lit *give his voice* [a]Ps 104:21; Hos 5:14; 11:10
5 [1]Or *striker-bar set*

2:7 *helpless . . . humble.* To care for them and to protect them from injustice were clearly commanded by Israel's law (Ex 23:6–8); also, throughout the ancient Near East, kings were supposed to defend such people. *a man and his father resort to the same girl.* Whether the girl in question was a household servant (in which case father and son used her as a family prostitute) is not clear. In any case, the law required that if there were sexual relations with a girl, marriage was obligatory (Ex 22:16; Deut 22:28–29). For a father and son to have sexual relations with the same girl or woman was strictly forbidden (Lev 18:7–8,15; 20:11–12). *profane My holy name.* Cf. Lev 18:21; 19:12; 20:3; 21:6; 22:2,32; Jer 34:16; Ezek 20:9,14,22,39; 36:20–23; 39:7.
2:8 *garments taken as pledges.* The law prohibited keeping a man's cloak overnight as a pledge (Ex 22:26–27; Deut 24:12–13), or taking a widow's cloak at all (Deut 24:17). *beside every altar . . . in the house of their God.* Israelites who broke the laws protecting the powerless brazenly used their wrongly gotten gains even in places supposed to be holy. *fined.* As restitution for damages suffered. Exorbitant claims or even false charges of damage seem to be suggested.
2:9 *I who destroyed.* Israel not only had known God's law but had been specially favored by His powerful help. *Amorite.* Here used for all the inhabitants of Canaan (see notes on Gen 10:16; 15:16; Judg 6:10; see also Deut 7:1 and note). *his fruit above and his root below.* That is, totally.
2:10 *I who brought you up.* See 3:1. God's great blessings to Israel in the past added to her guilt, and now they are recalled as a part of the Lord's indictment against His people.
2:11 *I raised up . . . prophets and . . . Nazirites.* Prophets, as God's faithful spokesmen (Deut 18:15–19), and Nazirites, as those uniquely dedicated to Him (Num 6:1–21; Judg 13:5), are singled out as special gifts to His people. These persons who were outside the priesthood were used by God through word and example to call His people to faithfulness.
2:12 *But you.* They showed utter disdain for God's faithful servants and thus betrayed their callous insensitivity to God's working among them (cf. 7:16).
2:13 A loaded cart crushes anything that falls beneath its wheels.
2:14–16 No one who might be expected to stand his ground or escape would be able to save himself.
2:16 *that day.* The day God comes in judgment—as He did through the Assyrian invasion that swept the northern kingdom away.
3:1–5:17 Oracles that underscore the certainty of God's judgment on Israel.
3:1 *Hear this word.* See 4:1; 5:1. The Lord calls His people to account because of their sins. *He.* Lit. "I" (see NASB marg.). He now speaks more directly than in 1:2–2:16.
3:2 *You only.* Israel's present strength and prosperity gave rise to complacency about her privileged status as the Lord's chosen people. She is shockingly reminded of the long-forgotten responsibilities her privileges entailed.
3:3–6 With these rhetorical questions (involving comparisons) Amos builds up to the statements of vv. 7–8, to explain why he is speaking such terrifying words. Each picture is of cause and effect, using figures drawn from daily life—and culminating in divine action (v. 6).

Does a trap spring up from the earth
when it captures nothing at all?
6 If a [a]trumpet is blown in a city will
not the people tremble?
If a [b]calamity occurs in a city has not
the LORD done it?
7 [1]Surely the Lord [2]GOD does nothing
Unless He [a]reveals His secret counsel
To His servants the prophets.
8 A [a]lion has roared! Who will not fear?
The [b]Lord [1]GOD has spoken! [c]Who can
but prophesy?

9 Proclaim on the citadels in [a]Ashdod
and on the citadels in the land of Egypt and
say, "Assemble yourselves on the [b]moun-
tains of Samaria and see *the* great tumults
within her and *the* [c]oppressions in her midst.
10 "But they [a]do not know how to do what
is right," declares the LORD, "these who
[b]hoard up [1]violence and devastation in their
citadels."

11 Therefore, thus says the Lord GOD,
"An [a]enemy, even one surrounding the
land,
Will pull down your [1]strength from
you
And your [b]citadels will be looted."
12 Thus says the LORD,
"Just as the shepherd [1a]snatches from
the lion's mouth a couple of legs or
a piece of an ear,
So will the sons of Israel dwelling in
Samaria be [2]snatched away—
With *the* [b]corner of a bed and *the*
[3c]cover of a couch!
13 "Hear and [a]testify against the house of
Jacob,"
Declares the Lord GOD, the God of
hosts.
14 "For on the day that I punish Israel's
transgressions,
I will also punish the altars of [a]Bethel;
The horns of the altar will be cut off
And they will fall to the ground.
15 "I will also smite the [1a]winter house
together with the [b]summer house;
The houses of [2c]ivory will also perish
And the [d]great houses will come to an
end,"
Declares the LORD.

"Yet You Have Not Returned to Me"

4 Hear this word, you cows of [a]Bashan
who are on the [b]mountain of Samaria,
Who [c]oppress the poor, who crush the
needy,
Who say to [1]your husbands, "Bring
now, that we may [d]drink!"
2 The Lord [1]GOD has [a]sworn by His
[b]holiness,
"Behold, the days are coming upon you
When [2]they will take you away with
[c]meat hooks,
And the last of you with [d]fish hooks.
3 "You will [a]go out *through* breaches *in*
the walls,
Each one straight before her,
And you [1]will be cast to Harmon,"
declares the LORD.

4 "Enter Bethel and transgress;

6 [a]Jer 4:5, 19, 21; 6:1; Hos 5:8; Zeph 1:16 [b]Is 14:24-27; 45:7 **7** [1]Or *For* [2]Heb *YHWH* [a]Gen 6:13; 18:17; Jer 23:22; Dan 9:22; John 15:15 **8** [1]Heb *YHWH*, usually rendered *LORD*, and so throughout the ch [a]Amos 1:2 [b]Jon 1:1-3; 3:1-3 [c]Jer 20:9; Acts 4:20 **9** [a]1 Sam 5:1 [b]Amos 4:1; 6:1 [c]Amos 5:11; 8:6 **10** [1]I.e. the booty from violence [a]Ps 14:4; Jer 4:22; Amos 5:7; 6:12 [b]Hab 2:8-10; Zeph 1:9; Zech 5:3, 4 **11** [1]Or *stronghold* [a]Amos 6:14 [b]Amos 2:5 **12** [1]Or *delivers* [2]Or *delivered* [3]Lit *damask* [a]1 Sam 17:34-37 [b]Ps 132:3 [c]Esth 1:6; 7:8; Amos 6:4 **13** [a]Ezek 2:7 **14** [a]2 Kin 23:15; Hos 10:5-8, 14, 15; Amos 4:4; 5:5, 6; 7:10, 13 **15** [1]Or *autumn* [2]I.e. ivory inlay [a]Jer 36:22 [b]Judg 3:20 [c]1 Kin 22:39; Ps 45:8 [d]Amos 2:5; 6:11 **4:1** [1]Lit *their lords* [a]Ps 22:12; Ezek 39:18 [b]Amos 3:9; 6:1 [c]Amos 5:11; 8:6 [d]Amos 2:8; 6:6 **2** [1]Heb *YHWH*, usually rendered *LORD*, and so throughout the ch [2]Lit *he* [a]Amos 6:8; 8:7 [b]Ps 89:35 [c]Is 37:29; Ezek 38:4 [d]Jer 16:16; Ezek 29:4; Hab 1:15 **3** [1]So Gr; M.T. reads *will cast* [a]Jer 52:7

3:8 *A lion.* Echoes 1:2. *Who can but prophesy?* Amos speaks because God has spoken.
3:9 The rich and powerful of Philistia and Egypt are summoned to witness the Lord's indictment against those who store up ill-gotten riches in the fortresses of Samaria (see v. 15). *citadels.* See note on 1:4. *great tumults.* The result of a violent, selfish power structure that was heedless of the justice called for in God's law.
3:10 *who hoard.* Cf. 2:6–8. The prosperity of Israel's wealthy depended on oppression and robbery. The following verses announce God's judgment on such greed (cf. Hab 2:6–11).
3:11 *enemy.* Assyria. *citadels will be looted.* Those that Samaria's wealthy had greedily filled with plunder.
3:12 *as the shepherd snatches . . . a couple of legs.* To prove to the owner that the sheep had been eaten by a wild animal, not stolen by the shepherd. *the sons . . . dwelling in Samaria.* In idle luxury (cf. 6:4). *be snatched away.* Only a mutilated remnant would survive. The nation as such would be more than wounded—it would be destroyed.
3:13 *Hear and testify.* Addressed to those summoned in v. 9. The rich and powerful of Philistia and Egypt are called upon to hear the Lord's indictment of the rich and powerful in Samaria and to testify that His indictment is true and that His judgment is warranted. Even these pagans will agree with God's judgment.
3:14 *altars of Bethel.* Israel's sins were rooted in the false shrine built by Jeroboam I at Bethel (1 Kin 12:26–33). *horns of the altar.* Even the last refuge for a condemned man (cf. 1 Kin 1:50–53) will afford Israel no protection.
3:15 *winter house . . . summer house.* Cf. 6:11; further signs of opulence that would not benefit their owners on the day of God's judgment—nor would expensive imported decorations, carvings and inlays of ivory (cf. 6:4; 1 Kin 22:39). Many examples of such carvings have been found in ruined palaces in Samaria and other cities.
4:1 *Hear this word.* See note on 3:1. *cows of Bashan.* Upper-class women, directly addressed, are compared with the best breed of cattle in ancient Canaan, which were raised (and pampered) in the pastures of northern Transjordan (cf. Ps 22:12; Ezek 39:18). Whether the metaphor was intended as an insult or as ironic flattery is uncertain.
4:2 *The Lord GOD has sworn.* Stresses the solemnity of the situation and the certainty of the events. *by His holiness.* Contrasts with Israel's sin, reminding them of what they could have been (Ex 19:6) if they had faithfully kept their side of the covenant—as God had His. *hooks.* According to Assyrian reliefs (pictures engraved on stone), prisoners of war were led away with a rope fastened to a hook that pierced the nose or lower lip (cf. 2 Kin 19:28; 2 Chr 33:11; Ezek 19:4,9; Hab 1:15). The Hebrew word here may, in fact, refer to ropes.
4:3 *breaches in the walls.* See 2 Kin 17:5. *Harmon.* Appears to be a place-name, though it is not otherwise known.
4:4–5 Spoken in irony.
4:4 *Bethel . . . Gilgal.* These towns had historical importance as places where God's help was commemorated (cf. Gen 35:1–15;

In Gilgal multiply transgression!
[a]Bring your sacrifices every morning,
Your tithes every three days.
5 "[1]Offer a [a]thank offering also from that
which is leavened,
And proclaim [b]freewill offerings, make
them known.
For so you [c]love *to do,* you sons of
Israel,"
Declares the Lord GOD.

6 "But I gave you also [a]cleanness of teeth
in all your cities
And lack of bread in all your places,
Yet you have [b]not returned to Me,"
declares the LORD.
7 "Furthermore, I [a]withheld the rain from
you
While *there were* still three months
until harvest.
Then I would send rain on one city
And on [b]another city I would not send
rain;
One part would be rained on,
While the part not rained on would
dry up.
8 "So two or three cities would stagger to
another city to drink [a]water,
But would [b]not be satisfied;
Yet you have [c]not returned to Me,"
declares the LORD.
9 "I [a]smote you with scorching *wind* and
mildew;
And the [b]caterpillar was devouring
Your many gardens and vineyards, fig
trees and olive trees;
Yet you have [c]not returned to Me,"
declares the LORD.
10 "I sent a [a]plague among you after the
manner of Egypt;
I [b]slew your young men by the sword
along with your [c]captured horses,
And I made the [d]stench of your camp
rise up in your nostrils;
Yet you have [e]not returned to Me,"
declares the LORD.
11 "I overthrew you, as [a]God overthrew
Sodom and Gomorrah,
And you were like a [b]firebrand
snatched from a blaze;
Yet you have [c]not returned to Me,"
declares the LORD.
12 "Therefore thus I will do to you, O Israel;
Because I will do this to you,
Prepare to [a]meet your God, O Israel."
13 For behold, He who [a]forms mountains
and [b]creates the wind
And [c]declares to man what are His
thoughts,
He who [d]makes dawn into darkness
And [e]treads on the high places of the
earth,
[f]The LORD God of hosts is His name.

"Seek Me that You May Live"

5 Hear this word which I take up for
you as a [a]dirge, O house of Israel:
2 She has fallen, she will [a]not rise
again—
The [b]virgin Israel.
She *lies* neglected on her land;
There is [c]none to raise her up.
3 For thus says the Lord [1]GOD,
"The city which goes forth a thousand
strong
Will have a [a]hundred left,
And the one which goes forth a
hundred *strong*
Will have [b]ten left to the house of
Israel."

4 For thus says the LORD to the house of
Israel,
"[a]Seek Me [b]that you may live.

4 [a]Num 28:3; Amos 5:21, 22 **5** [1]Lit *Offer up in smoke* [a]Lev 7:13 [b]Lev 22:18-21 [c]Jer 7:9, 10; Hos 9:1, 10 **6** [a]Is 3:1; Jer 14:18 [b]Is 9:13; Jer 5:3; Hag 2:17 **7** [a]Deut 11:17; 2 Chr 7:13; Is 5:6 [b]Ex 9:4, 26; 10:22, 23 **8** [a]1 Kin 18:5; Jer 14:4 [b]Ezek 4:16, 17; Hag 1:6 [c]Jer 3:7 **9** [a]Deut 28:22; Hag 2:17 [b]Joel 1:4, 7; Amos 7:1, 2 [c]Jer 3:10 **10** [a]Ex 9:3; Lev 26:25; Deut 28:27, 60; Ps 78:50 [b]Jer 11:22; 18:21; 48:15 [c]2 Kin 13:3, 7
10 [d]Joel 2:20 [e]Is 9:13 **11** [a]Gen 19:24, 25; Deut 29:23; Is 13:19 [b]Zech 3:2 [c]Jer 23:14 **12** [a]Is 32:11; 64:2; Jer 5:22 **13** [a]Job 38:4-7; Ps 65:6; Is 40:12 [b]Ps 135:7; Jer 10:13 [c]Dan 2:28, 30 [d]Jer 13:16; Joel 2:2; Amos 5:8 [e]Mic 1:3 [f]Is 47:4; Jer 10:16; Amos 5:8, 27; 9:6 **5:1** [a]Jer 7:29; 9:10, 17; Ezek 19:1 **2** [a]Amos 8:14 [b]Jer 14:17 [c]Is 51:18; Jer 50:32 **3** [1]Heb *YHWH,* usually rendered *LORD,* and so throughout the ch [a]Is 6:13 [b]Amos 6:9 **4** [a]Deut 4:29; 32:46, 47; Jer 29:13 [b]Is 55:3

Josh 4:20–24), and both were popular places of worship in Amos's day (5:5; cf. Hos 4:15; 9:15; 12:11). *sacrifices every morning.* See Ex 29:38–42. *tithes.* Apparently the special tithe that was to be brought every three years (cf. Deut 14:28; 26:12). *days.* Or "years" (the Hebrew for "days" sometimes stands for years).

4:5 *that which is leavened.* The burning of leavened bread in the sacrifices was strictly forbidden (see Lev 6:17; 7:12). Either Amos rebukes the Israelites for willful transgression of the law, or he speaks of burning in a general way for offering inappropriate gifts to the Lord. Leavened bread could accompany a peace offering (see Lev 7:13). *so you love to do.* They loved the forms and rituals of religion but did not love what God loves—goodness, mercy, kindness, justice (see 5:15; Is 5:7; 61:8; Hos 6:6; Mic 6:8).

4:6–11 In the past, God had used natural disasters to discipline and warn His people, but those lessons were soon forgotten (cf. Deut 28:22,39–40,42,48,56–57).

4:6 *I.* These were not simply natural disasters; they were direct acts of God (3:6). *Yet . . . Me.* See vv. 8–11.

4:7–8 Lack of rain three months before harvest would prevent full development of the grain.

4:9 *caterpillar.* Or "locust" (cf. 7:1; Joel 1:4).

4:10 *plague . . . after . . . Egypt.* See Ex 7:14–12:30.

4:11 *Sodom and Gomorrah.* Exemplified total destruction, God's judgment on those cities (see Gen 19:24–25) having already become proverbial (cf. Deut 29:23; Is 1:9; 13:19; Jer 49:18; 50:40; Zeph 2:9). *firebrand snatched from a blaze.* Saved only by God's grace (cf. Zech 3:2).

4:12 *Prepare to meet your God.* Devastated Israel, brought to her knees by the Assyrians, would meet the God she had covenanted with at Sinai and had now so grievously offended.

4:13 See note on 5:8–9. The God of such power and majesty is easily able to execute the judgment announced in v. 12.

5:1 *Hear this word.* See note on 3:1. *dirge.* Amos sorrowfully fashioned a lament as if Israel were already dead.

5:2 *virgin Israel.* See Jer 18:13; 31:4,21; see also notes on 2 Kin 19:21; Is 23:12. *neglected.* Left like a dead body on the open field (cf. Jer 9:22).

5:3 *city . . . one.* The Hebrew expression denotes communities of varying size, all of which would suffer.

5:4 *Seek.* See vv. 6,14. *live.* If they would seek the Lord, they (or at least a remnant, v. 15) could yet escape the violent death anticipated in Amos's lament.

5 "But do not [1]resort to [a]Bethel
And do not come to [b]Gilgal,
Nor cross over to [c]Beersheba;
For Gilgal will certainly go into captivity
And Bethel will [2]come to trouble.
6 "[a]Seek the LORD that you may live,
Or He will break forth like a [b]fire,
[1]O house of Joseph,
And it will consume with none to
quench *it* for Bethel,
7 *For* those who turn [a]justice into
wormwood
And [1]cast righteousness down to the
earth."

8 He who made the [a]Pleiades and Orion
And [b]changes deep darkness into
morning,
[1]Who also [c]darkens day *into* night,
Who [d]calls for the waters of the sea
And pours them out on the surface of
the earth,
The [e]LORD is His name.
9 It is He who [a]flashes forth *with*
destruction upon the strong,
So that [b]destruction comes upon the
fortress.

10 They hate him who [a]reproves in the
[1]gate,
And they [b]abhor him who speaks *with*
integrity.
11 Therefore because you [1]impose heavy
rent on the poor
And exact a tribute of grain from them,
Though you have built [a]houses of
well-hewn stone,
Yet you will not live in them;
You have planted pleasant vineyards,
yet you will [b]not drink their wine.
12 For I know your transgressions are
many and your sins are great,
You who [a]distress the righteous *and*
accept bribes
And [1]turn aside the poor in the [2]gate.
13 Therefore at [1]such a time the prudent
person [a]keeps silent, for it is an evil
time.

14 Seek good and not evil, that you may
live;
And thus may the LORD God of hosts
be with you,
[a]Just as you have said!
15 [a]Hate evil, love good,
And establish justice in the [1]gate!
Perhaps the LORD God of hosts
[b]May be gracious to the [c]remnant of
Joseph.

16 Therefore thus says the LORD God of
hosts, the Lord,
"There is [a]wailing in all the plazas,
And in all the streets they say, 'Alas!
Alas!'
They also call the [b]farmer to
mourning
And [1][c]professional mourners to
lamentation.
17 "And in all the [a]vineyards *there is*
wailing,

5 [1]Lit *seek* [2]Or *become iniquity* [a]1 Kin 12:28, 29; Amos 3:14; 4:4; 7:10, 13 [b]1 Sam 7:16; 11:14 [c]Gen 21:31-33; Amos 8:14
6 [1]Or in *the house* [a]Is 55:3, 6, 7; Amos 5:14 [b]Deut 4:24
7 [1]Lit *they have put down* [a]Amos 2:3; 5:12; 6:12
8 [1]Lit *And He darkened* [a]Job 9:9; 38:31 [b]Job 12:22; 38:12; Is 42:16 [c]Ps 104:20 [d]Ps 104:6-9; Amos 9:6 [e]Amos 4:13
9 [a]Is 29:5; Amos 2:14 [b]Mic 5:11
10 [1]I.e. the place where court was held [a]Is 29:21; Amos 5:15 [b]1 Kin 22:8; Is 59:15; Jer 17:16-18
11 [1]Another reading is *trample upon* [a]Amos 3:15; 6:11
11 [b]Mic 6:15
12 [1]Lit *they turn* [2]I.e. the place where court was held [a]Is 1:23; 5:23; Amos 2:6
13 [1]Lit *that time* [a]Eccl 3:7; Hos 4:4
14 [a]Mic 3:11
15 [1]I.e. the place where court was held [a]Ps 97:10; Rom 12:9 [b]Joel 2:14 [c]Mic 5:3, 7, 8
16 [1]Lit *those who know lamentation* [a]Jer 9:10, 18-20; Amos 8:3 [b]Joel 1:11 [c]2 Chr 35:25; Jer 9:17
17 [a]Is 16:10; Jer 48:33

5:5 *Bethel . . . Gilgal.* See note on 4:4. *Beersheba.* Located in the south of Judah, it also had evidently become a place of pilgrimage and idolatry (cf. 8:14). All shrines where the worship of God was abused would be destroyed.
5:6 The places of idolatry were doomed; yet if Israel turned to God, there was hope for her as a nation. Otherwise the people, too, would be destroyed. *house of Joseph.* The northern kingdom of Israel, dominated by the tribe of Ephraim, descendants of Joseph (also in v. 15; 6:6). *Bethel.* The main religious center of the northern kingdom (see 7:13; see also 3:14; 4:4; 7:10). The god the Israelites worshiped there would be powerless to save the place when the true God brought His judgment.
5:7 *those who turn justice into wormwood.* They corrupted the procedures and institutions of justice (the courts), making them instruments of injustice ("wormwood" was a synonym for bitterness = injustice; see Prov 5:4; Lam 3:19). Turning God's order upside down is inevitable in a society that ignores His law and despises true religion (see 6:12).
5:8–9 As in 4:13, a brief hymn is inserted (see 9:5–6). Here Amos highlights the contrast between "those who turn" good into bad (v. 7) and the One "who . . . changes" night into day and governs the order of the universe—and whose power can smash the walls His people hide behind.
5:8 *Pleiades.* A group of seven stars (part of the constellation Taurus); always mentioned in connection with Orion (see note on Job 9:9). *darkness into morning . . . day into night.* The orderly sequence of day and night (cf. Jer 31:35). *waters of the sea.* The waters above the expanse (see 9:6; Gen 1:7; see also notes on Ps 36:8; 42:7; 104:3,13); alternatively, waters evaporated from the sea and condensed as rain.
5:10 Continues the sentence begun in v. 7. This poetic paragraph is continued and completed in vv. 12b–13, which (in the Hebrew) use the third person, while the preceding passage (vv. 11–12a) uses the second person. The indictment of vv. 7,10,12b–13 is therefore more objective and descriptive, while that of vv. 11–12a is more direct and pointed. *reproves . . . speaks with integrity.* Those who are concerned that the courts uphold justice.
5:11 *Though you have built.* God would take away their prized possessions acquired through wrongful gain. Their prosperity would be turned to grief (cf. Deut 28:30,38–40).
5:13 *prudent person.* He knows he cannot change the state of affairs, and therefore only awaits judgment.
5:14 *Seek good.* Cf. "Seek Me" (v. 4); see Is 1:16–17 and note on Is 1:17. *that you may live.* The purpose is more definitely expressed than in vv. 4,6, and the way to change is explicit. *with you.* As your security and source of blessing.
5:15 *Perhaps.* Emphasizes the danger of presuming on God's grace. Even a widespread change of attitude would need the test of time to prove its genuineness. *remnant.* Implies that a change now would benefit the individual survivors of the disaster, though the nation as a whole would perish.
5:16–17 A return to the theme of lament with which this section began (vv. 1–2). *plazas . . . streets . . . farmer . . . vineyards.* All will be affected by God's punishment. Even farmers, usually too busy for such things, would join the professional mourners

Because I will pass through the midst
of you," says the LORD.

18 Alas, you who are longing for the [a]day
of the LORD,
For what purpose *will* the day of the
LORD *be* to you?
It *will be* [b]darkness and not light;
19 As when a man [a]flees from a lion
And a bear meets him,
[1]Or goes home, leans his hand against
the wall
And a snake bites him.
20 *Will* not the day of the LORD *be*
[a]darkness instead of light,
Even gloom with no brightness in it?

21 "I hate, I [a]reject your festivals,
Nor do I [1b]delight in your solemn
assemblies.
22 "Even though you [a]offer up to Me
burnt offerings and your grain
offerings,
I will not accept *them;*
And I will not *even* look at the [b]peace
offerings of your fatlings.
23 "Take away from Me the noise of your
songs;
I will not even listen to the sound of
your harps.
24 "But let [a]justice roll down like waters
And righteousness like an ever-
flowing stream.
25 "[1a]Did you present Me with sacrifices
and grain offerings in the wilderness for forty
years, O house of Israel?

18 [a]Is 5:19; Jer 30:7; Joel 1:15; 2:1, 11, 31 [b]Is 5:30; Joel 2:2
19 [1]Or *Then* [a]Job 20:24; Is 24:17, 18; Jer 15:2, 3; 48:44
20 [a]Is 13:10; Zeph 1:15
21 [1]Lit *like to smell* [a]Is 1:11-16; 66:3; Amos 4:4, 5; 8:10 [b]Lev 26:31; Jer 14:12; Hos 5:6
22 [a]Is 66:3; Mic 6:6, 7 [b]Lev 7:11-15; Amos 4:5
24 [a]Jer 22:3; Ezek 45:9; Mic 6:8
25 [1]Or *You presented Me with the sacrifices and a grain offering* [a]Deut 32:17; Josh 24:14; Neh 9:18-21; Acts 7:42, 43
26 [1]Or *Sakkuth (Saturn)* or *shrine of your Moloch* [2]Or *Kaiwan (Saturn)* or *stands of* [3]Or *your star gods* [a]Acts 7:43
6:1 [a]Is 32:9-11; Zeph 1:12; Luke 6:24 [b]Ex 19:5; Amos 3:2
2 [1]Or *you* [a]Gen 10:10; Is 10:9 [b]1 Kin 8:65; 2 Kin 18:34; Is 10:9 [c]1 Sam 5:8; 2 Chr 26:6

26 "[a]You also carried along [1]Sikkuth your
king and [2]Kiyyun, your images, [3]the star of
your gods which you made for yourselves.
27 "Therefore, I will make you go into exile
beyond Damascus," says the LORD, whose
name is the God of hosts.

"Those at Ease in Zion"

6 [a]Woe to those who are at ease in Zion
And to those who *feel* secure in the
mountain of Samaria,
The [b]distinguished men of the
foremost of nations,
To whom the house of Israel comes.
2 Go over to [a]Calneh and look,
And go from there to [b]Hamath the
great,
Then go down to [c]Gath of the
Philistines.
Are [1]they better than these kingdoms,
Or is their territory greater than yours?
3 Do you [a]put off the day of calamity,
And would you [b]bring near the seat of
violence?

4 Those who recline on beds of ivory
And sprawl on their [a]couches,
And [b]eat lambs from the flock
And calves from the midst of the stall,
5 Who improvise to the sound of the
harp,
And like David have [1]composed
[a]songs for themselves,

3 [a]Is 56:12; Amos 9:10 [b]Amos 3:10 4 [a]Amos 3:12 [b]Ezek 34:2, 3 5 [1]Or *invented musical instruments* [a]1 Chr 15:16; 23:5; Is 5:12

in lament, and mourning would overflow from the cities to the vineyards. When the holy God "will go through" (as He did in Egypt, Ex 12:12), punishment for the unholy and unjust will be inescapable (cf. Is 6:5).

5:18 *day of the LORD.* The time when God will show Himself the victor over the world, vindicating His claims to be the Lord over all the earth (see notes on 8:9; Is 2:11,17,20). Israel expected to be exalted as His people and longed for that day to come. Amos warned that the day would come, but not as Israel expected—it would be a day of "darkness instead of light" (v. 20) for her, because she had not been faithful to God. (Cf. "the day of our Lord Jesus Christ" and variations in 1 Cor 1:8; 3:12–15; 5:5; 2 Cor 1:14; Phil 1:6,10; 2:16.) Amos speaks primarily of an imminent and decisive judgment on Israel, not exclusively of the last day.

5:19–20 The two pictures (v. 19) emphasize vividly the inescapability of God's coming judgment.

5:21–27 Again God directly addresses Israel with the charge of unfaithfulness.

5:21–23 These three verses summarize and reject the current practice of religion in Israel. The institutions were not wrong in themselves; it was the worshipers and the ways they worshiped that were wrong. The people had no basis on which to come to God, because their conduct reflected disobedience to His law (see Is 1:11–15 and note).

5:21 *Nor do I delight in.* Lit. "I do not inhale with delight."

5:24 *justice . . . righteousness.* Prerequisites for acceptance by God; but these are what Israel had rejected and scorned (cf. vv. 7,10,12b). *waters . . . ever-flowing stream.* In contrast to stream beds that are dry much of the year. The simile is especially apt: As plant and animal life flourishes where there is water, so human life flourishes where there is justice and righteousness.

5:25 Israel's right relationship with the Lord was never established primarily by sacrifices. It was above all based on obedience (see 1 Sam 15:22–23; cf. Rom 1:5). *in the wilderness for forty years.* See Num 14:32–35.

5:26 The obscure language of this verse speaks of Israelite idolatry, but whether it was in the wilderness long ago or more recently in the promised land, or both, is not clear. The proper names are derived from Akkadian and refer to idolatrous objects of worship. The Septuagint (the Greek translation of the OT) represents a somewhat different text, which is followed by Acts 7:42–43.

5:27 This punishment is the final one—exile from the God-given land to remote foreign places.

6:1 *in Zion . . . in the mountain of Samaria.* Although Amos spoke primarily to Israel, Judah (Zion) also deserved his rebuke (cf. 2:4–5), for Israel properly comprised all 12 tribes. *foremost of nations.* In Israel's self-complacent eyes in this time of her newly recovered power and prosperity.

6:2 Perhaps Calneh and Hamath had fallen in Jeroboam II's campaign (2 Kin 14:28), and the wall of Gath had been broken down by Uzziah (2 Chr 26:6). These words may have been spoken by the "house of Israel" (v. 1, i.e., people of Israel) who, when they came before their notables, flattered their vanity and thus reinforced their arrogant complacency.

6:4 *ivory.* See 3:15 and note.

6:5 *like David.* See 1 Sam 16:15–23; 2 Sam 23:1.

6 Who [a]drink wine from [1]sacrificial
bowls
While they anoint themselves with the
finest of oils,
Yet they have not [b]grieved over the
ruin of Joseph.
7 Therefore, they will now [a]go into exile
at the head of the exiles,
And the [b]sprawlers' [1]banqueting will
[2]pass away.

8 The Lord [1]GOD has [a]sworn by Himself,
the LORD God of hosts has declared:
"I [b]loathe the arrogance of Jacob,
And [2]detest his [c]citadels;
Therefore I will [d]deliver up *the* city
and [3]all it contains."
9 And it will be, if [a]ten men are left in
one house, they will die.
10 Then one's [1]uncle, or his [2a]undertaker,
will lift him up to carry out *his* bones from
the house, and he will say to the one who is
in the innermost part of the house, "Is anyone else with you?" And that one will say,
"No one." Then he will [3]answer, "[b]Keep quiet. For [4]the name of the LORD is [c]not to be
mentioned."
11 For behold, the LORD is going to [a]com-
mand that the [b]great house be smashed to
pieces and the small house to fragments.
12 Do horses run on rocks?
Or does one plow [1]them with oxen?
Yet you have turned [a]justice into
poison
And the fruit of righteousness into
[2]wormwood,
13 You who rejoice in [1a]Lodebar,
[2]And say, "Have we not [b]by our *own*
strength taken [3]Karnaim for
ourselves?"

6 [1]Lit *sprinkling basins* [a]Amos 2:8; 4:1 [b]Ezek 9:4
7 [1]Or *cultic feasts* [2]Lit *turn aside* [a]Amos 7:11, 17 [b]1 Kin 20:16-21; Dan 5:4-6, 30
8 [1]Heb *YHWH*, usually rendered LORD [2]Lit *hate* [3]Lit *its fullness* [a]Gen 22:16; Jer 22:5; 51:14; Amos 4:2; 8:7 [b]Lev 26:30; Deut 32:19; Ps 106:40; Amos 5:21 [c]Amos 3:10, 11 [d]Hos 11:6
9 [a]Amos 5:3
10 [1]Or *beloved one* [2]Lit *one who burns him* [3]Lit *say* [4]Lit *not to make mention of the name of* [a]1 Sam 31:12 [b]Amos 5:13; 8:3 [c]Jer 44:26; Ezek 20:39
11 [a]Is 55:11 [b]2 Kin 25:9; Amos 3:15; 5:11
12 [1]Another reading is *the sea with oxen* [2]I.e. bitterness [a]1 Kin 21:7-13; Is 59:13, 14; Hos 10:4; Amos 5:7, 11, 12
13 [1]Lit *a thing of nothing* [2]Lit *Who* [3]Lit *a pair of horns* [a]Job 8:14, 15; Ps 2:2-4; Luke 12:19, 20 [b]Ps 75:4, 5; Is 28:14, 15
14 [a]Jer 5:15 [b]Num 34:7, 8; 1 Kin 8:65; 2 Kin 14:25

14 "For behold, [a]I am going to raise up a
nation against you,
O house of Israel," declares the LORD
God of hosts,
"And they will afflict you from the
[b]entrance of Hamath
To the [b]brook of the Arabah."

Warning Through Visions

7 Thus the Lord [1]GOD showed me, and
behold, He was forming a [a]locust-swarm
[2]when the spring crop began to sprout. And
behold, the spring crop *was* after the king's
[3]mowing.
2 And it came about, [1]when it had [a]fin-
ished eating the vegetation of the land, that I
said,
"[b]Lord GOD, please pardon!
[2]How can Jacob stand,
For he is [c]small?"
3 The LORD [1a]changed His mind about
this.
"It shall not be," said the LORD.
4 Thus the Lord GOD showed me, and
behold, the Lord GOD was calling to contend
with them by [a]fire, and it consumed the great
deep and began to consume the [1]farm land.
5 Then I said,
"[a]Lord GOD, please stop!
[b]How can Jacob stand, for he is
small?"
6 The LORD [1a]changed His mind about
this.
"This too shall not be," said the Lord
GOD.

7:1 [1]Heb *YHWH*, usually rendered *LORD*, and so throughout the ch [2]Lit *at the beginning of the coming up of* [3]Or *shearings* [a]Joel 1:4; Amos 4:9; Nah 3:15 **2** [1]Lit *if* [2]Lit *As who* [a]Ex 10:15 [b]Jer 14:7, 20, 21; Ezek 9:8; 11:13 [c]Is 37:4; Jer 42:2 **3** [1]Or *relented* [a]Deut 32:36; Jer 26:19; Hos 11:8; Amos 5:15; Jon 3:10 **4** [1]Lit *portion* [a]Deut 32:22; Is 66:15, 16; Amos 2:5 **5** [a]Ps 85:4; Joel 2:17 [b]Amos 7:2 **6** [1]Or *relented* [a]Ps 106:45; Amos 7:3; Jon 3:10

6:6 *Joseph.* See note on 5:6.
6:8 *sworn by Himself.* See note on Gen 22:16; cf. Heb 6:13–14. By this oath God declares that the verdict is final.
6:10–11 A fearful scene: Apparently a survivor is cowering inside the house, the relative forbidding him even to pray because God's wrath had fallen on the city.
6:10 *undertaker.* Lit. "one who burns him" (see NASB marg.). Reference may be to burning a memorial fire in honor of the dead (see Jer 34:5). Cremation was not generally practiced, being reserved primarily for serious offenders (see Lev 20:14; 21:9; Josh 7:15,25; cf. 1 Sam 31:11–13).
6:11 *great house . . . small house.* Cf. perhaps the "summer house" and "winter house" of 3:15.
6:12 *plow them with oxen.* The Hebrew for this phrase is sometimes translated (with a slight textual change) "plow the sea with oxen" (see NASB marg.). Israel's perversion of justice flies in the face of even common human wisdom about the right order of things.
6:13 *Lodebar . . . Karnaim.* See NASB marg. for Amos's ironic play on the meanings of these place names ("horn" signifies strength). They seem to have been regained from Hazael by Jehoash (2 Kin 10:32–33; 13:25), then taken by the Assyrians ("a nation," v. 14) soon after Amos's day (2 Kin 15:29)—beginning the sequence of events that would lead to the loss of all territory conquered by Jeroboam II.
6:14 *the entrance of Hamath To the brook of the Arabah.* From the Orontes River in north Lebanon to the Dead Sea—thus the whole land (cf. 2 Kin 14:25).
7:1 *showed me.* Introduces reports of visions that convey God's message through things seen as well as heard (see vv. 4,7; 8:1; cf. 9:1). *locust-swarm.* Cf. 4:9; Joel 1:4. *spring crop.* The growth that came up in the fields after the grains and early hay were harvested. On these the flocks and herds pastured until the summer drought stopped all growth (cf. 1 Kin 18:5). *king's mowing.* Apparently the earlier crop, from which the royal taxes were taken.
7:2 See v. 5. *How . . . stand?* Mass starvation would afflict all the people. *Jacob.* Israel. *small.* Powerless to withstand the calamity. Amos makes no appeal to the Lord's covenant with Israel—perhaps because Israel's unfaithfulness had removed all right to such an appeal.
7:3 See v. 6. *The LORD changed His mind.* In response to the prophetic intercession (cf. Gen 20:7)—but forgiveness is not offered.
7:4 *great deep.* Probably the Mediterranean Sea. *land.* Lit. "portion," probably referring to the promised land or, more precisely, to everything growing on the land (cf. Joel 1:19).
7:5 See note on v. 2.
7:6 See note on v. 3.

7 Thus He showed me, and behold, the
Lord was standing [1]by a [2]vertical wall with a
plumb line in His hand.
8 The LORD said to me, "[a]What do you
see, Amos?" And I said, "A plumb line."
Then the Lord said,
"Behold I am about to put a [b]plumb
line
In the midst of My people Israel.
I will [1c]spare them no longer.
9 "The [a]high places of Isaac will be
desolated
And the [b]sanctuaries of Israel laid
waste.
Then I will [c]rise up against the house
of Jeroboam with the sword."

Amos Accused, Answers

10 Then Amaziah, the [a]priest of Bethel,
sent *word* to [b]Jeroboam king of Israel, saying, "Amos has [c]conspired against you in the
midst of the house of Israel; the land is
unable to endure all his words.
11 "For thus Amos says, 'Jeroboam will die
by the sword and Israel will certainly go
from its land into exile.'"
12 Then Amaziah said to Amos, "[a]Go, you
seer, flee away to the land of Judah and there
eat bread and there do your prophesying!
13 "But [a]no longer prophesy at Bethel, for
it is a [b]sanctuary of the king and a royal [1]res-
idence."
14 Then Amos replied to Amaziah, "I am
not a prophet, nor am I the [a]son of a prophet; for I am a herdsman and a [1]grower of sycamore figs.
15 "But the LORD took me from [1]following
the flock and the LORD said to me, 'Go
[a]prophesy to My people Israel.'
16 "Now hear the word of the LORD: you
are saying, 'You [a]shall not prophesy against
Israel [b]nor shall you [1]speak against the
house of Isaac.'
17 "Therefore, thus says the LORD, 'Your
[a]wife will become a harlot in the city, your
[b]sons and your daughters will fall by the
sword, your land will be parceled up by a
measuring line and you yourself will die
[1]upon [c]unclean soil. Moreover, Israel will
certainly go from its land into exile.'"

Basket of Fruit and Israel's Captivity

8 Thus the Lord [1]GOD showed me, and
behold, *there was* a basket of summer
fruit.
2 He said, "What do you see, Amos?" And
[a]I said, "A basket of summer fruit." Then the
LORD said to me, "The [b]end has come for My
people Israel. I will [1c]spare them no longer.
3 "[1]The [a]songs of the palace will turn to
[b]wailing in that day," declares the Lord GOD.
"Many *will be* the [c]corpses; in every place
[2]they will cast them forth [3]in silence."
4 Hear this, you who [1a]trample the
needy, to do away with the humble of the
land,
5 saying,
"When will the [a]new moon [1]be over,

7 [1]Or *upon* [2]Lit *wall of a plumb line* **8** [1]Lit *pass him by* [a]Jer 1:11; Amos 8:2 [b]2 Kin 21:13; Is 28:17; 34:11; Lam 2:8 [c]Jer 15:6; Ezek 7:4-9; Amos 8:2 **9** [a]Gen 46:1; Hos 10:8; Mic 1:5 [b]Lev 26:31; Is 63:18; Jer 51:51; Amos 7:13 [c]2 Kin 15:8-10; Amos 7:11 **10** [a]1 Kin 12:31, 32; 13:33 [b]2 Kin 14:23, 24 [c]Jer 26:8-11; 38:4 **12** [a]Matt 8:34 **13** [1]Lit *house* [a]Amos 2:12; Acts 4:18 [b]1 Kin 12:29, 32; Amos 7:9 **14** [1]Or *nipper* [a]1 Kin 20:35; 2 Kin 2:3, 5; 4:38; 2 Chr 19:2 **15** [1]Lit *behind* [a]Jer 1:7; Ezek 2:3, 4 **16** [1]Lit *flow* [a]Amos 2:12; 7:13 [b]Deut 32:2; Ezek 20:46; 21:2 **17** [1]Or *in an unclean land* [a]Hos 4:13, 14 [b]Jer 14:16 [c]2 Kin 17:6; Ezek 4:13; Hos 9:3 **8:1** [1]Heb *YHWH*, usually rendered *LORD*, and so throughout the ch **2** [1]Lit *pass him by* [a]Jer 24:3 [b]Ezek 7:2, 3, 6 [c]Amos 7:8 **3** [1]Or *They will howl the palace songs* [2]Lit *he has thrown* [3]Or *hush!* [a]Amos 5:23; 6:4, 5; 8:10 [b]Amos 5:16 [c]Amos 6:8-10 **4** [1]Or *snap at* [a]Ps 14:4; Prov 30:14; Amos 2:7; 5:11, 12 **5** [1]Lit *pass by* [a]Num 28:11; 2 Kin 4:23

7:7 Israel is compared to a wall built true to plumb—what she should have been, after all the Lord had done for her.
7:8–9 In vv. 1–6 God proposed wholesale punishments amounting to total destruction, but relented at Amos's prayer—though without promise of forgiveness. Now the Lord is no longer open to such intercession (cf. Jer 7:16; 11:14; 14:11; 15:1).
7:8 *plumb line.* God's people had been built according to God's standards (v. 7). They were expected to be true to those standards, but were completely out of plumb when tested (cf. 2 Kin 21:13). *My people.* Here, for the first time in the book of Amos, the Lord calls Israel "My people" (see v. 15; 8:2; 9:10,14). *spare them no longer.* See 8:2.
7:9 *high places . . . sanctuaries . . . house.* The centers of religious and political pretension and of self-righteous pride would be wiped out. *Isaac.* Israel's (Jacob's) father, a way of referring to Israel found only in Amos (see v. 16). *Jeroboam.* The oracles of chs. 1–6 were spoken to the leading people of Israel and Samaria as a whole; here Amos names one man, the king.
7:11 Amaziah's words summarize Amos's message (see note on v. 17). *Jeroboam.* That is, his "house" (v. 9), the king's name also representing his dynasty. *will die.* Jeroboam died naturally (2 Kin 14:29), but his son and successor Zechariah (2 Kin 15:8) was assassinated (2 Kin 15:10).
7:12 *seer.* Amaziah dismissed Amos as a prophet for hire whom he need not take seriously.
7:13 *sanctuary of the king.* Amaziah served the king in Samaria, not Israel's heavenly King; hence he would not allow a prophetic word to be spoken against Jeroboam or his realm at the royal chapel.
7:14 *not a prophet, nor . . . the son of a prophet.* Amos denied any previous connection with the prophets or their disciples (see note on 1 Kin 20:35). No one had hired him to come and announce judgment on Jeroboam and Israel. *herdsman.* See note on 1:1, but the Hebrew uses a different word here—one not found elsewhere in the OT. The Hebrew for this word is, however, related to a word for "cattle," suggesting that Amos may also have tended cattle. *sycamore figs.* A large tree, yielding fig-like fruit as well as useful timber. To ensure good fruit, the gardener had to slit the top of each fig—which may be the procedure referred to by the obscure Hebrew word here rendered "took care of."
7:15 *following.* See 2 Sam 7:8. The Hebrew stresses the location of the shepherd rather than his activity. *Go.* Amos was in Bethel because God had sent him to prophesy there.
7:16 *You shall not prophesy.* Cf. 2:12.
7:17 Amos turned to condemn the priest personally. *harlot.* With the exile of Amaziah, the death of his children and the loss of the family estate, Amaziah's wife would be reduced to prostitution to survive. *your land.* Amaziah's private estate would be divided up and given to others. *unclean soil.* Where his ceremonial purity as a priest would be defiled. *Moreover, Israel . . . its land.* Amos repeats—verbatim in the Hebrew—the last two lines of Amaziah's earlier summary of Amos's message (v. 11).
8:1 *showed me.* See note on 7:1.
8:2 *summer fruit . . . The end has come.* A wordplay in Hebrew; Israel was ready to be plucked.
8:3 *that day.* See note on 5:18. *wailing . . . silence.* There would be no thanksgiving songs for this harvest (contrast Lev 23:39–41)—only the silence of despair.

So that we may sell grain,
And the [b]sabbath, that we may open
the wheat *market,*
To make the [2]bushel smaller and the
shekel bigger,
And to [c]cheat with [3]dishonest scales,
6 So as to [a]buy the helpless for [1]money
And the needy for a pair of sandals,
And *that* we may sell the refuse of the
wheat?"

7 The LORD has [a]sworn by the [b]pride of
Jacob,
"Indeed, I will [c]never forget any of
their deeds.
8 "Because of this will not the land
[a]quake
And everyone who dwells in it
[b]mourn?
Indeed, all of it will [c]rise up like the
Nile,
And it will be tossed about
And subside like the Nile of Egypt.
9 "It will come about in that day,"
declares the Lord GOD,
"That I will make the [a]sun go down at
noon
And [b]make the earth dark in [1]broad
daylight.
10 "Then I will [a]turn your festivals into
mourning
And all your songs into [1]lamentation;
And I will bring [b]sackcloth on
everyone's loins
And baldness on every head.
And I will make it [c]like *a time of*
mourning for an only son,
And the end of it will be like a bitter
day.

11 "Behold, days are coming," declares
the Lord GOD,
"When I will send a famine on the land,
Not a famine for bread or a thirst for
water,
But rather [a]for hearing the words of
the LORD.
12 "People will stagger from sea to sea
And from the north even to the east;
They will go to and fro to [a]seek the
word of the LORD,
But they will not find *it.*
13 "In that day the beautiful [a]virgins
And the young men will [b]faint from
thirst.
14 "*As for* those who swear by the [1a]guilt
of Samaria,
Who say, 'As your god lives, O [b]Dan,'
And, 'As the way of [c]Beersheba lives,'
They will fall and [d]not rise again."

God's Judgment Unavoidable

9 I saw the Lord standing beside the [a]altar,
and He said,
"Smite the capitals so that the
[b]thresholds will shake,
And [c]break them on the heads of
them all!
Then I will [d]slay the rest of them with
the sword;
They will [e]not have a fugitive who
will flee,
Or a refugee who will escape.
2 "Though they dig into [a]Sheol,
From there will My hand take them;
And though they [b]ascend to heaven,
From there will I bring them down.
3 "Though they hide on the summit of
Carmel,

5 [2]Lit *ephah* [3]Lit *balances of deception* [b]Ex 31:13-17; Neh 13:15 [c]Hos 12:7; Mic 6:11
6 [1]Lit *silver* [a]Amos 2:6
7 [a]Amos 4:2 [b]Deut 33:26, 29; Ps 68:34; Amos 6:8 [c]Ps 10:11; Hos 7:2; 8:13
8 [a]Ps 18:7; 60:2; Is 5:25 [b]Hos 4:3 [c]Jer 46:7, 8; Amos 9:5
9 [1]Lit *a day of light* [a]Job 5:14; Is 13:10; Jer 15:9; Mic 3:6 [b]Is 59:9, 10; Amos 4:13; 5:8
10 [1]Or *a dirge* [a]Job 20:23; Amos 5:21 [b]Is 15:2, 3; Jer 48:37; Ezek 7:18; 27:31 [c]Jer 6:26; Zech 12:10
11 [a]1 Sam 3:1; 2 Chr 15:3; Ps 74:9; Ezek 7:26; Mic 3:6
12 [a]Ezek 20:3, 31
13 [a]Lam 1:18; 2:21 [b]Is 41:17; Hos 2:3
14 [1]Or *Ashimah* [a]Hos 8:5 [b]1 Kin 12:28, 29 [c]Amos 5:5 [d]Amos 5:2
9:1 [a]Amos 3:14 [b]Zeph 2:14 [c]Ps 68:21; Hab 3:13 [d]Amos 7:17 [e]Jer 11:11
2 [a]Ps 139:8 [b]Jer 51:53; Obad 4

8:5 *new moon . . . sabbath.* The official religious festivals, when commerce ceased (cf. Num 28:9–15; 2 Kin 4:23). *bushel smaller . . . shekel bigger . . . dishonest scales.* See Lev 19:35–36; Deut 25:13–16; Prov 11:1; 16:11; 20:10,23.
8:6 See note on 2:6.
8:7 *sworn by the pride of Jacob.* Israel took pride in the fact that the Lord was her God.
8:8 *rise up like the Nile.* Because of the heavy seasonal rains in Ethiopia, the Nile in Egypt annually rose by as much as 25 feet, flooding the whole valley except for the towns and villages standing above it. Its waters carried a large amount of rich soil, which was deposited on the land—perhaps referred to by the words "stirred up."
8:9 *that day.* See note on 5:18. *earth dark.* As elsewhere, the "day of the LORD" is described as one in which the cosmic (world) order is disrupted and light is turned to darkness (see Is 13:10; 24:23; 34:4; 50:3; Ezek 32:7–8; Joel 2:10,31; Mic 3:6), as if creation is being undone (see Jer 4:23).
8:10 *mourning.* Illustrated by King David (2 Sam 18:33). *bring sackcloth . . . baldness on every head.* Signs of mourning (see Gen 37:34; Jer 47:5). *only son.* On whose life the future of the family depended (cf. 2 Sam 18:18). *bitter day.* The opposite of a "holiday" (Esth 9:22).
8:11 *days.* When God's judgment begins to take effect. *famine . . . for hearing the words of the LORD.* In times of great distress Israel turned to the Lord for a prophetic word of hope or guidance (see, e.g., 2 Kin 19:1–4,14; 22:13–14; Jer 21:2; Ezek 14:3,7), but in the coming judgment the Lord will answer all such appeals with silence—the awful silence of God (see 1 Sam 28:6; Ezek 7:26; 20:1–3; Mic 3:4,7).
8:12 *sea to sea . . . north . . . east.* Throughout the land of Israel, even to the Transjordan.
8:13 *thirst.* Both physical and spiritual. Their strength sapped, even the lovely girls and strong boys of the nation would faint and fall useless.
8:14 *those who swear.* By the gods of their various religious centers (see NASB marg.)—the false gods in which they trusted rather than in the Lord.
9:1 *I saw the Lord.* See note on 7:1. God is now poised on earth. *beside the altar.* God is about to initiate the destruction from the very place from which the people expect to hear a word of peace and blessing. *capitals.* God will shatter the temple completely, from the decorated capitals down to the heavy stone thresholds. The next lines depict the destruction. Whether the vision shows the Lord at Jerusalem or at Bethel is unclear, but we know of no temple structure at Bethel.
9:2–4 These verses emphasize the impossibility of escape from God's impending judgment. The imaginary extremes to which a person might go may be compared with those in Ps 139:7–12. God's domain includes every place, even the realm of the grave (v. 2).
9:3 *summit of Carmel.* See note on 1:2. *serpent.* In pagan

I will [a]search them out and take them
from there;
And though they [b]conceal themselves
from My sight on the floor of the
sea,
From there I will command the
[c]serpent and it will bite them.
4 "And though they go into [a]captivity
before their enemies,
From there I will command the sword
that it slay them,
And I will [b]set My eyes against them
for evil and not for good."

5 The Lord [1]GOD of hosts,
The One who [a]touches the land so
that it melts,
And [b]all those who dwell in it mourn,
And all of it rises up like the Nile
And subsides like the Nile of Egypt;
6 The One who builds His [1a]upper
chambers in the heavens
And has founded His vaulted dome
over the earth,
He who [b]calls for the waters of the sea
And [c]pours them out on the face of
the earth,
[d]The LORD is His name.

7 "Are you not as the sons of [a]Ethiopia to
Me,
O sons of Israel?" declares the LORD.
"Have I not brought up Israel from the
land of Egypt,
And the [b]Philistines from Caphtor and
the [c]Arameans from [d]Kir?
8 "Behold, the [a]eyes of the Lord GOD are
on the sinful kingdom,
And I will [b]destroy it from the face of
the earth;
Nevertheless, I will [c]not totally destroy
the house of Jacob,"
Declares the LORD.
9 "For behold, I am commanding,
And I will [a]shake the house of Israel
among all nations
As *grain* is shaken in a sieve,
But not a [1]kernel will fall to the
ground.
10 "All the [a]sinners of My people will die
by the sword,
Those who say, '[b]The calamity will
not overtake or confront us.'

3 [a]Jer 16:16 [b]Job 34:22; Ps 139:9, 10 [c]Is 27:1
4 [a]Lev 26:33 [b]Lev 17:10; Jer 21:10; 39:16; 44:11
5 [1]Heb *YHWH,* usually rendered LORD, and so throughout the ch [a]Ps 104:32; 144:5; Is 64:1; Mic 1:4 [b]Amos 8:8
6 [1]Or *stairs* [a]Ps 104:3, 13 [b]Amos 5:8 [c]Ps 104:6 [d]Amos 4:13
7 [a]2 Chr 14:9, 12; Is 20:4; 43:3 [b]Deut 2:23; Jer 47:4 [c]Amos 1:5 [d]2 Kin 16:9; Is 22:6
8 [a]Jer 44:27; Amos 9:4
8 [b]Amos 7:17; 9:10 [c]Jer 5:10; 30:11; 31:35, 36; Joel 2:32; Amos 3:12; Obad 17
9 [1]Or *pebble* [a]Is 30:28; Luke 22:31
10 [a]Is 33:14; Zech 13:8 [b]Amos 6:3
11 [1]Or *shelter* or *tabernacle* [a]Acts 15:16-18 [b]Is 16:5 [c]Ps 80:12 [d]Is 63:11; Jer 46:26
12 [1]Or *Gentiles* [a]Obad 19 [b]Num 24:18; Is 11:14 [c]Is 43:7
13 [a]Lev 26:5 [b]Joel 3:18 [c]Gen 49:11

The Restoration of Israel

11 "In that day I will [a]raise up the fallen
[1b]booth of David,
And wall up its [c]breaches;
I will also raise up its ruins
And rebuild it as in the [d]days of
old;
12 [a]That they may possess the remnant
of [b]Edom
And all the [1]nations who are [c]called
by My name,"
Declares the LORD who does this.

13 "Behold, days are coming," declares
the LORD,
"When the [a]plowman will overtake the
reaper
And the treader of grapes him who
sows seed;
When the [b]mountains will drip sweet
[c]wine
And all the hills will be dissolved.

mythology, the fierce monster of the sea. If someone should seek to escape by hiding in the depths, he could still not evade God, for even there all are subject to Him.

9:4 *go . . . before their enemies . . . I will command.* Even those dispersed among the nations will not escape God's judgment. *I will set My eyes . . . for evil.* Contrast Ps 33:18; 34:15.

9:5 *The Lord . . . who.* Introduces a hymnic reminder that Israel's God is the Creator and Sustainer of the universe, thus underlining the pronouncements of the previous verses (cf. 4:13; 5:8–9). *land . . . melts.* See note on Ps 46:6. *like the Nile.* See 8:8 and note.

9:6 *His upper chambers.* Contrasts the scale of God with the scale of man, whose structures fall at the movement of the earth (v. 5). See Ps 104:3 and note. *sea.* See 5:8 and note.

9:7 *sons of Ethiopia.* A dark-skinned people who lived south of Egypt, probably in the upper Nile region. *Have I not brought up Israel . . . ?* See note on Ex 20:2. Israel could not rely on God's past blessings as an assurance of His future benevolence. Her stubborn rebelliousness robbed the exodus of all special meaning for her; her journey from Egypt is reduced to no more significance than the movements of other peoples. *Philistines from Caphtor.* See note on Jer 47:4. *Kir.* See note on 1:5.

9:8 *sinful kingdom.* Israel, the chosen, whose disobedience was far worse than the sins of other nations (cf. 1:3–2:16; 3:1–2).

9:9 *sieve.* Separates the wheat from small stones and other refuse gathered with it when scooped up from the ground.

9:10 *All the sinners . . . will die.* For their persistent rebellion.

9:11 The verse is also regarded as Messianic in the Jewish Talmud. *I will raise up.* Raises a hope underlying Amos's words—one that runs through the whole OT from Gen 3:15 on: God will bring blessing after judgment and will not ultimately reject Israel. *booth.* Lit. "hut" (or rough booth)—either the dynasty ("house") of David or the united kingdom of the 12 tribes (David's kingdom). The word "hut" may have been chosen to recall David's humble beginnings. *as in the days of old.* In the days of David and Solomon.

9:12 *remnant of Edom.* Whatever is left of Israel's bitter enemy (see note on 1:11) after her punishment. *all the nations who are called by My name.* Refers to the extent of the rule of the Lord's anointed future King, recalling that David had reigned over many nations surrounding Israel. It represents the fulfillment of the Abrahamic and Davidic covenants. The Messiah will reign even over former enemies, of whom Edom is symbolic (see note on Is 34:5). *who does this.* God does what He says.

9:13–15 After all the forecasts of destruction, dearth and death (cf. 5:9,11,27), Amos's final words picture a glorious Edenic prosperity, when the seasons will run together so that sowing and reaping are without interval, and there will be a continuous supply of fresh produce (a reversal of the conditions portrayed in 4:6–11).

9:13 Note the similarity to Joel 3:18.

14 "Also I will [a]restore the [1]captivity of
My people Israel,
And they will [b]rebuild the ruined
cities and live *in them;*
They will also [c]plant vineyards and
drink their wine,
And make gardens and eat their fruit.
15 "I will also plant them on their land,
And [a]they will not again be rooted out
from their land
Which I have given them,"
Says the LORD your God.

14 [1]Or *fortunes* [a]Ps 53:6; Is 60:4; Jer 30:3, 18 [b]Is 61:4; 65:21 [c]Jer 24:6; 31:28
15 [a]Is 60:21; Ezek 34:28; 37:25

9:14–15 *I will restore . . . they will rebuild . . . They will also plant . . . I will also plant.* In the promised land, God will make His people productive, fruitful and secure.
9:14 *My people.* See note on 7:8; contrast Hos 1:9, but cf. Hos 2:23. *rebuild the ruined cities.* See Is 58:12 and note.
9:15 *not again.* When Israel is finally and fully restored, she will never again be destroyed. *your God.* Contrast Hos 1:9, but cf. Hos 2:23.

Obadiah

INTRODUCTION

Author

The author's name is Obadiah, which means "servant (or worshiper) of the LORD." His was a common name (see 1 Kin 18:3 – 16; 1 Chr 3:21; 7:3; 8:38; 9:16; 12:9; 27:19; 2 Chr 17:7; 34:12; Ezra 8:9; Neh 10:5; 12:25). Neither his father's name nor the place of his birth is given.

Date and Place of Writing

The date and place of composition are disputed. Dating the prophecy is mainly a matter of relating vv. 11 – 14 to one of two specific events in Israel's history:

1. The invasion of Jerusalem by Philistines and Arabs during the reign of Jehoram (853 – 841 B.C.); see 2 Kin 8:20 – 22; 2 Chr 21:8 – 20. In this case, Obadiah would be a contemporary of Elisha.
2. The Babylonian attacks on Jerusalem (605 – 586). Obadiah would then be a contemporary of Jeremiah. This alternative seems more likely.

The parallels between Obad 1 – 9 and Jer 49:7 – 22 have caused many to suggest some kind of interdependence between Obadiah and Jeremiah, but it may be that both prophets were drawing on a common source not otherwise known to us.

Unity and Theme

There is no compelling reason to doubt the unity of this brief prophecy. Its theme is that Edom, proud over her own security, has gloated over Israel's devastation by foreign powers. However, Edom's participation in that disaster will bring on God's wrath. She herself will be destroyed, but Mount Zion and Israel will be delivered, and God's kingdom will triumph.

Edom's hostile activities have spanned the centuries of Israel's existence. The following Biblical references are helpful in understanding the relation of Israel and Edom: Gen 27:41 – 45; 32:1 – 21; 33; 36; Ex 15:15; Num 20:14 – 21; Deut 2:1 – 6; 23:7; 1 Sam 22 with Ps 52; 2 Sam 8:13 – 14; 2 Kin 8:20 – 22; 14:7; Ps 83; Ezek 35; Joel 3:18 – 19; Amos 1:11 – 12; 9:12.

Since the Edomites are related to the Israelites (v. 10), their hostility is all the more reprehensible. Edom is fully responsible for her failure to assist Israel and for her open aggression. The fact that God rejected Esau (Gen 25:23; Mal 1:3; Rom 9:13) in no way exonerates the Edomites. Edom, smug in its mountain strongholds, will be dislodged and sacked. Israel will prosper because God is with her.

Outline

- I. Title and Introduction (1)
- II. Judgment on Edom (2 – 14)
  - A. Edom's Destruction Announced (2 – 7)
    - 1. The humbling of her pride (2 – 4)
    - 2. The completeness of her destruction (5 – 7)
  - B. Edom's Destruction Reaffirmed (8 – 14)
    - 1. Her shame and destruction (8 – 10)
    - 2. Her crimes against Israel (11 – 14)
- III. The Day of the Lord (15 – 21)
  - A. Judgment on the Nations but Deliverance for Zion (15 – 18)
  - B. The Lord's Kingdom Established (19 – 21)

Edom Will Be Humbled

1 The vision of Obadiah.
Thus says the Lord [1]GOD concerning [a]Edom—
[b]We have heard a report from the LORD,
And an [c]envoy has been sent among the nations *saying,*
"[d]Arise and let us go against her for battle"—
2 "Behold, I will make you [a]small among the nations;
You are greatly despised.
3 "The [a]arrogance of your heart has deceived you,
You who live in the clefts of [1]the [b]rock,
In the loftiness of your dwelling place,
Who say in your heart,
'[c]Who will bring me down to earth?'
4 "Though you [a]build high like the eagle,
Though you set your nest among the [b]stars,
From there I will bring you down,"
declares the LORD.
5 "If [a]thieves came to you,
If [1]robbers by night—
O how you will be ruined!—
Would they not steal *only* [2]until they had enough?
If grape gatherers came to you,
[b]Would they not leave *some* gleanings?
6 "O how Esau will be [a]ransacked,
And his hidden treasures searched out!
7 "All the [a]men [1]allied with you
Will send you forth to the border,
And the men at peace with you
Will deceive you and overpower you.
They who eat your [b]bread
Will set an ambush for you.
(There is [c]no understanding [2]in him.)
8 "Will I not on that day," declares the LORD,
"[a]Destroy wise men from Edom
And understanding from the mountain of Esau?
9 "Then your [a]mighty men will be dismayed, O [b]Teman,
So that everyone may be [c]cut off from the mountain of Esau by slaughter.

10 "Because of [a]violence to your brother Jacob,
[1]You will be covered *with* shame,
[b]And you will be cut off forever.
11 "On the day that you [a]stood aloof,
On the day that strangers carried off his wealth,
And foreigners entered his gate
And [b]cast lots for Jerusalem—
[c]You too were as one of them.
12 "[a]Do not [1]gloat over your brother's day,
The day of his misfortune.
And [b]do not rejoice over the sons of Judah
In the day of their destruction;
Yes, [c]do not [2]boast
In the day of *their* distress.
13 "Do not enter the gate of My people
In the [a]day of their disaster.
Yes, you, do not [1]gloat over their calamity

1:1 [1]Heb *YHWH,* usually rendered *LORD* [a]Ps 137:7; Is 21:11, 12; 34:1-17; 63:1-6; Jer 49:7-22; Ezek 25:12-14; 35:15; Joel 3:19; Amos 1:11, 12; Mal 1:4 [b]Jer 49:14-16; Obad 1-4 [c]Is 18:2; 30:4 [d]Jer 6:4, 5
2 [a]Num 24:18; Is 23:9
3 [1]Or *Sela* [a]Is 16:6; Jer 49:16 [b]2 Kin 14:7; 2 Chr 25:11f [c]Is 14:13-15; Rev 18:7
4 [a]Job 20:6, 7; Hab 2:9 [b]Is 14:12-15
5 [1]Lit *devastators of the night* [2]Lit *their sufficiency* [a]Jer 49:9 [b]Deut 24:21
6 [a]Jer 49:10
7 [1]Lit *of your covenant* [a]Jer 30:14
7 [2]I.e. in Esau; or *of it* [b]Ps 41:9 [c]Is 19:11; Jer 49:7
8 [a]Job 5:12-14; Is 29:14
9 [a]Jer 49:22 [b]Gen 36:11; 1 Chr 1:45; Job 2:11; Jer 49:7; Ezek 25:13; Amos 1:12; Hab 3:3 [c]Is 34:5-8; 63:1-3; Obad 5
10 [1]Lit *Shame will cover you* [a]Gen 27:41; Ezek 25:12; Joel 3:19; Amos 1:11 [b]Ezek 35:9
11 [a]Ps 83:5, 6; 137:7; Amos 1:6, 9 [b]Joel 3:3; Nah 3:10 [c]Ezek 35:10 **12** [1]Lit *look on* [2]Lit *make your mouth large* [a]Mic 4:11; 7:10 [b]Prov 17:5; Ezek 35:15; 36:5 [c]Ps 31:18; Ezek 35:12
13 [1]Lit *look on* [a]Ezek 35:5

---

1 *vision.* Commonly used in the OT to designate a revelation from God. *Obadiah.* See Introduction: Author. *We.* Either (1) the editorial "we," or (2) the prophet's association of Israel with himself, or (3) other prophets' pronouncements against Edom. In any case, the rest of the verse sets the stage for Obadiah's prophetic message, which begins with v. 2. *report.* An envoy had been sent to the nations, calling them to battle against Edom. Perhaps a conspiracy was under way between some of Edom's allies (v. 7). Although Edom feels secure (trusting in her mountain fortresses and her wise men, vv. 2–4,8–9), Obadiah announces God's judgment on her for her hostility to Israel.
2 *I will make you small.* Cf. the colloquial expression, "cut one down to size."
3 *rock.* See NASB marg. Sela was the capital of Edom. Perhaps the later Petra (both Sela and Petra mean "rock" or "cliff"), this rugged site is located some 50 miles south of the southern end of the Dead Sea. See note on 2 Kin 14:7.
4 *eagle.* A proud and regal bird, noted for strength, keenness of vision and power of flight. *stars.* Hyperbole for high, inaccessible places in the mountains.
5 *If thieves . . . If grape gatherers.* For a similar oracle against Edom see Jer 49:9.
6 *hidden treasures.* The ancient Greek historian Diodorus Siculus indicates that the Edomites put their wealth—accumulated from trade—in vaults in the rocks.
7 *set an ambush for you.* However the Hebrew for this expression is understood (its meaning is uncertain), it must indicate some act of treachery on the part of previously trusted close friends. Those who "eat bread with" are one's *com-panions* (Latin *cum,* "with," and *panis,* "bread"). See note on Ps 41:9.
8 *on that day.* The day of Edom's destruction; but the words also have an eschatological ring. Since in OT prophecy Edom was often emblematic of all the world powers hostile to God and His kingdom, her judgment anticipates God's complete removal of all such opposition in that day. *wise men.* In whom Edom put so much confidence for her security (see Jer 49:7). Eliphaz, one of Job's three friends, was a Temanite (see next note). *Esau.* Another name for Edom (see Gen 36:1).
9 *Teman.* A reference to all Edom, as in Jer 49:7,20 (see also Amos 1:12). Teman means "south," and the name probably refers to Edom as the southland. Some, however, identify Teman with Tawilan, a site about three miles east of Petra.
10 *your brother Jacob.* Edom's violent crimes are all the more reprehensible because they were committed against the brother nation. *covered with shame.* A striking expression since shame is usually associated with nakedness.
11 See Introduction: Date and Place of Writing. *strangers . . . foreigners.* These terms put in relief the sin of Edom: He did not act like a brother (v. 12) but was like one of the strangers.
12–14 A rebuke of Edom's hostile actions. The eight rebukes

In the day of their disaster.
And do not [b]loot their wealth
In the day of their disaster.
14 "Do not [a]stand at the fork of the road
To cut down their fugitives;
And do not imprison their survivors
In the day of their distress.

The Day of the LORD and the Future

15 "For the [a]day of the LORD draws near
on all the nations.
[b]As you have done, it will be done to
you.
Your [c]dealings will return on your
own head.
16 "Because just as you [a]drank on [b]My
holy mountain,
All the nations [c]will drink continually.
They will drink and [1]swallow
And become as if they had never
existed.
17 "But on Mount [a]Zion there will be
those who escape,
And it will be holy.
And the house of Jacob will [b]possess
their possessions.
18 "Then the house of Jacob will be a [a]fire
And the house of Joseph a flame;
But the house of Esau *will be* as
stubble.
And they will set [1]them on fire and
consume [1]them,
So that there will be [b]no survivor of
the house of Esau,"
For the LORD has spoken.
19 Then *those of* the [1]Negev will [a]possess
the mountain of Esau,
And *those of* the [2]Shephelah the
[b]Philistine *plain;*
Also, [c]possess the territory of Ephraim
and the territory of Samaria,
And Benjamin *will possess* Gilead.
20 And the exiles of this host of the sons
of Israel,
Who are *among* the Canaanites as far
as [a]Zarephath,
And the exiles of Jerusalem who are
in Sepharad
Will possess the [b]cities of the
Negev.
21 The [a]deliverers will ascend Mount
Zion
To judge the mountain of Esau,
And the [b]kingdom will be the LORD's.

13 [b]Ezek 35:10; 36:2, 3
14 [a]Is 16:3, 4
15 [a]Ezek 30:3; Joel 1:15; 2:1, 11, 31; Amos 5:18, 20 [b]Jer 50:29; 51:56; Hab 2:8 [c]Ezek 35:11
16 [1]Or *stagger* [a]Jer 49:12 [b]Joel 3:17 [c]Is 51:22, 23; Jer 25:15, 16
17 [a]Is 4:2, 3 [b]Is 14:1, 2; Amos 9:11-15
18 [a]Is 5:24; 9:18, 19; Zech 12:6
18 [1]I.e. the people of Esau [b]Jer 11:23; Amos 1:8
19 [1]I.e. South country [2]I.e. the foothills [a]Is 11:14; Amos 9:12 [b]Is 11:14 [c]Jer 31:5; 32:44
20 [a]1 Kin 17:9; Luke 4:26 [b]Jer 32:44; 33:13
21 [a]Neh 9:27 [b]Ps 22:28; 47:7-9; 67:4; Zech 14:9; Rev 11:15

in this section proceed from the general to the particular. See Ezek 35:13 and Ps 137 for examples of Edom's reactions to Judah's misfortunes.

15 *the day of the LORD draws near on all the nations.* If there was an eschatological glimmering in "on that day" (v. 8), it here becomes a strong ray. The day of the Lord brings judgment for the nations (including, but not limited to, Edom) and salvation for the house of Jacob. *on your own head.* The situation will be reversed in retribution for Edom's hostility against God's people detailed in vv. 11–14. Ezekiel's denunciation of Edom (ch. 35) reflects a similar punishment-fits-the-crime principle.

16 *just as you drank.* As the Edomites profaned the holy mountain by carousing, so the nations will drink and drink. Their drinking, however, is that of the bitter potion of God's judgment—which they will be compelled to keep on drinking. For drinking as punishment see Jer 25:15–16; 49:12.

17 *But on Mount Zion there will be . . . escape.* Beginning with this verse the blessings on the house of Jacob are mentioned. Eschatological references are twofold: judgment on God's enemies, blessing on God's people.

18 *Jacob . . . Joseph.* Previously it was stated that the Lord would destroy Edom, using other nations (v. 7); now it is to be done by God's people. *no survivor.* The final word to Esau is that his house (or nation) will be totally destroyed; there will be no Edomite survivors. Yet compare Amos 9:12 with Acts 15:17 and see note on Amos 9:12.

19 *those . . . will possess.* With Edom annihilated, others will occupy Edomite territory. Although not expressly identified, these are most likely the remnant of Israel referred to in the lines immediately following. *Negev.* See note on Gen 12:9. *Philistine.* See note on Gen 10:14. *Gilead.* See notes on Gen 31:21; Song 4:1.

20 *Zarephath.* See note on 1 Kin 17:9. *Sepharad.* Usually taken to refer to Sardis in Asia Minor (present-day Turkey), though some think that Sparta (the city in Greece) might be meant.

21 *deliverers.* Having developed the theme of possessing lands around Zion, the prophet now turns to the center. The "deliverers" come from Mount Zion and rule over the mountains of Esau. Mount Zion is exalted over the mountains of Esau. The Messiah, the Deliverer par excellence, may ultimately be in view. *the kingdom will be the LORD's.* The conclusion of the prophecy—and the final outcome of history. The last book of the Bible echoes this theme (Rev 11:15).

Jonah

INTRODUCTION

Title

The book is named after its principal character, whose name means "dove"; see the simile used of Ephraim in Hos 7:11 to portray the northern kingdom as "without sense." See also Ps 68:13; 74:19 and notes.

Author

Though the book does not identify its author, tradition has ascribed it to the prophet himself, Jonah son of Amittai (1:1), from Gath-hepher (2 Kin 14:25) in Zebulun (Josh 19:10,13). In view of its many similarities with the narratives about Elijah and Elisha, however, it may come from the same prophetic circles that originally composed the accounts about those prophets, perhaps in the eighth century B.C. (see Introduction to 1 Kings: Author, Sources and Date).

Background

In the half-century during which the prophet Jonah ministered (800 – 750 B.C.), a significant event affected the northern kingdom of Israel: King Jeroboam II (793 – 753) restored her traditional borders, ending almost a century of sporadic seesaw conflict between Israel and Damascus.

Jeroboam, in God's good providence (2 Kin 14:26 – 27), capitalized on Assyria's defeat of Damascus (in the latter half of the ninth century), which temporarily crushed that center of Aramean power. Prior to that time, not only had Israel been considerably reduced in size, but the king of Damascus had even been able to control internal affairs in the northern kingdom (2 Kin 13:7). However, after the Assyrian campaign against Damascus in 797, Jehoash, king of Israel, had been able to recover the territory lost to the king of Damascus (2 Kin 13:25). Internal troubles in Assyria subsequently allowed Jeroboam II to complete the restoration of Israel's northern borders. Nevertheless, Assyria remained the real threat from the north at this time.

The prophets of the Lord were speaking to Israel regarding these events. About 797 B.C. Elisha spoke to the king of Israel concerning future victories over Damascus (2 Kin 13:14 – 19). A few years later Jonah prophesied the restoration that Jeroboam II accomplished (2 Kin 14:25). But soon after Israel had triumphed, she began to gloat over her new-found power. Because she was relieved of foreign pressures — relief that had come in accordance with encouraging words from Elisha and Jonah — she felt jealously complacent about her favored status with God (Amos 6:1). She focused her religion on expectations of the "day of the LORD" (Amos 5:18 – 20), when God's darkness would engulf the other nations, leaving Israel to bask in His light.

It was in such a time that the Lord sent Amos and Hosea to announce to His people Israel that he would "spare them no longer" (Amos 7:8; 8:2) but would send them into exile "beyond Damascus" (Amos 5:27), i.e., to Assyria (Hos 9:3; 10:6; 11:5). During this time the Lord also sent Jonah to Nineveh to warn it of the imminent danger of divine judgment.

Since Jonah was a contemporary of Amos, see Introduction to Amos: Date and Historical Situation for additional details.

Date of Writing

For a number of reasons, including the preaching to Gentiles, the book is often assigned a postexilic date. At least, it is said, the book must have been written after the destruction of Nineveh in 612 B.C. But these considerations are not decisive. The similarity of this narrative to the Elijah-Elisha accounts has already been noted. One may also question whether mention of the repentance of Nineveh and the consequent averted destruction of the city would have had so much significance to the author after Nineveh's overthrow. And to suppose that proclaiming God's word to Gentiles had no relevance in the eighth century is to overlook the

fact that already in the previous century Elijah and Elisha had extended their ministries to foreign lands (1 Kin 17:7–24; 2 Kin 8:7–17). Moreover, the prophet Amos (c. 760–750) set God's redemptive work in behalf of Israel in the context of His dealings with the nations (Amos 1:3—2:16; 9:7,12). Perhaps the third quarter of the eighth century is the most likely date for the book, after the public ministries of Amos and Hosea and before the fall of Samaria to Assyria in 722–721.

Interpretation

Many have questioned whether the book of Jonah is historical. The supposed legendary character of some of the events (e.g., the episode involving the great fish) has caused them to suggest alternatives to the traditional view that the book is historical, biographical narrative. Although their specific suggestions range from fictional short story to allegory to parable, they share the common assumption that the account sprang essentially from the author's imagination, despite its serious and gracious message.

Such interpretations, often based in part on doubt about the miraculous as such, too quickly dismiss (1) the similarities between the narrative of Jonah and other parts of the OT and (2) the pervasive concern of the OT writers, especially the prophets, for history. They also fail to realize that OT narrators had a keen ear for recognizing how certain past events in Israel's pilgrimage with God illumine (by way of analogy) later events. (For example, the events surrounding the birth of Moses illumine the exodus, those surrounding Samuel's birth illumine the series of events narrated in the books of Samuel, and the ministries of Moses and Joshua illumine those of Elijah and Elisha.) Similarly, the prophets recognized that the future events they announced could be illumined by reference to analogous events of the past. Overlooking these features in OT narrative and prophecy, many have supposed that a story that too neatly fits the author's purpose must therefore be fictional.

On the other hand, it must be acknowledged that Biblical narrators were more than historians. They interpretatively recounted the past with the unswerving purpose of bringing it to bear on the present and the future. In the portrayal of past events, they used their materials to achieve this purpose effectively. Nonetheless, the integrity with which they treated the past ought not to be questioned. The book of Jonah recounts real events in the life and ministry of the prophet himself.

Literary Characteristics

Unlike most other prophetic parts of the OT, this book is a narrative account of a single prophetic mission. Its treatment of that mission is thus similar to the accounts of the ministries of Elijah and Elisha found in 1,2 Kings, and to certain narrative sections of Isaiah, Jeremiah and Ezekiel.

As is often the case in Biblical narratives, the author has compressed much into a small space; 40 verses tell the entire story (eight additional verses of poetry are devoted to Jonah's prayer of thanksgiving). In its scope (a single extended episode), compactness, vividness and character delineation, it is much like the book of Ruth.

Also as in Ruth, the author uses structural symmetry effectively. The story is developed in two parallel cycles that call attention to a series of comparisons and contrasts (see Outline). The story's climax is Jonah's grand prayer of confession, "Salvation is from the LORD"—the middle confession of three from his lips (1:9; 2:9; 4:2). The last sentence emphasizes that the Lord's word is final and decisive, while Jonah is left sitting in the hot, open country outside Nineveh.

The author uses the art of representative roles in a straightforward manner. In this story of God's loving concern for all people, Nineveh, the great menace to Israel, is representative of the Gentiles. Correspondingly, stubbornly reluctant Jonah represents Israel's jealousy of her favored relationship with God and her unwillingness to share the Lord's compassion with the nations.

The book depicts the larger scope of God's purpose for Israel: that she might rediscover the truth of His concern for the whole creation and that she might better understand her own role in carrying out that concern.

Outline

- I. Jonah Flees His Mission (chs. 1 — 2)
  - A. Jonah's Commission and Flight (1:1 – 3)
  - B. The Endangered Sailors' Cry to Their Gods (1:4 – 6)
  - C. Jonah's Disobedience Exposed (1:7 – 10)
  - D. Jonah's Punishment and Deliverance (1:11 — 2:1; 2:10)
  - E. His Prayer of Thanksgiving (2:2 – 9)
- II. Jonah Reluctantly Fulfills His Mission (chs. 3 — 4)
  - A. Jonah's Renewed Commission and Obedience (3:1 – 4)
  - B. The Endangered Ninevites' Repentant Appeal to the Lord (3:5 – 9)
  - C. The Ninevites' Repentance Acknowledged (3:10 — 4:4)
  - D. Jonah's Deliverance and Rebuke (4:5 – 11)

Jonah's Disobedience

1 The word of the LORD came to [a]Jonah the
son of Amittai saying,
2 "Arise, go to [a]Nineveh the great city and
[b]cry against it, for their [c]wickedness has
come up before Me."
3 But Jonah rose up to flee to [a]Tarshish
[b]from the presence of the LORD. So he went
down to [c]Joppa, found a ship which was
going to Tarshish, paid the fare and went
down into it to go with them to Tarshish
from the presence of the LORD.
4 The [a]LORD hurled a great wind on the
sea and there was a great storm on the sea so
that the ship was about to [1]break up.
5 Then the sailors became afraid and
every man cried to [a]his god, and they [b]threw
the [1]cargo which was in the ship into the sea
to lighten *it* [2]for them. But Jonah had gone
below into the hold of the ship, lain down
and fallen sound asleep.
6 So the captain approached him and said,
"How is it that you are sleeping? Get up, [a]call
on your god. Perhaps *your* [b]god will be concerned
about us so that we will not perish."
7 Each man said to his mate, "Come, let
us [a]cast lots so we may [1]learn on whose
account this calamity *has struck* us." So they
cast lots and the [b]lot fell on Jonah.

1:1 [a]2 Kin 14:25; Matt 12:39-41; 16:4; Luke 11:29, 30, 32
2 [a]Gen 10:11; 2 Kin 19:36; Is 37:37; Nah 1:1; Zeph 2:13 [b]Is 58:1 [c]Gen 18:20; Hos 7:2
3 [a]Is 23:1, 6, 10; Jer 10:9 [b]Gen 4:16; Ps 139:7, 9, 10 [c]Josh 19:46; 2 Chr 2:16; Ezra 3:7; Acts 9:36, 43
4 [1]Lit *be broken* [a]Ps 107:23-28; 135:6, 7
5 [1]Lit *vessels* [2]Lit *from upon* *them* [a]1 Kin 18:26 [b]Acts 27:18, 19, 38
6 [a]Ps 107:28 [b]2 Sam 12:22; Amos 5:15; Jon 3:9
7 [1]Lit *know* [a]Josh 7:14-18; 1 Sam 10:20, 21; 14:41, 42; Acts 1:23-26 [b]Num 32:23; Prov 16:33

1:1 *The word of the LORD came.* See 3:1; a common phrase used to indicate the divine source of the prophet's revelation (see, e.g., 1 Kin 17:8; Jer 1:2,4; Hos 1:1; Joel 1:1; Hag 1:1,3; Zech 1:1,7). *Jonah.* See Introduction: Title; Author.
1:2 *great city.* See 3:2; 4:11; see also note on 3:3. According to Gen 10:11–12, it was first built by Nimrod (perhaps along with Rehoboth Ir, Calah and Resen) and was traditionally known as the "great city." About 700 B.C. Sennacherib made it the capital of Assyria, which it remained until its fall in 612 (see Introduction to Nahum: Background). Nineveh is over 500 miles from Gath-hepher, Jonah's hometown. *their wickedness has come up.* Cf. Sodom and Gomorrah (Gen 18:20–21). Except for the violence (3:8) of Nineveh, her "wicked way" (3:8,10) is not described in Jonah. Nahum later states that Nineveh's sins included plotting evil against the Lord (Nah 1:11), cruelty and plundering in war (Nah 2:12–13; 3:1,19), prostitution and witchcraft (Nah 3:4) and commercial exploitation (Nah 3:16).
1:3 *rose up to flee.* The reason is found in 4:2. The futility of trying to run away from the Lord is acknowledged in Ps 139:7,9–10. *Tarshish.* Perhaps the city of Tartessus in southwest Spain, a Phoenician mining colony near Gibraltar. By heading in the opposite direction from Nineveh, to what seemed like the end of the world, Jonah intended to escape his divinely appointed task.
1:4–5 Although Jonah's mission was to bring God's warning of impending judgment to the pagan world, his refusal to go to Nineveh brings these pagan sailors into peril.
1:4 *The LORD hurled a great wind.* God's sovereign working in Jonah's mission is evident at several other points also: the fish (v. 17), the release of Jonah (2:10), the plant (4:6), the worm (4:7) and the wind (4:8).
1:5 *his god.* Apparently the sailors, who may have come from various ports, worshiped several pagan gods.
1:6 *the captain approached him.* The pagan captain's concern for everyone on board contrasts with the believing prophet's refusal to carry God's warning to Nineveh.
1:7 *let us cast lots.* The casting of lots was a custom widely practiced in the ancient Near East. The precise method is unclear, though it appears that, for the most part, sticks or marked pebbles were drawn from a receptacle into which they

The Book of Jonah

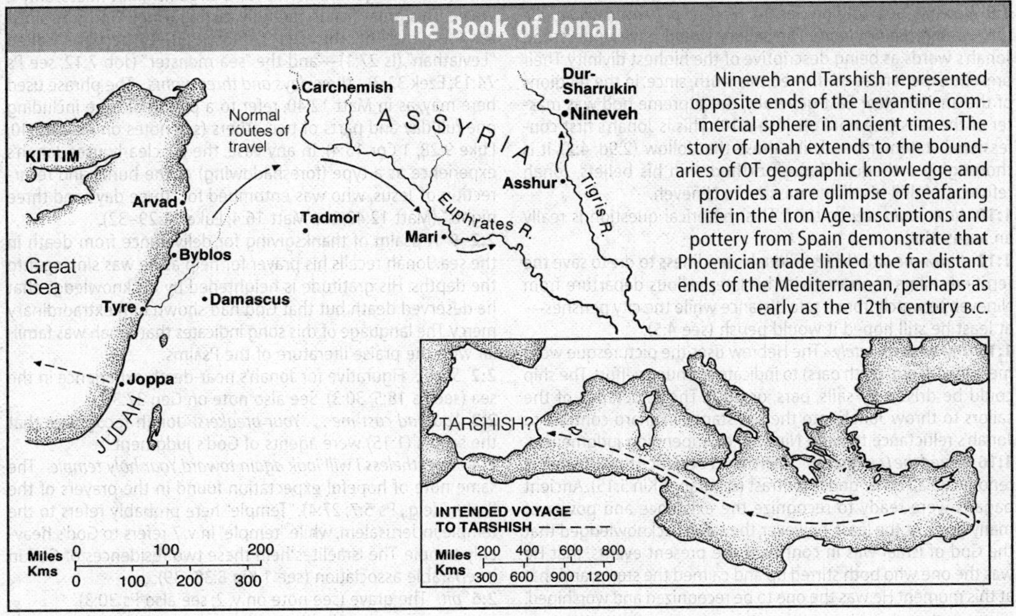

KITTIM
Arvad
Great Sea
Byblos
Tyre
Damascus
Joppa
JUDAH
Carchemish
Normal routes of travel
ASSYRIA
Tadmor
Mari
Euphrates R.
Dur-Sharrukin
Nineveh
Asshur
Tigris R.
Miles 0 100 200
Kms 0 100 200 300
TARSHISH?
INTENDED VOYAGE TO TARSHISH
Miles 200 400 600 800
Kms 300 600 900 1200

Nineveh and Tarshish represented opposite ends of the Levantine commercial sphere in ancient times. The story of Jonah extends to the boundaries of OT geographic knowledge and provides a rare glimpse of seafaring life in the Iron Age. Inscriptions and pottery from Spain demonstrate that Phoenician trade linked the far distant ends of the Mediterranean, perhaps as early as the 12th century B.C.

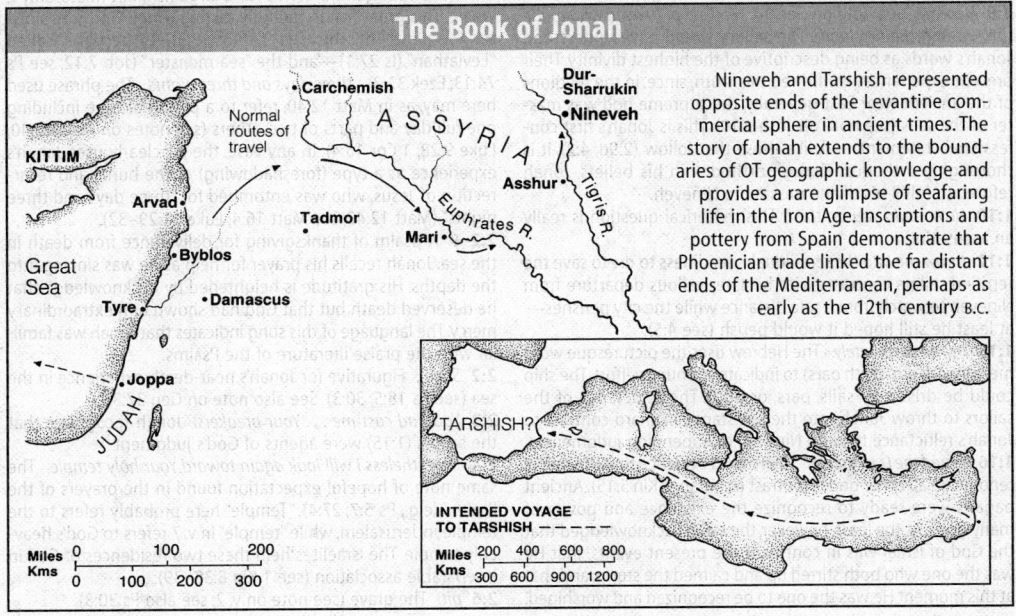

8 Then they said to him, "[a]Tell us, now!
On whose account *has* this calamity *struck*
us? What is your [b]occupation? And where do
you come from? What is your country? From
what people are you?"
9 He said to them, "I am a [a]Hebrew, and
I [b]fear the LORD [c]God of heaven who [d]made
the sea and the dry land."
10 Then the men became extremely frightened and they said to him, "[1]How could you
do this?" For the men knew that he was
[a]fleeing from the presence of the LORD,
because he had told them.
11 So they said to him, "What should we
do to you that the sea may become calm [1]for
us?"—for the sea was becoming increasingly
stormy.
12 He said to them, "Pick me up and throw
me into the sea. Then the sea will become
calm [1]for you, for I know that [a]on account of
me this great storm *has come* upon you."
13 However, the men [1]rowed *desperately* to
return to land but they could not, for the sea
was becoming *even* stormier against them.
14 Then they called on the [a]LORD and said,
"We earnestly pray, O LORD, do not let us
perish on account of this man's life and do
not put innocent blood on us; for [b]You, O
LORD, have done as You have pleased."
15 So they picked up Jonah, threw him
into the sea, and the sea [a]stopped its raging.
16 Then the men feared the LORD greatly,
and they offered a sacrifice to the LORD and
made [a]vows.
17 [1]And the LORD appointed a great fish to
swallow Jonah, and Jonah was in the [a]stom-
ach of the fish three days and three nights.

8 [a]Josh 7:19; 1 Sam 14:43 [b]Gen 47:3; 1 Sam 30:13 **9** [a]Gen 14:13; Ex 1:15; 2:13 [b]2 Kin 17:25, 28, 32, 33 [c]Ezra 1:2; Neh 1:4; Ps 136:26; Dan 2:18 [d]Neh 9:6; Ps 95:5; 146:6 **10** [1]Lit *What is this you have done* [a]Job 27:22; Jon 1:3 **11** [1]Lit *from upon us* **12** [1]Lit *from upon you* [a]2 Sam 24:17; 1 Chr 21:17 **13** [1]Lit *dug their oars into the water* **14** [a]Ps 107:28; Jon 1:16 [b]Ps 115:3; 135:6; Dan 4:34, 35 **15** [a]Ps 65:7; 93:3, 4; 107:29 **16** [a]Ps 50:14; 66:13, 14 **17** [1]Ch 2:1 in Heb

17 [a]Matt 12:40; 16:4 **2:1** [1]Ch 2:2 in Heb [a]Job 13:15; Ps 130:1, 2; Lam 3:53-56 **2** [1]Lit *belly* [a]1 Sam 30:6; Ps 18:4-6; 22:24; 120:1 [b]Ps 18:5, 6; 86:13; 88:1-7 **3** [1]Lit *surrounded* [a]Ps 69:1, 2, 14, 15; Lam 3:54 [b]Ps 42:7

Jonah's Prayer

2 [1]Then Jonah prayed to the LORD his God
[a]from the stomach of the fish,
2 and he said,
"I [a]called out of my distress to the LORD,
And He answered me.
I cried for help from the [1]depth of
[b]Sheol;
You heard my voice.
3 "For You had [a]cast me into the deep,
Into the heart of the seas,
And the current [1]engulfed me.
All Your [b]breakers and billows passed
over me.
4 "So I said, 'I have been [a]expelled from
Your sight.
Nevertheless I will look again [b]toward
Your holy temple.'
5 "[a]Water encompassed me to the [1]point
of death.
The great [b]deep [2]engulfed me,
Weeds were wrapped around my head.
6 "I [a]descended to the roots of the
mountains.
The earth with its [b]bars *was* around
me forever,
But You have [c]brought up my life from
[1]the pit, O LORD my God.

4 [1]Lit *before Your eyes* [a]Ps 31:22; Jer 7:15 [b]1 Kin 8:38; 2 Chr 6:38; Ps 5:7 **5** [1]Lit *soul* [2]Lit *surrounded* [a]Lam 3:54 [b]Ps 69:1, 2 **6** [1]Or *corruption* [a]Ps 18:5; 116:3 [b]Is 38:10; Matt 16:18 [c]Job 33:28; Ps 16:10; 30:3; Is 38:17

had been "cast." *lot fell on Jonah.* By the lot of judgment the Lord exposed the guilty one (cf. Josh 7:14–26; 1 Sam 14:38–44; Prov 16:33).

1:9 *Hebrew.* See note on Gen 14:13. *God of heaven who made the sea and the dry land.* The sailors would have understood Jonah's words as being descriptive of the highest divinity. Their present experiences confirmed this truth, since, in the religions of the ancient Near East generally, the supreme god was master of the seas (see note on Josh 3:10). This is Jonah's first confessional statement, and, like those that follow (2:9d; 4:2), it is thoroughly orthodox. Though orthodox in his beliefs, Jonah refuses to fulfill his divine mission to Nineveh.

1:10 *How could you do this?* This rhetorical question is really an accusation.

1:12 *throw me into the sea.* Jonah's readiness to die to save the terrified sailors contrasts with his later callous departure from Nineveh to watch from a safe distance while the city perishes—at least he still hoped it would perish (see 4:5).

1:13 *rowed desperately.* The Hebrew uses the picturesque word meaning "to dig" (with oars) to indicate strenuous effort. The ship could be driven by sails, oars, or both. The reluctance of the sailors to throw Jonah into the sea stands in sharp contrast to Jonah's reluctance to warn Nineveh of impending judgment.

1:16 *feared the LORD greatly.* There is no evidence that the sailors renounced all other gods (contrast Naaman, 2 Kin 5:15). Ancient pagans were ready to recognize the existence and power of many gods. At the least, however, the sailors acknowledged that the God of Israel was in control of the present events, that He was the one who both stirred up and calmed the storm, and that at this moment He was the one to be recognized and worshiped.

1:17 *the LORD appointed.* This characteristic phrase occurs also in 4:6–8. *great fish.* The Hebrew here and the Greek of Matt 12:40 are both general terms for a large fish, not necessarily a whale. This great fish is carefully distinguished from the sinister "serpent" of the sea (Amos 9:3)—otherwise called "Leviathan" (Is 27:1)—and the "sea monster" (Job 7:12; see Ps 74:13; Ezek 32:2). *three days and three nights.* The phrase used here may, as in Matt 12:40, refer to a period of time including one full day and parts of two others (see notes on Matt 12:40; Luke 9:28; 1 Cor 15:4). In any case, the NT clearly uses Jonah's experience as a type (foreshadowing) of the burial and resurrection of Jesus, who was entombed for "three days and three nights" (Matt 12:40; see Matt 16:4; Luke 11:29–32).

2:2–9 A psalm of thanksgiving for deliverance from death in the sea. Jonah recalls his prayer for help as he was sinking into the depths. His gratitude is heightened by his knowledge that he deserved death but that God had shown him extraordinary mercy. The language of this song indicates that Jonah was familiar with the praise literature of the Psalms.

2:2 *Sheol.* Figurative for Jonah's near-death experience in the sea (see Ps 18:5; 30:3). See also note on Gen 37:35.

2:3 *You had cast me . . . Your breakers.* Jonah recognizes that the sailors (1:15) were agents of God's judgment.

2:4 *Nevertheless I will look again toward Your holy temple.* The same note of hopeful expectation found in the prayers of the Psalms (e.g., Ps 5:7; 27:4). "Temple" here probably refers to the temple in Jerusalem, while "temple" in v. 7 refers to God's heavenly temple. The Israelites held these two residences of God in inseparable association (see 1 Kin 8:38–39).

2:6 *pit.* The grave (see note on v. 2; see also Ps 30:3).

7 "While [1]I was [a]fainting away,
I [b]remembered the LORD,
And my [c]prayer came to You,
Into [d]Your holy temple.
8 "Those who [a]regard [1]vain idols
Forsake their faithfulness,
9 But I will [a]sacrifice to You
With the voice of thanksgiving.
That which I have vowed I will [b]pay.
[c]Salvation is from the LORD."
10 Then the LORD commanded the [a]fish,
and it vomited Jonah up onto the dry land.

Nineveh Repents

3 Now the word of the LORD came to Jonah
the second time, saying,
2 "Arise, go to [a]Nineveh the great city and
[b]proclaim to it the proclamation which I am
going to tell you."
3 So Jonah arose and went to Nineveh
according to the word of the LORD. Now Nineveh was [1]an [a]exceedingly great city, a three
days' walk.
4 Then Jonah began to go through the
city one day's walk; and he [a]cried out and
said, "Yet forty days and Nineveh will be
overthrown."
5 Then the people of Nineveh believed in
God; and they called a [a]fast and put on sackcloth from the greatest to the least of them.
6 When the word reached the king of
Nineveh, he arose from his throne, laid aside
his robe from him, [a]covered *himself* with
sackcloth and sat on the [1]ashes.
7 He issued a [a]proclamation and it said,
"In Nineveh by the decree of the king and
his nobles: Do not let man, beast, herd, or
flock taste a thing. Do not let them eat or
drink water.
8 "But both man and beast must be covered with sackcloth; and let [1]men [a]call on
God earnestly that each may [b]turn from his
wicked way and from the violence which is
in [2]his hands.
9 "[a]Who knows, God may turn and relent
and withdraw His burning anger so that we
will not perish."
10 When God saw their deeds, that they
[a]turned from their wicked way, then [b]God
relented concerning the calamity which He
had declared He would [1]bring upon them.
And He did not do *it*.

Jonah's Displeasure Rebuked

4 But it greatly displeased Jonah and he
became [a]angry.
2 He [a]prayed to the LORD and said,
"Please LORD, was not this [1]what I said while
I was still in my *own* country? Therefore [2]in
order to forestall this I [b]fled to Tarshish, for I
knew that You are a [c]gracious and compassionate God, slow to anger and abundant in
lovingkindness, and one who relents concerning calamity.
3 "Therefore now, O LORD, please [a]take
my [1]life from me, for death is [b]better to me
than life."
4 The LORD said, "Do you have good reason to be angry?"
5 Then Jonah went out from the city
and sat east of [1]it. There he made a shelter
for himself and [a]sat under it in the shade
until he could see what would happen in
the city.
6 So the LORD God appointed a [1]plant
and it grew up over Jonah to be a shade over
his head to deliver him from his discomfort.

7 [1]Lit *my soul...within me* [a]Ps 142:3 [b]Ps 77:10, 11; 143:5 [c]2 Chr 30:27; Ps 18:6 [d]Ps 11:4; 65:4; Jon 2:4; Mic 1:2; Hab 2:20
8 [1]Lit *empty vanities* [a]2 Kin 17:15; Ps 31:6; Jer 10:8
9 [a]Ps 50:14, 23; Jer 33:11; Hos 14:2 [b]Job 22:27; Eccl 5:4, 5 [c]Ps 3:8; Is 45:17
10 [a]Jon 1:17
3:2 [a]Zeph 2:13 [b]Jer 1:17; Ezek 2:7
3 [1]Lit *a great city to God* [a]Jon 1:2; 4:11
4 [a]Matt 12:41; Luke 11:32
5 [a]Dan 9:3; Joel 1:14
6 [1]Or *dust* [a]Esth 4:1-4; Jer 6:26; Ezek 27:30, 31
7 [a]2 Chr 20:3; Ezra 8:21; Jon 3:5
8 [1]Lit *them* [2]Lit *their* [a]Ps 130:1; Jon 1:6, 14 [b]Is 1:16-19; 55:6, 7; Jer 18:11
9 [a]2 Sam 12:22; Joel 2:14
10 [1]Lit *do* [a]1 Kin 21:27-29; Jer 31:18 [b]Ex 32:14; Jer 18:8; Amos 7:3, 6
4:1 [a]Jon 4:4, 9; Matt 20:15; Luke 15:28
2 [1]Lit *my word* [2]Lit *I was beforehand in fleeing* [a]Jer 20:7 [b]Jon 1:3 [c]Ex 34:6; Num 14:18; Ps 86:5, 15; Joel 2:13

3 [1]Lit *soul* [a]1 Kin 19:4; Job 6:8, 9 [b]Job 7:15, 16; Eccl 7:1
5 [1]Lit *the city* [a]1 Kin 19:9, 13 **6** [1]Probably a castor oil plant, and so in vv 7, 9 and 10

2:9 *That which I have vowed.* In the book of Psalms, prayers were commonly accompanied by vows, usually involving thank offerings (e.g., Ps 50:14; 56:12; 61:8; 65:1; 66:13–14; 116:12–19). *Salvation is from the LORD.* The climax of Jonah's thanksgiving prayer. It is Jonah's second confessional statement (see note on 1:9) and stands at the literary midpoint of the book.

3:2 *proclaim to it the proclamation which I . . . tell you.* A prophet was the bearer of a message from God, not primarily a foreteller of coming events.

3:3 *arose and went.* But reluctantly, still wanting the Ninevites to be destroyed (4:1–5). *exceedingly great city.* See 4:11, which says the city had more than 120,000 inhabitants. Archaeological excavations indicate that the later imperial city of Nineveh was about eight miles around. The fact, however, that the city was a "three days' walk" may suggest a larger area, such as the four-city complex of Nineveh, Rehoboth Ir, Calah and Resen mentioned in Gen 10:11–12. Greater Nineveh covered an area of some 60 miles in circumference. On the other hand, "three days" may have been a conventional way of describing a medium-length distance (see Gen 30:36; Ex 3:18; Josh 9:16–17).

3:5–6 *fast . . . sackcloth . . . ashes.* Customary signs of humbling oneself in repentance (see 1 Kin 21:27; Neh 9:1).

3:5 *believed in God.* This may mean that the Ninevites genuinely turned to the Lord (cf. Matt 12:41). On the other hand, their belief in God may have gone no deeper than had the sailors' fear of God (see note on 1:16). At least they took the prophet's warning seriously and acted accordingly.

3:6 *king of Nineveh.* King of Assyria.

3:8 Inclusion of the domestic animals was unusual and expressed the urgency with which the Ninevites sought mercy.

3:9 God often responds in mercy to man's repentance by canceling threatened punishment (v. 10). See note on Jer 18:7–10.

4:1 *angry.* Jonah was angry that God would have compassion on an enemy of Israel. He wanted God's goodness to be shown only to Israelites, not to Gentiles.

4:2 *gracious . . . lovingkindness.* See Ex 34:6–7 and note. Jonah again uses a fixed, confessional formula (see note on 1:9). *slow to anger.* In contrast, Jonah became angry quickly (vv. 1,9).

4:3 *take my life.* Cf. 1 Kin 19:4 (Elijah). To Jonah, God's mercy to the Ninevites meant an end to Israel's favored standing with Him. Jonah shortly before had rejoiced in his deliverance from death, but now that Nineveh lives, he prefers to die.

4:5 *shelter.* Apparently this shelter did not provide enough shade since the next verse indicates that God provided a vine to give more shade. *until he could see.* Jonah still hoped that Nineveh would be destroyed.

4:6 *the LORD God appointed.* This characteristic phrase occurs also in vv. 7–8; 1:17. *plant.* Probably a castor oil plant, a shrub growing over 12 feet high with large, shady leaves. God graciously increased the comfort of His stubbornly defiant prophet.

And Jonah was [2]extremely happy about the
[1]plant.
7 But God appointed a worm when dawn
came the next day and it attacked the plant
and it [a]withered.
8 When the sun came up God appointed
a scorching [a]east wind, and the [b]sun beat
down on Jonah's head so that he became
faint and begged with *all* his soul to die, saying, "[c]Death is better to me than life."
9 Then God said to Jonah, "Do you have
good reason to be angry about the plant?"
And he said, "I have good reason to be
angry, even to death."
10 Then the LORD said, "You had compassion on the plant for which you did not
work and *which* you did not cause to grow,
which [1]came up overnight and perished
[2]overnight.
11 "Should I not [a]have compassion on Nineveh, the great city in which there are more
than 120,000 persons who do not [b]know *the*
difference between their right and left hand,
as well as many [c]animals?"

6 [1]Probably a castor oil plant, and so in vv 7, 9 and 10 [2]Lit *greatly*
7 [a]Joel 1:12
8 [a]Ezek 19:12; Hos 13:15 [b]Ps 121:6; Is 49:10 [c]Jon 4:3
10 [1]Lit *was a son of a night* [2]Lit *a son of a night*
11 [a]Jon 3:10 [b]Deut 1:39; Is 7:16 [c]Ps 36:6

4:8 *Death is better to me.* See note on v. 3.

4:10 *came up overnight and perished overnight.* Indicative of fleeting value.

4:11 *Should I not have compassion . . .?* God had the first word (1:1), and He also has the last. The commission He gave Jonah displayed His mercy and compassion to the Ninevites, and His last word to Jonah emphatically proclaimed that concern for every creature, both man and animal. Not only does the "LORD . . . preserve man and beast" (Ps 36:6; see Neh 9:6; Ps 145:16), but He takes "no pleasure in the death of the wicked, but (desires) rather that the wicked turn from his way and live" (Ezek 33:11; see Ezek 18:21–23). Jonah and his countrymen traditionally rejoiced in God's special mercies to Israel but wished only His wrath on their enemies. God here rebukes such hardness and proclaims His own gracious benevolence. *do not know . . . their right and left hand.* Like small children (cf. Deut 1:39; Is 7:15–16), the Ninevites needed God's fatherly compassion. *as well as many animals.* God's concern extended even to domestic animals.

Micah

INTRODUCTION

Author

Little is known about the prophet Micah beyond what can be learned from the book itself and Jer 26:18. Micah was from the town of Moresheth (1:1), probably Moresheth-gath (1:14) in southern Judah. The prophecy attests to Micah's deep sensitivity to the social ills of his day, especially as they affected the small towns and villages of his homeland.

Date

Micah prophesied sometime between 750 and 686 B.C. during the reigns of Jotham, Ahaz and Hezekiah, kings of Judah (1:1; Jer 26:18). He was therefore a contemporary of Isaiah (see Is 1:1) and Hosea (see Hos 1:1). Micah predicted the fall of Samaria (1:6), which took place in 722–721. This would place his early ministry in the reigns of Jotham (750–732) and Ahaz (735–715). (The reigns of Jotham and Ahaz overlapped.) Micah's message reflects social conditions prior to the religious reforms under Hezekiah (715–686). (The reigns of Ahaz and Hezekiah seem to have overlapped from c. 729 to 715; see 2 Kin 18:9 and note on Is 36:1.)

Background

The background of the book is the same as that found in the earlier portions of Isaiah, though Micah does not exhibit the same knowledge of Jerusalem's political life as Isaiah does. Perhaps this is because he, like Amos, was from a Judahite village.

Israel was in an apostate condition. Micah predicted the fall of her capital, Samaria (1:5–7), and also foretold the inevitable desolation of Judah (1:9–16).

Three significant historical events occurred during this period:

1. In 734–732 B.C. Tiglath-pileser III of Assyria led a military campaign against Aram (Syria), Philistia and parts of Israel and Judah. Ashkelon and Gaza were defeated. Judah, Ammon, Edom and Moab paid tribute to the Assyrian king, but Israel did not fare as well. According to 2 Kin 15:29 the northern kingdom lost most of its territory, including all of Gilead and much of Galilee. Damascus fell in 732 and was annexed to the Assyrian empire.

2. In 722–721 Samaria fell, and the northern kingdom of Israel was conquered by Assyria.

3. In 701 Judah joined a revolt against Assyria and was overrun by King Sennacherib and his army, though Jerusalem was spared.

Literary Characteristics

Micah's style is similar to that of Isaiah. Both prophets use vigorous language and many figures of speech; both show great tenderness in threatening punishment and in promising justice. Micah makes frequent use of plays on words, 1:10–15 (see NASB marg. notes there) being the classic example.

Theme and Message

As the Outline shows, Micah's message alternates between oracles of doom and oracles of hope. The theme is judgment and deliverance by God. Micah also stresses that God hates idolatry, injustice, rebellion and empty ritualism, but He delights in pardoning the penitent. Finally, the prophet declares that Zion will have greater glory in the future than ever before. The Davidic kingdom, though it will seem to come to an end, will reach greater heights through the coming Messianic deliverer.

Outline

I. Superscription (1:1)

II. Judgment against Israel and Judah (1:2—3:12)
   A. Introduction (1:2)
   B. The Predicted Destruction (1:3–7)
   C. Lamentation for the Destruction (1:8–16)
   D. Corruption in Micah's Society (2:1–11)
   E. Hope in the Midst of Gloom (2:12–13)
   F. The Leaders Condemned (ch. 3)

III. Hope for Israel and Judah (chs. 4—5)
   A. The Coming Kingdom (ch. 4)
   B. The Coming King (5:1–5a)
   C. Victory for the People of God (5:5b-15)

IV. The Lord's Case against Israel (ch. 6)
   A. The Lord's Accusation (6:1–8)
   B. The Coming Judgment (6:9–16)

V. Gloom Turns to Triumph (ch. 7)
   A. Micah Laments the Corruption of His Society (7:1–6)
   B. Micah's Assurance of Hope (7:7)
   C. A Bright Future for God's People (7:8–13)
   D. Victory for God's Kingdom (7:14–20)

Destruction in Israel and Judah

1 The [a]word of the LORD which came *to*
[b]Micah of Moresheth in the days of
[c]Jotham, [d]Ahaz *and* [e]Hezekiah, kings of
Judah, which he saw concerning Samaria
and Jerusalem.

2 Hear, O peoples, all of [1]you;
[a]Listen, O earth and [2]all it contains,
And let the Lord [3]GOD be a [b]witness
against you,
The Lord from His holy temple.
3 For behold, the LORD is [a]coming forth
from His place.
He will come down and [b]tread on the
high places of the [1]earth.
4 [a]The mountains will melt under Him
And the valleys will be split,
Like wax before the fire,
Like water poured down a steep place.
5 All this is for the rebellion of Jacob
And for the sins of the house of Israel.
What is the [a]rebellion of Jacob?
Is it not [b]Samaria?
What is the [c]high [1]place of Judah?
Is it not Jerusalem?
6 For I will make Samaria a [a]heap of
ruins [1]in the open country,
[b]Planting places for a vineyard.
I will [c]pour her stones down into the
valley
And will [d]lay bare her foundations.
7 All of her [a]idols will be smashed,
All of her earnings will be burned
with fire
And all of her images I will make
desolate,
For she collected *them* from a [b]harlot's
earnings,
And to the earnings of a harlot they
will return.
8 Because of this I must lament and
wail,
I must go [a]barefoot and naked;
I must make a lament like the [b]jackals
And a mourning like the ostriches.
9 For her [1a]wound is incurable,
For [b]it has come to Judah;
It has reached the [c]gate of my people,
Even to Jerusalem.
10 [a]Tell it not in Gath,
Weep not at all.
At [1]Beth-le-aphrah roll yourself in the
dust.
11 [1]Go on your way, inhabitant of
[2]Shaphir, in [a]shameful nakedness.
The inhabitant of [3b]Zaanan does not
[4]escape.
The lamentation of [5]Beth-ezel: "He
will take from you its [6]support."
12 For the inhabitant of [1]Maroth
Becomes weak [a]waiting for good,
Because a calamity has come down
from the LORD
To the [b]gate of Jerusalem.

1:1 [a]2 Pet 1:21 [b]Jer 26:18 [c]2 Kin 15:5, 32-38; 2 Chr 27:1-9; Is 1:1; Hos 1:1 [d]2 Kin 16:1-20; 2 Chr 28:1-27; Is 7:1-12 [e]2 Kin 18:1-20; 2 Chr 29:1-31
2 [1]Lit *them* [2]Lit *its fullness* [3]Heb *YHWH*, usually rendered *LORD* [a]Jer 6:19; 22:29 [b]Is 50:7
3 [1]Or *land* [a]Is 26:21 [b]Amos 4:13
4 [a]Ps 97:5; Is 64:1, 2; Nah 1:5
5 [1]Lit *places* [a]Jer 2:19 [b]Is 7:9; Amos 8:14 [c]2 Chr 34:3, 4
6 [1]Lit *of the field* [a]2 Kin 19:25; Mic 3:12 [b]Jer 31:5; Amos 5:11 [c]Lam 4:1 [d]Ezek 13:14
7 [a]Deut 9:21; 2 Chr 34:7
7 [b]Deut 23:18; Is 23:17
8 [a]Is 32:11 [b]Is 13:21, 22
9 [1]Lit *wounds* [a]Is 3:26; Jer 30:12, 15 [b]2 Kin 18:13; Is 8:7, 8 [c]Mic 1:12
10 [1]I.e. house of dust [a]2 Sam 1:20
11 [1]I.e. Go into captivity [2]I.e. pleasantness [3]I.e. going out [4]Lit *go out* [5]I.e. house of removal [6]Lit *standing place* [a]Ezek 23:29 [b]Josh 15:37
12 [1]I.e. bitterness [a]Is 59:9-11; Jer 14:19 [b]Mic 1:9

1:1 *Micah.* Means "Who is like the LORD?" *Moresheth.* See Introduction: Author. *Jotham, Ahaz and Hezekiah.* See Introduction: Date. For background on these kings and the book of Micah see 2 Kin 15:32–16:20; 18–20. Isaiah, Hosea and Micah prophesied at roughly the same time (see Is 1:1; Hos 1:1). *which he saw.* In a prophetic vision (see Is 1:1 and note). *Samaria and Jerusalem.* The capitals of Israel and Judah respectively. The judgment predicted by Micah involved these nations and not just their capital cities.

1:2 *Hear.* The Hebrew for this word introduces prophetic addresses also in 3:1 and 6:1 (see also 3:9; 6:2). *peoples . . . earth.* All nations—an announcement that the day of the Lord is at hand, when God will call the nations to account. In view of that day Micah speaks in his prophecy of the impending judgments on Israel and Judah. *holy temple.* Heaven (see v. 3), as in Ps 11:4; Jon 2:7; Hab 2:20.

1:3 *the LORD is coming.* An OT expression describing the Lord's intervention in history (see Ps 18:9; 96:13; 144:5; Is 26:21; 31:4; 64:1–3). *high places.* May refer to mountains as well as to pagan shrines, since both are cited here (vv. 4–5). Cf. Amos 4:13.

1:4 *mountains will melt.* See Ps 97:5; Nah 1:5.

1:5 *Jacob.* Jacob was an alternate name for Israel (see Gen 32:28 and note; 35:10). *Israel.* Here (and in v. 13) specifically the northern kingdom, but Micah uses the name also for the southern kingdom (see 3:1,8–9; 5:1,3) or for the whole covenant people (see vv. 14–15; 2:12; 5:2; 6:2). *high place.* Pagan center of idolatry (see 2 Chr 28:25).

1:6–7 God is the speaker. This prophecy was fulfilled during Micah's lifetime when Assyria destroyed Samaria in 722–721 B.C. (2 Kin 17:6).

1:6 *into the valley.* Samaria was built on a hill (1 Kin 16:24).

1:7 *harlot's.* Prostitution is often an OT symbol for idolatry or spiritual unfaithfulness (Ex 34:15–16; Judg 2:17; Ezek 23:29–30). *earnings.* The wealth that Samaria had gained from her idolatry will be taken by the Assyrians and placed in their own temples to be used again in the worship of idols.

1:8 *this.* The coming destruction of Samaria. *barefoot.* A sign of mourning (2 Sam 15:30). It is possible that Micah actually walked stripped and barefoot through Jerusalem (cf. Is 20:2). *naked.* Clothed only in a loincloth.

1:9 *wound.* The judgment about to overtake Samaria. *incurable.* See Is 17:11 and note; Jer 30:12. *gate.* The Assyrian destruction of the northern kingdom will spread like a malignant disease to the gate of Jerusalem (v. 12). The gate was where the process of town government was carried on (see Gen 19:1 and note; Ruth 4:1–4).

1:10–15 Micah employs several plays on words (see NASB marg. on these verses). The towns mentioned lie in the Shephelah, i.e., the foothills (500–1,500 feet high) between the Mediterranean coastal plain and the mountains of Judah.

1:10 *Tell it not in Gath.* These words introduce a funeral lament over Judah. Micah did not want the pagan people in Gath to gloat over the downfall of God's people. Cf. 2 Sam 1:20. *roll yourself in the dust.* As a sign of grief over the coming catastrophe. See Is 47:1 and note.

1:11 *shameful nakedness.* A reference to their future condition as prisoners (see Is 20:4). *does not escape.* Because of the invasion, the people will not dare to go outside their houses.

1:12 *has come.* Micah foresees the future so clearly that to him it seems as though it has already come.

13 Harness the chariot to the team of
horses,
O inhabitant of [a]Lachish—
She was the beginning of sin
To the daughter of Zion—
Because in you were found
The [b]rebellious acts of Israel.
14 Therefore you will give parting [a]gifts
On behalf of Moresheth-gath;
The houses of [b]Achzib *will* become a
[c]deception
To the kings of Israel.
15 Moreover, I will bring on you
The one who takes possession,
O inhabitant of [1a]Mareshah.
The glory of Israel will enter
[b]Adullam.
16 Make yourself [a]bald and cut off your
hair,
Because of the children of your
delight;
Extend your baldness like the eagle,
For they will [b]go from you into exile.

Woe to Oppressors

2 Woe to those who [a]scheme iniquity,
Who work out evil on their beds!
[1b]When morning comes, they do it,
For it is in the [c]power of their hands.
2 They [a]covet fields and then [b]seize
them,
And houses, and take *them* away.
They [1c]rob a man and his house,
A man and his inheritance.
3 Therefore thus says the LORD,
"Behold, I am [a]planning against this
[b]family a calamity
From which you [c]cannot remove your
necks;
And you will not walk [d]haughtily,
For it will be an [e]evil time.
4 "On that day they will [a]take up against
you a [1]taunt
And [2b]utter a bitter lamentation *and*
say,
'We are completely [c]destroyed!
He exchanges the portion of my
people;
How He removes it from me!
To the apostate He [d]apportions our
fields.'
5 "Therefore you will have no one
[1a]stretching a measuring line
For you by lot in the assembly of the
LORD.

6 '[a]Do not [1]speak out,' *so* they [1]speak
out.
But if [2]they do [b]not [1]speak out
concerning these things,
[c]Reproaches will not be turned back.
7 "Is it being said, O house of Jacob:
'Is the Spirit of the LORD [a]impatient?
Are these His doings?'
Do not My words [b]do good
To the one [c]walking uprightly?
8 "[1]Recently My people have arisen as an
[a]enemy—
You [b]strip the [2]robe off the garment
From [c]unsuspecting passers-by,
From those returned from war.
9 "The women of My people you [a]evict,
Each *one* from her pleasant house.
From her children you take My
[b]splendor forever.
10 "Arise and go,
For this is no place [a]of rest
Because of the [b]uncleanness that
brings on destruction,
A painful destruction.

13 [a]Josh 10:3; 2 Kin 14:19; Is 36:2 [b]Mic 1:5
14 [a]2 Kin 16:8 [b]Josh 15:44 [c]Jer 15:18
15 [1]I.e. possession [a]Josh 15:44 [b]Josh 12:15; 15:35; 2 Sam 23:13
16 [a]Is 22:12 [b]2 Kin 17:6; Amos 7:11, 17
2:1 [1]Lit *In the light of the morning* [a]Ps 36:4; Is 32:7; Nah 1:11 [b]Hos 7:6, 7 [c]Gen 31:29; Deut 28:32; Prov 3:27
2 [1]Lit *oppress* [a]Jer 22:17; Amos 8:4 [b]Is 5:8 [c]1 Kin 21:1-15
3 [a]Deut 28:48; Jer 18:11 [b]Jer 8:3; Amos 3:1, 2 [c]Lam 1:14; 5:5 [d]Is 2:11, 12 [e]Amos 5:13
4 [1]Or *proverb* [2]Lit *lament* [a]Hab 2:6 [b]Jer 9:10, 17-21; Mic 1:8 [c]Is 6:11; 24:3; Jer 4:13 [d]Jer 6:12; 8:10
5 [1]Lit *casting* [a]Num 34:13, 16-29; Deut 32:8; Josh 18:4, 10
6 [1]Lit *flow* [2]I.e. God's prophets [a]Is 30:10; Amos 2:12; 7:16 [b]Is 29:10; Mic 3:6 [c]Mic 6:16
7 [a]Is 50:2; 59:1 [b]Ps 119:65, 68, 116; Jer 15:16 [c]Ps 15:2; 84:11
8 [1]Lit *And yesterday* [2]Or *ornaments* [a]Jer 12:8 [b]Mic 3:2, 3; 7:2, 3 [c]Ps 120:6, 7 **9** [a]Jer 10:20 [b]Ezek 39:21; Hab 2:14 **10** [a]Deut 12:9 [b]Ps 106:38

1:13 *Lachish.* One of the largest towns in Judah (see Is 36:2 and note). Later, Sennacherib was so proud of capturing it that he decorated his palace at Nineveh with a relief picturing his exploits. *Harness . . . the team.* In order to escape. Lachish sounds like the Hebrew for "to the team." *daughter of Zion.* A personification of Jerusalem and its inhabitants.
1:14 *parting gifts.* The Hebrew for these words is translated "dowry" in 1 Kin 9:16. Jerusalem must give up Moresheth-gath, as a father gives a "dowry" to his daughter when she marries. *Achzib.* Achzib means "deception." The word "deceptive" is used in Jer 15:18 to describe a brook that has dried up in summer. Like such a brook, the city of Achzib will cease to exist. *Israel.* See note on 1:5.
1:15 Micah again represents God as speaking, as in vv. 6–7. *glory of Israel.* Either God Himself (see 1 Sam 15:29) or Israel's leaders (more likely in this context). *will enter Adullam.* In judgment (if reference is to God), or in flight (if reference is to Israel's leaders).
1:16 Israel was taken into exile by the Assyrians in 722–721 B.C., and Judah by the Babylonians in 586.
2:1–5 Directed primarily against wealthy landowners who oppressed the poor.
2:1 *power of their hands.* The rich, oppressing classes continued to get rich at the expense of the poor because they controlled the power structures of their society.
2:2 *They covet.* In violation of the tenth commandment (see Ex 20:17 and note; Deut 5:21). *inheritance.* Land that was to be the permanent possession of a particular family. See Lev 25:10,13 (year of jubilee); Num 27:1–11; 36:1–12 (Zelophehad's daughters); 1 Kin 21:1–19 (Naboth's vineyard).
2:3 *Therefore.* Because of the sins of Israel's influential classes, calamity will strike. *calamity.* The impending exile.
2:4 *We . . . me.* The rich landowners, on whom God's judgment will fall. *He.* God. *apostate.* The treacherous Assyrians (see Is 33:1 and note) who will capture the land.
2:5 *you.* The oppressing classes—the rich landowners. *no one stretching a measuring line.* They will be cut off from all the promises of the covenant people.
2:6 *they.* The false prophets whose words were addressed to Micah.
2:7 Verses 6–7a are spoken by Micah; vv. 7b–13 are spoken by God.
2:10 *place of rest.* A place that could be regarded as one's own possession, where a people could settle in security (cf. Josh 1:13–15; 21:43–44; 22:4).

11 "If a man walking after wind and
[a]falsehood
Had told lies *and said,*
'I will [1]speak out to you concerning
[b]wine and liquor,'
He would be [2]spokesman to [c]this
people.

12 "I will surely [a]assemble all of you,
Jacob,
I will surely gather the [b]remnant of
Israel.
I will put them together like sheep in
the fold;
Like a flock in the midst of its
pasture
They will be noisy with men.
13 "The breaker goes up before them;
They break out, pass through the gate
and go out by it.
So their king goes on before them,
And the LORD at their head."

Rulers Denounced

3 And I said,
"[a]Hear now, heads of Jacob
And rulers of the house of Israel.
Is it not for you to [b]know justice?
2 "You who hate good and love evil,
Who [a]tear off their skin from them
And their flesh from their bones,
3 Who [a]eat the flesh of my people,
Strip off their skin from them,
Break their bones
And [b]chop *them* up as for the pot
And as meat in a kettle."
4 Then they will [a]cry out to the LORD,
But He will not answer them.
Instead, He will [b]hide His face from
them at that time
Because they have [c]practiced evil
deeds.

5 Thus says the LORD concerning the
prophets who [a]lead my people astray;
When they have *something* to bite
with their teeth,
They [b]cry, "Peace,"
But against him who puts nothing in
their mouths
They declare holy war.
6 Therefore *it will be* [a]night for you—
without vision,
And darkness for you—without
divination.
The [b]sun will go down on the prophets,
And the day will become dark over
them.
7 The seers will be [a]ashamed
And the [b]diviners will be embarrassed.
Indeed, they will all [c]cover *their*
[1]mouths
Because there is [d]no answer from God.
8 On the other hand [a]I am filled with
power—
With the Spirit of the LORD—
And with justice and courage
To [b]make known to Jacob his
rebellious act,
Even to Israel his sin.
9 Now hear this, [a]heads of the house of
Jacob
And rulers of the house of Israel,
Who [b]abhor justice
And twist everything that is straight,
10 Who [a]build Zion with bloodshed
And Jerusalem with violent injustice.
11 Her leaders pronounce [a]judgment for
a bribe,
Her [b]priests instruct for a price
And her prophets divine for money.
Yet they lean on the LORD saying,
"[c]Is not the LORD in our midst?
Calamity will not come upon us."
12 Therefore, on account of you
[a]Zion will be plowed as a field,
[b]Jerusalem will become a heap of ruins,
And the [c]mountain of the [1]temple *will
become* high places of a forest.

Peaceful Latter Days

4 And it will come about in the [a]last days
That the [b]mountain of the house of
the LORD
Will be established [1]as the chief of the
mountains.

11 [1]Lit *flow* [2]Lit *one who flows oracles* [a]Jer 5:31 [b]Is 28:7 [c]Is 30:10, 11
12 [a]Mic 4:6, 7 [b]Mic 5:7, 8; 7:18
3:1 [a]Is 1:10; Mic 3:9 [b]Ps 82:1-5; Jer 5:5
2 [a]Ps 53:4; Ezek 22:27; Mic 2:8; 7:2, 3
3 [a]Ps 14:4; 27:2; Zeph 3:3 [b]Ezek 11:3, 6, 7
4 [a]Ps 18:41; Prov 1:28; Is 1:15; Jer 11:11 [b]Deut 31:17; Is 59:2 [c]Is 3:11; Mic 7:13
5 [a]Is 3:12; 9:15, 16; Jer 14:14, 15 [b]Jer 6:14
6 [a]Is 8:20-22; 29:10-12 [b]Is 59:10
7 [1]Lit *mustache* [a]Zech 13:4 [b]Is 44:25; 47:12-14 [c]Mic 7:16 [d]1 Sam 28:6; Mic 3:4
8 [a]Is 61:1, 2; Jer 1:18 [b]Is 58:1
9 [a]Mic 1:1 [b]Ps 58:1, 2; Is 1:23
10 [a]Jer 22:13, 17; Hab 2:12
11 [a]Is 1:23; Mic 7:3 [b]Jer 6:13 [c]Is 48:2
12 [1]Lit *house* [a]Jer 26:18 [b]Ps 79:1; Jer 9:11 [c]Mic 4:1
4:1 [1]Lit *on* [a]Is 2:2-4; Dan 2:28; 10:14; Hos 3:5 [b]Ezek 43:12; Mic 3:12; Zech 8:3

2:11 Anyone who promised greater affluence would gain a hearing.
2:12–13 Although Israel will be carried into captivity, a remnant will return (see note on Is 1:9).
2:12 *Jacob . . . Israel.* Here perhaps the entire nation, north and south. Contrast 1:5; 3:1,9–10.
3:1–12 Verses 1–4 deal with the sins of the leaders of Israel, vv. 5–7 with the false prophets and vv. 9–12 with the leaders, priests and prophets.
3:1 *Jacob . . . Israel.* Both names refer to Judah here (see vv. 9–10).
3:2–3 *tear off their skin . . . as meat in a kettle.* A series of figures of speech describing the cruel way the leaders treat the people.
3:2 *hate good and love evil.* Contrast Amos 5:15; Rom 12:9.
3:4 *they.* The leaders. *He will not answer.* See v. 7. *hide His face.* See Deut 31:17; Is 1:15 and note. Disobedience leads to separation from God.
3:5 *cry "Peace."* The false prophets predicted peace for Judah while Micah predicted destruction and captivity (see v. 12; 4:10). See also Jer 6:13–14; 8:10–11.
3:7 *seers.* An older term for "prophets" (see note on 1 Sam 9:9).
3:8 One of the chief purposes of Micah was to declare to Judah its sin. *filled . . . With the Spirit.* The prophets were Spirit-filled messengers (see Is 48:16).
3:11 *for a bribe.* See Is 1:23; 5:23.
3:12 The destruction of Jerusalem occurred in 586 B.C. This verse was quoted a century later in Jer 26:18. Jer 26:19 indicates that Micah's preaching may have been instrumental in the revival under King Hezekiah (see 2 Kin 18:1–6; 2 Chr 29–31).
4:1–3 See notes on Is 2:2–4, a passage that is almost the same as these verses.

It will be raised above the hills,
And the [c]peoples will stream to it.
2 [a]Many nations will come and say,
"[b]Come and let us go up to the mountain of the LORD
And to the house of the God of Jacob,
That [c]He may teach us about His ways
And that we may walk in His paths."
For [d]from Zion will go forth the law,
Even the word of the LORD from Jerusalem.
3 And He will [a]judge between many peoples
And render decisions for mighty, [1]distant nations.
Then they will hammer their swords [b]into plowshares
And their spears into pruning hooks;
Nation will not lift up sword against nation,
And never again will they [2]train for war.
4 Each of them will [a]sit under his vine
And under his fig tree,
With [b]no one to make *them* afraid,
For the [c]mouth of the LORD of hosts has spoken.
5 Though all the peoples walk
Each in the [a]name of his god,
As for us, [b]we will walk
In the name of the [c]LORD our God forever and ever.

6 "In that day," declares the LORD,
"I will assemble the [a]lame
And [b]gather the outcasts,
Even those whom I have afflicted.
7 "I will make the lame a [a]remnant
And the outcasts a strong nation,
And the [b]LORD will reign over them in Mount Zion
From now on and forever.
8 "As for you, [1][a]tower of the flock,
[2]Hill of the daughter of Zion,
To you it will come—
Even the [b]former dominion will come,
The kingdom of the daughter of Jerusalem.

9 "Now, why do you [a]cry out loudly?
Is there no king among you,
Or has your [b]counselor perished,
That agony has gripped you like a woman in childbirth?
10 "[a]Writhe and labor to give birth,
Daughter of Zion,
Like a woman in childbirth;
For now you will [b]go out of the city,
Dwell in the field,
And go to Babylon.
[c]There you will be rescued;
[d]There the LORD will redeem you
From the hand of your enemies.
11 "And now [a]many nations have been assembled against you
Who say, 'Let her be polluted,
And let our eyes [1]gloat over Zion.'
12 "But they do not [a]know the thoughts of the LORD,
And they do not understand His purpose;
For He has gathered them like sheaves to the threshing floor.
13 "Arise and [a]thresh, daughter of Zion,
For your horn I will make iron
And your hoofs I will make bronze,
That you may [b]pulverize many peoples,
That you may [c]devote to the LORD their unjust gain
And their wealth to the Lord of all the earth.

Birth of the King in Bethlehem

5 "[1]Now muster yourselves in troops, daughter of troops;
[2]They have laid siege against us;
With a rod they will [a]smite the judge of Israel on the cheek.
2 "[1]But as for [a]you, Bethlehem Ephrathah,
Too little to be among the clans of Judah,
From [b]you One will go forth for Me to be [c]ruler in Israel.
[2]His goings forth are [d]from long ago,
From the days of eternity."
3 Therefore He will [a]give them *up* until the time
When she [b]who is in labor has borne a child.

4:1 [c]Ps 22:27; 86:9; Jer 3:17
2 [a]Zech 2:11; 14:16 [b]Is 2:3; Jer 31:6 [c]Ps 25:8, 9, 12; Is 54:13 [d]Is 42:1-4; Zech 14:8, 9
3 [1]Lit *at a distance* [2]Lit *learn* [a]Is 2:4; 11:3-5 [b]Joel 3:10
4 [a]1 Kin 4:25; Zech 3:10 [b]Lev 26:6; Jer 30:10 [c]Is 1:20; 40:5
5 [a]2 Kin 17:29 [b]Zech 10:12 [c]Josh 24:15; Is 26:8, 13
6 [a]Zeph 3:19 [b]Ps 147:2; Ezek 34:13, 16; 37:21
7 [a]Mic 5:7, 8; 7:18 [b]Is 24:23
8 [1]Heb *Migdal-eder* [2]Heb *Ophel of* [a]Ps 48:3, 12; 61:3; Mic 2:12 [b]Is 1:26; Zech 9:10
9 [a]Jer 8:19
9 [b]Is 3:1-3
10 [a]Mic 5:3 [b]2 Kin 20:18; Hos 2:14 [c]Is 43:14; 45:13; Mic 7:8-12 [d]Is 48:20; 52:9-12
11 [1]Lit *look on* [a]Is 5:25-30; 17:12-14
12 [a]Ps 147:19, 20
13 [a]Is 41:15 [b]Jer 51:20-23 [c]Is 60:9
5:1 [1]Ch 4:14 in Heb [2]Lit *He has* [a]1 Kin 22:24; Job 16:10; Lam 3:30
2 [1]Ch 5:1 in Heb [2]Or *His appearances are from long ago, from days of old* [a]Gen 35:19; 48:7; Ruth 4:11; Matt 2:6 [b]Is 11:1; Luke 2:4; John 7:42 [c]Jer 30:21; Zech 9:9 [d]Ps 102:25; Prov 8:22, 23
3 [a]Hos 11:8; Mic 4:10; 7:13 [b]Mic 4:9, 10

4:4 *vine And . . . fig tree.* A reference to the peaceful security of the kingdom of God. See 1 Kin 4:25; Zech 3:10. *no one to make them afraid.* See Zeph 3:13. Fear will be a thing of the past.
4:5 *walk In the name of the LORD.* Confess, love, obey and rely on the Lord. Cf. Zech 10:12.
4:6 *In that day.* The Messianic period (see v. 1; see also note on Is 2:11,17,20).
4:7 *remnant.* The people of God (see 2:12; see also note on Is 1:9).
4:8 *tower of the flock.* The capital city of David, the shepherd-king. *former dominion.* The kingdom of David will be restored under the Messiah.
4:9–13 In vv. 9–10 Micah foresees the collapse of the monarchy and the impending exile in 586 B.C. as well as the restoration beginning in 538. Verses 11–13 are a prophecy of judgment against the gloating enemies of Jerusalem.
5:1 Jerusalem will be besieged, and her kings will be seized and taken to Babylon (the last king, Zedekiah, was blinded; see 2 Kin 25:7).
5:2 In contrast to the dire prediction of v. 1, Micah shifts to a positive note. *Ephrathah.* The region in which Bethlehem was located (see Ruth 1:2; 4:11; 1 Sam 17:12). *ruler.* Ultimately Christ, who will rule (see note on 4:8) for God the Father. *goings forth . . . long ago.* His beginnings were much earlier than His human birth (see John 8:58). *From . . . eternity.* Within history (cf. 2 Sam 7:12–16; Is 9:6–7; Amos 9:11), and even from eternity.
5:3 *He will give them up.* Until the Messiah is born and begins His rule. *Israel.* See note on 1:5.

Then the [c]remainder of His brethren
Will return to the sons of Israel.
4 And He will arise and [a]shepherd *His flock*
In the strength of the LORD,
In the majesty of the name of the LORD
His God.
And they will [1]remain,
Because [2]at that time He will be great
To the [b]ends of the earth.
5 This One [a]will be *our* peace.

When the [b]Assyrian invades our land,
When he tramples on our [1]citadels,
Then we will raise against him
Seven shepherds and eight leaders of
men.
6 They will [a]shepherd the land of
Assyria with the sword,
The land of [b]Nimrod at its entrances;
And He will [c]deliver *us* from the
Assyrian
When he attacks our land
And when he tramples our territory.

7 Then the [a]remnant of Jacob
Will be among many peoples
Like [b]dew from the LORD,
Like [c]showers on vegetation
Which do not wait for man
Or delay for the sons of men.
8 The remnant of Jacob
Will be among the nations,
Among many peoples
[a]Like a lion among the beasts of the
forest,
Like a young lion among flocks of
sheep,
Which, if he passes through,
[b]Tramples down and [c]tears,
And there is [d]none to rescue.
9 Your hand will be [a]lifted up against
your adversaries,
And all your enemies will be cut off.

10 "It will be in that day," declares the
LORD,
"[a]That I will cut off your [b]horses from
among you
And destroy your chariots.
11 "I will also cut off the [a]cities of your
land
And tear down all your [b]fortifications.
12 "I will cut off [a]sorceries from your hand,
And you will have fortune-tellers no
more.
13 "[a]I will cut off your carved images
And your *sacred* pillars from among
you,
So that you will no longer bow down
To the work of your hands.
14 "I will root out your [1a]Asherim from
among you
And destroy your cities.
15 "And I will [a]execute vengeance in
anger and wrath
On the nations which have not
obeyed."

God's Indictment of His People

6 Hear now what the LORD is saying,
"Arise, plead your case [1]before the
mountains,
And let the hills hear your voice.
2 "Listen, you mountains, to the
indictment of the LORD,
And you enduring [a]foundations of the
earth,
Because the [b]LORD has a case against
His people;
Even with Israel He will dispute.
3 "[a]My people, [b]what have I done to you,
And [c]how have I wearied you?
Answer Me.
4 "Indeed, I [a]brought you up from the
land of Egypt
And [b]ransomed you from the house of
slavery,
And I sent before you [c]Moses, Aaron
and [d]Miriam.
5 "My people, remember now
What [a]Balak king of Moab counseled
And what Balaam son of Beor
answered him,

3 [c]Is 10:20-22; Mic 5:7, 8
4 [1]Or *live* in safety [2]Lit *now* [a]Is 40:11; 49:9; Ezek 34:13-15, 23, 24; Mic 7:14 [b]Is 45:22; 52:10
5 [1]Or *palaces* [a]Is 9:6; Luke 2:14; Eph 2:14; Col 1:20 [b]Is 8:7, 8; 10:24-27
6 [a]Nah 2:11-13; Zeph 2:13 [b]Gen 10:8-11 [c]Is 14:25; 37:36, 37
7 [a]Mic 2:12; 4:7; 5:3; 7:18 [b]Deut 32:2; Ps 110:3; Hos 14:5 [c]Ps 72:6; Is 44:3
8 [a]Gen 49:9; Num 24:9 [b]Ps 44:5; Is 41:15, 16; Mic 4:13; Zech 10:5 [c]Hos 5:14 [d]Ps 50:22
9 [a]Ps 10:12; 21:8; Is 26:11
10 [a]Zech 9:10 [b]Deut 17:16; Is 2:7; Hos 14:3
11 [a]Is 1:7; 6:11 [b]Is 2:12-17; Hos 10:14; Amos 5:9
12 [a]Deut 18:10-12; Is 2:6; 8:19
13 [a]Is 2:18; 17:8; Ezek 6:9
14 [1]I.e. wooden symbols of a female deity [a]Ex 34:13; Is 17:8; 27:9
15 [a]Is 1:24; 65:12
6:1 [1]Lit *with*
2 [a]2 Sam 22:16; Ps 104:5 [b]Is 1:18; Hos 4:1; 12:2
3 [a]Ps 50:7 [b]Jer 2:5 [c]Is 43:22, 23
4 [a]Ex 12:51; 20:2 [b]Deut 7:8 [c]Ex 4:10-16; Ps 77:20 [d]Ex 15:20
5 [a]Num 22:5, 6

5:4 *strength . . . majesty.* The Messiah will shepherd and rule in the strength and majesty of God the Father.
5:5 *our peace.* Jesus is "our peace" (Eph 2:14). In addition to freedom from war, the Hebrew word for "peace" also connotes prosperity in the OT. See notes on Is 9:6 ("Prince of Peace"); Luke 2:14. *Assyrian.* Symbolic of all the enemies of God's people in every age. See Is 11:11; Zech 10:10–11. *we.* The people of God. *Seven . . . eight.* A figurative way of saying "many" (see note on Job 5:19).
5:6 *land of Nimrod.* Assyria. See Gen 10:8–11. *He.* The ruler of v. 2.
5:8 *lion.* Like the previous simile (v. 7) this pictures the inevitable progress of the people of God toward triumph over their enemies (v. 9).
5:10–14 In the Messianic era the people of God will not depend on weapons of war or pagan idols. The successes of His people are always achieved by dependence on Him.
6:1–16 This chapter depicts a courtroom scene in which the Lord lodges a legal complaint against Israel. In vv. 1–2 the Lord summons the people to listen to His accusation and to prepare their defense against the charges that follow in vv. 9–16. The Lord speaks in vv. 3–5, poignantly reminding the people of His gracious acts in their behalf. In vv. 6–7 Israel is speaking, and in v. 8 Micah responds directly to the nation, answering the questions of vv. 6–7. God charges the people with specific wrongs in vv. 9–16.
6:1–2 *mountains . . . foundations of the earth.* Inanimate objects were called on as third-party witnesses because of their enduring nature and because they were witnesses to His covenant (see Deut 32:1; Josh 24:27; Is 1:2 and note).
6:2 *Israel.* Primarily Judah here.
6:3 *My people.* Indicative of a tender rebuke (see also v. 5).
6:5 *Balak . . . Balaam.* See Num 22–24. *Shittim to Gilgal.* See Josh 3:1; 4:19.

And from [b]Shittim to [c]Gilgal,
So [1]that you might know the
[d]righteous acts of the LORD."

What God Requires of Man

6 [a]With what shall I come to the LORD
And bow myself before the God on
high?
Shall I come to Him with [b]burnt
offerings,
With yearling calves?
7 Does the LORD take delight in
[a]thousands of rams,
In ten thousand rivers of oil?
Shall I present my [b]firstborn *for* my
rebellious acts,
The fruit of my body for the sin of my
soul?
8 He has [a]told you, O man, what is
good;
And [b]what does the LORD require of
you
But to [c]do justice, to [d]love [1]kindness,
And to walk [2e]humbly with your God?

9 The voice of the LORD will call to the
city—
And it is sound wisdom to fear Your
name:
"Hear, O tribe. Who has appointed [1]its
time?
10 "Is there yet a man in the wicked house,
Along with treasures of [a]wickedness
And a [1b]short measure *that is* cursed?
11 "Can I justify wicked [a]scales
And a bag of deceptive weights?
12 "For the rich men of *the* [1]city are full of
[a]violence,
Her residents speak [b]lies,
And their [c]tongue is deceitful in their
mouth.
13 "So also I will make *you* [a]sick, striking
you down,
[b]Desolating *you* because of your sins.
14 "You will eat, but you will [a]not be
satisfied,
And your [1]vileness will be in your
midst.
You will *try to* remove *for safekeeping,*
But you will [b]not preserve *anything,*
And what you do preserve I will give
to the sword.
15 "You will sow but you will [a]not reap.
You will tread the olive but will not
anoint yourself with oil;
And the grapes, but you will [b]not
drink wine.
16 "The statutes of [a]Omri
And all the works of the house of
[b]Ahab are observed;
And in their devices you [c]walk.
Therefore I will give you up for
[d]destruction
And [1]your inhabitants for [e]derision,
And you will bear the [f]reproach of My
people."

The Prophet Acknowledges

7 Woe is me! For I am
Like the fruit pickers, like the [a]grape
gatherers.
There is not a cluster of grapes to eat,
Or a [b]first-ripe fig *which* [1]I crave.
2 The [1]godly person has [a]perished from
the land,
And there is no upright *person* among
men.
All of them lie in wait for
[b]bloodshed;
Each of them hunts the other with a
[c]net.
3 Concerning evil, both hands do it
[a]well.
The prince asks, also the judge, for a
[b]bribe,
And a great man speaks the desire of
his soul;
So they weave it together.
4 The best of them is like a [a]briar,
The most upright like a [b]thorn hedge.
The day when you post your
watchmen,
Your [c]punishment will come.
Then their [d]confusion will occur.
5 Do not [a]trust in a neighbor;
Do not have confidence in a friend.
From her who lies in your bosom
Guard [1]your lips.
6 For [a]son treats father contemptuously,
Daughter rises up against her mother,
Daughter-in-law against her mother-
in-law;
[b]A man's enemies are the men of his
own household.

5 [1]Lit *to know* [b]Num 25:1; Josh 2:1; 3:1 [c]Josh 4:19; 5:9, 10 [d]1 Sam 12:7; Is 1:27
6 [a]Ps 40:6-8 [b]Ps 51:16, 17
7 [a]Ps 50:9; Is 1:1; 40:16 [b]Lev 18:21; 20:1-5; 2 Kin 16:3; Jer 7:31
8 [1]Or *loyalty* [2]Or *circumspectly* [a]Deut 30:15 [b]Deut 10:12 [c]Is 56:1; Jer 22:3 [d]Hos 6:6 [e]Is 57:15; 66:2
9 [1]Lit *it*
10 [1]Lit *shrunken ephah* [a]Jer 5:26, 27; Amos 3:10 [b]Ezek 45:9, 10; Amos 8:5
11 [a]Lev 19:36; Hos 12:7
12 [1]Lit *her* [a]Is 1:23; 5:7; Amos 6:3, 4; Mic 2:1, 2 [b]Jer 9:2-6, 8; Hos 7:13; Amos 2:4 [c]Is 3:8
13 [a]Mic 1:9 [b]Is 1:7; 6:11
14 [1]Or possibly *garbage* or *excreta* [a]Is 9:20 [b]Is 30:6
15 [a]Deut 28:38-40; Jer 12:13 [b]Amos 5:11; Zeph 1:13
16 [1]Lit *her* [a]1 Kin 16:25, 26 [b]1 Kin 16:29-33 [c]Jer 7:24 [d]Jer 18:16; Mic 6:13 [e]Jer 19:8; 25:9, 18; 29:18 [f]Ps 44:13; Jer 51:51; Hos 12:14
7:1 [1]Lit *my soul* [a]Is 24:13 [b]Is 28:4; Hos 9:10
2 [1]Or *loyal* [a]Is 57:1 [b]Is 59:7; Mic 3:10 [c]Jer 5:26; Hos 5:1
3 [a]Prov 4:16, 17 [b]Amos 5:12; Mic 3:11
4 [a]Ezek 2:6; 28:24 [b]Nah 1:10 [c]Is 10:3; Hos 9:7 [d]Is 22:5
5 [1]Lit *openings of your mouth* [a]Jer 9:4
6 [a]Matt 10:21, 35; Luke 12:53 [b]Matt 10:36

6:6 The same thought is expressed in 1 Sam 15:22; Ps 51:16; Hos 6:6; Is 1:11–15 (see note there). Micah does not deny the desirability of sacrifices but shows that it does no good to offer them without obedience.
6:8 *man.* The use of the singular makes the accusation personal, though Micah is speaking to all Israel (see also Deut 10:12–13). *do justice . . . love kindness.* The kind of obedience God expects from His covenant people.
6:9 *city.* Jerusalem.
6:10 *measure.* About half a bushel.
6:11 See Prov 11:1; 20:23; Hos 12:7; Amos 8:5.
6:12 *Her.* Jerusalem's.
6:13 *So.* See note on 2:3.
6:16 *Omri . . . Ahab.* 1 Kin 16:25,30 says that they did more evil than all the kings who preceded them.
7:1–20 The speakers in this chapter are Micah (vv. 1–7), Zion (vv. 8–10), Micah (vv. 11–13), perhaps Zion (v. 14), God (v. 15), Micah (vv. 16–20). The chapter begins on a note of gloom but ends with a statement of hope.
7:1–2 Looking for the godly is like looking for summer fruit when the harvest has ended (see also Jer 8:20).
7:4 *day when . . . your watchmen.* The day of judgment that the prophets warned about (see Jer 6:17; Ezek 3:17–21).
7:6 The family unit was disintegrating.

God Is the Source of Salvation and Light

7 But as for me, I will [a]watch
expectantly for the LORD;
I will [b]wait for the God of my
salvation.
My [c]God will hear me.
8 [a]Do not rejoice over me, O [b]my enemy.
Though I fall I will [c]rise;
Though I dwell in darkness, the LORD
is a [d]light for me.

9 I will bear the indignation of the LORD
Because I have sinned against Him,
Until He [a]pleads my case and executes
justice for me.
He will bring me out to the [b]light,
And I will see His [1c]righteousness.
10 Then my enemy will see,
And shame will cover her who [a]said
to me,
"Where is the LORD your God?"
My eyes will look on her;
[1]At that time she will [2]be [b]trampled
down
Like mire of the streets.
11 *It will be* a day for [a]building your walls.
On that day will your boundary be
extended.
12 It *will be* a day when [1]they will [a]come
to you
From Assyria and the cities of Egypt,
From Egypt even to the [2]Euphrates,
Even from sea to sea and mountain to
mountain.
13 And the earth will become [a]desolate
because of her inhabitants,
On account of the [b]fruit of their deeds.

14 [a]Shepherd Your people with Your
[b]scepter,
The flock of Your [1]possession
Which dwells by itself in the
woodland,
In the midst of [2]a fruitful field.
Let them feed in [c]Bashan and Gilead
[d]As in the days of old.
15 "As in the days when you came out
from the land of Egypt,
I will show [1a]you miracles."
16 Nations [a]will see and be ashamed
Of all their might.
They will [b]put *their* hand on *their*
mouth,
Their ears will be deaf.
17 They will [a]lick the dust like a serpent,
Like [b]reptiles of the earth.
They will come [c]trembling out of their
[1]fortresses;
To the LORD our God they will come in
[d]dread
And they will be afraid before You.
18 Who is a God like You, who [a]pardons
iniquity
And passes over the rebellious act of
the [b]remnant of His [1]possession?
He does not [c]retain His anger forever,
Because He [d]delights in [2]unchanging
love.
19 He will again have compassion on us;
[a]He will tread our iniquities under
foot.
Yes, You will [b]cast all [1]their sins
Into the depths of the sea.
20 You will give [1a]truth to Jacob
And [2]unchanging love to Abraham,
Which You [b]swore to our forefathers
From the days of old.

7 [a]Hab 2:1 [b]Ps 130:5; Is 25:9 [c]Ps 4:3
8 [a]Prov 24:17; Obad 12 [b]Mic 7:10 [c]Amos 9:11 [d]Is 9:2
9 [1]I.e. right dealing [a]Jer 50:34 [b]Ps 37:6; Is 42:7, 16 [c]Is 46:13; 56:1
10 [1]Lit *Now* [2]Lit *become a trampled* place [a]Joel 2:17 [b]Is 51:23; Zech 10:5
11 [a]Is 54:11; Amos 9:11
12 [1]Lit *he* [2]Lit *River* [a]Is 19:23-25; 60:4, 9
13 [a]Jer 25:11; Mic 6:13 [b]Is 3:10, 11; Mic 3:4
14 [a]Ps 95:7; Is 40:11; 49:10; Mic 5:4 [b]Lev 27:32; Ps 23:4
14 [1]Or *inheritance* [2]Or *Carmel* [c]Jer 50:19 [d]Amos 9:11
15 [1]Lit *him* [a]Ex 3:20; 34:10; Ps 78:12
16 [a]Is 26:11 [b]Mic 3:7
17 [1]Lit *fastnesses* [a]Ps 72:9; Is 49:23 [b]Deut 32:24 [c]Ps 18:45 [d]Is 25:3; 59:19
18 [1]Or *inheritance* [2]Or *lovingkindness* [a]Ex 34:7, 9; Is 43:25 [b]Mic 2:12; 4:7; 5:7, 8 [c]Ps 103:8, 9, 13 [d]Jer 32:41
19 [1]Several ancient versions read *our* [a]Jer 50:20 [b]Is 38:17; 43:25; Jer 31:34 **20** [1]Or *faithfulness* [2]Or *lovingkindness* [a]Gen 24:27; 32:10 [b]Deut 7:8, 12

7:8 *me.* Zion. *my enemy.* Other nations. *Though I fall.* Micah foresees the destruction of Zion in 586 B.C.

7:14 *possession.* Israel (see also v. 18; Ps 94:14).

7:15–17 It is possible that these verses constitute a prayer that God will show His wonders again as in the exodus, that the nations will see and be ashamed, and that they will turn to the Lord in fear.

7:16 When the nations see God's power at the Messiah's coming, they will be amazed.

7:17 *lick the dust like a serpent.* A picture of defeat.

7:18–20 The conclusion to the whole book, not just to ch. 7.

7:18 *Who is a God like You . . . ?* Perhaps a pun on Micah's name (see note on 1:1). Cf. Ex 15:11; Ps 89:6.

7:19 *sins Into the depths of the sea.* See note on Is 38:17.

7:20 *Jacob . . . Abraham.* God had sworn to Abraham (Gen 22:17) and Jacob (Gen 28:14) that their descendants would be as numerous as the dust of the earth and the sand on the seashore, and He had promised Abraham that he would be the father of many nations (Gen 17:5; cf. Luke 1:54–55). All believers are ultimately included in this promise (Rom 4; Gal 3:6–29; Heb 11:12).

Nahum

INTRODUCTION

Author

The book contains the "vision of Nahum" (1:1), whose name means "comfort" and is related to the name Nehemiah, meaning "The LORD comforts" or "comfort of the LORD." (Nineveh's fall, which is Nahum's theme, would bring comfort to Judah.) Nothing is known about him except his hometown (Elkosh), and even its general location is uncertain.

Date

In 3:8–10 the author speaks of the fall of Thebes, which happened in 663 B.C., as already past. In all three chapters Nahum prophesied Nineveh's fall, which was fulfilled in 612. Nahum therefore uttered this oracle between 663 and 612, perhaps near the end of this period since he represents the fall of Nineveh as imminent (2:1; 3:14,19). This would place him during the reign of Josiah and make him a contemporary of Zephaniah and the young Jeremiah.

Background

Assyria (represented by Nineveh, 1:1) had already destroyed Samaria (722–721 B.C.), resulting in the captivity of the northern kingdom of Israel, and posed a present threat to Judah. The Assyrians were brutally cruel, their kings often being depicted as gloating over the gruesome punishments inflicted on conquered peoples. They conducted their wars with shocking ferocity, uprooted whole populations as state policy and deported them to other parts of their empire. The leaders of conquered cities were tortured and horribly mutilated before being executed (see note on 3:3). No wonder the dread of Assyria fell on all her neighbors!

About 700 B.C. King Sennacherib made Nineveh the capital of the Assyrian empire, and it remained the capital until it was destroyed in 612. Jonah had announced its destruction earlier (Jon 3:4), but the people repented and the destruction was temporarily averted. Not long after that, however, Nineveh reverted to its extreme wickedness, brutality and pride. The brutality reached its peak under Ashurbanipal (669–627), the last great ruler of the Assyrian empire. After his death, Assyria's influence and power waned rapidly until 612, when Nineveh was overthrown (see notes on 1:14; 2:1). (Further historical information is given in notes throughout the book.)

Recipients

Some words are addressed to Judah (see 1:12–13,15), but most are addressed to Nineveh (see 1:11,14; 2:1,13; 3:5–17,19) or its king (3:18). The book, however, was meant for Judahite readers.

Literary Style

The contents are primarily judicial (judgment oracles), with appropriate descriptions and vocabulary, as well as intense moods, sights and sounds. The language is poetic, with frequent use of metaphors and similes, vivid word pictures, repetition and many short—often staccato—phrases (see, e.g., 3:2–3). Rhetorical questions punctuate the flow of thought, which has a marked stress on moral indignation toward injustice.

Theological Themes

The focal point of the entire book is the Lord's judgment on Nineveh for her oppression, cruelty, idolatry and wickedness. The book ends with the destruction of the city.

According to Rom 11:22, God is not only kind but also stern. In Nahum, God is not only "slow to anger" (1:3) and "a stronghold . . . and He knows those who take refuge in Him" (1:7), but also one who "will by no

means leave the guilty unpunished" (1:3). God's righteous and just kingdom will ultimately triumph, for kingdoms built on wickedness and tyranny must eventually fall, as Assyria did.

In addition, Nahum declares the universal sovereignty of God. God is Lord of history and of all nations; as such He controls their destinies.

Outline

I. Title (1:1)

II. Nineveh's Judge (1:2–15)

- A. The Lord's Kindness and Sternness (1:2–8)
- B. Nineveh's Overthrow and Judah's Joy (1:9–15)

III. Nineveh's Judgment (ch. 2)

- A. Nineveh Besieged (2:1–10)
- B. Nineveh's Desolation Contrasted with Her Former Glory (2:11–13)

IV. Nineveh's Total Destruction (ch. 3)

- A. Nineveh's Sins (3:1–4)
- B. Nineveh's Doom (3:5–19)

God Is Awesome

1 The [1a]oracle of [b]Nineveh. The book of
the vision of Nahum the Elkoshite.
2 A [a]jealous and avenging God is the
LORD;
The LORD is [b]avenging and [1]wrathful.
The LORD takes [c]vengeance on His
adversaries,
And He reserves wrath for His
enemies.
3 The LORD is [a]slow to anger and great
in power,
And the LORD will by no means leave
the guilty unpunished.
In [b]whirlwind and storm is His way,
And [c]clouds are the dust beneath His
feet.
4 He [a]rebukes the sea and makes it dry;
He dries up all the rivers.
[b]Bashan and Carmel wither;
The blossoms of Lebanon wither.
5 Mountains [a]quake because of Him
And the hills [b]dissolve;
Indeed the earth is [c]upheaved by His
presence,
The [d]world and all the inhabitants in
it.
6 [a]Who can stand before His
indignation?
Who can endure the [b]burning of His
anger?
His [c]wrath is poured out like fire
And the [d]rocks are broken up by Him.
7 The LORD is [a]good,
A stronghold in the day of trouble,
And [b]He knows those who take refuge
in Him.
8 But with an [a]overflowing flood
He will make a complete end of [1]its
site,
And will pursue His enemies into
[b]darkness.

9 Whatever you [a]devise against the LORD,
He will make a [b]complete end of it.
Distress will not rise up twice.
10 Like tangled [a]thorns,
And like those who are [b]drunken with
their drink,
They are [c]consumed
As stubble completely withered.
11 From you has gone forth
One who [a]plotted evil against the LORD,
A [1b]wicked counselor.
12 Thus says the LORD,
"Though they are at full *strength* and
likewise many,
Even so, they will be [a]cut off and pass
away.
Though I have afflicted you,
I will afflict you [b]no longer.
13 "So now, I will [a]break his yoke bar
from upon you,
And I will tear off your shackles."

14 The LORD has issued a command
concerning [1]you:
"[2]Your name will [a]no longer be
perpetuated.
I will cut off [3b]idol and [4]image
From the house of your gods.
I will prepare your [c]grave,
For you are contemptible."

15 [1]Behold, [a]on the mountains the feet of
him who brings good news,
Who announces peace!

1:1 [1]Or *burden* [a]Is 13:1; 19:1; Jer 23:33, 34; Hab 1:1; Zech 9:1; Mal 1:1 [b]2 Kin 19:36; Jon 1:2; Nah 2:8; Zeph 2:13 **2** [1]Lit *a possessor of wrath* [a]Ex 20:5; Josh 24:19 [b]Deut 32:35, 41 [c]Ps 94:1 **3** [a]Ex 34:6, 7; Neh 9:17; Ps 103:8 [b]Ex 19:16; Is 29:6 [c]Ps 104:3; Is 19:1 **4** [a]Josh 3:15, 16; Ps 106:9; Is 50:2; Matt 8:26 [b]Is 33:9 **5** [a]Ex 19:18; 2 Sam 22:8; Ps 18:7 [b]Mic 1:4 [c]Is 24:1, 20 [d]Ps 98:7 **6** [a]Jer 10:10; Mal 3:2 [b]Is 13:13 [c]Is 66:15 [d]1 Kin 19:11 **7** [a]Ps 25:8; 37:39, 40; Jer 33:11 [b]Ps 1:6; John 10:14; 2 Tim 2:19 **8** [1]I.e. Nineveh's [a]Is 28:2, 17f; Amos 8:8

8 [b]Is 13:9, 10 **9** [a]Ps 2:1; Nah 1:11 [b]Is 28:22 **10** [a]2 Sam 23:6; Mic 7:4 [b]Is 56:12; Nah 3:11 [c]Is 5:24; 10:17; Mal 4:1 **11** [1]Or *worthless;* Heb *Belial* [a]Is 10:7-11; Nah 1:9 [b]Ezek 11:2 **12** [a]Is 10:16-19, 33, 34 [b]Lam 3:31, 32 **13** [a]Is 9:4; 10:27; Jer 2:20 **14** [1]I.e. the king of Nineveh [2]Lit *No more of your name will be sown* [3]Or *a graven image* [4]Lit *cast* metal *image* [a]Job 18:17; Ps 109:13; Is 14:22 [b]Is 46:1, 2; Mic 5:13, 14 [c]Ezek 32:22, 23 **15** [1]Ch 2:1 in Heb [a]Is 40:9; 52:7; Rom 10:15

1:1 The title of the book. *oracle.* See note on Is 13:1. *Nineveh.* See Introduction: Background; see also notes on Jon 1:2; 3:3. Here the capital city stands for the entire Assyrian empire. *vision.* See note on Is 1:1. *Nahum the Elkoshite.* See Introduction: Author.
1:2–3 The covenant name Yahweh ("the LORD") is emphasized.
1:2 *jealous.* See note on Ex 20:5. *avenging . . . avenging . . . vengeance.* God acts justly in judgment toward all who oppose Him and His kingdom. The repetition is for emphasis.
1:3 *the guilty.* Such as Nineveh. *whirlwind . . . storm . . . clouds.* See notes on Ps 18:7–15; 68:4; 77:16–19; 104:3–4.
1:4 *rebukes the sea and makes it dry.* As at the crossing of the Red Sea (Ex 14). *dries up all the rivers.* As at the crossing of the Jordan (Josh 3). *Bashan . . . Carmel . . . Lebanon.* See notes on Song 7:5; Is 2:13; 33:9; 35:2; Amos 4:1. These three places were noted for their fertility, vineyards and trees, but at the Lord's word they wither.
1:5 *mountains . . . hills . . . earth . . . world.* Emblems of stability and permanence.
1:6 *Who can stand . . . ? Who can endure . . . ?* Rhetorical questions. If mountains quake before the Lord (v. 5), what human being can think that he is not vulnerable? Cf. Rom 2:3–5.
1:7 *those who take refuge in Him.* Such as Judah.
1:8 *overflowing flood.* Symbolic of an invading army (see Is 8:7–8). *end . . . darkness.* In 612 B.C. that end came for Nineveh, and the darkness enveloped her. Through the ministry of Jonah, Nineveh had formerly experienced the light of God. But she later rejected it, and the result was the darkness of judgment.
1:9 *you devise.* See note on v. 11. *Distress will not rise up twice.* God never permitted the Assyrians a second victory over the Judahites; the first was the fall of Samaria (722–721 B.C.) and of the northern kingdom (Sennacherib's invasion in 701 was not a complete victory; see 2 Kin 18:13–19:37; Is 36–37).
1:10 *drunken with their drink.* See 3:11 and note.
1:11 *One who plotted evil.* Possibly the Assyrian king Ashurbanipal (669–627 B.C.), the last great Assyrian emperor, whose western expeditions succeeded in subduing Egypt and to whom King Manasseh had to submit as a vassal (see 2 Chr 33:11–13).
1:12 *they.* The Assyrians. *I have afflicted you.* God had used Assyria as the rod of His anger against His covenant-breaking people in the days of Ahaz (Is 10:5) and again in the time of Manasseh.
1:13 *I will break his yoke.* Judah was Assyria's vassal; that yoke would be broken.
1:14 *I will prepare your grave.* God used the Babylonians, the Medes and the Scythians to dig Nineveh's grave in 612 B.C. For the fulfillment of this prophecy see Ezek 32:22–23.
1:15 *mountains.* Of Jerusalem and Judah. *feet of him who*

[b]Celebrate your feasts, O Judah;
Pay your vows.
For [c]never again will the [2]wicked one
pass through you;
He is [d]cut off completely.

The Overthrow of Nineveh

2 [1]The one who [a]scatters has come up
against [2]you.
Man the fortress, watch the road;
[3]Strengthen your back, [4]summon all
your strength.
2 For the LORD will restore the [a]splendor
of Jacob
[b]Like the splendor of Israel,
Even though devastators have
devastated them
And [c]destroyed their vine branches.

3 The shields of [1]his mighty men are
colored red,
The warriors are dressed in [a]scarlet,
The chariots are *enveloped* in [2]flashing
steel
[3]When he is prepared *to march*,
And the cypress [b]*spears* are
brandished.
4 The [a]chariots race madly in the
streets,
They rush wildly in the [1]squares,
Their appearance is like torches,
They dash to and fro like lightning
flashes.
5 He remembers his [a]nobles;
They [b]stumble in their march,
They hurry to her wall,
And the [1]mantelet is set up.
6 The gates of the rivers are opened
And the palace is dissolved.
7 It is fixed:
She is stripped, she is carried away,
And her handmaids are [a]moaning like
the sound of doves,
[b]Beating on their [1]breasts.

8 Though Nineveh *was* like a pool of
water throughout her days,
Now they are fleeing;
"Stop, stop,"
But [a]no one turns back.
9 Plunder the silver!
Plunder the [a]gold!
For there is no limit to the
treasure—
Wealth from every kind of desirable
object.
10 She is [a]emptied! Yes, she is desolate
and waste!
[b]Hearts are melting and knees
knocking!
Also anguish is in [1]the whole body
And all their [c]faces are grown pale!
11 Where is the den of the lions
And the feeding place of the [a]young
lions,
Where the lion, lioness and lion's cub
prowled,
With nothing to disturb *them?*
12 The lion tore enough for his cubs,
[1]Killed *enough* for his lionesses,

15 [2]Or *worthless one;* Heb *Belial* [b]Lev 23:2, 4 [c]Is 52:1; Joel 3:17 [d]Is 29:7, 8
2:1 [1]Ch 2:2 in Heb [2]Lit *your face* [3]Lit *Make strong your loins* [4]Lit *strengthen power greatly* [a]Jer 51:20-23
2 [a]Is 60:15 [b]Ezek 37:21-23 [c]Ps 80:12, 13
3 [1]I.e. those attacking Nineveh [2]Lit *fire of steel* [3]Lit *On the day of his preparation* [a]Ezek 23:14, 15 [b]Job 39:23
4 [1]Lit *broad places* [a]Is 66:15; Jer 4:13; Ezek 26:10; Nah 3:2, 3
5 [a]Nah 3:18 [b]Jer 46:12
5 [1]Lit *covering used in a siege*
7 [1]Lit *hearts* [a]Is 38:14; 59:11 [b]Is 32:12
8 [a]Jer 46:5; 47:3
9 [a]Rev 18:12, 16
10 [1]Lit *all the loin* [a]Is 24:1; 34:10-13; Nah 2:2 [b]Ps 22:14; Is 13:7, 8; Ezek 21:7 [c]Joel 2:6
11 [a]Is 5:29
12 [1]Lit *Strangled*

brings good news. This verse sets forth a principle that is applicable in several contexts of deliverance. Here the reference is to the good news of deliverance from the Assyrian threat; in Is 52:7, deliverance from Babylonian exile; in Rom 10:15, deliverance from sin through the gospel ("good news") of Christ. *Celebrate your feasts.* In the joy of your deliverance. *Pay your vows.* Those you uttered in the time of distress (see note on Ps 7:17). *never again will the wicked one pass through you.* The Assyrian invasion in the days of Manasseh was the last. *wicked.* See note on Deut 13:13. *cut off completely.* Fulfilled in 612 when Nineveh fell (see note on v. 14).

2:1 *one who scatters.* Refers to the alliance of the Babylonians, the Medes and the Scythians—particularly the Medes under Cyaxares and the Babylonians under Nabopolassar. *Man the fortress . . . summon all your strength.* Probably irony, touched with sarcasm. *road.* By which the enemies will come.

2:2 *restore the splendor of Jacob . . . Israel.* The whole nation will be restored and united again.

2:3 *his mighty men.* Those of the attacker (v. 1), or perhaps those of Nineveh itself. *red.* Either (1) the color of the shields, or (2) a reference to blood on them, or (3) the result of the reflection of the sun shining on them. *brandished.* Ready to use.

2:4 *chariots . . . rush.* Refers to either (1) the Assyrian war chariots and their unprecedented speed as the Assyrians take frantic but vain steps to defend themselves, or (2) the chariots of Nineveh's invaders.

2:5 *He.* Perhaps the king of Assyria, though Nabopolassar is equally possible (see note on v. 1). *wall.* A moat 150 feet wide had to be filled in before reaching Nineveh's wall, which was almost 8 miles long with 15 gates. Then battering rams were moved up. *mantelet.* A defensive framework covered with hides to deflect stones and arrows.

2:6 *gates of the rivers.* Perhaps the dams on the Khoser River, which ran through the city to the Tigris River. They were either already in place, or quickly built, to back up the river water, then suddenly released so the flood would damage the walls. *palace is dissolved.* One ancient historian (the author of the *Babylonian Chronicles*) speaks of a flood that washed away some of the wall, making it easier for the invaders to enter the city.

2:7 *handmaids.* Possibly temple prostitutes, whose places of business and idols were being destroyed.

2:8 *like a pool . . . fleeing.* Some think that this refers to the Tigris and the smaller rivers encircling and running through parts of the city, and to a system of dams to make the city more impenetrable. Others take the language less literally as a reference to Nineveh's people fleeing, like water draining from a pool.

2:9 The cry of the invaders.

2:10 *emptied! . . . desolate and waste!* The Hebrew for all three words is similar. The *Babylonian Chronicles* confirms the fact that a great quantity of plunder was carried off by the invaders. *Hearts are melting . . . !* The powerful, insolent Ninevites become helpless with fear.

2:11–13 Nahum ironically contrasts the devastated and desolate city of Nineveh with its former glory and power, expressed in figurative terms.

2:11 *lion, lioness.* Cf. Is 5:29; Jer 4:7; Hos 5:14; Mic 5:8. The lion is an appropriate image to apply to Assyria because of the rapacious ways of the Assyrian monarchs and because Nineveh contained numerous lion sculptures.

And filled his lairs with prey
And his dens with torn flesh.
13 "Behold, [a]I am against you," declares
the LORD of hosts. "I will [b]burn up her chariots in smoke, a sword will devour your
young lions; I will [c]cut off your prey from the
land, and no longer will the voice of your
messengers be heard."

Nineveh's Complete Ruin

3 [a]Woe to the bloody city, completely
full of lies *and* pillage;
Her prey never departs.
2 The [a]noise of the whip,
The noise of the rattling of the wheel,
Galloping horses
And [1]bounding chariots!
3 Horsemen charging,
Swords flashing, [a]spears gleaming,
[b]Many slain, a mass of corpses,
And [1c]countless dead bodies—
They stumble over [2]the dead bodies!
4 *All* because of the [a]many harlotries of
the harlot,
The charming one, the [b]mistress of
sorceries,
Who [c]sells nations by her harlotries
And families by her sorceries.
5 "Behold, [a]I am against you," declares
the LORD of hosts;
"And I will [1b]lift up your skirts over
your face,
And [c]show to the nations your
nakedness
And to the kingdoms your disgrace.
6 "I will [a]throw [1]filth on you
And [b]make you vile,
And set you up as a [c]spectacle.
7 "And it will come about that all who
see you
Will [1]shrink from you and say,
'Nineveh is devastated!
[a]Who will grieve for her?'
Where will I seek comforters for you?"
8 Are you better than [1a]No-amon,
Which was situated by the [b]waters of
the Nile,
With water surrounding her,
Whose rampart *was* [2]the sea,
Whose wall *consisted* of [2]the sea?
9 [a]Ethiopia was *her* might,
And Egypt too, without limits.
[b]Put and [c]Lubim were among [1]her
helpers.
10 Yet she [a]became an exile,
She went into captivity;
Also her [b]small children were dashed
to pieces
[c]At the head of every street;
They [d]cast lots for her honorable men,
And all her great men were bound
with fetters.
11 You too will become [a]drunk,
You will be [b]hidden.
You too will search for a refuge from
the enemy.
12 All your fortifications are [a]fig trees
with [1b]ripe fruit—
When shaken, they fall into the eater's
mouth.
13 Behold, your people are [a]women in
your midst!
The gates of your land are [b]opened
wide to your enemies;
Fire consumes your gate bars.
14 [a]Draw for yourself water for the siege!
[b]Strengthen your fortifications!
Go into the clay and tread the mortar!
Take hold of the brick mold!
15 There [a]fire will consume you,

13 [a]Jer 21:13; Ezek 5:8; Nah 3:5 [b]Josh 11:6, 9; Ps 46:9 [c]Is 49:24, 25; Nah 3:1
3:1 [a]Ezek 24:6, 9
2 [1]Lit *skipping* [a]Job 39:22-25; Jer 47:3; Nah 2:3, 4
3 [1]Lit *there is no end to* [2]Lit *their* [a]Hab 3:11 [b]Is 34:3; 66:16 [c]Is 37:36; Ezek 39:4
4 [a]Is 23:17; Ezek 16:25-29; Rev 17:1, 2 [b]Is 47:9, 12, 13 [c]Rev 18:3
5 [1]Lit *uncover your* [a]Jer 50:31; Ezek 26:3; Nah 2:13 [b]Is 47:2, 3; Jer 13:26 [c]Ezek 16:37
6 [1]Lit *detestable things* [a]Job 9:31 [b]Job 30:8; Mal 2:9 [c]Is 14:16; Jer 51:37
7 [1]Lit *flee*
7 [a]Is 51:19; Jer 15:5
8 [1]I.e. the city of Amon: Thebes [2]I.e. the Nile [a]Jer 46:25; Ezek 30:14-16 [b]Is 19:6-8
9 [1]Lit *your* [a]Is 20:5 [b]Jer 46:9; Ezek 27:10; 30:5; 38:5 [c]2 Chr 12:3; 16:8
10 [a]Is 19:4; 20:4 [b]Ps 137:9; Is 13:16; Hos 13:16 [c]Lam 2:19 [d]Joel 3:3; Obad 11
11 [a]Is 49:26; Jer 25:27; Nah 1:10 [b]Is 2:10, 19; Hos 10:8
12 [1]Lit *first fruits* [a]Rev 6:13 [b]Is 28:4
13 [a]Is 19:16; Jer 50:37; 51:30 [b]Is 45:1, 2; Nah 2:6
14 [a]2 Chr 32:3, 4 [b]Nah 2:1 **15** [a]Is 66:15, 16; Nah 2:13; 3:13

2:12 *filled his lairs with prey.* Nineveh was filled with the spoils of war from many conquered nations.
2:13 *I will burn up.* Nineveh's fall will not be caused by merely natural forces or the superior power of her attackers; it will be an act of God. Nineveh had been put on trial, found guilty and sentenced to destruction. *no longer will the voice . . . be heard.* History has confirmed this prediction.
3:1 *bloody city.* Nineveh's bloody massacres of her conquered rivals were well known. *prey never departs.* The Assyrians were noted for their ruthlessness, brutality and terrible atrocities. Many of their victims were beheaded, impaled or burned.
3:3 *mass of corpses.* The Assyrian king Shalmaneser III boasted of erecting a pyramid of chopped-off heads in front of an enemy's city. Other Assyrian kings stacked corpses like cordwood by the gates of defeated cities. Nahum's description of the cruel Assyrians is apropos.
3:4 *harlot.* Probably a reference to the chief love goddess of Nineveh and, by extension, to the city as a whole. The lure of luxury and wealth brought multitudes to Nineveh. *sorceries . . . sorceries.* See Deut 18:10.
3:5 *lift up your skirts over your face.* The punishment of prostitutes and adulteresses.
3:6 Nineveh will be humiliated.
3:7 *Who . . . ? Where . . . ?* Rhetorical questions. Nineveh will receive no sympathy.
3:8 *No-amon.* Hebrew name for Thebes. *No-amon* means "city of (the god) Amon." Thebes was the great capital of Upper Egypt. Its site is occupied today by the towns of Luxor and Karnak. It was destroyed by the Assyrians in 663 B.C.
3:9 *Put.* A neighbor of Egypt, but its location is uncertain.
3:10 *her great men were bound with fetters.* Assyrian kings often did this; e.g., King Ashurbanipal gave this description of his treatment of a captured leader: "I . . . put a dog chain on him and made him occupy a kennel at the eastern gate of Nineveh."
3:11 *will become drunk.* Probably from the cup of God's wrath.
3:12 *fig trees with ripe fruit.* A metaphor for the eagerness with which the victors gather the rich loot of Nineveh. *they fall into the eater's mouth.* Nineveh's fortresses will finally fall just as easily.
3:13 *your people are women . . . !* They are weak and unable to stand against the invading armies.
3:14 *Draw . . . water.* A normal preparation for siege. *Strengthen your fortifications!* Irony, the point being that it will do no good (see note on 2:1).
3:15 *There.* Inside your strong fortifications. *fire will consume*

The sword will cut you down;
It will [b]consume you as the locust *does.*

Multiply yourself like the creeping
locust,
Multiply yourself like the swarming
locust.
16 You have increased your [a]traders more
than the stars of heaven—
The creeping locust [1]strips and flies
away.
17 Your [1a]guardsmen are like the
swarming locust.
Your [b]marshals are like hordes of
grasshoppers
Settling in the stone walls on a cold
day.
The sun rises and they flee,
And the place where they are is not
known.
18 Your shepherds are [a]sleeping, O [b]king
of Assyria;
Your [c]nobles are lying down.
Your people are [d]scattered on the
mountains
And there is no one to regather
them.
19 There is [a]no relief for your
breakdown,
Your [b]wound is incurable.
All who hear [1]about you
Will [c]clap *their* hands over you,
For on whom has not your evil passed
continually?

15 [b]Joel 1:4
16 [1]I.e. strips vegetation; or *molts* [a]Is 23:8
17 [1]Or *officials* [a]Rev 9:7 [b]Jer 51:27
18 [a]Ps 76:5, 6; Is 56:10; Jer 51:57 [b]Jer 50:18 [c]Nah 2:5 [d]1 Kin 22:17; Is 13:14
19 [1]Lit *your report* [a]Jer 46:11; Mic 1:9 [b]Jer 30:12 [c]Job 27:23; Lam 2:15

you. Confirmed by history and archaeology. Assyria's king died in the flames of his palace.

3:16 *your traders more than the stars.* Speaks of Assyria's vast trading and commercial enterprises. *creeping locust strips.* In the time of Nineveh's adversity the merchants stripped the land of its treasures, and the trade network was destroyed.

3:17 *locust.* Feared by the farmers of the ancient Near East, because they came in huge swarms and devoured everything in their path. Their activity provided an apt simile for the exploitative actions of Nineveh's officials during her destruction. *where . . . is not known.* Thus will Nineveh's officials disappear, without a trace. Interestingly, for centuries no one knew where Nineveh itself lay buried; in 1845 it was finally uncovered by archaeologists.

3:18 *shepherds.* Leaders. *O king.* The reigning king at the time of Nineveh's fall was Sin-shar-ishkun; so these words are prophetically addressed to him. *are lying down.* Die. *people are scattered.* The age-old scene of refugees fleeing a place of destruction is repeated at Nineveh.

3:19 *Your wound is incurable.* Nineveh was so totally destroyed that it was never rebuilt, and within a few centuries it was covered with windblown sand. So that "great city" (Jon 1:2; cf. 3:2) fell in 612 B.C., never to rise again—all in fulfillment of God's word through His prophet Nahum.

Habakkuk

INTRODUCTION

Author

Little is known about Habakkuk except that he was a contemporary of Jeremiah and a man of vigorous faith rooted deeply in the religious traditions of Israel. The account of his ministering to the needs of Daniel in the lions' den in the Apocryphal book *Bel and the Dragon* is legendary rather than historical.

Date

The prediction of the coming Babylonian invasion (1:6) indicates that Habakkuk lived in Judah toward the end of Josiah's reign (640 – 609 B.C.) or at the beginning of Jehoiakim's (609 – 598). The prophecy is generally dated a little before or after the battle of Carchemish (605), when Egyptian forces, who had earlier gone to the aid of the last Assyrian king, were routed by the Babylonians under Nabopolassar and Nebuchadnezzar and were pursued as far as the Egyptian border (Jer 46). Habakkuk, like Jeremiah, probably lived to see the initial fulfillment of his prophecy when Jerusalem was attacked by the Babylonians in 597.

Message

Among the prophetic writings, Habakkuk is somewhat unique in that it includes no oracle addressed to Israel. It contains, rather, a dialogue between the prophet and God (see Outline). (The book of Jonah, while narrative, presents an account of conflict between the Lord and one of his prophets.) In the first two chapters, Habakkuk argues with God over His ways that appear to Him unfathomable, if not unjust. Having received replies, he responds with a beautiful confession of faith (ch. 3).

This account of wrestling with God is, however, not just a fragment from a private journal that has somehow entered the public domain. It was composed for Israel. No doubt it represented the voice of the godly in Judah, struggling to comprehend the ways of God. God's answers therefore spoke to all who shared Habakkuk's troubled doubts. And Habakkuk's confession became a public expression — as indicated by its liturgical notations (see note on 3:1).

Habakkuk was perplexed that wickedness, strife and oppression were rampant in Judah but God seemingly did nothing. When told that the Lord was preparing to do something about it through the "fierce" Babylonians (1:6), his perplexity only intensified: How could God, who is "too pure to approve evil" (1:13), appoint such a nation "to judge" (1:12) "those more righteous than they" (1:13)?

God makes it clear, however, that eventually the corrupt destroyer will itself be destroyed. In the end, Habakkuk learns to rest in God's appointments and await his working in a spirit of worship.

Literary Features

The author wrote clearly and with great feeling, and penned many memorable phrases (2:2,4,14,20; 3:2,17 – 19). The book was popular during the intertestamental period; a complete commentary on its first two chapters has been found among the Dead Sea Scrolls (see "The Time between the Testaments," p. 1356).

Outline

I. Title (1:1)

II. Habakkuk's First Complaint: Why does the evil in Judah go unpunished? (1:2 – 4)

III. God's Answer: The Babylonians will punish Judah (1:5 – 11)

IV. Habakkuk's Second Complaint: How can a just God use wicked Babylon to punish a people more righteous than themselves? (1:12 — 2:1)

V. God's Answer: Babylon will be punished, and faith will be rewarded (2:2 – 20)

VI. Habakkuk's Prayer: After asking for manifestations of God's wrath and mercy (as he has seen in the past), he closes with a confession of trust and joy in God (ch. 3)

Chaldeans Used to Punish Judah

1 The [1][a]oracle which Habakkuk the prophet saw.

2 [a]How long, O LORD, will I call for help,
And You will not hear?
I cry out to You, "Violence!"
Yet You do [b]not save.
3 Why do You make me [a]see iniquity,
And cause *me* to look on wickedness?
Yes, [b]destruction and violence are before me;
[c]Strife exists and contention arises.
4 Therefore the [a]law is [1]ignored
And justice [2]is never upheld.
For the wicked [b]surround the righteous;
Therefore justice comes out [c]perverted.

5 "[a]Look among the nations! Observe!
Be astonished! [b]Wonder!
Because *I am* doing [c]something in your days—
You would not believe if [1]you were told.
6 "For behold, I am [a]raising up the Chaldeans,
That [1]fierce and impetuous people
Who march [2]throughout the earth
To [3][b]seize dwelling places which are not theirs.
7 "They are dreaded and [a]feared;
Their [b]justice and [1]authority [2]originate with themselves.
8 "Their [a]horses are swifter than leopards
And [1]keener than [b]wolves in the evening.
Their [2]horsemen come galloping,
Their horsemen come from afar;
They fly like an [c]eagle swooping *down* to devour.
9 "All of them come for violence.
[1]Their horde of [a]faces *moves* forward.
They collect captives like sand.
10 "They [a]mock at kings
And rulers are a laughing matter to them.
They [b]laugh at every fortress
And [c]heap up rubble to capture it.
11 "Then they will sweep through *like* the [a]wind and pass on.
But they will be held [b]guilty,
They whose [c]strength is their god."

12 Are You not from [a]everlasting,
O LORD, my God, my Holy One?
We will not die.
You, O LORD, have [b]appointed them to judge;
And You, O [c]Rock, have established them to correct.
13 *Your* eyes are too [a]pure to [1]approve evil,
And You can not look on wickedness *with favor.*
Why do You [b]look with favor
On those who deal [c]treacherously?
Why are You [d]silent when the wicked [e]swallow up
Those more righteous than they?
14 *Why* have You made men like the fish of the sea,
Like creeping things without a ruler over them?
15 *The Chaldeans* [a]bring all of them up with a hook,

1:1 [1]Or *burden* [a]Is 13:1; Nah 1:1 **2** [a]Ps 13:1, 2; 22:1, 2 [b]Jer 14:9 **3** [a]Ps 55:9-11; Jer 20:18 [b]Jer 20:8 [c]Jer 15:10 **4** [1]Or *ineffective;* lit *numbed* [2]Lit *never goes forth* [a]Ps 58:1, 2; 119:126; Is 59:12-14 [b]Ps 22:12; Is 1:21-23 [c]Is 5:20; Ezek 9:9 **5** [1]Lit *it* [a]Acts 13:41 [b]Is 29:9 [c]Is 29:14; Ezek 12:22-28 **6** [1]Lit *bitter* [2]Lit *the breadth of* [3]Lit *take possession of* [a]2 Kin 24:2; Jer 4:11-13 [b]Jer 8:10 **7** [1]Lit *eminence* [2]Lit *proceeds from* [a]Is 18:2, 7 [b]Jer 39:5-9 **8** [1]Or *more eager* to attack [2]Or *steeds paw* the ground [a]Jer 4:13 [b]Zeph 3:3

8 [c]Ezek 17:3; Hos 8:1 **9** [1]Or *The eagerness of their faces* [a]2 Kin 12:17; Dan 11:17 **10** [a]2 Chr 36:6, 10; Is 37:13 [b]Is 10:9; 14:16 [c]Jer 32:24; Ezek 26:8 **11** [a]Jer 4:11, 12 [b]Jer 2:3 [c]Dan 4:30; Hab 1:16 **12** [a]Deut 33:27; Ps 90:2; Mal 3:6 [b]Is 10:5, 6; Mal 3:5 [c]Deut 32:4 **13** [1]Lit *look at* [a]Ps 11:4-6; 34:15, 16 [b]Jer 12:1, 2 [c]Is 24:16 [d]Ps 50:21 [e]Ps 35:25 **15** [a]Jer 16:16; Amos 4:2

1:1 *oracle.* Such as the two found here (vv. 5–11; 2:2–20). Oracles were frequently received in visions. The Hebrew word for "oracle" (possibly meaning "burden," but perhaps only "pronouncement") often refers to revelations containing warnings of impending doom (cf. Is 15:1; 19:1; 22:1), but in Zech 9:1; 12:1; Mal 1:1 it refers to messages that also contain hope. *Habakkuk.* The name is probably Babylonian and refers to a kind of garden plant. *prophet.* Habakkuk is called a prophet also in 3:1, tying ch. 3 closely to chs. 1–2.
1:2–2:20 A dialogue between the prophet and God. The basic theme is age-old: Why does evil seem to go unpunished? Why does God not respond to prayer?
1:2 *Violence!* At this time Judah was probably under King Jehoiakim, who was ambitious, cruel and corrupt. Habakkuk describes the social corruption and spiritual apostasy of Judah in the late seventh century B.C.
1:3 *cause me to look on wickedness.* See v. 13. The prophet was amazed that God seemed to condone cruelty and violence.
1:4 *law is ignored . . . justice is never upheld.* Because wealthy landowners controlled the courts through bribery.
1:5 *would not believe.* To the people of Judah it was incredible that God would give them over to the arrogant Babylonians.
1:6 The apostate nation of Judah is to be punished by an invasion of the Babylonians, a powerful people who regained their independence from Assyria in 626 B.C., destroyed Assyrian power completely in 612–605, and flourished until 539. In this context, the Chaldeans are synonymous with the newly resurgent Babylonians. *seize dwelling places.* See 2:6–8.
1:7 *authority originate with themselves.* A mark of arrogance.
1:8 The speed with which Babylon conquered her enemies had become proverbial.
1:9 *collect captives like sand.* Like their Assyrian predecessors, the Babylonians deported conquered peoples as a matter of deliberate national policy (see 2:5).
1:10 *heap up rubble.* A siege method.
1:11 *whose strength is their god.* The Babylonians were so proud and confident of their military might that it had virtually become their god (see v. 16).
1:12 Habakkuk cannot see the justice in Judah's being punished by an even more wicked nation, and thinks that the Babylonians surely would not be allowed to conquer Judah completely. *from everlasting.* See Ps 90:2. *You, O LORD, have appointed them.* The prophet recognizes Babylon as God's agent of judgment (cf. Is 7:18–20; 44:28–45:1).
1:13 A classic statement of the problem of evil within the context of Israel's faith: Why does evil appear to flourish unchecked by a just and holy God? *treacherously . . . wicked.* The Babylonians. *Those more righteous.* Judah.
1:15 *hook.* See note on Amos 4:2. *Drag them away with their*

[b]Drag them away with their net,
And gather them together in their
fishing net.
Therefore they rejoice and are glad.
16 Therefore they offer a sacrifice to their
net
And [1]burn incense to their fishing net;
Because through [a]these things their
[2]catch is [3]large,
And their food is [4]plentiful.
17 Will they therefore empty their [a]net
And continually [b]slay nations without
sparing?

God Answers the Prophet

2 I will [a]stand on my guard post
And station myself on the rampart;
And I will [b]keep watch to see [c]what
He will speak to me,
And how I may reply [1]when I am
reproved.
2 Then the LORD answered me and
said,
"[a]Record the vision
And inscribe *it* on tablets,
That [1]the one who [2]reads it may run.
3 "For the vision is yet for the [a]appointed
time;
It [1]hastens toward the goal and it will
not [2]fail.
Though it tarries, [b]wait for it;
For it will certainly come, it [c]will not
delay.

4 "Behold, as for the [a]proud one,
His soul is not right within him;
But the [b]righteous will live by his
[1]faith.
5 "Furthermore, [a]wine betrays the
[b]haughty man,
So that he does not [c]stay at home.
He [d]enlarges his appetite like Sheol,
And he is like death, never satisfied.
He also gathers to himself all nations
And collects to himself all peoples.

6 "Will not all of these [a]take up a taunt-
song against him,
Even mockery *and* insinuations
against him
And say, '[b]Woe to him who increases
what is not his—
For how long—
And makes himself [1]rich with loans?'
7 "Will not [1]your creditors [a]rise up
suddenly,
And those who [2]collect from you
awaken?
Indeed, you will become plunder for
them.
8 "Because you have [a]looted many
nations,
All the remainder of the peoples will
loot you—
Because of human bloodshed and
violence [1]done to the land,
To the town and all its inhabitants.

9 "Woe to him who gets [a]evil gain for his
house
To [b]put his nest on high,
To be delivered from the hand of
calamity!
10 "You have devised a [a]shameful thing
for your house
By cutting off many peoples;
So you are [b]sinning against yourself.
11 "Surely the [a]stone will cry out from the
wall,

15 [b]Ps 10:9 **16** [1]Or *sacrifice* [2]Lit *portion* [3]Lit *fat;* or *plentiful* [4]Lit *the fat portion* [a]Jer 44:17 **17** [a]Is 19:8 [b]Is 14:5, 6 **2:1** [1]Lit *upon my reproof* [a]Is 21:8 [b]Ps 5:3 [c]Ps 85:8 **2** [1]Or *one may read it fluently* [2]Or *is to proclaim it* [a]Deut 27:8; Rom 15:4; Rev 1:19 **3** [1]Lit *pants* [2]Or *lie* [a]Dan 8:17, 19; 10:14 [b]Ps 27:14 [c]Ezek 12:25; Heb 10:37 **4** [1]Or *faithfulness* [a]Ps 49:18; Is 13:11 [b]Rom 1:17; Gal 3:11; Heb 10:38 **5** [a]Prov 20:1 [b]Prov 21:24 [c]2 Kin 14:10 [d]Prov 27:20; 30:16; Is 5:11-15 **6** [1]Lit *heavy* [a]Is 14:4-10; Jer 50:13 [b]Job 20:15-29; Hab 2:12 **7** [1]Lit *those who bite you* [2]Lit *violently shake you* [a]Prov 29:1 **8** [1]Lit *of the land* [a]Is 33:1; Jer 27:7; Zech 2:8 **9** [a]Jer 22:13; Ezek 22:27 [b]Jer 49:16 **10** [a]2 Kin 9:26; Nah 1:14; Hab 2:16 [b]Jer 26:19 **11** [a]Josh 24:27; Luke 19:40

net. Babylon's victims are as powerless as fish swimming into a net. Mesopotamian reliefs portray, in symbolic fashion, conquering rulers capturing the enemy in fishnets.

1:16 See note on v. 11.

2:1 *I will stand on my guard.* The figure of a guard looking out from a tower and expecting a response to his challenge. Any reproof would be for questioning God's justice. *rampart.* The walls of Jerusalem.

2:2–3 *vision.* See 1 Chr 17:15; Prov 29:18. The Hebrew for this word refers specifically to a prophet's vision (see, e.g., Is 1:1).

2:2 *That the one who reads it may run.* So that a messenger may run to deliver the message and read it to those to whom he has been sent.

2:3 *wait for it.* The following message deals with the fall of Babylon in 539 B.C., about 66 years after Habakkuk's prophecy. The Lord tells Habakkuk (and Judah) that fulfillment of the prophecy may "tarry," but that he and the people are to expect it (see 3:16).

2:4 *proud one.* Collective for the Babylonians, but with special reference to their king. *But.* In contrast to the Babylonians, whose desires are not upright. *the righteous will live by his faith.* See NASB marg.; see also Is 26, especially vv. 1–6. In light of God's revelation about how (and when) He is working, His people are to wait patiently and live by faith—trusting in their sovereign God. The clause is quoted frequently in the NT to support the teaching that people are saved by grace through faith (Rom 1:17; Gal 3:11; cf. Eph 2:8) and should live by faith (Heb 10:38–39). It became the rallying cry of the Protestant Reformation in the 16th century. The same principle that was applicable in the realm of national deliverance is applicable in the area of spiritual deliverance (salvation).

2:5 *enlarges his appetite like Sheol.* The grave never says, "Enough" (Prov 30:15–16; see note on Ps 49:14).

2:6–20 This taunt falls into two halves of ten (Hebrew) lines each (vv. 6–14 and vv. 15–20), each half concluding with a significant theological statement (vv. 14,20). Together these two statements set the five "woes" pronounced against Babylon (vv. 6,9,12,15,19; cf. Is 5:8–23; Matt 23:13–32; Luke 6:24–26; Rev 9:12; 11:14) in a larger frame of reference.

2:6 *all of these . . . against him.* The threatened victims of the Babylonian onslaught, especially Judah, will taunt ruthless Babylon. *Woe.* The Babylonians' greed for conquest is condemned.

2:8 *human bloodshed.* See v. 17. Therefore Babylon's blood would be shed (see note on Gen 9:6).

2:9 *Woe.* The Babylonians' pride in building is condemned. *nest on high.* Like the eagle building an inaccessible nest, the Babylonians thought their empire to be unconquerable (see Obad 3–4; cf. Is 14:4,13–15).

2:11 *the stone will cry out . . . And the rafter.* The stones and

And the rafter will answer it from the
[1]framework.

12 "Woe to him who [a]builds a city with
bloodshed
And founds a town with [1]violence!
13 "Is it not indeed from the LORD of hosts
That peoples [a]toil for fire,
And nations grow weary for nothing?
14 "For the earth will be [a]filled
With the knowledge of the glory of the
LORD,
As the waters cover the sea.

15 "Woe to you who make [1]your
neighbors drink,
Who mix in your venom even to make
them drunk
So as to look on their nakedness!
16 "You will be filled with disgrace rather
than honor.
Now you yourself [a]drink and [1]expose
your *own* nakedness.
The [b]cup in the LORD's right hand will
come around to you,
And [c]utter disgrace *will come* upon
your glory.
17 "For the [a]violence [1]done to Lebanon
will [2]overwhelm you,
And the devastation of *its* beasts [3]by
which you terrified them,
[b]Because of human bloodshed and
[c]violence [4]done to the land,
To the town and all its inhabitants.

18 "What [a]profit is the [1]idol when its
maker has carved it,
Or [2]an image, a [b]teacher of falsehood?
For *its* maker [c]trusts in his *own*
handiwork
When he fashions speechless idols.
19 "Woe to him who [a]says to a *piece of*
wood, '[b]Awake!'
To a mute stone, 'Arise!'
And that is *your* teacher?
Behold, it is overlaid with [c]gold and
silver,
And there is [d]no breath at all inside it.
20 "But the [a]LORD is in His holy temple.
[1]Let all the earth [b]be silent before Him."

God's Deliverance of His People

3 A prayer of Habakkuk the prophet,
according to [1]Shigionoth.
2 LORD, I have [a]heard [1]the report about
You *and* [2]I [b]fear.
O LORD, [c]revive [d]Your work in the
midst of the years,
In the midst of the years make it
known;
In wrath remember [3][e]mercy.

3 God comes from [a]Teman,
And the Holy One from Mount [b]Paran.
Selah.
His [c]splendor covers the heavens,
And the [d]earth is full of His praise.
4 *His* [a]radiance is like the sunlight;
He has rays *flashing* from His hand,
And there is the hiding of His [b]power.

11 [1]Lit *wood* **12** [1]Or *injustice* [a]Mic 3:10; Nah 3:1 **13** [a]Is 50:11; Jer 51:58 **14** [a]Ps 22:27; Is 11:9; Zech 14:9 **15** [1]Lit *his neighbor* **16** [1]Lit *show yourself uncircumcised;* or *stagger;* so DSS and ancient versions [a]Lam 4:21 [b]Jer 25:15, 17 [c]Nah 3:6 **17** [1]Lit *of Lebanon* [2]Lit *cover* [3]Lit which *terrified them* [4]Lit *of the land* [a]Joel 3:19; Zech 11:1 [b]Ps 55:23; Hab 2:8 [c]Jer 51:35; Hab 2:8 **18** [1]Or *a graven image* [a]Is 42:17; 44:9; Jer 2:27, 28
18 [2]Lit a *cast* metal *image* [b]Jer 10:8, 14; Zech 10:2 [c]Ps 115:4, 8 **19** [a]Jer 2:27, 28; 10:3 [b]1 Kin 18:26-29 [c]Ps 135:15-18; Jer 10:4, 9, 14 [d]Ps 135:17 **20** [1]Lit *Hush before Him, all the earth* [a]Mic 1:2 [b]Zeph 1:7; Zech 2:13 **3:1** [1]I.e. a highly emotional poetic form **2** [1]Or *Your report* [2]Or *I stand in awe of Your work, O* LORD*; In the midst of the years revive it,* [3]Or compassion [a]Job 42:5 [b]Ps 119:120; Jer 10:7 [c]Ps 71:20; 85:6 [d]Ps 44:1-8; Hab 1:5 [e]Num 14:19; 2 Sam 24:15-17; Is 54:8 **3** [a]Jer 49:7; Amos 1:12; Obad 9 [b]Gen 21:21; Deut 33:2 [c]Ps 113:4; 148:13 [d]Ps 48:10 **4** [a]Ps 18:12 [b]Job 26:14

beams in Babylonian houses were purchased with plunder, and thus testified against the occupants.

2:12 *Woe.* Babylonian injustice is condemned.

2:13 *toil for fire.* The cities built by the labor of the Babylonians (v. 12) will be burned.

2:14 The Lord's future destruction of proud Babylon and all her worldly glory will cause His greater glory to be known throughout the world (see Ex 14:4,17–18; Is 11:9; Rev 17:1–19:4).

2:15 Cf. Gen 9:20–22. *Woe.* Babylonian violence is condemned. Her rapacious treatment of her neighbors, which stripped them of all their wealth (cf. what she later did to Jerusalem, 2 Kin 25:8–21), is compared to one who makes his neighbor drunk so he can take lewd pleasure from the man's nakedness.

2:16 *be filled with disgrace . . . your own nakedness.* The Lord will do to Babylon what she has done to others. *cup in the LORD's right hand.* A symbol of divine retribution (see Is 51:17,22; Jer 25:15–17; Lam 4:21; Rev 14:10; 16:19).

2:17 *violence done to Lebanon.* The Babylonians apparently had ravaged the cedar forests of Lebanon to adorn their temples and palaces (cf. Is 14:8). *devastation of its beasts.* Assyrian inscriptions record hunting expeditions in the Lebanon range, and such sport may have been indulged in by the invading Babylonians as well. Babylonian violence was destructive of all forms of life, not only of lands and cities.

2:18 *idol.* The Hebrew for this word means "godlet" or "nonentity" (cf. Is 41:29; 44:9; Jer 10:15 and the condemnation of idolatry in Ex 20:4–5; Ps 115:4–8).

2:19 *Woe.* Babylonian idolatry is condemned.

2:20 *But.* The stone and wood idols of the nations (v. 19) are silent before people, but the people of the world are to be silent before the true God, who is about to judge (cf. Is 41:1; Zeph 1:7; Zech 2:13). *holy temple.* Heaven.

3:1 In the strict sense, petition is found in this prayer only in v. 2 but, as with many of the psalms, it is set in a larger context of recollection (vv. 3–15) and expression of confidence and trust (vv. 16–19). In fact, Habakkuk's prayer appears to have been used as a psalm; note the psalm-like heading (v. 1) and the musical and/or literary notations (vv. 1,3,9,13,19).

3:2 *heard the report about You.* In vv. 3–15 Habakkuk recalls a poetic celebration of God's mighty saving acts of old—perhaps one he had heard at the temple (see v. 16).

3:3 *God comes.* When celebrating the exodus, the OT poets (and poet-prophets) combined recollections of the mighty acts of God with conventional images of a fearsome manifestation of the Lord. He came down with His heavenly host and rode on the mighty thunderstorm as His chariot, with His arrows flying in all directions, a cloudburst of rain descending on the earth and the mountains quaking before Him (see Deut 33:2; Judg 5:4–5; Ps 18:7–15; 68:4–10,32–35; 77:16–19; Mic 1:3–4). Such figures characterize many of the references in the following verses. *Teman.* Means "southland." God is pictured as coming from the area south of Judah during the exodus. *Mount Paran.* See Deut 33:2; probably northwest of the Gulf of Aqaba and south of Kadesh-barnea, between Edom and Sinai. *earth is full.* See note on 2:14.

5 Before Him goes [a]pestilence,
And [b]plague comes [1]after Him.
6 He stood and surveyed the earth;
He looked and [a]startled the nations.
Yes, the perpetual mountains were
shattered,
The ancient hills [1]collapsed.
His ways are [b]everlasting.
7 I saw the tents of Cushan under
[a]distress,
The tent curtains of the land of
[b]Midian were trembling.

8 Did the LORD rage against the [a]rivers,
Or *was* Your anger against the rivers,
Or *was* Your wrath against the [b]sea,
That You [c]rode on Your horses,
On Your [d]chariots of salvation?
9 Your [a]bow was made bare,
The rods of [1]chastisement were
sworn. Selah.
You [b]cleaved the earth with rivers.
10 The mountains saw You *and* quaked;
The downpour of waters swept by.
The deep [a]uttered forth its voice,
It lifted high its hands.
11 [a]Sun *and* moon stood in their places;
They went away at the [b]light of Your
arrows,
At the radiance of Your gleaming spear.
12 In indignation You [a]marched through
the earth;
In anger You [1b]trampled the nations.
13 You went forth for the [a]salvation of
Your people,
For the salvation of Your [b]anointed.
You struck the [c]head of the house of
the evil
To lay him open from [1]thigh to neck.
Selah.

5 [1]Lit *at His feet* [a]Ex 12:29, 30; Num 16:46-49 [b]Num 11:1-3; Ps 18:12, 13
6 [1]Lit *bowed;* or *sank down* [a]Job 21:18; Ps 35:5 [b]Hab 1:12
7 [a]Ex 15:14-16 [b]Num 31:7, 8; Judg 7:24, 25; 8:12
8 [a]Ex 7:19, 20; Josh 3:16; Is 50:2 [b]Ex 14:16, 21; Ps 114:3, 5 [c]Deut 33:26; Ps 18:10; Hab 3:15 [d]Ps 68:17
9 [1]Lit *word* [a]Ps 7:12, 13; Hab 3:11 [b]Ps 78:16; 105:41
10 [a]Ps 93:3; 98:7, 8
11 [a]Josh 10:12-14 [b]Ps 18:14
12 [1]Or *thresh* [a]Ps 68:7 [b]Is 41:15; Jer 51:33; Mic 4:13
13 [1]Lit *foundation* [a]Ex 15:2; 2 Sam 5:20; Ps 68:19, 20 [b]Ps 20:6; 28:8 [c]Ps 68:21; 110:6
14 [1]Lit *shafts* [2]Or *warriors* or *villagers* [3]Lit *me* [a]Judg 7:22 [b]Dan 11:40; Zech 9:14 [c]Ps 10:8; 64:2-5
15 [a]Ps 77:19; Hab 3:8 [b]Ex 15:8
16 [1]Lit *belly* [2]Or *To come upon the people* who *will* [a]Dan 10:8; Hab 3:2 [b]Job 30:17, 30; Jer 23:9 [c]Luke 21:19 [d]Jer 5:15
17 [1]Lit *produce* [a]Joel 1:10-12; Amos 4:9; 2 Cor 4:8, 9 [b]Mic 6:15 [c]Joel 1:18 [d]Jer 5:17

14 You pierced with his [a]own [1]spears
The head of his [2]throngs.
They [b]stormed in to scatter [3]us;
Their exultation *was* like those
Who [c]devour the oppressed in secret.
15 You [a]trampled on the sea with Your
horses,
On the [b]surge of many waters.

16 I heard and my [1]inward parts
[a]trembled,
At the sound my lips quivered.
Decay enters my [b]bones,
And in my place I tremble.
Because I must [c]wait quietly for the
day of distress,
[2]For the [d]people to arise *who* will
invade us.
17 Though the [a]fig tree should not blossom
And there be no [1]fruit on the vines,
Though the yield of the [b]olive should
fail
And the fields produce no food,
Though the [c]flock should be cut off
from the fold
And there be [d]no cattle in the stalls,
18 Yet I will [a]exult in the LORD,
I will [b]rejoice in the [c]God of my
salvation.
19 The Lord [1]GOD is my [a]strength,
And [b]He has made my feet like hinds'
feet,
And makes me walk on my [c]high
places.

For the choir director, on my stringed instruments.

18 [a]Ex 15:1, 2; Job 13:15; Is 61:10; Rom 5:2, 3 [b]Ps 46:1-5; Phil 4:4 [c]Ps 25:5; 27:1; Is 12:2 **19** [1]Heb *YHWH,* usually rendered *LORD* [a]Ps 18:32, 33; 27:1; 46:1; Is 45:24 [b]2 Sam 22:34 [c]Deut 33:29

3:5 *pestilence . . . plague.* Means of divine punishment (cf. Ex 7:14–12:30; Lev 26:25; Ps 91:3,6).
3:6 God's presence was frequently marked by earthquakes (see Ex 19:18; Ps 18:7; Jer 4:24–26; 10:10). Landslides may also be alluded to here.
3:7 *Cushan . . . Midian.* Arab tribes living near Edom. *distress . . . trembling.* When Israel was delivered from Egypt under Moses, neighboring peoples were filled with fear (see Ex 15:14–16; Josh 2:9–10).
3:8 Poetic allusions to the plague on the Nile (Ex 7:20–24) and/or the stopping of the Jordan (Josh 3:15–17), and to the parting of the Red Sea (Ex 14:15–31). But see note on v. 3.
3:9 *rods of chastisement.* Probably thunderbolts unleashed by the heavenly archer. *cleaved the earth with rivers.* Caused by the accompanying thunderstorms.
3:11 *Sun and moon stood in their places.* Probably an allusion to the victory at Gibeon (Josh 10:12–13), indicating that God's triumph over His enemies would be just as complete as on that occasion.
3:12 *trampled.* See note on Amos 1:3.
3:13 *salvation of Your people.* God fought against the nations of Canaan (v. 12) but delivered His people. *salvation of.* Giving of victory to. *anointed.* The covenant nation, the "kingdom of priests" (Ex 19:6), which God came to deliver. He destroyed the enemy, and in this great act of wrath (v. 12) remembered mercy (v. 2). *head of the house of the evil.* Pharaoh (see Ex 14:5–9).
3:14–15 Another reference to the destruction of the Egyptians in the Red Sea. God will likewise vanquish present foes.
3:15 *horses.* See v. 8 and note.
3:16 Hearing the hymnic recollection of God's mighty deeds of old in Israel's behalf (vv. 3–15) fills the prophet with an awe so profound that he feels physically weak. Alternatively, it is possible that the message from the Lord that Babylon would be sent against Judah (1:5–11) had so devastated him that he felt ill—until he heard the Lord's further word. *wait quietly.* See note on 2:3. *people . . . who will invade us.* Babylonia.
3:17 Probably anticipates the awful results of the imminent Babylonian invasion and devastation.
3:18–19 Habakkuk has learned the lesson of faith (2:4)—to trust in God's providence regardless of circumstances. He declares that even if God should send suffering and loss, he would still rejoice in his Savior-God—one of the strongest affirmations of faith in all Scripture.
3:19 *made my feet like hinds' feet.* Gives me sure-footed confidence. *director.* Probably the conductor of the temple musicians. This chapter may have formed part of the temple prayers that were chanted with the accompaniment of instruments (see 1 Chr 16:4–7). *stringed instruments.* Including harp and lyre (Ps 33:2; 92:3; 144:9).

Zephaniah

INTRODUCTION

Author

The prophet Zephaniah was evidently a person of considerable social standing in Judah and was probably related to the royal line. The prophecy opens with a statement of the author's ancestry (1:1), which in itself is an unusual feature of the Hebrew prophetic tradition. Zephaniah was the fourth-generation descendant of Hezekiah, a notable king of Judah from 715 to 686 B.C. Apart from this statement, nothing more is said about his background. Whereas the prophet Micah dealt carefully and sympathetically with the problems of the common people of Judah, Zephaniah's utterances show a much greater familiarity with court circles and current political issues. Zephaniah was probably familiar with the writings of such prominent eighth-century prophets as Isaiah and Amos, whose utterances he reflects, and he may also have been aware of the ministry of the young Jeremiah.

Date

According to 1:1, Zephaniah prophesied during the reign of King Josiah (640–609 B.C.), making him a contemporary of Jeremiah, Nahum and perhaps Habakkuk. His prophecy is probably to be dated relatively early in Josiah's reign, before that king's attempt at reform (and while conditions brought about by the reigns of Manasseh and Amon still prevailed) and before the Assyrian king Ashurbanipal's death in 627 (while Assyria was still powerful, though threatened).

Background

See Introductions to Jeremiah and Nahum: Background; see also 2 Kin 22:1–23:30; 2 Chr 34–35 and notes.

Purpose and Theme

The intent of the author was to announce to Judah God's approaching judgment. A Scythian incursion into Canaan may have provided the immediate occasion. This fierce, horse-mounted people originated in what is now southern Russia, but by the seventh century B.C. had migrated across the Caucasus and settled in and along the northern territories of the Assyrian empire. Alternately the enemies and allies of Assyria, they seem to have thrust south along the Mediterranean sometime in the 620s, destroying Ashkelon and Ashdod and halting at the Egyptian border only because of a payoff by Pharaoh Psamtik (Psammetichus). Ultimately, however, the destruction prophesied by Zephaniah came at the hands of the Babylonians after they had overpowered Assyria and brought that ancient power to its end.

Zephaniah's main theme is the coming of the day of the Lord (see notes on Is 2:11,17,20; Joel 1:15; 2:2; Amos 5:18; 8:9), when God will severely punish the nations, including apostate Judah. He portrays the stark horror of that ordeal with the same graphic imagery found elsewhere in the prophets. But he also makes it clear that God will yet be merciful toward His people; like many other prophets, he ends his pronouncements of doom on the positive note of Judah's restoration.

Outline

I. Introduction (1:1–3)
   A. Title: The Prophet Identified (1:1)
   B. Prologue: Double Announcement of Total Judgment (1:2–3)
II. The Day of the Lord Coming on Judah and the Nations (1:4–18)
   A. Judgment on the Idolaters in Judah (1:4–9)
   B. Wailing throughout Jerusalem (1:10–13)

- C. The Inescapable Day of the Lord's Wrath (1:14–18)

III. God's Judgment on the Nations (2:1—3:8)
- A. Call to Repentance (2:1–3)
- B. Judgment on Philistia (2:4–7)
- C. Judgment on Moab and Ammon (2:8–11)
- D. Judgment on Cush (Ethiopia) (2:12)
- E. Judgment on Assyria (2:13–15)
- F. Judgment on Jerusalem (3:1–5)
- G. Jerusalem's Refusal to Repent (3:6–8)

IV. Redemption of the Remnant (3:9–20)
- A. The Nations Purified, the Remnant Restored, Jerusalem Purged (3:9–13)
- B. Rejoicing in the City (3:14–17)
- C. The Nation Restored (3:18–20)

Day of Judgment on Judah

1 The word of the LORD which came to
Zephaniah son of Cushi, son of Gedaliah,
son of Amariah, son of Hezekiah, in the days
of [a]Josiah son of [b]Amon, king of Judah:

2 "I will completely [a]remove all *things*
From the face of the [1]earth," declares
the LORD.
3 "I will remove [a]man and beast;
I will remove the [b]birds of the sky
And the fish of the sea,
And the [1c]ruins along with the wicked;
And I will cut off man from the face of
the [2]earth," declares the LORD.
4 "So I will [a]stretch out My hand against
Judah
And against all the inhabitants of
Jerusalem.
And I will [b]cut off the remnant of Baal
from this place,
And the names of the [c]idolatrous
priests along with the priests.
5 "And those who bow down on the
[a]housetops to the host of heaven,
And those who bow down *and* [b]swear
to the LORD and *yet* swear by
[1c]Milcom,
6 And those who have [a]turned back
from following the LORD,
And those who have [b]not sought the
LORD or inquired of Him."

7 [1a]Be silent before the Lord [2]GOD!
For the [b]day of the LORD is near,
For the LORD has prepared a [c]sacrifice,
He has [d]consecrated His guests.

8 "Then it will come about on the day of
the LORD's sacrifice
That I will [a]punish the princes, the
king's sons
And all who clothe themselves with
[b]foreign garments.
9 "And I will punish on that day all who
leap on the *temple* threshold,
Who fill the house of their [1]lord with
[a]violence and deceit.
10 "On that day," declares the LORD,
"There will be the sound of a cry from
the [a]Fish Gate,
A wail from the [1b]Second Quarter,
And a loud crash from the [c]hills.
11 "Wail, O inhabitants of the [1]Mortar,
For all the [2]people of [a]Canaan will be
silenced;
All who weigh out [b]silver will be cut
off.
12 "It will come about at that time
That I will [a]search Jerusalem with
lamps,
And I will punish the men
Who are [1b]stagnant in spirit,
Who say in their hearts,
'The LORD will [c]not do good or evil!'
13 "Moreover, their wealth will become
[a]plunder
And their houses desolate;
Yes, [b]they will build houses but not
inhabit *them*,

1:1 [a]2 Kin 22:1, 2; 2 Chr 34:1-33; Jer 1:2; 22:11 [b]2 Kin 21:18-26; 2 Chr 33:20-25 **2** [1]Lit *ground* [a]Gen 6:7; Jer 7:20; Ezek 33:27, 28 **3** [1]Or *stumbling blocks* [2]Lit *ground* [a]Is 6:11, 12 [b]Jer 4:25; 9:10 [c]Ezek 7:19; 14:3, 4, 8 **4** [a]Jer 6:12; Ezek 6:14 [b]Mic 5:13 [c]2 Kin 23:5; Hos 10:5 **5** [1]Or *their king;* M.T. *Malcam,* probably a variant spelling of Milcom [a]2 Kin 23:12; Jer 19:13 [b]Jer 5:2, 7; 7:9, 10 [c]1 Kin 11:5, 33; Jer 49:1 **6** [a]Is 1:4; Hos 7:10 [b]Is 9:13 **7** [1]Lit *Hush* [2]Heb *YHWH,* usually rendered *LORD* [a]Hab 2:20; Zech 2:13 [b]Zeph 1:14 [c]Is 34:6; Jer 46:10 [d]1 Sam 16:5; Is 13:3

8 [a]Is 24:21; Hab 1:10 [b]Is 2:6 **9** [1]Or *Lord* [a]Jer 5:27; Amos 3:10 **10** [1]I.e. a district of Jerusalem [a]2 Chr 33:14; Neh 3:3; 12:39 [b]2 Chr 34:22 [c]Ezek 6:13 **11** [1]I.e. a district of Jerusalem [2]Or *merchant people will* [a]Zeph 2:5; Zech 14:21 [b]Job 27:16, 17; Hos 9:6 **12** [1]Lit *thickening on their lees* [a]Jer 16:16, 17; Ezek 9:4-11; Amos 9:1-3 [b]Jer 48:11; Amos 6:1 [c]Ezek 8:12; 9:9 **13** [a]Jer 15:13; 17:3 [b]Amos 5:11; Mic 6:15

1:1 *The word of the LORD.* A common introductory phrase in the prophets (see, e.g., Jer 1:4; Hos 1:1; Mic 1:1). *Zephaniah.* Means "The LORD hides" or "The LORD protects," perhaps referring to God's protection of Zephaniah during the infamous reigns of Manasseh and Amon, the predecessors of good King Josiah. *son of Hezekiah.* From the author's pedigree, scholars suggest that he was in his early 20s when he began to prophesy. He is more closely identified with the ruling class than was Isaiah, although Isaiah also moved regularly in court circles and was perhaps of noble birth.
1:2 *completely remove.* See v. 3. Zephaniah speaks of the coming catastrophe in language reminiscent of God's utterances prior to the flood (Gen 6:7). But this time it will be by God's fire (v. 18; 3:8).
1:3 *ruins.* See NASB marg. Alternatively, the sense may be that God will place formidable obstacles in the paths of the wicked and destroy them completely.
1:4–6 Seems to indicate that Zephaniah's main ministry took place before 621 B.C., since the practices condemned here were abolished in Josiah's reforms (2 Kin 23:4–16). Perhaps Zephaniah's message was partly instrumental in motivating King Josiah and the people to undertake the reforms (cf. 2 Chr 34:1–7).
1:4 Judah is censured for its unrepentant participation in the gross idolatry of Baal worship. *Baal.* See note on Judg 2:13. *this place.* Jerusalem, where Zephaniah probably lived.
1:5 *on the housetops.* See 2 Kin 23:12; Jer 19:13. *bow down . . . to the host of heaven.* See Deut 4:15–19; 2 Kin 17:16; 21:3; Is 47:13. *swear to the LORD . . . by Milcom.* Syncretism (worship of one's own god along with other gods). *Milcom.* Worshiped by the Ammonites, his rituals sometimes involved child sacrifice. Molech worship (Milcom and Molech were variant names referring to the same god) was forbidden to the Israelites (Lev 18:21; 20:1–5). Despite this, Solomon set up an altar to Molech on the Mount of Olives (1 Kin 11:7). Manasseh established the rituals in the Valley of Ben-hinnom (2 Chr 33:6; Jer 7:31; 32:35).
1:7 *Be silent before the Lord GOD!* See Hab 2:20. *day of the LORD.* Zephaniah's main theme (see Introduction: Purpose and Theme); not of deliverance for Judah, but of divine vengeance on the idolatrous covenant nation. *sacrifice.* The victim is Judah. *consecrated.* Since the coming slaughter of judgment is called a sacrifice, God's preparation of His guests is called His consecration of them—in preparation for their feasting on the plunder. *His guests.* The pagan conquerors (mainly Babylon).
1:9 *leap on the temple threshold.* Or "leap over . . ."; perhaps referring to a pagan custom that began in the time of Samuel (1 Sam 5:5).
1:10–13 Wailing throughout the city (contrast 3:14–17).
1:10 Merchants who had grown rich through corrupt business practices would be destroyed. *Fish Gate.* See note on Neh 3:3. *Second Quarter.* See note on Neh 11:9.
1:11 *the Mortar.* May have been an area in the Tyropoeon Valley, just south of Mount Moriah, where some foreign merchants lived (see 1 Kin 20:34 and note; see also NASB marg. here).
1:12 *search Jerusalem with lamps.* The Babylonians later dragged people from houses, streets, sewers and tombs, where they had hidden. *The LORD will not do.* A typical depiction of the arrogance of the wicked (see note on Ps 10:11).
1:13 The assets of those who have become wealthy through

And plant vineyards but not drink
their wine."

14 Near is the [a]great [b]day of the LORD,
Near and coming very quickly;
Listen, the day of the LORD!
[1]In it the warrior [c]cries out bitterly.
15 A day of wrath is that day,
A day of [a]trouble and distress,
A day of destruction and desolation,
A day of [b]darkness and gloom,
A day of clouds and thick darkness,
16 A day of [a]trumpet and battle cry
Against the [b]fortified cities
And the high corner towers.
17 I will bring [a]distress on men
So that they will walk [b]like the blind,
Because they have sinned against the
LORD;
And their [c]blood will be poured out
like dust
And their [d]flesh like dung.
18 Neither their [a]silver nor their gold
Will be able to deliver them
On the day of the LORD's wrath;
And [b]all the earth will be devoured
In the fire of His jealousy,
For He will [c]make a complete end,
Indeed a terrifying one,
Of all the inhabitants of the earth.

Judgments on Judah's Enemies

2 Gather yourselves together, yes, [a]gather,
O nation [b]without [1]shame,
2 Before the decree [1]takes effect—
The day passes [a]like the chaff—
Before the [b]burning anger of the LORD
comes upon you,
Before the [c]day of the LORD's anger
comes upon you.
3 [a]Seek the LORD,
All you [b]humble of the [1]earth
Who have carried out His [2]ordinances;
[c]Seek righteousness, seek humility.
Perhaps you will be [d]hidden
In the day of the LORD's anger.

4 For [a]Gaza will be abandoned
And Ashkelon a desolation;
[a]Ashdod will be driven out at noon
And [a]Ekron will be uprooted.
5 Woe to the inhabitants of the seacoast,
The nation of the [1a]Cherethites!
The word of the LORD is [b]against you,
O [c]Canaan, land of the Philistines;
And I will [d]destroy you
So that there will be [e]no inhabitant.
6 So the seacoast will be [a]pastures,
With [1]caves for shepherds and folds
for flocks.
7 And the coast will be
For the [a]remnant of the house of Judah,
They will [b]pasture on it.
In the houses of Ashkelon they will lie
down at evening;
For the LORD their God will [c]care for
them
And [d]restore their fortune.

8 "I have heard the [1a]taunting of Moab
And the [b]revilings of the sons of
Ammon,
With which they have [2]taunted My
people
And [3c]become arrogant against their
territory.
9 "Therefore, as I live," declares the LORD
of hosts,
The God of Israel,
"Surely [a]Moab will be like [b]Sodom
And the sons of [c]Ammon like
[d]Gomorrah—
A place possessed by nettles and salt
pits,

14 [1]Lit *There* [a]Jer 30:7; Joel 2:11; Mal 4:5 [b]Ezek 7:7, 12; 30:3; Joel 1:15; 3:14; Zeph 1:7 [c]Ezek 7:16-18
15 [a]Is 22:5 [b]Joel 2:2, 31; Amos 5:18-20
16 [a]Is 27:13; Jer 4:19 [b]Is 2:12-15
17 [a]Jer 10:18 [b]Deut 28:29 [c]Ezek 24:7, 8 [d]Jer 8:2; 9:22
18 [a]Ezek 7:19 [b]Zeph 3:8 [c]Gen 6:7; Ezek 7:5-7
2:1 [1]Or *longing* [a]2 Chr 20:4; Joel 1:14 [b]Jer 3:3; 6:15
2 [1]Lit *is born* [a]Is 17:13; Hos 13:3 [b]Lam 4:11; Nah 1:6 [c]Zeph 1:18
3 [1]Or *land* [2]Or *justice* [a]Ps 105:4; Amos 5:6 [b]Ps 22:26; Is 11:4
3 [c]Amos 5:14, 15 [d]Ps 57:1; Is 26:20
4 [a]Amos 1:7, 8; Zech 9:5-7
5 [1]I.e. a segment of the Philistines with roots in Crete [a]Ezek 25:16 [b]Amos 3:1 [c]Zeph 1:11 [d]Is 14:29, 30 [e]Zeph 3:6
6 [1]Or *meadows* or *wells* [a]Is 5:17; 7:25
7 [a]Is 11:16 [b]Is 32:14 [c]Ex 4:31; Ps 80:14 [d]Jer 32:44; Zeph 3:20
8 [1]Lit *reproach* [2]Lit *reproached* [3]Lit *made themselves great* [a]Ezek 25:8 [b]Ezek 25:3 [c]Amos 1:13
9 [a]Is 15:1-9; Jer 48:1-47; Amos
2:1-3 [b]Gen 19:24 [c]Jer 49:1-6; Ezek 25:1-10 [d]Deut 29:23

dishonesty will be exposed and plundered (see Deut 28:30).
1:14–18 In a dramatic passage of great lyrical power, the Lord describes the destruction that will sweep the earth in the day of God's wrath.
1:15 *darkness . . . thick darkness.* See Amos 5:18–20.
1:17 *like the blind.* See Deut 28:28–29.
1:18 *Neither . . . silver nor . . . gold Will . . . deliver them.* In the day of God's judgment, material wealth cannot buy deliverance from punishment.
2:1–3 The prophet's exhortation to repent. This call to repentance and the later indictment of Jerusalem for refusal to repent (see 3:6–8 and note) frame the series of judgments that illustratively detail God's acts in the coming day of the Lord (2:4–3:5).
2:2 *like the chaff.* See note on Ps 1:4.
2:3 *Seek the LORD.* Even though destruction is imminent, there is still time to be sheltered from the calamity if only the nation will repent. *humble.* Those who abandon the arrogance of their idolatry and wickedness and humble themselves in repentance before God.
2:4–3:8 God's coming judgment on the nations—including Jerusalem (cf. Amos 1–2).
2:4 *Gaza . . . Ashkelon . . . Ashdod . . . Ekron.* See notes on Josh 13:3; Judg 3:3; Amos 1:6,8.
2:5 *Cherethites.* See note on 1 Sam 30:14. *Canaan.* See note on Gen 10:6. *I . . . no inhabitant.* The Lord's announced purpose.
2:6 The once-populous Philistine cities will revert to pastureland.
2:7 The faithful remnant of Judah will occupy this land and graze their flocks on it. *restore their fortune.* Or "bring back their captives." Here and in vv. 9,11 the prophet anticipates the ultimate outcome of the day of the Lord, which he spells out more fully in 3:9–20.
2:8 *Moab . . . sons of Ammon.* See notes on Gen 19:36–38; Amos 1:13. For the hostility of Ammon and Moab toward Israel see Amos 1:13–15; 2:1–3. They had often threatened to occupy Israelite territory (see Judg 11:12–13; Ezek 25:3–6).
2:9 *Sodom . . . Gomorrah.* See Gen 19. They were used in the OT to typify complete destruction at the hands of God (see Deut 29:23; Is 13:19; Jer 49:18), and their mention added ominous overtones to the prophet's description of the day of the Lord. *nettles.* A symbol of depopulation (see Is 7:23–25). *remnant . . . will inherit them.* See note on v. 7.

And a perpetual desolation.
The remnant of My people will
[e]plunder them
And the remainder of My nation will
inherit them."
10 This they will have in return for their
[a]pride, because they have [1b]taunted and
[2]become arrogant against the people of the
LORD of hosts.
11 The LORD will be [a]terrifying to them,
for He will [1]starve [b]all the gods of the earth;
and all the [c]coastlands of the nations will
[d]bow down to Him, everyone from his *own*
place.
12 "You also, O [a]Ethiopians, will be slain
by My sword."
13 And He will [a]stretch out His hand
against the north
And destroy [b]Assyria,
And He will make [c]Nineveh a
desolation,
Parched like the wilderness.
14 Flocks will lie down in her midst,
[1]All beasts which range in herds;
Both the [2a]pelican and the hedgehog
Will lodge in [3]the tops of her pillars;
[4]Birds will sing in the window,
Desolation *will be* on the threshold;
For He has laid bare the cedar work.
15 This is the [a]exultant city
Which [b]dwells securely,
Who says in her heart,
"[c]I am, and there is no one besides me."
How she has become a [d]desolation,
A resting place for beasts!
[e]Everyone who passes by her will hiss
And wave his hand *in contempt.*

Woe to Jerusalem and the Nations

3 Woe to her who is [a]rebellious and
[b]defiled,
The [c]tyrannical city!
2 She [a]heeded no voice,
She [b]accepted no instruction.
She did not [c]trust in the LORD,
She did not [d]draw near to her God.
3 Her [a]princes within her are roaring
lions,
Her judges are [b]wolves at evening;
They leave nothing for the morning.
4 Her prophets are [a]reckless,
treacherous men;
Her [b]priests have profaned the
sanctuary.
They have done violence to the law.
5 The LORD is [a]righteous [b]within her;
He will [c]do no injustice.
[d]Every morning He brings His justice
to light;
He does not fail.
But the unjust [e]knows no shame.
6 "I have cut off nations;
Their corner towers are in ruins.
I have made their streets [a]desolate,
With no one passing by;
Their [b]cities are laid waste,
Without a man, [c]without an
inhabitant.
7 "I said, 'Surely you will revere Me,
[a]Accept instruction.'
So her dwelling will [b]not be cut off
According to all that I have appointed
concerning her.
But they were eager to [c]corrupt all
their deeds.

8 "Therefore [a]wait for Me," declares the
LORD,
"For the day when I rise up as a witness.
Indeed, My decision is to [b]gather
nations,
To assemble kingdoms,
To pour out on them My indignation,
All My burning anger;
For [c]all the earth will be devoured
By the fire of My zeal.

9 [e]Is 11:14 **10** [1]Lit *reproached* [2]Lit *made* themselves *great* [a]Is 16:6 [b]Zeph 2:8 **11** [1]Lit *make lean* [a]Joel 2:11 [b]Zeph 1:4 [c]Is 24:15 [d]Ps 72:8-11; Zeph 3:9 **12** [a]Is 18:1-7; 20:4, 5; Ezek 30:4-9 **13** [a]Is 14:26; Zeph 1:4 [b]Is 10:16; Mic 5:6 [c]Nah 3:7 **14** [1]Or *All* kinds of *beasts in crowds;* lit *Every* kind of *beast of a nation* [2]Or *owl* or *jackdaw* [3]Lit *her capitals* [4]Lit *A voice* [a]Is 14:23; 34:11 **15** [a]Is 22:2 [b]Is 32:9, 11; 47:8 [c]Is 47:8; Ezek 28:2, 9 [d]Is 32:14 [e]Jer 18:16; 19:8 **3:1** [a]Jer 5:23 [b]Ezek 23:30 [c]Jer 6:6 **2** [a]Jer 7:23-28

2 [b]Jer 2:30; 5:3; 2 Tim 3:16 [c]Ps 78:22; Jer 13:25 [d]Ps 73:28 **3** [a]Ezek 22:27 [b]Jer 5:6; Hab 1:8 **4** [a]Judg 9:4 [b]Ezek 22:26; Mal 2:7, 8 **5** [a]Deut 32:4 [b]Zeph 3:15, 17 [c]Ps 92:15 [d]Job 7:18 [e]Zeph 2:1 **6** [a]Jer 9:12; Zech 7:14; Matt 23:38 [b]Lev 26:31; Is 6:11 [c]Zeph 2:5 **7** [a]Job 36:10; Ps 32:8; 1 Tim 1:5 [b]Jer 7:7 [c]Hos 9:9 **8** [a]Ps 27:14; Is 30:18; Hab 2:3 [b]Ezek 38:14-23; Joel 3:2 [c]Zeph 1:18

2:10 *in return for their pride . . . taunted . . . arrogant.* In reprisal, the faithful remnant will occupy Ammonite and Moabite territory.
2:11 *nations will bow down to Him.* See 3:9 and note.
2:12 *You also.* Without elaboration, the prophet simply announces God's purpose against Egypt (see v. 5 and note). *Ethiopians.* People from the upper (southern) Nile region. Egypt was ruled from 715 to 663 B.C. by a Cushite dynasty. *My sword.* Probably Babylon.
2:13 *north.* Although Nineveh was east of Judah, Assyrian armies normally invaded Canaan from the north, having first marched west along the Euphrates. *Nineveh.* See the books of Jonah and Nahum. Since Nineveh was destroyed in 612 B.C., Zephaniah's ministry had to be before that date. *desolation.* Even the site of Nineveh was later forgotten—until discovered through modern excavations.
2:15 *I am . . . no one besides me.* See Is 47:10. Assyria's boast belongs properly to God alone (see Is 45:5–6,18,21). *has become.* Anticipating Nineveh's impending destruction.
3:1 *tyrannical.* See Jer 22:3. *city.* Apostate Jerusalem is condemned for its sins.
3:3–4 *princes . . . judges . . . prophets . . . priests.* All classes of Judah's leaders are castigated for indulging in conduct completely opposed to their vocations and responsibilities (see Jer 1:18 and note).
3:3 *roaring lions . . . wolves at evening.* Those in power are rapacious.
3:4 *reckless, treacherous men.* Claiming to be prophets of the Lord, they proclaimed only lies (see Jer 5:31; 14:14; 23:16,32). *priests . . . have done violence to the law.* When they should have been teachers of the law (see Deut 31:9–13; 2 Chr 17:8–9; 19:8; Ezra 7:6; Jer 2:8; 18:18; Mal 2:7).
3:6–8 Jerusalem's refusal to repent (see 2:1–3 and note).
3:6 *I have cut off nations.* The destruction of other nations was meant to serve as a warning to wanton Judah, but to no avail (see v. 7).
3:7 *eager to corrupt.* See, e.g., Jer 7:13,25–26.
3:8 *wait.* A sarcastic statement to Judah to wait for the threatened catastrophe. *as a witness.* To lodge accusations (see Ps 50:7)—and then proceed to execute judgments. *My decision.* The Lord concludes His announcement of judgment with a general declaration of His intent.

9 "For then I will [1]give to the peoples
[a]purified lips,
That all of them may [b]call on the
name of the LORD,
To serve Him [2]shoulder to shoulder.
10 "From beyond the rivers of [a]Ethiopia
My [1]worshipers, [2]My dispersed ones,
Will [b]bring My offerings.
11 "In that day you will [a]feel no shame
Because of all your deeds
By which you have rebelled against
Me;
For then I will remove from your
midst
Your [b]proud, exulting ones,
And you will never again be haughty
On My [c]holy mountain.

A Remnant of Israel

12 "But I will leave among you
A [a]humble and lowly people,
And they will [b]take refuge in the name
of the LORD.
13 "The [a]remnant of Israel will [b]do no
wrong
And [c]tell no lies,
Nor will a deceitful tongue
Be found in their mouths;
For they will [d]feed and lie down
With no one to make them tremble."

14 Shout for joy, O daughter of Zion!
[a]Shout *in triumph,* O Israel!
Rejoice and exult with all *your* heart,
O daughter of Jerusalem!
15 The LORD has taken away [a]*His*
judgments against you,
He has cleared away your enemies.
The King of Israel, the LORD, is [b]in
your midst;
You will [c]fear disaster no more.
16 [a]In that day it will be said to
Jerusalem:
"[b]Do not be afraid, O Zion;
[c]Do not let your hands fall limp.
17 "The LORD your God is [a]in your midst,
A [1][b]victorious warrior.
He will [c]exult over you with joy,
He will [2]be quiet in His love,
He will rejoice over you with shouts of
joy.
18 "I will gather those who [a]grieve about
the appointed feasts—
They [1]came from you, *O Zion;*
The reproach *of exile* is a burden on
[2]them.
19 "Behold, I am going to deal at that time
With all your [a]oppressors,
I will save the [b]lame
And gather the outcast,
And I will turn their [c]shame into
[d]praise and renown
In all the earth.
20 "At that time I will [a]bring you in,
Even at the time when I gather you
together;
Indeed, I will give you [b]renown and
praise
Among all the peoples of the earth,
When I [c]restore your fortunes before
your eyes,"
Says the LORD.

9 [1]Lit *change* [2]Lit *with one shoulder* [a]Is 19:18; 57:19 [b]Ps 22:27; 86:9; Hab 2:14; Zeph 2:11
10 [1]Or *suppliants* [2]Lit *the daughter of My dispersed ones* [a]Ps 68:31; Is 18:1 [b]Is 60:6, 7
11 [a]Is 45:17; 54:4; Joel 2:26, 27 [b]Is 2:12; 5:15 [c]Is 11:9; 56:7; Ezek 20:40
12 [a]Is 14:30 [b]Is 14:32; 50:10; Nah 1:7; Zech 13:8, 9
13 [a]Is 10:20-22; Mic 4:7; Zeph 2:7 [b]Ps 119:3; Jer 31:33; Zeph 3:5 [c]Zech 8:3, 16; Rev 14:5 [d]Ezek 34:13-15
14 [a]Zech 9:9
15 [a]Ps 19:9; John 5:30; Rev 18:20
15 [b]Ezek 37:26-28; Zeph 3:5 [c]Is 54:14
16 [a]Is 25:9 [b]Is 35:3, 4 [c]Job 4:3; Heb 12:12
17 [1]Lit *A warrior who saves* [2]Or with some ancient versions, *renew* you *in* [a]Zeph 3:5, 15 [b]Is 63:1 [c]Is 62:5
18 [1]Lit *were* [2]Lit *her* [a]Ps 42:2-4; Ezek 9:4
19 [a]Is 60:14 [b]Ezek 34:16; Mic 4:6 [c]Ezek 16:27, 57 [d]Is 60:18; 62:7; Zech 8:23
20 [a]Ezek 37:12, 21 [b]Deut 26:18, 19; Is 56:5; 66:22 [c]Jer 29:14; Joel 3:1; Zeph 2:7

3:9–20 A three-part oracle (vv. 9–13, 14–17, 18–20) announcing redemption that will follow God's judgment.
3:9–13 The Lord gives assurance that the nations will be purified, the scattered remnant restored and Jerusalem purged.
3:9 God's fearful judgment of the nations will effect (or be followed by) their purification so that they will call on His name and serve Him. Israel's God will be acknowledged by the nations, and God's people will be held in honor by them (cf. vv. 19–20).
3:10 *Ethiopia.* The most distant area imaginable (see note on 2:12). The most widely dispersed will be restored. *bring My offerings.* Rather than Baal's and Molech's (cf. 1:4–5).
3:11 *For then.* This line begins the same as the first line of v. 9. Thus vv. 9–11a constitute a three-line unit (in Hebrew) and vv. 11b,c–12 a three-line unit. The latter speaks of a purified Jerusalem. Verse 13 is a summary conclusion. *My holy mountain.* Mount Zion (see Ps 2:6).
3:13 *no one to make them tremble.* See Mic 4:4.
3:14–17 Joy in the restored city (in two parts: vv. 14–15 and vv. 16–17)—the prophet's reassurance (contrast 1:10–13).
3:14 *daughter of Zion ... Jerusalem.* Personification of Jerusalem and its inhabitants.
3:15 *your enemies.* All those arrayed against Israel. *The King of Israel, the LORD.* See Is 44:6; see also Introduction to Psalms: Theology.
3:16 *Do not let your hands fall limp.* Do not be discouraged.
3:18–20 Summary announcement of restoration—the Lord's final assurance.
3:18 *appointed feasts.* See Lev 23.
3:20 *give you renown and praise.* See Gen 12:2–3.

Haggai

INTRODUCTION

Author

Haggai was a prophet who, along with Zechariah, encouraged the returned exiles to rebuild the temple (see Ezra 5:1 – 2; 6:14). "Haggai" means "festal," which may indicate that the prophet was born during one of the three pilgrimage feasts (Unleavened Bread, Pentecost or Weeks, and Booths; cf. Deut 16:16). Based on 2:3 (see note there) Haggai may have witnessed the destruction of Solomon's temple. If so, he must have been in his early 70s during his ministry.

Background

In 538 B.C. the conqueror of Babylon, Cyrus king of Persia, issued a decree allowing the Jews to return to Jerusalem and rebuild the temple (see Ezra 1:2 – 4; 6:3 – 5). Led by Zerubbabel (but see note on Ezra 1:8, "Sheshbazzar"), about 50,000 Jews journeyed home and began work on the temple. About two years later (536) they completed the foundation amid great rejoicing (Ezra 3:8 – 10). Their success aroused the Samaritans and other neighbors who feared the political and religious implications of a rebuilt temple in a thriving Jewish state. They therefore opposed the project vigorously and managed to halt work until Darius the Great became king of Persia in 522 B.C. (Ezra 4:1 – 5,24).

Darius was interested in the religions of his empire, and Haggai and Zechariah began to preach in his second year, 520 B.C. (see 1:1; Zech 1:1). The Jews were more to blame for their inactivity than their opponents, and Haggai tried to arouse them from their lethargy. When the governor of Trans-Euphrates and other officials tried to interfere with the rebuilding efforts, Darius fully supported the Jews (Ezra 5:3 – 6; 6:6 – 12). In 516 B.C. the temple was finished and dedicated (Ezra 6:15 – 18).

Date

The messages of Haggai were given during a four-month period in 520 B.C., the second year of King Darius. The first message was delivered on the first day of the sixth month (Aug. 29), the last on the 24th day of the ninth month (Dec. 18). See notes on 1:1; 2:1,10; see also Introduction to Zechariah: Dates.

Themes and Teaching

Next to Obadiah, Haggai is the shortest book in the OT, but its teachings are none the less significant. Haggai clearly shows the consequences of disobedience (1:6,11; 2:16 – 17) and obedience (2:7 – 9,19). When the people give priority to God and His house, they are blessed rather than cursed. Obedience brings the encouragement and strength of the Spirit of God (2:4 – 5).

Ch. 2 speaks of the coming of the Messiah, called the "desired of all nations" in v. 7 (see NASB marg. there). His coming would fill the rebuilt temple with glory (see 2:9 and note). The Lord made Zerubbabel his "signet ring" as a guarantee that the Messiah would come (see 2:23 and note). These passages are linked with the judgment of the nations at Christ's second coming, when the nations will be shaken and kingdoms overthrown (see 2:6 – 7,21 – 22 and notes; cf. Heb 12:25 – 29).

Literary Features

Like Malachi, Haggai uses a number of questions to highlight key issues (see 1:4,9; 2:3,19). He also makes effective use of repetition: "Consider your ways" occurs in 1:5,7; 2:15,18, and "I am with you" in 1:13; 2:4. "I am going to shake the heavens and the earth" is found in 2:6,21. The major sections of the book are marked off by the date on which the word of the Lord came "to" (or "by") Haggai (1:1; 2:1,10,20).

Several times the prophet appears to echo other Scriptures (compare 1:6 with Deut 28:38 – 39 and 2:17 with Deut 28:22). The threefold use of "take courage" in 2:4 (see note there) reflects the encouragement given in Josh 1:6 – 7,9,18.

Outline

I. First Message: The Call to Rebuild the Temple (1:1 – 11)
   A. The People's Lame Excuse (1:1 – 4)
   B. The Poverty of the People (1:5 – 6)
   C. The Reason God Has Cursed Them (1:7 – 11)
II. The Response of Zerubbabel and the People (1:12 – 15)
   A. The Leaders and Remnant Obey (1:12)
   B. The Lord Strengthens the Workers (1:13 – 15)
III. Second Message: The Temple to Be Filled with Glory (2:1 – 9)
   A. The People Encouraged (2:1 – 5)
   B. The Promise of Glory and Peace (2:6 – 9)
IV. Third Message: A Defiled People Purified and Blessed (2:10 – 19)
   A. The Rapid Spread of Sin (2:10 – 14)
   B. Poor Harvests because of Disobedience (2:15 – 17)
   C. Blessing to Come as the Temple Is Rebuilt (2:18 – 19)
V. Fourth Message: The Promise to Zerubbabel (2:20 – 23)
   A. The Judgment of the Nations (2:20 – 22)
   B. The Significance of Zerubbabel (2:23)

Haggai Begins Temple Building

1 In the [a]second year of Darius the king, on the first day of the sixth month, the word of the LORD came by the prophet [b]Haggai to [c]Zerubbabel the son of Shealtiel, [d]governor of Judah, and to [e]Joshua the son of Jehozadak, the high priest, saying,

2 "Thus says the LORD of [1]hosts, 'This people says, "The time has not come, *even* the time for the house of the LORD to be rebuilt." ' "

3 Then the word of the LORD came by Haggai the prophet, saying,

4 "Is it time for you yourselves to dwell in your paneled houses while this house [a]*lies* desolate?"

5 Now therefore, thus says the LORD of hosts, "[1]Consider your ways!

6 "You have [a]sown much, but [1]harvest little; *you* eat, but *there is* not *enough* to be satisfied; *you* drink, but *there is* [2]not *enough* to become drunk; *you* put on clothing, but no one is warm *enough;* and he who earns, earns wages *to put* into a purse with holes."

7 Thus says the LORD of hosts, "[1]Consider your ways!

8 "Go up to the [1]mountains, bring wood and [a]rebuild the [2]temple, that I may be [b]pleased with it and be [c]glorified," says the LORD.

9 "[a]*You* look for much, but behold, *it comes* to little; when you bring *it* home, I [b]blow it *away*. Why?" declares the LORD of hosts, "Because of My house which [c]*lies* desolate, while each of you runs to his own house.

10 "Therefore, because of you the [a]sky has withheld [1]its dew and the earth has withheld its produce.

11 "I called for a [a]drought on the land, on the mountains, on the grain, on the new wine, on the oil, on what the ground produces, on [b]men, on cattle, and on [c]all the labor of [1]your hands."

12 Then [a]Zerubbabel the son of Shealtiel, and [b]Joshua the son of Jehozadak, the high priest, with all the remnant of the people, [c]obeyed the voice of the LORD their God and the words of Haggai the prophet, as the LORD their God had sent him. And the people [1d]showed reverence for the LORD.

13 Then Haggai, the [a]messenger of the LORD, spoke [1]by the commission of the LORD to the people saying, " '[b]I am with you,' declares the LORD."

14 So the LORD stirred up the spirit of [a]Zerubbabel the son of Shealtiel, [a]governor of Judah, and the spirit of Joshua the son of Jehozadak, the high priest, and the spirit of all the [b]remnant of the people; and they came and [c]worked on the house of the LORD of hosts, their God,

15 on the twenty-fourth day of the sixth month in the second year of Darius the king.

The Builders Encouraged

2 On the twenty-first of the seventh month, the word of the LORD came by [a]Haggai the prophet saying,

2 "Speak now to [a]Zerubbabel the son of

1:1 [a]Ezra 4:24 [b]Ezra 5:1; 6:14; Hag 1:3, 12, 13; 2:1, 10, 20 [c]Ezra 2:2; Neh 7:7; Hag 1:12, 14; Zech 4:6; Matt 1:12, 13 [d]1 Kin 10:15; Ezra 5:3 [e]Zech 6:11
2 [1]Lit *hosts, saying*
4 [a]Jer 33:10, 12; Hag 1:9
5 [1]Lit *Set your heart on*
6 [1]Lit *bring in* [2]Lit *not becoming drunk* [a]Deut 28:38-40; Hos 8:7; Hag 1:9, 10; 2:16, 17
7 [1]Lit *Set your heart on*
8 [1]Lit *mountain* [2]Lit *house* [a]1 Kin 6:1 [b]Ps 132:13, 14 [c]Hag 2:7, 9
9 [a]Prov 27:20; Eccl 1:8 [b]Is 40:7 [c]Hag 1:4
10 [1]Lit *from dew* [a]Deut 28:23, 24; 1 Kin 17:1; Joel 1:18-20
11 [1]Lit *the palms* [a]Jer 14:2-6; Mal 3:9, 11 [b]Deut 28:22 [c]Hag 2:17
12 [1]Lit *feared before* [a]Hag 1:1 [b]Hag 1:14; 2:2 [c]Is 1:19; 1 Thess 2:13 [d]Deut 31:12, 13; Ps 112:1; Is 50:10
13 [1]Or *the message* [a]Is 44:26; Ezek 3:17; Mal 2:7; 3:1 [b]Ps 46:11; Is 41:10; 43:2 **14** [a]Hag 1:1; 2:2, 21 [b]Hag 1:12 [c]Ezra 5:2; Neh 4:6 **2:1** [a]Hag 1:1 **2** [a]Hag 1:1

1:1 *second year . . . first day . . . sixth month.* Aug. 29, 520 B.C. *Darius the king.* Darius Hystaspis (or Hystaspes) ruled Persia from 522 to 486 B.C. It was he who prepared the trilingual inscription on the Behistun (Bisitun) cliff wall (located in modern Iran), through which cuneiform languages were deciphered. *first day.* The new moon was the day on which prophets were sometimes consulted (see 2 Kin 4:22–23 and note on Is 1:14). *Zerubbabel.* See note on Ezra 1:8, "Sheshbazzar." *Shealtiel.* According to 1 Chr 3:17–19 he was Zerubbabel's grandfather (in Hebrew "son" sometimes means "grandson"). *Joshua.* Mentioned with Zerubbabel also in vv. 12,14; 2:2,4. *Jehozadak.* Had been taken captive by Nebuchadnezzar (1 Chr 6:15).
1:2 *LORD of hosts.* Used more than 90 times in Haggai, Zechariah and Malachi. See note on Is 13:4. *This people.* See 2:14. Because of their sin, the nation is not called "my people" (see Is 6:9; 8:6,11–12; Jer 14:10–11; see also note on Hos 1:9). *time has not come.* After the foundation of the temple had been laid in 536 B.C. (see Ezra 3:8–10), opposition hindered and then halted the work until 520 (see Ezra 4:1–5,24).
1:4 *paneled houses.* Usually connected with royal dwellings, which had cedar paneling (1 Kin 7:3,7; Jer 22:14).
1:6 *sown much . . . harvest little.* A curse for disobedience (see Deut 28:38–39). Lev 26:20 also describes the unfruitfulness of a land judged by God. *drink . . . drunk.* Cf. Is 55:1–2. The people experience futility in all their activities, legitimate or illegitimate (cf. Hos 4:10–11). *purse with holes.* Famine causes prices to rise sharply.
1:8 *mountains . . . wood.* Perhaps wood from the hills around Jerusalem was to supplement the cedar wood already purchased from Lebanon (see Ezra 3:7). *be pleased with it.* And with the sacrifices offered there (contrast Is 1:11). *be glorified.* An obedient nation would bring praise and honor to God (see Jer 13:11).
1:10 *dew.* Normally abundant, and often as valuable as rain (see 2 Sam 1:21; 1 Kin 17:1).
1:11 *mountains.* The hills were cultivated, especially through terracing (see Ps 104:13–15; Is 7:25; Joel 3:18). *the grain . . . the new wine . . . the oil.* The three basic crops of the land, often mentioned in a context of blessing or cursing (see Deut 7:13; 11:14; 28:51; Hos 2:8,22). Olive oil was used as food, ointment or medicine. *men, on cattle.* The drought affected men and cattle and so could be said to be "on" them too.
1:12 *remnant.* See note on Is 1:9. *showed reverence for the LORD.* Showing respect and obedience (see Deut 31:12–13; Mal 1:6; 3:5,16).
1:13 *messenger.* A title for prophets (see 2 Chr 36:15; Is 42:19 and note) or priests (see Mal 2:7). *I am with you.* A sure indication of success (see 2:4; Num 14:9; Gen 26:3 and note).
1:14 *stirred up the spirit.* See Ezra 1:5, where God stirred up many of these same people to return home and rebuild the temple.
1:15 *twenty-fourth day of the sixth month.* Sept. 21, 520 B.C.
2:1 *twenty-first of the seventh month.* Oct. 17, 520 B.C., the last day of the Feast of Booths. It was a time to celebrate the summer harvest (see Lev 23:34–43), though the crops were meager (see 1:11; cf. John 7:37). Solomon had dedicated the temple during this feast (1 Kin 8:2).

Shealtiel, [a]governor of Judah, and to [a]Joshua
the son of Jehozadak, the high priest, and to
the [b]remnant of the people saying,
3 'Who is [a]left among you who saw this
[1]temple in its [b]former glory? And how do
you see it now? Does it not [2]seem to you like
nothing [3]in comparison?
4 'But now [1][a]take courage, Zerubbabel,'
declares the LORD, 'take courage also, Joshua
son of Jehozadak, the high priest, and all
you people of the land take courage,' declares
the LORD, 'and work; for [b]I am with you,'
declares the LORD of hosts.
5 'As for the [1][a]promise which I [2]made
you when you came out of Egypt, [3]My [b]Spir-
it is abiding in your midst; [c]do not fear!'
6 "For thus says the LORD of hosts, '[a]Once
more [1]in a [b]little while, I am going to [c]shake
the heavens and the earth, the sea also and
the dry land.
7 'I will shake [a]all the nations; and [1]they
will come with the [b]wealth of all nations,
and I will [c]fill this house with glory,' says the
LORD of hosts.
8 'The [a]silver is Mine and the gold is
Mine,' declares the LORD of hosts.
9 'The latter [a]glory of this house will be
greater than the [b]former,' says the LORD of
hosts, 'and in this place I will give [c]peace,'
declares the LORD of hosts."
10 On the [a]twenty-fourth of the ninth
month, in the second year of Darius, the
word of the LORD came to Haggai the prophet, saying,
11 "Thus says the LORD of hosts, '[a]Ask now
the priests *for* a [1]ruling:
12 'If a man carries [a]holy meat in the [1]fold
of his garment, and touches bread with [2]this
fold, or cooked food, wine, oil, or any *other*
food, will it become holy?'" And the priests
answered, "No."
13 Then Haggai said, "[a]If one who is
unclean from a [1]corpse touches any of these,
will *the latter* become unclean?" And the
priests answered, "It will become unclean."
14 Then Haggai said, "'[a]So is this people.
And so is this nation before Me,' declares the
LORD, 'and so is every work of their hands;
and what they offer there is unclean.
15 'But now, do [1][a]consider from this day
[2]onward: before one [b]stone was placed on
another in the temple of the LORD,
16 [1]from that time *when* one came to a
grain heap of twenty *measures,* there would
be only ten; and *when* one came to the wine
vat to draw fifty [2]measures, there would be
only twenty.
17 'I smote you *and* every work of your

2 [a]Hag 1:1 [b]Hag 1:12
3 [1]Lit *house* [2]Lit *in your eyes* [3]Lit *like it* [a]Ezra 3:12 [b]Hag 2:9
4 [1]Lit *be strong* [a]Deut 31:23; 1 Chr 22:13; 28:20; Zech 8:9; Eph 6:10 [b]2 Sam 5:10; Acts 7:9
5 [1]Lit *word* [2]Lit *cut with* [3]Or *while...was standing* [a]Ex 19:4-6; 29:45, 46; 33:12-14; 34:8-10 [b]Neh 9:20; Is 63:11, 14 [c]Is 41:10, 13; Zech 8:13
6 [1]Lit *it is a little* [a]Heb 12:26 [b]Is 10:25; 29:17 [c]Hag 2:21
7 [1]Or *the desire of all nations will come* [a]Dan 2:44; Joel 3:9, 16 [b]Is 60:4-9 [c]1 Kin 8:11; Is 60:7
8 [a]1 Chr 29:14, 16; Is 60:17
9 [a]Zech 2:5 [b]Hag 2:3 [c]Is 9:6, 7; 66:12
10 [a]Hag 2:20
11 [1]Lit *law* [a]Deut 17:8-11; Mal 2:7
12 [1]Lit *wing* [2]Lit *his wing* [a]Ex 29:37; Lev 6:27, 29; 7:6; Ezek 44:19; Matt 23:19
13 [1]Lit *soul* [a]Lev 22:4-6; Num 19:22
14 [a]Prov 15:8; Is 1:11-15
15 [1]Lit *set your heart* [2]Or *backward* [a]Hag 1:5, 7; 2:18 [b]Ezra 3:10; 4:24
16 [1]Lit *since they were* [2]Or *troughs full*

2:3 *is left.* Some of the older exiles (perhaps including Haggai himself) had seen Solomon's magnificent temple, destroyed by the Babylonians 66 years earlier. *this temple in its former glory.* See vv. 7,9. Zerubbabel's temple was considered a continuation of Solomon's. *seem . . . like nothing.* Cf. the reaction when the foundation of the temple was finished (Ezra 3:12).

2:4 *take courage . . . work.* David used these words in 1 Chr 28:20 when he encouraged Solomon to build the temple. Joshua son of Nun had been exhorted with similar words (Josh 1:6–7,9,18). *I am with you.* See 1:13 and note; 1 Chr 28:20. The same God who helped Solomon will empower Zerubbabel and the people.

2:5 *My Spirit.* The Holy Spirit had rested on Moses and the 70 elders as they had led the people out of Egypt and through the wilderness (see Num 11:16–17,25; Is 63:11). See also Zech 4:6 and note. *do not fear!* See notes on v. 4; Josh 1:18; Is 41:10.

2:6 An announcement of the coming day of God's judgment on the nations—which the fall of Persia to Alexander the Great (333–330 B.C.) would foreshadow. Heb 12:26–27 relates this verse to the judgment of the nations at the second coming of Christ. The background for the shaking of the nations here and in vv. 21–22 is the judgment on Egypt at the Red Sea. Cf. also Is 14:16–17.

2:7 *they will come.* "They" (or "The Desire"; see NASB marg.) can refer to individuals, as in 1 Sam 9:20; Dan 9:23 (where the same Hebrew verb is translated "highly esteemed"); 11:37. Thus it may have Messianic significance (cf. Mal 3:1). The same Hebrew word can also refer to articles of value, however (see 2 Chr 20:25; 32:27)—such as the contribution of King Darius to the temple (Ezra 6:8). If that is the intent here, the bringing of the "wealth of the nations" to Zion in Is 60:5 is a close parallel (see note there). *fill . . . with glory.* "Glory" can refer to material splendor (see Is 60:7,13 and notes) or to the presence of God (Ex 40:34–35; 1 Kin 8:10–11). The latter references connect the glory of the Lord with the cloud that filled the sanctuary. When Christ came to the earthly temple, God's presence was evident as never before (see Luke 2:27,32).

2:8 *silver . . . gold.* God provided for Solomon's temple (1 Chr 29:2,7) and for Zerubbabel's (Ezra 6:5).

2:9 *glory . . . greater.* Ultimately because the Messiah would be present there (see v. 7 and note). *this place.* Probably Jerusalem (see Is 60:17 and note). *I will give peace.* Probably an allusion to the priestly benediction (see Num 6:26).

2:10 *twenty-fourth . . . ninth month.* Dec. 18, 520 B.C.—when winter crops were planted.

2:11 *priests.* They were consulted about the precise meaning of the law (see Jer 18:18; Mal 2:7–9).

2:12 *holy meat.* Meat from an animal set apart for a sacrifice. *will it become holy?* A question about transmitting holiness. Consecrated meat made the garment "holy" because it was in direct contact with that garment (see Lev 6:27), but the garment could not pass on that holiness to a third object. Cf. Ezek 46:20.

2:13 *will the latter become unclean?* Ceremonial uncleanness is transmitted much more easily than holiness. Anything touched by an unclean person becomes unclean (see Num 19:11–13,22).

2:14 *this people.* See 1:2 and note. *every work . . . is unclean.* Even though the people were back in the holy land, that holiness did not make them pure. They needed to obey the Lord, particularly with regard to rebuilding the temple. See notes on vv. 12–13.

2:15 *before one stone was placed.* Before the 24th day of the sixth month (1:15).

2:16 *grain heap.* See Jer 50:26. *only ten . . . only twenty.* The poor harvests were related to the sin of the people. See 1:11; Is 5:10 and note. *wine vat.* A trough into which grape juice flowed. See note on Is 16:10.

hands with [a]blasting wind, mildew and hail;
[1]yet you *did* not *come back* to Me,' declares
the LORD.
18 'Do [1a]consider from this day [2]onward,
from the [b]twenty-fourth day of the ninth
month; from the day when the temple of the
LORD was [c]founded, [1]consider:
19 'Is the seed still in the barn? Even
including the vine, the fig tree, the pomegranate and the olive tree, it has not borne
fruit. Yet from this day on I will [a]bless *you.*' "
20 Then the word of the LORD came a second time to Haggai on the [a]twenty-fourth
day of the month, saying,
21 "Speak to [a]Zerubbabel governor of
Judah, saying, 'I am going to [b]shake the
heavens and the earth.
22 'I will [a]overthrow the thrones of kingdoms and destroy the [b]power of the kingdoms of the [1]nations; and I will [c]overthrow
the chariots and their riders, and the [d]horses
and their riders will go down, [e]everyone by
the sword of another.'
23 'On that day,' declares the LORD of
hosts, 'I will take you, Zerubbabel, son of
Shealtiel, My servant,' declares the LORD,
'and I will make you like a [1a]signet *ring,* for
[b]I have chosen you,' " declares the LORD of
hosts.

17 [1]Or *but what did we have in common?* [a]Deut 28:22; 1 Kin 8:37; Amos 4:9 **18** [1]Lit *set your heart* [2]Or *backward* [a]Deut 32:29; Hag 2:15 [b]Hag 2:10 [c]Ezra 5:1, 2; Zech 8:9, 12 **19** [a]Ps 128:1-6; Jer 31:12, 14; Mal 3:10 **20** [a]Hag 2:10 **21** [a]Ezra 5:2; Hag 1:1; Zech 4:6-10 [b]Hag 2:6; Heb 12:26, 27

22 [1]Or *Gentiles* [a]Ezek 26:16; Zeph 3:8 [b]Mic 7:16 [c]Ps 46:9; Ezek 39:20; Mic 5:10 [d]Amos 2:15 [e]Judg 7:22; 2 Chr 20:23 **23** [1]Or *seal* [a]Song 8:6; Jer 22:24 [b]Is 42:1; 43:10

2:17 *blasting wind, mildew.* A scorching east wind resulted in blight on plant life (see Gen 41:6 and note). Blight and mildew are mentioned as a curse for disobedience in Deut 28:22. See also 1 Kin 8:37; Amos 4:9. *hail.* Sent to destroy the fields and livestock of Egypt (see Ex 9:25; Ps 78:47–48). *you did not come back.* See Amos 4:9.

2:18 *when the temple . . . was founded.* The same potential for blessing existed at the time when the foundation of the temple was laid in 536 B.C. (Ezra 3:11). This is a warning not to fail again.

2:19 *vine . . . fig tree . . . pomegranate . . . olive tree.* Grapes, figs and pomegranates ripened in August and September, and olives from September to November. These harvests, like the earlier grain crops, had produced little. See 1:11 and note. *I will bless you.* Because of their response to Haggai's message, future abundance is assured. Cf. Mal 3:10.

2:20 See note on v. 10.

2:21 *shake . . . the earth.* See v. 6 and note.

2:22 *overthrow . . . overthrow.* The Hebrew for these words is used with reference to Sodom and Gomorrah (see Gen 19:25; Amos 4:11). *chariots . . . horses . . . riders.* Cf. the destruction of Pharaoh's army at the Red Sea (Ex 15:1,4,19,21). *everyone by . . . another.* The plight of the armies of Midian (Judg 7:22), Gog (Ezek 38:21) and the nations fighting against Jerusalem in the last days (Zech 14:13).

2:23 *On that day.* The day of the Lord. See Is 2:11,17,20; 10:20,27; Zech 2:11 and notes. *My servant.* A term applied to prophets (see Is 20:3 and note), political leaders (Is 22:20) and the Messiah (see Is 41:8–9; 42:1 and notes). *signet ring.* A kind of seal that functioned as a signature (see Esth 8:8) and was worn on one's finger (Esth 3:10). Like other seals (cf. Gen 38:18) it could be used as a pledge or guarantee of full payment. Its mention here probably reverses the curse placed on King Jehoiachin in Jer 22:24 (cf. Judg 17:2). Zerubbabel would then be a guarantee that someday the Messiah descended from David will come (cf. Matt 1:1,12). In 2 Cor 1:22 the Holy Spirit is the seal guaranteeing the believer's future inheritance (cf. Eph 1:13–14). *chosen you.* See Is 41:8–9; 42:1 and notes.

Zechariah

INTRODUCTION

Background

Zechariah's prophetic ministry took place in the postexilic period, the time of the Jewish restoration from Babylonian captivity. For historical details see Introduction to Haggai: Background.

Author and Unity

Like Jeremiah (1:1) and Ezekiel (1:3), Zechariah was not only a prophet (1:1) but also a priest. He was born in Babylonia and was among those who returned to Judah in 538 B.C. under the leadership of Zerubbabel and Joshua (his grandfather Iddo is named among the returnees in Neh 12:4). At a later time, when Joiakim was high priest, Zechariah apparently succeeded Iddo (1:1,7) as head of that priestly family (Neh 12:10–16). Since the grandson succeeded the grandfather, it has been suggested that the father (Berekiah, 1:1,7) died at an early age.

Zechariah was a contemporary of Haggai (Ezra 5:1; 6:14) but continued his ministry long after him (compare 1:1 and 7:1 with Hag 1:1; see also Neh 12:1–16). His young age (see 2:4) in the early period of his ministry makes it possible that he ministered even into the reign of Artaxerxes I (465–424 B.C.).

Most likely Zechariah wrote the entire book that bears his name. Some have questioned his authorship of chs. 9 to 14 — citing differences in style and other compositional features, and giving historical and chronological references that allegedly require a different date and author from those of chs. 1 to 8. All these objections, however, can be explained in other satisfactory ways, so there is no compelling reason to question the unity of the book.

Dates

The dates of Zechariah's recorded messages are best correlated with those of Haggai and with other historical events as follows:

1. Haggai's first message (Hag 1:1–11; Ezra 5:1)	Aug. 29, 520 B.C.
2. Resumption of the building of the temple (Hag 1:12–15; Ezra 5:2) (The rebuilding seems to have been hindered from 536 to c. 530 [Ezra 4:1–5], and the work ceased altogether from c. 530 to 520 [Ezra 4:24].)	Sept. 21, 520
3. Haggai's second message (Hag 2:1–9)	Oct. 17, 520
4. Beginning of Zechariah's preaching (1:1–6)	Oct./Nov., 520
5. Haggai's third message (Hag 2:10–19)	Dec. 18, 520
6. Haggai's fourth message (Hag 2:20–23)	Dec. 18, 520
7. Tattenai's letter to Darius concerning the rebuilding of the temple (Ezra 5:3 — 6:14) (There must have been a lapse of time between the resumption of the building and Tattenai's appearance.)	519–518
8. Zechariah's eight night visions (chs. 1:7 — 6:8)	Feb. 15, 519
9. Joshua crowned (chs. 6:9 — 15)	Feb. 16 (?), 519
10. Repentance urged, blessings promised (chs. 7 — 8)	Dec. 7, 518
11. Dedication of the temple (Ezra 6:15–18)	Mar. 12, 516
12. Zechariah's final prophecy (chs. 9 — 14)	After 480 (?)

Occasion and Purpose

The occasion is the same as that of the book of Haggai (see Background; Dates). The chief purpose of Zechariah (and Haggai) was to rebuke the people of Judah and to encourage and motivate them to complete the rebuilding of the temple (Zech 4:8–10; Hag 1—2), though both prophets were clearly interested in spiritual renewal as well. In addition, the purpose of the eight night visions (1:7—6:8) is explained in 1:3,5–6: The Lord said that if Judah would return to him, he would return to them. Furthermore, His word would continue to be fulfilled.

Theological Teaching

The theological teaching of the book is related to its Messianic as well as its apocalyptic and eschatological motifs. Regarding the Messianic emphasis, Zechariah foretold Christ's coming in lowliness (6:12), His humanity (6:12; 13:7), His rejection and betrayal for 30 pieces of silver (11:12–13), His crucifixion (struck by the "sword" of the Lord; 13:7), His priesthood (6:13), His kingship (6:13; 9:9; 14:9,16), His coming in glory (14:4), His building of the Lord's temple (6:12–13), His reign (9:10; 14) and His establishment of enduring peace and prosperity (3:10; 9:9–10). These Messianic passages give added significance to Jesus' words in Luke 24:25–27,44.

Concerning the apocalyptic and eschatological emphasis, Zechariah foretold the siege of Jerusalem (12:1–3; 14:1–2), the initial victory of Judah's enemies (14:2), the Lord's defense of Jerusalem (14:3–4), the judgment on the nations (12:9; 14:3), the topographical changes in Judah (14:4–5), the celebration of the Feast of Booths in the Messianic kingdom age (14:16–19) and the ultimate holiness of Jerusalem and her people (14:20–21).

There is also theological significance in the prophet's name, which means "The LORD (Yahweh) remembers." "The LORD" is the personal, covenant name of God and is a perpetual testimony to His faithfulness to His promises (see note on Ex 3:14). He "remembers" His covenant promises and takes action to fulfill them. In the book of Zechariah God's promised deliverance from Babylonian exile, including a restored kingdom community and a functioning temple (the earthly throne of the divine King), leads into even grander pictures of the salvation and restoration to come through the Messiah.

Finally, the book as a whole teaches the sovereignty of God in history, over people and nations—past, present and future.

Literary Form and Themes

The book is primarily a mixture of exhortation (call to repentance, 1:2–6), prophetic visions (1:7—6:8) and judgment and salvation oracles (chs. 9—14). The prophetic visions of 1:7—6:8 are called apocalyptic (revelatory) literature, which is essentially a literature of encouragement to God's people. When the apocalyptic section is read along with the salvation (or deliverance) oracles in chs. 9—14, it becomes obvious that the dominant emphasis of the book is encouragement because of the glorious future that awaits the people of God.

In fact, encouragement is the book's central theme—primarily encouragement to complete the rebuilding of the temple. Various means are used to accomplish this end, and these function as subthemes. For example, great stress is laid on the coming of the Messiah and the overthrow of all anti-kingdom forces by Him so that God's rule can be finally and fully established on earth. The then-current local scene thus becomes the basis for contemplating the universal, eschatological picture.

Outline

Part I (chs. 1—8)

- I. Introduction (1:1–6)
  - A. The Date and the Author's Name (1:1)
  - B. A Call to Repentance (1:2–6)
- II. A Series of Eight Night Visions (1:7—6:8)
  - A. The Horseman among the Myrtle Trees (1:7–17)
  - B. The Four Horns and the Four Craftsmen (1:18–21)

C. A Man with a Measuring Line (ch. 2)
D. Clean Garments for the High Priest (ch. 3)
E. The Golden Lampstand and the Two Olive Trees (ch. 4)
F. The Flying Scroll (5:1–4)
G. The Woman in the Ephah (5:5–11)
H. The Four Chariots (6:1–8)

III. The Symbolic Crowning of Joshua the High Priest (6:9–15)

IV. The Problem of Fasting and the Promise of the Future (chs. 7—8)
A. The Question by the Delegation from Bethel (7:1–3)
B. The Rebuke by the Lord (7:4–7)
C. The Command to Repent (7:8–14)
D. The Restoration of Israel to God's Favor (8:1–17)
E. Kingdom Joy and Jewish Favor (8:18–23)

Part II (chs. 9 — 14)

V. Two Prophetic Oracles: The Great Messianic Future and the Full Realization of God's Kingdom (chs. 9—14)
A. The First Oracle: The Advent and Rejection of the Messiah (chs. 9—11)
1. The advent of the Messianic King (chs. 9—10)
2. The rejection of the Messianic Shepherd-King (ch. 11)
B. The Second Oracle: The Advent and Reception of the Messiah (chs. 12—14)
1. The deliverance and conversion of Israel (chs. 12—13)
2. The Messiah's coming and His kingdom (ch. 14)

A Call to Repentance

1 In the eighth month of the second year of
[a]Darius, the word of the LORD came to
[b]Zechariah the prophet, the son of Berechiah, the son of [c]Iddo saying,
2 "The LORD was very [a]angry with your
fathers.
3 "Therefore say to them, 'Thus says the
LORD of hosts, "[a]Return to Me," declares the
LORD of hosts, "that I may return to you,"
says the LORD of hosts.
4 "Do not be [a]like your fathers, to whom
the [b]former prophets proclaimed, saying,
'Thus says the LORD of hosts, "[c]Return now
from your evil ways and from your evil
deeds." ' But they did [d]not listen or give
heed to Me," declares the LORD.
5 "Your [a]fathers, where are they? And the
[b]prophets, do they live forever?
6 "But did not My words and My statutes,
which I commanded My servants the prophets, [a]overtake your fathers? Then they repented and said, '[b]As the LORD of hosts purposed
to do to us in accordance with our ways and
our deeds, so He has dealt with us.' " ' "

Patrol of the Earth

7 On the twenty-fourth day of the
eleventh month, which is the month Shebat,
in the second year of Darius, the word of the
LORD came to Zechariah the prophet, the son
of Berechiah, the son of Iddo, as follows:
8 I saw at night, and behold, a man was
riding on a [a]red horse, and he was standing
among the [b]myrtle trees which were in the
ravine, with red, sorrel and [c]white horses
behind him.
9 Then I said, "My [a]lord, what are
these?" And the [b]angel who was speaking
with me said to me, "I will show you what
these are."
10 And the man who was standing among
the myrtle trees answered and said, "These
are those whom the LORD has sent to [1][a]patrol
the earth."
11 So they answered the angel of the LORD
who was [a]standing among the myrtle trees
and said, "We have [1]patrolled the earth, and
behold, [b]all the earth is [2]peaceful and quiet."
12 Then the angel of the LORD said, "O
LORD of hosts, [a]how long will You [b]have no
compassion for Jerusalem and the cities of
Judah, with which You have been [c]indignant
these [d]seventy years?"
13 The LORD answered the [a]angel who
was speaking with me with [1]gracious words,
[b]comforting words.
14 So the angel who was speaking with
me said to me, "[a]Proclaim, saying, 'Thus
says the LORD of hosts, "I am [b]exceedingly
jealous for Jerusalem and Zion.
15 "But I am very [a]angry with the nations
who are [b]at ease; for while I was only a little
angry, they [1][c]furthered the disaster."

1:1 [a]Ezra 4:24; 6:15; Hag 1:15; 2:10; Zech 1:7; 7:1 [b]Ezra 5:1; 6:14; Zech 7:1; Matt 23:35; Luke 11:51 [c]Neh 12:4, 16 **2** [a]2 Chr 36:16; Jer 44:6; Ezek 8:18; Zech 1:15 **3** [a]Is 31:6; 44:22; Mal 3:7 **4** [a]Ps 78:8; 106:6, 7 [b]2 Chr 24:19; 36:15 [c]Is 1:16-19; Jer 4:1; Ezek 33:11 [d]Jer 6:17; 11:7, 8 **5** [a]Lam 5:7 [b]John 8:52 **6** [a]Jer 12:16, 17; 44:28, 29; Amos 9:10 [b]Lam 2:17 **8** [a]Zech 6:2; Rev 6:4 [b]Neh 8:15; Is 41:19; 55:13; Zech 1:10, 11 [c]Zech 6:3; Rev 6:2 **9** [a]Zech 1:19; 4:4, 5, 13; 6:4 [b]Zech 2:3; 5:5 **10** [1]Lit *walk about through* [a]Job 1:7; Zech 1:11; 4:10; 6:5-8 **11** [1]Lit *walked about through* [2]Lit *sitting* [a]Zech 1:8, 10 [b]Is 14:7 **12** [a]Ps 74:10; Jer 12:4; Hab 1:2 [b]Ps 102:13; Jer 30:18 [c]Ps 102:10; Jer 15:17 [d]Jer 25:11; 29:10; Dan 9:2; Zech 7:5 **13** [1]Lit *good* [a]Zech 1:9; 4:1 [b]Is 40:1, 2; 57:18 **14** [a]Is 40:2, 6; Zech 1:17 [b]Zech 8:2 **15** [1]Lit *helped for evil* [a]Zech 1:2 [b]Ps 123:4; Jer 48:11 [c]Amos 1:11

1:1 *eighth month of the second year.* October-November, 520 B.C. Haggai also began his prophetic ministry in Darius's second year, on the first day of the sixth month, i.e., on Aug. 29, 520 (Hag 1:1). *the word of the LORD.* A technical phrase for the prophetic word of revelation (see 9:1; 12:1; Jer 1:2; Ezek 1:3; Hos 1:1; Joel 1:1; Jon 1:1; 3:1; Mic 1:1; Zeph 1:1; Hag 1:1; Mal 1:1). See also note on 6:9. *prophet.* One called by God to be His spokesman (see note on Ex 7:1–2). *Iddo.* See v. 7; Ezra 5:1; 6:14; Neh 12:4,16; see also Introduction: Author.

1:2 *very angry with your fathers.* The Lord was angry because of the covenant-breaking sins of the Jews' preexilic forefathers, resulting in the destruction of Jerusalem and the temple in 586 B.C., followed by exile to Babylonia. God's anger should not be explained away, for to deny that God has genuine emotions is to deprive Him of one of the clear marks of personality.

1:3 *Return to Me . . . that I may return to you.* Cf. 7:13. If the people of Zechariah's day would change their course and go in the opposite direction from that of their forefathers (v. 4), the Lord would return to them with blessing instead of with a curse (see v. 16; see also Jer 18:7–10).

1:4 *former prophets.* Such as Isaiah (see Is 45:22), Jeremiah (see Jer 18:11) and Ezekiel (see Ezek 33:11). See also 7:7,12; Jer 25:4–5; 35:15.

1:5 *do they live forever?* No, but God's words through them live on to be fulfilled (see v. 6).

1:6 *did not My words . . . overtake your fathers?* Cf. Is 40:6–8; 55:10–11. For the imagery of "overtake" see Deut 28:2,15,45. *My servants the prophets.* See 2 Kin 9:7; 17:13,23; 21:10; 24:2; Ezra 9:11; Jer 7:25 and note; 25:4; Ezek 38:17; Dan 9:6,10; Amos 3:7. *they repented.* Apparently a reference to what happened to some of the preexilic forefathers and/or their offspring during the exile and immediately afterward (cf. Ezra 9; 10:1–17; Dan 9:1–19).

1:7–17 The first vision. Although God's covenant people are troubled while the oppressing nations are at ease, God is jealous (see note on Ex 20:5) for His people and will restore them and their towns and the temple. The imagery of the first vision is reflected in that of the eighth and final vision (6:1–8).

1:7 *twenty-fourth day of . . . Shebat.* Feb. 15, 519 B.C., about three months after the date of v. 1.

1:8 *I saw.* Not in a dream (see 4:1) but in a vision. The visions were given to Zechariah while he was fully awake. *at night.* Zechariah had all eight visions (1:7–6:8) in one night. *man was riding.* The angel of the Lord (v. 11). He must not be confused with the interpreting angel, who is mentioned in vv. 9,13–14,19; 2:3; 4:1,4–5; 5:5,10; 6:4–5. *horses.* Perhaps angelic messengers (v. 10).

1:11 *angel of the LORD.* See note on Gen 16:7. *peaceful.* Cf. 6:8. While the Persian empire as a whole was secure and at ease by this time (v. 15), the Jews in Judah were oppressed and still under foreign domination (v. 12).

1:12 *seventy years.* See 7:5 and note; Jer 25:11–12 and note; 29:10; cf. 2 Chr 36:21; Ezra 1:1; Dan 9:2.

1:13 *comforting words.* Those of vv. 14–17.

1:14 *jealous.* See 8:2. Through the use of such language the Lord's love for Judah is shown (see note on Ex 20:5; cf. James 4:4). The key idea is that of God vindicating Judah for the violations against her (v. 15).

1:15 *furthered the disaster.* God was angry with Israel and used the Assyrians (Is 10:5) and Babylonians (Is 47:6; Jer 25:9) to punish her, but they went too far by trying to destroy the Jews as a people.

16 'Therefore thus says the LORD, "I will
[a]return to Jerusalem with compassion; My
[b]house will be built in it," declares the LORD
of hosts, "and a measuring [c]line will be
stretched over Jerusalem."'
17 " Again, proclaim, saying, 'Thus says the
LORD of hosts, "My [a]cities will again overflow
with prosperity, and the LORD will again [b]comfort Zion and again [c]choose Jerusalem."'"
18 [1]Then I lifted up my eyes and looked,
and behold, *there were* four horns.
19 So I said to the angel who was speaking with me, "What are these?" And he
answered me, "These are the [a]horns which
have scattered Judah, Israel and Jerusalem."
20 Then the LORD showed me four [a]craftsmen.
21 I said, "What are these coming to do?"
And he said, "These are the [a]horns which
have scattered Judah so that no man lifts up
his head; but these *craftsmen* have come to
terrify them, to [b]throw down the horns of the
nations who have lifted up *their* horns against
the land of Judah in order to scatter it."

God's Favor to Zion

2 [1]Then I lifted up my eyes and looked, and
behold, *there was* a man with a [a]measuring line in his hand.
2 So I said, "Where are you going?" And
he said to me, "To [a]measure Jerusalem, to
see how wide it is and how long it is."
3 And behold, the [a]angel who was
speaking with me was going out, and another angel was coming out to meet him,
4 and said to him, "Run, speak to that
[a]young man, saying, '[b]Jerusalem will be
inhabited [1c]without walls because of the
[d]multitude of men and cattle within it.
5 'For I,' declares the LORD, 'will be a
[a]wall of fire [1]around her, and I will be the
[b]glory in her midst.'"
6 " [1]Ho there! [a]Flee from the land of the
north," declares the LORD, "for I have [b]dispersed you as the four winds of the heavens," declares the LORD.
7 "Ho, Zion! [a]Escape, you who are living
with the daughter of Babylon."
8 For thus says the LORD of hosts, "After
[1a]glory He has sent me against the nations
which plunder you, for he who touches you,
touches the [2b]apple of His eye.
9 "For behold, I will [a]wave My hand over
them so that they will be [b]plunder for their
slaves. Then you will know that the LORD of
hosts has sent Me.
10 " [a]Sing for joy and be glad, O daughter of
Zion; for behold I am coming and I will
[b]dwell in your midst," declares the LORD.
11 " [a]Many nations will join themselves to
the LORD in that day and will become My
people. Then I will [b]dwell in your midst, and
you will [c]know that the LORD of hosts has
sent Me to you.
12 "The LORD will [1a]possess Judah as His
portion in the holy land, and will again
[b]choose Jerusalem.
13 " [1a]Be silent, all flesh, before the LORD;
for He is [b]aroused from His holy habitation."

Joshua, the High Priest

3 Then he showed me [a]Joshua the high
priest standing before the angel of the
LORD, and [1b]Satan standing at his right hand
to accuse him.

16 [a]Is 54:8-10; Zech 2:10, 11 [b]Ezra 6:14, 15; Zech 4:9 [c]Jer 31:39; Zech 2:2, 4 **17** [a]Is 44:26; 61:4 [b]Is 51:3 [c]Zech 2:12 **18** [1]Ch 2:1 in Heb **19** [a]1 Kin 22:11; Ps 75:4, 5; Amos 6:13 mg **20** [a]Is 44:12; 54:16 **21** [a]Zech 1:19 [b]Ps 75:10 **2:1** [1]Ch 2:5 in Heb [a]Jer 31:39; Ezek 40:3; 47:3; Zech 1:16 **2** [a]Jer 31:39; Ezek 40:3; Rev 21:15-17 **3** [a]Zech 1:9 **4** [1]Lit like *unwalled villages;* or like *open country* [a]Jer 1:6; Dan 1:4; 1 Tim 4:12 [b]Zech 1:17; 8:4 [c]Ezek 38:11 [d]Is 49:20; Jer 30:19; 33:22 **5** [1]Lit *to her* [a]Is 4:5; 26:1; 60:18 [b]Hag 2:9; Zech 2:10, 11 **6** [1]Lit *Ho! Ho!* [a]Jer 3:18 [b]Jer 31:10; Ezek 11:16 **7** [a]Is 48:20; Jer 51:6 **8** [1]Or *the glory* [2]Lit *pupil* [a]Is 60:7-9 [b]Deut 32:10; Ps 17:8 **9** [a]Is 19:16 [b]Is 14:2 **10** [a]Is 65:18, 19; Zech 9:9 [b]Zech 2:5; 8:3 **11** [a]Mic 4:2 [b]Zech 2:5, 10 [c]Zech 2:9 **12** [1]Or *inherit* [a]Deut 32:9; Ps 33:12; Jer 10:16 [b]2 Chr 6:6; Ps 132:13, 14; Zech 1:17 **13** [1]Lit *Hush* [a]Hab 2:20; Zeph 1:7 [b]Ps 78:65; Is 51:9 **3:1** [1]Or the *Adversary* or *Accuser* [a]Ezra 5:2; Hag 1:1; Zech 6:11 [b]1 Chr 21:1; Job 1:6; Ps 109:6; Rev 12:10

1:16 *I will return.* See note on v. 3. *My house will be built.* See Ezra 6:14–16. *measuring line.* A symbol of restoration (cf. Jer 31:38–40).
1:17 *choose Jerusalem.* See 2:12; 3:2.
1:18–21 The second vision. The nations that devastated Israel (v. 19) will in turn be destroyed by other nations.
1:18 *four.* If the number is to be taken literally, the reference is probably to Assyria, Egypt, Babylonia and Medo-Persia. *horns.* Symbolic of strength in general (Ps 18:2), or the strength of a country, i.e., its king (Ps 89:17; Dan 7:7–8; 8:20–21; Rev 17:12), or, as here (see v. 21), the power of a nation in general.
1:20 *four craftsmen.* If the number is to be understood literally, probably the reference is to Egypt, Babylonia, Persia and Greece. What is clear is that all Judah's enemies will ultimately be defeated (v. 21).
2:1–13 The third vision. There will be full restoration and blessing for the covenant people, temple and city.
2:1 *measuring line.* See note on 1:16.
2:4 *young man.* Evidently Zechariah. *without walls.* The city's population will overflow to the point that it will be as though it had no walls (see 10:8,10; see also note on Is 49:19–20).
2:5 *wall of fire.* Here symbolic of divine protection (see Ex 13:21 and note; Is 4:5–6 and note). *glory.* See Ex 40:34.
2:6 *land of the north.* Babylon (v. 7) invaded Judah from the north (Jer 1:14; 4:6; 6:1,22; 10:22). *as the four winds.* In all directions. The exiles would return from north, south, east and west (Is 43:5–6; 49:12).
2:7 *Zion.* Jerusalem's exiles in Babylon. *Escape . . . Babylon.* Cf. Rev 18:4–8.
2:8 *apple of His eye.* See note on Deut 32:10.
2:9 *hand.* Power.
2:10 See 9:9. *I will dwell in your midst.* See v. 11; 8:3; Lev 26:11–12; Ezek 37:27; John 1:14; 2 Co 6:16; Rev 21:3.
2:11 *Many nations.* In fulfillment of the promise to Abraham (Gen 12:3; cf. Zec. 8:20–23; Gen 18:18; 22:18; Is 2:2–4; 60:3). *that day.* The day of the Lord (see 3:10; see also note on Is 2:11,17,20).
2:12 *holy land.* This designation occurs only here in Scripture. The land was rendered holy chiefly because it was the site of the earthly throne and sanctuary of the holy King, who dwelt there among His covenant people. See note on Ex 3:5. *choose Jerusalem.* See 1:17; 3:2.
2:13 *Be silent . . . before the LORD.* See Hab 2:20; Zeph 1:7. *aroused.* To judge (cf. v. 9).
3:1–10 The fourth vision. Israel will be cleansed and restored as a priestly nation (see Ex 19:6 and note).
3:1 *Joshua.* A variant of Jeshua, here and elsewhere in Zechariah and in Haggai. In Ezra 2:2 and Neh 7:7 he is referred to as Jeshua. Here he represents the sinful nation of Israel (see vv. 8–9). The names "Joshua" and "Jeshua" were common in ancient times. The Greek equivalent is spelled "Jesus" in English, and all three forms of the name mean "The LORD saves" (see note on Matt 1:21). *standing before.* Ministering before—as priest (see

2 The LORD said to Satan, "[a]The LORD
rebuke you, Satan! Indeed, the LORD who has
[b]chosen Jerusalem rebuke you! Is this not a
[c]brand plucked from the fire?"
3 Now Joshua was clothed with [a]filthy
garments and standing before the angel.
4 He spoke and said to those who were
standing before him, saying, "[a]Remove the
filthy garments from him." Again he said to
him, "See, I have [b]taken your iniquity away
from you and [1]will [c]clothe you with festal
robes."
5 Then I said, "Let them put a clean [a]turban on his head." So they put a clean turban
on his head and clothed him with garments,
while the angel of the LORD was standing by.
6 And the angel of the LORD admonished
Joshua, saying,
7 "Thus says the LORD of hosts, 'If you will
[a]walk in My ways and if you will perform
My service, then you will also [b]govern My
house and also have charge of My [c]courts,
and I will grant you [1]free access among these
who are standing *here.*

The Branch

8 'Now listen, Joshua the high priest, you
and your friends who are sitting in front of
you—indeed they are men who are a [a]symbol, for behold, I am going to bring in My
servant the [1b]Branch.
9 'For behold, the stone that I have set
before Joshua; on one stone are [a]seven eyes.
Behold, I will engrave an inscription on it,'
declares the LORD of hosts, 'and I will
[b]remove the iniquity of that land in one day.
10 'In that day,' declares the LORD of hosts,
'every one of you will invite his neighbor to
sit under *his* [a]vine and under *his* fig tree.'"

The Golden Lampstand and Olive Trees

4 Then [a]the angel who was speaking with
me returned and [b]roused me, as a man
who is awakened from his sleep.
2 He said to me, "[a]What do you see?"
And I said, "I see, and behold, a [b]lampstand
all of gold with its bowl on the top of it, and
its [c]seven lamps on it with seven spouts
belonging to each of the lamps which are on
the top of it;
3 also [a]two olive trees by it, one on the
right side of the bowl and the other on its
left side."
4 Then I said to the angel who was
speaking with me saying, "What are these,
[a]my lord?"

2 [a]Mark 9:25; Jude 9 [b]Zech 2:12 [c]Amos 4:11; Jude 23
3 [a]Ezra 9:15; Is 4:4; 64:6
4 [1]Lit *to clothe* [a]Is 43:25; Ezek 36:25 [b]Mic 7:18, 19; Zech 3:9 [c]Is 52:1; 61:10
5 [a]Job 29:14; Is 3:23
7 [1]Lit *goings* [a]1 Kin 3:14 [b]Deut 17:9, 12 [c]Is 62:9
8 [1]Lit *Sprout* [a]Is 8:18; 20:3; Ezek 12:11 [b]Is 11:1; 53:2; Jer 23:5; 33:15; Zech 6:12
9 [a]Zech 4:10 [b]Jer 31:34; 50:20; Zech 3:4
10 [a]1 Kin 4:25; Is 36:16; Mic 4:4
4:1 [a]Zech 1:9 [b]1 Kin 19:5-7; Jer 31:26
2 [a]Jer 1:13; Zech 5:2 [b]Ex 25:31, 37; Jer 52:19 [c]Rev 4:5
3 [a]Zech 4:11; Rev 11:4
4 [a]Zech 1:9; 4:5, 13; 6:4

Deut 10:8; 2 Chr 29:11; Ezek 44:15). *angel of the LORD.* See 1:11; see also note on Gen 16:7. *Satan.* See NASB marg.; cf. Job 1:6–12; 2:1–7; Rev 12:10. *right hand.* See Ps 109:6. *accuse.* The Hebrew for this word has the same root as the Hebrew for "Satan."

3:2 *rebuke . . . rebuke.* Repeated for emphasis (see 4:7; see also note on Is 40:1). *chosen Jerusalem.* See 1:17; 2:12. *brand plucked from the fire.* The Jews were retrieved from the fire of Babylonian exile to carry out God's future purpose for them (see Amos 4:11; see also Zech 13:8–9; Deut 4:20 and note; 7:7–8; 1 Kin 8:51; Is 48:10; Jer 11:4; 30:7; Rev 12:13–16).

3:4 *those who were standing before him.* Probably angels (see also v. 7). *Remove the filthy garments.* Thus depriving him of his priestly office. The act is here symbolic also of the removal of sin (see note on v. 9).

3:5 *put a clean turban on his head.* Thus reinstating him into his high-priestly function so that Israel once again has a divinely authorized priestly mediator. On the front of the turban were the words: "Holy to the LORD" (Ex 28:36; 39:30; cf. 14:20).

3:7 If Joshua and his priestly associates are faithful, they will be co-workers with the angels in the carrying out of God's purposes for Zion and Israel. *these . . . standing here.* See note on v. 4.

3:8 *friends.* Fellow priests. *My servant.* See notes on Ex 14:31; Ps 18 title; Is 41:8–9; 42:1–4; 42:1; Rom 1:1. *Branch.* A Messianic title (see 6:12; Is 4:2 and note; 11:1; Jer 23:5; 33:15).

3:9 *stone.* Probably another figure of the Messiah (cf. Ps 118:22–23; Is 8:13–15; 28:16 and note; Dan 2:35,45; Matt 21:42; Eph 2:19–22; 1 Pet 2:6–8). *seven eyes.* Perhaps symbolic of infinite intelligence (omniscience). See note on 4:10. *I will remove the iniquity of that land.* The symbolic act of v. 4 is now explained. "Land" stands for the people of Israel. For the cleansing spoken of here see also 12:10–13:1. *in one day.* Ultimately Good Friday, though some believe that the reference also includes Christ's second coming.

3:10 *that day.* The day of the Lord (see 2:11; see also note on Is 2:11,17,20). *sit under his vine and . . . fig tree.* A proverbial picture of peace, security and contentment (see 2 Kin 18:31; Mic 4:4 and note).

4:1–14 The fifth vision. The Jews are encouraged to rebuild the temple by being reminded of their divine resources. The light from the lampstand in the tabernacle/temple represents the reflection of God's glory in the consecration and the holy service of God's people (see note on Ex 25:31)—made possible only by the power of God's Spirit (see v. 6; the oil, v. 12). This enabling power will equip and sustain Zerubbabel in the rebuilding of the temple (vv. 6–10). And in the performance of their offices, Zerubbabel and Joshua (as representatives of the royal and priestly mediatorial offices) will channel the Spirit's enablement to God's people (vv. 11–14).

4:1 *roused me.* On the same night (see note on 1:8).

4:2 *What do you see?* See 5:2; see also Jer 1:11 and note. The vision here was probably of seven lamps arranged around a large bowl that served as a bountiful reservoir of oil. Each lamp had seven "spouts" or "lips" that held the wicks of the oil lamps. Each lamp had seven "spouts," meaning a total of 49 flames. Another possibility is that the "spouts" were "channels" conveying the oil from the bowl to the lamps. In any event, the bowl represents an abundant supply of oil, symbolizing the fullness of God's power through His Spirit, and the "seven . . . seven" represents the abundant light shining from the lamps (seven being the number of fullness or completeness).

4:3 *two olive trees.* Cf. Rev 11:4. The two olive trees stand for the priestly and royal offices and symbolize a continuing supply of oil. The two olive branches (v. 12) stand for Joshua the priest (ch. 3) and Zerubbabel from the royal house of David (ch. 4; cf. v. 14). These two leaders were to do God's work (e.g., on the temple and in the lives of the people) in the power of His Spirit (v. 6). The combination of the priestly and royal lines and their functions points ultimately to the Messianic King-Priest and His offices and functions (cf. 6:13).

4:4 *these.* The two olive trees of v. 3, as v. 11 makes clear. The answer to the question is postponed until v. 14.

5 So [a]the angel who was speaking with
me answered and said to me, "[b]Do you not
know what these are?" And I said, "No, my
lord."
6 Then he [1]said to me, "This is the word
of the LORD to [a]Zerubbabel saying, '[b]Not by
might nor by power, but by My [c]Spirit,' says
the LORD of hosts.
7 'What are you, O great [a]mountain?
Before Zerubbabel *you will become* a plain;
and he will bring forth the top stone with
[b]shouts of "Grace, grace to it!" ' "
8 Also the word of the LORD came to me,
saying,
9 "The hands of Zerubbabel have [a]laid the
foundation of this house, and his hands will
[b]finish *it*. Then you will know that the LORD
of hosts has sent me to [1]you.
10 "For who has despised the day of [a]small
things? [1]But these [b]seven will be glad when
they see the [2c]plumb line in the hand of
Zerubbabel—*these are* the [d]eyes of the LORD
which [e]range to and fro throughout the
earth."
11 Then I said to him, "What are these
[a]two olive trees on the right of the lampstand
and on its left?"
12 And I answered the second time and
said to him, "What are the two olive
[1]branches which are beside the two golden
pipes, which empty the golden *oil* from
themselves?"
13 So he answered me, saying, "[a]Do you
not know what these are?" And I said, "No,
[b]my lord."
14 Then he said, "These are the two
[1a]anointed ones who are [b]standing by the
[c]Lord of the whole earth."

The Flying Scroll

5 Then I lifted up my eyes again and
looked, and behold, *there was* a flying
[a]scroll.
2 And he said to me, "[a]What do you
see?" And I answered, "I see a flying scroll;
its length is twenty [1]cubits and its width ten
cubits."
3 Then he said to me, "This is the [a]curse
that is going forth over the face of the whole
[1]land; surely everyone who [b]steals will be
purged away according to [2]the writing on
one side, and everyone who [c]swears will be
purged away according to [2]the writing on the
other side.
4 "I will [a]make it go forth," declares the
LORD of hosts, "and it will [b]enter the house of
the [c]thief and the house of the one who
swears falsely by My name; and it will spend
the night within that house and [d]consume it
with its timber and stones."
5 Then [a]the angel who was speaking
with me went out and said to me, "Lift up

5 [a]Zech 1:9; 4:1 [b]Zech 4:13 **6** [1]Lit *said to me, saying* [a]Ezra 5:2; Hag 2:4, 5 [b]Is 11:2-4; 30:1; Hos 1:7 [c]2 Chr 32:7, 8; Eph 6:17 **7** [a]Ps 114:4, 6; Is 40:4; Jer 51:25; Nah 1:5; Zech 14:4, 5 [b]Ezra 3:10, 11; Ps 84:11 **9** [1]Lit *you* (plural) [a]Ezra 3:8-10; 5:16; Hag 2:18 [b]Ezra 6:14, 15; Zech 6:12, 13 **10** [1]Or *But they will rejoice when they see... Zerubbabel. These seven are the eyes of the* LORD [2]Lit *plummet stone* [a]Neh 4:2-4; Amos 7:2, 5; Hag 2:3 [b]Zech 3:9; Rev 8:2 [c]Amos 7:7, 8 [d]2 Chr 16:9; Prov 15:3; Jer 16:17 [e]Zech 1:10; Rev 5:6 **11** [a]Zech 4:3; Rev 11:4 **12** [1]Or *clusters* **13** [a]Zech 4:5

13 [b]Zech 4:4, 5 **14** [1]Lit *sons of fresh oil* [a]Ex 29:7; 40:15; 1 Sam 16:1, 12, 13; Is 61:1-3; Dan 9:24-26 [b]Zech 3:1-7 [c]Mic 4:13 **5:1** [a]Jer 36:2; Ezek 2:9; Rev 5:1 **2** [1]I.e. One cubit equals approx 18 in. [a]Zech 4:2 **3** [1]Or *earth* [2]Lit *it* [a]Is 24:6; 43:28; Jer 26:6 [b]Ex 20:15; Lev 19:11; Mal 3:8, 9 [c]Lev 19:12; Is 48:1; Jer 5:2; Zech 5:4 **4** [a]Mal 3:5 [b]Hos 4:2, 3 [c]Jer 2:26 [d]Lev 14:34, 35; Job 18:15 **5** [a]Zech 1:9

4:6 *Not by might nor by power.* Even though Zerubbabel does not possess the royal might and power that David and Solomon had enjoyed. *by My Spirit.* Interprets the symbolism of the oil (v. 12). The angel encouraged Zerubbabel to complete the rebuilding of the temple (vv. 7–10) and assured him of the Spirit's enablement.

4:7 *mountain . . . plain.* Faith in the power of God's Spirit can overcome mountainous obstacles. The figurative mountain probably included opposition (Ezra 4:1–5,24) and the people's unwillingness to persevere (Hag 1:14; 2:1–5). Cf. the same or similar imagery in Is 40:4; 41:15; 49:11; Matt 17:20; 21:21; Mark 11:23; 1 Cor 13:2; 2 Cor 10:4. *top stone.* The final stone to be put in place (see Ps 118:22), marking the completion of the restoration temple by Zerubbabel (see v. 9). *Grace, grace to it!* Repeated for emphasis (see 3:2; see also note on Is 40:1).

4:8 See note on 6:9.

4:9 *laid the foundation.* In 537–536 B.C. (Ezra 3:8–11; 5:16). *finish it.* In 516 (Ezra 6:14–16).

4:10 *day of small things.* Some thought the work on the temple was insignificant (Ezra 3:12; Hag 2:3), but God was in the rebuilding program and, by His Spirit (v. 6), would enable Zerubbabel to finish it. *plumb line.* The meaning of the Hebrew for this phrase is uncertain. If "plumb line" is correct, the text states that the people would rejoice when they saw this implement in Zerubbabel's hand to complete the task. But the Hebrew for these words may also be rendered "separated (i.e., chosen) stone," referring to the top stone of v. 7. *these . . . eyes.* See note on 3:9. God oversees the whole earth and is therefore in control of the situation in Judah.

4:14 The meaning of the vision is now explained. *two anointed.* Zerubbabel from the royal line of David and Joshua the priest. The oil (v. 12) used in anointing symbolizes the Holy Spirit (v. 6). The combination of ruler and priest points ultimately to the Messianic King-Priest (cf. 6:13; Ps 110; Heb 7). *Lord of the whole earth.* The master of the circumstances in which Zerubbabel and the people found themselves.

5:1–4 The sixth vision. Lawbreakers are condemned by the law they have broken; sinners will be purged from the land.

5:1 *flying.* Unrolled and waving like a banner, for all to read. *scroll.* See note on Ex 17:14.

5:2 *What do you see?* See 4:2; see also Jer 1:11 and note. *twenty . . . ten.* Thirty feet long and 15 feet wide; unusually large (especially in its width), for all to see. Such a bold, clear message of judgment against sin should spur the people on to repentance and righteousness.

5:3 *curse.* See Deut 27:26 and note. *on one side . . . on the other side.* Like the two tablets of the law (Ex 32:15), the scroll is inscribed on both sides (cf. Ezek 2:9–10; Rev 5:1). *everyone who steals.* He breaks the eighth commandment (Ex 20:15). *everyone who swears.* See 8:17. Such a person violates the third commandment (compare v. 4 with Ex 20:7). Although theft and perjury may have been the most common forms of lawbreaking at the time, they are probably intended as representative sins. The people of Judah had been guilty of infractions against the whole law (cf. James 2:10).

5:4 *it will enter . . . and consume.* "It" refers to the curse (v. 3). God's word, whether promise (ch. 4) or warning (as here), always accomplishes its purpose (cf. Ps 147:15; Is 55:10–11; Heb 4:12–13).

5:5–11 The seventh vision. Not only must flagrant, persistent sinners be removed from the land (vv. 1–4), but the whole sinful system will be removed—apparently to a more fitting place (Babylonia).

now your eyes and see what this is going forth."

6 I said, "What is it?" And he said, "This is the [1a]ephah going forth." Again he said, "This is their [2]appearance in all the [3]land

7 (and behold, a lead cover was lifted up); and this is a woman sitting inside the ephah."

8 Then he said, "This is [a]Wickedness!" And he threw her down into the middle of the ephah and cast the lead weight on its [1]opening.

9 Then I lifted up my eyes and looked, and there two women were coming out with the wind in their wings; and they had wings like the wings of a [a]stork, and they lifted up the ephah between the earth and the heavens.

10 I said to the angel who was speaking with me, "Where are they taking the ephah?"

11 Then he said to me, "To build a [1]temple for her in the land of [a]Shinar; and when it is prepared, she will be set there on her own pedestal."

The Four Chariots

6 Now I lifted up my eyes again and looked, and behold, [a]four chariots were coming forth from between the two mountains; and the mountains *were* bronze mountains.

2 With the first chariot *were* [a]red horses, with the second chariot [b]black horses,

3 with the third chariot [a]white horses, and with the fourth chariot strong [b]dappled horses.

4 Then I spoke and said to the angel who was speaking with me, "[a]What are these, my lord?"

5 The angel replied to me, "These are the [a]four spirits of heaven, going forth after standing before the Lord of all the earth,

6 with one of which the black horses are going forth to the [a]north country; and the white ones go forth after them, while the dappled ones go forth to the [b]south country.

7 "When the strong ones went out, they [1]were eager to go to [2a]patrol the earth." And He said, "Go, [2]patrol the earth." So they [3]patrolled the earth.

8 Then He cried out to me and spoke to me saying, "See, those who are going to the land of the north have [1a]appeased My wrath in the land of the north."

9 The [a]word of the LORD also came to me, saying,

10 "[a]Take *an offering* from the exiles, from Heldai, Tobijah and Jedaiah; and you go the same day and enter the house of Josiah the son of Zephaniah, where they have arrived from Babylon.

The Symbolic Crowns

11 "Take silver and gold, make an *ornate* [a]crown and set *it* on the head of [b]Joshua the son of Jehozadak, the high priest.

12 "Then say to him, 'Thus says the LORD of hosts, "Behold, a man whose name is [1a]Branch, for He will [2b]branch out from

6 [1]I.e. Approx one bu [2]Lit *eye;* some ancient versions read *iniquity* [3]Or *earth* [a]Lev 19:36; Amos 8:5
8 [1]Lit *mouth* [a]Hos 12:7; Amos 8:5; Mic 6:11
9 [a]Lev 11:13, 19; Ps 104:17; Jer 8:7
11 [1]Lit *house* [a]Gen 10:10; 11:2; 14:1; Is 11:11; Dan 1:2
6:1 [a]Dan 7:3; 8:22; Zech 1:18; 6:5
2 [a]Zech 1:8; Rev 6:4 [b]Rev 6:5
3 [a]Rev 6:2 [b]Rev 6:8
4 [a]Zech 1:9
5 [a]Jer 49:36; Ezek 37:9; Dan 7:2; 11:4; Matt 24:31; Rev 7:1
6 [a]Jer 1:14, 15; 4:6; 6:1; 25:9; 46:10; Ezek 1:4 [b]Is 43:6; Dan 11:5
7 [1]Lit *sought to go* [2]Lit *walk about through* [3]Lit *walked about through* [a]Zech 1:10
8 [1]Lit *caused My spirit to rest in* [a]Ezek 5:13; 24:13; Zech 1:15
9 [a]Zech 1:1; 7:1; 8:1
10 [a]Ezra 7:14-16; 8:26-30; Jer 28:6
11 [a]2 Sam 12:30; Ps 21:3; Song 3:11 [b]Ezra 3:2; Hag 1:1; Zech 3:1
12 [1]Lit *Sprout* [2]Lit *sprout up* [a]Is 4:2; 11:1; Jer 23:5; 33:15; Zech 3:8 [b]Is 53:2

5:6 *ephah.* A normal ephah-sized container would not be large enough to hold a person. This one was undoubtedly enlarged (like the flying scroll of vv. 1–2) for the purpose of the vision. *appearance.* See NASB marg. and v. 8 ("Wickedness").

5:7 *woman.* Perhaps the reason the people's wickedness was personified as a woman (cf. also Rev 17:3–6) is that the Hebrew word for "wickedness" (v. 8) is feminine in gender.

5:8 *Wickedness.* A general word denoting moral, religious and civil evil—frequently used as an antonym of righteousness (e.g., Prov 13:6; Ezek 33:12). The whole evil system was to be destroyed (cf. 2 Thess 2:6–8).

5:9 *two women.* Divinely chosen agents. *wind.* Also an instrument of God (Ps 104:3–4). The removal of wickedness would be the work of God alone.

5:11 *Shinar.* Babylonia (see Gen 10:10; 11:2; Rev 17–18). Babylonia, a land of idolatry, was an appropriate locale for wickedness—but not Israel, where God chose to dwell with His people. Only after purging it of its evil would the promised land truly be the "holy land" (2:12).

6:1–8 The eighth and last vision. It corresponds to the first (1:7–17), though there are differences in details, such as in the order and colors of the horses. As in the first vision, the Lord is depicted as the one who controls the events of history. He will conquer the nations that oppress Israel.

6:1 *four chariots.* Angelic spirits as agents of divine judgment (v. 5). *two mountains.* Possibly Mount Zion and the Mount of Olives, with the Kidron Valley between them. *bronze.* Perhaps symbolic of judgment (cf. Num 21:9).

6:2–3 *red . . . black . . . white . . . dappled.* The horses may signify various divine judgments on the earth (see note on v. 8). See also Rev 6:1–8 and note on Rev 6:2.

6:4 *these.* The chariots, with the horses harnessed to them.

6:5 *four spirits.* See note on v. 1. *Lord of all the earth.* See note on 4:14.

6:8 *north.* Primarily Babylonia, but also the direction from which most of Israel's foes invaded their nation (see note on 2:6). *have appeased My wrath.* The angelic beings dispatched to the north have triumphed and thus have pacified or appeased God's spirit (i.e., His anger). See 1:15, where God's displeasure was aroused against oppressive nations. Another view reads "have given My Spirit rest." In either case, since conquest was announced in the north, victory was assured over all enemies.

6:9–15 The fourth and fifth visions were concerned with the high priest and the civil governor (in the Davidic line). Zechariah now relates the message of those two visions to the Messianic King-Priest.

6:9 Introduces a prophetic oracle (see 4:8; 7:4,8; 8:1,18; see also note on 1:1).

6:10 *an offering.* Gifts (including "silver and gold," v. 11) for the temple (cf. Ezra 6:5; Hag 2:8).

6:11 *crown.* The Hebrew for this word is not the same as that used for the high priest's turban, but one referring to an ornate crown with many diadems (cf. Rev 19:12). The royal crowning of the high priest foreshadows the goal and consummation of prophecy—the crowning and reign of the Messianic King-Priest (see vv. 12–13; cf. Ps 110:4; Heb 7:1–3).

6:12 *Behold, a man.* Cf. Pilate's introduction of Jesus in John 19:5. *Branch.* See note on 3:8. According to the Aramaic Targum (a paraphrase), the Jerusalem Talmud (a collection of reli-

where He is; and He will [c]build the temple of
the LORD.
13 "Yes, it is He who will build the temple of
the LORD, and He who will [a]bear the honor
and sit and [b]rule on His throne. Thus, He will
be a [c]priest on His throne, and the counsel of
peace will be between the two [1]offices." '
14 "Now the [a]crown will become a reminder in the temple of the LORD to Helem,
Tobijah, Jedaiah and [1]Hen the son of Zephaniah.
15 "[a]Those who are far off will come and
[1]build the temple of the LORD." Then you
will [b]know that the LORD of hosts has sent
me to you. And it will take place if you completely [c]obey the LORD your God.

Hearts like Flint

7 In the fourth year of King Darius, the
word of the LORD came to Zechariah on
the fourth *day* of the ninth month, *which is*
[a]Chislev.
2 Now *the town of* Bethel had sent Sharezer and Regemmelech and [1]their men to
[2a]seek the favor of the LORD,
3 speaking to the [a]priests who belong to
the house of the LORD of hosts, and to the
prophets, saying, "Shall I weep in the [b]fifth
month [1]and abstain, as I have done these
many years?"
4 Then the word of the LORD of hosts
came to me, saying,
5 "Say to all the people of the land and to
the priests, 'When you fasted and mourned
in the fifth and seventh months [1]these [a]sev-
enty years, was it actually for [b]Me that you
fasted?
6 'When you eat and drink, [1]do you not
eat for yourselves and do you not drink for
yourselves?
7 'Are not *these* the words which the LORD
[a]proclaimed by the former prophets, when
Jerusalem was inhabited and [1b]prosperous
along with its cities around it, and the [2c]Neg-
ev and the [3]foothills were inhabited?' "
8 Then the word of the LORD came to
Zechariah saying,
9 "Thus has the LORD of hosts said, '[a]Dis-
pense true justice and practice [b]kindness and
compassion each to his brother;
10 and [a]do not oppress the widow or the
[1]orphan, the [2]stranger or the poor; and do
[b]not devise evil in your hearts against one
another.'
11 "But they [a]refused to pay attention and
[1b]turned a stubborn shoulder and [2c]stopped
their ears from hearing.
12 "They made their [a]hearts *like* [1b]flint [2]so
that they could not hear the law and the
[c]words which the LORD of hosts had sent by
His Spirit through the [d]former prophets;
therefore great [e]wrath came from the LORD of
hosts.
13 "And just as [a]He called and they would
not listen, so [b]they called and I would not
listen," says the LORD of hosts;
14 "but I [1a]scattered them with a [b]storm
wind among all the nations whom they have
not known. Thus the land is [c]desolated

12 [c]Ezra 3:8, 10; Amos 9:11; Zech 4:6-9 **13** [1]Lit *of them* [a]Is 9:6; 11:10; 22:24; 49:5, 6 [b]Is 9:7 [c]Ps 110:1, 4 **14** [1]I.e. Josiah [a]Zech 6:11 **15** [1]Lit *build in* [a]Is 56:6-8; 60:10 [b]Zech 2:9-11; 4:9 [c]Is 58:10-14; Jer 7:23; Zech 3:7
7:1 [a]Neh 1:1 **2** [1]Lit *his* [2]Lit *soften the face of* [a]1 Kin 13:6; Jer 26:19; Zech 8:21 **3** [1]Lit *abstaining;* or *dedicating myself* [a]Ezra 3:10-12 [b]Zech 8:19 **5** [1]Lit *and these* [a]Zech 1:12 [b]Is 1:11, 12; 58:5
6 [1]Lit *is it not you who eat and you who drink* **7** [1]Or *at ease* [2]I.e. South country [3]Heb *Shephelah* [a]Is 1:16-20; Jer 7:5, 23; Zech 1:4 [b]Jer 22:21 [c]Jer 13:19; 32:44 **9** [a]Ezek 18:8; 45:9; Zech 8:16 [b]2 Sam 9:7; Job 6:14; Mic 6:8 **10** [1]Or *fatherless* [2]Or *resident alien* [a]Ex 22:22; Ps 72:4; Jer 7:6 [b]Ps 21:11; Mic 2:1; Zech 8:17
11 [1]Lit *gave* [2]Lit *made heavy* [a]Jer 5:3; 8:5; 11:10 [b]Jer 7:26; 17:23 [c]Ps 58:4; Jer 5:21 **12** [1]Lit *corundum* [2]Lit *from hearing* [a]2 Chr 36:13; Ezek 2:4; 3:7-9 [b]Jer 17:1; Ezek 3:9 [c]Zech 7:7 [d]Neh 9:30 [e]2 Chr 36:16; Dan 9:11, 12 **13** [a]Jer 11:10, 14; 14:12 [b]Prov 1:24-28; Is 1:15 **14** [1]Lit *stormed them away upon all* [a]Deut 4:27; 28:64 [b]Jer 23:19 [c]Jer 44:6

gious instruction) and the Midrash (practical exposition), Jews early regarded this verse as Messianic. *branch out.* The NASB here reflects the wordplay in the Hebrew text. *temple.* Cf. Is 2:2–3; Ezek 40–43; Hag 2:6–9.

6:13 *His throne.* See 2 Sam 7:16; Is 9:7 and note; Luke 1:32. *priest on His throne.* The coming Davidic King will also be a priest. *two.* Probably the royal and priestly offices. Such a combination was not normally possible in Israel. For this reason, the sect of Qumran (see essay, p. 1356) expected two Messianic figures—a high-priest Messiah and a Davidic one. But the two offices and functions would in fact be united in the one person of the Messiah (cf. Ps 110; Heb 7).

6:14 *Hen.* Means "gracious one" perhaps another name for Josiah—to honor him for his hospitality (v. 10).

6:15 *Those who are far off will come and build.* Cf. Is 60:4–7.

7:1 *fourth year . . . fourth day . . . ninth month.* Dec. 7, 518 B.C.—not quite two years after the eight night visions (see note on 1:7).

7:3 *prophets.* Including Zechariah. *I.* The people of Bethel collectively. *weep in the fifth month.* See note on 8:19. *these many years.* "These seventy years" (v. 5).

7:4–7 A rebuke for selfish and insincere fasting on the part of the people and the priests.

7:4,8 See note on 6:9.

7:5 *fasted . . . fifth and seventh.* See note on 8:19. *seventy years.* See 1:12 and note. Since these fasts commemorated events related to the destruction of Jerusalem and the temple (see note on 8:19), the 70 years here are to be reckoned from 586 B.C. Strictly speaking, 68 years had transpired; 70 is thus a round number.

7:6 *for yourselves.* Cf. Is 1:11–17; 58:1–7,13–14.

7:7,12 *former prophets.* See note on 1:4.

7:7 *Negev.* See note on Gen 12:9. *foothills.* Sloping toward the Mediterranean.

7:9–10 Four tests of faithful covenant living, consisting of a series of social, moral and ethical commands.

7:9 *justice.* The proper ordering of all society (cf. 8:16; see Is 42:1,4; Mic 6:8). *kindness.* Cf. Hos 10:12; 12:6. *compassion.* See note on 1:16.

7:10 *oppress.* Oppression is denounced frequently in the OT (e.g., Amos 2:6–8; 4:1; 5:11–12,21–24; 8:4–6). *widow . . . orphan . . . stranger . . . poor.* For the Biblical concern for such people see, e.g., Deut 10:18; Is 1:17 and note; Jer 5:28; James 1:27; 1 John 3:16–18. In the ancient Near East, the ideal king was expected to protect the oppressed and needy members of society. *devise evil . . . against one another.* See 8:17.

7:11 *they.* The preexilic forefathers, as the reference to the "former prophets" in v. 12 shows. *turned a stubborn shoulder.* See Deut 9:6,13,27. *stopped their ears from hearing.* See Ps 58:4; Is 6:10 and note; cf. Is 33:15.

7:12 *like flint.* See Ezek 3:8–9. *words . . . sent by His Spirit.* The words of the prophets were inspired by God's Spirit (cf. Neh 9:30; 2 Pet 1:21). *great wrath.* See 1:2,15.

7:13 See note on 1:3.

7:14 *scattered them.* One of the curses for covenant disobedience (Deut 28:36–37,64–68; see note on Deut 28:64). *storm*

behind them [2]so that [d]no one went back and
forth, for they [e]made the pleasant land desolate."

The Coming Peace and Prosperity of Zion

8 Then the word of the LORD of hosts came,
saying,
2 "Thus says the LORD of hosts, 'I am
[a]exceedingly jealous for Zion, yes, with great
wrath I am jealous for her.'
3 "Thus says the LORD, 'I will return to
Zion and will [a]dwell in the midst of
Jerusalem. Then Jerusalem will be called the
City of [b]Truth, and the mountain of the LORD
of hosts *will be called* the Holy Mountain.'
4 "Thus says the LORD of hosts, '[a]Old men
and old women will again sit in the [1]streets
of Jerusalem, each man with his staff in his
hand because of [2]age.
5 'And the [1]streets of the city will be filled
with [a]boys and girls playing in its [1]streets.'
6 "Thus says the LORD of hosts, 'If it is
[1a]too difficult in the sight of the remnant of
this people in those days, will it also be [1b]too
difficult in My sight?' declares the LORD of
hosts.
7 "Thus says the LORD of hosts, 'Behold, I
am going to save My people from the land of
the [1a]east and from the land of the [2]west;
8 and I will [a]bring them *back* and they
will [b]live in the midst of Jerusalem; and they
shall be [c]My people, and I will be their God
in [1]truth and righteousness.'
9 "Thus says the LORD of hosts, 'Let your
hands be [a]strong, you who are listening in
these days to these words from the mouth of
the [b]prophets, *those* who *spoke* in the day
that the foundation of the house of the LORD
of hosts was laid, to the end that the temple
might be built.
10 'For before those days there was [a]no
wage for man or any wage for animal; and
for him who went out or came in there was
no [1b]peace because of [2]his enemies, and I
[c]set all men one against another.
11 'But now I will [a]not [1]treat the remnant
of this people as in the former days,' declares
the LORD of hosts.
12 'For *there will be* [a]peace for the seed:
the vine will yield its fruit, the land will yield
its produce and the heavens will give their
[b]dew; and I will cause the remnant of this
people to inherit [c]all these *things*.
13 'It will come about that just as you were
a [a]curse among the nations, O house of
Judah and house of Israel, so I will save you
that you may become a [b]blessing. Do not
fear; let your [c]hands be strong.'
14 "For thus says the LORD of hosts, 'Just as
I [a]purposed to do harm to you when your
fathers provoked Me to wrath,' says the LORD
of hosts, 'and I have not [b]relented,
15 so I have again purposed in these days
to [a]do good to Jerusalem and to the house of
Judah. [b]Do not fear!
16 'These are the things which you should
do: speak the [a]truth to one another; [b]judge
with truth and judgment for peace in your
[1]gates.
17 'Also let none of you [a]devise evil in

14 [2]Lit *from passing and from returning* [d]Is 60:15 [e]Jer 12:10
8:2 [a]Zech 1:14
3 [a]Zech 2:10, 11 [b]Zech 8:16, 19
4 [1]Or *squares* [2]Lit *the multitude of days* [a]Is 65:20
5 [1]Or *squares* [a]Jer 30:19, 20; 31:12, 13
6 [1]Or *wonderful* [a]Ps 118:23; 126:1-3 [b]Jer 32:17, 27
7 [1]Lit *rising* [2]Lit *setting sun* [a]Ps 107:3; Is 11:11; 27:12, 13; 43:5
8 [1]Or *faithfulness* [a]Zeph 3:20; Zech 10:10 [b]Jer 3:17; Ezek 37:25 [c]Ezek 11:20; 36:28; Zech 2:11
9 [a]1 Chr 22:13; Is 35:4; Hag 2:4 [b]Ezra 5:1; 6:14
10 [1]Or *safety* [2]Lit *the adversary* [a]Hag 2:15-19 [b]2 Chr 15:5 [c]Is 19:2; Amos 3:6; 9:4
11 [1]Lit *be to the* [a]Ps 103:9; Is 12:1; Hag 2:19
12 [a]Lev 26:3-6 [b]Gen 27:28; Deut 33:13, 28; Hos 13:3 [c]Is 61:7; Obad 17
13 [a]Jer 29:18; Dan 9:11 [b]Ps 72:17; Is 19:24, 25; Ezek 34:26; Zech 14:11 [c]Zech 8:9

14 [a]Jer 31:28 [b]Jer 4:28; Ezek 24:14 **15** [a]Jer 29:11; Mic 7:18-20 [b]Zech 8:13 **16** [1]I.e. the place where court was held [a]Ps 15:2; Prov 12:17-19; Zech 8:3; Eph 4:25 [b]Is 9:7; 11:4, 5; Zech 7:9 **17** [a]Prov 3:29; Jer 4:14; Zech 7:10

wind. See Prov 1:27; Is 40:24; Hos 4:19. *land . . . desolated.* See Deut 28:41–42,45–52. *for they made.* By their sins. *pleasant land.* Cf. Ps 106:24; Jer 3:19.

8:1–23 Ten promises of blessing, each beginning with "Thus says the LORD [of hosts]" (vv. 2,3,4,6,7,9,14,19,20,23).

8:1,18 See note on 6:9.

8:2 *jealous.* See 1:14; see also note on Ex 20:5.

8:3 *I will return.* See 1:3 and note; 1:16. *dwell.* See note on 2:10. *the City of Truth.* Cf. v. 16; see Is 1:26 and note. *the Holy Mountain.* Cf. 14:20–21.

8:4–5 See Is 11:6–9 and note; 65:20–25.

8:6,11–12 *remnant.* See notes on Is 1:9; 10:20–22.

8:6 *will it also be too difficult in My sight?* "Difficult" can be translated "wonderful" or "marvelous" in both instances in this verse (see NASB marg.; see also Gen 18:14 and note; Jer 32:17,27.

8:7 *save My people.* Deliver them from exile, bondage and dispersion (cf. Is 11:11–12; 43:5–7; Jer 30:7–11; 31:7–8). *from the land of the east and . . . the west.* Lit. "from the land of the sunrise and from the land of the going in of the sun," i.e., from everywhere—wherever the people are (cf. Ps 50:1; 113:3; Mal 1:11).

8:8 *they shall be My people, and I will be their God.* Covenant terminology, pertaining to intimate fellowship in a covenant relationship (see 13:9; Gen 17:7 and note; Ex 6:7; 29:45–46; Lev 11:45; 22:33; 25:38; 26:12 and note; 26:45; Num 15:41; Deut 29:13; Jer 24:7; 31:33; 32:38; Ezek 34:30–31; 36:28; 37:27; Hos 1:9–10; 2:23; 2 Cor 6:16; Heb 8:10; Rev 21:3). *truth and righteousness.* Judah's restoration to covenant favor and blessing rests on the faithfulness (truthfulness, dependability) and righteousness of God.

8:9 *hands be strong.* See v. 13. *prophets.* Including Haggai (1:1) and Zechariah (1:1; cf. Ezra 5:1–2).

8:10 *before those days.* Before the temple foundation was laid (see v. 9). *no wage.* See Hag 1:6–11; 2:15–19. *enemies.* For example, the Samaritans (Ezra 4:1–5).

8:11 *But now.* The reasons for discouragement have passed; God will now provide the grounds for encouragement.

8:12 Contrast with Hag 1:10–11. In Hag 2:19 God had predicted just such a reversal as is depicted here. Fertility and bounty are part of the covenant blessings for obedience promised in Lev 26:3–10; Deut 28:11–12; cf. Ezek 34:25–27.

8:13 *curse among the nations.* Part of the covenant curses for disobedience threatened in Deut 28:15–68 (see Deut 28:37); cf. Jer 24:9; 25:18. *Judah and . . . Israel.* The whole nation will experience this deliverance and blessing (cf. Jer 31:1–31; Ezek 37:15–28). *blessing.* See vv. 20–23; cf. Gen 12:2. *hands be strong.* See note on v. 9.

8:14–17 Verses 14–15 specify God's part in the people's restoration to favor and blessing; vv. 16–17 delineate their part.

8:14 *your fathers provoked Me to wrath.* See note on 1:2.

8:15 *do good.* See vv. 12–13.

8:16–17 See 7:9–10. Such moral and ethical behavior sums up the character of those who are in covenant relationship with the Lord.

8:16 *gates.* See Gen 19:1 and note; 2 Sam 18:24.

your heart against another, and do not love
[1b]perjury; for all these are what I [c]hate,'
declares the LORD."
18 Then the word of the LORD of hosts
came to me, saying,
19 "Thus says the LORD of hosts, 'The fast
of the [a]fourth, the fast of the [b]fifth, the fast
of the [c]seventh and the fast of the [d]tenth
months will become [e]joy, gladness, and
[1]cheerful feasts for the house of Judah; so
[f]love truth and peace.'
20 "Thus says the LORD of hosts, '*It will* yet
be that [a]peoples will come, even the inhabitants of many cities.
21 'The inhabitants of one will go to another, saying, "Let us go at once to [a]entreat the
favor of the LORD, and to seek the LORD of
hosts; [1]I will also go."
22 'So [a]many peoples and mighty nations
will come to seek the LORD of hosts in
Jerusalem and to [b]entreat the favor of the
LORD.'
23 "Thus says the LORD of hosts, 'In those
days ten men from all the [1]nations will
[2a]grasp the [3]garment of a Jew, saying, "Let
us go with you, for we have heard that God
is with you." ' "

Prophecies against Neighboring Nations

9 The [1]burden of the word of the LORD is
against the land of Hadrach, with
[a]Damascus as its resting place (for the eyes
of men, especially of all the tribes of Israel,
are toward the LORD),
2 And [a]Hamath also, which borders on
it;
[b]Tyre and [c]Sidon, [1]though [2]they are
[b]very wise.
3 For Tyre built herself a [a]fortress
And [b]piled up silver like dust,
And [c]gold like the mire of the streets.
4 Behold, the Lord will [a]dispossess her
And cast her wealth into the sea;
And she will be [b]consumed with fire.
5 Ashkelon will see *it* and be afraid.
Gaza too will writhe in great pain;
Also Ekron, for her expectation has
been confounded.
Moreover, the king will perish from
Gaza,
And Ashkelon will not be inhabited.
6 And a [1]mongrel race will dwell in
[a]Ashdod,
And I will cut off the pride of the
Philistines.
7 And I will remove their blood from
their mouth
And their detestable things from
between their teeth.
Then they also will be a remnant for
our God,
And be like a [1]clan in Judah,

17 [1]Lit *false oath* [b]Zech 5:4; Mal 3:5 [c]Prov 6:16-19; Hab 1:13
19 [1]Or *goodly* [a]2 Kin 25:3, 4; Jer 39:2 [b]Zech 7:3, 5 [c]2 Kin 25:25; Zech 7:5 [d]Jer 52:4 [e]Ps 30:11; Is 12:1 [f]Zech 8:16; Luke 1:74, 75
20 [a]Ps 117:1; Jer 16:19; Mic 4:2, 3; Zech 2:11; 14:16
21 [1]Or *let me go too* [a]Zech 7:2
22 [a]Is 2:2, 3; 25:7; 49:6, 22, 23; 60:3-12 [b]Zech 8:21
23 [1]Lit *languages of the nations* [2]Lit *grasp, and they will grasp* [3]Or *corner of the garment* [a]Is 45:14, 24; 60:14
9:1 [1]Or *oracle* [a]Is 17:1; Jer 49:23-27; Amos 1:3-5
2 [1]Or *because* [2]I.e. they think they are [a]Jer 49:23 [b]Ezek 28:2-5, 12 [c]Ezek 28:21
3 [a]Josh 19:29; 2 Sam 24:7 [b]Job 27:16; Ezek 27:33; 28:4, 5 [c]1 Kin 10:21, 27
4 [a]Ezek 26:3-5 [b]Ezek 28:18 **6** [1]Lit *bastard will* [a]Amos 1:8; Zeph 2:4 **7** [1]Or *chief*

8:17 *perjury.* See note on 5:3. *all these . . . I hate.* Prov 6:16–19 lists seven things the Lord hates, three of which relate directly to vv. 16–17 here: "a lying tongue," "a heart that devises wicked plans" and "a false witness who utters lies."
8:19 See 7:2–6. *fourth.* The fast that lamented the breaching of the walls of Jerusalem by Nebuchadnezzar (2 Ki 25:3–4; Jer 39:2; 52:6–7). *fifth.* Commemorated the burning of the temple and the other important buildings (2 Kin 25:8–10; Jer 52:12–14). *seventh.* Marked the anniversary of Gedaliah's assassination (2 Kin 25:22–25; Jer 41:1–3). *tenth.* Mourned the beginning of Nebuchadnezzar's siege of Jerusalem (2 Kin 25:1; Jer 39:1; 52:4; Ezek 24:1–2). *cheerful feasts.* Cf. Is 65:18–19; Jer 31:10–14.
8:20–23 For similar predictions about Gentiles seeking the Lord see 2:11 and note; Is 2:2–4; Mic 4:1–5.
8:22 *mighty nations.* Anticipates a fulfillment of the promise of Gentile blessing in the Abrahamic covenant (Gen 12:3; Gal 3:8,26–29; see also Is 55:5; 56:6–7; cf. Mark 11:17).
8:23 *ten.* One way of indicating a large or complete number in Hebrew (see Gen 31:7 and note; Lev 26:26; Num 14:22; 1 Sam 1:8; Neh 4:12). *Jew.* The word, used of the people of the kingdom of Judah after the exile, occurs first in Jer 32:12. *we have heard that God is with you.* True godliness attracts others to the Lord (see Gen 26:28; 30:27; see also notes on Gen 39:2–6; 1 Cor 14:24).
9:1–8 Probably a prophetic description of the Lord's march south to Jerusalem, destroying—as Divine Warrior—the traditional enemies of Israel. As history shows, the agent of His judgment was Alexander the Great (333 B.C.).
9:1 *The burden of the word of the LORD.* The Hebrew for this phrase occurs only two other times in the OT (12:1; Mal 1:1), making it likely that Zech 9–14 and Malachi were written during the same general period (see Introduction: Date). *Hadrach.* Hatarikka, north of Hamath on the Orontes River (see v. 2). *Damascus.* The leading city-state of the Arameans. *eyes . . . toward the LORD.* The thought may be that the eyes of men, especially all the tribes of Israel, are turned toward the Lord (for deliverance).
9:2 *And Hamath also.* Judgment will rest upon Hamath, just as upon Hadrach and Damascus. Hamath is modern Hama. See Amos 6:2. *it.* Damascus. *Tyre and Sidon.* Phoenician (modern Lebanese) coastal cities. Their judgment (vv. 3–4) is also foretold in Is 23; Ezek 26:3–14; 28:20–24; Amos 1:9–10.
9:3 *fortress.* The Hebrew for this word is a pun on the Hebrew for "Tyre" (meaning "rock"). The stronghold was Tyre's island fortress (Is 23:4; Ezek 26:5). It fell (v. 4) to Alexander in 332 B.C. *silver like dust . . . gold like the mire.* Cf. 1 Kin 10:21,27. Tyre was a center of trade and commerce, and her wealth was proverbial (see Is 23:2–3,8,18; Ezek 26:12; 27:3–27,33; 28:4–5,7,12–14, 16–18).
9:5–7 The Philistine cities were greatly alarmed at Alexander's steady advance.
9:5 *her expectation has been confounded.* As the northernmost city of Philistia, Ekron would be the first to suffer. Her hope that Tyre would stem the tide would meet with disappointment.
9:6 *mongrel race.* People of mixed nationality; they characterized the postexilic period (Neh 13:23–24). *I.* God. *Philistines.* See note on Gen 10:14. At one time their control of Canaan was so extensive that the land was eventually named after them ("Palestine").
9:7 *blood.* Of idolatrous sacrifices. *detestable things.* Ceremonially unclean food. *Jebusite.* These ancient inhabitants of Jerusalem (see note on Gen 10:16) were absorbed into Judah (e.g., Araunah in 2 Sam 24:16–24; 1 Chr 21:18–26). So would it be with a remnant of the Philistines.

And Ekron like a Jebusite.
8 But I will camp around My house
[1]because of an army,
Because of [a]him who passes by and
returns;
And [b]no oppressor will pass over
them anymore,
For now I have seen with My eyes.
9 [a]Rejoice greatly, O daughter of Zion!
Shout *in triumph,* O daughter of
Jerusalem!
Behold, your [b]king is coming to you;
He is [1c]just and [d]endowed with
salvation,
[e]Humble, and mounted on a donkey,
Even on a [f]colt, the [2]foal of a donkey.
10 I will [a]cut off the chariot from
Ephraim
And the [b]horse from Jerusalem;
And the [c]bow of war will be cut off.
And He will speak [d]peace to the
nations;
And His [e]dominion will be from sea to
sea,
And from the [1]River to the ends of the
earth.

Deliverance of Judah and Ephraim

11 As for you also, because of the [a]blood
of *My* covenant with you,
I have set your [b]prisoners free from
the [1]waterless pit.
12 Return to the [1a]stronghold, O
prisoners [2]who have the [b]hope;
This very day I am declaring that I
will restore [c]double to you.
13 For I will [a]bend Judah [1]as My bow,
I will fill the bow with Ephraim.
And I will stir up your sons, O Zion,
against your sons, O [b]Greece;
And I will make you like a [c]warrior's
sword.
14 Then the LORD will appear [a]over
them,
And His [b]arrow will go forth like
lightning;
And the Lord [1]GOD will blow the
[c]trumpet,
And will march in the [d]storm winds of
the south.
15 [a]The LORD of hosts will defend them.
And they will [b]devour and trample on
the [c]sling stones;
And they will drink *and* be
[d]boisterous as with wine;
And they will be filled like a *sacrificial*
basin,
Drenched like the [e]corners of the altar.
16 And the LORD their God will [a]save
them in that day
As the flock of His people;
For *they are as* the stones of a [b]crown,
[1]Sparkling in His land.
17 For what [1a]comeliness and [b]beauty
will be [2]theirs!
Grain will make the young men
flourish, and new wine the virgins.

God Will Bless Judah and Ephraim

10 Ask [a]rain from the LORD at the time of
the spring rain—
The LORD who [b]makes the [1]storm
clouds;

8 [1]Or *as a guard, so that none will go back and forth* [a]Is 52:1 [b]Is 54:14; 60:18
9 [1]Or *vindicated and victorious* [2]Lit *son of a female donkey* [a]Zeph 3:14, 15; Zech 2:10 [b]Ps 110:1; Is 9:6, 7; Jer 23:5, 6; Matt 21:5; John 12:15 [c]Zeph 3:5 [d]Is 43:3, 11 [e]Is 57:15 [f]Judg 10:4; Is 30:6
10 [1]I.e. Euphrates [a]Hos 1:7 [b]Mic 5:10 [c]Hos 2:18 [d]Is 57:19; Mic 4:2-4 [e]Ps 72:8; Is 60:12
11 [1]Lit *cistern in which there is no water* [a]Ex 24:8; Heb 10:2 [b]Is 24:22; 51:14
12 [1]Or *Stronghold* [2]Lit *of the hope* [a]Jer 16:19; Joel 3:16 [b]Jer 14:8; 17:13; Heb 6:18, 19 [c]Is 61:7
13 [1]Lit *for Me* [a]Jer 51:20
13 [b]Joel 3:6 [c]Ps 45:3
14 [1]Heb *YHWH,* usually rendered *LORD* [a]Is 31:5; Zech 2:5 [b]Ps 18:14; Hab 3:11 [c]Is 27:13 [d]Is 21:1; 66:15
15 [a]Is 37:35; Zech 12:8 [b]Zech 12:6 [c]Job 41:28 [d]Ps 78:65 [e]Ex 27:2
16 [1]Or *Displayed over* [a]Jer 31:10, 11 [b]Is 62:3 **17** [1]Lit *goodness* [2]Lit *his* [a]Jer 31:12, 14 [b]Ps 27:4; Is 33:17
10:1 [1]Or *thunderbolts* [a]Joel 2:23 [b]Jer 10:13

9:8 *camp around My house because of an army.* See 2:5. Alexander spared the temple and the city of Jerusalem. *oppressor.* The Hebrew for this word is translated "taskmaster(s)" in Ex 3:7; 5:6,10 and elsewhere; thus it echoes the Egyptian bondage motif. *I have seen with My eyes.* See Ex 3:7; Ps 32:8.
9:9 Quoted in the NT as Messianic and as referring ultimately to the Triumphal Entry of Jesus into Jerusalem (Matt 21:5; John 12:15). *daughter of Zion.* A personification of Jerusalem and its inhabitants. *your king.* The Davidic ("your") Messianic King. *just.* Conforming to the divine standard of morality and ethics, particularly as revealed in the Mosaic legislation; a characteristic of the ideal king (see 2 Sam 23:3–4; Ps 72:1–3; Is 9:7; 11:4–5; 53:11; Jer 23:5–6; 33:15–16). *Humble.* Cf. Is 53:2–3,7; Matt 11:29. *mounted on a donkey.* A suitable choice, since the donkey was a lowly animal of peace (contrast the war-horse of v. 10) as well as a princely mount (Judg 10:4; 12:14; 2 Sam 16:2) before the horse came into common use. The royal mount used by David and his sons was the mule (2 Sam 18:9; 1 Kin 1:33).
9:10 *cut off the chariot . . . horse . . . bow of war.* A similar era of disarmament is foreseen in Is 2:4; 9:5–7; 11:1–10; Mic 5:10–11. *Ephraim.* See note on v. 13. *peace to the nations.* In sharp contrast to Alexander's empire, which was founded on bloodshed, the Messianic King will establish a universal kingdom of peace as the ultimate fulfillment of the Abrahamic covenant (cf. 14:16; see Gen 12:3; 18:18; 22:18). *His dominion will be from . . . to.* It will be universal (see Ps 22:27–28; 72:8–11; Is 45:22; 52:10; 66:18).
9:11 *blood of My covenant with you.* Probably the Mosaic covenant (Ex 24:3–8). *prisoners.* Perhaps those still in Babylonia, the land of exile. *waterless pit.* Cf. Gen 37:24; Jer 38:6.
9:12 *stronghold.* Either (1) Jerusalem (Zion) and environs or (2) God Himself (cf. 2:5). *hope.* In the future delivering King (vv. 9–10). *double.* Full or complete restoration (cf. Is 61:7).
9:13 See note on 10:4. The Lord compares Himself to a warrior who uses Judah as His bow and Ephraim (the northern kingdom) as His arrow. *your sons, O Zion.* The Maccabees (see note on Dan 11:34). *your sons, O Greece.* The Seleucids of Syria (after the breakup of Alexander's empire).
9:14 See Ps 18:7–15; Hab 3:3–15. *trumpet.* Probably a reference to thunder (cf. Ex 19:16–19). *south.* In the region of Mount Sinai, where the Mosaic covenant was given (see v. 11) and where the Lord's dwelling was (see Judg 5:4–5; Ps 68:8; Hab 3:3).
9:15 The Apocryphal book 1 Maccabees (3:16–24; 4:6–16; 7:40–50) records a partial fulfillment of this verse. *sling stones.* Hurled at defenders on the city wall and onto the inhabitants inside. *sacrificial basin.* See Ex 27:1–3; Lev 4:6–7.
9:16 *that day.* See note on 2:11.
10:1 *The LORD . . . give them showers . . . vegetation.* The Lord, not the Canaanite god Baal, is the one who controls the weather and the rain, giving life and fertility to the land (see Jer 14:22; Amos 5:8). Therefore God's people are to pray to and trust in Him. See further Is 55:10–12; Hos 2:8; 6:3; Joel 2:21–27; Matt 5:45.

And He will give them [c]showers of
rain, vegetation in the field to *each*
man.
2 For the [a]teraphim speak [1]iniquity,
And the [b]diviners see [2]lying visions
And tell [c]false dreams;
They comfort in vain.
Therefore *the people* [3]wander like
[d]sheep,
They are afflicted, because there is no
shepherd.
3 "My [a]anger is kindled against the
shepherds,
And I will punish the [1]male goats;
For the LORD of hosts has [b]visited His
flock, the house of Judah,
And will make them like His majestic
horse in battle.
4 "From [1]them will come the
[a]cornerstone,
From [1]them the tent peg,
From [1]them the bow of [b]battle,
From [1]them every [2]ruler, *all* of them
together.
5 "They will be as mighty men,
[a]Treading down *the enemy* in the mire
of the streets in battle;
And they will fight, for the LORD *will
be* with them;
And the [b]riders on horses will be put
to shame.
6 "I will [a]strengthen the house of
Judah,
And I will [b]save the house of Joseph,
And I will [1c]bring them back,
Because I have had [d]compassion on
them;
And they will be as though I had [e]not
rejected them,
For I am the LORD their God and I will
[f]answer them.
7 "Ephraim will be like a mighty man,
And their heart will be glad as if *from*
wine;
Indeed, their [a]children will see *it* and
be glad,
[1]Their heart will rejoice in the LORD.
8 "I will [a]whistle for them to gather them
together,
For I have redeemed them;
And they will be as [b]numerous as they
[1c]were before.
9 "When I [1]scatter them among the
peoples,
They will [a]remember Me in far
countries,
And they with their children will live
and come back.
10 "I will [a]bring them back from the land
of Egypt
And gather them from Assyria;
And I will bring them into the land of
[b]Gilead and Lebanon
[1]Until [c]no *room* can be found for
them.
11 "And they will pass through the [a]sea *of*
distress
And He will strike the waves in the
sea,
So that all the depths of the [b]Nile will
dry up;
And the pride of [c]Assyria will be
brought down
And the scepter of [d]Egypt will depart.
12 "And I will [a]strengthen them in the
LORD,
And in His name [b]they will walk,"
declares the LORD.

The Doomed Flock

11 Open your doors, O Lebanon,
That a [a]fire may feed on your [b]cedars.

10:1 [c]Is 30:23
2 [1]Or *futility* [2]Lit a *lie* [3]Lit *journey* [a]Ezek 21:21; Hos 3:4 [b]Jer 27:9 [c]Jer 23:32 [d]Ezek 34:5, 8; Matt 9:36; Mark 6:34
3 [1]I.e. leaders [a]Jer 25:34-36 [b]Ezek 34:12
4 [1]Lit *him* [2]Or *oppressor* [a]Luke 20:17; Eph 2:20; 1 Pet 2:6 [b]Jer 51:20; Zech 9:10
5 [a]2 Sam 22:43 [b]Amos 2:15; Hag 2:22
6 [1]Or *make them dwell* [a]Zech 10:12 [b]Zech 8:7; 9:16 [c]Zech 8:8 [d]Is 54:8; Zech 1:16 [e]Is 54:4 [f]Zech 13:9
7 [1]Or *Let their heart rejoice* [a]Is 54:13; Ezek 37:25
8 [1]Lit *were numerous* [a]Is 5:26; 7:18, 19 [b]Jer 33:22; Rev 7:9 [c]Jer 30:20; Ezek 36:11
9 [1]Lit *sow* [a]1 Kin 8:47, 48; Ezek 6:9
10 [1]Lit *And* [a]Is 11:11 [b]Jer 50:19 [c]Is 49:19, 20
11 [a]Is 51:9, 10 [b]Is 19:5-7 [c]Zeph 2:13 [d]Ezek 30:13
12 [a]Zech 10:6 [b]Mic 4:5
11:1 [a]Jer 22:6, 7 [b]Ezek 31:3

10:2 *teraphim.* Household gods (see Gen 31:19 and note). They were used for divination during the period of the judges (Judg 17:5; 18:14–20). *diviners.* Included among false prophets, they were the occult counterpart to true prophets. Cf. Jer 23:30–32; 27:9–10. Resorting to such sources for information and guidance is expressly forbidden in Deut 18:9–14 because God provided true prophets (and ultimately the Messianic Prophet) for that purpose (Deut 18:15–22; see John 4:25; 6:14; Acts 3:22–23,26; see also note on Gen 30:27). *people wander like sheep.* See Is 53:6 and note. *there is no shepherd.* Spiritual leadership is missing (cf. Mark 6:34). "Shepherd" is primarily a royal motif, whether referring to human kings (2 Sam 5:2; Is 44:28; Jer 23:2–4) or to God as King (Ps 23:1; 100:3; Ezek 34:11–16) or to the Messianic, Davidic King (Ezek 34:23–24; John 10:11–16; Heb 13:20; 1 Pet 5:4).
10:3 *I will punish the male goats.* Cf. Ezek 34:1–10. *like His majestic horse.* Triumphant.
10:4 Probably Messianic (indicated by the Aramaic Targum). *From them.* See Gen 49:10; Jer 30:21; Mic 5:2. *cornerstone.* See note on 3:9; see especially Is 28:16; Eph 2:20. *tent peg.* The ruler as the support of the state (see note on Is 22:23; see also Is 22:24). *bow of battle.* Part of the Divine Warrior terminology (cf. 9:13; Ps 7:12; 45:5; Lam 2:4; 3:12; Hab 3:9).
10:5 *They.* Judah (v. 4), i.e., its people. *the LORD will be with them.* See Josh 1:5; Jer 1:8,19; 15:20. *put to shame.* Partly fulfilled in the Maccabean victories (during the period between the OT and the NT).
10:6 *Judah . . . Joseph.* The people of the southern and northern kingdoms will be reunited (see note on 8:13).
10:7 *Ephraim.* See note on 9:13. *glad as if from wine.* Cf. Ps 104:15.
10:8 *whistle.* A continuation of the shepherd metaphor (see Judg 5:16). *redeemed.* The Hebrew for this word is often used of ransoming from slavery or captivity (see Is 35:10; Mic 6:4; cf. 1 Pet 1:18–19). *as numerous as . . . before.* See Ex 1:6–20.
10:9 *They will remember Me.* According to the meaning of Zechariah's name, "the LORD remembers" (His covenant people and promises). Now they will remember Him.
10:10 *Egypt . . . Assyria.* See v. 11. Probably representing all the countries where the Israelites are dispersed, these two evoke memories of slavery and exile. *gather them.* See Is 11:11–16; Ezek 39:27–29. *Gilead.* See note on Gen 31:21; see also Song 6:5; Jer 50:19; Mic 7:14. *Lebanon.* See 2 Kin 19:23; Is 33:9 and note; 35:2 and note; Jer 22:6. *no room can be found.* See v. 8; 2:4; see also note on Is 49:19–20.
10:11 *pass through the sea of distress.* As at the Red Sea (see Ex 14:22 and note).
11:1–3 Some interpret this brief poem as a taunt song relat-

2 Wail, O [1]cypress, for the cedar has
fallen,
Because the glorious *trees* have been
destroyed;
Wail, O oaks of Bashan,
For the [2]impenetrable forest has come
down.
3 There is a sound of the shepherds'
[a]wail,
For their glory is ruined;
There is a [b]sound of the young lions'
roar,
For the [1]pride of the Jordan is ruined.

4 Thus says the Lord my God, "Pasture
the flock *doomed* to [a]slaughter.
5 "Those who buy them slay them and
[1]go [a]unpunished, and *each of* those who sell
them says, 'Blessed be the Lord, for [b]I have
become rich!' And their [c]own shepherds
have no pity on them.
6 "For I will [a]no longer have pity on the
inhabitants of the land," declares the Lord;
"but behold, I will [b]cause the men to [1]fall,
each into another's [2]power and into the
[2]power of his king; and they will strike the
land, and I will [c]not deliver *them* from their
[2]power."
7 So I [a]pastured the flock *doomed* to
slaughter, [1]hence the [b]afflicted of the flock.
And I took for myself two [c]staffs: the one I
called [2d]Favor and the other I called [3e]Union;
so I pastured the flock.
8 Then I annihilated the three shepherds
in [a]one month, for my soul was impatient
with them, and their soul also [1]was weary of
me.
9 Then I said, "I will not pasture you.
What is to [a]die, [1]let it die, and what is to be
annihilated, [2]let it be annihilated; and [3]let
those who are left eat one another's flesh."
10 I took my staff [1a]Favor and cut it in
pieces, to [2b]break my covenant which I had
made with all the peoples.
11 So it was [1]broken on that day, and
[2]thus the [a]afflicted of the flock who were
watching me realized that it was the word of
the Lord.
12 I said to them, "If it is good in your
sight, give *me* my [a]wages; but if not, [1]never
mind!" So they weighed out [b]thirty *shekels*
of silver as my wages.
13 Then the Lord said to me, "Throw it to
the [a]potter, *that* magnificent price at which I
was valued by them." So I took the thirty

2 [1]Or *juniper* [2]Another reading is *forest of the vintage* **3** [1]Or *jungle* [a]Jer 25:34-36 [b]Jer 2:15; 50:44 **4** [a]Ps 44:22; Zech 11:7 **5** [1]Lit *are not held guilty* [a]Jer 50:7 [b]Hos 12:8; 1 Tim 6:9 [c]Ezek 34:2, 3 **6** [1]Lit *find* [2]Lit *hand* [a]Jer 13:14 [b]Is 9:19-21; Mic 7:2-6; Zech 14:13 [c]Ps 50:22; Mic 5:8 **7** [1]Another reading is *for the sheep dealers* [a]Zech 11:4 [b]Jer 39:10; Zeph 3:12 **7** [2]Or *Pleasantness* [3]Or *Cords* [c]Ezek 37:16 [d]Ps 27:4; 90:17; Zech 11:10 [e]Ps 133:1; Ezek 37:16-23; Zech 11:14 **8** [1]Or *detested* [a]Hos 5:7 **9** [1]Or *will die* [2]Or *will be annihilated* [3]Or *those...will eat* [a]Jer 15:2 **10** [1]Or *Pleasantness* [2]Or *annul* [a]Zech 11:7 [b]Ps 89:39; Jer 14:21 **11** [1]Or *annulled* [2]Another reading is *the sheep dealers who* [a]Zeph 3:12 **12** [1]Lit *cease* [a]1 Kin 5:6; Mal 3:5 [b]Gen 37:28; Ex 21:32; Matt 26:15; 27:9, 10 **13** [a]Matt 27:3-10; Acts 1:18, 19

ed to the lament that will be sung over the destruction of the nations' power and arrogance (ch. 10), represented by the cedar, the pine and the oak (vv. 1–2). Their kings are represented by the shepherds and the lions (v. 3). Understood in this way, vv. 1–3 would provide the conclusion to the preceding section. Other interpreters, however, without denying the presence of figurative language, see the piece more literally as a description of the devastation of Syro-Palestine due to the rejection of the Messianic Good Shepherd (vv. 4–14). Verses 1–3 would then furnish the introduction to the next section. The geography of the text—Lebanon, Bashan and Jordan—would seem to favor this interpretation. Part of the fulfillment would be the destruction and further subjugation of the area by the Romans, including the fall of Jerusalem in A.D. 70 and of Masada in 73. Understood in this way, the passage is in sharp contrast with ch. 10 and its prediction of Israel's full deliverance and restoration to the covenant land. Now the scene is one of desolation for the land (vv. 1–3), followed by the threat of judgment and disaster for both land and people (vv. 4–6).

11:1 *Lebanon.* See 10:10 and note.

11:2 *Bashan.* See note on Is 2:13. The Israelites took this region from the Amorite king, Og, at the time of the conquest of Canaan (Num 21:33–35). It was allotted to the half-tribe of Manasseh (Josh 13:29–30; 17:5). *impenetrable forest.* Of Lebanon.

11:3 If the language is figurative, the shepherds and lions represent the rulers or leaders of the Jews (see v. 5; 10:3; cf. Jer 25:34–36). *pride of the Jordan.* Where the lions had their lairs.

11:4–14 The reason for the judgment on Israel in vv. 1–3 is now given, namely, the people's rejection of the Messianic Shepherd-King. Just as the Servant in the "servant songs" (see note on Is 42:1–4) is rejected, so here the Good Shepherd (a royal figure) is rejected. The same Messianic King is in view in both instances.

11:4 *says.* To Zechariah. *flock.* Israel.

11:5 *Those who buy.* The sheep (the Jews) are bought as slaves by outsiders. Part of the fulfillment came in A.D. 70 and the following years. *those who sell them.* "Their own shepherds (rulers or leaders)."

11:6 *land.* The Holy Land. *king.* Perhaps the Roman emperor (cf. John 19:15). *they.* Includes the Romans prophetically.

11:7 *I.* Zechariah, as a type (foreshadowing) of the Messianic Shepherd-King. *one I called Favor.* To ensure divine favor on the flock. *Union.* See Ezek 37:15–28. Such unity would be the result of the gracious leadership of the Good Shepherd. (For the significance of the subsequent breaking of the two staffs see vv. 10,14.)

11:8 *annihilated the three shepherds.* Although the three cannot be specifically identified, the Good Shepherd will dispose of all such unfit leaders. *my soul was impatient with them.* Cf. Is 1:13–14.

11:9 *What is to die, let it die.* The Good Shepherd terminates His providential care of the sheep. *eat one another's flesh.* According to Josephus, this actually happened during the Roman siege of Jerusalem in A.D. 70 (cf. also Lam 4:10).

11:10 *covenant.* Apparently a covenant of security and restraint, by which the Shepherd had been holding back the nations from His people (cf. Ezek 34:25; Hos 2:18). Now, however, the nations (e.g., the Romans) will be permitted to overrun them.

11:11 *the afflicted of the flock.* Probably the faithful few, who recognize the authoritative word of the Lord (see also v. 7). *it.* Probably Israel's affliction by the nations. *word of the Lord.* The faithful discern that what happens (e.g., the judgment on Jerusalem and the temple in A.D. 70) is a fulfillment of God's prophetic word—as a result of such actions as those denounced in Matt 23, which led to the rejection of the Good Shepherd.

11:12 *give me my wages.* Refers to the severance of the relationship. *never mind.* A more emphatic way of ending the relationship. *thirty shekels of silver.* The price of a slave among the Israelites in ancient times (see note on Ex 21:32); also, a way of indicating a trifling amount.

11:13 *magnificent price.* Irony and sarcasm. *threw them to the*

shekels of silver and threw them to the potter
in the house of the LORD.
14 Then I cut in pieces my second staff
[1][a]Union, to [b]break the brotherhood between
Judah and Israel.
15 The LORD said to me, "Take again for
yourself the equipment of a [1][a]foolish shepherd.
16 "For behold, I am going to raise up a
shepherd in the land who will [a]not care for
the perishing, seek the scattered, heal the
broken, or sustain the one standing, but will
[b]devour the flesh of the fat *sheep* and tear off
their hoofs.
17 "[a]Woe to the worthless shepherd
Who leaves the flock!
A [b]sword will be on his arm
And on his right eye!
His [c]arm will be totally withered
And his right eye will be [1]blind."

Jerusalem to Be Attacked

12 The [1]burden of the word of the LORD
concerning Israel.
Thus declares the LORD who [a]stretches out
the heavens, [b]lays the foundation of the earth,
and [c]forms the spirit of man within him,
2 "Behold, I am going to make Jerusalem
a [a]cup [1]that causes reeling to all the peoples
around; and when the siege is against
Jerusalem, it will also be against [b]Judah.
3 "It will come about in that day that I will
make Jerusalem a heavy [a]stone for all the
peoples; all who lift it will be [b]severely
[1]injured. And all the [c]nations of the earth
will be gathered against it.

14 [1]Or *Cords* [a]Zech 11:7 [b]Is 9:21; Zech 11:6
15 [1]Or *useless* [a]Is 6:10-12; Zech 11:17
16 [a]Jer 23:2 [b]Ezek 34:2-6
17 [1]Lit *completely dimmed* [a]Jer 23:1; Zech 10:2; 11:15 [b]Jer 50:35-37 [c]Ezek 30:21, 22
12:1 [1]Or *oracle* [a]Is 42:5; 44:24; Jer 51:15 [b]Job 26:7; Ps 102:25, 26; Heb 1:10-12 [c]Is 57:16; Heb 12:9
2 [1]Lit *of reeling* [a]Ps 75:8; Is 51:22, 23 [b]Zech 14:14
3 [1]Lit *scratched* [a]Dan 2:34, 35, 44, 45 [b]Matt 21:44 [c]Zech 14:2
4 [1]Lit *open My eyes*
5 [1]Lit *My strength is*
6 [a]Is 10:17, 18; Obad 18; Zech 11:1 [b]Zech 2:4; 8:3-5
7 [a]Jer 30:18 [b]Amos 9:11
8 [1]Or *stumbles* [a]Joel 3:16; Zech 9:14, 15 [b]Lev 26:8; Josh 23:10; Mic 7:8 [c]Ps 8:5; 82:6 [d]Ex 14:19; 33:2
9 [1]Lit *seek to* [a]Zech 14:2, 3

4 "In that day," declares the LORD, "I will
strike every horse with bewilderment and his
rider with madness. But I will [1]watch over
the house of Judah, while I strike every
horse of the peoples with blindness.
5 "Then the clans of Judah will say in
their hearts, '[1]A strong support for us are the
inhabitants of Jerusalem through the LORD of
hosts, their God.'
6 "In that day I will make the clans of
Judah like a [a]firepot among pieces of wood
and a flaming torch among sheaves, so they
will consume on the right hand and on the
left all the surrounding peoples, while the
[b]inhabitants of Jerusalem again dwell on
their own sites in Jerusalem.
7 "The LORD also will [a]save the tents of
Judah first, so that the glory of the house
of [b]David and the glory of the inhabitants of
Jerusalem will not be magnified above Judah.
8 "In that day the LORD will [a]defend the
inhabitants of Jerusalem, and the one who
[1][b]is feeble among them in that day will be like
David, and the house of David *will be* like
[c]God, like the [d]angel of the LORD before them.
9 "And in that day I will [1][a]set about to
destroy all the nations that come against
Jerusalem.
10 "I will [a]pour out on the house of David
and on the inhabitants of Jerusalem, [1]the
Spirit of grace and of supplication, so that
they will look on Me whom they have
[b]pierced; and they will mourn for Him, as
one [c]mourns for an only son, and they will

10 [1]Or *a spirit* [a]Is 44:3; Ezek 39:29; Joel 2:28, 29 [b]John 19:37; Rev 1:7 [c]Jer 6:26; Amos 8:10

potter in the house of the LORD. For the NT use of vv. 12–13 see Matt 26:14–15; 27:3–10; see also note on Matt 27:9.

11:14 *cut in pieces my second staff called Union.* Signifying the dissolution of the covenant nation, particularly of the unity between the south and the north. The breaking up of the nation into parties hostile to each other was characteristic of later Jewish history; it greatly hindered the popular cause in the war against Rome (cf. John 11:48).

11:15 *again.* See v. 7. *foolish shepherd.* With the Shepherd of the Lord's choice removed from the scene, a foolish and worthless (v. 17) shepherd replaces Him. A selfish, greedy, corrupt leader will arise and afflict the flock (the people of Israel).

11:16 *seek the scattered.* Cf. Gen 33:13; Is 40:11. *tear off their hoofs.* Apparently in a greedy search for the last edible piece.

11:17 *worthless shepherd.* See note on v. 15. This counterfeit shepherd may have found a partial historical fulfillment in such leaders as Simeon bar Kosiba or Kokhba (who led the Jewish revolt against the Romans in A.D. 132–135 and who was hailed as the Messiah by Rabbi Akiba). But it would seem that the final stage of the progressive fulfillment of the complete prophecy awaits the rise of the final antichrist (cf. Ezek 34:2–4; Dan 11:36–39; John 5:43; 2 Thess 2:3–10; Rev 13:1–8). *leaves the flock.* Contrast the Good Shepherd of John 10:11–16. *His arm will be totally withered.* His power will be paralyzed. *his right eye will be blind.* His intelligence will be nullified. Thus this leader will be powerless to fight.

12:1–14:21 This second oracle in Part II of the book revolves around two scenes: the final siege of Jerusalem, and the Messiah's return to defeat Israel's enemies and establish His kingdom.

12:1 *burden.* See note on 9:1. *Israel.* The whole nation, not just the northern kingdom. Judah and Jerusalem, however, are the main focus of attention. *the LORD who stretches . . . lays . . . forms.* This description of the Lord's creative power shows that He is able to perform what He predicts; it also strengthens the royal and sovereign authority of the message.

12:2 *cup that causes reeling to all.* See note on Is 51:17.

12:3 *that day.* See note on 2:11. The phrase is used often in chs. 12–14 (12:4,6,8–9,11; 13:1–2,4; 14:4,6,8–9,13,20–21). *all the nations . . . gathered against it.* See 14:2,12; Joel 3:9–16; cf. Rev 16:16–21.

12:4 *bewilderment . . . madness . . . blindness.* Listed in Deut 28:28 among Israel's curses for disobeying the stipulations of the covenant. Now these curses are turned against Israel's enemies. *watch over.* See Ps 32:8; 33:18.

12:6 Like a fire destroying wood and sheaves of grain, Judah's discerning leaders (see v. 5) will consume their enemies (cf. Judg 15:3–5; see note on Is 1:31).

12:8 *like David.* Like a great warrior. *like God.* Cf. Ex 4:16; 7:1. *like the angel of the LORD.* See Gen 48:16 and note; Ex 14:19; 23:20; 32:34; 33:2,14–15,22; Hos 12:3–4; see also Gen 16:7 and note.

12:10 *the Spirit.* See NASB marg.; see also Is 32:15 and note; 44:3; 59:20–21; Jer 31:31,33; Ezek 36:26–27; 39:29; Joel 2:28–29. *look on.* Or "look to." The emphasis seems to be on looking "to" the Messiah in faith (cf. Num 21:9; Is 45:22; John 3:14–15). *pierced.* Cf. Ps 22:16; Is 53:5; John 19:34; partly fulfilled in John 19:37. *mourns for an only son.* Cf. Jer 6:26. *like the bitter weeping over a firstborn.* Cf. Ex 11:5–6.

weep bitterly over Him like the bitter weeping over a firstborn.

11 "In that day there will be great [a]mourning in Jerusalem, like the mourning of Hadadrimmon in the [1]plain of [2]Megiddo.

12 "The land will mourn, every family by itself; the family of the house of David by itself and their wives by themselves; the family of the house of Nathan by itself and their wives by themselves;

13 the family of the house of Levi by itself and their wives by themselves; the family of the Shimeites by itself and their wives by themselves;

14 all the families that remain, every family by itself and their wives by themselves.

False Prophets Ashamed

13 "In that day a [a]fountain will be opened for the house of David and for the inhabitants of Jerusalem, for [b]sin and for [c]impurity.

2 "It will come about in that day," declares the LORD of hosts, "that I will [a]cut off the names of the idols from the land, and they will no longer be remembered; and I will also remove the [b]prophets and the [c]unclean spirit from the land.

3 "And if anyone still [a]prophesies, then his father and mother who gave birth to him will say to him, 'You shall [b]not live, for you have spoken [c]falsely in the name of the LORD'; and his [d]father and mother who gave birth to him will pierce him through when he prophesies.

4 "Also it will come about in that day that the prophets will each be [a]ashamed of his vision when he prophesies, and they will not put on a [b]hairy robe in order to deceive;

5 but he will say, 'I am [a]not a prophet; I am a tiller of the ground, for a man [1]sold me as a slave in my youth.'

6 "And one will say to him, 'What are these wounds [a]between your [1]arms?' Then he will say, '*Those* with which I was wounded in the house of [2]my friends.'

7 "Awake, O [a]sword, against My
[b]Shepherd,
And against the man, My
[c]Associate,"
Declares the LORD of hosts.
"[d]Strike the Shepherd that the sheep
may be scattered;
And I will [e]turn My hand [1]against the
little ones.
8 "It will come about in all the land,"
Declares the LORD,
"That [a]two parts in it will be cut off
and perish;
But the third will be left in it.
9 "And I will bring the third part through
the [a]fire,
Refine them as silver is refined,
And test them as gold is tested.
They will [b]call on My name,
And I will [c]answer them;
I will say, 'They are [d]My people,'
And they will say, 'The LORD is my
God.' "

11 [1]I.e. broad valley [2]Heb *Megiddon* [a]Matt 24:30; Rev 1:7
13:1 [a]Jer 2:13; 17:13 [b]Ps 51:2, 7; Is 1:16-18; John 1:29 [c]Num 19:17; Is 4:4; Ezek 36:25
2 [a]Ex 23:13; Hos 2:17 [b]Jer 23:14, 15 [c]1 Kin 22:22; Ezek 36:25, 29
3 [a]Jer 23:34 [b]Deut 18:20; Ezek 14:9 [c]Jer 23:25 [d]Deut 13:6-11; Matt 10:37
4 [a]Jer 6:15; 8:9; Mic 3:7 [b]2 Kin 1:8; Is 20:2; Matt 3:4
5 [1]Lit *caused another to buy me* [a]Amos 7:14
6 [1]Lit *hands* [2]Lit *those who love me* [a]2 Kin 9:24
7 [1]Or *upon* [a]Jer 47:6; Ezek 21:3-5 [b]Is 40:11; Ezek 34:23, 24; 37:24; Mic 5:2, 4 [c]Ps 2:2; Jer 23:5, 6 [d]Is 53:4, 5, 10; Matt 26:31; Mark 14:27 [e]Is 1:25
8 [a]Is 6:13; Ezek 5:2-4, 12
9 [a]Is 48:10; Mal 3:3 [b]Ps 34:15-17; 50:15; Zech 12:10 [c]Is 58:9; 65:24; Jer 29:11-13; Zech 10:6 [d]Hos 2:23

12:11 *Hadadrimmon.* The name of either (1) a place near Megiddo, where the people mourned the death of King Josiah (2 Chr 35:20–27; see v. 22 there for the plain of Megiddo and vv. 24–25 for the mourning), or (2) a Semitic storm god (see 2 Kin 5:18), whose name means "Hadad the thunderer" in Babylonian (as in the *Epic of Gilgamesh,* 11:98; see also Ezek 8:14 for an example of the practice of weeping for a Babylonian deity).
12:12 *Nathan.* David's son (2 Sam 5:14; cf. Luke 3:31).
12:13 *Shimeites.* Shimei was the son of Gershon, the son of Levi (Num 3:17–18,21). The repentance and mourning are led, then, by the civil (royal) and religious leaders.
13:1 *for sin and for impurity.* See 3:4–9; one of the provisions of the new covenant (Jer 31:34; Ezek 36:25).
13:2 *names of the idols.* The influence and fame, and even the very existence, of the idols. *prophets.* False prophecy was still a problem in the postexilic period (see Neh 6:12–14) and would again be a problem in the future (see Matt 24:4–5,11,23–24; 2 Thess 2:2–4).
13:3 *spoken falsely.* False prophecies. *father and mother . . . will pierce him.* In obedience to Deut 13:6–9. The Hebrew for "pierce" is the same as the verb for "pierced" in 12:10, perhaps indicating that the feelings and actions exhibited in piercing the Messiah will now be directed toward the false prophets.
13:4–6 Because of the stern measures just mentioned, a false prophet will be reluctant to identify himself as such and will be evasive in his responses to interrogation. To help conceal his true identity, he will not wear a "hairy robe" (v. 4), such as Elijah wore (2 Kin 1:8; see also Matt 3:4). Instead, to avoid the death penalty (v. 3), he will deny being a prophet and will claim to have been a farmer since his youth (v. 5). And if a suspicious person notices marks on his body and inquires about them (v. 6), he will claim he received them in a scuffle with friends (or perhaps as discipline from his parents during childhood). Apparently the accuser suspects that the false prophet's wounds were self-inflicted to arouse his prophetic ecstasy in idolatrous rites (as in 1 Kin 18:28; cf. also Lev 19:28; 21:5 and note; Deut 14:1; Jer 16:6; 41:5; 48:37).
13:6 Some take this verse as Messianic, but the interpretation given above seems preferable from the context (e.g., v. 5).
13:7 *My Shepherd.* The royal (Messianic) Good Shepherd (cf. the true Shepherd of 11:4–14; contrast the foolish and worthless shepherd of 11:15–17). *Strike the Shepherd.* In 11:17 it was the worthless shepherd who was to be struck; now it is the Good Shepherd (cf. also 12:10). *sheep may be scattered.* In fulfillment of the curses for covenant disobedience (Deut 28:64; 29:24–25). This part of the verse is quoted by Jesus not long before His arrest (Matt 26:31; Mark 14:27) and applied to the scattering of the apostles (Matt 26:56; Mark 14:49–50), who in turn are probably typological of the dispersion of the Jews in A.D. 70 and the subsequent years.
13:8–9 These verses depict a refining process for Israel (see note on Is 48:10).
13:8 *the third.* A remnant, thus revealing God's mercy in the midst of judgment.
13:9 *They are My people . . . The LORD is my God.* See note on 8:8. They will be restored to proper covenant relationship with the Lord (see also Ezek 20:30–44).

God Will Battle Jerusalem's Foes

14 Behold, a [a]day is coming for the LORD
when [b]the spoil taken from you will be
divided among you.
2 For I will [a]gather all the nations against
Jerusalem to battle, and the city will be captured, the [b]houses plundered, the women ravished and half of the city exiled, but the rest
of the people will not be cut off from the city.
3 Then the LORD will go forth and [a]fight
against those nations, as [1]when He fights on
a day of battle.
4 In that day His feet will [a]stand on the
Mount of Olives, which is in front of
Jerusalem on the east; and the Mount of
Olives will be [b]split in its middle from east to
west by a very large valley, so that half of the
mountain will move toward the north and
the other half toward the south.
5 You will flee by the valley of My mountains, for the valley of the mountains will
reach to Azel; yes, you will flee just as you fled
before the [a]earthquake in the days of Uzziah
king of Judah. [b]Then the LORD, my God, will
come, *and* all the holy ones with [1]Him!
6 In that day there will be [a]no light; the
[1]luminaries will dwindle.
7 For it will be [a]a unique day which is
[b]known to the LORD, neither day nor night,
but it will come about that at [c]evening time
there will be light.
8 And in that day [a]living waters will flow
out of Jerusalem, half of them toward the
eastern sea and the other half toward the
western sea; it will be in summer as well as
in winter.

God Will Be King over All

9 And the LORD will be [a]king over all the
earth; in that day the LORD will be *the only*
[b]one, and His name *the only* one.
10 All the land will be changed into a
plain from [a]Geba to [b]Rimmon south of Jerusalem; but [1]Jerusalem will [c]rise and [d]remain
on its site from [e]Benjamin's Gate as far as
the place of the First Gate to the [f]Corner
Gate, and from the [g]Tower of Hananel to the
king's wine presses.
11 [1]People will live in it, and there will
[a]no longer be a curse, for Jerusalem will
[b]dwell in security.
12 Now this will be the plague with which
the LORD will strike all the peoples who have
gone to war against Jerusalem; their flesh
will [a]rot while they stand on their feet, and
their eyes will rot in their sockets, and their
tongue will rot in their mouth.
13 It will come about in that day that a
great panic from the LORD will [1]fall on them;
and they will [a]seize one another's hand, and
the hand of one will [2]be lifted against the
hand of another.
14 [a]Judah also will fight at Jerusalem; and
the [b]wealth of all the surrounding nations
will be gathered, gold and silver and garments in great abundance.
15 So also like this [a]plague will be the
plague on the horse, the mule, the camel, the
donkey and all the cattle that will be in those
camps.
16 Then it will come about that any who
are left of all the nations that went against
Jerusalem will [a]go up from year to year to
worship the King, the LORD of hosts, and to
celebrate the [b]Feast of Booths.
17 And it will be that whichever of the

14:1 [a]Is 13:6, 9; Joel 2:1; Mal 4:1 [b]Zech 14:14
2 [a]Zech 12:2, 3 [b]Is 13:16
3 [1]Lit *His day of fighting* [a]Zech 9:14, 15
4 [a]Ezek 11:23 [b]Is 64:1, 2; Ezek 47:1-10; Mic 1:3, 4; Hab 3:6; Zech 4:7; 14:8
5 [1]So the versions; Heb *You* [a]Is 29:6; Amos 1:1 [b]Ps 96:13; Is 66:15, 16; Matt 16:27; 25:31
6 [1]Lit *glorious ones will congeal* [a]Is 13:10; Jer 4:23; Ezek 32:7, 8; Joel 2:30, 31; Acts 2:16, 19
7 [a]Jer 30:7; Amos 8:9 [b]Is 45:21; Acts 15:18 [c]Is 58:10; Rev 22:5
8 [a]Ezek 47:1-12; Joel 3:18; John 7:38; Rev 22:1, 2
9 [a]Is 2:2-4; 45:23; Zech 9:9; 14:16, 17
9 [b]Deut 6:4; Is 45:21-24
10 [1]Lit *it* [a]1 Kin 15:22 [b]Josh 15:32; Judg 20:45, 47 [c]Is 2:2; Amos 9:11 [d]Jer 30:18; Zech 12:6 [e]Jer 37:13; 38:7 [f]2 Kin 14:13 [g]Jer 31:38
11 [1]Lit *They* [a]Zech 8:13; Rev 22:3 [b]Jer 23:5, 6; Ezek 34:25-28
12 [a]Lev 26:16; Deut 28:21, 22
13 [1]Lit *be among* [2]Lit *rise up against*
[a]Zech 11:6 **14** [a]Zech 12:2, 5 [b]Is 23:18; Zech 14:1 **15** [a]Zech 14:12 **16** [a]Is 60:6-9; 66:18-21, 23 [b]Lev 23:34-44

14:1 *you . . . you.* Jerusalem (v. 2) is the object of the plunder.
14:2 *all the nations . . . to battle.* See v. 12; see also note on 12:3.
14:3 *day of battle.* Any occasion when the Lord supernaturally intervenes to deliver His people, such as at the Red Sea (see note on Ex 14:14).
14:4 *Mount of Olives.* Called by this name elsewhere in the OT only in 2 Sam 15:30. This prophecy is probably referred to in Acts 1:11–12. *east.* Thus it faced the temple mount and, being about 2,700 feet high, rose about 200 feet above it. Cf. Ezek 11:23; 43:1–2.
14:5 *Azel.* The name of a place east of Jerusalem, marking the eastern end of the newly formed valley. The location is unknown. *holy ones.* May include both believers and angels. They will accompany our Lord when He comes (cf. Matt 25:31; 1 Thess 3:13; Jude 14; Rev 19:14).
14:7 *unique day.* Due to the topographical, cosmic and cataclysmic changes. See also Is 60:19–20 and notes; cf. Rev 21:23–25; 22:5.
14:8 *living waters will flow.* Perhaps both literal and symbolic (cf. Ps 46:4; 65:9; Is 8:6; Jer 2:13; Ezek 47:1–12; Joel 3:18; John 4:10–14; 7:38; Rev 22:1–2).
14:9 *the LORD will be king over all the earth.* A pervasive theological theme in Scripture. *the LORD . . . the only one.* See Deut 6:4; Is 43:11 and notes.
14:10 *plain.* Hebrew *Arabah* (see note on Deut 1:1). All the land around Jerusalem is to be leveled. *Geba.* About six miles north-northeast of Jerusalem at the northern boundary of Judah (2 Kin 23:8). *Rimmon.* Also called En Rimmon (Neh 11:29; cf. Josh 15:32), it was about 35 miles south-southwest of Jerusalem, where the hill country of Judah slopes away into the Negev. *Jerusalem will rise.* See note on Is 2:2–4. The elevation may be both physical and in prominence. *Benjamin's Gate . . . First Gate . . . Tower of Hananel.* All were probably at the northeastern part of the city wall (cf. Jer 31:38; 37:12–13; 38:7). *Corner Gate.* At the northwest corner (cf. Jer 31:38). *king's wine presses.* Just south of the city. Thus the whole city is included.
14:11 *live in it.* See 2:4. *no longer . . . curse.* As at the time of the exile to Babylonia (see Is 43:28 and note). *Jerusalem will dwell in security.* See Jer 31:40.
14:12 *plague.* See Is 37:36 and note. *peoples . . . against Jerusalem.* See v. 2; see also note on 12:3.
14:13 *great panic . . . hand of one . . . against . . . another.* See note on Judg 7:22.
14:14 *gold and silver and garments.* The plunder of battle, thus reversing the situation in v. 1.
14:15 A similar plague will strike the beasts of burden, preventing the people from using them to escape.
14:16 See Is 2:2–4 and note. *Feast of Booths.* See notes on Ex 23:16; Ps 81:3. Of the three great pilgrimage festivals (see Ex

families of the earth does not go up to Jerusalem to worship the [a]King, the LORD of hosts, there will be [b]no rain on them.
18 If the family of Egypt does not go up or enter, then no *rain will fall* on them; it will be the [a]plague with which the LORD smites the nations who do not go up to celebrate the Feast of Booths.
19 This will be the [1]punishment of Egypt, and the [1]punishment of all the nations who do not go up to celebrate the Feast of Booths.
20 In that day there will *be inscribed* on the bells of the horses, "[a]HOLY TO THE LORD." And the [b]cooking pots in the LORD's house will be like the bowls before the altar.
21 Every cooking pot in Jerusalem and in Judah will be [a]holy to the LORD of hosts; and all who sacrifice will come and take of them and boil in them. And there will no longer be a [1b]Canaanite in the house of the LORD of hosts in that day.

17 [a]Zech 14:9, 16 [b]Jer 14:3-6; Amos 4:7
18 [a]Zech 14:12, 15
19 [1]Lit *sin*
20 [a]Ex 28:36-38 [b]Ezek 46:20
21 [1]Or *merchant* [a]Neh 8:10; Rom 14:6, 7; 1 Cor 10:31 [b]Zeph 1:11

23:14–17), perhaps Booths was selected as the one for representatives of the various Gentile nations because it was the last and greatest festival of the Hebrew calendar, gathering up into itself the year's worship. (See note on Ezek 45:25.) It was to be a time of grateful rejoicing (Lev 23:40; Deut 16:13–15; Neh 8:17). Beginning with the period of Ezra and Nehemiah, the reading and teaching of "the book of the law of God" became an integral part of the festivities (Neh 8:18; cf. Is 2:3). The festival seems to speak of the final, joyful regathering and restoration of Israel, as well as of the ingathering of the nations. See chart, pp. 164–165.

14:17 *no rain.* One of the curses for covenant disobedience (Deut 28:22–24; cf. Zech 9:11–10:1).

14:18 *family of Egypt . . . no rain will fall.* Another possible reading is, "enter, then the LORD will bring on them the plague with which He smites . . ." With either reading, the withholding of rain may still be included, for drought would cause even the Nile inundation to fail.

14:20 *HOLY TO THE LORD.* Engraved on the gold plate worn on the high priest's turban (Ex 28:36–38) as a reminder of his consecration to the Lord's service. See note on 3:5. God's original purpose for Israel (see Ex 19:6 and note) will be realized.

14:21 *Every cooking pot in Jerusalem . . . holy.* See Joel 3:17. Even common things become holy when they are used for God's service. *Canaanite.* Represents anyone who is morally or spiritually unclean—anyone who is not included among the chosen people of God (cf. Is 35:8; Ezek 43:7; 44:9; Rev 21:27).

Malachi

INTRODUCTION

Author

The book is ascribed to Malachi, whose name means "My messenger." Since the term occurs in 3:1, and since both prophets and priests were called messengers of the Lord (see 2:7; Hag 1:13), some have thought "Malachi" to be only a title that tradition has given the author. The view has been supported by appeal to the early Greek translation (the Septuagint), which translates the term in 1:1 "His messenger" rather than as a proper noun. The matter, however, remains uncertain, and it is still very likely that Malachi was in fact the author's name.

Background

Spurred on by the prophetic activity of Haggai and Zechariah, the returned exiles under the leadership of their governor Zerubbabel finished the temple in 516 B.C. In 458 the community was strengthened by the coming of Ezra the priest and several thousand more Jews. King Artaxerxes of Persia encouraged Ezra to develop the temple worship (Ezra 7:17) and to make sure the law of Moses was being obeyed (Ezra 7:25 – 26).

Thirteen years later (445) the same Persian king permitted his cupbearer Nehemiah to return to Jerusalem and rebuild the walls (Neh 6:15). As newly appointed governor, Nehemiah also spearheaded reforms to help the poor (Neh 5:2 – 13), and he convinced the people to shun mixed marriages, to keep the sabbath (Neh 10:30 – 31) and to bring their tithes and offerings faithfully (Neh 10:37 – 39).

In 433 B.C. Nehemiah returned to the service of the Persian king, and during his absence the Jews fell into sin once more. Later, however, Nehemiah came back to Jerusalem to discover that the tithes were ignored, the sabbath was broken, the people had intermarried with foreigners, and the priests had become corrupt (Neh 13:7 – 31). Several of these sins are condemned by Malachi (see 1:6 – 14; 2:14 – 16; 3:8 – 11).

Date

The similarity between the sins denounced in Nehemiah and those denounced in Malachi suggest that the two leaders were contemporaries. Malachi may have been written after Nehemiah returned to Persia in 433 B.C. or during his second period as governor. Since the governor mentioned in 1:8 (see note there) probably was not Nehemiah, the first alternative may be more likely. Malachi was most likely the last prophet of the OT era (though some place Joel later).

Themes and Theology

Although the Jews had been allowed to return from exile and rebuild the temple, several discouraging factors brought about a general religious malaise: (1) Their land remained but a small province in the backwaters of the Persian empire, (2) the glorious future announced by the prophets (including the other post-exilic prophets, Haggai and Zechariah) had not (yet) been realized, and (3) their God had not (yet) come to His temple (3:1) with majesty and power (as celebrated in Ps 68) to exalt His kingdom in the sight of the nations. Doubting God's covenant love (1:2) and no longer trusting His justice (2:17; 3:14 – 15), the Jews of the restored community began to lose hope. So their worship degenerated into a listless perpetuation of mere forms, and they no longer took the law seriously.

Malachi rebukes their doubt of God's love (1:2 – 5) and the faithlessness of both priests (1:6 — 2:9) and people (2:10 – 16). To their charge that God is unjust ("Where is the God of justice?" 2:17) because He has failed to come in judgment to exalt His people, Malachi answers with an announcement and a warning. The Lord they seek will come — but He will come "like a refiner's fire" (3:1 – 4). He will come to judge — but He will judge His people first (3:5).

Because the Lord does not change in His commitments and purpose, Israel has not been completely destroyed for her persistent unfaithfulness (3:6). But only through repentance and reformation will she again experience God's blessing (3:6–12). Those who honor the Lord will be spared when He comes to judge (3:16–18).

In conclusion, Malachi once more reassures and warns his readers that "the day ['the great and terrible day of the LORD,' 4:5] is coming" and that it will burn "like a furnace" (4:1). In that day the righteous will rejoice, and "you will tread down the wicked" (4:1–3). So "remember the law of Moses My servant" (4:4). To prepare His people for that day the Lord will send "Elijah the prophet" to call them back to the godly ways of their forefathers (4:5–6).

Literary Features

Malachi is called an "oracle" (see 1:1 and note) and is written in what might be called lofty prose. The text features a series of questions asked by both God and the people. Frequently the Lord's statements are followed by sarcastic questions introduced by "But you say" (1:2,6–7; 2:14,17; 3:7–8,13; cf. 1:13). In each case the Lord's response is given.

Repetition is a key element in the book. The name "LORD Almighty" occurs 20 times. The book begins with a description of the wasteland of Edom (1:3–4) and ends with a warning of Israel's destruction (4:6).

Several vivid figures are employed within the book of Malachi. The priests sniff contemptuously at the altar of the Lord (1:13), and the Lord spreads on their faces the offal from their sacrifices (2:3). As Judge, "He is like a refiner's fire and like fullers' soap" (3:2), but for the righteous "the sun of righteousness will rise with healing in its wings; and you will go forth and skip about like calves from the stall" (4:2).

Outline

I. Title (1:1)

II. Introduction: God's Covenant Love for Israel Affirmed (1:2–5)

III. Israel's Unfaithfulness Rebuked (1:6—2:16)
- A. The Unfaithfulness of the Priests (1:6—2:9)
  - 1. They dishonor God in their sacrifices (1:6–14)
  - 2. They do not faithfully teach the law (2:1–9)
- B. The Unfaithfulness of the People (2:10–16)

IV. The Lord's Coming Announced (2:17—4:6)
- A. The Lord Will Come to Purify the Priests and Judge the People (2:17—3:5)
- B. A Call to Repentance in View of the Lord's Coming (3:6–18)
  - 1. An exhortation to faithful giving (3:6–12)
  - 2. An exhortation to faithful service (3:13–18)
- C. The Day of the Lord Announced (ch. 4)

God's Love for Jacob

1 The [1][a]oracle of the word of the LORD to [b]Israel through [2]Malachi.

2 "I have [a]loved you," says the LORD. But you say, "How have You loved us?" "*Was* not Esau Jacob's brother?" declares the LORD. "Yet I [b]have loved Jacob;

3 but I have hated Esau, and I have [a]made his mountains a desolation and *appointed* his inheritance for the jackals of the wilderness."

4 Though Edom says, "We have been [a]beaten down, but we will [1][b]return and build up the ruins"; thus says the LORD of hosts, "They may [c]build, but I will tear down; and *men* will call them the [2]wicked territory, and the people [3]toward whom the LORD is indignant [d]forever."

5 Your eyes will see this and you will say, "[a]The LORD [1]be magnified beyond the [2]border of Israel!"

Sin of the Priests

6 " 'A son [a]honors *his* father, and a servant his master. Then if I am a [b]father, where is My honor? And if I am a master, where is My [1]respect?' says the LORD of hosts to you, O [c]priests who despise My name. But you say, 'How have we despised Your name?'

7 "*You* are presenting [a]defiled [1][b]food upon My altar. But you say, 'How have we defiled You?' In that you say, 'The [c]table of the LORD is to be despised.'

8 "But when you present the [a]blind for sacrifice, is it not evil? And when you present the lame and sick, is it not evil? [1]Why not offer it to your [b]governor? Would he be pleased with you? Or would he receive you kindly?" says the LORD of hosts.

9 "But now [1]will you not [a]entreat God's favor, that He may be gracious to us? [2]With such an offering on your part, will He [b]receive any of you kindly?" says the LORD of hosts.

10 "Oh that there were one among you who would [a]shut the [1]gates, that you might not uselessly kindle *fire on* My altar! I am not pleased with you," says the LORD of hosts, "[b]nor will I accept an offering from [2]you.

11 "For from the [a]rising of the sun even to its setting, [b]My name *will be* [c]great among the nations, and in every place [d]incense is going to be offered to My name, and a grain offering *that is* pure; for My name *will be* [e]great among the nations," says the LORD of hosts.

12 "But you are [a]profaning it, in that you say, 'The table of the Lord is defiled, and as for its fruit, its food is to be despised.'

13 "You also say, '[1]My, how [a]tiresome it is!' And you disdainfully sniff at it," says the LORD of hosts, "and you bring what was taken by [b]robbery and *what is* [c]lame or sick; so you bring the offering! Should I [d]receive that from your hand?" says the LORD.

14 "But cursed be the [a]swindler who has a male in his flock and vows it, but sacrifices a [b]blemished animal to the Lord, for I am a great [c]King," says the LORD of hosts, "and My name is [1][d]feared among the [2]nations."

Priests to Be Disciplined

2 "And now this commandment is for you, O priests.

2 "If you do [a]not listen, and if you do not

1:1 [1]Lit *burden* [2]Or *My messenger* [a]Is 13:1; Nah 1:1; Hab 1:1; Zech 9:1 [b]Mal 2:11 **2** [a]Deut 4:37; 7:8; 23:5; Is 41:8, 9; Jer 31:3; John 15:12 [b]Rom 9:13 **3** [a]Jer 49:10, 16-18; Ezek 35:3, 4, 7, 8, 15 **4** [1]Or *rebuild the ruins* [2]Lit *border of wickedness* [3]Or *whom the LORD has cursed* [a]Jer 5:17 [b]Is 9:9, 10 [c]Amos 3:15; 5:11; 6:11 [d]Ezek 35:9; Obad 10 **5** [1]Or *will be great* [2]Or *territory* [a]Ps 35:27; Mic 5:4 **6** [1]Lit *fear* [a]Ex 20:12; Prov 30:11, 17 [b]Deut 1:31; Is 1:2; Jer 3:4; Mal 2:10 [c]Zeph 3:4; Mal 2:1-9 **7** [1]Lit *bread* [a]Mal 1:8, 13 [b]Lev 3:11; 21:6, 8 [c]Mal 1:12 **8** [1]Lit *Offer it, please* [a]Lev 22:22; Deut 15:21 [b]Hag 1:1 **9** [1]Lit *entreat, please* [2]Lit *This has been from your hand* [a]Jer 27:18; Joel 2:12-14 [b]Amos 5:22 **10** [1]Or *doors* [2]Lit *your hand* [a]Is 1:13 [b]Jer 14:10, 12; Hos 5:6 **11** [a]Is 45:6 [b]Ps 111:9 [c]Is 66:18, 19 [d]Is 60:6 [e]Is 12:4, 5; 54:5; Jer 10:6, 7 **12** [a]Mal 1:7 **13** [1]Lit *Behold* it is *weariness* [a]Is 43:22 [b]Lev 6:4; Is 61:8 [c]Mal 1:8 [d]Mal 1:10 **14** [1]Or *revered* [2]Or *Gentiles* [a]Acts 5:1-4 [b]Lev 22:18-20 [c]Zech 14:9 [d]Zeph 2:11 **2:2** [a]Lev 26:14, 15; Deut 28:15

1:1 *oracle.* See Zech 9:1 and note; 12:1; see also Hab 1:1 and note.

1:2 *loved you.* The Lord's reassuring word to His disheartened people.

1:3 *I have hated Esau.* If Israel doubts God's covenant love, she should consider the contrast between God's ways with her and His ways with Jacob's brother Esau (Edom). Paul explains God's love for Jacob and hatred for Esau on the basis of election (Rom 9:10–13). God chose Jacob but not Esau. For the use of "love" and "hate" here, cf. how Leah was "hated" in that Jacob loved Rachel more (Gen 29:31,33; cf. Deut 21:16–17). Likewise, believers are to "hate" their parents (Luke 14:26) in the sense that they love Christ even more (Matt 10:37). *desolation.* Malachi's words about Edom echo those of the earlier prophets (see Is 34:5–15; Jer 49:7–22; Ezek 25:12–14; 35:1–15; Obadiah). Between c. 550 and 400 B.C. the Nabatean Arabs gradually forced the Edomites from their homeland.

1:4 *Though Edom says.* Her proud self-reliance has not assured her security and will not secure her future (cf. Jer 49:16).

1:5 *The LORD . . . Israel!* When she sees the ultimate fate of Edom, doubting Israel will acknowledge that the Lord is the great Ruler over all the nations.

1:6–2:9 The Lord rebukes the priests.

1:6 *son honors his father.* Cf. Is 1:2–3. *priests who despise My name.* Contrast 2:5; cf. Is 1:4.

1:7 *food.* The offerings (see v. 12; Lev 21:8,21). *defiled You.* By offering defiled sacrifices they defile the Lord Himself. *The table of the LORD.* The altar (see v. 12; Ezek 44:16). Since the priests ate from the sacrifices, the altar was also the table from which they got their food. *despised.* As the priests despised the Lord's altar and its sacrifices, so the Lord would cause the priests to be despised by the people (see 2:9 and note).

1:8 *blind . . . lame.* Animals with defects or serious flaws were unacceptable as sacrifices (see Deut 15:21). *governor.* Probably the Persian governor.

1:10 *shut the gates.* Better no sacrifices than sacrifices offered with contempt (cf. Is 1:11–15).

1:11 *great among the nations.* Cf. v. 14. God's judgment on Edom (v. 5) and other nations demonstrates His superiority over their gods, and it ultimately will evoke their recognition of Him (see Zeph 2:11). *incense . . . offering that is pure.* Cf. the acceptable offerings presented by foreigners in Is 56:6–7; 60:7. Some interpreters understand "incense" to mean "prayer" (cf. Rev 5:8) and "offerings" to mean "praise" (cf. Heb 13:15).

1:12 *defiled . . . despised.* See v. 7.

1:13 *disdainfully sniff at it.* Cf. the behavior of Eli's sons in 1 Sam 2:15–17. *taken by robbery . . . or sick.* See v. 8 and note.

1:14 *vows . . . a blemished animal.* An animal sacrificed in fulfillment of a vow had to be a male without defect or blemish (see Lev 22:18–23). *great King.* See Zech 14:9. *My name is feared.* More than the governor of v. 8 (see v. 11 and note).

take it to heart to give honor to My name,"
says the LORD of hosts, "then I will send the
[b]curse upon you and I will curse your blessings; and indeed, I have [c]cursed them
already, because you are not taking *it* to heart.
3 "Behold, I am going to [a]rebuke your
[1]offspring, and I will [b]spread [2]refuse on your
faces, the [2]refuse of your [c]feasts; and you
will be taken away [3]with it.
4 "Then you will know that I have sent
this commandment to you, [1]that My [a]cov-
enant may [2]continue with Levi," says the
LORD of hosts.
5 "My covenant with him was *one of* life
and [a]peace, and I gave them to him *as an*
object of [1]reverence; so he [2b]revered Me and
stood in awe of My name.
6 "[1a]True instruction was in his mouth
and unrighteousness was not found on his
lips; he walked [b]with Me in peace and
uprightness, and he [c]turned many back from
iniquity.
7 "For the lips of a priest should preserve
[a]knowledge, and [1]men should [b]seek [2]in-
struction from his mouth; for he is the [c]mes-
senger of the LORD of hosts.
8 "But as for you, you have turned aside
from the way; you have caused many to
[a]stumble [1]by the instruction; you have [2b]cor-
rupted the covenant of Levi," says the LORD
of hosts.
9 "So [a]I also have made you despised and
[b]abased [1]before all the people, just as you
are not keeping My ways but are showing
[c]partiality in the [2]instruction.

2:2 [b]Deut 28:16-20 [c]Mal 3:9
3 [1]Lit *seed* [2]Or *vomit* [3]Lit *to* [a]Lev 26:16; Deut 28:38 [b]Nah 3:6 [c]Ex 29:14
4 [1]Or *to be My covenant with* [2]Lit *be* [a]Num 3:11-13, 45; 18:21; Neh 13:29; Mal 3:1
5 [1]Or *fear* [2]Or *feared* [a]Num 25:12 [b]Num 25:7, 8, 13
6 [1]Or *Law of truth* [a]Ps 119:142, 151, 160 [b]Deut 33:8, 9; Ps 37:37 [c]Jer 23:22
7 [1]Lit *they* [2]Or *law* [a]Lev 10:11; Neh 8:7 [b]Num 27:21; Deut 17:8-11; Jer 18:18; Ezek 7:26 [c]Hag 1:13
8 [1]Or *in the law* [2]Or *violated* [a]Jer 18:15 [b]Num 25:12, 13; Neh 13:29; Ezek 44:10
9 [1]Lit *to* [2]Or *law* [a]Nah 3:6 [b]Ezek 7:26 [c]Deut 1:17; Mic 3:11

10 [a]Is 63:16; 64:8; Jer 31:9; 1 Cor 8:6; Eph 4:6 [b]Acts 17:24f [c]Jer 9:4, 5 [d]Ex 19:4-6; 24:3, 7, 8
11 [1]Or *in that He has loved and married*

Sin in the Family

10 "Do we not all have [a]one father? [b]Has
not one God created us? Why do we deal
[c]treacherously each against his brother so as
to profane the [d]covenant of our fathers?
11 "Judah has dealt [a]treacherously, and an
abomination has been committed in Israel
and in Jerusalem; for Judah has [b]profaned the
sanctuary of the LORD [1]which He loves and
has married the daughter of a foreign god.
12 "*As* for the man who does this, may the
[a]LORD cut off from the tents of Jacob *every-*
one who awakes and answers, or who [b]pres-
ents [1]an offering to the LORD of hosts.
13 "This is [1]another thing you do: you cover the altar of the LORD with tears, with
weeping and with groaning, because He [a]no
longer regards the [2]offering or accepts *it with*
favor from your hand.
14 "Yet you say, 'For what reason?' Because
the LORD has been a witness between you
and the [a]wife of your youth, against whom
you have dealt [b]treacherously, though she is
your companion and your wife by covenant.
15 "[1]But not one has [a]done *so* who has a
remnant of the Spirit. And [2]what did *that*
one *do* while he was seeking a [b]godly [3]off-
spring? Take heed then to your spirit, and let
no one deal [c]treacherously against the wife
of your youth.

[a]Jer 3:7-9 [b]Ezra 9:1, 2 **12** [1]Or *a grain offering* [a]Ezek 24:21; Hos 9:12 [b]Mal 1:10, 13 **13** [1]Lit *second* [2]Or *grain offering* [a]Jer 11:14; 14:12 **14** [a]Is 54:6 [b]Jer 9:2; Mal 3:5 **15** [1]Or *Did He not make one, although He had the remnant* [2]Or *why one? He sought a godly offspring* [3]Lit *seed* [a]Gen 2:24; Matt 19:4, 5 [b]Ruth 4:12; 1 Sam 2:20 [c]Ex 20:14; Lev 20:10

2:2 *curse your blessings.* It was the function of the priests to pronounce God's blessing on the people (see Num 6:23–27), but their blessings will become curses so that their uniquely priestly function will be worse than useless.

2:3 *spread refuse on your faces.* To disgrace you (see Nah 3:6). *refuse.* The entrails of an animal that were taken "outside the camp" and burned along with its hide and flesh (see Ex 29:14; Lev 8:17; 16:27).

2:4 *Levi.* The priests were chosen from the tribe of Levi (see Num 3:12–13; Neh 13:29).

2:5 *covenant . . . of life and peace.* An allusion to the covenant with Phinehas, Aaron's grandson, in Num 25:10–13. Phinehas defended God's honor by killing two offenders involved in the idolatry and immorality connected with the Baal of Peor (Num 25:1–3). *he revered Me.* Phinehas showed this by his zeal for God (see Num 25:13).

2:6–7 *instruction.* Priests were responsible to teach the law of Moses (see Lev 10:11; see also notes on Zeph 3:4; Hag 2:11).

2:6 *peace and uprightness.* Linked together also in Ps 37:37, but here "walked with me in peace and uprightness" probably refers to covenant loyalty.

2:7 *messenger.* As teacher of the law and as one through whom people could inquire of God (see notes on 3:1; Hag 1:13).

2:8 *corrupted the covenant.* By unfaithful teaching, but also, it seems, by intermarriage with foreigners (see Ezra 9:1; 10:18–22; Neh 13:27–29). *of Levi.* See v. 4 and note on v. 5.

2:9 *despised.* See 1:7,12 and note on 1:7. *showing partiality.* Forbidden in Lev 19:15. The priests were to be like God in this respect (see Deut 10:17).

2:10–16 Malachi rebukes the people—in a passage framed by references to "dealing treacherously." Two examples of their sin are specifically mentioned: marrying pagan women and divorce.

2:10 *one father.* See Is 63:16. *created us.* As His special people (see Is 43:1 and note). *deal treacherously.* One could not even trust his own fellow Israelites or the national leaders—like the priests. *covenant of our fathers.* The covenant God made with their forefathers at Mount Sinai.

2:11 *daughter of a foreign god.* A pagan woman. Such marriages were strictly forbidden in the covenant law because they would lead to apostasy (see Ex 34:15–16; Deut 7:3–4; 1 Kin 11:1–6; cf. Josh 23:12–13). Ezra and Nehemiah both wrestled with this problem (Ezra 9:1–2; Neh 13:23–29).

2:12 An alternative reading of the Hebrew text offers another possibility: If anyone "gives testimony" (instead of "awakes and answers") in behalf of one marrying a foreign woman, the one giving testimony is to be cut off. The verb for "gives testimony" is found in the same sense in Gen 30:33; Deut 5:20; Ruth 1:21; 1 Sam 12:3; 2 Sam 1:16; Is 3:9; Jer 14:7. On this reading, the one to be cut off is the one who speaks in defense of the wrongdoer. *tents of Jacob.* A figurative expression for the community (see Jer 30:18).

2:13 *weeping and . . . groaning.* Because the Lord does not respond to their sacrifices with blessing, they add wailing to their prayers.

2:14 *witness . . . wife by covenant.* Marriage was a covenant (see Prov 2:17; Ezek 16:8), and covenants were affirmed before witnesses (see notes on Deut 30:19; 1 Sam 20:23; Is 8:1–2).

2:15 Although the verse is difficult, it may refer to Abraham, who "married" the foreigner Hagar in order to have a son (Gen

16 “For [1]I hate [2a]divorce,” says the LORD, the God of Israel, “and [3]him who covers his garment with [4b]wrong,” says the LORD of hosts. “So take heed to your spirit, that you do not deal treacherously.”

17 You have [a]wearied the LORD with your words. Yet you say, “How have we wearied *Him?*” In that you say, “[b]Everyone who does evil is good in the sight of the LORD, and He [c]delights in them,” or, “[d]Where is the God of [e]justice?”

The Purifier

3 “[a]Behold, I am going to send [b]My [1]messenger, and he will [2c]clear the way before Me. And the Lord, whom you seek, will suddenly come to His temple; [3]and the [1d]messenger of the covenant, in whom you delight, behold, He is coming,” says the LORD of hosts.

2 “But who can [a]endure the day of His coming? And who can stand when He appears? For He is like a [b]refiner’s fire and like [1]fullers’ soap.

3 “He will sit as a smelter and purifier of silver, and He will [a]purify the sons of Levi and refine them like gold and silver, so that they may [b]present to the LORD [1]offerings in righteousness.

4 “Then the [1]offering of Judah and Jerusalem will be [a]pleasing to the LORD as in the [b]days of old and as in former years.

5 “Then I will draw near to you for judgment; and I will be a swift witness against the [a]sorcerers and against the [b]adulterers and against those who [c]swear falsely, and against those who oppress the [d]wage earner in his wages, the [e]widow and the [1]orphan, and those who turn aside the [2f]alien and do not [3]fear Me,” says the LORD of hosts.

6 “For [1]I, the LORD, [a]do not change; therefore you, O sons of Jacob, [2]are not consumed.

7 “From the [a]days of your fathers you have turned aside from My statutes and have not kept *them*. [b]Return to Me, and I will return to you,” says the LORD of hosts. “But you say, ‘How shall we return?’

You Have Robbed God

8 “Will a man [1]rob God? Yet you are robbing Me! But you say, ‘How have we robbed You?’ In [a]tithes and [2]offerings.

9 “You are [a]cursed with a curse, for you are [1]robbing Me, the whole nation *of you!*

10 “[a]Bring the whole tithe into the storehouse, so that there may be [1]food in My house, and test Me now in this,” says the LORD of hosts, “if I will not [b]open for you the windows of heaven and [c]pour out for you a blessing until [2d]it overflows.

11 “Then I will rebuke the [a]devourer for you, so that it will not [1]destroy the fruits of the ground; nor will your vine in the field cast *its grapes,*” says the LORD of hosts.

12 “[a]All the nations will call you blessed, for you shall be a [b]delightful land,” says the LORD of hosts.

13 “Your words have been [1]arrogant

16 [1]Lit *He hates* [2]Lit *sending away* [3]Lit *he covers* [4]Or *violence* [a]Deut 24:1; Matt 5:31; 19:6-8 [b]Ps 73:6; Is 59:6
17 [a]Is 43:22, 24 [b]Is 5:20; Zeph 1:12 [c]Job 9:24 [d]2 Pet 3:4 [e]Is 5:19; Jer 17:15
3:1 [1]Or *angel* [2]Or *prepare* [3]Or *even* [a]Matt 11:10, 14; Mark 1:2; Luke 1:76; 7:27 [b]Hag 1:13; John 1:6, 7 [c]Is 40:3 [d]Is 63:9
2 [1]Lit *laundrymen’s* [a]Is 33:14; Ezek 22:14; Rev 6:17 [b]Zech 13:9; Matt 3:10-12; 1 Cor 3:13-15
3 [1]Or *grain offerings* [a]Is 1:25; Dan 12:10 [b]Ps 4:5; 51:19
4 [1]Or *grain offering* [a]Ps 51:17-19 [b]2 Chr 7:1-3, 12
5 [a]Deut 18:10; Jer 27:9, 10 [b]Ezek 22:9-11 [c]Jer 5:2; 7:9; Zech 5:4 [d]Lev 19:13
5 [1]Or *fatherless* [2]Or *sojourner* [3]Or *revere* [e]Ex 22:22-24 [f]Deut 27:19
6 [1]Or *I am the LORD; I do not* [2]Or *have not come to an end* [a]Num 23:19; James 1:17
7 [a]Jer 7:25, 26; 16:11, 12 [b]Zech 1:3 **8** [1]Or *defraud* [2]Or *heave offerings* [a]Neh 13:11, 12 **9** [1]Or *defrauding* [a]Mal 2:2 **10** [1]Lit *prey* [2]Or *there is not* room *enough* [a]Lev 27:30; Num 18:21-24; Deut 12:6; 14:22-29; Neh 13:12 [b]Ps 78:23-29 [c]Ezek 34:26 [d]Lev 26:3-5 **11** [1]Lit *ruin* [a]Joel 1:4; 2:25 **12** [a]Is 61:9 [b]Is 62:4 **13** [1]Lit *strong*

16:1–4). But Abraham did not divorce Sarah, who had suggested the union with Hagar in the first place.

2:16 *I hate divorce.* See Is 50:1 and note. *wrong.* See 3:5.

2:17–4:6 The second half of Malachi’s prophecy speaks of God’s coming to His people. They had given up on God (see 2:17, which introduces this section) and had grown religiously cynical and morally corrupt. So God’s coming will mean judgment and purification as well as redemption.

2:17 *wearied the LORD with your words.* In Is 43:24 Israel’s sins had wearied God. *Everyone who does evil is good.* Such was the depth of their cynicism. *Where is . . . justice?* Cf. the sarcastic taunts of Is 5:19.

3:1 *My messenger.* The Hebrew for these words is *mal’aki;* it is normally used of a priest or prophet (see Hag 1:13 and note). This is fulfilled in John the Baptist (see Matt 11:10; Mark 1:2; Luke 1:76). *he will clear the way.* When the Lord comes, it will be to purify (v. 3) and judge (v. 5), but He will mercifully send one before Him to prepare His people (see 4:5–6 and notes; see also Is 40:3 and note). *the Lord, whom you seek . . . in whom you delight . . . is coming.* See Hag 2:7 and note. *messenger of the covenant.* The Messiah, who as the Lord’s representative will confirm and establish the covenant (see note on Is 42:6).

3:2 *day of His coming.* The day of the Lord (see 4:1; see also note on Is 2:11,17,20). Malachi announces the Lord’s coming to complete God’s work in history, especially the work he outlines in the rest of his book. His word is fulfilled in the accomplishments of the Messiah. *who can stand . . . ?* Those who desire the Lord’s coming must know that clean hands and a pure heart are required (cf. Ps 24:3–4; Is 33:14–15). *refiner’s fire.* See Is 1:25; Zech 13:8–9 and notes. *fullers’ soap.* See Is 7:3 and note. White clothes signified purity (cf. Mark 9:3; Rev 3:5).

3:3 *purify the sons of Levi.* Those who are supposed to be “messengers” of the Lord and who serve at the altar will be purged of their sins and unfaithfulness—such as the Lord has rebuked in 1:6–2:9.

3:4 *be pleasing.* See 1:8 and note. *days of old.* Probably the time of Moses and Phinehas (see note on 2:5).

3:5 When He comes, the Lord will both purify the Levites (vv. 3–4) and judge the people. *sorcerers.* Common in the ancient Near East (see Ex 7:11; Deut 18:10).

3:6 *do not change.* See James 1:17. Contrary to what many in Malachi’s day were thinking, God remains faithful to His covenant. *not consumed.* In contrast to Edom (1:3–5) and in spite of Israel’s history of unfaithfulness.

3:7 *Return . . . and I will return.* If the Lord is to come for Israel’s redemption, she must repent.

3:9 *curse.* See 2:2 and note.

3:10 *storehouse.* The treasury rooms of the sanctuary (see 1 Kin 7:51; 2 Chr 31:11–12; Neh 13:12). *windows of heaven.* Elsewhere the idiom refers to abundant provision of food (see 2 Kin 7:2,19; Ps 78:23–24). *pour out . . . blessing.* The promised covenant blessing (see Deut 28:12; cf. Is 44:3).

3:11 *devourer . . . cast its grapes.* Examples of the threatened covenant curses (see Deut 28:39–40).

3:12 *call you blessed.* In fulfillment of the promise to Abraham (see Gen 12:2–3; see also Is 61:9 and note).

against Me," says the LORD. "Yet you say,
'What have we spoken against You?'
14 "You have said, 'It is [a]vain to serve God;
and what [b]profit is it that we have kept His
charge, and that we have walked in mourning
before the LORD of hosts?
15 'So now we [a]call the arrogant blessed;
not only are the doers of wickedness built up
but they also test God and [b]escape.' "

The Book of Remembrance

16 Then those who [1]feared the LORD spoke
to one another, and the LORD [a]gave attention
and heard *it*, and a [b]book of remembrance
was written before Him for those who [1]fear
the LORD and who esteem His name.
17 "They will be [a]Mine," says the LORD of
hosts, "on the [b]day that I [1]prepare *My* [2c]own
possession, and I will [3]spare them as a man
[3d]spares his own son who serves him."
18 So you will again [a]distinguish between
the righteous and the wicked, between one
who serves God and one who does not serve
Him.

Final Admonition

4 "[1]For behold, the day is coming, [a]burning
like a furnace; and all the arrogant and
every evildoer will be [b]chaff; and the day
that is coming will [c]set them ablaze," says
the LORD of hosts, "so that it will leave them
neither root nor branch."
2 "But for you who [1]fear My name, the
[a]sun of righteousness will rise with [b]healing
in its wings; and you will go forth and [c]skip
about like calves from the stall.
3 "You will [a]tread down the wicked, for
they will be [b]ashes under the soles of your
feet [c]on the day [1]which I am preparing,"
says the LORD of hosts.
4 "[1a]Remember the law of Moses My servant,
even the statutes and ordinances
which I commanded him in Horeb for all
Israel.
5 "Behold, I am going to send you [a]Elijah
the prophet before the coming of the great
and terrible day of the LORD.
6 "He will [1a]restore the hearts of the
fathers to *their* children and the hearts of the
children to their fathers, so that I will not
come and [b]smite the land with a [2]curse."

14 [a]Jer 2:25; 18:12 [b]Is 58:3
15 [a]Is 2:22; Mal 4:1 [b]Jer 7:10
16 [1]Or *revere(d)* [a]Ps 34:15; Jer 31:18-20 [b]Is 4:3; Dan 12:1
17 [1]Lit *make* [2]Or *special treasure* [3]Or *have (has) compassion on* [a]Is 43:1 [b]Is 4:2 [c]Ex 19:5; Deut 7:6; Is 43:21; 1 Pet 2:9 [d]Ps 103:13
18 [a]Gen 18:25; Amos 5:15
4:1 [1]Ch 3:19 in Heb [a]Ps 21:9; Nah 1:5, 6; Mal 3:2, 3; 2 Pet 3:7
4:1 [b]Is 5:24; Obad 18 [c]Is 9:18, 19
2 [1]Or *revere* [a]2 Sam 23:4; Is 30:26; 60:1 [b]Jer 30:17; 33:6 [c]Is 35:6
3 [1]Or *when I act* [a]Job 40:12; Is 26:6; Mic 5:8 [b]Ezek 28:18 [c]Mal 3:17
4 [1]Ch 3:22 in Heb [a]Deut 4:23; 8:11, 19 13; Mark 9:11-13; Luke 1:17; John 1:21
5 [a]Matt 11:14; 17:10-13; Mark 9:11-13; Luke 1:17; John 1:21
6 [1]Or *turn* [2]Or *ban of destruction* [a]Luke 1:17 [b]Is 11:4; Rev 19:15

3:14 *It is vain to serve God.* Because the redemption they longed for had not yet been realized. *walked in mourning.* In sackcloth and ashes.

3:15 *arrogant.* Evildoers—those who challenge God (see note on Ps 10:11). *blessed.* In their unbelief, the Jews call blessed those whom the godly know to be cursed (see Ps 119:21)—but it is they who will be called blessed if they repent (v. 12). *doers of wickedness built up . . . escape.* Note the psalmist's struggle with the prosperity of the wicked in Ps 73:3,9–12.

3:16 *those who feared the LORD.* Those who had not given way to doubts and cynicism. *spoke to one another.* In the face of the widespread complaining against God (vv. 14–15), they sought mutual encouragement in fellowship. *book of remembrance.* Analogous to the records of notable deeds kept by earthly rulers (see Esth 6:1–3; Is 4:3; Dan 7:10; 12:1). *esteem His name.* Contrast the priests (1:12) and many among the people (vv. 14–15; 2:17).

3:17 *My own possession.* See note on Ex 19:5. *spare them.* In the day of judgment (see 4:1–2). *who serves him.* Cf. 1:6.

3:18 *you will again distinguish.* As they apparently do not now; hence their cynicism. *the righteous and the wicked.* See 2:17 and note.

4:1 *the day.* The day of the Lord (see v. 5; 3:2 and note). *burning like a furnace.* See 3:2–3; Is 1:31; 66:15–16 and notes. *arrogant.* See 3:15 and note. *chaff . . . ablaze.* See Is 47:14 and John the Baptist's prophecy about the work of Christ in Matt 3:12. *neither root nor branch.* Nothing of them will be left (see Ezek 17:8–9).

4:2 *sun of righteousness.* God and His glory are compared with the sun in Is 60:1,19 (see notes there). Christ is the "Sunrise" from heaven (see Luke 1:78–79; see also Is 9:2 and note). *righteousness . . . healing.* Salvation and renewal are intended (see Is 45:8; 46:13; 53:5; Jer 30:17 and notes). *its wings.* The sun's rays (cf. Ps 139:9). *like calves from the stall.* Frisky young calves often frolic about when released from confinement.

4:3 *tread down the wicked.* As one treads the wine press (see Is 63:2–3 and notes).

4:4 *Remember the law.* A final exhortation to those who impatiently wait for the Lord's coming. *My servant.* See Ex 14:31; Deut 34:5; Judg 2:8; Ps 18 title; Is 20:3; 41:8–9; 42:1 and notes. *Horeb.* Mount Sinai (cf. Ex 3:1).

4:5 See 3:1 and note. *Elijah.* As Elijah came before Elisha (whose ministry was one of judgment and redemption), so "Elijah" will be sent to prepare God's people for the Lord's coming. John the Baptist ministered "in the spirit and power of Elijah" (Luke 1:17; see Matt 11:13–14; 17:12–13; Mark 9:11–13). And some feel that Elijah may also be one of the two witnesses in Rev 11:3. *great and terrible day.* See v. 1; 3:2 and note; Joel 2:11,31.

4:6 *restore the hearts.* Cf. Gen 18:19; Deut 7:9–11. According to Luke 1:17 John the Baptist sought to accomplish this. *curse.* Total destruction. If Israel does not repent, she will be dealt with as God had dealt with Edom (see Is 34:5; cf. Mal 1:3–4).

From Malachi to Christ

THE PERSIAN PERIOD 450-330 B.C.

For about 200 years after Nehemiah's time the Persians controlled Judah, but the Jews were allowed to carry on their religious observances and were not interfered with. During this time Judah was ruled by high priests who were responsible to the Jewish government.

Rule of Alexander the Great

THE HELLENISTIC PERIOD 330-166 B.C.

In 333 B.C. the Persian armies stationed in Macedonia were defeated by Alexander the Great. He was convinced that Greek culture was the one force that could unify the world. Alexander permitted the Jews to observe their laws and even granted them exemption from tribute or tax during their sabbath years. When he built Alexandria in Egypt, he encouraged Jews to live there and gave them some of the same privileges he gave his Greek subjects.The Greek conquest prepared the way for the translation of the OT into Greek (Septuagint version) c.250 B.C.

Rule of the Ptolemies of Egypt

Rule of the Seleucids of Syria

THE HASMONEAN PERIOD 166-63 B.C.

When this historical period began, the Jews were being greatly oppressed. The Ptolemies had been tolerant of the Jews and their religious practices, but the Seleucid rulers were determined to force Hellenism on them. Copies of the Scriptures were ordered destroyed and laws were enforced with extreme cruelty. The oppressed Jews revolted, led by Judas the Maccabee.

Hasmonean Dynasty

THE ROMAN PERIOD 63 B.C. . . .

In the year 63 B.C. Pompey, the Roman general, captured Jerusalem, and the provinces of Palestine became subject to Rome. The local government was entrusted part of the time to princes and the rest of the time to procurators who were appointed by the emperors. Herod the Great was ruler of all Palestine at the time of Christ's birth.

Herod the Great rules as king; subject to Rome

Timeline: 410 — **400 B.C.** — 390 — 380 — 370 — 360 — 350 — 340 — 330 — 320 — 310 — **300** — 290 — 280 — 270 — 260 — 250 — 240 — 230 — 220 — 210 — **200** — 190 — 180 — 170 — 160 — 150 — 140 — 130 — 120 — 110 — **100** — 90 — 80 — 70 — 60 — 50 — 40 — 30 — 20 — 10 — 10 — 20 — A.D. 30

- Malachi c. 430 B.C.
- 334-323 Alexander the Great conquers the East
- 330-328 Alexander's years of power
- 320 Ptolemy (I) Soter conquers Jerusalem
- 311 Seleucus conquers Babylon; Seleucid dynasty begins
- 226 Antiochus III (the Great) of Syria overpowers Palestine
- 223-187 Antiochus becomes Seleucid ruler of Syria
- 198 Antiochus defeats Egypt and gains control of Palestine
- 175-164 Antiochus (IV) Epiphanes rules Syria; Judaism is prohibited
- 167 Mattathias and his sons rebel against Antiochus; Maccabean revolt begins
- 166-160 Judas Maccabeus's leadership
- 160-143 Jonathan is high priest
- 142 Tower of Jerusalem cleansed
- 142-134 Simon becomes high priest; establishes Hasmonean dynasty
- 134-104 John Hyrcanus enlarges the independent Jewish state
- 103 Aristobulus's rule
- 102-76 Alexander Janneus's rule
- 75-67 Rule of Salome Alexandra with Hyrcanus II as high priest
- 66-63 Battle between Aristobulus II and Hyrcanus II
- 63 Pompey invades Palestine; Roman rule begins
- 63-40 Hyrcanus II rules but is subject to Rome
- 40-37 Parthians conquer Jerusalem
- 37 Jerusalem besieged for six months
- 32 Herod defeated
- 19 Herod's temple begun
- 16 Herod visits Agrippa
- 4 Herod dies; Archelaus succeeds

The Time Between the Testaments

The time between the Testaments was one of ferment and change—a time of the realignment of traditional power blocs and the passing of a Near Eastern cultural tradition that had been dominant for almost 3,000 years.

In Biblical history, the approximately 400 years that separate the time of Nehemiah from the birth of Christ are known as the intertestamental period (c. 432–5 B.C.). Sometimes called the "silent" years, they were anything but silent. The events, literature and social forces of these years would shape the world of the NT.

History

With the Babylonian captivity, Israel ceased to be an independent nation and became a minor territory in a succession of larger empires. Very little is known about the latter years of Persian domination because the Jewish historian Josephus, our primary source for the intertestamental period, all but ignores them.

With Alexander the Great's acquisition of Palestine (332 B.C.), a new and more insidious threat to Israel emerged. Alexander was committed to the creation of a world united by Greek language and culture, a policy followed by his successors. This policy, called Hellenization, had a dramatic impact on the Jews.

At Alexander's death (323 B.C.) the empire he won was divided among his generals. Two of them founded dynasties—the Ptolemies in Egypt and the Seleucids in Syria and Mesopotamia—that would contend for control of Palestine for over a century.

The rule of the Ptolemies was considerate of Jewish religious sensitivities, but in 198 B.C. the Seleucids took control and paved the way for one of the most heroic periods in Jewish history.

The early Seleucid years were largely a continuation of the tolerant rule of the Ptolemies, but Antiochus IV Epiphanes (whose title means "God made manifest" and who ruled 175–164 B.C.) changed that when he attempted to consolidate his fading empire through a policy of radical Hellenization. While a segment of the Jewish aristocracy had already adopted Greek ways, the majority of Jews were outraged.

Antiochus's atrocities were aimed at the eradication of Jewish religion. He prohibited some of the central elements of Jewish practice, attempted to destroy all copies of the Torah (the Pentateuch) and required offerings to the Greek god Zeus. His crowning outrage was the erection of a statue of Zeus and the sacrificing of a pig in the Jerusalem temple itself.

Opposition to Antiochus was led by Mattathias, an elderly villager from a priestly family, and his five sons: Judas (Maccabeus), Jonathan, Simon, John and Eleazar. Mattathias destroyed a Greek altar established in his village, Modein, and killed Antiochus's emissary. This triggered the Maccabean revolt, a 24-year war (166–142 B.C.) that resulted in the independence of Judah until the Romans took control in 63 B.C.

The victory of Mattathias's family was Pyrrhic, however. With the death of his last son, Simon, the Hasmonean dynasty that they founded soon evolved into an aristocratic, Hellenistic regime sometimes hard to distinguish from that of the Seleucids. During the reign of Simon's son, John Hyrcanus, the orthodox Jews who had supported the Maccabees fell out of favor. With only a few exceptions, the rest of the Hasmoneans supported the Jewish Hellenizers. The Pharisees were actually persecuted by Alexander Janneus (102–76 B.C.).

The Hasmonean dynasty ended when, in 63 B.C., an expanding Roman empire intervened in a dynastic clash between the two sons of Janneus, Aristobulus II and Hyrcanus II. Pompey, the general who subdued the East for Rome, took Jerusalem after a three-month siege of the temple area, massacring priests in the performance of their duties and entering the holy of holies. This sacrilege began Roman rule in a way that Jews could neither forgive nor forget.

Literature

During these unhappy years of oppression and internal strife, the Jewish people produced a sizable body of literature that both recorded and addressed their era. Three of the more significant works are the Septuagint, the Apocrypha and the Dead Sea Scrolls.

Septuagint. Jewish legend says that 72 scholars, under the sponsorship of Ptolemy Philadelphus (c. 250 B.C.), were brought together on the island of Pharos, near Alexandria, where they produced a Greek translation of the OT in 72 days. From this tradition the Latin word for 70, "Septuagint," became the name attached to the translation. The Roman numeral for 70, LXX, is used as an abbreviation for it.

Behind the legend lies the probability that at least the Torah (the five books of Moses) was translated into Greek c. 250 B.C. for the use of the Greek-speaking Jews of Alexandria. The rest of the OT and some non-canonical books were also included in the LXX before the dawning of the Christian era, though it is difficult to be certain when.

The Septuagint quickly became the Bible of the Jews outside Palestine who, like the Alexandrians, no longer spoke Hebrew. It would be difficult to overestimate its influence. It made the Scriptures available both to the Jews who no longer spoke their ancestral language and to the entire Greek-speaking world. It later became the Bible of the early church. Also, its widespread popularity and use contributed to the retention of the Apocrypha by some branches of Christendom.

Apocrypha. Derived from a Greek word that means "hidden," Apocrypha has acquired the meaning "false," but in a technical sense it describes a specific body of writings. This collection consists of a variety of books and additions to canonical books that, with the exception of 2 Esdras (c. A.D. 90), were written during the intertestamental period. Their recognition as authoritative in Roman and Eastern Christianity is the result of a complex historical process.

The canon of the OT accepted by Protestants today was very likely established by the dawn of the second century A.D., though after the fall of Jerusalem and the destruction of the temple in 70. The precise scope of the OT was discussed among the Jews until the Council of Jamnia (c. 90). This Hebrew canon was not accepted by the early church, which used the Septuagint. In spite of disagreements among some of the church fathers as to which books were canonical and which were not, the Apocryphal books continued in common use by most Christians until the Reformation. During this period most Protestants decided to follow the original Hebrew canon while Rome, at the Council of Trent (1546) and more recently at the First Vatican Council (1869–70), affirmed the larger "Alexandrian" canon that includes the Apocrypha.

The Apocryphal books have retained their place primarily through the weight of ecclesiastical authority, without which they would not commend themselves as canonical literature. There is no clear evidence that Jesus or the apostles ever quoted any Apocryphal works as Scripture (but see note on Jude 14). The Jewish community that produced them repudiated them, and the historical surveys in the apostolic sermons recorded in Acts completely ignore the period they cover. Even the sober, historical account of 1 Maccabees is tarnished by numerous errors and anachronisms.

There is nothing of theological value in the Apocryphal books that cannot be duplicated in canonical Scripture, and they contain much that runs counter to its teachings. Nonetheless, this body of literature does provide a valuable source of information for the study of the intertestamental period.

Dead Sea Scrolls. In the spring of 1947 an Arab shepherd chanced upon a cave in the hills overlooking the southwestern shore of the Dead Sea that contained what has been called "the greatest manuscript discovery of modern times." The documents and fragments of documents found in those caves, dubbed the "Dead Sea Scrolls," included OT books, a few books of the Apocrypha, apocalyptic works, pseudepigrapha (books that purport to be the work of ancient heroes of the faith), and a number of books peculiar to the sect that produced them.

Approximately a third of the documents are Biblical, with Psalms, Deuteronomy and Isaiah—the books quoted most often in the NT—occurring most frequently. One of the most remarkable finds was a complete 24-foot-long scroll of Isaiah.

The Scrolls have made a significant contribution to the quest for a form of the OT texts most accurately reflecting the original manuscripts; they provide copies 1,000 years closer to the originals than were previously known. The understanding of Biblical Hebrew and Aramaic and knowledge of the development of Juda-

ism between the Testaments have been increased significantly. Of great importance to readers of the Bible is the demonstration of the care with which OT texts were copied, thus providing objective evidence for the general reliability of those texts.

Social Developments

The Judaism of Jesus' day is, to a large extent, the result of changes that came about in response to the pressures of the intertestamental period.

Diaspora. The Diaspora (dispersion) of Israel begun in the exile accelerated during these years until a writer of the day could say that Jews filled "every land and sea."

Jews outside Palestine, cut off from the temple, concentrated their religious life in the study of the Torah and the life of the synagogue (see below). The missionaries of the early church began their Gentile ministries among the Diaspora, using their Greek translation of the OT.

Sadducees. In Palestine, the Greek world made its greatest impact through the party of the Sadducees. Made up of aristocrats, it became the temple party. Because of their position, the Sadducees had a vested interest in the status quo.

Relatively few in number, they wielded disproportionate political power and controlled the high priesthood. They rejected all religious writings except the Torah, as well as any doctrine (such as the resurrection) not found in those five books.

Synagogue. During the exile, Israel was cut off from the temple, divested of nationhood and surrounded by pagan religious practices. Her faith was threatened with extinction. Under these circumstances, the exiles turned their religious focus from what they had lost to what they retained—the Torah and the belief that they were God's people. They concentrated on the law rather than nationhood, on personal piety rather than sacramental rectitude, and on prayer as an acceptable replacement for the sacrifices denied to them.

When they returned from the exile, they brought with them this new form of religious expression, as well as the synagogue (its center), and Judaism became a faith that could be practiced wherever the Torah could be carried. The emphases on personal piety and a relationship with God, which characterized synagogue worship, not only helped preserve Judaism but also prepared the way for the Christian gospel.

Pharisees. As the party of the synagogue, the Pharisees strove to reinterpret the law. They built a "hedge" around it to enable Jews to live righteously before God in a world that had changed drastically since the days of Moses. Although they were comparatively few in number, the Pharisees enjoyed the support of the people and influenced popular opinion if not national policy. They were the only party to survive the destruction of the temple in A.D. 70 and were the spiritual progenitors of modern Judaism.

Essenes. An almost forgotten Jewish sect until the discovery of the Dead Sea Scrolls, the Essenes were a small, separatist group that grew out of the conflicts of the Maccabean age. Like the Pharisees, they stressed strict legal observance, but they considered the temple priesthood corrupt and rejected much of the temple ritual and sacrificial system. Mentioned by several ancient writers, the precise nature of the Essenes is still not certain, though it is generally agreed that the Qumran community that produced the Dead Sea Scrolls was an Essene group.

Because they were convinced that they were the true remnant, these Qumran Essenes had separated themselves from Judaism at large and devoted themselves to personal purity and preparation for the final war between the "Sons of Light and the Sons of Darkness." They practiced an apocalyptic faith, looking back to the contributions of their "Teacher of Righteousness" and forward to the coming of two, and possibly three, Messiahs. The destruction of the temple in A.D. 70, however, seems to have delivered a death blow to their apocalyptic expectations.

Attempts have been made to equate aspects of the beliefs of the Qumran community with the origins of Christianity. Some have seen a prototype of Jesus in their "Teacher of Righteousness," and both John the Baptist and Jesus have been assigned membership in the sect. There is, however, only a superficial, speculative basis for these conjectures.

The New Testament

The Synoptic Gospels

A careful comparison of the four Gospels reveals that Matthew, Mark and Luke are noticeably similar, while John is quite different. The first three Gospels agree extensively in language, in the material they include, and in the order in which events and sayings from the life of Christ are recorded. (Chronological order does not appear to have been rigidly followed in any of the Gospels, however.) Because of this agreement, these three books are called the Synoptic Gospels (*syn,* "together with"; *optic,* "seeing"; thus "seeing together"). For an example of agreement in content see Matt 9:2–8; Mark 2:3–12; Luke 5:18–26. An instance of verbatim agreement is found in Matt 10:22a; Mark 13:13a; Luke 21:17. A mathematical comparison shows that 91 percent of Mark's Gospel is contained in Matthew, while 53 percent of Mark is found in Luke. Such agreement raises questions as to the origin of the Synoptic Gospels. Did the authors rely on a common source? Were they interdependent? Questions such as these constitute what is known as the Synoptic Problem. Several suggested solutions have been advanced:

1. *The use of oral tradition.* Some have thought that tradition had become so stereotyped that it provided a common source from which all the Gospel writers drew.

2. *The use of an early Gospel.* Some have postulated that the Synoptic authors all had access to an earlier Gospel, now lost.

3. *The use of written fragments.* Some have assumed that written fragments had been composed concerning various events from the life of Christ and that these were used by the Synoptic authors.

4. *Mutual dependence.* Some have suggested that the Synoptic writers drew from each other with the result that what they wrote was often very similar.

5. *The use of two major sources.* The most common view currently is that the Gospel of Mark and a hypothetical document, called *Quelle* (German for "source") or *Q,* were used by Matthew and Luke as sources for most of the materials included in their Gospels.

6. *The priority and use of Matthew.* Another view suggests that the other two Synoptics drew from Matthew as their main source.

7. *A combination of most of the above.* This theory assumes that the authors of the Synoptic Gospels made use of oral tradition, written fragments, mutual dependence on other Synoptic writers or on their Gospels, and the testimony of eyewitnesses.

Dating the Synoptic Gospels

MARK — MATTHEW — LUKE

ASSUMPTION A

Matthew and Luke used Mark as a major source

View No. 1

Mark written in the 50s or early 60s

(1) Matthew written in late 50s or the 60s

(2) Luke written 59–63

View No. 2

Mark written 65–70

(1) Matthew written in the 70s

(2) Luke written in the 70s

MARK | MATTHEW | LUKE

ASSUMPTION B

Matthew and Luke did not use Mark as a source

View No. 1

Mark could have been written anytime between 50 and 70

View No. 2

Mark written 65–70

(1) Matthew written in the 50s (see Introduction to Matthew: Date and Place of Writing)

(2) Luke written 59–63 (see Introduction to Luke: Date and Place of Writing)

Matthew

INTRODUCTION

See "The Synoptic Gospels," p. 1361.

Author

The early church fathers were unanimous in holding that Matthew, one of the 12 apostles, was the author of this Gospel. However, the results of modern critical studies—in particular those that stress Matthew's alleged dependence on Mark for a substantial part of his Gospel—have caused some Biblical scholars to abandon Matthean authorship. Why, they ask, would Matthew, an eyewitness to the events of our Lord's life, depend so heavily on Mark's account? The best answer seems to be that he agreed with it and wanted to show that the apostolic testimony to Christ was not divided.

Matthew, whose name means "gift of the LORD," was a tax collector who left his work to follow Jesus (9:9–13). In Mark and Luke he is called by his other name, Levi.

Date and Place of Writing

The Jewish nature of Matthew's Gospel may suggest that it was written in Palestine, though many think it may have originated in Syrian Antioch. Some have argued on the basis of its Jewish characteristics that it was written in the early church period, possibly the early part of A.D. 50, when the church was largely Jewish and the gospel was preached to Jews only (Ac 11:19). However, those who have concluded that both Matthew and Luke drew extensively from Mark's Gospel date it later—after the Gospel of Mark had been in circulation for a period of time. See chart, p. 1361. Accordingly, some feel that Matthew would have been written in the late 50s or in the 60s. Others, who assume that Mark was written between 65 and 70, place Matthew in the 70s or even later.

Recipients

Since his Gospel was written in Greek, Matthew's readers were obviously Greek-speaking. They also seem to have been Jews. Many elements point to Jewish readership: Matthew's concern with fulfillment of the OT (he has more quotations from and allusions to the OT than any other NT author); his tracing of Jesus' descent from Abraham (1:1–17); his lack of explanation of Jewish customs (especially in contrast to Mark); his use of Jewish terminology (e.g., "kingdom of heaven" and "Father in heaven," where "heaven" reveals the Jewish reverential reluctance to use the name of God); his emphasis on Jesus' role as "Son of David" (1:1; 9:27; 12:23; 15:22; 20:30–31; 21:9,15; 22:41–45). This does not mean, however, that Matthew restricts his Gospel to Jews. He records the coming of the magi (non-Jews) to worship the infant Jesus (2:1–12), as well as Jesus' statement that the "field is the world" (13:38). He also gives a full statement of the Great Commission (28:18–20). These passages show that, although Matthew's Gospel is Jewish, it has a universal outlook.

Purpose

Matthew's main purpose is to prove to his Jewish readers that Jesus is their Messiah. He does this primarily by showing how Jesus in His life and ministry fulfilled the OT Scriptures. Although all the Gospel writers quote the OT, Matthew includes nine additional proof texts (1:22–23; 2:15; 2:17–18; 2:23; 4:14–16; 8:17; 12:17–21; 13:35; 27:9–10) to drive home his basic theme: Jesus is the fulfillment of the OT predictions of the Messiah. Matthew even finds the history of God's people in the OT recapitulated in some aspects of Jesus' life (see, e.g., his quotation of Hos 11:1 in 2:15). To accomplish his purpose Matthew also emphasizes Jesus' Davidic lineage (see Recipients above).

Structure

The way the material is arranged reveals an artistic touch. The whole Gospel is woven around five great discourses: (1) chs. 5—7; (2) ch. 10; (3) ch. 13; (4) ch. 18; (5) chs. 24—25. That this is deliberate is clear from the refrain that concludes each discourse: "When Jesus had finished these words," or similar phrases (7:28; 11:1; 13:53; 19:1; 26:1). The narrative sections, in each case, appropriately lead up to the discourses. The Gospel has a fitting prologue (chs. 1—2) and a challenging epilogue (28:16–20).

The fivefold division may suggest that Matthew has modeled his book on the structure of the Pentateuch (the first five books of the OT). He may also be presenting the gospel as a new Torah and Jesus as a new and greater Moses.

Outline

- I. The Birth and Early Years of Jesus (chs. 1—2)
  - A. His Genealogy (1:1–17)
  - B. His Birth (1:18—2:12)
  - C. His Sojourn in Egypt (2:13–23)
- II. The Beginnings of Jesus' Ministry (3:1—4:11)
  - A. His Forerunner (3:1–12)
  - B. His Baptism (3:13–17)
  - C. His Temptation (4:1–11)
- III. Jesus' Ministry in Galilee (4:12—14:12)
  - A. The Beginning of the Galilean Campaign (4:12–25)
  - B. The Sermon on the Mount (chs. 5—7)
  - C. A Collection of Miracles (chs. 8—9)
  - D. The Commissioning of the 12 Apostles (ch. 10)
  - E. Ministry throughout Galilee (chs. 11—12)
  - F. The Parables of the Kingdom (ch. 13)
  - G. Herod's Reaction to Jesus' Ministry (14:1–12)
- IV. Jesus' Withdrawals from Galilee (14:13—17:20)
  - A. To the Eastern Shore of the Sea of Galilee (14:13—15:20)
  - B. To Phoenicia (15:21–28)
  - C. To the Decapolis (15:29—16:12)
  - D. To Caesarea Philippi (16:13—17:20)
- V. Jesus' Last Ministry in Galilee (17:22—18:35)
  - A. Prediction of Jesus' Death (17:22–23)
  - B. Temple Tax (17:24–27)
  - C. Discourse on Life in the Kingdom (ch. 18)
- VI. Jesus' Ministry in Judea and Perea (chs. 19—20)
  - A. Teaching concerning Divorce (19:1–12)
  - B. Teaching concerning Little Children (19:13–15)
  - C. The Rich Young Man (19:16–30)
  - D. The Parable of the Laborers in the Vineyard (20:1–16)
  - E. Prediction of Jesus' Death (20:17–19)
  - F. A Mother's Request (20:20–28)
  - G. Restoration of Sight at Jericho (20:29–34)
- VII. Passion Week (chs. 21—27)
  - A. The Triumphal Entry (21:1–11)
  - B. The Cleansing of the Temple (21:12–17)
  - C. The Last Controversies with the Jewish Leaders (21:18—23:39)
  - D. The Olivet Discourse concerning the End of the Age (chs. 24—25)
  - E. The Anointing of Jesus' Feet (26:1–13)
  - F. The Arrest, Trials and Death of Jesus (26:14—27:66)
- VIII. The Resurrection (ch. 28)

The Genealogy of Jesus the Messiah

1 The [1]record of the genealogy of [2]Jesus
[3]the Messiah, [a]the son of David, [b]the son
of Abraham:
2 Abraham [1]was the father of Isaac,
[2]Isaac the father of Jacob, and Jacob the
father of [3]Judah and his brothers.
3 Judah was the father of Perez and
Zerah by Tamar, [a]Perez was the father of
Hezron, and Hezron the father of [1]Ram.
4 Ram was the father of Amminadab,
Amminadab the father of Nahshon, and
Nahshon the father of Salmon.
5 Salmon was the father of Boaz by
Rahab, Boaz was the father of Obed by Ruth,
and Obed the father of Jesse.
6 Jesse was the father of David the king.
David [a]was the father of Solomon by
[1]Bathsheba who had been the wife of Uriah.
7 Solomon [a]was the father of Rehoboam,
Rehoboam the father of Abijah, and Abijah
the father of [1]Asa.
8 Asa was the father of Jehoshaphat,
Jehoshaphat the father of [1]Joram, and Joram
the father of Uzziah.
9 Uzziah was the father of [1]Jotham,
Jotham the father of Ahaz, and Ahaz the
father of Hezekiah.
10 Hezekiah was the father of Manasseh,
Manasseh the father of [1]Amon, and Amon
the [a]father of Josiah.
11 Josiah became the father of [1]Jeconiah
and his brothers, at the time of the [a]deporta-
tion to Babylon.
12 After the [a]deportation to Babylon: Jeconiah became the father of [1]Shealtiel, and
Shealtiel the father of Zerubbabel.
13 Zerubbabel was the father of [1]Abihud,
Abihud the father of Eliakim, and Eliakim
the father of Azor.
14 Azor was the father of Zadok, Zadok
the father of Achim, and Achim the father of
Eliud.
15 Eliud was the father of Eleazar, Eleazar
the father of Matthan, and Matthan the
father of Jacob.
16 Jacob was the father of Joseph the husband of Mary, by whom Jesus was born,
[a]who is called [1]the Messiah.
17 So all the generations from Abraham to
David are fourteen generations; from David
to the [a]deportation to Babylon, fourteen generations; and from the [a]deportation to Babylon to [1]the Messiah, fourteen generations.

Conception and Birth of Jesus

18 Now the birth of Jesus [1]Christ was as
follows: when His [a]mother Mary had been
[2]betrothed to Joseph, before they came
together she was [b]found to be with child by
the Holy Spirit.
19 And Joseph her husband, being a righteous man and not wanting to disgrace her,
planned [1a]to send her away secretly.

1:1 [1]Lit *book* [2]Heb *Yeshua* (*Joshua*), meaning *The LORD saves* [3]Gr *Christos* (*Christ*), Gr for *Messiah*, which means *Anointed One* [a]2 Sam 7:12-16; Ps 89:3f; 132:11; Is 9:6f; 11:1; Matt 9:27; Luke 1:32, 69; John 7:42; Acts 13:23; Rom 1:3; Rev 22:16 [b]Matt 1:1-6: *Luke 3:32-34;* Gen 22:18; Gal 3:16
2 [1]Lit *fathered*, and throughout the genealogy [2]Lit *and...*, and throughout the genealogy [3]Gr *Judas;* names of people in the Old Testament are given in their Old Testament form
3 [1]Gr *Aram* [a]Ruth 4:18-22; 1 Chr 2:1-15; Matt 1:3-6
6 [1]Lit *her of Uriah* [a]2 Sam 11:27; 12:24
7 [1]Gr *Asaph* [a]1 Chr 3:10ff
8 [1]Also Gr for *Jehoram* in 2 King 8:16; cf 1 Chron 3:11
9 [1]Gr *Joatham*
10 [1]Gr *Amos* [a]1 Chr 3:14
11 [1]*Jehoiachin* in 2 Kin 24:15 [a]2 Kin 24:14f; Jer 27:20; Matt 1:17

12 [1]Gr *Salathiel* [a]2 Kin 24:14f; Jer 27:20; Matt 1:17 **13** [1]Gr *Abioud*, usually spelled *Abiud* **16** [1]Gr *Christos (Christ)* [a]Matt 27:17, 22; Luke 2:11; John 4:25 **17** [1]Gr *Christos (Christ)* [a]2 Kin 24:14f; Jer 27:20; Matt 1:11, 12 **18** [1]I.e. The Messiah [2]The first stage of marriage in Jewish culture, usually lasting for a year before the wedding night, more legal than an engagement [a]Matt 12:46; Luke 1:27 [b]Luke 1:35 **19** [1]Or *to divorce her* [a]Deut 22:20-24; 24:1-4; John 8:4, 5

1:1–16 For a comparison of Matthew's genealogy with Luke's see note on Luke 3:23–38. The types of people mentioned in this genealogy reveal the broad scope of those who make up the people of God as well as the genealogy of Jesus.
1:1 *the son of David.* A Messianic title (see note on 9:27) found several times in this Gospel (in 1:20 it is not a Messianic title). *the son of Abraham.* Because Matthew was writing to Jews, it was important to identify Jesus in this way.
1:3 *Tamar.* In Matthew's genealogy four women are named: Tamar (here), Rahab (v. 5), Ruth (v. 5) and Bathsheba (v. 6). At least three of these women were Gentiles (Tamar, Rahab and Ruth). Bathsheba was probably an Israelite (1 Chr 3:5) but was closely associated with the Hittites because of Uriah, her Hittite husband. By including these women (contrary to custom) in his genealogy, Matthew may be indicating at the very outset of his Gospel that God's activity is not limited to men or the people of Israel.
1:4 *Amminadab.* Father-in-law of Aaron (Ex 6:23).
1:5 *Rahab.* See Josh 2. Since quite a long time had elapsed between Rahab and David and because of Matthew's desire for systematic organization (see note on v. 17), many of the generations between these two ancestors were assumed, but not listed, by Matthew.
1:8 *Joram the father.* Matthew calls Joram the father of Uzziah, but from 2 Chr 21:4–26:23 it is clear that, again, several generations were assumed (Ahaziah, Joash and Amaziah) and that "father" is used in the sense of "forefather."
1:11 *Josiah became the father.* Similarly (see note on v. 8), Josiah is called the father of Jeconiah (i.e., Jehoiachin; see NASB marg.), whereas he was actually the father of Jehoiakim and the grandfather of Jehoiachin (2 Chr 36:1–9).
1:12 *Shealtiel the father.* See note on 1 Chr 3:19.
1:16 Matthew does not say that Joseph was the father of Jesus but only that he was the husband of Mary and that Jesus was born of her. In this genealogy Matthew shows that, although Jesus is not the physical son of Joseph, He is the legal son and therefore a descendant of David.
1:17 *fourteen generations . . . fourteen . . . fourteen.* These divisions reflect two characteristics of Matthew's Gospel: (1) an apparent fondness for numbers and (2) concern for systematic arrangement. The number 14 may have been chosen because it is twice seven (the number of completeness) and/or because it is the numerical value of the name David (see note on Rev 13:17). For the practice of telescoping genealogies to achieve the desired number of names see Introduction to 1 Chronicles: Genealogies.
1:18 *had been betrothed.* There were no sexual relations during a Jewish betrothal period, but it was a much more binding relationship than a modern engagement and could be broken only by divorce (see v. 19). In Deut 22:24 a betrothed woman is called a "wife," though the preceding verse speaks of her as being "engaged to a man." Matthew uses the terms "husband" (v. 19) and "wife" (v. 24) of Joseph and Mary before they were married.
1:19 *righteous.* To Jews this meant being zealous in keeping the law. *send her away secretly.* He would sign the necessary legal papers but not have her judged publicly and stoned (see Deut 22:23–24).

20 But when he had considered this, behold, an angel of the Lord appeared to him in a dream, saying, "[a]Joseph, son of David, do not be afraid to take Mary as your wife; for [1]the Child who has been [2]conceived in her is of the Holy Spirit.

21 "She will bear a Son; and [a]you shall call His name Jesus, for [1]He [b]will save His people from their sins."

22 Now all this [1]took place to fulfill what was [a]spoken by the Lord through the prophet:

23 "[a]BEHOLD, THE VIRGIN SHALL BE WITH [b]CHILD AND SHALL BEAR A SON, AND THEY SHALL CALL HIS NAME [1]IMMANUEL," which translated means, "[c]GOD WITH US."

24 And Joseph [1]awoke from his sleep and did as the angel of the Lord commanded him, and took *Mary* as his wife,

25 [1]but kept her a virgin until she [a]gave birth to a Son; and [b]he called His name Jesus.

The Visit of the Magi

2 Now after Jesus was [a]born in Bethlehem of Judea in the days of [b]Herod the king, [1]magi from the east arrived in Jerusalem, saying,

2 "Where is He who has been born [a]King of the Jews? For we saw [b]His star in the east and have come to worship Him."

3 When Herod the king heard *this,* he was troubled, and all Jerusalem with him.

4 Gathering together all the chief priests and scribes of the people, he inquired of them where the [1]Messiah was to be born.

5 They said to him, "[a]In Bethlehem of Judea; for this is what has been written [1]by the prophet:

6 '[a]AND YOU, BETHLEHEM, LAND OF JUDAH,
ARE BY NO MEANS LEAST AMONG THE
LEADERS OF JUDAH;
FOR OUT OF YOU SHALL COME FORTH A
RULER
WHO WILL [b]SHEPHERD MY PEOPLE
ISRAEL.' "

7 Then Herod secretly called the magi and determined from them [1]the exact time [a]the star appeared.

8 And he sent them to Bethlehem and said, "Go and search carefully for the Child; and when you have found *Him,* report to me, so that I too may come and worship Him."

9 After hearing the king, they went their way; and the star, which they had seen in the east, went on before them until it came and stood over *the place* where the Child was.

10 When they saw the star, they rejoiced exceedingly with great joy.

11 After coming into the house they saw the Child with [a]Mary His mother; and they [1]fell to the ground and [b]worshiped Him.

20 [1]Lit *that which* [2]Lit *begotten* [a]Luke 2:4
21 [1]Lit *He Himself* [a]Luke 1:31; 2:21 [b]Luke 2:11; John 1:29; Acts 4:12; 5:31; 13:23, 38, 39; Col 1:20-23
22 [1]Lit *has happened* [a]Luke 24:44; Rom 1:2-4
23 [1]Or *Emmanuel* [a]Is 7:14 [b]Is 9:6, 7 [c]Is 8:10
24 [1]Lit *got up*
25 [1]Lit *and was not knowing her* [a]Luke 2:7 [b]Matt 1:21; Luke 2:21
2:1 [1]A caste of wise men specializing in astronomy, astrology, and natural science [a]Mic 5:2; Luke 2:4-7 [b]Luke 1:5
2 [a]Jer 23:5; 30:9; Zech 9:9; Matt 27:11; Luke 19:38; 23:38; John 1:49 [b]Num 24:17
4 [1]Gr *Christos (Christ)*
5 [1]Or *through* [a]John 7:42
6 [a]Mic 5:2; John 7:42 [b]John 21:16
7 [1]Lit *the time of the appearing star* [a]Num 24:17
11 [1]Lit *prostrated;* i.e. face down in a prone position to indicate worship [a]Matt 1:18; 12:46 [b]Matt 14:33

1:20 *in a dream.* The phrase occurs five times in the first two chapters of Matthew (here; 2:12–13,19,22) and indicates the means the Lord used for speaking to Joseph. *son of David.* Perhaps a hint that the message of the angel related to the expected Messiah. *take Mary as your wife.* They were legally bound to each other, but not yet living together as husband and wife. *the Child who has been conceived in her is of the Holy Spirit.* This agrees perfectly with the announcement to Mary (Luke 1:35), except that the latter is more specific (see note on Luke 1:26–35).
1:21 *Jesus . . . will save.* Jesus is the Greek form of Joshua, which means "The LORD saves".
1:22 *fulfill.* Twelve times (here; 2:15,23; 3:15; 4:14; 5:17; 8:17; 12:17; 13:14,35; 21:4; 27:9) Matthew speaks of the OT being fulfilled, i.e., of events in NT times that were prophesied in the OT—a powerful testimony to the divine origin of Scripture and its accuracy even in small details. In the fulfillments we also see the writer's concern for linking the gospel with the OT.
1:23 See note on Is 7:14. This is the first of at least 47 quotations, most of them Messianic, that Matthew takes from the OT (see marg. refs. throughout Matthew).
1:25 *kept her a virgin until she gave birth.* Both Matthew and Luke (1:26–35) make it clear that Jesus was born of a virgin. Although this doctrine is often ridiculed, it is an important part of the evangelical faith.
2:1 *Bethlehem of Judea.* A village about five miles south of Jerusalem. Matthew says nothing of the events in Nazareth (cf. Luke 1:26–56). Possibly wanting to emphasize Jesus' Davidic background, he begins with the events that happened in David's city. It is called "Bethlehem of Judea," not to distinguish it from the town of the same name about seven miles northwest of Nazareth, but to emphasize that Jesus came from the tribe and territory that produced the line of Davidic kings. That Jews expected the Messiah to be born in Bethlehem and to be from David's family is clear from John 7:42. *Herod the king.* Herod the Great (37–4 B.C.), to be distinguished from the other Herods in the Bible (see chart, p. 1367). Herod was a non-Jew, an Idumean, who was appointed king of Judea by the Roman Senate in 40 B.C. and gained control in 37. Like most rulers of the day, he was ruthless, murdering his wife, his three sons, mother-in-law, brother-in-law, uncle and many others—not to mention the babies in Bethlehem (v. 16). His reign was also noted for splendor, as seen in the many theaters, amphitheaters, monuments, pagan altars, fortresses and other buildings he erected or refurbished—including the greatest work of all, the rebuilding of the temple in Jerusalem, begun in 19 B.C. and finished 68 years after his death. *magi.* See NASB marg. Perhaps they were from Persia or southern Arabia, both of which are east of the Holy Land. *Jerusalem.* Since they were looking for the "King of the Jews" (v. 2), they naturally came to the Jewish capital city (see map No. 8 at the end of the study Bible).
2:2 *King of the Jews.* Indicates the magi were Gentiles. Matthew shows that people of all nations acknowledged Jesus as "King of the Jews" and came to worship Him as Lord. *star.* Probably not an ordinary star, planet or comet, though some scholars have identified it with the conjunction of Jupiter and Saturn.
2:4 *chief priests.* Sadducees (see note on 3:7) who were in charge of worship at the temple in Jerusalem. *scribes.* The Jewish scholars of the day, professionally trained in the development, teaching and application of OT law. Their authority was strictly human and traditional.
2:6 This prophecy from Micah had been given seven centuries earlier.
2:11 *house.* Contrary to tradition, the magi did not visit Jesus at the manger on the night of His birth as did the shepherds. They came some months later and visited Him as a "child" in His "house." *the Child with Mary His mother.* Every time the child

House of Herod

Mediterranean Sea
TRACONITIS
GALILEE
SAMARIA
PEREA
Herod the Great
JUDEA
IDUMEA

1st Generation

Mediterranean Sea
ITUREA
TRACONITIS
Herod Philip II
GALILEE
SAMARIA
Herod Antipas
PEREA
Archelaus
JUDEA
IDUMEA

2nd Generation

CHALCIS
ABILA
Mediterranean Sea
TRACONITIS
BATANEA
GALILEE
AURANITIS
Herod Agrippa I
PEREA
JUDEA
IDUMEA
ABILA

3rd Generation

Mediterranean Sea
TRA-CON-ITIS
BATA-NEA
TIBERIAS
AURA-NITIS
Herod Agrippa II
Ruled by Roman procurators
ABILA
This name appears in two locations
IDUMEA

4th Generation

Herod the Great

King of Judea, Galilee, Iturea, Traconitis (37-4 B.C.)
Birth of Jesus (Matt 2:1-19; Luke 1:5)

Herod Philip II

(MOTHER: CLEOPATRA)
Tetrach of Iturea and Traconitis (4 B.C.-A.D. 34)(Luke 3:1)

Archelaus

(MOTHER: MALTHACE)
Governor of Judea, Idumea and Samaria (4 B.C.-A.D. 6) When Mary and Joseph left Egypt, they avoided Judea and settled in Nazareth (Matt 2:19-23)

Aristobulus

(MOTHER: MARIAMNE)
(d. 10 B.C.) Not mentioned in the Bible

Herod Antipas

(MOTHER: MALTHACE)
Tetrarch of Galilee and Perea (4 B.C.-A.D. 39) (Luke 3:1) Second husband of Herodias. He put John the Baptist to death (Matt 14:1-12; Mark 6:14-29); Pilate sent Jesus to him (Luke 23:7-12)

Herod Philip I

(MOTHER: MARIAMNE)
He did not rule. First husband of Herodias (Matt 14:3; Mark 6:17) (d.c. A.D. 34)

Antipater

(MOTHER: DORIS)

Herod of Chalcis

Herod Agrippa I

King of Judea (A.D. 37-44)
Killed James; put Peter into prison. Struck down by an angel (Acts 12:1-24)

HERODIAS

Married her uncle Herod Philip I, and then a second uncle, Herod Antipas (Matt 14:3; Mark 6:17)

Felix (Governor of Judea)

DRUSILLA

Married Felix, governor of Judea (A.D. 52-59); Felix tried Paul (Acts 24:24)

Herod Agrippa II

King of Judea
Paul makes a legal defense before him (Acts 25:13–26:32)

BERNICE

With her brother at the time of Paul's defense (Acts 25:13)

SALOME

Daughter of Herodias and Herod Philip I. Danced for the head of John the Baptist (Matt 14:1-12; Mark 6:14-29)

KEY:
- King
- Tetrarch
- *BERNICE* — italic capitals denote females
- **Antipater** — bold type-blood line of Herod the Great
- Felix — light type-non blood line

. . . . . Denotes Herodias's marriage to Herod Antipas

— — Denotes Herodias's marriage to Herod Philip I and daughter of that marriage

Then, opening their treasures, they presented to Him gifts of gold, frankincense, and
myrrh.
12 And having been [a]warned *by God* [b]in a
dream not to return to Herod, the magi left
for their own country by another way.

The Flight to Egypt

13 Now when they had gone, behold, an
[a]angel of the Lord *[b]appeared to Joseph in a
dream and said, "Get up! Take the Child and
His mother and flee to Egypt, and remain
there until I tell you; for Herod is going to
search for the Child to destroy Him."
14 So [1]Joseph got up and took the Child
and His mother while it was still night, and
left for Egypt.
15 He [1]remained there until the death of
Herod. *This was* to fulfill what had been spoken by the Lord through the prophet: "[a]OUT
OF EGYPT I CALLED [b]MY SON."

Herod Slaughters Babies

16 Then when Herod saw that he had
been tricked by [a]the magi, he became very
enraged, and sent and [b]slew all the male
children who were in Bethlehem and all its
vicinity, from two years old and under,
according to the time which he had determined from the magi.
17 Then what had been spoken through
Jeremiah the prophet was fulfilled:
18 "[a]A VOICE WAS HEARD IN RAMAH,
WEEPING AND GREAT MOURNING,
RACHEL WEEPING FOR HER CHILDREN;
AND SHE REFUSED TO BE COMFORTED,
BECAUSE THEY WERE NO MORE."
19 But when Herod died, behold, an angel
of the Lord *[a]appeared in a dream to Joseph
in Egypt, and said,
20 "Get up, take the Child and His mother,
and go into the land of Israel; for those who
sought the Child's life are dead."
21 So [1]Joseph got up, took the Child and
His mother, and came into the land of Israel.
22 But when he heard that Archelaus was
reigning over Judea in place of his father
Herod, he was afraid to go there. Then after
being [a]warned *by God* in a dream, he left for
the regions of Galilee,
23 and came and lived in a city called
[a]Nazareth. *This was* to fulfill what was spoken through the prophets: "He shall be
called a [b]Nazarene."

The Preaching of John the Baptist

3 Now [a]in those days [b]John the Baptist
*[1]came, [2]preaching in the [c]wilderness of
Judea, saying,
2 "[a]Repent, for [b]the kingdom of heaven
[1]is at hand."
3 For this is the [a]one referred to [1]by Isaiah the prophet when he said,
"[b]THE VOICE OF ONE [2]CRYING IN THE
WILDERNESS,
'[c]MAKE READY THE WAY OF THE LORD,
MAKE HIS PATHS STRAIGHT!' "
4 Now John himself had [1a]a garment of

[a]2 Kin 1:8; Zech 13:4; Matt 11:8; Mark 1:6 [b]Lev 11:22

12 [a]Matt 2:13, 19, 22; Luke 2:26; Acts 10:22; Heb 8:5; 11:7 [b]Job 33:15, 16; Matt 1:20
13 [a]Acts 5:19; 10:7; 12:7-11 [b]Matt 2:12, 19
14 [1]Lit *he*
15 [1]Lit *was* [a]Hos 11:1; Num 24:8 [b]Ex 4:22f
16 [a]Matt 2:1 [b]Is 59:7
18 [a]Jer 31:15
19 [a]Matt 1:20; 2:12, 13, 22
21 [1]Lit *he*
22 [a]Matt 2:12, 13, 19
23 [a]Luke 1:26; 2:39; John 1:45, 46 [b]Mark 1:24; John 18:5, 7; 19:19
3:1 [1]Or *arrived,* or *appeared* [2]Or *proclaiming as a herald* [a]Matt 3:1-12: *Mark 1:3-8; Luke 3:2-17;* John 1:6-8, 19-28 [b]Matt 11:11-14; 16:14 [c]Josh 15:61; Judg 1:16
2 [1]Lit *has come near* [a]Matt 4:17 [b]Dan 2:44; Matt 4:17, 23; 6:10; 10:7; Mark 1:15; Luke 10:9f; 11:20; 21:31
3 [1]Or *through* [2]Or *shouting* [a]Luke 1:17, 76 [b]Is 40:3 [c]John 1:23
4 [1]Lit *his garment*

Jesus and His mother are mentioned together, He is mentioned first (vv. 11,13–14,20–21). *gold, frankincense, and myrrh.* The three gifts perhaps gave rise to the legend that there were three "wise men." But the Bible does not indicate the number of the magi, and they were almost certainly not kings. *myrrh.* See note on Gen 37:25.

2:15 *the death of Herod.* In 4 B.C. *OUT OF EGYPT I CALLED MY SON.* This quotation from Hos 11:1 originally referred to God's calling the nation of Israel out of Egypt in the time of Moses. But Matthew, under the inspiration of the Spirit, applies it also to Jesus. He sees the history of Israel (God's children) recapitulated in the life of Jesus (God's unique Son). Just as Israel as an infant nation went down into Egypt, so the child Jesus went there. And as Israel was led by God out of Egypt, so also was Jesus. How long Jesus and His parents were in Egypt is not known.

2:16 *slew all the male children . . . two years old and under.* The number killed has often been exaggerated as being in the thousands. In so small a village as Bethlehem, however (even with the surrounding area included), the number was probably not large—though the act, of course, was no less brutal.

2:18 See note on Jer 31:15.

2:22 *Archelaus.* This son of Herod the Great ruled over Judea and Samaria for only ten years (4 B.C.-A.D. 6). He was unusually cruel and tyrannical and so was deposed. Judea then became a Roman province, administered by prefects appointed by the emperor. *Galilee.* The northern part of the Holy Land in Jesus' day.

2:23 *Nazareth.* A rather obscure town, nowhere mentioned in the OT. It was Jesus' hometown (21:11; 26:71; see Luke 2:39; 4:16–24; John 1:45–46). *He shall be called a Nazarene.* These exact words are not found in the OT and probably refer to several OT prefigurations and/or predictions (note the plural, "prophets") that the Messiah would be despised (e.g., Ps 22:6; Is 53:3), for in Jesus' day "Nazarene" was virtually a synonym for "despised" (see John 1:45–46). Some hold that in speaking of Jesus as a "Nazarene," Matthew is referring primarily to the word "branch" (Hebrew *neṣer*) in Is 11:1.

3:1 *John the Baptist.* The forerunner of Jesus, born c. 7 B.C. to Zacharias, a priest, and his wife Elizabeth (see Luke 1:5–80). *wilderness of Judea.* An area that stretched some 20 miles from the Jerusalem-Bethlehem plateau down to the Jordan River and the Dead Sea, perhaps the same region where John lived (cf. Luke 1:80). The people of Qumran (often associated with the Dead Sea Scrolls) lived in this area too.

3:2 *Repent.* Make a radical change in one's life as a whole. *the kingdom of heaven.* A phrase found only in Matthew, where it occurs 32 times. See Introduction: Recipients. Mark and Luke refer to "the kingdom of God," a term Matthew uses only four times (see note on Mark 11:30). The kingdom of heaven is the rule of God and is both a present reality and a future hope. The idea of God's kingdom is central to Jesus' teaching and is mentioned 50 times in Matthew alone.

3:3 All three Synoptic Gospels quote Is 40:3 (Luke quotes two additional verses) and apply it to John the Baptist. *MAKE HIS PATHS STRAIGHT!* Equivalent to "MAKE READY THE WAY OF THE LORD" (see note on Luke 3:4). The preparation was to be moral and spiritual.

camel's hair and a leather belt around his
waist; and his food was [b]locusts and wild
honey.
5 Then Jerusalem [a]was going out to him,
and all Judea and all [b]the district around the
Jordan;
6 and they were being [a]baptized by him
in the Jordan River, as they confessed their
sins.
7 But when he saw many of the [a]Pharisees and [b]Sadducees coming for baptism, he
said to them, "You [c]brood of vipers, who
warned you to flee from [d]the wrath to come?
8 "[a]Therefore bear fruit [b]in keeping with
repentance;
9 and do not suppose that you can say to
yourselves, '[a]We have Abraham for our
father'; for I say to you that from these
stones God is able to raise up children to
Abraham.
10 "The [a]axe is already laid at the root of
the trees; therefore [b]every tree that does not
bear good fruit is cut down and thrown into
the fire.

5 [a]Mark 1:5 [b]Luke 3:3
6 [a]Matt 3:11, 13-16; Mark 1:5; John 1:25, 26; 3:23; Acts 1:5; 2:38-41; 10:37
7 [a]Matt 16:1ff; 23:13, 15 [b]Matt 22:23; Acts 4:1; 5:17; 23:6ff [c]Matt 12:34; 23:33 [d]1 Thess 1:10
8 [a]Luke 3:8; Eph 5:8, 9 [b]Acts 26:20
9 [a]Luke 3:8; 16:24; John 8:33, 39, 53; Acts 13:26; Rom 4:1; 9:7, 8; Gal 3:29
10 [a]Luke 3:9 [b]Ps 92:12-14; Matt 7:19; John 15:2

3:4 *leather belt.* Used to bind up the loose outer garments. *locusts and wild honey.* A man living in the wilderness did not hesitate to eat insects, and locusts were among the clean foods (Lev 11:21–22). John's simple food, clothing and life-style were a visual protest against self-indulgence.
3:6 *Jordan River.* See note on Mark 1:5.
3:7 *Pharisees and Sadducees.* The Pharisees (see notes on Mark 2:16; Luke 5:17) were a legalistic and separatistic group who strictly, but often hypocritically, kept the law of Moses and the unwritten "tradition of the elders" (15:2). The Sadducees (see notes on Mark 12:18; Luke 20:27; Acts 4:1) were more worldly and politically minded, and were theologically unorthodox—among other things denying the resurrection, angels and spirits (Acts 23:8). *baptism.* See note on Mark 1:4. *the wrath to come.* The arrival of the Messiah will bring repentance or judgment.
3:9 *We have Abraham for our father.* See John 8:39. Salvation does not come as a birthright (even for the Jews) but through faith in Christ (Rom 2:28–29; Gal 3:7,9,29). *these stones.* John may have pointed to the stones in the Jordan River. *children to Abraham.* The true people of God are not limited to the physical descendants of Abraham (cf. Ro. 9:6)
3:10 *The axe is already laid at the root of the trees.* Judgment is near.

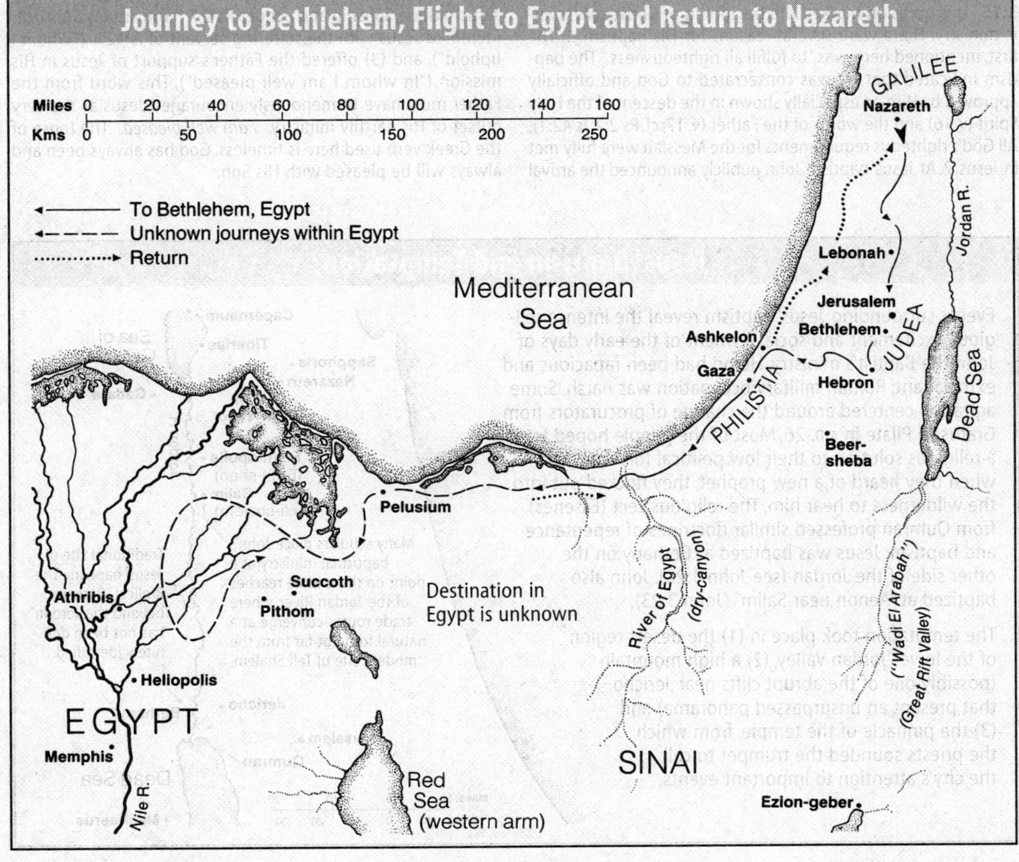
Journey to Bethlehem, Flight to Egypt and Return to Nazareth
Miles 0 20 40 60 80 100 120 140 160
Kms 0 50 100 150 200 250
To Bethlehem, Egypt
Unknown journeys within Egypt
Return
Mediterranean Sea
GALILEE
Nazareth
Jordan R.
Lebonah
Jerusalem
Bethlehem
Ashkelon
Gaza
JUDEA
Hebron
Dead Sea
PHILISTIA
Beer-sheba
Pelusium
Succoth
Pithom
Athribis
Heliopolis
Destination in Egypt is unknown
River of Egypt (dry-canyon)
("Wadi El Arabah") (Great Rift Valley)
EGYPT
Memphis
Nile R.
Red Sea (western arm)
SINAI
Ezion-geber

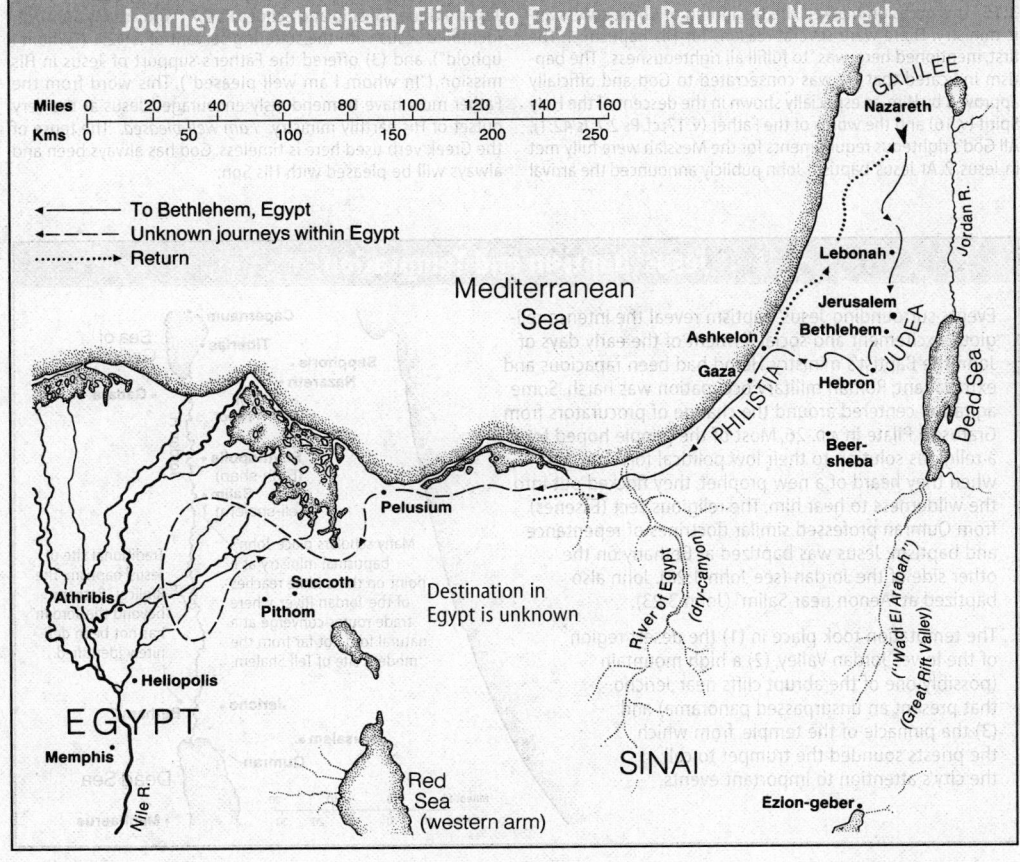

11 "As for me, [a]I baptize you [1]with water for repentance, but He who is coming after me is mightier than I, and I am not fit to remove His sandals; [b]He will baptize you [1]with the Holy Spirit and fire.

12 "His [a]winnowing fork is in His hand, and He will thoroughly clear His threshing floor; and He will [b]gather His wheat into the barn, but He will burn up the [c]chaff with [d]unquenchable fire."

The Baptism of Jesus

13 [a]Then Jesus *arrived [b]from Galilee at the Jordan *coming* to John, to be baptized by him.

14 But John tried to prevent Him, saying, "I have need to be baptized by You, and do You come to me?"

15 But Jesus answering said to him, "Permit *it* at this time; for in this way it is fitting for us [a]to fulfill all righteousness." Then he *permitted Him.

16 After being baptized, Jesus came up immediately from the water; and behold, the heavens were opened, and [1][a]he saw the Spirit of God descending as a dove *and* [2]lighting on Him,

17 and behold, a voice out of the heavens

11 [1]The Gr here can be translated *in, with* or *by* [a]Mark 1:4, 8; Luke 3:16; John 1:26f; Acts 1:5; 8:36, 38; 11:16 [b]John 1:33; Acts 2:3, 4; Titus 3:5 **12** [a]Is 30:24; 41:16; Jer 15:7; 51:2; Luke 3:17 [b]Matt 13:30 [c]Ps 1:4 [d]Is 66:24; Jer 7:20; Matt 13:41, 42; Mark 9:43, 48 **13** [a]Matt 3:13-17: *Mark 1:9-11; Luke 3:21, 22;* John 1:31-34 [b]Matt 2:22 **15** [a]Ps 40:7, 8; John 4:34; 8:29 **16** [1]Or *He* [2]Lit *coming upon Him* [a]Mark 1:10; Luke 3:22; John 1:32; Acts 7:56

3:11 *with water for repentance.* John's baptism presupposed repentance, and he would not baptize the Pharisees and Sadducees because they failed to give any evidence of repentance (vv. 7–8). *remove.* Mark (1:7) and Luke (3:16) have "untie." *with the Holy Spirit and fire.* Demonstrated in a dramatic way at Pentecost (Acts 1:5,8; 2:1–13; 11:16), though here "fire" may refer to judgment to come (see v. 12). The outpouring of the Holy Spirit on all God's people was promised in Joel 2:28–29.

3:12 *His winnowing fork.* For the process of winnowing see note on Ruth 1:22. Here it is figurative for the day of judgment at Christ's second coming. The OT prophets and NT writers sometimes compress the first and second comings of Christ so that they seem to be one event.

3:15 This occasion marked the beginning of Christ's Messianic ministry. There were several reasons for His baptism: 1. The first, mentioned here, was "to fulfill all righteousness." The baptism indicated that He was consecrated to God and officially approved by Him, as especially shown in the descent of the Holy Spirit (v. 16) and the words of the Father (v. 17; cf. Ps 2:7; Is 42:1). All God's righteous requirements for the Messiah were fully met in Jesus. 2. At Jesus' baptism John publicly announced the arrival of the Messiah and the inception of His ministry (John 1:31–34). 3. By His baptism Jesus completely identified Himself with man's sin and failure (though He Himself needed no repentance or cleansing from sin), becoming our substitute (2 Cor 5:21). 4. His baptism was an example to His followers.

3:16–17 All three persons of the Trinity are clearly seen here.

3:16 *Spirit of God.* The Holy Spirit came upon Jesus not to overcome sin (for He was sinless), but to equip Him (see note on Judg 3:10) for His work as the divine-human Messiah. *as a dove.* Either in the form of a dove or in a descent like a dove. See also note on Mark 1:10.

3:17 *a voice out of the heavens.* The voice (1) authenticated Jesus' unique Sonship and echoes Ps 2:7 ("You are My Son"), (2) identified Jesus with the suffering servant of Is 42:1 ("Whom I uphold"), and (3) offered the Father's support of Jesus in His mission ("In whom I am well pleased"). This word from the Father must have tremendously encouraged Jesus at the very outset of His earthly ministry. *I am well-pleased.* The tense of the Greek verb used here is timeless. God has always been and always will be pleased with His Son.

Jesus' Baptism and Temptation

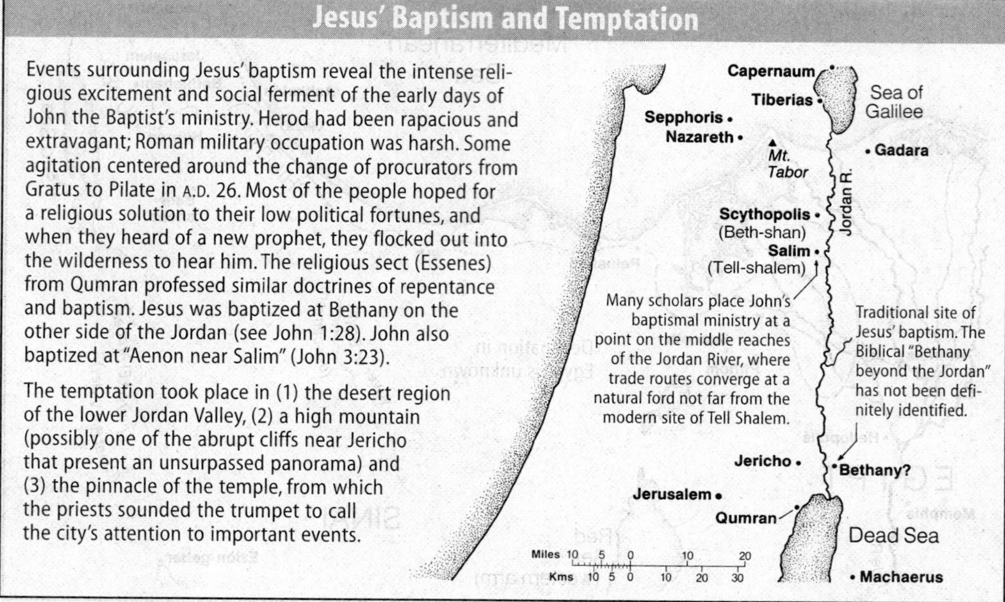

Capernaum
Tiberias
Sea of Galilee
Sepphoris
Nazareth
Mt. Tabor
Gadara
Jordan R.
Scythopolis (Beth-shan)
Salim (Tell-shalem)
Many scholars place John's baptismal ministry at a point on the middle reaches of the Jordan River, where trade routes converge at a natural ford not far from the modern site of Tell Shalem.
Traditional site of Jesus' baptism. The Biblical "Bethany beyond the Jordan" has not been definitely identified.
Jericho
Bethany?
Jerusalem
Qumran
Dead Sea
Machaerus
Miles 10 5 0 10 20
Kms 10 5 0 10 20 30

Events surrounding Jesus' baptism reveal the intense religious excitement and social ferment of the early days of John the Baptist's ministry. Herod had been rapacious and extravagant; Roman military occupation was harsh. Some agitation centered around the change of procurators from Gratus to Pilate in A.D. 26. Most of the people hoped for a religious solution to their low political fortunes, and when they heard of a new prophet, they flocked out into the wilderness to hear him. The religious sect (Essenes) from Qumran professed similar doctrines of repentance and baptism. Jesus was baptized at Bethany on the other side of the Jordan (see John 1:28). John also baptized at "Aenon near Salim" (John 3:23).

The temptation took place in (1) the desert region of the lower Jordan Valley, (2) a high mountain (possibly one of the abrupt cliffs near Jericho that present an unsurpassed panorama) and (3) the pinnacle of the temple, from which the priests sounded the trumpet to call the city's attention to important events.

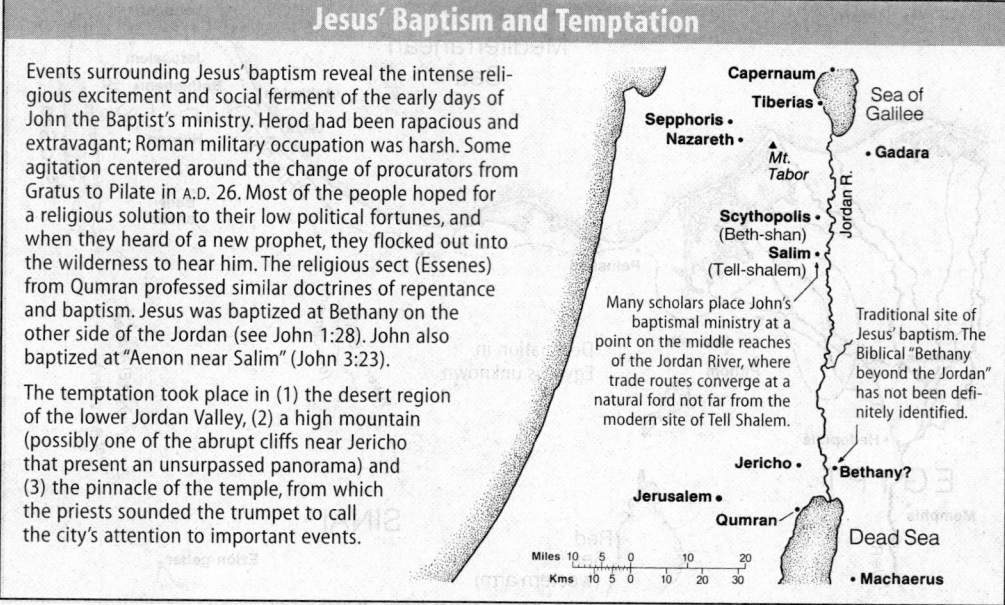

said, "[a]This is [1]My beloved Son, in whom I am well-pleased."

The Temptation of Jesus

4 [a]Then Jesus was led up by the Spirit into
the wilderness [b]to be tempted by the
devil.
2 And after He had [a]fasted forty days and
forty nights, He [1]then became hungry.
3 And [a]the tempter came and said to
Him, "If You are the [b]Son of God, command
that these stones become bread."
4 But He answered and said, "It is written,
'[a]MAN SHALL NOT LIVE ON BREAD ALONE, BUT
ON EVERY WORD THAT PROCEEDS OUT OF THE
MOUTH OF GOD.'"
5 Then the devil *took Him into [a]the
holy city and had Him stand on the pinnacle
of the temple,
6 and *said to Him, "If You are the Son of
God, throw Yourself down; for it is written,

'[a]HE WILL COMMAND HIS ANGELS
CONCERNING YOU';

and

'ON *their* HANDS THEY WILL BEAR YOU UP,
SO THAT YOU WILL NOT STRIKE YOUR FOOT
AGAINST A STONE.'"

7 Jesus said to him, "[1]On the other hand,
it is written, '[a]YOU SHALL NOT PUT THE LORD
YOUR GOD TO THE TEST.'"
8 [a]Again, the devil *took Him to a very
high mountain and *showed Him all the
kingdoms of the world and their glory;
9 and he said to Him, "[a]All these things I
will give You, if You fall down and [1]worship
me."
10 Then Jesus *said to him, "Go, Satan!
For it is written, '[a]YOU SHALL WORSHIP THE
LORD YOUR GOD, AND [1]SERVE HIM ONLY.'"
11 Then the devil *left Him; and behold,
[a]angels came and *began* to minister to Him.

Jesus Begins His Ministry

12 Now when Jesus heard that [a]John had
been taken into custody, [b]He withdrew into
Galilee;
13 and leaving Nazareth, He came and
[a]settled in Capernaum, which is by the sea,
in the region of Zebulun and Naphtali.
14 *This was* to fulfill what was spoken
through Isaiah the prophet:

17 [1]Or *My Son, the Beloved* [a]Ps 2:7; Is 42:1; Matt 12:18; 17:5; Mark 9:7; Luke 9:35; John 12:28
4:1 [a]Matt 4:1-11: *Mark 1:12, 13; Luke 4:1-13* [b]Heb 4:15; James 1:14
2 [1]Lit *later became;* or *afterward became* [a]Ex 34:28; 1 Kin 19:8
3 [a]1 Thess 3:5 [b]Matt 14:33; 26:63; Mark 3:11; 5:7; Luke 1:35; 4:41; John 1:34, 49; Acts 9:20
4 [a]Deut 8:3
5 [a]Neh 11:1, 18; Dan 9:24; Matt 27:53
6 [a]Ps 91:11, 12
7 [1]Lit *Again* [a]Deut 6:16
8 [a]Matt 16:26; 1 John 2:15-17
9 [1]Lit *prostrate Yourself* [a]1 Cor 10:20f
10 [1]Or *fulfill religious duty to Him* [a]Deut 6:13; 10:20
11 [a]Matt 26:53; Luke 22:43; Heb 1:14
12 [a]Matt 14:3; Mark 1:14; Luke 3:20; John 3:24 [b]Mark 1:14; Luke 4:14; John 1:43; 2:11
13 [a]Matt 11:23; Mark 1:21; 2:1; Luke 4:23, 31; John 2:12; 4:46f

4:1–11 The significance of Jesus' temptations, especially because they occurred at the outset of His public ministry, seems best understood in terms of the kind of Messiah He was to be. He would not accomplish His mission by using His supernatural power for His own needs (first temptation), by using His power to win a large following by miracles or magic (second temptation) or by compromising with Satan (third temptation). Jesus had no inward desire or inclination to sin, for these in themselves are sin (Matt 5:22,28). Because He was God He did not sin in any way, whether by actions or word or inner desire (2 Cor 5:21; Heb 7:26; 1 Pet 2:22; 1 John 3:5). Yet Jesus' temptation was real, not merely symbolic. He was "tempted in all things as we are, yet without sin" (Heb 4:15). He was confronted by the tempter with a real opportunity to sin. Although Jesus was the Son of God, He defeated Satan by using a weapon that everyone has at his or her disposal: the sword of the Spirit, which is the word of God (Eph 6:17). He met all three temptations with Scriptural truth (vv. 4,7,10) from Deuteronomy.

4:1 *led up by the Spirit . . . to be tempted.* This testing of Jesus (the Greek verb translated "tempted" can also be rendered "tested"), which was divinely intended, has as its primary background Deut 8:1–5, from which Jesus also quotes in His first reply to the devil (see v. 4 and text note). There Moses recalls how the Lord led the Israelites in the wilderness 40 years "that He might humble you, testing you, to know what was in your heart, whether you would keep His commandments or not." Here at the beginning of His ministry Jesus is subjected to a similar test and shows himself to be the true Israelite who lives "by everything that proceeds out of the mouth of the LORD." And whereas Adam failed the great test and plunged the whole race into sin (Gen 3), Jesus was faithful and thus demonstrated His qualification to become the Savior of all who receive Him. It was, moreover, important that Jesus be tested/tempted as Israel and we are, so that He could become our "merciful and faithful high priest" (Heb 2:17) and thus be "able to come to the aid of those who are tempted" (Heb 2:18; see Heb 4:15–16). Finally, as the one who remained faithful in temptation He became the model for all believers when they are tempted. *tempted by the devil.* God surely tests His people, but it is the devil who tempts to evil (see note on Gen 22:1; see also 1 John 3:8; Rev 2:9–10 and notes; Rev 12:9–10). Like the Hebrew for "Satan," the Greek for "devil" means "accuser" or "slanderer." The devil is a personal being, not a mere force or influence. He is the great archenemy of God and the leader of the hosts of darkness.

4:2 *forty days and forty nights.* The number recalls the experiences of Moses (Ex 24:18; 34:28) and Elijah (1 Kin 19:8), as well as the 40 years of Israel's temptation (testing) in the wilderness (Deut 8:2–3).

4:3 *If You are the Son of God.* Meaning "Since You are." The devil is not casting doubt on Jesus' divine sonship, but is tempting Him to use His supernatural powers as the Son of God for His own ends.

4:4 Just as God gave the Israelites manna in a supernatural way (Deut 8:3), so also man must rely on God for spiritual feeding. Jesus relied on His Father, not His own miracle power, for provision of food.

4:5 See note on Luke 4:2. *pinnacle of the temple.* See note on Luke 4:9. *temple.* The temple, including the entire temple area, had been rebuilt by Herod the Great (see note on 2:1; see also John 2:20). The courtyard had been greatly enlarged, to about 330 by 500 yards. To accomplish this a huge platform had been erected to compensate for the sharp falling off of the land to the southeast. An enormous retaining wall made of massive stones was built to support the platform. On the platform stood the temple building, porches and courtyards flanked by beautiful colonnades.

4:10 *Satan.* See note on v. 1.

4:12 See map No. 9 at the end of the study Bible. *John had been taken into custody.* See Mark 1:14 and note on Luke 3:20. The reason for John's imprisonment is given in 14:3–4.

4:13 *Capernaum.* Although not mentioned in the OT, it was evidently a sizable town in Jesus' day. Peter's house there became Jesus' base of operations during His extended ministry in Galilee (see Mark 2:1; 9:33). A fifth-century basilica now stands over the supposed site of Peter's house, and a fourth-century synagogue is located a short distance from it.

15 "[a]THE LAND OF ZEBULUN AND THE LAND OF
NAPHTALI,
[1]BY THE WAY OF THE SEA, BEYOND THE
JORDAN, GALILEE OF THE [2]GENTILES—
16 "[a]THE PEOPLE WHO WERE SITTING IN
DARKNESS SAW A GREAT LIGHT,
AND THOSE WHO WERE SITTING IN THE
LAND AND SHADOW OF DEATH,
UPON THEM A LIGHT DAWNED."
17 [a]From that time Jesus began to [1]preach
and say, "[b]Repent, for the kingdom of heav-
en is at hand."

The First Disciples

18 [a]Now as Jesus was walking by [b]the Sea
of Galilee, He saw two brothers, [c]Simon who
was called Peter, and Andrew his brother,
casting a net into the sea; for they were fishermen.
19 And He *said to them, "[1]Follow Me,
and I will make you fishers of men."
20 Immediately they left their nets and followed Him.

15 [1]Or *Toward the sea* [2]Lit *nations*, usually non-Jewish [a]Is 9:1
16 [a]Is 9:2; 60:1-3; Luke 2:32
17 [1]Or *proclaim* [a]Mark 1:14, 15 [b]Matt 3:2
18 [a]Matt 4:18-22: *Mark 1:16-20;* Luke 5:2-11; John 1:40-42 [b]Matt 15:29; Mark 7:31; Luke 5:1; John 6:1 [c]Matt 10:2; 16:18; John 1:40-42
19 [1]Lit *Come here after Me*

4:15–16 Another Messianic prophecy from Isaiah. Jesus spent most of His public ministry "in the region of Zebulun and Naphtali" (v. 13), which is north and west of the Sea of Galilee.
4:17 *From that time.* These words indicate an important turning point in the life of Jesus and occur three times in Matthew's Gospel (see also 16:21; 26:16, "From then on"). Some think these words mark the three main sections of the book. *Repent.* Jesus began His public ministry with the same message as that of John the Baptist (3:2). The people must repent because God's reign was drawing near in the person and ministry of Jesus Christ. Repentance is more than a change of mind or feeling sorry for one's sins. It is a radical and deliberate turning or returning to God that results in moral and ethical change and action. *kingdom of heaven.* See note on 3:2.
4:18 *Sea of Galilee.* See note on Mark 1:16. *net.* A circular casting net used either from a boat or while standing in shallow water.
4:19 *fishers of men.* Evangelism was at the heart of Jesus' call to His disciples.
4:20 See note on Mark 1:17.

Herod's Temple

20 B.C.–A.D. 70

Begun in 20 B.C., Herod's new structure towered 15 stories high, following the floor dimensions of the former temples in the Holy Place and the Most Holy Place. The high sanctuary shown here in a cutaway view was built on the site of the former temples of Solomon and Zerubbabel, and was completed in just 18 months.

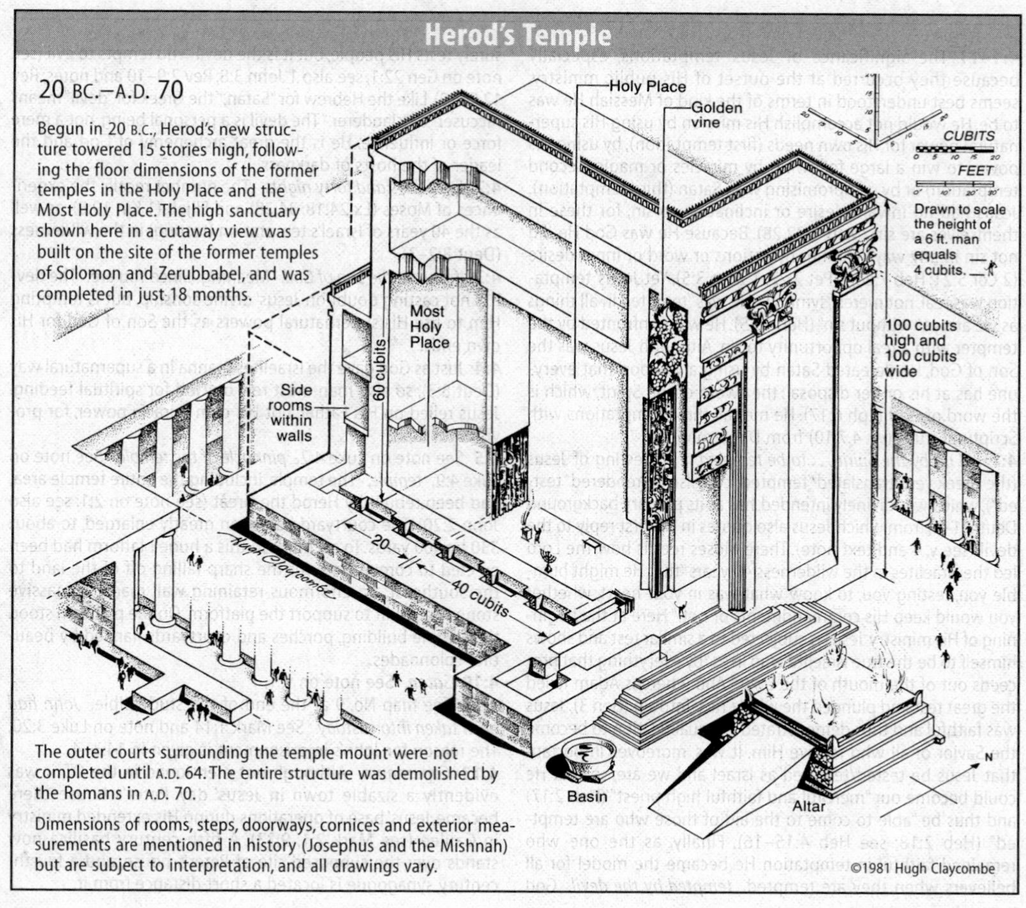

Holy Place
Golden vine
CUBITS
FEET
Drawn to scale the height of a 6 ft. man equals 4 cubits.
100 cubits high and 100 cubits wide
Most Holy Place
60 cubits
Side rooms within walls
20
40 cubits
Hugh Claycombe
Basin
Altar
N

The outer courts surrounding the temple mount were not completed until A.D. 64. The entire structure was demolished by the Romans in A.D. 70.

Dimensions of rooms, steps, doorways, cornices and exterior measurements are mentioned in history (Josephus and the Mishnah) but are subject to interpretation, and all drawings vary.

©1981 Hugh Claycombe

21 Going on from there He saw two other
brothers, [1a]James the *son* of Zebedee, and
[2]John his brother, in the boat with Zebedee
their father, mending their nets; and He
called them.
22 Immediately they left the boat and their
father, and followed Him.

Ministry in Galilee

23 Jesus was going [a]throughout all Galilee, [b]teaching in their synagogues and [c]pro-
claiming the [1]gospel of the kingdom, and
[d]healing every kind of disease and every
kind of sickness among the people.
24 The news about Him spread [a]through-
out all Syria; and they brought to Him all
who were ill, those suffering with various
diseases and pains, [b]demoniacs, [1c]epileptics,
[d]paralytics; and He healed them.
25 Large crowds [a]followed Him from Galilee and [b]*the* Decapolis and Jerusalem and
Judea and *from* [c]beyond the Jordan.

The Sermon on the Mount; The Beatitudes

5 [a]When Jesus saw the crowds, He went up
on [b]the [1]mountain; and after He sat
down, His disciples came to Him.
2 [a]He opened His mouth and *began* to
teach them, saying,

21 [1]Or *Jacob;* James is the Eng form of Jacob [2]Gr *Joannes,* Heb *Johanan* [a]Matt 10:2; 20:20
23 [1]Or *good news* [a]Mark 1:39; Luke 4:14, 44 [b]Matt 9:35; 13:54; Mark 1:21; 6:2; 10:1; Luke 4:15; 6:6; 13:10; John 6:59; 18:20 [c]Matt 3:2; 9:35; 24:14; Mark 1:14; Luke 4:43; 8:1; 16:16; Acts 20:25; 28:31 [d]Matt 8:16; 9:35; 14:14; 15:30; 19:2; 21:14; Mark 1:34; 3:10; Luke 4:40; 7:21; Acts 10:38
24 [1]Lit *moonstruck* [a]Mark 7:26; Luke 2:2; Acts 15:23; 18:18; 20:3; 21:3; Gal 1:21 [b]Matt 8:16, 28, 33; 9:32; 12:22; 15:22; Mark 1:32; 5:15, 16, 18; Luke 8:36; John 10:21 [c]Matt 17:15 [d]Matt 8:6; 9:2, 6; Mark 2:3-5, 9; Luke 5:24

3 "[1a]Blessed are the [2]poor in spirit, for
[b]theirs is the kingdom of heaven.
4 "Blessed are [a]those who mourn, for they
shall be comforted.
5 "Blessed are [a]the [1]gentle, for they shall
inherit the earth.
6 "Blessed are [a]those who hunger and
thirst for righteousness, for they shall be satisfied.
7 "Blessed are [a]the merciful, for they shall
receive mercy.
8 "Blessed are [a]the pure in heart, for [b]they
shall see God.
9 "Blessed are the peacemakers, for [a]they
shall be called sons of God.
10 "Blessed are those who have been [a]per-
secuted for the sake of righteousness, for
[b]theirs is the kingdom of heaven.
11 "Blessed are you when *people* [a]insult
you and persecute you, and falsely say all
kinds of evil against you because of Me.

25 [a]Mark 3:7, 8; Luke 6:17 [b]Mark 5:20; 7:31 [c]Matt 4:15
5:1 [1]Or *hill* [a]Matt ch 5-7; Luke 6:20-49 [b]Mark 3:13; Luke 6:17; 9:28; John 6:3, 15 2 [a]Matt 13:35; Acts 8:35; 10:34; 18:14
3 [1]I.e. fortunate or prosperous, and so through v 11 [2]I.e. those who are not spiritually arrogant [a]Matt 5:3-12; Luke 6:20-23 [b]Matt 5:10; 19:14; 25:34; Mark 10:14; Luke 6:20; 22:29f 4 [a]Is 61:2; John 16:20; Rev 7:17 5 [1]Or *humble, meek* [a]Ps 37:11 6 [a]Is 55:1, 2; John 4:14; 6:48ff; 7:37 7 [a]Prov 11:17; Matt 6:14, 15; 18:33-35 8 [a]Ps 24:4 [b]Heb 12:14; 1 John 3:2; Rev 22:4
9 [a]Matt 5:45; Luke 6:35; Rom 8:14 10 [a]1 Pet 3:14 [b]Matt 5:3; 19:14; 25:34; Mark 10:14; Luke 6:20; 22:29f 11 [a]1 Pet 4:14

4:21 *mending their nets.* Washing, mending and hanging the nets up to dry in preparation for the next day's work.
4:23 *teaching . . . proclaiming . . . healing.* Jesus' threefold ministry. The synagogues (see note on Mark 1:21) provided a place for Him to teach on the Sabbath. During the week He preached to larger crowds in the open air. *gospel.* See note on Mark 1:1.
4:24 *Syria.* The area north of Galilee and between Damascus and the Mediterranean Sea. *epileptics.* The Greek word for this expression originally meant "moonstruck" and reflects the ancient superstition that seizures were caused by changes of the moon. *paralytics.* A transliteration of the Greek that has come directly into English. Greek physicians were among the best in ancient times, and many of our medical terms come from their language.
4:25 *the Decapolis.* A league of free cities (Decapolis means "the Ten Cities") characterized by high Greek culture. All but one, Scythopolis (Beth Shan), were east of the Sea of Galilee and the Jordan River. The league stretched from a point northeast of the Sea of Galilee southward to Philadelphia (modern Amman).
5:1–7:29 The Sermon on the Mount is the first of five great discourses in Matthew (chs. 5–7; 10; 13; 18; 24–25). It contains three types of material: (1) beatitudes, i.e., declarations of blessedness (5:1–12), (2) ethical admonitions (5:13–20; 6:1–7:23) and (3) contrasts between Jesus' ethical teaching and Jewish legalistic traditions (5:21–48). The Sermon ends with a short parable stressing the importance of practicing what has just been taught (7:24–27) and an expression of amazement by the crowds at the authority with which Jesus spoke (7:28–29).
Opinion differs as to whether the Sermon is a summary of what Jesus taught on one occasion or a compilation of teachings presented on numerous occasions. Matthew possibly took a single sermon and expanded it with other relevant teachings of Jesus. Thirty-four of the verses in Matthew's Sermon occur in different contexts in Luke than the apparently parallel Sermon on the Plain (Luke 6:17–49).
The Sermon on the Mount's call to moral and ethical living is so high that some have dismissed it as being completely unrealistic or have projected its fulfillment to the future kingdom. There is no doubt, however, that Jesus (and Matthew) gave the Sermon as a standard for all Christians, realizing that its demands cannot be met in our own power. It is also true that Jesus occasionally used hyperbole to make His point (see, e.g., note on 5:29–30).
5:1 *mountain.* The exact location is uncertain. It may have been the gently sloping hillside at the northwest corner of the Sea of Galilee, not far from Capernaum (see note on Luke 6:20–49). The new law, like the old (Ex 19:3), was given from a mountain. *sat down.* It was the custom for Jewish rabbis to be seated while teaching (see Mark 4:1; 9:35; Luke 4:20; 5:3; John 8:2). *disciples.* Lit. "learners." Since at the end of the Sermon the "crowds" expressed amazement at Jesus' teaching (7:28), "disciples" may here be used in a broader sense than the Twelve. Or perhaps the Sermon is addressed to the Twelve with the crowds also listening.
5:3 *Blessed.* The word means more than "happy," because happiness is an emotion often dependent on outward circumstances. "Blessed" here refers to the ultimate well-being and distinctive spiritual joy of those who share in the salvation of the kingdom of God. See notes on Ps 1:1; Rev 1:3. *poor in spirit.* In contrast to the spiritually proud and self-sufficient. *theirs is the kingdom of heaven.* The kingdom is not something earned. It is more a gift than a recompense.
5:5 *gentle.* This beatitude is taken from Ps 37:11 and refers not so much to an attitude toward people as to a disposition before God, namely, humility. *the earth.* The new promised land (cf. Rev 21:1).
5:8 *heart.* The center of one's being, including mind, will and emotions (see note on Ps 4:7).
5:9 *peacemakers.* Those who promote peace, as far as it depends on them (Rom 12:18). In so doing, they reflect the character of their heavenly Father and so are called "sons of God."
5:10 *theirs is the kingdom of heaven.* A present reality as well as a future hope.

12 "Rejoice and be glad, for your reward in
heaven is great; for [a]in the same way they
persecuted the prophets who were before you.

Disciples and the World

13 "You are the salt of the earth; but [a]if the
salt has become tasteless, how [1]can it be
made salty *again*? It is no longer good for
anything, except to be thrown out and trampled under foot by men.
14 "You are [a]the light of the world. A city
set on a [1]hill cannot be hidden;
15 [a]nor does *anyone* light a lamp and put
it under a [1]basket, but on the lampstand,
and it gives light to all who are in the house.
16 "Let your light shine before men in such
a way that they may [a]see your good works,
and [b]glorify your Father who is in heaven.
17 "Do not think that I came to abolish the
[a]Law or the Prophets; I did not come to abolish but to fulfill.
18 "For truly I say to you, [a]until heaven
and earth pass away, not [1]the smallest letter
or stroke shall pass from the Law until all is
accomplished.
19 "Whoever then annuls one of the least
of these commandments, and teaches [1]oth-
ers *to do* the same, shall be called least [a]in
the kingdom of heaven; but whoever [2]keeps
and teaches *them*, he shall be called great in
the kingdom of heaven.
20 "For I say to you that unless your [a]righ-
teousness surpasses *that* of the scribes and
Pharisees, you will not enter the kingdom of
heaven.

Personal Relationships

21 "[a]You have heard that [1]the ancients
were told, '[b]YOU SHALL NOT COMMIT MURDER'
and 'Whoever commits murder shall be
[2]liable to [c]the court.'
22 "But I say to you that everyone who is
angry with his brother shall be [1]guilty before
[a]the court; and whoever says to his brother,
'[2]You good-for-nothing,' shall be [1]guilty
before [3b]the supreme court; and whoever
says, 'You fool,' shall be [1]guilty *enough to go*
into the [4c]fiery hell.
23 "Therefore if you are [a]presenting your
[1]offering at the altar, and there remember
that your brother has something against you,
24 leave your [1]offering there before the
altar and go; first be [a]reconciled to your
brother, and then come and present your
[1]offering.
25 "[a]Make friends quickly with your opponent at law while you are with him on the
way, so that your opponent may not hand
you over to the judge, and the judge to the
officer, and you be thrown into prison.
26 "Truly I say to you, [a]you will not come
out of there until you have paid up the last
[1]cent.
27 "[a]You have heard that it was said, '[b]YOU
SHALL NOT COMMIT ADULTERY';
28 but I say to you that everyone who

12 [a]2 Chr 36:16; Matt 23:37; Acts 7:52; 1 Thess 2:15; Heb 11:33ff; James 5:10 **13** [1]Lit *will* [a]Mark 9:50; Luke 14:34f **14** [1]Or *mountain* [a]Prov 4:18; John 8:12; 9:5; 12:36 **15** [1]Or *peck-measure* [a]Mark 4:21; Luke 8:16; 11:33; Phil 2:15 **16** [a]1 Pet 2:12 [b]Matt 9:8 **17** [a]Matt 7:12 **18** [1]Lit *one iota* (Heb yodh) or *one projection of a letter* (serif) [a]Matt 24:35; Luke 16:17 **19** [1]Gr *anthropoi* [2]Lit *does* [a]Matt 11:11 **20** [a]Luke 18:11, 12

21 [1]Lit *it was said to the ancients* [2]Or *guilty before* [a]Matt 5:27, 33, 38, 43 [b]Ex 20:13; Deut 5:17 [c]Deut 16:18; 2 Chr 19:5f **22** [1]Or *liable to* [2]Or *empty-head;* Gr *Raka (Raca)* fr Aram *reqa* [3]Lit *the Sanhedrin* [4]Lit *Gehenna of fire* [a]Deut 16:18; 2 Chr 19:5f [b]Matt 10:17; 26:59; Mark 13:9; 14:55; 15:1; Luke 22:66; John 11:47; Acts 4:15; 5:21; 6:12; 22:30; 23:1; 24:20 [c]Matt 5:29f; 10:28; 18:9; 23:15, 33; Mark 9:43ff; Luke 12:5; James 3:6 **23** [1]Or *gift* [a]Matt 5:24 **24** [1]Or *gift* [a]Rom 12:17, 18 **25** [a]Prov 25:8f; Luke 12:58 **26** [1]Lit *quadrans* (equaling two mites); i.e. 1/64 of a daily wage [a]Luke 12:59 **27** [a]Matt 5:21, 33, 38, 43 [b]Ex 20:14; Deut 5:18

5:13 *salt.* Used for flavoring and preserving. *has become tasteless.* Most of the salt used in Israel came from the Dead Sea and was full of impurities. This caused it to lose some of its flavor.
5:15 *lamp.* In Jesus' day people used small clay lamps that burned olive oil drawn up by a wick (see note on Ex 25:37). *basket.* A bowl that held about 8 quarts of ground meal or flour.
5:16 *Father who is in heaven.* Matthew uses the term "Father who is in heaven" or "heavenly Father" 19 times, Mark twice, Luke once, and John not at all.
5:17 *the Law.* The first five books of the Jewish Scriptures (our OT). *the Prophets.* Not only the Latter Prophets—Isaiah, Jeremiah and Ezekiel, which we call Major Prophets, and the 12 Minor Prophets (lumped together by the Jews as "the Book of the Twelve")—but also the so-called Former Prophets (Joshua, Judges, Samuel and Kings). Taken together, "the Law" and "the Prophets" designated the entire OT, including the Writings, the third section of the Hebrew Bible. See 13:35, where Matthew introduces a quotation from the Writings (Ps 78:2) with "what was spoken through the prophet." *fulfill.* Jesus fulfilled the Law in the sense that He gave it its full meaning. He emphasized its deep, underlying principles and total commitment to it rather than mere external acknowledgment and obedience.
5:18–20 Jesus is not speaking against observing all the requirements of the Law, but against hypocritical, Pharisaical legalism. Such legalism was not the keeping of all details of the Law but the hollow sham of keeping laws externally, to gain merit before God, while breaking them inwardly. It was following the letter of the Law while ignoring its spirit. Jesus repudiates the Pharisees' interpretation of the Law and their view of righteousness by works. He preaches a righteousness that comes only through faith in Him and His work. In the verses that follow, He gives six examples of Pharisaical externalism.
5:18 *smallest letter.* One word in Greek (*iota*), which we use when we say, "It doesn't make one iota of difference." It is the nearest Greek equivalent to the Hebrew *yodh,* the smallest letter of the Hebrew alphabet (see Ps 119:73 title). *stroke.* The Greek word means "horn" and was used to designate the slight embellishment or extension of certain letters of the Hebrew alphabet (somewhat like the bottom of a "j").
5:21 *the ancients were told.* The contrast that Jesus sets up (vv. 21,27,31,33,38,43) is not between the OT and His teaching (He has just established the validity of the OT Law). Rather, it is between externalistic interpretation of the rabbinic tradition on the one hand, and Jesus' correct interpretation of the Law on the other. *murder.* Several Hebrew and Greek verbs mean "kill." The ones used here and in Ex 20:13 specifically mean "murder."
5:22 *You good-for-nothing.* This phrase may be related to the Aramaic word for "empty" and mean "Empty-head!" *supreme court.* See note on Mark 14:55. *hell.* The Greek word is *ge(h)enna,* which derives its name from a deep ravine south of Jerusalem, the "Valley of (the Sons of) Hinnom" (Hebrew *ge hinnom*). During the reigns of the wicked Ahaz and Manasseh, human sacrifices to the Ammonite god Molech were offered there. Josiah desecrated the valley because of the pagan worship there (2 Kin 23:10; see Jer 7:31–32; 19:6). It became a sort of perpetually burning city dump and later a figure for the place of final punishment.
5:23–26 Two illustrations of dealing with anger by means of reconciliation.
5:26 *cent.* The smallest Roman copper coin.

looks at a woman [a]with lust for her has already committed adultery with her in his heart.

29 "[a]If your right eye makes you [1]stumble, tear it out and throw it from you; for it is better for you [2]to lose one of the parts of your body, [3]than for your whole body to be thrown into [4][b]hell.

30 "[a]If your right hand makes you [1]stumble, cut it off and throw it from you; for it is better for you [2]to lose one of the parts of your body, [3]than for your whole body to go into [4][b]hell.

31 "It was said, '[a]WHOEVER SENDS HIS WIFE AWAY, LET HIM GIVE HER A CERTIFICATE OF DIVORCE';

32 [a]but I say to you that everyone who [1]divorces his wife, except for *the* reason of unchastity, makes her commit adultery; and whoever marries a [2]divorced woman commits adultery.

33 "Again, [a]you have heard that [1]the ancients were told, '[2][b]YOU SHALL NOT [3]MAKE FALSE VOWS, BUT SHALL FULFILL YOUR [4]VOWS TO THE LORD.'

34 "But I say to you, [a]make no oath at all, either by heaven, for it is [b]the throne of God,

35 or by the earth, for it is the [a]footstool of His feet, or [1]by Jerusalem, for it is [b]THE CITY OF THE GREAT KING.

36 "Nor shall you make an oath by your head, for you cannot make one hair white or black.

37 "But let your statement be, 'Yes, yes' *or* 'No, no'; anything beyond these is [1]of [a]evil.

38 "[a]You have heard that it was said, '[b]AN EYE FOR AN EYE, AND A TOOTH FOR A TOOTH.'

39 "But I say to you, do not resist an evil person; but [a]whoever slaps you on your right cheek, turn the other to him also.

28 [a]2 Sam 11:2-5; Job 31:1; Matt 15:19; James 1:14, 15
29 [1]I.e. sin [2]Lit *that one...be lost* [3]Lit *not your whole body* [4]Gr *Gehenna* [a]Matt 18:9; Mark 9:47 [b]Matt 5:22
30 [1]I.e. sin [2]Lit *that one...be lost* [3]Lit *not your whole body* [4]Gr *Gehenna* [a]Matt 18:8; Mark 9:43 [b]Matt 5:22
31 [a]Deut 24:1, 3; Jer 3:1; Matt 19:7; Mark 10:4
32 [1]Or *sends away* [2]Or *sent away* [a]Matt 19:9; Mark 10:11f; Luke 16:18; 1 Cor 7:11f
33 [1]Lit *it was said to the ancients* [2]*you* and *your* are singular here [3]Or *break your vows* [4]Lit *oaths* [a]Matt 5:21, 27, 38, 43; 23:16ff [b]Lev 19:12; Num 30:2; Deut 23:21, 23
34 [a]James 5:12 [b]Is 66:1; Matt 23:22
35 [1]Or *toward* [a]Is 66:1; Acts 7:49 [b]Ps 48:2
37 [1]Or *from the evil one* [a]Matt 6:13; 13:19, 38; John 17:15; 2 Thess 3:3; 1 John 2:13f; 3:12; 5:18f
38 [a]Matt 5:21, 27, 33, 43 [b]Ex 21:24; Lev 24:20; Deut 19:21
39 [a]Matt 5:39-42: *Luke 6:29, 30;*1 Cor 6:7

40 "If anyone wants to sue you and take your [1]shirt, let him have your [2]coat also.

41 "Whoever [1]forces you to go one mile, go with him two.

42 "[a]Give to him who asks of you, and do not turn away from him who wants to borrow from you.

43 "[a]You have heard that it was said, '[b]YOU SHALL LOVE YOUR NEIGHBOR [c]and hate your enemy.'

44 "But I say to you, [a]love your enemies and pray for those who persecute you,

45 so that you may [1]be [a]sons of your Father who is in heaven; for He causes His sun to rise on *the* evil and *the* good, and sends rain on *the* righteous and *the* unrighteous.

46 "For [a]if you love those who love you, what reward do you have? Do not even the tax collectors do the same?

47 "If you greet only your brothers, what more are you doing *than others?* Do not even the Gentiles do the same?

48 "Therefore [1][a]you are to be perfect, as your heavenly Father is perfect.

Giving to the Poor and Prayer

6 "Beware of practicing your righteousness before men [a]to be noticed by them; otherwise you have no reward with your Father who is in heaven.

2 "So when you [1]give to the poor, do not sound a trumpet before you, as the hypocrites do in the synagogues and in the

40 [1]Lit *tunic;* i.e. a garment worn next to the body [2]Lit *cloak;* i.e. an outer garment **41** [1]Lit *will force* **42** [a]Deut 15:7-11; Luke 6:34f; 1 Tim 6:18 **43** [a]Matt 5:21, 27, 33, 38 [b]Lev 19:18 [c]Deut 23:3-6 **44** [a]Luke 6:27f; 23:34; Acts 7:60; Rom 12:20 **45** [1]Or *show yourselves to be* [a]Matt 5:9; Luke 6:35; Acts 14:17 **46** [a]Luke 6:32 **48** [1]Lit *you shall be* [a]Lev 19:2; Deut 18:13; 2 Cor 7:1; Phil 3:12-15 **6:1** [a]Matt 6:5, 16; 23:5 **2** [1]Or *give alms*

5:28 *looks at a woman with lust for her.* Not a passing glance but a willful, calculated stare that arouses sexual desire. According to Jesus this is a form of adultery even if it is only "in his heart."

5:29–30 Jesus is not teaching self-mutilation, for even a blind man can lust. The point is that we should deal as drastically with sin as necessary.

5:30 *hell.* See note on v. 22.

5:32 *except for the reason of unchastity.* See note on 19:3. Neither Mark 10:11–12 nor Luke 16:18 mentions this exception.

5:33–37 The OT allowed oaths except those that profaned the name of God. Jesus would do away with all oaths, in favor of always speaking the truth.

5:38 See notes on Ex 21:23–25; Lev 24:20.

5:39 *resist.* Here it probably means in a court of law. *slaps.* The Greek verb used here means "slaps you with the back of the hand." It was more of an insult than an act of violence. The point is that it is better to be insulted even twice than to take the matter to court.

5:40 *shirt . . . coat.* The first was an undergarment, the second a loose outer one.

5:41 *forces.* The Greek verb comes from a Persian word meaning "press into service" and is used in 27:32, where the Roman soldiers pressed Simon into service to carry Jesus' cross.

5:42 Probably not a general requirement to give to everyone who asks, but a reference to the poor (cf. Deut 15:7–11; Ps 112:5,9).

5:43 *hate your enemy.* Words not found anywhere in the OT. However, hatred for one's enemies was an accepted part of the Jewish ethic at that time.

5:44 *pray.* Prayer is one of the practical ways love expresses itself (cf. Job 42:8–10).

5:45 *that you may be sons of your Father who is in heaven.* Loving one's enemy does not make one a son of the heavenly Father. But it does make one known as a son. *the righteous and the unrighteous.* God shows His love to people without distinction.

5:46 *tax collectors.* Traditionally known as "publicans," these were local men employed by Roman tax contractors to collect taxes for them. Because they worked for Rome and often demanded unreasonable payments, the tax collectors gained a bad reputation and were generally hated and considered traitors.

5:48 *be perfect.* Christ sets up the high ideal of perfect love (see vv. 43–47)—not that we can fully attain it in this life. That, however, is God's high standard for us.

6:1 *righteousness.* This verse introduces the discussion of three acts of righteousness: (1) giving (vv. 2–4), (2) praying (vv. 5–15) and (3) fasting (vv. 16–18). *reward with your Father.* Spiritual growth and maturity or perhaps a heavenly reward of some kind.

6:2 *sound a trumpet before you.* Perhaps a reference to the noise

streets, so that they [a]may be honored by
men. [b]Truly I say to you, they have their
reward in full.
3 "But when you [1]give to the poor, do not
let your left hand know what your right hand
is doing,
4 so that your [1]giving will be in secret;
and [a]your Father who sees *what is done* in
secret will reward you.
5 "When you pray, you are not to be like
the hypocrites; for they love to [a]stand and
pray in the synagogues and on the street corners [1b]so that they may be seen by men. [c]Tru-
ly I say to you, they have their reward in full.
6 "But you, when you pray, [a]go into your
inner room, close your door and pray to your
Father who is in secret, and [b]your Father who
sees *what is done* in secret will reward you.
7 "And when you are praying, do not use
meaningless repetition as the Gentiles do, for
they suppose that they will be heard for their
[a]many words.
8 "So do not be like them; for [a]your Father
knows what you need before you ask Him.
9 "[a]Pray, then, in this way:
'Our Father who is in heaven,
Hallowed be Your name.
10 '[a]Your kingdom come.
[b]Your will be done,
On earth as it is in heaven.
11 '[a]Give us this day [1]our daily bread.
12 'And [a]forgive us our debts, as we also
have forgiven our debtors.
13 'And do not lead us into temptation,
but [a]deliver us from [1b]evil. [2][For
Yours is the kingdom and the power
and the glory forever. Amen.]'
14 "[a]For if you forgive [1]others for their
transgressions, your heavenly Father will
also forgive you.
15 "But [a]if you do not forgive [1]others, then
your Father will not forgive your transgressions.

Fasting, The True Treasure, Wealth (Mammon)

16 "[a]Whenever you fast, do not put on a
gloomy face as the hypocrites *do,* for they
[1]neglect their appearance so that they will be
noticed by men when they are fasting. [b]Tru-
ly I say to you, they have their reward in full.
17 "But you, when you fast, [a]anoint your
head and wash your face
18 so that your fasting will not be noticed
by men, but by your Father who is in secret;
and your [a]Father who sees *what is done* in
secret will reward you.
19 "[a]Do not store up for yourselves treasures on earth, where moth and rust destroy,
and where thieves break in and steal.
20 "But store up for yourselves [a]treasures
in heaven, where neither moth nor rust
destroys, and where thieves do not break in
or steal;
21 for [a]where your treasure is, there your
heart will be also.
22 "[a]The eye is the lamp of the body; so
then if your eye is [1]clear, your whole body
will be full of light.
23 "But if [a]your eye is [1]bad, your whole
body will be full of darkness. If then the light
that is in you is darkness, how great is the
darkness!
24 "[a]No one can serve two masters; for
either he will hate the one and love the other,
or he will be devoted to one and despise the
other. You cannot serve God and [1b]wealth.

The Cure for Anxiety

25 "[a]For this reason I say to you, [1]do not be
[b]worried about your [2]life, *as to* what you will
eat or what you will drink; nor for your
body, *as to* what you will put on. Is not life
more than food, and the body more than
clothing?
26 "[a]Look at the birds of the [1]air, that they

2 [a]Matt 6:5, 16; 23:5 [b]Matt 6:5, 16; Luke 6:24
3 [1]Or *give alms*
4 [1]Or *alms* [a]Jer 17:10; Matt 6:6, 18; Heb 4:13
5 [1]Lit *to be apparent to men* [a]Mark 11:25; Luke 18:11, 13 [b]Matt 6:1, 16 [c]Matt 6:2, 16; Luke 6:24
6 [a]Is 26:20; Matt 26:36-39; Acts 9:40 [b]Matt 6:4, 18
7 [a]1 Kin 18:26f
8 [a]Ps 38:9; 69:17-19; Matt 6:32; Luke 12:30
9 [a]Matt 6:9-13: *Luke 11:2-4*
10 [a]Matt 3:2; 4:17 [b]Matt 26:42; Luke 22:42; Acts 21:14
11 [1]Or *our bread for tomorrow* [a]Prov 30:8; Is 33:16; Luke 11:3
12 [a]Ex 34:7; Ps 32:1; 130:4; Matt 9:2; 26:28; Eph 1:7; 1 John 1:7-9
13 [1]Or *the evil one* [2]This clause not found in early mss [a]John 17:15; 1 Cor 10:13; 2 Thess 3:3; 2 Tim 4:18; 2 Pet 2:9; 1 John 5:18 [b]Matt 5:37
14 [1]Gr *anthropoi* [a]Matt 7:2; Mark 11:25f; Eph 4:32; Col 3:13
15 [1]Gr *anthropoi* [a]Matt 18:35
16 [a]Is 58:5

16 [1]Lit *distort their faces,* i.e. discolor their faces with makeup [b]Matt 6:2
17 [a]Ruth 3:3; 2 Sam 12:20
18 [a]Matt 6:4, 6
19 [a]Prov 23:4; Matt 19:21; Luke 12:21, 33; 18:22; 1 Tim 6:9, 10; Heb 13:5; James 5:2
20 [a]Matt 19:21; Luke 12:33; 1 Tim 6:19 **21** [a]Luke 12:34
22 [1]Or *healthy;* or *sincere* [a]Matt 6:22, 23: *Luke 11:34, 35*
23 [1]Or *evil* [a]Matt 20:15; Mark 7:22 **24** [1]*mamona,* Gr for Ara *mammon;* i.e. wealth, etc, personified as an object of worship [a]1 Kin 18:21; Luke 16:13; Gal 1:10; James 4:4 [b]Luke 16:9, 11, 13
25 [1]Or *stop being worried* [2]Lit *soul* [a]Matt 6:25-33: *Luke 12:22-31* [b]Matt 6:27, 28, 31, 34; Luke 10:41; 12:11, 22; Phil 4:6; 1 Pet 5:7
26 [1]Lit *heaven* [a]Job 35:11; 38:41; Ps 104:27, 28; Matt 10:29ff; Luke 12:24

made by coins as they were thrown into the temple treasury. Or the phrase may be used figuratively to mean "make a big show of it." *hypocrites.* The Greek word means "play-actor." Matthew uses the word 13 times (Mark, twice; Luke, three times). Here it refers to those who fake being pious. *their reward in full.* The honor they receive from people is all the reward they get.

6:3 *do not let your left hand know what your right hand is doing.* Not to be taken literally but as a way of emphasizing that one should not call attention to one's giving. Self-glorification is always a present danger.

6:6 *room.* The Greek word means "storeroom." Unlike most of the rooms in the house, it had a door that could be shut.

6:7 *use meaningless repetition as the Gentiles do.* They used long lists of the names of their gods in their prayers, hoping that by constantly repeating them they would call on the name of the god that could help them. Jesus is not necessarily condemning all long prayers, but meaningless verbiage in praying.

6:12 *debts.* Moral debts, i.e., sins (see note on Luke 11:4).

6:16 *fast.* See notes on Mark 2:18 and Luke 18:12.

6:17 *anoint your head and wash your face.* Jews put ashes on their heads when fasting. But Jesus told them to maintain their regular appearance. Fasting should not be done in an ostentatious way.

6:19–21 The dangers of riches are often mentioned in the NT (e.g., v. 24; 13:22; 19:22; Mark 10:17–30; Luke 12:16–21; 1 Tim 6:9–10,17–19; Heb 13:5), but nowhere are they condemned in and of themselves. What Jesus condemns here is greed and hoarding of money.

6:19 *moth and rust.* Representative of all agents and processes that destroy worldly possessions. *break in and steal.* Houses in the Holy Land had walls made of mud bricks and could be broken into easily.

6:20 *treasures in heaven.* Anything done in this life that has eternal value. The phrase is the equivalent of being "rich toward God" (Luke 12:21). In this context it probably more specifically refers to using one's material wealth for good causes.

do not sow, nor reap nor gather into barns, and *yet* your heavenly Father feeds them. Are you not worth much more than they?

27 "And who of you by being [a]worried can [b]add a *single* [1]hour to his [2]life?

28 "And why are you [a]worried about clothing? Observe how the lilies of the field grow; they do not toil nor do they spin,

29 yet I say to you that not even [a]Solomon in all his glory clothed himself like one of these.

30 "But if God so clothes the [a]grass of the field, which is *alive* today and tomorrow is thrown into the furnace, *will He* not much more *clothe* you? [b]You of little faith!

31 "Do not [a]worry then, saying, 'What will we eat?' or 'What will we drink?' or 'What will we wear for clothing?'

32 "For the Gentiles eagerly seek all these things; for [a]your heavenly Father knows that you need all these things.

33 "But [1]seek first [2]His kingdom and His righteousness, and [a]all these things will be [3]added to you.

34 "So do not [a]worry about tomorrow; for tomorrow will [1]care for itself. [2]Each day has enough trouble of its own.

Judging Others

7 "[a]Do not judge so that you will not be judged.

2 "For in the way you judge, you will be judged; and [1][a]by your standard of measure, it will be measured to you.

3 "Why do you [a]look at the speck that is in your brother's eye, but do not notice the log that is in your own eye?

4 "[a]Or how [1]can you say to your brother, 'Let me take the speck out of your eye,' and behold, the log is in your own eye?

5 "You hypocrite, first take the log out of your own eye, and then you will see clearly to take the speck out of your brother's eye.

6 "[a]Do not give what is holy to dogs, and do not throw your pearls before swine, or they will trample them under their feet, and turn and tear you to pieces.

27 [1]Lit *cubit* (approx 18 in.) [2]Or *height* [a]Matt 6:25, 28, 31, 34; Luke 10:41; 12:11, 22; Phil 4:6; 1 Pet 5:7 [b]Ps 39:5
28 [a]Matt 6:25, 27, 31, 34; Luke 10:41; 12:11, 22; Phil 4:6; 1 Pet 5:7
29 [a]1 Kin 10:4-7; 2 Chr 9:4-6, 20-22
30 [a]James 1:10, 11; 1 Pet 1:24 [b]Matt 8:26; 14:31; 16:8
31 [a]Matt 6:25, 27, 28, 34; Luke 10:41; 12:11, 22; Phil 4:6; 1 Pet 5:7
32 [a]Matt 6:8; Phil 4:19
33 [1]Or *continually seek* [2]Or *the kingdom* [3]Or *provided* [a]Matt 19:28; Mark 10:29f; Luke 18:29f; 1 Tim 4:8
34 [1]Lit *worry about itself* [2]Lit *Sufficient for the day is its evils* [a]Matt 6:25, 27, 28, 31; Luke 10:41; 12:11, 22; Phil 4:6; 1 Pet 5:7
7:1 [a]Matt 7:1-5: *Luke 6:37f, 41f;* Rom 14:10, 13
2 [1]Lit *by what measure you measure* [a]Mark 4:24; Luke 6:38
3 [a]Rom 2:1
4 [1]Lit *will* [a]Luke 6:42
6 [a]Matt 15:26

7 [1]Or *Keep asking* [2]Or *keep seeking* [3]Or *keep knocking* [a]Matt 7:7-11: *Luke 11:9-13* [b]Matt 18:19; 21:22; Mark 11:24; John 14:13; 15:7, 16; 16:23f; James 1:5f; 1 John 3:22; 5:14f

Prayer and the Golden Rule

7 "[1][a]Ask, and [b]it will be given to you; [2]seek, and you will find; [3]knock, and it will be opened to you.

8 "For everyone who asks receives, and he who seeks finds, and to him who knocks it will be opened.

9 "Or what man is there among you [1]who, when his son asks for a loaf, [2]will give him a stone?

10 "Or [1]if he asks for a fish, he will not give him a snake, will he?

11 "If you then, being evil, know how to give good gifts to your children, [a]how much more will your Father who is in heaven give what is good to those who ask Him!

12 "In everything, [a]therefore, [1]treat people the same way you want [2]them to treat you, for [b]this is the Law and the Prophets.

The Narrow and Wide Gates

13 "[a]Enter through the narrow gate; for the gate is wide and the way is broad that leads to destruction, and there are many who enter through it.

14 "For the gate is small and the way is narrow that leads to life, and there are few who find it.

A Tree and Its Fruit

15 "Beware of the [a]false prophets, who come to you in sheep's clothing, but inwardly are [b]ravenous wolves.

16 "You will [1][a]know them by their fruits. [2]Grapes are not gathered from thorn *bushes* nor figs from thistles, are they?

17 "So [a]every good tree bears good fruit, but the bad tree bears bad fruit.

18 "A good tree cannot produce bad fruit, nor can a bad tree produce good fruit.

9 [1]Lit *whom his son will ask* [2]Lit *he will not give him a stone, will he?* **10** [1]Lit *also will ask* **11** [a]Ps 84:11; Is 63:7; Rom 8:32; James 1:17 **12** [1]Lit *you, too, do so for them* [2]Lit *people;* Gr *anthropoi* [a]Luke 6:31 [b]Matt 22:40; Rom 13:8ff; Gal 5:14 **13** [a]Luke 13:24 **15** [a]Matt 24:11, 24; Mark 13:22; Luke 6:26; Acts 13:6; 2 Pet 2:1; 1 John 4:1; Rev 16:13; 19:20; 20:10 [b]Ezek 22:27; John 10:12; Acts 20:29 **16** [1]Or *recognize* [2]Lit *They do not gather* [a]Matt 7:20; 12:33; Luke 6:44; James 3:12 **17** [a]Matt 12:33, 35

6:28 *lilies.* Here represents flowers generally.

6:30 *thrown into the furnace.* Grass was commonly used to heat the clay ovens of the Holy Land.

7:1 The Christian is not to judge hypocritically or self-righteously, as can be seen from the context (v. 5). The same thought is expressed in 23:13–39 (cf. Rom 2:1). To obey Christ's commands in this chapter, we must first evaluate a person's character—whether he is a "dog" (v. 6) or a false prophet (v. 15), or whether his life shows fruit (v. 16). Scripture repeatedly exhorts believers to evaluate carefully and choose between good and bad people and things (sexually immoral, 1 Cor 5:9; those who masquerade as angels of light, 2 Cor 11:14; dogs, Phil 3:2; false prophets, 1 John 4:1). The Christian is to "examine everything" (1 Thess 5:21).

7:3 *speck . . . log.* An example of hyperbole in the teachings of Jesus (cf. 19:24, where Jesus speaks of a camel going through the eye of needle). Its purpose is to drive home a point.

7:6 Teaching should be given in accordance with the spiritual capacity of the learners. *dogs.* The unclean dogs of the street were held in low esteem.

7:8 *asks . . . seeks . . . knocks.* Greek present imperatives are used here, indicating constant asking, seeking and knocking. Persistent prayer is being emphasized.

7:12 The so-called Golden Rule is found in negative form in rabbinic Judaism and also in Hinduism, Buddhism and Confucianism. It occurred in various forms in Greek and Roman ethical teaching. Jesus stated it in positive form. *the Law and the Prophets.* See note on 5:17.

7:13 *narrow gate.* The gate that leads into the kingdom of heaven. It's synonymous with "life" (v. 14). *destruction.* Separation from God in hell.

7:15 *false prophets.* People who have not been sent by God but who claim that they have (see 24:24; Jer 23:16 and note).

19 "[a]Every tree that does not bear good fruit is cut down and thrown into the fire.

20 "So then, you will [1]know them [a]by their fruits.

21 "[a]Not everyone who says to Me, 'Lord, Lord,' will enter the kingdom of heaven, but he who does the will of My Father who is in heaven *will enter.*

22 "[a]Many will say to Me on [b]that day, 'Lord, Lord, did we not prophesy in Your name, and in Your name cast out demons, and in Your name perform many [1]miracles?'

23 "And then I will declare to them, 'I never knew you; [a]DEPART FROM ME, YOU WHO PRACTICE LAWLESSNESS.'

The Two Foundations

24 "Therefore [a]everyone who hears these words of Mine and [1]acts on them, [2]may be compared to a wise man who built his house on the rock.

25 "And the rain fell, and the [1]floods came, and the winds blew and slammed against that house; and *yet* it did not fall, for it had been founded on the rock.

26 "Everyone who hears these words of Mine and does not [1]act on them, will be like a foolish man who built his house on the sand.

27 "The rain fell, and the [1]floods came, and the winds blew and slammed against that house; and it fell—and great was its fall."

28 [1][a]When Jesus had finished these words, [b]the crowds were amazed at His teaching;

29 for He was teaching them as *one* having authority, and not as their scribes.

Jesus Cleanses a Leper; The Centurion's Faith

8 When [1]Jesus came down from the mountain, [2]large crowds followed Him.

2 And [a]a leper came to Him and [1][b]bowed down before Him, and said, "Lord, if You are willing, You can make me clean."

3 Jesus stretched out His hand and touched him, saying, "I am willing; be cleansed." And immediately his [a]leprosy was cleansed.

4 And Jesus *said to him, "[a]See that you tell no one; but [b]go, [c]show yourself to the priest and present the [1]offering that Moses commanded, as a testimony to them."

5 And [a]when [1]Jesus entered Capernaum, a centurion came to Him, imploring Him,

6 and saying, "[1]Lord, my [2]servant is [3]lying [a]paralyzed at home, fearfully tormented."

7 Jesus *said to him, "I will come and heal him."

8 But the centurion said, "[1]Lord, I am not worthy for You to come under my roof, but just [2]say the word, and my [3]servant will be healed.

9 "For I also am a man under [a]authority, with soldiers under me; and I say to this one, 'Go!' and he goes, and to another, 'Come!' and he comes, and to my slave, 'Do this!' and he does *it.*"

10 Now when Jesus heard *this,* He marveled and said to those who were following, "Truly I say to you, I have not found such great faith [1]with anyone in Israel.

11 "I say to you that many [a]will come from east and west, and [1]recline *at the table* with Abraham, Isaac and Jacob in the kingdom of heaven;

12 but [a]the sons of the kingdom will be cast out into [b]the outer darkness; in that place [c]there will be weeping and gnashing of teeth."

13 And Jesus said to the centurion, "Go; [1]it shall be done for you [a]as you have believed." And the [2]servant was healed that *very* [3]moment.

19 [a]Matt 3:10; Luke 3:9; 13:7; John 15:2, 6 **20** [1]Or *recognize* [a]Matt 7:16; 12:33; Luke 6:44; James 3:12 **21** [a]Luke 6:46 **22** [1]Or *works of power* [a]Matt 25:11f; Luke 13:25ff [b]Matt 10:15 **23** [a]Ps 6:8; Matt 25:41; Luke 13:27 **24** [1]Lit *does* [2]Lit *will* [a]Matt 7:24-27: *Luke 6:47-49;* Matt 16:18; James 1:22-25 **25** [1]Lit *rivers* **26** [1]Lit *do* **27** [1]Lit *rivers* **28** [1]Lit *And it happened when* [a]Matt 11:1; 13:53; 19:1; 26:1 [b]Matt 13:54; 22:33; Mark 1:22; 6:2; 11:18; Luke 4:32; John 7:46 **8:1** [1]Lit *He* [2]Lit *many* **2** [1]Or *worshiped* [a]Matt 8:2-4: *Mark 1:40-44; Luke 5:12-14* [b]Matt 9:18; 15:25; 18:26; 20:20; John 9:38; Acts 10:25

3 [a]Matt 11:5; Luke 4:27 **4** [1]Lit *gift* [a]Matt 9:30; 12:16; 17:9; Mark 1:44; 3:12; 5:43; 7:36; 8:30; 9:9; Luke 4:41; 8:56; 9:21 [b]Mark 1:44; Luke 5:14; 17:14 [c]Lev 13:49; 14:2ff **5** [1]Lit *He* [a]Matt 8:5-13: *Luke 7:1-10* **6** [1]Or *Sir* [2]Lit *boy* [3]Lit *thrown down* [a]Matt 4:24 **8** [1]Or *Sir* [2]Lit *say with a word* [3]Lit *boy* **9** [a]Mark 1:27; Luke 9:1 **10** [1]One early ms reads *not even in Israel* **11** [1]Or *dine* [a]Is 49:12; 59:19; Mal 1:11; Luke 13:29 **12** [a]Matt 13:38 [b]Matt 22:13; 25:30 [c]Matt 13:42, 50; 22:13; 24:51; 25:30; Luke 13:28 **13** [1]Or *let it be done;* i.e. a command [2]Lit *boy* [3]Lit *hour* [a]Matt 9:22, 29

7:21 *Lord.* A title that sometimes means only "sir" or "master" but here seems to mean more than that in view of the fact that Jesus is the One who makes the final decision about a person's eternal destiny. *kingdom of heaven.* See note on 3:2.

7:22 *that day.* The day of judgment (cf. Mal 3:17–18). *prophesy.* In the NT this verb primarily means to give a message from God, not necessarily to predict. *demons.* See note on Mark 1:23.

7:29 *authority.* The teachers of the law quoted other rabbis to support their own teaching (see note on 2:4), but Jesus spoke with divine authority.

8:2 *leper.* The Greek word was used for various diseases affecting the skin—not necessarily leprosy (see Lev 13–14 and note on Lev 13:2). *Lord.* See note on 7:21. *make me clean.* Leprosy made a person ceremonially unclean as well as physically afflicted (see note on Luke 5:12–16).

8:4 *tell no one.* Perhaps for several reasons: (1) Jesus did not want to be considered just a miracle worker, (2) He did not want His teaching ministry hindered by too much publicity being given to His healing miracles, and (3) He did not want His death to come prematurely, i.e., before He had finished His ministry. See 9:30; 12:16; Mark 1:44; 5:43; 7:36; Luke 8:56. *show yourself to the priest.* See note on Luke 5:14. *them.* The priests.

8:5–13 Although the incident in John 4:43–54 is similar, it probably is a separate episode in the life of Jesus.

8:5 *Capernaum.* See note on 4:13. *centurion.* A Roman military officer in charge of 100 soldiers. In Luke's account (Luke 7:1–5) Jewish elders and friends of the centurion came to Jesus on his behalf, but Matthew does not mention these intermediaries. A parallel situation was the flogging of Jesus by Pilate, in which the act was obviously not carried out by Pilate himself but by the Roman soldiers at Pilate's command (27:26, lit. "he flogged Jesus").

8:8 *I am not worthy for You to come under my roof.* In Greek the words "I am not worthy" are the same as those used by John the Baptist in 3:11 ("I am not fit"). The entire statement reveals how highly the centurion regarded Jesus. Or perhaps his response reflects his own sense of moral guilt in the presence of Jesus.

8:11 The universality of the gospel is one of Matthew's themes (see Introduction: Recipients). *table . . . in the kingdom of heaven.* The eschatological Messianic banquet that symbolizes the blessings of an intimate relationship with God (see Is 25:6–9).

8:12 *sons of the kingdom.* Jews who thought their Judaism was an inherited passport for entrance into the kingdom (see 3:9–10 and note on 3:9).

Peter's Mother-in-law and Many Others Healed

14 [a]When Jesus came into Peter's [1]home,
He saw his mother-in-law lying sick in bed
with a fever.
15 He touched her hand, and the fever left
her; and she got up and [1]waited on Him.
16 When evening came, they brought to
Him many [a]who were demon-possessed;
and He cast out the spirits with a word, and
[b]healed all who were ill.
17 *This was* to fulfill what was spoken
through Isaiah the prophet: "[a]HE HIMSELF
TOOK OUR INFIRMITIES AND [1]CARRIED AWAY OUR
DISEASES."

Discipleship Tested

18 Now when Jesus saw a crowd around
Him, [a]He gave orders to depart to the other
side *of the sea.*
19 [a]Then a scribe came and said to Him,
"Teacher, I will follow You wherever You
go."
20 Jesus *said to him, "The foxes have
holes and the birds of the [1]air *have* [2]nests,
but [a]the Son of Man has nowhere to lay His
head."
21 Another of the disciples said to Him,
"Lord, permit me first to go and bury my
father."
22 But Jesus *said to him, "[a]Follow Me,
and allow the dead to bury their own dead."
23 [a]When He got into the boat, His disciples followed Him.
24 And behold, there arose [1]a great storm
on the sea, so that the boat was being covered with the waves; but Jesus Himself was
asleep.
25 And they came to *Him* and woke Him,
saying, "[a]Save *us,* Lord; we are perishing!"
26 He *said to them, "Why are you
[1]afraid, [a]you men of little faith?" Then He
got up and rebuked the winds and the sea,
and [2]it became perfectly calm.
27 The men were amazed, and said,
"What kind of a man is this, that even the
winds and the sea obey Him?"

14 [1]Or *house* [a]Matt 8:14-16: *Mark 1:29-34; Luke 4:38-41*
15 [1]Or *served*
16 [a]Matt 4:24 [b]Matt 4:23; 8:33
17 [1]Or *removed* [a]Is 53:4
18 [a]Mark 4:35; Luke 8:22
19 [a]Matt 8:19-22: *Luke 9:57-60*
20 [1]Or *sky* [2]Or *roosting places* [a]Dan 7:13; Matt 9:6; 12:8, 32, 40; 13:41; 16:13, 27f; 17:9; 19:28; 26:64; Mark 8:38; Luke 12:8; 18:8; 21:36; John 1:51; 3:13f; 6:27; 12:34; Acts 7:56
22 [a]Matt 9:9; Mark 2:14; Luke 9:59, 60; John 1:43; 21:19
23 [a]Matt 8:23-27: *Mark 4:36-41; Luke 8:22-25*
24 [1]Lit *a shaking*
25 [a]Matt 8:2; 9:18
26 [1]Or *cowardly* [2]Lit *a great calm occurred* [a]Matt 6:30; 14:31; 16:8; 17:20
28 [a]Matt 8:28-34: *Mark 5:1-17; Luke 8:26-37* [b]Matt 4:24
29 [1]Lit *What is to us and to you* (a Heb idiom) [2]I.e. the appointed time of judgment [a]Judg 11:12; 2 Sam 16:10; 19:22; 1 Kin 17:18; 2 Kin 3:13; 2 Chr 35:21; Mark 1:24; 5:7; Luke 4:34; 8:28; John 2:4
33 [1]Lit *and the things of* [a]Matt 4:24
34 [a]Amos 7:12; Acts 16:39
9:1 [a]Matt 4:13; Mark 5:21

Jesus Casts Out Demons

28 [a]When He came to the other side into
the country of the Gadarenes, two men who
were [b]demon-possessed met Him as they
were coming out of the tombs. *They were* so
extremely violent that no one could pass by
that way.
29 And they cried out, saying, "[1][a]What
business do we have with each other, Son of
God? Have You come here to torment us
before [2]the time?"
30 Now there was a herd of many swine
feeding at a distance from them.
31 The demons *began* to entreat Him, saying, "If You *are going to* cast us out, send us
into the herd of swine."
32 And He said to them, "Go!" And they
came out and went into the swine, and the
whole herd rushed down the steep bank into
the sea and perished in the waters.
33 The herdsmen ran away, and went to
the city and reported everything, [1]including
what had happened to the [a]demoniacs.
34 And behold, the whole city came out to
meet Jesus; and when they saw Him, [a]they
implored Him to leave their region.

A Paralytic Healed

9 Getting into a boat, Jesus crossed over *the*
sea and came to [a]His own city.
2 [a]And they brought to Him a [b]paralytic
lying on a bed. Seeing their faith, Jesus said
to the paralytic, "[c]Take courage, [1]son; [d]your
sins are forgiven."
3 And some of the scribes said [1]to themselves, "This *fellow* [a]blasphemes."
4 And Jesus [a]knowing their thoughts
said, "Why are you thinking evil in your
hearts?
5 "Which is easier, to say, '[a]Your sins are
forgiven,' or to say, 'Get up, and walk'?
6 "But so that you may know that [a]the

2 [1]Lit *child* [a]Matt 9:2-8: *Mark 2:3-12; Luke 5:18-26* [b]Matt 4:24; 9:6 [c]Matt 9:22; 14:27; Mark 6:50; 10:49; John 16:33; Acts 23:11 [d]Mark 2:5, 9; Luke 5:20, 23; 7:48 **3** [1]Lit *among* [a]Mark 3:28, 29 **4** [a]Matt 12:25; Luke 6:8; 9:47 **5** [a]Matt 9:2, 6; Mark 2:5, 9; Luke 5:20, 23; 7:48 **6** [a]Matt 8:20; John 5:27

8:14 *Peter's . . . mother-in-law.* See notes on Mark 1:30 and Luke 4:38.
8:18 *the other side.* The east side.
8:19 *scribe.* See note on 2:4.
8:20 *Son of Man.* See note on Mark 8:31.
8:22 *allow the dead to bury their own dead.* Let the spiritually dead bury the physically dead. The time of Jesus' ministry was short and demanded full attention and commitment. This statement stresses the radical demands of Jesus' discipleship, since Jews placed great importance on the duty of children to bury their parents.
8:24 *great storm.* See note on Mark 4:37. *but Jesus Himself was asleep.* See note on Mark 4:38.
8:28 *country of the Gadarenes.* The region around the city of Gadara, six miles southeast of the Sea of Galilee. Mark and Luke identify the region by the capital city Gerasa, located about 35 miles southeast of the Sea. *two.* Mark (5:2) and Luke (8:27; see note there) mention only one Gadarene demoniac.
8:29 *time.* The time of their judgment (see notes on Mark 5:10 and Luke 8:31).
8:30 *herd of many swine.* Large numbers of Gentiles lived in Galilee. Normally Jews did not raise pigs, since they were considered the most "unclean" of all animals.
8:32 Though Jesus seemingly consented to the demons' request, the pigs carried the demons into the depths of the sea—perhaps symbolic of the Abyss (see Luke 8:31 and note).
8:34 *implored Him to leave.* They were probably more concerned about their financial loss than about the deliverance of the miserable demon-possessed man.
9:1 *crossed over.* The northern end of the Sea of Galilee. *His own city.* Capernaum (see note on 4:13).
9:2 *their faith.* The faith of the men who carried him as well as the faith of the paralytic.
9:3 *blasphemes.* Here the term includes usurping God's prerogative to forgive sins (see note on Mark 2:7).
9:5–6 See notes on Mark 2:9–10; 14:64.

Son of Man has authority on earth to forgive sins"—then He *said to the [b]paralytic, "Get up, pick up your bed and go home."

7 And he got up and [1]went home.

8 But when the crowds saw *this,* they were [1]awestruck, and [a]glorified God, who had given such authority to men.

Matthew Called

9 [a]As Jesus went on from there, He saw a man called [b]Matthew, sitting in the tax collector's booth; and He *said to him, "[c]Follow Me!" And he got up and followed Him.

10 Then it happened that as [1]Jesus was reclining *at the table* in the house, behold, many tax collectors and [2]sinners came and were dining with Jesus and His disciples.

11 When the Pharisees saw *this,* they said to His disciples, "[a]Why is your Teacher eating with the tax collectors and sinners?"

12 But when Jesus heard *this,* He said, "*It is* not [a]those who are healthy who need a physician, but those who are sick.

13 "But go and learn [1][a]what this means: '[b]I DESIRE [2]COMPASSION, [3]AND NOT SACRIFICE,' for [c]I did not come to call the righteous, but sinners."

The Question about Fasting

14 Then the disciples of John *came to Him, asking, "Why do we and [a]the Pharisees fast, but Your disciples do not fast?"

15 And Jesus said to them, "The [1]attendants of the bridegroom cannot mourn as long as the bridegroom is with them, can they? But the days will come when the bridegroom is taken away from them, and then they will fast.

16 "But no one puts [1]a patch of unshrunk cloth on an old garment; for [2]the patch pulls away from the garment, and a worse tear results.

17 "Nor do *people* put new wine into old wineskins; otherwise the wineskins burst, and the wine pours out and the wineskins are ruined; but they put new wine into fresh wineskins, and both are preserved."

6 [b]Matt 4:24; 9:2
7 [1]Or *departed*
8 [1]Lit *afraid* [a]Matt 5:16; 15:31; Mark 2:12; Luke 2:20; 5:25, 26; 7:16; 13:13; 17:15; 23:47; John 15:8; Acts 4:21; 11:18; 21:20; 2 Cor 9:13; Gal 1:24
9 [a]Matt 9:9-17: *Mark 2:14-22; Luke 5:27-38* [b]Matt 10:3; Mark 2:14; 3:18; Luke 6:15; Acts 1:13 [c]Matt 8:22
10 [1]Lit *He* [2]I.e. irreligious Jews
11 [a]Matt 11:19; Mark 2:16; Luke 5:30; 15:2
12 [a]Mark 2:17; Luke 5:31
13 [1]Lit *what is* [2]Or *mercy* [3]I.e. more than [a]Matt 12:7 [b]Hos 6:6 [c]Mark 2:17; Luke 5:32; 1 Tim 1:15
14 [a]Luke 18:12
15 [1]Lit *sons of the wedding place*
16 [1]Lit *that which is put on* [2]Lit *that which fills up*

18 [1]Or *one* [2]Lit *ruler* [3]Or *worshiped* [a]Matt 9:18-26: *Mark 5:22-43; Luke 8:41-56* [b]Matt 8:2
20 [1]I.e. tassel fringe with a blue cord [2]Or *outer garment* [a]Num 15:38; Deut 22:12; Matt 14:36; 23:5
21 [1]Lit *in herself* [2]Lit *be saved* [a]Matt 14:36; Mark 3:10; Luke 6:19
22 [1]Lit *saved you* [2]Lit *from that hour* [3]Lit *saved* [a]Matt 9:2 [b]Matt 9:29; 15:28; Mark 5:34; 10:52; Luke 7:50; 8:48; 17:19; 18:42
23 [1]Lit *ruler's* [a]2 Chr 35:25; Jer 9:17; 16:6; Ezek 24:17
24 [a]John 11:13; Acts 20:10
25 [1]Or *was raised up* [a]Acts 9:40 [b]Mark 9:27
26 [a]Matt 4:24; 9:31; 14:1; Mark 1:28, 45; Luke 4:14, 37; 5:15; 7:17
27 [a]Matt 1:1; 12:23; 15:22; 20:30, 31; 21:9, 15; 22:42; Mark 10:47, 48; 12:35; Luke 18:38, 39; 20:41f
29 [1]Or *Let it be done;* Gr command [a]Matt 8:13; 9:22
30 [a]Matt 8:4

Miracles of Healing

18 [a]While He was saying these things to them, [1]a *synagogue* [2]official came and [3][b]bowed down before Him, and said, "My daughter has just died; but come and lay Your hand on her, and she will live."

19 Jesus got up and *began* to follow him, and *so did* His disciples.

20 And a woman who had been suffering from a hemorrhage for twelve years, came up behind Him and touched [a]the [1]fringe of His [2]cloak;

21 for she was saying [1]to herself, "If I only [a]touch His garment, I will [2]get well."

22 But Jesus turning and seeing her said, "Daughter, [a]take courage; [b]your faith has [1]made you well." [2]At once the woman was [3]made well.

23 When Jesus came into the [1]official's house, and saw [a]the flute-players and the crowd in noisy disorder,

24 He said, "Leave; for the girl [a]has not died, but is asleep." And they *began* laughing at Him.

25 But [a]when the crowd had been sent out, He entered and [b]took her by the hand, and the girl [1]got up.

26 [a]This news spread throughout all that land.

27 As Jesus went on from there, two blind men followed Him, crying out, "Have mercy on us, [a]Son of David!"

28 When He entered the house, the blind men came up to Him, and Jesus *said to them, "Do you believe that I am able to do this?" They *said to Him, "Yes, Lord."

29 Then He touched their eyes, saying, "[1]It shall be done to you [a]according to your faith."

30 And their eyes were opened. And Jesus [a]sternly warned them: "See that no one knows *about this!*"

9:6 *Son of Man.* See note on Mark 8:31.
9:9 *Matthew.* Mark and Luke call this disciple Levi in the parallel accounts (but see also Mark 3:18; Luke 6:15; Acts 1:13). *tax collector's booth.* See note on Mark 2:14. *got up and followed Him.* See note on Luke 5:28.
9:10 *tax collectors.* See notes on 5:46 and Mark 2:16. *sinners.* See note on Mark 2:15.
9:11 *Pharisees.* See note on Mark 2:16.
9:13 *I did not come to call the righteous, but sinners.* See note on Mark 2:17.
9:14 *the disciples of John.* See notes on Mark 2:18 and Luke 5:33. *fast.* See notes on Mark 2:18 and Luke 5:33.
9:15 See notes on Mark 2:19–20.
9:17 *fresh wineskins.* In ancient times goatskins were used to hold wine. As the fresh grape juice fermented, the wine would expand, and the new wineskin would stretch. But a used skin, already stretched, would break. Jesus brings a newness that cannot be confined within the old forms.
9:18 *synagogue official.* From Mark and Luke we know that the official was Jairus (see note on Mark 5:22).
9:20 *suffering from a hemorrhage for twelve years.* See note on Mark 5:25.
9:21 See note on Mark 5:28.
9:22 *Daughter.* See notes on Luke 8:4–8. *made you well.* See note on Mark 5:34.
9:23 *flute-players.* Musicians hired to play in mourning ceremonies. *crowd in noisy disorder.* Mourners hired to wail and lament.
9:24 *not died, but is asleep.* See note on Luke 8:52.
9:27 *blind men.* Isaiah predicted the healing of the blind in the Messianic age (Is 35:5). *Son of David.* A popular Jewish title for the coming Messiah (e.g., 12:23; 20:30; 21:9; 22:41–45; see note on 1:1).
9:30 See notes on 8:4 and 16:20.

31 But they went out and [a]spread the news about Him throughout all that land.

32 As they were going out, [a]a mute, [b]demon-possessed man [1]was brought to Him.

33 After the demon was cast out, the mute man spoke; and the crowds were amazed, *and were* saying, "[a]Nothing like this has [1]ever been seen in Israel."

34 But the Pharisees were saying, "He [a]casts out the demons by the ruler of the demons."

35 Jesus was going through all the cities and villages, [a]teaching in their synagogues and proclaiming the gospel of the kingdom, and healing every kind of disease and every kind of sickness.

36 [a]Seeing the [1]people, He felt compassion for them, [b]because they were [2]distressed and [3]dispirited like sheep [4]without a shepherd.

37 Then He *said to His disciples, "[a]The harvest is plentiful, but the workers are few.

38 "Therefore beseech the Lord of the harvest to send out workers into His harvest."

The Twelve Disciples; Instructions for Service

10 Jesus [a]summoned His twelve disciples and gave them authority over unclean spirits, to cast them out, and to [b]heal every kind of disease and every kind of sickness.

2 [a]Now the names of the twelve apostles are these: The first, [b]Simon, who is called Peter, and [b]Andrew his brother; and [1c]James the son of Zebedee, and [2]John his brother;

3 [a]Philip and [1]Bartholomew; [b]Thomas and [c]Matthew the tax collector; [2d]James the son of Alphaeus, and [e]Thaddaeus;

4 Simon the [1]Zealot, and [a]Judas Iscariot, the one who betrayed Him.

5 [a]These twelve Jesus sent out after instructing them: "Do not [1]go [2]in *the* way of *the* Gentiles, and do not enter *any* city of the [b]Samaritans;

6 but rather go to [a]the lost sheep of the house of Israel.

7 "And as you go, [1]preach, saying, '[a]The kingdom of heaven [2]is at hand.'

8 "Heal *the* sick, raise *the* dead, cleanse *the* lepers, cast out demons. Freely you received, freely give.

9 "[a]Do not acquire gold, or silver, or copper for your money belts,

10 or a [1]bag for *your* journey, or even two [2]coats, or sandals, or a staff; for [a]the worker is worthy of his [3]support.

11 "And whatever city or village you enter, inquire who is worthy in it, and stay [1]at his house until you leave *that city.*

12 "As you enter the [1]house, [a]give it your [2]greeting.

13 "If the house is worthy, [1]give it your *blessing of* peace. But if it is not worthy, [2]take back your *blessing of* peace.

14 "Whoever does not receive you, nor heed your words, as you go out of that house or that city, [a]shake the dust off your feet.

15 "Truly I say to you, [a]it will be more tolerable for *the* land of [b]Sodom and Gomorrah in [c]the day of judgment than for that city.

A Hard Road before Them

16 "[a]Behold, I send you out as sheep in the midst of wolves; so [1]be [b]shrewd as serpents and [c]innocent as doves.

17 "But beware of men, for they will hand you over to *the* [a]courts and scourge you [b]in their synagogues;

18 and you will even be brought before governors and kings for My sake, as a testimony to them and to the Gentiles.

31 [a]Matt 4:24; 9:26; 14:1; Mark 1:28, 45; Luke 4:14, 37; 5:15; 7:17
32 [1]Lit *they brought* [a]Matt 12:22, 24 [b]Matt 4:24
33 [1]Lit *ever appeared* [a]Mark 2:12
34 [a]Matt 12:24; Mark 3:22; Luke 11:15; John 7:20f
35 [a]Matt 4:23; Mark 1:14
36 [1]Lit *crowds* [2]Or *harassed* [3]Lit *thrown down* [4]Lit *not having* [a]Matt 14:14; 15:32; Mark 6:34; 8:2 [b]Num 27:17; Ezek 34:5; Zech 10:2; Mark 6:34
37 [a]Luke 10:2
10:1 [a]Mark 3:13-15; 6:7 [b]Matt 9:35; Luke 9:1
2 [1]Or *Jacob;* James is the Eng form of Jacob [2]Gr *Joannes,* Heb *Johanan* [a]Matt 10:2-4: *Mark 3:16-19; Luke 6:14-16; Acts 1:13* [b]Matt 4:18 [c]Matt 4:21
3 [1]I.e. son of Talmai (Aram) [2]Or *Jacob* [a]John 1:43ff [b]John 11:16; 14:5; 20:24ff; 21:2 [c]Matt 9:9 [d]Mark 15:40 [e]Mark 3:18; Luke 6:16; Acts 1:13
4 [1]Or *Cananaean* [a]Matt 26:14; Luke 22:3; John 6:71; 13:2, 26
5 [1]Or *go off* [2]Or *on the road of* (Gr *hodos: way* or *road*) [a]Mark 6:7; Luke 9:2 [b]2 Kin 17:24ff; Luke 9:52; 10:33; 17:16; John 4:9, 39f; 8:48; Acts 8:25

6 [a]Matt 15:24 **7** [1]Or *proclaim* [2]Lit *has come near* [a]Matt 3:2
9 [a]Matt 10:9-15: *Mark 6:8-11; Luke 9:3-5; 10:4-12;* Luke 22:35
10 [1]Or *knapsack*, or *beggar's bag* [2]Or *inner garments* [3]Lit *nourishment* [a]1 Cor 9:14; 1 Tim 5:18 **11** [1]Lit *there until*
12 [1]Or *household* [2]I.e. the familiar Heb blessing, "Peace be to this house!" [a]1 Sam 25:6; Ps 122:7, 8 **13** [1]Lit *your peace is to come upon it* [2]Lit *your peace is to return to you* **14** [a]Acts 13:51 **15** [a]Matt 11:22, 24 [b]Matt 11:24; 2 Pet 2:6; Jude 7 [c]Matt 7:22; 11:22, 24; 12:36; Acts 17:31; 1 Thess 5:4; Heb 10:25; 2 Pet 2:9; 3:7; 1 John 4:17; Jude 6 **16** [1]Or *show yourselves to be* [a]Luke 10:3 [b]Gen 3:1; Matt 24:25; Rom 16:19 [c]Hos 7:11
17 [a]Matt 5:22 [b]Matt 23:34; Mark 13:9; Luke 12:11; Acts 5:40; 22:19; 26:11

9:32 *mute.* Isaiah also predicted that the mute would talk in the Messianic age (Is 35:6).

9:34 *ruler of demons.* See note on 10:25.

9:35 *synagogues.* See note on Mark 1:21. *gospel.* See note on Mark 1:1.

10:2–4 See notes on Luke 6:14–16.

10:2 *apostles.* The only occurrence of this word in Matthew's Gospel. See note on Mark 6:30.

10:4 *the Zealot.* Either a description of Simon's religious zeal or a reference to his membership in the party of the Zealots, a Jewish revolutionary group violently opposed to Roman rule over the Holy Land.

10:5 *Do not go.* The good news about the kingdom was to be proclaimed first to Jews only. After His death and resurrection, Jesus commanded the message to be taken to all nations (28:19; cf. 21:43). *Samaritans.* A mixed-blood race resulting from the intermarriage of Israelites left behind when the people of the northern kingdom were exiled and Gentiles brought into the land by the Assyrians (2 Kin 17:24). Bitter hostility existed between Jews and Samaritans in Jesus' day (see John 4:9).

10:7 *kingdom of heaven.* See note on 3:2.

10:8 *lepers.* The Greek word for leprosy was used for various diseases affecting the skin—not necessarily leprosy. See note on Lev 13:2.

10:9–10 See notes on Mark 6:8–9.

10:12 *your greeting.* The Jews' greeting was *shalom,* "peace."

10:14 *shake the dust off your feet.* A symbolic act practiced by the Pharisees when they left an "unclean" Gentile area. Here it represented an act of solemn warning to those who rejected God's message (see notes on Luke 9:5; Acts 13:51; cf. Acts 18:6).

10:15 *Sodom and Gomorrah.* See Gen 19:23–29.

10:16 Cf. Paul's statement in Rom 16:19: "I want you to be wise in what is good and innocent in what is evil."

10:17 *courts.* The lower courts, connected with local synagogues, that tried less serious cases and flogged those found guilty. *synagogues.* See notes on Mark 1:21 and Luke 21:12.

19 "[a]But when they hand you over, [b]do not worry about how or what you are to say; for it will be given you in that hour what you are to say.

20 "For [a]it is not you who speak, but *it is* the Spirit of your Father who speaks in you.

21 "[a]Brother will betray brother to death, and a father *his* child; and [b]children will rise up against parents and [1]cause them to be put to death.

22 "[a]You will be hated by all because of My name, but [b]it is the one who has endured to the end who will be saved.

23 "But whenever they [a]persecute you in [1]one city, flee to [2]the next; for truly I say to you, you will not finish *going through* the cities of Israel [b]until the Son of Man comes.

The Meaning of Discipleship

24 "[a]A [1]disciple is not above his teacher, nor a slave above his master.

25 "It is enough for the disciple that he become like his teacher, and the slave like his master. [a]If they have called the head of the house [1b]Beelzebul, how much more *will they malign* the members of his household!

26 "Therefore do not [a]fear them, [b]for there is nothing concealed that will not be revealed, or hidden that will not be known.

27 "[a]What I tell you in the darkness, speak in the light; and what you hear *whispered* in *your* ear, proclaim [b]upon the housetops.

28 "Do not fear those who kill the body but are unable to kill the soul; but rather [a]fear Him who is able to destroy both soul and body in [1b]hell.

29 "[a]Are not two sparrows sold for a [1]cent? And *yet* not one of them will fall to the ground apart from your Father.

30 "But [a]the very hairs of your head are all numbered.

31 "So do not fear; [a]you are more valuable than many sparrows.

32 "Therefore [a]everyone who [1]confesses Me before men, I will also confess [2]him before My Father who is in heaven.

33 "But [a]whoever [1]denies Me before men, I will also deny him before My Father who is in heaven.

34 "[a]Do not think that I came to [1]bring peace on the earth; I did not come to bring peace, but a sword.

35 "For I came to [a]SET A MAN AGAINST HIS FATHER, AND A DAUGHTER AGAINST HER MOTHER, AND A DAUGHTER-IN-LAW AGAINST HER MOTHER-IN-LAW;

36 and [a]A MAN'S ENEMIES WILL BE THE MEMBERS OF HIS HOUSEHOLD.

37 "[a]He who loves father or mother more than Me is not worthy of Me; and he who loves son or daughter more than Me is not worthy of Me.

38 "And [a]he who does not take his cross and follow after Me is not worthy of Me.

39 "[a]He who has found his [1]life will lose it, and he who has lost his [1]life for My sake will find it.

The Reward of Service

40 "[a]He who receives you receives Me, and [b]he who receives Me receives Him who sent Me.

41 "[a]He who receives a prophet in *the* name of a prophet shall receive a prophet's reward; and he who receives a righteous man in the name of a righteous man shall receive a righteous man's reward.

42 "And [a]whoever in the name of a disciple gives to one of these [1]little ones even a cup of cold water to drink, truly I say to you, he shall not lose his reward."

John's Questions

11 [a]When Jesus had finished [1]giving instructions to His twelve disciples, He departed from there [b]to teach and [2]preach in their cities.

19 [a]Matt 10:19-22: *Mark 13:11-13; Luke 21:12-17* [b]Matt 6:25; Luke 12:11, 12
20 [a]Luke 12:12; Acts 4:8; 13:9; 2 Cor 13:3
21 [1]Lit *put them to death* [a]Matt 10:35, 36; Mark 13:12 [b]Mic 7:6
22 [a]Matt 24:9; Luke 21:17; John 15:18ff [b]Matt 24:13; Mark 13:13
23 [1]Lit *this* [2]Lit *the other* [a]Matt 23:34 [b]Matt 16:27f
24 [1]Or *student* [a]Luke 6:40; John 13:16; 15:20
25 [1]Or *Beezebul:* ruler of demons [a]Matt 9:34 [b]2 Kin 1:2; Matt 12:24, 27; Mark 3:22; Luke 11:15, 18, 19
26 [a]Matt 10:26-33: *Luke 12:2-9* [b]Mark 4:22; Luke 8:17; 12:2; 1 Cor 4:5
27 [a]Luke 12:3 [b]Matt 24:17; Acts 5:20
28 [1]Gr *Gehenna* [a]Heb 10:31 [b]Matt 5:22; Luke 12:5
29 [1]Gr *assarion,* the smallest copper coin [a]Luke 12:6
30 [a]1 Sam 14:45; 2 Sam 14:11; 1 Kin 1:52; Luke 21:18; Acts 27:34
31 [a]Matt 12:12
32 [1]Lit *will confess in Me* [2]Lit *in him* [a]Luke 12:8; Rev 3:5
33 [1]Lit *will deny* [a]Mark 8:38; Luke 9:26; 2 Tim 2:12
34 [1]Lit *cast* [a]Matt 10:34, 35: *Luke 12:51-53*

35 [a]Mic 7:6; Matt 10:21; Luke 12:53 **36** [a]Mic 7:6; Matt 10:21 **37** [a]Deut 33:9; Luke 14:26 **38** [a]Matt 16:24; Mark 8:34; Luke 9:23; 14:27 **39** [1]Or *soul* [a]Matt 16:25; Mark 8:35; Luke 9:24; 17:33; John 12:25 **40** [a]Matt 18:5; Luke 10:16; John 13:20; Gal 4:14 [b]Mark 9:37; Luke 9:48; John 12:44 **41** [a]Matt 25:44, 45 **42** [1]I.e. humble [a]Matt 25:40; Mark 9:41 **11:1** [1]Or *commanding* [2]Or *proclaim* [a]Matt 7:28 [b]Matt 9:35; Luke 23:5

10:19 *do not worry about . . . what you are to say.* Not to be used by preachers as an excuse for lack of sermon preparation! See Luke 21:14–15.

10:22 *the one who has endured to the end . . . will be saved.* See note on Mark 13:13.

10:23 Jesus' saying here is probably best understood as referring to His coming in judgment on the Jews when Jerusalem and the temple were destroyed in A.D. 70.

10:25 *Beelzebul.* Satan, the ruler of demons (12:24); the Greek form of the Hebrew name Baal-Zebul ("Exalted Baal" or "Prince Baal"). The Hebrew epithet Baal-Zebub ("lord of flies"), is a parody on and mockery of the actual name (see Judg 10:6).

10:28 *soul.* The true self. Body and soul are closely related in this life but are separated at death and then reunited at the resurrection (cf. 2 Cor 5:1–10; Phil 1:23–24). *Him.* God. He alone determines the final destiny of us all. *hell.* See note on 5:22.

10:34 At first glance this saying sounds like a contradiction of Is 9:6 ("Prince of Peace"), Luke 2:14 ("on earth peace among men") and John 14:27 ("Peace I leave with you"). It is true that Christ came to bring peace—peace between the believer and God, and peace among men. Yet the inevitable result of Christ's coming is conflict—between Christ and the antichrist, between light and darkness, between Christ's children and the devil's children. This conflict can occur even between members of the same family (vv. 35–36).

10:38 *take his cross.* The first mention of the cross in Matthew's Gospel. The cross was an instrument of death and here symbolizes the necessity of total commitment—even unto death—on the part of Jesus' disciples (see note on Mark 8:34).

10:40–42 During times of persecution, hospitality was especially important and could be dangerous. So Jesus indicates that those who provide it and show kindness to God's people will receive a reward.

11:1 While the 12 apostles were carrying out their first mission, Jesus continued His ministry in Galilee.

2 [a]Now when [b]John, [1]while imprisoned,
heard of the works of Christ, he sent *word* by
his disciples
3 and said to Him, "Are You [a]the [1]Expect-
ed One, or shall we look for someone else?"
4 Jesus answered and said to them, "Go
and report to John what you hear and see:
5 [a]*the* BLIND RECEIVE SIGHT and *the* lame
walk, *the* lepers are cleansed and *the* deaf
hear, *the* dead are raised up, and *the* [b]POOR
HAVE THE [1]GOSPEL PREACHED TO THEM.
6 "And blessed is he [1]who [a]does not [2]take
offense at Me."

Jesus' Tribute to John

7 As these men were going *away,* Jesus
began to speak to the crowds about John,
"What did you go out into [a]the wilderness to
see? A reed shaken by the wind?
8 "[1]But what did you go out to see? A man
dressed in soft *clothing?* Those who wear soft
clothing are in kings' [2]palaces!
9 "[1]But what did you go out to see? [a]A
prophet? Yes, I tell you, and one who is more
than a prophet.
10 "This is the one about whom it [1]is written,

'[a]BEHOLD, I SEND MY MESSENGER [2]AHEAD
OF YOU,
WHO WILL PREPARE YOUR WAY BEFORE
YOU.'

11 "Truly I say to you, among those born of
women there has not arisen *anyone* greater
than John the Baptist! Yet the one who is
[1]least in the kingdom of heaven is greater
than he.
12 "[a]From the days of John the Baptist
until now the kingdom of heaven [1]suffers
violence, and violent men [2]take it by force.
13 "For all the prophets and the Law prophesied until John.
14 "And if you are willing to accept *it,* John
himself is [a]Elijah who [1]was to come.
15 "[a]He who has ears to hear, [1]let him hear.
16 "But to what shall I compare this generation? It is like children sitting in the market
places, who call out to the other *children,*
17 and say, 'We played the flute for you,
and you did not dance; we sang a dirge, and
you did not [1]mourn.'
18 "For John came neither [a]eating nor
[b]drinking, and they say, '[c]He has a demon!'
19 "The Son of Man came eating and drinking, and they say, 'Behold, a gluttonous man
and a [1]drunkard, [a]a friend of tax collectors
and [2]sinners!' Yet wisdom is vindicated by
her deeds."

The Unrepenting Cities

20 Then He began to denounce the cities
in which most of His [1a]miracles were done,
because they did not repent.
21 "[a]Woe to you, Chorazin! Woe to you,
[b]Bethsaida! For if the [1]miracles had occurred
in [c]Tyre and [c]Sidon which occurred in you,
they would have repented long ago in
[2d]sackcloth and ashes.
22 "Nevertheless I say to you, [a]it will be
more tolerable for Tyre and Sidon in [b]*the* day
of judgment than for you.
23 "And you, [a]Capernaum, will not be
exalted to heaven, will you? You will

2 [1]Lit *in prison* [a]Matt 11:2-19: *Luke 7:18-35;* Matt 4:12 [b]Matt 14:3; Mark 6:17; Luke 9:7ff
3 [1]Lit *Coming One* [a]Ps 118:26; Matt 11:10; John 6:14; 11:27; Heb 10:37
5 [1]Or *good news* [a]Is 35:5f; Matt 8:3; 12:13 [b]Is 61:1; Luke 4:18
6 [1]Lit *whoever* [2]Or *stumble over Me* [a]Matt 5:29; 13:57; 24:10; 26:31; Mark 6:3; John 6:61; 16:1
7 [a]Matt 3:1
8 [1]Or *Well then,* [2]Lit *houses*
9 [1]Or *Well then,* [a]Matt 14:5; 21:26; Luke 1:76; 20:6
10 [1]Lit *has been written* [2]Lit *before your face* [a]Mal 3:1; Mark 1:2
11 [1]Or *less*
12 [1]Or *is forcibly entered* [2]Or *seize it for themselves* [a]Luke 16:16
14 [1]Or *is going to come* [a]Mal 4:5; Matt 17:10-13; Mark 9:11-13; Luke 1:17; John 1:21
15 [1]Or *hear!* Or *listen!* [a]Matt 13:9, 43; Mark 4:9, 23; Luke 8:8; 14:35; Rev 2:7, 11, 17, 29; 3:6, 13, 22; 13:9
17 [1]Lit *beat the breast*
18 [a]Matt 3:4 [b]Luke 1:15 [c]Matt 9:34; John 7:20; 8:48f, 52; 10:20
19 [1]Or *wine-drinker* [2]I.e. irreligious Jews [a]Matt 9:11; Luke 5:29-32; 15:2
20 [1]Or *works of power* [a]Luke 10:13-15
21 [1]Or *works of power* [2]I.e. symbols of mourning [a]Matt 11:21-23: *Luke 10:13-15* [b]Mark 6:45; 8:22; Luke 9:10; John 1:44; 12:21 [c]Matt 11:22; 15:21; Mark 3:8; 7:24, 31; Luke 4:26; 6:17; Acts 12:20; 27:3 [d]Rev 11:3
22 [a]Matt 10:15; 11:24 [b]Matt 10:15; 12:36; Rev 20:11, 12
23 [a]Matt 4:13

11:3 *the Expected One.* The Messiah. *look for someone else.* See note on Luke 7:19.

11:4 *report to John what you hear and see.* See note on Luke 7:22.

11:5 *lepers.* See note on 8:2 and Lev 13:2. *the POOR HAVE THE GOSPEL PREACHED TO THEM.* See note on Luke 7:22.

11:6 *he who does not take offense.* See note on Luke 7:23.

11:11 *greater than he.* John belonged to the age of the old covenant, which was preparatory to Christ. The least NT saint has a higher privilege in Christ as a part of His bride (the church, Eph 5:25–27,32) than John the Baptist, who was only a friend of the bridegroom (John 3:29). Another view, however, stresses the expression "he who is least," holding that the key to its meaning is found in 18:4—"whoever . . . humbles himself as this child." Such a person, though "least," is regarded by God as even greater than John the Baptist.

11:12 *suffers violence.* The Greek here can be taken in either an active or a passive sense. In this context its passive meaning would be, "suffering violent attacks." The term "violent men," then, would be understood in a negative sense. The verse would then emphasize the ongoing persecution of the people of the kingdom.

11:13 *prophets and the Law.* The entire OT prophesied the coming of the kingdom. John represented the end of the old economy.

11:14 *John himself is Elijah who was to come.* A reference to Mal 4:5, which prophesied the reappearance of Elijah before the day of the Lord. Some of the people remembered the prophecy and asked John the Baptist, "Are you Elijah?" He answered, "I am not" (John 1:21). John was not literally the reincarnation of Elijah, but he did fulfill the function and role of the prophet (see Matt 17:10–13 and note on Luke 1:17).

11:16 *like children sitting in the market places.* See note on Luke 7:32.

11:17 *played the flute.* As at a wedding. *sang a dirge.* As at a funeral. The latter symbolized the ministry of John, the former that of Jesus. The people of Jesus' generation were like children who refused to respond on either occasion.

11:19 *Son of Man.* See note on Mark 8:31. *wisdom is vindicated by her deeds.* Apparently means that God (wisdom) had sent both John and Jesus in specific roles, and that this would be vindicated by the lasting works of both Jesus and John (see note on Luke 7:35).

11:21 *Chorazin.* Mentioned in the Bible only twice (here and in Luke 10:13), it was near the Sea of Galilee, probably about two miles north of Capernaum. *Bethsaida.* On the northeast shore of the Sea of Galilee. Philip the tetrarch rebuilt Bethsaida and named it "Julias," after Julia, daughter of Caesar Augustus. *Tyre and Sidon.* Cities on the Phoenician coast north of the Holy Land. *sackcloth.* Here a sign of repentance (see note on Gen 37:34). Cf. Rev 6:12. *ashes.* Also a sign of repentance.

11:23 *Capernaum.* See note on Luke 10:15.

[b]descend to [c]Hades; for if the [1]miracles had occurred in [d]Sodom which occurred in you, it would have remained to this day.

24 "Nevertheless I say to you that [a]it will be more tolerable for the land of [b]Sodom in *the* day of judgment, than for you."

Come to Me

25 [a]At that [1]time Jesus said, "I praise You, [b]Father, Lord of heaven and earth, that [c]You have hidden these things from *the* wise and intelligent and have revealed them to infants.

26 "Yes, [a]Father, for this way was well-pleasing in Your sight.

27 "[a]All things have been handed over to Me by My Father; and no one knows the Son except the Father; nor does anyone know the Father [b]except the Son, and anyone to whom the Son wills to reveal *Him.*

28 "[a]Come to Me, all [1]who are weary and heavy-laden, and I will give you rest.

29 "Take My yoke upon you and [a]learn from Me, for I am gentle and humble in heart, and [b]YOU WILL FIND REST FOR YOUR SOULS.

30 "For [a]My yoke is [1]easy and My burden is light."

Sabbath Questions

12 [a]At that [1]time Jesus went through the grainfields on the Sabbath, and His disciples became hungry and began to [b]pick the heads *of grain* and eat.

2 But when the Pharisees saw *this,* they said to Him, "Look, Your disciples do what [a]is not lawful to do on a Sabbath."

3 But He said to them, "Have you not read what David did when he became hungry, he and his companions,

4 how he entered the house of God, and [a]they ate the [1]consecrated bread, which was not lawful for him to eat nor for those with him, but for the priests alone?

5 "Or have you not read in the Law, that on the Sabbath the priests in the temple [1]break the Sabbath and are innocent?

6 "But I say to you that something [a]greater than the temple is here.

23 [1]Or *works of power* [a]Matt 4:13 [b]Is 14:13, 15; Ezek 26:20; 31:14; 32:18, 24 [c]Matt 16:18; Luke 10:15; 16:23; Acts 2:27, 31; Rev 1:18; 6:8; 20:13f [d]Matt 10:15
24 [a]Matt 10:15; 11:22 [b]Matt 10:15
25 [1]Or *occasion* [a]Matt 11:25-27: *Luke 10:21, 22* [b]Luke 22:42; 23:34; John 11:41; 12:27, 28 [c]Ps 8:2; 1 Cor 1:26ff
26 [a]Luke 22:42; 23:34; John 11:41; 12:27, 28
27 [a]Matt 28:18; John 3:35; 13:3; 17:2 [b]John 7:29; 10:15; 17:25
28 [1]Or *who work to exhaustion* [a]Jer 31:25; John 7:37
29 [a]John 13:15; Eph 4:20; Phil 2:5; 1 Pet 2:21; 1 John 2:6 [b]Jer 6:16
30 [1]Or *comfortable,* or *pleasant* [a]1 John 5:3
12:1 [1]Or *occasion* [a]Matt 12:1-8: *Mark 2:23-28; Luke 6:1-5* [b]Deut 23:25
2 [a]Matt 12:10; Luke 13:14; 14:3; John 5:10; 7:23; 9:16
4 [1]Or *showbread;* lit *loaves of presentation* [a]1 Sam 21:6
5 [1]Or *profane*
6 [a]2 Chr 6:18; Is 66:1, 2; Matt 12:41, 42

7 [1]Lit *is* [2]Or *mercy* [a]Hos 6:6; Matt 9:13
8 [a]Matt 8:20; 12:32, 40
9 [a]Matt 12:9-14: *Mark 3:1-6; Luke 6:6-11*

7 "But if you had known what this [1]means, '[a]I DESIRE [2]COMPASSION, AND NOT A SACRIFICE,' you would not have condemned the innocent.

Lord of the Sabbath

8 "For [a]the Son of Man is Lord of the Sabbath."

9 [a]Departing from there, He went into their synagogue.

10 And a man *was there* whose hand was withered. And they questioned [1]Jesus, asking, "[a]Is it lawful to heal on the Sabbath?"—so that they might accuse Him.

11 And He said to them, "[a]What man [1]is there among you who [2]has a sheep, and if it falls into a pit on the Sabbath, will he not take hold of it and lift it out?

12 "[a]How much more valuable then is a man than a sheep! So then, it is lawful to do [1]good on the Sabbath."

13 Then He *said to the man, "Stretch out your hand!" [a]He stretched it out, and it was restored to [1]normal, like the other.

14 But the Pharisees went out and [1][a]conspired against Him, *as to* how they might destroy Him.

15 But Jesus, [1]aware of *this,* withdrew from there. Many followed Him, and [a]He healed them all,

16 and [a]warned them not to [1]tell who He was.

17 *This was* to fulfill what was spoken through Isaiah the prophet:

18 "[a]BEHOLD, MY [1]SERVANT WHOM I [2]HAVE CHOSEN;
[b]MY BELOVED IN WHOM MY SOUL [3]is WELL-PLEASED;
[c]I WILL PUT MY SPIRIT UPON HIM,
[a]AND HE SHALL PROCLAIM [4]JUSTICE TO THE [5]GENTILES.

10 [1]Lit *Him* [a]Matt 12:2; Luke 13:14; 14:3; John 5:10; 7:23; 9:16 **11** [1]Lit *will be from you* [2]Lit *will have* [a]Luke 14:5 **12** [1]Lit *well* [a]Matt 10:31; Luke 14:1-6 **13** [1]Lit *health* [a]Matt 8:3; Acts 28:8 **14** [1]Lit *took counsel* [a]Matt 26:4; Mark 14:1; Luke 22:2; John 7:30, 44; 8:59; 10:31, 39; 11:53 **15** [1]Lit *knowing* [a]Matt 4:23 **16** [1]Lit *make Him known* [a]Matt 8:4; 9:30; 17:9 **18** [1]Lit *Child* [2]Lit *chose* [3]Or *took pleasure* [4]Or *judgment* [5]Or *nations* [a]Is 42:1 [b]Matt 3:17; 17:5 [c]Luke 4:18; John 3:34

11:25 *these things.* The "things" probably include an understanding of Jesus' mission. *the wise and intelligent.* The teachers of the law and the Pharisees. *infants.* The humble followers of Jesus.
12:1 *grainfields.* Of wheat or barley, the latter eaten by poorer people. *pick the heads of grain.* See note on Mark 2.23.
12:2 *Pharisees.* See note on Mark 2:16. *what is not lawful to do on a Sabbath.* See note on Mark 2:24.
12:3 *what David did.* See note on Mark 2:25.
12:4 *consecrated bread.* Each Sabbath, 12 fresh loaves of bread were to be set on a table in the holy place (Ex 25:30; Lev 24:5–9). The old loaves were eaten by the priests.
12:5 *break the Sabbath.* By doing work associated with the sacrifices.
12:8 *the Son of Man is Lord of the Sabbath.* See note on Luke 6:5.
12:9 *synagogue.* See note on Mark 1:21.
12:10 *heal on the Sabbath.* The rabbis prohibited healing on the Sabbath, unless it was feared the victim would die before the next day. Obviously the man with the withered hand was in no danger of this.
12:13 *"Stretch out your hand!" He stretched it out.* The fact that the man stretched out his withered hand shows there is a connection between faith and Jesus' healing power.
12:16 *not to tell who He was.* See note on 8:4.
12:18–21 Another fulfillment passage (see note on 1:22). This one is from Isaiah's first servant song (42:1–4) and is the longest OT quotation in Matthew's Gospel. It summarizes the quiet ministry of the Lord's servant, who will bring justice and hope to the nations.
12:18 *MY SERVANT.* Jesus is called God's servant only here and in Acts 3:13 (see note there), 26; 4:27,30. *MY BELOVED IN WHOM MY SOUL IS WELL-PLEASED.* See note on 3:17.

19 "[a]HE WILL NOT QUARREL, NOR CRY OUT;
NOR WILL ANYONE HEAR HIS VOICE IN THE STREETS.
20 "[a]A BATTERED REED HE WILL NOT BREAK OFF,
AND A SMOLDERING WICK HE WILL NOT PUT OUT,
UNTIL HE [1]LEADS [2]JUSTICE TO VICTORY.
21 "[a]AND IN HIS NAME THE [1]GENTILES WILL HOPE."

The Pharisees Rebuked

22 [a]Then a [b]demon-possessed man *who was* blind and mute was brought to [1]Jesus, and He healed him, so that the mute man spoke and saw.

23 All the crowds were amazed, and were saying, "This man cannot be the [a]Son of David, can he?"

24 But when the Pharisees heard *this,* they said, "This man [a]casts out demons only by [1]Beelzebul the ruler of the demons."

25 [a]And [b]knowing their thoughts Jesus said to them, "[1]Any kingdom divided against itself is laid waste; and [1]any city or house divided against itself will not stand.

26 "If [a]Satan casts out Satan, he [1]is divided against himself; how then will his kingdom stand?

27 "If I [a]by [1]Beelzebul cast out demons, [b]by whom do your sons cast *them* out? For this reason they will be your judges.

28 "But [a]if I cast out demons by the Spirit of God, then the kingdom of God has come upon you.

29 "Or how can anyone enter the strong man's house and carry off his property, unless he first binds the strong *man?* And then he will plunder his house.

The Unpardonable Sin

30 "[a]He who is not with Me is against Me; and he who does not gather with Me scatters.

31 "[a]Therefore I say to you, any sin and blasphemy shall be forgiven people, but blasphemy against the Spirit shall not be forgiven.

32 "[a]Whoever [1]speaks a word against the Son of Man, it shall be forgiven him; but whoever [1]speaks against the Holy Spirit, it shall not be forgiven him, either in [b]this age or in the *age* to come.

Words Reveal Character

33 "Either make the tree good and its fruit good, or make the tree bad and its fruit bad; for [a]the tree is known by its fruit.

34 "[a]You brood of vipers, how can you, being evil, speak [1]what is good? [b]For the mouth speaks out of that which fills the heart.

35 "[a]The good man brings out of *his* good treasure [1]what is good; and the evil man brings out of *his* evil treasure [2]what is evil.

36 "But I tell you that every [1]careless word that people [2]speak, they shall give an accounting for it in [a]the day of judgment.

37 "For [1]by your words you will be justified, and [1]by your words you will be condemned."

The Desire for Signs

38 Then some of the scribes and Pharisees said to Him, "Teacher, [a]we want to see a [1]sign from You."

39 But He answered and said to them, "[a]An evil and adulterous generation craves for a [1]sign; and *yet* no [1]sign will be given to it but the [1]sign of Jonah the prophet;

40 for just as [a]JONAH WAS THREE DAYS AND THREE NIGHTS IN THE BELLY OF THE SEA MONSTER, so will [b]the Son of Man be [c]three days and three nights in the heart of the earth.

41 "[a]The men of Nineveh will stand up with this generation at the judgment, and will condemn it because [b]they repented at the preaching of Jonah; and behold, [c]something greater than Jonah is here.

42 "[a]*The* Queen of *the* South will rise up with this generation at the judgment and will condemn it, because she came from the ends of the earth to hear the wisdom of Solomon; and behold, [b]something greater than Solomon is here.

43 "[a]Now when the unclean spirit goes out of a man, it passes through waterless places seeking rest, and does not find *it.*

44 "Then it says, 'I will return to my house from which I came'; and when it comes, it finds *it* unoccupied, swept, and put in order.

19 [a]Is 42:2 **20** [1]Or *puts forth* [2]Or *judgment* [a]Is 42:3 **21** [1]Or *nations* [a]Rom 15:12 **22** [1]Lit *Him* [a]Matt 12:22, 24: *Luke 11:14, 15;* Matt 9:32, 34 [b]Matt 4:24; 2 Thess 2:9 **23** [a]Matt 9:27 **24** [1]Or *Beezebul;* i.e. ruler of demons [a]Matt 9:34 **25** [1]Lit *Every* [a]Matt 12:25-29: *Mark 3:23-27; Luke 11:17-22* [b]Matt 9:4 **26** [1]Lit *was* [a]Matt 4:10; 13:19 **27** [1]V 24, note 1 [a]Matt 9:34 [b]Acts 19:13 **28** [a]1 John 3:8 **30** [a]Mark 9:40; Luke 9:50; 11:23 **31** [a]Matt 12:31, 32; Mark 3:28-30; Luke 12:10 **32** [1]Lit *will speak* [a]Luke 12:10 [b]Matt 13:22, 39; Mark 10:30; Luke 16:8; 18:30; 20:34, 35; Eph 1:21; 1 Tim 6:17; 2 Tim 4:10; Titus 2:12; Heb 6:5

33 [a]Matt 7:16-18; Luke 6:43, 44; John 15:4-7 **34** [1]Lit *good things* [a]Matt 3:7; 23:33; Luke 3:7 [b]1 Sam 24:13; Is 32:6; Matt 12:34, 35; 15:18; Luke 6:45; Eph 4:29; James 3:2-12 **35** [1]Lit *good things* [2]Lit *evil things* [a]Prov 10:20, 21; 25:11, 12; Matt 13:52; Col 4:6 **36** [1]Or *useless* [2]Lit *will speak* [a]Matt 10:15 **37** [1]Or *in accordance with* **38** [1]I.e. attesting miracle [a]Matt 16:1; Mark 8:11, 12; Luke 11:16; John 2:18; 6:30; 1 Cor 1:22 **39** [1]I.e. attesting miracle [a]Matt 12:39-42: *Luke 11:29-32;* Matt 16:4 **40** [a]Jon 1:17 [b]Matt 8:20 [c]Matt 16:21 **41** [a]Jon 1:2 [b]Jon 3:5 [c]Matt 12:6, 42 **42** [a]1 Kin 10:1; 2 Chr 9:1 [b]Matt 12:6, 41 **43** [a]Matt 12:43-45: *Luke 11:24-26*

12:20 Jesus mends broken lives (see v. 15; John 4:4–42; 8:3–11).

12:23 *the Son of David.* See note on 9:27.

12:24 *Beelzebul.* See note on 10:25.

12:28 *kingdom of God.* See note on 3:2.

12:31 *blasphemy against the Spirit shall not be forgiven.* The context (vv. 24,28,32) suggests that the "unpardonable sin" was attributing to Satan Christ's authenticating miracles done in the power of the Holy Spirit (see note on Mark 3:29).

12:38 *sign.* The Pharisees wanted to see a spectacular miracle, preferably in the sky (see Luke 11:16), as the sign that Jesus was the Messiah. Instead, He cites them a "sign" from history. See note on Luke 11:29.

12:39 *adulterous.* Referring to spiritual, not physical, adultery, in the sense that their generation had become unfaithful to its spiritual husband (God).

12:40 *THREE DAYS AND THREE NIGHTS.* Including at least part of the first day and part of the third day, a common Jewish reckoning of time. See note on Luke 24:46. *SEA MONSTER.* The Greek word does not mean "whale" but rather "sea creature," i.e., a huge fish (see note on Jon 1:17).

12:41–42 *something greater than Jonah . . . something greater than Solomon.* See note on Luke 11:31–32.

12:42 *Queen of the South.* In 1 Kin 10:1 she is called the queen of Sheba, a country in southwest Arabia, now called Yemen.

12:43–45 See note on Luke 11:24.

45 "Then it goes and takes along with it seven other spirits more wicked than itself, and they go in and live there; and [a]the last state of that man becomes worse than the first. That is the way it will also be with this evil generation."

Changed Relationships

46 [a]While He was still speaking to the crowds, behold, His [b]mother and [c]brothers were standing outside, seeking to speak to Him.

47 Someone said to Him, "Behold, Your mother and Your brothers are standing outside seeking to speak to You."

48 But [1]Jesus answered the one who was telling Him and said, "Who is My mother and who are My brothers?"

49 And stretching out His hand toward His disciples, He said, "Behold My mother and My brothers!

50 "For whoever does the will of My Father who is in heaven, he is My brother and sister and mother."

Jesus Teaches in Parables

13 That day Jesus went out of [a]the house and was sitting [b]by the sea.

2 And [1]large crowds gathered to Him, so [a]He got into a boat and sat down, and the whole crowd was standing on the beach.

3 And He spoke many things to them in [a]parables, saying, "Behold, the sower went out to sow;

4 and as he sowed, some *seeds* fell beside the road, and the birds came and ate them up.

5 "Others fell on the rocky places, where they did not have much soil; and immediately they sprang up, because they had no depth of soil.

6 "But when the sun had risen, they were scorched; and because they had no root, they withered away.

7 "Others fell [1]among the thorns, and the thorns came up and choked them out.

8 "And others fell on the good soil and *yielded a crop, some a [a]hundredfold, some sixty, and some thirty.

9 "[a]He who has ears, [1]let him hear."

45 [a]Mark 5:9; Luke 11:26; Heb 6:4-8; 2 Pet 2:20 **46** [a]Matt 12:46-50: *Mark 3:31-35; Luke 8:19-21* [b]Matt 1:18; 2:11ff; 13:55; Luke 1:43; 2:33f, 48, 51; John 2:1, 5, 12; 19:25f; Acts 1:14 [c]Matt 13:55; Mark 6:3; John 2:12; 7:3, 5, 10; Acts 1:14; 1 Cor 9:5; Gal 1:19 **48** [1]Lit *He* **13:1** [a]Matt 9:28; 13:36 [b]Matt 13:1-15: *Mark 4:1-12; Luke 8:4-10;* Mark 2:13 **2** [1]Lit *Many* [a]Luke 5:3 **3** [a]Matt 13:10ff; Mark 4:2ff **7** [1]Lit *upon* **8** [a]Gen 26:12; Matt 13:23 **9** [1]Or *hear!* Or *listen!* [a]Matt 11:15; Rev 2:7, 11, 17, 29; 3:6, 13, 22

11 [1]Lit *He* [a]Matt 19:11; 20:23; John 6:65; 1 Cor 2:10; Col 1:27; 1 John 2:20, 27 **12** [a]Matt 25:29; Mark 4:25; Luke 8:18; 19:26 **13** [a]Deut 29:4; Is 42:19, 20; Jer 5:21; Ezek 12:2 **14** [1]Lit *For them* [2]Lit *With a hearing you will hear* [3]Lit *and* [4]Lit *Seeing you will see* [a]Is 6:9; Mark 4:12; Luke 8:10; John 12:40; Acts 28:26, 27; Rom 10:16; 11:8 **15** [a]Is 6:10; Ps 119:70; Zech 7:11; Luke 19:42; John 8:43, 44; 2 Tim 4:4; Heb 5:11 **16** [a]Matt 13:16, 17: *Luke 10:23, 24;* Matt 16:17; John 20:29 **17** [a]John 8:56; Heb 11:13; 1 Pet 1:10-12 **18** [a]Matt 13:18-23: *Mark 4:13-20; Luke 8:11-15*

An Explanation

10 And the disciples came and said to Him, "Why do You speak to them in parables?"

11 [1]Jesus answered them, "[a]To you it has been granted to know the mysteries of the kingdom of heaven, but to them it has not been granted.

12 "[a]For whoever has, to him *more* shall be given, and he will have an abundance; but whoever does not have, even what he has shall be taken away from him.

13 "Therefore I speak to them in parables; because while [a]seeing they do not see, and while hearing they do not hear, nor do they understand.

14 "[1]In their case the prophecy of Isaiah is being fulfilled, which says,

'[2][a]YOU WILL KEEP ON HEARING, [3]BUT WILL NOT UNDERSTAND;
[4]YOU WILL KEEP ON SEEING, BUT WILL NOT PERCEIVE;

15 [a]FOR THE HEART OF THIS PEOPLE HAS BECOME DULL,
WITH THEIR EARS THEY SCARCELY HEAR,
AND THEY HAVE CLOSED THEIR EYES,
OTHERWISE THEY WOULD SEE WITH THEIR EYES,
HEAR WITH THEIR EARS,
AND UNDERSTAND WITH THEIR HEART AND RETURN,
AND I WOULD HEAL THEM.'

16 "[a]But blessed are your eyes, because they see; and your ears, because they hear.

17 "For truly I say to you that [a]many prophets and righteous men desired to see what you see, and did not see *it*, and to hear what you hear, and did not hear *it*.

The Sower Explained

18 "[a]Hear then the parable of the sower.

19 "When anyone hears [a]the [1]word of the kingdom and does not understand it, [b]the evil *one* comes and snatches away what has been sown in his heart. This is the one on whom seed was sown beside the road.

20 "The one on whom seed was sown on the rocky places, this is the man who hears the word and immediately receives it with joy;

19 [1]I.e. message [a]Matt 4:23 [b]Matt 5:37

12:46 *mother and brothers.* See note on Luke 8:19.
12:50 *whoever does the will of my Father.* See note on Mark 3:35.
13:2 *sat down.* See note on Mark 4:1.
13:3–9 See vv. 18–23 for the interpretation of this first parable.
13:3 *parables.* Our word "parable" comes from the Greek *parabole,* which means "a placing beside"—and thus a comparison or an illustration. Its most common use in the NT is for the illustrative stories that Jesus drew from nature and human life. The Synoptic Gospels contain about 30 of these stories. John's Gospel contains no parables but uses other figures of speech (see notes on Mark 4:2; Luke 8:4). *to sow.* See note on Luke 8:5.
13:4–6 See note on Mark 4:3–8.
13:5 *rocky places.* Not ground covered with small stones, but shallow soil on top of solid rock. See note on Luke 8:6.
13:8 *a hundredfold.* See note on Luke 8:8.
13:10 See note on Luke 8:9.
13:11 *mysteries of the kingdom of heaven.* See notes on Mark 4:11 and Luke 8:10.
13:13–14 Jesus speaks in parables because of the spiritual dullness of the people (see note on Luke 8:4).
13:13 *while seeing they do not see.* See notes on Mark 4:12 and Luke 8:10.
13:18 *Hear then the parable of the sower.* Jesus seldom interpreted His parables, but here He does.
13:19 *the evil one.* The devil.

21 yet he has no *firm* root in himself, but
is *only* temporary, and when affliction or persecution arises because of the [1]word, immediately he [2][a]falls away.
22 "And the one on whom seed was sown
among the thorns, this is the man who hears
the word, and the worry of [a]the [1]world and
the [b]deceitfulness of wealth choke the word,
and it becomes unfruitful.
23 "And the one on whom seed was sown
on the good soil, this is the man who hears
the word and understands it; who indeed
bears fruit and brings forth, some [a]a hundredfold, some sixty, and some thirty."

Tares among Wheat

24 Jesus presented another parable to
them, saying, "[a]The kingdom of heaven
[1]may be compared to a man who sowed
good seed in his field.
25 "But while his men were sleeping, his
enemy came and sowed [1]tares among the
wheat, and went away.
26 "But when the [1]wheat sprouted and
bore grain, then the tares became evident
also.
27 "The slaves of the landowner came and
said to him, 'Sir, did you not sow good seed
in your field? [1]How then does it have tares?'
28 "And he said to them, 'An [1]enemy has
done this!' The slaves *said to him, 'Do you
want us, then, to go and gather them up?'
29 "But he *said, 'No; for while you are
gathering up the tares, you may uproot the
wheat with them.
30 'Allow both to grow together until the
harvest; and in the time of the harvest I will
say to the reapers, "First gather up the tares
and bind them in bundles to burn them up;
but [a]gather the wheat into my barn." ' "

The Mustard Seed

31 He presented another parable to them,
saying, "[a]The kingdom of heaven is like [b]a
mustard seed, which a man took and sowed
in his field;
32 and this is smaller than all *other* seeds,
but when it is full grown, it is larger than the
garden plants and becomes a tree, so that
"[a]THE BIRDS OF THE [1]AIR come and NEST IN ITS
BRANCHES."

The Leaven

33 He spoke another parable to them,
"[a]The kingdom of heaven is like leaven,
which a woman took and hid in [b]three
[1]pecks of flour until it was all leavened."
34 All these things Jesus spoke to the
crowds in parables, and He did not speak to
them [a]without a parable.
35 *This was* to fulfill what was spoken
through the prophet:

"[a]I WILL OPEN MY MOUTH IN PARABLES;
I WILL UTTER THINGS HIDDEN SINCE THE
FOUNDATION OF THE WORLD."

The Tares Explained

36 Then He left the crowds and went into
[a]the house. And His disciples came to Him
and said, "[b]Explain to us the parable of the
[1]tares of the field."
37 And He said, "The one who sows the
good seed is [a]the Son of Man,
38 and the field is the world; and *as for*
the good seed, these are [a]the sons of the
kingdom; and the tares are [b]the sons of [c]the
evil *one;*
39 and the enemy who sowed them is the
devil, and the harvest is [a]the [1]end of the age;
and the reapers are angels.
40 "So just as the tares are gathered up and
burned with fire, so shall it be at [a]the [1]end of
the age.
41 "[a]The Son of Man [b]will send forth His
angels, and they will gather out of His kingdom [1]all [c]stumbling blocks, and those who
commit lawlessness,
42 and [a]will throw them into the furnace
of fire; in that place [b]there will be weeping
and gnashing of teeth.
43 "[a]Then THE RIGHTEOUS WILL SHINE FORTH AS

21 [1]I.e. message [2]Lit *is caused to stumble* [a]Matt 11:6
22 [1]Or *age* [a]Matt 12:32; 13:39; Mark 4:19; Rom 12:2; 1 Cor 1:20; 2:6, 8; 3:18; 2 Cor 4:4; Gal 1:4; Eph 2:2 [b]Matt 19:23; 1 Tim 6:9, 10, 17
23 [a]Matt 13:8
24 [1]Lit *was compared to* [a]Matt 13:31, 33, 45, 47; 18:23; 20:1; 22:2; 25:1; Mark 4:26-30; Luke 13:18, 20
25 [1]Or *darnel,* a weed resembling wheat
26 [1]Lit *grass*
27 [1]Lit *From where*
28 [1]Lit *enemy man*
30 [a]Matt 3:12
31 [a]Matt 13:31, 32: *Mark 4:30-32; Luke 13:18, 19;* Matt 13:24 [b]Matt 17:20; Luke 17:6
32 [1]Or *sky* [a]Ezek 17:23; Ps 104:12; Ezek 31:6; Dan 4:12
33 [1]Gr *sata* [a]Matt 13:33: *Luke 13:21;* Matt 13:24 [b]Gen 18:6; Judg 6:19; 1 Sam 1:24
34 [a]Mark 4:34; John 10:6; 16:25
35 [a]Ps 78:2
36 [1]Or *darnel,* a weed resembling wheat [a]Matt 13:1 [b]Matt 15:15
37 [a]Matt 8:20
38 [a]Matt 8:12 [b]John 8:44; Acts 13:10; 1 John 3:10 [c]Matt 5:37
39 [1]Or *consummation* [a]Matt 12:32; 13:22, 40, 49; 24:3; 28:20; 1 Cor 10:11; Heb 9:26
40 [1]Or *consummation* [a]Matt 12:32; 13:22, 39, 49; 24:3; 28:20; 1 Cor 10:11; Heb 9:26
41 [1]Or *everything that is offensive* [a]Matt 8:20 [b]Matt 24:31 [c]Zeph 1:3
42 [a]Matt 13:50 [b]Matt 8:12
43 [a]Dan 12:3

13:24–30 See vv. 36–43 for the interpretation.
13:24 *The kingdom of heaven may be compared to.* This phrase introduces six of the seven parables in this chapter (all but the parable of the sower).
13:25 *tares.* Probably darnel, which looks very much like wheat while it is young, but can later be distinguished. This parable does not refer to unbelievers in the professing church. The field is the world (v. 38). Thus the people of the kingdom live side by side with the people of the evil one.
13:31–32 Although the kingdom will seem to have an insignificant beginning, it will eventually spread throughout the world.
13:32 *smaller than . . . larger than.* The mustard seed is not the smallest seed known today, but it was the smallest seed used by farmers and gardeners in the Holy Land, and under favorable conditions the plant could reach some ten feet in height. *a tree . . . ITS BRANCHES.* Likely an allusion to Dan 4:21, suggesting that the kingdom of heaven will expand to world dominion and people from all nations will find rest in it (cf. Dan 2:35,44–45; 7:27; Rev 11:15).
13:33 In the Bible, leaven usually symbolizes that which is evil or unclean (see note on Mark 8:15). Here, however, it is a symbol of growth. As leaven permeates a batch of dough, so the kingdom of heaven spreads through a person's life. Or it may signify the growth of the kingdom by the inner working of the Holy Spirit (using God's word).
13:35 *spoken through the prophet.* The quotation is from Ps 78, a psalm ascribed to Asaph, who according to 2 Chr 29:30 was a "seer" (prophet).
13:37 *Son of Man.* See note on Mark 8:31.
13:42 *furnace of fire.* Often mentioned in connection with the final judgment in apocalyptic literature (see Rev 19:20; 20:14). *weeping and gnashing of teeth.* Occurs six times in Matthew's Gospel (8:12; here; 13:50; 22:13; 24:51; 25:30) and nowhere else in the NT.

THE SUN in the kingdom of their Father. [b]He who has ears, [1]let him hear.

Hidden Treasure

44 "[a]The kingdom of heaven is like a treasure hidden in the field, which a man found and hid *again;* and from joy over it he goes and [b]sells all that he has and buys that field.

A Costly Pearl

45 "Again, [a]the kingdom of heaven is like a merchant seeking fine pearls,

46 and upon finding one pearl of great value, he went and sold all that he had and bought it.

A Dragnet

47 "Again, [a]the kingdom of heaven is like a dragnet cast into the sea, and gathering *fish* of every kind;

48 and when it was filled, they drew it up on the beach; and they sat down and gathered the good *fish* into containers, but the bad they threw away.

49 "So it will be at [a]the [1]end of the age; the angels will come forth and [2]take out the wicked from among the righteous,

50 and [a]will throw them into the furnace of fire; in that place [b]there will be weeping and gnashing of teeth.

51 "Have you understood all these things?" They *said to Him, "Yes."

52 And [1]Jesus said to them, "Therefore every scribe who has become a disciple of the kingdom of heaven is like a head of a household, who brings out of his treasure things new and old."

Jesus Revisits Nazareth

53 [a]When Jesus had finished these parables, He departed from there.

54 [a]He came to [1]His hometown and [b]*began* teaching them in their synagogue, so that [c]they were astonished, and said, "Where *did* this man *get* this wisdom and *these* [2]miraculous powers?

55 "Is not this the carpenter's son? Is not [a]His mother called Mary, and His [a]brothers, James and Joseph and Simon and Judas?

56 "And [a]His sisters, are they not all with us? Where then *did* this man *get* all these things?"

57 And they took [a]offense at Him. But Jesus said to them, "[b]A prophet is not without honor except in his [1]hometown and in his *own* household."

58 And He did not do many [1]miracles there because of their unbelief.

John the Baptist Beheaded

14 [a]At that [1]time [b]Herod the tetrarch heard the news about Jesus,

2 and said to his servants, "[a]This is John the Baptist; [1]he has risen from the dead, and that is why miraculous powers are at work in him."

3 For when [a]Herod had John arrested, he bound him and put him [b]in prison because of [c]Herodias, the wife of his brother Philip.

4 For John had been saying to him, "[a]It is not lawful for you to have her."

5 Although Herod wanted to put him to death, he feared the crowd, because they regarded [1]John as [a]a prophet.

6 But when Herod's birthday came, the

43 [1]Or *hear!* Or *listen!* [b]Matt 11:15
44 [a]Matt 13:24 [b]Matt 13:46
45 [a]Matt 13:24
47 [a]Matt 13:44
49 [1]Or *consummation* [2]Or *separate* [a]Matt 13:39, 40
50 [a]Matt 13:42 [b]Matt 8:12
52 [1]Lit *He*
53 [a]Matt 7:28
54 [1]Or *His own part of the country* [2]Or *miracles* [a]Matt 13:54-58: *Mark 6:1-6* [b]Matt 4:23 [c]Matt 7:28
55 [a]Matt 12:46
56 [a]Mark 6:3
57 [1]Or *own part of the country* [a]Matt 11:6 [b]Mark 6:4; Luke 4:24; John 4:44
58 [1]Or *works of power*
14:1 [1]Or *occasion* [a]Matt 14:1-12: *Mark 6:14-29;* Matt 14:1, 2: *Luke 9:7-9* [b]Mark 8:15; Luke 3:1, 19; 8:3; 13:31; 23:7f, 11f, 15; Acts 4:27; 12:1
2 [1]Or *he, himself* [a]Matt 16:14; Mark 6:14; Luke 9:7
3 [a]Matt 14:1-12: *Mark 6:14-29;* Mark 8:15; Luke 3:1, 19; 8:3; 13:31; 23:7f, 11f, 15; Acts 4:27; 12:1 [b]Matt 4:12; 11:2 [c]Matt 14:6; Mark 6:17, 19, 22; Luke 3:19f
4 [a]Lev 18:16; 20:21
5 [1]Lit *him* [a]Matt 11:9

13:44–46 These two parables teach the same truth: The kingdom is of such great value that one should be willing to give up all he has in order to gain it. Jesus did not imply that one can purchase the kingdom with money or good deeds.

13:44 *treasure hidden in the field.* In ancient times it was common to hide treasure in the ground since there was no widespread equivalent of modern bank vaults for the safekeeping of funds—though there were "bankers" (see Matt 25:27 and note).

13:47–51 The parable of the dragnet teaches the same general lesson as the parable of the tares: There will be a final separation of the righteous and the wicked. The parable of the tares also emphasizes that we are not to try to make such a separation now and that this is entirely the Lord's business (vv. 28–30, 41–42).

13:53 Concludes a teaching section and introduces a narrative section (cf. 7:28–29).

13:54 *His hometown.* Nazareth (see note on 2:23). *teaching the people in their synagogue.* See note on Mark 1:21.

13:55 *carpenter's son.* The word translated "carpenter" could mean "stonemason." See note on Mark 6:3. (Apparently Joseph was not living at the time of this incident.) *brothers.* Sons born to Joseph and Mary after the virgin birth of Jesus (see note on Luke 8:19).

13:58 *unbelief.* The close relationship between faith and miracles is stressed in Matthew's Gospel (cf. 8:10,13; 9:2,22,28–29).

14:1 *tetrarch.* The ruler of a fourth part of a region. Herod the tetrarch (Herod Antipas) was one of several sons of Herod the Great. When Herod the Great died, his kingdom was divided among three of his sons. Herod Antipas ruled over Galilee and Perea (4 B.C.–A.D. 39). Matthew correctly refers to him as tetrarch here, as Luke regularly does (Luke 3:19; 9:7; Acts 13:1). But in v. 9 Matthew calls him "king"—as Mark also does (Mark 6:14)—because that was his popular title among the Galileans, as well as in Rome.

14:2 *John . . . risen from the dead.* See note on Mark 6:16.

14:3 *Herodias.* A granddaughter of Herod the Great. First she married her uncle, Herod Philip (Herod the Great also had another son named Philip), who lived in Rome. While a guest in their home, Herod Antipas persuaded Herodias to leave her husband for him. Marriage to one's brother's wife, while the brother was still living, was forbidden by the Mosaic law (Lev 18:16). *Philip.* The son of Herod the Great and Mariamne, the daughter of Simon the high priest, and thus a half-brother of Herod Antipas, born to Malthace (see chart, p. 1367).

14:6 *the daughter of Herodias.* Salome, according to Josephus. She later married her granduncle, the other Philip (son of Herod the Great), who ruled the northern territories (Luke 3:1). At this time Salome was a young woman of marriageable age. Her dance was undoubtedly lascivious, and the performance pleased both Herod and his guests.

daughter of [a]Herodias danced [1]before *them* and pleased [b]Herod,

7 so *much* that he promised with an oath to give her whatever she asked.

8 Having been prompted by her mother, she *said, "Give me here on a platter the head of John the Baptist."

9 Although he was grieved, the king commanded *it* to be given because of his oaths, and because of [1]his dinner guests.

10 He sent and had John beheaded in the prison.

11 And his head was brought on a platter and given to the girl, and she brought it to her mother.

12 His disciples came and took away the body and buried [1]it; and they went and reported to Jesus.

Five Thousand Fed

13 [a]Now when Jesus heard *about John,* He withdrew from there in a boat to a secluded place by Himself; and when the [1]people heard *of this,* they followed Him on foot from the cities.

14 When He went [1]ashore, He [a]saw a large crowd, and felt compassion for them and [b]healed their sick.

15 When it was evening, the disciples came to Him and said, "This place is desolate and the hour is already [1]late; so send the crowds away, that they may go into the villages and buy food for themselves."

16 But Jesus said to them, "They do not need to go away; you give them *something* to eat!"

17 They *said to Him, "We have here only [a]five loaves and two fish."

18 And He said, "Bring them here to Me."

19 Ordering the [1]people to [2]sit down on the grass, He took the five loaves and the two fish, and looking up toward heaven, He [a]blessed *the food,* and breaking the loaves He gave them to the disciples, and the disciples *gave them* to the crowds,

20 and they all ate and were satisfied. They picked up what was left over of the broken pieces, twelve full [a]baskets.

21 There were about five thousand men who ate, besides women and children.

Jesus Walks on the Water

22 [a]Immediately He [1]made the disciples get into the boat and go ahead of Him to the other side, while He sent the crowds away.

23 After He had sent the crowds away, [a]He went up on the mountain by Himself to pray; and when it was evening, He was there alone.

24 But the boat was already [1]a long distance from the land, [2]battered by the waves; for the wind was [3a]contrary.

25 And in [a]the [1]fourth watch of the night He came to them, walking on the sea.

26 When the disciples saw Him walking on the sea, they were terrified, and said, "It is [a]a ghost!" And they cried out [1]in fear.

27 But immediately Jesus spoke to them, saying, "[a]Take courage, it is I; [b]do not be afraid."

28 Peter said to Him, "Lord, if it is You, command me to come to You on the water."

29 And He said, "Come!" And Peter got out of the boat, and walked on the water and came toward Jesus.

30 But seeing the wind, he became frightened, and beginning to sink, he cried out, "Lord, save me!"

31 Immediately Jesus stretched out His hand and took hold of him, and *said to him, "[a]You of little faith, why did you doubt?"

32 When they got into the boat, the wind stopped.

33 And those who were in the boat worshiped Him, saying, "You are certainly [a]God's Son!"

34 [a]When they had crossed over, they came to land at [b]Gennesaret.

35 And when the men of that place [1]recognized Him, they sent *word* into all that surrounding district and brought to Him all who were sick;

36 and they implored Him that they might just touch [a]the fringe of His cloak; and as many as [b]touched *it* were cured.

6 [1]Lit *in the midst* [a]Matt 14:3; Mark 6:17, 19, 22; Luke 3:19 [b]Matt 14:1-12: *Mark 6:14-29;* Mark 8:15; Luke 3:1, 19; 8:3; 13:31; 23:7f, 11f, 15; Acts 4:27; 12:1
9 [1]Lit *those who reclined* at the table *with him*
12 [1]Lit *him*
13 [1]Lit *the crowds* [a]Matt 14:13-21: *Mark 6:32-44; Luke 9:10-17; John 6:1-13;* Matt 15:32-38
14 [1]Lit *out* [a]Matt 9:36 [b]Matt 4:23
15 [1]Lit *past*
17 [a]Matt 16:9
19 [1]Lit *crowds* [2]Lit *recline* [a]1 Sam 9:13; Matt 15:36; 26:26; Mark 6:41; 8:7; 14:22; Luke 24:30; Acts 27:35; Rom 14:6
20 [a]Matt 16:9; Mark 6:43; 8:19; Luke 9:17; John 6:13
22 [1]Lit *compelled* [a]Matt 14:22-33: *Mark 6:45-51; John 6:15-21*
23 [a]Mark 6:46; Luke 6:12; 9:28; John 6:15
24 [1]Lit *many stadia from;* a stadion was about 600 feet or about 182 meters [2]Lit *tormented* [3]Or *adverse* [a]Acts 27:4
25 [1]I.e. 3-6 a.m. [a]Matt 24:43; Mark 13:35
26 [1]Lit *from* [a]Luke 24:37
27 [a]Matt 9:2 [b]Matt 17:7; 28:5, 10; Mark 6:50; Luke 1:13, 30; 2:10; 5:10; 12:32; John 6:20; Rev 1:17
31 [a]Matt 6:30; 8:26; 16:8
33 [a]Matt 4:3
34 [a]Matt 14:34-36: *Mark 6:53-56; John 6:24, 25* [b]Mark 6:53; Luke 5:1
35 [1]Or *knew*
36 [a]Matt 9:20 [b]Matt 9:21; Mark 3:10; 6:56; 8:22; Luke 6:19

14:8 *platter.* A flat wooden dish on which meat was served.

14:13–21 See Mark 6:32–44; Luke 9:10–17; John 6:1–13 and notes.

14:21 *besides women and children.* Matthew alone notes this. He was writing to the Jews, who did not permit women and children to eat with men in public. So they were in a place by themselves.

14:22 *made.* The Greek word used here is strong. It means "to compel" and suggests a crisis. John records that after the miracle of the loaves and fish the crowds "were intending to come and take Him by force to make Him king" (6:15). This involved a complete misunderstanding of the mission of Jesus. The disciples may have been caught up in the enthusiasm and needed to be removed from the area quickly (cf. 16:5–12).

14:23 *to pray.* Matthew speaks of Jesus praying only here and in Gethsemane (cf. 26:36–46).

14:25 *fourth watch.* 3:00–6:00 A.M. According to Roman reckoning the night was divided into four watches: (1) 6:00–9:00 P.M., (2) 9:00–midnight, (3) midnight–3:00 A.M. and (4) 3:00–6:00 A.M. (see note on Mark 13:35). The Jews had only three watches during the night: (1) sunset–10:00 P.M., (2) 10:00 P.M.–2:00 A.M. and (3) 2:00 A.M.–sunrise (see Judg 7:19; 1 Sam 11:11). *walking on the sea.* See note on Mark 6:48.

14:34 *Gennesaret.* Either the narrow plain, about four miles long and less than two miles wide, on the west side of the Sea of Galilee near the north end (north of Magdala), or a town in the plain. The plain was considered a garden spot of the Holy Land, fertile and well watered.

14:36 *just touch the fringe of His cloak.* See note on Mark 5:28.

Tradition and Commandment

15 [a]Then some Pharisees and scribes *came
to Jesus [b]from Jerusalem and said,
2 "Why do Your disciples break the tradition of the elders? For they [a]do not wash
their hands when they eat bread."
3 And He answered and said to them,
"Why do you yourselves transgress the commandment of God for the sake of your tradition?
4 "For God said, '[a]HONOR YOUR FATHER AND
MOTHER,' and, '[b]HE WHO SPEAKS EVIL OF FATHER
OR MOTHER IS TO [1]BE PUT TO DEATH.'
5 "But you say, 'Whoever says to *his*
father or mother, "Whatever I have that
would help you has been [1]given *to God,*"
6 he is not to honor his father or his
mother[1].' And *by this* you invalidated the
word of God for the sake of your tradition.
7 "You hypocrites, rightly did Isaiah
prophesy of you:
8 '[a]THIS PEOPLE HONORS ME WITH THEIR LIPS,
BUT THEIR HEART IS FAR AWAY FROM ME.
9 'BUT IN VAIN DO THEY WORSHIP ME,
TEACHING AS [a]DOCTRINES THE PRECEPTS OF
MEN.'"
10 After Jesus called the crowd to Him, He
said to them, "Hear and understand.
11 "[a]*It is* not what enters into the mouth
that defiles the man, but what proceeds out
of the mouth, this defiles the man."
12 Then the disciples *came and *said to
Him, "Do You know that the Pharisees were
[1]offended when they heard this statement?"
13 But He answered and said, "[a]Every
plant which My heavenly Father did not
plant shall be uprooted.
14 "Let them alone; [a]they are blind guides
[1]of the blind. And [b]if a blind man guides a
blind man, both will fall into a pit."

The Heart of Man

15 Peter [1]said to Him, "[a]Explain the parable to us."
16 [1]Jesus said, "Are you still lacking in
understanding also?
17 "Do you not understand that everything
that goes into the mouth passes into the
stomach, and is [1]eliminated?
18 "But [a]the things that proceed out of the
mouth come from the heart, and those defile
the man.
19 "[a]For out of the heart come evil
thoughts, murders, adulteries, [1]fornications,
thefts, false witness, slanders.
20 "These are the things which defile the
man; but to eat with unwashed hands does
not defile the man."

The Syrophoenician Woman

21 [a]Jesus went away from there, and withdrew into the district of [b]Tyre and [b]Sidon.
22 And a Canaanite woman from that
region came out and *began* to cry out, saying, "Have mercy on me, Lord, [a]Son of
David; my daughter is cruelly [b]demon-pos-
sessed."
23 But He did not answer her a word. And
His disciples came and implored Him, saying, "Send her away, because she keeps
shouting [1]at us."
24 But He answered and said, "I was sent
only to [a]the lost sheep of the house of Israel."
25 But she came and [a]*began* [1]to bow
down before Him, saying, "Lord, help me!"
26 And He answered and said, "It is not
[1]good to take the children's bread and throw
it to the dogs."
27 But she said, "Yes, Lord; [1]but even the
dogs feed on the crumbs which fall from
their masters' table."
28 Then Jesus said to her, "O woman,
[a]your faith is great; it shall be done for you
as you wish." And her daughter was healed
[1]at once.

Healing Crowds

29 [a]Departing from there, Jesus went
along by [b]the Sea of Galilee, and having gone
up on the mountain, He was sitting there.
30 And [1]large crowds came to Him, bringing with them *those who were* lame, crippled,
blind, mute, and many others, and they laid
them down at His feet; and [a]He healed them.
31 So the crowd marveled as they saw the
mute speaking, the crippled [1]restored, and
the lame walking, and the blind seeing; and
they [a]glorified the God of Israel.

Four Thousand Fed

32 [a]And Jesus called His disciples to Him,
and said, "[b]I feel compassion for the [1]people,
because they [2]have remained with Me now
three days and have nothing to eat; and I do

15:1 [a]Matt 15:1-20: *Mark 7:1-23* [b]Mark 3:22; 7:1; John 1:19; Acts 25:7
2 [a]Luke 11:38
4 [1]Lit *die the death* [a]Ex 20:12; Deut 5:16 [b]Ex 21:17; Lev 20:9
5 [1]Lit *a gift;* i.e. an offering
6 [1]I.e. by supporting them with it
8 [a]Is 29:13
9 [a]Col 2:22
11 [a]Matt 15:18; Acts 10:14, 15; 1 Tim 4:3
12 [1]Lit *caused to stumble*
13 [a]Is 60:21; 61:3; John 15:2; 1 Cor 3:9
14 [1]Later mss add *of the blind* [a]Matt 23:16, 24 [b]Luke 6:39
15 [1]Lit *answered and said* [a]Matt 13:36
16 [1]Lit *and He*
17 [1]Lit *thrown out into the latrine*
18 [a]Matt 12:34; Mark 7:20
19 [1]I.e. sexual immorality [a]Gal 5:19ff
21 [a]Matt 15:21-28: *Mark 7:24-30* [b]Matt 11:21
22 [a]Matt 9:27 [b]Matt 4:24
23 [1]Lit *behind us*
24 [a]Matt 10:6
25 [1]Or *worshiped* [a]Matt 8:2
26 [1]Or *proper*
27 [1]Lit *for*
28 [1]Lit *from that hour* [a]Matt 9:22
29 [a]Matt 15:29-31; Mark 7:31-37 [b]Matt 4:18
30 [1]Lit *many* [a]Matt 4:23
31 [1]Or *healthy* [a]Matt 9:8
32 [1]Lit *crowd* [2]Lit *are remaining* [a]Matt 15:32-39: *Mark 8:1-10;* Matt 14:13-21 [b]Matt 9:36

15:2 *the tradition of the elders.* After the Babylonian captivity, the Jewish rabbis began to make meticulous rules and regulations governing the daily life of the people. These were interpretations and applications of the law of Moses, handed down from generation to generation. In Jesus' day this "tradition of the elders" was in oral form. It was not until c. A.D. 200 that it was put into writing in the Mishnah. *wash.* See Mark 7:1–4.
15:5–6 See notes on Mark 7:11,13.
15:7–20 See Mark 7:6–23 and notes.
15:21 *Tyre.* See note on Mark 7:24. *Sidon.* About 25 miles north of Tyre.
15:22 *Canaanite.* A term found many times in the OT but only here in the NT. In NT times there was no country known as Canaan. Some think this was the Semitic manner of referring to the people of Phoenicia at this time. Mark says the woman was "a Greek, born in Syrian Phoenicia" (7:26).
15:26 *children's.* "The lost sheep of the house of Israel" (v. 24). *the dogs.* The Greek says "little dogs," meaning a pet dog in the home, and Jesus' point was that the gospel was to be given first to Jews. The woman understood Jesus' implication and was willing to settle for "crumbs." Jesus rewarded her faith (v. 28).
15:27 *Yes, Lord.* See note on Mark 7:28.
15:29–39 See Mark 7:31–8:10 and notes.

not want to send them away hungry, for they might faint on the way."

33 The disciples *said to Him, "Where would we get so many loaves in *this* desolate place to satisfy such a large crowd?"

34 And Jesus *said to them, "How many loaves do you have?" And they said, "Seven, and a few small fish."

35 And He directed the [1]people to [2]sit down on the ground;

36 and He took the seven loaves and the fish; and [a]giving thanks, He broke them and started giving them to the disciples, and the disciples *gave them* to the people.

37 And they all ate and were satisfied, and they picked up what was left over of the broken pieces, seven large [a]baskets full.

38 And those who ate were four thousand men, besides women and children.

39 And sending away the crowds, Jesus got into [a]the boat and came to the region of [b]Magadan.

Pharisees Test Jesus

16 [a]The [b]Pharisees and Sadducees came up, and testing Jesus, they [c]asked Him to show them a [1]sign from heaven.

2 But He replied to them, "[1][a]When it is evening, you say, '*It will be* fair weather, for the sky is red.'

3 "And in the morning, '*There will be* a storm today, for the sky is red and threatening.' [a]Do you know how to discern the [1]appearance of the sky, but cannot *discern* the signs of the times?

4 "[a]An evil and adulterous generation seeks after a [1]sign; and a [1]sign will not be given it, except the sign of Jonah." And He left them and went away.

5 And the disciples came to the other side *of the sea*, but they had forgotten to bring *any* bread.

6 And Jesus said to them, "Watch out and [a]beware of the [1]leaven of the [b]Pharisees and Sadducees."

7 They began to discuss *this* among themselves, saying, "*He said that* because we did not bring *any* bread."

8 But Jesus, aware of this, said, "[a]You men of little faith, why do you discuss among yourselves that you have no bread?

9 "Do you not yet understand or remember [a]the five loaves of the five thousand, and how many baskets *full* you picked up?

10 "Or [a]the seven loaves of the four thousand, and how many large baskets *full* you picked up?

11 "How is it that you do not understand that I did not speak to you concerning bread? But [a]beware of the [1]leaven of the [b]Pharisees and Sadducees."

12 Then they understood that He did not say to beware of the leaven of bread, but of the teaching of the [a]Pharisees and Sadducees.

Peter's Confession of Christ

13 [a]Now when Jesus came into the district of [b]Caesarea Philippi, He was asking His disciples, "Who do people say that [c]the Son of Man is?"

14 And they said, "Some *say* [a]John the Baptist; and others, [1][b]Elijah; but still others, [2]Jeremiah, or one of the prophets."

15 He *said to them, "But who do you say that I am?"

16 Simon Peter answered, "You are [1][a]the Christ, [b]the Son of [c]the living God."

17 And Jesus said to him, "Blessed are you, [a]Simon [1]Barjona, because [b]flesh and blood did not reveal *this* to you, but My Father who is in heaven.

18 "I also say to you that you are [1][a]Peter, and upon this [2]rock I will build My church; and the gates of [b]Hades will not overpower it.

35 [1]Lit *crowd* [2]Lit *recline*
36 [a]Matt 14:19; 26:27; Luke 22:17, 19; John 6:11, 23; Acts 27:35; Rom 14:6
37 [a]Matt 16:10; Mark 8:8, 20; Acts 9:25
39 [a]Mark 3:9 [b]Mark 8:10
16:1 [1]Or *attesting miracle* [a]Matt 16:1-12: *Mark 8:11-21* [b]Matt 3:7; 16:6, 11, 12 [c]Matt 12:38; Luke 11:16
2 [1]Early mss do not contain the rest of v 2 and v 3 [a]Luke 12:54f
3 [1]Lit *face* [a]Luke 12:56
4 [1]Or *attesting miracle* [a]Matt 12:39; Luke 11:29
6 [1]Or *yeast* [a]Mark 8:15; Luke 12:1 [b]Matt 3:7
8 [a]Matt 6:30; 8:26; 14:31
9 [a]Matt 14:17-21
10 [a]Matt 15:34-38
11 [1]Or *yeast* [a]Matt 16:6; Mark 8:15; Luke 12:1 [b]Matt 3:7; 16:6, 12
12 [a]Matt 3:7; 5:20
13 [a]Matt 16:13-16: *Mark 8:27-29; Luke 9:18-20* [b]Mark 8:27 [c]Matt 8:20; 16:27, 28
14 [1]Gr *Elias* [2]Gr *Jeremias* [a]Matt 14:2 [b]Matt 17:10; Mark 6:15; Luke 9:8; John 1:21
16 [1]I.e. the Messiah [a]Matt 1:16; 16:20; John 11:27 [b]Matt 4:3 [c]Ps 42:2; Matt 26:63; Acts 14:15; Rom 9:26; 2 Cor 3:3; 6:16; 1 Thess 1:9; 1 Tim 3:15; 4:10; Heb 3:12; 9:14; 10:31; 12:22; Rev 7:2
17 [1]I.e. son of Jonah [a]John 1:42; 21:15-17 [b]1 Cor 15:50; Gal 1:16; Eph 6:12; Heb 2:14
18 [1]Gr *Petros,* a stone [2]Gr *petra,* large rock; bed-rock [a]Matt 4:18 [b]Matt 11:23

15:37 The feeding of the 5,000 is recorded in all four Gospels, but the feeding of the 4,000 is only in Matthew and Mark. The 12 baskets mentioned in the accounts of the feeding of the 5,000 were possibly the lunch baskets of the 12 apostles. The seven baskets mentioned here were possibly larger.

15:39 *Magadan.* Also called Magdala, the home of Mary Magdalene. Mark (8:10) has "Dalmanutha."

16:1 *sign from heaven.* See note on Mark 8:11.

16:4 *the sign of Jonah.* See 12:39–40 and note on Luke 11:30.

16:6 *leaven of the Pharisees and Sadducees.* See v. 12. Also see notes on 3:7; Mark 2:16; 8:15; 12:18.

16:12 Matthew often explains the meaning of Jesus' words (cf. 17:13).

16:13 *Caesarea Philippi.* To be distinguished from the magnificent city of Caesarea, which Herod the Great had built on the coast of the Mediterranean. Caesarea Philippi, rebuilt by Herod's son Philip (who named it after Tiberius Caesar and himself), was north of the Sea of Galilee, near the slopes of Mount Hermon. Originally it was called Paneas (the ancient name survives today as Banias) in honor of the Greek god Pan, whose shrine was located there. The region was especially pagan. *Son of Man.* See note on Mark 8:31.

16:16 *Christ.* Or *Messiah*; also in verse 20. Both mean "the Anointed One." The OT equivalent (*Messiah*) is used of anyone who was anointed with the holy oil, such as the priests and kings of Israel (e.g., Ex 29:7,21; 1 Sam 10;1,6; 16:13; 2 Sam 1:14,16). The word carries the idea of being chosen by God, consecrated to His service, and endued with His power to accomplish the assigned task. Toward the end of the OT period the word assumed a special meaning. It denoted the ideal king anointed and empowered by God to rescue His people from their enemies and establish His righteous kingdom (Dan 9:25–26). The ideas that clustered around the title *Messiah* tended to be political and national in nature. Probably for that reason Jesus seldom used the term. When He did accept it as applied to himself, He did so with reservations (cf. Mark 8:27–30; 14:61–63).

16:18 *Peter . . . rock . . . church.* In the Greek "Peter" is *petros* ("detached stone") and "rock" is *petra* ("bedrock"). Several interpretations have been given to these words. The "bedrock" on

19 "I will give you [a]the keys of the kingdom of heaven; and [b]whatever you bind on earth [1]shall have been bound in heaven, and whatever you loose on earth [2]shall have been loosed in heaven."

20 [a]Then He [1]warned the disciples that they should tell no one that He was [2b]the Christ.

Jesus Foretells His Death

21 [a]From that time [1]Jesus began to show His disciples that He must go to Jerusalem, and [b]suffer many things from the elders and chief priests and scribes, and be killed, and be raised up on the third day.

22 Peter took Him aside and began to rebuke Him, saying, "[1]God forbid *it*, Lord! This shall never [2]happen to You."

23 But He turned and said to Peter, "Get behind Me, [a]Satan! You are a stumbling block to Me; for you are not setting your mind on [1]God's interests, but man's."

Discipleship Is Costly

24 Then Jesus said to His disciples, "If anyone wishes to come after Me, he must deny himself, and [a]take up his cross and follow Me.

25 "For [a]whoever wishes to save his [1]life will lose it; but whoever loses his [1]life for My sake will find it.

26 "For what will it profit a man if he gains the whole world and forfeits his soul? Or what will a man give in exchange for his soul?

27 "For the [a]Son of Man [b]is going to come in the glory of His Father with His angels, and [c]WILL THEN [1]REPAY EVERY MAN ACCORDING TO HIS [2]DEEDS.

28 "Truly I say to you, there are some of those who are standing here who will not taste death until they see the [a]Son of Man [b]coming in His kingdom."

The Transfiguration

17 [a]Six days later Jesus *took with Him [b]Peter and [1]James and John his brother, and *led them up on a high mountain by themselves.

2 And He was transfigured before them; and His face shone like the sun, and His garments became as white as light.

3 And behold, Moses and Elijah appeared to them, talking with Him.

4 Peter said to Jesus, "Lord, it is good for

19 [1]Gr *estai dedemenon,* fut. pft. pass. [2]Gr *estai lelumenon,* fut. pft. pass. [a]Is 22:22; Rev 1:18; 3:7 [b]Matt 18:18; John 20:23
20 [1]Or *strictly admonished* [2]I.e. the Messiah [a]Matt 8:4; Mark 8:30; Luke 9:21 [b]Matt 1:16; 16:16; John 11:27
21 [1]Two early mss read *Jesus Christ* [a]Matt 16:21-28: *Mark 8:31-9:1; Luke 9:22-27* [b]Matt 12:40; 17:9, 12, 22f; 20:18f; 27:63; Mark 9:12, 31; Luke 17:25; 18:32; 24:7; John 2:19
22 [1]Lit (God be) *merciful to You* [2]Lit *be*
23 [1]Lit *the things of God* [a]Matt 4:10
24 [a]Matt 10:38; Luke 14:27
25 [1]Or *soul* [a]Matt 10:39
27 [1]Or *recompense* [2]Lit *doing* [a]Matt 8:20 [b]Matt 10:23; 24:3, 27, 37, 39; 26:64; Mark 8:38; 13:26; Luke 21:27; John 21:22; Acts 1:11; 1 Cor 15:23; 1 Thess 1:10; 4:16; 2 Thess 1:7, 10; 2:1, 8; James 5:7f; 2 Pet 1:16; 3:4, 12; 1 John 2:28; Rev 1:7 [c]Ps 62:12; Prov 24:12; Rom 2:6; 14:12; 1 Cor 3:13; 2 Cor 5:10; Eph 6:8; Col 3:25; Rev 2:23; 20:12; 22:12
28 [a]Matt 8:20 [b]Matt 10:23; 24:3, 27, 37, 39; 26:64; Mark 8:38; 13:26; Luke 21:27; John 21:22; Acts 1:11; 1 Cor 15:23; 1 Thess 1:10; 4:16; 2 Thess 1:7, 10; 2:1, 8; James 5:7f; 2 Pet 1:16; 3:4, 12; 1 John 2:28; Rev 1:7
17:1 [1]Or *Jacob* [a]Matt 17:1-8: *Mark 9:2-8; Luke 9:28-36* [b]Matt 26:37; Mark 5:37; 13:3

which the church is built is (1) Christ; (2) Peter's confession of faith in Jesus as the Messiah (v. 16); (3) Christ's teachings—one of the great emphases of Matthew's Gospel; (4) Peter himself, understood in terms of his role on the day of Pentecost (Acts 2), the Cornelius incident (Acts 10) and his leadership among the apostles. Eph 2:20 indicates that the church is "built on the foundation of the apostles and prophets." *church.* In the Gospels this word is used only by Matthew (here and twice in 18:17). In the Septuagint it is used for the congregation of Israel. In Greek circles of Jesus' day it indicated the assembly of free, voting citizens in a city (cf. Acts 19:32,39,41). *Hades.* The Greek name for the place of departed spirits, generally equivalent to the Hebrew *Sheol* (see note on Gen 37:35). The "gates of Hades" may mean the "powers of death," i.e., all forces opposed to Christ and His kingdom (but see note on Job 17:16).

16:19 *keys.* Perhaps Peter used these keys on the day of Pentecost (Acts 2) when he announced that the door of the kingdom was unlocked to Jews and proselytes and later when he acknowledged that it was also opened to Gentiles (Acts 10). *bind . . . loose.* Not authority to determine, but to announce, guilt or innocence (see 18:18 and the context there; cf. Acts 5:3,9).

16:20 *that they should tell no one.* Because of the false concepts of the Jews, who looked for an exclusively national and political Messiah, Jesus told His disciples not to publicize Peter's confession, lest it precipitate a revolution against Rome (see note on 8:4).

16:21 *began.* The beginning of a new emphasis in Jesus' ministry. Instead of teaching the crowds in parables, He concentrated on preparing the disciples for His coming suffering and death.

16:23 *Satan.* A loanword from Hebrew, meaning "adversary" or "accuser" (see note on Rev 2:9).

16:24 *take up his cross.* See notes on 10:38; Mark 8:34.

16:27 *Son of Man.* See note on Mark 8:31. *is going to come.* The *parousia,* the eschatological coming of Christ.

16:28 There are two main interpretations of this verse: 1. It is a prediction of the transfiguration, which happened a week later (17:1) and which demonstrated that Jesus will return in His Father's glory (16:27). 2. It refers to the Son of Man's authority and kingly reign in His post-resurrection church. Some of His disciples will witness—even participate in—this as described in the book of Acts. The context seems to favor the first view. See note on 2 Pet 1:16.

17:1–9 The transfiguration was: (1) a revelation of the glory of the Son of God, a glory hidden now but to be fully revealed when He returns; (2) a confirmation of the difficult teaching given to the disciples at Caesarea Philippi (16:13–20); and (3) a beneficial experience for the disciples, who were discouraged after having been reminded so recently of Jesus' impending suffering and death (16:21). See notes on Mark 9:2–7; Luke 9:28–35.

17:1 *Six days.* Mark also says "Six days" (Mark 9:2), counting just the days between Peter's confession and the transfiguration, whereas Luke, counting all the days involved, says, "Some eight days" (Luke 9:28). *Peter and James and John.* These three disciples had an especially close relationship to Jesus (see 26:37; Mark 5:37). *high mountain.* Its identity is unknown. However, the reference to Caesarea Philippi (16:13) may suggest that it was Mount Hermon, which was just northeast of Caesarea Philippi (see note on Luke 9:28). *by themselves.* Luke adds "to pray" (Luke 9:28).

17:2 *He was transfigured.* His appearance changed. The three disciples saw Jesus in His glorified state (see John 17:5; 2 Pet 1:17).

17:3 *Moses and Elijah.* Moses appears as the representative of the old covenant and the promise of salvation, which was soon to be fulfilled in the death of Jesus. Elijah appears as the appoint-

us to be here; if You wish, [a]I will make three [1]tabernacles here, one for You, and one for Moses, and one for Elijah."

5 While he was still speaking, a bright cloud overshadowed them, and behold, [a]a voice out of the cloud said, "[b]This is My beloved Son, with whom I am well-pleased; listen to Him!"

6 When the disciples heard *this,* they fell [1]face down to the ground and were terrified.

7 And Jesus came to *them* and touched them and said, "Get up, and [a]do not be afraid."

8 And lifting up their eyes, they saw no one except Jesus Himself alone.

9 [a]As they were coming down from the mountain, Jesus commanded them, saying, "[b]Tell the vision to no one until [c]the Son of Man has [d]risen from the dead."

10 And His disciples asked Him, "Why then do the scribes say that [a]Elijah must come first?"

11 And He answered and said, "Elijah is coming and will restore all things;

12 but I say to you that Elijah already came, and they did not recognize him, but did [1]to him whatever they wished. So also [a]the Son of Man is going to suffer [2]at their hands."

13 Then the disciples understood that He had spoken to them about John the Baptist.

The Demoniac

14 [a]When they came to the crowd, a man came up to Jesus, falling on his knees before Him and saying,

15 "[1]Lord, have mercy on my son, for he is a [2a]lunatic and is very ill; for he often falls into the fire and often into the water.

16 "I brought him to Your disciples, and they could not cure him."

17 And Jesus answered and said, "You unbelieving and perverted generation, how long shall I be with you? How long shall I put up with you? Bring him here to Me."

18 And Jesus rebuked him, and the demon came out of him, and the boy was cured [1]at once.

19 Then the disciples came to Jesus privately and said, "Why could we not drive it out?"

20 And He *said to them, "Because of the littleness of your faith; for truly I say to you, [a]if you have faith [1]the size of [b]a mustard seed, you will say to [c]this mountain, 'Move from here to there,' and it will move; and [d]nothing will be impossible to you.

21 ["[1a]But this kind does not go out except by prayer and fasting."]

22 [a]And while they were gathering together in Galilee, Jesus said to them, "The Son of Man is going to be [1]delivered into the hands of men;

23 and [a]they will kill Him, and He will be raised on the third day." And they were deeply grieved.

The Tribute Money

24 When they came to Capernaum, those who collected [a]the [1]two-drachma *tax* came to Peter and said, "Does your teacher not pay [a]the [1]two-drachma *tax?*"

25 He *said, "Yes." And when he came into the house, Jesus spoke to him first, saying, "What do you think, Simon? From whom do the kings of the earth collect [a]customs or [b]poll-tax, from their sons or from strangers?"

26 When Peter said, "From strangers," Jesus said to him, "Then the sons are [1]exempt.

27 "However, so that we do not [1a]offend them, go to the sea and throw in a hook, and take the first fish that comes up; and when you open its mouth, you will find [2]a shekel. Take that and give it to them for you and Me."

Rank in the Kingdom

18 [a]At that [1]time the disciples came to Jesus and said, "[b]Who then is greatest in the kingdom of heaven?"

4 [1]Or *sacred tents* [a]Mark 9:5; Luke 9:33
5 [a]Mark 1:11; Luke 3:22; 2 Pet 1:17f [b]Is 42:1; Matt 3:17; 12:18
6 [1]Lit *on their faces*
7 [a]Matt 14:27
9 [a]Matt 17:9-13: *Mark 9:9-13* [b]Matt 8:4 [c]Matt 8:20; 17:12, 22 [d]Matt 16:21
10 [a]Mal 4:5; Matt 11:14; 16:14
12 [1]Lit *in him;* or *in his case* [2]Lit *by them* [a]Matt 8:20; 17:9, 22
14 [a]Matt 17:14-19: *Mark 9:14-28;* Matt 17:14-18: *Luke 9:37-42*
15 [1]Or *Sir* [2]Or moonstruck; Gr *seleniazo* [a]Matt 4:24
18 [1]Lit *from that hour*
20 [1]Lit *as* [a]Matt 21:21f; Mark 11:23f; Luke 17:6 [b]Matt 13:31; Luke 17:6 [c]Matt 17:9; 1 Cor 13:2 [d]Mark 9:23; John 11:40
21 [1]Early mss do not contain this v [a]Mark 9:29
22 [1]Or *betrayed* [a]Matt 17:22, 23: *Mark 9:30-32; Luke 9:44, 45*
23 [a]Matt 16:21; 17:9
24 [1]Equivalent to two denarii or two days' wages, paid as a temple tax [a]Ex 30:13; 38:26
25 [a]Rom 13:7 [b]Matt 22:17, 19
26 [1]Or *free*
27 [1]Lit *cause them to stumble* [2]Lit *standard coin,* which was a shekel [a]Matt 5:29, 30; 18:6, 8, 9; Mark 9:42, 43, 45, 47; Luke 17:2; John 6:61; 1 Cor 8:13
18:1 [1]Lit *hour* [a]Matt 18:1-5: *Mark 9:33-37; Luke 9:46-48* [b]Luke 22:24

---

ed restorer of all things (Mal 4:5–6; Mark 9:11–13). Luke 9:31 says that they talked about Christ's death. See note on Luke 9:30.

17:4 *three tabernacles.* See notes on Mark 9:5; Luke 9:33.

17:5 *them.* Jesus, Moses and Elijah. *This is My beloved Son, with whom I am well-pleased.* The same words spoken from heaven at Jesus' baptism (3:17). No mere man, but the very Son of God, was transfigured.

17:6 *terrified.* Primarily with a sense of awe at the presence and majesty of God.

17:10 The traditional eschatology of the teachers of the law, based on Mal 4:5–6, held that Elijah must appear before the coming of the Messiah. The disciples reasoned that if Jesus really was the Messiah, as the transfiguration proved Him to be, why had not Elijah appeared?

17:12 *So also.* As John the Baptist was not recognized and was killed, so Jesus would be rejected and killed.

17:13 See note on 16:12.

17:18 Not all cases of lunacy were the result of demon possession, but this one was.

17:20 *littleness of your faith.* Not so much the quantity of their faith as its quality—a faith that is bathed in prayer (see Mark 9:29). *mustard seed.* See 13:31–32 and notes. *say to this mountain, 'Move from here to there.'* A proverbial statement meaning to remove great difficulties (cf. Is 54:10; 1 Cor 13:2). In this context it probably refers to removing the problems associated with the work of the kingdom.

17:22 The second prediction of Christ's death, the first being in 16:21.

17:24 *two-drachma tax.* The annual temple tax required of every male 20 years of age and older (Ex 30:13; 2 Chr 24:9; Neh 10:32). It was worth half a shekel (approximately two days' wages) and was used for the upkeep of the temple.

17:26 *the sons are exempt.* The implication is that Peter and the rest of the disciples belonged to God's royal household, but unbelieving Jews did not (see 21:43).

18:1 *Who then is greatest?* See note on Luke 9:46.

2 And He called a child to Himself and set him [1]before them,

3 and said, "Truly I say to you, unless you [1]are converted and [a]become like children, you will not enter the kingdom of heaven.

4 "Whoever then humbles himself as this child, he is the greatest in the kingdom of heaven.

5 "And whoever receives one such child in My name receives Me;

6 but [a]whoever [b]causes one of these little ones who believe in Me to stumble, it [1]would be better for him to have a [2]heavy millstone hung around his neck, and to be drowned in the depth of the sea.

Stumbling Blocks

7 "Woe to the world because of *its* stumbling blocks! For [a]it is inevitable that stumbling blocks come; but woe to that man through whom the stumbling block comes!

8 "[a]If your hand or your foot causes you to stumble, cut it off and throw it from you; it is better for you to enter life crippled or lame, than [1]to have two hands or two feet and be cast into the eternal fire.

9 "[a]If your eye causes you to stumble, pluck it out and throw it from you. It is better for you to enter life with one eye, than [1]to have two eyes and be cast into the [2b]fiery hell.

10 "See that you do not despise one of these little ones, for I say to you that [a]their angels in heaven continually see the face of My Father who is in heaven.

11 ["[1a]For the Son of Man has come to save that which was lost.]

Ninety-nine Plus One

12 "What do you think? [a]If any man has a hundred sheep, and one of them has gone astray, does he not leave the ninety-nine on the mountains and go and search for the one that is straying?

13 "If it turns out that he finds it, truly I say to you, he rejoices over it more than over the ninety-nine which have not gone astray.

14 "So it is not *the* will [1]of your Father who is in heaven that one of these little ones perish.

Discipline and Prayer

15 "[a]If your brother sins[1], go and [2]show him his fault [3]in private; if he listens to you, you have won your brother.

16 "But if he does not listen *to you,* take one or two more with you, so that [a]BY THE MOUTH OF TWO OR THREE WITNESSES EVERY [1]FACT MAY BE CONFIRMED.

17 "If he refuses to listen to them, [a]tell it to the church; and if he refuses to listen even to the church, [b]let him be to you as [1]a Gentile and [1]a tax collector.

18 "Truly I say to you, [a]whatever you [1]bind on earth [2]shall have been bound in heaven; and whatever you [3]loose on earth [2]shall have been loosed in heaven.

19 "Again I say to you, that if two of you agree on earth about anything that they may ask, [a]it shall be done for them [1]by My Father who is in heaven.

20 "For where two or three have gathered together in My name, [a]I am there in their midst."

Forgiveness

21 Then Peter came and said to Him, "Lord, [a]how often shall my brother sin against me and I forgive him? Up to [b]seven times?"

22 Jesus *said to him, "I do not say to you, up to seven times, but up to [a]seventy times seven.

23 "For this reason [a]the kingdom of heaven [1]may be compared to a king who wished to [b]settle accounts with his slaves.

24 "When he had begun to settle *them,* one who owed him [1]ten thousand talents was brought to him.

25 "But since he [1a]did not have *the means* to repay, his lord commanded him [b]to be sold, along with his wife and children and all that he had, and repayment to be made.

26 "So the slave fell *to the ground* and [a]prostrated himself before him, saying, 'Have patience with me and I will repay you everything.'

27 "And the lord of that slave felt compassion and released him and [a]forgave him the [1]debt.

2 [1]Lit *in their midst*
3 [1]Lit *are turned* [a]Matt 19:14; Mark 10:15; Luke 18:17; 1 Cor 14:20; 1 Pet 2:2
6 [1]Lit *is better* [2]Lit *millstone turned by a donkey* [a]Mark 9:42; Luke 17:2; 1 Cor 8:12 [b]Matt 17:27
7 [a]Luke 17:1; 1 Cor 11:19; 1 Tim 4:1
8 [1]Lit *having;* Gr part. [a]Matt 5:30; Mark 9:43
9 [1]Lit *having;* Gr part. [2]Lit *Gehenna of fire* [a]Matt 5:29; Mark 9:47 [b]Matt 5:22
10 [a]Luke 1:19; Acts 12:15; Rev 8:2
11 [1]Early mss do not contain this v [a]Luke 19:10
12 [a]Matt 18:12-14: *Luke 15:4-7*
14 [1]Lit *before*
15 [1]Late mss add *against you* [2]Or *reprove* [3]Lit *between you and him alone* [a]Lev 19:17; Luke 17:3; Gal 6:1; 2 Thess 3:15; James 5:19
16 [1]Lit *word* [a]Deut 19:15; John 8:17; 2 Cor 13:1; 1 Tim 5:19; Heb 10:28
17 [1]Lit *the* [a]1 Cor 6:1ff [b]2 Thess 3:6, 14f
18 [1]Or *forbid* [2]Gr fut. pft. pass. [3]Or *permit* [a]Matt 16:19; John 20:23
19 [1]Lit *from* [a]Matt 7:7
20 [a]Matt 28:20
21 [a]Matt 18:15 [b]Luke 17:4
22 [a]Gen 4:24
23 [1]Lit *was compared to* [a]Matt 13:24 [b]Matt 25:19
24 [1]A talent was worth more than fifteen years' wages of a laborer
25 [1]Or *was unable to* [a]Luke 7:42 [b]Ex 21:2; Lev 25:39; 2 Kin 4:1; Neh 5:5 **26** [a]Matt 8:2 **27** [1]Or *loan* [a]Luke 7:42

18:3 *like children.* Trusting and unpretentious.
18:6 *heavy millstone.* Lit. "a millstone of a donkey," i.e., a millstone turned by a donkey—far larger and heavier than the small millstones (24:41) used by women each morning in their homes.
18:8–9 See note on 5:29–30.
18:10 *their angels.* Guardian angels not exclusively for children, but for God's people in general (Ps 34:7; 91:11; Heb 1:14). *continually see the face of.* Have constant access to.
18:12–14 The parable of the lost sheep is also found in Luke 15:3–7. There it applies to unbelievers, here to believers. Jesus used the same parable to teach different truths in different situations.
18:12 *sheep.* See note on Luke 15:4.
18:15 *brother.* A fellow believer.
18:17 *church.* The local congregation. Here and 16:18 are the only two places where the Gospels speak of the "church." *Gentile.* For the Jews this meant any non-Jewish person. *tax collector.* See note on 5:46. This verse establishes one basis for excommunication.
18:18 See note on 16:19.
18:22 *seventy times seven.* Or "seventy-seven times." In either case the sense is "times without number" or "as many times as necessary."
18:23 *kingdom of heaven.* See note on 3:2.
18:25 For this practice of selling into slavery see Ex 21:2; Lev 25:39; 2 Kin 4:1; Neh 5:5; Is 50:1.

28 "But that slave went out and found one
of his fellow slaves who owed him a hundred
[1]denarii; and he seized him and *began* to
choke *him,* saying, 'Pay back what you owe.'
29 "So his fellow slave fell *to the ground*
and *began* to plead with him, saying, 'Have
patience with me and I will repay you.'
30 "But he was unwilling [1]and went and
threw him in prison until he should pay back
what was owed.
31 "So when his fellow slaves saw what
had happened, they were deeply grieved and
came and reported to their lord all that had
happened.
32 "Then summoning him, his lord *said to
him, 'You wicked slave, I forgave you all that
debt because you pleaded with me.
33 '[a]Should you not also have had mercy
on your fellow slave, in the same way that I
had mercy on you?'
34 "And his lord, moved with anger, handed him over to the torturers until he should
repay all that was owed him.
35 "[a]My heavenly Father will also do the
same to you, if each of you does not forgive
his brother from [1]your heart."

Concerning Divorce

19 [a]When Jesus had finished these words,
He departed from Galilee and [b]came
into the region of Judea beyond the Jordan;
2 and [1]large crowds followed Him, and
[a]He healed them there.
3 *Some* Pharisees came to [1]Jesus, testing
Him and asking, "[a]Is it lawful *for a man* to
[2]divorce his wife for any reason at all?"
4 And He answered and said, "Have you
not read [a]that He who created *them* from the
beginning MADE THEM MALE AND FEMALE,
5 and said, '[a]FOR THIS REASON A MAN SHALL
LEAVE HIS FATHER AND MOTHER AND BE JOINED TO
HIS WIFE, AND [b]THE TWO SHALL BECOME ONE
FLESH'?
6 "So they are no longer two, but one
flesh. What therefore God has joined together, let no man separate."
7 They *said to Him, "[a]Why then did
Moses command to GIVE HER A CERTIFICATE OF
DIVORCE AND SEND *her* AWAY?"
8 He *said to them, "Because of your
hardness of heart Moses permitted you to
[1]divorce your wives; but from the beginning
it has not been this way.
9 "And I say to you, [a]whoever [1]divorces
his wife, except for [2]immorality, and marries
another woman [3]commits adultery[4]."
10 The disciples *said to Him, "If the relationship of the man with his wife is like this,
it is better not to marry."
11 But He said to them, "[a]Not all men *can*
accept this statement, but [b]*only* those to
whom it has been given.
12 "For there are eunuchs who were born
that way from their mother's womb; and
there are eunuchs who were made eunuchs
by men; and there are *also* eunuchs who
made themselves eunuchs for the sake of the
kingdom of heaven. He who is able to accept
this, let him accept *it.*"

Jesus Blesses Little Children

13 [a]Then *some* children were brought to
Him so that He might lay His hands on them
and pray; and the disciples rebuked them.
14 But Jesus said, "[1][a]Let the children
alone, and do not hinder them from coming
to Me; for [b]the kingdom of heaven belongs
to such as these."
15 After laying His hands on them, He
departed from there.

The Rich Young Ruler

16 [a]And someone came to Him and said,
"Teacher, what good thing shall I do that I
may obtain [b]eternal life?"
17 And He said to him, "Why are you ask-

28 [1]The denarius was a day's wages
30 [1]Lit *but*
33 [a]Matt 6:12; Eph 4:32
35 [1]Lit *your hearts* [a]Matt 6:14
19:1 [a]Matt 7:28 [b]Matt 19:1-9: *Mark 10:1-12*
2 [1]Lit *many* [a]Matt 4:23
3 [1]Lit *Him* [2]Or *send away* [a]Matt 5:31
4 [a]Gen 1:27; 5:2
5 [a]Gen 2:24; Eph 5:31 [b]1 Cor 6:16
7 [a]Deut 24:1-4; Matt 5:31
8 [1]Or *send away*
9 [1]Or *sends away* [2]Lit *fornication* [3]Some early mss read *makes her commit adultery* [4]Some early mss add *and he who marries a divorced woman commits adultery* [a]Matt 5:32
11 [a]1 Cor 7:7ff [b]Matt 13:11
13 [a]Matt 19:13-15: *Mark 10:13-16; Luke 18:15-17*
14 [1]Or *Permit the children* [a]Matt 18:3; Mark 10:15; Luke 18:17; 1 Cor 14:20; 1 Pet 2:2 [b]Matt 5:3
16 [a]Matt 19:16-29: *Mark 10:17-30; Luke 18:18-30;* Luke 10:25-28 [b]Matt 25:46

18:35 *forgive.* The one main teaching of the parable.

19:1 *beyond the Jordan.* The east side, known later as Transjordan or Perea and today simply as Jordan. Jesus now began ministering there (see note on Luke 13:22).

19:3 *Pharisees.* See note on Mark 2:16. *for any reason at all.* This last part of the question is not in the parallel passage in Mark (10:2). Matthew possibly included it because he was writing to the Jews, who were aware of the dispute between the schools of Shammai and Hillel over the interpretation of Deut 24:1–4. Shammai held that "some indecency" (Deut 24:1) meant "immorality" (Matt 19:9)—the only allowable cause for divorce. Hillel (c. 60 B.C.-A.D. 20) emphasized the preceding clause, "she finds no favor in his eyes." He would allow a man to divorce his wife if she did anything he disliked—even if she burned his food while cooking it. Jesus clearly took the side of Shammai (see v. 9), but only after first pointing back to God's original ideal for marriage in Gen 1:27; 2:24.

19:10–12 See 1 Cor 7:7–8,26,32–35.

19:11 *this statement.* The disciples' conclusion in v. 10: "it is better not to marry." Not everyone can accept this teaching because it is not meant for everyone. Jesus then gives three examples of persons for whom it is meant in v. 12.

19:12 *made themselves eunuchs for the sake of the kingdom of heaven.* Those who have voluntarily adopted a celibate lifestyle in order to give themselves more completely to God's work. Under certain circumstances celibacy is recommended in Scripture (cf. 1Co. 7:25–38), but it is never presented as superior to marriage.

19:14 *kingdom of heaven.* See note on 3:2. *belongs to such as these.* See note on Mark 10:14.

19:16 *someone.* See note on Mark 10:17. *what good thing shall I do . . . ?* The rich man was thinking in terms of righteousness by works. Jesus had to correct this misunderstanding first before answering the question more fully. *eternal life.* The first use of this term in Matthew's Gospel (see v. 29; 25:46). In John it occurs much more frequently, often taking the place of the term "kingdom of God (or heaven)" used in the Synoptics, which treat the following three expressions as synonymous: (1) eternal life (v. 16; Mark 10:17; Luke 18:18), (2) entering the kingdom of heaven (v. 23; cf. Mark 10:24; Luke 18:24) and (3) being saved (vv. 25–26; Mark 10:26–27; Luke 18:26–27).

ing Me about what is good? There is *only*
One who is good; but [a]if you wish to enter
into life, keep the commandments."
18 *Then* he *said to Him, "Which ones?"
And Jesus said, "[a]YOU SHALL NOT COMMIT MUR-
DER; YOU SHALL NOT COMMIT ADULTERY; YOU
SHALL NOT STEAL; YOU SHALL NOT BEAR FALSE WIT-
NESS;
19 [a]HONOR YOUR FATHER AND MOTHER; and
[b]YOU SHALL LOVE YOUR NEIGHBOR AS YOURSELF."
20 The young man *said to Him, "All
these things I have kept; what am I still lacking?"
21 Jesus said to him, "If you wish to be
[1]complete, go *and* [a]sell your possessions and
give to *the* poor, and you will have [b]treasure
in heaven; and come, follow Me."
22 But when the young man heard this
statement, he went away grieving; for he
was one who owned much property.
23 And Jesus said to His disciples, "Truly I
say to you, [a]it is hard for a rich man to enter
the kingdom of heaven.
24 "Again I say to you, [a]it is easier for a
camel to go through the eye of a needle, than
for a rich man to enter the kingdom of God."
25 When the disciples heard *this,* they
were very astonished and said, "Then who
can be saved?"
26 And looking at *them* Jesus said to
them, "[a]With people this is impossible, but
with God all things are possible."

The Disciples' Reward

27 Then Peter said to Him, "Behold, we
have left everything and followed You; what
then will there be for us?"
28 And Jesus said to them, "Truly I say to
you, that you who have followed Me, in the
regeneration when [a]the Son of Man will sit
on [1]His glorious throne, [b]you also shall sit
upon twelve thrones, judging the twelve
tribes of Israel.

17 [a]Lev 18:5; Neh 9:29; Ezek 20:21
18 [a]Ex 20:13-16; Deut 5:17-20
19 [a]Ex 20:12; Deut 5:16 [b]Lev 19:18
21 [1]Or *perfect* [a]Luke 12:33; 16:9; Acts 2:45; 4:34f [b]Matt 6:20
23 [a]Matt 13:22; Mark 10:23f; Luke 18:24
24 [a]Mark 10:25; Luke 18:25
26 [a]Gen 18:14; Job 42:2; Jer 32:17; Zech 8:6; Mark 10:27; Luke 1:37; 18:27
28 [1]Lit *the throne of His glory* [a]Matt 25:31 [b]Luke 22:30; Rev 3:21; 4:4; 11:16; 20:4
29 [1]One early ms adds *or wife* [2]One early ms reads *a hundred times* [a]Matt 6:33; Mark 10:29f; Luke 18:29f
30 [a]Matt 20:16; Mark 10:31; Luke 13:30
20:1 [1]Lit *a man, a landowner* [a]Matt 13:24 [b]Matt 21:28, 33
2 [1]The denarius was a day's wages
3 [1]I.e. 9 a.m.
5 [1]I.e. noon and 3 p.m. [2]Lit *similarly*
6 [1]I.e. 5 p.m.
8 [1]Or *lord* [a]Lev 19:13; Deut 24:15 [b]Luke 8:3
9 [1]The denarius was a day's wages
10 [1]Lit *each one a denarius*

29 "And [a]everyone who has left houses or
brothers or sisters or father or mother [1]or
children or farms for My name's sake, will
receive [2]many times as much, and will inherit eternal life.
30 "[a]But many *who are* first will be last;
and *the* last, first.

Laborers in the Vineyard

20 "For [a]the kingdom of heaven is like [1]a
landowner who went out early in the
morning to hire laborers for his [b]vineyard.
2 "When he had agreed with the laborers
for a [1]denarius for the day, he sent them into
his vineyard.
3 "And he went out about the [1]third hour
and saw others standing idle in the market
place;
4 and to those he said, 'You also go into
the vineyard, and whatever is right I will give
you.' And *so* they went.
5 "Again he went out about the [1]sixth and
the ninth hour, and did [2]the same thing.
6 "And about the [1]eleventh *hour* he went
out and found others standing *around;* and
he *said to them, 'Why have you been standing here idle all day long?'
7 "They *said to him, 'Because no one
hired us.' He *said to them, 'You go into the
vineyard too.'
8 "When [a]evening came, the [1]owner of
the vineyard *said to his [b]foreman, 'Call the
laborers and pay them their wages, beginning with the last *group* to the first.'
9 "When those *hired* about the eleventh
hour came, each one received a [1]denarius.
10 "When those *hired* first came, they
thought that they would receive more; [1]but
each of them also received a denarius.
11 "When they received it, they grumbled
at the landowner,
12 saying, 'These last men have worked
only one hour, and you have made them

19:17 *There is only One who is good.* The good is not something to be done as meritorious in itself. God alone is good, and all other goodness derives from him—even the keeping of the commandments, which Jesus proceeded to enumerate (vv. 18–20). *if you wish to enter into life, keep the commandments.* "To enter into life" is the same as "obtain eternal life" (v. 16). The requirement to "keep the commandments" is not to establish one's merit before God but is to be an expression of true faith. The Bible always teaches that salvation is a gift of God's grace received through faith (see Eph 2:8).
19:20 *All these things I have kept.* See note on Mark 10:20.
19:21 *complete.* Greek *teleios,* "goal, end." His goal was eternal life, but wealth and lack of commitment stood in his way. *go and sell your possessions.* In His listing of the commandments, Jesus omitted "Do not covet." This was the rich man's main problem and was preventing him from entering life (see note on Mark 10:21).
19:22 *he went away grieving.* See note on Mark 10:22.
19:23 *kingdom of heaven.* See note on 3:2.
19:24 *camel to go through the eye of a needle.* See note on Mark 10:25.
19:26 See note on Mark 10:27.
19:28 *Truly I say to you.* See note on Mark 10:29. *Son of Man.* See note on Mark 8:31. *judging.* Governing or ruling (cf. the OT "judge"; see Introduction to Judges: Title).
19:29 *will receive many times as much.* Mark adds, "along with persecutions" (see note on Mark 10:30).
20:1–16 This parable occurs only in Matthew's Gospel. In its original setting, its main point seems to be the sovereign graciousness and generosity of God extended to "latecomers" (the poor and the outcasts of society) into God's kingdom. It is addressed to the grumblers (v. 11) who just cannot handle this amazing expression of God's grace. They almost certainly represent the religious leaders who opposed Jesus.
20:2 *a denarius.* The usual daily wage. A Roman soldier also received one denarius a day.
20:3 *third hour.* 9:00 A.M.
20:5 *sixth and the ninth hour.* Noon and 3:00 P.M. respectively.
20:6 *eleventh hour.* 5:00 P.M.
20:8 *When evening came.* Because farm workers were poor, the law of Moses required that they be paid at the end of each day (cf. Lev 19:13; Deut 24:14–15).

equal to us who have borne the burden and the [a]scorching heat of the day.'

13 "But he answered and said to one of them, '[a]Friend, I am doing you no wrong; did you not agree with me for a denarius?

14 'Take what is yours and go, but I wish to give to this last man the same as to you.

15 'Is it not lawful for me to do what I wish with what is my own? Or is your [a]eye [1]envious because I am [2]generous?'

16 "So [a]the last shall be first, and the first last."

Death, Resurrection Foretold

17 [a]As Jesus was about to go up to Jerusalem, He took the twelve *disciples* aside by themselves, and on the way He said to them,

18 "Behold, we are going up to Jerusalem; and the Son of Man [a]will be [1]delivered to the chief priests and scribes, and they will condemn Him to death,

19 and [a]will hand Him over to the Gentiles to mock and scourge and crucify *Him,* and on [b]the third day He will be raised up."

Preferment Asked

20 [a]Then the mother of [b]the sons of Zebedee came to [1]Jesus with her sons, [c]bowing down and making a request of Him.

21 And He said to her, "What do you wish?" She *said to Him, "Command that in Your kingdom these two sons of mine [a]may sit one on Your right and one on Your left."

22 But Jesus answered, "You do not know what you are asking. Are you able [a]to drink the cup that I am about to drink?" They *said to Him, "We are able."

23 He *said to them, "[a]My cup you shall drink; but to sit on My right and on *My* left, this is not Mine to give, [b]but it is for those for whom it has been [c]prepared by My Father."

24 And hearing *this,* the ten became indignant with the two brothers.

12 [a]Jon 4:8; Luke 12:55; James 1:11
13 [a]Matt 22:12; 26:50
15 [1]Lit *evil* [2]Lit *good* [a]Deut 15:9; Matt 6:23; Mark 7:22
16 [a]Matt 19:30; Mark 10:31; Luke 13:30
17 [a]Matt 20:17-19: *Mark 10:32-34; Luke 18:31-33*
18 [1]Or *betrayed* [a]Matt 16:21
19 [a]Matt 27:2; Acts 2:23; 3:13; 4:27; 21:11 [b]Matt 16:21; 17:23; Luke 18:32f
20 [1]Lit *Him* [a]Matt 20:20-28: *Mark 10:35-45* [b]Matt 4:21; 10:2 [c]Matt 8:2
21 [a]Matt 19:28
22 [a]Is 51:17, 22; Jer 49:12; Matt 26:39, 42; Luke 22:42; John 18:11
23 [a]Acts 12:2; Rev 1:9 [b]Matt 13:11 [c]Matt 25:34
25 [a]Matt 20:25-28; Luke 22:25-27
26 [a]Matt 23:11; Mark 9:35; 10:43; Luke 22:26
28 [1]Or *soul* [a]Matt 8:20 [b]Matt 26:28; John 13:13ff; 2 Cor 8:9; Phil 2:7; 1 Tim 2:6; Titus 2:14; Heb 9:28; Rev 1:5
29 [a]Matt 20:29-34: *Mark 10:46-52; Luke 18:35-43;* Matt 9:27-31
30 [a]Matt 9:27 [b]Matt 20:31
31 [a]Matt 9:27
21:1 [a]Matt 21:1-9: *Mark 11:1-10; Luke 19:29-38* [b]Matt 24:3; 26:30; Mark 11:1; 13:3; 14:26; Luke 19:29, 37; 21:37; 22:39; John 8:1; Acts 1:12

25 [a]But Jesus called them to Himself and said, "You know that the rulers of the Gentiles lord it over them, and *their* great men exercise authority over them.

26 "It is not this way among you, [a]but whoever wishes to become great among you shall be your servant,

27 and whoever wishes to be first among you shall be your slave;

28 just as [a]the Son of Man [b]did not come to be served, but to serve, and to give His [1]life a ransom for many."

Sight for the Blind

29 [a]As they were leaving Jericho, a large crowd followed Him.

30 And two blind men sitting by the road, hearing that Jesus was passing by, cried out, "Lord, [a]have mercy on us, [b]Son of David!"

31 The crowd sternly told them to be quiet, but they cried out all the more, "Lord, [a]Son of David, have mercy on us!"

32 And Jesus stopped and called them, and said, "What do you want Me to do for you?"

33 They *said to Him, "Lord, *we want* our eyes to be opened."

34 Moved with compassion, Jesus touched their eyes; and immediately they regained their sight and followed Him.

The Triumphal Entry

21 [a]When they had approached Jerusalem and had come to Bethphage, at [b]the Mount of Olives, then Jesus sent two disciples,

2 saying to them, "Go into the village opposite you, and immediately you will find a donkey tied *there* and a colt with her; untie them and bring them to Me.

3 "If anyone says anything to you, you

20:15 *is your eye envious . . . ?* Lit. "is your eye evil . . . ?" Apparently the evil eye was associated with jealousy and envy (cf. 1 Sam 18:9).
20:17–19 See Mark 10:32–34; Luke 18:31–33 and notes.
20:19 *and will hand Him over to the Gentiles to mock and scourge and crucify Him.* An additional statement in this third prediction of the passion. Jesus would not be killed by the Jews, which would have been by stoning, but would be crucified by the Romans. All three predictions include His resurrection on the third day (16:21; 17:23).
20:20 *mother of the sons of Zebedee.* Mark has "James and John, the two sons of Zebedee," asking the question (Mark 10:35–37), yet there is no contradiction. The three joined in making the petition.
20:21 *wish.* See note on Mark 10:35–36. *sit one on Your right and one on Your left.* See note on Mark 10:37.
20:22 *drink the cup.* A figure of speech meaning to "undergo" or "experience." Here the reference is to suffering (cf. 26:39). The same figure of speech is used in Jer 25:15; Ezek 23:32; Hab 2:16; Rev 14:10; 16:19; 18:6 for divine wrath or judgment. See note on Mark 10:38.
20:23 *is not Mine to give.* See note on Mark 10:40.
20:24 See note on Mark 10:41.
20:26 *It is not this way among you.* See note on Mark 10:43.
20:28 *ransom.* The Greek word was used most commonly for the price paid to redeem a slave. Similarly, Christ paid the ransom price of His own life to free us from the slavery of sin. *for.* Here the Greek for this preposition emphasizes the substitutionary nature of Christ's death. *many.* Christ "gave Himself as a ransom for all" (1 Tim 2:6). Salvation is offered to "all," but only the "many" (i.e., the elect) receive it. See note on Mark 10:45.
20:29 *Jericho.* See note on Mark 10:46.
20:30 *two blind men.* The other Synoptics mention only one (see note on Luke 18:35). *Son of David.* A Messianic title (see note on 9:27).
21:1 *Jerusalem.* See map No. 8 at the end of the study Bible. *Bethphage.* The name means "house of figs." It is not mentioned in the OT, and in the NT only in connection with the Triumphal Entry. In the Talmud it is spoken of as being near Jerusalem. *Mount of Olives.* See note on Mark 11:1.
21:2 *donkey.* An animal symbolic of humility, peace and Davidic royalty (see notes on Zech 9:9; Luke 19:30). See also note

shall say, 'The Lord has need of them,' and immediately he will send them."

4 [a]This [1]took place to fulfill what was spoken through the prophet:

5 "[a]SAY TO THE DAUGHTER OF ZION,
'BEHOLD YOUR KING IS COMING TO YOU,
GENTLE, AND MOUNTED ON A DONKEY,
EVEN ON A COLT, THE FOAL OF A BEAST OF BURDEN.' "

6 The disciples went and did just as Jesus had instructed them,

7 and brought the donkey and the colt, and laid their coats on them; and He sat on [1]the coats.

8 Most of the crowd [a]spread their coats in the road, and others were cutting branches from the trees and spreading them in the road.

9 The crowds going ahead of Him, and those who followed, were shouting,
"Hosanna to the [a]Son of David;
[b]BLESSED IS HE WHO COMES IN THE NAME OF THE LORD;
Hosanna [c]in the highest!"

10 When He had entered Jerusalem, all the city was stirred, saying, "Who is this?"

11 And the crowds were saying, "This is [a]the prophet Jesus, from [b]Nazareth in Galilee."

Cleansing the Temple

12 [a]And Jesus entered the temple and drove out all those who were buying and selling in the temple, and overturned the tables of the [b]money changers and the seats of those who were selling [c]doves.

13 And He *said to them, "It is written, '[a]MY HOUSE SHALL BE CALLED A HOUSE OF PRAYER'; but you are making it a [b]ROBBERS' [1]DEN."

14 And *the* blind and *the* lame came to Him in the temple, and [a]He healed them.

15 But when the chief priests and the scribes saw the wonderful things that He had done, and the children who were shouting in the temple, "Hosanna to the [a]Son of David," they became indignant

16 and said to Him, "Do You hear what these *children* are saying?" And Jesus *said to them, "Yes; have you never read, '[a]OUT OF THE MOUTH OF INFANTS AND NURSING BABIES YOU HAVE PREPARED PRAISE FOR YOURSELF'?"

17 And He left them and went out of the city to [a]Bethany, and spent the night there.

The Barren Fig Tree

18 [a]Now in the morning, when He was returning to the city, He became hungry.

19 Seeing a lone [a]fig tree by the road, He came to it and found nothing on it except leaves only; and He *said to it, "No longer shall there ever be *any* fruit from you." And at once the fig tree withered.

20 Seeing *this,* the disciples were amazed and asked, "How did the fig tree wither *all* at once?"

21 And Jesus answered and said to them, "Truly I say to you, [a]if you have faith and do not doubt, you will not only do what was done to the fig tree, but even if you say to this mountain, 'Be taken up and cast into the sea,' it will happen.

22 "And [a]all things you ask in prayer, believing, you will receive."

Authority Challenged

23 [a]When He entered the temple, the chief priests and the elders of the people came to Him [b]while He was teaching, and said, "By

4 [1]Lit *has happened* [a]Matt 21:4-9: *Mark 11:7-10; Luke 19:35-38; John 12:12-15*
5 [a]Is 62:11; Zech 9:9
7 [1]Lit *them*
8 [a]2 Kin 9:13
9 [a]Matt 9:27 [b]Ps 118:26 [c]Luke 2:14
11 [a]Matt 21:26; Mark 6:15; Luke 7:16, 39; 13:33; 24:19; John 1:21, 25; 4:19; 6:14; 7:40; 9:17; Acts 3:22f; 7:37 [b]Matt 2:23
12 [a]Matt 21:12-16: *Mark 11:15-18; Luke 19:45-47;* Matt 21:12, 13: *John 2:13-16* [b]Ex 30:13 [c]Lev 1:14; 5:7; 12:8
13 [1]Lit *cave* [a]Is 56:7 [b]Jer 7:11
14 [a]Matt 4:23
15 [a]Matt 9:27
16 [a]Ps 8:2; Matt 11:25
17 [a]Matt 26:6; Mark 11:1, 11, 12; 14:3; Luke 19:29; 24:50; John 11:1, 18; 12:1
18 [a]Matt 21:18-22: *Mark 11:12-14, 20-24*
19 [a]Luke 13:6-9
21 [a]Matt 17:20; Mark 11:23; Luke 17:6; James 1:6
22 [a]Matt 7:7
23 [a]Matt 21:23-27: *Mark 11:27-33; Luke 20:1-8* [b]Matt 26:55

on Mark 11:2. *colt.* See notes on Mark 11:2 and Luke 19:30.

21:3 *Lord.* See note on Luke 19:31.

21:7 *He sat on the coats.* We know from Mark (11:2) and Luke (19:30) that He rode the colt. Typically, a mother donkey followed her offspring closely. Matthew mentions two animals, while the other Gospels have only one (see note on Luke 19:30).

21:8 *spread their coats in the road.* An act of royal homage (see 2 Kin 9:13). *branches.* See note on Mark 11:8.

21:9 These are three separate quotations, not necessarily spoken at the same time. *Hosanna.* See note on Jer 31:7; both prayer and praise. *Son of David.* See note on 9:27. *in the highest.* That is, may those in heaven sing "Hosanna" (see Ps 148:1–2; Luke 2:14).

21:12–17 In the Synoptics the cleansing of the temple occurs during the last week of Jesus' ministry; in John it takes place during the first few months (John 2:12–16). Two explanations are possible: 1. There were two cleansings, one at the beginning and the other at the end of Jesus' public ministry. 2. There was only one cleansing, which took place during Passion Week but which John placed at the beginning of his account for theological reasons—to show that God's judgment was operative through the Messiah from the outset of His ministry. However, different details are present in the two accounts (the selling of cattle and sheep in John 2:14, the whip in John 2:15, and the statements of Jesus in Matt 21:13; John 2:16). From Matthew's and Luke's accounts we might assume that the cleansing of the temple took place on Sunday, following the so-called Triumphal Entry (21:1–11). But Mark (11:15–19) clearly indicates that it was on Monday. Matthew often compressed narratives.

21:12 *temple.* The "buying and selling" took place in the large outer court of the Gentiles, which covered several acres (see notes on Mark 11:15 and Luke 19:45).

21:13 *HOUSE OF PRAYER.* See note on Mark 11:17.

21:17 *Bethany.* A village on the eastern slope of the Mount of Olives, about two miles from Jerusalem and the final station on the road from Jericho to Jerusalem.

21:18–22 See note on vv. 12–17; another example of compressing narratives. Mark (11:12–14,20–25) places the cursing of the fig tree on Monday morning and the disciples' finding it withered on Tuesday morning. In Matthew's account the tree withered as soon as Jesus cursed it, emphasizing the immediacy of judgment. For the theological meaning of this event see note on Mark 11:14.

21:18 *city.* Jerusalem.

21:21 *say to this mountain, 'Be taken up and cast into the sea.'* See note on 17:20.

21:23 *chief priests.* See notes on 2:4; Mark 8:31; Luke 19:47. *By what authority . . . ?* See notes on Mark 11:28 and Luke 20:2.

what authority are You doing these things,
and who gave You this authority?”
24 Jesus said to them, “I will also ask you
one [1]thing, which if you tell Me, I will also
tell you by what authority I do these things.
25 “The baptism of John was from what
source, from heaven or from men?” And they
began reasoning among themselves, saying,
“If we say, ‘From heaven,’ He will say to us,
‘Then why did you not believe him?’
26 “But if we say, ‘From men,’ we fear the
[1]people; for they all regard John as [a]a
prophet.”
27 And answering Jesus, they said, “We
do not know.” He also said to them, “Neither will I tell you by what authority I do
these things.

Parable of Two Sons

28 “But what do you think? A man had two
[1]sons, and he came to the first and said,
‘[2]Son, go work today in the [a]vineyard.’
29 “And he answered, ‘I will not’; but afterward he regretted it and went.
30 “The man came to the second and said
the same thing; and he answered, ‘I *will,* sir’;
but he did not go.
31 “Which of the two did the will of his
father?” They *said, “The first.” Jesus *said
to them, “Truly I say to you that [a]the tax collectors and prostitutes [1]will get into the kingdom of God before you.
32 “For John came to you in the way of righteousness and you did not believe him; but
[a]the tax collectors and prostitutes did believe
him; and you, seeing *this,* did not even feel
remorse afterward so as to believe him.

Parable of the Landowner

33 “Listen to another parable. [a]There was a
[1]landowner who [b]PLANTED A [c]VINEYARD AND
PUT A WALL AROUND IT AND DUG A WINE PRESS IN
IT, AND BUILT A TOWER, and rented it out to
[2]vine-growers and [d]went on a journey.
34 “When the [1]harvest time approached,
he [a]sent his slaves to the vine-growers to
receive his produce.
35 “The vine-growers took his slaves and
beat one, and killed another, and stoned a
third.
36 “Again he [a]sent another group of slaves
larger than the first; and they did the same
thing to them.
37 “But afterward he sent his son to them,
saying, ‘They will respect my son.’
38 “But when the vine-growers saw the
son, they said among themselves, ‘This is
the heir; come, let us kill him and seize his
inheritance.’
39 “They took him, and threw him out of
the vineyard and killed him.
40 “Therefore when the [1]owner of the vineyard comes, what will he do to those vine-
growers?”
41 They *said to Him, “He will bring those
wretches to a wretched end, and [a]will rent
out the vineyard to other vine-growers who
will pay him the proceeds at the *proper* seasons.”
42 Jesus *said to them, “Did you never
read in the Scriptures,

‘[a]THE STONE WHICH THE BUILDERS
REJECTED,
THIS BECAME THE CHIEF CORNER *stone;*
THIS CAME ABOUT FROM THE LORD,
AND IT IS MARVELOUS IN OUR EYES’?

43 “Therefore I say to you, the kingdom of
God will be taken away from you and given
to a [1]people, producing the fruit of it.
44 “And [a]he who falls on this stone will be
broken to pieces; but on whomever it falls, it
will scatter him like dust.”
45 When the chief priests and the Pharisees heard His parables, they understood
that He was speaking about them.
46 When they sought to seize Him, they
[a]feared the [1]people, because they considered
Him to be a [b]prophet.

Parable of the Marriage Feast

22 Jesus spoke to them again in parables,
saying,
2 “[a]The kingdom of heaven [1]may be compared to [2]a king who [3]gave a [b]wedding feast
for his son.
3 “And he [a]sent out his slaves to call
those who had been invited to the wedding
feast, and they were unwilling to come.
4 “Again he [a]sent out other slaves saying,
‘Tell those who have been invited, “Behold,
I have prepared my dinner; my oxen and my
fattened livestock are *all* butchered and
everything is ready; come to the wedding
feast.” ’
5 “But they paid no attention and went
their way, one to his own [1]farm, another to
his business,
6 and the rest seized his slaves and mistreated them and killed them.
7 “But the king was enraged, and he sent

24 [1]Lit *word* **26** [1]Lit *crowd* [a]Matt 11:9; Mark 6:20 **28** [1]Lit *children* [2]Lit *Child* [a]Matt 20:1; 21:33 **31** [1]Lit *are getting into* [a]Luke 7:29, 37-50 **32** [a]Luke 3:12; 7:29f **33** [1]Lit *a man, head of a household* [2]Or *tenant farmers, also vv 34, 35, 38, 40* [a]Matt 21:33-46: *Mark 12:1-12; Luke 20:9-19* [b]Is 5:1, 2 [c]Matt 20:1; 21:28 [d]Matt 25:14 **34** [1]Lit *the fruit season* [a]Matt 22:3 **36** [a]Matt 22:4

40 [1]Lit *lord* **41** [a]Matt 8:11f; Acts 13:46; 18:6; 28:28 **42** [a]Ps 118:22f; Acts 4:11; Rom 9:33; 1 Pet 2:7 **43** [1]Lit *nation* **44** [a]Is 8:14, 15 **46** [1]Lit *crowds* [a]Matt 21:26 [b]Matt 21:11 **22:2** [1]Lit *was compared to* [2]Lit *a man, a king* [3]Lit *made* [a]Matt 13:24; 22:2-14; Luke 14:16-24 [b]Luke 12:36; John 2:2 **3** [a]Matt 21:34 **4** [a]Matt 21:36 **5** [1]Or *field*

21:25 *from heaven or from men?* See notes on Mark 11:30; Luke 20:4.
21:33–46 See notes on Mark 12:1–12 and Luke 20:9–19.
21:33 *TOWER.* For guarding the vineyard, especially when the grapes ripened, and for shelter. The rabbis specified that it was to be a raised wooden platform, 15 feet high and 6 feet square.
21:35–37 The vine-growers are the Jews, or their leaders. The slaves represent the OT prophets, many of whom were killed. The son represents Christ, who was condemned to death by the religious leaders.
21:41 *other vine-growers.* Gentiles, to whom Paul turned when the Jews, for the most part, rejected the gospel (Acts 13:46; 18:6). By the second century the church was composed almost entirely of Gentiles.
21:44 *will be broken to pieces.* See note on Luke 20:18.
21:45 *chief priests.* See notes on 2:4; Mark 8:31; Luke 19:47. *Pharisees.* See notes on 3:7, Mark 2:16; Luke 5:17. *parables.* See notes on 13:3; Mark 4:2; Luke 8:4.

his armies and destroyed those murderers and set their city on fire.

8 "Then he *said to his slaves, 'The wedding is ready, but those who were invited were not worthy.

9 'Go therefore to [a]the main highways, and as many as you find *there,* invite to the wedding feast.'

10 "Those slaves went out into the streets and gathered together all they found, both evil and good; and the wedding hall was filled with [1]dinner guests.

11 "But when the king came in to look over the dinner guests, he saw [a]a man there who was not dressed in wedding clothes,

12 and he *said to him, '[a]Friend, how did you come in here without wedding clothes?' And the man was speechless.

13 "Then the king said to the servants, 'Bind him hand and foot, and throw him into [a]the outer darkness; in that place there will be weeping and gnashing of teeth.'

14 "For many are [1][a]called, but few *are* [a]chosen."

Tribute to Caesar

15 [a]Then the Pharisees went and [1]plotted together how they might trap Him [2]in what He said.

16 And they *sent their disciples to Him, along with the [a]Herodians, saying, "Teacher, we know that You are truthful and teach the way of God in truth, and [1]defer to no one; for You are not partial to any.

17 "Tell us then, what do You think? Is it [1]lawful to give a [a]poll-tax to [b]Caesar, or not?"

18 But Jesus perceived their [1]malice, and said, "Why are you testing Me, you hypocrites?

19 "Show Me the [a]coin *used* for the poll-tax." And they brought Him a [1]denarius.

9 [a]Ezek 21:21; Obad 14
10 [1]Lit *those reclining* at the table
11 [a]2 Kin 10:22; Zech 3:3, 4
12 [a]Matt 20:13; 26:50
13 [a]Matt 8:12; 25:30; Luke 13:28
14 [1]Or *invited* [a]Matt 24:22; 2 Pet 1:10; Rev 17:14
15 [1]Lit *took counsel* [2]Lit *in word* [a]Matt 22:15-22: *Mark 12:13-17; Luke 20:20-26*
16 [1]Lit *it is not a concern to You about anyone;* i.e. You do not seek anyone's favor [a]Mark 3:6; 8:15; 12:13
17 [1]Or *permissible* [a]Matt 17:25 [b]Luke 2:1; 3:1
18 [1]Or *wickedness*
19 [1]The denarius was a day's wages [a]Matt 17:25
21 [a]Mark 12:17; Luke 20:25; Rom 13:7
22 [a]Mark 12:12
23 [a]Matt 22:23-33: *Mark 12:18-27; Luke 20:27-40* [b]Matt 3:7 [c]Acts 23:8
24 [a]Deut 25:5
29 [1]Or *knowing* [a]John 20:9
30 [a]Matt 24:38; Luke 17:27
32 [a]Ex 3:6
33 [a]Matt 7:28
34 [a]Matt 22:34-40: *Mark 12:28-31; Luke 10:25-37*

20 And He *said to them, "Whose likeness and inscription is this?"

21 They *said to Him, "Caesar's." Then He *said to them, "[a]Then render to Caesar the things that are Caesar's; and to God the things that are God's."

22 And hearing *this,* they were amazed, and [a]leaving Him, they went away.

Jesus Answers the Sadducees

23 [a]On that day *some* [b]Sadducees (who say [c]there is no resurrection) came to Jesus and questioned Him,

24 asking, "Teacher, Moses said, '[a]IF A MAN DIES HAVING NO CHILDREN, HIS BROTHER AS NEXT OF KIN SHALL MARRY HIS WIFE, AND RAISE UP CHILDREN FOR HIS BROTHER.'

25 "Now there were seven brothers with us; and the first married and died, and having no children left his wife to his brother;

26 so also the second, and the third, down to the seventh.

27 "Last of all, the woman died.

28 "In the resurrection, therefore, whose wife of the seven will she be? For they all had *married* her."

29 But Jesus answered and said to them, "You are mistaken, [a]not [1]understanding the Scriptures nor the power of God.

30 "For in the resurrection they neither [a]marry nor are given in marriage, but are like angels in heaven.

31 "But regarding the resurrection of the dead, have you not read what was spoken to you by God:

32 '[a]I AM THE GOD OF ABRAHAM, AND THE GOD OF ISAAC, AND THE GOD OF JACOB'? He is not the God of the dead but of the living."

33 When the crowds heard *this,* [a]they were astonished at His teaching.

34 [a]But when the Pharisees heard that

22:7 *set their city on fire.* A common military practice; here possibly an allusion to the destruction of Jerusalem in A.D. 70.

22:11 *not dressed in wedding clothes.* It has been conjectured that it may have been the custom for the host to provide the guests with wedding garments. This would have been necessary for the guests at this feast in particular, for they were brought in directly from the streets (vv. 9–10). The failure of the man in question to avail himself of a wedding garment was therefore an insult to the host, who had made the garments available.

22:13 *gnashing of teeth.* See note on 13:42.

22:14 A proverbial summary of the meaning of the parable. God invites "many" (perhaps "all" in view of the Semitic usage of "many") to be part of His kingdom, but only a "few" are chosen by Him. This does not mean that God chooses arbitrarily. The invitation must be accepted, followed by appropriate conduct. Proper behavior is evidence of being chosen.

22:15–17 The Pharisees were ardent nationalists, opposed to Roman rule, while the hated Herodians, as their name indicates, supported the Roman rule of the Herods. Now, however, the Pharisees enlisted the help of the Herodians to trap Jesus in His words. After trying to put Him off guard with flattery, they sprang their question: "Is it lawful to give a poll-tax to Caesar, or not?" (v. 17). If He said "No," the Herodians would report Him to the Roman governor and He would be executed for treason. If He said "Yes," the Pharisees would denounce Him to the people as disloyal to His nation.

22:19 *denarius.* The common Roman coin of that day (see note on 20:2). On one side was the portrait of Emperor Tiberius and on the other the inscription in Latin: "Tiberius Caesar Augustus, son of the divine Augustus." The coin was issued by Tiberius and was used for paying tax to him.

22:21 *to God the things that are God's.* In distinguishing clearly between Caesar and God, Jesus also protested against the false and idolatrous claims made on the coins (see previous note and note on Mark 12:17).

22:23 *Sadducess.* See notes on 3:7; Mark 12:18; Luke 20:27; Acts 4:1.

22:24 *Moses said.* Jesus quoted from the Pentateuch when arguing with the Sadducees, since those books had special authority for them (see note on Mark 12:18). The reference (Deut 25:5–6) is to the levirate law (from Latin *levir,* "brother-in-law"), which was given to protect the widow and guarantee continuance of the family line.

22:25–40 See Mark 12:18–31; Luke 20:27–40 and notes.

Jesus had silenced [b]the Sadducees, they
gathered themselves together.
35 One of them, [1][a]a lawyer, asked Him *a*
question, testing Him,
36 "Teacher, which is the great commandment in the Law?"
37 And He said to him, " '[a]YOU SHALL
LOVE THE LORD YOUR GOD WITH ALL YOUR HEART,
AND WITH ALL YOUR SOUL, AND WITH ALL YOUR
MIND.'
38 "This is the great and [1]foremost commandment.
39 "The second is like it, '[a]YOU SHALL LOVE
YOUR NEIGHBOR AS YOURSELF.'
40 "[a]On these two commandments depend
the whole Law and the Prophets."
41 [a]Now while the Pharisees were gathered together, Jesus asked them a question:
42 "What do you think about [1]the Christ,
whose son is He?" They *said to Him, "[a]*The*
son of David."
43 He *said to them, "Then how does
David [1][a]in the Spirit call Him 'Lord,' saying,
44 '[a]THE LORD SAID TO MY LORD,
"SIT AT MY RIGHT HAND,
UNTIL I PUT YOUR ENEMIES BENEATH YOUR
FEET" '?
45 "If David then calls Him 'Lord,' how is
He his son?"
46 [a]No one was able to answer Him a
word, nor did anyone dare from that day on
to ask Him [1]another question.

Pharisaism Exposed

23 [a]Then Jesus spoke to the crowds and
to His disciples,

34 [b]Matt 3:7 **35** [1]I.e. an expert in the Mosaic Law [a]Luke 7:30; 10:25; 11:45, 46, 52; 14:3; Titus 3:13 **37** [a]Deut 6:5 **38** [1]Or *first* **39** [a]Lev 19:18; Matt 19:19; Gal 5:14 **40** [a]Matt 7:12 **41** [a]Matt 22:41-46: *Mark 12:35-37; Luke 20:41-44* **42** [1]I.e. the Messiah **42** [a]Matt 9:27 **43** [1]Or *by inspiration* [a]2 Sam 23:2; Rev 1:10; 4:2 **44** [a]Ps 110:1; Matt 26:64; Mark 16:19; Acts 2:34f; 1 Cor 15:25; Heb 1:13; 10:13 **46** [1]Lit *any longer* [a]Mark 12:34; Luke 14:6; 20:40 **23:1** [a]Matt 23:1-7: *Mark 12:38, 39; Luke 20:45, 46*

22:37,39 LOVE. The Greek verb is not *phileo,* which expresses friendly affection, but *agapao,* the commitment of devotion that is directed by the will and can be commanded as a duty.
22:37 WITH ALL YOUR HEART . . . SOUL . . . MIND. With your whole being. The Hebrew of Deut 6:5 has "heart . . . soul . . . might," but some manuscripts of the Septuagint (the Greek translation of the OT) add "mind." Jesus combined all four terms in Mark 12:30.
22:40 *the whole Law and the Prophets.* The entire OT (see note on 5:17).
22:41-46 See notes on Mark 12:35-40; Luke 20:44-47.

Jewish Sects

PHARISEES

Their roots can be traced to the second century B.C.—to the Hasidim.

1. Along with the Torah, they accepted as equally inspired and authoritative all material contained within the oral tradition.
2. On free will and determination, they held to a mediating view that made it impossible for either free will or the sovereignty of God to cancel out the other.
3. They accepted a rather developed hierarchy of angels and demons.
4. They taught that there was a future for the dead.
5. They believed in the immortality of the soul and in reward and retribution after death.
6. They were champions of human equality.
7. The emphasis of their teaching was ethical rather than theological.

SADDUCEES

They probably had their beginning during the Hasmonean period (166-63 B.C.). Their demise occurred c. A.D. 70 with the fall of Jerusalem.

1. They denied that the oral law was authoritative and binding.
2. They interpreted Mosaic law more literally than did the Pharisees.
3. They were very exacting in Levitical purity.
4. They attributed all to free will.
5. They argued there is neither resurrection of the dead nor a future life.
6. They rejected a belief in angels and demons.
7. They rejected the idea of a spiritual world.
8. Only the books of Moses were canonical Scripture.

ESSENES

They probably originated among the Hasidim, along with the Pharisees, from whom they later separated (I Maccabees 2:42; 7:13). They were a group of very strict and zealous Jews who took part with the Maccabeans in a revolt against the Syrians, c. 165-155 B.C.

1. They followed a strict observance of the purity laws of the Torah.
2. They were notable for their communal ownership of property.
3. They had a strong sense of mutual responsibility.
4. Daily worship was an important feature along with a daily study of their sacred scriptures.
5. Solemn oaths of piety and obedience had to be taken.
6. Sacrifices were offered on holy days and during sacred seasons.
7. Marriage was not condemned in principle but was avoided.
8. They attributed all that happened to fate.

ZEALOTS

They originated during the reign of Herod the Great c. 6 B.C. and ceased to exist in A.D. 73 at Masada.

1. They opposed payment of tribute for taxes to a pagan emperor, saying that allegiance was due only to God.
2. They held a fierce loyalty to the Jewish traditions.
3. They were opposed to the use of the Greek language in Palestine.
4. They prophesied the coming of the time of salvation.

2 saying: "[a]The scribes and the Pharisees have seated themselves in the chair of Moses;

3 therefore all that they tell you, do and observe, but do not do according to their deeds; for they say *things* and do not do *them.*

4 "[a]They tie up heavy burdens and lay them on men's shoulders, but they themselves are unwilling to move them with *so much as* a finger.

5 "But they do all their deeds [a]to be noticed by men; for they [b]broaden their [1]phylacteries and lengthen [c]the tassels *of their garments.*

6 "They [a]love the place of honor at banquets and the chief seats in the synagogues,

7 and respectful greetings in the market places, and being called [a]Rabbi by men.

8 "But [a]do not be called [b]Rabbi; for One is your Teacher, and you are all brothers.

9 "Do not call *anyone* on earth your father; for [a]One is your Father, He who is in heaven.

10 "Do not be called [1]leaders; for One is your Leader, *that is,* Christ.

11 "[a]But the greatest among you shall be your servant.

12 "[a]Whoever exalts himself shall be humbled; and whoever humbles himself shall be exalted.

Eight Woes

13 "[a]But woe to you, scribes and Pharisees, hypocrites, [b]because you shut off the kingdom of heaven [1]from [2]people; for you do not enter in yourselves, nor do you allow those who are entering to go in.

14 ["[1]Woe to you, scribes and Pharisees, hypocrites, because [a]you devour widows' houses, and for a pretense you make long prayers; therefore you will receive greater condemnation.]

15 "Woe to you, scribes and Pharisees, hypocrites, because you travel around on sea and land to make one [1][a]proselyte; and when he becomes one, you make him twice as much a son of [2][b]hell as yourselves.

16 "Woe to you, [a]blind guides, who say, '[b]Whoever swears by the [1]temple, *that* is nothing; but whoever swears by the gold of the [1]temple is obligated.'

2 [a]Deut 33:3f; Ezra 7:6, 25; Neh 8:4
4 [a]Luke 11:46; Acts 15:10
5 [1]I.e. small cases containing Scripture texts worn on the left arm and forehead for religious purposes [a]Matt 6:1, 5, 16 [b]Ex 13:9; Deut 6:8; 11:18 [c]Matt 9:20
6 [a]Luke 11:43; 14:7; 20:46
7 [a]Matt 23:8; 26:25, 49; Mark 9:5; 10:51; 11:21; John 1:38, 49; 3:2, 26; 4:31; 6:25; 9:2; 11:8; 20:16
8 [a]James 3:1 [b]Matt 23:7; 26:25, 49; Mark 9:5; 10:51; 11:21; 14:45; John 1:38, 49; 3:2, 26; 4:31; 6:25; 9:2; 11:8; 20:16
9 [a]Matt 6:9; 7:11
10 [1]Or *teachers*
11 [a]Matt 20:26
12 [a]Luke 14:11; 18:14
13 [1]Lit *in front of* [2]Gr *anthropoi* [a]Matt 23:15, 16, 23, 25, 27, 29 [b]Luke 11:52
14 [1]This v not found in early mss [a]Mark 12:40; Luke 20:47
15 [1]Or *convert* [2]Gr *Gehenna* [a]Acts 2:10; 6:5; 13:43 [b]Matt 5:22
16 [1]Or *sanctuary* [a]Matt 15:14; 23:24 [b]Matt 5:33-35
17 [1]Lit *greater* [2]Or *sanctuary* [a]Ex 30:29
18 [1]Or *gift*
19 [1]Lit *greater* [2]Or *gift* [a]Ex 29:37
20 [1]Lit *he who* [2]Lit *it*
21 [1]Lit *he who* [2]Or *sanctuary* [3]Lit *it* [a]1 Kin 8:13; Ps 26:8; 132:14
22 [1]Lit *he who* [a]Is 66:1; Matt 5:34

17 "You fools and blind men! [a]Which is [1]more important, the gold or the [2]temple that sanctified the gold?

18 "And, 'Whoever swears by the altar, *that* is nothing, but whoever swears by the [1]offering on it, he is obligated.'

19 "You blind men, [a]which is [1]more important, the [2]offering, or the altar that sanctifies the [2]offering?

20 "Therefore, [1]whoever swears by the altar, swears *both* by [2]the altar and by everything on it.

21 "And [1]whoever swears by the [2]temple, swears *both* by [3]the temple and by Him who [a]dwells within it.

22 "And [1]whoever swears by heaven, [a]swears *both* by the throne of God and by Him who sits upon it.

23 "[a]Woe to you, scribes and Pharisees, hypocrites! For you tithe mint and dill and [1]cummin, and have neglected the weightier provisions of the law: justice and mercy and faithfulness; but these are the things you should have done without neglecting the others.

24 "You [a]blind guides, who strain out a gnat and swallow a camel!

25 "Woe to you, scribes and Pharisees, hypocrites! For [a]you clean the outside of the cup and of the dish, but inside they are full [1]of robbery and self-indulgence.

26 "You blind Pharisee, first [a]clean the inside of the cup and of the dish, so that the outside of it may become clean also.

27 "[a]Woe to you, scribes and Pharisees, hypocrites! For you are like whitewashed tombs which on the outside appear beautiful, but inside they are full of dead men's bones and all uncleanness.

28 "So you, too, outwardly appear righteous to men, but inwardly you are full of hypocrisy and lawlessness.

29 "[a]Woe to you, scribes and Pharisees, hypocrites! For you build the tombs of the prophets and adorn the monuments of the righteous,

30 and say, 'If we had been *living* in the

23 [1]Similar to caraway seeds [a]Matt 23:13; Luke 11:42
24 [a]Matt 23:16 25 [1]Or *as a result of* [a]Mark 7:4; Luke 11:39f
26 [a]Mark 7:4; Luke 11:39f 27 [a]Luke 11:44; Acts 23:3
29 [a]Luke 11:47f

23:2 *have seated themselves in the chair of Moses.* The authorized successors of Moses as teachers of the law.
23:5 *phylacteries.* These small boxes, worn on forehead and arm, contained four passages (Ex 13:1–10; 13:11–16; Deut 6:4–9; 11:13–21).
23:6 *chief seats in the synagogues.* See note on Mark 12:39.
23:8–10 The warning is against seeking titles of honor to foster pride. Obviously, we should avoid unreasonable literalism in applying such commands.
23:15 Jesus does not criticize the Pharisees for their evangelistic zeal. He objects to its results. The converts wound up "out-Phariseeing" the Pharisees, and that meant they became even more sons of hell (i.e., bound for hell) than their teachers. *hell.* See notes on 5:22 and Luke 12:5.
23:23 Jesus does not criticize the observance of the minutiae of the law (He says, "without neglecting" them), but He does criticize the hypocrisy often involved (see note on 5:18–20).
23:24 *strain out.* The strict Pharisee would carefully strain his drinking water through a cloth to be sure he did not swallow a gnat, the smallest of unclean animals. But, figuratively, he would swallow a camel—one of the largest.
23:27 *whitewashed tombs.* A person who stepped on a grave became ceremonially unclean (see Num 19:16), so graves were whitewashed to make them easily visible, especially at night. They appeared clean and beautiful on the outside, but they were dirty and rotten on the inside.

days of our fathers, we would not have been
partners with them in *shedding* the blood of
the prophets.'
31 "So you testify against yourselves, that
you [a]are [1]sons of those who murdered the
prophets.
32 "Fill up, then, the measure *of the guilt* of
your fathers.
33 "You serpents, [a]you brood of vipers,
how [1]will you escape the [2]sentence of [3b]hell?
34 "[a]Therefore, behold, [b]I am sending you
prophets and wise men and scribes; some of
them you will kill and crucify, and some of
them you will [c]scourge in your synagogues,
and [d]persecute from city to city,
35 so that upon you may fall *the guilt of* all
the righteous blood shed on earth, from the
blood of righteous [a]Abel to the blood of
Zechariah, the [b]son of Berechiah, whom [c]you
murdered between the [1]temple and the altar.
36 "Truly I say to you, all these things will
come upon [a]this generation.

Lament over Jerusalem

37 "[a]Jerusalem, Jerusalem, who [b]kills the
prophets and stones those who are sent to
her! How often I wanted to gather your children together, [c]the way a hen gathers her
chicks under her wings, and you were
unwilling.
38 "Behold, [a]your house is being left to you
desolate!
39 "For I say to you, from now on you will
not see Me until you say, '[a]BLESSED IS HE WHO
COMES IN THE NAME OF THE LORD!' "

Signs of Christ's Return

24 [a]Jesus [b]came out from the temple and
was going away [1]when His disciples
came up to point out the temple buildings to
Him.
2 And He said to them, "Do you not see
all these things? Truly I say to you, [a]not one
stone here will be left upon another, which
will not be torn down."

3 As He was sitting on [a]the Mount of
Olives, the disciples came to Him privately,
saying, "Tell us, when will these things happen, and what *will be* the sign of [b]Your coming, and of the [1]end of the age?"
4 And Jesus answered and said to them,
"[a]See to it that no one misleads you.
5 "For [a]many will come in My name, saying, 'I am the [1]Christ,' and will mislead many.
6 "You will be hearing of [a]wars and
rumors of wars. See that you are not frightened, for *those things* must take place, but
that is not yet the end.
7 "For [a]nation will rise against nation, and
kingdom against kingdom, and in various
places there will be [b]famines and earthquakes.
8 "[a]But all these things are *merely* the
beginning of birth pangs.
9 "[a]Then they will deliver you to tribulation, and will kill you, and [b]you will be hated by all nations because of My name.
10 "At that time many will [1a]fall away and
will [2]betray one another and hate one
another.
11 "Many [a]false prophets will arise and
will mislead many.
12 "Because lawlessness is increased,
[1]most people's love will grow cold.
13 "[a]But the one who endures to the end,
he will be saved.
14 "This [a]gospel of the kingdom [b]shall be
preached in the whole [1c]world as a testimony to all the nations, and then the end will
come.

Perilous Times

15 "Therefore when you see the [a]ABOMINA-
TION OF DESOLATION which was spoken of
through Daniel the prophet, standing in [b]the
holy place ([c]let the reader understand),

31 [1]Or *descendants* [a]Matt 23:34, 37; Acts 7:51f **33** [1]Lit *would* [2]Or *judgment* [3]Gr *Gehenna* [a]Matt 3:7; Luke 3:7 [b]Matt 5:22 **34** [a]Matt 23:34-36; Luke 11:49-51 [b]2 Chr 36:15, 16 [c]Matt 10:17 [d]Matt 10:23 **35** [1]Or *sanctuary* [a]Gen 4:8ff; Heb 11:4 [b]Zech 1:1 [c]2 Chr 24:21 **36** [a]Matt 10:23; 24:34 **37** [a]Matt 23:37-39: *Luke 13:34, 35* [b]Matt 5:12 [c]Ruth 2:12 **38** [a]1 Kin 9:7f; Jer 22:5 **39** [a]Ps 118:26; Matt 21:9 **24:1** [1]Lit *and* [a]Matt 24:1-51: *Mark 13; Luke 21:5-36* [b]Matt 21:23 **2** [a]Luke 19:44 **3** [1]Or *consummation* [a]Matt 21:1 [b]Matt 16:27f; 24:27, 37, 39 **4** [a]Jer 29:8 **5** [1]I.e. the Messiah [a]Matt 24:11, 24; Acts 5:36f; 1 John 2:18; 4:3 **6** [a]Rev 6:4 **7** [a]2 Chr 15:6; Is 19:2; Rev 6:8, 12 [b]Acts 11:28; Rev 6:5, 6 **8** [a]Matt 24:8-20; Luke 21:12-24 **9** [a]Matt 10:17; John 16:2 [b]Matt 10:22; John 15:18ff **10** [1]Lit *be caused to stumble* [2]Or *hand over* [a]Matt 11:6 **11** [a]Matt 7:15; 24:24 **12** [1]Lit *the love of many*

13 [a]Matt 10:22 **14** [1]Lit *inhabited earth* [a]Matt 4:23 [b]Rom 10:18; Col 1:6, 23 [c]Luke 2:1; 4:5; Acts 11:28; 17:6, 31; 19:27; Rom 10:18; Heb 1:6; 2:5; Rev 3:10; 16:14 **15** [a]Dan 9:27; 11:31; 12:11 [b]Mark 13:14; Luke 21:20; John 11:48; Acts 6:13f; 21:28 [c]Mark 13:14; Rev 1:3

23:33 *hell.* See notes on 5:22 and Luke 12:5.
23:35 *Abel to . . . Zechariah.* The murder of Abel is recorded in Gen 4:8 and that of Zechariah son of Jehoiada in 2 Chr 24:20–22 (Chronicles comes at the close of the OT according to the Hebrew arrangement). The expression was somewhat like our "from Genesis to Revelation." Jesus was summing up the history of martyrdom in the OT.
23:37–39 See notes on Luke 13:34–35.
24:1–25:46 The Olivet discourse, the fifth and last of the great discourses in Matthew's Gospel (see notes on 5:1–7:29; Mark 13:1–37).
24:2 *not one stone . . . left.* Fulfilled literally in A.D. 70, when the Romans under Titus completely destroyed Jerusalem and the temple buildings. Stones were even pried apart to collect the gold leaf that melted from the roof when the temple was set on fire. *stone.* See note on Mark 13:1. *torn down.* Excavations in 1968 uncovered large numbers of these stones, toppled from the walls by the invaders.
24:3 *Mount of Olives.* A ridge a little more than a mile long, beyond the Kidron Valley east of Jerusalem and rising about 200 feet above the city (see note on Mark 11:1). *when will these things happen, and what will be the sign of Your coming, and of the end of the age?* Jesus deals with these questions but does not distinguish them sharply. However, it appears that the description of the end of the age is discussed in vv. 4–14, the destruction of Jerusalem in vv. 15–22 (see Luke 21:20) and Christ's coming in vv. 23–31.
24:5 *Christ.* See note on 16:16.
24:8 *birth pangs.* The rabbis spoke of "birth pangs," i.e., sufferings, that would precede the coming of the Messiah.
24:15 *the ABOMINATION OF DESOLATION.* The detestable thing causing the desolation of the holy place. The primary reference in Daniel (9:27; 11:31; 12:11) was to 168 B.C., when Antiochus Epiphanes erected a pagan altar to Zeus on the sacred altar in the temple of Jerusalem. According to some, there were still two more stages in the progressive fulfillment of the predictions in Daniel and Matthew: (1) the Roman destruction of the temple in A.D. 70 and (2) the setting up of an image of the antichrist in Jerusalem (see 2 Thess 2:4; Rev 13:14–15; see also notes on Dan 9:25–27; 11:31).

16 then those who are in Judea must flee to the mountains.

17 "[1]Whoever is on [a]the housetop must not go down to get the things out that are in his house.

18 "[1]Whoever is in the field must not turn back to get his cloak.

19 "But [a]woe to those who are pregnant and to those who are nursing babies in those days!

20 "But pray that your flight will not be in the winter, or on a Sabbath.

21 "For then there will be a [a]great tribulation, such as has not occurred since the beginning of the world until now, nor ever will.

22 "Unless those days had been cut short, no [1]life would have been saved; but for [a]the sake of the [2]elect those days will be cut short.

23 "[a]Then if anyone says to you, 'Behold, here is the [1]Christ,' or '[2]There *He is,*' do not believe *him.*

24 "For false Christs and [a]false prophets will arise and will [1]show great [2b]signs and wonders, so as to mislead, if possible, even [c]the [3]elect.

25 "Behold, I have told you in advance.

26 "So if they say to you, 'Behold, He is in the wilderness,' do not go out, *or,* 'Behold, He is in the inner rooms,' do not believe *them.*

27 "[a]For just as the lightning comes from the east and flashes even to the west, so will the [b]coming of the [c]Son of Man be.

28 "[a]Wherever the corpse is, there the [1]vultures will gather.

The Glorious Return

29 "But immediately after the [a]tribulation of those days [b]THE SUN WILL BE DARKENED, AND THE MOON WILL NOT GIVE ITS LIGHT, AND [c]THE STARS WILL FALL from [1]the sky, and the powers of [1]the heavens will be shaken.

30 "And then [a]the sign of the Son of Man will appear in the sky, and then all the tribes of the earth will mourn, and they will see [b]the SON OF MAN COMING ON THE CLOUDS OF THE SKY with power and great glory.

31 "And [a]He will send forth His angels with [b]A GREAT TRUMPET and THEY WILL GATHER TOGETHER His [1c]elect from [d]the four winds, from one end of the sky to the other.

Parable of the Fig Tree

32 "Now learn the parable from the fig tree: when its branch has already become tender and puts forth its leaves, you know that summer is near;

33 so, you too, when you see all these things, [1]recognize that [2]He is near, *right* [a]at the [3]door.

34 "Truly I say to you, [a]this [1]generation will not pass away until all these things take place.

35 "[a]Heaven and earth will pass away, but My words will not pass away.

36 "But [a]of that day and hour no one knows, not even the angels of heaven, nor the Son, but the Father alone.

37 "For [1]the [a]coming of the Son of Man will be [b]just like the days of Noah.

38 "For as in those days before the flood they were eating and drinking, [a]marrying and giving in marriage, until the day that [b]Noah entered the ark,

39 and they did not [1]understand until the flood came and took them all away; so will the [a]coming of the Son of Man be.

40 "Then there will be two men in the field; one [1]will be taken and one [1]will be left.

41 "[a]Two women *will be* grinding at the [1b]mill; one [2]will be taken and one [2]will be left.

Be Ready for His Coming

42 "Therefore [a]be on the alert, for you do not know which day your Lord is coming.

43 "But [1]be sure of this, that [a]if the head of the house had known [b]at what time of the night the thief was coming, he would have

17 [1]Lit *He who* [a]1 Sam 9:25; 2 Sam 11:2; Matt 10:27; Luke 5:19; 12:3; 17:31; Acts 10:9 **18** [1]Lit *He who* **19** [a]Luke 23:29 **21** [a]Dan 12:1; Joel 2:2; Matt 24:29 **22** [1]Lit *flesh* [2]Or *chosen ones* [a]Matt 22:14; 24:24, 31; Luke 18:7 **23** [1]I.e. Messiah [2]Lit *here* [a]Luke 17:23f **24** [1]Lit *give* [2]Or *attesting miracles* [3]Or *chosen ones* [a]Matt 7:15; 24:11 [b]John 4:48; 2 Thess 2:9 [c]Matt 22:14; 24:22, 31; Luke 18:7 **27** [a]Luke 17:24 [b]Matt 24:3, 37, 39 [c]Matt 8:20 **28** [1]Or *eagles* [a]Job 39:30; Ezek 39:17; Hab 1:8; Luke 17:37 **29** [1]Or *heaven* [a]Matt 24:21 [b]Is 13:10; 24:23; Ezek 32:7; Joel 2:10, 31; 3:15f; Amos 5:20; 8:9; Zeph 1:15; Matt 24:29-35; Acts 2:20; Rev 6:12-17; 8:12 [c]Is 34:4; Rev 6:13 **30** [a]Matt 24:3; Rev 1:7 [b]Dan 7:13; Matt 16:27; 24:3, 37, 39

31 [1]Or *chosen ones* [a]Matt 13:41 [b]Ex 19:16; Deut 30:4; Is 27:13; Zech 9:14; 1 Cor 15:52; 1 Thess 4:16; Heb 12:19; Rev 8:2; 11:15 [c]Matt 24:22 [d]Dan 7:2; Zech 2:6; Rev 7:1 **33** [1]Or *know* [2]Or *it* [3]Lit *doors* [a]James 5:9; Rev 3:20 **34** [1]Or *race* [a]Matt 10:23; 16:28; 23:36 **35** [a]Matt 5:18; Mark 13:31; Luke 21:33 **36** [a]Mark 13:32; Acts 1:7 **37** [1]Lit *just as...were the days* [a]Matt 16:27; 24:3, 30, 39 [b]Gen 6:5; 7:6-23; Luke 17:26f **38** [a]Matt 22:30 [b]Gen 7:7 **39** [1]Lit *know* [a]Matt 16:27; 24:3, 30, 37 **40** [1]Lit *is* **41** [1]I.e. handmill [2]Lit *is* [a]Luke 17:35 [b]Ex 11:5; Deut 24:6; Is 47:2 **42** [a]Matt 24:43, 44; 25:10, 13; Luke 12:39f; 21:36 **43** [1]Lit *know this* [a]Matt 24:42, 44; 25:10, 13; Luke 12:39f; 21:36 [b]Matt 14:25; Mark 6:48; 13:35; Luke 12:38

24:16 *the mountains.* The Transjordan mountains, where Pella was located. Christians in Jerusalem fled to that area during the Roman siege shortly before A.D. 70. Some believe a similar fleeing will occur in a future tribulation period (identified with Daniel's 70th "week," Dan 9:27).

24:19 See note on Mark 13:17.

24:20 *in the winter.* See note on Mark 13:18. *or on a Sabbath.* Matthew alone includes this because he was writing to Jews, who were forbidden to travel more than about half a mile on the Sabbath.

24:21 *great tribulation.* Josephus, the Jewish historian who was there, describes the destruction of Jerusalem in almost identical language. Some believe the reference is also to a future period of great distress (see Dan 12:1).

24:22 *days . . . cut short.* Some hold that this statement means that the distress will be of such intensity that, if allowed to continue, it will destroy everyone. Others believe that Christ is referring to the cutting short of a previously determined time period (such as the 70th "seven" of Dan 9:27 or the 42 months of Rev 11:2; 13:5). *the elect.* The people of God.

24:28 *there the vultures will gather.* The coming of Christ will be as obvious as the gathering of vultures around a carcass (see note on Luke 17:37, where the saying is used in a slightly different sense).

24:29 See note on Mark 13:25.

24:30 *Son of Man.* See note on Mark 8:31.

24:34 *Truly I say to you.* See note on Mark 3:28. *this generation.* Or race; see also notes on Mark 13:30; Luke 21:32.

24:35 Jesus' words are more certain than the existence of the universe.

24:36 *nor the Son.* See note on Mark 13:32.

been on the alert and would not have allowed his house to be [2]broken into.

44 "For this reason [a]you also must be ready; for [b]the Son of Man is coming at an hour when you do not think *He will.*

45 "[a]Who then is the [b]faithful and [c]sensible slave whom his [1]master [d]put in charge of his household to give them their food at the proper time?

46 "Blessed is that slave whom his [1]master finds so doing when he comes.

47 "Truly I say to you that [a]he will put him in charge of all his possessions.

48 "But if that evil slave says in his heart, 'My [1]master [2]is not coming for a long time,'

49 and begins to beat his fellow slaves and eat and drink with drunkards;

50 the [1]master of that slave will come on a day when he does not expect *him* and at an hour which he does not know,

51 and will [1]cut him in pieces and [2]assign him a place with the hypocrites; in that place there will be [a]weeping and gnashing of teeth.

Parable of Ten Virgins

25 "Then [a]the kingdom of heaven will be comparable to ten virgins, who took their [b]lamps and went out to meet the bridegroom.

2 "Five of them were foolish, and five were [a]prudent.

3 "For when the foolish took their lamps, they took no oil with them,

4 but the [a]prudent took oil in flasks along with their lamps.

5 "Now while the bridegroom was delaying, they all got drowsy and *began* to sleep.

6 "But at midnight there was a shout, 'Behold, the bridegroom! Come out to meet *him.*'

7 "Then all those virgins rose and trimmed their lamps.

8 "The foolish said to the prudent, 'Give us some of your oil, for our lamps are going out.'

9 "But the [a]prudent answered, 'No, there will not be enough for us and you *too;* go instead to the dealers and buy *some* for yourselves.'

10 "And while they were going away to make the purchase, the bridegroom came, and those who were [a]ready went in with him to [b]the wedding feast; and [c]the door was shut.

11 "Later the other virgins also came, saying, '[a]Lord, lord, open up for us.'

12 "But he answered, 'Truly I say to you, I do not know you.'

13 "[a]Be on the alert then, for you do not know the day nor the hour.

Parable of the Talents

14 "[a]For *it is* just like a man [b]*about* to go on a journey, who called his own slaves and entrusted his possessions to them.

15 "To one he gave five [1a]talents, to another, two, and to another, one, each according to his own ability; and he [b]went on his journey.

16 "Immediately the one who had received the five [a]talents went and traded with them, and gained five more talents.

17 "In the same manner the one who *had received* the two *talents* gained two more.

18 "But he who received the one *talent* went away, and dug *a hole* in the ground and hid his [1]master's money.

19 "Now after a long time the master of those slaves *came and *[a]settled accounts with them.

20 "The one who had received the five [a]talents came up and brought five more talents, saying, 'Master, you entrusted five talents to me. See, I have gained five more talents.'

21 "His master said to him, 'Well done, good and [a]faithful slave. You were faithful with a few things, I will [b]put you in charge of many things; enter into the joy of your [1]master.'

22 "Also the one who *had received* the two [a]talents came up and said, 'Master, you entrusted two talents to me. See, I have gained two more talents.'

23 "His master said to him, 'Well done, good and [a]faithful slave. You were faithful with a few things, I will put you in charge of many things; enter into the joy of your master.'

24 "And the one also who had received the one [a]talent came up and said, 'Master, I knew you to be a hard man, reaping where you did not sow and gathering where you scattered no *seed.*

25 'And I was afraid, and went away and hid your talent in the ground. See, you have what is yours.'

26 "But his master answered and said to him, 'You wicked, lazy slave, you knew that I reap where I did not sow and gather where I scattered no *seed.*

27 'Then you ought to have put my money

43 [2]Lit *dug through*
44 [a]Matt 24:42, 43; 25:10, 13; Luke 12:39f; 21:36 [b]Matt 24:27
45 [1]Or *lord* [a]Matt 24:45-51: *Luke 12:42-46* [b]Matt 25:21, 23; Luke 16:10 [c]Matt 7:24; 10:16; 25:2ff [d]Matt 25:21, 23
46 [1]Or *lord*
47 [a]Matt 25:21, 23
48 [1]Or *lord* [2]Lit *lingers*
50 [1]Or *lord*
51 [1]Or *severely scourge him* [2]Lit *appoint his portion* [a]Matt 8:12
25:1 [a]Matt 13:24 [b]John 18:3; Acts 20:8; Rev 4:5; 8:10
2 [a]Matt 7:24; 10:16; 25:2ff
4 [a]Matt 7:24; 10:16; 25:2ff
9 [a]Matt 7:24; 10:16; 25:2ff
10 [a]Matt 24:42ff [b]Luke 12:35f [c]Matt 7:21ff; Luke 13:25
11 [a]Matt 7:21ff; Luke 13:25
13 [a]Matt 24:42ff
14 [a]Matt 25:14-30; Luke 19:12-27 [b]Matt 21:33
15 [1]A talent was worth about fifteen years' wages of a laborer [a]Matt 18:24; Luke 19:13 [b]Matt 21:33
16 [a]Matt 18:24; Luke 19:13
18 [1]Or *lord's*
19 [a]Matt 18:23
20 [a]Matt 18:24; Luke 19:13
21 [1]Or *lord* [a]Matt 24:45, 47; 25:23 [b]Luke 12:44; 22:29; Rev 3:21; 21:7
22 [a]Matt 18:24; Luke 19:13
23 [a]Matt 24:45, 47; 25:21
24 [a]Matt 18:24; Luke 19:13

24:51 *weeping and gnashing of teeth.* See note on 13:42.
25:1 *ten virgins.* The bridesmaids, who were responsible for preparing the bride to meet the bridegroom. *lamps.* Torches that consisted of a long pole with oil-drenched rags at the top. (Small clay lamps would have been of little use in an outdoor procession.)
25:3 *oil.* Olive oil.
25:7 *trimmed.* The charred ends of the rags were cut off and oil was added.
25:9 *there will not be enough.* Torches required large amounts of oil in order to keep burning, and the oil had to be replenished about every 15 minutes.
25:13 *Be on the alert.* The main point of the parable. *the day nor the hour.* Of the *parousia,* the coming of Christ.
25:15 *talents.* The term was first used for a unit of weight (about 75 pounds), then for a unit of coinage. The present-day use of "talent" to indicate an ability or gift is derived from this parable (see note on Luke 19:13).

[1]in the bank, and on my arrival I would have received my *money* back with interest.

28 'Therefore take away the talent from him, and give it to the one who has the ten talents.'

29 "[a]For to everyone who has, *more* shall be given, and he will have an abundance; but from the one who does not have, even what he does have shall be taken away.

30 "Throw out the worthless slave into [a]the outer darkness; in that place there will be weeping and gnashing of teeth.

The Judgment

31 "But when [a]the Son of Man comes in His glory, and all the angels with Him, then [b]He will sit on His glorious throne.

32 "All the nations will be [a]gathered before Him; and He will separate them from one another, [b]as the shepherd separates the sheep from the goats;

33 and He will put the sheep [a]on His right, and the goats [b]on the left.

34 "Then the King will say to those on His right, 'Come, you who are blessed of My Father, [a]inherit the kingdom prepared for you [b]from the foundation of the world.

35 'For [a]I was hungry, and you gave Me *something* to eat; I was thirsty, and you gave Me *something* to drink; [b]I was a stranger, and you invited Me in;

36 [a]naked, and you clothed Me; I was sick, and you [b]visited Me; [c]I was in prison, and you came to Me.'

37 "Then the righteous will answer Him, 'Lord, when did we see You hungry, and feed You, or thirsty, and give You *something* to drink?

38 'And when did we see You a stranger, and invite You in, or naked, and clothe You?

39 'When did we see You sick, or in prison, and come to You?'

40 "[a]The King will answer and say to them, 'Truly I say to you, [b]to the extent that you did it to one of these brothers of Mine, *even* the least *of them,* you did it to Me.'

41 "Then He will also say to those on His left, '[a]Depart from Me, accursed ones, into the [b]eternal fire which has been prepared for [c]the devil and his angels;

42 for I was hungry, and you gave Me *nothing* to eat; I was thirsty, and you gave Me nothing to drink;

43 I was a stranger, and you did not invite Me in; naked, and you did not clothe Me; sick, and in prison, and you did not visit Me.'

44 "Then they themselves also will answer, 'Lord, when did we see You hungry, or thirsty, or a stranger, or naked, or sick, or in prison, and did not [1]take care of You?'

45 "Then He will answer them, 'Truly I say to you, to the extent that you did not do it to one of the least of these, you did not do it to Me.'

46 "These will go away into [a]eternal punishment, but the righteous into [b]eternal life."

The Plot to Kill Jesus

26 [a]When Jesus had finished all these words, He said to His disciples,

2 "[a]You know that after two days [b]the Passover is coming, and the Son of Man is *to be* [c]handed over for crucifixion."

3 [a]Then the chief priests and the elders of the people were gathered together in [b]the court of the high priest, named [c]Caiaphas;

4 and they [a]plotted together to seize Jesus by stealth and kill Him.

5 But they were saying, "Not during the festival, [a]otherwise a riot might occur among the people."

The Precious Ointment

6 [a]Now when Jesus was in [b]Bethany, at the home of Simon the leper,

27 [1]Lit *to the bankers*
29 [a]Matt 13:12; Mark 4:25; Luke 8:18; John 15:2
30 [a]Matt 8:12; 22:13; Luke 13:28
31 [a]Matt 16:27f; 1 Thess 4:16; 2 Thess 1:7; Heb 9:28; Jude 14; Rev 1:7 [b]Matt 19:28
32 [a]Matt 13:49; 2 Cor 5:10 [b]Ezek 34:17, 20
33 [a]1 Kin 2:19; Ps 45:9 [b]Eccl 10:2
34 [a]Matt 5:3; 19:29; Luke 12:32; 1 Cor 6:9; 15:50; Gal 5:21; James 2:5 [b]Matt 13:35; Luke 11:50; John 17:24; Eph 1:4; Heb 4:3; 9:26; 1 Pet 1:20; Rev 13:8; 17:8
35 [a]Is 58:7; Ezek 18:7, 16; James 2:15, 16 [b]Job 31:32; Heb 13:2
36 [a]Is 58:7; Ezek 18:7, 16; James 2:15, 16 [b]James 1:27 [c]2 Tim 1:16f
40 [a]Matt 25:34; Luke 19:38; Rev 17:14; 19:16 [b]Prov 19:17; Matt 10:42; Heb 6:10
41 [a]Matt 7:23 [b]Mark 9:48; Luke 16:24; Jude 7 [c]Matt 4:10; Rev 12:9
44 [1]Or *serve*
46 [a]Dan 12:2; John 5:29; Acts 24:15 [b]Matt 19:29; John 3:15f, 36; 5:24; 6:27, 40, 47, 54; 17:2f; Acts 13:46, 48; Rom 2:7; 5:21; 6:23; Gal 6:8; 1 John 5:11
26:1 [a]Matt 7:28

2 [a]Matt 26:2-5: *Mark 14:1, 2; Luke 22:1, 2* [b]John 11:55; 13:1 [c]Matt 10:4 **3** [a]John 11:47 [b]Matt 26:58, 69; 27:27; Mark 14:54, 66; 15:16; Luke 22:55; John 18:15 [c]Matt 26:57; Luke 3:2; John 11:49; 18:13, 14, 24, 28; Acts 4:6 **4** [a]Matt 12:14 **5** [a]Matt 27:24 **6** [a]Matt 26:6-13: *Mark 14:3-9;* Luke 7:37-39; John 12:1-8 [b]Matt 21:17

25:27 *bank.* The Greek for this word comes from *trapeza* ("table"), a word seen on the front of banks in Greece today. Bankers sat at small tables and changed money (cf. 21:12). *interest.* The Greek for this word was first used in the sense of offspring, interest being the "offspring" of invested money.
25:29 The main point of the parable. Being ready for Christ's coming involves more than playing it safe and doing little or nothing. It demands the kind of service that produces results.
25:31–46 The two most widely accepted interpretations of this judgment are: 1. It will occur at the beginning of an earthly millennial kingdom (vv. 31,34). Its purpose will be to determine who will be allowed to enter the kingdom (v. 34). The criterion for judgment will be the kind of treatment shown to the Jewish people ("these brothers of mine," v. 40) during the preceding great tribulation period (vv. 35–40,42–45). Ultimately, how a person treats the Jewish people will reveal whether or not he is saved (vv. 41,46). 2. The judgment referred to occurs at the great white throne at the end of the age (Rev 20:11–15). Its purpose will be to determine who will be allowed to enter the eternal kingdom of the saved and who will be consigned to eternal punishment in hell (vv. 34,46). The basis for judgment will be whether love is shown to God's people (see 1 John 3:14–15).
25:34–40 Rewards in the kingdom of heaven are given to those who serve without thought of reward. There is no hint of merit here, for God gives out of grace, not debt.
26:2 *Passover.* See note on Mark 14:1. *Son of Man.* See note on Mark 8:31.
26:3 *chief priests and the elders of the people.* The clerical and lay leadership of the Sanhedrin (see note on 2:4). *Caiaphas.* High priest A.D. 18–36 and the son-in-law of Annas (John 18:13), a former high priest, who served 6–15.
26:5 *a riot might occur.* Hundreds of thousands of Jewish pilgrims came to Jerusalem for Passover, and riots were not unknown. The religious leaders (v. 3) knew that many people admired Jesus.
26:6–13 See note on John 12:1–11.
26:6 *Bethany.* See note on 21:17. *Simon the leper.* Mentioned elsewhere only in Mark 14:3, though Simon was a common Jewish name in the first century. He was probably a well-known victim of leprosy who had been healed by Jesus.

7 [a]a woman came to Him with an
alabaster vial of very costly perfume, and she
poured it on His head as He reclined *at the*
table.
8 But the disciples were indignant when
they saw *this,* and said, "Why this waste?
9 "For this *perfume* might have been sold
for a high price and *the money* given to the
poor."
10 But Jesus, aware of this, said to them,
"Why do you bother the woman? For she has
done a good deed to Me.
11 "For you always have [a]the poor with
you; but you do not always have Me.
12 "For when she poured this perfume on
My body, she did it [a]to prepare Me for burial.
13 "Truly I say to you, [a]wherever this
gospel is preached in the whole world, what
this woman has done will also be spoken of
in memory of her."

Judas's Bargain

14 [a]Then one of the twelve, named [b]Judas
Iscariot, went to the chief priests
15 and said, "What are you willing to give
me [1]to [2a]betray Him to you?" And [b]they
weighed out thirty [3]pieces of silver to him.
16 From then on he *began* looking for a
good opportunity to [1]betray [2]Jesus.
17 [a]Now on the first *day* of [b]Unleavened
Bread the disciples came to Jesus and asked,
"Where do You want us to prepare for You to
eat the Passover?"
18 And He said, "Go into the city to [a]a certain man, and say to him, 'The Teacher says,
"[b]My time is near; I *am to* keep the Passover
at your house with My disciples."' "
19 The disciples did as Jesus had directed
them; and they prepared the Passover.

The Last Passover

20 [a]Now when evening came, Jesus was
reclining *at the table* with the twelve disciples.
21 As they were eating, He said, "[a]Truly I
say to you that one of you will betray Me."
22 Being deeply grieved, they [1]each one
began to say to Him, "Surely not I, Lord?"
23 And He answered, "[a]He who dipped
his hand with Me in the bowl is the one who
will betray Me.
24 "The Son of Man *is to* go, [a]just as it is
written of Him; but woe to that man by
whom the Son of Man is betrayed! [b]It would
have been good [1]for that man if he had not
been born."
25 And [a]Judas, who was betraying Him,
said, "Surely it is not I, [b]Rabbi?" Jesus *said
to him, "[c]You have said *it* yourself."

The Lord's Supper Instituted

26 [a]While they were eating, Jesus took
some bread, and [1b]after a blessing, He broke
it and gave *it* to the disciples, and said,
"Take, eat; this is My body."
27 And when He had taken a cup and giv-
en thanks, He gave *it* to them, saying, "Drink
from it, all of you;
28 for [a]this is My blood of the covenant,
which is poured out for [b]many for forgiveness of sins.
29 "But I say to you, I will not drink of this
fruit of the vine from now on until that day
when I drink it new with you in My Father's
kingdom."
30 [a]After singing a hymn, they went out to
[b]the Mount of Olives.
31 Then Jesus *said to them, "You will all
[1a]fall away because of Me this night, for it is
written, '[b]I WILL STRIKE DOWN THE SHEPHERD,
AND THE SHEEP OF THE FLOCK SHALL BE [c]SCAT-
TERED.'
32 "But after I have been raised, [a]I will go
ahead of you to Galilee."

7 [a]Luke 7:37f **11** [a]Deut 15:11; Mark 14:7; John 12:8 **12** [a]John 19:40 **13** [a]Mark 14:9 **14** [a]Matt 26:14-16: *Mark 14:10, 11; Luke 22:3-6* [b]Matt 10:4; 26:25, 47; 27:3; John 6:71; 12:4; 13:26; Acts 1:16 **15** [1]Lit *and I will* [2]Or *deliver* [3]I.e. silver shekels [a]Matt 10:4 [b]Ex 21:32; Zech 11:12 **16** [1]Or *deliver* [2]Lit *Him* **17** [a]Matt 26:17-19: *Mark 14:12-16; Luke 22:7-13* [b]Ex 12:18-20 **18** [a]Mark 14:13; Luke 22:10 [b]John 7:6, 8 **20** [a]Matt 26:20-24: *Mark 14:17-21*

21 [a]Luke 22:21-23; John 13:21f **22** [1]Or *one after another* **23** [a]Ps 41:9; John 13:18, 26 **24** [1]Lit *for him if that man had not been born* [a]Matt 26:31, 54, 56; Mark 9:12; Luke 24:25-27, 46; Acts 17:2f; 26:22f; 1 Cor 15:3; 1 Pet 1:10f [b]Matt 18:7; Mark 14:21 **25** [a]Matt 26:14 [b]Matt 23:7; 26:49 [c]Matt 26:64; 27:11; Luke 22:70 **26** [1]Lit *having blessed* [a]Matt 26:26-29: *Mark 14:22-25; Luke 22:17-20; 1 Cor 11:23-25;* 1 Cor 10:16 [b]Matt 14:19 **28** [a]Ex 24:8; Heb 9:20 [b]Matt 20:28

30 [a]Matt 26:30-35: *Mark 14:26-31; Luke 22:31-34* [b]Matt 21:1 **31** [1]Or *stumble* [a]Matt 11:6 [b]Zech 13:7 [c]John 16:32 **32** [a]Matt 28:7, 10, 16; Mark 16:7

26:7 *alabaster vial.* Most "alabaster" of ancient times was actually marble (see note on Mark 14:3).
26:10 *good.* The Greek word has an aesthetic as well as an ethical meaning.
26:14 *Iscariot.* See note on Mark 3:19.
26:15 *thirty pieces of silver.* Equivalent to 120 denarii. Laborers customarily received one denarius for a day's work (see 20:1–16).
26:17 *the first day of Unleavened Bread.* The 14th of Nisan (March-April), it was also called the preparation of the Passover. The Passover meal was eaten the evening of the 14th after sunset—and therefore technically on the 15th, since the Jewish day ended at sunset. The Feast of Unleavened Bread lasted seven days, from the 15th to the 21st of Nisan (see Lev 23:5–6), but in the time of Christ the entire period, Nisan 14–21, was referred to under that name (see note on Mark 14:12).
26:18–30 These verses clearly indicate that Jesus ate the Passover meal with His disciples the night before His crucifixion. For more information on the Lord's Supper see notes on Mark 14:22,24.
26:18 *My time.* A reference to Jesus' crucifixion.
26:19 *prepared the Passover.* See note on Mark 14:15.
26:20 *reclining at the table.* See note on Mark 14:18.
26:21 *Truly I say to you.* See note on Mark 3:28.
26:23 *dipped his hand with Me in the bowl.* It was the custom—still practiced by some in the Middle East—to take a piece of bread, or a piece of meat wrapped in bread, and dip it into a bowl of sauce (made of stewed fruit) on the table. *will betray Me.* In that culture, as among Arabs today, to eat with a person was tantamount to saying, "I am your friend and will not hurt you." This fact made Judas's deed all the more despicable (cf. Ps 41:9).
26:24 *as it is written of Him.* See note on Mark 14:21. *Son of Man.* See note on Mark 8:31.
26:26–28 See note on Mark 14:22.
26:30 *hymn.* The Passover fellowship was concluded with the second half of the Hallel Psalms (Ps 115–118).
26:31 *all fall away.* Not Peter only, but all the eleven (Judas had previously withdrawn, John 13:30). The meaning of the words "fall away" is seen in Peter's denial (vv. 69–75) and in the terrified flight of the other disciples (v. 56). *I WILL STRIKE DOWN THE SHEPHERD.* See note on Zech 13:7.
26:32 *to Galilee.* Cf. 28:10,16–20; Mark 16:7; John 21:1–23.

The Life of Christ

CHILDHOOD

Birth of Jesus, BETHLEHEM, c. 6/5 B.C., Matt 1:18-25; Luke 2:1-7

Visit by shepherds, BETHLEHEM, Luke 2:8-20

Presentation in the temple, JERUSALEM, Luke 2:21-40

Visit by the Magi, BETHLEHEM, Matt 2:1-12

Escape to Egypt, NILE DELTA, Matt 2:13-18

Return to Nazareth, LOWER GALILEE, Matt 2:19-23

Visit to temple as a boy, JERUSALEM, c A.D. 7/8, Luke 2:41-52

YEAR OF INAUGURATION

YEAR OF POPULARITY

YEAR OF OPPOSITION

Begin less than full year of ministry

10 5 | 5 10 15 20 25 30 35

B.C. A.D.

Jesus baptized
JORDAN RIVER
c. A.D. 26
Matt 3:13-17; Mark 1:9-11; Luke 3:21-23; John 1:29-39

Jesus tempted by Satan
WILDERNESS
Matt 4:1-11; Mark 1:12-13; Luke 4:1-13

Jesus' first miracle
CANA
John 2:1-11

4 fishermen become Jesus' followers
SEA OF GALILEE AT CAPERNAUM
A.D. 27
Matt 4:18-22; Mark 1:16-20; Luke 5:1-11

Jesus heals Peter's mother-in-law
CAPERNAUM
Matt 8:14-17; Mark 1:29-34; Luke 4:38-41

YEAR OF INAUGURATION — YEAR OF POPULARITY

A.D. 27: FALL | WINTER | SPRING | SUMMER | FALL | 28 WINTER

Jesus' cleansing of the temple
A.D. 27
John 2:14-22

Jesus and Nicodemus
JERUSALEM
A.D. 27
John 3:1-21

Jesus talks to the Samaritan woman
SAMARIA
John 4:5-42

Jesus heals a nobleman's son
CANA
John 4:46-54

The people of Jesus' hometown try to kill Him
NAZARETH
Luke 4:16-31

Jesus begins His first preaching trip through Galilee
Matt 4:23-25; Mark 1:35-39; Luke 4:42-44

Matthew decides to follow Jesus
CAPERNAUM
Matt 9:9-13; Mark 2:13-17; Luke 5:27-32

Jesus chooses the 12 disciples
A.D. 28
Mark 3:13-19; Luke 6:12-15

Jesus preaches the "Sermon on the Mount"
Matt 5:1–7:29; Luke 6:20-49

A sinful woman anoints Jesus
CAPERNAUM
Luke 7:36-50

Jesus travels again through Galilee
Luke 8:1-3

Jesus tells parables about the kingdom
Matt 13:1-52; Mark 4:1-34; Luke 8:4-18

Jesus calms the storm
SEA OF GALILEE
Matt 8:23-27; Mark 4:35-41; Luke 8:22-25

Jesus feeds 5,000 people
NEAR BETHSAIDA
Spring, A.D. 29
Matt 14:13-21; Mark 6:30-44; Luke 9:10-17; John 6:1-14

Jesus walks on water
Matt 14:22-33; Mark 6:45-52; John 6:16-21

Jesus withdraws to Tyre and Sidon
Matt 15:21-28; Mark 7:24-30

Jesus feeds 4,000 people
Matt 15:32-39; Mark 8:1-9

Peter says that Jesus is the Son of God
Matt 16:13-20; Mark 8:27-30; Luke 9:18-21

Jesus tells His disciples He is going to die soon
CAESAREA PHILIPPI
Matt 16:21-26; Mark 8:31-37; Luke 9:22-25

Jesus is transfigured
Matt 17:1-13; Mark 9:2-13; Luke 9:28-36

Jesus pays His temple taxes
CAPERNAUM
Later in that year
Matt 17:24-27

YEAR OF OPPOSITION

SPRING | SUMMER | FALL | Oct. 29 | **29** | WINTER | SPRING | SUMMER | FALL

Jairus's daughter is brought back to life by Jesus
CAPERNAUM
Matt 9:18-26; Mark 5:21-43; Luke 8:40-56

Jesus sends His 12 followers out to preach and heal
Matt 9:35–11:1; Mark 6:6-13; Luke 9:1-6

John the Baptist is killed by Herod
MACHAERUS
A.D. 28
Matt 14:1-12; Mark 6:14-29; Luke 9:7-9

Jesus attends the Feast of Booths
JERUSALEM
October, A.D. 29
John 7:11-52

Jesus heals a man who was born blind
JERUSALEM
John 9:1-41

Jesus visits Mary and Martha
BETHANY
Luke 10:38-42

Jesus raises Lazarus from the dead
BETHANY
Winter, A.D. 29
John 11:1-44

Jesus begins His last trip to Jerusalem
A.D. 30
Luke 17:11

Jesus blesses the little children
ACROSS THE JORDAN
Matt 19:13-15; Mark 10:13-16; Luke 18:15-17

Jesus talks to the rich young man
ACROSS THE JORDAN
Matt 19:16-30; Mark 10:17-31; Luke 18:18-30

Jesus again tells about His death and resurrection
NEAR THE JORDAN
Matt 20:17-19; Mark 10:32-34; Luke 18:31-34

Jesus heals blind Bartimaeus
JERICHO
Matt 20:29-34; Mark 10:46-52; Luke 18:35-43

Jesus talks to Zacchaeus
JERICHO
Luke 19:1-10

Jesus returns to Bethany to visit Mary and Martha
BETHANY
John 11:55-12:1

THE LAST WEEK

The Triumphal Entry, JERUSALEM, Sunday
Matt 21:1-11; Mark 11:1-10; Luke 19:29-44; John 12:12-19

Jesus curses the fig tree, Monday
Matt 21:18-19; Mark 11:12-14

Jesus cleanses the temple, Monday
Matt 21:12-13; Mark 11:15-18

The authority of Jesus questioned, Tuesday
Matt 21:23-27; Mark 11:27-33; Luke 20:1-8

Jesus teaches in the temple, Tuesday
Matt 21:28–23:39; Mark 12:1-44; Luke 20:9–21:4

Jesus anointed, BETHANY, Tuesday
Matt 26:6-13; Mark 14:3-9; John 12:2-11

The plot against Jesus, Wednesday
Matt 26:14-16; Mark 14:10-11; Luke 22:3-6

The Last Supper, Thursday
Matt 26:17-29; Mark 14:12-25; Luke 22:7-20; John 13:1-38

Jesus comforts the disciples, Thursday
John 14:1–16:33

Gethsemane, Thursday
Matt 26:36-46; Mark 14:32-42; Luke 22:40-46

Jesus' arrest and trial, Thursday night and Friday
Matt 26:47–27:26; Mark 14:43–15:15;
Luke 22:47–23:25; John 18:2–19:16

Jesus' crucifixion and death, GOLGOTHA, Friday
Matt 27:27-56; Mark 15:16-41;
Luke 23:26-49; John 19:17-30

The burial of Jesus, JOSEPH'S TOMB, Friday
Matt 27:57-66; Mark 15:42-47;
Luke 23:50-56; John 19:31-42

30 WINTER | SPRING | SUMMER | FALL | A.D. 31 WINTER | SPRING | SUMMER

AFTER THE RESURRECTION

The empty tomb, JERUSALEM, Sunday
Matt 28:1-10; Mark 16:1-8; Luke 24:1-12; John 20:1-10

Mary Magdalene sees Jesus in the garden
JERUSALEM, Sunday
Matt 16:9-11; John 20:11-18

Jesus appears to the two going to Emmaus
Sunday
Mark 16:12-13; Luke 24:13-35

Jesus appears to 10 disciples
JERUSALEM, Sunday
Mark 16:14; Luke 24:36-43; John 20:19-25

Jesus appears to the 11 disciples
JERUSALEM, One week later
John 20:26-31

Jesus talks with some of His disciples
SEA OF GALILEE, One week later
John 21:1-25

Jesus ascends to His Father in Heaven
MATT OF OLIVES, 40 days later
Matt 28:16-20; Mark 16:19-20; Luke 24:44-53

Dotted lines leading to the timeline are meant to define sequence of events only. Exact dates, even year dates, are generally unknown.

33 But Peter said to Him, "*Even* though all may [1]fall away because of You, I will never fall away."

34 Jesus said to him, "[a]Truly I say to you that [b]this *very* night, before a rooster crows, you will deny Me three times."

35 Peter *said to Him, "[a]Even if I have to die with You, I will not deny You." All the disciples said the same thing too.

The Garden of Gethsemane

36 [a]Then Jesus *came with them to a place called [b]Gethsemane, and *said to His disciples, "Sit here while I go over there and pray."

37 And He took with Him [a]Peter and the two sons of Zebedee, and began to be grieved and distressed.

38 Then He *said to them, "[a]My soul is deeply grieved, to the point of death; remain here and [b]keep watch with Me."

39 And He went a little beyond *them,* and fell on His face and prayed, saying, "My Father, if it is possible, let [a]this cup pass from Me; [b]yet not as I will, but as You will."

40 And He *came to the disciples and *found them sleeping, and *said to Peter, "So, you *men* could not [a]keep watch with Me for one hour?

41 "[a]Keep watching and praying that you may not enter into temptation; [b]the spirit is willing, but the flesh is weak."

42 He went away again a second time and prayed, saying, "My Father, if this [a]cannot pass away unless I drink it, [b]Your will be done."

43 Again He came and found them sleeping, for their eyes were heavy.

44 And He left them again, and went away and prayed a third time, saying the same thing once more.

45 Then He *came to the disciples and *said to them, "[1]Are you still sleeping and resting? Behold, [a]the hour is at hand and the Son of Man is being betrayed into the hands of sinners.

46 "Get up, let us be going; behold, the one who betrays Me is at hand!"

Jesus' Betrayal and Arrest

47 [a]While He was still speaking, behold, [b]Judas, one of the twelve, came up [1]accompanied by a large crowd with swords and clubs, *who came* from the chief priests and elders of the people.

48 Now he who was betraying Him gave them a sign, saying, "Whomever I kiss, He is the one; seize Him."

49 Immediately Judas went to Jesus and said, "Hail, [a]Rabbi!" and kissed Him.

50 And Jesus said to him, "[a]Friend, *do* what you have come for." Then they came and laid hands on Jesus and seized Him.

51 And behold, [a]one of those who were with Jesus [1]reached and drew out his [b]sword, and struck the [a]slave of the high priest and [2]cut off his ear.

52 Then Jesus *said to him, "Put your sword back into its place; for [a]all those who take up the sword shall perish by the sword.

53 "Or do you think that I cannot appeal to My Father, and He will at once put at My disposal more than twelve [1a]legions of [b]angels?

54 "How then will [a]the Scriptures be fulfilled, *which say* that it must happen this way?"

55 At that time Jesus said to the crowds, "Have you come out with swords and clubs to arrest Me as *you would* against a robber? [a]Every day I used to sit in the temple teaching and you did not seize Me.

56 "But all this has taken place to fulfill [a]the Scriptures of the prophets." Then all the disciples left Him and fled.

Jesus before Caiaphas

57 [a]Those who had seized Jesus led Him away to [b]Caiaphas, the high priest, where the scribes and the elders were gathered together.

58 But [a]Peter was following Him at a distance as far as the [b]courtyard of the high priest, and entered in, and sat down with the [1c]officers to see the outcome.

59 Now the chief priests and the whole

33 [1]Or *stumble* **34** [a]Matt 26:75; John 13:38 [b]Mark 14:30 **35** [a]John 13:37 **36** [a]Matt 26:36-46: *Mark 14:32-42; Luke 22:40-46* [b]Mark 14:32; Luke 22:39; John 18:1 **37** [a]Matt 4:21; 17:1; Mark 5:37 **38** [a]John 12:27 [b]Matt 26:40, 41 **39** [a]Matt 20:22 [b]Matt 26:42; Mark 14:36; Luke 22:42; John 6:38 **40** [a]Matt 26:38 **41** [a]Matt 26:38 [b]Mark 14:38 **42** [a]Matt 20:22 [b]Matt 26:39; Mark 14:36; Luke 22:42; John 6:38 **45** [1]Or *Keep on sleeping therefore* [a]Mark 14:41; John 12:27; 13:1

47 [1]Lit *and with him* [a]Matt 26:47-56: *Mark 14:43-50; Luke 22:47-53; John 18:3-11* [b]Matt 26:14 **49** [a]Matt 23:7; 26:25 **50** [a]Matt 20:13; 22:12 **51** [1]Lit *extended the hand* [2]Lit *took off* [a]Mark 14:47; Luke 22:50; John 18:10 [b]Luke 22:38 **52** [a]Gen 9:6; Rev 13:10 **53** [1]A legion equaled 6,000 troops [a]Mark 5:9, 15; Luke 8:30 [b]Matt 4:11 **54** [a]Matt 26:24 **55** [a]Mark 12:35; 14:49; Luke 4:20; 19:47; 20:1; 21:37; John 7:14, 28; 8:2, 20; 18:20 **56** [a]Matt 26:24 **57** [a]Matt 26:57-68: *Mark 14:53-65; John 18:12f, 19-24* [b]Matt 26:3

58 [1]Or *servants* [a]John 18:15 [b]Matt 26:3 [c]Matt 5:25; John 7:32, 45f; 19:6; Acts 5:22, 26

26:34 *before a rooster crows.* The reference may be to the third of the Roman watches into which the night was divided (see note on 14:25; see also Mark 13:35). Or it may simply refer to early morning when the rooster crows.

26:36 *Gethsemane.* The name means "oil press," a place for squeezing the oil from olives (see note on Mark 14:32).

26:37 *Peter and the two sons of Zebedee.* The latter were James and John. These three disciples seem to have been especially close to Jesus (see note on Mark 5:37).

26:38–39 Jesus did not die serenely as many martyrs have. He was no mere martyr; He was the Lamb of God bearing the penalty of the sins of the entire human race. The wrath of God was turned loose on Him. Only this can adequately explain what took place at Gethsemane.

26:39 *cup.* A symbol of deep sorrow and suffering. Here it refers to His Father's face being turned away from Him when He who had no sin was made sin (i.e., a sin offering) for us (see 27:46; 2 Cor 5:21).

26:41 See note on Mark 14:38.

26:45 *Son of Man.* see note on Mark 8:31.

26:47 *a large crowd with swords and clubs.* See note on Mark 14:43. *chief priests and elders.* See notes on v. 3 and 2:4.

26:48 *Whomever I kiss.* See note on Luke 22:47.

26:49 *Rabbi.* Hebrew word for "(my) teacher." *kissed Him.* See notes on Mark 14:45 and Luke 22:47.

26:51 *one of those who were with Jesus.* Peter (see John 18:10). *slave of the high priest.* Malchus (see John 18:10).

26:53 *legions.* A Roman legion had 6,000 soldiers.

26:54 *Scriptures be fulfilled.* In view of v. 56 probably a reference to Zech 13:7.

26:57—27:26 For a summary of the two stages (religious and civil) of the trial of Jesus see note on Mark 14:53–15:15.

[1][a]Council kept trying to obtain false testimony against Jesus, so that they might put Him
to death.
60 They did not find *any,* even though
many false witnesses came forward. But later on [a]two came forward,
61 and said, "This man stated, '[a]I am able
to destroy the [1]temple of God and to rebuild
it [2]in three days.' "
62 The high priest stood up and said to
Him, "Do You not answer? What is it that
these men are testifying against You?"
63 But [a]Jesus kept silent. [b]And the high
priest said to Him, "I [1][c]adjure You by [d]the
living God, that You tell us whether You are
[2]the Christ, [e]the Son of God."
64 Jesus *said to him, "[a]You have said it
yourself; nevertheless I tell you, [1]hereafter
you will see [b]THE SON OF MAN SITTING AT THE
RIGHT HAND OF POWER, and [c]COMING ON THE
CLOUDS OF HEAVEN."
65 Then the high priest [a]tore his [1]robes
and said, "He has blasphemed! What further
need do we have of witnesses? Behold, you
have now heard the blasphemy;
66 what do you think?" They answered,
"[a]He deserves death!"
67 [a]Then they [b]spat in His face and beat
Him with their fists; and others [1]slapped
Him,
68 and said, "[a]Prophesy to us, You
[1]Christ; who is the one who hit You?"

Peter's Denials

69 [a]Now Peter was sitting outside in the
[b]courtyard, and a servant-girl came to him
and said, "You too were with Jesus the Galilean."
70 But he denied *it* before them all, saying, "I do not know what you are talking
about."
71 When he had gone out to the gateway,
another *servant-girl* saw him and *said to
those who were there, "This man was with
Jesus of Nazareth."
72 And again he denied *it* with an oath, "I
do not know the man."
73 A little later the bystanders came up
and said to Peter, "Surely you too are *one* of
them; [a]for even the way you talk [1]gives you
away."
74 Then he began to curse and swear, "I
do not know the man!" And immediately a
rooster crowed.
75 And Peter remembered the word which
Jesus had said, "[a]Before a rooster crows, you
will deny Me three times." And he went out
and wept bitterly.

Judas's Remorse

27 [a]Now when morning came, all the
chief priests and the elders of the people conferred together against Jesus to put
Him to death;
2 and they bound Him, and led Him
away and [a]delivered Him to [b]Pilate the governor.
3 Then when [a]Judas, who had betrayed
Him, saw that He had been condemned, he
felt remorse and returned [b]the thirty [1]pieces
of silver to the chief priests and elders,
4 saying, "I have sinned by betraying
innocent blood." But they said, "What is that
to us? [a]See *to that* yourself!"
5 And he threw the pieces of silver into
[a]the temple sanctuary and departed; and [b]he
went away and hanged himself.
6 The chief priests took the pieces of silver and said, "It is not lawful to put them
into the temple treasury, since it is the price
of blood."
7 And they conferred together and [1]with
the money bought the Potter's Field as a burial place for strangers.
8 [a]For this reason that field has been
called the Field of Blood to this day.
9 Then that which was spoken through
Jeremiah the prophet was fulfilled: "[a]AND
[1]THEY TOOK THE THIRTY PIECES OF SILVER, THE
PRICE OF THE ONE WHOSE PRICE HAD BEEN SET by
the sons of Israel;

59 [1]Or *Sanhedrin* [a]Matt 5:22
60 [a]Deut 19:15
61 [1]Or *sanctuary* [2]Or *after* [a]Matt 27:40; Mark 14:58; 15:29; John 2:19; Acts 6:14
63 [1]Or *charge You under oath* [2]I.e. the Messiah [a]Matt 27:12, 14; John 19:9 [b]Matt 26:63-66; Luke 22:67-71 [c]Lev 5:1 [d]Matt 16:16 [e]Matt 4:3
64 [1]Or *from now on* [a]Matt 26:25 [b]Ps 110:1; Mark 14:62 [c]Dan 7:13; Matt 16:27f
65 [1]Or *outer garments* [a]Num 14:6; Mark 14:63; Acts 14:14
66 [a]Lev 24:16; John 19:7
67 [1]Or *beat Him with rods* [a]Is 50:6; Matt 26:67, 68; Luke 22:63-65; John 18:22 [b]Matt 27:30; Mark 10:34
68 [1]I.e. the Messiah [a]Mark 14:65; Luke 22:64
69 [a]Matt 26:69-75: *Mark 14:66-72; Luke 22:55-62; John 18:16-18, 25-27* [b]Matt 26:3
73 [1]Lit *makes you evident* [a]Mark 14:70; Luke 22:59; John 18:26
75 [a]Matt 26:34
27:1 [a]Mark 15:1; Luke 22:66; John 18:28
2 [a]Matt 20:19 [b]Luke 3:1; 13:1; 23:12; Acts 3:13; 4:27; 1 Tim 6:13
3 [1]Or *silver shekels* [a]Matt 26:14 [b]Matt 26:15
4 [a]Matt 27:24 **5** [a]Matt 26:61; Luke 1:9, 21 [b]Acts 1:18
7 [1]Lit *from them* **8** [a]Acts 1:19 **9** [1]Or *I took;* cf Zech 11:13 [a]Zech 11:12

26:59 *Council.* See note on Mark 14:55.
26:61 *I am able to destroy the temple of God.* Evidently an intentional distortion of Jesus' words (John 2:19).
26:63 *I adjure You.* Jesus refused to answer the question of v. 62 (see v. 63a). But when the high priest used this form, He was legally obliged to reply. *Christ.* See note on 16:16.
26:65 *tore his robes.* Ordinarily the high priest was forbidden by law to do this (Lev 10:6; 21:10), but this was considered a highly unusual circumstance. The high priest interpreted Jesus' answer in v. 64 as blasphemy (see note on Mark 14:64).
26:67–68 Mark reports that they blindfolded Jesus (Mark 14:65), which explains the mocking command: "Prophesy . . . Who hit you?"
26:73 *the way you talk gives you away.* Peter had a decidedly Galilean accent that was conspicuous in Jerusalem.
27:1 *when morning came.* The Sanhedrin could not have a legal session at night, so at daybreak a special meeting was held to make the death sentence (see 26:66) official. See note on Mark 15:1.
27:2 *delivered Him to Pilate.* The Sanhedrin had been deprived by the Roman government of the right to carry out capital punishment, except in the case of a foreigner who invaded the sacred precincts of the temple. So Jesus had to be handed over to Pilate for execution. For additional information about Pilate see note on Mark 15:1.
27:3–10 See Acts 1:16–19.
27:5 *hanged himself.* See note on Acts 1:18.
27:8 *called the Field of Blood.* Cf. "the valley of Slaughter" in Jer 19:6.
27:9 *Jeremiah.* The quotation that follows seems to be a combining of Zech 11:12–13 and Jer 19:1–13 (or perhaps Jer 18:2–12 or Jer 32:6–9). But Matthew attributes it to the major prophet Jeremiah, just as Mark (1:2–3) quotes Mal 3:1 and Is 40:3 but attributes them to the major prophet Isaiah.

10 [a]AND [1]THEY GAVE THEM FOR THE POTTER'S FIELD, AS THE LORD DIRECTED ME."

Jesus before Pilate

11 [a]Now Jesus stood before the governor, and the governor questioned Him, saying, "Are You the [b]King of the Jews?" And Jesus said to him, "[c]*It is as* you say."

12 And while He was being accused by the chief priests and elders, [a]He did not answer.

13 Then Pilate *said to Him, "Do You not hear how many things they testify against You?"

14 And [a]He did not answer him with regard to even a *single* [1]charge, so the governor was quite amazed.

15 [a]Now at *the* feast the governor was accustomed to release for the [1]people *any* one prisoner whom they wanted.

16 At that time they were holding a notorious prisoner, called Barabbas.

17 So when the people gathered together, Pilate said to them, "Whom do you want me to release for you? Barabbas, or Jesus [a]who is called Christ?"

18 For he knew that because of envy they had handed Him over.

19 [a]While he was sitting on the judgment seat, his wife sent him *a message,* saying, "Have nothing to do with that [b]righteous Man; for [1]last night I suffered greatly [c]in a dream because of Him."

20 But the chief priests and the elders persuaded the crowds to [a]ask for Barabbas and to put Jesus to death.

21 But the governor [1]said to them, "Which of the two do you want me to release for you?" And they said, "Barabbas."

22 Pilate *said to them, "Then what shall I do with Jesus [a]who is called Christ?" They all *said, "[1]Crucify Him!"

23 And he said, "Why, what evil has He done?" But they kept shouting all the more, saying, "[1]Crucify Him!"

24 When Pilate saw that he was accomplishing nothing, but rather that [a]a riot was starting, he took water and [b]washed his hands in front of the crowd, saying, "I am innocent of [c]this Man's blood; [d]see *to that* yourselves."

25 And all the people said, "[a]His blood shall be on us and on our children!"

26 Then he released Barabbas [1]for them; but after having Jesus [a]scourged, he handed Him over to be crucified.

Jesus Is Mocked

27 [a]Then the soldiers of the governor took Jesus into [b]the [1]Praetorium and gathered the whole *Roman* [2c]cohort around Him.

28 They stripped Him and [a]put a scarlet robe on Him.

29 [a]And after twisting together a crown of thorns, they put it on His head, and a [1]reed in His right hand; and they knelt down before Him and mocked Him, saying, "[b]Hail, King of the Jews!"

30 [a]They spat on Him, and took the reed and *began* to beat Him on the head.

31 [a]After they had mocked Him, they took the *scarlet* robe off Him and put His *own* garments back on Him, and led Him away to crucify Him.

32 [a]As they were coming out, they found a man of [b]Cyrene named Simon, [1]whom they pressed into service to bear His cross.

The Crucifixion

33 [a]And when they came to a place called [b]Golgotha, which means Place of a Skull,

34 [a]they gave Him [b]wine to drink mixed with gall; and after tasting *it,* He was unwilling to drink.

35 And when they had crucified Him, [a]they divided up His garments among themselves by casting [1]lots.

36 And sitting down, they *began* to [a]keep watch over Him there.

37 And above His head they put up the charge against Him [1]which read, "[a]THIS IS JESUS THE KING OF THE JEWS."

10 [1]Some early mss read *I gave* [a]Zech 11:13 **11** [a]Matt 27:11-14: *Mark 15:2-5; Luke 23:2, 3; John 18:29-38* [b]Matt 2:2 [c]Matt 26:25 **12** [a]Matt 26:63; John 19:9 **14** [1]Lit *word* [a]Matt 27:12; Mark 15:5; Luke 23:9; John 19:9 **15** [1]Lit *crowd* [a]Matt 27:15-26: *Mark 15:6-15; Luke 23:17-25;* John 18:39-19:16 **17** [a]Matt 1:16; 27:22 **19** [1]Lit *today* [a]John 19:13; Acts 12:21; 18:12, 16f; 25:6, 10, 17 [b]Matt 27:24 [c]Gen 20:6; 31:11; Num 12:6; Job 33:15; Matt 1:20; 2:12f, 19, 22 **20** [a]Acts 3:14 **21** [1]Lit *answered and said to them* **22** [1]Lit *Let Him be crucified* [a]Matt 1:16 **23** [1]Lit *Let Him be crucified* **24** [a]Matt 26:5 [b]Deut 21:6-8 **24** [c]Matt 27:19 [d]Matt 27:4 **25** [a]Josh 2:19; Acts 5:28 **26** [1]Or *to them* [a]Mark 15:15; Luke 23:16; John 19:1 **27** [1]I.e. the governor's official residence [2]Or *battalion* [a]Matt 27:27-31: *Mark 15:16-20* [b]Matt 26:3; John 18:28, 33; 19:9 [c]Acts 10:1 **28** [a]Mark 15:17; John 19:2 **29** [1]Or *staff;* i.e. to mimic a king's scepter [a]Mark 15:17; John 19:2 [b]Mark 15:18; John 19:3 **30** [a]Matt 26:67; Mark 10:34; 14:65; 15:19 **31** [a]Mark 15:20 **32** [1]Lit *this one* [a]Matt 27:32: *Mark 15:21; Luke 23:26;* John 19:17 [b]Acts 2:10; 6:9; 11:20; 13:1 **33** [a]Matt 27:33-44: *Mark 15:22-32; Luke 23:33-43; John 19:17-24* [b]Luke 23:33; John 19:17 **34** [a]Ps 69:21 [b]Mark 15:23 **35** [1]Lit *a lot* [a]Ps 22:18 **36** [a]Matt 27:54 **37** [1]Lit *written* [a]Mark 15:26; Luke 23:38; John 19:19

27:15 *the governor was accustomed.* A custom of which nothing is known outside the Gospels.

27:16 *notorious.* The translation of a Greek word that here probably means "outstanding" or "notable" (cf. Rom 16:7). Barabbas had taken part in a rebellion (Luke 23:19; John 18:40), presumably against the Romans. So he would have been a folk hero among the Jews.

27:19 This incident is found only in Matthew's Gospel.

27:25 A chilling response by a bloodthirsty crowd. It has often been used to justify the persecution of the Jewish people. It should be noted, however, that it was not God but the people themselves who uttered these words. There is no evidence here that God granted their request. If there was a fulfillment, it was most likely seen in the destruction of Jerusalem in A.D. 70.

27:26 *scourged.* Roman floggings were so brutal that sometimes the victim died before crucifixion. See note on Mark 15:15.

27:27 *Praetorium.* The governor's official residence in Jerusalem (see note on Mark 15:16).

27:28 *scarlet robe.* The outer cloak of a Roman soldier.

27:29 *crown of thorns.* See note on Mark 15:17. *reed.* A mock scepter.

27:32 *Cyrene.* A city in North Africa. *Simon . . . to bear His cross.* See note on Mark 15:21.

27:33 *Golgotha.* See note on Mark 15:22.

27:34 *mixed with gall.* Tradition says that the women of Jerusalem customarily furnished this pain-killing narcotic to prisoners who were crucified. Jesus refused to drink it because He wanted to be fully conscious until His death (v. 50).

27:35 *crucified.* See note on Mark 15:24. *casting lots.* Explained more precisely in John 19:23–24.

27:37 See note on Mark 15:26.

38 At that time two robbers *were crucified with Him, one on the right and one on
the left.
39 And those passing by were [1]hurling
abuse at Him, [a]wagging their heads
40 and saying, "[a]You who *are going to*
destroy the temple and rebuild it in three
days, save Yourself! [b]If You are the Son of
God, come down from the cross."
41 In the same way the chief priests also,
along with the scribes and elders, were
mocking *Him* and saying,
42 "[a]He saved others; [1]He cannot save
Himself. [b]He is the King of Israel; let Him
now come down from the cross, and we will
believe in Him.
43 "[a]HE TRUSTS IN GOD; LET GOD RESCUE *Him*
now, IF HE [1]DELIGHTS IN HIM; for He said, 'I
am the Son of God.' "
44 [a]The robbers who had been crucified
with Him were also insulting Him with the
same words.
45 [a]Now from the [1]sixth hour darkness
[2]fell upon all the land until the [3]ninth hour.
46 About the ninth hour Jesus cried out
with a loud voice, saying, "[a]ELI, ELI, LAMA
SABACHTHANI?" that is, "MY GOD, MY GOD, WHY
HAVE YOU FORSAKEN ME?"
47 And some of those who were standing
there, when they heard it, *began* saying,
"This man is calling for Elijah."
48 [a]Immediately one of them ran, and taking a sponge, he filled it with sour wine and
put it on a reed, and gave Him a drink.
49 But the rest *of them* said, "[1]Let us see
whether Elijah will come to save Him[2]."
50 And Jesus [a]cried out again with a loud
voice, and yielded up His spirit.
51 [a]And behold, [b]the [1]veil of the temple
was torn in two from top to bottom; and [c]the
earth shook and the rocks were split.
52 The tombs were opened, and many
bodies of the [1]saints who had [a]fallen asleep
were raised;
53 and coming out of the tombs after His
resurrection they entered [a]the holy city and
appeared to many.
54 [a]Now the centurion, and those who
were with him [b]keeping guard over Jesus,
when they saw [c]the earthquake and the
things that were happening, became very
frightened and said, "Truly this was [1d]the
Son of God!"
55 [a]Many women were there looking on
from a distance, who had followed Jesus
from Galilee while [1b]ministering to Him.
56 Among them was [a]Mary Magdalene,
and Mary the mother of James and Joseph,
and [b]the mother of the sons of Zebedee.

Jesus Is Buried

57 [a]When it was evening, there came a
rich man from Arimathea, named Joseph,
who himself had also become a disciple of
Jesus.
58 This man went to Pilate and asked for
the body of Jesus. Then Pilate ordered it to
be given *to him.*
59 And Joseph took the body and
wrapped it in a clean linen cloth,
60 and laid it in his own new tomb, which
he had hewn out in the rock; and he rolled
[a]a large stone against the entrance of the
tomb and went away.
61 And [a]Mary Magdalene was there, and
the other Mary, sitting opposite the grave.
62 Now on the next day, [1]the day after
[a]the preparation, the chief priests and the
Pharisees gathered together with Pilate,
63 and said, "Sir, we remember that when
He was still alive that deceiver said, '[a]After
three days I *am to* rise again.'
64 "Therefore, give orders for the grave to
be made secure until the third day, otherwise
His disciples may come and steal Him away
and say to the people, 'He has risen from the
dead,' and the last deception will be worse
than the first."
65 Pilate said to them, "You have a

39 [1]Or *blaspheming* [a]Job 16:4; Ps 22:7; 109:25; Lam 2:15; Mark 15:29
40 [a]Matt 26:61; John 2:19 [b]Matt 27:42
42 [1]Or *can He not save Himself?* [a]Mark 15:31; Luke 23:35 [b]Matt 27:37; Luke 23:37; John 1:49; 12:13
43 [1]Or *takes pleasure in;* or *cares for him* [a]Ps 22:8
44 [a]Luke 23:39-43
45 [1]I.e. 12 noon [2]Or *occurred* [3]I.e. 3 p.m. [a]Matt 27:45-56: *Mark 15:33-41; Luke 23:44-49*
46 [a]Ps 22:1
48 [a]Ps 69:21; Mark 15:36; Luke 23:36; John 19:29
49 [1]Lit *Permit that we see* [2]Some early mss read *And another took a spear and pierced His side, and there came out water and blood* (cf John 19:34)
50 [a]Mark 15:37; Luke 23:46; John 19:30
51 [1]Or *curtain* [a]Matt 27:51-56: *Mark 15:38-41;* Luke 23:47-49 [b]Ex 26:31ff; Mark 15:38; Luke 23:45; Heb 9:3 [c]Matt 27:54
52 [1]Or *holy ones* [a]Acts 7:60
53 [a]Matt 4:5
54 [1]Or *a son of God* or *a son of a god* [a]Mark 15:39; Luke 23:47 [b]Matt 27:36 [c]Matt 27:51 [d]Matt 4:3; 27:43
55 [1]Or *caring for Him* [a]Mark 15:40f; Luke 23:49; John 19:25 [b]Mark 15:41; Luke 8:2, 3
56 [a]Matt 28:1; Mark 15:40, 47; 16:9; Luke 8:2; John 19:25; 20:1, 18 [b]Matt 20:20
57 [a]Matt 27:57-61: *Mark 15:42-47; Luke 23:50-56; John 19:38-42*
60 [a]Matt 27:66; 28:2; Mark 16:4
61 [a]Matt 27:56; 28:1
62 [1]Lit *which is after* [a]Mark 15:42; Luke 23:54; John 19:14, 31, 42
63 [a]Matt 16:21; 17:23; 20:19; Mark 8:31; 9:31; 10:34; Luke 9:22; 18:31-33

27:38 *two robbers.* See note on Mark 15:27.

27:45 *From the sixth hour . . . until the ninth hour.* From noon until 3:00 P.M.

27:46 *ELI, ELI, LAMA SABACHTHANI?* A mixture of Aramaic and Hebrew, translated by Matthew for his readers (see note on Mark 15:34).

27:49 See note on Mark 15:35.

27:51 *veil.* The inner curtain that separated the holy place from the most holy place. The tearing of the curtain signified Christ's making it possible for believers to go directly into God's presence (see Heb 9:1–14; 10:14–22).

27:52–53 An incident found only in Matthew's Gospel, perhaps symbolic of Christ's conquering death through His redemptive work on the cross.

27:54 *centurion.* See note on 8:5. *Son of God.* It cannot be determined whether the centurion made a fully Christian confession, or was only acknowledging that, since the gods had so obviously acted to vindicate this judicial victim, Jesus must be one especially favored by them (the Greek can also be translated "a son"). But in view of the ridicule voiced by "those passing by" (vv. 39–40), it seems probable that Matthew intended the former. See note on Luke 23:47.

27:56 See note on Mark 15:40.

27:57 *Arimathea.* A village in the hill country of Ephraim, about 20 miles northwest of Jerusalem.

27:58 *asked for the body of Jesus.* See note on Luke 23:52.

27:59–60 See note on Mark 15:46.

27:62 *the next day, the day after the preparation.* Saturday, the Sabbath. Friday was the preparation day for the Sabbath (sunset Friday to sunset Saturday).

27:64 *the last deception will be worse than the first.* The first would be that Jesus was the Messiah, the second that He had risen as the Son of God.

[a]guard; go, make it *as* secure as you know
how."
66 And they went and made the grave
secure, and along with [a]the guard they set a
[b]seal on [c]the stone.

Jesus Is Risen!

28 [a]Now after the Sabbath, as it began to
dawn toward the first *day* of the week,
[b]Mary Magdalene and the other Mary came
to look at the grave.
2 And behold, a severe earthquake had
occurred, for [a]an angel of the Lord descended from heaven and came and rolled away
[b]the stone and sat upon it.
3 And [a]his appearance was like lightning, and his clothing as white as snow.
4 The guards shook for fear of him and
became like dead men.
5 The angel said to the women, "[1][a]Do
not be afraid; for I know that you are looking
for Jesus who has been crucified.
6 "He is not here, for He has risen, [a]just as
He said. Come, see the place where He was
lying.
7 "Go quickly and tell His disciples that
He has risen from the dead; and behold, He
is going ahead of you [a]into Galilee, there you
will see Him; behold, I have told you."
8 And they left the tomb quickly with
fear and great joy and ran to report it to His
disciples.
9 And behold, Jesus met them [1]and
greeted them. And they came up and took
hold of His feet and worshiped Him.
10 Then Jesus *said to them, "[1][a]Do not be
afraid; go and take word to [b]My brethren to
leave [c]for Galilee, and there they will see Me."

65 [a]Matt 27:66; 28:11
66 [a]Matt 27:65; 28:11 [b]Dan 6:17 [c]Matt 27:60; 28:2; Mark 16:4
28:1 [a]Matt 28:1-8: *Mark 16:1-8; Luke 24:1-10;* John 20:1-8 [b]Matt 27:56, 61
2 [a]Luke 24:4; John 20:12 [b]Matt 27:66; Mark 16:4
3 [a]Dan 7:9; 10:6; Mark 9:3; John 20:12; Acts 1:10
5 [1]Or *Stop being afraid* [a]Matt 14:27; 28:10; Rev 1:17
6 [a]Matt 12:40; 16:21; 27:63
7 [a]Matt 26:32; 28:10, 16; Mark 16:7
9 [1]Lit *saying hello*
10 [1]Or *Stop being afraid* [a]Matt 14:27; 28:5 [b]John 20:17; Rom 8:29; Heb 2:11f, 17 [c]Matt 26:32; 28:7, 16
11 [a]Matt 27:65, 66
14 [1]Lit *make you free from care* [a]Matt 27:2
15 [a]Matt 9:31; Mark 1:45 [b]Matt 27:8
16 [a]Matt 26:32; 28:7, 10; Mark 15:41; 16:7
17 [a]Mark 16:11
18 [a]Dan 7:13f; Matt 11:27; 26:64; Rom 14:9; Eph 1:20-22; Phil 2:9f; Col 2:10; 1 Pet 3:22
19 [1]Or *Having gone;* Gr aorist part. [a]Mark 16:15f [b]Matt 13:52; Acts 1:8; 14:21 [c]Matt 25:32; Luke 24:47 [d]Acts 2:38; 8:16; Rom 6:3; 1 Cor 1:13, 15ff; Gal 3:27
20 [1]Lit *all the days* [a]Matt 18:20; Acts 18:10 [b]Matt 13:39

11 Now while they were on their way,
some of [a]the guard came into the city and
reported to the chief priests all that had happened.
12 And when they had assembled with
the elders and consulted together, they gave
a large sum of money to the soldiers,
13 and said, "You are to say, 'His disciples
came by night and stole Him away while we
were asleep.'
14 "And if this should come to [a]the governor's ears, we will win him over and [1]keep
you out of trouble."
15 And they took the money and did as
they had been instructed; and this story was
widely [a]spread among the Jews, *and is* [b]to
this day.

The Great Commission

16 But the eleven disciples proceeded [a]to
Galilee, to the mountain which Jesus had
designated.
17 When they saw Him, they worshiped
Him; but [a]some were doubtful.
18 And Jesus came up and spoke to them,
saying, "[a]All authority has been given to Me
in heaven and on earth.
19 "[1][a]Go therefore and [b]make disciples of
[c]all the nations, [d]baptizing them in the name
of the Father and the Son and the Holy Spirit,
20 teaching them to observe all that I commanded you; and lo, [a]I am with you [1]always,
even to [b]the end of the age."

27:65 *You have a guard.* Pilate granted them a guard of Roman soldiers (28:4,11–12).
28:1 *first day of the week.* See note on Luke 24:1. *the other Mary.* The wife of Clopas (see 27:56; John 19:25).
28:2 *behold . . . had occurred.* The sense is "Now there had been." It is clear from the parallel accounts (Mark 16:2–6; Luke 24:1–7; John 20:1) that the events of vv. 2–4 occurred before the women actually arrived at the tomb. *a severe earthquake.* Only Matthew mentions this earthquake and the one at Jesus' death (27:51,54).
28:11–15 Only Matthew tells of the posting of the guard (27:62–66), and he follows up by telling of their report.
28:16 *eleven.* Judas had committed suicide (27:5). *had designated.* See v. 10.
28:19 *all the nations.* Contrast 10:5–6. *baptizing them.* As a sign of their union with and commitment to Christ (see notes on Acts 2:38; Rom 6:3–4).
28:20 *with you.* Matthew ends with the reassuring and empowering words of Him who came to earth to be "God with us" (1:23).

Mark

INTRODUCTION

See "The Synoptic Gospels," p. 1361.

Author

Although there is no direct internal evidence of authorship, it was the unanimous testimony of the early church that this Gospel was written by John Mark. The most important evidence comes from Papias (c. A.D. 140), who quotes an even earlier source as saying: (1) Mark was a close associate of Peter, from whom he received the tradition of the things said and done by the Lord; (2) this tradition did not come to Mark as a finished, sequential account of the life of our Lord, but as the preaching of Peter—preaching directed to the needs of the early Christian communities; (3) Mark accurately preserved this material. The conclusion drawn from this tradition is that the Gospel of Mark largely consists of the preaching of Peter arranged and shaped by John Mark (see note on Acts 10:37).

John Mark in the NT

It is generally agreed that the Mark who is associated with Peter in the early non-Biblical tradition is also the John Mark of the NT. The first mention of him is in connection with his mother, who had a house in Jerusalem that served as a meeting place for believers (Acts 12:12). When Paul and Barnabas returned to Antioch from Jerusalem after the famine visit, Mark accompanied them (Acts 12:25). Mark next appears as a "helper" to Paul and Barnabas on their first missionary journey (Acts 13:5), but he deserted them at Perga, in Pamphylia, to return to Jerusalem (Acts 13:13). Paul must have been deeply disappointed with Mark's actions on this occasion, because when Barnabas proposed taking Mark on the second journey, Paul flatly refused, a refusal that broke up their working relationship (Acts 15:36–39). Barnabas took Mark, who was his cousin, and departed for Cyprus. No further mention is made of either of them in the book of Acts. Mark reappears in Paul's letter to the Colossians written from Rome. Paul sends a greeting from Mark and adds: "about whom you received instructions; if he comes to you, welcome him" (Col 4:10; see Phile 24, written about the same time). At this point Mark was apparently beginning to win his way back into Paul's confidence. By the end of Paul's life, Mark had fully regained Paul's favor (see 2 Tim 4:11).

Date of Composition

Some, who hold that Matthew and Luke used Mark as a major source, have suggested that Mark may have been composed in the 50s or early 60s. Others have felt that the content of the Gospel and statements made about Mark by the early church fathers indicate that the book was written shortly before the destruction of Jerusalem in A.D. 70. See chart, p. 1361.

Place of Origin

According to early church tradition, Mark was written "in the regions of Italy" (Anti-Marcionite Prologue) or, more specifically, in Rome (Irenaeus and Clement of Alexandria). These same authors closely associate Mark's writing of the Gospel with the apostle Peter. The above evidence is consistent with (1) the historical probability that Peter was in Rome during the last days of his life and was martyred there, and (2) the Biblical evidence that Mark also was in Rome about the same time and was closely associated with Peter (see 2 Tim 4:11; 1 Pet 5:13, where the word "Babylon" is probably a cryptogram for Rome).

Recipients

The evidence points to the church at Rome or at least to Gentile readers. Mark explains Jewish customs (7:2–4; 15:42), translates Aramaic words (3:17; 5:41; 7:11,34; 15:22) and seems to have a special interest in persecution and martyrdom (8:34–38; 13:9–13)—subjects of special concern to Roman believers. A Roman destination would explain the almost immediate acceptance of this Gospel and its rapid dissemination.

Occasion and Purpose

Since Mark's Gospel is traditionally associated with Rome, it may have been occasioned by the persecutions of the Roman church in the period c. A.D. 64–67. The famous fire of Rome in 64—probably set by Nero himself but blamed on Christians—resulted in widespread persecution. Even martyrdom was not unknown among Roman believers. Mark may be writing to prepare his readers for this suffering by placing before them the life of our Lord. There are many references, both explicit and veiled, to suffering and discipleship throughout his Gospel (see 1:12–13; 3:22,30; 8:34–38; 10:30,33–34,45; 13:8,11–13).

Emphases

1. *The cross.* Both the human cause (12:12; 14:1–2; 15:10) and the divine necessity (8:31; 9:31; 10:33) of the cross are emphasized by Mark.

2. *Discipleship.* Special attention should be paid to the passages on discipleship that arise from Jesus' predictions of His passion (8:34—9:1; 9:35—10:31; 10:42—45).

3. *The teachings of Jesus.* Although Mark records far fewer actual teachings of Jesus than the other Gospel writers, there is a remarkable emphasis on Jesus as teacher. The words "teacher," "teach" or "teaching," and "Rabbi" are applied to Jesus in Mark 37 times.

4. *The Messianic secret.* On several occasions Jesus warns His disciples or the person for whom He has worked a miracle to keep silent about who He is or what He has done (1:34,44; 3:12; 5:43; 7:36–37; 8:26,30; 9:9).

5. *Son of God.* Although Mark emphasizes the humanity of Jesus (see 3:5; 6:6,31,34; 7:34; 8:12,33; 10:14; 11:12), he does not neglect His deity (see 1:1,11; 3:11; 5:7; 9:7; 12:1–11; 13:32; 15:39).

Special Characteristics

Mark's Gospel is a simple, succinct, unadorned, yet vivid account of Jesus' ministry, emphasizing more what Jesus did than what He said. Mark moves quickly from one episode in Jesus' life and ministry to another, often using the adverb "immediately" (see note on 1:12). The book as a whole is characterized as "The beginning of the gospel" (1:1). The life, death and resurrection of Christ comprise the "beginning," of which the apostolic preaching in Acts is the continuation.

Outline

I. The Beginnings of Jesus' Ministry (1:1–13)
  A. His Forerunner (1:1–8)
  B. His Baptism (1:9–11)
  C. His Temptation (1:12–13)
II. Jesus' Ministry in Galilee (1:14—6:29)
  A. Early Galilean Ministry (1:14—3:12)
    1. Call of the first disciples (1:14–20)
    2. Miracles in Capernaum (1:21–34)
    3. A tour of Galilee (1:35–45)
    4. Ministry in Capernaum (2:1–22)
    5. Sabbath controversy (2:23—3:12)
  B. Later Galilean Ministry (3:13—6:29)
    1. Selection of the 12 apostles (3:13–19)
    2. Teachings in Capernaum (3:20–35)
    3. Parables of the kingdom (4:1–34)

4. Trip across the Sea of Galilee (4:35—5:20)
5. More Galilean miracles (5:21–43)
6. Unbelief in Jesus' hometown (6:1–6)
7. Six apostolic teams tour Galilee (6:7–13)
8. King Herod's reaction to Jesus' ministry (6:14–29)

III. Withdrawals from Galilee (6:30—9:32)
- A. To the Eastern Shore of the Sea of Galilee (6:30–52)
- B. To the Western Shore of the Sea of Galilee (6:53—7:23)
- C. To Phoenicia (7:24–30)
- D. To the Region of the Decapolis (7:31—8:10)
- E. To the Vicinity of Caesarea Philippi (8:11—9:32)

IV. Final Ministry in Galilee (9:33–50)

V. Jesus' Ministry in Judea and Perea (ch. 10)
- A. Teaching concerning Divorce (10:1–12)
- B. Teaching concerning Children (10:13–16)
- C. The Rich Young Man (10:17–31)
- D. Prediction of Jesus' Death (10:32–34)
- E. A Request of Two Brothers (10:35–45)
- F. Restoration of Bartimaeus's Sight (10:46–52)

VI. The Passion of Jesus (chs. 11—15)
- A. The Triumphal Entry (11:1–11)
- B. The Cleansing of the Temple (11:12–19)
- C. Concluding Controversies with Jewish Leaders (11:20—12:44)
- D. The Olivet Discourse concerning the End of the Age (ch. 13)
- E. The Anointing of Jesus (14:1–11)
- F. The Arrest, Trial and Death of Jesus (14:12—15:47)

VII. The Resurrection of Jesus (ch. 16)

Preaching of John the Baptist

1 The beginning of the gospel of Jesus Christ, [a]the Son of God.

2 [a]As it is written in Isaiah the prophet:

"[b]BEHOLD, I SEND MY MESSENGER [1]AHEAD OF YOU,
WHO WILL PREPARE YOUR WAY;

3 [a]THE VOICE OF ONE CRYING IN THE WILDERNESS,
'MAKE READY THE WAY OF THE LORD,
MAKE HIS PATHS STRAIGHT.' "

4 John the Baptist appeared in the wilderness [1a]preaching a baptism of repentance for the [b]forgiveness of sins.

5 And all the country of Judea was going out to him, and all the people of Jerusalem; and they were being baptized by him in the Jordan River, confessing their sins.

6 John was clothed with camel's hair and *wore* [a]a leather belt around his waist, and [1]his diet was locusts and wild honey.

7 And he was [1]preaching, and saying, "After me One is coming who is mightier than I, and I am not fit to stoop down and untie the thong of His sandals.

8 "I baptized you [1]with water; but He will baptize you [1]with the Holy Spirit."

The Baptism of Jesus

9 [a]In those days Jesus [b]came from Nazareth in Galilee and was baptized by John in the Jordan.

10 Immediately coming up out of the water, He saw the heavens [1]opening, and the Spirit like a dove descending upon Him;

11 and a voice came out of the heavens: "[a]You are My beloved Son, in You I am well-pleased."

12 [a]Immediately the Spirit *impelled Him *to go* out into the wilderness.

13 And He was in the wilderness forty days being tempted by [a]Satan; and He was with the wild beasts, and the angels were ministering to Him.

Jesus Preaches in Galilee

14 [a]Now after John had been [1]taken into custody, Jesus came into Galilee, [2b]preaching the gospel of God,

15 and saying, "[a]The time is fulfilled, and the kingdom of God [1]is at hand; [b]repent and [2]believe in the gospel."

16 [a]As He was going along by the Sea of

1:1 [a]Matt 4:3
2 [1]Lit *before your face* [a]Mark 1:2-8: *Matt 3:1-11; Luke 3:2-16* [b]Mal 3:1; Matt 11:10; Luke 7:27
3 [a]Is 40:3; Matt 3:3; Luke 3:4; John 1:23
4 [1]Or *proclaiming* [a]Acts 13:24 [b]Luke 1:77
6 [1]Lit *he was eating* [a]2 Kin 1:8
7 [1]Or *proclaiming*
8 [1]The Gr here can be translated *in, with* or *by*
9 [a]Mark 1:9-11: *Matt 3:13-17; Luke 3:21, 22* [b]Matt 2:23; Luke 2:51
10 [1]Or *being parted*
11 [a]Ps 2:7; Is 42:1; Matt 3:17; 12:18; Mark 9:7; Luke 3:22
12 [a]Mark 1:12, 13: *Matt 4:1-11; Luke 4:1-13*
13 [a]Matt 4:10
14 [1]Lit *delivered up* [2]Or *proclaiming* [a]Matt 4:12 [b]Matt 4:23
15 [1]Lit *has come near* [2]Or *put your trust in* [a]Gal 4:4; Eph 1:10; 1 Tim 2:6; Titus 1:3 [b]Matt 3:2; Acts 20:21
16 [a]Mark 1:16-20: *Matt 4:18-22;* Luke 5:2-11; John 1:40-42

1:1 *The beginning.* See Introduction: Special Characteristics; suggests the opening verse of Genesis (see John 1:1). *gospel.* From the Old English *godspel,* "good story" or "good news," which accurately translates the Greek. The good news is that God has provided salvation through the life, death and resurrection of Jesus Christ

1:2–3 *in Isaiah the prophet.* The quotation that immediately follows (see first two poetry lines) comes from Mal 3:1 but is followed by one from Is 40:3 (see note on Matt 27:9). Understanding the ministry of Jesus must begin with the OT. What Isaiah says about God applies to Jesus, His Son (v. 1). The passages cited speak of the messenger, the wilderness and the Lord, each of which is stressed in vv. 4–8.

1:4 *John . . . appeared.* Mark, like John, has no nativity narrative, but begins with the ministry of John the Baptist. The name John means "The LORD is gracious." *the Baptist.* John's practice of baptizing those who came to him in repentance was so characteristic of his ministry that he became known as "the Baptist" or "the Baptizer." *the wilderness.* The arid region west of the Dead Sea, whose inhabitants included those who wrote and preserved the Dead Sea Scrolls. *repentance.* Involves deliberate turning from sin to righteousness, and John's emphasis on repentance recalls the preaching of the prophets (e.g., Hos 3:4–5). God always grants forgiveness when there is repentance. *baptism.* John was preaching repentance-baptism, i.e., baptism that was preceded or accompanied by repentance. Baptism was not new to John's audience. They knew of baptism for Gentile converts, but had not heard that the descendants of Abraham (Jews) needed to repent and be baptized.

1:5 *all . . . all.* Obvious hyperbole, indicating the high interest created by John's preaching. For centuries Israel had had no prophet. *Jordan River.* The principal river in the Holy Land, beginning in the snows of Mount Hermon and ending in the Dead Sea. Its closest point to Jerusalem is about 20 miles.

1:6 *camel's hair . . . leather belt.* Worn by Elijah and other prophets (2 Kin 1:8; cf. Zech 13:4). *locusts and wild honey.* See note on Matt 3:4.

1:7 *preaching.* Mark's account of John's preaching is brief (cf. Matt 3:7–12; Luke 3:7–17) and focuses on the coming of the mighty One.

1:8 *baptize you with the Holy Spirit.* See note on Matt 3:11.

1:9 *In those days.* Jesus probably began His public ministry c. A.D. 27, when He was approximately 30 years old (Luke 3:23). As far as we know, He had spent most of His previous life in Nazareth. *Nazareth.* See note on Matt 2:23. *baptized by John.* For the significance of Jesus' baptism see Matt 3:15 and note.

1:10–11 All three persons of the Trinity are involved: (1) the Father speaks, (2) the Son is baptized, and (3) the Holy Spirit descends on the Son.

1:10 *the Spirit . . . descending on Him.* Jesus' anointing for ministry—an anointing He claimed in the synagogue at Nazareth (Luke 4:18). *like a dove.* Symbolizing the gentleness, purity and guilelessness of the Holy Spirit (see Matt 10:16).

1:11 An allusion to Ps 2:7 and Is 42:1. *a voice.* God sometimes spoke directly from heaven (see 9:7; John 12:28–29). *You are My beloved Son.* In v. 1 Mark proclaims Jesus as the Son of God; here God the Father Himself proclaims Jesus as His Son.

1:12 *Immediately.* A distinctive characteristic of Mark's style is his use (some 47 times) of this Greek word that is also translated as "just then" (v. 23).

1:13 *forty.* See note on Matt 4:2. *tempted.* See notes on Matt 4:1–11. *Satan.* See notes on Gen 3:1; Zech 3:1; Rev 2:9–10; 12:9–10. *wild beasts.* In Jesus' day there were many more wild animals—including lions—in Israel than today. Only Mark reports their presence in this connection; he emphasizes that God kept Jesus safe in the wilderness. *angels were ministering to Him.* As they had attended Israel in the wilderness (see Ex 23:20,23; 32:34).

1:14 *after John had been taken into custody.* See Matt 4:12 and note on Luke 3:20. *the gospel of God.* The good news from, as well as about, God.

1:15 *the kingdom of God.* See note on Matt 3:2. *is at hand.* The coming of Christ (the King) brings the kingdom near to the people.

Galilee, He saw Simon and Andrew, the
brother of Simon, casting a net in the sea; for
they were fishermen.
17 And Jesus said to them, "Follow Me,
and I will make you become fishers of men."
18 Immediately they left their nets and followed Him.
19 Going on a little farther, He saw [1]James
the son of Zebedee, and John his brother,
who were also in the boat mending the nets.
20 Immediately He called them; and they
left their father Zebedee in the boat with the
hired servants, and went away [1]to follow Him.
21 [a]They *went into Capernaum; and
immediately on the Sabbath [b]He entered the
synagogue and *began* to teach.
22 [a]They were amazed at His teaching; for
He was teaching them as *one* having authority, and not as the scribes.
23 Just then there was a man in their synagogue with an unclean spirit; and he cried
out,
24 saying, "[a]What [1]business do we have
with each other, Jesus [2]of [b]Nazareth? Have
You come to destroy us? I know who You
are—[c]the Holy One of God!"
25 And Jesus rebuked him, saying, "Be
quiet, and come out of him!"
26 Throwing him into convulsions, the
unclean spirit cried out with a loud voice
and came out of him.
27 They were all [a]amazed, so that they
debated among themselves, saying, "What is
this? A new teaching with authority! He
commands even the unclean spirits, and they
obey Him."

19 [1]Or *Jacob*
20 [1]Lit *after Him*
21 [a]Mark 1:21-28: *Luke 4:31-37* [b]Matt 4:23; Mark 1:39; 10:1
22 [a]Matt 7:28
24 [1]Lit *What to us and to You* (a Heb idiom) [2]Lit *the Nazarene* [a]Matt 8:29 [b]Matt 2:23; Mark 10:47; 14:67; 16:6; Luke 4:34; 24:19; Acts 24:5 [c]Luke 1:35; 4:34; John 6:69; Acts 3:14
27 [a]Mark 10:24, 32; 16:5, 6

29 [1]*Or Jacob* [a]Mark 1:29-31: *Matt 8:14, 15; Luke 4:38, 39* [b]Mark 1:21, 23
30 [1]Lit *Him*
31 [1]Or *served*
32 [a]Mark 1:32-34: *Matt 8:16, 17; Luke 4:40, 41* [b]Matt 8:16; Luke 4:40 [c]Matt 4:24
33 [a]Mark 1:21
34 [a]Matt 4:23
35 [a]Mark 1:35-38: *Luke 4:42, 43* [b]Matt 14:23; Luke 5:16

28 Immediately the news about Him
spread everywhere into all the surrounding
district of Galilee.

Crowds Healed

29 [a]And immediately after they came [b]out
of the synagogue, they came into the house
of Simon and Andrew, with [1]James and
John.
30 Now Simon's mother-in-law was lying
sick with a fever; and immediately they
*spoke to [1]Jesus about her.
31 And He came to her and raised her up,
taking her by the hand, and the fever left her,
and she [1]waited on them.
32 [a]When evening came, [b]after the sun
had set, they *began* bringing to Him all who
were ill and those who were [c]demon-pos-
sessed.
33 And the whole [a]city had gathered at
the door.
34 And He [a]healed many who were ill
with various diseases, and cast out many
demons; and He was not permitting the
demons to speak, because they knew who
He was.
35 [a]In the early morning, while it was still
dark, Jesus got up, left *the house,* and went
away to a secluded place, and [b]was praying
there.
36 Simon and his companions searched
for Him;
37 they found Him, and *said to Him,
"Everyone is looking for You."
38 He *said to them, "Let us go somewhere else to the towns nearby, so that I may

1:16 *Sea of Galilee.* A beautiful lake, almost 700 feet below sea level, 14 miles long and 6 miles wide, fed by the waters of the upper Jordan River. It was also called the Lake of Gennesaret (Luke 5:1) and the Sea of Tiberias (John 6:1; 21:1). In OT times it was known as the Sea of Chinnereth (e.g., Num 34:11). *Simon.* Probably a contraction of the OT name Simeon. Jesus gave Simon the name Peter (3:16; Matt 16:18; John 1:42). *net.* See note on Matt 4:18.

1:17 *Follow Me.* The call to discipleship is definite and demands a response of total commitment. This was not Jesus' first encounter with Simon and Andrew (see John 1:35–42). *fishers of men.* Evangelists (see Luke 5:10).

1:21 *Capernaum.* See note on Matt 4:13. *synagogue.* A very important religious institution among the Jews of that day. Originating during the exile, it provided a place where Jews could study the Scriptures and worship God. A synagogue could be established in any town where there were at least ten married Jewish men. *began to teach.* Jesus, like Paul (see Acts 13:15; 14:1; 17:2; 18:4), took advantage of the custom that allowed visiting teachers to participate in the worship service by invitation of the synagogue leaders.

1:22 *amazed.* Mark frequently reported the amazement that Jesus' teaching and actions produced (see 2:12; 5:20,42; 6:2,51; 7:37; 10:26; 11:18; see also 15:5). In these instances it was Christ's inherent authority that amazed. He did not quote human authorities, as did the teachers of the law, because his authority was directly from God. *scribes.* See note on Matt 2:4.

1:23 *a man in their synagogue . . . cried out.* It was actually the demon who cried out. *with an unclean spirit.* Demonic possession intended to torment and destroy those who are created in God's image, but the demon recognized that Jesus was a powerful adversary, capable of destroying the forces of Satan.

1:24 *the Holy One of God.* Apart from the parallel in Luke 4:34, the title is used elsewhere only in John 6:69 and points to Christ's divine origin rather than His Messiahship (see Luke 1:35). The name was perhaps used by the demons in accordance with the occult belief that the precise use of a person's name gave certain control over him. The man was possessed by more than one demon (see 5:9), but only one spoke.

1:25 *Be quiet.* Lit. "Be muzzled!" Jesus' superior power silences the shrieks of the demon-possessed man.

1:27 *with authority.* Jesus' authority in how He taught (v. 22) and in what He did (here) impressed the people.

1:29 *into the house of Simon and Andrew.* Jesus and the disciples probably went there for a meal, since the main Sabbath meal was served immediately following the synagogue service.

1:30 *Simon's mother-in-law.* 1 Cor 9:5 speaks of Peter's being married.

1:32 *they began bringing.* They waited until the Sabbath was over (after sunset) before carrying anything (see Jer 17:21–22).

1:34 *because they knew who He was.* Luke says, "because they knew Him to be the Christ" (Luke 4:41). Jesus probably wanted first to show by word and deed the kind of Messiah He was (in contrast to popular notions) before He clearly declared Himself, and He would not let the demons frustrate this intent.

1:36 *companions.* Andrew, James, John and perhaps Philip and Nathanael (cf. John 1:43–45).

[1]preach there also; for that is what I came for."

39 [a]And He went into their synagogues throughout all Galilee, [1]preaching and casting out the demons.

40 [a]And a leper *came to Jesus, beseeching Him and [b]falling on his knees before Him, and saying, "If You are willing, You can make me clean."

41 Moved with compassion, Jesus stretched out His hand and touched him, and *said to him, "I am willing; be cleansed."

42 Immediately the leprosy left him and he was cleansed.

43 And He sternly warned him and immediately sent him away,

44 and He *said to him, "[a]See that you say nothing to anyone; but [a]go, show yourself to the priest and [b]offer for your cleansing what Moses commanded, as a testimony to them."

45 But he went out and began to [a]proclaim it freely and to [a]spread the news around, to such an extent that [1]Jesus could no longer publicly enter a city, but [2]stayed out in unpopulated areas; and [b]they were coming to Him from everywhere.

The Paralytic Healed

2 When He had come back to Capernaum several days afterward, it was heard that He was at home.

2 And [a]many were gathered together, so that there was no longer room, not even near the door; and He was speaking the word to them.

3 [a]And they *came, bringing to Him a [b]paralytic, carried by four men.

38 [1]Or *proclaim*
39 [1]Or *proclaiming* [a]Matt 4:23; 9:35; Mark 1:23; 3:1
40 [a]Mark 1:40-44: *Matt 8:2-4; Luke 5:12-14* [b]Matt 8:2; Mark 10:17; Luke 5:12
44 [a]Matt 8:4 [b]Lev 14:1-32
45 [1]Lit *He* [2]Lit *was* [a]Matt 28:15; Luke 5:15 [b]Mark 2:2, 13; 3:7; Luke 5:17; John 6:2
2:2 [a]Mark 1:45; 2:13
3 [a]Mark 2:3-12: *Matt 9:2-8; Luke 5:18-26* [b]Matt 4:24
4 [1]Lit *bring to* [2]Lit *where He was* [a]Luke 5:19 [b]Matt 4:24
5 [1]Lit *child* [a]Matt 9:2
7 [1]Lit *if not one, God* [a]Is 43:25
8 [1]Lit *by*
9 [a]Matt 4:24
12 [a]Matt 9:8 [b]Matt 9:33
13 [1]Lit *crowd* [a]Mark 1:45
14 [1]also called *Matthew* [a]Mark 2:14-17: *Matt 9:9-13; Luke 5:27-32* [b]Matt 9:9

4 Being unable to [1]get to Him because of the crowd, they [a]removed the roof [2]above Him; and when they had dug an opening, they let down the pallet on which the [b]paralytic was lying.

5 And Jesus seeing their faith *said to the paralytic, "[1]Son, [a]your sins are forgiven."

6 But some of the scribes were sitting there and reasoning in their hearts,

7 "Why does this man speak that way? He is blaspheming; [a]who can forgive sins [1]but God alone?"

8 Immediately Jesus, aware [1]in His spirit that they were reasoning that way within themselves, *said to them, "Why are you reasoning about these things in your hearts?

9 "Which is easier, to say to the [a]paralytic, 'Your sins are forgiven'; or to say, 'Get up, and pick up your pallet and walk'?

10 "But so that you may know that the Son of Man has authority on earth to forgive sins"—He *said to the paralytic,

11 "I say to you, get up, pick up your pallet and go home."

12 And he got up and immediately picked up the pallet and went out in the sight of everyone, so that they were all amazed and [a]were glorifying God, saying, "[b]We have never seen anything like this."

13 And He went out again by the seashore; and [a]all the [1]people were coming to Him, and He was teaching them.

Levi (Matthew) Called

14 [a]As He passed by, He saw [1b]Levi the *son* of Alphaeus sitting in the tax booth, and

---

1:39 *throughout all Galilee.* The first of what seem to be three tours of Galilee (second tour, Luke 8:1; third tour, Mark 6:6 and Matt 11:1).
1:40 *leper.* See Lev 13–14.
1:41 *touched him.* An act that, according to Mosaic law, brought defilement (see Lev 13, especially vv. 45–46; cf. Lev 5:2). Jesus' compassion for the man superseded ceremonial considerations.
1:44 *say nothing to anyone.* See notes on Matt 8:4; 16:20. *go, show yourself to the priest.* See note on Luke 5:14. *a testimony to them.* The sacrifices were to be evidence to the priests and the people that the cure was real and that Jesus respected the law. The healing was also a testimony to Jesus' divine power, since Jews believed that only God could cure leprosy (see 2 Kin 5:1–14).
1:45 *no longer publicly enter a city.* Jesus' growing popularity with the people (see 1:28; 3:7–8; Luke 7:17) and the increasing opposition from Jewish leaders (see 2:6–7,16,23–24; 3:2,6,22) finally made it necessary for Him to withdraw from Galilee into surrounding territories.
2:1 *home.* When in Capernaum, Jesus probably made His home at Peter's house (see 1:21,29).
2:2 *many were gathered together.* The same enthusiasm that greeted Jesus earlier (1:32–33,37) was evident at His return.
2:3 *a paralytic.* Nothing definite can be said about the nature of the man's affliction beyond the fact that he could not walk. The determination of the four men to reach Jesus suggests that his condition was desperate.
2:4 *they removed the roof.* A typical Palestinian house had a flat roof accessible by means of an outside staircase. The roof was often made of a thick layer of clay (packed with a stone roller), supported by mats of branches across wood beams.
2:5 *And Jesus seeing their faith.* Jesus recognized that the bold action of the paralyzed man and his friends gave evidence of faith. *Son, your sins are forgiven.* Jesus first met the man's deepest need: forgiveness.
2:7 *He is blaspheming; who can forgive sins but God alone?* In Jewish theology even the Messiah could not forgive sins, and Jesus' forgiveness of sin was a claim to deity—which they considered to be blasphemous (see note on 14:64).
2:9 *Which is easier . . . ?* Jesus' point probably was that neither forgiving sins nor healing was easier. Both are equally impossible to men and equally easy to God.
2:10 *But so that you may know.* Probably spoken to the teachers of the law. The words "He said to the paralytic" are parenthetical to explain a change in the persons addressed. For a discussion of the title "Son of Man" see note on 8:31. It is clear that one purpose of miracles was to give evidence of Jesus' deity. See the use of miraculous signs in John's Gospel (2:11; 20:30–31).
2:12 *they were all amazed.* See note on 1:22.
2:14 *Levi the son of Alphaeus.* Matthew (see Matt 9:9; 10:3). His given name was probably Levi, and Matthew ("gift of the LORD") his apostolic name. *tax booth.* Levi was a tax collector (see note on Luke 3:12) under Herod Antipas, tetrarch of Galilee. The tax collector's booth where Jesus found Levi was probably a toll

He *said to him, "[c]Follow Me!" And he got
up and followed Him.
15 And it *[1]happened that He was reclining *at the table* in his house, and many tax
collectors and [2]sinners [3]were dining with
Jesus and His disciples; for there were many
of them, and they were following Him.
16 When [a]the scribes of the Pharisees saw
that He was eating with the sinners and tax
collectors, they said to His disciples, "[b]Why
is He eating and drinking with tax collectors
and [1]sinners?"
17 And hearing *this*, Jesus *said to them,
"[a]*It is* not those who are healthy who need a
physician, but those who are sick; I did not
come to call the righteous, but sinners."
18 [a]John's disciples and the Pharisees
were fasting; and they *came and *said to
Him, "Why do John's disciples and the disciples of the Pharisees fast, but Your disciples do not fast?"
19 And Jesus said to them, "While the
bridegroom is with them, [1]the attendants of
the bridegroom cannot fast, can they? So
long as they have the bridegroom with them,
they cannot fast.
20 "But the [a]days will come when the
bridegroom is taken away from them, and
then they will fast in that day.

14 [c]Matt 8:22
15 [1]Lit *happens* [2]I.e. irreligious Jews [3]Lit *were reclining with*
16 [1]I.e. irreligious Jews [a]Luke 5:30; Acts 23:9 [b]Matt 9:11
17 [a]Matt 9:12, 13; Luke 5:31, 32
18 [a]Mark 2:18-22: *Matt 9:14-17; Luke 5:33-38*
19 [1]Lit *sons of the bridal-chamber*
20 [a]Matt 9:15; Luke 17:22
21 [1]Lit *that which is put on* [2]Lit *that which fills up*
23 [a]Mark 2:23-28: *Matt 12:1-8; Luke 6:1-5* [b]Deut 23:25
24 [a]Matt 12:2
26 [1]Or *showbread;* lit *loaves of presentation* [a]1 Sam 21:1; 2 Sam 8:17; 1 Chr 24:6 [b]Lev 24:9
27 [1]Or *came into being* [2]Lit *because for the sake of* [a]Ex 23:12; Deut 5:14 [b]Col 2:16

21 "No one sews [1]a patch of unshrunk
cloth on an old garment; otherwise [2]the
patch pulls away from it, the new from the
old, and a worse tear results.
22 "No one puts new wine into old wineskins; otherwise the wine will burst the
skins, and the wine is lost and the skins *as*
well; but *one puts* new wine into fresh wineskins."

Question of the Sabbath

23 [a]And it happened that He was passing
through the grainfields on the Sabbath, and
His disciples began to make their way along
while [b]picking the heads *of grain.*
24 The Pharisees were saying to Him,
"Look, [a]why are they doing what is not lawful on the Sabbath?"
25 And He *said to them, "Have you never read what David did when he was in need
and he and his companions became hungry;
26 how he entered the house of God in the
time of [a]Abiathar *the* high priest, and ate the
[1]consecrated bread, which [b]is not lawful for
anyone to eat except the priests, and he also
gave it to those who were with him?"
27 Jesus said to them, "[a]The Sabbath
[1]was made [2]for man, and [b]not man [2]for the
Sabbath.

---

booth on the major international road that went from Damascus through Capernaum to the Mediterranean coast and to Egypt (see the "way of the sea," Is 9:1). *he got up and followed.* See note on Luke 5:28.

2:15 *sinners.* Notoriously evil people as well as those who refused to follow the Mosaic law as interpreted by the scribes. The term was commonly used of tax collectors, adulterers, robbers and the like. *were dining.* To eat with a person was a sign of friendship.

2:16 *scribes of the Pharisees.* Not all scribes were Pharisees—successors of the Hasidim, pious Jews who joined forces with the Maccabees during the struggle for freedom from Syrian oppression (166–142 B.C.). They first appear under the name Pharisees during the reign of John Hyrcanus (135–105). Although some, no doubt, were godly, most of those who came into conflict with Jesus were hypocritical, envious, rigid and formalistic. According to Pharisaism, God's grace extended only to those who kept his law. See notes on Matt 3:7; Luke 5:17. *tax collectors.* Jewish tax collectors were regarded as outcasts. They could not serve as witnesses or as judges and were expelled from the synagogue. In the eyes of the Jewish community their disgrace extended to their families. See note on Matt 5:46.

2:17 *I did not come to call the righteous, but sinners.* A self-righteous man does not realize his need for salvation, but an admitted sinner does.

2:18 *John's disciples.* John the Baptist's disciples may have been fasting because he was in prison (see 1:14), or this may have been a practice among them as an expression of repentance, intended to hasten the coming of redemption announced by John. *fasting.* In the Mosaic law only the fast of the day of atonement was required (Lev 16:29,31; 23:27–32; Num 29:7). After the Babylonian exile four other yearly fasts were observed by the Jews (Zech 7:5; 8:19). In Jesus' time the Pharisees fasted twice a week (see Luke 18:12). *disciples of the Pharisees.* Pharisees as such were not teachers, but some were also "scribes" (teachers of the law), who often had disciples. Or perhaps the phrase is used in a nontechnical way to refer to people influenced by the Pharisees.

2:19 *While the bridegroom is with them, the attendants of the bridegroom cannot fast, can they?* Jesus compared his disciples with the guests of a bridegroom. A Jewish wedding was a particularly joyous occasion, and the celebration associated with it often lasted a week. It was unthinkable to fast during such festivities, because fasting was associated with sorrow.

2:20 *when the bridegroom is taken away from them.* Jesus is the bridegroom, who would be taken from them by death, and then fasting would be in order.

2:22 *fresh wineskins.* See note on Matt 9:17.

2:23 *picking the heads of grain.* There was nothing wrong in the action itself, which comes under the provision of Deut 23:25.

2:24 *what is not lawful on the Sabbath.* According to Jewish tradition (in the Mishnah), harvesting (which is what Jesus' disciples technically were doing) was forbidden on the Sabbath. See Ex 34:21.

2:25 *what David did.* See 1 Sam 21:1–6. The relationship between the OT incident and the apparent infringement of the Sabbath by the disciples lies in the fact that on both occasions godly men did something forbidden. Since, however, it is always "lawful" to do good and to save life (even on the Sabbath), both David and the disciples were within the spirit of the law (see Is 58:6–7; Luke 6:6–11; 13:10–17; 14:1–6).

2:26 *in the time of Abiathar the high priest.* According to 1 Sam 21:1, Ahimelech, Abiathar's father, was then high priest (see note on 2 Sam 8:17). *consecrated bread.* See note on Matt 12:4.

2:27 *The Sabbath was made for man, and not man for the Sabbath.* Jewish tradition had so multiplied the requirements and restrictions for keeping the Sabbath that the burden had become intolerable. Jesus cut across these traditions and emphasized the God-given purpose of the Sabbath—a day intended for man (for spiritual, mental and physical restoration; see Ex 20:8–11).

28 "So the Son of Man is Lord even of the
Sabbath."

Jesus Heals on the Sabbath

3 [a]He [b]entered again into a synagogue; and
a man was there whose hand was withered.
2 [a]They were watching Him *to see* if He
would heal him on the Sabbath, [b]so that
they might accuse Him.
3 He *said to the man with the withered
hand, "[1]Get up and come forward!"
4 And He *said to them, "Is it lawful to
do good or to do harm on the Sabbath, to
save a life or to kill?" But they kept silent.
5 After [a]looking around at them with
anger, grieved at their hardness of heart, He
*said to the man, "Stretch out your hand."
And he stretched it out, and his hand was
restored.
6 The Pharisees went out and immediately *began* [1]conspiring with the [a]Herodians
against Him, *as to* how they might destroy
Him.
7 [a]Jesus withdrew to the sea with His
disciples; and [b]a great multitude from Galilee
followed; and *also* from Judea,
8 and from Jerusalem, and from [a]Idu-
mea, and beyond the Jordan, and the vicinity of [b]Tyre and Sidon, a great number of people heard of all that He was doing and came
to Him.
9 [a]And He told His disciples that a boat
should stand ready for Him because of the
crowd, so that they would not crowd Him;
10 for He had [a]healed many, with the
result that all those who had [b]afflictions
pressed around Him in order to [c]touch Him.
11 Whenever the unclean spirits saw Him,
they would fall down before Him and shout,
"You are [a]the Son of God!"
12 And He [a]earnestly warned them not to
[1]tell who He was.

The Twelve Are Chosen

13 And He *went up on [a]the mountain
and *[b]summoned those whom He Himself
wanted, and they came to Him.
14 And He appointed twelve, so that they
would be with Him and that He *could* send
them out to preach,
15 and to have authority to cast out the
demons.
16 And He appointed the twelve: [a]Simon
(to whom He gave the name Peter),
17 and [1]James, the *son* of Zebedee, and
John the brother of [1]James (to them He gave
the name Boanerges, which means, "Sons of
Thunder");
18 and Andrew, and Philip, and
Bartholomew, and Matthew, and Thomas,
and [1]James the son of Alphaeus, and Thaddaeus, and Simon the [2]Zealot;
19 and Judas Iscariot, who betrayed Him.
20 And He *came [1][a]home, and the [b]crowd
*gathered again, [c]to such an extent that they
could not even eat [2]a meal.

3:1 [a]Mark 3:1-6: *Matt 12:9-14; Luke 6:6-11* [b]Mark 1:21, 39
2 [a]Luke 6:7; 14:1; 20:20 [b]Matt 12:10; Luke 6:7; 11:54
3 [1]Lit *Arise into the midst*
5 [a]Luke 6:10
6 [1]Lit *giving counsel* [a]Matt 22:16; Mark 12:13
7 [a]Mark 3:7-12: *Matt 12:15, 16; Luke 6:17-19* [b]Matt 4:25; Luke 6:17
8 [a]Josh 15:1, 21; Ezek 35:15; 36:5 [b]Matt 11:21
9 [a]Mark 4:1; Luke 5:1-3
10 [a]Matt 4:23 [b]Mark 5:29, 34; Luke 7:21 [c]Matt 9:21; 14:36; Mark 6:56; 8:22
11 [a]Matt 4:3
12 [1]Lit *make Him known* [a]Matt 8:4
13 [a]Matt 5:1; Luke 6:12 [b]Matt 10:1; Mark 6:7; Luke 9:1
16 [a]Mark 3:16-19: *Matt 10:2-4; Luke 6:14-16;* Acts 1:13
17 [1]Or *Jacob*
18 [1]Or *Jacob* [2]Or *Cananaean*
20 [1]Lit *into a house* [2]Lit *bread* [a]Mark 2:1; 7:17; 9:28 [b]Mark 1:45; 3:7 [c]Mark 6:31

2:28 See note on Luke 6:5.

3:1–6 A demonstration that Jesus is Lord of the Sabbath (see 2:28).

3:2 *They.* The Pharisees (v. 6; cf. Luke 6:7). *to see if He would heal him on the Sabbath.* An indication that the Pharisees believed in Jesus' power to perform miracles. The question was not "Could he?" but "Would he?" Jewish tradition prescribed that aid could be given the sick on the Sabbath only when the person's life was threatened, which obviously was not the case here. See notes on 2:25; Luke 13:14. *might accuse Him.* Jesus' presence demanded a decision about His preaching, His acts and His person. The hostility, first seen in 2:6–7, continues to spread. See note on v. 6.

3:4 *to do good or to do harm on the Sabbath, to save a life or to kill?* Jesus asks: Which is better, to preserve life by healing or to destroy life by refusing to heal? The question is ironic since, whereas Jesus was ready to heal, the Pharisees were plotting to put Him to death. It is obvious who was guilty of breaking the Sabbath. *they kept silent.* See 12:34.

3:6 *The Pharisees . . . began conspiring.* The decision to seek Jesus' death was not the result of this incident alone, but was the response to a series of incidents (see 2:6–7,16–17,24). The plotting of the Pharisees and the Herodians is seen again on Tuesday of Passion Week (12:13). *Herodians.* Influential Jews who favored the Herodian dynasty, meaning they were supporters of Rome, from which the Herods received their authority. They joined the Pharisees in opposing Jesus because they feared He might have an unsettling political influence on the people. See note on Matt 22:15–17.

3:8 Here we see impressive evidence of Jesus' rapidly growing popularity among the people. This geographical list indicates that the crowds came not only from the areas in the vicinity of Capernaum but also from considerable distances. The regions mentioned included virtually all of Israel and its surrounding neighbors. Mark tells of Jesus' work in all these regions except Idumea (see 1:14, Galilee; 5:1 and 10:1, the region across the Jordan; 7:24,31, Tyre and Sidon; 10:1, Judea; 11:11, Jerusalem). *Idumea.* The Greek form of the Hebrew "Edom," but here referring to an area south of Judea, not to earlier Edomite territory. (See map, p. 1465.)

3:11 *the unclean spirits.* See note on 1:23. *You are the Son of God!* The evil spirits recognized who Jesus was, but they did not believe in Him (see note on 1:24).

3:12 *not to tell who He was.* The time for revealing Jesus' identity had not yet come (see 1:34 and note; see also notes on Matt 8:4; 16:20), and demons were hardly the proper channel for such disclosure.

3:14 *that they would be with Him.* The training of the twelve included not only instruction and practice in various forms of ministry but also continuous association and intimate fellowship with Jesus Himself.

3:16–19 See notes on Luke 6:14–16.

3:17 *Sons of Thunder.* Probably descriptive of their dispositions (see notes on 10:37; Luke 9:54–55).

3:18 *Thaddaeus.* Apparently the same as "Judas son of James" (see Luke 6:16; Acts 1:13). *the Zealot.* See note on Matt 10:4.

3:19 *Iscariot.* Probably means "the man from Kerioth," the town Kerioth-hezron (Josh 15:25), 12 miles south of Hebron (Jer 48:24). For Judas's betrayal of Jesus see 14:10–11,43–46.

3:20 *home.* Probably the home of Peter and Andrew (see 1:29; 2:1).

21 When [a]His own [1]people heard *of this,*
they went out to take custody of Him; for
they were saying, "[b]He has lost His senses."
22 The scribes who came down [a]from
Jerusalem were saying, "He is possessed by
[1b]Beelzebul," and "[c]He casts out the demons
by the ruler of the demons."
23 [a]And He called them to Himself and
began speaking to them in [b]parables, "How
can [c]Satan cast out Satan?
24 "If a kingdom is divided against itself,
that kingdom cannot stand.
25 "If a house is divided against itself, that
house will not be able to stand.
26 "If [a]Satan has risen up against himself
and is divided, he cannot stand, but [1]he is
finished!
27 "[a]But no one can enter the strong man's
house and plunder his property unless he
first binds the strong man, and then he will
plunder his house.
28 "[a]Truly I say to you, all sins shall be forgiven the sons of men, and whatever blasphemies they utter;
29 but [a]whoever blasphemes against the
Holy Spirit never has forgiveness, but is
guilty of an eternal sin"—
30 because they were saying, "He has an
unclean spirit."
31 [a]Then His mother and His brothers
*arrived, and standing outside they sent
word to Him and called Him.
32 A crowd was sitting around Him, and
they *said to Him, "Behold, Your mother and
Your brothers are outside looking for You."
33 Answering them, He *said, "Who are
My mother and My brothers?"
34 Looking about at those who were sitting around Him, He *said, "[a]Behold My
mother and My brothers!
35 "For whoever [a]does the will of God, he
is My brother and sister and mother."

21 [1]Or *kinsmen* [a]Mark 3:31f [b]John 10:20; Acts 26:24
22 [1]Or *Beezebul;* others read *Beelzebub* [a]Matt 15:1 [b]Matt 10:25; 11:18 [c]Matt 9:34
23 [a]Mark 3:23-27: *Matt 12:25-29; Luke 11:17-22* [b]Matt 13:3ff; Mark 4:2ff [c]Matt 4:10
26 [1]Lit *he has an end* [a]Matt 4:10
27 [a]Is 49:24, 25
28 [a]Matt 12:31, 32; Mark 3:28-30; Luke 12:10
29 [a]Luke 12:10
31 [a]Mark 3:31-35: *Matt 12:46-50; Luke 8:19-21*
34 [a]Matt 12:49
35 [a]Eph 6:6; Heb 10:36; 1 Pet 4:2; 1 John 2:17

4:1 [a]Mark 4:1-12: *Matt 13:1-15; Luke 8:4-10* [b]Mark 2:13; 3:7 [c]Luke 5:1-3
2 [a]Matt 13:3ff; Mark 3:23; 4:2ff
9 [1]Or *hear!;* or *listen!* [a]Matt 11:15; Mark 4:23; Rev 2:7, 11, 17, 29
10 [1]Lit *those about Him*
11 [a]1 Cor 5:12f; Col 4:5; 1 Thess 4:12; 1 Tim 3:7 [b]Mark 3:23; 4:2
12 [a]Is 6:9f; 43:8; Jer 5:21; Ezek 12:2; Matt 13:14; Luke 8:10; John 12:40; Rom 11:8

Parable of the Sower and Soils

4 [a]He began to teach again [b]by the sea.
And such a very large crowd gathered to
Him that [c]He got into a boat in the sea and
sat down; and the whole crowd was by the
sea on the land.
2 And He was teaching them many
things in [a]parables, and was saying to them
in His teaching,
3 "Listen *to this!* Behold, the sower went
out to sow;
4 as he was sowing, some *seed* fell
beside the road, and the birds came and ate
it up.
5 "Other *seed* fell on the rocky *ground*
where it did not have much soil; and immediately it sprang up because it had no depth
of soil.
6 "And after the sun had risen, it was
scorched; and because it had no root, it
withered away.
7 "Other *seed* fell among the thorns, and
the thorns came up and choked it, and it
yielded no crop.
8 "Other *seeds* fell into the good soil, and
as they grew up and increased, they yielded
a crop and produced thirty, sixty, and a hundredfold."
9 And He was saying, "[a]He who has ears
to hear, [1]let him hear."
10 As soon as He was alone, [1]His followers, along with the twelve, *began* asking Him
about the parables.
11 And He was saying to them, "To you
has been given the mystery of the kingdom
of God, but [a]those who are outside get
everything [b]in parables,
12 so that [a]WHILE SEEING, THEY MAY SEE AND
NOT PERCEIVE, AND WHILE HEARING, THEY MAY
HEAR AND NOT UNDERSTAND, OTHERWISE THEY
MIGHT RETURN AND BE FORGIVEN."

3:21 *His own people . . . went out to take custody of Him.* No doubt they had come to Capernaum from Nazareth, some 30 miles away (see v. 31).
3:22 *Beelzebul.* See note on Matt 10:25.
3:23 *parables.* In this context the word is used in the general sense of comparisons (see note on 4:2).
3:27 *enter the strong man's house and plunder his property.* Jesus was doing this very thing when He freed people from Satan's control.
3:28 *Truly I say to you.* A solemn affirmation used by Jesus to strengthen His assertions (see 8:12; 9:1,41; 10:15,29; 11:23; 12:43; 13:30; 14:9,18,25,30).
3:29 *whoever blasphemes against the Holy Spirit never has forgiveness.* Jesus identifies this sin in v. 30 (cf. v. 22)—the teachers of the law attributed Jesus' healing to Satan's power rather than to the Holy Spirit (see note on Matt 12:31).
3:31 *His mother and His brothers.* See note on Luke 8:19.
3:35 *whoever does the will of God.* Membership in God's spiritual family, evidenced by obedience to Him, is more important than membership in our human families (see note on 10:30).
4:1 *sat down.* Sitting was the usual position for Jewish teachers (see Matt 5:1; Luke 5:3; John 8:2).
4:2 *parables.* Usually stories out of ordinary life used to illustrate spiritual or moral truth, sometimes in the form of brief similes, comparisons (see note on 3:23), analogies or proverbial sayings. Ordinarily they had a single main point, and not every detail was meant to have significance. See notes on Matt 13:3; Luke 8:4.
4:3–8 In that day seed was broadcast by hand—which, by its nature, scattered some seed on unproductive ground (see note on Luke 8:5).
4:8 *produced . . . a hundredfold.* A hundredfold yield was an unusually productive harvest (see Gen 26:12). Harvest was a common figure for the consummation of God's kingdom (see Joel 3:13; Rev 14:14–20).
4:11 *mystery of the kingdom of God.* In the NT "mystery" refers to something God has revealed to His people. The mystery (that which was previously unknown) is proclaimed to all, but only those who have faith understand. In this context the mystery seems to be that the kingdom of God had drawn near in the coming of Jesus Christ.
4:12 *so that.* Jesus likens His preaching in parables to the ministry of Isaiah, which, while it gained some disciples (Is 8:16), was also to expose the hardhearted resistance of the many to God's warning and appeal.

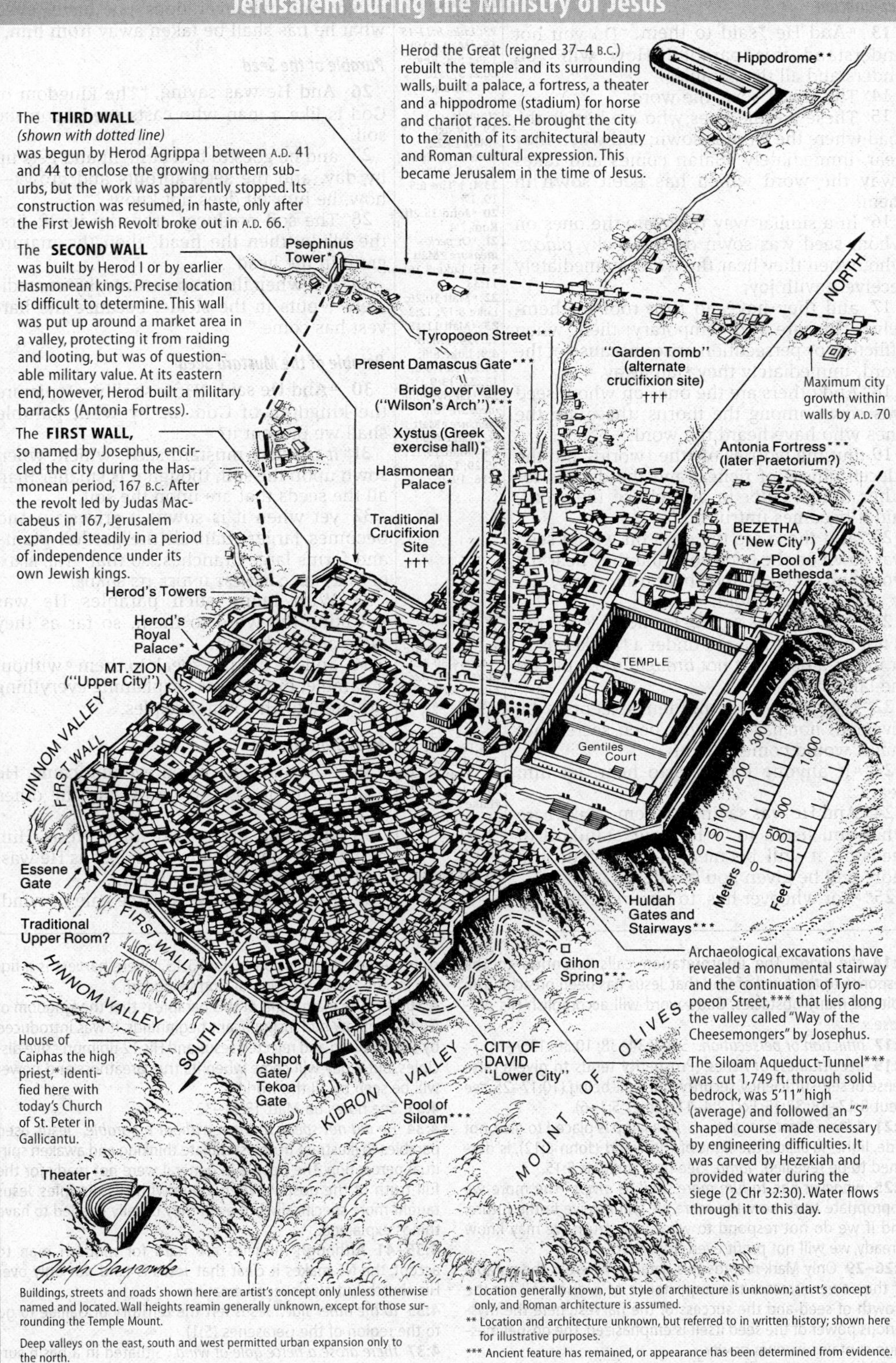

Jerusalem during the Ministry of Jesus
Herod the Great (reigned 37–4 B.C.) rebuilt the temple and its surrounding walls, built a palace, a fortress, a theater and a hippodrome (stadium) for horse and chariot races. He brought the city to the zenith of its architectural beauty and Roman cultural expression. This became Jerusalem in the time of Jesus.
Hippodrome**
The THIRD WALL (shown with dotted line) was begun by Herod Agrippa I between A.D. 41 and 44 to enclose the growing northern suburbs, but the work was apparently stopped. Its construction was resumed, in haste, only after the First Jewish Revolt broke out in A.D. 66.
The SECOND WALL was built by Herod I or by earlier Hasmonean kings. Precise location is difficult to determine. This wall was put up around a market area in a valley, protecting it from raiding and looting, but was of questionable military value. At its eastern end, however, Herod built a military barracks (Antonia Fortress).
The FIRST WALL, so named by Josephus, encircled the city during the Hasmonean period, 167 B.C. After the revolt led by Judas Maccabeus in 167, Jerusalem expanded steadily in a period of independence under its own Jewish kings.
Psephinus Tower*
NORTH
Tyropoeon Street***
Present Damascus Gate***
"Garden Tomb" (alternate crucifixion site) †††
Maximum city growth within walls by A.D. 70
Bridge over valley ("Wilson's Arch")***
Xystus (Greek exercise hall)*
Hasmonean Palace*
Antonia Fortress*** (later Praetorium?)
Traditional Crucifixion Site †††
BEZETHA ("New City")
Pool of Bethesda***
Herod's Towers
Herod's Royal Palace*
MT. ZION ("Upper City")
TEMPLE
Gentiles Court
HINNOM VALLEY
FIRST WALL
Essene Gate
FIRST WALL
Traditional Upper Room?
HINNOM VALLEY
SOUTH
House of Caiphas the high priest,* identified here with today's Church of St. Peter in Gallicantu.
Ashpot Gate/ Tekoa Gate
KIDRON VALLEY
Pool of Siloam***
CITY OF DAVID "Lower City"
MOUNT OF OLIVES
Gihon Spring***
Huldah Gates and Stairways***
Meters 0 100 200 300
Feet 0 100 500 1,000
Archaeological excavations have revealed a monumental stairway and the continuation of Tyropoeon Street,*** that lies along the valley called "Way of the Cheesemongers" by Josephus.
The Siloam Aqueduct-Tunnel*** was cut 1,749 ft. through solid bedrock, was 5'11" high (average) and followed an "S" shaped course made necessary by engineering difficulties. It was carved by Hezekiah and provided water during the siege (2 Chr 32:30). Water flows through it to this day.
Theater**
Hugh Claycombe

Buildings, streets and roads shown here are artist's concept only unless otherwise named and located. Wall heights reamin generally unknown, except for those surrounding the Temple Mount.

Deep valleys on the east, south and west permitted urban expansion only to the north.

* Location generally known, but style of architecture is unknown; artist's concept only, and Roman architecture is assumed.

** Location and architecture unknown, but referred to in written history; shown here for illustrative purposes.

*** Ancient feature has remained, or appearance has been determined from evidence.

Explanation

13 [a]And He *said to them, "Do you not understand this parable? How will you understand all the parables?

14" The sower sows the word.

15" These are the ones who are beside the road where the word is sown; and when they hear, immediately [a]Satan comes and takes away the word which has been sown in them.

16" In a similar way these are the ones on whom seed was sown on the rocky *places,* who, when they hear the word, immediately receive it with joy;

17 and they have no *firm* root in themselves, but are *only* temporary; then, when affliction or persecution arises because of the word, immediately they [1]fall away.

18" And others are the ones on whom seed was sown among the thorns; these are the ones who have heard the word,

19 but the worries of [a]the [1]world, and the [b]deceitfulness of riches, and the desires for other things enter in and choke the word, and it becomes unfruitful.

20" And those are the ones on whom seed was sown on the good soil; and they hear the word and accept it and [a]bear fruit, thirty, sixty, and a hundredfold."

21 And He was saying to them, "[a]A lamp is not brought to be put under a [1]basket, is it, or under a bed? Is it not *brought* to be put on the lampstand?

22" [a]For nothing is hidden, except to be revealed; nor has *anything* been secret, but that it would come to light.

23" [a]If anyone has ears to hear, let him hear."

24 And He was saying to them, "Take care what you listen to. [1a]By your standard of measure it will be measured to you; and more will be given you besides.

25" [a]For whoever has, to him *more* shall be given; and whoever does not have, even what he has shall be taken away from him."

Parable of the Seed

26 And He was saying, "The kingdom of God is like a man who casts seed upon the soil;

27 and he goes to bed at night and gets up by day, and the seed sprouts and grows—how, he himself does not know.

28" The soil produces crops by itself; first the blade, then the head, then the mature grain in the head.

29" But when the crop permits, he immediately [1a]puts in the sickle, because the harvest has come."

Parable of the Mustard Seed

30 [a]And He said, "How shall we [1b]picture the kingdom of God, or by what parable shall we present it?

31" *It is* like a mustard seed, which, when sown upon the soil, though it is smaller than all the seeds that are upon the soil,

32 yet when it is sown, it grows up and becomes larger than all the garden plants and forms large branches; so that [a]THE BIRDS OF THE [1]AIR can NEST UNDER ITS SHADE."

33 With many such parables He was speaking the word to them, so far as they were able to hear it;

34 and He did not speak to them [a]without a parable; but He was [b]explaining everything privately to His own disciples.

Jesus Stills the Sea

35 [a]On that day, when evening came, He *said to them, "Let us go over to the other side."

36 [1]Leaving the crowd, they *took Him along with them [a]in the boat, just as He was; and other boats were with Him.

37 And there *arose a fierce gale of wind,

13 [a]Mark 4:13-20: *Matt 13:18-23; Luke 8:11-15* **15** [a]Matt 4:10f; 1 Pet 5:8; Rev 20:2, 3, 7-10 **17** [1]Lit *are caused to stumble* **19** [1]Or *age* [a]Matt 13:22; Rom 12:2; Eph 2:2; 6:12 [b]Prov 23:4; 1 Tim 6:9, 10, 17 **20** [a]John 15:2ff; Rom 7:4 **21** [1]Or *peck-measure* [a]Matt 5:15; Luke 8:16; 11:33 **22** [a]Matt 10:26; Luke 8:17; 12:2 **23** [a]Matt 11:15; 13:9, 43; Mark 4:9; Luke 8:8; 14:35; Rev 3:6, 13, 22; 13:9 **24** [1]Lit *By what measure you measure* [a]Matt 7:2; Luke 6:38 **25** [a]Matt 13:12; 25:29; Luke 8:18; 19:26

29 [1]Lit *sends forth* [a]Joel 3:13 **30** [1]Lit *compare* [a]Mark 4:30-32: *Matt 13:31, 32; Luke 13:18, 19* [b]Matt 13:24 **32** [1]Or *sky* [a]Ezek 17:23; Ps 104:12; Ezek 31:6; Dan 4:12 **34** [a]Matt 13:34; John 10:6; 16:25 [b]Luke 24:27 **35** [a]Mark 4:35-41: *Matt 8:18, 23-27; Luke 8:22, 25* **36** [1]Or *Sending away* [a]Mark 3:9; 4:1; 5:2, 21

4:14 *the word.* The interpretation calls attention to the response to the word of God that Jesus has been preaching. In spite of many obstacles, God's word will accomplish His purpose.

4:17 *affliction or persecution.* See 8:34–38; 10:30; 13:9–13.

4:19 *deceitfulness of riches.* Prosperity tends to give a false sense of self-sufficiency, security and well-being (10:17–25; see Deut 8:17–18; 32:15; Eccl 2:4–11; James 5:1–6).

4:21 *A lamp is not brought . . .* As a lamp is placed to give, not hide, light, so Jesus, the light of the world (John 8:12), is destined to be revealed. *lamp.* See note on Matt 5:15.

4:25 *whoever has, to him more shall be given.* The more we appropriate truth now, the more we will receive in the future; and if we do not respond to what little truth we may know already, we will not profit even from that.

4:26–29 Only Mark records this parable. Whereas the parable of the sower stresses the importance of proper soil for the growth of seed and the success of the harvest, here the mysterious power of the seed itself is emphasized. The gospel message contains its own power.

4:29 *he immediately puts in the sickle, because the harvest has come.* A possible allusion to Joel 3:13, where harvest is a figure for the consummation of God's kingdom.

4:30–34 The main point of this parable is that the kingdom of God seemingly had insignificant beginnings. It was introduced by the despised and rejected Jesus and His 12 unimpressive disciples. But a day will come when its true greatness and power will be seen by all the world.

4:31 See notes on Matt 13:31–32.

4:34 *He did not speak to them without a parable.* Jesus used parables to illustrate truths, stimulate thinking and awaken spiritual perception. The people in general were not ready for the full truth of the gospel. When alone with His disciples Jesus taught more specifically, but even they usually needed to have things explained.

4:35–41 Although miracles are hard for modern man to accept, the NT makes it clear that Jesus is Lord not only over His church but also over all creation.

4:35 *to the other side.* Jesus left the territory of Galilee to go to the region of the Gerasenes (5:1).

4:37 *there arose a fierce gale of wind.* Situated in a basin surrounded by mountains, the Sea of Galilee is particularly sus-

and the waves were breaking over the boat
so much that the boat was already filling up.
38 Jesus Himself was in the stern, asleep
on the cushion; and they *woke Him and
*said to Him, "Teacher, do You not care that
we are perishing?"
39 And He got up and [a]rebuked the wind
and said to the sea, "Hush, be still." And the
wind died down and [1]it became perfectly
calm.
40 And He said to them, "Why are you
[1]afraid? [a]Do you still have no faith?"
41 They became very much afraid and
said to one another, "Who then is this, that
even the wind and the sea obey Him?"

The Gerasene Demoniac

5 [a]They came to the other side of the sea,
into the country of the Gerasenes.
2 When He got out of [a]the boat, immediately a man from the tombs [b]with an
unclean spirit met Him,
3 and he had his dwelling among the
tombs. And no one was able to bind him
anymore, even with a chain;
4 because he had often been bound with
shackles and chains, and the chains had
been torn apart by him and the shackles broken in pieces, and no one was strong enough
to subdue him.
5 Constantly, night and day, he was
screaming among the tombs and in the
mountains, and gashing himself with stones.
6 Seeing Jesus from a distance, he ran up
and bowed down before Him;
7 and shouting with a loud voice, he

39 [1]Lit *a great calm occurred* [a]Ps 65:7; 89:9; 107:29; Matt 8:26; Luke 8:24
40 [1]Or *cowardly* [a]Matt 14:31; Luke 8:25
5:1 [a]Mark 5:1-17: *Matt 8:28-34; Luke 8:26-37*
2 [a]Mark 3:9; 4:1, 36; 5:21 [b]Mark 1:23
7 [1]Lit *What to me and to you* (a Heb idiom) [a]Matt 8:29 [b]Matt 4:3 [c]Luke 8:28; Acts 16:17; Heb 7:1
9 [a]Matt 26:53; Mark 5:15; Luke 8:30
11 [1]Lit *there*
15 [a]Matt 4:24; Mark 5:16, 18 [b]Luke 8:27 [c]Luke 8:35 [d]Mark 5:9
16 [a]Matt 4:24; Mark 5:15
17 [a]Matt 8:34; Acts 16:39
18 [a]Mark 5:18-20: *Luke 8:38, 39*

*said, "[1][a]What business do we have with
each other, Jesus, [b]Son of [c]the Most High
God? I implore You by God, do not torment
me!"
8 For He had been saying to him, "Come
out of the man, you unclean spirit!"
9 And He was asking him, "What is your
name?" And he *said to Him, "My name is
[a]Legion; for we are many."
10 And he *began* to implore Him earnestly
not to send them out of the country.
11 Now there was a large herd of swine
feeding [1]nearby on the mountain.
12 *The demons* implored Him, saying,
"Send us into the swine so that we may enter
them."
13 Jesus gave them permission. And coming out, the unclean spirits entered the
swine; and the herd rushed down the steep
bank into the sea, about two thousand *of
them;* and they were drowned in the sea.
14 Their herdsmen ran away and reported
it in the city and in the country. And *the people* came to see what it was that had happened.
15 They *came to Jesus and *observed the
man who had been [a]demon-possessed sitting down, [b]clothed and [c]in his right mind,
the very man who had had the "[d]legion";
and they became frightened.
16 Those who had seen it described to
them how it had happened to the [a]demon-
possessed man, and *all* about the swine.
17 And they began to [a]implore Him to
leave their region.
18 [a]As He was getting into the boat, the

ceptible to sudden, violent storms. Cool air from the Mediterranean is drawn down through the narrow mountain passes and clashes with the hot, humid air lying over the lake.

4:38 *asleep on the cushion.* The picture of Jesus, exhausted and asleep on the cushion customarily kept under the coxswain's seat, is characteristic of Mark's human touch.

4:41 *Who then is this . . . ?* In view of what Jesus had just done, the only answer to this rhetorical question was: He is the very Son of God! God's presence, as well as His power, was demonstrated (see Ps 65:7; 107:25–30; Prov 30:4). Mark indicates his answer to this question in the opening line of his Gospel (1:1). By such miracles Jesus sought to establish and increase the disciples' faith in His deity.

5:1 *to the other side of the sea.* The east side of the lake, a territory largely inhabited by Gentiles, as indicated by the presence of the large herd of pigs—animals Jews considered "unclean" and therefore unfit to eat. *country of the Gerasenes.* Gerasa, located about 35 miles southeast of the Sea of Galilee, may have had holdings on the eastern shore of the Sea, giving its name to a small village there now known as Khersa. About one mile south is a fairly steep slope within 40 yards of the shore, and about two miles from there are cavern tombs that appear to have been used as dwellings.

5:3 *had his dwelling among the tombs.* It was not unusual for the same cave to provide burial for the dead and shelter for the living. Very poor people often lived in such caves.

5:4 *he had often been bound with shackles and chains.* Though the villagers no doubt chained him partly for their own protection, this harsh treatment added to his humiliation.

5:5 *he was screaming . . . and gashing himself with stones.* Every word in the story emphasizes the man's pathetic condition as well as the purpose of demonic possession—to torment and destroy the divine likeness with which man was created.

5:7 *What business do we have with each other . . . ?* A way of saying, "What do we have in common?" Similar expressions are found in the OT (e.g., 2 Sam 16:10; 19:22), where they mean, "Mind your own business!" The demon was speaking, using the voice of the possessed man. *Son of the Most High God.* See note on 1:24. *I implore You by God, do not torment me!* The demon sensed that he was to be punished and used the strongest basis for an oath that he knew, though his appeal to God was strangely ironic.

5:9 *My name is Legion; for we are many.* A Roman legion was made up of 6,000 men. Here the term suggests that the man was possessed by numerous demons and perhaps also represents the many powers opposed to Jesus, who embodies the power of God.

5:10 *not to send them out of the country.* The demons were fearful of being sent into eternal punishment, i.e., "into the abyss" (Luke 8:31).

5:13 *Jesus gave them permission.* See note on Matt 8:32.

5:16 *and all about the swine.* In addition to the remarkable change in the demon-possessed man, the drowning of the pigs seemed to be a major concern, no doubt because it was so dramatic and brought considerable financial loss to the owners.

5:17 *implore Him to leave their region.* Fear of further loss may have motivated this response, but also the fact that a powerful force was at work in their midst that they could not comprehend.

man who had been [b]demon-possessed was
imploring Him that he might [1]accompany
Him.
19 And He did not let him, but He *said to
him, "[a]Go home to your people and report to
them [1]what great things the Lord has done
for you, and *how* He had mercy on you."
20 And he went away and began to [a]pro-
claim in [b]Decapolis [1]what great things Jesus
had done for him; and everyone was amazed.

Miracles and Healing

21 [a]When Jesus had crossed over again in
[b]the boat to the other side, a large crowd
gathered around Him; and so He [1]stayed [c]by
the seashore.
22 [a]One of [b]the synagogue [1]officials
named Jairus *came up, and on seeing Him,
*fell at His feet
23 and *implored Him earnestly, saying,
"My little daughter is at the point of death;
please come and [a]lay Your hands on her, so
that she will [1]get well and live."
24 And He went off with him; and a large
crowd was following Him and pressing in on
Him.
25 A woman who had had a hemorrhage
for twelve years,
26 and had endured much at the hands of

18 [1]Lit *be with Him* [b]Matt 4:24; Mark 5:15, 16
19 [1]Or *everything that* [a]Luke 8:39
20 [1]Or *everything that* [a]Ps 66:16 [b]Matt 4:25; Mark 7:31
21 [1]Lit *was* [a]Matt 9:1; Luke 8:40 [b]Mark 4:36 [c]Mark 4:1
22 [1]Or *rulers* [a]Mark 5:22-43: *Matt 9:18-26; Luke 8:41-56* [b]Matt 9:18; Mark 5:35, 36, 38; Luke 8:49; 13:14; Acts 13:15; 18:8, 17
23 [1]Lit *be saved* [a]Mark 6:5; 7:32; 8:23; 16:18; Luke 4:40; 13:13; Acts 6:6; 9:17; 28:8

5:19 *report to them what great things the Lord has done for you.* This is in marked contrast to Jesus' exhortation to silence in the case of the man cleansed of leprosy (1:44; see 1:34; 3:12; see also note on Matt 8:4), perhaps because the healing of the demoniac was in Gentile territory, where there was little danger that Messianic ideas about Jesus might be circulated.
5:20 *Decapolis.* See note on Matt 4:25.
5:21 *the other side.* Jesus returned to the west side of the lake, perhaps to Capernaum.
5:22 *synagogue officials.* A ruler of the synagogue was a layman whose responsibilities were administrative and included such things as looking after the building and supervising the worship. Though there were exceptions (see Acts 13:15), most synagogues had only one ruler. Sometimes the title was honorary, with no administrative responsibilities assigned.
5:25 *had a hemorrhage for twelve years.* The precise nature of the woman's problem is not known. Her existence was wretched because people shunned her generally, since anyone

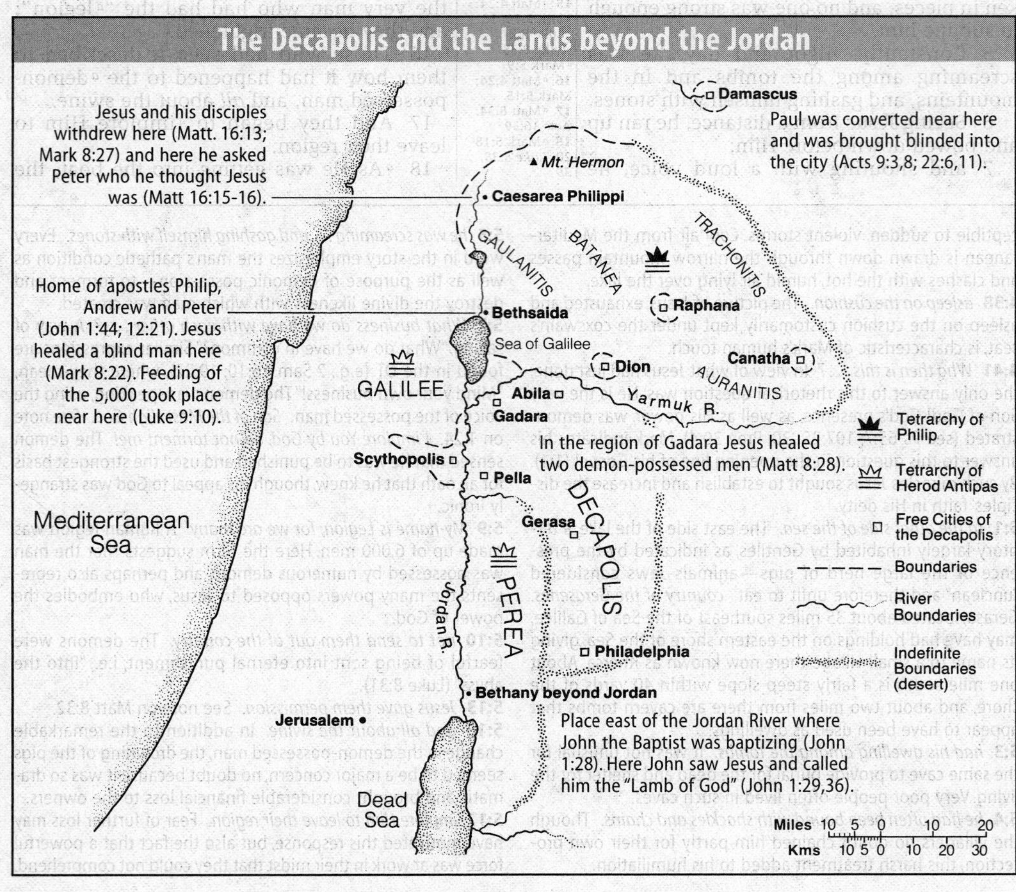

The Decapolis and the Lands beyond the Jordan
Jesus and his disciples withdrew here (Matt. 16:13; Mark 8:27) and here he asked Peter who he thought Jesus was (Matt 16:15-16).
Damascus
Paul was converted near here and was brought blinded into the city (Acts 9:3,8; 22:6,11).
Mt. Hermon
Caesarea Philippi
GAULANITIS
BATANEA
TRACHONITIS
Home of apostles Philip, Andrew and Peter (John 1:44; 12:21). Jesus healed a blind man here (Mark 8:22). Feeding of the 5,000 took place near here (Luke 9:10).
Raphana
Bethsaida
Sea of Galilee
Canatha
Dion
AURANITIS
GALILEE
Abila
Yarmuk R.
Gadara
In the region of Gadara Jesus healed two demon-possessed men (Matt 8:28).
Scythopolis
Pella
DECAPOLIS
Mediterranean Sea
Gerasa
PEREA
Jordan R.
Philadelphia
Bethany beyond Jordan
Jerusalem
Place east of the Jordan River where John the Baptist was baptizing (John 1:28). Here John saw Jesus and called him the "Lamb of God" (John 1:29,36).
Dead Sea
Tetrarchy of Philip
Tetrarchy of Herod Antipas
Free Cities of the Decapolis
Boundaries
River Boundaries
Indefinite Boundaries (desert)
Miles 10 5 0 10 20
Kms 10 5 0 10 20 30

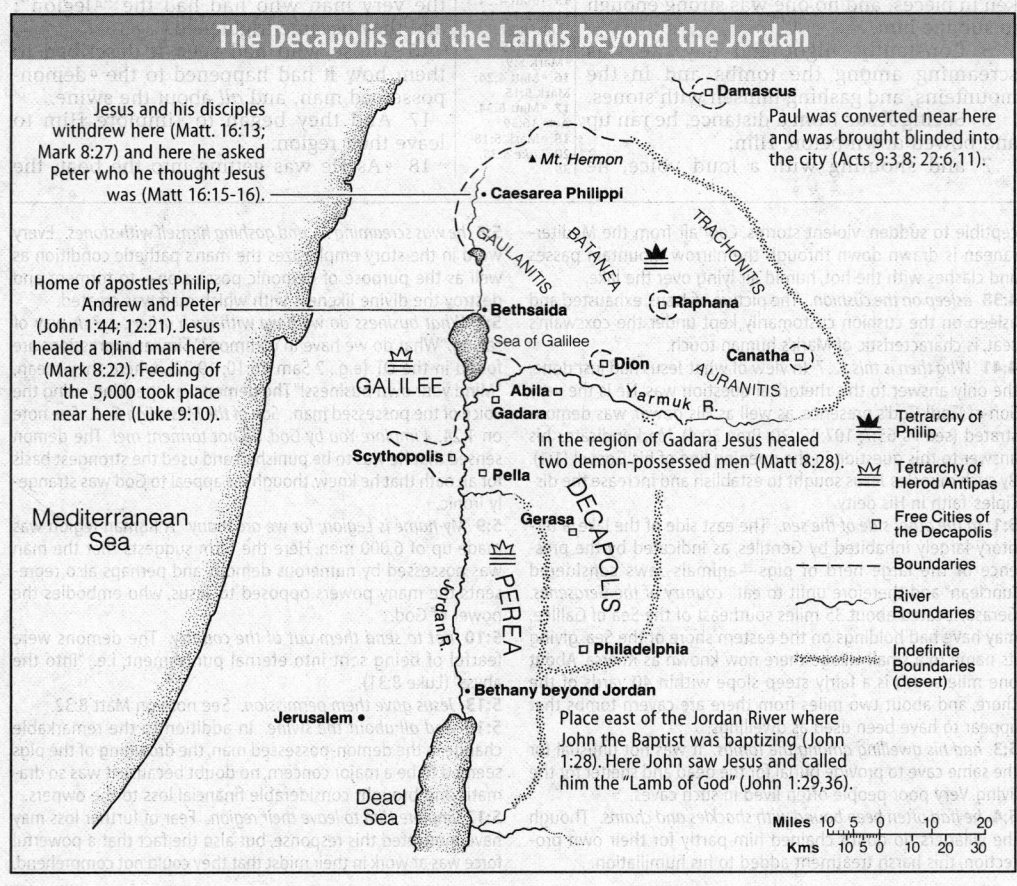

many physicians, and had spent all that she had and was not helped at all, but rather had grown worse—

27 after hearing about Jesus, she came up in the crowd behind *Him* and touched His [1]cloak.

28 For she [1]thought, "If I just touch His garments, I will [2]get well."

29 Immediately the flow of her blood was dried up; and she felt in her body that she was healed of her [a]affliction.

30 Immediately Jesus, perceiving in Himself that [a]the power *proceeding* from Him had gone forth, turned around in the crowd and said, "Who touched My garments?"

31 And His disciples said to Him, "You see the crowd pressing in on You, and You say, 'Who touched Me?' "

32 And He looked around to see the woman who had done this.

33 But the woman fearing and trembling, aware of what had happened to her, came and fell down before Him and told Him the whole truth.

34 And He said to her, "Daughter, [a]your faith has [1]made you well; [b]go in peace and be healed of your [c]affliction."

35 While He was still speaking, they *came from the *house of* the [a]synagogue official, saying, "Your daughter has died; why trouble the Teacher anymore?"

36 But Jesus, overhearing what was being spoken, *said to the [a]synagogue official, "[b]Do not be afraid *any longer,* only [1]believe."

37 And He allowed no one to accompany Him, except [a]Peter and [1]James and John the brother of [1]James.

38 They *came to the house of the [a]synagogue official; and He *saw a commotion, and *people* loudly weeping and wailing.

39 And entering in, He *said to them, "Why make a commotion and weep? The child has not died, but is asleep."

40 They *began* laughing at Him. But putting them all out, He *took along the child's father and mother and His own companions, and *entered *the room* where the child was.

41 Taking the child by the hand, He *said to her, "Talitha kum!" (which translated means, "Little girl, [a]I say to you, get up!").

42 Immediately the girl got up and *began* to walk, for she was twelve years old. And immediately they were completely astounded.

43 And He [a]gave them strict orders that no one should know about this, and He said that *something* should be given her to eat.

Teaching at Nazareth

6 [a]Jesus went out from there and *came into [1][b]His hometown; and His disciples *followed Him.

2 When the Sabbath came, He began [a]to teach in the synagogue; and the [b]many listeners were astonished, saying, "Where did this man *get* these things, and what is *this* wisdom given to Him, and such [1]miracles as these performed by His hands?

3 "Is not this [a]the carpenter, [b]the son of Mary, and brother of [1]James and Joses and Judas and Simon? Are not [c]His sisters here with us?" And they took [d]offense at Him.

4 Jesus said to them, "[a]A prophet is not without honor except in [1][b]his hometown and among his *own* relatives and in his *own* household."

5 And He could do no [1]miracle there

27 [1]Or *outer garment*
28 [1]Lit *was saying* [2]Lit *be saved*
29 [a]Mark 3:10; 5:34
30 [a]Luke 5:17
34 [1]Lit *saved you* [a]Matt 9:22 [b]Luke 7:50; 8:48; Acts 16:36; James 2:16 [c]Mark 3:10; 5:29
35 [a]Mark 5:22
36 [1]Or *keep on believing* [a]Mark 5:22 [b]Luke 8:50
37 [1]Or *Jacob;* James is the Eng form of Jacob [a]Matt 17:1; 26:37
38 [a]Mark 5:22
41 [a]Luke 7:14; Acts 9:40
43 [a]Matt 8:4
6:1 [1]Or *His own part of the country* [a]Mark 6:1-6: *Matt 13:54-58* [b]Matt 13:54, 57; Luke 4:16, 23
2 [1]Or *works of power* [a]Matt 4:23; Mark 10:1 [b]Matt 7:28
3 [1]Or *Jacob* [a]Matt 13:55 [b]Matt 12:46 [c]Matt 13:56 [d]Matt 11:6
4 [1]Or *his own part of the country* [a]Matt 13:57; John 4:44 [b]Mark 6:1
5 [1]Or *work of power*

having contact with her was made ceremonially unclean (Lev 15:25–33).

5:26 *had endured much at the hands of many physicians.* The Jewish Talmud preserves a record of medicines and treatments prescribed for illnesses of this sort.

5:28 *If I just touch His garments.* Although it needed to be bolstered by physical contact, her faith was rewarded (v. 34; cf. Acts 19:12).

5:30 *power proceeding from Him had gone forth.* The woman was healed because God graciously determined to heal her through the power then active in Jesus.

5:32 *looked around to see the woman who had done this.* Jesus would not allow the woman to recede into the crowd without publicly commending her faith and assuring her that she was permanently healed.

5:34 *made you well.* The Greek for "made you well" actually means "saved." Here both physical healing ("be healed of your affliction") and spiritual salvation ("go in peace") are meant. The two are often seen together in Mark's Gospel (see 2:1–12; 3:1–6).

5:37 *Peter and James and John.* These three disciples had an especially close relationship to Jesus (see note on Acts 3:1).

5:38 *people loudly weeping and wailing.* It was customary for professional mourners to be brought in at the time of death. In this case, however, it is not certain that enough time had elapsed for professional mourners to have been secured.

5:39 *not died, but is asleep.* See note on Luke 8:52.

5:41 *Talitha kum!* Mark is the only Gospel writer who here preserves the original Aramaic—one of the languages of the Holy Land in the first century A.D. and probably the language Jesus and His disciples ordinarily spoke (they may also have spoken Hebrew and Greek).

5:43 *that no one should know.* In the vicinity of Galilee Jesus often cautioned people whom He healed not to spread the story of the miracle. His great popularity with the people, coupled with the growing opposition from the religious leaders, could have precipitated a crisis before Jesus' ministry was completed (see 1:44; 5:19; 7:36; 8:26).

6:1 *His hometown.* Though Mark does not specifically mention Nazareth, it is obviously meant (see note on 1:9).

6:2 *teach in the synagogue.* See note on 1:21. *were astonished.* See note on 1:22.

6:3 *carpenter.* Matthew reports that Jesus was called "the carpenter's son" (Matt 13:55); only in Mark is Jesus Himself referred to as a carpenter. The Greek word can also apply to a mason or smith, but it seems to have its usual meaning ("carpenter") here. The question is derogatory, meaning, "Is He not a common worker with His hands like the rest of us?" *brother of James and Joses and Judas and Simon.* See note on Luke 8:19. *they took offense at Him.* They saw no reason to believe that He was different from them, much less that He was specially anointed by God.

6:5 *He could do no miracle there.* It was not that Jesus did not

except that He [a]laid His hands on a few sick people and healed them.

6 And He wondered at their unbelief.

[a]And He was going around the villages teaching.

The Twelve Sent Out

7 [a]And [b]He *summoned the twelve and began to send them out [c]in pairs, and gave them authority over the unclean spirits;

8 [a]and He instructed them that they should take nothing for *their* journey, except a mere staff—no bread, no [1]bag, no money in their belt—

9 but [1]*to* wear sandals; and *He added,* "Do not put on two [2]tunics."

10 And He said to them, "Wherever you enter a house, stay there until you [1]leave town.

11 "Any place that does not receive you or listen to you, as you go out from there, [a]shake the dust [1]off the soles of your feet for a testimony against them."

12 [a]They went out and [1]preached that *men* should repent.

13 And they were casting out many demons and [a]were anointing with oil many sick people and healing them.

John's Fate Recalled

14 [a]And King Herod heard *of it,* for His name had become well known; and *people* were saying, "[b]John the Baptist has risen from the dead, and that is why these miraculous powers are at work in Him."

15 But others were saying, "He is [a]Elijah." And others were saying, "*He is* [b]a prophet, like one of the prophets *of old.*"

16 But when Herod heard *of it,* he kept saying, "John, whom I beheaded, has risen!"

17 For Herod himself had sent and had John arrested and bound in prison on account of [a]Herodias, the wife of his brother Philip, because he had married her.

18 For John had been saying to Herod, "[a]It is not lawful for you to have your brother's wife."

19 [a]Herodias had a grudge against him and wanted to put him to death and could not *do so;*

20 for [a]Herod was afraid of John, knowing that he was a righteous and holy man, and he kept him safe. And when he heard him, he was very perplexed; [1]but he [2]used to enjoy listening to him.

21 A strategic day came when Herod on his birthday [a]gave a banquet for his lords and [1]military commanders and the leading men [b]of Galilee;

22 and when the daughter of [a]Herodias herself came in and danced, she pleased Herod and [1]his dinner guests; and the king said to the girl, "Ask me for whatever you want and I will give it to you."

23 And he swore to her, "Whatever you ask of me, I will give it to you; up to [a]half of my kingdom."

24 And she went out and said to her mother, "What shall I ask for?" And she said, "The head of John the Baptist."

25 Immediately she came in a hurry to the king and asked, saying, "I want you to give me at once the head of John the Baptist on a platter."

26 And although the king was very sorry, *yet* because of his oaths and because of [1]his dinner guests, he was unwilling to refuse her.

27 Immediately the king sent an executioner and commanded *him* to bring *back* his head. And he went and had him beheaded in the prison,

28 and brought his head on a platter, and gave it to the girl; and the girl gave it to her mother.

29 When his disciples heard *about this,* they came and took away his body and laid it in a tomb.

30 [a]The [b]apostles *gathered together with

5 [a]Mark 5:23
6 [a]Matt 9:35; Mark 1:39; 10:1; Luke 13:22
7 [a]Mark 6:7-11: *Matt 10:1, 9-14; Luke 9:1, 3-5;* Luke 10:4-11 [b]Matt 10:1, 5; Mark 3:13; Luke 9:1 [c]Luke 10:1
8 [1]Or *knapsack or beggar's bag* [a]Matt 10:10
9 [1]Lit *being shod with* [2]Or *inner garments*
10 [1]Lit *go out from there*
11 [1]Lit *under your feet* [a]Matt 10:14; Acts 13:51
12 [1]Or *proclaimed as a herald* [a]Matt 11:1; Luke 9:6
13 [a]James 5:14
14 [a]Mark 6:14-29: *Matt 14:1-12;* Mark 6:14-16: *Luke 9:7-9* [b]Matt 14:2; Luke 9:19
15 [a]Matt 16:14; Mark 8:28 [b]Matt 21:11
17 [a]Matt 14:3; Luke 3:19
18 [a]Matt 14:4
19 [a]Matt 14:3
20 [1]Lit *and* [2]Lit *was hearing him gladly* [a]Matt 21:26
21 [1]I.e. chiliarchs, in command of a thousand troops [a]Esth 1:3; 2:18 [b]Luke 3:1
22 [1]Lit *those who reclined at the table with him* [a]Matt 14:3
23 [a]Esth 5:3, 6; 7:2
26 [1]Lit *those reclining at the table*
30 [a]Luke 9:10 [b]Matt 10:2; Mark 3:14; Luke 6:13; 9:10; 17:5; 22:14; 24:10; Acts 1:2, 26

---

have power to perform miracles at Nazareth, but that He chose not to in such a climate of unbelief (v. 6).

6:6 *He wondered.* See note on Luke 7:9.

6:7 *in pairs.* The purpose of going in pairs may have been to bolster credibility by having the testimony of more than one witness (cf. Deut 17:6), as well as to provide mutual support during their training period.

6:8 *no bread, no bag, no money in their belt.* They were to depend entirely on the hospitality of those to whom they testified (see v. 10).

6:9 *Do not put on two tunics.* At night an extra tunic was helpful as a covering to protect from the cold night air, and the implication here is that the disciples were to trust in God to provide lodging each night.

6:11 *shake the dust off the soles of your feet.* See note on Matt 10:14.

6:12–13 *preached . . . were casting out many demons.* This mission marks the beginning of the disciples' own ministry in Jesus' name (see 3:14–15), and their message was precisely the same as his (1:15).

6:12 *repent.* See note on 1:4.

6:13 *anointing with oil many sick people.* In the ancient world olive oil was widely used as a medicine (see Is 1:6; Luke 10:34; James 5:14).

6:14 *King Herod.* See note on Matt 14:1. Mark may here have used the title "king" sarcastically (since Herod was actually a tetrarch), or perhaps he simply used Herod's popular title.

6:15 *He is Elijah.* See Mal 4:5.

6:16 *John . . . has risen!* Herod, disturbed by an uneasy conscience and disposed to superstition, feared that John had come back to haunt him.

6:17 *John arrested and bound in prison.* See 1:14; Luke 3:19–20. Josephus says that John was imprisoned at Machaerus, the fortress in Perea on the eastern side of the Dead Sea. *Herodias.* See note on Matt 14:3. *Philip.* See note on Matt 14:3.

6:22 *the daughter of Herodias.* See note on Matt 14:6.

6:23 *up to half of my kingdom.* A proverbial reference to generosity, not to be taken literally (see Esth 5:3,6). Generosity suited the occasion and would win the approval of the guests.

6:30 *apostles.* In Mark's Gospel the word occurs only here and

Jesus; and they reported to Him all that they
had done and taught.
31 And He *said to them, "Come away by
yourselves to a secluded place and rest a
while." (For there were many *people* coming
and going, and [a]they did not even have time
to eat.)
32 [a]They went away in [b]the boat to a
secluded place by themselves.

Five Thousand Fed

33 *The people* saw them going, and many
recognized *them* and ran there together on
foot from all the cities, and got there ahead
of them.
34 When Jesus went [1]ashore, He [a]saw a
large crowd, and He felt compassion for
them because [b]they were like sheep without
a shepherd; and He began to teach them
many things.
35 When it was already quite late, His disciples came to Him and said, "[1]This place is
desolate and it is already quite late;
36 send them away so that they may go
into the surrounding countryside and villages
and buy themselves [1]something to eat."
37 But He answered them, "You give them
something to eat!" [a]And they *said to Him,
"Shall we go and spend two hundred
[1b]denarii on bread and give them *something*
to eat?"
38 And He *said to them, "How many
loaves do you have? Go look!" And when
they found out, they *said, "Five, and two
fish."

31 [a]Mark 3:20
32 [a]Mark 6:32-44: *Matt 14:13-21; Luke 9:10-17; John 6:5-13;* Mark 8:2-9 [b]Mark 3:9; 4:36; 6:45
34 [1]Lit *out* [a]Matt 9:36 [b]Num 27:17; 1 Kin 22:17; 2 Chr 18:16; Zech 10:2
35 [1]Lit *The*
36 [1]Lit *what they may eat*
37 [1]The denarius was equivalent to one day's wage [a]John 6:7 [b]Matt 18:28; Luke 7:41
39 [1]Lit *recline*
40 [1]Lit *reclined*
41 [a]Matt 14:19
43 [a]Matt 14:20
44 [a]Matt 14:21
45 [a]Mark 6:45-51: *Matt 14:22-32; John 6:15-21* [b]Mark 6:32 [c]Matt 11:21; Mark 8:22
46 [a]Acts 18:18, 21; 2 Cor 2:13 [b]Matt 14:23
48 [1]Lit *harassed in rowing* [2]I.e. 3-6 a.m. [a]Matt 24:43; Mark 13:35
50 [1]Or *troubled*

39 And He commanded them all to [1]sit
down by groups on the green grass.
40 They [1]sat down in groups of hundreds
and of fifties.
41 And He took the five loaves and the
two fish, and looking up toward heaven, He
[a]blessed *the food* and broke the loaves and
He kept giving *them* to the disciples to set
before them; and He divided up the two fish
among them all.
42 They all ate and were satisfied,
43 and they picked up twelve full [a]baskets
of the broken pieces, and also of the fish.
44 There were [a]five thousand men who
ate the loaves.

Jesus Walks on the Water

45 [a]Immediately Jesus made His disciples
get into [b]the boat and go ahead of *Him* to the
other side to [c]Bethsaida, while He Himself
was sending the crowd away.
46 After [a]bidding them farewell, He left
[b]for the mountain to pray.
47 When it was evening, the boat was in
the middle of the sea, and He was alone on
the land.
48 Seeing them [1]straining at the oars, for
the wind was against them, at about the
[2a]fourth watch of the night He *came to
them, walking on the sea; and He intended
to pass by them.
49 But when they saw Him walking on the
sea, they supposed that it was a ghost, and
cried out;
50 for they all saw Him and were [1]terri-

in 3:14 (in some manuscripts). The apostles were Jesus' authorized agents or representatives (see note on Heb 3:1). In the NT the word is sometimes used quite generally (see John 13:16, where the Greek *apostolos* is translated "one who is sent"). In the technical sense it is used (1) of the twelve—in which sense it is also applied to Paul (Rom 1:1)—and (2) of a larger group including Barnabas (Acts 14:14), James the Lord's brother (Gal 1:19), and possibly Andronicus and Junias (Rom 16:7). *reported to Him all that they had done and taught.* Because He had commissioned them as His representatives. They were returning from a third preaching tour in Galilee (see note on 1:39).

6:32 *They went away in the boat . . . by themselves.* John reports that they went to the other side of the Sea of Galilee (John 6:1). Luke, more specifically, says they went to Bethsaida (Luke 9:10), which locates the feeding of the 5,000 on the northeast shore (see note on 7:24).

6:33 *ran there together on foot . . . and got there ahead of them.* Perhaps a strong headwind slowed down the boat so that the people had time to go on foot around the lake and arrive before the boat.

6:37 *two hundred denarii.* The usual pay for a day's work was one denarius (see Matt 20:2), meaning that about 200 denarii would be earned in eight months.

6:39 *green grass.* Grass is green around the Sea of Galilee after the late winter or early spring rains.

6:40 *groups of hundreds and of fifties.* Recalls the order of the Mosaic camp in the wilderness (e.g., Ex 18:21). The word translated "groups" means "garden plots," a picturesque figure (v. 39).

6:42 *all ate and were satisfied.* Attempts to explain away this miracle (e.g., by suggesting that Jesus and His disciples shared their lunch and the crowd followed their good example) are inadequate. If Jesus was, as He claimed to be, God incarnate, the miracle presents no difficulties. God had promised that when the true Shepherd came the wilderness would become rich pasture where the sheep would be gathered and fed (Ezek 34:23–31), and here the Messiah feasts with followers in the desert (cf. Is 25:6–9). Jesus is the Shepherd who provides for all our needs so that we lack nothing (cf. Ps 23:1).

6:43 *twelve full baskets of the broken pieces, and also of the fish.* Bread was regarded by Jews as a gift of God, and it was required that scraps that fell on the ground during a meal be picked up. The fragments were collected in small wicker baskets that were carried as a part of daily attire. Each of the disciples returned with his basket full (see 8:8; see also note on Matt 15:37).

6:44 *five thousand.* The size of the crowd is amazing in light of the fact that the neighboring towns of Capernaum and Bethsaida probably had a population of only 2,000–3,000 each. *men.* Lit. "males," as in all four Gospels. Matthew further emphasizes the point by adding "besides women and children" (Matt 14:21).

6:45 *go ahead of Him.* John indicates that the people were ready to take Jesus by force and make Him king (John 6:14–15), and Jesus therefore sent His disciples across the lake while He slipped away into the hills to pray.

6:48 *fourth watch.* 3:00–6:00 A.M. See 13:35; see also note on Matt 14:25. *walking on the sea.* A special display of the majestic presence and power of the transcendent Lord, who rules over the sea (see Ps 89:9; Is 51:10,15; Jer 31:35).

6:49 *a ghost.* Popular Jewish superstition held that the appearance of spirits during the night brought disaster. The disciples'

fied. But immediately He spoke with them and *said to them, "[a]Take courage; it is I, [b]do not be afraid."

51 Then He got into [a]the boat with them, and the wind stopped; and they were utterly astonished,

52 for [a]they [1]had not gained any insight from the *incident of* the loaves, but [2]their heart [b]was hardened.

Healing at Gennesaret

53 [a]When they had crossed over they came to land at Gennesaret, and moored to the shore.

54 When they got out of the boat, immediately *the people* recognized Him,

55 and ran about that whole country and began to carry here and there on their pallets those who were sick, to [1]the place they heard He was.

56 Wherever He entered villages, or cities, or countryside, they were laying the sick in the market places, and imploring Him that they might just [a]touch [b]the fringe of His cloak; and as many as touched it were being cured.

Followers of Tradition

7 [a]The Pharisees and some of the scribes gathered around Him when they had come [b]from Jerusalem,

2 and had seen that some of His disciples were eating their bread with [a]impure hands, that is, unwashed.

3 (For the Pharisees and all the Jews do not eat unless they [1]carefully wash their hands, *thus* observing the [a]traditions of the elders;

4 and *when they come* from the market place, they do not eat unless they [1]cleanse themselves; and there are many other things which they have received in order to observe, such as the [2]washing of [a]cups and pitchers and copper pots.)

5 The Pharisees and the scribes *asked Him, "Why do Your disciples not walk according to the [a]tradition of the elders, but eat their bread with [b]impure hands?"

6 And He said to them, "Rightly did Isaiah prophesy of you hypocrites, as it is written:

'[a]THIS PEOPLE HONORS ME WITH THEIR LIPS,
BUT THEIR HEART IS FAR AWAY FROM ME.
7 '[a]BUT IN VAIN DO THEY WORSHIP ME,
TEACHING AS DOCTRINES THE PRECEPTS OF MEN.'

8 "Neglecting the commandment of God, you hold to the [a]tradition of men."

9 He was also saying to them, "You are experts at setting aside the commandment of God in order to keep your [a]tradition.

10 "For Moses said, '[a]HONOR YOUR FATHER AND YOUR MOTHER'; and, '[b]HE WHO SPEAKS EVIL OF FATHER OR MOTHER, IS TO [1]BE PUT TO DEATH';

11 but you say, 'If a man says to *his* father or *his* mother, whatever I have that would help you is [a]Corban (that is to say, [1]given *to God*),'

12 you no longer permit him to do anything for *his* father or *his* mother;

13 *thus* invalidating the word of God by your [a]tradition which you have handed down; and you do many things such as that."

The Heart of Man

14 After He called the crowd to Him again, He *began* saying to them, "Listen to Me, all of you, and understand:

15 there is nothing outside the man which can defile him if it goes into him; but the

50 [a]Matt 9:2 [b]Matt 14:27
51 [a]Mark 6:32
52 [1]Lit *had not understood on the basis of* [2]Or *their mind was closed, made dull,* or *insensible* [a]Mark 8:17ff [b]Rom 11:7
53 [a]Mark 6:53-56: *Matt 14:34-36;* John 6:24, 25
55 [1]Lit *where they were hearing that He was*
56 [a]Mark 3:10 [b]Matt 9:20; Num 15:37-40
7:1 [a]Mark 7:1-23: *Matt 15:1-20* [b]Matt 15:1
2 [a]Matt 15:2; Mark 7:5; Luke 11:38; Acts 10:14, 28; 11:8; Rom 14:14; Heb 10:29; Rev 21:27
3 [1]Lit *with the fist* [a]Mark 7:5, 8, 9, 13; Gal 1:14
4 [1]Or *sprinkle*
4 [2]Lit *baptizing* [a]Matt 23:25
5 [a]Mark 7:3, 8, 9, 13; Gal 1:14 [b]Mark 7:2
6 [a]Is 29:13
7 [a]Is 29:13
8 [a]Mark 7:3, 5, 9, 13; Gal 1:14
9 [a]Mark 7:3, 5, 8, 13; Gal 1:14
10 [1]Lit *die the death* [a]Ex 20:12; Deut 5:16 [b]Ex 21:17; Lev 20:9
11 [1]Or *a gift,* i.e. an offering [a]Lev 1:2; Matt 27:6
13 [a]Mark 7:3, 5, 8, 9; Gal 1:14

---

terror was prompted by what they may have thought was a water spirit.

6:52 *they had not gained any insight from . . . the loaves.* Had they understood the feeding of the 5,000, they would not have been amazed at Jesus' walking on the water or His calming the waves. *their heart was hardened.* They were showing themselves to be similar to Jesus' opponents, who also exhibited hardness of heart (3:5). See 8:17–21; see also note on Ex 4:21.

6:53 *Gennesaret.* See note on Matt 14:34.

6:56 *touch the fringe of His cloak.* See note on 5:28.

7:1 *The Pharisees . . . had come from Jerusalem.* Another delegation of fact-finding religious leaders from Jerusalem (see 3:22) sent to investigate the Galilean activities of Jesus. See notes on 2:16; Matt 2:4.

7:3 *carefully wash their hands.* See note on John 2:6. *the traditions of the elders.* Considered to be binding (see v. 5 and note on Matt 15:2).

7:4 *market place.* Where Jews would come into contact with Gentiles, or with Jews who did not observe the ceremonial law, and thus become ceremonially unclean.

7:6 *Isaiah prophesy.* Isaiah roundly denounced the religious leaders of his day (Is 29:13), and Jesus uses a quotation from this prophet to describe the tradition of the elders as "the precepts of men" (v. 7).

7:8 *the commandment of God . . . the tradition of men.* Jesus clearly contrasts the two. God's commands are found in Scripture and are binding; the traditions of the elders (v. 3) are not Biblical and therefore not authoritative or binding.

7:10 The fifth commandment is cited in both its positive and negative forms.

7:11 *Corban.* The transliteration of a Hebrew word meaning "offering." By using this word in a religious vow an irresponsible Jewish son could formally dedicate to God (i.e., to the temple) his earnings that otherwise would have gone for the support of his parents. The money, however, did not necessarily have to go for religious purposes. The Corban formula was simply a means of circumventing the clear responsibility of children toward their parents as prescribed in the law. The teachers of the law held that the Corban oath was binding, even when uttered rashly. The practice was one of many traditions that adhered to the letter of the law while ignoring its spirit. *(that is to say, given to God).* By explaining this Hebrew word, Mark reveals that he is addressing Gentile readers, probably Romans primarily.

7:13 *thus invalidating the word of God by your tradition.* The teachers of the law appealed to Num 30:1–2 in support of the Corban vow, but Jesus categorically rejects the practice of using one Biblical teaching to nullify another. The scribal interpretation of Num 30:1–2 satisfied the letter of the passage but missed the meaning of the law as a whole. God never intend-

things which proceed out of the man are what defile the man.

16 ["[1]If anyone has ears to hear, let him hear."]

17 When he had left the crowd *and* entered [a]the house, [b]His disciples questioned Him about the parable.

18 And He *said to them, "Are you so lacking in understanding also? Do you not understand that whatever goes into the man from outside cannot defile him,

19 because it does not go into his heart, but into his stomach, and [1]is eliminated?" (*Thus He* declared [a]all foods [b]clean.)

20 And He was saying, "[a]That which proceeds out of the man, that is what defiles the man.

21 "For from within, out of the heart of men, proceed the evil thoughts, [1]fornications, thefts, murders, adulteries,

22 deeds of coveting *and* wickedness, *as well as* deceit, sensuality, [1][a]envy, slander, [2]pride *and* foolishness.

23 "All these evil things proceed from within and defile the man."

The Syrophoenician Woman

24 [a]Jesus got up and went away from there to the region of [b]Tyre[1]. And when He had entered a house, He wanted no one to know *of it;* [2]yet He could not escape notice.

25 But after hearing of Him, a woman whose little daughter had an unclean spirit immediately came and fell at His feet.

26 Now the woman was a [1]Gentile, of the Syrophoenician race. And she kept asking Him to cast the demon out of her daughter.

27 And He was saying to her, "Let the children be satisfied first, for it is not [1]good to take the children's bread and throw it to the dogs."

28 But she answered and *said to Him,

16 [1]Early mss do not contain this verse
17 [a]Mark 2:1; 3:20; 9:28 [b]Matt 15:15
19 [1]Lit *goes out into the latrine* [a]Rom 14:1-12; Col 2:16 [b]Luke 11:41; Acts 10:15; 11:9
20 [a]Matt 15:18; Mark 7:23
21 [1]I.e. acts of sexual immorality
22 [1]Lit *an evil eye* [2]Or *arrogance* [a]Matt 6:23; 20:15
24 [1]Two early mss add *and Sidon* [2]Lit *and* [a]Mark 7:24-30: *Matt 15:21-28* [b]Matt 11:21; Mark 7:31
26 [1]Lit *Greek*
27 [1]Or *proper*

ed obedience to one command to nullify another.

7:16 Although this verse is present in the majority of the Greek manuscripts, it does not occur in the most ancient ones. It appears to be a scribal addition derived from either 4:9 or 4:23.

7:19 *(Thus He declared all foods clean.)* Mark adds this parenthetical comment to help his readers see the significance of Jesus' pronouncement for them (see Acts 10:9–16).

7:20 *defiles.* Jesus replaced the normal Jewish understandings of defilement with the truth that defilement comes from an impure heart, not the violation of external rules. Fellowship with God is not interrupted by unclean hands or food, but by sin (see vv. 21–23).

7:24 *Tyre.* A Gentile city located in Phoenicia (modern Lebanon), which bordered Galilee to the northwest. A journey of about 30 miles from Capernaum would have brought Jesus to the vicinity of Tyre. *wanted no one to know.* Ever since the feeding of the 5,000 (6:30–44) Jesus and His disciples had been, for the most part, skirting the region of Galilee. His purpose was to avoid the opposition in Galilee and to secure opportunity to teach His disciples privately (9:30–31). The regions to which He withdrew were: (1) the northeastern shore of the Sea of Galilee (6:30–53), (2) Phoenicia (7:24–30), (3) the Decapolis (7:31–8:10) and (4) Caesarea Philippi (8:27–9:32).

7:26 *Syrophoenician.* At that time Phoenicia belonged administratively to Syria. Mark possibly used the term to distinguish this woman from the Libyan-Phoenicians of North Africa.

7:27 *the children's bread and throw it to the dogs.* See note on Matt 15:26.

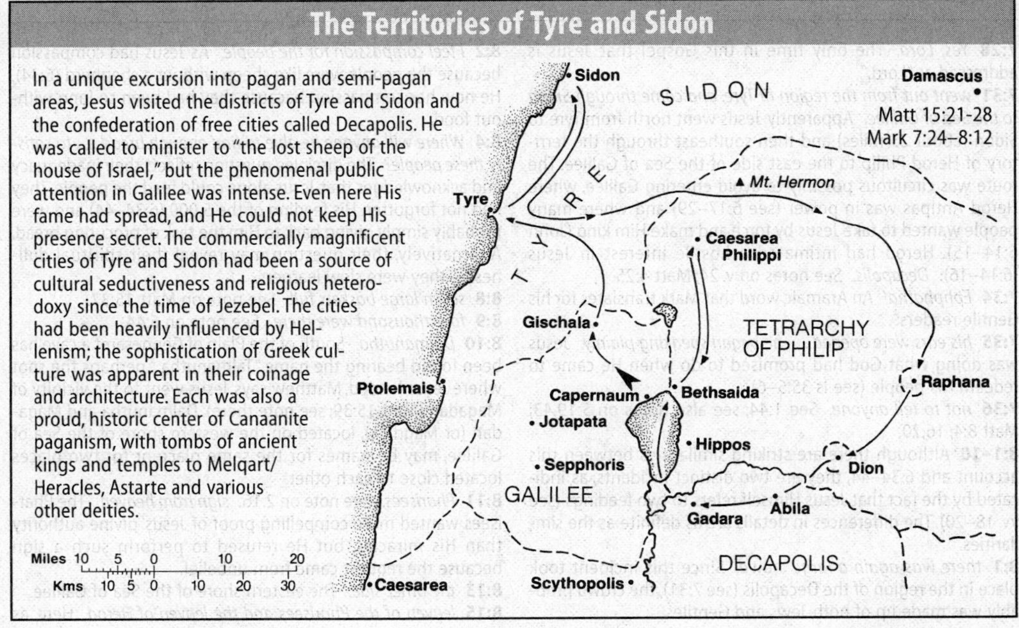
The Territories of Tyre and Sidon
In a unique excursion into pagan and semi-pagan areas, Jesus visited the districts of Tyre and Sidon and the confederation of free cities called Decapolis. He was called to minister to "the lost sheep of the house of Israel," but the phenomenal public attention in Galilee was intense. Even here His fame had spread, and He could not keep His presence secret. The commercially magnificent cities of Tyre and Sidon had been a source of cultural seductiveness and religious heterodoxy since the time of Jezebel. The cities had been heavily influenced by Hellenism; the sophistication of Greek culture was apparent in their coinage and architecture. Each was also a proud, historic center of Canaanite paganism, with tombs of ancient kings and temples to Melqart/Heracles, Astarte and various other deities.
Sidon
SIDON
Damascus
Matt 15:21-28
Mark 7:24-8:12
Mt. Hermon
Tyre
TYRE
Caesarea Philippi
Gischala
TETRARCHY OF PHILIP
Ptolemais
Capernaum
Bethsaida
Raphana
Jotapata
Hippos
Sepphoris
Dion
GALILEE
Gadara
Abila
DECAPOLIS
Caesarea
Scythopolis
Miles 10 5 0 10 20
Kms 10 5 0 10 20 30

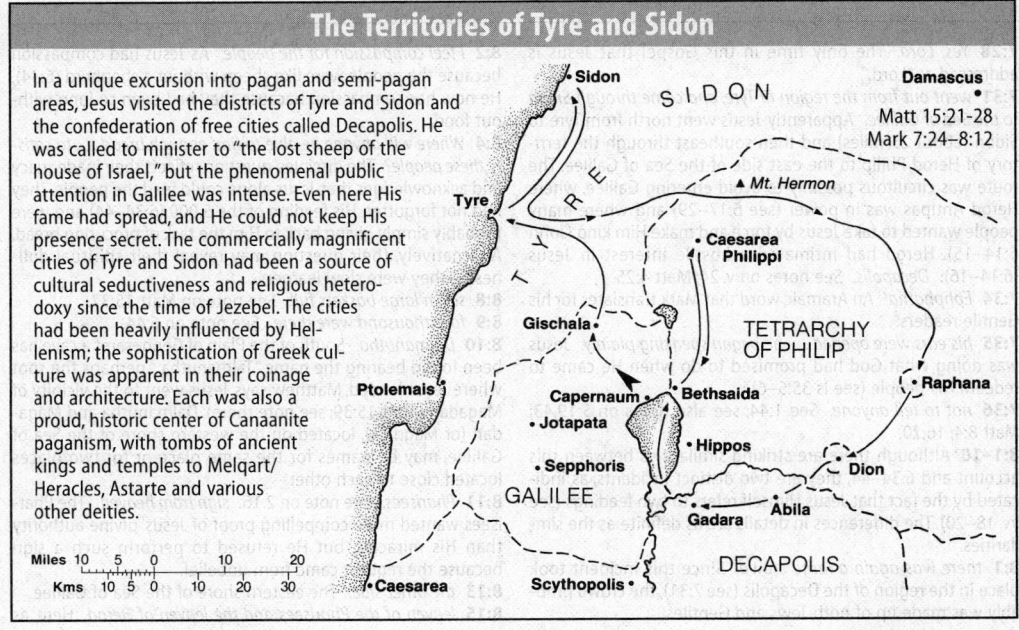

"Yes, Lord, *but* even the dogs under the table feed on the children's crumbs."

29 And He said to her, "Because of this [1]answer go; the demon has gone out of your daughter."

30 And going back to her home, she found the child [1]lying on the bed, the demon having left.

31 [a]Again He went out from the region of [b]Tyre, and came through Sidon to [c]the Sea of Galilee, within the region of [d]Decapolis.

32 They *brought to Him one who was deaf and spoke with difficulty, and they *implored Him to [a]lay His hand on him.

33 [a]Jesus took him aside from the crowd, by himself, and put His fingers into his ears, and after [a]spitting, He touched his tongue *with the saliva;*

34 and looking up to heaven with a deep [a]sigh, He *said to him, "Ephphatha!" that is, "Be opened!"

35 And his ears were opened, and the [1]impediment of his tongue [2]was removed, and he *began* speaking plainly.

36 And [a]He gave them orders not to tell anyone; but the more He ordered them, the more widely they [b]continued to proclaim it.

37 They were utterly astonished, saying, "He has done all things well; He makes even the deaf to hear and the mute to speak."

Four Thousand Fed

8 In those days, when there was again a large crowd and they had nothing to eat, [a]Jesus called His disciples and *said to them,

2 "[a]I feel compassion for the [1]people because they have remained with Me now three days and have nothing to eat.

3 "If I send them away hungry to their homes, they will faint on the way; and some of them have come from a great distance."

4 And His disciples answered Him, "Where will anyone be able *to find enough* [1]bread here in *this* desolate place to satisfy these people?"

5 And He was asking them, "How many loaves do you have?" And they said, "Seven."

6 And He *directed the [1]people to [2]sit down on the ground; and taking the seven loaves, He gave thanks and broke them, and started giving them to His disciples to [3]serve to them, and they served them to the [1]people.

7 They also had a few small fish; and [a]after He had blessed them, He ordered these to be [1]served as well.

8 And they ate and were satisfied; and they picked up seven large [a]baskets full of what was left over of the broken pieces.

9 About four thousand were *there;* and He sent them away.

10 And immediately He entered the boat with His disciples and came to the district of [a]Dalmanutha.

11 [a]The Pharisees came out and began to argue with Him, [b]seeking from Him a [1]sign from heaven, [2]to test Him.

12 [a]Sighing deeply [1]in His spirit, He *said, "Why does this generation seek for a [2]sign? Truly I say to you, [3][b]no [2]sign will be given to this generation."

13 Leaving them, He again embarked and went away to the other side.

14 And they had forgotten to take bread, and did not have more than one loaf in the boat with them.

15 And He was giving orders to them, saying, "[a]Watch out! Beware of the leaven of the Pharisees and the leaven of [b]Herod."

29 [1]Lit *word*
30 [1]Lit *thrown*
31 [a]Mark 7:31-37: *Matt 15:29-31* [b]Matt 11:21; Mark 7:24 [c]Matt 4:18 [d]Matt 4:25; Mark 5:20
32 [a]Mark 5:23
33 [a]Mark 8:23
34 [a]Mark 8:12
35 [1]Or *bond* [2]Lit *was loosed*
36 [a]Matt 8:4 [b]Mark 1:45
8:1 [a]Mark 8:1-9: *Matt 15:32-39;* Mark 6:34-44
2 [1]Lit *crowd* [a]Matt 9:36; Mark 6:34
4 [1]Lit *loaves*
6 [1]Lit *crowd* [2]Lit *recline* [3]Lit *set before*
7 [1]Lit *set before them* [a]Matt 14:19
8 [a]Matt 15:37; Mark 8:20
10 [a]Matt 15:39
11 [1]Or *attesting miracle* [2]Lit *testing Him* [a]Mark 8:11-21: *Matt 16:1-12* [b]Matt 12:38
12 [1]Or *to Himself* [2]Or *attesting miracle* [3]Lit *if a sign shall be given* [a]Mark 7:34 [b]Matt 12:39
15 [a]Matt 16:6; Luke 12:1 [b]Matt 14:1; 22:16

7:28 *Yes, Lord.* The only time in this Gospel that Jesus is addressed as "Lord."

7:31 *went out from the region of Tyre, and came through Sidon to the Sea of Galilee.* Apparently Jesus went north from Tyre to Sidon (about 25 miles) and then southeast through the territory of Herod Philip to the east side of the Sea of Galilee. The route was circuitous possibly to avoid entering Galilee, where Herod Antipas was in power (see 6:17–29) and where many people wanted to take Jesus by force and make Him king (John 6:14–15). Herod had intimated a hostile interest in Jesus (6:14–16). *Decapolis.* See notes on v. 24; Matt 4:25.

7:34 *Ephphatha!* An Aramaic word that Mark translates for his Gentile readers.

7:35 *his ears were opened . . . he began speaking plainly.* Jesus was doing what God had promised to do when He came to redeem His people (see Is 35:5–6).

7:36 *not to tell anyone.* See 1:44; see also notes on 5:19,43; Matt 8:4; 16:20.

8:1–10 Although there are striking similarities between this account and 6:34–44, they are two distinct incidents, as indicated by the fact that Jesus Himself refers to two feedings (see vv. 18–20). The differences in details are as definite as the similarities.

8:1 *there was again a large crowd.* Since this incident took place in the region of the Decapolis (see 7:31), the crowd probably was made up of both Jews and Gentiles.

8:2 *I feel compassion for the people.* As Jesus had compassion because the people were like sheep without a shepherd (6:34), He now has compassion because they had been so long without food.

8:4 *Where will anyone be able to find enough bread . . . to satisfy these people?* The disciples' question reflects their inadequacy and acknowledges that Jesus alone could feed the people. They had not forgotten His feeding of the 5,000 (6:34–44) and were probably simply giving back to Him the task of procuring bread. Alternatively, their question may reveal their spiritual dullness—they were slow learners.

8:8 *seven large baskets full.* See note on Matt 15:37.

8:9 *four thousand were there.* See note on 6:44.

8:10 *Dalmanutha.* South of the Plain of Gennesaret a cave has been found bearing the name "Talmanutha," perhaps the spot where Jesus landed. Matthew says Jesus went to the vicinity of Magadan (Matt 15:39; see note there). Dalmanutha and Magadan (or Magdala), located on the western shore of the Sea of Galilee, may be names for the same place or for two places located close to each other.

8:11 *Pharisees.* See note on 2:16. *sign from heaven.* The Pharisees wanted more compelling proof of Jesus' divine authority than His miracles, but He refused to perform such a sign because the request came from unbelief.

8:13 *the other side.* The eastern shore of the Sea of Galilee.

8:15 *leaven of the Pharisees and the leaven of Herod.* Here, as

16 They *began* to discuss with one another *the fact* that they had no bread.

17 And Jesus, aware of this, *said to them, "Why do you discuss *the fact* that you have no bread? [a]Do you not yet see or understand? Do you have a [1]hardened heart?

18 "[a]HAVING EYES, DO YOU NOT SEE? AND HAVING EARS, DO YOU NOT HEAR? And do you not remember,

19 when I broke [a]the five loaves for the five thousand, how many [b]baskets full of broken pieces you picked up?" They *said to Him, "Twelve."

20 "When *I broke* [a]the seven for the four thousand, how many large [b]baskets full of broken pieces did you pick up?" And they *said to Him, "Seven."

21 And He was saying to them, "[a]Do you not yet understand?"

22 And they *came to [a]Bethsaida. And they *brought a blind man to Jesus and *implored Him to [b]touch him.

23 Taking the blind man by the hand, He [a]brought him out of the village; and after [a]spitting on his eyes and [b]laying His hands on him, He asked him, "Do you see anything?"

24 And he [1]looked up and said, "I see men, for [2]I see *them* like trees, walking around."

25 Then again He laid His hands on his eyes; and he looked intently and was restored, and *began* to see everything clearly.

17 [1]Or *dull, insensible* [a]Mark 6:52
18 [a]Jer 5:21; Ezek 12:2; Mark 4:12
19 [a]Mark 6:41-44 [b]Matt 14:20
20 [a]Mark 8:6-9 [b]Mark 8:8
21 [a]Mark 6:52
22 [a]Matt 11:21; Mark 6:45 [b]Mark 3:10
23 [a]Mark 7:33 [b]Mark 5:23
24 [1]Or *gained sight* [2]Or *they look to me*
26 [a]Mark 8:23
27 [a]Mark 8:27-29: *Matt 16:13-16; Luke 9:18-20* [b]Matt 16:13
28 [a]Mark 6:14; Luke 9:7, 8
29 [1]I.e. the Messiah [a]John 6:68, 69
30 [1]Or *strictly admonished* [a]Matt 8:4; 16:20; Luke 9:21
31 [a]Mark 8:31-9:1: *Matt 16:21-28; Luke 9:22-27* [b]Matt 16:21
32 [a]John 10:24; 11:14; 16:25, 29; 18:20
33 [1]Lit *the things of God* [a]Matt 4:10
34 [a]Matt 10:38; Luke 14:27

26 And He sent him to his home, saying, "Do not even enter [a]the village."

Peter's Confession of Christ

27 [a]Jesus went out, along with His disciples, to the villages of [b]Caesarea Philippi; and on the way He questioned His disciples, saying to them, "Who do people say that I am?"

28 [a]They told Him, saying, "John the Baptist; and others *say* Elijah; but others, one of the prophets."

29 And He *continued* by questioning them, "But who do you say that I am?" [a]Peter *answered and *said to Him, "You are [1]the Christ."

30 And [a]He [1]warned them to tell no one about Him.

31 [a]And He began to teach them that [b]the Son of Man must suffer many things and be rejected by the elders and the chief priests and the scribes, and be killed, and after three days rise again.

32 And He was stating the matter [a]plainly. And Peter took Him aside and began to rebuke Him.

33 But turning around and seeing His disciples, He rebuked Peter and *said, "Get behind Me, [a]Satan; for you are not setting your mind on [1]God's interests, but man's."

34 And He summoned the crowd with His disciples, and said to them, "If anyone wishes to come after Me, he must deny himself, and [a]take up his cross and follow Me.

generally in the NT (Matt 16:6,11; Luke 12:1; 1 Cor 5:6–8; Gal 5:9; but Matt 13:33 seems to be an exception—see note there), leaven is a symbol of evil or corruption. The metaphor includes the idea of a tiny amount of leaven being able to ferment a large amount of dough. In this context it refers to the evil disposition of both the Pharisees and Herod Antipas (see Luke 23:8), who called for Jesus to produce a sign, i.e., a proof of His divine authority (see note on v. 11).

8:18–20 These verses imply two feeding narratives (see note on vv. 1–10).

8:22 *Bethsaida.* See note on Matt 11:21.

8:24 *like trees, walking around.* The man had no doubt bumped into trees in his blindness; now he dimly sees something like tree trunks moving about.

8:25 *Then again He laid His hands on his eyes.* This second laying on of hands is unique in Jesus' healing ministry. *began to see everything clearly.* Giving sight to the blind was another indication that Jesus was doing what God had promised to do when He came to bring salvation (Is 35:5).

8:26 *Do not even enter the village.* So as not to broadcast what Jesus had done for him and precipitate a crisis before Jesus had completed His ministry. See 1:44; see also notes on 5:19,43; Matt 8:4; 16:20.

8:27 *Caesarea Philippi.* See notes on 7:24; Matt 16:13.

8:29 *Christ.* See text note. Because popular Jewish ideas associated with the term "Christ" were largely political and national, Jesus seldom used it. Of its seven occurrences in Mark, only three appear in the sayings of Jesus (9:41; 12:35; 13:21), and in none of these does He use the title of Himself (with the possible exception of 9:41). Mark identifies Jesus as the Christ in 1:1.

8:30 *to tell no one about Him.* See 1:44; see also notes on 5:19,43; Matt 8:4; 16:20.

8:31–10:52 A new section begins in 8:31 and centers on three predictions of Jesus' death (8:31; 9:31; 10:33–34). It indicates a geographical shift from Galilee, where most of Jesus' public ministry reported by Mark took place, to Jerusalem and the closing days of Jesus' life on earth. In this section Jesus defines the true meaning of "Christ" as the title applies to Him.

8:31 *Son of Man.* Jesus' most common title for Himself, used 84 times in the Gospels and never used by anyone but Jesus. In Dan 7:13–14 the Son of Man is pictured as a heavenly figure who in the end times is entrusted by God with authority, glory and sovereign power. That Jesus used "Son of Man" as a Messianic title is evident by His use of it (v. 31) in juxtaposition to Peter's use of "Christ" (v. 29). See note on Dan 7:13. *must suffer.* As predicted in the Suffering Servant passage in Is 52:13–53:12 (see Mark 9:9,12,31; 10:33–34; 14:21,41). *elders.* The lay members of the Sanhedrin, the high court of the Jews. *chief priests.* See note on Matt 2:4. These included the ruling high priest, Caiaphas; the former high priest, Annas; and the high priestly families. *scribes.* See note on Matt 2:4. Representatives of the three groups mentioned here constituted the Sanhedrin.

8:32 *Peter . . . began to rebuke Him.* Suffering and rejection had no place in Peter's conception of the Messiah, and he rebuked Jesus for teaching what to him seemed not only inconceivable but terribly wrong.

8:33 *Satan.* Peter's attempt to dissuade Jesus from going to the cross held the same temptation Satan gave at the outset of Jesus' ministry (see Matt 4:8–10), so Jesus severely rebuked him.

8:34 *deny himself.* Cease to make self the object of his life and actions. *take up his cross.* The picture is of a man, already condemned, required to carry the beam of his own cross to the place of execution (see John 19:17). Cross-bearing is a willingness to suffer and die for the Lord's sake. *and follow Me.*

35 "For [a]whoever wishes to save his [1]life will lose it, but whoever loses his [1]life for My sake and the gospel's will save it.

36 "For what does it profit a man to gain the whole world, and forfeit his soul?

37 "For what will a man give in exchange for his soul?

38 "For [a]whoever is ashamed of Me and My words in this adulterous and sinful generation, [b]the Son of Man will also be ashamed of him when He [c]comes in the glory of His Father with the holy angels."

The Transfiguration

9 And Jesus was saying to them, "[a]Truly I say to you, there are some of those who are standing here who will not taste death until they see the kingdom of God after it has come with power."

2 [a]Six days later, Jesus *took with Him [b]Peter and [1]James and John, and *brought them up on a high mountain by themselves. And He was transfigured before them;

3 and [a]His garments became radiant and exceedingly white, as no launderer on earth can whiten them.

4 Elijah appeared to them along with Moses; and they were talking with Jesus.

5 Peter *said to Jesus, "[a]Rabbi, it is good for us to be here; [b]let us make three [1]tabernacles, one for You, and one for Moses, and one for Elijah."

6 For he did not know what to answer; for they became terrified.

7 Then a cloud [1]formed, overshadowing them, and [a]a voice [1]came out of the cloud, "[b]This is My beloved Son, [2]listen to Him!"

8 All at once they looked around and saw no one with them anymore, except Jesus alone.

9 [a]As they were coming down from the mountain, He [b]gave them orders not to relate to anyone what they had seen, [1]until the Son of Man rose from the dead.

10 They [1]seized upon [2]that statement, discussing with one another [3]what rising from the dead meant.

11 They asked Him, saying, "*Why is it* that the scribes say that [a]Elijah must come first?"

12 And He said to them, "Elijah does first come and restore all things. And *yet* how is it written of [a]the Son of Man that [b]He will suffer many things and be treated with contempt?

13 "But I say to you that Elijah has [1]indeed come, and they did to him whatever they wished, just as it is written of him."

All Things Possible

14 [a]When they came *back* to the disciples, they saw a large crowd around them, and *some* scribes arguing with them.

35 [1]Or *soul* [a]Matt 10:39; Luke 17:33; John 12:25
38 [a]Matt 10:33; Luke 9:26; Heb 11:16 [b]Matt 8:20 [c]Matt 16:27; Mark 13:26; Luke 9:26
9:1 [a]Matt 16:28; Mark 13:26; Luke 9:27
2 [1]Or *Jacob* [a]Mark 9:2-8: *Matt 17:1-8; Luke 9:28-36* [b]Mark 5:37
3 [a]Matt 28:3
5 [1]Or *sacred tents* [a]Matt 23:7 [b]Matt 17:4; Luke 9:33
7 [1]Or *occurred* [2]Or *give constant heed* [a]2 Pet 1:17f [b]Matt 3:17; Mark 1:11; Luke 3:22
9 [1]Lit *except when* [a]Mark 9:9-13: *Matt 17:9-13* [b]Matt 8:4; Mark 5:43; 7:36; 8:30
10 [1]Or *kept to themselves* [2]Lit *the statement* [3]Lit *what was the rising from the dead*
11 [a]Mal 4:5; Matt 11:14
12 [a]Mark 9:31 [b]Matt 16:21; 26:24 **13** [1]Lit *also* **14** [a]Mark 9:14-28: *Matt 17:14-19; Luke 9:37-42*

Implying that His own death would be by crucifixion.

8:35 *save his life.* Physical life may be saved by denying Jesus, but eternal life will be lost. Conversely, discipleship may result in the loss of physical life, but that loss is insignificant when compared with gaining eternal life.

8:36 *the whole world.* All the things that could possibly be achieved or acquired in this life. *soul.* That is, eternal life (also in v. 37).

8:38 *ashamed of Me and My words.* Contrast Rom 1:16. A person who is more concerned about fitting into and pleasing his own "adulterous and sinful generation" than about following and pleasing Christ will have no part in God's kingdom. *Son of Man.* See note on 8:31. *when He comes in the glory of His Father.* See 2 Thess 1:6–10. The situation in which Jesus is rejected, humiliated and put to death will be reversed when He returns in glory as the Judge of all people.

9:1 *Truly I say to you.* See note on 3:28. *not taste death until they see the kingdom of God after it has come with power.* See note on Matt 16:28. *kingdom of God.* See note on Matt 3:2.

9:2 *Six days later.* See note on Matt 17:1. *Peter and James and John.* See note on 5:37. *a high mountain.* See note on Luke 9:28. *transfigured.* See note on Matt 17:2.

9:4 *Elijah . . . along with Moses.* See notes on Matt 17:3; Luke 9:30.

9:5 *Rabbi.* Hebrew word for "(my) teacher." *three tabernacles.* Peter may have desired to erect new tents of meeting where God could again communicate with his people (see Ex 29:42). Or he may have been thinking of the booths used at the Feast of Booths (Lev 23:42). In any case, he seemed eager to find fulfillment of the promised glory then, prior to the sufferings that Jesus had announced as necessary.

9:7 *a voice came out of the cloud.* The cloud is frequently a symbol of God's presence to protect and guide (e.g., Ex 16:10; 19:9; 24:15–18; 33:9–10). *listen to Him!* The full sense includes obeying Him. When God is involved, the only true hearing is obedient hearing (see James 1:22–25).

9:9 *not to relate to anyone.* After Jesus' resurrection the disciples were to tell everyone what they had experienced, for Jesus' finished work would have demonstrated His true and full character as the Messiah. *Son of Man.* See note on 8:31.

9:10 *what rising from the dead meant.* As Jews they were familiar with the doctrine of the resurrection; it was the resurrection of the Son of Man that baffled them, because their theology had no place for a suffering and dying Messiah.

9:11 *Elijah must come first.* See note on Matt 17:10.

9:12 *Elijah does first come and restore all things.* A reference to the coming of Elijah, or one like him, in preparation for the coming of the Messiah (see note on Matt 17:10). *Son of Man.* See note on 8:31. *will suffer many things and be treated with contempt.* Just as "Elijah" (John the Baptist; see note on v. 13) has been rejected (see note on Matt 17:12).

9:13 *Elijah has indeed come.* A reference to John the Baptist (see Matt 17:13). *they.* Herod and Herodias (see 6:17–29). John, like Elijah, was opposed by a weak ruler and his wicked consort. *as it is written of him.* What Scripture says about Elijah in his relationship to Ahab and Jezebel (1 Kin 19:1–10). There is no prediction of suffering associated with Elijah's ministry in the end times. However, what happened to Elijah under the threats of Jezebel foreshadowed what would happen to John the Baptist. The order of events suggested in vv. 11–13 is as follows: (1) Elijah ministered in the days of wicked Jezebel; (2) Elijah was a type of John the Baptist, who in turn suffered at the hands of Herodias; (3) the Son of Man suffered and was rejected a short time after John was beheaded.

9:14 *the disciples.* The nine besides Peter, James and John (see v. 2).

15 Immediately, when the entire crowd saw Him, they were [a]amazed and *began* running up to greet Him.

16 And He asked them, "What are you discussing with them?"

17 And one of the crowd answered Him, "Teacher, I brought You my son, possessed with a spirit which makes him mute;

18 and [1]whenever it seizes him, it [2]slams him *to the ground* and he foams *at the mouth,* and grinds his teeth and [3]stiffens out. I told Your disciples to cast it out, and they could not *do it.*"

19 And He *answered them and *said, "O unbelieving generation, how long shall I be with you? How long shall I put up with you? Bring him to Me!"

20 They brought [1]the boy to Him. When he saw Him, immediately the spirit threw him into a convulsion, and falling to the ground, he *began* rolling around and foaming *at the mouth.*

21 And He asked his father, "How long has this been happening to him?" And he said, "From childhood.

22 "It has often thrown him both into the fire and into the water to destroy him. But if You can do anything, take pity on us and help us!"

23 And Jesus said to him, " 'If You can?' [a]All things are possible to him who believes."

24 Immediately the boy's father cried out and said, "I do believe; help my unbelief."

25 When Jesus saw that [a]a crowd was [1]rapidly gathering, He rebuked the unclean spirit, saying to it, "You deaf and mute spirit, I [2]command you, come out of him and do not enter him [3]again."

26 After crying out and throwing him into terrible convulsions, it came out; and *the boy* became so much like a corpse that most *of them* said, "He is dead!"

27 But Jesus took him by the hand and raised him; and he got up.

28 When He came [a]into *the* house, His disciples *began* questioning Him privately, "Why could we not drive it out?"

29 And He said to them, "This kind cannot come out by anything but prayer."

Death and Resurrection Foretold

30 [a]From there they went out and *began* to go through Galilee, and He did not want anyone to know *about it.*

31 For He was teaching His disciples and telling them, "[a]The Son of Man is to be [1]delivered into the hands of men, and they will kill Him; and when He has been killed, He will rise three days later."

32 But [a]they [1]did not understand *this* statement, and they were afraid to ask Him.

33 [a]They came to Capernaum; and when He [1]was in [b]the house, He *began* to question them, "What were you discussing on the way?"

34 But they kept silent, for on the way [a]they had discussed with one another which *of them was* the greatest.

35 Sitting down, He called the twelve and *said to them, "[a]If anyone wants to be first, [1]he shall be last of all and servant of all."

36 Taking a child, He set him [1]before them, and taking him in His arms, He said to them,

37 "[a]Whoever receives [1]one child like this in My name receives Me; and whoever receives Me does not receive Me, but Him who sent Me."

Dire Warnings

38 [a]John said to Him, "Teacher, we saw someone casting out demons in Your name, and [b]we tried to prevent him because he was not following us."

39 But Jesus said, "Do not hinder him, for there is no one who will perform a miracle in My name, and be able soon afterward to speak evil of Me.

40 "[a]For he who is not against us is [1]for us.

15 [a]Mark 14:33; 16:5, 6
18 [1]Or *wherever* [2]Or *tears him* [3]Or *withers away*
20 [1]Lit *him*
23 [a]Matt 17:20; John 11:40
25 [1]Or *running together* [2]Or *I Myself command* [3]Or *from now on* [a]Mark 9:15
28 [a]Mark 2:1; 7:17
30 [a]Mark 9:30-32: *Matt 17:22, 23; Luke 9:43-45*
31 [1]Or *betrayed* [a]Matt 16:21; Mark 8:31; 9:12
32 [1]Lit *were not knowing* [a]Luke 2:50; 9:45; 18:34; John 12:16
33 [1]Lit *had come* [a]Mark 9:33-37: *Matt 18:1-5; Luke 9:46-48* [b]Mark 3:19
34 [a]Matt 18:4; Mark 9:50; Luke 22:24
35 [1]Or *let him be* [a]Matt 20:26; 23:11; Mark 10:43, 44; Luke 22:26
36 [1]Lit *in their midst*
37 [1]Lit *one of such children* [a]Matt 10:40; Luke 10:16; John 13:20
38 [a]Mark 9:38-40: *Luke 9:49, 50* [b]Num 11:27-29
40 [1]Or *on our side* [a]Matt 12:30; Luke 11:23

9:18 Demonic possession was responsible for the boy's condition (see vv. 20,25–26).
9:22 *to destroy him.* See notes on 5:5,13.
9:23 *If You can? All things are possible to him who believes.* The question was not whether Jesus had the power to heal the boy but whether the father had faith to believe it. A person who truly believes will set no limits on what God can do.
9:24 *I do believe; help my unbelief.* Since faith is never perfect, belief and unbelief are often mixed.
9:25 *When Jesus saw that a crowd was rapidly gathering, He rebuked the unclean spirit.* As much as possible, Jesus wanted to avoid further publicity.
9:29 *This kind.* Seems to suggest that there are different kinds of demons. *cannot come out by anything but prayer.* The disciples apparently had taken for granted the power given to them or had come to believe that it was inherent in them. Lack of prayer indicated they had forgotten that their power over the demonic spirits was from Jesus (see 3:15; 6:7,13).
9:30 *began to go through Galilee.* Jesus' public ministry in and around Galilee was completed (see note on 7:24), and He was now on His way to Jerusalem to suffer and die (see 10:32–34). As He had been doing for several months, Jesus continued to focus His teaching ministry on the twelve (v. 31).
9:31 *Son of Man.* See note on 8:31.
9:32 *they did not understand.* See v. 10; 8:32–33.
9:33 *Capernaum.* See notes on 1:21; Matt 4:13. *the house.* Probably the one belonging to Peter and Andrew (see 1:29).
9:34 *they kept silent.* No doubt due to embarrassment. *which of them was the greatest.* Questions of rank and status are normal and played an important role in the life of Jewish groups at this time, but they had no place in Jesus' value system (see v. 35; 10:42–45).
9:35 *Sitting down.* See note on 4:1.
9:38 *not following us.* The man apparently was a believer, but he was not one of the exclusive company of the twelve. Nevertheless he acted in Jesus' name and had done what the disciples, on at least one occasion, had not been able to do (see vv. 14–18,28).
9:39 *Do not hinder him.* Jesus' view of discipleship was far more inclusive than the narrow view held by the twelve.

41 "For [a]whoever gives you a cup of water to drink [1]because of your name as *followers* of Christ, truly I say to you, he will not lose his reward.

42 "[a]Whoever causes one of these [1]little ones who believe to stumble, it [2]would be better for him if, with a heavy millstone hung around his neck, he [3]had been cast into the sea.

43 "[a]If your hand causes you to stumble, cut it off; it is better for you to enter life crippled, than, having your two hands, to go into [1][b]hell, into the [c]unquenchable fire,

44 [[1]where THEIR WORM DOES NOT DIE, AND THE FIRE IS NOT QUENCHED.]

45 "If your foot causes you to stumble, cut it off; it is better for you to enter life lame, than, having your two feet, to be cast into [1][a]hell,

46 [[1]where THEIR WORM DOES NOT DIE, AND THE FIRE IS NOT QUENCHED.]

47 "[a]If your eye causes you to stumble, throw it out; it is better for you to enter the kingdom of God with one eye, than, having two eyes, to be cast into [1][b]hell,

48 [a]where THEIR WORM DOES NOT DIE, AND [b]THE FIRE IS NOT QUENCHED.

49 "For everyone will be salted with fire.

50 "Salt is good; but [a]if the salt becomes unsalty, with what will you [1]make it salty *again?* [b]Have salt in yourselves, and [c]be at peace with one another."

41 [1]Lit *in a name that you are Christ's* [a]Matt 10:42
42 [1]I.e. humble [2]Lit *is better for him if a millstone turned by a donkey is hung* [3]Lit *has been thrown* [a]Matt 18:6; Luke 17:2; 1 Cor 8:12
43 [1]Gr *Gehenna* [a]Matt 5:30; 18:8 [b]Matt 5:22 [c]Matt 3:12; 25:41
44 [1]Vv 44 and 46, which are identical to v 48, are not found in the early mss
45 [1]Gr *Gehenna* [a]Matt 5:22
46 [1]See v 44, note
47 [1]Gr *Gehenna* [a]Matt 5:29; 18:9 [b]Matt 5:22
48 [a]Is 66:24 [b]Matt 3:12; 25:41
50 [1]Lit *season it* [a]Matt 5:13; Luke 14:34f [b]Col 4:6 [c]Mark 9:34; Rom 12:18; 2 Cor 13:11; 1 Thess 5:13

Jesus' Teaching about Divorce

10 [a]Getting up, He *went from there to the region of Judea and beyond the Jordan; crowds *gathered around Him again, and, [b]according to His custom, He once more *began* to teach them.

2 *Some* Pharisees came up to Jesus, testing Him, and *began* to question Him whether it was lawful for a man to [1]divorce a wife.

3 And He answered and said to them, "What did Moses command you?"

4 They said, "[a]Moses permitted *a man* TO WRITE A CERTIFICATE OF DIVORCE AND [1]SEND *her* AWAY."

5 But Jesus said to them, "[1][a]Because of your hardness of heart he wrote you this commandment.

6 "But [a]from the beginning of creation, *God* [b]MADE THEM MALE AND FEMALE.

7 "[a]FOR THIS REASON A MAN SHALL LEAVE HIS FATHER AND MOTHER[1],

8 [a]AND THE TWO SHALL BECOME ONE FLESH; so they are no longer two, but one flesh.

9 "What therefore God has joined together, let no man separate."

10 In the house the disciples *began* questioning Him about this again.

10:1 [a]Mark 10:1-12: *Matt 19:1-9* [b]Matt 4:23; 26:55; Mark 1:21; 2:13; 4:2; 6:2, 6, 34; 12:35; 14:49 **2** [1]Or *send away* **4** [1]Or *divorce her* [a]Deut 24:1, 3; Matt 5:31 **5** [1]Or *With reference to* [a]Matt 19:8 **6** [a]Mark 13:19; 2 Pet 3:4 [b]Gen 1:27; 5:2 **7** [1]Many late mss add *and shall cling to his wife* [a]Gen 2:24 **8** [a]Gen 2:24

9:41 *gives you a cup of water.* God remembers even small acts of kindness extended to believers because they are believers. *truly I say to you.* See note on 3:28. *his reward.* Including God's approval.

9:42 *one of these little ones who believe.* Perhaps the little children mentioned in vv. 36–37, or the man mentioned in v. 38. Jesus' point is clear: To cause even those whom we might consider to be the least of believers to sin will bring serious judgment. *millstone.* A heavy stone slab turned by a donkey in grinding grain.

9:43 *cut it off.* Hyperbole, a figure of speech that exaggerates to make its point, is used here to emphasize the need for drastic action. Often sin can be conquered only by radical "spiritual surgery." *life.* Eternal life in the presence of God. *hell.* See note on Matt 5:22.

9:44,46 Verses 44,46 are not found in important early manuscripts of the NT. Verses 44,46 are identical with v. 48.

9:47 *kingdom of God.* See note on Matt 3:2.

9:48 Is 66:24 speaks of the punishment for rebellion against God. As the final word of Isaiah's message, the passage became familiar as a picture of endless destruction. *WORM DOES NOT DIE.* Worms were always present in the rubbish dump (see note on Matt 5:22).

9:49 The saying may mean that everyone who enters hell will suffer its fire, or (if only loosely connected with the preceding) it may mean that every Christian in this life can expect to undergo the fire of suffering and purification.

9:50 *Salt is good.* The distinctive mark of discipleship typified by salt is allegiance to Jesus and the gospel (see 8:35,38; see also note on Matt 5:13). *be at peace with one another.* Strife is resolved and peace restored when we recognize in one another a common commitment to Jesus and the gospel.

10:1 *region of Judea.* The Greek and Roman equivalent to the OT land of Judah, essentially the southern part of the Holy Land (now exclusive of Idumea), which formerly had been the southern kingdom. For Jesus' ministry in Judea see note on Luke 9:51. *Jordan.* See note on 1:5. Jesus' journey took Him south from Capernaum, over the mountains of Samaria into Judea and then east across the Jordan into Perea, where He was in the territory of Herod Antipas (see note on Matt 14:1). For Jesus' ministry in Perea see note on Luke 13:22.

10:2 *Pharisees.* See note on 2:16. *came up to Jesus, testing Him.* The question of the Pharisees was hostile. It was for unlawful divorce and remarriage that John the Baptist denounced Herod Antipas and Herodias (see 6:17–18), and this rebuke cost him first imprisonment and then his life. Jesus was now within Herod's jurisdiction, and the Pharisees may have hoped that Jesus' reply would cause the tetrarch to seize Him as he had John. *whether it was lawful . . . to divorce a wife.* Jews of that day generally agreed that divorce was lawful, the only debated issue being the proper grounds for it (see note on Matt 19:3).

10:5 *Because of your hardness of heart.* Divorce was an accommodation to human weakness and was used to bring order in a society that had disregarded God's will, but it was not the standard God had originally intended, as vv. 6–9 clearly indicate. The purpose of Deut 24:1 was not to make divorce acceptable, but to reduce the hardship of its consequences.

10:6 *from the beginning of creation.* Jesus goes back to the time before human sin to show God's original intention. God instituted marriage as a great unifying blessing, bonding the male and female in His creation.

10:8 *no longer two, but one.* The deduction drawn by Jesus affirms the ideal of the permanence of marriage.

10:9 *What therefore God has joined together.* Jesus grounds the sanctity of marriage in the authority of God Himself, and His "No" to divorce safeguards against human selfishness, which always threatens to destroy marriage.

11 And He *said to them, "[a]Whoever [1]divorces his wife and marries another woman commits adultery against her;
12 and [a]if she herself [1]divorces her husband and marries another man, she is committing adultery."

Jesus Blesses Little Children

13 [a]And they were bringing children to Him so that He might touch them; but the disciples rebuked them.
14 But when Jesus saw this, He was indignant and said to them, "Permit the children to come to Me; do not hinder them; [a]for the kingdom of God belongs to such as these.
15 "Truly I say to you, [a]whoever does not receive the kingdom of God like a child will not enter it *at all.*"
16 And He [a]took them in His arms and *began* blessing them, laying His hands on them.

The Rich Young Ruler

17 [a]As He was setting out on a journey, a man ran up to Him and [b]knelt before Him, and asked Him, "Good Teacher, what shall I do to [c]inherit eternal life?"
18 And Jesus said to him, "Why do you call Me good? No one is good except God alone.
19 "You know the commandments, '[a]DO NOT MURDER, DO NOT COMMIT ADULTERY, DO NOT STEAL, DO NOT BEAR FALSE WITNESS, Do not defraud, HONOR YOUR FATHER AND MOTHER.' "
20 And he said to Him, "Teacher, I have kept [a]all these things from my youth up."
21 Looking at him, Jesus felt a love for him and said to him, "One thing you lack: go and sell all you possess and give to the poor, and you will have [a]treasure in heaven; and come, follow Me."
22 But at these words [1]he was saddened, and he went away grieving, for he was one who owned much property.
23 And Jesus, looking around, *said to His disciples, "[a]How hard it will be for those who are wealthy to enter the kingdom of God!"
24 The disciples [a]were amazed at His words. But Jesus *answered again and *said to them, "Children, how hard it is to enter the kingdom of God!
25 "[a]It is easier for a camel to go through the eye of a needle than for a rich man to enter the kingdom of God."
26 They were even more astonished and said to Him, "[1]Then who can be saved?"
27 Looking at them, Jesus *said, "[a]With people it is impossible, but not with God; for all things are possible with God."

11 [1]Or *sends away* [a]Matt 5:32 **12** [1]Or *sends away* [a]1 Cor 7:11, 13 **13** [a]Mark 10:13-16: *Matt 19:13-15; Luke 18:15-17* **14** [a]Matt 5:3 **15** [a]Matt 18:3; 19:14; Luke 18:17; 1 Cor 14:20; 1 Pet 2:2 **16** [a]Mark 9:36 **17** [a]Mark 10:17-31: *Matt 19:16-30; Luke 18:18-30* [b]Mark 1:40 [c]Matt 25:34; Luke 10:25; 18:18; Acts 20:32; Eph 1:18; 1 Pet 1:4

19 [a]Ex 20:12-16; Deut 5:16-20 **20** [a]Matt 19:20 **21** [a]Matt 6:20 **22** [1]Or *he became gloomy* **23** [a]Matt 19:23 **24** [a]Mark 1:27 **25** [a]Matt 19:24 **26** [1]Lit *And* **27** [a]Matt 19:26

10:11 *Whoever divorces his wife.* In Jewish practice divorce was effected by the husband himself, not by a judicial authority or court. *commits adultery against her.* A simple declaration of divorce on the part of a husband could not release him from the divine law of marriage and its moral obligations—this enduring force of the marriage bond was unrecognized in rabbinic courts. But see note on Matt 19:3; see also Matt 19:9, where an exception is mentioned. 1 Cor 7:15 may contain another exception (see notes on 1 Cor 7:12,15).
10:12 *she is committing adultery.* In this historical and geographical context, Jesus' pronouncements confirm the bold denunciation by John the Baptist and equally condemn Herod Antipas and Herodias.
10:14 *kingdom of God.* See note on Matt 3:2. *belongs to such as these.* The kingdom of God belongs to those who, like children, are prepared to receive the kingdom as a gift of God (see note on v. 15).
10:15 *Truly I say to you.* See note on 3:28. *like a child.* The point of comparison is the usual openness and receptivity of children. The kingdom of God must be received as a gift; it cannot be achieved by human effort. It may be entered only by those who know they are helpless, without claim or merit.
10:16 *and began blessing them.* Jesus visually demonstrated that the blessings of the kingdom are freely given.
10:17 *a man.* Mark does not identify the man, but Luke (18:18) calls him a "ruler," meaning he was probably a member of an official council or court, and Matthew (19:20) says he was "young." *what shall I do . . . ?* The rich man was thinking in terms of earning righteousness to merit eternal life, but Jesus taught that it was a gift to be received (see v. 15). *eternal life.* See note on Matt 19:16.
10:18 *Why do you call Me good?* Jesus was not denying His own goodness but was forcing the man to recognize that his only hope was in total reliance on God, who alone can give eternal life. He may also have been encouraging the young man to consider the full identity and nature of the One he was addressing.
10:19 *Do not defraud.* The prohibition of fraud may have represented the tenth commandment (against covetousness). If so, Jesus here mentions all six commandments that prohibit wrong actions and attitudes against one's fellowman (see Ex 20:12–16; Deut 5:16–21).
10:20 *I have kept all these things.* The man spoke sincerely, because for him keeping the law was a matter of external conformity. That the law also required inner obedience, which no one can fully satisfy, apparently escaped him completely. Paul speaks of having had a similar outlook before his conversion (Phil 3:6). *from my youth up.* Probably a reference to the age of 13, when a Jewish boy assumed personal responsibility for obeying the commandments.
10:21 *Jesus felt a love for him.* Jesus recognized the man's earnestness. His response was not intended to shame him by exposing failure to understand the spiritual depth of the commandments but was an expression of genuine love. *One thing you lack: go and sell all.* The young man's primary problem was his wealth (see v. 22), and therefore Jesus' prescription was to rid him of it. There is no indication that Jesus' command to him was meant for all Christians. It applies only to those who have the same spiritual problem. *treasure in heaven.* The gift of eternal life, or salvation. This treasure is not to be earned by self-denial or giving of one's material goods but is to be received by following Jesus. In giving away his wealth, the young man would have removed the obstacle that kept him from trusting in Jesus.
10:22 *he went away grieving, for he . . . owned much property.* The tragic decision to turn away reflected a greater love for his possessions than for eternal life (cf. 4:19).
10:25 *eye of a needle.* The camel was the largest animal found in the Holy Land. The vivid contrast between the largest animal and the smallest opening represents what, humanly speaking, is impossible.
10:27 *With people it is impossible, but not with God.* Salvation is totally the work of God. Every attempt to enter the kingdom

28 [a]Peter began to say to Him, "Behold, we have left everything and followed You."

29 Jesus said, "Truly I say to you, [a]there is no one who has left house or brothers or sisters or mother or father or children or farms, for My sake and for the gospel's sake,

30 [1]but that he will receive a hundred times as much now in [2]the present age, houses and brothers and sisters and mothers and children and farms, along with persecutions; and in [a]the age to come, eternal life.

31 "But [a]many *who are* first will be last, and the last, first."

Jesus' Sufferings Foretold

32 [a]They were on the road going up to Jerusalem, and Jesus was walking on ahead of them; and they [b]were amazed, and those who followed were fearful. And again He took the twelve aside and began to tell them what was going to happen to Him,

33 *saying,* "Behold, we are going up to Jerusalem, and [a]the Son of Man will be [1]delivered to the chief priests and the scribes; and they will condemn Him to death and will [2]hand Him over to the Gentiles.

34 "They will mock Him and [a]spit on Him, and scourge Him and kill *Him,* and three days later He will rise again."

35 [1a]James and John, the two sons of Zebedee, *came up to Jesus, saying, "Teacher, we want You to do for us whatever we ask of You."

36 And He said to them, "What do you want Me to do for you?"

37 They said to Him, "[1]Grant that we [a]may sit, one on Your right and one on *Your* left, in Your glory."

38 But Jesus said to them, "You do not know what you are asking. Are you able [a]to drink the cup that I drink, or [b]to be baptized with the baptism with which I am baptized?"

39 They said to Him, "We are able." And Jesus said to them, "The cup that I drink [a]you shall drink; and you shall be baptized with the baptism with which I am baptized.

40 "But to sit on My right or on *My* left, this is not Mine to give; [a]but it is for those for whom it has been prepared."

41 [a]Hearing *this,* the ten began to feel indignant with [1]James and John.

42 Calling them to Himself, Jesus *said to them, "You know that those who are recognized as rulers of the Gentiles lord it over them; and their great men exercise authority over them.

43 "But it is not this way among you, [a]but whoever wishes to become great among you shall be your servant;

44 and whoever wishes to be first among you shall be slave of all.

45 "For even the Son of Man [a]did not come to be served, but to serve, and to give His [1]life a ransom for many."

28 [a]Matt 4:20-22
29 [a]Matt 6:33; 19:29; Luke 18:29f
30 [1]Lit *if not* [2]Lit *this time* [a]Matt 12:32
31 [a]Matt 19:30; 20:16; Luke 13:30
32 [a]Mark 10:32-34: *Matt 20:17-19; Luke 18:31-33* [b]Mark 1:27
33 [1]Or *betrayed* [2]Or *betray* [a]Mark 8:31; 9:12
34 [a]Matt 16:21; 26:67; 27:30; Mark 9:31; 14:65
35 [1]Or *Jacob* [a]Mark 10:35-45: *Matt 20:20-28*
37 [1]Lit *Give to us* [a]Matt 19:28
38 [a]Matt 20:22 [b]Luke 12:50
39 [a]Acts 12:2; Rev 1:9
40 [a]Matt 13:11
41 [1]Or *Jacob* [a]Mark 10:42-45; Luke 22:25-27
43 [a]Matt 20:26; 23:11; Mark 9:35; Luke 22:26
45 [1]Or *soul* [a]Matt 20:28

on the basis of achievement or merit is futile. Apart from the grace of God, no one can be saved.

10:29 *Truly I say to you.* See note on 3:28. *gospel's.* See note on 1:1.

10:30 *the present age . . . the age to come.* These two terms take in all of time from the fall of man to the eternal state. The present age is evil (Gal 1:4), but the coming righteous age will begin with the second advent of Christ and continue forever. *a hundred times as much . . . along with persecutions.* The life of discipleship is a combination of promise and persecution, blessing and suffering. God takes nothing from a Christian without making multiplied restoration in a new and glorious form. Paradoxically, fellowship with other believers develops most deeply in persecution. *eternal life.* Beyond the conflicts of history is the triumph assured to those who belong to God.

10:31 *first will be last.* A warning against pride in sacrificial accomplishments such as Peter had manifested (v. 28).

10:32 *on the road going up to Jerusalem.* This last journey to Jerusalem began in a city called Ephraim (cf. John 11:54) and took Jesus into Galilee (Luke 17:11), south through Perea to Jericho (Luke 18:35), then to Bethany (Luke 19:29) and finally to Jerusalem (Luke 19:41). *those who followed.* Probably pilgrims on their way to the Passover in Jerusalem. *the twelve.* See 3:16–19 and notes on Luke 6:14–16.

10:33–34 *Gentiles. They will . . . kill Him.* The word "crucify" does not occur in any of the passion predictions in Mark's Gospel, but the statement that Jesus would be handed over to Gentiles to be killed by them suggests crucifixion, since this was the usual means of Roman execution of non-Romans.

10:33 *Son of Man . . . chief priests . . . scribes.* See notes on 8:31; Matt 2:4.

10:35–45 Parallel to 9:33–37. Both passages deal with true greatness and both follow a prediction of Jesus' suffering and death. Both also show how spiritually undiscerning the disciples were.

10:35–36 *want . . . want.* James's and John's desire for position and power would be realized only if they willingly submitted to servanthood (see "wishes . . . wishes" in vv. 43–44).

10:35 *James and John, the two sons of Zebedee.* See 1:19; 3:17.

10:37 *sit, one on Your right and one on Your left.* Positions of prestige and power.

10:38 *drink the cup that I drink.* A Jewish expression that meant to share someone's fate. In the OT the cup of wine was a common metaphor for God's wrath against human sin and rebellion (Ps 75:8; Is 51:17–23; Jer 25:15–28; 49:12; 51:7). Accordingly, the cup Jesus had to drink refers to divine punishment of sins that He bore in place of sinful mankind (see 10:45; 14:36). *be baptized with the baptism with which I am baptized.* The image of baptism is parallel to that of the cup, referring to His suffering and death as a baptism (see Luke 12:50; cf. Rom 6:3–4 for the figure).

10:40 *is not Mine to give.* Jesus would not usurp His Father's authority.

10:41 *the ten.* The other disciples. *indignant.* Possibly because they desired the positions of prestige and power for themselves.

10:43 *not this way among you.* Jesus overturns the value structure of the world. The life of discipleship is to be characterized by humble and loving service.

10:45 A key verse in Mark's Gospel. Jesus came to this world as a servant—indeed, the Servant—who would suffer and die for our redemption, as Isaiah clearly predicted (Is 52:13–53:12). *Son of Man.* See note on 8:31. *ransom.* Means "the price paid for release (from bondage)." Jesus gave His life to release us

Bartimaeus Receives His Sight

46 [a]Then they *came to Jericho. And [b]as
He was leaving Jericho with His disciples
and a large crowd, a blind beggar *named*
Bartimaeus, the son of Timaeus, was sitting
by the road.
47 When he heard that it was Jesus the
[a]Nazarene, he began to cry out and say,
"Jesus, [b]Son of David, have mercy on me!"
48 Many were sternly telling him to be
quiet, but he kept crying out all the more,
"[a]Son of David, have mercy on me!"
49 And Jesus stopped and said, "Call him
here." So they *called the blind man, saying
to him, "[a]Take courage, stand up! He is calling for you."
50 Throwing aside his cloak, he jumped
up and came to Jesus.
51 And answering him, Jesus said, "What
do you want Me to do for you?" And the
blind man said to Him, "[1][a]Rabboni, *I want* to
regain my sight!"
52 And Jesus said to him, "Go; [a]your faith
has [1]made you well." Immediately he
regained his sight and *began* following Him
on the road.

The Triumphal Entry

11 [a]As they *approached Jerusalem, at
Bethphage and [b]Bethany, near [c]the
Mount of Olives, He *sent two of His disciples,
2 and *said to them, "Go into the village
opposite you, and immediately as you enter
it, you will find a colt tied *there,* on which no
one yet has ever sat; untie it and bring it
here.
3 "If anyone says to you, 'Why are you
doing this?' you say, 'The Lord has need of
it'; and immediately he [1]will send it back
here."
4 They went away and found a colt tied
at the door, outside in the street; and they
*untied it.
5 Some of the bystanders were saying to
them, "What are you doing, untying the
colt?"
6 They spoke to them just as Jesus had
told *them,* and they gave them permission.
7 [a]They *brought the colt to Jesus and
put their coats on it; and He sat on it.
8 And many spread their coats in the
road, and others *spread* leafy branches
which they had cut from the fields.
9 Those who went in front and those
who followed were shouting:
"Hosanna!
[a]BLESSED IS HE WHO COMES IN THE NAME
OF THE LORD;
10 Blessed *is* the coming kingdom of our
father David;
Hosanna [a]in the highest!"
11 [a]Jesus entered Jerusalem *and came*
into the temple; and after looking around at
everything, [b]He left for Bethany with the
twelve, since it was already late.
12 [a]On the next day, when they had left
Bethany, He became hungry.
13 Seeing at a distance a fig tree in leaf, He
went *to see* if perhaps He would find any-

46 [a]Mark 10:46-52: *Matt 20:29-34; Luke 18:35-43* [b]Luke 18:35; 19:1
47 [a]Mark 1:24 [b]Matt 9:27
48 [a]Matt 9:27
49 [a]Matt 9:2
51 [1]I.e. My Master [a]Matt 23:7; John 20:16
52 [1]Lit *saved you* [a]Matt 9:22
11:1 [a]Mark 11:1-10: *Matt 21:1-9; Luke 19:29-38* [b]Matt 21:17 [c]Matt 21:1
3 [1]Lit *sends*
7 [a]Mark 11:7-10: *Matt 21:4-9; Luke 19:35-38; John 12:12-15*
9 [a]Ps 118:26; Matt 21:9
10 [a]Matt 21:9
11 [a]Matt 21:12 [b]Matt 21:17
12 [a]Mark 11:12-14, 20-24: *Matt 21:18-22*

from bondage to sin and death. *for.* That is, "in place of," pointing to Christ's substitutionary death. See note on Matt 20:28. *many.* In contrast to the one life given for our ransom.

10:46 *Jericho.* A very ancient city located five miles west of the Jordan and about 15 miles northeast of Jerusalem. In Jesus' time OT Jericho was largely abandoned, but a new city, south of the old one, had been built by Herod the Great. *leaving Jericho.* Luke says Jesus "approached the city" (Luke 18:35). He may have been referring to the new Jericho, while Matthew (20:29) and Mark may have meant the old city. *a blind beggar.* The presence of a blind beggar just outside the city gates, on a road pilgrims followed on the way to Jerusalem, was a common sight in that day.

10:47 *the Nazarene.* See note on Matt 2:23. *Son of David.* A Messianic title (see Is 11:1–3; Jer 23:5–6; Ezek 34:23–24; and notes on Matt 1:1; 9:27). Verses 47–48 are the only places in Mark where it is used to address Jesus. Its only other occurrence in Mark is in 12:35.

10:51 *Rabboni.* Hebrew word for "(my) teacher."

11:1–11 At this point a new section in the Gospel of Mark begins. Jesus arrives in Jerusalem, and the rest of his ministry takes place within the confines of the Holy City. The Triumphal Entry, which inaugurates Passion Week, is a deliberate Messianic action, and the clue to its understanding is found in Zech 9:9 (quoted in Matt 21:5; John 12:15). Jesus purposefully offers Himself as the Messiah, knowing that this will provoke Jewish leaders to take action against him.

11:1 *Bethphage.* See note on Matt 21:1. *Bethany.* See note on Matt 21:17. *Mount of Olives.* Directly east of Jerusalem, it rises to a height of about 2,700 feet, some 200 feet higher than Mount Zion. Its summit commands a magnificent view of the city and especially of the temple.

11:2 *the village opposite you.* Probably Bethphage. *colt.* The Greek word can mean the young of any animal, but here it means the colt of a donkey (see Matt 21:2; John 12:15). *on which no one yet has ever sat.* Unused animals were regarded as especially suitable for religious purposes (see Num 19:2; Deut 21:3; 1 Sam 6:7).

11:3 *If anyone says to you.* The message concerning the colt is not directed specifically to the owner but to anyone who might question the disciples' action. *Lord.* See note on Luke 19:31.

11:8 *leafy branches.* These were readily available in nearby fields. John identifies the branches as palm branches (John 12:13), which apparently came from Jericho, since they are not native to Jerusalem.

11:9 *Hosanna.* The English rendering of a Greek version of the Hebrew for 'save now!' as found in invocations such as Ps 118:25. *BLESSED IS HE WHO COMES.* A quotation of Ps 118:26, one of the Hallel ("Praise") Psalms sung at Passover and especially fitting for this occasion.

11:10 *the coming kingdom of our father David.* The Messianic kingdom promised to David's son (2 Sam 7:11–14).

11:11 *temple.* See note on Matt 4:5. *left for Bethany.* Apparently Jesus spent each night through Thursday of Passion Week in Bethany at the home of His friends Mary, Martha and Lazarus (see 11:19; 14:13; Matt 21:17; John 12:1–3). *the twelve.* See 3:16–19 and notes on Luke 6:14–16.

11:12 *On the next day.* Monday of Passion Week. *Bethany.* See note on Matt 21:17.

thing on it; and when He came to it, He
found nothing but leaves, for it was not the
season for figs.
14 He said to it, "May no one ever eat fruit
from you again!" And His disciples were listening.

Jesus Drives Money Changers from the Temple

15 [a]Then they *came to Jerusalem. And
He entered the temple and began to drive out
those who were buying and selling in the
temple, and overturned the tables of the
money changers and the seats of those who
were selling [1]doves;
16 and He would not permit anyone to
carry [1]merchandise through the temple.
17 And He *began* to teach and say to
them, "Is it not written, '[a]MY HOUSE SHALL BE
CALLED A HOUSE OF PRAYER FOR ALL THE NATIONS'?
[b]But you have made it a ROBBERS' [1]DEN."
18 The chief priests and the scribes heard
this, and [a]*began* seeking how to destroy
Him; for they were afraid of Him, for [b]the
whole crowd was astonished at His teaching.
19 [a]When evening came, [1]they would go
out of the city.
20 [a]As they were passing by in the morning, they saw the fig tree withered from the
roots *up.*
21 Being reminded, Peter *said to Him,
"[a]Rabbi, look, the fig tree which You cursed
has withered."
22 And Jesus *answered saying to them,
"[a]Have faith in God.
23 "[a]Truly I say to you, whoever says to
this mountain, 'Be taken up and cast into the
sea,' and does not doubt in his heart, but
believes that what he says is going to happen, it will be *granted* him.
24 "Therefore I say to you, [a]all things for
which you pray and ask, believe that you
have received them, and they will be *granted*
you.
25 " Whenever you [a]stand praying, [b]forgive,
if you have anything against anyone, so that
your Father who is in heaven will also forgive you your transgressions.
26 ["[1a]But if you do not forgive, neither
will your Father who is in heaven forgive
your transgressions."]

Jesus' Authority Questioned

27 They *came again to Jerusalem. [a]And
as He was walking in the temple, the chief
priests and the scribes and the elders *came
to Him,
28 and *began* saying to Him, "By what
authority are You doing these things, or who
gave You this authority to do these things?"
29 And Jesus said to them, "I will ask you
one question, and you answer Me, and *then*
I will tell you by what authority I do these
things.

15 [1]Lit *the doves* [a]Mark 11:15-18: *Matt 21:12-16; Luke 19:45-47;* John 2:13-16
16 [1]Lit *a vessel;* i.e. a receptacle or implement of any kind
17 [1]Lit *cave* [a]Is 56:7 [b]Jer 7:11
18 [a]Matt 21:46; Mark 12:12; Luke 20:19; John 7:1 [b]Matt 7:28
19 [1]I.e. Jesus and His disciples [a]Matt 21:17; Mark 11:11; Luke 21:37
20 [a]Mark 11:12-14, 20-24: *Matt 21:19-22*
21 [a]Matt 23:7
22 [a]Matt 17:20; 21:21f
23 [a]Matt 17:20; 1 Cor 13:2
24 [a]Matt 7:7f
25 [a]Matt 6:5 [b]Matt 6:14
26 [1]Early mss do not contain this v [a]Matt 6:15; 18:35
27 [a]Mark 11:27-33: *Matt 21:23-27; Luke 20:1-8*

11:13 *not the season for figs.* Fig trees around Jerusalem normally begin to get leaves in March or April but do not produce figs until their leaves are all out in June. This tree was an exception in that it was already, at Passover time, full of leaves.
11:14 *May no one ever eat fruit from you again!* Perhaps the incident was a parable of judgment, with the fig tree representing Israel (see Hos 9:10; Nah 3:12). A tree full of leaves normally should have fruit, but this one was cursed because it had none. The fact that the cleansing of the temple (vv. 15–19) is sandwiched between the two parts of the account of the fig tree (vv. 12–14 and vv. 20–25) may underscore the theme of judgment (see note on v. 21). The only application Jesus makes, however, is as an illustration of believing prayer (vv. 21–25).
11:15–19 All three Synoptic writers mention a cleansing of the temple at the end of Jesus' ministry. Only John has one at the beginning. See notes on Matt 21:12–17; John 2:14–17.
11:15 *the temple.* This refers to the court of the Gentiles, the only part of the temple in which Gentiles could worship God and gather for prayer (see v. 17). *buying and selling.* Pilgrims coming to the Passover Feast needed animals that met the ritual requirements for sacrifice, and the vendors set up their animal pens and money tables in the court of the Gentiles. *the tables of the money changers.* Pilgrims needed their money changed into the local currency because the annual temple tax had to be paid in that currency. Also, the Mishnah (see note on Matt 15:2) required Tyrian currency for some offerings. *those who were selling doves.* Doves were required for the purification of women (Lev 12:6; Luke 2:22–24), the cleansing of those with certain skin diseases (Lev 14:22), and other purposes (Lev 15:14,29). They were also the usual offering of the poor (Lev 5:7).
11:16 *to carry merchandise through the temple.* A detail found only in Mark. Apparently the temple area was being used as a shortcut between the city and the Mount of Olives. See note on v. 27.
11:17 *A HOUSE OF PRAYER FOR ALL THE NATIONS.* Is 56:7 assured godly non-Jews that they would be allowed to worship God in the temple. By allowing the court of the Gentiles to become a noisy, smelly marketplace, the Jewish religious leaders were interfering with God's provision. *A ROBBERS' DEN.* Not only because they took financial advantage of the people but because they robbed the temple of its sanctity.
11:18 *chief priests and the scribes.* See note on Matt 2:4. *began seeking how to destroy Him.* See note on 3:6. They regarded Jesus as a dangerous threat to their whole way of life.
11:19 *would go out of the city.* To Bethany (see note on v. 11).
11:20 *In the morning.* Tuesday morning of Passion Week. *withered from the roots up.* This detail indicates that the destruction was total (see Job 18:16) and that no one in the future would eat fruit from the tree. It served as a vivid warning of the judgment to come in A.D. 70 (see 13:2 and note on Matt 24:2).
11:21 *Rabbi.* Hebrew word for "(my) teacher." *fig tree which You cursed.* See note on v. 14. *has withered.* Perhaps prophetic of the fate of the Jewish authorities who were now about to reject their Messiah.
11:23 *Truly I say to you.* See note on 3:28. *this mountain . . . into the sea.* The Mount of Olives, from which the Dead Sea is visible.
11:26 This verse is not found in the earliest and best manuscripts of the NT, probably having been inserted from Matt 6:15.
11:27 *temple.* Several courts surrounded the main temple buildings, including the court of the women, the court of the men (Israelite), and the court of the Gentiles (see v. 16). *the chief priests and the scribes and the elders.* See note on 8:31.
11:28 *authority.* The Sanhedrin was asking why Jesus performed what appeared to be an official act if He possessed no official status (see note on Luke 20:2).

30 "Was the baptism of John from heaven,
or from men? Answer Me."
31 They *began* reasoning among themselves, saying, "If we say, 'From heaven,' He
will say, 'Then why did you not believe
him?'
32 "But [1]shall we say, 'From men'?"—they
were afraid of the people, for everyone considered John to have been a real prophet.
33 Answering Jesus, they *said, "We do
not know." And Jesus *said to them, "Nor
[1]will I tell you by what authority I do these
things."

Parable of the Vine-growers

12 [a]And He began to speak to them in parables: "[b]A man [c]PLANTED A VINEYARD AND
PUT A [1]WALL AROUND IT, AND DUG A VAT UNDER
THE WINE PRESS AND BUILT A TOWER, and rented
it out to [2]vine-growers and went on a journey.
2 "At the *harvest* time he sent a slave to
the vine-growers, in order to receive *some* of
the produce of the vineyard from the vine-
growers.
3 "They took him, and beat him and sent
him away empty-handed.
4 "Again he sent them another slave, and
they wounded him in the head, and treated
him shamefully.
5 "And he sent another, and that one they
killed; and *so with* many others, beating
some and killing others.
6 "He had one more *to send*, a beloved
son; he sent him last *of all* to them, saying,
'They will respect my son.'
7 "But those vine-growers said to one
another, 'This is the heir; come, let us kill
him, and the inheritance will be ours!'

32 [1]Or *if we say* **33** [1]Lit *do I tell* **12:1** [1]Or *fence* [2]Or *tenant farmers,* also vv 2, 7, 9 [a]Mark 3:23; 4:2ff [b]Mark 12:1-12: *Matt 21:33-46; Luke 20:9-19* [c]Is 5:1, 2

9 [1]Lit *lord* **10** [a]Ps 118:22 **11** [a]Ps 118:23 **12** [1]Lit *crowd* [a]Mark 11:18 [b]Matt 22:22 **13** [a]Mark 12:13-17: *Matt 22:15-22; Luke 20:20-26* [b]Matt 22:16 [c]Luke 11:54 **14** [1]Lit *it is not a concern to You about anyone;* i.e. You do not seek anyone's favor [2]Or *permissible* **15** [1]The denarius was a day's wages **17** [1]Or *were greatly marveling* [a]Matt 22:21 **18** [a]Mark 12:18-27: *Matt 22:23-33; Luke 20:27-38;* Acts 23:8

8 "They took him, and killed him and
threw him out of the vineyard.
9 "What will the [1]owner of the vineyard
do? He will come and destroy the vine-growers, and will give the vineyard to others.
10 "Have you not even read this Scripture:
'[a]THE STONE WHICH THE BUILDERS
REJECTED,
THIS BECAME THE CHIEF CORNER *stone;*
11 [a]THIS CAME ABOUT FROM THE LORD,
AND IT IS MARVELOUS IN OUR EYES'?"
12 [a]And they were seeking to seize Him,
and *yet* they feared the [1]people, for they
understood that He spoke the parable against
them. And *so* [b]they left Him and went away.

Jesus Answers the Pharisees, Sadducees and Scribes

13 [a]Then they *sent some of the Pharisees
and [b]Herodians to Him in order to [c]trap Him
in a statement.
14 They *came and *said to Him,
"Teacher, we know that You are truthful and
[1]defer to no one; for You are not partial to
any, but teach the way of God in truth. Is it
[2]lawful to pay a poll-tax to Caesar, or not?
15 "Shall we pay or shall we not pay?" But
He, knowing their hypocrisy, said to them,
"Why are you testing Me? Bring Me a [1]denar-
ius to look at."
16 They brought *one.* And He *said to
them, "Whose likeness and inscription is
this?" And they said to Him, "Caesar's."
17 And Jesus said to them, "[a]Render to
Caesar the things that are Caesar's, and to
God the things that are God's." And they
[1]were amazed at Him.
18 [a]*Some* Sadducees (who say that there
is no resurrection) *came to Jesus, and
began questioning Him, saying,

11:30 *from heaven, or from men?* "Heaven" was a common Jewish term for God, often substituted for the divine name to avoid a possible misuse of it (see Ex 20:7). Jesus' question implied that His authority, like that of John's baptism, came from God.
12:1–12 Most of Jesus' parables make one main point. This one is rather complex, and the details fit the social situation in Jewish Galilee in the first century. Large estates, owned by absentee landlords, were put in the hands of local peasants who cultivated the land as tenant farmers. The parable exposed the planned attempt on Jesus' life, and God's judgment on the planners. See notes on Matt 21:35–37,41.
12:1 *parables.* See note on 4:2. *A man PLANTED A VINEYARD.* The description reflects the language of Is 5:1–2 where the vineyard clearly symbolizes Israel. *TOWER.* See note on Matt 21:33.
12:7 *the inheritance will be ours!* Jewish law provided that a piece of property unclaimed by an heir would be declared "ownerless," and could be claimed by anyone. The vine-growers assumed that the son came as heir to claim his property, and that if he were slain, they could claim the land.
12:9 *others.* See note on Matt 21:41.
12:10 *CHIEF CORNER stone.* See note on Ps 118:22.
12:12 *against them.* The representatives of the Sanhedrin mentioned in 11:27.
12:13–17 This incident probably took place on Tuesday of Passion Week in one of the temple courts (see chart, pp. 1446–1447).
12:13 *Pharisees.* See note on 2:16. *Herodians.* See note on 3:6. The plan to destroy Jesus, which had originated early in His Galilean ministry, had now matured and was gaining momentum in Jerusalem.
12:14 *pay a poll-tax to Caesar.* Jews in Judea were required to pay tribute money to the emperor. The tax was highly unpopular, and some Jews flatly refused to pay it, believing that payment was an admission of Roman right to rule. See note on Matt 22:15–17.
12:15 *denarius.* See notes on 6:37; Matt 22:19.
12:17 *Render to Caesar the things that are Caesar's.* See note on Matt 22:21. There are obligations to the state that do not infringe on our obligations to God (see Rom 13:1–7; 1 Tim 2:1–6; Titus 3:1–2; 1 Pet 2:13–17).
12:18 *Sadducees.* A Jewish party that represented the wealthy and sophisticated classes. They were located largely in Jerusalem and made the temple and its administration their primary interest. Though they were small in number, in Jesus' time they exerted powerful political and religious influence. See notes on Matt 3:7; Luke 20:27; Acts 4:1. *(who say there is no resurrection).* They denied the resurrection, accepted only the five books of Moses as authoritative and flatly rejected the oral tradition (see note on Matt 15:2). These beliefs set them against the Pharisees and common Jewish piety.

19 "Teacher, Moses wrote for us that [a]IF A MAN'S BROTHER DIES and leaves behind a wife AND LEAVES NO CHILD, HIS BROTHER SHOULD [1]MARRY THE WIFE AND RAISE UP CHILDREN TO HIS BROTHER.

20 "There were seven brothers; and the first took a wife, and died leaving no children.

21 "The second one [1]married her, and died leaving behind no children; and the third likewise;

22 and *so* [1]all seven left no children. Last of all the woman died also.

23 "In the resurrection, [1]when they rise again, which one's wife will she be? For [2]all seven had married her."

24 Jesus said to them, "Is this not the reason you are mistaken, that you do not [1]understand the Scriptures or the power of God?

25 "For when they rise from the dead, they neither marry nor are given in marriage, but are like angels in heaven.

26 "But [1]regarding the fact that the dead rise again, have you not read in the book of Moses, [a]in the *passage* about *the burning* bush, how God spoke to him, saying, '[b]I AM THE GOD OF ABRAHAM, AND THE GOD OF ISAAC, and the God of Jacob'?

27 "[a]He is not the God [1]of the dead, but of the living; you are greatly mistaken."

28 [a]One of the scribes came and heard them arguing, and [b]recognizing that He had answered them well, asked Him, "What commandment is the [1]foremost of all?"

29 Jesus answered, "The foremost is, '[a]HEAR, O ISRAEL! THE LORD OUR GOD IS ONE LORD;

30 [a]AND YOU SHALL LOVE THE LORD YOUR GOD WITH ALL YOUR HEART, AND WITH ALL YOUR SOUL, AND WITH ALL YOUR MIND, AND WITH ALL YOUR STRENGTH.'

31 "The second is this, '[a]YOU SHALL LOVE YOUR NEIGHBOR AS YOURSELF.' There is no other commandment greater than these."

32 The scribe said to Him, "Right, Teacher; You have truly stated that [a]HE IS ONE, AND THERE IS NO ONE ELSE BESIDES HIM;

33 [a]AND TO LOVE HIM WITH ALL THE HEART AND WITH ALL THE UNDERSTANDING AND WITH ALL THE STRENGTH, AND TO LOVE ONE'S NEIGHBOR AS HIMSELF, [b]is much more than all burnt offerings and sacrifices."

34 When Jesus saw that he had answered intelligently, He said to him, "You are not far from the kingdom of God." [a]After that, no one would venture to ask Him any more questions.

35 [a]And Jesus *began* to say, as He [b]taught in the temple, "How *is it that* the scribes say that [1]the Christ is the [c]son of David?

36 "David himself said [1]in the Holy Spirit,

'[a]THE LORD SAID TO MY LORD,
"SIT AT MY RIGHT HAND,
UNTIL I PUT YOUR ENEMIES BENEATH YOUR FEET."'

37 "David himself calls Him 'Lord'; so in what sense is He his son?" And [a]the large crowd [1]enjoyed listening to Him.

38 [a]In His teaching He was saying: "Beware of the scribes who like to walk around in long robes, and *like* [b]respectful greetings in the market places,

39 and chief seats in the synagogues and places of honor at banquets,

40 [a]who devour widows' houses, and for appearance's sake offer long prayers; these will receive greater condemnation."

The Widow's Mite

41 [a]And He sat down opposite [b]the treasury, and *began* observing how the people were [c]putting [1]money into the treasury; and many rich people were putting in large sums.

42 A poor widow came and put in two

19 [1]Lit *take* [a]Deut 25:5 **21** [1]Lit *took* **22** [1]Lit *the seven* **23** [1]Early mss do not contain *when they rise again* [2]Lit *the seven* **24** [1]Or *know* **26** [1]Lit *concerning the dead, that they rise* [a]Luke 20:37; Rom 11:2 [b]Ex 3:6 **27** [1]Or *of corpses* [a]Matt 22:32; Luke 20:38 **28** [1]Or *first* [a]Mark 12:28-34: *Matt 22:34-40;* Luke 10:25-28; 20:39f [b]Matt 22:34; Luke 20:39 **29** [a]Deut 6:4 **30** [a]Deut 6:5 **31** [a]Lev 19:18

32 [a]Deut 4:35 **33** [a]Deut 6:5 [b]1 Sam 15:22; Hos 6:6; Mic 6:6-8; Matt 9:13; 12:7 **34** [a]Matt 22:46 **35** [1]I.e. the Messiah [a]Mark 12:35-37: *Matt 22:41-46; Luke 20:41-44* [b]Matt 26:55; Mark 10:1 [c]Matt 9:27 **36** [1]Or *by* [a]Ps 110:1 **37** [1]Lit *was gladly hearing Him* [a]John 12:9 **38** [a]Mark 12:38-40: *Matt 23:1-7; Luke 20:45-47* [b]Matt 23:7; Luke 11:43 **40** [a]Luke 20:47 **41** [1]I.e. copper coins [a]Mark 12:41-44: *Luke 21:1-4* [b]John 8:20 [c]2 Kin 12:9

12:19 See note on Matt 22:24.
12:26 *book of Moses.* The Pentateuch, the first five books of the OT. *in the passage about the burning bush.* A common way of referring to Ex 3:1–6 (see Rom 11:2, where "about Elijah" refers to 1 Kin 19:1–10).
12:28 *What commandment is the foremost of all?* Jewish rabbis counted 613 individual statutes in the law, and attempted to differentiate between "heavy" (or "great") and "light" (or "little") commands.
12:29 The first quotation came to be known as the Shema, named after the first word of Deut 6:4 in Hebrew, which means "hear." The Shema became the Jewish confession of faith, which was recited by pious Jews every morning and evening. To this day it begins every synagogue service.
12:31 To the Shema Jesus joined the commandment from Lev 19:18 to show that love for neighbor is a natural and logical outgrowth of love for God. *NEIGHBOR.* See Luke 10:25–37.
12:33 *all burnt offerings and sacrifices.* The comparison was undoubtedly suggested by the fact that the discussion took place in the temple courtyard (see 11:27).
12:34 *kingdom of God.* See note on Matt 3:2.
12:35 *temple.* See note on 11:27. *son of David.* See note on 10:47. Most of the people knew that the Messiah was to be from the family of David.
12:36 *THE LORD SAID TO MY LORD.* God said to David's Lord, i.e., David's superior—ultimately the Messiah (see note on Ps 110:1). The purpose of the quotation was to show that the Messiah was more than a descendant of David—he was David's Lord.
12:38 *long robes.* The scribes wore long, white linen robes that were fringed and almost reached to the ground.
12:39 *chief seats in the synagogues.* A reference to the bench in front of the "ark" that contained the sacred scrolls. Those who sat there could be seen by all the worshipers in the synagogue.
12:40 *devour widows' houses.* Since the scribes were not paid a regular salary, they were dependent on the generosity of patrons for their livelihood. Such a system was open to abuses, and widows were especially vulnerable to exploitation.
12:41 *the treasury.* Located in the court of the women. Both men and women were allowed in this court, but women could go no farther into the temple buildings. It contained 13 trumpet-shaped receptacles for contributions brought by worshipers.

[1]small copper coins, which amount to a [2]cent.

43 Calling His disciples to Him, He said to them, "Truly I say to you, this poor widow put in more than all [1]the contributors to the treasury;

44 for they all put in out of their [1]surplus, but she, out of her poverty, put in all she owned, [2]all she had [a]to live on."

Things to Come

13 [a]As He was going out of the temple, one of His disciples *said to Him, "Teacher, behold [1]what wonderful stones and [1]what wonderful buildings!"

2 And Jesus said to him, "Do you see these great buildings? [a]Not one stone will be left upon another which will not be torn down."

3 As He was sitting on [a]the Mount of Olives opposite the temple, [b]Peter and [1]James and John and Andrew were questioning Him privately,

4 "Tell us, when will these things be, and what *will be* the [1]sign when all these things are going to be fulfilled?"

5 And Jesus began to say to them, "See to it that no one misleads you.

6 "Many will come in My name, saying, '[a]I am *He!*' and will mislead many.

7 "When you hear of wars and rumors of wars, do not be frightened; *those things* must take place; but *that is* not yet the end.

8 "For nation will rise up against nation, and kingdom against kingdom; there will be earthquakes in various places; there will *also* be famines. These things are *merely* the beginning of birth pangs.

9 "But [1]be on your guard; for they will [a]deliver you to *the* [2]courts, and you will be flogged [a]in *the* synagogues, and you will stand before governors and kings for My sake, as a testimony to them.

10 "[a]The gospel must first be preached to all the nations.

11 "[a]When they [1]arrest you and hand you over, do not worry beforehand about what you are to say, but say whatever is given you in that hour; for it is not you who speak, but *it is* the Holy Spirit.

12 "Brother will betray brother to death, and a father *his* child; and children will rise up against parents and [1]have them put to death.

13 "[a]You will be hated by all because of My name, but the one who endures to the end, he will be saved.

14 "But [a]when you see the [b]ABOMINATION OF DESOLATION standing where it should not be (let the reader understand), then those who are in Judea must flee to the mountains.

15 "[a]The one who is on the housetop must not go down, or go in to get anything out of his house;

16 and the one who is in the field must not turn back to get his coat.

17 "But woe to those who are pregnant and to those who are nursing babies in those days!

18 "But pray that it may not happen in the winter.

19 "For those days will be a *time of* tribulation such as has not occurred [a]since the beginning of the creation which God created until now, and never will.

20 "Unless the Lord had shortened *those*

42 [1]Gr *lepta* [2]Gr *quadrans;* i.e. 1/64 of a denarius
43 [1]Lit *those who were putting in*
44 [1]Or *abundance* [2]Lit *her whole livelihood* [a]Luke 8:43; 15:12, 30; 21:4
13:1 [1]Lit *how great* [a]Mark 13:1-37: *Matt 24; Luke 21:5-36*
2 [a]Luke 19:44
3 [1]Or *Jacob* [a]Matt 21:1 [b]Matt 17:1
4 [1]Or *attesting miracle*
6 [a]John 8:24
9 [1]Lit *look to yourselves* [2]Or *Sanhedrin* or *Council* [a]Matt 10:17
10 [a]Matt 24:14
11 [1]Lit *lead* [a]Mark 13:11-13: *Matt 10:19-22; Luke 21:12-17*
12 [1]Lit *put them to death*
13 [a]Matt 10:22; John 15:21
14 [a]Matt 24:15f [b]Dan 9:27; 11:31; 12:11
15 [a]Luke 17:31
19 [a]Dan 12:1; Mark 10:6

12:42 *small copper coins.* The smallest coins then in circulation in the Holy Land. Though her offering was meager, the widow brought "all she had" (v. 44; see note on 2 Cor 8:12).
12:43 *Truly I say to you.* See note on 3:28.
13:1–37 The Olivet discourse, as this chapter of Mark is commonly called, falls into five sections: (1) Jesus' prophecy of the destruction of the temple and the questions of the disciples (vv. 1–4); (2) warnings against deceivers and false signs of the end (vv. 5–23); (3) the coming of the Son of Man (vv. 24–27); (4) the lesson of the fig tree (vv. 28–31); (5) exhortation to watchfulness (vv. 32–37).
13:1 *wonderful stones.* According to Josephus (*Antiquities,* 15.11.3), they were white, and some of them were 37 feet long, 12 feet high and 18 feet wide.
13:2 See note on Matt 24:2.
13:3 *Mount of Olives.* See note on 11:1. *Peter and James and John and Andrew.* See 1:16–20.
13:4 The disciples thought that the destruction of the temple would be one of the events that ushered in the end times (see Matt 24:3). *the sign.* The way by which the disciples might know that the destruction of the temple was about to take place and that the end of the age was approaching.
13:5 *See to it.* It is clear from such words as "See to it," "But be on your guard" (v. 9), "But take heed" (v. 23), "Take heed, keep on the alert" (v. 33), "Therefore, be on the alert" (v. 35) and "Be on the alert!" (v. 37) that one of the main purposes of the Olivet discourse was to alert the disciples to the danger of deception.
13:6 *I am He.* That is, the Messiah.
13:7 *the end.* Not the destruction of Jerusalem but the end of the age (see Matt 24:3).
13:8 *birth pangs.* See note on Matt 24:8.
13:9 *the courts.* The religious courts made up of the synagogue elders. *flogged.* Infraction of Jewish regulations was punishable by flogging, the maximum penalty being 39 strokes with the whip (see 2 Cor 11:23–24).
13:10 *first.* Before the end of the age (see Matt 24:14).
13:13 *endures to the end.* Such perseverance is a sure indication of salvation (cf. Heb 3:14; 6:11–12; 10:36).
13:14 *the* ABOMINATION OF DESOLATION. See notes on Dan 9:25–27; Matt 24:15. *standing where it should not be.* See 2 Thess 2:4. *those who are in Judea must flee to the mountains.* See note on Matt 24:16.
13:15 *the housetop.* See notes on 2:4; Luke 17:31.
13:16 *coat.* See note on Matt 5:40.
13:17 *those who are pregnant and to those who are nursing babies.* Representative of anyone forced to flee under especially difficult circumstances.
13:18 *in the winter.* The time when heavy rains caused streams to become swollen and impossible to cross, preventing many from reaching a place of refuge.
13:19 *a time of tribulation such as has not occurred.* See note on Matt 24:21.

Passion Week

Bethany, the Mount of Olives and Jerusalem

4. Clearing of the temple
MONDAY
Matt 21:10-17;
Mark 11:15-18;
Luke 19:45-48

The next day He returned to the temple and found the court of the Gentiles full of traders and money changers making a large profit as they gave out Jewish coins in exchange for "pagan" money. Jesus drove them out and overturned their tables.

Alternate "Gordon's Calvary"

NORTH

Present Damascus Gate

Traditional Crucifixion and Tomb Site

Jerusalem

Meters 0 100 200 300

Feet 0 500 1,000

SOUTH

KIDRON VALLEY

7. Passover Last Supper
THURSDAY
Matt 26:17-30; Mark 14:12-26;
Luke 22:7-23; John 13:1-30

In an upper room Jesus prepared both Himself and His disciples for His death. He gave the Passover meal a new meaning. The loaf of bread and cup of wine represented His body soon to be sacrificed and His blood soon to be shed. And so He instituted the "Lord's Supper." After singing a hymn they went to the Garden of Gethsemane, where Jesus prayed in agony, knowing what lay ahead for Him.

8. Crucifixion—FRIDAY
Matt 27:1-66; Mark 15:1-47; Luke 22:66—23:56; John 18:28—19:37

Following betrayal, arrest, desertion, false trials, denial, condemnation, beatings and mockery, Jesus was required to carry His cross to "The Place of the Skull," where He was crucified with two other prisoners.

9. In the tomb

Jesus' body was placed in the tomb before 6:00 p.m. Friday night, when the Sabbath began and all work stopped, and it lay in the tomb throughout the Sabbath.

10. Resurrection—SUNDAY Matt 28:1-13; Mark 16:1-20; Luke 24:1-49; John 20:1-31

Early in the morning, women went to the tomb and found that the stone closing the tomb's entrance had been rolled back. An angel told them Jesus was alive and gave them a message. Jesus appeared to Mary Magdalene in the garden, to Peter, to two disciples on the road to Emmaus, and later that day to all the disciples but Thomas. His resurrection was established as a fact.

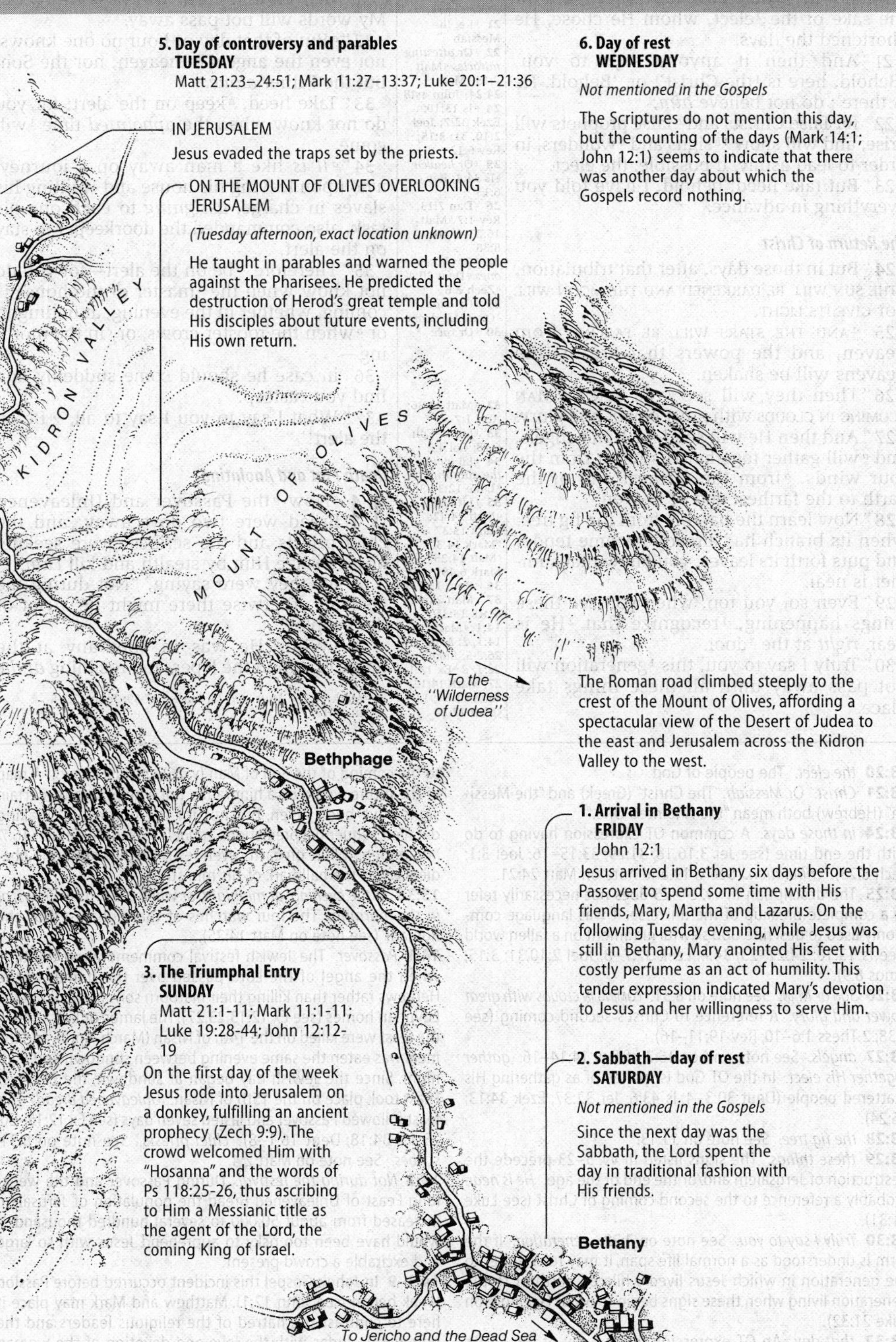

5. Day of controversy and parables
TUESDAY
Matt 21:23–24:51; Mark 11:27–13:37; Luke 20:1–21:36
IN JERUSALEM
Jesus evaded the traps set by the priests.
ON THE MOUNT OF OLIVES OVERLOOKING JERUSALEM
(Tuesday afternoon, exact location unknown)
He taught in parables and warned the people against the Pharisees. He predicted the destruction of Herod's great temple and told His disciples about future events, including His own return.
6. Day of rest
WEDNESDAY
Not mentioned in the Gospels
The Scriptures do not mention this day, but the counting of the days (Mark 14:1; John 12:1) seems to indicate that there was another day about which the Gospels record nothing.
KIDRON VALLEY
MOUNT OF OLIVES
To the "Wilderness of Judea"
The Roman road climbed steeply to the crest of the Mount of Olives, affording a spectacular view of the Desert of Judea to the east and Jerusalem across the Kidron Valley to the west.
Bethphage
1. Arrival in Bethany
FRIDAY
John 12:1
Jesus arrived in Bethany six days before the Passover to spend some time with His friends, Mary, Martha and Lazarus. On the following Tuesday evening, while Jesus was still in Bethany, Mary anointed His feet with costly perfume as an act of humility. This tender expression indicated Mary's devotion to Jesus and her willingness to serve Him.
3. The Triumphal Entry
SUNDAY
Matt 21:1-11; Mark 11:1-11; Luke 19:28-44; John 12:12-19
On the first day of the week Jesus rode into Jerusalem on a donkey, fulfilling an ancient prophecy (Zech 9:9). The crowd welcomed Him with "Hosanna" and the words of Ps 118:25-26, thus ascribing to Him a Messianic title as the agent of the Lord, the coming King of Israel.
2. Sabbath—day of rest
SATURDAY
Not mentioned in the Gospels
Since the next day was the Sabbath, the Lord spent the day in traditional fashion with His friends.
Bethany
To Jericho and the Dead Sea

days, no [1]life would have been saved; but for
the sake of the [2]elect, whom He chose, He
shortened the days.
21 "And then if anyone says to you,
'Behold, here is [1]the Christ'; or, 'Behold, *He*
is there'; do not believe *him;*
22 for false Christs and [a]false prophets will
arise, and will show [1b]signs and [b]wonders, in
order to lead astray, if possible, the elect.
23 "But take heed; behold, I have told you
everything in advance.

The Return of Christ

24 "But in those days, after that tribulation,
[a]THE SUN WILL BE DARKENED AND THE MOON WILL
NOT GIVE ITS LIGHT,
25 [a]AND THE STARS WILL BE FALLING from
heaven, and the powers that are in [1]the
heavens will be shaken.
26 "Then they will see [a]THE SON OF MAN
[b]COMING IN CLOUDS with great power and glory.
27 "And then He will send forth the angels,
and [a]will gather together His [1]elect from the
four winds, [b]from the farthest end of the
earth to the farthest end of heaven.
28 "Now learn the parable from the fig tree:
when its branch has already become tender
and puts forth its leaves, you know that summer is near.
29 "Even so, you too, when you see these
things happening, [1]recognize that [2]He is
near, *right* at the [3]door.
30 "Truly I say to you, this [1]generation will
not pass away until all these things take
place.
31 "Heaven and earth will pass away, but
My words will not pass away.
32 "[a]But of that day or hour no one knows,
not even the angels in heaven, nor the Son,
but the Father *alone.*
33 "Take heed, [a]keep on the alert; for you
do not know when the *appointed* time [1]will
come.
34 "[a]*It is* like a man away on a journey,
who upon leaving his house and [1]putting his
slaves in charge, *assigning* to each one his
task, also commanded the doorkeeper to stay
on the alert.
35 "Therefore, [a]be on the alert—for you do
not know when the [1]master of the house is
coming, whether in the evening, at midnight,
or [b]when the rooster crows, or [c]in the morning—
36 in case he should come suddenly and
find you [a]asleep.
37 "What I say to you I say to all, '[a]Be on
the alert!' "

Death Plot and Anointing

14 [a]Now [b]the Passover and Unleavened
Bread were two days away; and the
chief priests and the scribes [c]were seeking
how to seize Him by stealth and kill *Him;*
2 for they were saying, "Not during the
festival, otherwise there might be a riot of
the people."
3 [a]While He was in [b]Bethany at the
home of Simon the leper, and reclining *at the*

20 [1]Lit *flesh* [2]Or *chosen ones* **21** [1]I.e. the Messiah **22** [1]Or *attesting miracles* [a]Matt 7:15 [b]Matt 24:24; John 4:48 **24** [a]Is 13:10; Ezek 32:7; Joel 2:10, 31; 3:15; Rev 6:12 **25** [1]Or *heaven* [a]Is 34:4; Rev 6:13 **26** [a]Dan 7:13; Rev 1:7 [b]Matt 16:27; Mark 8:38 **27** [1]Or *chosen ones* [a]Deut 30:4 [b]Zech 2:6 **29** [1]Or *know* [2]Or *it* [3]Lit *doors* **30** [1]Or *race*

32 [a]Matt 24:36; Acts 1:7 **33** [1]Lit *is* [a]Eph 6:18; Col 4:2 **34** [1]Lit *giving the authority to* [a]Luke 12:36-38 **35** [1]Lit *lord* [a]Matt 24:42; Mark 13:37 [b]Mark 14:30 [c]Matt 14:25; Mark 6:48 **36** [a]Rom 13:11 **37** [a]Matt 24:42; Mark 13:35 **14:1** [a]Mark 14:1, 2: *Matt 26:2-5; Luke 22:1, 2* [b]Ex 12:1-27; Mark 14:12; John 11:55; 13:1 [c]Matt 12:14

3 [a]Mark 14:3-9: *Matt 26:6-13;* Luke 7:37-39; John 12:1-8 [b]Matt 21:17

13:20 *the elect.* The people of God.
13:21 *Christ.* Or *Messiah.* "The Christ" (Greek) and "the Messiah" (Hebrew) both mean "the Anointed One."
13:24 *in those days.* A common OT expression having to do with the end time (see Jer 3:16,18; 31:29; 33:15–16; Joel 3:1; Zech 8:23). *tribulation.* See v. 19 and note on Matt 24:21.
13:25 The description in vv. 24–25 does not necessarily refer to a complete breakup of the universe. It was language commonly used to describe God's awful judgment on a fallen world (see Is 13:10; 24:21–23; 34:4; Ezek 32:7–8; Joel 2:10,31; 3:15; Amos 8:9).
13:26 *SON OF MAN.* See note on 8:31. *COMING IN CLOUDS with great power and glory.* A reference to Christ's second coming (see 8:38; 2 Thess 1:6–10; Rev 19:11–16).
13:27 *angels.* See note on Gen 16:7; cf. Rev 14:14–16. *gather together His elect.* In the OT God is spoken of as gathering His scattered people (Deut 30:3–4; Is 43:6; Jer 32:37; Ezek 34:13; 36:24).
13:28 *the fig tree.* See note on 11:13.
13:29 *these things.* The signs listed in vv. 5–23 precede the destruction of Jerusalem and/or the end of the age. *He is near.* Probably a reference to the second coming of Christ (see Luke 21:31).
13:30 *Truly I say to you.* See note on 3:28. *generation.* If the term is understood as a normal life span, it may refer either to the generation in which Jesus lived while on earth or to the generation living when these signs begin to occur (see note on Luke 21:32).
13:32 *that day.* An OT expression for the day of the Lord's appearance (Amos 8:3,9,13; 9:11; Mic 4:6; 5:10; 7:11), referring to the coming of the Son of Man (v. 26). *no one knows.* A map of the future would be a hindrance, not a help, to faith. Certain signs have been given, but not for the purpose of making detailed, sequential predictions. *angels.* See note on Gen 16:7. *nor the Son.* While on earth, even Jesus lived by faith, and obedience was the hallmark of His ministry.
13:35 *in the evening, at midnight, or when the rooster crows, or in the morning.* The four watches of the night used by the Romans (see note on Matt 14:25).
14:1 *Passover.* The Jewish festival commemorating the time when the angel of the Lord passed over the homes of the Hebrews rather than killing their firstborn sons as he did in the Egyptian homes (see Ex 12:13,23,27). The lambs or kids used in the feast were killed on the 14th of Nisan (March-April), and the meal was eaten the same evening between sundown and midnight. Since the Jewish day began at sundown, the Passover Feast took place on the 15th of Nisan. *Unleavened Bread.* This feast followed Passover and lasted seven days (see Ex 12:15–20; 23:15; 34:18; Deut 16:1–8). *chief priests.* See note on 8:31. *scribes.* See note on Matt 2:4.
14:2 *Not during the festival.* During Passover and the week-long Feast of Unleavened Bread the population of Jerusalem increased from about 50,000 to several hundred thousand. It would have been too risky to apprehend Jesus with so large and excitable a crowd present.
14:3–9 In John's Gospel this incident occurred before Passion Week began (see John 12:1). Matthew and Mark may place it here to contrast the hatred of the religious leaders and the betrayal by Judas with the love and devotion of the woman who anointed Jesus.

table, there came a woman with an alabaster vial of very [c]costly perfume of pure [1]nard; *and* she broke the vial and poured it over His head.

4 But some were indignantly *remarking* to one another, “Why has this perfume been wasted?

5 “For this perfume might have been sold for over three hundred [1]denarii, and *the money* given to the poor.” And they were scolding her.

6 But Jesus said, “Let her alone; why do you bother her? She has done a good deed to Me.

7 “For you always have [a]the poor with you, and whenever you wish you can do good to them; but you do not always have Me.

8 “She has done what she could; [a]she has anointed My body beforehand for the burial.

9 “Truly I say to you, [a]wherever the gospel is preached in the whole world, what this woman has done will also be spoken of in memory of her.”

10 [a]Then Judas Iscariot, [b]who was one of the twelve, went off to the chief priests in order to [1]betray Him to them.

11 They were glad when they heard *this,* and promised to give him money. And he *began* seeking how to betray Him at an opportune time.

The Last Passover

12 [a]On the first day of [b]Unleavened Bread, when [1]the Passover *lamb* was being [c]sacrificed, His disciples *said to Him, “Where do You want us to go and prepare for You to eat the Passover?”

13 And He *sent two of His disciples and *said to them, “Go into the city, and a man will meet you carrying a pitcher of water; follow him;

14 and wherever he enters, say to the owner of the house, ‘The Teacher says, “Where is My [a]guest room in which I may eat the Passover with My disciples?” ’

15 “And he himself will show you a large upper room furnished *and* ready; prepare for us there.”

16 The disciples went out and came to the city, and found *it* just as He had told them; and they prepared the Passover.

17 [a]When it was evening He *came with the twelve.

18 As they were reclining *at the table* and eating, Jesus said, “Truly I say to you that one of you will [1]betray Me—[2]one who is eating with Me.”

19 They began to be grieved and to say to Him one by one, “Surely not I?”

20 And He said to them, “*It is* one of the twelve, [1]one who dips with Me in the bowl.

21 “For the Son of Man *is to* go just as it is written of Him; but woe to that man [1]by whom the Son of Man is betrayed! *It would have been* good [2]for that man if he had not been born.”

The Lord’s Supper

22 [a]While they were eating, He took *some*

3 [1]An aromatic oil extracted from an East Indian plant [c]Matt 26:6f; John 12:3
5 [1]The denarius was equivalent to a day’s wages
7 [a]Deut 15:11; Matt 26:11; John 12:8
8 [a]John 19:40
9 [a]Matt 26:13
10 [1]Or *hand Him over* [a]Mark 14:10, 11: *Matt 26:14-16; Luke 22:3-6* [b]John 6:71
12 [1]Lit *they were sacrificing* [a]Mark 14:12-16: *Matt 26:17-19; Luke 22:7-13* [b]Matt 26:17 [c]Deut 16:5; Mark 14:1; Luke 22:7; 1 Cor 5:7
14 [a]Luke 22:11
17 [a]Mark 14:17-21: *Matt 26:20-24; Luke 22:14, 21-23;* John 13:18ff
18 [1]Or *deliver Me over* [2]Or *the one*
20 [1]Or *the one*
21 [1]Or *through* [2]Lit *for him if that man had not been born*
22 [a]Mark 14:22-25: *Matt 26:26-29; Luke 22:17-20; 1 Cor 11:23-25;* Mark 10:16

14:3 *Bethany.* See note on Matt 21:17. *Simon the leper.* See note on Matt 26:6. *reclining at the table.* The usual posture for eating a banquet meal. *a woman.* We know from John’s Gospel (12:3) that she was Mary, the sister of Martha and Lazarus. *alabaster vial.* A sealed flask with a long neck that was broken off when the contents were used and that contained enough ointment for one application. *nard.* A perfume made from the aromatic oil extracted from the root of a plant grown chiefly in India. *poured it over His head.* Anointing was a common custom at feasts (see Ps 23:5; Luke 7:46). The woman’s action expressed her deep devotion to Jesus.

14:4 *some.* Matthew (26:8) identifies them as the disciples, while John (12:4–5) singles out Judas Iscariot.

14:5 *given to the poor.* It was a Jewish custom to give gifts to the poor on the evening of Passover (see John 13:29).

14:7 *you will always have the poor with you.* This did not express lack of concern for the poor, for their needs lay close to Jesus’ heart (see Matt 6:2–4; Luke 4:18; 6:20; 14:13,21; 18:22; John 13:29).

14:8 *for the burial.* It was a normal Jewish custom to anoint a body with aromatic oils in preparing it for burial (see 16:1). Jesus seems to anticipate suffering a criminal’s death, for only in that circumstance was there no anointing of the body.

14:9 *Truly I say to you.* See note on 3:28. *gospel.* See note on 1:1.

14:10 *Judas Iscariot.* See note on 3:19. *chief priests.* See note on 8:31. This was an unexpected opportunity that they seized, even though they had intended not to apprehend Jesus during the Feast (see v. 2).

14:11 *money.* Thirty silver coins (Matt 26:15).

14:12 *the first day of Unleavened Bread.* Ordinarily this would mean the 15th of Nisan, the day after Passover (see note on v. 1). However, the added phrase, “when the Passover lamb was being sacrificed,” makes it clear that the 14th of Nisan is meant because Passover lambs were killed on that day (Ex 12:6). The entire eight-day celebration was sometimes referred to as the Feast of Unleavened Bread, and there is evidence that the 14th of Nisan may have been loosely referred to as the “first day of Unleavened Bread.”

14:13 *two of His disciples.* Peter and John (Luke 22:8). *man . . . carrying a pitcher.* He would easily have been identified because customarily only women carried water jars.

14:14 *Where is My guest room . . . ?* It was a Jewish custom that anyone in Jerusalem who had a room available would give it upon request to a pilgrim to celebrate the Passover. It appears that Jesus had made previous arrangements with the owner of the house.

14:15 *prepare.* These would include food for the meal: unleavened bread, wine, bitter herbs, sauce and the lamb.

14:17 *When it was evening.* Thursday of Passion Week.

14:18 *reclining at the table and eating.* Originally the Passover meal was eaten standing (Ex 12:11), but in Jesus’ time it was customary to eat it while reclining. *Truly I say to you.* See note on 3:28.

14:20 *dips with Me in the bowl.* See note on Matt 26:23.

14:21 *Son of Man.* See note on 8:31. *as it is written of Him.* Jesus no doubt had the “suffering servant” passage of Is 53 in mind.

14:22 The NT gives four accounts of the Lord’s Supper (Matt 26:26–28; Mark 14:22–24; Luke 22:19–20; 1 Cor 11:23–25). Mat-

bread, and [1]after a [b]blessing He broke *it,* and
gave *it* to them, and said, "Take *it;* this is My
body."
23 And when He had taken a cup *and* giv-
en thanks, He gave *it* to them, and they all
drank from it.
24 And He said to them, "This is My
[a]blood of the [b]covenant, which is poured out
for many.
25 "Truly I say to you, I will never again
drink of the fruit of the vine until that day
when I drink it new in the kingdom of God."
26 [a]After singing a hymn, they went out to
[b]the Mount of Olives.
27 [a]And Jesus *said to them, "You will all
[1]fall away, because it is written, '[b]I WILL
STRIKE DOWN THE SHEPHERD, AND THE SHEEP
SHALL BE SCATTERED.'
28 "But after I have been raised, [a]I will go
ahead of you to Galilee."
29 But Peter said to Him, "*Even* though all
may [1]fall away, yet I will not."
30 And Jesus *said to him, "Truly I say to
you, that [1][a]this very night, before [b]a rooster
crows twice, you yourself will deny Me three
times."
31 But *Peter* kept saying insistently, "*Even*
if I have to die with You, I will not deny
You!" And they all were saying the same
thing also.

Jesus in Gethsemane

32 [a]They *came to a place named Gethsemane; and He *said to His disciples, "Sit
here until I have prayed."
33 And He *took with Him Peter and
[1]James and John, and began to be very [a]dis-
tressed and troubled.
34 And He *said to them, "[a]My soul is
deeply grieved to the point of death; remain
here and keep watch."
35 And He went a little beyond *them,* and
fell to the ground and *began* to pray that if it
were possible, [a]the hour might [1]pass Him by.
36 And He was saying, "[a]Abba! Father!
All things are possible for You; remove this
cup from Me; [b]yet not what I will, but what
You will."
37 And He *came and *found them sleeping, and *said to Peter, "Simon, are you
asleep? Could you not keep watch for one
hour?
38 "[a]Keep watching and praying that you
may not come into temptation; the spirit is
willing, but the flesh is weak."
39 Again He went away and prayed, saying the same [1]words.
40 And again He came and found them
sleeping, for their eyes were very heavy; and
they did not know what to answer Him.
41 And He *came the third time, and *said
to them, "[1]Are you still sleeping and resting?
It is enough; [a]the hour has come; behold,
the Son of Man is being [2]betrayed into the
hands of sinners.
42 "Get up, let us be going; behold, the one
who betrays Me is at hand!"

Betrayal and Arrest

43 [a]Immediately while He was still speaking, Judas, one of the twelve, *came up
[1]accompanied by a crowd with swords and
clubs, *who were* from the chief priests and
the scribes and the elders.
44 Now he who was betraying Him had
given them a signal, saying, "Whomever I
kiss, He is the one; seize Him and lead Him
away [1]under guard."

22 [1]Lit *having blessed* [b]Matt 14:19
24 [a]Ex 24:8 [b]Jer 31:31-34
26 [a]Matt 26:30 [b]Matt 21:1
27 [1]Or *stumble* [a]Mark 14:27-31: *Matt 26:31-35* [b]Zech 13:7
28 [a]Matt 28:16
29 [1]Or *stumble*
30 [1]Lit *today, on this night* [a]Matt 26:34 [b]Mark 14:68, 72; John 13:38
32 [a]Mark 14:32-42: *Matt 26:36-46; Luke 22:40-46*
33 [1]Or *Jacob* [a]Mark 9:15; 16:5, 6
34 [a]Matt 26:38; John 12:27
35 [1]Lit *pass from Him* [a]Matt 26:45; Mark 14:41
36 [a]Rom 8:15; Gal 4:6 [b]Matt 26:39
38 [a]Matt 26:41
39 [1]Lit *word*
41 [1]Or *Keep on sleeping therefore* [2]Or *delivered* [a]Mark 14:35
43 [1]Lit *and with him* [a]Mark 14:43-50: *Matt 26:47-56; Luke 22:47-53; John 18:3-11*
44 [1]Lit *safely*

thew's account is very much like Mark's, and Luke's and Paul's have similarities. All the accounts include the taking of the bread; the thanksgiving or blessing; the breaking of the bread; the saying, "This is My body"; the taking of the cup; and the explanation of the relation of blood to the covenant. Only Paul and Luke record Jesus' command to continue to celebrate the Supper. *this is My body.* The bread represented His body, given for them (see Luke 22:19; 1 Cor 11:24).

14:23 *given thanks.* The word "Eucharist" is derived from the Greek term used here.

14:24 *My blood of the covenant.* The cup represents the blood of Jesus, which, in turn, represents His poured-out life (i.e., His death). God's commitments to His people in the new covenant are possible only through Christ's atoning death (see Jer 31:31–34; Heb 8:8–12; see also notes on Luke 22:20; Ex 24:6,8). *for many.* See note on Rom 5:15.

14:25 *Truly I say to you.* See note on 3:28. *kingdom of God.* See note on Matt 3:2.

14:26 *a hymn.* See note on Matt 26:30. *Mount of Olives.* See note on 11:1.

14:30 *Truly I say to you.* See note on 3:28. *crows twice.* Some early manuscripts do not have *twice.*

14:32 *Gethsemane.* A garden or orchard on the lower slopes of the Mount of Olives, one of Jesus' favorite places (see Luke 22:39; John 18:2). The name is Hebrew and means "oil press," i.e., a place for squeezing the oil from olives.

14:33 *Peter and James and John.* See note on 5:37.

14:36 *Abba! Father!* Expressive of an especially close relationship to God. *this cup.* The chalice of death and of God's wrath that Jesus took from the Father's hand in fulfillment of His mission. What Jesus dreaded was not death as such, but the manner of His death as the One who was taking the sin of mankind upon Himself. See note on 10:38.

14:37 *Simon.* See note on 1:16. Perhaps Simon is singled out because of his bold assertion that he would not fail Jesus (see vv. 29–31).

14:38 *come into temptation.* Be attacked by temptation. Here the temptation is to be unfaithful in face of the threatening circumstances confronting them. *the spirit is willing.* When that part of man that is spirit is under God's control, it strives against human weakness. The expression is taken from Ps 51:12.

14:41 *Son of Man.* See note on 8:31.

14:43 *Judas.* See note on 3:19. *a crowd with swords and clubs.* Auxiliary police or servants of the court assigned to the task of maintaining public order beyond the precincts of the temple. John (18:3) indicates that at least some of the Roman cohort of soldiers were in the arresting group, along with officers of the temple guard. The fact that some carried clubs suggests that they were conscripted at the last moment. *chief priests . . . scribes . . . elders.* See notes on 8:31; Matt 2:4. The warrant for Jesus' arrest had been issued by the Sanhedrin.

45 After coming, Judas immediately went to Him, saying, "[a]Rabbi!" and kissed Him.

46 They laid hands on Him and seized Him.

47 But one of those who stood by drew his sword, and struck the slave of the high priest and [1]cut off his ear.

48 And Jesus said to them, "Have you come out with swords and clubs to arrest Me, as *you would* against a robber?

49 "Every day I was with you [a]in the temple teaching, and you did not seize Me; but *this has taken place* to fulfill the Scriptures."

50 And they all left Him and fled.

51 A young man was following Him, wearing *nothing but* a linen sheet over *his* naked *body;* and they *seized him.

52 But he [1]pulled free of the linen sheet and escaped naked.

Jesus before His Accusers

53 [a]They led Jesus away to the high priest; and all the chief priests and the elders and the scribes *gathered together.

54 Peter had followed Him at a distance, [a]right into [b]the courtyard of the high priest; and he was sitting with the [1]officers and [c]warming himself at the [2]fire.

55 Now the chief priests and the whole [1a]Council kept trying to obtain testimony against Jesus to put Him to death, and they were not finding any.

56 For many were giving false testimony against Him, but their testimony was not consistent.

57 Some stood up and *began* to give false testimony against Him, saying,

58 "We heard Him say, '[a]I will destroy this [1]temple made with hands, and in three days I will build another made without hands.' "

59 Not even in this respect was their testimony consistent.

60 The high priest stood up *and came* forward and questioned Jesus, saying, "Do You not answer? [1]What is it that these men are testifying against You?"

61 [a]But He kept silent and did not answer. [b]Again the high priest was questioning Him, and [1]saying to Him, "Are You [2]the Christ, the Son of the Blessed *One?*"

62 And Jesus said, "I am; and you shall see [a]THE SON OF MAN SITTING AT THE RIGHT HAND OF POWER, and [b]COMING WITH THE CLOUDS OF HEAVEN."

63 [a]Tearing his clothes, the high priest *said, "What further need do we have of witnesses?

64 "You have heard the [a]blasphemy; how does it seem to you?" And they all condemned Him to be deserving of death.

45 [a]Matt 23:7
47 [1]Lit *took off*
49 [a]Mark 12:35; Luke 19:47; 21:37
52 [1]Lit *left behind*
53 [a]Mark 14:53-65: *Matt 26:57-68; John 18:12f, 19-24*
54 [1]Or *servants* [2]Lit *light* [a]Mark 14:68 [b]Matt 26:3 [c]Mark 14:67; John 18:18
55 [1]Or *Sanhedrin* [a]Matt 5:22
58 [1]Or *sanctuary* [a]Matt 26:61; Mark 15:29; John 2:19
60 [1]Or *what do these testify?*
61 [1]Lit *says* [2]I.e. the Messiah [a]Matt 26:63 [b]Mark 14:61-63: *Matt 26:63ff; Luke 22:67-71*
62 [a]Ps 110:1; Mark 13:26 [b]Dan 7:13
63 [a]Num 14:6; Matt 26:65; Acts 14:14
64 [a]Lev 24:16

14:45 *Rabbi.* Hebrew word for "(my) teacher." *kissed Him.* A token of respect with which disciples customarily greeted their rabbi. See note on Luke 22:47.

14:47 *one of those who stood by.* We know from John that it was Peter, and the servant he struck was named Malchus (John 18:10).

14:49 *temple.* See note on 11:27. *to fulfill the Scriptures.* Perhaps a reference to Is 53, or more particularly to Zech 13:7, quoted by Jesus in v. 27 and fulfilled (at least in part) at this time.

14:50 *left Him.* In fulfillment of vv. 27–31.

14:51 *A young man.* Not specifically identified, but his anonymity may suggest that this was John Mark, writer of this Gospel. *a linen sheet.* Ordinarily the outer garment was made of wool. The fine linen garment left behind in the hand of a guard indicates that the youth was from a wealthy family.

14:52 *escaped naked.* The absence of an undergarment suggests that he had dressed hastily to follow Jesus.

14:53–15:15 Jesus' trial took place in two stages: a Jewish trial and a Roman trial, each of which had three episodes. For the Jewish trial these were: (1) the preliminary hearing before Annas, the former high priest (reported only in John 18:12–14, 19–23); (2) the trial before Caiaphas, the ruling high priest, and the Sanhedrin (14:53–65); and (3) the final action of the council, which terminated its all-night session (15:1). The three episodes of the Roman trial were: (1) the trial before Pilate (15:2–5); (2) the trial before Herod Antipas (only in Luke 23:6–12); and (3) the trial before Pilate continued and concluded (15:6–15). Since Mark gives no account of Jesus before Herod Antipas, the trial before Pilate forms a continuous and uninterrupted narrative in this Gospel (15:2–15).

14:53 *high priest.* Caiaphas, son-in-law of Annas, the former high priest. *all the chief priests and the elders and the scribes.* The entire Sanhedrin.

14:54 *courtyard of the high priest.* The Sanhedrin may have met at Caiaphas's house to ensure secrecy.

14:55 *Council.* The high court of the Jews. In NT times it was made up of three kinds of members: chief priests, elders, and scribes. Its total membership numbered 71, including the high priest, who was presiding officer. Under Roman jurisdiction the Council was given a great deal of authority, but they could not impose capital punishment (see John 18:31 and note on Matt 27:2).

14:56 *many were giving false testimony against Him.* In Jewish judicial procedure, witnesses functioned as the prosecution. *was not consistent.* According to Deut 19:15 a person could not be convicted unless two or more witnesses gave testimony, which assumes that their testimonies had to agree.

14:58 There is no statement by Jesus precisely like this in the Gospels. It is probably an allusion to what is reported in John 2:19.

14:61 *Christ.* Or *Messiah. Son of the Blessed One.* "The Blessed One" was a way of referring to God without pronouncing His name (see note on 11:30). The title was therefore equivalent to "Son of God," though in this context it would seem not to refer to deity but to royal Messiahship, since in popular Jewish belief the Messiah was to be a man, not God.

14:62 *Son of Man.* See note on 8:31. This Son of Man saying brings together Dan 7:13 and Ps 110:1.

14:63 *Tearing his clothes.* A sign of great grief or shock (see Gen 37:29; 2 Kin 18:37; 19:1). In the case of the high priest it was a form of judicial act expressing the fact that he regarded Jesus' answer as blasphemous (see note on Matt 26:65).

14:64 *blasphemy.* The sin of blasphemy not only involved reviling the name of God (see Lev 24:10–16) but also included any affront to His majesty or authority (see Mark 2:7; 3:28–29; John 5:18; 10:33). Jesus' claim to be the Messiah and, in fact, to have majesty and authority belonging only to God was therefore regarded by Caiaphas as blasphemy, for which the Mosaic law prescribed death by stoning (Lev 24:16).

65 Some began to [a]spit at Him, and [1][b]to blindfold Him, and to beat Him with their fists, and to say to Him, "[c]Prophesy!" And the officers [2]received Him with [3]slaps *in the face.*

Peter's Denials

66 [a]As Peter was below in [b]the courtyard, one of the servant-girls of the high priest *came,

67 and seeing Peter [a]warming himself, she looked at him and *said, "You also were with Jesus the [b]Nazarene."

68 But he denied *it,* saying, "I neither know nor understand what you are talking about." And he [a]went out onto the [1]porch, and a rooster crowed.[2]

69 The servant-girl saw him, and began once more to say to the bystanders, "This is *one* of them!"

70 But again [a]he denied it. And after a little while the bystanders were again saying to Peter, "Surely you are *one* of them, [b]for you are a Galilean too."

71 But he began to [1]curse and swear, "I do not know this man you are talking about!"

72 Immediately a rooster crowed a second time. And Peter remembered how Jesus had made the remark to him, "Before [a]a rooster crows twice, you will deny Me three times." [1]And he began to weep.

Jesus before Pilate

15 [a]Early in the morning the chief priests with the elders and scribes and the whole [1][b]Council, immediately held a consultation; and binding Jesus, they led Him away and delivered Him to Pilate.

2 [a]Pilate questioned Him, "Are You the King of the Jews?" And He *answered him, "*It is as* you say."

3 The chief priests *began* to accuse Him [1]harshly.

4 Then Pilate questioned Him again, saying, "Do You not answer? See how many charges they bring against You!"

5 But Jesus [a]made no further answer; so Pilate was amazed.

6 [a]Now at *the* feast he used to release for them *any* one prisoner whom they requested.

7 The man named Barabbas had been imprisoned with the insurrectionists who had committed murder in the insurrection.

8 The crowd went up and began asking him *to do* as he had been accustomed to do for them.

9 Pilate answered them, saying, "Do you want me to release for you the King of the Jews?"

10 For he was aware that the chief priests had handed Him over because of envy.

11 But the chief priests stirred up the crowd [a]*to ask* him to release Barabbas for them instead.

12 Answering again, Pilate said to them, "Then what shall I do with Him whom you call the King of the Jews?"

13 They shouted [1]back, "Crucify Him!"

14 But Pilate said to them, "Why, what evil has He done?" But they shouted all the more, "Crucify Him!"

15 Wishing to satisfy the crowd, Pilate released Barabbas for them, and after having Jesus [a]scourged, he handed Him over to be crucified.

Jesus Is Mocked

16 [a]The soldiers took Him away into [b]the [1]palace (that is, the Praetorium), and they *called together the whole *Roman* [2][c]cohort.

17 They *dressed Him up in purple, and

65 [1]Or *cover over His face* [2]Or *treated* [3]Or *blows with rods* [a]Matt 26:67; Mark 10:34 [b]Esth 7:8 [c]Matt 26:68; Luke 22:64
66 [a]Mark 14:66-72: *Matt 26:69-75; Luke 22:56-62; John 18:16-18, 25-27* [b]Mark 14:54
67 [a]Mark 14:54 [b]Mark 1:24
68 [1]Or *forecourt, gateway* [2]Later mss add *and a rooster crowed* [a]Mark 14:54
70 [a]Mark 14:68 [b]Matt 26:73; Luke 22:59
71 [1]Or *put himself under a curse*
72 [1]Or *Thinking of this, he began weeping* or *Rushing out, he began weeping* [a]Mark 14:30, 68
15:1 [1]Or *Sanhedrin* [a]Matt 27:1 [b]Matt 5:22
2 [a]Mark 15:2-5: *Matt 27:11-14; Luke 23:2, 3; John 18:29-38*
3 [1]Or *of many things*
5 [a]Matt 27:12
6 [a]Mark 15:6-15: *Matt 27:15-26; Luke 23:18-25; John 18:39-19:16*
11 [a]Acts 3:14
13 [1]Or *again*
15 [a]Matt 27:26
16 [1]Or *court* [2]Or *battalion* [a]Mark 15:16-20: *Matt 27:27-31* [b]Matt 26:3; 27:27 [c]Acts 10:1

14:65 *began to spit at Him . . . beat Him with their fists.* Conventional gestures of rejection and condemnation (Num 12:14; Deut 25:9; Job 30:10; Is 50:6). *blindfold Him.* An old interpretation of Is 11:2–4 held that the Messiah could judge by smell without the aid of sight. *Prophesy!* Say who it was who struck you!

14:66 *below.* While Jesus was being beaten in an upstairs room of Caiaphas's house, Peter was below in the courtyard. *one of the servant-girls.* The doorkeeper (John 18:16).

14:67 *Nazarene.* See note on Matt 2:23.

14:68 *I neither know nor understand what you are talking about.* Common in Jewish law for a formal, legal denial.

14:70 *Galilean.* Galileans were easily identified by their dialect. Peter's speech showed him to be a Galilean, and his presence among the Judeans in the courtyard suggested he was a follower of Jesus.

15:1 *Early in the morning.* The working day of a Roman official began at daylight. *morning.* Friday of Passion Week. *Council.* See note on 14:55. *held a consultation.* Apparently to accuse Jesus before the civil authority for treason rather than blasphemy (see Luke 23:1–14 and note on Luke 23:2). *Pilate.* The Roman governor of Judea from A.D. 26 to 36, whose official residence was in Caesarea, on the Mediterranean coast. (In 1961 archaeologists working at Caesarea unearthed a stone contemporary with Pilate and inscribed with his name.) When he came to Jerusalem, he stayed in the magnificent palace built by Herod the Great, located west and a little south of the temple area. Mark uses the word "Praetorium" to indicate this palace in v. 16, and it was here that the Roman trial of Jesus took place.

15:2 *Pilate questioned Him.* Judgment in a Roman court was the sole responsibility of the imperial magistrate.

15:3 *harshly.* Can also be translated as "many things." See note on Luke 23:2. Multiple charges were common in criminal cases.

15:4 *Do You not answer?* If Jesus made no defense, according to Roman law Pilate would have to pronounce against Him.

15:6 *he used to.* See note on John 18:39.

15:7 *Barabbas.* Probably a member of the Zealots, a revolutionary Jewish group. *in the insurrection.* Nothing from other sources is known about this insurrection, though Mark speaks of it as if it were well known. Under the Roman prefects such revolts were common (see Luke 13:1).

15:13 *Crucify.* See note on v. 24.

15:15 *scourged.* The Romans used a whip made of several strips of leather into which were embedded (near the ends) pieces of bone and lead. The Jews limited the number of stripes to a maximum of 40 (in practice to 39 in case of a miscount), but no such limitation was recognized by the Romans, and victims of Roman floggings often did not survive.

15:16 *Praetorium.* The word was used originally of a general's tent, or of the headquarters in a military camp (see note on v. 1).

after twisting a crown of thorns, they put it
on Him;
18 and they began to acclaim Him, "Hail,
King of the Jews!"
19 They kept beating His head with a
[1]reed, and spitting on Him, and kneeling and
bowing before Him.
20 After they had mocked Him, they took
the purple robe off Him and put His *own* garments on Him. And they *led Him out to
crucify Him.
21 [a]They *pressed into service a passer-by
coming from the country, Simon of Cyrene
(the father of Alexander and [b]Rufus), to bear
His cross.

The Crucifixion

22 [a]Then they *brought Him to the place
[b]Golgotha, which is translated, Place of a
Skull.
23 They tried to give Him [a]wine mixed
with myrrh; but He did not take it.
24 And they *crucified Him, and *[a]divid-
ed up His garments among themselves, casting [1]lots for them *to decide* [2]what each man
should take.
25 It was the [1a]third hour [2]when they crucified Him.
26 The inscription of the charge against
Him [1]read, "[a]THE KING OF THE JEWS."
27 They *crucified two robbers with Him,
one on His right and one on His left.
28 [[1]And the Scripture was fulfilled which
says, "And He was numbered with transgressors."]
29 Those passing by were [1]hurling abuse
at Him, [a]wagging their heads, and saying,
"Ha! You who *are going to* [b]destroy the temple and rebuild it in three days,
30 save Yourself, and come down from the
cross!"
31 In the same way the chief priests also,
along with the scribes, were mocking *Him*
among themselves and saying, "[a]He saved
others; [1]He cannot save Himself.
32 "Let *this* Christ, [a]the King of Israel, now
come down from the cross, so that we may
see and believe!" [b]Those who were crucified
with Him were also insulting Him.
33 [a]When the [1b]sixth hour came, darkness
[2]fell over the whole land until the [3b]ninth
hour.
34 At the [a]ninth hour Jesus cried out with
a loud voice, "[b]ELOI, ELOI, LAMA SABACH-
THANI?" which is translated, "MY GOD, MY
GOD, WHY HAVE YOU FORSAKEN ME?"

19 [1]Or *staff* (made of a reed) **21** [a]Mark 15:21: *Matt 27:32; Luke 23:26* [b]Rom 16:13 **22** [a]Mark 15:22-32: *Matt 27:33-44; Luke 23:33-43; John 19:17-24* [b]Luke 23:33; John 19:17 **23** [a]Matt 27:34 **24** [1]Lit *a lot upon* [2]Lit *who should take what* [a]Ps 22:18; John 19:24 **25** [1]I.e. 9 a.m. [2]Lit *and* [a]Mark 15:33 **26** [1]Lit *had been inscribed* [a]Matt 27:37 **28** [1]Early mss do not contain this v **29** [1]Or *blaspheming* [a]Ps 22:7; 109:25; Matt 27:39 [b]Mark 14:58; John 2:19 **31** [1]Or *can He not save Himself?* [a]Matt 27:42; Luke 23:35 **32** [a]Matt 27:42; Mark 15:26 [b]Matt 27:44; Mark 15:27; Luke 23:39-43 **33** [1]I.e. noon [2]Or *occurred* [3]I.e. 3 p.m. [a]Mark 15:33-41: *Matt 27:45-56; Luke 23:44-49* [b]Matt 27:45f; Mark 15:25; Luke 23:44 **34** [a]Matt 27:45f; Mark 15:25; Luke 23:44 [b]Ps 22:1; Matt 27:46

the whole Roman cohort. The soldiers quartered in the Praetorium were recruited from non-Jewish inhabitants of the Holy Land and assigned to the military governor.

15:17 *purple.* Probably an old military cloak, whose color suggested royalty (see Matt 27:28). *crown of thorns.* Made of a prickly plant (the Greek word means simply "briers"), of which there are many in the Holy Land. Both robe and crown were parts of the mock royal attire placed on Jesus.

15:18 *Hail, King of the Jews!* A mocking salutation that corresponded to "Hail, Caesar!"

15:19 *spiting on Him.* Probably a parody on the kiss of homage that was customary in the Near East when in the presence of royalty.

15:21 *Simon.* Probably a Jew who was in Jerusalem to celebrate the Passover (cf. "Cyrenians" in Acts 6:9). *Cyrene.* An important city of Libya in North Africa that had a large Jewish population. *Alexander and Rufus.* Only mentioned by Mark, but referred to in such a way as to suggest that they were known by those to whom he wrote. Rufus may be the same person spoken of in Rom 16:13. *bear His cross.* Men condemned to death were usually forced to carry a beam of the cross, often weighing 30 or 40 pounds, to the place of crucifixion. Jesus started out by carrying His (see John 19:17), but He had been so weakened by flogging that Simon was pressed into service.

15:22 *Place of a Skull.* It may have been a small hill (though the Gospels say nothing of a hill) that looked like a skull, or it may have been so named because of the many executions that took place there.

15:23 *wine mixed with myrrh.* The Talmud gives evidence that incense was mixed with wine to deaden pain (see Prov 31:6). Myrrh is a spice derived from plants native to the Arabian deserts and parts of Africa (see note on Gen 37:25).

15:24 *crucified.* A Roman means of execution in which the victim was nailed to a cross. Heavy, wrought-iron nails were driven through the wrists and the heel bones. If the life of the victim lingered too long, death was hastened by breaking his legs (see John 19:33). Archaeologists have discovered the bones of a crucified man, near Jerusalem, dating between A.D. 7 and 66, which shed light on the position of the victim when nailed to the cross. Only slaves, the basest of criminals, and offenders who were not Roman citizens were executed in this manner. First-century authors vividly describe the agony and disgrace of being crucified. *divided up His garments.* It was the accepted right of the executioner's squad to claim the minor possessions of the victim. Jesus' clothing probably consisted of an under and an outer garment, a belt, sandals and possibly a head covering.

15:25 *third hour.* See notes on Luke 23:44; John 19:14.

15:26 *charge against Him.* It was customary to write the charge on a wooden board that was carried before the victim as he walked to the place of execution, and then the board was affixed to the cross above his head. *THE KING OF THE JEWS.* The wording of the charge differs slightly in the Gospels, but all agree that Jesus was crucified for claiming to be the king of the Jews.

15:27 *two robbers.* According to Roman law, robbery was not a capital offense. Mark's term must signify men guilty of insurrection, crucified for high treason.

15:28 The earlier and more reliable Greek manuscripts do not have this verse. It was probably added from Luke 22:37 (quoting Is 53:12). Mark does not include many OT quotations.

15:29 See note on 14:58.

15:32 *Christ.* See note on 13:21. *Those who were crucified with Him.* One of the criminals later repented and asked to be included in Jesus' kingdom (Luke 23:39–43).

15:33 *sixth hour.* 12:00 noon. *ninth hour.* 3:00 P.M.

15:34 The words were spoken in Aramaic (but with some Hebrew characteristics), one of the languages commonly spoken in the Holy Land in Jesus' day. They reveal how deeply Jesus felt His abandonment by God as He bore the sins of mankind (but see introduction to Ps 22 and note on Ps 22:1).

35 When some of the bystanders heard it, they *began* saying, "Behold, He is calling for Elijah."

36 Someone ran and filled a sponge with sour wine, put it on a reed, and gave Him a drink, saying, "[1]Let us see whether Elijah will come to take Him down."

37 [a]And Jesus uttered a loud cry, and breathed His last.

38 [a]And the veil of the temple was torn in two from top to bottom.

39 [a]When the centurion, who was standing [1]right in front of Him, saw [2]the way He breathed His last, he said, "Truly this man was [3]the Son of God!"

40 [a]There were also *some* women looking on from a distance, among whom *were* Mary Magdalene, and Mary the mother of [1]James [b]the [2]Less and Joses, and [c]Salome.

41 When He was in Galilee, they used to follow Him and [1a]minister to Him; and *there were* many other women who came up with Him to Jerusalem.

Jesus Is Buried

42 [a]When evening had already come, because it was [b]the preparation day, that is, the day before the Sabbath,

43 Joseph of Arimathea came, a [a]prominent member of the Council, who himself was [b]waiting for the kingdom of God; and he [c]gathered up courage and went in before Pilate, and asked for the body of Jesus.

44 Pilate wondered if He was dead by this time, and summoning the centurion, he questioned him as to whether He was already dead.

45 And ascertaining this from [a]the centurion, he granted the body to Joseph.

46 Joseph bought a linen cloth, took Him down, wrapped Him in the linen cloth and laid Him in a tomb which had been hewn out in the rock; and he rolled a stone against the entrance of the tomb.

47 [a]Mary Magdalene and Mary the *mother* of Joses were looking on *to see* where He was laid.

The Resurrection

16 [a]When the Sabbath was over, [b]Mary Magdalene, and Mary the *mother* of [1]James, and Salome, [c]bought spices, so that they might come and anoint Him.

2 Very early on the first day of the week, they *came to the tomb when the sun had risen.

3 They were saying to one another, "Who will roll away [a]the stone for us from the entrance of the tomb?"

4 Looking up, they *saw that the stone had been rolled away, [1]although it was extremely large.

5 [a]Entering the tomb, they saw a young man sitting at the right, wearing a white robe; and they [b]were amazed.

6 And he *said to them, "[a]Do not be

36 [1]Lit *Permit that we see;* or *Hold off, let us see*
37 [a]Matt 27:50; Luke 23:46; John 19:30
38 [a]Ex 26:31-33; Matt 27:51; Luke 23:45
39 [1]Or *opposite Him* [2]Lit *that He thus* [3]Or *a son of God* or *son of a god* [a]Matt 27:54; Mark 15:45; Luke 23:47
40 [1]Or *Jacob* [2]Lit *little* (either in stature or age) [a]Mark 15:40, 41: *Matt 27:55f;* Luke 23:49; John 19:25 [b]Luke 19:3 [c]Mark 16:1
41 [1]Or *wait on* [a]Matt 27:55f
42 [a]Mark 15:42-47: *Matt 27:57-61; Luke 23:50-56; John 19:38-42* [b]Matt 27:62
43 [a]Matt 27:57; Luke 23:50, 51; Acts 13:50; 17:12 [b]Matt 27:57; Luke 2:25, 38; 23:51; John 19:38 [c]John 19:38
45 [a]Mark 15:39
47 [a]Matt 27:56; Mark 15:40; 16:1

16:1 [1]Or *Jacob* [a]Mark 16:1-8: *Matt 28:1-8; Luke 24:1-10;* John 20:1-8 [b]Mark 15:47 [c]Luke 23:56; John 19:39f **3** [a]Matt 27:60; Mark 15:46; 16:4 **4** [1]Lit *for* **5** [a]John 20:11, 12 [b]Mark 9:15 **6** [a]Mark 9:15

15:35 *Elijah.* The bystanders mistook the first words of Jesus' cry ("Eloi, Eloi") to be a cry for Elijah. It was commonly believed that Elijah would come in times of critical need to protect the innocent and rescue the righteous (v. 36).

15:36 *sour wine.* A type of wine used by laborers and soldiers.

15:37 *a loud cry.* The strength of the cry indicates that Jesus did not die the ordinary death of those crucified, who normally suffered long periods of complete agony, exhaustion and then unconsciousness before dying.

15:38 *veil of the temple.* The curtain that separated the holy place from the most holy place (Ex 26:31–33). The tearing of the curtain indicated that Christ had entered heaven itself for us so that we too may now enter God's very presence (Heb 9:8–10,12; 10:19–20).

15:39 *centurion.* A commander of 100 men in the Roman army. *saw the way He breathed His last.* See note on v. 37. *the Son of God.* See notes on Matt 27:54; Luke 23:47.

15:40 *Mary Magdalene.* From 16:9 and Luke 8:2 we learn that Jesus had driven seven demons from her. *Mary the mother of James the Less and Joses.* See v. 47; 16:1. *Salome.* Probably the wife of Zebedee and the mother of James and John (see Matt 27:56).

15:42 *preparation day.* Friday. Since it was now late in the afternoon, there was an urgency to get Jesus' body down from the cross before sundown, when the Sabbath began.

15:43 *Arimathea.* See note on Matt 27:57. *Council.* The Sanhedrin (see note on 14:55). *kingdom of God.* See note on Matt 3:2. *Pilate.* See note on v. I. *asked for the body of Jesus.* See note on Luke 23:52.

15:44 *wondered.* Crucified men often lived two or three days before dying, and the early death of Jesus was therefore extraordinary.

15:45 *he granted the body to Joseph.* The release of the body of one condemned for high treason, and especially to one who was not an immediate relative, was quite unusual.

15:46 *tomb which had been hewn out in the rock.* Matthew tells us that the tomb belonged to Joseph and that it was new, i.e., it had not been used before (Matt 27:60). The location of the tomb was in a garden very near the site of the crucifixion (see John 19:41). There is archaeological evidence that the traditional site of the burial of Jesus (the Church of the Holy Sepulchre in Jerusalem) was a cemetery during the first century A.D. *stone.* A disc-shaped stone that rolled in a sloped channel.

16:1 *Sabbath was over.* About 6:00 P.M. Saturday evening. No purchases were possible on the Sabbath. *Mary Magdalene, and Mary the mother of James, and Salome.* See note on 15:40. *spices.* Embalming was not practiced by the Jews. These spices were brought as an act of devotion and love. *so that they might come and anoint Him.* The women had no expectation of Jesus' resurrection.

16:3 *Who will roll away the stone . . . ?* Setting the large stone in place was a relatively easy task, but once it had slipped into the groove cut in bedrock in front of the entrance it was very difficult to remove.

16:5 *Entering the tomb.* Inside the large opening of the facade of the tomb was a forechamber, at the back of which a low rectangular opening led to the burial chamber. *young man . . . wearing a white robe.* Identified by Matthew (28:2) as an angel. See note on Luke 24:4.

amazed; you are looking for Jesus the [b]Naz-
arene, who has been crucified. [c]He has risen;
He is not here; behold, *here is* the place
where they laid Him.
7 "But go, tell His disciples and Peter, '[a]He
is going ahead of you to Galilee; there you
will see Him, just as He told you.' "
8 They went out and fled from the tomb,
for trembling and astonishment had gripped
them; and they said nothing to anyone, for
they were afraid.
9 [[1]Now after He had risen early on the
first day of the week, He first appeared to
[a]Mary Magdalene, from whom He had cast
out seven demons.
10 [a]She went and reported to those who
had been with Him, while they were mourning and weeping.
11 When they heard that He was alive and
had been seen by her, [a]they refused to
believe it.
12 After that, [a]He appeared in a different
form [b]to two of them while they were walking along on their way to the country.
13 They went away and reported it to the
others, but they [a]did not believe them either.

The Disciples Commissioned

14 Afterward [a]He appeared [b]to the eleven
themselves as they were reclining *at the
table;* and He reproached them for their
[c]unbelief and hardness of heart, because
they had not believed those who had seen
Him after He had risen.
15 And He said to them, "[a]Go into all the
world and preach the gospel to all creation.
16 "[a]He who has believed and has been
baptized shall be saved; but he who has dis-
believed shall be condemned.
17 "These [1]signs will accompany those
who have believed: [a]in My name they will
cast out demons, they will [b]speak with new
tongues;
18 they will [a]pick up serpents, and if they
drink any deadly *poison,* it will not hurt
them; they will [b]lay hands on the sick, and
they will recover."
19 So then, when the Lord Jesus had
[a]spoken to them, He [b]was received up into
heaven and [c]sat down at the right hand of
God.
20 And they went out and preached everywhere, while the Lord worked with them,
and confirmed the word by the [1]signs that
followed.]
[[2]*And they promptly reported all these
instructions to Peter and his companions. And
after that, Jesus Himself sent out through
them from east to west the sacred and imperishable proclamation of eternal salvation.*]

6 [b]Mark 1:24 [c]Matt 28:6; Luke 24:6
7 [a]Matt 26:32; Mark 14:28
9 [1]Later mss add vv 9-20 [a]Matt 27:56; John 20:14
10 [a]John 20:18
11 [a]Matt 28:17; Mark 16:13, 14; Luke 24:11, 41; John 20:25
12 [a]Mark 16:14; John 21:1, 14 [b]Luke 24:13-35
13 [a]Matt 28:17; Mark 16:11, 14; Luke 24:11, 41; John 20:25
14 [a]Mark 16:12; John 21:1, 14 [b]Luke 24:36; John 20:19, 26; 1 Cor 15:5 [c]Matt 28:17; Mark 16:11, 13; Luke 24:11, 41; John 20:25
15 [a]Matt 28:19; Acts 1:8
16 [a]John 3:18, 36; Acts 16:31
17 [1]Or *attesting miracles* [a]Mark 9:38; Luke 10:17; Acts 5:16; 8:7; 16:18; 19:12 [b]Acts 2:4; 10:46; 19:6; 1 Cor 12:10, 28, 30; 13:1; 14:2
18 [a]Luke 10:19; Acts 28:3-5 [b]Mark 5:23
19 [a]Acts 1:3 [b]Luke 9:51; 24:51; John 6:62; 20:17; Acts 1:2, 9-11; 1 Tim 3:16 [c]Ps 110:1; Luke 22:69; Acts 7:55f; Rom 8:34; Eph 1:20; Col 3:1; Heb 1:3; 8:1; 10:12; 12:2; 1 Pet 3:22
20 [1]Or *attesting miracles* [2]A few late mss and versions contain this paragraph, usually after v 8; a few have it at the end of ch

16:6 *crucified.* See note on 15:24. *He has risen.* The climax of Mark's Gospel is the resurrection, without which Jesus' death, though noble, would be indescribably tragic. But in the resurrection He is declared to be the Son of God with power (Rom 1:4).

16:7 *and Peter.* Jesus showed special concern for Peter, in view of his confident boasting and subsequent denials (14:29–31,66–72). *just as He told you.* See 14:28.

16:9–20 Serious doubt exists as to whether these verses belong to the Gospel of Mark. They are absent from important early manuscripts and display certain peculiarities of vocabulary, style and theological content that are unlike the rest of Mark. His Gospel probably ended at 16:8, or its original ending has been lost.

16:9 *Mary Magdalene.* See note on 15:40.

16:12–13 A shortened account of the two men going to Emmaus (see Luke 24:13–35).

16:14 *the eleven.* Judas Iscariot had committed suicide (see Matt 27:5).

16:16 *baptized.* See notes on 1:4; Rom 6:3–4.

16:18 *drink any deadly poison.* No occurrence of drinking deadly poison without harm is found in the NT.

16:19 *right hand of God.* A position of authority second only to God's (see 14:62; Ps 110:1).

Luke

INTRODUCTION

See "The Synoptic Gospels," p. 1361.

Author

The author's name does not appear in the book, but much unmistakable evidence points to Luke. This Gospel is a companion volume to the book of Acts, and the language and structure of these two books indicate that both were written by the same person. They are addressed to the same individual, Theophilus, and the second volume refers to the first (Acts 1:1). Certain sections in Acts use the pronoun "we" (Acts 16:10–17; 20:5–15; 21:1–18; 27:1—28:16), indicating that the author was with Paul when the events described in these passages took place. By process of elimination, "Luke, the beloved physician" (Col 4:14), and Paul's "fellow worker" (Philem 24) becomes the most likely candidate. His authorship is supported by the uniform testimony of early Christian writings (e.g., the Muratorian Canon, A.D. 170, and the works of Irenaeus, c. 180).

Luke was probably a Gentile by birth, well educated in Greek culture, a physician by profession, a companion of Paul at various times from his second missionary journey to his first imprisonment in Rome, and a loyal friend who remained with the apostle after others had deserted him (2Ti 4:11).

Antioch (of Syria) and Philippi are among the places suggested as his hometown.

Recipient and Purpose

The Gospel is specifically directed to Theophilus (1:3), whose name means "one who loves God" and almost certainly refers to a particular person rather than to lovers of God in general. The use of "most excellent" with the name further indicates an individual, and supports the idea that he was a Roman official or at least of high position and wealth. He was possibly Luke's patron, responsible for seeing that the writings were copied and distributed. Such a dedication to the publisher was common at that time.

Theophilus, however, was more than a publisher. The message of this Gospel was intended for his own instruction (1:4) as well as the instruction of those among whom the book would be circulated. The fact that the Gospel was initially directed to Theophilus does not narrow or limit its purpose. It was written to strengthen the faith of all believers and to answer the attacks of unbelievers. It was presented to displace disconnected and ill-founded reports about Jesus. Luke wanted to show that the place of the Gentile Christian in God's kingdom is based on the teaching of Jesus. He wanted to commend the preaching of the gospel to the whole world.

Date and Place of Writing

The two most commonly suggested periods for dating the Gospel of Luke are: (1) A.D. 59–63, and (2) the 70s or the 80s (see chart, p. 1361).

The place of writing was probably Rome, though Achaia, Ephesus and Caesarea also have been suggested. The place to which it was sent would, of course, depend on the residence of Theophilus. By its detailed designations of places in Palestine, the Gospel seems to be intended for readers who were unfamiliar with that land. Antioch, Achaia and Ephesus are possible destinations.

Style

Luke had outstanding command of the Greek language. His vocabulary is extensive and rich, and his style at times approaches that of classical Greek (as in the preface, 1:1–4), while at other times it is quite Semitic (1:5—2:52)—often like the Septuagint, Greek translation of the OT. His vocabulary seems to reveal geographical and cultural sensitivity, in that it varies with the particular land or people being described. When

Luke refers to Peter in a Jewish setting, he uses more Semitic language than when he refers to Paul in a Hellenistic setting.

Characteristics

The third Gospel presents the works and teachings of Jesus that are especially important for understanding the way of salvation. Its scope is complete from the birth of Christ to His ascension, its arrangement is orderly, and it appeals to both Jews and Gentiles. The writing is characterized by literary excellence, historical detail and warm, sensitive understanding of Jesus and those around him.

Since the Synoptic Gospels (Matthew, Mark and Luke) report many of the same episodes in Jesus' life, one would expect much similarity in their accounts. The dissimilarities reveal the distinctive emphases of the separate writers. Luke's characteristic themes include: (1) universality, recognition of Gentiles as well as Jews in God's plan; (2) emphasis on prayer, especially Jesus' praying before important occasions (see note on 3:21); (3) joy at the announcement of the gospel or "good news" (see note on 1:14); (4) special concern for the role of women; (5) special interest in the poor (some of the rich were included among Jesus' followers, but He seemed closest to the poor); (6) concern for sinners (Jesus was a friend to those deep in sin); (7) stress on the family circle (Jesus' activity included men, women and children, with the setting frequently in the home); (8) repeated use of the title "Son of Man" (e.g., 19:10); (9) emphasis on the Holy Spirit (see note on 4:1).

Sources

Although Luke acknowledges that many others had written of Jesus' life (1:1), he does not indicate that he relied on these reports for his own writing. He used personal investigation and arrangement, based on testimony from "eyewitnesses and servants of the word" (1:2)—including the preaching and oral accounts of the apostles. His language differences from the other Synoptics and his blocks of distinctive material (e.g., 10:1—18:14; 19:1–28) indicate independent work, though he obviously used some of the same sources.

Plan

Luke's account of Jesus' ministry can be divided into three major parts: (1) the events that occurred in and around Galilee (4:14—9:50), (2) those that took place in Judea and Perea (9:51—19:27), and (3) those of the final week in Jerusalem (19:28—24:53). Luke's uniqueness is especially seen in the amount of material devoted to Jesus' closing ministry in Judea and Perea. This material is predominantly made up of accounts of Jesus' discourses. Sixteen of the 23 parables that occur in Luke are found here (9:51—18:14; 19:1–28). Of the 20 miracles recorded in Luke, only 4 appear in these sections. Already in the ninth chapter (see note on 9:51), Jesus is seen anticipating His final appearance in Jerusalem and His crucifixion (see note on 13:22).

The main theme of the Gospel is the nature of Jesus' Messiahship and mission, and a key verse is 19:10.

Outline

- I. The Preface (1:1–4)
- II. The Coming of Jesus (1:5—2:52)
  - A. The Annunciations (1:5–56)
  - B. The Birth of John the Baptist (1:57–80)
  - C. The Birth and Childhood of Jesus (ch. 2)
- III. The Preparation of Jesus for His Public Ministry (3:1—4:13)
  - A. His Forerunner (3:1–20)
  - B. His Baptism (3:21–22)
  - C. His Genealogy (3:23–38)
  - D. His Temptation (4:1–13)
- IV. His Ministry in Galilee (4:14—9:9)
  - A. The Beginning of the Ministry in Galilee (4:14–41)
  - B. The First Tour of Galilee (4:42—5:39)
  - C. A Sabbath Controversy (6:1–11)
  - D. The Choice of the 12 Disciples (6:12–16)

E. The Sermon on the Plain (6:17–49)
F. Miracles in Capernaum and Nain (7:1–18)
G. The Inquiry of John the Baptist (7:19–29)
H. Jesus and the Pharisees (7:30–50)
I. The Second Tour of Galilee (8:1–3)
J. The Parables of the Kingdom (8:4–21)
K. The Trip across the Sea of Galilee (8:22–39)
L. The Third Tour of Galilee (8:40—9:9)

V. His Withdrawal to Regions around Galilee (9:10–50)
A. To the Eastern Shore of the Sea of Galilee (9:10–17)
B. To Caesarea Philippi (9:18–50)

VI. His Ministry in Judea (9:51—13:21)
A. Journey through Samaria to Judea (9:51–62)
B. The Mission of the 72 (10:1–24)
C. The Lawyer and the Parable of the Good Samaritan (10:25–37)
D. Jesus at Bethany with Mary and Martha (10:38–42)
E. Teachings in Judea (11:1—13:21)

VII. His Ministry in and around Perea (13:22—19:27)
A. The Narrow Door (13:22–30)
B. Warning concerning Herod (13:31–35)
C. At a Pharisee's House (14:1–23)
D. The Cost of Discipleship (14:24–35)
E. The Parables of the Lost Sheep, the Lost Coin and the Lost Son (ch. 15)
F. The Parable of the Shrewd Manager (16:1–18)
G. The Rich Man and Lazarus (16:19–31)
H. Miscellaneous Teachings (17:1–10)
I. Ten Healed of Leprosy (17:11–19)
J. The Coming of the Kingdom (17:20–37)
K. The Persistent Widow (18:1–8)
L. The Pharisee and the Tax Collector (18:9–14)
M. Jesus and the Children (18:15–17)
N. The Rich Young Ruler (18:18–30)
O. Christ Foretells His Death (18:31–34)
P. A Blind Beggar Given His Sight (18:35–43)
Q. Jesus and Zacchaeus (19:1–10)
R. The Parable of the Ten Minas (19:11–27)

VIII. His Last Days: Sacrifice and Triumph (19:28—24:53)
A. The Triumphal Entry (19:28–44)
B. The Cleansing of the Temple (19:45–48)
C. The Last Controversies with the Jewish Leaders (ch. 20)
D. The Olivet Discourse (ch. 21)
E. The Last Supper (22:1–38)
F. Jesus Praying in Gethsemane (22:39–46)
G. Jesus' Arrest (22:47–65)
H. Jesus on Trial (22:66—23:25)
I. The Crucifixion (23:26–56)
J. The Resurrection (24:1–12)
K. The Post-Resurrection Ministry (24:13–49)
L. The Ascension (24:50–53)

Introduction

1 Inasmuch as many have undertaken to
compile an account of the things
[1a]accomplished among us,
2 just as they were handed down to us
by those who [a]from the beginning [1]were
[b]eyewitnesses and [2c]servants of [d]the [3]word,
3 it seemed fitting for me as well, [a]hav-
ing [1]investigated everything carefully from
the beginning, to write *it* out for you [b]in con-
secutive order, [c]most excellent [d]Theophilus;
4 so that you may know the exact truth
about the things you have been [1a]taught.

Birth of John the Baptist Foretold

5 [a]In the days of Herod, king of Judea,
there was a priest named [1]Zacharias, of the
[b]division of [2]Abijah; and he had a wife [3]from
the daughters of Aaron, and her name was
Elizabeth.
6 They were both [a]righteous in the sight
of God, walking [b]blamelessly in all the commandments and requirements of the Lord.
7 But they had no child, because Elizabeth was barren, and they were both
advanced in [1]years.
8 Now it happened *that* while [a]he was
performing his priestly service before God in
the *appointed* order of his division,
9 according to the custom of the priestly
office, he was chosen by lot [a]to enter the
temple of the Lord and burn incense.
10 And the whole multitude of the people
were in prayer [a]outside at the hour of the
incense offering.
11 And [a]an angel of the Lord appeared to
him, standing to the right of the altar of
incense.
12 Zacharias was troubled when he saw
the angel, and [a]fear [1]gripped him.
13 But the angel said to him, "[a]Do not be
afraid, Zacharias, for your petition has been
heard, and your wife Elizabeth will bear you
a son, and [b]you will [1]give him the name
John.
14 "You will have joy and gladness, and
many will rejoice at his birth.
15 "For he will be great in the sight of the
Lord; and he will [a]drink no wine or liquor,
and he will be filled with the Holy Spirit
[1]while yet in his mother's womb.
16 "And he will [a]turn many of the sons of
Israel back to the Lord their God.
17 "It is he who will [a]go *as a forerunner*
before Him in the spirit and power of [b]Elijah,
[c]TO TURN THE HEARTS OF THE FATHERS BACK TO THE
CHILDREN, and the disobedient to the attitude
of the righteous, so as to [a]make ready a people prepared for the Lord."
18 Zacharias said to the angel, "How will

12 [1]Or *fell upon* [a]Luke 2:9 **13** [1]Lit *call his name* [a]Matt 14:27; Luke 1:30 [b]Luke 1:60, 63 **15** [1]Lit *from* [a]Num 6:3; Judg 13:4; Matt 11:18; Luke 7:33 **16** [a]Matt 3:2, 6; Luke 3:3 **17** [a]Luke 1:76 [b]Matt 11:14 [c]Mal 4:6

1:1 [1]Or *on which there is full conviction* [a]Rom 4:21; 14:5; Col 2:2; 4:12; 1 Thess 1:5; 2 Tim 4:17; Heb 6:11; 10:22
2 [1]Lit *became* [2]Or *ministers* [3]I.e. gospel [a]John 15:27; Acts 1:21f [b]2 Pet 1:16; 1 John 1:1 [c]Acts 26:16; 1 Cor 4:1; Heb 2:3 [d]Mark 4:14; 16:20; Acts 8:4; 14:25; 16:6; 17:11
3 [1]Or *followed* [a]1 Tim 4:6 [b]Acts 11:4; 18:23 [c]Acts 23:26; 24:3; 26:25 [d]Acts 1:1
4 [1]Or *orally instructed in* [a]Acts 18:25; Rom 2:18; 1 Cor 14:19; Gal 6:6
5 [1]I.e. Zechariah [2]Gr *Abia* [3]I.e. of priestly descent [a]Matt 2:1 [b]1 Chr 24:10
6 [a]Gen 7:1; Acts 2:25; 8:21 [b]Phil 2:15; 3:6; 1 Thess 3:13
7 [1]Lit *days*
8 [a]1 Chr 24:19; 2 Chr 8:14; 31:2
9 [a]Ex 30:7f
10 [a]Lev 16:17
11 [a]Luke 2:9; Acts 5:19

1:1–4 Using language similar to classical Greek, Luke begins with a formal preface, common to historical works of that time, in which he states his purpose for writing and identifies the recipient. He acknowledges other reports on the subject, shows the need for this new work and states his method of approach and sources of information.
1:1 *things accomplished among us.* Things prophesied in the OT and now fully accomplished.
1:2 *handed down.* A technical term for passing on information as authoritative tradition. *eyewitnesses and servants of the word.* Luke, though not an eyewitness himself, received testimony from those who were eyewitnesses and were dedicated to spreading the gospel. Apostolic preaching and interviews with other individuals associated with Jesus' ministry were available to him.
1:3 *investigated everything carefully.* Luke's account was exact in historical detail, having been checked in every way. Inspiration by the Holy Spirit did not rule out human effort. The account is complete, extending back to the very beginning of Jesus' earthly life. It has an orderly, meaningful arrangement that is generally chronological. *most excellent.* Paul used this respectful term for governors Felix (Acts 24:3) and Festus (Acts 26:25). *Theophilus.* See Introduction: Recipient and Purpose.
1:4 *so that you may know.* Cf. John's purpose for writing (John 20:31).
1:5 *Herod, king of Judea.* Herod the Great reigned 37–4 B.C., and his kingdom included Samaria, Galilee, much of Perea and Coele-Syria (see note on Matt 2:1). The time referred to here is probably c. 7–6 B.C. *Zacharias . . . Elizabeth.* Both were of priestly descent from the line of Aaron. *division of Abijah.* From the time of David the priests were organized into 24 divisions, and Abijah was one of the "priests, the heads of fathers' households" (Neh 12:12; see 1 Chr 24:10).
1:6 *righteous . . . blamelessly.* They were not sinless, but were faithful and sincere in keeping God's commandments. Simeon (2:25) and Joseph (Matt 1:19) are given similar praise.
1:7 *no child.* See note on v. 25.
1:9 It was one of the priest's duties to keep the incense burning on the altar in front of the most holy place. He supplied it with fresh incense before the morning sacrifice and again after the evening sacrifice (Ex 30:6–8). Ordinarily a priest would have this privilege very infrequently, and sometimes never, since duty assignments were determined by lot. *chosen by lot.* See notes on Neh 11:1; Prov 16:33; Jon 1:7; Acts 1:26.
1:11 *angel of the Lord.* See v. 19. *right of the altar.* The south side, since the altar faced east.
1:12 *fear.* A common reaction, as with Gideon (Judg 6:22–23) and Manoah (Judg 13:22).
1:13 *Do not be afraid.* This word of reassurance is given many times in both OT and NT (see, e.g., v. 30; 2:10 and note; 5:10; 8:50; 12:7,32; Gen 15:1; 21:17; 26:24; Deut 1:21; Josh 8:1). *John.* The name (derived from Hebrew) means "The LORD is gracious."
1:14 *joy.* A keynote of these opening chapters (vv. 14,44,47,58; 2:10).
1:15 *wine or liquor.* It appears likely that John was to be subject to the Nazirite vow of abstinence from alcoholic drinks (Num 6:1–4). If so, he was a lifelong Nazirite, as were Samson (Judg 13:4–7) and Samuel (1 Sam 1:11).
1:17 *Elijah.* John was not Elijah returning in the flesh (John 1:21), but he functioned like that OT preacher of repentance and was therefore a fulfillment of Mal 4:5–6 (see Matt 11:14; 17:10–13). *TO TURN THE HEARTS OF THE FATHERS BACK TO THE CHILDREN.* See note on Mal 4:6. *people prepared for the Lord.* John helped fulfill Isaiah's prophecy (Is 40:3–5), as Luke shows in 3:4–6.
1:18 *How will I know this for certain?* Like Abraham (Gen 15:8), Gideon (Judg 6:17) and Hezekiah (2 Kin 20:8), Zacharias asked for a sign (cf. 1 Cor 1:22).

I know this *for certain?* For [a]I am an old man and my wife is advanced in [1]years."

19 The angel answered and said to him, "I am [a]Gabriel, who [1b]stands in the presence of God, and I have been sent to speak to you and to bring you this good news.

20 "And behold, you shall be silent and unable to speak until the day when these things take place, because you did not believe my words, which will be fulfilled in their proper time."

21 The people were waiting for Zacharias, and were wondering at his delay in the temple.

22 But when he came out, he was unable to speak to them; and they realized that he had seen a vision in the temple; and he [a]kept [1]making signs to them, and remained mute.

23 When the days of his priestly service were ended, he went back home.

24 After these days Elizabeth his wife became pregnant, and she [1]kept herself in seclusion for five months, saying,

25 "This is the way the Lord has dealt with me in the days when He looked *with favor* upon *me,* to [a]take away my disgrace among men."

Jesus' Birth Foretold

26 Now in the sixth month the angel [a]Gabriel was sent from God to a city in Galilee called [b]Nazareth,

27 to [a]a virgin [1]engaged to a man whose name was Joseph, [b]of the [2]descendants of David; and the virgin's name was [3]Mary.

28 And coming in, he said to her, "Greetings, [1]favored one! The Lord [2]*is* with you."

29 But she [a]was very perplexed at *this* statement, and kept pondering what kind of salutation this was.

30 The angel said to her, "[a]Do not be afraid, Mary; for you have found favor with God.

31 "And behold, you will conceive in your womb and bear a son, and you [a]shall name Him Jesus.

32 "He will be great and will be called the Son of [a]the Most High; and the Lord God will give Him [b]the throne of His father David;

33 [a]and He will reign over the house of Jacob forever, [b]and His kingdom will have no end."

34 Mary said to the angel, "How [1]can this be, since I [2]am a virgin?"

35 The angel answered and said to her, "[a]The Holy Spirit will come upon you, and the power of [b]the Most High will overshadow you; and for that reason [c]the [1]holy Child shall be called [d]the Son of God.

36 "And behold, even your relative Elizabeth has also conceived a son in her old age; and [1]she who was called barren is now in her sixth month.

37 "For [1a]nothing will be impossible with God."

38 And Mary said, "Behold, the [1]bondslave of the Lord; may it be done to me according to your word." And the angel departed from her.

Mary Visits Elizabeth

39 Now [1]at this time Mary arose and went in a hurry to [a]the hill country, to a city of Judah,

40 and entered the house of Zacharias and greeted Elizabeth.

18 [1]Lit *days* [a]Gen 17:17
19 [1]Lit *stand beside* [a]Dan 8:16; 9:21; Luke 1:26 [b]Matt 18:10
22 [1]Or *beckoning to* or *nodding to* [a]Luke 1:62
24 [1]Lit *was hidden*
25 [a]Gen 30:23; Is 4:1; 25:8
26 [a]Luke 1:19 [b]Matt 2:23
27 [1]Or *betrothed;* i.e. the first stage of marriage in Jewish culture, usually lasting for a year before the wedding night. More legal than engagement [2]Lit *house* [3]Gr *Mariam;* i.e. Heb Miriam; so throughout Luke [a]Matt 1:18 [b]Matt 1:16, 20; Luke 2:4
28 [1]Or *woman richly blessed* [2]Or be
29 [a]Luke 1:12
30 [a]Matt 14:27; Luke 1:13
31 [a]Is 7:14; Matt 1:21, 25; Luke 2:21
32 [a]Mark 5:7; Luke 1:35, 76; 6:35; Acts 7:48 [b]2 Sam 7:12, 13, 16; Is 9:7
33 [a]Matt 1:1 [b]2 Sam 7:13, 16; Ps 89:36, 37; Dan 2:44; 7:14, 18, 27; Matt 28:18
34 [1]Lit *will* [2]Lit *know no man*
35 [1]Lit *the holy thing begotten* [a]Matt 1:18 [b]Luke 1:32 [c]Mark 1:24 [d]Matt 4:3; John 1:34, 49; 20:31
36 [1]Lit *this is the sixth month to her who* **37** [1]Lit *not any word* [a]Gen 18:14; Jer 32:17; Matt 19:26 **38** [1]I.e. female slave
39 [1]Lit *in these days* [a]Josh 20:7; 21:11; Luke 1:65

1:19 *Gabriel.* The name can mean "God is my hero" or "mighty man of God." Only two angels are identified by name in Scripture: Gabriel (Dan 8:16; 9:21) and Michael (Dan 10:13,21; Jude 9; Rev 12:7).

1:21 *The people were waiting for Zacharias.* They were waiting for him to come out of the holy place and pronounce the Aaronic blessing (Num 6:24–26).

1:23 *the days of his priestly service.* Each priest was responsible for a week's service at the temple once every six months. *home.* See v. 39.

1:24 *kept herself in seclusion.* In joy, devotion and gratitude that the Lord had taken away her childlessness.

1:25 *the Lord has . . . looked with favor upon me, to take away my disgrace.* Not only did lack of children deprive the parents of personal happiness, but it was generally considered to indicate divine disfavor and often brought social reproach (see Gen 16:2, Sarai; 25:21, Rebekah; 30:23, Rachel; 1 Sam 1:1–18, Hannah; see also Lev 20:20–21; Ps 128:3; Jer 22:30).

1:26–35 This section speaks clearly of the virginal conception of Jesus (vv. 27,34–35; see Matt 1:18–25). The conception was the work of the Holy Spirit; the eternal Second Person of the Trinity, while remaining God, also "became flesh" (John 1:14). From conception He was fully God and fully man.

1:26 *in the sixth month.* That is, from the time of John's conception. *Nazareth.* See note on Matt 2:23.

1:27 *engaged.* See note on Matt 1:18.

1:28 *Greetings. Ave* in the Latin Vulgate (from which comes "Ave Maria").

1:31 *Jesus.* See note on Matt 1:21 for the meaning of this name.

1:32 *the Son of the Most High.* This title has two senses: (1) the divine Son of God and (2) the Messiah born in time. His Messiahship is clearly referred to in the following context (vv. 32b–33). *Most High.* A title frequently used of God in both the OT and NT (see vv. 35,76; 6:35; 8:28; Gen 14:19 and note; 2 Sam 22:14). *throne.* Promised in the OT to the Messiah descended from David (2 Sam 7:13,16; Ps 2:6–7; 89:26–27; Is 9:6–7). *His father David.* Mary was a descendant of David, as was Joseph (see Matt 1:16); so Jesus could rightly be called a "son" of David.

1:33 *forever.* See Ps 45:6; Rev 11:15. *His kingdom will have no end.* Although Christ's role as mediator will one day be finished (see 1 Cor 15:24–28), the kingdom of the Father and Son, as one, will never end.

1:34 *How can this be . . . ?* Mary did not ask in disbelief, as Zacharias did (v. 20). See v. 45.

1:35 *holy Child.* Jesus never sinned (2 Cor 5:21; Heb 4:15; 7:26; 1 Pet 2:22; 1 John 3:5).

1:36 *your relative Elizabeth.* It is not known whether she was a cousin, aunt or other relation.

41 When Elizabeth heard Mary's greeting, the baby leaped in her womb; and Elizabeth was [a]filled with the Holy Spirit.

42 And she cried out with a loud voice and said, "Blessed *are* you among women, and blessed *is* the fruit of your womb!

43 "And [1]how has it *happened* to me, that the mother of [a]my Lord would come to me?

44 "For behold, when the sound of your greeting reached my ears, the baby leaped in my womb for joy.

45 "And [a]blessed *is* she who [1]believed that there would be a fulfillment of what had been spoken to her [2]by the Lord."

The Magnificat

46 And Mary said:
"[a]My soul [1b]exalts the Lord,
47 And [a]my spirit has rejoiced in [b]God
my Savior.
48 "For [a]He has had regard for the humble
state of His [1]bondslave;
For behold, from this time on all
generations will count me
[b]blessed.
49 "For the Mighty One has done great
things for me;
And holy is His name.
50 "[a]AND HIS MERCY IS [1]UPON GENERATION
AFTER GENERATION
TOWARD THOSE WHO FEAR HIM.
51 "[a]He has done [1]mighty deeds with His
arm;
He has scattered *those who were* proud
in the [2]thoughts of their heart.
52 "He has brought down rulers from *their*
thrones,
And has [a]exalted those who were
humble.
53 "[a]HE HAS FILLED THE HUNGRY WITH GOOD
THINGS;
And sent away the rich empty-
handed.
54 "He has given help to Israel His
servant,
[1]In remembrance of His mercy,
55 [a]As He spoke to our fathers,
[b]To Abraham and his [1]descendants
forever."

56 And Mary stayed with her about three months, and *then* returned to her home.

John Is Born

57 Now the time [1]had come for Elizabeth to give birth, and she gave birth to a son.

58 Her neighbors and her relatives heard that the Lord had [1a]displayed His great mercy toward her; and they were rejoicing with her.

59 And it happened that on [a]the eighth day they came to circumcise the child, and they were going to call him Zacharias, [1]after his father.

60 But his mother answered and said, "No indeed; but [a]he shall be called John."

61 And they said to her, "There is no one among your relatives who is called by that name."

62 And they [a]made signs to his father, as to what he wanted him called.

63 And he asked for a tablet and wrote as follows, "[a]His name is John." And they were all astonished.

64 [a]And at once his mouth was opened and his tongue *loosed,* and he *began* to speak in praise of God.

65 Fear came on all those living around them; and all these matters were being talked about in all [a]the hill country of Judea.

66 All who heard them kept them in mind, saying, "What then will this child *turn out to* be?" For [a]the hand of the Lord was certainly with him.

Zacharias's Prophecy

67 And his father Zacharias [a]was filled with the Holy Spirit, and [b]prophesied, saying:
68 "[a]Blessed *be* the Lord God of Israel,
For He has visited us and
accomplished [b]redemption for His
people,

41 [a]Luke 1:67; Acts 2:4; 4:8; 9:17 **43** [1]Lit *from where this to me* [a]Luke 2:11 **45** [1]Or *believed, because there will be* [2]Lit *from* [a]Luke 1:20, 48 **46** [1]Lit *makes great* [a]Luke 1:46-53: *1 Sam 2:1-10* [b]Ps 34:2f **47** [a]Ps 35:9; Hab 3:18 [b]1 Tim 1:1; 2:3; Titus 1:3; 2:10; 3:4; Jude 25 **48** [1]I.e. female slave [a]Ps 138:6 [b]Luke 1:45 **50** [1]Lit *unto generations and generations* [a]Ps 103:17 **51** [1]Lit *might* [2]Lit *thought, attitude* [a]Ps 98:1; 118:15 **52** [a]Job 5:11 **53** [a]Ps 107:9 **54** [1]Lit *So as to remember*

55 [1]Lit *seed* [a]Gen 17:19; Ps 132:11; Gal 3:16 [b]Gen 17:7 **57** [1]Lit *was fulfilled* **58** [1]Lit *magnified* [a]Gen 19:19 **59** [1]Lit *after the name of* [a]Gen 17:12; Lev 12:3; Luke 2:21; Phil 3:5 **60** [a]Luke 1:13, 63 **62** [a]Luke 1:22 **63** [a]Luke 1:13, 60 **64** [a]Luke 1:20 **65** [a]Luke 1:39 **66** [a]Acts 11:21 **67** [a]Luke 1:41; Acts 2:4, 8; 9:17 [b]Joel 2:28 **68** [a]1 Kin 1:48; Ps 41:13; 72:18; 106:48 [b]Luke 1:71; 2:38; Heb 9:12

1:44 *for joy.* In some mysterious way the Holy Spirit produced this remarkable response in the unborn baby.

1:46–55 One of four hymns preserved in Luke 1–2 (see vv. 68–79; 2:14; 2:29–32 and notes). This hymn of praise is known as the Magnificat because in the Latin Vulgate translation the opening word is *Magnificat,* which means "glorifies." This song is like a psalm, and should also be compared with the song of Hannah (1 Sam 2:1–10; see note on 1 Sam 2:1).

1:50 *THOSE WHO FEAR HIM.* Those who revere God and live in harmony with His will.

1:51 *His arm.* A figurative description of God's powerful acts. God does not have a body; He is spirit (John 4:24).

1:53 *HUNGRY.* Both physically and spiritually (Matt 5:6; John 6:35). The coming of God's kingdom will bring changes affecting every area of life.

1:54 *In remembrance of His mercy.* The song ends with an assurance that God will be true to His promises to His people (see Gen 22:16–18).

1:56 *three months.* Mary evidently remained with Elizabeth until John's birth and then returned to her home in Nazareth.

1:59 *call him . . . after his father.* An accepted practice in that day, as seen in Josephus (*Life*, 1).

1:62 *they made signs to his father.* Apparently assuming that since he was mute he was also deaf.

1:63 *a tablet.* Probably a small wooden board covered with wax.

1:67 *filled with the Holy Spirit . . . prophesied.* Prophecy not only predicts but also proclaims God's word. Both Zacharias and Elizabeth (vv. 41–45) were enabled by the Holy Spirit to express what otherwise they could not have formulated.

1:68–79 This hymn is called Benedictus ("Praise be") because the opening word in the Latin Vulgate translation is *Benedictus.* Whereas the Magnificat (see note on 1:46–55) is similar to a psalm, the Benedictus is more like a prophecy.

1:68 *accomplished redemption for His people.* Not limited to national security (v. 71), but including moral and spiritual salvation (vv. 75,77).

69 And has raised up a [a]horn of salvation for us
In the house of David [b]His servant—
70 [a]As He spoke by the mouth of His holy prophets [b]from of old—
71 [1a]Salvation [b]FROM OUR ENEMIES,
And FROM THE HAND OF ALL WHO HATE US;
72 [a]To show mercy toward our fathers,
[b]And to remember His holy covenant,
73 [a]The oath which He swore to Abraham our father,
74 To grant us that we, being rescued from the hand of our enemies,
Might serve Him without fear,
75 [a]In holiness and righteousness before Him all our days.
76 "And you, child, will be called the [a]prophet of [b]the Most High;
For you will go on [c]BEFORE THE LORD TO [d]PREPARE HIS WAYS;
77 To give to His people *the* knowledge of salvation
[1]By [a]the forgiveness of their sins,
78 Because of the tender mercy of our God,
With which [a]the Sunrise from on high will visit us,
79 [a]TO SHINE UPON THOSE WHO SIT IN DARKNESS AND THE SHADOW OF DEATH,
To guide our feet into the [b]way of peace."
80 [a]And the child continued to grow and
to become strong in spirit, and he lived in
the deserts until the day of his public appearance to Israel.

Jesus' Birth in Bethlehem

2 Now in those days a decree went out from
[a]Caesar Augustus, that a census be taken
of [b]all [1]the inhabited earth.
2 [1]This was the first census taken while
[2]Quirinius was governor of [a]Syria.
3 And everyone was on his way to register for the census, each to his own city.
4 Joseph also went up from Galilee, from
the city of Nazareth, to Judea, to the city of
David which is called Bethlehem, because
[a]he was of the house and family of David,
5 in order to register along with Mary,
who was engaged to him, and was with child.
6 While they were there, the days were
completed for her to give birth.
7 And she [a]gave birth to her firstborn
son; and she wrapped Him in cloths, and
laid Him in a [1]manger, because there was no
room for them in the inn.
8 In the same region there were *some*
shepherds staying out in the fields and keeping watch over their flock by night.
9 And [a]an angel of the Lord suddenly
[b]stood before them, and the glory of the Lord
shone around them; and they were terribly
frightened.
10 But the angel said to them, "[a]Do not be
afraid; for behold, I bring you good news of
great joy which will be for all the people;

69 [a]1 Sam 2:1, 10; Ps 18:2; 89:17; 132:17; Ezek 29:21 [b]Matt 1:1
70 [a]Rom 1:2 [b]Acts 3:21
71 [1]Or *Deliverance* [a]Luke 1:68 [b]Ps 106:10
72 [a]Mic 7:20 [b]Ps 105:8f, 42; 106:45
73 [a]Gen 22:16ff; Heb 6:13
75 [a]Eph 4:24
76 [a]Matt 11:9 [b]Luke 1:32 [c]Mal 3:1; Matt 11:10; Mark 1:2; Luke 7:27 [d]Luke 1:17
77 [1]Or *Consisting in* [a]Jer 31:34; Mark 1:4
78 [a]Mal 4:2; Eph 5:14; 2 Pet 1:19
79 [a]Is 9:2 [b]Is 59:8; Matt 4:16
80 [a]Luke 2:40

2:1 [1]I.e. the Roman empire [a]Matt 22:17; Luke 3:1 [b]Matt 24:14
2 [1]Or *This took place as a first census* [2]Gr *Kyrenios* [a]Matt 4:24
4 [a]Luke 1:27
7 [1]Or *feeding trough* [a]Matt 1:25
9 [a]Luke 1:11; Acts 5:19 [b]Luke 24:4; Acts 12:7
10 [a]Matt 14:27

1:69 *horn.* Here symbolizes strength, as in the horn of an animal (Deut 33:17; Ps 22:21; Mic 4:13). Jesus, the Messiah from the house of David, has the power to save.

1:74 *we, being rescued.* No doubt including liberation from all kinds of oppression and bondage as well as deliverance from sin.

1:76 *called the prophet of the Most High.* Whereas Jesus will be called "the Son of the Most High" (see v. 32 and note). *PREPARE HIS WAYS.* See note on 3:4.

1:78 *the Sunrise.* A reference to the coming of the Messiah (see also similar figures in Num 24:17; Is 9:2; 60:1; Mal 4:2). Zacharias not only praised his own son, the "prophet of the Most High" (vv. 76–77), but also gave honor to the coming Messiah (vv. 78–79).

1:79 *THOSE WHO SIT IN DARKNESS.* The lost, separated from God (Is 9:1–2; Matt 4:16). *peace.* See note on 2:14.

1:80 *lived in the deserts.* John's parents, old at his birth, probably died while he was young, and he apparently grew up in the Desert of Judea, which lies between Jerusalem and the Dead Sea. *until . . . his public appearance.* John's preaching and announcing the coming of the Messiah marked his public appearance. He was about 30 years old when he began his ministry (see note on 3:23).

2:1 Luke is the only Gospel writer who relates his narrative to dates of world history. *Caesar Augustus.* The first and (according to many) greatest Roman emperor (31 B.C.–A.D. 14). Having replaced the republic with an imperial form of government, he expanded the empire to include the entire Mediterranean world, established the famed *Pax Romana* ("Roman Peace") and ushered in the golden age of Roman literature and architecture. Augustus (which means "exalted") was a title voted to him by the Roman senate in 27 B.C. *census.* Used for military service and taxation. Jews, however, were exempt from Roman military service. God used the decree of a pagan emperor to fulfill the prophecy of Mic 5:2. *inhabited earth.* The Roman world. See map No. 13 at the end of the study Bible.

2:2 *Quirinius.* This official was possibly in office for two terms, first 6–4 B.C. and then A.D. 6–9. A census is associated with each term. This is the first; Acts 5:37 refers to the second.

2:3 *own city.* Probably the city of their ancestral origin.

2:4 *Nazareth . . . Bethlehem.* Bethlehem, the town where David was born (1 Sam 17:12; 20:6), was at least a three-day trip from Nazareth. *Judea.* The Greco-Roman designation for the southern part of the Holy Land, earlier included in the kingdom of Judah.

2:5 *with Mary.* Mary too was of the house of David and probably was required to enroll. In Syria, the Roman province in which the Holy Land was located, women 12 years of age and older were required to pay a poll tax and therefore to register. *engaged.* See note on Matt 1:18.

2:7 *cloths.* Strips of cloth were regularly used to wrap a newborn infant. *manger.* The feeding trough of the animals. This is the only indication that Christ was born in a stable. Very early tradition suggests that it was a cave, perhaps used as a stable.

2:8 *staying out in the fields.* Does not necessarily mean it was summer, the dry season. The flocks reserved for temple sacrifice were kept in the fields near Bethlehem throughout the year. *keeping watch.* Against thieves and predatory animals.

2:9 *an angel of the Lord.* A designation used throughout the birth narratives (see 1:11; Matt 1:20,24; 2:13,19). The angel in 1:11 is identified as Gabriel (1:19; see 1:26).

2:10 *Do not be afraid.* Fear was the common reaction to angelic appearances (see note on 1:13), and encouragement was needed.

11 for today in the city of David there has been born for you a [a]Savior, who is [1b]Christ [c]the Lord.

12 "[a]This *will be* a sign for you: you will find a baby wrapped in cloths and lying in a [1]manger."

13 And suddenly there appeared with the angel a multitude of the heavenly host praising God and saying,

14 "[a]Glory to God in the highest,
And on earth peace among men
[1b]with whom He is pleased."

15 When the angels had gone away from them into heaven, the shepherds *began* saying to one another, "Let us go straight to Bethlehem then, and see this thing that has happened which the Lord has made known to us."

16 So they came in a hurry and found their way to Mary and Joseph, and the baby as He lay in the [1]manger.

17 When they had seen this, they made known the statement which had been told them about this Child.

18 And all who heard it wondered at the things which were told them by the shepherds.

19 But Mary [a]treasured all these things, pondering them in her heart.

20 The shepherds went back, [a]glorifying and praising God for all that they had heard and seen, just as had been told them.

Jesus Presented at the Temple

21 And when [a]eight days had passed, [1]before His circumcision, [b]His name was *then* called Jesus, the name given by the angel before He was conceived in the womb.

22 [a]And when the days for their purification according to the law of Moses were completed, they brought Him up to Jerusalem to present Him to the Lord

23 (as it is written in the Law of the Lord, "[a]EVERY *firstborn* MALE THAT OPENS THE WOMB SHALL BE CALLED HOLY TO THE LORD"),

24 and to offer a sacrifice according to what was said in the Law of the Lord, "[a]A PAIR OF TURTLEDOVES OR TWO YOUNG PIGEONS."

25 And there was a man in Jerusalem whose name was Simeon; and this man was [a]righteous and devout, [b]looking for the consolation of Israel; and the Holy Spirit was upon him.

26 And [a]it had been revealed to him by the Holy Spirit that he would not [b]see death before he had seen the Lord's [1]Christ.

27 And he came in the Spirit into the temple; and when the parents brought in the child Jesus, [1a]to carry out for Him the custom of the Law,

28 then he took Him into his arms, and blessed God, and said,

29 "Now Lord, You are releasing Your
bond-servant to depart in peace,
[a]According to Your word;
30 For my eyes have [a]seen Your
salvation,
31 Which You have prepared in the
presence of all peoples,
32 [a]A LIGHT [1]OF REVELATION TO THE
GENTILES,
And the glory of Your people
Israel."

11 [1]I.e. Messiah [a]Matt 1:21; John 4:42; Acts 5:31 [b]Matt 1:16; 16:16, 20; John 11:27 [c]Luke 1:43; Acts 2:36; 10:36
12 [1]Or *feeding trough* [a]1 Sam 2:34; 2 Kin 19:29; 20:8f; Is 7:11, 14
14 [1]Lit *of good pleasure;* or *of good will* [a]Matt 21:9; Luke 19:38 [b]Luke 3:22; Eph 1:9; Phil 2:13
16 [1]Or *feeding trough*
19 [a]Luke 2:51
20 [a]Matt 9:8
21 [1]Lit *so as to circumcise Him* [a]Gen 17:12; Lev 12:3; Luke 1:59 [b]Matt 1:21, 25; Luke 1:31
22 [a]Lev 12:6-8
23 [a]Ex 13:2, 12; Num 3:13; 8:17
24 [a]Lev 5:11; 12:8
25 [a]Luke 1:6 [b]Mark 15:43; Luke 2:38; 23:51
26 [1]I.e. Messiah [a]Matt 2:12 [b]Ps 89:48; John 8:51; Heb 11:5
27 [1]Lit *to do for Him according to* [a]Luke 2:22
29 [a]Luke 2:26
30 [a]Ps 119:166, 174; Is 52:10; Luke 3:6
32 [1]Or *for* [a]Is 9:2; 42:6; 49:6, 9; 51:4; 60:1-3; Matt 4:16; Acts 13:47; 26:23

2:11 *city of David.* Bethlehem. *Savior.* Many Jews were looking for a political leader to deliver them from Roman rule, while others were hoping for a savior to deliver them from sickness and physical hardship. But this announcement concerns the Savior who would deliver from sin and death (see Matt 1:21; John 4:42). *Christ.* Or *Messiah*. "The Christ" (Greek) and "the Messiah" (Hebrew) both mean "the Anointed One." *the Lord.* A designation originally reserved for God but later applied to the Messiah as well (see Acts 2:36; Phil 2:11).

2:14 See note on 1:46–55. This brief hymn is called the Gloria in Excelsis Deo, from the first words of the Latin Vulgate translation (meaning "Glory to God in the Highest"). The angels recognized the glory and majesty of God by giving praise to Him. *in the highest.* A reference to heaven, where God dwells (cf. Matt 6:9). *peace among men with whom He is pleased.* Peace is not assured to all, but only to those pleasing to God—the objects of His good pleasure (see Luke's use of the words "well-pleased," "well-pleasing," and "gladly" elsewhere: 3:22; 10:21; 12:32). The Roman world was experiencing the *Pax Romana* ("Roman Peace"), marked by external tranquility. But the angels proclaimed a deeper, more lasting peace than that—a peace of mind and soul made possible by the Savior (v. 11). Peace with God is received by faith in Christ (Rom 5:1), and it is believers "with whom He is pleased." The Davidic Messiah was called "Prince of Peace" (Is 9:6), and Christ promised peace to His disciples (John 14:27). But Christ also brought conflict (the "sword"; see Matt 10:34–36; cf. Luke 12:49), for peace with God involves opposition to Satan and his work (James 4:4).

2:20 *praising God.* Terms of praise and giving glory to God often used by Luke (1:64; 2:13,28; 5:25–26; 7:16; 13:13; 17:15,18; 18:43; 19:37; 23:47; 24:53).

2:22 *their purification.* Following the birth of a son, the mother had to wait 40 days before going to the temple to offer sacrifice for her purification. If she could not afford a lamb and a pigeon (or dove), then two pigeons (or doves) would be acceptable (Lev 12:2–8; cf. Lev 5:11). *to Jerusalem.* The distance from Bethlehem to Jerusalem was only about six miles. *present Him to the Lord.* The firstborn of both man and animal were to be dedicated to the Lord (see v. 23; Ex 13:12–13). The animals were sacrificed, but the human beings were to serve God throughout their lives. The Levites actually served in the place of all the firstborn males in Israel (see Num 3:11–13; 8:17–18).

2:25 *the consolation of Israel.* The comfort the Messiah would bring to His people at His coming (see vv. 26,38; 23:51; 24:21; Is 40:1–2; Matt 5:4). *the Holy Spirit was upon him.* Not in the way common to all believers after Pentecost. Simeon was given a special insight by the Spirit so that he would recognize the "Christ."

2:29–32 See note on 1:46–55. This hymn of Simeon has been called the Nunc Dimittis, from the first words of the Latin Vulgate translation, meaning "[You] now dismiss."

2:31 *all peoples.* As a Gentile himself, Luke was careful to emphasize the truth that salvation was offered for the Gentiles (v. 32) as well as for Jews.

33 And His father and [a]mother were amazed at the things which were being said about Him.

34 And Simeon blessed them and said to Mary [a]His mother, "Behold, this *Child* is appointed for [b]the fall and [1]rise of many in Israel, and for a sign to be opposed—

35 and a sword will pierce even your own soul—to the end that thoughts from many hearts may be revealed."

36 And there was a [a]prophetess, [1]Anna the daughter of Phanuel, of [b]the tribe of Asher. She was advanced in [2]years [c]and had lived with *her* husband seven years after her [3]marriage,

37 and then as a widow to the age of eighty-four. She never left the temple, serving night and day with [a]fastings and prayers.

38 At that very [1]moment she came up and *began* giving thanks to God, and continued to speak of Him to all those who were [a]looking for the redemption of Jerusalem.

Return to Nazareth

39 When they had performed everything according to the Law of the Lord, they returned to Galilee, to [a]their own city of Nazareth.

40 [a]The Child continued to grow and become strong, [1]increasing in wisdom; and the grace of God was upon Him.

Visit to Jerusalem

41 Now His parents went to Jerusalem every year at [a]the Feast of the Passover.

42 And when He became twelve, they went up *there* according to the custom of the Feast;

43 and as they were returning, after spending the [a]full number of days, the boy Jesus stayed behind in Jerusalem. But His parents were unaware of it,

44 but supposed Him to be in the caravan, and went a day's journey; and they *began* looking for Him among their relatives and acquaintances.

45 When they did not find Him, they returned to Jerusalem looking for Him.

46 Then, after three days they found Him in the temple, sitting in the midst of the teachers, both listening to them and asking them questions.

47 And all who heard Him [a]were amazed at His understanding and His answers.

48 When they saw Him, they were astonished; and [a]His mother said to Him, "[1]Son, why have You treated us this way? Behold, [b]Your father and I [2]have been anxiously looking for You."

49 And He said to them, "Why is it that you were looking for Me? Did you not know that [a]I had to be in My Father's [1]*house?*"

50 But [a]they did not understand the statement which He [1]had made to them.

51 And He went down with them and came to [a]Nazareth, and He continued in subjection to them; and [b]His mother [c]treasured all *these* [1]things in her heart.

52 And Jesus kept increasing in wisdom and [1]stature, and in [a]favor with God and men.

John the Baptist Preaches

3 Now in the fifteenth year of the reign of Tiberius Caesar, when [a]Pontius Pilate was governor of Judea, and [b]Herod was tetrarch of Galilee, and his brother Philip was tetrarch of the region of Ituraea and

33 [a]Matt 12:46
34 [1]Or *resurrection* [a]Matt 12:46 [b]Matt 21:44; 1 Cor 1:23; 2 Cor 2:16; 1 Pet 2:8
36 [1]Or *Hannah* [2]Lit *days* [3]Lit *virginity* [a]Luke 2:38; Acts 21:9 [b]Josh 19:24 [c]1 Tim 5:9
37 [a]Luke 5:33; Acts 13:3; 14:23; 1 Tim 5:5
38 [1]Lit *hour* [a]Luke 1:68; 2:25
39 [a]Matt 2:23; Luke 1:26; 2:51; 4:16
40 [1]Lit *becoming full of* [a]Luke 1:80; 2:52
41 [a]Ex 12:11; 23:15; Deut 16:1-6
43 [a]Ex 12:15
47 [a]Matt 7:28; 13:54; 22:33; Mark 1:22; 6:2; 11:18; Luke 4:32; John 7:15
48 [1]Or *Child* [2]Lit *are looking* [a]Matt 12:46 [b]Luke 2:49; 3:23; 4:22
49 [1]Or *affairs;* lit *in the things of My Father* [a]John 4:34; 5:36
50 [1]Lit *had spoken* [a]Mark 9:32; Luke 9:45; 18:34
51 [1]Lit *words* [a]Luke 2:39 [b]Matt 12:46 [c]Luke 2:19
52 [1]Or *age* [a]Luke 2:40
3:1 [a]Matt 27:2 [b]Matt 14:1

2:33 *His father.* Luke, aware of the virgin birth of Jesus (1:26–35), is referring to Joseph as Jesus' legal father.

2:34 *fall and rise of many in Israel.* Christ raises up those who believe in Him, but is a stumbling block for those who disbelieve (see 20:17–18; 1 Cor 1:23; 1 Pet 2:6–8). *sign to be opposed.* Christ points to the Father and His love for sinners, and those who oppose Him also oppose the Father.

2:35 *sword will pierce even your own soul.* The word "even" indicates that Mary, as well as Jesus, would suffer deep anguish—the first reference in this Gospel to Christ's suffering and death.

2:36 *prophetess.* Other prophetesses were Miriam (Ex 15:20), Deborah (Judg 4:4), Huldah (2 Kin 22:14) and the daughters of Philip (Acts 21:9). *Anna.* Same name as OT Hannah (1 Sam 1:2), which means "gracious." Anna praised God for the child Jesus as Hannah had praised God for the child Samuel (1 Sam 2:1–10).

2:37 *never left the temple.* Herod's temple was quite large and included rooms for various uses, and Anna may have been allowed to live in one of them. This statement, however, probably means that she spent her waking hours attending and worshiping in the temple.

2:38 *Jerusalem.* The holy city of God's chosen people (Is 40:2; 52:9); here it stands for Israel as a whole.

2:39 *they returned to Galilee.* Luke does not mention the coming of the Magi, the danger from Herod, or the flight to and return from Egypt (cf. Matt 2:1–23).

2:41 *Feast of the Passover.* Annual attendance at three feasts by all adult males (normally accompanied by their families) was commanded in the law: Passover, Pentecost and Booths (see notes on Ex 23:14–17; Deut 16:16). Distance prevented many from attending all three, but most Jews tried to be at Passover.

2:42 *twelve.* At age 12 boys began preparing to take their places in the religious community the following year.

2:46 *three days.* One day traveling away from Jerusalem, a second traveling back and a third looking for Him. *the teachers.* The rabbis, experts in Judaism.

2:49 *in My Father's house.* Jesus pointed to His personal duty to His Father in heaven. He contrasted His "My Father" with Mary's "Your father" (v. 48). At 12 years of age He was aware of His unique relationship to God. But He was also obedient to His earthly parents (v. 51).

2:52 Luke appears to have borrowed the words of 1 Sam 2:26. *And Jesus kept increasing.* Although Jesus was God, there is no indication that He had all knowledge and wisdom from birth. He seems to have matured like any other boy.

3:1–2 Historians frequently dated an event by giving the year of the ruler's reign in which the event happened.

3:1 *fifteenth year.* Several possible dates could be indicated by this description, but the date A.D. 25–26 (Tiberius had authority in the provinces beginning in 11) best fits the chronology of the life of Christ. The other rulers named do not help pinpoint the beginning of John's ministry, but only serve to indicate the general historical period. *Pontius Pilate.* The Roman prefect

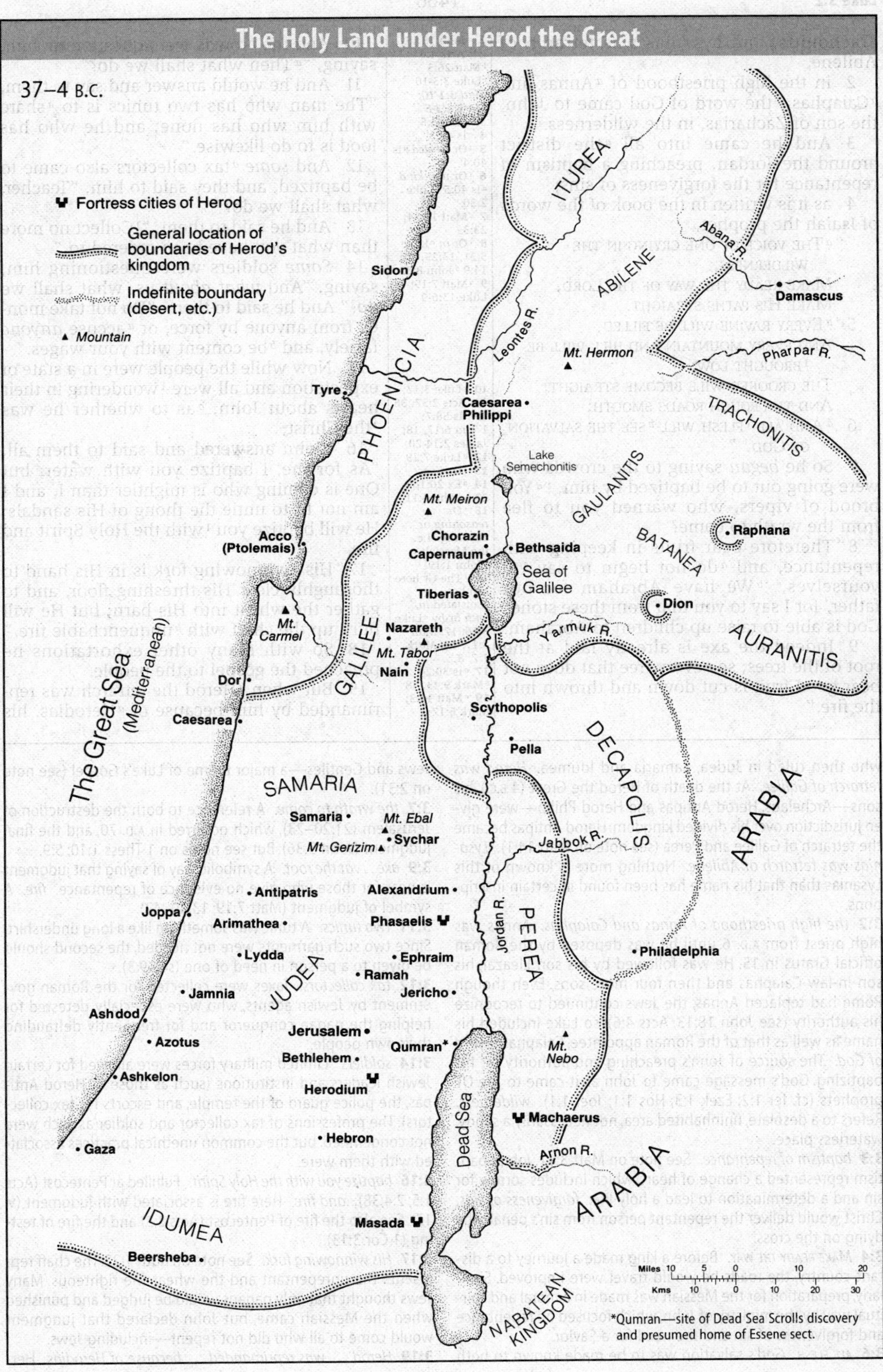

The Holy Land under Herod the Great
37–4 B.C.
Fortress cities of Herod
General location of boundaries of Herod's kingdom
Indefinite boundary (desert, etc.)
Mountain
ITUREA
ABILENE
Abana R.
Damascus
Sidon
Leontes R.
Mt. Hermon
Pharpar R.
PHOENICIA
Tyre
Caesarea Philippi
TRACHONITIS
Lake Semechonitis
GAULANITIS
Mt. Meiron
Acco (Ptolemais)
Chorazin
Capernaum
Bethsaida
Raphana
BATANEA
Sea of Galilee
Tiberias
Dion
Mt. Carmel
GALILEE
Nazareth
Mt. Tabor
Nain
Yarmuk R.
AURANITIS
The Great Sea (Mediterranean)
Dor
Caesarea
Scythopolis
Pella
DECAPOLIS
SAMARIA
Samaria
Mt. Ebal
Sychar
Mt. Gerizim
Jabbok R.
ARABIA
Antipatris
Alexandrium
Joppa
Arimathea
Phasaelis
Lydda
Ephraim
Ramah
JUDEA
Jordan R.
PEREA
Philadelphia
Jamnia
Jericho
Ashdod
Azotus
Jerusalem
Qumran*
Bethlehem
Mt. Nebo
Ashkelon
Herodium
Machaerus
Gaza
Hebron
Dead Sea
Arnon R.
ARABIA
Masada
IDUMEA
Beersheba
NABATEAN KINGDOM
Miles 10 5 0 10 20
Kms 10 0 10 20 30
*Qumran—site of Dead Sea Scrolls discovery and presumed home of Essene sect.

Trachonitis, and Lysanias was tetrarch of Abilene,

2 in the high priesthood of [a]Annas and [b]Caiaphas, [c]the word of God came to John, the son of Zacharias, in the wilderness.

3 And he came into all [a]the district around the Jordan, preaching a baptism of repentance for the forgiveness of sins;

4 as it is written in the book of the words of Isaiah the prophet,

"[a]THE VOICE OF ONE CRYING IN THE WILDERNESS,
'MAKE READY THE WAY OF THE LORD,
MAKE HIS PATHS STRAIGHT.
5 '[a]EVERY RAVINE WILL BE FILLED,
AND EVERY MOUNTAIN AND HILL WILL BE [1]BROUGHT LOW;
THE CROOKED WILL BECOME STRAIGHT,
AND THE ROUGH ROADS SMOOTH;
6 [a]AND ALL [1]FLESH WILL [b]SEE THE SALVATION OF GOD.' "

7 So he *began* saying to the crowds who were going out to be baptized by him, "[a]You brood of vipers, who warned you to flee from the wrath to come?

8 "Therefore bear fruits in keeping with repentance, and [a]do not begin to say [1]to yourselves, '[b]We have Abraham for our father,' for I say to you that from these stones God is able to raise up children to Abraham.

9 "Indeed the axe is already laid at the root of the trees; so [a]every tree that does not bear good fruit is cut down and thrown into the fire."

10 And the crowds were questioning him, saying, "[a]Then what shall we do?"

11 And he would answer and say to them, "The man who has two tunics is to [a]share with him who has none; and he who has food is to do likewise."

12 And *some* [a]tax collectors also came to be baptized, and they said to him, "Teacher, what shall we do?"

13 And he said to them, "[1]Collect no more than what you have been ordered to."

14 *Some* soldiers were questioning him, saying, "And *what about* us, what shall we do?" And he said to them, "Do not take money from anyone by force, or [a]accuse *anyone* falsely, and [b]be content with your wages."

15 Now while the people were in a state of expectation and all were [1]wondering in their hearts about John, [a]as to whether he was [2]the Christ,

16 [a]John answered and said to them all, "As for me, I baptize you with water; but One is coming who is mightier than I, and I am not fit to untie the thong of His sandals; He will baptize you [1]with the Holy Spirit and fire.

17 "His [a]winnowing fork is in His hand to thoroughly clear His threshing floor, and to gather the wheat into His barn; but He will burn up the chaff with [b]unquenchable fire."

18 So with many other exhortations he preached the gospel to the people.

19 But when [a]Herod the tetrarch was reprimanded by him because of [a]Herodias, his

2 [a]John 18:13, 24; Acts 4:6 [b]Matt 26:3 [c]Luke 3:3-10: *Matt 3:1-10; Mark 1:3-5*
3 [a]Matt 3:5
4 [a]Is 40:3
5 [1]Or *leveled* [a]Is 40:4
6 [1]Or *mankind* [a]Is 40:5 [b]Luke 2:30
7 [a]Matt 12:34; 23:33
8 [1]Or *in* [a]Luke 5:21; 13:25, 26; 14:9 [b]John 8:33
9 [a]Matt 7:19; Luke 13:6-9
10 [a]Luke 3:12, 14; Acts 2:37, 38
11 [a]Is 58:7; 1 Tim 6:17, 18; James 2:14-20
12 [a]Luke 7:29
13 [1]Or *Exact*
14 [a]Ex 20:16; 23:1 [b]Phil 4:11
15 [1]Or *reasoning* or *debating* [2]I.e. the Messiah [a]John 1:19f
16 [1]The Gr here can be translated *in*, *with* or *by* [a]Luke 3:16, 17: *Matt 3:11, 12; Mark 1:7, 8*
17 [a]Is 30:24 [b]Mark 9:43, 48
19 [a]Matt 14:3; Mark 6:17

---

who then ruled in Judea, Samaria and Idumea. *Herod was tetrarch of Galilee.* At the death of Herod the Great (4 B.C.), his sons—Archelaus, Herod Antipas and Herod Philip—were given jurisdiction over his divided kingdom. Herod Antipas became the tetrarch of Galilee and Perea (see note on Matt 14:1). *Lysanias was tetrarch of Abilene.* Nothing more is known of this Lysanias than that his name has been found in certain inscriptions.

3:2 *the high priesthood of Annas and Caiaphas.* Annas was high priest from A.D. 6 until he was deposed by the Roman official Gratus in 15. He was followed by his son Eleazar, his son-in-law Caiaphas and then four more sons. Even though Rome had replaced Annas, the Jews continued to recognize his authority (see John 18:13; Acts 4:6); so Luke included his name as well as that of the Roman appointee, Caiaphas. *word of God.* The source of John's preaching and authority for his baptizing. God's message came to John as it came to the OT prophets (cf. Jer 1:2; Ezek 1:3; Hos 1:1; Joel 1:1). *wilderness.* Refers to a desolate, uninhabited area, not necessarily a sandy, waterless place.

3:3 *baptism of repentance.* See note on Matt 3:11. John's baptism represented a change of heart, which includes sorrow for sin and a determination to lead a holy life. *forgiveness of sins.* Christ would deliver the repentant person from sin's penalty by dying on the cross.

3:4 *MAKE READY THE WAY.* Before a king made a journey to a distant country, the roads he would travel were improved. Similarly, preparation for the Messiah was made in a moral and spiritual way by the ministry of John, which focused on repentance and forgiveness of sin and the need for a Savior.

3:6 *ALL FLESH.* God's salvation was to be made known to both Jews and Gentiles—a major theme of Luke's Gospel (see note on 2:31).

3:7 *the wrath to come.* A reference to both the destruction of Jerusalem (21:20–23), which occurred in A.D. 70, and the final judgment (John 3:36). But see notes on 1 Thess 1:10; 5:9.

3:9 *axe . . . at the root.* A symbolic way of saying that judgment is near for those who give no evidence of repentance. *fire.* A symbol of judgment (Matt 7:19; 13:40–42).

3:11 *two tunics.* A tunic was something like a long undershirt. Since two such garments were not needed, the second should be given to a person in need of one (see 9:3).

3:12 *tax collectors.* Taxes were collected for the Roman government by Jewish agents, who were especially detested for helping the pagan conqueror and for frequently defrauding their own people.

3:14 *soldiers.* Limited military forces were allowed for certain Jewish leaders and institutions (such as those of Herod Antipas, the police guard of the temple, and escorts for tax collectors). The professions of tax collector and soldier as such were not condemned, but the common unethical practices associated with them were.

3:16 *baptize you with the Holy Spirit.* Fulfilled at Pentecost (Acts 1:5; 2:4,38). *and fire.* Here fire is associated with judgment (v. 17). See also the fire of Pentecost (Acts 2:3) and the fire of testing (1 Cor 3:13).

3:17 *His winnowing fork.* See note on Ruth 1:22. The chaff represents the unrepentant and the wheat the righteous. Many Jews thought that only pagans would be judged and punished when the Messiah came, but John declared that judgment would come to all who did not repent—including Jews.

3:19 *Herod . . . was reprimanded . . . because of Herodias.* Her-

brother's wife, and because of all the wicked things which [b]Herod had done,

20 Herod also added this to them all: [a]he locked John up in prison.

Jesus Is Baptized

21 [a]Now when all the people were baptized, Jesus was also baptized, and while He was [b]praying, heaven was opened,

22 and the Holy Spirit descended upon Him in bodily form like a dove, and a voice came out of heaven, "[a]You are My beloved Son, in You I am well-pleased."

Genealogy of Jesus

23 [a]When He began His ministry, Jesus Himself was about thirty years of age, being, [1]as was supposed, the son of [b]Joseph, [2]the son of [3]Eli,

24 the son of Matthat, the son of Levi, the son of Melchi, the son of Jannai, the son of Joseph,

25 the son of Mattathias, the son of Amos, the son of Nahum, the son of [1]Hesli, the son of Naggai,

26 the son of Maath, the son of Mattathias, the son of Semein, the son of Josech, the son of Joda,

27 the son of Joanan, the son of Rhesa, [a]the son of Zerubbabel, the son of [1]Shealtiel, the son of Neri,

28 the son of Melchi, the son of Addi, the son of Cosam, the son of Elmadam, the son of Er,

29 the son of [1]Joshua, the son of Eliezer, the son of Jorim, the son of Matthat, the son of Levi,

30 the son of Simeon, the son of [1]Judah, the son of Joseph, the son of Jonam, the son of Eliakim,

31 the son of Melea, the son of Menna, the son of Mattatha, the son of Nathan, the son of David,

32 [a]the son of Jesse, the son of Obed, the son of Boaz, the son of [1]Salmon, the son of [2]Nahshon,

33 the son of Amminadab, the son of Admin, the son of [1]Ram, the son of Hezron, the son of Perez, the son of Judah,

34 the son of Jacob, the son of Isaac, [a]the son of Abraham, the son of Terah, the son of Nahor,

35 the son of Serug, the son of [1]Reu, the son of Peleg, the son of [2]Heber, the son of Shelah,

36 the son of Cainan, the son of Arphaxad, the son of Shem, [a]the son of Noah, the son of Lamech,

37 the son of Methuselah, the son of Enoch, the son of Jared, the son of Mahalaleel, the son of Cainan,

38 the son of Enosh, the son of Seth, the son of Adam, the son of God.

The Temptation of Jesus

4 [a]Jesus, full of the Holy Spirit, [b]returned from the Jordan and was led around [1]by the Spirit in the wilderness

2 for [a]forty days, being tempted by the devil. And He ate nothing during those days, and when they had ended, He became hungry.

19 [b]Matt 14:1; Luke 3:1
20 [a]John 3:24
21 [a]Luke 3:21, 22: *Matt 3:13-17; Mark 1:9-11* [b]Matt 14:23; Luke 5:16; 9:18, 28f
22 [a]Ps 2:7; Is 42:1; Matt 3:17; 17:5; Mark 1:11; Luke 9:35; 2 Pet 1:17
23 [1]Lit *as it was being thought* [2]Lit *of Eli*, and so throughout the genealogy [3]Also spelled *Heli* [a]Matt 4:17; Acts 1:1 [b]Matt 1:16; Luke 3:23-27
25 [1]Also spelled *Esli*
27 [1]Gr *Salathiel;* names of people in the Old Testament are given in their Old Testament form through v 38 [a]Matt 1:12
29 [1]Gr *Jesus*
30 [1]Gr *Judas*
32 [1]Gr *Sala* [2]Gr *Naasson* [a]Luke 3:32-34: *Matt 1:1-6*
33 [1]Gr *Arni*
34 [a]Luke 3:34-36: *Gen 11:26-30; 1 Chr 1:24-27*
35 [1]Gr *Ragau* [2]Gr *Eber*
36 [a]Luke 3:36-38: *Gen 5:3-32; 1 Chr 1:1-4*

4:1 [1]Or *under the influence of;* lit *in* [a]Luke 4:1-13: *Matt 4:1-11; Mark 1:12, 13* [b]Luke 3:3 **2** [a]Ex 34:28; 1 Kin 19:8

od Antipas had married the daughter of Aretas IV of Arabia, but divorced her to marry his own niece, Herodias, who was already his brother's (Herod Philip's) wife (see Matt 14:3; Mark 6:17).

3:20 *locked John up in prison.* According to Josephus, John was imprisoned in Machaerus, east of the Dead Sea (*Antiquities*, 18.5.2). This did not occur until sometime after the beginning of Jesus' ministry (see John 3:22–24), but Luke mentions it here in order to conclude his section on John's ministry before beginning his account of the beginning of Jesus' ministry (see also Matt 4:12; Mark 1:14). He later briefly alludes to John's death (9:7–9).

3:21 *baptized.* See note on Matt 3:15. *while He was praying.* Only Luke notes Jesus' praying at the time of His baptism. Jesus in prayer is one of the special themes of Luke (see 5:16; 6:12; 9:18,28–29; 11:1; 22:32,41; 23:34,46).

3:22 *Holy Spirit descended.* Luke specifies "in bodily form." To John, it was a sign (see John 1:32–34; see also note on Mark 1:10). *You are My beloved Son.* See Ps 2:7; Is 42:1; Heb 1:5. Two other times the Gospel writers record the declarations of a voice from heaven addressing Jesus: (1) on the Mount of Transfiguration (9:35), and (2) in the temple area during Jesus' final week (John 12:28).

3:23–38 There are several differences between Luke's genealogy and Matthew's (1:2–16). Matthew begins with Abraham (the father of the Jewish people), while Luke traces the line in the reverse order and goes back to Adam, showing Jesus' relationship to the whole human race (see note on 2:31). From Abraham to David, the genealogies of Matthew and Luke are almost the same, but from David on they are different. Some scholars suggest that this is because Matthew traces the legal descent of the house of David using only heirs to the throne, while Luke traces the complete line of Joseph to David. A more likely explanation, however, is that Matthew follows the line of Joseph (Jesus' legal father), while Luke emphasizes that of Mary (Jesus' blood relative). Although tracing a genealogy through the mother's side was unusual, so was the virgin birth. Luke's explanation here that Jesus was the son of Joseph, "as was supposed" (v. 23), brings to mind his explicit virgin birth statement (1:34–35) and suggests the importance of the role of Mary in Jesus' genealogy.

3:23 *about thirty years of age.* Luke, a historian, relates the beginning of Jesus' public ministry both to world history (see vv. 1–2) and to the rest of Jesus' life. Thirty was the age when a Levite undertook his service (Num 4:47) and when a man was considered mature. *as was supposed.* Luke had already affirmed the virgin birth (1:34–35), and here makes clear again that Joseph was not Jesus' physical father.

4:1 *full of the Holy Spirit.* Luke emphasizes the Holy Spirit not only in his Gospel (1:35,41,67; 2:25–27; 3:16,22; 4:14,18; 10:21; 11:13; 12:10,12) but also in Acts, where the Spirit is mentioned 55 times. *in the wilderness.* The Desert of Judea (see Matt 3:1; see also note on 1:80).

4:2 *being tempted.* See notes on Matt 4:1–11; Heb 2:18; 4:15. Luke states that Jesus was tempted for the 40 days He was fasting, and the three specific temptations recounted in Matthew and Luke seem to have occurred at the close of this period—

3 And the devil said to Him, "If You are
the Son of God, tell this stone to become
bread."
4 And Jesus answered him, "It is written,
'[a]MAN SHALL NOT LIVE ON BREAD ALONE.' "
5 [a]And he led Him up and showed Him
all the kingdoms of [1][b]the world in a moment
of time.
6 And the devil said to Him, "I will give
You all this domain and [1]its glory; [a]for it has
been handed over to me, and I give it to
whomever I wish.
7 "Therefore if You [1]worship before me, it
shall all be Yours."
8 Jesus answered him, "It is written,
'[a]YOU SHALL WORSHIP THE LORD YOUR GOD AND
SERVE HIM ONLY.' "
9 [a]And he led Him to Jerusalem and had
Him stand on the pinnacle of the temple, and
said to Him, "If You are the Son of God,
throw Yourself down from here;
10 for it is written,
'[a]HE WILL COMMAND HIS ANGELS
CONCERNING YOU TO GUARD YOU,'
11 and,
'[a]ON *their* HANDS THEY WILL BEAR YOU UP,
SO THAT YOU WILL NOT STRIKE YOUR FOOT
AGAINST A STONE.' "
12 And Jesus answered and said to him,
"It is said, '[a]YOU SHALL NOT PUT THE LORD YOUR
GOD TO THE TEST.' "
13 When the devil had finished every
temptation, he left Him until an opportune
time.

Jesus' Public Ministry

14 And [a]Jesus returned to Galilee in the
power of the Spirit, and [b]news about Him
spread through all the surrounding district.
15 And He *began* [a]teaching in their synagogues and was praised by all.
16 And He came to [a]Nazareth, where He
had been brought up; and as was His custom, [b]He entered the synagogue on the Sabbath, and [c]stood up to read.
17 And the [1]book of the prophet Isaiah was
handed to Him. And He opened the [1]book
and found the place where it was written,
18 "[a]THE SPIRIT OF THE LORD IS UPON ME,
BECAUSE HE ANOINTED ME TO PREACH THE
GOSPEL TO THE POOR.
HE HAS SENT ME TO PROCLAIM RELEASE TO
THE CAPTIVES,
AND RECOVERY OF SIGHT TO THE BLIND,
TO SET FREE THOSE WHO ARE OPPRESSED,
19 [a]TO PROCLAIM THE FAVORABLE YEAR OF THE
LORD."
20 And He [a]closed the [1]book, gave it back
to the attendant and [b]sat down; and the eyes
of all in the synagogue were fixed on Him.
21 And He began to say to them, "Today
this Scripture has been fulfilled in your
[1]hearing."
22 And all were [1]speaking well of Him,
and wondering at the [2]gracious words which
[3]were falling from His lips; and they were
saying, "[a]Is this not Joseph's son?"
23 And He said to them, "No doubt you
will quote this proverb to Me, 'Physician,

4 [a]Deut 8:3
5 [1]Lit *the inhabited earth* [a]Matt 4:8-10 [b]Matt 24:14
6 [1]Lit *their* (referring to the kingdoms in v 5) [a]1 John 5:19
7 [1]Or *bow down before*
8 [a]Deut 6:13; 10:20; Matt 4:10
9 [a]Matt 4:5-7
10 [a]Ps 91:11
11 [a]Ps 91:12
12 [a]Deut 6:16

14 [a]Matt 4:12 [b]Matt 9:26; Luke 4:37
15 [a]Matt 4:23
16 [a]Luke 2:39, 51 [b]Matt 13:54; Mark 6:1f [c]Acts 13:14-16
17 [1]Or *scroll*
18 [a]Is 61:1; Matt 11:5; 12:18; John 3:34
19 [a]Is 61:2; Lev 25:10
20 [1]Or *scroll* [a]Luke 4:17 [b]Matt 26:55
21 [1]Lit *ears*
22 [1]Or *testifying* [2]Or *words of grace* [3]Lit *were proceeding out of His mouth* [a]Matt 13:55; Mark 6:3; John 6:42

when Jesus' hunger was greatest and His resistance lowest. The sequence of the second and third temptations differs in Matthew and Luke. Matthew probably followed the chronological order, since at the end of the mountain temptation (Matthew's third) Jesus told Satan to leave (Matt 4:10). To emphasize a certain point the Gospel writers often bring various events together, not intending to give chronological sequence. Perhaps Luke's focus here is geographical, as he concludes with Jesus in Jerusalem.

4:3 *If You are.* See note on Matt 4:3. *tell this stone to become bread.* The devil always makes his temptations seem attractive.

4:7 *worship before me.* The devil was tempting Jesus to avoid the sufferings of the cross, which He came specifically to endure (Mark 10:45). The temptation offered an easy shortcut to world dominion.

4:9 *the pinnacle of the temple.* Either the southeast corner of the temple colonnade, from which there was a drop of some 100 feet to the Kidron Valley below, or the pinnacle of the temple proper. *If You are.* See note on Matt 4:3. *throw Yourself down.* Satan was tempting Jesus to test God's faithfulness and to attract public attention dramatically.

4:10 *for it is written.* This time Satan also quoted Scripture, though he misused Ps 91:11–12.

4:12 Jesus answered with Scripture from Deuteronomy (6:16) as He did on the first (Deut 8:3) and second (Deut 6:13) temptations.

4:13 *he left Him until an opportune time.* Satan continued his testing throughout Jesus' ministry (see Mark 8:33), culminating in the supreme test at Gethsemane.

4:14 *in the power of the Spirit.* See note on v. 1.

4:15 *began teaching in their synagogues.* See note on Mark 1:21.

4:16 *He came to Nazareth.* Not at the start of His ministry but perhaps almost a year later (v. 23 presupposes that Jesus had already been ministering). Probably all the events of John 1:19–4:42 occurred between Luke 4:13 and 4:14. *as was His custom.* Jesus' custom of regular worship sets an example for all His followers. *to read.* Jesus probably read from Isaiah in Hebrew, and then He or someone else paraphrased it in Aramaic, one of the other common languages of the day.

4:17 *the book of the prophet Isaiah.* The books of the OT were written on scrolls, kept in a special place in the synagogue and handed to the reader by a special attendant. The passage Jesus read about the Messiah (Is 61:1–2) may have been one He chose to read, or it may have been the assigned passage for the day.

4:18 This verse tells of the Messiah's ministry of preaching and healing—to meet every human need. *HE ANOINTED ME.* Not with literal oil (see Ex 30:22–31), but with the Holy Spirit.

4:19 *THE FAVORABLE YEAR OF THE LORD.* Not a calendar year, but the period when salvation would be proclaimed—the Messianic age. This quotation from Is 61:1–2 alludes to the year of jubilee (Lev 25:8–55), when once every 50 years slaves were freed, debts were canceled and ancestral property was returned to the original family. Isaiah predicted primarily the liberation of Israel from the future Babylonian captivity, but Jesus proclaimed liberation from sin and all its consequences.

4:20 *sat down.* It was customary to stand while reading Scripture (v. 16) but to sit while teaching (see Matt 5:1; 26:55; John 8:2; Acts 16:13).

heal yourself! Whatever we heard was done
[a]at Capernaum, do here in [b]your hometown
as well.' "
24 And He said, "Truly I say to you, [a]no
prophet is welcome in his hometown.
25 "But I say to you in truth, there were
many widows in Israel [a]in the days of Elijah,
when the sky was shut up for three years
and six months, when a great famine came
over all the land;
26 and yet Elijah was sent to none of
them, but [a]only to [1]Zarephath, *in the land* of
[b]Sidon, to a woman who was a widow.
27 "And there were many lepers in Israel in
the time of Elisha the prophet; and none of
them was cleansed, but [a]only Naaman the
Syrian."
28 And all *the people* in the synagogue
were filled with rage as they heard these
things;
29 and they got up and [a]drove Him out of
the city, and led Him to the brow of the hill
on which their city had been built, in order
to throw Him down the cliff.
30 But [a]passing through their midst, He
went His way.

23 [a]Matt 4:13; Mark 1:21ff; 2:1ff; Luke 4:35ff; John 4:46ff [b]Mark 6:1; Luke 2:39, 51; 4:16
24 [a]Matt 13:57; Mark 6:4; John 4:44
25 [a]1 Kin 17:1; 18:1; James 5:17
26 [1]Gr *Sarepta* [a]1 Kin 17:9 [b]Matt 11:21
27 [a]2 Kin 5:1-14
29 [a]Num 15:35; Acts 7:58; Heb 13:12
30 [a]John 10:39

4:23 *Capernaum.* See note on Matt 4:13. *hometown.* Nazareth. Although Jesus was born in Bethlehem, He was brought up in Nazareth, in Galilee (1:26; 2:39,51; Matt 2:23).
4:26–27 Mention of Jesus' reference to God's helping two non-Israelites (1 Kin 17:1–15; 2 Kin 5:1–14) reflects Luke's special concern for the Gentiles. Jesus' point was that when Israel rejected God's messenger of redemption, God sent him to the Gentiles—and so it will be again if they refuse to accept Jesus (see 10:13–15; Rom 9–11).
4:26 *Sidon.* One of the oldest Phoenician cities, 20 miles north of Tyre. Jesus later healed a Gentile woman's daughter in this region (Matt 15:21–28).
4:28 *filled with rage.* Because of Jesus' inclusion of Gentiles as recipients of God's blessings.
4:30 *passing through their midst.* Luke does not explain whether the escape was miraculous or simply the result of Jesus' commanding presence. In any case, His time (to die) had not yet come (John 7:30).

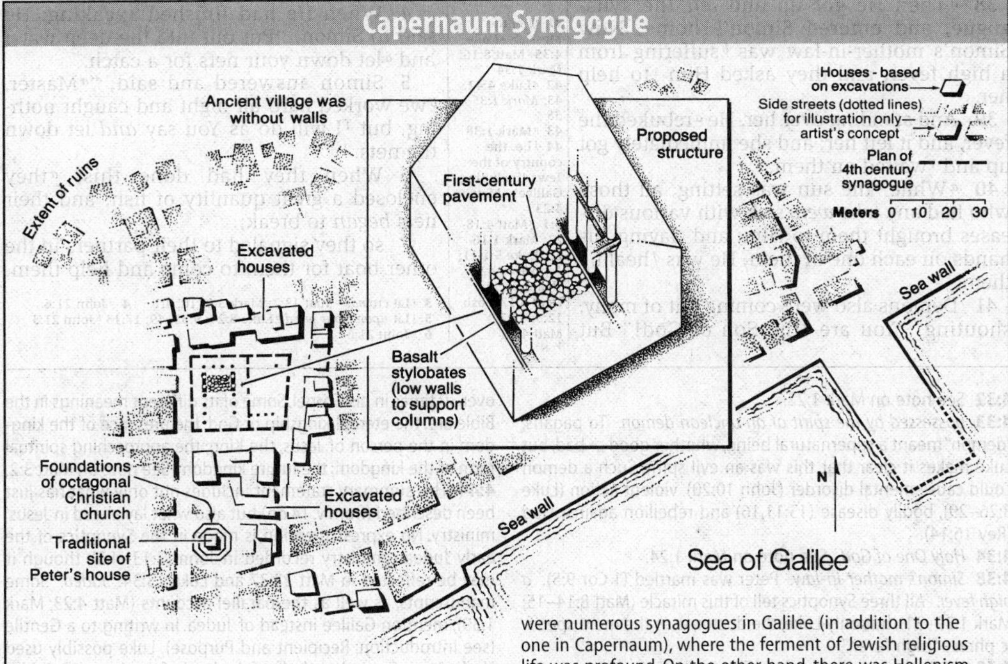
Capernaum Synagogue
Ancient village was without walls
Extent of ruins
Excavated houses
First-century pavement
Proposed structure
Houses - based on excavations
Side streets (dotted lines) for illustration only—artist's concept
Plan of 4th century synagogue
Meters 0 10 20 30
Basalt stylobates (low walls to support columns)
Foundations of octagonal Christian church
Excavated houses
Traditional site of Peter's house
Sea wall
Sea wall
N
Sea of Galilee

Capernaum was more than a seaside fishing village in the days of Jesus. It was the place that Christ chose to be the center of His ministry to the entire region of Galilee, and it possessed ideal characteristics as a point of dissemination for the gospel.

There were good reasons for this. The town itself was named *Kephar Nahum*, "village of (perhaps the prophet), Nahum" and was the centerpiece of a densely populated region having a bicultural flavor. On the one hand, there were numerous synagogues in Galilee (in addition to the one in Capernaum), where the ferment of Jewish religious life was profound. On the other hand, there was Hellenism, a pervasive culture already centuries old and potent in its paganism—a lifestyle that influenced manners, dress, architecture and political institutions as well.

Recent archaeological work at Capernaum has revealed a section of the pavement of a first-century synagogue below the still-existing ruins of the fourth-century one on the site. A private house later made into a church and a place of pilgrimage has yielded some evidence that may link it to the site of Simon Peter's house (Luke 4:38).

31 And [a]He came down to [b]Capernaum, a city of Galilee, and He was teaching them on the Sabbath;

32 and [a]they were amazed at His teaching, for [b]His [1]message was with authority.

33 In the synagogue there was a man [1]possessed by the spirit of an unclean demon, and he cried out with a loud voice,

34 "Let us alone! [1a]What business do we have with each other, Jesus [2]of [b]Nazareth? Have You come to destroy us? I know who You are—[b]the Holy One of God!"

35 But Jesus [a]rebuked him, saying, "Be quiet and come out of him!" And when the demon had thrown him down in the midst *of the people,* he came out of him without doing him any harm.

36 And amazement came upon them all, and they *began* talking with one another saying, "What is [1]this message? For [a]with authority and power He commands the unclean spirits and they come out."

37 And [a]the report about Him was spreading into every locality in the surrounding district.

Many Are Healed

38 [a]Then He got up and *left* the synagogue, and entered Simon's home. Now Simon's mother-in-law was [b]suffering from a high fever, and they asked Him [1]to help her.

39 And standing over her, He [a]rebuked the fever, and it left her; and she immediately got up and [1]waited on them.

40 [a]While [b]the sun was setting, all those who had any *who were* sick with various diseases brought them to Him; and [c]laying His hands on each one of them, He was [d]healing them.

41 Demons also were coming out of many, shouting, "You are [a]the Son of God!" But [b]rebuking them, He would [c]not allow them to speak, because they knew Him to be [1]the Christ.

42 [a]When day came, Jesus left and went to a secluded place; and the crowds were searching for Him, and came to Him and tried to keep Him from going away from them.

43 But He said to them, "I must preach the kingdom of God to the other cities also, [a]for I was sent for this purpose."

44 So He kept on preaching in the synagogues [a]of [1]Judea.

31 [a]Luke 4:31-37: *Mark 1:21-28* [b]Matt 4:13; Luke 4:23
32 [1]Lit *word* [a]Matt 7:28 [b]Luke 4:36; John 7:46
33 [1]Lit *having a spirit*
34 [1]Lit *What to us and to you* (a Heb idiom) [2]Lit *the Nazarene* [a]Matt 8:29 [b]Mark 1:24
35 [a]Matt 8:26; Mark 4:39; Luke 4:39, 41; 8:24
36 [1]Or *this word, that with authority...come out?* [a]Luke 4:32
37 [a]Luke 4:14
38 [1]Lit *about her* [a]Luke 4:38, 39: *Matt 8:14, 15; Mark 1:29-31* [b]Matt 4:24
39 [1]Or *served* [a]Luke 4:35, 41
40 [a]Luke 4:40, 41: *Matt 8:16, 17; Mark 1:32-34* [b]Mark 1:32 [c]Mark 5:23 [d]Matt 4:23
41 [a]Matt 4:3
41 [1]I.e. the Messiah [b]Luke 4:35 [c]Matt 8:16; Mark 1:34
42 [a]Luke 4:42, 43: *Mark 1:35-38*
43 [a]Mark 1:38
44 [1]I.e. the country of the Jews (including Galilee) [a]Matt 4:23
5:1 [a]Matt 4:18-22; Mark 1:16-20; Luke 5:1-11; John 1:40-42 [b]Num 34:11; Deut 3:17; Josh 12:3; 13:27; Matt 4:18

The First Disciples

5 [a]Now it happened that while the crowd was pressing around Him and listening to the word of God, He was standing by [b]the lake of Gennesaret;

2 and He saw two boats lying at the edge of the lake; but the fishermen had gotten out of them and were washing their nets.

3 And [a]He got into one of the boats, which was Simon's, and asked him to put out a little way from the land. And He sat down and *began* teaching the [1]people from the boat.

4 When He had finished speaking, He said to Simon, "Put out into the deep water and [a]let down your nets for a catch."

5 Simon answered and said, "[a]Master, [b]we worked hard all night and caught nothing, but [1]I will do as You say *and* let down the nets."

6 When they had done this, [a]they enclosed a great quantity of fish, and their nets *began* to break;

7 so they signaled to their partners in the other boat for them to come and help them.

3 [1]Lit *crowds* [a]Matt 13:2; Mark 3:9, 10; 4:1 **4** [a]John 21:6
5 [1]Lit *upon Your word* [a]Luke 8:24; 9:33, 49; 17:13 [b]John 21:3
6 [a]John 21:6

4:32 See note on Mark 1:22.
4:33 *possessed by the spirit of an unclean demon.* To pagans, "demon" meant a supernatural being, whether good or bad, but Luke makes it clear that this was an evil spirit. Such a demon could cause mental disorder (John 10:20), violent action (Luke 8:26–29), bodily disease (13:11,16) and rebellion against God (Rev 16:14).
4:34 *Holy One of God.* See note on Mark 1:24.
4:38 *Simon's mother-in-law.* Peter was married (1 Cor 9:5). *a high fever.* All three Synoptics tell of this miracle (Matt 8:14–15; Mark 1:29–31), but only Luke, the doctor, uses the more specific phrase "high fever."
4:40 *While the sun was setting.* The Sabbath (v. 31) was over at sundown (about 6:00 P.M.). Until then, according to the tradition of the elders, Jews could not travel more than about two-thirds of a mile or carry a burden. Only after sundown could they carry the sick to Jesus, and their eagerness is seen in the fact that they set out while the sun was still setting.
4:41 *because they knew Him to be the Christ.* See note on Mark 1:34.
4:42 *secluded place.* Mark includes the words "and was praying there" (Mark 1:35).
4:43 *kingdom of God.* Luke's first use of this phrase; it occurs over 30 times in his Gospel. Some of its different meanings in the Bible are: the eternal kingship of God; the presence of the kingdom in the person of Jesus, the King; the approaching spiritual form of the kingdom; the future kingdom. See note on Matt 3:2.
4:44 This summary statement includes not only what has just been described (from v. 14 on) but also what lay ahead in Jesus' ministry. No express mention is made in the Synoptics of the early Judean ministry recorded in John (2:13–4:3), though it may be reflected in Matt 23:37 and Luke 13:34. *Judea.* Some manuscripts, as well as the parallel accounts (Matt 4:23; Mark 1:39), mention Galilee instead of Judea. In writing to a Gentile (see Introduction: Recipient and Purpose), Luke possibly used "Judea" to refer to the whole of the land of the Jews (23:5; Acts 10:37; 11:1,29; 26:20).
5:1 *lake of Gennesaret.* Luke is the only one who calls it a lake. The other Gospel writers call it the Sea of Galilee, and John twice calls it the Sea of Tiberias (John 6:1; 21:1).
5:2 *washing their nets.* After each period of fishing, the nets were washed, stretched and prepared for use again.
5:3 *sat down.* The usual position for teaching (see note on 4:20). The boat provided an ideal arrangement, removed from the press of the crowd but near enough to be seen and heard.
5:7 *their partners.* See v. 10.

And they came and filled both of the boats,
so that they began to sink.
8 But when Simon Peter saw *that*, he fell
down at Jesus' [1]feet, saying, "Go away from
me Lord, for I am a sinful man, O Lord!"
9 For amazement had seized him and all
his companions because of the catch of fish
which they had taken;
10 and so also *were* [1]James and John, sons
of Zebedee, who were partners with Simon.
And Jesus said to Simon, "[a]Do not fear, from
now on you will be [b]catching men."
11 When they had brought their boats to
land, [a]they left everything and followed Him.

The Leper and the Paralytic

12 [a]While He was in one of the cities,
behold, *there was* a man [1]covered with leprosy; and when he saw Jesus, he fell on his
face and implored Him, saying, "Lord, if You
are willing, You can make me clean."
13 And He stretched out His hand and
touched him, saying, "I am willing; be
cleansed." And immediately the leprosy left
him.
14 And He ordered him to tell no one,
"But go and [a]show yourself to the priest
and make an offering for your cleansing,
just as Moses commanded, as a testimony
to them."
15 But [a]the news about Him was spreading even farther, and large crowds were
gathering to hear *Him* and to be healed of
their sicknesses.
16 But Jesus Himself would *often* slip
away [1]to the [2]wilderness and [a]pray.
17 [1]One day He was teaching; and [a]there
were *some* Pharisees and [b]teachers of the
law sitting *there,* who had [c]come from every
village of Galilee and Judea and *from* Jerusalem; and [d]the power of the Lord was *pres-*
ent for Him to perform healing.
18 [a]And *some* men *were* carrying on a
[1]bed a man who was paralyzed; and they
were trying to bring him in and to set him
down in front of Him.
19 But not finding any *way* to bring him in
because of the crowd, they went up on [a]the
roof and let him down [b]through the tiles
with his stretcher, into the middle *of the*
crowd, in front of Jesus.
20 Seeing their faith, He said, "[1]Friend,
[a]your sins are forgiven you."
21 The scribes and the Pharisees [a]began
to reason, saying, "[b]Who is this *man* who
speaks blasphemies? [c]Who can forgive sins,
but God alone?"
22 But Jesus, [1]aware of their reasonings,
answered and said to them, "Why are you
reasoning in your hearts?
23 "Which is easier, to say, 'Your sins have
been forgiven you,' or to say, 'Get up and
walk'?
24 "But, so that you may know that the Son
of Man has authority on earth to forgive
sins,"—He said to the [a]paralytic—"I say to
you, get up, and pick up your stretcher and
go home."
25 Immediately he got up before them,
and picked up what he had been lying on,
and went home [a]glorifying God.
26 [1]They were all struck with astonishment and *began* [a]glorifying God; and they
were filled [b]with fear, saying, "We have seen
remarkable things today."

Call of Levi (Matthew)

27 [a]After that He went out and noticed a
tax collector named [1b]Levi sitting in the tax
booth, and He said to him, "Follow Me."

8 [1]Lit *knees*
10 [1]Or *Jacob* [a]Matt 14:27 [b]2 Tim 2:26
11 [a]Matt 4:20, 22; 19:29; Mark 1:18, 20; Luke 5:28
12 [1]Lit *full of* [a]Luke 5:12-14: *Matt 8:2-4; Mark 1:40-44*
14 [a]Lev 13:49; 14:2ff
15 [a]Matt 9:26
16 [1]Lit *in* [2]Or *deserted places* [a]Matt 14:23; Mark 1:35; Luke 6:12
17 [1]Lit *On one of the days* [a]Matt 15:1 [b]Luke 2:46 [c]Mark 1:45
17 [d]Mark 5:30; Luke 6:19; 8:46
18 [1]Or *stretcher* [a]Luke 5:18-26: *Matt 9:2-8; Mark 2:3-12*
19 [a]Matt 24:17 [b]Mark 2:4
20 [1]Lit *Man* [a]Matt 9:2
21 [a]Luke 3:8 [b]Luke 7:49 [c]Is 43:25
22 [1]Or *perceiving*
24 [a]Matt 4:24
25 [a]Matt 9:8
26 [1]Lit *Astonishment took them all* [a]Matt 9:8 [b]Luke 1:65; 7:16
27 [1]Also called *Matthew* [a]Luke 5:27-39: *Matt 9:9-17; Mark 2:14-22* [b]Matt 9:9

5:8 *Go away from me Lord.* The nearer one comes to God, the more he feels his own sinfulness and unworthiness—as did Abraham (Gen 18:27), Job (42:6) and Isaiah (6:5).

5:11 *left everything and followed Him.* This was not the first time these men had been with Jesus (see John 1:40–42; 2:1–2). Their periodic and loose association now became a closely knit fellowship as they followed the Master. The scene is the same as Matt 4:18–22 and Mark 1:16–20, but the accounts relate events from different hours of the morning.

5:12–16 The healing of the man with leprosy is described in all three of the Synoptic Gospels, but the setting is different in each. In Matthew (8:1–4) it is part of a collection of miracles; in Mark (1:40–45) and Luke it is probably one incident that occurred on the first tour of Galilee.

5:12 *covered with leprosy.* Luke alone notes the extent of his disease. The Greek term for "leprosy" could refer to other skin diseases as well as leprosy, and was not used for leprosy in medical literature. See note on Lev 13:2

5:14 *tell no one.* See notes on Matt 8:4; 16:20. *But go and show yourself to the priest.* By this command Jesus urged the man to keep the law, to provide further proof for the actual healing, to testify to the authorities concerning His ministry and to supply ritual certification of cleansing so the man could be reinstated into society. *a testimony to them.* See note on Mark 1:44.

5:17 *Pharisees and teachers of the law.* See notes on Matt 2:4; 3:7; Mark 2:16. Opposition was rising in Galilee from these religious leaders. *Pharisees.* Mentioned here for the first time in Luke. Their name meaning "separated ones," they numbered about 6,000 and were spread over the whole of the Holy Land. They were teachers in the synagogues, religious examples in the eyes of the people and self-appointed guardians of the law and its proper observance. They considered the interpretations and regulations handed down by tradition to be virtually as authoritative as Scripture (Mark 7:8–13). Already Jesus had run counter to the Jewish leaders in Jerusalem (John 5:16–18). Now they came to a home in Capernaum (Mark 2:1–6) to hear and watch Him. *teachers of the law.* "Scribes," who studied, interpreted and taught the law (both written and oral). The majority of these teachers belonged to the party of the Pharisees.

5:19 *roof.* See note on Mark 2:4. *tiles.* Probably ceiling tiles.

5:21 *this man . . . speaks blasphemies.* See note on Mark 2:7. The Pharisees considered blasphemy to be the most serious sin a man could commit (see note on Mark 14:64).

5:23 *Which is easier, to say . . . ?* See notes on Mark 2:9–10.

5:24 *that you may know.* Jesus' power to heal was a visible affirmation of His power to forgive sins.

5:27 *a tax collector.* See note on 3:12. *tax booth.* The place where customs were collected (see note on Mark 2:14).

28 And he [a]left everything behind, and got up and *began* to follow Him.

29 And [a]Levi gave a big reception for Him in his house; and there was a great crowd of [b]tax collectors and other *people* who were reclining *at the table* with them.

30 [a]The Pharisees and their scribes *began* grumbling at His disciples, saying, "Why do you eat and drink with the tax collectors and [1]sinners?"

31 And Jesus answered and said to them, "[a]*It is* not those who are well who need a physician, but those who are sick.

32 "I have not come to call the righteous but sinners to repentance."

33 And they said to Him, "[a]The disciples of John often fast and offer prayers, the *disciples* of the Pharisees also do [1]the same, but Yours eat and drink."

34 And Jesus said to them, "You cannot make the [1]attendants of the bridegroom fast while the bridegroom is with them, can you?

35 "[a]But *the* days will come; and when the bridegroom is taken away from them, then they will fast in those days."

36 And He was also telling them a parable: "No one tears a piece of cloth from a new garment and puts it on an old garment; otherwise he will both tear the new, and the piece from the new will not match the old.

37 "And no one puts new wine into old wineskins; otherwise the new wine will burst the skins and it will be spilled out, and the skins will be ruined.

38 "But new wine must be put into fresh wineskins.

39 "And no one, after drinking old *wine* wishes for new; for he says, 'The old is good *enough*.' "

28 [a]Luke 5:11 **29** [a]Matt 9:9 [b]Luke 15:1 **30** [1]I.e. irreligious Jews [a]Mark 2:16; Luke 15:2; Acts 23:9 **31** [a]Matt 9:12, 13; Mark 2:17 **33** [1]Or *likewise* [a]Matt 9:14; Mark 2:18 **34** [1]Lit *sons of the bridal-chamber* **35** [a]Matt 9:15; Mark 2:20; Luke 17:22

Jesus Is Lord of the Sabbath

6 [a]Now it happened that He was passing through *some* grainfields on a Sabbath; and His disciples [b]were picking the heads of grain, rubbing them in their hands, and eating *the grain*.

2 But some of the Pharisees said, "Why do you do what [a]is not lawful on the Sabbath?"

3 And Jesus answering them said, "Have you not even read [a]what David did when he was hungry, he and those who were with him,

4 how he entered the house of God, and took and ate the [1]consecrated bread which [a]is not lawful for any to eat except the priests alone, and gave it to his companions?"

5 And He was saying to them, "The Son of Man is Lord of the Sabbath."

6 [a]On another Sabbath He entered [b]the synagogue and was teaching; and there was a man there [1]whose right hand was withered.

7 The scribes and the Pharisees [a]were watching Him closely *to see* if He healed on the Sabbath, so that they might find *reason* to accuse Him.

8 But He [a]knew [1]what they were thinking, and He said to the man with the withered hand, "Get up and [2]come forward!" And he got up and [3]came forward.

9 And Jesus said to them, "I ask you, is it lawful to do good or to do harm on the Sabbath, to save a life or to destroy it?"

10 After [a]looking around at them all, He said to him, "Stretch out your hand!" And he did *so;* and his hand was restored.

11 But they themselves were filled with [1]rage, and discussed together what they might do to Jesus.

6:1 [a]Luke 6:1-5: *Matt 12:1-8; Mark 2:23-28* [b]Deut 23:25 **2** [a]Matt 12:2 **3** [a]1 Sam 21:6 **4** [1]Or *showbread;* lit *loaves of presentation* [a]Lev 24:9 **6** [1]Lit *and his* [a]Luke 6:6-11: *Matt 12:9-14; Mark 3:1-6;* Luke 6:1 [b]Matt 4:23 **7** [a]Mark 3:2 **8** [1]Lit *their thoughts* [2]Lit *stand into the middle* [3]Lit *stood* [a]Matt 9:4 **10** [a]Mark 3:5 **11** [1]Lit *folly*

5:28 *left everything . . . and began to follow Him.* Since Jesus had been ministering in Capernaum for some time, Levi probably had known Him previously (see note on v. 11).

5:29 *a big reception.* When Levi began to follow Jesus, he did not do it secretly.

5:30 *Pharisees . . . began grumbling.* They probably stood outside and registered their complaints from a distance. *eat . . . with the tax collectors and sinners.* See note on Mark 2:15.

5:31 *not those who are well who need a physician, but those who are sick.* Not to imply that the Pharisees were "those who are well," but that a person must recognize himself as a sinner before he can be spiritually healed (see note on Mark 2:17).

5:33 *disciples of John . . . fast and offer prayers.* John the Baptist had grown up in the wilderness and learned to subsist on a meager, austere diet of locusts and wild honey. His ministry was characterized by a sober message and a strenuous schedule. For a contrast between Jesus' ministry and John the Baptist's see 7:24–28; Matt 11:1–19. The Pharisees also had rigorous lifestyles (see note on 18:12). But Jesus went to banquets, and His disciples enjoyed a freedom not known by the Pharisees. *fast.* See note on Mark 2:18. While Jesus rejected fasting legalistically for display (cf. Is 58:3–11), He Himself fasted privately and permitted its voluntary use for spiritual benefit (Matt 4:2; 6:16–18).

5:35 See notes on Mark 2:19–20.

5:36 *parable.* See notes on Matt 13:3; Mark 4:2.

5:37 *old wineskins.* See note on Matt 9:17.

5:39 *The old is good enough.* Jesus was indicating the reluctance of some people to change from their traditional religious ways and try the gospel.

6:1 *passing through some grainfields.* See note on Mark 2:23.

6:3 *what David did.* See note on Mark 2:25.

6:4 *consecrated bread.* See note on Matt 12:4.

6:5 *Son of Man.* See note on Mark 8:31. *Lord of the Sabbath.* Jesus has the authority to overrule laws concerning the Sabbath, particularly as interpreted by the Pharisees (see Matt 12:8; Mark 2:27).

6:8 *come forward.* So there would be no question about the healing.

6:9 *is it lawful . . . on the Sabbath . . . ?* Jesus had been enduring questions and attacks from the Pharisees and now took the initiative by putting the questions to everyone in the synagogue (see note on Mark 3:4).

6:10 *looking around at them.* Jesus wanted to see whether anyone objected to His question or the implied answer, but no one was bold enough to do so.

6:11 *they . . . were filled with rage.* Because they could not withstand Jesus' reasoning. Already they were plotting to take His life (John 5:18). See note on Mark 3:6.

Choosing the Twelve

12 It was [1]at this time that He went off to [a]the mountain to [b]pray, and He spent the whole night in prayer to God.

13 And when day came, [a]He called His disciples to Him and chose twelve of them, whom He also named as [b]apostles:

14 Simon, whom He also named Peter, and Andrew his brother; and [1]James and John; and Philip and Bartholomew;

15 and [a]Matthew and Thomas; James *the son* of Alphaeus, and Simon who was called the Zealot;

16 Judas *the son* of James, and Judas Iscariot, who became a traitor.

17 Jesus [a]came down with them and stood on a level place; and *there was* [b]a large crowd of His disciples, and a great throng of people from all Judea and Jerusalem and the coastal region of [c]Tyre and Sidon,

18 who had come to hear Him and to be healed of their diseases; and those who were troubled with unclean spirits were being cured.

19 And all the [1]people were trying to [a]touch Him, for [b]power was coming from Him and healing *them* all.

The Beatitudes

20 And turning His gaze toward His disciples, He *began* to say, "[a]Blessed *are* [1]you *who are* poor, for [b]yours is the kingdom of God.

21 "Blessed *are* [1]you who hunger now, for you shall be satisfied. Blessed *are* you who weep now, for you shall laugh.

22 "[a]Blessed are you when men hate you, and [b]ostracize you, and insult you, and scorn your name as evil, for the sake of the Son of Man.

23 "Be glad in that day and [a]leap *for joy,* for behold, your reward is great in heaven. For [b]in the same way their fathers used to [1]treat the prophets.

24 "But woe to [a]you who are rich, for [b]you are receiving your comfort in full.

25 "Woe to you who [1]are well-fed now, for you shall be hungry. Woe *to you* who laugh now, for you shall mourn and weep.

26 "Woe *to you* when all men speak well of you, for their fathers used to [1]treat the [a]false prophets in the same way.

27 "But I say to you who hear, [a]love your enemies, do good to those who hate you,

28 bless those who curse you, [a]pray for those who [1]mistreat you.

29 "[a]Whoever hits you on the cheek, offer him the other also; and whoever takes away your [1]coat, do not withhold your [2]shirt from him either.

30 "Give to everyone who asks of you, and whoever takes away what is yours, do not demand it back.

31 "[1a]Treat others the same way you want [2]them to treat you.

32 "[a]If you love those who love you, what credit is *that* to you? For even sinners love those who love them.

33 "If you do good to those who do good to you, what credit is *that* to you? For even sinners do the same.

34 "[a]If you lend to those from whom you expect to receive, what credit is *that* to you? Even sinners lend to sinners in order to receive back the same *amount.*

35 "But [a]love your enemies, and do good, and lend, [1]expecting nothing in return; and your reward will be great, and you will be [b]sons of [c]the Most High; for He Himself is kind to ungrateful and evil *men.*

12 [1]Lit *in these days* [a]Matt 5:1 [b]Matt 14:23; Luke 5:16; 9:18, 28
13 [a]Luke 6:13-16: *Matt 10:2-4; Mark 3:16-19; Acts 1:13* [b]Mark 6:30
14 [1]Or *Jacob,* also vv 15 and 16
15 [a]Matt 9:9
17 [a]Luke 6:12 [b]Matt 4:25; Mark 3:7, 8 [c]Matt 11:21
19 [1]Lit *crowd* [a]Matt 9:21; 14:36; Mark 3:10 [b]Luke 5:17
20 [1]Lit *the* [a]Matt 5:3-12; Luke 6:20-23 [b]Matt 5:3
21 [1]Lit *the*
22 [a]1 Pet 4:14 [b]John 9:22; 16:2
23 [a]Mal 4
23 [1]Lit *do to* [b]2 Chr 36:16; Acts 7:52
24 [a]Luke 16:25; James 5:1 [b]Matt 6:2
25 [1]Lit *having been filled*
26 [1]Lit *do to* [a]Matt 7:15
27 [a]Matt 5:44; Luke 6:35
28 [1]Or *revile* [a]Matt 5:44; Luke 6:35
29 [1]I.e. outer garment [2]Or *tunic;* i.e. garment worn next to body [a]Luke 6:29, 30: *Matt 5:39-42*
31 [1]Lit *Do to* [2]Lit *people* [a]Matt 7:12
32 [a]Matt 5:46
34 [a]Matt 5:42
35 [1]Or *not despairing at all* [a]Luke 6:27 [b]Matt 5:9 [c]Luke 1:32

6:12 Characteristically, Jesus spent the night in prayer before the important work of selecting His 12 apostles.

6:13 *He called His disciples.* Among those who came to hear Jesus was a group who regularly followed Him and were committed to His teachings. At least 70 men were included, since this many disciples were sent out on an evangelistic campaign (10:1,17). Later, 120 believers waited and worshiped in Jerusalem following the ascension (Acts 1:15). From such disciples Jesus at this time chose 12 to be His apostles, meaning "ones sent with a special commission" (see notes on Mark 6:30; 1 Cor 1:1; Heb 3:1).

6:14–16 Lists of the apostles appear also in Matt 10:2–4; Mark 3:16–19; Acts 1:13. Although the order of the names varies, Peter is always first and Judas Iscariot last.

6:14 *Bartholomew.* Seems to be (in the Synoptics) the same as Nathanael (in John). Nathanael is associated with Philip in John 1:45.

6:15 *Matthew.* Another name for Levi. *James the son of Alphaeus.* Probably the same as James the Less (Mark 15:40). *the Zealot.* See note on Matt 10:4.

6:16 *Judas the son of James.* Another name for Thaddaeus (Matt 10:3; Mark 3:18). *Judas Iscariot.* Probably the only one from Judea, the rest coming from Galilee (see note on Mark 3:19).

6:17 *stood on a level place.* Perhaps a plateau, which would satisfy both this context and that in Matt 5:1.

6:20–49 Luke's Sermon on the Plain, apparently parallel to Matthew's Sermon on the Mount (Matt 5–7). Although this sermon is much shorter than the one in Matthew, they both begin with the Beatitudes and end with the lesson of the builders. Some of Matthew's Sermon is found in other portions of Luke (e.g., 11:2–4; 12:22–31,33–34), suggesting that the material may have been given on various occasions in Jesus' preaching.

6:20–23 See Matt 5:3–12. The Beatitudes go deeper than material poverty (v. 20) and physical hunger (v. 21). Matthew's account indicates that Jesus spoke of poverty "in spirit" (Matt 5:3) and hunger "for righteousness" (Matt 5:6).

6:24–26 This section is a point-by-point negative counterpart of vv. 20–22.

6:27 *love your enemies.* The heart of Jesus' teaching is love. While the Golden Rule (v. 31) is sometimes expressed in negative form outside the Bible, Jesus not only forbids treating others spitefully but also commands that we love everyone—even our enemies.

6:29 *offer him the other.* We are not to have a retaliatory attitude. *coat . . . shirt.* The cloak was the outer coat, under which the tunic was worn.

36 "[1]Be merciful, just as your Father is merciful.

37 "[a]Do not judge, and you will not be judged; and do not condemn, and you will not be condemned; [1][b]pardon, and you will be pardoned.

38 "Give, and it will be given to you. They will [1]pour [a]into your lap a [b]good measure—pressed down, shaken together, *and* running over. For by your standard of measure it will be measured to you in return."

39 And He also spoke a parable to them: "[a]A blind man cannot guide a blind man, can he? Will they not both fall into a pit?

40 "[a]A [1]pupil is not above his teacher; but everyone, after he has been fully trained, will [2]be like his teacher.

41 "Why do you look at the speck that is in your brother's eye, but do not notice the log that is in your own eye?

42 "Or how can you say to your brother, 'Brother, let me take out the speck that is in your eye,' when you yourself do not see the log that is in your own eye? You hypocrite, first take the log out of your own eye, and then you will see clearly to take out the speck that is in your brother's eye.

43 "[a]For there is no good tree which produces bad fruit, nor, [1]on the other hand, a bad tree which produces good fruit.

44 "[a]For each tree is known by its own fruit. For men do not gather figs from thorns, nor do they pick grapes from a briar bush.

45 "[a]The good man out of the good [1]treasure of his heart brings forth what is good; and the evil *man* out of the evil *treasure* brings forth what is evil; [b]for his mouth speaks from [2]that which fills his heart.

Builders and Foundations

46 "[a]Why do you call Me, 'Lord, Lord,' and do not do what I say?

47 "[a]Everyone who comes to Me and hears My words and [1]acts on them, I will show you whom he is like:

48 he is like a man building a house, who [1]dug deep and laid a foundation on the rock; and when a flood occurred, the [2]torrent burst against that house and could not shake it, because it had been well built.

49 "But the one who has heard and has not acted *accordingly*, is like a man who built a house on the ground without any foundation; and the [1]torrent burst against it and immediately it collapsed, and the ruin of that house was great."

36 [1]Or *Become*
37 [1]Lit *release* [a]Luke 6:37-42: *Matt 7:1-5* [b]Matt 6:14; Luke 23:16; Acts 3:13
38 [1]Lit *give* [a]Mark 4:24 [b]Ps 79:12; Is 65:6, 7; Jer 32:18
39 [a]Matt 15:14
40 [1]Or *disciple* [2]Or *reach his teacher's level* [a]Matt 10:24; John 13:16; 15:20
43 [1]Lit *again* [a]Luke 6:43, 44: *Matt 7:16, 18, 20*
44 [a]Matt 7:16; 12:33
45 [1]Or *treasury, storehouse* [2]Lit *the abundance of* [a]Matt 12:35 [b]Matt 12:34
46 [a]Mal 1:6; Matt 7:21
47 [1]Lit *does* [a]Luke 6:47-49: *Matt 7:24-27;* James 1:22ff
48 [1]Lit *dug and went deep* [2]Lit *river*
49 [1]Lit *river*
7:1 [a]Matt 7:28 [b]Luke 7:1-10: *Matt 8:5-13*
2 [1]Lit *to whom he was honorable*
3 [1]Lit *elders of the Jews* [2]Lit *bring safely through, rescue* [a]Matt 8:5
6 [1]Or *Sir*
7 [1]Lit *say with a word* [2]Or *boy*
9 [a]Matt 8:10; Luke 7:50
11 [1]Lit *and*

Jesus Heals a Centurion's Servant

7 [a]When He had completed all His discourse in the hearing of the people, [b]He went to Capernaum.

2 And a centurion's slave, [1]who was highly regarded by him, was sick and about to die.

3 When he heard about Jesus, [a]he sent some [1]Jewish elders asking Him to come and [2]save the life of his slave.

4 When they came to Jesus, they earnestly implored Him, saying, "He is worthy for You to grant this to him;

5 for he loves our nation and it was he who built us our synagogue."

6 Now Jesus *started* on His way with them; and when He was not far from the house, the centurion sent friends, saying to Him, "[1]Lord, do not trouble Yourself further, for I am not worthy for You to come under my roof;

7 for this reason I did not even consider myself worthy to come to You, but *just* [1]say the word, and my [2]servant will be healed.

8 "For I also am a man placed under authority, with soldiers under me; and I say to this one, 'Go!' and he goes, and to another, 'Come!' and he comes, and to my slave, 'Do this!' and he does it."

9 Now when Jesus heard this, He marveled at him, and turned and said to the crowd that was following Him, "I say to you, [a]not even in Israel have I found such great faith."

10 When those who had been sent returned to the house, they found the slave in good health.

11 Soon afterwards He went to a city called Nain; and His disciples were going along with Him, [1]accompanied by a large crowd.

6:36 *just as your Father is merciful.* God's perfection should be our example and goal (see Matt 5:48).

6:37 *Do not judge.* Jesus did not relieve His followers of the need for discerning right and wrong (cf. vv. 43–45), but He condemned unjust and hypocritical judging of others.

6:38 *pour into your lap.* Probably refers to the way the outer garment was worn, leaving a fold over the belt that could be used as a large pocket to hold a measure of wheat.

6:41 *speck . . . log.* Jesus used hyperbole (a figure of speech that overstates for emphasis) to sharpen the contrast and to emphasize how foolish and hypocritical it is for us to criticize someone for a fault while remaining blind to our own considerable faults.

7:2 *centurion's slave.* The centurion was probably a member of Herod Antipas's forces, which were organized in Roman fashion, ordinarily in companies of 100 men. Roman centurions referred to in the NT showed characteristics to be admired (e.g., Acts 10:2; 23:17–18; 27:43). This centurion showed genuine concern for his slave, and he was admired by the Jews, who spoke favorably of him even though he was a Gentile (see vv. 5,9).

7:3 *Jewish elders.* Highly respected Jews of the community, though not necessarily rulers of the synagogue. They were willing to come and plead for the centurion. In Matthew's account (Matt 8:5–13) the centurion speaks with Jesus Himself, while in Luke's account he speaks with Jesus through his friends (see note on Matt 8:5).

7:6 *I am not worthy for You to come under my roof.* See note on Matt 8:8.

7:9 *He marveled.* The Greek word for "marvel" is used of Jesus is only mentioned twice. Here He "marveled" at faith while in Mark 6:6 He "wondered" (same Greek word) at a lack of faith.

12 Now as He approached the gate of the
city, [1]a dead man was being carried out, the
[2]only son of his mother, and she was a widow;
and a sizeable crowd from the city was
with her.
13 When [a]the Lord saw her, He felt compassion
for her, and said to her, "[1]Do not
weep."
14 And He came up and touched the coffin;
and the bearers came to a halt. And He
said, "Young man, I say to you, arise!"
15 The [1]dead man sat up and began to
speak. And *Jesus* gave him back to his mother.
16 [a]Fear gripped them all, and they *began*
[b]glorifying God, saying, "A great [c]prophet
has arisen among us!" and, "God has [1]visited
His people!"
17 [a]This report concerning Him went out
all over Judea and in all the surrounding district.

A Deputation from John

18 [a]The disciples of John reported to him
about all these things.
19 Summoning [1]two of his disciples, John
sent them to [a]the Lord, saying, "Are You the
[2]Expected One, or do we look for someone
else?"
20 When the men came to Him, they said,
"John the Baptist has sent us to You, to ask,
'Are You the [1]Expected One, or do we look
for someone else?' "
21 At that [1]very time He [a]cured many *people*
of diseases and [b]afflictions and evil spirits;
and He gave sight to many *who were* blind.
22 And He answered and said to them,
"Go and report to John what you have seen
and heard: *the* [a]BLIND RECEIVE SIGHT, *the* lame
walk, *the* lepers are cleansed, and *the* deaf
hear, *the* dead are raised up, *the* [b]POOR HAVE
THE GOSPEL PREACHED TO THEM.

12 [1]Lit *one who had died* [2]Or *only begotten*
13 [1]Or *Stop weeping* [a]Luke 7:19; 10:1; 11:1, 39; 12:42; 13:15; 17:5, 6; 18:6; 19:8; 22:61; 24:34; John 4:1; 6:23; 11:2
15 [1]Or *corpse*
16 [1]Or *cared for* [a]Luke 5:26 [b]Matt 9:8 [c]Matt 21:11; Luke 7:39
17 [a]Matt 9:26
18 [a]Luke 7:18-35: *Matt 11:2-19*
19 [1]Lit *a certain two* [2]Lit *Coming One* [a]Luke 7:13; 10:1; 11:1, 39; 12:42; 13:15; 17:5, 6; 18:6; 19:8; 22:61; 24:34; John 4:1; 6:23; 11:2
20 [1]Lit *Coming One*
21 [1]Lit *hour* [a]Matt 4:23 [b]Mark 3:10
22 [a]Is 35:5 [b]Is 61:1
23 [1]Lit *whoever*
25 [1]Or *Well then, what* [2]Or *garments*
27 [1]Lit *before Your face* [a]Mal 3:1; Matt 11:10; Mark 1:2
28 [1]Or *less*
29 [1]Or *justified God* [a]Luke 7:35 [b]Matt 21:32; Luke 3:12 [c]Acts 18:25; 19:3
30 [1]I.e. experts in the Mosaic Law [2]Lit *him* [a]Matt 22:35
33 [a]Luke 1:15

23 "Blessed is he [1]who does not take
offense at Me."
24 When the messengers of John had left,
He began to speak to the crowds about John,
"What did you go out into the wilderness to
see? A reed shaken by the wind?
25 "[1]But what did you go out to see? A man
dressed in soft [2]clothing? Those who are
splendidly clothed and live in luxury are
found in royal palaces!
26 "But what did you go out to see? A
prophet? Yes, I say to you, and one who is
more than a prophet.
27 "This is the one about whom it is written,

'[a]BEHOLD, I SEND MY MESSENGER [1]AHEAD OF YOU,
WHO WILL PREPARE YOUR WAY BEFORE YOU.'

28 "I say to you, among those born of
women there is no one greater than John; yet
he who is [1]least in the kingdom of God is
greater than he."
29 When all the people and the tax collectors
heard *this,* they [1]acknowledged [a]God's
justice, [b]having been baptized with [c]the baptism
of John.
30 But the Pharisees and the [1a]lawyers
rejected God's purpose for themselves, not
having been baptized by [2]John.
31 "To what then shall I compare the men
of this generation, and what are they like?
32 "They are like children who sit in the
market place and call to one another, and
they say, 'We played the flute for you, and
you did not dance; we sang a dirge, and you
did not weep.'
33 "For John the Baptist has come [a]eating
no bread and drinking no wine, and you say,
'He has a demon!'
34 "The Son of Man has come eating and

7:14 *coffin.* The man was probably carried in an open coffin, suggested by Jewish custom and the fact that he sat up in response to Jesus' command. This is the first of three instances of Jesus' raising someone from the dead, the others being Jairus's daughter (8:40–56) and Lazarus (John 11:38–44).
7:18 *disciples of John.* Despite John the Baptist's imprisonment, his disciples kept in contact with him and continued his ministry.
7:19 *do we look for someone else?* John had announced the coming of the Christ, but now he himself had been languishing in prison for months, and the work of Jesus had not brought the results John apparently expected. His disappointment was natural. He wanted reassurance—and perhaps also wanted to urge Jesus to further action.
7:22 *report to John what you have seen and heard.* In answer, Jesus pointed to His healing and life-restoring miracles. He did not give promises but clearly observable evidence—evidence that reflected the predicted ministry of the Messiah. *THE POOR HAVE THE GOSPEL PREACHED TO THEM.* In Jesus' review of His works, He used an ascending scale of impressive deeds, ending with the dead raised and the good news preached to the poor. In this way, Jesus reminded John that these were the things predicted of the Messiah in the Scriptures (see Is 29:18–21; 35:5–6; 61:1; see also Luke 4:18).
7:23 *he who does not take offense.* Jesus did not want discouragement and doubt to ensnare John.
7:24 *What did you go . . . to see?* John was not a weak messenger, swayed by the pressures of human opinion. On the contrary, he was a true prophet.
7:26 *more than a prophet.* John was the unique prophet sent to prepare the way for the Messiah.
7:28 *he who is least in the kingdom of God.* See note on Matt 11:11.
7:30 *lawyers.* A designation used by Luke (see 10:25; 11:45–46 ,52; 14:3; see also Matt 22:35) for the "scribes" (the teachers of the law), most of whom were Pharisees (see note on 5:17). *rejected God's purpose.* Tax collectors had shown their willingness to repent by accepting John's baptism, whereas the Pharisees showed their rejection of God's message by refusing to be baptized.
7:32 *like children who sit in the market place.* People had rejected both John and Jesus, but for different reasons—like children who refuse to play either a joyful game or a mournful one. They would not associate with John when he followed the strictest of rules or with Jesus when He freely associated with all kinds of people.

drinking, and you say, 'Behold, a gluttonous
man and a [1]drunkard, a friend of tax collectors and [2]sinners!'
35 "Yet wisdom [a]is vindicated by all her
children."
36 Now one of the Pharisees was requesting Him to [1]dine with him, and He entered
the Pharisee's house and reclined *at the*
table.
37 [a]And there was a woman in the city
who was a [1]sinner; and when she learned
that He was reclining *at the table* in the Pharisee's house, she brought an alabaster vial of
perfume,
38 and standing behind *Him* at His feet,
weeping, she began to wet His feet with her
tears, and kept wiping them with the hair of
her head, and kissing His feet and anointing
them with the perfume.
39 Now when the Pharisee who had invited Him saw this, he said to himself, "If this
man were [a]a prophet He would know who
and what sort of person this woman is who
is touching Him, that she is a [1]sinner."

Parable of Two Debtors

40 And Jesus answered him, "Simon, I
have something to say to you." And he
[1]replied, "Say it, Teacher."
41 "A moneylender had two debtors: one
owed five hundred [1a]denarii, and the other
fifty.
42 "When they [a]were unable to repay, he
graciously forgave them both. So which of
them will love him more?"
43 Simon answered and said, "I suppose
the one whom he forgave more." And He
said to him, "You have judged correctly."
44 Turning toward the woman, He said to
Simon, "Do you see this woman? I entered
your house; you [a]gave Me no water for My
feet, but she has wet My feet with her tears
and wiped them with her hair.
45 "You [a]gave Me no kiss; but she, since
the time I came in, has not ceased to kiss My
feet.
46 "[a]You did not anoint My head with oil,
but she anointed My feet with perfume.
47 "For this reason I say to you, her sins,
which are many, have been forgiven, for she
loved much; but he who is forgiven little,
loves little."
48 Then He said to her, "[a]Your sins have
been forgiven."
49 Those who were reclining *at the table*
with Him began to say [1]to themselves,
"[a]Who is this *man* who even forgives sins?"
50 And He said to the woman, "[a]Your
faith has saved you; [b]go in peace."

Ministering Women

8 Soon afterwards, He *began* going around
from one city and village to another, [a]pro-
claiming and preaching the kingdom of God.
The twelve were with Him,
2 and *also* [a]some women who had been
healed of evil spirits and sicknesses: [b]Mary
who was called Magdalene, from whom sev-
en demons had gone out,
3 and Joanna the wife of Chuza, [a]Her-
od's [b]steward, and Susanna, and many others who were contributing to their support
out of their private means.

Parable of the Sower

4 [a]When a large crowd was coming
together, and those from the various cities
were journeying to Him, He spoke by way of
a parable:
5 "The sower went out to sow his seed;

34 [1]Or *wine-drinker* [2]I.e. irreligious Jews
35 [a]Luke 7:29
36 [1]Lit *eat*
37 [1]I.e. an immoral woman [a]Matt 26:6-13; Mark 14:3-9; Luke 7:37-39; John 12:1-8
39 [1]I.e. an immoral woman [a]Luke 7:16; John 4:19
40 [1]Lit *says*
41 [1]The denarius was equivalent to a day's wages [a]Matt 18:28; Mark 6:37
42 [a]Matt 18:25
44 [a]Gen 18:4; 19:2; 43:24; Judg 19:21; 1 Tim 5:10
45 [a]2 Sam 15:5
46 [a]2 Sam 12:20; Ps 23:5; Eccl 9:8; Dan 10:3
48 [a]Matt 9:2; Mark 2:5, 9; Luke 5:20, 23
49 [1]Or *among* [a]Luke 5:21
50 [a]Matt 9:22; Luke 17:19; 18:42 [b]Mark 5:34; Luke 8:48
8:1 [a]Matt 4:23
2 [a]Matt 27:55; Mark 15:40, 41; Luke 23:49, 55 [b]Matt 27:56; Mark 16:9
3 [a]Matt 14:1 [b]Matt 20:8
4 [a]Luke 8:4-8: *Matt 13:2-9; Mark 4:1-9*

7:34 *a friend of tax collectors and sinners.* Jesus ate and talked with people who were religious and social outcasts. He even called a tax collector to be an apostle (5:27–32).
7:35 *wisdom is vindicated by all her children.* In contrast to the rejection by foolish critics, spiritually wise persons could see that the ministries of both John and Jesus were godly, despite their differences. See note on Matt 11:19.
7:36 *one of the Pharisees.* See note on 5:17. His motive may have been to entrap Jesus rather than to learn from Him.
7:37 *a woman . . . who was a sinner.* A prostitute. She must have heard Jesus preach, and in repentance she determined to lead a new life. She came out of love and gratitude, in the understanding that she could be forgiven. *alabaster vial.* A long-necked, globular bottle. *perfume.* A perfumed ointment.
7:38 *standing behind Him at His feet.* Jesus reclined on a couch with His feet extended away from the table, which made it possible for the woman to wipe His feet with her hair and still not disturb Him. *anointing them with the perfume.* The anointing, perhaps originally intended for Jesus' head, was instead applied to His feet. A similar act was performed by Mary of Bethany just over a week before the crucifixion (John 12:3).
7:41 *five hundred denarii.* A denarius was a coin worth about a day's wages.
7:44 *water for My feet.* The minimal gesture of hospitality.
7:47 *for she loved much.* Her love was evidence of her forgiveness, but not the basis for it. Verse 50 clearly states that she was saved by faith. See Eph 1:7.
7:50 *Your faith has saved you.* Her sins were forgiven and she could experience God's peace (see 1:79 and note on 2:14).
8:1 *He began going around.* Jesus' ministry had been centered in Capernaum, and much of His preaching was in synagogues, but now He traveled again from town to town on a second tour of the Galilean countryside. For the first tour see 4:43–44; Matt 4:23–25; Mark 1:38–39. For the third tour see note on 9:1–6. *kingdom of God.* See note on 4:43.
8:2 *Mary who was called Magdalene.* Her hometown was Magdala. She is not to be confused with the sinful woman of ch. 7 or Mary of Bethany (John 11:1).
8:3 *Susanna.* Nothing more is known of her. *contributing to their support.* Jesus and His disciples did not provide for themselves by miracles, but were supported by the service and means of such grateful people as these women.
8:4 *parable.* From this point on Jesus used parables (see notes on Matt 13:3; Mark 4:2) more extensively as a means of teaching. They were particularly effective and easy to remember because He used familiar scenes. Although parables clarified Jesus' teaching, they also included hidden meanings needing further explanation. These hidden meanings challenged the sincerely interested to further inquiry, and taught truths that Jesus wanted to conceal from unbelievers (see v. 10). From parables

and as he sowed, some fell beside the road, and it was trampled under foot and the birds of the [1]air ate it up.

6 "Other *seed* fell on rocky *soil,* and as soon as it grew up, it withered away, because it had no moisture.

7 "Other *seed* fell among the thorns; and the thorns grew up with it and choked it out.

8 "Other *seed* fell into the good soil, and grew up, and produced a crop a hundred times as great." As He said these things, He would call out, "[a]He who has ears to hear, [1]let him hear."

9 [a]His disciples *began* questioning Him as to what this parable meant.

10 And He said, "[a]To you it has been granted to know the mysteries of the kingdom of God, but to the rest *it is* in parables, so that [b]SEEING THEY MAY NOT SEE, AND HEARING THEY MAY NOT UNDERSTAND.

11 "Now the parable is this: [a]the seed is the word of God.

12 "Those beside the road are those who have heard; then the devil comes and takes away the word from their heart, so that they will not believe and be saved.

13 "Those on the rocky *soil are* those who, when they hear, receive the word with joy; and these have no *firm* root; [1]they believe for a while, and in time of temptation fall away.

14 "The *seed* which fell among the thorns, these are the ones who have heard, and as they go on their way they are choked with worries and riches and pleasures of *this* life, and bring no fruit to maturity.

15 "But the *seed* in the good soil, these are the ones who have heard the word in an honest and good heart, and hold it fast, and bear fruit with [1]perseverance.

Parable of the Lamp

16 "Now [a]no one after lighting a lamp covers it over with a container, or puts it under a bed; but he puts it on a lampstand, so that those who come in may see the light.

17 "[a]For nothing is hidden that will not become evident, nor *anything* secret that will not be known and come to light.

18 "So take care how you listen; [a]for whoever has, to him *more* shall be given; and whoever does not have, even what he [1]thinks he has shall be taken away from him."

19 [a]And His mother and brothers came to Him, and they were unable to get to Him because of the crowd.

20 And it was reported to Him, "Your mother and Your brothers are standing outside, wishing to see You."

21 But He answered and said to them, "My mother and My brothers are these [a]who hear the word of God and do it."

Jesus Stills the Sea

22 [a]Now on one of *those* days Jesus and His disciples got into a boat, and He said to

5 [1]Lit *heaven*
8 [1]Or *hear!* Or *listen!* [a]Matt 11:15; Mark 7:16; Luke 14:35; Rev 2:7, 11, 17, 29; 3:6, 13, 22; 13:9
9 [a]Luke 8:9-15: *Matt 13:10-23; Mark 4:10-20*
10 [a]Matt 13:11 [b]Is 6:9; Matt 13:14; Acts 28:26
11 [a]1 Pet 1:23
13 [1]Lit *who believe*
15 [1]Or *steadfastness*
16 [a]Matt 5:15; Mark 4:21; Luke 11:33
17 [a]Matt 10:26; Mark 4:22; Luke 12:2
18 [1]Or *seems to have* [a]Matt 13:12; 25:29; Luke 19:26
19 [a]Luke 8:19-21: *Matt 12:46-50; Mark 3:31-35*
21 [a]Luke 11:28
22 [a]Luke 8:22-25: *Matt 8:23-27; Mark 4:36-41*

Jesus' enemies could find no direct statements to use against Him. The parable of the sower is one of three parables recorded in each of the Synoptic Gospels (Matt 13:1–23; Mark 4:1–20). The others are those of the mustard seed (13:19; Matt 13:31–32; Mark 4:30–32) and of the vineyard (20:9–19; Matt 21:33–46; Mark 12:1–12).

8:5 *to sow his seed.* In Eastern practice the seed was sometimes sown first and the field plowed afterward. Roads and pathways went directly through many fields, and the traffic made much of the surface too hard for seed to take root in.

8:6 *on rocky soil.* On a thin layer of soil that covered solid rock. Any moisture that fell there soon evaporated, and the germinating seed withered and died (see Matt 13:5–6).

8:8 *a hundred times as great.* Luke's version is more abbreviated than Matthew's (13:8) and Mark's (4:8), but the point is the same: The quantity of increase depends on the quality of soil. *let him hear.* A challenge for listeners to understand the message and appropriate it for themselves.

8:9 *His disciples.* They included "His followers, along with the twelve" (Mark 4:10).

8:10 *mysteries of the kingdom of God.* Truths that can be known only by revelation from God (cf. Eph 3:2–5; 1 Pet 1:10–12). See note on Mark 4:11. *that* SEEING THEY MAY NOT SEE. This quotation from Isaiah (6:9) does not express a desire that some would not understand, but simply states the sad truth that those who are not willing to receive Jesus' message will find the truth hidden from them. Their ultimate fate is implied in the fuller quotation in Matt 13:14–15 (see note on Mark 4:12).

8:11 *the word of God.* The message that comes from God.

8:12 *will not believe.* The devil's purpose is that people will not hear with understanding and therefore will not appropriate the message and be saved.

8:13 *they believe for a while.* This kind of belief is superficial and does not save. It is similar to what James calls "dead" (James 2:17,26) or "useless" faith (James 2:20).

8:16 *lighting a lamp.* Although Jesus couched much of His message in parables, He intended that the disciples make the truths known as widely as possible (see note on 11:33). *puts it on a lampstand.* See note on Matt 5:15.

8:17 This verse explains v. 16. It is the destiny of the truth to be made known (cf. 12:2). The disciples were to begin a proclamation that would become universal.

8:18 *take care how you listen.* The disciples heard not only for themselves but also for those to whom they would minister (see Mark 4:24; cf. James 1:19–22). Truth that is not understood and appropriated will be lost (19:26), but truth that is used will be multiplied.

8:19 *His mother and brothers came.* See note on Mark 3:21. More is known about their motive from Mark 3:21,31–32. The family, thinking "He has lost His senses," probably wanted to get Him away from His heavy schedule. *brothers.* Did not believe in Jesus at this time (John 7:5). Various interpretations concerning their relationship to Jesus arose in the early church: They were sons of Joseph by a previous marriage (according to Epiphanius) or were cousins (said Jerome). The most natural conclusion (suggested by Helvidius) is that they were the sons of Joseph and Mary, younger half brothers of Jesus. Four of these brothers are named in Mark 6:3, where sisters are also mentioned. Since Joseph is not mentioned here, it is likely that he had died.

8:21 Jesus' reply was not meant to reject His natural family but to emphasize the higher priority of His spiritual relationship to those who believed in Him.

them, "Let us go over to the other side of
[b]the lake." So they launched out.
23 But as they were sailing along He fell
asleep; and a fierce gale of wind descended
on [a]the lake, and they *began* to be swamped
and to be in danger.
24 They came to Jesus and woke Him up,
saying, "[a]Master, Master, we are perishing!"
And He got up and [b]rebuked the wind and
the surging waves, and they stopped, and [1]it
became calm.
25 And He said to them, "Where is your
faith?" They were fearful and amazed, saying
to one another, "Who then is this, that He
commands even the winds and the water,
and they obey Him?"

The Demoniac Cured

26 [a]Then they sailed to the country of the
Gerasenes, which is opposite Galilee.
27 And when He came out onto the land,
He was met by a man from the city who was
possessed with demons; and who had not
put on any clothing for a long time, and was
not living in a house, but in the tombs.
28 Seeing Jesus, he cried out and fell
before Him, and said in a loud voice,
"[1a]What business do we have with each other,
Jesus, Son of [b]the Most High God? I beg
You, do not torment me."
29 For He had commanded the unclean
spirit to come out of the man. For it had
seized him many times; and he was bound
with chains and shackles and kept under
guard, and *yet* he would break his bonds and
be driven by the demon into the desert.
30 And Jesus asked him, "What is your
name?" And he said, "[a]Legion"; for many
demons had entered him.
31 They were imploring Him not to command
them to go away into [a]the abyss.
32 Now there was a herd of many swine
feeding there on the mountain; and *the
demons* implored Him to permit them to enter
[1]the swine. And He gave them permission.
33 And the demons came out of the man
and entered the swine; and the herd rushed
down the steep bank into [a]the lake and was
drowned.
34 When the herdsmen saw what had
happened, they ran away and reported it in
the city and *out* in the country.
35 *The people* went out to see what had
happened; and they came to Jesus, and
found the man from whom the demons had
gone out, sitting down [a]at the feet of Jesus,
clothed and in his right mind; and they
became frightened.
36 Those who had seen it reported to
them how the man who was [a]demon-possessed
had been [1]made well.
37 And all the people of the country of the
Gerasenes and the surrounding district asked
Him to leave them, for they were gripped
with great fear; and He got into a boat and
returned.
38 [a]But the man from whom the demons
had gone out was begging Him that he might
[1]accompany Him; but He sent him away,
saying,
39 "Return to your house and describe
what great things God has done for you." So
he went away, proclaiming throughout the
whole city what great things Jesus had done
for him.

Miracles of Healing

40 [a]And as Jesus returned, the [1]people
welcomed Him, for they had all been waiting
for Him.
41 [a]And there came a man named Jairus,
and he was an [1b]official of the synagogue;
and he fell at Jesus' feet, and *began* to
implore Him to come to his house;
42 for he had an [1]only daughter, about
twelve years old, and she was dying. But as
He went, the crowds were pressing against
Him.
43 And a woman who had a hemorrhage
for twelve years, and could not be healed by
anyone,
44 came up behind Him and touched the

22 [b]Luke 5:1f; 8:23
23 [a]Luke 5:1f; 8:22
24 [1]Lit *a calm occurred* [a]Luke 5:5 [b]Luke 4:39
26 [a]Luke 8:26-37: *Matt 8:28-34; Mark 5:1-17*
28 [1]Lit *What to me and to you* (a Heb idiom) [a]Matt 8:29 [b]Mark 5:7
30 [a]Matt 26:53
31 [a]Rom 10:7; Rev 9:1f, 11; 11:7; 17:8; 20:1, 3
32 [1]Lit *them*
33 [a]Luke 5:1f; 8:22
35 [a]Luke 10:39
36 [1]Or *saved* [a]Matt 4:24
38 [1]Lit *be with* [a]Luke 8:38, 39: *Mark 5:18-20*
40 [1]Lit *crowd* [a]Matt 9:1; Mark 5:21
41 [1]Lit *ruler* [a]Luke 8:41-56: *Matt 9:18-26; Mark 5:22-43* [b]Mark 5:22; Luke 8:49
42 [1]Or *only begotten*

8:23 *fierce gale of wind.* See note on Mark 4:37.
8:26 *country of the Gerasenes.* The Gospels describe the location of this event in two ways: (1) the region of the Gerasenes (see note on Mark 5:1); (2) the region of the Gadarenes (see note on Matt 8:28). Some manuscripts of Matthew, Mark and Luke read "Gergesenes," but this spelling may have been introduced in an attempt to resolve the differences.
8:27 *man . . . possessed with demons.* See note on 4:33. Matthew (8:28) refers to two demon-possessed men, but Mark (5:2) and Luke probably mention only the one who was prominent and did the talking. *tombs.* An isolated burial ground avoided by most people (but see note on Mark 5:3).
8:28 *Son of the Most High God.* Cf. 1:32; 4:34. The title "Most High God" was commonly used by Gentiles (see Gen 14:19 and note; Acts 16:17); its use here perhaps indicates that this man was not a Jew (but see note on Mark 1:24).
8:30 *What is your name?* Jesus asked the man his name, but it was the demons who replied, thus showing they were in control. *Legion.* See note on Mark 5:9.
8:31 *abyss.* A place of confinement for evil spirits and for Satan (see note on Rev 9:1).
8:32 *swine.* Pigs were unclean to Jews, and eating them was forbidden (Lev 11:7–8), but this was the Decapolis, a predominantly Gentile territory. *He gave them permission.* See note on Matt 8:32.
8:39 *Return to your house and describe what great things God has done for you.* Although the man wanted to follow Jesus, he was directed to make the miracle known in his own native territory. There was no danger here of interference with Jesus' ministry (see note on Mark 5:19).
8:41 *official of the synagogue.* The ruler was responsible for conducting services, selecting participants and maintaining order (see note on Mark 5:22).
8:43 *hemorrhage.* The hemorrhage had made her ceremonially unclean for 12 years (see Lev 15:19–30). *could not be healed by anyone.* Comparison with Mark 5:26 shows the restraint of Luke the physician in describing the failure of doctors to help her.

fringe of His [1]cloak, and immediately her
hemorrhage stopped.
45 And Jesus said, "Who is the one who
touched Me?" And while they were all denying it, Peter said, "[a]Master, the [1]people are
crowding and pressing in on You."
46 But Jesus said, "Someone did touch
Me, for I was aware that [a]power had gone
out of Me."
47 When the woman saw that she had not
escaped notice, she came trembling and fell
down before Him, and declared in the presence of all the people the reason why she
had touched Him, and how she had been
immediately healed.
48 And He said to her, "Daughter, [a]your
faith has [1]made you well; [b]go in peace."
49 While He was still speaking, someone
*came from *the house of* [a]the synagogue
official, saying, "Your daughter has died; do
not trouble the Teacher anymore."
50 But when Jesus heard *this,* He
answered him, "[a]Do not be afraid *any
longer;* only believe, and she will be [1]made
well."
51 When He came to the house, He did
not allow anyone to enter with Him, except
Peter and John and James, and the girl's
father and mother.
52 Now they were all weeping and
[a]lamenting for her; but He said, "Stop weeping, for she has not died, but [b]is asleep."
53 And they *began* laughing at Him,
knowing that she had died.
54 He, however, took her by the hand and
called, saying, "Child, arise!"
55 And her spirit returned, and she got up
immediately; and He gave orders for *something* to be given her to eat.
56 Her parents were amazed; but He

44 [1]Or *outer garment*
45 [1]Lit *crowds* [a]Luke 5:5
46 [a]Luke 5:17
48 [1]Or *saved you* [a]Matt 9:22 [b]Mark 5:34; Luke 7:50
49 [a]Luke 8:41
50 [1]Or *saved* [a]Mark 5:36
52 [a]Matt 11:17; Luke 23:27 [b]John 11:13
56 [a]Matt 8:4
9:1 [a]Matt 10:5; Mark 6:7
2 [a]Matt 10:7
3 [1]Or *knapsack or beggar's bag* [2]Or *inner garments* [a]Luke 9:3-5: *Matt 10:9-15; Mark 6:8-11;* Luke 10:4-12; 22:35 [b]Matt 10:10; Mark 6:8; Luke 22:35f
4 [1]Lit *and leave from there*
5 [a]Luke 10:11; Acts 13:51
6 [1]Or *from village to village* [a]Mark 6:12; Luke 8:1
7 [a]Luke 9:7-9: *Matt 14:1, 2;* Mark 6:14f [b]Matt 14:1; Luke 3:1; 13:31; 23:7 [c]Matt 14:2
8 [a]Matt 16:14
9 [a]Luke 23:8
10 [a]Mark 6:30 [b]Luke 9:10-17: *Matt 14:13-21; Mark 6:32-44; John 6:5-13* [c]Matt 11:21

[a]instructed them to tell no one what had
happened.

Ministry of the Twelve

9 [a]And He called the twelve together, and
gave them power and authority over all
the demons and to heal diseases.
2 And He sent them out to [a]proclaim the
kingdom of God and to perform healing.
3 And He said to them, "[a]Take nothing
for *your* journey, [b]neither a staff, nor a [1]bag,
nor bread, nor money; and do not *even* have
[2]two tunics apiece.
4 "Whatever house you enter, stay there
[1]until you leave that city.
5 "And as for those who do not receive
you, as you go out from that city, [a]shake the
dust off your feet as a testimony against
them."
6 Departing, they *began* going [1]through-
out the villages, [a]preaching the gospel and
healing everywhere.
7 [a]Now [b]Herod the tetrarch heard of all
that was happening; and he was greatly perplexed, because it was said by some that
[c]John had risen from the dead,
8 and by some that [a]Elijah had appeared,
and by others that one of the prophets of old
had risen again.
9 Herod said, "I myself had John beheaded; but who is this man about whom I hear
such things?" And [a]he kept trying to see
Him.
10 [a]When the apostles returned, they gave
an account to Him of all that they had done.
[b]Taking them with Him, He withdrew by
Himself to a city called [c]Bethsaida.
11 But the crowds were aware of this and
followed Him; and welcoming them, He
began speaking to them about the kingdom

8:45 *Who . . . touched me?* For the woman's good and for a testimony to the crowd, Jesus insisted that the miracle be made known.

8:46 *power had gone out.* See note on Mark 5:30.

8:48 *Daughter.* This woman is the only individual Jesus addressed with this tender term (cf. 23:28). *go in peace.* Cf. 7:50.

8:50 *will be made well.* See note on Mark 5:34.

8:52 *weeping and lamenting.* See note on Mark 5:38. *not died, but is asleep.* Jesus meant that she was not permanently dead (see John 11:11–14 for a similar statement about Lazarus).

8:56 *instructed them to tell no one.* See notes on Matt 8:4; Mark 5:43. Further publicity at this time concerning a raising from the dead would have been counterproductive to Jesus' ministry.

9:1–6 A new phase of Jesus' ministry began when He sent out the apostles to do the type of preaching, teaching and healing that they had observed Him doing (Matt 9:35). This was the third tour of Galilee by Jesus and His disciples (see note on 8:1). On the first tour Jesus traveled with the four fishermen; on the second all 12 were with Him; on the third Jesus traveled alone after sending out the twelve two by two.

9:1 *the twelve.* The apostles (see 6:13). *power and authority.* Special power to heal (see 5:17; 8:46) and authority in teaching and control over evil spirits. *demons.* Evil spirits (see note on 4:33).

9:3 *Take nothing.* No excess baggage that would encumber travel, not even the usual provisions. They were to be entirely dependent on the people with whom they were staying (see note on Mark 6:8).

9:4 *stay there.* They were not to move from house to house, seeking better lodging, but use only one home as headquarters while preaching in a community.

9:5 *shake the dust off your feet.* A sign of repudiation for their rejection of God's message and a gesture showing separation from everything associated with the place (see 10:11; see also notes on Matt 10:14; Acts 13:51).

9:7 *Herod the tetrarch.* See note on Matt 14:1. *John had risen from the dead.* See note on Mark 6:16. Luke does not give details about John's death (see Matt 14:1–12; Mark 6:17–29), which occurred about this time, but simply notes that it had taken place (v. 9).

9:8 *Elijah had appeared.* See notes on 1:17; Mark 9:12.

9:9 *he kept trying to see Him.* Herod's desire to see Jesus was not fulfilled until Jesus' trial (23:8–12).

9:10–17 The feeding of the 5,000 is the only miracle besides Jesus' resurrection that is reported in all four Gospels (see notes on Mark 6:30–44; John 6:1–14).

9:10 *Bethsaida.* See note on Matt 11:21. Jesus must have retired to a remote area near the town (v. 12).

of God and curing those who had need of
healing.

Five Thousand Fed

12 Now the day [1]was ending, and the
twelve came and said to Him, "Send the
crowd away, that they may go into the surrounding villages and countryside and find
lodging and get [2]something to eat; for here
we are in a desolate place."
13 But He said to them, "You give them
something to eat!" And they said, "We have
no more than five loaves and two fish, unless
perhaps we go and buy food for all these
people."
14 (For there were about five thousand
men.) And He said to His disciples, "Have
them [1]sit down *to eat* [a]in groups of about
fifty each."
15 They did so, and had them all [1]sit
down.
16 Then He took the five loaves and the
two fish, and looking up to heaven, He
blessed them, and broke *them*, and kept giving *them* to the disciples to set before the
[1]people.
17 And they all ate and were satisfied; and
[1]the broken pieces which they had left over
were picked up, twelve [a]baskets *full*.
18 [a]And it happened that while He was
[b]praying alone, the disciples were with Him,
and He questioned them, saying, "Who do
the [1]people say that I am?"
19 They answered and said, "John the
Baptist, and others *say* Elijah; but others,
that one of the prophets of old has risen
again."
20 And He said to them, "But who do you
say that I am?" And Peter answered and said,
"[a]The [1]Christ of God."
21 But He [1][a]warned them and instructed
them not to tell this to anyone,
22 [a]saying, "[b]The Son of Man must suffer
many things and be rejected by the elders
and chief priests and scribes, and be killed
and be raised up on the third day."
23 And He was saying to *them* all, "[a]If
anyone wishes to come after Me, he must
deny himself, and take up his cross daily and
follow Me.
24 "For [a]whoever wishes to save his [1]life
will lose it, but whoever loses his [1]life for My
sake, he is the one who will save it.
25 "For what is a man profited if he gains
the whole world, and [a]loses or forfeits himself?
26 "[a]For whoever is ashamed of Me and
My words, the Son of Man will be ashamed
of him when He comes in His glory, and *the
glory* of the Father and of the holy angels.
27 "But I say to you truthfully, [a]there are
some of those standing here who will not
taste death until they see the kingdom of
God."

The Transfiguration

28 [a]Some eight days after these sayings,
He took along [b]Peter and John and James,
and [c]went up on the mountain [d]to pray.
29 And while He was [a]praying, the
appearance of His face [b]became different,
and His clothing *became* white *and* [1]gleam-
ing.
30 And behold, two men were talking
with Him; and they were Moses and Elijah,
31 who, appearing in [1]glory, were speak-

12 [1]Lit *began to decline* [2]Lit *provisions*
14 [1]Lit *recline* [a]Mark 6:39
15 [1]Lit *recline*
16 [1]Lit *crowd*
17 [1]Lit *that which was left over to them of the broken pieces was* [a]Matt 14:20
18 [1]Lit *crowds* [a]Luke 9:18-20: *Matt 16:13-16; Mark 8:27-29* [b]Matt 14:23; Luke 6:12; 9:28
20 [1]I.e. Messiah [a]John 6:68f
21 [1]Or *strictly admonished* [a]Matt 8:4; 16:20; Mark 8:30
22 [a]Luke 9:22-27: *Matt 16:21-28; Mark 8:31-9:1* [b]Matt 16:21; Luke 9:44
23 [a]Matt 10:38; Luke 14:27
24 [1]Or *soul* [a]Matt 10:39; Luke 17:33; John 12:25
25 [a]Heb 10:34
26 [a]Matt 10:33; Luke 12:9
27 [a]Matt 16:28
28 [a]Luke 9:28-36: *Matt 17:1-8; Mark 9:2-8* [b]Matt 17:1 [c]Matt 5:1 [d]Luke 3:21; 5:16; 6:12; 9:18
29 [1]Lit *flashing like lightning* [a]Luke 3:21; 5:16; 6:12; 9:18 [b]Mark 16:12
31 [1]Or *splendor*

9:12 *the day was ending.* After the preaching and healing, the question was raised about food and lodging because they were in an isolated place. Jesus may have introduced the question (see John 6:5), but the Synoptics indicate that the disciples were also concerned.

9:14 *sit down to eat in groups of about fifty.* See note on Mark 6:40.

9:17 *the broken pieces . . . were picked up, twelve baskets full.* This act served as an example of avoiding wastefulness and as a demonstration that everyone had been adequately fed (see note on Mark 6:43).

9:18 *Who do the people say that I am?* The report brought by the disciples was the same as the one that reached Herod (see vv. 7–8). This event occurred to the north, outside Herod's territory, in the vicinity of Caesarea Philippi (see Matt 16:13 and note; see also note on Mark 7:24).

9:20 *Peter answered.* He was the spokesman for the disciples. *The Christ of God.* See note on 2:11. This predicted Deliverer (the Messiah) had been awaited for centuries (see John 4:25; see also notes on Matt 16:18; Mark 8:29).

9:21 *warned them . . . not to tell.* The people had false notions about the Messiah and needed to be taught further before Jesus identified Himself explicitly to the public. He had a crucial schedule to keep and could not be interrupted by premature reactions (see notes on Matt 8:4; 16:20; Mark 1:34).

9:22 *Son of Man.* See note on Mark 8:31. *must suffer.* Jesus' first explicit prediction of His death (for later references see v. 44; 12:50; 17:25; 18:31–33; cf. 24:7,25–27).

9:23 *take up his cross daily.* To follow Jesus requires self-denial, complete dedication and willing obedience. Luke emphasizes continued action, and "daily" is not mentioned explicitly in the parallel accounts (Matt 16:24–26; Mark 8:34). Disciples from Galilee knew what the cross meant, for hundreds of men had been executed by this means in their region.

9:24 *whoever loses his life for My sake.* A saying of Jesus found in all four Gospels and in two Gospels more than once (Matt 10:38–39; 16:24–25; Mark 8:34–35; Luke 14:26–27; 17:33; and, in slightly different form, John 12:25). No other saying of Jesus is given such emphasis.

9:26 *whoever is ashamed.* See 12:9; see also note on Mark 8:38.

9:27 See note on Matt 16:28. *kingdom of God.* See note on Matt 3:2.

9:28 *Some eight days.* Frequently used to indicate a week (cf. John 20:26; see note on Matt 17:1). *Peter and John and James.* These three were also with Jesus at the healing of Jairus's daughter (8:51) and in His last visit to Gethsemane (Mark 14:33). *on the mountain.* Although Mount Tabor is the traditional site of the Mount of Transfiguration, its distance from Caesarea Philippi (the vicinity of the last scene), its height (about 1,800 feet) and its occupation by a fortress make it unlikely. Mount Hermon fits the context much better by being both closer and higher (over 9,000 feet; see Mark 9:2). *pray.* Again Luke points out the place of prayer in an important event.

9:30 *Moses and Elijah.* Moses, the great OT deliverer and law-

ing of His [a]departure which He was about to
accomplish at Jerusalem.
32 Now Peter and his companions [a]had
been overcome with sleep; but when they
were fully awake, they saw His glory and the
two men standing with Him.
33 And as [1]these were leaving Him, Peter
said to Jesus, "[a]Master, it is good for us to be
here; [b]let us make three [2]tabernacles: one for
You, and one for Moses, and one for Elijah"—[c]not realizing what he was saying.
34 While he was saying this, a cloud
[1]formed and *began* to overshadow them; and
they were afraid as they entered the cloud.
35 Then [a]a voice came out of the cloud,
saying, "[b]This is My Son, *My* Chosen One;
listen to Him!"
36 And when the voice [1]had spoken,
Jesus was found alone. And [a]they kept
silent, and reported to no one in those days
any of the things which they had seen.
37 [a]On the next day, when they came
down from the mountain, a large crowd met
Him.
38 And a man from the crowd shouted,
saying, "Teacher, I beg You to look at my
son, for he is my [1]only *boy,*
39 and a spirit seizes him, and he suddenly screams, and it throws him into a convulsion with foaming *at the mouth;* and only
with difficulty does it leave him, mauling
him *as it leaves.*
40 "I begged Your disciples to cast it out,
and they could not."
41 And Jesus answered and said, "You
unbelieving and perverted generation, how
long shall I be with you and put up with
you? Bring your son here."
42 While he was still approaching, the
demon [1]slammed him *to the ground* and
threw him into a convulsion. But Jesus
rebuked the unclean spirit, and healed the
boy and gave him back to his father.
43 And they were all amazed at the
[1a]greatness of God.
[b]But while everyone was marveling at all
that He was doing, He said to His disciples,
44 "Let these words sink into your ears;
[a]for the Son of Man is going to be [1]delivered
into the hands of men."
45 But [a]they [1]did not understand this
statement, and it was concealed from them
so that they would not perceive it; and they
were afraid to ask Him about this statement.

The Test of Greatness

46 [a]An argument [1]started among them as
to which of them might be the greatest.
47 But Jesus, [a]knowing [1]what they were
thinking in their heart, took a child and
stood him by His side,
48 and said to them, "[a]Whoever receives
this child in My name receives Me, and whoever receives Me receives Him who sent Me;
[b]for the one who is least among all of you,
this is the one who is great."
49 [a]John answered and said, "[b]Master, we
saw someone casting out demons in Your
name; and we tried to prevent him because
he does not follow along with us."
50 But Jesus said to him, "Do not hinder
him; [a]for he who is not against you is [1]for
you."
51 When the days were approaching for
[a]His [1]ascension, He [2]was determined [b]to go
to Jerusalem;
52 and He sent messengers on ahead of
Him, and they went and entered a village of

31 [a]2 Pet 1:15
32 [a]Matt 26:43; Mark 14:40
33 [1]Lit *they* [2]Or *sacred tents* [a]Luke 5:5; 9:49 [b]Matt 17:4; Mark 9:5 [c]Mark 9:6
34 [1]Lit *occurred*
35 [a]2 Pet 1:17f [b]Is 42:1; Matt 3:17; 12:18; Mark 1:11; Luke 3:22
36 [1]Lit *occurred* [a]Matt 17:9; Mark 9:9f
37 [a]Luke 9:37-42: *Matt 17:14-18; Mark 9:14-27*
38 [1]Or *only begotten*
42 [1]Or *tore him*
43 [1]Or *majesty* [a]2 Pet 1:16 [b]Luke 9:43-45: *Matt 17:22f; Mark 9:30-32*
44 [1]Or *betrayed* [a]Luke 9:22
45 [1]Lit *were not knowing* [a]Mark 9:32
46 [1]Lit *entered in* [a]Luke 9:46-48: *Matt 18:1-5; Mark 9:33-37;* Luke 22:24
47 [1]Lit *the reasoning;* or *argument* [a]Matt 9:4
48 [a]Matt 10:40; Luke 10:16; John 13:20 [b]Luke 22:26
49 [a]Luke 9:49, 50: *Mark 9:38-40* [b]Luke 5:5; 9:33
50 [1]Or *on your side* [a]Matt 12:30; Luke 11:23
51 [1]Lit *taking up* [2]Lit *set His face* [a]Mark 16:19 [b]Luke 13:22; 17:11; 18:31; 19:11, 28

giver, and Elijah, the representative of the prophets. Moses' work had been finished by Joshua, Elijah's by Elisha (another form of the name Joshua). They now spoke with Jesus (whose Hebrew name was Joshua) about the "exodus" He was about to accomplish, by which He would deliver His people from the bondage of sin and bring to fulfillment the work of both Moses and Elijah (see note on 1 Kin 19:16).

9:31 *departure.* Greek *exodos,* a euphemism for Jesus' approaching death. It may also link Jesus' saving death and resurrection with God's saving of His people out of Egypt.

9:32 *overcome with sleep.* Perhaps the event was at night. *saw His glory.* See note on Ex 33:18.

9:33 *three tabernacles.* Temporary structures to prolong the visit of the three important persons: lawgiver, prophet and Messiah. The idea was not appropriate, however, because Jesus had a work to finish in His few remaining days on earth (see note on Mark 9:5).

9:35 *My Chosen One.* Related to a Jewish title found in Dead Sea Scrolls literature, and possibly echoing Is 42:1. See 23:35. "Chosen" parallels "beloved" in Matt 17:5 (see 2 Pet 1:17).

9:39 *a spirit seizes him.* This evil spirit was causing seizures (Matt 17:15) and a speechless condition (Mark 9:17). Evil spirits were responsible for many kinds of affliction (see note on 4:33).

9:44 Another prediction of Jesus' coming death (see note on v. 22), an indication of how it will be brought about (see 22:21).

9:46 *which . . . might be the greatest.* A subject that arose on a number of occasions (see 22:24; see also Mark 10:35–45).

9:48 *the one who is least . . . is great.* A person will become great as he sincerely and unpretentiously looks away from self to revere God.

9:49 *does not follow along with us.* Jesus shifts the pronoun to "you" in v. 50, which may mean that the man had a relationship to Jesus of which the disciples were unaware (see note on Mark 9:38).

9:50 *he who is not against you is for you.* Spoken in the context of opposition to the disciples' work (cf. 11:23, set in a different context).

9:51 *was determined to go to Jerusalem.* Lit. "set His face to go to Jerusalem" (cf. Is 50:7). Luke emphasizes Jesus' determination to complete His mission (see note on 13:22). This journey to Jerusalem, however, is not the one that led to His crucifixion but marks the beginning of a period of ministry in Judea, of which Jerusalem was the central city. Mark 10:1 notes this departure for Judea, which John more specifically describes as a journey to Jerusalem during the time of the Feast of Booths (John 7:1–10). The Judean ministry (see Introduction: Outline) is recounted in 9:51–13:21 and John 7:10–10:39.

9:52 *a village of the Samaritans.* Samaritans were particularly hostile to Jews who were on their way to observe religious festivals in Jerusalem. It was at least a three-day journey from Gal-

the [a]Samaritans to [1]make arrangements for Him.

53 But they did not receive Him, [a]because [1]He was traveling toward Jerusalem.

54 When His disciples [a]James and John saw *this,* they said, "Lord, do You want us to [b]command fire to come down from heaven and consume them?"

55 But He turned and rebuked them, [[1]and said, "You do not know what kind of spirit you are of;

56 for the Son of Man did not come to destroy men's lives, but to save them."] And they went on to another village.

Exacting Discipleship

57 [a]As they were going along the road, [b]someone said to Him, "I will follow You wherever You go."

58 And Jesus said to him, "The foxes have holes and the birds of the [1]air *have* [2]nests, but [a]the Son of Man has nowhere to lay His head."

59 And He said to another, "[a]Follow Me." But he said, "Lord, permit me first to go and bury my father."

60 But He said to him, "Allow the dead to bury their own dead; but as for you, go and [a]proclaim everywhere the kingdom of God."

61 Another also said, "I will follow You, Lord; but [a]first permit me to say good-bye to those at home."

62 But Jesus said to him, "[a]No one, after putting his hand to the plow and looking back, is fit for the kingdom of God."

The Seventy Sent Out

10 Now after this [a]the Lord appointed [1]seventy [b]others, and sent them [c]in pairs ahead of Him to every city and place where He Himself was going to come.

2 And He was saying to them, "[a]The harvest is plentiful, but the laborers are few; therefore beseech the Lord of the harvest to send out laborers into His harvest.

3 "Go; [a]behold, I send you out as lambs in the midst of wolves.

4 "[a]Carry no money belt, no [1]bag, no shoes; and greet no one on the way.

5 "Whatever house you enter, first say, 'Peace *be* to this house.'

6 "If a [1]man of peace is there, your peace will rest on him; but if not, it will return to you.

7 "Stay in [1]that house, eating and drinking [2]what they give you; for [a]the laborer is worthy of his wages. Do not keep moving from house to house.

8 "Whatever city you enter and they receive you, [a]eat what is set before you;

9 and heal those in it who are sick, and say to them, '[a]The kingdom of God has come near to you.'

10 "But whatever city you enter and they do not receive you, go out into its streets and say,

11 '[a]Even the dust of your city which clings to our feet we wipe off *in protest* against you; yet [1]be sure of this, that [b]the kingdom of God has come near.'

12 "I say to you, [a]it will be more tolerable in that day for [b]Sodom than for that city.

13 "[a]Woe to you, [b]Chorazin! Woe to you, [b]Bethsaida! For if the [1]miracles had been performed in [b]Tyre and Sidon which occurred in you, they would have repented long ago, sitting in [2c]sackcloth and ashes.

14 "But it will be more tolerable for [a]Tyre and Sidon in the judgment than for you.

15 "And you, [a]Capernaum, will not be exalted to heaven, will you? You will be brought down to Hades!

9:52 [1]Or *prepare* [a]Matt 10:5; Luke 10:33; 17:16; John 4:4
53 [1]Lit *His face was proceeding toward* [a]John 4:9
54 [a]Mark 3:17 [b]2 Kin 1:9-16
55 [1]Early mss do not contain bracketed portion
57 [a]Luke 9:51 [b]Luke 9:57-60: *Matt 8:19-22*
58 [1]Or *sky* [2]Or *roosting-places* [a]Matt 8:20
59 [a]Matt 8:22
60 [a]Matt 4:23
61 [a]1 Kin 19:20
62 [a]Phil 3:13
10:1 [1]Some mss read *seventy-two* [a]Luke 7:13 [b]Luke 9:1f, 52 [c]Mark 6:7
2 [a]Matt 9:37, 38; John 4:35
3 [a]Matt 10:16
4 [1]Or *knapsack or beggar's bag* [a]Matt 10:9-14; Mark 6:8-11; Luke 9:3-5; 10:4-12
6 [1]Lit *son of peace;* i.e. a person inclined toward peace
7 [1]Lit *the house itself* [2]Lit *the things from them* [a]Matt 10:10; 1 Cor 9:14; 1 Tim 5:18
8 [a]1 Cor 10:27
9 [a]Matt 3:2; 10:7; Luke 10:11
11 [1]Lit *know* [a]Matt 10:14; Mark 6:11; Luke 9:5; Acts 13:51 [b]Matt 3:2; 10:7; Luke 10:9
12 [a]Gen 19:24-28; Matt 10:15; 11:24 [b]Matt 10:15
13 [1]Or *works of power* [2]I.e. symbols of mourning [a]Luke 10:13-15: *Matt 11:21-23* [b]Is 23:1-18; Ezek 26:1-28:26; Joel 3:4-8; Matt 11:21 [c]Rev 11:3
14 [a]Matt 11:21
15 [a]Is 14:13-15; Matt 4:13; 11:23

---

ilee to Jerusalem through Samaria, and Samaritans refused overnight shelter for the pilgrims. Because of this antipathy, Jews traveling between Galilee and Jerusalem frequently went on the east side of the Jordan River.

9:54 *command fire to come down.* As Elijah had (2 Kin 1:9–16). James and John were known as "Sons of Thunder" (Mark 3:17).

9:55 *rebuked them.* See note on 2 Kin 1:10.

9:57 *As they were going along.* Continuing their journey through Samaria to Jerusalem.

9:59 *bury my father.* If his father had already died, the man would have been occupied with the burial then. But evidently he wanted to wait until after his father's death, which might have been years away. Jesus told him that the spiritually dead could bury the physically dead, and that the spiritually alive should be busy proclaiming the kingdom of God.

10:1 *appointed seventy.* Recorded only in Luke, though similar instructions were given to the twelve (Matt 9:37–38; 10:7–16; Mark 6:7–11; cf. Luke 9:3–5). Certain differences in early manuscripts make it unclear as to whether the number was 70 or 72. Jesus covered Judea with His message (see note on 9:51) as thoroughly as He had Galilee. *in pairs.* During His ministry in Galilee, Jesus had also sent out the twelve in pairs (see 9:1–6; Mark 6:7 and notes), a practice continued in the early church (Acts 13:2; 15:27,39–40; 17:14; 19:22).

10:4 *Carry no money belt, no bag, no shoes.* They were to travel light, without moneybag, luggage or extra sandals. *greet no one.* They were not to stop along the way to visit and exchange customary lengthy greetings. The mission was urgent.

10:7 *Do not keep moving.* See note on 9:4.

10:9 *The kingdom of God has come near.* The heart of Jesus' message (see notes on 4:43; Matt 3:2).

10:11 *dust . . . we wipe off.* See note on 9:5.

10:12 *more tolerable . . . for Sodom.* Although Sodom was so sinful that God destroyed it (Gen 19:24–28; Jude 7), the people who heard the message of Jesus and His disciples were even more accountable, because they had the gospel of the kingdom preached to them. *that day.* Judgment day.

10:13 *Chorazin . . . Bethsaida.* See note on Matt 11:21.

10:14 *Tyre and Sidon.* Gentile cities in Phoenicia, north of Galilee, which had not had opportunity to witness Jesus' miracles and hear His preaching as the people had in most of Galilee (see note on v. 12).

10:15 *Capernaum.* Jesus' headquarters on the north shore of Galilee (see Matt 4:13 and note), whose inhabitants had many

16 “[a]The one who listens to you listens to
Me, and [b]the one who rejects you rejects Me;
and he who rejects Me rejects the One who
sent Me.”

The Happy Results

17 The [1]seventy returned with joy, saying,
“Lord, even [a]the demons are subject to us in
Your name.”
18 And He said to them, “I was watching
[a]Satan fall from heaven like lightning.
19 “Behold, I have given you authority to
[a]tread on serpents and scorpions, and over
all the power of the enemy, and nothing will
injure you.
20 “Nevertheless do not rejoice in this, that
the spirits are subject to you, but rejoice that
[a]your names are recorded in heaven.”
21 [a]At that very [1]time He rejoiced greatly
in the Holy Spirit, and said, “I [2]praise You, O
Father, Lord of heaven and earth, that You
have hidden these things from *the* wise and
intelligent and have revealed them to infants.
Yes, Father, for this way was well-pleasing in
Your sight.
22 “[a]All things have been handed over to
Me by My Father, and [b]no one knows who
the Son is except the Father, and who the
Father is except the Son, and anyone to
whom the Son wills to reveal *Him*.”
23 [a]Turning to the disciples, He said privately, “Blessed *are* the eyes which see the
things you see,
24 for I say to you, that many prophets and
kings wished to see the things which you see,
and did not see *them*, and to hear the things
which you hear, and did not hear *them*.”
25 [a]And a [1b]lawyer stood up and put Him
to the test, saying, “Teacher, what shall I do
to inherit eternal life?”
26 And He said to him, “What is written
in the Law? [1]How does it read to you?”
27 And he answered, “[a]YOU SHALL LOVE THE
LORD YOUR GOD WITH ALL YOUR HEART, AND WITH
ALL YOUR SOUL, AND WITH ALL YOUR STRENGTH,
AND WITH ALL YOUR MIND; AND YOUR NEIGHBOR AS
YOURSELF.”
28 And He said to him, “You have answered correctly; [a]DO THIS AND YOU WILL LIVE.”
29 But wishing [a]to justify himself, he said
to Jesus, “And who is my neighbor?”

The Good Samaritan

30 Jesus replied and said, “A man was
[a]going down from Jerusalem to Jericho, and
fell among robbers, and they stripped him
and [1]beat him, and went away leaving him
half dead.
31 “And by chance a priest was going
down on that road, and when he saw him,
he passed by on the other side.
32 “Likewise a Levite also, when he came
to the place and saw him, passed by on the
other side.
33 “But a [a]Samaritan, who was on a journey, came upon him; and when he saw him,
he felt compassion,
34 and came to him and bandaged up his
wounds, pouring oil and wine on *them;* and
he put him on his own beast, and brought
him to an inn and took care of him.
35 “On the next day he took out two
[1]denarii and gave them to the innkeeper and
said, ‘Take care of him; and whatever more
you spend, when I return I will repay you.’
36 “Which of these three do you think
proved to be a neighbor to the man who fell
into the robbers’ *hands?*”
37 And he said, “The one who showed
mercy toward him.” Then Jesus said to him,
“Go and do [1]the same.”

Martha and Mary

38 Now as they were traveling along, He
entered a village; and a woman named [a]Mar-
tha welcomed Him into her home.

16 [a]Matt 10:40; Mark 9:37; Luke 9:48; John 13:20; Gal 4:14 [b]John 12:48; 1 Thess 4:8
17 [1]Some mss read *seventy-two* [a]Mark 16:17
18 [a]Matt 4:10
19 [a]Ps 91:13; Mark 16:18
20 [a]Ex 32:32; Ps 69:28; Is 4:3; Ezek 13:9; Dan 12:1; Phil 4:3; Heb 12:23; Rev 3:5; 13:8; 17:8; 20:12, 15; 21:27
21 [1]Lit *hour* [2]Or *acknowledge to You* [a]Luke 10:21, 22: *Matt 11:25-27*
22 [a]John 3:35 [b]John 10:15
23 [a]Luke 10:23, 24: *Matt 13:16, 17*
25 [1]I.e. an expert in the Mosaic Law [a]Luke 10:25-28: *Matt 22:34-40; Mark 12:28-31;* Matt 19:16-19 [b]Matt 22:35
26 [1]Lit *How do you read?*
27 [a]Deut 6:5; Lev 19:18
28 [a]Lev 18:5; Ezek 20:11; Matt 19:17
29 [a]Luke 16:15
30 [1]Lit *laid blows upon* [a]Luke 18:31; 19:28
33 [a]Matt 10:5; Luke 9:52
35 [1]The denarius was equivalent to a day's wages
37 [1]Or *likewise*
38 [a]Luke 10:40f; John 11:1, 5, 19ff, 30, 39; 12:2

opportunities to see and hear Jesus. Therefore the condemnation for their rejection was the greater.

10:18 *Satan fall.* Even the demons were driven out by the disciples (v. 17), which meant that Satan was suffering defeat.

10:19 *serpents and scorpions . . . power of the enemy.* The snakes and scorpions may represent evil spirits; the enemy is Satan himself.

10:20 Man's salvation is more important than power to overcome the evil one or escape his harm. *your names are recorded.* Salvation is recorded in heaven (see Ps 69:28; Dan 12:1; Phil 4:3; Heb 12:23; Rev 3:5).

10:25 *lawyer.* A scholar well versed in Scripture asked a common question (18:18; cf. Matt 22:35), either to take issue with Jesus or simply to see what kind of teacher He was. See note on 7:30.

10:27 *LOVE . . . GOD . . . YOUR NEIGHBOR.* Elsewhere Jesus uses these words in reply to another question (Matt 22:35–40; Mark 12:28–32), putting the same two Scriptures together (Deut 6:5; Lev 19:18). Whether a fourfold love (heart, soul, strength and mind, as here and in Mark 12:30) or threefold (Deut 6:5; Matt 22:37; Mark 12:33), the significance is that total devotion is demanded.

10:29 *to justify himself.* The answer to his first question was obviously one he knew, so to gain credibility he asked for an interpretation. In effect he said, "But the real question is: Who is my neighbor?"

10:30 *Jerusalem to Jericho.* A distance of 17 miles and a descent from about 2,500 feet above sea level to about 800 feet below sea level. The road ran through rocky, desert country, which provided places for robbers to waylay defenseless travelers.

10:31–33 *priest . . . Levite . . . Samaritan.* It is significant that the person Jesus commended was neither the religious leader nor the lay associate, but a hated foreigner. Jews viewed Samaritans as half-breeds, both physically (see note on Matt 10:5) and spiritually (see notes on John 4:20,22). Samaritans and Jews practiced open hostility (see note on 9:52), but Jesus asserted that love knows no national boundaries.

10:35 *two denarii.* Two days' wages, which would keep a man up to two months in an inn.

10:36 *Which . . . proved to be a neighbor to the man . . . ?* The question now became: Who proves he is the good neighbor by his actions?

10:38 *a village.* Bethany, about two miles from Jerusalem, was the home of Mary and Martha (John 12:1–3).

39 She had a sister called [a]Mary, who was
[b]seated at the Lord's feet, listening to His
word.
40 But [a]Martha was distracted with [1]all
her preparations; and she came up *to Him*
and said, "Lord, do You not care that my sister has left me to do all the serving alone?
Then tell her to help me."
41 But the Lord answered and said to her,
"[a]Martha, Martha, you are [b]worried and
bothered about so many things;
42 [a]but *only* one thing is necessary, for
[b]Mary has chosen the good part, which shall
not be taken away from her."

Instruction about Prayer

11 It happened that while [1]Jesus was praying in a certain place, after He had finished, one of His disciples said to Him,
"Lord, teach us to pray just as John also
taught his disciples."
2 And He said to them, "[a]When you
pray, say:
'[1]Father, hallowed be Your name.
Your kingdom come.
3 'Give us [a]each day our [1]daily bread.
4 'And forgive us our sins,
For we ourselves also forgive everyone
who [a]is indebted to us.
And lead us not into temptation.' "
5 Then He said to them, "[1]Suppose one
of you has a friend, and goes to him at midnight and says to him, 'Friend, lend me three
loaves;
6 for a friend of mine has come to me
from a journey, and I have nothing to set
before him';
7 and from inside he answers and says,
'Do not bother me; the door has already
been shut and my children [1]and I are in bed;
I cannot get up and give you *anything*.'
8 "I tell you, even though he will not get
up and give him *anything* because he is his
friend, yet [a]because of his [1]persistence he
will get up and give him as much as he
needs.
9 "So I say to you, [1][a]ask, and it will be
given to you; [2]seek, and you will find;
[3]knock, and it will be opened to you.
10 "For everyone who asks, receives; and
he who seeks, finds; and to him who knocks,
it will be opened.
11 "Now [1]suppose one of you fathers is
asked by his son for a [2]fish; he will not give
him a snake instead of a fish, will he?
12 "Or *if* he is asked for an egg, he will not
give him a scorpion, will he?
13 "[a]If you then, being evil, know how to
give good gifts to your children, how much
more will *your* [1]heavenly Father give the
Holy Spirit to those who ask Him?"

Pharisees' Blasphemy

14 [a]And He was casting out a demon, and
it was mute; when the demon had gone out,
the mute man spoke; and the crowds were
amazed.
15 But some of them said, "He casts out
demons [a]by [b]Beelzebul, the ruler of the
demons."
16 Others, [1]to test *Him*, [a]were demanding
of Him a [2]sign from heaven.
17 [a]But He knew their thoughts and said
to them, "[1]Any kingdom divided against
itself is laid waste; and a house *divided*
against [2]itself falls.
18 "If [a]Satan also is divided against himself, how will his kingdom stand? For you
say that I cast out demons by [b]Beelzebul.
19 "And if I by [a]Beelzebul cast out demons,
by whom do your sons cast them out? So
they will be your judges.
20 "But if I cast out demons by the [a]finger
of God, then [b]the kingdom of God has come
upon you.

39 [a]Luke 10:42; John 11:1f, 19f, 28, 31f, 45; 12:3 [b]Luke 8:35; Acts 22:3
40 [1]Lit *much service* [a]Luke 10:38, 41; John 11:1, 5, 19ff, 30, 39; 12:2
41 [a]Luke 10:38, 40; John 11:1, 5, 19ff, 30, 39; 12:2 [b]Matt 6:25
42 [a]Ps 27:4; John 6:27 [b]Luke 10:39; John 11:1f, 19f, 28, 31f, 45; 12:3
11:1 [1]Lit *He*
2 [1]Later mss add phrases from Matt 6:9-13 to make the two passages closely similar [a]Luke 11:2-4: *Matt 6:9-13*
3 [1]Or *bread for the coming day* or *needful bread* [a]Acts 17:11
4 [a]Luke 13:4 mg
5 [1]Lit *Which one of you will have*
7 [1]Lit *with me*
8 [1]Lit *shamelessness* [a]Luke 18:1-5
9 [1]Or *keep asking* [2]Or *keep seeking* [3]Or *keep knocking* [a]Luke 11:9-13: *Matt 7:7-11*
11 [1]Lit *which of you, a son, will ask the father* [2]Two early mss insert *loaf, he will not give him a stone, will he, or for a*
13 [1]Lit *Father from heaven* [a]Matt 7:11; Luke 18:7f
14 [a]Luke 11:14, 15: *Matt 12:22, 24;* Matt 9:32-34
15 [a]Matt 9:34 [b]Matt 10:25
16 [1]Lit *testing* [2]Or *attesting miracle* [a]Matt 12:38; 16:1; Mark 8:11
17 [1]Lit *every* [2]Lit *a house* [a]Luke 11:17-22: *Matt 12:25-29; Mark 3:23-27*
18 [a]Matt 4:10 [b]Matt 10:25
19 [a]Matt 10:25
20 [a]Ex 8:19 [b]Matt 3:2

11:1 *Jesus was praying.* Not only on special occasions (e.g., baptism, 3:21; choosing the twelve, 6:12; Gethsemane, 22:41) but also as a regular practice (5:16; Matt 14:23; Mark 1:35). *teach us to pray.* The Lord's model prayer was given here in answer to a request, and is similar to Matt 6:9–13, where it is a part of the Sermon on the Mount. Six petitions are included in the prayer as given in the Sermon on the Mount by Matthew (combining the last two petitions into one), whereas five appear in the prayer in Luke.

11:4 *forgive us our sins.* Matt 6:12 has "debts," but the meaning is the same as "sins." Jesus taught this truth on other occasions as well (Matt 18:35; Mark 11:25). The prayer is a pattern for believers, who have already been forgiven for their sins. Jesus speaks here of daily forgiveness, which is necessary to restore broken communion with God.

11:5–13 Jesus now urged persistence in prayer (vv. 5–8) and gave assurance that God answers prayer (vv. 9–13). The argument is from the lesser to the greater (see v. 13).

11:13 *give the Holy Spirit.* Matt 7:11 has "give what is good," probably referring to spiritual gifts. Luke emphasizes the work of the Spirit, the greatest of God's gifts.

11:14 *demon, and it was mute.* See note on 4:33. This evil spirit caused muteness. The probable parallel passage in Matthew (12:22–30; see also Mark 3:20–27) indicates that the man was also blind.

11:15 *Beelzebul, the ruler of the demons.* Satan (v. 18). See note on Matt 10:25.

11:16 *a sign from heaven.* Jesus had just healed a mute. Here was their sign, and they would not recognize it.

11:17 *kingdom divided against itself.* If Satan gave power to Jesus, who opposed Him in every way, Satan would be supporting an attack upon himself.

11:19 *by whom do your sons . . . ?* Jesus did not say whether the followers of the Pharisees (see Matt 12:24) actually drove out demons (see note on v. 24); but they claimed to drive them out by the power of God, and Jesus claimed the same. So to accuse Jesus of using Satanic power was implicitly to condemn their own followers as well. *your judges.* They will condemn you for your accusation against them.

11:20 *the kingdom of God has come.* In the sense that the King was present in the person of Jesus (see note on 4:43) and that the powers of evil were being overthrown.

21 "When [1]a strong *man,* fully armed,
guards his own house, his possessions are
[2]undisturbed.
22 "But when someone stronger than he
attacks him and overpowers him, he takes
away from him all his armor on which he
had relied and distributes his plunder.
23 "[a]He who is not with Me is against Me;
and he who does not gather with Me, scatters.
24 "[a]When the unclean spirit goes out of [1]a
man, it passes through waterless places
seeking rest, and not finding any, it says, 'I
will return to my house from which I came.'
25 "And when it comes, it finds it swept
and put in order.
26 "Then it goes and takes *along* seven other spirits more evil than itself, and they go in
and live there; and the last state of that man
becomes worse than the first."
27 While [1]Jesus was saying these things,
one of the women in the crowd raised her
voice and said to Him, "[a]Blessed is the
womb that bore You and the breasts at which
You nursed."
28 But He said, "On the contrary, blessed
are [a]those who hear the word of God and
observe it."

The Sign of Jonah

29 As the crowds were increasing, He
began to say, "[a]This generation is a wicked
generation; it [b]seeks for a [1]sign, and *yet* no
[1]sign will be given to it but the [1]sign of
Jonah.
30 "For just as [a]Jonah became a [1]sign to
the Ninevites, so will the Son of Man be to
this generation.
31 "The [a]Queen of the South will rise up
with the men of this generation at the judgment and condemn them, because she came
from the ends of the earth to hear the wisdom of Solomon; and behold, something
greater than Solomon is here.
32 "The men of Nineveh will stand up with
this generation at the judgment and condemn it, because [a]they repented at the
preaching of Jonah; and behold, something
greater than Jonah is here.
33 "[a]No one, after lighting a lamp, puts it
away in a cellar nor under a basket, but on
the lampstand, so that those who enter may
see the light.
34 "[a]The eye is the lamp of your body;
when your eye is [1]clear, your whole body
also is full of light; but when it is [2]bad, your
body also is full of darkness.
35 "Then watch out that the light in you is
not darkness.
36 "If therefore your whole body is full of
light, with no dark part in it, it will be wholly illumined, as when the lamp illumines you
with its rays."

Woes upon the Pharisees

37 Now when He had spoken, a Pharisee
*asked Him to have lunch with him; and He
went in, and reclined *at the table.*
38 When the Pharisee saw it, he was surprised that He had not first [1][a]ceremonially
washed before the [2]meal.
39 But [a]the Lord said to him, "Now [b]you
Pharisees clean the outside of the cup and of
the platter; but [1]inside of you, you are full of
robbery and wickedness.
40 "[a]You foolish ones, did not He who
made the outside make the inside also?

21 [1]Lit *the* [2]Lit *in peace*
23 [a]Matt 12:30; Mark 9:40
24 [1]Lit *the* [a]Luke 11:24-26: *Matt 12:43-45*
27 [1]Lit *He* [a]Luke 23:29
28 [a]Luke 8:21
29 [1]Or *attesting miracle* [a]Luke 11:29-32: *Matt 12:39-42;* Matt 16:4; Mark 8:12 [b]Matt 12:38; Luke 11:16
30 [1]Or *attesting miracle* [a]Jon 3:4
31 [a]1 Kin 10:1-10; 2 Chr 9:1-12
32 [a]Jon 3:5
33 [a]Matt 5:15; Mark 4:21; Luke 8:16
34 [1]Or *healthy* [2]Or *evil* [a]Luke 11:34, 35: *Matt 6:22, 23*
38 [1]Lit *baptized* [2]Or *lunch* [a]Matt 15:2; Mark 7:3f
39 [1]Lit *your inside is full* [a]Luke 7:13 [b]Matt 23:25f
40 [a]Luke 12:20; 1 Cor 15:36

11:22 *someone stronger . . . attacks.* Jesus was stronger than Beelzebub, and by His exorcism of demons He demonstrated that He had overpowered Satan and disarmed him. It was therefore foolish to suggest that Jesus had cast out demons by Satan's power.

11:23 The one who does not intentionally support Jesus opposes Him, making neutrality impossible. Even the worker in 9:50, whom the disciples said "does not follow along with us" (9:49), was apparently a believer, acting in Jesus' name (see note on Mark 9:38), and Jesus did not condemn him.

11:24 *unclean spirit goes out.* Jesus is perhaps referring to the work of Jewish exorcists, who claimed to cast out demons (cf. v. 19) but who rejected the kingdom of God and whose exorcisms were therefore ineffective. See Matt 12:43–45, where Jesus makes a similar comment about the Jewish nation of that day.

11:25 *finds it swept.* The place had been cleaned up but left unoccupied. A life reformed but lacking God's presence is open to reoccupancy by evil.

11:29 *seeks for a sign.* On several occasions Jews asked for miraculous signs (v. 16; Matt 12:38; Mark 8:11), but Jesus rejected their requests because they had wrong motives.

11:30 *as Jonah became a sign.* Jonah spent three days (see note on Matt 12:40) "buried" in the huge fish, just as Jesus would be buried for three days before His resurrection.

11:31–32 *something greater than Solomon . . . something greater than Jonah.* Jesus argued from the lesser to the greater. If the queen of Sheba responded positively to the wisdom of Solomon, and the men of Nineveh to the preaching of Jonah, how much more should the people of Jesus' day have responded to the ministry of Jesus, who is infinitely greater than Solomon or Jonah!

11:31 *The Queen of the South.* The queen of Sheba (see 1 Kin 10:1–10 and notes).

11:33 *a basket.* A container holding about one peck. *may see the light.* A lamp is meant to give light to those who are near it (see v. 36). Jesus had publicly exhibited the light of the gospel for all to see, but "a wicked generation" (v. 29) requested more spectacular signs. The problem was not with any failure on Jesus' part in giving light; it was with the faulty vision of his audience.

11:34 *your eye is clear.* Those asking for a sign do not need more light; they need clear eyes to allow the light to enter.

11:38 *had not first ceremonially washed.* Not commanded in the law but added in the tradition of the Pharisees (Mark 7:3; cf. Matt 15:9).

11:39 *clean the outside.* Engage in ceremonial washings of the body. *robbery and wickedness.* These Pharisees were more concerned about keeping ceremonies than about being moral (cf. Mark 7:20–23).

11:40 *make the inside also.* The inside of man (the "heart" and inner righteousness) is more important than the outside (ceremonial cleansing).

41 "But [a]give that which is within as charity, and [1]then all things are [b]clean for you.

42 "[a]But woe to you Pharisees! For you [b]pay tithe of mint and rue and every *kind of* garden herb, and *yet* disregard justice and the love of God; but these are the things you should have done without neglecting the others.

43 "Woe to you Pharisees! For you [a]love the chief seats in the synagogues and the respectful greetings in the market places.

44 "[a]Woe to you! For you are like [1]concealed tombs, and the people who walk over *them* are unaware *of it.*"

45 One of the [1][a]lawyers *said to Him in reply, "Teacher, when You say this, You insult us too."

46 But He said, "Woe to you [a]lawyers as well! For [b]you weigh men down with burdens hard to bear, [1]while you yourselves will not even touch the burdens with one of your fingers.

47 "[a]Woe to you! For you build the [1]tombs of the prophets, and *it was* your fathers *who* killed them.

48 "So you are witnesses and approve the deeds of your fathers; because it was they who killed them, and you build *their tombs.*

49 "For this reason also [a]the wisdom of God said, '[b]I will send to them prophets and apostles, and *some* of them they will kill and *some* they will [1]persecute,

50 so that the blood of all the prophets, shed [a]since the foundation of the world, may be [1]charged against this generation,

51 from [a]the blood of Abel to [b]the blood of Zechariah, who was killed between the altar and the house *of God;* yes, I tell you, it shall be [1]charged against this generation.'

52 "Woe to you [1][a]lawyers! For you have taken away the key of knowledge; [b]you yourselves did not enter, and you hindered those who were entering."

53 When He left there, the scribes and the Pharisees began to be very hostile and to question Him closely on many subjects,

54 [a]plotting against Him [b]to catch [1]*Him* in something He might say.

God Knows and Cares

12 Under these circumstances, after [1]so many thousands of [2]people had gathered together that they were stepping on one another, He began saying to His disciples first *of all,* "[a]Beware of the leaven of the Pharisees, which is hypocrisy.

2 "[a]But there is nothing covered up that will not be revealed, and hidden that will not be known.

3 "Accordingly, whatever you have said in the dark will be heard in the light, and what you have [1]whispered in the inner rooms will be proclaimed upon [a]the housetops.

4 "I say to you, [a]My friends, do not be afraid of those who kill the body and after that have no more that they can do.

5 "But I will [1]warn you whom to fear: [a]fear the One who, after He has killed, has authority to cast into [2][b]hell; yes, I tell you, fear Him!

6 "Are not [a]five sparrows sold for two [1]cents? *Yet* not one of them is forgotten before God.

7 "[a]Indeed, the very hairs of your head are all numbered. Do not fear; you are more valuable than many sparrows.

41 [1]Lit *behold* [a]Luke 12:33; 16:9 [b]Mark 7:19; Titus 1:15 **42** [a]Matt 23:23 [b]Lev 27:30; Luke 18:12 **43** [a]Matt 23:6f; Mark 12:38f; Luke 14:7; 20:46 **44** [1]Or *indistinct, unseen* [a]Matt 23:27 **45** [1]I.e. experts in the Mosaic Law [a]Matt 22:35; Luke 11:46, 52 **46** [1]Lit *and* [a]Matt 22:35; Luke 11:45, 52 [b]Matt 23:4 **47** [1]Or *monuments to* [a]Matt 23:29ff **49** [1]Or *drive out* [a]1 Cor 1:24, 30; Col 2:3 [b]Matt 23:34-36 **50** [1]Or *required of* [a]Matt 25:34 **51** [1]Or *required of* [a]Gen 4:8 [b]2 Chr 24:20, 21

52 [1]I.e. experts in the Mosaic Law [a]Matt 22:35; Luke 11:45, 46 [b]Matt 23:13 **54** [1]Lit *something out of His mouth* [a]Mark 3:2; Luke 20:20; Acts 23:21 [b]Mark 12:13 **12:1** [1]Lit *myriads* [2]Lit *the crowd* [a]Matt 16:6, 11f; Mark 8:15 **2** [a]Luke 12:2-9: *Matt 10:26-33;* Matt 10:26; Mark 4:22; Luke 8:17 **3** [1]Lit *spoken in the ear* [a]Matt 10:27; 24:17 **4** [a]John 15:13-15 **5** [1]Or *show* [2]Gr *Gehenna* [a]Heb 10:31 [b]Matt 5:22 **6** [1]Gr *assaria,* the smallest of copper coins [a]Matt 10:29 **7** [a]Matt 10:30

11:41 *all things are clean.* Giving from the heart makes everything else right. If one gives to the poor, his heart is no longer in the grip of "robbery and wickedness" (v. 39).

11:44 *concealed tombs.* The Jews whitewashed their tombs so that no one would accidentally touch them and be defiled (cf. Num 19:16; Matt 23:27). Just as touching a grave resulted in ceremonial uncleanness, being influenced by these corrupt religious leaders could lead to moral uncleanness.

11:45 *lawyers.* See note on 7:30.

11:46 *weigh men down.* By adding rules and regulations to the authentic law of Moses (see note on Matt 15:2) and doing nothing to help others keep them (Matt 23:4), while inventing ways for themselves to circumvent them.

11:47 *tombs of the prophets.* Outwardly these "lawyers" (v. 46) appeared to honor the prophets in building or rebuilding memorials, but inwardly they rejected the Christ the prophets announced. They lived in opposition to the teachings of the prophets, just as their forefathers had done.

11:49 *the wisdom of God said.* Not a quotation from the OT or any other known book. It may refer to God speaking through Jesus, or it may be referring in quotation form to God's decision to send prophets and apostles even though He knew they would be rejected.

11:51 *blood of Abel . . . Zechariah.* See note on Matt 23:35.

11:52 *the key of knowledge.* The very persons who should have opened the people's minds concerning the law obscured their understanding by faulty interpretation and an erroneous system of theology. They kept themselves and the people in ignorance of the way of salvation, or, as Matthew's account puts it, they "shut off the kingdom of heaven from people" (Matt 23:13).

11:54 *plotting . . . to catch Him.* The determination of the religious leaders to trap Jesus is evident throughout Luke (6:11; 19:47–48; 20:19–20; 22:2).

12:1 *leaven of the Pharisees.* See note on Mark 8:15.

12:2 *nothing covered up that will not be revealed.* In this context the meaning is that nothing hidden through hypocrisy will fail to be made known.

12:3 *inner rooms.* Storerooms were surrounded by other rooms so that no one could dig in from outside.

12:4 *after that have no more that they can do.* Encouragement in the face of persecution (see Matt 10:28).

12:5 *authority to cast into hell.* God alone has this power. The Greek word for "hell" is *ge(h)enna* (see note on Matt 5:22), not to be confused with Hades, the general name for the place of the dead. In the NT *ge(h)enna* is used only in Matthew, Mark, James 3:6 and here. *fear Him.* Respect His authority, stand in awe of His majesty and trust in Him. Verses 6–7 give the basis for trust.

12:6 *five sparrows sold for two cents.* God even cares for little birds, sold cheaply for food. Three words used for Roman coins are *denarius* (Matt 18:28), *assarion* (Matt 10:29, NASB marg.) and *quadrans* (Matt 5:26, NASB marg.), very loosely related to each other as are a 50-cent piece, nickel and penny. The coins here

8 "And I say to you, everyone who [a]confesses Me before men, the Son of Man will confess him also before the angels of God;

9 but [a]he who denies Me before men will be denied [b]before the angels of God.

10 "[a]And everyone who [1]speaks a word against the Son of Man, it will be forgiven him; but he who blasphemes against the Holy Spirit, it will not be forgiven him.

11 "When they bring you before [a]the synagogues and the rulers and the authorities, do not [b]worry about how or what you are to speak in your defense, or what you are to say;

12 for [a]the Holy Spirit will teach you in that very hour what you ought to say."

Covetousness Denounced

13 Someone [1]in the crowd said to Him, "Teacher, tell my brother to divide the *family* inheritance with me."

14 But He said to him, "[a]Man, who appointed Me a judge or arbitrator over you?"

15 Then He said to them, "[a]Beware, and be on your guard against every form of greed; for not *even* when one has an abundance does his life consist of his possessions."

16 And He told them a parable, saying, "The land of a rich man was very productive.

17 "And he began reasoning to himself, saying, 'What shall I do, since I have no place to store my crops?'

18 "Then he said, 'This is what I will do: I will tear down my barns and build larger ones, and there I will store all my grain and my goods.

19 'And I will say to my soul, "Soul, [a]you have many goods laid up for many years *to come;* take your ease, eat, drink *and* be merry." '

20 "But God said to him, '[a]You fool! This *very* night [1][b]your soul is required of you; and [c]*now* who will own what you have prepared?'

21 "So is the man who [a]stores up treasure for himself, and is not rich toward God."

22 And He said to His disciples, "[a]For this reason I say to you, [1]do not worry about *your* [2]life, *as to* what you will eat; nor for your body, *as to* what you will put on.

23 "For life is more than food, and the body more than clothing.

24 "Consider the [a]ravens, for they neither sow nor reap; they have no storeroom nor [b]barn, and *yet* God feeds them; how much more valuable you are than the birds!

25 "And which of you by worrying can add a *single* [1][a]hour to his [2]life's span?

26 "If then you cannot do even a very little thing, why do you worry about other matters?

27 "Consider the lilies, how they grow: they neither toil nor spin; but I tell you, not even [a]Solomon in all his glory clothed himself like one of these.

28 "But if God so clothes the grass in the field, which is *alive* today and tomorrow is thrown into the furnace, how much more *will He clothe* you? [a]You men of little faith!

29 "And do not seek what you will eat and what you will drink, and do not [a]keep worrying.

30 "For [1]all these things the nations of the world eagerly seek; but your Father knows that you need these things.

31 "But seek His kingdom, and [a]these things will be added to you.

32 "[a]Do not be afraid, [b]little flock, for [c]your Father has chosen gladly to give you the kingdom.

33 "[a]Sell your possessions and give to charity; make yourselves money belts which do not wear out, [b]an unfailing treasure in heaven, where no thief comes near nor moth destroys.

34 "For [a]where your treasure is, there your heart will be also.

Be in Readiness

35 "[1][a]Be dressed in [b]readiness, and *keep* your lamps lit.

36 "Be like men who are waiting for their master when he returns from the wedding feast, so that they may immediately open *the door* to him when he comes and knocks.

37 "Blessed are those slaves whom the master will find [a]on the alert when he comes; truly I say to you, that [b]he will gird

8 [a]Matt 10:32; Luke 15:10; Rom 10:9
9 [a]Matt 10:33; Luke 9:26 [b]Luke 15:10
10 [1]Lit *will speak* [a]Matt 12:31, 32; Mark 3:28-30
11 [a]Matt 10:17 [b]Matt 6:25; 10:19; Mark 13:11; Luke 12:22; 21:14
12 [a]Matt 10:20; Luke 21:15
13 [1]Lit *out of*
14 [a]Mic 6:8; Rom 2:1, 3; 9:20
15 [a]1 Tim 6:6-10
19 [a]Eccl 11:9
20 [1]Lit *they are demanding your soul from you* [a]Jer 17:11; Luke 11:40 [b]Job 27:8 [c]Ps 39:6
21 [a]Luke 12:33
22 [1]Or *stop being worried* [a]Luke 12:22-31: *Matt 6:25-33*
22 [2]Lit *soul*
24 [a]Job 38:41 [b]Luke 12:18
25 [1]Lit *cubit* (approx 18 in.) [2]Or *height* [a]Ps 39:5
27 [a]1 Kin 10:4-7; 2 Chr 9:3-6
28 [a]Matt 6:30
29 [a]Matt 6:31
30 [1]Or *these things all the nations of the world*
31 [a]Matt 6:33
32 [a]Matt 14:27 [b]John 21:15-17 [c]Eph 1:5, 9
33 [a]Matt 19:21; Luke 11:41; 18:22 [b]Matt 6:20; Luke 12:21
34 [a]Matt 6:21
35 [1]Lit *Let your loins be girded* [a]Matt 25:1ff [b]Eph 6:14; 1 Pet 1:13
37 [a]Matt 24:42 [b]Luke 17:8; John 13:4

are *assaria,* so the transaction would be something like five birds for two nickels.

12:8 *confesses Me.* When a person acknowledges that Jesus is the Messiah, the Son of God (Matt 16:16; 1 John 2:22), Jesus acknowledges that the individual is His loyal follower (cf. Matt 7:21).

12:9 *will be denied.* See 9:26; 2 Tim 2:12; cf. Matt 7:21; 25:41–46. The same word is used in Peter's denial (22:34, 61).

12:10 *blasphemes against the Holy Spirit.* See note on Matt 12:31; cf. Mark 3:28–29.

12:13 *divide the family inheritance.* Deut 21:17 gave the general rule that an elder son received double a younger one's portion. Disputes over such matters were normally settled by rabbis. This man's request of Jesus was selfish and materialistic. There is no indication that the man had been listening seriously to what Jesus had been saying (cf. vv. 1–11). Jesus replied with a parable about the consequences of greed.

12:16 *parable.* See note on 8:4.

12:20 *fool!* A strong word (11:40; Eph 5:17).

12:31 *seek His kingdom.* Since v. 32 suggests that Jesus is speaking to believers, who already possess the kingdom, this command probably means that Christians should seek the spiritual benefits of the kingdom rather than the material goods of the world (cf. Matt 6:33).

12:33 *give to charity.* The danger of riches and the need for giving are characteristic themes in Luke (3:11; 6:30; 11:41; 14:13–14; 16:9; 18:22; 19:8).

12:37 *gird himself to serve.* The master reverses the normal roles and serves the slaves (cf. 22:27; Mark 10:45; John 13:4–5, 12–16).

himself *to serve,* and have them recline *at the*
table, and will come up and wait on them.
38 "[a]Whether he comes in the [1]second
watch, or even in the [2]third, and finds *them*
so, blessed are those *slaves.*
39 "[a]But [1]be sure of this, that if the head of
the house had known at what hour the thief
was coming, he would not have allowed his
house to be [2b]broken into.
40 "[a]You too, be ready; for the Son of Man is
coming at an hour that you do not [1]expect."
41 Peter said, "Lord, are You addressing this
parable to us, or [a]to everyone *else* as well?"
42 And [a]the Lord said, "[b]Who then is the
faithful and sensible [c]steward, whom his
master will put in charge of his [1]servants, to
give them their rations at the proper time?
43 "Blessed is that [a]slave whom his [1]mas-
ter finds so doing when he comes.
44 "Truly I say to you that he will put him
in charge of all his possessions.
45 "But if that slave says in his heart, 'My
master [1]will be a long time in coming,' and
begins to beat the slaves, *both* men and
women, and to eat and drink and get drunk;
46 the master of that slave will come on a
day when he does not expect *him* and at an
hour he does not know, and will cut him in
pieces, and assign him a place with the
unbelievers.
47 "And that slave who knew his master's
will and did not get ready or act in accord
with his will, will [a]receive many lashes,
48 but the one who did not [a]know *it,* and
committed deeds worthy of [1]a flogging, will
receive but few. [b]From everyone who has
been given much, much will be required;
and to whom they entrusted much, of him
they will ask all the more.

Christ Divides Men

49 "I [1]have come to cast fire upon the earth;
and [2]how I wish it were already kindled!
50 "But I have a [a]baptism to [1]undergo, and
how distressed I am until it is accomplished!
51 "[a]Do you suppose that I came to grant
peace on earth? I tell you, no, but rather division;
52 for from now on five *members* in one
household will be divided, three against two
and two against three.
53 "They will be divided, [a]father against
son and son against father, mother against
daughter and daughter against mother,
mother-in-law against daughter-in-law and
daughter-in-law against mother-in-law."
54 And He was also saying to the crowds,
"[a]When you see a cloud rising in the west,
immediately you say, 'A shower is coming,'
and so it turns out.
55 "And when *you see* a south wind blowing, you say, 'It will be a [a]hot day,' and it
turns out *that way.*
56 "You hypocrites! [a]You know how to analyze the appearance of the earth and the sky,
but [1]why do you not analyze this present
time?
57 "And [a]why do you not even on your
own initiative judge what is right?
58 "For [a]while you are going with your
opponent to appear before the magistrate, on
your way *there* make an effort to [1]settle with
him, so that he may not drag you before the
judge, and the judge turn you over to the
officer, and the officer throw you into prison.
59 "I say to you, you will not get out of
there until you have paid the very last
[1a]cent."

Call to Repent

13 Now on the same occasion there were
some present who reported to Him
about the Galileans whose blood [a]Pilate had
[1]mixed with their sacrifices.
2 And Jesus said to them, "[a]Do you sup-

38 [1]I.e. 9 p.m. to midnight [2]I.e. midnight to 3 a.m. [a]Matt 24:43
39 [1]Lit *know* [2]Lit *dug through* [a]Luke 12:39, 40: *Matt 24:43, 44* [b]Matt 6:19
40 [1]Lit *think, suppose* [a]Mark 13:33; Luke 21:36
41 [a]Luke 12:47, 48
42 [1]Lit *service* [a]Luke 7:13 [b]Luke 12:42-46: *Matt 24:45-51* [c]Matt 24:45; Luke 16:1ff
43 [1]Or *lord* [a]Luke 12:42
45 [1]Lit *is delaying to come*
47 [a]Deut 25:2; James 4:17
48 [1]Lit *blows* [a]Lev 5:17; Num 15:29f [b]Matt 13:12
49 [1]Or *came* [2]Lit *what do I wish if...?*
50 [1]Lit *be baptized with* [a]Mark 10:38
51 [a]Luke 12:51-53: *Matt 10:34-36*
53 [a]Mic 7:6; Matt 10:21
54 [a]Matt 16:2f
55 [a]Matt 20:12
56 [1]Lit *how* [a]Matt 16:3
57 [a]Luke 21:30
58 [1]Lit *be released from him* [a]Luke 12:58, 59: *Matt 5:25, 26*
59 [1]Gr *lepton;* i.e. 1/128 of a denarius [a]Mark 12:42
13:1 [1]I.e. shed along with [a]Matt 27
2 [a]John 9:2f

12:38 *second watch, or even in the third.* Night was divided into four watches by the Romans (Mark 13:35) and three by the Jews (Judg 7:19); see note on Matt 14:25. These were probably the last two of the Jewish watches. The feast would have begun in the first watch.
12:40 Christ's return is certain, but the time is not known (cf. Matt 24:36).
12:41 Jesus taught the people in parables but used a more direct approach with the disciples. However, He did not intend these warnings of watchfulness just for the disciples (see Mark 13:37). In the following verses He emphasizes the duty to fulfill responsibilities.
12:42 *sensible steward.* An outstanding slave (v. 43) was sometimes left in charge of an estate (see 16:1).
12:46–48 *cut him in pieces . . . receive many lashes . . . will receive but few.* Three grades of punishment that the judge will mete out in proportion to both the privileges each person has enjoyed and his response to those privileges (see Rom 2:12–16).
12:49 *fire.* Applied figuratively in different ways in the NT (see note on 3:16). Here it is associated with judgment (v. 49) and division (v. 51). Judgment falls on the wicked, who are separated from the righteous.
12:50 *baptism.* The suffering that Jesus was to endure on the cross (see note on Mark 10:38). *until it is accomplished.* The words from the cross would pronounce the completion (John 19:28,30). Jesus wished that the hour of suffering were already past.
12:51 *division.* See note on Matt 10:34.
12:54–56 Wind from the west was from the Mediterranean Sea; from the south it was from the desert. Although people could use such indicators to forecast the weather, they could not recognize the signs of spiritual crisis, the coming of the Messiah, the threat of His death, the coming confrontation with Rome, and the eternal consequences these events would have for their own lives.
12:57 *on your own initiative judge.* Despite the insistence of the Pharisees, despite the Roman system, and even despite the pressure of family, a person must accept God on His terms. The signs of the times called for immediate decision—before judgment came on the Jewish nation.
12:58 *settle with him, so that.* Settle accounts before it is too late.
12:59 *last cent.* Greek *lepton.* If a *kodrantes* is compared to a penny (see note on v. 6), this coin corresponds to half a penny.
13:1 *the Galileans.* The incident is otherwise unknown, but having people killed while offering sacrifices in the temple fits

pose that these Galileans were *greater* sinners than all *other* Galileans because they
suffered this *fate*?
3 "I tell you, no, but unless you [1]repent,
you will all likewise perish.
4 "Or do you suppose that those eighteen
on whom the tower in [a]Siloam fell and killed
them were *worse* [1b]culprits than all the men
who live in Jerusalem?
5 "I tell you, no, but unless you repent,
you will all likewise perish."
6 And He *began* telling this parable: "A
man had [a]a fig tree which had been planted
in his vineyard; and he came looking for fruit
on it and did not find any.
7 "And he said to the vineyard-keeper,
'Behold, for three years I have come looking
for fruit on this fig tree [1]without finding any.
[a]Cut it down! Why does it even use up the
ground?'
8 "And he answered and said to him, 'Let
it alone, sir, for this year too, until I dig
around it and put in fertilizer;
9 and if it bears fruit next year, *fine;* but
if not, cut it down.' "

Healing on the Sabbath

10 And He was [a]teaching in one of the
synagogues on the Sabbath.
11 And there was a woman who for eighteen years had had [a]a sickness caused by a
spirit; and she was bent double, and could
not straighten up at all.
12 When Jesus saw her, He called her over
and said to her, "Woman, you are freed from
your sickness."
13 And He [a]laid His hands on her; and
immediately she was made erect again and
began [b]glorifying God.
14 But [a]the synagogue official, indignant
because Jesus [b]had healed on the Sabbath,
began saying to the crowd in response,
"[c]There are six days in which work should
be done; so come during them and get
healed, and not on the Sabbath day."
15 But [a]the Lord answered him and said,
"You hypocrites, [b]does not each of you on
the Sabbath untie his ox or his donkey from
the stall and lead him away to water *him*?
16 "And this woman, [a]a daughter of Abraham as she is, whom [b]Satan has bound for
eighteen long years, should she not have
been released from this bond on the Sabbath
day?"
17 As He said this, all His opponents were
being humiliated; and [a]the entire crowd was
rejoicing over all the glorious things being
done by Him.

Parables of Mustard Seed and Leaven

18 So [a]He was saying, "[b]What is the kingdom of God like, and to what shall I compare it?
19 "It is like a mustard seed, which a man
took and threw into his own garden; and it
grew and became a tree, and [a]THE BIRDS OF
THE [1]AIR NESTED IN ITS BRANCHES."
20 And again He said, "[a]To what shall I
compare the kingdom of God?
21 "[a]It is like leaven, which a woman took
and hid in [b]three [1]pecks of flour until it was
all leavened."

Teaching in the Villages

22 And He was passing through from one
city and village to another, teaching, and
[a]proceeding on His way to Jerusalem.
23 And someone said to Him, "Lord, are
there *just* a few who are being saved?" And
He said to them,

3 [1]Or *are repentant* **4** [1]Lit *debtors* [a]Neh 3:15; Is 8:6; John 9:7, 11 [b]Matt 6:12; Luke 11:4 **6** [a]Matt 21:19 **7** [1]Lit *and I do not find* [a]Matt 3:10; 7:19; Luke 3:9 **10** [a]Matt 4:23 **11** [a]Luke 13:16 **13** [a]Mark 5:23 [b]Matt 9:8 **14** [a]Mark 5:22

14 [b]Matt 12:2; Luke 14:3 [c]Ex 20:9; Deut 5:13 **15** [a]Luke 7:13 [b]Luke 14:5 **16** [a]Luke 19:9 [b]Matt 4:10; Luke 13:11 **17** [a]Luke 18:43 **18** [a]Luke 13:18, 19: *Matt 13:31, 32; Mark 4:30-32* [b]Matt 13:24; Luke 13:20 **19** [1]Or *sky* [a]Ezek 17:23 **20** [a]Matt 13:24; Luke 13:18 **21** [1]Gr *sata* [a]Luke 13:20, 21: *Matt 13:33* [b]Matt 13:33 **22** [a]Luke 9:51

the reputation of Pilate. These Galileans may have broken an important Roman regulation, which led to their bloody punishment.

13:2,4 *greater sinners . . . worse culprits.* In ancient times it was often assumed that a calamity would befall only those who were extremely sinful (see John 9:1–2; see also Job 4:7; 22:5, where Eliphaz falsely accused Job). But Jesus pointed out that all are sinners who must repent or face a fearful end.

13:4 *those eighteen.* Another unknown incident. *the tower in Siloam.* Built inside the southeast section of Jerusalem's wall.

13:6 *fig tree.* Probably refers to the Jewish nation (see note on Mark 11:14), but it may also apply to the individual soul.

13:7 *for three years.* A period of ample opportunity.

13:11 *caused by a spirit.* Various disorders were caused by evil spirits (see note on 4:33). The description of this woman's infirmity suggests that the bones of her spine were rigidly fused together.

13:12 *freed.* The spirit had been cast out, and the woman was freed from the bond of Satan and from her physical handicap.

13:14 *synagogue official.* See note on 8:41. *healed on the Sabbath.* A focal point of attack against Jesus was His conduct on the Sabbath (see 6:6–11; 14:1–6; Matt 12:1–8,11–12; John 5:1–18; see also Ex 20:9–10).

13:15 *untie his ox.* They had more regard for the needs of an animal than for the far greater need of a person. Jesus called His critics "hypocrites" because they pretended zeal for the law, but their motive was to attack Him and His healing.

13:19 *mustard seed.* See notes on Matt 13:31–32; Mark 4:31. Trees in Scripture are sometimes symbols of nations (see Ezek 17:23; 31:6; Dan 4:12,21).

13:21 *leaven.* See note on Matt 13:33. Its permeating quality is emphasized here as it works from the inside to affect all the dough. This parable speaks of the powerful influence of God's kingdom. *three pecks.* About one-half bushel or 20 quarts (22 liters); same amount as used by Sarah in Gen 18:6.

13:22 *from one city and village to another.* See chart, pp. 1408–1410. Somewhere between the events of 11:1 and 13:21 Jesus left Judea and began His work in and around Perea, which is recorded in 13:22–19:27; Matt 19:1–20:28; Mark 10; John 10:40–42. During the last part of the Perean ministry, it appears that He went north to Galilee and then traveled south again through Perea to Jericho and to Jerusalem. Some of Jesus' sayings that Luke attributes to the period of ministry in Perea are found in different settings in Matthew (7:13–14,22–23). Perhaps He repeated various sayings on different occasions. *proceeding on His way to Jerusalem.* Where He would die. Although Jesus was ministering throughout Perea, His eyes were constantly set on the Holy City and His ultimate destiny.

13:23 *just a few . . . saved?* Perhaps the questioner had observed that in spite of the very large crowds that came to

24 "[a]Strive to enter through the narrow
door; for many, I tell you, will seek to enter
and will not be able.
25 "Once the head of the house gets up and
[a]shuts the door, and you begin to stand outside and knock on the door, saying, '[b]Lord,
open up to us!' then He will answer and say
to you, '[c]I do not know where you are from.'
26 "Then you will [a]begin to say, 'We ate
and drank in Your presence, and You taught
in our streets';
27 and He will say, 'I tell you, [a]I do not
know where you are from; [b]DEPART FROM ME,
ALL YOU EVILDOERS.'
28 "[a]In that place there will be weeping
and gnashing of teeth when you see Abraham and Isaac and Jacob and all the prophets in the kingdom of God, but yourselves
being thrown out.
29 "And they [a]will come from east and
west and from north and south, and will
recline *at the table* in the kingdom of God.
30 "And behold, [a]*some* are last who will be
first and *some* are first who will be last."
31 Just at that time some Pharisees
approached, saying to Him, "Go away, leave
here, for [a]Herod wants to kill You."
32 And He said to them, "Go and tell that
fox, 'Behold, I cast out demons and perform
cures today and tomorrow, and the third *day*
I [1a]reach My goal.'
33 "Nevertheless [a]I must journey on today
and tomorrow and the next *day;* for it cannot
be that a [b]prophet would perish outside of
Jerusalem.
34 "[a]O Jerusalem, Jerusalem, *the city* that
kills the prophets and stones those sent to
her! How often I wanted to gather your children together, [b]just as a hen *gathers* her brood
under her wings, and you would not *have it!*
35 "Behold, your house is left to you *desolate;* and I say to you, you will not see Me
until *the time* comes when you say, '[a]BLESSED
IS HE WHO COMES IN THE NAME OF THE LORD!' "

24 [a]Matt 7:13 **25** [a]Matt 25:10 [b]Matt 7:22; 25:11 [c]Matt 7:23; 25:12; Luke 13:27 **26** [a]Luke 3:8 **27** [a]Luke 13:25 [b]Ps 6:8; Matt 25:41 **28** [a]Matt 8:12; 22:13; 25:30 **29** [a]Matt 8:11 **30** [a]Matt 19:30; 20:16; Mark 10:31 **31** [a]Matt 14:1; Luke 3:1; 9:7; 23:7 **32** [1]Or *am perfected* [a]Heb 2:10; 5:9; 7:28 **33** [a]John 11:9 [b]Matt 21:11 **34** [a]Luke 13:34, 35: *Matt 23:37-39;* Luke 19:41 [b]Matt 23:37 **35** [a]Ps 118:26; Matt 21:9; Luke 19:38 **14:1** [1]I.e. members of the Sanhedrin [a]Mark 3:2 **2** [1]Lit *behold* **3** [1]I.e. experts in Mosaic Law [a]Matt 22:35 [b]Matt 12:2; Luke 13:14 **5** [1]Lit *Whose son of you...will fall* [a]Matt 12:11; Luke 13:15 **6** [a]Matt 22:46; Luke 20:40 **7** [a]Matt 23:6 **8** [1]Lit *recline at* [a]Prov 25:6, 7 **9** [1]Lit *begin* [a]Luke 3:8 **10** [a]Prov 25:6, 7

Jesus Heals on the Sabbath

14 It happened that when He went into
the house of one of the [1]leaders of the
Pharisees on *the* Sabbath to eat bread, [a]they
were watching Him closely.
2 And [1]there in front of Him was a man
suffering from dropsy.
3 And Jesus answered and spoke to the
[1a]lawyers and Pharisees, saying, "[b]Is it lawful to heal on the Sabbath, or not?"
4 But they kept silent. And He took hold
of him and healed him, and sent him away.
5 And He said to them, "[1a]Which one of
you will have a son or an ox fall into a well,
and will not immediately pull him out on a
Sabbath day?"
6 [a]And they could make no reply to this.

Parable of the Guests

7 And He *began* speaking a parable to
the invited guests when He noticed how
[a]they had been picking out the places of
honor *at the table,* saying to them,
8 "When you are invited by someone to a
wedding feast, [a]do not [1]take the place of
honor, for someone more distinguished than
you may have been invited by him,
9 and he who invited you both will come
and say to you, 'Give *your* place to this man,'
and then [a]in disgrace you [1]proceed to occupy the last place.
10 "But when you are invited, go and
recline at the last place, so that when the one
who has invited you comes, he may say to
you, 'Friend, [a]move up higher'; then you

hear Jesus' preaching and be healed, there were only a few followers who were loyal. Jesus did not answer directly, but warned that many would try to enter after it was too late.

13:27 *I do not know where you are from.* See Matt 7:23; 25:12.

13:29 *they . . . from east and west and from north and south.* From the four corners of the world (Ps 107:3) and from among all people, including Gentiles.

13:31 *Herod wants to kill You.* See note on Matt 14:1. Jesus was probably in Perea, which was under Herod's jurisdiction (see note on 3:1). The Pharisees wanted to frighten Jesus into leaving this area and going to Judea.

13:32 *fox.* A crafty animal. *today and tomorrow.* In Semitic usage this phrase could refer to an indefinite but limited period of time. *reach My goal.* Jesus' life had a predetermined plan that would be carried out, and no harm could come to Him until His purpose was accomplished (cf. 4:43; 9:22).

13:33 *outside of Jerusalem.* Jesus' hour had not yet come (see 2:38; John 7:30; 8:20; cf. John 8:59; 10:39; 11:54). He would die in Jerusalem as had numerous prophets before Him.

13:34 *How often . . . !* This lament over Jerusalem may suggest that Jesus was in Jerusalem more often than the Synoptics indicate (cf. John 2:13; 4:45; 5:1; 7:10; 10:22). However, the statement in vv. 34–35 may have been uttered some distance from Jerusalem, i.e., in Perea. According to Matt 23:37–38, the same utterance was spoken on Tuesday of Passion Week. Jesus repeated many of His teachings and sayings.

13:35 *house is left . . . desolate.* God will abandon His temple and His city (see 21:20,24; Jer 12:7; 22:5). *not see Me until.* See Zech 12:10; Rev 1:7; cf. Is 45:23; Rom 14:11; Phil 2:10–11.

14:1 *on the Sabbath.* Of seven recorded miracles on the Sabbath, Luke includes five (4:31,38; 6:6; 13:14; 14:1); the other two are John 5:10; 9:14. Concerning the vigil of the Pharisees see note on 13:14. Sabbath meals were prepared the day before.

14:2 *dropsy.* An accumulation of fluid that would indicate illness affecting other parts of the body. The Greek for this word is a medical term found only here in the NT (see Introduction: Author).

14:3 *lawyers.* See notes on 5:17; 7:30. By questioning them before the miracle, Jesus made it difficult for them to protest afterward.

14:5 *have a son.* Some manuscripts read "donkey" instead of "son" The reading "donkey" matches well with having an "ox fall into a well." But in Deut 5:14 the law is specified for both humans and animals; one category opens with "son" and another with "ox." Jesus' action was "unlawful" only according to rabbinic interpretations, not according to the Mosaic law itself.

14:7 *places of honor.* Maneuvering for better seats may also have caused trouble at the Last Supper (22:24).

will have honor in the sight of all who [1]are at the table with you.

11 "[a]For everyone who exalts himself will be humbled, and he who humbles himself will be exalted."

12 And He also went on to say to the one who had invited Him, "When you give a luncheon or a dinner, do not invite your friends or your brothers or your relatives or rich neighbors, otherwise they may also invite you in return and *that* will be your repayment.

13 "But when you give a [1]reception, invite *the* poor, *the* crippled, *the* lame, *the* blind,

14 and you will be blessed, since they [1]do not have *the means* to repay you; for you will be repaid at [a]the resurrection of the righteous."

15 When one of those who were reclining *at the table* with Him heard this, he said to Him, "[a]Blessed is everyone who will eat bread in the kingdom of God!"

Parable of the Dinner

16 But He said to him, "[a]A man was giving a big dinner, and he invited many;

17 and at the dinner hour he sent his slave to say to those who had been invited, 'Come; for everything is ready now.'

18 "But they all alike began to make excuses. The first one said to him, 'I have bought a [1]piece of land and I need to go out and look at it; [2]please consider me excused.'

19 "Another one said, 'I have bought five yoke of oxen, and I am going to try them out; [1]please consider me excused.'

20 "Another one said, '[a]I have married a wife, and for that reason I cannot come.'

21 "And the slave came *back* and reported this to his master. Then the head of the household became angry and said to his slave, 'Go out at once into the streets and lanes of the city and bring in here the poor and crippled and blind and lame.'

22 "And the slave said, 'Master, what you commanded has been done, and still there is room.'

23 "And the master said to the slave, 'Go out into the highways and along the hedges, and compel *them* to come in, so that my house may be filled.

24 'For I tell you, none of those men who were invited shall taste of my dinner.' "

Discipleship Tested

25 Now [1]large crowds were going along with Him; and He turned and said to them,

26 "[a]If anyone comes to Me, and does not [1]hate his own father and mother and wife and children and brothers and sisters, yes, and even his own life, he cannot be My disciple.

27 "Whoever does not [a]carry his own cross and come after Me cannot be My disciple.

28 "For which one of you, when he wants to build a tower, does not first sit down and calculate the cost to see if he has enough to complete it?

29 "Otherwise, when he has laid a foundation and is not able to finish, all who observe it begin to ridicule him,

30 saying, 'This man began to build and was not able to finish.'

31 "Or what king, when he sets out to meet another king in battle, will not first sit down and [a]consider whether he is strong enough with ten thousand *men* to encounter the one coming against him with twenty thousand?

32 "Or else, while the other is still far away, he sends [1]a delegation and asks for terms of peace.

33 "So then, none of you can be My disciple who [a]does not give up all his own possessions.

34 "Therefore, salt is good; but [a]if even salt has become tasteless, with what will it be seasoned?

35 "It is useless either for the soil or for the manure pile; it is thrown out. [a]He who has ears to hear, [1]let him hear."

10 [1]Lit *recline at the table*
11 [a]2 Sam 22:28; Prov 29:23; Matt 23:12; Luke 1:52; 18:14; James 4:10
13 [1]Or *banquet*
14 [1]Or *are unable to* [a]John 5:29; Acts 24:15; Rev 20:4, 5
15 [a]Rev 19:9
16 [a]Matt 22:2-14; Luke 14:16-24
18 [1]Or *field* [2]Lit *I request you*
19 [1]Lit *I request you*
20 [a]Deut 24:5; 1 Cor 7:33
25 [1]Lit *many*
26 [1]I.e. by comparison of his love for Me [a]Matt 10:37
27 [a]Matt 10:38; 16:24; Mark 8:34; Luke 9:23
31 [a]Prov 20:18
32 [1]Or *an embassy*
33 [a]Phil 3:7; Heb 11:26
34 [a]Matt 5:13; Mark 9:50
35 [1]Or *hear!* Or *listen!* [a]Matt 11:15

14:11 *humbles himself will be exalted.* A basic principle repeated often in the Bible (see 11:43; 18:14; 20:46; 2 Chr 7:14–15; Prov 3:34; 25:6- 7; Matt 18:4; 23:12; James 4:10; 1 Pet 5:6).
14:14 *resurrection of the righteous.* All will be resurrected (Dan 12:2; John 5:28–29; Acts 24:15). Some hold that the resurrection of the righteous (1 Cor 15:23; 1 Thess 4:16; Rev 20:4–6) is distinct from the "general" resurrection (1 Cor 15:12,21; Heb 6:2; Rev 20:11–15). *the righteous.* Those who have been pronounced so by God on the basis of Christ's atonement and who have evidenced their faith by their actions (cf. Matt 25:34–40).
14:15 *eat bread in the kingdom.* The great Messianic banquet to come. Association of the future kingdom with a feast was common (13:29; Is 25:6; Matt 8:11; 25:1–10; 26:29; Rev 19:9).
14:16 *He said to him.* Jesus used the man's remark as the occasion for a parable warning that not everyone would enter the kingdom.
14:18 *bought a piece of land.* The initial invitation must have been accepted, but when the final invitation came (by Jewish custom the announcement that came when the dinner was ready), other interests took priority. None of the "reasons" given was genuine. For example, one did not buy a field without first seeing it, nor oxen without first trying them out (v. 19).
14:24 *those men who were invited.* Without explicitly mentioning them, Jesus warned "the lawyers and Pharisees" (v. 3) that those who refused the invitation to his Messianic banquet would not get one taste of it, but others would (see 20:9–19; see also note on Matt 21:41).
14:26 *hate his own father.* A vivid hyperbole, meaning that one must love Jesus even more than his immediate family (see Mal 1:2–3 for another use of the figure). See Matt 10:37.
14:27 *carry his own cross.* See 9:23; Matt 10:38 and notes.
14:28 *calculate the cost.* Jesus did not want a blind, naive commitment that expected only blessings. As a builder estimates costs or a king evaluates military strength (v. 31), so a person must consider what Jesus expects of His followers.
14:33 *give up all his own possessions.* The cost, Jesus warned, is complete surrender to Him.
14:34 *salt is good.* See note on Mark 9:50.

The Lost Sheep

15 Now all the [a]tax collectors and the [1]sinners were coming near Him to listen to Him.

2 Both the Pharisees and the scribes *began* to grumble, saying, "This man receives sinners and [a]eats with them."

3 So He told them this parable, saying,

4 "[a]What man among you, if he has a hundred sheep and has lost one of them, does not leave the ninety-nine in the [1]open pasture and go after the one which is lost until he finds it?

5 "When he has found it, he lays it on his shoulders, rejoicing.

6 "And when he comes home, he calls together his friends and his neighbors, saying to them, 'Rejoice with me, for I have found my sheep which was lost!'

7 "I tell you that in the same way, there will be *more* joy in heaven over one sinner who repents than over ninety-nine righteous persons who need no repentance.

The Lost Coin

8 "Or what woman, if she has ten [1]silver coins and loses one coin, does not light a lamp and sweep the house and search carefully until she finds it?

9 "When she has found it, she calls together her friends and neighbors, saying, 'Rejoice with me, for I have found the coin which I had lost!'

10 "In the same way, I tell you, there is joy [a]in the presence of the angels of God over one sinner who repents."

The Prodigal Son

11 And He said, "A man had two sons.

12 "The younger of them said to his father, 'Father, give me [a]the share of the estate that falls to me.' So he divided his [1b]wealth between them.

13 "And not many days later, the younger son gathered everything together and went on a journey into a distant country, and there he squandered his estate with loose living.

14 "Now when he had spent everything, a severe famine occurred in that country, and he began to be impoverished.

15 "So he went and [1]hired himself out to one of the citizens of that country, and he sent him into his fields to feed swine.

16 "And he would have gladly filled his stomach with the [1]pods that the swine were eating, and no one was giving *anything* to him.

17 "But when he came to [1]his senses, he said, 'How many of my father's hired men have more than enough bread, but I am dying here with hunger!

18 'I will get up and go to my father, and will say to him, "Father, I have sinned against heaven, and [1]in your sight;

19 I am no longer worthy to be called your son; make me as one of your hired men." '

20 "So he got up and came to [1]his father. But while he was still a long way off, his father saw him and felt compassion *for him*, and ran and [2a]embraced him and kissed him.

21 "And the son said to him, 'Father, I have sinned against heaven and in your sight; I am no longer worthy to be called your son.'

22 "But the father said to his slaves, 'Quickly bring out [a]the best robe and put it on him, and [b]put a ring on his hand and sandals on his feet;

23 and bring the fattened calf, kill it, and let us eat and celebrate;

24 for this son of mine was [a]dead and has come to life again; he was lost and has been found.' And they began to celebrate.

25 "Now his older son was in the field, and when he came and approached the house, he heard music and dancing.

15:1 [1]I.e. irreligious Jews [a]Luke 5:29
2 [a]Matt 9:11
4 [1]Lit *wilderness* [a]Matt 18:12-14; Luke 15:4-7
8 [1]Gr *drachmas*, one drachma was a day's wages
10 [a]Matt 10:32; Luke 15:7
12 [1]Lit *living* [a]Deut 21:17 [b]Mark 12:44; Luke 15:30
15 [1]Lit *was joined to*
16 [1]I.e. of the carob tree
17 [1]Lit *himself*
18 [1]Lit *before you*
20 [1]Lit *his own* [2]Lit *fell on his neck* [a]Gen 45:14; 46:29; Acts 20:37
22 [a]Zech 3:4; Rev 6:11 [b]Gen 41:42
24 [a]Matt 8:22; Luke 9:60; 15:32; Rom 11:15; Eph 2:1, 5; 5:14; Col 2:13; 1 Tim 5:6

15:1 *tax collectors and the sinners.* See notes on 3:12; Mark 2:15.

15:2 *began to grumble.* Complained among themselves, but not openly. *eats with them.* More than simple association, eating with a person indicated acceptance and recognition (cf. Acts 11:3; 1 Cor 5:11; Gal 2:12).

15:3 *this parable.* Jesus responded with a story that contrasted the love of God with the exclusiveness of the Pharisees.

15:4 *the one which is lost.* The shepherd theme was familiar from Ps 23; Is 40:11; Ezek 34:11–16.

15:7 *joy in heaven.* God's concern and joy at the sinner's repentance are set in stark contrast to the attitude of the Pharisees and the scribes (v. 2). *righteous . . . need no repentance.* Probably irony: those who think they are righteous (such as the Pharisees and the scribes) and feel no need to repent.

15:8 *ten silver coins.* Ten *drachmas*. A *drachma* was a Greek coin approximately equivalent to the Roman denarius, worth about an average day's wages (Matt 20:2). *search carefully.* Near Eastern houses frequently had no windows and only earthen floors, making the search for a single coin difficult.

15:12 *share of the estate.* The father might divide the inheritance (double to the older son; see Deut 21:17 and note on Luke 12:13) but retain the income from it until his death. But to give a younger son his portion of the inheritance upon request was highly unusual.

15:13 *gathered everything together.* The son's motive becomes apparent when he departs, taking with him all his possessions and leaving nothing behind to come back to. He wants to be free of parental restraint and to spend his share of the family wealth as he pleases. *loose living.* More specific in v. 30, though the older brother may have exaggerated because of his bitter attitude.

15:15 *to feed swine.* The ultimate indignity for a Jew; not only was the work distasteful but pigs were "unclean" animals (Lev 11:7).

15:16 *pods.* Seeds of the carob tree.

15:22–23 *best robe . . . ring . . . sandals . . . eat.* Each was a sign of position and acceptance (cf. Gen 41:42; Zech 3:4): a long robe of distinction, a signet ring of authority, sandals like a son (slaves went barefoot), and the fattened calf for a special occasion.

Parables of Jesus

PARABLE	MATTHEW	MARK	LUKE
Lamp under a basket	5:14-15	4:21-22	8:16; 11:33
Wise and foolish builders	7:24-27		6:47-49
New cloth on an old garment	9:16	2:21	5:36
New wine in old wineskins	9:17	2:22	5:37-38
Sower and the soils	13:3-8,18-23	4:3-8,14-20	8:5-8,11-15
Tares	13:24-30,36-43		
Mustard seed	13:31-32	4:30-32	13:18-19
Leaven	13:33		13:20-21
Hidden treasure	13:44		
Valuable pearl	13:45-46		
Dragnet	13:47-50		
Head of a household	13:52		
Lost sheep	18:12-14		15:4-7
Unmerciful slave	18:23-34		
Laborers in the vineyard	20:1-16		
Two sons	21:28-32		
Vine-growers	21:33-44	12:1-11	20:9-18
Wedding feast	22:2-14		
Fig tree	24:32-35	13:28-29	21:29-31
Faithful and sensible slave	24:45-51		12:42-48
Ten virgins	25:1-13		
Talents (minas)	25:14-30		19:12-27
Sheep and goats	25:31-46		
Growing seed		4:26-29	
Watchful slaves		13:35-37	12:35-40
Moneylender			7:41-43
Good Samaritan			10:30-37
Friend in need			11:5-8
Rich fool			12:16-21
Unfruitful fig tree			13:6-9
Lowest seat at the feast			14:7-14
Big dinner			14:16-24
Cost of discipleship			14:28-33
Lost coin			15:8-10
Lost (prodigal) son			15:11-32
Shrewd manager			16:1-8
Rich man and Lazarus			16:19-31
Master and his slave			17:7-10
Persistent widow			18:2-8
Pharisee and tax collector			18:10-14

26 "And he summoned one of the servants and *began* inquiring what these things could be.

27 "And he said to him, 'Your brother has come, and your father has killed the fattened calf because he has received him back safe and sound.'

28 "But he became angry and was not willing to go in; and his father came out and *began* pleading with him.

29 "But he answered and said to his father, 'Look! For so many years I have been serving you and I have never [1]neglected a command of yours; and *yet* you have never given me a young goat, so that I might celebrate with my friends;

30 but when this son of yours came, who has devoured your [1a]wealth with prostitutes, you killed the fattened calf for him.'

31 "And he said to him, 'Son, you [1]have always been with me, and all that is mine is yours.

32 'But we had to celebrate and rejoice, for this brother of yours was [a]dead and *has begun* to live, and *was* lost and has been found.' "

The Unrighteous Steward

16 Now He was also saying to the disciples, "There was a rich man who had a manager, and this *manager* was [1]reported to him as [a]squandering his possessions.

2 "And he called him and said to him, 'What is this I hear about you? Give an accounting of your management, for you can no longer be manager.'

3 "The manager said to himself, 'What shall I do, since my [1]master is taking the management away from me? I am not strong enough to dig; I am ashamed to beg.

4 'I know what I shall do, so that when I am removed from the management people will welcome me into their homes.'

5 "And he summoned each one of his [1]master's debtors, and he *began* saying to the first, 'How much do you owe my master?'

6 "And he said, 'A hundred [1]measures of oil.' And he said to him, 'Take your bill, and sit down quickly and write fifty.'

7 "Then he said to another, 'And how much do you owe?' And he said, 'A hundred [1]measures of wheat.' He *said to him, 'Take your bill, and write eighty.'

8 "And his [1]master praised the unrighteous manager because he had acted shrewdly; for the sons of [a]this age are more shrewd in relation to their own [2]kind than the [b]sons of light.

9 "And I say to you, [a]make friends for yourselves by means of the [1b]wealth of unrighteousness, so that when it fails, [c]they will receive you into the eternal dwellings.

10 "[a]He who is faithful in a very little thing is faithful also in much; and he who is unrighteous in a very little thing is unrighteous also in much.

11 "Therefore if you have not been faithful in the *use of* unrighteous [1a]wealth, who will entrust the true *riches* to you?

12 "And if you have not been faithful in *the use of* that which is another's, who will give you that which is your own?

13 "[a]No [1]servant can serve two masters;

29 [1]Or *disobeyed*
30 [1]Lit *living* [a]Prov 29:3; Luke 15:12
31 [1]Lit *are always with me*
32 [a]Luke 15:24
16:1 [1]Or *accused* [a]Luke 15:13
3 [1]Or *lord*
5 [1]Or *lord's*
6 [1]Gr *baths,* a Heb unit of measure equaling about 7 1/2 gal.
7 [1]Gr *kors,* one kor equals between 10 and 12 bu
8 [1]Or *lord* [2]Lit *generation* [a]Matt 12:32; Luke 20:34 [b]John 12:36; Eph 5:8; 1 Thess 5:5
9 [1]Gr *mammon,* fr Aram *mamona,* signifying riches, wealth, etc, personified as an object of worship [a]Matt 19:21; Luke 11:41; 12:33 [b]Matt 6:24; Luke 16:11, 13 [c]Luke 16:4
10 [a]Matt 25:21, 23
11 [1]Gr *mammon,* fr Aram *mamona,* signifying riches, wealth, etc, personified as an object of worship [a]Luke 16:9
13 [1]Or *house-servant* [a]Matt 6:24

15:28 *he.* The older brother's resentment is like the attitude of the Pharisees and teachers of the law who opposed Jesus, whereas the forgiving love of the father symbolizes the divine mercy of God.
15:29 *a young goat.* Cheaper food than a fattened calf.
15:30 *this son of yours.* The older brother would not even recognize him as his brother, so bitter was his hatred.
15:31 *all that is mine is yours.* The father's love included both brothers. The parable might better be called the parable of "The Father's Love" rather than "The Prodigal Son." It shows a contrast between the self-centered exclusiveness of the Pharisees, who failed to understand God's love, and the concern and joy of God at the repentance of sinners.
15:32 *dead and has begun to live.* A beautiful picture of the return of the younger son, which also pictures Christian conversion (see Rom 6:13; Eph 2:1,5). The words "lost and has been found" are often used to mean "perished and saved" (19:10; Matt 10:6; 18:10–14).
16:1 *disciples.* Perhaps more than just the twelve (see 6:13; 10:1). *manager.* A steward who handled all the business affairs of the owner. *squandering.* He had squandered his master's possessions, just as the prodigal ("wasteful") son (15:13).
16:3 *What shall I do . . . ?* The unrighteous manager (v. 8) had no scruples against using his position for his own benefit, even if it meant cheating his master. Knowing he would lose his job, the manager planned for his future by discounting the debts owed to his master in order to obligate the debtors to himself. Interpreters disagree as to whether his procedure of discounting was in itself dishonest. Was he giving away what really belonged to his master, or was he forgoing interest payments his master did not have a right to charge? Originally the manager may have overcharged the debtors, a common way of circumventing the Mosaic law that prohibited taking interest from fellow Jews (Deut 23:19). So, to reduce the debts, he may have returned the figures to their initial amounts, which would both satisfy his master and gain the good favor of the debtors. In any event, the point remains the same: He was shrewd enough to use the means at his disposal to plan for his future well-being.
16:6 *A hundred measures of oil.* The yield of about 450 olive trees.
16:7 *hundred measures of wheat.* The approximate yield of about 100 acres.
16:8 *sons of light.* God's people (John 12:36; Eph 5:8; 1 Thess 5:5).
16:9 *make friends.* By helping those in need, who in the future will show their gratitude when they welcome their benefactors into heaven ("eternal dwellings"). In this way worldly wealth may be wisely used to gain eternal benefit. *by means of the wealth of unrighteousness.* God's people should be alert to make use of what God has given them.
16:10 *faithful also in much.* Cf. 19:17; Matt 25:21. Faithfulness is not determined by the amount entrusted but by the character of the person who uses it.
16:11 *true riches.* The things of highest value, ultimately those of the spirit, the eternal.
16:13 *two masters.* See Matt 6:24; cf. James 4:4.

for either he will hate the one and love the other, or else he will be devoted to one and despise the other. You cannot serve God and [2b]wealth."

14 Now the Pharisees, who were [a]lovers of money, were listening to all these things and [b]were scoffing at Him.

15 And He said to them, "You are those who [a]justify yourselves [1]in the sight of men, but [b]God knows your hearts; for that which is highly esteemed among men is detestable [1]in the sight of God.

16 "[a]The Law and the Prophets *were proclaimed* until John; since that time [b]the gospel of the kingdom of God [1]has been preached, and everyone is forcing his way into it.

17 "[a]But it is easier for heaven and earth to pass away than for one [1]stroke of a letter of the Law to fail.

18 "[a]Everyone who [1]divorces his wife and marries another commits adultery, and he who marries one who is [2]divorced from a husband commits adultery.

The Rich Man and Lazarus

19 "Now there was a rich man, and he habitually dressed in purple and fine linen, joyously living in splendor every day.

20 "And a poor man named Lazarus [a]was laid at his gate, covered with sores,

21 and longing to be fed with the *crumbs* which were falling from the rich man's table; besides, even the dogs were coming and licking his sores.

22 "Now the poor man died and was carried away by the angels to [a]Abraham's bosom; and the rich man also died and was buried.

23 "In [a]Hades he lifted up his eyes, being in torment, and *saw Abraham far away and Lazarus in his bosom.

24 "And he cried out and said, '[a]Father Abraham, have mercy on me, and send Lazarus so that he may dip the tip of his finger in water and cool off my tongue, for I am in agony in [b]this flame.'

25 "But Abraham said, 'Child, remember that [a]during your life you received your good things, and likewise Lazarus bad things; but now he is being comforted here, and you are in agony.

26 'And [1]besides all this, between us and you there is a great chasm fixed, so that those who wish to come over from here to you will not be able, and *that* none may cross over from there to us.'

27 "And he said, 'Then I beg you, father, that you send him to my father's house—

28 for I have five brothers—in order that he may [a]warn them, so that they will not also come to this place of torment.'

29 "But Abraham *said, 'They have [a]Moses and the Prophets; let them hear them.'

30 "But he said, 'No, [a]father Abraham, but if someone goes to them from the dead, they will repent!'

31 "But he said to him, 'If they do not listen to Moses and the Prophets, they will not be persuaded even if someone rises from the dead.' "

Instructions

17 He said to His disciples, "[a]It is inevitable that [1]stumbling blocks come, but woe to him through whom they come!

2 "[a]It [1]would be better for him if a mill-

13 [2]Gr *mammon*, fr Aram *mamona*, signifying riches, wealth, etc, personified as an object of worship [b]Luke 16:9
14 [a]2 Tim 3:2 [b]Luke 23:35
15 [1]Lit *before* [a]Luke 10:29; 18:9, 14 [b]1 Sam 16:7; Prov 21:2; Acts 1:24; Rom 8:27
16 [1]Lit *is preached* [a]Matt 11:12f [b]Matt 4:23
17 [1]I.e. projection of a letter (serif) [a]Matt 5:18
18 [1]Or *sends away* [2]Or *sent away* [a]Matt 5:32; 1 Cor 7:10, 11
20 [a]Acts 3:2
22 [a]John 1:18; 13:23
23 [a]Matt 11:23
24 [a]Luke 3:8; 16:30; 19:9 [b]Matt 25:41
25 [a]Luke 6:24
26 [1]Lit *in all these things*
28 [a]Acts 2:40; 8:25; 10:42; 18:5; 20:21ff; 23:11; 28:23; Gal 5:3; Eph 4:17; 1 Thess 2:11; 4:6
29 [a]Luke 4:17; John 5:45-47; Acts 15:21
30 [a]Luke 3:8; 16:24; 19:9
17:1 [1]Or *temptations to sin* [a]Matt 18:7; 1 Cor 11:19; 1 Tim 4:1
2 [1]Lit *is* [a]Matt 18:6; Mark 9:42; 1 Cor 8:12

16:16 *until John.* The ministry of John the Baptist, which prepared the way for Jesus the Messiah, was the dividing line between the OT (the "Law and the Prophets") and the NT (see notes on Jer 31:31–34; Heb 8:6–12). *forcing his way.* The meaning is disputed, but it probably speaks of the fierce earnestness with which people were responding to the gospel of the kingdom. Multitudes were coming to hear Jesus and to receive His message.

16:17 The ministry of Jesus (introducing the new covenant era) was a fulfillment of the law (defining the old covenant era) in the most minute detail (cf. 21:33). *one stroke of a letter.* See notes on Matt 5:17–18.

16:18 *divorces his wife.* See Matt 5:31–32; 19:9; Mark 10:11–12; 1 Cor 7:10–11. Jesus affirms the continuing authority of the law: For example, adultery was still adultery, still unlawful and still sinful. Matthew's treatment is fuller in that (1) it shows that the law was given because of man's hardened heart in regard to divorce, and (2) it includes one exception as permissible grounds for divorce—marital unfaithfulness (Matt 19:9).

16:19 *a rich man.* Sometimes given the name Dives (from the Latin for "rich man"). *purple and fine linen.* Characteristic of costly garments.

16:20 *Lazarus.* Not the Lazarus Jesus raised from the dead (John 11:43–44). If this is a parable, it is the only one in which Jesus gave a name to one of the characters. *covered with sores.* The Greek for this phrase is a common medical term found only here in the NT (see Introduction: Author).

16:22 *Abraham's bosom.* The Talmud mentions both Paradise (see 23:43) and Abraham's bosom as the home of the righteous. Abraham's bosom refers to the place of blessedness to which the righteous dead go to await future vindication. Its bliss is the quality of blessedness reserved for people like Abraham.

16:23 *Hades.* Hades is the place to which the wicked dead go to await the final judgment. That torment begins in Hades is evident from the plight of the rich man. The location of Abraham's bosom is not specified, but it is separated from Hades by an impassable chasm. Hades includes the torment that characterizes hell (fire, Rev 20:10; agony, Rev 14:11; separation, Matt 8:12). Some understand Jesus' description of Abraham's side and Hades in a less literal way.

16:28 *I have five brothers.* For the first time the rich man showed concern for others.

16:29 *Moses and the Prophets.* A way of designating the whole OT. The rich man had failed to pay attention to Scripture and its teaching, and feared his brothers would do the same.

16:30 *someone . . . from the dead.* The story may suggest that Lazarus was intended, but Luke's account seems to imply that Jesus was speaking also of His own resurrection (cf. v. 31; 9:22). If a person's mind is closed and Scripture is rejected, no evidence—not even a resurrection—will change him.

17:2 *millstone.* A heavy stone for grinding grain. *one of these*

stone were hung around his neck and he were thrown into the sea, than that he would cause one of these little ones to stumble.

3 "[1]Be on your guard! [a]If your brother sins, rebuke him; and if he repents, forgive him.

4 "And if he sins against you [a]seven times a day, and returns to you seven times, saying, 'I repent,' [1]forgive him."

5 [a]The apostles said to [b]the Lord, "Increase our faith!"

6 And [a]the Lord said, "If you [1]had faith like [b]a mustard seed, you would say to this [c]mulberry tree, 'Be uprooted and be planted in the sea'; and it would [2]obey you.

7 "Which of you, having a slave plowing or tending sheep, will say to him when he has come in from the field, 'Come immediately and [1]sit down to eat'?

8 "But will he not say to him, '[a]Prepare something for me to eat, and *properly* [1]clothe yourself and serve me while I eat and drink; and [2]afterward you [3]may eat and drink'?

9 "He does not thank the slave because he did the things which were commanded, does he?

10 "So you too, when you do all the things which are commanded you, say, 'We are unworthy slaves; we have done *only* that which we ought to have done.' "

Ten Lepers Cleansed

11 While He was [a]on the way to Jerusalem, [b]He was passing [1]between Samaria and Galilee.

12 As He entered a village, ten leprous men who [a]stood at a distance met Him;

13 and they raised their voices, saying, "Jesus, [a]Master, have mercy on us!"

14 When He saw them, He said to them, "[a]Go and show yourselves to the priests." And as they were going, they were cleansed.

15 Now one of them, when he saw that he had been healed, turned back, [a]glorifying God with a loud voice,

16 and he fell on his face at His feet, giving thanks to Him. And he was a [a]Samaritan.

17 Then Jesus answered and said, "Were there not ten cleansed? But the nine—where are they?

18 "[1]Was no one found who returned to [a]give glory to God, except this foreigner?"

19 And He said to him, "Stand up and go; [a]your faith [1]has made you well."

20 Now having been questioned by the Pharisees [a]as to when the kingdom of God was coming, He answered them and said, "The kingdom of God is not coming with [1][b]signs to be observed;

21 nor will [a]they say, 'Look, here *it is!*' or, 'There *it is!*' For behold, the kingdom of God is [1]in your midst."

Second Coming Foretold

22 And He said to the disciples, "[a]The days will come when you will long to see one of the days of the Son of Man, and you will not see it.

23 "[a]They will say to you, 'Look there! Look here!' Do not go away, and do not run after *them.*

24 "[a]For just like the lightning, when it flashes out of one part [1]of the sky, shines to the other part [1]of the sky, so will the Son of Man be in His day.

25 "[a]But first He must suffer many things and be rejected by this generation.

26 "[a]And just as it happened [b]in the days

3 [1]Lit *Take heed to yourselves* [a]Matt 18:15
4 [1]Lit *you shall forgive* [a]Matt 18:21f
5 [a]Mark 6:30 [b]Luke 7:13
6 [1]Lit *have* [2]Lit *have obeyed* [a]Luke 7:13 [b]Matt 13:31; 17:20; Mark 4:31; Luke 13:19 [c]Luke 19:4
7 [1]Lit *recline*
8 [1]Lit *gird* [2]Lit *after these things* [3]Lit *will* [a]Luke 12:37
11 [1]Lit *through the middle of;* or *along the borders of* [a]Luke 9:51 [b]Luke 9:52ff; John 4:3f
12 [a]Lev 13:45f
13 [a]Luke 5:5
14 [a]Lev 14:1-32; Matt 8:4; Luke 5:14
15 [a]Matt 9:8
16 [a]Matt 10:5
18 [1]Lit *Were there not found those who* [a]Matt 9:8
19 [1]Lit *has saved you* [a]Matt 9:22; Luke 18:42
20 [1]Lit *observation* [a]Luke 19:11; Acts 1:6 [b]Luke 14:1
21 [1]Or *within you* [a]Luke 17:23
22 [a]Matt 9:15; Mark 2:20; Luke 5:35
23 [a]Matt 24:23; Mark 13:21; Luke 21:8
24 [1]Lit *under heaven* [a]Matt 24:27
25 [a]Matt 16:21; Luke 9:22
26 [a]Luke 17:26, 27: *Matt 24:37-39* [b]Gen 6:5-8; 7

little ones. Either young in the faith or young in age (cf. 10:21; Matt 18:6; Mark 10:24).

17:3 *your brother.* See Matt 18:15–17; cf. Matt 12:50.

17:4 *seven times.* That is, forgiveness is to be unlimited (cf. Ps 119:164; Matt 18:21–22).

17:5 *Increase our faith!* They felt incapable of measuring up to the standards set forth in vv. 1–4. They wanted greater faith to lay hold of the power to live up to Jesus' standards.

17:6 See Matt 17:20; Mark 11:23; see also notes on Matt 13:31–32; Mark 4:31.

17:7 *a slave.* A slave is used to illustrate performance of duty (cf. 12:37).

17:11 *between Samaria and Galilee.* From this point Jesus seems to have journeyed to Perea, where He ministered on His way south to Jerusalem (see notes on 9:51; 13:22).

17:14 *show yourselves to the priests.* Normal procedure after a cure (see Lev 13:2–3; 14:2–32).

17:16 *Samaritan.* See note on 10:31–33. Normally Jews did not associate with Samaritans (John 4:9), but leprosy broke down social barriers while erecting others (see notes on Lev 13:2,4,45–46).

17:19 *your faith has made you well.* See Matt 9:22. The phrase may also be rendered "your faith has saved you" (7:50). The fact that the Samaritan returned to thank Jesus may indicate that he had received salvation in addition to the physical healing all ten had received (cf. 7:50; 8:48,50).

17:21 *the kingdom of God is in your midst.* Probably indicating that the kingdom is present in the person of its King, Jesus (cf. 19:11; 21:7; Acts 1:6; see also note on 4:43). "In your midst" could also be rendered "within you," meaning that the kingdom is spiritual and eternal (Matt 23:26), rather than physical and external (cf. John 18:36). If this is the correct view, the pronoun "you" in the phrase "within you" is to be taken in a general sense rather than as referring to the unbelieving Pharisees personally. The kingdom certainly was not within them. If "you" is specific rather than general, it argues for the "in your midst" interpretation.

17:22 *long to see.* In time of trouble, believers will desire to experience the day when Jesus returns in His glory and delivers His people from their distress.

17:23 *Do not go away, and do not run after them.* Do not leave your work in order to pursue predictions of Christ's second advent.

17:24 *like the lightning.* His coming will be sudden, unexpected and public (cf. 12:40).

17:25 *He must suffer.* Jesus repeatedly foretold His coming death (5:35; 9:22,43–45; 12:50; 13:32–33; 18:32; 24:7; see Matt 16:21), which had to occur before His glorious return.

of Noah, so it will be also in the days of the
Son of Man:
27 they were eating, they were drinking,
they were marrying, they were being given in
marriage, until the day that Noah entered the
ark, and the flood came and destroyed them
all.
28 "[1]It was the same as happened in [a]the
days of Lot: they were eating, they were
drinking, they were buying, they were selling, they were planting, they were building;
29 but on the day that Lot went out from
Sodom it rained fire and [1]brimstone from
heaven and destroyed them all.
30 "It will be [1]just the same on the day that
the Son of Man [a]is revealed.
31 "On that day, the one who is [a]on the
housetop and whose goods are in the house
must not go down to take them out; and likewise the one who is in the field must not
turn back.
32 "[a]Remember Lot's wife.
33 "[a]Whoever seeks to keep his [1]life will
lose it, and whoever loses *his life* will preserve it.
34 "I tell you, on that night there will be
two in one bed; one will be taken and the
other will be left.
35 "[a]There will be two women grinding at
the same place; one will be taken and the
other will be left.
36 ["[1][a]Two men will be in the field; one
will be taken and the other will be left."]
37 And answering they *said to Him,
"Where, Lord?" And He said to them,
"[a]Where the body *is,* there also the [1]vultures
will be gathered."

Parables on Prayer

18 Now He was telling them a parable to
show that at all times they [a]ought to
pray and not to [b]lose heart,

28 [1]Lit *In the same way as* [a]Gen 19
29 [1]I.e. burning sulfur
30 [1]Lit *according to the same things* [a]Matt 16:27; 1 Cor 1:7; Col 3:4; 2 Thess 1:7; 1 Pet 1:7; 4:13; 1 John 2:28
31 [a]Matt 24:17, 18; Mark 13:15f; Luke 21:21
32 [a]Gen 19:26
33 [1]Or *soul* [a]Matt 10:39
35 [a]Matt 24:41
36 [1]Early mss do not contain this v [a]Matt 24:40
37 [1]Or *eagles* [a]Matt 24:28
18:1 [a]Luke 11:5-10 [b]2 Cor 4:1

2 [a]Luke 18:4; 20:13; Heb 12:9
3 [1]Lit *Do me justice*
4 [a]Luke 18:2; 20:13; Heb 12:9
5 [1]Lit *do her justice* [2]Lit *hit me under the eye* [a]Luke 11:8 [b]1 Cor 9:27
6 [a]Luke 7:13
7 [1]Or *and yet He is very patient toward them* [a]Rev 6:10 [b]Matt 24:22; Rom 8:33; Col 3:12; 2 Tim 2:10; Titus 1:1 [c]2 Pet 3:9
8 [1]Lit *the faith* [a]Luke 17:26ff
9 [a]Luke 16:15 [b]Rom 14:3, 10
10 [a]1 Kin 10:5; 2 Kin 20:5, 8; Acts 3:1
11 [a]Matt 6:5; Mark 11:25; Luke 22:41

2 saying, "In a certain city there was a
judge who did not fear God and did not
[a]respect man.
3 "There was a widow in that city, and she
kept coming to him, saying, '[1]Give me legal
protection from my opponent.'
4 "For a while he was unwilling; but afterward he said to himself, 'Even though I do
not fear God nor [a]respect man,
5 yet [a]because this widow bothers me, I
will [1]give her legal protection, otherwise by
continually coming she will [2][b]wear me
out.'"
6 And [a]the Lord said, "Hear what the
unrighteous judge *said;
7 now, will not God [a]bring about justice
for His [b]elect who cry to Him day and night,
[1]and will He [c]delay long over them?
8 "I tell you that He will bring about justice for them quickly. However, when the
Son of Man comes, [a]will He find [1]faith on
the earth?"

The Pharisee and the Publican

9 And He also told this parable to some
people who [a]trusted in themselves that they
were righteous, and [b]viewed others with
contempt:
10 "Two men [a]went up into the temple to
pray, one a Pharisee and the other a tax collector.
11 "The Pharisee [a]stood and was praying
this to himself: 'God, I thank You that I am
not like other people: swindlers, unjust,
adulterers, or even like this tax collector.
12 'I [a]fast twice a week; I [b]pay tithes of all
that I get.'
13 "But the tax collector, [a]standing some
distance away, [b]was even unwilling to lift up
his eyes to heaven, but [c]was beating his

12 [a]Matt 9:14 [b]Luke 11:42 13 [a]Matt 6:5; Mark 11:25; Luke 22:41 [b]Ezra 9:6 [c]Luke 23:48

17:28 *in the days of Lot.* See Gen 18:16–19:28.
17:30 *Son of Man is revealed.* At Jesus' second coming He will be plainly visible to all (1 Cor 1:7; 2 Thess 1:7; 1 Pet 1:7,13; 4:13).
17:31 *on the housetop.* It was customary to relax on the flat rooftop. When the final hour comes, however, the individual there should not be thinking of going into the house to retrieve some material objects. Matthew and Mark refer similarly to flight at the fall of Jerusalem, and indirectly to the end time (Matt 24:17–18; Mark 13:15), but here the reference is explicitly to Jesus' return (see v. 30; cf. 21:21).
17:33 *whoever loses his life will preserve it.* See note on 9:24 (cf. Matt 10:39).
17:35 *taken.* Could refer to being "taken to/from destruction" or "taken into the kingdom." What is clear is that no matter how close two people may be in life, they have no guarantee of the same eternal destiny. One may go to judgment and condemnation, the other to salvation, reward and blessing.
17:37 *Where . . . there also the vultures will be gathered.* A proverb. See note on Matt 24:28. In response to the disciples' question, Jesus explains that these things will take place wherever there are people to whom the event pertains.
18:2 *did not respect man.* Unconcerned about the needs of others or about their opinion of him.
18:3 *a widow.* Particularly helpless and vulnerable because she had no family to uphold her cause. Only justice and her own persistence were in her favor.
18:7 *will not God bring about justice . . .?* If an unworthy judge who feels no constraint of right or wrong is compelled by persistence to deal justly with a helpless individual, how much more will God answer prayer! *delay long over them.* God will not delay His support of the chosen ones when they are right. He is not like the unjust judge, who had to be badgered until he wearied and gave in.
18:8 *will He find faith . . . ?* Particularly faith that perseveres in prayer and loyalty (see Matt 24:12–13). Christ makes a second application that looks forward to the time of His second coming. A period of spiritual decline and persecution is assumed—a time that will require perseverance such as the widow demonstrated.
18:10 *to pray.* Periods for prayer were scheduled daily in connection with the morning and evening sacrifices. People could also go to the temple at any time for private prayer.
18:12 *fast twice a week.* Fasting was not commanded in the Mosaic law except for the fast on the day of atonement. However, the Pharisees also fasted on Mondays and Thursdays (see 5:33; Matt 6:16; 9:14; Mark 2:18; Acts 27:9). *tithes of all that I*

breast, saying, 'God, be [1]merciful to me, the
sinner!'
14 "I tell you, this man went to his house
justified rather than the other; [a]for everyone
who exalts himself will be humbled, but he
who humbles himself will be exalted."
15 [a]And they were bringing even their
babies to Him so that He would touch them,
but when the disciples saw it, they *began*
rebuking them.
16 But Jesus called for them, saying, "Permit the children to come to Me, and do not
hinder them, for the kingdom of God belongs
to such as these.
17 "Truly I say to you, [a]whoever does not
receive the kingdom of God like a child will
not enter it *at all.*"

The Rich Young Ruler

18 [a]A ruler questioned Him, saying,
"Good Teacher, what shall I do to inherit
eternal life?"
19 And Jesus said to him, "Why do you
call Me good? No one is good except God
alone.
20 "You know the commandments, '[a]DO
NOT COMMIT ADULTERY, DO NOT MURDER, DO NOT
STEAL, DO NOT BEAR FALSE WITNESS, HONOR YOUR
FATHER AND MOTHER.' "
21 And he said, "All these things I have
kept from *my* youth."
22 When Jesus heard *this,* He said to him,
"One thing you still lack; [a]sell all that you
possess and distribute it to the poor, and you
shall have [b]treasure in heaven; and come,
follow Me."
23 But when he had heard these things, he
became very sad, for he was extremely rich.
24 And Jesus looked at him and said,
"[a]How hard it is for those who are wealthy
to enter the kingdom of God!
25 "For [a]it is easier for a camel to [1]go
through the eye of a needle than for a rich
man to enter the kingdom of God."
26 They who heard it said, "Then who can
be saved?"
27 But He said, "[a]The things that are impossible with people are possible with God."
28 Peter said, "Behold, [a]we have left [1]our
own *homes* and followed You."
29 And He said to them, "Truly I say to
you, [a]there is no one who has left house or
wife or brothers or parents or children, for
the sake of the kingdom of God,
30 who will not receive many times as
much at this time and in [a]the age to come,
eternal life."
31 [a]Then He took the twelve aside and
said to them, "Behold, [b]we are going up to
Jerusalem, and [c]all things which are written
through the prophets about the Son of Man
will be accomplished.
32 "[a]For He will be [1]handed over to the
Gentiles, and will be mocked and mistreated
and spit upon,
33 and after they have scourged Him, they
will kill Him; and the third day He will rise
again."
34 But [a]the disciples understood none of
these things, and *the meaning of* this statement was hidden from them, and they did
not comprehend the things that were said.

Bartimaeus Receives Sight

35 [a]As [1b]Jesus was approaching Jericho, a
blind man was sitting by the road begging.
36 Now hearing a crowd going by, he
began to inquire what this was.
37 They told him that Jesus of Nazareth
was passing by.
38 And he called out, saying, "Jesus, [a]Son
of David, have mercy on me!"
39 Those who led the way were sternly
telling him to be quiet; but he kept crying
out all the more, "[a]Son of David, have mercy on me!"
40 And Jesus stopped and commanded
that he be brought to Him; and when he
came near, He questioned him,
41 "What do you want Me to do for you?"
And he said, "Lord, *I want* to regain my
sight!"
42 And Jesus said to him, "[1]Receive your
sight; [a]your faith has [2]made you well."
43 Immediately he regained his sight and
began following Him, [a]glorifying God; and

13 [1]Or *propitious*
14 [a]Matt 23:12; Luke 14:11
15 [a]Luke 18:15-17: *Matt 19:13-15; Mark 10:13-16*
17 [a]Matt 18:3; 19:14; Mark 10:15; 1 Cor 14:20; 1 Pet 2:2
18 [a]Luke 18:18-30: *Matt 19:16-29; Mark 10:17-30;* Luke 10:25-28
20 [a]Ex 20:12-16; Deut 5:16-20
22 [a]Matt 19:21; Luke 12:33 [b]Matt 6:20
24 [a]Matt 19:23; Mark 10:23f
25 [1]Lit *enter* [a]Matt 19:24; Mark 10:25
27 [a]Matt 19:26
28 [1]Lit *our own things* [a]Luke 5:11
29 [a]Matt 6:33; 19:29; Mark 10:29f
30 [a]Matt 12:32
31 [a]Luke 18:31-33: *Matt 20:17-19; Mark 10:32-34* [b]Luke 9:51 [c]Ps 22; Is 53
32 [1]Or *betrayed* [a]Matt 16:21
34 [a]Mark 9:32; Luke 9:45
35 [1]Lit *He* [a]Luke 18:35-43: *Matt 20:29-34; Mark 10:46-52* [b]Matt 20:29; Mark 10:46; Luke 19:1
38 [a]Matt 9:27; Luke 18:39
39 [a]Luke 18:38
42 [1]Lit *Regain your sight* [2]Lit *saved you* [a]Matt 9:22
43 [a]Matt 9:8

---

get. As a typical first-century Pharisee, he tithed all that he acquired, not merely what he earned.

18:13 *be merciful to me.* The verb used here means "to be propitiated" (see note on 1 John 2:2). The tax collector does not plead his good works but the mercy of God in forgiving his sin.

18:14 *justified.* God reckoned him to be righteous, i.e., his sins were forgiven and he was credited with righteousness—not his own (v. 9) but that which comes from God.

18:17 *like a child.* With total dependence, full trust, frank openness and complete sincerity (see Matt 18:3; 19:14; Mark 10:15; cf. 1 Pet 2:2). See note on Mark 10:15.

18:18–27 For this event see notes on Mark 10:17–27.

18:18 *eternal life.* See note on Matt 19:16.

18:30 *at this time . . . the age to come.* The present age of sin and misery and the future age to be inaugurated by the return of the Messiah.

18:31 *all things which are written through the prophets.* Sometimes referred to as the third prediction of Jesus' death, though the total number is more than three (see note on 17:25). The first distinct prediction is in 9:22 and the second in 9:43–45. The Messiah's death had been predicted and/or prefigured centuries before (e.g., Ps 22; Is 53; Zech 13:7; see Luke 24:27; Matt 26:24,31,54). *Son of Man.* See note on Mark 8:31.

18:35 *was approaching Jericho.* See note on Mark 10:46. *a blind man.* Bartimaeus (Mark 10:46). Matthew reports that two blind men were healed (see note on Matt 20:30). Probably since one was the spokesman and more outstanding, Mark and Luke did not record the presence of the other.

18:38–39 *Son of David.* A Messianic title (see Matt 22:41–45; Mark 12:35; John 7:42; see also 2 Sam 7:12–13; Ps 89:3–4; Amos 9:11; Matt 12:23; 21:15–16).

18:42 *your faith.* See note on 17:19.

when [b]all the people saw it, they gave praise
to God.

Zaccheus Converted

19 He [a]entered Jericho and was passing
through.
2 And there was a man called by the
name of Zaccheus; he was a chief tax collector and he was rich.
3 Zaccheus was trying to see who Jesus
was, and was unable because of the crowd,
for he was small in stature.
4 So he ran on ahead and climbed up
into a [1a]sycamore tree in order to see Him,
for He was about to pass through that way.
5 When Jesus came to the place, He
looked up and said to him, "Zaccheus, hurry
and come down, for today I must stay at
your house."
6 And he hurried and came down and
received Him [1]gladly.
7 When they saw it, they all *began* to
grumble, saying, "He has gone [1]to be the
guest of a man who is a sinner."
8 Zaccheus stopped and said to [a]the
Lord, "Behold, Lord, half of my possessions
I [1]will give to the poor, and if I have
[b]defrauded anyone of anything, I [1]will give
back [c]four times as much."
9 And Jesus said to him, "Today salvation has come to this house, because he, too,
is [a]a son of Abraham.
10 "For [a]the Son of Man has come to seek
and to save that which was lost."

Parable of Money Usage

11 While they were listening to these
things, Jesus went on to tell a parable,
because [a]He was near Jerusalem, and they

43 [b]Luke 9:43; 13:17; 19:37
19:1 [a]Luke 18:35
4 [1]I.e. fig-mulberry [a]1 Kin 10:27; 1 Chr 27:28; 2 Chr 1:15; 9:27; Ps 78:47; Is 9:10; Luke 17:6
6 [1]Lit *rejoicing*
7 [1]Or *to find lodging*
8 [1]Lit *am giving* [a]Luke 7:13 [b]Luke 3:14 [c]Ex 22:1; Lev 6:5; Num 5:7; 2 Sam 12:6
9 [a]Luke 3:8; 13:16; Rom 4:16; Gal 3:7
10 [a]Matt 18:11
11 [a]Luke 9:51
11 [b]Luke 17:20
12 [a]Matt 25:14-30; Luke 19:12-27
13 [1]A mina is equal to about 100 days' wages [2]Lit *while I am coming*
14 [1]Or *an embassy*
16 [1]Lit *Lord* [2]V 13, note 1
17 [a]Luke 16:10
18 [1]V 13, note 1 [2]Lit *lord*
22 [1]Lit *Out of your own mouth*

supposed that [b]the kingdom of God was
going to appear immediately.
12 So He said, "[a]A nobleman went to a
distant country to receive a kingdom for
himself, and *then* return.
13 "And he called ten of his slaves, and
gave them ten [1]minas and said to them, 'Do
business *with this* [2]until I come *back.*'
14 "But his citizens hated him and sent [1]a
delegation after him, saying, 'We do not
want this man to reign over us.'
15 "When he returned, after receiving the
kingdom, he ordered that these slaves, to
whom he had given the money, be called to
him so that he might know what business
they had done.
16 "The first appeared, saying, '[1]Master,
your [2]mina has made ten minas more.'
17 "And he said to him, 'Well done, good
slave, because you have been [a]faithful in a
very little thing, you are to be in authority
over ten cities.'
18 "The second came, saying, 'Your [1]mina,
[2]master, has made five minas.'
19 "And he said to him also, 'And you are
to be over five cities.'
20 "Another came, saying, 'Master, here is
your mina, which I kept put away in a hand-
kerchief;
21 for I was afraid of you, because you are
an exacting man; you take up what you did
not lay down and reap what you did not
sow.'
22 "He *said to him, '[1]By your own words
I will judge you, you worthless slave. Did
you know that I am an exacting man, taking
up what I did not lay down and reaping what
I did not sow?
23 'Then why did you not put my money

19:1 *entered Jericho.* See note on Mark 10:46.

19:2 *chief tax collector.* A position referred to only here in the Bible, probably designating one in charge of a district, with other tax collectors under him. The region was prosperous at this time, so it is no wonder that Zacchaeus had grown rich. See notes on 3:12; Mark 2:14–15.

19:4 *a sycamore tree.* A sturdy tree from 30 to 40 feet high, with a short trunk and spreading branches, capable of holding a grown man. (See note on Amos 7:14.)

19:5 *I must stay at your house.* Implies a divine necessity.

19:8 *four times.* Almost the extreme repayment required under the law in case of theft (Ex 22:1; 2 Sam 12:6; cf. Prov 6:31).

19:9 *son of Abraham.* A true Jew—not only of the lineage of Abraham but one who also walks "in the steps" of Abraham's faith (Rom 4:12). Jesus recognized the tax collector as such, though Jewish society excluded him.

19:10 A key verse in Luke's Gospel. *Son of Man.* A Messianic title (Dan 7:13) used only by Jesus in the four Gospels, by Stephen (Acts 7:56) and in John's vision (Rev 1:13). See Introduction: Plan; see also note on Mark 8:31. *to seek and to save.* An important summary of Jesus' purpose—to bring salvation, meaning eternal life (18:18), and the kingdom of God (18:25). See note on 15:32.

19:11 *kingdom . . . was going to appear.* They expected the Messiah to appear in power and glory and to set up His earthly kingdom, defeating all their political and military enemies.

19:12 *to receive a kingdom for himself.* A rather unusual procedure, but the Herods did just that when they went to Rome to be appointed rulers over the Jews. Similarly, Jesus was soon to depart and in the future is to return as King. During His absence, His servants are entrusted with their Master's affairs (for a similar parable see Matt 25:14–30).

19:13 *ten minas.* A mina was about three months' wages. One talent equaled 60 minas (see Matt 25:15) and a mina equaled 100 drachmas, each drachma being worth about a day's wages (see note on 15:8). Thus the total amount was valued at between two and three years' average wages, and a tenth would be about three months' wages. This was small, however, compared with the amounts mentioned in the parable recorded in Matthew. Here all ten are given the same amount.

19:14 *sent a delegation.* Such an incident had occurred over 30 years earlier in the case of Archelaus (Josephus, *Wars,* 2.6.1; *Antiquities,* 17.9.3), as well as in a number of other instances. This aspect of the story may have been included to warn the Jews against rejecting Jesus as King.

19:22 *you know that I am an exacting man . . . ?* The master did not admit to the statement of the servant, but repeated it in a question. If this was the opinion of the servant, he should have acted accordingly.

in the bank, and having come, I would have collected it with interest?'

24 "Then he said to the bystanders, 'Take the mina away from him and give it to the one who has the ten minas.'

25 "And they said to him, 'Master, he has ten minas *already.*'

26 "[a]I tell you that to everyone who has, more shall be given, but from the one who does not have, even what he does have shall be taken away.

27 "But [a]these enemies of mine, who did not want me to reign over them, bring them here and [b]slay them in my presence."

Triumphal Entry

28 After He had said these things, He [a]was going on ahead, [b]going up to Jerusalem.

29 [a]When He approached Bethphage and [b]Bethany, near the [1]mount that is called [c]Olivet, He sent two of the disciples,

30 saying, "Go into the village ahead of *you;* there, as you enter, you will find a colt tied on which no one yet has ever sat; untie it and bring it *here.*

31 "If anyone asks you, 'Why are you untying it?' you shall say, 'The Lord has need of it.'"

32 So those who were sent went away and found it just as He had told them.

33 As they were untying the colt, its [1]owners said to them, "Why are you untying the colt?"

34 They said, "The Lord has need of it."

35 They brought it to Jesus, [a]and they threw their coats on the colt and put Jesus *on it.*

36 As He was going, they were spreading their coats on the road.

37 As soon as He was approaching, near the descent of [a]the Mount of Olives, the whole crowd of the disciples began to [b]praise God [1]joyfully with a loud voice for all the [2]miracles which they had seen,

38 shouting:

"[a]BLESSED IS THE [b]KING WHO COMES IN THE NAME OF THE LORD;
Peace in heaven and [c]glory in the highest!"

39 [a]Some of the Pharisees [1]in the crowd said to Him, "Teacher, rebuke Your disciples."

40 But Jesus answered, "I tell you, if these become silent, [a]the stones will cry out!"

41 When He approached *Jerusalem,* He saw the city and [a]wept over it,

42 saying, "If you had known in this day, even you, the things which make for peace! But now they have been hidden from your eyes.

43 "For the days will come upon you [1]when your enemies will [a]throw up a [2]barricade against you, and [b]surround you and hem you in on every side,

44 and they will level you to the ground and your children within you, and [a]they will not leave in you one stone upon another, because you did not recognize [b]the time of your visitation."

Traders Driven from the Temple

45 [a]Jesus entered the temple and began to drive out those who were selling,

46 saying to them, "It is written, '[a]AND MY HOUSE SHALL BE A HOUSE OF PRAYER,' [b]but you have made it a ROBBERS' [1]DEN."

47 And [a]He was teaching daily in the temple; but the chief priests and the scribes and

26 [a]Matt 13:12; Mark 4:25; Luke 8:18
27 [a]Luke 19:14 [b]Matt 22:7; Luke 20:16
28 [a]Mark 10:32 [b]Luke 9:51
29 [1]Or *hill...Olive Grove;* Mount of Olives [a]Luke 19:29-38: *Matt 21:1-9; Mark 11:1-10* [b]Matt 21:17 [c]Luke 21:37; Acts 1:12
33 [1]Lit *lords*
35 [a]Luke 19:35-38: *Matt 21:4-9; Mark 11:7-10; John 12:12-15*
37 [1]Lit *rejoicing* [2]Or *works of power* [a]Matt 21:1; Luke 19:29 [b]Luke 18:43
38 [a]Ps 118:26 [b]Matt 2:2; 25:34 [c]Matt 21:9; Luke 2:14
39 [1]Lit *from* [a]Matt 21:15f
40 [a]Hab 2:11
41 [a]Luke 13:34, 35
43 [1]Lit *and* [2]I.e. a dirt wall or mound for siege purposes [a]Eccl 9:14; Is 29:3; 37:33; Jer 6:6; Ezek 4:2; 26:8 [b]Luke 21:20
44 [a]Matt 24:2; Mark 13:2; Luke 21:6 [b]1 Pet 2:12
45 [a]Luke 19:45, 46: *Matt 21:12, 13; Mark 11:15-17;* John 2:13-16
46 [1]Lit *cave* [a]Is 56:7; Jer 7:11; Matt 21:13; Mark 11:17 [b]Jer 7:11
47 [a]Matt 26:55; Luke 21:37

19:26 *more shall be given . . . what he does have shall be taken away.* See 8:18; 17:33; Matt 13:12. Those who seek spiritual gain in the gospel, for themselves and others, will become richer, and those who neglect or squander what is given them will become impoverished, losing even what they have.

19:27 *these enemies of mine . . . slay them.* Perhaps a reference to Jerusalem's destruction in A.D. 70. The punishment of those who rebelled and actively opposed the king (v. 14) was much more severe than that of the negligent servant.

19:28–44 The Triumphal Entry occurred on Sunday of Passion Week. See charts, p. 1408, 1446.

19:29 *Bethphage.* A village near the road going from Jericho to Jerusalem. *Bethany.* Another village about two miles southeast of Jerusalem (John 11:18), and the home of Mary, Martha and Lazarus. *mount that is called Olivet.* A ridge a little more than a mile long, separated from Jerusalem by the Kidron Valley—to the east of the city (see notes on Zech 14:4; Mark 11:1). *two of the disciples.* Not named here or in the parallel passages (Matt 21:1; Mark 11:1; cf. John 12:14).

19:30 *village.* Probably Bethphage. *colt.* In other accounts a donkey colt (John 12:15) is specified and the mother of the colt (Matt 21:7) with him. Luke uses a Greek word that the Septuagint frequently employed to translate the Hebrew word for "donkey." Jesus chooses to enter Jerusalem this time mounted on a donkey to claim publicly that He was the chosen Son of David to sit on David's throne (1 Kin 1:33,44), the one of whom the prophets had spoken (Zech 9:9). *on which no one yet has ever sat.* One that had not been put to secular use (Num 19:2; 1 Sam 6:7).

19:31 *The Lord.* Either God or, more likely, Jesus Himself, here claiming His own unique status as Israel's Lord.

19:37 *all the miracles.* The raising of Lazarus and the healing of blind Bartimaeus were recent examples, but included also would be the works recorded in John on various occasions in Jerusalem, as well as the whole of His ministry in Galilee (cf. Matt 21:14; John 12:17).

19:43 *your enemies will throw up a barricade.* See 21:20; fulfilled when the Romans took Jerusalem in A.D. 70, using an embankment to besiege the city. The description is reminiscent of OT predictions (Is 29:3; 37:33; Ezek 4:1–3).

19:44 *the time of your visitation.* God came to the Jews in the person of Jesus the Messiah, but they failed to recognize Him and rejected Him (see John 1:10–11; cf. Luke 20:13–16).

19:45 Mark (11:11–17) makes clear that this cleansing occurred the day after the Triumphal Entry, i.e., on Monday of Passion Week. *the temple.* The outer court (of the Gentiles), where animals for sacrifice were sold at unfair prices. John records a cleansing of the temple at the beginning of Jesus' ministry (John 2:13–25), but the Synoptics (see Matt 21:12–13; Mark 11:15–17) speak only of a cleansing at the close of Jesus' ministry (see notes on Matt 21:12–17; John 2:14–17).

19:47 *chief priests.* See 3:2; 22:52; 23:4; 24:20. They were part

the leading men among the people [b]were trying to destroy Him,
48 and they could not find [1]anything that
they might do, for all the people were hanging on to [2]every word He said.

Jesus' Authority Questioned

20 [a]On one of the days while [b]He was
teaching the people in the temple and
[c]preaching the gospel, the chief priests and
the scribes with the elders [d]confronted *Him,*
2 and they spoke, saying to Him, "Tell us
by what authority You are doing these
things, or who is the one who gave You this
authority?"
3 Jesus answered and said to them, "I will
also ask you a [1]question, and you tell Me:
4 "Was the baptism of John from heaven
or from men?"
5 They reasoned among themselves, saying, "If we say, 'From heaven,' He will say,
'Why did you not believe him?'
6 "But if we say, 'From men,' all the people will stone us to death, for they are convinced that John was a [a]prophet."
7 So they answered that they did not
know where *it came* from.
8 And Jesus said to them, "Nor [1]will I tell
you by what authority I do these things."

Parable of the Vine-growers

9 [a]And He began to tell the people this
parable: "A man planted a vineyard and
rented it out to [1]vine-growers, and went on a
journey for a long time.
10 "At the *harvest* time he sent a slave to
the vine-growers, so that they would give
him *some* of the produce of the vineyard; but
the vine-growers beat him and sent him
away empty-handed.
11 "And he proceeded to send another
slave; and they beat him also and treated
him shamefully and sent him away empty-
handed.
12 "And he proceeded to send a third; and
this one also they wounded and cast out.
13 "The [1]owner of the vineyard said, 'What
shall I do? I will send my beloved son; perhaps they will [a]respect him.'
14 "But when the vine-growers saw him,
they reasoned with one another, saying,
'This is the heir; let us kill him so that the
inheritance will be ours.'
15 "So they threw him out of the vineyard
and killed him. What, then, will the [1]owner
of the vineyard do to them?
16 "He will come and [a]destroy these vine-
growers and will give the vineyard to others." When they heard it, they said, "[b]May it
never be!"
17 But [1]Jesus looked at them and said,
"What then is this that is written:

'[a]THE STONE WHICH THE BUILDERS
REJECTED,
THIS BECAME [b]THE CHIEF CORNER *stone*'?

18 "[a]Everyone who falls on that stone will
be broken to pieces; but on whomever it
falls, it will scatter him like dust."

Tribute to Caesar

19 The scribes and the chief priests [a]tried
to lay hands on Him that very hour, and they
feared the people; for they understood that
He spoke this parable against them.
20 [a]So they watched Him, and sent spies
who [1]pretended to be righteous, in order
[b]that they might [2]catch Him in some statement, so that they *could* deliver Him to the
rule and the authority of [c]the governor.
21 They questioned Him, saying, "Teacher,

47 [b]Luke 20:19 **48** [1]Lit *what they would do* [2]Lit *Him, listening* **20:1** [a]Luke 20:1-8: *Matt 21:23-27; Mark 11:27-33* [b]Matt 26:55 [c]Luke 8:1 [d]Acts 4:1; 6:12 **3** [1]Lit *word* **6** [a]Matt 11:9; Luke 7:29, 30 **8** [1]Lit *do I tell* **9** [1]Or *tenant farmers,* also vv 10, 14, 16 [a]Luke 20:9-19: *Matt 21:33-46; Mark 12:1-12*

13 [1]Lit *lord* [a]Luke 18:2 **15** [1]Lit *lord* **16** [a]Matt 21:41; Mark 12:9; Luke 19:27 [b]Rom 3:4, 6, 31; 6:2, 15; 7:7, 13; 9:14; 11:1, 11; 1 Cor 6:15; Gal 2:17; 3:21; 6:14 **17** [1]Lit *He* [a]Ps 118:22 [b]Eph 2:20; 1 Pet 2:6 **18** [a]Matt 21:44 **19** [a]Luke 19:47 **20** [1]Lit *falsely represented themselves* [2]Lit *take hold of His word* [a]Luke 20:20-26: *Matt 22:15-22; Mark 12:13-17; Mark 3:2* [b]Luke 11:54; 20:26 [c]Matt 27:2

of the Sanhedrin, the ruling Jewish council (see note on Mark 14:55). *were trying to destroy Him.* See 20:19–20 (cf. John 7:1; 11:53–57).

20:1 The events of 20:1–21:36 all occurred on Tuesday of Passion Week—a long day of controversy. *one of the days.* Not specified, but Mark's parallel accounts (Mark 11:19–20,27–33) indicate that this day (Tuesday) followed the cleansing of the temple (Monday), which followed the Triumphal Entry (Sunday). *chief priests.* See 19:47 and note on Matt 2:4. *scribes.* See 5:30 and notes on 5:17; Matt 2:4. *elders.* See note on Matt 15:2. Each of these groups was represented in the Jewish council, the Sanhedrin (see 22:66).

20:2 *who . . . gave You this authority?* They had asked this of John the Baptist (John 1:19–25) and of Jesus early in His ministry (John 2:18–22). Here the reference is to the cleansing of the temple, which not only defied the authority of the Jewish leaders but also hurt their monetary profits. The leaders may also have been looking for a way to discredit Jesus in the eyes of the people or raise suspicion of Him as a threat to the authority of Rome.

20:4 *the baptism of John from heaven or from men?* By replying with a question, Jesus put the burden on His opponents—indicating only two alternatives: The work of John was either God-inspired or man-devised. By refusing to answer, they placed themselves in an awkward position. *from heaven.* See note on Mark 11:30.

20:10 *he sent a slave.* This parable (v. 9) is reminiscent of Is 5:1–7. The slaves who were sent to the vine-growers represent the prophets God sent in former times who were rejected (see Neh 9:26; Jer 7:25–26; 25:4–7; Matt 23:34; Acts 7:52; Heb 11:36–38). *give him some of the produce.* In accordance with a kind of sharecropping agreement, a fixed amount was due the landowner. At the proper time he would expect to receive his share.

20:13 *my beloved son.* The specific reference to the beloved son makes clearer the intended application of the son in the parable to the Son, Jesus Christ (see 3:22; Matt 17:5).

20:14 *inheritance will be ours.* See note on Mark 12:7.

20:16 *give the vineyard to others.* See note on Matt 21:41.

20:17 *THE CHIEF CORNER stone.* See note on Ps 118:22.

20:18 *will be broken to pieces.* As a pot dashed against a stone is broken, and as one lying beneath a falling stone is crushed, so those who reject Jesus the Messiah will be doomed (see Is 8:14; cf. Dan 2:34–35,44; Luke 2:34).

20:19 *scribes.* For their opposition to Jesus see 5:30; 9:22; 19:47; 22:2; 23:10.

20:20 *authority of the governor.* Fearing to take action themselves, the Jewish religious leaders hoped to draw from Jesus some statement that would bring action from the Roman officials and remove Him from His contact with the people.

we know that You speak and teach correctly,
and You [1]are not partial to any, but teach the
way of God in truth.
22 "Is it [1]lawful for us [a]to pay taxes to Caesar, or not?"
23 But He detected their trickery and said
to them,
24 "Show Me a [1]denarius. Whose [2]likeness
and inscription does it have?" They said,
"Caesar's."
25 And He said to them, "Then [a]render to
Caesar the things that are Caesar's, and to
God the things that are God's."
26 And they were unable to [1a]catch Him
in a saying in the presence of the people; and
being amazed at His answer, they became
silent.

Is There a Resurrection?

27 [a]Now there came to Him some of the
[b]Sadducees (who say that there is no resurrection),
28 and they questioned Him, saying,
"Teacher, Moses wrote for us that [a]IF A MAN'S
BROTHER DIES, having a wife, AND HE IS CHILD-
LESS, HIS BROTHER SHOULD [1]MARRY THE WIFE AND
RAISE UP CHILDREN TO HIS BROTHER.
29 "Now there were seven brothers; and
the first took a wife and died childless;
30 and the second
31 and the third [1]married her; and in the
same way [2]all seven [3]died, leaving no children.
32 "Finally the woman died also.
33 "In the resurrection therefore, which
one's wife will she be? For [1]all seven [2]had
married her."
34 Jesus said to them, "The sons of [a]this
age marry and are given in marriage,
35 but those who are considered worthy
to attain to [a]that age and the resurrection
from the dead, neither marry nor are given in
marriage;
36 for they cannot even die anymore,
because they are like angels, and are [a]sons of
God, being sons of the resurrection.
37 "But that the dead are raised, even
Moses showed, in [a]the *passage about the
burning* bush, where he calls the Lord [b]THE
GOD OF ABRAHAM, AND THE GOD OF ISAAC, AND
THE GOD OF JACOB.
38 "[a]Now He is not the God of the dead but
of the living; for [b]all live to Him."
39 Some of the scribes answered and said,
"Teacher, You have spoken well."
40 For [a]they did not have courage to question Him any longer about anything.
41 [a]Then He said to them, "How *is it that*
they say [1]the Christ is [b]David's son?
42 "For David himself says in the book of
Psalms,
'[a]THE LORD SAID TO MY LORD,
"SIT AT MY RIGHT HAND,
43 [a]UNTIL I MAKE YOUR ENEMIES A FOOTSTOOL
FOR YOUR FEET." '
44 "Therefore David calls Him 'Lord,' and
how is He his son?"
45 [a]And while all the people were listening, He said to the disciples,
46 "Beware of the scribes, [a]who like to
walk around in long robes, and love respectful greetings in the market places, and chief
seats in the synagogues and places of honor
at banquets,
47 who devour widows' houses, and for
appearance's sake offer long prayers. These
will receive greater condemnation."

The Widow's Gift

21 [a]And He looked up and saw the rich
putting their gifts into the treasury.

21 [1]Lit *do not receive a face*
22 [1]Or *permissible* [a]Matt 17:25; Luke 23:2
24 [1]The denarius was a day's wages [2]Lit *image*
25 [a]Matt 22:21; Mark 12:17
26 [1]Lit *catch His statement* [a]Luke 11:54
27 [a]Luke 20:27-40: *Matt 22:23-33; Mark 12:18-27* [b]Acts 23:8
28 [1]Lit *take* [a]Deut 25:5
31 [1]Lit *took* [2]Lit *the seven also* [3]Lit *left no children, and died*
33 [1]Lit *the* [2]Lit *had her as wife*
34 [a]Matt 12:32; Luke 16:8
35 [a]Matt 12:32; Luke 16:8
36 [a]Rom 8:16f; 1 John 3:1, 2
37 [a]Mark 12:26 [b]Ex 3:6
38 [a]Matt 22:32; Mark 12:27 [b]Rom 14:8
40 [a]Matt 22:46; Luke 14:6
41 [1]I.e. the Messiah [a]Luke 20:41-44: *Matt 22:41-46; Mark 12:35-37* [b]Matt 9:27
42 [a]Ps 110:1
43 [a]Ps 110:1
45 [a]Luke 20:45-47: *Matt 23:1-7; Mark 12:38-40*
46 [a]Luke 11:43; 14:7
21:1 [a]Luke 21:1-4: *Mark 12:41-44*

20:22 *taxes to Caesar.* To agree to the taxes demanded by Caesar would disappoint the people, but to advise no payment would disturb the Roman officials. The questioners hoped to trap Jesus with this dilemma.
20:24 *a denarius.* A Roman coin worth about a day's wages (see note on Matt 22:19).
20:25 *to God the things that are God's.* See note on Matt 22:21.
20:27 *Sadducees.* An aristocratic, politically minded group, willing to compromise with secular and pagan leaders. They controlled the high priesthood at this time and held the majority of the seats in the Sanhedrin. They did not believe in the resurrection or an afterlife, and they rejected the oral tradition taught by the Pharisees (Josephus, *Antiquities,* 13.10.6.). See notes on Matt 2:4; 3:7; Mark 12:18; Acts 4:1.
20:28 *HIS BROTHER SHOULD MARRY THE WIFE.* The levirate law (see note on Matt 22:24; cf. Gen 38:8).
20:34–35 *this age . . . that age.* See note on 18:30.
20:36 *like angels.* The resurrection order cannot be assumed to follow present earthly lines. In the new age there will be no marriage, no procreation and no death. *sons of the resurrection.* Those who are to take part in the resurrection of the righteous (cf. Matt 22:23–33; Mark 12:18–27; Acts 4:1–2; 23:6–10).
20:37 *passage about the burning bush.* Since Scripture chapters and verses were not used at the time of Christ, the passage was identified in this way, referring to Moses' experience with the burning bush (Ex 3:2).
20:39 *Teacher, You have spoken well.* Even though there was great animosity against Jesus, the scribes (who were Pharisees) sided with Jesus against the Sadducees on the matter of resurrection.
20:44 *David calls Him 'Lord.'* If the Messiah was a descendant of David, how could this honored king refer to his offspring as Lord? Unless Jesus' opponents were ready to admit that the Messiah was also the divine Son of God, they could not answer His question. See also note on Ps 110:1.
20:46 *long robes . . . chief seats.* See notes on Mark 12:38–39.
20:47 *devour widows' houses.* They take advantage of this defenseless group by fraud and schemes for selfish gain. *receive greater condemnation.* Cf. 12:47–48. The higher the esteem of men, the more severe the demands of true justice; and the more hypocrisy (Matt 23:1–36), the greater the condemnation.
21:1 *the treasury.* In the court of women 13 boxes, shaped like inverted megaphones, were positioned to receive the donations of the worshipers.

2 And He saw a poor widow putting [1]in
[a]two [2]small copper coins.
3 And He said, "Truly I say to you, this
poor widow put in more than all *of them;*
4 for they all out of their [1]surplus put
into the [2]offering; but she out of her poverty
put in all [3]that she had [a]to live on."
5 [a]And while some were talking about
the temple, that it was adorned with beautiful stones and votive gifts, He said,
6 "*As for* these things which you are looking at, the days will come in which [a]there
will not be left one stone upon another
which will not be torn down."
7 They questioned Him, saying, "Teacher,
when therefore will these things happen?
And what *will be* the [1]sign when these things
are about to take place?"
8 And He said, "See to it that you are not
misled; for many will come in My name, saying, '[a]I am *He,*' and, 'The time is near.' [b]Do
not go after them.
9 "When you hear of wars and disturbances, do not be terrified; for these things
must take place first, but the end *does* not
follow immediately."

Things to Come

10 Then He continued by saying to them,
"Nation will rise against nation and kingdom
against kingdom,
11 and there will be great earthquakes,
and in various places plagues and famines;
and there will be terrors and great [1]signs
from heaven.
12 "But before all these things, [a]they will
lay their hands on you and will persecute
you, delivering you to the synagogues and
prisons, [1]bringing you before kings and governors for My name's sake.
13 "[a]It will lead to [1]an opportunity for your
testimony.
14 "[a]So make up your minds not to prepare
beforehand to defend yourselves;
15 for [a]I will give you [1]utterance and wisdom which none of your opponents will be
able to resist or refute.
16 "But you will be betrayed even by parents and brothers and relatives and friends,
and they will put *some* of you to death,
17 and you will be hated by all because of
My name.
18 "Yet [a]not a hair of your head will perish.
19 "[a]By your endurance you will gain your
[1]lives.
20 "But when you see Jerusalem [a]sur-
rounded by armies, then [1]recognize that her
desolation is near.
21 "Then those who are in Judea must flee
to the mountains, and those who are in the
midst of [1]the city must leave, and [a]those
who are in the country must not enter [1]the
city;
22 because these are [a]days of vengeance,
so that all things which are written will be
fulfilled.
23 "Woe to those who are pregnant and to
those who are nursing babies in those days;
for [a]there will be great distress upon the
[1]land and wrath to this people;
24 and they will fall by [a]the edge of the
sword, and will be led captive into all the
nations; and [b]Jerusalem will be [c]trampled
under foot by the Gentiles until [d]the times of
the Gentiles are fulfilled.

2 [1]Lit *there* [2]Gr *lepta* [a]Mark 12:42
4 [1]Or *abundance* [2]Lit *gifts* [3]Lit *the living that she had* [a]Mark 12:44
5 [a]Luke 21:5-36: *Matt 24; Mark 13*
6 [a]Luke 19:44
7 [1]Or *attesting miracle*
8 [a]John 8:24 [b]Luke 17:23
11 [1]Or *attesting miracles*
12 [a]Luke 21:12-17: *Matt 10:19-22; Mark 13:11-13*
12 [1]Lit *being brought*
13 [1]Lit *a testimony for you* [a]Phil 1:12
14 [a]Luke 12:11
15 [1]Lit *a mouth* [a]Luke 12:12
18 [a]Matt 10:30; Luke 12:7
19 [1]Lit *souls* [a]Matt 10:22; 24:13; Rom 2:7; 5:3f; Heb 10:36; James 1:3; 2 Pet 1:6
20 [1]Lit *know* [a]Luke 19:43
21 [1]Lit *her* [a]Luke 17:31
22 [a]Is 63:4; Dan 9:24-27; Hos 9:7
23 [1]Or *earth* [a]Dan 8:19; 1 Cor 7:26
24 [a]Gen 34:26; Ex 17:13; Heb 11:34 [b]Is 63:18; Dan 8:13 [c]Rev 11:2 [d]Rom 11:25

21:2 *two small copper coins.* Jewish coins worth very little.
21:3–4 See note on 2 Cor 8:12.
21:5–36 See note on Mark 13:1–37.
21:5 *temple . . . was adorned.* One stone at the southwest corner was some 36 feet long. "Whatever was not overlaid with gold was purest white" (Josephus, *Jewish War,* 5.5.6.). Herod gave a golden vine for one of its decorations. Its grape clusters were as tall as a man. The full magnificence of the temple as elaborated and adorned by Herod has only recently come to light through archaeological investigations on the temple hill.
21:6 *not be left one stone.* Fulfilled in A.D. 70 when the Romans took Jerusalem and burned the temple (see note on Matt 24:2).
21:7 *when . . . ?* Mark reports that this question was asked by four disciples: Peter, James, John and Andrew (Mark 13:3). Matthew gives the question in a fuller form, including an inquiry for the sign of Jesus' coming and the end of the age (Matt 24:3). *what will be the sign . . . ?* What would be the indication that these things are about to happen?
21:8 *I am He.* I am Jesus the Messiah (having come a second time). *The time.* The end time.
21:9 *the end does not follow immediately.* Refers to the end of the age (see Matt 24:3,6). All the events listed in vv. 8–18 are characteristic of the entire present age, not just signs of the end of the age.
21:11 *signs from heaven.* See v. 25. For prophetic descriptions of celestial signs accompanying the day of the Lord see note on Mark 13:25.
21:12 *delivering you to the synagogues.* Synagogues were used not only for worship and school, but also for community administration and confinement while awaiting trial.
21:15 *none . . . will be able to resist.* See Acts 6:9–10.
21:18 Although persecution and death may come, God is in control, and the ultimate outcome will be eternal victory. *not a hair of your head will perish.* In view of v. 16 this cannot refer to physical safety. The figure indicates that there will be no real, i.e., spiritual, loss.
21:19 See note on Mark 13:13.
21:20 *surrounded by armies.* See 19:43. The sign that the end was near (cf. v. 7) would be the surrounding of Jerusalem with armies. Associated with this event would be the "abomination of desolation" (Matt 24:15).
21:21 *flee to the mountains.* When an army surrounds a city, it is natural to seek protection inside the walls, but Jesus directs His followers to seek the safety of the mountains because the city was doomed to destruction (see note on Matt 24:16).
21:22 *days of vengeance.* God's retributive justice as the consequence of faithlessness (cf. Is 63:4; Jer 5:29; Hos 9:7).
21:24 *times of the Gentiles.* The Gentiles would have both spiritual opportunities (Mark 13:10; cf. Luke 20:16; Rom 11:25) and domination of Jerusalem, but these times will end when God's purpose for the Gentiles has been fulfilled.

The Return of Christ

25 "There will be [1]signs in sun and moon and stars, and on the earth dismay among nations, in perplexity at the roaring of the sea and the waves,

26 men fainting from fear and the expectation of the things which are coming upon the [1]world; for the powers of [2]the heavens will be shaken.

27 "[a]Then they will see [b]THE SON OF MAN COMING IN A CLOUD with power and great glory.

28 "But when these things begin to take place, straighten up and lift up your heads, because [a]your redemption is drawing near."

29 Then He told them a parable: "Behold the fig tree and all the trees;

30 as soon as they put forth *leaves,* you see it and [a]know for yourselves that summer is now near.

31 "So you also, when you see these things happening, [1]recognize that [a]the kingdom of God is near.

32 "Truly I say to you, this [1]generation will not pass away until all things take place.

33 "[a]Heaven and earth will pass away, but My words will not pass away.

34 "[a]Be on guard, so that your hearts will not be weighted down with dissipation and drunkenness and the worries of life, and that day will not come on you suddenly like a trap;

35 for it will come upon all those who dwell on the face of all the earth.

36 "But [a]keep on the alert at all times, praying that you may have strength to escape all these things that are about to take place, and to [b]stand before the Son of Man."

37 Now [1]during the day He was [a]teaching in the temple, but [2b]at evening He would go out and spend the night on [3c]the mount that is called [4]Olivet.

38 And all the people would get up [a]early in the morning *to come* to Him in the temple to listen to Him.

Preparing the Passover

22 [a]Now the Feast of Unleavened Bread, which is called the [b]Passover, was approaching.

2 The chief priests and the scribes [a]were seeking how they might put Him to death; for they were afraid of the people.

3 [a]And [b]Satan entered into Judas who was called Iscariot, [1]belonging to the number of the twelve.

4 And he went away and discussed with the chief priests and [a]officers how he might betray Him to them.

5 They were glad and agreed to give him money.

6 So he consented, and *began* seeking a good opportunity to betray Him to them [1]apart from the crowd.

7 [a]Then came the *first* day of Unleavened Bread on which [b]the Passover *lamb* had to be sacrificed.

8 And Jesus sent [a]Peter and John, saying, "Go and prepare the Passover for us, so that we may eat it."

9 They said to Him, "Where do You want us to prepare it?"

25 [1]Or *attesting miracles* **26** [1]Lit *inhabited earth* [2]Or *heaven* **27** [a]Matt 16:27; 24:30; 26:64; Mark 13:26 [b]Dan 7:13; Rev 1:7 **28** [a]Luke 18:7 **30** [a]Luke 12:57 **31** [1]Lit *know* [a]Matt 3:2 **32** [1]Or *race* **33** [a]Matt 5:18; Luke 16:17 **34** [a]Matt 24:42-44; Mark 4:19; Luke 12:40, 45; 1 Thess 5:2ff **36** [a]Mark 13:33; Luke 12:40 [b]Luke 1:19; Rev 7:9; 8:2; 11:4

37 [1]Lit *days* [2]Lit *nights* [3]Or *the hill* [4]Or *Olive Grove* [a]Matt 26:55; Luke 19:47 [b]Mark 11:19 [c]Matt 21:1 **38** [a]John 8:2 **22:1** [a]Luke 22:1, 2: *Matt 26:2-5; Mark 14:1, 2;* Ex 12:1-27 [b]John 11:55; 13:1 **2** [a]Matt 12:14 **3** [1]Lit *being of* [a]Luke 22:3-6: *Matt 26:14-16; Mark 14:10, 11* [b]Matt 4:10; John 13:2, 27 **4** [a]1 Chr 9:11; Neh 11:11; Luke 22:52; Acts 4:1; 5:24, 26 **6** [1]Or *without a disturbance*

7 [a]Luke 22:7-13: *Matt 26:17-19; Mark 14:12-16* [b]Mark 14:12 **8** [a]Acts 3:1, 11; 4:13, 19; 8:14; Gal 2:9

21:27 *Then . . . SON OF MAN COMING.* The time of Christ's second coming (see Dan 7:13). Often the predictions in this discourse refer ultimately to the end times, while at the same time describing the more imminent destruction of Jerusalem in A.D. 70.
21:28 *lift up your heads.* Do not be downcast at the appearance of these signs, but look up in joy, hope and trust. *redemption.* Final, completed redemption.
21:29 *Behold the fig tree.* The coming of spring is announced by the greening of the trees (cf. Matt 24:32–35; Mark 13:28–31). In a similar way, one can anticipate the coming of the kingdom when its signs are seen. But "kingdom" is used in different ways (see note on 4:43). The reference in v. 31 is to the future kingdom.
21:32 *this generation.* If the reference is to the destruction of Jerusalem, which occurred about 40 years after Jesus spoke these words, "generation" is used in its ordinary sense of a normal life span. All these things were fulfilled in a preliminary sense in the A.D. 70 destruction of Jerusalem. If the reference is to the second coming of Christ, "generation" might indicate the Jewish people as a race (the word can also be translated "race"), who were promised existence to the very end. Or it might refer to the future generation alive at the beginning of these things. It does not mean that Jesus had a mistaken notion He was going to return immediately.
21:34 *that day.* When Christ returns and the future aspect of God's kingdom is inaugurated (cf. v. 31). *come on you suddenly.* Does not mean that Christ's second coming will be completely unannounced, since there will be introductory signs (vv. 28,31).
21:35 *all the earth.* The second coming of Christ will involve the whole of mankind, whereas the fall of Jerusalem did not.
21:37 *during the day.* Each day during the final week of His life, from His Triumphal Entry to the time of the Passover (Sunday-Thursday). *mount that is called Olivet.* See notes on 19:29; Matt 21:17.
22:1 *Feast of Unleavened Bread . . . Passover.* "Passover" was used in two different ways: (1) a specific meal begun at twilight on the 14th of Nisan (Lev 23:4–5), and (2) the week following the Passover meal (Ezek 45:21), otherwise known as the Feast of Unleavened Bread, a week in which no leaven was allowed (Ex 12:15–20; 13:3–7). By NT times the two names for the week-long festival were virtually interchangeable.
22:2 *The chief priests and the scribes.* See 20:1.
22:3 *Satan entered into Judas.* In the Gospels this expression is used on two separate occasions: (1) before Judas went to the chief priests and offered to betray Jesus (here), and (2) during the Last Supper (John 13:27). Thus the Gospel writers depict Satan's control over Judas, who had never displayed a high motive of service or commitment to Jesus.
22:4 *officers.* All of these were Jews selected mostly from the Levites.
22:7 *Passover lamb had to be sacrificed.* On the 14th of Nisan between 2:30 and 5:30 P.M. in the court of the priests—Thursday of Passion Week.

10 And He said to them, "When you have entered the city, a man will meet you carrying a pitcher of water; follow him into the house that he enters.

11 "And you shall say to the owner of the house, 'The Teacher says to you, "Where is the guest room in which I may eat the Passover with My disciples?"'

12 "And he will show you a large, furnished upper room; prepare it there."

13 And they left and found *everything* just as He had told them; and they prepared the Passover.

The Lord's Supper

14 [a]When the hour had come, He reclined *at the table,* and [b]the apostles with Him.

15 And He said to them, "I have earnestly desired to eat this Passover with you before I suffer;

16 for I say to you, I shall never again eat it [a]until it is fulfilled in the kingdom of God."

17 [a]And when He had taken a cup *and* [b]given thanks, He said, "Take this and share it among yourselves;

18 for [a]I say to you, I will not drink of the fruit of the vine from now on until the kingdom of God comes."

19 And when He had taken *some* bread *and* [a]given thanks, He broke it and gave it to them, saying, "This is My body which is given for you; do this in remembrance of Me."

20 And in the same way *He took* the cup after they had eaten, saying, "This cup which is [a]poured out for you is the [b]new covenant in My blood.

21 "[a]But behold, the hand of the one betraying Me is with [1]Mine on the table.

22 "For indeed, the Son of Man is going [a]as it has been determined; but woe to that man by whom He is betrayed!"

23 And they began to discuss among themselves which one of them it might be who was going to do this thing.

Who Is Greatest

24 And there arose also [a]a dispute among them *as to* which one of them was regarded to be greatest.

25 [a]And He said to them, "The kings of the Gentiles lord it over them; and those who have authority over them are called 'Benefactors.'

26 "But *it is* not this way with you, [a]but the one who is the greatest among you must become like [b]the youngest, and the leader like the servant.

27 "For [a]who is greater, the one who reclines *at the table* or the one who serves? Is it not the one who reclines *at the table*? But [b]I am among you as the one who serves.

28 "You are those who have stood by Me in My [a]trials;

29 and just as My Father has granted Me a [a]kingdom, I grant you

30 that you may [a]eat and drink at My table in My [b]kingdom, and [c]you will sit on thrones judging the twelve tribes of Israel.

14 [a]Matt 26:20; Mark 14:17 [b]Mark 6:30
16 [a]Luke 14:15; 22:18, 30; Rev 19:9
17 [a]Luke 22:17-20: *Matt 26:26-29; Mark 14:22-25; 1 Cor 11:23-25;* 1 Cor 10:16 [b]Matt 14:19
18 [a]Matt 26:29; Mark 14:25
19 [a]Matt 14:19
20 [a]Matt 26:28; Mark 14:24 [b]Ex 24:8; Jer 31:31; 1 Cor 11:25; 2 Cor 3:6; Heb 8:8, 13; 9:15
21 [1]Lit *Me* [a]Luke 22:21-23: *Matt 26:21-24; Mark 14:18-21;* Ps 41:9; John 13:18, 21, 22, 26
22 [a]Acts 2:23; 4:28; 10:42; 17:31
24 [a]Mark 9:34; Luke 9:46
25 [a]Luke 22:25-27: *Matt 20:25-28; Mark 10:42-45*
26 [a]Matt 23:11; Mark 9:35; Luke 9:48 [b]1 Pet 5:5
27 [a]Luke 12:37 [b]Matt 20:28; John 13:12-15
28 [a]Heb 2:18; 4:15
29 [a]Matt 5:3; 2 Tim 2:12
30 [a]Luke 22:16 [b]Matt 5:3; 2 Tim 2:12 [c]Matt 19:28

22:10 *a man . . . carrying a pitcher.* It was extraordinary to see a man carrying a pitcher of water, since this was normally women's work.
22:11 *The Teacher says.* This form of address may have been chosen because the owner was a follower already known to Jesus.
22:13 *as He had told them.* It may be that Jesus had made previous arrangements with the man in order to make sure that the Passover meal would not be interrupted. Since Jesus did not identify ahead of time just where He would observe Passover, Judas was unable to inform the enemy, who might have interrupted this important occasion.
22:14–30 It appears that Luke does not attempt to be strictly chronological in his account of the Last Supper. He records the most important part of the occasion first—the sharing of the bread and the cup. Then he tells of Jesus' comments about His betrayer and about the argument over who would be greatest, though both of these subjects seem to have been introduced earlier. John's Gospel (13:26–30), e.g., indicates that Judas had already left the room before the bread and cup of the Lord's Supper were shared, but Luke does not tell when he left.
22:14 *reclined at the table.* See note on Mark 14:3.
22:16 *until it is fulfilled.* Jesus yearned to keep this Passover with His disciples because it was the last occasion before He Himself was to be slain as the perfect Passover lamb (1 Cor 5:7) and thus fulfill this sacrifice for all time. Jesus would eat no more Passover meals until the coming of the future kingdom. After this He will renew fellowship with those who through the ages have commemorated the Lord's Supper. Finally the fellowship will be consummated in the great Messianic "marriage supper" to come (Rev 19:9).
22:17 *when He had taken a cup.* Either the first of the four cups shared during regular observance of the Passover meal, or the third cup.
22:18 *until the kingdom of God comes.* See notes on v. 16; 4:43.
22:19 *is.* Represents or signifies. *given for you.* Anticipating His substitutionary sacrifice on the cross. *in remembrance of Me.* Just as the Passover was a constant reminder and proclamation of God's redemption of Israel from bondage in Egypt, so the keeping of Christ's command would be a remembering and proclaiming of the deliverance of believers from the bondage of sin through Christ's atoning work on the cross.
22:20 *took the cup.* See note on Mark 14:24. *after they had eaten.* Mentioned only here and in 1 Cor 11:25; see note on 1 Cor 11:23–26. *new covenant.* Promised through the prophet Jeremiah (31:31–34)—the fuller administration of God's saving grace, founded on and sealed by the death of Jesus ("in My blood"). See note on 1 Cor 11:25.
22:25 *Benefactors.* A title assumed by or voted for rulers in Egypt, Syria and Rome as a display of honor, but frequently not representing actual service rendered.
22:26 *like the servant.* Jesus urges and exemplifies servant leadership—a trait that was as uncommon then as it is now.
22:28 *in My trials.* Including temptations (cf. 4:13), hardships (9:58) and rejection (John 1:11).
22:29 *a kingdom, I grant you.* The following context (v. 30) indicates that this kingdom is the future form of the kingdom (see notes on 4:43; Matt 3:2).
22:30 *sit on thrones.* As they shared in Jesus' trials, so they will share in His rule (2 Tim 2:12). *judging.* Leading or ruling. *the twelve tribes of Israel.* See Matt 19:28.

31 "Simon, Simon, behold, [a]Satan has [1]demanded *permission* to [b]sift you like wheat;

32 but I [a]have prayed for you, that your faith may not fail; and you, when once you have turned again, [b]strengthen your brothers."

33 [a]But he said to Him, "Lord, with You I am ready to go both to prison and to death!"

34 And He said, "I say to you, Peter, the rooster will not crow today until you have denied three times that you know Me."

35 And He said to them, "[a]When I sent you out without money belt and bag and sandals, you did not lack anything, did you?" They said, "*No,* nothing."

36 And He said to them, "But now, [1]whoever has a money belt is to take it along, likewise also a bag, and [1]whoever has no sword is to sell his [2]coat and buy one.

37 "For I tell you that this which is written must be fulfilled in Me, '[a]AND HE WAS NUMBERED WITH TRANSGRESSORS'; for [b]that which refers to Me has *its* [1]fulfillment."

38 They said, "Lord, look, here are two [a]swords." And He said to them, "It is enough."

The Garden of Gethsemane

39 [a]And He came out and proceeded [b]as was His custom to [c]the Mount of Olives; and the disciples also followed Him.

40 [a]When He arrived at the place, He said to them, "[b]Pray that you may not enter into temptation."

41 And He withdrew from them about a stone's throw, and He [a]knelt down and *began* to pray,

42 saying, "Father, if You are willing, remove this [a]cup from Me; [b]yet not My will, but Yours be done."

43 [1]Now an [a]angel from heaven appeared to Him, strengthening Him.

44 And [a]being in agony He was praying very fervently; and His sweat became like drops of blood, falling down upon the ground.

45 When He rose from prayer, He came to the disciples and found them sleeping from sorrow,

46 and said to them, "Why are you sleeping? Get up and [a]pray that you may not enter into temptation."

Jesus Betrayed by Judas

47 [a]While He was still speaking, behold, a crowd *came,* and the one called Judas, one of the twelve, was preceding them; and he approached Jesus to kiss Him.

48 But Jesus said to him, "Judas, are you betraying the Son of Man with a kiss?"

49 When those who were around Him saw what was going to happen, they said, "Lord, shall we strike with the [a]sword?"

50 And one of them struck the slave of the high priest and cut off his right ear.

51 But Jesus answered and said, "[1]Stop! No more of this." And He touched his ear and healed him.

52 Then Jesus said to the chief priests and [a]officers of the temple and elders who had come against Him, "Have you come out with swords and clubs [b]as you would against a robber?

53 "While I was with you daily in the temple, you did not lay hands on Me; but [1]this hour and the power of darkness are yours."

Jesus' Arrest

54 [a]Having arrested Him, they led Him

31 [1]Or *obtained by asking* [a]Job 1:6-12; 2:1-6; Matt 4:10 [b]Amos 9:9
32 [a]John 17:9, 15 [b]John 21:15-17
33 [a]Luke 22:33, 34: *Matt 26:33-35; Mark 14:29-31; John 13:37, 38*
35 [a]Matt 10:9f; Mark 6:8; Luke 9:3ff; 10:4
36 [1]Lit *he who* [2]Or *outer garment*
37 [1]Lit *end* [a]Is 53:12 [b]John 17:4; 19:30
38 [a]Luke 22:36, 49
39 [a]Matt 26:30; Mark 14:26; John 18:1 [b]Luke 21:37 [c]Matt 21:1
40 [a]Luke 22:40-46: *Matt 26:36-46; Mark 14:32-42* [b]Matt 6:13; Luke 22:46
41 [a]Matt 26:39; Mark 14:35; Luke 18:11
42 [a]Matt 20:22 [b]Matt 26:39
43 [1]Most early mss do not contain vv 43 and 44 [a]Matt 4:11
44 [a]Heb 5:7
46 [a]Luke 22:40
47 [a]Luke 22:47-53: *Matt 26:47-56; Mark 14:43-50; John 18:3-11*
49 [a]Luke 22:38
51 [1]Or *"Let Me at least do this," and He touched*
52 [a]Luke 22:4 [b]Luke 22:37
53 [1]Lit *this is your hour and power of darkness*
54 [a]Matt 26:57; Mark 14:53

22:31 *sift you.* The Greek for "you" is plural. Satan wanted to test the disciples, hoping to bring them to spiritual ruin.
22:36 *a money belt . . . a bag.* Cf. previous instructions (9:3; 10:4). Until now they had been dependent on generous hospitality, but future opposition would require them to be prepared to pay their own way. *buy one.* An extreme figure of speech used to warn them of the perilous times about to come. They would need defense and protection, as Paul did when he appealed to Caesar (Acts 25:11), and authority of God to "bear the sword" (Rom 13:4).
22:37 *NUMBERED WITH TRANSGRESSORS.* Jesus was soon to be arrested as a criminal, in fulfillment of prophetic Scripture, and His disciples would also be in danger for being His followers.
22:38 *". . . two swords.". . . "It is enough."* Sensing that the disciples had taken Him too literally, Jesus ironically closes the discussion with a curt "That's plenty!" Not long after this, Peter was rebuked for using a sword (v. 50).
22:39 *Mount of Olives.* See 21:37; John 18:2. Matthew specifies Gethsemane (Matt 26:36), and John, an olive grove (John 18:1). The place apparently was located on the lower slopes of the Mount of Olives.
22:40 *temptation.* Here refers to severe trial of the kind referred to in vv. 28–38, which might lead to a faltering of their faith.
22:42 *this cup.* The cup of suffering (Matt 20:22–23; cf. Is 51:17; Ezek 23:33). See note on Mark 14:36.
22:43 *an angel.* Matthew and Mark tell of angels ministering to Jesus at the close of His fasting and temptations (Matt 4:11; Mark 1:13), but Luke does not. Here Luke tells of the strengthening presence of an angel, but the other Gospels do not.
22:44 *drops of blood.* Probably perspiration in large drops like blood, or possibly hematidrosis, the actual mingling of blood and sweat as in cases of extreme anguish, strain or sensitivity.
22:47 *a crowd came.* They were sent by the chief priests, elders (Matt 26:47) and teachers of the law (Mark 14:43), and they carried swords and clubs. Included was a detachment of soldiers with officials of the Jews (v. 52; John 18:3). *to kiss Him.* This signal had been prearranged to identify Jesus to the authorities (Matt 26:48). It was unnecessary because Jesus identified Himself (John 18:5), but Judas acted out his plan anyway.
22:50 *the slave of the high priest.* Malchus by name; Simon Peter struck the blow (John 18:10).
22:51 *healed him.* Jesus rectified the wrong done by His follower. No faith on the part of Malchus was involved, but to allow such action would have been contrary to the teaching of Jesus.
22:53 *this hour . . . yours.* It was the time appointed for Jesus' enemies to apprehend Him, the time when the forces of darkness (the powers of evil) would do their worst to defeat God's plan.

away and brought Him to the house of the
high priest; but [b]Peter was following at a distance.
55 [a]After they had kindled a fire in the
middle of [b]the courtyard and had sat down
together, Peter was sitting among them.
56 And a servant-girl, seeing him as he sat
in the firelight and looking intently at him,
said, "This man was with Him too."
57 But he denied *it*, saying, "Woman, I do
not know Him."
58 A little later, [a]another saw him and
said, "You are *one* of them too!" But Peter
said, "Man, I am not!"
59 After about an hour had passed, another man *began* to insist, saying, "Certainly
this man also was with Him, [a]for he is a Galilean too."
60 But Peter said, "Man, I do not know
what you are talking about." Immediately,
while he was still speaking, a rooster
crowed.
61 [a]The Lord turned and looked at Peter.
And Peter remembered the word of the Lord,
how He had told him, "[b]Before a rooster
crows today, you will deny Me three times."
62 And he went out and wept bitterly.
63 [a]Now the men who were holding
[1]Jesus in custody were mocking Him and
beating Him,
64 and they blindfolded Him and were
asking Him, saying, "[a]Prophesy, who is the
one who hit You?"
65 And they were saying many other
things against Him, [a]blaspheming.

Jesus before the Sanhedrin

66 [a]When it was day, [b]the [1]Council of elders of the people assembled, both chief
priests and scribes, and they led Him away
to their [c]council *chamber*, saying,
67 "[a]If You are the [1]Christ, tell us." But He
said to them, "If I tell you, you will not
believe;
68 and if I ask a question, you will not
answer.
69 "[a]But from now on [b]THE SON OF MAN
WILL BE SEATED AT THE RIGHT HAND of the power OF GOD."
70 And they all said, "Are You [a]the Son of
God, then?" And He said to them, "[1][b]Yes, I
am."
71 Then they said, "What further need do
we have of testimony? For we have heard it
ourselves from His own mouth."

Jesus before Pilate

23 Then the whole body of them got up
and [a]brought Him before Pilate.
2 [a]And they began to accuse Him, saying, "We found this man [b]misleading our
nation and [c]forbidding to pay taxes to Caesar, and saying that He Himself is [1]Christ, a
King."
3 So Pilate asked Him, saying, "Are You
the King of the Jews?" And He answered him
and said, "[a]*It is as* you say."
4 Then Pilate said to the chief priests and
the crowds, "[a]I find no guilt in this man."
5 But they kept on insisting, saying, "He
stirs up the people, teaching all over Judea,
[a]starting from Galilee even as far as this
place."
6 When Pilate heard it, he asked whether
the man was a Galilean.
7 And when he learned that He belonged
to Herod's jurisdiction, he sent Him to [a]Her-
od, who himself also was in Jerusalem [1]at
that time.

Jesus before Herod

8 Now Herod was very glad when he saw
Jesus; for [a]he had wanted to see Him for a

54 [b]Matt 26:58; Mark 14:54; John 18:15
55 [a]Luke 22:55-62: *Matt 26:69-75; Mark 14:66-72; John 18:16-18, 25-27* [b]Matt 26:3
58 [a]John 18:26
59 [a]Matt 26:73; Mark 14:70
61 [a]Luke 7:13 [b]Luke 22:34
63 [1]Lit *Him* [a]Matt 26:67f; Mark 14:65; John 18:22f
64 [a]Matt 26:68; Mark 14:65
65 [a]Matt 27:39
66 [1]Or *Sanhedrin* [a]Matt 27:1f; Mark 15:1; John 18:28 [b]Acts 22:5 [c]Matt 5:22
67 [1]I.e. Messiah [a]Matt 26:63-66; Mark 14:61-63; Luke 22:67-71; John 18:19-21
69 [a]Matt 26:64; Mark 14:62; 16:19 [b]Ps 110:1
70 [1]Lit *You say that I am* [a]Matt 4:3 [b]Matt 26:64; 27:11; Luke 23:3
23:1 [a]Matt 27:2; Mark 15:1; John 18:28
2 [1]I.e. Messiah [a]Luke 23:2, 3: *Matt 27:11-14; Mark 15:2-5; John 18:29-37* [b]Luke 23:14 [c]Luke 20:22; John 18:33ff; 19:12; Acts 17:7
3 [a]Luke 22:70
4 [a]Matt 27:23; Mark 15:14; Luke 23:14, 22; John 18:38; 19:4, 6
5 [a]Matt 4:12
7 [1]Lit *in these days* [a]Matt 14:1; Mark 6:14; Luke 3:1; 9:7; 13:31
8 [a]Luke 9:9

22:54 *house of the high priest.* See notes on 3:2; Mark 14:53.
22:59 *he is a Galilean.* Recognized by his speech (Matt 26:73) and identified by a relative of Malchus, the high priest's slave (John 18:26).
22:61 *The Lord . . . looked at Peter.* Peter was outside in the enclosed courtyard, and perhaps Jesus was being taken from the trial by Caiaphas to the Sanhedrin when Jesus caught Peter's eye. *Peter remembered.* The words spoken by Jesus (v. 34).
22:66 *When it was day.* Only after daylight could a legal trial take place for the whole council (Sanhedrin) to pass the death sentence.
22:67 *If You are the Christ.* This demand is related to a question asked later: "Are You the Son of God, then?" (v. 70).
22:71 *we have heard it.* The reaction to Jesus' reply makes clear that His answer was a strong affirmative. Mark has simply, "I am" (Mark 14:62). It was blasphemy to claim to be the Messiah and the Son of God—unless, of course, the claim was true (see note on Mark 14:64).
23:1 *the whole body.* The body of the Sanhedrin (Matt 26:59; 27:1) who had met at the earliest hint of dawn (22:66). *brought Him before Pilate.* See note on Matt 27:2. *Pilate.* See note on Mark 15:1. The Roman governor had his main headquarters in Caesarea, but he was in Jerusalem during Passover to prevent trouble from the large number of Jews assembled for the occasion.
23:2 *misleading our nation.* Large crowds followed Jesus, but He was not misleading them or turning them against Rome. *forbidding to pay taxes.* Another untrue charge (see 20:25). *saying that He Himself is Christ, a King.* Jesus claimed to be the Messiah, but not a political or military king, the kind Rome would be anxious to eliminate.
23:3 *It is as you say.* Jesus affirms that He is a king, but then explains that His kingdom is not the kind that characterizes this world (John 18:33–38).
23:5 *Judea.* May here refer to the whole of the land of the Jews (including Galilee) or to the southern section only, where the region of Judea proper was governed by Pilate (see note on 4:44).
23:7 *Herod's jurisdiction.* See note on 3:1. Although Pilate and Herod were rivals, Pilate did not want to handle this case; so he sent Jesus to Herod (cf. v. 12). *in Jerusalem.* Herod's main headquarters was in Tiberias on the Sea of Galilee; but, like Pilate, he had come to Jerusalem because of the crowds at Passover.
23:8 *wanted to see Him.* Herod was worried about Jesus' iden-

long time, because he had been hearing
about Him and was hoping to see some [1]sign
performed by Him.
9 And he questioned Him [1]at some
length; but [a]He answered him nothing.
10 And the chief priests and the scribes
were standing there, accusing Him vehe-
mently.
11 And Herod with his soldiers, after treating Him with contempt and mocking Him,
[a]dressed Him in a gorgeous robe and sent
Him back to Pilate.
12 Now [a]Herod and Pilate became friends
with one another that very day; for before
they had been enemies with each other.

Pilate Seeks Jesus' Release

13 Pilate summoned the chief priests and
the [a]rulers and the people,
14 and said to them, "You brought this
man to me as one who [a]incites the people to
rebellion, and behold, having examined Him
before you, I [b]have found no guilt in this
man regarding the charges which you make
against Him.
15 "No, nor has [a]Herod, for he sent Him
back to us; and behold, nothing deserving
death has been done by Him.
16 "Therefore I will [a]punish Him and
release Him."
17 [[1]Now he was obliged to release to
them at the feast one prisoner.]
18 But they cried out all together, saying,
"[a]Away with this man, and release for us
Barabbas!"
19 (He was one who had been thrown into
prison for an insurrection made in the city,
and for murder.)
20 Pilate, wanting to release Jesus,
addressed them again,
21 but they kept on calling out, saying,
"Crucify, crucify Him!"
22 And he said to them the third time,
"Why, what evil has this man done? I have
found in Him no guilt *demanding* death;
therefore I will [a]punish Him and release
Him."
23 But they were insistent, with loud
voices asking that He be crucified. And their
voices *began* to prevail.
24 And Pilate pronounced sentence that
their demand be granted.
25 And he released the man they were
asking for who had been thrown into prison
for insurrection and murder, but he delivered
Jesus to their will.

Simon Bears the Cross

26 [a]When they led Him away, they seized
a man, Simon of [b]Cyrene, coming in from
the country, and placed on him the cross to
carry behind Jesus.
27 And following Him was a large crowd
of the people, and of women who were
[1a]mourning and lamenting Him.
28 But Jesus turning to them said,
"Daughters of Jerusalem, stop weeping for
Me, but weep for yourselves and for your
children.
29 "For behold, the days are coming when
they will say, '[a]Blessed are the barren, and
the wombs that never bore, and the breasts
that never nursed.'
30 "Then they will begin TO [a]SAY TO THE
MOUNTAINS, 'FALL ON US,' AND TO THE HILLS,
'COVER US.'
31 "For if they do these things [1]when the
tree is green, what will happen [2]when it is
dry?"
32 [a]Two others also, who were criminals,
were being led away to be put to death with
Him.

The Crucifixion

33 [a]When they came to the place called
[1]The Skull, there they crucified Him and the
criminals, one on the right and the other on
the left.

8 [1]Or *attesting miracle*
9 [1]Lit *in many words* [a]Matt 27:12, 14; Mark 15:5; John 19:9
11 [a]Matt 27:28
12 [a]Acts 4:27
13 [a]Luke 23:35; John 7:26, 48; 12:42; Acts 3:17; 4:5, 8; 13:27
14 [a]Luke 23:2 [b]Luke 23:4
15 [a]Luke 9:9
16 [a]Matt 27:26; Mark 15:15; Luke 23:22; John 19:1; Acts 16:37
17 [1]Early mss do not contain this v
18 [a]Luke 23:18-25: *Matt 27:15-26; Mark 15:6-15;* John 18:39-19:16
22 [a]Luke 23:16
26 [a]Luke 23:26: *Matt 27:32; Mark 15:21;* John 19:17 [b]Matt 27:32
27 [1]Lit *beating the breast* [a]Luke 8:52
29 [a]Matt 24:19; Luke 11:27; 21:23
30 [a]Hos 10:8; Is 2:19, 20; Rev 6:16
31 [1]Lit *in the green tree* [2]Lit *in the dry*
32 [a]Matt 27:38; Mark 15:27; John 19:18
33 [1]In Lat *Calvarius;* or *Calvary* [a]Luke 23:33-43: *Matt 27:33-44; Mark 15:22-32; John 19:17-24*

tity (9:7–9) and had desired to kill Him (13:31), though the two had never met. There is no record that Jesus ever preached in Tiberias, where Herod's residence was located.

23:11 *gorgeous robe.* See note on Mark 15:17.

23:16 *I will punish Him.* Although Pilate found Jesus "not guilty" as charged, he was willing to have Him illegally beaten in order to satisfy the chief priests and the people and to warn against any possible trouble in the future. Scourging, though not intended to kill, was sometimes fatal (see note on Mark 15:15).

23:18 *Barabbas.* Means "son of Abba." Pilate offered a choice between Jesus and an obviously evil, dangerous criminal (see Matt 27:15–20; Mark 15:6–11; John 18:39–40).

23:19 *insurrection . . . murder.* This particular uprising is otherwise unknown but, coupled with murder, it shows the gravity of his deeds (see John 18:40).

23:22 *third time.* See vv. 4,14.

23:25 *delivered Jesus.* Luke's account is abbreviated. Pilate had already handed Jesus over to the soldiers for scourging before He was convicted (John 19:1–5). He now handed Him over for crucifixion.

23:26 *Simon.* His sons, Rufus and Alexander (Mark 15:21), must have been known in Christian circles at a later time, and perhaps were associated with the church at Rome (Rom 16:13). *Cyrene.* A leading city of Libya, west of Egypt. *placed on him the cross.* See note on Mark 15:21.

23:28 *weep for yourselves and for your children.* Because of the terrible suffering to befall Jerusalem some 40 years later when the Romans would besiege the city and utterly destroy the temple.

23:29 *Blessed are the barren.* It would be better not to have children than to have them experience such suffering. Cf. Jer 16:1–4; 1 Cor 7:25–35.

23:30 *FALL ON US.* People would seek escape through destruction in death rather than endure continuing suffering and judgment (cf. Hos 10:8; Rev 6:16).

23:31 *tree is green . . . dry.* If they treat the Messiah this way when the "tree" is well-watered and green, what will their plight be when He is withdrawn from them and they suffer for their rejection in the dry period?

23:32 *who were criminals.* See note on v. 18.

23:33 *The Skull.* Latin *Calvaria,* hence the name "Calvary" (see note on Mark 15:22). *crucified.* See note on Mark 15:24.

34 [1]But Jesus was saying, "[a]Father, forgive them; for they do not know what they are doing." [b]And they cast lots, dividing up His garments among themselves.

35 And the people stood by, looking on. And even the [a]rulers were sneering at Him, saying, "He saved others; [b]let Him save Himself if this is the [1]Christ of God, His Chosen One."

36 The soldiers also mocked Him, coming up to Him, [a]offering Him sour wine,

37 and saying, "[a]If You are the King of the Jews, save Yourself!"

38 Now there was also an inscription above Him, "[a]THIS IS THE KING OF THE JEWS."

39 [a]One of the criminals who were hanged *there* was [1]hurling abuse at Him, saying, "Are You not the [2]Christ? [b]Save Yourself and us!"

40 But the other answered, and rebuking him said, "Do you not even fear God, since you are under the same sentence of condemnation?

41 "And we indeed *are suffering* justly, for we are receiving [1]what we deserve for our deeds; but this man has done nothing wrong."

42 And he was saying, "Jesus, remember me when You come [1]in Your kingdom!"

43 And He said to him, "Truly I say to you, today you shall be with Me in [a]Paradise."

44 [a]It was now about [1b]the sixth hour, and darkness [2]fell over the whole land until [3]the ninth hour,

45 [1]because the sun was obscured; and [a]the veil of the temple was torn [2]in two.

46 And Jesus, [a]crying out with a loud voice, said, "Father, [b]INTO YOUR HANDS I COMMIT MY SPIRIT." Having said this, He breathed His last.

47 [a]Now when the centurion saw what had happened, he *began* [b]praising God, saying, "Certainly this man was [1]innocent."

48 And all the crowds who came together for this spectacle, when they observed what had happened, *began* to return, [1a]beating their breasts.

49 [a]And all His acquaintances and [a]the women who accompanied Him from Galilee were standing at a distance, seeing these things.

Jesus Is Buried

50 [a]And a man named Joseph, who was a [b]member of the Council, a good and righteous man

51 (he had not consented to their plan and action), *a man* from Arimathea, a city of the Jews, who was [a]waiting for the kingdom of God;

52 this man went to Pilate and asked for the body of Jesus.

53 And he took it down and wrapped it in

34 [1]Some early mss do not contain *But Jesus was saying...doing* [a]Matt 11:25; Luke 22:42 [b]Ps 22:18; John 19:24
35 [1]I.e. Messiah [a]Luke 23:13 [b]Matt 27:43
36 [a]Matt 27:48
37 [a]Matt 27:43
38 [a]Matt 27:37; Mark 15:26; John 19:19
39 [1]Or *blaspheming* [2]I.e. Messiah [a]Matt 27:44; Mark 15:32; Luke 23:39-43 [b]Luke 23:35, 37
41 [1]Lit *things worthy of what we have done*
42 [1]Or *into*
43 [a]2 Cor 12:4; Rev 2:7
44 [1]I.e. noon [2]Or *occurred* [3]I.e. 3 p.m. [a]Luke 23:44-49: *Matt 27:45-56; Mark 15:33-41* [b]John 19:14
45 [1]Lit *the sun failing* [2]Lit *in the middle* [a]Ex 26:31-33; Matt 27:51
46 [a]Matt 27:50; Mark 15:37; John 19:30 [b]Ps 31:5
47 [1]Lit *righteous* [a]Matt 27:54; Mark 15:39 [b]Matt 9:8
48 [1]I.e. as a traditional sign of mourning or contrition [a]Luke 8:52; 18:13
49 [a]Matt 27:55f; Mark 15:40f; Luke 8:2; John 19:25
50 [a]Luke 23:50-56: *Matt 27:57-61; Mark 15:42-47; John 19:38-42* [b]Mark 15:43
51 [a]Mark 15:43; Luke 2:25

23:34 *dividing up His garments.* Any possessions an executed person had with him were taken by the executioners. Unwittingly the soldiers (cf. John 19:23–24) were fulfilling the words of Ps 22:18 (but see introduction to Ps 22 and notes on Ps 22:17,20–21).

23:35 *His Chosen One.* See note on 9:35.

23:36 *sour wine.* Or wine vinegar. A sour drink carried by the soldiers for the day. Jesus refused a sedative drink (Matt 27:34; Mark 15:23) but later was given the vinegar drink when He cried out in thirst (John 19:28–30). Luke shows that it was offered in mockery.

23:38 *inscription.* Indicated the crime for which a person was dying. This was Pilate's way of mocking the Jewish leaders as well as announcing what Jesus had been accused of. *KING OF THE JEWS.* See note on Mark 15:26.

23:39 *One of the criminals.* See note on Mark 15:32.

23:43 *Paradise.* In the Septuagint (the Greek translation of the OT) the word designated a garden (Gen 2:8–10) or forest (Neh 2:8), but in the NT (used only here and in 2 Cor 12:4; Rev 2:7) it refers to the place of bliss and rest between death and resurrection (cf. Luke 16:22; 2 Cor 12:2).

23:44 *about the sixth hour . . . the ninth hour.* From noon to three in the afternoon, by the Jewish method of designating time. Jesus had been put on the cross at the third hour (9:00 A.M., Mark 15:25). The "sixth hour" of John (John 19:14) may be Roman time (6:00 A.M.), when Pilate gave his decision (but see note on John 19:14).

23:45 *veil of the temple.* The curtain between the holy place and the most holy place. Its tearing symbolized Christ's opening the way directly to God (Heb 9:3,8; 10:19–22).

23:47 *began praising God.* Either for having seen God publicly vindicate Jesus by mighty signs from heaven, or out of fear (see Matt 27:54) to appease the heavenly Judge and thus ward off a divine penalty for having carried out an unjust judgment. *this man was innocent.* Or "this man was the Righteous One." Matthew and Mark report the centurion's words as "this man was the Son (or son) of God." "The Righteous One" and "the Son of God" would have been essentially equivalent terms. Similarly, "the son of God" and "a righteous man" would have been virtual equivalents. Which one the centurion intended is difficult to determine (see note on Matt 27:54). It seems clear, however, that the Gospel writers saw in his declaration a vindication of Jesus, and since the centurion was the Roman official in charge of the crucifixion, his testimony was viewed as significant (see also the declarations of Pilate: vv. 4,14–15,22; Matt 27:23–24).

23:48 *beating their breasts.* A sign of anguish, grief or contrition (cf. 18:13).

23:49 *the women . . . from Galilee.* See Matt 27:55–56; Mark 15:40–41; John 19:25; cf. Luke 24:10.

23:50 *Joseph . . . a member of the Council.* Either Joseph was not present at the meeting of the Sanhedrin (22:66), or he did not support the vote to have Jesus killed (see v. 51). Mark 14:64 suggests he was not present, for the decision was supported by "all."

23:51 *Arimathea.* See note on Matt 27:57. *waiting for the kingdom of God.* See 2:25.

23:52 The remains of an executed criminal often were left unburied or at best put in a dishonored place in a pauper's field. A near relative, such as a mother, might ask for the body, but it was a courageous gesture for Joseph, a member of the Sanhedrin, to ask for Jesus' body.

a linen cloth, and laid Him in a tomb cut into
the rock, where no one had ever lain.
54 It was [a]the [1]preparation day, and the
Sabbath was about to [2]begin.
55 Now [a]the women who had come with
Him out of Galilee followed, and saw the
tomb and how His body was laid.
56 Then they returned and [a]prepared
spices and perfumes.
And [b]on the Sabbath they rested according to the commandment.

The Resurrection

24 [a]But on the first day of the week, at
early dawn, they came to the tomb
bringing the spices which they had prepared.
2 And they found the stone rolled away
from the tomb,
3 but when they entered, they did not
find the body of [a]the Lord Jesus.
4 While they were perplexed about this,
behold, [a]two men suddenly [b]stood near
them in dazzling clothing;
5 and as *the women* were terrified and
bowed their faces to the ground, *the men*
said to them, "Why do you seek the living
One among the dead?
6 "He is not here, but He [a]has [1]risen.
Remember how He spoke to you [b]while He
was still in Galilee,
7 saying that [a]the Son of Man must be
delivered into the hands of sinful men, and
be crucified, and the third day rise again."
8 And [a]they remembered His words,
9 and returned from the tomb and reported all these things to the eleven and to all
the rest.
10 Now they were [a]Mary Magdalene and
Joanna and Mary the *mother* of James; also
the other women with them were telling
these things to [b]the apostles.
11 But these words appeared [1]to them as
nonsense, and they [a]would not believe them.
12 But Peter got up and [a]ran to the tomb;
stooping and looking in, he *saw the linen
wrappings [1]only; and he went away [b]to his
home, marveling at what had happened.

The Road to Emmaus

13 And behold, [a]two of them were going
that very day to a village named Emmaus,
which was [1]about seven miles from Jerusalem.
14 And they were talking with each other
about all these things which had taken place.
15 While they were talking and discussing, Jesus Himself approached and
began traveling with them.
16 But [a]their eyes were prevented from
recognizing Him.
17 And He said to them, "What are these
words that you are exchanging with one
another as you are walking?" And they stood
still, looking sad.
18 One *of them*, named Cleopas, answered
and said to Him, "Are You [1]the only one visiting Jerusalem and unaware of the things
which have happened here in these days?"
19 And He said to them, "What things?"
And they said to Him, "The things about
[a]Jesus the Nazarene, who was a [b]prophet

54 [1]I.e. preparation for the Sabbath [2]Lit *dawn* [a]Matt 27:62; Mark 15:42
55 [a]Luke 23:49
56 [a]Mark 16:1; Luke 24:1 [b]Ex 20:10f; Deut 5:14
24:1 [a]Luke 24:1-10: *Matt 28:1-8; Mark 16:1-8;* John 20:1-8
3 [a]Luke 7:13; Acts 1:21
4 [a]John 20:12 [b]Luke 2:9; Acts 12:7
6 [1]Or *been raised* [a]Mark 16:6 [b]Matt 17:22f; Mark 9:30f; Luke 9:44; 24:44
7 [a]Matt 16:21; Luke 24:46
8 [a]John 2:22
10 [a]Matt 27:56 [b]Mark 6:30
11 [1]Lit *in their sight* [a]Mark 16:11
12 [1]Or *by themselves* [a]John 20:3-6 [b]John 20:10
13 [1]Lit *60 stadia;* one stadion was about 600 ft [a]Mark 16:12
16 [a]Luke 24:31; John 20:14; 21:4
18 [1]Or *visiting Jerusalem alone*
19 [a]Mark 1:24 [b]Matt 21:11

23:53 *where no one had ever lain.* Rock-hewn tombs were usually made to accommodate several bodies. This one, though finished, had not yet been used. See notes on 19:30; Mark 15:46.

23:54 *preparation day.* Friday, the day before the Sabbath, when preparation was made for keeping the Sabbath. It could be used for Passover preparation, but since in this instance it is followed by the Sabbath, it indicates Friday.

23:55 *the women.* See v. 49; 24:10; cf. 8:2–3. They saw where Jesus was buried and would not mistake the location when they returned.

23:56 *spices and perfumes.* Yards of cloth and large quantities of spices were used in preparing a body for burial. "About a hundred pounds" of myrrh and aloes were already used on that first evening (John 19:39). More was purchased for the return of the women after the Sabbath.

24:1 *first day of the week.* Sunday began by Jewish time at sundown on Saturday. Spices could then be bought (Mark 16:1), and they were ready to set out early the next day. When the women started out, it was dark (John 20:1), and by the time they arrived at the tomb, it was still early dawn (see Matt 28:1; Mark 16:2).

24:2 *the stone rolled away.* A tomb's entrance was ordinarily closed to keep vandals and animals from disturbing the bodies. This stone, however, had been sealed by Roman authority for a different reason (see Matt 27:62–66).

24:4 *two men.* They looked like men, but their clothes were remarkable (see 9:29; Acts 1:10; 10:30). Other reports referring to them call them angels (v. 23; see also John 20:12). Although Matthew speaks of one angel (not two, Matt 28:2) and Mark of a young man in white (Mark 16:5), this is not strange because frequently only the spokesman is noted and an accompanying figure is not mentioned. Words and posture (seated, John 20:12; standing, Luke 24:4) often change in the course of events, so these variations are not necessarily contradictory. They are merely evidence of independent accounts.

24:6 *while . . . in Galilee.* Jesus had predicted His death and resurrection on a number of occasions (9:22), but the disciples failed to comprehend or accept what He was saying.

24:9 *to the eleven and to all the rest.* "Eleven" is sometimes used to refer to the group of apostles (Acts 1:26; 2:14) after the betrayal by Judas. Judas was dead at the time the apostles first met the risen Christ, but the group was still called the twelve (John 20:24). The "rest" included disciples who, for the most part, came from Galilee.

24:10 *Mary Magdalene.* See note on 8:2. She is named first in most of the lists of women (Matt 27:56; Mark 15:40; but cf. John 19:25) and was the first to see the risen Christ (John 20:13–18). *Joanna.* See 8:3. She is named by only Luke at this point (Mark is the only one who adds Salome at this time, Mark 16:1). *Mary the mother of James.* See Mark 16:1. She is the "other Mary" of Matt 28:1. The absence of the mother of Jesus is significant. She was probably with John (cf. John 19:27).

24:12 *Peter . . . ran.* John's Gospel (20:3–9) includes another disciple, John himself.

24:13 *two of them.* One was named Cleopas (v. 18.)

24:16 *prevented from recognizing Him.* By special divine intervention.

24:19 *a prophet.* They had respect for Jesus as a man of God,

mighty in deed and word in the sight of God
and all the people,
20 and how the chief priests and our
[a]rulers delivered Him to the sentence of
death, and crucified Him.
21 "But we were hoping that it was He who
was going to [a]redeem Israel. Indeed, besides
all this, it is the third day since these things
happened.
22 "But also some women among us
amazed us. [a]When they were at the tomb
early in the morning,
23 and did not find His body, they came,
saying that they had also seen a vision of
angels who said that He was alive.
24 "Some of those who were with us went
to the tomb and found it just exactly as the
women also had said; but Him they did not
see."

20 [a]Luke 23:13 21 [a]Luke 1:68 22 [a]Luke 24:1ff 25 [a]Matt 26:24 26 [1]I.e. Messiah [a]Luke 24:7, 44ff; Heb 2:10; 1 Pet 1:11 27 [1]Lit *from* [a]Gen 3:15; 12:3; Num 21:9 [John 3:14]; Deut 18:15 [John 1:45]; John 5:46 [b]2 Sam 7:12-16; Is 7:14 [Matt 1:23]; Is 9:1f [Matt 4:15f]; Is 42:1 [Matt 12:18ff]; Is 53:4 [Matt 8:17; Luke 22:37]; Dan 7:13 [Matt 24:30]; Mic 5:2 [Matt 2:6]; Zech 9:9 [Matt 21:5]; Acts 13:27

25 And He said to them, "O foolish men
and slow of heart to believe in all that [a]the
prophets have spoken!
26 "[a]Was it not necessary for the [1]Christ to
suffer these things and to enter into His glory?"
27 Then beginning [1]with [a]Moses and
[1]with all the [b]prophets, He explained to them
the things concerning Himself in all the
Scriptures.
28 And they approached the village where
they were going, and [a]He acted as though He
were going farther.
29 But they urged Him, saying, "Stay with
us, for it is *getting* toward evening, and the
day [1]is now nearly over." So He went in to
stay with them.

28 [a]Mark 6:48 29 [1]Lit *has now declined*

but after His death they apparently were reluctant to call Him the Messiah.

24:21 *to redeem Israel.* To set the Jewish nation free from bondage to Rome and usher in the kingdom of God (1:68; 2:38; 21:28,31; cf. Titus 2:14; 1 Pet 1:18). *the third day.* A reference either to the Jewish belief that after the third day the soul left the body or to Jesus' remark that He would be resurrected on the third day (9:22).

24:23 *vision of angels.* See note on v. 4.

24:24 *Some of those . . . with us.* See v. 12 and note.

24:27 *Moses and . . . all the prophets.* A way of designating the whole of the OT Scriptures.

24:28 *as though He were going farther.* If they had not invited Him in, He apparently would have continued on by Himself.

Resurrection Appearances

EVENT	PLACE	DAY OF THE WEEK	MATTHEW	MARK	LUKE	JOHN	ACTS	1 COR
The empty tomb	Jerusalem	Resurrection Sunday	28:1-10	16:1-8	24:1-12	20:1-9		
To Mary Magdalene in the garden	Jerusalem	Resurrection Sunday		16:9-11		20:11-18		
To other women	Jerusalem	Resurrection Sunday	28:9-10					
To two people going to Emmaus	Road to Emmaus	Resurrection Sunday		16:12-13	24:13-32			
To Peter	Jerusalem	Resurrection Sunday			24:34			15:5
To the ten disciples in the upper room	Jerusalem	Resurrection Sunday			24:36-43	20:19-25		
To the eleven disciples in the upper room	Jerusalem	Following Sunday		16:14		20:26-31		15:5
To seven disciples fishing	Sea of Galilee	Some time later				21:1-23		
To the eleven disciples on a mountain	Galilee	Some time later	28:16-20	16:15-18				
To more than five hundred	Unknown	Some time later						15:6
To James	Unknown	Some time later						15:7
To His disciples at His ascension	Mount of Olives	Forty days after Jesus' resurrection			24:44-49		1:3-8	
To Paul	Damascus	Several years later					9:1-19 22:3-16 26:9-18	9:1

30 When He had reclined *at the table* with them, He took the bread and [a]blessed *it,* and breaking *it,* He *began* giving *it* to them.

31 Then their [a]eyes were opened and they recognized Him; and He vanished from [1]their sight.

32 They said to one another, "[1]Were not our hearts burning within us while He was speaking to us on the road, while He [a]was [2]explaining the Scriptures to us?"

33 And they got up that very hour and returned to Jerusalem, and [a]found gathered together the eleven and [b]those who were with them,

34 saying, "[a]The Lord has really risen and [b]has appeared to Simon."

35 They *began* to relate [1]their experiences on the road and how [a]He was recognized by them in the breaking of the bread.

Other Appearances

36 While they were telling these things, [a]He Himself stood in their midst and *said to them, "Peace be to you."

37 But they were startled and frightened and thought that they were seeing [a]a spirit.

38 And He said to them, "Why are you troubled, and why do doubts arise in your [1]hearts?

39 "[a]See My hands and My feet, that it is I Myself; [b]touch Me and see, for a spirit does not have flesh and bones as you see that I have."

40 And when He had said this, He showed them His hands and His feet.

41 While they still [1a]could not believe *it* because of their joy and amazement, He said to them, "[b]Have you anything here to eat?"

42 They gave Him a piece of a broiled fish;

43 and He took it and [a]ate *it* before them.

44 Now He said to them, "[a]These are My words which I spoke to you while I was still with you, that all things which are written about Me in the [b]Law of Moses and the Prophets and [c]the Psalms must be fulfilled."

45 Then He [a]opened their [1]minds to understand the Scriptures,

46 and He said to them, "[a]Thus it is written, that the [1]Christ would suffer and [b]rise again from the dead the third day,

47 and that [a]repentance [1]for forgiveness of sins would be proclaimed [2]in His name to [b]all the nations, beginning from Jerusalem.

48 "You are [a]witnesses of these things.

49 "And behold, [a]I am sending forth the promise of My Father upon you; but [b]you are to stay in the city until you are clothed with power from on high."

The Ascension

50 And He led them out as far as [a]Bethany, and He lifted up His hands and blessed them.

51 While He was blessing them, He parted from them and was carried up into heaven.

52 And they, after worshiping Him, returned to Jerusalem with great joy,

53 and were continually in the temple [1]praising God.

30 [a]Matt 14:19 **31** [1]Lit *them* [a]Luke 24:16 **32** [1]Lit *Was not our heart* [2]Lit *opening* [a]Luke 24:45 **33** [a]Mark 16:13 [b]Acts 1:14 **34** [a]Luke 24:6 [b]1 Cor 15:5 **35** [1]Lit *the things* [a]Luke 24:30f **36** [a]Mark 16:14 **37** [a]Matt 14:26; Mark 6:49 **38** [1]Lit *heart* **39** [a]John 20:20, 27 [b]John 20:27; 1 John 1:1 **41** [1]Lit *were disbelieving* [a]Luke 24:11

41 [b]John 21:5 **43** [a]Acts 10:41 **44** [a]Luke 9:22, 44f; 18:31-34; 22:37 [b]Luke 24:27 [c]Ps 2:7ff [Acts 13:33]; Ps 16:10 [Acts 2:27]; Ps 22:1-18 [Matt 27:34-46]; Ps 69:1-21 [John 19:28ff]; Ps 72; 110:1 [Matt 22:43f]; Ps 118:22f [Matt 21:42] **45** [1]Lit *mind* [a]Luke 24:32; Acts 16:14; 1 John 5:20 **46** [1]I.e. Messiah [a]Luke 24:26, 44 [b]Luke 24:7 **47** [1]Later mss read *and forgiveness* [2]Or *on the basis of* [a]Acts 5:31; 10:43; 13:38; 26:18 [b]Matt 28:19 **48** [a]Acts 1:8, 22; 2:32; 3:15; 4:33; 5:32; 10:39, 41; 13:31; 1 Pet 5:1 **49** [a]John 14:26 [b]Acts 1:4 **50** [a]Matt 21:17; Acts 1:12 **53** [1]Lit *blessing*

24:31 *their eyes were opened.* Cf. v. 16; more than a matter of simple recognition.

24:33 *the eleven and those who were with them.* See note on v. 9.

24:36 *He Himself stood in their midst.* Behind locked doors (John 20:19), indicating that His body was of a different order. It was the glorified body of the resurrection (cf. Mark 16:12).

24:39 *My hands and My feet.* Indicating that Jesus' feet as well as His hands were nailed to the cross (see note on Mark 15:24; cf. John 20:20,27).

24:42 *a piece of a broiled fish.* Demonstrating that He had a physical body that could consume food.

24:44 *Law of Moses and the Prophets and the Psalms.* The three parts of the Hebrew OT (Psalms was the first book of the third section, called the Writings), indicating that Christ (the Messiah) was foretold in the whole OT.

24:45 *opened their minds.* By explaining the OT Scriptures (cf. v. 27).

24:46 *suffer . . . rise again from the dead . . . third day.* The OT depicts the Messiah as one who would suffer (Ps 22; Is 53) and rise from the dead on the third day (Ps 16:9–11; Is 53:10–11; compare Jon 1:17 with Matt 12:40).

24:47 *repentance for forgiveness of sins.* See Acts 5:31; 10:43; 13:38; 26:18. The prediction of Christ's death and resurrection (v. 46) is joined with the essence of man's response (repentance) and the resulting benefit (forgiveness; cf. Is 49:6; Acts 13:47; 26:22–23). *beginning from Jerusalem.* Cf. Acts 1:8.

24:49 *the promise of My Father.* Cf. Joel 2:28–29. The reference is to the coming power of the Spirit, fulfilled in Acts 2:4.

24:50 *Bethany.* A village on the Mount of Olives (see notes on 19:29; Matt 21:17).

24:51 *carried up into heaven.* Different from His previous disappearances (4:30; 24:3; John 8:59). They saw Him ascend into a cloud (Acts 1:9).

24:53 *in the temple.* During the period of time immediately following Christ's ascension the believers met continually in the temple (Acts 2:46; 3:1; 5:21,42), where many rooms were available for meetings (see note on 2:37).

John

INTRODUCTION

See "The Synoptic Gospels," p. 1361.

Author

The author is the apostle John, the disciple "whom Jesus loved" (13:23; 19:26; 20:2; 21:7,20,24). He was prominent in the early church but is not mentioned by name in this Gospel—which would be natural if he wrote it, but hard to explain otherwise. The author knew Jewish life well, as seen from references to popular Messianic speculations (e.g., 1:20–21; 7:40–42), to the hostility between Jews and Samaritans (4:9), and to Jewish customs, such as the duty of circumcision on the eighth day taking precedence over the prohibition of working on the Sabbath (see note on 7:22). He knew the geography of Palestine, locating Bethany about 15 stadia (about two miles) from Jerusalem (11:18) and mentioning Cana, a village not referred to in any earlier writing known to us (2:1; 21:2). The Gospel of John has many touches that were obviously based on the recollections of an eyewitness—such as the house at Bethany being filled with the fragrance of the broken perfume jar (12:3). Early writers such as Irenaeus and Tertullian say that John wrote this Gospel, and all other evidence agrees (see Introduction to 1 John: Author).

Date

In general, two views of the dating of this Gospel have been advocated:

1. The traditional view places it toward the end of the first century, c. A.D. 85 or later (see Introduction to 1 John: Date).

2. More recently, some scholars have suggested an earlier date, perhaps as early as the 50s and no later than 70.

The first view may be supported by reference to the statement of Clement of Alexandria that John wrote to supplement the accounts found in the other Gospels (Eusebius, *Ecclesiastical History,* 6.14.7), and thus his Gospel is later than the first three. It has also been argued that the seemingly more developed theology of the fourth Gospel indicates that it originated later.

The second view has found favor because it has been felt more recently that John wrote independently of the other Gospels. This does not contradict the statement of Clement referred to above. Also, those who hold this view point out that developed theology does not necessarily argue for a late origin. The theology of Romans (written c. 57) is every bit as developed as that in John. Further, the statement in 5:2 that there "is" (rather than "was") a pool "by the sheep gate" may suggest a time before 70, when Jerusalem was destroyed. Others, however, observe that John elsewhere sometimes used the present tense when speaking of the past.

Purpose and Emphases

Some interpreters have felt that John's aim was to set forth a version of the Christian message that would appeal to Greek thinkers. Others have seen a desire to supplement (or correct) the Synoptic Gospels, to combat some form of heresy, to oppose the continuing followers of John the Baptist or to achieve a similar goal. But the writer himself states his main purpose clearly: "These have been written so that you may believe that Jesus is the Christ, the Son of God; and that believing you may have life in His name" (20:31). He may have had Greek readers mainly in mind, some of whom were being exposed to heretical influence, but his primary intention was evangelistic. It is possible to understand "may believe" in the sense of "may continue to believe"—in which case the purpose would be to build up believers as well as to win new converts.

For the main emphases of the book see notes on 1:4,7,9,14,19,49; 2:4,11; 3:27; 4:34; 6:35; 13:1—17:26; 13:31; 17:1–2,5; 20:31.

Outline

- I. Prologue (1:1–18)
- II. Beginnings of Jesus' Ministry (1:19–51)
  - A. The Ministry of His Forerunner (1:19–34)
  - B. Jesus' Introduction to Some Future Disciples (1:35–51)
- III. Jesus' Public Ministry: Signs and Discourses (chs. 2—11)
  - A. Changing Water into Wine (2:1–11)
  - B. Cleansing the Temple (2:12–25)
  - C. Interview with Nicodemus (3:1–21)
  - D. Parallel Ministry with John the Baptist (3:22—4:3)
  - E. Journey through Samaria: The Woman at the Well (4:4–42)
  - F. Healing of the Official's Son (4:43–54)
  - G. Trip to Jerusalem for an Annual Feast (ch. 5)
  - H. The Feeding of the 5,000 and the Sermon on the Bread of Life (ch. 6)
  - I. Jesus at the Feast of Booths (chs. 7—8)
  - J. Healing of the Man Born Blind (ch. 9)
  - K. Parable of the Good Shepherd (10:1–21)
  - L. Debating at the Feast of Dedication (10:22–39)
  - M. Ministry in Perea (10:40–42)
  - N. The Raising of Lazarus (ch. 11)
- IV. The Passion Week (chs. 12—19)
  - A. The Anointing of Jesus' Feet (12:1–11)
  - B. The Triumphal Entry (12:12–19)
  - C. The Coming of the Greeks (12:20–36)
  - D. Continued Jewish Unbelief (12:37–50)
  - E. Farewell Discourses (chs. 13—17)
    - 1. Discourse at the Last Supper (chs. 13—14)
    - 2. Discourse on the way to Gethsemane (chs. 15—16)
    - 3. Jesus' prayer of intercession (ch. 17)
  - F. Jesus' Betrayal and Arrest (18:1–12)
  - G. The Trials of Jesus (18:13—19:15)
  - H. The Crucifixion and Burial (19:16—42)
- V. The Resurrection (20:1–29)
- VI. The Statement of Purpose (20:30–31)
- VII. Epilogue (ch. 21)

The Deity of Jesus Christ

1 [a]In the beginning was [b]the Word, and the
Word was [c]with God, and [d]the Word was
God.
2 [1]He was in the beginning with God.
3 [a]All things came into being through
Him, and apart from Him nothing came into
being that has come into being.
4 [a]In Him was life, and the life was [b]the
Light of men.
5 [a]The Light shines in the darkness, and
the darkness did not [1]comprehend it.

The Witness John

6 There [1]came a man sent from God,
whose name was [a]John.
7 [1]He came [2a]as a witness, to testify
about the Light, [b]so that all might believe
through him.
8 [1a]He was not the Light, but *he came* to
testify about the Light.
9 There was [a]the true Light [1]which, coming into the world, enlightens every man.
10 He was in the world, and [a]the world
was made through Him, and the world did
not know Him.
11 He came to His [1]own, and those who
were His own did not receive Him.
12 But as many as received Him, to them
He gave the right to become [a]children of God,
even [b]to those who believe in His name,
13 [a]who were [1]born, not of [2]blood nor of
the will of the flesh nor of the will of man,
but of God.

The Word Made Flesh

14 And [a]the Word [b]became flesh, and
[1c]dwelt among us, and [d]we saw His glory,
glory as of [2]the only begotten from the
Father, full of [e]grace and [f]truth.
15 John *[a]testified about Him and cried
out, saying, "This was He of whom I said,
'[b]He who comes after me [1]has a higher rank
than I, [c]for He existed before me.' "
16 For of His [a]fullness [1]we have all received, and [2]grace upon grace.
17 For [a]the Law was given through Moses;
[b]grace and [c]truth [1]were realized through
Jesus Christ.
18 [a]No one has seen God at any time; [b]the

1:1 [a]Gen 1:1; Col 1:17; 1 John 1:1 [b]John 1:14; Rev 19:13 [c]John 17:5; 1 John 1:2 [d]Phil 2:6 **2** [1]Lit *This one* **3** [a]John 1:10; 1 Cor 8:6; Col 1:16; Heb 1:2 **4** [a]John 5:26; 11:25; 14:6 [b]John 8:12; 9:5; 12:46 **5** [1]Or *overpower* [a]John 3:19 **6** [1]Or *came into being* [a]Matt 3:1 **7** [1]Lit *This one* [2]Lit *for testimony* [a]John 1:15, 19, 32; 3:26; 5:33 [b]John 1:12; Acts 19:4; Gal 3:26 **8** [1]Lit *That one* [a]John 1:20 **9** [1]Or *which enlightens every person coming into the world* [a]1 John 2:8 **10** [a]1 Cor 8:6; Col 1:16; Heb 1:2 **11** [1]Or *own things, possessions, domain* **12** [a]John 11:52; Gal 3:26 [b]John 1:7; 3:18; 1 John 3:23; 5:13

13 [1]Or *begotten* [2]Lit *bloods* [a]John 3:5f; James 1:18; 1 Pet 1:23; 1 John 2:29; 3:9 **14** [1]Or *tabernacled;* i.e. lived temporarily [2]Or *unique, only one of His kind* [a]Rev 19:13 [b]Rom 1:3; Gal 4:4; Phil 2:7f; 1 Tim 3:16; Heb 2:14; 1 John 1:1f; 4:2; 2 John 7 [c]Rev 21:3 [d]Luke 9:32; John 2:11; 17:22, 24; 2 Pet 1:16f; 1 John 1:1 [e]John 1:17; Rom 5:21; 6:14 [f]John 8:32; 14:6; 18:37 **15** [1]Lit *has become before me* [a]John 1:7 [b]Matt 3:11; John 1:27, 30 [c]John 1:30 **16** [1]Lit *we all received* [2]Lit *grace for grace* [a]Eph 1:23; 3:19; 4:13; Col 1:19; 2:9 **17** [1]Lit *came to be* [a]John 7:19 [b]John 1:14; Rom 5:21; 6:14 [c]John 8:32; 14:6; 18:37 **18** [a]Ex 33:20; John 6:46; Col 1:15; 1 Tim 6:16; 1 John 4:12 [b]John 3:16, 18; 1 John 4:9

1:1 *In the beginning.* See Gen 1:1. *Word.* Greeks used this term not only of the spoken word but also of the unspoken word, the word still in the mind—the reason. When they applied it to the universe, they meant the rational principle that governs all things. Jews, on the other hand, used it as a way of referring to God. Thus John used a term that was meaningful to both Jews and Gentiles. *with God.* The Word was distinct from the Father. *was God.* Jesus was God in the fullest sense (see note on Rom 9:5). The prologue (vv. 1–18) begins and ends with a ringing affirmation of His deity (see note on v. 18).

1:4 *life.* One of the great concepts of this Gospel. The Greek word for "life" (zoe) is found 36 times in John, while no other NT book uses it more than 17 times. Life is Christ's gift (10:28), and He, in fact, is "the life" (14:6). *Light of men.* This Gospel also links light with Christ, from whom comes all spiritual illumination. He is the "Light of the world," who holds out wonderful hope for man (8:12). For an OT link between life and light see Ps 36:9.

1:5 *darkness.* The stark contrast between light and darkness is a striking theme in this Gospel (see, e.g., 12:35).

1:6 *John.* In this Gospel the name John always refers to John the Baptist.

1:7 *as a witness, to testify.* John the Baptist's singular ministry was to testify to Jesus (10:41). "Witness" is another important concept in this Gospel. The Greek noun for "witness" or "testimony" is used 14 times (in Matthew not at all, in Mark three times, in Luke once) and the verb ("testify") 33 times (found once each in Matthew and Luke, not at all in Mark)—in both cases more often than anywhere else in the NT. John (the author) thereby emphasizes that the facts about Jesus are amply attested. *that all might believe through him.* People were not to believe "in" John the Baptist but "through" him. Similarly, the writer's purpose was to draw them to belief in Christ (20:31); he uses the Greek verb *pisteuo* ("believe") 98 times.

1:9 John is referring to the incarnation of Christ. *world.* Another common word in John's writings, the Greek *kosmos* is found 78 times in this Gospel and 24 times in his letters (only 47 times in all of Paul's writings). It can mean the universe, the earth, the people on earth, most people, people opposed to God, or the human system opposed to God's purposes. John emphasizes the word by repetition, and moves without explanation from one meaning to another (see, e.g., 17:5,14–15 and notes).

1:12 *He gave the right.* Membership in God's family is by grace alone—the gift of God (see Eph 2:8–9). It is never a human achievement, as v. 13 emphasizes; yet the imparting of the gift is dependent on man's reception of it, as the words "received" and "believe" make clear.

1:14 *became.* Indicates transition; the Word existed before He became man. *flesh.* A strong, almost crude, word that stresses the reality of Christ's manhood. *dwelt among us, and we saw His glory.* The Greek for "dwelt" is connected with the word for "tent/tabernacle"; the verse would have reminded John's Jewish readers of the tent of meeting, which was filled by the glory of God (Ex 40:34–35). Christ revealed His glory to His disciples by the miracles He performed (see 2:11) and by His death and resurrection. *grace and truth.* The corresponding Hebrew terms are often translated "(unfailing) love and faithfulness" (see notes on Ps 26:3; Prov 16:6). *grace.* A significant Christian concept (see notes on Jon 4:2; Gal 1:3; Eph 1:2), though John never uses the word after the prologue (vv. 1–18). *truth.* John uses this word, the Greek *aletheia*, 25 times and links closely with Jesus, who is the truth (14:6).

1:15 *cried out.* John characteristically uses present tense verbs in his writing. Here the Greek is in the present tense, even when John wrote it the action was in the past. The present tense in the original suggest the author John's sense that John the Baptist's message still sounded in people's ears beyond his death. *He existed before me.* In ancient times the older person was given respect and regarded as greater than the younger. People would normally have ranked Jesus lower in respect than John, who was older. John the Baptist explains that this is only apparent, since Jesus, as the Word, existed before he was born on earth.

only begotten God who is [c]in the bosom of
the Father, [d]He has explained *Him*.

The Testimony of John

19 This is [a]the testimony of John, when
[b]the Jews sent to him priests and Levites
[c]from Jerusalem to ask him, "Who are you?"
20 And he confessed and did not deny, but
confessed, "[a]I am not [1]the Christ."
21 They asked him, "What then? Are you
[a]Elijah?" And he *said, "I am not." "Are you
[b]the Prophet?" And he answered, "No."
22 Then they said to him, "Who are you,
so that we may give an answer to those
who sent us? What do you say about yourself?"
23 He said, "I am [a]A VOICE OF ONE CRYING IN
THE WILDERNESS, 'MAKE STRAIGHT THE WAY OF
THE LORD,' as Isaiah the prophet said."
24 Now they had been sent from the Pharisees.
25 They asked him, and said to him,
"Why then are you baptizing, if you are not
the [1]Christ, nor Elijah, nor [a]the Prophet?"
26 John answered them saying, "[a]I baptize
[1]in water, *but* among you stands One
whom you do not know.
27 "*It is* [a]He who comes after me, the
[b]thong of whose sandal I am not worthy to
untie."
28 These things took place in Bethany
[a]beyond the Jordan, where John was baptizing.
29 The next day he *saw Jesus coming to
him and *said, "Behold, [a]the Lamb of God
who [b]takes away the sin of the world!
30 "This is He on behalf of whom I said,
'[a]After me comes a Man who [1]has a higher
rank than I, [b]for He existed before me.'
31 "I did not recognize [1]Him, but so that
He might be manifested to Israel, I came
baptizing [2]in water."
32 John [a]testified saying, "[b]I have seen
the Spirit descending as a dove out of heaven, and He remained upon Him.
33 "I did not recognize [1]Him, but He who
sent me to baptize [2]in water said to me, 'He
upon whom you see the Spirit descending
and remaining upon Him, [a]this is the One
who baptizes [2]in the Holy Spirit.'

18 [c]Luke 16:22; John 13:23 [d]John 3:11
19 [a]John 1:7 [b]John 2:18, 20; 5:10, 15f, 18; 6:41, 52; 7:1, 11, 13, 15, 35; 8:22, 48, 52, 57; 9:18, 22; 10:24, 31, 33 [c]Matt 15:1
20 [1]I.e. the Messiah [a]Luke 3:15f; John 3:28
21 [a]Matt 11:14; 16:14 [b]Deut 18:15, 18; Matt 21:11; John 1:25
23 [a]Is 40:3; Matt 3:3; Mark 1:3; Luke 3:4
25 [1]I.e. Messiah [a]Deut 18:15, 18; Matt 21:11; John 1:21
26 [1]The Gr here can be translated *in, with* or *by* [a]Matt 3:11; Mark 1:8; Luke 3:16; Acts 1:5
27 [a]Matt 3:11; John 1:30
27 [b]Matt 3:11; Mark 1:7; Luke 3:16
28 [a]John 3:26; 10:40
29 [a]Is 53:7; John 1:36; Acts 8:32; 1 Pet 1:19; Rev 5:6, 8, 12f; 6:1 [b]Matt 1:21; 1 John 3:5
30 [1]Lit *has become before me* [a]Matt 3:11; John 1:27 [b]John 1:15
31 [1]I.e. as the Messiah [2]The Gr here can be translated *in, with* or *by*
32 [a]John 1:7 [b]Matt 3:16; Mark 1:10; Luke 3:22
33 [1]I.e. as the Messiah [2]The Gr here can be translated *in, with* or *by* [a]Matt 3:11; Mark 1:8; Luke 3:16; Acts 1:5

1:18 *the only begotten God.* An explicit declaration of Christ's deity (see vv. 1,14 and notes; 3:16). *has made Him known.* Sometimes in the OT people are said to have seen God (e.g., Ex 24:9–11). But we are also told that no one can see God and live (Ex 33:20). Therefore, since no human being can see God as He really is, those who saw God saw Him in a form He took on Himself temporarily for the occasion. Now, however, Christ has made Him known.

1:19 *the Jews.* The phrase occurs about 70 times in this Gospel. It is used in a favorable sense (e.g., 4:22) and in a neutral sense (e.g., 2:6). But generally John used it of the Jewish leaders who were hostile to Jesus (e.g., 8:48). Here it refers to the delegation sent by the Sanhedrin to look into the activities of an unauthorized teacher. *Levites.* Descendants of the tribe of Levi, who were assigned to specific duties in connection with the tabernacle and temple (Num 3:17–37). They also had teaching responsibilities (2 Chr 35:3; Neh 8:7–9), and it was probably in this role that they were sent with the priests to John the Baptist.

1:20 *I.* Emphatic, contrasting John the Baptist (or Baptizer) with someone else. Throughout the following verses this emphatic "I" occurs frequently, and almost invariably there is an implied contrast with Jesus, who is always given the higher place.

1:21 *Are you Elijah? . . . I am not.* The Jews remembered that Elijah had not died (2 Kin 2:11) and believed that the same prophet would come back to earth to announce the end time. In this sense, John properly denied that he was Elijah. When Jesus later said the Baptist was Elijah (Matt 11:14; 17:10–13), He meant it in the sense that John was a fulfillment of the prophecy of Mal 4:5 (cf. Luke 1:17). *the Prophet.* The prophet of Deut 18:15,18. The Jewish people expected a variety of persons to be associated with the coming of the Messiah. John the Baptist emphatically denies being the Prophet. He had come to testify about Jesus, yet they kept asking him about himself. His answers became progressively more terse.

1:23 The Baptist applied the prophecy of Is 40:3 to his own ministry of calling people to repent in preparation for the coming of the Messiah. The men of Qumran (the community that produced the Dead Sea Scrolls; see essay, p. 1356.) applied the same words to themselves, but they prepared for the Lord's coming by isolating themselves from the world to secure their own salvation. John concentrated on helping people come to the Messiah (the Christ).

1:24 *Pharisees.* The conservative religious party, who probed deeper than the rest of the delegation (v. 19). See notes on Matt 3:7; Mark 2:16; Luke 5:17.

1:25 *the Christ.* "The Christ" (Greek) and "The Messiah" (Hebrew) both mean "the Anointed One." In OT times anointing signified being set apart for service, particularly as king (cf. 1 Sam 16:1,13; 26:11) or priest (Ex 40:13–15; Lev 4:3). But people were looking for not just *an* anointed one but *the* Anointed One, the Messiah.

1:27 *the thong of whose sandal I am not worthy to untie.* A menial task, fit for a slave. Disciples would perform all sorts of service for their rabbis (teachers), but loosing sandal thongs was expressly excluded.

1:28 *Bethany.* The Bethany mentioned elsewhere in the Gospels was only about two miles from Jerusalem. The site of this other Bethany is not known, except that it was located on the east side of the Jordan.

1:29 *Lamb of God.* An expression found in the Bible only here and in v. 36. Many suggestions have been made as to its precise meaning (e.g., the lamb offered at Passover, or the lamb of Is 53:7, of Jer 11:19 or of Gen 22:8). But the expression seems to be a general reference to sacrifice, not the name for a particular offering. John was saying that Jesus would be the sacrifice that would atone for the sin of the world.

1:31 *I did not recognize Him.* John the Baptist, who "lived in the deserts until the day of his public appearance to Israel" (Luke 1:80), may not have known Jesus at all. But the words probably mean only that he did not know that Jesus was the Messiah until he saw the sign mentioned in vv. 32–33.

1:32 See note on Matt 3:15 for Jesus' baptism.

1:33 *the One who baptizes in the Holy Spirit.* John baptized with water, but Jesus would baptize with the Spirit. If a specific event

34 "I myself have seen, and have testified that this is [a]the Son of God."

Jesus' Public Ministry, First Converts

35 Again [a]the next day John was standing [1]with two of his disciples,

36 and he looked at Jesus as He walked, and *said, "Behold, [a]the Lamb of God!"

37 The two disciples heard him speak, and they followed Jesus.

38 And Jesus turned and saw them following, and *said to them, "What do you seek?" They said to Him, "[a]Rabbi (which translated means Teacher), where are You staying?"

39 He *said to them, "Come, and you will see." So they came and saw where He was staying; and they stayed with Him that day, for it was about the [1]tenth hour.

40 [a]One of the two who heard John *speak* and followed Him, was Andrew, Simon Peter's brother.

41 He *found first his own brother Simon and *said to him, "We have found the [a]Messiah" (which translated means [1]Christ).

42 He brought him to Jesus. Jesus looked at him and said, "You are Simon the son of [1a]John; you shall be called [b]Cephas" (which is translated [2c]Peter).

43 [a]The next day He purposed to go into [b]Galilee, and He *found [c]Philip. And Jesus *said to him, "[d]Follow Me."

44 Now [a]Philip was from [b]Bethsaida, of the city of Andrew and Peter.

45 [a]Philip *found [b]Nathanael and *said to him, "We have found Him of whom [c]Moses in the Law and *also* [c]the Prophets wrote—Jesus of [d]Nazareth, [e]the son of Joseph."

46 Nathanael said to him, "[a]Can any good thing come out of Nazareth?" [b]Philip *said to him, "Come and see."

47 Jesus saw Nathanael coming to Him, and *said of him, "Behold, an [a]Israelite indeed, in whom there is no deceit!"

48 Nathanael *said to Him, "How do You know me?" Jesus answered and said to him, "Before [a]Philip called you, when you were under the fig tree, I saw you."

49 Nathanael answered Him, "[a]Rabbi, You are [b]the Son of God; You are the [c]King of Israel."

50 Jesus answered and said to him, "Because I said to you that I saw you under the fig tree, do you believe? You will see greater things than these."

51 And He *said to him, "Truly, truly, I say to you, you will see [a]the heavens opened and [b]the angels of God ascending and descending on [c]the Son of Man."

Miracle at Cana

2 On [a]the third day there was a wedding in [b]Cana of Galilee, and the [c]mother of Jesus was there;

2 and both Jesus and His [a]disciples were invited to the wedding.

3 When the wine ran out, the mother of Jesus *said to Him, "They have no wine."

4 And Jesus *said to her, "[a]Woman, [1b]what does that have to do with us? [c]My hour has not yet come."

34 [a]Matt 4:3; John 1:49 **35** [1]Lit *and* [a]John 1:29 **36** [a]John 1:29 **38** [a]Matt 23:7f; John 1:49 **39** [1]Perhaps 10 a.m. (Roman time) **40** [a]Matt 4:18-22; Mark 1:16-20; Luke 5:2-11; John 1:40-42 **41** [1]Gr *Anointed One* [a]Dan 9:25; John 4:25 **42** [1]Gr *Joannes* [2]I.e. Rock or Stone [a]Matt 16:17; John 21:15-17 [b]1 Cor 1:12; 3:22; 9:5; 15:5; Gal 1:18; 2:9, 11, 14 [c]Matt 16:18 **43** [a]John 1:29, 35 [b]Matt 4:12; John 1:28; 2:11 [c]Matt 10:3; John 1:44-48; 6:5, 7; 12:21f; 14:8f [d]Matt 8:22 **44** [a]Matt 10:3; John 1:44-48; 6:5, 7; 12:21f; 14:8f [b]Matt 11:21 **45** [a]Matt 10:3; John 1:44-48; 6:5, 7; 12:21f; 14:8f [b]John 1:46-49; 21:2 [c]Luke 24:27 [d]Matt 2:23 [e]Luke 2:48; 3:23; 4:22; John 6:42 **46** [a]John 7:41, 52

46 [b]Matt 10:3; John 1:44-48; 6:5, 7; 12:21f; 14:8f **47** [a]Rom 9:4 **48** [a]Matt 10:3; John 1:44-48; 6:5, 7; 12:21f; 14:8f **49** [a]John 1:38 [b]John 1:34 [c]Matt 2:2; 27:42; Mark 15:32; John 12:13 **51** [a]Ezek 1:1; Matt 3:16; Luke 3:21; Acts 7:56; 10:11; Rev 19:11 [b]Gen 28:12 [c]Matt 8:20
2:1 [a]John 1:29, 35, 43 [b]John 2:11; 4:46; 21:2 [c]Matt 12:46
2 [a]John 1:40-49; 2:12, 17, 22; 3:22; 4:2, 8, 27; 6:8, 12, 16, 22, 24, 60f, 66; 7:3; 8:31 **4** [1]Lit *what to Me and to you* (a Hebrew idiom) [a]John 19:26 [b]Matt 8:29 [c]John 7:6, 8, 30; 8:20

---

is intended by these words, the fulfillment was the sending of the Holy Spirit on the day of Pentecost (Acts 2).

1:34 *Son of God.* See vv. 14,18; 3:16; 20:31.

1:35 *two.* One was Andrew (v. 40). The other is not named, but from early times it has been thought that he was the author of this Gospel. *his disciples.* In the sense that they had been baptized by John and looked to him as their religious teacher.

1:36 *Lamb of God.* See note on v. 29.

1:39 *tenth hour.* 4:00 P.M.

1:41 *the Messiah.* See note on v. 25.

1:42 *Peter.* Both Cephas (Aramaic) and Peter (Greek) mean "rock." In the Gospels, Peter was anything but a rock; he was impulsive and unstable. In Acts, he was a pillar of the early church. Jesus named him not for what he was but for what, by God's grace, he would become.

1:44 *Bethsaida.* See note on Matt 11:21.

1:45 *son of Joseph.* Not a denial of the virgin birth of Christ (Matt 1:18,20,23,25; Luke 1:35). Joseph was Jesus' legal, though not His natural, father.

1:46 *Nazareth.* See 7:52; see also note on Matt 2:23.

1:47 *an Israelite indeed.* See 2:24–25.

1:48 *fig tree.* Its shade was a favorite place for study and prayer in hot weather.

1:49 *Son of God.* See vv. 14,18,34; 3:16; 20:31. At the beginning of Jesus' ministry Nathanael acknowledged Jesus with this meaningful title; later it was used in mockery (Matt 27:40; cf. John 19:7). *King of Israel.* See 12:13. In Mark 15:32 "Christ" and "King of Israel" are equated.

1:51 *heavens opened.* In Jesus' ministry the disciples will see heaven's (God's) testimony to Jesus as plainly as if they heard an announcement from heaven concerning Him. *the angels of God ascending and descending.* As in Jacob's dream (see Gen 28:12 and note), thus marking Jesus as God's elect one through whom redemption comes to the world—perhaps identifying Jesus as *the* true Israelite (see v. 47). *Son of Man.* Jesus' favorite self-designation (see notes on Mark 8:31; Luke 6:5; 19:10).

2:1 *a wedding.* Little is known of how a wedding was performed in the Holy Land in the first century, but clearly the feast was very important and might go on for a week. To fail in proper hospitality was a serious offense. *Cana.* Mentioned only in John's Gospel (2:11; 4:46; 21:2). It was west of the Sea of Galilee, but the exact location is unknown.

2:3 *When the wine ran out.* More than a minor social embarrassment, since the family had an obligation to provide a feast of the socially required standard. There was no great variety in beverages, and people normally drank water or wine.

2:4 *My hour has not yet come.* Several similar expressions scattered through this Gospel (7:6,8,30; 8:20) picture Jesus moving inevitably toward the destiny for which He had come: the time of His sacrificial death on the cross. At the crucifixion and resurrection Jesus' time had truly come (12:23,27; 13:1; 16:32; 17:1).

Miracles of Jesus

HEALING MIRACLES	MATTHEW	MARK	LUKE	JOHN
Man with leprosy	8:2-4	1:40-42	5:12-13	
Roman centurion's servant	8:5-13		7:1-10	
Peter's mother-in-law	8:14-15	1:30-31	4:38-35	
Two men from Gadara	8:28-34	5:1-15	8:27-35	
Paralyzed man	9:2-7	2:3-12	5:18-25	
Woman with bleeding	9:20-22	5:25-29	8:43-48	
Two blind men	9:27-31			
Mute, demon-possessed man	9:32-33			
Man with a withered hand	12:10-13	3:1-5	6:6-10	
Blind, mute, demon-possessed man	12:22		11:14	
Canaanite woman's daughter	15:21-28	7:24-30		
Boy with a demon	17:14-18	9:17-29	9:38-43	
Two blind men (including Bartimaeus)	20:29-34	10:46-52	18:35-43	
Deaf mute		7:31-37		
Possessed man in synagogue		1:23-26	4:33-35	
Blind man at Bethsaida		8:22-26		
Crippled woman			13:11-13	
Man with dropsy			14:1-4	
Ten men with leprosy			17:11-19	
The high priest's servant			22:50-51	
Official's son at Capernaum				4:46-54
Sick man at pool of Bethesda				5:1-9
Man born blind				9:1-7

MIRACLES SHOWING POWER OVER NATURE	MATTHEW	MARK	LUKE	JOHN
Calming the storm	8:23-27	4:37-41	8:22-25	
Walking on water	14:25	6:48-51		6:19-21
Feeding of the 5,000	14:15-21	6:35-44	9:12-17	6:6-13
Feeding of the 4,000	15:32-38	8:1-9		
Coin in fish	17:24-27			
Fig tree withered	21:18-22	11:12-14,20-25		
Large catch of fish			5:4-11	
Water turned into wine				2:1-11
Another large catch of fish				21:1-11

MIRACLES OF RAISING THE DEAD	MATTHEW	MARK	LUKE	JOHN
Jairus's daughter	9:18-19,23-25	5:22-24,38-42	8:41-42,49-56	
Widow's son at Nain			7:11-15	
Lazarus				11:1-44

5 His [a]mother *said to the servants, "Whatever He says to you, do it."

6 Now there were six stone waterpots set there [a]for the Jewish custom of purification, containing [1]twenty or thirty gallons each.

7 Jesus *said to them, "Fill the waterpots with water." So they filled them up to the brim.

8 And He *said to them, "Draw *some* out now and take it to the [1]headwaiter." So they took it *to him.*

9 When the headwaiter tasted the water [a]which had become wine, and did not know where it came from (but the servants who had drawn the water knew), the headwaiter *called the bridegroom,

10 and *said to him, "Every man serves the good wine first, and when *the people* [a]have [1]drunk freely, *then he serves* the poorer *wine; but* you have kept the good wine until now."

11 This beginning of *His* [1a]signs Jesus did in Cana of [b]Galilee, and manifested His [c]glory, and His disciples believed in Him.

12 After this He went down to [a]Capernaum, He and His [b]mother and *His* [b]brothers and His [c]disciples; and they stayed there a few days.

First Passover—Cleansing the Temple

13 [a]The Passover of the Jews was near, and Jesus [b]went up to Jerusalem.

14 [a]And He found in the temple those who were selling oxen and sheep and doves, and the money changers seated *at their tables.*

15 And He made a scourge of cords, and drove *them* all out of the temple, with the sheep and the oxen; and He poured out the coins of the money changers and overturned their tables;

16 and to those who were selling [a]the doves He said, "Take these things away; stop

5 [a]Matt 12:46
6 [1]Lit *two or three measures* [a]Mark 7:3f; John 3:25
8 [1]Or *steward*
9 [a]John 4:46
10 [1]Or *have become drunk* [a]Matt 24:49; Luke 12:45; Acts 2:15; 1 Cor 11:21; Eph 5:18; 1 Thess 5:7; Rev 17:2, 6
11 [1]Or *attesting miracles;* i.e. one which points to the supernatural power of God in redeeming grace [a]John 2:23; 3:2; 4:54; 6:2, 14, 26, 30; 7:31; 9:16; 10:41; 11:47; 12:18, 37; 20:30 [b]John 1:43 [c]John 1:14
12 [a]Matt 4:13 [b]Matt 12:46 [c]John 2:2
13 [a]Deut 16:1-6; John 5:1; 6:4; 11:55 [b]Luke 2:41; John 2:23
14 [a]John 2:14-16: *Matt 21:12ff; Mark 11:15, 17; Luke 19:45f;* Mal 3:1ff
16 [a]Matt 21:12
16 [1]Lit *house* [b]Luke 2:49
17 [a]John 2:2 [b]Ps 69:9
18 [1]Lit *that You do these* [a]John 1:19 [b]Matt 12:38
19 [1]Or *sanctuary* [a]Matt 26:61; 27:40; Mark 14:58; 15:29; Acts 6:14
20 [1]Or *sanctuary* [a]John 1:19 [b]Ezra 5:16
21 [1]Or *sanctuary* [a]1 Cor 6:19
22 [a]John 2:2

making [b]My Father's house a [1]place of business."

17 His [a]disciples remembered that it was written, "[b]ZEAL FOR YOUR HOUSE WILL CONSUME ME."

18 [a]The Jews then said to Him, "[b]What sign do You show us [1]as your authority for doing these things?"

19 Jesus answered them, "[a]Destroy this [1]temple, and in three days I will raise it up."

20 [a]The Jews then said, "It took [b]forty-six years to build this [1]temple, and will You raise it up in three days?"

21 But He was speaking of [a]the [1]temple of His body.

22 So when He was raised from the dead, His [a]disciples [b]remembered that He said this; and they believed [c]the Scripture and the word which Jesus had spoken.

23 Now when He was in Jerusalem at [a]the Passover, during the feast, many believed in His name, [b]observing His signs which He was doing.

24 But Jesus, on His part, was not entrusting Himself to them, for [a]He knew all men,

25 and because He did not need anyone to testify concerning man, [a]for He Himself knew what was in man.

The New Birth

3 Now there was a man of the Pharisees, named [a]Nicodemus, a [b]ruler of the Jews;

2 this man came to Jesus by night and said to Him, "[a]Rabbi, we know that You have come from God *as* a teacher; for no one can do these [1b]signs that You do unless [c]God is with him."

[b]Luke 24:8; John 2:17; 12:16; 14:26 [c]Ps 16:10; Luke 24:26f; John 20:9; Acts 13:33 **23** [a]John 2:13 [b]John 2:11 **24** [a]Acts 1:24; 15:8 **25** [a]Matt 9:4; John 1:42, 47; 6:61, 64; 13:11
3:1 [a]John 7:50; 19:39 [b]Luke 23:13; John 7:26, 48 **2** [1]Or *attesting miracles* [a]Matt 23:7; John 3:26 [b]John 2:11 [c]John 9:33; 10:38; 14:10f; Acts 2:22; 10:38

2:6 *custom of purification.* Jews became ceremonially defiled during the normal circumstances of daily life, and were cleansed by pouring water over the hands. For a lengthy feast with many guests a large amount of water was required for this purpose. *containing.* Refers to capacity, not actual content.

2:11 *signs.* John always refers to Jesus' miracles as "signs," a word emphasizing the significance of the action rather than the marvel (see, e.g., 4:54; 6:14; 9:16; 11:47). They revealed Jesus' glory (see 1:14; cf. Is 35:1–2; Joel 3:18; Amos 9:13).

2:12 *went down.* Situated on the shore of the lake, Capernaum was at a lower level than Cana. *brothers.* See note on Luke 8:19.

2:13 *Passover.* See Ex 12 and notes on Ex 12:11–23; see also notes on Matt 26:17,18–30; Mark 14:1,12; Luke 22:1; and chart, pp. 164–165. Passover was one of the annual feasts that all Jewish men were required to celebrate in Jerusalem (Deut 16:16). See note on 5:1.

2:14–17 Matthew, Mark and Luke record a cleansing of the temple toward the end of Jesus' ministry (see note on Matt 21:12–17).

2:14 *oxen and sheep and doves.* Required for sacrifices. Jews who came great distances had to be able to buy sacrificial animals near the temple. The merchants, however, were selling them in the outer court of the temple itself, the one place where Gentiles could come to pray. *money changers.* Many coins had to be changed into currency acceptable to the temple authorities, which made money changers necessary (see note on Mark 11:15). They should not, however, have been working in the temple itself.

2:19 The Jews thought Jesus was referring to the literal temple, but John tells us that He was not (v. 21). Just a few years later Jesus was accused of saying that He would destroy the temple and raise it again (Matt 26:60–61; Mark 14:57–59), and mockers repeated the charge as He hung on the cross (Matt 27:40; Mark 15:29). The same misunderstanding may have been behind the charge against Stephen (Acts 6:14).

2:20 *forty-six years.* The temple was not finally completed until A.D. 64. The meaning is that work had been going on for 46 years. Since it had begun in 20 B.C., the year of the event recorded here is A.D. 26/27.

2:22 *remembered.* See 14:26.

2:23 *the Passover.* See note on v. 13. *name.* In ancient times an individual's "name" summed up his whole person.

3:1 *a man of the Pharisees.* See notes on Matt 3:7; Mark 2:16; Luke 5:17.

3:2 *by night.* Perhaps Nicodemus was afraid to come by day. Or he may have wanted a long talk, which would have been difficult in the daytime with the crowds around Jesus.

3 Jesus answered and said to him, "Truly, truly, I say to you, unless one [a]is born
[1]again he cannot see [b]the kingdom of God."
4 Nicodemus *said to Him, "How can a
man be born when he is old? He cannot
enter a second time into his mother's womb
and be born, can he?"
5 Jesus answered, "Truly, truly, I say to
you, unless one is born of [a]water and the
Spirit he cannot enter into [b]the kingdom of
God.
6 "[a]That which is born of the flesh is
flesh, and that which is born of the Spirit is
spirit.
7 "Do not be amazed that I said to you,
'You must be born [1]again.'
8 "[a]The wind blows where it wishes and
you hear the sound of it, but do not know
where it comes from and where it is going;
so is everyone who is born of the Spirit."
9 Nicodemus said to Him, "How can
these things be?"
10 Jesus answered and said to him, "Are
you [a]the teacher of Israel and do not understand these things?
11 "Truly, truly, I say to you, [a]we speak of
what we know and [b]testify of what we have
seen, and [b]you do not accept our testimony.
12 "If I told you earthly things and you do
not believe, how will you believe if I tell you
heavenly things?
13 "[a]No one has ascended into heaven, but
[b]He who descended from heaven: [c]the Son
of Man.
14 "As [a]Moses lifted up the serpent in the
wilderness, even so must [b]the Son of Man
[c]be lifted up;
15 so that whoever [1]believes will [a]in Him
have eternal life.
16 "For God so [a]loved the world, that He
[b]gave His [1c]only begotten Son, that whoever
[d]believes in Him shall not perish, but have
eternal life.

17 "For God [a]did not send the Son into the
world [b]to judge the world, but that the world
might be saved through Him.
18 "[a]He who believes in Him is not judged;
he who does not believe has been judged
already, because he has not believed in the
name of [b]the [1]only begotten Son of God.
19 "This is the judgment, that [a]the Light
has come into the world, and men loved the
darkness rather than the Light, for [b]their
deeds were evil.
20 "[a]For everyone who does evil hates the
Light, and does not come to the Light for fear
that his deeds will be exposed.
21 "But he who [a]practices the truth comes
to the Light, so that his deeds may be manifested as having been wrought in God."

John's Last Testimony

22 After these things Jesus and His [a]disci-
ples came into the land of Judea, and there
He was spending time with them and [b]bap-
tizing.
23 John also was baptizing in Aenon near
Salim, because there was much water there;
and *people* were coming and were being baptized—
24 for [a]John had not yet been thrown into
prison.
25 Therefore there arose a discussion on
the part of John's disciples with a Jew about
[a]purification.
26 And they came to John and said to
him, "[a]Rabbi, He who was with you [b]beyond
the Jordan, to whom you [c]have testified,
behold, He is baptizing and all are coming to
Him."
27 John answered and said, "[a]A man can

3 [1]Or *from above* [a]2 Cor 5:17; 1 Pet 1:23 [b]Matt 19:24; 21:31; Mark 9:47; 10:14f; John 3:5 **5** [a]Ezek 36:25-27; Eph 5:26; Titus 3:5 [b]Matt 19:24; 21:31; Mark 9:47; 10:14f; John 3:3 **6** [a]John 1:13; 1 Cor 15:50 **7** [1]Or *from above* **8** [a]Ps 135:7; Eccl 11:5; Ezek 37:9 **10** [a]Luke 2:46; 5:17; Acts 5:34 **11** [a]John 1:18; 7:16f; 8:26, 28; 12:49; 14:24 [b]John 3:32 **13** [a]Deut 30:12; Prov 30:4; Acts 2:34; Rom 10:6; Eph 4:9 [b]John 3:31; 6:38, 42 [c]Matt 8:20 **14** [a]Num 21:9 [b]Matt 8:20 [c]John 8:28; 12:34 **15** [1]Or *believes in Him will have eternal life* [a]John 20:31; 1 John 5:11-13 **16** [1]Or *unique*, only one of His kind [a]Rom 5:8; Eph 2:4; 2 Thess 2:16; 1 John 4:10; Rev 1:5 [b]Rom 8:32; 1 John 4:9 [c]John 1:18; 3:18; 1 John 4:9 [d]John 3:36; 6:40; 11:25f

17 [a]John 3:34; 5:36, 38; 6:29, 38, 57; 7:29; 8:42; 10:36; 11:42; 17:3, 8, 18, 21, 23, 25; 20:21 [b]Luke 19:10; John 8:15; 12:47; 1 John 4:14 **18** [1]Or *unique*, only one of His kind [a]Mark 16:16; John 5:24 [b]John 1:18; 1 John 4:9 **19** [a]John 1:4; 8:12; 9:5; 12:46 [b]John 7:7 **20** [a]John 3:20, 21; Eph 5:11, 13 **21** [a]1 John 1:6 **22** [a]John 2:2 [b]John 4:1, 2 **24** [a]Matt 4:12; 14:3; Mark 6:17; Luke 3:20 **25** [a]John 2:6 **26** [a]Matt 23:7; John 3:2 [b]John 1:28 [c]John 1:7 **27** [a]1 Cor 4:7; Heb 5:4

3:3 *born again.* The Greek here and in v. 7 may mean "born from above." Both meanings are consistent with Jesus' redeeming work.

3:5 *born of water and the Spirit.* A phrase understood in various ways: 1. It means much the same as "born of the Spirit" (v. 8; cf. Titus 3:5). 2. Water here refers to purification. 3. Water refers to baptism—that of John (1:31) or that of Jesus and His disciples (v. 22; 4:1–2). *kingdom of God.* See note on Matt 3:2.

3:7 *You.* This assertion applies to everyone, not just Nicodemus (the Greek for "you" is plural here). *must.* There are no exceptions. *born again.* See note on v. 3.

3:8 The Holy Spirit is sovereign. He works as He pleases in His renewal of the human heart.

3:11 *we.* The plural associates others, perhaps the disciples, with Jesus. The words are true of Christians as well as of Christ. *testimony.* See note on 1:7.

3:13 *the Son of Man.* Jesus' favorite self-designation (see notes on Mark 8:31; Luke 6:5; 19:10).

3:14 *must the Son of Man be lifted up.* See notes on 12:31–32.

3:15 *believes.* See note on 1:7. *eternal life.* An infinitely high quality of life in living fellowship with God—both now and forever.

3:16 *God so loved the world.* The great truth that motivated God's plan of salvation (cf. 1 John 4:9–10). *world.* All people on earth—or perhaps all creation (see note on 1:9). *that He gave.* See Is 9:6. *only begotten Son.* See 1:14,18; cf. Gen 22:2,16; Rom 8:32. Although believers are also called "sons of God" (2 Cor 6:18; Rev 21:7), Jesus is God's Son in a unique sense.

3:18 *believes . . . does not believe.* John is not speaking of momentary beliefs and doubts but of continuing, settled attitudes.

3:22 *baptizing.* According to 4:2 only the disciples actually baptized.

3:23 *Aenon.* Possibly about eight miles south of Scythopolis (Beth-shean), west of the Jordan.

3:25 *discussion . . . about purification.* The Dead Sea (Qumran) Scrolls (see essay, p. 1356) show that some Jews were deeply interested in the right way to achieve ceremonial purification.

3:26 *testified.* See note on 1:7. John's disciples knew that he had testified about Jesus, but they loved their master and were envious of Jesus' success.

receive nothing unless it [b]has been given
him from heaven.
28 "You yourselves [1]are my witnesses that I
said, '[a]I am not the [2]Christ,' but, 'I have been
sent ahead of Him.'
29 "He who has the bride is [a]the bridegroom; but the friend of the bridegroom,
who stands and hears him, rejoices greatly
because of the bridegroom's voice. So this
[b]joy of mine has been made full.
30 "He must increase, but I must decrease.
31 "[a]He who comes from above is above
all, [b]he who is of the earth is from the earth
and speaks of the earth. [a]He who comes
from heaven is above all.
32 "What He has seen and heard, of that He
[a]testifies; and [a]no one receives His testimony.
33 "He who has received His testimony
[a]has set his seal to *this,* that God is true.
34 "For He whom God has [a]sent speaks the
words of God; [1b]for He gives the Spirit without measure.
35 "[a]The Father loves the Son and [b]has giv-
en all things into His hand.
36 "He who [a]believes in the Son has eternal life; but he who [b]does not [1]obey the Son
will not see life, but the wrath of God abides
on him."

Jesus Goes to Galilee

4 Therefore when [a]the Lord knew that the
Pharisees had heard that Jesus was making and [b]baptizing more disciples than John
2 (although [a]Jesus Himself was not baptizing, but His [b]disciples were),
3 He left [a]Judea and went away [b]again
into Galilee.
4 And He had to pass through [a]Samaria.
5 So He *came to a city of [a]Samaria
called Sychar, near [b]the parcel of ground that
[c]Jacob gave to his son Joseph;
6 and Jacob's well was there. So Jesus,
being wearied from His journey, was sitting
thus by the well. It was about [1]the sixth
hour.

The Woman of Samaria

7 There *came a woman of Samaria to
draw water. Jesus *said to her, "Give Me a
drink."
8 For His [a]disciples had gone away into
[b]the city to buy food.
9 Therefore the [a]Samaritan woman *said
to Him, "How is it that You, being a Jew, ask
me for a drink since I am a Samaritan
woman?" (For [b]Jews have no dealings with
Samaritans.)
10 Jesus answered and said to her, "If you
knew the gift of God, and who it is who says
to you, 'Give Me a drink,' you would have
asked Him, and He would have given you
[a]living water."

27 [b]James 1:17 **28** [1]Lit *testify for me* [2]I.e. Messiah [a]John 1:20, 23 **29** [a]Matt 9:15; 25:1 [b]John 15:11; 16:24; 17:13; Phil 2:2; 1 John 1:4; 2 John 12 **31** [a]Matt 28:18; John 3:13; 8:23 [b]1 Cor 15:47; 1 John 4:5 **32** [a]John 3:11 **33** [a]John 6:27; Rom 4:11; 15:28; 1 Cor 9:2; 2 Cor 1:22; Eph 1:13; 4:30; 2 Tim 2:19; Rev 7:3-8 **34** [1]Lit *because He does not give the Spirit by measure* [a]John 3:17 [b]Matt 12:18; Luke 4:18; Acts 1:2; 10:38 **35** [a]Matt 28:18; John 5:20; 17:2 [b]Matt 11:27; Luke 10:22 **36** [1]Or *believe* [a]John 3:16 [b]Acts 14:2; Heb 3:18 **4:1** [a]Luke 7:13 [b]John 3:22, 26; 1 Cor 1:17

2 [a]John 3:22, 26; 1 Cor 1:17 [b]John 2:2 **3** [a]John 3:22 [b]John 2:11f **4** [a]Luke 9:52 **5** [a]Luke 9:52 [b]Gen 33:19; Josh 24:32 [c]Gen 48:22; John 4:12 **6** [1]Perhaps 6 p.m. Roman time or noon Jewish time **8** [a]John 2:2 [b]John 4:5, 39 **9** [a]Luke 9:52 [b]Ezra 4:3-6, 11ff; Matt 10:5; John 8:48; Acts 10:28 **10** [a]Jer 2:13; John 4:14; 7:37f; Rev 7:17; 21:6; 22:1, 17

3:27 The words are true of both Jesus and John (and of everyone). Both had what God had given them, so there was no place for envy. *given.* The Greek for "to give" is used frequently in this Gospel (75 times), especially of the things the Father gives the Son.

3:29 *the bridegroom.* The most important man at a wedding, referring here to Jesus. The friend (best man) is there only to help the bridegroom, which describes the role of John the Baptist. *rejoices greatly.* Not because he was on center stage, but because the bridegroom was there. John's joy was to hear of Jesus' success.

3:30 John the Baptist had been sent to prepare the way for the Messiah and here reaffirms his subordinate position.

3:31 *He who comes from above.* Jesus, whose heavenly origin (cf. 1 Cor 15:47) meant much to John. *he who is of the earth.* A general expression that could apply to anyone, but here it particularly refers to John the Baptist.

3:32 *what He has seen and heard.* Jesus taught from divine experience. *no one.* Does not mean that no person accepted what He said (see v. 33) but that people in general refused His teaching.

3:33 *set his seal.* When anyone accepts Christ's testimony, he accepts the truth that Jesus came from heaven and that God was acting in Him for the world's salvation. He thereby certifies that God is truthful.

3:34 *He whom God has sent.* Jesus. *without measure.* Some hold that it is only to Jesus that the Spirit is given without limit. Others take the second "He" as a reference to Christ's giving the Spirit without limit to believers.

3:36 *has.* Eternal life is a present possession, not something the believer will only obtain later (see note on v. 15). *wrath of God.* A strong expression, meaning that God is actively opposed to everything evil. The word "wrath" occurs only here in John's Gospel (see note on Rom 1:18). *abides.* A sinner cannot expect God's wrath eventually to fade away. God's opposition to evil is both total and permanent.

4:1 *Pharisees.* The religious leaders took a close interest in John the Baptist (see note on 1:24) and then also in Jesus.

4:2 The disciples did not baptize without Jesus' approval (3:22).

4:3 *left Judea.* Success (which aroused opposition; see 7:1), not failure, led Jesus to leave Judea.

4:4 *had to pass.* The necessity lay in Jesus' mission, not in geography. *Samaria.* Here the whole region, not simply the city. Jews often avoided Samaria by crossing the Jordan and traveling on the east side (see notes on Matt 10:5; Luke 9:52).

4:5 *Sychar.* A small village near Shechem. Jacob bought some land in the vicinity of Shechem (Gen 33:18–19), and it was apparently this land that he gave to Joseph (Gen 48:21–22). See map, p. 1522.

4:6 *Jacob's well.* Mentioned nowhere else in Scripture. *about the sixth hour.* About 12:00 noon.

4:7 *to draw water.* People normally drew water at the end of the day rather than in the heat of midday (see Gen 24:11 and note). But the practice is attested by Josephus, who says that the young ladies whom Moses helped (Ex 2:15–17) came to draw water at noon.

4:9 *have no dealings with.* The Greek implies the meaning, "do not use dishes Samaritans have used." A Jew would become ceremonially unclean if he used a drinking vessel handled by a Samaritan, since the Jews held that all Samaritans were "unclean."

4:10 *gift.* The Greek for this word is used only here in this Gospel and emphasizes God's grace through Christ. Jesus gave life and gave it freely. *living water.* In 7:38–39 the term is

Jesus in Judea and Samaria

Ptolemais

Mediterranean Sea

GALILEE

Capernaum

Sea of Galilee

Tiberias

Cana

Yarmuk R.

Nazareth

Mt. Tabor

Nain

Jordan R.

Scythopolis

Caesarea

The most important port in Judea in NT times.

Pella

Salim

Aenon

John the Baptist baptized here (John 3:23). It was also the probable location of John's ministry.

SAMARIA

Here Jesus talked with a Samaritan woman, at Jacob's well (John 4:5).

Samaria

Jabbok R.

Sychar

Mt. Gerizim

The mountain referred to by the Samaritan woman at the well as the worship center for the Samaritans (John 4:20-23).

Jordan R.

PEREA

JUDEA

Most important Biblical city. Jesus was crucified here as predicted (Matt 16:21; Mark 10:33; Luke 18:31).

The resurrected Jesus appeared to two people walking to Emmaus, and he ate with them there (Luke 24:13).

Jericho

Jesus healed a blind man here (Matt 20:29), and called Zacchaeus down from a tree (Luke 19:1). The Good Samaritan helped a traveler en route here (Luke 10:30).

Emmaus

Jerusalem

Bethany

Jesus raised Lazarus from the dead (John 11:43-44). Here Jesus was anointed in the house of Simon the Leper (Matt 26:6). It was also the scene of the ascension (Luke 24:50-51).

Bethlehem

The birthplace of Jesus (Matt 2:1; Luke 2:4).

Dead Sea

Machaerus

Arnon R.

Miles 5 0 10 20

Kms 5 0 10 20 30

11 She *said to Him, "[1]Sir, You have nothing to draw with and the well is deep; where then do You get that [a]living water?

12 "You are not greater than our father Jacob, are You, who [a]gave us the well, and drank of it himself and his sons and his cattle?"

13 Jesus answered and said to her, "Everyone who drinks of this water will thirst again;

14 but whoever drinks of the water that I will give him [a]shall never thirst; but the water that I will give him will become in him a well of water springing up to [b]eternal life."

15 The woman *said to Him, "[1]Sir, [a]give me this water, so I will not be thirsty nor come all the way here to draw."

16 He *said to her, "Go, call your husband and come here."

17 The woman answered and said, "I have no husband." Jesus *said to her, "You have correctly said, 'I have no husband';

18 for you have had five husbands, and the one whom you now have is not your husband; this you have said truly."

19 The woman *said to Him, "[1]Sir, I perceive that You are [a]a prophet.

20 "[a]Our fathers worshiped in [b]this mountain, and you *people* say that [c]in Jerusalem is the place where men ought to worship."

21 Jesus *said to her, "Woman, believe Me, [a]an hour is coming when [b]neither in this mountain nor in Jerusalem will you worship the Father.

22 "[a]You worship what you do not know; we worship what we know, for [b]salvation is from the Jews.

23 "But [a]an hour is coming, and now is, when the true worshipers will worship the Father [b]in spirit and truth; for such people the Father seeks to be His worshipers.

24 "God is [1]spirit, and those who worship Him must worship [a]in spirit and truth."

25 The woman *said to Him, "I know that [a]Messiah is coming ([b]He who is called Christ); when that One comes, He will declare all things to us."

26 Jesus *said to her, "[a]I who speak to you am *He.*"

27 At this point His [a]disciples came, and they were amazed that He had been speaking with a woman, yet no one said, "What do You seek?" or, "Why do You speak with her?"

28 So the woman left her waterpot, and went into the city and *said to the men,

29 "Come, see a man [a]who told me all the things that I *have* done; [b]this is not [1]the Christ, is it?"

30 They went out of the city, and were coming to Him.

31 Meanwhile the disciples were urging Him, saying, "[a]Rabbi, eat."

32 But He said to them, "I have food to eat that you do not know about."

33 So the [a]disciples were saying to one another, "No one brought Him *anything* to eat, did he?"

11 [1]Or *Lord* [a]Jer 2:13; John 4:14; 7:37f; Rev 7:17; 21:6; 22:1, 17
12 [a]John 4:6
14 [a]John 6:35; 7:38 [b]Matt 25:46; John 6:27
15 [1]Or *Lord* [a]John 6:35
19 [1]Or *Lord* [a]Matt 21:11; Luke 7:16, 39; 24:19; John 6:14; 7:40; 9:17
20 [a]Gen 33:20; John 4:12 [b]Deut 11:29; Josh 8:33 [c]Luke 9:53
21 [a]John 4:23; 5:25, 28; 16:2, 32 [b]Mal 1:11; 1 Tim 2:8
22 [a]2 Kin 17:28-41
22 [b]Is 2:3; Rom 3:1f; 9:4f
23 [a]John 4:21; 5:25, 28; 16:2, 32 [b]Phil 3:3
24 [1]Or *Spirit* [a]Phil 3:3
25 [a]Dan 9:25; John 1:41 [b]Matt 1:16; 27:17, 22; Luke 2:11
26 [a]John 8:24, 28, 58; 9:37; 13:19
27 [a]John 4:8
29 [1]I.e. the Messiah [a]John 4:17f [b]Matt 12:23; John 7:26, 31
31 [a]Matt 23:7; 26:25, 49; Mark 9:5; 11:21; 14:45; John 1:38, 49; 3:2, 26; 6:25; 9:2; 11:8
33 [a]Luke 6:13-16; John 1:40-49; 2:2

---

explained as meaning the Holy Spirit, but here it refers to eternal life (see v. 14).

4:11 *deep.* Christian pilgrim sources as early as the fourth century mention a well in this area that was about 100 feet deep. When the present well was cleaned out in 1935, it was found to be 138 feet deep.

4:12 *our father Jacob.* Respect for the past prevented her from seeing the great opportunity of the present.

4:14 *springing up.* The expression is a vigorous one, with a meaning like "leaping up." Jesus was speaking of vigorous, abundant life (cf. 10:10).

4:15 Cf. the misunderstanding of Nicodemus (3:4). In both cases the way was opened for further instruction.

4:18 *five husbands.* The Jews held that a woman might be divorced twice or at the most three times. If the Samaritans had the same standard, the woman's life had been exceedingly immoral. Apparently she had not married her present partner.

4:19 *a prophet.* Because of His special insight.

4:20 *this mountain.* Perhaps the woman did not like the way the conversation was going and so began to argue. The proper place of worship had long been a source of debate between Jews and Samaritans. Samaritans held that "this mountain" (Mount Gerizim) was especially sacred. Abraham and Jacob had built altars in the general vicinity (Gen 12:7; 33:20), and the people had been blessed from this mountain (Deut 11:29; 27:12). In the Samaritan Scriptures, Mount Gerizim (rather than Mount Ebal) was the mountain on which Moses had commanded an altar to be built (Deut 27:4–6). The Samaritans had built a temple on Mount Gerizim c. 400 B.C., which the Jews destroyed c. 128. Both actions, of course, increased hostility between the two groups. See map, p. 1522.

4:22 *worship what you do not know.* The Samaritan Bible contained only the Pentateuch. They worshiped the true God, but their failure to accept much of His revelation meant that they knew little of Him. *salvation is from the Jews.* The Messiah would be a Jew.

4:24 *God is spirit . . . worship in spirit and truth.* The place of worship is irrelevant, because true worship must be in keeping with God's nature, which is spirit. In John's Gospel truth is associated with Christ (14:6; see note on 1:14), a fact that has great importance for the proper understanding of Christian worship.

4:25 *Messiah . . . will declare all things.* The woman's last attempt to evade the issue. The matter was too important, she reasoned, for people like Jesus and herself to work out. Understanding would have to await the coming of the Messiah (see note on 1:25). The Samaritans expected a Messiah, but their rejection of all the inspired writings after the Pentateuch meant that they knew little about Him. They thought of Him mainly as a teacher.

4:26 *I . . . am He.* The only occasion before His trial on which Jesus specifically said that He was the Messiah (but see Mark 9:41). The term did not have the political overtones in Samaria that it had in Judea, which may be part of the reason Jesus used the designation here.

4:27 *were amazed.* Jewish religious teachers rarely spoke with women in public.

4:29 *all the things . . . I have done.* An exaggeration, but it shows the impression Jesus made on her. *this is not the Christ, is it?* Her question seems full of longing, as though she did not expect them to say "Yes," but she could not say "No."

4:33 A misunderstanding similar to that of the woman (v. 15).

34 Jesus *said to them, "My food is to [a]do the will of Him who sent Me and to [b]accomplish His work.

35 "Do you not say, 'There are yet four months, and *then* comes the harvest'? Behold, I say to you, lift up your eyes and look on the fields, that they are white [a]for harvest.

36 "Already he who reaps is receiving [a]wages and is gathering [b]fruit for [c]life eternal; so that he who sows and he who reaps may rejoice together.

37 "For in this *case* the saying is true, '[a]One sows and another reaps.'

38 "I sent you to reap that for which you have not labored; others have labored and you have entered into their labor."

The Samaritans

39 From [a]that city many of the Samaritans believed in Him because of the word of the woman who testified, "[b]He told me all the things that I *have* done."

40 So when the Samaritans came to Jesus, they were asking Him to stay with them; and He stayed there two days.

41 Many more believed because of His word;

42 and they were saying to the woman, "It is no longer because of what you said that we believe, for we have heard for ourselves and know that this One is indeed [a]the Savior of the world."

43 After [a]the two days He went forth from there into Galilee.

44 For Jesus Himself testified that [a]a prophet has no honor in his own country.

45 So when He came to Galilee, the Galileans received Him, [a]having seen all the things that He did in Jerusalem at the feast; for they themselves also went to the feast.

Healing a Nobleman's Son

46 Therefore He came again to [a]Cana of Galilee [b]where He had made the water wine. And there was a royal official whose son was sick at [c]Capernaum.

47 When he heard that Jesus had come [a]out of Judea into Galilee, he went to Him and was imploring *Him* to come down and heal his son; for he was at the point of death.

48 So Jesus said to him, "Unless you *people* see [1][a]signs and [a]wonders, you *simply* will not believe."

49 The royal official *said to Him, "[1]Sir, come down before my child dies."

50 Jesus *said to him, "[a]Go; your son lives." The man believed the word that Jesus spoke to him and started off.

51 As he was now going down, *his* slaves met him, saying that his [1]son was living.

52 So he inquired of them the hour when he began to get better. Then they said to him, "Yesterday at the [1]seventh hour the fever left him."

53 So the father knew that *it was* at that hour in which Jesus said to him, "Your son lives"; and he himself believed and [a]his whole household.

54 This is again a [a]second [1]sign that Jesus performed when He had [b]come out of Judea into Galilee.

The Healing at Bethesda

5 After these things there was [a]a feast of the Jews, and Jesus went up to Jerusalem.

2 Now there is in Jerusalem by [a]the

34 [a]John 5:30; 6:38 [b]John 5:36; 17:4; 19:28, 30
35 [a]Matt 9:37, 38; Luke 10:2
36 [a]Prov 11:18; 1 Cor 9:17f [b]Rom 1:13 [c]Matt 19:29; John 3:36; 4:14; 5:24; Rom 2:7; 6:23
37 [a]Job 31:8; Mic 6:15
39 [a]John 4:5, 30 [b]John 4:29
42 [a]Matt 1:21; Luke 2:11; John 1:29; Acts 5:31; 13:23; 1 Tim 4:10; 1 John 4:14
43 [a]John 4:40
44 [a]Matt 13:57; Mark 6:4; Luke 4:24
45 [a]John 2:23
46 [a]John 2:1 [b]John 2:9 [c]Luke 4:23; John 2:12
47 [a]John 4:3, 54
48 [1]Or *attesting miracles* [a]Dan 4:2f; 6:27; Matt 24:24; Mark 13:22; Acts 2:19, 22, 43; 4:30; 5:12; 6:8; 7:36; 14:3; 15:12; Rom 15:19; 1 Cor 1:22; 2 Cor 12:12; 2 Thess 2:9; Heb 2:4
49 [1]Or *Lord*
50 [a]Matt 8:13
51 [1]Or *boy*
52 [1]Perhaps 7 p.m. Roman time or 1 p.m. Jewish time
53 [a]Acts 11:14
54 [1]Or *attesting miracle* [a]John 2:11 [b]John 4:45f
5:1 [a]Deut 16:1; John 2:13
2 [a]Neh 3:1, 32; 12:39

4:34 *My food is to do the will of Him who sent Me.* John often mentions that Jesus depended on the Father and did the work the Father sent Him to do (e.g., 5:30; 6:38; 8:26; 9:4; 10:37–38; 12:49–50; 14:31; 15:10; 17:4).

4:35 *There are yet four months, and then comes the harvest.* Apparently a proverb that meant something like "Harvest cannot be rushed." But, while the crops must take their time ripening, in the fields that Jesus referred to the harvest is already ripe.

4:36 *is receiving wages.* The work, or at least part of it, had been done, and others were working hard. The disciples were not to think that the harvest was far off. Jesus was not speaking of grain but of "fruit for life eternal." There was urgency, for the crop would not wait. *rejoice together.* There is no competition among Christ's faithful servants, and sower and reaper share in the joy of the crop.

4:37 See 1 Cor 3:6–9.

4:38 *others.* May refer to John the Baptist and his supporters, on whose work the apostles would build. Or perhaps Jesus was looking further back, to the prophets and other godly men of old. Either way, He expected the apostles to be reapers as well as sowers.

4:42 *the Savior of the world.* In the NT the expression occurs only here and in 1John 4:14. It points to the facts (1) that Jesus not only teaches but also saves, and (2) that His salvation extends to the world (see note on 3:16).

4:44 *a prophet has no honor in his own country.* Nonetheless, Jesus went to Galilee, because He came to die for our salvation (cf. 1:29).

4:45 *received Him.* The welcome of the Galileans actually was a kind of rejection, for they were interested only in His miracles. They were not welcoming the Messiah who could save them, but only a miracle worker who could amaze them.

4:46 *royal official.* Evidently an officer in Herod's service.

4:48 *Unless you . . . see signs and wonders, you . . . will not believe.* The general attitude of Galileans, not that of the official.

4:50 *your son lives.* Not simply a prophecy, but words of power. Jesus was healing, not forecasting a happy ending (see vv. 51,53).

4:52 *seventh hour.* 1:00 p.m.

4:53 *believed.* Cf. the aim of this Gospel (20:31).

4:54 *a second sign.* There had, of course, already been many such signs (2:23; 3:2), but this was the second time Jesus performed a sign after coming from Judea to Galilee.

5:1 *After these things.* An indefinite expression (cf. 6:1; 7:1). *a feast of the Jews.* Probably one of the three pilgrimage feasts to which all Jewish males were expected to go—Passover, Pentecost or Booths. The identity of this feast is significant for the attempt to ascertain the number of Passovers included in Jesus' ministry, and thus the number of years His ministry lasted. John explicitly mentions at least three different Passovers: the first in 2:13,23 (see note on 2:13), the second in 6:4 and

sheep *gate* a pool, which is called [b]in
[1]Hebrew [2]Bethesda, having five porticoes.
3 In these lay a multitude of those who
were sick, blind, lame, and withered, [[1]wait-
ing for the moving of the waters;
4 for an angel of the Lord went down at
certain seasons into the pool and stirred up
the water; whoever then first, after the stirring up of the water, stepped in was made
well from whatever disease with which he
was afflicted.]
5 A man was there who had been [1]ill for
thirty-eight years.
6 When Jesus saw him lying *there,* and
knew that he had already been a long time *in
that condition,* He *said to him, "Do you
wish to get well?"
7 The sick man answered Him, "Sir, I
have no man to put me into the pool when
[a]the water is stirred up, but while I am coming, another steps down before me."
8 Jesus *said to him, "[a]Get up, pick up
your pallet and walk."
9 Immediately the man became well, and
picked up his pallet and *began* to walk.
[a]**N**ow it was the Sabbath on that day.
10 So [a]the Jews were saying to the man
who was cured, "It is the Sabbath, and [b]it is
not permissible for you to carry your pallet."
11 But he answered them, "He who made
me well was the one who said to me, 'Pick
up your pallet and walk.'"
12 They asked him, "Who is the man who
said to you, 'Pick up *your pallet* and walk'?"
13 But the man who was healed did not
know who it was, for Jesus had slipped away
while there was a crowd in *that* place.
14 Afterward Jesus *found him in the
temple and said to him, "Behold, you have
become well; do not [a]sin anymore, [b]so that
nothing worse happens to you."
15 The man went away, and told [a]the
Jews that it was Jesus who had made him
well.
16 For this reason [a]the Jews were persecuting Jesus, because He was doing these
things on the Sabbath.
17 But He answered them, "My Father is
working until now, and I Myself am working."

Jesus' Equality with God

18 For this reason therefore [a]the Jews
[b]were seeking all the more to kill Him,
because He not only was breaking the Sabbath, but also was calling God His own
Father, [c]making Himself equal with God.
19 Therefore Jesus answered and was saying to them, "Truly, truly, I say to you, [a]the
Son can do nothing of Himself, unless *it is*
something He sees the Father doing; for
whatever [1]the Father does, these things the
Son also does in like manner.
20 "[a]For the Father loves the Son, and

2 [1]I.e. Jewish Aramaic [2]Some early mss read *Bethsaida* or *Bethzatha* [b]John 19:13, 17, 20; 20:16; Acts 21:40; Rev 9:11; 16:16
3 [1]Early mss do not contain the remainder of v 3, nor v 4
5 [1]Lit *in his sickness*
7 [a]John 5:4
8 [a]Matt 9:6; Mark 2:11; Luke 5:24
9 [a]John 9:14
10 [a]John 1:19; 5:15, 16, 18 [b]Neh 13:19; Jer 17:21f; Matt 12:2; Luke 6:2; John 7:23; 9:16
14 [a]Mark 2:5; John 8:11 [b]Ezra 9:14
15 [a]John 1:19; 5:16, 18
16 [a]John 1:19; 5:10, 15, 18
18 [a]John 1:19; 5:15, 16 [b]John 5:16; 7:1 [c]John 10:33; 19:7
19 [1]Lit *that One* [a]Matt 26:39; John 5:30; 6:38; 8:28; 12:49; 14:10
20 [a]Matt 3:17; John 3:35; 2 Pet 1:17

the third several times (e.g., in 11:55; 12:1). If three Passovers are accepted, the length of Jesus' ministry was between two and three years. However, if the feast of 5:1 was a fourth Passover or assumes that a fourth Passover had come and gone, Jesus' ministry would have lasted between three and four years.

5:2 *there is.* Not "was." This may mean that the pool was still in existence at the time this was being written, i.e., that John wrote before the destruction of Jerusalem. However, this falls short of proving the time of writing (see Introduction: Date). *Bethesda.* The manuscripts have a variety of names (e.g., Bethzatha and Bethsaida), but one of the Dead Sea Scrolls seems to show that Bethesda is the right name. The site is generally identified with the twin pools near the present-day Saint Anne's Church. There would have been a colonnade on each of the four sides and another between the two pools.

5:3–4 Some manuscripts do not have 3b–4. They may have been added by a later copyist to explain why people waited by the pool in large numbers.

5:5 *ill.* John does not say what the trouble was, but it was a form of paralysis or at least lameness.

5:6 *Do you wish to get well?* The question was important. The man had not asked Jesus for help, and a beggar of that day could lose a sometimes profitable (and easy) income if he were cured. Or perhaps he had simply lost the will to be cured.

5:7 *when the water is stirred up.* The man did not see Jesus as a potential healer, and his mind was set on the supposed curative powers of the water.

5:9 *the man became well.* Ordinarily, faith in Jesus was essential to the cure (e.g., Mark 5:34), but here the man did not even know who Jesus was (v. 13). So while Jesus usually healed in response to faith, He was not limited by a person's lack of it.

5:10 *it is not permissible for you to carry your pallet.* It was not the law of Moses but their traditional interpretation of it that prohibited carrying loads of any kind on the Sabbath. The Jews had very strict regulations on keeping the Sabbath, but also had many curious loopholes that their lawyers made full use of (cf. Matt 23:4).

5:12 *the man.* The Jews were contrasting the authority of the law of God, which in their view prohibited the action, and that of a mere man (as they considered Jesus to be) who permitted it.

5:14 *nothing worse.* The eternal consequences of sin are more serious than any physical ailment.

5:16 *were persecuting.* John does not tell us what form the persecution took. *was doing.* The continuous action points to more than one incident, and the Jews apparently discerned a pattern.

5:17 *My Father is working until now.* Jesus' justification for His action was His close relation to His Father. The Jews did not refer to God as "My Father," regarding the term as too intimate—though they might have used "Our Father" or, in prayer, "My Father in heaven." Jesus also exemplified the way the Sabbath should be observed. God does not stop His deeds of compassion on that day and neither did Jesus.

5:18 *His own Father.* Referring to a special relationship. The Jews did not object to the idea that God is the Father of all, but they strongly objected to Jesus' claim that He stood in a special relationship to the Father—a relationship so close as to make Himself equal with God.

5:19 *can.* Because of who and what He was, it was not possible for Jesus to act except in dependence on the Father.

5:20 *the Father loves the Son.* Therefore the Father revealed to the Son His plans and purposes, and the Son obediently carried them out. *greater works.* The Son's activities in raising the dead and judging (see following verses).

shows Him all things that He Himself is
doing; and *the Father* will show Him [b]greater
works than these, so that you will marvel.
21 "For just as the Father raises the dead
and [a]gives them life, even so [b]the Son also
gives life to whom He wishes.
22 "For not even the Father judges anyone,
but [a]He has given all judgment to the Son,
23 so that all will honor the Son even as
they honor the Father. [a]He who does not
honor the Son does not honor the Father
who sent Him.
24 "Truly, truly, I say to you, he who hears
My word, and [a]believes Him who sent Me,
has eternal life, and [b]does not come into judgment, but has [c]passed out of death into life.

Two Resurrections

25 "Truly, truly, I say to you, [a]an hour is
coming and now is, when [b]the dead will
hear the voice of the Son of God, and those
who [c]hear will live.
26 "For just as the Father has life in Himself, even so He [a]gave to the Son also to have
life in Himself;
27 and He gave Him authority to [a]execute
judgment, because He is [1]*the* Son of Man.
28 "Do not marvel at this; for [a]an hour is
coming, in which [b]all who are in the tombs
will hear His voice,
29 and will come forth; [a]those who did
the good *deeds* to a resurrection of life, those
who committed the evil *deeds* to a resurrection of judgment.
30 "[a]I can do nothing on My own initiative.
As I hear, I judge; and [b]My judgment is just,
because I do not seek My own will, but [c]the
will of Him who sent Me.
31 "[a]If I *alone* testify about Myself, My testimony is not [1]true.
32 "There is [a]another who testifies of Me,
and I know that the testimony which He
gives about Me is true.

Witness of John

33 "You have sent to John, and he [a]has testified to the truth.
34 "But [a]the testimony which I receive is
not from man, but I say these things so that
you may be saved.
35 "He was [a]the lamp that was burning
and was shining and you [b]were willing to
rejoice for [1]a while in his light.

Witness of Works

36 "But the testimony which I have is
greater than *the testimony of* John; for [a]the
works which the Father has given Me [b]to
accomplish—the very works that I do—testify about Me, that the Father [c]has sent Me.

Witness of the Father

37 "And the Father who sent Me, [a]He has
testified of Me. You have neither heard His
voice at any time nor seen His form.
38 "You do not have [a]His word abiding in
you, for you do not believe Him whom He
[b]sent.

20 [b]John 14:12 **21** [a]Rom 4:17; 8:11 [b]John 11:25 **22** [a]John 5:27; 9:39; Acts 10:42; 17:31 **23** [a]Luke 10:16; 1 John 2:23 **24** [a]John 3:18; 12:44; 20:31; 1 John 5:13 [b]John 3:18 [c]1 John 3:14 **25** [a]John 4:21, 23; 5:28 [b]Luke 15:24 [c]John 6:60; 8:43, 47; 9:27 **26** [a]John 1:4; 6:57 **27** [1]Or *a son of man* [a]John 9:39; Acts 10:42; 17:31 **28** [a]John 4:21 [b]John 11:24; 1 Cor 15:52 **29** [a]Dan 12:2; Matt 25:46; Acts 24:15 **30** [a]John 5:19 **30** [b]John 8:16 [c]John 4:34; 6:38 **31** [1]I.e. admissible as legal evidence [a]John 8:14 **32** [a]John 5:37 **33** [a]John 1:7, 15, 19, 32; 3:26-30 **34** [a]John 5:32; 1 John 5:9 **35** [1]Lit *an hour* [a]2 Sam 21:17; 2 Pet 1:19 [b]Mark 1:5 **36** [a]Matt 11:4; John 2:23; 10:25, 38; 14:11; 15:24 [b]John 4:34 [c]John 3:17 **37** [a]Matt 3:17; Mark 1:11; Luke 3:22; 24:27; John 8:18; 1 John 5:9 **38** [a]1 John 2:14 [b]John 3:17

5:21 *the Father raises the dead.* A firm belief among the Jews. They also held that He did not give this privilege to anyone else. Jesus claimed a prerogative that, according to His opponents, belonged only to God. *the Son also gives life.* Probably refers to Christ's gift of abundant life here and now, though possibly also to the future resurrection (see 11:25–26).
5:22 *given all judgment to the Son.* The Jews believed that the Father is Judge of the world, so this teaching seemed heretical to them.
5:24 *believes Him . . . has eternal life.* Faith and life are connected (cf. 20:31). *has eternal life.* A present possession (see note on 3:15). *has passed.* The decisive action has taken place, and the believer no longer belongs to death.
5:25 *is coming and now is.* A reference not only to the future resurrection but also to the fact that Christ gives life now. The spiritually dead who hear Him receive life from Him.
5:26 *has life in Himself.* Must be understood against the background of the OT, where life is spoken of as belonging to God and as being His gift (Deut 30:20; Job 10:12; 33:4; Ps 16:11; 27:1; 36:9; etc.). The Son has been given the same kind of life that the Father possesses (cf. also 1 John 5:11 for the benefit to man).
5:27 *authority to execute judgment.* Granted to the Son by the Father. *Son of Man.* See note on 1:51.
5:28–29 A reference to the future raising of the dead.
5:29 *did the good deeds . . . life . . . committed the evil deeds . . . judgment.* As always in Scripture, judgment is on the basis of works, though salvation, of course, is a gift from God in response to faith (cf. v. 24).
5:30 *I can do nothing on My own initiative.* Jesus stresses His dependence on the Father (see note on v. 19). He judges only as He hears from the Father, which makes His judgment fair.
5:31–47 This section stresses the testimonies (see note on 1:7) of John the Baptist (v. 33), of the works of Jesus (v. 36), of God the Father (v. 37), of the Scriptures (v. 39) and of Moses (v. 46).
5:31 Jesus' testimony about Himself required the support of all God's revelation. Otherwise, it would have been unacceptable.
5:32 *another.* The Father testifies concerning the Son. The Jews might not accept this testimony, but it was the testimony that mattered most.
5:33 *You have sent to John.* A reference to the delegation from the Jewish leaders to John the Baptist (see 1:19). *he has testified.* The testimony of John was important, though not, of course, equal to the testimony of the Father. But had the Jews believed John, they would have believed Christ and would have been saved.
5:35 *He was.* The past tense may indicate that John was dead or at least imprisoned. In any case, his work was done. *was burning and was shining.* John's giving light was costly to him. *for a while.* The Jewish leaders never came to grips with John's message, and their responses to him were always at best tentative and superficial.
5:36 *works.* The miracles of Jesus, which testified to what He is and to His divine mission (see 10:25).
5:37 *the Father . . . He has testified . . . His voice.* Probably a reference to God's voice in the Scriptures (see vv. 38–39). God had also given His voice of approval at Jesus' baptism (see Matt 3:17). *nor seen His form.* Probably refers to their lack of spiritual perception of who Jesus really is.
5:38 *you do not believe.* The Jews did not recognize what God was saying, as their failure to believe Jesus shows.

Witness of the Scripture

39 "[1][a]You search the Scriptures because you think that in them you have eternal life; it is [b]these that testify about Me;

40 and you are unwilling to come to Me so that you may have life.

41 "[a]I do not receive glory from men;

42 but I know you, that you do not have the love of God in yourselves.

43 "I have come in My Father's name, and you do not receive Me; [a]if another comes in his own name, you will receive him.

44 "How can you believe, when you [a]receive [1]glory from one another and you do not seek [b]the [1]glory that is from [c]the *one and* only God?

45 "Do not think that I will accuse you before the Father; the one who accuses you is [a]Moses, in whom you have set your hope.

46 "For if you believed Moses, you would believe Me, for [a]he wrote about Me.

47 "But [a]if you do not believe his writings, how will you believe My words?"

Five Thousand Fed

6 After these things [a]Jesus went away to the other side of [b]the Sea of Galilee (or [c]Tiberias).

2 A large crowd followed Him, because they saw the [1][a]signs which He was performing on those who were sick.

3 Then [a]Jesus went up on the mountain, and there He sat down with His disciples.

4 Now [a]the Passover, the feast of the Jews, was near.

5 Therefore Jesus, lifting up His eyes and seeing that a large crowd was coming to Him, *said to [a]Philip, "Where are we to buy bread, so that these may eat?"

39 [1]Or (a command) *Search the Scriptures!* [a]John 7:52; Rom 2:17ff [b]Luke 24:25, 27; Acts 13:27
41 [a]John 5:44; 7:18; 1 Thess 2:6
43 [a]Matt 24:5
44 [1]Or *honor* or *fame* [a]John 5:41 [b]Rom 2:29 [c]John 17:3; 1 Tim 1:17
45 [a]John 9:28; Rom 2:17ff
46 [a]Luke 24:27
47 [a]Luke 16:29, 31
6:1 [a]John 6:1-13: *Matt 14:13-21; Mark 6:32-44; Luke 9:10-17* [b]Matt 4:18; Luke 5:1 [c]John 6:23; 21:1
2 [1]Or *attesting miracles* [a]John 2:11, 23; 3:2; 6:14, 30; 11:47; 12:18, 37; 20:30
3 [a]Matt 5:1; Mark 3:13; Luke 6:12; 9:28; John 6:15
4 [a]Deut 16:1; John 2:13
5 [a]John 1:43
6 [a]2 Cor 13:5; Rev 2:2
7 [1]The denarius was equivalent to a day's wages [a]John 1:43 [b]Mark 6:37
8 [a]John 2:2 [b]John 1:40
9 [a]John 6:11; 21:9, 10, 13
10 [1]Lit *recline(d)* [a]Mark 6:39 [b]Matt 14:21
11 [a]Matt 15:36; John 6:23 [b]John 6:9; 21:9, 10, 13
12 [a]John 2:2

6 This He was saying to [a]test him, for He Himself knew what He was intending to do.

7 [a]Philip answered Him, "[b]Two hundred [1]denarii worth of bread is not sufficient for them, for everyone to receive a little."

8 One of His [a]disciples, [b]Andrew, Simon Peter's brother, *said to Him,

9 "There is a lad here who has five barley loaves and two [a]fish, but what are these for so many people?"

10 Jesus said, "Have the people [1]sit down." Now there was [a]much grass in the place. So the men [1]sat down, in number about [b]five thousand.

11 Jesus then took the loaves, and [a]having given thanks, He distributed to those who were seated; likewise also of the [b]fish as much as they wanted.

12 When they were filled, He *said to His [a]disciples, "Gather up the leftover fragments so that nothing will be lost."

13 So they gathered them up, and filled twelve [a]baskets with fragments from the five barley loaves which were left over by those who had eaten.

14 Therefore when the people saw the [1]sign which He had performed, they said, "This is truly the [a]Prophet who is to come into the world."

Jesus Walks on the Water

15 So Jesus, perceiving that they were [1]intending to come and take Him by force [a]to make Him king, [b]withdrew again to [c]the mountain by Himself alone.

16 Now when evening came, His [a]disciples went down to the sea,

13 [a]Matt 14:20 **14** [1]Or *attesting miracle* [a]Matt 11:3; 21:11; John 1:21 **15** [1]Or *about* [a]John 18:36f [b]John 6:15-21: *Matt 14:22-33; Mark 6:45-51* [c]John 6:3 **16** [a]John 2:2

5:39 *You search.* The Jewish leaders studied Scripture in minute detail. Despite their reverence for the very letter of Scripture (see notes on Matt 5:18–21), they did not recognize the One to whom Scripture bears supreme testimony.

5:41 *glory from men.* Jesus did not accept human praise any more than human testimony (v. 34).

5:42 *love of God.* May mean God's love for them or theirs for God. Probably it is the latter, but people's love for God is in response to His prior love for them (1 John 4:19).

5:43–44 The Jews of v. 18 had their attention firmly fixed on people. Their emphasis on self-seeking and on human praise showed that they did not accept the One who came from God, and therefore they missed the praise that comes from God.

5:45 *the one who accuses you is Moses.* Jesus' listeners prided themselves on their attachment to Moses, their great lawgiver. So it was an unexpected thrust for Jesus to say that Moses himself would accuse them before God.

5:46 *he wrote about Me.* All the NT writers stressed, or assumed, that the OT, rightly read, points to Christ (cf. Luke 24:25–27,44). Jesus applied this truth specifically to the writings of Moses (see, e.g., notes on Gen 49:10; Ex 12:21; Lev 16:5; Num 24:17; Deut 18:15).

6:1–15 The feeding of the 5,000 is the one miracle, apart from the resurrection, found in all four Gospels. It shows Jesus as the supplier of human need, and sets the stage for His testimony that He is the bread of life (v. 35).

6:1 *After these things.* See 5:1 and note. *Tiberias.* Probably the official Roman name, while Sea of Galilee was the popular name. The name came from the town of Tiberias (named after the emperor), founded c. A.D. 20, and probably was not much in use during Jesus' ministry.

6:2 *signs.* See note on 2:11.

6:4 *Passover.* See note on 2:13.

6:5 *Philip.* Since he came from nearby Bethsaida (1:44), it was appropriate to ask him.

6:9 *barley loaves.* Cheap bread, the food of the poor.

6:10 *about five thousand.* The number of men; women and children were not included (Matt 14:21).

6:12 *Gather up the leftover fragments.* See note on Mark 6:43.

6:13 *twelve baskets . . . left over.* There was abundant supply.

6:14 *sign.* It pointed people to the Son of Man and the food for eternal life that He gives (v. 27), but they thought only of the Prophet, i.e., the prophet of Deut 18:15 who would be like Moses (see 1:21 and note). Through Moses, God had provided food and water for the people in the wilderness, and they expected the Prophet to do no more than this.

6:15 *take Him by force to make Him king.* Jesus rejected the world's version of kingship as a temptation of the devil (Matt 4:8–10; see note on John 18:36).

17 and after getting into a boat, they *started to* cross the sea [a]to Capernaum. It had
already become dark, and Jesus had not yet
come to them.
18 The sea *began* to be stirred up because
a strong wind was blowing.
19 Then, when they had rowed about
[1]three or four miles, they *saw Jesus walking
on the sea and drawing near to the boat; and
they were frightened.
20 But He *said to them, "It is I; [1][a]do not
be afraid."
21 So they were willing to receive Him
into the boat, and immediately the boat was
at the land to which they were going.
22 The next day [a]the crowd that stood on
the other side of the sea saw that there was
no other small boat there, except one, and
that Jesus [b]had not entered with His disciples into the boat, but *that* His disciples had
gone away alone.
23 There came other small boats from
[a]Tiberias near to the place where they ate
the bread after the [b]Lord [c]had given thanks.
24 So when the crowd saw that Jesus was
not there, nor His disciples, they themselves
got into the small boats, and [a]came to Capernaum seeking Jesus.
25 When they found Him on the other
side of the sea, they said to Him, "[a]Rabbi,
when did You get here?"

Words to the People

26 Jesus answered them and said, "Truly,
truly, I say to you, you [a]seek Me, not
because you saw [b]signs, but because you ate
of the loaves and were filled.
27 "Do not [a]work for the food which per-

17 [a]Mark 6:45; John 6:24, 59
19 [1]Lit *25 or 30 stadia*
20 [1]Or *stop being afraid*
[a]Matt 14:27
22 [a]John 6:2
[b]John 6:15ff
23 [a]John 6:1
[b]Luke 7:13
[c]John 6:11
24 [a]Matt 14:34; Mark 6:53; John 6:17, 59
25 [a]Matt 23:7
26 [a]John 6:24
[b]John 6:2, 14, 30
27 [a]Is 55:2

6:19 *three or four miles.* Mark says they were "in the middle of the sea" (Mark 6:47). *frightened.* They thought they were seeing a ghost (Matt 14:26).
6:21 *immediately the boat was at the land.* Some think that this was another miracle. In any event, the boat's safe arrival is implicitly credited to Jesus.
6:22–24 The crowd could not figure out what had happened to Jesus. But they wanted to see Him again, so they looked for Him in the most likely place, Capernaum.
6:27 *eternal life.* Not something to be achieved but to be

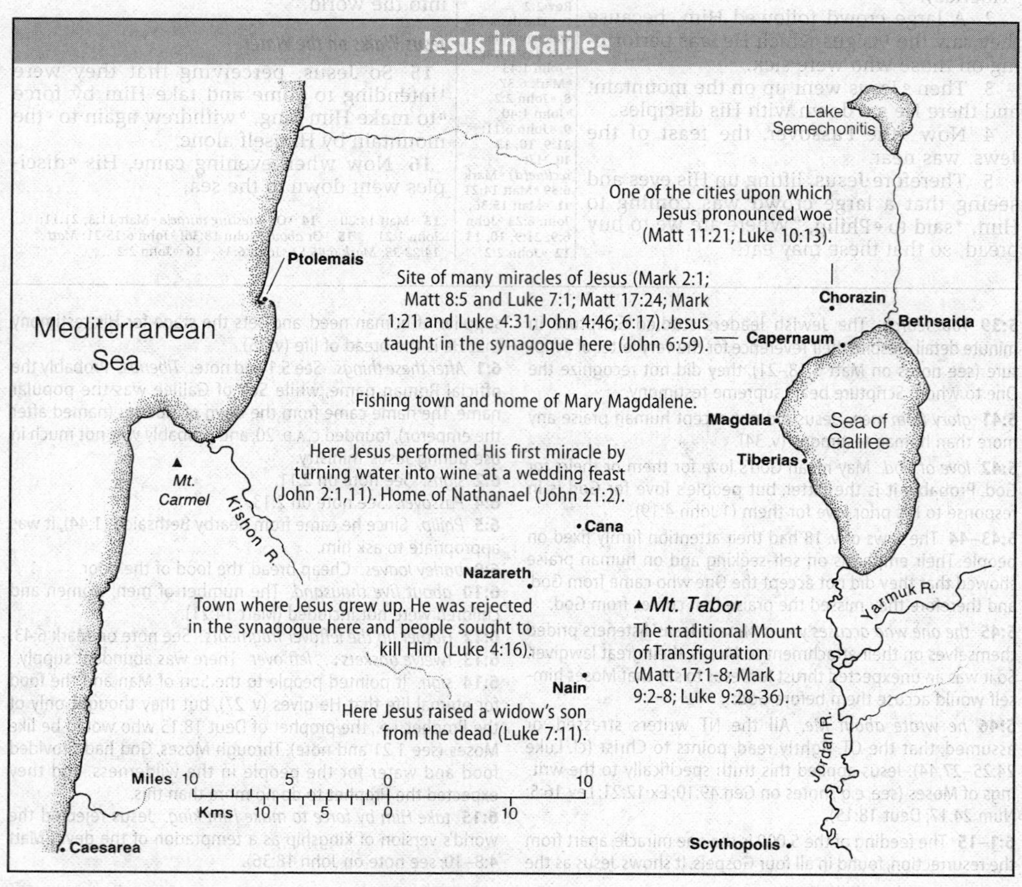
Jesus in Galilee
Lake Semechonitis
One of the cities upon which Jesus pronounced woe (Matt 11:21; Luke 10:13).
Ptolemais
Site of many miracles of Jesus (Mark 2:1; Matt 8:5 and Luke 7:1; Matt 17:24; Mark 1:21 and Luke 4:31; John 4:46; 6:17). Jesus taught in the synagogue here (John 6:59).
Chorazin
Bethsaida
Capernaum
Mediterranean Sea
Fishing town and home of Mary Magdalene.
Magdala
Sea of Galilee
Tiberias
Here Jesus performed His first miracle by turning water into wine at a wedding feast (John 2:1,11). Home of Nathanael (John 21:2).
Mt. Carmel
Kishon R.
Cana
Nazareth
Yarmuk R.
Mt. Tabor
Town where Jesus grew up. He was rejected in the synagogue here and people sought to kill Him (Luke 4:16).
The traditional Mount of Transfiguration (Matt 17:1-8; Mark 9:2-8; Luke 9:28-36).
Nain
Here Jesus raised a widow's son from the dead (Luke 7:11).
Jordan R.
Miles 10 5 0 10
Kms 10 5 0 10
Scythopolis
Caesarea

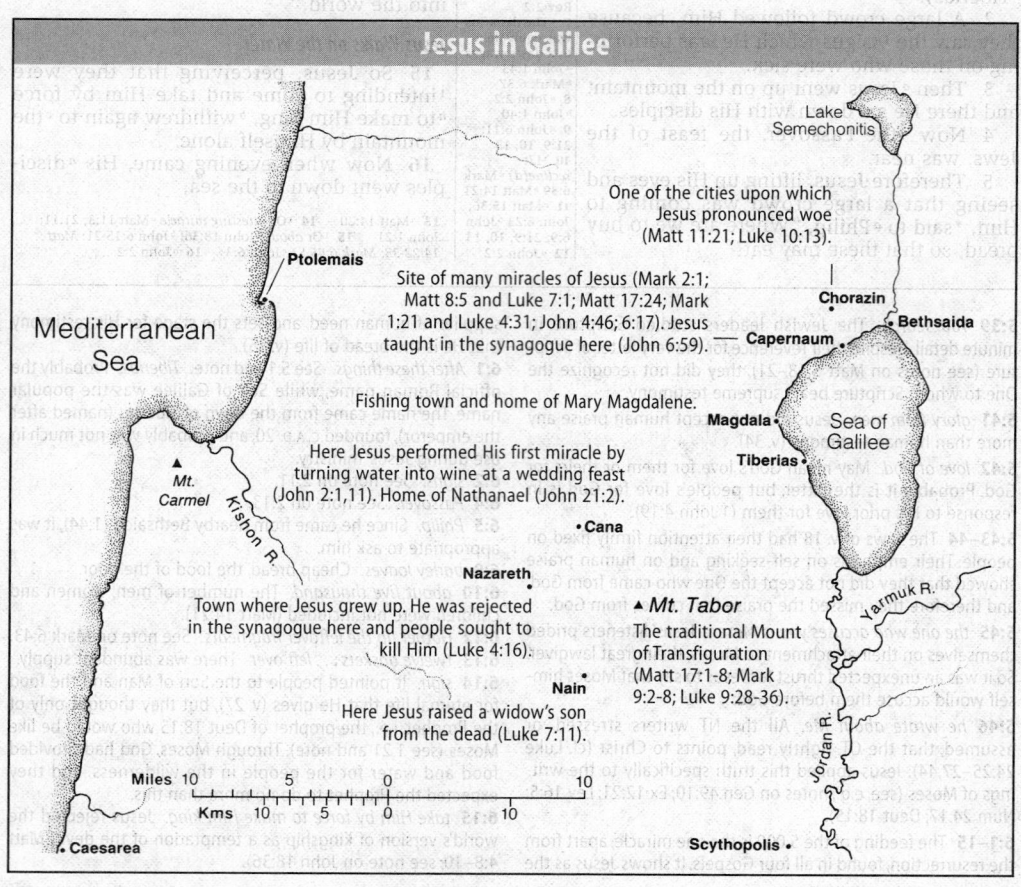

ishes, but for the food which endures to
[b]eternal life, which [c]the Son of Man will give
to you, for on Him the Father, God, [d]has set
His seal."
28 Therefore they said to Him, "What
shall we do, so that we may work the works
of God?"
29 Jesus answered and said to them, "This
is [a]the work of God, that you believe in Him
whom He [b]has sent."
30 So they said to Him, "[a]What then do
You do for a [b]sign, so that we may see, and
believe You? What work do You perform?
31 "[a]Our fathers ate the manna in the
wilderness; as it is written, '[b]HE GAVE THEM
BREAD OUT OF HEAVEN TO EAT.' "
32 Jesus then said to them, "Truly, truly, I
say to you, it is not Moses who has given you
the bread out of heaven, but it is My Father
who gives you the true bread out of heaven.
33 "For the bread of God is [1]that which
[a]comes down out of heaven, and gives life to
the world."
34 Then they said to Him, "Lord, always
[a]give us this bread."
35 Jesus said to them, "[a]I am the bread of
life; he who comes to Me will not hunger,
and he who believes in Me [b]will never thirst.
36 "But [a]I said to you that you have seen
Me, and yet do not believe.
37 "[a]All that the Father gives Me will come
to Me, and the one who comes to Me I will
certainly not cast out.
38 "For [a]I have come down from heaven,
[b]not to do My own will, but [c]the will of Him
who [d]sent Me.
39 "This is the will of Him who sent Me,
that of [a]all that He has given Me I [b]lose nothing,
but [c]raise it up on the last day.
40 "For this is the will of My Father, that
everyone who [a]beholds the Son and [b]believes
in Him will have eternal life, and I
Myself will [c]raise him up on the last day."

Words to the Jews

41 [a]Therefore the Jews were grumbling
about Him, because He said, "I am the bread
that [b]came down out of heaven."
42 They were saying, "[a]Is not this Jesus,
the son of Joseph, whose father and mother
[b]we know? How does He now say, '[c]I have
come down out of heaven'?"
43 Jesus answered and said to them, "Do
not grumble among yourselves.
44 "No one can come to Me unless the
Father who sent Me [a]draws him; and I will
[b]raise him up on the last day.
45 "It is written [a]in the prophets, '[b]AND
THEY SHALL ALL BE [c]TAUGHT OF GOD.' Everyone
who has heard and learned from the Father,
comes to Me.
46 "[a]Not that anyone has seen the Father,
except the One who is from God; He has
seen the Father.
47 "Truly, truly, I say to you, he who
believes [a]has eternal life.
48 "[a]I am the bread of life.
49 "[a]Your fathers ate the manna in the
wilderness, and they died.
50 "This is the bread which [a]comes down

27 [b]John 3:15f; 4:14; 6:40, 47, 54; 10:28; 17:2f [c]Matt 8:20; John 6:53, 62 [d]John 3:33 **29** [a]1 Thess 1:3; James 2:22; 1 John 3:23; Rev 2:26 [b]John 3:17 **30** [a]Matt 12:38 [b]John 6:2, 14, 26 **31** [a]Ex 16:4, 15, 21; Num 11:8; John 6:49, 58 [b]Ps 78:24; Ex 16:4, 15; Neh 9:15; Ps 105:40 **33** [1]Or *He who comes* [a]John 6:41, 50 **34** [a]John 4:15 **35** [a]John 6:48, 51 [b]John 4:14 **36** [a]John 6:26 **37** [a]John 6:39; 17:2, 24 **38** [a]John 3:13 [b]Matt 26:39 [c]John 4:34; 5:30 [d]John 6:29

39 [a]John 6:37; 17:2, 24 [b]John 17:12; 18:9 [c]Matt 10:15; John 6:40, 44, 54; 11:24 **40** [a]John 12:45; 14:17, 19 [b]John 3:16 [c]Matt 10:15; John 6:39, 44, 54; 11:24 **41** [a]John 1:19; 6:52 [b]John 6:33, 51, 58 **42** [a]Luke 4:22 [b]John 7:27f [c]John 6:38, 62 **44** [a]Jer 31:3; Hos 11:4; John 6:65; 12:32 [b]John 6:39

45 [a]Acts 7:42; 13:40; Heb 8:11 [b]Is 54:13; Jer 31:34 [c]Phil 3:15; 1 Thess 4:9; 1 John 2:27 **46** [a]John 1:18 **47** [a]John 3:36; 5:24; 6:51, 58; 11:26 **48** [a]John 6:35, 51 **49** [a]John 6:31, 58 **50** [a]John 6:33

received by faith in Christ (see vv. 28–29; see also note on 3:15). *Son of Man.* See note on Mark 8:31. Submission of the Son to the Father is one of John's major themes (see note on 4:34).

6:28 *What shall we do . . . ?* They missed the point that eternal life is Christ's gift and were thinking in terms of achieving it by pious works.

6:29 *work of God.* Believing in Jesus Christ is the indispensable "work" God calls for—the one that leads to eternal life.

6:30 *What work do You perform?* They seek from Jesus a sign greater than the gift of manna that had accompanied Moses' ministry.

6:31 *manna.* A popular Jewish expectation was that when the Messiah came he would renew the sending of manna. The crowd probably reasoned that Jesus had done little compared to Moses. He had fed 5,000; Moses had fed a nation. He did it once; Moses did it for 40 years. He gave ordinary bread; Moses gave "bread out of heaven."

6:32 Jesus corrected them, pointing out that the manna in the wilderness did not come from Moses but from God, and that the Father still "gives" (the present tense is important) the true bread from heaven (life through the Son).

6:33 *the bread of God.* Jesus moved the discussion to something (and Someone) much more important than manna.

6:34 *this bread.* Probably another misunderstanding, like that by the woman at the well (4:15; cf. also Nicodemus, 3:4). Their minds ran along materialistic lines.

6:35 *I am.* The first of seven self-descriptions of Jesus introduced by "I am" (see 8:12; 9:5; 10:7,9; 10:11,14; 11:25; 14:6; 15:1,5). In the Greek the words are solemnly emphatic and echo Ex 3:14. *the bread of life.* May mean "the bread that is living" and/or "the bread that gives life." What is implied in v. 33 is now made explicit and repeated with minor variations in vv. 41,48,51.

6:36 Contrast 20:29.

6:37 God's action (see v. 44; 10:29; 17:6; 18:9), not man's (v. 28), is primary in salvation, and Christ's mercy is unfailing (see vv. 31–40; 10:28; 17:9,12,15,19; 18:9).

6:38 *I have come down from heaven.* Repeated six times in this context (vv. 33,38,41,50–51,58), emphasizing Jesus' divine origin. *to do . . . the will of Him who sent Me.* See note on 4:34.

6:39 *I lose nothing.* The true believer will persevere because of Christ's firm hold on him (see Phil 1:6). *the last day.* An expression found only in John in the NT (see vv. 40,44,54).

6:40 *eternal life.* See note on 3:15. *raise him up on the last day.* Death cannot destroy the life that Christ gives.

6:41 *the Jews.* See note on 1:19.

6:44 *draws.* People do not come to Christ strictly on their own initiative; the Father draws them.

6:45 *the prophets.* The section of the OT from which the quotation is taken. *Everyone who has . . . learned from the Father, comes.* Only those who learn from God come to salvation, and all who learn from Him are saved.

6:49 *they died.* Jesus' opponents had set their hearts (cf. v. 31) on that which could neither give nor sustain spiritual life.

out of heaven, so that one may eat of it and [b]not die.

51 "[a]I am the living bread that [b]came down out of heaven; if anyone eats of this bread, [c]he will live forever; and the bread also which I will give [d]for the life of the world is [e]My flesh."

52 [a]Then the Jews [b]*began* to argue with one another, saying, "How can this man give us *His* flesh to eat?"

53 So Jesus said to them, "Truly, truly, I say to you, unless you eat the flesh of [a]the Son of Man and drink His blood, you have no life in yourselves.

54 "He who eats My flesh and drinks My blood has eternal life, and I will [a]raise him up on the last day.

55 "For My flesh is true food, and My blood is true drink.

56 "He who eats My flesh and drinks My blood [a]abides in Me, and I in him.

57 "As the [a]living Father [b]sent Me, and I live because of the Father, so he who eats Me, he also will live because of Me.

58 "This is the bread which [a]came down out of heaven; not as [b]the fathers ate and died; he who eats this bread [c]will live forever."

Words to the Disciples

59 These things He said [a]in the synagogue as He taught [b]in Capernaum.

60 Therefore many of His [a]disciples, when they heard *this* said, "[b]This is a difficult statement; who can listen to it?"

61 But Jesus, [a]conscious that His disciples grumbled at this, said to them, "Does this [b]cause you to stumble?

50 [b]John 3:36; 5:24; 6:47, 51, 58; 11:26 **51** [a]John 6:35, 48 [b]John 6:41, 58 [c]John 3:36; 5:24; 6:47, 58; 11:26 [d]John 1:29; 3:14f; Heb 10:10; 1 John 4:10 [e]John 6:53-56 **52** [a]John 1:19; 6:41 [b]John 9:16; 10:19 **53** [a]Matt 8:20; John 6:27, 62 **54** [a]John 6:39 **56** [a]John 15:4f; 17:23; 1 John 2:24; 3:24; 4:15f **57** [a]Matt 16:16; John 5:26 [b]John 3:17; 6:29, 38 **58** [a]John 6:33, 41, 51 [b]John 6:31, 49 [c]John 3:36; 5:24; 6:47, 51; 11:26 **59** [a]Matt 4:23 [b]John 6:24 **60** [a]John 2:2; 6:66; 7:3 [b]John 6:52 **61** [a]John 6:64 [b]Matt 11:6

62 [a]Matt 8:20; John 6:27, 53 [b]Mark 16:19; John 3:13 **63** [a]2 Cor 3:6 [b]John 6:68 **64** [1]Or *hand Him over* [a]John 6:60, 66 [b]John 2:25 [c]Matt 10:4; John 6:71; 13:11 **65** [a]John 6:37, 44 [b]Matt 13:11; John 3:27

62 "*What* then if you see [a]the Son of Man [b]ascending to where He was before?

63 "[a]It is the Spirit who gives life; the flesh profits nothing; [b]the words that I have spoken to you are spirit and are life.

64 "But there are [a]some of you who do not believe." For Jesus [b]knew from the beginning who they were who did not believe, and [c]who it was that would [1]betray Him.

65 And He was saying, "For this reason I have [a]said to you, that no one can come to Me unless [b]it has been granted him from the Father."

Peter's Confession of Faith

66 As a result of this many of His [a]disciples [b]withdrew and were not walking with Him anymore.

67 So Jesus said to [a]the twelve, "You do not want to go away also, do you?"

68 [a]Simon Peter answered Him, "Lord, to whom shall we go? You have [b]words of eternal life.

69 "We have believed and have come to know that You are [a]the Holy One of God."

70 Jesus answered them, "[a]Did I Myself not choose you, [b]the twelve, and *yet* one of you is [c]a devil?"

71 Now He meant Judas [a]*the son* of Simon Iscariot, for he, [b]one of [c]the twelve, [1]was going to betray Him.

66 [a]John 2:2; 7:3 [b]John 6:60, 64 **67** [a]Matt 10:2; John 2:2; 6:70f; 20:24 **68** [a]Matt 16:16 [b]John 6:63; 12:49f; 17:8 **69** [a]Mark 1:24; 8:29; Luke 9:20 **70** [a]John 15:16, 19 [b]Matt 10:2; John 2:2; 6:71; 20:24 [c]John 8:44; 13:2, 27; 17:12 **71** [1]Or *was intending to* [a]John 12:4; 13:2, 26 [b]Mark 14:10 [c]Matt 10:2; John 2:2; 6:70; 20:24

6:50 *eat . . . and not die.* Jesus' gift is in contrast; the life He gives is eternal.

6:51 *eats of this bread.* Appropriates Jesus as the sustenance of one's life. *which I will give . . . is My flesh.* Looking forward to Calvary. Providing eternal life would be costly to the Giver. *world.* See note on 4:42.

6:53–58 Jesus' absolute statement that "unless you eat the flesh of the Son of Man and drink His blood, you have no life in yourselves" (v. 53) precludes a direct reference to the Lord's Supper. He clearly does not teach that receiving that sacrament is the one requirement for eternal life or that it is the only ordinance through which Christ and His saving benefits are received. In this very discourse He emphasizes faith in response to testimony (see vv. 35,40,47,51). Flesh and blood here point to Christ as the crucified One and the source of life. Jesus speaks of faith's appropriation of Himself as God's appointed sacrifice, not—at least not directly—of any ritual requirement.

6:54 *the last day.* See note on v. 39.

6:58 *the bread which came down out of heaven.* As in v. 49, the value of the manna is limited and is contrasted with the heavenly food Christ gives. For the tenth time in this chapter reference is made to Jesus' coming down from heaven or to the bread from heaven.

6:60 *difficult.* Hard to accept, not hard to understand. The thought of eating the flesh of the Son of Man and drinking His blood was doubtless shocking to most of Jesus' Jewish hearers (see note on vv. 53–58).

6:62 *Son of Man.* See notes on Mark 8:31; Luke 6:5; 19:10. *ascending.* Probably refers to the series of events that began with the cross, where Jesus was glorified (see note on 7:39). *where He was before.* Referring to Jesus' heavenly preexistence.

6:63 Cf. 3:5–6,8. *are spirit and . . . life.* Are the Spirit at work producing life.

6:65 Coming to Christ for salvation is never a merely human achievement (see vv. 37,39,44–45).

6:66 *As a result of this.* May also mean "From this time" or both. *many . . . withdrew.* Jesus had already made clear what discipleship meant, and many were not ready to receive life in the way He taught.

6:68 As in the Synoptic Gospels, Peter acts as spokesman. *words of eternal life.* The expression is general. Peter was not speaking of a formula but of the thrust of Jesus' teaching. He perceived the truth of v. 63.

6:69 *We have believed and have come to know.* Since the Greek verbs are in the perfect tense, they mean, "We have entered a state of belief and knowledge that has continued until the present time." *the Holy One of God.* Applied to Jesus in Mark 1:24; Luke 4:34 (see Acts 2:27).

6:70 *a devil.* Judas (v. 71) would oppose Christ in the spirit of Satan.

6:71 *Iscariot.* Means "a man from Kerioth" (in Judea; see Josh 15:25) and would apply equally to the father and the son (cf. 12:4). Judas seems to have been the only non-Galilean among the Twelve. *one of the twelve.* And therefore one of the last persons likely to betray Jesus.

Jesus Teaches at the Feast

7 After these things Jesus [a]was walking in
Galilee, for He was unwilling to walk in
Judea because [b]the Jews [c]were seeking to
kill Him.
2 Now the feast of the Jews, [a]the Feast of
Booths, was near.
3 Therefore His [a]brothers said to Him,
"Leave here and go into Judea, so that Your
[b]disciples also may see Your works which
You are doing.
4 "For no one does anything in secret
[1]when he himself seeks to be *known* publicly. If You do these things, show Yourself to
the world."
5 For not even His [a]brothers were believing in Him.
6 So Jesus *said to them, "[a]My time is not
yet here, but your time is always opportune.
7 "[a]The world cannot hate you, but it
hates Me because I testify of it, that [b]its
deeds are evil.
8 "Go up to the feast yourselves; I do not
go up to this feast because [a]My time has not
yet fully come."
9 Having said these things to them, He
stayed in Galilee.
10 But when His [a]brothers had gone up to
the feast, then He Himself also went up, not
publicly, but as if, in secret.
11 [a]So the Jews [b]were seeking Him at the
feast and were saying, "Where is He?"

7:1 [a]John 4:3; 6:1; 11:54 [b]John 1:19; 7:11, 13, 15, 35 [c]John 5:18; 7:19; 8:37, 40; 11:53
2 [a]Lev 23:34; Deut 16:13, 16; Zech 14:16-19
3 [a]Matt 12:46; Mark 3:21; John 7:5, 10 [b]John 6:60
4 [1]Lit *and*
5 [a]Matt 12:46; Mark 3:21; John 7:3, 10
6 [a]Matt 26:18; John 2:4; 7:8, 30
7 [a]John 15:18f [b]John 3:19f
8 [a]John 7:6
10 [a]Matt 12:46; Mark 3:21; John 7:3, 5
11 [a]John 7:13, 15, 35 [b]John 11:56
12 [a]John 7:40-43
13 [a]John 9:22; 12:42; 19:38; 20:19
14 [a]Matt 26:55; John 7:28
15 [a]John 1:19; 7:11, 13, 35 [b]Acts 26:24
16 [a]John 3:11
17 [a]Ps 25:9, 14; Prov 3:32; Dan 12:10; John 3:21; 8:43f
18 [a]John 5:41; 8:50, 54; 12:43
19 [a]John 1:17 [b]Mark 11:18;

12 There was much grumbling among the
crowds concerning Him; [a]some were saying,
"He is a good man"; others were saying, "No,
on the contrary, He leads the people astray."
13 Yet no one was speaking openly of Him
for [a]fear of the Jews.
14 But when it was now the midst of the
feast Jesus went up into the temple, and
began to [a]teach.
15 [a]The Jews then were astonished, saying, "How has this man [b]become learned,
having never been educated?"
16 So Jesus answered them and said,
"[a]My teaching is not Mine, but His who sent
Me.
17 "[a]If anyone is willing to do His will, he
will know of the teaching, whether it is of
God or *whether* I speak from Myself.
18 "He who speaks from himself [a]seeks his
own glory; but He who is seeking the glory
of the One who sent Him, He is true, and
there is no unrighteousness in Him.
19 "[a]Did not Moses give you the Law, and
yet none of you carries out the Law? Why do
you [b]seek to kill Me?"
20 The crowd answered, "[a]You have a
demon! Who seeks to kill You?"
21 Jesus answered them, "I did [a]one
[1]deed, and you all marvel.
22 "For this reason [a]Moses has given you

John 7:1 **20** [a]Matt 11:18; John 8:48f, 52; 10:20 **21** [1]Or *work* [a]John 5:2-9, 16; 7:23 **22** [a]Lev 12:3

7:1–8:59 In chs. 7–8 John records strong opposition to Jesus, including repeated references to threats on His life (7:1,13,19,25, 30,32,44; 8:37,40,59). The apostle seems to have gathered the major arguments against the Messiahship of Jesus and here answers them.

7:1 *After these things.* As in 5:1 and 6:1 the time is indefinite. However, 6:4 refers to the Passover Feast and 7:2 to the Feast of Booths, making the interval about six months.

7:2 *Feast of Booths.* The great feast in the Jewish year, celebrating the completion of harvest and commemorating God's goodness to the people during the wilderness wanderings (see Lev 23:33–43; Deut 16:13–15; cf. Zech 14:16–19). The name came from the leafy shelters in which people lived throughout the seven days of the Feast.

7:3 *brothers.* See note on Luke 8:19.

7:4 It is not clear whether the brothers claimed some knowledge of Jesus' miracles that other people did not have or were suggesting that any claim to Messiahship must be decided in Jerusalem. Their advice was not given sincerely, for they did not yet believe in Jesus (v. 5).

7:6 *My time.* Jesus moved in accordance with the will of God (see note on 2:4).

7:7 *The world.* Either (1) people opposed to God or (2) the human system opposed to God's purposes (see note on 1:9). The brothers belonged to the world and therefore could not be the objects of its hatred. Jesus, however, rebuked the world and was hated accordingly.

7:8 *do not go up.* Jesus was not refusing to go to the Feast, but refusing to go in the way the brothers suggested—as a pilgrim. When He went, it would be to deliver a prophetic message from God, for which He awaited "His time" (see v. 6).

7:10 *not publicly.* Rejecting the brothers' suggestion to show Himself (v. 4).

7:12 *grumbling.* Because there was significant disagreement about who He was (cf. v. 13).

7:14 *the midst of the feast.* When the crowds would be at their maximum. Teaching in the temple courts at such a time would reach many.

7:15 *The Jews.* Distinct from "the crowds" (v. 12), who were also Jews (see note on 1:19). *having never been educated.* Under a rabbi. Jesus had never been the disciple of a recognized Jewish teacher.

7:16 *not Mine.* The Father, from whom He came, had been His "rabbi" (see note on 4:34).

7:17 *willing to do His will.* Reflecting a whole attitude of life. A person sincerely set on doing God's will welcomes Jesus' teaching and believes in Him (cf. 6:29). *he will know.* Augustine commented, "Understanding is the reward of faith . . . What is 'If any man be willing to do his will'? It is the same thing as to believe."

7:18 *He is true.* They should recognize that Jesus was not self-seeking. In this Gospel, no one is spoken of as being "true" except God the Father (3:33; 8:26) and Jesus (here). Once more John ranks Jesus with God.

7:19 *the Law.* The Jews congratulated themselves on being the chosen recipients of the law (cf. Rom 2:17), but Jesus told them that they all broke the law of which they were so proud.

7:20 *The crowd.* Probably the pilgrims who had come up to Jerusalem for the Feast—different from "the Jews" who were trying to kill Jesus (v. 1) and the Jerusalem mob that knew of the plot (v. 25). *You have a demon!* The accusation of demon possession is made elsewhere in John (e.g., 8:48–52; 10:20–21; cf. Matt 12:24–32; Mark 3:22–30).

7:21 *one deed.* Evidently that of healing the lame man (5:1–9), as the discussion about the Sabbath shows.

circumcision (not because it is from Moses,
but from [b]the fathers), and on *the* Sabbath
you circumcise a man.
23 "[a]If a man receives circumcision on *the*
Sabbath so that the Law of Moses will not be
broken, are you angry with Me because I
made an entire man well on *the* Sabbath?
24 "Do not [a]judge according to appearance,
but [1]judge with righteous judgment."
25 So some of the people of Jerusalem
were saying, "Is this not the man whom they
are seeking to kill?
26 "Look, He is speaking publicly, and they
are saying nothing to Him. [a]The rulers do not
really know that this is [1]the Christ, do they?
27 "However, [a]we know where this man is
from; but whenever the Christ may come, no
one knows where He is from."
28 Then Jesus cried out in the temple,
[a]teaching and saying, "[b]You both know Me
and know where I am from; and [c]I have not
come of Myself, but He who sent Me is true,
whom you do not know.
29 "[a]I know Him, because [b]I am from Him,
and [c]He sent Me."
30 So they [a]were seeking to seize Him;
and no man laid his hand on Him, because
His [b]hour had not yet come.
31 But [a]many of the crowd believed in
Him; and they were saying, "[b]When [1]the
Christ comes, He will not perform more
[2c]signs than those which this man has, will
He?"
32 The Pharisees heard the crowd mutter-
ing these things about Him, and the chief
priests and the Pharisees sent [a]officers to
[b]seize Him.

22 [b]Gen 17:10ff; 21:4; Acts 7:8
23 [a]Matt 12:2; John 5:9, 10
24 [1]Lit *judge the righteous judgment* [a]Lev 19:15; Is 11:3; Zech 7:9; John 8:15
26 [1]I.e. the Messiah [a]Luke 23:13; John 3:1
27 [a]John 6:42; 7:41f; 9:29
28 [a]John 7:14 [b]John 6:42; 7:14f; 9:29 [c]John 8:42
29 [a]Matt 11:27; John 8:55; 17:25 [b]John 6:46 [c]John 3:17
30 [a]Matt 21:46; John 7:32, 44; 10:39 [b]John 7:6; 8:20
31 [1]I.e. the Messiah [2]Or *attesting miracles* [a]John 2:23; 8:30; 10:42; 11:45; 12:11, 42 [b]John 7:26 [c]John 2:11
32 [a]Matt 26:58; John 7:45f [b]Matt 12:14
33 [a]John 12:35; 13:33; 14:19; 16:16-19 [b]John 14:12, 28; 16:5, 10, 17, 28; 20:17
34 [a]John 7:36; 8:21; 13:33
35 [a]John 7:1 [b]John 8:22 [c]Ps 147:2; Is 11:12; 56:8; Zeph 3:10; James 1:1; 1 Pet 1:1 [d]John 12:20; Acts 14:1; 17:4; 18:4; Rom 1:16

33 Therefore Jesus said, "[a]For a little
while longer I am with you, then [b]I go to
Him who sent Me.
34 "[a]You will seek Me, and will not find
Me; and where I am, you cannot come."
35 [a]The Jews then said to one another,
"[b]Where does this man intend to go that we
will not find Him? He is not intending to go
to [c]the Dispersion among [d]the Greeks, and
teach the Greeks, is He?
36 "What is this statement that He said,
'[a]You will seek Me, and will not find Me; and
where I am, you cannot come'?"
37 Now on [a]the last day, the great *day* of
the feast, Jesus stood and cried out, saying,
"[1b]If anyone is thirsty, [2]let him come to Me
and drink.
38 "He who believes in Me, [a]as the Scripture said, 'From [1]his innermost being will
flow rivers of [b]living water.' "
39 But this He spoke [a]of the Spirit, whom
those who believed in Him were to receive;
for [b]the Spirit was not yet *given*, because
Jesus was not yet [c]glorified.

Division of People over Jesus

40 *Some* of the people therefore, when
they heard these words, were saying, "This
certainly is [a]the Prophet."
41 Others were saying, "This is [1]the
Christ." Still others were saying, "[a]Surely

36 [a]John 7:34; 8:21; 13:33 **37** [1]Vv 37-38 may also be read: *If anyone is thirsty,...let him come..., he who believes in me as...* [2]Or *let him keep coming to Me and let him keep drinking* [a]Lev 23:36; Num 29:35; Neh 8:18 [b]John 4:10, 14; 6:35 **38** [1]Lit *out of his belly* [a]Is 44:3; 55:1; 58:11 [b]John 4:10 **39** [a]Joel 2:28; John 1:33 [b]John 20:22; Acts 1:4f; 2:4, 33; 19:2 [c]John 12:16, 23; 13:31f; 16:14; 17:1 **40** [a]Matt 21:11; John 1:21 **41** [1]I.e. the Messiah [a]John 1:46; 7:52

7:22 *circumcision.* The requirement of circumcision was included in the law Moses gave (Ex 12:44,48; Lev 12:3), yet it did not originate with Moses but went back to Abraham (Gen 17:9–14). The Jews took such regulations as that in Lev 12:3 to mean that circumcision must be performed on the eighth day even if it was the Sabbath, a day on which no work should be done. This exception is of critical importance in understanding the controversy (v. 23). Jesus was not saying that the Sabbath should not be observed or that the Jewish regulations were too harsh. He was saying that His opponents did not understand what the Sabbath meant. The command to circumcise showed that sometimes work not only might be done on the Sabbath but must be done then. Deeds of mercy were in this category.
7:25 *people of Jerusalem.* An expression found only here and in Mark 1:5 in the NT, probably referring to the Jerusalem mob (see note on v. 20). They did not originate the plot against Jesus, but they knew of it.
7:26 *The rulers do not really know . . . do they?* In Greek, the question is in a form that expects a negative answer. *the Christ.* See note on 1:25.
7:27 *no one knows where He is from.* Some Jews held that the OT gave the origin of the Messiah (cf. v. 42; Matt 2:4–6), but others believed that it did not.
7:28 *You . . . know Me.* Irony, because in a sense they knew Jesus and that He came from Nazareth, but in a deeper sense they did not know Jesus or the Father (8:19). Jesus mentioned again His dependence on the Father (cf. 4:34) and went on to declare that He had real knowledge of God and that they did not. Both His origin and mission were from God.
7:30 *they were seeking to seize Him.* Jesus' enemies were powerless against Him until His time came (see note on 2:4).
7:31 *crowd.* Of pilgrims (see note on v. 20). Many of them believed on the basis of the miraculous signs (cf. 6:26).
7:32 *The Pharisees.* See notes on Matt 3:7; Mark 2:16; Luke 5:17. *the chief priests.* There was only one ruling chief priest, but the Romans had deposed a number of chief priests, and these retained the title by courtesy.
7:33 *then I go.* Jesus changed the topic from His miracles to His death, to which He referred enigmatically (v. 34).
7:35 *Dispersion among the Greeks.* From the time of the exile, many Jews lived outside the Holy Land and were found in most cities throughout the Roman empire.
7:37 *the last . . . day of the feast.* Either the seventh or the eighth day: The Feast of Booths lasted seven days (Lev 23:34; Deut 16:13,15) but had a "holy convocation" on the eighth day (Lev 23:36). See note on Mark 14:12. *stood and cried out, saying.* Teachers usually sat, so Jesus drew special attention to His message.
7:38 *living water.* See note on 4:10.
7:39 *the Spirit.* Explaining the "living water" (v. 38). *was not yet given.* In the manner in which He would be given at Pentecost (see Acts 2). *glorified.* Here probably refers to Jesus' crucifixion, resurrection and exaltation (see note on 13:31). The fullness of the Spirit's work depends on Jesus' prior work of salvation.
7:40 *people.* The "crowd" of v. 20 (see note there).

[1]the Christ is not going to come from Galilee,
is He?
42 "Has not the Scripture said that the
Christ comes from [a]the descendants of
David, and from Bethlehem, the village
where David was?"
43 So [a]a division occurred in the crowd
because of Him.
44 [a]Some of them wanted to seize Him,
but no one laid hands on Him.
45 The [a]officers then came to the chief
priests and Pharisees, and they said to them,
"Why did you not bring Him?"
46 The [a]officers answered, "[b]Never has a
man spoken the way this man speaks."
47 The Pharisees then answered them,
"[a]You have not also been led astray, have
you?
48 "[a]No one of [b]the rulers or Pharisees has
believed in Him, has he?
49 "But this crowd which does not know
the Law is accursed."
50 [a]Nicodemus (he who came to Him
before, being one of them) *said to them,
51 "[a]Our Law does not judge a man unless
it first hears from him and knows what he is
doing, does it?"
52 They answered him, "[a]You are not also
from Galilee, are you? Search, and see that
no prophet arises out of Galilee."
53 [[1]Everyone went to his home.

41 [1]I.e. the Messiah
42 [a]Ps 89:4; Mic 5:2; Matt 1:1; 2:5f; Luke 2:4ff
43 [a]John 9:16; 10:19
44 [a]John 7:30
45 [a]John 7:32
46 [a]John 7:32 [b]Matt 7:28
47 [a]John 7:12
48 [a]John 12:42 [b]Luke 23:13; John 7:26
50 [a]John 3:1; 19:39
51 [a]Ex 23:1; Deut 17:6; 19:15; Prov 18:13; Acts 23:3
52 [a]John 1:46; 7:41
53 [1]Later mss add the story of the adulterous woman, numbering it as John 7:53-8:11

8:1 [a]Matt 21:1
2 [a]Matt 26:55; John 8:20
5 [a]Lev 20:10; Deut 22:22f
6 [a]Matt 16:1; 19:3; 22:18, 35; Mark 8:11; 10:2; 12:15; Luke 10:25; 11:16 [b]Mark 3:2
7 [a]John 8:10 [b]Matt 7:1; Rom 2:1 [c]Deut 17:7
10 [a]John 8:7

The Adulterous Woman

8 But Jesus went to [a]the Mount of Olives.
2 Early in the morning He came again
into the temple, and all the people were coming to Him; and [a]He sat down and *began* to
teach them.
3 The scribes and the Pharisees *brought
a woman caught in adultery, and having set
her in the center *of the court*,
4 they *said to Him, "Teacher, this woman
has been caught in adultery, in the very act.
5 "Now in the Law [a]Moses commanded
us to stone such women; what then do You
say?"
6 They were saying this, [a]testing Him,
[b]so that they might have grounds for accusing Him. But Jesus stooped down and with
His finger wrote on the ground.
7 But when they persisted in asking Him,
[a]He straightened up, and said to them, "[b]He
who is without sin among you, let him *be the*
[c]first to throw a stone at her."
8 Again He stooped down and wrote on
the ground.
9 When they heard it, they *began* to go
out one by one, beginning with the older
ones, and He was left alone, and the woman,
where she was, in the center *of the court*.
10 [a]Straightening up, Jesus said to her,
"Woman, where are they? Did no one condemn you?"

7:42 *Bethlehem.* There were different ideas about the Messiah's place of origin (cf. v. 27).
7:46 *The officers.* They knew they would be in trouble for failing to make the arrest, but did not mention the hostility of part of the crowd, which would have given them something of an excuse before the Pharisees. They were favorably impressed by the teaching of Jesus and were not inclined to cause Him trouble.
7:47 *The Pharisees then answered.* They must have been greatly irritated. Ordinarily the chief priests would have rebuked the temple guards.
7:49 *this crowd.* The pilgrim crowd again (see note on v. 20). *does not know.* The Pharisees exaggerated the people's ignorance of Scripture (cf. v. 42). But the average Jew paid little attention to the minutiae that mattered so much to the Pharisees. The "traditions of the elders" were too great a burden for people who earned their living by hard physical work, and consequently these regulations were widely disregarded.
7:50–51 There is irony here. The Pharisees implied that no leader believed in Jesus, yet Nicodemus, "a ruler of the Jews" (3:1), spoke up. They called for people to observe the law, but Nicodemus pointed to their own disregard for the law in this instance.
7:52 *no prophet arises out of Galilee.* See 1:46. They were angry—and wrong. Jonah came from Galilee, and perhaps other prophets as well. Moreover, the Pharisees overlooked the right of God to raise up prophets from wherever He chooses.
7:53–8:11 This story may not have belonged originally to the Gospel of John. It is absent from almost all the early manuscripts, and those that have it sometimes place it elsewhere (e.g., after Luke 21:38). But the story may well be authentic.
7:53 This verse (along with 8:1) shows that the story was originally attached to another narrative, since Jesus was not present at the meeting of the Sanhedrin described in vv. 45–52.
8:1 *Mount of Olives.* See note on Mark 11:1.
8:3 *scribes.* See notes on Matt 2:4; Luke 5:17. *a woman caught in adultery.* This sin cannot be committed alone, so the question arises as to why only one offender was brought. The incident was staged to trap Jesus (v. 6), and provision had been made for the man to escape. The woman's accusers must have been especially eager to humiliate her, since they could have kept her in private custody while they spoke to Jesus.
8:4 *caught . . . in the very act.* Compromising circumstances were not sufficient evidence, as Jewish law required witnesses who had seen the act.
8:5 *to stone such women.* They altered the law a little. The manner of execution was not prescribed unless the woman was a betrothed virgin (Deut 22:23–24). And the law required the execution of both parties (Lev 20:10; Deut 22:22), not just the woman.
8:6 *were saying this, testing Him.* The Romans did not allow the Jews to carry out death sentences (18:31), so if Jesus had said to stone her, He could have been in conflict with the Romans. If He had said not to stone her, He could have been accused of being unsupportive of the law. *wrote.* We can only guess what Jesus wrote on the ground.
8:7 *without sin.* The phrase is quite general and means "without any sin," not "without this sin." *let him be the first.* Jesus' answer disarmed them. Since He spoke of throwing a stone, He could not be accused of failure to uphold the law. But the qualification for throwing it prevented anyone from acting.
8:9 *began to go out.* Because they were not "without sin" (v. 7). *the older ones.* They were the first to realize what was involved. But all the men were either conscience-stricken or afraid, and in the end only Jesus and the woman remained.
8:10 *Woman.* Not a harsh form of address (cf. its use in 19:26).

11 She said, "No one, [1]Lord." And Jesus said, "[a]I do not condemn you, either. Go. From now on [b]sin no more."]

Jesus Is the Light of the World

12 Then Jesus again spoke to them, saying, "[a]I am the Light of the world; [b]he who follows Me will not walk in the darkness, but will have the Light of life."

13 So the Pharisees said to Him, "[a]You are testifying about Yourself; Your testimony is not [1]true."

14 Jesus answered and said to them, "[a]Even if I testify about Myself, My testimony is [1]true, for I know [b]where I came from and where I am going; but [c]you do not know where I come from or where I am going.

15 "[a]You judge [1]according to the flesh; [b]I am not judging anyone.

16 "But even [a]if I do judge, My judgment is true; for I am not alone *in it,* but I and the Father who sent Me.

17 "Even in [a]your law it has been written that the testimony of [b]two men is [1]true.

18 "I am He who testifies about Myself, and [a]the Father who sent Me testifies about Me."

19 So they were saying to Him, "Where is Your Father?" Jesus answered, "You know neither Me nor My Father; [a]if you knew Me, you would know My Father also."

20 These words He spoke in [a]the treasury, as [b]He taught in the temple; and no one seized Him, because [c]His hour had not yet come.

21 Then He said again to them, "I go away, and [a]you will seek Me, and [b]will die in your sin; where I am going, you cannot come."

22 So [a]the Jews were saying, "Surely He will not kill Himself, will He, since He says, '[b]Where I am going, you cannot come'?"

23 And He was saying to them, "[a]You are from below, I am from above; [b]you are of this world, [c]I am not of this world.

24 "Therefore I said to you that you [a]will die in your sins; for unless you believe that [1b]I am *He,* [a]you will die in your sins."

25 So they were saying to Him, "Who are You?" Jesus said to them, "[1]What have I been saying to you *from* the beginning?

26 "I have many things to speak and to judge concerning you, but [a]He who sent Me is true; and [b]the things which I heard from Him, these I speak to the world."

27 They did not realize that He had been speaking to them about the Father.

28 So Jesus said, "When you [a]lift up the Son of Man, then you will know that [1b]I am *He,* and [c]I do nothing on My own initiative, but I speak these things as the Father taught Me.

29 "And He who sent Me is with Me; [a]He [1]has not left Me alone, for [b]I always do the things that are pleasing to Him."

30 As He spoke these things, [a]many came to believe in Him.

The Truth Will Make You Free

31 So Jesus was saying to those Jews who had believed Him, "[a]If you continue in My word, *then* you are truly [b]disciples of Mine;

32 and [a]you will know the truth, and [b]the truth will make you free."

33 They answered Him, "[a]We are Abraham's descendants and have never yet been enslaved to anyone; how is it that You say, 'You will become free'?"

34 Jesus answered them, "Truly, truly, I

11 [1]Or *Sir* [a]John 3:17 [b]John 5:14
12 [a]John 1:4; 9:5; 12:35 [b]Matt 5:14
13 [1]Or *valid* [a]John 5:31
14 [1]Or *valid* [a]John 18:37; Rev 1:5; 3:14 [b]John 8:42; 13:3; 16:28 [c]John 7:28; 9:29
15 [1]I.e. by a carnal standard [a]1 Sam 16:7; John 7:24 [b]John 3:17
16 [a]John 5:30
17 [1]I.e. valid or admissible [a]Deut 17:6; 19:15 [b]Matt 18:16
18 [a]John 5:37; 1 John 5:9
19 [a]John 7:28; 8:55; 14:7, 9; 16:3
20 [a]Mark 12:41, 43; Luke 21:1 [b]John 7:14; 8:2 [c]John 7:30
21 [a]John 7:34 [b]John 8:24
22 [a]John 1:19; 8:48, 52, 57 [b]John 7:35
23 [a]John 3:31
23 [b]1 John 4:5 [c]John 17:14, 16
24 [1]Most authorities associate this with Ex 3:14, *I AM WHO I AM* [a]John 8:21 [b]Matt 24:5; Mark 13:6; Luke 21:8; John 4:26; 8:28, 58; 13:19
25 [1]Or *That which I have been saying to you from the beginning*
26 [a]John 3:33; 7:28 [b]John 8:40; 12:49; 15:15
28 [1]Lit *I AM* (v 24 note) [a]John 3:14; 12:32 [b]Matt 24:5; Mark 13:6; Luke 21:8; John 4:26; 8:24, 58; 13:19 [c]John 3:11; 5:19
29 [1]Or *did not leave* [a]John 8:16; 16:32 [b]John 4:34 **30** [a]John 7:31 **31** [a]John 15:7; 2 John 9 [b]John 2:2 **32** [a]John 1:14, 17 [b]John 8:36; Rom 8:2; 2 Cor 3:17; Gal 5:1, 13; James 2:12; 1 Pet 2:16 **33** [a]Matt 3:9; Luke 3:8; John 8:37, 39

8:11 *Go. From now on sin no more.* Jesus did not condone what the woman had done.

8:12 *I am.* See note on 6:35. *the Light.* See 1:4 and note; 9:5; 12:46. It is also true that "God is Light" (1 John 1:5). And as Jesus' followers reflect the light that comes from Him, they too are "the light of the world" (Matt 5:14; cf. Phil 2:15). *darkness.* Both the darkness of this world and that of Satan. *the Light of life.* "God is Light" (1 John 1:5); but Jesus is also the light from God that lights the way for life—as the pillar of fire lighted the way for the Israelites (see Ex 13:21; Neh 9:12).

8:13 *Pharisees.* See notes on Matt 3:7; Mark 2:16; Luke 5:17.

8:14 Jesus made two points in reply. First, He was qualified to bear testimony, whereas the Pharisees were not; and He knew both His origin and His destination, whereas they knew neither. (See note on vv. 16–18 for the second point.)

8:15 The judgment of the Pharisees was limited and worldly. In the sense they meant, Jesus made it clear that He did not judge at all. In the proper sense, of course, He did judge (v. 26).

8:16–18 Jesus' second point was that His testimony was not unsupported. The Father was with Him, so He and the Father were the two witnesses required by the law (Deut 17:6; 19:15).

8:16 *the Father who sent Me.* Jesus was always aware of His mission (see note on 4:34).

8:19 *if you knew Me.* John makes it clear that the Word (Jesus) was with God and was God (1:1) and reveals God (1:18). Jesus here stresses that the Father is known through the Son and that to know the one is to know the other.

8:20 *His hour.* See note on 2:4.

8:23 Things other than death divide people (cf., e.g., v. 47; 3:31; 15:19; 1 John 3:10 etc.). *of.* Here denotes origin. Jesus was certainly in the world, but He was not of the world. They belonged to "this world"—Satan's domain (1 John 5:19).

8:24 *believe.* See note on 1:7. *I am.* Jesus echoes God's great affirmation about Himself (see v. 58; see also notes on 6:35; Ex 3:14).

8:28 *lift up.* Normally used in the NT in the sense of "exalt," but John uses it of the crucifixion (see 3:14). *Son of Man.* See note on Mark 8:31. *I am.* See notes on vv. 24,58.

8:30 *believe.* Cf. 20:31.

8:31 *believed.* Here seems to mean "made a formal profession of faith." Their words show that these people were not true believers (see vv. 33,37).

8:32 *the truth.* Closely connected with Jesus (v. 36; 14:6), it is not philosophical truth but the truth that leads to salvation. *free.* Freedom from sin, not from ignorance (see v. 36).

8:33 *have never yet been enslaved.* An amazing disregard of their Roman overlords.

say to you, [a]everyone who commits sin is
the slave of sin.
35 "[a]The slave does not remain in the
house forever; [b]the son does remain forever.
36 "So if the Son [a]makes you free, you will
be free indeed.
37 "I know that you are [a]Abraham's descendants; yet [b]you seek to kill Me, because
My word [1]has no place in you.
38 "I speak the things which I have seen
[1]with *My* Father; therefore you also do the
things which you heard from [a]*your* father."
39 They answered and said to Him, "Abraham is [a]our father." Jesus *said to them, "[b]If
you are Abraham's children, do the deeds of
Abraham.
40 "But as it is, [a]you are seeking to kill Me,
a man who has [b]told you the truth, which I
heard from God; this Abraham did not do.
41 "You are doing the deeds of [a]your
father." They said to Him, "We were not born
of fornication; [b]we have one Father: God."
42 Jesus said to them, "If God were your
Father, [a]you would love Me, [b]for I proceeded
forth and have come from God, for I have
[c]not even come on My own initiative, but
[1d]He sent Me.
43 "Why do you not understand [1a]what I
am saying? *It is* because you cannot [b]hear
My word.
44 "[a]You are of [b]*your* father the devil, and
[c]you want to do the desires of your father.
[d]He was a murderer from the beginning, and
does not stand in the truth because [e]there is
no truth in him. Whenever he speaks [1]a lie,
he [f]speaks from his own *nature*, for he is a
liar and the father of [2]lies.
45 "But because [a]I speak the truth, you do
not believe Me.
46 "Which one of you convicts Me of sin? If
[a]I speak truth, why do you not believe Me?

34 [a]Rom 6:16; 2 Pet 2:19 **35** [a]Gen 21:10; Gal 4:30 [b]Luke 15:31 **36** [a]John 8:32 **37** [1]Or *makes no progress* [a]Matt 3:9; John 8:39 [b]John 7:1; 8:40 **38** [1]Or *in the presence of* [a]John 8:41, 44 **39** [a]Matt 3:9; John 8:37 [b]Rom 9:7; Gal 3:7 **40** [a]John 7:1; 8:37 [b]John 8:26 **41** [a]John 8:38, 44 [b]Deut 32:6; Is 63:16; 64:8 **42** [1]Lit *that One* [a]1 John 5:1 [b]John 13:3; 16:28, 30; 17:8 [c]John 7:28 [d]John 3:17 **43** [1]Or *My way of speaking* [a]John 8:33, 39, 41 [b]John 5:25 **44** [1]Lit *the lie* [2]Lit *it* [a]1 John 3:8 [b]John 8:38, 41 [c]John 7:17 [d]Gen 3:4; 1 John 3:8, 15 [e]1 John 2:4 [f]Matt 12:34 **45** [a]John 18:37 **46** [a]John 18:37

47 [a]1 John 4:6 **48** [a]John 1:19 [b]Matt 10:5; John 4:9 [c]John 7:20 **49** [a]John 7:20 **50** [a]John 5:41; 8:54 **51** [a]John 8:55; 14:23; 15:20; 17:6 [b]Matt 16:28; Luke 2:26; John 8:52; Heb 2:9; 11:5 **52** [a]John 1:19 [b]John 7:20 [c]John 8:55; 14:23; 15:20; 17:6 [d]John 8:51 **53** [a]John 4:12 **54** [a]John 8:50 [b]John 7:39

47 "[a]He who is of God hears the words of
God; for this reason you do not hear *them*,
because you are not of God."
48 [a]The Jews answered and said to Him,
"Do we not say rightly that You are a
[b]Samaritan and [c]have a demon?"
49 Jesus answered, "I do not [a]have a
demon; but I honor My Father, and you dishonor Me.
50 "But [a]I do not seek My glory; there is
One who seeks and judges.
51 "Truly, truly, I say to you, if anyone
[a]keeps My word he will never [b]see death."
52 [a]The Jews said to Him, "Now we know
that You [b]have a demon. Abraham died, and
the prophets *also;* and You say, 'If anyone
[c]keeps My word, he will never [d]taste of
death.'
53 "Surely You [a]are not greater than our
father Abraham, who died? The prophets
died too; whom do You make Yourself out *to
be?*"
54 Jesus answered, "[a]If I glorify Myself,
My glory is nothing; [b]it is My Father who
glorifies Me, of whom you say, 'He is our
God';
55 and [a]you have not come to know Him,
[b]but I know Him; and if I say that I do not
know Him, I will be [c]a liar like you, [b]but I do
know Him and [d]keep His word.
56 "[a]Your father Abraham [b]rejoiced [1]to see
My day, and he saw *it* and was glad."
57 [a]So the Jews said to Him, "You are not
yet fifty years old, and have You seen Abraham?"
58 Jesus said to them, "Truly, truly, I say
to you, before Abraham [1]was born, [a]I am."
59 Therefore they [a]picked up stones to

55 [a]John 8:19; 15:21 [b]John 7:29 [c]John 8:44 [d]John 8:51; 15:10 **56** [1]Lit *in order that he might see* [a]John 8:37, 39 [b]Matt 13:17; Heb 11:13 **57** [a]John 1:19 **58** [1]Lit *came into being* [a]Ex 3:14; John 1:1; 17:5, 24 **59** [a]Matt 12:14; John 10:31; 11:8

8:34 *the slave of sin.* Because the sinner cannot break free by his own strength.

8:37 *you seek to kill Me.* See note on 7:1–8:59.

8:38 Note the contrasts: "I . . . you"; "seen . . . heard"; "My Father . . . your father." Not until later (v. 44) did Jesus say who their father was, but it is clear even at this point that it was neither God nor Abraham as they claimed.

8:39–41 Their deeds revealed their parentage.

8:41 *born of fornication.* May have been a slander aimed at Jesus' virgin birth.

8:43 *what I am saying.* The form of expression—the actual words. *My word.* The content. These descendants of Abraham (v. 33) were so convinced of their own preconceptions that they did not really hear what Jesus was saying (cf. v. 47).

8:44 *your father the devil.* The Jews' relationship to Satan was now stated explicitly. Jesus clearly excluded the idea of the universal fatherhood of God. *you want.* Points to determination of will. Their problem was basically spiritual, not intellectual. Being oriented toward Satan, they were bent on murder (v. 37) and eventually would succeed (v. 28). *truth.* Foreign to Satan and those who are his (see 14:6).

8:46 *Which one . . . convicts Me of sin?* The asking of the question was more significant than the Jews' failure to answer, in that it showed Jesus had a perfectly clear conscience.

8:47 *hears the words of God.* See 10:3–4; 1 John 4:6.

8:48 *The Jews.* See note on 1:19. *a Samaritan.* Probably to suggest that He was lax in Jewish observances—"No better than a Samaritan." Or it may be a reflection on the birth of Jesus—perhaps claiming that His father was a Samaritan. *have a demon.* See 10:20 and note on 7:20.

8:51 *My word.* The whole of Jesus' message, which when accepted brings deliverance from death.

8:53 *Surely You are not greater . . . ?* The question was framed to expect the answer "No." This is ironic, since Jesus was indeed far greater than Abraham, even as He was greater than Moses (see 6:30–35 and notes).

8:56 *My day.* All that was involved in the incarnation. Jesus probably was not referring to any one occasion but to Abraham's general joy in the fulfilling of the purposes of God in Christ, by which all nations on earth would receive blessing (Gen 18:18). *he saw it.* In faith, from afar.

8:57 *not yet fifty years old.* A generous allowance for Jesus' maximum possible age. Jesus was "about" 30 when He began His ministry (Luke 3:23).

8:58 *I am.* A solemnly emphatic declaration echoing God's great affirmation in Ex 3:14 (see vv. 24,28; see also note on 6:35).

throw at Him, but Jesus [1b]hid Himself and went out of the temple.

Healing the Man Born Blind

9 As He passed by, He saw a man blind from birth.

2 And His disciples asked Him, "[a]Rabbi, who sinned, [b]this man or his [c]parents, that he would be born blind?"

3 Jesus answered, "*It was* neither *that* this man sinned, nor his parents; but *it was* so [a]that the works of God might be displayed in him.

4 "We must work the works of Him who sent Me [a]as long as it is day; night is coming when no one can work.

5 "While I am in the world, I am [a]the Light of the world."

6 When He had said this, He [a]spat on the ground, and made clay of the spittle, and applied the clay to his eyes,

7 and said to him, "Go, wash in [a]the pool of Siloam" (which is translated, Sent). So he went away and [b]washed, and [c]came *back* seeing.

8 Therefore the neighbors, and those who previously saw him as a beggar, were saying, "Is not this the one who used to [a]sit and beg?"

9 Others were saying, "This is he," *still* others were saying, "No, but he is like him." [1]He kept saying, "I am the one."

10 So they were saying to him, "How then were your eyes opened?"

11 He answered, "The man who is called Jesus made clay, and anointed my eyes, and said to me, 'Go to [a]Siloam and wash'; so I went away and washed, and I received sight."

12 They said to him, "Where is He?" He *said, "I do not know."

59 [1]Lit *was hidden* [b]John 12:36
9:2 [a]Matt 23:7 [b]Luke 13:2; John 9:34; Acts 28:4 [c]Ex 20:5
3 [a]John 11:4
4 [a]John 7:33; 11:9; 12:35; Gal 6:10
5 [a]Matt 5:14; John 1:4; 8:12; 12:46
6 [a]Mark 7:33; 8:23
7 [a]Neh 3:15; Is 8:6; Luke 13:4; John 9:11 [b]2 Kin 5:13f [c]Is 29:18; 35:5; 42:7; Matt 11:5; John 11:37
8 [a]Acts 3:2, 10
9 [1]Lit *That one*
11 [a]John 9:7

14 [a]John 5:9
15 [a]John 9:10
16 [1]Or *attesting miracles* [a]Matt 12:2; Luke 13:14; John 5:10; 7:23 [b]John 2:11 [c]John 6:52; 7:12, 43; 10:19
17 [a]John 9:15 [b]Deut 18:15; Matt 21:11
18 [a]John 1:19; 9:22
22 [1]I.e. the Messiah [a]John 7:13 [b]John 7:45-52 [c]Luke 6:22; John 12:42; 16:2

Controversy over the Man

13 They *brought to the Pharisees the man who was formerly blind.

14 [a]Now it was a Sabbath on the day when Jesus made the clay and opened his eyes.

15 [a]Then the Pharisees also were asking him again how he received his sight. And he said to them, "He applied clay to my eyes, and I washed, and I see."

16 Therefore some of the Pharisees were saying, "This man is not from God, because He [a]does not keep the Sabbath." But others were saying, "How can a man who is a sinner perform such [1b]signs?" And [c]there was a division among them.

17 So they *said to the blind man [a]again, "What do you say about Him, since He opened your eyes?" And he said, "He is a [b]prophet."

18 [a]The Jews then did not believe *it* of him, that he had been blind and had received sight, until they called the parents of the very one who had received his sight,

19 and questioned them, saying, "Is this your son, who you say was born blind? Then how does he now see?"

20 His parents answered them and said, "We know that this is our son, and that he was born blind;

21 but how he now sees, we do not know; or who opened his eyes, we do not know. Ask him; he is of age, he will speak for himself."

22 His parents said this because they [a]were afraid of the Jews; for the Jews [b]had already agreed that if anyone confessed Him to be [1]Christ, [c]he was to be put out of the synagogue.

Jesus did not say "I was" but "I am," expressing the eternity of His being and His oneness with the Father (see 1:1). With this climactic statement Jesus concludes His speech that began with the related claim, "I am the Light of the world" (v. 12).

8:59 *stones to throw at Him.* The Jews could not interpret Jesus' claim as other than blasphemy, for which stoning was the proper penalty (Lev 24:16).

9:1–12 Jesus performed more miracles of this kind than of any other. Giving sight to the blind was predicted as a Messianic activity (Is 29:18; 35:5; 42:7). Thus these miracles were additional evidence that Jesus was the Messiah (20:31).

9:2 *who sinned . . . ?* The rabbis had developed the principle that "There is no death without sin, and there is no suffering without iniquity." They were even capable of thinking that a child could sin in the womb or that its soul might have sinned in a preexistent state. They also held that terrible punishments came on certain people because of the sin of their parents. As the next verse shows, Jesus plainly contradicted these beliefs.

9:4 *We.* Not Jesus only.

9:5 *the Light of the world.* See note on 8:12.

9:6 Jesus used variety in His cures.

9:7 *Siloam.* Already an ancient name (see notes on 2 Kin 20:20; Neh 2:14; Job 28:10; Is 8:6). A rock-cut pool on the southern end of the main ridge on which Jerusalem was built, it served as part of the major water system developed by King Hezekiah. *Sent.* Or "one who has been sent."

9:8 *as a beggar.* Not mentioned previously, but it was about the only way a blind person of that day could support himself.

9:13 *Pharisees.* See notes on Matt 3:7; Mark 2:16; Luke 5:17.

9:14 *Sabbath.* Cf. 5:16 and the discussion that follows.

9:16 *some . . . others.* The first group started from their entrenched position and ruled out the possibility of Jesus' being from God. The second started from the fact of the "miraculous signs" and ruled out the possibility of His being a sinner (cf. vv. 31–33).

9:17 *What do you say about Him . . . ?* It is curious that they put such a question to such a person; their doing so reflected their perplexity. *a prophet.* Probably the highest designation of which the man could think. He progressed in his thinking about Jesus: from a man (v. 11), to a prophet (v. 17) who might be followed by disciples (v. 27), to one "from God" (v. 33), to one who was properly to be worshiped (v. 38).

9:18 *The Jews.* See note on 1:19. In their prejudice they did not learn from the sign but tried to discredit the miracle.

9:21 *he is of age.* There was much to which the parents could not testify, but their emphasis on the son's responsibility showed their fear of getting involved.

9:22 *put out of the synagogue.* Excommunication is reported as early as the time of Ezra (10:8), but there is practically no information about the way it was practiced in NT times. The syna-

23 For this reason his parents said, "[a]He is
of age; ask him."
24 So a second time they called the man
who had been blind, and said to him, "[a]Give
glory to God; we know that [b]this man is a
sinner."
25 He then answered, "Whether He is a
sinner, I do not know; one thing I do know,
that though I was blind, now I see."
26 So they said to him, "What did He do
to you? How did He open your eyes?"
27 He answered them, "[a]I told you already
and you did not [b]listen; why do you want to
hear *it* again? You do not want to become His
disciples too, do you?"
28 They reviled him and said, "You are His
disciple, but [a]we are disciples of Moses.
29 "We know that God has spoken to
Moses, but as for this man, [a]we do not know
where He is from."
30 The man answered and said to them,
"Well, here is an amazing thing, that you do
not know where He is from, and *yet* He
opened my eyes.
31 "We know that [a]God does not hear sinners; but if anyone is God-fearing and does
His will, He hears him.
32 "[1]Since the beginning of time it has never been heard that anyone opened the eyes
of a person born blind.
33 "[a]If this man were not from God, He
could do nothing."
34 They answered him, "[a]You were born
entirely in sins, and are you teaching us?" So
they [b]put him out.

Jesus Affirms His Deity

35 Jesus heard that they had [a]put him out,
and finding him, He said, "Do you believe in
the [b]Son of Man?"
36 He answered, "[a]Who is He, [1]Lord, that
I may believe in Him?"
37 Jesus said to him, "You have both seen
Him, and [a]He is the one who is talking with
you."
38 And he said, "Lord, I believe." And he
[a]worshiped Him.
39 And Jesus said, "[a]For judgment I came
into this world, so that [b]those who do not
see may see, and that [c]those who see may
become blind."
40 Those of the Pharisees who were with
Him heard these things and said to Him,
"[a]We are not blind too, are we?"
41 Jesus said to them, "[a]If you were blind,
you would have no sin; but [1]since you say,
'[b]We see,' your sin remains.

Parable of the Good Shepherd

10 "Truly, truly, I say to you, he who does
not enter by the door into the fold of
the sheep, but climbs up some other way, he
is [a]a thief and a robber.
2 "But he who enters by the door is [a]a
shepherd of the sheep.
3 "To him the doorkeeper opens, and the
sheep hear [a]his voice, and he calls his own
sheep by name and [b]leads them out.
4 "When he puts forth all his own, he
goes ahead of them, and the sheep follow
him because they know [a]his voice.
5 "A stranger they simply will not follow,
but will flee from him, because they do not
know [a]the voice of strangers."
6 This [a]figure of speech Jesus spoke to
them, but they did not understand what
those things were which He had been saying
to them.
7 So Jesus said to them again, "Truly, truly, I say to you, I am [a]the door of the sheep.

23 [a]John 9:21
24 [a]Josh 7:19; Ezra 10:11; Rev 11:13 [b]John 9:16
27 [a]John 9:15 [b]John 5:25
28 [a]John 5:45; Rom 2:17
29 [a]John 8:14
31 [a]Job 27:8f; 35:13; Ps 34:15f; 66:18; 145:19; Prov 15:29; 28:9; Is 1:15; James 5:16ff
32 [1]Lit *From the age it was not heard*
33 [a]John 3:2; 9:16
34 [a]John 9:2 [b]John 9:22, 35; 3 John 10
35 [a]John 9:22, 34; 3 John 10 [b]Matt 4:3
36 [1]Or *Sir* [a]Rom 10:14
37 [a]John 4:26
38 [a]Matt 8:2
39 [a]John 3:19; 5:22, 27 [b]Luke 4:18 [c]Matt 13:13; 15:14
40 [a]Rom 2:19
41 [1]Lit *now* [a]John 15:22, 24 [b]Prov 26:12
10:1 [a]John 10:8
2 [a]John 10:11f
3 [a]John 10:4f, 16, 27 [b]John 10:9
4 [a]John 10:5, 16, 27
5 [a]John 10:4, 16, 27
6 [a]John 16:25, 29; 2 Pet 2:22
7 [a]John 10:1f, 9

gogue was the center of Jewish community life, so excommunication cut a person off from many social relationships (though, in some of its forms, at least in later times, not from worship).
9:24 *we.* Emphatic in the Greek.
9:27 *His disciples too.* The man already counted himself a disciple.
9:30–33 Good reasoning from an unschooled man.
9:31 *God does not hear sinners.* Cf. the remark of some of the Pharisees in v. 16.
9:34 *put him out.* May mean "expelled him from their assembly" or, more probably, "excommunicated him" (see note on v. 22).
9:35 *finding him.* Jesus obviously had been looking for the man. *Son of Man.* See note on Mark 8:31.
9:36 The man was ready to follow any suggestion from his benefactor.
9:38 *Lord . . . he worshiped Him.* The man was giving Jesus the reverence due to God. *I believe.* See 20:31 and note on 1:7.
9:39 It is unlikely that the conversation of vv. 35–38 took place in the presence of the Pharisees. The incident of vv. 39–41, therefore, probably occurred a little later. *For judgment.* In a sense Jesus did not come for judgment (3:17; 12:47), but His coming divides people, and this always brings a type of judgment. Those who reject His gift end up "blind."
9:40 *Pharisees.* They found it incredible that anyone would consider them spiritually blind.
9:41 The Pharisees' claim to sight showed their complete unawareness of their spiritual blindness and need. And, though they claimed to have sight, their actions were evidence of their blindness.
10:1–30 Should be understood in light of the OT (and ancient Near Eastern) concept of "shepherd," symbolizing a royal caretaker of God's people. God Himself was called the "Shepherd of Israel" (Ps 80:1; cf. Ps 23:1; Is 40:10–11; Ezek 34:11–16), and He had given great responsibility to the leaders ("shepherds") of Israel, which they failed to respect. God denounced these false shepherds (see Is 56:9–12; Ezek 34) and promised to provide the true Shepherd, the Messiah, to care for the sheep (Ezek 34:23).
10:1 *fold of the sheep.* A court surrounded by walls but open to the sky, and with only one entrance. The walls kept the sheep from wandering and protected them from wild animals.
10:3 *the doorkeeper.* Apparently in charge of a large fold, where several flocks were kept. *his voice.* The sheep recognized the voice of their own shepherd and responded only to him. *his own sheep.* The shepherd did not call sheep randomly, but only those that belonged to him.
10:4 *he goes ahead.* The Palestinian shepherd led his sheep (he did not drive them), and the sheep followed because they knew his voice.
10:7 *I am.* See note on 6:35.

8 "All who came before Me are [a]thieves
and robbers, but the sheep did not hear them.
9 "[a]I am the door; if anyone enters
through Me, he will be saved, and will go in
and out and find pasture.
10 "The thief comes only to steal and kill
and destroy; I came that they [a]may have life,
and [1]have *it* abundantly.
11 "[a]I am the good shepherd; the good
shepherd [b]lays down His life for the sheep.
12 "He who is a hired hand, and not a
[a]shepherd, who is not the owner of the
sheep, sees the wolf coming, and leaves the
sheep and flees, and the wolf snatches them
and scatters *them*.
13 "*He flees* because he is a hired hand and
is not concerned about the sheep.
14 "[a]I am the good shepherd, and [b]I know
My own and My own know Me,
15 even as [a]the Father knows Me and I
know the Father; and [b]I lay down My life for
the sheep.
16 "I have [a]other sheep, which are not of
this fold; I must bring them also, and they
will hear My voice; and they will become
[b]one flock *with* [c]one shepherd.
17 "For this reason the Father loves Me,
because I [a]lay down My life so that I may
take it again.
18 "[a]No one has taken it away from Me,
but I [b]lay it down on My own initiative. I
have authority to lay it down, and I have
authority to take it up again. [c]This commandment I received from My Father."

19 [a]A division occurred again among the
Jews because of these words.
20 Many of them were saying, "He [a]has a
demon and [b]is insane. Why do you listen to
Him?"
21 Others were saying, "These are not the
sayings of one [a]demon-possessed. [b]A demon
cannot open the eyes of the blind, can he?"

Jesus Asserts His Deity

22 At that time the Feast of the Dedication
took place at Jerusalem;
23 it was winter, and Jesus was walking in
the temple in the portico of [a]Solomon.
24 [a]The Jews then gathered around Him,
and were saying to Him, "How long [1]will
You keep us in suspense? If You are [2]the
Christ, tell us [b]plainly."
25 Jesus answered them, "[a]I told you, and
you do not believe; [b]the works that I do in
My Father's name, these testify of Me.
26 "But you do not believe because [a]you
are not of My sheep.
27 "My sheep [a]hear My voice, and [b]I know
them, and they follow Me;
28 and I give [a]eternal life to them, and
they will never perish; and [b]no one will
snatch them out of My hand.
29 "[1]My Father, who has given *them* to Me,
is greater than all; and no one is able to
snatch *them* out of the Father's hand.

8 [a]Jer 23:1f; Ezek 34:2ff; John 10:1
9 [a]John 10:1f, 9
10 [1]Or *have abundance* [a]John 5:40
11 [a]Is 40:11; Ezek 34:11-16, 23; John 10:14; Heb 13:20; 1 Pet 5:4; Rev 7:17 [b]John 10:15, 17, 18; 15:13; 1 John 3:16
12 [a]John 10:2
14 [a]John 10:11 [b]John 10:27
15 [a]Matt 11:27; Luke 10:22 [b]John 10:11, 17, 18
16 [a]Is 56:8 [b]John 11:52; 17:20f; Eph 2:13-18; 1 Pet 2:25 [c]Ezek 34:23; 37:24
17 [a]John 10:11, 15, 18
18 [a]Matt 26:53; John 2:19; 5:26 [b]John 10:11, 15, 17 [c]John 14:31; 15:10; Phil 2:8; Heb 5:8
19 [a]John 7:43; 9:16
20 [a]John 7:20 [b]Mark 3:21
21 [a]Matt 4:24 [b]Ex 4:11; John 9:32f
23 [a]Acts 3:11; 5:12
24 [1]Lit *do You lift up our soul* [2]I.e. the Messiah [a]John 1:19; 10:31, 33 [b]Luke 22:67; John 16:25
25 [a]John 8:56, 58 [b]John 5:36; 10:38
26 [a]John 8:47
27 [a]John 10:4, 16 [b]John 10:14
28 [a]John 17:2f; 1 John 2:25; 5:11 [b]John 6:37, 39
29 [1]One early ms reads *What My Father has given Me is greater than all*

10:8 *All . . . before Me.* "False shepherds" like the Pharisees and the chief priests, not the true OT prophets (see note on vv. 1–30).
10:9 *the door.* The one way into salvation. Inside there is safety, and one is able to go out and find pasture, i.e., the supply of all needs.
10:10 *thief.* His interest is in himself. Christ's interest is in His sheep, whom He enables to have life to the full (see note on 1:4).
10:11 *I am.* See note on 6:35. *lays down His life.* A shepherd might risk danger for his sheep (see Gen 31:39; 1 Sam 17:34–37), but he expected to come through alive. Jesus said that the good shepherd will die for his sheep.
10:12 *hired hand.* He is interested in wages, not sheep. In time of danger he runs away because of what he is (v. 13) and abandons the flock to predators.
10:14 *I know . . . My own know.* A deep mutual knowledge, like that of the Father and the Son.
10:15 *I lay down My life.* See v. 11; the fact of central importance.
10:16 *other sheep.* These already belonged to Christ, though they had not yet been brought to Him. *not of this fold.* Those outside Judaism. Here is a glimpse of the future worldwide scope of the church. *one flock.* All God's people have the same Shepherd (see 17:20–23).
10:17–18 That Christ would die for His people runs through this section of John's Gospel. Both the love and the plan of the Father are involved, as well as the authority He gave to the Son. Christ obediently chose to die; otherwise, no one would have had the power to kill him.
10:19 *division.* See 7:43; 9:16.
10:20 *has a demon.* See note on 7:20.
10:21 Cf. 9:16.
10:22 *Feast of the Dedication.* The commemoration of the dedication of the temple by Judas Maccabeus in December, 165 B.C., after it had been profaned by Antiochus Epiphanes (see notes on Ezra 6:16; Dan 8:9–12). This was the last great deliverance the Jews had experienced.
10:23 *it was winter.* A description for those unfamiliar with the Jewish calendar. *portico of Solomon.* See Acts 3:11; 5:12. It was a roofed structure—somewhat similar to a Greek stoa—commonly but erroneously thought to date back to Solomon's time.
10:24 *the Christ.* See note on 1:25 and cf. 20:31. This was the critical question, but it was not easy to answer because of the different ideas of Messiahship then in vogue.
10:25 *I told you.* Jesus had not specifically affirmed His Messiahship except to the Samaritan woman (4:26). He may have meant here that the general thrust of His teaching made His claim clear or that such statements as that in 8:58 were sufficient. Or He may have been referring to the evidence of His whole manner of life (including the miracles)—all He had done in the Father's name (for the name see note on 2:23).
10:26 *not of My sheep.* Their failure to believe arose from what they were.
10:27 *voice.* Cf. vv. 3–5. *I know them.* Cf. v. 14. *they follow.* Cf. vv. 4–5.
10:28 *eternal life.* Christ's gift (see note on 3:15). *never perish.* The Greek construction here is a strong denial that the sheep will ever perish. The sheep's security is in the power of the shepherd, who will let no one take them from him.
10:29 *My Father.* See note on 5:17. *is able.* The Father's power ("hand") is greater than that of any enemy, making the sheep completely secure.

30"[a]I and the Father are [1]one."
31 The Jews [a]picked up stones again to stone Him.
32 Jesus answered them, "I showed you many good works from the Father; for which of them are you stoning Me?"
33 The Jews answered Him, "For a good work we do not stone You, but for [a]blasphemy; and because You, being a man, [b]make Yourself out *to be* God."
34 Jesus answered them, "Has it not been written in [a]your [b]Law, '[c]I SAID, YOU ARE GODS'?
35"If he called them gods, to whom the word of God came (and the Scripture cannot be broken),
36 do you say of Him, whom the Father [a]sanctified and [b]sent into the world, 'You are blaspheming,' because I said, '[c]I am the Son of God'?
37"[a]If I do not do the works of My Father, do not believe Me;
38 but if I do them, though you do not believe Me, believe [a]the works, so that you may [1]know and understand that [b]the Father is in Me, and I in the Father."
39 Therefore [a]they were seeking again to seize Him, and [b]He eluded their grasp.
40 And He went away [a]again beyond the Jordan to the place where John was first baptizing, and He was staying there.
41 Many came to Him and were saying, "While John performed no [a]sign, yet [b]everything John said about this man was true."
42 [a]Many believed in Him there.

The Death and Resurrection of Lazarus

11 Now a certain man was sick, Lazarus of [a]Bethany, the village of Mary and her sister [b]Martha.
2 It was the Mary who [a]anointed [b]the Lord with ointment, and wiped His feet with her hair, whose brother Lazarus was sick.
3 So the sisters sent *word* to Him, saying, "[a]Lord, behold, [b]he whom You love is sick."
4 But when Jesus heard *this*, He said, "This sickness is not to end in death, but for [a]the glory of God, so that the Son of God may be glorified by it."
5 Now Jesus loved [a]Martha and her sister and Lazarus.
6 So when He heard that he was sick, He then stayed two days *longer* in the place where He was.
7 Then after this He *said to the disciples, "[a]Let us go to Judea again."
8 The disciples *said to Him, "[a]Rabbi, the Jews were just now seeking [b]to stone You, and are You going there again?"
9 Jesus answered, "[a]Are there not twelve hours in the day? If anyone walks in the day, he does not stumble, because he sees the light of this world.
10"But if anyone walks in the night, he stumbles, because the light is not in him."

30 [1]Or *a unity; or one essence* [a]John 17:21ff **31** [a]John 8:59 **33** [a]Lev 24:16 [b]John 5:18 **34** [a]John 8:17 [b]John 12:34; 15:25; Rom 3:19; 1 Cor 14:21 [c]Ps 82:6 **36** [a]Jer 1:5; John 6:69 [b]John 3:17 [c]John 5:17f; 10:30 **37** [a]John 10:25; 15:24 **38** [1]Lit *know and continue knowing* [a]John 10:25; 14:11 [b]John 14:10f, 20; 17:21, 23 **39** [a]John 7:30 [b]Luke 4:30; John 8:59 **40** [a]John 1:28 **41** [a]John 2:11 [b]John 1:27, 30, 34; 3:27-30
42 [a]John 7:31 **11:1** [a]Matt 21:17; John 11:18 [b]Luke 10:38; John 11:5, 19ff **2** [a]Luke 7:38; John 12:3 [b]Luke 7:13; John 11:3, 21, 32; 13:13f **3** [a]Luke 7:13; John 11:2, 21, 32; 13:13f [b]John 11:5, 11, 36 **4** [a]John 9:3; 10:38; 11:40 **5** [a]John 11:1 **7** [a]John 10:40
8 [a]Matt 23:7 [b]John 8:59; 10:31 **9** [a]Luke 13:33; John 9:4; 12:35

10:30 *one.* The Greek is neuter—"one thing," not "one person." The two are one in essence or nature, but they are not identical persons. This great truth is what warrants Jesus' "I am" declarations (see 8:24,28,58 and note on 6:35; see also 17:21–22).
10:31 *The Jews.* See note on 1:19. *to stone Him.* They took Jesus' words as blasphemy, and therefore prepared to carry out the law (Lev 24:16), though without due process.
10:32 *good works.* Or "good deeds" (as, e.g., in Matt 5:16; 1 Tim 5:10,25; 6:18). Although the reference here includes Jesus' miracles, the underlying Greek words refer to works in general that are fine and noble in character first of all (see note on v. 38).
10:33 *blasphemy.* The Jewish leaders correctly understood the thrust of Jesus' words, but their preconceptions and unbelief prevented them from accepting His claim as true.
10:34 *your Law.* In its strictest sense the term meant the Pentateuch, but was often used, as here, of the whole OT. *you are gods.* The words Jesus quotes from Ps 82:6 refer to the judges (or other leaders or rulers), whose tasks were divinely appointed (see Ex 22:28 and note; Deut 1:17; 16:18; 2 Chr 19:6).
10:35 *Scripture cannot be broken.* Jesus testified to the complete authority and reliability of the OT.
10:36 If there is any sense in which men can be spoken of as "gods" (as Ps 82:6 speaks of human rulers or judges), how much more may the term be used of Him whom the Father set apart and sent!
10:37 *the works of My Father.* The kind of works of compassion that the Father Himself does.
10:38 *works.* The miracles were a part of Jesus' works. It was Jesus' quality of life, not people's inability to explain His marvels, that He primarily spoke of here (see note on v. 32).
10:39 *they were seeking . . . to seize Him.* It is not clear if this was to arrest Him for trial or to take Him out for stoning. *He eluded.* John does not say why they failed, but he often makes it clear that Jesus could not be killed before the appointed time (see note on 2:4; see also Luke 4:30).
10:41 *everything John said.* For John the Baptist as a witness see 1:7 and note.
11:1 *Lazarus.* Mentioned only in chs. 11–12 of John's Gospel (the name is found also in the parable of Luke 16:19–31). The sisters are mentioned in Luke 10:38–42.
11:2 *anointed . . . with ointment.* See 12:3.
11:3 *he whom You love.* The relationship must have been exceptionally close.
11:4 Cf. 9:3. *This sickness is not to end in death.* Thus predicting the raising of Lazarus (v. 44), since Jesus already knew of his death (v. 14). In fact, Lazarus must have died shortly after the messengers left Bethany, accounting for the "four days" of vv. 17,39: one day for the journey of the messengers, the two days when Jesus remained where He was (v. 6; see 10:40), and a day for Jesus' journey to Bethany. But see note on v. 17. *glory.* See notes on 7:39; 12:41; 13:31. Here God's Son would be glorified through what happened to Lazarus, partly because the miracle displays the glory of God (who alone can raise the dead; see 5:21) in Jesus (v. 40) and partly because it would help initiate events leading to the cross (vv. 46–53).
11:6 *He then stayed . . . where He was.* Jesus moved as the Father directed, not as people (here Mary and Martha) wished (cf. 2:3–4).
11:8 *the Jews.* See note on 1:19. *were . . . seeking to stone You.* See note on 10:31. There was clear danger in going into Judea.
11:9 *twelve hours.* Enough time for what must be done, but no time for waste.

11 This He said, and after that He *said to them, "Our [a]friend Lazarus [b]has fallen asleep; but I go, so that I may awaken him out of sleep."

12 The disciples then said to Him, "Lord, if he has fallen asleep, he will [1]recover."

13 Now [a]Jesus had spoken of his death, but they thought that He was speaking of [1]literal sleep.

14 So Jesus then said to them plainly, "Lazarus is dead,

15 and I am glad for your sakes that I was not there, so that you may believe; but let us go to him."

16 [a]Therefore Thomas, who is called [1b]Didymus, said to *his* fellow disciples, "Let us also go, so that we may die with Him."

17 So when Jesus came, He found that he had already been in the tomb [a]four days.

18 Now [a]Bethany was near Jerusalem, about [1]two miles off;

19 and many of [a]the Jews had come to [b]Martha and Mary, [c]to console them concerning *their* brother.

20 [a]Martha therefore, when she heard that Jesus was coming, went to meet Him, but [a]Mary [1]stayed at the house.

21 Martha then said to Jesus, "[a]Lord, [b]if You had been here, my brother would not have died.

22 "Even now I know that [a]whatever You ask of God, God will give You."

23 Jesus *said to her, "Your brother will rise again."

24 Martha *said to Him, "[a]I know that he will rise again in the resurrection on the last day."

25 Jesus said to her, "[a]I am the resurrection and the life; he who believes in Me will live even if he dies,

26 and everyone who lives and believes in Me [a]will never die. Do you believe this?"

27 She *said to Him, "Yes, Lord; I have believed that You are [1a]the Christ, the Son of God, *even* [2b]He who comes into the world."

28 When she had said this, she [a]went away and called Mary her sister, saying secretly, "[b]The Teacher is here and is calling for you."

29 And when she heard it, she *got up quickly and was coming to Him.

30 Now Jesus had not yet come into the village, but [a]was still in the place where Martha met Him.

31 [a]Then the Jews who were with her in the house, and [b]consoling her, when they saw that Mary got up quickly and went out, they followed her, supposing that she was going to the tomb to weep there.

32 Therefore, when Mary came where Jesus was, she saw Him, and fell at His feet, saying to Him, "[a]Lord, [b]if You had been here, my brother would not have died."

33 When Jesus therefore saw her weeping, and [a]the Jews who came with her *also* weeping, He [b]was deeply moved in spirit and [1c]was troubled,

34 and said, "Where have you laid him?" They *said to Him, "Lord, come and see."

35 Jesus [a]wept.

36 So [a]the Jews were saying, "See how He [b]loved him!"

37 But some of them said, "Could not this man, who [a]opened the eyes of the blind man, [1]have kept this man also from dying?"

38 So Jesus, again being deeply moved

11 [a]John 11:3 [b]Matt 27:52; Mark 5:39; John 11:13; Acts 7:60 **12** [1]Lit *be saved* **13** [1]Lit *the slumber of sleep* [a]Matt 9:24; Luke 8:52 **16** [1]I.e. the Twin [a]Matt 10:3; Mark 3:18; Luke 6:15; John 14:5; 20:26-28; Acts 1:13 [b]John 20:24; 21:2 **17** [a]John 11:39 **18** [1]Lit *15 stadia* (9,090 ft) [a]John 11:1 **19** [a]John 1:19; 11:8 [b]John 11:1 [c]1 Sam 31:13; 1 Chr 10:12; Job 2:11; John 11:31 **20** [1]Lit *was sitting* [a]Luke 10:38-42 **21** [a]John 11:2 [b]John 11:32, 37 **22** [a]John 9:31; 11:41f **24** [a]Dan 12:2; John 5:28f; Acts 24:15 **25** [a]John 1:4; 5:26; 6:39f; Rev 1:18

26 [a]John 6:47, 50, 51; 8:51 **27** [1]I.e. the Messiah [2]The Coming One was the Messianic title [a]Matt 16:16; Luke 2:11 [b]John 6:14 **28** [a]John 11:30 [b]Matt 26:18; Mark 14:14; Luke 22:11; John 13:13 **30** [a]John 11:20 **31** [a]John 11:19, 33 [b]John 11:19

32 [a]John 11:2 [b]John 11:21 **33** [1]Lit *troubled Himself* [a]John 11:19 [b]John 11:38 [c]John 12:27; 13:21 **35** [a]Luke 19:41; John 11:33 **36** [a]John 11:19 [b]John 11:3 **37** [1]Lit *have caused that this man also not die* [a]John 9:7

11:11 *fallen asleep.* A euphemism for death, used by the unbelieving world as well as by Christians.

11:15 *believe.* Cf. 20:31.

11:16 *Thomas . . . Didymus.* The Hebrew word from which we get "Thomas" and the Greek word *Didymus* both mean "twin." We usually remember Thomas for his doubting, but he was also capable of devotion and courage.

11:17 *four days.* See note on v. 4. Many Jews believed that the soul remained near the body for three days after death in the hope of returning to it. If this idea was in the minds of these people, they obviously thought all hope was gone—Lazarus was irrevocably dead.

11:19 *to console them.* Jewish custom provided for three days of very heavy mourning, then four of heavy mourning, followed by lighter mourning for the remainder of 30 days. It was usual for friends to visit the family to comfort them.

11:20 *she . . . went to meet Him.* Perhaps because as the elder she was hostess.

11:21 Repeated by Mary in v. 32. Perhaps the sisters had said this to one another often as they awaited Jesus' arrival.

11:22 *whatever You ask.* This comment seems to mean that Martha hoped for an immediate resurrection in spite of the fact that Lazarus's body had already begun to decay. Nothing is too difficult for God to do.

11:25 *I am.* See note on 6:35. *life.* See note on 1:4. Jesus was saying more than that He gives resurrection and life. In some way these are identified with Him, and His nature is such that final death is impossible for Him. He is life (cf. 14:6; Acts 3:15; Heb 7:16). *he who believes . . . will live.* See note on 1:7. Jesus not only is life but conveys life to the believer so that death will never triumph over him (cf. 1 Cor 15:54–57).

11:27 *I have believed.* Martha is often remembered for her shortcoming recorded in Luke 10:40–41. But she was a woman of faith, as this magnificent declaration shows.

11:28 *The Teacher.* A significant description to be given by a woman. The rabbis would not teach women (cf. 4:27), but Jesus taught them frequently.

11:31 *to weep there.* Wailing at a tomb was common, and the Jews immediately thought this was in Mary's mind. Because they followed her, Jesus got maximum publicity.

11:32 Cf. v. 21.

11:33 *weeping.* Both times the word denotes a loud expression of grief, i.e., "wailing." *troubled.* See note on 12:27; cf. 13:21.

11:35 *wept.* The Greek for this word is not the one for loud grief, as in v. 33, but one that denotes quiet weeping, i.e., "shed tears."

11:36 Cf. v. 5.

11:37 Their position was like that of Martha (v. 21) and Mary (v. 32), but they based it on Jesus' ability to give sight to the blind (cf. ch. 9).

within, *came to the tomb. Now it was a
[a]cave, and a stone was lying against it.
39 Jesus *said, "Remove the stone." Martha, the sister of the deceased, *said to Him,
"Lord, by this time [1]there will be a stench,
for he has been *dead* [a]four days."
40 Jesus *said to her, "[a]Did I not say to
you that if you believe, you will see the glory of God?"
41 So they removed the [a]stone. Then
Jesus [b]raised His eyes, and said, "[c]Father, I
thank You that You have heard Me.
42 "I knew that You always hear Me; but
[a]because of the [1]people standing around I
said it, so that they may believe that [b]You
sent Me."
43 When He had said these things, He
cried out with a loud voice, "Lazarus, come
forth."
44 The man who had died came forth,
[a]bound hand and foot with wrappings, and
[b]his face was wrapped around with a cloth.
Jesus *said to them, "Unbind him, and let
him go."
45 [a]Therefore many of the Jews [b]who
came to Mary, and [c]saw what He had done,
believed in Him.
46 But some of them went to the [a]Phar-
isees and told them the things which Jesus
had done.

Conspiracy to Kill Jesus

47 Therefore [a]the chief priests and the
Pharisees [b]convened a [c]council, and were
saying, "What are we doing? For this man is
performing many [1d]signs.
48 "If we let Him *go on* like this, all men
will believe in Him, and the Romans will
come and take away both our [a]place and our
nation."
49 But one of them, [a]Caiaphas, [b]who was
high priest that year, said to them, "You
know nothing at all,
50 nor do you take into account that [a]it is
expedient for you that one man die for the
people, and that the whole nation not perish."
51 Now he did not say this [1]on his own
initiative, but [a]being high priest that year, he
prophesied that Jesus was going to die for
the nation,
52 and not for the nation only, but in
order that He might also [a]gather together
into one the children of God who are scattered abroad.
53 So from that day on they [a]planned
together to kill Him.
54 Therefore Jesus [a]no longer continued
to walk publicly among the Jews, but went
away from there to the country near the
wilderness, into a city called [b]Ephraim; and
there He stayed with the disciples.
55 Now [a]the Passover of the Jews was
near, and many went up to Jerusalem out of
the country before the Passover [b]to purify
themselves.
56 So they [a]were seeking for Jesus, and
were saying to one another as they stood in
the temple, "What do you think; that He will
not come to the feast at all?"
57 Now [a]the chief priests and the Pharisees had given orders that if anyone knew
where He was, he was to report it, so that
they might seize Him.

38 [a]Matt 27:60; Mark 15:46; Luke 24:2; John 20:1
39 [1]Lit *he stinks* [a]John 11:17
40 [a]John 11:4, 23ff
41 [a]Matt 27:60; Mark 15:46; Luke 24:2; John 20:1 [b]John 17:1; Acts 7:55 [c]Matt 11:25
42 [1]Lit *crowd* [a]John 12:30; 17:21 [b]John 3:17
44 [a]John 19:40 [b]John 20:7
45 [a]John 7:31 [b]John 11:19; 12:17f [c]John 2:23
46 [a]John 7:32, 45; 11:57
47 [1]Or *attesting miracles* [a]John 7:32, 45; 11:57 [b]Matt 26:3 [c]Matt 5:22 [d]John 2:11
48 [a]Matt 24:15
49 [a]Matt 26:3 [b]John 11:51; 18:13
50 [a]John 18:14
51 [1]Lit *from himself* [a]John 18:13
52 [a]John 10:16
53 [a]Matt 26:4
54 [a]John 7:1 [b]2 Chr 13:19 mg
55 [a]Matt 26:1f; Mark 14:1; Luke 22:1; John 2:13; 12:1; 13:1 [b]Num 9:10; 2 Chr 30:17f; John 18:28
56 [a]John 7:11
57 [a]John 11:47

11:39 *four days.* See notes on vv. 4,17.
11:40 *glory.* See note on v. 4.
11:44 *wrappings.* Narrow strips, like bandages. Sometimes a shroud was used (see note on 19:40). *a cloth.* A separate item.
11:45 *many of the Jews . . . believed in Him.* Perhaps some who had been opposed to Jesus now came to believe (see note on 1:19; cf. 20:31).
11:46 *Pharisees.* See notes on Matt 3:7; Mark 2:16; Luke 5:17.
11:47 *the chief priests and the Pharisees.* In all four Gospels the Pharisees appear as Jesus' principal opponents throughout His public ministry. But they lacked political power, and it is the chief priests who were prominent in the events that led to Jesus' crucifixion. Here both groups are associated in a meeting of the Sanhedrin (see note on Mark 14:55). They did not deny the reality of the miraculous signs (see note on 2:11), but they did not understand their meaning, for they failed to believe.
11:48 *place.* Probably the temple (see Acts 6:13–14; 21:28), though sometimes the Jews used the expression to denote Jerusalem.
11:49 *Caiaphas.* High priest c. A.D. 18–36. He was the son-in-law of Annas (18:13), who had been deposed from the high priesthood by the Romans in A.D. 15. *high priest that year.* Means "high priest at that time." The high priesthood was not an annual office but one supposed to be held for life. *You know nothing at all.* A remark typical of Sadducean rudeness (Caiaphas, as high priest, was a Sadducee). Josephus says that Sadducees "in their intercourse with their peers are as rude as to aliens." For Sadducees see notes on Matt 2:4; 3:7; Mark 12:18; Luke 20:27; Acts 4:1.
11:50 *expedient.* Caiaphas was concerned with political expediency, not with guilt and innocence. He believed that one man, no matter how innocent, should perish rather than that the nation be put in jeopardy. Ironically, the Jews went ahead with their execution of Jesus, and in A.D. 70 the nation still perished.
11:51 *being high priest.* Caiaphas was not a private citizen but was God's high priest, and God overruled in what he said. *that year.* See note on v. 49. *prophesied.* His words were true in a way he could not imagine. Prophecy in Scripture is the impartation of divinely revealed truth. In reality Caiaphas's words meant that Jesus' death would be for the nation, not by way of removing political trouble, but by taking away the sins of those who believed in Him.
11:52 *the children of God . . . scattered abroad.* Jesus' death would have effects far beyond the nation (cf. 1:29; 3:16; 4:42; 10:16; etc.).
11:54 *went away.* Jesus was not to die before His "time" (see note on 2:4), but He would not act imprudently. Knowing the attitude of His opponents, He withdrew. He would die for others, but in His own time, not that of His enemies. *Ephraim.* If it was the city known as Ophrah, it was about 15 miles north of Jerusalem.
11:55 *Passover.* See notes on 2:13; 5:1. *to purify themselves.* Especially important at a time like Passover, because without it, it would not be possible to keep the Feast (cf. 18:28; see note on 2:6).

Mary Anoints Jesus

12 [a]Jesus, therefore, six days before [b]the Passover, came to [c]Bethany where Lazarus was, whom Jesus had raised from the dead.

2 So they made Him a supper there, and [a]Martha was serving; but Lazarus was one of those reclining *at the table* with Him.

3 [a]Mary then took a [1]pound of very costly [b]perfume of pure nard, and anointed the feet of Jesus and wiped His feet with her hair; and the house was filled with the fragrance of the perfume.

4 But [a]Judas Iscariot, one of His disciples, who was intending to [1]betray Him, *said,

5 "Why was this perfume not sold for [1]three hundred denarii and given to poor *people?*"

6 Now he said this, not because he was concerned about the poor, but because he was a thief, and as he [a]had the money box, he used to pilfer [b]what was put into it.

7 Therefore Jesus said, "Let her alone, so that she may keep [1]it for [a]the day of My burial.

8 "[a]For you always have the poor with you, but you do not always have Me."

9 The [a]large crowd of the Jews then learned that He was there; and they came, not for Jesus' sake only, but that they might also see Lazarus, [b]whom He raised from the dead.

10 But the chief priests planned to put Lazarus to death also;

11 because [a]on account of him [b]many of the Jews were going away and were believing in Jesus.

12:1 [a]John 12:1-8: *Matt 26:6-13; Mark 14:3-9; Luke 7:37-39* [b]John 11:55; 12:20 [c]Matt 21:17; John 11:43f
2 [a]Luke 10:38
3 [1]I.e. a Roman pound, equaling 12 oz [a]Luke 7:37f; John 11:2 [b]Mark 14:3
4 [1]Or *hand Him over* [a]John 6:71
5 [1]Equivalent to 11 months' wages
6 [a]John 13:29 [b]Luke 8:3
7 [1]I.e. the custom of preparing the body for burial [a]John 19:40
8 [a]Deut 15:11; Matt 26:11; Mark 14:7
9 [a]Mark 12:37; John 12:12 mg [b]John 11:43f; 12:1, 17f
11 [a]John 11:45f; 12:18 [b]John 7:31; 11:42
12 [a]John 12:12-15: *Matt 21:4-9; Mark 11:7-10; Luke 19:35-38* [b]John 12:1
13 [a]Ps 118:26 [b]John 1:49
15 [a]Zech 9:9
16 [a]Mark 9:32; John 2:22; 14:26 [b]John 7:39; 12:23
17 [1]Lit *crowd* [a]John 11:42
18 [1]Lit *crowd* [2]Or *attesting miracle* [a]Luke 19:37; John 12:12 [b]John 12:11
20 [a]John 7:35 [b]John 12:1
21 [a]John 1:44 [b]Matt 11:21

Jesus Enters Jerusalem

12 On the next day [a]the large crowd who had come to [b]the feast, when they heard that Jesus was coming to Jerusalem,

13 took the branches of the palm trees and went out to meet Him, and *began* to shout, "[a]Hosanna! BLESSED IS HE WHO COMES IN THE NAME OF THE LORD, even the [b]King of Israel."

14 Jesus, finding a young donkey, sat on it; as it is written,

15 "[a]FEAR NOT, DAUGHTER OF ZION; BEHOLD, YOUR KING IS COMING, SEATED ON A DONKEY'S COLT."

16 [a]These things His disciples did not understand at the first; but when Jesus [b]was glorified, then they remembered that these things were written of Him, and that they had done these things to Him.

17 So [a]the [1]people, who were with Him when He called Lazarus out of the tomb and raised him from the dead, continued to testify *about Him.*

18 [a]For this reason also the [1]people went and met Him, [b]because they heard that He had performed this [2]sign.

19 So the Pharisees said to one another, "You see that you are not doing any good; look, the world has gone after Him."

Greeks Seek Jesus

20 Now there were some [a]Greeks among those who were going up to worship at [b]the feast;

21 these then came to [a]Philip, who was from [b]Bethsaida of Galilee, and *began to* ask him, saying, "Sir, we wish to see Jesus."

12:1–11 All four Gospels have an account of a woman anointing Jesus. John's account seems to tell of the same incident recorded in Matt 26:6–13 and Mark 14:3–9, while that in Luke 7:36–50 is different.
12:1 *Bethany.* See note on Matt 21:17.
12:3 *nard.* The name of both a plant and the fragrant oil it yielded. Since it was very expensive, Mary's act of devotion was costly. It was also an unusual act, both because she poured the oil on Jesus' feet (normally it was poured on the head) and because she used her hair to wipe them (a respectable woman did not unbind her hair in public). Further, it showed her humility, for it was a servant's work to attend to the feet (see notes on 1:27; 13:5).
12:4 *Judas Iscariot.* See note on 6:71.
12:6 *a thief.* The one passage from which we learn that Judas was dishonest. Yet he must have been thought to be a man of some reliability, for he was keeper of the money bag.
12:7 *keep.* Probably the meaning is "save for this purpose." Perfume was normally associated with festivity, but it was also used in burials (see 19:39–40), and Jesus links it with His burial, which Mary's act unwittingly anticipates.
12:9 *Jews.* See note on 1:19.
12:10 The Jewish leaders previously had spoken of the death of one man (11:50), but now they wanted another death. Sin grows.
12:12 *large crowd.* Pilgrims who had come up from the country for the Passover Feast. Many of the pilgrims had doubtless seen and heard Jesus in Galilee, and they welcomed the opportunity to proclaim Him as Messiah.
12:13 *branches of the palm trees.* Used in celebration of victory. John saw a multitude with palm branches in heaven (Rev 7:9). *Hosanna!* A Hebrew expression meaning "Save!" that became an exclamation of praise (see note on Jer 31:7). *the name.* See note on 2:23. *even the King of Israel.* The people's addition to the words of the psalm, which John alone records. It reflects his special interest in Jesus' royalty, which he brings out throughout the passion narrative.
12:14 *donkey.* See notes on Zech 9:9; Matt 21:2,7; Mark 11:2; Luke 19:30.
12:16 An example of the meaning of 16:13. *glorified.* See notes on v. 41; 11:4; 13:31. Only after the crucifixion and the coming of the Holy Spirit did the disciples appreciate the meaning of the prophecy and its fulfillment.
12:19 *Pharisees.* See notes on Matt 3:7; Mark 2:16; Luke 5:17.
12:20 *Greeks.* Probably "God-fearers," people attracted to Judaism by its monotheism and morality, but repelled by its nationalism and requirements such as circumcision. They worshiped in the synagogues but did not become proselytes.
12:21 *Philip.* A Greek name, which may be why they came to this disciple (though he was not the only one of the Twelve to have a Greek name). *to see.* Means "to have an interview with." After v. 22 John records no more about these Greeks (yet see note on v. 32). He regarded their coming as important but not their conversation with Jesus. Jesus came to die for the world,

22 Philip *came and *told [a]Andrew;
Andrew and Philip *came and *told Jesus.
23 And Jesus *answered them, saying,
"[a]The hour has come for the Son of Man to
[b]be glorified.
24 "Truly, truly, I say to you, [a]unless a
grain of wheat falls into the earth and dies, it
remains alone; but if it dies, it bears much
fruit.
25 "[a]He who loves his [1]life loses it, and he
who [b]hates his [1]life in this world will keep it
to life eternal.
26 "If anyone [1]serves Me, he must follow
Me; and [a]where I am, there My servant will
be also; if anyone [1]serves Me, the Father will
[b]honor him.

Jesus Foretells His Death

27 "[a]Now My soul has become troubled;
and what shall I say, '[b]Father, save Me from
[c]this hour'? But for this purpose I came to
this hour.
28 "[a]Father, glorify Your name." Then a
[b]voice came out of heaven: "I have both glorified it, and will glorify it again."
29 So the crowd *of people* who stood by
and heard it were saying that it had thundered; others were saying, "[a]An angel has
spoken to Him."
30 Jesus answered and said, "[a]This voice
has not come for My sake, but for your
sakes.
31 "[a]Now judgment is upon this world;
now [b]the ruler of this world will be cast out.
32 "And I, if I [a]am lifted up from the earth,
will [b]draw all men to Myself."
33 But He was saying this [a]to indicate the
kind of death by which He was to die.
34 The crowd then answered Him, "We
have heard out of [a]the Law that [1][b]the Christ
is to remain forever; and how can You say,
'The [c]Son of Man must be [d]lifted up'? Who is
this [c]Son of Man?"
35 So Jesus said to them, "[a]For a little
while longer [b]the Light is among you. [c]Walk
while you have the Light, so that darkness
will not overtake you; he who [d]walks in the
darkness does not know where he goes.
36 "While you have the Light, [a]believe in
the Light, so that you may become [b]sons of
Light."
These things Jesus spoke, and He went
away and [1][c]hid Himself from them.
37 But though He had performed so many
[1]signs before them, *yet* they were not believing in Him.
38 *This was* to fulfill the word of Isaiah the
prophet which he spoke: "[a]LORD, WHO HAS
BELIEVED OUR REPORT? AND TO WHOM HAS THE
ARM OF THE LORD BEEN REVEALED?"
39 For this reason they could not believe,
for Isaiah said again,
40 "[a]HE HAS BLINDED THEIR EYES AND HE
[b]HARDENED THEIR HEART, SO THAT THEY WOULD
NOT SEE WITH THEIR EYES AND PERCEIVE WITH THEIR
HEART, AND [1]BE CONVERTED AND I HEAL THEM."
41 These things Isaiah said because [a]he
saw His glory, and [b]he spoke of Him.

22 [a]John 1:44 **23** [a]Matt 26:45; Mark 14:35, 41; John 13:1; 17:1 [b]John 7:39; 12:16; 13:32 **24** [a]Rom 14:9; 1 Cor 15:36 **25** [1]Lit *soul* [a]Matt 10:39; 16:25; Mark 8:35; Luke 9:24; 17:33 [b]Luke 14:26 **26** [1]Or *is serving* [a]John 14:3; 17:24; 2 Cor 5:8; Phil 1:23; 1 Thess 4:17 [b]1 Sam 2:30; Ps 91:15; Luke 12:37 **27** [a]Matt 26:38; Mark 14:34; John 11:33 [b]Matt 11:25 [c]John 12:23 **28** [a]Matt 11:25 [b]Matt 3:17; 17:5; Mark 1:11; 9:7; Luke 3:22; 9:35 **29** [a]Acts 23:9 **30** [a]John 11:42 **31** [a]John 3:19; 9:39; 16:11 [b]John 14:30; 16:11; 2 Cor 4:4; Eph 2:2; 6:12; 1 John 4:4; 5:19 **32** [a]John 3:14; 8:28; 12:34 [b]John 6:44

33 [a]John 18:32; 21:19 **34** [1]I.e. the Messiah [a]John 10:34 [b]Ps 110:4; Is 9:7; Ezek 37:25; Dan 7:14 [c]Matt 8:20 [d]John 3:14; 8:28; 12:32 **35** [a]John 7:33; 9:4 [b]John 12:46; 1 John 2:10 [c]Gal 6:10; Eph 5:8 [d]1 John 1:6; 2:11 **36** [1]Lit *was hidden* [a]John 12:46 [b]Luke 16:8; John 8:12 [c]John 8:59 **37** [1]Or *attesting signs* **38** [a]Is 53:1; Rom 10:16 **40** [1]Lit *be turned;* i.e. turn about [a]Is 6:10; Matt 13:14f [b]Mark 6:52 **41** [a]Is 6:1ff [b]Luke 24:27

and the coming of these Gentiles indicates the scope of the effectiveness of His approaching crucifixion.

12:23 *The hour has come.* The hour to which everything else led (see note on 2:4). *glorified.* Jesus was speaking about His death on the cross and His subsequent resurrection and exaltation (see notes on v. 41; 11:4; 13:31).

12:24 *if it dies, it bears.* The principle of life through death is seen in the plant world. The kernel must perish as a kernel if there is to be a plant.

12:25 *he who hates his life . . . will keep it.* To love one's life here and now—to concentrate on one's own success—is to lose what matters (cf. Matt 16:24–25; Mark 8:34–35; Luke 9:23–24). Supremely, of course, the principle is seen in the cross of Jesus. *hates.* Love for God must be such that all other loves are, by comparison, hatred. *life eternal.* See note on 3:15.

12:27 *troubled.* John's equivalent to the agony in Gethsemane described in the other Gospels. *this hour.* Jesus faced the prospect of becoming sin (or a sin offering) for sinful people (2 Cor 5:21). He considered praying for God to save Him from this death, but refused to pray it, because the very reason He had come was to die.

12:28 *Father, glorify Your name.* His prayer was not for deliverance but for the Father to be glorified. The voice from heaven gave the answer. *name.* See note on 2:23.

12:31 *upon this world.* The cross was God's judgment on the world. *the ruler of this world.* Satan (cf. 16:11). The cross would seem to be his triumph; in fact, it was his defeat. Out of it would flow the greatest good ever to come to the world.

12:32 *lifted up.* See note on 3:14. The cross was the supreme exaltation of Jesus (see notes on v. 41; 13:31). *all men.* Christ will draw people to Himself without regard for nationality, ethnic affiliation or status. It is significant that Greek Gentiles were present on this occasion (v. 20).

12:34 *the Law.* Here seems to mean OT Scripture in general (see note on 10:34), the reference being to passages such as Ps 89:36; 110:4; Is 9:7; Dan 7:14. *the Christ.* See note on 1:25. *Son of Man.* The only place in the Gospels where anyone other than Jesus used the expression, and even here Jesus is being quoted (see note on Mark 8:31).

12:35–36 *the Light.* Light is closely identified with Jesus, as seen from the call to believe in the light (see notes on 1:4; 8:12).

12:37 *they were not believing.* God's ancient people should have responded when God sent His Messiah. They should have seen the significance of the signs He did.

12:39 *could not believe.* Does not mean that the people in question had no choice. They purposely rejected God and chose evil, and v. 40 explains that God in turn brought on them a judicial blinding of eyes and hardening of hearts. Yet many Jewish leaders did believe in Jesus as the Messiah (v. 42).

12:40 These words from Is 6:10 are quoted by Jesus (Matt 13:14–15; Mark 4:12; Luke 8:10) and by Paul (Acts 28:26–27).

12:41 *saw His glory.* Isaiah spoke primarily of the glory of God (Is 6:3). John spoke of the glory of Jesus and made no basic distinction between the two, attesting Jesus' oneness with God. The thought of glory here is complex. There is the idea of majesty, and there is also the idea (which meant so much to John) that Jesus' death on the cross and His subsequent resurrection and exaltation show His real glory. Isaiah foresaw the

42 Nevertheless [a]many even of [b]the rulers
believed in Him, but [c]because of the Pharisees
they were not confessing *Him,* for fear that
they would be [1d]put out of the synagogue;
43 [a]for they loved the [1]approval of men
rather than the [1]approval of God.
44 And Jesus cried out and said, "[a]He
who believes in Me, does not believe in Me
but in Him who sent Me.
45 "[a]He who sees Me sees the One who
sent Me.
46 "[a]I have come *as* Light into the world,
so that everyone who believes in Me will not
remain in darkness.
47 "If anyone hears My sayings and does
not keep them, I do not judge him; for [a]I did
not come to judge the world, but to save the
world.
48 "[a]He who rejects Me and does not
receive My sayings, has one who judges him;
[b]the word I spoke is what will judge him at
[c]the last day.
49 "[a]For I did not speak [1]on My own initiative, but the Father Himself who sent Me
[b]has given Me a commandment *as to* what to
say and what to speak.
50 "I know that [a]His commandment is eternal life; therefore the things I speak, I speak
[b]just as the Father has told Me."

The Lord's Supper

13 Now before the Feast of [a]the Passover,
Jesus knowing that [b]His hour had
come that He would depart out of this world
[c]to the Father, having loved His own who
were in the world, He loved them [1]to the
end.
2 During supper, [a]the devil having
already put into the heart of [b]Judas Iscariot,
the son of Simon, to betray Him,
3 *Jesus,* [a]knowing that the Father had
given all things into His hands, and that [b]He
had come forth from God and was going
back to God,
4 *got up from supper, and *laid aside
His garments; and taking a towel, He [a]girded
Himself.

Jesus Washes the Disciples' Feet

5 Then He *poured water into the basin,
and began to [a]wash the disciples' feet and to
wipe them with the towel with which He
was girded.
6 So He *came to Simon Peter. He *said
to Him, "Lord, do You wash my feet?"
7 Jesus answered and said to him, "What
I do you do not realize now, but you will
understand [a]hereafter."
8 Peter *said to Him, "Never shall You
wash my feet!" Jesus answered him, "[a]If I
do not wash you, [b]you have no part with
Me."

42 [1]I.e. excommunicated [a]John 7:48; 12:11 [b]Luke 23:13 [c]John 7:13 [d]John 9:22
43 [1]Or *glory* [a]John 5:41, 44
44 [a]Matt 10:40; John 5:24
45 [a]John 14:9
46 [a]John 1:4; 3:19; 8:12; 9:5; 12:35f
47 [a]John 3:17; 8:15f
48 [a]Luke 10:16 [b]Deut 18:18f; John 5:45ff; 8:47 [c]Matt 10:15; John 6:39; Acts 17:31; 1 Pet 1:5; 2 Pet 3:3, 7; Heb 10:25
49 [1]Lit *of Myself* [a]John 3:11; 7:16; 8:26, 28, 38; 14:10, 24 [b]John 14:31; 17:8
50 [a]John 6:68 [b]John 5:19; 8:28
13:1 [a]John 2:13; 11:55 [b]John 12:23
13:1 [1]Or *to the uttermost;* or *eternally* [c]John 13:3; 16:28
2 [a]John 6:70; 13:27 [b]John 6:71
3 [a]John 3:35 [b]John 8:42
4 [a]Luke 12:37; 17:8 **5** [a]Gen 18:4; 19:2; 43:24; Judg 19:21; Luke 7:44; 1 Tim 5:10 **7** [a]John 13:12ff **8** [a]Ps 51:2, 7; Ezek 36:25; Acts 22:16; 1 Cor 6:11; Heb 10:22 [b]Deut 12:12; 2 Sam 20:1; 1 Kin 12:16

rejection of Christ, as the passages quoted (Is 53:1; 6:10) show. He spoke of the Messiah both in the words about blind eyes and hard hearts, on the one hand, and about healing, on the other. This is the cross and this is glory, for the cross and resurrection and exaltation portray both suffering and healing, rejection and triumph, humiliation and glory.

12:42 *many . . . rulers believed.* John does not give a picture of unrelieved gloom. Many Jewish leaders believed (see note on 1:7), though they remained secret believers for fear of excommunication (see note on 9:22).

12:44 *cried out.* The words are given special emphasis by being spoken in a loud voice. *believe in Me.* John ends his story of the public ministry of Jesus with an appeal for belief. He does not say when Jesus spoke these words (they may have been uttered earlier), but they are a fitting close to this part of his account. *Him who sent Me.* Jesus' mission, as well as the inseparability of the Father and the Son, is stressed throughout this Gospel.

12:46 *I have come . . . into the world.* Points to both Jesus' preexistence and His mission. *Light.* See notes on 1:4; 8:12.

12:47 *to judge.* Not the purpose of Jesus' coming, but judgment is the other side of salvation. It is not the purpose of the sun's shining to cast shadows, but when the sun shines, shadows are inevitable.

12:49 *the Father . . . has given Me a commandment . . . what to say.* Jesus' hearers have a great responsibility. His "word" (v. 48) is that which the Father commanded Him to say. To reject it, therefore, is to reject God.

12:50 *eternal life.* See note on 3:15. *therefore.* Jesus said what He did in order to fulfill the will of the Father—a wonderful note on which to end the account of Jesus' public ministry.

13:1–17:26 John has by far the longest account of the upper room, though curiously he says nothing about the institution of the Lord's Supper. Still we owe to him most of our information about what our Lord said to His disciples on that night. One feature of the discourse is Jesus' emphasis on love. The Greek noun *agape* ("love") and the verb *agapao* ("love") occur only eight times in chs. 1–12 but 31 times in chs. 13–17.

13:1 *Feast of the Passover.* See notes on 2:13; 5:1. *His hour.* See note on 2:4.

13:2 *supper.* Some believe that this feast was a fellowship meal eaten sometime before the Passover Feast. This would mean that the Last Supper could not have been the Passover meal as the Synoptic Gospels clearly indicate. However, this meal may have been the Passover Feast itself, in which case the accounts of the Synoptics and John would agree. *the devil.* See v. 27. *Judas Iscariot.* See note on 6:71.

13:3 *the Father had given all things into His hands.* John again emphasizes the fulfillment of God's plan and Jesus' control of the situation.

13:5 *began to wash the disciples' feet.* A menial task (see note on 1:27), normally performed by a servant. On this occasion there was no servant and no one else volunteered. Jesus' action was during the meal, not upon arrival, done deliberately to emphasize a point. It was a lesson in humility, but it also set forth the principle of selfless service that was so soon to be exemplified in the cross. John alone tells of this incident, but Luke says that in rebuking the disciples over a quarrel concerning who would be the greatest, Jesus said, "I am among you as the one who serves" (Luke 22:27). Jesus' life of service would culminate on the cross.

13:8 *Never.* Characteristically, Peter objected, though apparently no one else did. He was a mixture of humility (he did not want Jesus to perform this lowly service for him) and pride (he

9 Simon Peter *said to Him, "Lord, *then wash* not only my feet, but also my hands and my head."

10 Jesus *said to him, "He who has bathed needs only to wash his feet, but is completely clean; and [a]you are clean, but not all *of you.*"

11 For [a]He knew the one who was betraying Him; for this reason He said, "Not all of you are clean."

12 So when He had washed their feet, and [a]taken His garments and reclined *at the table* again, He said to them, "Do you know what I have done to you?

13 "You call Me [a]Teacher and [b]Lord; and [1]you are right, for *so* I am.

14 "If I then, [a]the Lord and the Teacher, washed your feet, you also ought to wash one another's feet.

15 "For I gave you [a]an example that you also should do as I did to you.

16 "Truly, truly, I say to you, [a]a slave is not greater than his master, nor *is* [b]one who is sent greater than the one who sent him.

17 "If you know these things, you are [a]blessed if you do them.

18 "[a]I do not speak of all of you. I know the ones I have [b]chosen; but *it is* [c]that the Scripture may be fulfilled, '[d]HE WHO EATS MY BREAD HAS LIFTED UP HIS HEEL AGAINST ME.'

19 "From now on [a]I am telling you before *it* comes to pass, so that when it does occur, you may believe that [b]I am *He.*

20 "Truly, truly, I say to you, [a]he who receives whomever I send receives Me; and he who receives Me receives Him who sent Me."

10 [a]John 15:3; Eph 5:26 **11** [a]John 6:64; 13:2 **12** [a]John 13:4 **13** [1]Lit *you say well* [a]John 11:28 [b]John 11:2; 1 Cor 12:3; Phil 2:11 **14** [a]John 11:2; 1 Cor 12:3; Phil 2:11 **15** [a]1 Pet 5:3 **16** [a]Matt 10:24; Luke 6:40; John 15:20 [b]2 Cor 8:23; Phil 2:25 **17** [a]Matt 7:24ff; Luke 11:28; James 1:25 **18** [a]John 13:10f [b]John 6:70; 15:16, 19 [c]John 15:25; 17:12; 18:32; 19:24, 36 [d]Ps 41:9; Matt 26:21ff; Mark 14:18f; Luke 22:21ff; John 13:21, 22, 26 **19** [a]John 14:29; 16:4 [b]John 8:24 **20** [a]Matt 10:40; Mark 9:37; Luke 9:48; 10:16; Gal 4:14

21 [1]Or *hand Me over* [a]John 11:33 [b]Matt 26:21f; Mark 14:18ff;

Jesus Predicts His Betrayal

21 When Jesus had said this, He [a]became troubled in spirit, and testified and said, "Truly, truly, I say to you, that [b]one of you will [1]betray Me."

22 The disciples *began* looking at one another, [a]at a loss *to know* of which one He was speaking.

23 There was reclining on [a]Jesus' bosom one of His disciples, [b]whom Jesus loved.

24 So Simon Peter *gestured to him, and *said to him, "Tell *us* who it is of whom He is speaking."

25 He, [a]leaning back thus on Jesus' bosom, *said to Him, "Lord, who is it?"

26 Jesus then *answered, "That is the one for whom I shall dip the morsel and give it to him." So when He had dipped the morsel, He *took and *gave it to Judas, [a]*the son* of Simon Iscariot.

27 After the morsel, [a]Satan then [b]entered into him. Therefore Jesus *said to him, "What you do, do quickly."

28 Now no one of those reclining *at the table* knew for what purpose He had said this to him.

29 For some were supposing, because Judas [a]had the money box, that Jesus was saying to him, "Buy the things we have need of [b]for the feast"; or else, that he should [c]give something to the poor.

Luke 22:21ff; John 13:18, 22, 26 **22** [a]Matt 26:21ff; Mark 14:18ff; Luke 22:21ff; John 13:18, 21, 26 **23** [a]John 1:18 [b]John 19:26; 20:2; 21:7, 20 **25** [a]John 21:20 **26** [a]John 6:71 **27** [a]Matt 4:10 [b]Luke 22:3; John 13:2 **29** [a]John 12:6 [b]John 13:1 [c]John 12:5

tried to dictate to Jesus). *If I do not wash you.* Jesus' reply looks beyond the incident to what it symbolizes: Peter needed a spiritual cleansing. The external washing was a picture of cleansing from sin, which Christians also sometimes need (see note on 1 John 1:9).

13:9 *my hands and my head.* Peter's response was wholehearted, but he was still dictating to Jesus.

13:10 *only to wash his feet.* A man would bathe himself before going to a feast. When he arrived, he only needed to wash his feet to be entirely clean again.

13:11 *He knew.* Again John emphasizes Jesus' command of the situation.

13:13 *Teacher . . . Lord.* An instructor would normally be called "Teacher," but "Lord" referred to one occupying the supreme place. Jesus accepted both titles.

13:14–15 Some Christians believe that Christ intended to institute a foot-washing ordinance to be practiced regularly. Most Christians, however, interpret Christ's action here as providing an example of humble service.

13:14 *wash one another's feet.* Christians should be willing to perform the most menial services for one another.

13:16 With minor variations this saying, which Jesus used often, is found in 15:20; Matt 10:24; Luke 6:40 (cf. Luke 22:27).

13:18 *do not speak of all of you.* Jesus was leading up to His prediction of the betrayal (v. 21). EATS MY BREAD. To eat bread together was a mark of close fellowship (see note on Ps 41:9). LIFTED UP HIS HEEL. May be derived from a horse's preparing to kick, or perhaps something like shaking off the dust from one's feet (Luke 9:5; 10:11).

13:19 *so that . . . you may believe.* See 20:31. Jesus' concern was for the disciples, not Himself. *I am He.* An emphatic form of speech, such as that in 8:58 (see note there).

13:20 *whomever I send . . . Him who sent Me.* Jesus' mission is a common theme in this Gospel, and now the mission of His followers is linked with it (cf. 20:21).

13:21 *troubled.* See 11:33. Though He knew of it long before it happened, Jesus was grieved by the betrayal of a friend.

13:22 *at a loss.* The disciples' astonishment shows that Judas had concealed his contacts with the high priests. No one suspected him (see v. 28), but all seem to have thought that the betrayal would be involuntary (see Mark 14:19).

13:23 *reclining.* At a dinner, guests reclined on couches, leaning on the left elbow with the head toward the table. *one of His disciples, whom Jesus loved.* Usually thought to be John, the author of this Gospel (see 19:26; 20:2; 21:7,20). The expression does not, of course, mean that Jesus did not love the others, but that there was a special bond with this man.

13:26 *the one for whom I shall dip the morsel and give it to him.* Evidently Judas was near Jesus, possibly in the seat of honor. John used Judas's full name (see note on 6:71) in recording this solemn moment.

13:27 *After the morsel.* Evidently the critical moment. If the giving of the bread to Judas was a mark of honor, it also seems to have been a final appeal—which Judas did not accept. *Satan.* The name is used only here in John (cf. v. 2). *do quickly.* Jesus' words once more indicate His control. He would die as He directed, not as His opponents determined.

13:29 *the feast.* See v. 1 and note on v. 2. *the poor.* See 12:5.

30 So after receiving the morsel he went
out immediately; and [a]it was night.
31 Therefore when he had gone out, Jesus
*said, "Now [1]is [a]the Son of Man [b]glorified,
and [c]God [1]is glorified in Him;
32 [1]if God is glorified in Him, [a]God will
also glorify Him in Himself, and will glorify
Him immediately.
33 "[a]Little children, I am with you [b]a little
while longer. [c]You will seek Me; and as I said
to the Jews, now I also say to you, 'Where I
am going, you cannot come.'
34 "A [a]new commandment I give to you,
[b]that you love one another, [c]even as I have
loved you, that you also love one another.
35 "[a]By this all men will know that you
are My disciples, if you have love for one
another."
36 Simon Peter *said to Him, "Lord,
where are You going?" Jesus answered,
"[a]Where I go, you cannot follow Me now;
but [b]you will follow later."
37 Peter *said to Him, "Lord, why can I
not follow You right now? [a]I will lay down
my life for You."
38 Jesus *answered, "Will you lay down
your life for Me? Truly, truly, I say to you, [a]a
rooster will not crow until you deny Me three
times.

Jesus Comforts His Disciples

14 "[a]Do not let your heart be troubled;
[1]believe in God, believe also in Me.
2 "In My Father's house are many
dwelling places; if it were not so, I would
have told you; for [a]I go to prepare a place for
you.
3 "If I go and prepare a place for you, [a]I
will come again and receive you to Myself,
that [b]where I am, *there* you may be also.
4 "And you know the way where I am
going."
5 [a]Thomas *said to Him, "Lord, we do
not know where You are going, how do we
know the way?"
6 Jesus *said to him, "I am [a]the way, and
[b]the truth, and [c]the life; no one comes to the
Father but through Me.

Oneness with the Father

7 "[a]If you had known Me, you would have
known My Father also; from now on you
[b]know Him, and have [c]seen Him."
8 [a]Philip *said to Him, "Lord, show us
the Father, and it is enough for us."
9 Jesus *said to him, "Have I been so
long with you, and *yet* you have not come to
know Me, Philip? [a]He who has seen Me has
seen the Father; how *can* you say, 'Show us
the Father'?
10 "Do you not believe that [a]I am in the
Father, and the Father is in Me? [b]The words
that I say to you I do not speak on My own
initiative, but the Father abiding in Me does
His works.
11 "Believe Me that [a]I am in the Father and
the Father is in Me; otherwise [b]believe
because of the works themselves.
12 "Truly, truly, I say to you, he who
believes in Me, the works that I do, he will

30 [a]Luke 22:53 **31** [1]Or *was* [a]Matt 8:20 [b]John 7:39 [c]John 14:13; 17:4; 1 Pet 4:11 **32** [1]Most early mss do not contain this phrase [a]John 17:1 **33** [a]1 John 2:1 [b]John 7:33 [c]John 7:34 **34** [a]John 15:12, 17; 1 John 2:7f; 3:11, 23; 2 John 5 [b]Lev 19:18; Matt 5:44; Gal 5:14; 1 Thess 4:9; Heb 13:1; 1 Pet 1:22; 1 John 4:7 [c]Eph 5:2; 1 John 4:10f **35** [a]1 John 3:14; 4:20 **36** [a]John 13:33; 14:2; 16:5 [b]John 21:18f; 2 Pet 1:14 **37** [a]John 13:37, 38: *Matt 26:33-35; Mark 14:29-31; Luke 22:33-34* **38** [a]Mark 14:30; John 18:27 **14:1** [1]Or *you believe in God* [a]John 14:27; 16:22, 24 **2** [a]John 13:33, 36 **3** [a]John 14:18, 28 [b]John 12:26 **5** [a]John 11:16 **6** [a]John 10:9; Rom 5:2; Eph 2:18; Heb 10:20 [b]John 1:14 [c]John 1:4; 11:25; 1 John 5:20 **7** [a]John 8:19 [b]1 John 2:13 [c]John 6:46 **8** [a]John 1:43 **9** [a]John 1:14; 12:45; Col 1:15; Heb 1:3 **10** [a]John 10:38; 14:11, 20 [b]John 5:19; 14:24 **11** [a]John 10:38; 14:10, 20 [b]John 5:36

13:30 *night.* In light of John's emphasis on the conflict between light and darkness, this may have been more than a time note—picturing also the darkness of Judas's soul.
13:31 *Son of Man.* See note on Mark 8:31. *glorified.* See v. 32 and note on 7:39. Here the idea of glory includes a reference to Jesus' sacrificial death on the cross and the glorious salvation that would result. *God is glorified in Him.* The glory of the Father is closely bound to that of the Son.
13:34 *A new commandment.* In a sense it was an old one (see Lev 19:18), but for Christ's disciples it was new, because it was the mark of their brotherhood, created by Christ's great love for them (cf. Matt 22:37–39; Mark 12:30–31; Luke 10:27). *as I have loved you.* Our standard is Christ's love for us.
13:35 *love.* The distinguishing mark of Christ's followers (cf. 1 John 3:23; 4:7–8,11–12,19–21).
13:36 *where are You going?* Peter seems to have ignored Jesus' words about love and was more concerned about his Master's departure. In Jesus' reply "you" is singular and thus personal to Peter, whereas in v. 33 the word is plural.
13:37 *I will lay down my life.* Words similar to those of the good shepherd in 10:11. Peter was characteristically sure of himself, when in fact he would not at this time lay down his life for Jesus. Exactly the opposite would be true.
13:38 *you deny Me three times.* Peter's denial is prophesied in all four Gospels (Matt 26:33–35; Mark 14:29–31; Luke 22:31–34).
14:1 *Do not . . . be troubled.* The apostles had just received disturbing news (13:33,36). *believe.* The antidote for a troubled heart.
14:2 *My Father's house.* Heaven. *dwelling places.* Implying permanence.
14:3 *I will come again.* Jesus comes in many ways, but the primary reference here is to His second advent.
14:4 *way.* See v. 6.
14:5 *Thomas.* He was honest, and plainly told the Lord he did not understand (see note on 11:16).
14:6 *I am.* See note on 6:35. *the way.* To God. Jesus is not one way among many, but the way (cf. Acts 4:12; Heb 10:19–20). In the early church, Christianity was sometimes called "the Way" (e.g., Acts 9:2; 19:9,23). *the truth.* A key emphasis in this Gospel (see note on 1:14). *the life.* See note on 1:4. Very likely the statement means "I am the way (to the Father) in that I am the truth and the life."
14:7 *Me . . . My Father.* Once more Jesus stresses the intimate connection between the Father and Himself. Jesus brought a full revelation of the Father (cf. 1:18), so that the apostles had real knowledge of Him.
14:10 *on My own initiative.* Jesus' teaching was not of human origin, and there was an inseparable connection between His words and His work.
14:11 *Believe . . . that I am in the Father and the Father is in Me.* Saving faith is trust in a person, but it must also have factual content. Faith includes believing that Jesus is one with the Father.
14:12 *greater works.* Miracles (see v. 11). These depended on Jesus' going to the Father, because they are works done in the strength of the Holy Spirit, whom Jesus would send from the Father (15:26; cf. 14:16–17).

do also; and [a]greater *works* than these he
will do; because [b]I go to the Father.
13 "[a]Whatever you ask in My name, that
will I do, so that [b]the Father may be glorified
in the Son.
14 "If you ask Me anything [a]in My name, I
will do *it*.
15 "[a]If you love Me, you will keep My commandments.

Role of the Spirit

16 "I will ask the Father, and He will give
you another [1a]Helper, that He may be with
you forever;
17 *that is* [a]the Spirit of truth, [b]whom the
world cannot receive, because it does not see
Him or know Him, *but* you know Him
because He abides with you and will be in
you.
18 "I will not leave you as orphans; [a]I will
come to you.
19 "[1a]After a little while [b]the world will no
longer see Me, but you *will* see Me; [c]because
I live, you will live also.
20 "[a]In that day you will know that [b]I am
in My Father, and you in Me, and I in you.
21 "[a]He who has My commandments and
keeps them is the one who loves Me; and [b]he
who loves Me will be loved by My Father,
and I will love him and will [c]disclose Myself
to him."
22 [a]Judas (not Iscariot) *said to Him,
"Lord, what then has happened [b]that You are
going to disclose Yourself to us and not to
the world?"
23 Jesus answered and said to him, "[a]If
anyone loves Me, he will [b]keep My word;
and [c]My Father will love him, and We [d]will
come to him and make Our abode with him.
24 "He who does not love Me [a]does not
keep My words; and [b]the word which you
hear is not Mine, but the Father's who sent
Me.
25 "These things I have spoken to you
while abiding with you.
26 "But the [a]Helper, the Holy Spirit,
[b]whom the Father will send in My name, [c]He
will teach you all things, and [d]bring to your
remembrance all that I said to you.
27 "[a]Peace I leave with you; My peace I
give to you; not as the world gives do I give
to you. [b]Do not let your heart be troubled,
nor let it be fearful.
28 "[a]You heard that I said to you, 'I go
away, and [b]I will come to you.' If you loved
Me, you would have rejoiced because [c]I go to
the Father, for [d]the Father is greater than I.
29 "Now [a]I have told you before it happens,
so that when it happens, you may believe.
30 "I will not speak much more with you,

12 [a]John 4:37f; 5:20 [b]John 7:33; 14:28 **13** [a]Matt 7:7 [b]John 13:31 **14** [a]John 15:16; 16:23f **15** [a]John 14:21, 23; 15:10; 1 John 5:3; 2 John 6 **16** [1]Gr *Paracletos*, one called alongside to help; or *Comforter, Advocate, Intercessor* [a]John 7:39; 14:26; 15:26; 16:7; Rom 8:26; 1 John 2:1 **17** [a]John 15:26; 16:13; 1 John 4:6; 5:7 [b]1 Cor 2:14 **18** [a]John 14:3, 28 **19** [1]Lit *Yet a little and the world* [a]John 7:33 [b]John 16:16, 22 [c]John 6:57 **20** [a]John 16:23, 26 [b]John 10:38; 14:11 **21** [a]John 14:15, 23; 15:10; 1 John 5:3; 2 John 6 [b]John 14:23; 16:27 [c]Ex 33:18f; Prov 8:17 **22** [a]Luke 6:16; Acts 1:13 [b]Acts 10:40, 41 **23** [a]John 14:15, 21; 15:10; 1 John 5:3; 2 John 6 [b]John 8:51; 1 John 2:5 [c]John 14:21 [d]2 Cor 6:16; Eph 3:17; 1 John 2:24; Rev 3:20; 21:3 **24** [a]John 14:23 [b]John 7:16; 14:10 **26** [a]John 14:16 [b]Luke 24:49; John 1:33; 15:26; 16:7; Acts 2:33 [c]John 16:13f; 1 John 2:20, 27 [d]John 2:22 **27** [a]John 16:33; 20:19; Phil 4:7; Col 3:15 [b]John 14:1 **28** [a]John 14:2-4 [b]John 14:3, 18 [c]John 14:12 [d]John 10:29; Phil 2:6 **29** [a]John 13:19

14:13 *in My name.* Not simply prayer that mentions Jesus' name but prayer in accordance with all that the person who bears the name is (see note on 2:23). It is prayer aimed at carrying forward the work Jesus did—prayer that He Himself will answer (see also v. 14).

14:15 *love . . . keep.* Love, like faith (James 2:14–26), cannot be separated from obedience.

14:16 *the Father . . . will give you.* The first of a series of important passages about the Holy Spirit (v. 26; 15:26; 16:7–15), the gift of the Father. *another.* Besides Jesus. *Helper.* Or "Counselor." It is a legal term, but with a broader meaning than "counsel for the defense" (see 1 John 2:1). It referred to any person who helped someone in trouble with the law. The Spirit will always stand by Christ's people.

14:17 *the Spirit of truth.* In essence and in action the Spirit is characterized by truth. He brings people to the truth of God. All three persons of the Trinity are linked with truth. See also the Father (4:23–24; cf. Ps 31:5; Is 65:16) and the Son (14:6). *the world.* Which takes no notice of the Spirit of God (cf. 1 Cor 2:14). But the Spirit was "with" Jesus' disciples and would be "in" them. Some believe the latter relationship (indwelling) specifically anticipates the coming of the Holy Spirit on the day of Pentecost (Acts 2; cf. Rom 8:9).

14:18 *I will come to you.* The words relate to the coming of the Spirit, but Jesus also speaks of His own appearances after the resurrection and at His second coming (see vv. 3, 19, 28; 16:22).

14:19 *the world . . . but you.* The cross separated the world (who would not see Jesus thereafter) from the disciples (who would). *because I live, you will live also.* The life of the Christian always depends on the life of Christ (cf. 1:4; 3:15).

14:20 *In that day you will know.* The resurrection would radically change their thinking.

14:21 *keeps . . . loves.* Love for Christ and keeping His commands cannot be separated (see note on v. 15). *loved by My Father . . . I will love him.* The love of the Father cannot be separated from that of the Son.

14:22 *what . . . ?* Judas (and, for that matter, the others) probably looked for Jesus to fulfill popular Messianic expectations. It was not easy, therefore, to understand how that would mean showing Himself to the disciples but not to the world.

14:23 *loves . . . keep . . . love.* Again love and obedience are linked (cf. vv. 15,21).

14:24 Once more the close relationship between Jesus' words and the Father's is stressed (see v. 10; 7:16).

14:26 *Helper.* See note on v. 16. *Holy Spirit.* His normal title in the NT (though only here and at 1:33; 20:22 in this Gospel)—emphasizing His holiness, rather than His power or greatness. *whom the Father will send.* Both the Father and the Son are involved in the sending (see 15:26). *name.* See notes on v. 13; 2:23. *bring to your remembrance all that I said to you.* Crucial for the life of the church—and for the writing of the NT.

14:27 *Peace . . . My peace.* A common Hebrew greeting (20:19,21,26), which Jesus uses here in an unusual way. The term speaks, in effect, of the salvation that Christ's redemptive work will achieve for His disciples—total well-being and inner rest of spirit, in fellowship with God. All true peace is His gift, which the repetition emphasizes. *not as the world gives do I give.* In its greetings of peace the world can only express a longing or wish. But Jesus' peace is real and present. *troubled.* See note on v. 1.

14:28 *heard that I said.* Cf. v. 3. *the Father is greater than I.* Revealing the subordinate role Jesus accepted as a necessary part of the incarnation. The statement must be understood in the light of the unity between the Father and the Son (10:30).

for [a]the ruler of the world is coming, and he
has nothing in Me;
31 but so that the world may know that I
love the Father, [1]I do exactly as [a]the Father
commanded Me. Get up, [b]let us go from
here.

Jesus Is the Vine—Followers Are Branches

15 "[a]I am the true vine, and My Father is
the [b]vinedresser.
2 "Every branch in Me that does not bear
fruit, He takes away; and every *branch* that
bears fruit, He [1]prunes it so that it may bear
more fruit.
3 "[a]You are already [1]clean because of the
word which I have spoken to you.
4 "[a]Abide in Me, and I in you. As the
branch cannot bear fruit [1]of itself unless it
abides in the vine, so neither *can* you unless
you abide in Me.
5 "I am the vine, you are the branches; he
who abides in Me and I in him, he [a]bears
much fruit, for apart from Me you can do
nothing.
6 "If anyone does not abide in Me, he is
[a]thrown away as a branch and dries up; and
they gather them, and cast them into the fire
and they are burned.
7 "If you abide in Me, and My words abide
in you, [a]ask whatever you wish, and it will
be done for you.
8 "My [a]Father is glorified by this, that you
bear much fruit, and *so* [1][b]prove to be My disciples.

30 [a]John 12:31
31 [1]Lit *and as the Father...so I do* [a]John 10:18; 12:49 [b]John 13:1; 18:1
15:1 [a]Ps 80:8ff; Is 5:1ff; Ezek 19:10ff; Matt 21:33ff [b]Matt 15:13; Rom 11:17; 1 Cor 3:9
2 [1]Lit *cleans;* used to describe pruning
3 [1]I.e. pruned like a branch [a]John 13:10; 17:17; Eph 5:26
4 [1]Lit *from* [a]John 6:56; 15:4-7; 1 John 2:6
5 [a]John 15:16
6 [a]John 15:2
7 [a]Matt 7:7; John 15:16
8 [1]Or *become My disciples* [a]Matt 5:16 [b]John 8:31
9 [a]John 3:35; 17:23, 24, 26
10 [a]John 14:15 [b]John 8:29
11 [a]John 17:13 [b]John 3:29
12 [a]John 13:34; 15:17; 1 John 3:23; 2 John 5
13 [a]Rom 5:7f [b]John 10:11

9 "Just as [a]the Father has loved Me, I have
also loved you; abide in My love.
10 "[a]If you keep My commandments, you
will abide in My love; just as [b]I have kept My
Father's commandments and abide in His
love.
11 "[a]These things I have spoken to you so
that My joy may be in you, and *that* your
[b]joy may be made full.

Disciples' Relation to Each Other

12 "This is [a]My commandment, that you
love one another, just as I have loved you.
13 "[a]Greater love has no one than this, that
one [b]lay down his life for his friends.
14 "You are My [a]friends if [b]you do what I
command you.
15 "No longer do I call you slaves, for the
slave does not know what his master is
doing; but I have called you friends, for [a]all
things that I have heard from My Father I
have made known to you.
16 "[a]You did not choose Me but I chose
you, and appointed you that you would go
and [b]bear fruit, and *that* your fruit would
remain, so that [c]whatever you ask of the
Father in My name He may give to you.
17 "This [a]I command you, that you love
one another.

14 [a]Luke 12:4 [b]Matt 12:50 **15** [a]John 8:26; 16:12
16 [a]John 6:70; 13:18; 15:19 [b]John 15:5 [c]John 14:13; 15:7; 16:23
17 [a]John 15:12

14:30 *ruler of the world.* See note on 12:31. *has nothing in Me.* Satan has a hold on people because of their fallen state. Since Christ was sinless, Satan could have no hold on Him.

14:31 *I do exactly as the Father commanded Me.* Jesus had stressed the importance of His followers being obedient (vv. 15,21,23), and He set the example. With these words He goes to fulfill His mission (chs. 18–19).

15:1 *I am.* See note on 6:35. *the true vine.* The vine is frequently used in the OT as a symbol of Israel (e.g., Ps 80:8–16; Is 5:1–7; Jer 2:21). When this imagery is used, Israel is often shown as lacking in some way. Jesus, however, is "the true vine."

15:2 *takes away.* A reference to judgment (see note on v. 6). *prunes.* Pruning produces fruitfulness. In the NT the figure of good fruit represents the product of a godly life (see Matt 3:8; 7:16–20) or virtues of character (see Gal 5:22–23; Eph 5:9; Phil 1:11).

15:3 *clean.* The Greek for "clean" is the same root word as "prunes" (v. 2). *the word.* Sums up the message of Jesus.

15:4 *Abide in Me.* The believer has no fruitfulness apart from his union and fellowship with Christ. A branch out of contact with the vine is lifeless.

15:5 *I am the vine.* See note on v. 1. The repetition gives emphasis. *abides in Me and I in him.* A living union with Christ is absolutely necessary; without it there is nothing.

15:6 *cast them into the fire and they are burned.* Judged (see note on v. 2). In light of such passages as 6:39; 10:27–28, these branches probably do not represent true believers. Genuine salvation is evidenced by a life of fruitfulness (see v. 10 and notes on vv. 2,4; see also Heb 6:9, "things that accompany salvation"; cf. Matt 7:19–23).

15:7 *My words abide in you.* It is impossible to pray correctly apart from knowing and believing the teachings of Christ. *ask whatever you wish.* See 14:13 and note.

15:8 *My Father is glorified.* The Father is glorified in the work of the Son (13:31–32), and He is also glorified in the fruit-bearing of disciples (see Matt 7:20; Luke 6:43–45).

15:10 *keep . . . as I have kept.* Again the importance of obedience (cf. 14:15,21,23), and again the example of Christ (cf. 14:31). *My love . . . His love.* See vv. 12,14. Obedience and love go together (see 1John 2:5; 5:2–3).

15:11 *joy.* Mentioned previously in this Gospel only in 3:29, but one of the characteristic notes of the upper room discourse (16:20–22,24; 17:13). The Christian way is never dreary, for Jesus desires His disciples' joy to be complete.

15:13 Christ's love was not only in words but also in His sacrificial death.

15:15 *slaves . . . friends.* A servant is simply an agent, doing what his master commands and often not understanding his master's purpose. But Jesus takes His friends into His confidence. *all things . . . I have made known to you.* From 16:12 we learn that though Jesus had let His disciples know as much as they were able to absorb of the Father's plan, the revelation was not yet complete. The Spirit would make other things known in due course.

15:16 *I chose you . . . bear fruit . . . ask.* Disciples normally chose the particular rabbi to whom they wanted to be attached, but it was not so with Jesus' disciples. He chose them, and for a purpose—the bearing of fruit. We usually desire a strong prayer life in order that we may be fruitful, but here it is the other way around. Jesus enables us to bear fruit, and then the Father will hear our prayers. *name.* See notes on 2:23; 14:13.

Disciples' Relation to the World

18 "[a]If the world hates you, [1]you know that it has hated Me before *it hated* you.

19 "If you were of the world, the world would love its own; but because you are not of the world, but [a]I chose you out of the world, [b]because of this the world hates you.

20 "Remember the word that I said to you, '[a]A slave is not greater than his master.' If they persecuted Me, [b]they will also persecute you; if they [c]kept My word, they will keep yours also.

21 "But all these things they will do to you [a]for My name's sake, [b]because they do not know the One who sent Me.

22 "[a]If I had not come and spoken to them, they would not have [1]sin, but now they have no excuse for their sin.

23 "He who hates Me hates My Father also.

24 "[a]If I had not done among them [b]the works which no one else did, they would not have [1]sin; but now they have both seen and hated Me and My Father as well.

25 "But *they have done this* to fulfill the word that is written in their [a]Law, '[b]THEY HATED ME WITHOUT A CAUSE.'

26 "When the [1][a]Helper comes, [b]whom I will send to you from the Father, *that is* [c]the Spirit of truth who proceeds from the Father, [d]He will testify about Me,

27 [1]and [a]you *will* testify also, because you have been with Me [b]from the beginning.

Jesus' Warning

16 "[a]These things I have spoken to you so that you may be kept from [b]stumbling.

18 [1]Or (imperative) *know that* [a]John 7:7; 1 John 3:13 **19** [a]John 15:16 [b]Matt 10:22; 24:9; John 17:14 **20** [a]Matt 10:24; John 13:16 [b]1 Cor 4:12; 2 Cor 4:9; 2 Tim 3:12 [c]John 8:51 **21** [a]Matt 10:22; 24:9; Mark 13:13; Luke 21:12, 17; Acts 4:17; 5:41; 9:14; 26:9; 1 Pet 4:14; Rev 2:3 [b]John 8:19, 55; 16:3; 17:25; Acts 3:17; 1 John 3:1 **22** [1]I.e. guilt [a]John 9:41; 15:24 **24** [1]I.e. guilt [a]John 9:41; 15:21 [b]John 5:36; 10:37 **25** [a]John 10:34 [b]Ps 35:19; 69:4 **26** [1]Gr *Paracletos*, one called alongside to help; or *Comforter, Advocate, Intercessor* [a]John 14:16 [b]John 14:26 [c]John 14:17 [d]1 John 5:7 **27** [1]Or (imperative) *and bear witness* [a]Luke 24:48; John 19:35; 21:24; 1 John 1:2; 4:14 [b]Luke 1:2
16:1 [a]John 15:18-27 [b]Matt 11:6

2 "[1]They will [a]make you outcasts from the synagogue, but [b]an hour is coming for everyone [c]who kills you to think that he is offering service to God.

3 "These things they will do [a]because they have not known the Father or Me.

4 "But these things I have spoken to you, [a]so that when their hour comes, you [1]may remember that I told you of them. These things I did not say to you [b]at the beginning, because I was with you.

The Holy Spirit Promised

5 "But now [a]I am going to Him who sent Me; and none of you asks Me, '[b]Where are You going?'

6 "But because I have said these things to you, [a]sorrow has filled your heart.

7 "But I tell you the truth, it is to your advantage that I go away; for if I do not go away, the [1][a]Helper will not come to you; but if I go, [b]I will send Him to you.

8 "And He, when He comes, will convict the world concerning sin and righteousness and judgment;

9 concerning sin, [a]because they do not believe in Me;

10 and concerning [a]righteousness, because [b]I go to the Father and you no longer see Me;

2 [1]Or *They will have you excommunicated* [a]John 9:22 [b]John 4:21; 16:25 [c]Is 66:5; Acts 26:9-11; Rev 6:9 **3** [a]John 8:19, 55; 15:21; 17:25; Acts 3:17; 1 John 3:1 **4** [1]Or *will remember them, that I told you* [a]John 13:19 [b]Luke 1:2 **5** [a]John 7:33; 16:10, 17, 28 [b]John 13:36; 14:5 **6** [a]John 14:1; 16:22 **7** [1]Gr *Paracletos*, one called alongside to help; or *Comforter, Advocate, Intercessor* [a]John 14:16 [b]John 14:26 **9** [a]John 15:22, 24 **10** [a]Acts 3:14; 7:52; 17:31; 1 Pet 3:18 [b]John 16:5

15:18–19 *world.* Here refers to the human system that opposes God's purpose (see note on 1:9).

15:19 *you are not of.* The believer's essential being, his new life, comes specially from God, and therefore he is not the same as those who oppose God.

15:21 *all these things they will do to you.* Because Christians do not belong to the world, persecution from the world is inevitable. The basic reason is the world's ignorance and rejection of the Father (cf. 16:3). *name's sake.* See note on 2:23.

15:22 *no excuse.* Privilege and responsibility go together. The Jews had had the great privilege of having the Son of God among them—in addition to having received God's special revelation in the OT. Their rejection of Jesus left them totally guilty and without excuse. Had He not come to them they would still have been sinners, but they would not have been guilty of rejecting Him directly (see v. 24).

15:25 *to fulfill the word that is written.* In the end God's purpose is always accomplished, despite the belief of sinful men that they have successfully opposed it. *Law.* See notes on 10:34; 12:34.

15:26 *Helper.* See note on 14:16. *I will send.* See notes on 14:16,26. *Spirit of truth.* See note on 14:17. *proceeds from the Father.* Probably refers to the Spirit's being sent to do the Father's work on earth rather than to His eternal relationship with the Father. *testify.* See note on 1:7.

15:27 *you . . . also.* Emphatic. Believers bear their testimony to Christ in the power of the Spirit. But it is their testimony, and they are responsible for bearing it. *from the beginning.* The apostles bore the definitive testimony, for they were uniquely chosen and taught by Christ and were eyewitnesses of His glory (see Luke 24:48; Acts 10:39,41).

16:2 *make you outcasts from the synagogue.* See note on 9:22. *service to God.* Religious people have often persecuted others in the strong conviction that this was right (see Acts 26:9–11; Gal 1:13–14).

16:3 *the Father.* See note on 5:17. *or Me.* Again the Father and the Son are linked. Not to know Christ is to be ignorant of the Father.

16:5 *none of you asks Me, 'Where are You going?'* Peter had asked such a question (13:36), but quickly turned his attention to another subject. His concern had been with what would happen to himself and the others and not for where Jesus was going.

16:6 *sorrow has filled your heart.* Because of His announced departure.

16:7 *if I do not go away.* Jesus did not say why the Spirit would not come until He went away, but clearly taught that His saving work on the cross was necessary before the sending of the Spirit. *Helper.* See note on 14:16. *I will send Him.* See note on 14:26.

16:8 *He . . . will convict the world.* The work the Spirit does in the world. The NT normally speaks of His work in believers. *convict.* Or "expose the guilt of."

16:9 *concerning sin.* Apart from the Spirit's convicting work, people can never see themselves as sinners. *because they do not believe.* May mean that their sin is their failure to believe, or that their unbelief is a classic example of sin. Typically, John may have had both of these in mind.

16:10 *concerning righteousness.* The righteousness brought

11 [a]and concerning judgment, because
the ruler of this world has been judged.
12 "I have many more things to say to you,
but you cannot bear *them* now.
13 "But when He, [a]the Spirit of truth,
comes, He will [b]guide you into all the truth;
for He will not speak on His own initiative,
but whatever He hears, He will speak; and
He will disclose to you what is to come.
14 "He will [a]glorify Me, for He will take of
Mine and will disclose *it* to you.
15 "[a]All things that the Father has are
Mine; therefore I said that He takes of Mine
and will disclose *it* to you.

Jesus' Death and Resurrection Foretold

16 "[a]A little while, and [b]you will no longer
see Me; and again a little while, and [c]you
will see Me."
17 *Some* of His disciples then said to one
another, "What is this thing He is telling us,
'[a]A little while, and you will not see Me; and
again a little while, and you will see Me';
and, 'because [b]I go to the Father'?"
18 So they were saying, "What is this that
He says, 'A little while'? We do not know
what He is talking about."
19 [a]Jesus knew that they wished to question Him, and He said to them, "Are you
deliberating together about this, that I said,
'A little while, and you will not see Me, and
again a little while, and you will see Me'?
20 "Truly, truly, I say to you, that [a]you will
weep and lament, but the world will rejoice;
you will grieve, but [b]your grief will be turned
into joy.
21 "[a]Whenever a woman is in labor she
has [1]pain, because her hour has come; but
when she gives birth to the child, she no
longer remembers the anguish because of
the joy that a [2]child has been born into the
world.
22 "Therefore [a]you too have grief now; but
[b]I will see you again, and your heart will
rejoice, and no one *will* take your joy away
from you.

Prayer Promises

23 "[a]In that day [b]you will not question Me
about anything. Truly, truly, I say to you, [c]if
you ask the Father for anything in My name,
He will give it to you.
24 "[a]Until now you have asked for nothing
in My name; ask and you will receive, so that
your [b]joy may be made full.
25 "These things I have spoken to you in
[1a]figurative language; [b]an hour is coming
when I will no longer speak to you in [1]figu-
rative language, but will tell you plainly of
the Father.
26 "[a]In that day [b]you will ask in My name,
and I do not say to you that I will request of
the Father on your behalf;
27 for [a]the Father Himself loves you,
because you have loved Me and [b]have
believed that [c]I came forth from the Father.

11 [a]John 12:31
13 [a]John 14:17 [b]John 14:26
14 [a]John 7:39
15 [a]John 17:10
16 [a]John 7:33 [b]John 14:18-24; 16:16-24 [c]John 16:22
17 [a]John 16:16 [b]John 16:5
19 [a]Mark 9:32; John 6:61
20 [a]Mark 16:10; Luke 23:27
20 [b]John 20:20
21 [1]Lit *grief* [2]Lit *human being* [a]Is 13:8; 21:3; 26:17; 66:7; Hos 13:13; Mic 4:9; 1 Thess 5:3
22 [a]John 16:6 [b]John 16:16
23 [a]John 14:20; 16:26 [b]John 16:19, 30 [c]John 15:16
24 [a]John 14:14 [b]John 3:29; 15:11
25 [1]Lit *proverbs;* or *figures of speech* [a]Matt 13:34; John 10:6; 16:29 [b]John 16:2
26 [a]John 14:20; 16:23 [b]John 16:19, 30
27 [a]John 14:21, 23 [b]John 2:11; 16:30 [c]John 8:42

about by Christ's sacrificial death (cf. Rom 1:17; 3:21–22). No one but the Holy Spirit can reveal to a person that a righteous status before God does not depend on good works but on Christ's death on the cross. *because I go to the Father.* The ascension, which as part of Christ's exaltation placed God's seal of approval on Christ's redemptive act.

16:11 *concerning judgment.* Jesus was speaking of the defeat of Satan, which was a form of judgment, not simply a victory. More than power is in question. God acts with justice. *ruler of this world.* See note on 12:31.

16:12 *you cannot bear them now.* This may mean "more than you can understand now," or "more than you can perform without the Spirit's help" (to live out Christ's teaching requires the enabling presence of the Spirit).

16:13 *Spirit of truth.* See note on 14:17. *whatever He hears.* We are not told whether He hears from the Father or the Son, but it obviously does not matter, for the verse stresses the close relationship among the three. *what is to come.* Probably means the whole Christian way or revelation (presented and preserved in the apostolic writings), still future at the time Jesus spoke.

16:14 *glorify Me.* See note on 1:14. The Spirit draws no attention to Himself but promotes the glory of Christ.

16:15 *All things that the Father has are Mine.* Cf. 17:10. The three Persons are closely related.

16:16 *A little while . . . a little while.* Few doubt that the first phrase refers to the interval before the crucifixion. But interpretations differ as to whether the second refers to the interval preceding the resurrection or the coming of the Spirit or the second coming of Christ. It seems that the language here best fits the resurrection.

16:17 *go to the Father.* See v. 10. Jesus had not linked this with "a little while," but the apostles saw them as connected.

16:20 *weep.* The same verb for loud wailing as in 11:33, which carries the idea of deep sorrow and its outward expression.

16:21 *a woman is in labor.* Giving birth usually causes both pain and joy (cf. Is 26:17–19; 66:7–14; Hos 13:13–14).

16:22 *I will see you again.* As in v. 16, probably a reference to Jesus' appearances after His resurrection. *no one will take your joy away.* The resurrection would change things permanently, bringing a joy that cannot be removed by the world's assaults.

16:23 *you will not question Me about anything.* Seems to mean asking for information (rather than asking in prayer), which would not be necessary after the resurrection. Jesus then moved on to the subject of prayer. However, Jesus may have been saying that His disciples previously had been praying to Christ, but after His death and resurrection they were to go directly to the Father and pray in Christ's name (see vv. 24,26–27 and notes). *name.* See notes on 2:23; 14:13.

16:24 *Until now.* Previously they had asked the Father or Christ, but they had not asked the Father in Christ's name. *your joy.* See note on 15:11.

16:25 *I have spoken to you in figurative language.* Throughout the discourse, not just in the immediately preceding words. *an hour is coming.* After the resurrection.

16:26 *in My name.* See notes on 2:23; 14:13. *I do not say to you that I will request.* Not a contradiction of Rom 8:34; Heb 7:25; 1 John 2:1. Those passages mean that Christ's presence in heaven as the crucified and risen Lord is itself an intercession. Here the teaching is that there will be no need for Him to make petitions in our behalf.

16:27 *the Father Himself loves you.* Christ is explaining why the disciples can come directly to the Father in prayer. It is because the disciples have loved and trusted in Jesus, and in love God will hear their requests in Jesus' name.

28 "[a]I came forth from the Father and have
come into the world; I am leaving the world
again and [b]going to the Father."
29 His disciples *said, "Lo, now You are
speaking plainly and are not [1]using [a]a figure
of speech.
30 "Now we know that You know all things,
and have no need for anyone to question You;
by this we [a]believe that You [b]came from God."
31 Jesus answered them, "Do you now
believe?
32 "Behold, [a]an hour is coming, and has
already come, for [b]you to be scattered, each
to [c]his own *home,* and to leave Me alone;
and *yet* [d]I am not alone, because the Father
is with Me.
33 "These things I have spoken to you, so
that [a]in Me you may have peace. [b]In the
world you have tribulation, but [c]take
courage; [d]I have overcome the world."

The High Priestly Prayer

17 Jesus spoke these things; and [a]lifting
up His eyes to heaven, He said, "Father,
the hour has come; [b]glorify Your Son, that
the Son may glorify You,
2 even as [a]You gave Him authority over
all flesh, that [b]to [1]all whom You have given
Him, [c]He may give eternal life.
3 "This is eternal life, that they may know
You, [a]the only true God, and Jesus Christ
whom [b]You have sent.
4 "[a]I glorified You on the earth, [1][b]having
accomplished the work which You have giv-
en Me to do.
5 "Now, Father, [a]glorify Me together with
Yourself, with the glory which I had [b]with
You before the world was.
6 "[a]I have manifested Your name to the
men whom [b]You gave Me out of the world;
they were [c]Yours and You gave them to Me,
and they have [d]kept Your word.
7 "Now they have come to know that
everything You have given Me is from You;
8 for [a]the words which You gave Me [b]I
have given to them; and they received *them*
and truly understood that [c]I came forth from
You, and they believed that [d]You sent Me.
9 "[a]I ask on their behalf; [b]I do not ask on
behalf of the world, but of those whom [c]You
have given Me; for [d]they are Yours;
10 and [a]all things that are Mine are Yours,
and Yours are Mine; and I have been glorified in them.
11 "I am no longer in the world; and *yet*
[a]they themselves are in the world, and [b]I
come to You. [c]Holy Father, keep them in Your
name, *the name* [d]which You have given Me,
that [e]they may be one even as We *are.*
12 "While I was with them, I was keeping
them in Your name [a]which You have given
Me; and I guarded them and [b]not one of
them perished but [c]the [1]son of perdition, so
that the [d]Scripture would be fulfilled.

28 [a]John 8:42; 16:30 [b]John 13:1, 3; 16:5, 10, 17
29 [1]Lit *saying a proverb* [a]Matt 13:34; John 10:6; 16:25
30 [a]John 2:11; 16:27 [b]John 8:42; 16:28
32 [a]John 4:23; 16:2, 25 [b]Zech 13:7; Matt 26:31 [c]John 19:27 [d]John 8:29
33 [a]John 14:27 [b]John 15:18ff [c]Matt 9:2 [d]Rom 8:37; 2 Cor 2:14; 4:7ff; 6:4ff; Rev 3:21; 12:11
17:1 [a]John 11:41 [b]John 7:39; 13:31f
2 [1]Lit *everything that You have given Him, to them He may* [a]John 3:35 [b]John 10:28 [c]John 6:37, 39; 17:6, 9, 24
3 [a]John 5:44 [b]John 3:17; 17:8, 21, 23, 25
4 [1]Or *by accomplishing* [a]John 13:31 [b]Luke 22:37; John 4:34
5 [a]John 17:1 [b]John 1:1; 8:58; 17:24; Phil 2:6
6 [a]John 17:26 [b]John 6:37, 39; 17:2, 9, 24 [c]John 17:9 [d]John 8:51
8 [a]John 6:68; 12:49 [b]John 15:15; 17:14, 26 [c]John 8:42; 16:27, 30 [d]John 3:17; 17:18, 21, 23, 25
9 [a]Luke 22:32; John 14:16 [b]Luke 23:34; John 17:20f [c]John 6:37, 39; 17:2, 6, 24 [d]John 17:6
10 [a]John 16:15
11 [a]John 13:1 [b]John 7:33; 17:13 [c]John 17:25 [d]John 17:6; Phil 2:9; Rev 19:12 [e]John 17:21f; Rom 12:5; Gal 3:28
12 [1]Heb idiom for one destined to perish [a]John 17:6; Phil 2:9; Rev 19:12 [b]John 6:39; 18:9 [c]John 6:70 [d]Ps 41:9; John 13:18

16:29 *not using a figure of speech.* See v. 25 and note.

16:30 *believe that You came from God.* Two recurring themes of this Gospel: believing (see note on 1:7) and Jesus' coming from God (see notes on 4:34; 17:3,8).

16:32 *you to be scattered.* The disciples had faith, but not enough to stand firm in face of disaster. Jesus knew they would fail; however, His church is not built on people's strength but on God's ability to use people even after they have failed.

16:33 Notice the contrasts: between "in Me" and "in this world" (see note on 1:9) and between "peace" and "tribulation." *I have overcome.* Just before His death Jesus affirms His final victory.

17:1–26 Jesus' longest recorded prayer.

17:1 *lifting up His eyes to heaven.* The customary attitude in prayer (11:41; Ps 123:1; Mark 7:34), though sometimes the person prostrated himself (see Matt 26:39). *Father.* Used of God in John's Gospel 116 times. *the hour.* See note on 2:4. *glorify . . . glorify.* See notes on 1:14; 7:39; 13:31. The glory of the Father and that of the Son are closely connected, and the death by which Jesus would glorify God would lead to eternal life for believers (v. 2).

17:2 *gave.* The thought of giving is stressed in this chapter (vv. 4,6–9,11–12,14,22,24); see note on 3:27. *all whom You have given Him.* Again God's initiative in salvation is stressed. *He may give eternal life.* See note on 3:15.

17:3 *sent.* Again the mission of Jesus is mentioned.

17:4 *I glorified You.* Christ's mission was not self-centered. *the work which You have given Me.* Jesus emphasized the supreme place of the Father.

17:5 *glorify Me . . . with the glory which I had with You.* Jesus asks the Father to return Him to His previous position of glory, to exchange humiliation for glorification. This occurred at Christ's resurrection and exaltation to God's right hand. *world.* The universe (see notes on v. 14; 1:9). "World" occurs 18 times in this prayer.

17:6 *I have manifested Your name.* See notes on 2:23; 14:13; cf. 1:18. *the men whom You gave Me.* Again the divine initiative (cf. 6:44).

17:7 *everything . . . is from You.* Only as people see the Father at work in Jesus do they have a proper concept of God. The disciples had at last reached this understanding.

17:8 Three things about the disciples are mentioned: 1. They accepted the teaching (unlike the Pharisees and others who heard it but did not receive it). 2. They knew with certainty Jesus' divine origin. Acceptance of the revelation led them further into truth. 3. They believed (see note on 1:7; cf. 1:12; 20:31).

17:9 *not . . . on behalf of the world.* The only prayer Jesus could pray for the world was that it cease to be worldly (i.e., opposed to God), and this He did pray (vv. 21,23).

17:11 *Holy Father.* A form of address found only here in the NT (but cf. 1 Pet 1:15–16; Rev 4:8; 6:10). The name suggests both remoteness and nearness; God is both awe-inspiring and loving. *that they may be one.* The latter part of the prayer strongly emphasizes unity. Here the unity is already given, not something to be achieved. The meaning is "that they continually be one" rather than "that they become one." The unity is to be like that between the Father and the Son. It is much more than unity of organization, but the church's present divisions are the result of the failures of Christians.

17:12 *I was keeping them.* Christ's power is adequate for every need. *the son of perdition.* Lit. "the son of destruction" (see

The Disciples in the World

13 "But now [a]I come to You; and [b]these things I speak in the world so that they may have My [c]joy made full in themselves.

14 "I have given them Your word; and [a]the world has hated them, because [b]they are not of the world, even as I am not of the world.

15 "I do not ask You to take them out of the world, but to keep them [1]from [2][a]the evil *one.*

16 "[a]They are not of the world, even as I am not of the world.

17 "[a]Sanctify them in the truth; Your word is truth.

18 "As [a]You sent Me into the world, [b]I also have sent them into the world.

19 "For their sakes I [a]sanctify Myself, that they themselves also may be [b]sanctified [c]in truth.

20 "I do not ask on behalf of these alone, but for those also who believe in Me through their word;

21 that they may all be one; [a]even as You, Father, *are* in Me and I in You, that they also may be in Us, [b]so that the world may [1]believe that [c]You sent Me.

Their Future Glory

22 "The [a]glory which You have given Me I have given to them, that they may be one, just as We are one;

23 [a]I in them and You in Me, that they may be perfected [1]in unity, so that the world may [2]know that [b]You sent Me, and [c]loved them, even as You have loved Me.

24 "Father, I desire that [a]they also, whom You have given Me, [b]be with Me where I am, so that they may see My [c]glory which You have given Me, for You loved Me before [d]the foundation of the world.

25 "O [a]righteous Father, [1]although [b]the world has not known You, yet I have known You; and these have known that [c]You sent Me;

26 and [a]I have made Your name known to them, and will make it known, so that [b]the love with which You loved Me may be in them, and I in them."

Judas Betrays Jesus

18 When Jesus had spoken these words, [a]He went forth with His disciples over [b]the [1]ravine of the Kidron, where there was [c]a garden, in which He entered [2]with His disciples.

2 Now Judas also, who was [1]betraying Him, knew the place, for Jesus had [a]often met there with His disciples.

3 [a]Judas then, having received [b]the

13 [a]John 7:33; 17:11 [b]John 15:11 [c]John 3:29 **14** [a]John 15:19 [b]John 8:23; 17:16 **15** [1]Or *out of* the power of [2]Or *evil* [a]Matt 5:37 **16** [a]John 17:14 **17** [a]John 15:3 **18** [a]John 3:17; 17:3, 8, 21, 23, 25 [b]Matt 10:5; John 4:38; 20:21 **19** [a]John 15:13 [b]John 15:3 [c]2 Cor 7:14; Col 1:6; 1 John 3:18 **21** [1]Gr tense indicates *continually believe* [a]John 10:38; 17:11, 23 [b]John 17:8 [c]John 3:17; 17:3, 8, 18, 23, 25 **22** [a]John 1:14; 17:24 **23** [a]John 10:38; 17:11, 21

23 [1]Lit *into one* [2]Gr tense indicates *continually know* [b]John 3:17; 17:3, 8, 18, 21, 25 [c]John 16:27 **24** [a]John 17:2 [b]John 12:26 [c]John 1:14; 17:22 [d]Matt 25:34; John 17:5 **25** [1]Lit *even the world* [a]John 17:11; 1 John 1:9 [b]John 7:29; 15:21 [c]John 3:17; 17:3, 8, 18, 21, 23 **26** [a]John 17:6 [b]John 15:9 **18:1** [1]Lit *winter-torrent* [2]Lit *and* [a]Matt 26:30, 36; Mark 14:26, 32; Luke 22:39 [b]2 Sam 15:23; 1 Kin 2:37; 15:13; 2 Kin 23:4, 6, 12; 2 Chr 15:16; 29:16; 30:14; Jer 31:40 [c]Matt 26:36; Mark 14:32; John 18:26 **2** [1]Or *handing Him over* [a]Luke 21:37; 22:39 **3** [a]John 18:3-11: *Matt 26:47-56; Mark 14:43-50; Luke 22:47-53* [b]John 18:12; Acts 10:1

2 Thess 2:3), i.e., one belonging to the sphere of damnation and destined for destruction (but predestination is not here in view). Reference is to Judas Iscariot.

17:13 *My joy.* See note on 15:11.

17:14 *the world.* The world that is hostile to God and God's people (see notes on v. 5; 1:9). *not of the world.* They do not have the mind-set of the world, i.e., hostility to God, for they have been "born of the Spirit" (3:8) and are "children of God" (1:12).

17:15 *not . . . take them out of the world.* The world is where Jesus' disciples are to do their work; Jesus does not wish them to be taken from it until that work is done (see v. 18). *the evil one.* Especially active in the world (1 John 5:19), making God's protection indispensable.

17:17 *Sanctify.* Means "to set apart for sacred use" or "to make holy"; also in v. 19. *the truth; Your word.* Sanctification and revelation (as recorded in God's word) go together. For the connection of Christ's teaching with truth cf. 8:31–32.

17:18 *As You sent Me . . . I also have sent them.* Jesus' mission is one of the dominant themes of this Gospel and is given as the pattern for His followers. *into the world.* We may long for heaven, but it is on earth that our work is done.

17:19 *I sanctify Myself.* This statement appears to be unparalleled. In the Septuagint (the Greek translation of the OT) the verb is used of consecrating priests (Ex 28:41) and sacrifices (Ex 28:38; Num 18:9). Jesus solemnly "sets himself apart to do God's will," which at this point meant His death. *that they . . . also . . . may be sanctified.* Jesus died on the cross not only to save us but also to consecrate us to God's service (see note on v. 17).

17:20 *those also who believe in Me.* Jesus had just spoken of the mission and the sanctification of His followers (vv. 18–19). He was confident that they would spread the gospel, and He prayed for those who would believe as a result. All future believers are included in this prayer.

17:21 *that they may all be one.* See note on v. 11. *Father.* See note on v. 1. *that the world may believe.* The unity of believers should have an effect on outsiders, to convince them of the mission of Christ. Jesus' prayer is a rebuke of the groundless and often bitter divisions among believers.

17:22 *The glory.* See note on v. l. Believers are to be characterized by humility and service, just as Christ was, and it is on them that God's glory rests. *they may be one, just as We are one.* Again the Lord emphasized the importance of unity among His followers, and again the standard is the unity of the Father and the Son.

17:23 *I in them and You in Me.* There are two indwellings: that of the Son in believers, and that of the Father in the Son. It is because the latter is a reality that the former can take place. *perfected in unity.* Again the emphasis on unity has an evangelistic aim. This time it is connected not only with the mission of Jesus but also with God's love for people and for Christ.

17:24 *Father.* See note on v. 1. *I desire.* Means "I will that." Jesus said, "I will"—His last will and testament for His followers. Where He Himself was concerned, He prayed, "not what I will, but what You will" (Mark 14:36). *be with Me.* The Christian's greatest blessing. *My glory.* Perhaps used here to refer to Jesus' eternal splendor (see 1 John 3:2). Or Jesus' prayer may have been that in the life to come they might fully appreciate the glory of His lowly service (cf. Eph 2:7).

17:25 *righteous Father.* A form of address found only here in the NT (cf. "Holy Father," v. 11). *these have known.* They did not know God directly and personally, but they knew God had sent Christ. To recognize God in Christ's mission is a great advance over anything the world can know.

18:1 *ravine of the Kidron.* East of Jerusalem and dry except during the rainy season.

18:3 *Judas.* See note on 6:71. *officers from the chief priests and the Pharisees.* Equivalent to the temple guard sent by the San-

Roman [1]cohort and [c]officers from the chief
priests and the Pharisees, *came there with
lanterns and [d]torches and weapons.
4 So Jesus, [a]knowing all the things that
were coming upon Him, went forth and
*said to them, "[b]Whom do you seek?"
5 They answered Him, "Jesus the Nazarene." He *said to them, "I am *He.*" And
Judas also, who was betraying Him, was
standing with them.
6 So when He said to them, "I am *He,*"
they drew back and fell to the ground.
7 Therefore He again asked them,
"[a]Whom do you seek?" And they said,
"Jesus the Nazarene."
8 Jesus answered, "I told you that I am
He; so if you seek Me, let these go their
way,"
9 to fulfill the word which He spoke,
"[a]Of those whom You have given Me I lost
not one."
10 Simon Peter then, [a]having a sword,
drew it and struck the high priest's slave,
and cut off his right ear; and the slave's
name was Malchus.
11 So Jesus said to Peter, "Put the sword
into the sheath; [a]the cup which the Father
has given Me, shall I not drink it?"

Jesus before the Priests

12 [a]So [b]the *Roman* [1]cohort and the [2]com-
mander and the [b]officers of the Jews, arrested Jesus and bound Him,

3 [1]Normally 600 men; *a battalion* [c]John 7:32; 18:12, 18 [d]Matt 25:1
4 [a]John 6:64; 13:1, 11 [b]John 18:7
7 [a]John 18:4
9 [a]John 17:12
10 [a]Matt 26:51; Mark 14:47
11 [a]Matt 20:22; 26:39; Mark 14:36; Luke 22:42
12 [1]Or *battalion* [2]I.e. chiliarch, in command of a thousand troops [a]John 18:12f: *Matt 26:57ff* [b]John 18:3
13 [a]Luke 3:2; John 18:24 [b]Matt 26:3; John 11:49, 51
14 [a]John 11:50
15 [a]Matt 26:58; Mark 14:54; Luke 22:54 [b]Matt 26:3; John 18:24, 28
16 [a]John 18:16-18: *Matt 26:69f; Mark 14:66-68; Luke 22:55-57*
17 [a]Acts 12:13 [b]John 18:25
18 [a]John 18:3 [b]John 21:9 [c]Mark 14:54, 67
19 [a]John 18:19-24: *Matt 26:59-68; Mark 14:55-65; Luke 22:63-71*

13 and led Him to [a]Annas first; for he was
father-in-law of [b]Caiaphas, who was high
priest that year.
14 Now Caiaphas was the one who had
advised the Jews that [a]it was expedient for
one man to die on behalf of the people.
15 [a]Simon Peter was following Jesus, and
so was another disciple. Now that disciple
was known to the high priest, and entered
with Jesus into [b]the court of the high priest,
16 [a]but Peter was standing at the door
outside. So the other disciple, who was
known to the high priest, went out and
spoke to the doorkeeper, and brought Peter
in.
17 [a]Then the slave-girl who kept the door
*said to Peter, "[b]You are not also *one* of this
man's disciples, are you?" He *said, "I am
not."
18 Now the slaves and the [a]officers were
standing *there,* having made [b]a charcoal fire,
for it was cold and they were [c]warming
themselves; and Peter was also with them,
standing and warming himself.
19 [a]The high priest then questioned Jesus
about His disciples, and about His teaching.
20 Jesus answered him, "I [a]have spoken
openly to the world; I always [b]taught in
[1]synagogues and [c]in the temple, where all
the Jews come together; and I spoke nothing
in secret.

20 [1]Lit *a synagogue* [a]John 7:26; 8:26 [b]Matt 4:23; John 6:59 [c]Matt 26:55

hedrin. *lanterns.* Terra-cotta holders into which household lamps could be inserted. *torches.* Resinous pieces of wood fastened together.

18:4 *knowing all the things that were coming upon Him.* Jesus was not taken by surprise.

18:5 *I am.* See 6:35; 8:58 and notes. *with them.* John does not let us forget where Judas belonged.

18:6 *fell to the ground.* They came to arrest a meek peasant and instead were met in the dim light by a majestic person.

18:8 *I am.* The threefold repetition (vv. 5,6,8) emphasizes the solemn words. *let these go their way.* Jesus cared for the disciples even as He was going to His death. Twice He had made the arresting party say plainly that He was the one they wanted (vv. 4–5,7).

18:9 *to fulfill the word.* Words normally used in quoting Scripture, and Jesus' words are on the same level. See 6:39; 17:12.

18:10 *Simon Peter.* It is to John that we owe the information that the man with the sword (the Greek for this word refers to a short sword) was Peter, and that the man he wounded was named Malchus.

18:11 *the cup.* Often points to suffering (Ps 75:8; Ezek 23:31–34) and the wrath of God (Is 51:17,22; Jer 25:15; Rev 14:10; 16:19). *the Father has given Me.* The Synoptic Gospels also speak of the cup at the time of Jesus' prayer at Gethsemane (Matt 26:39; Mark 14:36; Luke 22:42), and John says it came from the Father. God was in control.

18:12 *bound Him.* The reason for the bonds is not clear. Perhaps their use was standard procedure, much like the modern use of handcuffs.

18:13 *Annas.* Had been deposed from the high priesthood by the Romans in A.D. 15 but was probably still regarded by many as the true high priest. In Jewish law a man could not be sentenced on the day his trial was held. The two examinations—this one (mentioned only by John) and that before Caiaphas—may have been conducted to give some form of legitimacy to what was done. *high priest that year.* See note on 11:49.

18:14 *Caiaphas . . . had advised the Jews.* A reference to 11:49–50. For John it was this unconscious prophecy that mattered most about Caiaphas. John may also have been hinting that a fair trial could not be expected from a man who had already said that putting Jesus to death was expedient.

18:15 *another disciple.* Perhaps John himself. *known to the high priest.* Refers to more than casual acquaintance; he had entrée into the high priest's house and could bring Peter in.

18:17 *slave-girl who kept the door.* All four Gospels tell us that Peter's first challenge came from a slave girl, the most unimportant person imaginable. The form of the girl's question implied a negative answer, and Peter capitalized on her expectation by saying, "I am not." The other Gospels seem to indicate that the other denials followed immediately, but it is likely that there were intervals during which other things happened (see Luke 22:58–59).

18:18 *Peter was also with them, standing.* On a cold night he would have been conspicuous if he had stayed away from the fire.

18:19 *questioned.* Not legal, since witnesses were supposed to be brought in first to establish guilt. The accused was not required to prove his innocence. Perhaps Annas regarded this as a preliminary inquiry, not a trial.

18:20 *I have spoken openly.* It should not have been difficult to find witnesses (v. 21). *nothing in secret.* Not a denial that He taught the disciples privately, but a denial that He had secretly taught them subversive teaching different from His public message.

21 "Why do you question Me? Question
those who have heard what I spoke to them;
they know what I said."
22 When He had said this, one of the
[a]officers standing nearby [b]struck Jesus, saying, "Is that the way You answer the high
priest?"
23 [a]Jesus answered him, "If I have spoken
wrongly, testify of the wrong; but if rightly,
why do you strike Me?"
24 [a]So Annas sent Him bound to [a]Caia-
phas the high priest.

Peter's Denial of Jesus

25 [a]Now [b]Simon Peter was standing and
warming himself. So they said to him, "[c]You
are not also *one* of His disciples, are you?"
He denied *it,* and said, "I am not."
26 One of the slaves of the high priest,
being a relative of the one [a]whose ear Peter
cut off, *said, "Did I not see you in [b]the garden with Him?"
27 Peter then denied *it* again, and immediately [a]a rooster crowed.

Jesus before Pilate

28 [a]Then they *led Jesus from [b]Caiaphas
into [c]the [1]Praetorium, and it was early; and
they themselves did not enter into [c]the
[1]Praetorium so that [d]they would not be
defiled, but might eat the Passover.
29 [a]Therefore Pilate went out to them and
*said, "What accusation do you bring
against this Man?"
30 They answered and said to him, "If this
Man were not an evildoer, we would not
have delivered Him to you."
31 So Pilate said to them, "Take Him yourselves, and judge Him according to your
law." The Jews said to him, "We are not permitted to put anyone to death,"
32 to fulfill [a]the word of Jesus which He
spoke, signifying by what kind of death He
was about to die.
33 Therefore Pilate [a]entered again into the
Praetorium, and summoned Jesus and said
to Him, "[b]Are You the King of the Jews?"
34 Jesus answered, "Are you saying this
[1]on your own initiative, or did others tell you
about Me?"
35 Pilate answered, "I am not a Jew, am I?
Your own nation and the chief priests delivered You to me; what have You done?"
36 Jesus answered, "[a]My kingdom [1]is not
of this world. If My kingdom were of this
world, then My servants would be fighting
so that I would not be handed over to the
Jews; but as it is, My kingdom is not [2]of this
realm."
37 Therefore Pilate said to Him, "So You
are a king?" Jesus answered, "[a]You say *correctly* that I am a king. For this I have been

22 [a]John 18:3 [b]John 19:3
23 [a]Matt 5:39; Acts 23:2-5
24 [a]John 18:13
25 [a]John 18:25-27: *Matt 26:71-75; Mark 14:69-72; Luke 22:58-62* [b]John 18:18 [c]John 18:17
26 [a]John 18:10 [b]John 18:1
27 [a]John 13:38
28 [1]I.e. governor's official residence [a]Matt 27:2; Mark 15:1; Luke 23:1 [b]John 18:13 [c]Matt 27:27; John 18:33; 19:9 [d]John 11:55; Acts 11:3
29 [a]John 18:29-38: *Matt 27:11-14; Mark 15:2-5; Luke 23:2, 3*
32 [a]Matt 20:19; 26:2; Mark 10:33f; Luke 18:32f; John 3:14; 8:28; 12:32f
33 [a]John 18:28, 29; 19:9 [b]Luke 23:3; John 19:12
34 [1]Lit *from yourself*
36 [1]Or *is not derived from* [2]Lit *from here* [a]Matt 26:53; Luke 17:21; John 6:15
37 [a]Matt 27:11; Mark 15:2; Luke 22:70; 23:3

18:22 *struck.* Another illegality. The word apparently means a blow with the open hand—a slap.
18:23 *testify.* A legal term, indicating an invitation to act in proper legal form. John stresses the importance of testimony throughout his Gospel (see note on 1:7).
18:25 *they said to him.* Lit. "they asked him." Some find a difficulty in that Matt 26:71 says another girl asked this question, whereas Mark 14:69 says it was the same girl, and Luke 22:58 that it was a man. But with a group of servants talking around a fire, several would doubtless take up and repeat such a question, which could be the meaning of John's "they." As on the first occasion (v. 17) the question anticipated the answer "No." The servants probably did not really expect to find a follower of Jesus in the high priest's courtyard, but the question seemed worth asking.
18:26 *a relative.* Another piece of information we owe to John. A relative would have a deeper interest in the swordsman than other people had. But the light in the garden would have been dim, as in the courtyard (a charcoal fire glows, but does not have flames). *Did I not see you . . . ?* Expected the answer "Yes."
18:27 *a rooster crowed.* The fulfillment of the prophecy in 13:38.
18:28 *the Praetorium.* The palace of the Roman governor, Pilate. John says little about the Jewish phase of Jesus' trial but much about the Roman trial (see note on Mark 14:53–15:15). It is possible that John was in the Praetorium, the governor's official residence, for this trial. *early.* The chief priests evidently held a second session of the Sanhedrin after daybreak to give some appearance of legality to what they did (Mark 15:1). This occasion would have been immediately after that, perhaps between 6:00 A.M. and 7:00 A.M. *defiled.* A result of entering a Gentile residence. *eat the Passover.* Does not mean that the time of the Passover meal had not yet come, for this would contradict the Synoptic Gospels, which have Jesus eating the Passover meal the night before. The term "Passover" was used to refer to the whole festival of Passover and Unleavened Bread, which lasted seven days and included a number of meals.
18:29 *Pilate.* The Roman governor (see note on Mark 15:1). He showed himself tolerant of Jewish ways. *What accusation . . . ?* A normal question at the beginning of a trial, but it was difficult to answer, because the Jews had no charge that would stand up in a Roman court of law.
18:31 *Take Him yourselves.* In other words, no Roman charge, no Roman trial. *not permitted to put anyone to death.* They were looking for an execution, not a fair trial. The restriction was important, for otherwise Rome's supporters could be quietly removed by local legal executions. Sometimes the Romans seem to have condoned local executions (e.g., of Stephen, Acts 7), but normally they retained the right to inflict the death penalty.
18:32 *by what kind of death He was about to die.* Cf. 12:32–33 and "must" in 12:34. Jewish execution was by stoning, but Jesus' death was to be by crucifixion, whereby He would bear the curse (Deut 21:22–23). The Romans, not the Jews, had to put Jesus to death. God was overruling in the whole process.
18:33 *Are You the King of the Jews?* Pilate's first words to Jesus, identical in all four Gospels. One glance was enough to show him that a dangerous rebel existed only in the imaginations of Jesus' enemies.
18:34 *Are you saying this on your own initiative . . . ?* If so, Pilate's question (v. 33) had meant, "Are you a rebel?" If the question had originated with the Jews, it meant, "Are you the Messianic King?"
18:36 *My kingdom.* Jesus agrees that He has a kingdom, but asserts that it is not the kind of kingdom that has soldiers to fight for it. It was not built, nor is it maintained, by military might.

born, and for this I have come into the
world, [b]to testify to the truth. [c]Everyone who
is of the truth hears My voice."
38 Pilate *said to Him, "What is truth?"
And when he had said this, he [a]went out
again to the Jews and *said to them, "[b]I find
no guilt in Him.
39 "[a]But you have a custom that I release
someone [1]for you at the Passover; do you
wish then that I release [1]for you the King of
the Jews?"
40 So they cried out again, saying, "[a]Not
this Man, but Barabbas." Now Barabbas was
a robber.

The Crown of Thorns

19 Pilate then took Jesus and [1][a]scourged
Him.
2 [a]And the soldiers twisted together a
crown of thorns and put it on His head, and
put a purple robe on Him;
3 and they *began* to come up to Him and
say, "[a]Hail, King of the Jews!" and to [b]give
Him slaps *in the face.*
4 Pilate [a]came out again and *said to
them, "Behold, I am bringing Him out to you
so that you may know that [b]I find no guilt in
Him."
5 Jesus then came out, [a]wearing the
crown of thorns and the purple robe. *Pilate*
*said to them, "Behold, the Man!"
6 So when the chief priests and the [a]offi-
cers saw Him, they cried out saying, "Crucify, crucify!" Pilate *said to them, "Take Him
yourselves and crucify Him, for [b]I find no
guilt in Him."
7 The Jews answered him, "[a]We have a
law, and by that law He ought to die because
He [b]made Himself out *to be* the Son of God."
8 Therefore when Pilate heard this statement, he was *even* more afraid;
9 and he [a]entered into the [1]Praetorium
again and *said to Jesus, "Where are You
from?" But [b]Jesus gave him no answer.
10 So Pilate *said to Him, "You do not
speak to me? Do You not know that I have
authority to release You, and I have authority to crucify You?"
11 Jesus answered, "[a]You would have no
authority [1]over Me, unless it had been given
you from above; for this reason [b]he who
delivered Me to you has *the* greater sin."
12 As a result of this Pilate [1]made efforts
to release Him, but the Jews cried out saying,
"[a]If you release this Man, you are no friend
of Caesar; everyone who makes himself out
to be a king [2]opposes Caesar."
13 Therefore when Pilate heard these
words, he brought Jesus out, and [a]sat down
on the judgment seat at a place called [1]The
Pavement, but [b]in [2]Hebrew, Gabbatha.
14 Now it was [a]the day of preparation for
the Passover; it was about the [1][b]sixth hour.
And he *said to the Jews, "Behold, [c]your
King!"
15 So they cried out, "[a]Away with *Him,*

37 [b]John 1:14; 3:32; 8:14 [c]John 8:47; 1 John 4:6 **38** [a]John 18:33; 19:4 [b]Luke 23:4; John 19:4, 6 **39** [1]Or *to you* [a]John 18:39-19:16: *Matt 27:15-26; Mark 15:6-15; Luke 23:18-25* **40** [a]Acts 3:14 **19:1** [1]Or *had Him scourged* [a]Matt 27:26 **2** [a]Matt 27:27-30: *Mark 15:16-19* **3** [a]Matt 27:29; Mark 15:18 [b]John 18:22 **4** [a]John 18:33, 38 [b]Luke 23:4; John 18:38; 19:6 **5** [a]John 19:2 **6** [a]Matt 26:58; John 18:3
6 [b]Luke 23:4; John 18:38; 19:4 **7** [a]Lev 24:16; Matt 26:63-66 [b]John 5:18; 10:33 **9** [1]I.e. governor's official residence [a]John 18:33 [b]Matt 26:63; 27:12, 14; John 18:34-37 **11** [1]Lit *against* [a]Rom 13:1 [b]John 18:13f, 28ff; Acts 3:13 **12** [1]Lit *was seeking to* [2]Or *speaks against* [a]Luke 23:2; John 18:33ff

13 [1]Gr *The Lithostrotos* [2]I.e. Jewish Aramaic [a]Matt 27:19 [b]John 5:2; 19:17, 20 **14** [1]Perhaps 6 a.m. [a]Matt 27:62; John 19:31, 42 [b]Matt 27:45; Mark 15:25 [c]John 19:19, 21 **15** [a]Luke 23:18

18:37 *to testify to the truth.* Two of this Gospel's important ideas (see 1:7 and note; 1:14 and note; 14:6).

18:38 *What is truth?* Pilate may have been jesting, and meant, "What does truth matter?" Or he may have been serious, and meant, "It is not easy to find truth. What is it?" Either way, it was clear to him that Jesus was no rebel. *find no guilt in Him.* Teaching the truth was not a criminal offense.

18:39 *you have a custom.* Prisoners are known to have been released on special occasions in other places. *the King of the Jews.* John keeps his emphasis on the note of royalty. Pilate may have hoped that the use of the title would influence the people toward the way he wanted them to decide.

18:40 *Barabbas.* A rebel and a murderer (Luke 23:19). The name is Aramaic and means "son of Abba," i.e., "son of the father"; in place of this man, the "Son of the Father" died.

19:1 Pilate hoped a flogging would satisfy the Jews and enable him to release Jesus (see note on Mark 15:15).

19:2 *thorns.* A general term relating to any thorny plant. *purple.* A color used by royalty.

19:6 *Take Him . . . crucify Him.* The petulant utterance of an exasperated man, for the Jews could not carry out this form of execution. *I find no guilt.* For the third time Pilate proclaimed Jesus' innocence (see 18:38; 19:4). Luke also records this threefold proclamation (Luke 23:4,14,22).

19:7 *He ought to die.* Apparently referring to the penalty for blasphemy (Lev 24:16).

19:8 *even more afraid.* Pilate was evidently superstitious, and this charge frightened him.

19:9 *Jesus gave him no answer.* The reason is not clear since Jesus had answered other questions readily. Perhaps Pilate would not have understood the answer or would not have believed it.

19:10 *I have authority.* Pilate was incredulous and very conscious of his authority. His second question indicates his personal responsibility for crucifying Jesus.

19:11 Jesus' last words to Pilate. *from above.* All earthly authority comes ultimately from God. *the greater sin.* That of Caiaphas (not Judas, who was only a means). But "greater" implies that there was a lesser sin, so Pilate's sin was also real.

19:12 *no friend of Caesar.* Some people had official status as "Friends of Caesar," but the term seems to be used here in the general sense. There was an implied threat that if he released Jesus, Pilate would be accused before Caesar. His record was such that he could not face such a prospect without concern.

19:13 *The Pavement.* Not a translation of *Gabbatha,* which seems to mean "the hill of the house," but a different name for the same place.

19:14 *day of preparation.* Normally Friday was the day people prepared for the Sabbath. Here the meaning is Friday of Passover week. *about the sixth hour.* About noon. Mark 15:25 says that Jesus was crucified at "the third hour." It is possible that Mark's Gospel contains a copyist's error, for the Greek numerals for three and six could be confused. Or it may be that John was using Roman time, in which case the appearance before Pilate would have been at 6:00 A.M. and the crucifixion at 9:00 A.M. (the third hour according to Jewish reckoning; see Mark 15:33). For other time references see Matt 27:45–46; Mark 15:33–34; Luke 23:44. *the Jews.* See note on 1:19. *Behold, your King!* John does not let us forget the sovereignty of Jesus. Pilate did not mean the expression seriously, but John did.

away with *Him*, crucify Him!" Pilate *said
to them, "Shall I crucify your King?" The
chief priests answered, "We have no king
but Caesar."

The Crucifixion

16 So he then [a]handed Him over to them
to be crucified.
17 [a]They took Jesus, therefore, and He
went out, [1][b]bearing His own cross, to the
place called [c]the Place of a Skull, which is
called [d]in [2]Hebrew, Golgotha.
18 There they crucified Him, and with
Him [a]two other men, one on either side, and
Jesus in between.
19 Pilate also wrote an inscription and put
it on the cross. It was written, "[a]JESUS THE
NAZARENE, [b]THE KING OF THE JEWS."
20 Therefore many of the Jews read this
inscription, for the place where Jesus was
crucified was near the city; and it was written [a]in [1]Hebrew, Latin *and* in Greek.
21 So the chief priests of the Jews were
saying to Pilate, "Do not write, '[a]The King of
the Jews'; but that He said, 'I am [a]King of
the Jews.' "
22 Pilate answered, "[a]What I have written
I have written."
23 Then [a]the soldiers, when they had crucified Jesus, took His outer garments and
made [b]four parts, a part to every soldier and
also the [1]tunic; now the tunic was seamless,
woven [2]in one piece.
24 So they said to one another, "[a]Let us
not tear it, but cast lots for it, *to decide*
whose it shall be"; [b]*this was* to fulfill the
Scripture: "THEY [c]DIVIDED MY OUTER GARMENTS

16 [a]Matt 27:26; Mark 15:15; Luke 23:25
17 [1]Lit *bearing the cross for Himself* [2]I.e. Jewish Aramaic [a]John 19:17-24: *Matt 27:33-44; Mark 15:22-32; Luke 23:33-43* [b]Matt 27:32; Mark 15:21; Luke 14:27; 23:26 [c]Luke 23:33 [d]John 19:13
18 [a]Luke 23:32
19 [a]Matt 27:37; Mark 15:26; Luke 23:38 [b]John 19:14, 21
20 [1]I.e. Jewish Aramaic [a]John 19:13
21 [a]John 19:14, 19
22 [a]Gen 43:14; Esth 4:16
23 [1]Gr *khiton,* the garment worn next to the skin [2]Lit *from the upper part through the whole* [a]Matt 27:35; Mark 15:24; Luke 23:34 [b]Acts 12:4
24 [a]Ex 28:32; Matt 27:35; Mark 15:24; Luke 23:34 [b]John 19:28, 36f [c]Ps 22:18

24 [1]Lit *a lot*
25 [a]Matt 27:55f; Mark 15:40f; Luke 23:49 [b]Matt 12:46 [c]Luke 8:2; John 20:1, 18
26 [a]John 13:23 [b]John 2:4

AMONG THEM, AND FOR MY CLOTHING THEY CAST
[1]LOTS."
25 Therefore the soldiers did these things.
[a]But standing by the cross of Jesus were
[b]His mother, and His mother's sister, Mary
the *wife* of Clopas, and [c]Mary Magdalene.
26 When Jesus then saw His mother, and
[a]the disciple whom He loved standing nearby, He *said to His mother, "[b]Woman,
behold, your son!"
27 Then He *said to the disciple, "Behold,
your mother!" From that hour the disciple
took her into [a]his own *household.*
28 After this, Jesus, [a]knowing that all
things had already been accomplished, [b]to
fulfill the Scripture, *said, "[c]I am thirsty."
29 A jar full of sour wine was standing
there; so [a]they put a sponge full of the sour
wine upon *a branch of* hyssop and brought it
up to His mouth.
30 Therefore when Jesus had received the
sour wine, He said, "[a]It is finished!" And He
bowed His head and [b]gave up His spirit.

Care of the Body of Jesus

31 Then the Jews, because it was [a]the day
of preparation, so that [b]the bodies would not
remain on the cross on the Sabbath ([1]for that
Sabbath was a [c]high day), asked Pilate that
their legs might be broken, and *that* they
might be taken away.
32 So the soldiers came, and broke the

27 [a]Luke 18:28; John 1:11; 16:32; Acts 21:6 **28** [a]John 13:1; 17:4 [b]John 19:24, 36f [c]Ps 69:21 **29** [a]John 19:29, 30: *Matt 27:48, 50; Mark 15:36f; Luke 23:36* **30** [a]John 17:4 [b]Matt 27:50; Mark 15:37; Luke 23:46 **31** [1]Lit *for the day of that Sabbath was great* [a]John 19:14, 42 [b]Deut 21:23; Josh 8:29; 10:26f [c]Ex 12:16

19:15 *We have no king but Caesar.* More irony. They rejected any suggestion that they were rebels against Rome, but expressed the truth of their spiritual condition.

19:17 *bearing His own cross.* A cross might be shaped like a *T,* an *X,* a *Y,* or an *I,* as well as like the traditional form. A condemned man would normally carry a beam of it to the place of execution. Somewhere along the way Simon of Cyrene took Jesus' cross (Mark 15:21), probably because Jesus was weakened by the flogging. *Golgotha.* Aramaic for "the skull." The name of the site is given in both Greek and Aramaic ("Calvary" is from the Latin with the same meaning). See note on Mark 15:22.

19:18 *they crucified Him.* See note on Mark 15:24. As with the scourging, John describes this horror with one Greek word. None of the Gospel writers dwells on the physical sufferings of Jesus. *one on either side.* Perhaps meant as a final insult, but it brings out the important truth that in His death Jesus was identified with sinners.

19:19 *an inscription.* A placard stating the crime for which a man was executed was often fastened to his cross. *THE KING OF THE JEWS.* Again the royalty theme.

19:20 *Hebrew.* One of the languages of the Jewish people at that time (along with Hebrew). *Latin.* The official language of Rome. *Greek.* The common language of communication throughout the empire. The threefold inscription may account for the slight differences in wording in the four Gospels.

19:22 Pilate must have a sufficient reason for the execution, and he was not above mocking the Jews, but for John his insistence may also have served to underscore that Jesus' kingship is final and unalterable.

19:23 *tunic.* A type of shirt, reaching from the neck to the knees or ankles. *seamless.* Therefore too valuable to be cut up.

19:24 See introduction to Ps 22 and notes on Ps 22:17,20–21.

19:25 *Clopas.* Mentioned only here in the NT. *Mary Magdalene.* Appears in the crucifixion and resurrection story in all four Gospels, but apart from that we read of her only in Luke 8:2–3.

19:26 *disciple whom He loved.* John (see note on 13:23).

19:27 *took her into his own household.* And so took responsibility for her. It may be that Jesus' brothers still did not believe in Him (see 7:5).

19:28 *I am thirsty.* May refer to Ps 69:21 (cf. Ps 22:15).

19:29 *sour wine.* Equivalent to cheap wine, the drink of ordinary people. *a sponge.* A useful way of giving drink to one on a cross, and may indicate forethought and compassion on someone's part. *hyssop.* The name given to a number of plants. See also note on Ex 12:22.

19:30 *It is finished!* Apparently the loud cry of Matt 27:50; Mark 15:37. Jesus died as a victor and had completed what He came to do. *gave up His spirit.* An unusual way of describing death, perhaps suggesting an act of will.

19:31 *the Jews.* See note on 1:19. *preparation.* See note on v. 14. *a high day.* The Sabbath that fell at Passover time. The Passover meal had been eaten on Thursday evening, the day of Preparation was Friday, and the Sabbath came on Saturday. *legs might be broken.* To hasten death, because the victim then could not put any weight on his legs and breathing would be difficult.

legs of the first man and of the other who was [a]crucified with Him;

33 but coming to Jesus, when they saw that He was already dead, they did not break His legs.

34 But one of the soldiers pierced His side with a spear, and immediately [a]blood and water came out.

35 And he who has seen has [a]testified, and his testimony is true; and he knows that he is telling the truth, so that you also may believe.

36 For these things came to pass [a]to fulfill the Scripture, "[b]NOT A BONE OF HIM SHALL BE [1]BROKEN."

37 And again another Scripture says, "[a]THEY SHALL LOOK ON HIM WHOM THEY PIERCED."

38 [a]After these things Joseph of Arimathea, being a disciple of Jesus, but a [b]secret *one* for [c]fear of the Jews, asked Pilate that he might take away the body of Jesus; and Pilate granted permission. So he came and took away His body.

39 [a]Nicodemus, who had first come to Him by night, also came, [b]bringing a [1]mixture of [c]myrrh and aloes, about a [d]hundred [2]pounds *weight.*

40 So they took the body of Jesus and [a]bound it in [b]linen wrappings with the spices, as is the burial custom of the Jews.

41 Now in the place where He was crucified there was a garden, and in the garden a [a]new tomb [b]in which no one had yet been laid.

42 Therefore because of the Jewish day of [a]preparation, since the tomb was [b]nearby, they laid Jesus there.

32 [a]John 19:18
34 [a]1 John 5:6, 8
35 [a]John 15:27; 21:24
36 [1]Or *crushed* or *shattered* [a]John 19:24, 28 [b]Ex 12:46; Num 9:12; Ps 34:20
37 [a]Zech 12:10; Rev 1:7
38 [a]John 19:38-42: *Matt 27:57-61; Mark 15:42-47; Luke 23:50-56* [b]Mark 15:43 [c]John 7:13
39 [1]Two early mss read *package of* [2]Lit *100 litras* (12 oz each) [a]John 3:1 [b]Mark 16:1 [c]Ps 45:8; Prov 7:17; Song 4:14; Matt 2:11 [d]John 12:3
40 [a]Matt 26:12; Mark 14:8; John 11:44 [b]Luke 24:12; John 20:5, 7
41 [a]Matt 27:60 [b]Luke 23:53
42 [a]John 19:14, 31 [b]John 19:20, 41

20:1 [a]John 20:1-8: *Matt 28:1-8; Mark 16:1-8; Luke 24:1-10* [b]John 19:25; 20:18 [c]Matt 27:60, 66; 28:2; Mark 15:46; 16:3f; Luke 24:2; John 11:38
2 [a]John 13:23 [b]John 20:13
3 [a]Luke 24:12; John 20:3-10
5 [a]John 20:11 [b]John 19:40
7 [a]John 11:44 [b]John 19:40

The Empty Tomb

20 [a]Now on the first *day* of the week [b]Mary Magdalene *came early to the tomb, while it *was still dark, and *saw [c]the stone *already* taken away from the tomb.

2 So she *ran and *came to Simon Peter and to the other [a]disciple whom Jesus loved, and *said to them, "[b]They have taken away the Lord out of the tomb, and we do not know where they have laid Him."

3 [a]So Peter and the other disciple went forth, and they were going to the tomb.

4 The two were running together; and the other disciple ran ahead faster than Peter and came to the tomb first;

5 and [a]stooping and looking in, he *saw the [b]linen wrappings lying *there;* but he did not go in.

6 And so Simon Peter also *came, following him, and entered the tomb; and he *saw the linen wrappings lying *there,*

7 and [a]the face-cloth which had been on His head, not lying with the [b]linen wrappings, but rolled up in a place by itself.

8 So the other disciple who [a]had first come to the tomb then also entered, and he saw and believed.

9 For as yet [a]they did not understand the Scripture, [b]that He must rise again from the dead.

10 So the disciples went away again [a]to their own homes.

11 [a]But Mary was standing outside the tomb weeping; and so, as she wept, she [b]stooped and looked into the tomb;

8 [a]John 20:4 **9** [a]Matt 22:29; John 2:22 [b]Luke 24:26ff, 46
10 [a]Luke 24:12 **11** [a]Mark 16:5 [b]John 20:5

19:34 *pierced His side.* Probably to make doubly sure that Jesus was dead, but perhaps simply an act of brutality (see v. 37; Is 53:5; Zech 12:10; cf. Ps 22:16). *blood and water.* The result of the spear piercing the pericardium (the sac that surrounds the heart) and the heart itself.

19:35 *he who has seen.* Either John himself or someone he regarded as reliable. Obviously he considered the incident important, and comments that it was well attested. *knows ... believe.* See note on 1:7.

19:36–37 *Scripture.* Again John observes God's overruling in the fulfillment of Scripture. It was extraordinary that Jesus was the only one of the three whose legs were not broken and that He suffered an unusual spear thrust that did not break a bone.

19:38 *Joseph.* A rich disciple (Matt 27:57), and a member of the Sanhedrin who had not agreed to Jesus' condemnation (Luke 23:51). *Arimathea.* See note on Matt 27:57. *secret one.* It would have been hard for a member of the Sanhedrin to support Jesus' cause openly. Jesus' closest followers all ran away (Mark 14:50), and it was left to Joseph and Nicodemus to provide for His burial. *Pilate granted permission.* Otherwise people could take away their crucified friends before they died and revive them.

19:39 *Nicodemus.* John alone tells us that he joined Joseph in the burial. *a hundred pounds.* A very large amount, such as was used in royal burials (cf. 2 Chr 16:14).

19:40 *linen wrappings.* Thin strips like bandages. There was also a shroud, a large sheet (Matt 27:59; Mark 15:46; Luke 23:53).

19:41 *a new tomb.* Joseph's own tomb (Matt 27:60).

19:42 *preparation.* See note on v. 14. *nearby.* Haste was necessary, since it was near sunset, when the Sabbath would start and no work could be done.

20:1 *Mary Magdalene.* See note on 19:25; cf. Mark 16:9. *while it was still dark.* Mark says it was "when the sun had risen" (Mark 16:2). Perhaps the women came in groups, with Mary Magdalene coming very early. Or John may refer to the time of leaving home, Mark to that of arrival at the tomb.

20:2 *to Simon Peter.* Despite his denials, Peter was still the leading figure among the disciples. *disciple whom Jesus loved.* John (see note on 13:23). *we.* Indicates that there were others with Mary (see Matt 28:1; Mark 16:1; Luke 24:10), though John does not identify them. *have laid Him.* Mary had no thought of resurrection.

20:7 *rolled up.* An orderly arrangement, not in disarray, as would have resulted from a grave robbery.

20:8 *he saw and believed.* Cf. v. 29. John did not say what he believed, but it must have been that Jesus was resurrected.

20:9 *Scripture.* First they came to know of the resurrection through what they saw in the tomb; only later did they see it in Scripture. It is obvious they did not make up a story of resurrection to fit a preconceived understanding of Scriptural prophecy. *must rise.* It was in Scripture and thus the will of God.

20:11 *Mary.* Perhaps Jesus appeared first to Mary because she needed Him most at that time. *weeping.* As in 11:33, it means "wailing," a loud expression of grief.

12 and she *saw [a]two angels in white sitting, one at the head and one at the feet, where the body of Jesus had been lying.

13 And they *said to her, "[a]Woman, why are you weeping?" She *said to them, "Because [b]they have taken away my Lord, and I do not know where they have laid Him."

14 When she had said this, she turned around and *[a]saw Jesus standing *there,* and [b]did not know that it was Jesus.

15 Jesus *said to her, "[a]Woman, why are you weeping? Whom are you seeking?" Supposing Him to be the gardener, she *said to Him, "Sir, if you have carried Him away, tell me where you have laid Him, and I will take Him away."

16 Jesus *said to her, "Mary!" She turned and *said to Him [a]in [1]Hebrew, "[b]Rabboni!" (which means, Teacher).

17 Jesus *said to her, "Stop clinging to Me, for I have not yet ascended to the Father; but go to [a]My brethren and say to them, 'I [b]ascend to My Father and your Father, and My God and your God.' "

18 [a]Mary Magdalene *came, [b]announcing to the disciples, "I have seen the Lord," and *that* He had said these things to her.

Jesus among His Disciples

19 So when it was evening on that day, the first *day* of the week, and when the doors were shut where the disciples were, for [a]fear of the Jews, Jesus came and stood in their midst and *said to them, "[1][b]Peace *be* with you."

20 And when He had said this, [a]He showed them both His hands and His side. The disciples then [b]rejoiced when they saw the Lord.

21 So Jesus said to them again, "[a]Peace *be* with you; [b]as the Father has sent Me, I also send you."

22 And when He had said this, He breathed on them and *said to them, "Receive the Holy Spirit.

23 "[a]If you forgive the sins of any, *their sins* [1]have been forgiven them; if you retain the *sins* of any, they have been retained."

24 But [a]Thomas, one of [b]the twelve, called [1][a]Didymus, was not with them when Jesus came.

25 So the other disciples were saying to him, "We have seen the Lord!" But he said to them, "Unless I see in [a]His hands the imprint of the nails, and put my finger into the place of the nails, and put my hand into His side, [b]I will not believe."

26 [1]After eight days His disciples were again inside, and Thomas with them. Jesus *came, the doors having been [2]shut, and stood in their midst and said, "[a]Peace *be* with you."

27 Then He *said to Thomas, "[a]Reach here with your finger, and see My hands; and reach here your hand and put it into My side; and do not be unbelieving, but believing."

28 Thomas answered and said to Him, "My Lord and my God!"

29 Jesus *said to him, "Because you have seen Me, have you believed? [a]Blessed *are* they who did not see, and *yet* believed."

12 [a]Matt 28:2f; Mark 16:5; Luke 24:4
13 [a]John 20:15 [b]John 20:2
14 [a]Matt 28:9; Mark 16:9 [b]John 21:4
15 [a]John 20:13
16 [1]I.e. Jewish Aramaic [a]John 5:2 [b]Matt 23:7; Mark 10:51
17 [a]Matt 28:10 [b]Mark 12:26; 16:19; John 7:33
18 [a]John 20:1 [b]Mark 16:10; Luke 24:10, 23
19 [1]Lit *Peace to you* [a]John 7:13 [b]Luke 24:36; John 14:27; 20:21, 26
20 [a]Luke 24:39, 40; John 19:34 [b]John 16:20, 22
21 [a]Luke 24:36; John 14:27; 20:19, 26 [b]John 17:18
23 [1]I.e. have previously been forgiven [a]Matt 16:19; 18:18
24 [1]I.e. the Twin [a]John 11:16 [b]John 6:67
25 [a]John 20:20 [b]Mark 16:11
26 [1]Or *A week later* [2]Or *locked* [a]Luke 24:36; John 14:27; 20:19, 21
27 [a]Luke 24:40; John 20:25
29 [a]1 Pet 1:8

20:12 *two angels.* Matthew has one angel (Matt 28:2), Mark a young man (Mark 16:5) and Luke two men who were angels (Luke 24:4,23). See note on Luke 24:4.
20:14 *did not know that it was Jesus.* A number of times the risen Jesus was not recognized (21:4; Matt 28:17; Luke 24:16,37). He may have looked different, or He may intentionally have prevented recognition.
20:16 *Mary!* Cf. 10:3–4. *Rabboni!* A strengthened form of *Rabbi,* and in the NT found elsewhere only in Mark 10:51 (in the Greek). Although the word means "(my) teacher," there are few if any examples of its use in ancient Judaism as a form of address other than in calling on God in prayer. However, John's explanation casts doubt on any thought that Mary intended to address Jesus as God here.
20:17 *for I have not yet ascended.* The meaning appears to be that the ascension was still some time off. Mary would have opportunity to see Jesus again, so she need not cling to Him. Alternatively, Jesus may be reminding Mary that after His crucifixion she cannot have Him with her except through the Holy Spirit (see 16:5–16). *My brethren.* Probably the disciples (cf. v. 18; Matt 12:50). The members of His family did not believe in Him (7:5), though they became disciples not long after this (Acts 1:14). *My Father and your Father.* God is Father both of Christ and of believers, but in different senses (see 1:12,14,18,34).
20:19 *disciples.* Probably includes others besides the apostles, "the twelve" (v. 24). *the Jews.* See note on 1:19. *Peace be with you.* The normal Hebrew greeting (cf. Dan 10:19). Because of their behavior the previous Friday, they may have expected rebuke and censure; but Jesus calmed their fears (see note on 14:27).
20:20 *His hands and His side.* Where the wounds were (John does not refer to the wounds in the feet). According to Luke 24:37 they thought they were seeing a ghost. Jesus was clearly identifying Himself.
20:21 *Peace be with you.* See note on v. 19. *I also send you.* See note on 17:18.
20:22 *Receive the Holy Spirit.* Thus anticipating what happened 50 days later on the day of Pentecost (Acts 2). The disciples needed God's help to carry out the commission they had just been given.
20:23 Lit. "Those whose sins you forgive have already been forgiven; those whose sins you do not forgive have not been forgiven." God does not forgive people's sins because we do so, nor does He withhold forgiveness because we do. Rather, those who proclaim the gospel are in effect forgiving or not forgiving sins, depending on whether the hearers accept or reject Jesus Christ.
20:24 *Thomas.* See note on 11:16.
20:25 *Unless I see . . . and put . . . I will not believe.* Hardheaded skepticism can scarcely go further than this.
20:26 *Peace.* See vv. 19,21 and note on 14:27.
20:28 *My Lord and my God!* To acknowledge Jesus as one's Lord and God is the high point of faith (see note on 1:1).
20:29 *they who did not see, and yet believed.* Would have been very few at this time. All whom John mentions had seen in some sense. The words, of course, apply to future believers as well.

Why This Gospel Was Written

30 [a]Therefore many other [1b]signs Jesus
also performed in the presence of the disciples, which are not written in this book;
31 but these have been written [a]so that
you may believe that Jesus is [1]the Christ,
[b]the Son of God; and that [c]believing you may
have life in His name.

Jesus Appears at the Sea of Galilee

21 After these things Jesus [1a]manifested
Himself [b]again to the disciples at the
[c]Sea of Tiberias, and He manifested *Himself*
in this way.
2 Simon Peter, and [a]Thomas called [1]Did-
ymus, and [b]Nathanael of [c]Cana in Galilee,
and [d]the *sons* of Zebedee, and two others of
His disciples were together.
3 Simon Peter *said to them, "I am going
fishing." They *said to him, "We will also
come with you." They went out and got into
the boat; and [a]that night they caught nothing.
4 But when the day was now breaking,
Jesus stood on the beach; yet the disciples
did not [a]know that it was Jesus.
5 So Jesus *said to them, "Children, [a]you
do not have [1]any fish, do you?" They
answered Him, "No."
6 And He said to them, "[a]Cast the net on
the right-hand side of the boat and you will
find *a catch.*" So they cast, and then they
were not able to haul it in because of the
great number of fish.
7 [a]Therefore that disciple whom Jesus
loved *said to Peter, "It is the Lord." So
when Simon Peter heard that it was the Lord,
he put his outer garment on (for he was
stripped *for work)*, and threw himself into
the sea.
8 But the other disciples came in the little
boat, for they were not far from the land, but
about [1]one hundred yards away, dragging
the net *full* of fish.
9 So when they got out on the land, they
*saw a charcoal [a]fire *already* laid and [b]fish
placed on it, and bread.
10 Jesus *said to them, "Bring some of the
[a]fish which you have now caught."
11 Simon Peter went up and drew the net
to land, full of large fish, a hundred and fifty-
three; and although there were so many, the
net was not torn.

Jesus Provides

12 Jesus *said to them, "Come *and* have
[a]breakfast." None of the disciples ventured
to question Him, "Who are You?" knowing
that it was the Lord.
13 Jesus *came and *took [a]the bread and
*gave *it* to them, and the [b]fish likewise.
14 This is now the [a]third time that Jesus
[1]was manifested to the disciples, after He
was raised from the dead.

The Love Motivation

15 So when they had [a]finished breakfast,
Jesus *said to Simon Peter, "Simon, *son* of
John, do you [1b]love Me more than these?"
He *said to Him, "Yes, Lord; You know that I
[2]love You." He *said to him, "Tend [c]My
lambs."
16 He *said to him again a second time,

30 [1]Or *attesting miracles* [a]John 21:25 [b]John 2:11
31 [1]I.e. the Messiah [a]John 19:35 [b]Matt 4:3 [c]John 3:15
21:1 [1]Or *made Himself visible* [a]Mark 16:12; John 21:14 [b]John 20:19, 26 [c]John 6:1
2 [1]I.e. the Twin [a]John 11:16 [b]John 1:45ff [c]John 2:1 [d]Matt 4:21; Mark 1:19; Luke 5:10
3 [a]Luke 5:5
4 [a]Luke 24:16; John 20:14
5 [1]Lit *something eaten with bread* [a]Luke 24:41
6 [a]Luke 5:4ff
7 [a]John 13:23; 21:20
8 [1]Lit *200 cubits*
9 [a]John 18:18 [b]John 6:9, 11; 21:10, 13
10 [a]John 6:9, 11; 21:9, 13
12 [a]John 21:15
13 [a]John 21:9 [b]John 6:9, 11; 21:9, 10
14 [1]Or *made Himself visible* [a]John 20:19, 26
15 [1]Gr *agapao* [2]Gr *phileo* [a]John 21:12 [b]Matt 26:33; Mark 14:29; John 13:37 [c]Luke 12:32

20:30 *signs.* See note on 2:11. John had selected from among many. *in the presence of the disciples.* Those who could testify to what He had done. John again stresses testimony (see note on 1:7).
20:31 *that you may believe.* Expresses John's evangelistic purpose. *believe.* See note on 1:7. *Jesus is the Christ, the Son of God.* Faith has content. *the Christ.* See note on 1:25. This whole Gospel is written to show the truth of Jesus' Messiahship and to present Him as the Son of God, so that the readers may believe in Him. *that believing you may have life.* Another expression of purpose—to bring about faith that leads to life (see notes on 1:4; 3:15). *name.* Represents all that He is and stands for (see note on 2:23).
21:1 *Sea of Tiberias.* See note on 6:1.
21:2 *Simon Peter.* See note on Mark 1:16. *Thomas.* See note on 11:16. *sons of Zebedee.* Not named in this Gospel (see Matt 4:21).
21:3 *that night.* Nighttime was favored by fishermen in ancient times (as Aristotle, e.g., informs us).
21:4 *did not know that it was Jesus.* Cf. Mary Magdalene (see note on 20:14).
21:7 *disciple whom Jesus loved.* See note on 13:23. *his outer garment.* It is curious that he put on this garment (the word appears only here in the NT) preparatory to jumping into the water. But Jews regarded a greeting as a religious act that could be done only when one was clothed. Peter may have been preparing himself to greet the Lord.
21:11 *Peter . . . drew the net to land.* Appears to mean that Peter headed up the effort, for the whole group had not been able previously to haul the net into the boat (v. 6). *the net was not torn.* In contrast to the nets mentioned in Luke 5:6.
21:14 *the third time.* The third appearance to a group of disciples (20:19–23,24–29), though there had been other appearances to individuals.
21:15–17 *love.* The Greek word for "love" in Jesus' first two questions is different from the word for "love" in His third question, which is the same word Peter uses in all three answers. It is uncertain whether a distinction in meaning is intended since John often made slight word variations, apparently for stylistic reasons. Also, no distinction is made between these two words elsewhere in this Gospel. In this passage, however, they occur together, and the variations seem too deliberate to be explained on stylistic grounds. The "love" in Jesus' first two questions (*agapao*) refers to a love in which the entire personality, including the will, is involved. The "love" in Jesus' third question and in Peter's answers (*phileo*) refers to spontaneous natural affection or fondness in which emotion plays a more prominent role than will. Whatever interpretation is adopted, the important thing is that in so serious a matter as the reinstatement of Peter, the great question was whether he loved Jesus.
21:15 *more than these.* May mean "more than you love these men" or "more than these men love Me" or "more than you love these things" (i.e., the fishing gear). Perhaps the second is best, for Peter had claimed a devotion above that of the others (cf. 13:37; Matt 26:33; Mark 14:29). Peter did not take up the comparison, and Jesus did not explain it. *Tend My lambs.* Probably means much the same as "Shepherd My sheep" (v. 16) and "Tend My sheep" (v. 17).

"Simon, *son* of John, do you [1]love Me?" He
*said to Him, "Yes, Lord; You know that I
[2]love You." He *said to him, "[a]Shepherd My
sheep."
17 He *said to him the third time, "Simon,
son of John, do you [1]love Me?" Peter was
grieved because He said to him [a]the third
time, "Do you [1]love Me?" And he said to
Him, "Lord, [b]You know all things; You know
that I [1]love You." Jesus *said to him, "[c]Tend
My sheep.

Our Times Are in His Hand

18 "Truly, truly, I say to you, when you
were younger, you used to gird yourself and
walk wherever you wished; but when you
grow old, you will stretch out your hands
and someone else will gird you, and bring
you where you do not wish to *go.*"
19 Now this He said, [a]signifying by [b]what
kind of death he would glorify God. And
when He had spoken this, He *said to him,
"[c]Follow Me!"

20 Peter, turning around, *saw the [a]disci-
ple whom Jesus loved following *them;* the
one who also had [b]leaned back on His bosom at the supper and said, "Lord, who is the
one who betrays You?"
21 So Peter seeing him *said to Jesus,
"Lord, and what about this man?"
22 Jesus *said to him, "If I want him to
remain [a]until I come, what *is that* to you?
You [b]follow Me!"
23 Therefore this saying went out among
[a]the brethren that that disciple would not
die; yet Jesus did not say to him that he
would not die, but *only,* "If I want him to
remain [b]until I come, what *is that* to you?"
24 This is the disciple who [a]is testifying to
these things and wrote these things, and we
know that his testimony is true.
25 And there are also [a]many other things
which Jesus did, which if they *were written
in detail, I suppose that even the world itself
*would not contain the books that *would
be written.

16 [1]Gr *agapao* [2]Gr *phileo* [a]Matt 2:6; Acts 20:28; 1 Pet 5:2; Rev 7:17
17 [1]Gr *phileo* [a]John 13:38 [b]John 16:30 [c]John 21:15, 16
19 [a]John 12:33; 18:32 [b]2 Pet 1:14 [c]Matt 8:22; 16:24; John 21:22
20 [a]John 21:7 [b]John 13:25
22 [a]Matt 16:27f; 1 Cor 4:5; 11:26; James 5:7; Rev 2:25 [b]Matt 8:22; 16:24; John 21:19
23 [a]Acts 1:15 [b]Matt 16:27f; 1 Cor 4:5; 11:26; James 5:7; Rev 2:25
24 [a]John 15:27
25 [a]John 20:30

21:17 *You know all things.* Peter's replies stress Christ's knowledge, not his own grasp of the situation.

21:18 *stretch out your hands.* The early church understood this as a prophecy of crucifixion.

21:19 *what kind of death.* Peter would be a martyr. Tradition indicates that he was crucified upside down.

21:20 *disciple whom Jesus loved.* See note on 13:23. *following.* He was doing what Peter was twice told to do (vv. 19,22). *at the supper.* See 13:23–25.

21:22 *until I come.* A clear declaration of the second coming.

21:24 *disciple who is testifying.* Testimony is important throughout this Gospel (see note on 1:7). We now learn that it was the beloved disciple who was the witness behind the account. *these things.* Must refer to the whole book. *and wrote these things.* The beloved disciple was not only the witness but also the actual author. *we know.* Evidently written by contemporaries in a position to know the truth.

21:25 *many other things.* As in 20:30 we are assured that the author has been selective. *even the world itself would not contain.* Our historical knowledge of Jesus is at best partial, but we have been given all we need to know.

Major Archaeological Finds Relating to the NT

SITE OR ARTIFACT	LOCATION	RELATING SCRIPTURE
	ISRAEL	
Herod's temple	Jerusalem	Luke 1:9
Herod's winter palace	Jericho	Matt 2:4
The Herodium (possible site of Herod's tomb)	Near Bethlehem	Matt 2:19
Masada	Southwest of Dead Sea	Cf. Luke 21:20
Early synagogue	Capernaum	Mark 1:21
Pool of Siloam	Jerusalem	John 9:7
Pool of Bethesda	Jerusalem	John 5:2
Pilate inscription	Caesarea	Luke 3:1
Inscription: Gentile entrance of temple sanctuary	Jerusalem	Acts 21:27-29
Skeletal remains of crucified man	Jerusalem	Luke 23:33
Peter's house	Capernaum	Matt 8:14
Jacob's well	Nablus	John 4:5-6
	ASIA MINOR	
Derbe inscription	Kerti Hüyük	Acts 14:20
Sergius Paulus inscription	Antioch in Pisidia	Acts 13:6-7
Zeus altar (Satan's throne?)	Pergamum	Rev 2:13
Fourth-century B.C. walls	Assos	Acts 20:13-14
Artemis temple and altar	Ephesus	Acts 19:27-28
Ephesian theater	Ephesus	Acts 19:29
Silversmith shops	Ephesus	Acts 19:24
Artemis statues	Ephesus	Acts 19:35
	GREECE	
Erastus inscription	Corinth	Ro 16:23
Synagogue inscription	Corinth	Acts 18:4
Meat market inscription	Corinth	1 Cor 10:25
Cult dining rooms (in Asklepius and Demeter temples)	Corinth	1 Cor 8:10
Court (bema)	Corinth	Acts 18:12
Marketplace (bema)	Philippi	Acts 16:19
Starting gate for races	Isthmia	1 Cor 9:24,26
Gallio inscription	Delphi	Acts 18:12
Egnatian Way	Kavalla (Neapolis), Philippi, Apollonia, Thessalonica	Cf. Acts 16:11-12; 17:1
Politarch inscription	Thessalonica	Acts 17:6
	ITALY	
Tomb of Augustus	Rome	Luke 2:1
Mamertime Prison	Rome	2 Tim 1:16-17; 2:9; 4:6-8
Appian Way	Puteoli to Rome	Acts 28:13-16
Golden House of Nero	Rome	Cf. Acts 25:10; 1 Pet 2:13
Arch of Titus	Rome	Cf. Luke 19:43-44; 21:6,20

The Harmony of the Gospels

	MATTHEW	MARK	LUKE	JOHN
A PREVIEW OF WHO JESUS IS				
Luke's purpose in writing a gospel			1:1-4	
John's prologue: Jesus Christ, the preexistent Word incarnate				1:1-18
Jesus' legal lineage through Joseph and natural lineage through Mary	1:1-17		3:23b-38	
THE EARLY YEARS OF JOHN THE BAPTIST				
John's birth foretold to Zacharias			1:5-25	
Jesus' birth foretold to Mary			1:26-38	
Mary's visit to Elizabeth and Elizabeth's song			1:39-45	
Mary's song of joy			1:46-56	
John's birth			1:57-66	
Zacharias's prophetic song			1:67-79	
John's growth and early life			1:80	
THE EARLY YEARS OF JESUS CHRIST				
Circumstances of Jesus' birth explained to Joseph	1:18-25			
Birth of Jesus			2:1-7	
Praise of the angels and witness of the shepherds			2:8-20	
Circumcision of Jesus			2:21	
Jesus presented in the temple with the homage of Simeon and Anna			2:22-38	
Visit of the magi	2:1-12			
Escape into Egypt and murder of boys in Bethlehem	2:13-18			
Return to Nazareth	2:19-23		2:39	
Growth and early life of Jesus			2:40	
Jesus' first Passover in Jerusalem			2:41-50	
Jesus' growth to adulthood			2:51-52	
THE PUBLIC MINISTRY OF JOHN THE BAPTIST				
His ministry launched		1:1	3:1-2	
His person, proclamation, and baptism	3:1-6	1:2-6	3:3-6	
His messages to the Pharisees, Sadducees, crowds, tax collectors, and soldiers	3:7-10		3:7-14	
His description of Christ	3:11-12	1:7-8	3:15-18	
THE END OF JOHN'S MINISTRY AND THE BEGINNING OF CHRIST'S PUBLIC MINISTRY				
Jesus' baptism by John	3:13-17	1:9-11	3:21-23a	
Jesus' temptation in the wilderness	4:1-11	1:12-13	4:1-13	
John's testimony about himself to the priests and Levites				1:19-28
John's testimony to Jesus as the Son of God				1:29-34
Jesus' first followers				1:35-51
Jesus' first miracle: water becomes wine				2:1-11
Jesus' first stay in Capernaum with His relatives and early disciples				2:12
First cleansing of the temple at the Passover				2:13-22
Early response to Jesus' miracles				2:23-25
Nicodemus's interview with Jesus				3:1-21
John superseded by Jesus				3:22-36
Jesus' departure from Judea	4:12	1:14a	3:19-20; 4:14a	4:1-4
Discussion with a Samaritan woman				4:5-26
Challenge of a spiritual harvest				4:27-38
Evangelization of Sychar				4:39-42
Arrival in Galilee				4:43-45
THE MINISTRY OF CHRIST IN GALILEE				
Opposition at Home and a New Headquarters				
Nature of the Galilean ministry	4:17	1:14b-15	4:14b-15	
Child at Capernaum healed by Jesus while at Cana				4:46-54
Ministry and rejection at Nazareth			4:16-31a	
Move to Capernaum	4:13-16			

	MATTHEW	MARK	LUKE	JOHN
Disciples Called and Ministry Throughout Galilee				
Call of the four	4:18-22	1:16-20	5:1-11	
Teaching in the synagogue of Capernaum authenticated by healing a demoniac		1:21-28	4:31b-37	
Peter's mother-in-law and others healed	8:14-17	1:29-34	4:38-41	
Tour of Galilee with Simon and others	4:23-25	1:35-39	4:42-44	
Cleansing of a man with leprosy, followed by much publicity	8:2-4	1:40-45	5:12-16	
Forgiving and healing of a paralytic	9:1-8	2:1-12	5:17-26	
Call of Matthew	9:9	2:13-14	5:27-28	
Banquet at Matthew's house	9:10-13	2:15-17	5:29-32	
Jesus defends His disciples for feasting instead of fasting with three parables	9:14-17	2:18-22	5:33-39	
Sabbath Controversies and Withdrawals				
Jesus heals an invalid on the Sabbath				5:1-9
Effort to kill Jesus for breaking the Sabbath and saying He was equal with God				5:10-18
Discourse demonstrating the Son's equality with the Father				5:19-47
Controversy over disciples' picking grain on the Sabbath	12:1-8	2:23-28	6:1-5	
Healing of a man's withered hand on the Sabbath	12:9-14	3:1-6	6:6-11	
Withdrawal to the Sea of Galilee with large crowds from many places	12:15-21	3:7-12		
Appointment of the twelve and Sermon on the Mount				
Twelve apostles chosen		3:13-19	6:12-16	
Setting of the Sermon	5:1-2		6:17-19	
Blessings of those who inherit the kingdom and woes to those who do not	5:3-12		6:20-26	
Responsibility while awaiting the kingdom	5:13-16			
Law, righteousness, and the kingdom	5:17-20			
Six contrasts in interpreting the law	5:21-48		6:27-30, 32-36	
Three hypocritical "acts of righteousness" to be avoided	6:1-18			
Three prohibitions against avarice, harsh judgment, and unwise exposure of sacred things	6:19-7:6		6:37-42	
Application and conclusion	7:7-27		6:31, 43-49	
Reaction of the crowds	7:28-8:1			
Growing Fame and Emphasis on Repentance				
A centurion's faith and the healing of his servant	8:5-13		7:1-10	
A widow's son raised at Nain			7:11-17	
John the Baptist's relationship to the kingdom	11:2-19		7:18-35	
Woes upon Chorazin and Bethsaida for failure to repent	11:20-30			
Christ's feet anointed by a sinful but contrite woman			7:36-50	
First Public Rejection by Jewish Leaders				
A tour with the twelve and other followers			8:1-3	
Blasphemous accusation by the scribes and Pharisees	12:22-37	3:20-30		
Request for a sign refused	12:38-45			
Announcement of new spiritual kinship	12:46-50	3:31-35	8:19-21	
Secrets About the Kingdom Given in Parables				
TO THE CROWDS BY THE SEA				
The setting of the parables	13:1-3a	4:1-2	8:4	
The parable of the soils	13:3b-23	4:3-25	8:5-18	
The parable of the seed's spontaneous growth		4:26-29		
The parable of the tares	13:24-30			
The parable of the mustard tree	13:31-32	4:30-32		
The parable of the leavened loaf	13:33-35	4:33-34		
TO THE DISCIPLES IN THE HOUSE				
The parable of the tares explained	13:36-43			
The parable of the hidden treasure	13:44			

The Harmony of the Gospels –continued

	MATTHEW	MARK	LUKE	JOHN
The parable of the valuable pearl	13:45-46			
The parable of the dragnet	13:47-50			
The parable of the head of a household	13:51-53			
Continuing Opposition				
Crossing the lake and calming the storm	8:18, 23-27	4:35-41	8:22-25	
Healing the Gerasene demoniacs and resultant opposition	8:28-34	5:1-20	8:26-39	
Return to Galilee, healing of a woman who touched Jesus' garment, and raising of Jairus's daughter	9:18-26	5:21-43	8:40-56	
Three miracles of healing and another blasphemous accusation	9:27-34			
Final visit to unbelieving Nazareth	13:54-58	6:1-6a		
Final Galilean Campaign				
Shortage of workers	9:35-38	6:6b		
Commissioning of the twelve	10:1-42	6:7-11	9:1-5	
Workers sent out	11:1	6:12-13	9:6	
Antipas's mistaken identification of Jesus	14:1-2	6:14-16	9:7-9	
Earlier imprisonment and beheading of John the Baptist	14:3-12	6:17-29		
THE MINISTRY OF CHRIST AROUND GALILEE				
Lesson on the Bread of Life				
Return of the workers		6:30	9:10a	
Withdrawal from Galilee	14:13-14	6:31-34	9:10b-11	6:1-3
Feeding the five thousand	14:15-21	6:35-44	9:12-17	6:4-13
A premature attempt to make Jesus king blocked	14:22-23	6:45-46		6:14-15
Walking on the water during a storm on the lake	14:24-33	6:47-52		6:16-21
Healings at Gennesaret	14:34-36	6:53-56		
Discourse on the true bread of life				6:22-59
Defection among the disciples				6:60-71
Lesson on the Leaven of the Pharisees, Sadducees, and Herodians				
Conflict over the tradition of ceremonial uncleanness	15:1-3a, 7-9b, 3b-6, 10-20	7:1-23		7:1
Ministry to a believing Greek woman in Tyre and Sidon	15:21-28	7:24-30		
Healings in Decapolis	15:29-31	7:31-37		
Feeding the four thousand in Decapolis	15:32-38	8:1-9a		
Return to Galilee and encounter with the Pharisees and Sadducees	15:39-16:4	8:9b-12		
Warning about the error of the Pharisees, Sadducees, and Herodians	16:5-12	8:13-21		
Healing a blind man at Bethsaida		8:22-26		
Lesson of Messiahship Learned and Confirmed				
Peter's identification of Jesus as the Christ and first prophecy of the church	16:13-20	8:27-30	9:18-21	
First direct prediction of the rejection, crucifixion, and resurrection	16:21-26	8:31-37	9:22-25	
Coming of the Son of Man and judgment	16:27-28	8:38-9:1	9:26-27	
Transfiguration of Jesus	17:1-8	9:2-8	9:28-36a	
Discussion of resurrection, Elijah, and John the Baptist	17:9-13	9:9-13	9:36b	
Lessons on Responsibility to Others				
Healing of demoniac boy and unbelief rebuked	17:14-20	9:14-29	9:37-43a	
Second prediction of Jesus' death and resurrection	17:22-23	9:30-32	9:43b-45	
Payment of temple tax	17:24-27			
Rivalry over greatness in the kingdom	18:1-5	9:33-37	9:46-48	
Warning against causing believers to sin	18:6-14	9:38-50	9:49-50	
Treatment and forgiveness of a sinning brother	18:15-35			
Journey to Jerusalem for the Feast of Booths				
Complete commitment required of followers	8:19-22		9:57-62	
Ridicule by Jesus' half-brothers				7:2-9
Journey through Samaria			9:51-56	7:10

	MATTHEW	MARK	LUKE	JOHN
THE LATER JUDEAN MINISTRY OF CHRIST				
Ministry Beginning at the Feast of Booths				
Mixed reaction to Jesus' teaching and miracles				7:11-31
Frustrated attempt to arrest Jesus				7:32-52
Jesus' forgiveness of a woman caught in adultery				[7:53-8:11]
Conflict over Jesus' claim to be the light of the world				8:12-20
Jesus' relationship to God the Father				8:21-30
Jesus' relationship to Abraham, and attempted stoning				8:31-59
Healing of a man born blind				9:1-7
Response of the blind man's neighbors				9:8-12
Examination and excommunication of the blind man by the Pharisees				9:13-34
Jesus' identification of Himself to the blind man				9:35-38
Spiritual blindness of the Pharisees				9:39-41
Allegory of the good shepherd and the thief				10:1-18
Further division among the Jews				10:19-21
Private Lessons on Loving Service and Prayer				
Commissioning of the seventy			10:1-16	
Return of the seventy			10:17-24	
Story of the good Samaritan			10:25-37	
Jesus' visit with Mary and Martha			10:38-42	
Lesson on how to pray and parable of the bold friend			11:1-13	
Second Debate with the Scribes and the Pharisees				
A third blasphemous accusation and a second debate			11:14-36	
Woes to the Pharisees and the scribes while eating with a Pharisee			11:37-54	
Warning the disciples about hypocrisy			12:1-12	
Warning about greed and trust in wealth			12:13-34	
Warning against being unprepared for the Son of Man's coming			12:35-48	
Warning about the coming division			12:49-53	
Warning against failing to discern the present time			12:54-59	
Two alternatives: repent or perish			13:1-9	
Opposition from a synagogue ruler for healing a woman on the Sabbath			13:10-21	
Another attempt to stone or arrest Jesus for blasphemy at the Feast of Dedication				10:22-39
THE MINISTRY OF CHRIST IN AND AROUND PEREA				
Principles of Discipleship				
From Jerusalem to Perea				10:40-42
Question about salvation and entering the kingdom			13:22-30	
Anticipation of Jesus' coming death and His sorrow over Jerusalem			13:31-35	
Healing of a man with dropsy while eating with a prominent Pharisee on the Sabbath, and three parables suggested by the occasion			14:1-24	
Cost of discipleship			14:25-35	
Parables in defense of association with sinners			15:1-32	
Parable to teach the proper use of money			16:1-13	
Story to teach the danger of wealth			16:14-31	
Four lessons on discipleship			17:1-10	
Sickness and death of Lazarus				11:1-16
Lazarus raised from the dead				11:17-44
Decision of the Sanhedrin to put Jesus to death				11:45-54
Teaching While on Final Journey to Jerusalem				
Healing of ten lepers while passing through Samaria and Galilee			17:11-21	
Instructions regarding the Son of Man's coming			17:22-37	
Two parables on prayer: the persistent widow, and the Pharisee and the tax collector			18:1-14	
Conflict with Pharisaic teaching on divorce	19:1-12	10:1-12		

The Harmony of the Gospels –continued

	MATTHEW	MARK	LUKE	JOHN
Example of little children in relation to the kingdom	19:13-15	10:13-16	18:15-17	
Riches and the kingdom	19:16-30	10:17-31	18:18-30	
Parable of the landowner's sovereignty	20:1-16			
Third prediction of Jesus' death and resurrection	20:17-19	10:32-34	18:31-34	
Warning against ambitious pride	20:20-28	10:35-45		
Healing of blind Bartimaeus and his companion	20:29-34	10:46-52	18:35-43	
Salvation of Zacchaeus			19:1-10	
Parable to teach responsibility while the kingdom is delayed			19:11-28	
THE FORMAL PRESENTATION OF CHRIST TO ISRAEL AND THE RESULTING CONFLICT				
Triumphal Entry and the Fig Tree				
Arrival at Bethany				11:55-12:1, 9-11
Triumphal entry into Jerusalem	21:1-3, 6-7, 4-5, 8-11, 14-17	11:1-11	19:29-44	12:12-19
Cursing of the fig tree having leaves but no figs	21:18-19a	11:12-14		
Second cleansing of the temple	21:12-13	11:15-18	19:45-48	
Request of some Greeks to see Jesus and necessity of the Son of Man's being lifted up				12:20-36a
Different responses to Jesus and Jesus' response to the crowds				12:36b-50
Withered fig tree and the lesson on faith	21:19b-22	11:19-25	21:37-38	
Official Challenge to Christ's Authority				
Questioning of Jesus' authority by the chief priests, teachers of the law, and elders	21:23-27	11:27-33	20:1-8	
Jesus' response with His own question and three parables	21:28-22:14	12:1-12	20:9-19	
Attempts by Pharisees and Herodians to trap Jesus with a question about paying taxes to Caesar	22:15-22	12:13-17	20:20-26	
Sadducees' puzzling question about the resurrection	22:23-33	12:18-27	20:27-40	
A Pharisee's legal question	22:34-40	12:28-34		
Christ's Response to His Enemies' Challenges				
Christ's relationship to David as son and Lord	22:41-46	12:35-37	20:41-44	
Seven woes against the scribes and Pharisees	23:1-36	12:38-40	20:45-47	
Jesus' sorrow over Jerusalem	23:37-39			
A poor widow's gift of all she had		12:41-44	21:1-4	
PROPHECIES IN PREPARATION FOR THE DEATH OF CHRIST				
The Olivet Discourse: Jesus Speaks Prophetically About the Temple and His Own Second Coming				
Setting of the discourse	24:1-3	13:1-4	21:5-7	
Beginning of birth pains	24:4-14	13:5-13	21:8-19	
Abomination of desolation and subsequent distress	24:15-28	13:14-23	21:20-24	
Coming of the Son of Man	24:29-31	13:24-27	21:25-27	
Signs of nearness but unknown time	24:32-41	13:28-32	21:28-33	
Five parables to teach watchfulness and faithfulness	24:42-25:30	13:33-37	21:34-36	
Judgment at the Son of Man's coming	25:31-46			
Arrangements for Betrayal				
Plot by the Sanhedrin to arrest and kill Jesus	26:1-5	14:1-2	22:1-2	
Mary's anointing of Jesus for burial	26:6-13	14:3-9		12:2-8
Judas's agreement to betray Jesus	26:14-16	14:10-11	22:3-6	
The Last Supper				
Preparation for the Passover meal	26:17-19	14:12-16	22:7-13	
Beginning of the Passover meal and dissension among the disciples over greatness	26:20	14:17	22:14-16, 24-30	
Washing the disciples' feet				13:1-20
Identification of the betrayer	26:21-25	14:18-21	22:21-23	13:21-30

	MATTHEW	MARK	LUKE	JOHN
Prediction of Peter's denial	26:31-35	14:27-31	22:31-38	13:31-38
Conclusion of the meal and the Lord's Supper instituted (1 Cor 11:23-26)	26:26-29	14:22-25	22:17-20	
Discourse and Prayers from the Upper Room to Gethsemane				
Questions about His destination, the Father, and the Holy Spirit answered				14:1-31
The vine and the branches				15:1-17
Opposition from the world				15:18-16:4
Coming and ministry of the Spirit				16:5-15
Prediction of joy over His resurrection				16:16-22
Promise of answered prayer and peace				16:23-33
Jesus' prayer for His disciples and all who believe				17:1-26
Jesus' three agonizing prayers in Gethsemane	26:30, 36-46	14:26, 32-42	22:39-46	18:1
THE DEATH OF CHRIST				
Betrayal and Arrest				
Jesus betrayed, arrested, and forsaken	26:47-56	14:43-52	22:47-53	18:2-12
Trial				
First Jewish phase, before Annas				18:13-14, 19-23
Second Jewish phase, before Caiaphas and the Sanhedrin	26:57, 59-68	14:53, 55-65	22:54a, 63-65	18:24
Peter's denials	26:58, 69-75	14:54, 66-72	22:54b-62	18:15-18, 25-27
Third Jewish phase, before the Sanhedrin	27:1	15:1a	22:66-71	
Remorse and suicide of Judas Iscariot (Acts 1:18-19)	27:3-10			
First Roman phase, before Pilate	27:2, 11-14	15:1b-5	23:1-5	18:28-38
Second Roman phase, before Herod Antipas			23:6-12	
Third Roman phase, before Pilate	27:15-26	15:6-15	23:13-25	18:39-19:16a
Crucifixion				
Mockery by the Roman soldiers	27:27-30	15:16-19		
Journey to Golgotha	27:31-34	15:20-23	23:26-33a	19:16b-17
First three hours of crucifixion	27:35-44	15:24-32	23:33b-43	19:18, 23-24, 19-22, 25-27
Last three hours of crucifixion	27:45-50	15:33-37	23:44-45a, 46	19:28-30
Witness of Jesus' death	27:51-56	15:38-41	23:45b, 47-49	
Burial				
Certification of Jesus' death and procurement of His body	27:57-58	15:42-45	23:50-52	19:31-38
Jesus' body placed in a tomb	27:59-60	15:46	23:53-54	19:39-42
The tomb watched by the women and guarded by the soldiers	27:61-66	15:47	23:55-56	
THE RESURRECTION AND ASCENSION OF CHRIST				
The Empty Tomb				
The tomb visited by the women	28:1	16:1		
The stone rolled away	28:2-4			
The tomb found to be empty by the women	28:5-8	16:2-8	24:1-8	20:1
The tomb found to be empty by Peter and John			24:9-12	20:2-10
The Post Resurrection Appearances				
Appearance to Mary Magdalene		[16:9-11]		20:11-18
Appearance to the other women	28:9-10			
Report of the soldiers to the Jewish authorities	28:11-15			
Appearance to the two disciples traveling to Emmaus		[16:12-13]	24:13-32	
Report of the two disciples to the rest (1 Cor. 15:5a)			24:33-35	
Appearance to the ten assembled disciples		[16:14]	24:36-43	20:19-25
Appearance to the eleven assembled disciples (1 Cor. 15:5b)				20:26-31
Appearance to the seven disciples while fishing				21:1-25
Appearance to the Eleven in Galilee (1 Cor. 15:6)	28:16-20	[16:15-18]		
Appearance to James, Jesus' brother (1 Cor. 15:7)				
Appearance to the disciples in Jerusalem (Acts 1:3-8)			24:44-49	
The Ascension				
Christ's parting blessing and departure (Acts 1:9-12)		[16:19-20]	24:50-53	

Acts

INTRODUCTION

Author

Although the author does not name himself, evidence outside the Scriptures and inferences from the book itself lead to the conclusion that the author was Luke.

The earliest of the external testimonies appears in the Muratorian Canon (c. A.D. 170), where the explicit statement is made that Luke was the author of both the third Gospel and the "Acts of All the Apostles." Eusebius (c. 325) lists information from numerous sources to identify the author of these books as Luke (*Ecclesiastical History,* 3.4).

Within the writing itself are some clues as to who the author was:

1. *Luke, the companion of Paul.* In the description of the happenings in Acts, certain passages make use of the pronoun "we." At these points the author includes himself as a companion of Paul in his travels (16:10–17; 20:5—21:18; 27:1—28:16). A historian as careful with details as this author proves to be would have good reason for choosing to use "we" in some places and "they" elsewhere. The author was therefore probably present with Paul at the particular events described in the "we" sections.

These "we" passages include the period of Paul's two-year imprisonment at Rome (ch. 28). During this time Paul wrote, among other letters, Philemon and Colossians. In them he sends greetings from his companions, and Luke is included among them (Philem 23–24; Col 4:10–17). In fact, after eliminating those who, for one reason or another, would not fit the requirements for the author of Acts, Luke is left as the most likely candidate.

2. *Luke, the physician.* Although it cannot be proved that the author of Acts was a physician simply from his vocabulary, the words he uses and the traits and education reflected in his writings fit well his role as a physician (see, e.g., note on 28:6). It is true that the doctor of the first century did not have as specialized a vocabulary as that of doctors today, but there are some usages in Luke-Acts that seem to suggest that a medical man was the author of these books. And it should be remembered that Paul uses the term "physician" in describing Luke (Col 4:14).

Date

Two dates are possible for the writing of this book: (1) c. A.D. 63, soon after the last event recorded in the book, and (2) c. 70 or even later.

The earlier date is supported by:

1. *Silence about later events.* While arguments from silence are not conclusive, it is perhaps significant that the book contains no allusion to events that happened after the close of Paul's two-year imprisonment in Rome: e.g., the burning of Rome and the persecution of the Christians there (A.D. 64), the martyrdom of Peter and Paul (possibly 67) and the destruction of Jerusalem (70).

2. *No outcome of Paul's trial.* If Luke knew the outcome of the trial Paul was waiting for (28:30), why did he not record it at the close of Acts? Perhaps it was because he had brought the history up to date.

Those who prefer the later date hold that 1:8 reveals one of the purposes Luke had in writing his history, and that this purpose influenced the way the book ended. Luke wanted to show how the church penetrated the world of his day in ever-widening circles (Jerusalem, Judea, Samaria, the ends of the earth) until it reached Rome, the world's political and cultural center. On this understanding, mention of the martyrdom of Paul (c. A.D. 67) and of the destruction of Jerusalem (70) was not pertinent. This would allow for the writing of Acts c. 70 or even later.

Recipient

The recipient of the book, Theophilus, is the same person addressed in the first volume, the Gospel of Luke (see Introduction to Luke: Recipient and Purpose).

Importance

The book of Acts provides a bridge for the writings of the NT. As a second volume to Luke's Gospel, it joins what Jesus "began to do and teach" (1:1) as told in the Gospels with what He continued to do and teach through the apostles' preaching and the establishment of the church. Besides linking the Gospel narratives on the one hand and the apostolic letters on the other, it supplies an account of the life of Paul from which we can learn the setting for his letters. Geographically its story spans the lands between Jerusalem, where the church began, and Rome, the political center of the empire. Historically it recounts the first 30 years of the church. It is also a bridge that ties the church in its beginning with each succeeding age. This book may be studied to gain an understanding of the principles that ought to govern the church of any age.

Theme and Purpose

The theme of the work is best summarized in 1:8. It was ordinary procedure for a historian at this time to begin a second volume by summarizing the first volume and indicating the contents anticipated in his second volume. Luke summarized his first volume in 1:1–3; the theme of his second volume is presented in the words of Jesus: "You shall be My witnesses both in Jerusalem, and in all Judea and Samaria, and even to the remotest parts of the earth." This is, in effect, an outline of the book of Acts (see Plan and Outline).

The main purposes of the book appear to be:

1. *To present a history.* The significance of Acts as a historical account of Christian origins cannot be overestimated. It tells of the founding of the church, the spread of the gospel, the beginnings of congregations, and evangelistic efforts in the apostolic pattern. One of the unique aspects of Christianity is its firm historical foundation. The life and teachings of Jesus Christ are established in the four Gospel narratives, and the book of Acts provides a coordinated account of the beginnings of the church.

2. *To give a defense.* One finds embedded in Acts a record of Christian defenses made to both Jews (e.g., 4:8–12) and Gentiles (e.g., 25:8–11), with the underlying purpose of conversion. It shows how the early church coped with pagan and Jewish thought, the Roman government and Hellenistic society.

Luke probably wrote this work as Paul awaited trial in Rome. If his case came to court, what better court brief could Paul have had than a life of Jesus, a history of the beginnings of the church (including the activity of Paul) and an early collection of Paul's letters?

3. *To provide a guide.* Luke had no way of knowing how long the church would continue on this earth, but as long as it pursues its course, the book of Acts will be one of its major guides. In Acts we see basic principles being applied to specific situations in the context of problems and persecutions. These same principles continue to be applicable until Christ returns.

4. *To depict the triumph of Christianity in the face of bitter persecution.* The success of the church in carrying the gospel from Jerusalem to Rome and in planting local churches across the Roman empire demonstrated that Christianity was not a mere work of man. God was in it (see 5:35–39).

Characteristics

1. *Accurate historical detail.* Every page of Acts abounds with sharp, precise details, to the delight of the historian. The account covers a period of about 30 years and reaches across the lands from Jerusalem to Rome. Luke's description of these times and places is filled with all kinds of people and cultures, a variety of governmental administrations, court scenes in Caesarea, and dramatic events involving such centers as Antioch, Ephesus, Athens, Corinth and Rome. Barbarian country districts and Jewish centers are included as well. Yet in each instance archaeological findings reveal that Luke uses the proper terms for the time and place being described. Hostile criticism has not succeeded in disproving the detailed accuracy of Luke's political and geographical designations.

2. *Literary excellence.* Not only does Luke have a large vocabulary compared with other NT writers, but he also uses these words in literary styles that fit the cultural settings of the events he is recording. At times he

employs good, classical Greek; at other times the Aramaic of first-century Palestine shows through his expressions. This is an indication of Luke's careful practice of using language appropriate to the time and place being described. Aramaisms are used when Luke is describing happenings that took place in Palestine (chs. 1—12). When, however, Paul departs for Hellenistic lands beyond the territories where Aramaic-speaking people live, Aramaisms cease.

3. *Dramatic description.* Luke's skillful use of speeches contributes to the drama of his narrative. Not only are they carefully spaced and well balanced between Peter and Paul, but the speeches of a number of other individuals add variety and vividness to the account. Luke's use of details brings the action to life. Nowhere in ancient literature is there an account of a shipwreck superior to Luke's with its nautical details (ch. 27). The book is vivid and fast-moving throughout.

4. *Objective account.* Luke's careful arrangement of material need not detract from the accuracy of his record. He demonstrates the objectivity of his account by recording the failures as well as the successes, the bad as well as the good, in the early church. Not only is the discontent between the Grecian Jews and the Hebraic Jews recorded (6:1) but also the discord between Paul and Barnabas (15:39). Divisions and differences are recognized (15:2; 21:20–21).

Plan and Outline

Luke weaves together different interests and emphases as he relates the beginnings and expansion of the church. The design of his book revolves around (1) key persons: Peter and Paul; (2) important topics and events: the role of the Holy Spirit, pioneer missionary outreach to new fields, conversions, the growth of the church, and life in the Christian community; (3) significant problems: conflict between Jews and Gentiles, persecution of the church by some Jewish elements, trials before Jews and Romans, confrontations with Gentiles, and other hardships in the ministry; (4) geographical advances: five significant stages (see the quotations in the outline; see also map of "The Spread of the Gospel," p. 1598).

- I. Peter and the Beginnings of the Church in Palestine (chs. 1—12)
  - A. "Throughout all Judea and Galilee and Samaria" (1:1–9:31; see 9:31)
    1. Introduction (1:1–2)
    2. Christ's postresurrection ministry (1:3–11)
    3. The period of waiting for the Holy Spirit (1:12–26)
    4. The filling with the Spirit (ch. 2)
    5. The healing of the lame beggar and the resultant arrest of Peter and John (3:1—4:31)
    6. The community of goods (4:32—5:11)
    7. The arrest of the 12 apostles (5:12–42)
    8. The choice of the Seven (6:1–7)
    9. Stephen's arrest and martyrdom (6:8—7:60)
    10. The scattering of the Jerusalem believers (8:1–4)
    11. Philip's ministry (8:5–40)
        - a. In Samaria (8:5–25)
        - b. To the Ethiopian eunuch (8:26–40)
    12. Saul's conversion (9:1–31)
  - B. "To Phoenicia and Cyprus and Antioch" (9:32—12:25; see 11:19)
    1. Peter's ministry on the Mediterranean coast (9:32—11:18)
        - a. To Aeneas and Dorcas (9:32–43)
        - b. To Cornelius (10:1—11:18)
    2. The new Gentile church in Antioch (11:19–30)
    3. Herod's persecution of the church and his subsequent death (ch. 12)
- II. Paul and the Expansion of the Church from Antioch to Rome (chs. 13—28)
  - A. "Through the Phrygian and Galatian region" (13:1—15:35; see 16:6)
    1. Paul's first missionary journey (chs. 13—14)
    2. The Jerusalem council (15:1–35)
  - B. "Over to Macedonia" (15:36—21:16; see 16:9)

1. Paul's second missionary journey (15:36—18:22)
2. Paul's third missionary journey (18:23—21:16)

C. "To Rome" (21:17—28:31; see 28:14)

1. Paul's imprisonment in Jerusalem (21:17—23:35)
   a. Arrest (21:17—22:29)
   b. Trial before the Sanhedrin (22:30—23:11)
   c. Transfer to Caesarea (23:12–35)
2. Paul's imprisonment in Caesarea (chs. 24—26)
   a. Trial before Felix (ch. 24)
   b. Trial before Festus (25:1–12)
   c. Hearing before Festus and Agrippa (25:13—26:32)
3. Voyage to Rome (27:1—28:15)
4. Two years under house arrest in Rome (28:16–31)

Introduction

1 The first account I [1]composed, [a]Theoph-
ilus, about all that Jesus [b]began to do and
teach,
2 until the day when He [a]was taken up *to*
heaven, after He [b]had [1]by the Holy Spirit giv-
en orders to [c]the apostles whom He had
[d]chosen.
3 To [1]these [a]He also presented Himself
alive after His suffering, by many convincing
proofs, appearing to them over *a period of*
forty days and speaking of [b]the things concerning the kingdom of God.
4 [1]Gathering them together, He commanded them [a]not to leave Jerusalem, but
to wait for [2b]what the Father had promised,
"Which," *He said,* "you heard of from Me;
5 for [a]John baptized with water, but you
will be baptized [1]with the Holy Spirit [2b]not
many days from now."
6 So when they had come together, they
were asking Him, saying, "Lord, [a]is it at this
time You are restoring the kingdom to Israel?"
7 He said to them, "It is not for you to
know times or epochs which [a]the Father has
fixed by His own authority;
8 but you will receive power [a]when the
Holy Spirit has come upon you; and you
shall be [b]My witnesses both in Jerusalem,
and in all Judea and [c]Samaria, and even to
[d]the remotest part of the earth."

The Ascension

9 And after He had said these things,
[a]He was lifted up while they were looking
on, and a cloud received Him out of their
sight.
10 And as they were gazing intently into
[1]the sky while He was going, behold, [a]two
men in white clothing stood beside them.
11 They also said, "[a]Men of Galilee, why
do you stand looking into [1]the sky? This
Jesus, who [b]has been taken up from you into
heaven, will [c]come in just the same way as
you have watched Him go into heaven."

The Upper Room

12 Then they [a]returned to Jerusalem from
the [1b]mount called [2]Olivet, which is near
Jerusalem, a [3]Sabbath day's journey away.
13 When they had entered *the city,* they
went up to [a]the upper room where they were
staying; [b]that is, Peter and John and [1]James
and Andrew, Philip and Thomas, Bartholomew and Matthew, [1]James *the son* of
Alphaeus, and Simon the Zealot, and [c]Judas
the [2]*son* of [1]James.
14 These all with one mind [a]were continually devoting themselves to prayer, along

1:1 [1]Lit *made* [a]Luke 1:3 [b]Luke 3:23 **2** [1]Or *through* [a]Mark 16:19; Acts 1:9, 11, 22 [b]Matt 28:19f; Mark 16:15; John 20:21f; Acts 10:42 [c]Mark 6:30 [d]John 13:18; Acts 10:41 **3** [1]Lit *whom* [a]Matt 28:17; Mark 16:12, 14; Luke 24:34, 36; John 20:19, 26; 21:1, 14; 1 Cor 15:5-7 [b]Acts 8:12; 19:8; 28:23, 31 **4** [1]Or *eating with;* or *lodging with* [2]Lit *the promise of the Father* [a]Luke 24:49 [b]John 14:16, 26; 15:26; Acts 2:33 **5** [1]Or *in* [2]Lit *not long after these many days* [a]Matt 3:11; Mark 1:8; Luke 3:16; John 1:33; Acts 11:16 [b]Acts 2:1-4 **6** [a]Matt 17:11; Mark 9:12; Luke 17:20; 19:11 **7** [a]Matt 24:36; Mark 13:32 **8** [a]Acts 2:1-4 [b]Luke 24:48; John 15:27 [c]Acts 8:1, 5, 14 [d]Matt 28:19; Mark 16:15; Rom 10:18; Col 1:23 **9** [a]Luke 24:50, 51; Acts 1:2 **10** [1]Or *heaven* [a]Luke 24:4; John 20:12 **11** [1]Or *heaven* [a]Acts 2:7; 13:31 [b]Mark 16:19; Acts 1:9, 22 [c]Matt 16:27f; Acts 3:21 **12** [1]Or *hill* [2]Or *Olive Grove* [3]I.e. 2K cubits, or approx 3/5 mile [a]Luke 24:52 [b]Matt 21:1 **13** [1]Or *Jacob* [2]Or *brother* [a]Mark 14:15; Luke 22:12; Acts 9:37, 39; 20:8 [b]Acts 1:13: *Matt 10:2-4; Mark 3:16-19; Luke 6:14-16* [c]John 14:22 **14** [a]Acts 2:42; 6:4; Rom 12:12; Eph 6:18; Col 4:2

1:1 *The first account* The Gospel of Luke. Acts was addressed to the same patron, Theophilus (see Introduction to Luke: Recipient and Purpose). *began to do and teach.* An apt summation of Luke's Gospel, implying that Jesus' work continues in Acts through His own personal interventions and the ministry of the Holy Spirit.

1:2 *taken up to heaven.* The last scene of Luke's Gospel (24:50–52) and the opening scene of this second volume (vv. 6–11). The ascension occurred 40 days after the resurrection (v. 3). *by the Holy Spirit.* Jesus' postresurrection instruction of His apostles was carried on through the Holy Spirit, and succeeding statements make it clear that what the apostles were to accomplish was likewise to be done through the Spirit (vv. 4–5,8; see Luke 24:49; John 20:22; see also Introduction to Judges: Theme and Theology). Luke characteristically stresses the Holy Spirit's work and enabling power (e.g., v. 8; 2:4,17; 4:8,31; 5:3; 6:3,5; 7:55; 8:16; 9:17,31; 10:44; 13:2,4; 15:28; 16:6; 19:2,6; see note on Luke 4:1).

1:3 *many convincing proofs.* See the resurrection appearances (Matt 28:1–20; Luke 24:1–53; John 20:1–29; lCo 15:3–8). *kingdom of God.* The heart of Jesus' preaching (see notes on Matt 3:2; Luke 4:43).

1:4 *what the Father had promised.* The Holy Spirit (see John 14:26; 15:26–27; 16:12–13).

1:5 *John baptized with water.* See Luke 3:16. *not many days from now.* The day of Pentecost came ten days later, when the baptism with the Holy Spirit occurred (2:1–4).

1:6 *restoring the kingdom to Israel?* Like their fellow countrymen, they were looking for the deliverance of the people of Israel from foreign domination and for the establishment of an earthly kingdom. The reference to the coming of the Spirit had caused them to wonder if the new age was about to dawn.

1:7 *times or epochs.* The elapsing time or the character of coming events (see 1 Thess 5:1).

1:8 A virtual outline of Acts: The apostles were to be witnesses in Jerusalem (chs. 1–7), Judea and Samaria (chs. 8–9) and the ends of the earth—including Caesarea, Antioch, Asia Minor, Greece and Rome (chs. 10–28). However, they were not to begin this staggering task until they had been equipped with the power of the Spirit (vv. 4–5). *My witnesses.* An important theme throughout Acts (2:32; 3:15; 5:32; 10:39; 13:31; 22:15). *Judea.* The region in which Jerusalem was located. *Samaria.* The adjoining region to the north.

1:10 *two men in white clothing.* A common description of angels.

1:11 *Men of Galilee.* All the twelve were from Galilee except Judas, and he was no longer present. *in just the same way.* In the same resurrection body and in clouds and "great glory" (Matt 24:30).

1:12 *mount called Olivet.* The ascension occurred on the eastern slope of the mount between Jerusalem and Bethany (Luke 19:28–29,37; see notes on Zech 14:4; Mark 11:1; Luke 19:29). *Sabbath day's journey.* About 3/4 mile (1,100 meters). This distance was drawn from rabbinical reasoning based on several OT passages (Ex 16:29; Num 35:5; Josh 3:4). A faithful Jew was to travel no farther on the Sabbath.

1:13 *room.* Probably a room on the upper floor of a large house, such as the one where the Last Supper was held (Mark 14:15) or that of Mary, mother of Mark (see note on 12:12). *Bartholomew.* Apparently John calls him Nathanael (see John 1:45–49; 21:2). *James the son of Alphaeus.* The same as James the younger (Mark 15:40). *Zealot.* See note on Matt 10:4. *Judas the son of James.* Not Judas Iscariot, but the same as Thaddaeus (Matt 10:3; Mark 3:18).

with [b]*the* women, and Mary the [c]mother of
Jesus, and with His [c]brothers.
15 [1]At this time Peter stood up in the
midst of [a]the brethren (a gathering of about
one hundred and twenty [2]persons was there
together), and said,
16 "Brethren, [a]the Scripture had to be fulfilled, which the Holy Spirit foretold by the
mouth of David concerning Judas, [b]who
became a guide to those who arrested Jesus.
17 "For he was [a]counted among us and
received his share in [b]this ministry."
18 (Now this man [a]acquired a field with
[b]the price of his wickedness, and falling
headlong, he burst open in the middle and
all his intestines gushed out.
19 And it became known to all who were
living in Jerusalem; so that in [a]their own language that field was called Hakeldama, that
is, Field of Blood.)
20 "For it is written in the book of Psalms,
'[a]LET HIS HOMESTEAD BE MADE DESOLATE,
AND LET NO ONE DWELL IN IT';
and,
'[b]LET ANOTHER MAN TAKE HIS [1]OFFICE.'
21 "Therefore it is necessary that of the
men who have accompanied us all the time
that [a]the Lord Jesus went in and out [1]among
us—
22 [a]beginning [1]with the baptism of John
until the day that He [b]was taken up from
us—one of these *must* become a [c]witness
with us of His resurrection."
23 So they put forward two men, Joseph
called Barsabbas (who was also called Justus), and [a]Matthias.
24 And they [a]prayed and said, "You, Lord,
[b]who know the hearts of all men, show
which one of these two You have chosen
25 to [1]occupy [a]this ministry and [b]apostle-
ship from which Judas turned aside to go to
his own place."
26 And they [1][a]drew lots for them, and the
lot fell [2]to [b]Matthias; and he was [3]added to
[c]the eleven apostles.

The Day of Pentecost

2 When [a]the day of Pentecost [1]had come,
they were all together in one place.
2 And suddenly there came from heaven
a noise like a violent rushing wind, and it
filled [a]the whole house where they were sitting.
3 And there appeared to them tongues as
of fire [1]distributing themselves, and [2]they
[3]rested on each one of them.
4 And they were all [a]filled with the Holy

14 [b]Luke 8:2f [c]Matt 12:46 **15** [1]Lit *In these days* [2]Lit *names* [a]John 21:23; Acts 6:3; 9:30; 10:23; 11:1, 12, 26, 29; 12:17; 14:2; 15:1, 3, 22, 23, 32f, 40; 16:2, 40; 17:6, 10, 14; 18:18, 27; 21:7, 17; 22:5; 28:14f; Rom 1:13 **16** [a]John 13:18; 17:12; Acts 1:20 [b]Matt 26:47; Mark 14:43; Luke 22:47; John 18:3 **17** [a]John 6:70f [b]Acts 1:25; 20:24; 21:19 **18** [a]Matt 27:3-10 [b]Matt 26:14f **19** [a]Matt 27:8; Acts 21:40 **20** [1]Lit *position as overseer* [a]Ps 69:25 [b]Ps 109:8 **21** [1]Lit *to us* [a]Luke 24:3 **22** [1]Lit *from* [a]Matt 3:16; Mark 1:1-4, 9; Luke 3:21 [b]Mark 16:19; Acts 1:2 **22** [c]Acts 1:8; 2:32 **23** [a]Acts 1:26 **24** [a]Acts 6:6; 13:3; 14:23 [b]1 Sam 16:7; Jer 17:10; Acts 15:8; Rom 8:27 **25** [1]Lit *take the place of* [a]Acts 1:17 [b]Rom 1:5; 1 Cor 9:2; Gal 2:8 **26** [1]Lit *gave* [2]Or *upon* [3]Lit *voted together with* [a]Lev 16:8; Josh 14:2; 1 Sam 14:41f; Neh 10:34; 11:1; Prov 16:33 [b]Acts 1:23 [c]Acts 2:14 **2:1** [1]Lit *was being fulfilled* [a]Lev 23:15f; Acts 20:16; 1 Cor 16:8 **2** [a]Acts 4:31 **3** [1]Or *being distributed* [2]Lit *it* [3]Or *sat* **4** [a]Matt 10:20; Acts 1:5, 8; 4:8, 31; 6:3, 5; 7:55; 8:17; 9:17; 11:15; 13:9, 52

1:14 *with the women.* Possibly wives of the apostles (cf. 1 Cor 9:5) and those listed as ministering to Jesus (Matt 27:55; Luke 8:2–3; 24:22). *Mary the mother of Jesus.* Last mentioned here in Scripture. *brothers.* See note on Luke 8:19. These brothers would include James, who later became important in the church (12:17; 15:13; Gal 2:9).

1:16 *the Scripture had to be fulfilled.* The Scriptures referred to were Ps 69:25; 109:8 (see v. 20). Both before and after Christ came, numerous psalms were viewed as Messianic. What happened in the psalmist's experience was typical of the experiences of the Messiah. No doubt Jesus' instruction in Luke 24:27,45–47 included these Scriptures.

1:18 *this man acquired a field.* Judas bought the field indirectly: The money he returned to the priests (Matt 27:3) was used to purchase the potter's field (Matt 27:7). *falling headlong.* Matt 27:5 reports that Judas hanged himself. It appears that when the body finally fell, either because of decay or because someone cut it down, it was in a decomposed condition and so broke open in the middle. Another possibility is that "hanged" in Matt 27:5 means "impaled" (the Hebrew of Esth 2:23 can be translated "impaled"; see note there) and that the gruesome results of Judas's suicide are described here.

1:19 *Hakeldama.* An Aramaic term, no doubt adopted by people who knew the circumstances, for the field was purchased with Judas's blood money (Matt 27:3–8).

1:20 *it is written.* Two passages of Scripture (Ps 69:25; 109:8; see v. 16) were put together to suggest that Judas had left a vacancy that had to be filled.

1:21 *went in and out among us.* Ministered publicly.

1:22 *a witness with us of His resurrection.* Apparently several met this requirement. On this occasion, however, the believers were selecting someone to become an official witness to the resurrection—thus, a 12th apostle (v. 25).

1:23 *Barsabbas.* Means "son of (the) Sabbath." This patronymic was used for two early Jewish Christians, possibly brothers. One was Joseph (here); the other was Judas, a prophet in Jerusalem who was sent to Antioch with Silas (15:22,32). *Justus.* Joseph's Hellenistic name. Nothing more is known of him.

1:26 *drew lots.* See Prov 16:33. By casting lots they were able to allow God the right of choice. The use of rocks or sticks to designate the choice was common (see 1 Chr 26:13–16; see also notes on Neh 11:1; Jon 1:7). This is the Bible's last mention of casting lots.

2:1 *day of Pentecost.* The 50th day after the Sabbath of Passover week (Lev 23:15–16), thus the first day of the week. Pentecost is also called the Feast of Weeks (Deut 16:10), the Feast of the Harvest (Ex 23:16) and the day of the first fruits (Num 28:26). *they were all together.* The nearest antecedent of "they" is the 11 apostles (plus Matthias), but the reference is probably to all those mentioned in 1:13–15. *in one place.* Evidently not the upstairs room where they were staying (1:13) but perhaps some place in the temple precincts, for the apostles were "continually in the temple" when it was open (Luke 24:53; see note there).

2:2 *violent rushing wind.* Breath or wind is a symbol of the Spirit of God (see Ezek 37:9,14; John 3:8). The coming of the Spirit is marked by audible (wind) and visible (fire) signs. *whole house.* May refer to the temple (cf. 7:47).

2:3 *tongues.* A descriptive metaphor appropriate to the context, in which several languages are about to be spoken. *fire.* A symbol of the divine presence (see Ex 3:2 and note), it was also associated with judgment (see Matt 3:12).

2:4 *all.* Could refer either to the apostles or to the 120. Those holding that the 120 are meant point to the fulfillment of Joel's prophecy (vv. 17–18) as involving more than the 12 apostles. The nearest reference, however, is to the apostles (see note on v. 1), and the narrative continues with Peter and the 11 standing to address the crowd (v. 14). *filled with the Holy Spirit.* A

Spirit and began to [b]speak with other
[1]tongues, as the Spirit was giving them
[2]utterance.
5 Now there were Jews living in Jerusalem, [a]devout men from every nation under
heaven.
6 And when [a]this sound occurred, the
crowd came together, and were bewildered
because each one of them was hearing them
speak in his own [1]language.
7 [a]They were amazed and astonished,
saying, "[1]Why, are not all these who are
speaking [b]Galileans?
8 "And how is it that we each hear *them* in
our own [1]language [2]to which we were born?
9 "Parthians and Medes and Elamites, and
residents of Mesopotamia, Judea and [a]Cap-
padocia, [b]Pontus and [1c]Asia,
10 [a]Phrygia and [b]Pamphylia, Egypt and
the districts of Libya around [c]Cyrene, and
[1d]visitors from Rome, both Jews and [2e]pros-
elytes,

4 [1]Or *languages* [2]Or *ability to speak out* [b]Mark 16:17; 1 Cor 12:10f; 14:21
5 [a]Luke 2:25; Acts 8:2
6 [1]Or *dialect* [a]Acts 2:2
7 [1]Lit *Behold* [a]Acts 2:12 [b]Matt 26:73; Acts 1:11
8 [1]Or *dialect* [2]Lit *in*
9 [1]I.e. west coast province of Asia Minor [a]1 Pet 1:1 [b]Acts 18:2; 1 Pet 1:1 [c]Acts 6:9; 16:6; 19:10; 20:4; 21:27; 24:18; 27:2; Rom 16:5; 1 Cor 16:19; 2 Cor 1:8; 2 Tim 1:15; Rev 1:4
10 [1]Lit *the sojourning Romans* [2]I.e. Gentile converts to Judaism [a]Acts 16:6; 18:23 [b]Acts 13:13; 14:24; 15:38; 27:5 [c]Matt 27:32 [d]Acts 17:21 [e]Matt 23:15

fulfillment of 1:5,8; see also Jesus' promise in Luke 24:49. Their spirits were completely under the control of the Spirit; their words were His words. *with other tongues.* The Spirit enabled them to speak in languages they had not previously learned (the Greek can mean "tongues" or "languages"; also in v. 11). Two other examples of speaking in tongues are found in Acts (10:46; 19:6). One extended NT passage deals with this spiritual gift (1 Cor 12–14). Not all agree, however, that these other passages refer to speaking in known languages. The gift had particular relevance here, where people of different nationalities and languages were gathered.

2:5 *Jews . . . devout men.* Devout Jews from different parts of the world but assembled now in Jerusalem either as visitors or as current residents (cf. Luke 2:25).

2:6 *speak in his own language.* Jews from different parts of the world would understand the Aramaic of their homeland. Also the Greek language was common to all parts of the world. But more than this was occurring; they heard the apostles speak in languages native to the different places represented.

2:9 *Parthians.* Inhabitants of the territory from the Tigris to India. *Medes.* Media lay east of Mesopotamia, northwest of Persia and south-southwest of the Caspian Sea. *Elamites.* Elam was north of the Persian Gulf, bounded on the west by the Tigris. *Mesopotamia.* Between the Euphrates and Tigris rivers. *Judea.* The homeland of the Jews, perhaps used here in the OT sense "From the river of Egypt as far as the . . . Euphrates" (Gen 15:18), including Galilee. *Cappadocia, Pontus and Asia.* Districts in Asia Minor.

2:10 *Phrygia and Pamphylia.* Districts in Asia Minor. *Egypt.*

Countries of People Mentioned at Pentecost

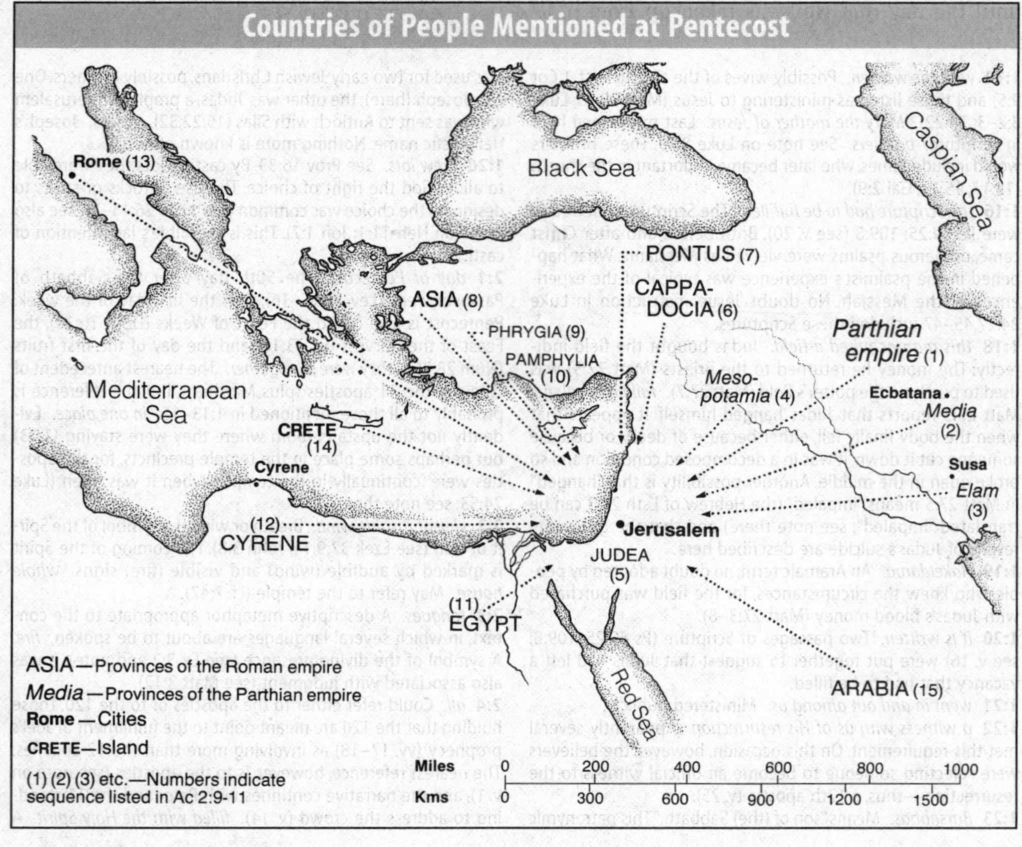

Rome (13)
Black Sea
Caspian Sea
PONTUS (7)
CAPPA-DOCIA (6)
ASIA (8)
PHRYGIA (9)
PAMPHYLIA (10)
Parthian empire (1)
Meso-potamia (4)
Ecbatana
Media (2)
Mediterranean Sea
CRETE (14)
Cyrene
Susa
Elam (3)
(12)
CYRENE
Jerusalem
JUDEA (5)
(11)
EGYPT
Red Sea
ARABIA (15)
ASIA—Provinces of the Roman empire
Media—Provinces of the Parthian empire
Rome—Cities
CRETE—Island
(1) (2) (3) etc.—Numbers indicate sequence listed in Ac 2:9-11
Miles 0 200 400 600 800 1000
Kms 0 300 600 900 1200 1500

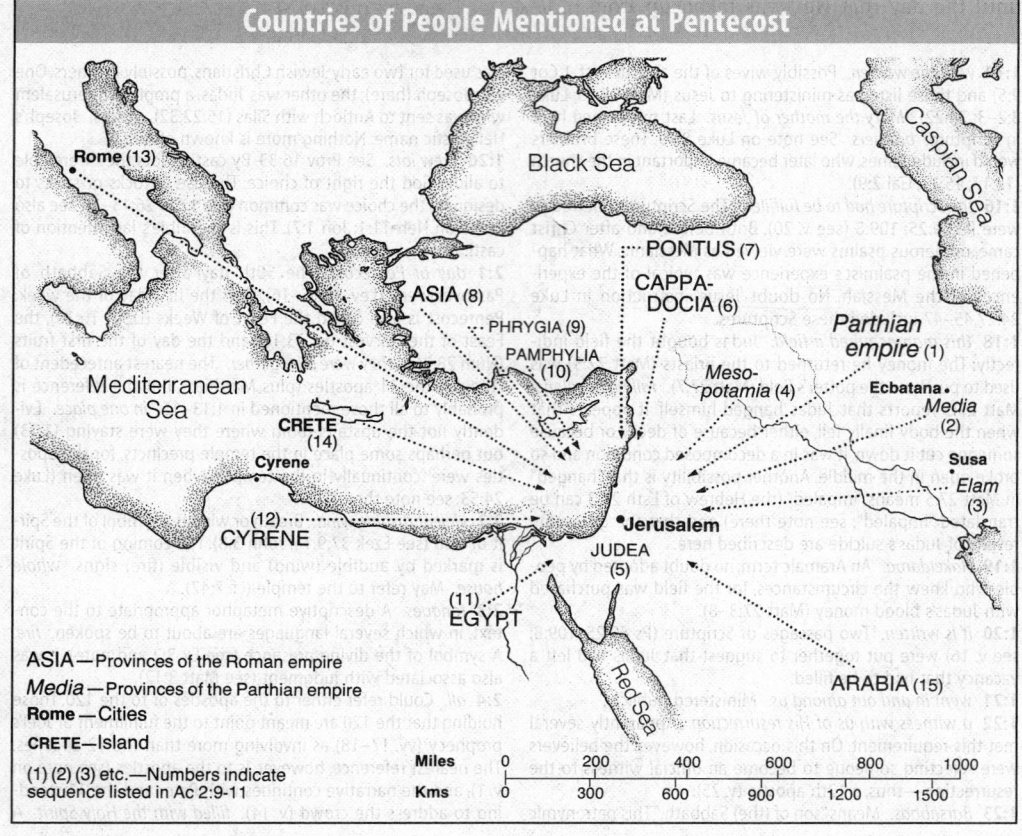

11 Cretans and Arabs—we hear them in
our *own* tongues speaking of the mighty
deeds of God."
12 And [a]they all continued in amazement
and great perplexity, saying to one another,
"What does this mean?"
13 But others were mocking and saying,
"[a]They are full of [1]sweet wine."

Peter's Sermon

14 But Peter, [1]taking his stand with [a]the
eleven, raised his voice and declared to
them: "Men of Judea and all you who live in
Jerusalem, let this be known to you and give
heed to my words.
15 "For these men are not drunk, as you
suppose, [a]for it is *only* the [1]third hour of the
day;
16 but this is what was spoken of through
the prophet Joel:
17 '[a]AND IT SHALL BE IN THE LAST DAYS,' God
says,
'THAT I WILL POUR FORTH OF MY SPIRIT ON
ALL [1]MANKIND;
AND YOUR SONS AND YOUR DAUGHTERS
SHALL PROPHESY,
AND YOUR YOUNG MEN SHALL SEE VISIONS,
AND YOUR OLD MEN SHALL DREAM DREAMS;
18 EVEN ON MY BONDSLAVES, BOTH MEN AND
WOMEN,
I WILL IN THOSE DAYS POUR FORTH OF MY
SPIRIT
And they shall prophesy.
19 'AND I WILL GRANT WONDERS IN THE SKY
ABOVE
AND SIGNS ON THE EARTH BELOW,
BLOOD, AND FIRE, AND VAPOR OF SMOKE.
20 'THE SUN WILL BE TURNED INTO DARKNESS
AND THE MOON INTO BLOOD,
BEFORE THE GREAT AND GLORIOUS DAY OF
THE LORD SHALL COME.
21 'AND IT SHALL BE THAT [a]EVERYONE WHO
CALLS ON THE NAME OF THE LORD WILL
BE SAVED.'
22 "Men of Israel, listen to these words:
[a]Jesus the Nazarene, [b]a man [1]attested to you
by God with [2]miracles and [c]wonders and
[3]signs which God performed through Him in
your midst, just as you yourselves know—
23 this *Man*, delivered over by the [a]prede-
termined plan and foreknowledge of God,
[b]you nailed to a cross by the hands of [1]god-
less men and put *Him* to death.
24 "[1]But [a]God raised Him up again, putting
an end to the [2]agony of death, since it [b]was
impossible for Him to be held [3]in its power.
25 "For David says of Him,
'[a]I SAW THE LORD ALWAYS IN MY PRESENCE;
FOR HE IS AT MY RIGHT HAND, SO THAT I
WILL NOT BE SHAKEN.
26 'THEREFORE MY HEART WAS GLAD AND MY
TONGUE EXULTED;
MOREOVER MY FLESH ALSO WILL LIVE IN
HOPE;
27 BECAUSE YOU WILL NOT ABANDON MY SOUL
TO [a]HADES,
[b]NOR [1]ALLOW YOUR [2]HOLY ONE TO
[3]UNDERGO DECAY.
28 'YOU HAVE MADE KNOWN TO ME THE WAYS
OF LIFE;
YOU WILL MAKE ME FULL OF GLADNESS
WITH YOUR PRESENCE.'
29 "[1]Brethren, I may confidently say to you
regarding the [a]patriarch David that he both
[b]died and [c]was buried, and [d]his tomb is
[2]with us to this day.

12 [a]Acts 2:7 **13** [1]I.e. new wine [a]1 Cor 14:23 **14** [1]Or *being put forward* as spokesman [a]Acts 1:26 **15** [1]I.e. 9 a.m. [a]1 Thess 5:7 **17** [1]Lit *flesh* [a]Joel 2:28-32 **21** [a]Rom 10:13 **22** [1]Or *exhibited* or *accredited* [2]Or *works of power* [3]Or *attesting miracles* [a]Acts 3:6; 4:10; 10:38 [b]John 3:2 [c]John 4:48; Acts 2:19, 43 **23** [1]Lit *men without the Law;* i.e. pagan [a]Luke 22:22; Acts 3:18; 4:28; 1 Pet 1:20 [b]Matt 27:35; Mark 15:24; Luke 23:33; 24:20; John 19:18; Acts 3:13 **24** [1]Lit *Whom God raised up* [2]Lit *birth pains* [3]Lit *by it* [a]Matt 28:5, 6; Mark 16:6; Luke 24:5, 6; Acts 2:32; 3:15, 26; 4:10; 5:30; 10:40; 13:30, 33, 34, 37; 17:31; Rom 4:24; 6:4; 8:11; 10:9; 1 Cor 6:14; 15:15; 2 Cor 4:14; Gal 1:1; Eph 1:20; Col 2:12; 1 Thess 1:10; Heb 13:20; 1 Pet 1:21 [b]John 20:9 **25** [a]Ps 16:8-11 **27** [1]Lit *give* [2]Or *devout* or *pious* [3]Lit *see corruption* [a]Matt 11:23; Acts 2:31 [b]Acts 13:35 **29** [1]Lit *Men brothers* [2]Lit *among* [a]Acts 7:8f; Heb 7:4 [b]Acts 13:36 [c]1 Kin 2:10 [d]Neh 3:16

Contained a great number of Jews. Two out of the five districts of Alexandria were Jewish. *Libya.* A region west of Egypt. *Cyrene.* The capital of a district of Libya called Cyrenaica. *Rome.* Thousands of Jews lived in Rome. *proselytes.* Gentiles who undertook the full observance of the Mosaic law were received into full fellowship with the Jews.

2:11 *Cretans.* Represented an island lying south-southeast of Greece. *Arabs.* From a region to the east. The kingdom of the Nabatean Arabs lay between the Red Sea and the Euphrates, with Petra as its capital. *we hear them . . . speaking.* Not a miracle of hearing but of speaking. The believers were declaring God's wonders in the native languages of the various visiting Jews.

2:14–40 The pattern and themes of the message that follows became common in the early church: (1) an explanation of events (vv. 14–21); (2) the gospel of Jesus Christ—His death, resurrection and exaltation (vv. 22–36); (3) an exhortation to repentance and baptism (vv. 37–40). The outline of this sermon is similar to those in chs. 3; 10; 13.

2:14 *with the eleven.* The apostles had been baptized with the Holy Spirit and had spoken in other languages to various groups. Now they stood with Peter, who served as their spokesman.

2:15 *only the third hour of the day.* On a festival day such as Pentecost, the Jew would not break his fast until at least 10:00 A.M. So it was extremely unlikely that a group of men would be drunk at such an early hour.

2:17–18 *ALL MANKIND . . . SONS . . . DAUGHTERS . . . YOUNG MEN . . . OLD MEN . . . MEN . . . WOMEN.* The Spirit is bestowed on all, irrespective of sex, age and rank.

2:17 *LAST DAYS.* See Is 2:2; Hos 3:5; Mic 4:1; see also notes on 1 Tim 4:1; 2 Tim 3:1; Heb 1:2; 1 Pet 1:20; 1 John 2:18. In the passage quoted from Joel the Hebrew has "after this" and the Septuagint "after these things." Peter interprets the passage as referring specifically to the latter days of the new covenant (see Jer 31:33–34; Ezek 36:26–27; 39:29) in contrast to the former days of the old covenant. The age of Messianic fulfillment has arrived. *MY SPIRIT.* See note on 1:2.

2:21 *EVERYONE WHO CALLS.* Cf. v. 39; includes faith and response rather than merely using words (Matt 7:21).

2:22 *attested . . . with miracles and wonders and signs.* The mighty works done by Jesus were signs that the Messiah had come.

2:23 *godless men.* The Greek has "those not having the law," i.e., Gentiles. The reference is to the Romans involved in the trial and crucifixion of Christ. Here, however, the Gentiles were acting in an evil way.

2:27 *NOT ABANDON MY SOUL TO HADES.* David referred ultimately to the Messiah (v. 31). God would not allow His physical body to decompose.

2:29 *his tomb is with us.* The tomb of David could be seen in Jerusalem. It still contained the remains of David's body. The words of Ps 16:8–11 did not fully apply to him.

30 "And so, because he was [a]a prophet and knew that [b]GOD HAD SWORN TO HIM WITH AN OATH TO SEAT *one* [1]OF HIS DESCENDANTS ON HIS THRONE,

31 he looked ahead and spoke of the resurrection of [1]the Christ, that [a]HE WAS NEITHER ABANDONED TO HADES, NOR DID His flesh [2]SUFFER DECAY.

32 "This Jesus [a]God raised up again, to which we are all [b]witnesses.

33 "Therefore having been exalted [1a]to the right hand of God, and [b]having received from the Father [c]the promise of the Holy Spirit, He has [d]poured forth this which you both see and hear.

34 "For it was not David who ascended into [1]heaven, but he himself says:

'[a]THE LORD SAID TO MY LORD,
"SIT AT MY RIGHT HAND,
35 UNTIL I MAKE YOUR ENEMIES A FOOTSTOOL FOR YOUR FEET." '

36 "Therefore let all the [a]house of Israel know for certain that God has made Him both [b]Lord and [1]Christ—this Jesus [c]whom you crucified."

The Ingathering

37 Now when they heard *this,* they were [1]pierced to the heart, and said to Peter and the rest of the apostles, "[2]Brethren, [3a]what shall we do?"

38 Peter *said* to them, "[a]Repent, and each of you be [b]baptized in the name of Jesus Christ for the forgiveness of your sins; and you will receive the gift of the Holy Spirit.

39 "For [a]the promise is for you and your children and for all who are [b]far off, as many as the Lord our God will call to Himself."

40 And with many other words he solemnly [a]testified and kept on exhorting them, saying, "[1]Be saved from this [b]perverse generation!"

41 So then, those who had received his word were baptized; and that day there were added about three thousand [1a]souls.

42 They were [a]continually devoting themselves to the apostles' teaching and to fellowship, to [b]the breaking of bread and [1a]to prayer.

43 [1]Everyone kept feeling a sense of awe; and many [a]wonders and [2]signs were taking place through the apostles.

44 And all those who had believed [1]were together and [a]had all things in common;

45 and they [a]*began* selling their property and possessions and were sharing them with all, as anyone might have need.

46 [a]Day by day continuing with one mind in the temple, and [b]breaking bread [1]from house to house, they were taking their [2]meals together with gladness and [3]sincerity of heart,

47 praising God and [a]having favor with all the people. And the Lord [b]was adding [1]to

30 [1]Lit *of the fruit of his loins* [a]Matt 22:43 [b]Ps 132:11; 2 Sam 7:12f; Ps 89:3f **31** [1]I.e. the Messiah [2]Lit *see corruption* [a]Matt 11:23; Acts 2:27 **32** [a]Acts 2:24; 3:15, 26; 4:10; 5:30; 10:40; 13:30, 33, 34, 37; 17:31; Rom 4:24; 6:4; 8:11; 10:9; 1 Cor 6:14; 15:15; 2 Cor 4:14; Gal 1:1; Eph 1:20; Col 2:12; 1 Thess 1:10; Heb 13:20; 1 Pet 1:21 [b]Acts 1:8 **33** [1]Or *by* [a]Mark 16:19; Acts 5:31 [b]Acts 1:4 [c]John 7:39; Gal 3:14 [d]Acts 2:17; 10:45 **34** [1]Lit *the heavens* [a]Ps 110:1; Matt 22:44f **36** [1]I.e. Messiah [a]Ezek 36:22, 32, 37; 45:6 [b]Acts 2:23 [c]Luke 2:11 **37** [1]Or *wounded in conscience* [2]Lit *Men brothers* [3]Or *what are we to do* [a]Luke 3:10, 12, 14 **38** [a]Mark 1:15; Luke 24:47; Acts 3:19; 5:31; 20:21 [b]Mark 16:16; Acts 8:12, 16; 22:16 **39** [a]Is 44:3; 54:13; 57:19; Joel 2:32; Rom 9:4; Eph 2:12 [b]Eph 2:13, 17 **40** [1]Or *Escape* [a]Luke 16:28 [b]Deut 32:5; Matt 17:17; Phil 2:15 **41** [1]I.e. persons [a]Acts 3:23; 7:14; 27:37; Rom 13:1; 1 Pet 3:20; Rev 16:3 **42** [1]Lit *the prayers* [a]Acts 1:14 [b]Luke 24:30; Acts 2:46; 20:7; 1 Cor 10:16 **43** [1]Lit *fear was occurring to every soul* [2]Or *attesting miracles* [a]Acts 2:22 **44** [1]One early ms does not contain *were* and *and* [a]Acts 4:32, 37; 5:2 **45** [a]Matt 19:21; Acts 4:34 **46** [1]Or *in the various private homes* [2]Lit *food* [3]Or *simplicity* [a]Acts 5:42 [b]Luke 24:30; Acts 2:42; 20:7; 1 Cor 10:16 **47** [1]Lit *together* [a]Acts 5:13 [b]Acts 2:41; 4:4; 5:14; 6:1, 7; 9:31, 35, 42; 11:21, 24; 14:1, 21; 16:5; 17:12

2:33 *promise of the Holy Spirit.* See note on 1:4. *has poured forth.* See v. 17; Joel 2:28.

2:34 *THE LORD SAID TO MY LORD.* The Lord (God) said to my Lord (the Son of David, the Messiah). According to Peter, David addressed his descendant with uncommon respect because he, through the inspiration of the Spirit, recognized how great and divine He would be (Matt 22:41–45). Not only was He to be resurrected (vv. 31–32) but He was to be exalted to God's right hand (vv. 33–35). And His presence there was now being demonstrated by the sending of the Holy Spirit (v. 33; John 16:7). See also note on Ps 110:1.

2:37 *pierced to the heart.* Reflects both belief in Jesus and regret over former rejection.

2:38 *Repent, and . . . be baptized.* Repentance was important in the message of the forerunner, John the Baptist (Mark 1:4; Luke 3:3), in the preaching of Jesus (Mark 1:15; Luke 13:3) and in the directions Jesus left just before His ascension (Luke 24:47). So also baptism was important to John the Baptizer (Mark 1:4), in the instructions of Jesus (Matt 28:18–19) and in the preaching recorded in Acts—where it was associated with belief (8:12; 18:8), acceptance of the word (v. 41) and repentance (here). *in the name of Jesus Christ.* Not a contradiction to the fuller formula given in Matt 28:19. In Acts the abbreviated form emphasizes the distinctive quality of this baptism, for Jesus is now included in a way that He was not in John's baptism (19:4–5). *for the forgiveness of your sins.* Not that baptism effects forgiveness. Rather, forgiveness comes through that which is symbolized by baptism (see Rom 6:3–4 and note). *Holy Spirit.* Two gifts are now given: the forgiveness of sins (see also 22:16) and the Holy Spirit. The promise of the indwelling gift of the Holy Spirit is given to all Christians (cf. Rom 8:9–11; 1 Cor 12:13).

2:41 *there were added.* Added to the number of believers.

2:42 *apostles' teaching.* Included all that Jesus Himself taught (Matt 28:20), especially the gospel, which was centered in His death, burial and resurrection (see vv. 23–24; 3:15; 4:10; 1 Cor 15:1–4). It was a unique teaching in that it came from God and was clothed with the authority conferred on the apostles (2 Cor 13:10; 1 Thess 4:2). Today it is available in the books of the NT. *fellowship.* The corporate fellowship of believers in worship. *breaking of bread.* Although this phrase is used of an ordinary meal in v. 46 (see Luke 24:30,35), the Lord's Supper seems to be indicated here (see note on 20:7; cf. 1 Cor 10:16; 11:20). *prayer.* Acts emphasizes the importance of prayer in the Christian life—private as well as public (1:14; 3:1; 6:4; 10:4,31; 12:5; 16:13,16).

2:44 *those who had believed were together.* The unity of the early church. *all things in common.* See 4:34–35. This was a voluntary sharing to provide for those who did not have enough for the essentials of living (see good and bad examples of sharing, 4:36–5:9).

2:46 *breaking bread from house to house.* Here the daily life of Christians is described, distinguishing their activity in the temple from that in their homes, where they ate their meals—not the Lord's Supper—with gladness and generosity. *gladness and sincerity of heart.* The fellowship, oneness and sharing enjoyed in the early church are fruits of the Spirit. Joy is to be the mood of the believer (see note on 16:34).

3:1 *Peter and John.* Among the foremost apostles (Gal 2:9).

their number day by day [c]those who were
being saved.

Healing the Lame Beggar

3 Now [a]Peter and John were going up to
the temple at the [1]ninth *hour,* [b]the hour
of prayer.
2 And [a]a man who had been lame from
his mother's womb was being carried along,
whom they [b]used to set down every day at
the gate of the temple which is called Beautiful, [c]in order to beg [1]alms of those who
were entering the temple.
3 When he saw [a]Peter and John about to
go into the temple, he *began* asking to
receive alms.
4 But Peter, along with John, [a]fixed his
gaze on him and said, "Look at us!"
5 And he *began* to give them his attention,
expecting to receive something from them.
6 But Peter said, "I do not possess silver
and gold, but what I do have I give to you:
[a]In the name of Jesus Christ the Nazarene—
walk!"
7 And seizing him by the right hand, he
raised him up; and immediately his feet and
his ankles were strengthened.
8 [1a]With a leap he stood upright and
began to walk; and he entered the temple
with them, walking and leaping and praising
God.
9 And [a]all the people saw him walking
and praising God;
10 and they were taking note of him as
being the one who used to [a]sit at the Beautiful Gate of the temple to *beg* alms, and they
were filled with wonder and amazement at
what had happened to him.

Peter's Second Sermon

11 While he was clinging to [a]Peter and
John, all the people ran together to them at
the so-called [1b]portico of Solomon, full of
amazement.
12 But when Peter saw *this,* he replied to
the people, "Men of Israel, why are you
amazed at this, or why do you gaze at us, as
if by our own power or piety we had made
him walk?
13 "[a]The God of Abraham, Isaac and Jacob,
[b]the God of our fathers, has glorified His
[1c]servant Jesus, *the one* whom [d]you delivered and disowned in the presence of [e]Pilate,
when he had [f]decided to release Him.
14 "But you disowned [a]the Holy and Righteous One and [b]asked for a murderer to be
granted to you,
15 but put to death the [1a]Prince of life, *the
one* whom [b]God raised from the dead, *a fact*
to which we are [c]witnesses.
16 "And on the basis of faith [a]in His name,
it is [1]the name of Jesus which has strengthened this man whom you see and know; and
the faith which *comes* through Him has giv-
en him this perfect health in the presence of
you all.
17 "And now, brethren, I know that you
acted [a]in ignorance, just as your [b]rulers did
also.
18 "But the things which [a]God announced
beforehand by the mouth of all the prophets,
[b]that His [1]Christ would suffer, He has thus
fulfilled.
19 "Therefore [a]repent and return, so that
your sins may be wiped away, in order that
[b]times of refreshing may come from the presence of the Lord;
20 and that He may send Jesus, the
[1]Christ appointed for you,
21 [a]whom heaven must receive until *the*
[1]period of [b]restoration of all things about

47 [c]1 Cor 1:18
3:1 [1]I.e. 3 p.m. [a]Luke 22:8; Acts 3:3, 4, 11 [b]Ps 55:17; Matt 27:45; Acts 10:30
2 [1]Or *a gift of charity* [a]Acts 14:8 [b]Luke 16:20 [c]John 9:8; Acts 3:10
3 [a]Luke 22:8; Acts 3:1, 4, 11
4 [a]Acts 10:4
6 [a]Acts 2:22; 3:16; 4:10
8 [1]Lit *leaping up* [a]Acts 14:10
9 [a]Acts 4:16, 21
10 [a]John 9:8; Acts 3:2
11 [a]Luke 22:8; Acts 3:3, 4
11 [1]Or *colonnade* [b]John 10:23; Acts 5:12
13 [1]Or *Son* [a]Matt 22:32 [b]Ex 3:13, 15; Acts 5:30; 7:32; 22:14 [c]Acts 3:26; 4:27, 30 [d]Matt 20:19; John 19:11; Acts 2:23 [e]Matt 27:2 [f]Luke 23:4
14 [a]Mark 1:24; Acts 4:27; 7:52; 2 Cor 5:21 [b]Matt 27:20; Mark 15:11; Luke 23:18, 25
15 [1]Or *Author* [a]Acts 5:31; Heb 2:10; 12:2 [b]Acts 2:24 [c]Luke 24:48
16 [1]Lit *His name* [a]Acts 3:6
17 [a]Luke 23:34; John 15:21; Acts 13:27; 26:9; Eph 4:18 [b]Luke 23:13
18 [1]Or *Anointed One;* i.e. Messiah [a]Acts 2:23 [b]Luke 24:27; Acts 17:3; 26:23

19 [a]Acts 2:38; 26:20 [b]2 Thess 1:7; Heb 4:1ff **20** [1]Or *Anointed One;* i.e. Messiah **21** [1]Lit *periods, times* [a]Acts 1:11 [b]Matt 17:11; Rom 8:21

Along with John's brother, James, they had been especially close to Jesus (Mark 9:2; 13:3; 14:33; Luke 22:8). Arrested together (4:3), they were also together in Samaria (8:14). *the hour of prayer.* The three stated times of prayer for later Judaism were midmorning (the third hour, 9:00 A.M.), the time of the evening sacrifice (the ninth hour, 3:00 P.M.) and sunset.

3:2 *gate . . . called Beautiful.* The favorite entrance to the temple court, it was probably the bronze-sheathed gate that is elsewhere called the Nicanor Gate. Apparently it led from the court of the Gentiles to the court of women, on the east wall of the temple proper.

3:6 *In the name of Jesus Christ.* Not by power of their own, but by the authority of the Messiah.

3:7 *he raised him up.* But he had faith to be healed (v. 16).

3:8 *entered the temple.* From the outer court (for Gentiles also) into the court of women, containing the treasury (Mark 12:41–44), and then into the court of Israel (see map No. 8 at the end of the Study Bible). From the outer court, nine gates led into the inner courts.

3:11 *portico of Solomon.* A porch along the inner side of the wall enclosing the outer court, with rows of 27-foot-high stone columns and a roof of cedar (see note on John 10:23).

3:12–26 See note on 2:14–40.

3:13 *His servant Jesus.* A reminder of the suffering servant prophesied in Is 52:13–53:12 (see Matt 12:18; Acts 4:27,30). *whom you . . . disowned.* Voted against Jesus, spurned Him, denied Him and refused to acknowledge Him as the true Messiah. *Pilate . . . had decided to release Him.* See John 19:12.

3:14 *Holy and Righteous One.* Blameless in relation to God and man.

3:15 *put to death . . . God raised . . . we are witnesses.* A recurring theme in the speeches of Acts (see 2:23–24; 4:10; 5:30–32; 10:39–41; 13:28–29; cf. 1 Cor 15:1–4).

3:18 *announced beforehand by . . . all the prophets.* Echoes what Jesus had said (Luke 24:26–27). The suffering was prophesied (compare Is 53:7–8 with Acts 8:32–33; Ps 2:1–2 with Acts 4:25–26; Ps 22:1 with Matt 27:46; see also 1 Pet 1:11).

3:19 *repent.* Repentance is a change of mind and will arising from sorrow for sin and leading to transformation of life (see note on 2:38). *return.* Subsequent to repentance and not completely identical with it. See 11:21 ("number who believed turned") and 26:20 ("repent and turn"; see also 9:35; 14:15; 15:19; 26:18; 28:27). In the strictest sense, repentance is turning from sin, and faith is turning to God. However, the word "turn" is not always used with such precision. *your sins . . . wiped away.* Your sins will be forgiven as a result of repentance.

which [c]God spoke by the mouth of His holy
prophets from ancient time.
22 "Moses said, '[a]THE LORD GOD WILL RAISE
UP FOR YOU A PROPHET [1]LIKE ME FROM YOUR
BRETHREN; TO HIM YOU SHALL GIVE HEED to
everything He says to you.
23 '[a]And it will be that every [b]soul that
does not heed that prophet [c]shall be utterly
destroyed from among the people.'
24 "And likewise, [a]all the prophets who
have spoken, from Samuel and *his* successors onward, also announced these days.
25 "It is you who are [a]the sons of the
prophets and of the [b]covenant which God
[1]made with your fathers, saying to Abraham,
'[c]AND IN YOUR SEED ALL THE FAMILIES OF THE
EARTH SHALL BE BLESSED.'
26 "For you [a]first, God [b]raised up His [1]Ser-
vant and sent Him to bless you by turning
every one *of you* from your wicked ways."

Peter and John Arrested

4 As they were speaking to the people, the
priests and [a]the captain of the temple
guard and [b]the Sadducees [c]came up to them,
2 being greatly disturbed because they
were teaching the people and proclaiming
[1a]in Jesus the resurrection from the dead.
3 And they laid hands on them and [a]put
them in jail until the next day, for it was
already evening.
4 But many of those who had heard the
[1]message believed; and [a]the number of the
men came to be about five thousand.
5 On the next day, their [a]rulers and elders and scribes were gathered together in
Jerusalem;
6 and [a]Annas the high priest *was there,*
and [b]Caiaphas and John and Alexander, and
all who were of high-priestly descent.
7 When they had placed them in the center, they *began to* inquire, "By what power,
or in what name, have you done this?"
8 Then Peter, [1a]filled with the Holy Spirit, said to them, "[2b]Rulers and elders of the
people,
9 if we are [1]on trial today for [a]a benefit
done to a sick man, [2]as to how this man has
been made well,
10 let it be known to all of you and to all
the people of Israel, that [1a]by the name of
Jesus Christ the Nazarene, whom you crucified, whom [b]God raised from the dead—[1]by
[2]this *name* this man stands here before you
in good health.
11 "[1a]He is the [b]STONE WHICH WAS [c]REJECTED
by you, THE BUILDERS, *but* WHICH BECAME THE
CHIEF CORNER *stone.*
12 "And there is salvation in [a]no one else;
for there is no other name under heaven that
has been given among men by which we
must be saved."

Threat and Release

13 Now as they observed the [a]confidence
of [b]Peter and John and understood that they
were uneducated and untrained men, they
were amazed, and [c]*began* to recognize them
[1]as having been with Jesus.
14 And seeing the man who had been
healed standing with them, they had nothing
to say in reply.
15 But when they had ordered them to

21 [c]Luke 1:70
22 [1]Or *as He raised up me* [a]Deut 18:15, 18; Acts 7:37
23 [a]Deut 18:19 [b]Acts 2:41 [c]Lev 23:29
24 [a]Luke 24:27; Acts 17:3; 26:23
25 [1]Lit *covenanted* [a]Acts 2:39 [b]Rom 9:4f [c]Gen 22:18
26 [1]Or *Son* [a]Matt 15:24; John 4:22; Acts 13:46; Rom 1:16; 2:9f [b]Acts 2:24
4:1 [a]Luke 22:4 [b]Matt 3:7 [c]Luke 20:1; Acts 6:12
2 [1]Or *in the case of* [a]Acts 3:15; 17:18
3 [a]Acts 5:18
4 [1]Lit *word* [a]Acts 2:41
5 [a]Luke 23:13; Acts 4:8
6 [a]Luke 3:2 [b]Matt 26:3
8 [1]Or *having just been filled* [2]Lit *Rulers of the people and elders* [a]Acts 2:4; 13:9 [b]Luke 23:13; Acts 4:5
9 [1]Lit *answering* [2]Or *by whom* [a]Acts 3:7f
10 [1]Or *in* [2]Or *Him* [a]Acts 2:22; 3:6 [b]Acts 2:24
11 [1]Lit *This One* [a]Matt 21:42 [b]Ps 118:22 [c]Mark 9:12
12 [a]Matt 1:21; Acts 10:43; 1 Tim 2:5
13 [1]Lit *that they had been* [a]Acts 4:31 [b]Luke 22:8; Acts 4:19 [c]John 7:15

3:22–26 RAISE UP . . . *raised up.* Christ is the fulfillment of prophecies made relative to Moses, David and Abraham. He was to be a prophet like Moses (vv. 22–23), He was foretold in Samuel's declarations concerning David (v. 24; see note there), and He was to bring blessing to all people as promised to Abraham (vv. 25–26).

3:24 *prophets . . . from Samuel . . . onward.* Samuel anointed David to be king and spoke of the establishment of his kingdom (1 Sam 16:13; cf. 13:14; 15:28; 28:17). Nathan's prophecy (2 Sam 7:12–16) was ultimately Messianic (see Acts 13:22–23, 34; Heb 1:5).

3:25 SEED. The word is singular, ultimately signifying Christ (see Gal 3:16).

4:1 *priests.* Those who were serving that week in the temple precincts (see note on Luke 1:23). *captain of the temple guard.* A member of one of the leading priestly families; next in rank to the high priest (see 5:24,26; Luke 22:4,52). *Sadducees.* A Jewish sect whose members came from the priestly line and controlled the temple. They did not believe in the resurrection or a personal Messiah, but held that the Messianic age—an ideal time—was then present and must be preserved. The high priest, one of their number, presided over the Sanhedrin (see 5:17; 23:6–8; Matt 22:23–33). See also notes on Matt 3:7; Mark 12:18; Luke 20:27.

4:3 *evening.* The evening sacrifices ended about 4:00 P.M., and the temple gates would be closed at that time. Any judgments involving life and death must be begun and concluded in daylight hours.

4:4 *men.* Lit. "males." *five thousand.* A growth from the 3,000 at Pentecost (2:41); see later growth (5:14; 6:7).

4:5 *rulers and elders and scribes.* The three groups making up the Sanhedrin, Israel's supreme court (see Luke 22:66; see also notes on Matt 2:4; 15:2; Mark 14:55; Luke 5:17).

4:6 *Annas.* High priest A.D. 6–15, but deposed by the Romans and succeeded by his son, Eleazar, then by his son-in-law, Caiaphas (18–36), who was also called Joseph. However, Annas was still recognized by the Jews as high priest (Luke 3:2; cf. John 18:13, 24). *John.* May be Jonathan son of Annas, who was appointed high priest in A.D. 36. Others suggest it was Johanan ben Zaccai, who became the president of the Great Synagogue after the fall of Jerusalem. *Alexander.* Not further identified.

4:8 *filled with the Holy Spirit.* See note on 2:4.

4:11 *the* STONE . . . REJECTED. Fulfillment of prophecy was an important element in early Christian sermons and defenses. Jesus had also used Ps 118:22 (Matt 21:42; see 1 Pet 2:7 and cf. Rom 9:33; Is 28:16).

4:12 *no other name.* See 10:43; John 14:6; 1 Tim 2:5; see also note on Matt 1:21.

4:13 *confidence.* A certain boldness characterized by the assurance, authority and forthrightness of the apostles (2:29; 4:29; 28:31), and shared by the believers (4:31). *uneducated and untrained men.* Peter and John had not been trained in the rabbinic schools, nor did they hold official positions in recognized religious circles.

leave the [1a]Council, they *began* to confer
with one another,
16 saying, "[a]What shall we do with these
men? For the fact that a [b]noteworthy [1]mira-
cle has taken place through them is apparent
to all who live in Jerusalem, and we cannot
deny it.
17 "But so that it will not spread any further among the people, let us warn them to
speak no longer to any man [a]in this name."
18 And when they had summoned them,
they [a]commanded them not to speak or
teach at all [1]in the name of Jesus.
19 But [a]Peter and John answered and said
to them, "[b]Whether it is right in the sight of
God to give heed to you rather than to God,
you be the judge;
20 for [a]we cannot stop speaking about
what we have seen and heard."
21 When they had threatened them further, they let them go (finding no basis on
which to punish them) [a]on account of the
people, because they were all [b]glorifying God
for what had happened;
22 for the man was more than forty years
old on whom this [1]miracle of healing had
been performed.
23 When they had been released, they
went to their own *companions* and reported
all that the chief priests and the elders had
said to them.
24 And when they heard *this*, they lifted
their voices to God with one accord and said,
"O [1]Lord, it is You who [a]MADE THE HEAVEN AND
THE EARTH AND THE SEA, AND ALL THAT IS IN
THEM,
25 who [a]by the Holy Spirit, *through* the
mouth of our father David Your servant,
said,

'[b]WHY DID THE [1]GENTILES RAGE,
AND THE PEOPLES DEVISE FUTILE THINGS?
26 '[a]THE KINGS OF THE EARTH [1]TOOK THEIR
STAND,
AND THE RULERS WERE GATHERED TOGETHER
AGAINST THE LORD AND AGAINST HIS
[2b]CHRIST.'

27 "For truly in this city there were gathered together against Your holy [1a]servant
Jesus, whom You anointed, both [b]Herod and
[c]Pontius Pilate, along with [d]the [2]Gentiles and
the peoples of Israel,
28 to do whatever Your hand and [a]Your
purpose predestined to occur.
29 "And [1]now, Lord, take note of their
threats, and grant that Your bond-servants
may [a]speak Your word with all [b]confidence,
30 while You extend Your hand to heal,
and [1a]signs and wonders take place through
the name of Your holy [2b]servant Jesus."
31 And when they had prayed, the [a]place
where they had gathered together was shak-
en, and they were all [b]filled with the Holy
Spirit and *began* to [c]speak the word of God
with [d]boldness.

Sharing among Believers

32 And the [1]congregation of those who
believed were of one heart and soul; and not
one *of them* [2]claimed that anything belonging to him was his own, but [a]all things were
common property to them.
33 And [a]with great power the apostles
were giving [b]testimony to the resurrection of
the Lord Jesus, and abundant grace was
upon them all.
34 For there was not a needy person
among them, for all who were owners of
land or houses [a]would sell them and bring
the [1]proceeds of the sales
35 and [a]lay them at the apostles' feet, and
they would be [b]distributed to each as any
had need.
36 Now Joseph, a Levite of [a]Cyprian birth,
who was also called [b]Barnabas by the apostles (which translated means Son of
[1c]Encouragement),
37 and who owned a tract of land, sold it
and brought the money and [a]laid it at the
apostles' feet.

15 [1]Or *Sanhedrin* [a]Matt 5:22
16 [1]Or *sign* [a]John 11:47 [b]Acts 3:7-10
17 [a]John 15:21
18 [1]Or *on the basis of* [a]Acts 5:28f
19 [a]Acts 4:13 [b]Acts 5:28f
20 [a]1 Cor 9:16
21 [a]Acts 5:26 [b]Matt 9:8
22 [1]Or *sign*
24 [1]Or *Master* [a]Ex 20:11; Neh 9:6; Ps 146:6
25 [1]Or *nations* [a]Acts 1:16 [b]Ps 2:1
26 [1]Or *approached* [2]Or *Anointed One;* i.e. Messiah [a]Ps 2:2 [b]Dan 9:24f; Luke 4:18; Acts 10:38; Heb 1:9
27 [1]Or *Son* [2]Or *nations* [a]Acts 3:13; 4:30 [b]Matt 14:1; Luke 23:7-11 [c]Matt 27:2; Mark 15:1; Luke 23:1, 12; John 18:28, 29 [d]Matt 20:19
28 [a]Acts 2:23
29 [1]Or *as for the present situation* [a]Phil 1:14 [b]Acts 4:13, 31; 14:3
30 [1]Or *attesting miracles* [2]Or *Son* [a]John 4:48 [b]Acts 3:13; 4:27
31 [a]Acts 2:1 [b]Acts 2:4 [c]Phil 1:14 [d]Acts 4:13; 14:3
32 [1]Or *multitude* [2]Lit *was saying* [a]Acts 2:44
33 [a]Acts 1:8 [b]Luke 24:48
34 [1]Lit *the prices of the things being sold* [a]Matt 19:21; Acts 2:45
35 [a]Acts 4:37; 5:2 [b]Acts 2:45; 6:1
36 [1]Or *Exhortation* or *Consolation* [a]Acts 11:19f; 13:4; 15:39; 21:3, 16; 27:4 [b]Acts 9:27; 11:22, 30; 12:25; 13:1, 2, 7; 1 Cor 9:6; Gal 2:1, 9, 13; Col 4:10 [c]Acts 2:40; 11:23; 13:15; 1 Cor 14:3; 1 Thess 2:3
37 [a]Acts 4:35; 5:2

4:20 *cannot stop speaking.* See 5:29.
4:23 *went.* Probably to the same upper room where the apostles had met before (1:13) and where the congregation may have continued to meet (12:12).
4:27 *Herod.* Herod Antipas, tetrarch of Galilee and Perea (Luke 23:7–15). *Pontius Pilate.* Roman procurator of Judea (Luke 23:1–24).
4:28 *predestined.* Not that God had compelled them to act as they did, but He willed to use them and their freely chosen acts to accomplish His saving purpose.
4:30 *holy servant.* See note on 3:13.
4:31 *was shaken.* An immediate sign that the prayers had been heard (see 16:26). *filled with the Holy Spirit.* See note on 2:4. *speak the word of God.* They continued preaching the gospel despite the warnings of the council (see note on v. 13).
4:32 *one in heart and soul.* In complete accord, extending to their attitude toward personal possessions (see 2:44).
4:33 *testimony to the resurrection.* As significant as the death of Christ was, the most compelling event was the resurrection—an event about which the disciples could not keep silent.
4:34 *all who were owners of land or houses would sell them.* See note on 2:44.
4:36 *Levite.* Although Levites owned no inherited land in the Holy Land, these regulations may not have applied to the Levites in other countries (Cyprus). So perhaps Barnabas sold land he owned in Cyprus and brought the proceeds to the apostles (v. 37). Or he may have been married, and the land sold may have been from his wife's property. It is also possible that the prohibition against Levite ownership of land in the Holy Land was no longer observed. *of Cyprian birth.* Cyprus was an island in the eastern part of the Mediterranean Sea. Jews had settled there from Maccabean times. *Barnabas.* Used here as a good example of giving. In this way Luke introduces the one who will become an important companion of Paul (see 13:1–4). For other significant contributions of this greathearted leader to the life and ministry of the early church see 9:27; 11:22,25; 15:37–39.

Fate of Ananias and Sapphira

5 But a man named Ananias, with his wife
Sapphira, sold a piece of property,
2 and [a]kept back *some* of the price for
himself, with his wife's [1]full knowledge, and
bringing a portion of it, he [b]laid it at the
apostles' feet.
3 But Peter said, "Ananias, why has
[a]Satan filled your heart to lie [b]to the Holy
Spirit and to [c]keep back *some* of the price of
the land?
4 "While it remained *unsold,* did it not
remain your own? And after it was sold, was
it not [1]under your control? Why is it that you
have [2]conceived this deed in your heart? You
have not lied to men but [a]to God."
5 And as he heard these words, Ananias
[a]fell down and breathed his last; and [b]great
fear came over all who heard of it.
6 The young men got up and [a]covered
him up, and after carrying him out, they
buried him.
7 Now there elapsed an interval of about
three hours, and his wife came in, not knowing what had happened.
8 And Peter responded to her, "Tell me
whether you sold the land [1a]for such and
such a price?" And she said, "Yes, [1]that was
the price."
9 Then Peter *said* to her, "Why is it that
you have agreed together to [a]put [b]the Spirit
of the Lord to the test? Behold, the feet of
those who have buried your husband are at
the door, and they will carry you out *as well.*"
10 And immediately she [a]fell at his feet
and breathed her last, and the young men
came in and found her dead, and they carried her out and buried her beside her husband.
11 And [a]great fear came over the whole
church, and over all who heard of these
things.
12 [1]At the hands of the apostles many
[a]signs and wonders were taking place
among the people; and they were all with
one accord in [b]Solomon's portico.
13 But none of the rest dared to associate
with them; however, [a]the people held them
in high esteem.
14 And all the more [a]believers in the Lord,
multitudes of men and women, were constantly [b]added to *their number,*
15 to such an extent that they even carried
the sick out into the streets and laid them on
cots and pallets, so that when Peter came by
[a]at least his shadow might fall on any one of
them.
16 Also the [1]people from the cities in the
vicinity of Jerusalem were coming together,
bringing people who were sick [2]or afflicted
with unclean spirits, and they were all being
healed.

Imprisonment and Release

17 But the high priest rose up, along with
all his associates (that is [a]the sect of [b]the
Sadducees), and they were filled with jealousy.
18 They laid hands on the apostles and
[a]put them in a public jail.
19 But during the night [a]an angel of the
Lord opened the gates of the prison, and taking them out he said,
20 "Go, stand and [1]speak to the people in
the temple [2a]the whole message of this Life."

5:2 [1]Or *collusion* [a]Acts 5:3 [b]Acts 4:35, 37
3 [a]Matt 4:10; Luke 22:3; John 13:2, 27 [b]Acts 5:4, 9 [c]Acts 5:2
4 [1]Or *in your authority* [2]Lit *placed* [a]Acts 5:3, 9
5 [a]Ezek 11:13; Acts 5:10 [b]Acts 2:43; 5:11
6 [a]John 19:40
8 [1]Lit *for so much* [a]Acts 5:2
9 [a]Acts 15:10 [b]Acts 5:3, 4
10 [a]Ezek 11:13; Acts 5:5
11 [a]Acts 2:43; 5:5
12 [1]Lit *Through* [a]John 4:48 [b]John 10:23; Acts 3:11
13 [a]Acts 2:47; 4:21
14 [a]2 Cor 6:15 [b]Acts 2:47; 11:24
15 [a]Acts 19:12
16 [1]Lit *multitude* [2]Lit *and*
17 [a]Acts 15:5 [b]Matt 3:7; Acts 4:1
18 [a]Acts 4:3
19 [a]Matt 1:20, 24; 2:13, 19; 28:2; Luke 1:11; 2:9; Acts 8:26; 10:3; 12:7, 23; 27:23
20 [1]Or *continue to speak* [2]Lit *all the words* [a]John 6:63, 68

5:1 *Ananias . . . Sapphira.* Given as bad examples of sharing (Barnabas was the good example; see note on 4:36). Love of praise for (pretended) generosity and love for money led to the first recorded sin in the life of the church. It is a warning to the readers that "God is not mocked" (Gal 6:7). Compare this divine judgment at the beginning of the church era with God's judgments on Nadab and Abihu (Lev 10:2), on Achan (Josh 7:25) and on Uzzah (2 Sam 6:7).
5:2 *kept back some.* They had a right to keep back whatever they chose, but to make it appear that they had given all when they had not was sinful.
5:3 *Satan filled your heart.* The continuing activity of Satan is noted (see Luke 22:3; John 13:2,27; 1 Pet 5:8). *lie to the Holy Spirit.* A comparison with v. 4 shows that the Holy Spirit is regarded as God Himself present with His people.
5:9 *to put the Spirit of the Lord to the test.* If no dire consequences had followed this act of sin, the results among the believers would have been serious when the deceit became known. Not only would dishonesty appear profitable, but the conclusion that the Spirit could be deceived would follow. It was important to set the course properly at the outset in order to leave no doubt that God will not tolerate such hypocrisy and deceit.
5:11 *church.* The first use of the term in Acts. It can denote either the local congregation (8:1; 11:22; 13:1) or the universal church (see 20:28). The Greek word for "church" (*ekklesia*) was already being used for political and other assemblies (see 19:32,40) and, in the Septuagint (the Greek translation of the OT), for Israel when gathered in religious assembly.
5:12 *Solomon's portico.* See note on 3:11.
5:13 *none of the rest dared to associate with them.* Because of the fate of Ananias and his wife, no pretenders or halfhearted followers risked identification with the believers. Luke cannot mean that no one joined the Christian community, since v. 14 indicates that many were coming to Christ.
5:14 *multitudes of men and women, were . . . added.* See 4:4. This is the first specific mention of women believing (cf. 8:3,12; 9:2; 13:50; 16:1,13–14; 17:4,12,34; 18:2; 21:5; but cf. also 1:14).
5:15 *Peter . . . his shadow.* Parallels such items as Paul's handkerchiefs (19:12) and the edge of Jesus' cloak (Matt 9:20)—not that any of these material objects had magical qualities, but the least article or shadow represented a direct means of contact with Jesus or His apostles.
5:17 *high priest.* The official high priest recognized by Rome was Caiaphas, but the Jews considered Annas, Caiaphas's father-in-law, to be the actual high priest since the high priesthood was to be held for life (see note on 4:6). *his associates.* His family members. *sect of the Sadducees.* See note on 4:1.
5:18 *in a public jail.* To await trial the next day.
5:19 *angel of the Lord.* This phrase is used four other times in Acts: (1) Stephen speaks of him (7:30–38); (2) he guides Philip (8:26); (3) he liberates Peter (12:7–10); (4) he strikes down Herod (12:23). See also Matt 1:20–24; 2:13,19; 28:2; Luke 1:11–38; 2:9.

21 Upon hearing *this,* they entered into the temple [a]about daybreak and *began* to teach.

Now when [b]the high priest and his associates came, they called [c]the [1]Council together, even all the Senate of the sons of Israel, and sent *orders* to the prison house for them to be brought.

22 But [a]the officers who came did not find them in the prison; and they returned and reported back,

23 saying, "We found the prison house locked quite securely and the guards standing at the doors; but when we had opened up, we found no one inside."

24 Now when [a]the captain of the temple *guard* and the chief priests heard these words, they were greatly perplexed about them as to what [1]would come of this.

25 But someone came and reported to them, "The men whom you put in prison are standing in the temple and teaching the people!"

26 Then [a]the captain went along with [b]the officers and *proceeded* to bring them *back* without violence (for [c]they were afraid of the people, that they might be stoned).

27 When they had brought them, they stood them [1]before [a]the Council. The high priest questioned them,

28 saying, "We gave you [a]strict orders not to continue teaching in this name, and [1]yet, you have filled Jerusalem with your teaching and [b]intend to bring this man's blood upon us."

29 But Peter and the apostles answered, "[a]We must obey God rather than men.

30 "[a]The God of our fathers [b]raised up Jesus, [1]whom you had [c]put to death by hanging Him on a [2]cross.

31 "[a]He is the one whom God exalted [1]to His right hand as a [2b]Prince and a [c]Savior, to grant [d]repentance to Israel, and forgiveness of sins.

32 "And we are [a]witnesses [1]of these things; and [b]*so is* the Holy Spirit, whom God has given to those who obey Him."

Gamaliel's Counsel

33 But when they heard this, they were [a]cut [1]to the quick and intended to kill them.

34 But a Pharisee named [a]Gamaliel, a [b]teacher of the Law, respected by all the people, stood up in [c]the Council and gave orders to put the men outside for a short time.

35 And he said to them, "Men of Israel, take care what you propose to do with these men.

36 "For some time ago Theudas rose up, [a]claiming to be somebody, and a group of about four hundred men joined up with him. [1]But he was killed, and all who [2]followed him were dispersed and came to nothing.

37 "After this man, Judas of Galilee rose up in the days of [a]the census and drew away *some* people after him; he too perished, and all those who [1]followed him were scattered.

38 "So in the present case, I say to you, stay away from these men and let them alone, for if this plan or [1]action [a]is of men, it will be overthrown;

39 but if it is of God, you will not be able to overthrow them; or else you may even be found [a]fighting against God."

40 They [1]took his advice; and after calling the apostles in, they [a]flogged them and ordered them not to [2]speak in the name of Jesus, and *then* released them.

41 So they went on their way from the presence of the [1a]Council, [b]rejoicing that they had been considered worthy to suffer shame [c]for *His* name.

42 [a]And every day, in the temple and [1]from house to house, they [2]kept right on teaching and [3b]preaching Jesus *as* the [4]Christ.

Choosing of the Seven

6 Now [1]at this time while the [a]disciples were [b]increasing *in number,* a complaint

21 [1]Or *Sanhedrin* [a]John 8:2 [b]Acts 4:6 [c]Matt 5:22; Acts 5:27, 34, 41
22 [a]Matt 26:58; Acts 5:26
24 [1]Lit *this would become* [a]Acts 4:1; 5:26
26 [a]Acts 5:24 [b]Acts 5:22 [c]Acts 4:21; 5:13
27 [1]Lit *in* [a]Matt 5:22; Acts 5:21, 34, 41
28 [1]Lit *behold* [a]Acts 4:18 [b]Matt 23:35; 27:25; Acts 2:23, 36; 3:14f; 7:52
29 [a]Acts 4:19
30 [1]Or *on whom you had laid violent hands* [2]Lit *wood* [a]Acts 3:13 [b]Acts 2:24 [c]Acts 10:39; 13:29; Gal 3:13; 1 Pet 2:24
31 [1]Or *by* [2]Or *Leader* [a]Acts 2:33 [b]Acts 3:15 [c]Luke 2:11 [d]Luke 24:47; Acts 2:38
32 [1]One early ms adds *in Him* [a]Luke 24:48 [b]John 15:26; Acts 15:28; Rom 8:16; Heb 2:4
33 [1]Or *in their hearts* [a]Acts 2:37; 7:54
34 [a]Acts 22:3 [b]Luke 2:46; 5:17 [c]Acts 5:21
36 [1]Lit *Who was killed* [2]Lit *were obeying* [a]Acts 8:9; Gal 2:6; 6:3
37 [1]Lit *were obeying* [a]Luke 2:2
38 [1]Or *work* [a]Mark 11:30
39 [a]Prov 21:30; Acts 11:17
40 [1]Lit *were persuaded by him* [2]Lit *be speaking* [a]Matt 10:17
41 [1]Or *Sanhedrin* [a]Acts 5:21 [b]1 Pet 4:14, 16 [c]John 15:21
42 [1]Or *in the various private homes* [2]Lit *were not ceasing to* [3]Lit *telling the good news of* [4]I.e. Messiah [a]Acts 2:46 [b]Acts 8:35; 11:20; 17:18; Gal 1:16
6:1 [1]Lit *in these days* [a]Acts 11:26 [b]Acts 2:47; 6:7

5:21 *Council.* The supreme Jewish court, consisting of 70 to 100 men (71 being the proper number). They sat in a semicircle, backed by three rows of disciples of the "learned men," with the clerks of the court standing in front.

5:24 *captain of the temple guard.* See note on 4:1.

5:28 *bring this man's blood upon us.* Probably a reference to the apostles' repeated declaration that some of the Jews and some of their leaders had killed Jesus (2:23; 3:13–15; 4:10–11; cf. Matt 27:25).

5:30 *cross.* Or "tree," used to describe the cross (1 Pet 2:24; see Deut 21:22–23). Like its Hebrew counterpart, the Greek for this word could refer to a tree, a pole, a wooden beam or some similar object.

5:32 *so is the Holy Spirit . . . given to those who obey Him.* See John 15:26–27. The disciples' testimony was directed and confirmed by the Holy Spirit, who convicts the world through the word (John 16:8–11) and is given to those who respond to God with "the obedience of faith" (Rom 1:5; see note on 6:7).

5:34 *a Pharisee named Gamaliel.* The most famous Jewish teacher of his time and traditionally listed among the "heads of the schools." Possibly he was the grandson of Hillel. Like Hillel (see note on Matt 19:3), he was moderate in his views, a characteristic that is apparent in his cautious recommendation on this occasion. Saul (Paul) was one of his students (22:3).

5:36 *Theudas.* We know of him from no other historical source.

5:37 *Judas of Galilee.* The Jewish historian Josephus refers to him as a man from Gamala in Gaulanitis who refused to give tribute to Caesar. His revolt was crushed, but a movement, started in his time, may have lived on in the party of the Zealots (see 1:13 and note on Matt 10:4). *days of the census.* Not the first census of Quirinius, noted by Luke in his Gospel (2:2), but the one in A.D. 6.

5:40 *flogged.* Beaten with the Jewish penalty of "thirty-nine lashes" (2 Cor 11:24).

6:1 *the disciples were increasing in number.* A considerable length of time may have transpired since the end of ch. 5. The

arose on the part of the [2c]Hellenistic *Jews*
against the *native* [d]Hebrews, because their
[e]widows were being overlooked in [f]the daily
serving *of food.*
2 So the twelve summoned the [1]congre-
gation of the disciples and said, "It is not
desirable for us to neglect the word of God in
order to serve tables.
3 "Therefore, [a]brethren, select from
among you seven men of good reputation,
[b]full of the Spirit and of wisdom, whom we
may put in charge of this task.
4 "But we will [a]devote ourselves to prayer
and to the [1]ministry of the word."
5 The statement found approval with the
whole [1]congregation; and they chose [a]Ste-
phen, a man [b]full of faith and of the Holy
Spirit, and [c]Philip, Prochorus, Nicanor,
Timon, Parmenas and [2]Nicolas, a [3d]proselyte
from [e]Antioch.
6 And these they brought before the
apostles; and after [a]praying, they [b]laid their
hands on them.
7 [a]The word of God kept on spreading;
and [b]the number of the disciples continued
to increase greatly in Jerusalem, and a great
many of the priests were becoming obedient
to [c]the faith.
8 And Stephen, full of grace and power,
was performing great [a]wonders and [1]signs
among the people.
9 But some men from what was called
the Synagogue of the Freedmen, *including*
both [a]Cyrenians and [b]Alexandrians, and
some from [c]Cilicia and [1d]Asia, rose up and
argued with Stephen.
10 But they were unable to cope with the
wisdom and the Spirit with which he was
speaking.
11 Then they secretly induced men to say,
"We have heard him speak blasphemous
words against Moses and *against* God."

6:1 [2]Jews who adopted the Gr language and much of Gr culture through acculturation [c]Acts 9:29; 11:20 [d]2 Cor 11:22; Phil 3:5 [e]Acts 9:39, 41; 1 Tim 5:3 [f]Acts 4:35; 11:29 **2** [1]Lit *multitude* **3** [a]John 21:23; Acts 1:15 [b]Acts 2:4 **4** [1]Or *service* [a]Acts 1:14 **5** [1]Lit *multitude* [2]Gr *Nikolaos* [3]I.e. a Gentile convert to Judaism [a]Acts 6:8ff; 11:19; 22:20 [b]Acts 6:3; 11:24 [c]Acts 8:5ff; 21:8 [d]Matt 23:15 [e]Acts 11:19 **6** [a]Acts 1:24 [b]Num 8:10; 27:18; Deut 34:9; Mark 5:23; Acts 8:17ff; 9:17; 13:3; 19:6; 1 Tim 4:14; 2 Tim 1:6; Heb 6:2 **7** [a]Acts 12:24; 19:20 [b]Acts 6:1 [c]Acts 13:8; 14:22; Gal 1:23; 6:10; Jude 3, 20 **8** [1]Or *attesting miracles* [a]John 4:48 **9** [1]I.e. west coast province of Asia Minor [a]Matt 27:32; Acts 2:10 [b]Acts 18:24 [c]Acts 15:23, 41; 21:39; 22:3; 23:34; 27:5; Gal 1:21 [d]Acts 16:6; 19:10; 21:27; 24:18

church continued to grow (see 5:14), but this gave rise to inevitable problems, both from within (6:1–7) and from without (6:8–7:60). At this stage of its development, the church was entirely Jewish in its composition. However, there were two groups of Jews within the fellowship: 1. *Hellenistic Jews.* Hellenists—those born in lands other than the Holy Land who spoke the Greek language and were more Grecian than Hebraic in their attitudes and outlook. 2. *native Hebrews.* Those who spoke the Aramaic and/or Hebrew language(s) of the Holy Land and preserved Jewish culture and customs. *daily serving of food.* Help was needed by widows who had no one to care for them and so became the church's responsibility (cf. 4:35; 11:28–29; see also 1 Tim 5:3–16).

6:2 *the twelve.* At this early stage, the apostles were responsible for church life in general, including the ministry of the word of God and the care of the needy. *tables.* The early church was concerned about a spiritual ministry ("word of God" and "prayer"; see v. 4) and a material ministry ("serve tables").

6:3 *select . . . seven men.* The church elected them (v. 5), and the apostles "ordained" them (v. 6). In this way they were appointed to their work. *full of the Spirit.* See note on 2:4.

6:5 *they chose Stephen . . . Nicolas.* It is significant that all seven of the men chosen had Greek names. The murmuring had come from the Greek-speaking segment of the church; so those elected to care for the work came from their number so as to represent their interests fairly. Only Stephen and Philip of the Seven receive further notice (Stephen, 6:8–7:60; Philip, 8:5–40; 21:8–9). *a proselyte from Antioch.* It is significant that a proselyte was included in the number and that Luke points out his place of origin as Antioch, the city to which the gospel was soon to be taken and which was to become the "headquarters" for the forthcoming Gentile missionary effort.

6:6 *praying, they laid their hands on them.* Laying on of hands was used in the OT period to confer blessing (Gen 48:13–20), to transfer guilt from sinner to sacrifice (Lev 1:4) and to commission a person for a new responsibility (Num 27:23). In the NT period, laying on of hands was observed in healing (28:8; Mark 1:41), blessing (Mark 10:16), ordaining or commissioning (Acts 6:6; 13:3; 1 Tim 5:22) and imparting of spiritual gifts (Acts 8:17; 19:6; 1 Tim 4:14; 2 Tim 1:6). These seven men were appointed to responsibilities turned over to them by the twelve apostles. The Greek word used to describe their responsibility ("serve," v. 2) is the verb from which the noun "deacon" comes. Later one reads of deacons in Phil 1:1; 1 Tim 3:8–13. The Greek noun for "deacon" can also be translated "minister" or "servant." The men appointed on this occasion were simply called "the seven" (21:8), just as the apostles were called "the twelve." It is disputed whether these seven were the first deacons or were later replaced by deacons (see note on 1 Tim 3:8).

6:7 One of a series of progress reports given periodically throughout the book of Acts (1:15; 2:41; 4:4; 5:14; 6:7; 9:31; 12:24; 16:5; 19:20; 28:31). *a great many of the priests.* Though involved by lineage and life service in the priestly observances of the old covenant, they accepted the preaching of the apostles, which proclaimed a sacrifice that made the old sacrifices unnecessary (Heb 8:13; 10:1–4, 11–14). *were becoming obedient to the faith.* Responded to the commands of the gospel. To believe is to obey God. Faith itself is obedience, but faith also produces obedience (Rom 1:5; Eph 2:8–10; James 2:14–26).

6:8 *great wonders and signs.* Until now, Acts told of only the apostles working miracles (2:43; 3:4–8; 5:12). But now, after the laying on of the apostles' hands, Stephen too is reported as working miraculous signs. Philip also will soon do the same (8:6).

6:9 *some men . . . rose up and argued.* Since Saul was from Tarsus, this may have been the synagogue he attended, and he may have been among those who argued with Stephen. He was present when Stephen was stoned (7:58). *Freedmen.* Persons who had been freed from slavery. They came from different Hellenistic areas. *Cyrenians.* Cyrene was the chief city in Libya and north Africa (see note on 2:10), halfway between Alexandria and Carthage. One of its population groups was Jewish (see 11:19–21). *Alexandrians.* Alexandria was the capital of Egypt and second only to Rome in the empire. Two out of five districts in Alexandria were Jewish. *Cilicia.* A Roman province in the southeast corner of Asia Minor adjoining Syria. Tarsus, the birthplace of Paul, was one of its principal towns. *Asia.* A Roman province in the western part of Asia Minor. Ephesus, where Paul later ministered for a few years, was its capital.

6:11 *blasphemous words against Moses and against God.* Since Stephen declared that the worship of God was no longer to be restricted to the temple (7:48–49), his opponents twisted these words to trump up an accusation that Stephen was attacking the temple, the law, Moses and, ultimately, God.

12 And they stirred up the people, the elders and the scribes, and they [a]came up to him and dragged him away and brought him [1]before [b]the [2]Council.

13 They put forward [a]false witnesses who said, "This man incessantly speaks against this [b]holy place and the Law;

14 for we have heard him say that [a]this Nazarene, Jesus, will destroy this place and alter [b]the customs which Moses handed down to us."

15 And fixing their gaze on him, all who were sitting in the [1a]Council saw his face like the face of an angel.

Stephen's Defense

7 The high priest said, "Are these things so?"

2 And he said, "Hear me, [a]brethren and fathers! [b]The God of glory [c]appeared to our father Abraham when he was in Mesopotamia, before he lived in [1]Haran,

3 and said to him, '[a]LEAVE YOUR COUNTRY AND YOUR RELATIVES, AND COME INTO THE LAND THAT I WILL SHOW YOU.'

4 "[a]Then he left the land of the Chaldeans and settled in [1]Haran. [b]From there, after his father died, *God* had him move to this country in which you are now living.

5 "But He gave him no inheritance in it, not even a foot of ground, and *yet,* even when he had no child, [a]He promised that HE WOULD GIVE IT TO HIM AS A POSSESSION, AND TO HIS DESCENDANTS AFTER HIM.

6 "But [a]God spoke to this effect, that his DESCENDANTS WOULD BE ALIENS IN A FOREIGN LAND, AND THAT THEY WOULD [1]BE ENSLAVED AND MISTREATED FOR FOUR HUNDRED YEARS.

7 " 'AND WHATEVER NATION TO WHICH THEY WILL BE IN BONDAGE I MYSELF WILL JUDGE,' said God, 'AND [a]AFTER THAT THEY WILL COME OUT AND [1]SERVE ME IN THIS PLACE.'

8 "And He [a]gave him [1]the covenant of circumcision; and so [b]*Abraham* became the father of Isaac, and circumcised him on the eighth day; and [c]Isaac *became the father of* Jacob, and [d]Jacob *of* the twelve [e]patriarchs.

9 "The patriarchs [a]became jealous of Joseph and sold him into Egypt. *Yet* God was with him,

10 and rescued him from all his afflictions, and [a]granted him favor and wisdom in the sight of Pharaoh, king of Egypt, and he made him governor over Egypt and all his household.

11 "Now [a]a famine came over all Egypt and Canaan, and great affliction *with it,* and our fathers [1]could find no food.

12 "But [a]when Jacob heard that there was grain in Egypt, he sent our fathers *there* the first time.

13 "On the second *visit* [a]Joseph [1]made himself known to his brothers, and [b]Joseph's family was disclosed to Pharaoh.

14 "Then [a]Joseph sent *word* and invited Jacob his father and all his relatives to come to him, [b]seventy-five [1c]persons *in all.*

15 "And [a]Jacob went down to Egypt and *there* he and our fathers died.

16 "*From there* they were removed to [1a]Shechem and laid in the tomb which Abraham had purchased for a sum of money from the sons of [2]Hamor in [1]Shechem.

12 [1]Lit *into* [2]Or *Sanhedrin* [a]Luke 20:1; Acts 4:1 [b]Matt 5:22 **13** [a]Matt 26:59-61; Acts 7:58 [b]Matt 24:15; Acts 21:28; 25:8 **14** [a]Matt 26:61 [b]Acts 15:1; 21:21; 26:3; 28:17 **15** [1]Or *Sanhedrin* [a]Matt 5:22 **7:2** [1]Gr *Charran* [a]Acts 22:1 [b]Ps 29:3; 1 Cor 2:8 [c]Gen 11:31; 15:7 **3** [a]Gen 12:1 **4** [1]Gr *Charran* [a]Gen 11:31; 15:7 [b]Gen 12:4, 5 **5** [a]Gen 12:7; 13:15; 15:18; 17:8 **6** [1]Lit *enslave them and mistreat them* [a]Gen 15:13f **7** [1]Or *worship* [a]Ex 3:12 **8** [1]Or *a* [a]Gen 17:10ff [b]Gen 21:2-4 [c]Gen 25:26 [d]Gen 29:31ff; 30:5ff; 35:23ff [e]Acts 2:29 **9** [a]Gen 37:11, 28; 39:2, 21f; 45:4 **10** [a]Gen 39:21; 41:40-46; Ps 105:21 **11** [1]Lit *were not finding* [a]Gen 41:54f; 42:5 **12** [a]Gen 42:2 **13** [1]Or *was made known* [a]Gen 45:1-4 [b]Gen 45:16 **14** [1]Lit *souls* [a]Gen 45:9, 10, 17, 18 [b]Gen 46:26f; Ex 1:5; Deut 10:22 [c]Acts 2:41 **15** [a]Gen 46:1-7; 49:33; Ex 1:6 **16** [1]Gr *Sychem* [2]Gr *Emmor* [a]Gen 23:16; 33:19; 50:13; Josh 24:32

6:12 *the elders and the scribes.* See notes on Matt 2:4; 15:2; Luke 5:17. *Council.* See note on Mark 14:55.
6:13 *speaks against this holy place and the Law.* Similar to the charges brought against Christ (see Matt 26:61). Stephen may have referred to Jesus' words as recorded in John 2:19, and the words may have been misunderstood or purposely misinterpreted (v. 14), as at the trial of Jesus.
7:1 *high priest.* Probably Caiaphas (see Matt 26:57–66), but see note on 4:6; cf. John 18:19, 24. *Are these things so?* See notes on 6:11,13.
7:2 *Abraham . . . in Mesopotamia, before he lived in Haran.* Abraham's call came in Ur, not Haran (cf. Gen 15:7; Neh 9:7). Or perhaps he was called first in Ur, and then later his call was renewed in Haran (see note on Jer 15:19–21).
7:4 *land of the Chaldeans.* A district in southern Babylonia, the name was later applied to a region that included all Babylonia. *after his father died.* Gen 11:26 does not mean that all three sons—Abraham, Nahor and Haran—were born to Terah in the same year when he was 70 years old. See Gen 11:26–12:1. It may be that Haran was Terah's firstborn and that Abraham was born 60 years later. Thus the death of Terah at 205 years of age could have occurred just before Abraham, at 75, left Haran.
7:6 *FOUR HUNDRED YEARS.* A round number for the length of Israel's stay in Egypt (Ex 12:40–41 has 430 years). That four generations would represent considerably less than 400 years is not a necessary conclusion (see note on Gen 15:16). Ex 6:16–20 makes Moses the great-grandson of Levi, son of Jacob and brother of Joseph. This would make four generations from Levi to Moses. But in 1 Chr 7:22–27 a list of ten names represents the generations between Ephraim, the son of Joseph, and Joshua. The ten generations at 40 years each would equal 400 years, the same period of time noted as four generations. But one list is abbreviated and the other gives a full genealogy.
7:8 *covenant of circumcision.* See notes on Gen 17:10–11. The essential conditions for the religion of Israel were already fulfilled long before the temple was built and their present religious customs began. *twelve patriarchs.* See Gen 35:23–26.
7:9 *patriarchs . . . sold him.* Israel consistently rejected God's favored individuals. Stephen builds his case about Jesus' rejection by noting Joseph's rejection by his brothers (Gen 37:12–36).
7:13 *second visit.* See Gen 43.
7:14 *Jacob . . . all his relatives . . . seventy-five persons in all.* Although the Hebrew Bible uses the number 70 (Gen 46:27; Ex 1:5; Deut 10:22), the Greek translation of the OT (the Septuagint) adds at Gen 46:20 the names of one son of Manasseh, two of Ephraim, and one grandson of each. This makes the number 75 and is the number that Stephen uses.
7:16 Stephen greatly compresses OT accounts of two land purchases (by Abraham and Jacob) and two burial places (at Hebron and Shechem). According to the OT, Abraham purchased land at Hebron (Gen 23:17–18), where he (Gen 25:9–11), Isaac (Gen 35:29) and Jacob (Gen 50:13) were buried. Jacob bought land at Shechem (Gen 33:19), where Joseph was later buried (Josh 24:32). Josephus preserves a tradition that Joseph's broth-

17 "But as the [a]time of the promise was
approaching which God had assured to
Abraham, [b]the people increased and multiplied in Egypt,
18 until [a]THERE AROSE ANOTHER KING OVER
EGYPT WHO KNEW NOTHING ABOUT JOSEPH.
19 "It was he who took [a]shrewd advantage
of our race and mistreated our fathers so that
they would [1b]expose their infants and they
would not survive.
20 "It was at this time that [a]Moses was
born; and he was lovely [1]in the sight of God,
and he was nurtured three months in his
father's home.
21 "And after he had been set outside,
[a]Pharaoh's daughter [1]took him away and
nurtured him as her own son.
22 "Moses was educated in all [a]the learning of the Egyptians, and he was a man of
power in words and deeds.
23 "But when he was approaching the age
of forty, [a]it entered his [1]mind to visit his
brethren, the sons of Israel.
24 "And when he saw one *of them* being
treated unjustly, he defended him and took
vengeance for the oppressed by striking
down the Egyptian.
25 "And he supposed that his brethren
understood that God was granting them
[1]deliverance [2]through him, but they did not
understand.
26 "[a]On the following day he appeared to
them as they were fighting together, and he
tried to reconcile them in peace, saying,
'Men, you are brethren, why do you injure
one another?'
27 "But the one who was injuring his
neighbor pushed him away, saying, '[a]WHO
MADE YOU A RULER AND JUDGE OVER US?
28 '[a]YOU DO NOT MEAN TO KILL ME AS YOU
KILLED THE EGYPTIAN YESTERDAY, DO YOU?'
29 "At this remark, [a]MOSES FLED AND BECAME
AN ALIEN IN THE LAND OF [1]MIDIAN, where he
[b]became the father of two sons.

30 "After forty years had passed, [a]AN ANGEL
APPEARED TO HIM IN THE WILDERNESS OF MOUNT
SINAI, IN THE FLAME OF A BURNING THORN BUSH.
31 "When Moses saw it, he marveled at the
sight; and as he approached to look *more*
closely, there came the voice of the Lord:
32 '[a]I AM THE GOD OF YOUR FATHERS, THE GOD
OF ABRAHAM AND ISAAC AND JACOB.' Moses
shook with fear and would not venture to
look.
33 "[a]BUT THE LORD SAID TO HIM, '[b]TAKE OFF
THE SANDALS FROM YOUR FEET, FOR THE PLACE ON
WHICH YOU ARE STANDING IS HOLY GROUND.
34 '[a]I HAVE CERTAINLY SEEN THE OPPRESSION OF
MY PEOPLE IN EGYPT AND HAVE HEARD THEIR
GROANS, AND I HAVE COME DOWN TO RESCUE THEM;
[1b]COME NOW, AND I WILL SEND YOU TO EGYPT.'
35 "This Moses whom they [a]disowned,
saying, 'WHO MADE YOU A RULER AND A JUDGE?'
is the one whom God [1]sent *to be* both a ruler
and a deliverer with the [2]help of the angel
who appeared to him in the thorn bush.
36 "[a]This man led them out, performing
[b]wonders and [1]signs in the land of Egypt and
in the Red Sea and in the [c]wilderness for
forty years.
37 "This is the Moses who said to the sons
of Israel, '[a]GOD WILL RAISE UP FOR YOU A PROPH-
ET [1]LIKE ME FROM YOUR BRETHREN.'
38 "This is the one who was in [a]the [1]con-
gregation in the wilderness together with [b]the
angel who was speaking to him on Mount
Sinai, and *who was* with our fathers; and he
received [c]living [d]oracles to pass on to you.
39 "Our fathers were unwilling to be obedient to him, but [a]repudiated him and in their
hearts turned back to Egypt,
40 [a]SAYING TO AARON, 'MAKE FOR US GODS
WHO WILL GO BEFORE US; FOR THIS MOSES WHO
LED US OUT OF THE LAND OF EGYPT—WE DO NOT
KNOW WHAT HAPPENED TO HIM.'
41 "[1]At that time [a]they made a [2]calf and
brought a sacrifice to the idol, and were
rejoicing in [b]the works of their hands.

17 [a]Gen 15:13 [b]Ex 1:7f
18 [a]Ex 1:8
19 [1]Or *put out to die* [a]Ex 1:10f, 16ff [b]Ex 1:22
20 [1]Lit *to God* [a]Ex 2:2; Heb 11:23
21 [1]Or *adopted him* [a]Ex 2:5f, 10
22 [a]1 Kin 4:30; Is 19:11
23 [1]Lit *heart* [a]Ex 2:11f; Heb 11:24-26
25 [1]Or *salvation* [2]Lit *through his hand*
26 [a]Ex 2:13f
27 [a]Ex 2:14; Acts 7:35
28 [a]Ex 2:14
29 [1]Gr *Madiam* [a]Ex 2:15, 22 [b]Ex 18:3, 4
30 [a]Ex 3:1f; Is 63:9
32 [a]Ex 3:6; Matt 22:32
33 [a]Ex 3:5 [b]Josh 5:15
34 [1]Lit *and now come!* [a]Ex 3:7f [b]Ex 3:10
35 [1]Lit *has sent* [2]Lit *hand* [a]Ex 2:14; Acts 7:27
36 [1]Or *attesting miracles* [a]Ex 12:41; 33:1; Heb 8:9 [b]Ex 7:3; 14:21; John 4:48 [c]Ex 16:35; Num 14:33; Ps 95:8-10; Acts 7:42; 13:18; Heb 3:8f
37 [1]Or *as He raised up me* [a]Deut 18:15, 18; Acts 3:22
38 [1]Gr *ekklesia* [a]Ex 19:17 [b]Acts 7:53 [c]Deut 32:47; Heb 4:12 [d]Rom 3:2; Heb 5:12; 1 Pet 4:11
39 [a]Num 14:3f
40 [a]Ex 32:1, 23
41 [1]Lit *in those days* [2]Or *young bull* [a]Ex 32:4, 6 [b]Rev 9:20

ers were buried at Hebron. Stephen's rhetorical device (by which he recalls that Jacob and the 12 patriarchs were not buried in Egypt but in Canaan) is strange to modern ears but would have been well understood by his hearers.

7:18 *another king . . . who knew nothing about Joseph.* See note on Ex 1:8.

7:22 *Moses was educated in all the learning of the Egyptians.* Not explicitly stated in the OT but to be expected if he grew up in the household of Pharaoh's daughter. Both Philo and Josephus speak of Moses' great learning.

7:23 *when he was . . . forty.* Moses was 80 years old when sent to speak before Pharaoh (Ex 7:7) and 120 years old when he died (Deut 34:7). Stephen's words agree with a tradition that at Moses' first departure from Egypt he was 40 years of age.

7:29 *FLED . . . MIDIAN.* Rejected by his own people, Moses feared that they would inform the Egyptians, and this led to his flight to Midian (Ex 2:15), the land flanking the Gulf of Aqaba on both sides. *became the father of two sons.* Gershom and Eliezer (Ex 2:22; 18:3–4; 1 Chr 23:15).

7:30 *After forty years.* Plus the 40 years of v. 23, making the 80 years of Ex 7:7. *Mount Sinai.* Called Horeb in Ex 3:1 (see note there).

7:35 *This Moses . . . sent to be both a ruler and a deliverer.* Israel rejected Moses, their deliverer, just as the Jews of Stephen's day were rejecting Jesus, their deliverer. Yet both were sent by God. *angel who appeared to him in the thorn bush.* See Ex 3:2.

7:37 *prophet like me.* See 3:22–23; see also note on Deut 18:15.

7:38 *angel who was speaking to him.* According to Jewish interpretation at that time, the law was given to Moses by angel mediation—after the manner of the original call of Moses (see Ex 3:2; see also v. 53; Gal 3:19; Heb 2:2). *he received living oracles to pass on to you.* Moses was the mediator between God and man on Mount Sinai.

7:39 *unwilling to be obedient to him.* Another rejection of God's representative and His commands.

7:40 *MAKE FOR US GODS.* While Moses was on Sinai receiving the law, the people made the golden calf, rejecting God and His representative (Ex 32:1). The people had not traveled far from the idolatry of Egypt.

42 "But God [a]turned away and delivered
them up to [1]serve the [2]host of heaven; as it is
written in the book of the prophets, '[b]IT WAS
NOT TO ME THAT YOU OFFERED VICTIMS AND SACRI-
FICES [c]FORTY YEARS IN THE WILDERNESS, WAS IT, O
HOUSE OF ISRAEL?
43 '[a]YOU ALSO TOOK ALONG THE TABERNACLE OF
MOLOCH AND THE STAR OF THE GOD [1]ROMPHA, THE
IMAGES WHICH YOU MADE TO WORSHIP. I ALSO WILL
REMOVE YOU BEYOND BABYLON.'
44 "Our fathers had [a]the tabernacle of testimony in the wilderness, just as He who
spoke to Moses directed *him* to make it
[b]according to the pattern which he had seen.
45 "And having received it in their turn, our
fathers [a]brought it in with [1]Joshua upon dispossessing the [2]nations whom God drove out
before our fathers, until the time of David.
46 "[a]*David* found favor in God's sight, and
[b]asked that he might find a dwelling place
for the [1]God of Jacob.
47 "But it was [a]Solomon who built a house
for Him.
48 "However, [a]the Most High does not
dwell in *houses* made by *human* hands; as
the prophet says:
49 '[a]HEAVEN IS MY THRONE,
AND EARTH IS THE FOOTSTOOL OF MY FEET;
WHAT KIND OF HOUSE WILL YOU BUILD FOR
ME?' says the Lord,
'OR WHAT PLACE IS THERE FOR MY REPOSE?
50 '[a]WAS IT NOT MY HAND WHICH MADE ALL
THESE THINGS?'
51 "You men who are [a]stiff-necked and
uncircumcised in heart and ears are always
resisting the Holy Spirit; you are doing just
as your fathers did.
52 "[a]Which one of the prophets did your
fathers not persecute? They killed those who
had previously announced the coming of
[b]the Righteous One, whose betrayers and
murderers [c]you have now become;
53 you who received the law as [a]ordained
by angels, and *yet* did not keep it."

Stephen Put to Death

54 Now when they heard this, they were
[a]cut to the quick, and they *began* gnashing
their teeth at him.
55 But being [a]full of the Holy Spirit, he
[b]gazed intently into heaven and saw the glory of God, and Jesus standing [c]at the right
hand of God;
56 and he said, "Behold, I see the [a]heav-
ens opened up and [b]the Son of Man standing
at the right hand of God."
57 But they cried out with a loud voice,
and covered their ears and rushed at him
with one impulse.
58 When they had [a]driven him out of the
city, they *began* stoning *him;* and [b]the witnesses [c]laid aside their robes at the feet of [d]a
young man named Saul.
59 They went on stoning Stephen as he
[a]called on *the Lord* and said, "Lord Jesus,
receive my spirit!"
60 Then [a]falling on his knees, he cried out
with a loud voice, "Lord, [b]do not hold this
sin against them!" Having said this, he [1c]fell
asleep.

Saul Persecutes the Church

8 [a]Saul was in hearty agreement with putting him to death.
And on that day a great persecution
[1]began against [b]the church in Jerusalem,
and they were all [c]scattered throughout the
regions of Judea and [d]Samaria, except the
apostles.

42 [1]Or *worship* [2]I.e. heavenly bodies [a]Josh 24:20; Is 63:10; Jer 19:13; Ezek 20:39 [b]Amos 5:25 [c]Acts 7:36
43 [1]Other mss spell it: *Romphan,* or *Rempham,* or *Raiphan,* or *Rephan* [a]Amos 5:26, 27
44 [a]Ex 25:8, 9; 38:21 [b]Ex 25:40
45 [1]Gr *Jesus* [2]Or *Gentiles* [a]Deut 32:49; Josh 3:14ff; 18:1; 23:9; 24:18; Ps 44:2f
46 [1]The earliest mss read *house* instead of *God;* the Septuagint reads *God* [a]2 Sam 7:8ff; Ps 132:1-5; Acts 13:22 [b]2 Sam 7:1-16; 1 Chr 17:1-14
47 [a]1 Kin 6:1-38; 8:20; 2 Chr 3:1-17
48 [a]Luke 1:32
49 [a]Is 66:1; Matt 5:34f
50 [a]Is 66:2
51 [a]Ex 32:9; 33:3, 5; Lev 26:41; Num 27:14; Is 63:10; Jer 6:10; 9:26
52 [a]2 Chr 36:15f; Matt 5:12; 23:31, 37 [b]Acts 3:14; 22:14; 1 John 2:1 [c]Acts 3:14; 5:28
53 [a]Deut 33:2; Acts 7:38; Gal 3:19; Heb 2:2
54 [a]Acts 5:33
55 [a]Acts 2:4 [b]John 11:41 [c]Mark 16:19
56 [a]John 1:51 [b]Matt 8:20
58 [a]Lev 24:14, 16; Luke 4:29 [b]Deut 13:9f; 17:7; Acts 6:13 [c]Acts 22:20 [d]Acts 8:1; 22:20; 26:10
59 [a]Acts 9:14, 21; 22:16; Rom 10:12-14; 1 Cor 1:2; 2 Tim 2:22
60 [1]I.e. died [a]Luke 22:41 [b]Matt 5:44; Luke 23:34 [c]Dan 12:2; Matt 27:52; John 11:11f; Acts 13:36; 1 Cor 15:6, 18, 20; 1 Thess 4:13ff; 2 Pet 3:4
8:1 [1]Lit *occurred* [a]Acts 7:58; 22:20; 26:10 [b]Acts 9:31 [c]Acts 8:4; 11:19 [d]Acts 1:8; 8:5, 14; 9:31

7:42 *God . . . delivered them up.* See note on Rom 1:24.
7:43 Stephen quotes Amos 5:25–27 as translated in the Septuagint, except that he replaces Damascus with Babylon in view of the fact that the final exile of Israel from the promised land was carried out by the Babylonians (Amos was speaking first of the Assyrian exile of the northern kingdom).
7:44–50 Because he had been accused of speaking against the "holy place" (6:13), Stephen concludes his recital with a word about the sanctuary. Presumably, he had been preaching that the risen Christ had now replaced the temple as the mediation of God's saving presence among His people and as the one (the "place") through whom they (and "all the nations," Mark 11:17) could come to God in prayer (see note on 6:13).
7:44 *tabernacle of testimony.* So called by Stephen because the primary contents of the wilderness tabernacle were the ark of the covenant and the two covenant tablets it contained, which were called "the testimony" (see Ex 25:16,21 and notes).
7:49 Isaiah reminded Israel that all creation is the temple that God Himself had made. Stephen recalls that word to remind his hearers that ultimately God builds His own temple.
7:51 *uncircumcised in heart and ears.* Though physically circumcised, they were acting like the uncircumcised pagan nations around them. They were not truly consecrated to the Lord.
7:53 *law as ordained by angels.* See note on v. 38.
7:55 *full of the Holy Spirit.* See note on 2:4; see also 6:5.
7:56 *Son of Man.* See note on Mark 8:31. Jesus used this title of Himself (see Mark 2:10) to emphasize His relationship to Messianic prediction (Matt 25:31; Dan 7:13–14). It is unusual for someone other than Jesus to apply this term to Christ (see also Rev 1:13).
7:58 *laid aside their robes at the feet of . . . Saul.* Some have thought that this marked Saul as being in charge of the execution. In any case, it is Luke's way of introducing the main character of the second section of the book.
7:60 *do not hold this sin against them.* Compare with Jesus' words (Luke 23:34).
8:1 *hearty agreement.* See 22:20. *scattered throughout . . . Judea and Samaria.* The beginning of the fulfillment of the commission in 1:8—not by the church's plan, but by events beyond the believers' control. See map, p. 1598. *except the apostles.* For the apostles to stay in Jerusalem would be an encouragement to those in prison and a center of appeal to those scattered. The church now went underground.

2 *Some* devout men buried Stephen, and
made loud lamentation over him.
3 But [a]Saul *began* ravaging the church,
entering house after house, and [b]dragging off
men and women, he would put them in
prison.

Philip in Samaria

4 Therefore, those [a]who had been scattered went about [1b]preaching the word.
5 [a]Philip went down to the city of Samaria and *began* proclaiming [1]Christ to them.
6 The crowds with one accord were giving attention to what was said by Philip, as
they heard and saw the [1]signs which he was
performing.
7 For *in the case of* many who had
[a]unclean spirits, they were coming out *of*
them shouting with a loud voice; and many
who had been [b]paralyzed and lame were
healed.
8 So there was [a]much rejoicing in that
city.
9 Now there was a man named Simon,
who formerly was practicing [a]magic in the
city and astonishing the people of Samaria,
[b]claiming to be someone great;
10 and they all, from smallest to greatest,
were giving attention to him, saying, "[a]This
man is what is called the Great Power of
God."
11 And they were giving him attention

3 [a]Acts 9:1, 13, 21; 22:4, 19; 26:10f; 1 Cor 15:9; Gal 1:13; Phil 3:6; 1 Tim 1:13 [b]James 2:6
4 [1]Or *bringing the good news of* [a]Acts 8:1 [b]Acts 8:12; 15:35
5 [1]I.e. the Messiah [a]Acts 6:5; 8:26, 30
6 [1]Or *attesting miracles*
7 [a]Mark 16:17 [b]Matt 4:24
8 [a]John 4:40-42; Acts 8:39
9 [a]Acts 8:11; 13:6 [b]Acts 5:36
10 [a]Acts 14:11; 28:6

8:3 *began ravaging.* See 22:4. The Greek underlying this phrase sometimes describes the ravages of wild animals.
8:4 *preaching the word.* Many witnesses to the gospel went everywhere proclaiming the good news. The number of witnesses multiplied, and the territory covered was expanded greatly (cf. 11:19–20).
8:5 *Philip.* One of the Seven in the Jerusalem church (6:3,5; see note on 6:6), who now becomes an evangelist, proclaiming the Christ (Messiah); see also 21:8. Philip is an example of one of those who were scattered. *the city of Samaria.* A reference to the old capital Samaria, renamed Sebaste or Neapolis (modern Nablus).
8:9 *Simon.* In early Christian literature the "sorcerer" (Simon Magus) is described as the arch-heretic of the church and the "father" of Gnostic teaching.
8:10 *the Great Power of God.* Simon claimed to be either God Himself or, more likely, His chief representative.
8:13 *Simon himself believed; . . . baptized.* It is difficult to know

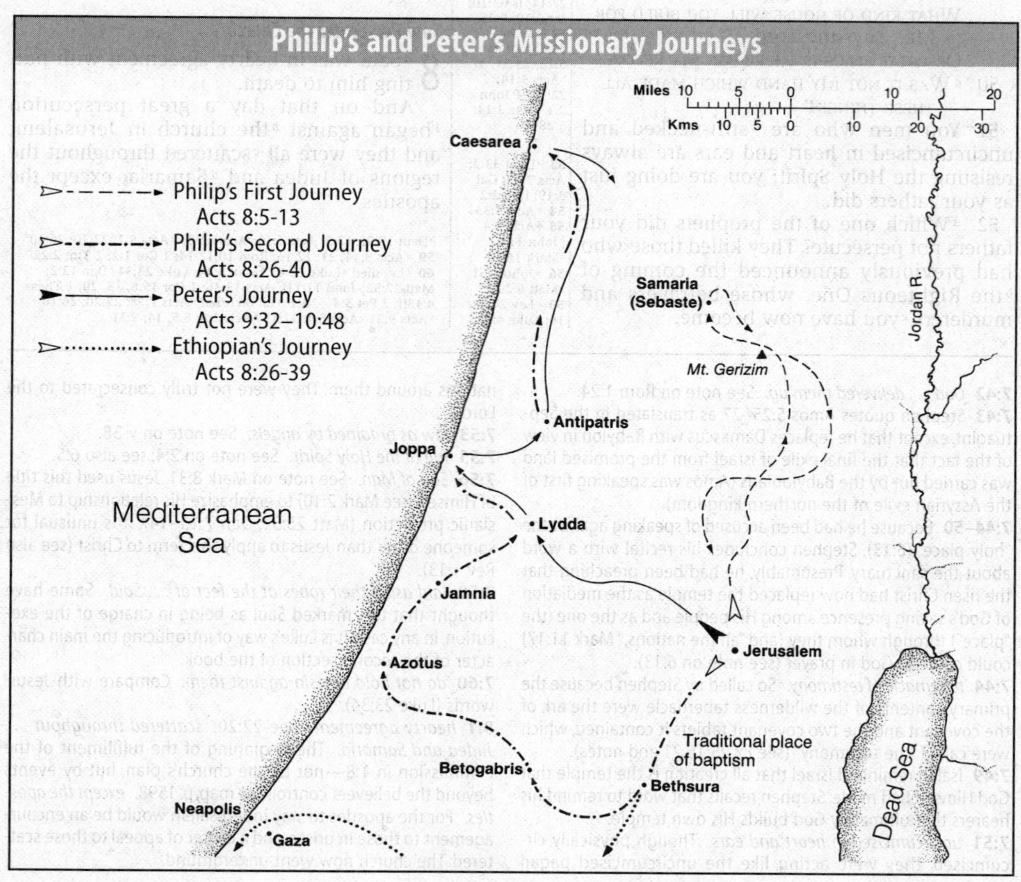
Philip's and Peter's Missionary Journeys
Miles 10 5 0 10 20
Kms 10 5 0 10 20 30
Philip's First Journey
Acts 8:5-13
Philip's Second Journey
Acts 8:26-40
Peter's Journey
Acts 9:32–10:48
Ethiopian's Journey
Acts 8:26-39
Caesarea
Samaria
(Sebaste)
Jordan R.
Mt. Gerizim
Antipatris
Joppa
Mediterranean
Sea
Lydda
Jamnia
Jerusalem
Azotus
Traditional place
of baptism
Betogabris
Bethsura
Dead Sea
Neapolis
Gaza

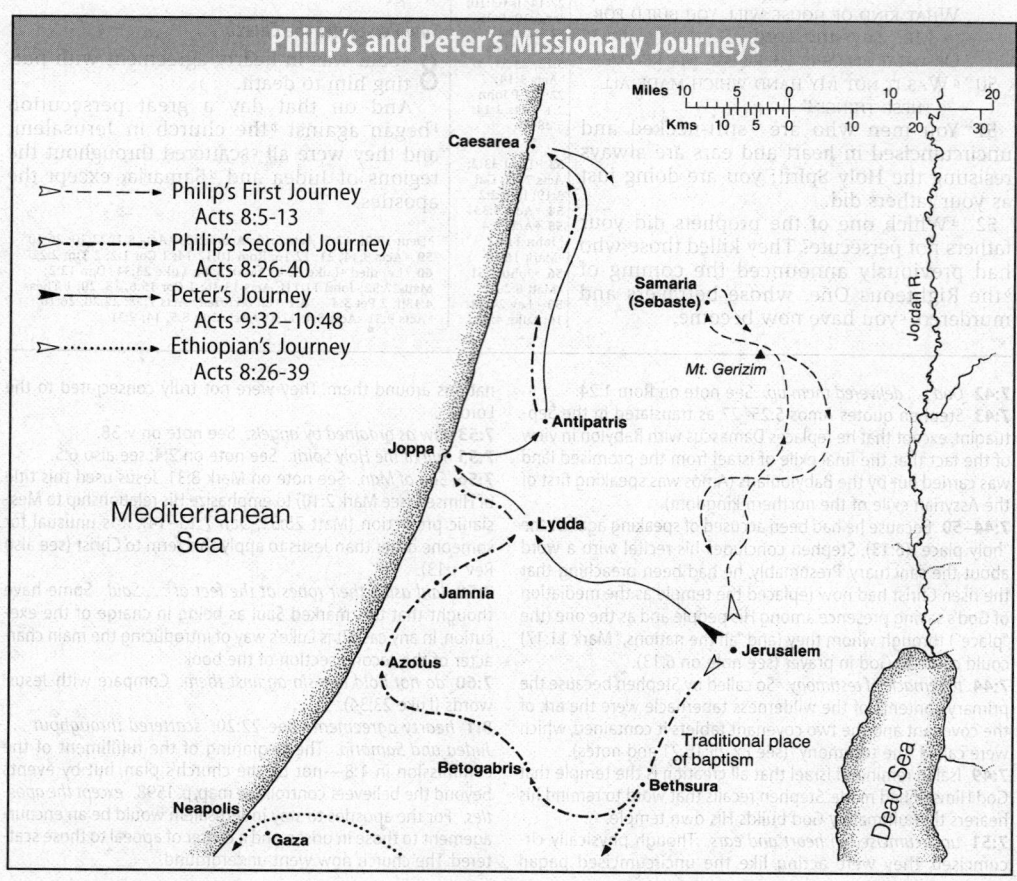

because he had for a long time astonished them with his [a]magic arts.

12 But when they believed Philip [a]preaching the good news about the kingdom of God and the name of Jesus Christ, they were being [b]baptized, men and women alike.

13 Even Simon himself believed; and after being baptized, he continued on with Philip, and as he observed [a]signs and [b]great miracles taking place, he was constantly amazed.

14 Now when [a]the apostles in Jerusalem heard that Samaria had received the word of God, they sent them [b]Peter and John,

15 who came down and prayed for them [a]that they might receive the Holy Spirit.

16 For He had [a]not yet fallen upon any of them; they had simply been [b]baptized [1]in the name of the Lord Jesus.

17 Then they [a]*began* laying their hands on them, and they were [b]receiving the Holy Spirit.

18 Now when Simon saw that the Spirit was bestowed through the laying on of the apostles' hands, he offered them money,

19 saying, "Give this authority to me as well, so that everyone on whom I lay my hands may receive the Holy Spirit."

20 But Peter said to him, "May your silver perish with you, because you thought you could [a]obtain the gift of God with money!

21 "You have [a]no part or portion in this [1]matter, for your heart is not [b]right before God.

22 "Therefore repent of this wickedness of yours, and pray the Lord that, [a]if possible, the intention of your heart may be forgiven you.

23 "For I see that you are in the gall of bitterness and in [a]the [1]bondage of iniquity."

24 But Simon answered and said, "[a]Pray to the Lord for me yourselves, so that nothing of what you have said may come upon me."

An Ethiopian Receives Christ

25 So, when they had solemnly [a]testified and spoken [b]the word of the Lord, they started back to Jerusalem, and were [c]preaching the gospel to many villages of the [d]Samaritans.

26 But [a]an angel of the Lord spoke to [b]Philip saying, "Get up and go south to the road that descends from Jerusalem to [c]Gaza." ([1]This is a desert *road*.)

27 So he got up and went; and [a]there was an Ethiopian eunuch, a court official of Candace, queen of the Ethiopians, who was in charge of all her treasure; and he [b]had come to Jerusalem to worship,

28 and he was returning and sitting in his [1]chariot, and was reading the prophet Isaiah.

29 Then [a]the Spirit said to Philip, "Go up and join this [1]chariot."

30 Philip ran up and heard him reading Isaiah the prophet, and said, "Do you understand what you are reading?"

31 And he said, "Well, how could I, unless someone guides me?" And he invited Philip to come up and sit with him.

32 Now the passage of Scripture which he was reading was this:

"[a]He was led as a sheep to slaughter;
And as a lamb before its shearer is silent,
So He does not open His mouth.

33 "[a]In humiliation His judgment was taken away;
Who will [1]relate His [2]generation?
For His life is removed from the earth."

34 The eunuch answered Philip and said, "Please *tell me*, of whom does the prophet say this? Of himself or of someone else?"

35 Then Philip [a]opened his mouth, and [b]beginning from this Scripture he [c]preached Jesus to him.

36 As they went along the road they came to some water; and the eunuch *said, "Look! Water! [a]What prevents me from being baptized?"

11 [a]Acts 8:9; 13:6 **12** [a]Acts 1:3; 8:4 [b]Acts 2:38 **13** [a]Acts 8:6 [b]Acts 19:11 **14** [a]Acts 8:1 [b]Luke 22:8 **15** [a]Acts 2:38; 19:2 **16** [1]Lit *into* [a]Matt 28:19; Acts 19:2 [b]Acts 2:38; 10:48 **17** [a]Mark 5:23; Acts 6:6 [b]Acts 2:4 **20** [a]2 Kin 5:16; Is 55:1; Dan 5:17; Matt 10:8; Acts 2:38 **21** [1]Or *teaching;* lit *word* [a]Deut 10:9; 12:12; Eph 5:5 [b]Ps 78:37 **22** [a]Is 55:7 **23** [1]Lit *bond* [a]Is 58:6 **24** [a]Gen 20:7; Ex 8:8; Num 21:7; James 5:16 **25** [a]Luke 16:28

25 [b]Acts 13:12 [c]Acts 8:40 [d]Matt 10:5 **26** [1]Or *This city is deserted* [a]Acts 5:19; 8:29 [b]Acts 8:5 [c]Gen 10:19 **27** [a]Ps 68:31; 87:4; Is 56:3ff [b]1 Kin 8:41f; John 12:20 **28** [1]Or *carriage* **29** [1]Or *carriage* [a]Acts 8:39; 10:19; 11:12; 13:2; 16:6, 7; 20:23; 21:11; 28:25; Heb 3:7 **32** [a]Is 53:7 **33** [1]Or *describe* [2]Or *family* or *origin* [a]Is 53:8 **35** [a]Matt 5:2 [b]Luke 24:27; Acts 17:2; 18:28; 28:23 [c]Acts 5:42 **36** [a]Acts 10:47

---

whether Simon's faith was genuine. Even though Luke says Simon believed, Peter's statement that Simon had no part in the apostles' ministry because his heart was not "right before God" (v. 21) casts some doubt.

8:14 *had received the word of God.* Were obedient to the gospel proclaimed by Philip. *sent them Peter and John.* The Jerusalem church assumed the responsibility of inspecting new evangelistic efforts and the communities of believers they produced (see 11:22).

8:16 *not yet fallen upon any of them.* Since the day of Pentecost, those who belong to Christ (see Rom 8:9) also have the Holy Spirit. But the Spirit had not yet been made manifest to the Christians in Samaria by the usual signs. This deficiency was now graciously supplied (v. 17).

8:17 *began laying their hands on them.* See v. 18; 19:1–7; cf. 2 Tim 1:6; see also note on 6:6.

8:18 *he offered them money.* Simon had boasted of having great powers before (see v. 10 and note), and now he tried to buy this magical power he believed the apostles possessed.

8:23 *in the gall of bitterness.* See Deut 29:18.

8:26 *an angel of the Lord.* Cf. v. 29; see note on 5:19. *from Jerusalem to Gaza.* A distance of about 50 miles.

8:27 *an Ethiopian.* Ethiopia corresponded in this period to Nubia, from the upper Nile region at the first cataract (Aswan) to Khartoum. *Candace.* The traditional title of the queen mother, responsible for performing the secular duties of the reigning king—who was thought to be too sacred for such activities. *come to Jerusalem to worship.* If not a full-fledged proselyte (Deut 23:1), the Ethiopian was a Gentile God-fearer.

8:30 *heard him reading.* It was customary practice to read aloud.

8:34 *of whom does the prophet say this?* Beginning with Is 53 (see v. 35), Philip may have identified the suffering servant with the Davidic Messiah of Is 11 or with the Son of Man (Dan 7:13).

8:35 *preached Jesus.* Proclaimed the way of salvation through Jesus Christ.

8:36 *they came to some water.* There were several possibilities: a brook in the Valley of Elah (which David crossed to meet Goliath, 1 Sam 17:40); the Wadi el-Hasi just north of Gaza; water from a spring or one of the many pools in the area.

37 [[1]And Philip said, "If you believe with all your heart, you may." And he answered and said, "I believe that Jesus Christ is the Son of God."]

38 And he ordered the [1]chariot to stop; and they both went down into the water, Philip as well as the eunuch, and he baptized him.

39 When they came up out of the water, [a]the Spirit of the Lord snatched Philip away; and the eunuch no longer saw him, [1]but went on his way rejoicing.

40 But Philip [1]found himself at [2a]Azotus, and as he passed through he [b]kept preaching the gospel to all the cities until he came to [c]Caesarea.

The Conversion of Saul

9 [a]Now [1]Saul, still [b]breathing [2]threats and murder against the disciples of the Lord, went to the high priest,

2 and asked for [a]letters from him to [b]the synagogues at [c]Damascus, so that if he found any belonging to [d]the Way, both men and women, he might bring them bound to Jerusalem.

3 As he was traveling, it happened that he was approaching Damascus, and [a]suddenly a light from heaven flashed around him;

4 and [a]he fell to the ground and heard a voice saying to him, "Saul, Saul, why are you persecuting Me?"

5 And he said, "Who are You, Lord?" And He *said*, "I am Jesus whom you are persecuting,

6 but get up and enter the city, and [a]it will be told you what you must do."

7 The men who traveled with him [a]stood speechless, [b]hearing the [1]voice but seeing no one.

8 Saul got up from the ground, and [a]though his eyes were open, he [1]could see nothing; and leading him by the hand, they brought him into [b]Damascus.

9 And he was three days without sight, and neither ate nor drank.

10 Now there was a disciple at [a]Damascus named [b]Ananias; and the Lord said to him in [c]a vision, "Ananias." And he said, "Here I am, Lord."

11 And the Lord *said* to him, "Get up and go to the street called Straight, and inquire at the house of Judas for a man from [a]Tarsus named Saul, for he is praying,

12 and he has seen [1]in a vision a man named Ananias come in and [a]lay his hands on him, so that he might regain his sight."

13 But Ananias answered, "Lord, I have heard from many about this man, [a]how much harm he did to [b]Your [1]saints at Jerusalem;

14 and here he [a]has authority from the chief priests to bind all who [b]call on Your name."

15 But the Lord said to him, "Go, for [a]he is a chosen [1]instrument of Mine, to bear My name before [b]the Gentiles and [c]kings and the sons of Israel;

16 for [a]I will show him how much he must suffer for My name's sake."

17 So Ananias departed and entered the

37 [1]Early mss do not contain this v
38 [1]Or *carriage*
39 [1]Lit *for he was going* [a]1 Kin 18:12; 2 Kin 2:16; Ezek 3:12, 14; 8:3; 11:1, 24; 43:5; 2 Cor 12:2
40 [1]Or *was found* [2]OT: Ashdod [a]Josh 11:22; 1 Sam 5:1 [b]Acts 8:25 [c]Acts 9:30; 10:1, 24; 11:11; 12:19; 18:22; 21:8, 16; 23:23, 33; 25:1, 4, 6, 13
9:1 [1]Later called Paul [2]Lit *threat* [a]Acts 9:1-22; 22:3-16; 26:9-18 [b]Acts 8:3; 9:13-21
2 [a]Acts 9:14, 21; 22:5; 26:10 [b]Matt 10:17 [c]Gen 14:15; 2 Cor 11:32; Gal 1:17 [d]John 14:6; Acts 18:25f; 19:9, 23; 22:4; 24:14, 22
3 [a]1 Cor 15:8
4 [a]Acts 22:7; 26:14
6 [a]Acts 9:16
7 [a]Acts 26:14
7 [1]Or *sound* [b]John 12:29f; Acts 22:9
8 [1]Lit *was seeing* [a]Acts 9:18; 22:11 [b]Gen 14:15; 2 Cor 11:32; Gal 1:17
10 [a]Gen 14:15; 2 Cor 11:32; Gal 1:17 [b]Acts 22:12 [c]Acts 10:3, 17, 19; 11:5; 12:9; 16:9f; 18:9
11 [a]Acts 9:30; 11:25; 21:39; 22:3
12 [1]A few early mss do not contain *in a vision* [a]Mark 5:23; Acts 6:6; 9:17
13 [1]Or *holy ones* [a]Acts 8:3 [b]Acts 9:32, 41; 26:10; Rom 1:7; 15:25, 26, 31; 16:2, 15; 1 Cor 1:2
14 [a]Acts 9:2, 21 [b]Acts 7:59
15 [1]Or *vessel* [a]Acts 13:2; Rom 1:1; 9:23; Gal 1:15; Eph 3:7 [b]Acts 22:21; 26:17; Rom 1:5; 11:13; 15:16; Gal 1:16; 2:7ff; Eph 3:1, 8; 1 Tim 2:7; 2 Tim 4:17 [c]Acts 25:22f; 26:1, 32; 2 Tim 4:17
16 [a]Acts 20:23; 21:4, 11, 13; 2 Cor 6:4f; 11:23-27; 1 Thess 3:3

8:39 *rejoicing.* Joy is associated with salvation in Acts (see note on 16:34).

8:40 *Azotus.* OT Ashdod (see 1 Sam 5:1), one of the five Philistine cities. It was about 19 miles from Gaza and 60 miles from Caesarea. *Caesarea.* Rebuilt by Herod and with an excellent harbor, it served as the headquarters of the Roman procurators. The account leaves Philip in Caesarea at this time; his next appearance is 20 years later, and he is still located in the same place (21:8).

9:1 *Saul.* Introduced at the stoning of Stephen (7:58), he was born in Tarsus and trained under Gamaliel (22:3). See note on Phil 3:4–14. *threats and murder.* We do not know that Saul was directly involved in the death of anyone other than Stephen (8:1), but there appear to have been similar cases (22:4; 26:10). *high priest.* Probably Caiaphas (see note on 4:6) and the members of the Sanhedrin, who had authority over Jews both in Judea and elsewhere.

9:2 *Damascus.* Located in the Roman province of Syria, it was the nearest important city outside the Holy Land. It also had a large Jewish population. The distance from Jerusalem to Damascus was about 150 miles, four to six days' travel. *the Way.* A name for Christianity occurring a number of times in Acts (16:17; 18:25–26; 19:9,23; 22:4; 24:14,22; see 2 Pet 2:2). Jesus called himself "the way" (John 14:6). *bound to Jerusalem.* Where the full authority of the Council could be exercised in trial for either acquittal or death.

9:3 *a light from heaven.* "At midday" (26:13).

9:4 *why are you persecuting Me?* To persecute the church is to persecute Christ, for the church is His body (see 1 Cor 12:27; Eph 1:22–23).

9:5 *Who are You, Lord?* In rabbinic tradition such a voice from heaven would have been understood as the voice of God Himself. The solemn repetition of Saul's name and the bright light suggested to him that he was in the presence of deity.

9:7 *hearing the voice.* Those with Saul heard the voice but "did not understand" (22:9) what it was saying (cf. Dan 10:7).

9:10 *Ananias.* This Ananias is mentioned elsewhere only in 22:12. His was a common name (5:1; 23:2). The Greek form is derived from the Hebrew name Hananiah, meaning "The LORD is gracious/shows grace" (see Dan 1:6).

9:11 *street called Straight.* Probably followed the same route of the long, straight street that today runs through the city from east to west. It is a decided contrast to the numerous crooked streets of the city (see map, p. 1589). *Tarsus.* See note on 22:3. *praying.* Prayer is often associated with visions in Luke and Acts (see 10:9–11; Luke 1:10; 3:21; 9:28).

9:13,32 *saints.* See notes on Rom 1:7; Phil 1:1.

9:15 *before the Gentiles.* See Rom 1:13–14. *kings.* Agrippa (26:1) and Caesar at Rome (25:11–12; 28:19).

9:17 *Jesus, who appeared to you.* The Damascus road experience was not merely a vision. The resurrected Christ actually appeared to Saul, and on this fact Saul based his qualification

house, and after [a]laying his hands on him
said, "[b]Brother Saul, the Lord Jesus, who
appeared to you on the road by which you
were coming, has sent me so that you may
regain your sight and be [c]filled with the Holy
Spirit."
18 And immediately there fell from his
eyes something like scales, and he regained
his sight, and he got up and was baptized;
19 and he took food and was strengthened.

Saul Begins to Preach Christ

Now [a]for several days he was with [b]the
disciples who were at Damascus,
20 and immediately he *began* to proclaim
Jesus [a]in the synagogues, [1]saying, "He is
[b]the Son of God."
21 All those hearing him continued to be
amazed, and were saying, "Is this not he
who in Jerusalem [a]destroyed those who
[b]called on this name, and *who* had come
here for the purpose of bringing them bound
before the chief priests?"
22 But Saul kept increasing in strength
and confounding the Jews who lived at
Damascus by proving that this *Jesus* is the
[1]Christ.
23 When [a]many days had elapsed, [b]the
Jews plotted together to do away with him,
24 but [a]their plot became known to Saul.
[b]They were also watching the gates day and
night so that they might put him to death;

17 [a]Mark 5:23; Acts 6:6; 9:12 [b]Acts 22:13 [c]Acts 2:4
19 [a]Acts 26:20 [b]Acts 9:26, 38; 11:26
20 [1]Lit *that* [a]Acts 13:5, 14; 14:1; 16:13; 17:2, 10; 18:4, 19; 19:8 [b]Matt 4:3; Acts 9:22; 13:33
21 [a]Acts 8:3; 9:13; Gal 1:13, 23 [b]Acts 9:14
22 [1]I.e. Messiah
23 [a]Gal 1:17, 18 [b]1 Thess 2:16
24 [a]Acts 20:3, 19; 23:12, 30; 25:3 [b]2 Cor 11:32f

to be an apostle (1 Cor 9:1; 15:8).
9:20 *immediately.* Following his baptism. *synagogues.* It became Saul's regular practice to preach at every opportunity in the synagogues (13:5; 14:1; 17:1–2,10; 18:4,19; 19:8). *He is the Son of God.* Saul's message was a declaration of what he himself had become convinced of on the Damascus road: Christ's deity and Messiahship (see v. 22 and note on Luke 2:11).
9:23 *When many days had elapsed.* Three years (Gal 1:17–18). It is probable that the major part of this period was spent in Arabia, away from Damascus, though the borders of Arabia extended to the environs of Damascus. *the Jews plotted together to do away with him.* Upon his return to Damascus, the governor under Aretas gave orders for his arrest (2 Cor 11:32). The absence of Roman coins struck in Damascus between A.D. 34 and 62 may indicate that Aretas was in control during that period.

Roman Damascus

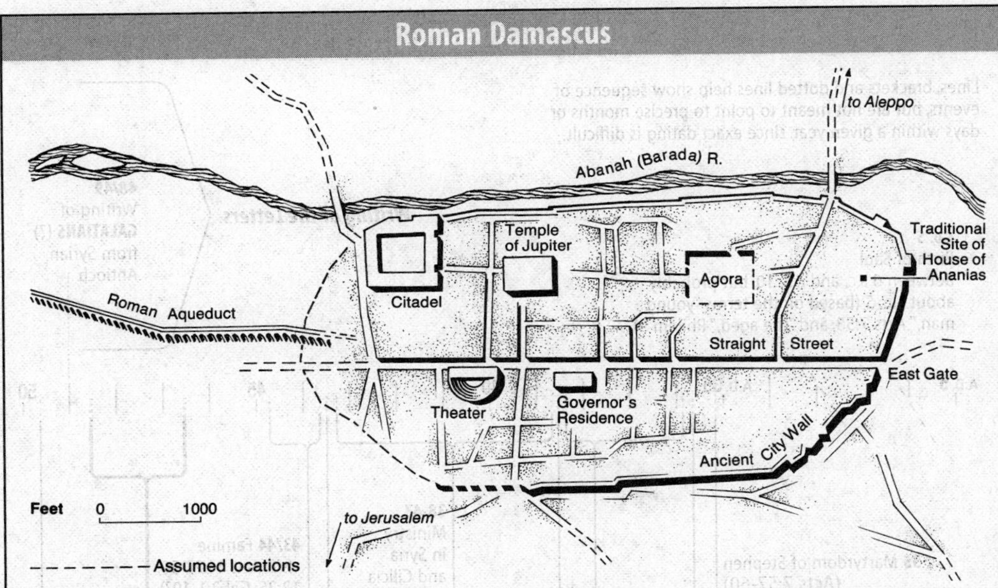

Damascus represented much more to Saul, the strict Pharisee, than any other stop on his campaign of repression. It was the hub of a vast commercial network with far-flung lines of caravan trade reaching into north Syria, Mesopotamia, Anatolia, Persia and Arabia. If the new "Way" of Christianity flourished in Damascus, it would quickly reach all these places. From the viewpoint of the Sanhedrin and of Saul, the arch-persecutor, it had to be stopped in Damascus.

The city itself was a veritable oasis, situated in a plain watered by the Biblical rivers Abanah and Pharpar.

Roman architecture overlaid the Hellenistic town plan with a great temple to Jupiter and a mile-long colonnaded street, the "street called Straight" of Acts 9:11. The city gates and a section of the town wall may still be seen today, as well as the lengthy bazaar that runs along the line of the ancient street.

The dominant political figure at the time of Paul's escape from Damascus (2 Cor 11:32-33) was Aretas IV, king of the Nabateans (9 B.C.-A.D. 40), though normally the Decapolis cities were attached to the province of Syria and were thus under the influence of Rome.

25 but his disciples took him by night and
let him down through *an opening in* the
wall, lowering him in a large basket.
26 [a]When he came to Jerusalem, he was
trying to associate with the disciples; [1]but
they were all afraid of him, not believing that
he was a disciple.
27 But [a]Barnabas took hold of him and
brought him to the apostles and described to
them how he had [b]seen the Lord on the
road, and that He had talked to him, and
how [c]at Damascus he had [d]spoken out boldly in the name of Jesus.
28 And he was with them, [1]moving about
freely in Jerusalem, [a]speaking out boldly in
the name of the Lord.
29 And he was talking and arguing with
the [1a]Hellenistic *Jews;* but they were
attempting to put him to death.
30 But when [a]the brethren learned *of it,*
they brought him down to [b]Caesarea and
[c]sent him away to [d]Tarsus.
31 So [a]the church throughout all Judea
and Galilee and Samaria [1]enjoyed peace,
being built up; and going on in the fear of

26 [1]Lit *and* [a]Acts 22:17-20; 26:20 **27** [a]Acts 4:36 [b]Acts 9:3-6 [c]Acts 9:20, 22 [d]Acts 4:13, 29; 9:29 **28** [1]Lit *going in and going out*

28 [a]Acts 4:13, 29; 9:29 **29** [1]Jews who adopted the Gr language and much of Gr culture through acculturation [a]Acts 6:1

30 [a]Acts 1:15 [b]Acts 8:40 [c]Gal 1:21 [d]Acts 9:11 **31** [1]Lit *was having* [a]Acts 5:11; 8:1; 16:5

9:25 *lowering him in a large basket.* See 2 Cor 11:33 (cf. Josh 2:15; 1 Sam 19:12).
9:26 *he came to Jerusalem.* From Gal 1:19 we learn that all the apostles were away except Peter and James, the Lord's brother. James was not one of the twelve, but he held a position in Jerusalem comparable to that of an apostle.
9:27 *Barnabas.* See note on 4:36.
9:29 *he was talking and arguing.* Formerly Saul was arguing against Christ; now he is forcefully presenting Jesus as the Messiah.
9:30 *Caesarea.* See note on 8:40. *Tarsus.* Saul's birthplace (see note on 22:3).
9:31 *the church.* The whole Christian body, including Christians in the districts of Judea, Galilee and Samaria. The singular thus does not here refer to the various congregations but to the church as a whole (see note on 5:11). *going on . . . in the comfort of the Holy Spirit.* The work of the Spirit is particularly noted throughout the book of Acts (see 13:2 and note on 1:2). This is why the book is sometimes called the Acts of the Holy Spirit.

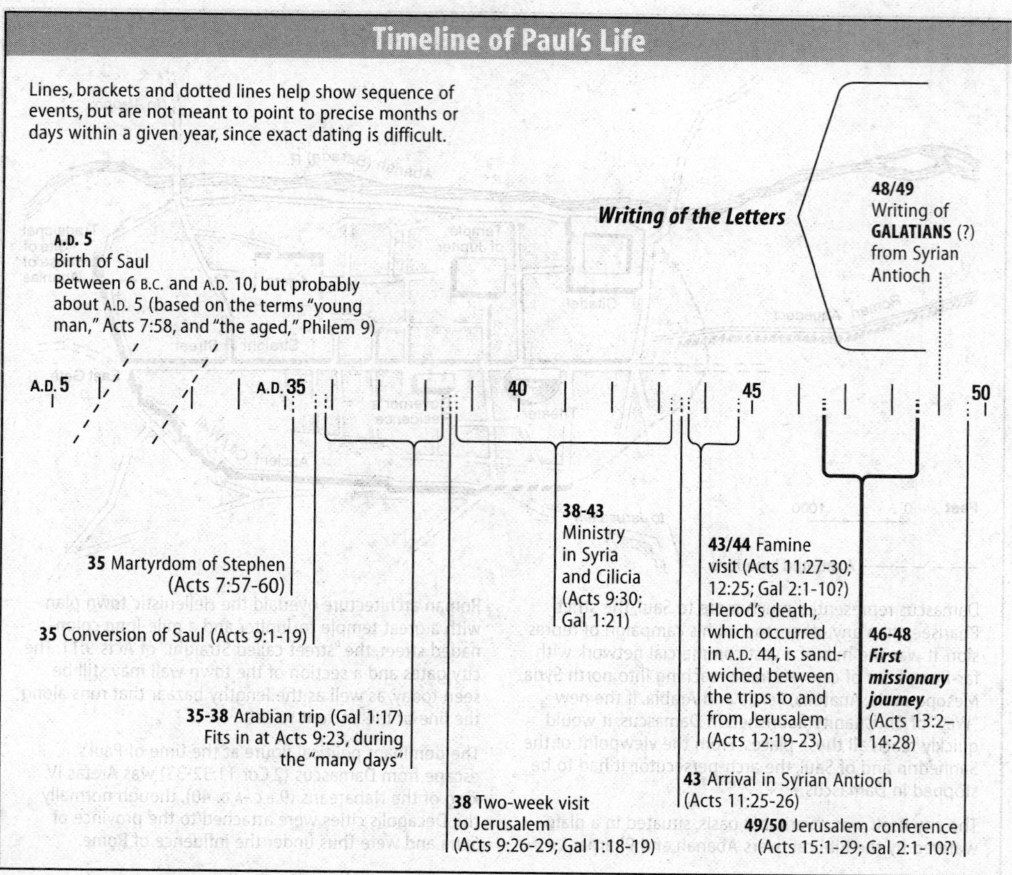
Timeline of Paul's Life
Lines, brackets and dotted lines help show sequence of events, but are not meant to point to precise months or days within a given year, since exact dating is difficult.
Writing of the Letters
48/49 Writing of GALATIANS (?) from Syrian Antioch
A.D. 5 Birth of Saul
Between 6 B.C. and A.D. 10, but probably about A.D. 5 (based on the terms "young man," Acts 7:58, and "the aged," Philem 9)
A.D. 5
A.D. 35
40
45
50
35 Martyrdom of Stephen (Acts 7:57-60)
35 Conversion of Saul (Acts 9:1-19)
35-38 Arabian trip (Gal 1:17) Fits in at Acts 9:23, during the "many days"
38 Two-week visit to Jerusalem (Acts 9:26-29; Gal 1:18-19)
38-43 Ministry in Syria and Cilicia (Acts 9:30; Gal 1:21)
43/44 Famine visit (Acts 11:27-30; 12:25; Gal 2:1-10?) Herod's death, which occurred in A.D. 44, is sandwiched between the trips to and from Jerusalem (Acts 12:19-23)
43 Arrival in Syrian Antioch (Acts 11:25-26)
46-48 First missionary journey (Acts 13:2–14:28)
49/50 Jerusalem conference (Acts 15:1-29; Gal 2:1-10?)

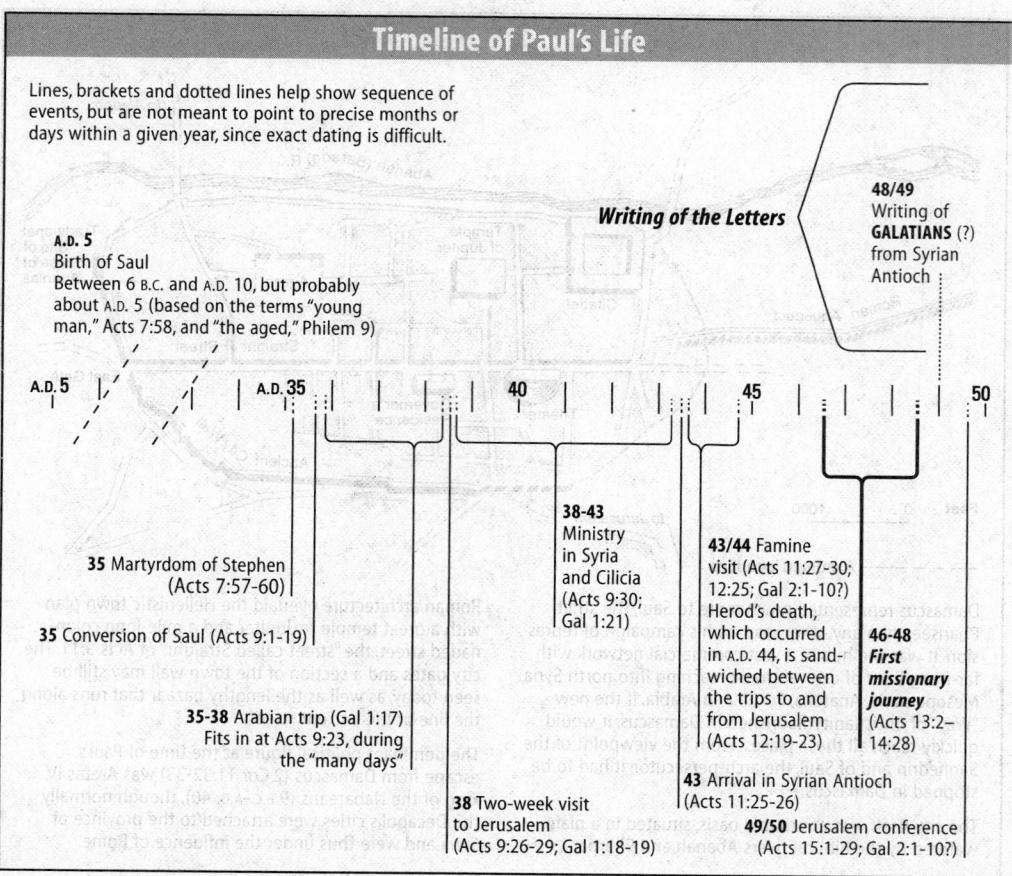

the Lord and in the comfort of the Holy Spirit, it continued to increase.

Peter's Ministry

32 Now as Peter was traveling through all
those regions, he came down also to [a]the
[1]saints who lived at [2b]Lydda.
33 There he found a man named Aeneas,
who had been bedridden eight years, for he
was paralyzed.
34 Peter said to him, "Aeneas, Jesus Christ
heals you; get up and make your bed."
Immediately he got up.
35 And all who lived at [1a]Lydda and
[b]Sharon saw him, and they [c]turned to the
Lord.
36 Now in [a]Joppa there was a disciple
named Tabitha (which translated *in Greek* is
called [1]Dorcas); this woman was abounding
with deeds of kindness and charity which
she continually did.
37 And it happened [1]at that time that she
fell sick and died; and when they had washed
her body, they laid it in an [a]upper room.
38 Since Lydda was near [a]Joppa, [b]the dis-

32 [1]Or *holy ones* [2]OT: Lod [a]Acts 9:13 [b]1 Chr 8:12; Ezra 2:33; Neh 7:37; 11:35 **35** [1]OT: Lod [a]1 Chr 8:12; Ezra 2:33; Neh 7:37; 11:35

35 [b]1 Chr 5:16; 27:29; Is 33:9; 35:2; 65:10 [c]Acts 2:47; 9:42; 11:21 **36** [1]I.e. Gazelle [a]Josh 19:46; 2 Chr 2:16; Ezra 3:7; Jon 1:3; Acts 9:38, 42f; 10:5, 8, 23, 32; 11:5, 13 **37** [1]Lit *in those days* [a]Acts 1:13; 9:39 **38** [a]Josh 19:46; 2 Chr 2:16; Ezra 3:7; Jon 1:3; Acts 9:36, 42f; 10:5, 8, 23, 32; 11:5, 13 [b]Acts 11:26

9:32 *Lydda.* A town two or three miles north of the road connecting Joppa and Jerusalem. Lydda is about 12 miles from Joppa.
9:33 *Aeneas.* Since Peter was there to visit the believers, Aeneas was probably one of the Christians.
9:35 *Sharon.* The fertile plain of Sharon runs about 50 miles along the Mediterranean coast, roughly from Joppa to Caesarea. The reference here, however, may be to a village in the neighborhood of Lydda instead of to a district (an Egyptian papyrus refers to a town by that name in the Holy Land).
9:36 *Joppa.* About 38 miles from Jerusalem, the main seaport of Judea. Today it is known as Jaffa and is a suburb of Tel Aviv.
9:37 *washed her body.* In preparation for burial, a custom common to both Jews (Purification of the Dead) and Greeks. *upper room.* If burial was delayed, it was customary to lay the body in an upper room. In Jerusalem the body had to be buried the day the person died, but outside Jerusalem up to three days might be allowed for burial.
9:38 *near Joppa.* See note on v. 32. *Do not delay in coming.* Whether for consolation or for a miracle, Peter was urged to

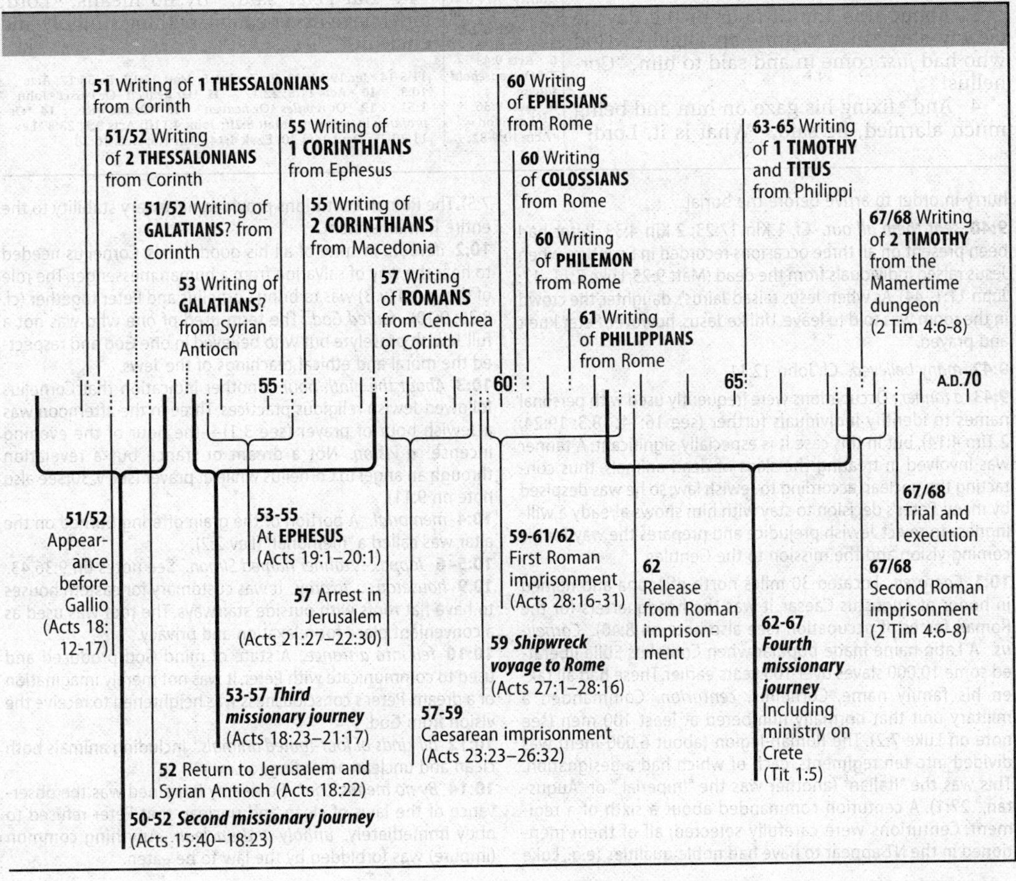

51 Writing of 1 THESSALONIANS from Corinth
51/52 Writing of 2 THESSALONIANS from Corinth
51/52 Writing of GALATIANS? from Corinth
55 Writing of 1 CORINTHIANS from Ephesus
55 Writing of 2 CORINTHIANS from Macedonia
53 Writing of GALATIANS? from Syrian Antioch
57 Writing of ROMANS from Cenchrea or Corinth
60 Writing of EPHESIANS from Rome
60 Writing of COLOSSIANS from Rome
60 Writing of PHILEMON from Rome
61 Writing of PHILIPPIANS from Rome
63-65 Writing of 1 TIMOTHY and TITUS from Philippi
67/68 Writing of 2 TIMOTHY from the Mamertime dungeon (2 Tim 4:6-8)
55
60
65
A.D.70
51/52 Appear-ance before Gallio (Acts 18:12-17)
53-55 At EPHESUS (Acts 19:1–20:1)
57 Arrest in Jerusalem (Acts 21:27–22:30)
53-57 Third missionary journey (Acts 18:23–21:17)
52 Return to Jerusalem and Syrian Antioch (Acts 18:22)
50-52 Second missionary journey (Acts 15:40–18:23)
59-61/62 First Roman imprisonment (Acts 28:16-31)
59 Shipwreck voyage to Rome (Acts 27:1–28:16)
57-59 Caesarean imprisonment (Acts 23:23–26:32)
62 Release from Roman imprison-ment
62-67 Fourth missionary journey Including ministry on Crete (Tit 1:5)
67/68 Trial and execution
67/68 Second Roman imprisonment (2 Tim 4:6-8)

ciples, having heard that Peter was there,
sent two men to him, imploring him, "Do
not delay in coming to us."
39 So Peter arose and went with them.
When he arrived, they brought him into the
[a]upper room; and all the [b]widows stood
beside him, weeping and showing all the
[1]tunics and garments that Dorcas used to
make while she was with them.
40 But Peter [a]sent them all out and [b]knelt
down and prayed, and turning to the body,
he said, "[c]Tabitha, arise." And she opened
her eyes, and when she saw Peter, she sat up.
41 And he gave her his hand and raised
her up; and calling [a]the [1]saints and [b]wid-
ows, he presented her alive.
42 It became known all over [a]Joppa, and
[b]many believed in the Lord.
43 And Peter stayed many days in [a]Joppa
with [b]a tanner *named* Simon.

Cornelius's Vision

10 Now *there was* a man at [a]Caesarea
named Cornelius, a centurion of what
was [b]called the Italian [1]cohort,
2 a devout man and [a]one who feared
God with all his household, and [b]gave many
[1]alms to the *Jewish* people and prayed to
God continually.
3 About [a]the [1]ninth hour of the day he
clearly saw [b]in a vision [c]an angel of God
who had *just* come in and said to him, "Cornelius!"
4 And [a]fixing his gaze on him and being
much alarmed, he said, "What is it, Lord?"
And he said to him, "Your prayers and [1]alms
[b]have ascended [c]as a memorial before God.
5 "Now dispatch *some* men to [a]Joppa and
send for a man *named* Simon, who is also
called Peter;
6 he is staying with a tanner *named*
[a]Simon, whose house is by the sea."
7 When the angel who was speaking to
him had left, he summoned two of his [1]ser-
vants and a devout soldier of those who
were his personal attendants,
8 and after he had explained everything
to them, he sent them to [a]Joppa.
9 On the next day, as they were on their
way and approaching the city, [a]Peter went
up on [b]the housetop about [c]the [1]sixth hour
to pray.
10 But he became hungry and was desiring to eat; but while they were making
preparations, he [a]fell into a trance;
11 and he *saw [a]the [1]sky opened up, and
an [2]object like a great sheet coming down,
lowered by four corners to the ground,
12 and there were in it all *kinds of* four-
footed animals and [1]crawling creatures of
the earth and birds of the [2]air.
13 A voice came to him, "Get up, Peter,
[1]kill and eat!"
14 But Peter said, "By no means, [a]Lord,
for [b]I have never eaten anything [1]unholy and
unclean."

39 [1]Or *inner garments* [a]Acts 1:13; 9:37 [b]Acts 6:1
40 [a]Matt 9:25 [b]Luke 22:41; Acts 7:60 [c]Mark 5:41
41 [1]Or *holy ones* [a]Acts 9:13, 32 [b]Acts 6:1
42 [a]Josh 19:46; 2 Chr 2:16; Jon 1:3; Acts 9:38, 42f; 10:5, 8, 23, 32; 11:5, 13 [b]Acts 9:35
43 [a]Josh 19:46; 2 Chr 2:16; Ezra 3:7; Jon 1:3; Acts 9:38, 42f; 10:5, 8, 23, 32; 11:13, 15 [b]Acts 10:6
10:1 [1]Or *battalion* [a]Acts 8:40; 10:24 [b]Matt 27:27; Mark 15:16; John 18:3, 12; Acts 21:31; 27:1
2 [1]Or *gifts of charity* [a]Acts 10:22, 35; 13:16, 26 [b]Luke 7:4f
3 [1]I.e. 3 p.m. [a]Acts 3:1 [b]Acts 9:10; 10:17, 19 [c]Acts 5:19
4 [a]Acts 3:4

4 [1]Or *deeds of charity* [b]Rev 8:4 [c]Matt 26:13; Phil 4:18; Heb 6:10
5 [a]Acts 9:36
6 [a]Acts 9:43
7 [1]Or *household slaves*
8 [a]Acts 9:36
9 [1]I.e. noon [a]Acts 10:9-32; 11:5-14 [b]Jer 19:13; 32:29; Zeph 1:5; Matt 24:17 [c]Ps 55:17; Acts 10:3
10 [a]Acts 11:5; 22:17
11 [1]Or *heaven* [2]Or *vessel* [a]John 1:51
12 [1]Or *reptiles* [2]Or *heaven*
13 [1]Or *sacrifice*
14 [1]Or *profane;* lit *common* [a]Matt 8:2ff; John 4:11ff; Acts 9:5; 22:8 [b]Lev 11:20-25; Deut 14:4-20; Ezek 4:14; Dan 1:8; Acts 10:28

hurry in order to arrive before the burial.

9:40 *sent them all out.* Cf. 1 Kin 17:23; 2 Kin 4:33. Peter had been present on all three occasions recorded in Scripture when Jesus raised individuals from the dead (Matt 9:25; Luke 7:11–17; John 11:1–44). As when Jesus raised Jairus's daughter, the crowd in the room was told to leave. Unlike Jesus, however, Peter knelt and prayed.

9:42 *many believed.* Cf. John 12:11.

9:43 *a tanner.* Occupations were frequently used with personal names to identify individuals further (see 16:14; 18:3; 19:24; 2 Tim 4:14), but in this case it is especially significant. A tanner was involved in treating the skins of dead animals, thus contacting the unclean according to Jewish law; so he was despised by many. Peter's decision to stay with him shows already a willingness to reject Jewish prejudice and prepares the way for his coming vision and the mission to the Gentiles.

10:1 *Caesarea.* Located 30 miles north of Joppa and named in honor of Augustus Caesar, it was the headquarters for the Roman forces of occupation (see also note on 8:40). *Cornelius.* A Latin name made popular when Cornelius Sulla liberated some 10,000 slaves over 100 years earlier. These had all taken his family name, Cornelius. *centurion.* Commanded a military unit that normally numbered at least 100 men (see note on Luke 7:2). The Roman legion (about 6,000 men) was divided into ten regiments, each of which had a designation. This was the "Italian" (another was the "Imperial," or "Augustan," 27:1). A centurion commanded about a sixth of a regiment. Centurions were carefully selected; all of them mentioned in the NT appear to have had noble qualities (e.g., Luke 7:5). The Roman centurions provided necessary stability to the entire Roman system.

10:2 *devout.* In spite of all his good deeds, Cornelius needed to hear the way of salvation from a human messenger. The role of the angel (v. 3) was to bring Cornelius and Peter together (cf. 8:26; 9:10). *feared God.* The term used of one who was not a full Jewish proselyte but who believed in one God and respected the moral and ethical teachings of the Jews.

10:3 *About the ninth hour.* Another indication that Cornelius followed Jewish religious practices. Three in the afternoon was a Jewish hour of prayer (see 3:1)—the hour of the evening incense. *a vision.* Not a dream or trance but a revelation through an angel to Cornelius while at prayer (see v. 30; see also note on 9:11).

10:4 *memorial.* A portion of the grain offering burned on the altar was called a "memorial" (Lev 2:2).

10:5–6 *Joppa . . . tanner named Simon.* See notes on 9:36,43.

10:9 *housetop . . . to pray.* It was customary for eastern houses to have flat roofs with outside stairways. The roof was used as a convenient place for relaxation and privacy.

10:10 *fell into a trance.* A state of mind God produced and used to communicate with Peter. It was not merely imagination or a dream. Peter's consciousness was heightened to receive the vision from God.

10:12 *all kinds of four-footed animals.* Including animals both clean and unclean according to Lev 11.

10:14 *By no means, Lord.* So deeply ingrained was the observance of the laws of clean and unclean that Peter refused to obey immediately. *unholy and unclean.* Anything common (impure) was forbidden by the law to be eaten.

15 Again a voice *came* to him a second
time, "[a]What God has cleansed, no *longer*
consider [1]unholy."
16 This happened three times, and immediately the [1]object was taken up into the
[2]sky.
17 Now while Peter was greatly perplexed
in [1]mind as to what [a]the vision which he
had seen might be, behold, [b]the men who
had been sent by Cornelius, having asked
directions for Simon's house, appeared at the
gate;
18 and calling out, they were asking
whether Simon, who was also called Peter,
was staying there.
19 While Peter was reflecting on [a]the
vision, [b]the Spirit said to him, "Behold,
[1]three men are looking for you.
20 "But get up, go downstairs and [a]accom-
pany them [1]without misgivings, for I have
sent them Myself."
21 Peter went down to the men and said,
"Behold, I am the one you are looking for;
what is the reason for which you have come?"
22 They said, "Cornelius, a centurion, a
righteous and [a]God-fearing man well spoken
of by the entire nation of the Jews, [b]was
divinely directed by a [c]holy angel to send for
you *to come* to his house and hear [1d]a message from you."
23 So he invited them in and gave them
lodging.

Peter at Caesarea

And on the next day he got up and went
away with them, and [a]some of [b]the brethren
from [c]Joppa accompanied him.
24 On the following day he entered [a]Caes-
area. Now Cornelius was waiting for them
and had called together his relatives and
close friends.
25 When Peter entered, Cornelius met
him, and fell at his feet and [1a]worshiped
him.
26 But Peter raised him up, saying,
"[a]Stand up; I too am *just* a man."
27 As he talked with him, he entered and
*found [a]many people assembled.
28 And he said to them, "You yourselves
know how [a]unlawful it is for a man who is a
Jew to associate with a foreigner or to visit
him; and *yet* [b]God has shown me that I
should not call any man [1]unholy or unclean.
29 "That is why I came without even raising any objection when I was sent for. So I
ask for what reason you have sent for me."
30 Cornelius said, "[a]Four days ago to this
hour, I was praying in my house during [b]the
[1]ninth hour; and behold, [c]a man stood
before me in shining garments,
31 and he *said, 'Cornelius, your prayer
has been heard and your [1]alms have been
remembered before God.
32 'Therefore send to [a]Joppa and invite
Simon, who is also called Peter, to come to
you; he is staying at the house of Simon *the*
tanner by the sea.'
33 "So I sent for you immediately, and you
have [1]been kind enough to come. Now then,
we are all here present before God to hear all
that you have been commanded by the
Lord."

Gentiles Hear Good News

34 [a]Opening his mouth, Peter said:
"**I** most certainly understand *now* that
[b]God is not one to show partiality,
35 but [a]in every nation the man who
[1b]fears Him and [2]does what is right is welcome to Him.
36 "The word which He sent to the sons of
Israel, [a]preaching [1b]peace through Jesus
Christ (He is [c]Lord of all)—
37 you yourselves know the thing which
took place throughout all Judea, starting
from Galilee, after the baptism which John
proclaimed.
38 "[1]*You know of* [a]Jesus of Nazareth, how

15 [1]Lit *make common* [a]Matt 15:11; Mark 7:19; Rom 14:14; 1 Cor 10:25ff; 1 Tim 4:4f; Titus 1:15 **16** [1]Or *vessel* [2]Or *heaven* **17** [1]Lit *himself* [a]Acts 10:3 [b]Acts 10:8 **19** [1]One early ms reads *two* [a]Acts 10:3 [b]Acts 8:29 **20** [1]Lit *doubting nothing* [a]Acts 15:7-9 **22** [1]Lit *words* [a]Acts 10:2 [b]Matt 2:12 [c]Mark 8:38; Luke 9:26; Rev 14:10 [d]Acts 11:14 **23** [a]Acts 10:45; 11:12 [b]Acts 1:15 [c]Acts 9:36 **24** [a]Acts 8:40; 10:1 **25** [1]Or *prostrated himself in reverence* [a]Matt 8:2 **26** [a]Acts 14:15; Rev 19:10; 22:8f

27 [a]Acts 10:24 **28** [1]Or *profane;* lit *common* [a]John 4:9; 18:28; Acts 11:3 [b]Acts 10:14f, 35; 15:9 **30** [1]I.e. 3 to 4 p.m. [a]Acts 10:9, 22f [b]Acts 3:1; 10:3 [c]Acts 10:3-6, 30-32 **31** [1]Or *deeds of charity* **32** [a]John 4:9; 18:28; Acts 11:3 **33** [1]Lit *done well in coming* **34** [a]Matt 5:2 [b]Deut 10:17; 2 Chr 19:7; Rom 2:11; Gal 2:6; Eph 6:9; Col 3:25; 1 Pet 1:17 **35** [1]Or *reverences* [2]Lit *works righteousness* [a]Acts 10:28 [b]Acts 10:2 **36** [1]Or *the gospel of peace* [a]Acts 13:32 [b]Luke 1:79; 2:14; Rom 5:1; Eph 2:17 [c]Matt 28:18; Acts 2:36; Rom 10:12 **38** [1]Or *How God anointed Jesus of Nazareth* [a]Acts 2:22

10:15 *God has cleansed.* Jesus had already laid the groundwork for setting aside the laws of clean and unclean food (Matt 15:11; see 1 Tim 4:3–5).

10:16 *three times.* To make a due impression on Peter.

10:23 *invited them in.* By providing lodging for them, Peter was already taking the first step toward accepting Gentiles. Such intimate relationship with Gentiles was contrary to prescribed Jewish practice. *the next day.* It was too late in the day to start out on the long journey to Caesarea (see note on v. 1). *some of the brethren.* Six in number (11:12), they were Jewish in background (10:45).

10:26 *I too am just a man.* Possibly Cornelius was only intending to honor Peter as one having a rank superior to his own, since he was God's messenger. But Peter allowed no chance for misunderstanding—he was not to be worshiped as more than a created being.

10:28 *God has shown me.* Peter recognized that his vision had deeper significance than declaring invalid the distinction between clean and unclean meat; he saw that the barrier between Jew and Gentile had been removed (see Eph 2:11–22).

10:30 *Four days ago.* The Jews counted a part of a day as a day: (1) the day the angel appeared to Cornelius, (2) the day the messengers came to Joppa and Peter received a vision, (3) the day the group set out from Joppa and (4) the day they arrived at Cornelius's house. *a man . . . in shining garments.* Common language to describe an angel when appearing in the form of a man.

10:34 *God is not one to show partiality.* God does not favor an individual because of his station in life, his nationality or his material possessions (see note on James 2:1). He does, however, respect his character and judge his work. This is evident because "in every nation the man who fears Him and does what is right is welcome to Him" (v. 35). Cornelius already worshiped the true God, but this was not enough: He lacked faith in Christ (v. 36).

10:36 *peace.* Between God and man (reconciliation). *Lord of all.* Lord of both Jew and Gentile (see vv. 34–35).

10:37 *after the baptism which John proclaimed.* Similar to the

God [b]anointed Him with the Holy Spirit and with power, [2c]and *how* He went about doing good and healing all who were oppressed by the devil, for [d]God was with Him.

39 "We are [a]witnesses of all the things He did both in the [1]land of the Jews and in Jerusalem. They also [b]put Him to death by hanging Him on a [2]cross.

40 "[a]God raised Him up on the third day and granted that He become visible,

41 [a]not to all the people, but to [b]witnesses who were chosen beforehand by God, *that is,* to us [c]who ate and drank with Him after He arose from the dead.

42 "And He [a]ordered us to [1]preach to the people, and solemnly to [b]testify that this is the One who has been [c]appointed by God as [d]Judge of the living and the dead.

43 "Of Him [a]all the prophets bear witness that through [b]His name everyone who believes in Him receives forgiveness of sins."

44 While Peter was still speaking these words, [a]the Holy Spirit fell upon all those who were listening to the [1]message.

45 [a]All the [1]circumcised believers who came with Peter were amazed, because the gift of the Holy Spirit had been [b]poured out on the Gentiles also.

46 For they were hearing them [a]speaking with tongues and exalting God. Then Peter answered,

47 "[a]Surely no one can refuse the water for these to be baptized who [b]have received the Holy Spirit just as we *did,* can he?"

48 And he [a]ordered them to be baptized [b]in the name of Jesus Christ. Then they asked him to stay on for a few days.

Peter Reports at Jerusalem

11 Now the apostles and [a]the brethren who were throughout Judea heard that the Gentiles also had received the word of God.

2 And when Peter came up to Jerusalem, [1a]those who were circumcised took issue with him,

3 saying, "[a]You [1]went to uncircumcised men and ate with them."

4 But Peter began *speaking* [1]and *proceeded* to explain to them [a]in orderly sequence, saying,

5 "[a]I was in the city of Joppa praying; and in a trance I saw [b]a vision, an [1]object coming down like a great sheet lowered by four corners from [2]the sky; and it came right down to me,

6 and when I had fixed my gaze on it and was observing it [1]I saw the four-footed animals of the earth and the wild beasts and the [2]crawling creatures and the birds of the [3]air.

7 "I also heard a voice saying to me, 'Get up, Peter; [1]kill and eat.'

8 "But I said, 'By no means, Lord, for nothing [1]unholy or unclean has ever entered my mouth.'

9 "But a voice from heaven answered a second time, '[a]What God has cleansed, no longer [1]consider unholy.'

10 "This happened three times, and everything was drawn back up into [1]the sky.

11 "And behold, at that moment three men appeared at the house in which we were *staying,* having been sent to me from [a]Caesarea.

12 "[a]The Spirit told me to go with them [1b]without misgivings. [c]These six brethren also went with me and we entered the man's house.

13 "And he reported to us how he had seen the angel [1]standing in his house, and saying, 'Send to Joppa and have Simon, who is also called Peter, brought here;

14 and he will speak [a]words to you by which you will be saved, you and [b]all your household.'

38 [2]Lit *who went* [b]Acts 4:26 [c]Matt 4:23 [d]John 3:2
39 [1]Or *countryside* [2]Lit *wood* [a]Luke 24:48; Acts 10:41 [b]Acts 5:30
40 [a]Acts 2:24
41 [a]John 14:19, 22; 15:27 [b]Luke 24:48; Acts 10:39 [c]Luke 24:43; Acts 1:4 mg
42 [1]Or *proclaim* [a]Acts 1:2 [b]Luke 16:28 [c]Luke 22:22 [d]John 5:22, 27; Acts 17:31; 2 Tim 4:1; 1 Pet 4:5
43 [a]Acts 3:18 [b]Luke 24:47; Acts 2:38; 4:12
44 [1]Lit *word* [a]Acts 11:15; 15:8
45 [1]Lit *believers from among the circumcision;* i.e. Jewish Christians [a]Acts 10:23 [b]Acts 2:33, 38
46 [a]Mark 16:17; Acts 2:4; 19:6
47 [a]Acts 8:36 [b]Acts 2:4; 10:44f; 11:17; 15:8
48 [a]1 Cor 1:14-17 [b]Acts 2:38; 8:16; 19:5
11:1 [a]Acts 1:15
2 [1]Lit *those of the circumcision;* i.e. Jewish Christians [a]Acts 10:45
3 [1]Or *entered the house of* [a]Matt 9:11; Acts 10:28; Gal 2:12
4 [1]Lit *and was explaining* [a]Luke 1:3
5 [1]Or *vessel* [2]Or *heaven* [a]Acts 10:9-32; 11:5-14 [b]Acts 9:10
6 [1]Lit *and I saw* [2]Or *reptiles* [3]Or *heaven*
7 [1]Or *sacrifice*
8 [1]Or *profane;* lit *common* **9** [1]Lit *make common* [a]Acts 10:15
10 [1]Or *heaven* **11** [a]Acts 8:40 **12** [1]Or *without making any distinction* [a]Acts 8:29 [b]Acts 15:9; Rom 3:22 [c]Acts 10:23
13 [1]Or *after he had stood in his house and said* **14** [a]Acts 10:22 [b]John 4:53; Acts 10:2; 16:15, 31-34; 18:8; 1 Cor 1:16

---

outline of Mark's Gospel, Peter's sermon begins with John's baptism and continues to the resurrection of Jesus. This is significant since the early church fathers viewed Mark as the "interpreter" of Peter (see Introduction to Mark: Author). See previous summaries of Peter's preaching (2:14–41; 3:12–26; 4:8–12; 5:29–32); see also note on 2:14–40.

10:38 *how God anointed Him.* See Is 61:1–3; Luke 4:18–21.

10:39 *hanging him on a cross.* See note on 5:30.

10:41 *who ate and drank.* Those who ate with Jesus after He rose from the dead received unmistakable evidence of His bodily resurrection (see Luke 24:42–43; John 21:12–15).

10:44 *the Holy Spirit fell upon.* See 8:16 and note.

10:45 *amazed . . . on the Gentiles also.* Apparently the early Jewish Christians failed to understand that the gospel was for the Gentiles as well as for the Jews, and that they would share alike in the benefits of redemption. Gentile proselytes to Judaism, however, were accepted (see 6:5).

10:47 *Surely no one can refuse the water for these to be baptized . . . ?* The Gentiles had received the same gift (11:17) as the Jewish believers; they spoke in tongues as did the Jewish Christians on the day of Pentecost. This was unavoidable evidence that the invitation to the kingdom was open to Gentiles as well as to Jews.

11:1 *the apostles and the brethren.* At times "brethren" is used to refer to those of common Jewish lineage (2:29; 7:2), but in Christian contexts it denotes those united in Christ (6:3; 10:23). In matters of deep concern, the apostles did not act alone. The divine will gave guidance, and the apostles interpreted and exhorted, but the consent of the whole church was sought ("the whole congregation," 6:5; "apostles and the brethren," 11:1; "the church," 11:22; "the church and the apostles and the elders," 15:4; cf. 15:22).

11:2 *those . . . circumcised.* Jewish Christians.

11:3 *uncircumcised men.* The Gentiles who would not observe the laws of clean and unclean food and would violate Jewish regulations concerning food preparation.

11:4–17 See notes on 10:1–23,28–33.

11:14 *you and all your household.* Not only the family but also slaves and employed individuals under Cornelius's authority (see note on Gen 6:18).

15 "And as I began to speak, [a]the Holy Spirit fell upon them just [b]as *He did* upon us at the beginning.

16 "And I remembered the word of the Lord, how He used to say, '[a]John baptized with water, but you will be baptized [1]with the Holy Spirit.'

17 "Therefore if [a]God gave to them the same gift as *He gave* to us also after believing in the Lord Jesus Christ, [b]who was I that I could [1]stand in God's way?"

18 When they heard this, they [1]quieted down and [a]glorified God, saying, "Well then, God has granted to the Gentiles also the [b]repentance *that leads* to life."

The Church at Antioch

19 [a]So then those who were scattered because of the [1]persecution that occurred in connection with Stephen made their way [2]to [b]Phoenicia and [c]Cyprus and [d]Antioch, speaking the word to no one except to Jews alone.

20 But there were some of them, men of [a]Cyprus and [b]Cyrene, who came to [c]Antioch and *began* speaking to the [1d]Greeks also, [2e]preaching the Lord Jesus.

21 And [a]the hand of the Lord was with them, and [b]a large number who believed turned to the Lord.

22 The [1]news about them [2]reached the ears of the church at Jerusalem, and they sent [a]Barnabas off [3]to [b]Antioch.

23 Then when he arrived and [1]witnessed [a]the grace of God, he rejoiced and *began* to encourage them all with [2]resolute heart to remain *true* to the Lord;

24 for he was a good man, and [a]full of the Holy Spirit and of faith. And [b]considerable [1]numbers were [2]brought to the Lord.

25 And he left for [a]Tarsus to look for Saul;

26 and when he had found him, he brought him to [a]Antioch. And for an entire year they [1]met with the church and taught considerable [2]numbers; and [b]the disciples were first called [c]Christians in [a]Antioch.

27 Now [1]at this time [a]some prophets came down from Jerusalem to [b]Antioch.

28 One of them named [a]Agabus stood up and *began* to indicate [1]by the Spirit that there would certainly be a great famine [b]all over the [2]world. [3]And this took place in the *reign* of [c]Claudius.

29 And in the proportion that any of [a]the disciples had means, each of them determined to send *a contribution* for the [1]relief of [b]the brethren living in Judea.

30 [a]And this they did, sending it [1]in charge of [b]Barnabas and Saul to the [c]elders.

Peter's Arrest and Deliverance

12 Now about that time [1]Herod the king laid hands on some who belonged to the church in order to mistreat them.

15 [a]Acts 10:44 [b]Acts 2:4 **16** [1]Or *in* [a]Acts 1:5 **17** [1]Lit *prevent God* [a]Acts 10:45, 47 [b]Acts 5:39 **18** [1]Lit *became silent* [a]Matt 9:8 [b]2 Cor 7:10 **19** [1]Lit *tribulation* [2]Lit *as far as* [a]Acts 8:1, 4 [b]Acts 15:3; 21:2 [c]Acts 4:36 [d]Acts 6:5; 11:20, 22, 27; 13:1; 14:26; 15:22f, 30, 35; 18:22; Gal 2:11 **20** [1]Lit *Hellenists;* people who lived by Greek customs and culture [2]Or *bringing the good news of* [a]Acts 4:36 [b]Matt 27:32; Acts 2:10; 6:9; 13:1 [c]Acts 6:5; 11:19, 22, 27; 13:1; 14:26; 15:22f, 30, 35; 18:22; Gal 2:11 [d]John 7:35; Acts 6:1 [e]Acts 5:42 **21** [a]Luke 1:66 [b]Acts 2:47 **22** [1]Lit *word* [2]Lit *was heard in* [3]Lit *as far as* [a]Acts 4:36 [b]Acts 6:5; 11:19, 20, 27; 13:1; 18:22; Gal 2:11 **23** [1]Lit *saw* [2]Lit *purpose of heart* [a]Acts 13:43; 14:26; 15:40; 20:24, 32 **24** [1]Lit *crowd was* [2]Lit *added* [a]Acts 2:4 [b]Acts 2:47; 5:14; 11:21 **25** [a]Acts 9:11 **26** [1]Or *were gathered together* [2]Lit *crowd* [a]Acts 6:5; 11:20, 22, 27 [b]John 2:2; Acts 1:15 [c]Acts 26:28; 1 Pet 4:16 **27** [1]Lit *in these days* [a]Luke 11:49; Acts 2:17; 13:1; 1 Cor 12:10, 28f [b]Acts 6:5; 11:20, 22, 26; 13:1; 14:26; 15:22f, 30, 35; 18:22; Gal 2:11 **28** [1]Or *through* [2]Lit *inhabited earth* [3]Lit *which* [a]Acts 21:10 [b]Matt 24:14 [c]Acts 18:2 **29** [1]Lit *service* [a]John 2:2; Acts 1:15; 6:1f; 9:19, 25, 26, 38; 11:26; 13:52; 14:20, 22, 28 [b]Acts 11:1 **30** [1]Lit *by the hand of* [a]Acts 12:25 [b]Acts 4:36 [c]Acts 14:23; 15:2, 4, 6, 22f; 16:4; 20:17; 21:18; 1 Tim 5:17, 19; Titus 1:5; James 5:14; 1 Pet 5:1; 2 John 1; 3 John 1 **12:1** [1]I.e. Herod Agrippa I

11:17 *stand in God's way.* Peter could not deny the Gentiles the invitation to be baptized (10:47) and to enjoy full fellowship in Christ with all believers. The Jewish believers were compelled to recognize that God was going to save Gentiles on equal terms with Jews. By divine action rather than by human choice, the door was being opened to Gentiles.

11:18 *repentance that leads to life.* A change of one's attitude toward sin, which leads to a turning from sin to God and results in eternal life (see note on 2:38).

11:19 *Phoenicia.* A country about 15 miles wide and 120 miles long stretching along the northeastern Mediterranean coast (modern Lebanon). Its important cities were Tyre and Sidon. *Cyprus.* An island in the northeastern Mediterranean; the home of Barnabas (4:36). *Antioch.* The third city of the Roman empire (after Rome and Alexandria). It was 15 miles inland from the northeast corner of the Mediterranean. The first largely Gentile local church was located here, and it was from this church that Paul's three missionary journeys were launched (13:1–4; 15:40; 18:23).

11:20 *Cyrene.* See note on 2:10. *Greeks.* Not Greek-speaking Jews, but Gentiles.

11:21 *hand of the Lord.* Cf. 4:30; 13:11; cf. also Luke 1:66. It indicates divine approval and blessing, sometimes evidenced by signs and wonders (see Ex 8:19).

11:22 *Barnabas.* See notes on 4:36; 9:27. *Antioch.* See note on v. 19. The sending of Barnabas was apparently in keeping with the Jerusalem church's policy of sending leaders to check on new ministries that came to their attention (see 8:14).

11:24 *full of the Holy Spirit and of faith.* See the description of Stephen (6:5).

11:25 *Tarsus.* See 9:11,30 and note on 22:3.

11:26 *entire year.* Luke notes definite periods of time (18:11; 19:8,10; 24:27; 28:30). *Christians.* Whether adopted by believers or invented by enemies as a term of reproach, it is an apt title for those "belonging to Christ" (the meaning of the term).

11:27 *prophets.* The first mention of the gift of prophecy in Acts. Prophets preach, exhort, explain or, as in this case, foretell (see 13:1; 15:32; 19:6; 21:9–10; Rom 12:6; 1 Cor 12:10; 13:2,8; 14:3,6,29–37; see also notes on Jon 3:2; Zech 1:1; Eph 4:11).

11:28 *Agabus.* Later foretells Paul's imprisonment (21:10). In Acts, prophets are engaged in foretelling (v. 27; 21:9–10) at least as often as in "forthtelling" (15:32).

11:30 *elders.* First reference to them in Acts (see notes on 1 Tim 3:1; 5:17). Since the apostles are not mentioned, they may have been absent from Jerusalem at this time.

12:1 *about that time.* Some hold that the events recorded in ch. 12 group together matters concerning Herod and may not be in strict chronological order. For example, the arrival of Barnabas and Saul in Jerusalem (11:30) may have followed Herod's persecution and Peter's release from prison. Since the date of Herod's death was A.D. 44, these events would probably have occurred in 43. According to this view, the famine of 11:28 occurred c. 46, following Herod's death (v. 23). Others hold that such juggling of events is not necessary. Thus the relief gift of 11:30 came before Herod's death in 44, and the return of Barnabas and Saul (v. 25) followed Herod's death. According to the former view, the Jerusalem visit of Gal 2:1–10 was the famine visit of v. 25; 11:30. According to the latter view, the Gal 2:1 vis-

2 And he [a]had James the brother of John [b]put to death with a sword.

3 When he saw that it [a]pleased the Jews, he proceeded to arrest Peter also. Now [1]it was during [b]the days of Unleavened Bread.

4 When he had seized him, he put him in prison, delivering him to four [1a]squads of soldiers to guard him, intending after [b]the Passover to bring him out before the people.

5 So Peter was kept in the prison, but prayer for him was being made fervently by the church to God.

6 On [1]the very night when Herod was about to bring him forward, Peter was sleeping between two soldiers, [a]bound with two chains, and guards in front of the door were watching over the prison.

7 And behold, [a]an angel of the Lord suddenly [b]appeared and a light shone in the cell; and he struck Peter's side and woke him up, saying, "Get up quickly." And [c]his chains fell off his hands.

8 And the angel said to him, "Gird yourself and [1]put on your sandals." And he did so. And he *said to him, "Wrap your cloak around you and follow me."

9 And he went out and continued to follow, and he did not know that what was being done by the angel was real, but thought he was seeing [a]a vision.

10 When they had passed the first and second guard, they came to the iron gate that leads into the city, which [a]opened for them by itself; and they went out and went along one street, and immediately the angel departed from him.

11 When Peter [a]came [1]to himself, he said, "Now I know for sure that [b]the Lord has sent forth His angel and rescued me from the hand of Herod and from all [2]that the Jewish people were expecting."

12 And when he realized *this,* he went to the house of Mary, the mother of [a]John who was also called Mark, where many were gathered together and [b]were praying.

13 When he knocked at the door of the gate, [a]a servant-girl named Rhoda came to answer.

14 When she recognized Peter's voice, [a]because of her joy she did not open the gate, but ran in and announced that Peter was standing in front of the gate.

15 They said to her, "You are out of your mind!" But she kept insisting that it was so. They kept saying, "It is [a]his angel."

16 But Peter continued knocking; and when they had opened *the door,* they saw him and were amazed.

17 But [a]motioning to them with his hand to be silent, he described to them how the Lord had led him out of the prison. And he said, "Report these things to [1b]James and [c]the brethren." Then he left and went to another place.

18 Now when day came, there was no small disturbance among the soldiers *as to* [1]what could have become of Peter.

19 When Herod had searched for him and had not found him, he examined the guards and ordered that they [a]be led away *to execution.* Then he went down from Judea to [b]Caesarea and was spending time there.

Death of Herod

20 Now he was very angry with the people of [a]Tyre and Sidon; and with one accord they came to him, and having won over Blastus the king's chamberlain, they were asking for peace, because [b]their country was fed by the king's country.

21 On an appointed day Herod, having put on his royal apparel, took his seat on the

2 [a]Matt 4:21; 20:23 [b]Mark 10:39
3 [1]Lit *they were the days* [a]Acts 24:27; 25:9 [b]Ex 12:15; 23:15; Acts 20:6
4 [1]Lit *quaternions;* a quaternion was composed of four soldiers [a]John 19:23 [b]Ex 12:1-27; Mark 14:1; Acts 12:3
6 [1]Lit *that night* [a]Acts 21:33
7 [a]Acts 5:19 [b]Luke 2:9; 24:4 [c]Acts 16:26
8 [1]Lit *bind*
9 [a]Acts 9:10
10 [a]Acts 5:19; 16:26
11 [1]Lit *in himself* [2]Lit *the expectation of the people of the Jews* [a]Luke 15:17 [b]Dan 3:28; 6:22
12 [a]Acts 12:25; 13:5, 13; 15:37, 39; Col 4:10; 2 Tim 4:11; Philem 24; 1 Pet 5:13 [b]Acts 12:5
13 [a]John 18:16f
14 [a]Luke 24:41
15 [a]Matt 18:10
17 [1]Or *Jacob* [a]Acts 13:16; 19:33; 21:40 [b]Mark 6:3; Acts 15:13; 21:18; 1 Cor 15:7; Gal 1:19; 2:9, 12 [c]Acts 1:15
18 [1]Lit *what therefore had become*
19 [a]Acts 16:27; 27:42 [b]Acts 8:40
20 [a]Matt 11:21 [b]1 Kin 5:11; Ezra 3:7; Ezek 27:17

it was the Jerusalem council visit of 15:1–29. *Herod the king.* Agrippa I, grandson of Herod the Great (see notes on Matt 2:1; 14:1) and son of Aristobulus. He was a nephew of Herod Antipas, who had beheaded John the Baptist (Matt 14:3–12) and had tried Jesus (Luke 23:8–12). When Antipas was exiled, Agrippa received his tetrarchy as well as those of Philip and Lysanias (see Luke 3:1). In A.D. 41 Judea and Samaria were added to his realm.

12:2 *James.* Brother of John the apostle and son of Zebedee (Matt 4:21). This event took place about ten years after Jesus' death and resurrection. Jesus had warned of their coming suffering (Matt 20:23). *death with a sword.* Beheaded, like John the Baptist.

12:3 *days of Unleavened Bread.* See note on Luke 22:1.

12:4 *four squads.* One company of four soldiers for each of the four watches of the night. *Passover.* Another way of referring to the whole week of the festival (see note on Luke 22:1).

12:7 *a light shone.* The glory of the Lord (see Luke 2:9).

12:9 *he went out.* Out of the prison, probably the tower of Antonia, located at the northwest corner of the temple—the "barracks" where Paul was later held (see 21:34).

12:12 *Mary.* The aunt of Barnabas (see Col 4:10). Apparently her home was a gathering place for Christians. It may have been the location of the upper room where the Last Supper was held (see Mark 14:13–15; see also Acts 1:13) and the place of prayer in 4:31. *John . . . Mark.* See note on v. 25.

12:13 *Rhoda.* A hired servant, but in sympathy with the family and the church.

12:15 *his angel.* Reflects the belief that everyone has a personal angel who ministers to him (cf. Matt 18:10; Heb 1:14), adding the idea that such an angel occasionally showed himself and that his appearance resembled the person under his care.

12:16 *they . . . were amazed.* Though "prayer for him was being made fervently by the church" (v. 5).

12:17 *James.* The Lord's brother, a leader in the Jerusalem church (Gal 1:19). James, the brother of John had been killed (see v. 2).

12:19 *Caesarea.* Not only a headquarters for Roman procurators, but Agrippa used it as his capital when no procurators were assigned to Judea (see notes on 8:40; 10:1).

12:20 *Tyre and Sidon.* The leading cities of Phoenicia (Lebanon today). They were dependent on the grainfields of Galilee for their food. *Blastus.* The treasurer; not otherwise known.

12:21 *On an appointed day.* A festival Herod was celebrating in honor of Claudius Caesar (Josephus, *Antiquities,* 19.8.2). *royal*

[1]rostrum and *began* delivering an address to
them.
22 The people kept crying out, "The voice
of a god and not of a man!"
23 And immediately [a]an angel of the Lord
struck him because he did not give God the
glory, and he was eaten by worms and [1]died.
24 But [a]the word of the Lord continued to
grow and to be multiplied.
25 And [a]Barnabas and [a]Saul returned
[1]from Jerusalem [b]when they had fulfilled
their [2]mission, taking along with *them*
[c]John, who was also called Mark.

First Missionary Journey

13 Now there were at [a]Antioch, in the
[b]church that was *there,* [c]prophets and
[d]teachers: [e]Barnabas, and Simeon who was
called Niger, and Lucius of [f]Cyrene, and
Manaen who had been brought up with
[g]Herod the tetrarch, and Saul.
2 While they were ministering to the
Lord and fasting, [a]the Holy Spirit said, "Set
apart for Me [b]Barnabas and Saul for [c]the
work to which I have called them."
3 Then, when they had fasted and
[a]prayed and [b]laid their hands on them, [c]they
sent them away.
4 So, being [a]sent out by the Holy Spirit,
they went down to Seleucia and from there
they sailed to [b]Cyprus.

21 [1]Or *judgment seat* **23** [1]Lit *breathed his last breath* [a]2 Sam 24:16; 2 Kin 19:35; Acts 5:19 **24** [a]Acts 6:7; 19:20 **25** [1]Two early mss read *to Jerusalem* [2]Lit *ministry* [a]Acts 4:36; 13:1ff [b]Acts 11:30 [c]Acts 12:12 **13:1** [a]Acts 11:19 [b]Acts 11:26 [c]Acts 11:27; 15:32; 19:6; 21:9; 1 Cor 11:4f; 13:2, 8f; 14:29, 32, 37 [d]Rom 12:6f; 1 Cor 12:28f; Eph 4:11; James 3:1 [e]Acts 4:36 [f]Matt 27:32; Acts 11:20 [g]Matt 14:1 **2** [a]Acts 8:29; 13:4 [b]Acts 4:36 [c]Acts 9:15 **3** [a]Acts 1:24 [b]Acts 6:6 [c]Acts 13:4; 14:26 **4** [a]Acts 13:2f [b]Acts 4:36 **5** [a]Acts 9:20; 13:14 [b]Acts 12:12 **6** [a]Acts 8:9 [b]Matt 7:15 **7** [a]Acts 13:8, 12; 18:12; 19:38

5 When they reached Salamis, they
began to proclaim the word of God in [a]the
synagogues of the Jews; and they also had
[b]John as their helper.
6 When they had gone through the
whole island as far as Paphos, they found a
[a]magician, a Jewish [b]false prophet whose
name was Bar-Jesus,
7 who was with the [a]proconsul, Sergius
Paulus, a man of intelligence. This man
summoned Barnabas and Saul and sought to
hear the word of God.
8 But Elymas the [a]magician (for so his
name is translated) was opposing them,
seeking to turn the [b]proconsul away from
[c]the faith.
9 But Saul, who was also *known as* Paul,
[1a]filled with the Holy Spirit, fixed his gaze
on him,
10 and said, "You who are full of all deceit
and fraud, you [a]son of the devil, you enemy
of all righteousness, will you not cease to
make crooked [b]the straight ways of the Lord?
11 "Now, behold, [a]the hand of the Lord is
upon you, and you will be blind and not see
the sun for a time." And immediately a mist
and a darkness fell upon him, and he went

8 [a]Acts 8:9 [b]Acts 13:7, 12; 18:12; 19:38 [c]Acts 6:7 **9** [1]Or *having just been filled* [a]Acts 2:4; 4:8 **10** [a]Matt 13:38; John 8:44 [b]Hos 14:9; 2 Pet 2:15 **11** [a]Ex 9:3; 1 Sam 5:6f; Job 19:21; Ps 32:4; Heb 10:31

apparel. The historian Josephus describes a silver robe, dazzling bright, that Herod wore that day. When people acclaimed him a god, he did not deny it. He was seized with violent pains, was carried out and died five days later (Josephus, *Antiquities,* 19.8.2).

12:23 *angel of the Lord.* See note on v. 7. *eaten by worms.* A miserable death associated with Herod's acceptance of acclaim to be divine, but may also be seen as divine retribution for his persecution of the church.

12:24 *the word of the Lord . . . multiplied.* Third summary report of progress (see 6:7; 9:31). Three more follow (16:5; 19:20; 28:31).

12:25 *John . . . Mark.* See v. 12. He was perhaps the young man who fled on the night of Jesus' arrest (Mark 14:51–52). He wrote the second Gospel (see Introduction to Mark: Author; John Mark in the NT) and accompanied Barnabas and Saul on the first part of their first missionary journey (see notes on 15:38–39).

13:1 *prophets.* See note on 11:27. The special gift of inspiration experienced by OT prophets (Deut 18:18–20; 2 Pet 1:21) was known in the NT as well (2:17–18; 1 Cor 14:29–32; Eph 3:5). The prophets are second to the apostles in Paul's lists (1 Cor 12:28–29; Eph 2:20; 4:11; but cf. Luke 11:49; Rom 12:6; 1 Cor 12:10). *teachers.* See 11:26; 15:35; 18:11; 20:20; 28:31; 1 Cor 12:28–29; Eph 4:11. *Barnabas . . . Saul.* The church leaders at Antioch, perhaps listed in the order of their importance. *Barnabas.* See note on 4:36. He was sent originally to Antioch by the church in Jerusalem (11:22), had recently returned from taking alms to Jerusalem (12:25) and was a recognized leader in the church at Antioch. *Simeon who was called Niger.* "Simeon" suggests Jewish background; in that case, Niger (Latin for "black") may indicate his dark complexion. *Lucius of Cyrene.* Lucius is a Latin name. In the second group of preachers coming to Antioch, some were from Cyrene (11:20), capital of Libya (see 6:9 and note). *Manaen.* In Hebrew, Menahem. Since he was the foster brother of Herod Antipas, he would be able to tell of the thoughts and actions of Herod (see Luke 9:7–9).

13:2 *ministering to the Lord and fasting.* Paul's first missionary journey did not result from a planning session but from the Spirit's initiative as the leaders worshiped (see v. 4). The communication from the Holy Spirit may have come through the prophets.

13:3 *laid their hands on them.* For the purpose of separating the two for the designated work (see 14:26 for the completion of the mission). Fasting and prayer accompany this appointment (see 14:23; cf. Luke 2:37).

13:4 See map No. 11 at the end of the study Bible. *Seleucia.* The seaport of Antioch (16 miles to the west, and 5 miles upstream from the mouth of the Orontes River). *Cyprus.* Many Jews lived there, and the gospel had already been preached there (11:19–20; see note on 11:19).

13:5 *Salamis.* A town on the east coast of the central plain of Cyprus, near modern Famagusta. *John.* John Mark, a cousin of Barnabas (see Col 4:10); see also note on 12:25.

13:6 *Paphos.* At the western end of Cyprus, nearly 100 miles from Salamis. It was the headquarters for Roman rule. *Bar-jesus.* "Bar" is Aramaic for "son of"; "Jesus" is derived from the Greek for "Joshua" (see note on Matt 1:21).

13:7 *proconsul.* Since Cyprus was a Roman senatorial province, a proconsul was assigned to it.

13:8 *Elymas.* A Semitic name meaning "sorcerer" or "magician" or "wise man" (probably a self-assumed designation).

13:9 *Saul . . . known as Paul.* The names mean "asked [of God]" and "little" respectively. It was customary to have a given name, in this case Saul (Hebrew, Jewish background), and a later name, in this case Paul (Roman, Hellenistic background). From now on Saul is called Paul in Acts. This may be due to Saul's success in preaching to Paulus or to the fact that he is now entering the Gentile phase of his ministry. The order in which they are mentioned now changes from "Barnabas and Saul" to "Paul and Barnabas." Upon their return to the Jerusalem church,

The Spread of the Gospel

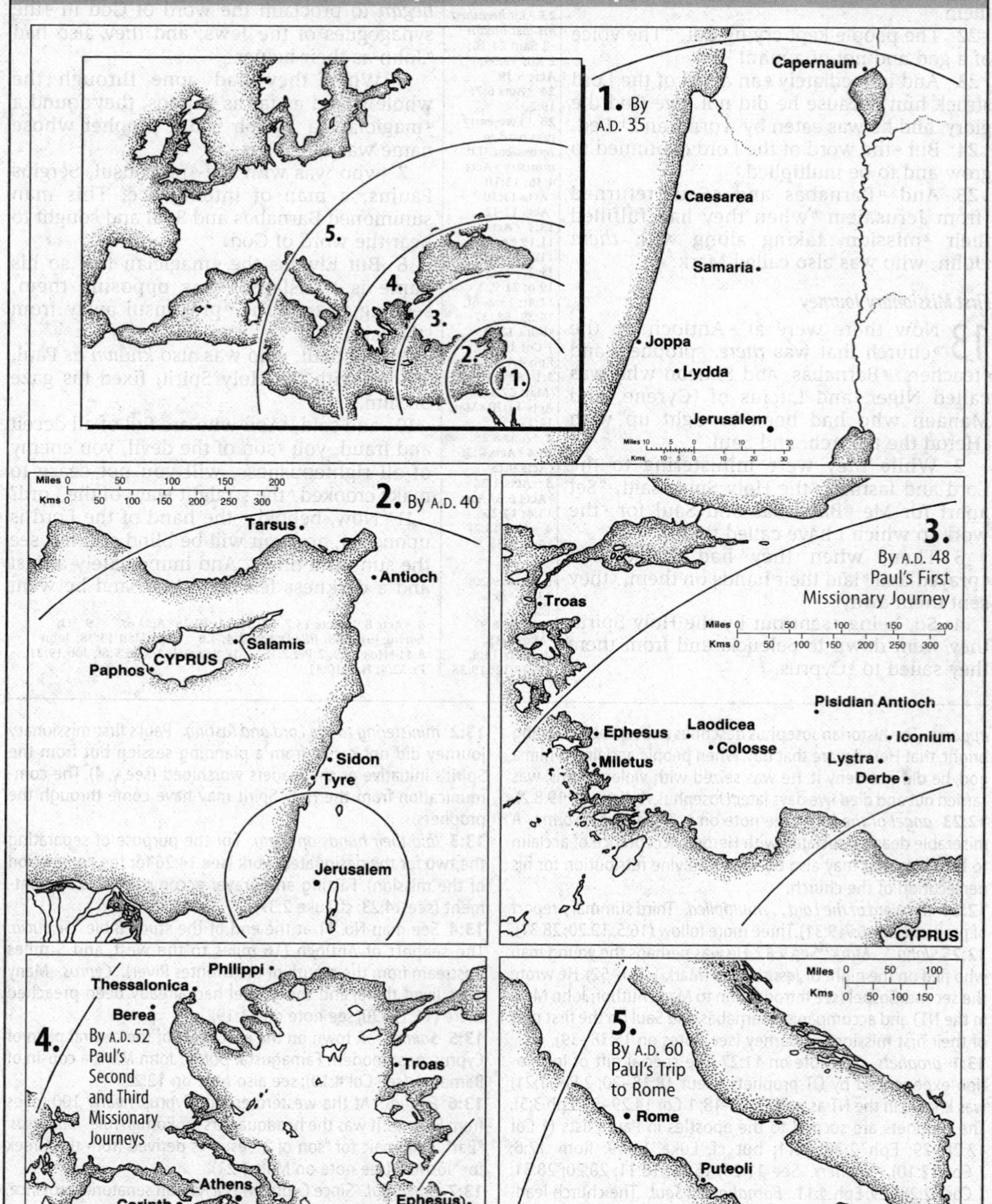

1. By A.D. 35

Capernaum
Caesarea
Samaria
Joppa
Lydda
Jerusalem

Miles 10 5 0 10 20
Kms 10 5 0 10 20 30

2. By A.D. 40

Miles 0 50 100 150 200
Kms 0 50 100 150 200 250 300

Tarsus
Antioch
Salamis
CYPRUS
Paphos
Sidon
Tyre
Jerusalem

3. By A.D. 48
Paul's First
Missionary Journey

Miles 0 50 100 150 200
Kms 0 50 100 150 200 250 300

Troas
Pisidian Antioch
Ephesus
Laodicea
Colosse
Iconium
Miletus
Lystra
Derbe
CYPRUS

4. By A.D. 52
Paul's
Second
and Third
Missionary
Journeys

Philippi
Thessalonica
Berea
Troas
Athens
Corinth
Ephesus
CRETE

Miles 0 50 100
Kms 0 50 100 150 200

5. By A.D. 60
Paul's Trip
to Rome

Miles 0 50 100
Kms 0 50 100 150

Rome
Puteoli
Rhegium
SICILY
Syracuse

about seeking those who would lead him by
the hand.
12 Then the [a]proconsul believed when he
saw what had happened, being amazed at
[b]the teaching of the Lord.
13 Now Paul and his companions put out
to sea from [a]Paphos and came to [b]Perga in
[c]Pamphylia; but [d]John left them and
returned to Jerusalem.
14 But going on from Perga, they arrived at
[a]Pisidian [b]Antioch, and on [c]the Sabbath day
they went into [d]the synagogue and sat down.
15 After [a]the reading of the Law and [b]the
Prophets [c]the synagogue officials sent to
them, saying, "Brethren, if you have any
word of exhortation for the people, say it."
16 Paul stood up, and [a]motioning with his
hand said,
"Men of Israel, and [b]you who fear God,
listen:
17 "The God of this people Israel [a]chose
our fathers and [1b]made the people great during their stay in the land of Egypt, and with
an uplifted arm [c]He led them out from it.
18 "For [a]a period of about forty years [b]He
put up with them in the wilderness.
19 "[a]When He had destroyed [b]seven nations in the land of Canaan, He [c]distributed
their land as an inheritance—*all of which
took* [d]about four hundred and fifty years.
20 "After these things He [a]gave *them*
judges until [b]Samuel the prophet.

12 [a]Acts 13:7, 8; 18:12; 19:38 [b]Acts 8:25; 13:49; 15:35f; 19:10, 20 **13** [a]Acts 13:6 [b]Acts 14:25 [c]Acts 2:10; 14:24; 15:38; 27:5 [d]Acts 12:12 **14** [a]Acts 14:24 [b]Acts 14:19, 21; 2 Tim 3:11 [c]Acts 13:42, 44; 16:13; 17:2; 18:4 [d]Acts 9:20; 13:5 **15** [a]Acts 15:21; 2 Cor 3:14f [b]Acts 13:27 [c]Mark 5:22 **16** [a]Acts 12:17 **16** [b]Acts 10:2; 13:26 **17** [1]Or *exalted* [a]Ex 6:1, 6; 13:14, 16; Deut 7:6-8; Acts 7:17ff [b]Ex 1:7 [c]Ex 12:51 **18** [a]Num 14:34; Acts 7:36 [b]Deut 1:31 **19** [a]Acts 7:45 [b]Deut 7:1 [c]Josh 14:1; 19:51; Ps 78:55 [d]Judg 11:26; 1 Kin 6:1 **20** [a]Judg 2:16 [b]1 Sam 3:20; Acts 3:24

however, the order reverts to "Barnabas and Paul" (15:12).

13:12 *proconsul believed.* He was convinced by the miracle and the message.

13:13 *Perga in Pamphylia.* Perga was the capital of Pamphylia, a coastal province of Asia Minor between the provinces of Lycia and Cilicia, and was 5 miles inland and 12 miles east of the important seaport Attalia. *John left them.* Homesickness to get back to Jerusalem, an illness of Paul necessitating a change in plans and a trip to Galatia, and a change in leadership from Barnabas to Paul have all been suggested as reasons for John Mark's return. Paul's dissatisfaction with his departure is noted later (15:37–39).

13:14 *Pisidian.* See note on 14:24. *Antioch.* Named after Antiochus, king of Syria after the death of Alexander the Great. It was 110 miles from Perga and was at the hub of good roads and trade. The city had a large Jewish population. It was a Roman colony, which meant that a contingent of retired military men was settled there. They were given free land and were made citizens of the city of Rome, with all the accompanying privileges. *synagogue.* Paul's regular practice was to begin his preaching in the synagogue as long as the Jews would allow it (see v. 5; 14:1; 17:1,10,17; 18:4,19; 19:8). His reason for doing so was grounded in his understanding of God's redemptive plan (see v. 46; Rom 1:16; 2:9–10; see also Rom 9–11). He was not neglecting his Gentile mission, for the God-fearers (Gentiles committed to worshiping the one true God) were part of the audience. Moreover, the synagogue provided a ready-made preaching situation with a building, regularly scheduled meetings and a people who knew the OT Scriptures. It was customary to invite visitors, and especially visiting rabbis (such as Paul), to address the gathering.

13:15 *the Law and the Prophets.* Sections from the OT were read, followed by exposition and exhortation. *officials.* Those who were responsible for calling readers and preachers, arranging the service and maintaining order.

13:16 *you who fear God.* See note on 10:2.

13:19 *about four hundred and fifty years.* The 400 years of the

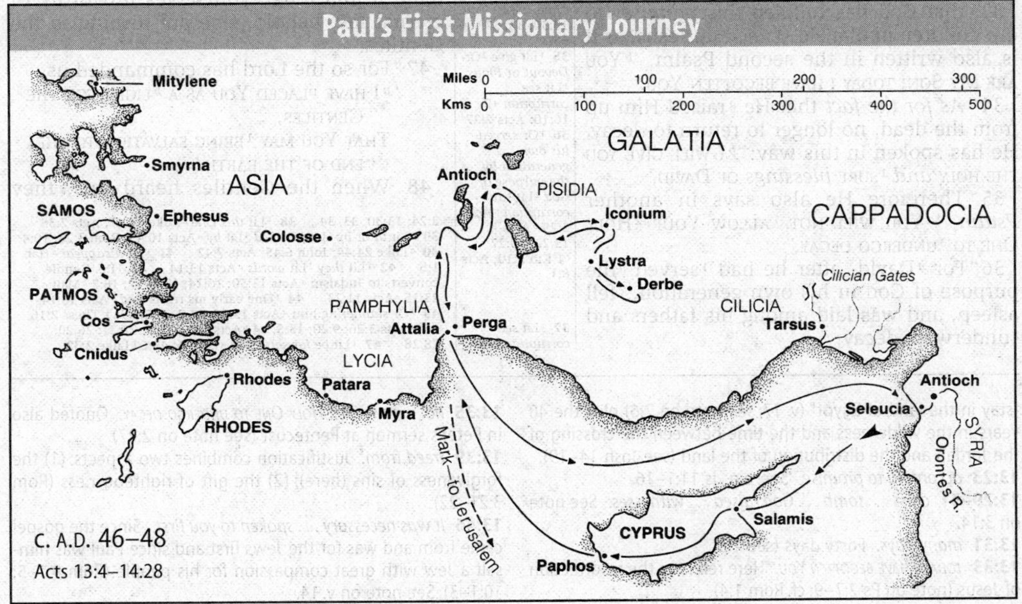

Paul's First Missionary Journey
Miles 0 100 200 300
Kms 0 100 200 300 400 500
Mitylene
Smyrna
ASIA
SAMOS
Ephesus
Colosse
PATMOS
Cos
Cnidus
Rhodes
RHODES
Patara
Myra
LYCIA
PAMPHYLIA
Attalia
Perga
Antioch
PISIDIA
Iconium
Lystra
Derbe
GALATIA
CAPPADOCIA
Cilician Gates
CILICIA
Tarsus
Antioch
Seleucia
SYRIA
Orontes R.
Salamis
CYPRUS
Paphos
Mark—to Jerusalem
C. A.D. 46–48
Acts 13:4–14:28

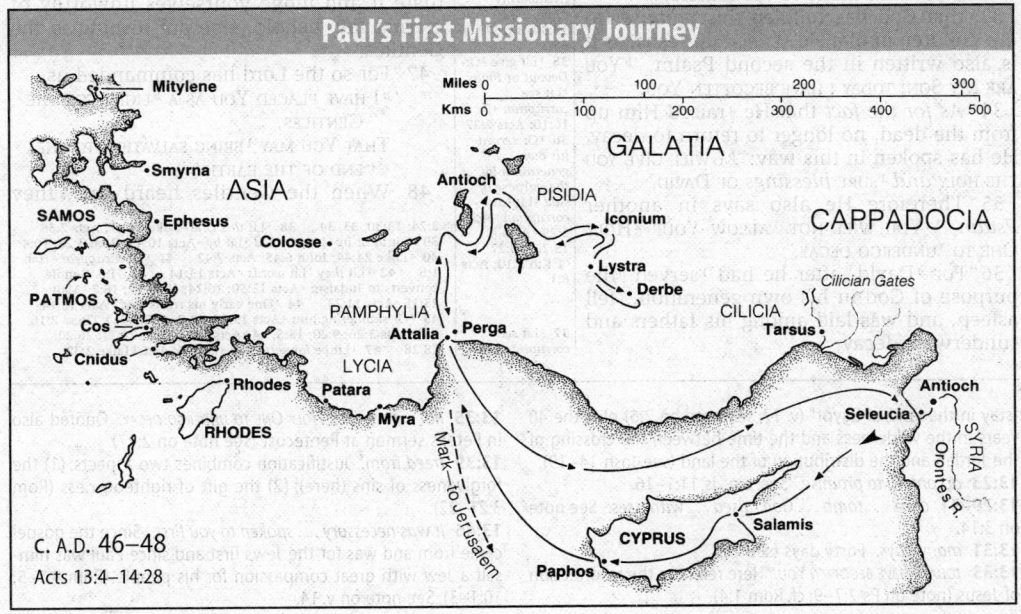

21 "Then they [a]asked for a king, and God gave them [b]Saul the son of Kish, a man of the tribe of Benjamin, for forty years.

22 "After He had [a]removed him, He raised up David to be their king, concerning whom He also testified and said, '[b]I HAVE FOUND DAVID the son of Jesse, A MAN AFTER MY HEART, who will do all My [1]will.'

23 "[a]From the descendants of this man, [b]according to promise, God has brought to Israel [c]a Savior, Jesus,

24 after [a]John had proclaimed before [1]His coming a [b]baptism of repentance to all the people of Israel.

25 "And while John [a]was completing his course, [b]he kept saying, 'What do you suppose that I am? I am not *He.* But behold, one is coming after me the sandals of whose feet I am not worthy to untie.'

26 "Brethren, sons of Abraham's family, and those among you who fear God, to us the message of [a]this salvation has been sent.

27 "For those who live in Jerusalem, and their [a]rulers, [b]recognizing neither Him nor the [1]utterances of [c]the prophets which are [d]read every Sabbath, fulfilled *these* by condemning *Him.*

28 "And though they found no ground for *putting Him to* death, they [a]asked Pilate that He be [1]executed.

29 "When they had [a]carried out all that was written concerning Him, [b]they took Him down from [c]the [1]cross and [d]laid Him in a tomb.

30 "But God [a]raised Him from the dead;

31 and for many days [a]He appeared to those who came up with Him from Galilee to Jerusalem, the very ones who are now [b]His witnesses to the people.

32 "And we [a]preach to you the good news of [b]the promise made to the fathers,

33 that God has fulfilled this *promise* [1]to our children in that He [a]raised up Jesus, as it is also written in the second Psalm, '[b]YOU ARE MY SON; TODAY I HAVE BEGOTTEN YOU.'

34 "*As for the fact* that He [a]raised Him up from the dead, no longer to return to decay, He has spoken in this way: '[b]I WILL GIVE YOU THE HOLY *and* [1]SURE *blessings* OF DAVID.'

35 "Therefore He also says in another *Psalm,* '[a]YOU WILL NOT [1]ALLOW YOUR [2]HOLY ONE TO [3]UNDERGO DECAY.'

36 "For [a]David, after he had [1]served [b]the purpose of God in his own generation, [c]fell asleep, and was laid among his fathers and [2]underwent decay;

37 but He whom God [a]raised did not [1]undergo decay.

38 "Therefore let it be known to you, brethren, that [a]through [1]Him forgiveness of sins is proclaimed to you,

39 and [1]through Him [a]everyone who believes is [2]freed [3]from all things, from which you could not be [2]freed [3]through the Law of Moses.

40 "Therefore take heed, so that the thing spoken of [a]in the Prophets may not come upon *you:*

41 '[a]BEHOLD, YOU SCOFFERS, AND MARVEL, AND [1]PERISH;
FOR I AM ACCOMPLISHING A WORK IN YOUR DAYS,
A WORK WHICH YOU WILL NEVER BELIEVE,
THOUGH SOMEONE SHOULD DESCRIBE IT TO YOU.' "

42 As [1]Paul and Barnabas were going out, the people kept begging that these [2]things might be spoken to them the next [a]Sabbath.

43 Now when *the meeting of* the synagogue had broken up, many of the Jews and of the [a]God-fearing [1][b]proselytes followed Paul and Barnabas, who, speaking to them, were urging them to continue in [c]the grace of God.

Paul Turns to the Gentiles

44 The next [a]Sabbath nearly the whole city assembled to hear the word of [1]the Lord.

45 But when [a]the Jews saw the crowds, they were filled with jealousy and *began* contradicting the things spoken by Paul, and were [1]blaspheming.

46 Paul and Barnabas spoke out boldly and said, "It was necessary that the word of God be spoken to you [a]first; since you repudiate it and judge yourselves unworthy of eternal life, behold, [b]we are turning to the Gentiles.

47 "For so the Lord has commanded us,
'[a]I HAVE PLACED YOU AS A [b]LIGHT FOR THE GENTILES,
THAT YOU MAY [1]BRING SALVATION TO THE END OF THE EARTH.' "

48 When the Gentiles heard this, they

21 [a]1 Sam 8:5 [b]1 Sam 9:1f; 10:1, 21 **22** [1]Lit *wishes* [a]1 Sam 15:23, 26, 28; 16:1, 13 [b]1 Sam 13:14; Ps 89:20; Acts 7:46 **23** [a]Matt 1:1 [b]Acts 13:32f [c]Luke 2:11; John 4:42 **24** [1]Lit *the face of His entering* [a]Mark 1:1-4; Acts 1:22; 19:4 [b]Luke 3:3 **25** [a]Acts 20:24 [b]Matt 3:11; Mark 1:7; Luke 3:16; John 1:20, 27 **26** [a]John 6:68; Acts 4:12; 5:20; 13:46; 28:28 **27** [1]Lit *voices* [a]Luke 23:13 [b]Acts 3:17 [c]Luke 24:27 [d]Acts 13:15 **28** [1]Lit *destroyed* [a]Matt 27:22, 23; Mark 15:13, 14; Luke 23:21-23; John 19:15; Acts 3:14 **29** [1]Lit *wood* [a]Acts 26:22 [b]Luke 23:53 [c]Acts 5:30 [d]Matt 27:57-61; Mark 15:42-47; Luke 23:50-56; John 19:38-42 **30** [a]Acts 2:24; 13:33, 34, 37 **31** [a]Acts 1:3 [b]Luke 24:48 **32** [a]Acts 5:42; 14:15 [b]Acts 13:23; 26:6; Rom 1:2; 4:13; 9:4 **33** [1]Late mss read *to us their children* [a]Acts 2:24; 13:30, 34, 37 [b]Ps 2:7 **34** [1]Lit *trustworthy* [a]Acts 2:24; 13:30, 33, 37 [b]Is 55:3 **35** [1]Lit *give* [2]Or *Devout* or *Pious* [3]Lit *see corruption* [a]Ps 16:10; Acts 2:27 **36** [1]Or *served his own generation by the purpose of God* [2]Lit *saw corruption* [a]Acts 2:29 [b]Acts 13:22; 20:27 [c]1 Kin 2:10; Acts 8:1 **37** [1]Lit *see corruption* [a]Acts 2:24; 13:30, 33, 34 **38** [1]Lit *this One* [a]Luke 24:47; Acts 2:38 **39** [1]Lit *in* or *by* [2]Lit *justified* [3]Lit *by* [a]Acts 10:43; Rom 3:28; 10:4 **40** [a]Luke 24:44; John 6:45; Acts 7:42 **41** [1]Lit *disappear* [a]Hab 1:5 **42** [1]Lit *they* [2]Lit *words* [a]Acts 13:14 **43** [1]I.e. Gentile converts to Judaism [a]Acts 13:50; 16:14; 17:4, 17; 18:7 [b]Matt 23:15 [c]Acts 11:23 **44** [1]One early ms reads *God* [a]Acts 13:14 **45** [1]Or *slandering* him [a]Acts 13:50; 14:2, 4, 5, 19; 1 Thess 2:16 **46** [a]Acts 3:26; 9:20; 13:5, 14 [b]Acts 18:6; 19:9; 22:21; 26:20; 28:28 **47** [1]Lit *be for salvation* [a]Is 42:6; 49:6 [b]Luke 2:32

"stay in the land of Egypt" (v. 17; see note on 7:6) plus the 40 years in the wilderness and the time between the crossing of the Jordan and the distribution of the land (see Josh 14–19).

13:23 *according to promise.* See, e.g., Is 11:1–16.

13:29–31 *cross . . . tomb . . . God raised . . . witnesses.* See note on 3:14.

13:31 *many days.* Forty days (see 1:3).

13:33 *TODAY I HAVE BEGOTTEN YOU.* Here refers to the resurrection of Jesus (note on Ps 2:7–9; cf. Rom 1:4).

13:35 *NOT ALLOW YOUR HOLY ONE TO UNDERGO DECAY.* Quoted also in Peter's sermon at Pentecost (see note on 2:27).

13:39 *freed from.* Justification combines two aspects: (1) the forgiveness of sins (here); (2) the gift of righteousness (Rom 3:21–22).

13:46 *It was necessary . . . spoken to you first.* Since the gospel came from and was for the Jews first and since Paul was himself a Jew with great compassion for his people (Rom 9:1–5; 10:1–3). See note on v. 14.

began rejoicing and glorifying [a]the word of
[1]the Lord; and as many as [b]had been
appointed to eternal life believed.
49 And [a]the word of the Lord was being
spread through the whole region.
50 But [a]the Jews incited the [1b]devout
women [c]of prominence and the leading men
of the city, and instigated a persecution
against Paul and Barnabas, and drove them
out of their [2]district.
51 But [a]they shook off the dust of their
feet *in protest* against them and went to [b]Ico-
nium.
52 And the disciples were continually
[a]filled with joy and with the Holy Spirit.

Acceptance and Opposition

14 In [a]Iconium [b]they entered the synagogue of the Jews together, and spoke
in such a manner [c]that a large number
of people believed, both of Jews and of
[d]Greeks.
2 But [a]the Jews who [1b]disbelieved stirred
up the [2]minds of the Gentiles and embittered
them against [c]the brethren.
3 Therefore they spent a long time *there*
[a]speaking boldly *with reliance* upon the
Lord, who was testifying to the word of His
grace, granting that [1b]signs and wonders be
done by their hands.
4 [a]But the [1]people of the city were divided; and some [2]sided with [b]the Jews, and
some with [c]the apostles.
5 And when an attempt was made by
both the Gentiles and [a]the Jews with their
rulers, to mistreat and to [b]stone them,
6 they became aware of it and fled to the
cities of [a]Lycaonia, [b]Lystra and [c]Derbe, and
the surrounding region;
7 and there they continued to [a]preach
the gospel.
8 At [a]Lystra [b]a man was sitting who had
no strength in his feet, lame from his mother's womb, who had never walked.
9 This man was listening to Paul as he
spoke, who, [a]when he had fixed his gaze on
him and had seen that he had [b]faith to be
[1]made well,
10 said with a loud voice, "Stand upright
on your feet." [a]And he leaped up and *began*
to walk.
11 When the crowds saw what Paul had
done, they raised their voice, saying in the
[a]Lycaonian language, "[b]The gods have become like men and have come down to us."
12 And they *began* calling Barnabas,
[1]Zeus, and Paul, [2]Hermes, because he was
[3]the chief speaker.
13 The priest of Zeus, whose *temple* was
[1]just outside the city, brought oxen and gar-
lands to the gates, and [a]wanted to offer sacrifice with the crowds.
14 But when [a]the apostles Barnabas and
Paul heard of it, they [b]tore their [1]robes and
rushed out into the crowd, crying out
15 and saying, "Men, why are you doing
these things? We are also [a]men of the same
nature as you, and [b]preach the gospel to you
that you should turn from these [1c]vain things
to a [d]living God, [e]WHO MADE THE HEAVEN AND
THE EARTH AND THE SEA AND ALL THAT IS IN THEM.

48 [1]Two early mss read *God* [a]Acts 13:12 [b]Rom 8:28ff; Eph 1:4f, 11 **49** [a]Acts 13:12 **50** [1]Or *worshiping* [2]Lit *boundaries* [a]Acts 13:45; 14:2, 4, 5, 19; 1 Thess 2:14ff [b]Acts 13:43; 16:14; 17:4, 17; 18:7 [c]Mark 15:43 **51** [a]Matt 10:14; Mark 6:11; Luke 9:5; 10:11; Acts 18:6 [b]Acts 14:1, 19, 21; 16:2; 2 Tim 3:11 **52** [a]Acts 2:4 **14:1** [a]Acts 13:51; 14:19, 21; 16:2; 2 Tim 3:11 [b]Acts 13:5 [c]Acts 2:47 [d]John 7:35; Acts 18:4 **2** [1]Or *disobeyed* [2]Lit *souls* [a]Acts 13:45, 50; 14:4, 5, 19; 1 Thess 2:14ff [b]John 3:36 [c]Acts 1:15 **3** [1]Or *attesting miracles* [a]Acts 4:29f; 20:32; Heb 2:4 [b]John 4:48 **4** [1]Lit *multitude* [2]Lit *were* [a]Acts 17:4f; 19:9; 28:24 [b]Acts 13:45, 50; 14:2, 5, 19; 1 Thess 2:14ff [c]Acts 14:14 **5** [a]Acts 13:45, 50; 14:2, 4, 19; 1 Thess 2:14ff [b]Acts 14:19 **6** [a]Acts 14:11 [b]Acts 14:8, 21; 16:1f; 2 Tim 3:11 [c]Acts 14:20; 16:1; 20:4 **7** [a]Acts 14:15, 21; 16:10

8 [a]Acts 14:6, 21; 16:1f; 2 Tim 3:11 [b]Acts 3:2 **9** [1]Lit *saved* [a]Acts 3:4; 10:4 [b]Matt 9:28 **10** [a]Acts 3:8 **11** [a]Acts 14:6 [b]Acts 8:10; 28:6 **12** [1]Lat *Jupiter*, the chief pagan god [2]Lat *Mercury*, considered the messenger or spokesman for the pagan gods of Greece and Rome [3]Lit *the leader of the speaking* **13** [1]Lit *in front of* [a]Dan 2:46 **14** [1]Or *outer garments* [a]Acts 14:4 [b]Num 14:6; Matt 26:65; Mark 14:63 **15** [1]I.e. idols [a]Acts 10:26; James 5:17 [b]Acts 13:32; 14:7, 21 [c]Deut 32:21; 1 Sam 12:21; Jer 8:19; 14:22; 1 Cor 8:4 [d]Matt 16:16 [e]Ex 20:11; Ps 146:6; Acts 4:24; 17:24; Rev 14:7

13:48 *as many as had been appointed to eternal life believed.* Possession of eternal life involves both human faith and divine appointment.

13:51 *shook off the dust.* To show the severance of responsibility and the repudiation of those who had rejected their message and had brought suffering to the servants of the Lord (see note on Luke 9:5). *Iconium.* Modern Konya; it was an important crossroads and agricultural center in the central plain of the province of Galatia.

13:52 *filled . . . with the Holy Spirit.* See note on 2:4.

14:1 *large number.* At first there was good success, then bitter opposition from the Jews (v. 2). But these evidently failed in their initial attempt, for Paul and Barnabas remained there a considerable time (v. 3). A second wave of persecution was planned, involving violence (v. 5).

14:3 *was testifying . . . granting that signs and wonders.* A major purpose of miracles was to confirm the truth of the words and the approval of God.

14:4 *apostles.* Both Paul and Barnabas are called apostles (see v. 14; see also note on Mark 6:30). The term is used here not of the twelve but in the broader sense to refer to persons sent on a mission, i.e., missionaries (see 13:2–3).

14:5 *stone them.* A Jewish mode of execution for blasphemy. Probably mob action was planned here.

14:6 *cities of Lycaonia.* Lycaonia was a district east of Pisidia, north of the Taurus Mountains. It was part of the Roman province of Galatia. *Lystra.* A Roman colony (see note on 13:14) and probable home of Timothy (though he was known in Iconium as well), it was about 20 miles from Iconium and 130 miles from Antioch. *Derbe.* About 60 miles from Lystra; home of Gaius (see 20:4 and note on 14:20).

14:12 *Zeus . . . Hermes.* Zeus was the patron god of the city, and his temple was there. People who came to bring sacrifices to Zeus apparently decided to make an offering to Paul and Barnabas instead. The identification of Zeus with Barnabas may indicate that his appearance was more imposing, and Paul was identified as the god Hermes (the Roman Mercury) because he was the spokesman (see 28:6). This incident may have been occasioned by an ancient legend that told of a supposed visit to the same general area by Zeus and Hermes. They were, however, not recognized by anyone except an old couple. So the people of Lystra were determined not to allow such an oversight to happen again.

14:13 *gates.* The Greek for this expression can refer to the temple gates, the city gates or house gates.

14:14 *tore their robes.* A Jewish way of expressing great anguish (see Gen 37:29,34).

14:15 *vain things.* Used in the OT to denote false gods (see 1 Sam 12:21).

16 "[1]In the generations gone by He [a]per-
mitted all the [2]nations to [b]go their own
ways;
17 and yet [a]He did not leave Himself without witness, in that He did good and [b]gave
you rains from heaven and fruitful seasons,
[1]satisfying your hearts with food and gladness."
18 *Even* saying these things, with difficulty they restrained the crowds from offering
sacrifice to them.
19 But [a]Jews came from [b]Antioch and
[c]Iconium, and having won over the crowds,
they [d]stoned Paul and dragged him out of the
city, supposing him to be dead.
20 But while [a]the disciples stood around
him, he got up and entered the city. The next
day he went away with Barnabas to [b]Derbe.
21 After they had [a]preached the gospel to
that city and had [b]made many disciples, they
returned to [c]Lystra and to [d]Iconium and to
[e]Antioch,
22 strengthening the souls of [a]the disciples, encouraging them to continue in [b]the
faith, and *saying*, "[c]Through many tribulations we must enter the kingdom of God."
23 When [a]they had appointed [b]elders for
them in every church, having [c]prayed with
fasting, they [d]commended them to the Lord
in whom they had believed.
24 They passed through [a]Pisidia and came
into [b]Pamphylia.
25 When they had spoken the word in
[a]Perga, they went down to Attalia.
26 From there they sailed to [a]Antioch,
from [b]which they had been [c]commended to
the grace of God for the work that they had
[1]accomplished.

16 [1]Lit *Who in the generations gone by permitted* [2]Or *Gentiles* [a]Acts 17:30 [b]Ps 81:12; Mic 4:5
17 [1]Lit *filling* [a]Acts 17:26f; Rom 1:19f [b]Deut 11:14; Job 5:10; Ps 65:10f; Ezek 34:26f; Joel 2:23
19 [a]Acts 13:45, 50; 14:2, 4, 5; 1 Thess 2:14ff [b]Acts 13:14; 14:21, 26 [c]Acts 13:51; 14:1, 21 [d]Acts 14:5; 2 Cor 11:25; 2 Tim 3:11
20 [a]Acts 11:26; 14:22, 28 [b]Acts 14:6
21 [a]Acts 14:7 [b]Acts 2:47 [c]Acts 14:6 [d]Acts 13:51; 14:1, 19 [e]Acts 13:14; 14:19, 26
22 [a]Acts 11:26; 14:28 [b]Acts 6:7 [c]Mark 10:30; John 15:18, 20; 16:33; Acts 9:16; 1 Thess 3:3; 2 Tim 3:12; 1 Pet 2:21; Rev 1:9
23 [a]2 Cor 8:19; Titus 1:5 [b]Acts 11:30 [c]Acts 1:24; 13:3 [d]Acts 20:32
24 [a]Acts 13:14 [b]Acts 13:13
25 [a]Acts 13:13
26 [1]Lit *fulfilled* [a]Acts 11:19 [b]Acts 13:3 [c]Acts 11:23; 15:40
27 [1]Lit *that* [a]Acts 15:3, 4, 12; 21:19 [b]1 Cor 16:9; 2 Cor 2:12; Col 4:3; Rev 3:8

27 When they had arrived and gathered
the church together, they *began* to [a]report all
things that God had done with them and
[1]how He had opened a [b]door of faith to the
Gentiles.
28 And they spent [1]a long time with [a]the
disciples.

The Council at Jerusalem

15 [a]Some men came down from Judea
and *began* teaching [b]the brethren,
"Unless you are [c]circumcised according to
[d]the custom of Moses, you cannot be saved."
2 And when Paul and Barnabas had
[1]great dissension and [a]debate with them,
[b]*the brethren* determined that Paul and Barnabas and some others of them should go up
to Jerusalem to the [c]apostles and elders concerning this issue.
3 Therefore, being [a]sent on their way by
the church, they were passing through both
[b]Phoenicia and Samaria, [c]describing in detail
the conversion of the Gentiles, and were
bringing great joy to all [d]the brethren.
4 When they arrived at Jerusalem, they
were received by the church and [a]the apostles and the elders, and they [b]reported all
that God had done with them.
5 But some of [a]the sect of the [b]Pharisees
who had believed stood up, saying, "It is
necessary to [c]circumcise them and to direct
them to observe the Law of Moses."

28 [1]Lit *not a little* [a]Acts 11:26; 14:22 **15:1** [a]Acts 15:24 [b]Acts 1:15; 15:3, 22, 32 [c]Lev 12:3; Acts 15:5; 1 Cor 7:18; Gal 2:11, 14; 5:2f [d]Acts 6:14 **2** [1]Lit *not a little* [a]Acts 15:7 [b]Gal 2:2 [c]Acts 11:30; 15:4, 6, 22, 23; 16:4 **3** [a]Acts 20:38; 21:5; Rom 15:24; 1 Cor 16:6, 11; 2 Cor 1:16; Titus 3:13; 3 John 6 [b]Acts 11:19 [c]Acts 14:27; 15:4, 12 [d]Acts 1:15; 15:22, 32 **4** [a]Acts 11:30; 15:6, 22, 23; 16:4 [b]Acts 14:27; 15:12 **5** [a]Acts 5:17; 24:5, 14; 26:5; 28:22 [b]Matt 3:7; Acts 26:5 [c]1 Cor 7:18; Gal 2:11, 14; 5:2f

14:19 *they stoned Paul.* Inside the city rather than at the usual place of execution outside the walls (cf. 2 Cor 12:2).
14:20 *disciples stood around him.* Young Timothy may have been present (see 2 Tim 3:10–11). *Derbe.* A border town in the southeastern part of the Lycaonian region of Galatia (see note on v. 6). An inscription naming the city has been discovered about 30 miles east of what was previously thought to be the city site.
14:23 *appointed.* The Greek for this word (used also in 2 Cor 8:19) can mean (1) to stretch out the hand, (2) to appoint by show of hands or (3) to appoint or elect without regard to the method. In 6:6 the appointment of the seven included selection by the church and presentation to the apostles, who prayed and laid their hands on them. Because these were new churches, at least partly pagan in background, Paul and Barnabas may have both selected and appointed the elders.
14:24 *Pisidia.* A district about 120 miles long and 50 miles wide, north of Pamphylia (13:13–14). Bandits frequented the region (see perhaps 2 Cor 11:26). *Pamphylia.* A district 80 miles long and 20 miles at the widest part, on the southern coast of Asia Minor. After A.D. 74 Pisidia was included in the Roman province of Pamphylia (see 13:13).
14:25 *Perga.* See note on 13:13. *Attalia.* The best harbor on the coast of Pamphylia (see 13:13).
14:26 *Antioch.* See 11:20; see also note on 11:19.
14:27 *opened a door of faith.* God had brought Gentiles to faith—had, as it were, opened the door for them to believe (cf. 11:18).
14:28 *long time.* Probably more than a year.
15:1 *Some men.* Probably from "the sect of the Pharisees" (v. 5). These were believers who insisted that before a person could become a true Christian he must keep the law of Moses, and the test of such compliance was circumcision. *from Judea.* Meant that these Judaizers (or legalists) were given a hearing, not that they correctly represented the apostles and elders of Jerusalem (cf. v. 24).
15:2 *go up to Jerusalem.* See notes on 12:1; Gal 2:1. Those who hold that Gal 2:1–10 refers to the famine visit of 11:27–30; 12:25 argue that since Gal 2:2 says that the visit mentioned there was occasioned by a revelation, it must refer to Agabus's prediction of the coming famine (11:27–28). Those who believe that Gal 2:1–10 refers to the Jerusalem council visit of 15:1–22 assert that the famine visit occurred at the time of Herod Agrippa's death in A.D. 44 (11:27–30; 12:25). Thus Saul's conversion, which was 14 years earlier (Gal 2:1), would have occurred in 30, the probable year of Christ's crucifixion—which obviously seems too early.
15:4–22 The sequence of meetings described in vv. 4–22 is: (1) a general meeting of welcome and report (vv. 4–5); (2) a meeting of the leaders (perhaps to one side) while the church was still assembled (vv. 6–11); (3) a meeting of the apostles, the elders and the whole assembly (vv. 12–22).
15:4 The first meeting was a report, cordially received, about the work done among the Gentiles.
15:5 *some of the sect of the Pharisees . . . believed.* Some Phar-

6 [a]The apostles and the elders came
together to [1]look into this [2]matter.
7 After there had been much [a]debate,
Peter stood up and said to them, "Brethren,
you know that [1]in the early days [b]God made
a choice among you, that by my mouth the
Gentiles would hear the word of [c]the gospel
and believe.
8 "And God, [a]who knows the heart, testified to them [b]giving them the Holy Spirit,
just as He also did to us;
9 and [a]He made no distinction between
us and them, [b]cleansing their hearts by faith.
10 "Now therefore why do you [a]put God to
the test by placing upon the neck of the disciples a yoke which [b]neither our fathers nor
we have been able to bear?
11 "But we believe that we are saved
through [a]the grace of the Lord Jesus, in the
same way as they also are."
12 All the people kept silent, and they
were listening to Barnabas and Paul as they
were [a]relating what [b]signs and wonders God
had done through them among the Gentiles.

James's Judgment

13 After they had stopped speaking,
[1a]James answered, saying, "Brethren, listen
to me.
14 "[a]Simeon has related how God first concerned Himself about taking from among the
Gentiles a people for His name.
15 "With this the words of [a]the Prophets
agree, just as it is written,
16 '[a]AFTER THESE THINGS [b]I will return,
AND I WILL REBUILD THE [1]TABERNACLE OF
DAVID WHICH HAS FALLEN,
AND I WILL REBUILD ITS RUINS,
AND I WILL RESTORE IT,
17 [a]SO THAT THE REST OF [1]MANKIND MAY SEEK
THE LORD,
AND ALL THE GENTILES [2b]WHO ARE CALLED
BY MY NAME,'
18 [a]SAYS THE LORD, WHO [1b]MAKES THESE
THINGS KNOWN FROM LONG AGO.
19 "Therefore it is [a]my judgment that we
do not trouble those who are turning to God
from among the Gentiles,
20 but that we write to them that they
abstain from [1a]things contaminated by idols
and from [b]fornication and from [c]what is
strangled and from blood.
21 "For [a]Moses from ancient generations
has in every city those who preach him, since
[1]he is read in the synagogues every Sabbath."
22 Then it seemed good to [a]the apostles
and the elders, with the whole church, to
choose men from among them to send to
[b]Antioch with Paul and Barnabas—Judas
called Barsabbas, and [c]Silas, leading men
among [d]the brethren,
23 and they [1]sent this letter by them,
"[a]The apostles and the brethren who are
elders, to [b]the brethren in [c]Antioch and

6 [1]Lit *see about* [2]Lit *word* [a]Acts 11:30; 15:4, 22, 23; 16:4 **7** [1]Lit *from days of old* [a]Acts 15:2 [b]Acts 10:19f [c]Acts 20:24 **8** [a]Acts 1:24 [b]Acts 2:4; 10:44, 47 **9** [a]Acts 10:28, 34; 11:12 [b]Acts 10:43 **10** [a]Acts 5:9 [b]Matt 23:4; Gal 5:1 **11** [a]Rom 3:24; 5:15; 2 Cor 13:14; Eph 2:5-8 **12** [a]Acts 14:27; 15:3, 4 [b]John 4:48 **13** [1]Or *Jacob* [a]Acts 12:17 **14** [a]Acts 15:7; 2 Pet 1:1 **15** [a]Acts 13:40 **16** [a]Amos 9:11 [b]Jer 12:15

16 [1]Or *tent* **17** [1]Gr *anthropoi* [2]Lit *upon whom My name is called* [a]Amos 9:12 [b]Deut 28:10; Is 63:19; Jer 14:9; Dan 9:19; James 2:7 **18** [1]Or *does these things which were known* [a]Amos 9:12 [b]Is 45:21 **19** [a]Acts 15:28; 21:25 **20** [1]Lit *the pollutions of* [a]Ex 34:15-17; Dan 1:8; Acts 15:29; 1 Cor 8:7, 13; 10:7f, 14-28; Rev 2:14, 20 [b]Lev 18:6-23 [c]Gen 9:4; Lev 3:17; 7:26; 17:10, 14; 19:26; Deut 12:16, 23; 15:23; 1 Sam 14:33 **21** [1]I.e. the books of Moses, Gen through Deut [a]Acts 13:15; 2 Cor 3:14f **22** [a]Acts 15:2 [b]Acts 11:20 [c]Acts 15:27, 32, 40; 16:19, 25, 29; 17:4, 10, 14f; 18:5; 2 Cor 1:19; 1 Thess 1:1; 2 Thess 1:1; 1 Pet 5:12 [d]Acts 15:1 **23** [1]Lit *wrote by their hand* [a]Acts 15:2 [b]Acts 15:1 [c]Acts 11:20

isees became Christians and brought their Judaic beliefs with them. They believed that Gentiles must first become converts to Judaism and be circumcised (see v. 1), and then they would be eligible to be saved by faith. Perhaps some of them had gone to Antioch and now returned to present their case.

15:7 *Peter stood up.* After a period of considerable discussion by the apostles and elders, Peter addressed them. *Gentiles would hear.* Peter's argument was his own experience: God had sent him to preach to the Gentiles (10:28–29).

15:8 *giving them the Holy Spirit.* The irrefutable proof of God's acceptance (see 10:44,47; 11:17–18).

15:9 *cleansing their hearts by faith.* Peter's way of saying what Paul affirmed (Rom 5:1; cf. Gal 2:15–16).

15:10 *a yoke.* The law (see Gal 5:1; cf. Matt 11:28–29).

15:11 *we are saved . . . as they also are.* See Rom 3:9. *through the grace of the Lord.* No circumcision was required.

15:12 *people kept silent.* See note on vv. 4–22. Apparently the people had remained in place while the apostles and elders met. The assembly had not remained quiet during that time, but now they became silent to listen to the leaders. *Barnabas and Paul.* The order here puts Barnabas first (perhaps reflecting his importance in Jerusalem), whereas in the account of the missionary journey the order was "Paul and Barnabas" after the events on the island of Cyprus (13:7,9,13,42). *signs and wonders.* See 8:19–20; 14:3.

15:13 *James.* The brother of the Lord. His argument added proof from Scripture.

15:14 *Simeon.* Peter (see v. 7). James uses Peter's Hebrew name in its Hebrew form (Simeon is a variant of Simon). *a people for His name.* A new community largely made up of Gentiles but including Jews as well (John 10:16; cf. 1 Pet 2:9–10).

15:15 *Prophets.* Specifically Amos 9:11–12.

15:16 *AFTER THESE THINGS I will return.* Some have taken this quotation from Amos as setting forth a sequence of the end times, including (1) the church age (taking out "a people for His name," v. 14), (2) the restoration of Israel as a nation (v. 16) and (3) the final salvation of the Gentiles (vv. 17–18). Others declare that the quotation merely confirms God's intent to save Gentiles.

15:19 *do not trouble.* Circumcision was not required, but four stipulations were laid down (see note on v. 20). These were in areas where the Gentiles had particular weaknesses and where the Jews were particularly repulsed by Gentile violations. It would help both the individual and the relationship between Gentile and Jew if these requirements were observed. They involved divine directives that the Jews believed were given before the Mosaic laws.

15:20 *things contaminated by idols.* See v. 29; 1 Cor 8:7–13; Rev 2:14,20. *fornication.* A sin taken too lightly by the Greeks and also associated with certain pagan religious festivals. *what is strangled.* Thus retaining the blood that was forbidden to be eaten (see Gen 9:4). *blood.* Expressly forbidden in Jewish law (see Lev 17:10–12). Reference here may be to consuming blood apart from meat.

15:22 *apostles and the elders, with the whole church.* Apparently there was unanimous agreement with the choice of messengers and with the contents of the letter (vv. 23–29). *Judas called Barsabbas.* The same surname as that of Joseph Barsabbas (see 1:23 and note). The two may have been brothers. *Silas.* A leader in the Jerusalem church, a prophet (v. 32) and a Roman citizen (16:37).

[d]Syria and [e]Cilicia who are from the
Gentiles, [f]greetings.
24 "Since we have heard that [a]some [1]of our
number to whom we gave no instruction have [b]disturbed you with *their*
words, unsettling your souls,
25 [a]it seemed good to us, having [1]become
of one mind, to select men to send to
you with our beloved Barnabas and
Paul,
26 men who have [1a]risked their lives for
the name of our Lord Jesus Christ.
27 "Therefore we have sent [a]Judas and
[b]Silas, who themselves will also report
the same things by word *of mouth.*
28 "For [a]it seemed good to [b]the Holy Spirit
and to [c]us to lay upon you no greater
burden than these essentials:
29 that you abstain from [a]things sacrificed
to idols and from [a]blood and from
[a]things strangled and from [a]fornication;
[1]if you keep yourselves free from such
things, you will do well. Farewell."
30 So when they were sent away, [a]they
went down to Antioch; and having gathered
the [1]congregation together, they delivered
the letter.
31 When they had read it, they rejoiced
because of its [1]encouragement.
32 [a]Judas and [b]Silas, also being [c]prophets
themselves, [1]encouraged and strengthened
[d]the brethren with a lengthy message.
33 After they had spent time *there,* they
were sent away from the brethren [a]in peace
to those who had [b]sent them out.

23 [d]Matt 4:24; Acts 15:41; Gal 1:21 [e]Acts 6:9 [f]Acts 23:26; James 1:1; 2 John 10f
24 [1]Lit *from us* [a]Acts 15:1 [b]Gal 1:7; 5:10
25 [1]Or *met together* [a]Acts 15:28
26 [1]Lit *given over* [a]Acts 9:23ff; 14:19
27 [a]Acts 15:22, 32 [b]Acts 15:22
28 [a]Acts 15:25 [b]Acts 5:32; 15:8 [c]Acts 15:19, 25
29 [a]Acts 15:20
29 [1]Lit *from which keeping yourselves free* [a]Acts 15:20
30 [1]Or *multitude* [a]Acts 15:22f
31 [1]Or *exhortation*
32 [1]Or *exhorted* [a]Acts 15:22, 27 [b]Acts 15:22 [c]Acts 13:1 [d]Acts 15:1
33 [a]Mark 5:34; Acts 16:36; 1 Cor 16:11; Heb 11:31 [b]Acts 15:22

15:23 *in Antioch and Syria and Cilicia.* Antioch was the leading city of the combined provinces of Syria and Cilicia.
15:28 *seemed good to the Holy Spirit and to us.* Prior authority is given to the Spirit (whose working in the assembly is thus claimed), but there was also agreement among the apostles, elders and brothers (vv. 22–23).
15:29 *abstain from things . . . fornication.* See note on v. 20.
15:32 *prophets.* One of the primary functions of prophets in the early church was, as here indicated, to encourage and strengthen the brothers.
15:33 *those who had sent them.* The Jerusalem church (see v. 22).

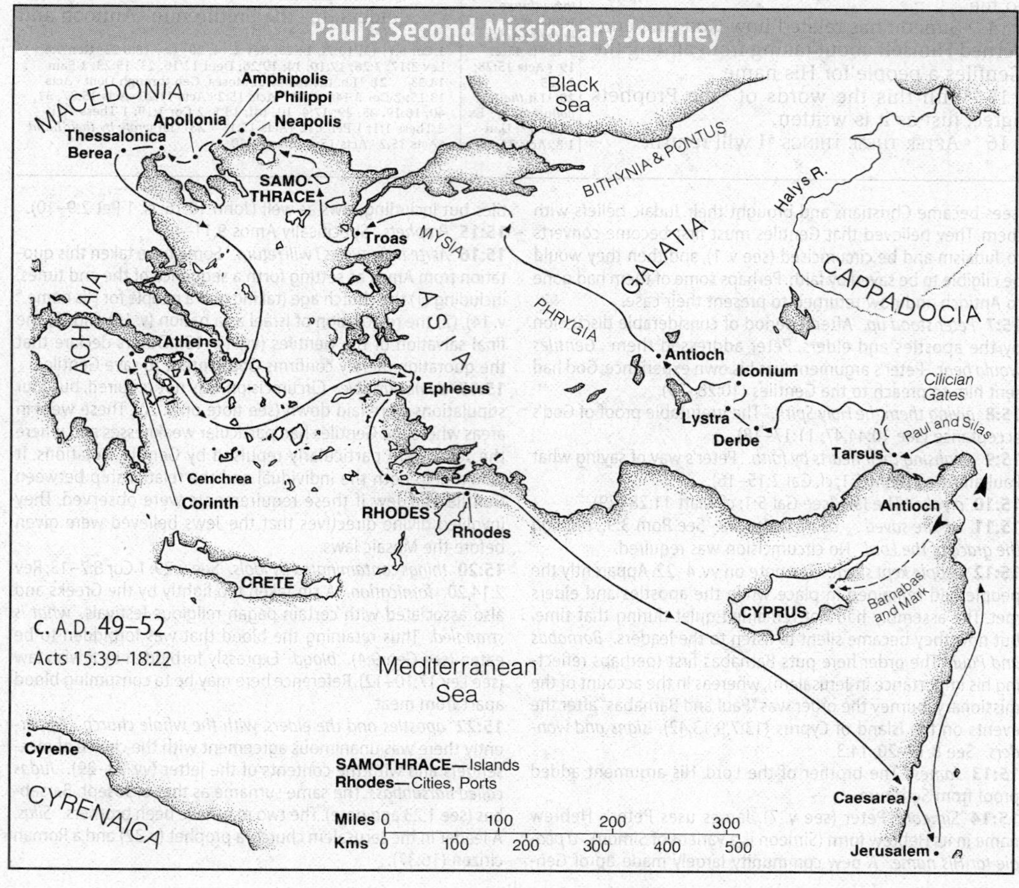
Paul's Second Missionary Journey
MACEDONIA
Amphipolis
Philippi
Apollonia
Neapolis
Thessalonica
Berea
SAMOTHRACE
Black Sea
BITHYNIA & PONTUS
Halys R.
Troas
MYSIA
GALATIA
CAPPADOCIA
ASIA
PHRYGIA
ACHAIA
Athens
Antioch
Iconium
Cilician Gates
Ephesus
Lystra
Derbe
Paul and Silas
Tarsus
Cenchrea
Corinth
RHODES
Rhodes
Antioch
CRETE
CYPRUS
Barnabas and Mark
C. A.D. 49–52
Acts 15:39–18:22
Mediterranean Sea
Cyrene
SAMOTHRACE—Islands
Rhodes—Cities, Ports
CYRENAICA
Caesarea
Miles 0 100 200 300
Kms 0 100 200 300 400 500
Jerusalem

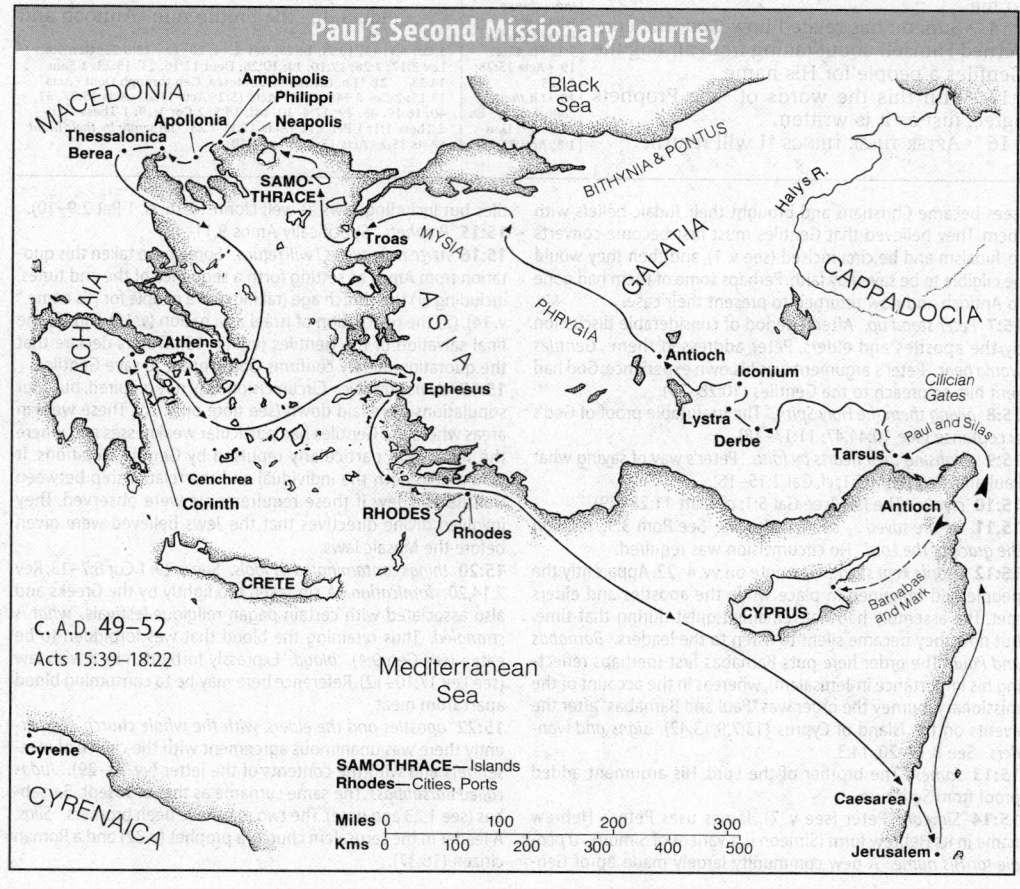

34 [[1]But it seemed good to Silas to remain there.]

35 But [a]Paul and Barnabas stayed in Antioch, teaching and [b]preaching with many others also, [c]the word of the Lord.

Second Missionary Journey

36 After some days Paul said to Barnabas, "Let us return and visit the brethren in [a]every city in which we proclaimed [b]the word of the Lord, *and see* how they are."

37 Barnabas wanted to take [a]John, called Mark, along with them also.

38 But Paul kept insisting that they should not take him along who had [a]deserted them [1]in Pamphylia and had not gone with them to the work.

39 And there occurred such a sharp disagreement that they separated from one another, and Barnabas took [a]Mark with him and sailed away to [b]Cyprus.

40 But Paul chose [a]Silas and left, being [b]committed by the brethren to the grace of the Lord.

41 And he was traveling through [a]Syria and [b]Cilicia, strengthening the churches.

The Macedonian Vision

16 Paul came also to [a]Derbe and to [a]Lystra. And a disciple was there, named [b]Timothy, the son of a [c]Jewish woman who was a believer, but his father was a Greek,

2 and he was well spoken of by [a]the brethren who were in [b]Lystra and [c]Iconium.

3 Paul wanted this man to [1]go with him; and he [a]took him and circumcised him because of the Jews who were in those parts, for they all knew that his father was a Greek.

4 Now while they were passing through the cities, they were delivering [a]the decrees which had been decided upon by [b]the apostles and [c]elders who were in Jerusalem, for them to observe.

5 So [a]the churches were being strengthened [1]in the faith, and were [b]increasing in number daily.

6 They passed through the [1a]Phrygian and [b]Galatian region, having been forbidden by the Holy Spirit to speak the word in [2c]Asia;

7 and after they came to [a]Mysia, they were trying to go into [b]Bithynia, and the [c]Spirit of Jesus did not permit them;

8 and passing by [a]Mysia, they came down to [b]Troas.

9 [a]A vision appeared to Paul in the night: a man of [b]Macedonia was standing and appealing to him, and saying, "Come over to Macedonia and help us."

34 [1]Early mss do not contain this v
35 [a]Acts 12:25 [b]Acts 8:4 [c]Acts 13:12
36 [a]Acts 13:4, 13, 14, 51; 14:6, 24f [b]Acts 13:12
37 [a]Acts 12:12
38 [1]Lit *from* [a]Acts 13:13
39 [a]Acts 12:12; 15:37; Col 4:10 [b]Acts 4:36
40 [a]Acts 15:22 [b]Acts 11:23; 14:26
41 [a]Matt 4:24; Acts 15:23 [b]Acts 6:9
16:1 [a]Acts 14:6 [b]Acts 17:14f; 18:5; 19:22; 20:4; Rom 16:21; 1 Cor 4:17; 16:10; 2 Cor 1:1, 19; Phil 1:1; 2:19; Col 1:1; 1 Thess 1:1; 3:2, 6; 2 Thess 1:1; 1 Tim 1:2, 18; 6:20; 2 Tim 1:2; Philem 1; Heb 13:23 [c]2 Tim 1:5; 3:15
2 [a]Acts 16:40 [b]Acts 14:6 [c]Acts 13:51
3 [1]Lit *go out* [a]Gal 2:3
4 [a]Acts 15:28f [b]Acts 15:2 [c]Acts 11:30
5 [1]Or *in faith* [a]Acts 9:31 [b]Acts 2:47
6 [1]Or *Phrygia and the Galatian region* [2]I.e. west coast province of Asia Minor [a]Acts 2:10; 18:23 [b]Acts 18:23; 1 Cor 16:1; Gal 1:2; 3:1; 2 Tim 4:10; 1 Pet 1:1 [c]Acts 2:9
7 [a]Acts 16:8 [b]1 Pet 1:1 [c]Luke 24:49; Acts 8:29; Rom 8:9; Gal 4:6; Phil 1:19; 1 Pet 1:11
8 [a]Acts 16:7 [b]Acts 16:11; 20:5f; 2 Cor 2:12; 2 Tim 4:13
9 [a]Acts 9:10 [b]Acts 16:10, 12; 18:5; 19:21f, 29; 20:1, 3; 27:2; Rom 15:26

15:36 *every city in which we proclaimed the word.* Towns of the first missionary journey (see 13:4–14:26).

15:38 *who had deserted them.* Mark had turned back at Perga and did not go to Antioch, Iconium, Lystra and Derbe (see note on 13:13).

15:39 *they separated from one another.* Barnabas and Mark do not appear again in Acts. However, in 1 Cor 9:6 Paul names Barnabas as setting a noble example in working to support himself. Also in Gal 2:11–13 another scene is described in Antioch that includes Barnabas. Mark evidently returned from his work with Barnabas and became associated with Peter (see 1 Pet 5:13). During Paul's first imprisonment, Mark was included in Paul's group (see Col 4:10; Philem 24). By the end of Paul's life he came to admire Mark so much that he requested him to come to be with him during his final days (2 Tim 4:11; see Introduction to Mark: John Mark in the NT). *Cyprus.* The island of Barnabas's birthplace (cf. 4:36).

15:40 *Silas.* Had returned to Jerusalem with Judas after delivering the Jerusalem letter (vv. 32–33). His presence in Antioch now indicates that, after reporting to those who had sent him, he came back to Antioch to participate in the church's work there.

16:1 See map No. 11 at the end of the study Bible. *Derbe.* See notes on 14:6,20. Paul had approached Derbe on the first trip from the opposite direction, so the order of towns is reversed here. *Lystra.* See note on 14:6. *Timothy.* Since Paul addressed him as a young man some 15 years later (see 1 Tim 4:12), he must have been in his teens at this time. *father was a Greek.* Statements concerning his mother's faith (here and in 2 Tim 1:5) and silence concerning any faith on his father's part suggest that the father was neither a convert to Judaism nor a believer in Christ.

16:3 *he . . . circumcised him.* As a matter of expediency so that his work among the Jews might be more effective. This was different from Titus's case (see Gal 2:3), where circumcision was refused because some were demanding it as necessary for salvation.

16:6 *They.* Paul, Silas and Timothy. *Phrygian. . . . region.* The district was formerly the Hellenistic territory of Phrygia, but it had more recently been divided between the Roman provinces of Asia and Galatia. Iconium and Antioch were in Galatian Phrygia. *Galatian region.* The name had been used to denote the Hellenistic kingdom, but in 25 B.C. it had been expanded considerably to become the Roman province of that name. *Asia.* This, too, had been a smaller area formerly but now was a Roman province including the Hellenistic districts of Mysia, Lydia, Caria and parts of Phrygia.

16:7 *Mysia.* In the northwest part of the province of Asia. Luke uses these old Hellenistic names, but Paul preferred the provincial (Roman) names. *Bithynia.* A senatorial province formed after 74 B.C., it was east of Mysia. *Spirit of Jesus.* As the "Holy Spirit" was used at times interchangeably with "God" (see 5:3–4), so here "Holy Spirit" is used interchangeably with "Spirit of Jesus." *not permit.* The Spirit may have led in any of a number of ways: vision, circumstances, good sense or use of the prophetic gift.

16:8 *Troas.* Located ten miles from ancient Troy. Alexandria Troas (its full name) was a Roman colony and an important seaport for connections between Macedonia and Greece on the one hand and Asia Minor on the other. Paul returned to Troas following his work in Ephesus on his third journey (see 2 Cor 2:12). At some time—on Paul's second journey or on his third—a church was started there, for Paul ministered to believers in Troas when he returned from his third journey on his way to Jerusalem (20:5–12).

16:9 *vision.* One of the ways God gave direction (cf. 10:3). *man of Macedonia.* Macedonia had become a Roman province in

10 When he had seen [a]the vision, immediately [b]we sought to [1]go into Macedonia,
concluding that God had called us to [c]preach
the gospel to them.
11 So putting out to sea from [a]Troas, we
ran [b]a straight course to Samothrace, and on
the day following to Neapolis;
12 and from there to [a]Philippi, which is a
leading city of the district of [b]Macedonia, [c]a
Roman colony; and we were staying in this
city for some days.
13 And on [a]the Sabbath day we went outside the gate to a riverside, where we were
supposing that there would be a place of
prayer; and we sat down and began speaking
to the women who had assembled.

First Convert in Europe

14 A woman named Lydia, from the city
of [a]Thyatira, a seller of purple fabrics, [b]a
worshiper of God, was listening; [1]and the
Lord [c]opened her heart to respond to the
things spoken by Paul.
15 And when she and [a]her household had
been baptized, she urged us, saying, "If you
have judged me to be faithful to the Lord,
come into my house and stay." And she prevailed upon us.
16 It happened that as we were going to
[a]the place of prayer, a slave-girl having [b]a
spirit of divination met us, who was bringing
her masters much profit by fortune-telling.
17 Following after Paul and us, she kept
crying out, saying, "These men are bond-servants of [a]the Most High God, who are proclaiming to you [1]the way of salvation."
18 She continued doing this for many
days. But Paul was greatly annoyed, and
turned and said to the spirit, "I command you
[a]in the name of Jesus Christ to come out of
her!" And it came out at that very [1]moment.
19 But when her masters saw that their
hope of [a]profit was [1]gone, they seized [b]Paul
and Silas and [c]dragged them into the market
place before the authorities,
20 and when they had brought them to
the chief magistrates, they said, "These men
are throwing our city into confusion, being
Jews,
21 and [a]are proclaiming customs which it
is not lawful for us to accept or to observe,
being [b]Romans."

Paul and Silas Imprisoned

22 The crowd rose up together against
them, and the chief magistrates tore their
[1]robes off them and proceeded to order
[2]*them* to be [a]beaten with rods.
23 When they had struck them with many
blows, they threw them into prison, commanding [a]the jailer to guard them securely;
24 [1]and he, having received such a command, threw them into the inner prison and
fastened their feet in [a]the [2]stocks.
25 But about midnight [a]Paul and Silas were
praying and [b]singing hymns of praise to God,
and the prisoners were listening to them;
26 and suddenly [a]there came a great
earthquake, so that the foundations of the
prison house were shaken; and immediately

10 [1]Lit *go out* [a]Acts 9:10 [b][we] Acts 16:10-17; 20:5-15; 21:1-18; 27:1-28:16 [c]Acts 14:7
11 [a]Acts 16:8; 20:5f; 2 Cor 2:12; 2 Tim 4:13 [b]Acts 21:1
12 [a]Acts 20:6; Phil 1:1; 1 Thess 2:2 [b]Acts 16:9, 10; 18:5; 19:21f, 29; 20:1, 3; 27:2; Rom 15:26 [c]Acts 16:21
13 [a]Acts 13:14
14 [1]Lit *whose heart the Lord opened* [a]Rev 1:11; 2:18, 24 [b]Acts 13:43; 18:7 [c]Luke 24:45
15 [a]Acts 11:14
16 [a]Acts 16:13 [b]Lev 19:31; 20:6, 27; Deut 18:11; 1 Sam 28:3, 7; 2 Kin 21:6; 1 Chr 10:13; Is 8:19
17 [1]Lit *a way* [a]Mark 5:7
18 [1]Lit *hour* [a]Mark 16:17
19 [1]Lit *gone out* [a]Acts 16:16; 19:25f [b]Acts 15:22, 40; 16:25, 29 [c]Acts 8:3; 17:6f; 21:30; James 2:6
21 [a]Esth 3:8 [b]Acts 16:12
22 [1]Or *outer garments* [2]Lit *to beat with rods* [a]2 Cor 11:25; 1 Thess 2:2
23 [a]Acts 16:27, 36
24 [1]Lit *who* [2]Lit *wood* [a]Job 13:27; 33:11; Jer 20:2f; 29:26
25 [a]Acts 16:19 [b]Eph 5:19
26 [a]Acts 4:31

148 B.C. There is no indication that the man of the vision is Luke, as some have suggested, but he does join the group at this point.
16:10 *we sought to go.* This is where the "we" passages of Acts begin (see Introduction: Author). The conclusion is that Luke is informing the reader that he had joined the party at Troas.
16:11 *Samothrace.* An island in the northeastern Aegean Sea. It was a convenient place for boats to anchor rather than risk sailing at night. *Neapolis.* The seaport for Philippi, ten miles away; modern Kavalla.
16:12 *Philippi.* A city in eastern Macedonia named after Philip II, father of Alexander the Great (see map, p. 1729). Since it was a Roman colony, it was independent of provincial administration and had a governmental organization modeled after that of Rome (see note on 13:14). Many retired legionnaires from the Roman army settled there, but few Jews. See Introduction to Philippians: Recipients. *leading city.* Thessalonica was the capital of Macedonia. But Macedonia had four districts, and Philippi was in the first of these.
16:13 *a place of prayer.* There were so few Jews in Philippi that there was no synagogue, so the Jews who were there met for prayer along the banks of the Gangites River (see map, p. 1729). It was customary for such places of prayer to be located outdoors near running water.
16:14 *Lydia.* A businesswoman. Her name may be associated with her place of origin, the Hellenistic district of Lydia. *Thyatira.* In the Roman province of Asia, 20 miles southeast of Pergamum (in the Hellenistic kingdom of Lydia). It was famous for its dyeing works, especially royal purple (crimson). See Rev 1:11 and note on Rev 2:18. *worshiper of God.* Lydia was a Gentile who, like Cornelius (see 10:2), believed in the true God and followed the moral teachings of Scripture. She had not, however, become a full convert to Judaism. *opened her heart.* After the resurrection the minds of the disciples were opened to understand the Scriptures (Luke 24:45); similarly, Lydia's heart was opened to respond to the gospel message of Paul.
16:16 *a spirit of divination.* A "python" spirit, a demonic spirit. The python was a mythical snake worshiped at Delphi and associated with the Delphic oracle. The term "python" came to be used of the persons through whom the python spirit supposedly spoke. Since such persons spoke involuntarily, the term "ventriloquist" was used to describe them. To what extent she actually predicted the future is not known.
16:17 *us.* The "we" section (see note on v. 10) ends here and begins again in 20:5. *Most High God.* A title used by the man possessed by an evil spirit (Mark 5:7). It was a common title among both Jews (see Num 24:16; Is 14:14; Dan 3:26) and Greeks (found in inscriptions). But the title is not used of God in the NT by Christians or Jews (cf. Acts 7:48).
16:20 *magistrates.* The Greek term *strategos* (Latin *praetor*), not the usual word but a term of courtesy used in some Roman colonies, such as Philippi.
16:21 *customs . . . not lawful.* If a religion failed to receive Roman approval, it was considered *religio illicita.* Judaism had legal recognition, but Christianity did not.
16:22 *beaten.* With rods.
16:24 *inner prison . . . stocks.* Used not only for extra security but also for torture.

[b]all the doors were opened and everyone's [c]chains were unfastened.

27 When [a]the jailer awoke and saw the prison doors opened, he drew his sword and was about [b]to kill himself, supposing that the prisoners had escaped.

28 But Paul cried out with a loud voice, saying, "Do not harm yourself, for we are all here!"

29 And he called for lights and rushed in, and trembling with fear he fell down before [a]Paul and Silas,

30 and after he brought them out, he said, "Sirs, [a]what must I do to be saved?"

The Jailer Converted

31 They said, "[a]Believe in the Lord Jesus, and you will be saved, you and [b]your household."

32 And they spoke the word of [1]the Lord to him together with all who were in his house.

33 And he took them [a]that *very* hour of the night and washed their wounds, and immediately he was baptized, he and all his *household*.

34 And he brought them into his house and set [1]food before them, and rejoiced [2]greatly, having believed in God with [a]his whole household.

35 Now when day came, the chief magistrates sent their policemen, saying, "Release those men."

36 And [a]the jailer reported these words to Paul, *saying*, "The chief magistrates have sent to release you. Therefore come out now and go [b]in peace."

37 But Paul said to them, "They have beaten us in public without trial, [a]men who are Romans, and have thrown us into prison; and now are they sending us away secretly?

26 [b]Acts 12:10 [c]Acts 12:7
27 [a]Acts 16:23, 36 [b]Acts 12:19
29 [a]Acts 16:19
30 [a]Acts 2:37; 22:10
31 [a]Mark 16:16 [b]Acts 11:14; 16:15
32 [1]Two early mss read *God*
33 [a]Acts 16:25
34 [1]Lit *a table* [2]Or *greatly with his whole household, having believed in God* [a]Acts 11:14; 16:15
36 [a]Acts 16:27 [b]Acts 15:33
37 [a]Acts 22:25-29
38 [a]Acts 22:29
39 [a]Matt 8:34
40 [1]Or *exhorted* [a]Acts 16:14 [b]Acts 1:15; 16:2
17:1 [a]Acts 17:11, 13; 20:4; 27:2; Phil 4:16; 1 Thess 1:1; 2 Thess 1:1; 2 Tim 4:10
2 [a]Acts 9:20; 17:10, 17 [b]Acts 13:14 [c]Acts 8:35
3 [1]Lit *opening* [2]Lit *placing before* [3]I.e. Messiah [a]Acts 3:18 [b]John 20:9 [c]Acts 9:22; 18:5, 28
4 [1]Lit *and a large* [2]Lit *not a few* [a]Acts 14:4 [b]Acts 15:22, 40; 17:10, 14f [c]Acts 13:43; 17:17 [d]John 7:35 [e]Acts 13:50
5 [a]Acts 17:13; 1 Thess 2:14ff [b]Acts 17:6, 7, 9; Rom 16:21
6 [1]Lit *the inhabited earth* [a]Acts 16:19f [b]Matt 24:14; Acts 17:31

No indeed! But let them come themselves and bring us out."

38 The policemen reported these words to the chief magistrates. [a]They were afraid when they heard that they were Romans,

39 and they came and appealed to them, and when they had brought them out, they kept begging them [a]to leave the city.

40 They went out of the prison and entered *the house of* [a]Lydia, and when they saw [b]the brethren, they [1]encouraged them and departed.

Paul at Thessalonica

17 Now when they had traveled through Amphipolis and Apollonia, they came to [a]Thessalonica, where there was a synagogue of the Jews.

2 And [a]according to Paul's custom, he went to them, and for three [b]Sabbaths reasoned with them from [c]the Scriptures,

3 [1]explaining and [2]giving evidence that the [3]Christ [a]had to suffer and [b]rise again from the dead, and *saying*, "[c]This Jesus whom I am proclaiming to you is the [3]Christ."

4 [a]And some of them were persuaded and joined [b]Paul and Silas, [1]along with a large number of the [c]God-fearing [d]Greeks and [2]a number of the [e]leading women.

5 But [a]the Jews, becoming jealous and taking along some wicked men from the market place, formed a mob and set the city in an uproar; and attacking the house of [b]Jason, they were seeking to bring them out to the people.

6 When they did not find them, they *began* [a]dragging Jason and some brethren before the city authorities, shouting, "These men who have upset [1b]the world have come here also;

16:27 *about to kill himself.* If a prisoner escaped, the life of the guard was demanded in his place (see 12:19). To take his own life would shorten the shame and distress.
16:30 *what must I do to be saved?* The jailer had heard that these were preachers of a way of salvation (v. 17). Now with the earthquake and his own impending death, he wanted to know about the way.
16:31 *Believe in the Lord Jesus.* A concise statement of the way of salvation (see 10:43).
16:32 *word of the Lord.* See 10:36. Paul and Silas explained the gospel more thoroughly to the jailer and to all the other members of his household, and they all believed in Christ and were saved (v. 34).
16:34 *rejoiced greatly.* The consistent consequence of conversion, regardless of circumstances (see note on 8:39).
16:35 *magistrates.* See note on v. 20.
16:37 *without trial.* Public beating for a Roman citizen (see v. 38) would have been illegal, let alone beating without a trial. *let them come themselves.* Paul and Silas were not asking for an escort to salve their injured pride as much as they were establishing their innocence for the sake of the church in Philippi and its future.
17:1 *Amphipolis . . . Thessalonica.* The Egnatian Way crossed the whole of present-day northern Greece east-west and included Philippi, Amphipolis, Apollonia and Thessalonica on its route. At several locations, such as Kavalla (Neapolis), Philippi and Apollonia, the road is still visible today. If a person traveled about 30 miles a day, each city could be reached after one day's journey. *Thessalonica.* About 100 miles from Philippi. It was the capital of the province of Macedonia and had a population of more than 200,000, including a colony of Jews (and a synagogue). All these contributed to Paul's decision to preach there. See Introduction to 1 Thessalonians: The City and the Church.
17:2 *went to them.* To the synagogue (v. 1; see note on 13:14). *three Sabbaths.* These two weeks represent the time spent in the synagogue reasoning with the Jews, not Paul's total time in Thessalonica. An analysis of the Thessalonian letters reveals that Paul had taught them much more doctrine than would have been possible in two or three weeks.
17:4 *God-fearing Greeks.* See notes on 10:2; 16:14. *leading women.* Perhaps the wives of the leading men of the city, but women who deserve notice and position in their own right (see also v. 12).
17:5 *becoming jealous.* Because of the large number of people (including some Jews, many God-fearing Gentiles and many prominent women) who responded to Paul's ministry (cf. 13:45). *house of Jason.* Paul had probably been staying there.
17:6 *city authorities.* The Greek term *politarch* (lit. "city ruler"),

7 [1]and Jason [a]has welcomed them, and they all act [b]contrary to the decrees of Caesar, saying that there is another king, Jesus."

8 They stirred up the crowd and the city authorities who heard these things.

9 And when they had received a [1]pledge from [a]Jason and the others, they released them.

Paul at Berea

10 [a]The brethren immediately sent [b]Paul and Silas away by night to [c]Berea, [1]and when they arrived, they went into [d]the synagogue of the Jews.

11 Now these were more noble-minded than those in [a]Thessalonica, [1]for they received the word with [2]great eagerness, examining the Scriptures daily *to see* whether these things were so.

12 Therefore [a]many of them believed, [1]along with a number of [b]prominent Greek [c]women and men.

13 But when the Jews of [a]Thessalonica found out that the word of God had been proclaimed by Paul in [b]Berea also, they came there as well, agitating and stirring up the crowds.

14 Then immediately [a]the brethren sent Paul out to go as far as the sea; and [b]Silas and [c]Timothy remained there.

15 Now [a]those who escorted Paul brought him as far as [b]Athens; and receiving a command for [c]Silas and Timothy to [d]come to him as soon as possible, they left.

7 [1]Lit *whom Jason has welcomed* [a]Luke 10:38; James 2:25 [b]Luke 23:2
9 [1]Or *bond* [a]Acts 17:5
10 [1]Lit *who when...arrived went* [a]Acts 1:15; 17:6, 14f [b]Acts 17:4 [c]Acts 17:13; 20:4 [d]Acts 17:1f
11 [1]Lit *who received* [2]Lit *all* [a]Acts 17:1
12 [1]Lit *and not a few* [a]Acts 2:47 [b]Mark 15:43 [c]Acts 13:50
13 [a]Acts 17:1 [b]Acts 17:10; 20:4
14 [a]Acts 1:15; 17:6, 10 [b]Acts 15:22; 17:4, 10 [c]Acts 16:1
15 [a]Acts 15:3 [b]Acts 17:16, 21f; 18:1; 1 Thess 3:1 [c]Acts 17:14 [d]Acts 18:5
16 [a]Acts 17:15, 21f; 18:1; 1 Thess 3:1
17 [a]Acts 9:20; 17:2 [b]Acts 17:4
18 [1]Or *disputing* [2]I.e. one who makes his living by picking up scraps [a]1 Cor 1:20; 4:10 [b]Acts 4:2; 17:31f
19 [1]Or *before* [2]Or *Hill of Ares, god of war* [3]Lit *which is being spoken by you* [a]Acts 23:19

Paul at Athens

16 Now while Paul was waiting for them at [a]Athens, his spirit was being provoked within him as he was observing the city full of idols.

17 So he was reasoning [a]in the synagogue with the Jews and [b]the God-fearing *Gentiles,* and in the market place every day with those who happened to be present.

18 And also some of the Epicurean and Stoic philosophers were [1]conversing with him. Some were saying, "What would [a]this [2]idle babbler wish to say?" Others, "He seems to be a proclaimer of strange deities,"—because he was preaching [b]Jesus and the resurrection.

19 And they [a]took him and brought him [1]to the [2b]Areopagus, saying, "May we know what [c]this new teaching is [3]which you are proclaiming?

20 "For you are bringing some strange things to our ears; so we want to know what these things mean."

21 (Now all the Athenians and the strangers [a]visiting there used to spend their time in nothing other than telling or hearing something new.)

Sermon on Mars Hill

22 So Paul stood in the midst of the [1]Areopagus and said, "Men of [a]Athens, I observe that you are very [b]religious in all respects.

[b]Acts 17:22 [c]Mark 1:27 **21** [a]Acts 2:10 **22** [1]Or *the Council of the Areopagus* [a]Acts 17:15 [b]Acts 25:19

used here and in v. 8, is found nowhere else in Greek literature, but it was discovered in 1835 in a Greek inscription on an arch that had spanned the Egnatian Way on the west side of Thessalonica. (The arch was destroyed in 1867, but the block with the inscription was rescued and is now in the British Museum in London.) The term has since been found in 16 other inscriptions in surrounding towns of Macedonia, and elsewhere.

17:7 *act contrary to the decrees of Caesar.* Blasphemy was the gravest accusation for a Jew, but treason—to support a rival king above Caesar—was the worst accusation for a Roman.

17:9 *received a pledge.* Jason was forced to guarantee a peaceful, quiet community, or he would face the confiscation of his properties and perhaps even death.

17:10 *Paul and Silas.* It has been suggested that Timothy was left at Philippi and rejoined Paul and Silas at Berea (compare v. 10 with v. 14). *Berea.* Modern Verria, located 50 miles from Thessalonica in another district of Macedonia. *synagogue.* See note on 13:14.

17:14 *as far as the sea.* One might conclude that Paul went by boat to Athens. But the road to Athens is also a coast road, and Paul may have walked the distance after having been escorted to the coast (some 20 miles). In any event, Christian companions stayed with him until reaching Athens.

17:15 *Athens.* Five centuries before Paul, Athens had been at the height of its glory in art, philosophy and literature. She had retained her reputation in philosophy through the years and still maintained a leading university in Paul's day.

17:17 *synagogue.* See note on 13:14. *God-fearing Gentiles.* See note on 10:2.

17:18 *Epicurean . . . philosophers.* Originally they taught that the supreme good is happiness—but not mere momentary pleasure or temporary gratification. By Paul's time, however, this philosophy had degenerated into a more sensual system of thought. *Stoic philosophers.* They taught that people should live in accord with nature, recognize their own self-sufficiency and independence, and suppress their desires. At its best, Stoicism had some admirable qualities, but, like Epicureanism, by Paul's time it had degenerated into a system of pride. *babbler.* The Greek word meant "seed picker," a bird picking up seeds here and there. Then it came to refer to the loafer in the marketplace who picked up whatever scraps of learning he could find and paraded them without digesting them himself.

17:19 *Areopagus.* Means "hill of Ares." Ares was the Greek god of thunder and war (the Roman equivalent was Mars). The Areopagus was located just west of the acropolis and south of the Agora and had once been the site of the meeting of the Court or Council of the Areopagus. Earlier the Council governed a Greek city-state, but by NT times the Areopagus retained authority only in the areas of religion and morals and met in the Royal Portico at the northwest corner of the Agora. They considered themselves the custodians of teachings that introduced new religions and foreign gods.

17:22 *religious.* Or "superstitious." The Greek for this word could be used to congratulate a person or to criticize him, depending on whether the person using it included himself in the circle of individuals he was describing. The Athenians would not know which meaning to take until Paul continued. In this context it is clear that Paul wanted to be complimentary in order to gain a hearing.

23 "For while I was passing through and
examining the [a]objects of your worship, I
also found an altar with this inscription, 'TO
AN UNKNOWN GOD.' Therefore what [b]you
worship in ignorance, this I proclaim to you.
24 "[a]The God who made the world and all
things in it, since He is [b]Lord of heaven and
earth, does not [c]dwell in temples made with
hands;
25 nor is He served by human hands, [a]as
though He needed anything, since He Himself gives to all *people* life and breath and all
things;
26 and [a]He made from one *man* every
nation of mankind to live on all the face of
the earth, having [b]determined *their* appointed times and the boundaries of their habitation,
27 that they would seek God, if perhaps
they might grope for Him and find Him,
[a]though He is not far from each one of us;
28 for [a]in Him we live and move and
[1]exist, as even some of your own poets have
said, 'For we also are His children.'
29 "Being then the children of God, we
[a]ought not to think that the Divine Nature is
like gold or silver or stone, an image formed
by the art and thought of man.
30 "Therefore having [a]overlooked [b]the
times of ignorance, God is [c]now declaring to
men that all *people* everywhere should repent,
31 because He has fixed [a]a day in which
[b]He will judge [1][c]the world in righteousness
[2]through a Man whom He has [d]appointed,
having furnished proof to all men [3]by [e]rais-
ing Him from the dead."

23 [a]2 Thess 2:4 [b]John 4:22 **24** [a]Is 42:5; Acts 14:15 [b]Deut 10:14; Ps 115:16; Matt 11:25 [c]1 Kin 8:27; Acts 7:48 **25** [a]Job 22:2; Ps 50:10-12 **26** [a]Mal 2:10 [b]Deut 32:8; Job 12:23 **27** [a]Deut 4:7; Jer 23:23f; Acts 14:17 **28** [1]Lit *are* [a]Job 12:10; Dan 5:23 **29** [a]Is 40:18ff; Rom 1:23 **30** [a]Acts 14:16; Rom 3:25 [b]Acts 17:23 [c]Luke 24:47; Acts 26:20; Titus 2:11f **31** [1]Lit *the inhabited earth* [2]Lit *by* or *in* [3]Or *when He raised* [a]Matt 10:15 [b]Ps 9:8; 96:13; 98:9; John 5:22, 27; Acts 10:42 [c]Matt 24:14; Acts 17:6 [d]Luke 22:22 [e]Acts 2:24

32 [1]Lit *also again* [a]Acts 17:18, 31 **34** [a]Acts 17:19, 22 **18:1** [a]Acts 17:15 [b]Acts 18:8; 19:1; 1 Cor 1:2; 2 Cor 1:1, 23; 6:11; 2 Tim 4:20 **2** [a]Acts 18:18, 26; Rom 16:3;

32 Now when they heard of [a]the resurrection of the dead, some *began* to sneer, but
others said, "We shall hear you [1]again concerning this."
33 So Paul went out of their midst.
34 But some men joined him and believed, among whom also were Dionysius
the [a]Areopagite and a woman named Damaris and others with them.

Paul at Corinth

18 After these things he left [a]Athens and
went to [b]Corinth.
2 And he found a Jew named [a]Aquila, a
native of [b]Pontus, having recently come from
[c]Italy with his wife [a]Priscilla, because [d]Clau-
dius had commanded all the Jews to leave
Rome. He came to them,
3 and because he was of the same trade,
he stayed with them and [a]they were working, for by trade they were tent-makers.
4 And he was reasoning [a]in the synagogue every [b]Sabbath and trying to persuade
[c]Jews and Greeks.
5 But when [a]Silas and Timothy [b]came
down from [c]Macedonia, Paul *began* devoting
himself completely to the word, solemnly
[d]testifying to the Jews that [e]Jesus was the
[1]Christ.
6 But when they resisted and blasphemed, he [a]shook out his garments and

1 Cor 16:19; 2 Tim 4:19 [b]Acts 2:9 [c]Acts 27:1, 6; Heb 13:24 [d]Acts 11:28 **3** [a]Acts 20:34; 1 Cor 4:12; 9:14f; 2 Cor 11:7; 12:13; 1 Thess 2:9; 4:11; 2 Thess 3:8 **4** [a]Acts 9:20; 18:19 [b]Acts 13:14 [c]Acts 14:1 **5** [1]I.e. Messiah [a]Acts 15:22; 16:1; 17:14 [b]Acts 17:15 [c]Acts 16:9 [d]Luke 16:28; Acts 20:21 [e]Acts 17:3; 18:28 **6** [a]Neh 5:13; Acts 13:51

17:23 *TO AN UNKNOWN GOD.* The Greeks were fearful of offending any god by failing to give him attention; so they felt they could cover any omissions by the label "unknown god." Other Greek writers confirm that such altars could be seen in Athens—a striking point of contact for Paul.

17:24 *The God who made the world.* Thus a personal Creator, in contrast with the views of pantheistic Stoicism.

17:26 *He made from one man every nation.* All people are of one family (whether Athenians or Romans, Greeks or barbarians, Jews or Gentiles). *determined their appointed times.* He planned the exact times when nations should emerge and decline. *boundaries of their habitation.* He also planned the specific area to be occupied by each nation. He is God, the Designer (things were not left to Chance, as the Epicureans thought).

17:28 *some of your own poets.* There are two quotations here: (1) "In Him we live and move and exist," from the Cretan poet Epimenides (c. 600 B.C.) in his *Cretica,* and (2) "For we also are His children," from the Cilician poet Aratus (c. 315–240) in his *Phaenomena,* as well as from Cleanthes (331–233) in his *Hymn to Zeus.* Paul quotes Greek poets elsewhere as well (see 1 Cor 15:33; Titus 1:12 and notes).

17:30 *overlooked the times of ignorance.* God had not judged them for worshiping false gods in their ignorance (see v. 31).

17:31 *a Man whom He has appointed.* Jesus, the Son of Man (see Dan 7:13; cf. Matt 25:31–46; Acts 10:42).

17:32 *resurrection of the dead.* Immortality of the soul was accepted by the Greeks, but not resurrection of a dead body.

17:33 *their midst.* The meeting of the Areopagites.

17:34 *Dionysius.* Later tradition states, though it cannot be proved, that he became bishop of Athens. *Damaris.* Some have suggested that she must have been a foreign, educated woman to have been present at a public meeting such as the Areopagus. It is also possible that she was a God-fearing Gentile who had heard Paul at the synagogue (v. 17).

18:1 *went to Corinth.* Either by land along the isthmus (a distance of about 50 miles) or by sea from Piraeus, the port of Athens, to Cenchrea, on the eastern shore of the isthmus of Corinth. See Introduction to 1 Corinthians: The City of Corinth; see also map, p. 1661.

18:2 *Pontus.* In the northeastern region of Asia Minor, a province lying along the Black Sea between Bithynia and Armenia (see 2:9). *Priscilla.* The diminutive form of Prisca. Since no mention is made of a conversion and since a partnership is established in work (see v. 3), it is likely that they were already Christians. They may have been converted in Rome by those returning from Pentecost or by others at a later time. *Claudius.* Emperor of Rome (A.D. 41–54). *commanded all the Jews to leave Rome.* Recorded in Suetonius (*Claudius,* 25). The expulsion order was given, Suetonius writes, because of "their [the Jews'] continual tumults instigated by Chrestus" (a common misspelling of "Christ"). If "Chrestus" refers to Christ, the riots obviously were "about" Him rather than led "by" Him.

18:3 *tent-makers.* Paul would have been taught this trade as a youth. It was the Jewish custom to provide manual training for sons, whether rich or poor.

18:4 *synagogue.* See note on 13:14.

18:5 *Silas and Timothy came down from Macedonia.* Paul instructed these two to come to him at Athens (17:15). Evidently

said to them, "Your [b]blood *be* on your own
heads! I am clean. From now on I will go [c]to
the Gentiles."
7 Then he left there and went to the
house of a man named [1]Titius Justus, [a]a
worshiper of God, whose house was next to
the synagogue.
8 [a]Crispus, [b]the leader of the synagogue,
believed in the Lord [c]with all his household,
and many of the [d]Corinthians when they
heard were believing and being baptized.
9 And the Lord said to Paul in the night
by [a]a vision, "Do not be afraid *any longer*,
but go on speaking and do not be silent;
10 for I am with you, and no man will
attack you in order to harm you, for I have
many people in this city."
11 And he settled *there* a year and six
months, teaching the word of God among
them.
12 But while Gallio was [a]proconsul of
[b]Achaia, [c]the Jews with one accord rose up
against Paul and brought him before [d]the
judgment seat,
13 saying, "This man persuades men to
worship God contrary to [a]the law."
14 But when Paul was about to [a]open his
mouth, Gallio said to the Jews, "If it were a
matter of wrong or of vicious crime, O Jews,
it would be reasonable for me to put up with
you;
15 but if there are [a]questions about words
and names and your own law, look after it
yourselves; I am unwilling to be a judge of
these matters."
16 And he drove them away from [a]the
judgment seat.
17 And they all took hold of [a]Sosthenes,
[b]the leader of the synagogue, and *began*
beating him in front of [c]the judgment seat.
But Gallio was not concerned about any of
these things.
18 Paul, having remained many days
longer, [a]took leave of [b]the brethren and put
out to sea for [c]Syria, and with him were
[d]Priscilla and [d]Aquila. In [e]Cenchrea [1]he [f]had
his hair cut, for he was keeping a vow.
19 They came to [a]Ephesus, and he left
them there. Now he himself entered [b]the
synagogue and reasoned with the Jews.
20 When they asked him to stay for a
longer time, he did not consent,
21 but [a]taking leave of them and saying,
"I will return to you again [b]if God wills," he
set sail from [c]Ephesus.
22 When he had landed at [a]Caesarea, he
went up and greeted the church, and went
down to [b]Antioch.

Third Missionary Journey

23 And having spent some time *there*, he
left and passed successively through the
[a]Galatian region and Phrygia, strengthening
all the disciples.

6 [b]2 Sam 1:16; 1 Kin 2:33; Ezek 18:13; 33:4, 6, 8; Matt 27:25; Acts 20:26 [c]Acts 13:46
7 [1]One early ms reads *Titus;* two other early mss omit the name [a]Acts 13:43; 16:14
8 [a]1 Cor 1:14 [b]Mark 5:22 [c]Acts 11:14 [d]Acts 18:1; 19:1; 1 Cor 1:2; 2 Cor 1:1, 23; 6:11; 2 Tim 4:20
9 [a]Acts 9:10
12 [a]Acts 13:7 [b]Acts 18:27; 19:21; Rom 15:26; 1 Cor 16:15; 2 Cor 1:1; 9:2; 11:10; 1 Thess 1:7f [c]1 Thess 2:14ff [d]Matt 27:19
13 [a]John 19:7; Acts 18:15
14 [a]Matt 5:2
15 [a]Acts 23:29; 25:19
16 [a]Matt 27:19
17 [a]1 Cor 1:1 [b]Acts 18:8 [c]Matt 27:19
18 [1]Lit *having his hair cut* [a]Mark 6:46 [b]Acts 1:15; 18:27 [c]Matt 4:24 [d]Acts 18:2, 26 [e]Rom 16:1 [f]Num 6:2, 5, 9, 18; Acts 21:24
19 [a]Acts 18:21, 24; 19:1, 17, 26, 28, 34f; 20:16f; 21:29; 1 Cor 15:32; 16:8; Eph 1:1; 1 Tim 1:3; 2 Tim 1:18; 4:12; Rev 1:11; 2:1 [b]Acts 18:4
21 [a]Mark 6:46 [b]Rom 1:10; 15:32; 1 Cor 4:19; 16:7; Heb 6:3; James 4:15; 1 Pet 3:17 [c]Acts 18:19, 24; 19:1, 17, 26, 28, 34f; 20:16f; 21:29; 1 Cor 15:32; 16:8; Eph 1:1; 1 Tim 1:3; 2 Tim 1:18; 4:12; Rev 1:11; 2:1
22 [a]Acts 8:40 [b]Acts 11:19
23 [a]Acts 16:6

---

they did (1 Thess 3:1), but they may have been sent back to Macedonia almost immediately to check on the churches—perhaps Silas to Philippi and Timothy to Thessalonica.

18:7 *Titius Justus.* Titius was a common Roman name. Justus is used to distinguish him from the Titus of 2 Cor 2:13; 7:13–14; 8:16,23. *worshiper of God.* Like Titus, an uncircumcised Gentile, but attending the synagogue.

18:8 *Crispus.* Paul baptized him (1 Cor 1:14). *leader of the synagogue.* See note on 13:15. *believing and being baptized.* The response to the gospel, a process going on daily, as the tense of the Greek verbs indicates.

18:9 *by a vision.* Paul had seen the Lord in a resurrection body at his conversion (9:4–6; 1 Cor 15:8) and in the temple at Jerusalem in a trance (22:17–18). Now he sees Him in a vision (see 23:11).

18:11 *a year and six months.* During this time he may also have taken the gospel to the neighboring districts of Achaia (2 Cor 1:1).

18:12 *Gallio.* The brother of Seneca, the philosopher, who was the tutor of Nero. Gallio was admired as a man of exceptional fairness and calmness. From an inscription found at Delphi, it is known that Gallio was proconsul of Achaia in A.D. 51–52. This information enables us to date Paul's visit to Corinth on his second journey as well as his writing of the Thessalonian letters.

18:13 *contrary to the law.* The Jews were claiming that Paul was advocating a religion not recognized by Roman law as Judaism was. If he had been given the opportunity to speak, he could have argued that the gospel he was preaching was the faith of his fathers (see 24:14–15; 26:6–7) and thus authorized by Roman law.

18:17 *they all took hold of Sosthenes.* It is not clear whether the Greeks beat Sosthenes, seeing the occasion as an opportunity to vent their feelings against the Jews, or the Jews beat their own synagogue ruler because he was unsuccessful in presenting their case—probably the former. A Sosthenes is included with Paul in the writing of 1 Corinthians (1:1). Perhaps he was the second ruler of the synagogue at Corinth to become a Christian in response to Paul's preaching (see v. 8).

18:18 *Priscilla and Aquila.* The order of the names used here (but cf. v. 2) may indicate the prominent role of Priscilla or her higher social position (see Rom 16:3; 2 Tim 4:19). *he was keeping a vow.* Grammatically this could refer to Aquila, but the emphasis on Paul and his activity makes Paul more probable. It was probably a temporary Nazirite vow (see Num 6:1–21). Different vows were frequently taken to express thanks for deliverance from grave dangers. Shaving the head marked the end of a vow.

18:19 *Ephesus.* Leading commercial city of Asia Minor, the capital of provincial Asia and the warden of the temple of Artemis (Diana). See Introduction to Ephesians: The City of Ephesus; see also map, p. 1716. *he left them there.* Priscilla and Aquila would give valuable aid upon Paul's return, providing advice as to where and how the work there could be started. *synagogue.* See note on 13:14.

18:22 *greeted the church.* Could refer to a congregation in Caesarea, but the explanation that "he went up" makes it more likely that it was the church in Jerusalem, some 2,500 feet above sea level.

18:23 See map No. 11 at the end of the study Bible. *Galatian region and Phrygia.* The same route he had taken when starting on his second missionary journey, but in the reverse order

24 Now a Jew named [a]Apollos, an [b]Alex-
andrian by birth, [1]an eloquent man, came to
[c]Ephesus; and he was mighty in the Scriptures.
25 This man had been instructed in [a]the
way of the Lord; and being fervent in spirit,
he was speaking and teaching accurately the
things concerning Jesus, being acquainted
only with [b]the baptism of John;
26 and [1]he began to speak out boldly in the
synagogue. But when [a]Priscilla and Aquila
heard him, they took him aside and explained
to him [b]the way of God more accurately.
27 And when he wanted to go across to
[a]Achaia, [b]the brethren encouraged him and
wrote to [c]the disciples to welcome him; and
when he had arrived, he greatly [1]helped
those who had believed through grace,
28 for he powerfully refuted the Jews in
public, demonstrating [a]by the Scriptures that
[b]Jesus was the [1]Christ.

Paul at Ephesus

19 It happened that while [a]Apollos was at
[b]Corinth, Paul passed through the
[c]upper country and came to [d]Ephesus, and
found some disciples.

24 [1]Or *a learned man* [a]Acts 19:1; 1 Cor 1:12; 3:5, 6, 22; 4:6; 16:12; Titus 3:13 [b]Acts 6:9 [c]Acts 18:19
25 [a]Acts 9:2; 18:26 [b]Luke 7:29; Acts 19:3
26 [1]Lit *this man* [a]Acts 18:2, 18 [b]Acts 18:25
27 [a]Acts 18:12; 19:1 [b]Acts 18:18
27 [1]Or *helped greatly through grace those who had believed* [c]Acts 11:26
28 [1]I.e. Messiah [a]Acts 8:35 [b]Acts 18:5

19:1 [a]Acts 18:24; 1 Cor 1:12; 3:5, 6, 22; 4:6; 16:12; Titus 3:13 [b]Acts 18:1 [c]Acts 18:23 [d]Acts 18:21, 24; 19:17, 26, 28, 34f; 20:16f; 21:29; 1 Cor 15:32; 16:8; Eph 1:1; 1 Tim 1:3; 2 Tim 1:18; 4:12; Rev 1:11; 2:1

(16:6). The use of the phrase may indicate the southern part of Galatia in the Phrygian area (see note on 16:6).

18:24 *Alexandrian.* Alexandria, in Egypt, was the second most important city in the Roman empire and had a large Jewish population.

18:25 *baptism of John.* It was not in the name of Jesus (see also 19:2–4). Apollos knew something about Jesus, but basically he, like John, was still looking forward to the coming of the Messiah. His baptism was based on repentance rather than on faith in the finished work of Christ.

18:27 *Achaia.* The Roman province with Corinth as its capital.

19:1 *Apollos was at Corinth.* Apollos was introduced at Ephesus (18:24) in the absence of Paul; he moved to Corinth before Paul returned to Ephesus. But later Apollos came back to Ephesus during Paul's ministry there (see 1 Cor 16:12). *through the upper country.* Not the lower direct route down the Lycus and Meander valleys but the upper Phrygian route approaching Ephesus from a more northerly direction. If Paul got to northern Galatia, which is unlikely, it must have been on one of these trips through the interior (see 16:6; 18:23). *Ephesus.* See note

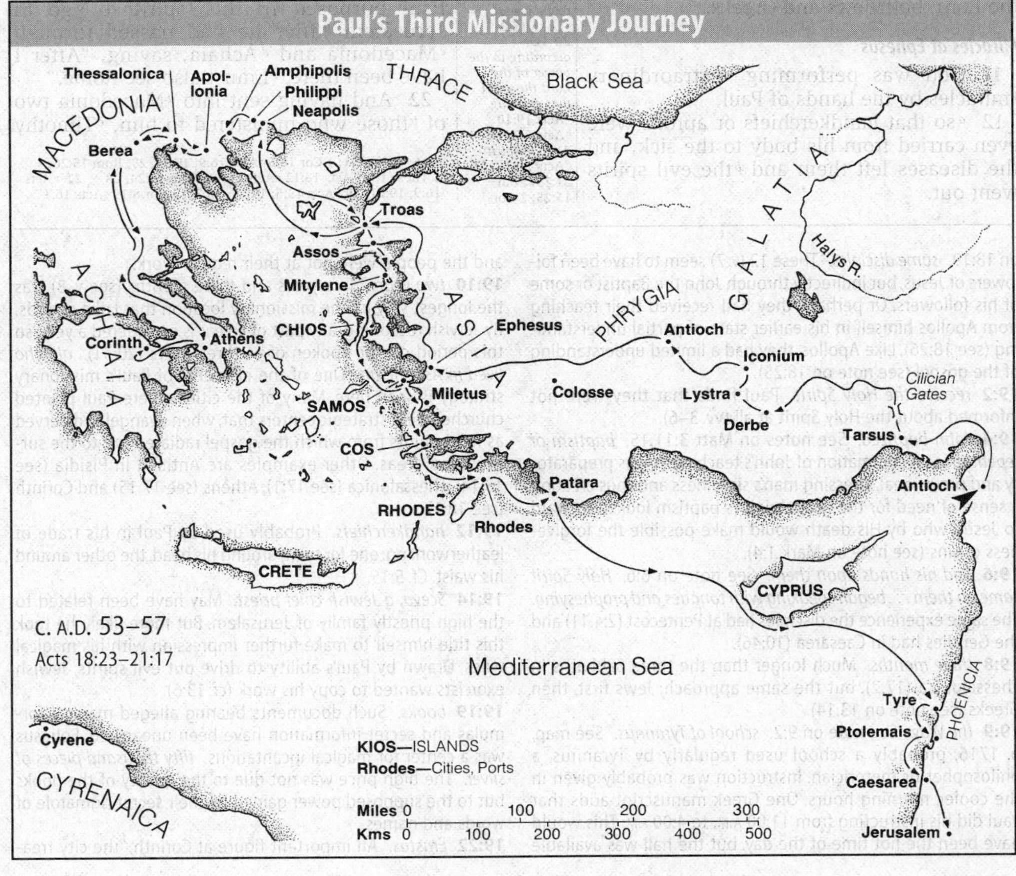

2 He said to them, "[a]Did you receive the Holy Spirit when you believed?" And they *said* to him, "No, [b]we have not even heard whether [1]there is a Holy Spirit."

3 And he said, "Into what then were you baptized?" And they said, "[a]Into John's baptism."

4 Paul said, "[a]John baptized with the baptism of repentance, telling the people [b]to believe in Him who was coming after him, that is, in Jesus."

5 When they heard this, they were [a]baptized [1]in the name of the Lord Jesus.

6 And when Paul had [a]laid his hands upon them, the Holy Spirit came on them, and they *began* [b]speaking with tongues and [c]prophesying.

7 There were in all about twelve men.

8 And he entered [a]the synagogue and continued speaking out boldly for three months, reasoning and persuading *them* [b]about the kingdom of God.

9 But when [a]some were becoming hardened and disobedient, speaking evil of [b]the Way before the [1]people, he withdrew from them and took away [c]the disciples, reasoning daily in the school of Tyrannus.

10 This took place for [a]two years, so that all who lived in [1b]Asia heard [c]the word of the Lord, both Jews and Greeks.

Miracles at Ephesus

11 God was performing [a]extraordinary [1]miracles by the hands of Paul,

12 [a]so that handkerchiefs or aprons were even carried from his body to the sick, and the diseases left them and [b]the evil spirits went out.

13 But also some of the Jewish [a]exorcists, who went from place to place, attempted to name over those who had the evil spirits the name of the Lord Jesus, saying, "I adjure you by Jesus whom Paul preaches."

14 Seven sons of one Sceva, a Jewish chief priest, were doing this.

15 And the evil spirit answered and said to them, "I recognize Jesus, and I know about Paul, but who are you?"

16 And the man, in whom was the evil spirit, leaped on them and subdued all of them and overpowered them, so that they fled out of that house naked and wounded.

17 This became known to all, both Jews and Greeks, who lived in [a]Ephesus; and fear fell upon them all and the name of the Lord Jesus was being magnified.

18 Many also of those who had believed kept coming, confessing and disclosing their practices.

19 And many of those who practiced magic brought their books together and *began* burning them in the sight of everyone; and they counted up the price of them and found it [1]fifty thousand [a]pieces of silver.

20 So [1a]the word of the Lord [b]was growing mightily and prevailing.

21 Now after these things were finished, Paul purposed in the [1]spirit to [a]go to Jerusalem [b]after he had passed through [c]Macedonia and [d]Achaia, saying, "After I have been there, [e]I must also see Rome."

22 And having sent into [a]Macedonia two of [b]those who ministered to him, [c]Timothy

2 [1]Or *the Holy Spirit has been given* [a]Acts 8:15f; 11:16f [b]John 7:39 **3** [a]Luke 7:29; Acts 18:25 **4** [a]Matt 3:11; Mark 1:4, 7, 8; Luke 3:16; John 1:26, 27; Acts 13:24 [b]John 1:7 **5** [1]Lit *into* [a]Acts 8:12, 16; 10:48 **6** [a]Acts 6:6; 8:17 [b]Mark 16:17; Acts 2:4; 10:46 [c]Acts 13:1 **8** [a]Acts 9:20; 18:26 [b]Acts 1:3 **9** [1]Lit *multitude* [a]Acts 14:4 [b]Acts 9:2; 19:23 [c]Acts 11:26; 19:30 **10** [1]I.e. west coast province of Asia Minor [a]Acts 19:8; 20:31 [b]Acts 16:6; 19:22, 26, 27 [c]Acts 13:12; 19:20 **11** [1]Or *works of power* [a]Acts 8:13 **12** [a]Acts 5:15 [b]Mark 16:17 **13** [a]Matt 12:27; Luke 11:19 **17** [a]Acts 18:19 **19** [1]Probably fifty thousand Greek drachmas; a drachma approximated a day's wage [a]Luke 15:8 **20** [1]Or *according to the power of the Lord the word was growing* [a]Acts 19:10 [b]Acts 6:7; 12:24 **21** [1]Or *Spirit* [a]Acts 20:16, 22; 21:15; Rom 15:25; 2 Cor 1:16 [b]Acts 20:1; 1 Cor 16:5 [c]Acts 16:9; 19:22, 29; Rom 15:26; 1 Thess 1:7f [d]Acts 18:12 [e]Acts 23:11; Rom 15:24, 28 **22** [a]Acts 16:9; 19:21, 29 [b]Acts 13:5; 19:29; 20:34; 2 Cor 8:19 [c]Acts 16:1

on 18:19. *some disciples.* These 12 (v. 7) seem to have been followers of Jesus, but indirectly through John the Baptist or some of his followers. Or perhaps they had received their teaching from Apollos himself in his earlier state of partial understanding (see 18:26). Like Apollos, they had a limited understanding of the gospel (see note on 18:25).

19:2 *receive the Holy Spirit.* Paul finds that they were not informed about the Holy Spirit at all (vv. 3–6).

19:4 *John baptized.* See notes on Matt 3:11,15. *baptism of repentance.* A summation of John's teaching. It was preparatory and provisional, stressing man's sinfulness and thus creating a sense of need for the gospel. John's baptism looked forward to Jesus, who by His death would make possible the forgiveness of sins (see note on Mark 1:4).

19:6 *laid his hands upon them.* See note on 6:6. *Holy Spirit came on them . . . began speaking with tongues and prophesying.* The same experience the disciples had at Pentecost (2:4,11) and the Gentiles had in Caesarea (10:46).

19:8 *three months.* Much longer than the three Sabbaths in Thessalonica (17:2), but the same approach: Jews first, then Greeks (see note on 13:14).

19:9 *the Way.* See note on 9:2. *school of Tyrannus.* See map, p. 1716; probably a school used regularly by Tyrannus, a philosopher or rhetorician. Instruction was probably given in the cooler, morning hours. One Greek manuscript adds that Paul did his instructing from 11:00 A.M. to 4:00 P.M. This would have been the hot time of the day, but the hall was available and the people were not at their regular work.

19:10 *two years.* Two years and three months (see v. 8) was the longest stay in one missionary location that Luke records. By Jewish reckoning, any part of a year is considered a year; so this period can be spoken of as three years (20:31). *all who lived in Asia heard.* One of the elements of Paul's missionary strategy is seen here. Many of the cities where Paul planted churches were strategic centers that, when evangelized, served as focal points from which the gospel radiated out to the surrounding areas. Other examples are Antioch in Pisidia (see 13:14), Thessalonica (see 17:1), Athens (see 17:15) and Corinth (see 18:1).

19:12 *handkerchiefs.* Probably used by Paul in his trade of leatherworking: one for tying around his head, the other around his waist. Cf. 5:15.

19:14 *Sceva, a Jewish chief priest.* May have been related to the high priestly family of Jerusalem. But more likely he took this title himself to make further impression with his magical wiles. Drawn by Paul's ability to drive out evil spirits, Jewish exorcists wanted to copy his work (cf. 13:6).

19:19 *books.* Such documents bearing alleged magical formulas and secret information have been unearthed. Ephesus was a center for magical incantations. *fifty thousand pieces of silver.* The high price was not due to the quality of the books but to the supposed power gained by their secret rigmarole of words and names.

19:22 *Erastus.* An important figure at Corinth, "the city trea-

and [d]Erastus, he himself stayed in [1][e]Asia for a while.

23 About that time there occurred no small disturbance concerning [a]the Way.

24 For a man named Demetrius, a silversmith, who made silver shrines of [1]Artemis, [a]was bringing no little [2]business to the craftsmen;

25 these he gathered together with the workmen of similar *trades,* and said, "Men, you know that our prosperity [1]depends upon this business.

26 "You see and hear that not only in [a]Ephesus, but in almost all of [1][b]Asia, this Paul has persuaded and turned away a considerable number of people, saying that [2][c]gods made with hands are no gods *at all.*

27 "Not only is there danger that this trade of ours fall into disrepute, but also that the temple of the great goddess [1]Artemis be regarded as worthless and that she whom all of [2][a]Asia and [b]the [3]world worship will even be dethroned from her magnificence."

28 When they heard *this* and were filled with rage, they *began* crying out, saying, "Great is [1]Artemis of the [a]Ephesians!"

29 The city was filled with the confusion, and they rushed [1]with one accord into the theater, dragging along [a]Gaius and [b]Aristarchus, Paul's traveling [c]companions from [d]Macedonia.

30 And when Paul wanted to go into the [1]assembly, [a]the disciples would not let him.

31 Also some of the [1]Asiarchs who were friends of his sent to him and repeatedly urged him not to [2]venture into the theater.

32 [a]So then, some were shouting one thing and some another, for the [1]assembly was in confusion and the majority did not know [2]for what reason they had come together.

33 Some of the crowd [1]concluded *it was* Alexander, since the Jews had put him forward; and having [a]motioned with his hand, Alexander was intending to make a defense to the [2]assembly.

34 But when they recognized that he was a Jew, a *single* outcry arose from them all as they shouted for about two hours, "Great is [1]Artemis of the Ephesians!"

35 After quieting the crowd, the town clerk *said, "Men of [a]Ephesus, what man is there after all who does not know that the city of the Ephesians is guardian of the temple of the great [1]Artemis and of the *image* which fell down from [2]heaven?

36 "So, since these are undeniable facts, you ought to keep calm and to do nothing rash.

37 "For you have brought these men *here* who are neither [a]robbers of temples nor blasphemers of our goddess.

38 "So then, if Demetrius and the craftsmen who are with him have a complaint against any man, the courts are in session and [1][a]proconsuls are *available;* let them bring charges against one another.

39 "But if you want anything beyond this, it shall be settled in the [1]lawful [2]assembly.

40 "For indeed we are in danger of being accused of a riot in connection with today's events, since there is no *real* cause *for it,* and in this connection we will be unable to account for this disorderly gathering."

41 After saying this he dismissed the [1]assembly.

Paul in Macedonia and Greece

20 After the uproar had ceased, Paul sent for [a]the disciples, and when he had

22 [1]I.e. west coast province of Asia Minor [d]Rom 16:23; 2 Tim 4:20 [e]Acts 19:10
23 [a]Acts 19:9
24 [1]Lat *Diana* [2]Or *profit* [a]Acts 16:16, 19f
25 [1]Lit *is from*
26 [1]V 22, note 1 [2]Lit *those* [a]Acts 18:19 [b]Acts 19:10 [c]Deut 4:28; Ps 115:4; Is 44:10-20; Jer 10:3ff; Acts 17:29; 1 Cor 8:4; 10:19; Rev 9:20
27 [1]Lat *Diana* [2]V 22, note 1 [3]Lit *the inhabited earth* [a]Acts 19:10 [b]Matt 24:14
28 [1]Lat *Diana* [a]Acts 18:19
29 [1]Or *together* [a]Acts 20:4 [b]Acts 20:4; 27:2; Col 4:10; Philem 24 [c]Acts 13:5; 19:22; 20:34; 2 Cor 8:19 [d]Acts 16:9; 19:22
30 [1]Lit *people* [a]Acts 19:9
31 [1]I.e. political or religious officials of the province of Asia [2]Lit *give himself*
32 [1]Gr *ekklesia* [2]Or *on whose account* [a]Acts 21:34
33 [1]Or *advised Alexander* [2]Lit *people* [a]Acts 12:17
34 [1]Lat *Diana*
35 [1]Lat *Diana* [2]Lit *Zeus;* Lat *Jupiter* [a]Acts 18:19
37 [a]Rom 2:22
38 [1]Or *provincial governors* [a]Acts 13:7
39 [1]Or *regular* [2]Gr *ekklesia* **41** [1]Gr *ekklesia* **20:1** [a]Acts 11:26

surer" at one time (see note on Rom 16:23). He is located later at Corinth also (2 Tim 4:20). Just now he returns to Corinth by way of Macedonia with Timothy.

19:24 *Demetrius, a silversmith.* Each trade had its guild, and Demetrius was probably a responsible leader of the guild for the manufacture of silver shrines and images. *Artemis.* The Greek name for the Roman goddess Diana. The Ephesian Artemis, however, was very different from the Greco-Roman goddess. She had taken on the characteristics of Cybele, the mother goddess of fertility worshiped in Asia Minor and served by many prostitute priestesses. A meteorite may be the basis of the many-breasted image of heavenly workmanship claimed for Artemis (v. 35). (Some have identified the objects that cover the torso of the image as ostrich eggs.) Reproductions of the original image from the time of the emperor Domitian (A.D. 81–96) have been found in Ephesus.

19:25 *prosperity.* Since the temple of Artemis was one of the seven wonders of the ancient world, people came from far and wide to view it. Their purchase of silver shrines and images produced a lucrative business for the craftsmen.

19:27 *temple of the great goddess.* See map, p. 1716; the glory of Ephesus: 425 feet long and 220 feet wide, having 127 white marble columns 62 feet high and less than 4 feet apart. In the inner sanctuary was the many-breasted image supposedly dropped from heaven.

19:29 *Aristarchus.* Traveled later with Paul from Corinth to Jerusalem (20:3–4), and also accompanied Paul on the voyage from Jerusalem to Rome (27:1–2; Col 4:10).

19:31 *Asiarchs.* Greek *Asiarchon,* members of a council of men of wealth and influence elected to promote the worship of the emperor. Paul had friends in this highest circle.

19:33 *Alexander.* Pushed forward by the Jews either to make clear the disassociation of the Jews from the Christians and/or to accuse the Christians further of an offense against the Greeks. The crowd recognized that the Jews were not worshipers of Artemis any more than the Christians.

19:35 *town clerk.* The secretary of the city who published the decisions of the civic assembly. He was the most important local official and the chief executive officer of the assembly, acting as go-between for Ephesus and the Roman authorities.

19:38 *courts ... proconsuls.* Probably general terms, not intended to refer to more than one court or one proconsul. As capital city of the province of Asia, Ephesus was the headquarters for the proconsul.

19:39 *lawful assembly.* The regular civil meeting ordinarily held three times a month.

exhorted them and taken his leave of them,
he left [b]to go to [c]Macedonia.

2 When he had gone through those districts and had given them much exhortation,
he came to Greece.

3 And *there* he spent three months, and
when [a]a plot was formed against him by the
Jews as he was about to set sail for [b]Syria, he
decided to return through [c]Macedonia.

4 And [1]he was accompanied by Sopater
of [a]Berea, *the son* of Pyrrhus, and by
[b]Aristarchus and Secundus of the [c]Thessalo-
nians, and [b]Gaius of [d]Derbe, and [e]Timothy,
and [f]Tychicus and [g]Trophimus of [2h]Asia.

5 But these had gone on ahead and were
waiting for [a]us at [b]Troas.

6 [a]We sailed from [b]Philippi after [c]the
days of Unleavened Bread, and came to them
at [d]Troas within five days; and there we
stayed seven days.

7 On [a]the first day of the week, when
[b]we were gathered together to [c]break bread,
Paul *began* talking to them, intending to
leave the next day, and he prolonged his
[1]message until midnight.

8 There were many [a]lamps in the [b]upper
room where we were gathered together.

9 And there was a young man named
[1]Eutychus sitting [2]on the window sill, sinking
into a deep sleep; and as Paul kept on talking,
he was overcome by sleep and fell down from
the third floor and was picked up dead.

10 But Paul went down and [a]fell upon
him, and after embracing him, he [b]said,
"[1]Do not be troubled, for his life is in him."

11 When he had gone *back* up and had
[a]broken the bread and [1]eaten, he talked with
them a long while until daybreak, and then
left.

12 They took away the boy alive, and were
[1]greatly comforted.

Troas to Miletus

13 But [a]we, going ahead to the ship, set
sail for Assos, intending from there to take
Paul on board; for so he had arranged it,
intending himself to go [1]by land.

14 And when he met us at Assos, we took
him on board and came to Mitylene.

15 Sailing from there, we arrived the following day opposite Chios; and the next day
we crossed over to Samos; and the day following we came to [a]Miletus.

20:1 [b]Acts 19:21 [c]Acts 16:9; 20:3
3 [a]Acts 9:23f; 20:19 [b]Matt 4:24 [c]Acts 16:9; 20:1
4 [1]Lit *there accompanied him* [2]I.e. west coast province of Asia Minor [a]Acts 17:10 [b]Acts 19:29 [c]Acts 17:1 [d]Acts 14:6 [e]Acts 16:1 [f]Eph 6:21; Col 4:7; 2 Tim 4:12; Titus 3:12 [g]Acts 21:29; 2 Tim 4:20 [h]Acts 16:6; 20:16, 18
5 [a]Acts 16:10; 20:5-15 [b]Acts 16:8
6 [a]Acts 16:10; 20:5-15 [b]Acts 16:12 [c]Acts 12:3 [d]Acts 16:8
7 [1]Lit *word, speech* [a]1 Cor 16:2; Rev 1:10 [b]Acts 16:10; 20:5-15 [c]Acts 2:42; 20:11
8 [a]Matt 25:1 [b]Acts 1:13
9 [1]*Eutychus* means *Good fortune*, i.e. *'Lucky'* [2]Or *at the window*
10 [1]Or *Stop being troubled*

[a]1 Kin 17:21; 2 Kin 4:34 [b]Matt 9:23f; Mark 5:39 **11** [1]Lit *tasted* [a]Acts 2:42; 20:7 **12** [1]Lit *not moderately* **13** [1]Or *on foot* [a]Acts 16:10; 20:5-15 **15** [a]Acts 20:17; 2 Tim 4:20

20:1 *taken his leave . . . he left.* Paul wanted to: (1) leave Ephesus, (2) preach in Troas on his way to Macedonia, (3) meet Titus at Troas with a report from Corinth (see 2 Cor 2:12–13) and (4) continue collecting the offering for Judea (see 1 Cor 16:1–4; 2 Co 8:1–9:15; Rom 15:25–28).
20:2 *he had gone through those districts.* May cover a considerable period. He may have gone to Illyricum (see Rom 15:19) at this time.
20:3 *three months.* Probably a reference to the stay in Corinth, the capital of Achaia. These would be the winter months when ships did not sail regularly. Paul probably wrote Romans at this time (see Introduction to Romans: Occasion). *a plot . . . against him.* The Jews were determined to take Paul's life; also, at this time he was carrying the offering for the Christians in Judea, so there would have been a temptation for theft as well. The port at Cenchrea would have provided a convenient place for Paul's enemies to detect him as he entered a ship to embark for Syria.
20:4 These men seem to be the delegates appointed to accompany Paul and the money given for the needy in Judea (see note on 2 Cor 8:23). Three were from Macedonia, two from Galatia and two from Asia. Luke may have joined them at Philippi ("We sailed," v. 6; see note on 16:10). *Sopater.* May be the same as Sosipater (Rom 16:21). *Aristarchus.* See note on 19:29. *Secundus.* Not mentioned elsewhere. His name means "second," as Tertius (see Rom 16:22) means "third" and Quartus (see Rom 16:23) means "fourth." *Gaius from Derbe.* A Gaius from Macedonia was associated with Aristarchus (see 19:29), but the grouping of the names in pairs (after the reference to Sopater) indicates that this Gaius was associated with Roman Galatia and is different from the Macedonian Gaius. *Timothy.* May have represented more than one particular church. He was from Lystra but had been responsible for working in other churches (1 Cor 16:10–11; Phil 2:19–23). He had been sent to Macedonia before Paul left Ephesus (19:22). *Tychicus.* A constant help to Paul, especially in association with the churches of Asia (Eph 6:21–22; Col 4:7–9; 2 Tim 4:12; Titus 3:12). *Trophimus.* Appears again in 21:29 (see 2 Tim 4:20). He was an Ephesian, and it is implied that he was a Gentile.
20:5 *Troas.* Was to be the rendezvous for Paul and those who went on ahead by sea from Neapolis, the seaport of Philippi (16:11). Paul and his immediate companions stayed in Philippi before sailing a week later.
20:6 *from Philippi.* From the seaport, Neapolis, about ten miles away. *days of Unleavened Bread.* Began with Passover and lasted a week. Paul spent the period in Philippi. Formerly he had hoped to reach Jerusalem sooner (see 19:21), but now he hoped to arrive there for Pentecost (see 20:16). *within five days.* The voyage from Neapolis to Troas took five days. It had taken about two days the other direction (16:11). *seven days.* Although Paul was in a hurry to arrive at Jerusalem by Pentecost, he remained seven days at Troas. This might have been because of a ship schedule, but more likely the delay was in order to meet with the believers on the first day of the week to break bread.
20:7 *first day of the week.* Sunday. Although some maintain that they met on Saturday evening since the Jewish day began at six o'clock the previous evening, there is no indication that Luke is using the Jewish method of reporting time to tell of happenings in this Hellenistic city. *to break bread.* Here indicates the Lord's Supper, since breaking bread was the expressed purpose for this formal gathering. The Lord's Supper had been commanded (Luke 22:19), and it was observed regularly (see 2:42).
20:9 *Eutychus.* A name common among the freedman class (see note on 6:9).
20:10 *his life is in him.* As Peter had raised Tabitha (9:40), so Paul raised Eutychus.
20:13 *Assos.* On the opposite side of the peninsula from Troas—about 20 miles away by land. The coastline, however, was about 40 miles. Thus Paul was not far behind the ship that sailed around the peninsula.
20:14 *Mitylene.* After the first day of sailing, they put into this harbor on the southeast shore of the island of Lesbos.
20:15 *Chios.* The second night they spent off the shore of this larger island, which lay along the west coast of Asia Minor.

16 For Paul had decided to sail past [a]Eph-
esus so that he would not have to spend time
in [1][b]Asia; for he was hurrying [c]to be in Jerusalem, if possible, [d]on the day of Pentecost.

Farewell to Ephesus

17 From Miletus he sent to [a]Ephesus and
called to him [b]the elders of the church.
18 And when they had come to him, he
said to them,
"You yourselves know, [a]from the first day
that I set foot in [1]Asia, how I was with you
the whole time,
19 serving the Lord with all humility and
with tears and with trials which came upon
me [1]through [a]the plots of the Jews;
20 how I [a]did not shrink from declaring to
you anything that was profitable, and teaching you publicly and [1]from house to house,
21 solemnly [a]testifying to both Jews and
Greeks of [b]repentance toward God and [c]faith
in our Lord Jesus Christ.
22 "And now, behold, bound in [1]spirit, [a]I
am on my way to Jerusalem, not knowing
what will happen to me there,
23 except that [a]the Holy Spirit solemnly
[b]testifies to me in every city, saying that
[c]bonds and afflictions await me.
24 "But [a]I do not consider my life of any
account as dear to myself, so that I may [b]fin-
ish my course and [c]the ministry which I
received from the Lord Jesus, to [d]testify
solemnly of the gospel of [e]the grace of God.
25 "And now, behold, I know that all of
you, among whom I went about [a]preaching
the kingdom, will no longer see my face.
26 "Therefore, I [1]testify to you this day that
[a]I am [2]innocent of the blood of all men.
27 "For I [a]did not shrink from declaring to
you the whole [b]purpose of God.
28 "Be on guard for yourselves and for all
[a]the flock, among which the Holy Spirit has
made you [1]overseers, to shepherd [b]the
church of God which [c]He [2]purchased [3]with
His own blood.
29 "I know that after my departure [a]savage
wolves will come in among you, not sparing
[b]the flock;
30 and from among your own selves men
will arise, speaking perverse things, to draw
away [a]the disciples after them.
31 "Therefore be on the alert, remembering
that night and day for a period of [a]three
years I did not cease to admonish each one
[b]with tears.
32 "And now I [a]commend you to God and
to [b]the word of His grace, which is able to
[c]build *you* up and to give *you* [d]the inheritance among all those who are sanctified.
33 "[a]I have coveted no one's silver or gold
or clothes.
34 "You yourselves know that [a]these hands
ministered to my *own* needs and to the [b]men
who were with me.
35 "In everything I showed you that by
working hard in this manner you must help
the weak and remember the words of the
Lord Jesus, that He Himself said, 'It is more
blessed to give than to receive.' "
36 When he had said these things, he
[a]knelt down and prayed with them all.
37 And [1]they *began* to weep aloud and
[2][a]embraced Paul, and repeatedly kissed him,

16 [1]I.e. west coast province of Asia Minor [a]Acts 18:19 [b]Acts 16:6; 20:4, 18 [c]Acts 19:21; 20:6, 22; 1 Cor 16:8 [d]Acts 2:1
17 [a]Acts 18:19 [b]Acts 11:30
18 [1]V 16, note 1 [a]Acts 18:19; 19:1, 10; 20:4, 16
19 [1]Lit *by* [a]Acts 20:3
20 [1]Or *in the various private homes* [a]Acts 20:27
21 [a]Luke 16:28; Acts 18:5; 20:23, 24 [b]Acts 2:38; 11:18; 26:20 [c]Acts 24:24; 26:18; Eph 1:15; Col 2:5; Philem 5
22 [1]Or *the Spirit* [a]Acts 17:16; 20:16
23 [a]Acts 8:29 [b]Luke 16:28; Acts 18:5; 20:21, 24 [c]Acts 9:16; 21:33
24 [a]Acts 21:13 [b]Acts 13:25; 2 Tim 4:7 [c]Acts 1:17 [d]Luke 16:28; Acts 18:5; 20:21 [e]Acts 11:23; 20:32
25 [a]Matt 4:23; Acts 28:31
26 [1]Or *call you to witness* [2]Lit *pure from* [a]Acts 18:6
27 [a]Acts 20:20 [b]Acts 13:36
28 [1]Or *bishops* [2]Lit *acquired* [3]Lit *through* [a]Luke 12:32; John 21:15-17; Acts 20:29; 1 Pet 5:2f [b]Matt 16:18; Rom 16:16; 1 Cor 10:32 [c]Eph 1:7, 14; Titus 2:14; 1 Pet 1:19; 2:9; Rev 5:9
29 [a]Ezek 22:27; Matt 7:15 [b]Luke 12:32; John 21:15-17; Acts 20:28; 1 Pet 5:2f
30 [a]Acts 11:26
31 [a]Acts 19:8, 10; 24:17 [b]Acts 20:19
32 [a]Acts 14:23 [b]Acts 14:3; 20:24 [c]Acts 9:31 [d]Acts 26:18; Eph 1:14; 5:5; Col 1:12; 3:24; Heb 9:15; 1 Pet 1:4
33 [a]1 Cor 9:4-18; 2 Cor 11:7-12; 12:14-18; 1 Thess 2:5f
34 [a]Acts 18:3 [b]Acts 19:22
36 [a]Acts 9:40; 21:5; Luke 22:41
37 [1]Lit *a considerable weeping of all occurred* [2]Lit *threw themselves on Paul's neck* [a]Luke 15:20

Samos. Crossing the mouth of the bay that leads to Ephesus, they came on the third day to Samos, one of the most important islands in the Aegean. *Miletus.* Thirty miles south of Ephesus, the destination of the ship Paul was on. He would have had to change ships to put into Ephesus, which would have lost time (see v. 16). If he had come to Ephesus, he would have had to visit a number of families, which would have taken more time. If trouble should arise, as the riot of a year ago (19:23–41), even more time would be lost. It could not be risked.

20:16 *on the day of Pentecost.* Fifty days from Passover. Five days plus seven days (v. 6) plus four days (vv. 13–15) had already gone by, leaving only about two-thirds of the time for the remainder of the trip.

20:17 *elders of the church.* The importance of the leadership of elders has been evident throughout Paul's ministry. He had delivered the famine gift from the church at Antioch to the elders of the Jerusalem church (11:30). He had appointed elders on his first missionary journey (see 14:23) and had addressed the holders of this office later in Philippi (Phil 1:1, "overseers"). He requested the Ephesian elders to meet with him on this solemn occasion (see v. 28). Some years later he wrote down instruction about the elders' qualifications (1 Tim 3; Titus 1).

20:19 *with tears.* See v. 31. Paul's ministry at Ephesus was conducted with emotional fervency and a sense of urgency.

20:22 *bound in spirit.* Paul did not go to Jerusalem against the direction of the Spirit, as some have suggested, but because of the guidance of the Spirit. People pleaded with him not to go (21:4,12), not because the Spirit prohibited his going but because the Spirit revealed the capture that awaited him there (21:11–12).

20:25 *all of you . . . will no longer see my face.* Not a message from God but what Paul anticipated. He had been mistaken before in his plans: He had intended to stay in Ephesus until Pentecost, but he had to leave earlier (see v. 1; 1 Cor 16:8–9). His prophetic power was not used to foresee his own future, just as his healing power was not used to heal his own disease (see 2 Cor 12:7–9). As it turned out, it seems that Paul did revisit Ephesus (see 1 Tim 1:3).

20:28 *overseers, to shepherd.* The "elders" (v. 17) were called "overseers" and told to pastor ("shepherd") the flock—demonstrating that the same men could be called "elders," "overseers" or "pastors." *His own blood.* Lit. "the blood of his own one," a term of endearment (such as "his own dear one," referring to His own Son).

20:31 *three years.* See note on 19:10.

20:32 *are sanctified.* Positional sanctification (see 26:18; see also note on 1 Cor 1:2).

20:34 *ministered to my own needs.* Paul had worked in Thessalonica (1 Thess 2:9) and Corinth (Acts 18:3).

20:35 *remember the words . . . that He Himself said.* A formula

38 [1]grieving especially over [a]the word which he had spoken, that they would not see his face again. And they were [b]accompanying him to the ship.

Paul Sails from Miletus

21 When [a]we had parted from them and had set sail, we ran [b]a straight course to Cos and the next day to Rhodes and from there to Patara;

2 and having found a ship crossing over to [a]Phoenicia, we went aboard and set sail.

3 When we came in sight of [a]Cyprus, leaving it on the left, we kept sailing to [b]Syria and landed at [c]Tyre; for there the ship was to unload its cargo.

4 After looking up [a]the disciples, we stayed there seven days; and they kept telling Paul [1b]through the Spirit not to set foot in Jerusalem.

5 When [1]our days there were ended, we left and started on our journey, while they all, with wives and children, [a]escorted us until *we were* out of the city. After [b]kneeling down on the beach and praying, we said farewell to one another.

6 Then we went on board the ship, and they returned [a]home again.

7 When we had finished the voyage from [a]Tyre, we arrived at Ptolemais, and after greeting [b]the brethren, we stayed with them for a day.

8 On the next day we left and came to [a]Caesarea, and entering the house of [b]Philip the [c]evangelist, who was [b]one of the seven, we stayed with him.

9 Now this man had four virgin daughters who were [a]prophetesses.

10 As we were staying there for some days, a prophet named [a]Agabus came down from Judea.

11 And coming to us, he [a]took Paul's belt and bound his own feet and hands, and said, "This [b]is what the Holy Spirit says: 'In this way the Jews at Jerusalem will [c]bind the man who owns this belt and [d]deliver him into the hands of the Gentiles.' "

12 When we had heard this, we as well as the local residents *began* begging him [a]not to go up to Jerusalem.

13 Then Paul answered, "What are you doing, weeping and breaking my heart? For [a]I am ready not only to be bound, but even to die at Jerusalem for [b]the name of the Lord Jesus."

14 And since he would not be persuaded, we fell silent, remarking, "[a]The will of the Lord be done!"

Paul at Jerusalem

15 After these days we got ready and [a]started on our way up to Jerusalem.

16 *Some* of [a]the disciples from [b]Caesarea also came with us, taking us to Mnason of [c]Cyprus, a [d]disciple of long standing with whom we were to lodge.

17 After we arrived in Jerusalem, [a]the brethren received us gladly.

18 And the following day Paul went in with us to [1a]James, and all [b]the elders were present.

19 After he had greeted them, he [a]*began* to relate one by one the things which God had done among the Gentiles through his [b]ministry.

20 And when they heard it they *began* [a]glorifying God; and they said to him, "You

38 [1]Lit *suffering pain* [a]Acts 20:25 [b]Acts 15:3
21:1 [a][we] Acts 16:10; 21:1-18 [b]Acts 16:11
2 [a]Acts 11:19; 21:3
3 [a]Acts 4:36; 21:16 [b]Matt 4:24 [c]Acts 12:20; 21:7
4 [1]I.e. because of impressions made by the Spirit [a]Acts 11:26; 21:16 [b]Acts 20:23; 21:11
5 [1]Lit *we had completed the days* [a]Acts 15:3 [b]Luke 22:41; Acts 9:40; 20:36
6 [a]John 19:27
7 [a]Acts 12:20; 21:3 [b]Acts 1:15; 21:17
8 [a]Acts 8:40; 21:16 [b]Acts 6:5; 8:5 [c]Eph 4:11; 2 Tim 4:5
9 [a]Luke 2:36; Acts 13:1; 1 Cor 11:5
10 [a]Acts 11:28
11 [a]1 Kin 22:11; Is 20:2; Jer 13:1-11; 19:1, 11; John 18 [b]Acts 8:29 [c]Acts 9:16; 21:33 [d]Matt 20:19
12 [a]Acts 21:15
13 [a]Acts 20:24 [b]Acts 5:41; 9:16
14 [a]Luke 22:42
15 [a]Acts 21:12
16 [a]Acts 21:4 [b]Acts 8:40 [c]Acts 4:36; 21:3 [d]Acts 15:7
17 [a]Acts 1:15; 21:7
18 [1]Or *Jacob* [a]Acts 12:17 [b]Acts 11:30
19 [a]Acts 14:27 [b]Acts 1:17
20 [a]Matt 9:8

regularly used in the early church to introduce a quotation from Jesus (1 Clement 46:7). This is a rare instance of a saying of Jesus not found in the canonical Gospels.

21:1 *ran a straight course to Cos.* Favorable winds took them to a stopping place for the night at this island. *Rhodes.* The leading city on the island of Rhodes, once noted for its harbor colossus, one of the seven wonders of the ancient world (but demolished over two centuries before Paul arrived there). It took them a day to get to Rhodes. *Patara.* On the southern coast of Lycia. Paul changed ships from a vessel that hugged the shore of Asia Minor to one going directly to Tyre and Phoenicia.

21:3 *Cyprus.* See 13:4. *Tyre.* Paul had passed through this Phoenician area at least once before (15:3; cf. Mark 7:24).

21:4 *seven days.* These, added to the 29 days since the Passover in Philippi, would leave only two weeks until Pentecost. *kept telling Paul . . . not to set foot.* The Spirit warned of the coming trials in store for Paul at Jerusalem. Because of these warnings, Paul's brothers urged him not to go on, knowing that trials lay ahead. But Paul felt "bound in spirit" to go (20:22).

21:7 *Ptolemais.* The modern city of Acco, north of and across the bay from Mount Carmel. It was one day's journey from Tyre on the north and another 35 miles to Caesarea on the south.

21:8 *Caesarea.* A Gentile city, the capital of Roman Judea (see note on 10:1). *Philip the evangelist.* Philip's evangelistic work may have focused on Caesarea for almost 25 years (see note on 8:40). "Evangelist" is a title used only here and in Eph 4:11; 2 Tim 4:5.

21:9 *virgin daughters.* They may have been dedicated in a special way to serving the Lord. *prophetesses.* See 1 Cor 11:5; 12:8–10; cf. Luke 2:36. For OT prophetesses see Ex 15:20; Judg 4:4; 2 Kin 22:14; Neh 6:14.

21:10 *prophet named Agabus.* Evidently he held the office of prophet, as Philip held the office of evangelist (v. 8). This is the same prophet who had been in Antioch prophesying the coming famine in Jerusalem some 15 years earlier (11:27–29).

21:12 *we as well as the local residents.* Now Luke, in the company of travelers with Paul, joins in urging Paul not to go to Jerusalem.

21:14 *will of the Lord be done!* May mean that they finally recognized that it was the Lord's will for Paul to go to Jerusalem.

21:16 *Mnason.* Must have been a disciple of some means to be able to accommodate Paul and a group of about nine men traveling with him.

21:17 *arrived in Jerusalem.* No more than a day or two before Pentecost. *the brethren received us gladly.* May indicate the grateful reception of the offering as well.

21:18 *James.* The brother of the Lord, author of the letter of James and leader of the church in Jerusalem (see Gal 1:19; 2:9). He is called an apostle but was not one of the twelve.

21:23 *under a vow.* They were evidently under the temporary

see, brother, how many [1]thousands there are
among the Jews of those who have believed,
and they are all [b]zealous for the Law;
21 and they have been told about you,
that you are [a]teaching all the Jews who are
among the Gentiles to forsake Moses, telling
them [b]not to circumcise their children nor to
[1]walk according to [c]the customs.
22 "What, then, is *to be done*? They will
certainly hear that you have come.
23 "Therefore do this that we tell you. We
have four men who [1a]are under a vow;
24 take them and [a]purify yourself along
with them, and [1]pay their expenses so that
they may [b]shave their [2]heads; and all will
know that there is nothing to the things
which they have been told about you, but
that you yourself also walk orderly, keeping
the Law.
25 "But concerning the Gentiles who have
believed, we wrote, [a]having decided that
they should abstain from [1]meat sacrificed to
idols and from blood and from what is strangled and from fornication."
26 Then Paul [1]took the men, and the next
day, [a]purifying himself along with them,
[b]went into the temple giving notice of the
completion of the days of purification, until
the sacrifice was offered for each one of
them.

Paul Seized in the Temple

27 When [a]the seven days were almost
over, [b]the Jews from [1c]Asia, upon seeing him
in the temple, *began* to stir up all the crowd
and laid hands on him,
28 crying out, "Men of Israel, come to our
aid! [a]This is the man who preaches to all
men everywhere against our people and the
Law and this place; and besides he has even
brought Greeks into the temple and has
[b]defiled this holy place."
29 For they had previously seen [a]Trophi-
mus the [b]Ephesian in the city with him, and
they supposed that Paul had brought him
into the temple.
30 Then all the city was provoked, and
[1]the people rushed together, and taking hold
of Paul they [a]dragged him out of the temple,
and immediately the doors were shut.
31 While they were seeking to kill him, a
report came up to the [1]commander of the
[a]*Roman* [2]cohort that all Jerusalem was in
confusion.
32 At once he [a]took along *some* soldiers
and centurions and ran down to them; and
when they saw the [1]commander and the soldiers, they stopped beating Paul.
33 Then the [1]commander came up and
took hold of him, and ordered him to be
[a]bound with [b]two chains; and he *began* asking who he was and what he had done.
34 But among the crowd [a]some were
shouting one thing *and* some another, and
when he could not find out the [1]facts
because of the uproar, he ordered him to be
brought into [b]the barracks.
35 When he got to [a]the stairs, he was carried by the soldiers because of the violence
of the [1]mob;
36 for the multitude of the people kept following them, shouting, "[a]Away with him!"
37 As Paul was about to be brought into
[a]the barracks, he said to the [1]commander,
"May I say something to you?" And he *said,
"Do you know Greek?
38 "Then you are not [a]the Egyptian who
some [1]time ago stirred up a revolt and led
the four thousand men of the Assassins out
[b]into the wilderness?"

20 [1]Lit *ten thousands* [b]Acts 15:1; 22:3; Rom 10:2; Gal 1:14
21 [1]I.e. observe or live by [a]Acts 21:28 [b]Acts 15:19ff; 1 Cor 7:18f [c]Acts 6:14
23 [1]Lit *have a vow on them* [a]Num 6:13-21; Acts 18:18
24 [1]Lit *spend on them* [2]Lit *head* [a]John 11:55; Acts 21:26; 24:18 [b]Acts 18:18
25 [1]Lit *the thing* [a]Acts 15:19f, 29
26 [1]Or *took the men the next day, and purifying himself* [a]John 11:55; Acts 21:24; 24:18 [b]Num 6:13; Acts 24:18
27 [1]I.e. west coast province of Asia Minor [a]Num 6:9, 13-20 [b]Acts 20:19; 24:18 [c]Acts 16:6
28 [a]Acts 6:13 [b]Matt 24:15; Acts 6:13f; 24:6
29 [a]Acts 20:4 [b]Acts 18:19
30 [1]Lit *a running together of the people occurred* [a]2 Kin 11:15; Acts 16:19; 26:21
31 [1]I.e. chiliarch, in command of one thousand troops [2]Or *battalion* [a]Acts 10:1
32 [1]V 31, note 1 [a]Acts 23:27
33 [1]V 31, note 1 [a]Acts 20:23; 21:11; 22:29; 26:29; 28:20; Eph 6:20; 2 Tim 1:16; 2:9 [b]Acts 12:6
34 [1]Lit *certainty* [a]Acts 19:32 [b]Acts 21:37; 22:24; 23:10, 16, 32
35 [1]Lit *crowd* [a]Acts 21:40 **36** [a]Luke 23:18; John 19:15; Acts 22:22 **37** [1]V 31, note 1 [a]Acts 21:34; 22:24; 23:10, 16, 32
38 [1]Lit *days* [a]Acts 5:36 [b]Matt 24:26

Nazirite vow and became unclean before the completion time of the vow (perhaps from contact with a dead body); cf. Num 6:2–12.

21:24 *purify yourself.* In some instances the rites included the offering of sacrifices. Such rites were observed by choice by some Jewish Christians but were not required of Christians, whether Jew or Gentile. *pay their expenses.* Paul's part in sponsoring these men would include (1) paying part or all of the expenses of the sacrificial victims (in this case eight pigeons and four lambs, Num 6:9–12) and (2) going to the temple to notify the priest when their days of purification would be fulfilled so the priests would be prepared to sacrifice their offerings (v. 26). *keeping the Law.* Paul had earlier taken a vow himself (18:18), he had been a Jew to the Jews (see 1 Cor 9:20–21), and Timothy had been circumcised (16:3). However, Paul was very careful not to sacrifice Christian principle in any act of obedience to the law (he would not have Titus circumcised, Gal 2:3).

21:27 *seven days.* Cf. Num 6:9. These were the days required for purification, shaving their heads at the altar, the sacrifice of a sin offering and burnt offering for each, and announcing the completion to the priests. *Jews from Asia.* Paul had suffered already from the hands of Asian Jews (20:19).

21:28 *brought Greeks into the temple.* Explicitly forbidden according to inscribed stone markers (still in existence). Any Gentiles found within the bounds of the court of Israel would be killed. But there is no evidence that Paul had brought anyone other than Jews into the area.

21:29 *Trophimus.* Paul probably did not take him into the forbidden area. If he had, they should have attacked Trophimus rather than Paul.

21:30 *doors were shut.* By order of the temple officer to prevent further trouble inside the sacred precincts.

21:31 *commander.* Greek *chiliarch,* a commander of 1,000 (a regiment), Claudius Lysias by name (23:26), who was stationed at the Fortress of Antonia (see note on v. 37).

21:32 *some ... centurions.* Since the plural is used, it is likely that at least two centurions and 200 soldiers were involved.

21:33 *two chains.* Probably his hands were chained to a soldier on either side.

21:37 *barracks.* The Fortress of Antonia was connected to the northern end of the temple area by two flights of steps. The tower overlooked the temple area.

21:38 *the Egyptian who . . . stirred up a revolt.* Josephus tells of an Egyptian false prophet who some years earlier had led 4,000 (Josephus, through a misreading of a Greek capital letter, says 30,000) out to the Mount of Olives. Roman soldiers killed hun-

39 But Paul said, "[a]I am a Jew of Tarsus in
[b]Cilicia, a citizen of no insignificant city; and
I beg you, allow me to speak to the people."
40 When he had given him permission,
Paul, standing on [a]the stairs, [b]motioned to
the people with his hand; and when there
[1]was a great hush, he spoke to them in the
[2c]Hebrew dialect, saying,

Paul's Defense before the Jews

22 "[a]Brethren and fathers, hear my
defense which I now *offer* to you."
2 And when they heard that he was
addressing them in the [1a]Hebrew dialect,
they became even more quiet; and he *said,
3 "[a]I am [b]a Jew, born in [c]Tarsus of [d]Cili-
cia, but brought up in this city, educated
[1]under [e]Gamaliel, [2f]strictly according to the
law of our fathers, being zealous for God just
as [g]you all are today.
4 "[a]I persecuted this [b]Way to the death,
binding and putting both men and women
into prisons,
5 as also [a]the high priest and all [b]the
Council of the elders [1]can testify. From them
I also [c]received letters to [d]the brethren, and
started off for [c]Damascus in order to bring
even those who were there to Jerusalem [2]as
prisoners to be punished.
6 "[a]But it happened that as I was on my
way, approaching Damascus about noontime, a very bright light suddenly flashed
from heaven all around me,
7 and I fell to the ground and heard a
voice saying to me, 'Saul, Saul, why are you
persecuting Me?'
8 "And I answered, 'Who are You, Lord?'
And He said to me, 'I am [a]Jesus the Nazarene, whom you are persecuting.'
9 "And those who were with me [a]saw the
light, to be sure, but [b]did not [1]understand the
voice of the One who was speaking to me.
10 "And I said, '[a]What shall I do, Lord?'
And the Lord said to me, 'Get up and go on
into Damascus, and there you will be told of
all that has been appointed for you to do.'
11 "But since I [a]could not see because of
the [1]brightness of that light, I was led by the
hand by those who were with me and came
into Damascus.
12 "A certain [a]Ananias, a man who was
devout by the standard of the Law, *and* [b]well
spoken of by all the Jews who lived there,
13 came to me, and standing near said to
me, '[a]Brother Saul, receive your sight!' And
[1b]at that very time I looked up at him.
14 "And he said, '[a]The God of our fathers
has [b]appointed you to know His will and to
[c]see the [d]Righteous One and to hear an
[1]utterance from His mouth.
15 'For you will be [a]a witness for Him to
all men of [b]what you have seen and heard.
16 'Now why do you delay? [a]Get up and
be baptized, and [b]wash away your sins,
[c]calling on His name.'
17 "It happened when I [a]returned to
Jerusalem and was praying in the temple,
that I [b]fell into a trance,
18 and I saw Him saying to me, '[a]Make
haste, and get out of Jerusalem quickly,
because they will not accept your testimony
about Me.'
19 "And I said, 'Lord, they themselves

39 [a]Acts 9:11; 22:3 [b]Acts 6:9 **40** [1]Lit *occurred* [2]I.e. Jewish Aramaic [a]Acts 21:35 [b]Acts 12:17 [c]John 5:2; Acts 1:19; 22:2; 26:14
22:1 [a]Acts 7:2 **2** [1]I.e. Jewish Aramaic [a]Acts 21:40
3 [1]Lit *at the feet of* [2]Lit *according to the strictness of the ancestral law* [a]Acts 9:1-22; 22:3-16; 26:9-18 [b]Acts 21:39 [c]Acts 9:11 [d]Acts 6:9 [e]Acts 5:34 [f]Acts 23:6; 26:5; Phil 3:6 [g]Acts 21:20
4 [a]Acts 8:3; 22:19f; 26:9-11 [b]Acts 9:2
5 [1]Lit *testifies for me* [2]Lit *having been bound* [a]Acts 9:1 [b]Luke 22:66; Acts 5:21; 1 Tim 4:14 [c]Acts 9:2 [d]Acts 2:29; 3:17; 13:26; 23:1; 28:17, 21; Rom 9:3
6 [a]Acts 22:6-11: *Acts 9:3-8; 26:12-18*
8 [a]Acts 26:9
9 [1]Or *hear* (with comprehension) [a]Acts 26:13 [b]Acts 9:7
10 [a]Acts 16:30
11 [1]Lit *glory* [a]Acts 9:8
12 [a]Acts 9:10 [b]Acts 6:3; 10:22
13 [1]Or *instantly;* lit *at the very hour* [a]Acts 9:17 [b]Acts 9:18
14 [1]Or *message;* lit *voice* [a]Acts 3:13 [b]Acts 9:15; 26:16 [c]Acts 9:17; 26:16; 1 Cor 9:1; 15:8 [d]Acts 7:52 **15** [a]Acts 23:11; 26:16 [b]Acts 22:14 **16** [a]Acts 9:18 [b]Acts 2:38; 1 Cor 6:11; Eph 5:26; Heb 10:22 [c]Acts 7:59 **17** [a]Acts 9:26; 26:20 [b]Acts 10:10
18 [a]Acts 9:29

dreds, but the leader escaped. *men of the Assassins.* The Greek here is a loanword from Latin *sicarii,* meaning "dagger-men," who were violent assassins.

21:39 *Tarsus.* See note on 22:3.

21:40 *the Hebrew dialect.* More likely Aramaic than Hebrew, since Aramaic was the most commonly used language among Palestinian Jews.

22:1 *Brethren.* See note on 11:1.

22:2 *the Hebrew dialect.* See note on 21:40. Actually, if he had spoken in Hebrew, they would have become quieter in order not to miss a single word, because it would have been more difficult for them to understand.

22:3 *born in Tarsus.* Paul had citizenship in Tarsus (21:39) as well as being a Roman citizen. "No insignificant city" (21:39) was used by Euripides to describe Athens. Tarsus was 10 miles inland on the Cydnus River and 30 miles from the mountains, which were cut by a deep, narrow gorge called the Cilician Gates. It was an important commercial center, university city and crossroads of travel. *brought up in this city.* Paul must have come to Jerusalem at an early age. Another translation ("brought up in this city at the feet of Gamaliel, being thoroughly trained according to the law of our fathers") would suggest that Paul came to Jerusalem when he was old enough to begin training under Gamaliel. *Gamaliel.* The most honored rabbi of the first century. Possibly he was the grandson of Hillel (see also 5:34–40).

22:4 *I persecuted this Way.* See 9:1–4.

22:5 *high priest.* Caiaphas, the high priest over 20 years earlier, was now dead, and Ananias was high priest (see 23:2); but the records of the high priest would show Paul's testimony to be true.

22:6 *about noontime.* A detail not included in the earlier account (9:1–22).

22:8 *Who are You, Lord?* See note on 9:5. *persecuting.* See note on 9:4.

22:9 *did not understand the voice.* They heard the sound (9:7) but did not understand what was said.

22:12 *Ananias . . . devout by the standard of the Law.* Important to this audience (see note on Luke 1:6).

22:14 *to see the Righteous One.* Cf. 3:14. To see the resurrected Jesus was all-important to Paul (see 26:16; 1 Cor 9:1; 15:8). It was that experience that had convinced him of the truth of the gospel and that became the foundation of his theology.

22:16 *wash away your sins.* Baptism is the outward sign of an inward work of grace. The reality and the symbol are closely associated in the NT (see 2:38; Titus 3:5; 1 Pet 3:21). The outward rite, however, does not produce the inward grace (cf. Rom 2:28–29; Eph 2:8–9; Phil 3:4–9). See note on Rom 6:3–4.

22:17 *when I returned to Jerusalem.* Refers to the visit described in 9:26; Gal 1:17–18. *in the temple, that I fell into a trance.* See Peter's trance (10:10; 11:5; cf. 2 Cor 12:3). Paul was not a blasphemer of the temple but continued to hold it in high honor.

understand that in one synagogue after another [a]I used to imprison and [b]beat those who believed in You.

20 'And [a]when the blood of Your witness Stephen was being shed, I also was standing by approving, and watching out for the coats of those who were slaying him.'

21 "And He said to me, 'Go! For I will send you far away [a]to the Gentiles.' "

22 They listened to him up to this statement, and *then* they raised their voices and said, "[a]Away with such a fellow from the earth, for [b]he should not be allowed to live!"

23 And as they were crying out and [a]throwing off their cloaks and [b]tossing dust into the air,

24 the [1]commander ordered him to be brought into [a]the barracks, stating that he should be [b]examined by scourging so that he might find out the reason why they were shouting against him that way.

25 But when they stretched him out [1]with thongs, Paul said to the centurion who was standing by, "Is it [2]lawful for you to scourge [a]a man who is a Roman and uncondemned?"

26 When the centurion heard *this,* he went to the [1]commander and told him, saying, "What are you about to do? For this man is a Roman."

27 The [1]commander came and said to him, "Tell me, are you a Roman?" And he said, "Yes."

28 The [1]commander answered, "I acquired this citizenship with a large sum of money." And Paul said, "But I was actually born *a citizen.*"

29 Therefore those who were about to [a]examine him immediately [1]let go of him; and the [2]commander also [b]was afraid when he found out that he was a Roman, and because he had [3c]put him in chains.

30 But on the next day, [a]wishing to know for certain why he had been accused by the Jews, he [b]released him and ordered the chief priests and all [c]the [1]Council to assemble, and brought Paul down and set him before them.

Paul before the Council

23 Paul, looking intently at [a]the [1]Council, said, "[b]Brethren, [c]I have [2]lived my life with a perfectly good conscience before God up to this day."

2 The high priest [a]Ananias commanded those standing beside him [b]to strike him on the mouth.

3 Then Paul said to him, "God is going to strike you, [a]you whitewashed wall! Do you [b]sit to try me according to the Law, and in violation of the Law order me to be struck?"

4 But the bystanders said, "Do you revile God's high priest?"

5 And Paul said, "I was not aware, brethren, that he was high priest; for it is written, '[a]YOU SHALL NOT SPEAK EVIL OF A RULER OF YOUR PEOPLE.' "

6 But perceiving that one group were [a]Sadducees and the other Pharisees, Paul *began* crying out in [b]the [1]Council, "[c]Brethren, [d]I am a Pharisee, a son of Pharisees; I am on trial for [e]the hope and resurrection of the dead!"

19 [a]Acts 8:3; 22:4 [b]Matt 10:17; Acts 26:11
20 [a]Acts 7:58f; 8:1; 26:10
21 [a]Acts 9:15
22 [a]Acts 21:36; 1 Thess 2:16 [b]Acts 25:24
23 [a]Acts 7:58 [b]2 Sam 16:13
24 [1]I.e. chiliarch, in command of one thousand troops [a]Acts 21:34 [b]Acts 22:29
25 [1]Or *for the whip* [2]Interrogation by torture was a procedure used with slaves [a]Acts 16:37
26 [1]V 24, note 1
27 [1]V 24, note 1
28 [1]V 24, note 1
29 [1]Lit *withdrew from* [2]V 24, note 1 [3]Lit *bound him* [a]Acts 22:24 [b]Acts 16:38 [c]Acts 21:33
30 [1]Or *Sanhedrin* [a]Acts 23:28 [b]Acts 21:33 [c]Matt 5:22
23:1 [1]Or *Sanhedrin* [2]Or *conducted myself as a citizen* [a]Acts 22:30; 23:6, 15, 20, 28 [b]Acts 22:5 [c]Acts 24:16; 2 Cor 1:12; 2 Tim 1:3
2 [a]Acts 24:1 [b]John 18:22
3 [a]Matt 23:27 [b]Lev 19:15; Deut 25:2; John 7:51
5 [a]Ex 22:28 **6** [1]Or *Sanhedrin* [a]Matt 3:7; 22:23 [b]Acts 22:30; 23:1, 15, 20, 28 [c]Acts 22:5 [d]Acts 26:5; Phil 3:5 [e]Acts 24:15, 21; 26:8

22:20 *standing by approving.* Does not necessarily mean that Paul had to be a member of the Sanhedrin, though some have thought so (see note on 26:10). He could show his approval by allowing them to put their cloaks at his feet.

22:24 *commander.* See note on 21:31. *barracks.* See note on 21:37. *examined by scourging.* Not with the rod, as at Philippi (16:22–24), but with the scourge, a merciless instrument of torture. It was legal to use it to force a confession from a slave or alien but never from a Roman citizen. The scourge consisted of a whip of leather thongs with pieces of bone or metal attached to the ends.

22:25 *they stretched him out.* The Greek word used for tying a person to a post for whipping. *centurion.* See note on 10:1. *Roman.* According to Roman law, all Roman citizens were assured exclusion from all degrading forms of punishment: beating with rods, scourging, crucifixion.

22:28 *acquired . . . large sum of money.* There were three ways to obtain Roman citizenship: (1) receive it as a reward for some outstanding service to Rome; (2) buy it at a considerable price; (3) be born into a family of Roman citizens. How Paul's father or an earlier ancestor had gained citizenship, no one knows. By 171 B.C. a large number of Jews were citizens of Tarsus, and in the time of Pompey (106–48) some of these could have received Roman citizenship as well. Cf. 16:37.

22:30 *he released him.* Paul was no longer bound, and presumably he would have been free completely if the Council had not wished to detain him. *chief priests.* Those of the high priestly line of descent (mainly Sadducees), but the Council now included a considerable number of Pharisees. These men constituted the ruling body of the Jews. The Jewish court was respected by the Roman governor, whose approval had to be obtained before sentencing to capital punishment.

23:1 *Council.* See note on 5:21. *Brethren.* Fellow Jews (see note on 11:1). *good conscience.* A consistent claim of Paul.

23:2 *Ananias.* High priest A.D. 47–59, son of Nebedaeus. He is not to be confused with the high priest Annas (A.D. 6–15; see note on Luke 3:2). Ananias was noted for cruelty and violence. When the revolt against Rome broke out, he was assassinated by his own people.

23:3 *whitewashed wall!* Having an attractive exterior but filled with unclean contents, such as tombs holding dead bodies (see Matt 23:27); or walls that look substantial but fall before the winds (see Ezek 13:10–12). It is a metaphor for a hypocrite.

23:5 *I was not aware . . . that he was high priest.* Explained in different ways: 1. Paul had poor eyesight (suggested by such passages as Gal 4:15; 6:11) and failed to see that the one who presided was the high priest. 2. He failed to discern that the one who presided was the high priest because on some occasions others had sat in his place. 3. He was using pure irony: A true high priest would not give such an order. 4. He refused to acknowledge that Ananias was the high priest under these circumstances.

23:6 *Sadducees.* See notes on 4:1; Matt 3:7; Mark 12:18; Luke 20:27. They denied the resurrection and angels and spirits (v. 8). *Pharisees.* See notes on Matt 3:7; Mark 2:16; Luke 5:17.

7 As he said this, there occurred a dissension between the Pharisees and Sadducees, and the assembly was divided.

8 For [a]the Sadducees say that there is no resurrection, nor an angel, nor a spirit, but the Pharisees acknowledge them all.

9 And there occurred a great uproar; and some of [a]the scribes of the Pharisaic party stood up and *began* to argue heatedly, saying, "[b]We find nothing wrong with this man; [c]suppose a spirit or an angel has spoken to him?"

10 And as a great dissension was developing, the [1]commander was afraid Paul would be torn to pieces by them and ordered the troops to go down and take him away from them by force, and bring him into [a]the barracks.

11 But on [a]the night *immediately* following, the Lord stood at his side and said, "[b]Take courage; for [c]as you have [d]solemnly witnessed to My cause at Jerusalem, so you must witness at Rome also."

A Conspiracy to Kill Paul

12 When it was day, [a]the Jews formed a [1]conspiracy and [b]bound themselves under an oath, saying that they would neither eat nor drink until they had killed Paul.

13 There were more than forty who formed this plot.

14 They came to the chief priests and the elders and said, "We have [a]bound ourselves under a solemn oath to taste nothing until we have killed Paul.

15 "Now therefore, you [1]and [a]the [2]Council notify the [3]commander to bring him down to you, as though you were going to determine his case by a more thorough investigation; and we for our part are ready to slay him before he comes near *the place.*"

16 But the son of Paul's sister heard of their ambush, [1]and he came and entered [a]the barracks and told Paul.

17 Paul called one of the centurions to him and said, "Lead this young man to the [1]commander, for he has something to report to him."

18 So he took him and led him to the [1]commander and *said, "Paul [a]the prisoner called me to him and asked me to lead this young man to you since he has something to tell you."

19 The [1]commander took him by the hand and stepping aside, *began* to inquire of him privately, "What is it that you have to report to me?"

20 And he said, "[a]The Jews have agreed to ask you to bring Paul down tomorrow to [b]the [1]Council, as though they were going to inquire somewhat more thoroughly about him.

21 "So do not [1]listen to them, for more than forty of them are [a]lying in wait for him who have [b]bound themselves under a curse not to eat or drink until they slay him; and now they are ready and waiting for the promise from you."

22 So the [1]commander let the young man go, instructing him, "Tell no one that you have notified me of these things."

Paul Moved to Caesarea

23 And he called to him two of the centurions and said, "Get two hundred soldiers ready by [1]the third hour of the night to proceed to [a]Caesarea, [2]with seventy horsemen and two hundred [3]spearmen."

24 *They were* also to provide mounts to put Paul on and bring him safely to [a]Felix the governor.

25 And he wrote a letter having this form:

26 "Claudius Lysias, to the [a]most excellent governor Felix, [b]greetings.

27 "When this man was arrested by the Jews and was about to be slain by them, [a]I came up to them with the troops and rescued him, [b]having learned that he was a Roman.

28 "And [a]wanting to ascertain the charge for which they were accusing him, I [b]brought him down to their [1c]Council;

29 and I found him to be accused over [a]questions about their Law, but [1]under [b]no accusation deserving death or [2]imprisonment.

30 "When I was [a]informed that there would be [b]a plot against the man, I sent him to you at once, also instructing [c]his accusers to [1]bring charges against him before you."

[a]Acts 23:20f [b]Acts 9:24; 23:12 [c]Acts 23:35; 24:19; 25:16

8 [a]Matt 22:23; Mark 12:18; Luke 20:27
9 [a]Mark 2:16; Luke 5:30 [b]Acts 23:29 [c]John 12:29; Acts 22:6ff
10 [1]I.e. chiliarch, in command of one thousand troops [a]Acts 21:34; 23:16, 32
11 [a]Acts 18:9 [b]Matt 9:2 [c]Acts 19:21 [d]Luke 16:28; Acts 28:23
12 [1]Or *mob* [a]Acts 9:23; 23:30; 1 Thess 2:16 [b]Acts 23:14, 21
14 [a]Acts 23:12, 21
15 [1]Lit *with* [2]Or *Sanhedrin* [3]V 10, note 1 [a]Acts 22:30; 23:1, 6, 20, 28
16 [1]Or *having been present* with them, *and he entered* [a]Acts 21:34; 23:10, 32
17 [1]V 10, note 1
18 [1]V 10, note 1 [a]Eph 3:1
19 [1]V 10, note 1
20 [1]Or *Sanhedrin* [a]Acts 23:14f [b]Acts 22:30; 23:1, 6, 15, 28
21 [1]Lit *be persuaded by them* [a]Acts 23:12, 14 [b]Luke 11:54
22 [1]V 10, note 1
23 [1]I.e. 9 p.m. [2]Lit *and* [3]Or *slingers* or *bowmen* [a]Acts 8:40; 23:33
24 [a]Acts 23:26, 33; 24:1, 3, 10; 25:14
26 [a]Luke 1:3; Acts 24:3; 26:25 [b]Acts 15:23
27 [a]Acts 21:32f [b]Acts 22:25-29
28 [1]Or *Sanhedrin* [a]Acts 22:30 [b]Acts 23:10 [c]Acts 23:1
29 [1]Lit *having* [2]Lit *bonds* [a]Acts 18:15; 25:19 [b]Acts 23:9; 25:25; 26:31; 28:18
30 [1]Lit *speak against him*

23:10 *commander.* See note on 21:31. *barracks.* See note on 21:37.

23:11 *the Lord stood at his side.* In times of crisis and need for strength, Paul was given help (see 18:9; 22:18; 27:23).

23:12 *bound themselves under an oath.* Probably these were from the Zealots or the "terrorists" (see note on 21:38) later responsible for revolt against Rome.

23:17 *centurions.* See note on 10:1. *commander.* See note on 21:31.

23:22 *Tell no one.* For the boy's own safety and because of the commander's plans to transfer Paul under cover of night (see v. 23).

23:23 *soldiers . . . horsemen . . . spearmen.* Heavily armed infantry, cavalry and lightly armed soldiers. The commander assigned 470 men to protect Paul, the Roman citizen (cf. 22:25–29)—but the Greek for "spearmen" is an obscure word and could perhaps be translated "additional mounts and pack animals."

23:27 *having learned that he was a Roman.* Inserted to gain the commander's favor with Rome, but not a true statement, because the commander did not learn of Paul's citizenship until he was about to scourge him to gain information.

23:30 *instructing his accusers to bring . . . before you.* He anticipated that the order would be given by the time the letter was delivered.

31 So the soldiers, in accordance with their orders, took Paul and brought him by night to Antipatris.

32 But the next day, leaving [a]the horsemen to go on with him, they returned to [b]the barracks.

33 When these had come to [a]Caesarea and delivered the letter to [b]the governor, they also presented Paul to him.

34 When he had read it, he asked from what [a]province he was, and when he learned that [b]he was from Cilicia,

35 he said, "I will give you a hearing after your [a]accusers arrive also," giving orders for him to be [b]kept in Herod's [1]Praetorium.

Paul before Felix

24 After [a]five days the high priest [b]Ananias came down with some elders, [1]with an [2]attorney *named* Tertullus, and they [3]brought charges to [c]the governor against Paul.

2 After *Paul* had been summoned, Tertullus began to accuse him, saying *to the governor,*

"Since we have through you attained much peace, and since by your providence reforms are being carried out for this nation,

3 we acknowledge *this* in every way and everywhere, [a]most excellent Felix, with all thankfulness.

4 "But, that I may not weary you any further, I beg you [1]to grant us, by your kindness, a brief hearing.

5 "For we have found this man a real pest and a fellow who stirs up dissension among all the Jews throughout [1]the world, and a ringleader of the [a]sect of the Nazarenes.

6 "And he even tried to [a]desecrate the temple; and [1]then we arrested him. [[2]We wanted to judge him according to our own Law.

7 "But Lysias the commander came along, and with much violence took him out of our hands,

8 ordering his accusers to come before you.] By examining him yourself concerning all these matters you will be able to ascertain the things of which we accuse him."

9 [a]The Jews also joined in the attack, asserting that these things were so.

10 When [a]the governor had nodded for him to speak, Paul responded:

"Knowing that for many years you have been a judge to this nation, I cheerfully make my defense,

11 since you can take note of the fact that no more than [a]twelve days ago I went up to Jerusalem to worship.

12 "[a]Neither in the temple, nor in the synagogues, nor in the city *itself* did they find me carrying on a discussion with anyone or [b]causing [1]a riot.

13 "[a]Nor can they prove to you *the charges* of which they now accuse me.

14 "But this I admit to you, that according to [a]the Way which they call a [b]sect I do serve [1][c]the God of our fathers, [d]believing everything that is in accordance with the Law and that is written in the Prophets;

32 [a]Acts 23:23 [b]Acts 23:10
33 [a]Acts 8:40; 23:23 [b]Acts 23:24, 26; 24:1, 3, 10; 25:14
34 [a]Acts 25:1 [b]Acts 6:9; 21:39
35 [1]I.e. governor's official residence [a]Acts 23:30; 24:19; 25:16 [b]Acts 24:27
24:1 [1]Lit *and* [2]Lit *orator* [3]Or *presented their evidence* or *case* [a]Acts 24:11 [b]Acts 23:2 [c]Acts 23:24
3 [a]Acts 23:26; 26:25
4 [1]Lit *to hear...briefly*
5 [1]Lit *the inhabited earth* [a]Acts 15:5; 24:14
6 [1]Lit *also* [2]The early mss do not contain the remainder of v 6, v 7, nor the first part of v 8 [a]Acts 21:28
9 [a]1 Thess 2:16
10 [a]Acts 23:24
11 [a]Acts 21:18, 27; 24:1
12 [1]Lit *an attack of a mob* [a]Acts 25:8 [b]Acts 24:18
13 [a]Acts 25:7
14 [1]Lit *the ancestral God* [a]Acts 9:2; 24:22 [b]Acts 15:5; 24:5 [c]Acts 3:13 [d]Acts 25:8; 26:4ff, 22f; 28:23

23:31 *Antipatris.* Rebuilt by Herod the Great and named for his father. It was a military post between Samaria and Judea—30 miles from Jerusalem.

23:33 *Caesarea.* The headquarters of Roman rule for Samaria and Judea—28 miles from Antipatris.

23:34 *he.* Antonius Felix. The emperor Claudius had appointed him governor of Judea c. A.D. 52, a time when Felix's brother was the emperor's favorite minister. The brothers had formerly been slaves, then freedmen, then high officials in government. The historian Tacitus said of Felix, "He held the power of a tyrant with the disposition of a slave." He married three queens in succession, one of whom was Drusilla (see note on 24:24). *from Cilicia.* If Paul had come from a province nearby, Felix might have turned him over for trial under another's jurisdiction.

23:35 *Herod's Praetorium.* Erected as a royal residence by Herod the Great but now used as a Roman government center (praetorium)—the place for the official business of the emperor and/or to house personnel directly responsible to the emperor. Praetoria were located in Rome (Phil 1:13), Ephesus, Jerusalem (John 18:28), Caesarea and other parts of the empire.

24:1 *After five days.* After the departure from Jerusalem. This would allow just enough time for a messenger to go from Caesarea to Jerusalem, the Council to appoint their representatives, and the appointees to make the return journey to Caesarea. *Ananias.* See note on 23:2. The high priest himself made the 60-mile journey to supervise the case personally. *elders.* The Council was made up of 71 elders. The designation was used of both the religious and the political councils. See notes on Ex 3:16; 2 Sam 3:17; Joel 1:2; Matt 15:2. *attorney.* Lit. "orator." In a court trial one trained in forensic rhetoric would serve as an attorney at law. *Tertullus.* A common variant of the name Tertius. Possibly he was a Roman but more likely a Hellenistic Jew familiar with the procedures of the Roman court.

24:2–3 *much peace . . . with all thankfulness.* The expected eulogy with which to introduce a speech before a judge. In his six years in office Felix had eliminated bands of robbers, thwarted organized assassins and crushed a movement led by an Egyptian (see note on 21:38). But in general his record was not good. He was recalled by Rome two years later because of misrule. His reforms and improvements are hard to identify historically.

24:5 *pest . . . ringleader of the sect of the Nazarenes.* To excite dissension in the empire was treason against Caesar. To be a leader of a religious sect without Roman approval was contrary to law. *the sect of the Nazarenes.* Christianity.

24:6 *tried to desecrate the temple.* The charge is now qualified by "an attempt," rather than the former claim (see note on 21:28).

24:10 Paul's reserved introduction lacks the flattery employed by Tertullus (vv. 2–4).

24:11 *twelve days ago.* Paul answers each accusation. He was not a troublemaker, and he had not been involved in disturbances. He had but recently arrived in Jerusalem. He had spent five days in Caesarea and nearly seven in Jerusalem.

24:14 *according to the Way . . . I do serve . . . God.* Paul admits to his part in the Way, but he still believes the Law and the Prophets. He shares the same hope as the Jews—resurrection and judgment (v. 15).

15 having a hope in God, which [a]these men cherish themselves, that there shall certainly be a resurrection of both the righteous and the wicked.

16 "In view of this, [a]I also [1]do my best to maintain always a blameless conscience *both* before God and before men.

17 "Now [a]after several years I [b]came to bring [1]alms to my nation and to present offerings;

18 in which they found me *occupied* in the temple, having been [a]purified, without *any* [b]crowd or uproar. But *there were* some [c]Jews from [1]Asia—

19 who ought to have been present before you and to [a]make accusation, if they should have anything against me.

20 "Or else let these men themselves tell what misdeed they found when I stood before [a]the [1]Council,

21 other than for this one statement which [a]I shouted out while standing among them, 'For the resurrection of the dead I am on trial before you today.' "

22 But Felix, [1]having a more exact knowledge about [a]the Way, put them off, saying, "When Lysias the [2]commander comes down, I will decide your case."

23 Then he gave orders to the centurion for him to be [a]kept in custody and *yet* [b]have *some* freedom, and not to prevent any of [c]his friends from ministering to him.

24 But some days later Felix arrived with Drusilla, his [1]wife who was a Jewess, and sent for Paul and heard him *speak* about [a]faith in Christ Jesus.

25 But as he was discussing [a]righteousness, [b]self-control and [c]the judgment to come, Felix became frightened and said, "Go away for the present, and when I find time I will summon you."

26 At the same time too, he was hoping that [a]money would be given him by Paul; therefore he also used to send for him quite often and converse with him.

27 But after two years had passed, Felix [1]was succeeded by Porcius [a]Festus, and [b]wishing to do the Jews a favor, Felix left Paul [c]imprisoned.

Paul before Festus

25 Festus then, having arrived in [a]the province, three days later went up to Jerusalem from [b]Caesarea.

2 And the chief priests and the leading men of the Jews [a]brought charges against Paul, and they were urging him,

3 requesting a [1]concession against [2]Paul, that he might [3]have him brought to Jerusalem (*at the same time,* [a]setting an ambush to kill him on the way).

4 Festus then [a]answered that Paul [b]was being kept in custody at [c]Caesarea and that he himself was about to leave shortly.

5 "Therefore," he *said, "let the influential men among you [1]go there with me, and if there is anything wrong [2]about the man, let them [3]prosecute him."

6 After he had spent not more than eight or ten days among them, he went down to [a]Caesarea, and on the next day he took his seat on [b]the tribunal and ordered Paul to be brought.

15 [a]Dan 12:2; John 5:28f; 11:24; Acts 23:6 **16** [1]Lit *practice myself* [a]Acts 23:1 **17** [1]Or *gifts to charity* [a]Acts 20:31 [b]Acts 11:29f; Rom 15:25-28; 1 Cor 16:1-4; 2 Cor 8:1-4; 9:1, 2, 12; Gal 2:10 **18** [1]I.e. west coast province of Asia Minor [a]Acts 21:26 [b]Acts 24:12 [c]Acts 21:27 **19** [a]Acts 23:30 **20** [1]Or *Sanhedrin* [a]Matt 5:22 **21** [a]Acts 23:6; 24:15 **22** [1]Lit *knowing more accurately* [2]I.e. chiliarch, in command of one thousand troops [a]Acts 24:14 **23** [a]Acts 23:35 [b]Acts 28:16 [c]Acts 23:16; 27:3 **24** [1]Lit *own wife* [a]Acts 20:21 **25** [a]Titus 2:12 [b]Gal 5:23; Titus 1:8; 2 Pet 1:6 [c]Acts 10:42

26 [a]Acts 24:17 **27** [1]Lit *received a successor, Porcius Festus* [a]Acts 25:1, 4, 9, 12; 26:24f, 32 [b]Acts 12:3; 25:9 [c]Acts 23:35; 25:14 **25:1** [a]Acts 23:34 [b]Acts 8:40; 25:4, 6, 13 **2** [a]Acts 24:1; 25:15 **3** [1]Or *favor* [2]Lit *him* [3]Lit *send for him to Jerusalem* [a]Acts 9:24 **4** [a]Acts 25:16 [b]Acts 24:23 [c]Acts 8:40; 25:1, 6, 13 **5** [1]Lit *go down* [2]Lit *in* [3]Or *accuse* **6** [a]Acts 8:40; 25:1, 4, 13 [b]Matt 27:19; Acts 25:10, 17

24:16 *blameless conscience.* See note on 23:1.
24:17 *to bring alms to my nation.* The only explicit reference in Acts to the collection that was so important to Paul (see note on 20:4). *to present offerings.* May refer to Paul's help in sponsoring those who were fulfilling their vows (see 21:24). He also may have intended to present offerings for himself.
24:18 *Jews from Asia.* See 21:27–29. The absence of these Asian Jews would seem to suggest that they could not substantiate their accusations.
24:21 *For the resurrection.* Paul again introduces the point of contention between the Pharisees and Sadducees.
24:22 *having . . . exact knowledge about the Way.* Felix could not have governed Judea and Samaria for six years without becoming familiar with the place and activities of the Christians.
24:23 *yet have some freedom.* Perhaps Paul was under house arrest similar to what he experienced while waiting trial in Rome (28:30–31)—in recognition of the fact that he was a Roman citizen who had not been found guilty of any crime.
24:24 *Drusilla.* Felix's third wife, daughter of Herod Agrippa I. At age 15 she married Azizus, king of Emesa, but deserted him for Felix a year later. Her son, also named Agrippa, died in the eruption of Vesuvius (A.D. 79).
24:25 *Felix became frightened.* Hearing of righteousness, self-control and the judgment, Felix looked at his past life and was filled with fear. He had a spark of sincerity and concern. *when I find time.* Lust, pride, greed and selfish ambition made it continually inconvenient to change.
24:26 *money would be given him.* Felix supposed that Paul had access to considerable funds. He had heard of his bringing an offering to the Jewish Christians in Jerusalem (see v. 17). So he wanted Paul to give him money in order to secure his release. Paul no longer had the money, nor would he offer a bribe if he had it.
24:27 *Felix was succeeded by . . . Festus.* Felix was recalled to Rome in A.D. 59/60 to answer for disturbances and irregularities in his rule, such as his handling of riots between Jewish and Syrian inhabitants. Festus is not mentioned in existing historical records before his arrival in Judea. He died in office after two years, but his record for that time shows wisdom and honesty superior to both his predecessor, Felix, and his successor, Albinus. *to do the Jews a favor.* Felix did not want to incite more anger among the Jews, whom he would be facing in Roman court shortly. To release Paul from prison would do just that.
25:1 *to Jerusalem from Caesarea.* Sixty miles, a two-day trip. Festus was anxious to go immediately to the center of Jewish rule and worship.
25:2 *chief priests and . . . leading . . . Jews.* The Council (see note on Mark 14:55).
25:3 *an ambush.* Probably the same group that had earlier made a vow to take Paul's life (see note on 23:12).
25:6 *took his seat on the tribunal.* To make his decision binding as a formal ruling.

7 After Paul arrived, the Jews who had
come down from Jerusalem stood around
him, bringing [a]many and serious charges
against him [b]which they could not prove,
8 while Paul said in his own defense, "[a]I
have committed no offense either against the
Law of the Jews or against the temple or
against Caesar."
9 But Festus, [a]wishing to do the Jews a
favor, answered Paul and said, "[b]Are you
willing to go up to Jerusalem and [1]stand trial before me on these *charges?*"
10 But Paul said, "I am standing before
Caesar's [a]tribunal, where I ought to be tried.
I have done no wrong to *the* Jews, as you
also very well know.
11 "If, then, I am a wrongdoer and have
committed anything worthy of death, I do
not refuse to die; but if none of those things
is *true* of which these men accuse me, no
one can hand me over to them. I [a]appeal to
Caesar."
12 Then when Festus had conferred with
[1]his council, he answered, "You have
appealed to Caesar, to Caesar you shall go."
13 Now when several days had elapsed,
King Agrippa and Bernice arrived at [a]Caesa-
rea [1]and paid their respects to Festus.
14 While they were spending many days
there, Festus laid Paul's case before the king,
saying, "There is a man who was [a]left as a
prisoner by Felix;
15 and when I was at Jerusalem, the chief
priests and the elders of the Jews [a]brought
charges against him, asking for a sentence of
condemnation against him.
16 "I [a]answered them that it is not the custom of the Romans to hand over any man
before [b]the accused meets his accusers face
to face and has an opportunity to make his
defense against the charges.
17 "So after they had assembled here, I did
not delay, but on the next day took my seat
on [a]the tribunal and ordered the man to be
brought before me.
18 "When the accusers stood up, they
began bringing charges against him not of
such crimes as I was expecting,
19 but they *simply* had some [a]points of
disagreement with him about their own
[1b]religion and about a dead man, Jesus,
whom Paul asserted to be alive.
20 "[a]Being at a loss how to investigate
[1]such matters, I asked whether he was willing to go to Jerusalem and there stand trial
on these matters.
21 "But when Paul [a]appealed to be held in
custody for [1]the Emperor's decision, I
ordered him to be kept in custody until I
send him to Caesar."
22 Then [a]Agrippa *said* to Festus, "I also
would like to hear the man myself." "Tomorrow," he *said, "you shall hear him."

Paul before Agrippa

23 So, on the next day when [a]Agrippa
came [1]together with [a]Bernice amid great
pomp, and entered the auditorium [2]accom-
panied by the [3]commanders and the prominent men of the city, at the command of Festus, Paul was brought in.
24 Festus *said, "King Agrippa, and all

7 [a]Acts 24:5f [b]Acts 24:13
8 [a]Acts 6:13; 24:12; 28:17
9 [1]Lit *be judged* [a]Acts 12:3; 24:27 [b]Acts 25:20
10 [a]Matt 27:19; Acts 25:6, 17
11 [a]Acts 25:21, 25; 26:32; 28:19
12 [1]A different group from that mentioned in Acts 4:15 and 24:20
13 [1]Lit *greeting Festus* [a]Acts 8:40; 25:1, 4, 6
14 [a]Acts 24:27
15 [a]Acts 24:1; 25:2
16 [a]Acts 25:4f [b]Acts 23:30
17 [a]Matt 27:19; Acts 25:6, 10
19 [1]Or *superstition* [a]Acts 18:15; 23:29 [b]Acts 17:22
20 [1]Lit *these* [a]Acts 25:9
21 [1]Lit *the Augustus's* (in this case Nero) [a]Acts 25:11f
22 [a]Acts 9:15
23 [1]Lit *and Bernice* [2]Lit *and with* [3]I.e. chiliarchs, in command of one thousand troops [a]Acts 25:13; 26:30

25:7 *which they could not prove.* Again, as in the first hearing, Paul's adversaries produced no witnesses or evidence of any kind.
25:8 *no offense . . . against the Law.* Paul had respect for the law (see Rom 7:12; 8:3–4; 1 Cor 9:20). *against the temple.* See notes on 21:28–29. Paul had not defied its customs by taking Trophimus into forbidden areas (21:29). Jesus had prophesied its destruction, but He was not responsible for its plight (Luke 21:5–6). *against Caesar.* Paul proclaimed the kingdom of God but not as a political rival of Rome (cf. 17:6–7). He advocated respect for law and order (see Rom 13:1–7) and prayer for civil rulers (see 1 Tim 2:2).
25:9 *Are you willing to go up to Jerusalem . . . ?* Obviously not. Festus had said that the trial would be before him; so Paul insisted that he was then standing in the Roman civil court (v. 10). He wanted to keep his trial there rather than suffer at the hands of a Jewish religious court. As a Roman citizen, he could refuse to go to a local provincial court; instead he looked to a higher Roman court.
25:11 *I appeal to Caesar.* Nero had become the emperor by this time. It was the right of every Roman citizen to have his case heard before Caesar himself (or his representative) in Rome. This was the highest court of appeal, and winning such a case could have led to more than just Paul's acquittal. It could have resulted in official recognition of Christianity as distinct from Judaism.
25:12 *his council.* The officials and legal experts who made up the advisory council for the Roman governor.
25:13 *King Agrippa.* Herod Agrippa II. He was 17 years old at the death of his father in A.D. 44 (12:23). Being too young to succeed his father, he was replaced by Roman procurators. Eight years later, however, a gradual extension of territorial authority began. Ultimately he ruled over territory north and northeast of the Sea of Galilee, over several Galilean cities and over some cities in Perea. At the Jewish revolt, when Jerusalem fell, he was on the side of the Romans. He died c. A.D. 100—the last of the Herods. *Bernice.* The oldest daughter of Agrippa I, she was 16 years old at his death. When only 13, she married her uncle, Herod of Chalcis, and had two sons. When Herod died, she lived with her brother, Agrippa II. To silence rumors that she was living in incest with her brother, she married Polemon, king of Cilicia, but left him soon to return to Agrippa. She became the mistress of the emperor Vespasian's son Titus but was later ignored by him. *paid their respects.* It was customary for rulers to pay a complimentary visit to a new ruler at the time of his assignment. It was advantageous to each that they get along (cf. Herod Antipas and Pilate, Luke 23:6–12).
25:19 *religion.* Or "superstition," the same word used by Paul in 17:22 (see note there).
25:22 *I also would like to hear.* Agrippa had been wishing to hear Paul (cf. Antipas wanting to see Jesus, Luke 9:9; 23:8).
25:23 *auditorium.* Not the judgment hall, for this was not a court trial. It was in an auditorium appropriate for the pomp of the occasion, with a king, his sister, the Roman governor and the outstanding leaders of both the Jews and the Roman government present. *commanders.* Five regiments were stationed at Caesarea, so their five commanders would be in attendance (see note on 21:31).

you gentlemen here present with us, you see this man about whom [a]all the people of the Jews appealed to me, both at Jerusalem and here, loudly declaring that [b]he ought not to live any longer.

25 "But I found that he had committed [a]nothing worthy of death; and since he himself [b]appealed to [1]the Emperor, I decided to send him.

26 "[1]Yet I have nothing definite about him to write to my lord. Therefore I have brought him before you *all* and especially before you, King Agrippa, so that after the investigation has taken place, I may have something to write.

27 "For it seems absurd to me in sending a prisoner, not to indicate also the charges against him."

Paul's Defense before Agrippa

26 [a]Agrippa said to Paul, "You are permitted to speak for yourself." Then Paul stretched out his hand and *proceeded* to make his defense:

2 "In regard to all the things of which I am accused by the Jews, I consider myself fortunate, King Agrippa, that I am about to make my defense before you today;

3 [1]especially because you are an expert in all [a]customs and [2]questions among *the* Jews; therefore I beg you to listen to me patiently.

4 "So then, all Jews know [a]my manner of life from my youth up, which from the beginning was spent among my *own* nation and at Jerusalem;

5 since they have known about me for a long time, if they are willing to testify, that I lived *as* a [a]Pharisee [b]according to the strictest [c]sect of our religion.

6 "And now I am [1]standing trial [a]for the hope of [b]the promise made by God to our fathers;

24 [a]Acts 25:2, 7 [b]Acts 22:22
25 [1]V 21, note 1 [a]Luke 23:4; Acts 23:29 [b]Acts 25:11f
26 [1]Lit *About whom I have nothing definite*
26:1 [a]Acts 9:15
3 [1]Or *because you are especially expert* [2]Or *controversial issues* [a]Acts 6:14; 25:19; 26:7
4 [a]Gal 1:13f; Phil 3:5
5 [a]Acts 23:6; Phil 3:5 [b]Acts 22:3 [c]Acts 15:5
6 [1]Lit *being tried* [a]Acts 24:15; 28:20 [b]Acts 13:32
7 [a]James 1:1 [b]Acts 24:15; 28:20 [c]Acts 26:2
8 [a]Acts 23:6
9 [a]John 16:2; 1 Tim 1:13 [b]John 15:21
10 [1]Lit *also* [2]Or *holy ones* [a]Acts 8:3; 9:13 [b]Acts 9:1f [c]Acts 22:20
11 [1]Or *outlying* [a]Matt 10:17; Acts 22:19 [b]Acts 9:1 [c]Acts 22:5
12 [1]Lit *In which things* [a]Acts 26:12-18: *9:3-8; 22:6-11*
13 [1]Lit *above the brightness of*
14 [1]I.e. Jewish Aramaic [2]An idiom referring to an animal's futile resistance to being prodded with goads [a]Acts 9:7 [b]Acts 21:40
16 [1]Two early mss read *seen Me* [a]Ezek 2:1; Dan 10:11 [b]Acts 22:14 [c]Luke 1:2 [d]Acts 22:15
17 [a]Jer 1:8, 19 [b]1 Chr 16:35; Acts 9:15

7 *the promise* [a]to which our twelve tribes hope to attain, as they earnestly serve *God* night and day. And for this [b]hope, O King, I am being [c]accused by Jews.

8 "Why is it considered incredible among you *people* [a]if God does raise the dead?

9 "So then, [a]I thought to myself that I had to do many things hostile to [b]the name of Jesus of Nazareth.

10 "And this is [1]just what I [a]did in Jerusalem; not only did I lock up many of the [2]saints in prisons, having [b]received authority from the chief priests, but also when they were being put to death I [c]cast my vote against them.

11 "And [a]as I punished them often in all the synagogues, I tried to force them to blaspheme; and being [b]furiously enraged at them, I kept pursuing them [c]even to [1]foreign cities.

12 "[1]While so engaged [a]as I was journeying to Damascus with the authority and commission of the chief priests,

13 at midday, O King, I saw on the way a light from heaven, [1]brighter than the sun, shining all around me and those who were journeying with me.

14 "And when we had [a]all fallen to the ground, I heard a voice saying to me in the [1b]Hebrew dialect, 'Saul, Saul, why are you persecuting Me? [2]It is hard for you to kick against the goads.'

15 "And I said, 'Who are You, Lord?' And the Lord said, 'I am Jesus whom you are persecuting.

16 'But get up and [a]stand on your feet; for this purpose I have appeared to you, to [b]appoint you a [c]minister and [d]a witness not only to the things which you have [1]seen, but also to the things in which I will appear to you;

17 [a]rescuing you [b]from the *Jewish* people and from the Gentiles, to whom I am sending you,

---

25:26 *I have nothing definite.* Festus was required to send Caesar an explicit report on the case when an appeal was made. He hoped for some help from Agrippa in this matter. This was not an official trial but a special hearing to satisfy the curiosity of Agrippa and provide an assessment for Festus. *especially before you, King Agrippa.* He would be sensitive to differences between Pharisees and Sadducees, expectations of the Messiah, differences between Jews and Christians, and Jewish customs pertinent to these problems.

26:1 *permitted to speak.* Agrippa gave the permission because Festus allowed him to have charge of the hearing.

26:3 *an expert in all customs and questions among the Jews.* Agrippa as king controlled the temple treasury and the investments of the high priest, and could appoint the high priest. He was consulted by the Romans on religious matters. This is one of the reasons Festus wanted him to assess Paul.

26:5 *I lived as a Pharisee.* Cf. Gal 1:14.

26:6 *the hope of the promise made by God.* Including God's kingdom, the Messiah and the resurrection (see v. 8).

26:8 Paul had been speaking to Agrippa but at this point must have addressed others as well, such as Festus and the commanders (see note on 21:31), who did not believe in the resurrection. Agrippa was also allied with the Sadducees, whom he appointed high priests, and was likely to reject both the resurrection of Christ and resurrection in general.

26:10 *I cast my vote against them.* Does not necessarily mean that Paul was a member of the Council (see note on 22:20). He may have been appointed to a commission to carry out the prosecution (see v. 12), where his vote was given.

26:11 *force them to blaspheme.* He tried to force them either to curse Jesus or to confess publicly that Jesus is the Son of God, in which case they could be condemned for blasphemy, a sufficient cause for death (see Matt 26:63–66).

26:12 *I was journeying to Damascus.* Again Paul gives an account of his conversion (see 9:1–19; 22:4–21 and notes).

26:14 *I heard a voice.* See notes on 9:7; 22:9. *to kick against the goads.* A Greek proverb for useless resistance—the ox succeeds only in hurting itself.

26:17 *to whom I am sending you.* Not only to the Jews but also to the Gentiles (see 22:21; Gal 1:15–16). His mission was from God (Gal 1:1).

18 to [a]open their eyes so that they may turn from [b]darkness to light and from the dominion of [c]Satan to God, that they may receive [d]forgiveness of sins and an [e]inheritance among those who have been sanctified by [f]faith in Me.'

19 "So, King Agrippa, I did not prove disobedient to the heavenly vision,

20 but *kept* declaring both [a]to those of Damascus first, and *also* [b]at Jerusalem and *then* throughout all the region of Judea, and *even* [c]to the Gentiles, that they should [d]repent and turn to God, performing deeds [e]appropriate to repentance.

21 "For this reason *some* Jews [a]seized me in the temple and tried [b]to put me to death.

22 "So, having obtained help from God, I stand to this day [a]testifying both to small and great, stating nothing but what [b]the Prophets and Moses said was going to take place;

23 [1][a]that [2]the Christ was [3]to suffer, *and* [1]that [b]by reason of *His* resurrection from the dead He would be the first to proclaim [c]light both to the *Jewish* people and to the Gentiles."

24 While *Paul* was saying this in his defense, Festus *said in a loud voice, "Paul, you are out of your mind! [1]*Your* great [a]learning is [2]driving you mad."

25 But Paul *said, "I am not out of my mind, [a]most excellent Festus, but I utter words [1]of sober truth.

26 "For the king [1][a]knows about these matters, and I speak to him also with confidence, since I am persuaded that none of these things escape his notice; for this has not been done in a [2]corner.

27 "King Agrippa, do you believe the Prophets? I know that you [1]do."

28 Agrippa *replied* to Paul, "[1]In a short time you [2]will persuade me to [3]become a [a]Christian."

29 And Paul *said,* "[1]I would wish to God, that whether [2]in a short or long time, not only you, but also all who hear me this day, might become such as I am, except for these [a]chains."

30 [a]The king stood up and the governor and Bernice, and those who were sitting with them,

31 and when they had gone aside, they *began* talking to one another, saying, "[a]This man is not doing anything worthy of death or [1]imprisonment."

32 And Agrippa said to Festus, "This man might have been [a]set free if he had not [b]appealed to Caesar."

Paul Is Sent to Rome

27 When it was decided that [a]we [b]would sail for [c]Italy, they proceeded to deliver Paul and some other prisoners to a centurion of the Augustan [1][d]cohort named Julius.

2 And embarking in an Adramyttian ship, which was about to sail to the regions along the coast of [1][a]Asia, we put out to sea accompanied by [b]Aristarchus, a [c]Macedonian of [d]Thessalonica.

3 The next day we put in at [a]Sidon; and Julius [b]treated Paul with consideration and [c]allowed him to go to his friends and receive care.

4 From there we put out to sea and sailed under the shelter of [a]Cyprus because [b]the winds were contrary.

5 When we had sailed through the sea

18 [a]Is 35:5; 42:7, 16; Eph 5:8; Col 1:13; 1 Pet 2:9 [b]John 1:5; Eph 5:8; Col 1:12f; 1 Thess 5:5; 1 Pet 2:9 [c]Matt 4:10 [d]Luke 24:47; Acts 2:38 [e]Acts 20:32 [f]Acts 20:21
20 [a]Acts 9:19ff [b]Acts 9:26-29; 22:17-20 [c]Acts 9:15; 13:46 [d]Acts 3:19 [e]Matt 3:8; Luke 3:8
21 [a]Acts 21:27, 30 [b]Acts 21:31
22 [a]Luke 16:28 [b]Acts 10:43; 24:14
23 [1]Lit *whether* [2]I.e. the Messiah [3]Lit *subject to suffering* [a]Matt 26:24; Acts 3:18 [b]1 Cor 15:20, 23; Col 1:18; Rev 1:5 [c]Is 42:6; 49:6; Luke 2:32; 2 Cor 4:4
24 [1]Lit *The many letters* [2]Lit *turning you to madness* [a]John 7:15; 2 Tim 3:15
25 [1]Lit *of truth and rationality* [a]Acts 23:26; 24:3
26 [1]Or *understands* [2]I.e. a hidden or secret place [a]Acts 26:3
27 [1]Lit *believe*
28 [1]Or *With a little*
28 [2]Or *are trying to convince* [3]Lit *make* [a]Acts 11:26
29 [1]Or *I would pray to* [2]Or *with a little or with much* [a]Acts 21:33
30 [a]Acts 25:23 **31** [1]Lit *bonds* [a]Acts 23:29 **32** [a]Acts 28:18 [b]Acts 25:11 **27:1** [1]Or *battalion* [a][we] Acts 16:10; 27:1-28 [b]Acts 25:12, 25 [c]Acts 18:2; 27:6 [d]Acts 10:1 **2** [1]I.e. west coast province of Asia Minor [a]Acts 2:9 [b]Acts 19:29 [c]Acts 16:9 [d]Acts 17:1 **3** [a]Matt 11:21 [b]Acts 27:43 [c]Acts 24:23 **4** [a]Acts 4:36 [b]Acts 27:7

26:18 *from darkness to light.* A figure especially characteristic of Paul (see Rom 13:12; 2 Cor 4:6; Eph 5:8–14; Col 1:13; 1 Thess 5:5). *have been sanctified.* Positional sanctification (see notes on 20:32; 1 Cor 1:2).

26:22 *the Prophets and Moses.* The OT Scriptures (Luke 24:27,44).

26:23 *the Gentiles.* Cf. Isa 49:6.

26:24 *you are out of your mind!* See John 10:20; 1 Cor 14:23. The governor felt that Paul's education and reading of the sacred Scriptures had led him to a mania about prophecy and resurrection.

26:26 *not been done in a corner.* This gospel is based on actual events, lived out in historical times and places. The king must himself attest to the truth of what Paul has affirmed.

26:27 *do you believe the Prophets?* King Agrippa was faced with a dilemma. If he said "Yes," Paul would press him to recognize their fulfillment in Jesus; if he said "No," he would be in trouble with the devout Jews, who accepted the message of the prophets as the very word of God.

26:28 *In a short time you will persuade me to become a Christian.* His answer is an evasion of Paul's question and an answer to what he anticipates Paul's next question to be. His point is that he will not be persuaded by such a brief statement.

26:29 *these chains.* Paul was still bound as a prisoner.

27:1 See map No. 11 at the end of the study Bible. *we would sail.* The "we" narrative (see note on 16:10) begins again (the last such reference appeared in 21:18). Probably Luke has spent the two years of Paul's Caesarean imprisonment nearby, and now he joins those ready to sail. *centurion . . . named Julius.* Otherwise unknown. Perhaps he was given the specific duties of an imperial courier, which included delivering prisoners for trial. *Augustan cohort.* The Roman legions were designated by number, and each of the regiments also had designations. The identification "Augustan," or "Imperial" (belonging to the empire), was common (see note on 10:1).

27:2 *Adramyttian.* A harbor on the west coast of the province of Asia, southeast of Troas, east of Assos. *regions along the coast.* At one of these stops, Julius would plan to transfer to a ship going to Rome. *Aristarchus.* See 19:29; 20:4; see also Philem 24 and Col 4:10, indicating he was in Rome with Paul later.

27:3 *Sidon.* About 70 miles north of Caesarea.

27:4 *the shelter of Cyprus.* They sought the protecting shelter of the island by sailing north on the eastern side of the island, then west along the northern side. *the winds were contrary.* Prevailing winds in summer were westerly.

along the coast of [a]Cilicia and [b]Pamphylia, we landed at Myra in Lycia.

6 There the centurion found an [a]Alexandrian ship sailing for [b]Italy, and he put us aboard it.

7 When we had sailed slowly for a good many days, and with difficulty had arrived off Cnidus, [a]since the wind did not permit us *to go* farther, we sailed under the shelter of [b]Crete, off Salmone;

8 and with difficulty [a]sailing past it we came to a place called Fair Havens, near which was the city of Lasea.

9 When considerable time had passed and the voyage was now dangerous, since even [a]the [1]fast was already over, Paul *began* to admonish them,

10 and said to them, "Men, I perceive that the voyage will certainly be with [a]damage and great loss, not only of the cargo and the ship, but also of our lives."

11 But the centurion was more persuaded by the [a]pilot and the [1]captain of the ship than by what was being said by Paul.

12 Because the harbor was not suitable for wintering, the majority reached a decision to put out to sea from there, if somehow they could reach Phoenix, a harbor of [a]Crete, facing southwest and northwest, and spend the winter *there.*

13 [1]When a moderate south wind came up, supposing that they had attained their purpose, they weighed anchor and *began* [a]sailing along [b]Crete, close *inshore.*

5 [a]Acts 6:9 [b]Acts 13:13
6 [a]Acts 28:11 [b]Acts 18:2; 27:1
7 [a]Acts 27:4 [b]Acts 2:11; 27:12f, 21; Titus 1:5, 12
8 [a]Acts 27:13
9 [1]I.e. Day of Atonement in September or October, which was a dangerous time of year for navigation [a]Lev 16:29-31; 23:27-29; Num 29:7
10 [a]Acts 27:21
11 [1]Or *owner* [a]Rev 18:17
12 [a]Acts 2:11; 27:13, 21; Titus 1:5, 12
13 [1]Lit *a south wind having gently blown* [a]Acts 27:8 [b]Acts 2:11; 27:12f, 21; Titus 1:5, 12

14 [1]Lit *it* [2]I.e. a northeaster [a]Mark 4:37
16 [1]Or *skiff:* a small boat in tow or carried on board for emergency use, transportation to and from shore, etc
17 [1]Lit *helps* [2]Or *gear* [a]Acts 27:26, 29
18 [1]Lit *they were doing a throwing out* [a]Jon 1:5; Acts 27:38

Shipwreck

14 But before very long there [a]rushed down from [1]the land a violent wind, called [2]Euraquilo;

15 and when the ship was caught *in it* and could not face the wind, we gave way *to it* and let ourselves be driven along.

16 Running under the shelter of a small island called Clauda, we were scarcely able to get the *ship's* [1]boat under control.

17 After they had hoisted it up, they used [1]supporting cables in undergirding the ship; and fearing that they might [a]run aground on *the shallows* of Syrtis, they let down the [2]sea anchor and in this way let themselves be driven along.

18 The next day as we were being violently storm-tossed, [1]they began to [a]jettison the cargo;

19 and on the third day they threw the ship's tackle overboard with their own hands.

20 Since neither sun nor stars appeared for many days, and no small storm was assailing *us,* from then on all hope of our being saved was gradually abandoned.

21 [1]When they had gone a long time without food, then Paul stood up in their midst and said, "[a]Men, you ought to have [2]followed my advice and not to have set sail from [b]Crete and [3]incurred this [a]damage and loss.

21 [1]Lit *there being much abstinence from food* [2]Lit *obeyed me* [3]Lit *gained* [a]Acts 27:10 [b]Acts 27:7

27:5 *Cilicia and Pamphylia.* Adjoining provinces on the southern shore of Asia Minor. From Sidon to Myra along this coast would normally be a voyage of 10 to 15 days. *Myra in Lycia.* The growing importance of the city of Myra was associated with the development of navigation. Instead of hugging the coast from point to point, more ships were daring to run directly from Alexandria in Egypt to harbors like Myra on the southern coast of Asia Minor. It was considerably out of the way on the trip to Rome from Egypt, but the prevailing westerly wind would not allow a direct voyage toward the west. Myra became an important grain-storage city as well.

27:6 *Alexandrian ship.* A ship from Egypt (with grain cargo, v. 38) bound for Rome. Paul and the others could have remained on the first ship and continued up the coast to Macedonia, then taken the land route over the Egnatian Way across Greece and on to Rome, entering Italy at the port of Brundisium. But Julius chose to change ships here, accepting the opportunity of a voyage direct to Rome. Some suggest that Aristarchus from Macedonia stayed with the first ship and went to his home area to tell of Paul's coming imprisonment in Rome. If so, he later joined Paul in Rome (see note on v. 2).

27:7 *Cnidus.* From Myra to Cnidus at the southwest point of Asia Minor was about 170 miles. The trip probably took another 10 to 15 days. *Crete.* An island 160 miles long. Rather than cross the open sea to Greece, the ship was forced to bear south, seeking to sail west with the protection of the island of Crete on the north ("under the shelter of Crete"). *Salmone.* A promontory on the northeast point of Crete.

27:8 *Fair Havens . . . Lasea.* The former was a port about midway on the southern coast of Crete, and the latter was a city about five miles away.

27:9 *the fast.* The Jewish day of atonement fell in the latter part of September or in October. The usual sailing season by Jewish calculation lasted from Pentecost (May-June) to Booths, which was five days after the Fast. The Romans considered sailing after Sept. 15 doubtful and after Nov. 11 suicidal.

27:12 *Phoenix.* A major city that served as a wintering place, having a harbor with protection against the storms.

27:14 *Euraquilo.* A typhoon-like, east-northeast wind (a "northeaster"), which drove the ship away from their destination.

27:16 *Clauda.* About 23 miles from Crete. This provided enough shelter to make preparation against the storm. *to get the ship's boat under control.* A small boat was being towed behind the ship. It was interfering with the progress of the ship and with the steering. It may also have been in danger of being crushed against the ship in the wind and the waves. It had to be taken aboard (v. 17).

27:17 *used supporting cables in undergirding the ship.* Probably crosswise, in order to keep the ship from being broken apart by the storm. *Syrtis.* A long stretch of desolate banks of quicksand along northern Africa off the coast of Tunis and Tripoli—still far away, but in such a storm the ship could be driven a great distance. *sea anchor.* Lowered apparently to keep the ship from running onto the sandbars of Syrtis, but the Greek for this expression should perhaps be rendered "mainsail."

27:18 *jettison the cargo.* To lighten the ship. They kept some bags of grain, however (see v. 38).

27:19 *ship's tackle.* Spars, planks and perhaps the yardarm with the mainsail attached. At times these were dragged behind, serving as a brake.

27:21 *ought to have followed my advice.* Although they had not done so, Paul had good news for everyone (vv. 22–26).

22 "*Yet* now I urge you to [a]keep up your
courage, for there will be no loss of life
among you, but *only* of the ship.
23 "For this very night [a]an angel of the God
to whom I belong and [b]whom I serve [c]stood
before me,
24 saying, 'Do not be afraid, Paul; [a]you
must stand before Caesar; and behold, God
has granted you [b]all those who are sailing
with you.'
25 "Therefore, [a]keep up your courage,
men, for I believe God that [1]it will turn out
exactly as I have been told.
26 "But we must [a]run aground on a certain
[b]island."
27 But when the fourteenth night came, as
we were being driven about in the Adriatic
Sea, about midnight the sailors *began* to surmise that [1]they were approaching some land.
28 They took soundings and found *it to be*
twenty fathoms; and a little farther on they
took another sounding and found *it to be* fifteen fathoms.
29 Fearing that we might [a]run aground
somewhere on the [1]rocks, they cast four
anchors from the stern and [2]wished for daybreak.
30 But as the sailors were trying to escape
from the ship and had let down [a]the *ship's*
boat into the sea, on the pretense of intending to lay out anchors from the bow,
31 Paul said to the centurion and to the
soldiers, "Unless these men remain in the
ship, you yourselves cannot be saved."
32 Then the soldiers cut away the [a]ropes
of the *ship's* boat and let it fall away.
33 Until the day was about to dawn, Paul
was encouraging them all to take some food,
saying, "Today is the fourteenth day that you
have been constantly watching and going
without eating, having taken nothing.
34 "Therefore I encourage you to take some
food, for this is for your preservation, for
[a]not a hair from the head of any of you will
perish."
35 Having said this, he took bread and
[a]gave thanks to God in the presence of all,
and he broke it and began to eat.
36 All [a]of them [1]were encouraged and
they themselves also took food.

22 [a]Acts 27:25, 36
23 [a]Acts 5:19 [b]Rom 1:9 [c]Acts 18:9; 23:11; 2 Tim 4:17
24 [a]Acts 23:11 [b]Acts 27:31, 42, 44
25 [1]Lit *it will be* [a]Acts 27:22, 36
26 [a]Acts 27:17, 29 [b]Acts 28:1
27 [1]Lit *some land was approaching them*
29 [1]Lit *rough places* [a]Acts 27:17, 26
29 [2]Lit *they were praying for it to become day*
30 [a]Acts 27:16
32 [a]John 2:15
34 [a]Matt 10:30
35 [a]Matt 14:19
36 [1]Lit *became cheerful* [a]Acts 27:22, 25

27:27 *fourteenth night.* After leaving Fair Havens. *Adriatic Sea.* The sea between Italy, Malta, Crete and Greece. In ancient times the Adriatic Sea extended as far south as Sicily and Crete. (Some think this sea included all the area between Greece, Italy and Africa and that it was known as the Adrian, not the Adriatic, Sea.) Its extent now has been considerably reduced. *began to surmise.* By the sound of breakers.

27:28 *took another sounding.* Measured the depth of the sea by letting down a weighted line.

27:30 *trying to escape.* Without a port for the ship, the sailors felt their chance for survival was better in the single lifeboat, unencumbered by the many passengers.

27:31 *Unless these men remain.* If the sailors had been allowed to desert the ship in seeking to save themselves, the passengers would have been unable to beach the ship the following day.

27:33 *having taken nothing.* No provisions had been distributed nor regular meals eaten since the storm began.

27:35 *took bread and gave thanks.* Paul gave two good examples: He ate food for physical nourishment and gave thanks to God. To give thanks before a meal was common practice among God's people (see Luke 9:16; 24:30; 1 Tim 4:4–5).

Paul's Journey to Rome

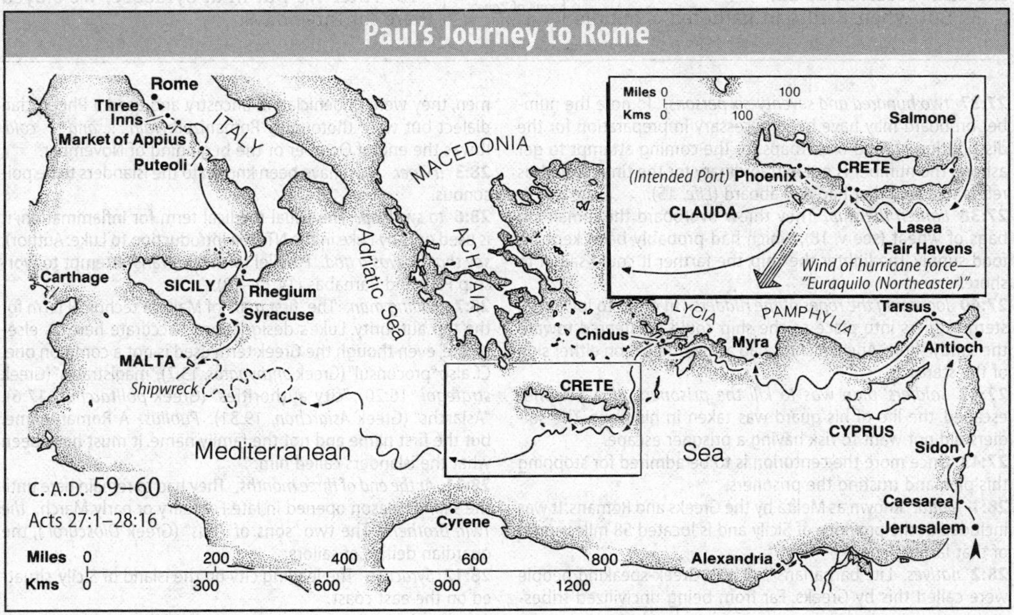

Rome
Three Inns
Market of Appius
Puteoli
ITALY
MACEDONIA
ACHAIA
Adriatic Sea
Carthage
SICILY
Rhegium
Syracuse
MALTA
Shipwreck
CRETE
Cnidus
LYCIA
PAMPHYLIA
Myra
Tarsus
Antioch
CYPRUS
Sidon
Caesarea
Jerusalem
Mediterranean
Sea
Cyrene
Alexandria
C. A.D. 59–60
Acts 27:1–28:16
Miles 0 200 400 600 800
Kms 0 300 600 900 1200
Miles 0 100
Kms 0 100
Salmone
(Intended Port) Phoenix
CRETE
CLAUDA
Lasea
Fair Havens
Wind of hurricane force—
"Euraquilo (Northeaster)"

37 All of us in the ship were two hundred
and seventy-six [1][a]persons.
38 When they had eaten enough, they
began to lighten the ship by [a]throwing out
the wheat into the sea.
39 When day came, [a]they [1]could not recognize the land; but they did observe a bay
with a beach, and they resolved to drive the
ship onto it if they could.
40 And casting off [a]the anchors, they left
them in the sea while at the same time they
were loosening the ropes of the rudders; and
hoisting the foresail to the wind, they were
heading for the beach.
41 But striking a [1]reef where two seas
met, they ran the vessel aground; and the
prow stuck fast and remained immovable,
but the stern *began* to be broken up by the
force *of the waves.*
42 The soldiers' plan was to [a]kill the prisoners, so that none *of them* would swim
away and escape;
43 but the centurion, [a]wanting to bring
Paul safely through, kept them from their
intention, and commanded that those who
could swim should [1]jump overboard first
and get to land,
44 and the rest *should follow,* some on
planks, and others on various things from
the ship. And so it happened that [a]they all
were brought safely to land.

Safe at Malta

28 When [a]they had been brought safely
through, [b]then we found out that [c]the
island was called [1]Malta.
2 [a]The [1]natives showed us extraordinary
kindness; for because of the rain that had set
in and because of the cold, they kindled a
fire and [b]received us all.
3 But when Paul had gathered a bundle
of sticks and laid them on the fire, a viper
came out [1]because of the heat and fastened
itself on his hand.
4 When [a]the [1]natives saw the creature
hanging from his hand, they *began* saying to
one another, "[b]Undoubtedly this man is a
murderer, and though he has been saved
from the sea, [2]justice has not allowed him to
live."
5 However [a]he shook the creature off
into the fire and suffered no harm.
6 But they were expecting that he was
about to swell up or suddenly fall down
dead. But after they had waited a long time
and had seen nothing unusual happen to
him, they changed their minds and [a]*began* to
say that he was a god.
7 Now in the neighborhood of that place
were lands belonging to the leading man of
the island, named Publius, who welcomed
us and entertained us courteously three
days.
8 And it happened that the father of Publius was lying *in bed* afflicted with *recurrent*
fever and dysentery; and Paul went in *to see*
him and after he had [a]prayed, he [b]laid his
hands on him and healed him.
9 After this had happened, the rest of the
people on the island who had diseases were
coming to him and getting cured.
10 They also honored us with many
[1]marks of respect; and when we were setting
sail, they [2]supplied *us* with [3]all we needed.

Paul Arrives at Rome

11 At the end of three months we set sail
on [a]an Alexandrian ship which had wintered
at the island, and which had [1]the Twin
Brothers for its figurehead.
12 After we put in at Syracuse, we stayed
there for three days.

37 [1]Lit *souls* [a]Acts 2:41
38 [a]Jon 1:5; Acts 27:18
39 [1]Lit *were not recognizing* [a]Acts 28:1
40 [a]Acts 27:29
41 [1]Lit *place*
42 [a]Acts 12:19
43 [1]Lit *throw themselves* [a]Acts 27:3
44 [a]Acts 27:22, 31
28:1 [1]Or *Melita* [a][they] Acts 16:10; 27:1 [b]Acts 27:39 [c]Acts 27:26
2 [1]Lit *barbarians* [a]Acts 28:4; Rom 1:14; 1 Cor 14:11; Col 3:11 [b]Rom 14:1
3 [1]Or *from the heat*
4 [1]Lit *barbarians* [2]Or *Justice,* i.e. the personification of a goddess [a]Acts 28:2 [b]Luke 13:2, 4
5 [a]Mark 16:18
6 [a]Acts 14:11
8 [a]Acts 9:40; James 5:14f [b]Matt 9:18; Mark 5:23; 6:5
10 [1]Lit *honors* [2]Or *put on board* [3]Lit *the things pertaining to the needs*
11 [1]Gr *the Dioscuri;* i.e. Castor and Pollux, twin sons of Zeus [a]Acts 27:6

27:37 *two hundred and seventy-six persons.* To note the number on board may have been necessary in preparation for the distribution of food or perhaps for the coming attempt to get ashore. The number is not extraordinary for the time. Josephus refers to a ship that had 600 aboard (*Life,* 15).
27:38 *lighten the ship.* They threw overboard the remaining bags of wheat (see v. 18), which had probably been kept for food supply. The lighter the ship, the farther it could sail in to shore.
27:40 *loosening the ropes of the rudders.* In order to lower the stern rudders into place so the ship could be steered toward the sandy shore. Ancient ships had a steering oar on either side of the stern.
27:42 *soldiers' plan was to kill the prisoners.* If a prisoner escaped, the life of his guard was taken in his place. The soldiers did not want to risk having a prisoner escape.
27:43 Once more the centurion is to be admired for stopping this plan and trusting the prisoners.
28:1 *Malta.* Known as Melita by the Greeks and Romans. It was included in the province of Sicily and is located 58 miles south of that large island.
28:2 *natives.* Lit. "barbarians"; all non-Greek-speaking people were called this by Greeks. Far from being uncivilized tribesmen, they were Phoenician in ancestry and used a Phoenician dialect but were thoroughly Romanized. *rain . . . and . . . cold.* It was the end of October or the beginning of November.
28:3 *a viper.* Must have been known to the islanders to be poisonous.
28:6 *to swell up.* The usual medical term for inflammation; it is used only by Luke in the NT (see Introduction to Luke: Author). *say that he was a god.* Parallel to the Lystrans' attempt to worship Paul and Barnabas (14:11–18).
28:7 *leading man.* The "first man" of Malta, a technical term for the top authority. Luke's designation is accurate here, as elsewhere, even though the Greek term used is not a common one. Cf. also "proconsul" (Greek *anthypatos,* 13:7), "magistrates" (Greek *strategoi,* 16:20), "city authorities" (Greek *politarchas,* 17:6), "Asiarchs" (Greek *Asiarchon,* 19:31). *Publius.* A Roman name, but the first name and not the family name. It must have been what the islanders called him.
28:11 *At the end of three months.* They had to remain here until the sailing season opened in late February or early March. *the Twin Brothers.* The two "sons of Zeus" (Greek *Dioscuroi*), the guardian deities of sailors.
28:12 *Syracuse.* The leading city on the island of Sicily, situated on the east coast.

13 From there we sailed around and arrived at Rhegium, and a day later a south wind sprang up, and on the second day we came to Puteoli.

14 [1]There we found *some* [a]brethren, and were invited to stay with them for seven days; and thus we came to Rome.

15 And the [a]brethren, when they heard about us, came from there as far as the [1]Market of Appius and [2]Three Inns to meet us; and when Paul saw them, he thanked God and took courage.

16 When we entered Rome, Paul was [a]allowed to stay by himself, with the soldier who was guarding him.

17 After three days [1]Paul called together those who were [a]the leading men of the Jews, and when they came together, he *began* saying to them, "[b]Brethren, [c]though I had done nothing against our people or [d]the customs of our [2]fathers, yet I was delivered as a prisoner from Jerusalem into the hands of the Romans.

18 "And when they had [a]examined me, they [b]were willing to release me because there was [c]no ground [1]for putting me to death.

19 "But when the Jews [1]objected, I was forced to [a]appeal to Caesar, not that I had any accusation against my nation.

20 "For this reason, therefore, I [1]requested to see you and to speak with you, for I am wearing [a]this chain for [b]the sake of the hope of Israel."

21 They said to him, "We have neither received letters from Judea concerning you, nor have any of [a]the brethren come here and reported or spoken anything bad about you.

22 "But we desire to hear from you what [1]your views are; for concerning this [a]sect, it is known to us that [b]it is spoken against everywhere."

23 When they had set a day for Paul, they came to him at [a]his lodging in large numbers; and he was explaining to them by solemnly [b]testifying about the kingdom of God and trying to persuade them concerning Jesus, [c]from both the Law of Moses and from the Prophets, from morning until evening.

24 [a]Some were being persuaded by the things spoken, but others would not believe.

25 And when they did not agree with one another, they *began* leaving after Paul had spoken one *parting* word, "The Holy Spirit rightly spoke through Isaiah the prophet to your fathers,

26 saying,

'[a]GO TO THIS PEOPLE AND SAY,
"[1][b]YOU WILL KEEP ON HEARING, [2]BUT WILL NOT UNDERSTAND;
AND [3]YOU WILL KEEP ON SEEING, BUT WILL NOT PERCEIVE;
27 [a]FOR THE HEART OF THIS PEOPLE HAS BECOME DULL,
AND WITH THEIR EARS THEY SCARCELY HEAR,
AND THEY HAVE CLOSED THEIR EYES;
OTHERWISE THEY MIGHT SEE WITH THEIR EYES,
AND HEAR WITH THEIR EARS,
AND UNDERSTAND WITH THEIR HEART AND RETURN,
AND I WOULD HEAL THEM." '

28 "Therefore let it be known to you that [a]this salvation of God has been sent [b]to the Gentiles; they will also listen."

29 [[1]When he had spoken these words, the Jews departed, having a great dispute among themselves.]

14 [1]Lit *Where* [a]John 21:23; Acts 1:15; 6:3; 9:30; 28:15; Rom 1:13; **15** [1]Lat *Appii Forum*, a station about 43 miles from Rome [2]Lat *Tres Tabernae*, a station about 33 miles from Rome [a]Acts 1:15; 10:23; 11:1, 12, 29; 12:17 **16** [a]Acts 24:23 **17** [1]Lit *he* [2]Or *forefathers* [a]Acts 13:50; 25:2 [b]Acts 22:5 [c]Acts 25:8 [d]Acts 6:14 **18** [1]Lit *of death in me* [a]Acts 22:24 [b]Acts 26:32 [c]Acts 23:29; 25:25; 26:31 **19** [1]Lit *spoke against* [a]Acts 25:11, 21, 25; 26:32 **20** [1]Or *invited you to see me and speak with me* [a]Acts 21:33 [b]Acts 26:6f **21** [a]Acts 3:17; 22:5; 28:14; Rom 9:3 **22** [1]Lit *you think* [a]Acts 24:14

22 [b]1 Pet 2:12; 3:16; 4:14, 16 **23** [a]Philem 22 [b]Luke 16:28; Acts 1:3; 23:11 [c]Acts 8:35 **24** [a]Acts 14:4 **26** [1]Lit *with a hearing* [2]Lit *and* [3]Lit *seeing you will see* [a]Is 6:9 [b]Matt 13:14f **27** [a]Is 6:10 **28** [a]Ps 98:3; Luke 2:30; Acts 13:26 [b]Acts 9:15; 13:46

29 [1]Early mss do not contain this v

28:13 *Rhegium.* A town on the coast of Italy, near the southwestern tip and close to the narrowest point of the strait separating that country from Sicily, opposite Messina. Around the promontory north of the town was the whirlpool of Charybdis and the rock of Scylla. Coming from his triumph in Judea, the general Titus landed here on his way to Rome. *Puteoli.* Modern Pozzuoli, almost 200 miles from Rhegium. It was situated in the northern part of the Bay of Naples and was the chief port of Rome, though 75 miles away. The population included Jews as well as Christians.

28:14 *stay . . . for seven days.* As at Troas (20:6) and Tyre (21:4), Paul was with them for one or perhaps two Sundays to observe the keeping of the Lord's Supper and to teach and preach. Either the centurion had business to care for or he was free to delay the journey at Paul's request (see 27:42–43; see also 27:3). *Rome.* See map, p. 1631.

28:15 *Market of Appius.* A small town 43 miles from Rome, noted for its wickedness. Some Roman Christians came this far to meet Paul. Beyond this they would not be certain of the way he would come. *Three Inns.* A town 33 miles from Rome. Other Roman believers met Paul here. The term "inn" was used to designate any kind of shop.

28:16 *stay by himself.* "In his own rented quarters" (v. 30). He had committed no flagrant crime and was not a politically dangerous rival. So he was allowed to have his own living quarters, but a guard was with him at all times, perhaps chained to him (Eph 6:20; Phil 1:13–14,17; Col 4:3,18; Philem 10,13).

28:17 *leading men of the Jews.* The decree of the emperor Claudius (see 18:2) had been allowed to lapse, and Jews had returned to Rome with their leaders. *Brethren.* An epithet that recognized the common Jewish blood he shared with them. Cf. the usage in v. 15, referring to brothers in Christ.

28:20 *the hope of Israel.* See note on 26:6.

28:22 *we desire to hear . . . your views.* The Jews in Rome were well aware of the dispute over whether Jesus was the Messiah. They wanted to hear Paul's presentation, and he was eager to present it before the arrival of adverse opinions from the Jewish leaders of Jerusalem.

28:23 *Law of Moses . . . Prophets.* The OT Scriptures (see Luke 24:27,44).

28:28 *salvation of God has been sent to the Gentiles.* The main thought of the book of Acts. The gospel is meant for all. And Paul was a chosen vessel to carry the message to Gentiles as well as to Jews.

30 And he stayed two full years [1]in his
own rented quarters and was welcoming all
who came to him,
31 [1a]preaching the kingdom of God and
teaching concerning the Lord Jesus Christ
[b]with all openness, unhindered.

30 [1]Or *at his own expense*
31 [1]Or *proclaiming*
[a]Matt 4:23; Acts 20:25; 28:23
[b]2 Tim 2:9

28:30 *two full years.* Paul served the Lord (v. 31) during the full period of waiting for his accusers to press the trial in Rome. There are a number of indications that he was released from this imprisonment: 1. Acts stops abruptly at this time. 2. Paul wrote to churches expecting to visit them soon; so he must have anticipated a release (see Phil 2:24; Philem 22). 3. A number of the details in the Pastoral Letters do not fit into the historical setting given in the book of Acts. Following the close of the book, these details indicate a return to Asia Minor, Crete and Greece. 4. Tradition indicates that Paul went to Spain. Even if he did not go, the very fact that a tradition arose suggests a time when he could have taken that journey. See map, pp. 1762–1763.

Rome in the Time of Paul

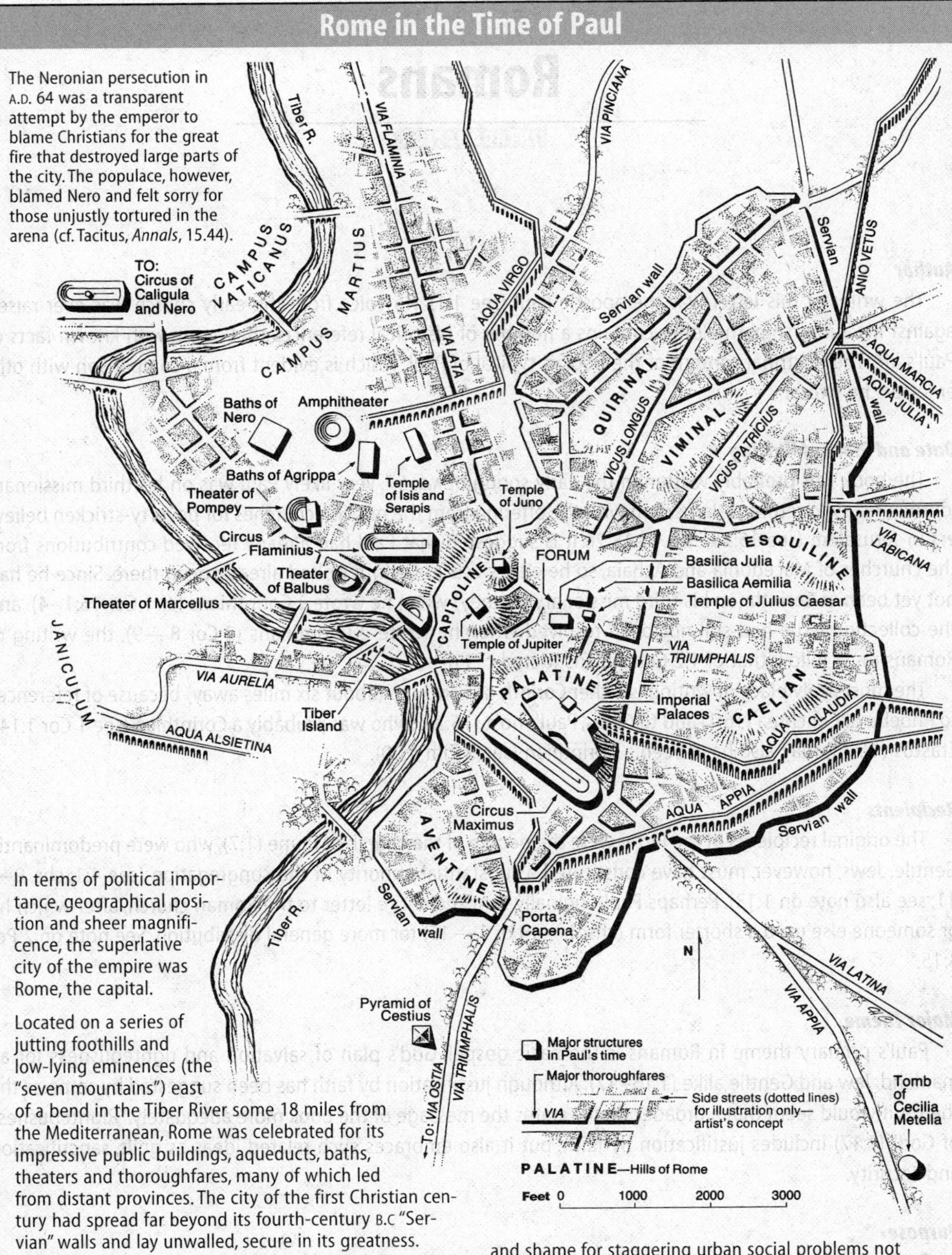

TO: Circus of Caligula and Nero
Tiber R.
VIA FLAMINIA
VIA PINCIANA
CAMPUS VATICANUS
CAMPUS MARTIUS
AQUA VIRGO
VIA LATA
Servian wall
Servian
ANIO VETUS
AQUA MARCIA
AQUA JULIA
wall
QUIRINAL
VICUS LONGUS
VIMINAL
VICUS PATRICIUS
Baths of Nero
Amphitheater
Baths of Agrippa
Temple of Isis and Serapis
Theater of Pompey
Temple of Juno
Circus Flaminius
FORUM
ESQUILINE
VIA LABICANA
Theater of Balbus
Basilica Julia
Basilica Aemilia
Theater of Marcellus
CAPITOLINE
Temple of Julius Caesar
JANICULUM
Temple of Jupiter
VIA TRIUMPHALIS
VIA AURELIA
PALATINE
Imperial Palaces
CAELIAN
Tiber Island
AQUA CLAUDIA
AQUA ALSIETINA
Circus Maximus
AQUA APPIA
Servian wall
AVENTINE
Servian wall
Tiber R.
Porta Capena
N
VIA LATINA
VIA APPIA
Pyramid of Cestius
To: VIA OSTIA
VIA TRIUMPHALIS
Major structures in Paul's time
Major thoroughfares
VIA
Side streets (dotted lines) for illustration only—artist's concept
Tomb of Cecilia Metella
PALATINE—Hills of Rome
Feet 0 1000 2000 3000

The Neronian persecution in A.D. 64 was a transparent attempt by the emperor to blame Christians for the great fire that destroyed large parts of the city. The populace, however, blamed Nero and felt sorry for those unjustly tortured in the arena (cf. Tacitus, *Annals*, 15.44).

In terms of political importance, geographical position and sheer magnificence, the superlative city of the empire was Rome, the capital.

Located on a series of jutting foothills and low-lying eminences (the "seven mountains") east of a bend in the Tiber River some 18 miles from the Mediterranean, Rome was celebrated for its impressive public buildings, aqueducts, baths, theaters and thoroughfares, many of which led from distant provinces. The city of the first Christian century had spread far beyond its fourth-century B.C "Servian" walls and lay unwalled, secure in its greatness.

The most prominent features were the Capitoline hill, with temples to Jupiter and Juno, and the nearby Palatine, adorned with imperial palaces, including Nero's "Golden House." Both hills overlooked the Roman Forum, the hub of the entire empire.

Alternatively described as the glorious crowning achievement of mankind and as the sewer of the universe where all the scum from every corner of the empire gathered, Rome had reasons for both civic pride in its architecture and shame for staggering urban social problems not unlike those of cities today.

The apostle Paul entered the city from the south on the Via Appia. He first lived under house arrest and then, after a period of freedom, as a condemned prisoner in the Mamertime dungeon near the Forum. Remarkably, Paul was able to proclaim the gospel among all classes of people, from the palace to the prison. According to tradition, he was executed at a spot on the Ostian Way outside Rome in A.D. 68.

Romans

INTRODUCTION

Author

The writer of this letter was the apostle Paul (see 1:1). No voice from the early church was ever raised against his authorship. The letter contains a number of historical references that agree with known facts of Paul's life. The doctrinal content of the book is typical of Paul, which is evident from a comparison with other letters he wrote.

Date and Place of Writing

The book was probably written in the early spring of A.D. 57. Very likely Paul was on his third missionary journey, ready to return to Jerusalem with the offering from the mission churches for poverty-stricken believers in Jerusalem (see 15:25–27). In 15:26 it is suggested that Paul had already received contributions from the churches of Macedonia and Achaia, so he either was at Corinth or had already been there. Since he had not yet been at Corinth (on his third missionary journey) when he wrote 1 Corinthians (cf. 1 Cor 16:1–4) and the collection issue had still not been resolved when he wrote 2 Corinthians (2 Cor 8—9), the writing of Romans must follow that of 1,2 Corinthians (dated c. 55).

The most likely place of writing is either Corinth or Cenchrea (about six miles away) because of references to Phoebe of Cenchrea (16:1) and to Gaius, Paul's host (16:23), who was probably a Corinthian (see 1 Cor 1:14). Erastus (16:23) may also have been a Corinthian (see 2 Tim 4:20).

Recipients

The original recipients of the letter were the people of the church at Rome (1:7), who were predominantly Gentile. Jews, however, must have constituted a substantial minority of the congregation (see 4:1; chs. 9—11; see also note on 1:13). Perhaps Paul originally sent the entire letter to the Roman church, after which he or someone else used a shorter form (chs. 1—14 or 1—15) for more general distribution. See note on 2 Pet 3:15.

Major Theme

Paul's primary theme in Romans is the basic gospel, God's plan of salvation and righteousness for all mankind, Jew and Gentile alike (1:16–17). Although justification by faith has been suggested by some as the theme, it would seem that a broader theme states the message of the book more adequately. "Righteousness of God" (1:17) includes justification by faith, but it also embraces such related ideas as guilt, sanctification and security.

Purpose

Paul's purposes for writing this letter were varied:

1. He wrote to prepare the way for his coming visit to Rome and his proposed mission to Spain (1:10–15; 15:22–29).

2. He wrote to present the basic system of salvation to a church that had not received the teaching of an apostle before.

3. He sought to explain the relationship between Jew and Gentile in God's overall plan of redemption. The Jewish Christians were being rejected by the larger Gentile group in the church (14:1) because the Jewish believers still felt constrained to observe dietary laws and sacred days (14:2–6).

Occasion

When Paul wrote this letter, he was probably at Corinth (Acts 20:2–3) on his third missionary journey. His work in the eastern Mediterranean was almost finished (see 15:18–23), and he greatly desired to visit the Roman church (see 1:11–12; 15:23–24). At this time, however, he could not go to Rome because he felt he must personally deliver the collection taken among the Gentile churches for the poverty-stricken Christians of Jerusalem (see 15:25–28). So instead of going to Rome, he sent a letter to prepare the Christians there for his intended visit in connection with a mission to Spain (see 15:23–24). For many years Paul had wanted to visit Rome to minister there (see 1:13–15), and this letter served as a careful and systematic theological introduction to that hoped-for personal ministry. Since he was not acquainted directly with the Roman church, he says little about its problems (but see 14:1—15:13; cf. also 13:1–7; 16:17–18).

Content

Paul begins by surveying the spiritual condition of all mankind. He finds Jews and Gentiles alike to be sinners and in need of salvation. That salvation has been provided by God through Jesus Christ and His redemptive work on the cross. It is a provision, however, that must be received by faith—a principle by which God has always dealt with mankind, as the example of Abraham shows. Since salvation is only the beginning of Christian experience, Paul moves on to show how the believer is freed from sin, law and death—a provision made possible by his union with Christ in both death and resurrection and by the indwelling presence and power of the Holy Spirit. Paul then shows that Israel too, though presently in a state of unbelief, has a place in God's sovereign redemptive plan. Now she consists of only a remnant, allowing for the conversion of the Gentiles, but the time will come when "all Israel will be saved" (11:26). The letter concludes with an appeal to the readers to work out their Christian faith in practical ways, both in the church and in the world. None of Paul's other letters states so profoundly the content of the gospel and its implications for both the present and the future.

Special Characteristics

1. *The most systematic of Paul's letters.* It reads more like an elaborate theological essay than a letter.
2. *Emphasis on Christian doctrine.* The number and importance of the theological themes touched upon are impressive: sin, salvation, grace, faith, righteousness, justification, sanctification, redemption, death and resurrection.
3. *Widespread use of OT quotations.* Although Paul regularly quotes from the OT in his letters, in Romans the argument is sometimes carried along by such quotations (see especially chs. 9—11).
4. *Deep concern for Israel.* Paul writes about her present status, her relationship to the Gentiles and her final salvation.

Outline

I. Introduction (1:1–15)
II. Theme: Righteousness of God (1:16–17)
III. The Unrighteousness of All Mankind (1:18—3:20)
   A. Gentiles (1:18–32)
   B. Jews (2:1—3:8)
   C. Summary: All People (3:9–20)
IV. Righteousness Imputed: Justification (3:21—5:21)
   A. Through Christ (3:21–26)
   B. Received by Faith (3:27—4:25)
      1. The principle established (3:27–31)
      2. The principle illustrated (ch. 4)
   C. The Fruits of Righteousness (5:1–11)
   D. Summary: Man's Unrighteousness Contrasted with God's Gift of Righteousness (5:12–21)
V. Righteousness Imparted: Sanctification (chs. 6—8)
   A. Freedom from Sin's Tyranny (ch. 6)

B. Freedom from the Law's Condemnation (ch. 7)
C. Life in the Power of the Holy Spirit (ch. 8)
VI. God's Righteousness Vindicated: The Problem of the Rejection of Israel (chs. 9—11)
A. The Justice of the Rejection (9:1–29)
B. The Cause of the Rejection (9:30—10:21)
C. Facts That Lessen the Difficulty (ch. 11)
1. The rejection is not total (11:1–10)
2. The rejection is not final (11:11–24)
3. God's ultimate purpose is mercy (11:25–36)
VII. Righteousness Practiced (12:1—15:13)
A. In the Body—the Church (ch. 12)
B. In the World (ch. 13)
C. Among Weak and Strong Christians (14:1—15:13)
VIII. Conclusion (15:14–33)
IX. Commendation and Greetings (ch. 16)

The Gospel Exalted

1 Paul, a bond-servant of Christ Jesus, [1][a]called *as* an apostle, [b]set apart for [c]the gospel of God,

2 which He [a]promised beforehand through His [b]prophets in the holy Scriptures,

3 concerning His Son, who was born [a]of a [1]descendant of David [b]according to the flesh,

4 who was declared [a]the Son of God with power [1]by the resurrection from the dead, according to the [2]Spirit of holiness, Jesus Christ our Lord,

5 through whom we have received grace and [a]apostleship [1]to bring about *the* [b]obedience of faith among [c]all the Gentiles for His name's sake,

6 among whom you also are the [a]called of Jesus Christ;

7 to all who are [a]beloved of God in Rome, called *as* [1][b]saints: [c]Grace to you and peace from God our Father and the Lord Jesus Christ.

8 First, [a]I thank my God through Jesus Christ [1]for you all, because [b]your faith is being proclaimed throughout the whole world.

9 For [a]God, whom I [b]serve in my spirit in the *preaching of the* gospel of His Son, is my witness *as to* how unceasingly [c]I make mention of you,

10 always in my prayers making request, if perhaps now at last by [a]the will of God I may succeed in coming to you.

11 For [a]I long to see you so that I may impart some spiritual gift to you, that you may be [1]established;

12 that is, that I may be encouraged together with you *while* among you, each of us by the other's faith, both yours and mine.

13 [a]I do not want you to be unaware, [b]brethren, that often I [c]have planned to come to you (and have been prevented so far) so that I may obtain some [d]fruit among you also, even as among the rest of the Gentiles.

14 [a]I am [1]under obligation both to Greeks and to [b]barbarians, both to the wise and to the foolish.

15 So, for my part, I am eager to [a]preach the gospel to you also who are in Rome.

16 For I am not [a]ashamed of the gospel, for [b]it is the power of God for salvation to everyone who believes, to the [c]Jew first and also to [d]the Greek.

17 For in it [a]*the* righteousness of God is revealed [1]from faith to faith; as it is written, "[2][b]BUT THE RIGHTEOUS *man* SHALL LIVE BY FAITH."

Unbelief and Its Consequences

18 For [a]the wrath of God is revealed from heaven against all ungodliness and unrighteousness of men who [b]suppress the truth [1]in unrighteousness,

1:1 [1]Lit *a called apostle* [a]1 Cor 1:1; 9:1; 2 Cor 1:1 [b]Acts 9:15; 13:2; Gal 1:15 [c]Mark 1:14; Rom 15:16 **2** [a]Titus 1:2 [b]Luke 1:70; Rom 3:21; 16:26 **3** [1]Lit *seed* [a]Matt 1:1 [b]John 1:14; Rom 4:1; 9:3, 5; 1 Cor 10:18 **4** [1]Or *as a result of* [2]Or *spirit* [a]Matt 4:3 **5** [1]Lit *for obedience* [a]Acts 1:25; Gal 1:16 [b]Acts 6:7; Rom 16:26 [c]Acts 9:15 **6** [a]Jude 1; Rev 17:14 **7** [1]Or *holy ones* [a]Rom 5:5ff; 8:39 [b]Acts 9:13; Rom 8:28ff; 1 Cor 1:2, 24 [c]Num 6:25f; 1 Cor 1:3; 2 Cor 1:2; Gal 1:3; Eph 1:2; Phil 1:2; Col 1:2; 1 Thess 1:1; 2 Thess 1:2 **8** [1]Or *concerning you all, that...* [a]1 Cor 1:4; Eph 1:15f; Phil 1:3f; Col 1:3f; 1 Thess 1:2; 2:13 [b]Acts 28:22; Rom 16:19 **9** [a]Rom 9:1 [b]Acts 24:14; 2 Tim 1:3 [c]Eph 1:16; Phil 1:3f **10** [a]Acts 18:21; Rom 15:32 **11** [1]Or *strengthened* [a]Acts 19:21; Rom 15:23 **13** [a]Rom 11:25; 1 Cor 10:1; 12:1; 2 Cor 1:8; 1 Thess 4:13 [b]Acts 1:15; Rom 7:1; 1 Cor 1:10; 14:20, 26; Gal 3:15 [c]Acts 19:21; Rom 15:22f [d]John 4:36; 15:16; Phil 1:22; Col 1:6 **14** [1]Lit *debtor* [a]1 Cor 9:16 [b]Acts 28:2 **15** [a]Rom 15:20 **16** [a]Mark 8:38; 2 Tim 1:8, 12, 16 [b]1 Cor 1:18, 24 [c]Acts 3:26; Rom 2:9 [d]John 7:35 **17** [1]Or *by* [2]Or *But he who is righteous by faith shall live* [a]Rom 3:21; 9:30; Phil 3:9 [b]Hab 2:4; Gal 3:11; Heb 10:38 **18** [1]Or *by* [a]Rom 5:9; Eph 5:6; Col 3:6 [b]2 Thess 2:6f

1:1 *Paul.* In ancient times writers put their names at the beginning of letters. For more information on Paul see notes on Acts 9:1; Phil 3:4–14. *bond-servant.* The Greek for this word means (1) a "slave," who completely belongs to his owner and has no freedom to leave, and (2) a "servant," who willingly chooses to serve his master. See notes on Ex 14:31; Ps 18 title; Is 41:8–9; 42:1. *apostle.* One specially commissioned by Christ (see notes on Mark 6:30; 1 Cor 1:1; Heb 3:1). *gospel.* See note on Mark 1:1.

1:2 *prophets.* Not just the writers of the prophetic books, for the whole OT prophesied about Jesus (see Luke 24:27,44). *holy Scriptures.* The OT.

1:7 *saints.* The basic idea of the Greek for this word is "holiness." All Christians are saints in that they are positionally "set apart" to God and are experientially being made increasingly "holy" by the Holy Spirit (see note on 1 Cor 1:2). *Grace.* See notes on Jon 4:2; Gal 1:3; Eph 1:2. *peace.* See notes on John 14:27; 20:19; Gal 1:3; Eph 1:2.

1:8 *thank.* Paul often began his letters with thanks (see 1 Cor 1:4; Eph 1:16; Phil 1:3; Col 1:3; 1 Thess 1:2; 2 Thess 1:3; 2 Tim 1:3; Philem 4). *through Jesus Christ.* The Christian must go through Christ not only for requests to God (see John 15:16) but also to give thanks. *throughout the whole world.* Every place where the gospel has been preached.

1:9 *gospel of His Son.* The same as the "gospel of God" (v. 1).

1:12 *together.* Paul's genuine humility is seen in his desire to be ministered to by the believers at Rome as well as to minister to them.

1:13 *fruit.* New converts as well as spiritual growth by those already converted. *among you . . . among the rest of the Gentiles.* Suggests that the church at Rome was predominantly Gentile.

1:14 *Greeks.* Those Gentiles who spoke Greek or followed the Greek way of life, even though they may have been Latin-speaking citizens of the Roman empire. *barbarians.* Lit. "barbarians," a word that probably imitated the unintelligible sound of their languages to Greek ears. They were the other Gentiles to whom Paul ministered.

1:16–17 The theme of the entire book.

1:16 *not ashamed.* Not even in the capital city of the Roman empire (see v. 15). *gospel.* See note on Mark 1:1. *first.* Not only in time but also in privilege. "Salvation is from the Jews" (John 4:22), and the Messiah was a Jew. The "oracles of God" (3:2), the covenants, law, temple worship, revelation of the divine glory, and Messianic prophecies came to them (9:3–5). These privileges, however, were not extended to the Jews because of their superior merit or because of God's partiality toward them. It was necessary that the invasion of this world by the gospel begin at a particular point with a particular people, who in turn were responsible to carry that gospel to the other nations.

1:17 *righteousness.* The state of being "in the right" in relation to God (see notes on 2:13; 3:21,24).

1:18–3:20 In developing the theme of righteousness from God (1:17; 3:21–5:21), Paul sets the stage by showing that all have sinned and therefore need the righteousness that only God can provide. He shows the sin of the Gentiles (1:18–32) and the sin of the Jews (2:1–3:8) and then summarizes the sin of all—Gentile and Jew alike (3:9–20).

1:18–20 No one—not even one who has not heard of the Bible or of Christ—has an excuse for not honoring God, because the whole created world reveals Him.

1:18 *wrath of God.* Not a petulant, irrational burst of anger, such

19 because [a]that which is known about God is evident [1]within them; for God made it evident to them.

20 For [a]since the creation of the world His invisible attributes, His eternal power and divine nature, have been clearly seen, [b]being understood through what has been made, so that they are without excuse.

21 For even though they knew God, they did not [1]honor Him as God or give thanks, but they became [a]futile in their speculations, and their foolish heart was darkened.

22 [a]Professing to be wise, they became fools,

23 and [a]exchanged the glory of the incorruptible God for an image in the form of corruptible man and of birds and four-footed animals and [1]crawling creatures.

24 Therefore [a]God gave them over in the lusts of their hearts to impurity, so that their bodies would be [b]dishonored among them.

25 For they exchanged the truth of God for [1]a [a]lie, and worshiped and served the creature rather than the Creator, [b]who is blessed [2]forever. Amen.

26 For this reason [a]God gave them over to [b]degrading passions; for their women exchanged the natural function for that which is [1]unnatural,

27 and in the same way also the men abandoned the natural function of the woman and burned in their desire toward one another, [a]men with men committing [1]indecent acts and receiving in [2]their own persons the due penalty of their error.

28 And just as they did not see fit [1]to acknowledge God any longer, [a]God gave them over to a depraved mind, to do those things which are not proper,

29 being filled with all unrighteousness, wickedness, greed, evil; full of envy, murder, strife, deceit, malice; *they are* [a]gossips,

30 slanderers, [1a]haters of God, insolent, arrogant, boastful, inventors of evil, [b]disobedient to parents,

31 without understanding, untrustworthy, [a]unloving, unmerciful;

32 and although they know the ordinance of God, that those who practice such things are worthy of [a]death, they not only do the same, but also [b]give hearty approval to those who practice them.

The Impartiality of God

2 Therefore you have [a]no excuse, [1b]everyone of you who passes judgment, for in that which [c]you judge another, you condemn yourself; for you who judge practice the same things.

2 And we know that the judgment of God [1]rightly falls upon those who practice such things.

3 But do you suppose this, [a]O man, [1]when you pass judgment on those who practice such things and do the same *yourself*, that you will escape the judgment of God?

4 Or do you think lightly of [a]the riches of His [b]kindness and [c]tolerance and [d]patience, not knowing that the kindness of God leads you to repentance?

5 But [1]because of your stubbornness and unrepentant heart [a]you are storing up wrath for yourself [b]in the day of wrath and revelation of the righteous judgment of God,

6 [a]who WILL RENDER TO EACH PERSON ACCORDING TO HIS DEEDS:

19 [1]Or *among* [a]Acts 14:17; 17:24ff **20** [a]Mark 10:6 [b]Job 12:7-9; Ps 19:1-6; Jer 5:21f **21** [1]Lit *glorify* [a]2 Kin 17:15; Jer 2:5; Eph 4:17f **22** [a]Jer 10:14; 1 Cor 1:20 **23** [1]Or *reptiles* [a]Deut 4:16-18; Ps 106:20; Jer 2:11; Acts 17:29 **24** [a]Rom 1:26, 28; Eph 4:19 [b]Eph 2:3 **25** [1]Lit *the lie* [2]Lit *unto the ages* [a]Is 44:20; Jer 10:14; 13:25; 16:19 [b]Rom 9:5; 2 Cor 11:31 **26** [1]Lit *against nature* [a]Rom 1:24 [b]1 Thess 4:5 **27** [1]Lit *the shameless deed* [2]Lit *themselves* [a]Lev 18:22; 20:13; 1 Cor 6:9 **28** [1]Lit *to have God in knowledge* [a]Rom 1:24

29 [a]2 Cor 12:20 **30** [1]Or *hateful to God* [a]Ps 5:5 [b]2 Tim 3:2 **31** [a]2 Tim 3:3 **32** [a]Rom 6:21 [b]Luke 11:48; Acts 8:1; 22:20 **2:1** [1]Lit *O man, everyone who* [a]Rom 1:20 [b]Luke 12:14; Rom 2:3; 9:20 [c]2 Sam 12:5-7; Matt 7:1; Luke 6:37; Rom 14:22 **2** [1]Lit *is according to truth against* **3** [1]Lit *who passes judgment* [a]Luke 12:14; Rom 2:1; 9:20 **4** [a]Rom 9:23; 11:33; 2 Cor 8:2; Eph 1:7, 18; 2:7; Phil 4:19; Col 1:27; 2:2; Titus 3:6 [b]Rom 11:22 [c]Rom 3:25 [d]Ex 34:6; Rom 9:22; 1 Tim 1:16; 1 Pet 3:20; 2 Pet 3:9, 15 **5** [1]Or *in accordance with* [a]Deut 32:34f; Prov 1:18 [b]Ps 110:5; 2 Cor 5:10; 2 Thess 1:5; Jude 6 **6** [a]Ps 62:12; Prov 24:12; Matt 16:27

as humans often exhibit, but a holy, just revulsion against what is contrary to and opposes His holy nature and will. *is revealed.* God's wrath is not limited to the end-time judgment of the wicked (1 Thess 1:10; Rev 19:15; 20:11–15). Here the wrath of God is His abandonment of the wicked to their sins (vv. 24–32). *the truth.* The truth about God revealed in the creation order.

1:21 *knew God.* From seeing His revelation in creation (vv. 19–20). The fact that these people were idolaters (v. 23) and knew God only through the creation order indicates that they were Gentiles. *give thanks.* For earthly blessings, such as sun, rain and crops (see Matt 5:45; Acts 14:17).

1:23 *glory.* God's unique majesty (see Is 48:11), which fallen mankind has lost sight of and for which they have substituted deities of their own devising, patterned after various creatures.

1:24,26,28 *God gave them over.* God allowed sin to run its course as an act of judgment.

1:25 *Amen.* Can mean either "Yes indeed, it is so" or "So be it" (see 9:5; 11:36; 15:33; 16:27; see also note on Deut 27:15; cf. 1 Kin 1:36).

1:26 *their women.* Not necessarily their wives.

1:27 Homosexual practice is sinful in God's eyes. The OT also condemns the practice (see Lev 18:22).

1:28 *acknowledge God.* See vv. 19,21. *a depraved mind.* The intent precedes the act (see v. 21; Mark 7:20–23).

1:32 *they know.* Their outrageous conduct was not due to total ignorance of what God required but to self-will and rebellion. *hearty approval.* The extreme of sin is applauding, rather than regretting, the sins of others.

2:1–16 In this section Paul sets forth principles that govern God's judgment. God judges (1) according to truth (v. 2), (2) according to deeds (vv. 6–11) and (3) according to the light a person has (vv. 12–15). These principles lay the groundwork for Paul's discussion of the guilt of the Jews (vv. 17–29).

2:1 *no excuse.* Paul's teaching about judging agrees with that of Jesus (see note on Matt 7:1), who did not condemn judging as such, but hypocritical judging. *one . . . who passes judgment.* A warning that had special relevance for Jews, who were inclined to look down on Gentiles because of their ignorance of God's revelation in the OT and because of their immoral lives.

2:2 *we know.* An expression Paul frequently used that assumed the persons addressed agreed with the statement that followed (see 3:19; 7:14; 8:22,28; 1 Cor 8:1,4; 2 Cor 5:1; 1 Tim 1:8).

2:3 Jesus also condemned this attitude (Matt 7:3; cf. Luke 18:9).

2:4 The purpose of God's kindness is to give opportunity for repentance (2 Pet 3:9). The Jews had misconstrued His patience to be a lack of intent to judge.

2:5 *day of wrath.* Judgment at the end of time in contrast to the judgment discussed in 1:18–32.

7 to those who by [a]perseverance in doing good seek for [b]glory and honor and [c]immortality, [d]eternal life;

8 but to those who are [a]selfishly ambitious and [b]do not obey the truth, but obey unrighteousness, wrath and indignation.

9 *There will be* [a]tribulation and distress [1]for every soul of man who does evil, of the Jew [b]first and also of the Greek,

10 but [a]glory and honor and peace to everyone who does good, to the Jew [b]first and also to the Greek.

11 For [a]there is no partiality with God.

12 For all who have sinned [1a]without the Law will also perish [1]without the Law, and all who have sinned [2]under the Law will be judged [3]by the Law;

13 for *it is* [a]not the hearers [1]of the Law *who* are [2]just before God, but the doers [1]of the Law will be justified.

14 For when Gentiles who do not have [1]the Law do [2a]instinctively the things of the Law, these, not having [1]the Law, are a law to themselves,

15 in that they show [a]the work of the Law written in their hearts, their conscience bearing witness and their thoughts alternately accusing or else defending them,

16 on the day when, [a]according to my gospel, [b]God will judge the secrets of men through Christ Jesus.

The Jew Is Condemned by the Law

17 But if you bear the name "Jew" and [a]rely [1]upon the Law and boast in God,

18 and know *His* will and [1a]approve the things that are essential, being instructed out of the Law,

19 and are confident that you yourself are a guide to the blind, a light to those who are in darkness,

20 a [1]corrector of the foolish, a teacher of [2]the immature, having in the Law [a]the embodiment of knowledge and of the truth,

21 you, therefore, [a]who teach another, do you not teach yourself? You who [1]preach that one shall not steal, do you steal?

22 You who say that one should not commit adultery, do you commit adultery? You who abhor idols, do you [a]rob temples?

23 You who [a]boast [1]in the Law, through your breaking the Law, do you dishonor God?

24 For "[a]THE NAME OF GOD IS BLASPHEMED AMONG THE GENTILES [b]BECAUSE OF YOU," just as it is written.

25 For indeed circumcision is of value if you [a]practice [1]the Law; but if you are a transgressor [2]of the Law, [b]your circumcision has become uncircumcision.

26 [a]So if [b]the [1]uncircumcised man [c]keeps the requirements of the Law, will not his uncircumcision be regarded as circumcision?

27 And [a]he who is physically uncircumcised, if he keeps the Law, will he not [b]judge you who [1]though having the letter *of the Law* and circumcision are a transgressor [2]of the Law?

28 For [a]he is not a Jew who is one outwardly, nor is circumcision that which is outward in the flesh.

29 But [a]he is a Jew who is one inwardly; and [b]circumcision is that which is of the heart, by the [c]Spirit, not by the letter; [d]and his praise is not from men, but from God.

7 [a]Luke 8:15; Heb 10:36 [b]Rom 2:10; Heb 2:7; 1 Pet 1:7 [c]1 Cor 15:42, 50, 53f; Eph 6:24; 2 Tim 1:10 [d]Matt 25:46 **8** [a]2 Cor 12:20; Gal 5:20; Phil 1:17; 2:3; James 3:14, 16 [b]2 Thess 2:12 **9** [1]Lit *upon* [a]Rom 8:35 [b]Acts 3:26; Rom 1:16; 1 Pet 4:17 **10** [a]Rom 2:7; Heb 2:7; 1 Pet 1:7 [b]Rom 2:9 **11** [a]Deut 10:17; Acts 10:34 **12** [1]Or *without law* [2]Or *under law* [3]Or *by law* [a]Acts 2:23; 1 Cor 9:21 **13** [1]Or *of law* [2]Or *righteous* [a]Matt 7:21, 24ff; John 13:17; James 1:22f, 25 **14** [1]Or *law* [2]Lit *by nature* [a]Acts 10:35; Rom 1:19; 2:15 **15** [a]Rom 2:14, 27 **16** [a]Rom 16:25; 1 Cor 15:1; Gal 1:11; 1 Tim 1:11; 2 Tim 2:8 [b]Acts 10:42; 17:31; Rom 3:6; 14:10 **17** [1]Or *upon law* [a]Mic 3:11; John 5:45; Rom 2:23; 9:4 **18** [1]Or *distinguish between the things which differ* [a]Phil 1:10 **20** [1]Or *instructor* [2]Lit *infants* [a]Rom 3:31; 2 Tim 1:13 **21** [1]Or *proclaim* [a]Matt 23:3ff **22** [a]Acts 19:37

23 [1]Or *in law* [a]Mic 3:11; John 5:45; Rom 2:17; 9:4 **24** [a]Is 52:5; Ezek 36:20ff [b]2 Pet 2:2 **25** [1]Or *law* [2]Or *of law* [a]Rom 2:13f, 27 [b]Jer 4:4; 9:25f **26** [1]Lit *uncircumcision* [a]1 Cor 7:19 [b]Rom 3:30; Eph 2:11 [c]Rom 2:25, 27; 8:4 **27** [1]Lit *through the letter* [2]Or *of law* [a]Rom 3:30; Eph 2:11 [b]Matt 12:41 **28** [a]John 8:39; Rom 2:17; 9:6; Gal 6:15 **29** [a]Phil 3:3; Col 2:11 [b]Deut 30:6 [c]Rom 2:27; 7:6; 2 Cor 3:6 [d]John 5:44; 12:43; 1 Cor 4:5; 2 Cor 10:18

2:6–7 Paul is not contradicting his continual emphasis in all his writings, including Romans, that a person is saved not by what he does but by faith in what Christ does for him. Rather, he is discussing the principle of judgment according to deeds (see note on vv. 1–16). If anyone persists in doing good deeds (i.e., lives a perfect life), he will receive eternal life. No one can do this, but if anyone could, God would give him life, since God judges according to what a person does.
2:9 *of the Jew first.* With spiritual privilege comes spiritual responsibility (see Amos 3:2; Luke 12:48).
2:11 A basic teaching of both the OT and the NT.
2:12 *Law.* The Mosaic Law. "For all who have sinned without the Law" refers to Gentiles. God judges according to the light available to people. Gentiles will not be condemned for not obeying a Law they did not possess. Their judgment will be on other grounds (see 1:18–20; 2:15; cf. Amos 1:3–2:3).
2:13 *will be justified.* At God's pronouncement of acquittal on judgment day (see note on 3:24).
2:14 *instinctively.* By natural impulse without the external constraint of the Mosaic Law. *things of the Law.* Does not mean that pagans fulfilled the requirements of the Mosaic Law but refers to practices in pagan society that agreed with the Law, such as caring for the sick and elderly, honoring parents and condemning adultery. *law to themselves.* The moral nature of pagans, enlightened by conscience (v. 15), functioned for them as the Mosaic Law did for the Jews.
2:16 This verse picks up Paul's thought from v. 13, vv. 14–15 being parenthetical in Paul's argument.
2:17–24 The presentation takes the form of a dialogue. Paul knew how a self-righteous Jew thought, for he had been one himself. He cites one advantage after another that Jews considered to be unqualified assets. But those assets became liabilities when there was no correspondence between profession and practice. Paul applied to the Jew the principles of judgment set forth in vv. 1–16 (see note on those verses).
2:19–20 *the blind . . . immature.* Gentiles, to whom Jews regarded themselves as vastly superior because they (the Jews) possessed the Mosaic law.
2:22 *do you rob temples?* See Acts 19:37. Large amounts of wealth were often stored in pagan temples.
2:25 *circumcision.* A sign of the covenant that God made with Israel (see Lev 12:3) and a pledge of the covenant blessing (see Gen 17 and notes on Gen 17:10–11). The Jews had come to regard circumcision as a guarantee of God's favor.
2:27 If a Gentile's deeds excelled those of a Jew in righteousness, that very fact condemned the Jew, who had an immeasurably better set of standards in the Law of Moses.
2:29 *by the Spirit.* The true sign of belonging to God is not an

All the World Guilty

3 Then what [1]advantage has the Jew? Or
what is the benefit of circumcision?
2 Great in every respect. First of all, that
[a]they were entrusted with the [b]oracles of
God.
3 What then? If [a]some [1]did not believe,
their [2]unbelief will not nullify the faithfulness of God, will it?
4 [a]May it never be! Rather, let God be
found true, though every man *be found* [b]a
liar, as it is written,
"[c]THAT YOU MAY BE JUSTIFIED IN YOUR
WORDS,
AND PREVAIL WHEN YOU [1]ARE JUDGED."
5 But if our unrighteousness [1a]demon-
strates the righteousness of God, [b]what shall
we say? The God who inflicts wrath is not
unrighteous, is He? ([c]I am speaking in human
terms.)
6 [a]May it never be! For otherwise, how
will [b]God judge the world?
7 But if through my lie [a]the truth of God
abounded to His glory, [b]why am I also still
being judged as a sinner?
8 And why not *say* (as we are slanderously reported and as some claim that we
say), "[a]Let us do evil that good may come"?
[1]Their condemnation is just.
9 What then? [1a]Are we better than they?
Not at all; for we have already charged that
both [b]Jews and [c]Greeks are [d]all under sin;
10 as it is written,
"[a]THERE IS NONE RIGHTEOUS, NOT EVEN
ONE;
11 THERE IS NONE WHO UNDERSTANDS,
THERE IS NONE WHO SEEKS FOR GOD;
12 ALL HAVE TURNED ASIDE, TOGETHER THEY
HAVE BECOME USELESS;
THERE IS NONE WHO DOES GOOD,
THERE IS NOT EVEN ONE."
13 "[a]THEIR THROAT IS AN OPEN GRAVE,
WITH THEIR TONGUES THEY KEEP
DECEIVING,"
"[b]THE POISON OF ASPS IS UNDER THEIR LIPS";
14 "[a]WHOSE MOUTH IS FULL OF CURSING AND
BITTERNESS";
15 "[a]THEIR FEET ARE SWIFT TO SHED BLOOD,
16 DESTRUCTION AND MISERY ARE IN THEIR
PATHS,
17 AND THE PATH OF PEACE THEY HAVE NOT
KNOWN."
18 "[a]THERE IS NO FEAR OF GOD BEFORE THEIR
EYES."
19 Now we know that whatever the [a]Law
says, it speaks to [b]those who are [1]under the
Law, so that every mouth may be closed and
[c]all the world may become accountable to
God;
20 because [a]by the works [1]of the Law no
flesh will be justified in His sight; for
[2b]through the Law *comes* the knowledge of
sin.

Justification by Faith

21 But now apart [1]from the Law [a]*the* righteousness of God has been manifested, being
[b]witnessed by the Law and the Prophets,
22 even *the* [a]righteousness of God through
[b]faith [c]in Jesus Christ for [d]all those [1]who
believe; for [e]there is no distinction;

3:1 [1]Lit *is the advantage of the Jew*
2 [a]Deut 4:8; Ps 147:19; Rom 9:4 [b]Acts 7:38
3 [1]Or *were unfaithful* [2]Or *unfaithfulness* [a]Rom 10:16; Heb 4:2
4 [1]Lit *in Your judging* [a]Luke 20:16; Rom 3:6, 31 [b]Ps 116:11; Rom 3:7 [c]Ps 51:4
5 [1]Or *commends* [a]Rom 5:8; 2 Cor 6:4; 7:11 [b]Rom 4:1; 7:7; 8:31; 9:14, 30 [c]Rom 6:19; 1 Cor 9:8; 15:32; Gal 3:15
6 [a]Luke 20:16; Rom 3:4, 31 [b]Rom 2:16
7 [a]Rom 3:4 [b]Rom 9:19
8 [1]Lit *Whose* [a]Rom 6:1
9 [1]Or *Are we worse* [a]Rom 3:1 [b]Rom 2:1-29 [c]Rom 1:18-32 [d]Rom 3:19, 23; 11:32; Gal 3:22
10 [a]Ps 14:1-3; 53:1-3
13 [a]Ps 5:9 [b]Ps 140:3
14 [a]Ps 10:7
15 [a]Is 59:7f
18 [a]Ps 36:1
19 [1]Lit *in* [a]John 10:34 [b]Rom 2:12 [c]Rom 3:9
20 [1]Or *of law* [2]Or *through law* [a]Ps 143:2; Acts 13:39; Gal 2:16 [b]Rom 4:15; 5:13, 20; 7:7
21 [1]Or *from law* [a]Rom 1:17; 9:30 [b]Acts 10:43; Rom 1:2
22 [1]Or *who believe For there is no distinction, since they all have sinned...and are being justified* [a]Rom 1:17; 9:30 [b]Rom 4:5 [c]Acts 3:16; Gal 2:16, 20; 3:22; Eph 3:12 [d]Rom 4:11, 16; 10:4 [e]Rom 10:12; Gal 3:28; Col 3:11

outward mark on the physical body, but the regenerating power of the Holy Spirit within—what Paul meant by "circumcision . . . of the heart" (see Deut 30:6).

3:2 *First of all.* Paul does not discuss the other advantages of being a Jew until 9:4–5. *entrusted.* The advantage of having the very words of God involves a duty.

3:3 *faithfulness of God.* God is faithful to His promises and would punish Israel for its unbelief (v. 5; see 2 Tim 2:13).

3:4 God's punishment of sin exhibits His faithfulness to His righteous character.

3:5 *demonstrates the righteousness of God.* By contrast, in showing it up against the dark background of man's sin. *in human terms.* "Human" in the sense of its weakness and absurdity.

3:6 *judge.* On judgment day. *the world.* All moral creatures (also in v. 19)—a more limited reference than in 1:20.

3:9 *Are we better than they?* Are Jews better than Gentiles in the sight of God? *all.* Nine times in four verses (vv. 9–12) Paul mentions the universality of sin ("all," two times; "none," four times; "not even one," two times; "together," once). *under sin.* Under its power and condemnation.

3:10–18 A collection of OT quotations that underscores Paul's charge that both Jews and Gentiles are under the power of sin. Several factors explain why the citations are not always verbatim: 1. NT quotations sometimes gave the general sense and were not meant to be word-for-word. 2. Quotation marks were not used in Greek. 3. The quotations were often taken from the Greek translation (the Septuagint) of the Hebrew OT, because Greek readers were not familiar with the Hebrew Bible. 4. Sometimes the NT writer, in order to drive home his point, would purposely (under the inspiration of the Holy Spirit) enlarge, abbreviate or adapt an OT passage or combine two or more passages.

3:11 *UNDERSTANDS.* About God and what is right.

3:13 *OPEN GRAVE.* Expressing the corruption of the heart.

3:18 *FEAR OF GOD.* Awesome reverence for God; the source of all godliness (see note on Gen 20:11).

3:19 *we know.* See note on 2:2. *Law.* The OT (as in John 10:34; 15:25; 1 Cor 14:21). *those who are under the Law.* Jews. *every mouth . . . all the world.* Jews as well as Gentiles are guilty.

3:20 *justified.* See notes on v. 24; 2:13.

3:21–5:21 Having shown that all (both Gentiles and Jews) are unrighteous (1:18–3:20), Paul now shows that God has provided a righteousness for mankind.

3:21 *But now.* There are two possible meanings: (1) temporal—all of time is divided into two periods, and in the "now" period the righteousness from God has been made known; (2) logical—the contrast is between the righteousness gained by observing the law (which is impossible, v. 20) and the righteousness provided by God. *witnessed by the Law and the Prophets.* See Gen 15:6; Ps 32:1–2; Hab 2:4.

3:22–23 *there is no distinction . . . glory of God.* A parenthetical thought: "All those who believe" (v. 22) are "justified as a gift" (v. 24), not "all have sinned" (v. 23) are "justified as a gift" (v. 24). Thus "justified" goes with "believe" not with "sinned".

3:22 *no distinction.* Between Jews and Gentiles (see 10:12).

23 for all [1][a]have sinned and fall short of
the glory of God,
24 being justified as a gift [a]by His grace
through [b]the redemption which is in Christ
Jesus;
25 whom God displayed publicly as [a]a
[1]propitiation [2][b]in His blood through faith.
This was to demonstrate His righteousness,
[3]because in the [c]forbearance of God He
[d]passed over the sins previously committed;
26 for the demonstration, *I say,* of His
righteousness at the present time, so that He
would be just and the justifier of the one
who [1]has faith in Jesus.
27 Where then is [a]boasting? It is excluded.
By [b]what kind of law? Of works? No, but by
a law of faith.
28 [1]For [a]we maintain that a man is justified by faith apart from works [2]of the Law.
29 Or [a]is God *the God* of Jews only? Is He
not *the God* of Gentiles also? Yes, of Gentiles
also,
30 since indeed [a]God [b]who will justify the
[1]circumcised [2]by faith and the [3]uncircum-
cised through faith [c]is one.
31 Do we then nullify [1]the Law through
faith? [a]May it never be! On the contrary, we
[b]establish the Law.

23 [1]Or *sinned* [a]Rom 3:9 **24** [a]Rom 4:4f, 16; Eph 2:8 [b]1 Cor 1:30; Eph 1:7; Col 1:14; Heb 9:15 **25** [1]Or *a propitiatory sacrifice* [2]Or *by* [3]Lit *because of the passing over of the sins previously committed in the forbearance of God* [a]1 John 2:2; 4:10 [b]1 Cor 5:7; Heb 9:14, 28; 1 Pet 1:19; Rev 1:5 [c]Rom 2:4 [d]Acts 14:16; 17:30 **26** [1]Lit *is of the faith of Jesus* **27** [a]Rom 2:17, 23; 4:2; 1 Cor 1:29ff [b]Rom 9:31 **28** [1]One early ms reads *Therefore* [2]Or *of law* [a]Acts 13:39; Rom 3:20, 21; Eph 2:9; James 2:20, 24, 26 **29** [a]Acts 10:34f; Rom 9:24; 10:12; 15:9; Gal 3:28 **30** [1]Lit *circumcision* [2]Lit *out of* [3]Lit *uncircumcision* [a]Rom 10:12; Gal 3:20 [b]Rom 3:22; 4:11f, 16; Gal 3:8 [c]Deut 6:4 **31** [1]Or *law* [a]Luke 20:16; Rom 3:4 [b]Matt 5:17; Rom 3:4, 6; 8:4

Justification by Faith Evidenced in Old Testament

4 What then shall we say that Abraham,
[1]our forefather [a]according to the flesh,
has found?
2 For if Abraham was justified [1]by works,
he has something to boast about, but [a]not
[2]before God.
3 For what does the Scripture say?
"[a]ABRAHAM BELIEVED GOD, AND IT WAS CREDITED
TO HIM AS RIGHTEOUSNESS."
4 Now to the one who [a]works, his wage
is not credited as a favor, but as what is due.
5 But to the one who does not work, but
[a]believes in Him who justifies the ungodly,
his faith is credited as righteousness,
6 just as David also speaks of the blessing on the man to whom God credits righteousness apart from works:
7 "[a]BLESSED ARE THOSE WHOSE LAWLESS
DEEDS HAVE BEEN FORGIVEN,
AND WHOSE SINS HAVE BEEN COVERED.
8 "[a]BLESSED IS THE MAN WHOSE SIN THE LORD
WILL NOT [b]TAKE INTO ACCOUNT."

4:1 [1]Or *our forefather, has found according to the flesh* [a]Rom 1:3 **2** [1]Lit *out of* [2]Lit *toward* [a]1 Cor 1:31 **3** [a]Gen 15:6; Rom 4:9, 22; Gal 3:6; James 2:23 **4** [a]Rom 11:6 **5** [a]John 6:29; Rom 3:22 **7** [a]Ps 32:1 **8** [a]Ps 32:2 [b]2 Cor 5:19

3:23 *glory of God.* What God intended man to be. The glory that man had before the fall (see Gen 1:26–28; Ps 8:5–6; cf. Eph 4:24; Col 3:10) the believer will again have through Christ (see Heb 2:5–9).

3:24 *justified.* Paul uses the Greek verb for "justified" 27 times, mostly in Romans and Galatians. It is translated by some form of the English word "justify" 24 times, by "freed" three times (6:7,18,22), by "acquitted" once (1 Cor 4:4) and by "vindicated" once (1 Tim 3:16). The term describes what happens when someone believes in Christ as his Savior: From the negative viewpoint, God declares the person to be not guilty; from the positive viewpoint, He declares him to be righteous. He cancels the guilt of the person's sin and credits righteousness to him. Paul emphasizes two points in this regard: 1. No one lives a perfectly good, holy, righteous life. On the contrary, "there is none righteous" (v. 10), and "all have sinned and fall short of the glory of God" (v. 23). "By the works of the Law no flesh will be justified in His sight" (v. 20). 2. But even though all are sinners and not sons, God will declare everyone who puts his trust in Jesus not guilty but righteous. This legal declaration is valid because Christ died to pay the penalty for our sin and lived a life of perfect righteousness that can in turn be imputed to us. This is the central theme of Romans and is stated in the theme verse, 1:17 ("the righteousness of God"). Christ's righteousness (His obedience to God's law and His sacrificial death) will be credited to believers as their own. Paul uses the word "credited" nine times in ch. 4 alone. *as a gift by His grace.* The central thought in justification is that, although man clearly and totally deserves to be declared guilty (vv. 9–19), because of his trust in Christ God declares him righteous. This is stated in several ways here: (1) "as a gift" (for nothing), (2) "by His grace," (3) "through the redemption which is in Christ Jesus" and (4) "through faith" (v. 25). *redemption.* A word taken from the slave market—the basic idea is that of obtaining release by payment of a ransom. Paul uses this word to refer to release from guilt, with its liability for judgment, and to deliverance from slavery to sin, because Christ in His death paid the ransom for us.

3:25 *propitiation.* The Greek for this phrase speaks of a sacrifice that satisfies the righteous wrath of God: "One who would turn aside God's wrath, taking away sin." Without this appeasement all people are justly destined for eternal punishment. See also note on 1 John 2:2. *His blood through faith.* Saving faith looks to Jesus Christ in His sacrificial death for us.

3:25b–26 The sins of God's people, punished symbolically in the animal sacrifices of the OT period, would be totally punished in the once-for-all sacrifice of Christ on the cross.

3:28 *by faith.* When Luther translated this passage, he added the word "alone," which, though not in the Greek, accurately reflects the meaning (see note on James 2:14–26).

3:30 *God . . . is one.* By appealing to the first article of Jewish faith ("the LORD is one!" Deut 6:4), Paul argues that there is only one way of salvation for both Jew and Gentile, namely, faith in Christ.

3:31 Paul anticipated being charged with antinomianism (against law): If justification comes by faith alone, then is not the law rejected? He gives a more complete answer in chs. 6–7 and reasserts the validity of the law in 13:8–10.

4:1 *Abraham, our forefather.* The great patriarch of the Jewish nation, the true example of a justified person (see James 2:21–23). The Jews of Jesus' time used Abraham as an example of justification by works, but Paul holds him up as a shining example of righteousness by faith (see Gal 3:6–9).

4:3 The reference is to Gen 15:6, where nothing is mentioned about works. *credited.* Abraham had kept no law, rendered no service and performed no ritual that earned credit to his account before God. His belief in God, who had made promises to him, was credited to him as righteousness.

4:6–8 God does not continue to credit unrighteousness to the sinner who repents, but forgives him when he confesses (see Ps 32:3–5; Ezek 18:23,27–28,32; 33:14–16).

9 Is this blessing then on [1a]the circumcised, or on [2]the uncircumcised also? For [b]we say, "[c]FAITH WAS CREDITED TO ABRAHAM AS RIGHTEOUSNESS."

10 How then was it credited? While he was [1]circumcised, or [2]uncircumcised? Not while [1]circumcised, but while [2]uncircumcised;

11 and he [a]received the sign of circumcision, [b]a seal of the righteousness of the faith which [1]he had while uncircumcised, so that he might be [c]the father of [d]all who believe without being circumcised, that righteousness might be credited to them,

12 and the father of circumcision to those who not only are of the circumcision, but who also follow in the steps of the faith of our father Abraham which [1]he had while uncircumcised.

13 For [a]the promise to Abraham or to his [1]descendants [b]that he would be heir of the world was not [2]through the Law, but through the righteousness of faith.

14 For [a]if those who are [1]of the Law are heirs, faith is made void and the promise is nullified;

15 for [a]the Law brings about wrath, but [b]where there is no law, there also is no violation.

16 For this reason *it is* [1]by faith, in order that *it may be* in accordance with [a]grace, so that the promise will be guaranteed to [b]all the [2]descendants, not only to [3]those who are of the Law, but also to [3c]those who are of the faith of Abraham, who is [d]the father of us all,

17 (as it is written, "[a]A FATHER OF MANY NATIONS HAVE I MADE YOU") in the presence of Him whom he believed, *even* God, [b]who gives life to the dead and [1c]calls into being [d]that which does not exist.

18 In hope against hope he believed, so that he might become [a]a father of many nations according to that which had been spoken, "[b]SO SHALL YOUR [1]DESCENDANTS BE."

19 Without becoming weak in faith he contemplated his own body, now [a]as good as dead since [b]he was about a hundred years old, and [c]the deadness of Sarah's womb;

20 yet, with respect to the promise of God, he did not waver in unbelief but grew strong in faith, [a]giving glory to God,

21 and [a]being fully assured that [b]what God had promised, He was able also to perform.

22 Therefore [a]IT WAS ALSO CREDITED TO HIM AS RIGHTEOUSNESS.

23 Now [a]not for his sake only was it written that it was credited to him,

9 [1]Lit *circumcision* [2]Lit *uncircumcision* [a]Rom 3:30 [b]Rom 4:3 [c]Gen 15:6
10 [1]Lit *in circumcision* [2]Lit *in uncircumcision*
11 [1]Lit *was in uncircumcision* [a]Gen 17:10f [b]John 3:33 [c]Luke 19:9; Rom 4:16f [d]Rom 3:22; 4:16
12 [1]Lit *was in uncircumcision*
13 [1]Lit *seed* [2]Or *through law* [a]Rom 9:8; Gal 3:16, 29 [b]Gen 17:4-6; 22:17f
14 [1]Or *of law* [a]Gal 3:18
15 [a]Rom 7:7, 10-25; 1 Cor 15:56; Gal 3:10 [b]Rom 3:20
16 [1]Or *out of* [a]Rom 3:24
16 [2]Lit *seed* [3]Lit *that which is* [b]Rom 4:11; 9:8; 15:8 [c]Gal 3:7 [d]Luke 19:9; Rom 4:11
17 [1]Lit *calls the things which do not exist as existing* [a]Gen 17:5 [b]John 5:21 [c]Is 48:13; 51:2 [d]1 Cor 1:28
18 [1]Lit *seed* [a]Rom 4:17 [b]Gen 15:5
19 [a]Heb 11:12 [b]Gen 17:17 [c]Gen 18:11
20 [a]Matt 9:8
21 [a]Rom 14:5 [b]Gen 18:14; Heb 11:19
22 [a]Gen 15:6; Rom 4:3
23 [a]Rom 15:4; 1 Cor 9:9f; 10:11; 2 Tim 3:16f

4:9 *circumcised.* Jews. *uncircumcised.* Gentiles.

4:10 *Not while . . . but while.* Abraham was declared righteous (Gen 15) some 14 years before he was circumcised (Gen 17). See Gal 3:17 for a similar statement.

4:11 *sign.* Circumcision was, among other things, the outward sign of the righteousness that God had credited to Abraham for his faith. *so that.* Abraham is the "father" of believing Gentiles (the uncircumcised), because he believed and was justified before the rite of circumcision (the mark of Jews) was instituted.

4:12 *father of circumcision.* Abraham is also the father of believing Jews. Thus his story shows that for Jew and Gentile alike there is only one way of justification—the way of faith.

4:13 *not through the Law.* Not on the condition that the promise be merited by works of the Law. *his descendants.* All those of whom Abraham is said to be father (vv. 11–12). *heir of the world.* "World" here refers to the creation, as in 1:20. No express mention of this heirship is made in the Genesis account of Abraham. He is promised "descendants as the dust of the earth" (Gen 13:16) and possession of the land of Canaan (Gen 12:7; 13:14–15; 15:7,18–21; 17:8), and that all the peoples on earth will be blessed through him (Gen 12:3; 18:18) or his offspring (Gen 22:18). But since, as Genesis already makes clear, God purposed through Abraham and his offspring to work out the destiny of the whole world, it was implicit in the promises to Abraham that he and his offspring would "inherit the earth" (see Ps 37:9,11,22,29,34; Matt 5:5). The full realization of this awaits the consummation of the Messianic kingdom at Christ's return.

4:14 *those who are of the Law.* Those whose claim to the inheritance is based on the fulfillment of the Law. *promise.* See note on v. 13.

4:15 *Law brings about wrath.* The Law, because it reveals sin and even stimulates it (see 7:7–11), produces wrath, not promise. *violation.* Overstepping a clearly defined line. Where there is no Law there is still sin, but it does not have the character of transgression.

4:16 A summary of the thought of vv. 11–12. For the close correlation between faith and grace see 3:24–25; Eph 2:8. *those who are of the Law.* Jewish Christians. *those who are of the faith of Abraham.* Gentile Christians who share Abraham's faith but who, like Abraham, do not possess the Law.

4:17 *in the presence of Him.* God considers Abraham the father of Jews and believing Gentiles alike, no matter how others (especially the Jews) may see him. *God, who gives life to the dead.* The main reference is to the birth of Isaac through Abraham and Sarah, both of whom were far past the age of childbearing (see Gen 18:11). Secondarily Paul alludes also to the resurrection of Christ (see vv. 24–25). *calls . . . that which does not exist.* God has the ability to create out of nothing, as He demonstrated in the birth of Isaac.

4:18 *In hope against hope he believed.* When all hope, as a human possibility, failed, Abraham placed his hope in God.

4:19 *Without becoming weak in faith.* Abraham had some anxious moments (see Gen 17:17–18), but God did not count these against him. *contemplated.* Faith does not refuse to face reality but looks beyond all difficulties to God and His promises. *deadness of Sarah's womb.* Sarah was ten years younger than Abraham (see Gen 17:17) but well past the age of bearing children.

4:20 *giving glory to God.* Because Abraham had faith to believe that God would do what He promised. Whereas works are man's attempt to establish a claim on God, faith brings glory to Him.

4:22 *Therefore.* Abraham's faith was "credited to him as righteousness" because it was true faith, i.e., complete confidence in God's promise.

4:23 *not for his sake only.* Abraham's experience was not private or individual but had broad implications. If justification by faith was true for him, it is universally true.

24 but for our sake also, to whom it will
be credited, as those [a]who believe in Him
who [b]raised Jesus our Lord from the dead,
25 *He* who was [a]delivered over because of
our transgressions, and was [b]raised because
of our justification.

Results of Justification

5 [a]Therefore, having been justified by faith,
[1b]we have peace with God through our
Lord Jesus Christ,
2 through whom also we have [a]obtained
our introduction by faith into this grace [b]in
which we stand; and [1]we exult in hope of
the glory of God.
3 [a]And not only this, but [1]we also [b]exult
in our tribulations, knowing that tribulation
brings about [c]perseverance;
4 and [a]perseverance, [b]proven character;
and proven character, hope;
5 and hope [a]does not disappoint,
because the love of God has been [b]poured
out within our hearts through the Holy Spirit who was given to us.
6 For while we were still [a]helpless, [b]at
the right time [c]Christ died for the ungodly.
7 For one will hardly die for a righteous
man; [1]though perhaps for the good man
someone would dare even to die.
8 But God [a]demonstrates [b]His own love
toward us, in that while we were yet sinners,
[c]Christ died for us.
9 Much more then, having now been justified [1a]by His blood, we shall be saved
[b]from the wrath *of God* through Him.
10 For if while we were [a]enemies we were
reconciled to God through the death of His
Son, much more, having been reconciled, we
shall be saved [1b]by His life.
11 [a]And not only this, [1]but we also exult
in God through our Lord Jesus Christ,
through whom we have now received [b]the
reconciliation.
12 Therefore, just as through [a]one man
sin entered into the world, and [b]death
through sin, and [c]so death spread to all men,
because all sinned—

24 [a]Rom 10:9; 1 Pet 1:21 [b]Acts 2:24
25 [a]Is 53:4, 5; Rom 5:6, 8; 8:32; Gal 2:20; Eph 5:2 [b]Rom 5:18; 1 Cor 15:17; 2 Cor 5:15
5:1 [1]Two early mss read *let us have* [a]Rom 3:28 [b]Rom 5:11
2 [1]Or *let us exult* [a]Eph 2:18; 3:12; Heb 10:19f; 1 Pet 3:18 [b]1 Cor 15:1
3 [1]Or *let us also exult* [a]Rom 5:11; 8:23; 9:10; 2 Cor 8:19 [b]Matt 5:12; James 1:2f [c]Luke 21:19
4 [a]Luke 21:19 [b]Phil 2:22; James 1:12
5 [a]Ps 119:116; Rom 9:33; Heb 6:18f [b]Acts 2:33; 10:45; Gal 4:6; Titus 3:6
6 [a]Rom 5:8, 10 [b]Gal 4:4 [c]Rom 4:25; 5:8; 8:32; Gal 2:20; Eph 5:2
7 [1]Lit *for*
8 [a]Rom 3:5 [b]John 3:16; 15:13; Rom 8:39 [c]Rom 4:25; 5:6; 8:32; Gal 2:20; Eph 5:2 **9** [1]Or *in* [a]Rom 3:25 [b]Rom 1:18; 1 Thess 1:10 **10** [1]Or *in* [a]Rom 11:28; 2 Cor 5:18f; Eph 2:3; Col 1:21f [b]Rom 8:34; Heb 7:25; 1 John 2:1 **11** [1]Lit *but also exulting* [a]Rom 5:3; 8:23; 9:10; 2 Cor 8:19 [b]Rom 5:10; 11:15; 2 Cor 5:18f **12** [a]Gen 2:17; 3:6, 19; Rom 5:15-17; 1 Cor 15:21f [b]Rom 6:23; 1 Cor 15:56; James 1:15 [c]Rom 5:14, 19, 21; 1 Cor 15:22

4:24 *but for our sake also.* As Abraham was justified because he believed in a God who brought life from the dead, so we will be justified by believing "in Him who raised Jesus our Lord from the dead."

4:25 These words, which reflect the Septuagint (Greek) translation of Is 53:12, are probably quoted from a Christian confessional formula.

5:1 *peace with God.* Not merely a subjective feeling (peace of mind) but primarily an objective status, a new relationship with God: Once we were His enemies, but now we are His friends (see v. 10; Eph 2:16; Col 1:21–22).

5:2 *introduction.* Jesus ushers us into the presence of God. The heavy curtain (of the temple) that separated man from God and God from man has been removed (see note on Matt 27:51). *hope of the glory of God.* The Christian's confidence that the purpose for which God created him will be ultimately realized (see note on 3:23).

5:3 *exult in our tribulations.* Not "because of" but "in." Paul does not advocate a morbid view of life but a joyous and triumphant one.

5:4 A Christian can rejoice in suffering because he knows that it is not meaningless. Part of God's purpose is to produce character in His children.

5:5 *hope does not disappoint.* The believer's hope is not to be equated with unfounded optimism. On the contrary, it is the blessed assurance of our future destiny and is based on God's love, which is revealed to us by the Holy Spirit and objectively demonstrated to us in the death of Christ. Paul has moved from faith (v. 1) to hope (vv. 2,4–5) to love (v. 5; see 1 Cor 13:13; see also note on 1 Thess 1:3). *has been poured out.* The verb indicates a present status resulting from a past action. When we first believed in Christ, the Holy Spirit poured out His love in our hearts, and His love for us continues to dwell in us.

5:6 *the right time.* The appointed moment in God's redemptive plan (Mark 1:15; Gal 4:4). *Christ died for the ungodly.* Christ's love is grounded in God's free grace and is not the result of any inherent worthiness found in its objects (mankind). In fact, it is lavished on us in spite of our undesirable character.

5:7 *righteous man . . . good man.* We were neither righteous nor good, but sinners, when Christ died for us (see v. 8; 3:10–12).

5:9 *by His blood.* By laying down His life as a sacrifice—a reference to Christ's death for our sins (see 3:25). *wrath of God.* The final judgment, as the verb "shall be saved" makes clear (cf. 1 Thess 1:9–10).

5:10 *enemies.* Man is the enemy of God, not the reverse. Thus the hostility must be removed from man if reconciliation is to be accomplished. God took the initiative in bringing this about through the death of His Son (see v. 11; Col 1:21–22). *reconciled.* To reconcile is "to put an end to hostility," and is closely related to the term "justify," as the parallelism in vv. 9–10 indicates:

v. 9	v. 10
justified	reconciled
by His blood	through the death of His Son
we shall be saved	we shall be saved

saved by His life. A reference to the unending life and ministry of the resurrected Christ for His people (see Heb 7:25). Since we were reconciled when we were God's enemies, we will be saved because Christ lives to keep us.

5:11 *we have now received the reconciliation.* Reconciliation, like justification (v. 1), is a present reality for Christians and is something to rejoice about.

5:12–21 A contrast between Adam and Christ. Adam introduced sin and death into the world; Christ brought righteousness and life. The comparison begun in v. 12 is completed in v. 18; these two verses summarize the whole passage. These two men also sum up the message of the book up to this point. Adam stands for man's condemnation (1:18–3:20); Christ stands for the believer's justification (3:21–5:11).

5:12 *death.* Physical death is the penalty for sin. It is also the symbol of spiritual death, man's ultimate separation from God. *because all sinned.* Not a repetition of 3:23. The context shows that Adam's sin involved the rest of mankind in condemnation (vv. 18–19) and death (v. 15). We do not start life with even the possibility of living it sinlessly; we begin it with a sinful nature (see Gen 8:21; Ps 51:5; 58:3; Eph 2:3).

13 for [1]until the Law sin was in the world, but [a]sin is not imputed when there is no law.

14 Nevertheless death reigned from Adam until Moses, even over those who had not sinned [a]in the likeness of the offense of Adam, who is a [1b]type of Him who was to come.

15 But [1]the free gift is not like the transgression. For if by the transgression of [a]the one [b]the many died, much more did the grace of God and the gift by [c]the grace of the one Man, Jesus Christ, abound to the many.

16 The gift is not like *that which came* through the one who sinned; for on the one hand [a]the judgment *arose* from one *transgression* [1]resulting in condemnation, but on the other hand the free gift *arose* from many transgressions [2]resulting in justification.

17 For if by the transgression of the one, death reigned [a]through the one, much more those who receive the abundance of grace and of the gift of righteousness will [b]reign in life through the One, Jesus Christ.

18 So then as through [a]one transgression [1]there resulted condemnation to all men, even so through one [b]act of righteousness [2]there resulted [c]justification of life to all men.

19 For as through the one man's disobedience [a]the many [b]were made sinners, even so through [c]the obedience of the One [a]the many will be made righteous.

20 [1a]The Law came in so that the transgression would increase; but where sin increased, [b]grace abounded all the more,

21 so that, as [a]sin reigned in death, even so [b]grace would reign through righteousness to eternal life through Jesus Christ our Lord.

Believers Are Dead to Sin, Alive to God

6 [a]What shall we say then? Are we to [b]continue in sin so that grace may increase?

2 [a]May it never be! How shall we who [b]died to sin still live in it?

3 Or do you not know that all of us who have been [a]baptized into [b]Christ Jesus have been baptized into His death?

4 Therefore we have been [a]buried with Him through baptism into death, so that as Christ was [b]raised from the dead through the [c]glory of the Father, so we too might walk in [d]newness of life.

5 For [a]if we have become [1]united with *Him* in the likeness of His death, certainly we shall also be [2]*in the likeness* of His resurrection,

6 knowing this, that our [a]old [1]self was [b]crucified with *Him,* in order that our [c]body of sin might be [2]done away with, so that we would no longer be slaves to sin;

13 [1]Or *until law* [a]Rom 4:15 **14** [1]Or *foreshadowing* [a]Hos 6:7 [b]1 Cor 15:45 **15** [1]Lit *not as the transgression, so also is the free gift* [a]Rom 5:12, 18, 19 [b]Rom 5:19 [c]Acts 15:11 **16** [1]Lit *to condemnation* [2]Lit *to an act of righteousness* [a]1 Cor 11:32 **17** [a]Gen 2:17; 3:6, 19; Rom 5:12, 15, 16; 1 Cor 15:21f [b]2 Tim 2:12; Rev 22:5 **18** [1]Lit *to condemnation* [2]Lit *to justification* [a]Rom 5:12, 15 [b]Rom 3:25 [c]Rom 4:25 **19** [a]Rom 5:15, 18 [b]Rom 5:12; 11:32 [c]Phil 2:8 **20** [1]Or *law* [a]Rom 3:20; 7:7f; Gal 3:19 **20** [b]Rom 6:1; 1 Tim 1:14 **21** [a]Rom 5:12, 14 [b]John 1:17; Rom 6:23 **6:1** [a]Rom 3:5 [b]Rom 3:8; 6:15 **2** [a]Luke 20:16; Rom 6:15 [b]Rom 6:11; 7:4, 6; Gal 2:19; Col 2:20; 3:3; 1 Pet 2:24 **3** [a]Matt 28:19 [b]Acts 2:38; 8:16; 19:5; Gal 3:27 **4** [a]Col 2:12 [b]Acts 2:24; Rom 6:9 [c]John 11:40; 2 Cor 13:4 [d]Rom 7:6; 2 Cor 5:17; Gal 6:15; Eph 4:23f; Col 3:10 **5** [1]Or *united with the likeness* [2]Or *with* [a]2 Cor 4:10; Phil 3:10f; Col 2:12; 3:1 **6** [1]Gr *anthropos* [2]Or *made powerless* [a]Eph 4:22; Col 3:9 [b]Gal 2:20; 5:24; 6:14 [c]Rom 7:24

5:13 *sin is not imputed.* In the period when there was no (Mosaic) law, sin was not charged against man (see 4:15). Death, however, continued to occur (v. 14). Since death is the penalty for sin, people between Adam and Moses were involved in the sin of someone else, namely, Adam (see note on v. 12).

5:14 *type.* Adam by his sin brought universal ruin on the human race. In this act he is the prototype of Christ, who through one righteous act (v. 18) brought universal blessing. The analogy is one of contrast.

5:15 *the many.* The same as "all men" in v. 12 (see Is 53:11; Mark 10:45). *much more.* A theme that runs through this section. God's grace is infinitely greater for good than is Adam's sin for evil.

5:16 *gift.* Salvation. *many transgressions.* The sins of the succeeding generations.

5:17 *will reign in life.* The future reign of believers with Jesus Christ (2 Tim 2:12; Rev 22:5).

5:18 *life to all men.* Does not mean that everyone eventually will be saved, but that salvation is available to all. To be effective, God's gracious gift must be received (see v. 17).

5:19 *made righteous.* A reference to a standing (status) before God (see 2 Cor 5:21), not to a change in character. The latter (the doctrine of sanctification) is developed in chs. 6–8.

5:20 *Law came in.* Not to bring about redemption but to point up the need for it. The Law made sin even more sinful by revealing what sin is in stark contrast to God's holiness.

6:1–8:39 In 3:21–5:21 Paul explains how God has provided for our redemption and justification. He next explains the doctrine of sanctification—the process by which believers grow to maturity in Christ. He treats this subject in three parts: (1) freedom from sin's tyranny (ch. 6), (2) freedom from the Law's condemnation (ch. 7) and (3) life in the power of the Holy Spirit (ch. 8).

6:1 *Are we to continue in sin so that grace may increase?* This question arose out of what Paul had just said in 5:20: "Where sin increased, grace abounded all the more." Such a question expresses an antinomian (against law) viewpoint. Apparently some objected to Paul's teaching of justification by faith alone because they thought it would lead to moral irresponsibility.

6:2 *died to sin.* The reference is to an event in the past and is explained in v. 3.

6:3–4 The when and how of the Christian's death to sin. In NT times baptism so closely followed conversion that the two were considered part of one event (see Acts 2:38 and note). So although baptism is not a means by which we enter into a vital faith relationship with Jesus Christ, it is closely associated with faith. Baptism depicts graphically what happens as a result of the Christian's union with Christ, which comes with faith—through faith we are united with Christ, just as through our natural birth we are united with Adam. As we fell into sin and became subject to death in father Adam, so we now have died and been raised again with Christ—which baptism symbolizes.

6:4 *buried with Him through baptism into death.* Amplified in vv. 5–7. *through the glory of the Father.* By the power of God. God's glory is His divine excellence, His perfection. Any one of His attributes is a manifestation of His excellence. Thus His power is a manifestation of His glory, as is His righteousness (see 3:23). Glory and power are often closely related in the Bible (see Ps 145:11; Col 1:11; 1 Pet 4:11; Rev 1:6; 4:11; 5:12–13; 7:12; 19:1). *walk in newness of life.* Amplified in vv. 8–10.

6:6 *our old self.* Our unregenerate self; what we once were. *body of sin.* The self in its pre-Christian state, dominated by sin. This is a figurative expression in which the old self is personified. It is a "body" that can be put to death. For the believer, this old self has been rendered powerless so that it can no longer enslave us to sin—whatever lingering vitality it may yet exert in its death throes.

7 for [a]he who has died is [1]freed from sin.
8 Now [a]if we have died with Christ, we
believe that we shall also live with Him,
9 knowing that Christ, having been
[a]raised from the dead, [1]is never to die again;
[b]death no longer is master over Him.
10 For the death that He died, He died to
sin once for all; but the life that He lives, He
lives to God.
11 Even so consider yourselves to be
[a]dead to sin, but alive to God in Christ Jesus.
12 Therefore do not let sin [a]reign in your
mortal body so that you obey its lusts,
13 and do not go on [a]presenting [1]the
members of your body to sin *as* [2]instruments
of unrighteousness; but [b]present yourselves
to God as those alive from the dead, and
your members *as* [2]instruments of righteousness to God.
14 For [a]sin shall not [b]be master over you,
for [c]you are not under law but [d]under grace.
15 What then? [a]Shall we sin because we
are not under law but under grace? [b]May it
never be!
16 Do you not [a]know that when you present yourselves to someone *as* [b]slaves for
obedience, you are slaves of the one whom
you obey, either of [c]sin [1]resulting in death,
or of obedience [2]resulting in righteousness?
17 But [a]thanks be to God that [1]though you
were slaves of sin, you became obedient
from the heart to that [b]form of teaching to
which you were committed,
18 and having been [a]freed from sin, you
became slaves of righteousness.
19 [a]I am speaking in human terms because
of the weakness of your flesh. For just [b]as you
presented your members as slaves to impurity and to lawlessness, [1]resulting in *further*
lawlessness, so now present your members as
slaves to righteousness, [2]resulting in sanctification.
20 For [a]when you were slaves of sin, you
were free in regard to righteousness.
21 Therefore what [1a]benefit were you
then [2]deriving [3]from the things of which you
are now ashamed? For the outcome of those
things is [b]death.
22 But now having been [a]freed from sin
and [b]enslaved to God, you [1]derive your
[2c]benefit, [3]resulting in sanctification, and
[d]the outcome, eternal life.
23 For the wages of [a]sin is death, but the
free gift of God is [b]eternal life in Christ Jesus
our Lord.

7 [1]Or *acquitted* [a]1 Pet 4:1 **8** [a]Rom 6:4; 2 Cor 4:10; 2 Tim 2:11 **9** [1]Lit *no longer dies* [a]Acts 2:24; Rom 6:4 [b]Rev 1:18 **11** [a]Rom 6:2; 7:4, 6; Gal 2:19; Col 2:20; 3:3; 1 Pet 2:24 **12** [a]Rom 6:14 **13** [1]Lit *your members to sin* [2]Or *weapons* [a]Rom 6:16, 19; 7:5; Col 3:5 [b]Rom 12:1; 2 Cor 5:14f; 1 Pet 2:24 **14** [a]Rom 8:2, 12 [b]Rom 6:12 [c]Rom 5:18; 7:4, 6; Gal 4:21 [d]Rom 5:17, 21 **15** [a]Rom 6:1 [b]Luke 20:16; Rom 6:2 **16** [1]Lit *to death* [2]Lit *to righteousness* [a]Rom 11:2; 1 Cor 3:16; 5:6; 6:2, 3, 9, 15, 16, 19; 9:13, 24 [b]John 8:34; 2 Pet 2:19 [c]Rom 6:21, 23 **17** [1]Lit *you were slaves...but you became* [a]Rom 1:8; 2 Cor 2:14

17 [b]2 Tim 1:13

18 [a]John 8:32; Rom 6:22; 8:2 **19** [1]Lit *to lawlessness* [2]Lit *to sanctification* [a]Rom 3:5 [b]Rom 6:13 **20** [a]Matt 6:24; Rom 6:16 **21** [1]Lit *fruit* [2]Lit *having* [3]Lit *in* [a]Jer 12:13; Ezek 16:63; Rom 7:5 [b]Rom 1:32; 5:12; 6:16, 23; 8:6, 13; Gal 6:8 **22** [1]Lit *have* [2]Lit *fruit* [3]Lit *to sanctification* [a]John 8:32; Rom 6:18; 8:2 [b]1 Cor 7:22; 1 Pet 2:16 [c]Rom 7:4 [d]1 Pet 1:9 **23** [a]Rom 1:32; 5:12; 6:16, 21; 8:6, 13; Gal 6:8 [b]Matt 25:46; Rom 5:21; 8:38, 39

6:7 *has died.* The believer's death with Christ to sin's ruling power. *freed from sin.* Set free from its shackles and power.

6:8 As resurrection followed death in the experience of Christ, so the believer who dies with Christ is raised to a new quality of moral life here and now. Resurrection in the sense of a new birth is already a fact, and it increasingly exerts itself in the believer's life.

6:10 *He died to sin once for all.* In His death Christ (for the sake of sinners) submitted to the "reign" of sin (5:21); but His death broke the judicial link between sin and death, and He passed forever from the sphere of sin's "reign." Having been raised from the dead, He now lives forever to glorify God. *to God.* For the glory of God.

6:11 *consider yourselves.* The first step toward victory over sin in the believer's life (for the succeeding steps see note on vv. 12–13). He is dead to sin and alive to God, and by faith he is to live in the light of this truth. *in Christ.* The first occurrence in Romans of this phrase, which is found often in Paul's writings. True believers are "in Christ" because they have died with Christ and have been raised to new life with Him.

6:12–13 A call for the Christian to become in experience what he already is in position—dead to sin (see vv. 5–7) and alive to God (see vv. 8–10). The second step toward the Christian's victory over sin is refusal to let sin reign in his life (v. 12). The third step is to offer himself to God (v. 13).

6:13 *presenting.* Put yourselves in the service of, perhaps also echoing the language of sacrifice. *members of your body.* All the separate capacities of your being (also in v. 19).

6:14 *sin shall not be master over you.* Paul conceived of sin as a power that enslaves, and so personified it. *not under law.* The meaning is not that the Christian has been freed from all moral authority. He has, however, been freed from the law in the manner in which God's people were under law in the OT era. Law provides no enablement to resist the power of sin; it only condemns the sinner. But grace enables. *under grace.* For the disciplinary aspect of grace see Titus 2:11–12.

6:15–23 The question raised here seems to come from those who are afraid that the doctrine of justification by faith alone will remove all moral restraint. Paul rejects such a suggestion and shows that a Christian does not throw morality to the winds. To the contrary, he exchanges sin for righteousness as his master.

6:16 The contrast between sin and obedience suggests that sin is by nature disobedience to God.

6:17 *obedient from the heart.* Christian obedience is not forced or legalistic, but willing. *form of teaching.* May refer to a summary of the moral and ethical teachings of Christ that was given to new converts in the early church.

6:18 *slaves of righteousness.* A Christian has changed masters. Whereas he was formerly a slave to sin, he becomes a slave (a willing servant) to righteousness.

6:19 *I am speaking in human terms.* An apology for using an imperfect analogy. The word "slave" when applied to Christians, who are free in Christ, naturally presents problems.

6:22 *freed from sin.* See note on v. 6. *sanctification.* Slavery to God produces holiness, and the end of the process is eternal life (viewed not in its present sense but in its final, future sense). There is no eternal life without holiness (see Heb 12:14). Anyone who has been justified will surely give evidence of that fact by the presence of holiness in his life. For other uses of various forms of the word "sanctification" see v. 19; 1 Cor 1:30; 1 Thess 4:3–4,7; 2 Thess 2:13; 1 Tim 2:15; Heb 12:14; 1 Pet 1:2.

6:23 Two kinds of servitude are contrasted here. One brings death as its wages; the other results in eternal life, not as wages earned or merited, but as a gift of God. For the contrast between wages and gift see 4:4.

Believers United to Christ

7 Or do you not know, [a]brethren (for I am speaking to those who know the law), that the law has jurisdiction over a person as long as he lives?

2 For [a]the married woman is bound by law to her [1]husband while he is living; but if her husband dies, she is released from the law [2]concerning the husband.

3 So then, if while her husband is living she is joined to another man, she shall be called an adulteress; but if her husband dies, she is free from the law, so that she is not an adulteress though she is joined to another man.

4 Therefore, my brethren, you also were [a]made to die [b]to the Law [c]through the body of Christ, so that you might be joined to another, to Him who was raised from the dead, in order that we might bear fruit for God.

5 For while we were [a]in the flesh, the sinful passions, which were [b]*aroused* by the Law, were at work [c]in [1]the members of our body to bear fruit for death.

6 But now we have been [a]released from the Law, having [b]died to that by which we were bound, so that we serve in [c]newness of [d]the [1]Spirit and not in oldness of the letter.

7 [a]What shall we say then? Is the Law sin? [b]May it never be! On the contrary, [c]I would not have come to know sin except [1]through the Law; for I would not have known about [2]coveting if the Law had not said, "[d]YOU SHALL NOT [2]COVET."

8 But sin, [a]taking opportunity [b]through the commandment, produced in me [1]coveting of every kind; for [c]apart [2]from the Law sin *is* dead.

9 I was once alive apart [1]from the Law; but when the commandment came, sin became alive and I died;

10 and this commandment, which was [1][a]to result in life, proved [2]to result in death for me;

11 for sin, [a]taking an opportunity [b]through the commandment, [c]deceived me and through it killed me.

12 [a]So then, the Law is holy, and the commandment is holy and righteous and good.

13 Therefore did that which is good become *a cause of* death for me? [a]May it never be! Rather it was sin, in order that it might be shown to be sin by effecting my death through that which is good, so that through the commandment sin would become utterly sinful.

7:1 [a]Rom 1:13
2 [1]Lit *living husband* [2]Lit *of* [a]1 Cor 7:39
4 [a]Rom 6:2; 7:6 [b]Rom 8:2; Gal 2:19; 5:18 [c]Col 1:22
5 [1]Lit *our members to bear* [a]Rom 8:8f; 2 Cor 10:3 [b]Rom 7:7f [c]Rom 6:13, 21, 23
6 [1]Or *spirit* [a]Rom 7:2 [b]Rom 6:2 [c]Rom 6:4 [d]Rom 2:29
7 [1]Or *through law* [2]Or *lust* [a]Rom 3:5 [b]Luke 20:16 [c]Rom 3:20; 4:15; 5:20 [d]Ex 20:17; Deut 5:21
8 [1]Or *lust* [2]Or *from law* [a]Rom 7:11 [b]Rom 3:20; 7:11 [c]1 Cor 15:56
9 [1]Or *from law*
10 [1]Lit *to life* [2]Lit *to death* [a]Lev 18:5; Luke 10:28; Rom 10:5; Gal 3:12
11 [a]Rom 7:8 [b]Rom 3:20; 7:8 [c]Gen 3:13
12 [a]Rom 7:16; 1 Tim 1:8
13 [a]Luke 20:16

7:1 *law.* Perhaps Paul has in mind the Mosaic law, but his concern here is with the fundamental character of law as such.
7:2–3 These verses illustrate the principle set down in v. 1. Death decisively changes a person's relationship to the law.
7:4 *Therefore.* Paul now draws the conclusion from the principle stated in v. 1 and illustrated in vv. 2–3. *die to the Law.* The Law's power to condemn no longer threatens the Christian, whose death here is to be understood in terms of 6:2–7. There, however, he dies to sin; here he dies to the Law. The result is that the Law has no more hold on him. *through the body of Christ.* His physical body (self) crucified. *joined to another.* The resurrected Christ (see 6:5). The purpose of this union is to produce the fruit of holiness.
7:5 *in the flesh.* A condition, so far as Christians are concerned, that belongs to the past—the unregenerate state. *aroused by the Law.* The Law not only reveals sin; it also stimulates it. The natural tendency in man is to desire the forbidden thing. *death.* Physical death and, beyond that, spiritual death—final separation from God—were the fruit of our "union" with the Law.
7:6 *released from the Law.* In the sense of its condemnation (see note on v. 4). *by which we were bound.* The Law; see vv. 4,6. *newness of the Spirit.* See note on 8:4. *oldness of the letter.* Life under the OT Law.
7:7 *Is the Law sin?* This question was occasioned by the remarks about the Law in vv. 4–6. *I.* Paul seems to be using the first person pronoun of himself, but also as representative of mankind in general (vv. 7–12) and of Christians in particular (vv. 13–25). *I would not have come to know sin.* The Law fulfilled the important function of revealing the presence and fact of sin.
7:8 *opportunity through the commandment.* See note on v. 5. *sin is dead.* Not nonexistent but not fully perceived.
7:9 *I was once alive.* Paul reviews his own experience from the vantage point of his present understanding. Before he realized that the Law condemned him to death, he was alive. Reference is to the time either before his *bar mitzvah* (see below) or before his conversion, when the true rigor of the Law became clear to him (see Luke 18:20–21; Phil 3:6). *when the commandment came.* When Paul came to the realization that he stood guilty before the law—a reference either to his *bar mitzvah,* when he, at age 13, assumed full responsibility for the Law, or to the time when he became aware of the full force of the Law (at his conversion). *I died.* Paul came to realize he was condemned to death, because Law reveals sin, and sin's wages is death (6:23).
7:10 *to result in life.* See Lev 18:5. As it worked out, Law became the avenue through which sin entered—both in Paul's experience and in that of mankind. Instead of giving life, the Law brought condemnation; instead of producing holiness, it stimulated sin.
7:12 *the Law is holy.* Despite the despicable use that sin made of the Law, the Law was not to blame. The Law is God's and as such is holy, righteous and good.
7:13–25 Whether Paul is describing a Christian or non-Christian experience has been hotly debated through the centuries. That he is speaking of the non-Christian life is suggested by: (1) the use of phrases such as "sold into bondage to sin" (v. 14), "I know that nothing good dwells in me" (v. 18) and "Wretched man that I am!" (v. 24)—which do not seem to describe Christian experience; (2) the contrast between ch. 7 and ch. 8, making it difficult for the other view to be credible; (3) the problem of the value of conversion if one ends up in spiritual misery. In favor of the view that Paul is describing Christian experience are: (1) the use of the present tense throughout the passage; (2) Paul's humble opinion of himself (v. 18); (3) his high regard for God's Law (vv. 14,16); (4) the location of this passage in the section of Romans where Paul is dealing with sanctification—the growth of the Christian in holiness.
7:13 Sin used a holy thing (law) for an unholy end (death). By this fact the contemptible nature of sin is revealed.
7:14 *spiritual.* The Law had its origin in God. *I am.* The personal pronoun and the verb, taken together, suggest that Paul

The Conflict of Two Natures

14 For we know that the Law is [a]spiritual,
but I am [a]of flesh, [b]sold [1c]into bondage to
sin.
15 For what I am doing, [a]I do not understand; for I am not practicing [b]what I *would*
like to *do,* but I am doing the very thing I
hate.
16 But if I do the very thing I do not want
to do, I agree with [a]the Law, *confessing* that
the Law is good.
17 So now, [a]no longer am I the one doing
it, but sin which dwells in me.
18 For I know that nothing good dwells in
me, that is, in my [a]flesh; for the willing is
present in me, but the doing of the good *is*
not.
19 For [a]the good that I want, I do not do,
but I practice the very evil that I do not want.
20 But if I am doing the very thing I do not
want, [a]I am no longer the one doing it, but
sin which dwells in me.
21 I find then [a]the [1]principle that evil is
present in me, the one who wants to do good.
22 For I joyfully concur with the law of
God [1]in [a]the inner man,
23 but I see [a]a different law in [1]the members of my body, waging war against the
[b]law of my mind and making me a prisoner
[2]of [c]the law of sin which is in my members.
24 Wretched man that I am! Who will set
me free from [1a]the body of this [b]death?
25 [a]Thanks be to God through Jesus
Christ our Lord! So then, on the one hand I
myself with my mind am serving the law of
God, but on the other, with my flesh [b]the law
of sin.

Deliverance from Bondage

8 Therefore there is now no [a]condemnation
for those who are [b]in [c]Christ Jesus.
2 For [a]the law of the Spirit of life [1]in
[b]Christ Jesus [c]has set you free from the law
of sin and of death.
3 For [a]what the Law could not do,
[1b]weak as it was through the flesh, God *did:*
sending His own Son in [c]the likeness of [2]sin-
ful flesh and *as an offering* for sin, He condemned sin in the flesh,
4 so that the [a]requirement of the Law
might be fulfilled in us, who [b]do not walk
according to the flesh but according to the
Spirit.
5 For those who are according to the flesh
set their minds on [a]the things of the flesh,
but those who are according to the Spirit,
[b]the things of the Spirit.
6 [a]For the mind set on the flesh is [b]death,
but the mind set on the Spirit is life and
peace,
7 because the mind set on the flesh is

14 [1]Lit *under sin* [a]1 Cor 3:1 [b]1 Kin 21:20, 25; 2 Kin 17:17; Rom 6:6; Gal 4:3 [c]Rom 3:9 **15** [a]John 15:15 [b]Rom 7:19; Gal 5:17 **16** [a]Rom 7:12; 1 Tim 1:8 **17** [a]Rom 7:20 **18** [a]John 3:6; Rom 7:25; 8:3 **19** [a]Rom 7:15 **20** [a]Rom 7:17 **21** [1]Lit *law* [a]Rom 7:23, 25; 8:2 **22** [1]Or *concerning* [a]2 Cor 4:16; Eph 3:16; 1 Pet 3:4 **23** [1]Lit *my members* [2]Lit *in* [a]Rom 6:19; Gal 5:17; James 4:1; 1 Pet 2:11 [b]Rom 7:25 [c]Rom 7:21, 25; 8:2 **24** [1]Or *this body of death* [a]Rom 6:6; Col 2:11 [b]Rom 8:2 **25** [a]1 Cor 15:57 [b]Rom 7:21, 23; 8:2 **8:1** [a]Rom 5:16; 8:34 [b]Rom 8:9f [c]Rom 8:2, 11, 39; 16:3 **2** [1]Or *has set you free in Christ Jesus* [a]1 Cor 15:45 [b]Rom 8:1, 11, 39; 16:3 [c]John 8:32, 36; Rom 6:14, 18; 7:4 **3** [1]Lit *in which it was weak* [2]Lit *flesh of sin* [a]Acts 13:39; Heb 10:1ff [b]Rom 7:18f; Heb 7:18 [c]Phil 2:7; Heb 2:14, 17; 4:15 **4** [a]Luke 1:6; Rom 2:26 [b]Gal 5:16, 25 **5** [a]Gal 5:19-21 [b]Gal 5:22-25 **6** [a]Gal 6:8 [b]Rom 6:21; 8:13

---

is describing his present (Christian) experience. *of flesh.* Even a believer has the seeds of rebellion in his heart. *sold into bondage to sin.* A phrase so strong that many refuse to accept it as descriptive of a Christian. However, it may graphically point out the failure even of Christians to meet the radical ethical and moral demands of the gospel. It also points up the persistent nature of sin.

7:15 *I do not understand.* The struggle within creates tension, ambivalence and confusion.

7:16 *I agree . . . that the Law is good.* Even when Paul is rebellious and disobedient, the Holy Spirit reveals to him the essential goodness of the Law.

7:17 *no longer am I the one doing it.* Not an attempt to escape moral responsibility but a statement of the great control sin can have over a Christian's life.

7:18 *nothing good dwells in me.* A reference to man's fallen nature, as the last phrase of the sentence indicates. Paul is not saying that no goodness at all exists in Christians.

7:20 *sin . . . in me.* See note on v. 17.

7:22 *I joyfully concur with the law of God.* The Mosaic Law or God's law generally. It is difficult to see how a non-Christian could say this.

7:23 *different law.* A principle or force at work in Paul preventing him from giving obedience to God's law. *law of my mind.* His desire to obey God's law. *law of sin.* Essentially the same as "another law," mentioned above.

7:24 *body of this death.* Figurative for the body of sin (6:6) that hung on him like a corpse and from which he could not gain freedom.

7:25 The first half of this verse is the answer to the question stated in v. 24—deliverance comes, not through legalistic effort, but through Christ. The last half is a summary of vv. 13–24. *I myself.* The real self—the inner being that delights in God's law (v. 22).

8:1 *condemnation.* The law brings condemnation because it points out, stimulates and condemns sin. But the Christian is no longer "under law" (6:14). *in Christ Jesus.* United with him, as explained in 6:1–10 (see note on 6:11).

8:2 *the law of the Spirit of life.* The controlling power of the Holy Spirit, who is life-giving. Paul uses the word "law" in several different ways in Romans—to mean, e.g., a controlling power (here); God's law (2:17–20; 9:31; 10:3–5); the Pentateuch (3:21b); the OT as a whole (3:19); a principle (3:27). *law of sin and of death.* The controlling power of sin, which ultimately produces death.

8:3 *could not do.* The law was not able to overcome sin. It could point out, condemn and even stimulate sin, but it could not remove it. *in the likeness of sinful flesh.* Christ in His incarnation became truly a man, but, unlike all other men, was sinless. *in the flesh.* "Flesh" may refer either to man's flesh or to Christ's. If the latter, it states where God condemned sin, namely, in Christ's human (but not sinful) nature—the interpretation that seems more consistent with Paul's teaching.

8:4 *requirement of the Law.* The Law still plays a role in the life of a believer—not, however, as a means of salvation but as a moral and ethical guide, obeyed out of love for God and by the power that the Spirit provides. This is the fulfillment of Jer 31:33–34 (a prophecy of the new covenant). *fulfilled.* God's aim in sending His Son was that believers might be enabled to embody the true and full intentions of the law. *according to the Spirit.* How the law's righteous requirements can be fully met—by no longer letting the sinful nature hold sway but by yielding to the directing and empowering ministry of the Holy Spirit.

8:5–8 Two mind-sets are described here: that of the sinful nature and that of the Spirit. The former leads to death, the latter to life and peace. The sinful nature is bound up with death

[a]hostile toward God; for it does not subject
itself to the law of God, for it is not even able
to do so,
8 and those who are [a]in the flesh cannot
please God.
9 However, you are not [a]in the flesh but
in the Spirit, if indeed the Spirit of God
[b]dwells in you. But [c]if anyone does not have
the Spirit of Christ, he does not belong to
Him.
10 [a]If Christ is in you, though the body is
dead because of sin, yet the spirit is [1]alive
because of righteousness.
11 But if the Spirit of Him who [a]raised
Jesus from the dead dwells in you, [b]He who
raised [c]Christ Jesus from the dead will also
give life to your mortal bodies [1]through His
Spirit who dwells in you.
12 So then, brethren, we are under obligation, not to the flesh, to live according to the
flesh—
13 for [a]if you are living according to the
flesh, you [1]must die; but if by the Spirit you
are [b]putting to death the deeds of the body,
you will live.
14 For all who are [a]being led by the Spirit
of God, these are [b]sons of God.
15 For you [a]have not received a spirit of
slavery [1]leading to fear again, but you [b]have
received [2]a spirit of adoption as sons by
which we cry out, "[c]Abba! Father!"

7 [a]James 4:4 **8** [a]Rom 7:5 **9** [a]Rom 7:5 [b]John 14:23; Rom 8:11; 1 Cor 3:16; 6:19; 2 Cor 6:16; Gal 4:6; Phil 1:19; 2 Tim 1:14; 1 John 4:13 [c]John 14:17 **10** [1]Lit *life* [a]John 17:23; Gal 2:20; Eph 3:17; Col 1:27 **11** [1]One early ms reads *because of* [a]Acts 2:24; Rom 6:4 [b]John 5:21 [c]Rom 8:1, 2, 39; 16:3 **13** [1]Or *are going to* [a]Rom 8:6 [b]Col 3:5 **14** [a]Gal 5:18 [b]Hos 1:10; Matt 5:9; John 1:12; Rom 8:16, 19; 9:8, 26; 2 Cor 6:18; Gal 3:26; 1 John 3:1; Rev 21:7 **15** [1]Lit *for fear again* [2]Or *the Spirit* [a]2 Tim 1:7; Heb 2:15 [b]Rom 8:23; Gal 4:5f [c]Mark 14:36; Gal 4:6

16 [a]Acts 5:32 [b]Hos 1:10; Matt 5:9; John 1:12; Rom 8:14, 19; 9:8, 26; 2 Cor 6:18; Gal 3:26; 1 John 3:1; Rev 21:7

16 The Spirit Himself [a]testifies with our
spirit that we are [b]children of God,
17 and if children, [a]heirs also, heirs of
God and fellow heirs with Christ, [b]if indeed
we suffer with *Him* so that we may also be
glorified with *Him.*
18 For I consider that the sufferings of this
present time [a]are not worthy to be compared
with the [b]glory that is to be revealed to us.
19 For the [a]anxious longing of the creation
waits eagerly for [b]the revealing of the [c]sons
of God.
20 For the creation [a]was subjected to
[b]futility, not willingly, but [c]because of Him
who subjected it, [1]in hope
21 that [a]the creation itself also will be set
free from its slavery to corruption into the
freedom of the glory of the children of God.
22 For we know that the whole creation
[a]groans and suffers the pains of childbirth
together until now.
23 [a]And not only this, but also we ourselves, having [b]the first fruits of the Spirit,
even we ourselves [c]groan within ourselves,

17 [a]Acts 20:32; Gal 3:29; 4:7; Eph 3:6; Titus 3:7; Heb 1:14; Rev 21:7 [b]2 Cor 1:5, 7; Phil 3:10; Col 1:24; 2 Tim 2:12; 1 Pet 4:13 **18** [a]2 Cor 4:17; 1 Pet 4:13 [b]Col 3:4; Titus 2:13; 1 Pet 1:5; 5:1 **19** [a]Phil 1:20 [b]Rom 8:18; 1 Cor 1:7f; Col 3:4; 1 Pet 1:7, 13; 1 John 3:2 [c]Hos 1:10; Matt 5:9; John 1:12; Rom 8:14, 16; 9:8, 26; 2 Cor 6:18; Gal 3:26; 1 John 3:1; Rev 21:7 **20** [1]Or *in hope; because the creation* [a]Gen 3:17-19 [b]Ps 39:5f; Eccl 1:2 [c]Gen 3:17; 5:29 **21** [a]Acts 3:21; 2 Pet 3:13; Rev 21:1 **22** [a]Jer 12:4, 11 **23** [a]Rom 5:3 [b]Rom 8:16; 2 Cor 1:22 [c]2 Cor 5:2, 4

(v. 6), hostility to God (v. 7), insubordination (v. 7) and unacceptability to God (v. 8).

8:10 *though the body is dead because of sin.* Even a Christian's body is subject to physical death, the consequence of sin. *the spirit is alive.* Or "the Spirit is life" (see v. 2). On this reading, "body" is understood as in 7:24. *because of righteousness.* Because the spirit of the Christian has been justified, it is not subject to death as is his body. The Christian is indwelt by the life-giving Spirit as a result of his justification.

8:11 For the close connection between the resurrection of Christ and that of believers see 1 Cor 6:14; 15:20,23; 2 Cor 4:14; Phil 3:21; 1 Thess 4:14. *give life to your mortal bodies.* The resurrection of our bodies, guaranteed to believers by the indwelling presence of the Holy Spirit—whose presence is evidenced by a Spirit-controlled life (vv. 4–9), which in turn provides assurance that our resurrection is certain even now.

8:14 *sons of God.* God is the Father of all in the sense that He created all and His love and providential care are extended to all (see Matt 5:45). But not all are His children. Jesus said to the unbelieving Jews of His day, "You are of your father the devil" (John 8:44). People become children of God through faith in God's unique Son (see John 1:12–13), and being led by God's Spirit is the hallmark of this relationship.

8:15 *adoption.* The underlying Greek term for "adoption" occurs four other times in the NT (v. 23; 9:4; Gal 4:5 [see note there]; Eph 1:5). Adoption was common among the Greeks and Romans, who granted the adopted son all the privileges of a natural son, including inheritance rights. Christians are adopted sons by grace; Christ, however, is God's Son by nature. *Abba! Father!* Abba (Aramaic for "Father") is expressive of an especially close relationship to God.

8:16 *testifies with our spirit.* The inner testimony of the Holy Spirit to our relationship to Christ. *children of God.* The same as "sons of God," terms that in the NT are synonymous.

8:17 *heirs.* Those who have already entered, at least partially, into the possession of their inheritance. *fellow heirs with Christ.* Everything really belongs to Christ, but by grace we share in what is His. *if indeed we suffer with Him.* The Greek construction used here does not set forth a condition but states a fact. The meaning, then, is not that there is some doubt about sharing Christ's glory. Rather, despite the fact that Christians presently suffer, they are assured a future entrance into their inheritance.

8:19 *the creation.* Both animate and inanimate, but exclusive of human beings (see vv. 22–23, where "whole creation" and "we ourselves" are contrasted). *the revealing of the sons of God.* Christians are already sons of God, but the full manifestation of all that this means will not come until the end (see 1 John 3:1–2).

8:20 *was subjected to futility.* A reference to Gen 3:17–19. *in hope.* A possible allusion to the promise of Gen 3:15.

8:21 *will be set free from its slavery to corruption.* The physical universe is not destined for destruction (annihilation) but for renewal (see 2 Pet 3:13; Rev 21:1). And living things will no longer be subject to death and decay, as they are today.

8:22 *groans.* Creation is personified as a woman in labor waiting for the birth of her child.

8:23 *first fruits of the Spirit.* The Christian's possession of the Holy Spirit is not only evidence of his present salvation (vv. 14,16) but is also a pledge of his future inheritance—and not only a pledge but also the down payment on that inheritance (see 2 Cor 1:22; 5:5; Eph 1:14). *adoption as sons.* See note on v. 15. Christians are already God's children, but this is a reference to the full realization of our inheritance in Christ. *redemption of our body.* The resurrection, as the final stage of our adoption. The first stage was God's predestination of our adoption (see Eph 1:5); the second is our present inclusion as children of God (see v. 14; Gal 3:26).

[d]waiting eagerly for *our* adoption as sons,
[e]the redemption of our body.
24 For [a]in hope we have been saved, but
[b]hope that is seen is not hope; for who hopes
for what he *already* sees?
25 But [a]if we hope for what we do not see,
with perseverance we wait eagerly for it.

Our Victory in Christ

26 In the same way the Spirit also helps
our weakness; for [a]we do not know how to
pray as we should, but [b]the Spirit Himself
intercedes for *us* with groanings too deep for
words;
27 and [a]He who searches the hearts knows
what [b]the mind of the Spirit is, because He
[c]intercedes for the [1]saints according to *the*
will of God.
28 And we know that [1]God causes [a]all
things to work together for good to those
who love God, to those who are [b]called
according to *His* purpose.
29 For those whom He [a]foreknew, He also
[b]predestined *to become* [c]conformed to the
image of His Son, so that He would be the
[d]firstborn among many brethren;
30 and these whom He [a]predestined, He
also [b]called; and these whom He called, He
also [c]justified; and these whom He justified,
He also [d]glorified.
31 [a]What then shall we say to these
things? [b]If God *is* for us, who *is* against us?
32 He who [a]did not spare His own Son,
but [b]delivered Him over for us all, how will
He not also with Him freely give us all
things?
33 Who will bring a charge against [a]God's
elect? [b]God is the one who justifies;
34 who is the one who [a]condemns? Christ
Jesus is He who [b]died, yes, rather who was
[1c]raised, who is [d]at the right hand of God,
who also [e]intercedes for us.
35 Who will separate us from [a]the love of
[1]Christ? Will [b]tribulation, or distress, or [c]per-
secution, or [c]famine, or [c]nakedness, or [c]per-
il, or sword?
36 Just as it is written,

"[a]FOR YOUR SAKE WE ARE BEING PUT TO
DEATH ALL DAY LONG;
WE WERE CONSIDERED AS SHEEP TO BE
SLAUGHTERED."

37 But in all these things we overwhelmingly [a]conquer through [b]Him who loved us.
38 For I am convinced that neither [a]death,
nor life, nor [b]angels, nor principalities, nor
[a]things present, nor things to come, nor
powers,
39 nor height, nor depth, nor any other
created thing, will be able to separate us
from [a]the love of God, which is [b]in Christ
Jesus our Lord.

Solicitude for Israel

9 [a]I am telling the truth in Christ, I am not
lying, my conscience testifies with me in
the Holy Spirit,

23 [d]Rom 8:15, 19, 25; Gal 5:5 [e]Rom 7:24 **24** [a]Rom 8:20; 1 Thess 5:8; Titus 3:7 [b]Rom 4:18; 2 Cor 5:7; Heb 11:1 **25** [a]1 Thess 1:3 **26** [a]Matt 20:22; 2 Cor 12:8 [b]John 14:16; Rom 8:15f; Eph 6:18 **27** [1]Or *holy ones* [a]Ps 139:1f; Luke 16:15; Acts 1:24; Rev 2:23 [b]Rom 8:6 [c]Rom 8:34 **28** [1]One early ms reads *all things work together for good* [a]Rom 8:32 [b]Rom 8:30; 9:24; 11:29; 1 Cor 1:9; Gal 1:6, 15; 5:8; Eph 1:11; 3:11; 2 Thess 2:14; Heb 9:15; 1 Pet 2:9; 3:9 **29** [a]Rom 11:2; 1 Cor 8:3; 2 Tim 1:9; 1 Pet 1:2, 20 [b]Rom 9:23; 1 Cor 2:7; Eph 1:5, 11 [c]1 Cor 15:49; Phil 3:21 [d]Col 1:18; Heb 1:6 **30** [a]Rom 9:23; 11:29; 1 Cor 2:7; Eph 1:5, 11 [b]Rom 8:28; 9:24; 1 Cor 1:9; Gal 1:6, 15; 5:8; Eph 1:11; 3:11; 2 Thess 2:14; Heb 9:15; 1 Pet 2:9; 3:9 [c]1 Cor 6:11 [d]John 17:22; Rom 8:21; 9:23 **31** [a]Rom 3:5; 4:1 [b]Ps 118:6; Matt 1:23

32 [a]John 3:16; Rom 5:8 [b]Rom 4:25 **33** [a]Luke 18:7 [b]Is 50:8f **34** [1]One early ms reads *raised from the dead* [a]Rom 8:1 [b]Rom 5:6f [c]Acts 2:24 [d]Mark 16:19 [e]Rom 8:27; Heb 7:25 **35** [1]Two early mss read *God* [a]Rom 8:37f [b]Rom 2:9; 2 Cor 4:8 [c]1 Cor 4:11; 2 Cor 11:26f **36** [a]Ps 44:22; Acts 20:24; 1 Cor 4:9; 15:30f; 2 Cor 1:9; 4:10f; 6:9; 11:23 **37** [a]John 16:33; 1 Cor 15:57 [b]Gal 2:20; Eph 5:2; Rev 1:5 **38** [a]1 Cor 3:22 [b]1 Cor 15:24; Eph 1:21; 1 Pet 3:22 **39** [a]Rom 5:8 [b]Rom 8:1 **9:1** [a]2 Cor 11:10; Gal 1:20; 1 Tim 2:7

8:24 *in hope.* We are saved by faith (see Eph 2:8), not hope; but hope accompanies salvation.
8:26 *In the same way.* As hope sustains the believer in suffering, so the Holy Spirit helps him in prayer. *with groanings too deep for words.* In v. 23 it is the believer who groans; here it is the Holy Spirit. Whether Paul means words that are unspoken or words that cannot be expressed in human language is not clear—probably the former, though v. 27 seems to suggest the latter.
8:27 The relationship between the Holy Spirit and God the Father is so close that the Holy Spirit's prayers need not be audible. God knows His every thought.
8:28 *good.* That which conforms us "to the image of His Son" (v. 29). *called.* Effectual calling: the call of God to which there is invariably a positive response.
8:29 *foreknew.* Some insist that the knowledge here is not abstract but is couched in love and mixed with purpose. They hold that God not only knew us before we had any knowledge of Him but that He also knew us, in the sense of choosing us by His grace, before the foundation of the world (see Eph 1:4; 2 Tim 1:9 and notes). Others believe that Paul here refers to the fact that in eternity past God knew those who by faith would become His people. *predestined.* Predestination here is to moral conformity to the likeness of His Son. *that He would be the firstborn among many brethren.* The reason God foreknew, predestined and conformed believers to Christ's likeness is that the Son might hold the position of highest honor in the great family of God.
8:30 *predestined . . . glorified.* The sequence by which God carries out His predestination. *glorified.* Since this final stage is firmly grounded in God's set purpose, it is as certain as if it had already happened.
8:31 *If God is for us.* The form of the condition makes it clear that there is no doubt about it.
8:32 The argument (from the greater to the lesser) here is similar to that in 5:9–10. If God gave the supreme gift of His Son to save us, He will certainly also give whatever is necessary to bring to fulfillment the work begun at the cross. See note on Gen 22:16.
8:33–34 A court of law is in mind. No charge can be brought against the Christian because God has already pronounced a verdict of not guilty.
8:34 Three reasons are given as to why no one can condemn God's elect: (1) Christ died for us; (2) He is alive and seated at the right hand of God, the position of power; (3) He is interceding for us.
8:35–39 Paul wanted to show his readers that suffering does not separate believers from Christ but actually carries them along toward their ultimate goal.
8:36 Ps 44:22 is quoted to show that suffering has always been part of the experience of God's people.
8:37 *who loved us.* Referring especially to Christ's death on the cross.
8:39 *nor height, nor depth.* It is impossible to get beyond God's loving reach. *nor any other created thing.* Includes all created things. Only God is not included, and He is the one who has justified us (v. 33).
9:1 *in the Holy Spirit.* Conscience is a reliable guide only when enlightened by the Holy Spirit.

2 that I have great sorrow and unceasing
grief in my heart.
3 For [a]I could [1]wish that I myself were
[b]accursed, *separated* from Christ for the sake
of my brethren, my kinsmen [c]according to
the flesh,
4 who are [a]Israelites, to whom belongs
[b]the adoption as sons, and [c]the glory and
[d]the covenants and [e]the giving of the Law
and [f]the *temple* service and [g]the promises,
5 whose are [a]the fathers, and [b]from
whom is [1]the Christ according to the flesh,
[c]who is over all, [d]God [e]blessed [2]forever.
Amen.
6 But *it is* not as though [a]the word of
God has failed. [b]For they are not all Israel
who are *descended* from Israel;
7 nor are they all children [a]because they
are Abraham's [1]descendants, but: "[2][b]THROUGH
ISAAC YOUR [1]DESCENDANTS WILL BE NAMED."
8 That is, it is not the children of the flesh
who are [a]children of God, but the [b]children
of the promise are regarded as [1]descendants.
9 For this is the word of promise: "[a]AT
THIS TIME I WILL COME, AND SARAH SHALL HAVE A
SON."
10 [a]And not only this, but there was
[b]Rebekah also, when she had conceived
twins by one man, our father Isaac;

3 [1]Lit *pray* [a]Ex 32:32 [b]1 Cor 12:3; 16:22; Gal 1:8f [c]Rom 1:3; 11:14; Eph 6:5 **4** [a]Deut 7:6; 14:1f; Rom 9:6 [b]Ex 4:22; Rom 8:15 [c]Ex 40:34; 1 Kin 8:11; Ezek 1:28; Heb 9:5 [d]Gen 17:2; Deut 29:14; Luke 1:72; Acts 3:25; Eph 2:12 [e]Deut 4:13f; Ps 147:19 [f]Heb 9:1, 6 [g]Acts 2:39; 13:32; Eph 2:12 **5** [1]I.e. the Messiah [2]Lit *unto the ages* [a]Acts 3:13; Rom 11:28 [b]Matt 1:1-16; Rom 1:3 [c]Col 1:16-19 [d]John 1:1 [e]Rom 1:25 **6** [a]Num 23:19 [b]John 1:47; Rom 2:28f; Gal 6:16 **7** [1]Lit *seed* [2]Lit *in* [a]John 8:33, 39; Gal 4:23 [b]Gen 21:12; Heb 11:18 **8** [1]Lit *seed* [a]Rom 8:14 [b]Rom 4:13, 16; Gal 3:29; 4:28; Heb 11:11 **9** [a]Gen 18:10 **10** [a]Rom 5:3 [b]Gen 25:21

11 for though *the twins* were not yet born
and had not done anything good or bad, so
that [a]God's purpose according to *His* choice
would [1]stand, not [2]because of works but
[2]because of Him who calls,
12 it was said to her, "[a]THE OLDER WILL
SERVE THE YOUNGER."
13 Just as it is written, "[a]JACOB I LOVED, BUT
ESAU I HATED."
14 [a]What shall we say then? [b]There is no
injustice with God, is there? [c]May it never
be!
15 For He says to Moses, "[a]I WILL HAVE MER-
CY ON WHOM I HAVE MERCY, AND I WILL HAVE
COMPASSION ON WHOM I HAVE COMPASSION."
16 So then it *does* not *depend* on the man
who wills or the man who [a]runs, but on
[b]God who has mercy.
17 For the Scripture says to Pharaoh,
"[a]FOR THIS VERY PURPOSE I RAISED YOU UP, TO
DEMONSTRATE MY POWER IN YOU, AND THAT MY
NAME MIGHT BE PROCLAIMED [1]THROUGHOUT THE
WHOLE EARTH."
18 So then He has mercy on whom He
desires, and He [a]hardens whom He desires.

11 [1]Lit *remain* [2]Lit *from* [a]Rom 4:17; 8:28 **12** [a]Gen 25:23 **13** [a]Mal 1:2f **14** [a]Rom 3:5 [b]2 Chr 19:7; Rom 2:11 [c]Luke 20:16 **15** [a]Ex 33:19 **16** [a]Gal 2:2 [b]Eph 2:8 **17** [1]Lit *in* [a]Ex 9:16 **18** [a]Ex 4:21; 7:3; 9:12; 10:20, 27; 11:10; 14:4, 17; Deut 2:30; Josh 11:20; John 12:40; Rom 11:7, 25

9:3 *accursed.* The Greek for this word is *anathema,* and it means delivered over to the wrath of God for eternal destruction (see 1 Cor 12:3; 16:22; Gal 1:8–9). Such was Paul's great love for his fellow Jews. For a similar expression of love see Ex 32:32.
9:4 *Israelites.* The descendants of Jacob (who was renamed Israel by God; see Gen 32:28). The name was used of the entire nation (see Judg 5:7), then of the northern kingdom after the nation was divided (see 1 Kin 12), the southern kingdom being called Judah. During the intertestamental period and later in NT times, Palestinian Jews used the title to indicate that they were the chosen people of God. Its use here is especially relevant because Paul is about to show that, despite Israel's unbelief and disobedience, God's promises to her are still valid. *adoption.* Israel had been accepted as God's son (see Ex 4:22–23; Jer 31:9; Hos 11:1). *glory.* The evidence of the presence of God among His people (see Ex 16:7,10; Lev 9:6,23; Num 16:19). *covenants.* For example, the Abrahamic (Gen 15:17–21; 17:1–8); the Mosaic (Ex 19:5; 24:1–4), renewed on the plains of Moab (Deut 29:1–15), at Mounts Ebal and Gerizim (Josh 8:30–35) and at Shechem (Josh 24); the Levitical (Num 25:12–13; Jer 33:21; Mal 2:4–5); the Davidic (2 Sam 7; 23:5; Ps 89:3–4,28–29; 132:11–12); and the new (prophesied in Jer 31:31–40). *promises.* Especially those made to Abraham (Gen 12:7; 13:14–17; 17:4–8; 22:16–18) but also including the many OT Messianic promises (e.g., 2 Sam 7:12,16; Is 9:6–7; Jer 23:5; 31:31–34; Ezek 34:23–24; 37:24–28).
9:5 *fathers.* Abraham, Isaac, Jacob and his sons. *Christ . . . who is over all, God.* One of the clearest statements of the deity of Jesus Christ found in the entire NT, assuming that "God" refers to "Christ." See also 1:4; Matt 1:23; 28:19; Luke 1:35; 5:20–21; John 1:1,3,10,14,18; 5:18; 20:28; 2 Cor 13:14; Phil 2:6; Col 1:15–20; 2:9; Titus 2:13; Heb 1:3,8; 2 Pet 1:1; Rev 1:13–18; 22:13.
9:6 *word of God.* His clearly stated purpose, which has not failed, because "they are not all Israel who are descended from Israel." Paul is not denying the election of all Israel (as a nation) but stating that within Israel there is a separation, that of unbelieving Israel and believing Israel. Physical descent is no guarantee of a place in God's family.
9:7 *descendants.* Physical descendants (e.g., Ishmael and his offspring).
9:8 *children of the flesh.* Those merely biologically descended from Abraham. *children of God.* See v. 4. Not all Israelites were God's children. The reference is to the Israel of faith.
9:11 *done anything good or bad.* God's choice of Jacob was based on sovereign freedom, not on the fulfillment of any prior conditions. *God's purpose according to His choice.* God's purpose embodied in His election (see note on Eph 1:4). *not because of works but because of Him who calls.* Before Rebekah's children were even born, God made a choice—a choice obviously not based on works. *calls.* See 8:28 and note.
9:13 *JACOB I LOVED, BUT ESAU I HATED.* Equivalent to "Jacob I chose, but Esau I rejected." In vv. 6–13 Paul is clearly dealing with personal and not national election—he is not portraying the nation Israel (Jacob) over the nation Edom (Esau)—though Mal 1:2–3 does speak of the nations. Paul's intention is evident in light of the problem he is addressing: How can God's promise stand when so many who comprise Israel (in the OT collective sense) are unbelieving and therefore cut off?
9:14 *There is no injustice with God, is there?* Unjust to elect on the basis of His sovereign freedom, as with Jacob and Esau.
9:15 Paul denies injustice in God's dealing with Isaac and Ishmael, and Jacob and Esau, by appealing to God's sovereign right to dispense mercy as He chooses.
9:16 *it.* God's choice, which is not controlled in any way by man. However, Paul makes it clear that the basis for Israel's rejection was her unbelief (see vv. 30–32).
9:17 *Pharaoh.* Pharaoh of the exodus. *RAISED YOU UP.* Made you ruler of Egypt. *MY NAME.* The character of God, particularly as revealed in the exodus (see Ex 15:13–18; Josh 2:10–11; 9:9; 1 Sam 4:8).
9:18 The first part of this verse again echoes Ex 33:19 (see v. 15) and the last part such texts as Ex 7:3; 9:12; 14:4,17, in which

19 [a]You will say to me then, "[b]Why does
He still find fault? For [c]who resists His will?"
20 On the contrary, who are you, [a]O man,
who [b]answers back to God? [c]The thing mold-
ed will not say to the molder, "Why did you
make me like this," will it?
21 Or does not the potter have a right over
the clay, to make from the same lump one
vessel [1]for honorable use and another [2]for
common use?
22 [1]What if God, although willing to
demonstrate His wrath and to make His
power known, endured with much [a]patience
vessels of wrath [b]prepared for destruction?
23 And *He did so* to make known [a]the
riches of His glory upon [b]vessels of mercy,
which He [c]prepared beforehand for glory,
24 *even* us, whom He also [a]called, [b]not
from among Jews only, but also from among
Gentiles.
25 As He says also in Hosea,
"[a]I WILL CALL THOSE WHO WERE NOT MY
PEOPLE, 'MY PEOPLE,'
AND HER WHO WAS NOT BELOVED,
'BELOVED.' "
26 "[a]AND IT SHALL BE THAT IN THE PLACE
WHERE IT WAS SAID TO THEM, 'YOU ARE
NOT MY PEOPLE,'
THERE THEY SHALL BE CALLED SONS OF
[b]THE LIVING GOD."
27 Isaiah cries out concerning Israel,
"[a]THOUGH THE NUMBER OF THE SONS OF ISRAEL BE
[b]LIKE THE SAND OF THE SEA, IT IS [c]THE REMNANT
THAT WILL BE SAVED;

19 [a]Rom 11:19; 1 Cor 15:35; James 2:18 [b]Rom 3:7 [c]2 Chr 20:6; Job 9:12; Dan 4:35
20 [a]Rom 2:1 [b]Job 33:13 [c]Is 29:16; 45:9; 64:8; Jer 18:6; Rom 9:22f; 2 Tim 2:20
21 [1]Lit *for honor* [2]Lit *for dishonor*
22 [1]Lit *But* [a]Rom 2:4 [b]Prov 16:4; 1 Pet 2:8
23 [a]Rom 2:4; Eph 3:16 [b]Acts 9:15 [c]Rom 8:29f
24 [a]Rom 8:28 [b]Rom 3:29
25 [a]Hos 2:23; 1 Pet 2:10
26 [a]Hos 1:10 [b]Matt 16:16
27 [a]Is 10:22 [b]Gen 22:17; Hos 1:10 [c]Rom 11:5
28 [1]Lit *finishing it* [2]Lit *cutting it short* [a]Is 10:23
29 [1]I.e. Hosts [2]Lit *seed* [3]Lit *been made like* [a]Is 1:9 [b]James 5:4 [c]Deut 29:23; Is 13:19; Jer 49:18; 50:40; Amos 4:11
30 [1]Lit *out of* [a]Rom 9:14 [b]Rom 1:17; 3:21f; 10:6; Gal 2:16; 3:24; Phil 3:9; Heb 11:7
31 [a]Is 51:1; Rom 9:30; 10:2f, 20; 11:7 [b]Gal 5:4

28 [a]FOR THE LORD WILL EXECUTE HIS WORD ON
THE EARTH, [1]THOROUGHLY AND [2]QUICKLY."
29 And just as Isaiah foretold,
"[a]UNLESS [b]THE LORD OF [1]SABAOTH HAD
LEFT TO US A [2]POSTERITY,
[c]WE WOULD HAVE BECOME LIKE SODOM,
AND WOULD HAVE [3]RESEMBLED
GOMORRAH."
30 [a]What shall we say then? That Gentiles, who did not pursue righteousness,
attained righteousness, even [b]the righteousness which is [1]by faith;
31 but Israel, [a]pursuing a law of righteousness, did not [b]arrive at *that* law.
32 Why? Because *they did* not *pursue it*
[1]by faith, but as though *it were* [1]by works.
They stumbled over [a]the stumbling stone,
33 just as it is written,
"[a]BEHOLD, I LAY IN ZION [b]A STONE OF
STUMBLING AND A ROCK OF OFFENSE,
[c]AND HE WHO BELIEVES IN HIM [d]WILL NOT
BE [1]DISAPPOINTED."

The Word of Faith Brings Salvation

10 Brethren, my heart's desire and my
prayer to God for them is for *their* salvation.
2 For I testify about them that they have
[a]a zeal for God, but not in accordance with
knowledge.
3 For not knowing about [a]God's righ-

32 [1]Lit *out of* [a]Is 8:14; 1 Pet 2:6, 8 [b]Is 8:14 [c]Rom 10:11 [d]Rom 5:5
33 [1]Lit *put to shame* [a]Is 28:16 [b]Is 8:14 [c]Rom 10:11 [d]Rom 5:5
3 [a]Rom 1:17
10:2 [a]Acts 21:20

God is said to harden the hearts of Pharaoh and the Egyptians. *on whom He desires.* Cannot mean that God is arbitrary in His mercy, because Paul ultimately bases God's rejection of Israel on her unbelief (see vv. 30–32).

9:19 Someone may object: "If God determines whose heart is hardened and whose is not, how can God blame anyone for hardening his heart?"

9:20 *who are you, O man, who answers back to God?* Paul is not silencing all questioning of God by man, but he is speaking to those with an impenitent, God-defying attitude who want to make God answerable to man for what He does and who, by their questions, defame the character of God.

9:21 The analogy between God and the potter and between man and the pot should not be pressed to the extreme. The main point is the sovereign freedom of God in dealing with man.

9:22–23 An illustration of the principle stated in v. 21. The emphasis is on God's mercy, not His wrath.

9:22 No one can call God to account for what He does. But He does not exercise His freedom of choice arbitrarily, and He shows great patience even toward the objects of His wrath. In light of 2:4, the purpose of such patience is to bring about repentance.

9:23 *glory.* See note on 3:23.

9:25–26 In the original context these passages from Hosea refer to the spiritual restoration of Israel. But Paul finds in them the principle that God is a saving, forgiving, restoring God, who delights to take those who are "not My people" and make them "My people." Paul then applies this principle to Gentiles, whom God makes His people by sovereignly grafting them into covenant relationship (see ch. 11).

9:27–29 The two passages from Isaiah indicate that only a small remnant will survive from the great multitude of Israelites. God's calling includes both Jews and Gentiles (see v. 24), but the vast majority are Gentiles, as v. 30 suggests.

9:30–32 A new step in Paul's argument: The reason for Israel's rejection lay in the nature of her disobedience—she failed to obey her own God-given law, which in reality was pointing to Christ. She pursued the law—yet not by faith but by works. Thus the real cause of Israel's rejection was that she failed to believe.

9:31 *law of righteousness.* The law that prescribed the way to righteousness. Paul does not reject obedience to the law but righteousness by works, the attempt to use the law to put God in one's debt.

9:32 *not . . . by faith.* The failure of Israel was not that she pursued the wrong thing (i.e., righteous standing before God), but that she pursued it by works in a futile effort to merit God's favor rather than pursuing it by faith. *the stumbling stone.* Jesus, the Messiah. God's rejection of Israel was not arbitrary but was based on Israel's rejection of God's way of gaining righteousness (faith).

9:33 The two passages from Isaiah, which are here combined, apparently were commonly used by early Christians in defense of Jesus' Messiahship (see 1 Pet 2:4,6–8; see also Ps 118:22; Luke 20:17–18).

10:1 *prayer to God for them.* Paul often prayed for the churches (see Eph 1:15–23; Col 1:3; 1 Thess 1:2–3; 2 Thess 1:3). Here he prays for the salvation of his fellow countrymen.

10:2 *zeal for God.* The Jews' zeal for God (see Acts 21:20; 22:3; Gal 1:14) was commendable in that God was its object, but it was flawed because it was not based on right knowledge about God's way of salvation. Paul, before his conversion, was an example of such zeal (see Gal 1:14).

teousness and [b]seeking to establish their
own, they did not subject themselves to the
righteousness of God.
4 For [a]Christ is the [1]end of the law for
righteousness to [b]everyone who believes.
5 For Moses writes that the man who
practices the righteousness which is [1]based
on law [a]shall live [2]by that righteousness.
6 But [a]the righteousness [1]based on faith
speaks as follows: "[b]DO NOT SAY IN YOUR
HEART, 'WHO WILL ASCEND INTO HEAVEN?' (that
is, to bring Christ down),
7 or 'WHO WILL DESCEND INTO THE [a]ABYSS?'
(that is, to [b]bring Christ up from the dead)."
8 But what does it say? "[a]THE WORD IS
NEAR YOU, in your mouth and in your
heart"—that is, the word of faith which we
are preaching,
9 [1]that [a]if you confess with your mouth
Jesus *as* Lord, and [b]believe in your heart that
[c]God raised Him from the dead, you will be
saved;
10 for with the heart a person believes,
[1]resulting in righteousness, and with the
mouth he confesses, [2]resulting in salvation.
11 For the Scripture says, "[a]WHOEVER
BELIEVES IN HIM WILL NOT BE [1]DISAPPOINTED."
12 For [a]there is no distinction between Jew
and Greek; for the same *Lord* is [b]Lord of [c]all,
abounding in riches for all who call on Him;
13 for "[a]WHOEVER WILL CALL ON THE NAME OF
THE LORD WILL BE SAVED."
14 How then will they call on Him in
whom they have not believed? How will they
believe in Him [a]whom they have not heard?
And how will they hear without [b]a preacher?
15 How will they preach unless they are
sent? Just as it is written, "[a]HOW BEAUTIFUL
ARE THE FEET OF THOSE WHO [1b]BRING GOOD NEWS
OF GOOD THINGS!"
16 However, they [a]did not all heed the
[1]good news; for Isaiah says, "[b]LORD, WHO HAS
BELIEVED OUR REPORT?"
17 So faith *comes* from [a]hearing, and hearing by [b]the word [1]of Christ.
18 But I say, surely they have never heard,
have they? Indeed they have;

"[a]THEIR VOICE HAS GONE OUT INTO ALL THE
EARTH,
AND THEIR WORDS TO THE ENDS OF THE
[1]WORLD."

3 [b]Is 51:1; Rom 10:2f, 20; 11:7 **4** [1]Or *goal* [a]Rom 7:1-4; Gal 3:24; 4:5 [b]Rom 3:22 **5** [1]Lit *out of, from* [2]Lit *by it* [a]Lev 18:5; Neh 9:29; Ezek 20:11, 13, 21; Rom 7:10 **6** [1]Lit *out of, from* [a]Rom 9:30 [b]Deut 30:12 **7** [a]Luke 8:31 [b]Heb 13:20 **8** [a]Deut 30:14 **9** [1]Or *because* [a]Matt 10:32; Luke 12:8; Rom 14:9; 1 Cor 12:3; Phil 2:11 [b]Acts 16:31; Rom 4:24 [c]Acts 2:24 **10** [1]Lit *to righteousness* [2]Lit *to salvation* **11** [1]Lit *put to shame* [a]Is 28:16; Rom 9:33

12 [a]Rom 3:22, 29 [b]Acts 10:36 [c]Rom 3:29 **13** [a]Joel 2:32; Acts 2:21 **14** [a]Eph 2:17; 4:21 [b]Acts 8:31; Titus 1:3

15 [1]Or *preach the gospel* [a]Is 52:7 [b]Rom 1:15; 15:20 **16** [1]Or *gospel* [a]Rom 3:3 [b]Is 53:1; John 12:38 **17** [1]Or *concerning Christ* [a]Gal 3:2, 5 [b]Col 3:16 **18** [1]Or *inhabited earth* [a]Ps 19:4; Rom 1:8; Col 1:6, 23; 1 Thess 1:8

10:3 *their own.* Righteous standing based on mere human effort. *righteousness of God.* Righteous standing based on faith (see 1:17), which comes from God as a gift and cannot be earned by man's works.
10:4 *Christ is the end of the law.* Although the Greek word for "end" (*telos*) can mean either (1) "termination," "cessation," or (2) "goal," "culmination," "fulfillment," it seems best here to understand it in the latter sense. Christ is the fulfillment of the law (see Matt 5:17) in the sense that He brought it to completion by obeying perfectly its demands and by fulfilling its types and prophecies. The Christian is no longer "under law" (6:15), since Christ has freed him from its condemnation, but the law still plays a role in his life. He is liberated by the Holy Spirit to fulfill its moral demands (see 8:4). *righteousness.* The righteous standing before God that Christ makes available to everyone who believes (see notes on 1:17; 3:24).
10:5 *the man who practices . . . righteousness . . . shall live by that righteousness.* Lev 18:5 (see note there; see also Deut 6:25) speaks of the righteousness to which Israel was called under the Sinai covenant. Some understand Paul's purpose in quoting it here as describing the way of obtaining righteousness ("shall live") by keeping the law (see 2:6–10). Others think that the reference is to Christ, who perfectly fulfilled the law's demands and thus makes salvation available to all who believe (see Heb 5:9).
10:6–7 The purpose of the OT quotation is to explain the nature of the righteousness that is by faith. It does not require heroic feats such as bringing Christ down from heaven or up from the grave. Deut 30:12–13 in its original context refers to the law, and Paul here applies the basic principle to Christ.
10:8 *THE WORD IS NEAR YOU.* In the OT passage the "word" is God's word as found in the law. Paul takes the passage and applies it to the gospel, "the word of faith"—the main point being the accessibility of the gospel. Righteousness is gained by faith, not by deeds, and is readily available to anyone who will receive it freely from God through Christ.
10:9 *Jesus as Lord.* The earliest Christian confession of faith (cf. 1 Cor 12:3), probably used at baptisms. In view of the fact that "Lord" (Greek *kyrios*) is used over 6,000 times in the Septuagint (the Greek translation of the OT) to translate the name of Israel's God (Yahweh), it is clear that Paul, when using this word of Jesus, is ascribing deity to him. *in your heart.* In Biblical terms the heart is not merely the seat of the emotions and affections, but also of the intellect and will. *God raised Him from the dead.* A bedrock truth of Christian doctrine (see 1 Cor 15:4,14,17) and the central thrust of apostolic preaching (see, e.g., Acts 2:31–32; 3:15; 4:10; 10:40). Christians believe not only that Jesus lived but also that He still lives. *will be saved.* In the future tense. Paul is thinking of final salvation—salvation at the last day.
10:10 Salvation involves inward belief ("with the heart") as well as outward confession ("with the mouth").
10:12 *no distinction between Jew and Greek.* In the sense that both are on the same footing as far as salvation is concerned (see v. 13).
10:13 Peter cited this same passage (Joel 2:32) on the day of Pentecost (Acts 2:21).
10:14–15 Since it might be argued that Jews had never had a fair opportunity to hear and respond to the gospel, Paul, by means of a series of rhetorical questions, states (in reverse order) the conditions necessary to call on Christ and be saved: (1) a preacher sent from God, (2) proclamation of the message, (3) hearing the message, (4) believing the message.
10:15 *HOW BEAUTIFUL ARE THE FEET OF THOSE WHO BRING GOOD NEWS.* The quotation is from Is 52:7, which refers to those who bring the exiles the good news of their imminent release from captivity in Babylon. Here it is applied to gospel preachers, who bring the good news of release from captivity to sin.
10:17 *word of Christ.* Either (1) the gospel concerning Christ, or (2) Christ speaking His message through His messengers.
10:18 *THEIR VOICE.* The quotation is from Ps 19:4, which refers to the testimony of the heavens to the glory of God. Here "their voice" is applied to gospel preachers and is used to show that Israel cannot offer the excuse that she did not have opportunity to hear, since preachers went everywhere. These words (originally used to describe God's revelation in nature) aptly describe the widespread preaching of the gospel, and Paul uses

19 But I say, surely Israel did not know,
did they? First Moses says,
"[a]I WILL [b]MAKE YOU JEALOUS BY THAT
WHICH IS NOT A NATION,
BY A NATION WITHOUT UNDERSTANDING
WILL I ANGER YOU."
20 And Isaiah is very bold and says,
"[a]I WAS FOUND BY THOSE WHO DID NOT SEEK
ME,
I BECAME MANIFEST TO THOSE WHO DID NOT
ASK FOR ME."
21 But as for Israel He says, "[a]ALL THE DAY
LONG I HAVE STRETCHED OUT MY HANDS TO A DIS-
OBEDIENT AND OBSTINATE PEOPLE."

Israel Is Not Cast Away

11 I say then, God has not [a]rejected His
people, has He? [b]May it never be! For [c]I
too am an Israelite, [1]a descendant of Abraham, of the tribe of Benjamin.
2 God [a]has not rejected His people
whom He [b]foreknew. [c]Or do you not know
what the Scripture says in *the passage about*
Elijah, how he pleads with God against Israel?
3 "Lord, [a]THEY HAVE KILLED YOUR PROPHETS,
THEY HAVE TORN DOWN YOUR ALTARS, AND I ALONE
AM LEFT, AND THEY ARE SEEKING MY LIFE."
4 But what [1]is the divine response to
him? "[a]I HAVE KEPT for Myself SEVEN THOUSAND
MEN WHO HAVE NOT BOWED THE KNEE TO BAAL."
5 In the same way then, there has also
come to be at the present time [a]a remnant
according to *God's* [1]gracious choice.
6 But [a]if it is by grace, it is no longer [1]on
the basis of works, otherwise grace is no
longer grace.
7 What then? What [a]Israel is seeking, it
has not obtained, but [1]those who were chosen obtained it, and the rest were [b]hardened;
8 just as it is written,
"[a]GOD GAVE THEM A SPIRIT OF STUPOR,
EYES TO SEE NOT AND EARS TO HEAR NOT,
DOWN TO THIS VERY DAY."
9 And David says,
"[a]LET THEIR TABLE BECOME A SNARE AND A
TRAP,
AND A STUMBLING BLOCK AND A
RETRIBUTION TO THEM.
10 "[a]LET THEIR EYES BE DARKENED TO SEE NOT,
AND BEND THEIR BACKS FOREVER."
11 [a]I say then, they did not stumble so as
to fall, did they? [b]May it never be! But by
their transgression [c]salvation *has come* to the
Gentiles, to [d]make them jealous.
12 Now if their transgression is riches for
the world and their failure is riches for the
Gentiles, how much more will their [1a]fulfill-
ment be!
13 But I am speaking to you who are Gentiles. Inasmuch then as [a]I am an apostle of
Gentiles, I magnify my ministry,
14 if somehow I might [a]move to jealousy
[b]my [1]fellow countrymen and [c]save some of
them.
15 For if their rejection is the [a]reconcilia-
tion of the world, what will *their* acceptance
be but [b]life from the dead?

19 [a]Deut 32:21 [b]Rom 11:11, 14 **20** [a]Is 65:1; Rom 9:30 **21** [a]Is 65:2 **11:1** [1]Lit *of the seed of Abraham* [a]1 Sam 12:22; Jer 31:37; 33:24-26 [b]Luke 20:16 [c]2 Cor 11:22; Phil 3:5 **2** [a]Ps 94:14 [b]Rom 8:29 [c]Rom 6:16 **3** [a]1 Kin 19:10, 14 **4** [1]Lit *says* [a]1 Kin 19:18 **5** [1]Lit *choice of grace* [a]2 Kin 19:4; Rom 9:27 **6** [1]Lit *out of* [a]Rom 4:4 **7** [1]Lit *the election* [a]Rom 9:31 [b]Mark 6:52; Rom 9:18; 11:25; 2 Cor 3:14 **8** [a]Deut 29:4; Is 29:10; Matt 13:13f **9** [a]Ps 69:22 **10** [a]Ps 69:23 **11** [a]Rom 11:1 [b]Luke 20:16 [c]Acts 28:28 [d]Rom 11:14 **12** [1]Or *fullness* [a]Rom 11:25 **13** [a]Acts 9:15 **14** [1]Lit *flesh* [a]Rom 11:11 [b]Gen 29:14; 2 Sam 19:12f; Rom 9:3 [c]1 Cor 1:21; 7:16; 9:22; 1 Tim 1:15; 2:4; 2 Tim 1:9; Titus 3:5 **15** [a]Rom 5:11 [b]Luke 15:24, 32

them to show that Jews had ample opportunity to hear the message of redemption.

10:19 *surely Israel did not know, did they?* The quotation that follows (from Deut 32:21) answers this question by suggesting that the Gentiles, whom the Jews considered to be spiritually unenlightened, understood. Surely if they understood the message, the Jews could have. *THAT WHICH IS NOT A NATION.* The Gentiles, those who are not a nation of God's forming in the sense that Israel was.

10:21 The responsibility for Israel's rejection as a nation rested with Israel herself. She had failed to meet God's requirement, namely, faith.

11:1 *rejected.* Totally rejected. There has always been a faithful remnant among the Jewish people.

11:2 *whom He foreknew.* See note on 8:29.

11:5 *remnant.* As it was in Elijah's day, so it was in Paul's day. Despite widespread apostasy, a faithful remnant of Jews remained. *according to God's gracious choice.* The grounds for the existence of the remnant was not their good works but God's grace.

11:7 *What Israel is seeking.* A righteous standing before God, which eluded the greater part of Israel. *those who were chosen.* The faithful remnant among the Jews. *were hardened.* Because they refused the way of faith (see 9:31–32), God made them impervious to spiritual truth (see notes on Is 6:8–10)—a judicial hardening of Israel.

11:8 *TO THIS VERY DAY.* The spiritual dullness of the Jews had continued from Isaiah's day to Paul's day.

11:9–10 The passage from Ps 69:22–23 was probably originally spoken by David concerning his enemies; Paul uses it to describe the results of the divine hardening.

11:11 *their transgression.* The Jews' rejection of the gospel. *make them jealous.* See v. 14; 10:19.

11:12 *riches for the world.* Equivalent to "riches for the Gentiles," a reference to the abundant benefits of salvation already enjoyed by believing Gentiles, which had come about because of the rejection of the gospel by the Jews. That rejection caused the apostles to turn to the Gentiles (see Acts 13:46–48; 18:6). *their failure.* Equivalent to "their transgression" (see note on v. 11), but focusing on the loss that this transgression entailed. *how much more.* See note on v. 15. *their fulfillment.* The salvation of Israel (see vv. 26–27; see also the "fullness of the Gentiles," v. 25).

11:13 *apostle of Gentiles.* See 1:5; Acts 9:15; Gal 1:16; 2:7,9.

11:15 *their rejection.* God's temporary and partial exclusion of the Jews. *reconciliation of the world.* Somewhat equivalent to "riches for the world" (see note on v. 12). *life from the dead.* Equivalent to "how much more" in v. 12. The sequence of redemptive events is: The "transgression" and "failure" (v. 12) of Israel leads to the salvation of the Gentiles, which leads to the jealousy or envy of Israel, which leads to the "fulfillment" (v. 12) of Israel when the hardening is removed, which leads to even more riches for the Gentiles. But to what does the "how much more" (v. 12) for the Gentiles refer, which Paul describes here as "life from the dead"? Three views may be suggested: (1) an unprecedented spiritual awakening in the world; (2) the consummation of redemption at the resurrection of the dead; (3) a figurative expression describing the conversion of the Jews as a joyful and glorious event (like resurrection)—which will result in even greater blessing for the world. Of these three

16 If the [a]first piece *of dough* is holy, the
lump is also; and if the root is holy, the
branches are too.
17 But if some of the [a]branches were broken off, and [b]you, being a wild olive, were
grafted in among them and became partaker
with them of the [1]rich root of the olive tree,
18 do not be arrogant toward the
branches; but if you are arrogant, *remember*
that [a]it is not you who supports the root, but
the root *supports* you.
19 [a]You will say then, "Branches were
broken off so that I might be grafted in."
20 Quite right, they were broken off for
their unbelief, but you [a]stand by your faith.
[b]Do not be conceited, but fear;
21 for if God did not spare the natural
branches, He will not spare you, either.
22 Behold then the kindness and severity
of God; to those who fell, severity, but to
you, God's [a]kindness, [b]if you continue in His
kindness; otherwise you also [c]will be cut off.
23 And they also, [a]if they do not continue
in their unbelief, will be grafted in, for God is
able to graft them in again.
24 For if you were cut off from what is by
nature a wild olive tree, and were grafted
contrary to nature into a cultivated olive tree,
how much more will these who are the natural *branches* be grafted into their own olive
tree?
25 For [a]I do not want you, brethren, to be
uninformed of this [b]mystery—so that you
will not be [c]wise in your own estimation—
that a partial [d]hardening has happened to
Israel until the [e]fullness of the Gentiles has
come in;
26 and so all Israel will be saved; just as it
is written,

"[a]THE DELIVERER WILL COME FROM ZION,
HE WILL REMOVE UNGODLINESS FROM
JACOB."
27 "[a]THIS IS [1]MY COVENANT WITH THEM,
[b]WHEN I TAKE AWAY THEIR SINS."

16 [a]Num 15:18ff; Neh 10:37; Ezek 44:30
17 [1]Lit *root of the fatness* [a]Jer 11:16; John 15:2 [b]Eph 2:11ff
18 [a]John 4:22
19 [a]Rom 9:19
20 [a]Rom 5:2; 1 Cor 10:12; 2 Cor 1:24 [b]Rom 12:16; 1 Tim 6:17; 1 Pet 1:17
22 [a]Rom 2:4 [b]1 Cor 15:2; Heb 3:6, 14 [c]John 15:2
23 [a]2 Cor 3:16
25 [a]Rom 1:13 [b]Matt 13:11; Rom 16:25; 1 Cor 2:7-10; Eph 3:3-5, 9 [c]Rom 12:16 [d]Rom 11:7 [e]Luke 21:24; John 10:16; Rom 11:12
26 [a]Is 59:20
27 [1]Lit *the covenant from Me* [a]Is 59:21; Jer 31:33, 34; Heb 8:10 [b]Is 27:9; Heb 8:12

views the first seems least likely, since, before Israel's spiritual rebirth, the fullness of the Gentiles will already have come in (see v. 25). Since the Gentile mission will then be complete, there seems to be no place for a period of unprecedented spiritual awakening. The second view also seems unlikely, since the context suggests nothing of bodily resurrection.

11:16 The first half of this verse is a reference to Num 15:17–21. Part of the dough made from the first of the harvested grain (first fruits) was offered to the Lord. This consecrated the whole batch. *first piece of dough.* The patriarchs. *lump.* The Jewish people. *holy.* Not that all Jews are righteous (i.e., saved) but that God will be true to His promises concerning them (see 3:3–4). Paul foresaw a future for Israel, even though she was for a time set aside. *root.* The patriarchs. *branches.* The Jewish people.

11:17 *branches.* Individual Jews. *wild olive.* Gentile Christians. *grafted in.* The usual procedure was to insert a shoot or slip of a cultivated tree into a common or wild one. In vv. 17–24, however, the metaphor is used, "contrary to nature" (v. 24), of grafting a wild olive branch (the Gentiles) into the cultivated olive tree. Such a procedure is unnatural, which is precisely the point. Normally, such a graft would be unfruitful. *rich root.* The patriarchs. The whole olive tree represents the people of God.

11:18 *the root supports you.* The salvation of Gentile Christians is dependent on the Jews, especially the patriarchs (e.g., the Abrahamic covenant). See John 4:22.

11:19 *Branches.* Unbelieving Jews.

11:20 *fear.* On the fear of God see note on Gen 20:11; see also Prov 3:7; Phil 2:12–13; Heb 4:1, "be careful"; 1 Pet 1:17.

11:22 *kindness and severity of God.* Any adequate doctrine of God must include these two elements. When we ignore His kindness, God seems a ruthless tyrant; when we ignore His sternness, He seems a doting Father.

11:23 *God is able to graft them in again.* Paul holds out hope for the Jews—God is able (see Matt 19:26; Mark 10:27; Luke 18:27).

11:24 *contrary to nature.* Paul recognized that such grafting was not commonly practiced (see note on v. 17). The inclusion of Gentiles in the family of God is "contrary to nature" (cf. Eph 2:12). Obviously, the reasoning in this verse is more theological than horticultural. It would be difficult horticulturally to graft broken branches back into the parent tree, but the Jews really "belong" (historically and theologically) to the parent tree. Thus they will "much more . . . be grafted into their own olive tree."

11:25 *mystery.* The so-called mystery religions of Paul's day used the Greek word (*mysterion*) in the sense of something that was to be revealed only to the initiated. Paul himself, however, used it to refer to something formerly hidden or obscure but now revealed by God for all to know and understand (see 16:25; 1 Cor 2:7; 4:1; 13:2; 14:2; 15:51; Eph 1:9; 3:3–4,9; 5:32; 6:19; Col 1:26–27; 2:2; 4:3; 2 Thess 2:7; 1 Tim 3:9,16). The word is used of (1) the incarnation (1 Tim 3:16; see note there), (2) the death of Christ (1 Cor 2:7, "God's wisdom is a mystery"), (3) God's purpose to sum up all things in Christ (Eph 1:9) and especially to include both Jews and Gentiles in the NT church (Eph 3:3–6), (4) the change that will take place at the resurrection (1 Cor 15:51), and (5) the plan of God by which both Jew and Gentile, after a period of disobedience by both, will by His mercy be included in His kingdom (v. 25). *so that you will not be wise in your own estimation.* God's merciful plan to include the Gentiles in His great salvation plan should humble them, not fill them with arrogance. *partial.* Israel's hardening is partial, not total. *until.* Israel's hardening is temporary, not permanent. *fullness of the Gentiles.* The total number of the elect Gentiles.

11:26 *and so.* An emphatic statement that this is the way all Israel will be saved. *all Israel.* Three main interpretations of this phrase are: (1) the total number of elect Jews of every generation (equivalent to the "fulfillment" of Israel [v. 12], which is analogous to the "fullness ['full number'] of the Gentiles" [v. 25]); (2) the total number of the elect, both Jews and Gentiles, of every generation; (3) the great majority of Jews of the final generation. *will be saved.* The salvation of the Jews will, of course, be on the same basis as anyone's salvation: personal faith in Jesus Christ, crucified and risen from the dead. *THE DELIVERER WILL COME FROM ZION.* The quotation is from Is 59:20, where the deliverer ("Redeemer") seems to refer to God. The Talmud understood the text to be a reference to the Messiah, and Paul appears to use it in this way. *ZION.* See note on Gal 4:26.

11:27 *COVENANT.* The new covenant of Jer 31:31–34. *WHEN I TAKE AWAY THEIR SINS.* See Jer 31:34; Zech 13:1. Just as salvation for Gentiles involves forgiveness of sins, so the Jews, when they are saved, are forgiven by the mercy of God—His forgiveness based only on their repentance and faith (see v. 23; Zech 12:10–13:1).

28 [1]From the standpoint of the gospel they are [a]enemies for your sake, but [2]from the standpoint of *God's* choice they are beloved for [b]the sake of the fathers;

29 for the gifts and the [a]calling of God [b]are irrevocable.

30 For just as you once were disobedient to God, but now have been shown mercy because of their disobedience,

31 so these also now have been disobedient, that because of the mercy shown to you they also may now be shown mercy.

32 For [a]God has shut up all in disobedience so that He may show mercy to all.

33 Oh, the depth of [a]the riches [1]both of the [b]wisdom and knowledge of God! [c]How unsearchable are His judgments and unfathomable His ways!

34 For [a]WHO HAS KNOWN THE MIND OF THE LORD, OR WHO BECAME HIS COUNSELOR?

35 Or [a]WHO HAS FIRST GIVEN TO HIM [1]THAT IT MIGHT BE PAID BACK TO HIM AGAIN?

36 For [a]from Him and through Him and to Him are all things. [b]To Him *be* the glory [1]forever. Amen.

Dedicated Service

12 Therefore [a]I urge you, brethren, by the mercies of God, to [b]present your bodies a living and holy sacrifice, [1]acceptable to God, *which is* your [2]spiritual service of worship.

2 And do not [a]be conformed to [b]this [1]world, but be transformed by the [c]renewing of your mind, so that you may [2d]prove what the will of God is, that which is good and [3]acceptable and perfect.

3 For through [a]the grace given to me I say to everyone among you [b]not to think more highly of himself than he ought to think; but to think so as to have sound judgment, as God has allotted to [c]each a measure of faith.

4 For [a]just as we have many members in one body and all the members do not have the same function,

5 so we, [a]who are many, are [b]one body in Christ, and individually members one of another.

6 Since we have gifts that [a]differ according to the grace given to us, *each of us is to exercise them accordingly:* if [b]prophecy, [1]according to the proportion of his faith;

7 if [1a]service, in his serving; or he who [b]teaches, in his teaching;

8 or he who [a]exhorts, in his exhortation;

28 [1]Lit *According to the gospel* [2]Lit *according to the election* [a]Rom 5:10 [b]Deut 7:8; 10:15; Rom 9:5 **29** [a]Rom 8:28; 1 Cor 1:26; Eph 1:18; 4:1, 4; Phil 3:14; 2 Thess 1:11; 2 Tim 1:9; Heb 3:1; 2 Pet 1:10 [b]Heb 7:21 **32** [a]Rom 3:9; Gal 3:22f **33** [1]Or *and the wisdom* [a]Rom 2:4; Eph 3:8 [b]Eph 3:10; Col 2:3 [c]Job 5:9; 11:7; 15:8 **34** [a]Is 40:13f; 1 Cor 2:16 **35** [1]Lit *and it will be paid back* [a]Job 35:7; 41:11 **36** [1]Lit *to the ages* [a]1 Cor 8:6; 11:12; Col 1:16; Heb 2:10 [b]Rom 16:27; Eph 3:21; Phil 4:20; 1 Tim 1:17; 2 Tim 4:18; 1 Pet 4:11; 5:11; 2 Pet 3:18; Jude 25; Rev 1:6; 5:13; 7:12 **12:1** [1]Or *well-pleasing* [2]Or *rational* [a]1 Cor 1:10; 2 Cor 10:1-4; Eph 4:1; 1 Pet 2:11 [b]Rom 6:13, 16, 19; 1 Cor 6:20; Heb 13:15; 1 Pet 2:5 **2** [1]Or *age* [2]Or *approve* [3]Or *well-pleasing* [a]1 Pet 1:14 [b]Matt 13:22; Gal 1:4; 1 John 2:15 [c]Eph 4:23; Titus 3:5 [d]Eph 5:10, 17; Col 1:9 **3** [a]Rom 1:5; 15:15; 1 Cor 3:10; 15:10; Gal 2:9; Eph 3:7f [b]Rom 11:20; 12:16 [c]1 Cor 7:17; 2 Cor 10:13; Eph 4:7; 1 Pet 4:11 **4** [a]1 Cor 12:12-14; Eph 4:4, 16 **5** [a]1 Cor 10:17, 33 [b]1 Cor 12:20, 27; Eph 4:12, 25 **6** [1]Or *in agreement with the faith* [a]Rom 12:3; 1 Cor 7:7; 12:4; 1 Pet 4:10 [b]Acts 13:1; 1 Cor 12:10 **7** [1]Or *office of service* [a]Acts 6:1; 1 Cor 12:5, 28 [b]Acts 13:1; 1 Cor 12:28; 14:26 **8** [a]Acts 4:36; 11:23; 13:15

11:28 *they are enemies.* Only temporarily. *for your sake.* Explained in v. 11. *beloved for the sake of the fathers.* Not because any merit was passed on from the patriarchs to the Jewish people as a whole, but because God in love chose Israel and that choice was irrevocable.

11:29 *the gifts and the calling of God are irrevocable.* God does not change His mind with reference to His call. Even though Israel is presently in a state of unbelief, God's purpose will be fulfilled in her.

11:32 *all.* Both groups under discussion (Jews and Gentiles). There has been a period of disobedience for each in order that God may have mercy on them all. Paul is in no way teaching universal salvation.

11:33–36 The doxology that ends this section of Romans is the natural outpouring of Paul's praise to God, whose wisdom and knowledge brought about His great plan for the salvation of both Jews and Gentiles.

12:1–16:27 Paul now turns to the practical application of all he has said previously in the letter. This does not mean that he has not said anything about Christian living up to this point. Chs. 6–8 have touched on this already, but now Paul goes into detail to show that Jesus Christ is to be Lord of every area of life. These chapters are not a postscript to the great theological discussions in chs. 1–11. In a real sense the entire letter has been directed toward the goal of showing that God demands our action as well as our believing and thinking. Faith expresses itself in obedience.

12:1 *Therefore I urge you.* Paul draws an important inference from the truth set forth in chs. 1–11. *mercies of God.* Much of the letter has been concerned with demonstrating this. *your bodies.* See 6:13 and note. *living . . . sacrifice.* In contrast to dead animal sacrifices, or perhaps "living" in the sense of having the new life of the Holy Spirit (see 6:4). *spiritual service.* Not merely ritual activity but the involvement of heart, mind and will. *worship.* Obedient service.

12:2 *this world.* With all its evil and corruption (see Gal 1:4). *be transformed.* Here a process, not a single event. The same word is used in the transfiguration narratives (Matt 17:2–8; Mark 9:2–8) and in 2 Cor 3:18. *mind.* Thought and will as they relate to morality (see 1:28). *so that.* After the spiritual transformation just described has taken place. *will of God.* What God wants from the believer here and now. *good.* That which leads to the spiritual and moral growth of the Christian. *acceptable.* To God, not necessarily to us. *perfect.* No improvement can be made on the will of God.

12:3 *God has allotted.* Since the power comes from God, there can be no basis for a superior attitude or self-righteousness. *measure of faith.* The power given by God to each believer to fulfill various ministries in the Church (see vv. 4–8).

12:4–8 Paul likens Christians to members of a human body. There are many members and each has a different function, but all are needed for the health of the body. The emphasis is on unity within diversity (see 1 Cor 12:12–31).

12:5 *in Christ.* The key to Paul's concept of Christian unity. It is only in Jesus Christ that any unity in the church is possible. True unity is spiritually based. See note on 6:11.

12:6 *gifts.* Greek *charismata,* referring to special gifts of grace—freely given by God to His people to meet the needs of the body (see notes on 1 Cor 1:7; 12:4). *prophecy.* See note on 1 Cor 12:10. *according to.* There is to be no false modesty that denies the existence of gifts or refuses to use them. *to the proportion of his faith.* Probably means about the same thing as "measure of faith" in v. 3 (see note there).

12:7 *service.* Any kind of service needed by the body of Christ or by any of its members. *teaches.* See notes on 1 Cor 12:28; Eph 4:11.

12:8 *exhorts.* Exhorting others with an uplifting, cheerful call to worthwhile accomplishment. The teacher often carried out

he who gives, with [1b]liberality; [c]he who [2]leads, with diligence; he who shows mercy, with [d]cheerfulness.

9 *Let* [a]love *be* without hypocrisy. [b]Abhor what is evil; cling to what is good.

10 *Be* [a]devoted to one another in brotherly love; [1]give preference to one another [b]in honor;

11 not lagging behind in diligence, [a]fervent in spirit, [b]serving the Lord;

12 [a]rejoicing in hope, [b]persevering in tribulation, [c]devoted to prayer,

13 [a]contributing to the needs of the [1]saints, [2b]practicing hospitality.

14 [a]Bless those who persecute [1]you; bless and do not curse.

15 [a]Rejoice with those who rejoice, and weep with those who weep.

16 [a]Be of the same mind toward one another; [b]do not be haughty in mind, but [1]associate with the lowly. [c]Do not be wise in your own estimation.

17 [a]Never pay back evil for evil to anyone. [1b]Respect what is right in the sight of all men.

18 If possible, [a]so far as it depends on you, [b]be at peace with all men.

19 [a]Never take your own revenge, beloved, but [1]leave room for the wrath *of God*, for it is written, "[b]VENGEANCE IS MINE, I WILL REPAY," says the Lord.

8 [1]Or *simplicity* [2]Or *gives aid* [b]2 Cor 8:2; 9:11, 13 [c]1 Cor 12:28; 1 Tim 5:17 [d]2 Cor 9:7
9 [a]2 Cor 6:6; 1 Tim 1:5 [b]1 Thess 5:21f
10 [1]Or *outdo one another in showing honor* [a]John 13:34; 1 Thess 4:9; Heb 13:1; 2 Pet 1:7 [b]Rom 13:7; Phil 2:3; 1 Pet 2:17
11 [a]Acts 18:25 [b]Acts 20:19
12 [a]Rom 5:2 [b]Heb 10:32, 36 [c]Acts 1:14
13 [1]Or *holy ones* [2]Lit *pursuing* [a]Rom 15:25; 1 Cor 16:15; 2 Cor 9:1; Heb 6:10 [b]Matt 25:35; 1 Tim 3:2
14 [1]Two early mss do not contain *you* [a]Matt 5:44; Luke 6:28; 1 Cor 4:12
15 [a]Job 30:25; Heb 13:3
16 [1]Or *accommodate yourself to lowly things* [a]Rom 15:5; 2 Cor 13:11; Phil 2:2; 4:2; 1 Pet 3:8 [b]Rom 11:20; 12:3 [c]Prov 3:7; Rom 11:25

20 "[a]BUT IF YOUR ENEMY IS HUNGRY, FEED HIM, AND IF HE IS THIRSTY, GIVE HIM A DRINK; FOR IN SO DOING YOU WILL HEAP BURNING COALS ON HIS HEAD."

21 Do not be overcome by evil, but overcome evil with good.

Be Subject to Government

13 Every [1a]person is to be in [b]subjection to the governing authorities. For [c]there is no authority except [2]from God, and those which exist are established by God.

2 Therefore [1]whoever resists authority has opposed the ordinance of God; and they who have opposed will receive condemnation upon themselves.

3 For [a]rulers are not a cause of fear for [1]good behavior, but for evil. Do you want to have no fear of authority? Do what is good and you will have praise from the same;

4 for it is a minister of God to you for good. But if you do what is evil, be afraid; for it does not bear the sword for nothing; for it is a minister of God, an [a]avenger who brings wrath on the one who practices evil.

17 [1]Lit *Take thought for* [a]Prov 20:22; 24:29; Rom 12:19 [b]2 Cor 8:21 **18** [a]Rom 1:15 [b]Mark 9:50; Rom 14:19 **19** [1]Lit *give a place* [a]Prov 20:22; 24:29; Rom 12:17 [b]Deut 32:35; Ps 94:1; 1 Thess 4:6; Heb 10:30 **20** [a]2 Kin 6:22; Prov 25:21f; Matt 5:44; Luke 6:27 **13:1** [1]Or *soul* [2]Lit *by* [a]Acts 2:41 [b]Titus 3:1; 1 Pet 2:13f [c]Dan 2:21; 4:17; John 19:11 **2** [1]Lit *he who* **3** [1]Lit *good work* [a]1 Pet 2:14 **4** [a]1 Thess 4:6

this function. In teaching, the believer is shown what he must do; in encouraging, he is helped to do it. *gives.* Giving what is one's own, or possibly distributing what has been given by others. *who leads.* Possibly a reference to an elder. The Ephesian church had elders by about this time (see Acts 20:17; 1 Thess 5:12; 1 Tim 5:17). *shows mercy.* Caring for the sick, the poor and the aged. *with cheerfulness.* Serving the needy should be a delight, not a chore.

12:9 *love.* The Christian's love for fellow Christians and perhaps also for his fellowman. *without hypocrisy.* True love, not pretense. In view of the preceding paragraph, with its emphasis on social concern, the love Paul speaks of here is not mere emotion but is active love.

12:10 *brotherly love.* Love within the family of God. *give preference to one another in honor.* Only a mind renewed by the Holy Spirit (see v. 2) could possibly do this (see Phil 2:3).

12:11 *fervent in spirit.* If "spirit" means "Holy Spirit" here the reference would be to the fervor the Holy Spirit provides.

12:12 *rejoicing in hope.* The certainty of the Christian's hope is a cause for joy (see 5:5; see also 8:16–25; 1 Pet 1:3–9). *persevering.* Enduring triumphantly—necessary for a Christian, because affliction is his inevitable experience (see John 16:33). *devoted to prayer.* One must not only pray in hard times, but also maintain communion with God through prayer at all times (see Luke 18:1; 1 Thess 5:17).

12:13 *contributing to . . . the saints.* The Christian has social responsibility to all people, but especially to other believers (see Gal 6:10).

12:14 *Bless those who persecute you.* Paul is echoing Jesus' teaching in Matt 5:44; Luke 6:28.

12:15 Identification with others in their joys and in their sorrows is a Christian's privilege and responsibility.

12:17 *Never pay back evil for evil to anyone.* See Matt 5:39–42,44–45; 1 Thess 5:15; 1 Pet 3:9. *Respect what is right in the sight of all men.* A possible reflection of Prov 3:4 in the Septuagint (the Greek translation of the OT). Christian conduct should never betray the high moral standards of the gospel, or it will provoke the disdain of unbelievers and bring the gospel into disrepute (see 2 Cor 8:21; 1 Tim 3:7).

12:18 *If possible . . . be at peace.* Jesus pronounced a blessing on peacemakers (Matt 5:9), and believers are to cultivate peace with everyone to the extent that it depends on them.

12:20 *HEAP BURNING COALS ON HIS HEAD.* Doing good to one's enemy (v. 21), instead of trying to take revenge, may bring about his repentance (see note on Prov 25:22).

13:1 *be in subjection.* A significant word in vv. 1–7. *governing authorities.* The civil rulers, all of whom were probably pagans at the time Paul was writing. Christians may have been tempted not to submit to them and to claim allegiance only to Christ. *established by God.* Even the possibility of a persecuting state did not shake Paul's conviction that civil government is ordained by God.

13:2 *condemnation.* Either divine judgment or, more likely, punishment by the governing authorities, since v. 3 ("For") explains this verse; see also v. 4.

13:3 *Do what is good and you will have praise.* Paul is not stating that this will always be true but is describing the proper, ideal function of rulers. When civil rulers overstep their proper function, the Christian is to obey God rather than man (see Acts 4:19; 5:29).

13:4 *it is a minister of God.* In the order of divine providence the ruler is God's servant (see Is 45:1). *good.* Rulers exist for the benefit of society—to protect the general public by maintaining good order. *the sword.* The symbol of Roman authority on both the national and the international levels. Here we find the Biblical principle of using force for the maintenance of good order.

5 Therefore it is necessary to be in subjection, not only because of wrath, but also [a]for conscience' sake.

6 For because of this you also pay taxes, for *rulers* are servants of God, devoting themselves to this very thing.

7 [a]Render to all what is due them: [b]tax to whom tax *is due;* [c]custom to whom custom; fear to whom fear; honor to whom honor.

8 Owe nothing to anyone except to love one another; for [a]he who loves [1]his neighbor has fulfilled *the* law.

9 For this, "[a]YOU SHALL NOT COMMIT ADULTERY, YOU SHALL NOT MURDER, YOU SHALL NOT STEAL, YOU SHALL NOT COVET," and if there is any other commandment, it is summed up in this saying, "[b]YOU SHALL LOVE YOUR NEIGHBOR AS YOURSELF."

10 Love [1]does no wrong to a neighbor; therefore [a]love is the fulfillment of *the* law.

11 *Do* this, knowing the time, that it is [a]already the hour for you to [b]awaken from sleep; for now [1]salvation is nearer to us than when we believed.

12 [a]The night is almost gone, and [b]the day is near. Therefore let us lay aside [c]the deeds of darkness and put on [d]the armor of light.

13 Let us [1a]behave properly as in the day, [b]not in carousing and drunkenness, not in sexual promiscuity and sensuality, not in strife and jealousy.

14 But [a]put on the Lord Jesus Christ, and make no provision for the flesh [b]in regard to *its* lusts.

Principles of Conscience

14 Now [a]accept the one who is [b]weak in faith, *but* not for *the purpose of* passing judgment on his opinions.

2 [a]One person has faith that he may eat all things, but he who is [b]weak eats vegetables *only.*

3 The one who eats is not to [a]regard with contempt the one who does not eat, and the one who does not eat is not to [b]judge the one who eats, for God has [c]accepted him.

4 [a]Who are you to judge the [1]servant of another? To his own [2]master he stands or falls; and he will stand, for the Lord is able to make him stand.

5 [a]One person [1]regards one day above

5 [a]Eccl 8; 1 Pet 2:13, 19
7 [a]Matt 22:21; Mark 12:17; Luke 20:25 [b]Luke 20:22; 23:2 [c]Matt 17:25
8 [1]Lit *the other* [a]Matt 7:12; 22:39f; John 13:34; Rom 13:10; Gal 5:14; James 2:8
9 [a]Ex 20:13ff; Deut 5:17ff [b]Lev 19:18; Matt 19:19
10 [1]Lit *works no evil* [a]Matt 7:12; 22:39f; John 13:34; Rom 13:8; Gal 5:14; James 2:8
11 [1]Or *our salvation is nearer than when* [a]1 Cor 7:29f; 10:11; James 5:8; 1 Pet 4:7; 2 Pet 3:9, 11; 1 John 2:18; Rev 1:3; 22:10 [b]Mark 13:37; 1 Cor 15:34; Eph 5:14; 1 Thess 5:6
12 [a]1 Cor 7:29f; 10:11; James 5:8; 1 Pet 4:7; 2 Pet 3:9, 11; 1 John 2:18; Rev 1:3; 22:10 [b]Heb 10:25; 1 John 2:8; Rev 1:3; 22:10 [c]Eph 5:11 [d]2 Cor 6:7; 10:4; Eph 6:11, 13; 1 Thess 5:8
13 [1]Lit *walk* [a]1 Thess 4:12 [b]Luke 21:34; Gal 5:21; Eph 5:18; 1 Pet 4:3
14 [a]Job 29:14; Gal 3:27; Eph 4:24; Col 3:10, 12 [b]Gal 5:16; 1 Pet 2:11
14:1 [a]Acts 28:2; Rom 11:15; 14:3; 15:7 [b]Rom 14:2; 15:1; 1 Cor 8:9ff; 9:22
2 [a]Rom 14:14 [b]Rom 14:1; 15:1; 1 Cor 8:9ff; 9:22
3 [a]Luke 18:9; Rom 14:10 [b]Rom 14:10, 13; Col 2:16 [c]Acts 28:2; Rom 11:15; 14:1; 15:7
4 [1]Or *house-servant* [2]Lit *lord* [a]Rom 9:20; James 4:12
5 [1]Lit *judges* [a]Gal 4:10

13:5 *for conscience' sake.* Civil authorities are ordained by God, and in order to maintain a good conscience Christians must duly honor them.

13:6 *you also pay taxes.* Because rulers are God's agents, who function for the benefit of society in general.

13:8 *except to love.* To love is the one debt that is never paid off. No matter how much one has loved, he is under obligation to keep on loving. *one another.* Includes not only fellow Christians but all people, as the second half of the verse makes clear ("neighbor"). *the law.* The Mosaic law, which lays down both moral and social responsibilities.

13:9 Further explains the last statement of v. 8, namely, that love of neighbor encompasses all our social responsibilities. *YOUR NEIGHBOR.* Jesus taught that our neighbor is anyone in need (see Luke 10:25–37), which is probably the idea Paul has in mind here. *AS YOURSELF.* Not a command to love ourselves but a recognition of the fact that we naturally do so.

13:11–14 In this section, as in other NT passages, the certain coming of the end of the present age is used to provide motivation for godly living (see, e.g., Matt 25:31–46; Mark 13:33–37; James 5:7–11; 2 Pet 3:11–14).

13:11 *the time.* The time of salvation, the closing period of the present age, before the consummation of the kingdom. *the hour.* The time for action. *salvation.* The full realization of salvation at the second coming of Jesus Christ (see 8:23; Heb 9:28; 1 Pet 1:5). *is nearer.* Every day brings us closer to the second advent of Christ.

13:12 *The night.* The present evil age. *is almost gone, and the day is near.* A clear example of the NT teaching of the "nearness" of the end times (see Matt 24:33; 1 Cor 7:29; Phil 4:5; James 5:8–9; 1 Pet 4:7; 1 John 2:18). These texts do not mean that the early Christians believed that Jesus would return within a few years (and thus were mistaken). Rather, they regarded the death and resurrection of Christ as the crucial events of history that began the last days. Since the next great event in God's redemptive plan is the second coming of Jesus Christ, "the night," no matter how long chronologically it may last, is "almost gone." *the day.* The appearing of Jesus Christ, which ushers in the consummation of the kingdom.

13:14 *put on the Lord Jesus Christ.* See Gal 3:27. Paul exhorts believers to display outwardly what has already taken place inwardly—including practicing all the virtues associated with Christ.

14:1 *who is weak in faith.* Probably Jewish Christians at Rome who were unwilling to give up the observance of certain requirements of the law, such as dietary restrictions and the keeping of the Sabbath and other special days. Their concern was not quite the same as that of the Judaizers of Galatia. The Judaizers thought they could put God in their debt by works of righteousness and were trying to force this heretical teaching on the Galatian churches, but the "weak" Roman Christians did neither. They were not yet clear as to the status of OT regulations under the new covenant inaugurated by the coming of Christ. *not for . . . passing judgment on his opinions.* Fellowship among Christians is not to be based on everyone's agreement on disputable questions. Christians do not agree on all matters pertaining to the Christian life, nor do they need to.

14:2 *One person has faith.* In contrast, Paul now describes the "strong" Christian. Here faith is used in the sense of assurance or confidence. The strong Christian's understanding of the gospel allows him to recognize that one's diet has no spiritual significance.

14:4 *of another.* God's. A Christian must not reject a fellow Christian, who is also a servant of God. *To his own master he stands or falls.* The "weak" Christian is not the master of his "strong" brother, nor is the "strong" the master of the "weak." God is Master, and to Him alone all believers are responsible.

14:5 *one day above another.* Some feel that this refers primarily to the Sabbath, but it is probably a reference to all the special days of the OT ceremonial law. *regards every day alike.* All days are to be dedicated to God through holy living and godly service. *fully convinced in his own mind.* The importance of per-

another, another regards every day *alike.*
Each person must be [b]fully convinced in his
own mind.
6 He who observes the day, observes it
for the Lord, and he who eats, [1]does so for
the Lord, for he [a]gives thanks to God; and he
who eats not, for the Lord he does not eat,
and gives thanks to God.
7 For not one of us [a]lives for himself, and
not one dies for himself;
8 for if we live, we live for the Lord, or
if we die, we die for the Lord; therefore
[a]whether we live or die, we are the Lord's.
9 For to this end [a]Christ died and lived
again, that He might be [b]Lord both of the
dead and of the living.
10 But you, why do you judge your brother? Or you again, why do you [a]regard your
brother with contempt? For [b]we will all stand
before the judgment seat of God.
11 For it is written,

"[a]As I LIVE, SAYS THE LORD, [b]EVERY KNEE
SHALL BOW TO ME,
AND EVERY TONGUE SHALL [1]GIVE PRAISE TO
GOD."

12 So then [a]each one of us will give an
account of himself to God.
13 Therefore let us not [a]judge one another anymore, but rather determine this—[b]not
to put an obstacle or a stumbling block in a
brother's way.
14 I know and am convinced [1]in the Lord
Jesus that [a]nothing is unclean in itself; but to
him who [b]thinks anything to be unclean, to
him it is unclean.
15 For if because of food your brother is
hurt, you are no longer [a]walking according
to love. [b]Do not destroy with your food him
for whom Christ died.
16 Therefore [a]do not let what is for you a
good thing be [1]spoken of as evil;
17 for the kingdom of God [a]is not eating
and drinking, but righteousness and [b]peace
and [b]joy in the Holy Spirit.
18 For he who in this *way* [a]serves Christ is
[b]acceptable to God and approved by men.
19 So then [1]we [a]pursue the things which
make for peace and the [b]building up of one
another.
20 [a]Do not tear down the work of God for
the sake of food. [b]All things indeed are
clean, but [c]they are evil for the man who
eats [1]and gives offense.
21 [a]It is good not to eat meat or to drink
wine, or *to do anything* by which your
brother stumbles.
22 The faith which you have, have [1]as
your own conviction before God. Happy is
he who [a]does not condemn himself in what
he approves.
23 But [a]he who doubts is condemned if he
eats, because *his eating is* not from faith; and
whatever is not from faith is sin.

5 [b]Luke 1:1; Rom 4:21; 14:23 **6** [1]Lit *eats* [a]Matt 14:19; 15:36; 1 Cor 10:30; 1 Tim 4:3f **7** [a]Rom 8:38f; 2 Cor 5:15; Gal 2:20; Phil 1:20f **8** [a]Luke 20:38; Phil 1:20; 1 Thess 5:10; Rev 14:13 **9** [a]Rev 1:18; 2:8 [b]Matt 28:18; John 12:24; Phil 2:11; 1 Thess 5:10 **10** [a]Luke 18:9; Rom 14:3 [b]Rom 2:16; 2 Cor 5:10 **11** [1]Or *confess* [a]Is 45:23 [b]Phil 2:10f **12** [a]Matt 12:36; 16:27; 1 Pet 4:5 **13** [a]Matt 7:1; Rom 14:3 [b]1 Cor 8:13 **14** [1]Lit *through* [a]Acts 10:15; Rom 14:2, 20 [b]1 Cor 8:7 **15** [a]Eph 5:2 [b]Rom 14:20; 1 Cor 8:11 **16** [1]Lit *blasphemed* [a]1 Cor 10:30; Titus 2:5 **17** [a]1 Cor 8:8 [b]Rom 15:13; Gal 5:22 **18** [a]Rom 16:18 [b]2 Cor 8:21; Phil 4:8; 1 Pet 2:12 **19** [1]Later mss read *let us pursue* [a]Ps 34:14; Rom 12:18; 1 Cor 7:15; 2 Tim 2:22; Heb 12:14 [b]Rom 15:2; 1 Cor 10:23; 14:3f, 26; 2 Cor 12:19; Eph 4:12, 29 **20** [1]Lit *with offense* [a]Rom 14:15 [b]Acts 10:15; Rom 14:2, 14 [c]1 Cor 8:9-12 **21** [a]1 Cor 8:13 **22** [1]Lit *according to yourself* [a]1 John 3:21 **23** [a]Rom 14:5

sonal conviction in disputable matters of conduct runs through this passage (see vv. 14,16,22–23).

14:6 The motivation behind the actions of both the strong and the weak is to be the same: Both should want to serve the Lord and give thanks for His provision.

14:7 *not one of us lives for himself.* The reference is to "us" Christians. We do not live to please ourselves but the Lord. *not one dies for himself.* Even in death the important thing is one's relationship to the Lord. Paul repeats the truths of this verse in v. 8.

14:9 *Lord.* See note on 10:9. Christ's Lordship over both the dead and the living arises out of His death and resurrection.

14:10 *why do you judge your brother?* Addressed to weak Christians. *why do you regard your brother with contempt?* Addressed to strong Christians. *we will all.* Refers to every Christian. *judgment seat of God.* All Christians will be judged, and the judgment will be based on works (see 2 Cor 5:10; cf. 1 Cor 3:10–15).

14:13 *but rather.* The words that immediately follow are addressed to strong Christians. *obstacle.* Something that causes one to fall into sin.

14:14 *I know and am convinced in the Lord Jesus.* Now that Paul was a Christian, the old food taboos no longer applied (see Matt 15:10–11,16–20; Mark 7:14–23). *nothing is unclean in itself.* For Paul's teaching elsewhere on this subject see 1 Tim 4:4; Titus 1:15. *to him who thinks anything to be unclean, to him it is unclean.* Not to be generalized to mean that sin is only a matter of subjective opinion or conscience. Paul is not discussing conduct that in the light of Scripture is clearly sinful, but conduct concerning which Christians may legitimately differ (in this case, food regulations). With regard to such matters, decisions should be guided by conscience.

14:15 *love.* The key to proper settlement of disputes. *him for whom Christ died.* Christ so valued the weak brother as to die for him. Surely the strong Christian ought to be willing to make adjustments in his own behavior for the sake of such brothers.

14:16 *what is for you a good thing.* From your own understanding of Christian liberty. *be spoken of as evil.* To exercise freedom without responsibility can lead to evil results.

14:17 *kingdom of God.* See notes on Matt 3:2; Luke 4:43. *is not eating and drinking.* To be concerned with such trivial matters is to miss completely the essence of Christian living. *righteousness.* Righteous living. Paul's concern for the moral and ethical dimension of the Christian life stands out in all his letters. *peace.* See 5:1 and note. *joy in the Holy Spirit.* Joy given by the Holy Spirit.

14:19 *the building up of one another.* The spiritual building up of individual Christians and of the church (see 1:11–12).

14:20 *work of God.* The weak Christian brother who as a redeemed person is God's work and in whom God continues to work (cf. Eph 2:10). *gives offense.* Paul recognizes a strong Christian's right to certain freedoms, but qualifies it with the principle of regard for a weak brother's scruples.

14:22 *have as your own conviction before God.* The strong Christian is not required to go against his convictions or change his standards. Yet he is not to flaunt his Christian freedom but keep it a private matter. *what he approves.* Probably a reference to the eating of certain foods.

14:23 *whatever.* The matters discussed above, namely, conduct about which there can be legitimate differences of opinion between Christians.

Self-denial on Behalf of Others

15 Now we who are strong ought to bear
the weaknesses of [a]those without
strength and not *just* please ourselves.
2 Each of us is to [a]please his neighbor
[1]for his good, to his [b]edification.
3 For even [a]Christ did not please Himself; but as it is written, "[b]THE REPROACHES OF
THOSE WHO REPROACHED YOU FELL ON ME."
4 For [a]whatever was written in earlier
times was written for our instruction, so that
through perseverance and the encouragement of the Scriptures we might have hope.
5 Now may the [a]God [1]who gives perseverance and encouragement grant you [b]to be
of the same mind with one another according to Christ Jesus,
6 so that with one accord you may with
one [1]voice glorify [a]the God and Father of our
Lord Jesus Christ.
7 Therefore, [a]accept one another, just as
Christ also accepted [1]us to the glory of God.
8 For I say that Christ has become a servant to [a]the circumcision on behalf of the
truth of God to confirm [b]the promises *given*
to the fathers,
9 and for [a]the Gentiles to [b]glorify God for
His mercy; as it is written,
"[c]THEREFORE I WILL [1]GIVE PRAISE TO YOU
AMONG THE GENTILES,
AND I WILL SING TO YOUR NAME."
10 Again he says,
"[a]REJOICE, O GENTILES, WITH HIS PEOPLE."
11 And again,
"[a]PRAISE THE LORD ALL YOU GENTILES,
AND LET ALL THE PEOPLES PRAISE HIM."
12 Again Isaiah says,
"[a]THERE SHALL COME [b]THE ROOT OF JESSE,
AND HE WHO ARISES TO RULE OVER THE
GENTILES,
[c]IN HIM SHALL THE GENTILES HOPE."
13 Now may the God of hope fill you with
all [a]joy and peace in believing, so that you
will abound in hope [b]by the power of the
Holy Spirit.
14 And concerning you, my brethren, I
myself also am convinced that you yourselves are full of [a]goodness, filled with [b]all
knowledge and able also to admonish one
another.
15 But I have written very boldly to you
on some points so as to remind you again,
because of [a]the grace that was given me
[1]from God,
16 to be [a]a minister of Christ Jesus to the
Gentiles, ministering as a priest the [b]gospel
of God, so that *my* [c]offering of the Gentiles
may become acceptable, sanctified by the
Holy Spirit.
17 Therefore in Christ Jesus I have found
[a]reason for boasting in [b]things pertaining to
God.
18 For I will not presume to speak of any-

15:1 [a]Rom 14:1; Gal 6:2; 1 Thess 5:14
2 [1]Lit *for what is good to edification* [a]1 Cor 9:22; 10:24, 33; 2 Cor 13:9 [b]Rom 14:19; 1 Cor 10:23; 14:3f, 26; 2 Cor 12:19; Eph 4:12, 29
3 [a]2 Cor 8:9 [b]Ps 69:9
4 [a]Rom 4:23f; 2 Tim 3:16
5 [1]Lit *of perseverance* [a]2 Cor 1:3 [b]Rom 12:16
6 [1]Lit *mouth* [a]Rev 1:6
7 [1]One early ms reads *you* [a]Rom 14:1
8 [a]Matt 15:24; Acts 3:26 [b]Rom 4:16; 2 Cor 1:20
9 [1]Or *confess* [a]Rom 3:29; 11:30f [b]Matt 9:8 [c]2 Sam 22:50; Ps 18:49
10 [a]Deut 32:43
11 [a]Ps 117:1
12 [a]Is 11:10 [b]Rev 5:5; 22:16 [c]Matt 12:21
13 [a]Rom 14:17 [b]Rom 15:19; 1 Cor 2:4; 1 Thess 1:5
14 [a]Eph 5:9; 2 Thess 1:11 [b]1 Cor 1:5; 8:1, 7, 10; 12:8; 13:2
15 [1]One early ms reads *by God* [a]Rom 12:3 **16** [a]Acts 9:15; Rom 11:13 [b]Rom 1:1; 15:19, 20 [c]Rom 12:1; Eph 5:2; Phil 2:17 **17** [a]Phil 3:3 [b]Heb 2:17; 5:1

15:1 *we who are strong.* Paul identifies himself with the strong Christians, those whose personal convictions allow them more freedom than the weak. *to bear.* Not merely to tolerate or put up with but to uphold lovingly. *weaknesses.* Not sins, since in the matters under discussion there is no clear guidance in Scripture. *not just please ourselves.* Not that a Christian should never please himself, but that he should not insist on doing what he wants without regard to the scruples of other Christians.
15:3 *Christ did not please Himself.* He came to do the will of the Father, not His own will. This involved suffering and even death (see Matt 20:28; Mark 10:45; 1 Cor 10:33–11:1; 2 Cor 8:9; Phil 2:5–8). *THE REPROACHES OF THOSE WHO REPROACHED YOU FELL ON ME.* In the psalm quoted (69:9) "you" refers to God and "me" refers to the righteous sufferer, whom Paul identifies with Christ. The quotation serves to show how Christ did not please himself, but voluntarily bore man's hostility toward God.
15:4 Here Paul defends his application of Ps 69:9 to Christ. In so doing, he states a great truth concerning the purpose of Scripture: It was written for our instruction, so that as we patiently endure we might be encouraged to hold fast our hope in Christ (see 1 Cor 10:6,11).
15:5 *to be of the same mind.* Not that believers should all come to the same conclusions on the matters of conscience discussed above, but that they might agree to disagree in love.
15:7 *just as Christ also accepted us.* See 14:3,4,15.
15:8 *Christ has become a servant to the circumcision.* Clearly revealed in His earthly ministry. He was sent to the Jewish people and largely limited His ministry to them (see Matt 15:24). God gave a special priority, so far as the gospel is concerned, to the Jews (see 3:1–8). *promises given to the fathers.* The covenant promises made to Abraham (Gen 12:1–3; 17:7; 18:19; 22:18), Isaac (Gen 26:3–4) and Jacob (Gen 28:13–15; 46:2–4).
15:9 *for the Gentiles to glorify God.* From the beginning, God's redemptive work in and for Israel had in view the redemption of the Gentiles (see Gen 12:3). They would both see God's mighty and gracious acts for His people and hear the praises of God's people as they celebrated what God had done for them (a common theme in the Psalms; see Paul's quotations in vv. 9b–12 and note on Ps 9:1). Thus they would come to know the true God and glorify Him for His mercy (see notes on Ps 46:10; 47:9). God's greatest and climactic act for Israel's salvation was the sending of the Messiah to fulfill the promises made to the patriarchs and so to gather in the great harvest of the Gentiles.
15:12 *ROOT OF JESSE.* Jesse was the father of David (see 1 Sam 16:5–13; Matt 1:6), and the Messiah was the "Son of David" (Matt 21:9). See Is 11:1; Rev 5:5. *IN HIM SHALL THE GENTILES HOPE.* The Gentile mission of the early church was a fulfillment of this prophecy, as is the continuing evangelization of the nations.
15:13 *God of hope.* Any hope the Christian has comes from God. See note on 5:5. *by the power of the Holy Spirit.* Hope cannot be conjured up by man's effort; it is God's gift by His Spirit (see 8:24–25).
15:15 *so as to remind you again.* Since Paul had never preached or taught in Rome, he may be referring to Christian doctrine generally known in the church.
15:16 *minister of Christ Jesus to the Gentiles.* See note on 11:13. *ministering as a priest the gospel.* Paul's priestly function was different from that of the Levitical priests. They were involved with the rituals of the temple, whereas he preached the gospel. *my offering . . . may become acceptable, sanctified by the Holy Spirit.* The offering Paul brought to God was the Gentile church.
15:17 *I have found reason for boasting.* Paul was not boasting of his own achievements but of what Christ had accomplished through him.

thing [1]except what [a]Christ has accomplished
through me, [2]resulting in the obedience of
the Gentiles by word and deed,
19 in the power of [1a]signs and wonders,
[b]in the power of the Spirit; so that [c]from
Jerusalem and round about as [d]far as
Illyricum I have [2]fully preached the gospel of
Christ.
20 And thus I aspired to [a]preach the
gospel, not where Christ was *already* named,
[b]so that I would not build on another man's
foundation;
21 but as it is written,

"[a]THEY WHO HAD NO NEWS OF HIM SHALL SEE,
AND THEY WHO HAVE NOT HEARD SHALL UNDERSTAND."

22 For this reason [a]I have often been prevented from coming to you;
23 but now, with no further place for me
in these regions, and since I [a]have had for
many years a longing to come to you
24 whenever I [a]go to Spain—for I hope to
see you in passing, and to be [b]helped on my
way there by you, when I have first [c]enjoyed
your company [1]for a while—
25 but now, [a]I am going to Jerusalem
[b]serving the [1]saints.
26 For [a]Macedonia and [b]Achaia have been
pleased to make a contribution for the poor
among the [1]saints in Jerusalem.
27 Yes, they were pleased *to do so,* and
they are indebted to them. For [a]if the Gentiles have shared in their spiritual things,
they are indebted to minister to them also in
material things.
28 Therefore, when I have finished this,
and [a]have [1]put my seal on this fruit of theirs,
I will [b]go on by way of you to Spain.
29 I know that when [a]I come to you, I will
come in the fullness of the blessing of Christ.
30 Now I urge you, brethren, by our Lord
Jesus Christ and by [a]the love of the Spirit, to
[b]strive together with me in your prayers to
God for me,
31 that I may be [a]rescued from those who
are disobedient in Judea, and *that* my [b]ser-
vice for Jerusalem may prove acceptable to
the [1c]saints;
32 so that [a]I may come to you in joy by
[b]the will of God and find *refreshing* rest in
your company.
33 Now [a]the God of peace be with you all.
Amen.

Greetings and Love Expressed

16 I [a]commend to you our sister Phoebe,
who is a [1]servant of the church which
is at [b]Cenchrea;
2 that you [a]receive her in the Lord in a
manner worthy of the [1b]saints, and that you
help her in whatever matter she may have
need of you; for she herself has also been a
helper of many, [2]and of myself as well.
3 Greet [a]Prisca and Aquila, my fellow
workers [b]in [c]Christ Jesus,
4 who for my life risked their own necks,
to whom not only do I give thanks, but also
all the churches of the Gentiles;
5 also *greet* [a]the church that is in their
house. Greet Epaenetus, my beloved, who is
the [b]first convert to Christ from [1c]Asia.

18 [1]Lit *which Christ has not accomplished* [2]Lit *to the obedience* [a]Acts 15:12; 21:19; Rom 1:5; 2 Cor 3:5
19 [1]Or *attesting miracles* [2]Lit *fulfilled* [a]John 4:48 [b]Rom 15:13; 1 Cor 2:4; 1 Thess 1:5 [c]Acts 22:17-21 [d]Acts 20:1f
20 [a]Rom 1:15; 10:15; 15:16 [b]1 Cor 3:10; 2 Cor 10:15f
21 [a]Is 52:15
22 [a]Rom 1:13; 1 Thess 2:18
23 [a]Acts 19:21; Rom 1:10f; 15:29, 32
24 [1]Lit *in part* [a]Rom 15:28 [b]Acts 15:3 [c]Rom 1:12
25 [1]Or *holy ones* [a]Acts 19:21 [b]Acts 24:17
26 [1]V 25, note 1 [a]Acts 16:9; 1 Cor 16:5; 2 Cor 1:16; 2:13; 7:5; 8:1; 9:2, 4; 11:9; Phil 4:15; 1 Thess 1:7f; 4:10; 1 Tim 1:3 [b]Acts 18:12; 19:21
27 [a]1 Cor 9:11
28 [1]Lit *sealed to them this fruit* [a]John 3:33 [b]Rom 15:24
29 [a]Acts 19:21; Rom 1:10f; 15:23, 32
30 [a]Gal 5:22; Col 1:8 [b]2 Cor 1:11; Col 4:12
31 [1]V 25, note 1 [a]2 Cor 1:10; 2 Thess 3:2; 2 Tim 3:11; 4:17 [b]Rom 15:25f; 2 Cor 8:4; 9:1 [c]Acts 9:13, 15
32 [a]Rom 15:23 [b]Acts 18:21; Rom 1:10
33 [a]Rom 16:20; 2 Cor 13:11; Phil 4:9; 1 Thess 5:23; 2 Thess 3:16; Heb 13:20
16:1 [1]Or *deaconess* [a]2 Cor 3:1 [b]Acts 18:18
2 [1]Or *holy ones* [2]Lit *and of me, myself* [a]Phil 2:29 [b]Acts 9:13, 15
3 [a]Acts 18:2 [b]Rom 8:1ff; 16:7, 9, 10; 2 Cor 5:17; 12:2; Gal 1:22 [c]Rom 8:1
5 [1]I.e. west coast province of Asia Minor [a]1 Cor 16:19; Col 4:15; Philem 2 [b]1 Cor 16:15 [c]Acts 16:6

15:19 *signs and wonders.* See Acts 14:8–10; 16:16–18,25–26; 20:9–12; 28:8–9; 2 Cor 12:12; Heb 2:3–4. *from Jerusalem.* The home of the mother church, where the gospel originated and its dissemination began (see Acts 1:8). *Illyricum.* A Roman province north of Macedonia (present-day Albania and Yugoslavia). Acts mentions nothing of his ministry there, and perhaps all he means is that he reached the border. *I have fully preached the gospel.* Not everyone had heard the gospel in the eastern Mediterranean, but Paul believed that his work there had been completed and it was time to move on to other places.

15:22 *prevented from coming to you.* Paul's great desire to complete the missionary task in the eastern Mediterranean had prevented him from making a trip to Rome.

15:23 *no further place for me.* Because of the principle stated in v. 20. *for many years a longing to come to you.* See 1:11–15.

15:24 *to be helped on my way there by you.* Paul wanted to use the Roman church as a base of operations for a mission to Spain. *enjoyed your company for a while.* More than a quick stop at Rome was contemplated (see 1:11–12).

15:25 *serving the saints.* Paul wanted to present the gift (see v. 26) personally to the Jerusalem church. The gift needed interpretation. It was not merely money; it represented the love and concern of the Gentile churches for their Jewish brothers and sisters. *saints.* Refers generally to believers in Jesus Christ (see note on 1:7).

15:26 *contribution.* See 1 Cor 16:1–4; 2 Cor 8–9.

15:27 *their spiritual things.* Especially Christ and the gospel.

15:28 *this fruit.* The collection from the Gentile churches.

15:31 *that I may be rescued from those . . . disobedient in Judea.* Paul wanted to go to Jerusalem. The delivery of the collection was important to him, but he had received warnings about what might happen to him there (see Acts 20:22–23). *may prove acceptable.* Perhaps a reference to the way in which the money was to be distributed—often a delicate and difficult task.

15:32 *find refreshing.* See 1:11–12.

15:33 *God of peace.* See notes on 5:1; 1 Thess 5:23.

16:1 *our sister.* In the sense of being a fellow believer. *Phoebe.* Probably the carrier of the letter to Rome. *servant.* One who serves or ministers in any way. When church related, as it is here, it probably refers to a specific office—woman deacon or deaconess. *Cenchrea.* A port located about six miles east of Corinth on the Saronic Gulf.

16:3 *Prisca and Aquila.* Close friends of Paul who worked in the same trade of tentmaking (see Acts 18:2–3).

16:4 *for my life risked their own necks.* There is no other record of this in the NT or elsewhere, but it must have been widely known, as the last part of the verse indicates.

6 Greet Mary, who has worked hard for
you.

7 Greet Andronicus and [1]Junias, my
[a]kinsmen and my [b]fellow prisoners, who are
outstanding among the apostles, who also
[2]were [c]in Christ before me.

8 Greet Ampliatus, my beloved in the Lord.

9 Greet Urbanus, our fellow worker [a]in
Christ, and Stachys my beloved.

10 Greet Apelles, the approved [a]in Christ.
Greet those who are of the *household* of Aristobulus.

11 Greet Herodion, my [a]kinsman. Greet
those of the *household* of Narcissus, who are
in the Lord.

12 Greet Tryphaena and Tryphosa, workers in the Lord. Greet Persis the beloved,
who has worked hard in the Lord.

13 Greet [a]Rufus, a choice man in the Lord,
also his mother and mine.

14 Greet Asyncritus, Phlegon, Hermes, Pat-
robas, Hermas and the brethren with them.

15 Greet Philologus and Julia, Nereus and
his sister, and Olympas, and all [a]the [1]saints
who are with them.

16 [a]Greet one another with a holy kiss. All
the churches of Christ greet you.

17 Now I urge you, brethren, keep your
eye on those who cause dissensions and
[1]hindrances [a]contrary to the teaching which
you learned, and [b]turn away from them.

18 For such men are [a]slaves, not of our
Lord Christ but of [b]their own [1]appetites; and
by their [c]smooth and flattering speech they
deceive the hearts of the unsuspecting.

19 For the report of your obedience [a]has
reached to all; therefore I am rejoicing over
you, but [b]I want you to be wise in what is
good and innocent in what is evil.

20 [a]The God of peace will soon crush
[b]Satan under your feet.

[c]The grace of our Lord Jesus be with you.

21 [a]Timothy my fellow worker greets you,
and *so do* [b]Lucius and [c]Jason and [d]Sosipater,
my [e]kinsmen.

22 I, Tertius, who [a]write this letter, greet
you in the Lord.

23 [a]Gaius, host to me and to the whole
church, greets you. [b]Erastus, the city treasurer greets you, and Quartus, the brother.

24 [[1]The grace of our Lord Jesus Christ be
with you all. Amen.]

25 [a]Now to Him who is able to establish
you [b]according to my gospel and the preaching of Jesus Christ, according to the revelation of [c]the mystery which has been kept
secret for [d]long ages past,

26 but now is manifested, and by [a]the
Scriptures of the prophets, according to the
commandment of the eternal God, has been
made known to all the nations, *leading* to
[b]obedience of faith;

27 to the only wise God, through Jesus
Christ, [a]be the glory forever. Amen.

7 [1]Or *Junia* (fem) [2]Lit *have become* [a]Rom 9:3; 16:11, 21 [b]Col 4:10; Philem 23 [c]Rom 8:11ff; 16:3, 9, 10; 2 Cor 5:17; 12:2; Gal 1:22
9 [a]Rom 8:11ff; 16:3, 7, 10; 2 Cor 5:17; 12:2; Gal 1:22
10 [a]Rom 8:11ff; 16:3, 7, 9; 2 Cor 5:17; 12:2; Gal 1:22
11 [a]Rom 9:3; 16:7, 21
13 [a]Mark 15:21
15 [1]V 2, note 1 [a]Rom 16:2, 14
16 [a]1 Cor 16:20; 2 Cor 13:12; 1 Thess 5:26; 1 Pet 5:14
17 [1]Lit *occasions of stumbling* [a]1 Tim 1:3; 6:3 [b]Matt 7:15; Gal 1:8f; 2 Thess 3:6, 14; Titus 3:10; 2 John 10
18 [1]Lit *belly* [a]Rom 14:18 [b]Phil 3:19 [c]Col 2:4; 2 Pet 2:3
19 [a]Rom 1:8 [b]Jer 4:22; Matt 10:16; 1 Cor 14:20
20 [a]Rom 15:33 [b]Matt 4:10 [c]1 Cor 16:23; 2 Cor 13:14; Gal 6:18; Phil 4:23; 1 Thess 5:28; 2 Thess 3:18; Rev 22:21
21 [a]Acts 16:1 [b][Acts 13:1] [c][Acts 17:5] [d][Acts 20:4] [e]Rom 9:3; 16:7, 11
22 [a]1 Cor 16:21; Gal 6:11; Col 4:18; 2 Thess 3:17; Philem 19
23 [a][Acts 19:29; 20:4]; 1 Cor 1:14 [b]Acts 19:22; 2 Tim 4:20
24 [1]Early mss do not contain this v **25** [a]Eph 3:20; Jude 24 [b]Rom 2:16 [c]Matt 13:35; Rom 11:25; 1 Cor 2:1, 7; 4:1; Eph 1:9; 3:3, 9; 6:19; Col 1:26f; 2:2; 4:3; 1 Tim 3:16 [d]2 Tim 1:9; Titus 1:2
26 [a]Rom 1:2 [b]Rom 1:5 **27** [a]Rom 11:36

16:6 *Mary.* Six persons are known by this name in the NT. This one is unknown apart from this reference.
16:7 *Junias.* A feminine name. *among the apostles.* Two interpretations are given: 1. "Apostles" is used in a wider sense than the twelve—to include preachers of the gospel recognized by the churches (see Acts 14:4,14; 1 Thess 2:6). 2. "Apostles" is preceded by the definite article, which may indicate that the twelve are in view. In this case, the meaning would be that these two persons were outstanding "in the opinion of" the apostles.
16:8–10 *Ampliatus . . . Urbanus . . . Stachys . . . Apelles.* All common slave names found in the imperial household.
16:10 *Aristobulus.* Perhaps refers to the grandson of Herod the Great and brother of Herod Agrippa I.
16:11 *my kinsman.* Perhaps a reference to his being a Jew. *Narcissus.* Sometimes identified with Tiberius Claudius Narcissus, a wealthy freedman of the Roman emperor Tiberius.
16:12 *Tryphaena and Tryphosa.* Perhaps sisters, even twins, because it was common for such persons to be given names from the same root. *Persis.* Means "Persian woman."
16:14–15 None of these persons can be further identified, except that they were slaves or freedmen in the Roman church.
16:16 *holy kiss.* See 1 Cor 16:20; 2 Cor 13:12; 1 Thess 5:26; 1 Pet 5:14. Justin Martyr (A.D. 150) tells us that the holy kiss was a regular part of the worship service in his day. It is still a practice in some churches.
16:17–20 A theological application of the story of man's fall (Gen 3).
16:17 *those who cause dissensions and hindrances.* Who these people were we cannot tell, but some of their characteristics are mentioned in v. 18.
16:19 *wise in what is good.* Christians are to be experts in doing good.
16:20 *God of peace.* See 15:33. *will soon crush Satan.* A reference to Satan's final doom (cf. Gen 3:15). For "soon" see note on 13:12.
16:21 *Jason.* Possibly the Jason mentioned in Acts 17:5–9. *Sosipater.* Probably Sopater son of Pyrrhus from Berea (see Acts 20:4).
16:22 *I, Tertius, who write this letter.* Not mentioned elsewhere in the NT. He had functioned as Paul's secretary.
16:23 *Gaius.* Usually identified with Titius Justus, a God-fearer, in whose house Paul stayed while in Corinth (see Acts 18:7; 1 Cor 1:14). His full name would be Gaius Titius Justus. *whole church.* In Corinth. *Erastus.* At Corinth archaeologists have discovered a reused block of stone in a paved square, with the Latin inscription: "Erastus, commissioner of public works, bore the expense of this pavement." This may refer to the Erastus mentioned here. If it does, it is the earliest reference to a Christian by name outside the NT. He may also be the same person referred to in Acts 19:22 and 2 Tim 4:20, though it is difficult to be certain because the name was fairly common. *Quartus.* Means "fourth (son)."
16:25 *my gospel.* Not a gospel different from that preached by others, but a gospel Paul received by direct revelation (see Gal 1:12). *preaching of Jesus Christ.* A description of the gospel; it is about Jesus Christ, who is its content. *mystery.* See note on 11:25. *for long ages.* From eternity past (see 1 Cor 2:6–10).
16:26 *manifested, and by the Scriptures of the prophet.* See 1:2. *all the nations.* The universality of the gospel (see Matt 28:19).
16:27 *to . . . God . . . be the glory.* The ultimate purpose of all things.

1 Corinthians

INTRODUCTION

Author and Date

Paul is acknowledged as the author both by the letter itself (1:1–2; 16:21) and by the early church fathers. His authorship was attested by Clement of Rome as early as A.D. 96, and today practically all NT scholars concur. The letter was written c. 55 toward the close of Paul's three-year residency in Ephesus (see 16:5–9; Acts 20:31). It is clear from his reference to staying at Ephesus until Pentecost (16:8) that he intended to remain there somewhat less than a year when he wrote 1 Corinthians.

The City of Corinth

It has been estimated that in Paul's day Corinth had a population of about 250,000 free persons, plus as many as 400,000 slaves. In a number of ways it was the chief city of Greece.

1. *Its commerce.* Located just off the Corinthian isthmus, it was a crossroads for travelers and traders. It had two harbors: (1) Cenchrea, six miles to the east on the Saronic Gulf, and (2) Lechaion, a mile and a half to the west on the Corinthian Gulf. Goods flowed across the isthmus on the Diolkos, a road by which smaller ships could be hauled fully loaded across the isthmus, and by which cargoes of larger ships could be transported by wagons from one side to the other. Goods flowed through the city from Italy and Spain to the west and from Asia Minor, Phoenicia and Egypt to the east.

2. *Its culture.* Although Corinth was not a university town like Athens, it was characterized nevertheless by typical Greek culture. Its people were interested in Greek philosophy and placed a high premium on wisdom.

3. *Its religion.* Corinth contained at least 12 temples. Whether they were all in use during Paul's time is not known for certain. One of the most infamous was the temple dedicated to Aphrodite, the goddess of love, whose worshipers practiced religious prostitution. About a fourth of a mile north of the theater stood the temple of Asclepius, the god of healing, and in the middle of the city the sixth-century B.C. temple of Apollo was located. In addition, the Jews had established a synagogue; the inscribed lintel of it has been found and placed in the museum at old Corinth.

4. *Its immorality.* Like any large commercial city, Corinth was a center for open and unbridled immorality. The worship of Aphrodite fostered prostitution in the name of religion. At one time 1,000 sacred prostitutes served her temple. So widely known did the immorality of Corinth become that the Greek verb "to Corinthianize" came to mean "to practice sexual immorality." In a setting like this it is no wonder that the Corinthian church was plagued with numerous problems.

Occasion and Purpose

Paul had received information from several sources concerning the conditions existing in the church at Corinth. Some members of the household of Chloe had informed him of the factions that had developed in the church (1:11). There were three individuals—Stephanas, Fortunatus and Achaicus—who had come to Paul in Ephesus to make some contribution to his ministry (16:17), but whether these were the ones from Chloe's household we do not know.

Some of those who had come had brought disturbing information concerning moral irregularities in the church (chs. 5—6). Immorality had plagued the Corinthian assembly almost from the beginning. From 5:9–10 it is apparent that Paul had written previously concerning moral laxness. He had urged believers "not to associate with immoral people" (5:9). Because of misunderstanding he now finds it necessary to clarify his instruction (5:10–11) and to urge immediate and drastic action (5:3–5,13).

Other Corinthian visitors had brought a letter from the church that requested counsel on several subjects (see 7:1; cf. 8:1; 12:1; 16:1).

It is clear that, although the church was gifted (see 1:4–7), it was immature and unspiritual (3:1–4). Paul's purposes for writing were: (1) to instruct and restore the church in its areas of weakness, correcting erroneous practices such as divisions (1:10—4:21), immorality (ch. 5; 6:12–20), litigation in pagan courts (6:1–8) and abuse of the Lord's Supper (11:17–34); (2) to correct false teaching concerning the resurrection (ch. 15); and (3) to give instruction concerning the offering for poverty-stricken believers in Jerusalem (16:1–4).

Theme

The letter revolves around the theme of problems in Christian conduct in the church. It thus has to do with progressive sanctification, the continuing development of holiness of character. Obviously Paul was personally concerned with the Corinthians' problems, revealing a true pastor's (shepherd's) heart.

Relevance

This letter is timely for the church today, both to instruct and to inspire. Most of the questions and problems that confronted the church at Corinth are still very much with us—problems like immaturity, instability, divisions, jealousy and envy, lawsuits, marital difficulties, sexual immorality and misuse of spiritual gifts. Yet in spite of this concentration on problems, the book contains some of the most familiar and beloved chapters in the entire Bible—e.g., ch. 13 (on love) and ch. 15 (on resurrection).

Corinth in the Time of Paul

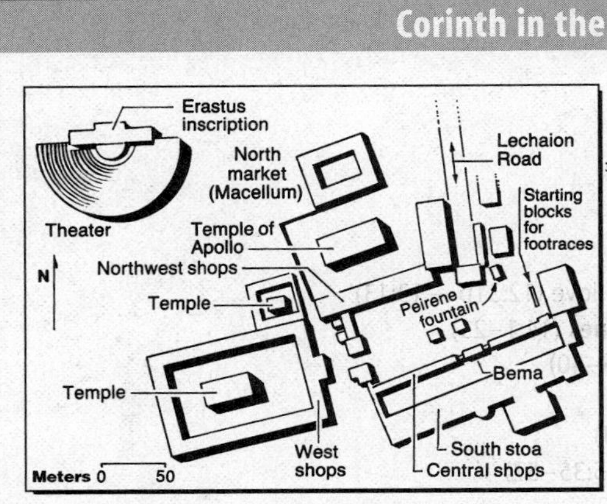

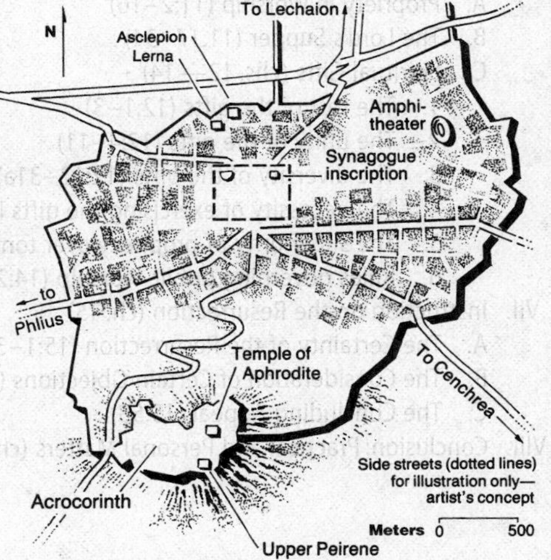

The city of Corinth, perched like a one-eyed Titan astride the narrow isthmus connecting the Greek mainland with the Peloponnese, was one of the dominant commercial centers of the Hellenic world as early as the eighth century B.C.

No city in Greece was more favorably situated for land and sea trade. With a high, strong citadel at its back, it lay between the Saronic Gulf and the Ionian Sea and ports at Lechaion and Cenchrea. A *diolkos*, or stone tramway for the overland transport of ships, linked the two seas. Crowning the Acrocorinth was the temple of Aphrodite, served, according to Strabo, by more than 1,000 pagan priestess-prostitutes.

By the time the gospel reached Corinth in the spring of A.D. 52, the city had a proud history of leadership in the Achaian League, and a spirit of revived Hellenism under Roman domination following the destruction of the city by Mummius in 146 B.C.

Paul's lengthy stay in Corinth brought him directly in contact with the major monuments of the *agora*, many of which still survive. The fountain-house of the spring *Peirene*, the temple of Apollo, the *macellum* or meat market (1 Cor 10:25) and the theater, the *bema* (Acts 18:12), and the unimpressive synagogue all played a part in the experience of the apostle. An inscription from the theater names the city official Erastus, probably the friend of Paul mentioned in Rom 16:23.

Outline

I. Introduction (1:1–9)

II. Divisions in the Church (1:10—4:21)
   A. The Fact of the Divisions (1:10–17)
   B. The Causes of the Divisions (1:18—4:13)
      1. A wrong conception of the Christian message (1:18–3:4)
      2. A wrong conception of Christian ministry and ministers (3:5—4:5)
      3. A wrong conception of the Christian (4:6–13)
   C. The Exhortation to End the Divisions (4:14–21)

III. Moral and Ethical Disorders in the Life of the Church (chs. 5—6)
   A. Laxity in Church Discipline (ch. 5)
   B. Lawsuits before Non-Christian Judges (6:1–11)
   C. Licentiousness or Sexual Immorality (6:12–20)

IV. Instruction on Marriage (ch. 7)
   A. The Prologue: General Principles (7:1–7)
   B. The Problems of the Married (7:8–24)
   C. The Problems of the Unmarried (7:25–40)

V. Instruction on Questionable Practices (8:1—11:1)
   A. The Principles Involved (ch. 8)
   B. The Principles Illustrated (ch. 9)
   C. A Warning from the History of Israel (10:1–22)
   D. The Principles Applied (10:23—11:1)

VI. Instruction on Public Worship (11:2—14:40)
   A. Propriety in Worship (11:2–16)
   B. The Lord's Supper (11:17–34)
   C. Spiritual Gifts (chs. 12—14)
      1. The test of the gifts (12:1–3)
      2. The unity of the gifts (12:4–11)
      3. The diversity of the gifts (12:12–31a)
      4. The necessity of exercising the gifts in love (12:31b—13:13)
      5. The superiority of prophecy over tongues (14:1–25)
      6. Rules governing public worship (14:26–40)

VII. Instruction on the Resurrection (ch. 15)
   A. The Certainty of the Resurrection (15:1–34)
   B. The Consideration of Certain Objections (15:35–57)
   C. The Concluding Appeal (15:58)

VIII. Conclusion: Practical and Personal Matters (ch. 16)

Appeal to Unity

1 Paul, [a]called *as* an apostle of Jesus Christ [1]by [b]the will of God, and [c]Sosthenes our [d]brother,

2 To [a]the church of God which is at [b]Corinth, to those who have been sanctified in Christ Jesus, [1]saints [c]by calling, with all who in every place [d]call on the name of our Lord Jesus Christ, their *Lord* and ours:

3 [a]Grace to you and peace from God our Father and the Lord Jesus Christ.

4 [a]I thank [1]my God always concerning you for the grace of God which was given you in Christ Jesus,

5 that in everything you were [a]enriched in Him, in all [b]speech and [b]all knowledge,

6 even as [a]the testimony concerning Christ was confirmed [1]in you,

7 so that you are not lacking in any gift, [a]awaiting eagerly the revelation of our Lord Jesus Christ,

8 [a]who will also confirm you to the end, blameless in [b]the day of our Lord Jesus Christ.

9 [a]God is faithful, through whom you were [b]called into [c]fellowship with His Son, Jesus Christ our Lord.

10 Now [a]I exhort you, [b]brethren, by the name of our Lord Jesus Christ, that you all [1]agree and that there be no [2][c]divisions among you, but that you be [3]made complete in [d]the same mind and in the same judgment.

1:1 [1]Lit *through* [a]Rom 1:1 [b]Rom 1:10; 2 Tim 1:1 [c]Acts 18:17 [d]Acts 1:15
2 [1]Or *holy ones* [a]1 Cor 10:32 [b]Acts 18:1 [c]Rom 1:7; 8:28 [d]Acts 7:59
3 [a]Rom 1:7
4 [1]Two early mss do not contain *my* [a]Rom 1:8
5 [a]2 Cor 9:11 [b]Rom 15:14; 2 Cor 8:7
6 [1]Or *among* [a]2 Thess 1:10; 1 Tim 2:6; 2 Tim 1:8; Rev 1:2
7 [a]Luke 17:30; Rom 8:19, 23; Phil 3:20; 2 Pet 3:12
8 [a]Rom 8:19; Phil 1:6; Col 2:7; 1 Thess 3:13; 5:23 [b]Luke 17:24, 30; 1 Cor 5:5; 2 Cor 1:14; Phil 1:6, 10; 2:16; 1 Thess 5:2; 2 Thess 2:2
9 [a]Deut 7:9; Is 49:7; 1 Cor 10:13; 2 Cor 1:18; 1 Thess 5:24; 2 Thess 3:3 [b]Rom 8:28 [c]1 John 1:3
10 [1]Lit *speak the same thing* [2]Lit *schisms* [3]Or *united* [a]Rom 12:1 [b]Rom 1:13 [c]1 Cor 11:18 [d]Rom 12:16; Phil 1:27

11 For I have been informed concerning you, my brethren, by Chloe's *people,* that there are quarrels among you.

12 Now I mean this, that [a]each one of you is saying, "I am of Paul," and "I of [b]Apollos," and "I of [c]Cephas," and "I of Christ."

13 [1]Has Christ been divided? Paul was not crucified for you, was he? Or were you [a]baptized [2]in the name of Paul?

14 [1]I thank God that I [a]baptized none of you except [a]Crispus and [b]Gaius,

15 so that no one would say you were baptized [1]in my name.

16 Now I did baptize also the [a]household of Stephanas; beyond that, I do not know whether I baptized any other.

17 [a]For Christ did not send me to baptize, but to preach the gospel, [b]not in [1]cleverness of speech, so that the cross of Christ would not be made void.

The Wisdom of God

18 For the word of the cross is [a]foolishness to [b]those who [1]are perishing, but to us who [2]are being saved it is [c]the power of God.

19 For it is written,

"[a]I WILL DESTROY THE WISDOM OF THE WISE,

12 [a]Matt 23:8-10; 1 Cor 3:4 [b]Acts 18:24; 1 Cor 3:22 [c]John 1:42; 1 Cor 3:22; 9:5; 15:5 **13** [1]Or *Christ has been divided!* or *Christ is divided!* [2]Lit *into* [a]Matt 28:19; Acts 2:38 **14** [1]Two early mss read *I give thanks that* [a]Acts 18:8 [b]Rom 16:23 **15** [1]Lit *into* **16** [a]1 Cor 16:15, 17 **17** [1]Lit *wisdom* [a]John 4:2; Acts 10:48 [b]1 Cor 2:1, 4, 13; 2 Cor 10:10; 11:6 **18** [1]Or *perish* [2]Or *are saved* [a]1 Cor 1:21, 23, 25; 2:14; 4:10 [b]Acts 2:47; 2 Cor 2:15; 4:3; 2 Thess 2:10 [c]Rom 1:16; 1 Cor 1:24 **19** [a]Is 29:14

1:1 *Paul.* The Greek custom was to begin a letter with the writer's name. For more information on Paul see notes on Acts 9:1; Phil 3:4–14. *apostle of Jesus Christ.* See notes on Mark 6:30; Heb 3:1. Paul uses this title in all his letters (except Philippians, 1,2 Thessalonians and Philemon) to establish his authority as Christ's messenger—an authority that had been challenged (see ch. 9; 2 Cor 11). He reinforces his authority by adding "by the will of God," i.e., by divine initiative. *Sosthenes.* Perhaps the synagogue ruler at Corinth who was assaulted by the Greeks (Acts 18:17). If so, he obviously became a Christian—possibly while Paul was preaching at Corinth (Acts 18:18) or during Apollos's ministry there (Acts 19:1).

1:2 *church of God.* Used only by Paul and only in Acts 20:28, here and 2 Cor 1:1. Its OT counterpart is the expression "assembly (or community) of the LORD" (see Deut 23:1; see also Num 16:3; 20:4; 1 Chr 28:8). *sanctified.* Set apart for the Lord. It can also mean "made holy," which is done by (1) being declared holy through faith in Christ's atoning death on the cross (sometimes called positional sanctification), and (2) being made holy by the work of the Holy Spirit in the lives of Christians (sometimes called progressive sanctification). In spite of the fact that Paul found much in the Corinthian Christians to criticize, he still called them "sanctified"—not because of their conduct, but because of their relationship to Christ (positional sanctification).

1:3 *Grace . . . and peace.* See notes on Jon 4:2; John 14:27; 20:19; Gal 1:3; Eph 1:2.

1:4 *thank.* See Rom 1:8.

1:5 *speech and . . . knowledge.* Gifts of the Spirit (see 12:8; also 2 Cor 8:7).

1:6 *confirmed.* Paul's preaching about Christ had been accepted by the Corinthians, and they had proved it to be true.

1:7 *any gift.* Probably refers to the spiritual gifts of chs. 12–14. According to those chapters, a spiritual gift is a manifestation of the Holy Spirit enabling one to minister to the needs of Christ's body, the church (see 12:7–11; 14:3,12,17). The Greek word used here stresses that it is a gift of grace.

1:8 *who.* God the Father. *the end.* Of the age, when Christ comes again. *in the day of our Lord Jesus Christ.* When He returns (v. 7; Phil 1:6).

1:9 *God is faithful.* He may be trusted to do what He has promised (1 Thess 5:24), namely, to "confirm you to the end" (v. 8).

1:10 *brethren.* In Christ believers have a unity similar to that of blood brothers and sisters. Paul is referring to both men and women (see 16:20; Rom 16:3,6–7,12–13,15).

1:11 *quarrels.* See Gal 5:20; James 4:1–2.

1:12 *Apollos.* He had carried on a fruitful ministry in Corinth (Acts 18:24–28; 19:1). *Cephas.* Peter. It has been suggested that those who followed Peter in Corinth were Jewish Christians.

1:13 *Has Christ been divided?* See 12:12–13. *in the name of Paul?* Implies becoming a follower or intimate associate.

1:16 *household.* Other examples of households being baptized are those of Cornelius (Acts 10:24, 48), Lydia (Acts 16:15) and the Philippian jailer (Acts 16:33–34). The term may include family members, servants or anyone who lived in the house. *Stephanas.* See 16:15,17.

1:17 *not . . . to baptize.* Paul is not minimizing baptism; rather, he is asserting that his God-given task was primarily to preach. Jesus (John 4:2) and Peter (Acts 10:48) also had others baptize for them. *cleverness of speech.* Lit. "wisdom of speech." Paul's mission was not to couch the gospel in the language of the trained orator, who had studied the techniques of influencing people by persuasive arguments.

1:19 The quotation is from Is 29:14, where God denounced the policy of the "wise" in Judah in seeking an alliance with Egypt

AND THE CLEVERNESS OF THE CLEVER I WILL
SET ASIDE."
20 [a]Where is the wise man? Where is the
scribe? Where is the debater of [b]this age?
Has not God [c]made foolish the wisdom of
[d]the world?
21 For since in the wisdom of God [a]the
world through its wisdom did not *come to*
know God, [b]God was well-pleased through
the [c]foolishness of the [1]message preached to
[d]save those who believe.
22 For indeed [a]Jews ask for [1]signs and
Greeks search for wisdom;
23 but we preach [1][a]Christ crucified, [b]to
Jews a stumbling block and to Gentiles [c]fool-
ishness,
24 but to those who are [a]the called, both
Jews and Greeks, Christ [b]the power of God
and [c]the wisdom of God.
25 Because the [a]foolishness of God is wiser than men, and [b]the weakness of God is
stronger than men.
26 For [1]consider your [a]calling, brethren,
that there were [b]not many wise according to
[2]the flesh, not many mighty, not many noble;
27 but [a]God has chosen the foolish things
of [b]the world to shame the wise, and God
has chosen the weak things of [b]the world to
shame the things which are strong,
28 and the base things of [a]the world and
the despised God has chosen, [b]the things
that are not, so that He may [c]nullify the
things that are,
29 so that [a]no [1]man may boast before
God.
30 But [1]by His doing you are in [a]Christ
Jesus, who became to us [b]wisdom from God,
[2]and [c]righteousness and [d]sanctification, and
[e]redemption,
31 so that, just as it is written, "[a]LET HIM
WHO BOASTS, BOAST IN THE LORD."

Paul's Reliance upon the Spirit

2 And when I came to you, brethren, I [a]did
not come with superiority of speech or of
wisdom, proclaiming to you [b]the [1]testimony
of God.
2 For I determined to know nothing
among you except [a]Jesus Christ, and Him
crucified.
3 I was with you in [a]weakness and in
[b]fear and in much trembling,
4 and my [1]message and my preaching
were [a]not in persuasive words of wisdom, but
in demonstration of [b]the Spirit and of power,
5 so that your faith would not [1]rest on
the wisdom of men, but on [a]the power of
God.
6 Yet we do speak wisdom among those
who are [a]mature; a wisdom, however, not of
[b]this age nor of the rulers of [b]this age, who
are [c]passing away;
7 but we speak God's wisdom in a [a]mys-
tery, the hidden *wisdom* which God [b]predes-
tined before the [c]ages to our glory;

20 [a]Job 12:17; Is 19:11f; 33:18 [b]Matt 13:22; 1 Cor 2:6, 8; 3:18, 19 [c]Rom 1:20ff [d]John 12:31; 1 Cor 1:27f; 6:2; 11:32; James 4:4
21 [1]Lit *preaching* [a]John 12:31; 1 Cor 1:27f; 6:2; 11:32; James 4:4 [b]Luke 12:32; Gal 1:15; Col 1:19 [c]1 Cor 1:18, 23, 25; 2:14; 4:10 [d]Rom 11:14; James 5:20
22 [1]Or *attesting miracles* [a]Matt 12:38
23 [1]I.e. Messiah [a]1 Cor 2:2; Gal 3:1; 5:11 [b]Luke 2:34; 1 Pet 2:8 [c]1 Cor 1:18, 21, 25; 2:14; 4:10
24 [a]Rom 8:28 [b]Rom 1:16; 1 Cor 1:18 [c]Luke 11:49; 1 Cor 1:30
25 [a]1 Cor 1:18, 21, 23; 2:14; 4:10 [b]2 Cor 13:4
26 [1]Lit *see* [2]I.e. human standards [a]Rom 11:29 [b]Matt 11:25; 1 Cor 1:20; 2:8
27 [a]James 2:5 [b]1 Cor 1:20
28 [a]1 Cor 1:20 [b]Rom 4:17 [c]Job 34:19; 1 Cor 2:6; 2 Thess 2:8; Heb 2:14
29 [1]Lit *flesh* [a]Eph 2:9
30 [1]Lit *of Him* [a]Rom 8:1; 1 Cor 4:15
30 [2]Or *both* [b]1 Cor 1:24 [c]Jer 23:5f; 33:16; 2 Cor 5:21; Phil 3:9 [d]1 Cor 1:2; 6:11; 1 Thess 5:23 [e]Rom 3:24; Eph 1:7, 14; Col 1:14
31 [a]Jer 9:23f; 2 Cor 10:17
2:1 [1]One early ms reads *mystery* [a]1 Cor 1:17; 2:4, 13 [b]1 Cor 2:7
2 [a]1 Cor 1:23; Gal 6:14
3 [a]1 Cor 4:10; 2 Cor 11:30; 12:5, 9f; 13:9 [b]Is 19:16; 2 Cor 7:15; Eph 6:5
4 [1]Lit *word* [a]1 Cor 1:17; 2:1, 13 [b]Rom 15:19; 1 Cor 4:20
5 [1]Lit *be* [a]2 Cor 4:7; 6:7; 12:9
6 [a]Eph 4:13; Phil 3:15; Heb 5:14; 6:1 [b]Matt 13:22; 1 Cor 1:20 [c]1 Cor 1:28
7 [a]Rom 11:25; 16:25f; 1 Cor 2:1 [b]Rom 8:29f [c]Heb 1:2; 11:3

when threatened by King Sennacherib of Assyria. *THE WISE.* Aristides said that on every street in Corinth one met a so-called wise man, who had his own solutions to the world's problems.

1:20 *wise man.* Probably a reference to Gentile philosophers in general. *scribe.* Probably the Jewish teacher of the law (see note on Matt 2:4). *debater of this age.* Probably refers to the Greek sophists, who engaged in long and subtle disputes. *God made foolish the wisdom of the world.* All humanly devised philosophical systems end in meaninglessness because they have a wrong concept of God and His revelation.

1:21 *wisdom . . . foolishness.* Jesus expresses a similar thought in Luke 10:21. It is God's intention that worldly wisdom should not be the means of knowing Him. *foolishness of the message preached.* Not that preaching is foolish, but that the message being preached (Christ crucified) is viewed by the world as foolish.

1:22 *Greeks search for wisdom.* True of Greeks in general, but especially of the Greek philosophers.

1:23 *Christ crucified.* See 2:2. *to Jews a stumbling block.* They expected a triumphant, political Messiah (Acts 1:6), not a crucified one. *to Gentiles foolishness.* Greeks and Romans were sure that no reputable person would be crucified, so it was unthinkable that a crucified criminal could be the Savior.

1:24 *power.* See Rom 1:4,16; Mark 12:24. *wisdom.* See v. 30. The crucified Christ is the power that saves and the wisdom that transforms seeming folly into ultimate and highest discernment.

1:26–31 The Corinthian Christians themselves were living proof that salvation does not depend on anything in man, so that when someone is saved, he must boast in the Lord (v. 31).

1:30 *by His doing you are in Christ.* It is God who has called you to union and communion with Christ. *righteousness.* It is by faith in Christ that we are justified (declared righteous); see Rom 5:19. *sanctification.* See note on v. 2. *redemption.* See note on Rom 3:24.

2:1 *when I came to you.* On his initial trip to Corinth c. A.D. 51 (Acts 18). *with superiority of speech or of wisdom.* See note on 1:17. Perhaps Apollos (Acts 18:24–28) had influenced the Corinthians in such a way that they were placing undue emphasis on eloquence and intellectual ability.

2:2 *know nothing . . . except Jesus Christ.* Paul resolved to make Christ the sole subject of his teaching and preaching while he was with them. *Jesus Christ.* See 1:30. *Him crucified.* See 1:17–18,23.

2:4 *not in persuasive words of wisdom.* This does not give preachers a license to neglect study and preparation. Paul's letters reveal a great deal of knowledge in many areas of learning, and his eloquence is apparent in his address before the Areopagus (see Acts 17:22–31 and notes). Paul's point is that unless the Holy Spirit works in a listener's heart, the wisdom and eloquence of a preacher are ineffective. Paul's confidence as a preacher did not rest on intellectual and oratorical ability, as did that of the Greek orators (see note on 1:17). *demonstration.* The Greek word is used of producing proofs in an argument in court. Paul's preaching was marked by the convincing demonstration of the power of the Holy Spirit.

2:6 *mature.* Wise, developed Christians; contrast the "infants" mentioned in 3:1 (see Heb 5:13–6:3).

2:7 *mystery.* Cf. Rom 16:25–26; Eph 3:4–5; 1 Tim 3:16. The mys-

8 *the wisdom* [a]which none of the rulers of [b]this age has understood; for if they had understood it they would not have crucified [c]the Lord of glory;

9 but just as it is written,

"[a]THINGS WHICH EYE HAS NOT SEEN AND EAR HAS NOT HEARD,
AND *which* HAVE NOT ENTERED THE HEART OF MAN,
ALL THAT GOD HAS PREPARED FOR THOSE WHO LOVE HIM."

10 [1][a]For to us God revealed *them* [b]through the Spirit; for the Spirit searches all things, even the [c]depths of God.

11 For who among men knows the *thoughts* of a man except the [a]spirit of the man which is in him? Even so the *thoughts* of God no one knows except the Spirit of God.

12 Now we [a]have received, not the spirit of [b]the world, but the Spirit who is from God, so that we may know the things freely given to us by God,

13 which things we also speak, [a]not in words taught by human wisdom, but in those taught by the Spirit, [1]combining spiritual *thoughts* with spiritual *words.*

14 But [1]a [a]natural man [b]does not accept the things of the Spirit of God, for they are [c]foolishness to him; and he cannot understand them, because they are spiritually [2]appraised.

15 But he who is [a]spiritual appraises all things, yet he himself is appraised by no one.

16 For [a]WHO HAS KNOWN THE MIND OF THE LORD, THAT HE WILL INSTRUCT HIM? But [b]we have the mind of Christ.

8 [a]1 Cor 1:26; 2:6 [b]Matt 13:22; 1 Cor 1:20 [c]Acts 7:2; James 2:1
9 [a]Is 64:4; 65:17
10 [1]One early ms reads *But* [a]Matt 11:25; 13:11; 16:17; Gal 1:12; Eph 3:3, 5 [b]John 14:26 [c]Rom 11:33ff
11 [a]Prov 20:27
12 [a]Rom 8:15 [b]1 Cor 1:27
13 [1]Or *interpreting spiritual* things *for spiritual* men [a]1 Cor 1:17; 2:1, 4
14 [1]Or *an unspiritual* [2]Or *examined* [a]1 Cor 15:44, 46; James 3:15; Jude 19 mg [b]John 14:17 [c]1 Cor 1:18
15 [a]1 Cor 3:1; 14:37; Gal 6:1
16 [a]Is 40:13; Rom 11:34 [b]John 15:15

3:1 [a]1 Cor 2:15; 14:37; Gal 6:1 [b]Rom 7:14; 1 Cor 2:14 [c]1 Cor 2:6; Eph 4:14; Heb 5:13
2 [a]Heb 5:12f; 1 Pet 2:2 [b]John 16:12
3 [1]Lit *according to man* [a]Rom 13:13; 1 Cor 1:10f; 11:18 [b]1 Cor 3:4
4 [a]1 Cor 1:12 [b]1 Cor 3:3
5 [a]Rom 15:16; 2 Cor 3:3, 6; 4:1; 5:18; 6:4; Eph 3:7; Col 1:25; 1 Tim 1:12

Foundations for Living

3 And I, brethren, could not speak to you as to [a]spiritual men, but as to [b]men of flesh, as to [c]infants in Christ.

2 I gave you [a]milk to drink, not solid food; for you [b]were not yet able *to receive it.* Indeed, even now you are not yet able,

3 for you are still fleshly. For since there is [a]jealousy and strife among you, are you not fleshly, and are you not walking [1][b]like mere men?

4 For when [a]one says, "I am of Paul," and another, "I am of Apollos," are you not *mere* [b]men?

5 What then is Apollos? And what is Paul? [a]Servants through whom you believed, even [b]as the Lord gave *opportunity* to each one.

6 [a]I planted, [b]Apollos watered, but [c]God was causing the growth.

7 So then neither the one who plants nor the one who waters is anything, but God who causes the growth.

8 Now he who plants and he who waters are one; but each will [a]receive his own [1]reward according to his own labor.

9 For we are God's [a]fellow workers; you are God's [1][b]field, God's [c]building.

10 According to [a]the grace of God which was given to me, like a wise master builder [b]I laid a foundation, and [c]another is building on it. But each man must be careful how he builds on it.

[b]Rom 12:6; 1 Cor 3:10 **6** [a]1 Cor 4:15; 9:1; 15:1; 2 Cor 10:14f [b]Acts 18:24-27; 1 Cor 1:12 [c]1 Cor 15:10 **8** [1]Or *wages* [a]1 Cor 3:14; 4:5; 9:17; Gal 6:4 **9** [1]Or *cultivated land* [a]Mark 16:20; 2 Cor 6:1 [b]Is 61:3; Matt 15:13 [c]1 Cor 3:16; Eph 2:20-22; Col 2:7; 1 Pet 2:5 **10** [a]Rom 12:3; 1 Cor 15:10 [b]Rom 15:20; 1 Cor 3:11f [c]1 Thess 3:2

tery, or secret, was once hidden but is now known because God has revealed it to His people (v. 10). To unbelievers it is still hidden. *to our glory.* God's wisdom will cause every believer to share eventually in Christ's glory (Rom 8:17).

2:8 *rulers of this age.* Such as the chief priests (Luke 24:20), Pilate and Herod Antipas (cf. Acts 4:27). *crucified the Lord of glory.* The cross is here contrasted with the majesty of the victim.

2:9 *ALL THAT GOD HAS PREPARED.* Probably not to be limited to either present or future blessing; both are involved (cf. vv. 7, 12).

2:10 *Spirit searches all things.* Not in order to know them, for He knows all things. Instead He comprehends the depth of God's nature and His plans of grace; so He is fully competent to make the revelation claimed here.

2:12 *spirit of the world.* Cf. v. 6 ("wisdom . . . of this age"); the spirit of human wisdom as alienated from God—the attitude of the sinful nature (Rom 8:6–7).

2:13 *those taught by the Spirit.* The message Paul proclaimed was expressed in words given by the Holy Spirit. Thus spiritual truth was aptly combined with fitting spiritual words.

2:14–3:4 This passage explains why many fail to apprehend true wisdom (2:9). It is because such wisdom is perceived by the spiritual (mature) Christian (2:14–16; cf. v. 6). The Corinthians, however, were worldly (infant) believers (3:1–4), and the proof of their immaturity was their division over human leaders (3:3–4).

2:14 *natural man.* Described in Jude 19 as one who is "worldly-minded" (cf. Rom 8:9). The non-Christian is basically dominated by the merely physical, worldly or natural life. Because he does not possess the Holy Spirit, he is not equipped to receive appreciatively truth that comes from the Spirit. Such a person needs the new birth (John 3:1–8; Titus 3:5–6). *foolishness.* See 1:18.

2:15 *spiritual.* Mature (v. 6). *appraised by no one.* One who does not have the Spirit is not qualified to judge the spiritual person. Thus believers are not rightfully subject to the opinions of unbelievers.

3:1 *brethren.* See note on 1:10. *spiritual.* See note on 2:15. *men of flesh.* See note on 2:14–3:4.

3:2 *milk . . . not solid food.* See notes on Heb 5:12–14.

3:3 *like mere men.* Like men of the world instead of men of God. They were following merely human standards.

3:4 *I am of Paul . . . Apollos.* See 1:12.

3:6 *I planted.* See Acts 18:4–11. Paul's work was of a pioneer nature, preaching where no one had ever preached before. *Apollos watered.* See Acts 18:24–28. Apollos worked in the established church, edifying the converts Paul had won.

3:9 *God's field.* The people are God's farm. *God's building.* They are also depicted as God's temple (vv. 16–17). He owns the farm and the building where both Paul and Apollos worked.

3:10 *I laid a foundation.* By preaching Christ and Him crucified (2:2). *another.* Apollos.

11 For no man can lay a [a]foundation other than the one which is laid, which is Jesus
Christ.
12 Now if any man builds on the foundation with gold, silver, [1]precious stones,
wood, hay, straw,
13 [a]each man's work will become evident;
for [b]the day will show it because it is *to be*
revealed with fire, and the fire itself will test
[1]the quality of each man's work.
14 If any man's work which he has built
on it remains, he will [a]receive a reward.
15 If any man's work is burned up, he will
suffer loss; but he himself will be saved, yet
[a]so as through fire.
16 [a]Do you not know that [b]you are a
[1]temple of God and *that* the Spirit of God
dwells in you?
17 If any man destroys the [1]temple of God,
God will destroy him, for the [1]temple of God
is holy, and [2]that is what you are.
18 [a]Let no man deceive himself. [b]If any
man among you thinks that he is wise in
[c]this age, he must become foolish, so that he
may become wise.
19 For [a]the wisdom of this world is foolishness before God. For it is written, *"He is*
[b]THE ONE WHO CATCHES THE WISE IN THEIR CRAFTI-
NESS";
20 and again, "[a]THE LORD KNOWS THE REA-
SONINGS of the wise, THAT THEY ARE USELESS."
21 So then [a]let no one boast in men. For
[b]all things belong to you,
22 [a]whether Paul or Apollos or Cephas or
the world or [b]life or death or things present
or things to come; all things belong to you,
23 and [a]you belong to Christ; and [b]Christ
belongs to God.

11 [a]Is 28:16; Eph 2:20; 1 Pet 2:4ff
12 [1]Or *costly*
13 [1]Lit *of what sort each man's work is* [a]1 Cor 4:5 [b]Matt 10:15; 1 Cor 1:8; 2 Thess 1:7-10; 2 Tim 1:12, 18; 4:8
14 [a]1 Cor 3:8; 4:5; 9:17; Gal 6:4
15 [a]Job 23:10; Ps 66:10, 12; Jude 23
16 [1]Or *sanctuary* [a]Rom 6:16 [b]Rom 8:9; 1 Cor 6:19; 2 Cor 6:16; Eph 2:21f
17 [1]Or *sanctuary* [2]Lit *who you are*
18 [a]Is 5:21 [b]1 Cor 8:2; Gal 6:3 [c]1 Cor 1:20
19 [a]1 Cor 1:20 [b]Job 5:13
20 [a]Ps 94:11
21 [a]1 Cor 4:6 [b]Rom 8:32
22 [a]1 Cor 1:12; 3:5, 6 [b]Rom 8:38
23 [a]1 Cor 15:23; 2 Cor 10:7; Gal 3:29 [b]1 Cor 11:3; 15:28

4:1 [a]Luke 1:2 [b]1 Cor 9:17; Titus 1:7; 1 Pet 4:10 [c]Rom 11:25; 16:25
2 [1]Lit *in*
3 [1]Lit *day*
4 [a]Acts 23:1; 2 Cor 1:12 [b]Ps 143:2; Rom 2:13
5 [1]Lit *judging anything* [2]I.e. the appointed time of judgment [a]Matt 7:1; Rom 2:1 [b]John 21:22; Rom 2:16 [c]1 Cor 3:13 [d]Rom 2:29; 1 Cor 3:8; 2 Cor 10:18
6 [1]Lit *puffed up* [a]1 Cor 1:19, 31; 3:19f [b]1 Cor 4:18f; 8:1; 13:4 [c]1 Cor 1:12; 3:4
7 [a]John 3:27; Rom 12:3, 6; 1 Pet 4:10
8 [a]Rev 3:17f

Servants of Christ

4 Let a man regard us in this manner, as
[a]servants of Christ and [b]stewards of [c]the
mysteries of God.
2 In this case, moreover, it is required [1]of
stewards that one be found trustworthy.
3 But to me it is a very small thing that I
may be examined by you, or by *any* human
[1]court; in fact, I do not even examine myself.
4 For I [a]am conscious of nothing against
myself, yet I am not by this [b]acquitted; but
the one who examines me is the Lord.
5 Therefore [a]do not go on [1]passing judgment before [2]the time, *but wait* [b]until the
Lord comes who will both [c]bring to light the
things hidden in the darkness and disclose
the motives of *men's* hearts; and then each
man's [d]praise will come to him from God.
6 Now these things, brethren, I have figuratively applied to myself and Apollos for
your sakes, so that in us you may learn not
to exceed [a]what is written, so that no one of
you will [b]become [1]arrogant [c]in behalf of one
against the other.
7 For who regards you as superior?
[a]What do you have that you did not receive?
And if you did receive it, why do you boast
as if you had not received it?
8 You are [a]already filled, you have
already become rich, you have become kings
without us; and indeed, *I* wish that you had
become kings so that we also might reign
with you.
9 For, I think, God has exhibited us apos-

3:12 *gold, silver, precious stones.* Precious, durable work that stands the test of divine judgment; symbolic of pure Christian doctrine and living. *wood, hay, straw.* Worthless work that will not stand the test; symbolic of weak, insipid teaching and life.
3:13 Cf. 4:5; 2 Cor 5:10. *the day.* See note on 1:8. *fire.* God's judgment. The work of some believers will stand the test while that of others will disappear—emphasizing the importance of teaching the pure word of God.
3:15 *loss.* Of reward (v. 14). *as through fire.* Perhaps a Greek proverbial phrase, meaning "by a narrow escape," with one's work burned up by the fire of God's pure justice and judgment.
3:16 *temple of God.* God's church. Paul does not mean here that each of his readers is a temple of the Holy Spirit. He says, "You yourselves (plural) are God's temple (singular)." In 6:19 he speaks of each Christian as a temple of the Holy Spirit.
3:17 *God will destroy him.* Strong language, indicating that such a foolish laborer is not one of the Lord's true servants. This is in contrast to the thought of v. 15, where the faulty Christian worker is saved, but his work is destroyed (he suffers loss of reward). In the context of chs. 1–4 Paul here refers to people who tear the local church apart by factions and quarrels (1:11–12). *holy.* Sacred, set apart for God's use and glory; so do not desecrate the church by breaking it up into various factions.
3:18 *become foolish.* Turn away from human wisdom (from being "wise in this age"). Cf. 1:18. *become wise.* Cf. 1:21, 24.
3:21 *in men.* About being some man's disciple (see 1:12; 3:4; cf. 1:31; 4:6). *all things belong to you.* All these Christian leaders belong to the whole church. No group can call one leader its very own (see vv. 22–23).
3:23 *you belong to Christ.* You are united with and belong to Christ. *Christ belongs to God.* Christ is in union with God the Father (John 10:30) and with God the Holy Spirit (2 Cor 13:14). Similarly, Christians are in union with the church's true leaders (v. 22) and with Christ (v. 23), who in turn is in union with the other members of the Trinity.
4:1 *stewards.* The Greek underlying this phrase means "house manager." *mysteries.* Things that human wisdom cannot discover but that are now revealed by God to His people (see note on Rom 11:25).
4:3 *not even examine myself.* His judgment was merely human, and his conscience may be mistaken (v. 4). Only God is fully qualified to judge.
4:5 *the time.* When God will judge believers (see 3:13). *disclose the motives.* Cf. Ps 19:12; 139:23–24; Heb 4:12–13.
4:6 *these things.* See 3:5–4:5. *learn not to exceed what is written.* Perhaps a proverb common among the rabbis. *what is written.* In Scripture. Our view of man should be Biblical (cf. v. 7; 1:9, 31; 3:19–20; Rom 12:3). We should recognize man's weakness and ever-present limitations. *become arrogant.* One of the root causes of divisions.
4:8 Paul uses irony and sarcasm here to get the Corinthians to see how poor they really are because of their haughtiness and spiritual immaturity in comparison with apostles.

tles last of all, as men [a]condemned to death;
because we [b]have become a spectacle to the
world, [1]both to angels and to men.
10 We are [a]fools for Christ's sake, but
[b]you are prudent in Christ; [c]we are weak,
but you are strong; you are distinguished,
but we are without honor.
11 To this present hour we are both [a]hun-
gry and thirsty, and are poorly clothed, and
are roughly treated, and are homeless;
12 and we toil, [a]working with our own
hands; when we are [b]reviled, we bless; when
we are [c]persecuted, we endure;
13 when we are slandered, we try to [1]con-
ciliate; we have [a]become as the scum of the
world, the dregs of all things, *even* until now.
14 I do not write these things to [a]shame
you, but to admonish you as my beloved
[b]children.
15 For if you were to have countless
[a]tutors in Christ, yet *you would* not *have*
many fathers, for in [b]Christ Jesus I [c]became
your father through the [d]gospel.
16 Therefore I exhort you, be [a]imitators of
me.
17 For this reason I [a]have sent to you
[b]Timothy, who is my [c]beloved and faithful
child in the Lord, and he will remind you of
my ways which are in Christ, [d]just as I teach
everywhere in every church.
18 Now some have become [1a]arrogant, as
though I were not [b]coming to you.
19 But I [a]will come to you soon, [b]if the
Lord wills, and I shall find out, not the
[1]words of those who are [c]arrogant but their
power.

9 [1]Or *and to angels and to men* [a]Rom 8:36; 1 Cor 15:31; 2 Cor 11:23 [b]Heb 10:33 **10** [a]Acts 17:18; 26:24; 1 Cor 1:18 [b]1 Cor 1:19f; 3:18; 2 Cor 11:19 [c]1 Cor 2:3; 2 Cor 13:9 **11** [a]Rom 8:35; 2 Cor 11:23-27 **12** [a]Acts 18:3 [b]1 Pet 3:9 [c]John 15:20; Rom 8:35 **13** [1]Or *console* [a]Lam 3:45 **14** [a]1 Cor 6:5; 15:34 [b]2 Cor 6:13; 12:14; 1 Thess 2:11; 1 John 2:1; 3 John 4 **15** [a]Gal 3:24f [b]1 Cor 1:30 [c]Num 11:12; 1 Cor 3:8; Gal 4:19; Philem 10 [d]1 Cor 9:12, 14, 18, 23; 15:1 **16** [a]1 Cor 11:1; Phil 3:17; 4:9; 1 Thess 1:6; 2 Thess 3:9 **17** [a]1 Cor 16:10 [b]Acts 16:1 [c]1 Cor 4:14; 1 Tim 1:2, 18; 2 Tim 1:2 [d]1 Cor 7:17; 14:33; 16:1; Titus 1:5 **18** [1]Lit *puffed up* [a]1 Cor 4:6 [b]1 Cor 4:21 **19** [1]Lit *word* [a]Acts 19:21; 20:2; 1 Cor 11:34; 16:5f; 16:7-9; 2 Cor 1:15f [b]Acts 18:21 [c]1 Cor 4:6

20 For the kingdom of God does [a]not consist in [1]words but in power.
21 What do you desire? [a]Shall I come to
you with a rod, or with love and a spirit of
gentleness?

Immorality Rebuked

5 It is actually reported that there is
immorality among you, and immorality of
such a kind as does not exist even among the
Gentiles, that someone has [a]his father's wife.
2 [1]You [a]have become [2]arrogant and
[1]have not [b]mourned instead, so that the one
who had done this deed would be [c]removed
from your midst.
3 For I, on my part, though [a]absent in
body but present in spirit, have already
judged him who has so committed this, as
though I were present.
4 [a]In the name of our Lord Jesus, when
you are assembled, and [1]I with you in spirit,
[b]with the power of our Lord Jesus,
5 *I have decided* to [a]deliver such a one to
[b]Satan for the destruction of his flesh, so that
his spirit may be saved in [c]the day of the
Lord [1]Jesus.
6 [a]Your boasting is not good. [b]Do you
not know that [c]a little leaven leavens the
whole lump *of dough?*
7 Clean out the old leaven so that you

20 [1]Lit *word* [a]1 Cor 2:4 **21** [a]2 Cor 1:23; 2:1, 3; 12:20; 13:2, 10 **5:1** [a]Lev 18:8; Deut 22:30; 27:20 **2** [1]Or *have you...?* [2]Lit *puffed up* [a]1 Cor 4:6 [b]2 Cor 7:7-10 [c]1 Cor 5:13 **3** [a]Col 2:5; 1 Thess 2:17 **4** [1]Lit *my spirit, with the power* [a]2 Thess 3:6 [b]John 20:23; 2 Cor 2:10; 13:3, 10 **5** [1]Two early mss do not contain *Jesus* [a]Prov 23:14; Luke 22:31; 1 Tim 1:20 [b]Matt 4:10 [c]1 Cor 1:8 **6** [a]1 Cor 5:2; James 4:16 [b]Rom 6:16 [c]Hos 7:4; Matt 16:6, 12; Gal 5:9

4:9 *apostles.* See note on 1:1. *spectacle.* "Theater" is derived from the Greek word used here. Paul refers to the gladiatorial contests in the arena (or perhaps to the triumphal procession of a victorious Roman general). He pictures all the world and even angels looking on while the apostles are brought in last to fight to the death.

4:10 More irony.

4:11–13 A graphic description of Paul's condition in Ephesus right up to the writing of this letter.

4:12 *we toil, working with our own hands.* Paul was a tentmaker by trade (Acts 18:3; cf. 20:34–35; 1 Cor 9:6,18). *we bless.* See Matt 5:44. *endure.* Instead of retaliating.

4:14 *my beloved children.* See v. 15.

4:15 *your father.* See 3:6,10.

4:18 *some.* Some of the Corinthians who were trying to undercut Paul's authority (see 9:1–3) were teaching that he was unstable (2 Cor 1:17) and that his ministry was not important (2 Cor 10:10).

4:19 *arrogant.* See 5:2.

4:20 *kingdom of God.* God's present reign in the lives of His people—that dynamic new life in Christ (2 Cor 5:17), the power of the new birth (John 3:3–8), showing itself in a humble life, dedicated to Christ and His church. *not . . . in words but in power.* Idle, empty talk is contrasted with the genuine power of the Holy Spirit.

5:1 *not . . . even among the Gentiles.* The Roman orator Cicero states that incest was practically unheard of in Roman society. *his father's wife.* That this expression was used rather than "his mother" suggests that the woman was his stepmother. The OT prohibited such sexual relations (Lev 18:8; Deut 27:20).

5:2 *arrogant.* Evidently proud of their liberty—a distortion of grace. *removed from your midst.* Excommunicated from the church (cf. John 9:22).

5:4 *In the name of our Lord Jesus, when you are assembled.* The Corinthians are to pass judgment on the man by the authority of the Lord Jesus. *the power of our Lord Jesus.* Jesus' power is present through His word and His Holy Spirit.

5:5 *deliver such a one to Satan.* Abandon this sinful man to the devil that he may afflict the man as he pleases. This abandonment to Satan was to be accomplished, not by some magical incantation, but by expelling the man from the church (see v. 13; also vv. 2,7,11). To expel him was to put him out in the devil's territory, severed from any connection with God's people. *for the destruction of his flesh.* Satan is allowed to bring physical affliction on the man, which would bring him to repentance. *his spirit may be saved.* Cf. 3:15. The person put out of the church may well be a Christian. *day of the Lord Jesus.* When Christ returns (see 1:7).

5:6 *a little leaven . . . the whole lump of dough.* To illustrate Christian holiness and discipline, Paul alludes to the prohibition against the use of leaven (or yeast) in the bread eaten in the Passover Feast (see Ex 12:15). Leaven in Scripture usually symbolizes evil or sin (see note on Mark 8:15), and the church here is called on to get rid of the leaven of sin (v. 8) because they are an unleavened batch of dough—new creations in Christ (2 Cor 5:17).

5:7 *Clean out the old leaven.* Perhaps refers to the Passover custom of sweeping all the (leavened) bread crumbs out of one's

may be a new lump, just as you are *in fact*
unleavened. For Christ our [a]Passover also
has been sacrificed.
8 Therefore let us celebrate the feast,
[a]not with old leaven, nor with the leaven of
malice and wickedness, but with the unleavened bread of sincerity and truth.
9 I wrote you in my letter [a]not to associate with immoral people;
10 I *did* not at all *mean* with the immoral
people of this world, or with the covetous
and swindlers, or with [a]idolaters, for then
you would have to go out of the world.
11 But [1]actually, I wrote to you not to
associate [2]with any so-called [a]brother if he is
an immoral person, or covetous, or [b]an idolater, or a reviler, or a drunkard, or a
swindler—not even to eat with such a one.
12 For what have I to do with judging
[a]outsiders? [b]Do you not judge those who are
within *the church?*
13 But those who are outside, God
[1]judges. [a]REMOVE THE WICKED MAN FROM AMONG
YOURSELVES.

Lawsuits Discouraged

6 Does any one of you, when he has a [1]case
against his neighbor, dare to go to law
before the unrighteous and [a]not before the
[2]saints?
2 Or [a]do you not know that [b]the [1]saints
will judge [c]the world? If the world is judged
by you, are you not competent *to* [2]*constitute*
the smallest law courts?
3 [a]Do you not know that we will judge
angels? How much more matters of this life?
4 So if you have law courts dealing with
matters of this life, [1]do you appoint them as
judges who are of no account in the church?
5 [a]I say *this* to your shame. *Is it* so, *that*
there is not among you one wise man who
will be able to decide between his [b]breth-
ren,
6 but brother goes to law with brother,
and that before [a]unbelievers?
7 Actually, then, it is already a defeat for
you, that you have lawsuits with one another. [a]Why not rather be wronged? Why not
rather be defrauded?
8 On the contrary, you yourselves wrong
and defraud. *You do* this even to *your* [a]breth-
ren.
9 Or [a]do you not know that the unrighteous will not [b]inherit the kingdom of God?
[c]Do not be deceived; [d]neither fornicators,
nor idolaters, nor adulterers, nor [1]effeminate,
nor homosexuals,
10 nor thieves, nor *the* covetous, nor

7 [a]Mark 14:12; 1 Pet 1:19 **8** [a]Ex 12:19; 13:7; Deut 16:3 **9** [a]2 Cor 6:14; Eph 5:11; 2 Thess 3:6 **10** [a]1 Cor 10:27 **11** [1]Lit *now* [2]Lit *together if any man called a brother is* [a]Acts 1:15; 2 Thess 3:6 [b]1 Cor 10:7, 14, 20f **12** [a]Mark 4:11 [b]1 Cor 5:3-5; 6:1-4 **13** [1]Or *will judge* [a]Deut 13:5; 17:7, 12; 21:21; 22:21; 1 Cor 5:2 **6:1** [1]Lit *matter* [2]Or *holy ones* [a]Matt 18:17 **2** [1]V 1, note 2 [a]Rom 6:16 [b]Dan 7:18, 22, 27; Matt 19:28

2 [2]Or try *the trivial cases?* [c]1 Cor 1:20 **3** [a]Rom 6:16 **4** [1]Or *appoint them...church* **5** [a]1 Cor 4:14; 15:34 [b]Acts 1:15; 9:13; 1 Cor 6:1 **6** [a]2 Cor 6:14f; 1 Tim 5:8

7 [a]Matt 5:39f **8** [a]1 Thess 4:6 **9** [1]I.e. effeminate by perversion [a]Rom 6:16 [b]Acts 20:32; 1 Cor 15:50; Gal 5:21; Eph 5:5 [c]Luke 21:8; 1 Cor 15:33; Gal 6:7; James 1:16; 1 John 3:7 [d]Rom 13:13; 1 Cor 5:11; Gal 5:19-21; Eph 5:5; 1 Tim 1:10; Rev 21:8; 22:15

house before preparing the Passover meal. *as you are in fact unleavened.* Positionally they were a new batch, already sanctified in God's sight (see 1:2; 6:11), but Paul calls on them to become holy also in conduct (see note on 1:2). *Christ our Passover.* In His death on the cross, Christ fulfilled the true meaning of the Jewish sacrifice of the Passover lamb (Is 53:7; John 1:29). Christ, the Lamb of God, was crucified on Passover day, a celebration that began the evening before when the Passover meal was eaten (cf. Ex 12:8).

5:8 *let us celebrate the feast.* Keeping the Feast of Unleavened Bread (which followed Passover) symbolizes living the Christian life in holy dedication to God (cf. Rom 12:1–2; 1 Pet 2:5) and not getting involved in such sins as malice and wickedness and incestuous relations.

5:9 *I wrote you in my letter.* Paul here clarifies a previous letter (one not preserved). The Corinthians mistook that letter to mean that, on separating from sin, they should disassociate themselves from all immoral persons, including non-Christian people. Instead, Paul meant that they should separate from immoral persons in the church who claimed to be Christian brothers (vv. 10–11).

5:11 *not even to eat with such a one.* Calling oneself a Christian while continuing to live an immoral life is reprehensible and degrading, and gives a false testimony to Christ. If the true Christian has intimate association with someone who does this, the non-Christian world may assume that the church approves such immoral, ungodly living and thus the name of Christ would be dishonored. Questions could arise concerning the true character of the Christian's own testimony (cf. Rom 16:17–18; 2 Thess 3:6, 14–15).

5:12 *judge those who are within.* The church is to exercise spiritual discipline over the professing believers in the church (cf. Matt 18:15–18), but it is not to attempt to judge the unsaved world. There are governing authorities to do that (Rom 13:1–5), and the ultimate judgment of the world is to be left to God (v. 13; cf. Rev 20:11–15).

6:1 *a case against his neighbor.* Paul seems to be talking about various kinds of property court cases here (cf. the phrase "rather be cheated," v. 7), not criminal cases that should be handled by the state (Rom 13:3–4). *before the saints.* The Corinthians should take their property cases before qualified Christians for settlement. In Paul's day the Romans allowed the Jews to apply their own law in property matters, and since the Romans did not yet consider Christians as a separate class from the Jews, Christians no doubt had the same rights.

6:2 *saints will judge the world.* With Christ. Cf. Matt 19:28; 2 Tim 2:12; Rev 20:4. *competent to constitute the smallest law courts.* Paul views believers as fully competent to judge cases where Christians have claims against each other, because they view matters from a godly vantage point. In comparison with their future role in the judgment of the world and of angels, judgments concerning things of this life are insignificant.

6:3 *we will judge angels.* Cf. 2 Pet 2:4,9; Jude 6.

6:4 *judges who are of no account.* Either the verse suggests that the least in the church are capable of judging such small matters, or it asks ironically if believers should submit their cases to pagan judges, who really are not qualified to decide on cases between Christians.

6:7 *already a defeat.* Most likely by greed, retaliation and hatred, instead of practicing unselfishness, forgiveness and love—even willingness to suffer loss.

6:9 *not inherit the kingdom of God.* Cf. John 3:3–5. *fornicators.* Paul here identifies three kinds of sexually immoral persons: adulterers, male prostitutes and males who practice homosexuality. In Rom 1:26 he adds the category of females who practice homosexuality. People who engage in such practices, as well as the other offenders listed in vv. 9–10, are explicitly excluded from God's kingdom (but see next note).

drunkards, nor revilers, nor swindlers, will
[a]inherit the kingdom of God.
11 [a]Such were some of you; but you were
[b]washed, but you were [c]sanctified, but you
were [d]justified in the name of the Lord Jesus
Christ and in the Spirit of our God.

The Body Is the Lord's

12 [a]All things are lawful for me, but not all
things are profitable. All things are lawful for
me, but I will not be mastered by anything.
13 [a]Food is for the [1]stomach and the
[1]stomach is for food, but God will [b]do away
with both [2]of them. Yet the body is not for
immorality, but [c]for the Lord, and [d]the Lord
is for the body.
14 Now God has not only [a]raised the
Lord, but [b]will also raise us up through His
power.
15 [a]Do you not know that [b]your bodies
are members of Christ? Shall I then take
away the members of Christ and make them
members of a prostitute? [c]May it never be!
16 Or [a]do you not know that the one who
joins himself to a prostitute is one body *with
her*? For He says, "[b]THE TWO SHALL BECOME ONE
FLESH."
17 But the one who joins himself to the
Lord is [a]one spirit *with Him.*

10 [a]Acts 20:32; 1 Cor 15:50; Gal 5:21; Eph 5:5
11 [a]1 Cor 12:2; Eph 2:2f; Col 3:5-7; Titus 3:3-7 [b]Acts 22:16; Eph 5:26 [c]1 Cor 1:2, 30 [d]Rom 8:30
12 [a]1 Cor 10:23
13 [1]Lit *belly* [2]Lit *it and them* [a]Matt 15:17 [b]Col 2:22 [c]1 Cor 6:15, 19 [d]Gal 5:24; Eph 5:23
14 [a]Acts 2:24 [b]John 6:39f; 1 Cor 15:23
15 [a]1 Cor 6:3 [b]Rom 12:5; 1 Cor 6:13; 12:27; Eph 5:30 [c]Luke 20:16
16 [a]1 Cor 6:3 [b]Gen 2:24; Matt 19:5; Mark 10:8; Eph 5:31
17 [a]John 17:21-23; Rom 8:9-11; 1 Cor 6:15; Gal 2:20
18 [1]Or *one who practices immorality* [a]1 Cor 6:9; 2 Cor 12:21; Eph 5:3; Col 3:5; Heb 13:4
19 [1]Or *sanctuary* [2]Or

18 [a]Flee immorality. Every *other* sin that a
man commits is outside the body, but the
[1]immoral man sins against his own body.
19 Or [a]do you not know that [b]your body is
a [1]temple of the Holy Spirit who is in you,
whom you have from [2]God, and that [c]you
are not your own?
20 For [a]you have been bought with a
price: therefore glorify God in [b]your body.

Teaching on Marriage

7 Now concerning the things about which
you wrote, it is [a]good for a man not to
touch a woman.
2 But because of immoralities, each man
is to have his own wife, and each woman is
to have her own husband.
3 The husband must [1]fulfill his duty to
his wife, and likewise also the wife to her
husband.
4 The wife does not have authority over
her own body, but the husband *does;* and
likewise also the husband does not have
authority over his own body, but the wife
does.

God? And you...own [a]1 Cor 6:3 [b]John 2:21; 1 Cor 3:16; 2 Cor 6:16 [c]Rom 14:7f **20** [a]Acts 20:28; 1 Cor 7:23; 1 Pet 1:18f; 2 Pet 2:1; Rev 5:9 [b]Rom 12:1; Phil 1:20 **7:1** [a]1 Cor 7:8, 26 **3** [1]Lit *render*

6:11 *Such were some of you.* God, however, does save and sanctify people like those described in vv. 9–10.

6:12 *All things are lawful for me.* Paul is probably quoting some in the Corinthian congregation who boasted that they had a right to do anything they pleased. The apostle counters by observing that such "freedom" of action may not benefit the Christian. *not be mastered by anything.* One may become enslaved by those actions in which he "freely" indulges (see note on 10:23).

6:13 *Food is for the stomach and the stomach is for food.* Paul quotes some Corinthians again who were claiming that as the physical acts of eating and digesting food have no bearing on one's inner spiritual life, so the physical act of promiscuous sexual activity does not affect one's spiritual life. *the body is not for immorality, but for the Lord.* Paul here declares the dignity of the human body: It is intended for the Lord. Although granting that food and the stomach are transitory, Paul denies that what one does with his body is unimportant. This is particularly true of the use of sex, which the Lord has ordained in wedlock for the good of mankind (cf. Heb 13:4).

6:14 *God . . . raised the Lord . . . also raise us.* As an illustration of God's high regard for the body, Paul cites the resurrection of Christ's body and, eventually, the believer's body (15:51–53; 1 Thess 4:16–17). A body destined for resurrection should not be used for immorality.

6:15 *members of Christ.* See 12:27. It is not merely the spirit that is a member of Christ's body; it is the whole person, consisting of spirit and body. This fact gives dignity to the human body.

6:16 *one body with her.* In a sexual relationship the two bodies become one (cf. Gen 2:24; Matt 19:5), and a new human being may emerge from the sexual union. Sexual relations outside the marriage bond are a gross perversion of the divinely established marriage union.

6:17 *one spirit with Him.* There is a higher union than the marriage bond: the believer's spiritual union with Christ, which is the perfect model for the kind of unity that should mark the marriage relationship (cf. Eph 5:21–33).

6:18 *other sin . . . is outside the body.* Perhaps means that in a unique way, sexual immorality gratifies one's physical body. Or, since the word "other" does not occur in the Greek text, Paul may be quoting a Corinthian slogan (see note on v. 12), which he refutes in the second half of the verse. *the immoral man sins against his own body.* The body is a temple of the Holy Spirit (v. 19); thus to use it in prostitution disgraces God's temple. Furthermore, the prostitutes of Corinth were dedicated to the service of Aphrodite, the goddess of love and sex. See note on 7:2.

6:19 *your body is a temple of the Holy Spirit.* The Christian should value his body as a sacred place where God dwells and should realize that by the Spirit's presence and power he can be helped against such sins as sexual immorality (Rom 8:9). *not your own.* Cf. 1 Pet 2:9.

6:20 *glorify God in your body.* Cf. 10:31; Rom 6:12–13; Col 3:17.

7:1 *things about which you wrote.* The Corinthians had written Paul, asking him a number of vexing questions (see 8:1; 12:1). *good for a man not to touch a woman.* Because of the crisis at Corinth (v. 26). Elsewhere (Eph 5:22–33; Col 3:18–19; 1 Tim 3:2,12; 5:14) Paul spoke strongly in favor of the married state, and in 1 Tim 4:1–3 he taught that forbidding to marry would be a sign of the end-time apostasy. Another possible interpretation is that Paul is again (see notes on 6:12–13,18) quoting a slogan of the Corinthians suggesting it was good for a man not to have sexual relations with a woman. He refutes this idea in v. 2 by stating that sexual relations have their proper expression in marriage.

7:2 *immoralities.* Example: The temple to Aphrodite on the Acrocorinth, the rocky eminence above Corinth, at one time had in service 1,000 prostitute priestesses.

7:3 *fulfill his duty to his wife.* Married couples should have normal sexual relations. Permanent abstention deprives the other partner of his or her natural right and may be conducive to temptation.

7:4 *likewise.* Both husband and wife have conjugal rights and exclusive possession of the other in this area.

5 [a]Stop depriving one another, except by
agreement for a time, so that you may devote
yourselves to prayer, and [1]come together
again so that [b]Satan will not tempt you
because of your lack of self-control.
6 But this I say by way of concession,
[a]not of command.
7 [1]Yet I wish that all men were [a]even as I
myself am. However, [b]each man has his own
gift from God, one in this manner, and
another in that.
8 But I say to the unmarried and to widows that it is [a]good for them if they remain
[b]even as I.
9 But if they do not have self-control, [a]let
them marry; for it is better to marry than to
burn *with passion*.
10 But to the married I give instructions,
[a]not I, but the Lord, that the wife should not
[1]leave her husband
11 (but if she does leave, she must remain
unmarried, or else be reconciled to her husband), and that the husband should not
[1]divorce his wife.
12 But to the rest [a]I say, not the Lord, that
if any brother has a wife who is an unbeliever, and she consents to live with him, he
must not [1]divorce her.
13 And a woman who has an unbelieving
husband, and he consents to live with her,
she must not [1]send her husband away.
14 For the unbelieving husband is sanctified through his wife, and the unbelieving
wife is sanctified through [1]her believing husband; for otherwise your children are
unclean, but now they are [a]holy.
15 Yet if the unbelieving one leaves, let
him leave; the brother or the sister is not
under bondage in such *cases,* but God has
called [1]us [2a]to peace.
16 For how do you know, O wife, whether
you will [a]save your husband? Or how do you
know, O husband, whether you will save
your wife?
17 Only, [a]as the Lord has assigned to each
one, as God has called each, in this manner
let him walk. And [b]so I direct in [c]all the
churches.
18 Was any man called *when he was
already* circumcised? He is not to become
uncircumcised. Has anyone been called in
uncircumcision? [a]He is not to be circumcised.
19 [a]Circumcision is nothing, and uncircumcision is nothing, but *what matters is*
[b]the keeping of the commandments of God.
20 [a]Each man must remain in that [1]condi-
tion in which he was called.
21 Were you called while a slave? [1]Do not
worry about it; but if you are able also to
become free, rather [2]do that.
22 For he who was called in the Lord
while a slave, is [a]the Lord's freedman; likewise he who was called while free, is
[b]Christ's slave.

5 [1]Lit *be* [a]Ex 19:15; 1 Sam 21:5 [b]Matt 4:10
6 [a]2 Cor 8:8
7 [1]One early ms reads *For* [a]1 Cor 7:8; 9:5 [b]Matt 19:11f; Rom 12:6; 1 Cor 12:4, 11
8 [a]1 Cor 7:1, 26 [b]1 Cor 7:7; 9:5
9 [a]1 Tim 5:14
10 [1]Lit *depart from* [a]Mal 2:16; Matt 5:32; 19:3-9; Mark 10:2-12; Luke 16:18; 1 Cor 7:6
11 [1]Or *leave his wife*
12 [1]Or *leave her* [a]1 Cor 7:6; 2 Cor 11:17
13 [1]Or *leave her husband*
14 [1]Lit *the brother*
14 [a]Ezra 9:2; Mal 2:15
15 [1]One early ms reads *you* [2]Lit *in* [a]Rom 14:19
16 [a]Rom 11:14; 1 Pet 3:1
17 [a]Rom 12:3 [b]1 Cor 4:17 [c]1 Cor 11:16; 14:33; 2 Cor 8:18; 11:28; Gal 1:22; 1 Thess 2:14; 2 Thess 1:4
18 [a]Acts 15:1ff
19 [a]Rom 2:27, 29; Gal 3:28; 5:6; 6:15; Col 3:11 [b]Rom 2:25

20 [1]Lit *calling* [a]1 Cor 7:24 **21** [1]Lit *Let it not be a care to you* [2]Lit *use* **22** [a]John 8:32, 36; Philem 16 [b]Eph 6:6; Col 3:24; 1 Pet 2:16

7:5 *Stop depriving one another.* Of sexual fulfillment. *Satan . . . not tempt you because of your lack of self-control.* The Christian deprived of normal sexual activity with his or her marriage partner may be tempted by Satan to sexual immorality. The normal God-given sexual drive in the human being is strong.

7:6 *concession, not of command.* Although marriage is desirable and according to God's plan, it was not mandatory under the difficult circumstances at Corinth (see v. 26). In another situation (1 Tim 5:14) Paul urges "the younger widows to marry."

7:10 *I give instructions, not I, but the Lord).* Paul is citing a command from the Lord Jesus during His earthly ministry that married couples must stay together (Matt 5:32; 19:3–9; Mark 10:2–12; Luke 16:18). Paul probably heard such commands from other disciples (cf. Gal 1:18–19) or from Jesus Himself by a special revelation.

7:11 *but if she does leave, she must remain unmarried, or else be reconciled.* Paul argues that in the light of Christ's command she (or he) is not to marry again. Rather, the separated or divorced couple are to be reconciled. Clearly the ideal is that marriage should not be permanently disrupted.

7:12 *I say, not the Lord.* Paul is not quoting a direct command from Jesus here. *any brother has a wife . . . an unbeliever.* The apostle is talking here (and in v. 13) about couples already married, when one of them becomes a Christian. If at all possible, they should remain together, unless the unbeliever, whether man or woman, refuses to remain (v. 15).

7:14 *the unbelieving husband . . . wife is sanctified.* The unbelieving partner is influenced by the godly life of the Christian partner; so that family is under the holy influence of the believer and in that sense is sanctified. *your children . . . are holy.* They at least have the advantage of being under the sanctifying influence of one Christian parent (see v. 16) and so may be called holy. Some believe that such children are called holy because they are included with their parents in the new covenant in Christ, just as the children of Abraham were included in the covenant with their father (and so were circumcised).

7:15 *the brother or the sister is not under bondage in such cases.* The believer is not under obligation to try to continue living with the unbeliever. *peace.* If the unbeliever were forced to live with the believer, there would be no peace in the home.

7:17 *as the Lord has assigned to each one . . . let him walk.* Each Christian is to live contentedly for the Lord in whatever economic, social and religious station in life God has placed him. See v. 18 for an example.

7:18 *circumcised . . . uncircumcised.* Jew . . . Gentile. In the religious sphere, Christian Jews should not try to obliterate physically the fact that they are Jews, and Christian Gentiles should not yield to Jewish pressure for circumcision (cf. Acts 15:1–5; Gal 5:1–3).

7:21 *Were you . . . a slave?* In the social and economic sphere, the Christian slave should live contentedly in his situation, realizing that he has become free in Christ (v. 22; John 8:32, 36). *if you are able . . . to become free . . . do that.* If a Christian slave has an opportunity to get his freedom, he should take advantage of it. In the Roman empire slaves were sometimes freed by Roman patricians. There is nothing wrong with seeking to improve your condition, but be content at every stage.

7:22 *he who was . . . free, is Christ's slave.* A man who was not a Roman slave should realize that in a spiritual sense he belonged to Christ, and, because of his allegiance to Christ, he must not oppress the underprivileged slave. Cf. Eph 6:5,9; Col 3:22; 4:1.

23 [a]You were bought with a price; do not become slaves of men.

24 Brethren, [a]each one is to remain with God in that *condition* in which he was called.

25 Now concerning virgins I have [a]no command of the Lord, but I give an opinion as one who [1b]by the mercy of the Lord is trustworthy.

26 I think then that this is good in view of the [1]present [a]distress, that [b]it is good for a man [2]to remain as he is.

27 Are you bound to a wife? Do not seek to be released. Are you released from a wife? Do not seek a wife.

28 But if you marry, you have not sinned; and if a virgin marries, she has not sinned. Yet such will have [1]trouble in this life, and I am trying to spare you.

29 But this I say, brethren, [a]the time has been shortened, so that from now on those who have wives should be as though they had none;

30 and those who weep, as though they did not weep; and those who rejoice, as though they did not rejoice; and those who buy, as though they did not possess;

31 and those who use the world, as though they did not [a]make full use of it; for [b]the form of this world is passing away.

32 But I want you to be free from concern. One who is [a]unmarried is concerned about the things of the Lord, how he may please the Lord;

33 but one who is married is concerned about the things of the world, how he may please his wife,

34 and *his interests* are divided. The woman who is unmarried, and the virgin, is concerned about the things of the Lord, that she may be holy both in body and spirit; but one who is married is concerned about the things of the world, how she may please her husband.

35 This I say for your own benefit; not to put a restraint upon you, but [1]to promote what is appropriate and *to secure* undistracted devotion to the Lord.

36 But if any man thinks that he is acting unbecomingly toward his virgin *daughter*, if she is past her youth, and if it must be so, let him do what he wishes, he does not sin; let [1]her marry.

37 But he who stands firm in his heart, [1]being under no constraint, but has authority [2]over his own will, and has decided this in his own heart, to keep his own virgin *daughter*, he will do well.

38 So then both he who gives his own virgin *daughter* in marriage does well, and he who does not give her in marriage will do better.

39 [a]A wife is bound as long as her husband lives; but if her husband [1]is dead, she is free to be married to whom she wishes, only [b]in the Lord.

40 But [a]in my opinion she is happier if she remains as she is; and I think that I also have the Spirit of God.

Take Care with Your Liberty

8 Now concerning [a]things sacrificed to idols, we know that we all have [b]knowledge. Knowledge [1c]makes arrogant, but love [d]edifies.

2 [a]If anyone supposes that he knows

23 [a]1 Cor 6:20
24 [a]1 Cor 7:20
25 [1]Lit *has had mercy shown on him by the Lord to be trustworthy* [a]1 Cor 7:6 [b]2 Cor 4:1; 1 Tim 1:13, 16
26 [1]Or *impending* [2]Lit *so to be* [a]Luke 21:23; 2 Thess 2:2 [b]1 Cor 7:1, 8
28 [1]Lit *tribulation in the flesh*
29 [a]Rom 13:11f; 1 Cor 7:31
31 [a]1 Cor 9:18 [b]1 Cor 7:29; 1 John 2:17
32 [a]1 Tim 5:5
35 [1]Lit *for what is seemly*
36 [1]Lit *them*
37 [1]Lit *having no necessity* [2]Lit *pertaining to*
39 [1]Lit *falls asleep* [a]Rom 7:2 [b]2 Cor 6:14
40 [a]1 Cor 7:6, 25
8:1 [1]Lit *puffs up* [a]Acts 15:20; 1 Cor 8:4, 7, 10 [b]Rom 15:14; 1 Cor 8:7, 10; 10:15 [c]1 Cor 4:6 [d]Rom 14:19
2 [a]1 Cor 3:18

7:23 *bought with a price . . . not . . . slaves of men.* Christians in all stations of life should realize that their ultimate allegiance is not to men but to Christ, who bought them with His blood (6:20; 1 Pet 1:18–19).

7:25 *Now concerning virgins.* Paul answers another major question the Corinthians had asked (v. 1). *I give an opinion as one who . . . is trustworthy.* Paul is not giving a direct command from Jesus here (as in v. 10; cf. Acts 20:35). In this matter, which is not a question of right and wrong, Paul expresses his own judgment. Even though he put it this way, he is certainly not denying that he wrote under the influence of divine inspiration (see v. 40). And since he writes under inspiration, what he recommends is clearly the better course of action.

7:26 *present distress.* Probably a reference to the pressures of the Christian life in an immoral and particularly hostile environment (cf. vv. 2,28; 5:1; 2 Tim 3:12). Paul's recommendation here does not apply to all times and all situations.

7:28 *trouble.* Times of suffering and persecution for Christ, when being married would mean even greater hardship in taking care of one's mate.

7:29 *time has been shortened.* The time for doing the Lord's work has become increasingly short. Life is fleeting, as times of persecution remind us. Do not be unduly concerned with the affairs of this world (vv. 29–31) because material things are changing and disappearing (v. 31). Some think the reference is to the Lord's second coming.

7:34 *his interests are divided.* He cannot give undistracted service to Christ (v. 35). This is particularly true in times of persecution.

7:36 *he is acting unbecomingly toward his virgin daughter . . . past her youth . . . let her marry.* In the light of hostility toward believers in Corinth, a man might refrain from giving his daughter in marriage. But if he then realizes that his daughter is getting beyond her prime marriageable age and the situation thus seems unfair to her, it is perfectly proper for him to give her in marriage.

7:37 *has authority over his own will . . . will do well.* The man who determines that there is no need for him to give his daughter in marriage under the circumstances has made a good decision too (v. 38).

7:39 *bound as long as her husband lives.* Marriage is a lifelong union (yet see the exception clause in Matt 19:9). *if her husband is dead.* Death breaks the marriage bond, and a Christian is then free to marry another Christian ("only in the Lord").

7:40 *as she is.* A widow. *I think that I also have the Spirit of God.* Paul writes as one convinced that he is guided by the Holy Spirit.

8:1 *Now concerning things sacrificed to idols.* Another matter the Corinthians had written about (see note on 7:1). *sacrificed to idols.* Offered on pagan altars. Meat left over from a sacrifice might be eaten by the priests, eaten by the offerer and his friends at a feast in the temple (see note on v. 10) or sold in the public meat market. Some Christians felt that if they ate such meat, they participated in pagan worship and thus com-

anything, he has not yet [b]known as he ought
to know;
3 but if anyone loves God, he [a]is known
by Him.
4 Therefore concerning the eating of
[a]things sacrificed to idols, we know that
[1]there is [b]no such thing as an idol in the
world, and that [c]there is no God but one.
5 For even if [a]there are so-called gods
whether in heaven or on earth, as indeed
there are many gods and many lords,
6 yet for us [a]there is *but* one God, [b]the
Father, [c]from whom are all things and we
exist for Him; and [d]one Lord, Jesus Christ,
[e]by whom are all things, and we *exist*
through Him.
7 However not all men [a]have this knowledge; but [b]some, being accustomed to the
idol until now, eat *food* as if it were sacrificed to an idol; and their conscience being
weak is defiled.
8 But [a]food will not [1]commend us to
God; we are neither [2]the worse if we do not
eat, nor [3]the better if we do eat.
9 But [a]take care that this [1]liberty of yours
does not somehow become a stumbling
block to the [b]weak.
10 For if someone sees you, who have
[a]knowledge, dining in an idol's temple, will
not his conscience, if he is weak, be
strengthened to eat [b]things sacrificed to
idols?
11 For through [a]your knowledge he who
is weak [b]is ruined, the brother for whose
sake Christ died.
12 [a]And so, by sinning against the
brethren and wounding their conscience
when it is weak, you sin [b]against Christ.
13 Therefore, [a]if food causes my brother
to stumble, I will never eat meat again, so
that I will not cause my brother to stumble.

Paul's Use of Liberty

9 Am I not [a]free? Am I not an [b]apostle?
Have I not [c]seen Jesus our Lord? Are you
not [d]my work in the Lord?
2 If to others I am not an apostle, at least
I am to you; for you are the [a]seal of my
[b]apostleship in the Lord.
3 My defense to those who examine me
is this:
4 [1][a]Do we not have a right to eat and
drink?

2 [b]1 Cor 13:8-12; 1 Tim 6:4 **3** [a]Ps 1:6; Jer 1:5; Amos 3:2; Rom 8:29; 11:2; Gal 4:9 **4** [1]Lit *nothing is an idol in the world;* i.e. an idol has no real existence [a]Acts 15:20; 1 Cor 8:1, 7, 10 [b]Acts 14:15; 1 Cor 10:19; Gal 4:8 [c]Deut 4:35, 39; 6:4; 1 Cor 8:6 **5** [a]2 Thess 2:4 **6** [a]Deut 4:35, 39; 6:4; Is 46:9; Jer 10:6, 7; 1 Cor 8:4 [b]Mal 2:10; Eph 4:6 [c]Rom 11:36 [d]John 13:13; 1 Cor 1:2; Eph 4:5; 1 Tim 2:5 [e]John 1:3; Col 1:16 **7** [a]1 Cor 8:4ff [b]Rom 14:14, 22f **8** [1]Or *present* [2]Lit *lacking* [3]Lit *abounding* [a]Rom 14:17 **9** [1]Lit *right* [a]Rom 14:13, 21; 1 Cor 10:28; Gal 5:13 [b]Rom 14:1; 1 Cor 8:10f **10** [a]1 Cor 8:4ff

10 [b]Acts 15:20; 1 Cor 8:1, 4, 7 **11** [a]1 Cor 8:4ff [b]Rom 14:15, 20 **12** [a]Matt 18:6; Rom 14:20 [b]Matt 25:45 **13** [a]Rom 14:21; 1 Cor 10:32; 2 Cor 6:3; 11:29 **9:1** [a]1 Cor 9:19; 10:29 [b]Acts 14:14; Rom 1:1; 2 Cor 12:12; 1 Thess 2:6; 1 Tim 2:7; 2 Tim 1:11 [c]Acts 9:3, 17; 18:9; 22:14, 18; 23:11; 1 Cor 15:8 [d]1 Cor 3:6; 4:15 **2** [a]John 3:33; 2 Cor 3:2f [b]Acts 1:25 **4** [1]Lit *It is not that we have no right to eat and drink, is it?* [a]1 Cor 9:14; 1 Thess 2:6, 9; 2 Thess 3:8f

promised their testimony for Christ. Other Christians did not feel this way. *knowledge.* Explained in vv. 2–6. *Knowledge makes arrogant.* It fills one with false pride. *love edifies.* Explained in vv. 7–13. The Christian should love his brother who doubts.

8:2 *has not yet known.* The wisest and most knowledgeable Christian realizes that his knowledge is limited. God is the only one who knows all (cf. Rom 11:33–36).

8:3 *if anyone loves God, he is known by Him.* A person who tempers his knowledge with love toward God shows that he is really known and thus accepted by God as one of God's own redeemed (Gal 4:8–9; 1John 4:7–8).

8:4 *no such thing as an idol.* It represents no real god and possesses no power (see Ps 115:4–7; 135:15–17; Is 44:12–20). But there are demons behind them (10:20).

8:5 *so-called gods.* The alleged gods of Greek and Roman mythology. *many gods and many lords.* Not that there actually are many gods and lords. This would contradict the consistent and emphatic teaching of Scripture that there is but one God (Deut 6:4). Paul is recognizing the obvious fact that there are many who are worshiped as gods—though they do not actually exist, to say nothing of being deities.

8:6 *from whom are all things . . . by whom are all things.* See Heb 2:10. God the Father is the ultimate source of all creation (Acts 4:24). God the Son is the dynamic one through whom, with the Father, all things came into existence (John 1:3; Col 1:16).

8:7 *have this knowledge.* Knows that an idol has no personal reality. *their conscience being weak is defiled.* Christians who conceive of an idol as being real cannot rid themselves of this idea. Consequently, they think that in eating meat sacrificed on pagan altars they have involved themselves in pagan worship and thus have sinned against Christ.

8:9 *this liberty of yours.* To eat meat sacrificed to idols because you know that an idol is nothing (v. 4). *the weak.* Those Christians whose consciences are weak, who think it is wrong to eat meat sacrificed to idols.

8:10 *dining in an idol's temple.* At the site of ancient Corinth, archaeologists have discovered two temples containing rooms apparently used for pagan feasts where meat offered to idols was eaten. To such feasts Christians may have been invited by pagan friends.

8:11 *through your knowledge he who is weak is ruined.* The weak Christian is influenced by the example of the stronger Christian and, though he feels it to be wrong, eats the meat that has been offered to an idol. The spiritual destruction that follows is explained in v. 12.

8:12 *wounding their conscience when it is weak.* Eating meat offered to idols when they feel it is wrong tends to blunt their consciences, so that doing what is wrong becomes much easier. The result may be moral tragedy. *you sin against Christ.* Because Christ died for your brother (v. 11), even as He died for you. It is also a sin against Christ because it breaks the unity of the members of His body (the church).

8:13 *I will never eat meat again.* Paul will forever refrain from engaging in the harmless practice of eating meat sacrificed to idols if it will cause his weak Christian brother, who feels it is wrong, also to eat that meat.

9:1 *Am I not free?* Do I not have the rights that any Christian has? *Am I not an apostle?* Some at Corinth (2 Cor 12:11–12) and elsewhere (Gal 1:1; 1:15–2:10) questioned Paul's genuine apostleship. To certify his apostleship Paul gives this proof: that he has seen the Lord Jesus (Acts 9:1–9; 22:6–16; 26:12–18), as was true of the other apostles (Acts 1:21–22). Furthermore, he adds that his ministry has produced true spiritual fruit (the Corinthians) for the Lord, which should confirm to them that he is indeed an apostle.

9:4 *right to eat and drink.* Paul and Barnabas, as God's workers, have a right to have their food and other physical needs supplied at the church's expense (cf. vv. 6,13–14).

5 [1][a]Do we not have a right to take along a
[2]believing wife, even as the rest of the apostles
and the [b]brothers of the Lord and [c]Cephas?
6 Or do only [1][a]Barnabas and I not have a
right to refrain from working?
7 Who at any time serves [a]as a soldier at
his own expense? Who [b]plants a vineyard and
does not eat the fruit of it? Or who tends a
flock and does not [1]use the milk of the flock?
8 I am not speaking these things [a]according
to [1]human judgment, am I? Or does not
the Law also say these things?
9 For it is written in the Law of Moses,
"[a]YOU SHALL NOT MUZZLE THE OX WHILE HE IS
THRESHING." God is not concerned about
[b]oxen, is He?
10 Or is He speaking altogether for our
sake? Yes, [a]for our sake it was written,
because [b]the plowman ought to plow in
hope, and the thresher *to thresh* in hope of
sharing *the crops.*
11 [a]If we sowed spiritual things in you, is it
too much if we reap material things from you?
12 If others share the right over you, do we
not more? Nevertheless, we [a]did not use this
right, but we endure all things [b]so that we will
cause no hindrance to the [c]gospel of Christ.
13 [a]Do you not know that those who [b]per-
form sacred services eat the *food* of the temple, *and* those who attend regularly to the
altar have their share [1]from the altar?
14 So also [a]the Lord directed those who
proclaim the [b]gospel to [c]get their living from
the gospel.
15 But I have [a]used none of these things.
And I am not writing these things so that it
will be done so in my case; for it would be
better for me to die than have any man make
[b]my boast an empty one.
16 For if I preach the gospel, I have nothing to boast of, for [a]I am under compulsion;
for woe is me if I do not preach [b]the gospel.
17 For if I do this voluntarily, I have a
[a]reward; but if against my will, I have a
[b]stewardship entrusted to me.
18 What then is my [a]reward? That, when
I preach the gospel, I may offer the gospel
[b]without charge, so as [c]not to make full use
of my right in the gospel.
19 For though I am [a]free from all *men,* I
have made myself [b]a slave to all, so that I
may [c]win more.
20 [a]To the Jews I became as a Jew, so that
I might win Jews; to those who are under
[1]the Law, as under [1]the Law though [b]not
being myself under [1]the Law, so that I might
win those who are under [1]the Law;
21 to those who are [a]without law, [b]as
without law, though not being without the
law of God but [c]under the law of Christ, so
that I might win those who are without law.
22 To the [a]weak I became weak, that I
might win the weak; I have become [b]all
things to all men, [c]so that I may by all means
save some.
23 I do all things for the sake of the
gospel, so that I may become a fellow partaker of it.
24 [a]Do you not know that those who run
in a race all run, but *only* one receives [b]the
prize? [c]Run in such a way that you may win.

5 [1]Lit *It is not that we have no right to take along...Cephas, is it?* [2]Lit *sister, as wife* [a]1 Cor 7:7f [b]Matt 12:46 [c]Matt 8:14; John 1:42 **6** [1]Lit *I and Barnabas* [a]Acts 4:36 **7** [1]Lit *eat of* [a]2 Cor 10:4; 1 Tim 1:18; 2 Tim 2:3f [b]Deut 20:6; Prov 27:18; 1 Cor 3:6, 8 **8** [1]Lit *man* [a]Rom 3:5 **9** [a]Deut 25:4; 1 Tim 5:18 [b]Deut 22:1-4; Prov 12:10 **10** [a]Rom 4:23f [b]2 Tim 2:6 **11** [a]Rom 15:27; 1 Cor 9:14 **12** [a]Acts 18:3; 20:33; 1 Cor 9:15, 18 [b]2 Cor 6:3; 11:12 [c]1 Cor 4:15; 9:14, 16, 18, 23; 2 Cor 2:12 **13** [1]Lit *with* [a]Rom 6:16 [b]Lev 6:16, 26; 7:6, 31ff; Num 5:9f; 18:8-20, 31; Deut 18:1 **14** [a]Matt 10:10; Luke 10:7; 1 Tim 5:18 [b]1 Cor 4:15; 9:12, 16, 18, 23; 2 Cor 2:12 [c]Luke 10:8; 1 Cor 9:4 **15** [a]Acts 18:3; 20:33; 1 Cor 9:12, 18 [b]2 Cor 11:10 **16** [a]Acts 9:15; Rom 1:14 [b]1 Cor 4:15; 9:12, 14, 18, 23; 2 Cor 2:12 **17** [a]John 4:36; 1 Cor 3:8; 9:18 [b]1 Cor 4:1; Gal 2:7; Eph 3:2; Phil 1:16; Col 1:25 **18** [a]John 4:36; 1 Cor 3:8; 9:17 [b]Acts 18:3; 2 Cor 11:7; 12:13 [c]1 Cor 7:31; 9:12 **19** [a]1 Cor 9:1 [b]2 Cor 4:5; Gal 5:13 [c]Matt 18:15; 1 Pet 3:1 **20** [1]Or *law* [a]Acts 16:3; 21:23-26; Rom 11:14 [b]Gal 2:19 **21** [a]Rom 2:12, 14 [b]Gal 2:3; 3:2 [c]1 Cor 7:22; Gal 6:2 **22** [a]Rom 14:1; 15:1; 2 Cor 11:29 [b]1 Cor 10:33 [c]Rom 11:14 **24** [a]1 Cor 9:13 [b]Phil 3:14; Col 2:18 [c]Gal 2:2; 2 Tim 4:7; Heb 12:1

9:5 *take along a believing wife.* Paul asserts his right to be married, if he wishes. This does not mean that he was married, as some have imagined (see 7:7). Other apostles, including Peter (see Mark 1:30), had wives.

9:11 *reap material things.* Food, lodging and pay supplied by the Corinthians (cf. Gal 6:6). Paul here sets forth the principle that Christian workers should be paid for their labors.

9:12 *did not use this right.* The point of Paul's discussion in ch. 9. He had numerous rights that he did not claim because of his love for the Corinthians. Thus ch. 9 is an extended personal illustration of the practice advocated in ch. 8. Because of love for others, believers should be ready to surrender their rights.

9:13 *those who perform sacred services.* The Corinthian believers would understand this illustration not only from their knowledge of the OT (cf. Lev 7:28–36; Num 18:8–20) but also from the practice in pagan temples in Greece and Rome.

9:15 *my boast.* That he had preached the gospel without charge, so that they could not say that they had paid him for it.

9:16 *I am under compulsion.* The Lord had laid on Paul the necessity of preaching the gospel (Acts 9:1–16; 26:16–18; see also Jer 20:9 and note).

9:18 *my reward . . . when I preach the gospel.* Paul's reward in preaching is not material things but the boasting that he has preached to the Corinthians without charge and has not taken advantage of the rights he deserves: food and drink, shelter and pay (vv. 3–12).

9:19 *I have made myself a slave to all.* Not only did Paul not use his right to material support in preaching the gospel but he also deprived himself—curtailed his personal privileges and social and religious rights—in dealing with different kinds of people. *that I may win.* To bring to Christ.

9:20 *those who are under the Law.* Those under the OT Law and religious practices (the Jews). *as under the Law.* For the Jews' sake Paul conformed to the Jewish Law (Acts 16:3; 18:18; 21:20–26).

9:21 *those who are without law.* Those who have not been raised under the OT law (the Gentiles). *as without law.* Paul accommodated himself to Gentile culture when it did not violate his allegiance to Christ, though he still reckoned that he was under God's law and Christ's law. (By "Christ's law" Paul is probably referring to Christ's teachings, though the term is not necessarily restricted to them.)

9:22 *the weak.* Those whose consciences are weak (8:9–12). *I became weak.* Paul did not exercise his Christian freedom in such things as eating meat sacrificed to idols (8:9,13).

9:23 *become a . . . partaker.* The blessings of realizing that he has been faithful to Christ in preaching, of hearing the Lord's "Well done" (Matt 25:21; Luke 19:17) and of seeing others come to Christ.

9:24 *race all run.* The Corinthians were familiar with the foot races in their own Isthmian games, which occurred every other year and were second only to the Olympic games in impor-

25 Everyone who [a]competes in the games exercises self-control in all things. They then *do it* to receive a perishable [b]wreath, but we an imperishable.

26 Therefore I [a]run in such a way, as not without aim; I box in such a way, as not [b]beating the air;

27 but I [1]discipline [a]my body and make it my slave, so that, after I have preached to others, I myself will not be disqualified.

Avoid Israel's Mistakes

10 For [a]I do not want you to be unaware, brethren, that our fathers were all [b]under the cloud and all [c]passed through the sea;

2 and all were [a]baptized into Moses in the cloud and in the sea;

3 and all [a]ate the same spiritual food;

4 and all [a]drank the same spiritual drink, for they were drinking from a spiritual rock which followed them; and the rock was [1]Christ.

5 Nevertheless, with most of them God was not well-pleased; for [a]they were laid low in the wilderness.

6 Now these things happened as [a]examples for us, so that we would not crave evil things as [b]they also craved.

7 Do not be [a]idolaters, as some of them were; as it is written, "[b]THE PEOPLE SAT DOWN TO EAT AND DRINK, AND STOOD UP TO [c]PLAY."

8 Nor let us act immorally, as [a]some of them [1]did, and [b]twenty-three thousand fell in one day.

9 Nor let us try the Lord, as [a]some of them [1]did, and were destroyed by the serpents.

10 Nor [a]grumble, as some of them [1]did, and [b]were destroyed by the [c]destroyer.

11 Now these things happened to them as an [a]example, and [b]they were written for our instruction, upon whom [c]the ends of the ages have come.

12 Therefore let him who [a]thinks he stands take heed that he does not fall.

13 No temptation has overtaken you but such as is common to man; and [a]God is faithful, who will not allow you to be [b]tempted beyond what you are able, but with the temptation will provide the way of escape also, so that you will be able to endure it.

14 Therefore, my [a]beloved, flee from [b]idolatry.

15 I speak as to wise men; you judge what I say.

16 Is not the [a]cup of blessing which we bless a sharing in the blood of Christ? Is not the [1b]bread which we break a sharing in the body of Christ?

25 [a]Eph 6:12; 1 Tim 6:12; 2 Tim 2:5; 4:7 [b]2 Tim 4:8; James 1:12; 1 Pet 5:4; Rev 2:10; 3:11 **26** [a]Gal 2:2; 2 Tim 4:7; Heb 12:1 [b]1 Cor 14:9 **27** [1]Lit *bruise* [a]Rom 8:13 **10:1** [a]Rom 1:13 [b]Ex 13:21; Ps 105:39 [c]Ex 14:22, 29; Neh 9:11; Ps 66:6 **2** [a]Rom 6:3; 1 Cor 1:13; Gal 3:27 **3** [a]Ex 16:4, 35; Deut 8:3; Neh 9:15, 20; Ps 78:24f; John 6:31 **4** [1]I.e. the Messiah [a]Ex 17:6; Num 20:11; Ps 78:15 **5** [a]Num 14:29ff, 37; 26:65; Heb 3:17; Jude 5 **6** [a]1 Cor 10:11 [b]Num 11:4, 34; Ps 106:14 **7** [a]Ex 32:4; 1 Cor 5:11; 10:14 [b]Ex 32:6 [c]Ex 32:19

8 [1]Lit *acted immorally* [a]Num 25:1ff [b]Num 25:9 **9** [1]Lit *made trial* [a]Num 21:5f **10** [1]Lit *grumbled* [a]Num 16:41; 17:5, 10 [b]Num 16:49 [c]Ex 12:23; 2 Sam 24:16; 1 Chr 21:15; Heb 11:28 **11** [a]1 Cor 10:6 [b]Rom 4:23 [c]Rom 13:11 **12** [a]Rom 11:20; 2 Pet 3:17 **13** [a]1 Cor 1:9 [b]2 Pet 2:9 **14** [a]Heb 6:9 [b]1 Cor 10:7, 19f; 1 John 5:21 **16** [1]Lit *loaf* [a]Matt 26:27f; Mark 14:23f; Luke 22:20; 1 Cor 11:25 [b]Matt 26:26; Luke 22:19; Acts 2:42; 1 Cor 11:23f

tance. *prize.* In ancient times the prize was a perishable wreath (v. 25).

9:25 *wreath . . . imperishable.* See 2 Tim 4:8; James 1:12; 1 Pet 5:4; Rev 2:10; 3:11; 4:10 and notes.

9:26 *run . . . not without aim.* See Phil 3:14.

9:27 *I discipline my body and make it my slave.* Here Paul uses the figure of boxing to represent the Christian life. He does not aimlessly beat the air, but he severely disciplines his own body in serving Christ. *will not be disqualified.* Paul realizes that he must with rigor serve the Lord and battle against sin. If he fails in this, he may be excluded from the reward (see 3:10–15).

10:1 *under the cloud.* Under God's leadership and guidance (Ex 13:21–22; Num 9:15–23; 14:14; Deut 1:33; Ps 78:14). His guidance did not fail them—He successfully led them through the sea (Ex 14:22,29).

10:2 As a people, they were united under God's redemptive program, and they submitted to Moses, God's appointed leader (Ex 14:31). *baptized.* A figure used to depict their submission to Moses as their deliverer and leader, just as Christian baptism depicts the believer's submission to Christ as Savior and Lord.

10:3–4 *spiritual food . . . spiritual drink.* The manna and the water from the rock are used as figures representing the spiritual sustenance that God continually provides for His people (Ex 16:2–36; 17:1–7; Num 20:2–11; 21:16).

10:4 *the rock was Christ.* The rock, from which the water came, and the manna were symbolic of supernatural sustenance through Christ, the bread of life and the water of life (John 4:14; 6:30–35).

10:5 *with most of them God was not well-pleased.* In spite of the remarkable privileges given to Israel (vv. 1–4), they failed to obey God, thus incurring His displeasure. Of the adults who came out of Egypt, only Caleb and Joshua were allowed to enter Canaan (Num 14:22–24, 28–35; Josh 1:1–2).

10:6 *as they also craved.* What Paul has in mind is described in vv. 7–10.

10:7 *idolaters.* Referring to the incident of the golden calf (Ex 32:1–6). The people ate a ritual meal sacrificed to an idol (cf. ch. 8).

10:8 Refers to Israel's joining herself to Baal of Peor (Num 25:1–9), participating in the worship of this god of the Moabites and engaging in sexual immorality with the prostitute virgins who worshiped this god. *twenty-three thousand.* The Hebrew and Greek (Septuagint) texts of Num 25:9 have 24,000. It is clear that Paul is not striving for exactness. He is only speaking approximately. First-century writers were not as concerned about being precise as 20th-century authors often are.

10:10 *Nor grumble.* As in Num 16:41. *destroyer.* Paul links the angel who brought the plague of Num 16:46–50—because of the grumbling of the Israelites against Moses and Aaron (Num 16:41)—with the destroying angel of Ex 12:23.

10:11 *written for our instruction.* See note on Rom 15:4. *the ends of the ages.* The period of time inaugurated by Christ's death and resurrection and continuing into the future until Christ's second coming and beyond. It is the period of fulfillment when all that God has been doing for His people throughout all previous ages comes to its fruition in the Messiah.

10:13 *temptation.* Temptation in itself is not sin. Jesus was tempted (Matt 4:1–11). Yielding to the temptation is sin. *endure it.* Through God's enablement to resist the temptation to sin.

10:14 *flee from idolatry.* Like that described in Ex 32:1–6. Corinthian Christians had come out of a background of paganism. Temples for the worship of Apollo, Asclepius, Demeter, Aphrodite and other pagan gods and goddesses were seen daily by the Corinthians as they engaged in the activities of everyday life. The worship of Aphrodite, with its many sacred prostitutes, was a particularly strong temptation.

10:16 *cup of blessing.* One of the cups drunk at the Jewish

17 Since there is one [1]bread, we [a]who are many are one body; for we all partake of the one [1]bread.

18 Look at [1]the nation [a]Israel; are not those who [b]eat the sacrifices sharers in the altar?

19 What do I mean then? That a thing sacrificed to idols is anything, or [a]that an idol is anything?

20 *No,* but *I say* that the things which the Gentiles sacrifice, they [a]sacrifice to demons and not to God; and I do not want you to become sharers in demons.

21 [a]You cannot drink the cup of the Lord and the cup of demons; you cannot partake of the table of the Lord and [b]the table of demons.

22 Or do we [a]provoke the Lord to jealousy? We are not [b]stronger than He, are we?

23 [a]All things are lawful, but not all things are profitable. All things are lawful, but not all things [b]edify.

24 Let no one [a]seek his own *good,* but that of his [1]neighbor.

25 [a]Eat anything that is sold in the meat market without asking questions for conscience' sake;

26 [a]FOR THE EARTH IS THE LORD'S, AND [1]ALL IT CONTAINS.

27 If [a]one of the unbelievers invites you and you want to go, [b]eat anything that is set before you without asking questions for conscience' sake.

28 But [a]if anyone says to you, "This is meat sacrificed to idols," do not eat *it,* for the sake of the one who informed *you,* and for conscience' sake;

29 I mean not your own conscience, but the other *man's;* for [a]why is my freedom judged by another's conscience?

30 If I partake with thankfulness, [a]why am I slandered concerning that for which I [b]give thanks?

31 Whether, then, you eat or drink or [a]whatever you do, do all to the glory of God.

32 [a]Give no offense either to Jews or to Greeks or to [b]the church of God;

33 just as I also [a]please all men in all things, [b]not seeking my own profit but the *profit* of the many, [c]so that they may be saved.

Christian Order

11 [a]Be imitators of me, just as I also am of Christ.

17 [1]Lit *loaf* [a]Rom 12:5; 1 Cor 12:12f, 27; Eph 4:4, 16; Col 3:15 **18** [1]Lit *Israel according to the flesh* [a]Rom 1:3 [b]Lev 7:6, 14f; Deut 12:17f **19** [a]1 Cor 8:4 **20** [a]Deut 32:17; Ps 106:37; Gal 4:8; Rev 9:20 **21** [a]2 Cor 6:16 [b]Is 65:11 **22** [a]Deut 32:21 [b]Eccl 6:10; Is 45:9 **23** [a]1 Cor 6:12 [b]Rom 14:19 **24** [1]Lit *the other* [a]Rom 15:2; 1 Cor 10:33; 13:5; 2 Cor 12:14; Phil 2:21 **25** [a]Acts 10:15; 1 Cor 8:7 **26** [1]Lit *its fullness* [a]Ps 24:1; 50:12; 1 Tim 4:4

27 [a]1 Cor 5:10 [b]Luke 10:8 **28** [a]1 Cor 8:7, 10-12 **29** [a]Rom 14:16; 1 Cor 9:19 **30** [a]1 Cor 9:1 [b]Rom 14:6 **31** [a]Col 3:17; 1 Pet 4:11

32 [a]Acts 24:16; 1 Cor 8:13 [b]Acts 20:28; 1 Cor 1:2; 7:17; 11:22; 15:9; 2 Cor 1:1; Gal 1:13; Phil 3:6; 1 Tim 3:5, 15 **33** [a]Rom 15:2; 1 Cor 9:22; Gal 1:10 [b]Rom 15:2; 1 Cor 13:5; 2 Cor 12:14; Phil 2:21 [c]Rom 11:14; 1 Thess 2:16 **11:1** [a]1 Cor 4:16; Phil 3:17

Passover, at which time the Lord's Supper was instituted (Matt 26:17–30; Mark 14:12–26; Luke 22:7–23). *sharing in the blood of Christ.* A memorial symbol of fellowship with the crucified Christ, not a literal drinking of His blood. When the Lord's Supper was instituted, Christ had not yet poured out His blood. The Lord's Supper is to remind us of Him (11:25).

10:17 *one bread.* The act of many believers partaking of one loaf of bread symbolizes the unity of the body of Christ, the church, which is nourished by the one bread of life (see John 6:33–58).

10:18 *those who eat the sacrifices sharers in the altar.* When the people of Israel ate part of the sacrifice made at the altar (Lev 7:15; 8:31; Deut 12:17–18), they participated in the worship of God, who established the sacrifices and whose altar it was. Likewise when the pagans sacrificed, they did so to demons (vv. 20–21). Paul denies that the idol is anything, i.e., that it is a real deity (v. 19). Nor is a sacrifice offered to a so-called god anything, because the idol is nothing and the god being worshiped is no god at all. In reality, demons (not gods) were the objects of idol worship. God's people are warned that if they do eat meat sacrificed to idols, they should not eat it with pagans in their temple feasts, for to do so is to become "sharers in demons" (v. 20).

10:22 *provoke the Lord to jealousy.* By sharing in pagan idolatry and worship (cf. Ex 20:5; Deut 32:21; Ps 78:58).

10:23 *not all things are profitable.* See note on 6:12. Personal freedom and desire for one's rights are not the only considerations. One must also consider the good "of his neighbor" (v. 24; cf. 8:1; Gal 6:2).

10:25 *Eat anything that is sold in the meat market.* Even if it has been sacrificed to an idol, because out in the public market it has lost its pagan religious significance.

10:26 A quotation from Ps 24:1 used at Jewish mealtimes as a blessing (cf. Ps 50:12; 89:11).

10:27 *eat anything that is set before you.* Whether or not it might be meat sacrificed to idols, ask no questions. As long as the subject has not been brought up, you are free to eat the meat, even if it had been offered to an idol.

10:28 *for the sake of the one who informed you.* If the meat has been identified as meat sacrificed to idols and you eat it, the man—whether a believer or an unbeliever—might think you condone, or even are willing to participate in, the worship of the idols the meat has been offered to. *for conscience' sake.* In eating meat that has publicly been declared to have been sacrificed to idols, you may offend "the other man's" conscience (v. 29) by causing him to think it is all right to eat meat sacrificed to idols even though he has doubts about it. Or if he is an unbeliever, he may think that the Christian worships both God and a pagan idol.

10:29 *my freedom.* Cf. Rom 14:16. The exercise of one's personal freedom is to be governed by whether it will bring glory to God, whether it will build up the church of God and whether it will encourage the unsaved to receive Christ as Savior and Lord (vv. 31–33).

10:30 *that for which I give thanks.* Paul could thank God for meat sacrificed to idols, for the idol is nothing and the meat is a part of God's created world.

10:31 *all to the glory of God.* The all-inclusive principle that governs the discussion in chs. 8–10 is that God should be glorified in everything that is done.

10:32 *Give no offense.* The particular cause of stumbling Paul had in mind was that of eating meat offered to idols (see 8:13). Living to glorify God will result in doing what is beneficial for others, whether Christians ("the church of God") or non-Christians ("Jews, Greeks").

10:33 *please all men in all things.* Paul does not mean that he will compromise the truths of the gospel in order to please everybody, but that he will consider his fellowman and not cause anyone's conscience to be offended by his daily life, thus keeping that person from receiving the gospel. *that they may be saved.* See 9:22.

11:1 Notice the order: (1) Christ is the supreme example (cf.

2 Now [a]I praise you because you [b]remember me in everything and [c]hold firmly to the traditions, just as I delivered them to you.

3 But I want you to understand that [1]Christ is the [a]head of every man, and [b]the man is the head of a woman, and God is the [c]head of [1]Christ.

4 Every man who has *something* on his head while praying or [a]prophesying disgraces his head.

5 But every [a]woman who has her head uncovered while praying or prophesying disgraces her head, for she is one and the same as the woman [1]whose head is [b]shaved.

6 For if a woman does not cover [1]her head, let her also [2]have her hair cut off; but if it is disgraceful for a woman to [2]have her hair cut off or [1]her head shaved, let her cover [1]her head.

7 For a man ought not to have his head covered, since he is the [a]image and glory of God; but the woman is the glory of man.

8 For [a]man [1]does not originate from woman, but woman from man;

9 for indeed man was not created for the woman's sake, but [a]woman for the man's sake.

10 Therefore the woman ought to have *a symbol of* authority on her head, because of the angels.

11 However, in the Lord, neither is woman [1]independent of man, nor is man [1]independent of woman.

12 For as the woman [1]originates from the man, so also the man *has his birth* through the woman; and [a]all things [2]originate [b]from God.

13 [a]Judge [1]for yourselves: is it proper for a woman to pray to God *with her head* uncovered?

14 Does not even nature itself teach you that if a man has long hair, it is a dishonor to him,

15 but if a woman has long hair, it is a glory to her? For her hair is given to her for a covering.

16 But if one is inclined to be contentious, [a]we have no [1]other practice, nor have [b]the churches of God.

17 But in giving this instruction, [a]I do not praise you, because you come together not for the better but for the worse.

18 For, in the first place, when you come together [1]as a church, I hear that [2a]divisions exist among you; and in part I believe it.

2 [a]1 Cor 11:17, 22 [b]1 Cor 4:17; 15:2; 1 Thess 1:6; 3:6 [c]2 Thess 2:15; 3:6
3 [1]I.e. the Messiah [a]Eph 1:22; 4:15; 5:23; Col 1:18; 2:19 [b]Gen 3:16; Eph 5:23 [c]1 Cor 3:23
4 [a]Acts 13:1; 1 Thess 5:20
5 [1]Lit *who is shaved* [a]Luke 2:36; Acts 21:9; 1 Cor 14:34 [b]Deut 21:12
6 [1]Lit *herself* [2]Lit *shear herself*
7 [a]Gen 1:26; 5:1; 9:6; James 3:9
8 [1]Lit *is not from* [a]Gen 2:21-23; 1 Tim 2:13
9 [a]Gen 2:18
11 [1]Lit *without*
12 [1]Lit *is* [2]Lit *are* [a]2 Cor 5:18 [b]Rom 11:36
13 [1]Lit *in* [a]Luke 12:57
16 [1]Lit *such* [a]1 Cor 4:5; 9:1-3, 6 [b]1 Cor 7:17
17 [a]1 Cor 11:2, 22
18 [1]Lit *in church* [2]Lit *schisms* [a]1 Cor 1:10; 3:3

1 Pet 2:21); (2) Christ's apostle follows His example ("just as I also am of Christ"); (3) we are to follow the apostle's example.

11:3–16 The subject of this section is propriety in public worship, not male-female relations in general. Paul is concerned, however, that the proper relationship between husbands and wives be reflected in public worship. As in the previous section, he desires that all be done to the glory of God (10:31).

11:3 Some understand the term "head" to refer primarily to the concept of honor, in that one's physical head is the seat of his honor (cf. vv. 4–5). Thus as Christ honored God, man is to honor Christ, and woman is to honor her husband. Others see in the word "head" the idea of authority (which would also include the concept of honor). They point out that Paul clearly uses the term in the sense of authority in Eph 1:21–22 ("under His feet"; "head over everything"), in Eph 5:22–23 (where headship is seen in a context of submission) and in Col 1:18; 2:10. Thus as Christ is in authority over man and is therefore to be honored by man, so the husband is in a position of authority and is therefore to be honored by his wife. See note on 15:28.

11:4 The first use of "head" in this verse refers to man's physical head; the second refers to his spiritual Head (Christ)—or perhaps is intended in a double sense. In the culture of Paul's day, men uncovered their heads in worship to signify their respect for and submission to deity. When a man prayed or prophesied with his head covered, he failed to show the proper attitude toward Christ.

11:5–6 For a woman, taking off her head covering in public and exposing her hair was a sign of loose morals and sexual promiscuity. Paul says she might as well have her hair cut or shaved off. The shaved head indicated that the woman either had been publicly disgraced because of some shameful act or was openly flaunting her independence and her refusal to be in submission to her husband. Paul's message to her was: Show your respect for and submission to your husband by covering your head during public worship.

Some do not see in these verses a temporary cultural significance to the covering/uncovering of the head. They insist that, since Paul referred to the order of creation (vv. 7–9), his directive is not to be restricted to his time. Thus women of all times should wear a head covering.

Others find a lasting principle in the passage requiring wives, in all ways, to show respect for their husbands by submitting to their authority—not merely by a particular style of attire, but by godly lives. Man, who was created first, is to have authority over his wife (see 1 Tim 2:11–14). The wife was made out of his body (Gen 2:21–24) to be his helper and companion (Gen 2:20). She is to honor her husband by submitting to him as her head (see v. 3).

Still others see these verses, not as a mandate for all marriages, but as reflecting marriage relationships at that time in Corinth and therefore giving a reason why the women there should have covered their heads (v. 10). They point to vv. 11–12 as a contrast, emphasizing equality and mutual dependence between men and women who are "in the Lord" (v. 11; see Gal 3:28; 1 Pet 3:7).

11:10 *symbol of authority.* Understood by some to refer to the woman's authority as co-ruler with man in the creation (Gen 1:26–27). Others take the phrase to refer to the man's authority as properly recognized by the woman in her head covering. *angels.* Perhaps mentioned here because they are interested in all aspects of the Christian's salvation and are sensitive to decorum in worship (cf. Eph 3:10; 1 Tim 5:21).

11:13–14 *proper . . . nature itself.* Believers must be conscious of how their actions appear in their culture, in light of what is considered to be honorable behavior.

11:16 In worship services, Paul and the churches in general followed the common custom of the men wearing short hair and the women long hair. Paul was basing his remarks, particularly in vv. 13–16, on common custom in the churches.

11:17 *do not praise.* Contrast v. 2.

11:18 *divisions.* Paul had already dealt with one aspect of these divisions (1:10–17).

19 For there [a]must also be factions among you, [b]so that those who are approved may become [1]evident among you.

20 Therefore when you meet together, it is not to eat the Lord's Supper,

21 for in your eating each one takes his own supper first; and one is hungry and [a]another is drunk.

22 What! Do you not have houses in which to eat and drink? Or do you despise the [a]church of God and [b]shame those who have nothing? What shall I say to you? Shall [c]I praise you? In this I will not praise you.

The Lord's Supper

23 For [a]I received from the Lord that which I also delivered to you, that [b]the Lord Jesus in the night in which He was betrayed took bread;

24 and when He had given thanks, He broke it and said, "This is My body, which is for you; do this in remembrance of Me."

25 In the same way *He took* [a]the cup also after supper, saying, "This cup is the [b]new covenant in My blood; do this, as often as you drink *it*, in remembrance of Me."

26 For as often as you eat this bread and drink the cup, you proclaim the Lord's death [a]until He comes.

19 [1]Or *manifest* [a]Matt 18:7; Luke 17:1; 1 Tim 4:1; 2 Pet 2:1 [b]Deut 13:3; 1 John 2:19
21 [a]Jude 12
22 [a]1 Cor 10:32 [b]James 2:6 [c]1 Cor 11:2, 17
23 [a]1 Cor 15:3; Gal 1:12; Col 3:24 [b]1 Cor 11:23-25: *Matt 26:26-28; Mark 14:22-24; Luke 22:17-20;* 1 Cor 10:16
25 [a]1 Cor 10:16 [b]Ex 24:6-8; Luke 22:20; 2 Cor 3:6
26 [a]John 21:22; 1 Cor 4:5

27 Therefore whoever eats the bread or drinks the cup of the Lord in an unworthy manner, shall be [a]guilty of the body and the blood of the Lord.

28 But a man must [a]examine himself, and in so doing he is to eat of the bread and drink of the cup.

29 For he who eats and drinks, eats and drinks judgment to himself if he does not judge the body rightly.

30 For this reason many among you are weak and sick, and a number [1a]sleep.

31 But if we judged ourselves rightly, we would not be judged.

32 But when we are judged, we are [a]disciplined by the Lord so that we will not be condemned along with [b]the world.

33 So then, my brethren, when you come together to eat, wait for one another.

34 If anyone is [a]hungry, let him eat [b]at home, so that you will not come together for judgment. The remaining matters I will [c]arrange [d]when I come.

The Use of Spiritual Gifts

12 Now concerning [a]spiritual *gifts*, brethren, [b]I do not want you to be unaware.

27 [a]Heb 10:29
28 [a]Matt 26:22; 2 Cor 13:5; Gal 6:4
30 [1]I.e. are dead [a]Acts 7:60
32 [a]2 Sam 7:14; Ps 94:12; Heb 12:7-10; Rev 3:19 [b]1 Cor 1:20
34 [a]1 Cor 11:21 [b]1 Cor 11:22 [c]1 Cor 4:17; 7:17; 16:1 [d]1 Cor 4:19

12:1 [a]1 Cor 12:4; 14:1 [b]Rom 1:13

11:19 *those who are approved.* As deplorable as factions may be, they serve one good purpose: They distinguish those who are faithful and true in God's sight.
11:20 *not to eat the Lord's Supper.* Their intention was to eat the Lord's Supper, but it was profaned by their gluttony and discrimination.
11:21 *is hungry . . . is drunk.* The early church held the *agape* ("love") feast in connection with the Lord's Supper (cf. 2 Pet 2:13; Jude 12). Perhaps the meal was something like a present-day potluck dinner. In good Greek style they brought food for all to share, the rich bringing more and the poor less, but because of their cliques the rich ate much and the poor were left hungry.
11:22 *Shall I praise you?* See v. 17.
11:23–26 Observe the similarity of Paul's words here with Matt 26:26–29; Mark 14:22–25; and especially Luke 22:17–20.
11:23 *I received from the Lord.* Paul does not necessarily mean that he received the message about the Lord's Supper directly from Christ. The information probably was passed on to him by others who had heard it from Jesus.
11:24 *had given thanks.* The Jewish practice at meals. This makes it a true Eucharist ("thanksgiving"). *My body.* The broken bread is a symbol of Christ's body given for sinners (Luke 22:19). *in remembrance of Me.* As the Feast of Passover was a commemorative meal (see Ex 12:14), so also the Lord's Supper is a memorial supper, recalling and portraying Christ's death for sinners.
11:25 *the cup.* A symbol of the new covenant in Jesus' blood (Luke 22:20; cf. Jer 31:31–34). (The old covenant was the Mosaic or Sinaitic covenant; see Ex 24:3–8.) By the use of this covenant sign God signifies His bestowal of salvation upon His people, sealed and paid for by the shedding of Jesus' blood. *after supper.* After the Passover supper. The Lord's Supper was first celebrated by Jesus in connection with the Passover meal (cf. Matt 26:18–30 and parallels in Mark and Luke).
11:26 *as often as you eat . . . and drink.* The Lord's Supper should be held periodically, but there is no explicit instruction as to how often. *until He comes.* Cf. Matt 26:29.
11:27 *in an unworthy manner.* In the irreverent and self-centered manner that characterized some of the Corinthians at their unruly *agape* supper (vv. 19–22; see note on v. 21).
11:28 *examine himself.* A person should test the attitude of his own heart and actions and his awareness of the significance of the Supper, thus making the Supper, under God, a spiritual means of grace.
11:29 *judgment.* Not God's eternal judgment, which is to come on the unbeliever, but such disciplinary judgment as physical sickness and death (v. 30). *if he does not judge the body rightly.* The word "body" may refer to either the Lord's physical body or the church as the body of Christ (see 12:13,27). The first view means that the person partakes of the Lord's Supper without recognizing that it symbolizes Christ's crucified body. But in that case, why is the blood not mentioned? The second view means that the participant is not aware of the nature of the church as the body of Christ, resulting in the self-centered actions of vv. 20–21.
11:30 *sleep.* A common first-century figure of speech for death.
11:32 *disciplined.* As God's redeemed children we are disciplined—just as a human father disciplines his child—so that we might repent of our sins (cf. 2 Cor 7:10) and grow in grace (2 Pet 3:18; Heb 12:7–11).
11:33 *come together to eat.* Another reference to the *agape* fellowship meal (see note on v. 21). Each person was to exercise restraint and wait to eat with the others. If a person was too hungry, he should satisfy his hunger at home and not bring selfish and discriminatory practices into the church.
11:34 *remaining matters . . . when I come.* Paul suggests that they had other problems concerning the Lord's Supper that needed his attention, but he would take care of these later.
12:1 *Now concerning.* Suggests Paul is answering another question raised by the Corinthians in their letter (cf. 7:1; 8:1; 16:1). *spiritual gifts.* For a definition see note on 1:7, though a different Greek word is used there.

2 [a]You know that when you were pagans, *you were* [b]led astray to the [c]mute idols, however you were led.

3 Therefore I make known to you that no one speaking [1a]by the Spirit of God says, "Jesus is [2b]accursed"; and no one can say, "Jesus is [c]Lord," except [1a]by the Holy Spirit.

4 Now there are [a]varieties of gifts, but the same Spirit.

5 And there are varieties of ministries, and the same Lord.

6 There are varieties of effects, but the same [a]God who works all things in all *persons.*

7 But to each one is given the manifestation of the Spirit [a]for the common good.

8 For to one is given the word of [a]wisdom through the Spirit, and to another the word of [b]knowledge according to the same Spirit;

9 to another [a]faith [1]by the same Spirit, and to another [b]gifts of [2]healing [1]by the one Spirit,

10 and to another the [1]effecting of [2a]miracles, and to another [b]prophecy, and to another the [3c]distinguishing of spirits, to another *various* [d]kinds of tongues, and to another the [e]interpretation of tongues.

11 But one and the same Spirit works all these things, [a]distributing to each one individually just as He wills.

12 For even [a]as the body is one and *yet* has many members, and all the members of the body, though they are many, are one body, [b]so also is Christ.

13 For [1a]by one Spirit we were all baptized into one body, whether [b]Jews or Greeks, whether slaves or free, and we were all made to [c]drink of one Spirit.

14 For [a]the body is not one member, but many.

15 If the foot says, "Because I am not a hand, I am not *a part* of the body," it is not for this reason [1]any the less *a part* of the body.

2 [a]1 Cor 6:11; Eph 2:11f; 1 Pet 4:3 [b]1 Thess 1:9 [c]Ps 115:5; Is 46:7; Jer 10:5; Hab 2:18f
3 [1]Or *in* [2]Gr *anathema* [a]Matt 22:43; 1 John 4:2f; Rev 1:10 [b]Rom 9:3 [c]John 13:13; Rom 10:9
4 [a]Rom 12:6f; 1 Cor 12:11; Eph 4:4ff, 11; Heb 2:4
6 [a]1 Cor 15:28; Eph 1:23; 4:6
7 [a]1 Cor 12:12-30; 14:26; Eph 4:12
8 [a]1 Cor 2:6; 2 Cor 1:12 [b]Rom 15:14; 1 Cor 2:11, 16; 2 Cor 2:14; 4:6; 8:7; 11:6
9 [1]Or *in* [2]Lit *healings* [a]1 Cor 13:2; 2 Cor 4:13 [b]1 Cor 12:28, 30
10 [1]Lit *effects* [2]Or *works of power* [a]1 Cor 12:28f; Gal 3:5

10 [3]Lit *distinguishings* [b]1 Cor 11:4; 13:2, 8 [c]1 Cor 14:29; 1 John 4:1 [d]Mark 16:17; 1 Cor 12:28, 30; 13:1; 14:2ff [e]1 Cor 12:30; 14:26
11 [a]1 Cor 12:4 **12** [a]Rom 12:4f; 1 Cor 10:17 [b]1 Cor 12:27
13 [1]Or *in* [a]Eph 2:18 [b]Rom 3:22; Gal 3:28; Eph 2:13-18; Col 3:11 [c]John 7:37-39 **14** [a]1 Cor 12:20 **15** [1]Lit *not* a part

---

12:2 *led astray to the mute idols.* At one time the Corinthians had been led by various influences to worship mute idols (cf. 10:19–20), but now they are to be led by the Holy Spirit.

12:3 *"Jesus is accursed" . . . "Jesus is Lord."* One who is regenerated by the Holy Spirit cannot pronounce a curse on Jesus; rather, he is the only one who from the heart can confess, "Jesus is Lord" (cf. John 20:28; also 1 John 4:2–3). The Greek word for "Lord" here is used in the Greek translation of the OT (the Septuagint) to translate the Hebrew name *Yahweh* ("the LORD").

12:4–6 *same Spirit . . . same Lord . . . same God.* These verses, reflecting the Trinity, show the diversity and unity of spiritual gifts.

12:4 *gifts.* Gifts of grace produced by the indwelling Holy Spirit. See note on v. 1.

12:5 *ministries.* The Greek word in its various forms is used to indicate service to the Christian community, such as serving tables (Acts 6:2–3); it is also the word used a little later in the first-century Christian church for the office of deacon (Phil 1:1).

12:6 *effects.* The Greek word indicates power that is in operation. Spiritual gifts produce results that are obvious.

12:7 *to each one is given the manifestation . . . for the common good.* Every member of the body of Christ has been given some spiritual gift that is an evidence of the Spirit's working in his life. All the gifts are intended to build up the members of the Christian community (see 1 Pet 4:10–11). They are not to be used for selfish advantage, as some in the Corinthian community apparently were doing.

12:8 *to one . . . to another.* Not everyone has the same gift or all the gifts. *word of wisdom . . . knowledge.* Gifts that meet the need of the Christian community when knowledge or wisdom is required to make decisions or to choose proper courses of action.

12:9 *faith.* Not saving faith, which all Christians have, but faith to meet a specific need within the body of Christ. *gifts of healing.* Lit. "gifts of healings." The double plural may suggest different kinds of illnesses and the various ways God heals them.

12:10 *effecting of miracles.* Lit. "deeds of power." In Scripture a miracle is an action that cannot be explained by natural means. It is an act of God intended as evidence of His power and purpose. *prophecy.* A communication of the mind of God imparted to a believer by the Holy Spirit. It may be a prediction (cf. Agabus, Acts 11:28; 21:10–11) or an indication of the will of God in a given situation (cf. 14:29–30; Acts 13:1–2). *distinguishing of spirits.* Since there can also be false prophecies that come from evil spirits, this gift is necessary in order to distinguish the true from the false (cf. 1John 4:1–6). *various kinds of tongues.* Since the Greek word for "tongues" means "languages" or "dialects," some understand it to refer to the ability to speak in unlearned human languages, as the apostles did on the day of Pentecost (Acts 2:4,6,11; cf. also 1 Cor 14:9–10). Others believe that in chs. 12–14 the term "tongues" refers to both earthly and heavenly languages, including ecstatic languages of praise and prayer (13:1; 14:2,10). *interpretation of tongues.* The communication of the message spoken in a tongue so that hearers can understand and be edified (cf. 14:5, 13,27–28).

12:11 *as He wills.* The Holy Spirit sovereignly determines which gift or gifts each believer should have.

12:12 *one . . . many members.* This example illustrates the unity and diversity of the different spiritual gifts exercised by God's people, who are all members of the one body of Christ. *is Christ.* Is Christ's body, the church, of which He is the head (Eph 1:22–23).

12:13 *by one Spirit . . . all baptized into one body.* Spiritually baptized, regenerated by the Holy Spirit (John 3:3,5) and united with Christ as part of His body. *Jews or Greeks.* In Christ there is no racial or cultural distinction. *slaves or free.* No social distinction. *all made to drink of one Spirit.* God has given all His people the Holy Spirit to indwell them (6:19) so that their lives may overflow with the fruit of the Spirit (Gal 5:22–23; cf. John 7:37–39).

12:14–20 Addressed mainly to those who feel that their gifts are inferior and unimportant. Apparently the more spectacular gifts (such as tongues) had been glorified in the Corinthian church, making those who did not have them feel inferior.

12:14 As the human body must have diversity to work effectively as a whole, so the members of Christ's body have diverse gifts, the use of which can help bring about the accomplishment of Christ's united purpose. Each must properly exercise his gifts or effectively use his position for the good of the whole: e.g., the gift of the message of wisdom, the message of knowledge, the position of apostle, elder (1 Pet 5:1), deacon (Acts 6:1–6).

16 And if the ear says, "Because I am not an eye, I am not *a part* of the body," it is not for this reason [1]any the less *a part* of the body.

17 If the whole body were an eye, where would the hearing be? If the whole were hearing, where would the sense of smell be?

18 But now God has [a]placed the members, each one of them, in the body, [b]just as He desired.

19 If they were all one member, where would the body be?

20 But now [a]there are many members, but one body.

21 And the eye cannot say to the hand, "I have no need of you"; or again the head to the feet, "I have no need of you."

22 On the contrary, [1]it is much truer that the members of the body which seem to be weaker are necessary;

23 and those *members* of the body which we [1]deem less honorable, [2]on these we bestow more abundant honor, and our less presentable members become much more presentable,

24 whereas our more presentable members have no need *of it.* But God has *so* composed the body, giving more abundant honor to that *member* which lacked,

25 so that there may be no [1]division in the body, but *that* the members may have the same care for one another.

26 And if one member suffers, all the members suffer with it; if *one* member is [1]honored, all the members rejoice with it.

27 Now you are [a]Christ's body, and [b]individually members of it.

28 And God has [1a]appointed in [b]the church, first [c]apostles, second [d]prophets, third [e]teachers, then [2f]miracles, then [g]gifts of healings, helps, [h]administrations, *various* [i]kinds of tongues.

29 All are not apostles, are they? All are not prophets, are they? All are not teachers, are they? All are not *workers of* [1]miracles, are they?

30 All do not have gifts of healings, do they? All do not speak with tongues, do they? All do not [a]interpret, do they?

31 But [a]earnestly desire the greater gifts.

And I show you a still more excellent way.

The Excellence of Love

13 If I speak with the [a]tongues of men and of [b]angels, but do not have love, I have become a noisy gong or a [c]clanging cymbal.

16 [1]Lit *not a* part
18 [a]1 Cor 12:28 [b]Rom 12:6; 1 Cor 12:11
20 [a]1 Cor 12:12, 14
22 [1]Lit *to a much greater degree the members*
23 [1]Or *think to be* [2]Or *these we clothe with*
25 [1]Lit *schism*
26 [1]Lit *glorified*
27 [a]1 Cor 1:2; 12:12; Eph 1:23; 4:12; Col 1:18, 24; 2:19 [b]Rom 12:5; Eph 5:30
28 [1]Lit *set some in* [2]Or *works of power* [a]1 Cor 12:18 [b]1 Cor 10:32 [c]Eph 4:11 [d]Acts 13:1; Eph 2:20; 3:5 [e]Acts 13:1 [f]1 Cor 12:10, 29 [g]1 Cor 12:9, 30 [h]Rom 12:8 [i]1 Cor 12:10
29 [1]Or *works of power*
30 [a]1 Cor 12:10
31 [a]1 Cor 14:1, 39
13:1 [a]1 Cor 12:10 [b]2 Cor 12:4; Rev 14:2 [c]Ps 150:5

12:18 Paul stresses the sovereign purpose of God in diversifying the parts of the body; by implication he is saying that God has arranged that different Christians in the body of Christ exercise different spiritual gifts, not the same gift. And this diversity is intended to accomplish God's unified purpose. God's method employs diversity to create unity.
12:21–26 Addressed mainly to those who feel that their gifts are superior and most important. These verses provide another indication that some gifts, like tongues, had been magnified as being preeminent.
12:21 The principle here is the interdependence of the parts of the body in the one whole. Christians in the body of Christ are mutually dependent as they exercise their distinctive functions.
12:22 *weaker are necessary.* Christians who seem to have less important functions in the body of Christ are actually indispensable.
12:23 *those members of the body which we deem less honorable, on these we bestow more abundant honor.* Just as we give food to the stomach, though it is a less attractive part of the body, so we should give honor and support to the Christians in the church who have ordinary gifts (in their functions). *our less presentable members become much more presentable.* Christians whose functions may be very obscure in the church are to be given special respect.
12:24 Persons with more spectacular gifts do not need to be given special honor.
12:25 *no division.* See 1:10–12.
12:26 *all the members suffer.* In the body of Christ if one Christian suffers, all the Christians are affected (cf. Acts 12:1–5—the martyrdom of James and the imprisonment of Peter).
12:27 *you are Christ's body.* Addressed to the local church at Corinth. Each local church is the body of Christ just as the universal church is Christ's body.
12:28 The list here differs somewhat from that in vv. 8–10 (see notes there). Paul notes three of the gifted individuals of Eph 4:11, then five of the spiritual gifts listed in vv. 8–10. The apostles and prophets were part of the foundation of the church (Eph 2:20), and teaching was associated with the pastoral office (Eph 4:11; 1 Tim 3:2). These three gifted individuals are listed as "first," "second" and "third," indicating their importance in the church. The rest of the list is introduced with "then," indicating the variety that follows. Paul's lists of spiritual gifts seem to be largely random samples. Apart from v. 28a he does not rank them in importance since he has already insisted that all gifts are important (vv. 21–26). *apostles.* Those chosen by Christ during His earthly ministry to be with Him and to go out and preach (Mark 3:14). They were also to be witnesses of the resurrection (Acts 1:21–22). The term may occasionally have been used in a broader sense (Rom 16:7; Gal 1:19). *miracles . . . healings . . . tongues.* See notes on vv. 9–10. *helps.* Any act of helping others may be the product of a spiritual gift (cf. Rom 12:6–8), though the primary reference here is probably to a ministry to the poor, needy, sick and distressed (cf. Acts 6:1–6). *administrations.* Those with gifts of administration were enabled by the Holy Spirit to organize and project plans and spiritual programs in the church.
12:29–30 *All are not apostles.* Christians have different gifts, and no one gift should be expected by everyone.
12:31 *earnestly desire the greater gifts.* See v. 28; 14:1,5,12,39. An alternative translation could be "you are eagerly desiring . . . ." If this is correct, the Corinthians were apparently seeking status through the exercise of the gifts that seemed to them to be more important. *a still more excellent way.* Paul now shows the right way to exercise all spiritual gifts—the way of love. He does not identify love as a gift; rather, it is a fruit of the Spirit (Gal 5:22).
13:1–3 *tongues . . . prophecy . . . faith . . . give.* Paul selects four gifts as examples. He declares that even their most spectacular manifestations mean nothing unless motivated by love.
13:1 *tongues of men and of angels.* Paul uses hyperbole. Even if he could speak not only the various languages that human beings speak but even the languages used by angels—if he did not speak in love, it would be nothing but noise. *love.* The

2 If I have *the gift of* [a]prophecy, and
know all [b]mysteries and all [c]knowledge; and
if I have [d]all faith, so as to [e]remove mountains, but do not have love, I am nothing.
3 And if I [a]give all my possessions to
feed *the poor,* and if I [b]surrender my body
[1]to be burned, but do not have love, it profits me nothing.
4 Love [a]is patient, love is kind *and* [b]is
not jealous; love does not brag *and* is not
[c]arrogant,
5 does not act unbecomingly; it [a]does
not seek its own, is not provoked, [b]does not
take into account a wrong *suffered,*
6 [a]does not rejoice in unrighteousness,
but [b]rejoices with the truth;
7 [1a]bears all things, believes all things,
hopes all things, endures all things.
8 Love never fails; but if *there are gifts of*
[1a]prophecy, they will be done away; if *there*
are [b]tongues, they will cease; if *there is*
knowledge, it will be done away.
9 For we [a]know in part and we prophesy
in part;
10 but when the perfect comes, the partial
will be done away.
11 When I was a child, I used to speak like
a child, think like a child, reason like a child;
when I [1]became a man, I did away with
childish things.
12 For now we [a]see in a mirror [1]dimly, but
then [b]face to face; now I know in part, but
then I will know fully just as I also [c]have
been fully known.
13 But now faith, hope, love, abide these
three; but the [1]greatest of these is [a]love.

Prophecy a Superior Gift

14 [a]Pursue love, yet [b]desire earnestly
[c]spiritual *gifts,* but especially that you
may [d]prophesy.
2 For one who [a]speaks in a tongue does
not speak to men but to God; for no one
[1]understands, but [2]in *his* spirit he speaks
[b]mysteries.
3 But one who prophesies speaks to men
for [a]edification and [b]exhortation and consolation.
4 One who [a]speaks in a tongue [b]edifies
himself; but one who [c]prophesies [b]edifies
the church.

2 [a]Matt 7:22; Acts 13:1; 1 Cor 11:4; 13:8; 14:1, 39 [b]1 Cor 14:2; 15:51 [c]Rom 15:14 [d]1 Cor 12:9 [e]Matt 17:20; 21:21; Mark 11:23 **3** [1]Early mss read *that I may boast* [a]Matt 6:2 [b]Dan 3:28 **4** [a]Prov 10:12; 17:9; 1 Thess 5:14; 1 Pet 4:8 [b]Acts 7:9 [c]1 Cor 4:6 **5** [a]1 Cor 10:24; Phil 2:21 [b]2 Cor 5:19 **6** [a]2 Thess 2:12 [b]2 John 4; 3 John 3f **7** [1]Or *covers* [a]1 Cor 9:12 **8** [1]Lit *prophecies* [a]1 Cor 13:2 [b]1 Cor 13:1 **9** [a]1 Cor 8:2; 13:12 **11** [1]Lit *have become...have done away with* **12** [1]Lit *in a riddle* [a]2 Cor 5:7; Phil 3:12; James 1:23 [b]Gen 32:30; Num 12:8; 1 John 3:2 [c]1 Cor 8:3 **13** [1]Lit *greater* [a]Gal 5:6 **14:1** [a]1 Cor 16:14 [b]1 Cor 12:31; 14:39 [c]1 Cor 12:1 [d]1 Cor 13:2 **2** [1]Lit *hears* [2]Or *by the Spirit* [a]Mark 16:17; 1 Cor 12:10, 28, 30; 13:1; 14:18ff [b]1 Cor 13:2 **3** [a]Rom 14:19; 1 Cor 14:5, 12, 17, 26 [b]Acts 4:36 **4** [a]Mark 16:17; 1 Cor 12:10, 28, 30; 13:1; 14:18ff, 26f [b]Rom 14:19; 1 Cor 14:5, 12, 17, 26 [c]1 Cor 13:2

Greek for this word indicates a selfless concern for the welfare of others that is not called forth by any quality of lovableness in the person loved, but is the product of a will to love in obedience to God's command. It is like Christ's love manifested on the cross (cf. John 13:34–35; 1 John 3:16).

13:2 *all mysteries and all knowledge.* Again Paul uses hyperbole to express the amount of understanding possessed. Even if one's gift is unlimited knowledge, if one does not possess and exercise that knowledge in love, he is nothing. *faith, so as to remove mountains.* A special capacity to trust God to meet outstanding needs. Again Paul uses hyperbole.

13:3 *surrender my body to be burned.* A reference to suffering martyrdom through burning at the stake, as many early Christians experienced. Even the supreme sacrifice, if not motivated by love, accomplishes nothing.

13:4–7 Love is now described both positively and negatively.

13:4 *not arrogant.* See 8:1.

13:5 *not act unbecomingly.* Perhaps an indirect reference to their unruly conduct in worship (11:18–22).

13:6 *does not rejoice in unrighteousness.* As they were doing in ch. 5.

13:8 *prophecy . . . will be done away; . . . tongues . . . will cease; . . . knowledge . . . will be done away.* These three will cease because they are partial in nature (v. 9) and will be unnecessary when what is complete has come (v. 10).

13:10 *the perfect.* The Greek for this word can mean "end," "fulfillment," "completeness" or "maturity." In this context the contrast is between the partial and the complete. Some refer the verse to the return of Christ, others to the death of the Christian, others to the maturity (or establishment) of the church (see the illustration in v. 11), still others to the completion of the canon of NT Scripture. Verse 12, however, seems to indicate that Paul is here speaking of Christ's second coming.

13:12 *we see in a mirror dimly.* The imagery is of a polished metal (probably bronze) mirror in which one could receive only an imperfect reflection (cf. James 1:23)—in contrast to seeing the Lord directly and clearly in heaven. *know fully . . . fully known.* The Christian will know the Lord to the fullest extent possible for a finite being, similar to the way the Lord knows the Christian fully and infinitely. This will not be true until the Lord returns.

13:13 *faith, hope and love.* See note on 1 Thess 1:3. *abide.* Now and forever. *the greatest of these is love.* Because God is love (1John 4:8) and has communicated His love to us (1John 4:10) and commands us to love one another (John 13:34–35). Love supersedes the gifts because it outlasts them all. Long after these sought-after gifts are no longer necessary, love will still be the governing principle that controls all that God and His redeemed people are and do.

14:1–5 The basic principle Paul insists on is that whatever is done in the church must contribute to the edification (building up) of the body. This is in keeping with the declaration in 12:7 that gifts are "given for the common good." It also is in agreement with the principle of love (ch. 13). What is spoken in the church, then, must be intelligible—it must be spoken in the vernacular language or at least be interpreted in the vernacular. Prophecy is therefore more desirable than tongues (unless an interpreter is present) because prophecy is spoken in the native language of the listeners.

14:1 *Pursue love . . . spiritual gifts.* Love is the means by which spiritual gifts are made effective. *especially that you may prophesy.* See note on 12:10.

14:2 *tongue.* Or "another language" (also in vv. 4,13,14,19, 26,27). The hearers cannot understand what the person who speaks in a tongue is saying. Therefore what he says is a mystery unless it is interpreted. Only God understands it. *in his spirit.* It is not spoken from his mind (see vv. 14–17).

14:3 In prophesying the speaker can edify and encourage others (12:7).

14:4 *edifies himself.* This edification does not involve the mind since the speaker does not understand what he has said. It is a personal edification in the area of the emotions, of deepening conviction, of fuller commitment and greater love.

5 Now I wish that you all [a]spoke in tongues, but [b]*even* more that you would prophesy; and greater is one who prophesies than one who [a]speaks in tongues, unless he interprets, so that the church may receive [c]edifying.

6 But now, brethren, if I come to you speaking in tongues, what will I profit you unless I speak to you either by way of [a]revelation or of [b]knowledge or of [c]prophecy or of [d]teaching?

7 Yet *even* lifeless things, either flute or harp, in producing a sound, if they do not produce a distinction in the tones, how will it be known what is played on the flute or on the harp?

8 For if [a]the [1]bugle produces an indistinct sound, who will prepare himself for battle?

9 So also you, unless you utter by the tongue speech that is clear, how will it be known what is spoken? For you will be [a]speaking into the air.

10 There are, perhaps, a great many kinds of [1]languages in the world, and no *kind* is without meaning.

11 If then I do not know the meaning of the language, I will be to the one who speaks a [1a]barbarian, and the one who speaks will be a [1]barbarian [2]to me.

12 So also you, since you are zealous of [1]spiritual *gifts,* seek to abound for the [a]edification of the church.

13 Therefore let one who speaks in a tongue pray that he may interpret.

14 For if I pray in a tongue, my spirit prays, but my mind is unfruitful.

15 [a]What is *the outcome* then? I will pray with the spirit and I will pray with the mind also; I will [b]sing with the spirit and I will sing with the mind also.

16 Otherwise if you bless [1]in the spirit *only,* how will the one who fills the place of the [2]ungifted say [a]the "Amen" at your [b]giving of thanks, since he does not know what you are saying?

17 For you are giving thanks well enough, but the other person is not [a]edified.

18 I thank God, I speak in tongues more than you all;

19 however, in the church I desire to speak five words with my mind so that I may instruct others also, rather than ten thousand words in a tongue.

Instruction for the Church

20 [a]Brethren, [b]do not be children in your thinking; yet in evil [c]be infants, but in your thinking be mature.

21 In [a]the Law it is written, "[b]BY MEN OF STRANGE TONGUES AND BY THE LIPS OF STRANGERS I WILL SPEAK TO THIS PEOPLE, AND EVEN SO THEY WILL NOT LISTEN TO ME," says the Lord.

22 So then tongues are for a sign, not to those who believe but to unbelievers; but [a]prophecy *is for a sign,* not to unbelievers but to those who believe.

23 Therefore if the whole church assembles together and all speak in tongues, and

5 [a]Mark 16:17; 1 Cor 12:10, 28, 30; 13:1; 14:18ff, 26f [b]Num 11:29 [c]Rom 14:19; 1 Cor 14:4, 12, 17, 26
6 [a]1 Cor 14:26; Eph 1:17 [b]1 Cor 12:8 [c]1 Cor 13:2 [d]Acts 2:42; Rom 6:17; 1 Cor 14:26
8 [1]Lit *trumpet* [a]Num 10:9; Jer 4:19; Ezek 33:3-6; Joel 2:1
9 [a]1 Cor 9:26
10 [1]Lit *voices*
11 [1]Or *foreigner* [2]Or *in my estimation* [a]Acts 28:2
12 [1]Lit *spirits* [a]Rom 14:19; 1 Cor 14:4, 5, 17, 26
15 [a]Acts 21:22; 1 Cor 14:26 [b]Eph 5:19; Col 3:16
16 [1]Or *with the* [2]I.e. unversed in spiritual gifts [a]Deut 27:15-26; 1 Chr 16:36; Neh 5:13; 8:6; Ps 106:48; Jer 11:5; 28:6; Rev 5:14; 7:12 [b]Matt 15:36
17 [a]Rom 14:19; 1 Cor 14:4, 5, 12, 26
20 [a]Rom 1:13 [b]Eph 4:14; Heb 5:12f [c]Ps 131:2; Matt 18:3; Rom 16:19; 1 Pet 2:2
21 [a]John 10:34; 1 Cor 14:34 [b]Is 28:11f
22 [a]1 Cor 14:1

14:5 *wish that you all spoke in tongues.* Paul was not opposed to tongues-speaking if it was practiced properly. *greater is the one who prophesies.* Because he serves the common good more effectively since what he says can be understood and thus edifies the church. *unless he interprets.* If the tongues-speaker also has the gift of interpretation, his speaking is as beneficial as prophecy, for then it can be understood (see v. 13).
14:6 *what will I profit you . . . ?* It would be useless for a person to speak in tongues unless, by interpretation, he brings the church something understandable and edifying.
14:7 *flute or harp.* Instruments that were well known in Greece. *distinction in the tones.* For a person to recognize the tune and to understand and appreciate it, there must be a variety of notes so arranged as to create a meaningful tune. One note repeated monotonously cannot accomplish this.
14:8 *the bugle . . . prepare himself for battle.* All Greeks would be acquainted with the use of the trumpet for battle signals (cf. Homer's *Iliad,* 18.219), and the Jews would be familiar with the use of the ram's horn (Num 10:9; Josh 6:4,9). Again, the notes sounded must convey a message.
14:9 *speech that is clear.* Speak in the vernacular language of the listeners rather than in a tongue (or else provide an interpretation).
14:10 *many kinds of languages.* Some see vv. 10–11 as an indication that the tongues of chs. 12–14 were unlearned foreign languages.
14:12 *abound for the edification of the church.* The basic principle of ch. 14.
14:14 *mind is unfruitful.* When a person speaks in tongues or prays in tongues, the human mind does not produce the language.
14:15–17 *pray . . . sing . . . bless . . . say the "Amen" . . . giving of thanks.* Elements employed in OT (1 Chr 16:36; Neh 5:13; 8:6; Ps 104:33; 136:1; 148:1) and NT worship (Rom 11:36; Eph 5:18–20). "Amen," meaning "It is true" or "So be it," is the believer's confession of agreement with the words spoken (cf. Gal 1:5). Thus it is important that a message in tongues be interpreted.
14:15 *pray with the spirit . . . with the mind . . . sing with the spirit . . . with the mind.* May mean that Paul will sometimes pray or sing with his spirit in a tongue; at other times he will pray or sing with his mind in his own language. Others believe that Paul was declaring his intention to pray or sing with both mind and spirit at the same time.
14:19 *however, in the church.* Some believe that an interpretation is unnecessary when the gift of tongues is being used as a private prayer language. They base such a distinction on v. 18 (see v. 14) when compared with the phrase quoted here.
14:20 *in evil be infants.* Just as in the case of infants, have no evil desires or wrong motives in wanting to excel in spiritual gifts (such as speaking in tongues) as an end in itself.
14:21–22 The passage from Is 28 indicates that the foreign language of the Assyrians was a sign to unbelieving Israel that judgment was coming on them. Paul deduced from this fact that tongues were intended to be a sign for unbelievers (v. 22), as, e.g., in Acts 2:4–12. Similarly, prophecy was for believers (v. 22) since it communicated revealed truth to those disposed to receive it (cf. Matt 13:11–16).
14:21 *In the Law.* Cf. Rom 3:10–19, where Paul quotes from a number of passages from the OT, including Isaiah, and then in v. 19 collectively calls them "the Law."

[1]ungifted men or unbelievers enter, will they
not say that [a]you are mad?
24 But if all [a]prophesy, and an unbeliever
or an [1]ungifted man enters, he is [b]convicted
by all, he is called to account by all;
25 [a]the secrets of his heart are disclosed;
and so he will [b]fall on his face and worship
God, [c]declaring that God is certainly among
you.
26 [a]What is *the outcome* then, [b]brethren?
When you assemble, [c]each one has a [d]psalm,
has a [e]teaching, has a [e]revelation, has a
[f]tongue, has an [g]interpretation. Let [h]all
things be done for edification.
27 If anyone speaks in a [a]tongue, *it should
be* by two or at the most three, and *each* in
turn, and one must [b]interpret;
28 but if there is no interpreter, he must
keep silent in the church; and let him speak
to himself and to God.
29 Let two or three [a]prophets speak, and
let the others [b]pass judgment.
30 But if a revelation is made to another
who is seated, the first one must keep silent.
31 For you can all prophesy one by one, so
that all may learn and all may be exhorted;
32 and the spirits of prophets are subject
to prophets;
33 for God is not *a God* of [a]confusion but
of [1]peace, as in [b]all the churches of the
[c]saints.
34 The women are to [a]keep silent in the
churches; for they are not permitted to
speak, but [b]are to subject themselves, just as
[c]the Law also says.
35 If they desire to learn anything, let
them ask their own husbands at home; for
it is [1]improper for a woman to speak in
church.
36 [1]Was it from you that the word of God
first went forth? Or has it come to you only?
37 [a]If anyone thinks he is a prophet or

23 [1]V 16, note 2 [a]Acts 2:13 **24** [1]V 16, note 2 [a]1 Cor 14:1 [b]John 16:8 **25** [a]John 4:19 [b]Luke 17:16 [c]Is 45:14; Dan 2:47; Zech 8:23; Acts 4:13 **26** [a]1 Cor 14:15 [b]Rom 1:13 [c]1 Cor 12:8-10 [d]Eph 5:19 [e]1 Cor 14:6 [f]1 Cor 14:2 [g]1 Cor 12:10; 14:5, 13, 27f [h]Rom 14:19 **27** [a]1 Cor 14:2 [b]1 Cor 12:10; 14:5, 13, 26ff **29** [a]1 Cor 13:2; 14:32, 37 [b]1 Cor 12:10

33 [1]Or *peace. As in all...saints, let* [a]1 Cor 14:40 [b]1 Cor 4:17; 7:17 [c]Acts 9:13 **34** [a]1 Cor 11:5, 13 [b]1 Tim 2:11f; 1 Pet 3:1 [c]1 Cor 14:21 **35** [1]Or *disgraceful* **36** [1]Lit *Or was* **37** [a]2 Cor 10:7

14:23 *ungifted men.* Perhaps those untaught in spiritual gifts (see 12:1), or perhaps inquirers into the Christian faith. *unbelievers.* Those who have made no movement toward saving faith. The context is a meeting of the church in which everyone is speaking in tongues with the result that general confusion reigns. *you are mad.* The visitors will be repulsed by the confusion, and the phenomenon meant to be an impressive sign will have a negative effect on the unsaved.

14:24 *all prophesy.* Prophecy, spoken in the vernacular language and intended for believers, turns out to have a positive effect on unbelievers because they hear and understand and are convicted of their sins. (Yet see restrictions on prophesying in vv. 29–32 and notes there.)

14:26–27 *each one . . . anyone . . . one.* The stress here is again on the diversity and yet complementary nature of spiritual gifts. It is also apparent that every member could participate, not just certain leaders or officers.

14:26 *a psalm . . . a teaching . . . a revelation . . . a tongue . . . an interpretation.* Elements that made up the worship service at Corinth. Some of these elements (the hymn and the word of instruction) came from OT and synagogue worship (cf. Matt 26:30; Luke 4:16–22). All parts of Christian worship should be edifying to the church.

14:27–28 Three restrictions are placed on speaking in a tongue "in the church" (v. 28): 1. Only two or three should do so in a meeting. 2. They should do so one at a time. 3. There must be interpretation.

14:28 *he must keep silent.* The implication seems to be that it was up to the one speaking in a tongue in the Corinthian church to make certain that there was in the audience someone to interpret his message.

14:29 *Let two or three prophets speak.* Apparently in turn (v. 31), as with the tongues-speakers (v. 27). *pass judgment.* The prophets themselves were to decide whether the messages of their fellow prophets were valid (see note on v. 32).

14:30 *a revelation.* Not an inspired revelation intended to become a part of written Scripture. In OT times, Scriptural revelation came through prophets, and in NT times through apostles or close associates of apostles. Prophecy referred to in chs. 12–14 could come through any member of the church (vv. 26,29–31). It could be a prediction (Agabus, Acts 11:28; 21:10–11), a divine directive (Acts 13:1–2) or a message designed to strengthen, encourage or comfort (v. 3).

14:32 *subject to prophets.* Prophecy (and tongues as well) was not an uncontrollable emotional ecstasy. Paul insists that these gifts should be controlled by the recipients themselves (vv. 15, 26–32). See notes on vv. 27–29.

14:33 *God . . . of peace.* See note on 1 Thess 5:23. *confusion.* Paul was concerned that disorderly and unregulated worship at Corinth would bring discredit on the name of the God who had called them in Christ to peace and unity. *in all the churches of the saints.* A unique expression in the NT that stresses the universality and commonality of the whole visible church of God on earth. All congregations are to obey the directives that follow.

14:34–35 See note on 11:3–16. Some believe that in light of 11:3 there is a God-ordained order that is to be the basis for administration and authority. Women are to be in submission to their husbands both at home (see Eph 5:22) and in the church (see v. 34; 1 Tim 2:11–12) regardless of their particular culture. According to this view, a timeless order was established at creation (see note on 11:5–6).

Others maintain that Paul's concern is that the church be strengthened (v. 26) by believers showing respect for others (see vv. 30–31) and for God (see v. 33) as they exercise their spiritual gifts. Such respect must necessarily take account of accepted social practices. If within a particular social order, it is disgraceful for a woman to speak in church—and it was in this case (v. 35)—then she shows disrespect by doing so and should remain silent. There were occasions, though—even in this culture—for women to speak in church. For example, in 11:5 Paul assumes that women pray and prophesy in public worship. Thus his purpose, according to this view, was not to define the role of women but to establish a fitting (vv. 34–35) and orderly (vv. 27–31) way of worship (v. 40).

Still others say that in this context Paul is discussing primarily the disruption of worship by women who become involved in noisy discussions surrounding tongues-speaking and prophecy. Instead of publicly clamoring for explanations, the wives were to discuss matters with their husbands at home (cf. v. 35). Paul does not altogether forbid women to speak in church (see 11:5). What he is forbidding is the disorderly speaking indicated in these verses.

14:36 Paul asks these rhetorical questions sarcastically, suggesting that the Corinthians were following their own practice in these matters rather than conforming to God's word.

[b]spiritual, let him recognize that the things
which I write to you [c]are the Lord's commandment.
38 But if anyone does not recognize *this,*
he [1]is not recognized.
39 Therefore, my brethren, [a]desire
earnestly to [b]prophesy, and do not forbid to
speak in tongues.
40 But [a]all things must be done properly
and in an orderly manner.

The Fact of Christ's Resurrection

15 Now [a]I make known to you, brethren,
the [b]gospel which I preached to you,
which also you received, [c]in which also you
stand,
2 by which also you are saved, [a]if you
hold fast [1]the word which I preached to you,
[b]unless you believed in vain.
3 For [a]I delivered to you [1]as of first
importance what I also received, that Christ
died [b]for our sins [c]according to the Scriptures,
4 and that He was buried, and that He
was [a]raised on the third day [b]according to
the Scriptures,

37 [b]1 Cor 2:15 [c]1 John 4:6
38 [1]Two early mss read *is not to be recognized*
39 [a]1 Cor 12:31 [b]1 Cor 13:2; 14:1
40 [a]1 Cor 14:33
15:1 [a]Rom 2:16; Gal 1:11 [b]Rom 2:16; 1 Cor 3:6; 4:15 [c]Rom 5:2; 11:20; 2 Cor 1:24
2 [1]Lit *to what word I* [a]Rom 11:22 [b]Gal 3:4
3 [1]Lit *among the first* [a]1 Cor 11:23 [b]John 1:29; Gal 1:4; Heb 5:1, 3; 1 Pet 2:24 [c]Is 53:5-12; Matt 26:24; Luke 24:25-27; Acts 8:32f; 17:2f; 26:22
4 [a]Matt 16:21; John 2:20ff; Acts 2:24 [b]Ps 16:8ff; Acts 2:31; 26:22f
5 [a]Luke 24:34 [b]1 Cor 1:12 [c]Mark 16:14; Luke 24:36; John 20:19
6 [a]Acts 7:60; 1 Cor 15:18, 20

5 and that [a]He appeared to [b]Cephas,
then [c]to the twelve.
6 After that He appeared to more than
five hundred brethren at one time, most of
whom remain until now, but some [a]have
fallen asleep;
7 then He appeared to [1a]James, then to
[b]all the apostles;
8 and last of all, as [1]to one untimely
born, [a]He appeared to me also.
9 For I am [a]the least of the apostles, [1]and
not fit to be called an apostle, because I [b]per-
secuted the church of God.
10 But by [a]the grace of God I am what I
am, and His grace toward me did not prove
vain; but I [b]labored even more than all of
them, yet [c]not I, but the grace of God with
me.
11 Whether then *it was* I or they, so we
preach and so you believed.
12 Now if Christ is preached, that He has
been raised from the dead, how do some

7 [1]Or *Jacob* [a]Acts 12:17 [b]Luke 24:33, 36f; Acts 1:3f **8** [1]Lit *to an untimely birth* [a]Acts 9:3-8; 22:6-11; 26:12-18; 1 Cor 9:1
9 [1]Lit *who am* [a]2 Cor 12:11; Eph 3:8; 1 Tim 1:15 [b]Acts 8:3
10 [a]Rom 12:3 [b]2 Cor 11:23; Col 1:29; 1 Tim 4:10 [c]1 Cor 3:6; 2 Cor 3:5; Phil 2:13

14:37 *the Lord's commandment.* Paul's commands are the Lord's commands and are to be followed. In a situation where so much stress was being placed on gifts, Paul insists that any genuinely gifted person will recognize the apostle's God-given authority.

14:38 *he is not recognized.* Paul and the churches will ignore such a disobedient person, and so he will be regarded as an unbeliever.

14:39 *do not forbid to speak in tongues.* Paul's solution to the tongues problem in the Corinthian church was not to forbid tongues, but to correct the improper use of the gift.

14:40 *properly and in an orderly manner.* As spelled out in vv. 26–35.

15:2 *if you hold fast.* See note on Heb 3:14. *believed in vain.* If you are not persevering in the Christian faith, this is an evidence that you did not have saving faith in the first place (cf. Judas Iscariot, who eventually showed that he was not a true believer).

15:3–5 Two lines of evidence for the death and resurrection of Christ are given here: (1) the testimony of the OT (e.g., Ps 16:8–11; Is 53:5–6,11) and (2) the testimony of eyewitnesses (Acts 1:21–22). Six resurrection appearances are listed here. The Gospels give more.

15:3 *I delivered to you as of first importance what I also received.* Here Paul links himself with early Christian tradition. He was not its originator, nor did he receive it directly from the Lord. His source was other Christians. The verbs he uses are technical terms for receiving and transmitting tradition (see note on 11:23). What follows is the heart of the gospel: that Christ died for our sins (not for His own sins; cf. Heb 7:27), that He was buried (confirmation that He had really died) and that He was raised from the dead.

15:4 *on the third day.* Cf. Matt 12:40. The Jews counted parts of days as whole days. Thus the three days would include part of Friday afternoon, all of Saturday, and Sunday morning. A similar way of reckoning time is seen in John 20:26 (lit. "after eight days," NASB "a week later"); two Sundays are implied, one at each end of the expression.

15:5 *Cephas . . . the twelve.* The appearance to Peter is the one mentioned in Luke 24:34, which occurred on Easter Sunday. The appearance to the twelve seems to have taken place on Sunday evening (see Luke 24:36–43; John 20:19–23). "The twelve" seems to have been used to refer to the group of original apostles, even though Judas was no longer with them (notice, however, that the 11 disciples, the 11 apostles or "the eleven" are referred to in Matt 28:16; Mark 16:14; Luke 24:9,33; Acts 1:26).

15:6 *more than five hundred . . . at one time.* The appearance to this large group may be mentioned to help bolster the faith of those Corinthians who evidently had some doubts about the resurrection of Christ (cf. v. 12). This appearance may be the one in Galilee recorded in Matt 28:10,16–20, where the eleven and possibly more met the risen Lord. *some have fallen asleep.* A common expression at that time for physical death (cf. Acts 7:60).

15:7 *James.* Since this James is listed in addition to the apostles, he is not James son of Zebedee or James son of Alphaeus (Matt 10:2–3). This is James, the half-brother of Jesus (Matt 13:55), who did not believe in Christ before the resurrection (John 7:5) but afterward joined the apostolic band (Acts 1:14) and later became prominent in the Jerusalem church (Acts 15:13). It is not clear in Scripture when and where this appearance to James occurred. *to all the apostles.* For example, Acts 1:6–11.

15:8 *last of all.* See Acts 9:1–8. This appearance to Paul came several years after the resurrection (perhaps c. A.D. 33). *one untimely born.* Paul was not part of the original group of apostles. He had not lived with Christ as the others had. His entry into the apostolic office was not at the same time ("untimely") as the others. Furthermore, at his conversion he was abruptly snatched from his former way of life (Acts 9:3–6).

15:9 *church of God.* In persecuting the church, he was actually persecuting Christ (see Acts 9:4–5).

15:12–19 Some at Corinth were saying that there was no resurrection of the body, and Paul draws a number of conclusions from this false contention. If the dead do not rise from the grave, then (1) "not even Christ has been raised" (v. 13); (2) "our preaching is vain" (v. 14); (3) "your faith also is vain" (v. 14); (4) we are "false witnesses" that God raised Christ from the dead (v. 15);

among you say that there [a]is no resurrection
of the dead?
13 But if there is no resurrection of the
dead, not even Christ has been raised;
14 and [a]if Christ has not been raised, then
our preaching is vain, your faith also is vain.
15 Moreover we are even found *to be* false
witnesses of God, because we testified
[1]against God that He [a]raised [2]Christ, whom
He did not raise, if in fact the dead are not
raised.
16 For if the dead are not raised, not even
Christ has been raised;
17 and if Christ has not been raised, your
faith is worthless; [a]you are still in your sins.
18 Then those also who [a]have fallen
asleep in Christ have perished.
19 If we have hoped in Christ in this life
only, we are [a]of all men most to be pitied.

The Order of Resurrection

20 But now Christ [a]has been raised from
the dead, the [b]first fruits of those who [c]are
asleep.
21 For since [a]by a man *came* death, by a
man also *came* the resurrection of the dead.
22 For [a]as in Adam all die, so also in
[1]Christ all will be made alive.
23 But each in his own order: Christ [a]the
first fruits, after that [b]those who are Christ's
at [c]His coming,
24 then *comes* the end, when He hands
over [a]the kingdom to the [b]God and Father,
when He has abolished [c]all rule and all
authority and power.
25 For He must reign [a]until He has put all
His enemies under His feet.
26 The last enemy that will be [a]abolished
is death.
27 For [a]HE HAS PUT ALL THINGS IN SUBJECTION
UNDER HIS FEET. But when He says, "[b]All
things are put in subjection," it is evident
that He is excepted who put all things in subjection to Him.
28 When [a]all things are subjected to Him,
then the Son Himself also will be subjected
to the One who subjected all things to Him,
so that [b]God may be all in all.
29 Otherwise, what will those do who are
baptized for the dead? If the dead are not
raised at all, why then are they baptized for
them?
30 Why are we also [a]in danger every
hour?

12 [a]Acts 17:32; 23:8; 2 Tim 2:18 **14** [a]1 Thess 4:14 **15** [1]Or *concerning* [2]I.e. the Messiah [a]Acts 2:24 **17** [a]Rom 4:25 **18** [a]1 Cor 15:6; 1 Thess 4:16; Rev 14:13 **19** [a]1 Cor 4:9; 2 Tim 3:12 **20** [a]Acts 2:24; 1 Pet 1:3 [b]Acts 26:23; 1 Cor 15:23; Rev 1:5 [c]1 Cor 15:6; 1 Thess 4:16; Rev 14:13 **21** [a]Rom 5:12 **22** [1]I.e. the Messiah [a]Rom 5:14-18

23 [a]Acts 26:23; 1 Cor 15:20; Rev 1:5 [b]1 Cor 6:14; 15:52; 1 Thess 4:16 [c]1 Thess 2:19 **24** [a]Dan 2:44; 7:14, 27; 2 Pet 1:11 [b]Eph 5:20 [c]Rom 8:38 **25** [a]Ps 110:1; Matt 22:44 **26** [a]2 Tim 1:10; Rev 20:14; 21:4

27 [a]Ps 8:6 [b]Matt 11:27; 28:18; Eph 1:22; Heb 2:8 **28** [a]Phil 3:21 [b]1 Cor 3:23; 12:6 **30** [a]2 Cor 11:26

(5) "your faith is worthless" (v. 17); (6) "you are still in your sins" (v. 17) and still carry the guilt and condemnation of sin; (7) "those also who have fallen asleep [have died] in Christ have perished" (v. 18); and (8) "we are . . . most to be pitied" who "have hoped in Christ in this life only" (v. 19) and put up with persecution and hardship.

15:12 *He has been raised.* Christ was raised historically on the third day. Paul uses this same verb form (that expresses the certainty of Christ's bodily resurrection) a total of seven times in this passage (vv. 4,12–14,16–17,20).

15:20 *now Christ has been raised.* Paul's categorical conclusion based on his evidence set forth in vv. 3–8. *first fruits.* The first sheaf of the harvest given to the Lord (Lev 23:10–11,17,20) as a token that all the harvest belonged to the Lord and would be dedicated to Him through dedicated lives. So Christ, who has been raised, is the guarantee of the resurrection of all of God's redeemed people (cf. 1 Thess 4:13–18).

15:21 *by a man came death.* Through Adam (Gen 3:17–19). *by a man also came the resurrection of the dead.* Through Christ, the second Adam, "the last Adam" (v. 45; cf. Rom 5:12–21).

15:22 *in Adam all die.* All who are "in Adam"—i.e., his descendants—suffer death. *in Christ all will be made alive.* All who are "in Christ"—i.e., who are related to Him by faith—will be made alive at the resurrection (cf. John 5:25; 1 Thess 4:16–17; Rev 20:6).

15:23 *each in his own order.* Christ, the first fruits, was raised in His own time in history (c. A.D. 30), and those who are identified with Christ by faith will be raised at His second coming. His resurrection is the pledge that ours will follow.

15:24 *the end.* The second coming of Christ and all the events accompanying it. This includes His handing over the kingdom to the Father, following His destroying all dominion, authority and power of the persons and forces who oppose Him.

15:25 *For He must reign.* During this process of Christ's destroying all dominion and handing over the kingdom to the Father, Christ must reign (Rev 20:1–6). Some take this to mean that Christ will literally reign with His saints for 1,000 years on the earth (cf. Is 2:2–4; Mic 4:1–5). Others believe that this refers to Christ's reign over the course of history and in the lives of His people, who are spiritually raised, or born again. This reign is viewed as continuing throughout the present age. *under His feet.* An OT figure for complete conquest. Verse 25 is an allusion to Ps 110:1 (cf. Matt 22:44).

15:26 This destruction of death will occur at the end of the second-coming events after Christ conquers His enemies (Rev 19:11–21; 20:5–14), at the great white throne judgment (when death and Hades will be thrown into the lake of fire).

15:28 *the Son Himself also will be subjected to the One.* The Son will be made subject to the Father in the sense that administratively, after He subjects all things to His power, He will then turn it all over to God the Father, the administrative head. This is not to suggest that the Son is in any way inferior to the Father. All three persons of the Trinity are equal in deity and in dignity. The subordination referred to is one of function (see note on 11:3). The Father is supreme in the Trinity; the Son carries out the Father's will (e.g., in creation, redemption); the Spirit is sent by the Father and the Son to vitalize life, communicate God's truth, apply His salvation to people and enable them to obey God's will (or word). *so that God may be all in all.* The triune God will be shown to be supreme and sovereign in all things.

15:29 *those . . . who are baptized for the dead.* The present tense suggests that at Corinth people were currently being baptized for the dead. But because Paul does not give any more information about the practice, many attempts have been made to interpret the concept. Three of these are: 1. Living believers were being baptized for believers who died before they were baptized, so that they too, in a sense, would not miss out on baptism. 2. Christians were being baptized in anticipation of the resurrection of the dead. 3. New converts were being baptized to fill the ranks of Christians who had died. At any rate, Paul mentions this custom almost in passing, using it in his arguments substantiating the resurrection of the dead, but without necessarily approving the practice. Probably the passage will always remain obscure.

15:30 *Why are we also in danger every hour?* If there is no res-

31 I affirm, brethren, by the boasting in
you which I have in Christ Jesus our Lord, [a]I
die daily.
32 If [1]from human motives I [a]fought with
wild beasts at [b]Ephesus, what does it profit
me? If the dead are not raised, [c]LET US EAT AND
DRINK, FOR TOMORROW WE DIE.
33 [a]Do not be deceived: "Bad company
corrupts good morals."
34 [a]Become sober-minded [1]as you ought,
and stop sinning; for some have [b]no knowledge of God. [c]I speak *this* to your shame.
35 But [a]someone will say, "How are [b]the
dead raised? And with what kind of body do
they come?"
36 [a]You fool! That which you [b]sow does
not come to life unless it dies;
37 and that which you sow, you do not
sow the body which is to be, but a bare grain,
perhaps of wheat or of [1]something else.
38 But God gives it a body just as He
wished, and [a]to each of the seeds a body of
its own.
39 All flesh is not the same flesh, but there
is one *flesh* of men, and another flesh of
beasts, and another flesh of birds, and
another of fish.
40 There are also heavenly bodies and
earthly bodies, but the glory of the heavenly
is one, and the *glory* of the earthly is another.
41 There is one glory of the sun, and
another glory of the moon, and another glory of the stars; for star differs from star in
glory.
42 [a]So also is the resurrection of the dead.
It is sown [1b]a perishable *body*, it is raised
[2c]an imperishable *body;*
43 it is sown in dishonor, it is raised in
[a]glory; it is sown in weakness, it is raised in
power;
44 it is sown a [a]natural body, it is raised a
[b]spiritual body. If there is a natural body,
there is also a spiritual *body.*
45 So also it is written, "The first [a]MAN,
Adam, BECAME A LIVING SOUL." The [b]last Adam
became a [c]life-giving spirit.
46 However, the spiritual is not first, but
the natural; then the spiritual.
47 The first man is [a]from the earth,
[1b]earthy; the second man is from heaven.
48 As is the earthy, so also are those who
are earthy; and as is the heavenly, [a]so also
are those who are heavenly.
49 Just as we have [a]borne the image of
the earthy, [1]we [b]will also bear the image of
the heavenly.

The Mystery of Resurrection

50 Now I say this, brethren, that [a]flesh
and blood cannot [b]inherit the kingdom of
God; nor does [1]the perishable inherit [2c]the
imperishable.

31 [a]Rom 8:36
32 [1]Lit *according to man* [a]2 Cor 1:8 [b]Acts 18:19; 1 Cor 16:8 [c]Is 22:13; 56:12; Luke 12:19
33 [a]1 Cor 6:9
34 [1]Lit *righteously* [a]Rom 13:11 [b]Matt 22:29; Acts 26:8 [c]1 Cor 6:5
35 [a]Rom 9:19 [b]Ezek 37:3
36 [a]Luke 11:40 [b]John 12:24
37 [1]Lit *some of the rest*
38 [a]Gen 1:11
42 [1]Lit *in corruption* [2]Lit *in incorruption* [a]Dan 12:3; Matt 13:43 [b]Rom 8:21; 1 Cor 15:50; Gal 6:8 [c]Rom 2:7
43 [a]Phil 3:21; Col 3:4
44 [a]1 Cor 2:14 [b]1 Cor 15:50
45 [a]Gen 2:7 [b]Rom 5:14 [c]John 5:21; 6:57f; Rom 8:2
47 [1]Lit *made of dust* [a]John 3:31 [b]Gen 2:7; 3:19
48 [a]Phil 3:20f
49 [1]Two early mss read *let us also* [a]Gen 5:3 [b]Rom 8:29

50 [1]Lit *corruption* [2]Lit *incorruption* [a]Matt 16:17; John 3:5f [b]1 Cor 6:9 [c]Rom 2:7

urrection, why should we suffer persecution and privation for Christ every day (cf. 2 Cor 11:23–29)?

15:32 *I fought with wild beasts at Ephesus.* This statement can be taken literally or figuratively. But since from Acts 19 we have no evidence of Paul suffering imprisonment and having to face the lions, it is more likely that the expression means that the enemies in Ephesus were as ferocious as wild beasts. *LET US EAT AND DRINK, FOR TOMORROW WE DIE.* See Is 22:13; a fitting philosophy of life if there is no resurrection.

15:33 A quotation from the Greek comedy *Thais* written by the Greek poet Menander, whose writings the Corinthians would know. The application of the quotation is that those who are teaching that there is no resurrection (v. 12) are the "bad company," and they are corrupting the "good morals" of those who hold to the correct doctrine. Cf. Prov 13:20.

15:34 *stop sinning.* The sin of denying that there is a resurrection and thus doubting even the resurrection of Christ, all of which had a negative effect on the lives they were living. *some have no knowledge of God.* Even in the Corinthian church. This, Paul says, is a shameful situation.

15:35–49 In discussing the nature of the resurrection body, Paul compares it to plant life (vv. 36–38), to fleshly beings (v. 39) and to celestial and earthly physical bodies (vv. 40–41).

15:36–38 Plant organisms, though organized similarly in their own order, are different; the seed sown is related to the new plant that sprouts, but the new sprout has a different and genuinely new body that God has given it.

15:39 *All flesh is not the same.* Although there is much that is similar in the organizational character of fleshly beings, each species is different: man, animals, birds, fish.

15:40–41 Here the analogy involves inanimate objects of creation: the sun, moon and stars with their differing splendor, and the earthly bodies (possibly the great mountains, canyons and seas) with their splendor. In it all, God can take similar physical material and organize it differently to accomplish His purpose.

15:42–44 In applying these analogies, the apostle says that in the case of the resurrection of the dead, God will take a perishable, dishonorable, weak (and sinful) body—"a natural body" characterized by sin—and in the resurrection make it an imperishable, glorious, powerful body. "Spiritual body" does not mean a nonmaterial body but, from the analogies, a physical one similar to the present natural body organizationally, but radically different in that it will be imperishable, glorious and powerful, fit to live eternally with God. There is continuity, but there is also change.

15:44–49 The contrast here between the natural body and the spiritual body again follows from their two representatives (see notes on vv. 21–22). One is the first Adam, who had a natural body of the dust of the ground (Gen 2:7) and through whom a natural body is given to his descendants. The other is the last Adam, Christ, the life-giving spirit (cf. John 5:26) who through His death and resurrection will at the second coming give His redeemed people a spiritual body—physical, yet imperishable, without corruption, and adaptable to live with God forever (cf. Phil 3:21). It will be a body similar to Christ's resurrected, glorified physical body (cf. Luke 24:36–43).

15:46 Adam, the earthly man, and his descendants received natural, earthly bodies. Christ, the last Adam, the man from heaven who became incarnate in a human body, received a glorified, spiritual body following His resurrection. Similarly, His redeemed people will receive a spiritual body.

15:50 Paul's final argument about the resurrection of the body: God's redeemed people must have newly organized, imperishable bodies to live with him. "Flesh and blood" stands for perishable, corrupt, weak, sinful human beings.

51 Behold, I tell you a [a]mystery; we will
not all sleep, but we will all be [b]changed,
52 in a moment, in the twinkling of an
eye, at the last trumpet; for [a]the trumpet will
sound, and [b]the dead will be raised [1]imper-
ishable, and [c]we will be changed.
53 For this [1]perishable must put on [2][a]the
imperishable, and this [b]mortal must put on
immortality.
54 But when this [1]perishable will have put
on [2]the imperishable, and this mortal will
have put on immortality, then will come
about the saying that is written, "[a]DEATH IS
SWALLOWED UP in victory.
55 "[a]O DEATH, WHERE IS YOUR VICTORY? O
DEATH, WHERE IS YOUR STING?"
56 The sting of [a]death is sin, and [b]the
power of sin is the law;
57 but [a]thanks be to God, who gives us
the [b]victory through our Lord Jesus Christ.
58 [a]Therefore, my beloved brethren, be
steadfast, immovable, always abounding in
[b]the work of the Lord, knowing that your toil
is not *in* vain in the Lord.

Instructions and Greetings

16 Now concerning [a]the collection for [b]the
saints, as [c]I directed the churches of
[d]Galatia, so do you also.
2 On [a]the first day of every week each
one of you is to [1]put aside and save, as he
may prosper, so that [b]no collections be made
when I come.
3 When I arrive, [a]whomever you may
approve, I will send them with letters to carry your gift to Jerusalem;
4 and if it is fitting for me to go also, they
will go with me.
5 But I [a]will come to you after I go
through [b]Macedonia, for I [c]am going through
Macedonia;
6 and perhaps I will stay with you, or
even spend the winter, so that you may
[a]send me on my way wherever I may go.
7 For I do not wish to see you now [a]*just*
in passing; for I hope to remain with you for
some time, [b]if the Lord permits.
8 But I will remain in [a]Ephesus until
[b]Pentecost;
9 for a [a]wide door [1]for effective *service*
has opened to me, and [b]there are many
adversaries.
10 Now if [a]Timothy comes, see that he is
with you without [1]cause to be afraid, for he
is doing [b]the Lord's work, as I also am.
11 [a]So let no one despise him. But [b]send

51 [a]1 Cor 13:2 [b]2 Cor 5:2, 4 **52** [1]Lit *incorruptible* [a]Matt 24:31 [b]John 5:28 [c]1 Thess 4:15, 17 **53** [1]Lit *corruptible* [2]Lit *incorruption* [a]Rom 2:7 [b]2 Cor 5:4 **54** [1]V 53, note 1 [2]V 53, note 2 [a]Is 25:8 **55** [a]Hos 13:14 **56** [a]Rom 5:12 [b]Rom 3:20; 4:15; 7:8 **57** [a]Rom 7:25; 2 Cor 2:14 [b]Rom 8:37; Heb 2:14f; 1 John 5:4; Rev 21:4 **58** [a]2 Pet 3:14 [b]1 Cor 16:10 **16:1** [a]Acts 24:17; Rom 15:25f [b]Acts 9:13 [c]1 Cor 4:17 [d]Acts 16:6 **2** [a]Acts 20:7

2 [1]Lit *put by himself* [b]2 Cor 9:4f **3** [a]2 Cor 3:1; 8:18f **5** [a]1 Cor 4:19 [b]Rom 15:26 [c]Acts 19:21 **6** [a]Acts 15:3; 1 Cor 16:11

7 [a]2 Cor 1:15f [b]Acts 18:21 **8** [a]Acts 18:19 [b]Acts 2:1 **9** [1]Lit *and* [a]Acts 14:27 [b]Acts 19:9 **10** [1]Lit *fear; for* [a]Acts 16:1; 1 Cor 4:17; 2 Cor 1:1 [b]1 Cor 15:58 **11** [a]1 Tim 4:12; Titus 2:15 [b]Acts 15:3; 1 Cor 16:6

15:51 *mystery.* Things about the resurrection body that were not understood but are now revealed (see note on Rom 11:25). *we will not all sleep.* Some believers will not experience death and the grave. *we will all be changed.* All believers, whether alive when Jesus comes again or in the grave, will receive changed, imperishable bodies.
15:52 *in a moment.* The change to an imperishable body will occur instantly at the last trumpet call. Some refer this to the "loud trumpet call" of Matt 24:31 or the seventh trumpet of Rev 11:15, others to the rapture (the snatching away) of God's people (cf. 1 Thess 4:16), which they hold will take place before Christ's (and their) return to reign on earth (cf. Rev 19:11–16; 20:1–6). *we will be changed.* Paul lived in anticipation of Christ's return, as all believers should.
15:56 *The sting of death is sin.* It was sin that brought us under death's power—it was Adam's sin that brought his death and ultimately ours (see Rom 5:12). *the power of sin is the law.* The law of God gives sin its power, for it reveals our sin and condemns us because of our sin.
15:57 *victory through our Lord Jesus Christ.* Victory over the condemnation for sin that the law brought (v. 56) and over death and the grave (vv. 54–55), through the death and resurrection of Christ (cf. Rom 4:25).
15:58 *Therefore.* Because of Christ's resurrection and ours, we know that serving Him is not empty, useless activity. *your toil is not in vain in the Lord.* Our effort is invested in the Lord's winning cause. He will also reward us at His second coming (Matt 25:21; cf. Luke 19:17).
16:1 *Now concerning.* Again an answer to one of the questions of the Corinthians (cf. 7:1; 8:1; 12:1). *the saints.* God's people at Jerusalem (cf. v. 3; Rom 15:26). *churches of Galatia.* The fact that the Galatian and Macedonian churches (2 Cor 8:1; 9:1–4) are involved, along with the Corinthians, indicates that the collection of this offering was quite widespread. The Jerusalem saints may have become poverty-stricken because of the famine recorded in Acts 11:28 (c. A.D. 44 or 46), or because of the persecution of Jerusalem Christians (cf. Acts 8:1).
16:2 *On the first day of every week each one of you is to put aside.* Every Sunday each person was to bring what he had set aside for the Lord's work—an amount proportionate to his income. Since it was to be brought on Sunday, the new day for worship (cf. Acts 20:7; Rev 1:10), probably it was collected at the worship service, not at home. Justin Martyr indicates (in his *Apology,* 1.67–68) that in his time (c. A.D. 150) offerings were brought to the church on Sundays.
16:3 For proper financial accountability and responsibility these approved men would act as auditors and guardians of the funds the Corinthians gave (cf. 2 Cor 8:16–21).
16:4 *if it is fitting for me to go also.* Possibly to take care of important missionary business, or to be there to explain about the gift when it arrives.
16:5 *after I go through Macedonia.* After leaving Ephesus (v. 8), where he was when he wrote 1 Corinthians, Paul planned to go up to Macedonia, no doubt to visit the Philippians and others in northern Greece, and then to Corinth. He had originally planned to go to Corinth first and then to Macedonia but thought it best to change his plans (see 2 Cor 1:12–2:4).
16:6 *even spend the winter.* Probably the three-month stay in Greece mentioned in Acts 20:3. *send me on my way.* With supplies and equipment, and certainly with prayers and goodwill. However, Paul had indicated earlier in the letter (9:7–12) that he did not want to be a financial burden to them.
16:8 *until Pentecost.* The 50th day (Pentecost means "50") after Passover, when the Jews celebrated the Feast of First fruits (Lev 23:10–16)—late spring.
16:9 *many adversaries.* Probably a reference to the pagan craftsmen who made the silver shrines of Artemis and to the general populace whom they had stirred up (Acts 19:23–34).
16:10 *if Timothy comes.* In Acts 19:22 Paul sends Timothy (and Erastus) into Macedonia, after which Timothy was to go on to

him on his way [c]in peace, so that he may
come to me; for I expect him with the brethren.
12 But concerning [a]Apollos our brother, I
encouraged him greatly to come to you with
the brethren; and it was not at all *his* desire
to come now, but he will come when he has
opportunity.
13 [a]Be on the alert, [b]stand firm in the
faith, [c]act like men, [d]be strong.
14 Let all that you do be done [a]in love.
15 Now I urge you, brethren (you know
the [a]household of Stephanas, that [1]they were
the [b]first fruits of [c]Achaia, and that they have
devoted themselves for [d]ministry to [e]the
saints),
16 that [a]you also be in subjection to such
men and to everyone who helps in the work
and labors.
17 I rejoice over the [1a]coming of Stephanas and Fortunatus and Achaicus, because
they have [2]supplied [b]what was lacking on
your part.
18 For they [a]have refreshed my spirit and
yours. Therefore [b]acknowledge such men.
19 The churches of [a]Asia greet you. [b]Aqui-
la and Prisca greet you heartily in the Lord,
with [c]the church that is in their house.
20 All the brethren greet you. [a]Greet one
another with a holy kiss.
21 The greeting is in [a]my own hand—
[1]Paul.
22 If anyone does not love the Lord, he is
to be [1a]accursed. [2b]Maranatha.
23 [a]The grace of the Lord Jesus be with
you.
24 My love be with you all in Christ Jesus.
Amen.

11 [c]Acts 15:33 **12** [a]Acts 18:24; 1 Cor 1:12; 3:5f **13** [a]Matt 24:42 [b]1 Cor 15:1; Gal 5:1; Phil 1:27; 4:1; 1 Thess 3:8; 2 Thess 2:15 [c]1 Sam 4:9; 2 Sam 10:12 [d]Ps 31:24; Eph 3:16; 6:10; Col 1:11 **14** [a]1 Cor 14:1 **15** [1]Lit *it was* [a]1 Cor 1:16 [b]Rom 16:5 [c]Acts 18:12 [d]Rom 15:31 [e]1 Cor 16:1 **16** [a]1 Thess 5:12; Heb 13:17 **17** [1]Or *presence* [a]2 Cor 7:6f **17** [2]Or *made up for your absence* [b]2 Cor 11:9; Phil 2:30 **18** [a]2 Cor 7:13; Philem 7, 20 [b]Phil 2:29; 1 Thess 5:12 **19** [a]Acts 16:6 [b]Acts 18:2 [c]Rom 16:5 **20** [a]Rom 16:16 **21** [1]Lit *Paul's* [a]Rom 16:22; Gal 6:11; Col 4:18; 2 Thess 3:17; Philem 19 **22** [1]Gr *anathema* [2]I.e. O [our] Lord come! [a]Rom 9:3 [b]Phil 4:5; Rev 22:20 **23** [a]Rom 16:20

Corinth (1 Cor 4:17). *see that he is with you without cause to be afraid.* Timothy seems to have been somewhat timid (1 Tim 4:12; 2 Tim 1:7), and Paul wants the Corinthians to treat him kindly.

16:11 *brethren.* Possibly including Erastus (cf. Acts 19:22), who was a believer from Corinth and "city treasurer" (Rom 16:23; see note there).

16:12 *But concerning Apollos.* The Corinthians had asked Paul about Apollos (cf. the similar words, "now concerning," in 7:1; 8:1; 12:1; 16:1) and his coming to see them.

16:15 *household of Stephanas.* Evidently the Corinthians had little respect for this household that Paul had baptized (1:16). They were among the first converts in Achaia (Greece), along with the few individuals in Athens who had believed a short time earlier (Acts 17:34). *ministry.* The whole household of Stephanas was serving.

16:17 Probably the ones who had brought to the apostle the letter from the Corinthians referred to in 7:1. Their coming "supplied what was lacking" from the Corinthians, i.e., the affection of these three brothers supplied the affection Paul desired from the whole Corinthian church.

16:18 *refreshed my spirit and yours.* Perhaps through their willingness to come to get Paul's advice and to bring it back to them. At least a new relationship between Paul and the Corinthians was in the making.

16:19 *of Asia.* The Roman province (presently in western Turkey) in which Ephesus and the surrounding cities were located (cf. Acts 19:10). During Paul's long ministry in Ephesus all in the province of Asia heard the word. The churches of Colosse, Laodicea and Hierapolis (cf. Col 4:13–16; Rev 1:11), which were located on the border of the province of Asia, may be included in the greetings, along with the other churches of Rev 2–3. *Aquila and Prisca.* They had helped Paul found the church at Corinth (Acts 18:1–4). *heartily in the Lord.* Enthusiastically as fellow believers. *the church that is in their house.* Aquila and Priscilla had left Corinth with Paul and had gone to Ephesus (Acts 18:18–19). Evidently they were still there, and a church was meeting at their house; it now sends greetings. House churches were common in this early period (cf. Rom 16:3–5; Philem 2).

16:20 *holy kiss.* The kiss of mutual respect and love in the Lord was evidently the public practice of early Christians—from a practice that was customary in the ancient East. Such a practice may have been used in the first-century A.D. synagogue—men kissing men, and women kissing women—and it would have been natural for the practice to have been continued in the early Jewish-Gentile churches.

16:21 *greeting is in my own hand.* Paul now signs this letter, as was his habit (see Col 4:18; Philem 19), a mark of the authenticity of the letter (2 Thess 3:17). Someone else had been penning the letter for him up to this point (cf. Rom 16:22).

16:22 *he is to be accursed.* May this person experience God's displeasure and wrath, since he has declared himself an unbeliever (John 3:36). This is not a curse based on things God has created (e.g., heaven and earth), an oath that Jesus forbids. Rather, it is a curse based on God as witness to the unbeliever's essential lack of love and obedience to God (see also Gal 1:8–9). *Maranatha.* An expression meaning "O Lord come!", used by the early church as a cry that the second coming of Christ may soon take place.

16:23 The apostle's usual benediction (see Gal 6:18; Eph 6:24; Phil 4:23); a longer Trinitarian benediction is found in 2 Cor 13:14.

16:24 Although he has been severe with the Corinthians, Paul wants them to know that he loves them as believers in Christ Jesus.

2 Corinthians

INTRODUCTION

Author

Paul is the author of this letter (see 1:1; 10:1). It is stamped with his style and it contains more autobiographical material than any of his other writings.

Date

The available evidence indicates that the year A.D. 55 is a reasonable estimate for the writing of this letter. From 1 Cor 16:5–8 we conclude that 1 Corinthians was written from Ephesus before Pentecost (in the spring) and that 2 Corinthians was written later that same year before the onset of winter. 2 Cor 2:13; 7:5 indicate that it was written from Macedonia.

Recipients

The opening salutation of the letter states that it was addressed to the church in Corinth and to the Christians throughout Achaia (the Roman province comprising all the territory of Greece south of Macedonia).

Purpose

The Corinthian church had been infiltrated by false teachers who were challenging both Paul's personal integrity and his authority as an apostle. Because he had announced a change in his itinerary, with the result that he would now pay the Corinthians one (long) visit instead of two (short) visits, these adversaries were asserting that his word was not to be trusted. They were also saying that he was not a genuine apostle and that he was putting into his own pocket the money they had collected for the poverty-stricken believers in Jerusalem. Paul asks the Corinthians to consider that his personal life in their midst was always honorable and that his life-transforming message of salvation was true. He urges them to prepare for his impending visit by completing the collection they had started a year previously and by dealing with the troublemakers in their midst. He warns them that he means what he writes.

Structure

The structure of the letter relates primarily to Paul's impending third visit to Corinth. The letter falls naturally into three sections:

1. Paul explains the reason for the change of itinerary (chs. 1—7).
2. Paul encourages the Corinthians to complete the collection in preparation for his arrival (chs. 8—9).
3. Paul stresses the certainty of his coming, his authenticity as an apostle and his readiness as an apostle to exercise discipline if necessary (chs. 10—13).

Unity

Some have questioned the unity of this letter (see note on 2:3–4), but it forms a coherent whole, as the structure (above) shows. Tradition has been unanimous in affirming its unity (the early church fathers, e.g., knew the letter only in its present form). Furthermore, none of the early Greek manuscripts breaks up the book.

Outline

I. Primarily Apologetic: Paul's Explanation of His Conduct and Apostolic Ministry (chs. 1—7)
   A. Salutation (1:1–2)
   B. Thanksgiving for Divine Comfort in Affliction (1:3–11)

- C. The Integrity of Paul's Motives and Conduct (1:12—2:4)
- D. Forgiving the Offender at Corinth (2:5–11)
- E. God's Direction in the Ministry (2:12–17)
- F. The Corinthian Believers—a Letter from Christ (3:1–11)
- G. Seeing the Glory of God with Unveiled Faces (3:12—4:6)
- H. Treasure in Earthen Vessels (4:7–16a)
- I. The Prospect of Death and What It Means for the Christian (4:16b—5:10)
- J. The Ministry of Reconciliation (5:11—6:10)
- K. A Spiritual Father's Appeal to His Children (6:11—7:4)
- L. The Meeting with Titus (7:5–16)

II. Hortatory: The Collection for the Christians at Jerusalem (chs. 8—9)
- A. Generosity Encouraged (8:1–15)
- B. Titus and His Companions Sent to Corinth (8:16—9:5)
- C. Results of Generous Giving (9:6–15)

III. Polemical: Paul's Vindication of His Apostolic Authority (chs. 10—13)
- A. Paul's Defense of His Apostolic Authority and the Area of His Mission (ch. 10)
- B. Paul Forced into Foolish Boasting (chs. 11—12)
- C. Final Warnings (13:1–10)
- D. Conclusion (13:11–14)

Introduction

1 Paul, [a]an apostle of [b]Christ Jesus [c]by the
will of God, and [d]Timothy *our* brother,
To [e]the church of God which is at [f]Cor-
inth with all the [1]saints who are throughout
[g]Achaia:
2 [a]Grace to you and peace from God our
Father and the Lord Jesus Christ.
3 [a]Blessed *be* the God and Father of our
Lord Jesus Christ, the Father of mercies and
[b]God of all comfort,
4 who [a]comforts us in all our affliction
so that we will be able to comfort those who
are in [1]any affliction with the comfort with
which we ourselves are comforted by God.
5 For just [a]as the sufferings of Christ are
[1]ours in abundance, so also our comfort is
abundant through Christ.
6 But if we are afflicted, it is [a]for your
comfort and salvation; or if we are comforted, it is for your comfort, which is effective
in the patient enduring of the same sufferings which we also suffer;
7 and our hope for you is firmly grounded, knowing that [a]as you are sharers of our
sufferings, so also you are *sharers* of our
comfort.
8 For [a]we do not want you to be
unaware, brethren, of our [b]affliction which
came *to us* in [1c]Asia, that we were burdened
excessively, beyond our strength, so that we
despaired even of life;
9 [1]indeed, we had the sentence of death
within ourselves so that we would not trust
in ourselves, but in God who raises the dead;
10 who [a]delivered us from so great a *peril*
of death, and will deliver *us,* [1]He [b]on whom
we have set our hope. And He will yet deliver us,
11 you also joining in [a]helping us through
your prayers, so that thanks may be given by
[b]many persons on our behalf for the favor
bestowed on us through *the prayers of* many.

Paul's Integrity

12 For our [1]proud confidence is this: the
testimony of [a]our conscience, that in holiness and [b]godly sincerity, [c]not in fleshly wisdom but in the grace of God, we have conducted ourselves in the world, and especially
toward you.
13 For we write nothing else to you than
what you read and understand, and I hope
you will understand [a]until the end;
14 just as you also partially did understand
us, that we are your reason to be proud as you
also are ours, in [a]the day of our Lord Jesus.
15 In this confidence I intended at first to
[a]come to you, so that you might [1]twice
receive a [2b]blessing;
16 [1]that is, to [a]pass [2]your way into [b]Mace-
donia, and again from Macedonia to come to
you, and by you to be [c]helped on my journey
to Judea.
17 Therefore, I was not vacillating when I
intended to do this, was I? Or what I purpose, do I purpose [a]according to the flesh,
so that with me there will be yes, yes and
no, no *at the same time?*

1:1 [1]Or *holy ones* [a]Rom 1:1; Gal 1:1; Eph 1:1; Col 1:1; 2 Tim 1:1; Titus 1:1 [b]Gal 3:26 [c]1 Cor 1:1 [d]Acts 16:1; 1 Cor 16:10; 2 Cor 1:19 [e]1 Cor 10:32 [f]Acts 18:1 [g]Acts 18:12
2 [a]Rom 1:7
3 [a]Eph 1:3; 1 Pet 1:3 [b]Rom 15:5
4 [1]Lit *every* [a]Is 51:12; 66:13; 2 Cor 7:6, 7, 13
5 [1]Lit *to us* [a]2 Cor 4:10; Phil 3:10; Col 1:24
6 [a]2 Cor 4:15; 12:15; Eph 3:1, 13; 2 Tim 2:10
7 [a]Rom 8:17
8 [1]I.e. west coast province of Asia Minor [a]Rom 1:13 [b]Acts 19:23; 1 Cor 15:32 [c]Acts 16:6
9 [1]Lit *but we ourselves*
10 [a]Rom 15:31
10 [1]One early ms reads *on whom we have set our hope that He will also* [b]1 Tim 4:10
11 [a]Rom 15:30; Phil 1:19; Philem 22 [b]2 Cor 4:15; 9:11f
12 [1]Lit *boasting* [a]Acts 23:1; 1 Thess 2:10; Heb 13:18 [b]2 Cor 2:17 [c]1 Cor 1:17; James 3:15
13 [a]1 Cor 1:8
14 [a]1 Cor 1:8 **15** [1]Lit *have a second grace* [2]One early ms reads *joy* [a]1 Cor 4:19 [b]Rom 1:11; 15:29 **16** [1]Lit *and* [2]Lit *through you into* [a]Acts 19:21; 1 Cor 16:5-7 [b]Acts 19:21; Rom 15:26 [c]Acts 15:3; 1 Cor 16:6, 11 **17** [a]2 Cor 10:2f; 11:18

1:1 *apostle.* One specially commissioned by Christ (see notes on Mark 6:30; 1 Cor 1:1; Heb 3:1). *Timothy.* Evidently with Paul when this letter was written, but not necessarily a co-author. *our brother.* Our fellow believer, our brother in Christ (cf. Acts 9:17; Heb 2:11). *church of God.* The community of believers, the local representatives of the universal church (see note on 1 Cor 1:2). *saints.* Another term for God's people; it means "those who have been set apart as holy to the Lord" (see note on Rom 1:7). *Achaia.* Greece, as distinct from Macedonia in the north. Though the letter deals particularly with the situation in Corinth, it was also intended for Christians elsewhere in Greece. Presumably copies of the letter would be made in Corinth and circulated to them.

1:2 *Grace to you and peace.* See notes on Jon 4:2; John 14:27; 20:19; Gal 1:3; Eph 1:2.

1:3 *God.* The source of our comfort. *comfort.* Consolation and encouragement. This comfort flows to believers when they suffer for Jesus' sake, and it equips them to comfort others who are in trouble (vv. 4–7).

1:8 *our affliction.* Throughout this letter Paul uses the editorial plural (we, us, our, ourselves). Except where the context plainly indicates otherwise, these plurals should be understood as referring to Paul alone. *Asia.* The Roman province of that name in western Asia Minor, now Turkish territory. The precise location where Paul's hardships occurred is not given, nor is the nature of affliction.

1:9 Paul's hardships were so life-threatening that he regarded his survival and recovery as tantamount to being raised from the dead. *trust . . . in God.* A key principle of this letter. God's grace is all-sufficient, and our weakness is precisely the opportunity for His power to be displayed (cf. 12:9–10).

1:12 In defending his trustworthiness against the slanders being spread about him, Paul appeals to the witness of his own conscience and to the Corinthians' firsthand knowledge of his character. He had spent 18 months with them when he first came to Corinth (Acts 18:11), so they could not plead ignorance of his integrity.

1:13 In keeping with their knowledge of Paul's character, they can trust what he writes from a distance: He means what he says.

1:14 *partially.* Some in Corinth had allowed their confidence in Paul and his apostolic authority to be shaken by the false apostles who had penetrated their ranks. *day of our Lord Jesus.* His return (cf. 1 Thess 2:19–20).

1:15 *that you might twice receive a blessing.* Here and in v. 16 Paul refers to his change of itinerary. Originally he had planned to cross over by sea from Ephesus to Corinth, visiting the Corinthians before traveling north to Macedonia, and then, returning from Macedonia, to visit them a second time, thus giving them the benefit of two short visits. This was when he was on good terms with them. What probably occurred was that he paid them a quick visit directly from Ephesus, a visit he had not contemplated and one that he made "in sorrow" (2:1). That visit then gave rise to his letter that caused them sorrow (see 7:8–9).

1:17 *I was not vacillating . . . was I?* Paul's opponents in Corinth had been attempting to persuade the Christians there that this change of plan was evidence that his word was not to be

18 But as [a]God is faithful, [b]our word to
you is not yes and no.
19 For [a]the Son of God, Christ Jesus, who
was preached among you by us—by me and
[b]Silvanus and [c]Timothy—was not yes and
no, but is yes [d]in Him.
20 For [a]as many as are the promises of
God, [b]in Him they are yes; therefore also
through Him is [c]our Amen to the glory of
God through us.
21 Now He who [a]establishes us with you
in Christ and [b]anointed us is God,
22 who also [a]sealed us and [b]gave *us* the
Spirit in our hearts as a [1]pledge.
23 But [a]I call God as witness [1]to my soul,
that [b]to spare you I did not come again to
[c]Corinth.
24 Not that we [a]lord it over your faith, but
are workers with you for your joy; for in your
faith you are [b]standing firm.

Reaffirm Your Love

2 But I determined this [1]for my own sake,
that I [a]would not come to you in sorrow
again.
2 For if I [a]cause you sorrow, who then
makes me glad but the one whom I made
sorrowful?
3 This is the very thing I [a]wrote you, so
that [b]when I came, I would not have sorrow
from those who ought to make me rejoice;
having [c]confidence in you all that my joy
would be *the joy* of you all.
4 For out of much affliction and anguish
of heart I [a]wrote to you with many tears; not
so that you would be made sorrowful, but
that you might know the love which I have
especially for you.
5 But [a]if any has caused sorrow, he has
caused sorrow not to me, but in some
degree—[1]in order not to say too much—to
all of you.
6 Sufficient for such a one is [a]this punishment which *was inflicted* by the majority,
7 so that on the contrary you should
rather [a]forgive and comfort *him,* otherwise
such a one might be overwhelmed by excessive sorrow.
8 Wherefore I urge you to reaffirm *your*
love for him.
9 For to this end also [a]I wrote, so that I
might [1b]put you to the test, whether you are
[c]obedient in all things.
10 But one whom you forgive anything, I
forgive also; for indeed what I have forgiven,
if I have forgiven anything, *I did it* for your
sakes [a]in the presence of Christ,
11 so that no advantage would be taken of
us by [a]Satan, for [b]we are not ignorant of his
schemes.
12 Now when I came to [a]Troas for the

18 [a]1 Cor 1:9 [b]2 Cor 2:17 **19** [a]Matt 4:3; 16:16; 26:63 [b]Acts 15:22; 1 Thess 1:1; 2 Thess 1:1; 1 Pet 5:12 [c]Acts 18:5; 2 Cor 1:1 [d]Heb 13:8 **20** [a]Rom 15:8 [b]Heb 13:8 [c]1 Cor 14:16; Rev 3:14 **21** [a]1 Cor 1:8 [b]1 John 2:20, 27 **22** [1]Or *down payment* [a]John 3:33 [b]Rom 8:16; 2 Cor 5:5; Eph 1:14 **23** [1]Lit *upon* [a]Rom 1:9; Gal 1:20 [b]1 Cor 4:21; 2 Cor 2:1, 3 [c]2 Cor 1:1 **24** [a]2 Cor 4:5; 11:20; 1 Pet 5:3 [b]Rom 11:20; 1 Cor 15:1 **2:1** [1]Or *as far as I am concerned* [a]1 Cor 4:21; 2 Cor 12:21 **2** [a]2 Cor 7:8 **3** [a]2 Cor 2:9; 7:8, 12 [b]1 Cor 4:21; 2 Cor 12:21 [c]Gal 5:10; 2 Thess 3:4; Philem 21

4 [a]2 Cor 2:9; 7:8, 12

5 [1]Lit *so that I not be burdensome* [a]1 Cor 5:1f **6** [a]1 Cor 5:4f; 2 Cor 7:11 **7** [a]Gal 6:1; Eph 4:32 **9** [1]Lit *know the proof of you* [a]2 Cor 2:3f [b]2 Cor 8:2; Phil 2:22 [c]2 Cor 7:15; 10:6 **10** [a]1 Cor 5:4; 2 Cor 4:6 **11** [a]Matt 4:10 [b]Luke 22:31; 2 Cor 4:4; 1 Pet 5:8 **12** [a]Acts 16:8

trusted, that he was fickle and unreliable. The two rhetorical questions are in effect his denial that he acts lightly and that he says "Yes" and "No" at the same time so that it is impossible to know what he means. In any case, his plan to visit the Corinthians had not been abandoned; it had simply been modified.
1:18 *not yes and no.* Paul now (vv. 18–20) appeals to the gospel message he had preached to them: Believing it, they had found it to be altogether true and entirely free from ambiguity, and by their experience of its dynamic power they had proved it to be one great affirmative in Christ, in whom all God's promises are "Yes."
1:20 *Amen.* The "Amen" uttered by the congregation at the end of an offering of prayer or praise (cf. 1 Cor 14:16).
1:22 *sealed.* See notes on Hag 2:23; Eph 1:13. *pledge.* A part given as a guarantee that the whole will be forthcoming. The part is of the same kind as the whole. The first installment of a sum of money that has been inherited, e.g., assures the recipient that the whole will be received. This justifies the expansion of a single Greek word into several English words: "a deposit, guaranteeing what is to come."
1:23 *to spare you.* Paul's change of plans for visiting the Corinthian Christians had been motivated, not by a fickle and insensitive attitude, but by love and concern for them.
2:1 *come . . . in sorrow again.* Paul had already made one painful visit to Corinth, and he wanted to avoid another such visit, though he was ready to exert his authority should it prove necessary (cf. 13:2). The occasion of this former painful visit is not known to us. It could not have been his original visit to Corinth at the time when the church there was founded in response to the preaching of the gospel. Therefore he must have paid a second visit, which is confirmed by 12:14; 13:1, where he states that the visit he is now about to make will be his third. The second visit probably took place between the writing of 1 and 2 Corinthians, though some hold that it occurred before 1 Corinthians was written.
2:3–4 *I wrote you . . . out of much affliction and anguish.* This passage refers to a previous letter that had been sent to the Corinthians. The consensus of the church from the earliest times has been that this previous letter is 1 Corinthians. In more recent times, however, the hypothesis that the reference is to an intermediate letter, written after 1 Corinthians and before 2 Corinthians, has been widely accepted. Some advocates of this theory hold that the letter in question is now lost; others have identified it, in whole or in part, with the last four chapters of 2 Corinthians, contending that these chapters are out of harmony with the earlier ones and that they fit the description of a letter written "out of great distress and anguish." There is, however, no historical evidence that the unity of 2 Corinthians was questioned or that its integrity was doubted prior to modern times.
2:5–11 Speaks of a particular person who has been the cause of serious offense in Corinth and upon whom church discipline has been imposed. Paul admonishes the Corinthians that because the offender has shown genuine sorrow and repentance for his sin the punishment should be discontinued and he should be lovingly restored to their fellowship. Church discipline, important as it is, should not be allowed to develop into a form of graceless rigor in which there is no room for pardon and restoration. The offense in question probably took place during Paul's intermediate visit to Corinth (see note on v. 1) and was the occasion for his writing the severe letter demanding the punishment of the offender (see note on vv. 3–4). Another view is that Paul refers to the incident recorded in 1 Cor 5.
2:12 *when I came to Troas.* Paul had traveled up from Ephesus

[b]gospel of Christ and when a [c]door was
opened for me in the Lord,
13 I [a]had no rest for my spirit, not finding
[b]Titus my brother; but [c]taking my leave of
them, I went on to [d]Macedonia.
14 [a]But thanks be to God, who always
[b]leads us in triumph in Christ, and manifests
through us the [c]sweet aroma of the [d]knowl-
edge of Him in every place.
15 For we are a [a]fragrance of Christ to God
among [b]those who are being saved and
among those who are perishing;
16 [a]to the one an aroma from death to
death, to the other an aroma from life to life.
And who is [b]adequate for these things?
17 For we are not like many, [1a]peddling
the word of God, but [b]as from sincerity, but
as from God, we speak in Christ [c]in the sight
of God.

Ministers of a New Covenant

3 Are we beginning to [a]commend ourselves
again? Or do we need, as some, [b]letters of
commendation to you or from you?

12 [b]Rom 1:1; 2 Cor 4:3, 4; 8:18; 9:13; 10:14; 11:4, 7; 1 Thess 3:2 [c]Acts 14:27 **13** [a]2 Cor 7:5 [b]2 Cor 7:6, 13f; 8:6, 16, 23; 12:18; Gal 2:1, 3; 2 Tim 4:10; Titus 1:4 [c]Mark 6:46 [d]Rom 15:26 **14** [a]Rom 1:8; 6:17; 1 Cor 15:57; 2 Cor 8:16; 9:15 [b]Col 2:15 [c]Song 1:3; Ezek 20:41; Eph 5:2; Phil 4:18 [d]1 Cor 12:8 **15** [a]Song 1:3; Ezek 20:41; Eph 5:2; Phil 4:18 [b]1 Cor 1:18 **16** [a]Luke 2:34; John 9:39; 1 Pet 2:7f [b]2 Cor 3:5f **17** [1]Or *corrupting* [a]2 Cor 4:2; Gal 1:6-9 [b]1 Cor 5:8; 2 Cor 1:12; 1 Thess 2:4; 1 Pet 4:11 [c]2 Cor 12:19

2 [a]You are our letter, written in our
hearts, known and read by all men;
3 being manifested that you are a letter
of Christ, [1a]cared for by us, written not with
ink but with the Spirit of [b]the living God, not
on [c]tablets of stone but on [d]tablets of
[2e]human hearts.
4 Such [a]confidence we have through
Christ toward God.
5 Not that we are adequate in ourselves
to consider anything as *coming* from ourselves, but [a]our adequacy is from God,
6 who also made us adequate *as* [a]ser-
vants of a [b]new covenant, not of [c]the letter
but of the Spirit; for the letter kills, but [d]the
Spirit gives life.
7 But if the [a]ministry of death, [b]in letters
engraved on stones, came [1]with glory, [c]so

3:1 [a]2 Cor 5:12; 10:12, 18; 12:11 [b]Acts 18:27; 1 Cor 16:3 **2** [a]1 Cor 9:2 **3** [1]Lit *served* [2]Lit *hearts of flesh* [a]2 Cor 3:6 [b]Matt 16:16 [c]Ex 24:12; 31:18; 32:15f; 2 Cor 3:7 [d]Prov 3:3; 7:3; Jer 17:1 [e]Jer 31:33; Ezek 11:19; 36:26 **4** [a]Eph 3:12 **5** [a]1 Cor 15:10 **6** [a]1 Cor 3:5 [b]Jer 31:31; Luke 22:20 [c]Rom 2:29 [d]John 6:63; Rom 7:6 **7** [1]Or *in glory* [a]Rom 4:15; 5:20; 7:5f; 2 Cor 3:9; Gal 3:10, 21f [b]Ex 24:12; 31:18; 32:15f; 2 Cor 3:3 [c]Ex 34:29-35; 2 Cor 3:13

---

to Troas, a city on the Aegean coast opposite the island of Tenedos, hoping to find Titus there and to receive news from him about the Corinthian church. But Titus, who presumably Paul knew would be following the same route in reverse, did not arrive in Troas; so Paul, anxious for news from Corinth, "went on to Macedonia" (v. 13), perhaps to the city of Philippi.

2:13 *my brother.* Cf. 8:23. Paul held Titus in high esteem; he entrusted Titus with the organization of the collection of funds in Corinth for the relief of the poverty-stricken Christians of Jerusalem (8:6), and he chose him to bear this letter to the Corinthian Christians (8:16–17).

2:14 At this point Paul breaks off the narrative of his itinerary and in a characteristic manner allows his spontaneous spirit to carry him into a lengthy digression (the narrative is not resumed until 7:5). The digression, however, is quite relevant to the main tenor of this letter, for it is an immensely rich outpouring of triumphant faith in praise of the unfailing adequacy of the grace of God for every conceivable situation, no matter how threatening and destructive it may seem to be. *leads us in triumph.* The imagery is that of a Roman triumph in which the victorious general would lead his soldiers and the captives they had taken in festive procession, while the people watched and applauded and the air was filled with the sweet smell released by the burning of spices in the streets. So the Christian, called to spiritual warfare, is triumphantly led by God in Christ, and it is through Him that God spreads everywhere the "sweet aroma" of the knowledge of Christ.

2:16 *an aroma from death . . . an aroma from life.* As the gospel aroma is released in the world through Christian testimony, it is always sweet-smelling, even though it may be differently received. The two ultimate categories of mankind are "those who are being saved and . . . those who are perishing" (v. 15). To the latter, testifying Christians are the smell of death, not because the gospel message has become evil-smelling or death-dealing, but because in rejecting the life-giving grace of God unbelievers choose death for themselves. To those who welcome the gospel of God's grace, Christians with their testimony are the fragrance of life. *who is adequate for these things?* For the answer see 3:5.

2:17 *we are not . . . peddling the word of God.* Paul is referring to false teachers who had infiltrated the Corinthian church. Such persons—themselves insincere, self-sufficient and boastful—artfully presented themselves in a persuasive manner, and their chief interest was to take money from gullible church members. Paul, by contrast, had preached the gospel sincerely and free of charge, taking care not to be a financial burden to the Corinthian believers (see 11:7–12; 1 Cor 9:7–15).

3:1 *Are we beginning to commend ourselves again?* Paul is sensitive to the fact that virtually everything he wrote or said was liable to be twisted and used in a hostile manner by the false teachers in Corinth. *letters of commendation.* The appearance of vagrant impostors, who claimed to be teachers of apostolic truth, led to the need for letters of recommendation. Paul needed no such confirmation; but others, including the Corinthian intruders, did need authentication and, being themselves false, often resorted to unscrupulous methods for obtaining or forging letters of recommendation.

3:2 *known and read by all men.* Because of the power of the gospel demonstrated by their transformed lives.

3:3 *letter of Christ.* Paul is no more than the instrument in the hands of the Master. *written not with ink.* As a parchment or papyrus document would be. *with the Spirit of the living God.* As though the Spirit were a substitute for ink! Ink fades and may easily be deleted or blocked out since it is no more than an inanimate fluid. But the Spirit of the living God is Himself life and therefore life-giving (v. 6), and the life He gives is eternal and without defect. *not on tablets of stone.* As at Sinai (see note on v. 6). *on tablets of human hearts.* See Jer 31:33; Ezek 11:19; 36:26. Paul explains the significance of this contrast between the old and the new covenants in vv. 7–18.

3:5 *our adequacy is from God.* Answers the question in 2:16: "And who is adequate for these things?"

3:6 *servants of.* Those who serve the cause of (see Rom 15:16; Col 1:7; 4:7; 1 Tim 4:6). Paul will return to the theme of "this ministry" in 4:1. *new covenant.* Here Paul takes up the theme suggested by the mention of "tablets of human hearts" (v. 3). See Heb 8–10 and note on Heb 7:22. Paul's reference to ministers of a new covenant in contrast to the "ministry of death" (v. 7) may have been occasioned by his opponents in Corinth who were Judaizers, perhaps those who claimed to be associated with Peter (1 Cor 1:12) and who are referred to as Hebrews in 11:22 (see note there). *the letter.* The "tablets of stone" on

that the sons of Israel could not look intently at the face of Moses because of the glory
of his face, fading *as* it was,
8 how will the ministry of the Spirit fail
to be even more with glory?
9 For if [a]the ministry of condemnation
has glory, much more does the [b]ministry of
righteousness abound in glory.
10 For indeed what had glory, in this case
has no glory because of the glory that surpasses *it.*
11 For if that which fades away *was* [1]with
glory, much more that which remains *is* in
glory.
12 [a]Therefore having such a hope, [b]we
use great boldness in *our* speech,
13 and *are* not like Moses, [a]*who* used to
put a veil over his face so that the sons of
Israel would not look intently at the end of
what was fading away.
14 But their minds were [a]hardened; for
until this very day at the [b]reading of [c]the old
covenant the same veil [1]remains unlifted,
because it is removed in Christ.
15 But to this day whenever Moses is
read, a veil lies over their heart;
16 [a]but whenever a person turns to the
Lord, the veil is taken away.
17 Now the Lord is the Spirit, and where
[a]the Spirit of the Lord is, [b]*there* is liberty.
18 But we all, with unveiled face, [a]behold-
ing as in a mirror the [b]glory of the Lord, are
being [c]transformed into the same image from
glory to glory, just as from [d]the Lord, the
Spirit.

Paul's Apostolic Ministry

4 Therefore, since we have this [a]ministry,
as we [b]received mercy, we [c]do not lose
heart,
2 but we have renounced the [a]things hidden because of shame, not walking in crafti-

9 [a]Deut 27:26; 2 Cor 3:7; Heb 12:18-21 [b]Rom 1:17; 3:21f
11 [1]Lit *through*
12 [a]2 Cor 7:4 [b]Acts 4:13, 29; 2 Cor 7:4; Eph 6:19; 1 Thess 2:2
13 [a]Ex 34:33-35; 2 Cor 3:7
14 [a]Rom 11:7; 2 Cor 4:4 [b]Acts 13:15 [c]2 Cor 3:6
14 [1]Or *remains, it not being revealed that it is done away in Christ*
16 [a]Ex 34:34; Rom 11:23
17 [a]Is 61:1f; Gal 4:6 [b]John 8:32; Gal 5:1, 13
18 [a]1 Cor 13:12 [b]John 17:22, 24; 2 Cor 4:4, 6 [c]Rom 8:29 [d]2 Cor 3:17
4:1 [a]1 Cor 3:5 [b]1 Cor 7:25 [c]Luke 18:1; 2 Cor 4:16; Gal 6:9; Eph 3:13; 2 Thess 3:13
2 [a]Rom 6:21; 1 Cor 4:5

which the letter of the law was originally written (see Ex 24:12; 31:18; 32:15–16). *the Spirit.* The writing of the law "with the Spirit of the living God . . . on tablets of human hearts," which was the promise of the new covenant as foretold by the prophets (see Jer 31:31–34; 32:39–40; Ezek 11:19; 36:26). *the letter kills, but the Spirit gives life.* Does not mean that the external, literal sense of Scripture is deadly or unprofitable while the inner, spiritual (mystical or mythical) sense is vital. "The letter" is synonymous with the law as an external standard before which all people, because they are lawbreakers, stand guilty and condemned to death. Therefore it is described as the "ministry of death" and the "ministry of condemnation" (vv. 7,9). On the other hand, the Spirit who gives life is the "Spirit of the living God" who, in fulfillment of the promise of the new covenant, writes that same law inwardly "on tablets of human hearts" (v. 3). He thus provides the believer with love for God's law, which previously he had hated, and with power to keep it, which previously he had not possessed.

3:7–18 Paul is defending his "ministry" of the new covenant in Christ (cf. v. 6; 4:1) and here compares the experiences of Moses, who mediated the old covenant of Sinai, and his own as a minister of the new covenant. But he now applies the word "ministry" to the law that was "engraved in letters on stone" and to the Spirit, who writes "on tablets of human hearts" (v. 3). The point of comparison is the fading glory that shone on Moses' face and the "ever-increasing glory" reflected in the faces of those who minister the new covenant. This contrast in regard to glory serves to highlight the temporary and inadequate character of the old covenant and the permanent and effective character of the new covenant.

3:7 *came with glory.* The law of the old covenant given at Sinai was in no way bad or evil; on the contrary, Paul describes it elsewhere as holy, righteous, good and spiritual (Rom 7:12,14). The evil is in the hearts and deeds of people who, as lawbreakers, bring upon themselves the condemnation of the law and the penalty of death—and the law engraved on stone could not purge away that evil. *glory of his face.* The glory of God surrounded the giving of the law and was reflected on the face of Moses when he descended from the mountain (see Ex 34:29–30).

3:8–9 *ministry of the Spirit . . . ministry of righteousness.* The ministry of the Spirit gives life instead of death. "Righteousness" is here both objective (justification) and personal (sanctification).

3:11 *that which fades away.* Paul here applies the fading to the old covenant of Sinai, which was not to endure forever. In due course it was superseded by the unfading and much more glorious radiance belonging to the new covenant.

3:13 *Moses, who used to put a veil over his face.* See Ex 34:33–35. The purpose of the veil was to prevent the Israelites from seeing the fading of the glory.

3:14 *until this very day . . . the same veil remains.* The veil that prevented them from seeing the fading of the glory on Moses' face is still with them, preventing them from recognizing the temporary and inadequate character of the old covenant—a "veil" that is removed only in Christ. Only those who have received the new covenant in Christ have the power to see how the new covenant has transcended and replaced the old covenant—because of its greater glory.

3:17 *the Lord is the Spirit.* This statement should be linked with what was said at the end of v. 6: "the Spirit gives life." It is only by turning to the Lord (v. 16) that the condemnation and the sentence of death pronounced by the law on the lawbreaker are annulled and replaced by the free life-giving grace of the new covenant. There is a close relationship between the Spirit of Christ and the Holy Spirit. Both are said to dwell in the believer (Rom 8:9; Gal 2:20). In Rom 8:9–10 the Spirit, the Spirit of God, the Spirit of Christ, and Christ all seem to be used interchangeably. In Acts 16:6–7 the Holy Spirit and the Spirit of Jesus appear to be one and the same. Perhaps this is because the Holy Spirit proceeds from the Father and the Son, and the first two persons of the Trinity accomplish their purposes through the Spirit.

3:18 *with unveiled face.* In contrast to Moses. *being transformed into the same image from glory to glory.* Christ Himself is the glory of God in the fullness of its radiance (Heb 1:3); His is the eternal and unfading glory, which He had with the Father before the world began (John 17:5). We who believe are made partakers of this glory by being gradually transformed into the likeness of Christ. The reference here is to the process of Christian sanctification.

4:1 *this ministry.* See 3:6 and note. *we do not lose heart.* When God through His mercy calls and commissions His servants, He also supplies the strength necessary for them to persevere in the face of hardships and persecutions.

4:2 *we have renounced the things hidden because of shame.* Paul is referring to the false teachers in Corinth. By contrast, he is able to appeal to the conscience of every one of them and

ness or [b]adulterating the word of God, but
by the manifestation of truth [c]commending
ourselves to every man's conscience in the
sight of God.
3 And even if our [a]gospel is [b]veiled, it is
veiled [1]to [c]those who are perishing,
4 in whose case [a]the god of [b]this [1]world
has [c]blinded the minds of the unbelieving
[2]so that they might not see the [d]light of the
gospel of the [e]glory of Christ, who is the
[f]image of God.
5 For we [a]do not preach ourselves but
Christ Jesus as Lord, and ourselves as your
bond-servants [1]for Jesus' sake.
6 For God, who said, "[a]Light shall shine
out of darkness," is the One who has [b]shone
in our hearts to give the [c]Light of the knowledge of the glory of God in the face of Christ.
7 But we have this treasure in [a]earthen
vessels, so that the surpassing greatness of
[b]the power will be of God and not from ourselves;
8 *we are* [a]afflicted in every way, but not
[b]crushed; [c]perplexed, but not despairing;
9 [a]persecuted, but not [b]forsaken; [c]struck
down, but not destroyed;
10 [a]always carrying about in the body the
dying of Jesus, so that [b]the life of Jesus also
may be manifested in our body.

2 [b]2 Cor 2:17 [c]2 Cor 5:11f
3 [1]Lit *in* [a]2 Cor 2:12 [b]1 Cor 2:6ff; 2 Cor 3:14 [c]1 Cor 1:18; 2 Cor 2:15
4 [1]Lit *age* [2]Or *that the light...image of God, would not dawn* upon them [a]John 12:31 [b]Matt 13:22 [c]2 Cor 3:14 [d]Acts 26:18; 2 Cor 4:6 [e]2 Cor 3:18; 4:6 [f]John 1:18; Phil 2:6; Col 1:15; Heb 1:3
5 [1]Two early mss read *through Jesus* [a]1 Cor 4:15f; 1 Thess 2:6f
6 [a]Gen 1:3 [b]2 Pet 1:19 [c]Acts 26:18; 2 Cor 4:4
7 [a]Job 4:19; 10:9; 33:6; Lam 4:2; 2 Cor 5:1; 2 Tim 2:20 [b]Judg 7:2; 1 Cor 2:5
8 [a]2 Cor 1:8; 7:5 [b]2 Cor 6:12 [c]Gal 4:20
9 [a]John 15:20; Rom 8:35f [b]Ps 129:2; Heb 13:5 [c]Ps 37:24; Prov 24:16; Mic 7:8

11 For we who live are constantly being
delivered over to death for Jesus' sake, so
that the life of Jesus also may be manifested
in our mortal flesh.
12 So death works in us, but life in you.
13 But having the same [a]spirit of faith,
according to what is written, "[b]I BELIEVED,
THEREFORE I SPOKE," we also believe, therefore
we also speak,
14 knowing that He who [a]raised the Lord
Jesus [b]will raise us also with Jesus and will
[c]present us with you.
15 For all things *are* [a]for your sakes, so
that the grace which is [1][b]spreading to more
and more people may cause the giving of
thanks to abound to the glory of God.
16 Therefore we [a]do not lose heart, but
though our outer man is decaying, yet our
[b]inner man is [c]being renewed day by day.
17 For momentary, [a]light affliction is producing for us an eternal weight of glory far
beyond all comparison,
18 while we [a]look not at the things which
are seen, but at the things which are not

10 [a]Rom 6:5; 8:36; Gal 6:17 [b]Rom 6:8 **13** [a]1 Cor 12:9 [b]Ps 116:10 **14** [a]Acts 2:24 [b]1 Thess 4:14 [c]Luke 21:36; Eph 5:27; Col 1:22; Jude 24 **15** [1]Lit *being multiplied through the many* [a]Rom 8:28; 2 Cor 1:6 [b]1 Cor 9:19; 2 Cor 1:11 **16** [a]2 Cor 4:1 [b]Rom 7:22 [c]Is 40:29, 31; Col 3:10 **17** [a]Rom 8:18 **18** [a]Rom 8:24; 2 Cor 5:7; Heb 11:1, 13

also to his integrity in the sight of God, because his practice was always that of setting forth the truth plainly, i.e., without veiling it or resorting to deception (cf. 1:12,18–24).

4:3 *if our gospel is veiled.* See 3:13–18.

4:4 *god of this world.* The devil, who is the archenemy of God and the unseen power behind all unbelief and ungodliness. Those who follow him have in effect made him their god. *this world.* Used in contrast to the future eternal age when God's creation will be forever purged of all that now mars and defiles it. In Gal 1:4 it is called the "present evil age." *blinded the minds of the unbelieving.* Paul continues to use the imagery of the veil that covers the divine glory so that those who reject the gospel fail to see that glory (3:12–18). *image of God.* Christ, who is both the incarnate Son and the Second Person of the Trinity, authentically displays God to us, for He is the very radiance of divine glory (Heb 1:3). He is the image of God in which man was originally created and into which redeemed mankind is being gloriously transformed (3:18), until at last, when Christ comes again at the end of this age, we who believe will be like Him (1 John 3:2).

4:5 *we do not preach ourselves.* As did the false teachers, puffed up with self-importance. Paul does not lord it over their faith (1:24), for there is only one Lord, Jesus Christ, and He is the theme of Paul's preaching.

4:6 *Light shall shine out of darkness.* God said this at the creation (Gen 1:2–4), and God says it again in the new creation or new birth (see 5:17; John 3:3,7; 1 Pet 1:3) as the darkness of sin is dispelled by the light of the gospel. *the Light of the knowledge of the glory of God.* The light that now shines in Paul's heart (qualifying him to be a proclaimer of Christ) is the knowledge of the glory of God as it was displayed in the face of Christ—who has come, not just from an earthly tabernacle, but from the glorious presence of God in heaven itself (see John 1:14).

4:7 *this treasure.* The gospel. *earthen vessels.* It was customary to conceal treasure in clay jars, which had little value or beauty and did not attract attention to themselves and their precious contents. Here they represent Paul's human frailty and unworthiness. *surpassing greatness of the power will be of God and not from ourselves.* The idea that the absolute insufficiency of man reveals the total sufficiency of God pervades this letter.

4:10 *always carrying about in the body the dying of Jesus.* The frailty of the "earthen vessel" of Paul's humanity (v. 7) is plainly seen in the constant hardships and persecutions with which he is buffeted for the sake of the gospel and through which he shares in Christ's suffering (see 1:5; Rom 8:17; Phil 3:10; Col 1:24).

4:11 *that the life of Jesus also may be manifested in our mortal flesh.* The reference is to Christ's resurrection life and power. Once again (see note on v. 7), human weakness provides the occasion for the triumph of divine power, and daily "dying" magnifies the wonder of daily resurrection life (see 1:9).

4:13 *I believed, therefore I spoke.* Faith leads to testimony. Paul therefore tirelessly labored and journeyed to bring the gospel message to others.

4:16 *Therefore we do not lose heart.* Repeating the statement in v. 1. The intervening paragraphs explain why the apostle continues to have a cheerful heart, and the remaining verses of the chapter summarize the argument he has developed. *decaying.* Because of the hardships to which he is subjected. *being renewed.* Because of the inextinguishable flame of the resurrection life of Jesus burning within. Moreover, the inward renewal overcomes the outward destruction, and ultimately overcomes even death itself.

4:17 *momentary, light affliction.* Seen in the perspective of eternity, the Christian's difficulties, whatever they may be, diminish in importance. *eternal weight of glory far beyond all comparison.* By comparison, the eternal glory is far greater than all the suffering one may face in this life (cf. Rom 8:18).

4:18 *things which are seen . . . things which are not seen.* The experiences and circumstances of this present life, often painful and perplexing, are what is visible to the Christian; but these are merely phenomena in the passing parade of our fallen age

seen; for the things which are seen are temporal, but the things which are not seen are
eternal.

The Temporal and Eternal

5 For we know that if [1]the [a]earthly [b]tent
which is our house is torn down, we have
a building from God, a house [c]not made with
hands, eternal in the heavens.
2 For indeed in this *house* we [a]groan,
longing to be [b]clothed with our dwelling
from heaven,
3 inasmuch as we, having put it on, will
not be found naked.
4 For indeed while we are in this tent, we
[a]groan, being burdened, because we do not
want to be unclothed but to be [b]clothed, so
that what is [c]mortal will be swallowed up by
life.
5 Now He who prepared us for this very
purpose is God, who [a]gave to us the Spirit as
a [1]pledge.
6 Therefore, being always of good
courage, and knowing that [a]while we are at
home in the body we are absent from the
Lord—

5:1 [1]Lit *our earthly house of the tent* [a]Job 4:19; 1 Cor 15:47; 2 Cor 4:7 [b]2 Pet 1:13f [c]Mark 14:58; Acts 7:48; Heb 9:11, 24
2 [a]Rom 8:23; 2 Cor 5:4 [b]1 Cor 15:53f; 2 Cor 5:4
4 [a]2 Cor 5:2 [b]1 Cor 15:53f; 2 Cor 5:2 [c]1 Cor 15:54
5 [1]Or *down payment* [a]Rom 8:23; 2 Cor 1:22
6 [a]Heb 11:13f
7 [1]Or *appearance* [a]1 Cor 13:12; 2 Cor 4:18
8 [a]Phil 1:23 [b]John 12:26; Phil 1:23
9 [a]Rom 14:18; Col 1:10; 1 Thess 4:1
10 [1]Lit *the things through the body* [a]Matt 16:27; Acts 10:42; Rom 2:16; 14:10, 12; Eph 6:8

7 for [a]we walk by faith, not by [1]sight—
8 we are of good courage, I say, and [a]pre-
fer rather to be absent from the body and [b]to
be at home with the Lord.
9 Therefore we also have as our ambition, whether at home or absent, to be
[a]pleasing to Him.
10 For we must all appear before [a]the
judgment seat of Christ, so that each one
may be recompensed for [1]his deeds in the
body, according to what he has done,
whether good or bad.
11 Therefore, knowing the [a]fear of the
Lord, we persuade men, but we are made
manifest to God; and I hope that we are
[b]made manifest also in your consciences.
12 We are not [a]again commending ourselves to you but *are* giving you an [b]occasion
to be proud of us, so that you will have *an
answer* for those who take pride in appearance and not in heart.
13 For if we [1]are [a]beside ourselves, it is for
God; if we are of sound mind, it is for you.

11 [a]Heb 10:31; 12:29; Jude 23 [b]2 Cor 4:2 **12** [a]2 Cor 3:1 [b]2 Cor 1:14; Phil 1:26 **13** [1]Lit *were* [a]Mark 3:21; 2 Cor 11:1, 16ff; 12:11

and are therefore temporary and fleeting. To fix our eyes on these visible things would cause us to lose heart (vv. 1,16). By contrast the unseen realities, which are no less real for being invisible (cf. Heb 11:1,7, 26–27), are eternal and imperishable. Accordingly, we look up and away from the impermanent appearances of this present world scene (see Phil 3:20; Heb 12:2).

5:1 *earthly tent which is our house.* Our present body (see 2 Pet 1:13). As a tent is a temporary and flimsy abode, so our bodies are frail, vulnerable and wasting away (4:10–12,16). *a building from God, a house . . . eternal in the heavens.* A solid structure—permanent, not temporary. This is one of the eternal realities that are as yet unseen (4:18). *not made with hands.* The work of God, and therefore perfect and permanent (see Heb 9:11).

5:2 *we groan.* Because we long for the perfection that will be ours when we put on the glorious spiritual body (cf. 1 Cor 15:42–49). *clothed with our dwelling from heaven.* The eternal dwelling provided by God is pictured as something the Christian puts on like a garment.

5:3 *naked.* Without the clothing of a body, which is the state of those whose earthly tent-dwelling has been dismantled by death (see note on v. 8).

5:4 *what is mortal.* Our present mortal body. *swallowed up by life.* By our participation in the resurrection life of Jesus (4:10) our mortal being is swallowed up by life, not by death. Paul reverses the age-old imagery of death and the grave being the great swallower (see Ps 69:15; Prov 1:12), as did Isaiah (see Is 25:8; see also 1 Cor 15:54).

5:5 *God, who gave to us the Spirit.* The Holy Spirit, poured out by the risen and exalted Savior, applies the benefits of Christ's redeeming work to the believer's heart and makes the resurrection power of Jesus a reality of his daily experience (cf. 4:14,16). This guarantees his eventual total transformation into the likeness of Christ's glorified body (Phil 3:21). *pledge.* See note on 1:22.

5:6 *at home in the body . . . absent from the Lord.* Still living here in our earthly tent-dwelling (v. 1); it does not mean that we are deprived of the Lord's spiritual presence with us in our daily pilgrimage.

5:8 *absent from the body . . . at home with the Lord.* The situation of the Christian after death, when he is no longer living in his "earthly tent" (v. 1). This is an intermediate state between death and resurrection and, apparently, a disembodied state; but it is not a limbo of oblivion, for the believer who has died is at home with his Lord, and that is preferable to our present life in the body (cf. Phil 1:23).

5:9 *whether at home or absent.* Whether we will be alive or will have already died at His coming.

5:10 *appear before the judgment seat of Christ.* This accounting has nothing to do with justification, which is credited to the Christian fully and forever through faith in Christ; instead, it refers to what we have done with our lives as Christians (cf. 1 Cor 3:11–15). *deeds in the body . . . what he has done.* Although the body is wasting away, we are responsible for our actions while in it. Non-Christians, too, are morally responsible and liable to God's judgment (see Rom 2:5,16), but Paul has believers in mind here.

5:11 *fear of the Lord.* As the one to whom we are accountable (v. 10). *we persuade men.* Paul needs to persuade some members of the Corinthian church that he, not any of the false teachers who have invaded their ranks, is their authentic apostle.

5:12 *take pride in appearance.* The pretension of the false apostles is a superficial front; their concern is not with spirituality that is true and deep, but with money and popularity and self-importance.

5:13 *beside ourselves . . . of sound mind.* Probably Paul's enemies were asserting that he was suffering from religious mania, pointing perhaps to the sensational conversion he claimed to have experienced on the road to Damascus and to what they regarded as his insane way of life. If this is to be out of his mind, Paul does not deny it, for this whole letter shows how willingly and joyfully he endured affliction for the gospel (cf. 12:10). That, however, was essentially a matter between him and God. On the other hand, there was nothing that could be called eccentric about his manner of presenting the gospel to the Corinthians, for in this he had been, and continued to be, sensible and sober-minded, avoiding flowery rhetoric and all forms of sensationalism (cf. 1 Cor 2:1–5).

14 For the love of Christ [a]controls us, having concluded this, that [b]one died for all, therefore all died;

15 and He died for all, so that they who live might no longer [a]live for themselves, but for Him who died and rose again on their behalf.

16 Therefore from now on we recognize no one [1a]according to the flesh; even though we have known Christ [1]according to the flesh, yet now we know *Him in this way* no longer.

17 Therefore if anyone is [a]in Christ, [1]*he is* [b]a new creature; [c]the old things passed away; behold, new things have come.

18 Now [a]all *these* things are from God, [b]who reconciled us to Himself through Christ and gave us the [c]ministry of reconciliation,

19 namely, that [a]God was in Christ reconciling the world to Himself, [b]not counting their trespasses against them, and [1]He has [2]committed to us the word of reconciliation.

20 Therefore, we are [a]ambassadors for Christ, [b]as though God were making an appeal through us; we beg you on behalf of Christ, be [c]reconciled to God.

21 He made Him who [a]knew no sin *to be* [b]sin on our behalf, so that we might become the [c]righteousness of God in Him.

Their Ministry Commended

6 And [a]working together *with Him*, [b]we also urge you not to receive [c]the grace of God in vain—

2 for He says,

"[a]AT THE ACCEPTABLE TIME I LISTENED TO YOU,
AND ON THE DAY OF SALVATION I HELPED YOU."

Behold, now is "THE ACCEPTABLE TIME," behold, now is "THE DAY OF SALVATION"—

3 [a]giving no cause for offense in anything, so that the ministry will not be discredited,

4 but in everything [a]commending ourselves as [1b]servants of God, [c]in much endurance, in afflictions, in hardships, in distresses,

5 in [a]beatings, in imprisonments, in [b]tumults, in labors, in sleeplessness, in [c]hunger,

6 in purity, in [a]knowledge, in [b]patience, in kindness, in the [c]Holy Spirit, in [d]genuine love,

7 in [a]the word of truth, in [b]the power of God; by [c]the weapons of righteousness for the right hand and the left,

8 by glory and [a]dishonor, by [b]evil report and good report; *regarded* as [c]deceivers and yet [d]true;

9 as unknown [1]yet well-known, as [a]dying [1]yet behold, [b]we live; as [2]punished [1]yet not put to death,

14 [a]Acts 18:5 [b]Rom 5:15; 6:6f; Gal 2:20; Col 3:3
15 [a]Rom 14:7-9
16 [1]I.e. by what he is in the flesh [a]John 8:15; 2 Cor 11:18; Phil 3:4
17 [1]Or there is *a new creation* [a]Rom 16:7 [b]John 3:3; Rom 6:4; Gal 6:15 [c]Is 43:18f; 65:17; Eph 4:24; Rev 21:4f
18 [a]1 Cor 11:12 [b]Rom 5:10; Col 1:20 [c]1 Cor 3:5
19 [1]Lit *having* [2]Lit *placed in us* [a]Col 2:9 [b]Rom 4:8; 1 Cor 13:5
20 [a]Mal 2:7; Eph 6:20 [b]2 Cor 6:1 [c]Rom 5:10; Col 1:20
21 [a]Acts 3:14; Heb 4:15; 7:26; 1 Pet 2:22; 1 John 3:5 [b]Rom 3:25; 4:25; 8:3; Gal 3:13 [c]Rom 1:17; 3:21f; 1 Cor 1:30
6:1 [a]1 Cor 3:9 [b]2 Cor 5:20 [c]Acts 11:23
2 [a]Is 49:8
3 [a]1 Cor 8:9, 13; 9:12
4 [1]Or *ministers* [a]Rom 3:5 [b]1 Cor 3:5; 2 Tim 2:24f [c]Acts 9:16; 2 Cor 4:8-11; 6:4ff; 11:23-27; 12:10
5 [a]Acts 16:23 [b]Acts 19:23ff [c]1 Cor 4:11
6 [a]1 Cor 12:8; 2 Cor 11:6 [b]2 Cor 1:23; 2:10; 13:10 [c]1 Cor 2:4; 1 Thess 1:5 [d]Rom 12:9
7 [a]2 Cor 2:17; 4:2 [b]1 Cor 2:5 [c]Rom 13:12; 2 Cor 10:4; Eph 6:11ff
8 [a]1 Cor 4:10 [b]Rom 3:8; 1 Cor 4:13; 2 Cor 12:16 [c]Matt 27:63 [d]2 Cor 1:18; 4:2; 1 Thess 2:3f
9 [1]Lit *and* [2]Or *disciplined* [a]Rom 8:36 [b]2 Cor 1:8, 10; 4:11

5:14 *love of Christ.* As shown in His death for us, though some hold that the meaning here is "our love for Christ." *one.* The incarnate Son. *for all.* For all mankind. *therefore all died.* Because Christ died for all, He involved all in His death. For some His death would confirm their own death, but for others (those who by faith would become united with Him) His death was their death to sin and self, so that they now live in and with the resurrected Christ (v. 15). However, some hold that Paul is not speaking specifically here about the scope of Christ's atonement but about the effect of Christ's death on the Christian life. Thus "all" would refer not to mankind in general but only to the church.

5:16 *we have known Christ according to the flesh.* Paul is admitting that before his conversion he held views of Christ that were "according to the flesh"—based on purely human considerations.

5:17 *in Christ.* United with Christ through faith in Him and commitment to Him. *new creature.* Redemption is the restoration and fulfillment of God's purposes in creation (see note on 4:6), and this takes place in Christ, through whom all things were made (see John 1:3; Col 1:16; Heb 1:2) and in whom all things are restored or created anew (cf. Rom 8:18–23; Eph 2:10).

5:18 *all these things are from God.* God takes the initiative in redemption (see Rom 5:8; John 3:16), and He sustains it and brings it to completion. *ministry of reconciliation.* We who are the recipients of divine reconciliation have the privilege and obligation of now being, like Paul in a sense, the heralds and instruments in God's hands to minister the message of reconciliation throughout the world (v. 19).

5:21 *knew no sin . . . sin on our behalf.* A summary of the gospel and its logic. Christ, the only entirely righteous one, at Calvary took our sin upon himself and endured the punishment we deserved, namely, death and separation from God. Thus, by a marvelous exchange, He made it possible for us to receive His righteousness and thereby be reconciled to God. Our standing and our acceptance before God are solely in Him (cf. 1 Cor 1:30). Again, all this is God's doing; all this is freely available to us because of the initiative of divine grace. *be sin.* Or "be a sin offering."

6:1 *to receive the grace of God in vain.* To live for oneself (see 5:15) is one way to do this.

6:2 *THE ACCEPTABLE TIME . . . THE DAY OF SALVATION.* An affirmation that is true in a general sense of all God's saving acts in the history of His people, but that finds its particular fulfillment in this present age of grace between the two comings of Christ. This understanding does not exclude from grace and salvation those who lived before Christ's coming, for the believers of the OT period received the promises that in due course were fulfilled in Christ (1:20) and they saw and welcomed their fulfillment from a distance (see John 8:56; Heb 11:13).

6:3 *giving no cause for offense in anything.* Paul is concerned that he live an exemplary life because he does not want the ministry discredited.

6:4–10 Cf. 4:8–12.

6:4 *commending ourselves as servants of God.* Paul commends himself again inasmuch as the gospel he preached in Corinth is at stake; but, in contrast to the false apostles who were no better than self-servers, he does so as God's servant. His life, with all its trials and afflictions, could not have been more starkly different from that of these intruders whose concern was for their own comfort and prestige.

10 as [a]sorrowful yet always [a]rejoicing, as
[b]poor yet making many rich, as [c]having
nothing [1]yet possessing [d]all things.
11 [a]Our mouth [1]has spoken freely to you,
O Corinthians, our [b]heart is opened wide.
12 You are not restrained [1]by us, but [a]you
are restrained in your own [2]affections.
13 Now in a like [a]exchange—I speak as to
[b]children—open wide *to us* also.
14 [a]Do not be [1]bound together with
[b]unbelievers; for what [c]partnership have
righteousness and lawlessness, or what fellowship has light with darkness?
15 Or what [a]harmony has Christ with
[1]Belial, or [2]what has a [b]believer in common
with an [c]unbeliever?
16 Or [a]what agreement has the temple of
God with idols? For we are [b]the temple of
[c]the living God; just as God said,

"[d]I WILL [e]DWELL IN THEM AND [f]WALK
AMONG THEM;
AND I WILL BE THEIR GOD, AND THEY
SHALL BE MY PEOPLE.
17 "[a]Therefore, [b]COME OUT FROM THEIR MIDST
AND BE SEPARATE," says the Lord.
"AND DO NOT TOUCH WHAT IS UNCLEAN;
And I will welcome you.
18 "[a]And I will be a father to you,
And you shall be [b]sons and daughters
to Me,"
Says the Lord Almighty.

Paul Reveals His Heart

7 Therefore, having these promises,
[a]beloved, [b]let us cleanse ourselves from
all defilement of flesh and spirit, perfecting
holiness in the fear of God.
2 [a]Make room for us *in your hearts;* we
wronged no one, we corrupted no one, we
took advantage of no one.
3 I do not speak to condemn you, for I
have said [a]before that you are [b]in our hearts
to die together and to live together.
4 Great is my [a]confidence [1]in you; great
is my [b]boasting on your behalf. I am filled
with [c]comfort; I am overflowing with [d]joy in
all our affliction.
5 For even when we came into [a]Macedo-
nia our flesh had no rest, but we were
[b]afflicted on every side: [c]conflicts without,
fears within.
6 But [a]God, who comforts the [1]depressed,
[b]comforted us by the coming of [c]Titus;
7 and not only by his coming, but also by
the comfort with which he was comforted in
you, as he reported to us your longing, your
mourning, your zeal for me; so that I
rejoiced even more.
8 For though I [a]caused you sorrow by my
letter, I do not regret it; though I did regret
it—*for* I see that that letter caused you sorrow, though only for a while—
9 I now rejoice, not that you were made
sorrowful, but that you were made sorrowful
to *the point of* repentance; for you were
made sorrowful according to *the will of* God,

10 [1]Lit *and* [a]John 16:22; 2 Cor 7:4; Phil 2:17; 4:4; Col 1:24; 1 Thess 1:6 [b]1 Cor 1:5; 2 Cor 8:9 [c]Acts 3:6 [d]Rom 8:32; 1 Cor 3:21
11 [1]Lit *is open to you* [a]Ezek 33:22; Eph 6:19 [b]Is 60:5; 2 Cor 7:3
12 [1]Or *in us* [2]Lit *inward parts* [a]2 Cor 7:2
13 [a]Gal 4:12 [b]1 Cor 4:14
14 [1]Lit *unequally yoked* [a]Deut 22:10; 1 Cor 5:9f [b]1 Cor 6:6 [c]Eph 5:7, 11; 1 John 1:6
15 [1]Gr *Beliar* [2]Lit *what part has a believer with an unbeliever* [a]1 Cor 10:21 [b]Acts 5:14; 1 Pet 1:21 [c]1 Cor 6:6
16 [a]1 Cor 10:21 [b]1 Cor 3:16; 6:19 [c]Matt 16:16 [d]Ex 29:45; Lev 26:12; Jer 31:1; Ezek 37:27 [e]Ex 25:8; John 14:23 [f]Rev 2:1
17 [a]Is 52:11 [b]Rev 18:4
18 [a]2 Sam 7:14; 1 Chr 17:13; Is 43:6; Hos 1:10 [b]Rom 8:14

7:1 [a]Heb 6:9 [b]1 Pet 1:15f
2 [a]2 Cor 6:12f; 12:15
3 [a]2 Cor 6:11f [b]Phil 1:7 **4** [1]Lit *toward* [a]2 Cor 3:12 [b]2 Cor 7:14; 8:24; 9:2f; 10:8; Phil 1:26; 2 Thess 1:4 [c]2 Cor 1:4 [d]2 Cor 6:10 **5** [a]Rom 15:26; 2 Cor 2:13 [b]2 Cor 4:8 [c]Deut 32:25
6 [1]Or *humble* [a]2 Cor 1:3f [b]2 Cor 7:13 [c]2 Cor 2:13; 7:13f
8 [a]2 Cor 2:2

6:10 *making many rich.* In Christ. True wealth does not consist in worldly possessions but in being "rich toward God" (Luke 12:15,21). The believer, even if he has nothing of this world's goods, nevertheless has everything in Him who is Lord of all (cf. 1 Cor 1:4–5; 3:21–23; Eph 2:7; 3:8; Phil 4:19; Col 2:3).

6:11–13 Paul has always been completely open and sincere in his relations with the Christians in Corinth (cf. 1:12–14; 4:2), but the false apostles among them have been trying to persuade them that Paul does not really love them. Now the apostle tenderly appeals to these Corinthians, who are the beneficiaries of his love for them (cf. 11:11).

6:14 *Do not be bound together with unbelievers.* Doubtless Paul has in mind the OT prohibition of "mixtures" as in Deut 22:10. For the Corinthian believers to cooperate with false teachers, who are in reality servants of Satan, notwithstanding their charming and persuasive ways (see notes on 11:13–14), is to become unequally yoked, destroying the harmony and fellowship that unite them in Christ.

6:15 *Belial.* A term (from Hebrew) used to designate Satan (see note on Deut 13:13).

6:16 *agreement has the temple of God and idols.* There can be no reversion to or compromise with the idolatry they have forsaken for the gospel (cf. 1 Thess 1:9). *temple of the living God.* Built of "living stones," namely, Christian believers (1 Pet 2:5); therefore it is all the more important that they form no defiling and unholy alliances (cf. 1 Cor 6:19–20).

7:1 *holiness.* See 1 Thess 4:7; 1John 3:3.

7:2 *we wronged no one.* Implies that Paul had been accused by the false teachers of being unjust, destructive and fraudulent—the very things they themselves were guilty of.

7:3 Again he declares the depth of his affection for the Corinthian believers and appeals to them to respond, contrary to the wishes of the false teachers, by displaying their love for him, their genuine apostle (cf. 6:11–13).

7:4 *Great is my confidence . . . overflowing with joy.* The long digression that started at 2:14 concludes here on this note of exhilaration. The news he had been so anxiously awaiting from Corinth has turned out to be good and reassuring, and Paul is overjoyed to receive it.

7:5–6 *when we came into Macedonia . . . God . . . comforted us by the coming of Titus.* Here Paul resumes the account he began in 2:12–13, where he described how his hopes of meeting Titus in Troas were disappointed and how, restless for news, he had decided to press on into Macedonia. He now explains that on reaching Macedonia, he was at last comforted by the arrival of Titus, who brought the news he most wanted to hear concerning the situation in Corinth. Titus himself had been well received in that city and was able to assure Paul (see v. 7) of the "longing" and "zeal" of the Corinthian Christians for him and of the "mourning" they had expressed because of the grief they had caused him. Consequently, he "rejoiced even more."

7:8–9 *I do not regret it . . . I did regret it . . . I now rejoice.* Paul did regret the necessity of writing a letter to the Corinthians that caused sorrow to them. However, it was not the actual writing that he regretted, but the situation that required the writing. Moreover, the fact that the letter had the desired effect made him happy, for their sorrow did not leave them embittered and hostile but led them to repentance. They became sorrowful as God intended, and so were benefited, not harmed, by the letter.

so that you might not suffer loss in anything
[1]through us.
10 For the sorrow that is according to *the*
will of God produces a [a]repentance [1]without
regret, *leading* to salvation, but the sorrow
of the world produces death.
11 For behold what earnestness this very
thing, this [1]godly sorrow, has produced in
you: what vindication of yourselves, what
indignation, what fear, what [a]longing, what
zeal, what [b]avenging of wrong! In everything
you [c]demonstrated yourselves to be innocent
in the matter.
12 So although [a]I wrote to you, *it was* not
for the sake of [b]the offender nor for the sake
of the one offended, but that your earnestness on our behalf might be made known to
you in the sight of God.
13 For this reason we have been [a]com-
forted.
And besides our comfort, we rejoiced even
much more for the joy of [b]Titus, because his
[c]spirit has been refreshed by you all.
14 For if in anything I have [a]boasted to
him about you, I was not put to shame; but
as we spoke all things to you in truth, so also
our boasting before [b]Titus proved to be *the*
truth.
15 His [1]affection abounds all the more
toward you, as he remembers the [a]obedience
of you all, how you received him with [b]fear
and trembling.
16 I rejoice that in everything [a]I have confidence in you.

Great Generosity

8 Now, brethren, we *wish to* make known
to you the grace of God which has been
[a]given in the churches of [b]Macedonia,
2 that in a great ordeal of affliction their
abundance of joy and their deep poverty
overflowed in the [a]wealth of their liberality.
3 For I testify that [a]according to their
ability, and beyond their ability, *they gave* of
their own accord,
4 begging us with much urging for the
[a]favor [1]of participation in the [2b]support of
the [3]saints,
5 and *this,* not as we had [1]expected, but
they first [a]gave themselves to the Lord and to
us by [b]the will of God.
6 So we [a]urged [b]Titus that as he had previously [c]made a beginning, so he would also
complete in you [d]this gracious work as well.
7 But just as you [a]abound [b]in everything,
in faith and utterance and knowledge and in
all earnestness and in the [1]love we inspired
in you, *see* that you [a]abound in this gracious
work also.
8 I [a]am not speaking *this* as a command,
but as proving through the earnestness of
others the sincerity of your love also.
9 For you know [a]the grace of our Lord
Jesus Christ, that [b]though He was rich, yet
for your sake He became poor, so that you
through His poverty might become rich.
10 I [a]give *my* opinion in this matter, for
this is to your advantage, who were the first
to begin [b]a year ago not only to do *this,* but
also to desire *to do it.*
11 But now finish [1]doing it also, so that
just as *there was* the [a]readiness to desire it,
so *there may be* also the completion of it by
your ability.
12 For if the readiness is present, it is
acceptable [a]according to what *a person* has,
not according to what he does not have.

9 [1]Lit *from* **10** [1]Or *leading to a salvation without regret* [a]Acts 11:18 **11** [1]Lit *sorrow according to God* [a]2 Cor 7:7 [b]2 Cor 2:6 [c]Rom 3:5 **12** [a]2 Cor 2:3, 9; 7:8 [b]1 Cor 5:1f **13** [a]2 Cor 7:6 [b]2 Cor 2:13; 7:6, 14 [c]1 Cor 16:18 **14** [a]2 Cor 7:4; 8:24; 9:2f; 10:8; Phil 1:26; 2 Thess 1:4 [b]2 Cor 2:13; 7:6, 13 **15** [1]Lit *inward parts* [a]2 Cor 2:9 [b]1 Cor 2:3; Phil 2:12 **16** [a]2 Cor 2:3 **8:1** [a]2 Cor 8:5 [b]Acts 16:9

2 [a]Rom 2:4 **3** [a]1 Cor 16:2; 2 Cor 8:11 **4** [1]Lit *and* [2]Lit *service to the saints* [3]Or *holy ones* [a]Acts 24:17; Rom 15:25f [b]Rom 15:31; 2 Cor 8:19f; 9:1, 12f **5** [1]Lit *hoped* [a]2 Cor 8:1 [b]1 Cor 1:1 **6** [a]2 Cor 8:17; 12:18 [b]2 Cor 2:13; 8:16, 23 [c]2 Cor 8:10 [d]Acts 24:17; Rom 15:25f **7** [1]Lit *love from us in you;* one early ms reads *your love for us* [a]2 Cor 9:8 [b]Rom 15:14; 1 Cor 1:5; 12:8 **8** [a]1 Cor 7:6 **9** [a]2 Cor 13:14 [b]Matt 20:28; 2 Cor 6:10; Phil 2:6f **10** [a]1 Cor 7:25, 40 [b]1 Cor 16:2f; 2 Cor 9:2 **11** [1]Lit *the doing* [a]2 Cor 8:12, 19; 9:2 **12** [a]Mark 12:43f; Luke 21:3, 4; 2 Cor 9:7

7:10 *sorrow that is according to the will of God . . . sorrow of the world.* The former manifests itself by repentance and the experience of divine grace; the latter brings death because, instead of being God-centered sorrow over the wickedness of sin, it is self-centered sorrow over the painful consequences of sin. The letter's primary purpose was not to deal with the notorious offender in Corinth or the person he had injured, but to test their loyalty and devotion to Paul as their apostle.

8:1–9:15 Paul addresses the question of the collection of money for the distressed Christians in Jerusalem, which the Corinthians had started but not completed.

8:1 *grace.* The "gracious work" of giving on the part of believers (v. 7) is more than matched by the self-giving "grace of our Lord Jesus Christ" (v. 9).

8:2 *abundance of joy.* In the blessings of the gospel.

8:5 *they first gave themselves to the Lord.* The true principle of all Christian giving. These Macedonian Christians are an amazing example to the Corinthian believers and to the church in every age of the dynamic difference that God's grace makes in the lives and attitudes of His people—a central theme of this letter (cf. 12:9–10).

8:6 *we urged Titus.* The collection had been started in Corinth under the direction of Titus during the previous year (see v. 10; 9:2), but, no doubt because of the troubles in the Corinthian church, had slowed down or come to a standstill. Paul is now sending Titus back to them, taking with him this present letter, for the purpose of completing this good work, which he describes as a "gracious work" (cf. the link between the grace of God and the selfless generosity of the Macedonian churches in vv. 1–5).

8:7 *you abound in everything.* Cf. 1 Cor 1:4–7.

8:8 *I am not speaking this as a command.* True charity and generosity cannot be commanded. *earnestness of others.* The remarkable example of the Macedonian churches (vv. 1–5). *sincerity of your love.* They can prove this by giving selflessly and spontaneously.

8:9 *though He was rich . . . He became poor.* The eternal Son, in His incarnation and His atoning death in our place on the cross, emptied Himself of His riches (see Phil 2:7). *through His poverty might become rich.* The supreme and inescapable incentive of all genuine Christian generosity.

8:11 *now finish doing it.* The work they had started "a year ago" with desire (v. 10) needs to be completed (see note on v. 6).

8:12 *according to what a person has.* What matters is the willingness, which is the motive of true generosity, no matter how small the amount that can be afforded. An outstanding example of one who put this principle into practice is the poor widow (see Mark 12:41–44). The mechanics of the collection being made in Corinth had been proposed by Paul in his earlier letter (see 1 Cor 16:1–2).

13 For *this* is not for the ease of others *and*
for your affliction, but by way of equality—
14 at this present time your abundance
being a supply for [a]their need, so that their
abundance also may become *a supply* for
[a]your need, that there may be equality;
15 as it is written, "[a]HE WHO *gathered*
MUCH DID NOT HAVE TOO MUCH, AND HE WHO
gathered LITTLE HAD NO LACK."
16 But [a]thanks be to God who [b]puts the
same earnestness on your behalf in the heart
of [c]Titus.
17 For he not only accepted our [a]appeal,
but being himself very earnest, he has gone
to you of his own accord.
18 We have sent along with him [a]the
brother whose fame in *the things of* the
[b]gospel *has spread* through [c]all the churches;
19 [a]and not only *this,* but he has also been
[b]appointed by the churches to travel with us
in [c]this gracious work, which is being
administered by us for the glory of the Lord
Himself, and *to show* our [d]readiness,
20 [1]taking precaution so that no one will
discredit us in our administration of this generous gift;
21 for we [a]have regard for what is honorable, not only in [b]the sight of the Lord, but
also in the sight of men.
22 We have sent with them our brother,
whom we have often tested and found diligent in many things, but now even more diligent because of *his* great confidence in you.
23 As for [a]Titus, *he is* my [b]partner and
fellow worker [1]among you; as for our
[c]brethren, *they are* [2d]messengers of the
churches, [e]a glory to Christ.
24 Therefore [1]openly before the churches,
[2]show them the proof of your love and of our
[a]reason for boasting about you.

God Gives Most

9 For [a]it is superfluous for me to write to
you about this [b]ministry to the [1]saints;

14 [a]Acts 4:34; 2 Cor 9:12 **15** [a]Ex 16:18 **16** [a]2 Cor 2:14 [b]Rev 17:17 [c]2 Cor 2:13; 8:6, 23 **17** [a]2 Cor 8:6; 12:18 **18** [a]1 Cor 16:3; 2 Cor 12:18 [b]2 Cor 2:12 [c]1 Cor 4:17; 7:17 **19** [a]Rom 5:3 [b]Acts 14:23; 1 Cor 16:3f [c]2 Cor 8:4, 6 [d]2 Cor 8:11, 12; 9:2 **20** [1]Lit *avoiding this* **21** [a]Rom 12:17 [b]Prov 3:4; Rom 14:18 **23** [1]Lit *for you* [2]Lit *apostles* [a]2 Cor 8:6 [b]Philem 17 [c]2 Cor 8:18, 22 [d]John 13:16; Phil 2:25 [e]1 Cor 11:7 **24** [1]Lit *in the face of the churches* [2]Or *show the proof...for boasting to them about you* [a]2 Cor 7:4 **9:1** [1]Or *holy ones* [a]1 Thess 4:9 [b]2 Cor 8:4

2 [a]2 Cor 7:4 [b]Rom 15:26 [c]Acts 18:12 [d]2 Cor 8:10 **3** [a]2 Cor 7:4 [b]1 Cor 16:2 **4** [a]Rom 15:26 **5** [1]Lit *blessing* [2]Lit *as covetousness* [a]2 Cor 9:3 [b]Gen 33:11; Judg 1:15; 2 Cor 9:6 [c]Phil 4:17 [d]2 Cor 12:17f **6** [1]Lit *with blessings* [a]Prov 11:24f; 22:9; Gal 6:7, 9 **7** [a]Deut 15:10; 1 Chr 29:17; Rom 12:8; 2 Cor 8:12 [b]Ex 25:2

2 for I know your readiness, of which I
[a]boast about you to the [b]Macedonians,
namely, that [c]Achaia has been prepared
since [d]last year, and your zeal has stirred up
most of them.
3 But I have sent the brethren, in order
that our [a]boasting about you may not be
made empty in this case, so that, [b]as I was
saying, you may be prepared;
4 otherwise if any [a]Macedonians come
with me and find you unprepared, we—not
to speak of you—will be put to shame by this
confidence.
5 So I thought it necessary to urge the
[a]brethren that they would go on ahead to
you and arrange beforehand your previously
promised [1b]bountiful gift, so that the same
would be ready as a [1c]bountiful gift and not
[2d]affected by covetousness.
6 Now this *I say,* [a]he who sows sparingly will also reap sparingly, and he who sows
[1]bountifully will also reap [1]bountifully.
7 Each one *must do* just as he has purposed in his heart, not [a]grudgingly or under
compulsion, for [b]God loves a cheerful giver.
8 And [a]God is able to make all grace
abound to you, so that always having all sufficiency in everything, you may have an
abundance for every good deed;
9 as it is written,
"[a]HE SCATTERED ABROAD, HE GAVE TO THE
POOR,
HIS RIGHTEOUSNESS [1]ENDURES FOREVER."
10 Now He who supplies [a]seed to the
sower and bread for food will supply and
multiply your seed for sowing and [b]increase
the harvest of your righteousness;
11 you will be [a]enriched in everything for
all liberality, which through us is producing
[b]thanksgiving to God.
12 For the ministry of this service is not
only fully supplying [a]the needs of the

8 [a]Eph 3:20 **9** [1]Lit *abides* [a]Ps 112:9 **10** [a]Is 55:10 [b]Hos 10:12 **11** [a]1 Cor 1:5 [b]2 Cor 1:11 **12** [a]2 Cor 8:14

8:15 The reference is to the gathering by the Israelites of the manna in the wilderness. Though in the daily gathering the aged and weak might collect less than the prescribed amount and the young and vigorous might collect more, there was an equal distribution, so that the excess of some ministered to the deficiency of others.

8:16 *Titus.* Had established a relationship of trust and affection with the Corinthians (see 7:6–7,13–15). He had organized the collection when it was started the previous year (see note on v. 6).

8:18 *the brother.* Probably Luke, but possibly Barnabas. In any case, it was someone who was widely known for the faithfulness of his ministry.

8:19 *appointed by the churches.* Paul provides a good example of the care that church leaders should take in handling money.

8:20 It is important not only that God sees (cf. vv. 19,21) but also that people see that one is carrying on the Lord's work in a proper, ethical and honest manner.

8:21 *we have regard for what is honorable.* Even so, Paul is the victim of disgraceful slander (implied by 12:17–18; see Introduction: Purpose); but the integrity of his representatives (see note on v. 23) reflects well on his own integrity.

8:22 *our brother.* This second brother is anonymous, like the one already mentioned (see v. 18 and note).

8:23 *partner and fellow worker.* See note on 2:13. *messengers of the churches.* Duly elected delegates of the churches at large (so that they could not be dismissed as cronies chosen by Paul alone); see note on Acts 20:4. *a glory to Christ.* Christians of outstanding faithfulness.

9:6 Probably a well-known proverb—but not taken from the OT book of Proverbs.

9:7 See Luke 6:38.

9:8 *always having all sufficiency in everything.* Through His abounding grace, God can enable each Christian to abound in generous deeds (see v. 11).

9:9–10 *RIGHTEOUSNESS.* See note on Ps 1:5.

9:12 *not only fully supplying the needs of the saints.* The effect of generous giving on the part of the Corinthians will extend beyond Jerusalem, the destination of their gift, to the church as a whole, causing widespread prayer and praise to be offered (see vv. 13–14).

[1]saints, but is also overflowing [b]through
many thanksgivings to God.
13 Because of the proof given by this
[a]ministry, they will [b]glorify God for *your*
obedience to your [c]confession of the [d]gospel
of Christ and for the liberality of your [1]con-
tribution to them and to all,
14 while they also, by prayer on your
behalf, yearn for you because of the surpassing grace of God in you.
15 [a]Thanks be to God for His indescribable [b]gift!

Paul Describes Himself

10 Now [a]I, Paul, myself [b]urge you by the
[c]meekness and gentleness of Christ—I
who [d]am [1]meek when face to face with you,
but bold toward you when absent!
2 I ask that [a]when I am present I *need*
not be bold with the confidence with which
I propose to be courageous against [b]some,
who regard us as if we walked [c]according to
the flesh.
3 For though we walk in the flesh, we do
not war [a]according to the flesh,
4 for the [a]weapons of our warfare are not
of the flesh, but [1]divinely powerful [b]for the
destruction of fortresses.
5 *We are* destroying speculations and
every [a]lofty thing raised up against the
knowledge of God, and *we are* taking every
thought captive to the [b]obedience of Christ,
6 and we are ready to punish all disobedience, whenever [a]your obedience is complete.
7 [1][a]You are looking at [2]things as they are
outwardly. [b]If anyone is confident in himself
that he is Christ's, let him consider this again
within himself, that just as he is Christ's, [c]so
also are we.
8 For even if [a]I boast somewhat [1]further
about our [b]authority, which the Lord gave
for building you up and not for destroying
you, I will not be put to shame,
9 [1]for I do not wish to seem as if I would
terrify you by my letters.
10 For they say, "His letters are weighty
and strong, but his [1]personal presence
is [a]unimpressive and [b]his speech contemptible."
11 Let such a person consider this, that
what we are in word by letters when absent,
such persons *we are* also in deed when present.
12 For we are not bold to class or compare
ourselves with [1]some of those who [a]com-
mend themselves; but when they measure
themselves by themselves and compare

12 [1]Or *holy ones* [b]2 Cor 1:11 **13** [1]Or *sharing with them* [a]Rom 15:31; 2 Cor 8:4 [b]Matt 9:8 [c]1 Tim 6:12f; Heb 3:1; 4:14; 10:23 [d]2 Cor 2:12 **15** [a]2 Cor 2:14 [b]Rom 5:15f **10:1** [1]Lit *lowly* [a]Gal 5:2; Eph 3:1; Col 1:23 [b]Rom 12:1 [c]Matt 11:29; 1 Cor 4:21; Phil 4:5 [d]1 Cor 2:3f; 2 Cor 10:10 **2** [a]1 Cor 4:21; 2 Cor 13:2, 10 [b]1 Cor 4:18f [c]Rom 8:4; 2 Cor 1:17 **3** [a]Rom 8:4; 2 Cor 1:17 **4** [1]Or *mighty before God* [a]1 Cor 9:7; 2 Cor 6:7; 1 Tim 1:18 [b]Jer 1:10; 2 Cor 10:8; 13:10 **5** [a]Is 2:11f

5 [b]2 Cor 9:13 **6** [a]2 Cor 2:9 **7** [1]Or *Look at…*or *Do you look at…?* [2]Lit *what is before your face* [a]John 7:24; 2 Cor 5:12 [b]1 Cor 1:12; 14:37 [c]1 Cor 9:1; 2 Cor 11:23; Gal 1:12 **8** [1]Or *more abundantly* [a]2 Cor 7:4 [b]2 Cor 13:10 **9** [1]Lit *so that I may not seem* **10** [1]Lit *bodily presence is weak* [a]1 Cor 2:3; 2 Cor 12:7; Gal 4:13f [b]1 Cor 1:17; 2 Cor 11:6 **12** [1]Or *any* [a]2 Cor 3:1; 10:18

9:14 *the surpassing grace of God in you.* Displayed in this unselfish demonstration of their loving concern for fellow believers who are in desperate need.

9:15 *indescribable gift.* His own Son (John 3:16). God is the first giver; He first selflessly gives Himself to us in the person of His Son, and all true Christian giving is our response of gratitude for this gift that is beyond description (cf. 8:9; 1 John 4:9–11).

10:1 *meek when face to face . . . bold . . . when absent!* From the mild tone of the first nine chapters of Paul's letter, it appears that the majority of the Corinthian believers had been won over to Paul (cf. 7:6–13), after having been alienated by his Corinthian opponents. In this final section (chs. 10–13), however, Paul deals firmly with the slanders that have been spread against him in Corinth by the remaining opposition. Those who wish to discredit him have been saying that he is bold at a distance, threatening to take severe disciplinary action, especially in his letters (cf., e.g., his warning that, if necessary, he will come "with a rod" in 1 Cor 4:18–21). But they say that he will not dare to be anything but weak and indecisive if he is present with them in person—in short, that he does not have the apostolic authority he claims to have. Paul is ready to prove otherwise, should the occasion demand, when he comes to Corinth for the third time (see vv. 6,10–11). His appeal to the meekness and gentleness of Christ is an indication of his own affectionate desire to show these same qualities when present with them. In any case, though weak in himself, Paul is strong in the Lord—as this whole letter explains—and those who are rebellious can expect to feel the force of his divinely given authority.

10:4 *weapons of our warfare.* Paul is prepared for warfare; his weapons, however, are not the weapons prized by this fallen world and fashioned by human pride and arrogance. *fortresses.* Of "speculations" and "every lofty thing" (v. 5) defiantly raised "against the knowledge of God" (cf. Rom 1:18–23), among which are the faulty reasonings by which the false apostles have been trying to shake the faith of the Christians in Corinth (see 1 Cor 2:13–14).

10:5 *every thought . . . obedience of Christ.* The center of man's being thus becomes fully subject to the lordship of Christ.

10:7 *he is Christ's.* Probably echoes the claim to superior spirituality by the Christ party (1 Cor 1:12) and the false teachers in Corinth. Paul, who had dramatically encountered and been commissioned by the risen Lord (see Acts 9:3–9; 22:6–11; 26:12–18) and who received the gospel he preached "through a revelation of Jesus Christ" (Gal 1:12; cf. 2 Cor 12:2–7), asserts that he belongs to Christ just as much.

10:8 *authority . . . for building you up.* The primary purpose of Paul's apostolic authority is constructive, for building up, not destructive, for pulling down (the same statement is made again in 13:10). The demands he makes in his letters are written so that they may put right what is amiss and so that things may be in order for his arrival, thus removing the need for severe action (pulling down) and preparing the way for edification (building up).

10:9 *terrify you by my letters.* See 2:3–4; 7:8–9; chs. 10–13; 1 Cor 4:18–21.

10:10 *his speech contemptible.* See note on v. 1. Paul's adversaries used a professional type of oratory as their stock in trade, designed to extract money from their gullible audiences. But Paul's manner of speaking was quite different; it was plain, straightforward and free from artificiality—and it was also free of charge (see note on 11:7), which meant, if his slanderous opponents were to be believed, that what he said was worthless. But in coming to Corinth Paul had purposely disdained academic eloquence and wisdom and was determined to proclaim the message of Christ crucified, and the transformed lives of the Corinthian believers testified to the divine power with which he spoke (cf. 1 Cor 2:1–5).

10:12 *they measure themselves by themselves.* The false teach-

themselves with themselves, they are without understanding.
13 But we will not boast [a]beyond *our*
measure, but [1b]within the measure of the
sphere which God apportioned to us as a
measure, to reach even as far as you.
14 For we are not overextending ourselves, as if we did not reach to you, for [a]we
were the first to come even as far as you in
the [b]gospel of Christ;
15 not boasting [a]beyond *our* measure, *that*
is, in [b]other men's labors, but with the hope
that as [c]your faith grows, we will be, [1]within
our sphere, [d]enlarged even more by you,
16 so as to [a]preach the gospel even to [b]the
regions beyond you, *and* not to boast [1c]in
what has been accomplished in the sphere
of another.
17 But [a]HE WHO BOASTS IS TO BOAST IN THE
LORD.
18 For it is not he who [a]commends himself that is approved, but he [b]whom the Lord
commends.

Paul Defends His Apostleship

11 I wish that you would [a]bear with me in
a little [b]foolishness; but [1]indeed you
are bearing with me.
2 For I am jealous for you with a godly
jealousy; for I [a]betrothed you to one husband, so that to Christ I might [b]present you
as a pure virgin.
3 But I am afraid that, as the [a]serpent
deceived Eve by his craftiness, your minds
will be led astray from the simplicity and
purity *of devotion* to Christ.
4 For if [1]one comes and preaches [a]anoth-
er Jesus whom we have not preached, or you
receive a [b]different spirit which you have not
received, or a [c]different gospel which you
have not accepted, you [d]bear *this* [e]beautifully.
5 For I consider myself [a]not in the least
inferior to the [1]most eminent apostles.
6 But even if I am [a]unskilled in speech,
yet I am not *so* in [b]knowledge; in fact, in
every way we have [c]made *this* evident to you
in all things.
7 Or [a]did I commit a sin in humbling
myself so that you might be exalted, because
I preached the [b]gospel of God to you [c]with-
out charge?
8 I robbed other churches by [a]taking
wages *from them* to serve you;
9 and when I was present with you and
was in need, I was [a]not a burden to anyone;
for when [b]the brethren came from [c]Macedo-
nia they fully supplied my need, and in
everything I kept myself from [a]being a burden to you, [1]and will continue to do so.
10 [a]As the truth of Christ is in me, [b]this
boasting of mine will not be stopped in the
regions of [c]Achaia.

13 [1]Lit *according to the measure* [a]2 Cor 10:15 [b]Rom 12:3; 2 Cor 10:15f
14 [a]1 Cor 3:6 [b]2 Cor 2:12
15 [1]Lit *according to our sphere* [a]2 Cor 10:13 [b]Rom 15:20 [c]2 Thess 1:3 [d]Acts 5:13
16 [1]Lit *to the things prepared in the* [a]2 Cor 11:7 [b]Acts 19:21 [c]Rom 15:20
17 [a]Jer 9:24; 1 Cor 1:31
18 [a]2 Cor 10:12 [b]Rom 2:29; 1 Cor 4:5
11:1 [1]Or *do indeed bear with me* [a]Matt 17:17; 2 Cor 11:4, 16, 19f [b]2 Cor 5:13; 11:17, 21
2 [a]Hos 2:19f; Eph 5:26f [b]2 Cor 4:14
3 [a]Gen 3:4, 13; John 8:44; 1 Thess 3:5; 1 Tim 2:14; Rev 12:9, 15
4 [1]Lit *the one who comes preaches* [a]1 Cor 3:11 [b]Rom 8:15 [c]Gal 1:6 [d]2 Cor 11:1 [e]Mark 7:9
5 [1]Or *super-apostles* [a]2 Cor 12:11; Gal 2:6
6 [a]1 Cor 1:17 [b]1 Cor 12:8; Eph 3:4 [c]2 Cor 4:2
7 [a]2 Cor 12:13 [b]Rom 1:1; 2 Cor 2:12 [c]Acts 18:3; 1 Cor 9:18
8 [a]1 Cor 4:12; 9:6; Phil 4:15, 18
9 [1]Lit *and I will keep* [a]2 Cor 12:13f, 16 [b]Acts 18:5 [c]Rom 15:26; Phil 4:15-18
10 [a]Rom 1:9; 9:1; 2 Cor 1:23; Gal 2:20 [b]1 Cor 9:15 [c]Acts 18:12

ers in Corinth behave as though there is no standard of comparison higher than themselves, but Paul boasts only in the Lord (see vv. 13–18; cf. 1 Cor 1:31).

10:13 *the sphere which God apportioned to us.* The picture Paul has in mind may be that of an athletic contest in which lanes are marked out for the different runners. In that case "sphere" should be rendered "lane" (also in vv. 15–16). In intruding themselves into Corinth, the false apostles had crossed into Paul's lane, which was the lane that God had marked out and that had brought him to the Corinthians as their genuine apostle. He has no intention of invading the territory marked out for others and claiming their work as his own, as these false teachers were doing. Others understand the Greek word in question to refer to an assigned sphere of authority.

10:16 *regions beyond.* Spain is probably in his thoughts (see Rom 15:24,28).

11:1 *foolishness.* In order to compare his own ministry with that of the false apostles who have invaded the Corinthian church, Paul has to speak about himself, which inevitably seems like foolish boasting.

11:2 *godly jealousy.* Paul cannot bear the thought that there might be any rival to Christ and His gospel. *I betrothed you to one husband.* As their spiritual father (cf. 6:13), Paul has promised the Corinthian believers to Christ, who is frequently depicted in the NT as the bridegroom, with the church portrayed as His bride (Matt 9:15; John 3:29; Rom 7:4; 1 Cor 6:15; Eph 5:23–32; Rev 19:7–9; 21:2). *pure virgin.* Undefiled by the doctrines of false teachers (see vv. 3–4).

11:4 *another Jesus whom we have not preached.* They presented a Jesus cast in the mold of Judaistic teachings (Paul's opponents were Jews; see v. 22). *different spirit.* A spirit of bondage, fear and worldliness (cf. Rom 8:15; 1 Cor 2:12; Gal 2:4; 4:24; Col 2:20–23) instead of a spirit of freedom, love, joy, peace and power (cf. 3:17; Rom 14:17; Gal 2:4; 5:1,22; Eph 3:20; Col 1:11; 2 Tim 1:7). *different gospel.* Cf. Gal 1:6–9. *you bear this beautifully.* They have been undiscerningly tolerant of these deceivers in their midst.

11:5 *the most eminent apostles.* Paul's sarcastic way of referring to the false apostles who had infiltrated the Corinthian church and were in reality not apostles at all, except in their own arrogantly inflated opinion of themselves (cf. 10:12).

11:6 *even if I am unskilled in speech.* Using the skills, references and flourishes of professional rhetoric (see note on 10:10). *I am not so in knowledge.* As the Corinthian believers well knew, Paul had knowledge of Christ that was true, powerful and God-given, totally distinct from the powerless human wisdom the false teachers were attempting to deceive them with (cf. 1 Cor 2:6–10).

11:7 *without charge.* Another slanderous criticism made by Paul's adversaries was that his refusal to accept payment for his instruction proved that it was worth nothing. This accusation at the same time helped to cloak their own grasping character, since their method of operation, like that of first-century traveling philosophers and religious teachers, was to demand payment for their "professional" services. Paul, his enemies said, was lowering himself and committing a sin by breaking the rule that a teacher should receive payment in proportion to the worth of his performance.

11:8 *robbed other churches.* Accepted freely given support from established congregations.

11:9 *burden.* A financial liability (see note on 2:17). This reinforced his teaching that the gospel of Jesus Christ is a free gift. *brethren came from Macedonia.* They brought gifts from the churches in that province (Acts 18:5), particularly from the church at Philippi (Phil 4:15).

11 Why? [a]Because I do not love you? [b]God
knows *I do!*
12 But what I am doing I will continue to
do, [a]so that I may cut off opportunity from
those who desire an opportunity to be
[1]regarded just as we are in the matter about
which they are boasting.
13 For such men are [a]false apostles,
[b]deceitful workers, disguising themselves as
apostles of Christ.
14 No wonder, for even [a]Satan disguises
himself as an [b]angel of light.
15 Therefore it is not surprising if his servants also disguise themselves as servants of
righteousness, [a]whose end will be according
to their deeds.
16 [a]Again I say, let no one think me foolish; but if *you do,* receive me even as foolish,
so that I also may boast a little.
17 What I am saying, I am not saying [1a]as
the Lord would, but as [b]in foolishness, in
this confidence of boasting.
18 Since [a]many boast [b]according to the
flesh, I will boast also.
19 For you, [a]being *so* wise, tolerate the
foolish gladly.
20 For you tolerate it if anyone [a]enslaves
you, anyone [b]devours you, anyone [c]takes
advantage of you, anyone [d]exalts himself,
anyone [e]hits you in the face.
21 To *my* [a]shame I *must* say that we have
been [b]weak *by comparison.*

But in whatever respect anyone *else* [c]is
bold—I [d]speak in foolishness—I am just as
bold myself.
22 Are they [a]Hebrews? [b]So am I. Are they
[c]Israelites? [c]So am I. Are they [1d]descendants
of Abraham? [e]So am I.
23 Are they [a]servants of Christ?—I speak
as if insane—I more so; in [1b]far more labors,
in [1c]far more imprisonments, [2d]beaten times
without number, often in [e]danger of death.
24 Five times I received from the Jews
[a]thirty-nine *lashes.*
25 Three times I was [a]beaten with rods,
once I was [b]stoned, three times I was shipwrecked, a night and a day I have spent in
the deep.
26 *I have been* on frequent journeys, in
dangers from rivers, dangers from robbers,
dangers from *my* [a]countrymen, dangers from
the [b]Gentiles, dangers in the [c]city, dangers in
the wilderness, dangers on the sea, dangers
among [d]false brethren;
27 *I have been* in [a]labor and hardship,
[1]through many sleepless nights, in [b]hunger
and thirst, often [c]without food, in cold and
[2d]exposure.

11 [a]2 Cor 12:15 [b]Rom 1:9; 2 Cor 2:17; 11:31; 12:2f **12** [1]Lit *found* [a]1 Cor 9:12 **13** [a]Acts 20:30; Gal 1:7; 2:4; Phil 1:15; Titus 1:10f; 2 Pet 2:1; Rev 2:2 [b]Phil 3:2 **14** [a]Matt 4:10; Eph 6:12; Col 1:13 [b]Col 1:12 **15** [a]Rom 2:6; 3:8 **16** [a]2 Cor 11:1 **17** [1]Lit *in accordance with the Lord* [a]1 Cor 7:12, 25 [b]2 Cor 11:21 **18** [a]Phil 3:3f [b]2 Cor 5:16 **19** [a]1 Cor 4:10 **20** [a]2 Cor 1:24; Gal 2:4; 4:3, 9; 5:1 [b]Mark 12:40 [c]2 Cor 11:3; 12:16 [d]2 Cor 10:5 [e]1 Cor 4:11 **21** [a]2 Cor 6:8 [b]2 Cor 10:10

21 [c]2 Cor 10:2 [d]2 Cor 11:17 **22** [1]Lit *seed* [a]Acts 6:1 [b]Phil 3:5 [c]Rom 9:4 [d]Gal 3:16 [e]Rom 11:1 **23** [1]Lit *more abundant* [2]Lit *exceedingly in stripes* [a]1 Cor 3:5; 2 Cor 3:6; 10:7 [b]1 Cor 15:10 [c]2 Cor 6:5 [d]Acts 16:23; 2 Cor 6:5 [e]Rom 8:36 **24** [a]Deut 25:3 **25** [a]Acts 16:22 [b]Acts 14:19 **26** [a]Acts 9:23; 13:45, 50; 14:5; 17:5, 13; 18:12; 20:3, 19; 21:27; 23:10, 12; 25:3; 1 Thess 2:15 [b]Acts 14:5, 19; 19:23ff; 27:42 [c]Acts 21:31 [d]Gal 2:4 **27** [1]Lit *often in wakefulness* [2]Lit *nakedness;* i.e. lack of clothing [a]1 Thess 2:9; 2 Thess 3:8 [b]1 Cor 4:11; Phil 4:12 [c]2 Cor 6:5 [d]1 Cor 4:11

11:12 *I will continue.* Paul will not be deterred from presenting the gospel without charge. Actually, this practice made his adversaries look bad. They were greedy for gain, and it would have suited them better if Paul had been willing to accept money for his teaching, for this would have put him on a level with their practice. *just as we are.* In financial matters.
11:13 *disguising themselves as apostles of Christ.* Now Paul exposes these would-be "eminent apostles" (v. 5) as false apostles and servants of Satan (v. 14) who are covering up their true identity.
11:14 *as an angel of light.* Though he is in reality the prince of darkness.
11:16 *let no one think me foolish.* See note on v. 1.
11:18 *boast.* By speaking of the nature of his apostolic ministry.
11:19 *you . . . tolerate the foolish gladly.* Resumes the implied rebuke of v. 4, and has the same ironic tone. There it was a matter of their readiness to tolerate false teaching; here it is a matter of their willingness to put up with disgraceful treatment by these false teachers, who are described as fools because of their self-centered boasting.
11:20 *enslaves you.* By the imposition of tyrannical man-made rules and prohibitions (cf. Gal 5:1). *devours you.* See Mark 12:40. *takes advantage of you.* Thanks to the Corinthians' lack of discernment and their readiness to be impressed by outward show and clever talk. *exalts himself.* For the purpose of lording it over the members of the church (cf. 1:24). *hits you in the face.* Using physical violence to cow them into submission.
11:21 *weak by comparison.* Compared with the crude self-seeking roughness of the impostors, Paul's conduct may well be considered weak, but he is probably speaking ironically here.
11:22 *Hebrews . . . Israelites . . . descendants of Abraham.* The claims implied here on the part of the false apostles indicate that they were Jews who felt superior to Gentile Christians. From this there follows the probability that they were Judaizers, i.e., they wished to impose distinctive Jewish practices and observances as required for Gentile converts. This, of course, was not Paul's position (see Rom 2:28–29; 1 Cor 12:13; Gal 3:28–29; Eph 2:11–18; Col 3:11). For Paul's claim see Acts 22:3–5; 26:4–5; Phil 3:5–6.
11:23 *servants of Christ.* Paul is not granting their claim to be servants of Christ. Indeed, the consideration of the nature of his ministry and its cost to him in suffering will show that he is more Christ's servant than any or all of them. *often in danger of death.* Cf. 4:8–11. He means this literally, for the sufferings he lists here and in the verses that follow were life-threatening. The catalogue that follows makes it clear that Luke's account in Acts is selective.
11:24–25 *lashes . . . rods.* Eight floggings are mentioned here, five at the hands of the Jews (cf. Deut 25:1–3) and three at the hands of the Roman authorities, who used rods on these occasions (see Acts 16:22–23). The three beatings with rods took place despite the fact that Paul, being a Roman citizen, was legally protected from such punishment (cf. Acts 16:37–39; 22:25–29).
11:25 *stoned.* A traditional manner of Jewish execution (cf. Acts 14:19–20). *shipwrecked.* Only one shipwreck is recorded in Acts, but it took place after the writing of this letter (Acts 27:39–44). The three shipwrecks referred to here could have taken place during the voyages mentioned in Acts 9:30; 11:25–26; 13:4,13; 14:25–26; 16:11; 17:14; 18:18–19, 21–22. *a night and a day . . . in the deep.* Probably as a result of one of the shipwrecks.
11:26 *in dangers.* Apart from the specific incidents referred to in the preceding verses, Paul constantly faced situations of danger as well as labors and hardships (see note on Acts 14:24).

28 Apart from *such* [1]external things, there
is the daily pressure on me *of* concern for
[a]all the churches.
29 Who is [a]weak without my being weak?
Who is [1]led into sin [2]without my intense
concern?
30 If I have to boast, I will boast of what
pertains to my [a]weakness.
31 The God and Father of the Lord Jesus,
[a]He who is blessed forever, [b]knows that I am
not lying.
32 In [a]Damascus the ethnarch under Aretas the king was [b]guarding the city of the
Damascenes in order to seize me,
33 and I was let down in a basket [a]through
a window [1]in the wall, and *so* escaped his
hands.

Paul's Vision

12 [a]Boasting is necessary, though it is not
profitable; but I will go on to visions
and [b]revelations [1]of the Lord.
2 I know a man [a]in Christ who fourteen
years ago—whether in the body I do not
know, or out of the body I do not know,
[b]God knows—such a man was [c]caught up to
the [d]third heaven.
3 And I know how such a man—whether
in the body or apart from the body I do not
know, [a]God knows—
4 was [a]caught up into [b]Paradise and
heard inexpressible words, which a man is
not permitted to speak.
5 [a]On behalf of such a man I will boast;
but on my own behalf I will not boast,
except in regard to *my* [b]weaknesses.
6 For if I do wish to boast I will not be
[a]foolish, [b]for I will be speaking the truth; but
I refrain *from this,* so that no one will credit
me with more than he sees *in* me or hears
from me.

A Thorn in the Flesh

7 Because of the surpassing greatness of
the [a]revelations, for this reason, to keep me
from exalting myself, there was given me a
[b]thorn in the flesh, a [c]messenger of Satan to
[1]torment me—to keep me from exalting
myself!
8 Concerning this I implored the Lord
[a]three times that it might leave me.
9 And He has said to me, "My grace is
sufficient for you, for [a]power is perfected in
weakness." Most gladly, therefore, I will
rather [b]boast [1]about my weaknesses, so that
the power of Christ may dwell in me.
10 Therefore [a]I am well content with weaknesses, with [1]insults, with [b]distresses, with
[c]persecutions, with [b]difficulties, [d]for Christ's
sake; for [e]when I am weak, then I am strong.
11 I have become [a]foolish; you yourselves
compelled me. Actually I should have been
commended by you, for [b]in no respect was I
inferior to the [1]most eminent apostles, even
though [c]I am a nobody.

28 [1]Or *the things unmentioned* [a]1 Cor 7:17
29 [1]Lit *made to stumble* [2]Lit *and I do not burn* [a]1 Cor 8:9, 13; 9:22
30 [a]1 Cor 2:3
31 [a]Rom 1:25 [b]2 Cor 11:11
32 [a]Acts 9:2 [b]Acts 9:24
33 [1]Lit *through* [a]Acts 9:25
12:1 [1]Or *from* [a]2 Cor 11:16, 18, 30; 12:5, 9 [b]1 Cor 14:6; 2 Cor 12:7; Gal 1:12; 2:2; Eph 3:3
2 [a]Rom 16:7 [b]2 Cor 11:11 [c]Ezek 8:3; Acts 8:39; 2 Cor 12:4; 1 Thess 4:17; Rev 12:5 [d]Deut 10:14; Ps 148:4; Eph 4:10; Heb 4:14
3 [a]2 Cor 11:11
4 [a]Ezek 8:3; Acts 8:39; 2 Cor 12:2; 1 Thess 4:17; Rev 12:5 [b]Luke 23:43
5 [a]2 Cor 12:1
5 [b]1 Cor 2:3; 2 Cor 12:9f
6 [a]2 Cor 5:13; 11:16f; 12:11 [b]2 Cor 7:14
7 [1]Lit *beat* [a]2 Cor 12:1 [b]Num 33:55; Ezek 28:24; Hos 2:6 [c]Job 2:6; Matt 4:10; 1 Cor 5:5
8 [a]Matt 26:44 **9** [1]Lit *in* [a]1 Cor 2:5; Eph 3:16; Phil 4:13 [b]1 Cor 2:3; 2 Cor 12:5 **10** [1]Or *mistreatment* [a]Rom 5:3; 8:35 [b]2 Cor 6:4 [c]2 Thess 1:4; 2 Tim 3:11 [d]2 Cor 5:15, 20 [e]2 Cor 13:4
11 [1]Or *super-apostles* [a]2 Cor 5:13; 11:16f; 12:6 [b]1 Cor 15:10; 2 Cor 11:5 [c]1 Cor 3:7; 13:2; 15:9

11:29 So closely did Paul identify himself with them that he felt the weakness of any member who was weak. If anyone was led into sin, he not only burned with indignation against the person responsible but also experienced the shame of the offense and longed for the restoration of the one who had stumbled.
11:30 *I will boast of what pertains to my weakness.* His weakness opens the way for him to experience the superabundant strength of God's grace. Therefore his boasting in its entirety, unlike that of the false apostles, is not in what he has done but in what God has done.
11:32 *Aretas the king.* Aretas IV, father-in-law of Herod Antipas, ruled over the Nabatean Arabs from c. 9 B.C. to A.D. 40. The Roman emperor Caligula may have given Damascus to Aretas since it was once part of his territory.
12:1 *visions and revelations.* If his adversaries falsely claimed to have received their teaching directly from God through visions and revelations, Paul could claim that this was truly so in his case. But he mentions this here to show that the supreme height to which he was raised through these ecstatic experiences was counterbalanced by the humbling depth of a particular affliction he was given to bear (see v. 7), so that he should continue to glory not in self but only in the "God of all grace" (1 Pet 5:10).
12:2–4 *caught up to the third heaven . . . caught up into Paradise.* Paul is sure of this remarkable experience, but he is unsure whether this rapture (being "caught up") was one that included the body or one that took place in separation from the body. The third heaven designates a place beyond the immediate heaven of the earth's atmosphere and beyond the further heaven of outer space and its constellations into the presence of God himself. Thus the risen and glorified Lord is said to have passed "through the heavens" (Heb 4:14), and now, having "ascended far above all the heavens" (Eph 4:10), to be "exalted above the heavens" (Heb 7:26). The term "Paradise" is synonymous with the third heaven, where those believers who have died are even now "at home with the Lord" (5:8; cf. "with Christ," Phil 1:23). The nature of the inexpressible things that Paul heard remains unknown to us because this is something Paul was not permitted to tell. It was an experience that must have given incalculable strength to his apostleship, which involved him in such constant and extreme suffering. Moreover, as this experience was not self-induced, it afforded him no room for self-glorification (vv. 5–6).
12:5 *On behalf of such a man I will boast.* Some believe that the man "caught up to the third heaven" (v. 2) was not Paul and that Paul here insists that he will not boast about such a glorious experience but only about his weakness.
12:7 *thorn in the flesh.* The precise nature of this severe affliction remains unknown. *messenger of Satan.* A further description of Paul's thorn (cf. 1 Cor 5:5; 11:30; 1 Tim 1:20; see Job 2:10).
12:9 *My grace is sufficient for you.* A better solution than to remove Paul's thorn. Human weakness provides the ideal opportunity for the display of divine power.
12:10 Cf. Eph 3:16; Phil 4:13.
12:11 *have become foolish.* See note on 11:1. *you . . . compelled me.* The Corinthian Christians have put Paul under pressure to write about himself as he did because they had accepted the claims of the "eminent apostles" who had invaded their ranks, challenging Paul's apostolic authority.

12 The [1][a]signs [2]of a true apostle were performed among you with all perseverance, by
[1]signs and wonders and [3]miracles.
13 For in what respect were you treated as
inferior to the rest of the churches, except
that [a]I myself did not become a burden to
you? Forgive me [b]this wrong!
14 Here [a]for this third time I am ready to
come to you, and I [b]will not be a burden to
you; for I [c]do not seek what is yours, but [d]you;
for [e]children are not responsible to save up for
their parents, but [f]parents for *their* children.
15 I will [a]most gladly spend and be
expended for your souls. If [b]I love you more,
am I to be loved less?
16 But be that as it may, I [a]did not burden
you myself; nevertheless, crafty fellow that I
am, I [b]took you in by deceit.
17 [a]*Certainly* I have not taken advantage
of you through any of those whom I have
sent to you, have I?
18 I [a]urged [b]Titus *to go,* and I sent [c]the
brother with him. Titus did not take any
advantage of you, did he? Did we not [1]con-
duct ourselves [2]in the same [d]spirit *and walk*
[e]in the same steps?
19 All this time [1]you have been thinking
that we are defending ourselves to you. *Actually,* [a]it is in the sight of God that we have
been speaking in Christ; and [b]all for your
upbuilding, [c]beloved.
20 For I am afraid that perhaps [a]when I
come I may find you to be not what I wish
and may be found by you to be not what you
wish; that perhaps *there will be* [b]strife, jealousy, [c]angry tempers, [d]disputes, [e]slanders,
[f]gossip, [g]arrogance, [h]disturbances;
21 I am afraid that when I come again my
God may humiliate me before you, and I may
mourn over many of those who have [a]sinned
in the past and not repented of the [b]impuri-
ty, [1]immorality and sensuality which they
have practiced.

Examine Yourselves

13 [a]This is the third time I am coming to
you. [b]EVERY [1]FACT [2]IS TO BE CONFIRMED BY
THE [3]TESTIMONY OF TWO OR THREE WITNESSES.
2 I have previously said when present the
second time, and though now absent I say in
advance to those who have [a]sinned in the
past and to all the rest *as well,* that [b]if I come
again I will not [c]spare *anyone,*
3 since you are [a]seeking for proof of the
[b]Christ who speaks in me, and who is not
weak toward you, but [c]mighty in you.
4 For indeed He was [a]crucified because
of weakness, yet He lives [b]because of the
power of God. For we also are [c]weak [1]in
Him, yet [d]we will live with Him because of
the power of God *directed* toward you.
5 [a]Test yourselves *to see* if you are in the
faith; [b]examine yourselves! Or do you not
recognize this about yourselves, that Jesus
Christ is in you—unless indeed you [1][c]fail the
test?
6 But I trust that you will realize that we
ourselves [1]do not fail the test.

12 [1]Or *attesting miracles* [2]Lit *of the apostle* [3]Or *works of power* [a]John 4:48; Rom 15:19; 1 Cor 9:1 **13** [a]1 Cor 9:12, 18; 2 Cor 11:9; 12:14 [b]2 Cor 11:7 **14** [a]2 Cor 1:15; 13:1, 2 [b]1 Cor 9:12, 18; 2 Cor 11:9; 12:13 [c]1 Cor 10:24, 33 [d]1 Cor 9:19 [e]1 Cor 4:14f; Gal 4:19 [f]Prov 19:14; Ezek 34:2 **15** [a]Rom 9:3; 2 Cor 1:6; Phil 2:17; Col 1:24; 1 Thess 2:8; 2 Tim 2:10 [b]2 Cor 11:11 **16** [a]2 Cor 11:9 [b]2 Cor 11:20 **17** [a]2 Cor 9:5 **18** [1]Lit *walk* [2]Or *by the same Spirit* [a]2 Cor 8:6 [b]2 Cor 2:13 [c]2 Cor 8:18 [d]1 Cor 4:21 [e]Rom 4:12 **19** [1]Or *have you been thinking...?* [a]Rom 9:1; 2 Cor 2:17 [b]Rom 14:19; 2 Cor 10:8; 1 Thess 5:11 [c]Heb 6:9 **20** [a]1 Cor 4:21; 2 Cor 2:1-4 [b]1 Cor 1:11; 3:3 [c]Gal 5:20 [d]Rom 2:8; 1 Cor 11:19 [e]Rom 1:30; James 4:11; 1 Pet 2:1 [f]Rom 1:29 [g]1 Cor 4:6, 18; 5:2 [h]1 Cor 14:33

21 [1]I.e. sexual immorality [a]2 Cor 13:2 [b]1 Cor 6:9, 18; Gal 5:19; Col 3:5 **13:1** [1]Lit *word* [2]Lit *shall be* [3]Lit *mouth* [a]2 Cor 12:14 [b]Deut 17:6; 19:15; Matt 18:16 **2** [a]2 Cor 12:21 [b]1 Cor 4:21; 2 Cor 13:10 [c]2 Cor 1:23; 10:11 **3** [a]2 Cor 10:1, 10 [b]Matt 10:20; 1 Cor 5:4; 7:40 [c]2 Cor 9:8; 10:4 **4** [1]One early ms reads *with Him* [a]Phil 2:7f; 1 Pet 3:18 [b]Rom 1:4; 6:4; 1 Cor 6:14 [c]1 Cor 2:3; 2 Cor 13:9 [d]Rom 6:8 **5** [1]Lit *are unapproved* [a]John 6:6 [b]1 Cor 11:28 [c]1 Cor 9:27 **6** [1]Lit *are not unapproved*

12:12 *signs of a true apostle.* Extraordinary gifts and powers had been displayed in their midst. By implication, the false teachers had come to them without these apostolic signs (cf. Heb 2:3–4).

12:13 *I myself did not become a burden to you.* See note on 11:9. Paul's refusal to accept any payment when preaching the gospel to the Corinthians had been slanderously twisted by his adversaries (see notes on 11:7,12). They, who had grasped at all they could get, were saying that it was he who had sinned against the Corinthians. *Forgive me this wrong!* Irony—resuming the line of discussion in 11:7–12.

12:14 *third time.* See note on 2:1. *not be a burden.* Chiefly now, so that the falsity and greed of the "eminent apostles" may be clearly exposed (see 11:12). *children.* Paul is their spiritual father (cf. 6:13).

12:15 His paternal devotion to them is shown not merely in his readiness to spend whatever money he has for them but, much more deeply, in his joyful willingness to spend himself completely for their sake.

12:16 *I took you in by deceit.* Sarcastically echoes another of the slanders being made against Paul by the false apostles: that he was exploiting them by the trick of organizing a collection for the poverty-stricken Christians in Jerusalem—contributions that would never reach the mother-city because they went into Paul's own pocket (v. 17). No wonder, then, that he could afford not to be a burden to them! The fact is, however, that it is these false apostles who are the "deceitful workmen" masquerading as "servants of righteousness" (11:13–15). Paul is unblemished both in conduct and in conscience, and the Corinthians are fully aware of this.

12:18 *Titus . . . the brother.* See notes on 8:6,16,18–23.

12:19 *in the sight of God . . . speaking in Christ.* Paul's concern in speaking of himself is not for his own personal prestige and reputation before people (cf. 1 Cor 4:3–4). It is before God that he stands, and his standing before God is in Christ. Far from being self-centered, his concern is for the Corinthians, his dear friends—for their strengthening as they too stand before God in Christ. His entire ministry, with its sufferings, is directed to this end (cf. 10:8).

13:2 *I will not spare anyone.* Paul will not hesitate to take stern disciplinary action against offenders when he comes to Corinth for the third time, as he is about to do.

13:3 *seeking for proof of the Christ who speaks in me.* See note on 10:10. They will be given ample proof when he comes, unless they show a change of heart. *who is not weak.* Rebellion against Paul is rebellion against Christ, who appointed him as His apostle. The authority of the apostle is the authority of his Master. Any who imagine that Paul is weak will find that Christ, the Lord who speaks through His apostle, is not weak but powerful.

13:4 *we will live with Him because of the power of God.* Paul is referring to his present apostolic authority, and to the fact that divine power will be displayed by the punishment of any who resist that authority.

13:5 *Test yourselves . . . examine yourselves!* Instead of demanding proof that Christ was speaking through him (v. 3), as the

7 Now we pray to God that you do no
wrong; not that we ourselves may appear
approved, but that you may do what is right,
even though we may [1]appear unapproved.
8 For we can do nothing against the
truth, but *only* for the truth.
9 For we rejoice when we ourselves are
[a]weak but you are strong; this we also pray
for, [1]that you be [b]made complete.
10 For this reason I am writing these
things while absent, so that when present [a]I
need not use [b]severity, in accordance with
the [c]authority which the Lord gave me for
building up and not for tearing down.

11 [a]Finally, brethren, [1]rejoice, [2b]be made
complete, be comforted, [c]be like-minded,
[d]live in peace; and [e]the God of love and
peace will be with you.
12 [a]Greet one another with a holy kiss.
13 [a]All the [1]saints greet you.
14 [a]The grace of the Lord Jesus Christ,
and the [b]love of God, and the [c]fellowship of
the Holy Spirit, be with you all.

7 [1]Lit *be as*
9 [1]Lit *your completion* [a]2 Cor 12:10; 13:4 [b]1 Cor 1:10; 2 Cor 13:11; Eph 4:12; 1 Thess 3:10
10 [a]2 Cor 2:3 [b]Titus 1:13 [c]1 Cor 5:4; 2 Cor 10:8
11 [1]Or *farewell* [2]Or *put yourselves in order* [a]1 Thess 4:1; 2 Thess 3:1 [b]1 Cor 1:10; 2 Cor 13:9; Eph 4:12; 1 Thess 3:10 [c]Rom 12:16 [d]Mark 9:50 [e]Rom 15:33; Eph 6:23
12 [a]Rom 16:16 **13** [1]Or *holy ones* [a]Phil 4:22 **14** [a]Rom 16:20; 2 Cor 8:9 [b]Rom 5:5; Jude 21 [c]Phil 2:1

false apostles were inciting them to do, they should look into their own hearts.
13:7 *do what is right.* Then there will be no need for Paul to give evidence of his authority by taking disciplinary action when he comes to them.
13:8 *we can do nothing against the truth.* Paul can exercise his apostolic authority only in a way that supports the truth. Consequently, if the truth is acknowledged when he arrives in Corinth, there will be no need for him to take disciplinary action.
13:9 *weak.* To have no need to give proof of his apostolic strength. *strong.* In the truth.
13:11–14 These concluding exhortations and salutations exhibit a note of confidence.
13:11 *God of . . . peace.* See note on 1 Thess 5:23.
13:12 *kiss.* A token of mutual trust and affection, still in common use in the Near East—corresponding to the handshake of the Western world. For Christians it must be a holy kiss, for all greetings should be purely and sincerely exchanged in Christ (see 1:2).
13:14 The benediction is Trinitarian in form and has ever since been a part of Christian worship tradition. It serves to remind us that the mystery of the Holy Trinity is known to be true not through rational or philosophical explanation but through Christian experience, whereby the believer knows firsthand the grace, the love, and the fellowship that freely flow to him from the three Persons of the one Lord God.

Galatians

INTRODUCTION

Author

The opening verse identifies the author of Galatians as the apostle Paul. Apart from a few 19th-century scholars, no one has seriously questioned his authorship.

Date and Destination

The date of Galatians depends to a great extent on the destination of the letter. There are two main views:

1. *The North Galatian theory.* This older view holds that the letter was addressed to churches located in north-central Asia Minor (Pessinus, Ancyra and Tavium), where the Gauls had settled when they invaded the area in the third century B.C. It is held that Paul visited this area on his second missionary journey, though Acts contains no reference to such a visit. Galatians, it is maintained, was written between A.D. 53 and 57 from Ephesus or Macedonia.

2. *The South Galatian theory.* According to this view, Galatians was written to churches in the southern area of the Roman province of Galatia (Antioch, Iconium, Lystra and Derbe) that Paul had founded on his first missionary journey. Some believe that Galatians was written from Syrian Antioch in 48–49 after Paul's first journey and before the Jerusalem council meeting (Acts 15). Others say that Galatians was written in Syrian Antioch or Corinth between 51 and 53.

Occasion and Purpose

Judaizers were Jewish Christians who believed, among other things, that a number of the ceremonial practices of the OT were still binding on the NT church. Following Paul's successful campaign in Galatia, they insisted that Gentile converts to Christianity abide by certain OT rites, especially circumcision. They may have been motivated by a desire to avoid the persecution of Zealot Jews who objected to their fraternizing with Gentiles (see 6:12). The Judaizers argued that Paul was not an authentic apostle and that out of a desire to make the message more appealing to Gentiles he had removed from the gospel certain legal requirements.

Paul responded by clearly establishing his apostolic authority and thereby substantiating the gospel he preached. By introducing additional requirements for justification (e.g., works of the law) his adversaries had perverted the gospel of grace and, unless prevented, would bring Paul's converts into the bondage of legalism. It is by grace through faith alone that man is justified, and it is by faith alone that he is to live out his new life in the freedom of the Spirit.

Theological Teaching

Galatians stands as an eloquent and vigorous apologetic for the essential NT truth that man is justified by faith in Jesus Christ—by nothing less and nothing more—and that he is sanctified not by legalistic works but by the obedience that comes from faith in God's work for him, in him and through him by the grace and power of Christ and the Holy Spirit. It was the rediscovery of the basic message of Galatians that brought about the Reformation. Galatians is often referred to as "Luther's book," because Martin Luther relied so strongly on this letter in his writings and arguments against the prevailing theology of his day. A key verse is 2:16 (see note there).

Outline

- I. Introduction (1:1–9)
  - A. Salutation (1:1–5)
  - B. Denunciation (1:6–9)

- II. Personal: Authentication of the Apostle of Liberty and Faith (1:10—2:21)
  - A. Paul's Gospel Was Received by Special Revelation (1:10–12)
  - B. Paul's Gospel Was Independent of the Jerusalem Apostles and the Judean Churches (1:13—2:21)
    1. Evidenced by his early activities as a Christian (1:13–17)
    2. Evidenced by his first post-Christian visit to Jerusalem (1:18–24)
    3. Evidenced by his second post-Christian visit to Jerusalem (2:1–10)
    4. Evidenced by his rebuke of Peter at Antioch (2:11–21)
- III. Doctrinal: Justification of the Doctrine of Liberty and Faith (chs. 3—4)
  - A. The Galatians' Experience of the Gospel (3:1–5)
  - B. The Experience of Abraham (3:6–9)
  - C. The Curse of the Law (3:10–14)
  - D. The Priority of the Promise (3:15–18)
  - E. The Purpose of the Law (3:19–25)
  - F. Sons, Not Slaves (3:26—4:11)
  - G. Appeal to Enter into Freedom from Law (4:12–20)
  - H. The Allegory of Hagar and Sarah (4:21–31)
- IV. Practical: Practice of the Life of Liberty and Faith (5:1—6:10)
  - A. Exhortation to Freedom (5:1–12)
  - B. Life by the Spirit, Not by the Flesh (5:13–26)
  - C. Call for Mutual Help (6:1–10)
- V. Conclusion (6:11–18)

Introduction

1 Paul, [a]an apostle ([b]not *sent* from men nor through the agency of man, but [c]through Jesus Christ and God the Father, who [d]raised Him from the dead),

2 and all [a]the brethren who are with me, To [b]the churches of Galatia:

3 [a]Grace to you and peace from [1]God our Father and the Lord Jesus Christ,

4 who [a]gave Himself for our sins so that He might rescue us from [b]this present evil [1]age, according to the will of [c]our God and Father,

5 [a]to whom *be* the glory forevermore. Amen.

Perversion of the Gospel

6 I am amazed that you are so quickly deserting [a]Him who called you [1]by the grace of Christ, for a [b]different gospel;

7 which is *really* not another; only there are some who are [a]disturbing you and want to distort the gospel of Christ.

8 But even if we, or [a]an angel from heaven, should preach to you a gospel [1]contrary to what we have preached to you, he is to be [2b]accursed!

9 As we [a]have said before, so I say again now, [b]if any man is preaching to you a gospel [1]contrary to what you received, he is to be [2c]accursed!

10 For am I now [a]seeking the favor of men, or of God? Or am I striving to please men? If I were still trying to please men, I would not be a [b]bond-servant of Christ.

Paul Defends His Ministry

11 For [a]I would have you know, brethren, that the gospel which was preached by me is [b]not according to man.

12 For [a]I neither received it from man, nor was I taught it, but *I received it* through a [b]revelation of Jesus Christ.

13 For you have heard of [a]my former manner of life in Judaism, how I [b]used to persecute [c]the church of God beyond measure and [d]tried to destroy it;

14 and I [a]was advancing in Judaism beyond many of my contemporaries among my [1]countrymen, being more extremely zealous for my [b]ancestral traditions.

15 But when God, who had set me apart *even* from my mother's womb and [a]called me through His grace, was pleased

16 to reveal His Son in me so that I might [a]preach Him among the Gentiles, [b]I did not immediately consult with [1c]flesh and blood,

17 [a]nor did I go up to Jerusalem to those who were apostles before me; but I went

1:1 [a]2 Cor 1:1 [b]Gal 1:11f [c]Acts 9:15; Gal 1:15f [d]Acts 2:24 **2** [a]Phil 4:21 [b]Acts 16:6; 1 Cor 16:1 **3** [1]Two early mss read *God the Father, and our Lord Jesus Christ* [a]Rom 1:7 **4** [1]Or *world* [a]Gal 2:20 [b]Matt 13:22; Rom 12:2; 2 Cor 4:4 [c]Phil 4:20 **5** [a]Rom 11:36 **6** [1]Lit *in* [a]Rom 8:28; Gal 1:15; 5:8 [b]2 Cor 11:4; Gal 1:7, 11; 2:2, 7; 5:14; 1 Tim 1:3 **7** [a]Acts 15:24; Gal 5:10 **8** [1]Or *other than, more than* [2]Gr *anathema* [a]2 Cor 11:14 [b]Rom 9:3 **9** [1]Or *other than, more than* [2]Gr *anathema* [a]Acts 18:23 [b]Rom 16:17 [c]Rom 9:3 **10** [a]1 Cor 10:33; 1 Thess 2:4 **10** [b]Rom 1:1; Phil 1:1 **11** [a]Rom 2:16; 1 Cor 15:1 [b]1 Cor 3:4; 9:8 **12** [a]1 Cor 11:23; Gal 1:1 [b]1 Cor 2:10; 2 Cor 12:1; Gal 1:16; 2:2 **13** [a]Acts 26:4f [b]Acts 8:3; 22:4, 5 [c]1 Cor 10:32 [d]Acts 9:21 **14** [1]Lit *race* [a]Acts 22:3 [b]Jer 9:14; Matt 15:2; Mark 7:3; Col 2:8 **15** [a]Is 49:1, 5; Jer 1:5; Acts 9:15; Rom 1:1; Gal 1:6 **16** [1]I.e. human beings [a]Acts 9:15; Gal 2:9 [b]Acts 9:20 [c]Matt 16:17 **17** [a]Acts 9:19-22

1:1 *Paul.* Writers of this time customarily put their names at the beginning of letters. For more information on Paul see notes on Acts 9:1; Phil 3:4–14. *apostle.* One sent on a mission with full authority of representation; an ambassador (see note on 1 Cor 1:1). *raised Him from the dead.* The resurrection is the central affirmation of the Christian faith (see Acts 17:18; Rom 1:4; 1 Cor 15:20; 1 Pet 1:3), and because Paul had seen the risen Christ he was qualified to be an apostle (see Acts 1:22 and note; 2:32; 1 Cor 15:8).

1:2 *brethren.* Fellow Christians (see 3:15; 4:12; 5:11; 6:18). *churches.* This was a circular letter to several congregations. *Galatia.* The term occurs four times in the NT. In 2 Tim 4:10 the reference is uncertain. In 1 Pet 1:1 it refers to the northern area of Asia Minor occupied by the Gauls. Here (and in 1 Cor 16:1) Paul probably uses the term to refer to the Roman province of Galatia and an additional area to the south, through which he traveled on his first missionary journey (Acts 13:14–14:23). See Introduction: Date and Destination.

1:3 *Grace.* The Christian adaptation of a common Greek form of greeting (see notes on Jon 4:2; Eph 1:2). *peace.* The common Hebrew form of greeting (see notes on John 14:27; 20:19; Eph 1:2).

1:4 *for our sins.* See Matt 1:21; John 1:29; 1 Cor 15:3; 1 Pet 2:24. *present evil age.* The present period of the world's history (see note on 2 Cor 4:4). In contrast to the age to come (the climax of the Messianic age), this present age is characterized by wickedness (Eph 2:2; 6:12).

1:5 For other doxologies see Rom 9:5; 11:36; 16:27; Eph 3:21; 1 Tim 1:17.

1:6 *so quickly.* So soon after your conversion. *Him who called you.* God. *grace of Christ.* The test of a pure, unadulterated gospel.

1:7 *some.* The Judaizers (see Introduction: Occasion and Purpose).

1:8 *accursed.* The Greek word (*anathema*) originally referred to a pagan temple offering in payment for a vow. Later it came to represent a curse (see v. 9; 1 Cor 12:3; 16:22; Rom 9:3).

1:10 *bond-servant of Christ.* Paul once wore the "yoke of slavery" (5:1) but, having been set free from sin by the redemption that is in Christ, he became a slave of righteousness, a slave of God (see Rom 6:18,22).

1:11 *I would have you know, brethren.* A similar phrase is found in 1 Cor 15:1, where Paul sets forth the gospel he received. *the gospel . . . preached by me.* Called "my gospel" in Rom 2:16; 16:25. Salvation is for all and is received by faith in Christ.

1:12 *received it through a revelation.* See Eph 3:2–6.

1:13 *Judaism.* The Jewish faith and way of life that developed during the period between the OT and the NT. The term is derived from Judah, the southern kingdom that came to an end in the sixth century B.C. with the exile into Babylonia. *church of God.* The NT counterpart of the OT assembly (see Num 16:21) or community of the Lord (Num 20:4).

1:14 *zealous.* See Phil 3:6. *ancestral traditions.* Traditions orally transmitted from previous generations and contrasted with the written law of Moses. Cf. the "tradition of the elders" (see note on Matt 15:2).

1:15 *set me apart even from my mother's womb.* See Is 49:1; Jer 1:5; Rom 1:1.

1:16 *Gentiles.* Lit. "nations" or "peoples." The term commonly designated foreigners—hence pagans, or the non-Jewish world. *flesh and blood.* In the NT always with the implication of human weakness or ignorance (see Matt 16:17; 1 Cor 15:50; Eph 6:12). Paul received his message from God.

1:17 *Jerusalem.* The religious center of Judaism and the birthplace of Christianity. *Arabia.* The Nabatean kingdom in Trans-

away to Arabia, and returned once more to
[b]Damascus.
18 Then [a]three years later I went up [b]to
Jerusalem to [1]become acquainted with
[c]Cephas, and stayed with him fifteen days.
19 But I did not see any other of the apostles except [1a]James, the Lord's brother.
20 (Now in what I am writing to you, [1]I
assure you [a]before God that I am not lying.)
21 Then [a]I went into the regions of [b]Syria
and [c]Cilicia.
22 I was *still* unknown by [1]sight to [a]the
churches of Judea which were [b]in Christ;
23 but only, they kept hearing, "He who
once persecuted us is now preaching [a]the
faith which he once [b]tried to destroy."
24 And they [a]were glorifying God [1]be-
cause of me.

The Council at Jerusalem

2 Then after an interval of fourteen years I
[a]went up again to Jerusalem with [b]Bar-
nabas, taking [c]Titus along also.
2 [1]It was because of a [a]revelation that I
went up; and I submitted to them the [b]gospel
which I preach among the Gentiles, but *I did*
so in private to those who were of reputation, for fear that I might be [c]running, or had
run, in vain.
3 But not even [a]Titus, who was with me,
though he was a Greek, was [b]compelled to
be circumcised.
4 But *it was* because of the [a]false
brethren secretly brought in, who [b]had
sneaked in to spy out our [c]liberty which we
have in Christ Jesus, in order to [d]bring us
into bondage.
5 But we did not yield in subjection to
them for even an hour, so that [a]the truth of
the gospel would remain with you.
6 But from those who [1]were of high [a]rep-
utation (what they were makes no difference
to me; [b]God [2]shows no partiality)—well,
those who were of reputation contributed
nothing to me.
7 But on the contrary, seeing that I had
been [a]entrusted with the [b]gospel [1]to the
uncircumcised, just as [c]Peter *had been* [2]to
the circumcised
8 (for He who effectually worked for
Peter in *his* [a]apostleship [1]to the circumcised
effectually worked for me also to the Gentiles),
9 and recognizing [a]the grace that had
been given to me, [1b]James and [c]Cephas and
John, who were [d]reputed to be [e]pillars, gave
to me and [f]Barnabas the [g]right [2]hand of fellowship, so that we *might* [h]*go* to the Gentiles
and they to the circumcised.
10 *They* only *asked* us to remember the
poor—[a]the very thing I also was eager to do.

Peter (Cephas) Opposed by Paul

11 But when [a]Cephas came to [b]Antioch, I
opposed him to his face, because he [1]stood
condemned.
12 For prior to the coming of certain men
from [1a]James, he used to [b]eat with the Gen-

17 [b]Acts 9:2
18 [1]Or *visit Cephas* [a]Acts 9:22f [b]Acts 9:26 [c]John 1:42; Gal 2:9, 11, 14
19 [1]Or *Jacob* [a]Matt 12:46; Acts 12:17
20 [1]Lit *behold before God* [a]Rom 9:1; 2 Cor 1:23; 11:31
21 [a]Acts 9:30 [b]Acts 15:23, 41 [c]Acts 6:9
22 [1]Lit *face* [a]1 Cor 7:17; 1 Thess 2:14 [b]Rom 16:7
23 [a]Acts 6:7; Gal 6:10 [b]Acts 9:21
24 [1]Lit *in me* [a]Matt 9:8
2:1 [a]Acts 15:2 [b]Acts 4:36; Gal 2:9, 13 [c]2 Cor 2:13; Gal 2:3
2 [1]Lit *according to revelation I went up* [a]Acts 15:2; Gal 1:12 [b]Gal 1:6 [c]Rom 9:16; 1 Cor 9:24ff; Gal 5:7; Phil 2:16; 2 Tim 4:7; Heb 12:1
3 [a]2 Cor 2:13; Gal 2:1 [b]Acts 16:3; 1 Cor 9:21
4 [a]Acts 15:1, 24; 2 Cor 11:13, 26; Gal 1:7 [b]2 Pet 2:1; Jude 4 [c]Gal 5:1, 13; James 1:25 [d]Rom 8:15; 2 Cor 11:20
5 [a]Gal 1:6; 2:14; Col 1:5
6 [1]Lit *seemed to be something* [2]Lit *does not receive a face* [a]2 Cor 11:5; 12:11; Gal 2:9; 6:3 [b]Acts 10:34
7 [1]Lit *of the uncircumcision* [2]Lit *of the circumcision* [a]1 Cor 9:17; 1 Thess 2:4; 1 Tim 1:11 [b]Acts 9:15; Gal 1:16 [c]Gal 1:18; 2:9, 11, 14
8 [1]Lit *of the circumcision* [a]Acts 1:25
9 [1]Or *Jacob* [2]Lit *hands* [a]Rom 12:3 [b]Acts 12:17; Gal 2:12 [c]Luke 22:8; Gal 1:18; 2:7, 11, 14 [d]2 Cor 11:5; 12:11; Gal 2:2, 6; 6:3 [e]1 Tim 3:15; Rev 3:12 [f]Acts 4:36; Gal 2:1, 13 [g]2 Kin 10:15 [h]Gal 1:16
10 [a]Acts 24:17
11 [1]Or *was to be condemned;* lit *was one who was condemned,* or, *was self-condemned* [a]Gal 1:18; 2:7, 9, 14 [b]Acts 11:19; 15:1
12 [1]Or *Jacob* [a]Acts 12:17; Gal 2:9 [b]Acts 11:3

---

jordan stretching from Damascus southwest to the Suez. *Damascus.* Ancient capital of Syria (Aram in the OT). Paul had been converted en route from Jerusalem to Damascus (Acts 9:1–9).

1:18 *three years later.* From the time of his departure into Arabia. The text does not say he spent the three years in Arabia. *I went up to Jerusalem.* Probably the visit referred to in Acts 9:26–30, though some equate it with the one in Acts 11:30. *Cephas.* Peter; from the Aramaic word for "stone" (see Matt 16:18 and note). The name designates a like quality in the bearer (see note on John 1:42).

1:19 *James.* See Introduction to James: Author. In Acts 21:18 this James appears to be the leader of the elders in the Jerusalem church. *the Lord's brother.* See note on Luke 8:19.

1:21 *Syria and Cilicia.* Provinces in Asia Minor. Specifically Paul went to Tarsus (see Acts 9:30), his hometown.

2:1 *after . . . fourteen years.* Probably from the date of Paul's conversion. *I went up again to Jerusalem.* According to some, the visit mentioned in Acts 11:30; according to others, the one in Acts 15:1–4 (see notes on Acts 12:1; 15:2). *Barnabas.* Means "one who encourages." His given name was Joseph, and he was a Levite from the island of Cyprus (see Acts 4:36 and note). He was Paul's companion on the first missionary journey (Acts 13:1–14:28). *Titus.* A Gentile Christian who served as Paul's delegate to Corinth and later was left in Crete to oversee the church there (see Titus 1:5).

2:2 *those who were of reputation.* Paul recognized their authority, and is probably referring to James, Peter and John (v. 9; cf. v. 6). *had run, in vain.* See 1 Cor 15:58; Phil 2:16.

2:4 *false brethren.* Judaizers who held that Gentile converts should be circumcised and obey the law of Moses (cf. Acts 15:5; 2 Cor 11:26). *to spy out.* Used in the Septuagint (the Greek translation of the OT) in 2 Sam 10:3 and 1 Chr 19:3 of spying out a territory. *liberty.* See 5:1,13; Rom 6:18,20,22; 8:2.

2:6 *those who were of high reputation.* See note on v. 2. *shows no partiality.* Cf. Deut 10:17; 1 Sam 16:7; Luke 20:21; James 2:1.

2:7 *to the uncircumcised.* Paul's ministry was not exclusively to the Gentiles. In fact, he regularly went first to the synagogue when arriving in a new location (see note on Acts 13:14). He did, however, consider himself to be foremost an apostle to the Gentiles (see Rom 11:13 and note).

2:9 *James.* See note on 1:19. *pillars.* A common metaphor for those who represent and strongly support an institution. *right hand of fellowship.* A common practice among both Hebrews and Greeks, indicating a pledge of friendship.

2:11 *Antioch.* The leading city of Syria and third leading city of the Roman empire (after Rome and Alexandria). From it Paul had been sent out on his missionary journeys (see Acts 13:1–3; 14:26). *stood condemned.* For yielding to the pressure of the circumcision party (the Judaizers), thus going against what he knew to be right.

2:12 *party of the circumcision.* Judaizers, who believed that circumcision was necessary for salvation (cf. Acts 10:45; 11:2; Rom 4:12).

tiles; but when they came, he *began* to withdraw and hold himself aloof, [c]fearing [2]the party of the circumcision.

13 The rest of the Jews joined him in hypocrisy, with the result that even [a]Barnabas was carried away by their hypocrisy.

14 But when I saw that they [a]were not [1]straightforward about [b]the truth of the gospel, I said to [c]Cephas in the presence of all, "If you, being a Jew, [d]live like the Gentiles and not like the Jews, how *is it that* you compel the Gentiles to live like Jews? [2]

15 "We *are* [a]Jews by nature and not [b]sinners from among the Gentiles;

16 nevertheless knowing that [a]a man is not justified by the works of [1]the Law but through faith in Christ Jesus, even we have believed in Christ Jesus, so that we may be justified by [b]faith in Christ and not by the works of [1]the Law; since [c]by the works of [1]the Law no [2]flesh will be justified.

17 "But if, while seeking to be justified in Christ, we ourselves have also been found [a]sinners, is Christ then a minister of sin? [b]May it never be!

18 "For if I rebuild what I have *once* destroyed, I [a]prove myself to be a transgressor.

19 "For through [1]the Law I [a]died to [1]the Law, so that I might live to God.

20 "I have been [a]crucified with Christ; and it is no longer I who live, but [b]Christ lives in me; and [1]the *life* which I now live in the flesh I live by faith in [c]the Son of God, who [d]loved me and [e]gave Himself up for me.

21 "I do not nullify the grace of God, for [a]if righteousness *comes* through [1]the Law, then Christ died needlessly."

12 [2]Or *converts from the circumcised;* lit *those from the circumcision* [c]Acts 11:2
13 [a]Acts 4:36; Gal 2:1, 9
14 [1]Or *progressing toward;* lit *walking straightly* [2]Some close the direct quotation here, others extend it through v 21 [a]Heb 12:13 [b]Gal 1:6; 2:5; Col 1:5 [c]Gal 1:18; 2:7, 9, 11 [d]Acts 10:28; Gal 2:12
15 [a]Phil 3:4f [b]1 Sam 15:18; Luke 24:7
16 [1]Or *law* [2]Or *mortal man* [a]Acts 13:39; Gal 3:11 [b]Rom 3:22; 9:30 [c]Ps 143:2; Rom 3:20
17 [a]Gal 2:15 [b]Luke 20:16; Gal 3:21
18 [a]Rom 3:5
19 [1]Or *law* [a]Rom 6:2; 7:4; 1 Cor 9:20
20 [1]Or *insofar as I* [a]Rom 6:6; Gal 5:24; 6:14 [b]Rom 8:10 [c]Matt 4:3 [d]Rom 8:37 [e]Gal 1:4
21 [1]Or *law* [a]Gal 3:21

3:1 [1]Lit *O* [a]Gal 1:2 [b]1 Cor 1:23; Gal 5:11
2 [1]Or *law* [2]Lit *the hearing of faith* [a]Rom 10:17

Faith Brings Righteousness

3 [1]You foolish [a]Galatians, who has bewitched you, before whose eyes Jesus Christ [b]was publicly portrayed *as* crucified?

2 This is the only thing I want to find out from you: did you receive the Spirit by the works of [1]the Law, or by [2a]hearing with faith?

3 Are you so foolish? Having begun [1]by the Spirit, are you now [2]being perfected by the flesh?

4 Did you [1]suffer so many things in vain—[a]if indeed it was in vain?

5 So then, does He who [a]provides you with the Spirit and [b]works [1]miracles among you, do it by the works of [2]the Law, or by [3c]hearing with faith?

6 [1]Even so [a]Abraham [b]BELIEVED GOD, AND IT WAS RECKONED TO HIM AS RIGHTEOUSNESS.

7 Therefore, [1]be sure that [a]it is those who are of faith who are [b]sons of Abraham.

8 The Scripture, foreseeing that God [1]would justify the [2]Gentiles by faith, preached the gospel beforehand to Abraham, *saying,* "[a]ALL THE NATIONS WILL BE BLESSED IN YOU."

9 So then [a]those who are of faith are blessed with [1]Abraham, the believer.

10 For as many as are of the works of [1]the Law are under a curse; for it is written, "[a]CURSED IS EVERYONE WHO DOES NOT ABIDE BY ALL THINGS WRITTEN IN THE BOOK OF THE LAW, TO PERFORM THEM."

11 Now that [a]no one is justified [1]by [2]the

3 [1]Or *with* [2]Or *ending with* **4** [1]Or *experience* [a]1 Cor 15:2
5 [1]Or *works of power* [2]Or *law* [3]Lit *the hearing of faith* [a]2 Cor 9:10; Phil 1:19 [b]1 Cor 12:10 [c]Rom 10:17 **6** [1]Lit *Just as* [a]Rom 4:3 [b]Gen 15:6 **7** [1]Lit *know* [a]Rom 4:16; Gal 3:9 [b]Luke 19:9; Gal 6:16 **8** [1]Lit *justifies* [2]Lit *nations* [a]Gen 12:3 **9** [1]Lit *the believing Abraham* [a]Gal 3:7 **10** [1]Or *law* [a]Deut 27:26
11 [1]Or *in* [2]Or *law* [a]Gal 2:16

2:13 *rest of the Jews.* Jewish Christians not associated with the circumcision party but whom Peter's behavior had led astray.
2:14 *live like the Gentiles.* You do not observe Jewish customs, especially dietary restrictions (see v. 12).
2:16 A key verse in Galatians (see Introduction: Theological Teaching). Three times it tells us that no one is justified by observing the law, and three times it underscores the indispensable requirement of placing one's faith in Christ. *justified by faith.* The essence of the gospel message (see Rom 3:20,28; Phil 3:9; see also notes on Rom 3:24,28). Faith is the means by which justification is received, not its basis. *by the works of the Law.* Paul is not depreciating the Law itself, for he clearly maintained that God's Law is "holy and righteous and good" (Rom 7:12). He is arguing against an illegitimate use of the OT Law that made the observance of that Law the grounds of acceptance with God.
2:19 *I died to the Law.* See v. 20; see also note on Rom 7:4.
2:20 *crucified with Christ.* See 5:24; 6:14; Rom 6:8–10; 7:6; see also note on Rom 6:7. *gave Himself up for me.* See 1:4; 1 Tim 2:6; Titus 2:14.
2:21 *Christ died needlessly.* To mingle legalism with grace distorts grace and makes a mockery of the cross.
3:1 *foolish.* They were not mentally deficient but simply failed to use their powers of perception (see Luke 24:25; Rom 1:14; 1 Tim 6:9; Titus 3:3). *who . . . ?* Obviously legalistic Judaizers. *portrayed as crucified.* See 1 Cor 1:23; 2:2. The verb means "to publicly portray or placard." Cf. the bronze serpent that Moses displayed on a pole (Num 21:9).
3:2 *the Spirit.* From this point on in Galatians Paul refers to the Holy Spirit 16 times.
3:3 *begun by the Spirit . . . being perfected.* Both salvation and sanctification are the work of the Holy Spirit. *by the flesh.* A reference to human nature in its unregenerate weakness. Trying to achieve righteousness by works, including circumcision, was a part of life in the "flesh."
3:4 Paul hopes that those who have been misled will return to the true gospel.
3:7 *sons of Abraham.* Abraham was the physical and spiritual father of the Jewish race (see John 8:33,39,53; Acts 7:2; Rom 4:12). Here all believers (Jews and Gentiles) are called his spiritual children (see notes on Rom 4:11–12). They are also referred to as the "seed" or "descendants" of Abraham (v. 16; Heb 2:16).
3:8 *Scripture, foreseeing.* A personification of Scripture that calls attention to its divine origin (see 1 Tim 5:18).
3:9 *Abraham, the believer.* Paul develops this theme at length in Rom 4; see also Heb 11:8–19.
3:10 *are the works of the Law.* The reference is to legalists—those who refuse God's offer of grace and insist on pursuing righteousness through works. *under a curse.* Because no one under the law ever perfectly kept the Law. God's blessing has never been earned, but has always been freely given. *ALL THINGS.* See James 2:10.

Law before God is evident; for, "[3][b]THE RIGH-
TEOUS MAN SHALL LIVE BY FAITH."
12 [1]However, the Law is not [2]of faith; on
the contrary, "[a]HE WHO PRACTICES THEM SHALL
LIVE [3]BY THEM."
13 Christ [a]redeemed us from the curse of
the Law, having become a curse for us—for
it is written, "[b]CURSED IS EVERYONE WHO HANGS
ON [c]A [1]TREE"—
14 in order that [a]in Christ Jesus the blessing of Abraham might [1]come to the Gentiles,
so that we [b]would receive [c]the promise of
the Spirit through faith.

Intent of the Law

15 [a]Brethren, [b]I speak [1]in terms of human
relations: [c]even though it is *only* a man's
[2]covenant, yet when it has been ratified, no
one sets it aside or adds [3]conditions to it.
16 Now the promises were spoken [a]to
Abraham and to his seed. He does not say,
"And to seeds," as *referring* to many, but
rather to one, "[b]And to your seed," that is,
Christ.
17 What I am saying is this: the Law, which
came [a]four hundred and thirty years later,
does not invalidate a covenant previously ratified by God, so as to nullify the promise.
18 For [a]if the inheritance is [1]based on law,
it is no longer [1]based on a promise; but [b]God
has granted it to Abraham by means of a
promise.
19 [a]Why the Law then? It was added
[1]because of transgressions, having been
[b]ordained through angels [c]by the [2]agency of
a mediator, until [d]the seed would come to
whom the promise had been made.
20 Now [a]a mediator is not [1]for one *party*
only; whereas God is *only* one.
21 Is the Law then contrary to the promises of God? [a]May it never be! For [b]if a law
had been given which was able to impart
life, then righteousness [1]would indeed have
been [2]based on law.
22 But the Scripture has [a]shut up [1]every-
one under sin, so that the promise by faith in
Jesus Christ might be given to those who
believe.
23 But before faith came, we were kept in
custody under the law, [a]being shut up to the
faith which was later to be revealed.
24 Therefore the Law has become our
[a]tutor *to lead us* to Christ, so that [b]we may
be justified by faith.
25 But now that faith has come, we are no
longer under a [1][a]tutor.
26 For you are all [a]sons of God through
faith in [b]Christ Jesus.
27 For all of you who were [a]baptized into
Christ have [b]clothed yourselves with Christ.
28 [a]There is neither Jew nor Greek, there
is neither slave nor free man, there is [1]nei-
ther male nor female; for [b]you are all one in
[c]Christ Jesus.
29 And if [a]you [1]belong to Christ, then you
are Abraham's [2]descendants, heirs according
to [b]promise.

11 [3]Or *But he who is righteous by faith shall live* [b]Hab 2:4; Rom 1:17; Heb 10:38
12 [1]Or *And* [2]Or *based on* [3]Or *in* [a]Lev 18:5; Rom 10:5
13 [1]Or *cross;* lit *wood* [a]Gal 4:5 [b]Deut 21:23 [c]Acts 5:30
14 [1]Or *occur* [a]Rom 4:9, 16; Gal 3:28 [b]Gal 3:2 [c]Acts 2:33; Eph 1:13
15 [1]Lit *according to man* [2]Or *will* or *testament* [3]Or *a codicil* [a]Acts 1:15; Rom 1:13; Gal 6:18 [b]Rom 3:5 [c]Heb 6:16
16 [a]Luke 1:55; Rom 4:13, 16; 9:4 [b]Acts 3:25
17 [a]Gen 15:13f; Ex 12:40; Acts 7:6
18 [1]Lit *out of, from* [a]Rom 4:14 [b]Heb 6:14
19 [1]Or *for the sake of defining* [2]Lit *hand* [a]Rom 5:20 [b]Acts 7:53 [c]Ex 20:19; Deut 5:5 [d]Gal 3:16
20 [1]Lit *of one* [a]1 Tim 2:5; Heb 8:6; 9:15; 12:24
21 [1]Or *would indeed be* [2]Lit *out of, from* [a]Luke 20:16; Gal 2:17 [b]Gal 2:21
22 [1]Lit *things* [a]Rom 11:32
23 [a]Rom 11:32
24 [a]1 Cor 4:15 [b]Gal 2:16 **25** [1]Lit *child-conductor* [a]1 Cor 4:15
26 [a]Rom 8:14; Gal 4:5 [b]Rom 8:1; Gal 3:28; 4:14; 5:6, 24; Eph 1:1; Phil 1:1; Col 1:4; 1 Tim 1:12; 2 Tim 1:1; Titus 1:4
27 [a]Matt 28:19; Rom 6:3; 1 Cor 10:2 [b]Rom 13:14 **28** [1]Lit *not male and female* [a]Rom 3:22; 1 Cor 12:13; Col 3:11 [b]John 17:11; Eph 2:15 [c]Rom 8:1; Gal 3:26; 4:14; 5:6, 24; Eph 1:1; Phil 1:1; Col 1:4; 1 Tim 1:12; 2 Tim 1:1; Titus 1:4 **29** [1]Lit *are Christ's* [2]Lit *seed* [a]Rom 4:13; 1 Cor 3:23 [b]Rom 9:8; Gal 3:18; 4:28

3:11 SHALL LIVE. Means here (and in v. 12) almost the same thing as "will be justified."
3:13 *Christ redeemed us from the curse of the Law.* See 4:5; Rom 8:3. TREE. Used in classical Greek of stocks and poles on which bodies were impaled, here of the cross (see Acts 5:30; 10:39; 1 Pet 2:24).
3:14 *the blessing of Abraham.* See v. 8; Rom 4:1–5. *promise of the Spirit.* See Ezek 36:26; 37:14; 39:29; John 14:16; cf. Eph 1:13.
3:15 *Brethren.* See note on 1:2. *man's covenant.* The Greek word normally indicates a last will or testament, which is probably the legal instrument Paul is referring to here. But in the Septuagint (the Greek translation of the OT) it had been widely used of God's covenant with His people (see also Matt 26:28; Luke 1:72; Acts 3:25; 7:8; 2 Cor 3:14; Heb 8:9), so Paul's choice of analogy was apt for his purpose.
3:16 *promises.* See notes on Rom 4:13; 9:4.
3:17 *four hundred and thirty years.* See Ex 12:40–41. The period in Egypt is designated in round numbers as "400 years" in Gen 15:13; Acts 7:6.
3:19 *was added.* From the time of Abraham, the promise covenanted to him (Gen 12:2–3,7; 15:18–20; 17:4–8) had stood at the center of God's relationship with His people. After the exodus the law contained in the Sinaitic covenant (Ex 19–24) became an additional element in that relationship—what Jeremiah by implication called the "old covenant" when he brought God's promise of a "new covenant" (Jer 31:31–34). *through angels.* See Deut 33:2; Acts 7:38,53; Heb 2:2. *the seed.* Christ.
3:20 The Mosaic covenant was a formal arrangement of mutual commitments between God and Israel, with Moses as the mediator. But since the promise God covenanted with Abraham involved commitment only from God's side (and God is one; see note on Deut 6:4), no mediator was involved.
3:21 The reason the law is not opposed to the promise is that, although in itself it cannot save, it serves to reveal sin, which alienates God from man, and to show the need for the salvation that the promise offers.
3:23 *faith.* In Christ (v. 22). *kept in custody under the law.* To be a prisoner of sin (v. 22) and a prisoner of law amounts to much the same, because law reveals and stimulates sin (see 4:3; Rom 7:8; Col 2:20).
3:24 *has become our tutor.* The expression translates the Greek *paidagogos* (from which "pedagogue" is derived). It refers to the personal slave-attendant who accompanied a freeborn boy wherever he went and exercised a certain amount of discipline over him. His function was more like that of a baby-sitter than a teacher (see 1 Cor 4:15, "tutors").
3:25–26 By adoption, the justified believer is a full adult and heir in God's family, with all the attendant rights and privileges (4:1–7; Rom 8:14–17).
3:27 *baptized into Christ.* See Rom 6:3–11; 1 Cor 12:13.
3:28 Unity in Christ transcends ethnic, social and sexual distinctions (see Rom 10:12; 1 Cor 12:13; Eph 2:15–16). *free.* See 5:1,13; Rom 6:18,20,22; 8:2. "Free" and "freedom" are key words in Galatians, occurring ten times (here; 4:22–23,26,30–31; 5:1,13; cf. "liberty" in 2:4).
3:29 Christians are Abraham's true, spiritual descendants.

Sonship in Christ

4 Now I say, as long as the heir is a [1]child,
he does not differ at all from a slave
although he is [2]owner of everything,
2 but he is under guardians and [1]man-
agers until the date set by the father.
3 So also we, while we were children,
were held [a]in bondage under the [1b]elemental
things of the world.
4 But when [a]the fullness of the time
came, God sent forth His Son, [b]born of a
woman, born [c]under [1]the Law,
5 so that He might redeem those who
were under [1]the Law, that we might receive
the adoption as [a]sons.
6 Because you are sons, [a]God has sent
forth the Spirit of His Son into our hearts,
crying, "[b]Abba! Father!"
7 Therefore you are no longer a slave, but
a son; and [a]if a son, then an heir [1]through
God.
8 However at that time, [a]when you did
not know God, you were [b]slaves to [c]those
which by nature are no gods.
9 But now that you have come to know
God, or rather to be [a]known by God, [b]how is
it that you turn back again to the weak and
worthless [1c]elemental things, to which you
desire to be enslaved all over again?
10 You [a]observe days and months and
seasons and years.

4:1 [1]Or *minor* [2]Lit *lord*
2 [1]Or *stewards*
3 [1]Or *rudimentary teachings* or *principles* [a]Gal 2:4; 4:8f, 24f [b]Gal 4:9; Col 2:8, 20; Heb 5:12
4 [1]Or *law* [a]Mark 1:15 [b]John 1:14; Rom 1:3; 8:3; Phil 2:7 [c]Luke 2:21f, 27
5 [1]Or *law* [a]Rom 8:14; Gal 3:26
6 [a]Acts 16:7; Rom 5:5; 8:9, 16; 2 Cor 3:17 [b]Mark 14:36; Rom 8:15
7 [1]I.e. through the gracious act of [a]Rom 8:17
8 [a]1 Cor 1:21; Eph 2:12; 1 Thess 4:5; 2 Thess 1:8 [b]Gal 4:3 [c]2 Chr 13:9; Is 37:19; Jer 2:11; 1 Cor 8:4f; 10:20
9 [1]Or *rudimentary teachings* or *principles* [a]1 Cor 8:3 [b]Col 2:20 [c]Gal 4:3
10 [a]Rom 14:5; Col 2:16
11 [1]Or *for*
12 [a]Gal 6:18 [b]2 Cor 6:11, 13

11 I fear for you, that perhaps I have
labored [1]over you in vain.
12 I beg of you, [a]brethren, [b]become as I
am, for I also *have become* as you *are*. You
have done me no wrong;
13 but you know that it was because of a
[1]bodily illness that I preached the gospel to
you the [2]first time;
14 and that which was a [1]trial to you in
my [2]bodily condition you did not despise or
[3]loathe, but [a]you received me as an angel of
God, as [b]Christ Jesus *Himself*.
15 Where then is [1]that sense of blessing
you had? For I bear you witness that, if possible, you would have plucked out your eyes
and given them to me.
16 So have I become your enemy [a]by
[1]telling you the truth?
17 They eagerly seek you, not commend-
ably, but they wish to shut you out so that
you will seek them.
18 But it is good always to be eagerly
sought in a commendable [1]manner, and [a]not
only when I am present with you.
19 [a]My children, with whom [b]I am again
in labor until [c]Christ is formed in you—
20 but I could wish to be present with you

13 [1]Lit *weakness of the flesh* [2]Or *former* **14** [1]Or *temptation* [2]Lit *flesh* [3]Lit *spit out at* [a]Matt 10:40; 1 Thess 2:13 [b]Gal 3:26
15 [1]Lit *the congratulation of yourselves* **16** [1]Or *dealing truthfully with you* [a]Amos 5:10 **18** [1]Or *thing* [a]Gal 4:13f
19 [a]1 John 2:1 [b]1 Cor 4:15 [c]Eph 4:13

4:1 *child.* A minor. Contrast with "mature" in 1 Cor 14:20 ("perfect" in Phil 3:15).
4:2 *guardians.* A broader term than "tutor" in 3:24. See Matt 20:8 ("foreman"); Luke 8:3 ("steward").
4:3 *in bondage.* See note on 3:23. *elemental things.* The Greek term meant essentially "things placed side by side in a row" (as the ABCs) and then came to mean fundamental principles or basic elements of various kinds. The context here suggests that it refers to the elemental forms of religion, whether those of the Jews (under the law, v. 5) or those of the Gentiles (under their old religious bondage, v. 8). *of the world.* In the sense that these principles do not come from the "new creation" (6:15).
4:4 *fullness of the time came.* The time "set" (v. 2) by God for His children to become adult sons and heirs. *God sent forth His Son.* See John 1:14; 3:16; Rom 1:1–6; 1John 4:14. *born of a woman.* Showing that Christ was truly human. *born under the Law.* Subject to the Jewish Law.
4:5 *the adoption as sons.* Lit. "adoption [of a son]." See Rom 8:15, where the "spirit of adoption as sons" is contrasted with the "spirit of slavery" (cf. Eph 1:5). God takes into His family as fully recognized sons and heirs both Jews (those who had been under law) and Gentiles who believe in Christ.
4:6 *Spirit of His Son.* A new "guardian" (v. 2), identified as the "Spirit of God" in Rom 8:9 (see Rom 8:2; Eph 1:13–14). *crying.* The Greek for this phrase is a vivid verb expressing deep emotion, often used of an inarticulate cry. In Matt 27:50 it is used of Jesus' final cry. *Abba! Father!* "Abba," expressive of an especially close relationship to God, is Aramaic for "Father."
4:8 *when you did not know God.* See 1 Cor 12:2; 1 Thess 4:5. *are no gods.* When the Galatians were pagans, they thought that the beings they worshiped were gods; but when they became Christians, they learned better.
4:9 *turn back.* See 3:1–3. *weak and worthless elemental things.* See note on v. 3. *enslaved . . . again.* Legalistic trust in rituals, in moral achievement, in law, in good works, or even in cold, dead orthodoxy may indicate a relapse into second childhood on the part of those who should be knowing and enjoying the freedom of full-grown sons.
4:10 *days.* Such as the sabbath and the day of atonement (tenth day of Tishri; see Lev 16:29–34), which had never been, and can never be, in themselves means of salvation or sanctification. *months and seasons.* Such as New Moons (see Num 28:11–15; Is 1:13–14), Passover (Ex 12:18) and First fruits (Lev 23:10). *years.* Such as the sabbath year (see Lev 25:4). The Pharisees meticulously observed all these to gain merit before God.
4:11 *in vain.* Due to their return to the old covenant law.
4:12 *brethren.* See note on 1:2.
4:13 *illness.* On the basis of v. 15; 6:11 some suggest it was eye trouble. Others have suggested malaria or epilepsy. *preached . . . the first time.* When Paul visited Galatia on his first missionary journey (Acts 13:14–14:23).
4:14 *you received me.* He implies that under the influence of Judaizers they have changed their attitude toward him.
4:15 *Where . . . is that sense of blessing you had?* Because of the restraints of legalistic Judaism they had lost their blessing and joy. *plucked out your eyes.* A hyperbole indicating their willingness, for his benefit, to part with that which was most precious to them. See Mark 2:4, where the same verb is used of digging through a roof.
4:16 *your enemy.* Telling the truth sometimes results in loss of friends.
4:17 *They.* Judaizers (see 2:4,12).
4:19 *My children.* For Paul's affectionate relationship to his converts see Acts 20:37–38; Phil 4:1; 1 Thess 2:7–8. The expression occurs only here in Paul's writings, but is common in John's (e.g., John 13:33; 1 John 2:1; 3:7). *until Christ is formed in you.* The goal of Paul's ministry (see Rom 8:29; Eph 4:13,15; Col 1:27).

now and to change my tone, for [a]I am perplexed about you.

Bond and Free

21 Tell me, you who want to be under law,
do you not [a]listen to the law?
22 For it is written that Abraham had two
sons, [a]one by the bondwoman and [b]one by
the free woman.
23 But [a]the son by the bondwoman [1]was
born according to the flesh, and [b]the son by
the free woman through the promise.
24 [1][a]This is allegorically speaking, for
these *women* are two covenants: one *proceeding* from [b]Mount Sinai bearing children
[2]who are to be [c]slaves; [3]she is Hagar.
25 Now this Hagar is Mount Sinai in Arabia and corresponds to the present Jerusalem, for she is in slavery with her children.
26 But [a]the Jerusalem above is free; [1]she
is our mother.
27 For it is written,
"[a]REJOICE, BARREN WOMAN WHO DOES NOT
BEAR;
BREAK FORTH AND SHOUT, YOU WHO ARE
NOT IN LABOR;
FOR MORE NUMEROUS ARE THE CHILDREN OF
THE DESOLATE
THAN OF THE ONE WHO HAS A HUSBAND."
28 And you brethren, [a]like Isaac, are [b]chil-
dren of promise.
29 But as at that time [a]he who was born
according to the flesh [b]persecuted him *who
was born* according to the Spirit, [c]so it is now
also.

20 [a]2 Cor 4:8
21 [a]Luke 16:29
22 [a]Gen 16:15 [b]Gen 21:2
23 [1]Lit *has been born* [a]Rom 9:7; Gal 4:29 [b]Gen 17:16ff; 18:10ff; 21:1; Gal 4:28; Heb 11:11
24 [1]Lit *Which* [2]Lit *into slavery* [3]Lit *which* [a]1 Cor 10:11 [b]Deut 33:2 [c]Gal 4:3
26 [1]Lit *which* [a]Heb 12:22; Rev 3:12; 21:2, 10
27 [a]Is 54:1
28 [a]Gal 4:23 [b]Rom 9:7ff; Gal 3:29
29 [a]Gal 4:23 [b]Gen 21:9 [c]Gal 5:11
30 [a]Gen 21:10, 12 [b]John 8:35
31 [1]V 5:1, note 1
5:1 [1]Some authorities prefer to join with 4:31 and render *but with the freedom of the free woman Christ set us free* [a]John 8:32, 36; Rom 8:15; 2 Cor 3:17; Gal 2:4; 5:13 [b]1 Cor 16:13 [c]Acts 15:10; Gal 2:4
2 [a]2 Cor 10:1 [b]Acts 15:1; Gal 5:3, 6, 11
3 [a]Luke 16:28 [b]Acts 15:1; Gal 5:2, 6, 11 [c]Rom 2:25

30 But what does the Scripture say?
"[a]CAST OUT THE BONDWOMAN AND HER
SON,
FOR [b]THE SON OF THE BONDWOMAN SHALL
NOT BE AN HEIR WITH THE SON OF THE
FREE WOMAN."
31 So then, brethren, we are not children
of a bondwoman, [1]but of the free woman.

Walk by the Spirit

5 [1][a]It was for freedom that Christ set us
free; therefore [b]keep standing firm and do
not be subject again to a [c]yoke of slavery.
2 Behold I, [a]Paul, say to you that if you
receive [b]circumcision, Christ will be of no
benefit to you.
3 And I [a]testify again to every man who
receives [b]circumcision, that he is under obligation to [c]keep the whole Law.
4 You have been severed from Christ, you
who [1]are seeking to be justified by law; you
have [a]fallen from grace.
5 For we [1]through the Spirit, [2]by faith,
are [a]waiting for the hope of righteousness.
6 For in [a]Christ Jesus [b]neither circumcision nor uncircumcision means anything,
but [c]faith working through love.
7 You were [a]running well; who hindered
you from obeying the truth?
8 This persuasion *did* not *come* from
[a]Him who calls you.

4 [1]Or *would be* [a]Heb 12:15; 2 Pet 3:17 **5** [1]Lit *by* [2]Lit *out of* [a]Rom 8:23; 1 Cor 1:7 **6** [a]Gal 3:26 [b]1 Cor 7:19; Gal 6:15 [c]Col 1:4f; 1 Thess 1:3; James 2:18, 20, 22 **7** [a]Gal 2:2 **8** [a]Rom 8:28; Gal 1:6

4:22 *two sons.* Ishmael was born to the slave woman, Hagar (Gen 16:1–16), and Isaac to the free woman, Sarah (Gen 21:2–5).
4:24 *allegorically speaking.* The Sarah-Hagar account is not an allegory in the sense that it was nonhistorical, but in the sense that Paul uses the events to illustrate a theological truth. *covenants.* See note on 3:15. *Mount Sinai.* Where the old covenant was established, with its law governing Israel's life (see Ex 19:2; 20:1–17).
4:25 *corresponds to the present Jerusalem.* Jerusalem can be equated with Mount Sinai because it represents the center of Judaism, which is still under bondage to the law issued at Mount Sinai.
4:26 *the Jerusalem above.* Rabbinical teaching held that the Jerusalem above was the heavenly archetype that in the Messianic period would be let down to earth (cf. Rev 21:2). Here it refers to the heavenly city of God, in which Christ reigns and of which Christians are citizens, in contrast to the "present Jerusalem" (v. 25). *our mother.* As citizens of the heavenly Jerusalem, Christians are her children.
4:27 Paul applies Isaiah's joyful promise to exiled Jerusalem (in her exile "barren" of children) to the ingathering of believers through the gospel, by which "Jerusalem's" children have become many.
4:28 *children of promise.* Children by virtue of God's promise (see 3:29; Rom 9:8).
4:29 *persecuted him who was born according to the Spirit.* Suggested by Gen 21:9; cf. Ps 83:5–6. *so it is now.* See Acts 13:50; 14:2–5,19; 1 Thess 2:14–16.
4:30 *CAST OUT THE BONDWOMAN.* Sarah's words in Gen 21:10 were used by Paul as the Scriptural basis for teaching the Galatians to put the Judaizers out of the church.
4:31 *we are not children of a bondwoman.* The believer is not enslaved to the law but is a child of promise and lives by faith (cf. 3:7,29).
5:1 *freedom.* Emphasized by its position in the Greek sentence. The freedom spoken of here is freedom from the yoke of the law. *subject.* In classical Greek the verb meant "to be caught or entangled in." *yoke of slavery.* The burden of the rigorous demands of the law as the means for gaining God's favor—an intolerable burden for sinful man (see Acts 15:10–11).
5:2 *circumcision.* As a condition for God's acceptance.
5:3 *obligation to keep the whole Law.* The OT Law is a unit; submission to it cannot be selective.
5:4 *fallen from grace.* Placed yourself outside the scope of divine favor, because gaining God's favor by observing the law and receiving it by grace are mutually exclusive (see 2 Pet 3:17).
5:5 *the hope of righteousness.* A reference to God's final verdict of "not guilty," assured presently to the believer by faith and by the sanctifying work of the Holy Spirit. This is one of the few eschatological statements in Galatians.
5:6 *neither circumcision nor uncircumcision means anything.* See v. 2; 2:21; 6:15; 1 Cor 7:19. *faith working through love.* Faith is not mere intellectual assent (see James 2:18–19) but a living trust in God's grace that expresses itself in acts of love (see 1 Thess 1:3).
5:7 *were running well.* Before the Judaizers hindered them. Paul was fond of depicting the Christian life as a race (see, e.g., 2:2; Phil 2:16).
5:8 *persuasion.* By the Judaizers.

9 [a]A little leaven leavens the whole lump
of dough.
10 [a]I have confidence [1]in you in the Lord
that you [b]will adopt no other view; but the
one who is [c]disturbing you will bear his
judgment, whoever he is.
11 But I, brethren, if I still preach circumcision, why am I still [a]persecuted? Then [b]the
stumbling block of the cross has been abolished.
12 I wish that [a]those who are troubling
you would even [1b]mutilate themselves.
13 For you were called to [a]freedom,
brethren; [b]only *do* not *turn* your freedom
into an opportunity for the flesh, but through
love [c]serve one another.
14 For [a]the whole Law is fulfilled in one
word, in the *statement,* "[b]YOU SHALL LOVE
YOUR NEIGHBOR AS YOURSELF."
15 But if you [a]bite and devour one another, take care that you are not consumed by
one another.
16 But I say, [a]walk by the Spirit, and you
will not carry out [b]the desire of the flesh.
17 For [a]the flesh [1]sets its desire against
the Spirit, and the Spirit against the flesh; for
these are in opposition to one another, [b]so
that you may not do the things that you
[2]please.
18 But if you are [a]led by the Spirit, [b]you
are not under the Law.
19 Now the deeds of the flesh are evident,
which are: [1a]immorality, impurity, sensuality,
20 idolatry, [a]sorcery, enmities, [b]strife, jealousy, outbursts of anger, [c]disputes, dissensions, [1d]factions,
21 envying, [a]drunkenness, carousing, and
things like these, of which I forewarn you,
just as I have forewarned you, that those
who practice such things will not [b]inherit the
kingdom of God.
22 But [a]the fruit of the Spirit is [b]love, joy,
peace, patience, kindness, goodness, faithfulness,
23 gentleness, [a]self-control; against such
things [b]there is no law.
24 Now those who [1]belong to [a]Christ
Jesus have [b]crucified the flesh with its passions and [c]desires.
25 If we live by the Spirit, let us also [1]walk
[a]by the Spirit.
26 Let us not become [a]boastful, challenging one another, envying one another.

Bear One Another's Burdens

6 [a]Brethren, even if [1]anyone is caught in
any trespass, you who are [b]spiritual,
[c]restore such a one [d]in a spirit of gentleness;
each one looking to yourself, so that you too
will not be tempted.
2 [a]Bear one another's burdens, and
thereby fulfill [b]the law of Christ.
3 For [a]if anyone thinks he is something
when he is nothing, he deceives himself.
4 But each one must [a]examine his own
work, and then he will have *reason for*
[b]boasting in regard to himself alone, and not
in regard to another.
5 For [a]each one will bear his own load.

9 [a]1 Cor 5:6 **10** [1]Lit *toward* [a]2 Cor 2:3 [b]Gal 5:7; Phil 3:15 [c]Gal 1:7; 5:12 **11** [a]Gal 4:29; 6:12 [b]Rom 9:33; 1 Cor 1:23 **12** [1]Or *cut themselves off* [a]Gal 2:4; 5:10 [b]Deut 23:1 **13** [a]Gal 5:1 [b]1 Cor 8:9; 1 Pet 2:16 [c]1 Cor 9:19; Eph 5:21 **14** [a]Matt 7:12; 22:40; Rom 13:8, 10; Gal 6:2 [b]Lev 19:18; Matt 19:19; John 13:34 **15** [a]Gal 5:20; Phil 3:2 **16** [a]Rom 8:4; 13:14; Gal 5:24f [b]Rom 13:14; Eph 2:3 **17** [1]Lit *lusts against* [2]Lit *wish* [a]Rom 7:18, 23; 8:5ff [b]Rom 7:15ff **18** [a]Rom 8:14 [b]Rom 6:14; 7:4; 1 Tim 1:9 **19** [1]I.e. sexual immorality [a]1 Cor 6:9, 18; 2 Cor 12:21 **20** [1]Or *heresies* [a]Rev 21:8 [b]2 Cor 12:20 [c]Rom 2:8; James 3:14ff [d]1 Cor 11:19 **21** [a]Rom 13:13

21 [b]1 Cor 6:9 **22** [a]Matt 7:16ff; Eph 5:9 [b]Rom 5:1-5; 1 Cor 13:4; Col 3:12-15 **23** [a]Acts 24:25 [b]Gal 5:18

24 [1]Lit *are of Christ Jesus* [a]Gal 3:26 [b]Rom 6:6; Gal 2:20; 6:14 [c]Gal 5:16f **25** [1]Or *follow the Spirit* [a]Gal 5:16 **26** [a]Phil 2:3
6:1 [1]Gr *anthropos* [a]Gal 6:18; 1 Thess 4:1 [b]1 Cor 2:15 [c]2 Cor 2:7; 2 Thess 3:15; Heb 12:13; James 5:19f [d]1 Cor 4:21 **2** [a]Rom 15:1 [b]Rom 8:2; 1 Cor 9:21; James 1:25; 2:12; 2 Pet 3:2 **3** [a]Acts 5:36; 1 Cor 3:18; 2 Cor 12:11 **4** [a]1 Cor 11:28 [b]Phil 1:26 **5** [a]Prov 9:12; Rom 14:12; 1 Cor 3:8

5:9 A proverb used here to stress the pervasive effect of Judaism. When the word "leaven" in the Bible is used as a symbol, it indicates evil or false teaching (see note on Mark 8:15), except in Matt 13:33.

5:11 *brethren.* See note on 1:2. *stumbling block of the cross.* See Rom 9:32–33; 1 Cor 1:23.

5:12 *mutilate themselves.* The Greek word means "to cut off," or "to castrate." In Phil 3:2 Paul uses a related word to describe the same sort of people as "the false circumcision." His sarcasm is evident.

5:13 *do not turn your freedom into an opportunity for the flesh.* See Rom 6:1; 1 Pet 2:16. Liberty is not license but freedom to serve God and each other in love.

5:14 *whole Law is fulfilled.* Doing to others what you would have them do to you expresses the spirit and intention of "the Law and the Prophets" (Matt 7:12; cf. Mark 12:31).

5:15 *bite and devour one another.* Opposite of vv. 13–14. Seeking to attain status with God and man by mere observance of law breeds a self-righteous, critical spirit.

5:16 *walk by.* Present tense—"go on living" (used of habitual conduct). Living by the promptings and power of the Spirit is the key to conquering sinful desires (see v. 25; Rom 8:2–4).

5:17 *in opposition to one another.* See Rom 7:15–23; 1 Pet 2:11.

5:18 *led by the Spirit.* See Rom 8:14. *not under the Law.* Not under the bondage of trying to please God by minute observance of the Law for salvation or sanctification (see note on Rom 6:14).

5:19–21 For other lists of vices see 1 Cor 6:9–10; Eph 5:5; Rev 22:15.

5:22–23 For other lists of virtues see 2 Cor 6:6; Eph 4:2; 5:9; Col 3:12–15. Christian character is produced by the Holy Spirit, not by the mere moral discipline of trying to live by law. Paul makes it clear that justification by faith does not result in libertinism. The indwelling Holy Spirit produces Christian virtues in the believer's life.

5:22 *fruit of the Spirit.* Compare the singular "fruit" with the plural "deeds" (v. 19).

5:23 *no law.* See 1 Tim 1:9.

5:24 *crucified the flesh.* See 2:20; 6:14.

5:25 *walk by.* Or "walk in line with," a different Greek verb from "walk by" in v. 16.

6:1 *Brethren.* See note on 1:2. *you who are spiritual.* Contrast with 1 Cor 3:1–3. *restore.* The Greek for this verb is used elsewhere for setting bones, mending nets, or bringing factions together.

6:2 *Bear one another's burdens.* The emphasis is on moral burdens or weaknesses (see v.1; Rom 15:1–3). *law of Christ.* See note on 1 Cor 9:21.

6:4 *each one must examine his own work.* The emphasis here is on personal responsibility (see 1 Cor 11:28; 2 Cor 13:5).

6:5 *bear his own load.* The "for" at the beginning of the verse connects it with v. 4. Each of us is responsible before God. The reference may be to the future judgment (the verb is in the

6 [a]The one who is taught [b]the word is to
share all good things with the one who
teaches *him.*
7 [a]Do not be deceived, [b]God is not
mocked; for [c]whatever a man sows, this he
will also reap.
8 [a]For the one who sows to his own flesh
will from the flesh reap [b]corruption, but [c]the
one who sows to the Spirit will from the Spirit reap eternal life.
9 [a]Let us not lose heart in doing good,
for in due time we will reap if we [b]do not
grow weary.
10 So then, [1][a]while we have opportunity,
let us do good to all people, and especially to
those who are of the [b]household of [c]the
faith.
11 See with what large letters I [1]am writing to you [a]with my own hand.
12 Those who desire [a]to make a good
showing in the flesh try to [b]compel you to be
circumcised, simply so that they [c]will not be
persecuted [1]for the cross of Christ.
13 For those who [1]are circumcised do not
even [a]keep [2]the Law themselves, but they
desire to have you circumcised so that they
may [b]boast in your flesh.
14 But [a]may it never be that I would
boast, [b]except in the cross of our Lord Jesus
Christ, [c]through [1]which the world has been
crucified to me, and [d]I to the world.
15 For [a]neither is circumcision anything,
nor uncircumcision, but a [b]new [1]creation.
16 And those who will [1]walk by this rule,
peace and mercy *be* upon them, and upon
the [a]Israel of God.
17 From now on let no one cause trouble
for me, for I bear on my body the [a]brand-
marks of Jesus.
18 [a]The grace of our Lord Jesus Christ be
[b]with your spirit, [c]brethren. Amen.

6 [a]1 Cor 9:11, 14 [b]2 Tim 4:2 **7** [a]1 Cor 6:9 [b]Job 13:9 [c]2 Cor 9:6 **8** [a]Job 4:8; Hos 8:7; Rom 6:21 [b]1 Cor 15:42 [c]Rom 8:11; James 3:18 **9** [a]1 Cor 15:58; 2 Cor 4:1 [b]Matt 10:22; Heb 12:3, 5; James 5:7f **10** [1]Or *as* [a]Prov 3:27; John 12:35 [b]Eph 2:19; Heb 3:6; 1 Pet 2:5; 4:17 [c]Acts 6:7; Gal 1:23 **11** [1]Or *have written* [a]1 Cor 16:21 **12** [1]Or *because of* [a]Matt 23:27f [b]Acts 15:1 [c]Gal 5:11 **13** [1]Two early mss read *have been* [2]Or *law* [a]Rom 2:25 [b]Phil 3:3

14 [1]Or *whom* [a]Luke 20:16; Gal 2:17; 3:21 [b]1 Cor 2:2 [c]Gal 2:20; Col 2:20 [d]Rom 6:2, 6; Gal 2:19f; 5:24 **15** [1]Or *creature* [a]Rom 2:26, 28; 1 Cor 7:19; Gal 5:6 [b]2 Cor 5:17; Eph 2:10, 15; 4:24; Col 3:10 **16** [1]Or *follow this rule* [a]Rom 9:6; Gal 3:7, 29; Phil 3:3 **17** [a]Is 44:5; Ezek 9:4; 2 Cor 4:10; 11:23; Rev 13:16 **18** [a]Rom 16:20 [b]2 Tim 4:22 [c]Acts 1:15; Rom 1:13; Gal 3:15; 4:12, 28, 31

future tense), when every person will give an account to God (Rom 14:12; 2 Cor 5:10).
6:6 *share all good things.* See Phil 4:14–19.
6:7 *whatever a man sows, this he will also reap.* See 2 Cor 9:6. As vv. 8–9 show, the principle applies not only negatively but also positively.
6:8 See Rom 8:13. *corruption.* See 5:19–21. *eternal life.* In 5:21 Paul speaks of inheriting "the kingdom of God," here of reaping "eternal life." The first focuses on the realm (sphere, context) that will be inherited (as Israel inherited the promised land); the second focuses on the blessed life that will be enjoyed in that realm.
6:10 *especially to those who are of the household of the faith.* See 1 Tim 5:8.
6:11 *large letters.* May have been for emphasis or, as some have suggested, because he had poor eyesight (see note on 4:13). *with my own hand.* The letter up to this point had probably been dictated to a scribe, after which Paul took the pen in his own hand and finished the letter.
6:12 *compel you to be circumcised.* Cf. 2:3. *that they will not be persecuted.* By advocating circumcision (see 5:11) the Judaizers were less apt to experience opposition from the Jewish opponents of Christianity. They were thinking only of themselves. See Introduction: Occasion and Purpose.
6:14 *boast, except in the cross.* See 1 Cor 1:31; 2:2. *the world.* All that is against God. *crucified to me, and I to the world.* See 2:19–20; 5:24; see also notes on James 4:4; 1John 2:15.
6:15 *new creation.* In Christ man undergoes a transformation that results in an entirely new being. Creation again takes place (see 2 Cor 5:17).
6:16 *this rule.* See vv. 14–15. *peace and mercy.* Cf. Ps 125:5; 128:6. *Israel of God.* Christian Jews. If the conjunction is translated as "even" instead of "and," the phrase stands in contrast to "Israel according to flesh" (a literal rendering of the Greek for "nation Israel" in 1 Cor 10:18). The NT church, made up of believing Jews and Gentiles, is the new seed of Abraham and the heir according to the promise (3:29; cf. Rom 9:6; Phil 3:3).
6:17 *brand-marks of Jesus.* In ancient times the Greek word was used of the brand-marks that identified slaves or animals. Paul's suffering (stoning, Acts 14:19; beatings, Acts 16:22; 2 Cor 11:25; illness, 2 Cor 12:7; Gal 4:13–14) marked him as a "bond-servant of Christ" (1:10; cf. 2 Cor 4:10).
6:18 *Amen.* A word of confirmation often used at the close of a doxology or benediction.

Ephesians

INTRODUCTION

Author, Date and Place of Writing

The author identifies himself as Paul (1:1; 3:1; cf. 3:7,13; 4:1; 6:19–20). Some have taken the absence of the usual personal greetings and the verbal similarity of many parts to Colossians, among other reasons, as grounds for doubting authorship by the apostle Paul. However, this was probably a circular letter, intended for other churches in addition to the one in Ephesus (see notes on 1:1,15; 6:21–23). Paul may have written it about the same time as Colossians, c. A.D. 60, while he was in prison at Rome (see 3:1; 4:1; 6:20).

The City of Ephesus

Ephesus was the most important city in western Asia Minor (now Turkey). It had a harbor that at that time opened into the Cayster River, which in turn emptied into the Aegean Sea. Because it was also at an inter-

Ephesus in the Time of Paul

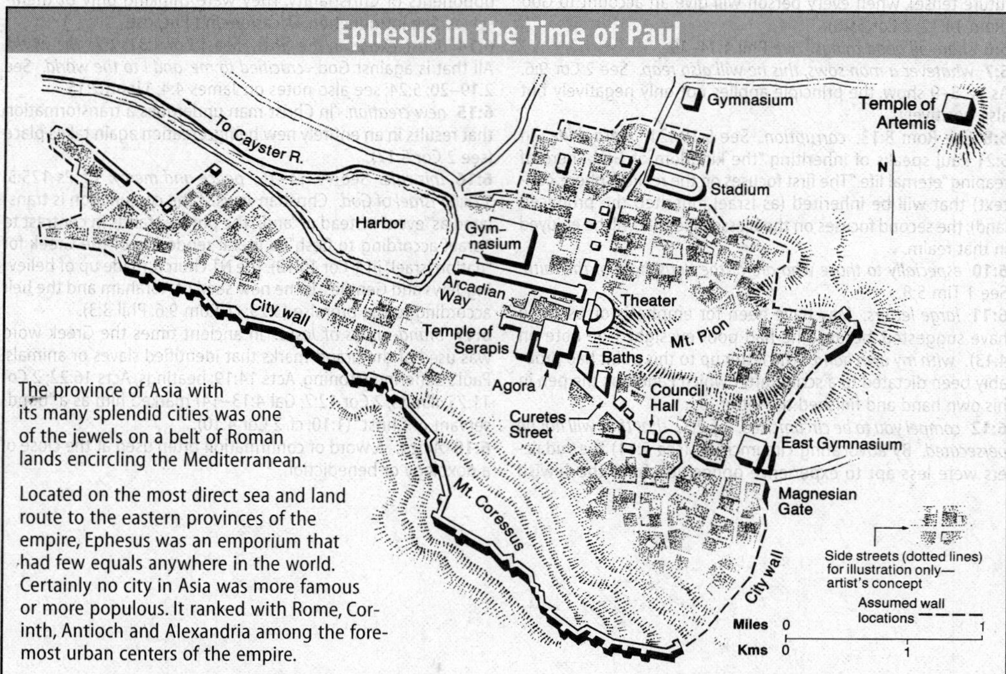

The province of Asia with its many splendid cities was one of the jewels on a belt of Roman lands encircling the Mediterranean.

Located on the most direct sea and land route to the eastern provinces of the empire, Ephesus was an emporium that had few equals anywhere in the world. Certainly no city in Asia was more famous or more populous. It ranked with Rome, Corinth, Antioch and Alexandria among the foremost urban centers of the empire.

Situated on an inland harbor (now silted up), the city was connected by a narrow channel via the Cayster River with the Aegean Sea some three miles away. Ephesus boasted impressive civic monuments, including, most prominently, the temple of Artemis (Diana), one of the seven wonders of the ancient world. Coins of the city proudly displayed the slogan Neokoros, "temple-warden."

Here in Ephesus Paul preached to large crowds of people. The silversmiths complained that he had influenced large numbers of people here in Ephesus and in practically the whole province of Asia (Ac 19:26). In one of the most dramatic events recorded in the NT, the apostle escaped a huge mob in the theater. This structure, located on the slope of Mt. Pion at the end of the Arcadian Way, could seat 25,000 people!

Other places doubtless familiar to the apostle were the Commercial Agora, the Magnesian Gate, the Town Hall or "Council House," and the Street of the Curetes. The location of the lecture hall of Tyrannus, where Paul taught, is unknown.

section of major trade routes, Ephesus became a commercial center. It boasted a pagan temple dedicated to the Roman goddess Diana (Greek *Artemis*); cf. Acts 19:23–31. Paul made Ephesus a center for evangelism for about three years (see note on Acts 19:10), and the church there apparently flourished for some time, but later needed the warning of Rev 2:1–7.

Message

Unlike several of the other letters Paul wrote, Ephesians does not address any particular error or heresy. Paul wrote to expand the horizons of his readers, so that they might understand better the dimensions of God's eternal purpose and grace and come to appreciate the high goals God has for the church.

The letter opens with a sequence of statements about God's blessings, which are interspersed with a remarkable variety of expressions drawing attention to God's wisdom, forethought and purpose. Paul emphasizes that we have been saved, not only for our personal benefit, but also to bring praise and glory to God. The climax of God's purpose, in the "fullness of the times," is to bring all things in the universe together under Christ (1:10). It is crucially important that Christians realize this, so in 1:15–23 Paul prays for their understanding (a second prayer occurs in 3:14–21).

Having explained God's great goals for the church, Paul proceeds to show the steps toward their fulfillment. First, God has reconciled individuals to Himself as an act of grace (2:1–10). Second, God has reconciled these saved individuals to each other, Christ having broken down the barriers through His own death (2:11–22). But God has done something even beyond this: He has united these reconciled individuals in one body, the church. This is a "mystery" not fully known until it was revealed to Paul (3:1–6). Now Paul is able to state even more clearly what God has intended for the church, namely, that it be the means by which He displays His "manifold wisdom" to the "rulers and the authorities in the heavenly places" (3:7–13). It is clear through the repetition of "heavenly places" (1:3,20; 2:6; 3:10; 6:12) that Christian existence is not merely on an earthly plane. It receives its meaning and significance from heaven, where Christ is exalted at the right hand of God (1:20).

Nevertheless, that life is lived out on earth, where the practical daily life of the believer continues to work out the purposes of God. The ascended Lord gave "gifts" to the members of His church to enable them to minister to one another and so promote unity and maturity (4:1–16). The unity of the church under the headship of Christ foreshadows the uniting of "all things . . . in the heavens and things on the earth" under Christ (1:10). The new life of purity and mutual deference stands in contrast to the old way of life without Christ (4:17—6:9). Those who are "strong in the Lord" have victory over the evil one in the great spiritual conflict, especially through the power of prayer (6:10–20).

Outline

I. Greetings (1:1–2)
II. The Divine Purpose: The Glory and Headship of Christ (1:3–14)
III. Prayer That Christians May Realize God's Purpose and Power (1:15–23)
IV. Steps Toward the Fulfillment of God's Purpose (chs. 2–3)
  A. Salvation of Individuals by Grace (2:1–10)
  B. Reconciliation of Jew and Gentile through the Cross (2:11–18)
  C. Uniting of Jew and Gentile in One Household (2:19–22)
  D. Revelation of God's Wisdom through the Church (3:1–13)
  E. Prayer for Deeper Experience of God's Fullness (3:14–21)
V. Practical Ways to Fulfill God's Purpose in the Church (4:1—6:20)
  A. Unity (4:1–6)
  B. Maturity (4:7–16)
  C. Renewal of Personal Life (4:17—5:20)
  D. Deference in Personal Relationships (5:21—6:9)
    1. Principle (5:21)
    2. Husbands and wives (5:22–33)
    3. Children and parents (6:1–4)
    4. Slaves and masters (6:5–9)
  E. Strength in the Spiritual Conflict (6:10–20)
VI. Conclusion, Final Greetings and Benediction (6:21–24)

The Blessings of Redemption

1 Paul, [a]an apostle of [b]Christ Jesus [1][c]by the
will of God,
To the [2][d]saints who are [3]at [e]Ephesus and
[f]*who are* faithful in [b]Christ Jesus:
2 [a]Grace to you and peace from God our
Father and the Lord Jesus Christ.
3 [a]Blessed *be* the God and Father of our
Lord Jesus Christ, who has blessed us with
every spiritual blessing in [b]the heavenly
places in Christ,
4 just as [a]He chose us in Him before [b]the
foundation of the world, that we would be
[c]holy and blameless before [1]Him. [d]In love
5 [1]He [a]predestined us to [b]adoption as
sons through Jesus Christ to Himself,
[c]according to the [2]kind intention of His will,
6 [a]to the praise of the glory of His grace,
which He freely bestowed on us in [b]the
Beloved.
7 [a]In [1]Him we have [b]redemption [c]through
His blood, the [d]forgiveness of our trespasses,
according to [e]the riches of His grace
8 which He [1]lavished on [2]us. In all wisdom and insight
9 He [1][a]made known to us the mystery of
His will, [b]according to His [2]kind intention
which He [c]purposed in Him
10 with a view to an administration [1]suit-
able to [a]the fullness of the times, *that is,* [b]the
summing up of all things in Christ, things [2]in
the heavens and things on the earth. In Him
11 [1]also we [2][a]have obtained an inheritance, having been [b]predestined [c]according
to His purpose who works all things [d]after
the counsel of His will,
12 to the end that we who were the first to
hope in [1]Christ would be [a]to the praise of
His glory.
13 In [1]Him, you also, after listening to

1:1 [1]Lit *through* [2]Or *holy ones* [3]Three early mss do not contain *at Ephesus* [a]2 Cor 1:1 [b]Rom 8:1 [c]1 Cor 1:1 [d]Acts 9:13 [e]Acts 18:19 [f]Col 1:2
2 [a]Rom 1:7
3 [a]2 Cor 1:3 [b]Eph 1:20; 2:6; 3:10; 6:12
4 [1]Or *Him, in love* [a]Eph 2:10; 2 Thess 2:13f [b]Matt 25:34 [c]Eph 5:27; Col 1:22 [d]Eph 4:2, 15, 16; 5:2
5 [1]Lit *having predestined* [2]Lit *good pleasure* [a]Acts 13:48; Rom 8:29f [b]Rom 8:14ff [c]Phil 2:13; Col 1:19
6 [a]Eph 1:12, 14 [b]Matt 3:17
7 [1]Lit *whom* [a]Col 1:14 [b]Rom 3:24; 1 Cor 1:30; Eph 1:14 [c]Acts 20:28; Rom 3:25 [d]Acts 2:38 [e]Rom 2:4; Eph 1:18; 2:7; 3:8, 16
8 [1]Lit *made abundant toward* [2]Or *us, in all wisdom and insight*
9 [1]Lit *making known* [2]Lit *good pleasure* [a]Rom 11:25; Eph 3:3 [b]1 Cor 1:21; Gal 1:15 [c]Rom 8:28; Eph 1:11
10 [1]Lit *of* [2]Lit *upon* [a]Mark 1:15 [b]Eph 3:15; Phil 2:9f; Col 1:16, 20
11 [1]Lit *in whom also* [2]Or *were made a heritage* [a]Deut 4:20; Eph 1:14; Titus 2:14 [b]Eph 1:5 [c]Rom 8:28f; Eph 3:11 [d]Rom 9:11; Heb 6:17
12 [1]I.e. the Messiah [a]Eph 1:6, 14
13 [1]Lit *whom*

1:1 *apostle.* One specially commissioned by Christ (see notes on Mark 6:30; 1 Cor 1:1; Heb 3:1). *by the will of God.* Paul not only stresses his authority under God, but also anticipates the strong emphasis he will make later in this chapter and book on God's sovereign plan and purpose. *at Ephesus.* The book may have been intended as a circular letter to several churches, including the one at Ephesus (see notes on v. 15; 6:21–23; Acts 19:10). *in Christ.* This phrase (or a similar one) occurs 11 times in vv. 1–13. It refers to the spiritual union of Christ with believers, which Paul often symbolizes by the metaphor "body (of Christ)" (see, e.g., v. 23; 2:16; 4:4,12,16; 5:23,30).

1:2 *Grace to you and peace.* Although these words were commonly used in the greetings of secular letters, the words that follow show that Paul intended a spiritual dimension. He uses the word "grace" 12 times and "peace" 8 times in Ephesians.

1:3–14 All one sentence in Greek, this section is often called a "doxology" because it recites what God has done and is an expression of worship to honor Him. Paul speaks first of the blessings we have through the Father (v. 3), then of those that come through the Son (vv. 4–13a) and finally of those through the Holy Spirit (1:13b–14).

1:3 *Father of our Lord Jesus Christ.* Jesus' relation to God the Father is unique (see John 20:17 and note). *blessed . . . blessing.* Jewish people used the word "bless" to express both God's kindness to us and our thanks or praise to him. *heavenly places.* Occurs five times in Ephesians, emphasizing Paul's perception that in the exaltation of Christ (His resurrection and enthronement at God's right hand) and in the Christian's union with the exalted Christ ultimate issues are involved—issues that pertain to the divine realm and that in the final analysis are worked out in and from that realm. At stake are God's eternal eschatological purpose (3:11) and the titanic conflict between God and the powerful spiritual forces arrayed against Him—a purpose and a conflict that come to focus in the history of redemption. Here (v. 3) Paul asserts that, through their union with the exalted Christ, Christians have already been made beneficiaries of every spiritual blessing that belongs to and comes from the heavenly places. In vv. 20–22, he proclaims Christ's exaltation to that realm and His elevation over all other powers and titles so that He rules over all for the sake of His church. According to 2:6, those who have been made alive with Christ (2:5) share in Christ's exaltation and enthronement in heaven. Thus (3:10) by the gathering of Gentiles and Jews into one body of Christ (the church), God triumphantly displays His "manifold wisdom" to the "the rulers and the authorities" in the heavenly realm. As a result, the spiritual struggle of the saints here and now is not so much against "flesh and blood" as against the great spiritual forces that war against God in heaven (6:12).

1:4 *chose.* Divine election is a constant theme in Paul's letters (Rom 8:29–33; 9:6–26; 11:5,7,28; 16:13; Col 3:12; 1 Thess 1:4; 2 Thess 2:13; Titus 1:1). In this chapter it is emphasized in the following ways: (1) "He chose us" (here); (2) "He predestined us" (v. 5); (3) "also we have obtained an inheritance" (v. 11); (4) "having been predestined" (v. 11). *before the foundation of the world.* See John 17:24. *holy and blameless.* See 5:27 for the same pair of words. Holiness is the result—not the basis—of God's choosing. It refers both to the holiness imparted to the believer because of Christ and to the believer's personal sanctification (see note on 1 Cor 1:2). *In love.* Cf. 3:17; 4:2,15–16; 5:2.

1:5 *adoption.* See note on Rom 8:23.

1:6 *to the praise.* See vv. 12,14. Election is for God's glory.

1:7 *redemption.* See v. 14; 4:30; Rom 3:24; Titus 2:14. The Ephesians were familiar with the Greco-Roman practice of redemption: Slaves were freed by the payment of a ransom. Similarly, the ransom necessary to free sinners from the bondage of sin and the resulting curse imposed by the law (see Gal 3:13) was the death of Christ (called here "His blood"). *through His blood.* Cf. 2:13; 1 Pet 1:18–19.

1:9 *mystery.* See notes on Rom 11:25; Col 1:26.

1:10 *the summing up . . . in Christ.* Paul uses a significant term here that not only has the idea of leadership but also was often used of adding up a column of figures. A contemporary way of putting it might be to say that in a world of confusion, where things do not "add up" or make sense, we look forward to the time when everything will be brought into meaningful relationship under the headship of Christ. *In Him.* Christ is the center of God's plan. Whether the universe or the individual Christian is in view, it is only in relationship to Christ that there is a meaningful future destiny. Paul goes on to speak, not of the world as a whole, but of those who respond to God's call.

1:12 *we who were the first to hope in Christ.* Probably a reference to those Jews who, like Paul, had become believers before many Gentiles had.

1:13 *you also.* Probably refers to the majority of the Ephesians,

[a]the message of truth, the gospel of your salvation—having also [2]believed, you were
[b]sealed in [1]Him with [c]the Holy Spirit of
promise,
14 who is [1][a]given as a pledge of [b]our
inheritance, with a view to the [c]redemption
of [d]*God's own* possession, [e]to the praise of
His glory.
15 For this reason I too, [a]having heard of
the faith in the Lord Jesus which *exists*
among you and [1]your love for [b]all the [2]saints,
16 [a]do not cease giving thanks for you,
[b]while making mention *of you* in my prayers;
17 that the [a]God of our Lord Jesus Christ,
[b]the Father of glory, may give to you a spirit
of [c]wisdom and of [d]revelation in the [1]knowl-
edge of Him.
18 *I pray that* [a]the eyes of your heart [1]may
be enlightened, so that you will know what
is the [b]hope of His [c]calling, what are [d]the
riches of the glory of [e]His inheritance in [f]the
[2]saints,
19 and what is the surpassing greatness of
His power toward us who believe. [a]*These are*
in accordance with the working of the
[b]strength of His might
20 which He brought about in Christ,
when He [a]raised Him from the dead and
[b]seated Him at His right hand in [c]the heavenly *places*,
21 far above [a]all rule and authority and
power and dominion, and every [b]name that
is named, not only in [c]this age but also in
the one to come.
22 And He [a]put all things in subjection
under His feet, and gave Him as [b]head over
all things to the church,
23 which is His [a]body, the [b]fullness of
Him who [c]fills [d]all in all.

13 [2]Or *believed in Him, you were sealed* [a]Eph 4:21; Col 1:5 [b]Eph 4:30 [c]Acts 2:33
14 [1]Or *a down payment* [a]2 Cor 1:22 [b]Acts 20:32 [c]Eph 1:7 [d]Eph 1:11 [e]Eph 1:6, 12
15 [1]Three early mss do not contain *your love* [2]V 1, note 2 [a]Col 1:4; Philem 5 [b]Eph 1:1; 3:18
16 [a]Rom 1:8f; Col 1:9 [b]Rom 1:9
17 [1]Or *true knowledge* [a]John 20:17; Rom 15:6 [b]Acts 7:2; 1 Cor 2:8 [c]Col 1:9 [d]1 Cor 14:6
18 [1]Lit *being* [2]Or *holy ones* [a]Acts 26:18; 2 Cor 4:6; Heb 6:4 [b]Eph 4:4 [c]Rom 11:29 [d]Eph 1:7 [e]Eph 1:11 [f]Col 1:12
19 [a]Eph 3:7; Col 1:29 [b]Eph 6:10
20 [a]Acts 2:24 [b]Mark 16:19 [c]Eph 1:3
21 [a]Matt 28:18; Col 1:16 [b]Phil 2:9; Rev 19:12 [c]Matt 12:32
22 [a]Ps 8:6; 1 Cor 15:27
22 [b]1 Cor 11:3; Eph 4:15; Col 1:18
23 [a]1 Cor 12:27; Eph 4:12; Col 1:18, 24 [b]John 1:16; Eph 3:19 [c]Eph 4:10 [d]Col 3:11

Made Alive in Christ

2 And you [1]were [a]dead [2]in your trespasses
and sins,
2 in which you [a]formerly walked according to the [1]course of [b]this world, according
to [c]the prince of the power of the air, of the
spirit that is now working in [d]the sons of disobedience.
3 Among them we too all [a]formerly lived
in [b]the lusts of our flesh, [1]indulging the
desires of the flesh and of the [2]mind, and
were [c]by nature [d]children of wrath, [e]even as
the rest.
4 But God, being [a]rich in mercy, because
of [b]His great love with which He loved us,
5 even when we were [a]dead [1]in our
transgressions, made us alive together [2]with
Christ ([b]by grace you have been saved),
6 and [a]raised us up with Him, and [b]seat-
ed us with Him in [c]the heavenly *places* in
[d]Christ Jesus,
7 so that in the ages to come He might
show the surpassing [a]riches of His grace in
[b]kindness toward us in Christ Jesus.

2:1 [1]Lit *being* [2]Or *by reason of* [a]Eph 2:5; Col 2:13
2 [1]Lit *age* [a]1 Cor 6:11; Eph 2:3 [b]Eph 1:21 [c]John 12:31; Eph 6:12 [d]Eph 5:6
3 [1]Lit *doing* [2]Lit *thoughts* [a]Eph 2:2 [b]Gal 5:16f [c]Rom 2:14; Gal 2:15 [d]Rom 5:9; Col 1:21; 2 Pet 2:14 [e]Rom 5:12
4 [a]Eph 1:7 [b]John 3:16
5 [1]Or *by reason of* [2]Two early mss read *in Christ* [a]Eph 2:1 [b]Acts 15:11
6 [a]Col 2:12 [b]Eph 1:20 [c]Eph 1:3 [d]Eph 1:1; 2:10, 13
7 [a]Rom 2:4; Eph 1:7 [b]Titus 3:4

---

who were Gentiles. *sealed.* In those days a seal denoted ownership.

1:14 *pledge.* See note on Rom 8:23.

1:15 *having heard.* This sounds strange from one who had spent a few years in Ephesus. He may be referring to a greatly enlarged church there, many of whom Paul did not know, or, if Ephesians was intended as a circular letter (see note on v. 1), he may be referring to news from the whole area, only a part of which he had visited.

1:17 *God of our Lord Jesus Christ.* See note on v. 3. *Him.* God the Father.

1:18 *eyes of your heart.* Your mind or understanding or inner awareness. *hope.* Has an objective quality of certainty (see Rom 8:25). It is the assurance of eternal life guaranteed by the present possession of the Holy Spirit (see v. 14). *calling.* See Phil 3:14; 2 Tim 1:9; Heb 3:1. *the glory of His inheritance in the saints.* Either the inheritance we have from God (see v. 14; Col 1:12) or the inheritance God receives, i.e., the saints themselves. *saints.* Those whom God has called to be His own people, i.e., all Christians (see vv. 1,15). The word carried the idea of dedication to a deity.

1:19 In this verse Paul piles term upon term to emphasize that the extraordinary divine force by which Jesus Christ was raised (v. 20) is the same power at work in and through believers.

1:20 *right hand.* The symbolic place of highest honor and authority.

1:21 *all rule . . . every name that is named.* Including whatever supernatural beings his contemporaries might conceive of, for in his day many people believed not only in the existence of angels and demons, but also in that of other beings. Christ is above them all. *this age . . . the one to come.* Like the rabbinic teachers of his day, Paul distinguishes between the present age, which is evil, and the future age when the Messiah will consummate His kingdom and there will be a completely righteous society on earth.

1:22 *under His feet.* Ps 8:5–6 emphasizes the destiny of man, and Heb 2:6–9 shows that ultimately it is the Son of Man who rules over everything (cf. Heb 10:13). *head.* Christ is not only head of the church, but also head over everything (see note on v. 10).

1:23 *His body.* See 2:16; 4:4,12,16; 5:23,30. *fullness . . . fills.* The church is the fullness of Christ probably in the sense that it is filled by Him who fills all things.

2:1–10 In ch. 1 Paul wrote of the great purposes and plan of God, culminating in the universal headship of Christ (1:10), all of which is to be for "the praise of His glory" (1:14). He now proceeds to explain the steps by which God will accomplish His purposes, beginning with the salvation of individuals.

2:1 A description of their past moral and spiritual condition, separated from the life of God.

2:2 *prince.* Satan (cf. John 14:30, "ruler"). *air.* Satan is no mere earthbound enemy (cf. 6:12). *spirit.* Satan is a created, but not a human, being (cf. Job 1:6; Ezek 28:15; see note on Is 14:12–15).

2:3 *we . . . all.* Jews and Gentiles. *children of wrath.* See Rom 1:18–20; 2:5; 9:22.

2:5 *made us alive together with Christ.* This truth is expanded in Rom 6:1–10.

2:6 *heavenly places.* See note on 1:3. *in Christ Jesus.* Through our union with Christ.

2:7 *ages to come.* Cf. 1:21; probably refers to the future of eternal blessing with Christ. *show.* Or "exhibit" or "prove."

8 For [a]by grace you have been saved [b]through faith; and [1]that not of yourselves, *it is* [c]the gift of God;

9 [a]not as a result of works, so that [b]no one may boast.

10 For we are His workmanship, [a]created in [b]Christ Jesus for [c]good works, which God [d]prepared beforehand so that we would [e]walk in them.

11 Therefore remember that [a]formerly [b]you, the Gentiles in the flesh, who are called "[c]Uncircumcision" by the so-called "[c]Circumcision," *which is* performed in the flesh by human hands—

12 *remember* that you were at that time separate from Christ, [1a]excluded from the commonwealth of Israel, and strangers to [b]the covenants of promise, having [c]no hope and [d]without God in the world.

13 But now in [a]Christ Jesus you who [b]formerly were [c]far off [1]have [c]been brought near [2d]by the blood of Christ.

14 For He Himself is [a]our peace, [b]who made both *groups into* one and broke down the [1]barrier of the dividing wall,

15 [1]by [a]abolishing in His flesh the enmity, *which is* [b]the Law of commandments *contained* in ordinances, so that in Himself He might [2c]make the two into [d]one new man, *thus* establishing [e]peace,

16 and might [a]reconcile them both in [b]one body to God through the cross, [1]by it having [c]put to death the enmity.

17 AND [a]HE CAME AND PREACHED [b]PEACE TO YOU WHO WERE [c]FAR AWAY, AND PEACE TO THOSE WHO WERE [c]NEAR;

18 for through Him we both have [a]our access in [b]one Spirit to [c]the Father.

19 So then you are no longer [a]strangers and aliens, but you are [b]fellow citizens with the [1]saints, and are of [c]God's household,

20 having been [a]built on [b]the foundation of [c]the apostles and prophets, [d]Christ Jesus Himself being the [e]corner *stone*,

21 [a]in whom the whole building, being fitted together, is growing into [b]a holy [1]temple in the Lord,

8 [1]I.e. that salvation [a]Acts 15:11; Eph 2:5 [b]1 Pet 1:5 [c]John 4:10
9 [a]Rom 3:28; 2 Tim 1:9 [b]1 Cor 1:29
10 [a]Eph 2:15; 4:24; Col 3:10 [b]Eph 1:1; 2:6, 13 [c]Titus 2:14 [d]Eph 1:4 [e]Eph 4:1
11 [a]Eph 2:2 [b]1 Cor 12:2; Eph 5:8 [c]Rom 2:28f; Col 2:11
12 [1]Or *alienated* [a]Rom 9:4; Col 1:21 [b]Gal 3:17; Heb 8:6 [c]1 Thess 4:13 [d]Gal 4:8; 1 Thess 4:5
13 [1]Lit *became;* or *were made* [2]Or *in* [a]Eph 1:1; 2:6 [b]Eph 2:2 [c]Is 57:19; Acts 2:39; Eph 2:17 [d]Rom 3:25; Col 1:20
14 [1]Lit *the dividing wall of the barrier* [a]Is 9:6; Eph 2:15; Col 3:15 [b]1 Cor 12:13; Gal 3:28; Col 3:11
15 [1]Or *the enmity, by abolishing in His flesh the Law* [2]Lit *create* [a]Eph 2:16; Col 1:21f [b]Col 2:14, 20 [c]Gal 3:28; Eph 2:10; Col 3:10, 11 [d]Gal 3:28; Col 3:10f [e]Is 9:6; Eph 2:14; Col 3:15
16 [1]Or *in Himself* [a]2 Cor 5:18; Col 1:20, 22 [b]1 Cor 10:17; Eph 4:4 [c]Eph 2:15
17 [a]Is 57:19; Rom 10:14 [b]Acts 10:36; Eph 2:14 [c]Eph 2:13
18 [a]Rom 5:2; Eph 3:12 [b]1 Cor 12:13; Eph 4:4 [c]Col 1:12
19 [1]Or *holy ones* [a]Eph 2:12; Heb 11:13; 1 Pet 2:11 [b]Phil 3:20; Heb 12:22f [c]Gal 6:10
20 [a]1 Cor 3:9 [b]Matt 16:18; 1 Cor 3:10; Rev 21:14 [c]1 Cor 12:28; Eph 3:5 [d]1 Cor 3:11 [e]Ps 118:22; Luke 20:17
21 [1]Or *sanctuary* [a]Eph 4:15f; Col 2:19 [b]1 Cor 3:16f

2:8 A major passage for understanding God's grace, i.e., His kindness, unmerited favor and forgiving love. *you have been saved.* "Saved" has a wide range of meanings. It includes salvation from God's wrath, which we all had incurred by our sinfulness. The tense of the verb (also in v. 5) suggests a completed action with emphasis on its present effect. *through faith.* See Rom 3:21–31 (and notes on that passage), which establishes the necessity of faith in Christ as the only means of being made right with God. *not of yourselves.* No human effort can contribute to our salvation; it is the gift of God.

2:9 *not as a result of works.* One cannot earn salvation by the "works of the Law" (Rom 3:20, 28). Such a legalistic approach to salvation (or sanctification) is consistently condemned in Scripture. *no one may boast.* No one can take credit for his or her salvation.

2:10 *workmanship.* The Greek for this word sometimes has the connotation of a "work of art." *prepared beforehand.* Carries forward the theme of God's sovereign purpose and planning, seen in ch. 1.

2:11–22 From the salvation of individuals, Paul moves to another aspect of salvation in which God reconciles Jews and Gentiles, previously hostile peoples, not only to Himself but also to each other through Christ (vv. 11–16). Even more than that, God unites these now reconciled people in one body, a truth introduced in vv. 19–22 and explained in ch. 3.

2:11 *Therefore.* Refers to the state of those without Christ, described in vv. 1–10. *you, the Gentiles.* Most of the Ephesians (cf. 1:13, "you also"). *"Uncircumcision" . . . "Circumcision."* The rite of circumcision was applied to all Jewish male babies; so this physical act ("performed in the flesh by human hands") was a clear mark of distinction between Jew and Gentile, in which Jewish people naturally took pride.

2:12 *at that time.* Before salvation, in contrast to "But now" (v. 13). *separate from Christ . . . without God.* All these expressions emphasize the distance of unbelieving Gentiles from Israel, as well as from Christ. *covenants.* God had promised blessings to and through the Jewish people (see note on Rom 9:4).

2:13 *But now.* Not only contrasts with "at that time" (v. 12) but also introduces the contrast between "from Christ" (v. 12) and "in Christ" (here). *blood of Christ.* Expresses the violent death of Christ as He poured out His lifeblood as a sacrifice for us (cf. 1:7).

2:14 *both.* Believing Jews and believing Gentiles. *barrier . . . dividing wall.* Vivid description of the total religious isolation Jews and Gentiles experienced from each other.

2:15 *abolishing . . . the Law.* Since Matt 5:17 and Rom 3:31 teach that God's moral standard expressed in the OT law is not changed by the coming of Christ, what is abolished here is probably the effect of the specific "commandments contained in ordinances" in separating Jews from Gentiles, whose nonobservance of the Jewish law renders them ritually unclean. *in His flesh.* Probably refers to the death of Christ. *one new man.* The united body of believers, the church.

2:16 *one body.* While this could possibly mean the body of Christ offered on the cross (cf. "in His flesh," v. 15), it probably refers to the "one new man" just mentioned, the body of believers.

2:17 *FAR AWAY . . . NEAR.* Gentiles and Jews respectively.

2:19 *So then.* Paul indicates that the unity described in vv. 19–22 is based on what Christ did through His death, described in vv. 14–18. *you.* The Gentiles at Ephesus are particularly in mind here. *citizens . . . household.* Familiar imagery. The household in ancient times was what we today might call an "extended family."

2:20 *foundation.* Further metaphorical language to convey the idea of a solid, integrated structure. *apostles and prophets.* Probably refers to the founding work of the early Christian apostles and prophets as they preached and taught God's word (cf. 1 Cor 3:10–11). *corner stone.* Is 28:16, which uses the same term in its pre-Christian Greek translation (the Septuagint), refers to a foundation with a "tested" stone at the corner.

2:21 *fitted together.* Cf. 4:16 for the same word. Both passages speak of the close relationship between believers. *growing.* The description of a building under construction conveys the sense of the dynamic growth of the church. *holy temple.* Paul now uses the metaphor of a temple, thereby indicating the purpose ("to become") for which God has established His church.

22 in whom you also are being [a]built together into a [b]dwelling of God in the Spirit.

Paul's Stewardship

3 For this reason I, Paul, [a]the prisoner of
[b]Christ Jesus [c]for the sake of you [d]Gentiles—
2 if indeed you have heard of the [a]stewardship of God's grace which was given to
me for you;
3 [a]that [b]by revelation there was [c]made
known to me [d]the mystery, [e]as I wrote
before in brief.
4 [1]By referring to this, when you read
you can understand [a]my insight [2]into the
[b]mystery of Christ,
5 which in other generations was not
made known to the sons of men, as it has
now been revealed to His holy [a]apostles and
prophets [1]in the Spirit;
6 *to be specific,* that the Gentiles are [a]fellow heirs and [b]fellow members of the body,
and [c]fellow partakers of the promise in
[d]Christ Jesus through the gospel,
7 [a]of which I was made a [b]minister,
according to the gift of [c]God's grace which
was given to me [d]according to the working
of His power.
8 To me, [a]the very least of all [1]saints, this
grace was given, to [b]preach to the Gentiles
the unfathomable [c]riches of Christ,
9 and to [1]bring to light what is the
administration of the [a]mystery which for
ages has been [b]hidden in God [c]who created
all things;
10 so that the manifold [a]wisdom of God
might now be [b]made known through the
church to the [c]rulers and the authorities in
[d]the heavenly *places.*
11 *This was* in [a]accordance with the [1]eternal purpose which He [2]carried out in [b]Christ
Jesus our Lord,
12 in whom we have boldness and [1a]confident [b]access through faith [2]in Him.
13 Therefore I ask [1]you not [a]to lose heart
at my tribulations [b]on your behalf, [2]for they
are your glory.
14 For this reason I [a]bow my knees before
the Father,

22 [a]1 Cor 3:9, 16; 2 Cor 6:16 [b]Eph 3:17 **3:1** [a]Acts 23:18; Eph 4:1; 2 Tim 1:8; Philem 1, 9, 23 [b]Gal 5:24 [c]2 Cor 1:6; Eph 3:13 [d]Eph 3:8 **2** [a]Eph 1:10; 3:9; Col 1:25; 1 Tim 1:4 **3** [a]Acts 22:17, 21; 26:16ff [b]Gal 1:12 [c]Eph 1:9; 3:4, 6, 9 [d]Rom 11:25; 16:25; Eph 3:4, 9; 6:19; Col 1:26f; 4:3 [e]Eph 1:9f; Heb 13:22; 1 Pet 5:12 **4** [1]Lit *To which, when you read* [2]Lit *in* [a]2 Cor 11:6 [b]Rom 11:25; 16:25; Eph 3:3, 9; 6:19; Col 1:26f; 4:3 **5** [1]Or *by* [a]1 Cor 12:28; Eph 2:20 **6** [a]Gal 3:29 [b]Eph 2:16 [c]Eph 5:7 [d]Gal 5:24 **7** [a]Col 1:23, 25 [b]1 Cor 3:5 [c]Acts 9:15; Rom 12:3; Eph 3:2 [d]Eph 1:19; 3:20 **8** [1]Or *holy ones* [a]1 Cor 15:9 [b]Acts 9:15; Eph 3:1f [c]Rom 2:4; Eph 1:7; 3:16 **9** [1]Two early mss read *make all know* [a]Rom 11:25; 16:25; Eph 3:3, 4; 6:19; Col 1:26f; 4:3 [b]Col 3:3 [c]Rev 4:11 **10** [a]Rom 11:33; 1 Cor 2:7 [b]Eph 1:23; 1 Pet 1:12 [c]Eph 1:21; 6:12; Col 2:10, 15 [d]Eph 1:3 **11** [1]Lit *purpose of the ages* [2]Or *formed* [a]Eph 1:11 [b]Gal 5:24; Eph 3:1 **12** [1]Lit *access in confidence* [2]Lit *of Him* [a]2 Cor 3:4; Heb 4:16; 10:19, 35; 1 John 2:28; 3:21 [b]Eph 2:18 **13** [1]Or *that I may not lose* [2]Lit *which are* [a]2 Cor 4:1 [b]Eph 3:1 **14** [a]Phil 2:10

2:22 *dwelling.* The church is to be a people or community in whom the Holy Spirit dwells.

3:1–13 Having saved people individually by His grace (2:1–10), and having reconciled them to each other as well as to Himself through the sacrificial death of Christ (2:11–22), God also now unites them on an equal basis in one body, the church. This step in God's eternal plan was not fully revealed in previous times. Paul calls it a "mystery."

3:1 *For this reason.* Because of all that God has done, explained in the preceding several verses. *prisoner.* Apparently Paul was under house arrest at this time (see Acts 28:16,30). *of Christ.* Paul's physical imprisonment was because he obeyed Christ in spite of opposition. After this verse Paul breaks his train of thought to explain the "mystery" (v. 4). He resumes his initial thought in v. 14.

3:2 *if indeed you have heard.* Most of the Ephesians would have heard of Paul's ministry because of his long stay there earlier. However, if this was a circular letter (see note on 1:1), the other churches may not have known much about it. *stewardship.* Paul unfolds God's administrative plan for the church and for the universe in this letter (see especially 1:3–12). He has been given a significant responsibility in the execution of this plan.

3:3 *mystery.* A truth known only by divine revelation (v. 5; see Rom 16:25; see also notes on Rom 11:25; Col 1:26). Here the word "mystery" has the special meaning of the private, wise plan of God, which in Ephesians relates primarily to the unification of believing Jews and Gentiles in the new body, the church (see v. 6). It may be thought of as a secret that is temporarily hidden, but more than that, it is a plan God is actively working out and revealing stage by stage (cf. 1:9–10; Rev 10:7). *as I wrote before in brief.* May refer to 1:9–10.

3:5 *not made known to the sons of men.* See note on v. 6. *holy.* Set apart for God's service. *apostles and prophets.* See note on 2:20. Although Paul was the chief recipient, others received this revelation also.

3:6 *fellow . . . fellow . . . fellow.* The repetition of this word indicates the unique aspect of the mystery that was not previously known: the equality and mutuality that Gentiles had with Jews in the church, the one body. That Gentiles would turn to the God of Israel and be saved was prophesied in the OT (see Rom 15:9–12); that they would come into an organic unity with believing Jews on an equal footing was unexpected. *heirs.* See note on 1:18.

3:8 *the very least.* Cf. 1 Tim 1:15. Paul never ceased to be amazed that one so unworthy as he should have been chosen for so high a task. His modesty was genuine, even though we may disagree with his self-evaluation. *grace.* In this case, a special endowment that brings responsibility for service. *to preach.* Lit. "to gospelize"; parallels "to bring to light" (v. 9). *unfathomable.* Far beyond what we can know, but not beyond our appreciation—at least in part (cf. Rom 11:33).

3:10 *manifold.* Variegated or multifaceted (in the way that many facets of a diamond reflect and enhance its beauty). *now.* In contrast to the previous "ages" (v. 9). *through the church.* The fact that God had done the seemingly impossible—reconciling and organically uniting Jews and Gentiles in the church—makes the church the perfect means of displaying God's wisdom. *rulers and the authorities.* Christ had ascended over all these (1:20–21). It is a staggering thought that the church on earth is observed, so to speak, by these spiritual powers and that to the degree the church is spiritually united it portrays to them the wisdom of God. This thought may be essential in understanding the meaning of "calling" in 4:1. *heavenly places.* See note on 1:3.

3:11 *eternal purpose.* The effective headship of Christ over a united church is in preparation for His ultimate assumption of headship over the universe (1:10).

3:14–21 Paul now expresses a prayer that grows out of his awareness of all that God is doing in believers. God's key gifts are "power" (vv. 16,20) and "love" (vv. 17–19).

3:14 *For this reason.* Resumes the thought of v. 1. *I bow my knees.* Expresses deep emotion and reverence, as people in Paul's day usually stood to pray.

15 from whom [1]every family in heaven and on earth derives its name,

16 that He would grant you, according to [a]the riches of His glory, to be [b]strengthened with power through His Spirit in [c]the inner man,

17 so that [a]Christ may dwell in your hearts through faith; *and* that you, being [b]rooted and [c]grounded in love,

18 may be able to comprehend with [a]all the [1]saints what is [b]the breadth and length and height and depth,

19 and to know [a]the love of Christ which [b]surpasses knowledge, that you may be [c]filled up to all the [d]fullness of God.

20 [a]Now to Him who is [b]able to do far more abundantly beyond all that we ask or think, [c]according to the power that works within us,

21 [a]to Him *be* the glory in the church and in Christ Jesus to all generations [1]forever and ever. Amen.

Unity of the Spirit

4 Therefore I, [a]the prisoner of the Lord, [b]implore you to [c]walk in a manner worthy of the [d]calling with which you have been [e]called,

2 with all [a]humility and gentleness, with patience, showing tolerance for one another [b]in love,

3 being diligent to preserve the unity of the Spirit in the [a]bond of peace.

4 *There is* [a]one body and one Spirit, just as also you were called in one [b]hope of your calling;

5 [a]one Lord, one faith, one baptism,

6 one God and Father of all [a]who is over all and through all and in all.

7 But [a]to each one of us [b]grace was given [c]according to the measure of Christ's gift.

8 Therefore [1]it says,

"[a]WHEN HE ASCENDED ON HIGH,
HE [b]LED CAPTIVE A HOST OF CAPTIVES,
AND HE GAVE GIFTS TO MEN."

9 (Now this *expression,* "He [a]ascended," what [1]does it mean except that He also [2]had descended into [b]the lower parts of the earth?

10 He who descended is Himself also He who ascended [a]far above all the heavens, so that He might [b]fill all things.)

11 And He [a]gave [b]some *as* apostles, and

15 [1]Or *the whole*
16 [a]Eph 1:18; 3:8 [b]1 Cor 16:13; Phil 4:13; Col 1:11 [c]Rom 7:22
17 [a]John 14:23; Rom 8:9f; 2 Cor 13:5; Eph 2:22 [b]1 Cor 3:6; Col 2:7 [c]Col 1:23
18 [1]V 8, note 1 [a]Eph 1:15 [b]Job 11:8f
19 [a]Rom 8:35, 39 [b]Phil 4:7 [c]Col 2:10 [d]Eph 1:23
20 [a]Rom 16:25 [b]2 Cor 9:8 [c]Eph 3:7
21 [1]Lit *of the age of the ages* [a]Rom 11:36
4:1 [a]Eph 3:1 [b]Rom 12:1 [c]Eph 2:10; Col 1:10; 2:6; 1 Thess 2:12 [d]Rom 11:29 [e]Rom 8:28f
2 [a]Col 3:12f [b]Eph 1:4
3 [a]Col 3:14f
4 [a]1 Cor 12:4ff; Eph 2:16, 18 [b]Eph 1:18
5 [a]1 Cor 8:6
6 [a]Rom 11:36
7 [a]1 Cor 12:7, 11 [b]Eph 3:2 [c]Rom 12:3 **8** [1]Or *He* [a]Ps 68:18 [b]Col 2:15 **9** [1]Lit *is it except* [2]One early ms reads *had first descended* [a]John 3:13 [b]Is 44:23 **10** [a]Eph 1:20f; Heb 4:14; 7:26 [b]Eph 1:23 **11** [a]Eph 4:8 [b]Acts 13:1; 1 Cor 12:28

3:15 *family.* The word in Greek is similar to the word for "father," so it can be said that the "family" derives its name (and being) from the "father." God is our Father, and we can commit our prayers to Him in confidence.

3:17 *dwell.* Be completely at home. Christ was already present in the Ephesian believers' lives (cf. Rom 8:9). *hearts.* The whole inner being.

3:19 *surpasses knowledge.* Not unknowable, but so great that it cannot be completely known. *fullness.* God, who is infinite in all His attributes, allows us to draw on His resources—in this case, His love.

3:20 *more abundantly beyond.* Has specific reference to the matters presented in this section of Ephesians but is not limited to these. *power.* See 1:19–21.

3:21 *to Him be the glory.* The ultimate goal of our existence (see 1:6 and note). *in the church and in Christ Jesus.* A remarkable parallel. God has called the church to an extraordinary position and vocation (cf. v. 10; 4:1).

4:1–32 The chapter begins (v. 2) and ends (v. 32) with exhortations to love and forgive one another.

4:1–16 So far Paul has taught that God brought Jew and Gentile into a new relationship to each other in the church and that he called the church to display his wisdom. Paul now shows how God made provision for those in the church to live and work together in unity and to grow together into maturity.

4:1 *prisoner.* See note on 3:1. *calling.* See 3:10,21 and notes.

4:3 *preserve the unity.* Which God produced through the reconciling death of Christ (see 2:14–22). It is the heavy responsibility of Christians to keep that unity from being disturbed.

4:4 *one hope.* Has different aspects (e.g., 1:5,10; 2:7), but it is still one hope, tied to the glorious future of Christ, in which all believers share.

4:5 *one baptism.* Probably not the baptism of the Spirit (see 1 Cor 12:13), which was inward and therefore invisible, but water baptism (see note on Rom 6:3–4). Since Paul apparently has in mind that which identifies all believers as belonging together, he would naturally refer to that church ordinance in which every new convert participated publicly. At that time it was a more obvious common mark of identification of Christians than it is now, when it is celebrated in different ways and often only seen by those in the church.

4:7 *grace.* See 3:7–8.

4:8 Ps 68:18 (see note there) speaks of God's triumphant ascension to His throne in the temple at Jerusalem (symbol of His heavenly throne). Paul applies this to Christ's triumphal ascension into heaven. Where the psalm states further that God "received gifts among men," Paul apparently takes his cue from certain rabbinic interpretations current in his day that read the Hebrew preposition for "among" in the sense of "to" (a meaning it often has) and the verb for "received" in the sense of "take and give" (a meaning it sometimes has—but with a different preposition; see Gen 15:9; 18:5; 27:13; Ex 25:2; 1 Kin 17:10–11). CAPTIVES. Probably Paul applies this to the spiritual enemies Christ defeated at the cross.

4:9 *ascended . . . descended.* Although Paul quoted from the psalm to introduce the idea of the "gifts to men," he takes the opportunity to remind his readers of Christ's coming to earth (His incarnation) and His subsequent resurrection and ascension. This passage probably does not teach, as some think and as some translations suggest, that Christ descended into hell.

4:11 *He gave.* The quotation from Ps 68 has its ultimate meaning when applied to Christ as the ascended Lord, who Himself has given gifts. *apostles.* Mentioned here because of their role in establishing the church (see 2:20). For qualifications of the initial group of apostles see Acts 1:21–22; see also notes on Mark 6:30; Rom 1:1; 1 Cor 1:1; Heb 3:1. In a broader sense, Paul was also an apostle (see 1:1). *prophets.* People to whom God made known a message for His people that was appropriate to their particular need or situation (see 1 Cor 14:3–4; see also note on 1 Cor 12:10). *evangelists.* See Acts 21:8; 1 Cor 1:17. While the other gifted people helped the church grow through edification, the evangelists helped the church grow by augmentation. Since the objective mentioned in v. 12 is "for the equipping of the saints for the work of service," we may assume

some *as* prophets, and some *as* [c]evangelists,
and some *as* pastors and [d]teachers,
12 [a]for the equipping of the [1]saints for the
work of service, to the building up of [b]the
body of Christ;
13 until we all attain to [a]the unity of the
faith, and of the [1b]knowledge of the Son of
God, to a [c]mature man, to the measure of the
stature [2]which belongs to the [d]fullness of
Christ.
14 [1]As a result, we are [a]no longer to be
children, [b]tossed here and there by waves
and carried about by every wind of doctrine,
by the trickery of men, by [c]craftiness [2]in
[d]deceitful scheming;
15 but [1]speaking the truth [a]in love, [2]we
are to [b]grow up in all *aspects* into Him who
is the [c]head, *even* Christ,
16 from whom [a]the whole body, being fitted and held together [1]by what every joint
supplies, according to the [2]proper working of
each individual part, causes the growth of
the body for the building up of itself [b]in love.

The Christian's Walk

17 [a]So this I say, and affirm together with
the Lord, [b]that you walk no longer just as the
Gentiles also walk, in the [c]futility of their
mind,
18 being [a]darkened in their understanding, [1b]excluded from the life of God because
of the [c]ignorance that is in them, because of
the [d]hardness of their heart;
19 and they, having [a]become callous,
[b]have given themselves over to [c]sensuality
[1]for the practice of every kind of impurity
with greediness.
20 But you did not [a]learn [1]Christ in this
way,
21 if indeed you [a]have heard Him and
have [b]been taught in Him, just as truth is in
Jesus,
22 that, in reference to your former manner of life, you [a]lay aside the [b]old [1]self,
which is being corrupted in accordance with
the [c]lusts of deceit,
23 and that you be [a]renewed in the spirit
of your mind,
24 and [a]put on the [b]new [1]self, which [2c]in
the likeness of God has been created in righteousness and holiness of the truth.

11 [c]Acts 21:8 [d]Acts 13:1 **12** [1]Or *holy ones* [a]2 Cor 13:9 [b]1 Cor 12:27; Eph 1:23 **13** [1]Or *true knowledge* [2]Lit *of the fullness* [a]Eph 4:3, 5 [b]John 6:69; Eph 1:17; Phil 3:10 [c]1 Cor 14:20; Col 1:28; Heb 5:14 [d]John 1:16; Eph 1:23 **14** [1]Lit *So that we will no longer be* [2]Lit *with regard to the scheming of deceit* [a]1 Cor 14:20 [b]James 1:6; Jude 12 [c]1 Cor 3:19; 2 Cor 4:2; 11:3 [d]Eph 6:11 **15** [1]Or *holding to or being truthful in* [2]Or *let us grow up* [a]Eph 1:4 [b]Eph 2:21 [c]Eph 1:22 **16** [1]Lit *through every joint of the supply* [2]Lit *working in measure* [a]Rom 12:4f; Col 2:19 [b]Eph 1:4 **17** [a]Col 2:4 [b]Eph 2:2; 4:22 [c]Rom 1:21; Col 2:18; 1 Pet 1:18; 2 Pet 2:18 **18** [1]Or *alienated* [a]Rom 1:21 [b]Eph 2:1, 12 [c]Acts 3:17; 17:30; 1 Cor 2:8; Heb 5:2; 9:7; 1 Pet 1:14 [d]Mark 3:5; Rom 11:7, 25; 2 Cor 3:14 **19** [1]Or *greedy for the practice of every kind of impurity* [a]1 Tim 4:2 [b]Rom 1:24 [c]Col 3:5 **20** [1]I.e. the Messiah [a]Matt 11:29 **21** [a]Rom 10:14; Eph 1:13; 2:17; Col 1:5 [b]Col 2:7 **22** [1]Lit *man* [a]Eph 4:25, 31; Col 3:8; Heb 12:1; James 1:21; 1 Pet 2:1 [b]Rom 6:6 [c]2 Cor 11:3; Heb 3:13 **23** [a]Rom 12:2 **24** [1]Lit *man* [2]Lit *according to God* [a]Rom 13:14 [b]Rom 6:4; 7:6; 12:2; 2 Cor 5:17; Col 3:10 [c]Eph 2:10

that evangelists, among their various ministries, helped other Christians in their testimony. *pastors and teachers.* Because of the Greek grammatical construction (also, the word "some" introduces both words together), it is clear that these groups of gifted people are closely related. Those who have pastoral care for God's people (the image is that of shepherding) will naturally provide "food" from the Scriptures (teaching). They will be especially gifted as teachers (cf. 1 Tim 3:2).

4:12 *for the equipping of the saints for the work of service.* Those mentioned in v. 11 were not to do all the work for the people, but were to train the people to do the work themselves. *to the building up of the body of Christ.* See v. 16. Spiritual gifts are for the body, the church, and are not to be exercised individualistically. "Building up" reflects the imagery of 2:19–22. Both concepts—body and building—occurring together emphasize the key idea of growth.

4:13 *until.* Expresses not merely duration but also purpose. *unity.* Carries forward the ideal of vv. 1–6. *of the faith.* Here "faith" refers to the Christians' common conviction about Christ and the doctrines concerning Him, as the following words make clear (cf. also "the apostles' teaching" in Acts 2:42). *knowledge of the Son of God.* Unity is not just a matter of a loving attitude or religious feeling, but of truth and a common understanding about God's Son. *mature . . . fullness of Christ.* Not the maturity of doctrinal conviction just mentioned, nor a personal maturity that includes the ability to relate well to other people (cf. vv. 2–3), but the maturity of the perfectly balanced character of Christ.

4:14 *children.* Contrast the maturity of v. 13. *tossed.* The nautical imagery pictures the instability of those who are not strong Christians. *doctrine.* Then, as now, there were many distorted teachings and heresies that would easily throw the immature off course. *trickery . . . craftiness . . . deceitful scheming.* Sometimes those who try to draw people away from the Christian faith are not innocently misguided but deliberately deceitful and evil (cf. 1 Tim 4:1–2).

4:15 *speaking the truth in love.* A truthful and loving manner of life is implied. *grow up . . . head.* A slightly different restatement of v. 13, based now on the imagery of Christ as the Head of the body, which is the church. Paul thus speaks primarily of corporate maturity. It is the "body of Christ" that needs "building up" (v. 12). In v. 13 "we all" are to become "mature".

4:16 Further details of the imagery of the body growing under the direction of the Head. The parts of the body help each other in the growing process, picturing the mutual ministries of God's people spoken of in vv. 11–13. *love.* Maturity and unity are impossible without it (cf. vv. 2,15).

4:17–5:20 Paul has just discussed unity and maturity as twin goals for the church, which God has brought into existence through the death of Christ. He now goes on to show that purity is also essential among those who belong to Him.

4:17 *futility of their mind.* Life without God is intellectually frustrating, useless and meaningless (see, e.g., Eccl 1:2; Rom 1:21).

4:18 *darkened in their understanding.* Continues the idea of a futile thought life. *hardness of their heart.* Moral unresponsiveness.

4:19 *have given themselves over.* Just as Pharaoh's heart was hardened reciprocally by himself and by God (see Ex 7–11), so here the Gentiles have given themselves over to a sinful kind of life, while Rom 1:24,26,28 says that God gave them over to that life.

4:20 *you.* Emphatic.

4:21 *truth is in Jesus.* The wording and the use of the name Jesus (rather than Christ) suggest that Paul is referring to the embodiment of truth in Jesus' earthly life.

4:22 *old self.* Probably means the kind of person the Christian used to be. The old life-style resulted from deceitful desires.

4:23 *mind.* Cf. the evil thoughts of unbelievers (vv. 17–18).

4:24 *new self . . . in the likeness of God.* Since the new self is created, it cannot refer to the indwelling Christ, but rather to the kind of person He produces in the new believer. Nor is it some kind of new essential nature the believer has, because

25 Therefore, [a]laying aside falsehood, [b]SPEAK TRUTH EACH ONE *of you* WITH HIS NEIGHBOR, for we are [c]members of one another.

26 [a]BE ANGRY, AND *yet* DO NOT SIN; do not let the sun go down on your anger,

27 and do not [a]give the devil [1]an opportunity.

28 He who steals must steal no longer; but rather [a]he must labor, [b]performing with his own hands what is good, [c]so that he will have *something* to share with [1]one who has need.

29 Let no [1][a]unwholesome word proceed from your mouth, but only such *a word* as is good for [b]edification [2]according to the need *of the moment,* so that it will give grace to those who hear.

30 [a]Do not grieve the Holy Spirit of God, [1]by whom you were [b]sealed for the day of redemption.

31 [a]Let all bitterness and wrath and anger and clamor and slander be [b]put away from you, along with all [c]malice.

32 [a]Be kind to one another, tender-hearted, forgiving each other, [b]just as God in Christ also has forgiven [1]you.

25 [a]Eph 4:22, 31; Col 3:8; Heb 12:1; James 1:21; 1 Pet 2:1 [b]Zech 8:16; Eph 4:15; Col 3:9 [c]Rom 12:5
26 [a]Ps 4:4
27 [1]Lit *a place* [a]Rom 12:19; James 4:7
28 [1]Lit *the one* [a]Acts 20:35; 1 Cor 4:12; Gal 6:10 [b]1 Thess 4:11; 2 Thess 3:8, 11f; Titus 3:8, 14 [c]Luke 3:11; 1 Thess 4:12
29 [1]Lit *rotten* [2]Lit *of the need* [a]Matt 12:34; Eph 5:4; Col 3:8 [b]Eccl 10:12; Rom 14:19; Col 4:6
30 [1]Lit *in* [a]Is 63:10; 1 Thess 5:19 [b]John 3:33; Eph 1:13
31 [a]Rom 3:14; Col 3:8, 19 [b]Eph 4:22 [c]1 Pet 2:1
32 [1]Two early mss read *us* [a]1 Cor 13:4; Col 3:12f; 1 Pet 3:8 [b]Matt 6:14f; 2 Cor 2:10
5:1 [a]Matt 5:48; Luke 6:36; Eph 4:32
2 [a]Rom 14:15; Col 3:14

Be Imitators of God

5 [a]Therefore be imitators of God, as beloved children;

2 and [a]walk in love, just as Christ also [b]loved [1]you and [c]gave Himself up for us, an [d]offering and a sacrifice to God [2]as a [e]fragrant aroma.

3 But [a]immorality [1]or any impurity or greed must not even be named among you, as is proper among [2]saints;

4 and *there must be no* [a]filthiness and silly talk, or coarse jesting, which [b]are not fitting, but rather [c]giving of thanks.

5 For this you know with certainty, that [a]no [1]immoral or impure person or covetous man, who is an idolater, has an inheritance in the kingdom [b]of Christ and God.

6 [a]Let no one deceive you with empty words, for because of these things [b]the wrath of God comes upon [c]the sons of disobedience.

7 Therefore do not be [a]partakers with them;

8 for [a]you were formerly [b]darkness, but now you are Light in the Lord; walk as [c]children of Light

9 (for [a]the fruit of the Light *consists* in all [b]goodness and righteousness and truth),

2 [1]One early ms reads *us* [2]Lit *for an odor of fragrance* [b]John 13:34; Rom 8:37 [c]John 6:51; Rom 4:25; Gal 2:20; Eph 5:25 [d]Heb 7:27; 9:14; 10:10, 12 [e]Ex 29:18, 25; 2 Cor 2:14 **3** [1]Lit *and all* [2]Or *holy ones* [a]Col 3:5 **4** [a]Matt 12:34; Eph 4:29; Col 3:8 [b]Rom 1:28 [c]Eph 5:20 **5** [1]I.e. one who commits sexual immorality [a]1 Cor 6:9; Col 3:5 [b]Col 1:13 **6** [a]Col 2:8 [b]Rom 1:18; Col 3:6 [c]Eph 2:2 **7** [a]Eph 3:6 **8** [a]Eph 2:2 [b]Acts 26:18; Col 1:12f [c]John 12:36; Rom 13:12 **9** [a]Gal 5:22 [b]Rom 15:14

---

that would have been brought into existence at his new birth. In contrast, this is a new way of life that one not only "puts on" positionally at conversion (note the past tense in the parallel in Col 3:9–10) but is also urged to "put on" experientially as a Christian (see note on Rom 6:12–13).

4:25 *TRUTH.* Cf. vv. 15,21. *NEIGHBOR.* Probably means fellow Christians in this context.

4:26 *BE ANGRY.* Christians do not lose their emotions at conversion, but their emotions should be purified. Some anger is sinful, some is not. *do not let the sun go down.* No anger is to outlast the day.

4:27 *the devil.* Personal sin is usually due to our evil desires (see James 1:14) rather than to direct tempting by the devil. However, Satan can use our sins—especially those, like anger, that are against others—to bring about greater evil, such as divisions among Christians.

4:28 *steal no longer . . . labor . . . have something to share.* It is not enough to cease from sin; one must do good. The former thief must now help those in need.

4:29 *only such . . . as is good for edification.* An exhortation parallel to the previous one. The Christian not only stops saying unwholesome things; he also begins to say things that will help build others up.

4:30 *grieve.* By sin, such an "unwholesome word" (v. 29) and the sins mentioned in v. 31. The verb also demonstrates that the Holy Spirit is a person, not just an influence, for only a person can be grieved. *sealed.* See note on 1:13. *day of redemption.* See 1:14; 1 Pet 1:5 and notes.

4:31 *bitterness . . . malice.* Such things grieve the Holy Spirit. This continues the instruction concerning one's speech (v. 29).

4:32 *kind . . . tender-hearted.* The opposite of the negative qualities of v. 31. *forgiving.* This basic Christian attitude, which is a result of being forgiven in Christ, along with being kind and compassionate, brings to others what we have received from God.

5:1 *be imitators.* One way of imitating God is to have a forgiving spirit (4:32). The way we imitate our Lord is to act "just as" (v. 2; 4:32) He did. The sacrificial way Jesus expressed His love for us is not only the means of salvation (as seen in ch. 2) but also an example of the way we are to live for the sake of others.

5:2 *offering . . . fragrant aroma.* In the OT the offering of a sacrifice pleased the Lord so much that it was described as a "soothing aroma" (Gen 8:21; Ex 29:18,25,41; Lev 1:9,13,17).

5:3 *any impurity or greed.* Paul moves from specifically sexual sins to more general sins, such as greed. These include sexual lust but refer to other kinds of excessive desire as well. *not even be named.* See v. 12. *saints.* We are also a "holy temple" (2:21; cf. 2 Cor 6:16; 1 Pet 2:5,9).

5:4 *silly talk, or coarse jesting.* The context and the word "obscenity" indicate that it is not humor as such but dirty jokes and the like that are out of place. *giving of thanks.* By being grateful for all that God has given us, we can displace evil thoughts and words.

5:5 *immoral or impure . . . or covetous.* See v. 3. *idolater.* Cf. Col 3:5. The greedy person wants things more than he wants God, and puts things in place of God, thereby committing idolatry. *inheritance.* The person who persists in sexual and other kinds of greed has excluded God, who therefore excludes him from the kingdom (but see notes on 1 Cor 6:9,11).

5:7 *partakers.* Although Christians live in normal social relationships with others, as did the Lord Jesus (Luke 5:30–32; 15:1–2), they are not to participate in the sinful life-style of unbelievers.

5:8 *darkness . . . Light.* This section emphasizes the contrast between light and darkness, showing that those who belong to Him who is "Light" (1 John 1:5), i.e., pure and true, not only have their lives illumined by Him but also are the means of introducing that light into the dark areas of human conduct (cf. Matt 5:14).

5:9 *fruit of the Light.* A mixed metaphor, but the meaning is clear. Light is productive (consider the effect of light on plant

10 [1a]trying to learn what is pleasing to the
Lord.
11 [a]Do not participate in the unfruitful
[b]deeds of [c]darkness, but instead even
[1d]expose them;
12 for it is disgraceful even to speak of the
things which are done by them in secret.
13 But all things become visible [a]when
they are [1]exposed by the light, for everything
that becomes visible is light.
14 For this reason [1]it says,
"[a]Awake, sleeper,
And arise from [b]the dead,
And Christ [c]will shine on you."
15 Therefore [1]be careful how you [a]walk,
not [b]as unwise men but as wise,
16 [1a]making the most of your time,
because [b]the days are evil.
17 So then do not be foolish, but [a]under-
stand what the will of the Lord is.
18 And [a]do not get drunk with wine, [1]for
that is [b]dissipation, but be [c]filled with the
Spirit,
19 [a]speaking to [1]one another in [b]psalms
and [c]hymns and spiritual [d]songs, [e]singing
and making melody with your heart to the
Lord;
20 [a]always giving thanks for all things in
the name of our Lord Jesus Christ to [1b]God,
even the Father;
21 [1a]and be subject to one another in the
[2b]fear of Christ.

Marriage Like Christ and the Church

22 [a]Wives, [b]*be subject* to your own husbands, [c]as to the Lord.
23 For [a]the husband is the head of the
wife, as Christ also is the [b]head of the church,
He Himself [c]*being* the Savior of the body.
24 But as the church is subject to Christ,
so also the wives *ought to be* to their husbands in everything.
25 [a]Husbands, love your wives, just as
Christ also loved the church and [b]gave Himself up for her,

10 [1]Lit *proving what* [a]Rom 12:2 **11** [1]Or *reprove* [a]1 Cor 5:9; 2 Cor 6:14 [b]Rom 13:12 [c]Acts 26:18; Col 1:12f [d]1 Tim 5:20 **13** [1]Or *reproved* [a]John 3:20f **14** [1]Or *He* [a]Is 26:19; 51:17; 52:1; 60:1; Rom 13:11 [b]Eph 2:1 [c]Luke 1:78f **15** [1]Lit *look carefully* [a]Eph 5:2 [b]Col 4:5 **16** [1]Lit *redeeming the time* [a]Col 4:5 [b]Gal 1:4; Eph 6:13 **17** [a]Rom 12:2; Col 1:9; 1 Thess 4:3 **18** [1]Lit *in which is* [a]Prov 20:1; 23:31f; Rom 13:13; 1 Cor 5:11; 1 Thess 5:7 [b]Titus 1:6; 1 Pet 4:4 [c]Luke 1:15 **19** [1]Or *yourselves* [a]Col 3:16 [b]1 Cor 14:26 [c]Acts 16:25 [d]Rev 5:9 [e]1 Cor 14:15 **20** [1]Lit *the God and Father* [a]Rom 1:8; Eph 5:4; Col 3:17 [b]1 Cor 15:24 **21** [1]Lit *being subject* [2]Or *reverence* [a]Gal 5:13; Phil 2:3; 1 Pet 5:5 [b]2 Cor 5:11 **22** [a]Eph 5:22-6:9: *Col 3:18-4:1* [b]1 Cor 14:34f; Titus 2:5; 1 Pet 3:1 [c]Eph 6:5 **23** [a]1 Cor 11:3 [b]Eph 1:22 [c]1 Cor 6:13 **25** [a]Eph 5:28, 33; Col 3:19; 1 Pet 3:7 [b]Eph 5:2

growth), and those who live in God's light produce the fruit of moral and ethical character (cf. Gal 5:22–23), while those who live in darkness do not (see v. 11).

5:11 *Do not participate in.* See v. 7. *expose.* Light, by nature, exposes what is in darkness, and the contrast shows sin for what it really is.

5:12 *disgraceful . . . to speak of.* Christians should not dwell on the evils that their lives are exposing in others.

5:13–14 *all things . . . visible . . . everything . . . visible.* By the repetition of these words, Paul seems to be stressing the all-pervasive nature of the light of God and its inevitable effect.

5:14 *it says.* What follows may well be a hymn used by the early Christians (see note on Col 3:16). *sleeper . . . dead.* Two images that describe a sinner (cf. 2:1). *Christ will shine on you.* With His life-giving light.

5:15 *unwise . . . wise.* Having emphasized the contrast between light and darkness, Paul now turns to the contrast between wisdom and foolishness.

5:16 *time.* The foolish person has no strategy for life and misses opportunities to live for God in an evil environment.

5:17 *foolish . . . understand.* The contrast continues. The foolish person not only misses opportunities to make wise use of time; he has a more fundamental problem: He does not understand what are God's purposes for mankind and for Christians. God's purposes are a basic theme in Ephesians (see ch. 1).

5:18 *do not get drunk . . . be filled with the Spirit.* The Greek present tense is used to indicate that the filling of the Spirit is not a once-for-all experience. Repeatedly, as the occasion requires, the Spirit empowers for worship, service and testimony. The contrast between being filled with wine and filled with the Spirit is obvious. But there is something in common that enables Paul to make the contrast, namely, that one can be under an influence that affects him, whether of wine or of the Spirit. Since Col 3:15–4:1 is very similar to Eph 5:18–6:9, we may assume that Paul intends to convey a basically similar thought in the introductory sentences to each passage. When he speaks here of being filled with the Spirit and when he speaks in Colossians of being under the rule of the peace of Christ and indwelt by the "word" of Christ, he means to be under God's control. The effect of this control is essentially the same in both passages: a happy, mutual encouragement to praise God and a healthy, mutual relationship with people.

5:19 *psalms . . . songs.* Every kind of appropriate song—whether psalms like those of the OT, or hymns directed to God or to others that Christians were accustomed to singing—could provide a means for praising and thanking God (v. 20). Actually, however, all three terms may refer to different types of psalms.

5:21–6:9 In chs. 2–4 Paul showed the way God brought believing Jews and Gentiles together into a new relationship in Christ. In 4:1–6 he stressed the importance of unity. Now he shows how believers, filled with the Spirit, can live together in a practical way in various human relationships. This list of mutual responsibilities is similar to the pattern found in Col 3:18–4:1; 1 Pet 2:13–3:12; cf. Rom 13:1–10.

5:21 *be subject to one another.* Basic to the following paragraphs. Paul will show how, in each relationship, each partner can have a conciliatory attitude that will help that relationship. The grammar indicates that this mutual submission is associated with the filling of the Spirit in v. 18. The command "be filled" (v. 18) is followed by a series of participles in the Greek: speaking (v. 19), singing (v. 19), making melody (v. 19), giving thanks (v. 20) and submitting (v. 21).

5:22 *Wives, be subject.* An aspect of the mutual submission taught in v. 21. To be subject meant to yield one's own rights. If the relationship called for it, as in the military, the term could connote obedience, but that meaning is not called for here. In fact, the word "obey" does not appear in Scripture with respect to wives, though it does with respect to children (6:1) and slaves (6:5). *as to the Lord.* Does not put a woman's husband in the place of the Lord, but shows rather that a woman ought to submit to her husband as an act of submission to the Lord.

5:23 *head of the wife.* See note on 1 Cor 11:3. *as Christ.* The analogy between the relationship of Christ to the church and that of the husband to the wife is basic to the entire passage. *He . . . body.* See 2:16; 4:4,12,16. *Savior.* Christ earned, so to speak, the right to His special relationship to the church.

5:25 *Husbands.* Paul now shows that this is not a one-sided submission, but a reciprocal relationship. *love.* Explained by what follows. *gave Himself up for her.* Not only the expression

26 [a]so that He might sanctify her, having
[b]cleansed her by the [c]washing of water with
[d]the word,
27 that He might [a]present to Himself the
church [1]in all her glory, having no spot or
wrinkle or any such thing; but that she
would be [b]holy and blameless.
28 So husbands ought also to [a]love their
own wives as their own bodies. He who
loves his own wife loves himself;
29 for no one ever hated his own flesh,
but nourishes and cherishes it, just as Christ
also *does* the church,
30 because we are [a]members of His
[b]body.
31 [a]FOR THIS REASON A MAN SHALL LEAVE HIS
FATHER AND MOTHER AND SHALL BE JOINED TO HIS
WIFE, AND THE TWO SHALL BECOME ONE FLESH.
32 This mystery is great; but I am speaking with reference to Christ and the church.
33 Nevertheless, each individual among
you also is to [a]love his own wife even as
himself, and the wife must *see to it* that she
[1b]respects her husband.

Family Relationships

6 [a]Children, obey your parents in the Lord,
for this is right.
2 [a]HONOR YOUR FATHER AND MOTHER (which
is the first commandment with a promise),
3 SO THAT IT MAY BE WELL WITH YOU, AND
THAT YOU MAY LIVE LONG ON THE EARTH.
4 [a]Fathers, do not provoke your children
to anger, but [b]bring them up in the discipline
and instruction of the Lord.
5 [a]Slaves, be obedient to those who are
your [1]masters according to the flesh, with
[b]fear and trembling, in the sincerity of your
heart, [c]as to Christ;
6 [a]not [1]by way of eyeservice, as [b]men-
pleasers, but as [c]slaves of Christ, [d]doing the
will of God from the [2]heart.
7 With good will [1]render service, [a]as to
the Lord, and not to men,
8 [a]knowing that [b]whatever good thing
each one does, this he will receive back from
the Lord, [c]whether slave or free.
9 And masters, do the same things to
them, and [a]give up threatening, knowing
that [b]both their Master and yours is in heav-
en, and there is [c]no partiality with Him.

The Armor of God

10 Finally, [a]be strong in the Lord and in
[b]the strength of His might.
11 [a]Put on the full armor of God, so that
you will be able to stand firm against the
[b]schemes of the devil.
12 For our [a]struggle is not against [1b]flesh
and blood, but [c]against the rulers, against
the powers, against the [d]world forces of this
[e]darkness, against the [f]spiritual *forces* of
wickedness in [g]the heavenly *places.*
13 Therefore, take up [a]the full armor of
God, so that you will be able to [b]resist in [c]the
evil day, and having done everything, to
stand firm.
14 Stand firm therefore, [a]HAVING GIRDED

26 [a]Titus 2:14; Heb 10:10, 14, 29; 13:12 [b]2 Pet 1:9 [c]Acts 22:16; 1 Cor 6:11; Titus 3:5 [d]John 15:3; 17:17; Rom 10:8f; Eph 6:17
27 [1]Lit *glorious* [a]2 Cor 4:14; 11:2; Col 1:22 [b]Eph 1:4
28 [a]Eph 5:25, 33; 1 Pet 3:7
30 [a]1 Cor 6:15; 12:27 [b]Eph 1:23
31 [a]Gen 2:24; Matt 19:5; Mark 10:7f
33 [1]Lit *fear* [a]Eph 5:25, 28; 1 Pet 3:7 [b]1 Pet 3:2, 5f
6:1 [a]Prov 6:20; 23:22; Col 3:20
2 [a]Ex 20:12; Deut 5:16
4 [a]Col 3:21 [b]Gen 18:19; Deut 6:7; 11:19; Ps 78:4; Prov 22:6; 2 Tim 3:15
5 [1]I.e. earthly masters, with fear [a]Col 3:22; 1 Tim 6:1; Titus 2:9
5 [b]1 Cor 2:3 [c]Eph 5:22
6 [1]Lit *according to* [2]Lit *soul* [a]Col 3:22 [b]Gal 1:10 [c]1 Cor 7:22 [d]Mark 3:35
7 [1]Lit *rendering* [a]Col 3:23
8 [a]Col 3:24 [b]Matt 16:27; 2 Cor 5:10; Col 3:24f [c]1 Cor 12:13; Col 3:11
9 [a]Lev 25:43 [b]Job 31:13ff; John 13:13; Col 4:1 [c]Deut 10:17; Acts 10:34; Col 3:25
10 [a]1 Cor 16:13; 2 Tim 2:1 [b]Eph 1:19
11 [a]Rom 13:12; Eph 6:13 [b]Eph 4:14
12 [1]Lit *blood and flesh* [a]1 Cor 9:25 [b]Matt 16:17 [c]Eph 1:21; 2:2; 3:10 [d]John 12:31 [e]Acts 26:18; Col 1:13 [f]Eph 3:10 [g]Eph 1:3
13 [a]Eph 6:11 [b]James 4:7 [c]Eph 5:16
14 [a]Is 11:5; Luke 12:35; 1 Pet 1:13

of our Lord's love, but also an example of how the husband ought to devote himself to his wife's good. To give oneself up to death for the beloved is a more extreme expression of devotion than the wife is called on to make.

5:26 *washing of water with the word.* Many attempts have been made to see marriage customs or liturgical symbolism in these words. One thing is clear: The Lord Jesus died not only to bring forgiveness, but also to effect a new life of holiness in the church, which is His "bride." A study of the concepts of washing, of water and of the word should include reference to John 3:5; 15:3; Titus 3:5; James 1:18; 1 Pet 1:23; 3:21.

5:27 *holy and blameless.* See 1:4.

5:28–29 *as their own bodies . . . loves himself . . . his own flesh.* The basis for such expressions and for the teaching of these verses is the quotation from Gen 2:24 in v. 31. If the husband and wife become "one flesh," then for the man to love his wife is to love one who has become part of himself.

5:32 *mystery.* See note on Rom 11:25. The profound truth of the union of Christ and his "bride," the church, is beyond unaided human understanding. It is not that the relationship of husband and wife provides an illustration of the union of Christ and the church, but that the basic reality is the latter, with marriage a human echo of that relationship.

5:33 *love . . . respects.* A rephrasing and summary of the whole passage.

6:3 *ON THE EARTH.* In Deut 5:16 (see Ex 20:12), where this commandment occurs, the "promise" (v. 2) was expressed in terms of the anticipated occupation of the "land," i.e., Canaan. That specific application was, of course, not appropriate to the Ephesians, so the more general application is made here.

6:4 *do not provoke.* Fathers must surrender any right they may feel they have to act unreasonably toward their children.

6:5 *Slaves.* Both the OT and the NT included regulations for societal situations such as slavery and divorce (see Deut 24:1–4), which were the results of the hardness of hearts (Matt 19:8). Such regulations did not encourage or condone such situations but were divinely-given, practical ways of dealing with the realities of the day.

6:9 *masters.* Once again Paul stresses reciprocal attitudes (cf. 5:21–6:4). See note on Titus 2:9.

6:10–20 Paul's scope in Ephesians has been cosmic. From the very beginning he has drawn attention to the unseen world (see note on 1:3; see also 1:10,20–23; 2:6; 6:10), and now he describes the spiritual battle that takes place against evil "in the heavenly places" (v. 12).

6:10 *strong . . . might.* Implies that human effort is inadequate but God's power is invincible.

6:12 *not against flesh and blood.* A caution against lashing out against human opponents as though they were the real enemy and also against assuming that the battle can be fought using merely human resources. *rulers . . . forces.* Cf. Paul's earlier allusions to powerful beings in the unseen world (see notes on 1:21; 3:10). *heavenly places.* See note on 1:3.

6:13–14 *resist . . . Stand firm.* In this context the imagery is not that of a massive invasion of the domain of evil, but of individual soldiers withstanding assault.

YOUR LOINS WITH TRUTH, and HAVING [b]PUT ON THE
BREASTPLATE OF RIGHTEOUSNESS,
15 and having [a]shod YOUR FEET WITH THE
PREPARATION OF THE GOSPEL OF PEACE;
16 [1]in addition to all, taking up the [a]shield
of faith with which you will be able to extinguish all the [b]flaming arrows of [c]the evil *one.*
17 And take [a]THE HELMET OF SALVATION, and
the [b]sword of the Spirit, which is [c]the word
of God.
18 [1]With all [a]prayer and petition [2b]pray at
all times [c]in the Spirit, and with this in view,
[3d]be on the alert with all [e]perseverance and
[f]petition for all the saints,
19 and [a]*pray* on my behalf, that utterance
may be given to me [b]in the opening of my
mouth, to make known with [c]boldness [d]the
mystery of the gospel,
20 for which I am an [a]ambassador [b]in
[1]chains; that [2]in *proclaiming* it I may speak
[c]boldly, [d]as I ought to speak.

14 [b]Is 59:17; Rom 13:12; Eph 6:13; 1 Thess 5:8
15 [a]Is 52:7; Rom 10:15
16 [1]Lit *in all* [a]1 Thess 5:8 [b]Ps 7:13; 120:4 [c]Matt 5:37
17 [a]Is 59:17 [b]Is 49:2; Hos 6:5; Heb 4:12 [c]Eph 5:26; Heb 6:5
18 [1]Lit *Through* [2]Lit *praying* [3]Lit *being* [a]Phil 4:6 [b]Luke 18:1; Col 1:3; 4:2; 1 Thess 5:17 [c]Rom 8:26f [d]Mark 13:33 [e]Acts 1:14 [f]1 Tim 2:1
19 [a]Col 4:3; 1 Thess 5:25 [b]2 Cor 6:11 [c]2 Cor 3:12 [d]Eph 3:3
20 [1]Lit *a chain* [2]Two early mss read *I may speak boldly* [a]2 Cor 5:20; Philem 9 mg [b]Acts 21:33; 28:20; Eph 3:1; Phil 1:7; Col 4:3 [c]2 Cor 3:12 [d]Col 4:4 **21** [1]Lit *what* [a]Eph 6:21, 22: *Col 4:7-9* [b]Acts 20:4; 2 Tim 4:12 [c]Col 4:7 **22** [1]Lit *Whom I have sent to you* [2]Lit *the things about us* [a]Col 4:8 [b]Col 2:2; 4:8 **23** [a]Rom 15:33; Gal 6:16; 2 Thess 3:16; 1 Pet 5:14 [b]Gal 5:6; 1 Thess 5:8 **24** [1]Lit *in incorruption*

21 [a]But that you also may know about my
circumstances, [1]how I am doing, [b]Tychicus,
[c]the beloved brother and faithful minister in
the Lord, will make everything known to
you.
22 [1a]I have sent him to you for this very
purpose, so that you may know [2]about us,
and that he may [b]comfort your hearts.
23 [a]Peace be to the brethren, and [b]love
with faith, from God the Father and the Lord
Jesus Christ.
24 Grace be with all those who love our
Lord Jesus Christ [1]with incorruptible *love.*

6:14 *GIRDED YOUR LOINS WITH TRUTH.* Cf. the symbolic clothing of the Messiah in Is 11:5. Character, not brute force, wins the battle, just as in the case of the Messiah. *BREASTPLATE OF RIGHTEOUSNESS.* Here again, the warrior's character is his defense. God himself is symbolically described as putting on a breastplate of righteousness when He goes forth to bring about justice (see Is 59:17).

6:15 *shod YOUR FEET WITH THE PREPARATION.* Whereas the description of the messenger's feet in Is 52:7 reflects the custom of running barefooted, here the message of the gospel is picturesquely connected with the protective and supportive footgear of the Roman soldier.

6:16 *shield of faith . . . extinguish . . . flaming arrows.* Describes the large Roman shield covered with leather, which could be soaked in water and used to put out flame-tipped arrows.

6:17–18 *sword of the Spirit . . . pray . . . in the Spirit.* Reminders that the battle is spiritual and must be fought in God's strength, depending on the word and on God through prayer.

6:17 *HELMET OF SALVATION.* Is 59:17 has similar language, along with the breastplate imagery (see note on v. 14). The helmet both protected the soldier and provided a striking symbol of military victory.

6:21–23 Paul concludes with greetings that lack personal references such as are usually found in his letters. This is understandable if Ephesians is a circular letter (see note on 1:1).

6:21 *Tychicus.* An associate of Paul who traveled as his representative (cf. Col 4:7; 2 Tim 4:12; Titus 3:12).

Philippians

INTRODUCTION

Author, Date and Place of Writing

The early church was unanimous in its testimony that Philippians was written by the apostle Paul (see 1:1). Internally the letter reveals the stamp of genuineness. The many personal references of the author fit what we know of Paul from other NT books.

It is evident that Paul wrote the letter from prison (see 1:13–14). Some have argued that this imprisonment took place in Ephesus, perhaps c. A.D. 53–55; others put it in Caesarea c. 57–59. Best evidence, however, favors Rome as the place of origin and the date as c. 61. This fits well with the account of Paul's house arrest in Acts 28:14–31. When he wrote Philippians, he was not in the Mamertime dungeon as he was when he wrote 2 Timothy. He was in his own rented house, where for two years he was free to impart the gospel to all who came to him.

Purpose

Paul's primary purpose in writing this letter was to thank the Philippians for the gift they had sent him upon learning of his detention at Rome (1:5; 4:10–19). However, he makes use of this occasion to fulfill several other desires: (1) to report on his own circumstances (1:12–26; 4:10–19); (2) to encourage the Philippians to stand firm in the face of persecution and rejoice regardless of circumstances (1:27–30; 4:4); (3) to exhort them to humility and unity (2:1–11; 4:2–5); (4) to commend Timothy and Epaphroditus to the Philippian church (2:19–30); and (5) to warn the Philippians against the Judaizers (legalists) and antinomians (libertines) among them (ch. 3).

Recipients

The city of Philippi was named after King Philip II of Macedon, father of Alexander the Great. It was a prosperous Roman colony, which meant that the citizens of Philippi were also citizens of the city of Rome itself. They prided themselves on being Romans (see Acts 16:21), dressed like Romans and often spoke Latin. No doubt this was the background for Paul's reference to the believer's heavenly citizenship (3:20–21). Many of the Philippians were retired military men who had been given land in the vicinity and who in turn served as a military presence in this frontier city. That Philippi was a Roman colony may explain why there were not enough Jews there to permit the establishment of a synagogue and why Paul does not quote the OT in the Philippian letter.

Characteristics

1. Philippians contains no OT quotations.
2. It is a missionary thank-you letter in which the missionary reports on the progress of his work.
3. It manifests a particularly vigorous type of Christian living: (1) self-humbling (2:1–4); (2) pressing toward the goal (3:13–14); (3) lack of anxiety (4:6); (4) ability to do all things (4:13).
4. It is outstanding as the NT letter of joy; the word "joy" in its various forms occurs some 16 times.
5. It contains one of the most profound Christological passages in the NT (2:5–11). Yet, profound as it is, Paul includes it mainly for illustrative purposes.

Outline

I. Salutation (1:1–2)
II. Thanksgiving and Prayer for the Philippians (1:3–11)
III. Paul's Personal Circumstances (1:12–26)

- IV. Exhortations (1:27—2:18)
  - A. Living a Life Worthy of the Gospel (1:27–30)
  - B. Following the Servant Attitude of Christ (2:1–18)
- V. Paul's Associates in the Gospel (2:19–30)
  - A. Timothy (2:19–24)
  - B. Epaphroditus (2:25–30)
- VI. Warnings against Judaizers and Antinomians (3:1—4:1)
  - A. Against Judaizers or Legalists (3:1–16)
  - B. Against Antinomians or Libertines (3:17—4:1)
- VII. Final Exhortations, Thanks and Conclusion (4:2–23)
  - A. Exhortations concerning Various Aspects of the Christian Life (4:2–9)
  - B. Concluding Testimony and Repeated Thanks (4:10–20)
  - C. Greetings and Benediction (4:21–23)

Philippi in the Time of Paul

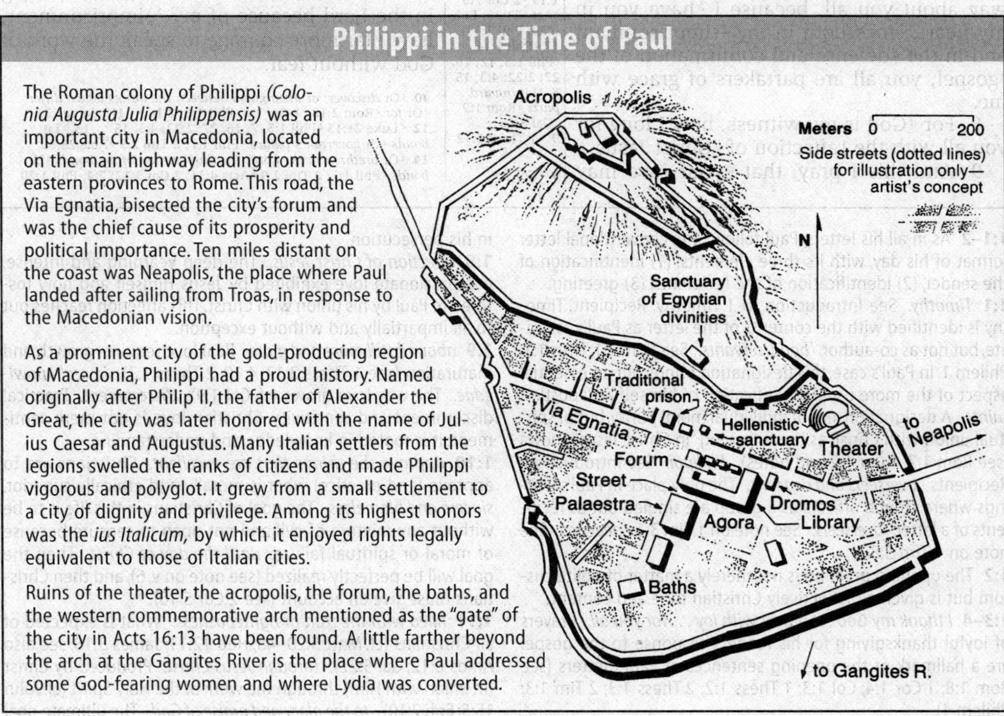

The Roman colony of Philippi *(Colonia Augusta Julia Philippensis)* was an important city in Macedonia, located on the main highway leading from the eastern provinces to Rome. This road, the Via Egnatia, bisected the city's forum and was the chief cause of its prosperity and political importance. Ten miles distant on the coast was Neapolis, the place where Paul landed after sailing from Troas, in response to the Macedonian vision.

As a prominent city of the gold-producing region of Macedonia, Philippi had a proud history. Named originally after Philip II, the father of Alexander the Great, the city was later honored with the name of Julius Caesar and Augustus. Many Italian settlers from the legions swelled the ranks of citizens and made Philippi vigorous and polyglot. It grew from a small settlement to a city of dignity and privilege. Among its highest honors was the *ius Italicum,* by which it enjoyed rights legally equivalent to those of Italian cities.

Ruins of the theater, the acropolis, the forum, the baths, and the western commemorative arch mentioned as the "gate" of the city in Acts 16:13 have been found. A little farther beyond the arch at the Gangites River is the place where Paul addressed some God-fearing women and where Lydia was converted.

Thanksgiving

1 [a]Paul and [b]Timothy, [c]bond-servants of [d]Christ Jesus,

To [e]all the [1f]saints in Christ Jesus who are in [g]Philippi, [2]including the [h]overseers and [i]deacons:

2 [a]Grace to you and peace from God our Father and the Lord Jesus Christ.

3 [a]I thank my God in all my remembrance of you,

4 always offering prayer with joy in [a]my every prayer for you all,

5 in view of your [1a]participation in the [b]gospel [c]from the first day until now.

6 *For I am* confident of this very thing, that He who began a good work in you will perfect it until [a]the day of Christ Jesus.

7 [1]For [a]it is only right for me to feel this way about you all, because I [b]have you in my heart, since both in my [2c]imprisonment and in the [d]defense and confirmation of the [e]gospel, you all are partakers of grace with me.

8 For [a]God is my witness, how I long for you all with the [1]affection of [b]Christ Jesus.

9 And this I pray, that [a]your love may abound still more and more in [b]real knowledge and all discernment,

10 so that you may [1a]approve the things that are excellent, in order to be sincere and blameless [2]until [b]the day of Christ;

11 having been filled with the [a]fruit of righteousness which *comes* through Jesus Christ, to the glory and praise of God.

The Gospel Is Preached

12 Now I want you to know, brethren, that my circumstances [a]have turned out for the greater progress of the [b]gospel,

13 so that my [1a]imprisonment in *the cause of* Christ has become well known throughout the whole [2]praetorian guard and to [b]everyone else,

14 and that most of the [1]brethren, trusting in the Lord because of my [2a]imprisonment, have [b]far more courage to speak the word of God without fear.

1:1 [1]Or *holy ones* [2]Lit *with* [a]2 Cor 1:1 [b]Acts 16:1 [c]Rom 1:1; Gal 1:10 [d]Gal 3:26 [e]2 Cor 1:1; Col 1:2 [f]Acts 9:13 [g]Acts 16:12 [h]Acts 20:28; 1 Tim 3:1f; Titus 1:7 [i]1 Tim 3:8ff
2 [a]Rom 1:7
3 [a]Rom 1:8
4 [a]Rom 1:9
5 [1]Or *sharing in the preaching of the gospel* [a]Acts 2:42; Phil 4:15 [b]Phil 1:7; 2:22; 4:3, 15 [c]Acts 16:12-40; Phil 2:12; 4:15
6 [a]1 Cor 1:8; Phil 1:10; 2:16
7 [1]Lit *Just as it is right* [2]Lit *bonds* [a]2 Pet 1:13 [b]2 Cor 7:3 [c]Acts 21:33; Eph 6:20; Phil 1:13f, 17 [d]Phil 1:16 [e]Phil 1:5, 12, 16, 27; 2:22; 4:3, 15
8 [1]Lit *inward parts* [a]Rom 1:9 [b]Gal 3:26
9 [a]1 Thess 3:12
9 [b]Col 1:9

10 [1]Or *discover;* or *distinguish between the things which differ* [2]Or *for* [a]Rom 2:18 [b]1 Cor 1:8; Phil 1:6; 2:16 **11** [a]James 3:18 **12** [a]Luke 21:13 [b]Phil 1:5, 7, 16, 27; 2:22; 4:3, 15 **13** [1]Lit *bonds* [2]Or *governor's palace* [a]Phil 1:7; 2 Tim 2:9 [b]Acts 28:30 **14** [1]Or *brethren in the Lord, trusting because of my bonds* [2]Lit *bonds* [a]Phil 1:7; 2 Tim 2:9 [b]Acts 4:31; 2 Cor 3:12; 7:4; Phil 1:20

1:1–2 As in all his letters, Paul follows the conventional letter format of his day, with its three elements: (1) identification of the sender, (2) identification of the recipients, (3) greeting.

1:1 *Timothy.* See Introduction to 1 Timothy: Recipient. Timothy is identified with the contents of the letter as Paul's associate, but not as co-author. *bond-servants.* See Rom 1:1; Titus 1:1; Philem 1. In Paul's case, this designation brings out an essential aspect of the more usual identification of himself as "apostle." *saints.* A designation, not of individual moral purity, but of spiritual union with Christ, as the following "in Christ Jesus" shows (see Rom 1:7; 1 Cor 1:2 and notes). *Philippi.* See Introduction: Recipients. *overseers and deacons.* The only place in Paul's writings where church officers as a group are singled out as recipients of a letter. *overseers.* See note on 1 Tim 3:1. *deacons.* See note on 1 Tim 3:8.

1:2 The opening greeting is not merely a matter of polite custom but is given a distinctively Christian tone and content.

1:3–4 *I thank my God . . . prayer with joy . . . for you all.* Prayers of joyful thanksgiving for his readers' response to the gospel are a hallmark of the opening sentences of Paul's letters (see Rom 1:8; 1 Cor 1:4; Col 1:3; 1 Thess 1:2; 2 Thess 1:3; 2 Tim 1:3; Philem 4).

1:5 *your participation in the gospel.* The basis of Paul's prayerful thanksgiving is not only their reception of the gospel but also their active support of his ministry (see 4:15). *from the first day.* When Paul first came to Philippi (see Acts 16:12). *now.* Toward the close (see 2:24) of Paul's first Roman imprisonment (see Acts 28:16–31).

1:6 *work in you.* Paul is confident, not only of what God has done "for" the readers in forgiving their sins, but also of what he has done "in" them (see v. 11). "Work" refers to God's activity in saving them. *day of Christ Jesus.* His return, when their salvation will be brought to completion (see 1:10; 2:16; 1 Cor 1:8; 5:5; 2 Cor 1:14). It is God who initiates salvation, who continues it and who will one day bring it to its consummation.

1:7 *partakers of grace.* Not even imprisonment and persecution can change such sharing. Even in Paul's imprisonment they willingly identified themselves with Paul by sending Epaphroditus and their financial gifts. They had become one with Paul in his persecution.

1:8 *affection of Christ Jesus.* The deep yearning and intense, compassionate love exhibited by Jesus Himself and now fostered in Paul by his union with Christ. This affection reaches out to all impartially and without exception.

1:9 *abound still more and more.* Real love requires growth and maturation (see 1 Thess 3:12; 4:10; 2 Thess 1:3). *in real knowledge.* The way love grows (cf. Col 1:9). *discernment.* Practical discernment and sensitivity. Christian love is not mere sentiment; it is rooted in knowledge and understanding.

1:10 *approve the things that are excellent.* Christians are to approve (and practice) what is morally and ethically superior. *sincere and blameless.* The goal of Christians in this life is to be without any mixture of evil and not open to censure because of moral or spiritual failure. *until the day of Christ.* Then the goal will be perfectly realized (see note on v. 6), and then Christians must give an account (see 2 Cor 5:10).

1:11 *filled with the fruit of righteousness.* What is expected of all Christians (cf. Matt 5:20–48; Heb 12:11; James 3:18; see also Amos 6:12; Gal 5:22). *through Jesus Christ.* Produced by Christ (in union with Him) through the work of the Holy Spirit (cf. John 15:5; Eph 2:10). *to the glory and praise of God.* The ultimate goal of all that God does in believers (see Eph 1:6,12,14).

1:12 *my circumstances.* Paul's detainment in prison. *greater progress of the gospel.* Instead of hindering the gospel, Paul's imprisonment had served to make it known.

1:13 *imprisonment in the cause of Christ . . . well known.* It has become apparent to all who know of Paul's situation that he is imprisoned, not because he is guilty of some crime, but on account of his stand for the gospel. *imprisonment.* Either actual chains or a broader reference to his sufferings and imprisonment (see v. 14).*whole praetorian guard.* A contingent of soldiers, numbering several thousand, many of whom would have had personal contact with Paul or would have been assigned individually to guard him during the course of his imprisonment (see Acts 28:16,30).

1:14 *have . . . courage to speak.* The unexpected result of Paul's imprisonment is that others, encouraged by his example, are forcefully proclaiming the gospel.

15 [a]Some, to be sure, are preaching Christ
even [1]from envy and strife, but some also
[1]from good will;
16 the latter *do it* out of love, knowing that
I am appointed for the defense of the [a]gospel;
17 the former proclaim Christ [a]out of selfish ambition [1]rather than from pure motives,
thinking to cause me distress in my [2b]impris-
onment.
18 What then? Only that in every way,
whether in pretense or in truth, Christ is proclaimed; and in this I rejoice.
Yes, and I will rejoice,
19 for I know that this will turn out for my
[1]deliverance [a]through your [2]prayers and the
provision of [b]the Spirit of Jesus Christ,
20 according to my [a]earnest expectation
and [b]hope, that I will not be put to shame in
anything, but *that* with [c]all boldness, Christ
will even now, as always, be [d]exalted in my
body, [e]whether by life or by death.

To Live Is Christ

21 For to me, [a]to live is Christ and to die is
gain.
22 [1]But if *I am* to live *on* in the flesh, this
will mean [a]fruitful labor for me; and I do not
know [2]which to choose.
23 But I am hard-pressed from both *directions,* having the [a]desire to depart and [b]be
with Christ, for *that* is very much better;
24 yet to remain on in the flesh is more
necessary for your sake.
25 [a]Convinced of this, I know that I will
remain and continue with you all for your
progress and joy [1]in the faith,
26 so that your [a]proud confidence in me
may abound in Christ Jesus through my
coming to you again.
27 Only conduct yourselves in a manner
[a]worthy of the [b]gospel of Christ, so that
whether I come and see you or remain
absent, I will hear of you that you are [c]stand-
ing firm in [d]one spirit, with one [1]mind [e]striv-
ing together for the faith of the gospel;
28 in no way alarmed by *your* opponents—
which is a [a]sign of destruction for them, but
of salvation for you, and that *too,* from God.
29 For to you [a]it has been granted for
Christ's sake, not only to believe in Him, but
also to [b]suffer for His sake,
30 experiencing the same [a]conflict which
[b]you saw in me, and now hear *to be* in me.

15 [1]Lit *because of* [a]2 Cor 11:13 **16** [a]Phil 1:5, 7, 12, 27; 2:22; 4:3, 15 **17** [1]Lit *not sincerely* [2]Lit *bonds* [a]Rom 2:8; Phil 2:3 [b]Phil 1:7; 2 Tim 2:9 **19** [1]Or *salvation* [2]Lit *supplication* [a]2 Cor 1:11 [b]Acts 16:7 **20** [a]Rom 8:19 [b]Rom 5:5; 1 Pet 4:16 [c]Acts 4:31; 2 Cor 3:12; 7:4; Phil 1:14 [d]1 Cor 6:20 [e]Rom 14:8 **21** [a]Gal 2:20 **22** [1]Or *But if to live in the flesh, this will be fruitful labor for me, then I* [2]Lit *what I shall choose* [a]Rom 1:13 **23** [a]2 Cor 5:8; 2 Tim 4:6 [b]John 12:26 **25** [1]Lit *of* [a]Phil 2:24 **26** [a]2 Cor 5:12; 7:4; Phil 2:16 **27** [1]Lit *soul* [a]Eph 4:1 [b]Phil 1:5 [c]1 Cor 16:13; Phil 4:1 [d]Acts 4:32 [e]Jude 3 **28** [a]2 Thess 1:5 **29** [a]Matt 5:11, 12 [b]Acts 14:22 **30** [a]Col 1:29; 2:1; 1 Thess 2:2; 1 Tim 6:12; 2 Tim 4:7; Heb 10:32; 12:1 [b]Acts 16:19-40; Phil 1:13

1:15 *from envy and strife . . . from good will.* The gospel preaching stimulated by Paul's imprisonment stems from either one of two sharply opposed motives.
1:16 *the latter do it out of love.* Those who preach with a right motive recognize the true reason for Paul's imprisonment, already expressed earlier in v. 13, and are encouraged to take the same bold stand that he has taken.
1:17 *the former proclaim Christ out of selfish ambition.* Those who preach with wrong, insincere motives do so out of a sense of competition with Paul and so think they are making his imprisonment more difficult to bear. *rather than from pure motives.* Not all preaching of the gospel is based on proper motives.
1:18 *whether in pretense or in truth, Christ is proclaimed.* These preachers are not to be viewed as being heretical. Their message is true, even though their motives are not pure. The gospel has its objectivity and validity apart from those who proclaim it; the message is more than the medium. *I rejoice . . . I will rejoice.* An example of the kind of vigorous Christian experience Paul expressed. He was under arrest, and fellow Christians sought, by their preaching, to add to his difficulties; yet he kept on rejoicing.
1:19 *deliverance.* Either Paul's release from prison (see v. 25; 2:24) or, in view of the immediately following verses, the deliverance brought to the believer by death (cf. Rom 8:28). Verse 25, however, seems to point to the former interpretation. *Spirit of Jesus Christ.* The Holy Spirit is not only the Spirit of God the Father (Rom 8:9,14; 1 Cor 2:10–11,14) but also the Spirit of Christ, the second person of the Trinity (Acts 16:7; Rom 8:9; Gal 4:6). He is sent by the Father (John 14:16–17,26; Gal 4:6) and by the Son (John 15:26; 16:7).
1:20 *be put to shame . . . with all boldness.* The circumstances of imprisonment, with all its attendant suffering and oppression, constitute a real temptation for Paul to abandon the gospel and his resolute service for Christ. *my body.* Where the exalted Christ dwells by His Spirit and is at work (cf. Rom 8:9–10), and so is exalted by what Paul does. *whether by life or by death.* Whether his service for Christ continues or ends in death.
1:21 *to live is Christ.* Christ was the source and secret of Paul's continual joy (even in prison), for Paul's life found all its meaning in Christ. *gain.* Verse 23 specifies that the gain brought by death is "being with Christ," so that here Paul is saying that his ultimate concern and most precious possession, both now and forever, is Christ and his relationship to Him.
1:22 *fruitful labor.* The spread of the gospel and the upbuilding of the church.
1:23–24 *depart and be with Christ . . . remain on in the flesh.* Either alternative was a good one. While mysteries remain, this passage clearly teaches that when believers die they are with Christ, apart from the body.
1:23 *very much better.* Being with Christ after death must involve some kind of conscious presence and fellowship (cf. 2 Cor 5:6,8).
1:24 *necessary for your sake.* Paul puts the needs of those he ministers to ahead of his personal preference.
1:25 *I will remain.* Possibly Paul was later released from prison (see map, pp. 1762–1763). *progress . . . in the faith.* The Christian life is to be one of joyful growth and advance (see note on v. 9 and the verses cited there).
1:27 *worthy of the gospel.* Appropriate to the standards and goals given with the gospel. *in one spirit.* Having a common disposition and purpose. *with one mind striving.* Particularly where the gospel is under attack, Christians need each other and must stand together.
1:28 *a sign.* Persistent opposition to the church and the gospel is a sure sign of eventual destruction, since it involves rejection of the only way of salvation. By the same token, when Christians are persecuted for their faith, this is a sign of the genuineness of their salvation (see 2 Thess 1:5).
1:29 *granted . . . to suffer.* Given as a gift or privilege. Christian suffering, as well as faith, is a blessing (cf. Matt 5:11–12; Acts 5:41; James 1:2; 1 Pet 4:14). The Christian life is to be a "not only . . . but also" proposition: not only believing but also suffering.
1:30 *same conflict.* Their common involvement with Paul in conflict with those who oppose the gospel. *you saw.* When

Be Like Christ

2 Therefore if there is any encouragement
in Christ, if there is any consolation of
love, if there is any [a]fellowship of the Spirit,
if any [1b]affection and compassion,
2 [a]make my joy complete [1]by [b]being of
the same mind, maintaining the same love,
united in spirit, intent on one purpose.
3 Do nothing [1]from [2a]selfishness or
[b]empty conceit, but with humility of mind
[c]regard one another as more important than
yourselves;
4 [a]do not *merely* look out for your own
personal interests, but also for the interests
of others.
5 [a]Have this attitude [1]in yourselves
which was also in [b]Christ Jesus,
6 who, although He [a]existed in the [b]form
of God, [c]did not regard equality with God a
thing to be [1]grasped,
7 but [1a]emptied Himself, taking the form
of a [b]bond-servant, *and* [c]being made in the
likeness of men.
8 Being found in appearance as a man,
[a]He humbled Himself by becoming [b]obedi-
ent to the point of death, even [c]death [1]on a
cross.
9 [a]For this reason also, God [b]highly
exalted Him, and bestowed on Him [c]the
name which is above every name,
10 so that at the name of Jesus [a]EVERY KNEE
WILL BOW, of [b]those who are in heaven and on
earth and under the earth,
11 and that every tongue will confess that
Jesus Christ is [a]Lord, to the glory of God the
Father.
12 So then, my beloved, [a]just as you have
always obeyed, not as in my presence only,
but now much more in my absence, work
out your [b]salvation with [c]fear and trembling;
13 for it is [a]God who is at work in you,

2:1 [1]Lit *inward parts* [a]2 Cor 13:14 [b]Col 3:12 **2** [1]Lit *that you be* [a]John 3:29 [b]Rom 12:16; Phil 4:2 **3** [1]Lit *according to* [2]Or *contentiousness* [a]Rom 2:8; Phil 1:17 [b]Gal 5:26 [c]Rom 12:10; Eph 5:21 **4** [a]Rom 15:1f **5** [1]Or *among* [a]Matt 11:29; Rom 15:3 [b]Phil 1:1 **6** [1]I.e. utilized or asserted [a]John 1:1 [b]2 Cor 4:4 [c]John 5:18; 10:33; 14:28 **7** [1]I.e. laid aside His privileges [a]2 Cor 8:9 [b]Matt 20:28 [c]John 1:14; Rom 8:3; Gal 4:4; Heb 2:17 **8** [1]Lit *of* [a]2 Cor 8:9 [b]Matt 26:39; John 10:18; Rom 5:19; Heb 5:8 [c]Heb 12:2 **9** [a]Heb 1:9 [b]Matt 28:18; Acts 2:33; Heb 2:9 [c]Eph 1:21 **10** [a]Is 45:23; Rom 14:11 [b]Eph 1:10 **11** [a]John 13:13; Rom 10:9; 14:9 **12** [a]Phil 1:5, 6; 4:15 [b]Heb 5:9 [c]2 Cor 7:15 **13** [a]Rom 12:3; 1 Cor 12:6; 15:10; Heb 13:21

Paul and Silas first visited Philippi and were imprisoned (see Acts 16:19–40).

2:1 *in Christ.* Or "united in Christ." In Paul's teaching, this personal union is the basic reality of salvation. To be in Christ is to be saved. It is to be in intimate personal relationship with Christ the Savior. From this relationship flow all the particular benefits and fruits of salvation, like encouragement (see, e.g., 3:8–10; Rom 8:1; 2 Cor 5:17; Gal 2:20). *consolation of love.* The comforting knowledge and assurance that come from God's love in Christ, demonstrated especially in Christ's death for the forgiveness of sins and eternal life (see John 3:16; Rom 5:8; 8:38–39; 1 John 3:16; 4:9–10,16). *fellowship of the Spirit.* The fellowship among believers produced by the Spirit, who indwells each of them (see 2 Cor 13:14). *affection and compassion.* Christians are to have intense care and deep sympathy for each other (see 1:8; Col 3:12). All these benefits—encouragement, comfort, fellowship, tenderness and compassion—are viewed by Paul as present realities for the Philippians.

2:2 *same mind . . . same love . . . united in spirit . . . one purpose.* Emphasizes the unity that should exist among Christians. *same mind.* Not uniformity in thought but the common disposition to work together and serve one another—the "attitude" of Christ (v. 5; see 4:2; Rom 12:16; 15:5; 2 Cor 13:11).

2:3 *selfishness or empty conceit.* The mortal enemies of unity and harmony in the church (cf. 1:17; see Gal 5:20, where the Greek for "selfishness" is rendered "disputes" and listed among the "deeds of the flesh"). *humility.* The source of Christian unity. This is the mind-set of the person who is not conceited but who has a right attitude toward himself. *regard one another as more important than yourselves.* Not that everyone else is superior or more talented, but that Christian love sees others as worthy of preferential treatment (see Rom 12:10; Gal 5:13; Eph 5:21; 1 Pet 5:5).

2:4 *your own personal interests.* These are proper, but only if there is equal concern for the interests of others (cf. Rom 15:1).

2:5 *Have this attitude . . . which was in Christ.* In spite of all that is unique and radically different about the person and work of Christ (see vv. 6–11), Christians are to have His attitude of self-sacrificing humility and love for others (see vv. 2–4; Matt 11:29; John 13:12–17).

2:6–11 The poetic, even lyric, character of these verses is apparent. Many view them as an early Christian hymn (see note on Col 3:16), taken over and perhaps modified by Paul. If so, they nonetheless express his convictions. The passage treats Christ's humiliation (vv. 6–8) and exaltation (vv. 9–11).

2:6 *in the form of God.* Affirming that Jesus is fully God (see note on Rom 9:5). *form.* Essential form, the sum of those qualities that make God specifically God. *equality with God.* The status and privileges that inevitably follow from being in very nature God. *a thing to be grasped.* Perhaps something to be forcibly retained—the glory Christ had with the Father before His incarnation. But He did not consider that high position to be something He could not give up. On the other hand, it may be something still to be attained, like a prize, as if He did not yet possess it.

2:7 *emptied Himself.* He did this, not by giving up deity, but by laying aside His glory (see John 17:5) and submitting to the humiliation of becoming man (see 2 Cor 8:9). Jesus is truly God and truly man. Another view is that He emptied Himself, not of deity itself, but of its prerogatives—the high position and glory of deity. *form of a bond-servant.* Emphasizes the full reality of His servant identity (see Matt 20:28). As a servant, He was always submissive to the will of the Father.

2:8 *appearance as a man.* Not only was Jesus "like" a human being (v. 7), but He also took on the actual outward characteristics of a man (see John 1:14; Rom 8:3; Heb 2:17). *humbled Himself.* See v. 7; 2 Cor 8:9. *obedient.* How Jesus humbled himself (cf. Heb 5:7–8). A "bond-servant" (v. 7) obeys. *of death.* Stresses both the totality and the climax of Jesus' obedience. *on a cross.* Heightens Jesus' humiliation; He died as someone cursed (see Gal 3:13; Heb 12:2). Crucifixion was the most degrading kind of execution that could be inflicted on a person.

2:9 *exalted.* See Matt 28:18; Acts 2:33; cf. Is 52:13. *the name . . . above every name.* Reference doubtless is to the office or rank conferred on Jesus—His glorious position, not His proper name (cf. Eph 1:21; Heb 1:4–5).

2:10–11 *BOW . . . confess.* Cf. Is 45:23. God's design is that all people everywhere should worship and serve Jesus as Lord. Ultimately all will acknowledge Him as Lord (see Rom 14:9), whether willingly or not.

2:12 *So then.* Because of Christ's incomparable example (vv. 5–11). *obeyed.* The commands of God as passed on to the Philippians by Paul (see Rom 1:5; 15:18; 2 Cor 10:5–6). *my presence.* During the course of Paul's second (see Acts 16:12–40)

both to will and to work [b]for *His* good pleasure.
14 Do all things without [a]grumbling or disputing;
15 so that you will [1]prove yourselves to be [a]blameless and innocent, [b]children of God above reproach in the midst of a [c]crooked and perverse generation, among whom you [2d]appear as [3]lights in the world,
16 holding [1]fast the word of life, so that in [a]the day of Christ I will have reason to glory because I did not [b]run in vain nor [c]toil in vain.
17 But even if I am being [a]poured out as a drink offering upon [b]the sacrifice and service of your faith, I rejoice and share my joy with you all.
18 You too, *I urge you*, rejoice in the same way and share your joy with me.

Timothy and Epaphroditus

19 But I hope [1]in the Lord Jesus to [a]send [b]Timothy to you shortly, so that I also may be encouraged when I learn of your condition.
20 For I have no one *else* [a]of kindred spirit who will genuinely be concerned for your welfare.
21 For they all [a]seek after their own interests, not those of Christ Jesus.
22 But you know [a]of his proven worth, that [b]he served with me in the furtherance of the gospel [c]like a child *serving* his father.
23 [a]Therefore I hope to send him immediately, as soon as I see how things *go* with me;
24 and [a]I trust in the Lord that I myself also will be coming shortly.
25 But I thought it necessary to send to you [a]Epaphroditus, my brother and [b]fellow worker and [c]fellow soldier, who is also your [1d]messenger and [a]minister to my need;
26 because he was longing [1]for you all and was distressed because you had heard that he was sick.
27 For indeed he was sick to the point of death, but God had mercy on him, and not on him only but also on me, so that I would not have sorrow upon sorrow.
28 Therefore I have sent him all the more eagerly so that when you see him again you may rejoice and I may be less concerned *about you.*
29 [a]Receive him then in the Lord with all joy, and [b]hold men like him in high regard;
30 because he came close to death [1a]for the work of Christ, risking his life to [b]complete [2]what was deficient in your service to me.

The Goal of Life

3 Finally, my brethren, [a]rejoice in the Lord. To write the same things *again* is no trouble to me, and it is a safeguard for you.

13 [b]Eph 1:5 **14** [a]1 Cor 10:10; 1 Pet 4:9 **15** [1]Or *become* [2]Or *shine* [3]Or *luminaries, stars* [a]Luke 1:6; Phil 3:6 [b]Matt 5:45; Eph 5:1 [c]Deut 32:5; Acts 2:40 [d]Matt 5:14-16 **16** [1]Or *forth* [a]Phil 1:6 [b]Gal 2:2 [c]Is 49:4; Gal 4:11; 1 Thess 3:5 **17** [a]2 Cor 12:15; 2 Tim 4:6 [b]Num 28:6, 7; Rom 15:16 **19** [1]Or *trusting in* [a]Phil 2:23 [b]Phil 1:1 **20** [a]1 Cor 16:10; 2 Tim 3:10 **21** [a]1 Cor 10:24; 13:5; Phil 2:4 **22** [a]Rom 5:4; Acts 16:2 [b]Acts 16:3; 1 Cor 16:10; 2 Tim 3:10 [c]1 Cor 4:17 **23** [a]Phil 2:19 **24** [a]Phil 1:25 **25** [1]Lit *apostle* [a]Phil 4:18 [b]Rom 16:3, 9, 21; Phil 4:3; Philem 1, 24 [c]Philem 2 [d]John 13:16; 2 Cor 8:23 **26** [1]One early ms reads *to see you all* **29** [a]Rom 16:2 [b]1 Cor 16:18 **30** [1]Lit *because of* [2]Lit *your deficiency of service* [a]Acts 20:24 [b]1 Cor 16:17; Phil 4:10 **3:1** [a]Phil 2:18; 4:4

and third (see Acts 20:1–3,6) missionary journeys. *work out your salvation.* Work it out to the finish; not a reference to the attempt to earn one's salvation by works, but to the expression of one's salvation in spiritual growth and development. Salvation is not merely a gift received once for all; it expresses itself in an ongoing process in which the believer is strenuously involved (cf. Matt 24:13; 1 Cor 9:24–27; Heb 3:14; 6:9–11; 2 Pet 1:5–8)—the process of perseverance, spiritual growth and maturation. *fear and trembling.* Not because of doubt or anxiety; rather, the reference is to an active reverence and a singleness of purpose in response to God's grace.

2:13 *to will and to work.* Intention, or faith, and our obedience cannot be separated (cf. Gal 5:6; James 2:18,20,22).

2:14–17 Some things involved in working out our salvation.

2:14 *grumbling.* Being discontented with God's will is an expression of unbelief that prevents one from doing what pleases God (v. 13; cf. 1 Cor 10:10). *disputing.* Over debatable points that do not need to be settled for the good of the church (see 2 Tim 2:23; Titus 3:9).

2:15 *blameless and innocent . . . above reproach.* Not absolute, sinless perfection, but wholehearted, unmixed devotion to doing God's will. *crooked and perverse generation.* A description of the unbelieving world (see Acts 2:40; Eph 2:1–3; cf. Matt 17:17). *appear as lights.* The contrast, like light in darkness, that Christians are to be to the world around them (cf. Matt 5:15–16).

2:16 *glory.* Not out of pride or a sense of self-accomplishment, but because of what God has done through Paul (see 1 Thess 2:19). *day of Christ.* See note on 1:6. *in vain.* Cf. 1 Cor 9:24–27.

2:17–18 *I . . . rejoice . . . You too . . . rejoice.* Christian joy ought always to be mutual.

2:17 *I am being poured out.* The reference may be to his entire ministry as one large thanksgiving sacrifice. However, it is more probable that Paul refers to his present imprisonment, which may end in a martyr's death. His life would then be poured out as a drink offering accompanying the sacrificial service of the Philippians. *as a drink offering.* The OT background is the daily sacrifices in Ex 29:38–41. *of your faith.* Genuine faith is active and working (see note on v. 13).

2:19–23 Paul plans to send Timothy, who is with him in Rome (see 1:1), to discover and report on conditions in the Philippian church.

2:20 *I have no one else of kindred spirit.* Timothy was a good example of the kind of person envisioned in the exhortation of v. 4.

2:21 A sharp contrast between Timothy and Paul's other associates—an outstanding commendation for one so young.

2:22 *like a child serving his father.* This relationship between Timothy and Paul is developed at length in 1,2 Timothy. *serving.* Like Jesus and Paul, Timothy had a servant attitude.

2:24 Paul anticipates his release in the near future (see 1:25).

2:25–30 Epaphroditus, too, after a close brush with death (vv. 27,30), is being sent home to Philippi.

2:25 *messenger.* A broader use of the Greek word often translated "apostle," applied here to Epaphroditus as a representative of the Philippian church (cf. 2 Cor 8:23).

2:27 Cf. 1:21–26.

2:28 *concerned.* The legitimate cares and concerns that come with the Christian life and the gospel ministry (see note on 4:6; cf. 2 Cor 4:8; 11:28).

3:1 *Finally.* Marks a transition to a new section as Paul moves toward his conclusion; this does not mark the close of the letter, however (cf. 4:8). *rejoice in the Lord.* See 4:4. *same things again.* Matters taken up in the verses that follow, which Paul had previously dealt with either orally when he was in Philippi or perhaps in an earlier letter. *safeguard.* Where serious error is present, there is safety in repetition.

2 Beware of the [a]dogs, beware of the [b]evil workers, beware of the [1]false circumcision;

3 for [a]we are the *true* [1]circumcision, who [b]worship in the Spirit of God and [c]glory in [d]Christ Jesus and put no confidence in the flesh,

4 although [a]I myself might have confidence even in the flesh. If anyone else has a mind to put confidence in the flesh, I far more:

5 [a]circumcised the eighth day, of the [b]nation of Israel, of the [c]tribe of Benjamin, a [b]Hebrew of Hebrews; as to the Law, [d]a Pharisee;

6 as to zeal, [a]a persecutor of the church; as to the [b]righteousness which is in the Law, found [c]blameless.

7 But [a]whatever things were gain to me, those things I have counted as loss for the sake of Christ.

8 More than that, I count all things to be loss [1]in view of the surpassing value of [2][a]knowing [b]Christ Jesus my Lord, [1]for whom I have suffered the loss of all things, and count them but rubbish so that I may gain Christ,

9 and may be found in Him, not having [a]a righteousness of my own derived from *the* Law, but that which is through faith in Christ, [b]the righteousness which *comes* from God on the basis of faith,

10 that I may [a]know Him and [b]the power of His resurrection and [1][c]the fellowship of His sufferings, being [d]conformed to His death;

11 [1]in order that I may [a]attain to the resurrection from the dead.

12 Not that I have already [a]obtained *it* or have already [b]become perfect, but I press on [1]so that I may [c]lay hold of that [2]for which also I [d]was laid hold of by [e]Christ Jesus.

13 Brethren, I do not regard myself as having laid hold of *it* yet; but one thing *I do:* [a]forgetting what *lies* behind and reaching forward to what *lies* ahead,

14 I [a]press on toward the goal for the prize of the [b]upward call of God in [c]Christ Jesus.

2 [1]Lit *mutilation;* Gr *katatome* [a]Ps 22:16, 20; Gal 5:15; Rev 22:15 [b]2 Cor 11:13 **3** [1]Gr *peritome* [a]Rom 2:29; 9:6; Gal 6:15 [b]Gal 5:25 [c]Rom 15:17; Gal 6:14 [d]Rom 8:39; Phil 1:1; 3:12 **4** [a]2 Cor 5:16; 11:18 **5** [a]Luke 1:59 [b]Rom 11:1; 2 Cor 11:22 [c]Rom 11:1 [d]Acts 22:3; 23:6; 26:5 **6** [a]Acts 8:3; 22:4, 5; 26:9-11 [b]Phil 3:9 [c]Phil 2:15 **7** [a]Luke 14:33 **8** [1]Lit *because of* [2]Lit *the knowledge of* [a]Jer 9:23f; John 17:3; Eph 4:13; Phil 3:10; 2 Pet 1:3 [b]Rom 8:39; Phil 1:1; 3:12 **9** [a]Rom 10:5; Phil 3:6 [b]Rom 9:30; 1 Cor 1:30 **10** [1]Or *participation in* [a]Jer 9:23f; John 17:3; Eph 4:13; Phil 3:8; 2 Pet 1:13 [b]Rom 6:5 [c]Rom 8:17 [d]Rom 6:5; 8:36; Gal 6:17 **11** [1]Lit *if somehow* [a]Acts 26:7; 1 Cor 15:23; Rev 20:5f **12** [1]Lit *if I may even* [2]Or *because also* [a]1 Cor 9:24f; 1 Tim 6:12, 19 [b]1 Cor 13:10 [c]1 Tim 6:12, 19 [d]Acts 9:5f [e]Rom 8:39; Phil 1:1; 3:3, 8 **13** [a]Luke 9:62 **14** [a]1 Cor 9:24; Heb 6:1 [b]Rom 8:28; 11:29; 2 Tim 1:9 [c]Phil 3:3

3:2 *dogs.* A harsh word for Paul's opponents, showing their aggressive opposition to the gospel and the seriousness of their error and its destructive, "devouring" results (cf. Gal 5:15). Their teaching was probably similar to what Paul had to oppose in the Galatian churches (see Introduction to Galatians: Occasion and Purpose). *false circumcision.* Again a strong, painfully vivid term; the false teachers have so distorted the meaning of circumcision (cf. v. 3) that it has become nothing more than a useless cutting of the body.

3:3 *circumcision.* Its true, inner meaning is realized only in believers, who worship God with genuine spiritual worship and who glory in Christ as their Savior rather than trusting in their own human effort (cf. Rom 2:28–29; Col 2:12–13; see also Deut 30:6; Ezek 36:26). *glory . . . no confidence.* Everyone is a "boaster," either in Christ or in himself. *flesh.* Weak human nature. Although the term "flesh" in Paul's letters often refers to sinful human nature, it speaks here of the frailty of human nature: It is not worthy of our confidence; it cannot save.

3:4–14 Paul's personal testimony, a model for every believer; one of the most significant autobiographical sections in his letters (see Gal 1:13–24; 1 Tim 1:12–16; cf. Acts 22:1–21; 26:1–23).

3:4–6 Paul's pre-Christian confidence, rooted in his Jewish pedigree, privileges and attainments.

3:5 *eighth day.* See Gen 17:12. *of the nation of Israel.* Paul was born a Jew and was not a proselyte. *tribe of Benjamin.* His Jewish roots are deep and unambiguous. Jerusalem, the Holy City, lay on the border of the tribal territory of Benjamin. *Hebrew of Hebrews.* In language, attitudes and life-style (see Acts 22:2–3; Gal 1:14). *Pharisee.* See Acts 22:3; 23:6; 26:5.

3:6 *righteousness . . . in the Law.* Righteousness produced by using the Law as an attempt to merit God's approval and blessing (cf. v. 9)—a use of the Law strongly opposed by Paul as contrary to the gospel itself (see Rom 3:27–28; 4:1–5; Gal 2:16; 3:10–12). *blameless.* In terms of legalistic standards of scrupulous external conformity to the Law.

3:7–14 Paul's confidence in Christ.

3:7 *whatever.* The things mentioned in vv. 5–6. *gain . . . loss.* The great reversal in Paul—begun on the road to Damascus (see Acts 9:3–16)—from being self-centered to being centered in Christ.

3:8 *knowing Christ Jesus.* Not only a knowledge of facts but a knowledge gained through experience that, in its surpassing greatness, transforms the entire person. The following verses spell this out. *rubbish.* What Paul now has as a Christian is not merely preferable or a better alternative; in contrast, his former way of life was worthless and despicable.

3:9 *be found in Him.* Union with Christ (see note on 2:1; cf. 1 Cor 1:30)—not simply an experience in the past, but a present, continuing relationship. *righteousness . . . from the Law.* See note on v. 6. *righteousness . . . of faith.* A principal benefit of union with Christ (see Rom 3:21–22; 1 Cor 1:30; Gal 2:16).

3:10 *know Him.* As in v. 8, this knowledge is not merely factual; it includes the experience of the power of His resurrection (see Eph 1:17–20), of fellowship in His sufferings (cf. Acts 9:16) and of being like Him in His death (see 2 Cor 4:7–12; 12:9–10). Believers already share positionally in Christ's death and resurrection (cf. Rom 6:2–13; Gal 2:20; 5:24; 6:14; Eph 2:6; Col 2:12–13; 3:1). In v. 10, however, Paul speaks of the actual experience of Christ's resurrection power and of suffering with and for Him, even to the point of death.

3:11 *that I may.* Not an indication of doubt or uncertainty, but of intense concern and involvement. *resurrection.* The great personal anticipation of every believer (see Dan 12:2; John 5:29; Acts 24:15; 1 Cor 15:23; 1 Thess 4:16).

3:12–14 The Christian life is like a race; elsewhere Paul uses athletic imagery in a similar way (1 Cor 9:24–27; 1 Tim 6:12; 2 Tim 4:7–8; cf. Matt 24:13; Heb 12:1).

3:12 *lay hold . . . I was laid hold of.* Paul's goal is Christ's goal for him, and Christ supplies the resources for him to "press on toward the goal" (v. 14; cf. 2:12–13).

3:13 *forgetting.* Not losing all memory of his sinful past (see vv. 4–6), but leaving it behind him as done with and settled.

3:14 *prize.* The winner of the Greek races received a wreath of leaves and sometimes a cash award; the Christian receives an award of everlasting glory. *upward.* Paul's ultimate aspirations are found not in this life but in heaven, because Christ is there (see Col 3:1–2).

15 Let us therefore, as many as are [1a]per-
fect, have this attitude; and if in anything
you have a [b]different attitude, [c]God will
reveal that also to you;
16 however, let us keep [1a]living by that
same *standard* to which we have attained.
17 Brethren, [a]join in following my example, and observe those who walk according
to the [b]pattern you have in us.
18 For [a]many walk, of whom I often told
you, and now tell you even [b]weeping, *that*
they are enemies of [c]the cross of Christ,
19 whose end is destruction, whose god is
their [1a]appetite, and *whose* [b]glory is in their
shame, who [c]set their minds on earthly
things.
20 For [a]our [1]citizenship is in heaven, from
which also we eagerly [b]wait for a Savior, the
Lord Jesus Christ;
21 who will [a]transform [1]the body of our
humble state into [b]conformity with [2]the
[c]body of His glory, [d]by the exertion of the
power that He has even to [e]subject all things
to Himself.

15 [1]Or *mature* [a]Matt 5:48; 1 Cor 2:6 [b]Gal 5:10 [c]John 6:45; Eph 1:17; 1 Thess 4:9 **16** [1]Lit *following in line* [a]Gal 6:16 **17** [a]1 Cor 4:16; 11:1; Phil 4:9 [b]1 Pet 5:3 **18** [a]2 Cor 11:13 [b]Acts 20:31 [c]Gal 6:14 **19** [1]Lit *belly* [a]Rom 16:18; Titus 1:12 [b]Rom 6:21; Jude 13 [c]Rom 8:5f; Col 3:2 **20** [1]Lit *commonwealth* [a]Eph 2:19; Phil 1:27; Col 3:1; Heb 12:22 [b]1 Cor 1:7 **21** [1]Or *our lowly body* [2]Or *His glorious body* [a]1 Cor 15:43-53 [b]Rom 8:29; Col 3:4 [c]1 Cor 15:43, 49 [d]Eph 1:19 [e]1 Cor 15:28

Think of Excellence

4 Therefore, my beloved brethren [1]whom I
[a]long *to see,* my joy and crown, in this
way [b]stand firm in the Lord, my beloved.
2 I urge Euodia and I urge Syntyche to
[1a]live in harmony in the Lord.
3 Indeed, true companion, I ask you also
to help these women who have shared my
struggle in *the cause of* the gospel, together
with Clement also and the rest of my [a]fellow
workers, whose [b]names are in the book of life.
4 [a]Rejoice in the Lord always; again I will
say, rejoice!
5 Let your gentle *spirit* be known to all
men. [a]The Lord is [1]near.
6 [a]Be anxious for nothing, but in everything by [b]prayer and supplication with
thanksgiving let your requests be made
known to God.
7 And [a]the peace of God, which sur-

4:1 [1]Lit *and longed for* [a]Phil 1:8 [b]1 Cor 16:13; Phil 1:27 **2** [1]Or *be of the same mind* [a]Phil 2:2 **3** [a]Phil 2:25 [b]Luke 10:20 **4** [a]Phil 3:1 **5** [1]Or *at hand* [a]1 Cor 16:22 mg; Heb 10:37; James 5:8f **6** [a]Matt 6:25 [b]Eph 6:18; 1 Tim 2:1; 5:5 **7** [a]Is 26:3; John 14:27; Phil 4:9; Col 3:15

3:15 *perfect.* Those who have made reasonable progress in spiritual growth and stability (see 1 Cor 2:6; 3:1–3; Heb 5:14). *this attitude.* That expressed in vv. 12–14: There are heights yet to be scaled; do not become complacent. *have a different attitude.* If the readers accept the view set forth in vv. 12–14 and yet fail to agree in some lesser point, God will clarify the matter for them.

3:16 *keep living by . . . have attained.* Put into practice the truth they have already comprehended. We are responsible for the truth we currently possess.

3:17 *following my example.* As Paul follows the example of Christ. *observe those who walk.* The life-styles Christians lead ought to be models worth following.

3:18 *often told you.* See v. 1. *weeping.* See Acts 20:19,31. *they are enemies of the cross.* In glaring contrast to Paul's conduct (v. 10) and to the truth of the gospel.

3:19 *destruction.* The opposite of salvation. *god . . . appetite.* A deep self-centeredness; their appetites and desires come first. *earthly things.* They have set their minds on the things of this life; they are antinomians (libertines), the opposite of the legalists of v. 2.

3:20 *citizenship.* In this world Christians are aliens, fully involved in it, yet not of it (cf. John 17:14–16; 1 Cor 7:29–31; 1 Pet 2:11). *in heaven.* Where Christ is and where believers are—in union with Him; contrast the "earthly things" of v. 19 (see Eph 2:6; Col 3:1–4). *from which . . . eagerly wait.* See Rom 8:19; 1 Cor 1:7; 1 Thess 1:9–10; 2 Tim 4:8.

3:21 *will transform.* By the Holy Spirit at the resurrection (see Rom 8:11; 1 Cor 6:14; 15:50–53). *the body of our humble state.* Subject to weakness, decay and death, due to sin (see Rom 8:10,20–23; 1 Cor 15:42–44). *conformity with the body of His glory.* See Rom 8:29; 1 John 3:2. The resurrection body, received already by Christ, who is the "first fruits," will be received by believers in the future resurrection "harvest" (see 1 Cor 15:20,49). It is "spiritual," i.e., transformed by the power of the Holy Spirit (see 1 Cor 15:44,46). *power . . . to subject.* Christ's present power, earned by His obedience to death (see 2:8) and received in His resurrection and ascension, is universal and absolute (see Matt 28:18; 1 Cor 15:27; Eph 1:20–22).

4:1 *beloved . . . long to see.* See notes on 1:8; 2:1. *my joy and crown.* True not only now, but especially when Christ returns (see 1 Thess 2:19). *in this way.* Refers to the closing statements of ch. 3. In the face of libertine practices (3:18–19), the Philippians should follow Paul's example (3:17), having their minds set on heavenly things (3:20–21). *stand firm.* In the midst of present struggles for the sake of the gospel (cf. 1:27–30; 1 Cor 15:58).

4:2–3 The disagreement between Euodia and Syntyche is serious enough to be mentioned in a letter to be read publicly, but Paul seems confident that "these women" (v. 3) will be reconciled. His handling of the situation is a model of tact—he does not take sides but encourages others closer to the situation to promote reconciliation (see 2:2).

4:3 *shared my struggle . . . my fellow workers.* Those associated with the apostle in the cause of the gospel (women as well as men) are his equals, not subordinates (cf. 2:25; Rom 16:3,9,21; Philem 24). *Clement.* Not mentioned elsewhere in the NT. *the rest of my fellow workers.* Not mentioned individually because they are known to God and their names are entered in the book of life, the heavenly register of the elect (see note on Rev 3:5).

4:4 *Rejoice in the Lord.* See 3:1. *always.* Under all kinds of circumstances, including suffering (see Hab 3:17–18; James 1:2; 1 Pet 4:13).

4:5 *gentle spirit.* Christlike consideration for others (cf. 2 Cor 10:1). It is especially essential in church leaders (see 1 Tim 3:3; Titus 3:2, "showing every consideration"). *near.* See Rom 13:11; cf. James 5:8–9; Rev 22:7,12,20. The next great event in God's prophetic schedule is Christ's return. The whole period from Christ's first coming to the consummation of the kingdom is viewed in the NT as the last time (1 John 2:18). From God's vantage point, a thousand years are as a day. Thus there is a sense in which, for every generation, the Lord's coming is near.

4:6 *anxious.* Self-centered, counterproductive worry, not legitimate cares and concerns for the spread of the gospel (see 2:28 and note; 2 Cor 11:28; see also Matt 6:25–31; 1 Pet 5:7). *in everything, by prayer.* Anxiety and prayer are two great opposing forces in Christian experience. *thanksgiving.* The antidote to worry (along with prayer and petition).

4:7 *peace of God.* Not merely a psychological state of mind, but an inner tranquillity based on peace with God—the peace-

passes all [1]comprehension, will [b]guard your
hearts and your [c]minds in [d]Christ Jesus.
8 Finally, brethren, [a]whatever is true,
whatever is honorable, whatever is right,
whatever is pure, whatever is [1]lovely, whatever is of good repute, if there is any excellence and if anything worthy of praise,
[2]dwell on these things.
9 The things you have learned and
received and heard and seen [a]in me, practice
these things, and [b]the God of peace will be
with you.

God's Provisions

10 But I rejoiced in the Lord greatly, that
now at last [a]you have revived your concern
for me; indeed, you were concerned *before,*
but you lacked opportunity.
11 Not that I speak [1]from want, for I have
learned to be [2a]content in whatever circumstances I am.
12 I know how to get along with humble
means, and I also know how to live in prosperity; in any and every circumstance I have
learned the secret of being filled and going
[a]hungry, both of having abundance and
[b]suffering need.
13 I can do all things [1]through Him who
[a]strengthens me.

7 [1]Lit *mind* [b]1 Pet 1:5 [c]2 Cor 10:5 [d]Phil 1:1; 4:19, 21
8 [1]Or *lovable and gracious* [2]Lit *ponder these things* [a]Rom 14:18; 1 Pet 2:12
9 [a]Phil 3:17 [b]Rom 15:33
10 [a]2 Cor 11:9; Phil 2:30
11 [1]Lit *according to* [2]Or *self-sufficient* [a]2 Cor 9:8; 1 Tim 6:6, 8; Heb 13:5
12 [a]1 Cor 4:11 [b]2 Cor 11:9
13 [1]Lit *in* [a]2 Cor 12:9; Eph 3:16; Col 1:11
14 [a]Heb 10:33; Rev 1:9

14 Nevertheless, you have done well to
[a]share *with me* in my affliction.
15 You yourselves also know, Philippians,
that at the [1a]first preaching of the gospel,
after I left [b]Macedonia, no church [c]shared
with me in the matter of giving and receiving
but you alone;
16 for even in [a]Thessalonica you sent *a*
gift more than once for my needs.
17 [a]Not that I seek the gift itself, but I seek
for the [1]profit which increases to your
account.
18 But I have received everything in full
and have an abundance; I am [1]amply supplied, having received from [a]Epaphroditus
[2]what you have sent, [3b]a fragrant aroma, an
acceptable sacrifice, well-pleasing to God.
19 And [a]my God will supply [1]all your
needs according to His [b]riches in glory in
Christ Jesus.
20 Now to [a]our God and Father [b]*be* the
glory [1]forever and ever. Amen.

15 [1]Lit *beginning of* [a]Phil 1:5 [b]Rom 15:26 [c]2 Cor 11:9
16 [a]Acts 17:1; 1 Thess 2:9 17 [1]Lit *fruit* [a]1 Cor 9:11f; 2 Cor 9:5 18 [1]Lit *made full* [2]Lit *the things from you* [3]Lit *an odor of fragrance* [a]Phil 2:25 [b]Ex 29:18; 2 Cor 2:14; Eph 5:2 19 [1]Or *every need of yours* [a]2 Cor 9:8 [b]Rom 2:4 20 [1]Lit *to the ages of the ages* [a]Gal 1:4 [b]Rom 11:36

---

ful state of those whose sins are forgiven (cf. John 14:27; Rom 5:1). The opposite of anxiety, it is the tranquillity that comes when the believer commits all his cares to God in prayer and worries about them no more. *surpasses all comprehension.* The full dimensions of God's love and care are beyond human comprehension (see Eph 3:18–20). *guard . . . hearts . . . minds.* A military concept depicting a sentry standing guard. God's "protective custody" of those who are in Christ Jesus extends to the core of their beings and to their deepest intentions (cf. 1 Pet 1:5).

4:8 *Finally.* See note on 3:1. *true . . . worthy of praise.* Paul understood the influence of one's thoughts on one's life. What a person allows to occupy his mind will sooner or later determine his speech and his action. Paul's exhortation to "dwell on these things" is followed by a second exhortation, "practice these things" (v. 9). The combination of virtues listed in vv. 8–9 is sure to produce a wholesome thought pattern, which in turn will result in a life of moral and spiritual excellence.

4:9 *seen in me.* See note on 3:17. *God of peace.* See note on 1 Thess 5:23; cf. the "peace of God" (v. 7).

4:10 *at last . . . lacked opportunity.* The delay in sending gifts to Paul was not the fault of the Philippians, nor was it because they were lacking in concern for him (cf. 2 Cor 11:9). Perhaps Paul's uncertain itinerary prior to his arrival at Rome or the lack of an available messenger had prevented the Philippians from showing their concern.

4:11 *content in whatever circumstances.* Paul genuinely appreciates the gifts from Philippi (see vv. 14,18) but he is not ultimately dependent on them (cf. 1 Tim 6:6–8).

4:12 *secret of being filled . . . having abundance.* Prosperity, too, can be a source of discontent.

4:13 *all things.* Everything pleasing to God. *Him who strengthens me.* Christ. Union with the living, exalted Christ is the secret of being content (v. 12) and the source of Paul's abiding strength (see especially 2 Cor 12:9–10; see also John 15:5; Eph 3:16–17; Col 1:11).

4:14 *share.* The Philippians' gifts are a means of involving them in Paul's troubles (cf. Heb 10:33).

4:15 *first preaching.* During Paul's second missionary journey, when he first preached in Philippi (see Acts 16:12–40). *left.* For the south (Achaia), where Athens and Corinth were located (see Acts 17:14–16; 18:1–4). *Macedonia.* The northern part of modern-day Greece, where Berea and Thessalonica, as well as Philippi, were located. *shared with me in the matter of.* Or "participated with me in an account of." Paul uses commercial language to describe "giving and receiving" (credit and debit) between the Philippians and himself (see "increases to your account," v. 17). Yet this commercial imagery is plainly transcended by the mutual concern and self-sacrifice of their relationship. *but you alone.* The generosity of the Philippian church is unique and unmatched (cf. 2 Cor 8:1–5).

4:16 *even in Thessalonica.* While he was still in Macedonia (see Acts 17:1–9). *gift more than once.* The gifts sent to Rome through Epaphroditus are the latest in a long and consistent pattern of generosity (cf. 2 Cor 8:1–5).

4:17 *increases to your account.* See note on v. 15. The "investment value" of the Philippians' gift is not primarily what Paul received, but the "spiritual dividends" they received.

4:18 *a fragrant aroma, an acceptable sacrifice.* The OT background is the sacrifice, not of atonement for sin, but of thanksgiving and praise (cf. Lev 7:12–15; Rom 12:1; Eph 5:2; Heb 13:15–16). *acceptable . . . well-pleasing to God.* Because of Christ's work for us (see 1 Pet 2:5) and God's work in us (see Phil 2:13).

4:19 *my.* A personal touch (cf. "my God" in 1:3). *will supply.* A promise given to a church that had sacrificially given to meet Paul's need. *your needs.* Paul is concerned not only about his own situation but also about that of the Philippians. *His riches in glory in Christ Jesus.* The true measure of God's blessings to the church (cf. Eph 1:18; 3:16–20).

4:20 Paul cannot hold back a doxology, especially as he considers the truth of v. 19.

21 Greet every [1]saint in Christ Jesus. [a]The
brethren who are with me greet you.
22 [a]All the [1b]saints greet you, especially
those of Caesar's household.
23 [a]The grace of the Lord Jesus Christ [b]be
with your spirit.

21 [1]Or *holy one* [a]Gal 1:2
22 [1]V 21, note 1 [a]2 Cor 13:13 [b]Acts 9:13
23 [a]Rom 16:20 [b]2 Tim 4:22

4:21–22 Final greetings are a typical feature of Paul's letters (see, e.g., Rom 16:3–16,21–23; 1 Cor 16:19–20; 2 Cor 13:12–13; Col 4:10–12,14–15,18).
4:21 *every saint.* See note on 1:1. *brethren who are with me.* Paul's fellow workers at Rome, especially Timothy (see 1:1,14,16).
4:22 *Caesar's household.* Not blood relatives of the emperor, but those employed (slaves or freedmen) in or around the palace area (cf. "praetorian guard," 1:13).
4:23 A typical closing benediction of Paul. *your spirit.* Not one part of man to the exclusion of other parts, but the whole person seen from his inner side, at the core of his being (cf. Gal 6:18; 2 Tim 4:22; Philem 25).

Colossians

INTRODUCTION

Author, Date and Place of Writing

That Colossians is a genuine letter of Paul is not usually disputed. In the early church, all who speak on the subject of authorship ascribe it to Paul. In the 19th century, however, some thought that the heresy refuted in ch. 2 was second-century Gnosticism. But a careful analysis of ch. 2 shows that the heresy referred to there is noticeably less developed than the Gnosticism of leading Gnostic teachers of the second and third centuries. Also, the seeds of what later became the full-blown Gnosticism of the second century were present in the first century and already making inroads into the churches. Consequently, it is not necessary to date Colossians in the second century at a time too late for Paul to have written the letter.

Instead, it is to be dated during Paul's first imprisonment in Rome, where he spent at least two years under house arrest (see Acts 28:16–31). Some have argued that Paul wrote Colossians from Ephesus or Caesarea, but most of the evidence favors Rome as the place where Paul penned all the Prison Letters (Ephesians, Colossians, Philippians and Philemon). Colossians should be dated c. A.D. 60, in the same year as Ephesians and Philemon.

Colosse: The Town and the Church

Several hundred years before Paul's day, Colosse had been a leading city in Asia Minor (present-day Turkey). It was located on the Lycus River and on the great east-west trade route leading from Ephesus on the Aegean Sea to the Euphrates River. By the first century A.D. Colosse was diminished to a second-rate market town, which had been surpassed long ago in power and importance by the neighboring towns of Laodicea and Hierapolis (see 4:13).

What gave Colosse NT importance, however, was the fact that, during Paul's three-year ministry in Ephesus, Epaphras had been converted and had carried the gospel to Colosse (cf. 1:7–8; Acts 19:10). The young church that resulted then became the target of heretical attack, which led to Epaphras's visit to Paul in Rome and ultimately to the penning of the Colossian letter.

Perhaps as a result of the efforts of Epaphras or other converts of Paul, Christian churches had also been established in Laodicea and Hierapolis. Some of them were house churches (see 4:15; Philem 2). Most likely all of them were primarily Gentile.

The Colossian Heresy

Paul never explicitly describes the false teaching he opposes in the Colossian letter. The nature of the heresy must be inferred from statements he made in opposition to the false teachers. An analysis of his refutation suggests that the heresy was diverse in nature. Some of the elements of its teachings were:

1. *Ceremonialism.* It held to strict rules about the kinds of permissible food and drink, religious festivals (2:16–17) and circumcision (2:11; 3:11).

2. *Asceticism.* "Do not handle, do not taste, do not touch!" (2:21; cf. 2:23).

3. *Angel worship.* See 2:18.

4. *Depreciation of Christ.* This is implied in Paul's stress on the supremacy of Christ (1:15–20; 2:2–3,9).

5. *Secret knowledge.* The Gnostics boasted of this (see 2:18 and Paul's emphasis in 2:2–3 on Christ, "in whom are hidden all the treasures of wisdom").

6. *Reliance on human wisdom and tradition.* See 2:4,8.

These elements seem to fall into two categories, Jewish and Gnostic. It is likely, therefore, that the Colossian heresy was a mixture of an extreme form of Judaism and an early stage of Gnosticism (see Introduction to 1 John: Gnosticism; see also note on 2:23).

Purpose and Theme

Paul's purpose is to refute the Colossian heresy. To accomplish this goal, he exalts Christ as the very image of God (1:15), the Creator (1:16), the preexistent sustainer of all things (1:17), the head of the church (1:18), the first to be resurrected (1:18), the fullness of deity in bodily form (1:19; 2:9) and the reconciler (1:20–22). Thus Christ is completely adequate. We "have been made complete" in Christ (2:10). On the other hand, the Colossian heresy was altogether inadequate. It was a hollow and deceptive philosophy (2:8), lacking any ability to restrain the old sinful nature (2:23).

The theme of Colossians is the complete adequacy of Christ as contrasted with the emptiness of mere human philosophy.

Outline

I. Introduction (1:1–14)
   A. Greetings (1:1–2)
   B. Thanksgiving (1:3–8)
   C. Prayer (1:9–14)
II. The Supremacy of Christ (1:15–23)
III. Paul's Labor for the Church (1:24—2:7)
   A. A Ministry for the Sake of the Church (1:24–29)
   B. A Concern for the Spiritual Welfare of His Readers (2:1–7)
IV. Freedom from Human Regulations through Life with Christ (2:8–23)
   A. Warning to Guard against the False Teachers (2:8–15)
   B. Pleas to Reject the False Teachers (2:16–19)
   C. An Analysis of the Heresy (2:20–23)
V. Rules for Holy Living (3:1—4:6)
   A. The Old Self and the New Self (3:1–17)
   B. Rules for Christian Households (3:18—4:1)
   C. Further Instructions (4:2–6)
VI. Final Greetings (4:7–18)

Thankfulness for Spiritual Attainments

1 [a]Paul, [b]an apostle of Jesus Christ [1c]by the
will of God, and [d]Timothy [2]our brother,
2 To the [1a]saints and faithful brethren in
Christ *who are* at Colossae: [b]Grace to you
and peace from God our Father.
3 [a]We give thanks to God, [b]the Father of
our Lord Jesus Christ, praying always for
you,
4 [a]since we heard of your faith in Christ
Jesus and the [b]love which you have [1]for [c]all
the [2]saints;
5 because of the [a]hope [b]laid up for you
in [1]heaven, of which you previously [c]heard
in the word of truth, [2]the gospel
6 which has come to you, just as [1a]in all
the world also it is constantly bearing [b]fruit
and [2]increasing, even as *it has been doing* in
you also since the day you [c]heard *of it* and
[3]understood the grace of God in truth;
7 just as you learned *it* from [a]Epaphras,
our [b]beloved fellow bond-servant, who is a
faithful servant of Christ on our behalf,
8 and he also informed us of your [a]love
in the Spirit.
9 For this reason also, [a]since the day we
heard *of it,* [b]we have not ceased to pray for
you and to ask that you may be filled with
the [1c]knowledge of His will in all spiritual
[d]wisdom and understanding,
10 so that you will [a]walk in a manner
worthy of the Lord, [1b]to please *Him* in all
respects, [c]bearing fruit in every good work
and [2]increasing in the [3]knowledge of God;
11 [a]strengthened with all power, according to [1]His glorious might, [2]for the attaining
of all steadfastness and [3]patience; [b]joyously
12 giving thanks to [a]the Father, who has
qualified us [1]to share in [b]the inheritance of
the [2]saints in [c]Light.

The Incomparable Christ

13 [1]For He rescued us from the [2a]domain
of darkness, and transferred us to the kingdom of [3b]His beloved Son,
14 [a]in whom we have redemption, the forgiveness of sins.
15 [1]He is the [a]image of the [b]invisible God,
the [c]firstborn of all creation.

1:1 [1]Lit *through* [2]Lit *the* [a]Phil 1:1 [b]2 Cor 1:1 [c]1 Cor 1:1 [d]2 Cor 1:1; 1 Thess 3:2 **2** [1]Or *holy ones* [a]Acts 9:13 [b]Rom 1:7 **3** [a]Rom 1:8 [b]Rom 15:6; 2 Cor 1:3 **4** [1]Or *toward* [2]Or *holy ones* [a]Eph 1:15 [b]Gal 5:6 [c]Eph 6:18 **5** [1]Lit *the heavens* [2]Or *of the gospel* [a]Acts 23:6 [b]2 Tim 4:8 [c]Eph 1:13 **6** [1]Or *it is in the world* [2]Or *spreading abroad* [3]Or *came really to know* [a]Rom 10:18 [b]Rom 1:13 [c]Eph 4:21 **7** [a]Col 4:12 [b]Col 4:7 **8** [a]Rom 15:30 **9** [a]Col 1:4 [b]Eph 1:16

9 [1]Or *real knowledge* [c]Phil 1:9 [d]Eph 1:17 **10** [1]Lit *unto all pleasing* [2]Or *growing by the knowledge* [3]Or *real knowledge* [a]Eph 4:1 [b]Eph 5:10 [c]Rom 1:13 **11** [1]Lit *the might of His glory* [2]Lit *unto all* [3]Or *patience with joy* [a]1 Cor 16:13 [b]Eph 4:2 **12** [1]Lit *unto the portion of* [2]Or *holy ones* [a]Eph 2:18 [b]Acts 20:32 [c]Acts 26:18 **13** [1]Lit *Who rescued* [2]Lit *authority* [3]Lit *the Son of His love* [a]Eph 6:12 [b]Eph 1:6 **14** [a]Rom 3:24 **15** [1]Lit *Who is* [a]2 Cor 4:4 [b]John 1:1 [c]Rom 8:29

1:1 *Paul.* It was customary to put the writer's name at the beginning of a letter. For more information on Paul see notes on Acts 9:1; Phil 3:4–14. *Christ.* Paul is very Christ-centered, as seen by this short letter, in which he uses the title "Christ" 25 times and the title "Lord" (alone) 9 times. *Timothy.* Paul also mentions Timothy in 2 Corinthians, Philippians, 1,2 Thessalonians and Philemon, but Paul is really the sole author, as seen by the constant use of "I" (see especially 4:18).

1:2 *saints.* Because of Christ's substitutionary death for the Colossian believers, they are declared holy in the sight of God, and because of the Holy Spirit's work, they are continuing to be made holy in their lives. *faithful.* See 1:7; 4:7,9. *in Christ.* Paul mentions the spiritual union with Christ 11 times in Colossians (see note on Eph 1:3). *Grace . . . and peace.* See notes on Jon 4:2; John 14:27; 20:19; Gal 1:3; Eph 1:2.

1:3 *We.* Paul and Timothy. *give thanks to God.* Every one of Paul's letters, except Galatians, begins with thanks or praise (see note on Phil 1:3–4). In Colossians thanks is an important theme (see v. 12; 2:7; 3:15–17; 4:2). The Bible never thanks man for his faith and love, but rather God, who is the source of these virtues.

1:5 The three great Christian virtues of faith, love and hope appear also in Rom 5:2–5; 1 Cor 13:13; Gal 5:5–6; 1 Thess 1:3; 5:8; Heb 10:22–24. *hope.* Not wishful thinking but a firm assurance. For this unusual thought of faith and love coming from hope see Titus 1:2.

1:6 *in all the world.* Hyperbole, to dramatize the rapid spread of the gospel into every quarter of the Roman empire within three decades of Pentecost (see v. 23; Rom 1:8; 10:18; 16:19). In refutation of the charge of the false teachers, Paul insists that the Christian faith is not merely local or regional but worldwide.

1:7 *Epaphras.* A native (4:12) and probably founder of the Colossian church, and an evangelist in nearby Laodicea and Hierapolis (4:13). Paul loved and admired him, calling him a "fellow prisoner" (Philem 23), his dear fellow servant and a faithful minister of Christ. Epaphras was the one who told Paul at Rome about the Colossian church problem and thereby stimulated him to write this letter (vv. 4,8). His name, a shortened form of Epaphroditus (from "Aphrodite," the Greek goddess of love), suggests that he was a convert from paganism. He is not the Epaphroditus of Phil 2:25; 4:18.

1:8 *your love in the Spirit.* The Holy Spirit is the source of all Christian love.

1:9 *the knowledge of His will.* Biblical knowledge is not merely the possession of facts. Rather, knowledge and wisdom in the Bible are practical, having to do with godly living. This is borne out by vv. 10–12, where knowledge, wisdom and understanding result in a life worthy of the Lord.

1:12 *Light.* Symbolizes holiness (Matt 5:14; 6:23; Acts 26:18; 1 John 1:5), truth (Ps 36:9; 119:105,130; 2 Cor 4:6), love (James 1:17; 1 John 2:9–10), glory (Is 60:1–3; 1 Tim 6:16) and life (John 1:4). Accordingly, God (1 John 1:5), Christ (John 8:12) and the Christian (Eph 5:8) are characterized by light. The "Light" is the opposite of the "domain of darkness" (v. 13).

1:13 *kingdom.* Does not here refer to a territory but to the authority, rule or sovereign power of a king. Here it means that the Christian is no longer under the dominion of evil (darkness) but under the benevolent rule of God's Son.

1:14 *redemption.* Deliverance and freedom from the penalty of sin by the payment of a ransom—the substitutionary death of Christ.

1:15–20 Perhaps an early Christian hymn (see note on 3:16) on the supremacy of Christ—used here by Paul to counteract the false teaching at Colossae. It is divided into two parts: (1) Christ's supremacy in creation (vv. 15–17); (2) Christ's supremacy in redemption (vv. 18–20).

1:15 *image.* Christ is called the "image of God" here and in 2 Cor 4:4. In Heb 1:3 He is described as the "radiance of His glory and the exact representation of His nature." This figure of the image suggests two truths: (1) God is invisible ("No one has seen God at any time," John 1:18); (2) Christ, who is the eternal Son of God and who became the God-man, reflects and reveals Him (see also John 1:18; 14:9). *firstborn of all creation.* Just as the firstborn son had certain privileges and rights in the Biblical world, so also Christ has certain rights in relation to all creation—priority, preeminence and sovereignty (vv. 16–18).

16 For [1a]by Him all things were created, [a]*both* in the heavens and on earth, visible and invisible, whether [b]thrones or dominions or rulers or authorities—[c]all things have been created through Him and for Him.

17 He [1a]is before all things, and in Him all things [2]hold together.

18 He is also [a]head of [b]the body, the church; and He is [c]the beginning, [d]the firstborn from the dead, so that He Himself will come to have first place in everything.

19 For [1]it was [a]the *Father's* good pleasure for all [b]the [2]fullness to dwell in Him,

20 and through Him to [a]reconcile all things to Himself, having made [b]peace through [c]the blood of His cross; through Him, *I say,* [d]whether things on earth or things in [1]heaven.

21 And although you were [a]formerly alienated and hostile in mind, *engaged* in evil deeds,

22 yet He has now [a]reconciled you in His fleshly [b]body through death, in order to [c]present you before Him [d]holy and blameless and beyond reproach—

23 if indeed you continue in [1]the faith firmly [a]established and steadfast, and not moved away from the [b]hope of the gospel that you have heard, which was proclaimed [c]in all creation under heaven, [d]and of which I, Paul, [2]was made a [3e]minister.

24 [a]Now I rejoice in my sufferings for your sake, and in my flesh [b]I [1]do my share on behalf of [c]His body, which is the church, in filling up what is lacking [2]in Christ's afflictions.

25 [a]Of *this church* I [1]was made a minister according to the [b]stewardship from God bestowed on me for your benefit, so that I might [2]fully carry out the *preaching of* the word of God,

26 *that is,* [a]the mystery which has been hidden from the *past* ages and generations, but has now been manifested to His [1]saints,

27 to whom [a]God willed to make known what is [b]the riches of the glory of this mystery among the Gentiles, which is [c]Christ in you, the [d]hope of glory.

28 We proclaim Him, [a]admonishing every man and teaching every man [1]with all [b]wisdom, so that we may [c]present every man [2d]complete in Christ.

29 For this purpose also I [a]labor, [b]striving [c]according to His [1]power, which [2]mightily works within me.

You Are Built Up in Christ

2 For I want you to know how great a [a]struggle I have on your behalf and for those who are at [b]Laodicea, and for all those who have not [1]personally seen my face,

16 [1]Or *in* [a]Eph 1:10 [b]Eph 1:20f; Col 2:15 [c]John 1:3; Rom 11:36; 1 Cor 8:6 **17** [1]Or *has existed prior to* [2]Or *endure* [a]John 1:1; 8:58 **18** [a]Eph 1:22 [b]Eph 1:23; Col 1:24; 2:19 [c]Rev 3:14 [d]Acts 26:23 **19** [1]Or *all the fullness was pleased to dwell* [2]I.e. fullness of deity [a]Eph 1:5 [b]John 1:16 **20** [1]Lit *the heavens* [a]2 Cor 5:18; Eph 2:16 [b]Rom 5:1; Eph 2:14 [c]Eph 2:13 [d]Col 1:16 **21** [a]Rom 5:10; Eph 2:3, 12 **22** [a]2 Cor 5:18; Eph 2:16 [b]Rom 7:4 [c]Eph 5:27; Col 1:28 [d]Eph 1:4 **23** [1]Or *in faith* [2]Lit *became* [3]Or *servant* [a]Eph 3:17; Col 2:7 [b]Col 1:5 [c]Mark 16:15; Acts 2:5; Col 1:6 [d]Eph 3:7; Col 1:25 [e]1 Cor 3:5 **24** [1]Or *representatively ...fill up* [a]Rom 8:17; 2 Cor 1:5; 12:15; Phil 2:17 [b]2 Tim 1:8; 2:10

24 [2]Lit *of* [c]Col 1:18 **25** [1]Lit *became* [2]Lit *make full the word of God* [a]Col 1:23 [b]Eph 3:2 **26** [1]Or *holy ones* [a]Rom 16:25f; Eph 3:3f; Col 2:2; 4:3 **27** [a]Matt 13:11 [b]Eph 1:7, 18; 3:16 [c]Rom 8:10 [d]1 Tim 1:1 **28** [1]Lit *in* [2]Or *perfect* [a]Acts 20:31; Col 3:16 [b]1 Cor 2:6f; Col 2:3 [c]Col 1:22 [d]Matt 5:48; Eph 4:13 **29** [1]Lit *working* [2]Lit *in power* [a]1 Cor 15:10 [b]Col 2:1; 4:12 [c]Eph 1:19; Col 2:12 **2:1** [1]Lit *in the flesh* [a]Col 1:29; 4:12 [b]Col 4:13, 15f; Rev 1:11

1:16 *by Him all things were created.* See John 1:3. Seven times in vv. 15–20 Paul mentions "all creation," "all things" and "everything," thus stressing that Christ is supreme over all. *thrones or dominions or rulers or authorities.* Angels. An angelic hierarchy figured prominently in the Colossian heresy (see Introduction: The Colossian Heresy).

1:17 *He is before all things.* Referring to time, as in John 1:1–2; 8:58.

1:18 *beginning.* Of the new creation. *firstborn.* Christ was the first to rise from the dead with a resurrection body. Elsewhere Paul calls Him the "first fruits of those who are asleep" (1 Cor 15:20). Others who were raised from the dead (2 Kin 4:35; Luke 7:15; John 11:44; Acts 9:36–41; 20:7–11) were raised only to die again.

1:19 *fullness.* Part of the technical vocabulary of some Gnostic philosophies. In these systems it meant the sum of the supernatural forces controlling the fate of people. For Paul "fullness" meant the totality of God with all His powers and attributes (2:9).

1:20 *reconcile all things to Himself.* Does not mean that Christ by His death has saved all people. Scripture speaks of an eternal hell and makes clear that only believers are saved. When Adam and Eve sinned, not only was the harmony between God and man destroyed, but also disorder came into creation (Rom 8:19–22). So when Christ died on the cross, He made peace possible between God and man, and He restored in principle the harmony in the physical world, though the full realization of the latter will come only when Christ returns (Rom 8:21).

1:22 *death.* Christ's death.

1:23 *all creation.* See note on v. 6.

1:24 *my sufferings.* By preaching the gospel to the Gentiles, Paul experienced all kinds of affliction, but here he was probably referring especially to his imprisonment. *filling up what is lacking.* Does not mean that there was a deficiency in the atoning sacrifice of Christ. Rather, it means that Paul suffered afflictions because he was preaching the good news of Christ's atonement. Christ suffered on the cross to atone for sin, and Paul filled up Christ's afflictions by experiencing the added sufferings necessary to carry this good news to a lost world.

1:25 *fully carry out the preaching of the word of God.* The meaning seems to be that the word of God is brought to completion, i.e., to its intended purpose, only when it is proclaimed (cf. Is 55:11). Paul's commission to bring the word to completion, therefore, required him to make the word of God heard in Colossae as well as elsewhere. See Rom 15:19 for a similar statement.

1:26 *mystery.* The purpose of God, unknown to man except by revelation. This word was a popular, pagan religious term, used in the mystery religions to refer to secret information available only to an exclusive group of people. Paul changes that meaning radically by always combining it with words such as "manifested" (here), "made known" (Eph 1:9), "bring to light" (Eph 3:9) and "revelation" (Rom 16:25). The Christian mystery is not secret knowledge for a few. It is a revelation of divine truths—once hidden but now openly proclaimed.

1:27 *Gentiles . . . Christ in you.* The mystery is the fact that Christ indwells Gentiles, for it had not been previously revealed that the Gentiles would be admitted to the church on equal terms with Israel (see note on Eph 3:6).

1:28 *complete.* Employed by the mystery religions and the Gnostics to describe those who had become possessors of the secrets or knowledge boasted of by the particular religion (see Introduction to 1 John: Gnosticism). But in Christ every believer is one of the perfect.

2:1 *Laodicea.* This letter was to be read to the church there

2 that their [a]hearts may be encouraged,
having been [b]knit together in love, and
attaining to all [c]the wealth [1]that comes from
the full assurance of understanding, *result-*
ing in a [d]true knowledge of [e]God's mystery,
that is, Christ *Himself,*
3 in whom are hidden all [a]the treasures
of wisdom and knowledge.
4 [a]I say this so that no one will delude
you with [b]persuasive argument.
5 For even though I am [a]absent in body,
nevertheless I am with you in spirit, rejoicing
[1]to see [2]your [b]good discipline and the [c]sta-
bility of your faith in Christ.
6 Therefore as you have received [a]Christ
Jesus the Lord, *so* [1b]walk in Him,
7 having been firmly [a]rooted *and now*
being [b]built up in Him and [c]established [1]in
your faith, just as you [d]were instructed, *and*
overflowing [2]with gratitude.
8 [a]See to it that no one takes you captive
through [b]philosophy and empty deception,
according to the tradition of men, according
to the [c]elementary principles of the world,
[1]rather than according to Christ.
9 For in Him all the [a]fullness of Deity
dwells in bodily form,
10 and in Him you have been [a]made
[1]complete, and [b]He is the head [2]over all [c]rule
and authority;
11 and in Him [a]you were also circumcised
with a circumcision made without hands, in
the removal of [b]the body of the flesh by the
circumcision of Christ;
12 having been [a]buried with Him in baptism, in which you were also [b]raised up with
Him through faith in the working of God,
who [c]raised Him from the dead.
13 When you were [a]dead [1]in your transgressions and the uncircumcision of your
flesh, He [b]made you alive together with Him,
having forgiven us all our transgressions,
14 having canceled out [a]the certificate of
debt consisting of decrees against us, which
was hostile to us; and [b]He has taken it out of
the way, having nailed it to the cross.
15 When He had [1a]disarmed the [b]rulers
and authorities, He [a]made a public display of
them, having [c]triumphed over them through
[2]Him.
16 Therefore no one is to [1a]act as your
judge in regard to [b]food or [b]drink or in
respect to a [c]festival or a [d]new moon or a
[e]Sabbath [2]day—
17 things which are [a]a *mere* shadow of
what is to come; but the [1]substance [2]belongs
to Christ.
18 Let no one keep [1a]defrauding you of
your prize by [b]delighting in [2]self-abasement
and the worship of the angels, [3]taking his
stand on *visions* he has seen, [4c]inflated without cause by his [d]fleshly mind,

2 [1]Lit *of the full assurance* [a]1 Cor 14:31; Eph 6:22; Col 4:8 [b]Col 2:19 [c]Eph 1:7, 18; 3:16 [d]Matt 13:11 [e]Rom 16:25f; Eph 3:3f; Col 1:26; 4:3 **3** [a]Is 11:2; Rom 11:33 **4** [a]Eph 4:17 [b]Rom 16:18 **5** [1]Lit *and seeing* [2]Or *your good order* [a]1 Cor 5:3 [b]1 Cor 14:40 [c]1 Pet 5:9 **6** [1]Or *lead your life* [a]Gal 3:26 [b]Col 1:10 **7** [1]Or *by* [2]One early ms reads *in it with* [a]Eph 3:17 [b]1 Cor 3:9; Eph 2:20 [c]1 Cor 1:8 [d]Eph 4:21 **8** [1]Lit *and not* [a]1 Cor 8:9; 10:12; Gal 5:15; Heb 3:12 [b]Eph 5:6; Col 2:23; 1 Tim 6:20 [c]Gal 4:3; Col 2:20 **9** [a]2 Cor 5:19; Col 1:19 **10** [1]Lit *full* [2]Lit *of* [a]Eph 3:19 [b]Eph 1:21f [c]1 Cor 15:24; Eph 3:10; Col 2:15 **11** [a]Rom 2:29; Eph 2:11 [b]Rom 6:6; 7:24; Gal 5:24; Col 3:5 **12** [a]Rom 6:4f **12** [b]Rom 6:5; Eph 2:6; Col 2:13; 3:1 [c]Acts 2:24 **13** [1]Or *by reason of* [a]Eph 2:1 [b]Eph 2:5; Col 2:12 **14** [a]Eph 2:15; Col 2:20 [b]1 Pet 2:24 **15** [1]Or *divested Himself of* [2]Or *it;* i.e. the cross [a]Eph 4:8 [b]John 12:31; 1 Cor 15:24; Eph 3:10; Col 2:10 [c]2 Cor 2:14 **16** [1]Lit *judge you* [2]Or *days* [a]Rom 14:3 [b]Mark 7:19; Rom 14:17; Heb 9:10 [c]Lev 23:2; Rom 14:5 [d]1 Chr 23:31; 2 Chr 31:3; Neh 10:33 [e]Mark 2:27f; Gal 4:10 **17** [1]Lit *body* [2]Lit *of Christ* [a]Heb 8:5; 10:1 **18** [1]Or *deciding against you* [2]Or *humility* [3]Or *going into detail about* [4]Or *conceited* [a]1 Cor 9:24; Phil 3:14 [b]Col 2:23 [c]1 Cor 4:6 [d]Rom 8:7

too (4:16). Laodicea (near modern Denizli) was only about 11 miles from Colossae.

2:2 *mystery.* See notes on 1:26; Rom 11:25.

2:3 *knowledge.* Paul stressed knowledge in this letter (v. 2; 1:9–10) because he was refuting a heresy that emphasized knowledge as the means of salvation (see Introduction to 1 John: Gnosticism). Paul insisted that the Christian, not the Gnostic, possessed genuine knowledge.

2:5 *absent in body, . . . with you in spirit.* Similar to 1 Cor 5:3.

2:6 *walk in Him.* The believer's intimate, spiritual, living union with Christ is mentioned repeatedly in this letter (see, e.g., vv. 7,10–13,20; 1:2,27–28; 3:1,3).

2:8 *elementary principles of the world.* This term (which occurs also in v. 20 and Gal 4:3,9) means false, worldly, religious, elementary teachings. Paul was counteracting the Colossian heresy, which, in part, taught that for salvation one needed to combine faith in Christ with secret knowledge and with man-made regulations concerning such physical and external practices as circumcision, eating and drinking, and observance of religious festivals.

2:9 *fullness of Deity.* See note on 1:19. The declaration that the very essence of deity was present in totality in Jesus' human body was a direct refutation of Gnostic teaching.

2:10–15 Here Paul declares that the Christian is complete in Christ, rather than being deficient as the Gnostics claimed. This completeness includes the putting off of the sinful nature (v. 11), resurrection from spiritual death (vv. 12–13), forgiveness (v. 13) and deliverance from legalistic requirements (v. 14) and from evil spirit beings (v. 15).

2:11–12 *circumcision . . . baptism.* In the Israelite faith, circumcision was a sign that the individual stood in covenant relation with God. While this is the only reference where circumcision is associated with baptism, some see the passage as implying that, for the Christian, water baptism is the parallel sign of the covenant relationship.

2:14 *certificate of debt.* A business term, meaning a certificate of indebtedness in the debtor's handwriting. Paul uses it as a designation for the Mosaic law, with all its regulations, under which everyone is a debtor to God.

2:15 *When He had disarmed.* Not only did God cancel out the accusations of the law against the Christian, but He also conquered and disarmed the evil angels (powers and authorities, 1:16; Eph 6:12), who entice people to follow asceticism and false teachings about Christ. The picture is of conquered soldiers stripped of their clothes as well as their weapons to symbolize their total defeat. *having triumphed over them.* Lit. "leading them in a triumphal procession." The metaphor recalls a Roman general leading his captives through the streets of his city for all the citizens to see as evidence of his complete victory (see 2 Cor 2:14 and note). That Christ triumphed over the devil and his cohorts is seen from Matt 12:29; Luke 10:18; Rom 16:20.

2:17 *shadow . . . substance.* The ceremonial laws of the OT are here referred to as shadows (cf. Heb 8:5; 10:1) because they symbolically depicted the coming of Christ; so any insistence on the observance of such ceremonies is a failure to recognize that their fulfillment has already taken place. This element of the Colossian heresy was combined with a rigid asceticism, as vv. 20–21 reveal.

2:18 *defrauding.* This term pictures an umpire or referee who excludes from competition any athlete who fails to follow the

19 and not holding fast to [a]the head, from
whom [b]the entire body, being supplied and
held together by the joints and [1]ligaments,
grows with a growth [2]which is from God.
20 [a]If you have died with Christ [1]to the
[b]elementary principles of the world, [c]why, as
if you were living in the world, do you submit yourself to [d]decrees, such as,
21 "Do not handle, do not taste, do not
touch!"
22 (which all *refer* [a]*to* things destined to
perish [1]with use)—in accordance with the
[b]commandments and teachings of men?
23 These are matters which have, to be
sure, the [1]appearance of wisdom in [2a]self-
made religion and self-abasement and
[b]severe treatment of the body, *but are* of no
value against [c]fleshly indulgence.

Put On the New Self

3 Therefore if you have been [a]raised up
with Christ, keep seeking the things
above, where Christ is, [b]seated at the right
hand of God.
2 [1a]Set your mind on the things above,
not on the things that are on earth.
3 For you have [a]died and your life is hidden with Christ in God.
4 When Christ, [a]who is our life, is
revealed, [b]then you also will be revealed
with Him in glory.
5 [a]Therefore [1]consider [b]the members of
your earthly body as dead to [2c]immorality,
impurity, passion, evil desire, and greed,
which [3]amounts to idolatry.
6 For it is because of these things that
[a]the wrath of God will come [1]upon the sons
of disobedience,
7 and [a]in them you also once walked,
when you were living [1]in them.
8 But now you also, [a]put them all aside:
[b]anger, wrath, malice, slander, *and* [c]abusive
speech from your mouth.
9 [1a]Do not lie to one another, since you
[b]laid aside the old [2]self with its *evil* practices,
10 and have [a]put on the new self who is
being [1b]renewed to a true knowledge
[c]according to the image of the One who [d]cre-
ated him—
11 *a renewal* in which [a]there is no *distinction between* Greek and Jew, [b]circumcised
and uncircumcised, [1c]barbarian, Scythian,
[d]slave and freeman, but [e]Christ is all, and in
all.
12 So, as those who have been [a]chosen of
God, holy and beloved, [b]put on a [c]heart of
compassion, kindness, [d]humility, gentleness
and [1e]patience;

19 [1]Lit *bonds* [2]Lit *of God* [a]Eph 1:22 [b]Eph 1:23; 4:16
20 [1]Lit *from* [a]Rom 6:2 [b]Col 2:8 [c]Gal 4:9 [d]Col 2:14, 16
22 [1]Or *by being consumed* [a]1 Cor 6:13 [b]Is 29:13; Matt 15:9; Titus 1:14
23 [1]Lit *report;* Gr *logos* [2]Or *would-be religion* [a]Col 2:18 [b]1 Tim 4:3 [c]Rom 13:14; 1 Tim 4:8
3:1 [a]Col 2:12 [b]Ps 110:1; Mark 16:19
2 [1]Or *Be intent on* [a]Matt 16:23; Phil 3:19, 20
3 [a]Rom 6:2; 2 Cor 5:14; Col 2:20
4 [a]John 11:25; Gal 2:20 [b]1 Cor 1:7; Phil 3:21; 1 Pet 1:13; 1 John 2:28; 3:2
5 [1]Lit *put to death the members which are upon the earth* [2]Lit *fornication* [a]Rom 8:13 [b]Col 2:11 [c]Mark 7:21f; 1 Cor 6:9f, 18; 2 Cor 12:21; Gal 5:19f; Eph 4:19; 5:3, 5
5 [3]Lit *is*

6 [1]Two early mss do not contain *upon the sons of disobedience* [a]Rom 1:18; Eph 5:6 **7** [1]Or *among these* [a]Eph 2:2 **8** [a]Eph 4:22 [b]Eph 4:31 [c]Eph 4:29 **9** [1]Or *Stop lying* [2]Gr *anthropos* [a]Eph 4:25 [b]Eph 4:22 **10** [1]Lit *renovated* [a]Eph 4:24 [b]Rom 12:2; 2 Cor 4:16; Eph 4:23 [c]Gen 1:26; Rom 8:29 [d]Eph 2:10 **11** [1]I.e. those who were not Greeks, either by birth or by culture [a]Rom 10:12; 1 Cor 12:13; Gal 3:28 [b]1 Cor 7:19; Gal 5:6 [c]Acts 28:2 [d]Eph 6:8 [e]Eph 1:23 **12** [1]I.e. forbearance toward others [a]Luke 18:7 [b]Eph 4:24 [c]Luke 1:78; Gal 5:22f; Phil 2:1 [d]Eph 4:2; Phil 2:3 [e]1 Cor 13:4; 2 Cor 6:6

rules. The Colossians were not to permit any false teacher to deny the reality of their salvation because they were not delighting in mock humility and in the worship of angelic beings. *self-abasement.* Humility in which one delights is of necessity mock humility. Paul may refer to a professed humility in view of the absolute God, who was believed to be so far above man that He could only be worshiped in the form of angels He had created. Second-century Gnosticism conceived of a list of spirit beings who had emanated from God and through whom God may be approached. *he has seen.* Probably refers to professed visions by the false teachers.

2:19 *not holding fast to the head.* The central error of the Colossian heresy is a defective view of Christ, in which He is believed to be less than deity (see v. 9; 1:19).

2:20 *elementary principles.* See note on v. 8.

2:21 *Do not handle . . . taste . . . touch!* The strict ascetic nature of the heresy is seen here. These prohibitions seem to carry OT ceremonial laws to the extreme.

2:23 A rather detailed analysis of the Colossian heresy: 1. It appeared to set forth an impressive system of religious philosophy. 2. It was, however, a system created by the false teachers themselves ("self-made"), rather than being of divine origin. 3. The false teachers attempted to parade their humility. 4. This may have been done by a harsh asceticism that brutally misused the body. Paul's analysis is that such practices are worthless because they totally fail to control sinful desires. *self-made religion.* The false teachers themselves had created the regulations of their heretical system. They were not from God.

3:1 *Therefore.* "Therefore" links the doctrinal section of the letter with the practical section, just as it does in Rom 12:1; Eph 4:1; Phil 4:1. *you have been raised up.* Verses 1–10 set forth what has been described as the indicative and the imperative (standing and state) of the Christian. The indicative statements describe the believer's position in Christ: He is dead (v. 3); he has been raised with Christ (v. 1); he is with Christ in heaven ("hidden with Christ," v. 3); he has "laid aside the old self" (v. 9); and he has "put on the new self" (v. 10). The imperative statements indicate what the believer is to do as a result: He is to set his heart (or mind) on things above (vv. 1–2); he is to put to death practices that belong to his earthly nature (v. 5); and he is to rid himself of practices that characterized his unregenerate self (v. 8). In summary, he is called upon to become in daily experience what he is positionally in Christ (cf. Rom 6:1–13).

3:4 *is revealed.* Refers to Christ's second coming.

3:6 *wrath of God.* See note on Zech 1:2. God is unalterably opposed to sin and will invariably make sure that it is justly punished.

3:9–10 *laid aside . . . put on.* As one takes off dirty clothes and puts on clean ones, so the Christian is called upon to renounce his evil ways and live in accordance with the rules of Christ's kingdom (see vv. 12–14; cf. Gal 3:27).

3:10 *renewed.* See 2 Co 5:17. *knowledge.* See 1:10; 2:2–3. *image of the One who created him.* See note on Gen 1:26.

3:11 *barbarian.* Someone who did not speak Greek and was thought to be uncivilized. *Scythian.* Scythians were known especially for their brutality and were considered by others as little better than wild beasts. They came originally from what is today south Russia. *Christ is all, and in all.* Christ transcends all barriers and unifies people from all cultures, races and nations. Such distinctions are no longer significant. Christ alone matters.

3:12 *chosen of God.* Israel was called this (Deut 4:37), and so is the Christian community (1 Pet 2:9). Divine election is a constant theme in Paul's letters (see note on Eph 1:4), but the Bible never teaches that it dulls human responsibility. On the con-

13 [a]bearing with one another, and [b]forgiving each other, whoever has a complaint against anyone; [b]just as the Lord forgave you, so also should you.

14 Beyond all these things *put on* love, which is [1a]the perfect bond of [b]unity.

15 Let [a]the peace of Christ [1]rule in your hearts, to which [2]indeed you were called in [b]one body; and [3]be thankful.

16 Let [a]the word of [1]Christ richly dwell within you, [2]with all wisdom [b]teaching and admonishing [3]one another [c]with psalms *and* hymns *and* spiritual songs, [d]singing [4]with thankfulness in your hearts to God.

17 [a]Whatever you do in word or deed, *do* all in the name of the Lord Jesus, [b]giving thanks through Him to God the Father.

Family Relations

18 [a]Wives, [b]be subject to your husbands, as is fitting in the Lord.

19 [a]Husbands, love your wives and do not be embittered against them.

20 [a]Children, be obedient to your parents in all things, for this is well-pleasing [1]to the Lord.

21 [a]Fathers, do not exasperate your children, so that they will not lose heart.

22 [a]Slaves, in all things obey those who are your masters [1]on earth, [b]not with [2]external service, as those who *merely* please men, but with sincerity of heart, fearing the Lord.

23 Whatever you do, do your work [1]heartily, [a]as for the Lord [2]rather than for men,

24 [a]knowing that from the Lord you will receive the reward [1]of [b]the inheritance. It is the Lord Christ whom you [c]serve.

25 For [a]he who does wrong will receive the consequences of the wrong which he has done, and [1b]that without partiality.

Fellow Workers

4 Masters, grant to your slaves justice and fairness, [a]knowing that you too have a Master in heaven.

2 [a]Devote yourselves to prayer, keeping alert in it with *an attitude of* thanksgiving;

3 praying at the same time [a]for us as well, that God will open up to us a [b]door for [c]the word, so that we may speak forth [d]the mystery of Christ, for which I have also [e]been imprisoned;

4 that I may make it clear [a]in the way I ought to speak.

5 [1a]Conduct yourselves with wisdom toward [b]outsiders, [2c]making the most of the opportunity.

6 [a]Let your speech always be [1]with grace, *as though* seasoned with [b]salt, so that you will know how you should [c]respond to each person.

7 [a]As to all my affairs, [b]Tychicus, *our* [c]beloved brother and faithful servant and fellow bond-servant in the Lord, will bring you information.

8 [a]*For* I have sent him to you for this very purpose, that you may know about our circumstances and that he may [b]encourage your hearts;

9 [1]and with him [a]Onesimus, *our* faithful and [b]beloved brother, [c]who is one of your *number.* They will inform you about the whole situation here.

10 [a]Aristarchus, my [b]fellow prisoner, sends you his greetings; and *also* [c]Barnabas's cousin Mark (about whom you received

13 [a]Eph 4:2 [b]Rom 15:7; Eph 4:32 **14** [1]Lit *the uniting bond of perfection* [a]Eph 4:3 [b]John 17:23; Heb 6:1 **15** [1]Or *act as arbiter* [2]Lit *also* [3]Or *show yourselves thankful* [a]John 14:27 [b]Eph 2:16 **16** [1]One early ms reads *the Lord* [2]Or *in* [3]Or *one another, singing with psalms...* [4]Or *by;* lit *in His grace* [a]Rom 10:17; Eph 5:26; 1 Thess 1:8 [b]Col 1:28 [c]Eph 5:19 [d]1 Cor 14:15 **17** [a]1 Cor 10:31 [b]Eph 5:20; Col 3:15 **18** [a]Col 3:18-4:1: *Eph 5:22-6:9* [b]Eph 5:22 **19** [a]Eph 5:25; 1 Pet 3:7 **20** [1]Lit *in* [a]Eph 6:1 **21** [a]Eph 6:4 **22** [1]Lit *according to the flesh* [2]Lit *eyeservice* [a]Eph 6:5 [b]Eph 6:6 **23** [1]Lit *from the soul* [2]Lit *and not* [a]Eph 6:7 **24** [1]I.e. consisting of [a]Eph 6:8 [b]Acts 20:32; 1 Pet 1:4 [c]1 Cor 7:22 **25** [1]Lit *there is no partiality* [a]Eph 6:8 [b]Deut 10:17; Acts 10:34; Eph 6:9

4:1 [a]Eph 6:9 **2** [a]Acts 1:14; Eph 6:18 **3** [a]Eph 6:19 [b]Acts 14:27 [c]2 Tim 4:2 [d]Eph 3:3, 4; 6:19 [e]Eph 6:20 **4** [a]Eph 6:20 **5** [1]Lit *Walk* [2]Lit *redeeming the time* [a]Eph 5:15 [b]Mark 4:11 [c]Eph 5:16 **6** [1]Or *gracious* [a]Eph 4:29 [b]Mark 9:50 [c]1 Pet 3:15 **7** [a]Col 4:7-9: *Eph 6:21, 22* [b]Acts 20:4; 2 Tim 4:12 [c]Eph 6:21; Col 1:7 **8** [a]Eph 6:22 [b]Col 2:2 **9** [1]Lit *along with Onesimus* [a]Philem 10 [b]Col 1:7 [c]Col 4:12 **10** [a]Acts 19:29; 27:2; Philem 24 [b]Rom 16:7 [c]Acts 4:36; 12:12, 25; 15:37, 39

---

trary, as this verse shows, it is precisely because the Christian has been elected to eternal salvation that he must put forth every effort to live the godly life. For Paul, divine sovereignty and human responsibility go hand in hand.

3:15 *peace of Christ.* The attitude of peace that Christ alone gives—in place of the attitude of bitterness and quarrelsomeness. This attitude is to "rule" (lit. "function like an umpire") in all human relationships.

3:16 *word of Christ.* Refers especially to Christ's teaching, which in the time of the Colossians was transmitted orally. But by implication it includes the OT as well as the NT. *psalms and hymns and spiritual songs.* Some of the most important doctrines were expressed in Christian hymns preserved for us now only in Paul's letters (1:15–20; Eph 5:14; Phil 2:6–11; 1 Tim 3:16). "Psalms" refers to the OT psalms (see Luke 20:42; 24:44; Acts 1:20; 13:33), some of which may have been set to music by the church. "Psalm" could also describe a song newly composed for Christian worship (cf. 1 Cor 14:26, where "hymn" is lit. "psalm" in the Greek text). A "hymn" was a song of praise, especially used in a celebration (see Mark 14:26; Heb 2:12; see also Acts 16:25), much like the OT psalms that praised God for all that He is. A "song" recounted the acts of God and praised Him for them (see Rev 5:9; 14:3; 15:3), much like the OT psalms that thanked God for all that He had done. See note on Eph 5:19.

3:18–4:1 See notes on Eph 5:22–6:9.

3:20 *in all things.* In everything not sinful (see Acts 5:29).

3:22–4:1 Paul neither condones slavery nor sanctions revolt against masters. Rather, he calls on both slaves and masters to show Christian principles in their relationship and thus to attempt to change the institution from within. The reason Paul writes more about slaves and masters than about wives, husbands, children and fathers may be that the slave Onesimus (4:9) is going along with Tychicus to deliver this Colossian letter and the letter to Philemon, Onesimus's master, who also lived in Colossae.

4:6 *seasoned with salt.* Salt is a preservative and is tasty. Similarly, the Christian's conversation is to be wholesome (see 3:8; Eph 4:29).

4:7 *Tychicus.* See note on Eph 6:21.

4:9–17 Onesimus (v. 9), Aristarchus (v. 10), Mark (v. 10), Epaphras (v. 12), Luke (v. 14), Demas (v. 14) and Archippus (v. 17) are mentioned in Philemon. This suggests that the letters to Colossae and Philemon were written at the same time and place.

4:9 *Onesimus.* See Introduction to Philemon: Recipient, Background and Purpose.

4:10 *Aristarchus.* A Macedonian, who is mentioned three times

[1]instructions; [d]if he comes to you, welcome
him);
11 and *also* Jesus who is called Justus;
these are the only [a]fellow workers for the
kingdom of God [b]who are from the circumcision, and they have proved to be an
encouragement to me.
12 [a]Epaphras, [b]who is one of your number, a bondslave of Jesus Christ, sends you
his greetings, always [c]laboring earnestly for
you in his prayers, that you may [1]stand
[2d]perfect and [3]fully assured in all the will of
God.
13 For I testify for him that he has [1]a deep
concern for you and for those who are in
[a]Laodicea and Hierapolis.
14 [a]Luke, the beloved physician, sends
you his greetings, and *also* [b]Demas.
15 Greet the brethren who are in [a]Laodi-
cea and also [1]Nympha and [b]the church that
is in [2]her house.
16 [a]When [1]this letter is read among you,
have it also read in the church of the Laodiceans; and you, for your part [a]read [1]my letter *that is coming* from [b]Laodicea.
17 Say to [a]Archippus, "Take heed to the
[b]ministry which you have received in the
Lord, that you may [1]fulfill it."
18 [1]I, Paul, [a]write this greeting with my
own hand. [b]Remember my [2c]imprisonment.
[d]Grace be with you.

10 [1]Or *orders* [d]2 Tim 4:11 **11** [a]Rom 16:3 [b]Acts 11:2 **12** [1]Or *stand firm* [2]Or *complete* or *mature* [3]Or *made complete* [a]Col 1:7; Philem 23 [b]Col 4:9 [c]Rom 15:30 [d]Col 1:28 **13** [1]Or *much toil* or *great pain* [a]Col 2:1; 4:15f **14** [a]2 Tim 4:11; Philem 24 [b]2 Tim 4:10; Philem 24 **15** [1]Or *Nymphas* (masc) [2]One early ms reads *their* [a]Col 2:1; 4:13, 16 [b]Rom 16:5 **16** [1]Lit *the* [a]1 Thess 5:27; 2 Thess 3:14 [b]Col 2:1; 4:13, 15 **17** [1]Or *continually fulfill* [a]Philem 2 [b]2 Tim 4:5 **18** [1]Lit *The greeting by my hand of Paul* [2]Lit *bonds* [a]1 Cor 16:21 [b]Heb 13:3 [c]Phil 1:7; Col 4:3 [d]1 Tim 6:21; 2 Tim 4:22; Titus 3:15; Heb 13:25

in Acts: 1. He was with Paul during the Ephesian riot (Acts 19:29) and therefore was known in Colossae. 2. Both he and Tychicus (Acts 20:4) were with Paul in Greece. 3. He accompanied Paul on his trip to Rome (Acts 27:2). *Mark.* The author of the second Gospel. Against Barnabas's advice, Paul refused to take Mark on the second missionary journey because Mark had "deserted" him at Pamphylia (Acts 15:38). But now—about 12 years later—the difficulties seem to have been ironed out, because Paul, both here and in Philem 24 (sent at the same time to Philemon, who was in Colossae), sends Mark's greetings. About five years later, Paul even writes that Mark "is useful to me for service" (2 Tim 4:11). See note on Acts 15:39.

4:13 *Hierapolis.* A town in Asia Minor (present-day Turkey), about 6 miles from Laodicea and 14 miles from Colossae. Its church may have been founded during Paul's three-year stay in Ephesus (Acts 19), but probably not by Paul himself (cf. 2:1).

4:14 *Luke.* Wrote about Paul in the book of Acts, having often accompanied him on his travels (see note on Acts 16:10). He was with Paul in Rome during his imprisonment (Acts 28), where this letter was written. *Demas.* A Christian worker who would later desert Paul (2 Tim 4:10).

4:15 *Nympha.* Probably a Laodicean. *church that is in her house.* For the most part, the early church had no buildings, so it usually met for worship and instruction in homes. It often centered around one family, as, e.g., Priscilla and Aquila (Rom 16:5; 1 Cor 16:19), Philemon (Philem 2) and Mary the mother of John (Acts 12:12).

4:16 *When this letter is read among you.* The practice of the early church was to read Paul's letters aloud to the assembled congregation. *letter . . . from Laodicea.* Does not necessarily mean a letter by the Laodiceans. Rather, it could have been a letter that the Laodiceans were to lend to the Colossians—a letter that Paul had originally written to the Laodiceans. This may have been a fourth letter that Tychicus carried to this area in what is present-day Turkey, in addition to Ephesians, Colossians and Philemon. Or this letter could have been Paul's letter to the Ephesians—a circular letter making the rounds from Ephesus to Laodicea to Colossae (see Introduction to Ephesians: Author, Date and Place of Writing).

4:17 *Archippus.* Philem 2 calls him Paul's "fellow soldier."

4:18 Paul's custom was to dictate his letters (see Rom 16:22) and pen a few greetings himself (1 Cor 16:21; Gal 6:11; 2 Thess 3:17; Philem 19). His personal signature was the guarantee of the genuineness of the letter.

1 Thessalonians

INTRODUCTION

Background of the Thessalonian Letters

It is helpful to trace the locations of Paul and his companions that relate to the Thessalonian correspondence. The travels were as follows:

1. Paul and Silas fled from Thessalonica to Berea (see Acts 17:10). Since Timothy is not mentioned, it is possible that he stayed in Thessalonica or went back to Philippi and then rejoined Paul and Silas in Berea (Acts 17:14).
2. Paul fled to Athens from Berean persecution, leaving Silas and Timothy in Berea (see Acts 17:14).
3. Paul sent word back, instructing Silas and Timothy to come to him in Athens (see Acts 17:15; see also note on 3:1–2).
4. Timothy rejoined Paul at Athens and was sent back to Thessalonica (see 3:1–5). Since Silas is not mentioned, it has been conjectured that he went back to Philippi when Timothy went to Thessalonica.
5. Paul moved on to Corinth (see Acts 18:1).
6. Silas and Timothy came to Paul in Corinth (see 3:6; Acts 18:5).
7. Paul wrote 1 Thessalonians and sent it to the church.
8. About six months later (A.D. 51/52) he sent 2 Thessalonians in response to further information about the church there.

Author, Date and Place of Writing

Both external and internal evidence (see 1:1; 2:18) support the view that Paul wrote 1 Thessalonians (from Corinth; see note on 3:1–2). Early church writers are agreed on the matter, with testimonies beginning as early as A.D. 140 (Marcion). Paul's known characteristics are apparent in the letter (3:1–2,8–11 compared with Acts 15:36; 2 Cor 11:28). Historical allusions in the book fit Paul's life as recounted in Acts and in his own letters (2:14–16 compared with Acts 17:5–10; 3:6 compared with Acts 17:16). In the face of such evidence, few have ever rejected authorship by Paul.

It is generally dated c. A.D. 51. Weighty support for this date was found in an inscription discovered at Delphi, Greece, that dates Gallio's proconsulship to c. 51–52 and thus places Paul at Corinth at the same time (see Acts 18:12–17). Except for the possibility of an early date for Galatians (48–49?), 1 Thessalonians is Paul's earliest canonical letter.

Thessalonica: The City and the Church

Thessalonica was a bustling seaport city at the head of the Thermaic Gulf. It was an important communication and trade center, located at the junction of the great Egnatian Way and the road leading north to the Danube. Its population numbered about 200,000, making it the largest city in Macedonia. It was also the capital of its province.

The background of the Thessalonian church is found in Acts 17:1–9. Since Paul began his ministry there in the Jewish synagogue, it is reasonable to assume that the new church included some Jews. However, 1:9–10; Acts 17:4 seem to indicate that the church was largely Gentile in membership.

Purpose

Paul had left Thessalonica abruptly (see Acts 17:5–10) after a rather brief stay. Recent converts from paganism (1:9) were thus left with little external support in the midst of persecution. Paul's purpose in writing this letter was to encourage the new converts in their trials (3:3–5), to give instruction concerning godly living

(4:1–8), to urge some not to neglect daily work (4:11–12) and to give assurance concerning the future of believers who die before Christ returns (see Theme; see also notes on 4:13,15).

Theme

Although the thrust of the letter is varied (see Purpose), the subject of eschatology (doctrine of last things) seems to be predominant in both Thessalonian letters. Every chapter of 1 Thessalonians ends with a reference to the second coming of Christ, with ch. 4 giving it major consideration (1:9–10; 2:19–20; 3:13; 4:13–18; 5:23–24). Thus, the second coming seems to permeate the letter and may be viewed in some sense as its theme. The two letters are often designated as the eschatological letters of Paul.

Outline

- I. The Thanksgiving for the Thessalonians (ch. 1)
  - A. The Grounds for the Thanksgiving (1:1–4)
  - B. The Genuineness of the Grounds (1:5–10)
- II. The Defense of the Apostolic Actions and Absence (chs. 2—3)
  - A. The Defense of the Apostolic Actions (2:1–16)
  - B. The Defense of the Apostolic Absence (2:17—3:10)
  - C. The Prayer (3:11–13)
- III. The Exhortations to the Thessalonians (4:1—5:22)
  - A. Primarily concerning Personal Life (4:1–12)
  - B. Concerning the Coming of Christ (4:13—5:11)
  - C. Primarily concerning Church Life (5:12–22)
- IV. The Concluding Prayer, Greetings and Benediction (5:23–28)

Thanksgiving for These Believers

1 [a]Paul and [b]Silvanus and [c]Timothy,
To the [d]church of the Thessalonians in
God the Father and the Lord Jesus Christ:
[e]Grace to you and peace.
2 [a]We give thanks to God always for all
of you, [b]making mention of *you* in our
prayers;
3 constantly bearing in mind your [a]work
of faith and labor of [b]love and [1c]steadfast-
ness of hope [2]in our Lord Jesus Christ in the
presence of [d]our God and Father,
4 knowing, [a]brethren beloved by God,
[b]*His* choice of you;
5 for our [a]gospel did not come to you in
word only, but also [b]in power and in the
Holy Spirit and with [c]full conviction; just as
you know [d]what kind of men we [1]proved to
be among you for your sake.
6 You also became [a]imitators of us and
of the Lord, [b]having received [c]the word in
much tribulation with the [d]joy of the Holy
Spirit,
7 so that you became an example to all
the believers in [a]Macedonia and in [b]Achaia.
8 For [a]the word of the Lord has [b]sounded
forth from you, not only in [c]Macedonia and
[d]Achaia, but also [e]in every place your faith

1:1 [a]2 Thess 1:1 [b]2 Cor 1:19 [c]Acts 16:1 [d]Acts 17:1 [e]Rom 1:7 **2** [a]Rom 1:8; 2 Thess 1:3 [b]Rom 1:9 **3** [1]Or *perseverance* [2]Lit *of* [a]John 6:29 [b]1 Cor 13:13 [c]Rom 8:25; 15:4 [d]Gal 1:4 **4** [a]Rom 1:7; 2 Thess 2:13 [b]2 Pet 1:10 **5** [1]Or *became* [a]1 Cor 9:14 [b]Rom 15:19 [c]Luke 1:1; Col 2:2 [d]1 Thess 2:10 **6** [a]1 Cor 4:16; 11:1f [b]Acts 17:5-10 [c]2 Tim 4:2 [d]Acts 13:52; 2 Cor 6:10; Gal 5:22 **7** [a]Rom 15:26 [b]Acts 18:12 **8** [a]Col 3:16; 2 Thess 3:1 [b]Rom 10:18 [c]Rom 15:26 [d]Acts 18:12 [e]Rom 1:8; 16:19; 2 Cor 2:14

9 [1]Lit *entrance* [2]Lit *to* [3]Or *the idols* [4]Or *the*

toward God has gone forth, so that we have
no need to say anything.
9 For they themselves report about us
what kind of a [1a]reception we had [2]with
you, and how you [b]turned to God [c]from
[3]idols to serve [4d]a living and true God,
10 and to [a]wait for His Son from [1]heaven,
whom He [b]raised from the dead, *that is* Jesus,
who [c]rescues us from [d]the wrath to come.

Paul's Ministry

2 For you yourselves know, brethren, that
our [1a]coming to you [b]was not in vain,
2 but after we had already suffered and
been [a]mistreated in [b]Philippi, as you know,
we had the boldness in our God [c]to speak to
you the [d]gospel of God amid much [1e]opposi-
tion.
3 For our [a]exhortation does not *come*
from [b]error or [c]impurity or [1]by way of
[d]deceit;
4 [a]but just as we have been approved by
God to be [b]entrusted with the gospel, so we

[a]1 Thess 2:1 [b]Acts 14:15 [c]1 Cor 12:2 [d]Matt 16:16 **10** [1]Lit *the heavens* [a]Matt 16:27f; 1 Cor 1:7 [b]Acts 2:24 [c]Rom 5:9 [d]Matt 3:7; 1 Thess 2:16; 5:9 **2:1** [1]Lit *entrance* [a]1 Thess 1:9 [b]2 Thess 1:10 **2** [1]Or *struggle, conflict* [a]Acts 14:5; 16:19-24; Phil 1:30 [b]Acts 16:22-24 [c]Acts 17:1-9 [d]Rom 1:1 [e]Phil 1:30 **3** [1]Lit *in deceit* [a]Acts 13:15 [b]2 Thess 2:11 [c]1 Thess 4:7 [d]2 Cor 4:2 **4** [a]2 Cor 2:17 [b]Gal 2:7

1:1 *Paul.* See notes on Acts 9:1; 13:9; Phil 3:4–14. *Silvanus.* See note on Acts 15:22. He accompanied Paul on most of his second missionary journey. *Timothy.* See Introduction to 1 Timothy: Recipient. Both he and Silas helped Paul found the Thessalonian church (see Acts 17:1–14). *in.* Indicates the vital union and living relationship that Christians have with the Father and the Son (see John 14:23; 17:21). The close connection between the Father and the Son points to the Trinitarian relationship (see 3:11; 2 Thess 1:2,8,12; 2:16; 3:5). *Grace . . . and peace.* See notes on Jon 4:2; John 14:27; 20:19; Gal 1:3; Eph 1:2.

1:2 *thanks.* See note on Phil 1:3–4.

1:3 The triad of faith, hope and love is found often in the NT (5:8; Rom 5:2–5; 1 Cor 13:13; Gal 5:5–6; Col 1:4–5; Heb 6:10–12; 10:22–24; 1 Pet 1:3–8,21–22). *work of faith.* Faith produces action (see Rom 1:5; 16:26; Gal 5:6; 2 Thess 1:11; James 2:14–26). *hope.* Not unfounded wishful thinking, but firm confidence in our Lord Jesus Christ and His return (v. 10). See Heb 6:18–20 and note on Col 1:5.

1:4 *knowing.* The reasons for Paul's conviction regarding their election are stated in vv. 5–10. *brethren.* United to each other through union with Christ. This term (including its singular form) is used 28 times in the two letters to the Thessalonians. *beloved . . . His choice.* Both words speak of God's electing love (see Col 3:12; 2 Thess 2:13; see also note on Eph 1:4).

1:5 *our gospel.* The gospel preached by Paul, Silas and Timothy and that they themselves had received by faith. It is first of all God the Father's (2:8) because He originated it, and Christ's (3:2) because it springs from His atoning death. *power.* The power that delivered them from spiritual bondage. That power is of the Holy Spirit (see Rom 15:13,18–19; 1 Cor 2:4–5), but it also resides in the gospel itself (see Rom 1:16). *full conviction.* Such conviction, on the part of both the preachers and the Thessalonians, was also of the Holy Spirit.

1:6 *imitators.* The order in Christian imitation: (1) Believers in Macedonia and Achaia imitated the Thessalonians (v. 7), just as the Thessalonians imitated the churches in Judea (2:14); (2) the Thessalonians imitated Paul, just as the Corinthians did (1 Cor 4:6; 11:1) and just as all believers were to imitate their leaders (2 Thess 3:7,9; 1 Tim 4:12; Titus 2:7; 1 Pet 5:3); (3) Paul imitated Christ (1 Cor 11:1) as did the Thessalonians (v. 6); (4) all were to imitate God (Eph 5:1). *much tribulation.* Such as recorded in Acts 17:5–14 (see also 1 Thess 2:14).

1:7 *Macedonia and Achaia.* The two Roman provinces into which Greece was then divided (see Acts 19:21; Rom 15:26).

1:8 *every place.* In every place they visited or knew about (see Rom 1:8; 1 Cor 1:2; 2 Cor 2:14; 1 Tim 2:8). The news spread because Thessalonica was on the important Egnatian Way; it was also a busy seaport and the capital of the Roman province of Macedonia.

1:9–10 Three marks of true conversion: (1) turning from idols, (2) serving God and (3) waiting for Christ to return. In his two short letters to the Thessalonians, Paul speaks much of the second coming of Christ (v. 10; 2:19; 3:13; 4:13–5:4; 2 Thess 1:7–10; 2:1–12).

1:10 *Jesus.* See note on Matt 1:21. *wrath.* Some see a reference here to the final judgment (see note on Rom 1:18), while others think it refers to a future period of tribulation.

2:1–12 A "manual" for a minister: 1. His message is God's good news ("gospel," v. 2). 2. His motive is not impurity (v. 3), pleasing people (v. 4), greed (v. 5) or seeking praise from people (v. 6), but pleasing God (v. 4). 3. His manner is not one of trickery (v. 3), flattery (v. 5) or a cover-up (v. 5), but of courage (v. 2), gentleness (v. 7), love (vv. 8,11), toil (v. 9) and holiness (v. 10).

2:1 *you yourselves know.* The local church could refute the accusation of insincerity that evidently had been leveled against Paul (v. 3).

2:2 *mistreated.* Paul was deeply hurt by the way he had been treated in the city of Philippi (see Acts 16:19–40).

2:3 *deceit.* The Greek for this word was originally used of a lure for catching fish; it came to be used of any sort of cunning used for profit.

2:4 *our hearts.* Not simply our emotions, but also our intellects and wills.

speak, [c]not as pleasing men, but God who
[1d]examines our hearts.
5 For we never came [1]with flattering
speech, as you know, nor with [a]a pretext for
greed—[b]God is witness—
6 nor did we [a]seek glory from men,
either from you or from others, even though
as [b]apostles of Christ [1]we might have
[2]asserted our authority.
7 But we [1]proved to be [2a]gentle [3]among
you, [b]as a nursing *mother* [4]tenderly cares for
her own children.
8 Having so fond an affection for you, we
were well-pleased to [a]impart to you not only
the [b]gospel of God but also our own [1]lives,
because you had become [2]very dear to us.
9 For you recall, brethren, our [a]labor and
hardship, *how* [b]working night and day so as
not to be a [c]burden to any of you, we proclaimed to you the [d]gospel of God.
10 You are witnesses, and *so is* [a]God,
[b]how devoutly and uprightly and blamelessly we [1]behaved toward you [2]believers;
11 just as you know how we *were* [a]exhort-
ing and encouraging and [1b]imploring each one
of you as [c]a father *would* his own children,
12 so that you would [a]walk in a manner
worthy of the God who [b]calls you into His
own kingdom and [c]glory.
13 For this reason we also constantly
[a]thank God that when you received the
[b]word of God which you heard from us, you
accepted *it* [c]not *as* the word of men, but *for*
what it really is, the word of God, [d]which
also performs its work in you who believe.
14 For you, brethren, became [a]imitators of
[b]the churches of God in Christ Jesus that are
[c]in Judea, for [d]you also endured the same
sufferings at the hands of your own countrymen, [e]even as they *did* from the Jews,
15 [a]who both killed the Lord Jesus and
[b]the prophets, and [1]drove us out. [2]They are
not pleasing to God, [2]but hostile to all men,
16 [a]hindering us from speaking to the
Gentiles [b]so that they may be saved; with the
result that they always [c]fill up the measure of
their sins. But [d]wrath has come upon them
[1]to the utmost.
17 But we, brethren, having been taken
away from you for a [1]short while—[a]in [2]per-
son, not in [3]spirit—were all the more eager
with great desire [b]to see your face.
18 [1]For [a]we wanted to come to you—I,
Paul, [2b]more than once—and *yet* [c]Satan
[d]hindered us.
19 For who is our hope or [a]joy or crown of
exultation? Is it not even you, in the presence
of our Lord Jesus at His [1b]coming?
20 For you are [a]our glory and joy.

Encouragement of Timothy's Visit

3 Therefore [a]when we could endure *it* no
longer, we thought it best to be left
behind at [b]Athens alone,
2 and we sent [a]Timothy, our brother and
God's fellow worker in the gospel of Christ,
to strengthen and encourage you as to your
faith,
3 so that no one would be [1]disturbed by
these afflictions; for you yourselves know
that [a]we have been destined for this.
4 For indeed when we were with you, we

4 [1]Or *approves* [c]Gal 1:10 [d]Rom 8:27 **5** [1]Lit *in a word of flattery* [a]Acts 20:33; 2 Pet 2:3 [b]Rom 1:9; 1 Thess 2:10 **6** [1]Lit *being able to* [2]Or *be burdensome* [a]John 5:41, 44; 2 Cor 4:5 [b]1 Cor 9:1f **7** [1]Or *became gentle* [2]Three early mss read *babes* [3]Lit *in the midst of you* [4]Or *cherishes* [a]2 Tim 2:24 [b]Gal 4:19; 1 Thess 2:11 **8** [1]Or *souls* [2]Lit *beloved* [a]2 Cor 12:15; 1 John 3:16 [b]Rom 1:1 **9** [a]Phil 4:16; 2 Thess 3:8 [b]Acts 18:3 [c]1 Cor 9:4f; 2 Cor 11:9 [d]Rom 1:1 **10** [1]Lit *became* [2]Or who *believe* [a]1 Thess 2:5 [b]2 Cor 1:12; 1 Thess 1:5 **11** [1]Or *testifying to* [a]1 Thess 5:14 [b]Luke 16:28; 1 Thess 4:6 [c]1 Cor 4:14; 1 Thess 2:7 **12** [a]Eph 4:1 [b]Rom 8:28; 1 Thess 5:24; 2 Thess 2:14 [c]2 Cor 4:6; 1 Pet 5:10 **13** [a]Rom 1:8; 1 Thess 1:2 [b]Rom 10:17; Heb 4:2 [c]Matt 10:20; Gal 4:14 [d]Heb 4:12 **14** [a]1 Thess 1:6 [b]1 Cor 7:17; 10:32 [c]Gal 1:22 [d]Acts 17:5; 1 Thess 3:4; 2 Thess 1:4f [e]Heb 10:33f **15** [1]Or *persecuted us* [2]Lit *and* [a]Luke 24:20; Acts 2:23 [b]Matt 5:12; Acts 7:52 **16** [1]Or *forever* or *altogether;* lit *to the end* [a]Acts 9:23; 13:45, 50; 14:2, 5, 19; 17:5, 13; 18:12; 21:21f, 27; 25:2, 7 [b]1 Cor 10:33 [c]Gen 15:16; Dan 8:23; Matt 23:32 [d]1 Thess 1:10 **17** [1]Lit *occasion of an hour* [2]Lit *face* [3]Lit *heart* [a]1 Cor 5:3 [b]1 Thess 3:10 **18** [1]Or *Because* [2]Lit *both once and twice* [a]Rom 15:22 [b]Phil 4:16 [c]Matt 4:10 [d]Rom 1:13; 15:22 **19** [1]Or *presence* [a]Phil 4:1 [b]Matt 16:27; Mark 8:38; John 21:22; 1 Thess 3:13; 4:15; 5:23 **20** [a]2 Cor 1:14
3:1 [a]1 Thess 3:5 [b]Acts 17:15f **2** [a]2 Cor 1:1; Col 1:1
3 [1]Or *deceived* [a]Acts 9:16; 14:22

2:5 *pretext.* Personal profit was never Paul's aim.
2:6 *asserted our authority.* Apostles were entitled to be supported by the church (see 1 Cor 9:3–14; 2 Cor 11:7–11). Paul did not always take advantage of the right, but insisted that he had it.
2:9 *labor and hardship.* Greeks despised manual labor and viewed it as fit only for slaves, but Paul was not ashamed of doing any sort of work that would help further the gospel. He did not want to be unduly dependent on others.
2:12 *walk in a manner worthy of . . . God.* See Eph 4:1. *calls.* See note on 1:4. *kingdom.* The chief subject of Jesus' teaching. Paul did not use this term often, but used it once to sum up the message of his preaching (Acts 20:25).
2:13 *not as the word of men.* Not tailored to fit the popular knowledge of the day.
2:14 *you also endured . . . at the hands of . . . countrymen.* At the time of Paul's initial visit to Thessalonica, persecution instigated by the Jews apparently was carried out by Gentiles (see Acts 17:5–9). *Jews.* Although Paul had great love and deep concern for the salvation of those of his own race (see Rom 9:1–3; 10:1), he did not fail to rebuke harshly Jews who persecuted the church.
2:15 *prophets.* Throughout OT history, Israelites had persecuted their prophets (cf. Acts 7:52).
2:16 *wrath has come.* The eschatological wrath, the final outpouring of God's anger upon sinful mankind (see 1:10). It is spoken of as already present, either because it had been partially experienced by the Jews or because of its absolute certainty.
2:17 *taken away.* Lit. "orphaned." Paul is like a mother (v. 7), a father (v. 11) and now an orphan.
2:19 *crown.* Not a royal crown, but a wreath used on festive occasions or as the prize in the Greek games. *at His coming.* The expression was used regarding the arrival of a great person, as on a royal visit.
2:20 *you are our glory and joy.* True both now (cf. Phil 4:1) and when Christ returns.
3:1–2 Paul first went to Athens alone, then sent to Berea for Silas and Timothy (Acts 17:14–15). It is not clear whether Silas, as instructed (Acts 17:15), came to Athens with Timothy. However, when Timothy later returned from Thessalonica to Paul, who was now at Corinth, Silas came with him (Acts 18:5). See Introduction: Background of the Thessalonian Letters.
3:1 *we.* An editorial "we," referring to Paul alone.
3:2 *God's fellow worker.* A striking way of viewing Christian service, found also in 1 Cor 3:9. *gospel of Christ.* See notes on 1:5; Mark 1:1. *strengthen.* In Greek classical literature the word was generally used in the literal sense of putting a buttress on a building. In the NT it is mainly used figuratively, as here.
3:3 *afflictions.* The opposition and persecution suffered by the Thessalonian converts. Christians must expect troubles (see Mark 4:17; John 16:33; Acts 14:22; 2 Tim 3:12; 1 Pet 4:12), but

kept telling you in advance that we were
going to suffer affliction; [1a]and so it came to
pass, [2]as you know.
5 For this reason, [a]when I could endure
it no longer, I also [b]sent to [1]find out about
your faith, for fear that [c]the tempter might
have tempted you, and [d]our labor would be
in vain.
6 But now that [a]Timothy has come to us
from you, and has brought us good news of
[b]your faith and love, and that you always
[c]think kindly of us, longing to see us just as
we also long to see you,
7 for this reason, brethren, in all our distress and affliction we were comforted about
you through your faith;
8 for now we *really* live, if you [a]stand
firm in the Lord.
9 For [a]what thanks can we render to God
for you in return for all the joy with which
we rejoice before our God on your account,
10 as we [a]night and day keep praying
most earnestly that we may [b]see your face,
and may [c]complete what is lacking in your
faith?
11 [a]Now may [b]our God and Father [c]Him-
self and Jesus our Lord [d]direct our way to
you;
12 and may the Lord cause you to increase
and [a]abound in love for one another, and for
all people, just as we also *do* for you;
13 so that He may [a]establish your hearts
[b]without blame in holiness before [c]our God
and Father at the [1d]coming of our Lord Jesus
[e]with all His [2]saints.

4 [1]Lit *just as* [2]Lit *and* [a]1 Thess 2:14
5 [1]Or *to know, to ascertain* [a]Phil 2:19; 1 Thess 3:1 [b]1 Thess 3:2 [c]Matt 4:3 [d]2 Cor 6:1; Phil 2:16
6 [a]Acts 18:5 [b]1 Thess 1:3 [c]1 Cor 11:2
8 [a]1 Cor 16:13
9 [a]1 Thess 1:2
10 [a]2 Tim 1:3 [b]1 Thess 2:17 [c]2 Cor 13:9
11 [a]2 Thess 2:16 [b]Gal 1:4; 1 Thess 3:13 [c]1 Thess 4:16; 5:23; 2 Thess 2:16; 3:16; Rev 21:3 [d]2 Thess 3:5
12 [a]Phil 1:9; 1 Thess 4:1, 10; 2 Thess 1:3
13 [a]1 Cor 1:8; 1 Thess 3:2 [b]Luke 1:6 [c]Gal 1:4; 1 Thess 3:11

13 [1]Or *presence* [2]Or *holy ones* [d]1 Thess 2:19 [e]Matt 25:31; Mark 8:38; 1 Thess 4:17; 2 Thess 1:7
4:1 [1]Or *conduct yourselves* [a]2 Cor 13:11; 2 Thess 3:1 [b]Gal 6:1; 1 Thess 5:12; 2 Thess 1:3; 2:1; 3:1, 13

Sanctification and Love

4 [a]Finally then, [b]brethren, we request and
exhort you in the Lord Jesus, that as you
received from us *instruction* as to how you
ought to [1c]walk and [d]please God (just as you
actually do [1]walk), that you [e]excel still more.
2 For you know what commandments we
gave you [1]by *the authority of* the Lord Jesus.
3 For this is the will of God, your sanctification; *that is,* that you [a]abstain from [1]sex-
ual immorality;
4 that [a]each of you know how to [1]pos-
sess his own [2b]vessel in sanctification and
[c]honor,
5 not in [1a]lustful passion, like the Gentiles who [b]do not know God;
6 *and* that no man transgress and
[a]defraud his brother [b]in the matter because
[c]the Lord is *the* avenger in all these things,
just as we also [d]told you before and solemnly warned *you.*
7 For [a]God has not called us for [b]the
purpose of impurity, but [1]in sanctification.
8 So, he who rejects *this* is not rejecting

[c]Eph 4:1 [d]2 Cor 5:9 [e]Phil 1:9; 1 Thess 3:12; 4:10; 2 Thess 1:3
2 [1]Lit *through the Lord* **3** [1]Or *fornication* [a]1 Cor 6:18
4 [1]Or *acquire* [2]I.e. body; or wife [a]1 Cor 7:2, 9 [b]2 Cor 4:7; 1 Pet 3:7 [c]Rom 1:24 **5** [1]Lit *passion of lust* [a]Rom 1:26 [b]Gal 4:8
6 [a]1 Cor 6:8 [b]2 Cor 7:11 [c]Rom 12:19; 13:4; Heb 13:4 [d]Luke 16:28; 1 Thess 2:11; Heb 2:6 **7** [1]I.e. in the state or sphere of [a]1 Pet 1:15 [b]1 Thess 2:3

---

these are not disasters, for they advance God's purposes (see Acts 11:19; Rom 5:3; 2 Cor 1:4; 4:17).

3:5 *I.* Paul uses the Greek emphatic pronoun (elsewhere used only in 2:18) to bring out his deep concern. *tempter.* Satan is spoken of in every major division of the NT. He is supreme among evil spirits (see John 16:11; Eph 2:2). His activities can affect the physical (see 2 Cor 12:7) and the spiritual (see Matt 13:39; Mark 4:15; 2 Cor 4:4). He tempted Jesus (Matt 4:1–11), and he continues to tempt Jesus' servants (see Luke 22:3; 1 Cor 7:5). He hinders missionary work (2:18). But he has already been defeated (see Col 2:15), and Christians need not be overwhelmed by him (see Eph 6:16). His final overthrow is certain (see Rev 20:10).

3:6 *brought us good news.* The only place where the Greek for this phrase is used by Paul for anything other than the gospel. Three things caused him joy: (1) "your faith"—a right attitude toward God; (2) "your . . . love"—a right attitude toward man; (3) "you . . . longing to see us"—a right attitude toward Paul.

3:9 *thanks . . . to God.* The preceding shows that Paul's work of evangelism had been effective. He might have congratulated himself on work well done, but instead he thanked God for the joy he had from what God had done.

3:10 *night and day.* Not prayer at two set times, but frequent prayer (see 1:2–3). *most earnestly.* Translates a strong and unusual Greek compound word (found elsewhere in the NT only in 5:13; Eph 3:20) that brings out Paul's passionate longing. *what is lacking.* Some of the things lacking were of a practical nature, such as moral (4:1–12) and disciplinary matters (5:12–24). Others were doctrinal, such as confusion over Christ's return (4:13–5:11). *your faith.* The fifth time in the chapter that Paul speaks of their faith (see vv. 2,5–7).

3:11 In the middle of a letter Paul frequently breaks into prayer (e.g., Eph 1:15–23; 3:14–21; Phil 1:9–11; Col 1:9–12). For the link between Father and Son see note on 1:1.

3:12 *the Lord.* In Paul's writings this usually means Jesus rather than the Father.

3:13 *establish.* See note on v. 2. *holiness.* The basic idea is "set apart [for God]." Here it refers to the completed process of sanctification (see note on 1 Cor 1:2). *saints.* Used of the saints (Christians) in many NT passages. Here it may mean the departed saints who will return with Jesus, or it may mean the angels or, probably, both.

4:1 *Finally.* The main section of the letter is finished, though much is yet to come (see Phil 3:1 and note). *we request and exhort you.* Paul is not arrogant, but he does speak with authority in the Lord Jesus. He has the "mind of Christ" (1 Cor 2:16). *walk.* Paul uses this metaphor often of the Christian way (see Rom 6:4; 2 Cor 5:7; Eph 4:1; 5:15; Col 1:10; 2:6; 4:5, "conduct yourselves"). It points to steady progress.

4:2 *commandments.* Used of authoritative commands and has a military ring (see Acts 5:28; 16:24).

4:3 *sanctification.* See note on 3:13. *sexual immorality.* In the first century moral standards were generally very low, and chastity was regarded as an unreasonable restriction. Paul, however, would not compromise God's clear and demanding standards. The warning was needed, for Christians were not immune to the temptation (see 1 Cor 5:1).

4:5 *like the Gentiles.* The Christian is to be different.

4:6 *transgress.* Sexual sin harms others besides those who engage in it. In adultery, e.g., the spouse is always wronged. Premarital sex wrongs the future partner by robbing him or her of the virginity that ought to be brought to marriage. *the Lord is the avenger.* A motive for chastity.

4:7 Another reason for chastity is God's call to holiness.

man but the God who [a]gives His Holy Spirit
to you.
9 Now as to the [a]love of the brethren,
you [b]have no need for *anyone* to write to
you, for you yourselves are [c]taught by God to
love one another;
10 for indeed [a]you do practice it toward
all the brethren who are in all Macedonia.
But we urge you, brethren, to [b]excel still
more,
11 and to make it your ambition [a]to lead a
quiet life and [b]attend to your own business
and [c]work with your hands, just as we commanded you,
12 so that you will [1a]behave properly
toward [b]outsiders and [2c]not be in any need.

Those Who Died in Christ

13 But [a]we do not want you to be uninformed, brethren, about those who [b]are
asleep, so that you will not grieve as do [c]the
rest who have [d]no hope.
14 For if we believe that Jesus died and
rose again, [a]even so God will bring with Him
[b]those who have fallen asleep [1]in Jesus.
15 For this we say to you [a]by the word of
the Lord, that [b]we who are alive [1]and remain
until [c]the coming of the Lord, will not precede [d]those who have fallen asleep.
16 For the Lord [a]Himself [b]will descend
from heaven with a [1c]shout, with the voice
of [d]*the* archangel and with the [e]trumpet of
God, and [f]the dead in Christ will rise first.
17 Then [a]we who are alive [1]and remain
will be [b]caught up together with them [c]in the
clouds to meet the Lord in the air, and so we
shall always [d]be with the Lord.
18 Therefore comfort one another with
these words.

The Day of the Lord

5 Now as to the [a]times and the epochs,
brethren, you [b]have no need of anything
to be written to you.
2 For you yourselves know full well that
[a]the day of the Lord [1]will come [b]just like a
thief in the night.

8 [a]Rom 5:5; 2 Cor 1:22; Gal 4:6; 1 John 3:24 **9** [a]John 13:34; Rom 12:10 [b]2 Cor 9:1; 1 Thess 5:1 [c]Jer 31:33f; John 6:45; 1 John 2:27 **10** [a]1 Thess 1:7 [b]1 Thess 3:12 **11** [a]2 Thess 3:12 [b]1 Pet 4:15 [c]Acts 18:3; Eph 4:28; 2 Thess 3:10-12 **12** [1]Lit *walk* [2]Lit *have need of nothing* [a]Rom 13:13; Col 4:5 [b]Mark 4:11 [c]Eph 4:28 **13** [a]Rom 1:13 [b]Acts 7:60 [c]Eph 2:3; 1 Thess 5:6 [d]Eph 2:12 **14** [1]Lit *through* [a]Rom 14:9; 2 Cor 4:14 [b]1 Cor 15:18; 1 Thess 4:13 **15** [a]1 Kin 13:17f; 20:35; 2 Cor 12:1; Gal 1:12 **15** [1]Lit *who* [b]1 Cor 15:52; 1 Thess 5:10 [c]1 Thess 2:19 [d]1 Cor 15:18; 1 Thess 4:13 **16** [1]Or *cry of command* [a]1 Thess 3:11 [b]1 Thess 1:10; 2 Thess 1:7 [c]Joel 2:11 [d]Jude 9 [e]Matt 24:31 [f]1 Cor 15:23; 2 Thess 2:1; Rev 14:13 **17** [1]Lit *who* [a]1 Cor 15:52; 1 Thess 5:10 [b]2 Cor 12:2 [c]Dan 7:13; Acts 1:9; Rev 11:12 [d]John 12:26 **5:1** [a]Acts 1:7 [b]1 Thess 4:9 **2** [1]Lit *is coming* [a]1 Cor 1:8 [b]Luke 21:34; 1 Thess 5:4; 2 Pet 3:10; Rev 3:3; 16:15

4:8 *God who gives His Holy Spirit.* Still another reason for chastity is that sexual sin is against God, who gives the Holy Spirit to believers for their sanctification. To live in sexual immorality is to reject God, specifically in regard to the Holy Spirit.

4:9 *love of the brethren.* Translates *philadelphia,* a Greek word that outside the NT almost without exception denoted the mutual love of children of the same father. In the NT it always means love of fellow believers in Christ, all of whom have the same heavenly Father. *taught by God.* Cf. Is 54:13; John 6:45; 1 Cor 2:13.

4:11 Some Thessalonians, probably because of idleness, were taking undue interest in other people's affairs. *work with your hands.* The Greeks in general thought manual labor degrading and fit only for slaves. Christians took seriously the need for earning their own living, but some of the Thessalonians, perhaps as a result of their belief in the imminent return of Christ (see 2 Thess 3:11), were neglecting work and relying on others to support them.

4:12 *not be in any need.* Or "have need of nothing." Both meanings are true and significant. Christians in need because of their idleness are not obedient Christians.

4:13 *those who are asleep.* For the Christian, sleep is a particularly apt metaphor for death, since death's finality and horror are removed by the assurance of resurrection. Some of the Thessalonians seem to have misunderstood Paul and thought all believers would live until Christ returns. When some died, the question arose, "Will those who have died have part in that great day?" See note on v. 15. *who have no hope.* Inscriptions on tombs and references in literature show that first-century pagans viewed death with horror, as the end of everything. The Christian attitude was in strong contrast (see 1 Cor 15:55–57; Phil 1:21–23).

4:14 *died.* Paul does not say that Christ "slept," perhaps to underscore the fact that He bore the full horror of death so that those who believe in Him would not have to. *rose again.* For the importance of the resurrection see 1 Cor 15, especially vv. 14,17–22. *those who have fallen asleep in Jesus.* Believers who have died, trusting in Jesus.

4:15 *by the word of the Lord.* The doctrine mentioned here is not recorded in the Gospels and was either a direct revelation to Paul or something Jesus said that Christians passed on orally. *we who are alive.* Those believers who will be alive when Christ returns. "We" does not necessarily mean that Paul thought that he would be alive then. He often identified himself with those he wrote to or about. Elsewhere he says that God will raise "us" at that time (1 Cor 6:14; 2 Cor 4:14). *will not precede.* The Thessalonians had evidently been concerned that those among them who died would miss their place in the great events when the Lord comes, and Paul assures them this will not be the case.

4:16 *the Lord Himself.* See Acts 1:11. *archangel.* The only named archangel in the Bible is Michael (Jude 9; see Dan 10:13). In Scripture, Gabriel is simply called an angel (Luke 1:19,26). *will rise first.* Before the ascension of believers mentioned in the next verse.

4:17 *we who are alive.* See note on v. 15. *caught up.* The only place in the NT where a "rapture" (from the Latin Vulgate rendering) is clearly referred to. Some hold that this will be secret, but Paul seems to be describing something open and public, with loud voices and a trumpet blast. *with the Lord.* The chief hope of the believer (see 5:10; John 14:3; 2 Cor 5:8; Phil 1:23; Col 3:4).

4:18 *comfort one another.* The primary purpose of vv. 13–18 is not to give a chronology of future events, though that is involved, but to urge mutual encouragement, as shown here and in v. 13.

5:1 *times and the epochs.* See Acts 1:6–7. There have always been some Christians who try to fix the date of our Lord's return, but apparently the Thessalonians were not among them.

5:2 *day of the Lord.* See 1 Cor 5:5. The expression goes back to Amos 5:18. In the OT it is a time when God will come and intervene with judgment and/or blessing. In the NT the thought of judgment continues (see Rom 2:5; 2 Pet 2:9), but it is also the "day of redemption" (Eph 4:30); the "day of God" (2 Pet 3:12), or of Christ (1 Cor 1:8; Phil 1:6); and the "last day" (John 6:39), the "great Day" (Jude 6) or simply "that day" (2 Thess 1:10). It is the consummation of all things. There will be some preliminary signs (e.g., 2 Thess 2:3), but the coming will be as unexpected

3 While they are saying, "[a]Peace and safety!" then [1][b]destruction [2]will come upon them suddenly like [c]labor pains upon a woman with child, and they will not escape.

4 But you, brethren, are not in [a]darkness, that the day would overtake you [1][b]like a thief;

5 for you are all [a]sons of light and sons of day. We are not of night nor of [b]darkness;

6 so then let us not [a]sleep as [1][b]others do, but let us be alert and [2][c]sober.

7 For those who sleep do their sleeping at night, and those who get drunk get [a]drunk at night.

8 But since [a]we are of *the* day, let us [b]be [1]sober, having put on the [c]breastplate of [d]faith and love, and as a [e]helmet, the [f]hope of salvation.

9 For God has not destined us for [a]wrath, but for [b]obtaining salvation through our Lord Jesus Christ,

10 [a]who died for us, so that whether we are awake or asleep, we will live together with Him.

11 Therefore [1]encourage one another and [a]build up one another, just as you also are doing.

3 [1]Or *sudden destruction* [2]Lit *comes upon* [a]Jer 6:14; 8:11; Ezek 13:10 [b]2 Thess 1:9 [c]John 16:21
4 [1]One early ms reads *like thieves* [a]Acts 26:18; 1 John 2:8 [b]Luke 21:34; 1 Thess 5:2; 2 Pet 3:10; Rev 3:3; 16:15
5 [a]Luke 16:8 [b]Acts 26:18; 1 John 2:8
6 [1]Lit *the remaining ones* [2]Or *self-controlled* [a]Rom 13:11; 1 Thess 5:10 [b]Eph 2:3; 1 Thess 4:13 [c]1 Pet 1:13
7 [a]Acts 2:15; 2 Pet 2:13
8 [1]Or *self-controlled* [a]1 Thess 5:5 [b]1 Pet 1:13 [c]Is 59:17; Eph 6:14 [d]Eph 6:23 [e]Eph 6:17 [f]Rom 8:24
9 [a]1 Thess 1:10 [b]2 Thess 2:13f
10 [a]Rom 14:9
11 [1]Or *comfort* [a]Eph 4:29.
12 [1]Lit *know*

Christian Conduct

12 But we request of you, brethren, that you [1][a]appreciate those [b]who diligently labor among you, and [c]have charge over you in the Lord and give you [2]instruction,

13 and that you esteem them very highly in love because of their work. [a]Live in peace with one another.

14 We urge you, brethren, admonish [a]the [1]unruly, encourage [b]the fainthearted, help [c]the weak, be [d]patient with everyone.

15 See that [a]no one repays another with evil for evil, but always [b]seek after that which is good for one another and for all people.

16 [a]Rejoice always;

17 [a]pray without ceasing;

18 in everything [a]give thanks; for this is God's will for you in Christ Jesus.

19 [a]Do not quench the Spirit;

20 do not despise [a]prophetic [1]utterances.

[2]Or *admonition* [a]1 Cor 16:18; 1 Tim 5:17 [b]Rom 16:6, 12; 1 Cor 15:10; 16:16 [c]Heb 13:17 **13** [a]Mark 9:50 **14** [1]Or *undisciplined* [a]2 Thess 3:6, 7, 11 [b]Is 35:4 [c]Rom 14:1f; 1 Cor 8:7ff; Rom 15:1 [d]1 Cor 13:4 **15** [a]Matt 5:44; Rom 12:17; 1 Pet 3:9 [b]Rom 12:9; Gal 6:10; 1 Thess 5:21 **16** [a]Phil 4:4 **17** [a]Eph 6:18 **18** [a]Eph 5:20 **19** [a]Eph 4:30 **20** [1]Or *gifts* [a]Acts 13:1; 1 Cor 14:31

---

as that of a thief in the night (cf. Matt 24:43–44; Luke 12:39–40; 2 Pet 3:10; Rev 3:3; 16:15).

5:3 *destruction.* Not annihilation, but exclusion from the Lord's presence (2 Thess 1:9); thus the ruin of life and all its proud accomplishments. *suddenly.* Paul stresses the surprise of unbelievers. He uses a word found elsewhere in the NT only in Luke 21:34. *labor pains.* Here the idea is not the pain of childbirth so much as the suddenness and inevitability of such pains. *not.* An emphatic double negative in the Greek, a construction Paul uses only four times in all his writings.

5:4 *darkness.* Believers no longer live in darkness, nor are they of the darkness (v. 5). See John 1:5; Acts 26:18. *thief.* See note on v. 2.

5:5 In Semitic languages (such as Hebrew) to be the "son of" a quality meant to be characterized by that quality. Christians do not simply live in the light; they are characterized by light.

5:6 *sleep.* Unbelievers are spiritually insensitive, but this kind of sleep is not for "sons of the light." *be alert.* Lit. "watch," which is in keeping with the emphasis Paul is placing on Christ's coming (cf. Matt 24:42–43; 25:13; Mark 13:34–37). *sober.* A contrast with the conduct mentioned in v. 7.

5:8 *the day.* A reference to the light that characterizes Christians; perhaps it refers also to the coming of Christ (see v. 2 and note). *breastplate . . . helmet.* Paul also uses the metaphor of armor in Rom 13:12; 2 Cor 6:7; 10:4; Eph 6:13–17. He does not consistently attach a particular virtue to each piece of armor; it is the general idea of equipment for battle that is pictured. For the triad of faith, hope and love see note on 1:3.

5:9 *destined.* God's appointment, not man's choice, is the significant thing. *wrath.* See note on 1:10. *salvation.* Our final, completed salvation.

5:10 *are awake or asleep.* That is, "live or die"; or, if the sense is moral, "are alert or carnal" (see v. 6). *with Him.* To be Christ's is to have entered a relationship that nothing can destroy.

5:11 *build up.* The verb basically applies to building houses, but Paul frequently used it for Christians being edified.

5:12 *those who diligently labor among you.* Not much is known about the organization and leadership of the church at this period, but the reference is possibly to elders.

5:13 *because of their work.* Not merely because of personal attachment or respect for their high position, but in appreciation for their work. *Live in peace.* The words apply to Christian relationships in general, but here they probably refer especially to right relations between leaders and those under them.

5:14 *the unruly.* Or "those who are idle"; they were loafers. It seems that some Thessalonians were so sure that the second coming was close that they had given up their jobs in order to prepare for it, but Paul says they should work (see 2 Thess 3:10–11 and notes). *the fainthearted . . . the weak.* These are to be helped, not rejected, by the strong (cf. Rom 14:1–15; 1 Cor 8:13).

5:15 *repays.* Retaliation is never a Christian option (cf. Rom 12:17; 1 Pet 3:9). Christians are called to forgive (see Matt 5:38–42; 18:21–35).

5:16 People are naturally happy on some occasions, but the Christian's joy is not dependent on circumstances. It comes from what Christ has done, and it is constant.

5:17 For the practice of continual (or regular) prayer see 1:3; 2:13; Rom 1:9–10; Eph 6:18; Col 1:3; 2 Tim 1:3.

5:18 As in v. 16, Christians are differentiated from the natural man. Because of what God has done, they are continually thankful whatever the circumstances (cf. Eph 5:20).

5:19 *quench the Spirit.* There is a warmth, a glow, about the Spirit's presence that makes this language appropriate. The kind of conduct Paul is opposing may include loafing, immorality and the other sins he has denounced. On the other hand, he may be warning against a mechanical attitude toward worship that discourages the expression of the gifts of the Spirit in the local assembly (see v. 20).

5:20 *prophetic utterances.* For the gift of prophecy see Rom 12:6; 1 Cor 12:10,28; 13:2; 14; Eph 4:11. For the function of prophecies see 1 Cor 14:3.

21 But [a]examine everything *carefully;*
[b]hold fast to that which is good;
22 abstain from every [1]form of evil.
23 Now [a]may the God of peace [b]Himself
sanctify you entirely; and may your [c]spirit
and soul and body be preserved complete,
[d]without blame at [e]the coming of our Lord
Jesus Christ.
24 [a]Faithful is He who [b]calls you, and He
also will bring it to pass.
25 Brethren, [a]pray for us[1].
26 [a]Greet all the brethren with a holy kiss.
27 I adjure you by the Lord to [a]have this
letter read to all the [b]brethren.
28 [a]The grace of our Lord Jesus Christ be
with you.

21 [a]1 Cor 14:29; 1 John 4:1 [b]Rom 12:9; Gal 6:10; 1 Thess 5:15 **22** [1]Or *appearance* **23** [a]Rom 15:33 [b]1 Thess 3:11 [c]Luke 1:46f; Heb 4:12 [d]James 1:4; 2 Pet 3:14 [e]1 Thess 2:19 **24** [a]1 Cor 1:9; 2 Thess 3:3 [b]1 Thess 2:12 **25** [1]Two early mss add *also* [a]Eph 6:19; 2 Thess 3:1; Heb 13:18 **26** [a]Rom 16:16 **27** [a]Col 4:16 [b]Acts 1:15 **28** [a]Rom 16:20; 2 Thess 3:18

5:21 *examine everything.* The approval of prophecy (v. 20) does not mean that anyone who claims to speak in the name of the Lord is to be accepted without question. Paul does not say what specific tests are to be applied, but he is clear that every teaching must be tested—surely they must be in agreement with his gospel.

5:23 A typical prayer. *God of peace.* A fitting reference to God in view of vv. 12–15. But Paul often refers to God in this way near the end of his letters (see Rom 15:33; 16:20; 1 Cor 14:33; 2 Cor 13:11; Phil 4:9; cf. 2 Thess 3:16). *your spirit and soul and body.* Paul is emphasizing the whole person, not attempting to differentiate the parts.

5:24 Paul's confidence rests in the nature of God (cf. Gen 18:25), who can be relied on to complete what He begins (see Num 23:19; Phil 1:6).

5:26 *all.* Paul sent a warm greeting to everyone, even those he had corrected. *holy kiss.* A kiss was a normal greeting of that day, similar to our modern handshake (cf. Rom 16:16; 1 Cor 16:20; 2 Cor 13:12; and a "kiss of love," 1 Pet 5:14).

5:27 *I adjure you.* Surprisingly strong language, meaning "I put you on oath." Paul clearly wanted every member of the church to read or hear his letter and to know of his concern and advice for them.

5:28 Paul always ended his letters with a benediction of grace for his readers, sometimes adding other blessings, as in 2 Cor 13:14.

2 Thessalonians

INTRODUCTION

See Introduction to 1 Thessalonians.

Author, Date and Place of Writing

Paul's authorship of 2 Thessalonians has been questioned more often than that of 1 Thessalonians, in spite of the fact that it has more support from early Christian writers. Objections are based on internal factors rather than on the adequacy of the statements of the church fathers. It is thought that there are differences in the vocabulary (ten words not used elsewhere), in the style (it is said to be unexpectedly formal) and in the eschatology (the doctrine of the "man of lawlessness" is not taught elsewhere). However, such arguments have not convinced current scholars. A majority still hold to Paul's authorship of 2 Thessalonians.

Because of its similarity to 1 Thessalonians, it must have been written not long after the first letter—perhaps about six months. The situation in the church seems to have been much the same. Paul probably penned it (see 1:1; 3:17) c. A.D. 51 or 52 in Corinth, after Silas and Timothy had returned from delivering 1 Thessalonians.

Purpose

Inasmuch as the situation in the Thessalonian church has not changed substantially, Paul's purpose in writing is very much the same as in his first letter to them. He writes (1) to encourage persecuted believers (1:4–10), (2) to exhort the Thessalonians to be steadfast and to work for a living (2:13—3:15) and (3) to correct a misunderstanding concerning the Lord's return (2:1–12).

Theme

Like 1 Thessalonians, this letter deals extensively with eschatology (see Introduction to 1 Thessalonians: Theme). In fact, in 2 Thessalonians 18 out of 47 verses (38 percent) deal with this subject.

Outline

I. Introduction (ch. 1)
   - A. Salutation (1:1–2)
   - B. Thanksgiving for Their Faith, Love and Perseverance (1:3–10)
   - C. Intercession for Their Spiritual Progress (1:11–12)

II. Instruction (ch. 2)
   - A. Prophecy regarding the Day of the Lord (2:1–12)
   - B. Thanksgiving for Their Election and Calling (Their Position) (2:13–15)
   - C. Prayer for Their Service and Testimony (Their Practice) (2:16–17)

III. Injunctions (ch. 3)
   - A. Call to Prayer (3:1–3)
   - B. Charge to Discipline for the Disorderly and Lazy (3:4–15)
   - C. Conclusion, Greeting and Benediction (3:16–18)

Thanksgiving for Faith and Perseverance

1 [a]Paul and [b]Silvanus and [c]Timothy,
To the [d]church of the Thessalonians in
God our Father and the Lord Jesus Christ:
2 [a]Grace to you and peace from God the
Father and the Lord Jesus Christ.
3 We ought always [a]to give thanks to
God for you, [b]brethren, as is *only* fitting,
because your faith is greatly enlarged, and
the [c]love of each one of you toward one
another grows *ever* greater;
4 therefore, we ourselves [a]speak proudly
of you among [b]the churches of God for your
[1]perseverance and faith [b]in the midst of all
your persecutions and afflictions which you
endure.
5 *This is* a [a]plain indication of God's
righteous judgment so that you will be [b]con-
sidered worthy of the kingdom of God, for
which indeed you are suffering.
6 [1]For after all [a]it is *only* just [2]for God to
repay with affliction those who afflict you,
7 and *to give* relief to you who are afflicted [1]and to us as well [2a]when the Lord Jesus
will be revealed [b]from heaven [c]with [3]His
mighty angels [d]in flaming fire,
8 dealing out retribution to those who
[a]do not know God and to those who [b]do not
obey the gospel of our Lord Jesus.
9 These will pay the penalty of [a]eternal
destruction, [b]away from the presence of the
Lord and from the glory of His power,
10 when He comes to be [a]glorified [1]in His
[2]saints on that [b]day, and to be marveled at
among all who have believed—for our [c]testi-
mony to you was believed.
11 To this end also we [a]pray for you
always, that our God will [1b]count you worthy of your [c]calling, and fulfill every desire
for [d]goodness and the [e]work of faith with
power,
12 so that the [a]name of our Lord Jesus
will be glorified in you, and you in Him,
according to the grace of our God and *the*
Lord Jesus Christ.

Man of Lawlessness

2 Now we request you, [a]brethren, with
regard to the [1b]coming of our Lord Jesus
Christ and our [c]gathering together to Him,
2 that you not be quickly shaken from
your [1]composure or be disturbed either by a
[a]spirit or a [2b]message or a [c]letter as if from

1:1 [a]1 Thess 1:1 [b]2 Cor 1:19 [c]Acts 16:1 [d]Acts 17:1; 1 Thess 1:1 **2** [a]Rom 1:7 **3** [a]Rom 1:8; Eph 5:20; 1 Thess 1:2; 2 Thess 2:13 [b]1 Thess 4:1; 2 Thess 2:1 [c]1 Thess 3:12 **4** [1]Or *steadfastness* [a]2 Cor 7:4; 1 Thess 2:19 [b]1 Cor 7:17; 1 Thess 2:14 **5** [a]Phil 1:28 [b]Luke 20:35; 2 Thess 1:11 **6** [1]Lit *If indeed* [2]Or *in the sight of* [a]Ex 23:22; Col 3:25; Heb 6:10 **7** [1]Lit *along with us* [2]Lit *at the revelation of the Lord Jesus* [3]Lit *the angels of His power* [a]Luke 17:30 [b]1 Thess 4:16 [c]Jude 14 [d]Ex 3:2; 19:18; Is 66:15; Ezek 1:13; Dan 7:9; Matt 25:41; 1 Cor 3:13; Heb 10:27; 12:29; 2 Pet 3:7; Jude 7; Rev 14:10 **8** [a]Gal 4:8 [b]Rom 2:8

9 [a]Phil 3:19; 1 Thess 5:3 [b]Is 2:10, 19, 21; 2 Thess 2:8 **10** [1]Or *in the persons of* [2]Or *holy ones* [a]Is 49:3; John 17:10; 1 Thess 2:12 [b]Is 2:11ff; 1 Cor 3:13 [c]1 Cor 1:6; 1 Thess 2:1 **11** [1]Or *make* [a]Col 1:9 [b]2 Thess 1:5 [c]Rom 11:29 [d]Rom 15:14 [e]1 Thess 1:3 **12** [a]Is 24:15; 66:5; Mal 1:11; Phil 2:9ff **2:1** [1]Or *presence* [a]2 Thess 1:3 [b]1 Thess 2:19 [c]Mark 13:27; 1 Thess 4:15-17 **2** [1]Lit *mind* [2]Lit *word* [a]1 Cor 14:32; 1 John 4:1 [b]1 Thess 5:2; 2 Thess 2:15 [c]2 Thess 3:17

1:1–2 See note on 1 Thess 1:1.
1:3 *ought.* Paul is obliged to give thanks where it is due (cf. 1 Thess 1:7–8; see note on Phil 1:3–4). *brethren.* See note on 1 Thess 1:4. *faith . . . love.* Two virtues that Paul had been pleased to acknowledge in the Thessalonian church (see 1 Thess 3:6–7), but that were also somewhat lacking (1 Thess 3:10,12). *grows ever greater.* The same verb Paul had used in his prayer that their love might grow (1 Thess 3:12). He is recording an exact answer to prayer.
1:4 *we.* Emphatic, "we ourselves." Paul seems to imply that it was unusual for the founders of a church to boast about it, though others might do so (cf. 1 Thess 1:9). But the Thessalonians were so outstanding that Paul departed from normal practice. *persecutions and afflictions.* See 1 Thess 1:6; 2:14; 3:3.
1:5 *plain indication of God's righteous judgment.* The evidence was in the way the Thessalonians endured trials. The judgment on them was right because God did not leave them to their own resources. He provided strength to endure, and this in turn produced spiritual and moral character. It also proved that God was on their side and gave a warning to their persecutors (cf. Phil 1:28). *kingdom of God.* See notes on 1 Thess 2:12; Matt 3:2. *for which.* That is, "in the interest of which" or "in behalf of which."
1:6 *just for God.* The justice of God brings punishment on unrepentant sinners (cf. Mark 9:47–48; Luke 13:3–5), and it may be in the here and now (see Rom 1:24,26,28) as well as on judgment day.
1:7 *give relief.* Retribution not only involves punishment of the evil but also relief for the righteous. *us as well.* Paul was no academic theologian writing in comfort from a distance; rather, he was suffering just as they were. *revealed.* Christ is now hidden, and many people even deny His existence. But at His second coming He will be seen by everyone for who He is. *flaming fire.* He comes to punish wickedness (cf. Is 66:15; Rev 1:14). *His mighty angels.* Perhaps a class of angels (such a group is mentioned in apocalyptic writings) given special power to do God's will.
1:8 *do not know God.* Does not refer to those who have never heard of the true God but to those who refuse to recognize Him (cf. 2:10,12; Rom 1:28). *do not obey.* The gospel invites acceptance, and rejection is disobedience to a royal invitation.
1:9 *destruction.* Not annihilation (see note on 1 Thess 5:3). Paul uses the word in 1 Cor 5:5, possibly of the destruction of the "flesh" for the purpose of salvation. Since, however, salvation implies resurrection of the body, annihilation cannot be in mind. The word means something like "complete ruin." Here it means being shut out from Christ's presence. This eternal separation is the penalty of sin and the essence of hell.
1:10 *glorified in His saints.* Not simply "among" but "in" them. His glory is seen in what they are. *saints.* See note on 1 Thess 3:13. *that day.* See note on 1 Thess 5:2. *our testimony.* The preaching of the gospel is essentially bearing testimony to what God has done in Christ.
1:11 *pray for you always.* See note on 1 Thess 5:17. *desire for goodness.* Lit. "resolve of goodness." God initiates every good purpose and every act prompted by faith; Paul prays accordingly that He will bring them to fulfillment.
1:12 *name.* In ancient times one's name was often more than a personal label; it summed up what a person was. Paul looks for glory to be ascribed to Christ for all He will do in the lives of the Thessalonian Christians.
2:1 *coming.* See note on 1 Thess 2:19. The second coming of Christ is the principal topic of 2 Thessalonians. What Paul wrote was supplemental to his oral teaching and the instructions contained in his earlier letter. *gathering together to Him.* See note on 1 Thess 4:17.
2:2 *shaken.* The Greek for this verb was often used of a ship adrift from its mooring, and suggests lack of stability. *disturbed.* Jesus issued a similar instruction, using the same verb (Mark 13:7). *a spirit.* Paul seems to be uncertain about what was disturbing them, so he uses a general expression denoting any inspired revelation. *message.* Lit. "word," perhaps referring to a sermon or other oral communication. *a letter as if from us.* A

us, to the effect that [d]the day of the Lord
[e]has come.

3 [a]Let no one in any way deceive you, for
it will not come unless the [1b]apostasy comes
first, and the [c]man of lawlessness is
revealed, the [d]son of destruction,

4 who opposes and exalts himself above
[1a]every so-called god or object of worship,
so that he takes his seat in the temple of
God, [b]displaying himself as being God.

5 Do you not remember that [a]while I was
still with you, I was telling you these things?

6 And you know [a]what restrains him
now, so that in his time he will be revealed.

7 For [a]the mystery of lawlessness is
already at work; only [b]he who now restrains
will do so until he is taken out of the way.

8 Then that lawless one [a]will be revealed
whom the Lord will slay [b]with the breath of
His mouth and bring to an end by the
[c]appearance of His [1]coming;

9 *that is,* the one whose [1]coming is in
accord with the activity of [a]Satan, with all
power and [2b]signs and false wonders,

10 and with [1]all the deception of wickedness for [a]those who perish, because they did
not receive the love of [b]the truth so as to be
saved.

11 For this reason [a]God [1]will send upon
them [2]a [b]deluding influence so that they will
believe [3]what is false,

12 in order that they all may be [1]judged
who [a]did not believe the truth, but [2b]took
pleasure in wickedness.

13 [a]But we should always give thanks to
God for you, [b]brethren beloved by the Lord,
because [c]God has chosen you [1]from the
beginning [d]for salvation [2e]through sanctification [3]by the Spirit and faith in the truth.

14 It was for this He [a]called you through
[b]our gospel, [1]that you may gain the glory of
our Lord Jesus Christ.

15 So then, brethren, [a]stand firm and
[b]hold to the traditions which you were
taught, whether [c]by word *of mouth* or [c]by
letter [1]from us.

16 [a]Now may our Lord Jesus Christ [a]Him-
self and God our Father, who has [b]loved us
and given us eternal comfort and [c]good hope
by grace,

2 [d]1 Cor 1:8 [e]1 Cor 7:26 **3** [1]Or *falling away* from the faith [a]Eph 5:6 [b]1 Tim 4:1 [c]Dan 7:25; 8:25; 11:36; 2 Thess 2:8; Rev 13:5ff [d]John 17:12 **4** [1]Or *everyone who is called God* [a]1 Cor 8:5 [b]Is 14:14; Ezek 28:2 **5** [a]1 Thess 3:4 **6** [a]2 Thess 2:7 **7** [a]Rev 17:5, 7 [b]2 Thess 2:6 **8** [1]Or *presence* [a]Dan 7:25; 8:25; 11:36; 2 Thess 2:3; Rev 13:5ff [b]Is 11:4; Rev 2:16; 19:15 [c]1 Tim 6:14; 2 Tim 1:10; 4:1, 8; Titus 2:13 **9** [1]Or *presence* [2]Or *attesting miracles* [a]Matt 4:10 [b]Matt 24:24; John 4:48 **10** [1]Or *every deception* [a]1 Cor 1:18 [b]2 Thess 2:12, 13 **11** [1]Lit *is sending* [2]Lit *an activity of error* [3]Or *the lie* [a]1 Kin 22:22; Rom 1:28 [b]1 Thess 2:3; 2 Tim 4:4 **12** [1]Or *condemned* [2]Or *approved* [a]Rom 2:8 [b]Rom 1:32; 1 Cor 13:6 **13** [1]One early ms reads *first fruits* [2]Lit *in* [3]Lit *of* [a]2 Thess 1:3 [b]1 Thess 1:4 [c]Eph 1:4ff [d]1 Cor 1:21; 1 Thess 2:12; 5:9; 1 Pet 1:5 [e]1 Thess 4:7; 1 Pet 1:2 **14** [1]Lit *to the gaining of* [a]1 Thess 2:12 [b]1 Thess 1:5 **15** [1]Lit *of* [a]1 Cor 16:13 [b]1 Cor 11:2; 2 Thess 3:6 [c]2 Thess 2:2 **16** [a]1 Thess 3:11 [b]John 3:16 [c]Titus 3:7; 1 Pet 1:3

forgery. *day of the Lord.* See note on 1 Thess 5:2. *has come.* Obviously Christ's climactic return had not occurred, but Paul was combating the idea that the final days had begun and their completion would be imminent.

2:3 *the apostasy.* At the last time there will be a falling away from the faith (see Matt 24:10–12; 1 Tim 4:1). But here Paul is speaking of active rebellion, the supreme opposition of evil to the things of God. *the man of lawlessness.* The leader of the forces of evil at the last time. Only here is he called by this name. John tells us of many "antichrists" (1 John 2:18), and this may be the worst of them—the antichrist of Rev 13—though Paul's description of the man of lawlessness has some distinctive features. He is not Satan, because he is clearly distinguished from him in v. 9. *revealed.* Since the Greek for this word is from the same root as that used of Jesus Christ in 1:7, it may indicate something supernatural. *son of destruction.* For all his proud claims, his final overthrow is certain. The same Greek expression is used of Judas Iscariot in John 17:12, where it is translated "son of perdition."

2:4 *every so-called god or object of worship.* He is not merely a political or military man, but claims a place above every god and everything associated with worship. He even claims to be God. *temple of God.* Apparently refers to a physical building (cf. Mark 13:14) from which he makes his blasphemous pronouncements (cf. Dan 11:36–45; Rev 13:1–15).

2:6 *what restrains him.* The expression is neuter, but the masculine equivalent is in v. 7. There have been many suggestions as to the identity of this restrainer: the Roman state with its emperor, Paul's missionary work, the Jewish state, the principle of law and government embodied in the state, the Holy Spirit or the restraining ministry of the Holy Spirit through the church, and others.

2:7 *mystery.* In the NT a mystery usually denotes something people could not know by themselves but that God has revealed (see note on Rom 11:25). It is most often used in reference to the gospel or some aspect of it. The expression here indicates that we know some things about evil only as God reveals them. This evil is already at work and will continue until the restrainer is removed at the end time.

2:8 *that lawless one will be revealed.* Evidently refers to some supernatural aspects of his appearing (see v. 9). *slay with the breath of His mouth.* Despite his impressiveness (v. 4), the man of lawlessness will easily be destroyed by Christ (cf. Dan 11:45; Rev 19:20). *appearance.* In 2 Tim 1:10 ("appearing") the Greek for this word refers to Jesus' first coming, but everywhere else in the NT to His second coming.

2:9 *coming.* The same word used of Christ's coming in v. 8. Satan empowers him with miracles, signs and wonders (cf. Matt 24:24). *false.* Not "bogus," but "producing false impressions."

2:10 *deception.* The aim of the miracles of v. 9. *did not receive.* Their unbelief was willing and intentional. *truth.* Often closely connected with Jesus (see John 14:6; Eph 4:21) and with the gospel (see Gal 2:5; Eph 1:13).

2:11 *For this reason.* Because of their deliberate rejection of the truth (v. 10). *God will send upon them a deluding influence.* God uses sin to punish the sinful (cf. Rom 1:24–28). *what is false.* Not just any lie, but the great lie that the man of lawlessness is God (v. 4).

2:13 *beloved by the Lord . . . God has chosen.* For the connection between God's love and election see Col 3:12; 1 Thess 1:4; see also note on Eph 1:4. *from the beginning.* Election is from eternity (see Eph 1:4). *sanctification.* A necessary aspect of salvation, not something reserved for special Christians (see 1 Thess 3:13; 4:3 and notes). *truth.* See note on v. 10. All three persons of the Trinity are mentioned in this verse (see note on 1 Thess 1:1).

2:14 *called . . . through our gospel.* The past tense refers to the time when the Thessalonians were converted; but the divine call is a present reality in 1 Thess 2:12; 5:24. *our gospel.* See note on 1 Thess 1:5. *glory of our Lord Jesus Christ.* Cf. 1 Thess 2:12. Ultimately there is no glory other than God's.

2:15 *traditions.* Until the NT was written, essential Christian teaching was passed on in the "traditions," just as rabbinic law was (see note on Matt 15:2); it could be either oral or written.

17 [a]comfort and [b]strengthen your hearts
in every good work and word.

Exhortation

3 [a]Finally, brethren, [b]pray for us that [c]the
word of the Lord will [1]spread rapidly and
be glorified, just as *it did* also with you;
2 and that we will be [a]rescued from [1]per-
verse and evil men; for not all have [2]faith.
3 But [a]the Lord is faithful, [1]and He will
strengthen and protect you [2]from [b]the evil
one.
4 We have [a]confidence in the Lord concerning you, that you [b]are doing and will
continue to do what we command.
5 May the Lord [a]direct your hearts into
the love of God and into the steadfastness of
Christ.
6 Now we command you, brethren, [a]in
the name of our Lord Jesus Christ, that you
[1b]keep away from every brother who [2]leads
an [3c]unruly life and not according to [d]the tradition which [4]you received from us.
7 For you yourselves know how you
ought to [1a]follow our example, because we
did not act in an undisciplined manner
among you,
8 nor did we [a]eat [1]anyone's bread [2]with-
out paying for it, but with [b]labor and hardship we *kept* [c]working night and day so that
we would not be a burden to any of you;
9 not because we do not have [a]the right
to this, but in order to offer ourselves [b]as a
model for you, so that you would [1]follow our
example.
10 For even [a]when we were with you, we
used to give you this order: [b]if anyone is not
willing to work, then he is not to eat, either.
11 For we hear that some among you are
[a]leading an undisciplined life, doing no work
at all, but acting like [b]busybodies.
12 Now such persons we command and
[a]exhort in the Lord Jesus Christ to [b]work in
quiet fashion and eat their own bread.
13 But as for you, [a]brethren, [b]do not grow
weary of doing good.
14 If anyone does not obey our [1]instruc-
tion [2a]in this letter, take special note of that
person [3b]and do not associate with him, so
that he will be [c]put to shame.
15 *Yet* [a]do not regard him as an enemy,
but [1b]admonish him as a [c]brother.
16 Now [a]may the Lord of peace [b]Himself
continually grant you peace in every [1]cir-
cumstance. [c]The Lord be with you all!
17 [1]I, Paul, write this greeting [a]with my
own hand, and this is a distinguishing mark
in every letter; this is the way I write.
18 [a]The grace of our Lord Jesus Christ be
with you all.

17 [a]1 Thess 3:2, 13 [b]2 Thess 3:3 **3:1** [1]Lit *run* [a]1 Thess 4:1 [b]1 Thess 5:25 [c]1 Thess 1:8 **2** [1]Lit *improper* [2]Or *the faith* [a]Rom 15:31 **3** [1]Lit *who will* [2]Or *from evil* [a]1 Cor 1:9; 1 Thess 5:24 [b]Matt 5:37 **4** [a]2 Cor 2:3 [b]1 Thess 4:10 **5** [a]1 Thess 3:11 **6** [1]Or *avoid* [2]Lit *walks disorderly* [3]Or *undisciplined* [4]One early ms reads *they* [a]1 Cor 5:4 [b]Rom 16:17; 1 Cor 5:11; 2 Thess 3:14 [c]1 Thess 5:14; 2 Thess 3:7, 11 [d]1 Cor 11:2; 2 Thess 2:15 **7** [1]Lit *imitate us* [a]1 Thess 1:6; 2 Thess 3:9 **8** [1]Lit *from anyone* [2]Lit *freely* [a]1 Cor 9:4 [b]1 Thess 2:9 [c]Acts 18:3; Eph 4:28 **9** [a]1 Cor 9:4ff [b]2 Thess 3:7

9 [1]Lit *imitate us* **10** [a]1 Thess 3:4 [b]1 Thess 4:11 **11** [a]2 Thess 3:6 [b]1 Tim 5:13; 1 Pet 4:15 **12** [a]1 Thess 4:1 [b]1 Thess 4:11 **13** [a]1 Thess 4:1 [b]2 Cor 4:1; Gal 6:9 **14** [1]Lit *word* [2]Lit *through* [3]Lit *not to associate* [a]Col 4:16 [b]2 Thess 3:6 [c]1 Cor 4:14 **15** [1]Or *keep admonishing* [a]Gal 6:1 [b]1 Thess 5:14 [c]2 Thess 3:6, 13 **16** [1]Lit *way* [a]Rom 15:33 [b]1 Thess 3:11 [c]Ruth 2:4 **17** [1]Lit *The greeting by my hand of Paul* [a]1 Cor 16:21 **18** [a]Rom 16:20; 1 Thess 5:28

In 1 Cor 15:3 Paul uses the technical words for receiving and handing on traditions.

2:16–17 There is a similar prayer in about the same place in the first letter (1 Thess 3:11–13).

2:17 *comfort and strengthen.* Also used together in 1 Thess 3:2. The prayer is for inner strength that will produce results in both action and speech.

3:1 *Finally.* See note on 1 Thess 4:1. In 1 Thess 5:25 Paul simply asked for prayer; here he mentions specifics. *just as it did also with you.* Lit. "just as also with you." The expression is general enough to cover the present as well as the past (cf. 1 Thess 2:13).

3:2 *perverse.* The Greek for this word means "out of place," and elsewhere in the NT it is used only of things (see Luke 23:41; Acts 25:5). Perverseness is always out of place. For Paul's difficulties at Corinth (where he wrote this letter) see Acts 18:12–13.

3:3 *faithful.* In the Greek text, "faithful" immediately follows "faith" (v. 2), putting the faithfulness of God in sharp contrast with the lack of faith in people (cf. 1 Cor 1:9; 10:13; 2 Cor 1:18).

3:5 *hearts.* See note on 1 Thess 2:4. *love of God.* Paul is about to rebuke the idle, and is here reminding them of God's love. There should be no hard feelings among those who owe everything to the love of God.

3:6 *command.* An authoritative word with a military ring. *the name.* See note on 1:12. *keep away.* Not withdrawal of all contact but withholding of close fellowship. Idleness is sinful and disruptive, but those guilty of it are still brothers (v. 15). *leads an unruly life.* The problem was mentioned in the first letter (4:11–12; 5:14; see notes there), and evidently had worsened. Paul takes it seriously and gives more attention to it in this letter than to anything else but the second coming. *tradition.* See note on 2:15.

3:7 *follow our example.* See note on 1 Thess 1:6.

3:8 *eat . . . bread.* A Hebraism for "make a living" (see, e.g., Gen 3:19; Amos 7:12). Paul is not saying that he never accepted hospitality but that he had not depended on other people for his living (see 1 Thess 2:9 and note).

3:9 *the right.* See note on 1 Thess 2:6.

3:10 Pagan parallels are in the form, "He who does not work does not eat." But Paul gives an imperative: lit. "let him not eat." The Christian must not be a loafer.

3:11 *busybodies.* Worse than idle, they were interfering with other people's affairs, a problem to which an unruly or idle life often leads.

3:14 Paul realizes that some may not heed his letter. *associate with.* The Greek for this phrase is an unusual double compound, meaning "mix up together with" (used elsewhere in the NT only in 1 Cor 5:9,11—of a similar withdrawal of close fellowship). It indicates a disassociation that will bring the person back to a right attitude. *put to shame.* And repent. The aim is not punishment but restoration to fellowship.

3:15 Discipline in the church should be brotherly, never harsh. *admonish.* See 1 Thess 5:12.

3:16 *Lord of peace.* The more usual phrase is "God of peace" (see note on 1 Thess 5:23). *you all.* Even the disorderly.

3:17 Paul normally dictated his letters (cf. Rom 16:22), but toward the end he added something in his own handwriting (see 1 Cor 16:21; Gal 6:11; Col 4:18). Here he tells us that this practice was his distinguishing mark.

3:18 See note on 1 Thess 5:28. Paul has criticized his offenders, but his last prayer is for everyone.

The Pastoral Letters

1,2 Timothy and Titus are known as the Pastoral Letters because they give instruction to Timothy and Titus concerning the pastoral care of churches. All three letters probably were written not long after the events of Acts 28.

After his imprisonment in Rome (c. A.D. 60–62), Paul most likely began his fourth missionary journey (see "Paul's Fourth Missionary Journey," pp. 1762–1763). During this trip he commissioned Titus to remain as his representative in Crete, and he left Timothy in charge of the church at Ephesus. Paul then moved on to Philippi in northern Greece (Macedonia), where he wrote his first letter to Timothy and his letter to Titus (c. 63–65). Later he traveled to Rome, where he was imprisoned for the second time and where he wrote 2 Timothy shortly before he was executed (67 or 68).

Certain themes and phrases recur throughout the Pastoral Letters: (1) God the Savior (see note on Titus 1:3); (2) sound doctrine, faith and teaching (see note on Titus 1:9); (3) godliness (see note on 1 Tim 2:2); (4) controversies (1 Tim 1:4; 6:4; 2 Tim 2:23; Titus 3:9); (5) trustworthy sayings (see note on 1 Tim 1:15).

1 Timothy

INTRODUCTION

Author

Both early tradition and the salutations of the Pastoral Letters themselves confirm Paul as their author. Some objections have been raised in recent years on the basis of an alleged uncharacteristic vocabulary and style (e.g., see notes on 1:15; 2:2), but evidence is still convincingly supportive of Paul's authorship.

Background and Purpose

During his fourth missionary journey, Paul had instructed Timothy to care for the church at Ephesus (1:3) while he went on to Macedonia (see "The Pastoral Letters," p. 1758). When he realized that he might not return to Ephesus in the near future (3:14–15), he wrote this first letter to Timothy to develop the charge he had given his young assistant (1:3,18), to refute false teachings (1:3–7; 4:1–8; 6:3–5,20–21) and to supervise the affairs of the growing Ephesian church (church worship, 2:1–15; the appointment of qualified church leaders, 3:1–13; 5:17–25).

A major problem in the Ephesian church was a heresy that combined Gnosticism (see Introduction to 1 John: Gnosticism), decadent Judaism (1:3–7) and false asceticism (4:1–5).

Date

1 Timothy was written sometime after the events of Acts 28 (c. 63–65), at least eight years after Paul's three-year stay in Ephesus (Acts 19:8,10; 20:31).

Recipient

As the salutation indicates (1:2), Paul is writing to Timothy, a native of Lystra (in modern Turkey). Timothy's father was Greek, while his mother was a Jewish Christian (Acts 16:1). From childhood he had been taught the OT (2 Tim 1:5; 3:15). Paul called him "my true child in the faith" (1:2), perhaps having led him to Christ during his first visit to Lystra. At the time of his second visit Paul invited Timothy to join him on his missionary travels, and circumcised him so that his Greek ancestry would not be a liability in working with the Jews (Acts 16:3). Timothy shared in the evangelization of Macedonia and Achaia (Acts 17:14–15; 18:5) and was with Paul during much of his long preaching ministry at Ephesus (Acts 19:22). He traveled with Paul from Ephesus to Macedonia, to Corinth, back to Macedonia, and to Asia Minor (Acts 20:1–6). He seems even to have accompanied him all the way to Jerusalem. He was with Paul during the apostle's first imprisonment (Phil 1:1; Col 1:1; Philem 1).

Following Paul's release (after Acts 28), Timothy again traveled with him but eventually stayed at Ephesus to deal with the problems there, while Paul went on to Macedonia. Paul's closeness to and admiration of Timothy are seen in Paul's naming him as the co-sender of six of his letters (2 Corinthians, Philippians, Colossians, 1,2 Thessalonians and Philemon) and in his speaking highly of him to the Philippians (Phil 2:19–22). At the end of Paul's life he requested Timothy to join him at Rome (2 Tim 4:9,21). According to Heb 13:23, Timothy himself was imprisoned and subsequently released—whether at Rome or elsewhere, we do not know.

Timothy was not an apostle, and he was probably not an overseer since he was given instructions about overseers (3:1–7; 5:17–22). It may be best to regard him as an apostolic representative, delegated to carry out special work (see Titus 1:5).

Outline

- I. Salutation (1:1–2)
- II. Warning against False Teachers (1:3–11)
    - A. The Nature of the Heresy (1:3–7)
    - B. The Purpose of the Law (1:8–11)
- III. The Lord's Grace to Paul (1:12–17)
- IV. The Purpose of Paul's Instructions to Timothy (1:18–20)
- V. Instructions concerning the Administration of the Church (chs. 2—3)
    - A. Public Worship (ch. 2)
        - 1. Prayer in public worship (2:1–8)
        - 2. Women in public worship (2:9–15)
    - B. Qualifications for Church Officers (3:1–13)
        - 1. Overseers (3:1–7)
        - 2. Deacons (3:8–13)
    - C. Purpose of These Instructions (3:14–16)
- VI. Methods of Dealing with False Teaching (ch. 4)
    - A. False Teaching Described (4:1–5)
    - B. Methods of Dealing with It Explained (4:6–16)
- VII. Methods of Dealing with Different Groups in the Church (5:1—6:2)
    - A. The Older and Younger (5:1–2)
    - B. Widows (5:3–16)
    - C. Elders (5:17–25)
    - D. Slaves (6:1–2)
- VIII. Miscellaneous Matters (6:3–19)
    - A. False Teachers (6:3–5)
    - B. Love of Money (6:6–10)
    - C. Charge to Timothy (6:11–16)
    - D. The Rich (6:17–19)
- IX. Concluding Appeal (6:20–21)

Misleadings in Doctrine and Living

1 Paul, [a]an apostle of [b]Christ Jesus [c]accord-
ing to the commandment of [c]God our
Savior, and of [b]Christ Jesus, *who is* our
[d]hope,
2 To [a]Timothy, [a]*my* true child in *the*
faith: [b]Grace, mercy *and* peace from God the
Father and [c]Christ Jesus our Lord.
3 As I urged you [1]upon my departure for
[a]Macedonia, [2]remain on at [b]Ephesus so that
you may instruct certain men not to [c]teach
strange doctrines,
4 nor to [1]pay attention to [a]myths and
endless [b]genealogies, which give rise to mere
[c]speculation rather than [d]*furthering* [2]the
administration of God which is by faith.
5 But the goal of our [1a]instruction is love
[b]from a pure heart and a [c]good conscience
and a sincere [d]faith.
6 For some men, straying from these
things, have turned aside to [a]fruitless discussion,
7 [a]wanting to be [b]teachers of the Law,
even though they do not understand either
what they are saying or the matters about
which they make confident assertions.
8 But we know that [a]the Law is good, if
one uses it lawfully,
9 realizing the fact that [a]law is not made
for a righteous person, but for those who are
lawless and [b]rebellious, for the [c]ungodly and
sinners, for the unholy and [d]profane, for
those who kill their fathers or mothers, for
murderers
10 [1]and [2a]immoral men [1]and [b]homosexu-
als [1]and [c]kidnappers [1]and [d]liars [1]and [e]per-
jurers, and whatever else is contrary to
[f]sound teaching,
11 according to [a]the glorious gospel of
[b]the blessed God, with which I have been
[c]entrusted.
12 I thank [a]Christ Jesus our Lord, who has
[b]strengthened me, because He considered
me faithful, [c]putting me into service,
13 even though I was formerly a blasphemer and a [a]persecutor and a violent aggressor. Yet I was [b]shown mercy because [c]I acted
ignorantly in unbelief;
14 and the [a]grace of our Lord was more
than abundant, with the [b]faith and love
which are *found* in Christ Jesus.
15 [a]It is a trustworthy statement, deserving full acceptance, that [b]Christ Jesus came
into the world to [c]save sinners, among
whom [d]I am foremost *of all*.
16 Yet for this reason I [a]found mercy, so
that in me as the foremost, Jesus Christ
might [b]demonstrate His perfect patience as
an example for those [1]who would believe in
Him for eternal life.
17 Now to the [a]King [1]eternal, [b]immortal,
[c]invisible, the [d]only God, [e]*be* honor and glory [2]forever and ever. Amen.
18 This [a]command I entrust to you, Timothy, [b]*my* [1]son, in accordance with the
[c]prophecies previously made concerning
you, that by them you [d]fight the good fight,
19 keeping [a]faith and a good conscience,

1:1 [a]2 Cor 1:1 [b]1 Tim 1:12 [c]Titus 1:3 [d]Col 1:27
2 [a]2 Tim 1:2 [b]Rom 1:7; 2 Tim 1:2; Titus 1:4 [c]1 Tim 1:12
3 [1]Lit *while going to* [2]Lit *to remain* [a]Rom 15:26 [b]Acts 18:19 [c]Rom 16:17; 2 Cor 11:4; Gal 1:6f; 1 Tim 6:3
4 [1]Or *occupy themselves with* [2]Lit *God's provision* [a]1 Tim 4:7; 2 Tim 4:4; Titus 1:14; 2 Pet 1:16 [b]Titus 3:9 [c]2 Tim 2:23 [d]Eph 3:2
5 [1]Lit *commandment* [a]1 Tim 1:18 [b]2 Tim 2:22 [c]1 Tim 1:19; 3:9; 2 Tim 1:3; 1 Pet 3:16, 21 [d]2 Tim 1:5
6 [a]Titus 1:10
7 [a]James 3:1 [b]Luke 2:46
8 [a]Rom 7:12, 16
9 [a]Gal 5:23 [b]Titus 1:6, 10 [c]1 Pet 4:18; Jude 15 [d]1 Tim 4:7; 6:20; Heb 12:16
10 [1]Lit *for* [2]Or *fornicators* [a]1 Cor 6:9 [b]Lev 18:22 [c]Ex 21:16; Rev 18:13 [d]Rev 21:8, 27; 22:15 [e]Matt 5:33 [f]1 Tim 4:6; 6:3; 2 Tim 4:3; Titus 1:9, 13; 2:1, 2
11 [a]2 Cor 4:4 [b]1 Tim 6:15 [c]Gal 2:7
12 [a]Gal 3:26 [b]Acts 9:22; Phil 4:13; 2 Tim 4:17 [c]Acts 9:15
13 [a]Acts 8:3 [b]1 Cor 7:25 [c]Acts 26:9
14 [a]Rom 5:20; 1 Cor 3:10; 2 Cor 4:15; Gal 1:13-16 [b]1 Thess 1:3; 1 Tim 2:15; 4:12; 6:11; 2 Tim 1:13; 2:22; Titus 2:2
15 [a]1 Tim 3:1; 4:9; 2 Tim 2:11; Titus 3:8 [b]Mark 2:17; Luke 15:2ff; 19:10 [c]Rom 11:14 [d]1 Cor 15:9; Eph 3:8
16 [1]Or *destined to* [a]1 Cor 7:25; 1 Tim 1:13 [b]Eph 2:7
17 [1]Lit *of the ages* [2]Lit *to the ages of the ages* [a]Rev 15:3 [b]1 Tim 6:16 [c]Col 1:15 [d]John 5:44; 1 Tim 6:15; Jude 25 [e]Rom 2:7, 10; 11:36; Heb 2:7
18 [1]Or *child* [a]1 Tim 1:5 [b]1 Tim 1:2 [c]1 Tim 4:14 [d]2 Cor 10:4; 1 Tim 6:12; 2 Tim 2:3f; 4:7
19 [a]1 Tim 1:5

1:1 *apostle.* One specially commissioned by Christ (see notes on Mark 6:30; 1 Cor 1:1; Heb 3:1). *Christ Jesus . . . our hope.* See Titus 2:13. *hope.* Expresses absolute certainty, not a mere wish.

1:2 *my true child in the faith.* My spiritual son (see 1:18; 1 Cor 4:17; 2 Tim 1:2; 2:1; Philem 10). *Grace.* See notes on Jon 4:2; Gal 1:3; Eph 1:2. *mercy.* See Rom 9:23. *peace.* See notes on John 14:27; 20:19; Gal 1:3; Eph 1:2.

1:3–11 In this section, along with 4:1–8; 6:3–5,20–21, Paul warns against heretical teachers in the Ephesian church. They are characterized by (1) teaching false doctrines (1:3; 6:3); (2) teaching Jewish myths (Titus 1:14); (3) wanting to be teachers of the OT law (1:7); (4) building up endless, far-fetched, fictitious stories based on obscure genealogical points (1:4; 4:7; Titus 3:9); (5) being conceited (1:7; 6:4); (6) being argumentative (1:4; 6:4; 2 Tim 2:23; Titus 3:9); (7) using talk that was meaningless (1:6) and foolish (2 Tim 2:23; Titus 3:9); (8) not knowing what they were talking about (1:7; 6:4); (9) teaching ascetic practices (4:3); and (10) using their positions of religious leadership for personal financial gain (6:5). These heretics probably were forerunners of the Gnostics (6:20–21; see Introduction to 1 John: Gnosticism).

1:3 *upon my departure for Macedonia.* Since this incident is not recorded in Acts, it probably occurred after Acts 28, between Paul's first and second Roman imprisonments (see Introduction: Recipient). *remain on at Ephesus.* The Ephesian church was well established by this time. Paul had had an extensive ministry there on his third missionary journey about eight years earlier (Acts 19:1–20:1). After his release from prison in Rome (after Acts 28), he revisited the church, leaving Timothy in charge while he journeyed on to Macedonia.

1:4 *myths and endless genealogies.* Probably mythical stories built on OT history (genealogies) that later developed into intricate Gnostic philosophical systems (see Introduction to 1 John: Gnosticism).

1:8 *the Law is good.* See Rom 7:7–12.

1:10 *sound teaching.* See note on Titus 1:9.

1:11 *gospel.* See note on Mark 1:1. *entrusted.* See 6:20; 1 Cor 9:17; Gal 2:7; 1 Thess 2:4; 2 Tim 1:12,14; 2:2.

1:13 *a blasphemer and a persecutor and a violent aggressor.* See Acts 9:1; 22:4–5,19; 26:10–11.

1:15 *It is a trustworthy statement.* A clause found nowhere else in the NT but used five times in the Pastorals (here; 3:1; 4:9; 2 Tim 2:11; Titus 3:8) to identify a key saying.

1:18 *prophecies previously made concerning you.* In the early church God revealed His will in various matters through prophets (see Acts 13:1–3, where prophets had an active role in the sending of Paul and Barnabas on their mission to the Gentiles). In Timothy's case this prophecy may have occurred at the time of or before his ordination (4:14), perhaps about 12 years earlier on Paul's second missionary journey (see Acts 16:3). Prophecies about Timothy seem to have pointed to the significant leadership role he was to have in the church.

which some have rejected and suffered shipwreck in regard to [1][b]their faith.
20 [1]Among these are [a]Hymenaeus and
[b]Alexander, whom I have [c]handed over to
Satan, so that they will be [d]taught not to
blaspheme.

A Call to Prayer

2 First of all, then, I urge that [a]entreaties
and prayers, petitions *and* thanksgivings,
be made on behalf of all men,
2 [a]for kings and all who are in [1]authori-
ty, so that we may lead a tranquil and quiet
life in all godliness and [2]dignity.
3 This is good and acceptable in the sight
of [a]God our Savior,
4 [a]who desires all men to be [b]saved and
to [c]come to the [1]knowledge of the truth.

19 [1]Lit *the* [b]1 Tim 6:12, 21; 2 Tim 2:18
20 [1]Lit *Of* [a]2 Tim 2:17 [b]2 Tim 4:14 [c]1 Cor 5:5 [d]1 Cor 11:32; Heb 12:5ff
2:1 [a]Eph 6:18
2 [1]Or *a high position* [2]Or *seriousness* [a]Ezra 6:10; Rom 13:1 **3** [a]Luke 1:47; 1 Tim 1:1; 4:10 **4** [1]Or *recognition* [a]Ezek 18:23, 32; John 3:17; 1 Tim 4:10; Titus 2:11; 2 Pet 3:9 [b]Rom 11:14 [c]2 Tim 2:25; 3:7; Titus 1:1; Heb 10:26

1:20 *Hymenaeus.* See 2 Tim 2:17–18. *Alexander.* Perhaps the Alexander of 2 Tim 4:14 (but see note there). *handed over to Satan.* The reference is to church discipline (see note on Matt 18:17). Paul had excluded these two men from the church, which was considered a sanctuary from Satan's power. Out in the world, away from the fellowship and care of the church, they would be "taught" (the word means basically "to discipline") not to blaspheme. The purpose of such drastic action was more remedial than punitive. For a similar situation see 1 Cor 5:5,13; see also note on 1 Cor 5:5.

2:2 *kings and all who are in authority.* See Jer 29:7. The notorious Roman emperor Nero (A.D. 54–68) was in power when Paul wrote these words. *godliness.* A key word (along with "godly") in the Pastorals, the Greek term occurs eight times in 1 Timothy (here; 3:16; 4:7–8; 6:3,5–6,11), once in 2 Timothy (3:5) and once in Titus (1:1), but nowhere else in the writings of Paul. It implies a good and holy life, with special emphasis on its source, a deep reverence for God.

2:4 *who desires all men to be saved.* God desires the salvation of all people. On the other hand, the Bible indicates that God chooses some (not all) people to be saved (e.g., 1 Pet 1:2). Some interpreters understand such passages to teach that God has chosen those He, in His foreknowledge, knew would believe when confronted with the gospel and enabled to believe. Other interpreters hold that, though human reasoning cannot resolve the seeming inconsistency, the Bible teaches both truths and thus there can be no actual contradiction. Certainly there is none in the mind of God. See note on Rom 8:29.

Paul's Fourth Missionary Journey

c. A.D. 62–68

Atlantic Ocean
GALLIA
Massilia
HISPANIA
Tarraco
Toletum
Carthage Nova
Gades
Tingis

It is clear from Acts 13:1–21:17 that Paul went on three missionary journeys. There is also reason to believe that he made a fourth journey after his release from the Roman imprisonment recorded in Acts 28. The conclusion that such a journey did indeed take place is based on: (1) Paul's declared intention to go to Spain (Rom 15:24,28), (2) Eusebius's implication that Paul was released following his first Roman imprisonment (*Ecclesiastical History*, 2.22.2-3) and (3) statements in early Christian literature that he took the gospel as far as Spain (Clement of Rome, *Epistle to the Corinthians*, ch. 5; *Actus Petri Vercellenses*, chs. 1-3; Muratorian Canon, lines 34-39).

The places Paul may have visited after his release from prison are indicated by statements of intention in his earlier writings and by subsequent mention in the Pastoral Letters. The order of his travel cannot be determined with certainty, but the itinerary at the right seems likely.

1. **Rome**—released from prison in A.D. 62
2. **Spain**—62-64 (Rom 15:24,28)
3. **Crete**—64-65 (Titus 1:5)
4. **Miletus**—65 (2 Tim 4:20)
5. **Colosse**—66 (Philem 22)
6. **Ephesus**—66 (1 Tim 1:3)
7. **Philippi**—66 (Phil 2:23-24; 1 Tim 1:3)
8. **Nicopolis**—66-67 (Titus 3:12)
9. **Rome**—67
10. Martyrdom—67/68

5 For there is [a]one God, *and* [b]one mediator also between God and men, *the* [c]man
Christ Jesus,
6 who [a]gave Himself as a ransom for all,
the [b]testimony [1]*given* at [2c]the proper time.
7 [a]For this I was appointed a [1]preacher
and [b]an apostle ([c]I am telling the truth, I am
not lying) as a teacher of [d]the Gentiles in
faith and truth.
8 Therefore [a]I want the men [b]in every
place to pray, [c]lifting up [d]holy hands, without wrath and dissension.

5 [a]Rom 3:30; 10:12; 1 Cor 8:4 [b]1 Cor 8:6; Gal 3:20 [c]Matt 1:1; Rom 1:3
6 [1]Or *to be given* [2]Lit *its own times* [a]Matt 20:28; Gal 1:4 [b]1 Cor 1:6 [c]Mark 1:15; Gal 4:4; 1 Tim 6:15; Titus 1:3
7 [1]Or *herald* [a]Eph 3:8; 1 Tim 1:11; 2 Tim 1:11 [b]1 Cor 9:1 [c]Rom

Women Instructed

9 Likewise, *I want* [a]women to adorn
themselves with proper clothing, [1]modestly
and discreetly, not with braided hair and
gold or pearls or costly garments,
10 but rather by means of good works, as
is proper for women making a claim to godliness.

9:1 [d]Acts 9:15 **8** [a]Phil 1:12; 1 Tim 5:14; Titus 3:8 [b]John 4:21; 1 Cor 1:2; 2 Cor 2:14; 1 Thess 1:8 [c]Ps 63:4; Luke 24:50 [d]Ps 24:4; James 4:8 **9** [1]Lit *with modesty* [a]1 Pet 3:3

2:5 *there is one God.* The basic belief of Judaism (Deut 6:4), which every Jew confessed daily in the *Shema* (see note on Mark 12:29).

2:6 *ransom.* See note on Matt 20:28. *testimony.* The apostolic testimony that Christ gave Himself as the ransom. *proper time.* See note on Gal 4:4.

2:7 *For this.* To testify that, through His death, Christ has bridged the gap between God and man and made salvation available to all. *preacher.* One who with authority makes a public proclamation. *apostle.* See notes on Mark 6:30; 1 Cor 1:1.

2:8–14 Some maintain that Paul's teaching about women here is historically conditioned, not universal and timeless. Others view these verses as unaffected by the historical situation and therefore applicable to every age.

2:8 *men.* The Greek for this word does not refer to mankind (as in vv. 5–6) but to male as distinct from female. That women also prayed in public, however, seems evident from 1 Cor 11:5.

2:9 Not a total ban on the wearing of jewelry or braided hair. Rather, Paul was expressing caution in a society where such things were signs of extravagant luxury and proud personal display.

2:10 See 1 Pet 3:3–4.

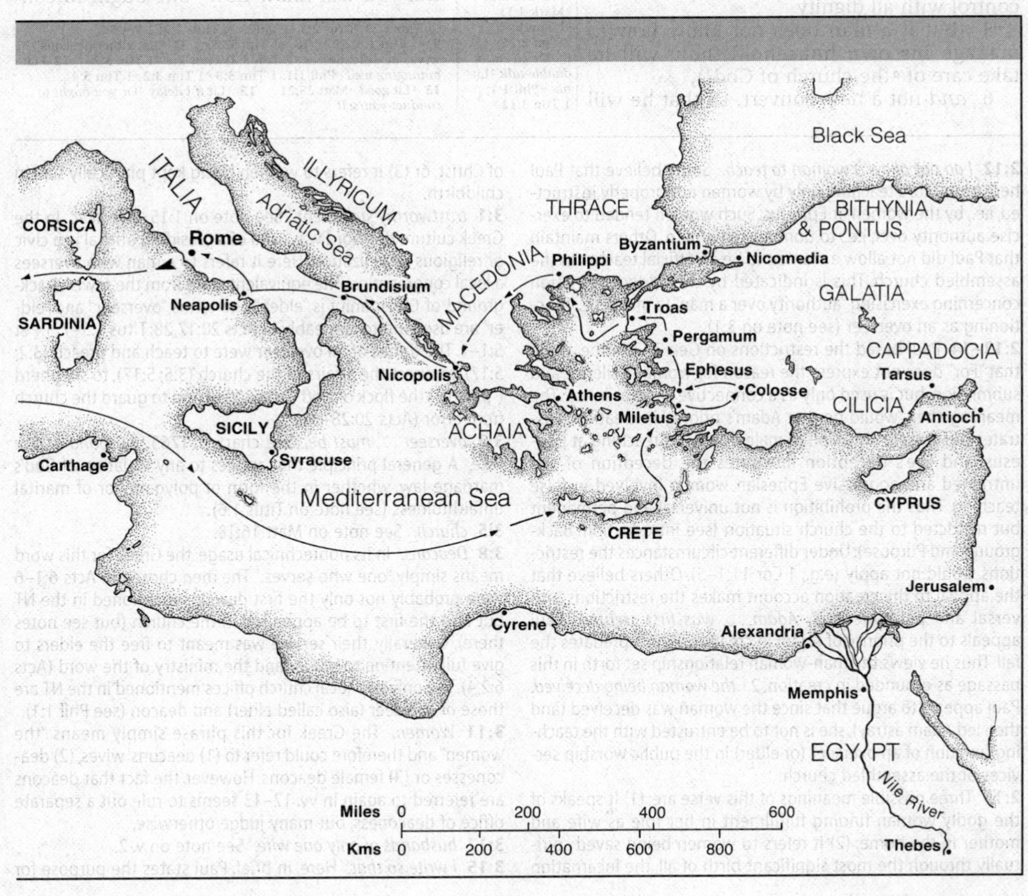

11 [a]A woman must quietly receive instruction with entire submissiveness.
12 [a]But I do not allow a woman to teach
or exercise authority over a man, but to
remain quiet.
13 [a]For it was Adam who was first [1]creat-
ed, *and* then Eve.
14 And *it was* not Adam *who* was deceived, but [a]the woman being deceived, [1]fell
into transgression.
15 But *women* will be [1]preserved through
the bearing of children if they continue in
[a]faith and love and sanctity with [2]self-
restraint.

Overseers and Deacons

3 [a]It is a trustworthy statement: if any man
aspires to the [b]office of [1]overseer, it is a
fine work he desires *to do*.
2 [1][a]An overseer, then, must be above
reproach, [b]the husband of one wife, [c]tem-
perate, prudent, respectable, [d]hospitable,
[e]able to teach,
3 [a]not addicted to wine [1]or pugnacious,
but gentle, peaceable, [b]free from the love of
money.
4 *He must be* one who [a]manages his own
household well, keeping his children under
control with all dignity
5 (but if a man does not know how to
manage his own household, how will he
take care of [a]the church of God?),
6 *and* not a new convert, so that he will
not become [a]conceited and fall into the
[b]condemnation [1]incurred by the devil.
7 And he must [a]have a good reputation
with [b]those outside *the church,* so that he
will not fall into reproach and [c]the snare of
the devil.
8 [a]Deacons likewise *must be* men of dignity, not [1]double-tongued, [2b]or addicted to
much wine [2c]or fond of sordid gain,
9 [a]*but* holding to the mystery of the faith
with a clear conscience.
10 [a]These men must also first be tested;
then let them serve as deacons if they are
beyond reproach.
11 [1]Women *must* likewise *be* dignified,
[a]not malicious gossips, but [b]temperate, faithful in all things.
12 [a]Deacons must be [b]husbands of *only*
one wife, *and* [1c]good managers of *their* children and their own households.
13 For those who have served well as deacons [a]obtain for themselves a [1]high standing
and great confidence in the faith that is in
Christ Jesus.
14 I am writing these things to you, hoping to come to you before long;
15 but [1]in case I am delayed, *I write* so
that you will know how [2]one ought to con-

11 [a]1 Cor 14:34; Titus 2:5
12 [a]1 Cor 14:34; Titus 2:5
13 [1]Or *formed* [a]Gen 2:7, 22; 3:16; 1 Cor 11:8ff
14 [1]Lit *has come* [a]Gen 3:6, 13; 2 Cor 11:3
15 [1]Lit *saved* [2]Or *discretion* [a]1 Tim 1:14
3:1 [1]Or *bishop* [a]1 Tim 1:15 [b]Acts 20:28; Phil 1:1
2 [1]Lit *The* [a]1 Tim 3:2-4; Titus 1:6-8 [b]Luke 2:36f; 1 Tim 5:9; Titus 1:6 [c]1 Tim 3:8, 11; Titus 2:2 [d]Rom 12:13; Titus 1:8; Heb 13:2; 1 Pet 4:9 [e]2 Tim 2:24
3 [1]Lit *not* [a]Titus 1:7 [b]1 Tim 3:8; 6:10; Titus 1:7; Heb 13:5
4 [a]1 Tim 3:12
5 [a]1 Cor 10:32; 1 Tim 3:15
6 [1]Lit *of the devil* [a]1 Tim 6:4; 2 Tim 3:4 [b]1 Tim 3:7
7 [a]2 Cor 8:21 [b]Mark 4:11 [c]1 Tim 6:9; 2 Tim 2:26
8 [1]Or *given to double-talk* [2]Lit *not* [a]Phil 1:1; 1 Tim 3:12 [b]1 Tim 5:23; Titus 2:3 [c]1 Tim 3:3; Titus 1:7; 1 Pet 5:2
9 [a]1 Tim 1:5, 19 **10** [a]1 Tim 5:22 **11** [1]I.e. either deacons' wives or deaconesses [a]2 Tim 3:3; Titus 2:3 [b]1 Tim 3:2 **12** [1]Lit *managing well* [a]Phil 1:1; 1 Tim 3:8 [b]1 Tim 3:2 [c]1 Tim 3:4
13 [1]Lit *good* [a]Matt 25:21 **15** [1]Lit *if I delay* [2]Or *you ought to conduct yourself*

2:12 *I do not allow a woman to teach.* Some believe that Paul here prohibited teaching only by women not properly instructed, i.e., by the women at Ephesus. Such women tended to exercise authority over, i.e., to domineer, the men. Others maintain that Paul did not allow a woman to be an official teacher in the assembled church. This is indicated by the added restriction concerning exercising "authority over a man" (a male), i.e., functioning as an overseer (see note on 3:1).

2:13–14 Paul based the restrictions on Gen 2–3. Some argue that "For" does not express the reason for woman's silence and submission, but is used only as a connective word as in v. 5. The meaning, then, would be that Adam's priority in creation illustrates the present situation of male priority in teaching at Ephesus, and Eve's deception illustrates the deception of the untrained and aggressive Ephesian women involved in false teaching. Thus the prohibition is not universal and permanent but restricted to the church situation (see Introduction: Background and Purpose). Under different circumstances the restrictions would not apply (e.g., 1 Cor 11:1–5). Others believe that the appeal to the creation account makes the restrictions universal and permanent: 1. *Adam . . . was first created.* Paul appeals to the priority of Adam in creation, which predates the fall. Thus he views the man-woman relationship set forth in this passage as grounded in creation. 2. *the woman being deceived.* Paul appears to argue that since the woman was deceived (and then led Adam astray), she is not to be entrusted with the teaching function of an overseer (or elder) in the public worship services of the assembled church.

2:15 Three possible meanings of this verse are: (1) It speaks of the godly woman finding fulfillment in her role as wife and mother in the home; (2) it refers to women being saved spiritually through the most significant birth of all, the incarnation of Christ; or (3) it refers to women being kept physically safe in childbirth.

3:1 *trustworthy statement.* See note on 1:15. *overseer.* In the Greek culture the word was used of a presiding official in a civic or religious organization. Here it refers to a man who oversees a local congregation. The equivalent word from the Jewish background of Christianity is "elder." The terms "overseer" and "elder" are used interchangeably in Acts 20:17,28; Titus 1:5–7; 1 Pet 5:1–2. The duties of an overseer were to teach and preach (3:2; 5:17), to direct the affairs of the church (3:5; 5:17), to shepherd ("pastor") the flock of God (Acts 20:28) and to guard the church from error (Acts 20:28–31).

3:2 *overseer . . . must be.* See chart, p. 1765. *husband of one wife.* A general principle that applies to any violation of God's marriage law, whether in the form of polygamy or of marital unfaithfulness (see note on Titus 1:6).

3:5 *church.* See note on Matt 16:18.

3:8 *Deacons.* In its nontechnical usage, the Greek for this word means simply "one who serves." The men chosen in Acts 6:1–6 were probably not only the first deacons mentioned in the NT but also the first to be appointed in the church (but see notes there). Generally, their service was meant to free the elders to give full attention to prayer and the ministry of the word (Acts 6:2,4). The only two local church offices mentioned in the NT are those of overseer (also called elder) and deacon (see Phil 1:1).

3:11 *Women.* The Greek for this phrase simply means "the women" and therefore could refer to (1) deacons' wives, (2) deaconesses or (3) female deacons. However, the fact that deacons are referred to again in vv. 12–13 seems to rule out a separate office of deaconess, but many judge otherwise.

3:12 *husbands of only one wife.* See note on v. 2.

3:15 *I write so that.* Here, in brief, Paul states the purpose for

duct himself in [a]the household of God,
which is the [b]church of [c]the living God, the
[d]pillar and support of the truth.
16 By common confession, great is [a]the
mystery of godliness:

> He who was [b]revealed in the flesh,
> Was [1c]vindicated [2]in the Spirit,
> [d]Seen by angels,
> [e]Proclaimed among the nations,
> [f]Believed on in the world,
> [g]Taken up in glory.

Apostasy

4 But [a]the Spirit explicitly says that [b]in later times some will [1]fall away from the
faith, paying attention to [c]deceitful spirits
and [d]doctrines of demons,
2 by means of the hypocrisy of liars
[a]seared in their own conscience as with a
branding iron,
3 *men* who [a]forbid marriage *and advocate* [b]abstaining from foods which [c]God has
created to be [d]gratefully shared in by those
who believe and know the truth.
4 For [a]everything created by God is good,
and nothing is to be rejected if it is [b]received
with gratitude;
5 for it is sanctified by means of [a]the
word of God and prayer.

A Good Minister's Discipline

6 In pointing out these things to [a]the
brethren, you will be a good [b]servant of
Christ Jesus, *constantly* nourished on the
words of the faith and of the [1c]sound doctrine which you [d]have been following.
7 But [1]have nothing to do with [a]worldly
[b]fables fit only for old women. On the other
hand, discipline yourself for the purpose of
[c]godliness;

15 [a]1 Cor 3:16; 2 Cor 6:16; Eph 2:21f; 1 Pet 2:5; 4:17 [b]1 Tim 3:5 [c]Matt 16:16; 1 Tim 4:10 [d]Gal 2:9; 2 Tim 2:19
16 [1]Or *justified* [2]Or *by* [a]Rom 16:25 [b]John 1:14; 1 Pet 1:20; 1 John 3:5, 8 [c]Rom 3:4 [d]Luke 2:13; 24:4; 1 Pet 1:12 [e]Rom 16:26; 2 Cor 1:19; Col 1:23 [f]2 Thess 1:10 [g]Mark 16:19; Acts 1:9
4:1 [1]I.e. apostacize [a]John 16:13; Acts 20:23; 21:11; 1 Cor 2:10f [b]2 Thess 2:3ff; 2 Tim 3:1; 2 Pet 3:3; Jude 18 [c]1 John 4:6 [d]James 3:15
2 [a]Eph 4:19
3 [a]Heb 13:4 [b]Col 2:16, 23 [c]Gen 1:29; 9:3 [d]Rom 14:6; 1 Cor 10:30f; 1 Tim 4:4
4 [a]1 Cor 10:26 [b]Rom 14:6; 1 Cor 10:30f; 1 Tim 4:3 **5** [a]Gen 1:25, 31; Heb 11:3 **6** [1]Lit *good* [a]Acts 1:15 [b]2 Cor 11:23 [c]1 Tim 1:10 [d]Luke 1:3; Phil 2:20, 22; 2 Tim 3:10 **7** [1]Or *reject* [a]1 Tim 1:9 [b]1 Tim 1:4 [c]1 Tim 4:8; 6:3, 5f; 2 Tim 3:5

writing the letter—to give instructions concerning church conduct (v. 15).

3:16 *mystery of godliness.* See notes on Rom 11:25; Col 1:26. The phrase means the "revealed secret of true piety," i.e., the secret that produces piety in people. That secret, as the following words indicate, is none other than Jesus Christ. His incarnation, in all its aspects (particularly His saving work), is the source of genuine piety. The words are printed in poetic form and probably come from an early creedal hymn (see note on Col 3:16). *vindicated in the Spirit.* The Holy Spirit enabled Jesus to drive out demons (see Matt 12:28) and perform miracles. Most importantly, the Spirit raised Jesus from the dead (see Rom 1:4; 1 Pet 3:18) and thereby vindicated Him, showing that He was indeed the Son of God. *Seen by angels.* At His resurrection (Matt 28:2) and ascension (Acts 1:10).

4:1 *the Spirit explicitly says.* As, e.g., in Matt 24:11; Mark 13:22; Acts 20:29–30; 2 Thess 2:3. Paul, however, is perhaps speaking here of a specific revelation made to him by the Spirit. *in later times.* The time beginning with the first coming of Christ (see note on Heb 1:1). That Paul is not referring only to the time immediately prior to Christ's second coming is obvious from his assumption in v. 7 that the false teachings were already present at the time of his writing.

4:3 This unbiblical asceticism arose out of the mistaken belief that the material world was evil—a central belief of the Gnostic heresy (see Introduction to 1 John: Gnosticism).

4:7 *fables.* See note on 1:4. *discipline yourself for . . . godliness.* See note on 2:2. Godliness requires self-discipline.

Qualifications for Elders/Overseers and Deacons

Qualification	Office	Reference
Self-controlled	**ELDER**	1 Tim 3:2; Titus 1:8
Hospitable	**ELDER**	1 Tim 3:2; Titus 1:8
Able to teach	**ELDER**	1 Tim 3:2; 5:17; Titus 1:9
Not violent but gentle	**ELDER**	1 Tim 3:3; Titus 1:7
Not quarrelsome	**ELDER**	1 Tim 3:3
Not a lover of money	**ELDER**	1 Tim 3:3
Not a recent convert	**ELDER**	1 Tim 3:6
Has a good reputation with outsiders	**ELDER**	1 Tim 3:7
Not overbearing	**ELDER**	Titus 1:7
Not quick-tempered	**ELDER**	Titus 1:7
Loves what is good	**ELDER**	Titus 1:8
Upright, holy	**ELDER**	Titus 1:8
Disciplined	**ELDER**	Titus 1:8
Above reproach (blameless)	**ELDER**	1 Tim 3:2; Titus 1:6
	DEACON	1 Tim 3:9
Husband of one wife	**ELDER**	1 Tim 3:2; Titus 1:6
	DEACON	1 Tim 3:12
Temperate	**ELDER**	1 Tim 3:2; Titus 1:7
	DEACON	1 Tim 3:8
Respectable	**ELDER**	1 Tim 3:2
	DEACON	1 Tim 3:8
Not given to drunkenness	**ELDER**	1 Tim 3:3; Titus 1:7
	DEACON	1 Tim 3:8
Manages his own family well	**ELDER**	1 Tim 3:4
	DEACON	1 Tim 3:12
Sees that his children obey him	**ELDER**	1 Tim 3:4-5; Titus 1:6
	DEACON	1 Tim 3:12
Does not pursue dishonest gain	**ELDER**	Titus 1:7
	DEACON	1Ti 3:8
Holds to the truth	**ELDER**	Titus 1:9
	DEACON	1 Tim 3:9
Sincere	***DEACON***	1 Tim 3:8
Tested	***DEACON***	1 Tim 3:10

8 for [a]bodily discipline is only of little profit, but [b]godliness is profitable for all things, since it [c]holds promise for the [d]present life and *also* for the *life* to come.

9 [a]It is a trustworthy statement deserving full acceptance.

10 For it is for this we labor and strive, because we have fixed [a]our hope on [b]the living God, who is [c]the Savior of all men, especially of believers.

11 [1a]Prescribe and teach these things.

12 [a]Let no one look down on your youthfulness, but *rather* in speech, conduct, [b]love, faith *and* purity, show yourself [c]an example [1]of those who believe.

13 [a]Until I come, give attention to the *public* [b]reading *of Scripture,* to exhortation and teaching.

14 Do not neglect the spiritual gift within you, which was bestowed on you through [a]prophetic utterance with [b]the laying on of hands by the [1c]presbytery.

15 Take pains with these things; be *absorbed* in them, so that your progress will be evident to all.

16 [a]Pay close attention to yourself and to your teaching; persevere in these things, for as you do this you will [1b]ensure salvation both for yourself and for those who hear you.

Honor Widows

5 [a]Do not sharply rebuke an [b]older man, but *rather* appeal to *him* as a father, *to* [c]the younger men as brothers,

2 the older women as mothers, *and* the younger women as sisters, in all purity.

3 Honor widows who are [a]widows indeed;

4 but if any widow has children or grandchildren, [a]they must first learn to practice piety in regard to their own family and to [1]make some return to their parents; for this is [b]acceptable in the sight of God.

5 Now she who is a [a]widow indeed and who has been left alone, [b]has fixed her hope on God and continues in [c]entreaties and prayers night and day.

6 But she who [a]gives herself to wanton pleasure is [b]dead even while she lives.

7 [1a]Prescribe these things as well, so that they may be above reproach.

8 But if anyone does not provide for his own, and especially for those of his household, he has [a]denied the faith and is worse than an unbeliever.

9 A widow is to be [a]put on the list only if she is not less than sixty years old, *having been* [b]the wife of one man,

10 having a reputation for [a]good works; *and* if she has brought up children, if she has [b]shown hospitality to strangers, if she [c]has washed the [1]saints' feet, if she has [d]assisted those in distress, *and* if she has devoted herself to every good work.

11 But refuse *to put* younger widows *on the list,* for when they feel [a]sensual desires in disregard of Christ, they want to get married,

12 *thus* incurring condemnation, because they have set aside their previous [1]pledge.

13 At the same time they also learn *to be* idle, as they go around from house to house; and not merely idle, but also [a]gossips and [b]busybodies, talking about [c]things not proper *to mention.*

14 Therefore, I want younger *widows* to get [a]married, bear children, [b]keep house, *and* [c]give the enemy no occasion for reproach;

15 for some [a]have already turned aside to follow [b]Satan.

16 If any woman who is a believer [a]has

8 [a]Col 2:23 [b]1 Tim 4:7; 6:3, 5f; 2 Tim 3:5 [c]Ps 37:9, 11; Prov 19:23; 22:4; Matt 6:33 [d]Matt 6:33; 12:32; Mark 10:30
9 [a]1 Tim 1:15
10 [a]2 Cor 1:10; 1 Tim 6:17 [b]1 Tim 3:15 [c]John 4:42; 1 Tim 2:4
11 [1]Or *Keep commanding and teaching* [a]1 Tim 5:7; 6:2
12 [1]Or *to* [a]1 Cor 16:11; Titus 2:15 [b]Titus 2:7; 1 Pet 5:3 [c]1 Tim 1:14
13 [a]1 Tim 3:14 [b]2 Tim 3:15ff
14 [1]Or *board of elders* [a]1 Tim 1:18 [b]Acts 6:6; 1 Tim 5:22; 2 Tim 1:6 [c]Acts 11:30
16 [1]Lit *save both yourself and those* [a]Acts 20:28 [b]1 Cor 1:21
5:1 [a]Lev 19:32 [b]Titus 2:2 [c]Titus 2:6
3 [a]Acts 6:1; 9:39, 41; 1 Tim 5:5, 16
4 [1]Lit *give back recompenses* [a]Eph 6:2 [b]1 Tim 2:3
5 [a]Acts 6:1; 9:39, 41; 1 Tim 5:3, 16 [b]1 Cor 7:34; 1 Pet 3:5 [c]Luke 2:37; 1 Tim 2:1; 2 Tim 1:3
6 [a]James 5:5 [b]Luke 15:24; 2 Tim 3:6; Rev 3:1
7 [1]Or *Keep commanding* [a]1 Tim 4:11
8 [a]2 Tim 2:12; Titus 1:16; 2 Pet 2:1; Jude 4
9 [a]1 Tim 5:16 [b]1 Tim 3:2 **10** [1]Or *holy ones* [a]Acts 9:36; 1 Tim 6:18; Titus 2:7; 3:8; 1 Pet 2:12 [b]1 Tim 3:2 [c]Luke 7:44; John 13:14 [d]1 Tim 5:16 **11** [a]Rev 18:7 **12** [1]Lit *faith* **13** [a]3 John 10 [b]2 Thess 3:11 [c]Titus 1:11 **14** [a]1 Cor 7:9; 1 Tim 4:3 [b]Titus 2:5 [c]1 Tim 6:1 **15** [a]1 Tim 1:20 [b]Matt 4:10 **16** [a]1 Tim 5:4

4:9 *trustworthy statement.* See note on 1:15. It is possible that the expression in this instance refers back to the seemingly proverbial statement in v. 8. The words "labor and strive" in v. 10 may refer to the training mentioned in vv. 7b–8.
4:10 *hope.* See note on 1:1. *Savior of all.* Obviously this does not mean that God saves every person from eternal punishment, for such universalism would contradict the clear testimony of Scripture. God is, however, the Savior of all in that He offers salvation to all and saves all who come to him.
4:12 *your youthfulness.* Timothy was probably in his mid–30s or younger, and in that day, such an influential position was not usually held by a man so young. For this reason, perhaps his leadership had been called into question.
4:13 *Until I come.* Paul's journey had taken him from Ephesus to Macedonia (see map, pp. 1762–1763), but he hoped to rejoin Timothy soon at Ephesus (3:14).
4:14 *prophetic utterance.* See note on 1:18.
4:16 *you will ensure salvation . . . for those who hear you.* God alone saves, but Christians can be God's instruments to bring about the salvation of others. *will ensure salvation.* Salvation is both an event and a process. We are saved at the time of conversion but are still being saved in the sense of being made more conformed to Christ's image (1 Cor 1:18).
5:3 *Honor widows . . . indeed.* Probably means taking care of them, including the giving of material support. Widows were particularly vulnerable in ancient societies because no pensions, government assistance, life insurance, or the like were available to them.
5:6 *dead even while she lives.* Dead spiritually while living physically.
5:9 *the list.* The church in Ephesus seems to have maintained a list of widows supported by the church. While there is no evidence of an order of widows comparable to that of the overseers, it appears that those on the list were expected to devote themselves to prayer (v. 5) and good deeds (v. 10).
5:10 *washed the saints' feet.* A menial task, but necessary because of dusty roads and the wearing of sandals (see John 13:14).
5:12 *set aside their previous pledge.* Perhaps when a widow was added to the list she pledged special devotion to Christ, which would be diminished by remarriage. Or Paul may be referring to the believer's basic trust in Christ, which a widow would compromise by marrying outside the faith.
5:15 *Satan.* See notes on Zech 3:1; Matt 16:23; Rev 12:10.

dependent widows, she must [b]assist them
and the church must not be burdened, so
that it may assist those who are [c]widows
indeed.

Concerning Elders

17 [a]The elders who [b]rule well are to be
considered worthy of double honor, especially those who [c]work hard [1]at preaching and
teaching.
18 For the Scripture says, "[a]YOU SHALL NOT
MUZZLE THE OX WHILE HE IS THRESHING," and
"[b]The laborer is worthy of his wages."
19 Do not receive an accusation against an
[a]elder except on the basis of [b]two or three
witnesses.
20 Those who continue in sin, [a]rebuke in
the presence of all, [b]so that the rest also will
be fearful *of sinning.*
21 [a]I solemnly charge you in the presence
of God and of Christ Jesus and of *His* chosen
angels, to maintain these *principles* without
bias, doing nothing in a *spirit of* partiality.
22 [a]Do not lay hands upon anyone *too*
hastily and [1]thereby share [b]*responsibility for*
the sins of others; keep yourself [2]free from
sin.
23 No longer drink water *exclusively,* but
[a]use a little wine for the sake of your stomach and your frequent ailments.
24 The sins of some men are quite evident, going before them to judgment; for
others, their *sins* [a]follow after.
25 Likewise also, deeds that are good are
quite evident, and [a]those which are otherwise cannot be concealed.

Instructions to Those Who Minister

6 [a]All who are under the yoke as slaves are
to regard their own masters as worthy of
all honor so [b]that the name of God and *our*
doctrine will not be [1]spoken against.
2 Those who have believers as their masters must not be disrespectful to them
because they are [a]brethren, but must serve
them all the more, because those who [1]par-
take of the benefit are believers and beloved.
[b]Teach and [2]preach these *principles.*
3 If anyone [a]advocates a different doctrine and does not [1]agree with [b]sound
words, those of our Lord Jesus Christ, and
with the doctrine [c]conforming to godliness,
4 he is [a]conceited *and* understands nothing; but he [1]has a morbid interest in [b]con-
troversial questions and [c]disputes about
words, out of which arise envy, strife, abusive language, evil suspicions,
5 and constant friction between [a]men of
depraved mind and deprived of the truth,
who [b]suppose that [1]godliness is a means of
gain.
6 [a]But godliness *actually* is a means of
[b]great gain when accompanied by [c]content-
ment.
7 For [a]we have brought nothing into the
world, so we cannot take anything out of it
either.
8 If we [a]have food and covering, with
these we shall be content.
9 [a]But those who want to get rich fall
into temptation and [b]a snare and many foolish and harmful desires which plunge men
into ruin and destruction.
10 For [a]the love of money is a root of all
[1]sorts of evil, and some by longing for it have
[b]wandered away from the faith and pierced
themselves with many griefs.
11 But [a]flee from these things, you [b]man
of God, and pursue righteousness, godliness,
[c]faith, [d]love, [1]perseverance *and* gentleness.
12 [a]Fight the good fight of [b]faith; [c]take
hold of the eternal life [d]to which you were
called, and you made the good [e]confession
in the presence of [f]many witnesses.

16 [b]1 Tim 5:10 [c]1 Tim 5:3 **17** [1]Lit *in word* [a]Acts 11:30; 1 Tim 4:14; 5:19 [b]Rom 12:8 [c]1 Thess 5:12 **18** [a]Deut 25:4; 1 Cor 9:9 [b]Lev 19:13; Deut 24:15; Matt 10:10; Luke 10:7; 1 Cor 9:14 **19** [a]Acts 11:30; 1 Tim 4:14; 5:17 [b]Deut 17:6; 19:15; Matt 18:16 **20** [a]Gal 2:14; Eph 5:11; 2 Tim 4:2 [b]2 Cor 7:11 **21** [a]Luke 9:26; 1 Tim 6:13; 2 Tim 2:14; 4:1 **22** [1]Lit *do not share* [2]Lit *pure* [a]1 Tim 3:10; 4:14 [b]Eph 5:11; 1 Tim 3:2-7 **23** [a]1 Tim 3:8 **24** [a]Rev 14:13 **25** [a]Prov 10:9 **6:1** [1]Or *blasphemed* [a]Eph 6:5; Titus 2:9; 1 Pet 2:18 [b]Titus 2:5 **2** [a]Acts 1:15; Gal 3:28; Philem 16

2 [1]Or *devote themselves to kindness* [2]Lit *exhort, urge* [b]1 Tim 4:11 **3** [1]Lit *come to;* or *come with* [a]1 Tim 1:3 [b]1 Tim 1:10 [c]Titus 1:1 **4** [1]Lit *is sick about* [a]1 Tim 3:6 [b]1 Tim 1:4 [c]Acts 18:15; 2 Tim 2:14 **5** [1]Or *religion* [a]2 Tim 3:8; Titus 1:15 [b]Titus 1:11; 2 Pet 2:3 **6** [a]Luke 12:15-21; 1 Tim 6:6-10 [b]1 Tim 4:8 [c]Phil 4:11; Heb 13:5 **7** [a]Job 1:21; Eccl 5:15 **8** [a]Prov 30:8 **9** [a]Prov 15:27; 23:4; 28:20; Luke 12:21; 1 Tim 6:17 [b]1 Tim 3:7 **10** [1]Lit *the evils* [a]Col 3:5; 1 Tim 3:3; 6:9 [b]James 5:19 **11** [1]Or *steadfastness* [a]2 Tim 2:22 [b]2 Tim 3:17 [c]1 Tim 1:14 [d]2 Tim 3:10 **12** [a]1 Cor 9:25f; Phil 1:30; 1 Tim 1:18 [b]1 Tim 1:19 [c]Phil 3:12; 1 Tim 6:19 [d]Col 3:15 [e]2 Cor 9:13; 1 Tim 6:13 [f]1 Tim 4:14; 2 Tim 2:2

5:17 All elders were to exercise leadership (3:4–5) and to teach and preach (3:2), and all were to receive honor. But those who excelled in leadership were to be counted worthy of double honor. This was especially true of those who labored at teaching and preaching. (The Greek word translated "work" refers to toil.) That such honor should include financial support is indicated by the two illustrations in v. 18.

5:18 *Scripture.* The use of this term for both an OT (Deut 25:4) and a NT (Luke 10:7) passage shows that by this time portions of the NT (or what ultimately became a part of the NT) were considered to be equal in authority to the OT Scriptures.

5:20 *Those who continue in sin.* The context indicates that Paul is speaking of the discipline of elders.

5:21 *chosen angels.* Chosen angels, in contrast to Satan and the other fallen angels.

5:22 *Do not lay hands upon anyone too hastily.* Paul is speaking of the ordination of an elder, which should not be performed until the candidate has had time to prove himself. *thereby share . . . the sins of others.* Do not ordain a person unworthy of the office of elder. *keep yourself free from sin.* Probably refers to refusal to become involved in the ordination of an unworthy man.

5:23 *No longer drink water exclusively.* A parenthetical comment in Paul's discussion of elders. In view of Timothy's physical ailments, and perhaps because safe drinking water was often difficult to find, Paul advised him to drink a little wine.

5:24–25 *sins of some men . . . deeds that are good.* Paul advises being alert to hidden sins as well as to good deeds in the lives of candidates for ordination.

6:1 *slaves.* See notes on Eph 6:5; Col 3:22–4:1.

6:2 *preach these principles.* Refers to the instructions to slaves.

6:3–5 Paul returns to the subject of 1:3. See note on 1:3–11.

6:5 *deprived of the truth.* They had once known the truth but had been led into error. *who suppose that godliness is a means of gain.* See note on 2 Cor 11:7.

6:11 *godliness.* See note on 2:2.

6:12 *take hold of the eternal life.* Timothy had possessed eternal life since he had first been saved, but Paul urges him to claim its benefits in greater fullness (see vv. 17–19 and note on 4:16). *you made the good confession.* Probably a reference

13 [a]I charge you in the presence of God, who [1]gives life to all things, and of [b]Christ Jesus, who testified the [c]good confession [d]before Pontius Pilate,

14 that you keep the commandment without stain or reproach until the [a]appearing of our Lord Jesus Christ,

15 which He will [1]bring about at [a]the proper time—He who is [b]the blessed and [c]only Sovereign, [d]the King of [2]kings and [e]Lord of [3]lords,

16 [a]who alone possesses immortality and [b]dwells in unapproachable light, [c]whom no man has seen or can see. [a]To Him *be* honor and eternal dominion! Amen.

17 Instruct those who are rich in [a]this present world [b]not to be conceited or to [c]fix their hope on the uncertainty of riches, but on God, [d]who richly supplies us with all things to enjoy.

18 *Instruct them* to do good, to be rich in [a]good [1]works, [b]to be generous and ready to share,

19 [a]storing up for themselves the treasure of a good foundation for the future, so that they may [b]take hold of that which is life indeed.

20 O [a]Timothy, guard [b]what has been entrusted to you, avoiding [c]worldly *and* empty chatter *and* the opposing arguments of what is falsely called "knowledge"—

21 which some have professed and thus [a]gone astray [1]from [b]the faith.

[c]Grace be with you.

13 [1]Or *preserves alive* [a]1 Tim 5:21 [b]Gal 3:26; 1 Tim 1:12, 15; 2:5 [c]2 Cor 9:13; 1 Tim 6:12 [d]Matt 27:2; John 18:37 **14** [a]2 Thess 2:8 **15** [1]Lit *show* [2]Lit *those who reign as kings* [3]Lit *those who rule as lords* [a]1 Tim 2:6 [b]1 Tim 1:11 [c]1 Tim 1:17 [d]Deut 10:17; Rev 17:14; 19:16 [e]Ps 136:3 **16** [a]1 Tim 1:17 [b]Ps 104:2; James 1:17; 1 John 1:5 [c]John 1:18 **17** [a]Matt 12:32; 2 Tim 4:10; Titus 2:12 [b]Ps 62:10; Luke 12:20; Rom 11:20; 1 Tim 6:9 [c]1 Tim 4:10 [d]Acts 14:17 **18** [1]Or *deeds* [a]1 Tim 5:10 [b]Rom 12:8; Eph 4:28 **19** [a]Matt 6:20 [b]1 Tim 6:12 **20** [a]1 Tim 1:2 [b]2 Tim 1:12, 14 [c]1 Tim 1:9; 2 Tim 2:16 **21** [1]Lit *concerning* [a]2 Tim 2:18 [b]1 Tim 1:19 [c]Col 4:18

to Timothy's confession of faith at his baptism during Paul's first missionary journey.

6:13 *who testified the good confession before Pontius Pilate.* Probably a reference to Jesus' statements recorded in John 18:33–37; 19:10–11.

6:14 *the commandment.* Perhaps the whole charge given to Timothy to preach the gospel and care for the church (see v. 20)—though the preceding context may indicate that Paul used the singular "command" to sum up the various commands listed in vv. 11–12.

6:15 *at the proper time.* Just as Jesus' first coming occurred at the precise time God wanted (Gal 4:4), so also His second coming will be at God's appointed time. *King of kings and Lord of lords.* See Rev 19:16.

6:16 *whom no man has seen or can see.* See note on John 1:18.

6:19 *take hold of that which is life.* See note on v. 12.

6:20 *what has been entrusted to you.* The gospel. The same command is found in 2 Tim 1:14. *what is falsely called "knowledge."* A reference to an early form of the heresy of Gnosticism, which taught that one may be saved by knowledge. (The term "Gnosticism" comes from the Greek word for knowledge; see Introduction to 1 John: Gnosticism.)

6:21 *Grace be with you.* The Greek for "you" here is plural, indicating that, although Paul is writing to Timothy, he expects the letter to be read to the entire Ephesian congregation.

2 Timothy

INTRODUCTION

See "The Pastoral Letters," p. 1758.

Author, Date and Setting

After Paul's release from prison in Rome in A.D. 62/63 (Acts 28) and after his fourth missionary journey (see "Paul's Fourth Missionary Journey," pp. 1762–1763), during which he wrote 1 Timothy and Titus, Paul was again imprisoned under Emperor Nero c. 66–67. It was during this time that he wrote 2 Timothy. In contrast to his first imprisonment, when he lived in a rented house (Acts 28:30), he now languished in a cold dungeon (4:13), chained like a common criminal (1:16; 2:9). His friends even had a hard time finding out where he was being kept (1:17). Paul knew that his work was done and his life was nearly at an end (4:6–8).

Reasons for Writing

Paul had three reasons for writing to Timothy at this time:

1. He was lonely. Phygelus and Hermogenes, "everyone in the province of Asia" (1:15), and Demas (4:10) had deserted him. Crescens, Titus and Tychicus were away (4:10–12), and only Luke was with him (4:11). Paul wanted very much for Timothy to join him also. Timothy was his "fellow worker" (Rom 16:21), who "as a son with his father" had served closely with Paul (Phil 2:22; see 1 Cor 4:17). Of him Paul could say, "I have no one else like him" (Phil 2:20). Paul longed for Timothy (1:4) and twice asked him to come soon (4:9,21). For more information on Timothy see Introduction to 1 Timothy: Recipient.

2. Paul was concerned about the welfare of the churches during this time of persecution under Nero, and he admonishes Timothy to guard the gospel (1:14), to persevere in it (3:14), to keep on preaching it (4:2) and, if necessary, to suffer for it (1:8; 2:3).

3. He wanted to write to the Ephesian church through Timothy (see note on 4:22).

Outline

- I. Introduction (1:1–4)
- II. Paul's Concern for Timothy (1:5–14)
- III. Paul's Situation (1:15–18)
- IV. Special Instructions to Timothy (ch. 2)
  - A. Call for Endurance (2:1–13)
  - B. Warning about Foolish Controversies (2:14–26)
- V. Warning about the Last Days (ch. 3)
  - A. Terrible Times (3:1–9)
  - B. Means of Combating Them (3:10–17)
- VI. Paul's Departing Remarks (4:1–8)
  - A. Charge to Preach the Word (4:1–5)
  - B. Paul's Victorious Prospect (4:6–8)
- VII. Final Requests and Greetings (4:9–22)

Timothy Charged to Guard His Trust

1 Paul, [a]an apostle of [b]Christ Jesus [1c]by the
will of God, according to the promise of
[d]life in Christ Jesus,
2 To [a]Timothy, my beloved [1b]son:
[c]Grace, mercy *and* peace from God the
Father and Christ Jesus our Lord.
3 [a]I thank God, whom I [b]serve with a
[c]clear conscience [1]the way my forefathers
did, [d]as I constantly remember you in my
[2]prayers night and day,
4 [a]longing to see you, [b]even as I recall
your tears, so that I may be filled with joy.
5 [1]For I am mindful of the [a]sincere faith
within you, which first dwelt in your grandmother Lois and [b]your mother Eunice, and I
am sure that *it is* in you as well.
6 For this reason I remind you to kindle
afresh [a]the gift of God which is in you
through [a]the laying on of my hands.
7 For God has not given us a [a]spirit of
[1]timidity, but of power and love and [2]disci-
pline.
8 Therefore [a]do not be ashamed of the
[b]testimony of our Lord or of me [c]His prisoner, but join with *me* in [d]suffering for the
[e]gospel according to the power of God,
9 who has [a]saved us and [b]called us with
a holy [c]calling, [d]not according to our works,
but according to His own [b]purpose and grace
which was granted us in [e]Christ Jesus from
[f]all eternity,
10 but [a]now has been revealed by the
[b]appearing of our Savior [c]Christ Jesus, who
[d]abolished death and brought life and
immortality to light through the gospel,
11 [a]for which I was appointed a preacher
and an apostle and a teacher.
12 For this reason I also suffer these
things, but [a]I am not ashamed; for I know
[b]whom I have believed and I am convinced
that He is able to [c]guard what I have entrusted to Him [1]until [d]that day.
13 [1a]Retain the [b]standard of [c]sound words
[d]which you have heard from me, in the [e]faith
and love which are in [f]Christ Jesus.
14 Guard, through the Holy Spirit who
[a]dwells in us, the [1b]treasure which has been
entrusted to *you.*
15 You are aware of the fact that all who
are in [1a]Asia [b]turned away from me, among
whom are Phygelus and Hermogenes.
16 The Lord grant mercy to [a]the house of
Onesiphorus, for he often refreshed me and
[b]was not ashamed of my [1c]chains;
17 but when he was in Rome, he eagerly
searched for me and found me—
18 the Lord grant to him to find mercy
from the Lord on [a]that day—and you know
very well what services he rendered at [b]Eph-
esus.

Be Strong

2 You therefore, my [1a]son, [b]be strong in the
grace that is in [c]Christ Jesus.
2 The things [a]which you have heard
from me in the presence of [b]many witnesses,
[c]entrust these to [d]faithful men who will be
[e]able to teach others also.

1:1 [1]Lit *through* [a]2 Cor 1:1 [b]Gal 3:26 [c]1 Cor 1:1 [d]1 Tim 6:19 **2** [1]Or *child* [a]Acts 16:1; 1 Tim 1:2 [b]1 Tim 1:2; 2 Tim 2:1; Titus 1:4 [c]Rom 1:7 **3** [1]Lit *from my forefathers* [2]Or *petitions* [a]Rom 1:8 [b]Acts 24:14 [c]Acts 23:1; 24:16; 1 Tim 1:5 [d]Rom 1:9 **4** [a]2 Tim 4:9, 21 [b]Acts 20:37 **5** [1]Lit *Receiving remembrance of* [a]1 Tim 1:5 [b]Acts 16:1; 2 Tim 3:15 **6** [a]1 Tim 4:14 **7** [1]Or *cowardice* [2]Or *sound judgment* [a]John 14:27; Rom 8:15 **8** [a]Mark 8:38; Rom 1:16; 2 Tim 1:12, 16 [b]1 Cor 1:6 [c]Eph 3:1; 2 Tim 1:16 [d]2 Tim 2:3, 9; 4:5 [e]2 Tim 1:10; 2:8 **9** [a]Rom 11:14 [b]Rom 8:28ff [c]Rom 11:29 [d]Eph 2:9 [e]2 Tim 1:1 [f]Rom 16:25; Eph 1:4; Titus 1:2 **10** [a]Rom 16:26 [b]2 Thess 2:8; 2 Tim 4:1, 8; Titus 2:11 [c]2 Tim 1:1 [d]1 Cor 15:26; Heb 2:14f **11** [a]1 Tim 2:7 **12** [1]Or *for* [a]2 Tim 1:8, 16 [b]Titus 3:8 [c]1 Tim 6:20; 2 Tim 1:14 [d]1 Cor 1:8; 3:13; 2 Tim 1:18; 4:8 **13** [1]Or *Hold the example* [a]2 Tim 3:14; Titus 1:9 [b]Rom 2:20; 6:17 [c]1 Tim 1:10 [d]2 Tim 2:2 [e]1 Tim 1:14 [f]2 Tim 1:1 **14** [1]Lit *good deposit* [a]Rom 8:9 [b]1 Tim 6:20; 2 Tim 1:12 **15** [1]I.e. the province of Asia [a]Acts 2:9 [b]2 Tim 4:10, 11, 16 **16** [1]Lit *chain* [a]2 Tim 4:19 [b]2 Tim 1:8 [c]Eph 6:20 **18** [a]1 Cor 1:8; 3:13; 2 Tim 1:12; 4:8 [b]Acts 18:19; 1 Tim 1:3 **2:1** [1]Or *child* [a]2 Tim 1:2 [b]Eph 6:10 [c]2 Tim 1:1 **2** [a]2 Tim 1:13 [b]1 Tim 6:12 [c]1 Tim 1:18 [d]1 Tim 1:12 [e]2 Cor 2:14ff; 3:5

1:1 *apostle.* One specially commissioned by Christ (see notes on Mark 6:30; 1 Cor 1:1; Heb 3:1). *according to the promise of life.* Paul's being chosen to be an apostle was in keeping with that promise because apostles were appointed to preach and explain the good news that eternal life is available to all who will receive it through faith in Christ.

1:2 *Timothy, my beloved son.* See note on 1 Tim 1:2. *Grace . . . peace.* See notes on Jon 4:2; John 14:27; 20:19; Gal 1:3; Eph 1:2.

1:3 *thank God . . . in my prayers.* See note on Phil 1:3–4.

1:4 *longing to see you.* See 4:9,21. *recall your tears.* Probably refers to Timothy's tears when Paul left for Macedonia (1 Tim 1:3).

1:5 *your grandmother Lois . . . your mother Eunice.* According to Acts 16:1, Timothy's mother was a Jewish Christian. Here we learn that his grandmother too was a Christian. Timothy's father, however, was a Greek and apparently an unbeliever (Acts 16:1). It was probably because of him that Timothy had not been circumcised as a child.

1:6 *kindle afresh the gift of God.* Gifts are not given in full bloom; they need to be developed through use. *through the laying on of my hands.* Paul was God's instrument, through whom the gift came from the Holy Spirit to Timothy (see note on 1 Tim 1:18).

1:7 *God has not given us a spirit of timidity.* Apparently lack of confidence was a serious problem for Timothy (see 1 Cor 16:10–11; 1 Tim 4:12).

1:9 *not according to our works, but according to His own purpose and grace.* Salvation is by grace alone and is based not on human effort but on God's saving plan and the gracious gift of His Son (see Rom 3:28; Eph 2:8–9; Titus 3:5). *from all eternity.* God's plan to save lost sinners was made in eternity past (see Eph 1:4; 1 Pet 1:20; Rev 13:8).

1:11 *preacher and an apostle.* See note on 1 Tim 2:7.

1:12 *that day.* The day of judgment.

1:13 *sound words.* See note on Titus 1:9. *faith and love . . . in Christ.* Faith and love through union with Christ—another way of saying "Christian faith and love" (see 1 Tim 1:14).

1:14 *the treasure . . . entrusted to you.* The gospel. Paul gives the same command in 1 Tim 6:20.

1:15 *all.* Probably hyperbole, a deliberate exaggeration to express widespread desertion. *Asia.* Timothy was in Ephesus, the capital of the province of Asia, which is in western Turkey today. *Phygelus and Hermogenes.* Nothing more is known about these two people.

1:16 *Onesiphorus.* Probably he and his family lived in Ephesus (v. 18; 4:19).

1:17 *Rome.* See Introduction: Author, Date and Setting; see also v. 8; 2:9.

1:18 *that day.* The day of judgment. *services he rendered at Ephesus.* Either on Paul's third missionary journey (Acts 19) or on his fourth (see map, pp. 1762–1763).

2:1 *my son.* See note on 1 Tim 1:2.

2:2 *in the presence of many witnesses.* Refers to Paul's preach-

3 [a]Suffer hardship with *me*, as a good
[b]soldier of [c]Christ Jesus.
4 No soldier in active service [a]entangles
himself in the affairs of everyday life, so that
he may please the one who enlisted him as a
soldier.
5 Also if anyone [a]competes as an athlete,
he [1]does not win the prize unless he com-
petes according to the rules.
6 [a]The hard-working farmer ought to be
the first to receive his share of the crops.
7 Consider what I say, for the Lord will
give you understanding in everything.
8 Remember Jesus Christ, [a]risen from
the dead, [b]descendant of David, [c]according
to my gospel,
9 [1]for which I [a]suffer hardship even to
[b]imprisonment as a [c]criminal; but [d]the word
of God [e]is not imprisoned.
10 For this reason [a]I endure all things for
[b]the sake of those who are chosen, [c]so that
they also may obtain the [d]salvation which is
in [e]Christ Jesus *and* with *it* [f]eternal glory.
11 [a]It is a trustworthy statement:
For [b]if we died with Him, we will also
live with Him;
12 If we endure, [a]we will also reign with
Him;
If we [1b]deny Him, He also will deny
us;
13 If we are faithless, [a]He remains
faithful, for [b]He cannot deny
Himself.

An Unashamed Workman

14 Remind *them* of these things, and
solemnly [a]charge *them* in the presence of
God not to [b]wrangle about words, which is
useless *and leads* to the ruin of the hearers.

3 [a]2 Tim 1:8 [b]1 Cor 9:7; 1 Tim 1:18 [c]2 Tim 1:1
4 [a]2 Pet 2:20
5 [1]Lit *is not crowned* [a]1 Cor 9:25
6 [a]1 Cor 9:10
8 [a]Acts 2:24 [b]Matt 1:1 [c]Rom 2:16
9 [1]Lit *in which* [a]2 Tim 1:8; 2:3 [b]Phil 1:7 [c]Luke 23:32 [d]1 Thess 1:8 [e]Acts 28:31; 2 Tim 4:17
10 [a]Col 1:24 [b]Luke 18:7; Titus 1:1 [c]2 Cor 1:6; 1 Thess 5:9 [d]1 Cor 1:21 [e]2 Tim 1:1; 2:1, 3 [f]2 Cor 4:17; 1 Pet 5:10
11 [a]1 Tim 1:15 [b]Rom 6:8; 1 Thess 5:10
12 [1]Lit *will deny* [a]Matt 19:28; Luke 22:29; Rom 5:17; 8:17 [b]Matt 10:33; Luke 12:9; 1 Tim 5:8
13 [a]Rom 3:3; 1 Cor 1:9 [b]Num 23:19; Titus 1:2
14 [a]1 Tim 5:21; 2 Tim 4:1 [b]1 Tim 6:4; 2 Tim 2:23; Titus 3:9
15 [a]Rom 6:13; James 1:12 [b]Eph 1:13; James 1:18
16 [1]Lit *they will make further progress in ungodliness* [a]Titus 3:9 [b]1 Tim 1:9; 6:20
17 [1]Lit *word* [2]Or *cancer* [a]1 Tim 1:20
18 [a]1 Cor 15:12

15 Be diligent to [a]present yourself
approved to God as a workman who does
not need to be ashamed, accurately handling
[b]the word of truth.
16 But [a]avoid [b]worldly *and* empty chatter,
for [1]it will lead to further ungodliness,
17 and their [1]talk will spread like [2]gan-
grene. Among them are [a]Hymenaeus and
Philetus,
18 *men* who have gone astray from the
truth saying that [a]the resurrection has
already taken place, and they upset [b]the faith
of some.
19 Nevertheless, the [a]firm foundation of
God stands, having this [b]seal, "[c]The Lord
knows those who are His," and, "[d]Everyone
who names the name of the Lord is to
abstain from wickedness."
20 Now in a large house there are not only
gold and silver vessels, but also vessels of
wood and of earthenware, and [a]some to
honor and some to dishonor.
21 Therefore, if anyone cleanses himself
from [a]these *things,* he will be a vessel for
honor, sanctified, useful to the Master, [b]pre-
pared for every good work.
22 Now [a]flee from youthful lusts and pursue righteousness, [b]faith, love *and* peace,
with those who [c]call on the Lord [d]from a
pure heart.
23 But refuse foolish and ignorant [a]specu-
lations, knowing that they [b]produce [1]quar-
rels.
24 [a]The Lord's bond-servant must not be

[b]1 Tim 1:19; Titus 1:11 **19** [a]Is 28:16f; 1 Tim 3:15 [b]John 3:33 [c]John 10:14; 1 Cor 8:3 [d]Luke 13:27; 1 Cor 1:2 **20** [a]Rom 9:21
21 [a]1 Tim 6:11; 2 Tim 2:16-18 [b]2 Cor 9:8; Eph 2:10; 2 Tim 3:17
22 [a]1 Tim 6:11 [b]1 Tim 1:14 [c]Acts 7:59 [d]1 Tim 1:5 **23** [1]Lit *fightings* [a]1 Tim 6:4; 2 Tim 2:14; Titus 3:9 [b]Titus 3:9; James 4:1
24 [a]1 Tim 3:3; Titus 1:7

ing and teaching, which Timothy had heard repeatedly on all three missionary journeys.

2:3–6 Paul gives three examples for Timothy to follow: (1) a soldier who wants to please his commander; (2) an athlete who follows the rules of the game; and (3) a farmer who works hard.

2:6 *to receive his share of the crops.* In this illustration, as in the previous two (soldier, vv. 3–4; athlete, v. 5), the main lesson is that dedicated effort will be rewarded—not necessarily monetarily, but in enjoyment of seeing the gospel produce changed lives.

2:8 *risen from the dead, descendant of David.* Christ's resurrection proclaims His deity, and His descent from David shows His humanity; both truths are basic to the gospel. Since Christ is God, His death has infinite value; since He is man, He could rightfully become our substitute.

2:9 *imprisonment as a criminal.* Apparently Paul was awaiting execution (see 4:6).

2:10 *I endure all things for the . . . chosen.* No suffering is too great if it brings about the salvation of God's chosen ones who will yet believe. *in Christ Jesus.* See note on 1:13. *eternal glory.* The final state of salvation.

2:11–13 Probably an early Christian hymn. The point to which Paul appeals is that suffering for Christ will be followed by glory.

2:11 *trustworthy statement.* See note on 1 Tim 1:15. *if we died with Him, we will also live with Him.* The Greek grammatical construction here assumes that we died with Christ in the past, when He died for us on the cross. We are therefore assured that we will also live with Him eternally.

2:12 *If we endure, we will also reign.* Faithfully bearing up under suffering and trial will result in reward when Christ returns. *If we deny Him.* See Matt 10:33.

2:14–18 The wording of vv. 14–16 indicates that the heresy mentioned here is an early form of Gnosticism—the same as that dealt with in 1 Timothy and Titus (see note on 1 Tim 1:3–11 and Introduction to 1 John: Gnosticism). Two leaders of this heresy, Hymenaeus (see 1 Tim 1:20) and Philetus, denied the bodily resurrection and probably asserted that there is only a spiritual resurrection (similar to the error mentioned in 1 Cor 15:12–19). Gnosticism interpreted the resurrection allegorically, not literally.

2:15 *Be diligent.* See 4:9,21. *word of truth.* The gospel.

2:19 *firm foundation of God.* The church, which upholds the truth (1 Tim 3:15). In spite of the heresy of Hymenaeus and Philetus, Timothy should be heartened to know that the church is God's solid foundation. There are two seals on it: One stresses the security of the church ("The Lord knows those who are His"; here "know," as often in the Bible, means to be intimately acquainted with), while the other emphasizes human responsibility ("Everyone who names the name of the Lord is to abstain from wickedness"). *seal.* The church is owned and securely protected by God (see note on Eph 1:13).

2:22 *youthful.* See note on 1 Tim 4:12.

quarrelsome, but be kind to all, [b]able to
teach, patient when wronged,
25 [a]with gentleness correcting those who
are in opposition, [b]if perhaps God may grant
them repentance leading to [c]the knowledge
of the truth,
26 and they may come to their senses *and*
escape from [a]the snare of the devil, having
been [b]held captive [1]by him to do his will.

"Difficult Times Will Come"

3 But realize this, that [a]in the last days difficult times will come.
2 For men will be [a]lovers of self, [b]lovers
of money, [c]boastful, [c]arrogant, [d]revilers,
[e]disobedient to parents, [e]ungrateful, [f]unholy,
3 [a]unloving, irreconcilable, [b]malicious
gossips, without self-control, brutal, [1c]haters
of good,
4 [a]treacherous, [b]reckless, [c]conceited,
[d]lovers of pleasure rather than lovers of God,
5 holding to a form of [1a]godliness,
although they have [b]denied its power; [c]Avoid
such men as these.
6 For among them are those who [1a]enter
into households and captivate [2b]weak
women weighed down with sins, led on by
[c]various impulses,
7 always learning and never able to
[a]come to the [1]knowledge of the truth.
8 Just as [a]Jannes and Jambres [b]opposed
Moses, so these *men* also oppose the truth,
[c]men of depraved mind, rejected in regard to
the faith.
9 But they will not make further progress;
for their [a]folly will be obvious to all, just [b]as
[1]Jannes's and Jambres's folly was also.
10 Now you [a]followed my teaching, conduct, purpose, faith, patience, [b]love, [1]perse-
verance,

24 [b]1 Tim 3:2
25 [a]Gal 6:1; Titus 3:2; 1 Pet 3:15 [b]Acts 8:22 [c]1 Tim 2:4
26 [1]Or *by him, to do His will* [a]1 Tim 3:7 [b]Luke 5:10
3:1 [a]1 Tim 4:1
2 [a]Phil 2:21 [b]Luke 16:14; 1 Tim 3:3; 6:10 [c]Rom 1:30 [d]2 Pet 2:10-12 [e]Luke 6:35 [f]1 Tim 1:9
3 [1]Lit *not loving good* [a]Rom 1:31 [b]1 Tim 3:11 [c]Titus 1:8
4 [a]Acts 7:52 [b]Acts 19:36 [c]1 Tim 3:6 [d]Phil 3:19
5 [1]Or *religion* [a]1 Tim 4:7 [b]1 Tim 5:8 [c]Matt 7:15; 2 Thess 3:6
6 [1]Or *creep into* [2]Or *idle* [a]Jude 4 [b]1 Tim 5:6; Titus 3:3 [c]Titus 3:3
7 [1]Or *recognition* [a]2 Tim 2:25
8 [a]Ex 7:11 [b]Acts 13:8 [c]1 Tim 6:5
9 [1]Lit *that of those* [a]Luke 6:11 [b]Ex 7:11, 12; 8:18; 9:11
10 [1]Or *steadfastness* [a]Phil 2:20, 22; 1 Tim 4:6 [b]1 Tim 6:11
11 [a]2 Cor 12:10 [b]2 Cor 1:5, 7 [c]Acts 13:14, 45, 50 [d]Acts 14:1-7, 19 [e]Acts 14:8-20 [f]2 Cor 11:23-27 [g]Rom 15:31
12 [a]John 15:20; Acts 14:22; 2 Cor 4:9f

11 [a]persecutions, *and* [b]sufferings, such as
happened to me at [c]Antioch, at [d]Iconium
and at [e]Lystra; what [f]persecutions I endured,
and out of them all [g]the Lord rescued me!
12 Indeed, all who desire to live godly in
Christ Jesus [a]will be persecuted.
13 But evil men and impostors [a]will proceed *from bad* to worse, [b]deceiving and
being deceived.
14 You, however, [a]continue in the things
you have learned and become convinced of,
knowing from whom you have learned *them,*
15 and that [a]from childhood you have
known [b]the sacred writings which are able
to [c]give you the wisdom that leads to [d]salva-
tion through faith which is in [e]Christ Jesus.
16 [a]All Scripture is [1]inspired by God and
profitable for teaching, for reproof, for correction, for [2]training in righteousness;
17 so that [a]the man of God may be adequate, [b]equipped for every good work.

"Preach the Word"

4 [a]I solemnly charge *you* in the presence of
God and of Christ Jesus, who is to [b]judge
the living and the dead, and by His [c]appear-
ing and His kingdom:
2 preach [a]the word; be ready in season
and out of season; [b]reprove, rebuke, exhort,
with [1]great [c]patience and instruction.
3 For [a]the time will come when they will
not endure [b]sound doctrine; but *wanting* to
have their ears tickled, they will accumulate
for themselves teachers in accordance to
their own desires,

13 [a]2 Tim 2:16 [b]Titus 3:3 **14** [a]2 Tim 1:13; Titus 1:9 **15** [a]2 Tim 1:5 [b]John 5:47; Rom 2:27 [c]Ps 119:98f [d]1 Cor 1:21 [e]2 Tim 1:1 **16** [1]Lit *God-breathed* [2]Lit *training which is in* [a]Rom 4:23f; 15:4; 2 Pet 1:20f **17** [a]1 Tim 6:11 [b]2 Tim 2:21; Heb 13:21 **4:1** [a]1 Tim 5:21; 2 Tim 2:14 [b]Acts 10:42 [c]2 Thess 2:8; 2 Tim 1:10; 4:8 **2** [1]Lit *all* [a]Gal 6:6; Col 4:3; 1 Thess 1:6 [b]1 Tim 5:20; Titus 1:13; 2:15 [c]2 Tim 3:10 **3** [a]2 Tim 3:1 [b]1 Tim 1:10; 2 Tim 1:13

3:1 *last days.* The Messianic era, the time beginning with Christ's first coming (see notes on Acts 2:17; 1 Tim 4:1; Heb 1:2; 1 Pet 1:20; 1 John 2:18). That "the last days" in this passage does not refer only to the time just prior to Christ's return is apparent from Paul's command to Timothy to have nothing to do with the unbelieving and unfaithful people who characterize this time (v. 5).

3:6 *weak women.* Unstable women who are guilt-ridden because of their sins, torn by lust, and victims of various false teachers ("always learning," v. 7, but never coming to a saving knowledge of Christ).

3:8 *Jannes and Jambres.* Neither of these men is mentioned in the OT, but according to Jewish tradition they were the Egyptian court magicians who opposed Moses (see Ex 7:11 and note).

3:11 *Antioch, at Iconium and at Lystra.* Three cities in the Roman province of Galatia, which Paul visited on his first and second missionary journeys (Acts 13:14–14:23; 16:1–6). Since Timothy was from Lystra, he would have known firsthand of Paul's sufferings in that region. *out of them all the Lord rescued me!* Even from execution by stoning (Acts 14:19–20).

3:12 A principle repeated elsewhere in the NT (see Matt 10:22; Acts 14:22; Phil 1:29; 1 Pet 4:12). *in Christ.* See note on 1:13.

3:14 *from whom you have learned them.* Perhaps a reference to Paul as well as to Timothy's mother and grandmother (1:5).

3:15 *from childhood you have known the sacred writings.* A Jewish boy formally began to study the OT when he was five years old. Timothy was taught at home by his mother and grandmother even before he reached this age.

3:16 *All Scripture.* The primary reference is to the OT, since some of the NT books had not even been written at this time. (See 1 Tim 5:18; 2 Pet 3:15–16 for indications that some NT books—or material ultimately included in the NT—were already considered equal in authority to the OT Scriptures.) *inspired by God.* Paul affirms God's active involvement in the writing of Scripture, an involvement so powerful and pervasive that what is written is the infallible and authoritative word of God (see 2 Pet 1:20–21 and notes).

4:1 *I solemnly charge you.* Paul states his charge to Timothy, aware that he does so in the presence of God the Father and of Christ, who will judge all men. He is also keenly aware of the twin facts of Christ's return and the coming establishment of God's kingdom in its fullest expression. Timothy was to view a charge so given as of utmost importance.

4:2 *be ready.* Be ready in any situation to speak the needed word, whether of correction, of rebuke or of encouragement.

4:3 *sound doctrine.* See note on Titus 1:9. *have their ears tickled.* Ears that want to be "satisfied" by words in keeping with one's evil desires.

4 and [a]will turn away their ears from the
truth and [b]will turn aside to myths.
5 But you, [a]be sober in all things,
[b]endure hardship, do the work of an [c]evan-
gelist, fulfill your [d]ministry.
6 For I am already being [a]poured out as a
drink offering, and the time of [b]my departure
has come.
7 [a]I have fought the good fight, I have
finished [b]the course, I have kept [c]the faith;
8 in the future there [a]is laid up for me
[b]the crown of righteousness, which the Lord,
the righteous Judge, will award to me on
[c]that day; and not only to me, but also to [d]all
who have loved His [e]appearing.

Personal Concerns

9 [a]Make every effort to come to me soon;
10 for [a]Demas, having loved [b]this present
[1]world, has deserted me and gone to [c]Thes-
salonica; Crescens *has gone* to [2][d]Galatia,
[e]Titus to Dalmatia.
11 [a]Only [b]Luke is with me. Pick up [c]Mark
and bring him with you, [d]for he is useful to
me for service.
12 But [a]Tychicus I have sent to [b]Ephesus.
13 When you come bring the cloak which
I left at [a]Troas with Carpus, and the books,
especially the parchments.
14 [a]Alexander the coppersmith did me
much harm; [b]the Lord will repay him according to his deeds.
15 Be on guard against him yourself, for
he vigorously opposed our [1]teaching.
16 At my first defense no one supported
me, but all deserted me; [a]may it not be
counted against them.
17 But the Lord stood with me and
[a]strengthened me, so that through me [b]the
proclamation might [1]be [c]fully accomplished,
and that all [d]the Gentiles might hear; and I
was [e]rescued out of [f]the lion's mouth.
18 The Lord will rescue me from every evil
deed, and will [1][a]bring me safely to His
[b]heavenly kingdom; [c]to [2]Him *be* the glory
forever and ever. Amen.
19 Greet Prisca and [a]Aquila, and [b]the
household of Onesiphorus.
20 [a]Erastus remained at [b]Corinth, but
[c]Trophimus I left sick at [d]Miletus.
21 [a]Make every effort to come before
[b]winter. Eubulus greets you, also Pudens and
Linus and Claudia and all the brethren.
22 [a]The Lord be with your spirit. [b]Grace
be with you.

4 [a]2 Thess 2:11; Titus 1:14 [b]1 Tim 1:4 **5** [a]1 Pet 1:13 [b]2 Tim 1:8 [c]Acts 21:8 [d]Eph 4:12; Col 4:17 **6** [a]Phil 2:17 [b]Phil 1:23; 2 Pet 1:14 **7** [a]1 Cor 9:25f; Phil 1:30; 1 Tim 1:18; 6:12 [b]Acts 20:24; 1 Cor 9:24 [c]2 Tim 3:10 **8** [a]Col 1:5; 1 Pet 1:4 [b]1 Cor 9:25; 2 Tim 2:5; James 1:12 [c]2 Tim 1:12 [d]Phil 3:11 [e]2 Tim 4:1 **9** [a]2 Tim 1:4; 4:21; Titus 3:12 **10** [1]Or *age* [2]One early ms reads *Gaul* [a]Col 4:14 [b]1 Tim 6:17 [c]Acts 17:1 [d]Acts 16:6 [e]2 Cor 2:13; 8:23; Gal 2:3; Titus 1:4 **11** [a]2 Tim 1:15 [b]Col 4:14; Philem 24 [c]Acts 12:12, 25; 15:37-39; Col 4:10 [d]2 Tim 2:21 **12** [a]Acts 20:4; Eph 6:21, 22; Col 4:7f [b]Acts 18:19 **13** [a]Acts 16:8 **14** [a]Acts 19:33; 1 Tim 1:20

14 [b]Ps 62:12; Rom 2:6; 12:19 **15** [1]Lit *words* **16** [a]Acts 7:60; 1 Cor 13:5 **17** [1]Or *be fulfilled* [a]1 Tim 1:12; 2 Tim 2:1 [b]Titus 1:3 [c]2 Tim 4:5 [d]Acts 9:15; Phil 1:12ff [e]Rom 15:31; 2 Tim 3:11 [f]1 Sam 17:37; Ps 22:21 **18** [1]Or *save me for* [2]Lit *Whom* [a]1 Cor 1:21 [b]1 Cor 15:50; 2 Tim 4:1; Heb 11:16; 12:22 [c]Rom 11:36; 2 Pet 3:18 **19** [a]Acts 18:2 [b]2 Tim 1:16 **20** [a]Acts 19:22; Rom 16:23 [b]Acts 18:1 [c]Acts 20:4; 21:29 [d]Acts 20:15 **21** [a]2 Tim 4:9 [b]Titus 3:12 **22** [a]Gal 6:18; Phil 4:23; Philem 25 [b]Col 4:18

4:4 *myths.* See note on 1 Tim 1:4.

4:6 *drink offering.* The offering of wine poured around the base of the altar (see Num 15:1–12; 28:7,24). Paul views his approaching death as the pouring out of his life as an offering to Christ (see Phil 2:17). *my departure.* His impending death (cf. Phil 1:23).

4:7 In this verse Paul looks back over 30 years of labor as an apostle (c. A.D. 36–66). Like an athlete who had engaged successfully in a contest ("fought the good fight"), he had "finished the course" and had "kept the faith," i.e., had carefully observed the rules (the teachings) of the Christian faith (see 2:5). Or, in view of the Pastorals' emphasis on sound doctrine, perhaps "the faith" refers to the deposit of Christian truth. Paul has kept (guarded) it.

4:8 *crown of righteousness.* Continuing with the same figure of speech, Paul uses the metaphor of the wreath given to the winner of a race (1 Cor 9:25). He could be referring to (1) a crown given as a reward for a righteous life, (2) a crown consisting of righteousness or (3) a crown given righteously (justly) by the righteous Judge. *that day.* The day of Christ's second coming ("appearing").

4:10 *Crescens.* Mentioned only here in the NT. *Galatia.* Either the northern area of Asia Minor (Gaul) or a Roman province in what is now central Turkey (see note on Gal 1:2). *Titus to Dalmatia.* See Introduction to Titus: Recipient. *Dalmatia.* Present-day Albania and a portion of Yugoslavia, also known in Scripture as Illyricum (Rom 15:19).

4:11 *Mark.* John Mark had deserted Paul and Barnabas on their first missionary journey (Acts 13:13). After Paul refused to take Mark on the second journey, Barnabas separated from Paul, taking Mark with him on a mission to Cyprus (Acts 15:36–41). Ultimately Mark proved himself to Paul, indicated by his presence with Paul during Paul's first Roman imprisonment (Col 4:10; Philem 24) and by Paul's request here for Timothy to bring Mark with him to Rome.

4:13 *cloak.* For protection against the cold dampness (see Introduction: Author, Date and Setting). It was probably a heavy, sleeveless, outer garment, circular in shape and with a hole in the middle for one's head. *Carpus.* Not mentioned elsewhere. *the books, especially the parchments.* The scrolls (see note on Ex 17:14) were made of papyrus, and the parchments were made of the skins of animals. The latter may have been copies of parts of the OT.

4:14 *Alexander the coppersmith.* Possibly the Alexander mentioned in 1 Tim 1:20.

4:16 *my first defense.* The first court hearing of Paul's present case, not his defense on the occasion of his first imprisonment (Acts 28).

4:17 *so that through me the proclamation might be fully accomplished.* Even in these dire circumstances Paul used the occasion to testify about Jesus Christ in the imperial court. *I was rescued out of the lion's mouth.* Since, as a Roman citizen, Paul could not be thrown to the lions in the amphitheater, this must be a figurative way of saying that his first hearing did not result in an immediate guilty verdict.

4:18 *The Lord will rescue me from every evil deed.* Since Paul fully expected to die soon (v. 6), the rescue he speaks of here is spiritual, not physical. *heavenly kingdom.* Heaven itself.

4:19 *Onesiphorus.* See note on 1:16.

4:20 *Erastus.* See note on Rom 16:23. *Miletus.* A seaport on the coast of Asia Minor about 50 miles south of Ephesus.

4:21 *Linus.* Early tradition says he was bishop of Rome after the deaths of Peter and Paul.

4:22 *Grace.* See notes on Jon 4:2; Gal 1:3; Eph 1:2. *you.* As at the end of 1 Timothy, "you" here is plural, showing that the letter was intended for public use. The word "your" in the first part of the verse, however, is singular, indicating that it was addressed to Timothy alone. In view of Paul's impending death and the solemn charge he gave to his timid young friend, Timothy needed such encouragement.

Titus

INTRODUCTION

See "The Pastoral Letters," p. 1758.

Author

The author is Paul (see Introduction to 1 Timothy: Author).

Recipient

The letter is addressed to Titus, one of Paul's converts (1:4) and a considerable help to Paul in his ministry. When Paul left Antioch to discuss "his" gospel (2 Tim 2:8) with the Jerusalem leaders, he took Titus with him (Gal 2:1–3); acceptance of Titus (a Gentile) as a Christian without circumcision vindicated Paul's stand there (Gal 2:3–5). Presumably Titus, who is not referred to in Acts (but is mentioned 13 times in the rest of the NT), worked with Paul at Ephesus during the third missionary journey. From there the apostle sent him to Corinth to help that church with its work (see notes on 2 Cor 2:12–13; 7:5–6; 8:6).

Following Paul's release from his first Roman imprisonment (Acts 28), he and Titus worked briefly in Crete (1:5), after which he commissioned Titus to remain there as his representative and complete some needed work (1:5; 2:15; 3:12–13). Paul asked Titus to meet him at Nicopolis (on the west coast of Greece) when a replacement arrived (3:12). Later, Titus went on a mission to Dalmatia (modern Yugoslavia; see note on 2 Tim 4:10), the last word we hear about him in the NT. Considering the assignments given him, he obviously was a capable and resourceful leader.

Crete

The fourth largest island of the Mediterranean, Crete lies directly south of the Aegean Sea (see note on 1 Sam 30:14; cf. Paul's experiences there in Acts 27:7–13). In NT times life in Crete had sunk to a deplorable moral level. The dishonesty, gluttony and laziness of its inhabitants were proverbial (1:12).

Occasion and Purpose

Apparently Paul introduced Christianity in Crete when he and Titus visited the island, after which he left Titus there to organize the converts. Paul sent the letter with Zenas and Apollos, who were on a journey that took them through Crete (3:13), to give Titus personal authorization and guidance in meeting opposition (1:5; 2:1,7–8,15; 3:9), instructions about faith and conduct, and warnings about false teachers. Paul also informed Titus of his future plans for him (3:12).

Place and Date of Writing

Paul possibly wrote from Macedonia, for he had not yet reached Nicopolis (see 3:12). The letter was written after his release from the first Roman imprisonment (Acts 28), probably between A.D. 63 and 65—or possibly at a later date if he wrote after his assumed trip to Spain.

Distinctive Characteristics

Especially significant, considering the nature of the Cretan heresy, are the repeated emphases on "good deeds" (1:16; 2:7,14; 3:1,8,14) and the classic summaries of Christian doctrine (2:11–14; 3:4–7).

Outline

I. Salutation (1:1–4)
II. Concerning Elders (1:5–9)
  A. Reasons for Leaving Titus in Crete (1:5)
  B. Qualifications of Elders (1:6–9)
III. Concerning False Teachers (1:10–16)
IV. Concerning Various Groups in the Congregations (ch. 2)
  A. The Instructions to Different Groups (2:1–10)
  B. The Foundation for Christian Living (2:11–14)
  C. The Duty of Titus (2:15)
V. Concerning Believers in General (3:1–8)
  A. Obligations as Citizens (3:1–2)
  B. Motives for Godly Conduct (3:3–8)
VI. Concerning Response to Spiritual Error (3:9–11)
VII. Conclusion (3:12–15)

Salutation

1 Paul, [a]a bond-servant of God and an
[b]apostle of Jesus Christ, [1]for the faith of
those [c]chosen of God and [d]the knowledge of
the truth which is [e]according to godliness,
2 in [a]the hope of eternal life, which God,
[b]who cannot lie, [c]promised [1][d]long ages ago,
3 but [a]at the proper time manifested,
even His word, in [b]the proclamation [c]with
which I was entrusted [d]according to the
commandment of [e]God our Savior,
4 To [a]Titus, [b]my true child [1]in a [c]com-
mon faith: [d]Grace and peace from God the
Father and [e]Christ Jesus our Savior.

Qualifications of Elders

5 For this reason I left you in [a]Crete, that
you would set in order what remains and
[b]appoint [c]elders in every city as I directed
you,
6 *namely,* [a]if any man is above reproach,
the [b]husband of one wife, having children
who believe, not accused of [c]dissipation or
[d]rebellion.
7 For the [1][a]overseer must be above
reproach as [b]God's steward, not [c]self-willed,
not quick-tempered, not [d]addicted to wine,
not pugnacious, [e]not fond of sordid gain,
8 but [a]hospitable, [b]loving what is good,
sensible, just, devout, self-controlled,
9 [a]holding fast the faithful word which is
in accordance with the teaching, so that he
will be able both to exhort in [b]sound doctrine and to refute those who contradict.
10 [a]For there are many [b]rebellious men,
[c]empty talkers and deceivers, especially
[d]those of the circumcision,
11 who must be silenced because they are
upsetting [a]whole families, teaching [b]things
they should not *teach* [c]for the sake of sordid
gain.
12 One of themselves, a prophet of their
own, said, "[a]Cretans are always liars, evil
beasts, lazy gluttons."
13 This testimony is true. For this reason
[a]reprove them [b]severely so that they may be
[c]sound in the faith,

1:1 [1]Or *according to* [a]Rom 1:1; James 1:1; Rev 1:1 [b]2 Cor 1:1 [c]Luke 18:7 [d]1 Tim 2:4 [e]1 Tim 6:3
2 [1]Lit *before times eternal* [a]2 Tim 1:1; Titus 3:7 [b]2 Tim 2:13; Heb 6:18 [c]Rom 1:2 [d]2 Tim 1:9
3 [a]1 Tim 2:6 [b]Rom 16:25; 2 Tim 4:17 [c]1 Tim 1:11 [d]1 Tim 1:1 [e]Luke 1:47; 1 Tim 1:1; Titus 2:10; 3:4
4 [1]Lit *according to* [a]2 Cor 2:13; 8:23; Gal 2:3; 2 Tim 4:10 [b]2 Tim 1:2 [c]2 Pet 1:1 [d]Rom 1:7 [e]1 Tim 1:12; 2 Tim 1:1
5 [a]Acts 27:7; Titus 1:12 [b]Acts 14:23 [c]Acts 11:30
6 [a]1 Tim 3:2-4; Titus 1:6-8 [b]1 Tim 3:2 [c]Eph 5:18 [d]Titus 1:10
7 [1]Or *bishop* [a]1 Tim 3:2 [b]1 Cor 4:1 [c]2 Pet 2:10 [d]1 Tim 3:3 [e]1 Tim 3:3, 8
8 [a]1 Tim 3:2 [b]2 Tim 3:3 **9** [a]2 Thess 2:15; 1 Tim 1:19; 2 Tim 1:13 [b]1 Tim 1:10; Titus 2:1 **10** [a]2 Cor 11:13 [b]Titus 1:6 [c]1 Tim 1:6 [d]Acts 11:2 **11** [a]1 Tim 5:4; 2 Tim 3:6 [b]1 Tim 5:13 [c]1 Tim 6:5 **12** [a]Acts 2:11; 27:7 **13** [a]1 Tim 5:20; 2 Tim 4:2; Titus 2:15 [b]2 Cor 13:10 [c]Titus 2:2

1:1 *bond-servant of God.* Only here does Paul call himself a servant of God; elsewhere he says "bond-servant of Christ" (Rom 1:1; Gal 1:10; Phil 1:1). James uses both terms of himself (James 1:1). *bond-servant.* See note on Rom 1:1. *apostle.* One specially commissioned by Christ (see notes on Mark 6:30; 1 Cor 1:1; Heb 3:1). *for the faith . . . and the knowledge.* Paul's appointed mission as God's servant and Christ's apostle—further explained in v. 2 (see Acts 9:15; 22:15; 26:16–18).

1:2 *hope.* See note on Col 1:5. *cannot lie.* In contrast to the Cretans (v. 12)—and the devil (John 8:44).

1:3 *proper time.* Crucial events in God's program occur at His designated times in history (1 Tim 2:6; 6:15). *His word.* The authoritative message that centers in Christ. *God our Savior.* Three times in the letter God the Father is called Savior (here; 2:10; 3:4; see also 1 Tim 1:1; 2:3; 4:10), and three times Jesus is called Savior (v. 4; 2:13; 3:6; see also 2 Tim 1:10).

1:4 *my true child.* Titus, like Timothy (1 Tim 1:2), was a spiritual son, having been converted through Paul's ministry. Onesimus was also called a son by Paul (Philem 10). *true.* Genuine. *a common faith.* The faith shared by all true believers. *Savior.* In all of Paul's other salutations Jesus is called "Lord." Paul uses "Savior" 12 times in all his letters, half of the references being in Titus.

1:5 *left you in Crete.* Implies that Paul and Titus had been together in Crete, a ministry not mentioned in Acts. On his voyage to Rome, Paul visited Crete briefly as a prisoner (Acts 27:7–8), but now that he had been released from his first Roman imprisonment he was free to travel wherever he wished (see 3:12). *appoint elders.* Though Paul and Titus perhaps had already preached in Crete, they had not had time to organize churches. The appointing of elders is consistent with Paul's usual practice (Acts 14:23).

1:6–9 1 Tim 3:1–7 gives a parallel list of qualifications for elders, but the two lists reflect the different situations in which Timothy and Titus ministered. See chart, p. 1765.

1:6 *husband of one wife.* Since elders, by definition, were chosen from among the older men of the congregation, Paul assumed they already would be married and have children. A qualified unmarried man was not necessarily barred. It is also improbable that the standard forbids an elder to remarry if his wife dies (cf. Rom 7:2–3; 1 Cor 7:39; 1 Tim 5:14). The most likely meaning is simply that a faithful monogamous married life must be maintained. See note on 1 Tim 3:2.

1:7 *the overseer.* The use of "elder" in v. 5 and "overseer" (or "bishop") in v. 7 indicates that the terms were used interchangeably (cf. Acts 20:17,28; 1 Pet 5:1–2). "Elder" indicates qualification (maturity and experience), while "overseer" indicates responsibility (watching over God's flock).

1:8 *sensible.* A virtue much needed in Crete (see vv. 10–14); Paul refers to it five times in two chapters (here; 2:2,5–6,12). *self-controlled.* Possessing the inner strength to control one's desires and actions.

1:9 *sound doctrine.* Correct teaching, in keeping with that of the apostles (see 1 Tim 1:10; 6:3; 2 Tim 1:13; 4:3). The teaching is called "sound" not only because it builds up in the faith, but because it protects against the corrupting influence of false teachers. Soundness of doctrine, faith and speech is a basic concern in all the Pastoral Letters (1,2 Timothy; Titus). In them the word "sound" occurs ten times (see also "sound' in Rom 12:3, 2 Cor 5:13).

1:10 *rebellious.* Against the word of God and against Paul and Titus as the Lord's authoritative ministers. *men.* These troublemakers had three main characteristics: 1. They belonged to the "circumcision," like the people of Gal 2:12, believing that, for salvation or sanctification or both, it was necessary to be circumcised and to keep the Jewish ceremonial law (see Introduction to Galatians: Occasion and Purpose). 2. They held to unscriptural Jewish myths (v. 14) and genealogies (3:9; see 1 Tim 1:4 and note there). 3. They were ascetics (vv. 14–15), having scruples against things that God declared to be good. *empty talkers.* Paul used similar language in writing to Timothy about this kind of person (1 Tim 1:6).

1:12 The quotation is from the poet Epimenides (a sixth-century B.C. native of Knossos, Crete), who was held in high esteem by the Cretans. Several fulfilled predictions were ascribed to him. For other uses of pagan sayings by Paul see Acts 17:28; 1 Cor 15:33 and notes. In Greek literature "to Cretanize" meant to lie.

14 not paying attention to Jewish [a]myths
and [b]commandments of men who [c]turn
away from the truth.
15 [a]To the pure, all things are pure; but [b]to
those who are defiled and unbelieving, nothing is pure, but both their [c]mind and their
conscience are defiled.
16 [a]They profess to know God, but by
their deeds they [b]deny *Him,* being [c]detest-
able and [d]disobedient and [e]worthless [f]for
any good deed.

Duties of the Older and Younger

2 But as for you, speak the things which are
fitting for [a]sound doctrine.
2 [a]Older men are to be [b]temperate, dignified, sensible, [c]sound [d]in faith, in love, in
[1]perseverance.
3 Older women likewise are to be reverent in their behavior, [a]not malicious gossips
nor [b]enslaved to much wine, teaching what
is good,
4 so that they may [1]encourage the young
women to love their husbands, to love their
children,
5 *to be* sensible, pure, [a]workers at home,
kind, being [b]subject to their own husbands,
[c]so that the word of God will not be dishonored.
6 Likewise urge [a]the young men to be
[1]sensible;
7 in all things show yourself to be [a]an
example of good deeds, *with* [1]purity in doctrine, dignified,
8 sound *in* speech which is beyond
reproach, so [a]that the opponent will be put
to shame, having nothing bad to say about
us.
9 *Urge* [a]bondslaves to be subject to their
own masters in everything, to be well-pleasing, not [1]argumentative,
10 not pilfering, but showing all good faith
so that they will adorn the doctrine of [a]God
our Savior in every respect.
11 For the grace of God has [a]appeared,
[1][b]bringing salvation to all men,
12 [1]instructing us to deny ungodliness and
[a]worldly desires and [b]to live sensibly, righteously and godly [c]in the present age,
13 looking for the blessed hope and the

14 [a]1 Tim 1:4 [b]Col 2:22 [c]2 Tim 4:4
15 [a]Luke 11:41; Rom 14:20 [b]Rom 14:14, 23 [c]1 Tim 6:5
16 [a]1 John 2:4 [b]1 Tim 5:8 [c]Rev 21:8 [d]Titus 3:3 [e]2 Tim 3:8 [f]2 Tim 3:17; Titus 3:1
2:1 [a]Titus 1:9
2 [1]Or *steadfastness* [a]Philem 9 [b]1 Tim 3:2 [c]Titus 1:13 [d]1 Tim 1:2, 14
3 [a]1 Tim 3:11 [b]1 Tim 3:8
4 [1]Or *train*
5 [a]1 Tim 5:14 [b]Eph 5:22
5 [c]1 Tim 6:1
6 [1]Or *sensible in all things; show* [a]1 Tim 5:1
7 [1]Or *soundness;* lit *uncorruptness* [a]1 Tim 4:12
8 [a]2 Thess 3:14; 1 Pet 2:12
9 [1]Lit *contradicting* [a]Eph 6:5; 1 Tim 6:1
10 [a]Titus 1:3
11 [1]Or *to all men, bringing* [a]2 Tim 1:10; Titus 3:4 [b]1 Tim 2:4
12 [1]Or *disciplining* [a]1 Tim 6:9; Titus 3:3 [b]2 Tim 3:12 [c]1 Tim 6:17

1:14 *Jewish myths.* See note on v. 10.
1:15 *To the pure, all things are pure.* To Christians, who have been purified by the atoning death of Christ, "everything created by God is good, and nothing is to be rejected if it is received with gratitude" (1 Tim 4:4). *to those who are defiled and unbelieving, nothing is pure.* Unbelievers, especially ascetics with unbiblical scruples against certain foods, marriage and the like (cf. 1 Tim 4:3; Col 2:21), do not enjoy the freedom of true Christians, who receive all God's creation with thanksgiving. Instead, they set up arbitrary, man-made prohibitions against what they consider to be impure (see Matt 15:10–11,16–20; Mark 7:14–19; Acts 10:9–16; Rom 14:20). The principle of this verse does not conflict with the many NT teachings against practices that are morally and spiritually wrong. *conscience.* See 1 Tim 4:2–3.
1:16 *by their deeds they deny Him.* The false teachers stood condemned by the test of personal conduct. *good.* See Introduction: Distinctive Characteristics. Right knowledge is extremely important because it leads to godliness (v. 1). Paul maintained a remarkable balance between doctrine and practice.
2:1 *you.* Emphatic, contrasting the work of Titus with that of the false teachers just denounced (1:10–16).
2:2–10 Sound doctrine demands right conduct of all believers, regardless of age, sex or position.
2:2 Older men, as leaders, were to be moral and spiritual examples. *temperate.* Instead of being "lazy gluttons," as were Cretans in general (1:12), these older believers were to be responsible and sensible.
2:3 *likewise.* The same moral standards applied to women as to men. *not malicious gossips.* Slanderous talk apparently was a common vice among Cretan women.
2:4 *love their husbands.* Just as husbands are exhorted (Eph 5:25) to love their wives (though different Greek words for "love" are used in the two passages).
2:5 *that the word of God will not be dishonored.* Indicating Paul's deep spiritual concern behind these ethical instructions. See also vv. 8,10, dealing with his concern that Christian living should help rather than hinder the spread of the gospel.
2:7–8 Perhaps Titus was still a young man and was not yet well respected by the Cretan churches. The demands on a leader are all-inclusive, involving not only his word but also his life-style (James 3:1).
2:7 *good.* See Introduction: Distinctive Characteristics.
2:9–10 Instructions for a distinct group in the churches. Slavery was a basic element of Roman society, and the impact of Christianity upon slaves was a vital concern. Guidance for the conduct of Christian slaves was essential (see note on Eph 6:5).
2:9 *masters.* The Greek for this word, from which our English term "despot" is derived, indicates the owner's absolute authority over his slave. Roman slaves had no legal rights, their fates being entirely in their masters' hands.
2:10 *adorn the doctrine.* Christian slaves could give a unique and powerful testimony to the gospel by their willing faithfulness and obedience to their masters.
2:11–14 Briefly describes the effect grace should have on believers. It encourages rejection of ungodliness and leads to holier living—in keeping with Paul's repeated insistence that profession of Christ be accompanied by godly living (vv. 1–2,4–5,10; 3:8).
2:11 *For.* Introduces the doctrinal basis for the ethical demands just stressed. Right conduct must be founded on right doctrine. *grace of God.* The undeserved love God showed us in Christ while we were still sinners and His enemies (Rom 5:6–10) and by which we are saved apart from any moral achievements or religious acts on our part (see 3:5; Eph 2:8–9). But this same grace instructs us that our salvation should produce good works (see note on v. 14; see also Eph 2:10).
2:12 *instructing us.* The word translated "teaches" refers to more than instruction; it includes the whole process of training a child—instruction, encouragement, correction and discipline. *the present age.* See note on 2 Cor 4:4.
2:13 *the blessed hope and the . . . glory.* The second coming (see 1 Tim 6:14; 2 Tim 4:1; see also note on 2 Tim 4:8). *our great God and Savior, Christ Jesus.* It is possible to translate this phrase "the great God and our Saviour, Jesus Christ" (KJV), but the NASB rendering better represents the Greek construction. It is an explicit testimony to the deity of Christ (see note on Rom 9:5).

[a]appearing of the glory of [1][b]our great God
and Savior, Christ Jesus,
14 who [a]gave Himself for us [b]to redeem
us from every lawless deed, and to [c]purify
for Himself a [d]people for His own possession, [e]zealous for good deeds.
15 These things speak and [a]exhort and
[a]reprove with all [1]authority. [b]Let no one disregard you.

Godly Living

3 [a]Remind them [b]to be subject to rulers, to
authorities, to be obedient, to be [c]ready
for every good deed,
2 to malign no one, [a]to be peaceable,
[a]gentle, [b]showing every consideration for all
men.
3 [a]For we also once were foolish ourselves, [b]disobedient, [c]deceived, [d]enslaved to
[e]various lusts and pleasures, spending our
life in [f]malice and [f]envy, hateful, hating one
another.
4 But when the [a]kindness of [b]God our
Savior and *His* love for mankind [c]appeared,
5 [a]He saved us, [b]not on the basis of
deeds which we have done in righteousness,
but [c]according to His mercy, by the [d]washing
of regeneration and [e]renewing by the Holy
Spirit,
6 [a]whom He poured out upon us [b]richly
through Jesus Christ our Savior,
7 so that being justified by His grace we
would be made [a]heirs [1]according to *the* hope
of eternal life.
8 [a]This is a trustworthy statement; and
concerning these things I [b]want you to
speak confidently, so that those who have
[c]believed God will be careful to [d]engage in
good deeds. These things are good and profitable for men.
9 But [a]avoid [b]foolish controversies and
[c]genealogies and strife and [d]disputes about
the Law, for they are [e]unprofitable and
worthless.
10 [a]Reject a [b]factious man [c]after a first
and second warning,
11 knowing that such a man is [a]perverted
and is sinning, being self-condemned.

Personal Concerns

12 When I send Artemas or [a]Tychicus to
you, [b]make every effort to come to me at
Nicopolis, for I have decided to [c]spend the
winter there.
13 Diligently help Zenas the [a]lawyer and
[b]Apollos on their way so that nothing is lacking for them.
14 [a]Our people must also learn to [b]engage
in good [1]deeds to meet [c]pressing needs, so
that they will not be [d]unfruitful.
15 [a]All who are with me greet you. Greet
those who love us [b]in *the* faith.
[c]**G**race be with you all.

13 [1]Or *the great God and our Savior* [a]2 Thess 2:8 [b]1 Tim 1:1; 2 Tim 1:2; Titus 1:4; 2 Pet 1:1 **14** [a]1 Tim 2:6 [b]Ps 130:8; 1 Pet 1:18f [c]Ezek 37:23; Heb 1:3; 9:14; 1 John 1:7 [d]Ex 19:5; Deut 4:20; 7:6; 14:2; Eph 1:11; 1 Pet 2:9 [e]Eph 2:10; Titus 3:8; 1 Pet 3:13 **15** [1]Lit *command* [a]1 Tim 4:13; 5:20; 2 Tim 4:2 [b]1 Tim 4:12 **3:1** [a]2 Tim 2:14 [b]Rom 13:1 [c]2 Tim 2:21 **2** [a]1 Tim 3:3; 1 Pet 2:18 [b]2 Tim 2:25 **3** [a]Rom 11:30; Col 3:7 [b]Titus 1:16 [c]2 Tim 3:13 [d]Rom 6:6, 12 [e]2 Tim 3:6; Titus 2:12 [f]Rom 1:29 **4** [a]Rom 2:4; Eph 2:7; 1 Pet 2:3 [b]Titus 2:10 [c]Titus 2:11 **5** [a]Rom 11:14; 2 Tim 1:9 [b]Eph 2:9 [c]Eph 2:4; 1 Pet 1:3 [d]John 3:5; Eph 5:26; 1 Pet 3:21 [e]Rom 12:2 **6** [a]Rom 5:5 [b]Rom 2:4; 1 Tim 6:17 **7** [1]Or *of eternal life according to hope* [a]Matt 25:34; Mark 10:17; Rom 8:17, 24; Titus 1:2 **8** [a]1 Tim 1:15 [b]1 Tim 2:8 [c]2 Tim 1:12 [d]Titus 2:7, 14; 3:14 **9** [a]2 Tim 2:16 [b]1 Tim 1:4; 2 Tim 2:23 [c]1 Tim 1:4 [d]James 4:1 [e]2 Tim 2:14 **10** [a]2 John 10 [b]Rom 16:17 [c]Matt 18:15f **11** [a]Titus 1:14 **12** [a]Acts 20:4; Eph 6:21f; Col 4:7f; 2 Tim 4:12 [b]2 Tim 4:9 [c]2 Tim 4:21 **13** [a]Matt 22:35 [b]Acts 18:24; 1 Cor 16:12 **14** [1]Or *occupations* [a]Titus 2:8 [b]Titus 3:8 [c]Rom 12:13; Phil 4:16 [d]Matt 7:19; Phil 1:11; Col 1:10 **15** [a]Acts 20:34 [b]1 Tim 1:2 [c]Col 4:18

2:14 Salvation involves the double work of redeeming us from guilt and judgment and of producing moral purity and helpful service to others (see Introduction: Distinctive Characteristics).
2:15 A summary of Titus's responsibility and authority. *things.* The content of the whole chapter.
3:1–2 NT teaching is not confined to the area of personal salvation but includes much instruction about practical living. Although believers are citizens of heaven (Phil 3:20), they must also submit themselves to earthly government (see Rom 13:1–7; 1 Pet 2:13–17) and help promote the well-being of the community.
3:1 *to rulers, to authorities.* The terms refer to all forms and levels of human government (cf. Eph 3:10; 6:12 for application to angels). *good.* See Introduction: Distinctive Characteristics.
3:4 *kindness . . . and His love.* The reasons why God did not simply banish fallen man but acted to save him (cf. 2:11). The Greek here for "love" is *philanthropia,* "love for mankind."
3:5 *saved us . . . according to His mercy.* Salvation is not achieved by human effort or merit but comes through God's mercy alone. *washing of regeneration.* A reference to new birth, of which baptism (among other things) is a sign. It cannot mean that baptism is necessary for regeneration, since the NT plainly teaches that the new birth is an act of God's Spirit (see, e.g., John 3:5) and is not effected or achieved by ceremony. *renewing by the Holy Spirit.* Also a reference to new birth.
3:8 *trustworthy statement.* A reference to the doctrinal summary in vv. 4–7. This phrase, which occurs only here in Titus, appears four other times in the Pastoral Letters (1 Tim 1:15; 3:1; 4:9; 2 Tim 2:11) and nowhere else in the NT. *good.* See Introduction: Distinctive Characteristics.
3:9 *about the Law.* A reference to the situation described in 1:10–16. A similar problem existed in Ephesus (see 1 Tim 1:3–7).
3:10 *factious man.* The Greek for this phrase became a technical term in the early church for a type of "heretic" who promoted dissension by propagating extreme views of legitimate Christian truths.
3:11 Stubborn refusal to listen to correction reveals inner perversion.
3:12 *Tychicus.* Paul's trusted co-worker, who on various occasions traveled with or for Paul (Acts 20:4; Eph 6:21–22; Col 4:7–8; 2 Tim 4:12). *Nicopolis.* Means "city of victory." Several cities had this name, but the reference here apparently is to the city in Epirus on the western shore of Greece. *decided to spend the winter there.* Indicates that Paul had not arrived there when he wrote and that he was still free to travel at will, not yet having been imprisoned in Rome for the second time.
3:13 *Zenas the lawyer.* Mentioned only here in the NT. If he was a Jewish convert, "lawyer" means that he was an expert in the Mosaic law; if he was a Gentile convert, that he was a Roman jurist. *Apollos.* A native of Alexandria and one of Paul's well-known co-workers (Acts 18:24–28; 19:1; 1 Cor 1:12; 3:4–6,22; 16:12). The two travelers apparently brought the letter from Paul.
3:14 *good.* See Introduction: Distinctive Characteristics.

Philemon

INTRODUCTION

Author, Date and Place of Writing

Paul wrote this short letter (see vv. 1, 9, 19) probably at the same time as Colossians (c. A.D. 60; see Introduction to Colossians: Author, Date and Place of Writing) and sent it to Colosse with the same travelers, Onesimus and Tychicus. He apparently wrote both letters from prison in Rome, though possibly from Ephesus (see Introduction to Philippians: Author, Date and Place of Writing).

Recipient, Background and Purpose

Paul wrote this letter to Philemon, a believer in Colosse who, along with others, was a slave owner (cf. Col 4:1; for slavery in the NT see note on Eph 6:5). One of his slaves, Onesimus, had apparently stolen from him (cf. v. 18) and then run away, which under Roman law was punishable by death. But Onesimus met Paul and through his ministry became a Christian (see v. 10). Now he was willing to return to his master, and Paul writes this personal appeal to ask that he be accepted as a Christian brother (see v. 16).

Approach and Structure

To win Philemon's willing acceptance of Onesimus, Paul writes very tactfully and in a lighthearted tone, which he creates with a wordplay (see note on v. 11). The appeal (vv. 4–21) is organized in a way prescribed by ancient Greek and Roman teachers: to build rapport (vv. 4–10), to persuade the mind (vv. 11–19) and to move the emotions (vv. 20–21). The name Onesimus is not mentioned until the rapport has been built (v. 10), and the appeal itself is stated only near the end of the section to persuade the mind (v. 17).

Outline

I. Greetings (1–3)
II. Thanksgiving and Prayer (4–7)
III. Paul's Plea for Onesimus (8–21)
IV. Final Request, Greetings and Benediction (22–25)

Salutation

1 [a]Paul, [b]a prisoner of [c]Christ Jesus, and
[d]Timothy [1]our brother,
To Philemon our beloved *brother* and [e]fel-
low worker,
2 and to Apphia [1][a]our sister, and to
[b]Archippus our [c]fellow soldier, and to [d]the
church in your house:
3 [a]Grace to you and peace from God our
Father and the Lord Jesus Christ.

Philemon's Love and Faith

4 [a]I thank my God always, making mention of you in my prayers,
5 because I [a]hear of your love and of the
faith which you have toward the Lord Jesus
and toward all the [1]saints;
6 *and I pray* that the fellowship of your
faith may become effective [1]through the
[a]knowledge of every good thing which is in
you [2]for Christ's sake.
7 For I have come to have much [a]joy and
comfort in your love, because the [1]hearts of
the [2]saints have been [b]refreshed through
you, brother.
8 Therefore, [a]though I have [1]enough
confidence in Christ to order you *to do* what
is [b]proper,
9 yet for love's sake I rather [a]appeal *to
you*—since I am such a person as Paul, [1]the
[b]aged, and now also [c]a prisoner of [d]Christ
Jesus—

Plea for Onesimus, a Free Man

10 I [a]appeal to you for my [b]child [1][c]Onesi-
mus, whom I have begotten in my [2]impris-
onment,
11 who formerly was useless to you, but
now is useful both to you and to me.
12 I have sent him back to you in person,
that is, *sending* my very heart,
13 whom I wished to keep with me, so
that on your behalf he might minister to me
in my [1][a]imprisonment for the gospel;
14 but without your consent I did not
want to do anything, so that your goodness
would [a]not be, in effect, by compulsion but
of your own free will.
15 For perhaps [a]he was for this reason
separated *from you* for a while, that you
would have him back forever,
16 [a]no longer as a slave, but more than a
slave, [b]a beloved brother, especially to me,
but how much more to you, both [c]in the
flesh and in the Lord.
17 If then you regard me a [a]partner, accept
him as *you would* me.
18 But if he has wronged you in any way
or owes you anything, charge that to my
account;
19 [a]I, Paul, am writing this with my own
hand, I will repay it ([b]not to [1]mention to you
that you owe to me even your own self as
well).
20 Yes, brother, let me benefit from you in
the Lord; [a]refresh my heart in Christ.
21 [a]Having confidence in your obedience,
I write to you, since I know that you will do
even more than what I say.
22 At the same time also prepare me a
[a]lodging, for [b]I hope that through [c]your
prayers [d]I will be given to you.
23 [a]Epaphras, my [b]fellow prisoner in
Christ Jesus, greets you,
24 *as do* [a]Mark, [b]Aristarchus, [c]Demas,
[c]Luke, my [d]fellow workers.
25 [a]The grace of the Lord Jesus Christ be
[b]with your spirit.[1]

1:1 [1]Lit *the* [a]Phil 1:1 [b]Eph 3:1 [c]Gal 3:26 [d]2 Cor 1:1; Col 1:1 [e]Phil 2:25; Philem 24
2 [1]Lit *the* [a]Rom 16:1 [b]Col 4:17 [c]Phil 2:25; 2 Tim 2:3 [d]Rom 16:5
3 [a]Rom 1:7
4 [a]Rom 1:8f
5 [1]Or *holy ones* [a]Eph 1:15; Col 1:4; 1 Thess 3:6
6 [1]Or *in* [2]Lit *toward Christ* [a]Phil 1:9; Col 1:9; 3:10
7 [1]Lit *inward parts* [2]Or *holy ones* [a]2 Cor 7:4, 13 [b]1 Cor 16:18; Philem 20
8 [1]Lit *much* [a]2 Cor 3:12; 1 Thess 2:6 [b]Eph 5:4
9 [1]Or *an ambassador* [a]Rom 12:1 [b]Titus 2:2 [c]Philem 1 [d]Gal 3:26; 1 Tim 1:12; Philem 23
10 [1]I.e. useful [2]Lit *bonds* [a]Rom 12:1 [b]1 Cor 4:14f [c]Col 4:9
13 [1]Lit *bonds* [a]Phil 1:7; Philem 10
14 [a]2 Cor 9:7; 1 Pet 5:2
15 [a]Gen 45:5, 8
16 [a]1 Cor 7:22 [b]Matt 23:8; 1 Tim 6:2 [c]Eph 6:5; Col 3:22
17 [a]2 Cor 8:23
19 [1]Lit *say* [a]1 Cor 16:21; 2 Cor 10:1; Gal 5:2 [b]2 Cor 9:4
20 [a]Philem 7
21 [a]2 Cor 2:3
22 [a]Acts 28:23 [b]Phil 1:25; 2:24 [c]2 Cor 1:11 [d]Acts 27:24; Heb 13:19
23 [a]Col 1:7; 4:12 [b]Rom 16:7; Philem 1
24 [a]Acts 12:12, 25; 15:37-39; Col 4:10 [b]Acts 19:29; 27:2; Col 4:10 [c]Col 4:14; 2 Tim 4:10f [d]Philem 1
25 [1]One early ms adds *Amen* [a]Gal 6:18 [b]2 Tim 4:22

1–2 Although Paul writes together with Timothy and although he addresses the entire church in Colossae, in this very personal letter to Philemon he uses "I" rather than "we," and "you" (singular except in vv. 22,25).

1 *prisoner.* See notes on Eph 3:1; Phil 1:13. *Timothy.* See note on Col 1:1; see also Introduction to 1 Timothy: Recipient. *Philemon.* A Christian living in Colossae or nearby and the owner of the slave Onesimus.

2 *Apphia.* Probably Philemon's wife. *Archippus.* See Col 4:17.

4 *thank . . . making mention of you in my prayers.* See note on Phil 1:3–4.

5 *love and . . . faith . . . toward the Lord Jesus and . . . all the saints.* See Col 1:4.

7 *hearts.* The English equivalent of the Greek for "intestines"—the part of the body that is figurative for the emotions of pity and love (see vv. 12,20).

10 *my child.* See note on 1 Tim 1:2. *Onesimus.* See Introduction: Recipient, Background and Purpose.

11 *useless . . . useful.* A play on the meaning of Onesimus's name ("useful").

17–19 Luther said, "Even as Christ did for us with God the Father, thus Paul also does for Onesimus with Philemon."

20 *me . . . my.* Both pronouns are emphatic, making an obvious allusion to v. 7. *benefit.* The Greek for this word is another play on the name Onesimus.

22 *At the same time also.* It was not unusual for an ancient letter, though occasioned by one matter, to also include another matter. Often, as here, the second matter had to do with how and when the author planned to meet the recipient again.

23 *Epaphras.* See Col 4:12.

24 *Mark, Aristarchus.* See note on Col 4:10. *Demas, Luke.* See note on Col 4:14.

Hebrews

INTRODUCTION

Author

The writer of this letter does not identify himself, but he was obviously well known to the original recipients. Though for some 1,200 years (from c. A.D. 400 to 1600) the book was commonly called "The Epistle of Paul to the Hebrews," there was no agreement in the earliest centuries regarding its authorship. Since the Reformation it has been widely recognized that Paul could not have been the writer. There is no disharmony between the teaching of Hebrews and that of Paul's letters, but the specific emphases and writing styles are markedly different. Contrary to Paul's usual practice, the author of Hebrews nowhere identifies himself in the letter—except to indicate that he was a man (see note on 11:32). Moreover, the statement "After it was at the first spoken through the Lord, it was confirmed to us by those who heard" (2:3), indicates that the author had neither been with Jesus during his earthly ministry nor received special revelation directly from the risen Lord, as had Paul (Gal 1:11–12).

The earliest suggestion of authorship is found in Tertullian's *De Pudicitia,* 20 (c. 200), in which he quotes from "an epistle to the Hebrews under the name of Barnabas." From the letter itself it is clear that the writer must have had authority in the apostolic church and was an intellectual Hebrew Christian well versed in the OT. Barnabas meets these requirements. He was a Jew of the priestly tribe of Levi (Acts 4:36) who became a close friend of Paul after the latter's conversion. Under the guidance of the Holy Spirit, the church at Antioch commissioned Barnabas and Paul for the work of evangelism and sent them off on the first missionary journey (Acts 13:1–4).

The other leading candidate for authorship is Apollos, whose name was first suggested by Martin Luther and who is favored by many scholars today. Apollos, an Alexandrian by birth, was also a Jewish Christian with notable intellectual and oratorical abilities. Luke tells us that Apollos was "an eloquent man . . . and he was mighty in the Scriptures" (Acts 18:24). We also know that Apollos was associated with Paul in the early years of the church in Corinth (1 Cor 1:12; 3:4–6,22).

Date

Hebrews must have been written before the destruction of Jerusalem and the temple in A.D. 70 because: (1) had it been written after this date, the author surely would have mentioned the temple's destruction and the end of the Jewish sacrificial system; and (2) the author consistently uses the Greek present tense when speaking of the temple and the priestly activities connected with it (see 5:1–3; 7:23,27; 8:3–5; 9:6–9,13,25; 10:1,3–4,8,11; 13:10–11).

Recipients

The letter was addressed primarily to Jewish converts who were familiar with the OT and who were being tempted to revert to Judaism or to Judaize the gospel (cf. Gal 2:14). Some have suggested that these professing Jewish Christians were thinking of merging with a Jewish sect, such as the one at Qumran near the Dead Sea. It has also been suggested that the recipients were from the large number of priests who "were becoming obedient to the faith" (Acts 6:7).

Theme

The theme of Hebrews is the absolute supremacy and sufficiency of Jesus Christ as revealer and as mediator of God's grace. The prologue (1:1–4) presents Christ as God's full and final revelation, far surpassing the limited preliminary revelation given in the OT. The prophecies and promises of the OT are fulfilled in the "new covenant" (or "new testament"), of which Christ is the mediator. From the OT itself, Christ is shown to be supe-

rior to the ancient prophets, to angels, to Moses (the mediator of the former covenant) and to Aaron and the priestly succession descended from Him. Hebrews could be called "the book of better things" since the two Greek words for "better" and "superior" occur 15 times in the letter.

Practical applications of this theme are given throughout the book. The readers are told that there can be no turning back to or continuation in the old Jewish system, which has been superseded by the unique priesthood of Christ. God's people now must look only to Him, whose atoning death, resurrection and ascension have opened the way into the true, heavenly sanctuary of God's presence. Resisting temptations to give up the struggle, believers must persevere in the spiritual contest to which they have committed themselves. Otherwise they may meet with judgment as did the rebellious generation of Israelites in the wilderness.

Outline

I. Prologue: The Superiority of God's New Revelation (1:1–4)

II. The Superiority of Christ to Leaders of the Old Covenant (1:5—7:28)

- A. Christ Is Superior to the Angels (1:5—2:18)
  1. Scriptural proof of superiority (1:5–14)
  2. Exhortation not to ignore the revelation of God in His Son (2:1–4)
  3. Further Scriptural proof of superiority over the angels (2:5–18)
- B. Christ Is Superior to Moses (3:1—4:13)
  1. Demonstration of Christ's superiority (3:1–6)
  2. Exhortation to enter salvation-rest (3:7—4:13)
- C. Christ Is Superior to the Aaronic Priests (4:14—7:28)
  1. Exhortation to hold fast (4:14–16)
  2. Qualifications of a priest (5:1–10)
  3. Exhortation to abandon spiritual lethargy (5:11—6:12)
  4. Certainty of God's promise (6:13–20)
  5. Christ's superior priestly order (ch. 7)

III. The Superior Sacrificial Work of Our High Priest (chs. 8—10)

- A. A Better Covenant (ch. 8)
- B. A Better Sanctuary (9:1–12)
- C. A Better Sacrifice (9:13—10:18)
- D. Exhortations (10:19–39)

IV. Final Plea for Persevering Faith (chs. 11—12)

- A. Examples of Past Heroes of the Faith (ch. 11)
- B. Encouragement for Persevering Faith (12:1–11)
- C. Exhortations for Persevering Faith (12:12–17)
- D. Motivation for Persevering Faith (12:18–29)

V. Conclusion (ch. 13)

- A. Practical Rules for Christian Living (13:1–17)
- B. Request for Prayer (13:18–19)
- C. Benediction (13:20–21)
- D. Personal Remarks (13:22–23)
- E. Greetings and Final Benediction (13:24–25)

God's Final Word in His Son

1 God, after He [a]spoke long ago to the
fathers in [b]the prophets in many portions
and [c]in many ways,
2 [1a]in these last days [b]has spoken to us
[2]in [c]His Son, whom He appointed [d]heir of all
things, [e]through whom also He made the
[3f]world.
3 [1]And He is the radiance of His glory
and the exact [a]representation of His nature,
and [2b]upholds all things by the word of His
power. When He had made [c]purification of
sins, He [d]sat down at the right hand of the
[e]Majesty on high,
4 having become as much better than the
angels, as He has inherited a more excellent
[a]name than they.
5 For to which of the angels did He ever
say,

"[a]YOU ARE MY SON,
TODAY I HAVE BEGOTTEN YOU"?

And again,

"[b]I WILL BE A FATHER TO HIM
AND HE SHALL BE A SON TO ME"?

6 And [1]when He again [a]brings the firstborn into [2b]the world, He says,

"[c]AND LET ALL THE ANGELS OF GOD
WORSHIP HIM."

7 And of the angels He says,

"[a]WHO MAKES HIS ANGELS WINDS,
AND HIS MINISTERS A FLAME OF FIRE."

8 But of the Son *He says,*

"[a]YOUR THRONE, O GOD, IS FOREVER AND
EVER,
AND THE RIGHTEOUS SCEPTER IS THE
SCEPTER OF [1]HIS KINGDOM.
9 "[a]YOU HAVE LOVED RIGHTEOUSNESS AND
HATED LAWLESSNESS;
[b]THEREFORE GOD, YOUR GOD, HAS
[c]ANOINTED YOU
WITH THE OIL OF GLADNESS ABOVE YOUR
COMPANIONS."

10 And,

"[a]YOU, LORD, IN THE BEGINNING LAID THE
FOUNDATION OF THE EARTH,
AND THE HEAVENS ARE THE WORKS OF
YOUR HANDS;
11 [a]THEY WILL PERISH, BUT YOU REMAIN;
[b]AND THEY ALL WILL BECOME OLD LIKE A
GARMENT,
12 [a]AND LIKE A MANTLE YOU WILL ROLL THEM
UP;

1:1 [a]John 9:29; 16:13; Heb 2:2f; 3:5; 4:8; 5:5; 11:18; 12:25 [b]Acts 2:30; 3:21 [c]Num 12:6, 8; Joel 2:28 **2** [1]Or *at the end of these days* [2]Lit *in Son;* or in the person of a Son [3]Lit *ages* [a]Matt 13:39; 1 Pet 1:20 [b]John 9:29 [c]John 5:26, 27; Heb 3:6; 5:8; 7:28 [d]Ps 2:8; Matt 28:18; Mark 12:7; Rom 8:17; Heb 2:8 [e]John 1:3; 1 Cor 8:6; Col 1:16 [f]1 Cor 2:7; Heb 11:3 **3** [1]Lit *Who being* [2]Lit *upholding* [a]2 Cor 4:4 [b]Col 1:17 [c]Titus 2:14; Heb 9:14 [d]Mark 16:19; Heb 8:1; 10:12; 12:2 [e]2 Pet 1:17 **4** [a]Eph 1:21 **5** [a]Ps 2:7; Acts 13:33; Heb 5:5 [b]2 Sam 7:14 **6** [1]Or *again when He brings* [2]Lit *the inhabited earth* [a]Heb 10:5 [b]Matt 24:14 [c]Ps 97:7 **7** [a]Ps 104:4 **8** [1]Late mss read *Your* [a]Ps 45:6 **9** [a]Ps 45:7 [b]John 10:17; Phil 2:9; Heb 2:9 [c]Is 61:1, 3 **10** [a]Ps 102:25 **11** [a]Ps 102:26 [b]Is 51:6; Heb 8:13 **12** [a]Ps 102:26, 27

1:1 *He spoke.* Cf. "has spoken" (v. 2). God is the ultimate author of both the OT and the NT. *long ago.* Prior to Christ's coming, in contrast to "in these last days" (v. 2), the Messianic era inaugurated by the incarnation (see notes on Acts 2:17; 1 Tim 4:1; 1 John 2:18). *to the fathers.* In contrast to "to us" (v. 2). *in the prophets.* All OT writers are here viewed as prophets in that their testimony was preparation for the coming of Christ; cf. "in His Son" (v. 2), a new and unique category of revelation in contrast to that of the prophets. *in many portions and in many ways.* The OT revelation was fragmentary and occasional, lacking fullness and finality.

1:2–3 The superiority of the Son's revelation is demonstrated by seven great descriptive statements about Him: 1. *appointed heir of all things.* The incarnate Son, having performed the work of redemption, was gloriously exalted to the position of the firstborn heir of God, i.e., He received the inheritance of God's estate ("all things"). See Rom 8:17. 2. *through whom also He made the world.* See John 1:3; Col 1:16. 3. *radiance of His glory.* As the brilliance of the sun is inseparable from the sun itself, so the Son's radiance is inseparable from deity, for He Himself is God, the second person of the Trinity (John 1:14,18). 4. *exact representation of His nature.* Jesus is not merely an image or reflection of God. Because the Son Himself is God, He is the absolutely authentic representation of God's being (cf. John 14:9; Col 1:15). 5. *upholds all things.* Christ is not like Atlas, the mythical Greek god who held the world on his shoulders. The Son dynamically holds together all that has been created through Him (Col 1:17). 6. *made purification of sins.* Through His redeeming death on the cross. 7. *sat down at the right hand of the Majesty on high.* Being seated at God's right hand indicates that the work of redemption is complete and that Christ is actively ruling with God as Lord over all (see v. 13; 8:1; 10:12; 12:2; Eph 1:20; Col 3:1; 1 Pet 3:22; see also note on Mark 16:19).

1:4 *much better than the angels.* To most Jews angels were exalted beings, especially revered because they were involved in giving the law at Sinai (see note on 2:2) and to the Jews the law was God's supreme revelation. The Dead Sea Scrolls reflect the expectation that the archangel Michael would be the supreme figure in the Messianic kingdom. Whether the recipients of Hebrews were tempted to assign angels a place above Christ (Messiah) is not known. *name.* To Jews a name stood for the full character of a person in all he was and did (see note on Gen 17:5). The section that follows indicates that this name was "Son"—a name to which no angel could lay claim.

1:5–14 Christ's superiority to angels is documented by seven OT quotations, showing that He is God's Son, that He is worshiped by angels and that, though He is God, He is distinguished from the Father.

1:5 *YOU ARE MY SON, TODAY I HAVE BEGOTTEN YOU.* This passage (Ps 2:7) is quoted in Acts 13:33 as fulfilled in Christ's resurrection (cf. Rom 1:4). *I WILL BE A FATHER TO HIM AND HE SHALL BE A SON TO ME.* Jews acknowledged 2 Sam 7:14 (of which this passage is a quotation) and Ps 2 to be Messianic in their ultimate application (see Luke 1:32–33). This royal personage is neither an angel nor an archangel; He is God's Son.

1:6 *firstborn.* See note on Col 1:15. *LET ALL THE ANGELS OF GOD WORSHIP HIM.* Possibly quoted from Ps 97:7. This statement, which in the OT refers to the Lord God (Yahweh), is here applied to Christ, giving clear indication of His full deity. The very beings with whom Christ is being compared are commanded to proclaim His superiority by worshiping Him.

1:7 *WHO MAKES HIS ANGELS WINDS, AND HIS MINISTERS A FLAME OF FIRE.* Ps 104:4 speaks of the storm wind and the lightning as agents of God's purposes. The Septuagint (the Greek translation of the OT), which the author of Hebrews quotes as the version familiar to his readers, reflects the developing doctrine of angels during the period between the OT and the NT.

1:8 *BUT OF THE SON HE SAYS, "YOUR THRONE, O GOD, IS FOREVER."* The author selects a passage that intimates the deity of the Messianic (and Davidic) King, further demonstrating the Son's superiority over angels.

1:10 *YOU, LORD, IN THE BEGINNING LAID THE FOUNDATION OF THE EARTH.* As in v. 6, a passage addressed to Yahweh ("You, Lord") is applied to the Son.

LIKE A GARMENT THEY WILL ALSO BE
CHANGED.
BUT YOU ARE [b]THE SAME,
AND YOUR YEARS WILL NOT COME TO AN
END."

13 But to which of the angels has He ever
said,
"[a]SIT AT MY RIGHT HAND,
[b]UNTIL I MAKE YOUR ENEMIES
A FOOTSTOOL FOR YOUR FEET"?
14 Are they not all [a]ministering spirits,
sent out to render service for the sake of
those who will [b]inherit [c]salvation?

Give Heed

2 For this reason we must pay much closer
attention to [1]what we have heard, so that
[a]we do not drift away *from it.*
2 For if the word [a]spoken through [b]an-
gels proved [1]unalterable, and [c]every transgression and disobedience received a just
[2d]penalty,
3 [a]how will we escape if we neglect so
great a [b]salvation? [1]After it was at the first
[c]spoken through the Lord, it was [d]confirmed
to us by those who heard,
4 God also testifying with them, both by
[a]signs and wonders and by [b]various [1]mira-
cles and by [2c]gifts of the Holy Spirit [d]accord-
ing to His own will.

Earth Subject to Man

5 For He did not subject to angels [1a]the
world to come, concerning which we are
speaking.
6 But one has testified [a]somewhere, saying,
"[b]WHAT IS MAN, THAT YOU REMEMBER HIM?
OR THE SON OF MAN, THAT YOU ARE
CONCERNED ABOUT HIM?
7 "[a]YOU HAVE MADE HIM [1]FOR A LITTLE WHILE
LOWER THAN THE ANGELS;
YOU HAVE CROWNED HIM WITH GLORY AND
HONOR,
[2]AND HAVE APPOINTED HIM OVER THE
WORKS OF YOUR HANDS;
8 [a]YOU HAVE PUT ALL THINGS IN SUBJECTION
UNDER HIS FEET."
For in subjecting all things to him, He left
nothing that is not subject to him. But now
[b]we do not yet see all things subjected to
him.

Jesus Briefly Humbled

9 But we do see Him who was [a]made
[1]for a little while lower than the angels,
namely, Jesus, [b]because of the suffering of
death [c]crowned with glory and honor, so
that [d]by the grace of God He might [e]taste
death [f]for everyone.
10 For [a]it was fitting for Him, [b]for whom
are all things, and through whom are all
things, in bringing many sons to glory, to

12 [b]Heb 13:8 **13** [a]Ps 110:1; Matt 22:44; Heb 1:3 [b]Josh 10:24; Heb 10:13 **14** [a]Ps 103:20f; Dan 7:10 [b]Matt 25:34; Mark 10:17; Titus 3:7; Heb 6:12 [c]Rom 11:14; 1 Cor 1:21; Heb 2:3; 5:9; 9:28 **2:1** [1]Lit *the things that have been heard* [a]Prov 3:21 **2** [1]Or *steadfast* [2]Or *recompense* [a]Heb 1:1 [b]Acts 7:53 [c]Heb 10:28 [d]Heb 10:35; 11:26 **3** [1]Lit *Which was* [a]Heb 10:29; 12:25 [b]Rom 11:14; 1 Cor 1:21; Heb 1:14; 5:9; 9:28 [c]Heb 1:1 [d]Mark 16:20; Luke 1:2; 1 John 1:1 **4** [1]Or *works of power* [2]Lit *distributions* [a]John 4:48 [b]Mark 6:14 [c]1 Cor 12:4, 11; Eph 4:7 [d]Eph 1:5 **5** [1]Lit *the inhabited earth* [a]Matt 24:14; Heb 6:5 **6** [a]Heb 4:4 [b]Ps 8:4 **7** [1]Or *...him a little lower than...* [2]Two early mss do not contain *And...hands* [a]Ps 8:5, 6 **8** [a]Ps 8:6; 1 Cor 15:27 [b]1 Cor 15:25 **9** [1]Or *a little lower* [a]Heb 2:7 [b]Acts 2:33; 3:13; 1 Pet 1:21 [c]Phil 2:9; Heb 1:9 [d]John 3:16 [e]Matt 16:28; John 8:52 [f]Heb 7:25 **10** [a]Luke 24:26 [b]Rom 11:36

1:13 SIT AT MY RIGHT HAND. See note on vv. 2–3. Ps 110 is applied repeatedly to Jesus in Hebrews (vv. 3,13; 5:6,10; 6:20; 7:3,11, 17,21; 8:1; 10:12–13; 12:2).

1:14 *ministering spirits.* Christ reigns; angels minister as those sent to serve.

2:1–4 The first of five warnings strategically positioned throughout the letter (see 3:7–4:13; 5:11–6:12; 10:19–39; 12:14–29).

2:1 *what we have heard.* The message of the gospel, including that of Christ's person as the God-man and His redemptive work on the cross. *drift away.* From the greater revelation given through the Son.

2:2 *the word spoken through angels.* The law given to Moses at Sinai. That angels were active in giving the law is indicated by Deut 33:2 ("ten thousand holy ones"); Ps 68:17; Acts 7:38,53; Gal 3:19.

2:3 *so great a salvation.* The argument here is from the lesser to the greater, and assumes that the gospel is greater than the law. Thus, if disregard for the law brought certain punishment, disregard for the gospel will bring even greater punishment. *confirmed to us by those who heard.* The eyewitnesses, chiefly the apostles (see 2 Pet 1:16; 1 John 1:1), had vouched for the message first announced by Christ. The author himself apparently was neither an apostle nor an eyewitness (see Introduction: Author).

2:4 *signs and wonders and by various miracles.* God added His confirmation to the gospel message through supernatural acts such as healing the sick (see Acts 3:7–9,11–12,16). *gifts of the Holy Spirit.* Such as the gift of tongues (see Acts 2:4–12). *according to His own will.* See 1 Cor 12:4–11.

2:5–18 An exposition of Ps 8:4–6, which continues to show Christ's superiority over the angels—in fulfilling man's role as sovereign over the earth and in redeeming fallen man, not fallen angels. To accomplish all this, Christ assumed human nature (see vv. 11,14).

2:5 *He did not subject to angels the world to come.* Some think the readers were being enticed to believe that the future kingdom would be under the rule of angelic beings (see note on 1:4). Others see the author trying to dissuade his readers from turning back to Judaism. He shows that Christ, as bearer of the new revelation, is superior to angels who had participated in bringing the revelation at Sinai.

2:6a *one has testified somewhere.* Such a well-known passage as Ps 8:4–6 did not need precise identification.

2:6b–8 Awed by the marvelous order and immensity of God's handiwork in the celestial universe, the psalmist marveled at the high dignity God had bestowed on puny man by entrusting him with dominion over the other creatures (see Gen 1:26–28 and notes).

2:7 ANGELS. See note on Ps 8:5.

2:8 *all things.* God's purpose from the beginning was that man should be sovereign in the creaturely realm, subject only to God. Due to sin, that purpose of God has not yet been fully realized. Indeed, men are themselves "subject to slavery" (v. 15).

2:9 *Him . . . crowned with glory and honor.* See 10:13. Ps 8 is here applied to Jesus in particular. As forerunner of man's restored dominion over the earth, He was made lower than the angels for a while but is now crowned with glory and honor at God's right hand. By His perfect life, His death on the cross and His exaltation, He has made possible for redeemed man the ultimate fulfillment of Ps 8 in the future kingdom, when man will regain sovereignty over creation.

2:10 *many sons to glory.* Those who believe in Christ are made God's children through His only Son (cf. John 1:12–13). *perfect*

[c]perfect the [1][d]author of their salvation
through sufferings.
11 For both He who [a]sanctifies and those
who [b]are [1]sanctified are all [c]from one *Father;*
for which reason He is not ashamed to call
them [d]brethren,
12 saying,
"[a]I WILL PROCLAIM YOUR NAME TO MY
BRETHREN,
IN THE MIDST OF THE CONGREGATION I WILL
SING YOUR PRAISE."
13 And again,
"[a]I WILL PUT MY TRUST IN HIM."
And again,
"[b]BEHOLD, I AND THE CHILDREN WHOM GOD
HAS GIVEN ME."
14 Therefore, since the children share in
[1][a]flesh and blood, [b]He Himself likewise also
partook of the same, that [c]through death He
might render powerless [d]him who had the
power of death, that is, the devil,
15 and might free those who through [a]fear
of death were subject to slavery all their
lives.
16 For assuredly He does not [1]give help to
angels, but He gives help to the [2]descendant
of Abraham.
17 Therefore, He [1]had [a]to be made like
His brethren in all things, so that He might
[b]become a merciful and faithful [c]high priest
in [d]things pertaining to God, to [e]make propitiation for the sins of the people.
18 For since He Himself was [a]tempted in
that which He has suffered, He is able to
come to the aid of those who are tempted.

Jesus Our High Priest

3 Therefore, [a]holy brethren, partakers of a
[b]heavenly calling, consider Jesus, [c]the
Apostle and [d]High Priest of our [e]confession;
2 [1]He was faithful to Him who appointed
Him, as [a]Moses also was in all His house.
3 [a]For He has been counted worthy of
more glory than Moses, by just so much as
the builder of the house has more honor
than the house.
4 For every house is built by someone,
but the builder of all things is God.
5 Now [a]Moses was faithful in all His
house as [b]a servant, [c]for a testimony of those
things [d]which were to be spoken later;
6 but Christ *was faithful* as [a]a Son over
His house—[b]whose house we are, [c]if we

10 [1]Or *leader* [c]Heb 5:9; 7:28 [d]Acts 3:15; 5:31
11 [1]Or *being sanctified* [a]Heb 13:12 [b]Heb 10:10 [c]Acts 17:28 [d]Matt 25:40; Mark 3:34f; John 20:17
12 [a]Ps 22:22
13 [a]Is 8:17 [b]Is 8:18
14 [1]Lit *blood and flesh* [a]Matt 16:17 [b]John 1:14 [c]1 Cor 15:54-57; 2 Tim 1:10 [d]John 12:31; 1 John 3:8
15 [a]Rom 8:15
16 [1]Lit *take hold of angels, but He takes hold of* [2]Lit *seed*
17 [1]Lit *was obligated to be* [a]Phil 2:7; Heb 2:14
17 [b]Heb 4:15f; 5:2 [c]Heb 3:1; 4:14f; 5:5, 10; 6:20; 7:26, 28; 8:1, 3; 9:11; 10:21 [d]Rom 15:17; Heb 5:1 [e]Dan 9:24; 1 John 2:2; 4:10
18 [a]Heb 4:15
3:1 [a]Acts 1:15; Heb 2:11; 3:12; 10:19; 13:22 [b]Phil 3:14 [c]John 17:3 [d]Heb 2:17; 4:14f; 5:5, 10; 6:20; 7:26, 28; 8:1, 3; 9:11; 10:21 [e]2 Cor 9:13; Heb 4:14; 10:23
2 [1]Lit *Being faithful* [a]Ex 40:16; Num 12:7; Heb 3:5
3 [a]2 Cor 3:7-11
5 [a]Ex 40:16; Num 12:7; Heb 3:2 [b]Ex 14:31; Num 12:7 [c]Deut 18:18f [d]Heb 1:1
6 [a]Heb 1:2 [b]1 Cor 3:16; 1 Tim 3:15 [c]Rom 11:22; Heb 3:14; 4:14

. . . *through sufferings.* Christ had not been morally or spiritually imperfect, but His incarnation was completed (perfected) when He experienced suffering. He identified with us on the deepest level of anguish, and so became qualified to pay the price for our sinful imperfection and to become our sympathetic high priest. *author.* The Greek word occurs only four times in the NT: here; 12:2; Acts 3:15; 5:31 ("Prince").

2:11 *who sanctifies . . . who are sanctified.* Christ became man to identify Himself with man and, by His substitutionary sacrifice on the cross, to restore the holiness man had lost. *to call them brethren.* Our brotherhood with Jesus is the brotherhood of the Redeemer with the redeemed, who are truly one with Him.

2:12 *I WILL PROCLAIM YOUR NAME TO MY BRETHREN.* A quotation from Ps 22:22, a psalm describing the sufferings and triumph of God's righteous servant (see introduction to Ps 22). The key phrase is "my brethren," seen here as coming from the lips of the triumphant Messiah.

2:13 *I WILL PUT MY TRUST IN HIM.* An expression of true dependence on God perfectly exemplified in Christ. In Him humanity is seen as it was intended to be. *BEHOLD, I AND THE CHILDREN WHOM GOD HAS GIVEN ME.* Also seen ultimately as an utterance of the incarnate Son. The Father's children are given to the Son to be His brothers (see v. 11).

2:14 *him who had the power of death.* Satan wields the power of death only insofar as he induces people to sin and to come under sin's penalty, which is death (see Ezek 18:4; Rom 5:12; 6:23).

2:15 *free.* See 1 Cor 15:54–57; Rev 1:18.

2:16 *descendant of Abraham.* Christ assumed not angelic nature but human nature, characterized by the descendants of Abraham.

2:17 *a merciful and faithful high priest.* Christ could represent mankind before God only if He became one with them. *make propitiation.* Making propitiation meant turning away God's wrath. See notes on Lev 16:20–22; 17:11. In order for Christ to turn aside the wrath of God against guilty sinners, He had to become one with them and die as a substitute for them.

2:18 *He Himself was tempted.* See note on 4:15.

3:1–4:13 An exposition of Ps 95:7–11, stressing Christ's superiority over Moses and warning against disobedience and unbelief.

3:1 *partakers.* See note on v. 14. *a heavenly calling.* The invitation that comes from heaven and leads to heaven. *Apostle.* Means "one who is sent" (see notes on Mark 6:30; 1 Cor 1:1). Jesus repeatedly spoke of Himself as having been sent into the world by the Father (e.g., Matt 10:40; 15:24; Mark 9:37; Luke 9:48; John 4:34; 5:24,30,36–38; 6:38). He is the supreme apostle, the one from whom all other apostleship flows.

3:2 A comparison of Christ and Moses, both of whom were sent by the Father to lead His people—the one to lead them from bondage under Pharaoh to the promised land, the other to lead them from bondage under the devil (2:14–15) to the Sabbath-rest promised to those who believe (4:3,9). The Sabbath-rest may be heaven, though many hold that it refers primarily to the salvation-rest of Christ's redemption. The analogy focuses on faithful stewardship.

3:3 *the builder . . . has more honor than the house.* Jesus is the actual builder of the house (or household), whereas Moses was simply a part of it.

3:4 *the builder of all things is God.* Jesus is here equated with God, making it beyond question that Christ is greater than Moses.

3:5–6 *in all His house as a servant . . . a Son over His house.* The superiority of Christ over Moses is shown in two comparisons: (1) Moses was a servant, whereas Christ is a son, and (2) Moses was in God's house, i.e., a part of it, whereas Christ is over God's house.

3:6 *whose house we are.* The house is made up of God's people, His household (see Eph 2:19; 1 Pet 2:5). *if we hold fast our confidence and the . . . hope.* Failure to persevere reveals that a person is actually not a child of God, whereas perseverance

hold fast our [d]confidence and the boast of
our [e]hope firm until the end.
7 Therefore, just as [a]the Holy Spirit says,
"[b]TODAY IF YOU HEAR HIS VOICE,
8 [a]DO NOT HARDEN YOUR HEARTS AS [1]WHEN
THEY PROVOKED ME,
AS IN THE DAY OF TRIAL IN THE
WILDERNESS,
9 [a]WHERE YOUR FATHERS TRIED *Me* BY
TESTING *Me*,
AND SAW MY WORKS FOR [b]FORTY YEARS.
10 "[a]THEREFORE I WAS ANGRY WITH THIS
GENERATION,
AND SAID, 'THEY ALWAYS GO ASTRAY IN
THEIR HEART,
AND THEY DID NOT KNOW MY WAYS';
11 [a]AS I SWORE IN MY WRATH,
'THEY SHALL NOT ENTER MY REST.' "

The Peril of Unbelief

12 [a]Take care, brethren, that there not be
in any one of you an evil, unbelieving heart
[1]that falls away from [b]the living God.
13 But [a]encourage one another day after
day, as long as it is *still* called "Today," so
that none of you will be hardened by the
[b]deceitfulness of sin.
14 For we have become partakers of
Christ, [a]if we hold fast the beginning of our
[b]assurance firm until the end,
15 while it is said,
"[a]TODAY IF YOU HEAR HIS VOICE,
DO NOT HARDEN YOUR HEARTS, AS [1]WHEN
THEY PROVOKED ME."
16 For who [a]provoked *Him* when they had
heard? Indeed, [b]did not all those who came
out of Egypt *led* by Moses?
17 And with whom was He angry for forty
years? Was it not with those who sinned,
[a]whose bodies fell in the wilderness?
18 And to whom did He swear [a]that they
would not enter His rest, but to those who
were [b]disobedient?
19 *So* we see that they were not able to
enter because of [a]unbelief.

The Believer's Rest

4 Therefore, let us fear if, while a promise
remains of entering His rest, any one of
you may seem to have [a]come short of it.
2 For indeed we have had good news
preached to us, just as they also; but [a]the
word [1]they heard did not profit them,
because [2]it was not united by faith in those
who heard.
3 For we who have believed enter that
rest, just as He has said,
"[a]AS I SWORE IN MY WRATH,
THEY SHALL NOT ENTER MY REST,"
although His works were finished [b]from the
foundation of the world.
4 For He has said [a]somewhere concerning the seventh *day:* "[b]AND GOD [c]RESTED ON
THE SEVENTH DAY FROM ALL HIS WORKS";
5 and again in this *passage,* "[a]THEY SHALL
NOT ENTER MY REST."
6 Therefore, since it remains for some to
enter it, and those who formerly had good
news preached to them failed to enter
because of [a]disobedience,
7 He again fixes a certain day, "Today,"
saying [1]through David after so long a time
just [a]as has been said before,
"[b]TODAY IF YOU HEAR HIS VOICE,
DO NOT HARDEN YOUR HEARTS."
8 For [a]if [1]Joshua had given them rest, He
would not have spoken of another day after
that.

6 [d]Eph 3:12; Heb 4:16; 10:19, 35 [e]Heb 6:11; 7:19; 10:23; 11:1; 1 Pet 1:3
7 [a]Acts 28:25; Heb 9:8; 10:15 [b]Ps 95:7; Heb 3:15; 4:7
8 [1]Lit *in the provocation* [a]Ps 95:8
9 [a]Ps 95:9-11 [b]Acts 7:36
10 [a]Ps 95:10
11 [a]Ps 95:11; Heb 4:3, 5
12 [1]Lit *in falling* [a]Col 2:8; Heb 12:25 [b]Matt 16:16; Heb 9:14; 10:31; 12:22
13 [a]Heb 10:24f [b]Eph 4:22
14 [a]Heb 3:6 [b]Heb 11:1
15 [1]Lit *in the rebellion* [a]Ps 95:7f; Heb 3:7; 4:7
16 [a]Jer 32:29; 44:3, 8 [b]Num 14:2, 11, 30; Deut 1:35, 36, 38
17 [a]Num 14:29; 1 Cor 10:5
18 [a]Num 14:23; Deut 1:34f; Heb 4:2 [b]Rom 11:30-32; Heb 4:6, 11
19 [a]John 3:18, 36; Rom 11:23; Heb 3:12
4:1 [a]2 Cor 6:1; Gal 5:4; Heb 12:15
2 [1]Lit *of hearing* [2]Two early mss read *they were...faith with those who heard* [a]Rom 10:17; Gal 3:2; 1 Thess 2:13
3 [a]Ps 95:11; Heb 3:11 [b]Matt 25:34
4 [a]Heb 2:6 [b]Gen 2:2 [c]Ex 20:11; 31:17
5 [a]Ps 95:11; Heb 3:11
6 [a]Heb 3:18; 4:11
7 [1]Or *in* [a]Heb 3:7f [b]Ps 95:7f
8 [1]Gr *Jesus* [a]Josh 22:4

---

is the hallmark of His children.

3:7–11 This quotation from Ps 95:7–11 summarizes the inglorious history of Israel under Moses' leadership in the wilderness. Three time periods are alluded to: that of the exodus, that of the psalmist and that of the writing of Hebrews. The example of Israel under Moses was used by the psalmist to warn the Israelites of his day against unbelief and disobedience. In a similar way the author of Hebrews applied the psalmist's warning to the recipients of this letter. The warning also applies today.

3:12 *that falls away from the living God.* To turn away rebelliously (lit. "to become apostate") from God is to turn away from life and to choose death, just as did some of the Israelites who came out of Egypt.

3:13 *as long as it is still called "Today."* See 4:7. This is still the day of divine grace and opportunity to trust God, but it will not last indefinitely.

3:14 *partakers of Christ.* To belong to Him and participate in the blessings (cf. v. 1). *hold fast the beginning of our assurance firm until the end.* Salvation is evidenced by continuing in faith to the end. Such perseverance reveals those who share in Christ (see note on v. 6).

3:16–19 The argument is pursued with a series of rhetorical questions. The important truths are that the people who failed to enter Canaan were the ones who had heard God's promise concerning the land and that they refused to believe what God had promised (v. 19)—an action described as rebellion (v. 16), sin (v. 17) and disobedience (v. 18). Consequently, God in His anger closed the doors of Canaan in the face of that whole generation of Israelites (Num 14:21–35). First-century readers of Hebrews faced a similar danger spiritually.

4:1 *a promise remains of entering His rest.* Salvation is still available. "His rest" cannot refer ultimately to the rest in Canaan offered to the Israelites. That temporary, earthly rest gained under Joshua (see v. 8; see also note on Josh 1:13) pointed to a rest that is spiritual and eternal.

4:3 *we who have believed enter that rest.* Just as entering physical rest in Canaan demanded faith in God's promise, so salvation-rest is entered only by faith in the person and work of Jesus Christ. *His works were finished from the foundation of the world.* God rested from His work on the seventh day of creation (see v. 4; Gen 2:2), and thus His rest is already a reality. The rest God calls us to enter (vv. 10–11) is not our rest but His rest, which He invites us to share.

4:6–8 Israel's going into Canaan under Joshua was a partial and temporary entering of God's rest. That, however, was not the end of entering, as shown in the continuing invitation of Ps 95:7–8.

4:7 *"Today."* See note on 3:13.

9 So there remains a Sabbath rest for the people of God.

10 For the one who has entered His rest has himself also [a]rested from his works, as [b]God did from His.

11 Therefore let us be diligent to enter that rest, so that no one will fall, through *following* the same [a]example of [b]disobedience.

12 For [a]the word of God is [b]living and [c]active and sharper than any two-edged [d]sword, and piercing as far as the division of [e]soul and [e]spirit, of both joints and marrow, and [f]able to judge the thoughts and intentions of the heart.

13 And [a]there is no creature hidden from His sight, but all things are [b]open and laid bare to the eyes of Him with whom we have to do.

14 Therefore, since we have a great [a]high priest who has [b]passed through the heavens, Jesus [c]the Son of God, let us hold fast our [d]confession.

15 For we do not have [a]a high priest who cannot sympathize with our weaknesses, but One who has been [b]tempted in all things as *we are, yet* [c]without sin.

16 Therefore let us [a]draw near with [b]confidence to the throne of grace, so that we may receive mercy and find grace to help in time of need.

10 [a]Rev 14:13 [b]Gen 2:2; Heb 4:4
11 [a]2 Pet 2:6 [b]Heb 3:18; 4:6
12 [a]Jer 23:29; Eph 5:26; Heb 6:5; 1 Pet 1:23 [b]Acts 7:38 [c]1 Thess 2:13 [d]Eph 6:17 [e]1 Thess 5:23 [f]John 12:48; 1 Cor 14:24f
13 [a]2 Chr 16:9; Ps 33:13-15 [b]Job 26:6
14 [a]Heb 2:17 [b]Eph 4:10; Heb 6:20; 8:1; 9:24 [c]Matt 4:3; Heb 1:2; 6:6; 7:3; 10:29 [d]Heb 3:1
15 [a]Heb 2:17 [b]Heb 2:18 [c]2 Cor 5:21; Heb 7:26
16 [a]Heb 7:19 [b]Heb 3:6

5:1 [a]Ex 28:1 [b]Heb 2:17 [c]Heb 7:27; 8:3f; 9:9; 10:11 [d]1 Cor 15:3; Heb 7:27; 10:12
2 [1]Lit *being able to* [2]Or *subject to weakness* [a]Heb 2:18; 4:15 [b]Eph 4:18; Heb 9:7 mg [c]James 5:19; 1 Pet 2:25 [d]Heb 7:28
3 [a]1 Cor 15:3; Heb 7:27; 10:12

The Perfect High Priest

5 For every high priest [a]taken from among men is appointed on behalf of men in [b]things pertaining to God, in order to [c]offer both gifts and sacrifices [d]for sins;

2 [1a]he can deal gently with the [b]ignorant and [c]misguided, since he himself also is [2d]beset with weakness;

3 and because of it he is obligated to offer *sacrifices* [a]for sins, [b]as for the people, so also for himself.

4 And [a]no one takes the honor to himself, but *receives it* when he is called by God, even [b]as Aaron was.

5 So also Christ [a]did not glorify Himself so as to become a [b]high priest, but He who [c]said to Him,

"[d]You are My Son,
Today I have begotten You";

6 just as He says also in another *passage,*

"[a]You are a priest forever
According to [b]the order of
Melchizedek."

7 [1]In the days of His flesh, [2a]He offered up both prayers and supplications with [b]loud

[b]Lev 9:7; 16:6; Heb 7:27; 9:7 **4** [a]Num 16:40; 18:7; 2 Chr 26:18 [b]Ex 28:1; 1 Chr 23:13 **5** [a]John 8:54 [b]Heb 2:17; 5:10 [c]Heb 1:1, 5 [d]Ps 2:7 **6** [a]Ps 110:4; Heb 7:17 [b]Heb 5:10; 6:20; 7:11, 17
7 [1]I.e. during Christ's earthly life [2]Lit *who having offered up* [a]Matt 26:39, 42, 44; Mark 14:36, 39; Luke 22:41, 44 [b]Matt 27:46, 50; Mark 15:34, 37; Luke 23:46

4:9 *there remains a Sabbath rest.* God's rest may still be entered by faith in His Son.

4:10 *rested from his works.* Whereas God rested from the work of creation, the believer ceases his efforts to gain salvation by his own works and rests in the finished work of Christ on the cross. According to some, however, the believer's final rest is in view here (see Rev 14:13).

4:11 *be diligent.* Not a call to earn one's salvation by works, but an exhortation to enter salvation-rest by faith and not follow Israel's sad example in the wilderness.

4:12–13 The reasons for giving serious attention to the exhortation of v. 11.

4:12 *word of God.* God's truth was revealed by Jesus (the incarnate Word; see John 1:1,14), but it has also been given verbally, the word referred to here. This dynamic word of God, active in accomplishing God's purposes, appears in both the OT and the NT (see Ps 107:20; 147:18; Is 40:8; 55:11; Gal 3:8; Eph 5:26; James 1:18; 1 Pet 1:23). The author of Hebrews describes it as a living power that judges as with an all-seeing eye, penetrating a person's innermost being. *soul and spirit . . . joints and marrow.* The totality and depth of one's being.

4:13 *there is no creature hidden from His sight.* The author associates the activity of the word with the activity of God as though they are one and the same—which in a sense they are.

4:14–7:28 An exposition of Ps 110:4, stressing Christ's superiority over Aaron because of a better priesthood.

4:14 *great high priest.* See 2:17; 3:1. The author here begins an extended discussion of the superior priesthood of Christ. *through the heavens.* As the Aaronic high priest on the day of atonement passed from the sight of the people into the most holy place (see Lev 16:15,17), so Jesus passed from the sight of His watching disciples, ascending through the heavens into the heavenly sanctuary, His work of atonement accomplished (Acts 1:9–11). *hold fast our confession.* Suggests that the readers were in danger of letting their faith slip (see similar admonitions in 2:1; 3:6,14).

4:15 *tempted in all things as we are.* See 2:18. The author stresses the parallel between Christ's temptations and ours. He did not have each temptation we have but experienced every kind of temptation a person can have. *yet without sin.* The way in which Christ's temptations were completely different from ours was in the results—His temptations never led to sin (see Matt 4:1–11).

4:16 *Therefore let us draw near.* Because Christ our high priest has experienced human temptation, He stands ready to give immediate and sympathetic help when we are tempted.

5:1–4 The high-priestly office had two specific qualifications: (1) A candidate had to be "taken from among men" (v. 1) and thus be able to represent them before God; and (2) he had to be "called by God" (v. 4).

5:1 *gifts and sacrifices.* See 8:3; 9:9; see also notes on Lev 1:2; 2:1.

5:2 *the ignorant and misguided.* See Is 53:6. Contrast the unintentional sin (as in Lev 4; Num 15:27–29) with defiant rebellion against God (see Num 15:30–31; cf. Heb 6:4–6; 10:26–31).

5:4 *no one takes the honor to himself.* In Christ's day the high-priestly office was in the hands of a family that had bought control of it.

5:5 *Christ did not glorify Himself so as to become a high priest.* The Son was appointed by the Father, as the two prophetic statements cited here show (Ps 2:7; 110:4). His high priesthood, however, was "according to the order of Melchizedek" (v. 6), not in the order of Aaron. *Today I have begotten You.* See notes on 1:5; Ps 2:7–9; cf. Rom 1:4.

5:7 *days of His flesh.* The principal reference here is to Christ's agony in the Garden of Gethsemane. *to the One able to save Him from death.* To the Father. Jesus did not shrink from physical suffering and death but from the indescribable agony of taking mankind's sin on Himself (see Matt 27:46). Although He asked that the cup of suffering might be taken from Him, He

crying and tears to the One [c]able to save Him [3]from death, and He [4]was heard because of His [d]piety.

8 Although He was [a]a Son, He learned [b]obedience from the things which He suffered.

9 And having been made [a]perfect, He became to all those who obey Him the source of eternal salvation,

10 being designated by God as [a]a high priest according to [b]the order of Melchizedek.

11 Concerning [1]him we have much to say, and *it is* hard to explain, since you have become dull of hearing.

12 For though [1]by this time you ought to be teachers, you have need again for someone to teach you [a]the [2b]elementary principles of the [c]oracles of God, and you have come to need [d]milk and not solid food.

13 For everyone who partakes *only* of milk is not accustomed to the word of righteousness, for he is an [a]infant.

14 But solid food is for [a]the mature, who because of practice have their senses [b]trained to [c]discern good and evil.

The Peril of Falling Away

6 Therefore [a]leaving [b]the [1]elementary teaching about the [2]Christ, let us press on to [3c]maturity, not laying again a foundation of repentance from [d]dead works and of faith toward God,

2 of [a]instruction about washings and [b]laying on of hands, and the [c]resurrection of the dead and [c]eternal judgment.

3 And this we will do, [a]if God permits.

4 For in the case of those who have once been [a]enlightened and have tasted of [b]the heavenly gift and have been made [c]partakers of the Holy Spirit,

5 and [a]have tasted the good [b]word of God and the powers of [c]the age to come,

6 and *then* have fallen away, it is [a]impossible to renew them again to repentance, [1b]since they again crucify to themselves the Son of God and put Him to open shame.

7 For ground that drinks the rain which often [1]falls on it and brings forth vegetation useful to those [a]for whose sake it is also tilled, receives a blessing from God;

8 but if it yields thorns and thistles, it is worthless and [a]close [1]to being cursed, and [2]it ends up being burned.

7 [3]Or *out of* [4]Lit *having been heard* [c]Mark 14:36 [d]Heb 11:7; 12:28 **8** [a]Heb 1:2 [b]Phil 2:8 **9** [a]Heb 2:10 **10** [a]Heb 2:17; 5:5 [b]Heb 5:6 **11** [1]Lit *whom* or *which* **12** [1]Lit *because of the time* [2]Lit *elements of the beginning* [a]Gal 4:3 [b]Heb 6:1 [c]Acts 7:38 [d]1 Cor 3:2; 1 Pet 2:2 **13** [a]1 Cor 3:1; 14:20; 1 Pet 2:2 **14** [a]1 Cor 2:6; Eph 4:13; Heb 6:1 [b]1 Tim 4:7 [c]Rom 14:1ff **6:1** [1]Lit *word of the beginning* [2]I.e. Messiah [a]Phil 3:13f [b]Heb 5:12

6:1 [3]Or *perfection* [c]Heb 5:14 [d]Heb 9:14 **2** [a]John 3:25; Acts 19:3f [b]Acts 6:6 [c]Acts 17:31f **3** [a]Acts 18:21

4 [a]2 Cor 4:4, 6; Heb 10:32 [b]John 4:10; Eph 2:8 [c]Gal 3:2; Heb 2:4 **5** [a]1 Pet 2:3 [b]Eph 6:17 [c]Heb 2:5 **6** [1]Or *while* [a]Matt 19:26; Heb 10:26f; 2 Pet 2:21; 1 John 5:16 [b]Heb 10:29 **7** [1]Lit *comes* [a]2 Tim 2:6 **8** [1]Lit *near to a curse* [2]Lit *whose end is for burning* [a]Gen 3:17f; Deut 29:22ff

did not waver in His determination to fulfill the Father's will (see Matt 26:36–46). *He was heard.* His prayer was granted by the Father, who saved Him from death—through resurrection.

5:8 *He learned obedience from the things which He suffered.* He was made "perfect" (v. 9) through suffering (see note on 2:10), namely, His temptation in the wilderness and His ordeal on the cross. Though He was the eternal Son of God, it was necessary for Him as the incarnate Son to learn obedience—not that He was ever disobedient, but that He was called on to obey to an extent He had never before experienced. The temptations He faced were real and the battle for victory was difficult, but where Adam failed and fell, Jesus resisted and prevailed. His humanity was thereby completed, "made perfect" (v. 9), and on the basis of this perfection He could become "the source of eternal salvation" (v. 9; see also 9:12).

5:11 *Concerning him we have much to say.* See ch. 7. *dull of hearing.* Instead of progressing in the Christian life, the readers had become spiritually sluggish and mentally lazy (6:12).

5:12 *by this time.* They were not recent converts. *elementary principles of the oracles of God.* These are listed in 6:1–2 (see note there). Having taken the first steps toward becoming (mature) Christians, they had slipped back to where they started. *solid food.* Advanced teaching such as that given in ch. 7.

5:14 *the mature.* Those who had progressed in spiritual life and had become Christians of sound judgment and discernment. *discern good and evil.* Something neither physical nor spiritual infants can do.

6:1–2 *not laying again a foundation.* Six fundamental doctrines are mentioned: 1. *repentance.* The change of mind that causes one to turn away from sin and/or useless rituals. 2. *faith toward God.* The counterpart of repentance. As repentance is turning away from the darkness of sin, faith is turning to the light of God. 3. *instruction about washings.* Probably refers to different baptisms with which the readers were familiar, such as Jewish baptism of proselytes, John the Baptist's baptism, and the baptism commanded by Jesus (Matt 28:19). 4. *laying on of hands.* Sometimes followed baptism (Acts 8:16–17; 19:5–6). Otherwise laying on of hands was practiced in connection with ordaining or commissioning (see Acts 6:6; 13:3; 1 Tim 5:22; 2 Tim 1:6), healing the sick (see Mark 6:5; 16:18; Luke 4:40; Acts 28:8) and bestowal of blessing (see Matt 19:13–15). 5. *resurrection of the dead.* The resurrection of all people in the last days (see John 5:25–29; 11:25; 2 Cor 4:14). 6. *eternal judgment.* The destiny of those who reject God's saving grace and persist in their sinful ways.

6:1 *elementary teaching about the Christ.* See note on 5:12.

6:3 A common expression of dependence on the will of God (cf. 1 Cor 16:7). Only the Lord can open minds and hearts and bring spiritual maturity.

6:4–6 The most common interpretations of this difficult passage are: 1. It refers to Christians who actually lose their salvation. 2. It is a hypothetical argument to warn immature Hebrew Christians (5:11–14) that they must progress to maturity (see v. 1) or else experience divine discipline or judgment (see vv. 7–8). 3. It refers to professing Christians whose apostasy proves that their faith was not genuine (cf. 1 John 2:19). This view sees chs. 3–4 as a warning based on the rebellion of the Israelites in the wilderness. As Israel could not enter the promised land after spying out the region and tasting its fruit, so the professing Hebrew Christians would not be able to repent if they adamantly turned against "the light" they had received. According to this interpretation, such expressions as "enlightened," "tasted of the heavenly gift" and "partakers of the Holy Spirit" indicate that such persons had come under the influence of God's covenant blessings and had professed to turn from darkness to light but were in danger of a public and final rejection of Christ, proving they had never been regenerated (see 10:26–31 and notes).

6:5 *the age to come.* See Mark 10:30 and note; 1 Tim 6:19.

6:7–8 A short parable graphically illustrating the warning just given (see John 15:5–6; 2 Pet 2:20–22; 1 John 5:16).

Better Things for You

9 But, [a]beloved, we are convinced of better things concerning you, and things that [1]accompany salvation, though we are speaking in this way.

10 For [a]God is not unjust so as to forget [b]your work and the love which you have shown toward His name, in having [c]ministered and in still ministering to the [1]saints.

11 And we desire that each one of you show the same diligence [1]so as to realize the [a]full assurance of [b]hope until the end,

12 so that you will not be sluggish, but [a]imitators of those who through [b]faith and patience [c]inherit the promises.

13 For [a]when God made the promise to Abraham, since He could swear by no one greater, He [b]swore by Himself,

14 saying, "[a]I WILL SURELY BLESS YOU AND I WILL SURELY MULTIPLY YOU."

15 And so, [a]having patiently waited, he obtained the promise.

16 [a]For men swear by [1]one greater *than themselves,* and with them [b]an oath *given* as confirmation is an end of every dispute.

17 [1]In the same way God, desiring even more to show to [a]the heirs of the promise [b]the unchangeableness of His purpose, [2]interposed with an oath,

18 so that by two unchangeable things in which [a]it is impossible for God to lie, we who have [1]taken refuge would have strong encouragement to take hold of [b]the hope set before us.

19 [1]This [a]hope we have as an anchor of the soul, a *hope* both sure and steadfast and one which [b]enters [2]within the veil,

20 [a]where Jesus has entered as a forerunner for us, having become a [b]high priest forever according to the order of Melchizedek.

Melchizedek's Priesthood Like Christ's

7 For this [a]Melchizedek, king of Salem, priest of the [b]Most High God, who met Abraham as he was returning from the slaughter of the kings and blessed him,

2 to whom also Abraham apportioned a tenth part of all *the spoils,* was first of all, by the translation *of his name,* king of righteousness, and then also king of Salem, which is king of peace.

3 Without father, without mother, [a]without genealogy, having neither beginning of days nor end of life, but made like [b]the Son of God, he remains a priest perpetually.

4 Now observe how great this man was to whom Abraham, the [a]patriarch, [b]gave a tenth of the choicest spoils.

5 And those indeed of [a]the sons of Levi who receive the priest's office have commandment [1]in the Law to collect [2]a tenth from the people, that is, from their brethren, although these [3]are descended from Abraham.

6 But the one [a]whose genealogy is not traced from them [b]collected [1]a tenth from

9 [1]Or *belong to* [a]1 Cor 10:14; 2 Cor 7:1; 12:19; 1 Pet 2:11; 2 Pet 3:1; 1 John 2:7; Jude 3 **10** [1]Or *holy ones* [a]Prov 19:17; Matt 10:42; 25:40; Acts 10:4 [b]1 Thess 1:3 [c]Rom 15:25; Heb 10:32-34 **11** [1]Lit *to the full* [a]Heb 10:22 [b]Heb 3:6 **12** [a]Heb 13:7 [b]2 Thess 1:4; James 1:3; Rev 13:10 [c]Heb 1:14 **13** [a]Gal 3:15, 18 [b]Gen 22:16; Luke 1:73 **14** [a]Gen 22:17 **15** [a]Gen 12:4; 21:5 **16** [1]Or *Him who is greater* [a]Gal 3:15 [b]Ex 22:11 **17** [1]Lit *In which* [2]Or *guaranteed* [a]Heb 11:9 [b]Ps 110:4; Prov 19:21; Heb 6:18 **18** [1]Lit *in which* [a]Num 23:19; Titus 1:2 [b]Heb 3:6; 7:19 **19** [1]Lit *Which* hope *we have* [a]Ps 39:7; 62:5; Acts 23:6; Rom 4:18; 5:4, 5; 1 Cor 13:13; Col 1:27; 1 Pet 1:3

19 [2]Or *inside* [b]Lev 16:2, 15; Heb 9:3, 7 **20** [a]John 14:2; Heb 4:14 [b]Ps 110:4; Heb 2:17; 5:6 **7:1** [a]Gen 14:18-20; Heb 7:6 [b]Mark 5:7 **3** [a]Heb 7:6 [b]Matt 4:3; Heb 7:1, 28 **4** [a]Acts 2:29; 7:8f [b]Gen 14:20 **5** [1]Lit *according to* [2]Or *tithes* [3]Lit *have come out of the loins of* [a]Num 18:21, 26; 2 Chr 31:4f **6** [1]Or *tithes* [a]Heb 7:3 [b]Heb 7:1f

6:9 *convinced of better things . . . that accompany salvation.* Although the author has suggested the possibility that some of his readers may still be unsaved, he is confident that God has been at work among them. Changed lives and works of love (v. 10) suggest that many of these persons were indeed regenerated.

6:11 *the full assurance of hope.* See 11:1; 2 Pet 1:10. *until the end.* A call for perseverance in faith as an evidence of salvation.

6:12 *those who through faith and patience inherit the promises.* For examples see ch. 11.

6:13 *God made the promise to Abraham.* The promise of many descendants was made with an oath to emphasize its unchanging character (see Gen 22:16–18). Ordinarily the swearing of an oath belongs to our fallen human situation, in which a man's word is not always trustworthy. God's swearing of an oath was a condescension to human frailty, thus making His word, which in itself is absolutely trustworthy, doubly dependable (see v. 18).

6:15 *having patiently waited.* For 25 years (see Gen 12:3–4; 21:5). *obtained the promise.* The birth of his son Isaac (Gen 17:2; 18:10; 21:5).

6:18 *two unchangeable things.* God's promise, which in itself is absolutely trustworthy, and God's oath confirming that promise. *would have strong encouragement.* Since we look back on the fulfillment of the promise that Abraham saw only in anticipation (11:13; John 8:56).

6:19 *as an anchor of the soul . . . sure and steadfast.* Like an anchor holding a ship safely in position, our hope in Christ guarantees our safety. *within the veil.* Whereas the ship's anchor goes down to the ocean bed, the Christian's anchor goes up into the true, heavenly sanctuary, where he is moored to God himself.

6:20 *a high priest forever according to the order of Melchizedek.* The grand theme that the author is about to develop (ch. 7).

7:1 *Melchizedek.* See Gen 14:18–20 and notes. *king . . . priest.* Of particular significance is Melchizedek's holding both offices, one of the ways in which he prefigured Christ. *Salem.* Jerusalem (see note on Gen 14:18).

7:2 *king of righteousness . . . king of peace.* Messianic titles (see Is 9:6–7; Jer 23:5–6; 33:15–16).

7:3 *Without father . . . nor end of life.* Gen 14:18–20, contrary to the practice elsewhere in the early chapters of Genesis, does not mention Melchizedek's parentage and children, or his birth and death. That he was a real, historical figure is clear, but the author of Hebrews (in accordance with Jewish interpretation) uses the silence of Scripture about Melchizedek's genealogy to portray him as a prefiguration of Christ. Melchizedek's priesthood anticipates Christ's eternal existence and His unending priesthood. Some believe the appearance of Melchizedek to Abraham was a manifestation of Christ before His incarnation, but the comparison "like the Son of God" argues against such an interpretation.

7:4 *observe how great this man was.* The one who collects a tithe is greater than the one who pays it, and "the lesser is blessed by the greater" (v. 7). In both ways Melchizedek was greater than Abraham.

Abraham and [2b]blessed the one who [c]had
the promises.
7 But without any dispute the lesser is
blessed by the greater.
8 In this case mortal men receive tithes,
but in that case one *receives them,* [a]of whom
it is witnessed that he lives on.
9 And, so to speak, through Abraham
even Levi, who received tithes, paid tithes,
10 for he was still in the loins of his father
when Melchizedek met him.
11 [a]Now if perfection was through the
Levitical priesthood (for on the basis of it
[b]the people received the Law), what further
need *was there* for another priest to arise
[c]according to the order of Melchizedek, and
not be designated according to the order of
Aaron?
12 For when the priesthood is changed, of
necessity there takes place a change of law
also.
13 For [a]the one concerning whom [b]these
things are spoken belongs to another tribe,
from which no one has officiated at the altar.
14 For it is evident that our Lord [1]was
[a]descended from Judah, a tribe with reference to which Moses spoke nothing concerning priests.
15 And this is clearer still, if another priest
arises according to the likeness of Melchizedek,
16 who has become *such* not on the basis
of a law of [1a]physical requirement, but
according to the power of [b]an indestructible
life.
17 For it is attested *of Him,*

"[a]YOU ARE A PRIEST FOREVER
ACCORDING TO THE ORDER OF
MELCHIZEDEK."

6 [2]Lit *has blessed* [c]Rom 4:13
8 [a]Heb 5:6; 6:20
11 [a]Heb 7:18f; 8:7 [b]Heb 9:6; 10:1 [c]Heb 5:6; 7:17
13 [a]Heb 7:14 [b]Heb 7:11
14 [1]Lit *has arisen from* [a]Num 24:17; Is 11:1; Mic 5:2; Matt 2:6; Rev 5:5
16 [1]Lit *fleshly commandment;* i.e. to be a descendant of Levi [a]Heb 9:10 [b]Heb 9:14
17 [a]Ps 110:4; Heb 5:6; 6:20; 7:21
18 [a]Rom 8:3; Gal 3:21; Heb 7:11
19 [a]Acts 13:39; Rom 3:20; 7:7f; Gal 2:16; 3:21; Heb 9:9; 10:1 [b]Heb 3:6 [c]Lam 3:57; Heb 4:16; 7:25; 10:1, 22; James 4:8
21 [a]Ps 110:4; Heb 5:6; 7:17 [b]Num 23:19; 1 Sam 15:29; Rom 11:29 [c]Heb 7:23f, 28
22 [a]Ps 119:122; Is 38:14 [b]Heb 8:6
23 [1]Lit *The greater number have become priests...*
24 [a]Is 9:7; John 12:34; Rom 9:5; Heb 7:23f, 28
25 [1]Or *completely* [a]1 Cor 1:21 [b]Heb 7:19 [c]Rom 8:34; Heb 9:24

18 For, on the one hand, there is a setting
aside of a former commandment [a]because of
its weakness and uselessness
19 (for [a]the Law made nothing perfect),
and on the other hand there is a bringing in
of a better [b]hope, through which we [c]draw
near to God.
20 And inasmuch as *it was* not without an
oath
21 (for they indeed became priests without an oath, but He with an oath through the
One who said to Him,

"[a]THE LORD HAS SWORN
AND [b]WILL NOT CHANGE HIS MIND,
'YOU ARE A PRIEST [c]FOREVER' ");

22 so much the more also Jesus has
become the [a]guarantee of [b]a better covenant.
23 [1]The *former* priests, on the one hand,
existed in greater numbers because they
were prevented by death from continuing,
24 but Jesus, on the other hand, because
He continues [a]forever, holds His priesthood
permanently.
25 Therefore He is able also to [a]save [1]for-
ever those who [b]draw near to God through
Him, since He always lives to [c]make intercession for them.
26 For it was fitting for us to have such a
[a]high priest, [b]holy, [c]innocent, undefiled,
separated from sinners and [d]exalted above
the heavens;
27 who does not need daily, like those
high priests, to [a]offer up sacrifices, [b]first for
His own sins and then for the *sins* of the people, because this He did [c]once for all when
He [d]offered up Himself.

26 [a]Heb 2:17 [b]2 Cor 5:21; Heb 4:15 [c]1 Pet 2:22 [d]Heb 4:14
27 [a]Heb 5:1 [b]Lev 9:7; Heb 5:3 [c]Heb 9:12, 28; 10:10 [d]Eph 5:2; Heb 9:14, 28; 10:10, 12

7:11 *on the basis of it.* The Levitical priesthood. *the people received the Law.* The Law of Moses and the priesthood went together. All the people without exception were sinners, subject to the Law's condemnation, and thus were in need of a priestly system to mediate between them and God. *according to . . . Melchizedek . . . not . . . according to . . . Aaron.* Implies that the Aaronic (or Levitical) priesthood was imperfect but that Melchizedek's was perfect. The announcement of the coming one who would be a priest forever (Ps 110:4) was written midway in the history of the Levitical priesthood, which could only mean that the existing system was to give way to something better.

7:16 *become such not on the basis of . . . physical requirement.* In the Law of Moses the priestly function was restricted to the tribe of Levi (Deut 18:1), but Jesus came from the nonpriestly tribe of Judah (vv. 14–15). *the power of an indestructible life.* According to Ps 110:4 the priest in the order of Melchizedek is "a priest forever."

7:18 *a former commandment . . . weakness and uselessness.* The law is holy and good (Rom 7:12), but it is not able to make right those who sin by breaking it, nor can it give the power necessary to fulfill its demands (v. 19a).

7:19 The law was only preparatory (see Gal 3:23–25) and brought nothing to fulfillment (see Matt 5:17). *better hope.* The new covenant is better because it assures us of complete redemption and brings us into the very presence of God. See note on Col 1:5.

7:20 No divine oath was associated with the establishment of the Levitical priesthood. The priesthood pledged in Ps 110 is superior because it was divinely affirmed with an oath.

7:22 *better covenant.* See chs. 8–10.

7:23 *they were prevented by death from continuing.* Impermanence was further evidence of the imperfection of the Levitical order.

7:25 *forever.* May include the ideas of completeness and permanence. Jesus is a perfect high priest forever; so He is able to save completely and for all time. *always lives to make intercession.* His people will never be without a priestly representative (see John 17; 1John 2:1).

7:26 *such a high priest.* One who meets our need for salvation from sin and its consequences.

7:27 *daily.* A reference to the endless repetition of sacrifices throughout the year (see Ex 29:36–42), evidence that these sacrifices never effectively and finally dealt with sin. *first for His own sins.* Christ's priesthood is superior because He has no personal sins for which sacrifice must be made. *once for all.* A key concept in Hebrews (see 9:12,26; 10:2,10). The Levitical priests had to bring daily offerings to the Lord, whereas Jesus sacrificed Himself once for all. *offered up Himself.* Levitical priests offered up only animals; our high priest offered Himself, the perfect substitute—Man for man.

28 For the Law appoints men as high priests [a]who are weak, but the word of the oath, which came after the Law, *appoints* [b]a Son, [c]made perfect forever.

A Better Ministry

8 Now the main point in what has been said *is this:* we have such a [a]high priest, who has taken His seat at [b]the right hand of the throne of the [b]Majesty in the heavens,

2 a [a]minister [1]in the sanctuary and [1]in the [b]true [2]tabernacle, which the Lord [c]pitched, not man.

3 For every [a]high priest is appointed [b]to offer both gifts and sacrifices; so it is necessary that this *high priest* also have something to offer.

4 Now if He were on earth, He would not be a priest at all, since there are those who [a]offer the gifts according to the Law;

5 who serve [a]a copy and [b]shadow of the heavenly things, just as Moses [1]was [c]warned *by God* when he was about to erect the [2]tabernacle; for, "[d]SEE," He says, "THAT YOU MAKE all things ACCORDING TO THE PATTERN WHICH WAS SHOWN YOU ON THE MOUNTAIN."

6 But now He has obtained a more excellent ministry, by as much as He is also the [a]mediator of [b]a better covenant, which has been enacted on better promises.

A New Covenant

7 For [a]if that first *covenant* had been faultless, there would have been no occasion sought for a second.

8 For finding fault with them, He says,

"[a]BEHOLD, DAYS ARE COMING, SAYS THE LORD,
[1]WHEN I WILL EFFECT [b]A NEW COVENANT
WITH THE HOUSE OF ISRAEL AND WITH THE HOUSE OF JUDAH;
9 [a]NOT LIKE THE COVENANT WHICH I MADE WITH THEIR FATHERS
ON THE DAY WHEN I TOOK THEM BY THE HAND
TO LEAD THEM OUT OF THE LAND OF EGYPT;
FOR THEY DID NOT CONTINUE IN MY COVENANT,
AND I DID NOT CARE FOR THEM, SAYS THE LORD.
10 "[a]FOR THIS IS THE COVENANT THAT I WILL MAKE WITH THE HOUSE OF ISRAEL
AFTER THOSE DAYS, SAYS THE LORD:
[1]I WILL PUT MY LAWS INTO THEIR MINDS,
AND I WILL WRITE THEM [b]ON THEIR HEARTS.
AND I WILL BE THEIR GOD,
AND THEY SHALL BE MY PEOPLE.
11 "[a]AND THEY SHALL NOT TEACH EVERYONE HIS FELLOW CITIZEN,
AND EVERYONE HIS BROTHER, SAYING,
'KNOW THE LORD,'
FOR [b]ALL WILL KNOW ME,
FROM [1]THE LEAST TO THE GREATEST OF THEM.
12 "[a]FOR I WILL BE MERCIFUL TO THEIR INIQUITIES,
[b]AND I WILL REMEMBER THEIR SINS NO MORE."

13 [1]When He said, "[a]A new *covenant,*" He

28 [a]Heb 5:2 [b]Heb 1:2 [c]Heb 2:10
8:1 [a]Col 3:1; Heb 2:17; 3:1 [b]Ps 110:1; Heb 1:3
2 [1]Or *of* [2]Or *sacred tent* [a]Heb 10:11 [b]Heb 9:11, 24 [c]Ex 33:7
3 [a]Heb 2:17 [b]Rom 4:25; 5:6, 8; Gal 2:20; Eph 5:2; Heb 5:1; 8:4
4 [a]Heb 5:1; 7:27; 8:3; 9:9; 10:11
5 [1]Lit *has been* [2]Or *sacred tent* [a]Heb 9:23 [b]Col 2:17; Heb 10:1 [c]Matt 2:12; Heb 11:7; 12:25 [d]Ex 25:40
6 [a]1 Tim 2:5 [b]Luke 22:20; Heb 7:22; 8:8; 9:15; 12:24
7 [a]Heb 7:11
8 [1]Lit *And* [a]Jer 31:31 [b]Luke 22:20; 2 Cor 3:6; Heb 7:22; 8:6, 13; 9:15; 12:24
9 [a]Ex 19:5; 24:6-8; Deut 5:2, 3; Jer 31:32
10 [1]Lit *Putting my laws into...* [a]Jer 31:33; Rom 11:27; Heb 10:16 [b]2 Cor 3:3
11 [1]Lit *small to great of them* [a]Jer 31:34 [b]Is 54:13; John 6:45; 1 John 2:27
12 [a]Is 43:25; Jer 31:34; 50:20; Mic 7:18, 19 [b]Heb 10:17
13 [1]Or *In His saying* [a]Luke 22:20; 2 Cor 3:6; Heb 7:22; 8:6, 8; 9:15; 12:24

7:28 *men . . . who are weak.* Because (1) they are mortal and therefore impermanent, v. 23; (2) they are sinful, v. 27; and (3) they could only offer animals, which could never provide a genuine substitute for man, who is made in the image of God (see Gen 1:26–28 and notes). *made perfect forever.* Christ was made perfect in that He faced temptation without succumbing to sin (see notes on 2:10; 5:8). Instead He perfectly obeyed the Father, thereby establishing a perfection that is eternal.

8:1–10:39 The argument of this section grows out of an exposition of Jer 31:31–34 and demonstrates that Christ is the mediator of a "better covenant" (7:22).

8:1 See note on 1:2–3. *the Majesty in the heavens.* A Jewish expression for God (see 1:3).

8:2 *true tabernacle.* In contrast to the tabernacle erected by Moses, which was an imperfect and impermanent copy of the heavenly one. *which the Lord pitched, not man.* The heavenly sanctuary built by God corresponds to the most holy place, the innermost sanctuary in Moses' tabernacle, into which the high priest briefly entered with the blood of atonement once a year (see Lev 16:13–15,34). In the heavenly sanctuary, however, our great high priest dwells eternally as our intercessor (7:25).

8:3 *gifts and sacrifices.* See note on 5:1.

8:4 *He would not be a priest.* By His human birth Jesus belonged to the tribe of Judah, which was not the priestly tribe (see 7:12–14). *those who offer the gifts.* Members of the tribe of Levi. The present tense of the verb "offer," here and elsewhere in the letter, indicates that the temple in Jerusalem was still standing. This letter, therefore, must have been written prior to the temple's destruction in A.D. 70 (see Introduction: Date).

8:5 *a copy and shadow of the heavenly things.* The heavenly reality is the sanctuary of God's presence, into which Christ our high priest entered with His own blood (see 9:11–12). *MAKE all things ACCORDING TO THE PATTERN.* Because both the tabernacle and its ministry were intended to illustrate symbolically the only way sinners may approach a holy God and find forgiveness.

8:6 *He is . . . mediator of a better covenant.* See 9:15; 12:24; 1 Tim 2:5. The new covenant (see vv. 8–12; Jer 31:31–34) that Jesus mediates is superior to the covenant God made through Moses at Sinai (see Ex 24:7–8). *enacted on better promises.* See vv. 10–12.

8:7 *if that first covenant had been faultless.* The line of argument here is similar to that in 7:11, where the Levitical priestly order is shown to be inferior because it was replaced by the order of Melchizedek. Similarly, if the Mosaic covenant were without defect, there would have been no need to replace it with a new covenant. Concerning the fact that there was nothing essentially "wrong" with the Mosaic covenant see note on 7:18.

8:8–12 A quotation from Jer 31:31–34 containing a prophetic announcement and definition of the new covenant, which was to be different from the Mosaic covenant (v. 9). Its superior benefits are: (1) God's laws will become inner principles (v. 10a) that enable His people to delight in doing His will (cf. Ezek 36:26–27; Rom 8:2–4); (2) God and His people will have intimate fellowship (v. 10b); (3) sinful ignorance of God will be removed forever (v. 11); and (4) forgiveness of sins will be an everlasting reality (v. 12).

has made the first obsolete. [b]But whatever is becoming obsolete and growing old is [2]ready to disappear.

The Old and the New

9 Now even the first *covenant* had [a]regulations of divine worship and [b]the earthly sanctuary.

2 For there was [a]a [1]tabernacle prepared, the [2]outer one, in which *were* [b]the lampstand and [c]the table and [d]the [3]sacred bread; this is called the holy place.

3 Behind [a]the second veil there was a [1]tabernacle which is called the [b]Holy of Holies,

4 having a golden [1a]altar of incense and [b]the ark of the covenant covered on all sides with gold, in which was [c]a golden jar holding the manna, and [d]Aaron's rod which budded, and [e]the tables of the covenant;

5 and above it *were* the [a]cherubim of glory [b]overshadowing the mercy seat; but of these things we cannot now speak in detail.

6 Now when these things have been so prepared, the priests [a]are continually entering the [1]outer [2]tabernacle performing the divine worship,

7 but into [a]the second, only [b]the high priest *enters* [c]once a year, [d]not without *taking* blood, which he [e]offers for himself and for the [1f]sins of the people committed in ignorance.

8 [a]The Holy Spirit *is* signifying this, [b]that the way into the holy place has not yet been disclosed while the [1]outer tabernacle is still standing,

9 which *is* a symbol for the present time. Accordingly [a]both gifts and sacrifices are offered which [b]cannot make the worshiper perfect in conscience,

10 since they *relate* only to [a]food and [b]drink and various [c]washings, [d]regulations for the [1]body imposed until [e]a time of reformation.

11 But when Christ appeared *as* a [a]high priest of the [b]good things [1]to come, *He entered* through [c]the greater and more perfect [2]tabernacle, [d]not made with hands, that is to say, [e]not of this creation;

12 and not through [a]the blood of goats and calves, but [b]through His own blood, He [c]entered the holy place [d]once for all, [1]having obtained [e]eternal redemption.

13 For if [a]the blood of goats and bulls and [b]the ashes of a heifer sprinkling those who have been defiled sanctify for the [1]cleansing of the flesh,

14 how much more will [a]the blood of Christ, who through [1b]the eternal Spirit [c]offered Himself without blemish to God, [d]cleanse [2]your conscience from [e]dead works to serve [f]the living God?

15 For this reason [a]He is the [b]mediator of

13 [2]Or *near* [b]2 Cor 5:17; Heb 1:11
9:1 [a]Heb 9:10 [b]Ex 25:8; Heb 8:2; 9:11, 24
2 [1]Or *sacred tent* [2]Lit *first* [3]Lit *loaves of presentation* [a]Ex 25:8, 9; 26:1-30 [b]Ex 25:31-39 [c]Ex 25:23-29 [d]Ex 25:30; Lev 24:5ff; Matt 12:4
3 [1]Or *sacred tent* [a]Ex 26:31-33; 40:3 [b]Ex 26:33
4 [1]Or *censer* [a]Ex 30:1-5; 37:25f [b]Ex 25:10ff; 37:1ff [c]Ex 16:32f [d]Num 17:10 [e]Ex 25:16; 31:18; 32:15; Deut 9:9, 11, 15; 10:3-5
5 [a]Ex 25:18ff [b]Ex 25:17, 20; Lev 16:2; 1 Kin 8:7
6 [1]Lit *first* [2]Or *sacred tent* [a]Num 18:2-6; 28:3
7 [1]Lit *ignorance of the people* [a]Heb 9:3 [b]Lev 16:12ff [c]Ex 30:10; Lev 16:34; Heb 10:3 [d]Lev 16:11, 14 [e]Heb 5:3 [f]Num 15:25; Heb 5:2
8 [1]Lit *first* [a]Heb 3:7 [b]John 14:6; Heb 10:20
9 [a]Heb 5:1 [b]Heb 7:19
10 [1]Lit *flesh* [a]Lev 11:2ff; Col 2:16 [b]Num 6:3 [c]Lev 11:25; Num 19:13; Mark 7:4 [d]Heb 7:16 [e]Heb 7:12
11 [1]Two early mss read *that have come* [2]Or *sacred tent* [a]Heb 2:17 [b]Heb 10:1 [c]Heb 8:2; 9:24 [d]Mark 14:58; 2 Cor 5:1 [e]2 Cor 4:18; Heb 12:27; 13:14
12 [1]Or *obtaining* [a]Lev 4:3; 16:6, 15; Heb 9:19 [b]Heb 9:14; 13:12 [c]Heb 9:24 [d]Heb 7:27 [e]Heb 5:9; 9:15
13 [1]Lit *purity* [a]Lev 16:15; Heb 9:19; 10:4 [b]Num 19:9, 17f
14 [1]Or His *eternal spirit* [2]One early ms reads *our* [a]Heb 9:12; 13:12 [b]1 Cor 15:45; 1 Pet 3:18 [c]Eph 5:2; Heb 7:27; 10:10, 12 [d]Acts 15:9; Titus 2:14; Heb 1:3; 10:2, 22 [e]Heb 6:1 [f]Matt 16:16; Heb 3:12
15 [a]Rom 3:24 [b]1 Tim 2:5; Heb 8:6; 12:24

8:13 *obsolete and growing old.* The announcement of the new covenant clearly proved the impermanence of the one already in existence. To return to the old system would be to return to what is no longer valid or effective.

9:2 *there was a tabernacle prepared.* The tabernacle built under Moses. *lampstand.* Made of hammered gold and placed at the south side of the holy place (Ex 40:24), it had seven lamps that were kept burning every night (Ex 25:31–40). *the table and the sacred bread.* Made of acacia wood overlaid with gold, it stood on the north side of the holy place (Ex 40:22). On it were twelve loaves, arranged in two rows of six (Lev 24:5–6).

9:4 *having a golden altar of incense.* Although the altar of incense stood in the holy place, the author describes it as belonging to the most holy place. His purpose was to show its close relationship to the inner sanctuary and the ark of the covenant (cf. Ex 40:5; 1 Kin 6:22). On the day of atonement the high priest took incense from this altar, along with the blood of the sin offering, into the most holy place (Lev 16:12–14). *ark of the covenant.* A chest made of acacia wood, overlaid inside and out with gold (Ex 25:10–16). *manna . . . rod . . . tables.* See notes on Ex 16:33–34; see also Num 17:8–10.

9:5 *cherubim of glory.* Two winged figures made of pure gold, of one piece with the atonement cover, or mercy seat, and standing at either end of it. It was between them that the glory of God's presence appeared (Ex 25:17–22; Lev 16:2; Num 7:89). *mercy seat.* Fitting exactly over the top of the ark of the covenant, it was a slab of pure gold on which the blood of the sin offering was sprinkled by the high priest on the day of atonement (Lev 16:14–15).

9:7 *once a year.* On the day of atonement (*Yom Kippur*), the tenth day of the seventh month (Lev 16:29,34). For a description of its ritual see Lev 16 and notes.

9:8 *while the outer tabernacle is still standing.* As long as the Mosaic system with its imperfect priesthood and sacrifice remained in effect (8:7–8,13).

9:9 *a symbol for the present time.* The Mosaic tabernacle, though superseded, still provided instruction through its typical (symbolic) significance and was a reminder that returning to the old order was useless, since it could not deal effectively with sin. *gifts and sacrifices.* See note on 5:1.

9:10 *a time of reformation.* The new covenant, with its new priesthood, new sanctuary and new sacrifice, all introduced by Christ.

9:11 *not of this creation.* It was not an earthly tabernacle, but the heavenly sanctuary of God's presence (v. 24; 8:2).

9:12 *He entered . . . once for all.* Not repeatedly year after year as did the Levitical high priests. Christ's sacrifice was perfect, because it was completely effective and did not need to be repeated. After He had obtained eternal redemption, Christ ascended into the true heavenly sanctuary.

9:13 *blood of goats and bulls.* As on the day of atonement. *ashes of a heifer.* As prescribed in Num 19 for those who became ceremonially unclean as a result of contact with a corpse. *cleansing of the flesh.* Such sprinkling, since it was only external, could not cleanse a person from sin.

9:14 *offered Himself.* He was the one who offered the sacrifice, and He was the sacrifice itself. *without blemish.* In the entirety of Christ's being, not just superficially. *cleanse your conscience.* Remove sin's defilement from the very core of our beings.

9:15 *mediator.* See 8:6 and note; 12:24; 1 Tim 2:5. *new cov-*

a [c]new covenant, so that, since a death has
taken place for the redemption of the transgressions that were *committed* under the first
covenant, those who have been [d]called may
[e]receive the promise of [f]the eternal inheritance.
16 For where a [1]covenant is, there must of
necessity [2]be the death of the one who made
it.
17 For a [1]covenant is valid *only* when
[2]men are dead, [3]for it is never in force while
the one who made it lives.
18 Therefore even the first *covenant* was
not inaugurated without blood.
19 For when every commandment had
been [a]spoken by Moses to all the people
according to the Law, [b]he took the [c]blood of
the calves and the goats, with [d]water and
scarlet wool and hyssop, and sprinkled both
[e]the book itself and all the people,
20 saying, "[a]THIS IS THE BLOOD OF THE COV-
ENANT WHICH GOD COMMANDED YOU."
21 And in the same way he [a]sprinkled
both the [1]tabernacle and all the vessels of
the ministry with the blood.
22 And according to the [1]Law, *one may*
[a]almost *say,* all things are cleansed with
blood, and [b]without shedding of blood there
is no forgiveness.
23 Therefore it was necessary for the
[a]copies of the things in the heavens to be
cleansed with these, but [a]the heavenly
things themselves with better sacrifices than
these.
24 For Christ [a]did not enter a holy place
made with hands, a *mere* copy of [b]the true
one, but into [c]heaven itself, now [d]to appear
in the presence of God for us;

15 [c]Heb 8:8 [d]Matt 22:3ff; Rom 8:28f; Heb 3:1 [e]Heb 6:15; 10:36; 11:39 [f]Acts 20:32
16 [1]Or *testament* [2]Lit *be brought*
17 [1]Or *testament* [2]Lit *over the dead* [3]Two early mss read *for is it then...lives?*
19 [a]Heb 1:1 [b]Ex 24:6ff [c]Heb 9:12 [d]Lev 14:4, 7; Num 19:6, 18 [e]Ex 24:7
20 [a]Ex 24:8; Matt 26:28
21 [1]Or *sacred tent* [a]Ex 24:6; 40:9; Lev 8:15, 19; 16:14-16
22 [1]Or *Law, almost all things* [a]Lev 5:11f [b]Lev 17:11
23 [a]Heb 8:5
24 [a]Heb 4:14; 9:12 [b]Heb 8:2 [c]Heb 9:12 [d]Matt 18:10; Heb 7:25
25 [a]Heb 9:7 [b]Heb 9:2; 10:19
26 [1]Or *by His sacrifice* [a]Matt 25:34; Heb 4:3 [b]Heb 7:27; 9:12 [c]Matt 13:39; Heb 1:2 [d]1 John 3:5, 8 [e]Heb 9:12, 14
27 [1]Lit *laid up* [a]Gen 3:19 [b]2 Cor 5:10; 1 John 4:17
28 [a]Heb 7:27 [b]Is 53:12; 1 Pet 2:24 [c]Acts 1:11 [d]Heb 5:9 [e]Heb 4:15 [f]1 Cor 1:7; Titus 2:13
10:1 [1]Lit *image* [2]Two early mss read *they can*

25 nor was it that He would offer Himself
often, as [a]the high priest enters [b]the holy
place [a]year by year with blood that is not his
own.
26 Otherwise, He would have needed to
suffer often since [a]the foundation of the
world; but now [b]once at [c]the consummation
of the ages He has been [d]manifested to put
away sin [1][e]by the sacrifice of Himself.
27 And inasmuch as [a]it is [1]appointed for
men to die once and after this [b]*comes* judgment,
28 so Christ also, having been [a]offered
once to [b]bear the sins of many, will appear
[c]a second time for [d]salvation [e]without *reference to* sin, to those who [f]eagerly await Him.

One Sacrifice of Christ Is Sufficient

10 For the Law, since it has *only* [a]a shadow of [b]the good things to come *and* not
the very [1]form of things, [2]can [c]never, by the
same sacrifices which they offer continually
year by year, [d]make perfect those who draw
near.
2 Otherwise, would they not have ceased
to be offered, because the worshipers, having once been cleansed, would no longer
have had [a]consciousness of sins?
3 But [a]in [1]those *sacrifices* there is a
reminder of sins year by year.
4 For it is [a]impossible for the [b]blood of
bulls and goats to take away sins.
5 Therefore, [a]when He comes into the
world, He says,
"[b]SACRIFICE AND OFFERING YOU HAVE NOT
DESIRED,

[a]Heb 8:5 [b]Heb 9:11 [c]Rom 8:3; Heb 9:9; 10:4, 11 [d]Heb 7:19
2 [a]1 Pet 2:19 **3** [1]Lit *them there is* [a]Heb 9:7 **4** [a]Heb 10:1, 11 [b]Heb 9:12f **5** [a]Heb 1:6 [b]Ps 40:6

enant. See 7:22; 8:6,13. *for the redemption of the transgressions.* Cf. Mark 10:45 and note. By shedding His blood, He paid the necessary price to set them free from the sins committed under the first covenant, i.e., violations of Mosaic law. *the promise of the eternal inheritance.* Defined in the passage from Jeremiah (31:31–34) quoted in 8:8–12. On the basis of Christ's atoning death, this inheritance has become real for those who are called by God (cf. Rom 8:28).

9:16 *covenant.* Here and in v. 17 "covenant" is used in the sense of a last will and testament. (Verse 18 returns to the concept of covenant.) Beneficiaries have no claim on the benefits assigned to them in a will until the testator dies (v. 17). Since Christ's death has been duly attested, "the promise of the eternal inheritance" (v. 15) is available to His beneficiaries.

9:18 *without blood.* Without death—the death of the calves from which Moses took blood to seal the old covenant.

9:19–20 For the ceremony referred to here see Ex 24:4–8.

9:21 See, e.g., Lev 8:10,19,30.

9:23 *copies of the things in the heavens.* See 8:5. Whereas it was necessary for the earthly sanctuary to be purified with animal sacrifices, it was necessary for the heavenly sanctuary to be purified with the better sacrifice of Christ Himself.

9:24 *now to appear in the presence of God for us.* See 7:25; 1 John 2:1.

9:26 *consummation of the ages.* His coming has ushered in the great Messianic era, toward which all history has moved (see note on 1:2; cf. 1 Pet 1:20).

9:27 *appointed . . . to die once and after this comes judgment.* As in the natural order man dies once (v. 27; as a consequence of sin, Rom 5:12), so Christ died once as the perfect sacrifice for sin (v. 28). And as, after death, man faces judgment, so Christ, after His death, will appear again, bringing salvation (see next note) from sin and its judgment.

9:28 *for salvation.* The consummation, in all its glorious fullness, of the salvation purchased for us on the cross (see Rom 8:29–30; Phil 3:20–21; 1 John 3:2–3). *eagerly await Him.* As the Israelites waited for the high priest while he was in the most holy place on the day of atonement (see 2 Tim 4:8; Titus 2:13).

10:1 *the Law.* Together with the Levitical priesthood to which it was closely linked under the Mosaic system (see note on 7:11). *only a shadow.* The sacrifices prescribed by the law prefigured Christ's ultimate sacrifice. Thus they were repeated year after year, the very repetition bearing testimony that the perfect, sin-removing sacrifice had not yet been offered.

10:4 *impossible for the blood of bulls and goats to take away sins.* An animal cannot possibly be a completely adequate substitute for a human being, who is made in God's image.

10:5–6 The different terms used for Levitical sacrifices represent four of the five types of offerings prescribed by the Mosaic Law (Lev 1–7), namely, fellowship, grain, burnt and sin.

10:5 *when He comes into the world, He says.* The words of this psalm of David (40:6–8) express Christ's obedient submission

But [c]A body You have prepared for Me;
6 [a]In whole burnt offerings and
sacrifices for sin You have taken no
pleasure.
7 "[a]Then I said, 'Behold, I have come
(In [b]the scroll of the book it is
written of Me)
To do Your will, O God.' "
8 After saying above, "[a]Sacrifices and
offerings and [b]whole burnt offerings and
sacrifices [c]for sin You have not desired, nor
have You taken pleasure *in them*" (which are
offered according to the Law),
9 then He [1]said, "[a]Behold, I have come to
do Your will.." He takes away the first in
order to establish the second.
10 By [1]this will we have been [a]sanctified
through [b]the offering of [c]the body of Jesus
Christ [d]once for all.
11 Every priest stands daily ministering
and [a]offering time after time the same sacrifices, which [b]can never take away sins;
12 but He, having offered one sacrifice
[a]for [1]sins [b]for all time, [c]sat down at the right
hand of God,
13 waiting from that time onward [a]until
His enemies be made a footstool for His feet.
14 For by one offering He has [a]perfected
[b]for all time those who are [1]sanctified.
15 And [a]the Holy Spirit also testifies to us;
for after saying,
16 "[a]This is the covenant that I will make
with them
After those days, says the Lord:
I will put My laws upon their heart,
And on their mind I will write them,"
He then says,
17 "[a]And their sins and their lawless deeds
I will remember no more."
18 Now where there is forgiveness of
these things, there is no longer *any* offering
for sin.

A New and Living Way

19 Therefore, brethren, since we [a]have
confidence to [b]enter the holy place by the
blood of Jesus,
20 by [a]a new and living way which He
inaugurated for us through [b]the veil, that is,
His flesh,
21 and since *we have* [a]a great priest [b]over
the house of God,
22 let us [a]draw near with a [1]sincere heart
in [b]full assurance of faith, having our hearts
[c]sprinkled *clean* from an evil conscience and
our bodies [d]washed with pure water.
23 Let us hold fast the [a]confession of our
[b]hope without wavering, for [c]He who promised is faithful;
24 and let us consider how [a]to stimulate
one another to love and [b]good deeds,
25 not forsaking our own [a]assembling to-

5 [c]Heb 2:14; 5:7; 1 Pet 2:24
6 [a]Ps 40:6
7 [a]Ps 40:7, 8 [b]Ezra 6:2; Jer 36:2; Ezek 2:9; 3:1f
8 [a]Ps 40:6; Heb 10:5f [b]Mark 12:33 [c]Rom 8:3
9 [1]Lit *has said* [a]Ps 40:7, 8; Heb 10:7
10 [1]Lit *which* [a]John 17:19; Eph 5:26; Heb 2:11; 10:14, 29; 13:12 [b]John 6:51; Eph 5:2; Heb 7:27; 9:14, 28; 10:12 [c]Heb 2:14; 5:7; 1 Pet 2:24 [d]Heb 7:27
11 [a]Heb 5:1 [b]Mic 6:6-8; Heb 10:1, 4
12 [1]Or *sins, forever sat down* [a]Heb 5:1 [b]Heb 10:14 [c]Ps 110:1; Heb 1:3
13 [a]Ps 110:1; Heb 1:13
14 [1]Or *being sanctified* [a]Heb 10:1 [b]Heb 10:12
15 [a]Heb 3:7
16 [a]Jer 31:33; Heb 8:10
17 [a]Jer 31:34; Heb 8:12
19 [a]Heb 3:6; 10:35 [b]Heb 9:25
20 [a]Heb 9:8 [b]Heb 6:19; 9:3
21 [a]Heb 2:17 [b]1 Tim 3:15; Heb 3:6
22 [1]Lit *true* [a]Heb 7:19; 10:1 [b]Heb 6:11 [c]Ezek 36:25; Heb 9:19; 12:24; 1 Pet 1:2 [d]Acts 22:16; 1 Cor 6:11; Eph 5:26; Titus 3:5; 1 Pet 3:21 **23** [a]Heb 3:1 [b]Heb 3:6 [c]1 Cor 1:9; 10:13; Heb 11:11
24 [a]Heb 13:1 [b]Titus 3:8 **25** [a]Acts 2:42

---

to the Father in coming to earth. The Mosaic sacrifices are replaced by submissive obedience to the will of God (v. 7).

10:6 *You have taken no pleasure.* These offerings were only preparatory and temporary, looking forward to the one perfect and final offering—that of the incarnate Son of God.

10:7 *To do Your will.* The will of the Father was the Son's consuming concern (see Luke 22:42; John 4:34).

10:9 *He takes away the first in order to establish the second.* His perfect sacrifice, offered in complete submission, supersedes and therefore replaces all previous sacrifices.

10:10 *been sanctified.* Justified, set apart in consecration to God, and now experiencing the process of continuing sanctification (see "are sanctified," v. 14; see also note on 1 Cor 1:2).

10:11–14 A contrast between "standing" and "sitting." The Levitical priest always stood, because his work was never finished.

10:11 *offering . . . the same sacrifices.* Because these sacrifices were unable to accomplish what they signified. They could not remove sin, and thus had to be offered over and over again.

10:12 *He . . . sat down at the right hand of God.* In contrast to the work of the Levitical priests, which was never done (v. 11; see notes on 1:3,13), Christ's work was completed. His one sacrifice atoned for all sins of all time, making any further sacrifice unnecessary (v. 14).

10:15–18 The two quotations included in these verses are from Jer 31:31–34 (already cited in 8:8–12). The new covenant guarantees that sins will be effectively and completely forgiven (v. 17), with the result that no additional sacrifice for sins is needed (v. 18).

10:19 Another section of practical application and exhortation begins here (see note on 2:1–4). *confidence to enter the holy place.* The way into the sanctuary of God's presence was closed to the people under the former covenant because the blood of animal sacrifices could never completely atone for their sins. Now, however, believers can come to the throne of grace since the perfect priest has offered the perfect sacrifice, atoning for sin once for all.

10:20 *the veil, that is, His flesh.* When Jesus died, the curtain separating the holy place from the most holy place was "torn in two from top to bottom" (Mark 15:38). The curtain symbolizes the body of Christ in terms of suffering: Like the curtain, His body was torn to open the way into the divine presence.

10:22–25 Five exhortations spring from Jesus' provision for our reconciliation to His Father: 1. "Let us draw near." 2. "Let us hold fast the confession of our hope without wavering." 3. "Let us consider how to stimulate one another." 4. "Not forsaking our own assembling together." 5. "Encouraging one another."

10:22 Four conditions are given for drawing "near' to God: 1. *a sincere heart.* Undivided allegiance in the inner being. 2. *full assurance of faith.* Faith that knows no hesitation in trusting in and following Christ. 3. *hearts sprinkled . . . from an evil conscience.* Total freedom from a sense of guilt, a freedom based on the once-for-all sacrifice of Christ. 4. *bodies washed with pure water.* Not an external ceremony such as baptism but a figure for inner cleansing, of which the washing of the priests under the old covenant was a symbol (see Ex 30:19–21; Lev 8:6; see also Ezek 36:25, where a similar expression is used figuratively for the cleansing resulting from the new covenant).

10:23 *without wavering.* Without doubt or hesitation. Some of the readers were tempted to give up the struggle and turn back to a form of Judaism. *confession of our hope.* See 6:18–20. *He who promised is faithful.* Cf. 2 Tim 2:13.

10:25 *not forsaking our own assembling together.* The Greek word translated "forsaking" speaks of desertion and abandon-

gether, as is the habit of some, but [b]encour-
aging *one another;* and all the more as you
see [c]the day drawing near.

Christ or Judgment

26 For if we go on [a]sinning willfully after
receiving [b]the knowledge of the truth, there
no longer remains a sacrifice for sins,
27 but a terrifying expectation of [a]judg-
ment and [b]THE FURY OF A FIRE WHICH WILL CON-
SUME THE ADVERSARIES.
28 [a]Anyone who has set aside the Law of
Moses dies without mercy on *the testimony
of* two or three witnesses.
29 [a]How much severer punishment do
you think he will deserve [b]who has trampled
under foot the Son of God, and has regarded
as unclean [c]the blood of the covenant [d]by
which he was sanctified, and has [e]insulted
the Spirit of grace?
30 For we know Him who said, "[a]VEN-
GEANCE IS MINE, I WILL REPAY." And again,
"[b]THE LORD WILL JUDGE HIS PEOPLE."
31 It is a [a]terrifying thing to fall into the
hands of the [b]living God.
32 But remember [a]the former days, [1]when,
after being [b]enlightened, you endured a great
[c]conflict of sufferings,
33 partly by being [a]made a public spectacle through reproaches and tribulations, and
partly by becoming [b]sharers with those who
were so treated.
34 For you [a]showed sympathy to the prisoners and accepted [b]joyfully the seizure of
your property, knowing that you have for
yourselves [c]a better possession and a lasting
one.
35 Therefore, do not throw away your
[a]confidence, which has a great [b]reward.
36 For you have need of [a]endurance, so

25 [b]Heb 3:13 [c]1 Cor 3:13 **26** [a]Num 15:30; Heb 6:4-8; 2 Pet 2:20f [b]1 Tim 2:4 **27** [a]John 5:29; Heb 9:27 [b]Is 26:11; 2 Thess 1:7 **28** [a]Deut 17:2-6; 19:15; Matt 18:16; Heb 2:2 **29** [a]Heb 2:3 [b]Heb 6:6 [c]Ex 24:8; Matt 26:28; Heb 13:20 [d]Eph 5:26; Heb 9:13f; Rev 1:5 [e]1 Cor 6:11; Eph 4:30; Heb 6:4 **30** [a]Deut 32:35; Rom 12:19 [b]Deut 32:36 **31** [a]2 Cor 5:11 [b]Matt 16:16; Heb 3:12 **32** [1]Lit *in which* [a]Heb 5:12 [b]Heb 6:4 [c]Phil 1:30 **33** [a]1 Cor 4:9; Heb 12:4 [b]Phil 4:14; 1 Thess 2:14 **34** [a]Heb 13:3 [b]Matt 5:12 [c]Heb 9:15; 11:16; 13:14; 1 Pet 1:4f **35** [a]Heb 10:19 [b]Heb 2:2 **36** [a]Luke 21:19; Heb 12:1

36 [1]Lit *the promise* [b]Mark 3:35 [c]Heb 9:15 **37** [a]Hab 2:3; Heb 10:25; Rev 22:20 [b]Matt 11:3 **38** [a]Hab 2:4; Rom 1:17; Gal 3:11 **39** [1]Lit *we are not of shrinking back...but of faith* [2]Or *possessing* **11:1** [1]Or *substance* [2]Or *expected* [3]Or *evidence* [a]Heb

that when you have [b]done the will of God,
you may [c]receive [1]what was promised.
37 [a]FOR YET IN A VERY LITTLE WHILE,
[b]HE WHO IS COMING WILL COME, AND WILL
NOT DELAY.
38 [a]BUT MY RIGHTEOUS ONE SHALL LIVE BY
FAITH;
AND IF HE SHRINKS BACK, MY SOUL HAS NO
PLEASURE IN HIM.
39 But [1]we are not of those who shrink
back to destruction, but of those who have
faith to the [2]preserving of the soul.

The Triumphs of Faith

11 Now faith is the [1a]assurance of *things*
[2b]hoped for, the [3]conviction of [c]things
not seen.
2 For by it the [a]men of old [1b]gained
approval.
3 By faith we understand that the
[1a]worlds were prepared [b]by the word of God,
so that what is seen [c]was not made out of
things which are visible.
4 By faith [a]Abel offered to God a better
sacrifice than Cain, through which he
[b]obtained the testimony that he was righteous, God testifying [1]about his [c]gifts, and
through [2]faith, though [d]he is dead, he still
speaks.
5 By faith [a]Enoch was taken up so that
he would not [b]see death; AND HE WAS NOT
FOUND BECAUSE GOD TOOK HIM UP; for he
obtained the witness that before his being
taken up he was pleasing to God.
6 And without faith it is impossible to
please *Him,* for he who [a]comes to God must

3:14 [b]Heb 3:6 [c]Rom 8:24; 2 Cor 4:18; 5:7; Heb 11:7, 27 **2** [1]Lit *obtained a* good *testimony* [a]Heb 1:1 [b]Heb 11:4, 39 **3** [1]Lit *ages* [a]John 1:3; Heb 1:2 [b]Gen ch 1; Ps 33:6, 9; Heb 6:5; 2 Pet 3:5 [c]Rom 4:17 **4** [1]I.e. by receiving his gifts [2]Lit *it* [a]Gen 4:4; Matt 23:35; 1 John 3:12 [b]Heb 11:2 [c]Heb 5:1 [d]Gen 4:8-10; Heb 12:24 **5** [a]Gen 5:21-24 [b]Luke 2:26; John 8:51; Heb 2:9 **6** [a]Heb 7:19

ment (see Matt 27:46; 2 Cor 4:9; 2 Tim 4:10,16). *the day.* Of the Lord's return (see 1 Thess 5:2,4; 2 Thess 1:10; 2:2; 2 Pet 3:10).

10:26–31 That these verses are a warning to persons ("some," v. 25) deserting the Christian assembly is apparent from the Greek word *gar* ("for") at the beginning of v. 26. See notes on 6:4–8, where the same spiritual condition is discussed.

10:26 *go on sinning willfully.* Committing the sin of apostasy (see v. 29; see also note on 5:2). The OT background is Num 15:27–31. *there no longer remains a sacrifice for sins.* To reject Christ's sacrifice for sins is to reject the only sacrifice; there is no other.

10:27 *judgment and* THE FURY OF A FIRE. See 2 Thess 1:6–9.

10:28 See Deut 17:2–7.

10:29 *blood of the covenant.* See 9:20; 13:20; Ex 24:8; Matt 26:28; Mark 14:24.

10:31 See 12:29.

10:32 *the former days.* Presumably following their first enthusiastic response to the gospel, when they had unflinchingly suffered loss and persecution and were deeply concerned for each other.

10:34 *better possession and a lasting one.* Such as salvation in Christ and future reward (11:10,13–16,26,35; 13:14; Matt 5:11–12; 6:19–21; Rom 8:18).

10:38 *my righteous one shall live by faith.* See note on Hab 2:4.

10:39 *shrink back to destruction.* The opposite of "believe and are saved." The author is confident that those to whom he is writing are, for the most part, among the saved (see note on 6:9).

11:1–12:29 Exhortations based on the preceding expositions of OT passages.

11:2 *men of old.* Heroes of faith in the pre-Christian era, such as those listed in this chapter.

11:4 See Gen 4:2–5. *obtained the testimony that he was righteous.* Both brothers brought offerings to the Lord: Cain from the fruits of the soil, and Abel from the firstborn of his flock. The chief reason for the acceptance of Abel's sacrifice was that he offered it "by faith." It is implied that Cain's sacrifice was rejected because he offered it without faith, as a mere formality (see note on Gen 4:3–4; see also 1 John 3:12).

11:5 *Enoch.* See Gen 5:18–24. TOOK HIM UP. To God's presence (see note on Gen 5:24; cf. Ps 49:15; 73:24).

11:6 *without faith it is impossible to please Him.* That Enoch pleased God is proof of his faith. *believe that He is.* Faith must have an object, and the proper object of genuine faith is God. *who seek Him.* See Jer 29:13.

believe that He is and *that* He is a rewarder
of those who seek Him.
7 By faith [a]Noah, being [b]warned *by God*
about [c]things not yet seen, [1][d]in reverence
[e]prepared an ark for the salvation of his
household, by which he condemned the
world, and became an heir of [f]the righteousness which is according to faith.
8 By faith [a]Abraham, when he was
called, obeyed [1]by going out to a place which
he was to [b]receive for an inheritance; and he
went out, not knowing where he was going.
9 By faith he lived as an alien in [a]the
land of promise, as in a foreign *land,*
[b]dwelling in tents with Isaac and Jacob, [c]fel-
low heirs of the same promise;
10 for he was looking for [a]the city which
has [b]foundations, [c]whose architect and
builder is God.
11 By faith even [a]Sarah herself received
[1]ability to conceive, even beyond the proper
time of life, since she considered Him [b]faith-
ful who had promised.
12 Therefore there was born even of one
man, and [a]him as good as dead [1]at that, *as*
many descendants [b]AS THE STARS OF HEAVEN IN
NUMBER, AND INNUMERABLE AS THE SAND WHICH IS
BY THE SEASHORE.
13 [a]All these died in faith, [b]without
receiving the promises, but [c]having seen
them and having welcomed them from a distance, and [d]having confessed that they were
strangers and exiles on the earth.
14 For those who say such things make it
clear that they are seeking a country of their
own.
15 And indeed if they had been [1]thinking

7 [1]Lit *having become reverent* [a]Gen 6:13-22 [b]Heb 8:5 [c]Heb 11:1 [d]Heb 5:7 [e]1 Pet 3:20 [f]Gen 6:9; Ezek 14:14, 20; Rom 4:13; 9:30
8 [1]Lit *to go out* [a]Gen 12:1-4; Acts 7:2-4 [b]Gen 12:7
9 [a]Acts 7:5 [b]Gen 12:8; 13:3, 18; 18:1, 9 [c]Heb 6:17
10 [a]Heb 12:22; 13:14 [b]Rev 21:14ff [c]Heb 11:16
11 [1]Lit *power for the laying down of seed* [a]Gen 17:19; 18:11-14; 21:2 [b]Heb 10:23
12 [1]Lit *in these things* [a]Rom 4:19 [b]Gen 15:5; 22:17; 32:12
13 [a]Matt 13:17 [b]Heb 11:39 [c]John 8:56; Heb 11:27 [d]Gen 23:4; 47:9; 1 Chr 29:15; Ps 39:12; Eph 2:19; 1 Pet 1:1; 2:11
15 [1]Or *remembering*

15 [a]Gen 24:6-8
16 [1]Lit *ashamed of them, to be* [a]2 Tim 4:18 [b]Mark 8:38; Heb 2:11 [c]Gen 26:24; 28:13; Ex 3:6, 15; 4:5 [d]Heb 11:10; Rev 21:2
17 [a]Gen 22:1-10; James 2:21 [b]Heb 11:13
18 [1]Lit *seed*

of that *country* from which they went out,
[a]they would have had opportunity to return.
16 But as it is, they desire a better *country,*
that is, a [a]heavenly one. Therefore [b]God is
not [1]ashamed to be [c]called their God; for [d]He
has prepared a city for them.
17 By faith [a]Abraham, when he was tested, offered up Isaac, and he who had
[b]received the promises was offering up his
only begotten *son;*
18 *it was he* to whom it was said, "[a]IN
ISAAC YOUR [1]DESCENDANTS SHALL BE CALLED."
19 [1]He considered that [a]God is able to
raise *people* even from the dead, from which
he also received him back [2]as a [b]type.
20 By faith [a]Isaac blessed Jacob and Esau,
even regarding things to come.
21 By faith [a]Jacob, as he was dying,
blessed each of the sons of Joseph, and
[b]worshiped, *leaning* on the top of his staff.
22 By faith [a]Joseph, when he was dying,
made mention of the exodus of the sons of
Israel, and gave orders concerning his bones.
23 By faith [a]Moses, when he was born,
was hidden for three months by his parents,
because they saw he was a beautiful child;
and they were not afraid of the [b]king's edict.
24 By faith Moses, [a]when he had grown
up, refused to be called the son of Pharaoh's
daughter,
25 choosing rather to [a]endure ill-treatment
with the people of God than to enjoy the
passing pleasures of sin,

[a]Gen 21:12; Rom 9:7 **19** [1]Lit *Considering* [2]Or *figuratively speaking;* lit *in a parable* [a]Rom 4:21 [b]Heb 9:9 **20** [a]Gen 27:27-29, 39f **21** [a]Gen 48:1, 5, 16, 20 [b]Gen 47:31; 1 Kin 1:47 **22** [a]Gen 50:24f; Ex 13:19 **23** [a]Ex 2:2 [b]Ex 1:16, 22 **24** [a]Ex 2:10, 11ff **25** [a]Heb 11:37

11:7 *Noah.* See Gen 5:28–9:29. *by which he condemned.* When the flood came, God's word was proved to be true, Noah's faith was vindicated, and the world's unbelief was judged. *righteousness which is according to faith.* Noah expressed complete trust in God and His word, even when it related to "things not seen" (v. 1), namely, the coming flood. Thus Noah also fitted the description of God's righteous ones who live by faith (10:38). His faith in God's word moved him to build the ark in a dry, landlocked region where it was inconceivable that there would ever be enough water to float the vessel.
11:8 *Abraham.* Presented in the NT as the outstanding example of those who live "by faith" and as the "father of all who believe" (Rom 4:11–12,16; Gal 3:7,9,29). *called.* See Gen 12:1–3. His faith expressed itself in obedience (see note on Gen 12:4). *a place which he was to receive.* Canaan. *not knowing where he was going.* He did not go in blind faith, but in complete confidence in God's trustworthiness.
11:10 *city which has foundations.* Speaks of permanence in contrast to the tents in which the patriarch lived (v. 9). This city is "the heavenly Jerusalem" (12:22), "the city which is to come" (13:14) and the "new Jerusalem" (Rev 21:2–4, 9–27). *builder.* Cf. Ps 147:2.
11:11 *Sarah . . . received ability to conceive.* Probably referring to the fact that she was far past childbearing (Gen 18:11–12; see note on Gen 11:30).
11:12 *as good as dead.* Because he was 100 years old (see Gen 21:5; Rom 4:19). *STARS OF HEAVEN . . . SAND . . . BY THE SEASHORE.* See Gen 13:16 and note; 15:5; 22:17; 26:4; 1 Kin 4:20.
11:13 *having seen them and welcomed them from a distance.* By faith they saw—dimly—these heavenly realities and were sure that what they hoped for would ultimately be theirs (see v. 1). *strangers and exiles on the earth.* Their true home was in heaven.
11:14 *country of their own.* That better, heavenly country (v. 16).
11:16 *prepared a city for them.* City (v. 10) and country are interchangeable in the concluding chapters of this letter (vv. 9–10,14–16; 13:14). The ultimate reality is represented by the new Jerusalem in John's vision of the believer's eternal state (see Rev 21:2).
11:17 See Gen 22. *his only begotten son.* See Gen 22:2,12,16; John 3:16; Rom 8:32.
11:19 *God is able to raise . . . the dead.* So strong was Abraham's faith that he actually believed that God would raise Isaac from the dead if necessary, an event that did occur figuratively when the substitute ram was provided (Gen 22:13).
11:20 See Gen 27:27–40.
11:21 See Gen 47:29–31; 48:8–20.
11:22 See Gen 50:24–25. Jacob (v. 21) and Joseph are additional examples of those whose faith is no less strong at death than in life (v. 13).
11:23–29 See Acts 7:20–44.
11:23 *his parents.* See Ex 6:20; Num 26:58–59. *a beautiful child.* See note on Ex 2:2. *the king's edict.* To kill all Israelite males at birth (Ex 1:16,22).
11:25 *pleasures of sin.* The luxury and prestige in Egypt's royal palace.

26 [a]considering the reproach of [1]Christ greater riches than the treasures of Egypt; for he was looking to the [b]reward.

27 By faith he [a]left Egypt, not [b]fearing the wrath of the king; for he endured, as [c]seeing Him who is unseen.

28 By faith he [1a]kept the Passover and the sprinkling of the blood, so that [b]he who destroyed the firstborn would not touch them.

29 By faith they [a]passed through the Red Sea as though *they were passing* through dry land; and the Egyptians, when they attempted it, were [1]drowned.

30 By faith [a]the walls of Jericho fell down [b]after they had been encircled for seven days.

31 By faith [a]Rahab the harlot did not perish along with those who were disobedient, after she had welcomed the spies [1]in peace.

32 And what more shall I say? For time will fail me if I tell of [a]Gideon, [b]Barak, [c]Samson, [d]Jephthah, of [e]David and [f]Samuel and the prophets,

33 who by faith [a]conquered kingdoms, [b]performed *acts of* righteousness, [c]obtained promises, [d]shut the mouths of lions,

34 [a]quenched the power of fire, [b]escaped the edge of the sword, from weakness were made strong, [c]became mighty in war, [c]put foreign armies to flight.

35 [a]Women received *back* their dead by resurrection; and others were tortured, not accepting their [1]release, so that they might obtain a better resurrection;

36 and others [1]experienced mockings and scourgings, yes, also [a]chains and imprisonment.

37 They were [a]stoned, they were [b]sawn in two, [1]they were tempted, they were [c]put to death with the sword; they went about [d]in sheepskins, in goatskins, being destitute, afflicted, [e]ill-treated

38 (*men* of whom the world was not worthy), [a]wandering in deserts and mountains and caves and holes [1]in the ground.

39 And all these, having [1a]gained approval through their faith, [b]did not receive [2]what was promised,

40 because God had [1]provided [a]something better for us, so that [b]apart from us they would not be made perfect.

26 [1]I.e. the Messiah [a]Luke 14:33; Phil 3:7f [b]Heb 2:2 **27** [a]Ex 2:15; 12:50f; 13:17f [b]Ex 2:14; 10:28f [c]Col 1:15; Heb 11:1, 13 **28** [1]Lit *has kept* [a]Ex 12:21ff [b]Ex 12:23, 29f; 1 Cor 10:10 **29** [1]Lit *swallowed up* [a]Ex 14:22-29 **30** [a]Josh 6:20 [b]Josh 6:15f **31** [1]Lit *with* [a]Josh 2:9ff; 6:23; James 2:25 **32** [a]Judg ch 6-8 [b]Judg ch 4, 5 [c]Judg ch 13-16 [d]Judg ch 11, 12 [e]1 Sam 16:1, 13 [f]1 Sam 1:20 **33** [a]Judg ch 4, 7, 11, 14; 2 Sam 5:17-20; 8:1f; 10:12 [b]1 Sam 12:4; 2 Sam 8:15 [c]2 Sam 7:11f [d]Judg 14:6; 1 Sam 17:34ff; Dan 6:22 **34** [a]Dan 3:23ff [b]Ex 18:4; 1 Sam 18:11; 19:10; 1 Kin ch 19; 2 Kin ch 6; Ps 144:10 [c]Judg 7:21; 15:8, 15f; 1 Sam 17:51f; 2 Sam 8:1-6; 10:15ff **35** [1]Lit *redemption* [a]1 Kin 17:23; 2 Kin 4:36f **36** [1]Lit *received the trial of* [a]Gen 39:20; 1 Kin 22:27; 2 Chr 18:26; Jer 20:2; 37:15 **37** [1]One early ms does not contain *they were tempted* [a]1 Kin 21:13; 2 Chr 24:21 [b]2 Sam 12:31; 1 Chr 20:3 [c]1 Kin 19:10; Jer 26:23 [d]1 Kin 19:13, 19; 2 Kin 2:8, 13f; Zech 13:4 [e]Heb 11:25; 13:3 **38** [1]Lit *of* [a]1 Kin 18:4, 13; 19:9 **39** [1]Lit *obtained a testimony* [2]Lit *the promise* [a]Heb 11:2 [b]Heb 10:36; 11:13 **40** [1]Or *foreseen* [a]Heb 11:16 [b]Rev 6:11

11:26 *of Christ.* Although Moses' understanding of the details of the Messianic hope was extremely limited, he chose to be associated with the people through whom that hope was to be realized. *treasures of Egypt.* The priceless treasures of King Tutankhamun's tomb alone included several thousand pounds of pure gold.

11:27 *By faith he left Egypt.* Probably referring to his flight to Midian in the Sinai peninsula when he was 40 years old (Ex 2:11–15; Acts 7:23–29). *not fearing the wrath of the king.* Exodus indicates that Moses was afraid (Ex 2:14) but does not expressly say of whom. And it tells us that he fled from Pharaoh when Pharaoh tried to kill him (Ex 2:15) but does not expressly say that he fled out of fear. The author of Hebrews capitalizes on these features of the account to highlight the fact that, in his fleeing from Pharaoh, Moses was sustained by his trust in God that the liberation of Israel would come and that he would have some part in it. *he endured.* For 40 years in Midian (Acts 7:30). *seeing Him who is unseen.* See vv. 1,6.

11:28 See Ex 12.

11:29 See Ex 14–15. The third and final 40-year period of Moses' life was spent leading the Israelites through the wilderness. At the age of 120 years he died in Moab (Deut 34:1–7).

11:30 Moses' place as leader was taken by Joshua, who brought the people of Israel into the land of promise. *Jericho.* The first great obstacle to their conquest of the land was captured by faith without a battle (Josh 6).

11:31 *Rahab the harlot.* A designation describing her way of life prior to her newly found faith (Josh 2:8–11; 6:22–25); also a testimony to God's boundless grace that can reach down and redeem and raise any sinner to eternal dignity. *welcomed the spies.* See James 2:25.

11:32–38 There were many more heroes of faith before the coming of Christ, and much more could be written of them. Only a small sampling is given, representing all types of men and women of faith. The great quality they had in common was that of overcoming "by faith" (v. 33).

11:32 *if I tell.* Translates the masculine form of a Greek verb, indicating that the author of Hebrews was a man (see Introduction: Author). *Gideon, Barak, Samson, Jephthah.* See Judg 4:6–5:15; 6:11–8:35; 11:1–12:7; 13:24–16:31; 1 Sam 12:11, where Gideon is called Jerubbaal (see Judg 6:32 and note). *Samuel and the prophets.* See Ps 99:6; Jer 15:1; Acts 3:24; 13:20.

11:33 *mouths of lions.* Cf. Daniel in the lions' den (Dan 6).

11:34 *quenched the power of fire.* Cf. Daniel's friends, Shadrach, Meshach and Abednego, in the fiery furnace (Dan 3). *weakness were made strong.* Through God's help (see Rom 8:26; 2 Cor 12:9).

11:35 *Women received back their dead.* Cf. the widow of Zarephath (1 Kin 17:17–24) and the Shunammite woman (2 Kin 4:8–36). *were tortured, not accepting their release, so that they might obtain a better resurrection.* Strongly reminiscent of the heroic Maccabean Jewish patriots of the second century B.C. (see 2 Maccabees 7). But the description applies also to countless believers, known and unknown, who demonstrated their faith in God by persevering in the face of harsh trials and afflictions.

11:37 *They were stoned.* Men like Zechariah, the son of Jehoiada the priest, who were put to death for declaring the truth (2 Chr 24:20–22; Luke 11:51). See also Introduction to Jeremiah: Author and Date. *sawn in two.* Perhaps refers to Isaiah, who, according to tradition, met this kind of death under wicked King Manasseh (see Introduction to Isaiah: Author).

11:39 *all . . . gained approval through their faith.* Not all the heroes of faith experienced immediate triumph over their circumstances, but all were blessed by God.

11:40 *God had provided something better.* The fulfillment for them, as for us, is in Christ who is "the resurrection and the life" (John 11:25–26). *apart from us they would not be made perfect.* All persons of faith who had gone before focused their faith on God and His promises. The fulfillment of God's promises to them has now come in Jesus Christ, and their redemption too is now complete in Him.

Jesus, the Example

12 Therefore, since we have so great a cloud of witnesses surrounding us, let us also [a]lay aside every encumbrance and the sin which so easily entangles us, and let us [b]run with [c]endurance the race that is set before us,

2 [1]fixing our eyes on Jesus, the [2a]author and perfecter of faith, who for the joy set before Him [b]endured the cross, [c]despising the shame, and has [d]sat down at the right hand of the throne of God.

3 For [a]consider Him who has endured such hostility by sinners against Himself, so that you will not grow weary [1b]and lose heart.

A Father's Discipline

4 [a]You have not yet resisted [1b]to the point of shedding blood in your striving against sin;

5 and you have forgotten the exhortation which is addressed to you as sons,

"[a]MY SON, DO NOT REGARD LIGHTLY THE
DISCIPLINE OF THE LORD,
NOR [b]FAINT WHEN YOU ARE REPROVED BY
HIM;

6 [a]FOR THOSE [b]WHOM THE LORD LOVES HE
DISCIPLINES,
AND HE SCOURGES EVERY SON WHOM HE
RECEIVES."

7 It is for discipline that you endure; [a]God deals with you as with sons; for what son is there whom *his* father does not discipline?

8 But if you are without discipline, [a]of which all have become partakers, then you are illegitimate children and not sons.

9 Furthermore, we had [1]earthly fathers to discipline us, and we [a]respected them; shall we not much rather be subject to [b]the Father of [2]spirits, and [c]live?

10 For they disciplined us for a short time as seemed best to them, but He *disciplines us* for *our* good, [a]so that we may share His holiness.

11 All discipline [a]for the moment seems not to be joyful, but sorrowful; yet to those who have been trained by it, afterwards it yields the [b]peaceful fruit of righteousness.

12 Therefore, [1a]strengthen the hands that are weak and the knees that are feeble,

13 and [a]make straight paths for your feet, so that *the limb* which is lame may not be put out of joint, but rather [b]be healed.

14 [a]Pursue peace with all men, and the [b]sanctification without which no one will [c]see the Lord.

15 See to it that no one [a]comes short of the grace of God; that no [b]root of bitterness springing up causes trouble, and by it many be [c]defiled;

16 that *there be* no [a]immoral or [b]godless person like Esau, [c]who sold his own birthright for a *single* meal.

17 For you know that even afterwards, [a]when he desired to inherit the blessing, he

12:1 [a]Rom 13:12; Eph 4:22 [b]1 Cor 9:24; Gal 2:2 [c]Heb 10:36
2 [1]Lit *looking to* [2]Or *leader* [a]Heb 2:10 [b]Phil 2:8f; Heb 2:9 [c]1 Cor 1:18, 23; Heb 13:13 [d]Heb 1:3
3 [1]Lit *fainting in your souls* [a]Rev 2:3 [b]Gal 6:9; Heb 12:5
4 [1]Lit *as far as blood* [a]Heb 10:32ff; 13:13 [b]Phil 2:8
5 [a]Job 5:17; Prov 3:11 [b]Heb 12:3
6 [a]Prov 3:12 [b]Ps 119:75; Rev 3:19
7 [a]Deut 8:5; 2 Sam 7:14; Prov 13:24; 19:18; 23:13f
8 [a]1 Pet 5:9
9 [1]Lit *fathers of our flesh* [2]Or *our spirits* [a]Luke 18:2 [b]Num 16:22; 27:16; Rev 22:6 [c]Is 38:16
10 [a]2 Pet 1:4
11 [a]1 Pet 1:6 [b]Is 32:17; 2 Tim 4:8; James 3:17f
12 [1]Lit *make straight* [a]Is 35:3
13 [a]Prov 4:26; Gal 2:14 [b]Gal 6:1; James 5:16
14 [a]Rom 14:19 [b]Rom 6:22; Heb 12:10 [c]Matt 5:8; Heb 9:28
15 [a]2 Cor 6:1; Gal 5:4; Heb 4:1 [b]Deut 29:18 [c]Titus 1:15
16 [a]Heb 13:4 [b]1 Tim 1:9 [c]Gen 25:33f
17 [a]Gen 27:30-40

12:1 *so great a cloud of witnesses surrounding us.* The imagery suggests an athletic contest in a great amphitheater. The witnesses are the heroes of the past who have just been mentioned (ch. 11). They are not spectators but inspiring examples. The Greek word translated "witnesses" is the origin of the English word "martyr" and means "testifiers, witnesses." They bear testimony to the power of faith and to God's faithfulness. *run with endurance.* See Acts 20:24; 1 Cor 9:24–26; Gal 2:2; 5:7; Phil 2:16; 2 Tim 4:7. The Christian life is pictured as a long-distance race rather than a short sprint. Some Hebrew Christians were tempted to drop out of the contest because of persecution.
12:2 *fixing our eyes on Jesus.* Just as a runner concentrates on the finish line, we should concentrate on Jesus, the goal and objective of our faith (Phil 3:13–14). *author.* See note on 2:10. *perfecter of faith.* Our faith, which has its beginning in Him, is also completed in Him; He is both the start and the end of the race. He is also the supreme witness who has already run the race and overcome. *joy set before Him.* His accomplishing our eternal redemption and His glorification at the Father's "right hand" (see note on 1:3; cf. Is 53:10–12). *endured the cross.* See Phil 2:5–8. *despising the shame.* As with Christ, the humiliation of our present suffering for the gospel's sake is far outweighed by the prospect of future glory (see 11:26; Matt 5:10–12; Rom 8:18; 2 Cor 4:17; 1 Pet 4:13; 5:1,10).
12:3 *consider Him.* He suffered infinitely more than any of His disciples is asked to suffer—a great encouragement for us when we are weary and tempted to become discouraged. *not grow weary.* See Is 40:28–31.
12:4 *not yet resisted to the point of shedding blood.* Though they had suffered persecution and loss of possessions (10:32–34), they had not had to die for the faith.
12:5 *THE DISCIPLINE OF THE LORD.* Suffering and persecution should be seen as corrective and instructive training for our spiritual development as His children.
12:6 *scourges.* The Greek for this verb means "to whip." God chastens us in order to correct our faults.
12:7 *deals with you as with sons.* God's discipline is evidence that we are His children. Far from being a reason for despair, discipline is a basis for encouragement and perseverance (v. 10).
12:11 *it yields the peaceful fruit of righteousness.* When received submissively (see v. 9), discipline is wholesome and beneficial.
12:13 *make straight paths.* A call for upright conduct that will help, rather than hinder, the spiritual and moral welfare of others, especially the "lame" who waver in the Christian faith.
12:14 *sanctification without which no one will see the Lord.* Cf. 1 Pet 1:15–16; 1 John 3:2–3.
12:15 *comes short of the grace of God.* "Falls short of" or "fails to lay hold of" God's grace. Such an experience is described in 2:1–4; 6:4–8. *root of bitterness.* Pride, animosity, rivalry or anything else harmful to others.
12:16 *godless person like Esau.* See Gen 25:29–34. He had no appreciation for true values and was profane in his outlook on life (cf. Phil 3:18–19). He "despised his birthright" (Gen 25:34) by valuing food for his stomach more highly than his birthright.
12:17 *the blessing.* Of the firstborn. The readers were thinking of compromising their faith in order to gain relief from persecution. But to trade their spiritual birthright for temporary ease in this world would deprive them of Christ's blessing. *he was rejected.* Because he only regretted his loss, and did not repent

was rejected, for he found no place for
repentance, though he sought for it with
tears.

Contrast of Sinai and Zion

18 [a]For you have not come to [b]*a mountain*
that can be touched and to a blazing fire, and
to darkness and gloom and whirlwind,
19 and to the [a]blast of a trumpet and the
[b]sound of words which *sound was such that*
those who heard [c]begged that no further
word be spoken to them.
20 For they could not bear the command,
"[a]IF EVEN A BEAST TOUCHES THE MOUNTAIN, IT
WILL BE STONED."
21 And so terrible was the sight, *that* Moses said, "[a]I AM FULL OF FEAR and trembling."
22 But [a]you have come to Mount Zion and
to [b]the city of [c]the living God, [d]the heavenly
Jerusalem, and to [e]myriads of [1]angels,
23 to the general assembly and [a]church of
the firstborn who [b]are enrolled in heaven,
and to God, [c]the Judge of all, and to the
[d]spirits of *the* righteous made perfect,
24 and to Jesus, the [a]mediator of a new
covenant, and to the [b]sprinkled blood, which
speaks better than [c]*the blood* of Abel.

The Unshaken Kingdom

25 [a]See to it that you do not refuse Him
who is [b]speaking. For [c]if those did not
escape when they [d]refused him who
[e]warned *them* on earth, [1]much less *will* we
escape who turn away from Him who [e]*warns*
from heaven.
26 And [a]His voice shook the earth then,
but now He has promised, saying, "[b]YET
ONCE MORE I WILL SHAKE NOT ONLY THE EARTH,
BUT ALSO THE HEAVEN."
27 This *expression,* "Yet once more,"
denotes [a]the removing of those things which
can be shaken, as of created things, so that
those things which cannot be shaken may
remain.
28 Therefore, since we receive a [a]kingdom
which cannot be shaken, let us [1]show gratitude, by which we may [b]offer to God an
acceptable service with reverence and awe;
29 for [a]our God is a consuming fire.

The Changeless Christ

13 Let [a]love of the brethren continue.
2 Do not neglect to [a]show hospitality to
strangers, for by this some have [b]entertained
angels without knowing it.
3 [a]Remember [b]the prisoners, as though
in prison with them, *and* those who are ill-
treated, since you yourselves also are in the
body.
4 [a]Marriage *is to be held* in honor among
all, and the *marriage* bed *is to be* undefiled;
[b]for fornicators and adulterers God will
judge.
5 *Make sure that* your character is [a]free
from the love of money, [b]being content with

18 [a]2 Cor 3:7-13; Heb 12:18ff [b]Ex 19:12, 16ff; 20:18; Deut 4:11; 5:22
19 [a]Ex 19:16, 19; 20:18; Matt 24:31 [b]Ex 19:19; Deut 4:12 [c]Ex 20:19; Deut 5:25; 18:16
20 [a]Ex 19:12f
21 [a]Deut 9:19
22 [1]Or *angels in festive gathering, and to the church* [a]Rev 14:1 [b]Eph 2:19; Phil 3:20; Heb 11:10; Rev 21:2 [c]Heb 3:12 [d]Gal 4:26; Heb 11:16 [e]Rev 5:11
23 [a]Ex 4:22; Heb 2:12 [b]Luke 10:20 [c]Gen 18:25; Ps 50:6; 94:2 [d]Heb 11:40; Rev 6:9, 11
24 [a]1 Tim 2:5; Heb 8:6; 9:15 [b]Heb 9:19; 10:22; 1 Pet 1:2 [c]Gen 4:10; Heb 11:4
25 [1]Lit *much rather we* will not escape... [a]Heb 3:12 [b]Heb 1:1 [c]Heb 2:2f; 10:28f [d]Heb 12:19 [e]Ex 20:22; Heb 8:5; 11:7
26 [a]Ex 19:18; Judg 5:4f [b]Hag 2:6
27 [a]Is 34:4; 54:10; 65:17; Rom 8:19, 21; 1 Cor 7:31; Heb 1:10ff
28 [1]Lit *have* [a]Dan 2:44 [b]Heb 13:15, 21 **29** [a]Deut 4:24; 9:3; Is 33:14; 2 Thess 1:7; Heb 10:27, 31 **13:1** [a]Rom 12:10; 1 Thess 4:9; 1 Pet 1:22 **2** [a]Matt 25:35; Rom 12:13; 1 Pet 4:9 [b]Gen 18:1ff; 19:1f **3** [a]Col 4:18 [b]Matt 25:36; Heb 10:34 **4** [a]1 Cor 7:38; 1 Tim 4:3 [b]1 Cor 6:9; Gal 5:19, 21; 1 Thess 4:6 **5** [a]Eph 5:3; Col 3:5; 1 Tim 3:3 [b]Phil 4:11

---

of his sin (Gen 27, especially v. 41). His sorrow was not "sorrow that is according to the will of God" that "produces a repentance . . . leading to salvation," but "the sorrow of the world" that "produces death" (2 Cor 7:10). *with tears.* See Gen 27:34–38.

12:18–21 These verses describe the awesome occasion when the law was given at Mount Sinai (see Ex 19:10–25; Deut 4:11–12; 5:22–26), a description focusing on the old covenant's tangible mountain, ordinances, terrifying warnings and severe penalties. Believers in Jesus Christ do not have such a threatening covenant, and should not consider returning to it.

12:22 *Mount Zion.* Not the literal Mount Zion (Jerusalem, or its southeast portion), but the heavenly city of God and those who dwell there with Him (see 11:10,13–16; 13:14; Phil 3:20). The circumstances under which the old covenant was given (vv. 18–21) and the features of the new covenant (vv. 22–24) point up the utter contrast between the two covenants, and lay the foundation for one more warning and exhortation to those still thinking of going back to Judaism. *myriads of angels.* See Rev 5:11–12.

12:23 *church of the firstborn.* Believers in general who make up the church: (1) They cannot be angels since these have just been mentioned (v. 22); (2) "firstborn" cannot refer to Christ (though He is called firstborn, 1:6; Rom 8:29; Col 1:15–18; Rev 1:5), since here the Greek word is plural; (3) that their names are recorded in heaven reminds us of the redeemed (see Rev 3:5; 13:8; 17:8; 20:12; 21:27). The designation "firstborn" suggests their privileged position as heirs together with Christ, the supreme firstborn and "heir of all things" (Heb 1:2). *God, the Judge of all.* See 4:13; Rom 14:10–12; 1 Cor 3:10–15; 2 Cor 5:10; Rev 20:11–15. *spirits of the righteous made perfect.* For the most part, these were pre-Christian believers such as Abel (11:4) and Noah (11:7). They are referred to as "spirits" because they are waiting for the resurrection and as "righteous" because God credited their faith to them as righteousness, as He did to Abraham (see Rom 4:3). Actual justification was not accomplished, however, until Christ made it complete by His death on the cross (see 11:40; Rom 3:24–26; 4:23–25).

12:24 *mediator of a new covenant.* See 7:22; 8:6 and note; 8:13; 9:15; 1 Tim 2:5. *speaks better than the blood of Abel.* Abel's blood cried out for justice and retribution (see note on Gen 4:10), whereas the blood of Jesus shed on the cross speaks of forgiveness and reconciliation (9:12; 10:19; Col 1:20; 1 John 1:7).

12:25 *Him who is speaking.* God. *warned them on earth.* At Sinai. *Him who warns from heaven.* Christ, who is both from and in heaven (1:1–3; 4:14; 6:20; 7:26; 9:24). Since we have greater revelation, we have greater responsibility and therefore greater danger (2:2–4).

12:26 *shook the earth.* See Ex 19:18; Judg 5:5; Ps 68:7–8.

12:27 *once more.* During the great end-time upheavals associated with the second advent of Christ. *which cannot be shaken.* The kingdom (v. 28).

12:28 *offer to God . . . acceptable service.* See John 4:19–24; Rom 12:1.

12:29 Cf. Ex 24:17; Deut 9:3.

13:2 *entertained angels without knowing it.* As did Abraham (Gen 18), Gideon (Judg 6) and Manoah (Judg 13).

13:3 *Remember the prisoners . . . and those who are ill-treated.* See 10:32–34; 1 Cor 12:26.

13:5 *love of money.* See Luke 12:15,21; Phil 4:10–13; 1 Tim 6:6–10,17–19. *being content.* See Phil 4:11–12; 1 Tim 6:8.

what you have; for He Himself has said, "[c]I WILL NEVER DESERT YOU, NOR WILL I EVER FORSAKE YOU,"

6 so that we confidently say,

"[a]THE LORD IS MY HELPER, I WILL NOT BE AFRAID.
WHAT WILL MAN DO TO ME?"

7 Remember [a]those who led you, who spoke [b]the word of God to you; and considering the [1]result of their conduct, [c]imitate their faith.

8 [a]Jesus Christ *is* the same yesterday and today and forever.

9 [a]Do not be carried away by varied and strange teachings; for it is good for the heart to [b]be strengthened by grace, not by [c]foods, [d]through which those who [1]were so occupied were not benefited.

10 We have an altar [a]from which those [b]who serve the [1]tabernacle have no right to eat.

11 For [a]the bodies of those animals whose blood is brought into the holy place by the high priest *as an offering* for sin, are burned outside the camp.

12 Therefore Jesus also, [a]that He might sanctify the people [b]through His own blood, suffered [c]outside the gate.

13 So, let us go out to Him outside the camp, [a]bearing His reproach.

14 For here [a]we do not have a lasting city, but we are seeking [b]*the city* which is to come.

God-pleasing Sacrifices

15 [a]Through Him then, let us continually offer up a [b]sacrifice of praise to God, that is, [c]the fruit of lips that [1]give thanks to His name.

16 And do not neglect doing good and [a]sharing, for [b]with such sacrifices God is pleased.

17 [a]Obey your leaders and submit *to them,* for [b]they keep watch over your souls as those who will give an account. [1]Let them do this with joy and not [2]with grief, for this would be unprofitable for you.

18 [a]Pray for us, for we are sure that we have a [b]good conscience, desiring to conduct ourselves honorably in all things.

19 And I urge *you* all the more to do this, [a]so that I may be restored to you the sooner.

Benediction

20 Now [a]the God of peace, who [b]brought up from the dead the [c]great Shepherd of the sheep [1]through [d]the blood of the [e]eternal covenant, *even* Jesus our Lord,

21 [a]equip you in every good thing to do His will, [b]working in us that [c]which is pleasing in His sight, through Jesus Christ, [d]to whom *be* the glory forever and ever. Amen.

22 But [a]I urge you, [b]brethren, [1]bear with

5 [c]Deut 31:6, 8; Josh 1:5 **6** [a]Ps 118:6 **7** [1]Or *end of their life* [a]Heb 13:17, 24 [b]Luke 5:1 [c]Heb 6:12 **8** [a]2 Cor 1:19; Heb 1:12 **9** [1]Lit *walked* [a]Eph 4:14; 5:6; Jude 12 [b]2 Cor 1:21; Col 2:7 [c]Col 2:16 [d]Heb 9:10 **10** [1]Or *sacred tent* [a]1 Cor 10:18 [b]Heb 8:5 **11** [a]Ex 29:14; Lev 4:12, 21; 9:11; 16:27; Num 19:3, 7 **12** [a]Eph 5:26; Heb 2:11 [b]Heb 9:12 [c]John 19:17 **13** [a]Luke 9:23; Heb 11:26; 12:2 **14** [a]Heb 10:34; 12:27 [b]Eph 2:19; Heb 2:5; 11:10, 16; 12:22

15 [1]Lit *confess* [a]1 Pet 2:5 [b]Lev 7:12 [c]Is 57:19; Hos 14:2 **16** [a]Rom 12:13 [b]Phil 4:18 **17** [1]Lit *in order that they may do this* [2]Lit *groaning* [a]1 Cor 16:16; Heb 13:7, 24 [b]Is 62:6; Ezek 3:17; Acts 20:28 **18** [a]1 Thess 5:25 [b]Acts 24:16; 1 Tim 1:5 **19** [a]Philem 22 **20** [1]Lit *in* [a]Rom 15:33 [b]Acts 2:24; Rom 10:7 [c]Is 63:11; John 10:11; 1 Pet 2:25 [d]Zech 9:11; Heb 10:29 [e]Is 55:3; Jer 32:40; Ezek 37:26 **21** [a]1 Pet 5:10 [b]Phil 2:13 [c]Heb 12:28; 1 John 3:22 [d]Rom 11:36 **22** [1]Or *listen to* [a]Acts 13:15; Heb 3:13; 10:25; 12:5; 13:19 [b]Heb 3:1

13:7 *those who led you, who spoke the word of God.* See 2:3; 5:12. *considering the result of their conduct.* Probably indicates that these exemplary leaders were now dead. *imitate their faith.* See 6:12; 1 Cor 4:16; Eph 5:1; 1 Thess 1:6–7; 2:14; 3 John 11.

13:8 *Jesus Christ is the same.* A confession of the changelessness of Christ, no doubt related to the preceding verse. The substance of their former leaders' faith was the unchanging Christ. *yesterday.* Probably the days of Christ's life on earth, when the eyewitnesses observed Him (2:3). *today.* The Christ whom the eyewitnesses saw was still the same, and what they had said about Him was still true. *forever.* And it will always be true. To compromise His absolute supremacy by returning to the inferior Aaronic priesthood and sacrifices (see chs. 5–10) is to undermine the gospel.

13:9 *not by foods.* As the legalistic Judaizers were teaching. The old Mosaic order was done away with at the cross and must not be revived.

13:10 *We have an altar.* Probably refers to the cross, which marked the end of the whole Aaronic priesthood and its replacement by the order of Melchizedek, of which Christ is the unique and only priest. *no right to eat.* The priests could not eat of the sacrifice on the day of atonement, but we can partake of our sacrifice, so to speak—through spiritual reception of Christ by faith (see John 6:48–58). We have a higher privilege than the priests under the old covenant had.

13:11 *burned outside the camp.* See Lev 4:12 and note; 16:27.

13:12 *Jesus also . . . suffered outside the gate.* Christ's death outside Jerusalem represented the removal of sin, as had the removal of the bodies of sacrificial animals outside the camp of Israel.

13:13 *go out to Him outside the camp.* Calls for separation from Judaism to Christ. As He died in disgrace outside the city, so the readers should be willing to be disgraced by turning unequivocally from Judaism to Christ.

13:14 *city that is to come.* See notes on 11:10,14,16.

13:15 *sacrifice of praise.* "Sacrifice" is used metaphorically here to represent an offering to God (see Rom 12:1; Phil 4:18). Animal offerings are now obsolete.

13:17 *your leaders.* Their present leaders, as distinct from their first ones, now dead, mentioned in v. 7. *submit to them.* Dictatorial leadership is not condoned by this command (see 3 John 9–10), but respect for authority, orderliness and discipline in the church are taught throughout the NT.

13:19 *restored to you.* The identity and whereabouts of the writer are not known to us, but "restored" suggests that somehow he had been delayed in visiting those to whom he was writing, perhaps by his current ministry. That he was not under arrest is clear from v. 23.

13:20–21 This benediction provides a fitting conclusion to the letter. *God of peace.* A title for God used frequently in benedictions (see Rom 15:33; 16:20; Phil 4:9; 1 Thess 5:23).

13:20 *great Shepherd.* See, e.g., Ps 23; Is 40:11; Ezek 34:11–16, 23; 37:24; John 10:2–3,11,14,27; 1 Pet 2:25; 5:4. *eternal covenant.* The new covenant (see note on 8:8–12). What Jeremiah designates as the new covenant in 31:31 he describes as everlasting in 32:40 (see also Is 55:3 and note; 61:8). On the blood of the covenant see note on 10:29.

13:21 *every good thing.* Such as faith, faithfulness, obedience and perseverance.

13:22–25 A postscript.

13:22 *word of exhortation.* The main thrust of the letter is to go on in Christian maturity and not fall away from Christ. *briefly.*

[2]this [b]word of exhortation, for [c]I have written to you briefly.
23 [1]Take notice that [a]our brother Timothy
has been released, with whom, if he comes
soon, I will see you.
24 Greet [a]all of your leaders and all the
[1b]saints. Those from [c]Italy greet you.
25 [a]Grace be with you all.

22 [2]Lit *the* [b]Heb 3:1 [c]1 Pet 5:12 **23** [1]Lit *Know* [a]Acts 16:1; Col 1:1 **24** [1]Or *holy ones* [a]1 Cor 16:16; Heb 13:7, 17 [b]Acts 9:13 [c]Acts 18:2 **25** [a]Col 4:18

Compared to the lengthy treatise that would be necessary to explain adequately the superiority of Christ.

13:23 *Timothy has been released.* Timothy, who was well known to the recipients of the letter, had recently been released from prison.

13:24 *leaders.* Mentioned in v. 17. *Those from Italy.* Does not mean that this letter was written either to or from Italy. The writer is passing on greetings from some Italian believers.

The General Letters

The seven letters following Hebrews—James, 1,2 Peter, 1,2,3 John and Jude—have often been designated as the General Letters. This term goes back to the early church historian Eusebius (c. A.D. 265–340), who in his *Ecclesiastical History* (2.23–25) first referred to these seven letters as Catholic Letters, using the word "catholic" to mean "universal."

The letters so designated may be said to be, for the most part, addressed to general audiences rather than to specific persons or localized groups. 2 and 3 John, the two letters that seem most obviously addressed to individuals, have long been viewed as appendages of 1 John, which is clearly general in its address. However, when compared with Paul's letters, all these letters except 3 John are clearly general in nature. By contrast, Paul addresses his letters to such recipients as the saints at Philippi, or the churches of Galatia, or Timothy or Titus.

As Eusebius noted long ago, one interesting fact connected with the General Letters is that most of them were at one time among the disputed books of the NT. James, 2 Peter, 2 John, 3 John and Jude were all questioned extensively before being admitted to the canon of Scripture.

James

INTRODUCTION

Author

The author identifies himself as James (1:1), and he was probably the brother of Jesus and leader of the Jerusalem council (Acts 15). Four men in the NT have this name. The author of this letter could not have been the apostle James, who died too early (A.D. 44) to have written it. The other two men named James had neither the stature nor the influence that the writer of this letter had.

James was one of several brothers of Christ and was probably the oldest since he heads the list in Matt 13:55. At first he did not believe in Jesus and even challenged Him and misunderstood His mission (John 7:2–5). Later he became very prominent in the church:

1. He was one of the select individuals Christ appeared to after His resurrection (1 Cor 15:7).
2. Paul called him a "pillar" of the church (Gal 2:9).
3. Paul, on his first post-conversion visit to Jerusalem, saw James (Gal 1:19).
4. Paul did the same on his last visit (Acts 21:18).
5. When Peter was rescued from prison, he told his friends to tell James (Acts 12:17).
6. James was a leader in the important council of Jerusalem (Acts 15:13).
7. Jude could identify himself simply as a "brother of James" (Jude 1:1), so well known was James.

He was martyred c. A.D. 62.

Date

Some date the letter in the early 60s. There are indications, however, that it was written before A.D. 50:

1. Its distinctively Jewish nature suggests that it was composed when the church was still predominantly Jewish.
2. It reflects a simple church order—officers of the church are called "elders" (5:14) and "teachers" (3:1).
3. No reference is made to the controversy over Gentile circumcision.
4. The Greek term *synagoge* ("synagogue," "meeting," or "assembly") is used to designate the meeting or meeting place of the church (2:2).

If this early dating is correct, this letter is the earliest of all the NT writings—with the possible exception of Galatians.

Recipients

The recipients are identified explicitly only in 1:1: "the twelve tribes who are dispersed abroad." Some hold that this expression refers to Christians in general, but the term "twelve tribes" would more naturally apply to Jewish Christians. Furthermore, a Jewish audience would be more in keeping with the obviously Jewish nature of the letter (e.g., the use of the Hebrew title for God, *kyrios sabaoth,* "Lord of Sabaoth," 5:4). That the recipients were Christians is clear from 2:1; 5:7–8. It has been plausibly suggested that these were believers from the early Jerusalem church who, after Stephen's death, were scattered as far as Phoenicia, Cyprus and Syrian Antioch (Acts 8:1; 11:19). This would account for James's references to trials and oppression, his intimate knowledge of the readers and the authoritative nature of the letter. As leader of the Jerusalem church, James wrote as pastor to instruct and encourage his dispersed people in the face of their difficulties.

Distinctive Characteristics

Characteristics that make the letter distinctive are: (1) its unmistakably Jewish nature; (2) its emphasis on vital Christianity, characterized by good deeds and a faith that works (genuine faith must and will be accompanied by a consistent life-style); (3) its simple organization; (4) its familiarity with Jesus' teachings preserved

in the Sermon on the Mount (compare 2:5 with Matt 5:3; 3:10–12 with Matt 7:15–20; 3:18 with Matt 5:9; 5:2–3 with Matt 6:19–20; 5:12 with Matt 5:33–37); (5) its similarity to OT wisdom writings such as Proverbs; (6) its excellent Greek.

Outline

- I. Greetings (1:1)
- II. Trials and Temptations (1:2–18)
  - A. The Testing of Faith (1:2–12)
  - B. The Source of Temptation (1:13–18)
- III. Listening and Doing (1:19–27)
- IV. Favoritism Forbidden (2:1–13)
- V. Faith and Deeds (2:14–26)
- VI. Taming the Tongue (3:1–12)
- VII. Two Kinds of Wisdom (3:13–18)
- VIII. Warning against Worldliness (ch. 4)
  - A. Quarrelsomeness (4:1–3)
  - B. Spiritual Unfaithfulness (4:4)
  - C. Pride (4:5–10)
  - D. Slander (4:11–12)
  - E. Boasting (4:13–17)
- IX. Warning to Rich Oppressors (5:1–6)
- X. Miscellaneous Exhortations (5:7–20)
  - A. Concerning Patience in Suffering (5:7–11)
  - B. Concerning Oaths (5:12)
  - C. Concerning the Prayer of Faith (5:13–18)
  - D. Concerning Those Who Wander from the Truth (5:19–20)

Testing Your Faith

1 [1a]James, a [b]bond-servant of God and [c]of the Lord Jesus Christ,

To [d]the twelve tribes who are [2e]dispersed abroad: [f]Greetings.

2 [a]Consider it all joy, my brethren, when you encounter [b]various [1]trials,

3 knowing that [a]the testing of your [b]faith produces [1c]endurance.

4 And let [1a]endurance have *its* perfect [2]result, so that you may be [3b]perfect and complete, lacking in nothing.

5 But if any of you [a]lacks wisdom, let him ask of God, who gives to all generously and [1]without reproach, and [b]it will be given to him.

6 But he must [a]ask in faith [b]without any doubting, for the one who doubts is like the surf of the sea, [c]driven and tossed by the wind.

7 For that man ought not to expect that he will receive anything from the Lord,

8 *being* a [1a]double-minded man, [b]unstable in all his ways.

9 [a]But the [1]brother of humble circumstances is to glory in his high position;

10 and the rich man *is to glory* in his humiliation, because [a]like [1]flowering grass he will pass away.

11 For the sun rises with [1a]a scorching wind and [b]withers the grass; and its flower falls off and the beauty of its appearance is destroyed; so too the rich man in the midst of his pursuits will fade away.

12 [a]Blessed is a man who perseveres under trial; for once he has [1]been approved, he will receive [b]the crown of life which *the Lord* [c]has promised to those who [d]love Him.

13 Let no one say when he is tempted, "[a]I am being tempted [1]by God"; for God cannot be tempted [2]by evil, and He Himself does not tempt anyone.

14 But each one is tempted when he is carried away and enticed by his own lust.

15 Then [a]when lust has conceived, it gives birth to sin; and when [b]sin [1]is accomplished, it brings forth death.

16 [a]Do not be [1]deceived, [b]my beloved brethren.

17 Every good thing given and every perfect gift is [a]from above, coming down from [b]the Father of lights, [c]with whom there is no variation or [1]shifting shadow.

18 In the exercise of [a]His will He [b]brought us forth by [c]the word of truth, so that we would be [1]a kind of [d]first fruits [2]among His creatures.

19 [1]*This* [a]you know, [b]my beloved brethren. But everyone must be quick to hear, [c]slow to speak *and* [d]slow to anger;

20 for [a]the anger of man does not achieve the righteousness of God.

21 Therefore, [a]putting aside all filthiness and *all* [1]that remains of wickedness, in [2]humility receive [b]the word implanted, which is able to save your souls.

22 [a]But prove yourselves doers of the word, and not merely hearers who delude themselves.

23 For if anyone is a hearer of the word

1:1 [1]Or *Jacob* [2]Lit *in the Dispersion* [a]Acts 12:17 [b]Titus 1:1 [c]Rom 1:1 [d]Luke 22:30 [e]John 7:35 [f]Acts 15:23
2 [1]Or *temptations* [a]Matt 5:12; James 1:12; 5:11 [b]1 Pet 1:6
3 [1]Or *steadfastness* [a]1 Pet 1:7 [b]Heb 6:12 [c]Luke 21:19
4 [1]V 3, note 1 [2]Lit *work* [3]Or *mature* [a]Luke 21:19 [b]Matt 5:48; Col 4:12
5 [1]Lit *does not reproach* [a]1 Kin 3:9ff; James 3:17 [b]Matt 7:7
6 [a]Matt 21:21 [b]Mark 11:23; Acts 10:20 [c]Matt 14:28-31; Eph 4:14
8 [1]Or *doubting, hesitating* [a]James 4:8 [b]2 Pet 2:14
9 [1]I.e. church member [a]Luke 14:11
10 [1]Lit *the flower of the grass* [a]1 Cor 7:31; 1 Pet 1:24
11 [1]Lit *the* [a]Matt 20:12 [b]Ps 102:4, 11; Is 40:7f
12 [1]Or *passed the test* [a]Luke 6:22; James 5:11; 1 Pet 3:14; 4:14 [b]1 Cor 9:25 [c]Ex 20:6; James 2:5 [d]1 Cor 2:9; 8:3
13 [1]Lit *from* [a]Gen 22:1
13 [2]Lit *of evil things*
15 [1]Lit *is brought to completion* [a]Job 15:35; Ps 7:14; Is 59:4 [b]Rom 5:12; 6:23 **16** [1]Or *misled* [a]1 Cor 6:9 [b]Acts 1:15; James 1:2, 19; 2:1, 5, 14; 3:1, 10; 4:11; 5:12, 19 **17** [1]Lit *shadow of turning* [a]John 3:3; James 3:15, 17 [b]Ps 136:7; 1 John 1:5 [c]Mal 3:6
18 [1]Or *a certain first fruits* [2]Lit *of* [a]John 1:13 [b]James 1:15; 1 Pet 1:3, 23 [c]2 Cor 6:7; Eph 1:13; 2 Tim 2:15 [d]Jer 2:3; Rev 14:4
19 [1]Or *Know* this [a]1 John 2:21 [b]Acts 1:15; James 1:2, 16; 2:1, 5, 14; 3:1, 10; 4:11; 5:12, 19 [c]Prov 10:19; 17:27 [d]Prov 16:32; Eccl 7:9 **20** [a]Matt 5:22; Eph 4:26 **21** [1]Lit *abundance of malice* [2]Or *gentleness* [a]Eph 4:22; 1 Pet 2:1 [b]Eph 1:13; 1 Pet 1:22f
22 [a]Matt 7:24-27; Luke 6:46-49; Rom 2:13; James 1:22-25; 2:14-20

1:1 *James.* See Introduction: Author. *bond-servant.* See note on Rom 1:1. *twelve tribes.* See Introduction: Recipients.

1:2 *joy.* See Matt 5:11–12; Rom 5:3; 1 Pet 1:6. *brethren.* James addresses the readers as brothers 15 times in this short letter. He has many rebukes for them, but he chides them in brotherly love. *trials.* The same Greek root lies behind the word "trials" here and the word "tempted" in v. 13. In vv. 2–3 the emphasis is on difficulties that come from outside; in vv. 13–15 it is on inner moral trials such as temptation to sin.

1:5 *wisdom.* Enables one to face trials with "joy" (v. 2). Wisdom is not just acquired information but practical insight with spiritual implications (see Prov 1:2–4; 2:10–15; 4:5–9; 9:10–12).

1:6 *surf of the sea.* See Eph 4:14.

1:9–10 *brother of humble circumstances . . . rich man.* Since James's discussions of wisdom (vv. 5–8) and of the poor man and the rich man (vv. 9–11) appear between the two sections on trials (vv. 2–4 and v. 12), vv. 5–11 may also have to do with trials. The Christian who suffers the trial of poverty is to take pride in his high position (v. 9) as a believer (see 2:5), and the wealthy Christian is to take pride (v. 10) in trials that bring him low, perhaps including the loss of his wealth.

1:12 *Blessed.* See Jer 17:7–8; Matt 5:3–12; see also notes on Ps 1:1; Matt 5:3; Rev 1:3. *crown.* The Greek for this word was the usual term for the wreath placed on the head of a victorious athlete or military leader (see 2 Tim 4:8; 1 Pet 5:4; Rev 2:10 and note). *life.* Eternal life, as the future tense of the verb ("will receive") indicates.

1:13 *tempted.* In vv. 13–14 the verb refers to temptations that test one's moral strength to resist sin (see note on Matt 4:1). *God cannot be tempted.* Because God in His very nature is holy, there is nothing in Him for sin to appeal to. *He Himself does not tempt anyone.* See note on Gen 22:1.

1:15 The three stages—desire, sin, death—are seen in the temptations of Eve (Gen 3:6–22) and David (2 Sam 11:2–17).

1:17 *Every good thing . . . and every perfect gift is from above.* See v. 5; 3:17. *Father of . . . lights.* God is the Creator of the heavenly bodies, which give light to the earth, but, unlike them, He does not change.

1:18 *brought us forth.* Not a reference to creation but to regeneration (see John 3:3–8). *word of truth.* The proclamation of the gospel (see 1 Pet 1:23–25). *first fruits.* See Lev 23:9–14. Just as the first sheaf of the harvest was an indication that the whole harvest would eventually follow, so the early Christians were an indication that a great number of people would eventually be born again.

1:19 *everyone must be . . . slow to speak.* See v. 26.

1:21 *word.* Of God.

and not a doer, he is like a man who looks at his [1]natural face [a]in a mirror;

24 for *once* he has looked at himself and gone away, [1]he has immediately forgotten what kind of person he was.

25 But one who looks intently at the perfect law, [a]the *law* of liberty, and abides by it, not having become a forgetful hearer but [1]an effectual doer, this man will be [b]blessed in [2]what he does.

26 If anyone thinks himself to be religious, and yet does not [1a]bridle his tongue but deceives his *own* heart, this man's religion is worthless.

27 Pure and undefiled religion [a]in the sight of *our* God and Father is this: to [b]visit [c]orphans and widows in their distress, *and* to keep oneself unstained [1]by [d]the world.

The Sin of Partiality

2 [a]My brethren, [b]do not hold your faith in our [c]glorious Lord Jesus Christ with *an attitude of* [d]personal favoritism.

2 For if a man comes into your [1]assembly with a gold ring and dressed in [2a]fine clothes, and there also comes in a poor man in [b]dirty clothes,

3 and you [1]pay special attention to the one who is wearing the [a]fine clothes, and say, "You sit here in a good place," and you say to the poor man, "You stand over there, or sit down by my footstool,"

4 have you not made distinctions among yourselves, and become judges [a]with evil [1]motives?

5 Listen, [a]my beloved brethren: did not [b]God choose the poor [1]of this world *to be* [c]rich in faith and [d]heirs of the kingdom which He [e]promised to those who love Him?

6 But you have dishonored the poor man. Is it not the rich who oppress you and [1]personally [a]drag you into [2]court?

7 [a]Do they not blaspheme the fair name [1]by which you have been called?

8 If, however, you [a]are fulfilling the [1]royal law according to the Scripture, "[b]You SHALL LOVE YOUR NEIGHBOR AS YOURSELF," you are doing well.

9 But if you [a]show partiality, you are committing sin *and* are convicted by the [1]law as transgressors.

10 For whoever keeps the whole [1]law and yet [a]stumbles in one *point,* he has become [b]guilty of all.

11 For He who said, "[a]DO NOT COMMIT ADULTERY," also said, "[b]DO NOT COMMIT MURDER." Now if you do not commit adultery, but do commit murder, you have become a transgressor of the [1]law.

12 So speak and so act as those who are to be judged by [a]*the* law of liberty.

13 For [a]judgment *will be* merciless to one who has shown no mercy; mercy [1]triumphs over judgment.

Faith and Works

14 [a]What use is it, [b]my brethren, if someone says he has faith but he has no works? Can [1]that faith save him?

15 [a]If a brother or sister is without clothing and in need of daily food,

16 and one of you says to them, "[a]Go in

23 [1]Lit *the face of his birth;* or *nature* [a]1 Cor 13:12 **24** [1]Lit *and he* **25** [1]Lit *a doer of a work* [2]Lit *his doing* [a]John 8:32; Rom 8:2; Gal 2:4; 6:2; James 2:12; 1 Pet 2:16 [b]John 13:17 **26** [1]Or *control* [a]Ps 39:1; 141:3; James 3:2-12 **27** [1]Lit *from* [a]Rom 2:13; Gal 3:11 [b]Matt 25:36 [c]Deut 14:29; Job 31:16, 17, 21; Ps 146:9; Is 1:17, 23 [d]Matt 12:32; Eph 2:2; Titus 2:12; James 4:4; 2 Pet 1:4; 2:20; 1 John 2:15-17 **2:1** [a]James 1:16 [b]Heb 12:2 [c]Acts 7:2; 1 Cor 2:8 [d]Acts 10:34; James 2:9 **2** [1]Or *synagogue* [2]Or *bright* [a]Luke 23:11; James 2:3 [b]Zech 3:3f **3** [1]Lit *look at* [a]Luke 23:11 **4** [1]Lit *reasonings* [a]Luke 18:6; John 7:24 **5** [1]Lit *to the* [a]James 1:16 [b]Job 34:19; 1 Cor 1:27f [c]Luke 12:21; Rev 2:9 [d]Matt 5:3; 25:34 [e]James 1:12 **6** [1]Lit *they themselves* [2]Lit *courts* [a]Acts 8:3; 16:19 **7** [1]Lit *which has been called upon you* [a]Acts 11:26; 1 Pet 4:16 **8** [1]Or *law of* our *King* [a]Matt 7:12 [b]Lev 19:18 **9** [1]Or *Law* [a]Acts 10:34; James 2:1 **10** [1]Or *Law* [a]James 3:2; 2 Pet 1:10; Jude 24 [b]Matt 5:19; Gal 5:3 **11** [1]Or *Law* [a]Ex 20:14; Deut 5:18 [b]Ex 20:13; Deut 5:17 **12** [a]James 1:25 **13** [1]Lit *boasts against* [a]Prov 21:13; Matt 5:7; 18:32-35; Luke 6:37f **14** [1]Lit *the* [a]James 1:22ff [b]James 1:16 **15** [a]Matt 25:35f; Luke 3:11 **16** [a]1 John 3:17f

1:25 *perfect law.* The moral and ethical teaching of Christianity, which is based on the OT moral law, as embodied in the Ten Commandments (see Ps 19:7), but brought to completion (perfection) by Jesus Christ. *liberty.* In contrast to the sinner, who is a slave to sin (John 8:34), obeying the moral law gives the Christian the joyous freedom to be what he was created for (see 2:12).

1:26 *religious.* Refers to the outward acts of religion: e.g., giving to the needy, fasting and public acts of praying and worshiping.

1:27 See Jer 22:16. *world.* Not the world of nature but the world of people in their rebellion against and alienation from God (see 1John 2:15).

2:1 *faith . . . with an attitude of personal favoritism.* God does not show favoritism—nor should believers.

2:2 *assembly.* The Greek for this term is the origin of the English word "synagogue."

2:5–13 James gives three arguments against showing favoritism to the rich: 1. The rich persecute the poor—the believers (vv. 5–7). 2. Favoritism violates the royal law of love and thus is sin (vv. 8–11). 3. Favoritism will be judged (vv. 12–13).

2:5 *did not God choose the poor?* See Luke 6:20; 1 Cor 1:26–31. *the kingdom.* The kingdom that is entered by the new birth (John 3:3,5) and that will be consummated in the future (Matt 25:34,46).

2:8 *royal law.* The law of love (Lev 19:18) is called "royal" because it is the supreme law that is the source of all other laws governing human relationships. It is the summation of all such laws (Matt 22:36–40; Rom 13:8–10).

2:10 *guilty of all.* The law is the expression of the character and will of God; therefore to violate one part of the law is to violate God's will and thus His whole law (cf. Matt 5:18–19; 23:23).

2:12 *judged.* This judgment is not for determining eternal destiny, for James is speaking to believers (v. 1), whose destiny is already determined (John 5:24). Rather, it is for giving rewards to believers (1 Cor 3:12–15; 2 Cor 5:10; Rev 22:12).

2:13 *mercy triumphs over judgment.* If man is merciful, God will be merciful on the Day of Judgment (see Prov 21:13; Matt 5:7; 6:14–15; 18:21–35).

2:14–26 In vv. 14–20,24,26 "faith" is not used in the sense of genuine, saving faith. Rather, it is demonic (v. 19), useless (v. 20) and dead (v. 26). It is a mere intellectual acceptance of certain truths without trust in Christ as Savior. James is also not saying that a person is saved by works and not by genuine faith. Rather, he is saying, to use Martin Luther's words, that a man is justified (declared righteous before God) by faith alone, but not by a faith that is alone. Genuine faith will produce good deeds, but only faith in Christ saves. (For more information on justification see note on Rom 3:24.)

2:15–16 This illustration of false faith is parallel to the illustration of false love found in 1 John 3:17. The latter passage calls for love in action; this one calls for faith in action.

peace, [1]be warmed and be filled," and yet
you do not give them what is necessary for
their body, what use is that?
17 Even so [a]faith, if it has no works, is
[1]dead, *being* by itself.
18 [a]But someone [1]may *well* say, "You
have faith and I have works; show me your
[b]faith without the works, and I will [c]show
you my faith [d]by my works."
19 You believe that [1a]God is one. [b]You do
well; [c]the demons also believe, and shudder.
20 But are you willing to recognize, [a]you
foolish fellow, that [b]faith without works is
useless?
21 [a]Was not Abraham our father justified
by works when he offered up Isaac his son
on the altar?
22 You see that [a]faith was working with
his works, and [1]as a result of the [b]works,
faith was [2]perfected;
23 and the Scripture was fulfilled which
says, "[a]AND ABRAHAM BELIEVED GOD, AND IT
WAS RECKONED TO HIM AS RIGHTEOUSNESS," and
he was called [b]the friend of God.
24 You see that a man is justified by works
and not by faith alone.
25 In the same way, was not [a]Rahab the
harlot also justified by works [b]when she
received the messengers and sent them out
by another way?
26 For just as the body without *the* spirit is
dead, so also [a]faith without works is dead.

The Tongue Is a Fire

3 [a]Let not many *of you* become teachers,
[b]my brethren, knowing that as such we
will incur a [1]stricter judgment.
2 For we all [a]stumble in many *ways.* [b]If
anyone does not stumble in [1]what he says,
he is a [c]perfect man, able to [d]bridle the
whole body as well.
3 Now [a]if we put the bits into the horses'
mouths so that they will obey us, we direct
their entire body as well.
4 Look at the ships also, though they are
so great and are driven by strong winds, are
still directed by a very small rudder wherever the inclination of the pilot desires.
5 So also the tongue is a small part of the
body, and *yet* it [a]boasts of great things.
[b]See how great a forest is set aflame by
such a small fire!
6 And [a]the tongue is a fire, the *very*
world of iniquity; the tongue is set among
our members as that which [b]defiles the
entire body, and sets on fire the course of *our*
[1]life, and is set on fire by [2c]hell.
7 For every [1]species of beasts and birds,
of reptiles and creatures of the sea, is tamed
and has been tamed by the human [1]race.
8 But no one can tame the tongue; *it is* a
restless evil *and* full of [a]deadly poison.
9 With it we bless [a]*our* Lord and Father,
and with it we curse men, [b]who have been
made in the likeness of God;
10 from the same mouth come *both* blessing and cursing. My brethren, these things
ought not to be this way.
11 Does a fountain send out from the
same opening *both* [1]fresh and bitter *water?*
12 [a]Can a fig tree, my brethren, produce
olives, or a vine produce figs? Nor *can* salt
water produce [1]fresh.

Wisdom from Above

13 Who among you is wise and understanding? [a]Let him show by his [b]good
behavior his deeds in the gentleness of wisdom.
14 But if you have bitter [a]jealousy and
[1]selfish ambition in your heart, do not be
arrogant and *so* lie against [b]the truth.
15 This wisdom is not that which comes

16 [1]Or *warm yourselves and fill yourselves* **17** [1]Or *dead by its own standards* [a]Gal 5:6; James 2:20, 26 **18** [1]Lit *will* [a]Rom 9:19 [b]Rom 3:28; 4:6; Heb 11:33 [c]James 3:13 [d]Matt 7:16f; Gal 5:6 **19** [1]One early ms reads *there is one God* [a]Deut 6:4; Mark 12:29 [b]James 2:8 [c]Matt 8:29; Mark 1:24; 5:7; Luke 4:34; Acts 19:15 **20** [a]Rom 9:20; 1 Cor 15:36 [b]Gal 5:6; James 2:17, 26 **21** [a]Gen 22:9, 10, 12, 16-18 **22** [1]Or *by the deeds* [2]Or *completed* [a]John 6:29; Heb 11:17 [b]1 Thess 1:3 **23** [a]Gen 15:6; Rom 4:3 [b]2 Chr 20:7; Is 41:8 **25** [a]Heb 11:31 [b]Josh 2:4, 6, 15 **26** [a]Gal 5:6; James 2:17, 20 **3:1** [1]Or *greater condemnation* [a]Matt 23:8; Rom 2:20f; 1 Tim 1:7 [b]James 1:16; 3:10 **2** [1]Lit *word* [a]James 2:10 [b]Matt 12:34-37; James 3:2-12 [c]James 1:4 [d]James 1:26 **3** [a]Ps 32:9 **5** [a]Ps 12:3f; 73:8f [b]Prov 26:20f **6** [1]Or *existence, origin* [2]Gr *Gehenna* [a]Ps 120:2, 3; Prov 16:27 [b]Matt 12:36f; 15:11, 18f [c]Matt 5:22 **7** [1]Lit *nature* **8** [a]Ps 140:3; Eccl 10:11; Rom 3:13 **9** [a]James 1:27 [b]Gen 1:26; 1 Cor 11:7 **11** [1]Lit *sweet* **12** [1]V 11, note 1 [a]Matt 7:16 **13** [a]James 2:18 [b]1 Pet 2:12 **14** [1]Or *strife* [a]Rom 2:8; 2 Cor 12:20; James 3:16 [b]1 Tim 2:4; James 1:18; 5:19

2:18 *You have faith and I have works.* The false claim is that there are "faith" Christians and "works" Christians, i.e., that faith and deeds can exist independently of each other. *show me your faith without the works.* Irony; James denies the possibility of this.

2:19 *God is one.* A declaration of monotheism that reflects the well-known Jewish creed called in Hebrew the *Shema,* "Hear" (Deut 6:4; Mark 12:29).

2:21 Apart from its context, this verse might seem to contradict the Biblical teaching that people are saved by faith and not by good deeds (Rom 3:28; Gal 2:15–16). But James means only that righteous action is evidence of genuine faith—not that it saves, for the verse (Gen 15:6) that he cites (v. 23) to substantiate his point says, "Then he believed in the LORD; and He reckoned it [i.e., faith, not works] to him as righteousness." Furthermore, Abraham's act of faith recorded in Gen 15:6 occurred before he offered up Isaac, which was only a proof of the genuineness of his faith. As Paul wrote, the only thing that matters is "faith working through love" (Gal 5:6). Faith that saves produces deeds.

2:23 *the friend of God.* This designation (see 2 Chr 20:7) further describes Abraham's relationship to God as one of complete acceptance.

2:24 *not by faith alone.* Not by an intellectual assent to certain truths (see note on 2:14–26).

2:25 *Rahab the harlot.* James does not approve Rahab's occupation. He merely commends her for her faith (see also Heb 11:31), which she demonstrated by helping the spies (Josh 2).

3:1 *stricter judgment.* Because a teacher has great influence, he will be held more accountable (see Luke 20:47; cf. Matt 23:1–33).

3:2 *perfect man.* Since the tongue is so difficult to control, anyone who controls it perfectly gains control of himself in all other areas of life as well.

3:6 *world of iniquity.* Like the world in its fallenness. *set on fire by hell.* A figurative way of saying that the source of the tongue's evil is the devil (see John 8:44). See notes on Matt 5:22; Luke 16:23.

3:9 *likeness of God.* Since man has been made like God (Gen 1:26–27), to curse man is like cursing God (see Gen 9:6). See note on Gen 1:26.

3:13 *wisdom.* See note on 1:5.

down [a]from above, but is [b]earthly, [1][c]natural, [d]demonic.

16 For where [a]jealousy and [1]selfish ambition exist, [2]there is disorder and every evil thing.

17 But the wisdom [a]from above is first [b]pure, then [c]peaceable, [d]gentle, [1]reasonable, [e]full of mercy and good fruits, [f]unwavering, without [g]hypocrisy.

18 And the [1][a]seed whose fruit is righteousness is sown in peace [2]by those who make peace.

Things to Avoid

4 [1]What is the source of quarrels and [a]conflicts among you? [2]Is not the source your pleasures that wage [b]war in your members?

2 You lust and do not have; *so* you [a]commit murder. You are envious and cannot obtain; *so* you fight and quarrel. You do not have because you do not ask.

3 You ask and [a]do not receive, because you ask [1]with wrong motives, so that you may spend *it* [2]on your pleasures.

4 You [a]adulteresses, do you not know that friendship with [b]the world is [c]hostility toward God? [d]Therefore whoever wishes to be a friend of the world makes himself an enemy of God.

5 Or do you think that the Scripture [a]speaks to no purpose: "[1]He [2]jealously desires [b]the Spirit which He has made to dwell in us"?

6 But [a]He gives a greater grace. Therefore *it* says, "[b]GOD IS OPPOSED TO THE PROUD, BUT GIVES GRACE TO THE HUMBLE."

7 [a]Submit therefore to God. [b]Resist the devil and he will flee from you.

8 [a]Draw near to God and He will draw near to you. [b]Cleanse your hands, you sinners; and [c]purify your hearts, you [d]double-minded.

9 [a]Be miserable and mourn and weep; let your laughter be turned into mourning and your joy to gloom.

10 [a]Humble yourselves in the presence of the Lord, and He will exalt you.

11 [a]Do not speak against one another, [b]brethren. He who speaks against a brother or [c]judges his brother, speaks against [d]the law and judges the law; but if you judge the law, you are not [e]a doer of the law but a judge *of it.*

12 There is *only* one [a]Lawgiver and Judge, the One who is [b]able to save and to destroy; but [c]who are you who judge your neighbor?

13 [a]Come now, you who say, "[b]Today or tomorrow we will go to such and such a city, and spend a year there and engage in business and make a profit."

14 [1]Yet you do not know [2]what your life will be like tomorrow. [a]You are *just* a vapor that appears for a little while and then vanishes away.

15 [1]Instead, *you ought* to say, "[a]If the Lord wills, we will live and also do this or that."

16 But as it is, you boast in your [1]arrogance; [a]all such boasting is evil.

17 Therefore, [a]to one who knows *the* [1]right thing to do and does not do it, to him it is sin.

Misuse of Riches

5 [a]Come now, [b]you rich, [c]weep and howl for your miseries which are coming upon you.

2 [a]Your riches have rotted and your garments have become moth-eaten.

3 Your gold and your silver have rusted; and their rust will be a witness against you

15 [1]Or *unspiritual* [a]James 1:17 [b]1 Cor 2:6; 3:19 [c]2 Cor 1:12; Jude 19 [d]2 Thess 2:9f; 1 Tim 4:1; Rev 2:24 **16** [1]V 14, note 1 [2]I.e. in that place [a]Rom 2:8; 2 Cor 12:20; James 3:14 **17** [1]Or *willing to yield* [a]James 1:17 [b]2 Cor 7:11; James 4:8 [c]Matt 5:9; Heb 12:11 [d]Titus 3:2 [e]Luke 6:36; James 2:13 [f]James 2:4 [g]Rom 12:9; 2 Cor 6:6 **18** [1]Lit *fruit of righteousness* [2]Or *for* [a]Prov 11:18; Is 32:17; Hos 10:12; Amos 6:12; Gal 6:8; Phil 1:11 **4:1** [1]Lit *From where wars and from where fightings* [2]Lit Are they *not from here,* from your [a]Titus 3:9 [b]Rom 7:23 **2** [a]James 5:6; 1 John 3:15 **3** [1]Lit *wickedly* [2]Lit *in* [a]1 John 3:22; 5:14 **4** [a]Jer 2:2; Ezek 16:32 [b]James 1:27 [c]Rom 8:7; 1 John 2:15 [d]Matt 6:24; John 15:19 **5** [1]Or *The spirit which He has made to dwell in us lusts with envy* [2]Lit *desires to jealousy* [a]Num 23:19 [b]1 Cor 6:19; 2 Cor 6:16 **6** [a]Is 54:7f; Matt 13:12 [b]Ps 138:6; Prov 3:34; Matt 23:12; 1 Pet 5:5 **7** [a]1 Pet 5:6 [b]Eph 4:27; 6:11f; 1 Pet 5:8f **8** [a]2 Chr 15:2; Zech 1:3; Mal 3:7; Heb 7:19 [b]Job 17:9; Is 1:16; 1 Tim 2:8 [c]Jer 4:14; James 3:17; 1 Pet 1:22; 1 John 3:3 [d]James 1:8 **9** [a]Neh 8:9; Prov 14:13; Luke 6:25 **10** [a]Job 5:11; Ezek 21:26; Luke 1:52; James 4:6 **11** [a]2 Cor 12:20; James 5:9; 1 Pet 2:1 [b]James 1:16; 5:7, 9, 10 [c]Matt 7:1; Rom 14:4 [d]James 2:8 [e]James 1:22 **12** [a]Is 33:22; James 5:9 [b]Matt 10:28 [c]Rom 14:4 **13** [a]James 5:1 [b]Prov 27:1; Luke 12:18-20 **14** [1]Lit *Who do not* [2]Or *what* will happen *tomorrow. What kind of life is yours?* [a]Job 7:7; Ps 39:5; 102:3; 144:4 **15** [1]Lit *Instead of your saying* [a]Acts 18:21 **16** [1]Or *pretensions* [a]1 Cor 5:6 **17** [1]Or *good* [a]Luke 12:47; John 9:41; 2 Pet 2:21 **5:1** [a]James 4:13 [b]Luke 6:24; 1 Tim 6:9 [c]Is 13:6; 15:3; Ezek 30:2 **2** [a]Job 13:28; Is 50:9; Matt 6:19f

---

3:15 *from above.* From God (see 1:5,17; 1 Cor 2:6–16).

3:16 *disorder.* "God is not a God of confusion but of peace" (1 Cor 14:33).

3:17 *unwavering.* See 2:1–13.

3:18 *those who make peace.* Contrast v. 16. Discord cannot produce righteousness.

4:1 *pleasures.* The Greek for this term is the source of our word "hedonism."

4:2 *murder.* Figurative (hyperbole) for "hate."

4:4 *adulteresses.* Those who are spiritually unfaithful, who love the world rather than God. For spiritual adultery see, e.g., Jer 31:32. *world.* See note on 1:27.

4:5 *Scripture.* The passage James had in mind is not known. *Spirit.* Or "spirit." Then the meaning would be that God "jealously desires" our faithfulness and love (see v. 4). In this case the "Scripture" referred to may be Ex 20:5.

4:6 See 1 Pet 5:5, which also quotes Prov 3:34.

4:7–10 These verses contain ten commands, each of which is so stated in Greek that it calls for immediate action in rooting out the sinful attitude of pride.

4:7 *Resist the devil.* See Eph 6:11–18; 1 Pet 5:8–9.

4:8 *Cleanse your hands.* Before the OT priests approached God at the tabernacle, they had to wash their hands and feet at the bronze basin as a symbol of spiritual cleansing (Ex 30:17–21). See Ps 24:4 for the imagery of "clean hands and a pure heart."

4:9 *Be miserable and mourn and weep.* Repent.

4:10 See Matt 23:12.

4:11 *speaks against a brother . . . speaks against the law.* See note on 2:8; see also Ex 20:16; Ps 15:3; 50:19–20; Prov 6:16,19. To speak against a brother is to scorn the law of love.

5:1 *rich.* These (as also in 2:2,6) are not Christians, for James warns them to repent and weep because of the coming misery. Verses 1–6 are similar to OT declarations of judgment against pagan nations, interspersed in books otherwise addressed to God's people (Is 13–23; Jer 46–51; Ezek 25–32; Amos 1:3–2:16; Zeph 2:4–15).

5:2 *garments.* One of the main forms of wealth in the ancient world (see Acts 20:33).

5:3 *rust.* The result of hoarding. It will both testify against

and will consume your flesh like fire. It is [a]in
the last days that you have stored up your
treasure!
4 Behold, [a]the pay of the laborers who
mowed your fields, *and* which has been
withheld by you, cries out *against you;* and
[b]the outcry of those who did the harvesting
has reached the ears of [c]the Lord of [1]Sabaoth.
5 You have [a]lived luxuriously on the earth
and led a life of wanton pleasure; you have
[1]fattened your hearts in [b]a day of slaughter.
6 You have condemned and [1a]put to
death [b]the righteous *man;* he does not resist
you.

Exhortation

7 Therefore be patient, [a]brethren, [b]until
the coming of the Lord. [c]The farmer waits
for the precious produce of the soil, being
patient about it, until [1]it gets [d]the early and
late rains.
8 [a]You too be patient; [b]strengthen your
hearts, for [c]the coming of the Lord is [d]near.
9 [a]Do not [1]complain, [b]brethren, against
one another, so that you yourselves may not
be judged; behold, [c]the Judge is standing
[2d]right at the [3]door.
10 As an example, [a]brethren, of suffering
and patience, take [b]the prophets who spoke
in the name of the Lord.
11 We count those [a]blessed who endured.
You have heard of [b]the [1]endurance of Job
and have seen [c]the [2]outcome of the Lord's
dealings, that [d]the Lord is full of compassion
and *is* merciful.
12 But above all, [a]my brethren, [b]do not
swear, either by heaven or by earth or with
any other oath; but [1]your yes is to be yes,
and your no, no, so that you may not fall
under judgment.
13 Is anyone among you [a]suffering? [b]*Then*
he must pray. Is anyone cheerful? He is to
[c]sing praises.
14 Is anyone among you sick? *Then* he
must call for [a]the elders of the church and
they are to pray over him, [1b]anointing him
with oil in the name of the Lord;
15 and the [a]prayer [1]offered in faith will
[2b]restore the one who is sick, and the Lord
will [c]raise him up, and if he has committed
sins, [3]they will be forgiven him.
16 Therefore, [a]confess your sins to one
another, and pray for one another so that
you may be [b]healed. [c]The effective [1]prayer of
a righteous man can accomplish much.
17 Elijah was [a]a man with a nature like
ours, and [b]he prayed [1]earnestly that it would
not rain, and it did not rain on the earth for
[c]three years and six months.
18 Then he [a]prayed again, and [b]the [1]sky
[2]poured rain and the earth produced its fruit.
19 My brethren, [a]if any among you strays
from [b]the truth and one turns him back,
20 let him know that [1]he who turns a sinner from the error of his way will [a]save his
soul from death and will [b]cover a multitude
of sins.

3 [a]James 5:7, 8 **4** [1]I.e. Hosts [a]Lev 19:13; Job 24:10f; Jer 22:13; Mal 3:5 [b]Ex 2:23; Deut 24:15; Job 31:38f [c]Rom 9:29; Is 5:9 **5** [1]Lit *nourished* [a]Ezek 16:49; Luke 16:19; 1 Tim 5:6; 2 Pet 2:13 [b]Jer 12:3; 25:34 **6** [1]Or *murdered* [a]James 4:2 [b]Heb 10:38; 1 Pet 4:18 **7** [1]Or *he* [a]James 4:11; 5:9, 10 [b]John 21:22; 1 Thess 2:19 [c]Gal 6:9 [d]Deut 11:14; Jer 5:24; Joel 2:23 **8** [a]Luke 21:19 [b]1 Thess 3:13 [c]John 21:22; 1 Thess 2:19 [d]Rom 13:11, 12; 1 Pet 4:7 **9** [1]Lit *groan* [2]Lit *before* [3]Lit *doors* [a]James 4:11 [b]James 5:7, 10 [c]1 Cor 4:5; James 4:12; 1 Pet 4:5 [d]Matt 24:33; Mark 13:29 **10** [a]James 4:11; 5:7, 9 [b]Matt 5:12 **11** [1]Or *steadfastness* [2]Lit *end of the Lord* [a]Matt 5:10; 1 Pet 3:14 [b]Job 1:21f; 2:10 [c]Job 42:10, 12 [d]Ex 34:6; Ps 103:8 **12** [1]Lit *yours is to be yes, yes, and no, no* [a]James 1:16 [b]Matt 5:34-37

13 [a]James 5:10 [b]Ps 50:15 [c]1 Cor 14:15; Col 3:16 **14** [1]Lit *having anointed* [a]Acts 11:30 [b]Mark 6:13; 16:18 **15** [1]Lit *of* [2]Or *save* [3]Lit *it* [a]James 1:6 [b]1 Cor 1:21; James 5:20 [c]John 6:39; 2 Cor 4:14 **16** [1]Lit *supplication* [a]Matt 3:6; Mark 1:5; Acts 19:18 [b]Heb 12:13; 1 Pet 2:24 [c]Gen 18:23-32; John 9:31 **17** [1]Lit *with prayer* [a]Acts 14:15 [b]1 Kin 17:1; 18:1 [c]Luke 4:25 **18** [1]Lit *heaven* [2]Lit *gave* [a]1 Kin 18:42 [b]1 Kin 18:45 **19** [a]Matt 18:15; Gal 6:1 [b]James 3:14 **20** [1]Lit *he who has turned* [a]Rom 11:14; 1 Cor 1:21; James 1:21 [b]Prov 10:12; 1 Pet 4:8

and judge the selfish rich. *last days.* See notes on Acts 2:17; 1 Tim 4:1; 2 Tim 3:1; Heb 1:2; 1 John 2:18.

5:4 *the Lord of Sabaoth.* See notes on Gen 17:1; 1 Sam 1:3.

5:5 *luxuriously . . . wanton pleasure.* See Luke 16:19–31. *a day of slaughter.* The day of judgment. The wicked rich are like cattle that continue to fatten themselves on the very day they are to be slaughtered, totally unaware of coming destruction.

5:7 *Therefore.* Refers back to vv. 1–6. Since the believers are suffering at the hands of the wicked rich, they are to look forward patiently to the Lord's return. *early and late rains.* In Israel the autumn rain comes in October and November soon after the grain is sown, and the spring rain comes in March and April just prior to harvest (Deut 11:14; Jer 5:24; Hos 6:3; Joel 2:24).

5:9 *Do not complain.* James calls for patience toward believers as well as unbelievers (vv. 7–8). *the Judge is standing right at the door.* A reference to Christ's second coming (see vv. 7–8) and the judgment associated with it. The NT insistence on imminence (e.g., in Rom 13:12; Heb 10:25; 1 Pet 4:7; Rev 22:20) arises from the teaching that the "last days" began with the incarnation. We have been living in the "last days" (v. 3) ever since (see note on Heb 1:1). The next great event in redemptive history is Christ's second coming. The NT does not say when it will take place, but its certainty is never questioned and believers are consistently admonished to watch for it. It was in this light that James expected the imminent return of Christ.

5:11 *endurance of Job.* Not "patience." Job was not patient (Job 3; 12:1–3; 16:1–3; 21:4), but he persevered (Job 1:20–22; 2:9–10; 13:15). This is the only place in the NT where Job is mentioned, though Job 5:13 is quoted in 1 Cor 3:19.

5:12 *do not swear.* James's words are very close to Christ's (Matt 5:33–37). James is not condemning the taking of solemn oaths, such as God's before Abraham (Heb 6:13) or Jesus' before Caiaphas (Matt 26:63–64) or Paul's (Rom 1:9; 9:1) or a man's before the Lord (Ex 22:11). Rather, he is condemning the flippant use of God's name or a sacred object to guarantee the truth of what is spoken.

5:14 *elders.* See notes on 1 Tim 3:1; 5:17. *church.* See note on Matt 16:18. *oil.* One of the best-known ancient medicines (referred to by Philo, Pliny and the physician Galen; see also Is 1:6; Luke 10:34). Some believe that James may be using the term medicinally in this passage. Others, however, regard its use here as an aid to faith, an outward sign of the healing to be brought about by God in response to "prayer offered in faith" (v. 15; see Mark 6:13).

5:17 *Elijah . . . prayed.* That Elijah prayed may be assumed from 1 Kin 17:1; 18:41–46. The three and a half years (see also Luke 4:25) are probably a round number (half of seven), based on 1 Kin 18:1 (see note there; cf. Rev 11:1–6).

5:19 *strays from the truth.* The wanderer is either a professing Christian, whose faith is not genuine (cf. Heb 6:4–8; 2 Pet 2:20–21), or a sinning Christian, who needs to be restored. For the former, the death spoken of in v. 20 is the "second death" (Rev 21:8); for the latter, it is physical death (cf. 1 Cor 11:30). See note on 1 John 5:16.

5:20 *cover a multitude of sins.* The sins of the wanderer will be forgiven by God.

1 Peter

INTRODUCTION

Author and Date

The author identifies himself as the apostle Peter (1:1), and the contents and character of the letter support his authorship (see notes on 1:12; 4:13; 5:1–2,5,13). Moreover, the letter reflects the history and terminology of the Gospels and Acts (notably Peter's speeches); its themes and concepts reflect Peter's experiences and his associations in the period of our Lord's earthly ministry and in the apostolic age. That he was acquainted, e.g., with Paul and his letters is made clear in 2 Pet 3:15–16; Gal 1:18; 2:1–21 and elsewhere; coincidences in thought and expression with Paul's writings are therefore not surprising.

From the beginning, 1 Peter was recognized as authoritative and as the work of the apostle Peter. The earliest reference to it may be 2 Pet 3:1, where Peter himself refers to a former letter he had written. 1 Clement (A.D. 95) seems to indicate acquaintance with 1 Peter. Polycarp, a disciple of the apostle John, makes use of 1 Peter in his letter to the Philippians. The author of the Gospel of Truth (140–150) was acquainted with 1 Peter. Eusebius (fourth century) indicated that it was universally received.

The letter was explicitly ascribed to Peter by that group of church fathers whose testimonies appear in the attestation of so many of the genuine NT writings, namely, Irenaeus (A.D. 140–203), Tertullian (150–222), Clement of Alexandria (155–215) and Origen (185–253). It is thus clear that Peter's authorship of the book has early and strong support.

Nevertheless some claim that the idiomatic Greek of this letter is beyond Peter's competence. But in his time Aramaic, Hebrew and Greek were used in Palestine, and he may well have been acquainted with more than one language. That he was not a professionally trained scribe (Acts 4:13) does not mean that he was unacquainted with Greek; in fact, as a Galilean fisherman he in all likelihood did use it. Even if he had not known it in the earliest days of the church, he may have acquired it as an important aid to his apostolic ministry in the decades that intervened between then and the writing of 1 Peter.

It is true, however, that the Greek of 1 Peter is good literary Greek, and even though Peter could no doubt speak Greek, as so many in the Mediterranean world could, it is unlikely that he would write such polished Greek. But it is at this point that Peter's remark in 5:12 concerning Silas may be significant. Here the apostle claims that he wrote "through" (or more lit. "by means of") Silas. This phrase cannot refer merely to Silas as a letter carrier. Thus Silas was the intermediate agent in writing. Some have claimed that Silas's qualifications for recording Peter's letter in literary Greek are found in Acts 15:22–29. It is known that a secretary in those days often composed documents in good Greek for those who did not have the language facility to do so. Thus in 1 Peter Silas's Greek may be seen, while in 2 Peter it may be Peter's rough Greek that appears.

Some also maintain that the book reflects a situation that did not exist until after Peter's death, suggesting that the persecution referred to in 4:14–16; 5:8–9 is descriptive of Domitian's reign (A.D. 81–96). However, the situation that was developing in Nero's time (54–68) is just as adequately described by those verses. The book can be satisfactorily dated in the early 60s. It cannot be placed earlier than 60 since it shows familiarity with Paul's Prison Letters (e.g., Colossians and Ephesians, which are to be dated no earlier than 60): Compare 1:1–3 with Eph 1:1–3; 2:18 with Col 3:22; 3:1–6 with Eph 5:22–24. Furthermore, it cannot be dated later than 67/68, since Peter was martyred during Nero's reign.

Place of Writing

In 5:13 Peter indicates that he was in Babylon when he wrote 1 Peter. Among the interpretations that have been suggested are that he was writing from (1) Egyptian Babylon, which was a military post, (2) Mesopotamian Babylon, (3) Jerusalem and (4) Rome. Peter may well be using the name "Babylon" symbolically, as it seems to be used in the book of Revelation (see, e.g., notes on Rev 17:9–10). Tradition connects

him in the latter part of his life with Rome, and certain early writers held that 1 Peter was written there. On the other hand, it is known that Babylon existed in the first century as a small town on the Euphrates. Furthermore, it is pointed out that (1) there is no evidence that the term Babylon was used figuratively to refer to Rome until Revelation was written (c. A.D. 95), and (2) the context of 5:13 is not at all figurative or cryptic.

Recipients

See note on 1:1.

Themes

Although 1 Peter is a short letter, it touches on various doctrines and has much to say about Christian life and duties. It is not surprising that different readers have found it to have different principal themes. For example, it has been characterized as a letter of separation, of suffering and persecution, of suffering and glory, of hope, of pilgrimage, of courage, and as a letter dealing with the true grace of God. Peter says that he has written "exhorting you and testifying that this is the true grace of God" (5:12). This is a definitive general description of the letter, but it does not exclude the recognition of numerous subordinate and contributory themes. The letter is composed also of a series of exhortations (imperatives) that run from 1:13 to 5:11.

Outline

- I. Salutation (1:1–2)
- II. Praise to God for His Grace and Salvation (1:3–12)
- III. Exhortations to Holiness of Life (1:13—5:11)
  - A. The Requirement of Holiness (1:13—2:3)
  - B. The Position of Believers (2:4–12)
    - 1. A spiritual house (2:4–8)
    - 2. A chosen people (2:9–10)
    - 3. Aliens and strangers (2:11–12)
  - C. Submission to Authority (2:13—3:7)
    - 1. Submission to rulers (2:13–17)
    - 2. Submission to masters (2:18–20)
    - 3. Christ's example of submission (2:21–25)
    - 4. Submission of wives to husbands (3:1–6)
    - 5. The corresponding duty of husbands (3:7)
  - D. Duties of All (3:8–17)
  - E. Christ's Example (3:18—4:6)
  - F. Conduct in View of the End of All Things (4:7–11)
  - G. Conduct of Those Who Suffer for Christ (4:12–19)
  - H. Conduct of Elders (5:1–4)
  - I. Conduct of Young Men (5:5–11)
- IV. The Purpose of the Letter (5:12)
- V. Closing Greetings (5:13–14)

A Living Hope, and a Sure Salvation

1 [a]Peter, an apostle of Jesus Christ,
To those who reside as [b]aliens, [c]scattered
throughout [d]Pontus, [e]Galatia, [d]Cappadocia,
[d]Asia, and [f]Bithynia, [g]who are chosen
2 according to the [a]foreknowledge of
God the Father, [b]by the sanctifying work of
the Spirit, [1]to [c]obey Jesus Christ and be
[d]sprinkled with His blood: [e]May grace and
peace [2]be yours in the fullest measure.
3 [a]Blessed be the God and Father of our
Lord Jesus Christ, who [b]according to His
great mercy [c]has caused us to be born again
to [d]a living hope through the [e]resurrection of
Jesus Christ from the dead,
4 to *obtain* an [a]inheritance *which is*
imperishable and undefiled and [b]will not
fade away, [c]reserved in heaven for you,
5 who are [a]protected by the power of
God [b]through faith for [c]a salvation ready [d]to
be revealed in the last time.
6 [a]In this you greatly rejoice, even
though now [b]for a little while, [c]if necessary,
you have been distressed by [d]various [1]trials,
7 so that the [1][a]proof of your faith, *being*
more precious than gold which [2]is perishable, [b]even though tested by fire, [c]may be
found to result in praise and glory and hon-
or at [d]the revelation of Jesus Christ;
8 and [a]though you have not seen Him,
you [b]love Him, and though you do not see
Him now, but believe in Him, you greatly
rejoice with joy inexpressible and [1]full of
glory,
9 obtaining as [a]the outcome of your faith
the salvation of [1]your souls.
10 [a]As to this salvation, the prophets who
[b]prophesied of the [c]grace that *would come* to
you made careful searches and inquiries,
11 [1]seeking to know what person or time
[a]the Spirit of Christ within them was indicating as He [b]predicted the sufferings of
Christ and the glories [2]to follow.
12 It was revealed to them that they were
not serving themselves, but you, in these
things which now have been announced to
you through those who [a]preached the gospel
to you by [b]the Holy Spirit sent from heav-
en—things into which [c]angels long to [1]look.

1:1 [a]2 Pet 1:1 [b]1 Pet 2:11 [c]James 1:1 [d]Acts 2:9 [e]Acts 16:6 [f]Acts 16:7 [g]Matt 24:22; Luke 18:7 **2** [1]Lit *unto obedience and sprinkling* [2]Lit *be multiplied for you* [a]Rom 8:29; 1 Pet 1:20 [b]2 Thess 2:13 [c]1 Pet 1:14, 22 [d]Heb 10:22; 12:24 [e]2 Pet 1:2 **3** [a]2 Cor 1:3 [b]Gal 6:16; Titus 3:5 [c]James 1:18; 1 Pet 1:23 [d]1 Pet 1:13, 21; 3:5, 15; 1 John 3:3 [e]1 Cor 15:20; 1 Pet 3:21 **4** [a]Acts 20:32; Rom 8:17; Col 3:24 [b]1 Pet 5:4 [c]2 Tim 4:8 **5** [a]John 10:28; Phil 4:7 [b]Eph 2:8 [c]1 Cor 1:21; 2 Thess 2:13 [d]1 Pet 4:13; 5:1 **6** [1]Or *temptations* [a]Rom 5:2 [b]1 Pet 5:10 [c]1 Pet 3:17 [d]James 1:2; 1 Pet 4:12 **7** [1]Or *genuineness* [2]Lit *perishes* [a]James 1:3 [b]1 Cor 3:13 [c]Rom 2:7 [d]Luke 17:30; 1 Pet 1:13; 4:13 **8** [1]Lit *glorified* [a]John 20:29 [b]Eph 3:19 **9** [1]One early ms does not contain *your* [a]Rom 6:22 **10** [a]Matt 13:17; Luke 10:24 [b]Matt 26:24 [c]1 Pet 1:13 **11** [1]Or *inquiring* [2]Lit *after these* [a]2 Pet 1:21 [b]Matt 26:24 **12** [1]Or *gain a clear glimpse* [a]1 Pet 1:25; 4:6 [b]Acts 2:2-4 [c]1 Tim 3:16

1:1 *Peter.* See notes on Matt 16:18; John 1:42. *apostle.* See notes on Mark 6:30; 1 Cor 1:1; Heb 3:1. *chosen.* See note on Eph 1:4. *reside as aliens.* People temporarily residing on earth but whose home is in heaven (cf. 1 Chr 29:15; Ps 39:12; Heb 13:14). *scattered throughout Pontus . . . Bithynia.* Jewish and Gentile Christians scattered throughout much of Asia Minor. People from this area were in Jerusalem on the day of Pentecost (see Acts 2:9–11). Paul preached and taught in some of these provinces (see, e.g., Acts 16:6; 18:23; 19:10,26).

1:2 *foreknowledge.* See note on Rom 8:29. *Father . . . Spirit . . . Jesus Christ.* All three persons of the Trinity are involved in the redemption of the elect. *sanctifying work.* See note on 2 Thess 2:13. The order of the terms employed suggests that the sanctifying work of the Spirit referred to here is the influence of the Spirit that draws one from sin toward holiness. Peter says it is "to" (or "for") obedience and sprinkling of Christ's blood, i.e., the Spirit's sanctifying leads to obedient saving faith and cleansing from sin (see note on 1 Cor 7:14). *to obey Jesus Christ.* God's choice or election is designed to bring this about. *sprinkled with His blood.* The benefits of Christ's redemption are applied to His people (cf. Ex 24:4–8; Is 52:15; Heb 9:11–14,18–28). *grace and peace.* See notes on Jon 4:2; John 14:27; 20:19; Gal 1:3; Eph 1:2.

1:3 *living hope.* In spite of the frequent suffering and persecution mentioned in this letter (v. 6; 2:12,18–25; 3:13–18; 4:1,4,12–19; 5:1,7–10), hope is such a key thought in it (the word itself is used here and in vv. 13,21; 3:5,15) that it may be called a letter of hope in the midst of suffering (see Introduction: Themes). In the Bible, hope is not wishful thinking but a firm conviction, much like faith that is directed toward the future. *resurrection of Jesus Christ.* Secures for His people their new birth and the hope that they will be resurrected just as He was.

1:4 *to obtain an inheritance.* Believers are born again not only to a hope but also to the inheritance that is the substance of the hope. The inheritance is eternal—in its essence (it is not subject to decay) and in its preservation (it is divinely kept for us).

1:5 *by the power of God through faith.* There are two sides to the perseverance of the Christian. He is shielded (1) by God's power and (2) by his own faith. Thus he is never kept contrary to his will nor apart from God's activity. *salvation.* See note on 2 Tim 1:9. The Bible speaks of salvation as (1) past—when a person first believes (see, e.g., Titus 3:5), (2) present—the continuing process of salvation, or sanctification (see v. 9; 1 Cor 1:18), and (3) future—when Christ returns and salvation, or sanctification, is completed through glorification (here; see also Rom 8:23,30; 13:11).

1:7 *that the proof of your faith . . . may be found.* See Rom 5:3; James 1:2–4. Not only is the faith itself precious, but Peter's words indicate that the trial of faith is also valuable. *glory.* A key word in 1,2 Peter.

1:8 *though you do not see Him now, but believe.* Similar to Jesus' saying in John 20:29, on an occasion when Peter was present.

1:9 *souls.* Implies the whole person. Peter is not excluding the body from heaven.

1:10 *prophets . . . made careful searches.* Inspiration (see 2 Pet 1:21) did not bestow omniscience. The prophets probably did not always understand the full significance of all the words they spoke.

1:11 *Spirit of Christ.* The Holy Spirit is called this because Christ sent Him (see John 16:7) and ministered through Him (see Luke 4:14,18). *the sufferings of Christ and the glories.* A theme running through the Bible (see, e.g., Ps 22; Is 52:13–53:12; Zech 9:9–10; 13:7; Matt 16:21–23; 17:22; 20:19; Luke 24:26,46; John 2:19; Acts 3:17–21), and a basic concept in this letter (vv. 18–21; 3:17–22; 4:12–16; 5:1,4,9–10). Those who are united to Christ will also, after suffering, enter into glory. And they will benefit in the midst of their present sufferings from His having already entered into glory (vv. 3,8,21; 3:21–22).

1:12 *Holy Spirit sent from heaven.* By Christ, on the day of Pentecost (see Acts 2:33), at which Peter was present. God the Father also sent the Spirit (see John 14:16,26). *into which angels long to look.* Their intense desire is highlighted by the Greek word rendered "to look into." It means "to stoop and look intently" (see John 20:5,11).

13 Therefore, [1a]prepare your minds for
action, [2b]keep sober *in spirit,* fix your [c]hope
completely on the [d]grace [3]to be brought to
you at [e]the revelation of Jesus Christ.
14 As [1a]obedient children, do not [2b]be
conformed to the former lusts *which were*
yours in your [c]ignorance,
15 but [1a]like the Holy One who called
you, [2b]be holy yourselves also [c]in all *your*
behavior;
16 because it is written, "[a]YOU SHALL BE
HOLY, FOR I AM HOLY."
17 If you [a]address as Father the One who
[b]impartially [c]judges according to each one's
work, conduct yourselves [d]in fear during the
time of your [e]stay *on earth;*
18 knowing that you were not [1a]redeemed
with perishable things like silver or gold
from your [b]futile way of life inherited from
your forefathers,
19 but with precious [a]blood, as of a [b]lamb
unblemished and spotless, *the blood* of Christ.
20 For He was [a]foreknown before [b]the
foundation of the world, but has [c]appeared
[1]in these last times [d]for the sake of you
21 who through Him are [a]believers in
God, who raised Him from the dead and
[b]gave Him glory, so that your faith and [c]hope
are in God.
22 Since you have [a]in obedience to the
truth [b]purified your souls for a [1c]sincere love
of the brethren, fervently love one another
from [2]the heart,
23 for you have been [a]born again [b]not of
seed which is perishable but imperishable,
that is, through the living and enduring
[c]word of God.
24 For,
"[a]ALL FLESH IS LIKE GRASS,
AND ALL ITS GLORY LIKE THE FLOWER OF
GRASS.
THE GRASS WITHERS,
AND THE FLOWER FALLS OFF,
25 [a]BUT THE WORD OF THE LORD ENDURES
FOREVER."
And this is [b]the word which was [1]preached
to you.

As Newborn Babes

2 Therefore, [a]putting aside all [1]malice and
all deceit and [2]hypocrisy and [2]envy and
all [2b]slander,
2 [a]like newborn babies, long for the

13 [1]Lit *gird the loins of your mind* [2]Lit *be sober* [3]Or *which is announced* [a]Eph 6:14 [b]1 Thess 5:6, 8; 2 Tim 4:5; 1 Pet 4:7; 5:8 [c]1 Pet 1:3 [d]1 Pet 1:10 [e]1 Pet 1:7 **14** [1]Lit *children of obedience* [2]Or *conform yourselves* [a]1 Pet 1:2 [b]Rom 12:2; 1 Pet 4:2f [c]Eph 4:18 **15** [1]Lit *according to* [2]Or *become* [a]1 Thess 4:7; 1 John 3:3 [b]2 Cor 7:1 [c]James 3:13 **16** [a]Lev 11:44f; 19:2; 20:7 **17** [a]Ps 89:26; Jer 3:19; Matt 6:9 [b]Acts 10:34 [c]Matt 16:27 [d]2 Cor 7:1; Heb 12:28; 1 Pet 3:15 [e]1 Pet 2:11 **18** [1]Or *ransomed* [a]Is 52:3; 1 Cor 6:20; Titus 2:14; Heb 9:12 [b]Eph 4:17 **19** [a]Acts 20:28; 1 Pet 1:2 [b]John 1:29 **20** [1]Lit *at the end of the times* [a]Acts 2:23; Eph 1:4; 1 Pet 1:2; Rev 13:8 [b]Matt 25:34 [c]Heb 9:26 [d]Heb 2:14 **21** [a]Rom 4:24; 10:9 [b]John 17:5, 24; 1 Tim 3:16; Heb 2:9 [c]1 Pet 1:3 **22** [1]Lit *unhypocritical* [2]Two early mss read *a clean heart* [a]1 Pet 1:2 [b]James 4:8 [c]John 13:34; Rom 12:10; Heb 13:1; 1 Pet 2:17; 3:8 **23** [a]John 3:3; 1 Pet 1:3 [b]John 1:13 [c]Heb 4:12 **24** [a]Is 40:6ff; James 1:10f **25** [1]Lit *preached as good news to you* [a]Is 40:8 [b]Heb 6:5 **2:1** [1]Or *wickedness* [2]plural nouns [a]Eph 4:22, 25, 31; James 1:21 [b]James 4:11 **2** [a]Matt 18:3; 19:14; Mark 10:15; Luke 18:17; 1 Cor 14:20

1:13 *prepare . . . for action.* The first of a long series of exhortations (actually imperatives) that end at 5:11. This one is a graphic call for action. In the language of the first century it meant that the reader should literally gather up his long, flowing garments and be ready for physical action. *grace to be brought to you.* The final state of complete blessedness and deliverance from sin. Peter later indicates that a major purpose of this letter is to encourage and testify regarding the true grace of God (5:12).
1:14 *children.* Christians, born into the family of God (see v. 23), are children of their heavenly Father (v. 17) and can pray, "Our Father who is in heaven" (Matt 6:9). Believers are also described as being adopted into God's family (see Rom 8:15 and note).
1:16 BE HOLY, FOR I AM HOLY. To be holy is to be set apart—set apart from sin and impurity, and set apart to God. The complete moral perfection of God, whose eyes are too pure to look on evil with favor (Hab 1:13), should move His people to strive for moral purity. 1 Peter is a letter of practical earnestness, filled with exhortations and encouragements.
1:17 *impartially.* See Rom 2:11; James 2:1. *your stay on earth.* See note on v. 1. *fear.* Not terror, but wholesome reverence and respect for God, which is the basis for all godly living (cf. Prov 1:7; 8:13; 16:6).
1:18 *redeemed.* In the Bible, to redeem means to free someone from something bad by paying a penalty, or a ransom (see e.g., Ex 21:30 and note; see also Ex 13:13). Likewise, in the Greek world slaves could be redeemed by the payment of a price, either by someone else or by the slave himself. Similarly, Jesus redeems believers from the "curse of the Law" (Gal 3:13) and "every lawless deed" (Titus 2:14). The ransom price is not silver or gold, but Christ's blood (Eph 1:7; 1 Pet 1:19; Rev 5:9), i.e., His death (Matt 20:28; Mark 10:45; Heb 9:15) or Christ Himself (Gal 3:13). The result is the "forgiveness of sins" (Col 1:14) and "being justified" (Rom 3:24; see note there). *futile way of life inherited from your forefathers.* Some maintain that the recipients must have been pagans because the NT stresses the emptiness of pagan life (Rom 1:21; Eph 4:17). Others think they were Jews since Jews were traditionalists who stressed the influence of the father as teacher in the home. In the light of the context of the whole letter, probably both Jews and Gentiles are addressed.
1:19 *lamb.* The OT sacrifices were types (foreshadowings) of Christ, depicting the ultimate and only effective sacrifice. Thus Christ is the Passover lamb (1 Cor 5:7), who takes away the sin of the world (John 1:29). *unblemished and spotless.* See Heb 9:14 and note; see also Introduction to Leviticus: Themes.
1:20 *foreknown.* God knew before creation that it would be necessary for Christ to redeem man (cf. Rev 13:8), but He has revealed Christ in these last times. Or the Greek for "foreknown" may also be rendered "chosen." Then the meaning would be that in eternity past God "chose" Christ as Redeemer. *these last times.* See notes on Acts 2:17; 1 Tim 4:1; 2 Tim 3:1; Heb 1:1; 1 John 2:18.
1:22 *sincere love.* See Rom 12:9. *love one another.* A command no doubt based on John 13:34–35. See also 1 Thess 4:9–10, where, like Peter, Paul commends his readers for their love of fellow believers and then urges them to love still more.
1:23 *born again . . . through the . . . word of God.* The new birth comes about through the direct action of the Holy Spirit (Titus 3:5), but the word of God also plays an important role (see James 1:18), for it presents the gospel to the sinner and calls on him to repent and believe in Christ (see v. 25). *seed which is perishable . . . imperishable.* In this context the seed is doubtless the word of God, which is imperishable, living and enduring.
1:25 THE WORD . . . ENDURES FOREVER. The main point of the quotation here.
2:1 *Therefore.* Connects the exhortations that follow with 1:23–25; compare "born again" (1:23) with "newborn babies" (2:2).
2:2 *long for.* The unrestrained hunger of a healthy baby provides an example of the kind of eager desire for spiritual food

[1][b]pure [2]milk of the word, so that by it you
may [c]grow [3]in respect to salvation,
3 if you have [a]tasted [1][b]the kindness of
the Lord.

As Living Stones

4 And coming to Him as to a living stone
which has been [a]rejected by men, but is
[1]choice and precious in the sight of God,
5 [a]you also, as living stones, [1]are being
built up as a [b]spiritual house for a holy
[c]priesthood, to [d]offer up spiritual sacrifices
acceptable to God through Jesus Christ.
6 For *this* is contained in [1]Scripture:
"[a]BEHOLD, I LAY IN ZION A CHOICE STONE, A
[b]PRECIOUS CORNER *stone*,
AND HE WHO BELIEVES IN [2]HIM WILL NOT
BE [3]DISAPPOINTED."
7 [a]This precious value, then, is for you
who believe; but for those who disbelieve,
"[b]THE STONE WHICH THE BUILDERS
[c]REJECTED,
THIS BECAME THE VERY CORNER *stone*,"
8 and,
"[a]A STONE OF STUMBLING AND A ROCK OF
OFFENSE";
[b]for they stumble because they are disobedient to the word, [c]and to this *doom* they were
also appointed.
9 But you are [a]A CHOSEN RACE, A royal
[b]PRIESTHOOD, A [c]HOLY NATION, [d]A PEOPLE FOR
God's OWN POSSESSION, so that you may proclaim the excellencies of Him who has called
you [e]out of darkness into His marvelous
light;
10 [a]for you once were NOT A PEOPLE, but
now you are THE PEOPLE OF GOD; you had NOT
RECEIVED MERCY, but now you have RECEIVED
MERCY.
11 [a]Beloved, [b]I urge you as [c]aliens and
strangers to abstain from [d]fleshly lusts which
wage [e]war against the soul.
12 [a]Keep your behavior excellent among
the Gentiles, so that in the thing in which
they [b]slander you as evildoers, they may
[1]because of your good deeds, as they
observe *them*, [c]glorify God [d]in the day of
[2]visitation.

2 [1]Or *unadulterated* [2]Or *spiritual* (Gr *logikos*) *milk* [3]Or *up to salvation* [b]1 Cor 3:2 [c]Eph 4:15f
3 [1]Lit *that the Lord is kind* [a]Heb 6:5 [b]Ps 34:8; Titus 3:4
4 [1]Lit *chosen;* or *elect* [a]1 Pet 2:7
5 [1]Or *allow yourselves to be built up;* or *build yourselves up* [a]1 Cor 3:9 [b]Gal 6:10; 1 Tim 3:15 [c]Is 61:6; 66:21; 1 Pet 2:9; Rev 1:6 [d]Rom 15:16; Heb 13:15
6 [1]Or *a scripture* [2]Or *it* [3]Or *put to shame* [a]Is 28:16; Rom 9:32, 33; 10:11; 1 Pet 2:8 [b]Eph 2:20
7 [a]2 Cor 2:16; 1 Pet 2:7, 8 [b]Ps 118:22; Matt 21:42; Luke 2:34 [c]1 Pet 2:4
8 [a]Is 8:14 [b]1 Cor 1:23; Gal 5:11 [c]Rom 9:22
9 [a]Is 43:20f; Deut 10:15 [b]Is 61:6; 66:21; 1 Pet 2:5; Rev 1:6 [c]Ex 19:6; Deut 7:6 [d]Ex 19:5; Deut 4:20; 14:2; Titus 2:14 [e]Is 9:2; 42:16; Acts 26:18; 2 Cor 4:6
10 [a]Hos 1:10; 2:23; Rom 9:25; 10:19
11 [a]Heb 6:9; 1 Pet 4:12 [b]Rom 12:1 [c]Lev 25:23; Ps 39:12; Eph 2:19; Heb 11:13; 1 Pet 1:17 [d]Rom 13:14; Gal 5:16, 24 [e]James 4:1
12 [1]Or *as a result of* [2]I.e. Christ's coming again in judgment [a]2 Cor 8:21; Phil 2:15; Titus 2:8; 1 Pet 2:15; 3:16 [b]Acts 28:22 [c]Matt 5:16; 9:8; John 13:31; 1 Pet 4:11, 16 [d]Is 10:3; Luke 19:44

that ought to mark the believer. *pure milk of the word.* Probably referring to God's word (1:23,25). The author is speaking figuratively. Milk is not to be understood here as in 1 Cor 3:2; Heb 5:12–14—in unfavorable contrast to solid food—but as an appropriate nourishment for babies. *grow.* The Greek for this phrase is the standard term for the desirable growth of children.

2:3 *have tasted.* The tense of the Greek verb used here suggests that an initial act of tasting is referred to. Since this taste has proved satisfactory, the believers are urged to long for additional spiritual food.

2:4 *living stone.* Christ (see vv. 6–8; cf. Matt 21:42; Mark 12:10–11; Luke 20:17; Acts 4:11; Rom 9:33). The stone is living in that it is personal. Furthermore He is a life-giving stone. Christ as the Son of God has life in Himself (John 1:4; 5:26). See also "living water" (John 4:10–14; 7:38), "living bread" (John 6:51) and "living way" (Heb 10:20). *rejected by men, but is choice . . . in the sight of God.* Peter repeatedly makes a contrast in Acts between the hostility of unbelieving men toward Jesus and God's exaltation of Him (Acts 2:22–36; 3:13–15; 4:10–11; 10:39–42).

2:5 *living stones.* Believers are not literal pieces of rock, but are persons. In addition, they derive their life from Christ, who is the original living Stone to whom they have come (v. 4), the "life-giving spirit" (1 Cor 15:45). These references to stones may well reflect Jesus' words to Peter in Matt 16:18. *spiritual house.* The house is spiritual in a metaphorical sense, but also in that it is formed and indwelt by the Spirit of God. Every stone in the house has been made alive by the Holy Spirit, sent by the exalted living Stone, Jesus Christ (cf. Acts 2:33). The OT temple provides the background of this passage (cf. John 2:19; 1 Cor 3:16; Eph 2:19–22). *holy priesthood.* The whole body of believers. As priests, believers are to (1) reflect the holiness of God and that of their high priest (see 1:15; Heb 7:26; 10:10), (2) offer spiritual sacrifices (here), (3) intercede for man before God and (4) represent God before man. *spiritual sacrifices.* The NT refers to a variety of offerings: bodies offered to God (Rom 12:1), offerings of money or material goods (Phil 4:18; Heb 13:16), sacrifices of praise to God (Heb 13:15) and sacrifices of doing good (Heb 13:16). *acceptable to God.* Through the work of our Mediator, Jesus Christ (cf. John 14:6). Believers are living stones that make up a spiritual temple in which, as a holy priesthood, they offer up spiritual sacrifices.

2:6 *PRECIOUS CORNER stone.* See Ps 118:22; Matt 21:42; Mark 12:10; Luke 20:17; Acts 4:11. This is an obvious reference to Christ, as vv. 6b–8 make clear. The corner stone, which determined the design and orientation of the building, was the most significant stone in the structure. The picture that Peter creates is of a structure made up of believers (living stones, v. 5), the design and orientation of which are all in keeping with Christ, the corner stone. *HE WHO BELIEVES IN HIM.* Two attitudes toward the corner stone are evident: (1) Some trust in Him; (2) others reject Him (v. 7) and, as a result, stumble and fall (v. 8).

2:8 *to this doom they were also appointed.* Some see here an indication that some people are destined to fall and be lost. Others say that unbelievers are destined to be lost because God in His foreknowledge (cf. 1:2) saw them as unbelievers. Still others hold that Peter means that unbelief is destined to result in eternal destruction.

2:9 *CHOSEN RACE.* See Eph 1:4 and note; Is 43:10,20; 44:1–2. As Israel was called God's chosen people in the OT, so in the NT believers are designated as chosen, or elect. *royal PRIESTHOOD.* See note on v. 5; see also Is 61:6. *HOLY NATION.* See Deut 28:9. *PEOPLE FOR God's OWN POSSESSION.* See Deut 4:20; 7:6; 14:2; Is 43:21; Mal 3:17. Though once not the people of God, they are now the recipients of God's mercy (see Hos 1:6–10; Rom 9:25–26; 10:19). *proclaim the excellencies of Him.* See Is 43:21; Acts 2:11.

2:10 See notes on Hos 1:6,9; 2:1,22; Rom 9:25–26. In Hosea it is Israel who is not God's people; in Romans it is the Gentiles to whom Paul applies Hosea's words; in 1 Peter the words are applied to both.

2:11 *aliens and strangers.* See note on 1:1. As aliens and strangers on earth, whose citizenship is in heaven, they are to be separated from the corruption of the world, not yielding to its destructive sinful desires.

2:12 *good deeds, as they observe them.* Deeds that can be seen

Honor Authority

13 [a]Submit yourselves for the Lord's sake
to every human institution, whether to a
king as the one in authority,
14 or to governors as sent [1]by him [a]for the
punishment of evildoers and the [b]praise of
those who do right.
15 For [1a]such is the will of God that by
doing right you may [b]silence the ignorance
of foolish men.
16 *Act* as [a]free men, and [1]do not use your
freedom as a covering for evil, but *use it* as
[b]bondslaves of God.
17 [a]Honor all people, [b]love the brotherhood, [c]fear God, [d]honor the [1]king.
18 [a]Servants, be submissive to your masters with all respect, not only to those who
are good and [b]gentle, but also to those who
are [1]unreasonable.
19 For this *finds* [1]favor, if for the sake of
[a]conscience toward God a person bears up
under sorrows when suffering unjustly.
20 For what credit is there if, when you
sin and are harshly treated, you endure it
with patience? But if [a]when you do what is
right and suffer *for it* you patiently endure it,
this *finds* [1]favor with God.

Christ Is Our Example

21 For [a]you have been called for this purpose, [b]since Christ also suffered for you,
leaving you [c]an example for you to follow in
His steps,
22 WHO [a]COMMITTED NO SIN, NOR WAS ANY
DECEIT FOUND IN HIS MOUTH;
23 [1]and while being [a]reviled, He did not
revile in return; while suffering, He uttered
no threats, but kept entrusting *Himself* to
Him who judges righteously;
24 and He Himself [1a]bore our sins in His
body on the [2b]cross, so that we [c]might die to
[3]sin and live to righteousness; for [d]by His
[4]wounds you were [e]healed.
25 For you were [a]continually straying like
sheep, but now you have returned to the
[b]Shepherd and [1]Guardian of your souls.

13 [a]Rom 13:1
14 [1]Lit *through* [a]Rom 13:4 [b]Rom 13:3
15 [1]Lit *so* [a]1 Pet 3:17 [b]1 Pet 2:12
16 [1]Lit *not having* [a]John 8:32; James 1:25 [b]Rom 6:22; 1 Cor 7:22
17 [1]Or *emperor* [a]Rom 12:10; 13:7 [b]1 Pet 1:22 [c]Prov 24:21 [d]Matt 22:21; 1 Pet 2:13
18 [1]Or *perverse* [a]Eph 6:5 [b]James 3:17
19 [1]Or *grace* [a]Rom 13:5; 1 Pet 3:14, 16f
20 [a]1 Pet 3:17
20 [1]V 19, note 1
21 [a]Acts 14:22; 1 Pet 3:9 [b]1 Pet 3:18; 4:1, 13 [c]Matt 11:29; 16:24
22 [a]Is 53:9; 2 Cor 5:21

23 [1]Lit *who* [a]Is 53:7; Heb 12:3; 1 Pet 3:9 **24** [1]Or *carried...up to the cross* [2]Lit *wood* [3]Lit *sins* [4]Lit *wound;* or *welt* [a]Is 53:4, 11; 1 Cor 15:3; Heb 9:28 [b]Acts 5:30 [c]Rom 6:2, 13 [d]Is 53:5 [e]Heb 12:13; James 5:16 **25** [1]Or *Bishop, Overseer* [a]Is 53:6 [b]John 10:11; 1 Pet 5:4

---

to be good (cf. Matt 5:16). The Greek word translated "observe" refers to a careful watching, over a period of time. The pagans' evaluation is not a "snap judgment." *the day of visitation.* Perhaps the day of judgment and ensuing punishment, or possibly the day when God visits a person with salvation. The believer's good life may then influence the unbeliever to repent and believe.

2:13–3:6 Peter urges that Christians submit to all legitimate authorities, whether or not the persons exercising authority are believers. The recognition of properly constituted authority is necessary for the greatest good of the largest number of people, and it is necessary to best fulfill the will of God in the world.

2:13 *every human institution.* Authority established among men depends on God for its existence (Rom 13:1–2). Indirectly, when one disobeys a human ruler he disobeys God, who ordained the system of human government (cf. Rom 13:2). *to a king.* When Peter wrote, the emperor was the godless, brutal Nero, who ruled from A.D. 54 to 68 (see Introduction: Author and Date). Of course, obedience to the emperor must never be in violation of the law of God (to see this basic principle in action cf. Acts 4:19; 5:29).

2:15 *silence the ignorance.* Good citizenship counters false charges made against Christians and thus commends the gospel to unbelievers.

2:16 *Act as free men.* Does not authorize rebellion against constituted authority, but urges believers freely to submit to God and to earthly authorities (as long as such submission does not conflict with the law of God). *as a covering for evil.* Genuine freedom is the freedom to serve God, a freedom exercised under law. Liberty is not license to do as we please.

2:17 *Honor all people.* Because every human being bears the image of God. *fear God.* See note on 1:17.

2:18 *Servants.* Household servants, whatever their particular training and functions. The context indicates that Peter is addressing Christian slaves. NT writers do not attack slavery as an institution (see note on Eph 6:5), but the NT contains the principles that ultimately uprooted slavery. Peter's basic teachings on the subject may apply to employer-employee relations today (see Eph 6:5–8; Col 3:22–25; 1 Tim 6:1–2; Titus 2:9–10).

2:19 *conscience toward God.* As submission to duly constituted authority is "for the Lord's sake" (v. 13; cf. Eph 6:7–8), so one will submit to the point of suffering unjustly if it is God's will.

2:21 *you have been called for this purpose.* The patient endurance of injustice is part of God's plan for the Christian. It was an important feature of the true grace of God experienced by the readers (5:12). *Christ also suffered for you.* Cf. Is 52:13–53:12. Christ is the supreme example of suffering evil for doing good. His experience as the suffering Servant-Savior transforms the sufferings of His followers from misery into privilege.

2:22 Scripture declares the sinlessness of Christ in the clearest of terms, allowing for no exception (see 1:19; Acts 3:14; 2 Cor 5:21; Heb 4:15; 7:26; 1 John 3:5). *ANY DECEIT.* Cf. v. 1; 3:10.

2:23 Prominent examples of our Lord's silent submission are found in Matt 27:12–14,34–44 and parallels. *entrusting Himself.* Cf. 4:19.

2:24 *bore our sins.* See Is 53:12. Although dealing with the example set by Christ, Peter touches also on the redemptive work of Christ, which has significance far beyond that of setting an example. Peter here points to the substitutionary character of the atonement. Christ, like the sacrificial lamb of the OT, died for our sins, the innocent for the guilty. *cross.* See Acts 5:30 and note; see also Acts 10:39; 13:29; Gal 3:13 and note. *that we might die to sin and live to righteousness.* Cf. Rom 6:3–14. Peter stresses the bearing of the cross on our sanctification. As a result of Christ's death on the cross, believers are positionally dead to sin so that they may live new lives and present themselves to God as instruments of righteousness (see note on Rom 6:11–13). *you were healed.* See Is 53:5; not generally viewed as a reference to physical healing, though some believe that such healing was included in the atonement (cf. Matt 8:16–17). Others see spiritual healing in this passage. It is another way of asserting that Christ's death brings salvation to those who trust in Him.

2:25 *Shepherd.* A concept raised here in connection with the allusion to the wandering sheep of Is 53. The sheep had wandered from their shepherd, and to their Shepherd (Christ) they have now returned. See note on Ps 23:1; see also John 10:11,14 and note on Heb 13:20. *Guardian.* Christ (cf. 5:2,4; Acts 20:28). Elders are to be both shepherds and guardians, i.e., they are to

Godly Living

3 [a]In the same way, you wives, [b]be submissive to your own husbands so that even if any *of them* are disobedient to the word, they may be [c]won without a word by the behavior of their wives,

2 as they observe your chaste and [1]respectful behavior.

3 [a]Your adornment must not be *merely* external—braiding the hair, and wearing gold jewelry, or putting on dresses;

4 but *let it be* [a]the hidden person of the heart, with the imperishable quality of a gentle and quiet spirit, which is precious in the sight of God.

5 For in this way in former times the holy women also, [a]who hoped in God, used to adorn themselves, being submissive to their own husbands;

6 just as Sarah obeyed Abraham, [a]calling him lord, and you have become her children if you do what is right [1b]without being frightened by any fear.

7 [a]You husbands in the same way, live with *your wives* in an understanding way, as with [1b]someone weaker, since she is a woman; and show her honor as a fellow heir of the grace of life, so that your prayers will not be hindered.

8 [1]To sum up, [a]all of you be harmonious, sympathetic, [b]brotherly, [c]kindhearted, and [d]humble in spirit;

9 [a]not returning evil for evil or [b]insult for insult, but [1]giving a [c]blessing instead; for [d]you were called for the very purpose that you might [e]inherit a blessing.

10 For,

"[a]THE ONE WHO DESIRES LIFE, TO LOVE AND SEE GOOD DAYS,
MUST KEEP HIS TONGUE FROM EVIL AND HIS LIPS FROM SPEAKING DECEIT.
11 "[a]HE MUST TURN AWAY FROM EVIL AND DO GOOD;
HE MUST SEEK PEACE AND PURSUE IT.
12 "[a]FOR THE EYES OF THE LORD ARE TOWARD THE RIGHTEOUS,
AND HIS EARS ATTEND TO THEIR PRAYER,
BUT THE FACE OF THE LORD IS AGAINST THOSE WHO DO EVIL."

13 [a]Who is [1]there to harm you if you prove zealous for what is good?

14 But even if you should [a]suffer for the sake of righteousness, [b]you [1]are blessed. [c]AND DO NOT FEAR THEIR [2]INTIMIDATION, AND DO NOT BE TROUBLED,

15 but [1]sanctify [a]Christ as Lord in your hearts, always *being* ready [b]to make a [2]defense to everyone who asks you to give an account for the [a]hope that is in you, yet [c]with gentleness and [3d]reverence;

16 [1]and keep a [a]good conscience so that in the thing in which [b]you are slandered,

3:1 [a]1 Pet 3:7 [b]Eph 5:22; Col 3:18 [c]1 Cor 9:19
2 [1]Lit *with respect*
3 [a]Is 3:18ff; 1 Tim 2:9
4 [a]Rom 7:22
5 [a]1 Tim 5:5; 1 Pet 1:3
6 [1]Lit *and are not* [a]Gen 18:12 [b]1 Pet 3:14
7 [1]Lit *a weaker vessel* [a]Eph 5:25; Col 3:19 [b]1 Thess 4:4
8 [1]Or *Finally* [a]Rom 12:16 [b]1 Pet 1:22 [c]Eph 4:32 [d]Eph 4:2; Phil 2:3; 1 Pet 5:5
9 [1]Lit *blessing instead* [a]Rom 12:17; 1 Thess 5:15 [b]1 Cor 4:12; 1 Pet 2:23 [c]Luke 6:28; Rom 12:14; 1 Cor 4:12 [d]1 Pet 2:21 [e]Gal 3:14; Heb 6:14; 12:17
10 [a]Ps 34:12, 13
11 [a]Ps 34:14
12 [a]Ps 34:15, 16
13 [1]Lit *the one who will harm you* [a]Prov 16:7
14 [1]Or would be [2]Lit *fear* [a]Matt 5:10; 1 Pet 2:19ff; 4:15f [b]James 5:11 [c]Is 8:12f; 1 Pet 3:6
15 [1]I.e. set apart [2]Or *argument;* or *explanation* [3]Or *fear* [a]1 Pet 1:3 [b]Col 4:6 [c]2 Tim 2:25 [d]1 Pet 1:17
16 [1]Lit *having a good* [a]1 Tim 1:5; Heb 13:18; 1 Pet 3:21 [b]1 Pet 2:12, 15

look out for the welfare of the flock. These are not two separate offices or functions; the second term is a further explanation of the first.

3:1–6 Instructions to wives (cf. Gen 3:16; 1 Cor 11:3; Eph 5:22–24; Col 3:18; 1 Tim 2:9–10; Titus 2:5).

3:1 *In the same way.* As believers are to submit to government authorities (2:13–17), and as slaves are to submit to masters (2:18–25). *be submissive.* The same Greek verb as is used in 2:13,18, a term that calls for submission to a recognized authority. Inferiority is not implied by this passage. The submission is one of role or function necessary for the orderly operation of the home. *the word.* The gospel message. *without a word.* Believing wives are not to rely on argumentation to win their unbelieving husbands, but on the quality of their lives. "Actions speak louder than words."

3:2 *chaste and respectful behavior.* Their lives are to be marked by a moral purity that springs from reverence toward God.

3:3 *hair . . . jewelry.* Extreme coiffures and gaudy exhibits of jewelry. Christian women should not rely on such extremes of adornment for beauty. *dresses.* The Greek for this word simply means "garment," but in this context expensive garments are meant.

3:5 *former times . . . holy women.* The standards stated by Peter are not limited to any particular time or culture.

3:6 *lord.* An expression of the submission called for in v. 1. *her children . . . fear.* Christian women become daughters of Sarah as they become like her in doing good and in not fearing any potential disaster, but trusting in God (cf. Prov 3:25–27).

3:7 *someone weaker.* Not a reference to moral stamina, strength of character or mental capacity, but most likely to sheer physical strength. *fellow heir of the grace of life.* Women experience the saving grace of God on equal terms with men (see Gal 3:28). *prayers will not be hindered.* Spiritual fellowship, with God and with one another, may be hindered by disregarding God's instruction concerning husband-wife relationships.

3:8–12 In 2:11–17 Peter addressed all his readers, and in 2:18–25 he spoke directly to slaves; in 3:1–6 he addressed wives, and in 3:7 husbands. Now he encourages all his readers to develop virtues appropriate in their relations with others (see "all of you," v. 8).

3:8 *be harmonious.* See Rom 12:16; Phil 2:2. *sympathetic.* See Rom 12:15; 1 Cor 12:26. *brotherly.* See 1 Thess 4:9–10; Heb 13:1. *kindhearted.* See Col 3:12. *humble.* See Phil 2:6–8.

3:9 See Rom 12:17–21.

3:10–12 Peter introduces this quotation from Ps 34 with the explanatory conjunction "For," showing that he views the quotation as giving reasons for obeying the exhortation of v. 9. According to the psalmist, (1) the one who does such things will find life to be most gratifying (v. 10), (2) his days will be good (v. 10), (3) God's eyes will ever be on him to bless him (v. 12), and (4) God's ears will be ready to hear his prayer (v. 12).

3:13 *Who . . . harm you . . . ?* As a general rule, people are not harmed for acts of kindness. This is especially true if one is an enthusiast ("eager") for doing good.

3:14 *even if you should suffer.* In the Greek, this conditional clause is the furthest removed from stating a reality. Suffering for righteousness is a remote possibility, but even if it does occur, it brings special blessing to the sufferer (see Matt 5:10–12). *THEIR INTIMIDATION.* In Isaiah's context God's people are not to view things as unbelievers do. They are not to make worldly judgments or be afraid of the enemies of God. Instead, they are to fear God (see Is 8:13).

3:15 *sanctify Christ as Lord.* An exhortation to the readers to make an inner commitment to Christ. Then they need not be

those who revile your good behavior in
Christ will be put to shame.
17 For [a]it is better, [b]if [1]God should will it
so, that you suffer for doing what is right
rather than for doing what is wrong.
18 For [a]Christ also died for sins [b]once for
all, *the* just for *the* unjust, so that He might
[c]bring us to God, having been put to death
[d]in the flesh, but made alive [e]in the [1]spirit;
19 in [1]which also He went and made
proclamation to the spirits *now* in prison,
20 who once were disobedient, when the
[a]patience of God [b]kept waiting in the days of
Noah, during the construction of [c]the ark, in
which a few, that is, [d]eight [e]persons, were
brought safely through *the* [1]water.
21 [a]Corresponding to that, baptism now
saves you—[b]not the removal of dirt from the
flesh, but an appeal to God [1]for a [c]good conscience—through [d]the resurrection of Jesus
Christ,
22 [a]who is at the right hand of God, [b]hav-
ing gone into heaven, [c]after angels and
authorities and powers had been subjected
to Him.

17 [1]Lit *the will of God* [a]1 Pet 2:20; 4:15f [b]Acts 18:21; 1 Pet 1:6; 2:15; 4:19
18 [1]Or *Spirit* [a]1 Pet 2:21 [b]Heb 9:26, 28; 10:10 [c]Rom 5:2; Eph 3:12 [d]Col 1:22; 1 Pet 4:1 [e]1 Pet 4:6
19 [1]Or *whom*
20 [1]I.e. the great flood [a]Rom 2:4 [b]Gen 6:3, 5, 13f [c]Heb 11:7 [d]Gen 8:18; 2 Pet 2:5 [e]Acts 2:41; 1 Pet 1:9, 22; 2:25; 4:19
21 [1]Or *from* [a]Acts 16:33; Titus 3:5 [b]Heb 9:14; 10:22 [c]1 Tim 1:5; Heb 13:18; 1 Pet 3:16 [d]1 Pet 1:3
22 [a]Mark 16:19 [b]Heb 4:14; 6:20
22 [c]Rom 8:38f; Heb 1:6

Keep Fervent in Your Love

4 Therefore, since [a]Christ has [1]suffered in
the flesh, [b]arm yourselves also with the
same purpose, because [c]he who has [1]suf-
fered in the flesh has ceased from sin,
2 [a]so as to live [b]the rest of the time in the
flesh no longer for the lusts of men, but for
the [c]will of God.
3 For [a]the time already past is sufficient
for you to have carried out the desire of the
Gentiles, [1][b]having pursued a course of sensuality, lusts, drunkenness, carousing, drinking parties and [2]abominable idolatries.
4 In *all* this, they are surprised that you

4:1 [1]I.e. suffered death [a]1 Pet 2:21 [b]Eph 6:13 [c]Rom 6:7
2 [a]Rom 6:2; Col 3:3 [b]1 Pet 1:14 [c]Mark 3:35 **3** [1]Lit *having gone in* [2]Lit *lawless* [a]1 Cor 12:2 [b]Rom 13:13; Eph 2:2; 4:17ff

speechless when called on to defend their faith. Instead, there will be a readiness to answer. *with gentleness and reverence.* The Christian is always to be a gentleman or gentle woman, even when opposed by unbelievers. Our apologetic ("defense") is always to be given with love, never in degrading terms.

3:16 *put to shame.* Because it is shown to be obviously untrue and because the believer's loving attitude puts the opponent's bitterness in a bad light.

3:18 *once for all.* See Heb 9:28. *the just for the unjust.* Peter, like Paul in Phil 2:5–11, refers to Jesus as an example of the type of conduct that should characterize the Christian. We are to be ready to suffer for doing good (vv. 13–14,17). The thought of Christ's suffering and death, however, leads Peter to comment on what occurred after Christ's death—which leads to tangential remarks about preaching to the spirits in prison and about baptism (see vv. 19–21). *made alive in the spirit.* Referring to Christ's own spirit, through which "He went and made proclamation to the spirits now in prison" (v. 19).

3:19–20a Three main interpretations of this passage have been suggested: 1. Some hold that in His preincarnate state Christ went and preached through Noah to the wicked generation of that time. 2. Others argue that between His death and resurrection Christ went to the prison where fallen angels are incarcerated and there preached to the angels who are said to have left their proper state and married human women during Noah's time (cf. Gen 6:1–4; 2 Pet 2:4; Jude 6). The "sons of God" in Gen 6:2,4 are said to have been angels, as they are in Job 1:6; 2:1. The message He preached to these evil angels was probably a declaration of victory. 3. Still others say that between death and resurrection Christ went to the place of the dead and preached to the spirits of Noah's wicked contemporaries. What He proclaimed may have been the gospel, or it may have been a declaration of victory for Christ and doom for His hearers.

The weakness of the first view is that it does not relate the event to Christ's death and resurrection, as the context seems to do. The main problem with the second view is that it assumes sexual relations between angels and women, and such physical relations may not be possible for angels since they are spirits. A major difficulty with the third view is that the term "spirits" is only used of human beings when qualifying terms are added. Otherwise the term seems restricted to supernatural beings.

3:21 *Corresponding to that, baptism.* There is a double figure here. The flood symbolizes baptism, and baptism symbolizes salvation. The flood was a figure of baptism in that in both instances the water that spoke of judgment (in the flood the death of the wicked, in baptism the death of Christ and the believer) is the water that saves. Baptism is a symbol of salvation in that it depicts Christ's death, burial and resurrection and our identification with Him in these experiences (see Rom 6:4). *now saves you.* In reality, believers are saved by what baptism symbolizes—Christ's death and resurrection. The symbol and the reality are so closely related that the symbol is sometimes used to refer to the reality (see note on Rom 6:3–4). *appeal to God for a good conscience.* The act of baptism is a commitment on the part of the believer in all good conscience to make sure that what baptism symbolizes will become a reality in his life. *saves you . . . through the resurrection of Jesus Christ.* In the final analysis people are saved not by any ritual, but by the supernatural power of the resurrection.

3:22 *at the right hand of God.* See Heb 1:3; 12:2. *gone into heaven.* See Acts 1:9–11. *angels and authorities and powers.* See Eph 1:21; 6:12.

4:1 *Therefore.* Since 3:19–22 is parenthetical, 4:1 ties directly back to 3:18. The aspect of Christ's suffering that these passages stress is suffering unjustly because one has done good. Furthermore, it is physical suffering—"in the flesh." *arm yourselves also with the same purpose.* Believers are to be prepared also to suffer unjustly, and to face such abuse with Christ's attitude—with His willingness to suffer for doing good. (For a similar principle in Paul's writings see Phil 2:5–11.) *because . . . has ceased from sin.* Such suffering enables one to straighten out his priorities. Sinful desires and practices that once seemed important now seem insignificant when one's life is in jeopardy. Serious suffering for Christ advances the progress of sanctification. (Some see a parallel between this passage and Rom 6:1–14, but Peter is not referring to being dead to sin in Paul's sense.)

4:2 *for the lusts of men . . . for the will of God.* Now that Christ's attitude prevails, God's will is the determining factor in life.

4:3 *time already past.* The time before conversion. *the Gentiles.* This, along with the term "idolatries," suggests that at least some of the readers were non-Jews (see note on 1:1), converted from pagan backgrounds.

4:4 *they are surprised . . . and they malign you.* One of the reasons for the suffering the readers were undergoing.

do not run with *them* into the same excesses of [a]dissipation, and they [b]malign *you;*

5 but they will give account to Him who is ready to judge [a]the living and the dead.

6 For [a]the gospel has for this purpose been [1]preached even to those who are dead, that though they are judged in the flesh as men, they may live in the spirit according to *the will of* God.

7 [a]The end of all things [1]is near; therefore, [b]be of sound judgment and sober *spirit* for the purpose of [2]prayer.

8 Above all, [a]keep fervent in your love for one another, because [b]love covers a multitude of sins.

9 [a]Be hospitable to one another without [b]complaint.

10 [a]As each one has received a *special* gift, employ it in serving one another as good [b]stewards of the manifold grace of God.

11 [a]Whoever speaks, *is to do so* [1]as one who is speaking the [b]utterances of God; whoever serves *is to do so* as one who is serving [2c]by the strength which God supplies; so that [d]in all things God may be glorified through Jesus Christ, [e]to whom belongs the glory and dominion forever and ever. Amen.

Share the Sufferings of Christ

12 [a]Beloved, do not be surprised at the [b]fiery ordeal among you, which comes upon you for your testing, as though some strange thing were happening to you;

13 but to the degree that you [a]share the sufferings of Christ, keep on rejoicing, so that also at the [b]revelation of His glory [c]you may rejoice with exultation.

14 If you are reviled [1a]for the name of Christ, [b]you are blessed, [c]because the Spirit of glory and of God rests on you.

15 Make sure that [a]none of you suffers as a murderer, or thief, or evildoer, or a [1b]troublesome meddler;

16 but if *anyone suffers* as a [a]Christian, he is not to be ashamed, but is to [b]glorify God in this name.

17 For *it is* time for judgment [a]to begin [1]with [b]the household of God; and if *it* [c]*begins* with us first, what *will be* the outcome for those [d]who do not obey the [e]gospel of God?

18 [a]AND IF IT IS WITH DIFFICULTY THAT THE RIGHTEOUS IS SAVED, [1]WHAT WILL BECOME OF THE [b]GODLESS MAN AND THE SINNER?

19 Therefore, those also who suffer according to [a]the will of God shall entrust their souls to a faithful Creator in doing what is right.

4 [a]Eph 5:18 [b]1 Pet 3:16 **5** [a]Acts 10:42; Rom 14:9; 2 Tim 4:1 **6** [1]I.e. preached in their lifetimes [a]1 Pet 3:18 **7** [1]Lit *has come near* [2]Lit *prayers* [a]Rom 13:11; Heb 9:26; James 5:8; 1 John 2:18 [b]1 Pet 1:13 **8** [a]1 Pet 1:22 [b]Prov 10:12; 1 Cor 13:4ff; James 5:20 **9** [a]1 Tim 3:2; Heb 13:2 [b]Phil 2:14 **10** [a]Rom 12:6f [b]1 Cor 4:1 **11** [1]Lit *as utterances* [2]Lit *from* [a]1 Thess 2:4; Titus 2:1, 15; Heb 13:7 [b]Acts 7:38 [c]Eph 1:19; 6:10 [d]1 Cor 10:31; 1 Pet 2:12 [e]Rom 11:36; 1 Pet 5:11; Rev 1:6; 5:13 **12** [a]1 Pet 2:11 [b]1 Pet 1:6f **13** [a]Rom 8:17; 2 Cor 1:5; 4:10; Phil 3:10 [b]2 Tim 2:12 [c]1 Pet 1:7; 5:1 **14** [1]Lit *in* [a]John 15:21; Heb 11:26; 1 Pet 4:16 [b]Matt 5:11; Luke 6:22; Acts 5:41 [c]2 Cor 4:10f, 16 **15** [1]Lit *one who oversees others' affairs* [a]1 Pet 2:19f; 3:17 [b]1 Thess 4:11; 2 Thess 3:11; 1 Tim 5:13 **16** [a]Acts 5:41; 28:22; James 2:7 [b]1 Pet 4:11 **17** [1]Lit *from* [a]Jer 25:29; Ezek 9:6; Amos 3:2 [b]1 Tim 3:15; Heb 3:6; 1 Pet 2:5 [c]Rom 2:9 [d]2 Thess 1:8 [e]Rom 1:1 **18** [1]Lit *where will appear* [a]Prov 11:31; Luke 23:31 [b]1 Tim 1:9 **19** [a]1 Pet 3:17

4:5 *will give account.* See Acts 17:31; Rom 2:5,16. *Him who is ready to judge.* In the NT both the Father and the Son are said to be judge on the great, final judgment day. The Father is the ultimate source of judgment, but He will delegate judgment to the Son (cf. John 5:27; Acts 17:31). *the living and the dead.* Those alive and those dead when the final judgment day dawns.

4:6 *for this purpose.* The reason referred to is expressed in the latter part of the verse (in the "so that" clause), not in the preceding verse. *has . . . been preached even to those who are dead.* That is, to those who are *now* dead. This preaching was a past event. The word "now" does not occur in the Greek, but it is necessary to make it clear that the preaching was done not after these people had died, but while they were still alive. (There will be no opportunity for people to be saved after death; see Heb 9:27.) *though they are judged in the flesh as men.* The first reason that the gospel was preached to those now dead. Some say that this judgment is that to which all people must submit, either in this life (see John 5:24) or in the life to come (see v. 5). The gospel is preached to people in this life so that in Christ's death they may receive judgment now and avoid judgment to come. Others hold that these people are judged according to human standards by the pagan world, which does not understand why God's people no longer follow its sinful way of life (see vv. 2–4). So also the world misunderstood Christ (see Acts 2:22–24,36; 3:13–15; 5:30–32; 7:51–53). *may live in the spirit according to the will of God.* The second reason that the gospel was preached to those now dead. Some believe this means that all gospel preaching has as its goal that the hearers may live as God lives—eternally—and that this life is given by the Holy Spirit. Others maintain that it means that the ultimate reason for the preaching of the gospel is that God's people, even though the wicked world may abuse them and put them to death, will have eternal life, which the Holy Spirit imparts.

4:7 *The end . . . is near.* See note on James 5:9. *therefore.* Anticipating the end times, particularly Christ's return, should influence believers' attitudes, actions and relationships (see 2 Pet 3:11–14). *of sound judgment.* Christians are to be characterized by reason; are to make wise, mature decisions; and are to have a clearly defined, decisive purpose in life. *sober spirit.* See Gal 5:23. *prayer.* Cf. 3:7; Luke 18:1; 1 Cor 7:5; Eph 6:18; 1 Thess 5:17; 1 John 5:14–15.

4:8 *keep fervent in your love.* See 1 Thess 4:9–10; 2 Pet 1:7; 1 John 4:7–11. *love covers a multitude of sins.* Love forgives again and again (see Matt 18:21–22; 1 Cor 13:5; Eph 4:32).

4:9 *Be hospitable.* See Rom 12:13; 1 Tim 3:2; 5:10; Titus 1:8; 3 John 5–8.

4:10 *As each one has received a special gift, employ it.* See Rom 12:4–8; 1 Cor 12:7–11.

4:11 *utterances.* The Greek for this phrase is used to refer to the Scriptures or to words God has spoken (see Acts 7:38; Rom 3:2). *to whom belongs the glory.* See 1 Cor 1:26–31; Jude 24–25.

4:12 *Beloved.* Or "Loved ones" (see 2:11). *do not be surprised at the fiery ordeal.* See 1:6–7; 2:20–21.

4:13 *share the sufferings of Christ, keep on rejoicing.* See note on Col 1:24. Peter once rebelled against the idea that Christ would suffer (see Matt 16:21–23).

4:14 *reviled for the name of Christ.* See Matt 5:11–12; John 15:18–20; Acts 5:41; 14:22; Rom 8:17; 2 Cor 1:5; Phil 3:10; 2 Tim 3:12.

4:17 *judgment to begin with the household of God.* The persecutions that believers were undergoing were divinely sent judgment intended to purify God's people. *the outcome for those who do not obey the gospel.* If God brings judgment on His own people, how much more serious will the judgment be that He will bring on unbelievers!

Serve God Willingly

5 [a]Therefore, I exhort the elders among
you, as *your* [b]fellow elder and [c]witness of
the sufferings of Christ, and a [d]partaker also
of the glory that is to be revealed,
2 shepherd [a]the flock of God among
you, exercising oversight [b]not under compulsion, but voluntarily, according to *the*
will of God; and [c]not for sordid gain, but
with eagerness;
3 nor yet as [a]lording it over [1]those allotted to your charge, but [2]proving to be [b]exam-
ples to the flock.
4 And when the Chief [a]Shepherd
appears, you will receive the [b]unfading
[1c]crown of glory.
5 [a]You younger men, likewise, [b]be subject to *your* elders; and all of you, clothe
yourselves with [c]humility toward one another, for [d]GOD IS OPPOSED TO THE PROUD, BUT GIVES
GRACE TO THE HUMBLE.
6 Therefore [a]humble yourselves under
the mighty hand of God, that He may exalt
you at the proper time,
7 casting all your [a]anxiety on Him,
because He cares for you.
8 [a]Be of sober *spirit*, [b]be on the alert.
Your adversary, [c]the devil, prowls around like
a roaring [d]lion, seeking someone to devour.
9 [1a]But resist him, [b]firm in *your* faith,
knowing that [c]the same experiences of suffering are being accomplished by your
[2]brethren who are in the world.
10 After you have suffered [a]for a little
while, the [b]God of all grace, who [c]called you
to His [d]eternal glory in Christ, will Himself
[e]perfect, [f]confirm, strengthen *and* establish
you.
11 [a]To Him *be* dominion forever and ever.
Amen.
12 Through [a]Silvanus, our faithful brother
[1](for so I regard *him*), [b]I have written to you
briefly, exhorting and testifying that this is
[c]the true grace of God. [d]Stand firm in it!
13 She who is in Babylon, chosen together with you, sends you greetings, and *so does*
my son, [a]Mark.
14 [a]Greet one another with a kiss of love.
[b]Peace be to you all who are in Christ.

5:1 [a]Acts 11:30 [b]2 John 1; 3 John 1 [c]Luke 24:48; Heb 12:1 [d]1 Pet 1:5, 7; 4:13; Rev 1:9 **2** [a]John 21:16; Acts 20:28 [b]Philem 14 [c]1 Tim 3:8 **3** [1]Lit *the allotments* [2]Or *becoming* [a]Ezek 34:4; Matt 20:25f [b]John 13:15; Phil 3:17; 1 Thess 1:7; 2 Thess 3:9; 1 Tim 4:12; Titus 2:7 **4** [1]Lit *wreath* [a]1 Pet 2:25 [b]1 Pet 1:4 [c]1 Cor 9:25 **5** [a]Luke 22:26; 1 Tim 5:1 [b]Eph 5:21 [c]1 Pet 3:8 [d]Prov 3:34; James 4:6 **6** [a]Matt 23:12; Luke 14:11; 18:14; James 4:10 **7** [a]Ps 55:22; Matt 6:25 **8** [a]1 Pet 1:13 [b]Matt 24:42

8 [c]James 4:7 [d]2 Tim 4:17

9 [1]Lit *whom resist* [2]Lit *brotherhood* [a]James 4:7 [b]Col 2:5 [c]Acts 14:22 **10** [a]1 Pet 1:6 [b]1 Pet 4:10 [c]1 Cor 1:9; 1 Thess 2:12 [d]2 Cor 4:17; 2 Tim 2:10 [e]1 Cor 1:10; Heb 13:21 [f]Rom 16:25; 2 Thess 2:17; 3:3 **11** [a]Rom 11:36; 1 Pet 4:11 **12** [1]Lit *(as I consider)* [a]2 Cor 1:19 [b]Heb 13:22 [c]Acts 11:23; 1 Pet 1:13; 4:10 [d]1 Cor 15:1 **13** [a]Acts 12:12, 25; 15:37, 39; Col 4:10; Philem 24 **14** [a]Rom 16:16 [b]Eph 6:23

5:1 *fellow elder.* See notes on Acts 20:17; 1 Tim 3:1; 5:17. Peter, who identified himself as an apostle at the beginning of his letter (1:1), chooses now to identify himself with the elders of the churches (cf. 2 John 1; 3 John 1). This would be heartening to them in light of their great responsibilities and the difficult situation faced by the churches. The churches for which these elders were responsible were scattered across much of Asia Minor (see 1:1), so if Peter was a local church officer, he must have been officially related to one of them. *witness of the sufferings of Christ.* Peter had been with Jesus from the early days of His ministry and was a witness of all its phases and aspects, including the climactic events of His suffering (cf. Matt 26:58; Mark 14:54; Luke 22:60–62; John 18:10–11,15–16). In this letter he bears notable witness to Christ's sufferings (see 2:21–24) and obeys His command in Acts 1:8. *partaker also of the glory . . . to be revealed.* Peter witnessed Christ's glory in His ministry in general (see John 1:14; 2:11), and, as one present at the transfiguration (see Matt 16:27; 17:8), he had already seen the glory of Christ's coming kingdom. In God's appointed time, just as Christ suffered and entered into glory, so all His people, after their sufferings, will participate in His future glory.

5:2 *shepherd the flock of God.* A metaphor that our Lord Himself had employed (John 10:1–18; Luke 15:3–7) and that must have been etched on Peter's mind (see John 21:15–17; cf. 1 Pet 2:25). Peter is fulfilling Christ's command to feed His sheep as he writes this letter. What he writes to the elders is reminiscent of Paul's farewell address to the Ephesian elders (especially Acts 20:28). The term "shepherd" is an OT metaphor as well (see Ezek 34:1–10, where the Lord holds the leaders of Israel responsible for failing to care for the flock). *exercising oversight.* The same term is used in Acts 20:28; Phil 1:1; 1 Tim 3:2; Titus 1:7. See note on 1 Tim 3:1. It is clear from this passage, as well as from Acts 20:17,28, that the three terms "elder," "overseer" and "shepherd" all apply to one office (see note on Titus 1:7).

5:3 *nor . . . lording it over those allotted to your charge.* Cf. Matt 16:24–27; Mark 10:42–45; Phil 2:6–11; 2 Thess 3:9. Although Peter has full apostolic authority (see v. 1), he does not lord it over his readers in this letter, but exemplifies the virtues he recommends.

5:4 *Chief Shepherd.* Christ. When He returns, He will reward those who have served as shepherds under Him. *unfading.* See 1:4.

5:5 *be subject.* The theme that runs throughout 2:13–3:6. Here it applies to church leaders. *clothe yourselves with humility toward one another.* Peter may have had in mind the footwashing scene of John 13, in which he figured prominently. Although he was at first rebellious, he writes now with understanding (see John 13:7).

5:6 See Luke 14:11. *exalt you at the proper time.* His help will come at just the right time.

5:7 Cf. Phil 4:6–7.

5:8 *Be of sober spirit.* See 1 Thess 5:6,8. *alert.* Perhaps Peter remembered his own difficulty in keeping awake during our Lord's agony in Gethsemane (see Matt 26:36–46).

5:9 *your brethren.* They are not isolated; they belong to a fellowship of suffering.

5:10 *grace.* See notes on Gal 1:3; Eph 1:2.

5:12 *Through Silvanus.* Silvanus (Silas) may have been the bearer of the letter to its destination. He may also have been a scribe who recorded what Peter dictated or who aided, as an informed and intelligent secretary, in the phrasing of Peter's thoughts (see Introduction: Author and Date). *exhorting . . . grace of God.* See Introduction: Themes.

5:13 *Babylon.* See Introduction: Place of Writing. *chosen.* See note on Eph 1:4. *my son, Mark.* Peter regards Mark with such warmth and affection that he calls him his son. It is possible that Peter had led Mark to Christ (see 1 Tim 1:2 and note). Early Christian tradition closely associates Mark and Peter (see Introduction to Mark: Author).

5:14 *kiss.* See note on 1 Cor 16:20. *Peace be to you all . . . in Christ.* Spiritual well-being and blessedness to all who are united to Christ. Peter thus ends with a reference to the union of believers with Christ, a concept fundamental to the understanding of the whole letter.

2 Peter

INTRODUCTION

Author

The author identifies himself as Simon Peter (1:1). He uses the first person singular pronoun in a highly personal passage (1:12–15) and claims to be an eyewitness of the transfiguration (1:16–18; cf. Matt 17:1–5). He asserts that this is his second letter to the readers (3:1) and refers to Paul as "our beloved brother" (3:15; see note there). In short, the letter claims to be Peter's, and its character is compatible with that claim.

Although 2 Peter was not as widely known and recognized in the early church as 1 Peter, some may have used and accepted it as authoritative as early as the second century and perhaps even in the latter part of the first century (1 Clement [A.D. 95] may allude to it). It was not ascribed to Peter until Origen's time (185–253), and he seems to reflect some doubt concerning it. Eusebius (265–340) placed it among the questioned books, though he admits that most accept it as from Peter. After Eusebius's time, it seems to have been quite generally accepted as canonical.

In recent centuries, however, its genuineness has been challenged by a considerable number of scholars. One of the objections that has been raised is the difference in style from that of 1 Peter. But the difference is not absolute; there are noteworthy similarities in vocabulary and in other matters. In fact, no other known writing is as much like 1 Peter as 2 Peter. The differences that do exist may be accounted for by variations in subject matter, in the form and purpose of the letters, in the time and circumstances of writing, in sources or models, and in scribes who may have been employed. Perhaps most significant is the statement in 1 Pet 5:12 that Silas assisted in the writing of 1 Peter. No such statement is made concerning 2 Peter, which may explain its noticeable difference in style (see Introduction to 1 Peter: Author and Date).

Other objections arise from a naturalistic reconstruction of early Christian history or misunderstandings or misconstructions of the available data. For example, some argue that the reference to Paul's letters in 3:15–16 indicates an advanced date for this book—beyond Peter's lifetime. But it is quite possible that Paul's letters were gathered at an early date, since some of them had been in existence and perhaps in circulation for more than ten years (Thessalonians by as much as 15 years) prior to Peter's death. Besides, what Peter says may only indicate that he was acquainted with some of Paul's letters (communication in the Roman world and in the early church was good), not that there was a formal, ecclesiastical collection of them.

Date

2 Peter was written toward the end of Peter's life (cf. 1:12–15), after he had written a prior letter (3:1) to the same readers (probably 1 Peter). Since Peter was martyred during the reign of Nero, his death must have occurred prior to A.D. 68; so it is very likely that he wrote 2 Peter between 65 and 68.

Some have argued that this date is too early for the writing of 2 Peter, but nothing in the book requires a later date. The error combated is comparable to the kind of heresy present in the first century. To insist that the second chapter was directed against second-century Gnosticism is to assume more than the contents of the chapter warrant. While the heretics referred to in 2 Peter may well have been among the forerunners of second-century Gnostics, nothing is said of them that would not fit into the later years of Peter's life.

Some have suggested a later date because they interpret the reference to the fathers in 3:4 to mean an earlier Christian generation. However, the word is most naturally interpreted as the OT patriarchs (cf. John 6:31, "fathers"; Acts 3:13; Heb 1:1). Similarly, reference to Paul and his letters (3:15–16; see Author) does not require a date beyond Peter's lifetime.

2 Peter and Jude

There are conspicuous similarities between 2 Peter and Jude (compare 2 Pet 2 with Jude 4–18), but there are also conspicuous differences. It has been suggested that one borrowed from the other or that they both drew on a common source. If there is borrowing, it is not a slavish borrowing but one that adapts to suit the writer's purpose. While many have insisted that Jude used Peter, it is more reasonable to assume that the longer letter (Peter) incorporated much of the shorter (Jude). Such borrowing is fairly common in ancient writings. For example, many believe that Paul used parts of early hymns in Phil 2:6–11 and 1 Tim 3:16.

Purpose

In his first letter Peter feeds Christ's sheep by instructing them how to deal with persecution from outside the church (see, e.g., 1 Pet 4:12); in this second letter he teaches them how to deal with false teachers and evildoers who have come into the church (see 2:1; 3:3–4). While the particular situations naturally call for variations in content and emphasis, in both letters Peter as a pastor ("shepherd") of Christ's sheep (John 21:15–17) seeks to commend to his readers a wholesome combination of Christian faith and practice. More specifically, his purpose is threefold: (1) to stimulate Christian growth (ch. 1), (2) to combat false teaching (ch. 2) and (3) to encourage watchfulness in view of the Lord's certain return (ch. 3).

Outline

- I. Introduction (1:1–2)
- II. Exhortation to Growth in Christian Virtues (1:3–11)
  - A. The Divine Enablement (1:3–4)
  - B. The Call for Growth (1:5–7)
  - C. The Value of Such Growth (1:8–11)
- III. The Purpose and Authentication of Peter's Message (1:12–21)
  - A. His Aim in Writing (1:12–15)
  - B. The Basis of His Authority (1:16–21)
- IV. Warning against False Teachers (ch. 2)
  - A. Their Coming Predicted (2:1–3a)
  - B. Their Judgment Assured (2:3b-9)
  - C. Their Characteristics Set Forth (2:10–22)
- V. The Fact of Christ's Return (3:1–16)
  - A. Peter's Purpose in Writing Restated (3:1–2)
  - B. The Coming of Scoffers (3:3–7)
  - C. The Certainty of Christ's Return (3:8–10)
  - D. Exhortations Based on the Fact of Christ's Return (3:11–16)
- VI. Concluding Remarks (3:17–18)

Growth in Christian Virtue

1 [1]Simon Peter, a [a]bond-servant and [b]apostle of Jesus Christ,

To those who have received [c]a faith of the same [2]kind as ours, [3]by [d]the righteousness of [e]our God and Savior, Jesus Christ:

2 [a]Grace and peace be multiplied to you in [b]the knowledge of God and of Jesus our Lord;

3 seeing that His [a]divine power has granted to us everything pertaining to life and godliness, through the true [b]knowledge of Him who [c]called us [1]by His own glory and [2]excellence.

4 [1]For by these He has granted to us His precious and magnificent [a]promises, so that by them you may become [b]partakers of *the* divine nature, having [c]escaped the [d]corruption that is in [e]the world by lust.

5 Now for this very reason also, applying all diligence, in your faith [a]supply [b]moral [1]excellence, and in *your* moral excellence, [c]knowledge,

6 and in *your* knowledge, [a]self-control, and in *your* self-control, [b]perseverance, and in *your* perseverance, [c]godliness,

7 and in *your* godliness, [a]brotherly kindness, and in *your* brotherly kindness, love.

8 For if these *qualities* are yours and are increasing, they render you neither useless nor [a]unfruitful in the true [b]knowledge of our Lord Jesus Christ.

9 For he who lacks these *qualities* is [a]blind *or* short-sighted, having forgotten *his* [b]purification from his former sins.

10 Therefore, brethren, be all the more diligent to make certain about His [a]calling and [b]choosing you; for as long as you practice these things, you will never [c]stumble;

11 for in this way the entrance into [a]the eternal kingdom of our [b]Lord and Savior Jesus Christ will be [c]abundantly [d]supplied to you.

12 Therefore, [a]I will always be ready to remind you of these things, even though you *already* know *them,* and have been established in [b]the truth which is present with *you.*

13 I consider it [a]right, as long as I am in [b]this *earthly* dwelling, to [c]stir you up by way of reminder,

14 knowing that [a]the laying aside of my

1:1 [1]Two early mss read *Simeon* [2]Or *value* [3]Or *in* [a]Rom 1:1; Phil 1:1; James 1:1; Jude 1 [b]1 Pet 1:1 [c]Rom 1:12; 2 Cor 4:13; Titus 1:4 [d]Rom 3:21-26 [e]Titus 2:13
2 [a]Rom 1:7; 1 Pet 1:2 [b]John 17:3; Phil 3:8; 2 Pet 1:3, 8; 2:20; 3:18
3 [1]Or *to* [2]Or *virtue* [a]1 Pet 1:5 [b]John 17:3; Phil 3:8; 2 Pet 1:2, 8; 2:20; 3:18 [c]1 Thess 2:12; 2 Thess 2:14; 1 Pet 5:10
4 [1]Lit *Through which* (things) [a]2 Pet 3:9, 13 [b]Eph 4:13, 24; Heb 12:10; 1 John 3:2 [c]2 Pet 2:18, 20 [d]2 Pet 2:19 [e]James 1:27
5 [1]Or *virtue* [a]2 Pet 1:11 [b]2 Pet 1:3 [c]Col 2:3; 2 Pet 1:2
6 [a]Acts 24:25 [b]Luke 21:19 [c]2 Pet 1:3
7 [a]Rom 12:10; 1 Pet 1:22
8 [a]Col 1:10 [b]John 17:3; Phil 3:8; 2 Pet 1:2, 3; 2:20; 3:18
9 [a]1 John 2:11 [b]Eph 5:26; Titus 2:14
10 [a]Matt 22:14; Rom 11:29; 2 Pet 1:3 [b]1 Thess 1:4 [c]James 2:10; 2 Pet 3:17; Jude 24
11 [a]2 Tim 4:18 [b]2 Pet 2:20; 3:18 [c]Rom 2:4; 1 Tim 6:17 [d]2 Pet 1:5
12 [a]Phil 3:1; 1 John 2:21; Jude 5 [b]Col 1:5f; 2 John 2
13 [a]Phil 1:7 [b]2 Cor 5:1, 4; 2 Pet 1:14 [c]2 Pet 3:1
14 [a]2 Cor 5:1; 2 Tim 4:6

1:1 *Simon Peter.* See notes on Matt 16:18; John 1:42. *bond-servant.* See note on Rom 1:1. *apostle.* See notes on Mark 6:30; 1 Cor 1:1; Heb 3:1. *To those.* Probably the same people as those in 1 Pet 1:1. *have received.* God in His justice ("righteousness") imparts to people the ability to believe. *a faith.* Not here a body of truth to be believed—the faith—but the act of believing, or the God-given capacity to trust in Christ for salvation. *God and Savior, Jesus Christ.* Assumes that Jesus is both God and Savior. For other passages that ascribe deity to Christ see note on Rom 9:5.

1:2 *Grace and peace.* See notes on Jon 4:2; John 14:27; 20:19; Gal 1:3; Eph 1:2. *knowledge of God and of Jesus.* The concept of Christian knowledge is prominent in 2 Peter (see 1:3,5,8; 3:18). Peter was combating heretical teaching, and one of the best antidotes for heresy is the statement of true knowledge.

1:3 *everything pertaining to life and godliness.* God has made available all that we need spiritually through our knowledge of Him. If indeed 2 Peter was written to combat an incipient Gnosticism, the apostle may be insisting that the knowledge possessed by those in apostolic circles was entirely adequate to meet their spiritual needs. No secret, esoteric knowledge is necessary for salvation (see Introduction to 1 John: Gnosticism). *glory and excellence.* The excellence of God: "Glory" expresses the excellence of His being—His attributes and essence; "excellence" depicts excellence expressed in deeds—virtue in action.

1:4 *by these.* Through God's excellence—internal and external—He has given us great promises. Their nature is suggested in the words that follow: participation in the divine nature and escape from worldly corruption. *partakers of the divine nature.* Does not indicate that Christians become divine in any sense, but only that we are indwelt by God through His Holy Spirit (see John 14:16–17). Our humanity and His deity, as well as the human personality and the divine, remain distinct and separate.

1:5–9 The virtues that will produce a well-rounded, fruitful Christian life.

1:5 *faith.* The root of the Christian life (see v. 1 and note). *moral excellence.* Cf. v. 3. *knowledge.* See notes on vv. 2–3.

1:6 *self-control.* According to many of the false teachers, knowledge made self-control unnecessary; according to Peter, Christian knowledge leads to self-control. *godliness.* A genuine reverence toward God that governs one's attitude toward every aspect of life.

1:7 *brotherly kindness.* Warmhearted affection toward all in the family of faith. *love.* The kind of outgoing, selfless attitude that leads one to sacrifice for the good of others (see note on 1 Pet 4:8).

1:8 *if these qualities are yours.* Peter does not mean to imply that the believer is to cultivate each listed quality in turn, one after the other until all have been perfected. Instead, they are all to be cultivated simultaneously. *are increasing.* Peter has continuing spiritual growth in mind. *neither useless nor unfruitful in the true knowledge.* The Christian's knowledge should affect the way he lives. It does not set him free from moral restraints, as the heretics taught (see Introduction to 1 John: Gnosticism). Rather, it produces holiness and all such virtues (cf. Col 1:9–12).

1:9 *blind or short-sighted.* Since one cannot be both at the same time, Peter may have in mind a possible alternative meaning for "blind," namely, "to shut the eyes." Such a person is blind because he has closed his eyes to the truth.

1:10 *make certain about His calling and choosing you.* By cultivating the qualities listed in vv. 5–7, they and others can be assured that God has chosen them and called them (cf. Matt 7:20). The genuineness of their profession will be demonstrated as they express these virtues (cf. Gal 5:6; James 2:18). When God elects and calls, it is to obedience and holiness (1 Pet 1:2; Eph 1:3–6), and these fruits confirm their divine source. *never stumble.* Those who in this way give evidence of their faith will never cease to persevere.

1:11 *eternal kingdom.* Eternal life (cf. Matt 25:46). *entrance . . . will be abundantly supplied.* By producing the fruits Peter is commending to them (see vv. 5–10).

1:13 *earthly dwelling.* See John 1:14; 2 Cor 5:1 and notes.

earthly dwelling is imminent, [b]as also our
Lord Jesus Christ has made clear to me.
15 And I will also be diligent that at any
time after my [a]departure you will be able to
call these things to mind.

Eyewitnesses

16 For we did not follow cleverly devised
[a]tales when we made known to you the
[b]power and coming of our Lord Jesus Christ,
but we were [c]eyewitnesses of His majesty.
17 For when He received honor and glory
from God the Father, such an [1a]utterance as
this was [2]made to Him by the [b]Majestic Glory, "This is My beloved Son with whom I am
well-pleased"—
18 and we ourselves heard this [1]utterance
made from heaven when we were with Him
on the [a]holy mountain.
19 [1]*So* we have [a]the prophetic word *made*
more [b]sure, to which you do well to pay
attention as to [c]a lamp shining in a dark
place, until the [d]day dawns and the [e]morn-
ing star arises [f]in your hearts.
20 But [a]know this first of all, that [b]no
prophecy of Scripture is *a matter* of one's
own interpretation,
21 for [a]no prophecy was ever made by an
act of human will, but men [b]moved by the
Holy Spirit spoke from God.

The Rise of False Prophets

2 But [a]false prophets also arose among the
people, just as there will also be [b]false
teachers [c]among you, who will [d]secretly
introduce [e]destructive heresies, even [f]deny-
ing the [g]Master who [h]bought them, bringing
swift destruction upon themselves.
2 Many will follow their [a]sensuality, and
because of them [b]the way of the truth will be
[c]maligned;
3 and in *their* [a]greed they will [b]exploit
you with [c]false words; [d]their judgment from
long ago is not idle, and their destruction is
not asleep.
4 For [a]if God did not spare angels when
they sinned, but cast them into hell and
[b]committed them to pits of darkness,
reserved for judgment;

14 [b]John 13:36; 21:19 **15** [a]Luke 9:31 **16** [a]1 Tim 1:4; 2 Pet 2:3 [b]Mark 13:26; 14:62; 1 Thess 2:19 [c]Matt 17:1ff; Mark 9:2ff; Luke 9:28ff **17** [1]Lit *voice* [2]Lit *brought* [a]Matt 17:5; Mark 9:7; Luke 9:35 [b]Heb 1:3 **18** [1]Lit *voice brought* [a]Ex 3:5; Josh 5:15 **19** [1]Or *We have the* even *more sure prophetic word* [a]1 Pet 1:10f [b]Heb 2:2 [c]Ps 119:105 [d]Luke 1:78 [e]Rev 22:16 [f]2 Cor 4:6 **20** [a]2 Pet 3:3 [b]Rom 12:6 **21** [a]Jer 23:26; 2 Tim 3:16 [b]2 Sam 23:2; Luke 1:70; Acts 1:16; 3:18; 1 Pet 1:11

2:1 [a]Deut 13:1ff; Jer 6:13 [b]2 Cor 11:13 [c]Matt 7:15; 1 Tim 4:1 [d]Gal 2:4; Jude 4 [e]1 Cor 11:19; Gal 5:20 [f]Jude 4 [g]Rev 6:10 [h]1 Cor 6:20 **2** [a]Gen 19:5ff; 2 Pet 2:7, 18; Jude 4 [b]Acts 16:17; 22:4; 24:14 [c]Rom 2:24 **3** [a]1 Tim 6:5; 2 Pet 2:14; Jude 16 [b]2 Cor 2:17; 1 Thess 2:5 [c]Rom 16:18; 2 Pet 1:16 [d]Deut 32:35 **4** [a]Jude 6 [b]Rev 20:1f

1:14 *Christ has made clear to me.* Either the revelation recorded in John 21:18–19 or a subsequent one.
1:15 *will be able to call these things to mind.* An aim that was realized, whether intentionally or unintentionally, through the Gospel of Mark, which early tradition connected with Peter.
1:16 *cleverly devised tales.* Peter's message was based on his eyewitness account of the supernatural events that marked the life of Jesus. It was not made up of myths and imaginative stories as was the message of the heretics of 2:3. *coming of our Lord Jesus Christ.* In Christ's transfiguration the disciples received a foretaste of what His coming will be like when He returns to establish His eternal kingdom (Matt 16:28). *eyewitnesses of His majesty.* A reference to Christ's transfiguration (see vv. 17–18; Matt 16:28–17:8).
1:19–21 Peter's message rests on two solid foundations: (1) the voice from God at the transfiguration (vv. 16–18) and (2) the still more significant testimony of Scripture (vv. 19–21). An alternative, but less probable, view is that the apostles' testimony to the transfiguration fulfills and thus confirms the Scriptures that predicted such things.
1:19 *more sure.* Or "very certain."
1:20 Two major views of this verse are: 1. No prophecy is to be privately or independently interpreted (cf. the false teachers in 3:16). The Holy Spirit, Scripture itself and the church should be included in the interpretative process. 2. No prophecy originated through the prophet's own interpretation. The preceding and following contexts indicate that this view is probably to be preferred. In vv. 16–19 the subject discussed is the origin of the apostolic message. Did it come from human imaginings, or was it from God? In v. 21 again the subject is origin. No prophecy of Scripture arose from a merely human interpretation of things. This understanding of v. 20 is further supported by the explanatory "for" with which v. 21 begins. Verse 21 explains v. 20 by restating its content and then affirming God as the origin of prophecy.
1:21 *moved by the Holy Spirit.* See note on 2 Tim 3:16. In the production of Scripture both God and man were active participants. God was the source of the content of Scripture, so that what it says is what God has said. But the human author also actively spoke; he was more than a recorder. Yet what he said came from God. Although actively speaking, he was carried along by the Holy Spirit.
2:1 *false prophets.* See 2 Kin 18:19; Is 9:13–17; Jer 5:31; 14:14; 23:30–32. *there will also be false teachers among you.* Numerous NT passages warn of false teachers who are already present or yet to come (see Matt 24:4–5,11; Acts 20:29–30; Gal 1:6–9; Phil 3:2; Col 2:4,8,18,20–23; 2 Thess 2:1–3; 1 Tim 1:3–7; 4:1–3; 2 Tim 3:1–8; 1 John 2:18–19,22–23; 2 John 7–11; Jude 3–4). *destructive heresies.* Divisive opinions or teachings that result in the moral and spiritual destruction of those who accept them. *the Master who bought them.* Does not necessarily mean that the false teachers were believers. Christ's death paid the penalty for their sin, but it would not become effective for their salvation unless they trusted in Christ as Savior. (However, see vv. 20–22, where it is obvious that the heretics had at least professed knowing the Lord.) *swift destruction.* Not immediate physical calamity, but sudden doom, whether at death or at the Lord's second coming (cf. Matt 24:50–51; 2 Thess 1:9).
2:2 *sensuality.* Open, extreme immorality not held in check by any sense of shame. *way of the truth.* See Ps 119:30. The Christian faith is not only correct doctrine but also correct living.
2:3 *in their greed.* They will be motivated by a desire for money and will commercialize the Christian faith to their own selfish advantage. *false words.* See note on 1:16. *from long ago is not idle.* Long ago, in OT times, their condemnation was declared (see vv. 4–9 for OT examples of the fact that judgment is coming on the wicked). *destruction is not asleep.* Although delay makes it seem that they have escaped God's judgment, destruction is a reality that is sure to come upon them.
2:4–8 Three examples showing that God will rescue the godly and destroy the wicked.
2:4 *angels when they sinned.* Some believe this sin was the one referred to in Gen 6:2, where the sons of God are said to have intermarried with the daughters of men, meaning (according to this view) that angels married human women. The offspring of those marriages are said to have been the Nephilim (Gen 6:4;

5 and did not spare [a]the ancient world, but preserved [b]Noah, a [1]preacher of righteousness, with seven others, when He brought a [c]flood upon the world of the ungodly;

6 and *if* He [a]condemned the cities of Sodom and Gomorrah to destruction by reducing *them* to ashes, having made them an [b]example to those who would [c]live ungodly *lives* thereafter;

7 and *if* He [a]rescued righteous Lot, oppressed by the [b]sensual conduct of [c]unprincipled men

8 (for by what he saw and heard *that* [a]righteous man, while living among them, felt *his* righteous soul tormented day after day by *their* lawless deeds),

9 [a]*then* the Lord knows how to rescue the godly from [1]temptation, and to keep the unrighteous under punishment for the [b]day of judgment,

10 and especially those who [1a]indulge the flesh in *its* corrupt desires and [b]despise authority.

Daring, [c]self-willed, they do not tremble when they [b]revile angelic [2]majesties,

11 [a]whereas angels who are greater in might and power do not bring a reviling judgment against them before the Lord.

12 But [a]these, like unreasoning animals, [b]born as creatures of instinct to be captured and killed, reviling where they have no knowledge, will in [1]the destruction of those creatures also be destroyed,

13 suffering wrong as [a]the wages of doing wrong. They count it a pleasure to [b]revel in the [c]daytime. They are stains and blemishes, [b]reveling in their [1]deceptions, as they [d]carouse with you,

14 having eyes full of adultery that never cease from sin, [a]enticing [b]unstable souls, having a heart trained in [c]greed, [d]accursed children;

15 forsaking [a]the right way, they have gone astray, having followed [b]the way of Balaam, the *son* of Beor, who loved [c]the wages of unrighteousness;

16 but he received a rebuke for his own

5 [1]Or *herald* [a]Ezek 26:20; 2 Pet 3:6 [b]Gen 6:8, 9; 1 Pet 3:20 [c]2 Pet 3:6
6 [a]Gen 19:24; Jude 7 [b]Is 1:9; Matt 10:15; 11:23; Rom 9:29; Jude 7 [c]Jude 15
7 [a]Gen 19:16, 29 [b]Gen 19:5ff; 2 Pet 2:2, 18; Jude 4 [c]2 Pet 3:17
8 [a]Heb 11:4
9 [1]Lit *trial;* or *temptation* [a]1 Cor 10:13; Rev 3:10 [b]Matt 10:15; Jude 6
10 [1]Lit *go after* [2]Lit *glories* [a]2 Pet 3:3; Jude 16, 18 [b]Ex 22:28; Jude 8 [c]Titus 1:7
11 [a]Jude 9
12 [1]Lit *their destruction also* [a]Jude 10 [b]Jer 12:3; Col 2:22
13 [1]One early ms reads *love feasts* [a]2 Pet 2:15 [b]Rom 13:13 [c]1 Thess 5:7 [d]1 Cor 11:21; Jude 12
14 [a]2 Pet 2:18 [b]James 1:8; 2 Pet 3:16 [c]2 Pet 2:3 [d]Eph 2:3
15 [a]Acts 13:10 [b]Num 22:5, 7; Deut 23:4; Neh 13:2; Jude 11; Rev 2:14 [c]2 Pet 2:13

---

see notes on Gen 6:2,4). But since it appears impossible for angels, who are spirits, to have sexual relations with women, the sin referred to in this verse probably occurred before the fall of Adam and Eve. The angels who fell became the devil and the evil angels (probably the demons and evil spirits referred to in the NT). *cast them into hell.* The Greek for "hell" is "Tartarus," the term used by the Greeks to designate the place where the most wicked spirits were sent to be punished. Why some evil angels are imprisoned and others are free to serve Satan as demons is not explained in Scripture. *judgment.* The final judgment, probably associated with the great white throne judgment of Rev 20:11–15.

2:5 *preacher of righteousness.* A description of Noah found nowhere else in Scripture. However, similar descriptions are used of him in Josephus (*Antiquities,* 1.3.1), *1 Clement* (7.6; 9.4) and the *Sibylline Oracles* (1.128–29). *seven others.* Noah's wife, three sons and three daughters-in-law (Noah was the eighth; see 1 Pet 3:20). *the ungodly.* See Gen 6:5,11–12.

2:6 *condemned the cities of Sodom and Gomorrah.* See Gen 19.

2:7 *oppressed by the sensual conduct.* See Gen 19:4–9. How Lot could be so distressed, how he could be called a "righteous man," and yet offer to turn his two daughters over to the wicked townsmen to be sexually abused is difficult to understand apart from a knowledge of the code of honor characteristic of that day (see note on Gen 19:8).

2:9 States the point made in vv. 4–8—the wicked whose coming Peter predicts will surely be punished.

2:10 *especially those.* The heretics of Peter's day are certain to come under judgment for two main reasons: 1. They follow the corrupt desire of the sinful nature, perhaps referring to homosexuality, the sin of the Sodomites (see Gen 19:5). At least the author has in mind a similar inordinate sexual practice. 2. They despise authority. *revile angelic majesties.* A specific example of despising authority. This could refer to the slander of earthly dignitaries such as church leaders, which might well be expected from such shameless peddlers of error. On the other hand, it could refer to the blaspheming of angels, as the NASB text suggests. This view seems more likely since the parallel passage in Jude 8–10 is speaking of angels.

2:11 *angels . . . do not bring a reviling judgment.* Even good angels, who might have more right to do so because of their greater power, do not bring such accusations against inferior evil angels.

2:12 *like unreasoning animals.* A scathing denunciation. They are like irrational animals, whose lives are guided by mere instinct and who are born merely to be slaughtered. Destruction is their final lot. *where they have no knowledge.* The heresy to which Peter refers may have been an early form of second-century Gnosticism (see Introduction to 1 John: Gnosticism) that claimed to possess special, esoteric knowledge. If so, it is ironic that those who professed special knowledge acted out of abysmal ignorance, and the result was arrogant blasphemy.

2:13 *revel in the daytime.* See 1 Thess 5:7. Even the pagan world carried on their corrupt practices under cover of darkness, but these heretics were utterly shameless. *in their deceptions, as they carouse with you.* Jude 12 without doubt reads "love feasts," which may well have been the intended reading here. These false teachers seem to have been involved in the sacred feasts of brotherly love that, in the early church, accompanied the Lord's Supper. In fact, it appears that they injected their carousing into these holy observances and delighted in their shameless acts.

2:14 *eyes full of adultery.* Lit. "eyes full of an adulteress," which means that they desired every woman they saw, viewing her as a potential sex partner. *never cease from sin.* Their eyes serve as constant instruments of lust. *enticing unstable souls.* For a parallel use of the Greek word for "enticing" see James 1:14. It depicts the fisherman who attempts to lure and catch fish with bait. *trained in greed.* The Greek text implies that they had exercised themselves like an athlete, not in physical activity but in greed.

2:15 *way of Balaam, the son of Beor.* See Num 22–24. Balaam was bent on cursing Israel, though God had forbidden it. He wanted the money Balak offered him. Similarly these false teachers apparently were guilty of attempting to extract money from naive listeners. For a donkey to rebuke the prophet's madness reflects not only on the foolishness of Balaam but also on that of the false teachers of Peter's day.

transgression, [a]*for* a mute donkey, speaking
with a voice of a man, restrained the madness of the prophet.
17 These are [a]springs without water and
mists driven by a storm, [b]for whom the
[1]black darkness has been reserved.
18 For speaking out [a]arrogant *words* of
[b]vanity they [c]entice by fleshly desires, by
[d]sensuality, those who barely [e]escape from
the ones who live in error,
19 promising them freedom while they
themselves are slaves of corruption; for [a]by
what a man is overcome, by this he is
enslaved.
20 For if, after they have [a]escaped the
defilements of the world by [b]the knowledge
of the [c]Lord and Savior Jesus Christ, they are
again [d]entangled in them and are overcome,
[e]the last state has become worse for them
than the first.
21 [a]For it would be better for them not to
have known the way of righteousness, than
having known it, to turn away from [b]the
holy commandment [c]handed on to them.
22 [1]It has happened to them according to
the true proverb, "[a]A DOG RETURNS TO ITS OWN
VOMIT," and, "A sow, after washing, *returns*
to wallowing in the mire."

Purpose of This Letter

3 This is now, [a]beloved, the second letter I
am writing to you in which I am [b]stirring
up your sincere mind by way of reminder,
2 that you should [a]remember the words
spoken beforehand by [b]the holy prophets
and [c]the commandment of the Lord and Savior *spoken* by your apostles.

The Coming Day of the Lord

3 [a]Know this first of all, that [b]in the last
days [c]mockers will come with *their* mocking,
[d]following after their own lusts,
4 and saying, "[a]Where is the promise of
His [b]coming? For *ever* since the fathers [c]fell
asleep, all continues just as it was [d]from the
beginning of creation."

16 [a]Num 22:21, 23, 28, 30ff **17** [1]Lit *blackness of darkness* [a]Jude 12 [b]Jude 13 **18** [a]Jude 16 [b]Eph 4:17 [c]2 Pet 2:14 [d]2 Pet 2:2 [e]2 Pet 1:4; 2:20 **19** [a]John 8:34; Rom 6:16 **20** [a]2 Pet 2:18 [b]2 Pet 1:2 [c]2 Pet 1:11; 3:18 [d]2 Tim 2:4 [e]Matt 12:45; Luke 11:26 **21** [a]Ezek 18:24; Heb 6:4ff; 10:26f; James 4:17 [b]Gal 6:2; 1 Tim 6:14; 2 Pet 3:2 [c]Jude 3 **22** [1]Lit *The thing of the true proverb has happened to them*

22 [a]Prov 26:11 **3:1** [a]1 Pet 2:11; 2 Pet 3:8, 14, 17 [b]2 Pet 1:13 **2** [a]Jude 17 [b]Luke 1:70; Acts 3:21; Eph 3:5 [c]Gal 6:2; 1 Tim 6:14; 2 Pet 2:21 **3** [a]2 Pet 1:20 [b]1 Tim 4:1; Heb 1:2 [c]Jude 18 [d]2 Pet 2:10 **4** [a]Is 5:19; Jer 17:15; Ezek 11:3; 12:22, 27; Mal 2:17; Matt 24:48 [b]1 Thess 2:19; 2 Pet 3:12 [c]Acts 7:60 [d]Mark 10:6

2:17 *springs without water.* A picture of cruel deception. The thirsty traveler comes to the spring expecting cool, refreshing water but finds it dry. So the false teachers promise satisfying truth but in reality have nothing to offer. *mists driven by a storm.* Gone before a drop of moisture falls. *black darkness.* Their destiny is hell.

2:18 *speaking out arrogant words of vanity.* Words that sound impressive to the new convert but in reality have nothing to offer. *entice.* See note on v. 14 ("enticing"). *those who barely escape.* New converts who have just broken away from pagan friends. Thus the depraved false teachers prey on new converts, who have not yet had a chance to develop spiritual resistance.

2:19 *promising them freedom.* Probably freedom from moral restraint (cf. 1 Cor 6:12–13; Gal 5:13). The very ones who promise freedom from bondage to rules and regulations are themselves slaves of depravity. Freedom from law resulted in bondage to sin, and liberty was turned into license.

2:20–22 Some point to this passage as clear proof that a genuinely saved person may lose his salvation. He knows the Lord; he escapes the world's corruption; he knows the way of righteousness. Then he turns away from the message and goes back to his old way of life. His knowledge is said to have been genuine; his change of life was real; and his return to his old way of life was not superficial. Others insist that the knowledge of the Lord and of the way of righteousness could not have been genuine. If the person had been truly regenerated, he would have persevered in his faith. It is argued that the teaching of John 10:27–30 (especially v. 28) and Rom 8:28–39 makes it clear that no genuinely saved person can be lost. Thus, according to this view, the persons described here could not have been genuinely saved.

2:20 *if, after they have escaped the defilements of the world.* A reference to false teachers who had once apparently been believers in Christ. Their professed knowledge of Christ had at least produced a change in life-style. *again entangled in them and are overcome.* A complete return to the old sinful pattern of life.

2:21 *better . . . not to have known the way of righteousness.* Knowledge of the way increases one's responsibility and his hardness of heart if he then rejects it. In its early days, Christianity was known as "the way" (Acts 9:2; 18:25; 19:9,23; 22:4; 24:14,22). *holy commandment.* The whole Christian message that people are commanded to receive.

2:22 *A DOG RETURNS . . . A sow . . . returns.* In both cases the nature of the animal is not changed. The sow returns to the mud because by nature it is still a sow. The change was merely cosmetic.

3:1 *beloved.* Or "Loved ones" (see vv. 8,14,17; 1 Pet 2:11; 4:12). *second letter.* The first letter may have been 1 Peter, though there is some reason to doubt this identification. For example, 1 Peter cannot be very accurately described as a reminder. *reminder.* See 1:12–13,15.

3:2 *holy prophets.* OT personages. *commandment.* See note on 2:21. *your apostles.* Peter places the OT prophets and the NT apostles on an equal plane. Both are vehicles of God's sacred truth. Peter, being one of the apostles, can speak with knowledge and authority as a representative of the apostolic group.

3:3 *first of all.* This expression is used in 1:20 to call attention to a matter of great importance. *last days.* An expression that refers to the whole period introduced by Christ's first coming. These days are last in comparison to OT days, which were preliminary and preparatory. Also, the Christian era is the time of the beginnings of prophetic fulfillment. *mockers will come.* Perhaps the same false teachers described in ch. 2 (e.g., they follow their own evil desires; cf. 2:10,18–19). In ch. 3, however, the emphasis is on Christ's return. These people may have been early Gnostics who resisted the idea of a time of judgment and moral accountability.

3:4 *His.* Christ's. *ever since the fathers fell asleep.* Either the first Christians to die after Christ's death and resurrection (e.g., Stephen, James the brother of John, and other early Christian leaders who had died; cf. Heb 13:7) or the OT patriarchs (see Introduction: Date). *all continues just as it was.* Their argument against Christ's return was: Since it has not occurred up to this time, it will never occur. That nature is not subject to divine intervention, they say, has been proved by observation (1) of the period since the fathers died—perhaps 30 years—and (2) of the period since creation.

5 For [1]when they maintain this, it
escapes their notice that [a]by the word of God
the heavens existed long ago and *the* earth
was [b]formed out of water and by water,
6 through which [a]the world at that time
was [b]destroyed, being flooded with water.
7 But by His word [a]the present heavens
and earth are being reserved for [b]fire, kept
for [c]the day of judgment and destruction of
ungodly men.
8 But do not let this one *fact* escape your
notice, [a]beloved, that with the Lord one day
is like a thousand years, and [b]a thousand
years like one day.
9 [a]The Lord is not slow about His promise, as some count slowness, but [b]is patient
toward you, [c]not wishing for any to perish
but for all to come to repentance.

A New Heaven and Earth

10 But [a]the day of the Lord [b]will come like
a thief, in which [c]the heavens [d]will pass
away with a roar and the [e]elements will be
destroyed with intense heat, and [f]the earth
and [1]its works will be [2]burned up.
11 Since all these things are to be
destroyed in this way, what sort of people
ought you to be in holy conduct and godliness,
12 [a]looking for and hastening the coming
of the day of God, because of which [b]the
heavens will be destroyed by burning, and
the [c]elements will melt with intense heat!
13 But according to His [a]promise we are
looking for [b]new heavens and a new earth,
[c]in which righteousness dwells.
14 [a]Therefore, [b]beloved, since you look
for these things, be diligent to be [c]found by
Him in peace, [d]spotless and blameless,
15 and regard the [a]patience of our Lord *as*
salvation; just as also [b]our beloved brother

5 [1]Or *they are willfully ignorant of this fact, that* [a]Gen 1:6, 9; Heb 11:3 [b]Ps 24:2; 136:6
6 [a]2 Pet 2:5 [b]Gen 7:11, 12, 21f
7 [a]2 Pet 3:10, 12 [b]Is 66:15; Dan 7:9f; 2 Thess 1:7; Heb 12:29 [c]Matt 10:15; 1 Cor 3:13; Jude 7
8 [a]2 Pet 3:1 [b]Ps 90:4
9 [a]Hab 2:3; Rom 13:11; Heb 10:37 [b]Rom 2:4; Rev 2:21 [c]1 Tim 2:4; Rev 2:21
10 [a]1 Cor 1:8 [b]Matt 24:43; Luke 12:39; 1 Thess 5:2; Rev 3:3; 16:15 [c]Is 34:4; 2 Pet 3:7, 12 [d]Matt 24:35; Rev 21:1 [e]Is 24:19; Mic 1:4

10 [1]Lit *the works in it* [2]Two early mss read *discovered* [f]2 Pet 3:7
12 [a]1 Cor 1:7 [b]2 Pet 3:7, 10 [c]Is 24:19; 34:4; Mic 1:4 **13** [a]Is 65:17; 66:22 [b]Rom 8:21; Rev 21:1 [c]Is 60:21; 65:25; Rev 21:27
14 [a]1 Cor 15:58; 2 Pet 1:10 [b]2 Pet 3:1 [c]1 Pet 1:7 [d]Phil 2:15; 1 Thess 5:23; 1 Tim 6:14; James 1:27 **15** [a]2 Pet 3:9 [b]Acts 9:17; 15:25; 2 Pet 3:2

3:5 *it escapes their notice.* Ignoring the flood as a divine intervention was not an oversight; it was deliberate. They did not want to face up to the fallacy in their argument. *the word of God.* Of command, such as "Let there be light" (Gen 1:3). *earth was formed out of water and by water.* See Gen 1:6–10, where the waters on earth were separated from the atmospheric waters of the heavens, and the mountains then appeared, causing the earthly waters to be gathered into oceans.

3:6 *through which the world at that time was destroyed, being flooded.* Peter points out the fallacy of the scoffers' argument. There has been a divine intervention since the time of creation, namely, the flood. The term "world" may refer to the earth or, more probably, to the world of people (cf. John 3:16). All the people except Noah and his family were overcome by the flood and perished. This does not necessarily mean that the flood was universal. It may simply have extended to all the inhabited areas of earth (see note on Gen 6:17).

3:7 *by His word.* The word of God that brought the world into existence (v. 5) and that brought watery destruction on the wicked of Noah's day will bring fiery destruction on the world that exists today and on its wicked people.

3:8 *a thousand years like one day.* Cf. Ps 90:4. God does not view time as humans do. He stands above time, with the result that when time is seen in the light of eternity, an age appears no longer than one short day, and a day seems no shorter than a long age. Since time is purely relative with God, He waits patiently while human beings stew with impatience.

3:9 God's seeming delay in bringing about the consummation of all things is a result not of indifference but of patience in waiting for all who will come to repentance. Thus the scoffers are wrong on two points: 1. They fail to recognize that all things have not continued without divine intervention since creation (the flood was an intervention, vv. 4–6). 2. They misunderstand the reason for apparent divine delay (God is a long-suffering God).

3:10 *day of the Lord.* See notes on Is 2:11,17,20; Amos 5:18; 1 Thess 5:2. *like a thief.* Suddenly and unexpectedly. *the heavens will pass away with a roar.* Apocalyptic language, common to books like Daniel and Revelation. Due to the figurative nature of such writings, we must not expect complete literalism but recognize it as an attempt to describe the indescribable, a task as impossible as it would have been for a first-century writer to describe the phenomena of our atomic age. What may be referred to is the destruction of the atmospheric heavens with a great rushing sound (see v. 12). *elements.* Refers either to the heavenly bodies or to the physical elements—in the first century, such things as earth, air, fire and water; in today's more precise scientific terminology, hydrogen, oxygen, carbon, etc. *intense heat.* See vv. 7,12. *earth . . . burned up.* Either the earth and its contents will disappear and not be seen anymore, or the earth and all man's works will appear before God's judgment seat.

3:11 *Since all these things are to be destroyed.* The transitory nature of the material universe ought to make a difference in one's system of values and one's priorities. The result should be lives of holiness (separated from sin and to God) and godliness (devoted to the worship and service of God). Cf. Matt 25:13; 1 Thess 5:6,8,11; 2 Pet 1:13–16.

3:12 *hastening the coming.* That day may be hastened by God's people as they speed up the accomplishment of His purposes. Since He is waiting for all who will come to repentance (v. 9), the sooner believers bring others to the Savior the sooner that day will dawn (cf. Acts 3:19–20). Prayer also serves to hasten the day (Matt 6:10), as does holy living (v. 11). *the day of God.* Apparently synonymous with "the day of the Lord" (v. 10) since it is characterized by the same kind of events. Cf. Rev 16:14. *heavens will be destroyed.* See v. 10. *elements will melt with intense heat!* See v. 10; Is 34:4.

3:13 *His promise.* New heavens and a new earth are promised by Isaiah (65:17; 66:22). This promise is confirmed by Rev 21:1. *in which righteousness dwells.* Righteousness will dwell there as a permanent resident. Cf. Is 11:4–5; 45:8; Dan 9:24.

3:14 *spotless and blameless.* Cf. 1 Pet 1:19, where the same two Greek words are applied to Christ.

3:15 *regard the patience of the Lord as salvation.* See v. 9. *our beloved brother Paul.* Peter expresses warmth in his reference to Paul. The unity of teaching and purpose that governed their relationship, abundantly attested in Paul's letters and the book of Acts, is confirmed here by Peter. It has been suggested that what Paul wrote to the recipients of 2 Peter may have been a copy of Romans, which was sent to the churches as a circular letter (cf. Rom 16:4; see Introduction to Romans: Recipients; see also note on 1 Pet 1:1).

Paul, [c]according to the wisdom given him,
wrote to you,
16 as also in all *his* letters, speaking in
them of [a]these things, [b]in which are some
things hard to understand, which the
untaught and [c]unstable distort, as *they do*
also [d]the rest of the Scriptures, to their own
destruction.
17 You therefore, [a]beloved, knowing this
beforehand, [b]be on your guard so that you
are not carried away by [c]the error of [d]unprin-
cipled men and [e]fall from your own steadfastness,
18 but grow in the grace and [a]knowledge
of our [b]Lord and Savior Jesus Christ. [c]To
Him *be* the glory, both now and to the day of
eternity. Amen.

15 [c]1 Cor 3:10; Eph 3:3
16 [a]2 Pet 3:14 [b]Heb 5:11 [c]2 Pet 2:14 [d]2 Pet 3:2
17 [a]2 Pet 3:1 [b]1 Cor 10:12
17 [c]2 Pet 2:18 [d]2 Pet 2:7 [e]Rev 2:5
18 [a]2 Pet 1:2 [b]2 Pet 1:11; 2:20 [c]Rom 11:36; 2 Tim 4:18; Rev 1:6

3:16 *as also in all his letters.* Peter may be referring in general to the exhortations to holy living in vv. 11–14, which parallel many passages in Paul's writings. *the untaught and unstable.* The untaught are simply the unlearned who have not been taught basic apostolic teaching and thus may be easily led astray (cf. 2:14). *the rest of the Scriptures.* Peter placed Paul's writings on the same level of authority as the God-breathed writings of the OT (see 1:21; 2 Tim 3:16).

3:17 *knowing this beforehand.* That false teachers are coming (cf. ch. 2).

3:18 *grow in . . . knowledge.* Peter concludes by again stressing knowledge (see 1:2–3 and notes; see also 1:5), probably as an antidote to the false teachers who boasted in their esoteric knowledge.

1 John

INTRODUCTION

Author

The author is John son of Zebedee (see Mark 1:19–20)—the apostle and the author of the Gospel of John and Revelation (see Introductions to both books: Author). He may have been a first cousin of Jesus (his mother may have been Salome, possibly a sister of Mary; cf. Matt 27:56; Mark 15:40; 16:1; John 19:25—this view assumes that "His mother's sister" in this verse refers to Salome; some further assume that "Mary the wife of Clopas" in this verse stands in apposition to "His mother's sister," which would mean that this Mary and Salome were one and the same person); he was a fisherman, one of Jesus' inner circle (together with James and Peter) and the disciple "whom Jesus loved" (John 13:23).

Unlike most NT letters, 1 John does not tell us who its author is. The earliest identification of him comes from the church fathers: Irenaeus (c. A.D. 140–203), Clement of Alexandria (c. 150–215), Tertullian (c. 155–222) and Origen (c. 185–253) all designated the writer as the apostle John. As far as we know, no one else was suggested by the early church.

This traditional identification is confirmed by evidence in the letter itself:

1. The style of the Gospel of John is markedly similar to that of this letter. Both are written in simple Greek and use contrasting figures, such as light and darkness, life and death, truth and lies, love and hate.

2. Similar phrases and expressions, such as those found in the following passages, are striking:

1 John	Gospel of John
1:1	1:1,14
1:4	16:24
1:6–7	3:19–21
2:7	13:34–35
3:8	8:44
3:14	5:24
4:6	8:47
4:9	1:14,18; 3:16
5:9	5:32,37
5:12	3:36

3. The mention of eyewitness testimony (1:1–4) harmonizes with the fact that John was a follower of Christ from the earliest days of His ministry.

4. The authoritative manner that pervades the letter (seen in its commands, 2:15,24,28; 4:1; 5:21; its firm assertions, 2:6; 3:14; 4:12; and its pointed identification of error, 1:6,8; 2:4,22) is what would be expected from an apostle.

5. The suggestions of advanced age (addressing his readers as "children," 2:1,28; 3:7) agree with early church tradition concerning John's age when he wrote the books known to be his.

6. The description of the heretics as antichrists (2:18), liars (2:22) and children of the devil (3:10) is consistent with Jesus' characterization of John as a son of thunder (Mark 3:17).

7. The indications of a close relationship with the Lord (1:1; 2:5–6,24,27–28) fit the descriptions of "the disciple whom Jesus loved" and the one who reclined "next to him" (John 13:23).

Date

The letter is difficult to date with precision, but factors such as (1) evidence from early Christian writers (Irenaeus and Clement of Alexandria), (2) the early form of Gnosticism reflected in the denunciations of the letter and (3) indications of the advanced age of John suggest the end of the first century. Since the author

of 1 John seems to build on concepts and themes found in the fourth Gospel (see 1 John 2:7–11), it is reasonable to date the letter somewhere between A.D. 85 and 95, after the writing of the Gospel, which may have been written c. 85 (see Introduction to John: Date).

Recipients

1 John 2:12–14,19; 3:1; 5:13 make it clear that this letter was addressed to believers. But the letter itself does not indicate who they were or where they lived. The fact that it mentions no one by name suggests it was a circular letter sent to Christians in a number of places. Evidence from early Christian writers places the apostle John in Ephesus during most of his later years (c. A.D. 70–100). The earliest confirmed use of 1 John was in the province of Asia (in modern Turkey), where Ephesus was located. Clement of Alexandria indicates that John ministered in the various churches scattered throughout that province. It may be assumed, therefore, that 1 John was sent to the churches of the province of Asia (see map No. 12 at the end of the Study Bible).

Gnosticism

One of the most dangerous heresies of the first two centuries of the church was Gnosticism. Its central teaching was that spirit is entirely good and matter is entirely evil. From this unbiblical dualism flowed five important errors:

1. Man's body, which is matter, is therefore evil. It is to be contrasted with God, who is wholly spirit and therefore good.

2. Salvation is the escape from the body, achieved not by faith in Christ but by special knowledge (the Greek word for "knowledge" is *gnosis,* hence Gnosticism).

3. Christ's true humanity was denied in two ways: (1) Some said that Christ only seemed to have a body, a view called Docetism, from the Greek *dokeo* ("to seem"), and (2) others said that the divine Christ joined the man Jesus at baptism and left him before he died, a view called Cerinthianism, after its most prominent spokesman, Cerinthus. This view is the background of much of 1 John (see 1:1; 2:22; 4:2–3).

4. Since the body was considered evil, it was to be treated harshly. This ascetic form of Gnosticism is the background of part of the letter to the Colossians (2:21–23).

5. Paradoxically, this dualism also led to licentiousness. The reasoning was that, since matter—and not the breaking of God's law (1 John 3:4)—was considered evil, breaking his law was of no moral consequence.

The Gnosticism addressed in the NT was an early form of the heresy, not the intricately developed system of the second and third centuries. In addition to that seen in Colossians and in John's letters, acquaintance with early Gnosticism is reflected in 1,2 Timothy, Titus, and 2 Peter and perhaps 1 Corinthians.

Occasion and Purpose

John's readers were confronted with an early form of Gnostic teaching of the Cerinthian variety (see Gnosticism). This heresy was also libertine, throwing off all moral restraints.

Consequently, John wrote this letter with two basic purposes in mind: (1) to expose false teachers (2:26) and (2) to give believers assurance of salvation (5:13). In keeping with his intention to combat Gnostic teachers, John specifically struck at their total lack of morality (3:8–10); and by giving eyewitness testimony to the incarnation, he sought to confirm his readers' belief in the incarnate Christ (1:3). Success in this would give the writer joy (1:4).

*Outline**

I. Introduction: The Reality of the Incarnation (1:1–4)
II. The Christian Life as Fellowship with the Father and the Son (1:5–2:28)
  A. Ethical Tests of Fellowship (1:5—2:11)
    1. Moral likeness (1:5–7)
    2. Confession of sin (1:8—2:2)
    3. Obedience (2:3–6)
    4. Love for fellow believers (2:7–11)

B. Two Digressions (2:12–17)
C. Christological Test of Fellowship (2:18–28)
1. Contrast: apostates versus believers (2:18–21)
2. Person of Christ: the crux of the test (2:22–23)
3. Persistent belief: key to continuing fellowship (2:24–28)

III. The Christian Life as Divine Sonship (2:29—4:6)
A. Ethical Tests of Sonship (2:29—3:24)
1. Righteousness (2:29—3:10a)
2. Love (3:10b-24)
B. Christological Tests of Sonship (4:1–6)

IV. The Christian Life as an Integration of the Ethical and the Christological (4:7—5:12)
A. The Ethical Test: Love (4:7—5:5)
1. The source of love (4:7–16)
2. The fruit of love (4:17–19)
3. The relationship of love for God and love for one's spiritual brother (4:20—5:1)
4. Obedience: the evidence of love for God's children (5:2–5)
B. The Christological Test (5:6–12)

V. Conclusion: Great Christian Certainties (5:13–21)

*Copyright © 1985, the Moody Bible Institute of Chicago.

Introduction, The Incarnate Word

1 What was [a]from the beginning, what we
have [b]heard, what we have [c]seen with
our eyes, what we [d]have looked at and
[e]touched with our hands, concerning the
[f]Word of Life—
2 and [a]the life was manifested, and we
have [b]seen and [c]testify and proclaim to you
[d]the eternal life, which was [e]with the Father
and was [a]manifested to us—
3 what we have [a]seen and [b]heard we
proclaim to you also, so that you too may
have fellowship with us; and indeed our [c]fel-
lowship is with the Father, and with His Son
Jesus Christ.
4 [a]These things we write, so that our [b]joy
may be made complete.

God Is Light

5 [a]This is the message we have heard
from Him and announce to you, that [b]God is
Light, and in Him there is no darkness at all.
6 [a]If we say that we have fellowship with
Him and *yet* walk in the darkness, we [b]lie
and [c]do not practice the truth;
7 but if we [a]walk in the Light as [b]He
Himself is in the Light, we have fellowship
with one another, and [c]the blood of Jesus
His Son cleanses us from all sin.

1:1 [a]John 1:1f; 1 John 2:13, 14 [b]Acts 4:20; 1 John 1:3 [c]John 19:35; 2 Pet 1:16; 1 John 1:2 [d]John 1:14; 1 John 4:14 [e]Luke 24:39; John 20:27 [f]John 1:1, 4 **2** [a]John 1:4; 1 John 3:5, 8; 5:20 [b]John 19:35; 1 John 1:1 [c]John 15:27; 1 John 4:14 [d]John 10:28; 17:3; 1 John 2:25; 5:11, 13, 20 [e]John 1:1 **3** [a]John 19:35; 2 Pet 1:16; 1 John 1:1 [b]Acts 4:20; 1 John 1:1 [c]John 17:3, 21; 1 Cor 1:9 **4** [a]1 John 2:1 [b]John 3:29 **5** [a]John 1:19; 1 John 3:11 [b]1 Tim 6:16; James 1:17 **6** [a]John 8:12; 1 John 2:11 [b]John 8:55; 1 John 2:4; 4:20 [c]John 3:21 **7** [a]Is 2:5 [b]1 Tim 6:16 [c]Titus 2:14

8 [a]Job 15:14; Prov 20:9; Rom

8 [a]If we say that we have no sin, we are
deceiving ourselves and the [b]truth is not in us.
9 [a]If we confess our sins, He is faithful
and righteous to forgive us our sins and [b]to
cleanse us from all unrighteousness.
10 [a]If we say that we have not sinned, we
[b]make Him a liar and [c]His word is not in us.

Christ Is Our Advocate

2 [a]My little children, I am [b]writing these
things to you so that you may not sin.
And if anyone sins, [c]we have an [1d]Advocate
with the Father, Jesus Christ the righteous;
2 and He Himself is [a]the [1]propitiation for
our sins; and not for ours only, but also [b]for
those of the whole world.
3 [a]By this we know that we have come to
[b]know Him, if we [c]keep His commandments.
4 The one who says, "[a]I have come to
[b]know Him," and does not keep His commandments, is a [c]liar, and [d]the truth is not in
him;

3:10ff; James 3:2 [b]John 8:44; 1 John 2:4 **9** [a]Ps 32:5; Prov 28:13 [b]Titus 2:14 **10** [a]Job 15:14 [b]John 3:33; 1 John 5:10 [c]1 John 2:14 **2:1** [1]Gr *Paracletos,* one called alongside to help; or *Intercessor* [a]John 13:33; Gal 4:19; 1 John 2:12, 28; 3:7, 18; 4:4; 5:21 [b]1 John 1:4 [c]Rom 8:34; 1 Tim 2:5; Heb 7:25; 9:24 [d]John 14:16 **2** [1]Or *satisfaction* [a]Rom 3:25; Heb 2:17; 1 John 4:10 [b]John 4:42; 11:51f; 1 John 4:14 **3** [a]1 John 2:5; 3:24; 4:13; 5:2 [b]1 John 2:4; 3:6; 4:7f [c]John 14:15; 15:10; 1 John 3:22, 24; 5:3; Rev 12:17; 14:12 **4** [a]Titus 1:10 [b]1 John 3:6; 4:7f [c]1 John 1:6 [d]1 John 1:8

1:1–4 The introduction to this letter deals with the same subject and uses several of the same words as the introduction to John's Gospel (1:1–4)—"beginning," "Word," "life," "with."

1:1 *was from the beginning.* Has always existed. *we.* John and the other apostles. *heard . . . seen . . . looked at . . . touched.* The apostle had made a careful examination of the Word of Life. He testifies that the one who has existed from eternity "became flesh" (John 1:14)—i.e., a flesh-and-blood man. He was true God and true man. At the outset, John contradicts the heresy of the Gnostics (see Introduction: Gnosticism). *Word of Life.* The one who is life and reveals life (see v. 2 and note). "Word" here speaks of revelation (see note on John 1:1).

1:2 *the life . . . the eternal life.* Christ. He is called "the life" because He is the living one who has life in Himself (see John 11:25; 14:6). He is also the source of life and sovereign over life (5:11). The letter begins and ends (5:20) with the theme of eternal life.

1:3 *fellowship with us.* Participation with us (vicariously) in our experience of hearing, seeing and touching the incarnate Christ (v. 1). Fellowship (Greek *koinonia*) is the spiritual union of the believer with Christ—as described in the figures of the vine and branches (John 15:1–5) and the body and the head (1 Cor 12:12; Col 1:18)—as well as communion with the Father and with fellow believers.

1:4 *our joy . . . complete.* John's joy in the Lord could not be complete unless his readers shared the true knowledge of the Christ (see 2 John 12).

1:5 *from Him.* From Christ. *Light . . . darkness.* Light represents what is good, true and holy, while darkness represents what is evil and false (see John 3:19–21).

1:6–7 *walk in the darkness . . . in the Light.* Two life-styles—one characterized by wickedness and error, the other by holiness and truth.

1:6 *we.* John and his readers. *we have fellowship with Him.* To be in living, spiritual union with God. *walk.* A metaphor for living. *truth.* See note on John 1:14.

1:7 *sin.* A key word in 1 John, occurring 27 times in the Greek.

1:9 *faithful and righteous.* Here the phrase is virtually a single concept (faithful-and-just). It indicates that God's response toward those who confess their sins will be in accordance with His nature and His gracious commitment to His people (see Ps 143:1; Zech 8:8). *faithful.* To His promise to forgive (see Jer 31:34; Mic 7:18–20; Heb 10:22–23). *to forgive us.* Will provide the forgiveness that restores the communion with God that had been interrupted by sin (as requested in the Lord's Prayer, Matt 6:12).

1:10 *we have not sinned.* Gnostics denied that their immoral actions were sinful.

2:1 *little children.* John, the aged apostle, often used this expression of endearment (vv. 12–13,28; 3:7,18; 4:4; 5:21; the term in 2:18 translates a different Greek word). *an Advocate.* The Greek word refers to someone who speaks in court in behalf of a defendant (see note on John 14:16). *the righteous.* In God's court the defender must be, and is, sinless.

2:2 *propitiation for our sins.* Propitiation refers to turning away God's wrath (see also 4:10). God's holiness demands punishment for man's sin. God, therefore, out of love (4:10; John 3:16), sent His Son to make substitutionary atonement for the believer's sin. In this way the Father's wrath is propitiated (satisfied, appeased); His wrath against the Christian's sin has been turned away and directed toward Christ. See note on Rom 3:25. *for those of the whole world.* Forgiveness through Christ's atoning sacrifice is not limited to one particular group only; it has worldwide application (see John 1:29). It must, however, be received by faith (see John 3:16). Thus this verse does not teach universalism (that all people ultimately will be saved), but that God is an impartial God.

2:3 Forty-two times 1 John uses two Greek verbs normally translated "know." One of these verbs is related to the name of the Gnostics, the heretical sect that claimed to have a special knowledge (Greek *gnosis*) of God (see Introduction: Gnosticism). *keep His commandments.* Does not mean that only those who

5 but whoever [a]keeps His word, in him
the [b]love of God has truly been perfected.
[c]By this we know that we are in Him:
6 the one who says he [a]abides in Him
[b]ought himself to walk in the same manner
as He walked.
7 [a]Beloved, I am [b]not writing a new commandment to you, but an old commandment
which you have had [c]from the beginning; the
old commandment is the word which you
have heard.
8 [1]On the other hand, I am writing [a]a
new commandment to you, which is true in
Him and in you, because [b]the darkness is
passing away and [c]the true Light is already
shining.
9 The one who says he is in the Light and
yet [a]hates his [b]brother is in the darkness
until now.
10 [a]The one who loves his brother abides
in the Light and there is no cause for stumbling in him.
11 But the one who [a]hates his brother is
in the darkness and [b]walks in the darkness,
and does not know where he is going
because the darkness has [c]blinded his eyes.
12 I am writing to you, [a]little children,
because [b]your sins have been forgiven you
for His name's sake.
13 I am writing to you, fathers, because
you know Him [a]who has been from the

5 [a]John 14:23 [b]1 John 4:12 [c]1 John 2:3; 3:24; 4:13; 5:2 **6** [a]John 15:4 [b]John 13:15; 15:10; 1 Pet 2:21 **7** [a]Heb 6:9; 1 John 3:2, 21; 4:1, 7, 11 [b]John 13:34; 1 John 3:11, 23; 4:21; 2 John 5 [c]1 John 2:24; 3:11; 2 John 5, 6 **8** [1]Lit *Again* [a]John 13:34 [b]Rom 13:12; Eph 5:8; 1 Thess 5:4f [c]John 1:9 **9** [a]1 John 2:11; 3:15; 4:20 [b]Acts 1:15; 1 John 3:10, 16; 4:20f **10** [a]John 11:9; 1 John 2:10, 11 **11** [a]1 John 2:9; 3:15; 4:20 [b]John 12:35; 1 John 1:6 [c]2 Cor 4:4; 2 Pet 1:9 **12** [a]1 John 2:1 [b]Acts 13:38; 1 Cor 6:11 **13** [a]1 John 1:1

13 [b]John 16:33; 1 John 2:14; 4:4; 5:4f; Rev 2:7 [c]Matt 5:37; 1 John 2:14; 3:12; 5:18f [d]John 14:7; 1 John 2:3 **14** [a]1 John 1:1 [b]Eph 6:10 [c]John

beginning. I am writing to you, young men,
because [b]you have overcome [c]the evil one. I
have written to you, children, because [d]you
know the Father.
14 I have written to you, fathers, because
you know Him [a]who has been from the
beginning. I have written to you, young men,
because you are [b]strong, and the [c]word of
God abides in you, and [d]you have overcome
the evil one.

Do Not Love the World

15 Do not love [a]the world nor the things
in the world. [b]If anyone loves the world, the
love of the Father is not in him.
16 For all that is in the world, [a]the lust of
the flesh and [b]the lust of the eyes and [c]the
boastful pride of life, is not from the Father,
but is from the world.
17 [a]The world is passing away, and *also*
its lusts; but the one who [b]does the will of
God lives forever.
18 Children, [a]it is the last hour; and just
as you heard that [b]antichrist is coming,
[c]even now many antichrists have appeared;
from this we know that it is the last hour.
19 [a]They went out from us, but they were

5:38; 8:37; 1 John 1:10 [d]1 John 2:13 **15** [a]Rom 12:2; James 1:27 [b]James 4:4 **16** [a]Rom 13:14; Eph 2:3; 1 Pet 2:11 [b]Prov 27:20 [c]James 4:16 **17** [a]1 Cor 7:31 [b]Mark 3:35 **18** [a]Rom 13:11; 1 Tim 4:1; 1 Pet 4:7 [b]Matt 24:5, 24; 1 John 2:22; 4:3; 2 John 7 [c]Mark 13:22; 1 John 4:1, 3 **19** [a]Acts 20:30

never disobey (1:8–9) know God, but simply refers to those whose lives are generally characterized by obedience.

2:5 *in him the love of God has truly been perfected.* Means either that God's love for the believer is made complete when it moves the believer to acts of obedience (see 4:12), or that our love for God becomes complete when it expresses itself in acts of obedience (see 3:16–18). *in Him.* Spiritual union with God (see John 17:21).

2:7–8 *new commandment.* See John 13:34–35. The Biblical command to love was old (see Lev 19:18; also Matt 22:39–40). But its newness is seen in: (1) the new and dramatic illustration of divine love on the cross; (2) Christ's exposition of the OT law (see Matt 5), which seemed new to Christ's hearers; and (3) the daily experience of believers as they grow in love for each other.

2:7 *Beloved.* Like "little children" (see note on v. 1), a favorite term of John's (used ten times in two letters: here; 3:2,21; 4:1,7,11; 3 John 1–2,5,11). *from the beginning.* The beginning of their Christian experience, when they first heard the gospel.

2:8 *true Light.* Used in the NT only here and in John 1:9, this phrase refers to the gospel of Jesus Christ, who is the light of the world (John 8:12), and to its saving effects in the lives of believers.

2:9–10 *hates . . . loves.* In the Bible hatred and love as moral qualities are not primarily emotions, but attitudes expressed in actions (see 3:15–16).

2:9 *Light . . . darkness.* See note on 1:5. *brother.* Fellow believer.

2:10 *stumbling.* Into sin.

2:12–14 *I am writing to you . . . because.* By extended repetition in these verses, John assures his readers that, in spite of the rigorous tests contained in the letter, he is confident of their salvation. *little children . . . fathers . . . young men.* As elsewhere in this letter, "little children" probably refers to all John's readers (see note on v. 1), including fathers and young men. The terms "fathers" and "young men" may, however, describe two different levels of spiritual maturity. Some hold that all three terms refer to levels of spiritual maturity.

2:12 *His name's.* Jesus (see 3:23; 5:13; see also note on Acts 4:12).

2:13–14 *Him who has been from the beginning.* Christ (see note on 1:1).

2:15 *the world.* Not the world of people (John 3:16) or the created world (John 17:24), but the world, or realm, of sin (v. 16; James 4:4), which is controlled by Satan and organized against God and righteousness (see note on John 1:9). *love of the Father.* Love for the Father.

2:18 *last hour.* With other NT writers, John viewed the whole period beginning with Christ's first coming as the last days (see Acts 2:17; 2 Tim 3:1; Heb 1:2; 1 Pet 1:20). They understood this to be the "last" of the days because neither former prophecy nor new revelation concerning the history of salvation indicated the coming of another era before the return of Christ. The word "last" in "last days," "last times" and "last hour" also expresses a sense of urgency and imminence. The Christian is to be alert, waiting for the return of Christ (Matt 25:1–13). *antichrist . . . many antichrists.* John assumed his readers knew that a great enemy of God and His people will arise before Christ's return. That person is called "antichrist" (v. 18), "the man of lawlessness" (2 Thess 2:3; but see note there) and "the beast" (Rev 13:1–10). But prior to him, there will be many antichrists. These are characterized by the following: (1) They deny the incarnation (4:2; 2 John 7) and that Jesus is the divine Christ (v. 22); (2) they deny the Father (v. 22); (3) they do not have the Father (v. 23); (4) they are liars (v. 22) and deceivers (2 John 7); (5) they are many (v. 18); (6) in John's day they left the church because they had nothing in common with believers (v. 19). The antichrists referred to in John's letter were the early Gnostics.

not *really* of us; for if they had been of us, they would have remained with us; but *they went out,* [b]so that [1]it would be shown that they all are not of us.

20 [1]But you have an [a]anointing from [b]the Holy One, and [c]you all know.

21 I have not written to you because you do not know the truth, but [a]because you do know it, and [1]because no lie is [b]of the truth.

22 Who is the liar but [a]the one who denies that Jesus is the [1]Christ? This is [b]the antichrist, the one who denies the Father and the Son.

23 [a]Whoever denies the Son does not have the Father; the one who confesses the Son has the Father also.

24 As for you, let that abide in you which you heard [a]from the beginning. If what you heard from the beginning abides in you, you also [b]will abide in the Son and in the Father.

The Promise Is Eternal Life

25 [a]This is the promise which He Himself [1]made to us: eternal life.

26 These things I have written to you concerning those who are trying to [a]deceive you.

27 As for you, the [a]anointing which you received from Him abides in you, and you have no need for anyone to teach you; but as His anointing [b]teaches you about all things, and is [c]true and is not a lie, and just as it has taught you, [1]you abide in Him.

28 Now, [a]little children, abide in Him, so that when He [b]appears, we may have [c]confidence and [d]not [1]shrink away from Him in shame [2]at His [e]coming.

29 If you know that [a]He is righteous, you know that everyone also who practices righteousness [b]is [1]born of Him.

Children of God Love One Another

3 See [1a]how great a love the Father has bestowed on us, that we would be called [b]children of God; and *such* we are. For this reason the world does not know us, because [c]it did not know Him.

2 [a]Beloved, now we are [b]children of God, and [c]it has not appeared as yet what we will be. We know that when He [d]appears, we will be [e]like Him, because we will [f]see Him just as He is.

3 And everyone who has this [a]hope *fixed* on Him [b]purifies himself, just as He is pure.

4 Everyone who practices sin also practices lawlessness; and [a]sin is lawlessness.

5 You know that He [a]appeared in order to [b]take away sins; and [c]in Him there is no sin.

6 No one who abides in Him [a]sins; no one who sins has seen Him or [1b]knows Him.

7 [a]Little children, make sure no one [b]deceives you; [c]the one who practices righteousness is righteous, just as He is righteous;

8 the one who practices sin is [a]of the devil; for the devil [1]has sinned from the beginning. [b]The Son of God [c]appeared for this purpose, [d]to destroy the works of the devil.

9 No one who is [1a]born of God [b]practices

19 [1]Lit *they would be revealed* [b]1 Cor 11:19 **20** [1]Lit *And* [a]2 Cor 1:21; 1 John 2:27 [b]Mark 1:24; Acts 10:38 [c]Prov 28:5; Matt 13:11; John 14:26; 1 Cor 2:15f; 1 John 2:27 **21** [1]Or know *that* [a]James 1:19; 2 Pet 1:12; Jude 5 [b]John 8:44; 18:37; 1 John 3:19 **22** [1]I.e. Messiah [a]1 John 4:3; 2 John 7 [b]Matt 24:5, 24; 1 John 2:18; 4:3; 2 John 7 **23** [a]John 8:19; 16:3; 17:3; 1 John 4:15; 5:1; 2 John 9 **24** [a]1 John 2:7 [b]John 14:23; 1 John 1:3; 2 John 9 **25** [1]Lit *promised us* [a]John 3:15; 6:40; 1 John 1:2 **26** [a]1 John 3:7; 2 John 7 **27** [1]Or *abide in Him;* Gr command [a]John 14:16; 1 John 2:20 [b]John 14:26; 1 Cor 2:12; 1 Thess 4:9 [c]John 14:17 **28** [1]Lit *be put to shame from Him* [2]Or *in His presence* [a]1 John 2:1 [b]Luke 17:30; Col 3:4; 1 John 3:2 [c]Eph 3:12; 1 John 3:21; 4:17; 5:14 [d]Mark 8:38 [e]1 Thess 2:19 **29** [1]Or *begotten* [a]John 7:18; 1 John 3:7 [b]John 1:13; 3:3; 1 John 3:9; 4:7; 5:1, 4, 18; 3 John 11 **3:1** [1]Lit *what kind of love* [a]John 3:16; 1 John 4:10 [b]John 1:12; 11:52; Rom 8:16; 1 John 3:2, 10 [c]John 15:18, 21; 16:3 **2** [a]1 John 2:7 [b]John 1:12; 11:52; Rom 8:16; 1 John 3:1, 10 [c]Rom 8:19, 23f [d]Luke 17:30; Col 3:4; 1 John 2:28 [e]Rom 8:29; 2 Pet 1:4 [f]John 17:24; 2 Cor 3:18 **3** [a]Rom 15:12; 1 Pet 1:3 [b]John 17:19; 2 Cor 7:1 **4** [a]Rom 4:15; 1 John 5:17 **5** [a]1 John 1:2; 3:8 [b]John 1:29; 1 Pet 1:18-20; 1 John 2:2 [c]2 Cor 5:21; 1 John 2:29 **6** [1]Or *has known* [a]1 John 3:9 [b]1 John 2:3; 3 John 11 **7** [a]1 John 2:1 [b]1 John 2:26 [c]1 John 2:29 **8** [1]Lit *sins* [a]Matt 13:38; John 8:44; 1 John 3:10 [b]Matt 4:3 [c]1 John 3:5 [d]John 12:31; 16:11 **9** [1]Or *begotten* [a]John 1:13; 3:3; 1 John 2:29; 4:7; 5:1, 4, 18; 3 John 11 [b]1 Pet 1:23; 1 John 3:6; 5:18

The "anti" in antichrist means "against" (cf. 2 Thess 2:4; Rev 13:6–7).

2:20 *anointing.* The Holy Spirit (see v. 27; Acts 10:38). *Holy One.* Either Jesus Christ (Mark 1:24; John 6:69; Acts 2:27; 3:14; 22:14) or the Father (2 Kin 19:22; Job 6:10).

2:22 *Jesus is the Christ.* The man Jesus is the divine Christ (see the parallel confession in 5:5; see also Introduction: Gnosticism and note on 5:6).

2:23 See 2 John 9 for the same thought.

2:26 One of the statements of purpose for the letter (see Introduction: Occasion and Purpose).

2:27 *anointing.* See note on v. 20. *have no need for anyone to teach you.* Since the Bible constantly advocates teaching (Matt 28:20; 1 Cor 12:28; Eph 4:11; Col 3:16; 1 Tim 4:11; 2 Tim 2:2,24), John is not ruling out human teachers. At the time when he wrote, however, Gnostic teachers were insisting that the teaching of the apostles was to be supplemented with the "higher knowledge" that they (the Gnostics) claimed to possess. John's response was that what the readers were taught under the Spirit's ministry through the apostles not only was adequate but was the only reliable truth. *teaches you.* The teaching ministry of the Holy Spirit (what is commonly called illumination) does not involve revelation of new truth or the explanation of all difficult passages of Scripture to our satisfaction. Rather, it is the development of the capacity to appreciate and appropriate God's truth already revealed—making the Bible meaningful in thought and daily living. *all things.* All things necessary to know for salvation and Christian living.

2:28 *abide in Him.* See "abides in" (vv. 24,27). *confidence.* See 3:21; 4:17; 5:14.

2:29 *He . . . Him.* God the Father. *practices righteousness.* Members of God's family are marked by holy living.

3:1 *children of God.* See note on John 1:12.

3:2 *He . . . Him.* Christ.

3:3 *hope.* Not a mere wish, but unshakable confidence concerning the future (see note on Rom 5:2). *Him.* Christ. *purifies himself.* By turning from sin.

3:6 *sins.* John is not asserting sinless perfection (see 1:8–10; 2:1), but explaining that the believer's life is characterized not by sin but by doing what is right.

3:8 *devil.* In this short letter John says much about the devil: 1. He is called "the devil" (here) and "the evil one" (v. 12; 2:13–14; 5:18–19). 2. He "has sinned from the beginning" (here), i.e., from the time he first rebelled against God, before the fall of Adam and Eve (John 8:44). 3. He is the instigator of human sin, and those who continue to sin belong to him (vv. 8,12) and are his children (v. 10). 4. He is in the world (4:3) and has "the whole world" of unbelievers under his control (5:19). 5. But he cannot lay hold of the believer to harm him (5:18). 6. On the contrary, the Christian will overcome him (2:13–14; 4:4), and Christ will destroy his work.

sin, because His seed abides in him; and he
cannot sin, because he is [1]born of God.
10 By this the [a]children of God and the
[b]children of the devil are obvious: [1]anyone
who does not practice righteousness is not
of God, nor the one who [c]does not love his
[d]brother.
11 [a]For this is the message [b]which you
have heard from the beginning, [c]that we
should love one another;
12 not as [a]Cain, *who* was of [b]the evil one
and slew his brother. And for what reason
did he slay him? Because [c]his deeds were
evil, and his brother's were righteous.
13 Do not be surprised, brethren, if [a]the
world hates you.
14 We know that we have [a]passed out of
death into life, [b]because we love the brethren. He who does not love abides in death.
15 Everyone who [a]hates his brother is a
murderer; and you know that [b]no murderer
has eternal life abiding in him.
16 We know love by this, that [a]He laid
down His life for us; and [b]we ought to lay
down our lives for the [c]brethren.
17 But [a]whoever has the world's goods,
and sees his brother in need and [b]closes his
[1]heart [2]against him, [c]how does the love of
God abide in him?
18 [a]Little children, let us not love with
word or with tongue, but in deed and [b]truth.
19 We will know by this that we are [a]of
the truth, and will [1]assure our heart before
Him
20 [1]in whatever our heart condemns us;
for God is greater than our heart and knows
all things.
21 [a]Beloved, if our heart does not condemn us, we have [b]confidence [1]before God;
22 and [a]whatever we ask we receive from
Him, because we [b]keep His commandments
and do [c]the things that are pleasing in His
sight.
23 This is His commandment, that we
[1][a]believe in [b]the name of His Son Jesus
Christ, and love one another, just as [c]He
[2]commanded us.
24 The one who [a]keeps His commandments [b]abides in Him, and He in him. [c]We
know by this that [d]He abides in us, by the
Spirit whom He has given us.

Testing the Spirits

4 [a]Beloved, do not believe every [b]spirit, but
test the spirits to see whether they are
from God, because [c]many false prophets
have gone out into the world.
2 By this you know the Spirit of God:
[a]every spirit that [b]confesses that [c]Jesus
Christ has come in the flesh is from God;
3 and every spirit that [a]does not confess
Jesus is not from God; this is the *spirit* of the
[b]antichrist, of which you have heard that it is
coming, and [c]now it is already in the world.
4 You are from God, [a]little children, and
[b]have overcome them; because [c]greater is He
who is in you than [d]he who is in the world.
5 [a]They are from the world; therefore
they speak *as* from the world, and the world
listens to them.
6 [a]We are from God; [b]he who knows God
listens to us; [c]he who is not from God does

9 [1]Or *begotten* **10** [1]Lit *everyone* [a]John 1:12; 11:52; Rom 8:16; 1 John 3:1, 2 [b]Matt 13:38; John 8:44; 1 John 3:8 [c]Rom 13:8ff; Col 3:14; 1 Tim 1:5; 1 John 4:8 [d]1 John 2:9 **11** [a]1 John 1:5 [b]1 John 2:7 [c]John 13:4f; 15:12; 1 John 4:7, 11f, 21; 2 John 5 **12** [a]Gen 4:8 [b]Matt 5:37; 1 John 2:13f [c]Ps 38:20; Prov 29:10; John 8:40, 41 **13** [a]John 15:18; 17:14 **14** [a]John 5:24 [b]John 13:35; 1 John 2:10 **15** [a]Matt 5:21f; John 8:44 [b]Gal 5:20f; Rev 21:8 **16** [a]John 10:11; 15:13 [b]Phil 2:17; 1 Thess 2:8 [c]1 John 2:9 **17** [1]Lit *inward parts* [2]Lit *from* [a]James 2:15f [b]Deut 15:7 [c]1 John 4:20 **18** [a]1 John 2:1; 3:7 [b]2 John 1; 3 John 1 **19** [1]Lit *persuade* [a]1 John 2:21 **20** [1]Or *that if our heart condemns us, that God...* **21** [1]Lit *toward* [a]1 John 3:2 [b]1 John 2:28; 5:14 **22** [a]Job 22:26f; Matt 7:7; 21:22; John 9:31
22 [b]1 John 2:3 [c]John 8:29; Heb 13:21 **23** [1]Or *believe the name* [2]Lit *gave us a commandment* [a]John 6:29 [b]John 1:12; 2:23; 3:18 [c]John 13:34; 15:12; 1 John 2:8 **24** [a]1 John 2:3 [b]John 6:56; 10:38; 1 John 2:6, 24; 4:15 [c]John 14:17; Rom 8:9, 14, 16; 1 Thess 4:8; 1 John 4:13 [d]1 John 2:5 **4:1** [a]3 John 11 [b]Jer 29:8; 1 Cor 12:10; 1 Thess 5:20f; 2 Thess 2:2 [c]Jer 14:14; 2 Pet 2:1; 1 John 2:18
2 [a]1 Cor 12:3 [b]1 John 2:23 [c]John 1:14; 1 John 1:2 **3** [a]1 John 2:22; 2 John 7 [b]1 John 2:18, 22 [c]2 Thess 2:3-7; 1 John 2:18
4 [a]1 John 2:1 [b]1 John 2:13 [c]Rom 8:31; 1 John 3:20 [d]John 12:31
5 [a]John 15:19; 17:14, 16 **6** [a]John 8:23; 1 John 4:4 [b]John 8:47; 10:3ff; 18:37 [c]1 Cor 14:37

3:9 *His seed.* The picture is of human reproduction, in which the sperm (the Greek for "seed" is *sperma*) bears the life principle and transfers the paternal characteristics. *cannot sin.* Not a complete cessation of sin, but a life that is not characterized by sin.
3:11 *from the beginning.* See note on 2:7.
3:12 *Cain.* See Heb 11:4.
3:14 *brethren.* Fellow believers.
3:15 *hates.* See note on 2:9–10.
3:17–18 See James 2:14–17.
3:17 *love of God.* God's kind of love, which He pours out in the believer's heart (Rom 5:5) and which in turn enables the Christian to love fellow believers. Or it may speak of the believer's love for God.
3:20 *God is greater than our heart.* An oversensitive conscience can be quieted by the knowledge that God Himself has declared active love to be an evidence of salvation. He knows the hearts of all—whether, in spite of shortcomings, they have been born of Him.
3:23 This command has two parts: (1) Believe in Christ (see John 6:29), and (2) love each other (see John 13:34–35). The first part is developed in 4:1–6 and the second part in 4:7–12.
4:1 *spirit.* A person moved by a spirit, whether by the Holy Spirit or an evil one. *test the spirits.* Cf. 1 Thess 5:21. (Matt 7:1 does not refer to such testing or judgment; it speaks of self-righteous moral judgment of others.) *false prophets.* A true prophet speaks from God, being "moved by the Holy Spirit' (2 Pet 1:21). False prophets, such as the Gnostics of John's day, speak under the influence of spirits alienated from God. Christ warned against false prophets (Matt 7:15; 24:11), as did Paul (1 Tim 4:1) and Peter (2 Pet 2:1).
4:2 *confesses.* Not only knows intellectually—for demons know, and shudder (James 2:19; cf. Mark 1:24)—but also confesses publicly. *Jesus Christ has come in the flesh.* See note on 1:1. Thus John excludes the Gnostics, especially the Cerinthians, who taught that the divine Christ came upon the human Jesus at his baptism and then left him at the cross, so that it was only the man Jesus who died (see Introduction: Gnosticism).
4:3 *does not confess Jesus.* The incarnate Jesus Christ of 1:2 (see note on 2:18).
4:4 *from God.* An abbreviated form of the expression "born of God" (2:29; 3:9–10). *them.* The false prophets (v. 1), who were inspired by the spirit of the antichrist (v. 3). *he who is in the world.* The devil (John 12:31; 16:11). In v. 3 "world" means the inhabited earth; in vv. 4–5 it means the community, or system, of those not born of God—including the antichrists (see note on John 1:9).
4:6 *spirit of truth.* Cf. 5:6; see note on John 14:17.

not listen to us. By this we know [d]the spirit
of truth and [e]the spirit of error.

God Is Love

7 [a]Beloved, let us [b]love one another, for
love is from God; and [c]everyone who loves is
[1d]born of God and [e]knows God.
8 The one who does not love does not
know God, for [a]God is love.
9 By this the love of God was manifested
[1a]in us, that [b]God has sent His [2]only begotten Son into the world so that we might live
through Him.
10 In this is love, [a]not that we loved God,
but that [b]He loved us and sent His Son *to be*
[c]the propitiation for our sins.
11 [a]Beloved, if God so loved us, [b]we also
ought to love one another.
12 [a]No one has seen God at any time; if
we love one another, God abides in us, and
His [b]love is perfected in us.
13 [a]By this we know that we abide in Him
and He in us, because He has given us of His
Spirit.
14 We have seen and [a]testify that the
Father has [b]sent the Son *to be* the Savior of
the world.
15 [a]Whoever confesses that [b]Jesus is the
Son of God, God [c]abides in him, and he in
God.
16 [a]We have come to know and have
believed the love which God has [1b]for us.
[c]God is love, and the one who [d]abides in
love abides in God, and God abides in him.
17 By this, [a]love is perfected with us, so
that we may have [b]confidence in [c]the day of
judgment; because [d]as He is, so also are we
in this world.
18 There is no fear in love; but [a]perfect
love casts out fear, because fear [1]involves
punishment, and the one who fears is not
[b]perfected in love.
19 [a]We love, because He first loved us.
20 [a]If someone says, "I love God," and
[b]hates his brother, he is a [c]liar; for [d]the one
who does not love his brother whom he has
seen, [e]cannot love God whom he has not
seen.
21 And [a]this commandment we have from
Him, that the one who loves God [b]should
love his brother also.

Overcoming the World

5 [a]Whoever believes that Jesus is the
[1]Christ is [2b]born of God, and whoever
loves the [3]Father [c]loves the *child* [2]born of
Him.
2 [a]By this we know that [b]we love the
children of God, when we love God and
[1]observe His commandments.
3 For [a]this is the love of God, that we
[b]keep His commandments; and [c]His commandments are not burdensome.
4 For whatever is [1a]born of God [b]over-
comes the world; and this is the victory that
has overcome the world—our faith.
5 Who is the one who overcomes the
world, but he who [a]believes that Jesus is the
Son of God?
6 This is the One who came [a]by water
and blood, Jesus Christ; not [1]with the water
only, but [1]with the water and [1]with the
blood. It is [b]the Spirit who testifies, because
the Spirit is the truth.

6 [d]John 14:17 [e]1 Tim 4:1 **7** [1]Or *begotten* [a]1 John 2:7 [b]1 John 3:11 [c]1 John 5:1 [d]1 John 2:29 [e]1 Cor 8:3; 1 John 2:3 **8** [a]1 John 4:7, 16 **9** [1]Or *in our case* [2]Or *unique, only one of His kind* [a]John 9:3; 1 John 4:16 [b]John 3:16f; 1 John 4:10; 5:11 **10** [a]Rom 5:8, 10; 1 John 4:19 [b]John 3:16f; 1 John 4:9; 5:11 [c]1 John 2:2 **11** [a]1 John 2:7 [b]1 John 4:7 **12** [a]John 1:18; 1 Tim 6:16; 1 John 4:20 [b]1 John 2:5; 4:17f **13** [a]Rom 8:9; 1 John 3:24 **14** [a]John 15:27; 1 John 1:2 [b]John 3:17; 4:42; 1 John 2:2 **15** [a]1 John 2:23 [b]Rom 10:9; 1 John 3:23; 4:2; 5:1, 5 [c]1 John 2:24; 3:24 **16** [1]Lit *in* [a]John 6:69 [b]John 9:3; 1 John 4:9 [c]1 John 4:7, 8 [d]1 John 4:12f **17** [a]1 John 2:5; 4:12 [b]1 John 2:28 [c]Matt 10:15 [d]John 17:22; 1 John 2:6; 3:1, 7, 16 **18** [1]Lit *has* [a]Rom 8:15

18 [b]1 John 4:12 **19** [a]1 John 4:10 **20** [a]1 John 1:6, 8, 10; 2:4 [b]1 John 2:9, 11 [c]1 John 1:6 [d]1 John 3:17 [e]1 Pet 1:8; 1 John 4:12 **21** [a]Lev 19:18; Matt 5:43f; 22:37ff; John 13:34 [b]1 John 3:11 **5:1** [1]I.e. Messiah [2]Or *begotten* [3]Lit *one who begets* [a]1 John 2:22f; 4:2, 15 [b]John 1:3; 3:3; 1 John 2:29; 5:4, 18 [c]John 8:42 **2** [1]Lit *do* [a]1 John 2:5 [b]1 John 3:14 **3** [a]John 14:15; 2 John 6 [b]1 John 2:3 [c]Matt 11:30; 23:4 **4** [1]Or *begotten* [a]John 1:13; 3:3; 1 John 2:29; 5:1, 18 [b]1 John 2:13; 4:4 **5** [a]1 John 4:15; 5:1 **6** [1]Lit *in* [a]John 19:34 [b]Matt 3:16f; John 15:26; 16:13-15

4:7–5:3 The word "love" in its various forms is used 43 times in the letter, 32 times in this short section.
4:8 *does not know God.* Only those who are to some degree like Him truly know Him. *God is love.* In His essential nature and in all His actions, God is loving. John similarly affirms that God is spirit (John 4:24) and light (1:5), as well as holy, powerful, faithful, true and just.
4:9 *only begotten Son.* See note on John 1:18.
4:10 *propitiation for our sins.* See note on 2:2.
4:12 *No one has seen God at any time.* See note on John 1:18. Since our love has its source in God's love, His love reaches full expression (is made complete) when we love fellow Christians. Thus the God whom "no one has seen" is seen in those who love, because God lives in them.
4:16 *God is love.* See note on v. 8.
4:17 *so also are we.* Like Christ. The fact that we are like Christ in love is a sign that God, who is love, lives in us; therefore we may have confidence on the day of judgment that we are saved.
4:18 *no fear in love.* There is no fear of God's judgment because genuine love confirms salvation.
4:19 All love comes ultimately from God; genuine love is never self-generated by His creatures.
4:21 *this commandment.* See John 13:34.
5:1 *Whoever believes that Jesus is the Christ is born of God.* Faith in Jesus as the Christ is a sign of being born again, just as love is (4:7). *the Christ.* See note on 2:22. *whoever loves the Father loves the child born of Him.* John wrote at a time when members of a family were closely associated as a unit under the headship of the father. He could therefore use the family as an illustration to show that anyone who loves God the Father will naturally love God's children.
5:3 *His commandments are not burdensome.* Not because the commands themselves are light or easy to obey but, as John explains in v. 4, because of the new birth. The one born of God by faith is enabled by the Holy Spirit to obey.
5:4 *overcomes . . . has overcome.* To overcome the world is to gain victory over its sinful pattern of life, which is another way of describing obedience to God (v. 3). Such obedience is not impossible for the believer because he has been born again and the Holy Spirit dwells within him and gives him strength. John speaks of two aspects of victory: (1) the initial victory of turning in faith from the world to God ("has overcome"); (2) the continuing day-by-day victory of Christian living ("overcomes"). *world.* See note on 2:15.
5:5 *Son of God.* For parallel confessions see 2:22; 4:2; 5:1.
5:6 Water symbolizes Jesus' baptism, and blood symbolizes His death. These are mentioned because Jesus' ministry began at His baptism and ended at His death. John is reacting to the heretics of his day (see Introduction: Gnosticism) who said that

7 For there are [a]three that testify:
8 [1]the Spirit and the water and the blood;
and the three are [2]in agreement.
9 [a]If we receive the testimony of men,
the testimony of God is greater; for the testimony of God is this, that [b]He has testified
concerning His Son.
10 The one who believes in the Son of
God [a]has the testimony in himself; the one
who does not believe God has [b]made Him a
liar, because he has not believed in the testimony that God has given concerning His
Son.
11 And the testimony is this, that God has
given us [a]eternal life, and [b]this life is in His
Son.
12 [a]He who has the Son has the life; he
who does not have the Son of God does not
have the life.

This Is Written That You May Know

13 [a]These things I have written to you
who [b]believe in the name of the Son of God,
so that you may know that you have [c]eternal
life.
14 This is [a]the confidence which we have
[1]before Him, that, [b]if we ask anything
according to His will, He hears us.
15 And if we know that He hears us *in*
whatever we ask, [a]we know that we have
the requests which we have asked from Him.
16 If anyone sees his brother [1]committing
a sin not *leading* to death, [a]he shall ask and
[2]*God* will for him give life to those who commit sin not *leading* to death. [b]There is a sin
leading to death; [c]I do not say that he should
make request for this.
17 [a]All unrighteousness is sin, and [b]there
is a sin not *leading* to death.
18 [a]We know that [b]no one who is [1]born of
God sins; but He who was [1]born of God
[c]keeps him, and [d]the evil one does not
[e]touch him.
19 [a]We know that [b]we are of God, and
that [c]the whole world lies in *the power of* the
evil one.
20 And [a]we know that [b]the Son of God
has come, and has [c]given us understanding
so that we may know [d]Him who is true; and
we [e]are in Him who is true, in His Son Jesus
Christ. [f]This is the true God and [g]eternal life.
21 [a]Little children, guard yourselves from
[b]idols.

7 [a]Matt 18:16 **8** [1]A few late mss add ...*in heaven, the Father, the Word, and the Holy Spirit, and these three are one. And there are three that testify on earth, the Spirit* [2]Lit *for the one thing* **9** [a]John 5:34, 37; 8:18 [b]Matt 3:17; John 5:32, 37 **10** [a]Rom 8:16; Gal 4-6; Rev 12:17 [b]John 3:18, 33; 1 John 1:10 **11** [a]John 3:36; 1 John 1:2; 2:25; 4:9; 5:13, 20 [b]John 1:4 **12** [a]John 3:15f, 36 **13** [a]John 20:31 [b]1 John 3:23 [c]1 John 1:2; 2:25; 4:9; 5:11, 20 **14** [1]Lit *toward* [a]1 John 2:28; 3:21f [b]Matt 7:7; John 14:13; 1 John 3:22 **15** [a]1 John 5:18-20 **16** [1]Lit *sinning* [2]Or *God will give him life,* that is, *to those who...* [a]James 5:15 [b]Num 15:30; Heb 6:4-6; 10:26 [c]Jer 7:16; 14:11 **17** [a]1 John 3:4 [b]1 John 2:1f; 5:16 **18** [1]Or *begotten* [a]1 John 5:15, 19, 20 [b]1 John 3:9 [c]James 1:27; Jude 21 [d]1 John 2:13 [e]John 14:30 **19** [a]1 John 5:15, 18, 20 [b]1 John 4:6 [c]John 12:31; 17:15; Gal 1:4 **20** [a]1 John 5:15, 18, 19 [b]John 8:42; 1 John 5:5 [c]Luke 24:45 [d]John 17:3; Rev 3:7 [e]John 1:18; 14:9; 1 John 2:23; Rev 3:7 [f]1 John 1:2 [g]1 John 5:11 **21** [a]1 John 2:1 [b]1 Cor 10:7, 14; 1 Thess 1:9

Jesus was born only a man and remained so until His baptism. At that time, they maintained, the Christ (the Son of God) descended on the human Jesus, but left him before his suffering on the cross—so that it was only the man Jesus who died. Throughout this letter John has been insisting that Jesus Christ is God as well as man (1:1–4; 4:2; 5:5). He now asserts that it was this God-man Jesus Christ who came into our world, was baptized and died. Jesus was the Son of God not only at His baptism but also at His death (v. 6b). This truth is extremely important, because, if Jesus died only as a man, His sacrificial atonement (2:2; 4:10) would not have been sufficient to take away the guilt of man's sin. *the Spirit who testifies.* The Holy Spirit testifies that Jesus is the Son of God in two ways: (1) The Spirit descended on Jesus at His baptism (John 1:32–34), and (2) He continues to confirm in the hearts of believers the apostolic testimony that Jesus' baptism and death verify that He is the Christ, the Son of God (2:27; 1 Cor 12:3).

5:7 *three.* The OT law required "two or three witnesses" (Deut 17:6; 19:15; see 1 Tim 5:19).

5:9 *testimony of God.* The Holy Spirit's testimony, mentioned in vv. 6–8.

5:11 *has given us eternal life.* As a present possession (see notes on John 3:15,36).

5:13 Another statement of the letter's purpose (see 2:26). See Introduction: Occasion and Purpose.

5:14 *if we ask anything according to His will.* For another condition for prayer see 3:21–22.

5:16 Verses 16–17 illustrate the kind of petition we can be sure God will answer (see vv. 14–15). *sin leading to death.* In the context of this letter directed against Gnostic teaching, which denied the incarnation and threw off all moral restraints, it is probable that the "sin leading to death" refers to the Gnostics' adamant and persistent denial of the truth and to their shameless immorality. This kind of unrepentant sin leads to spiritual death. Another view is that this is sin that results in physical death. It is held that, because a believer continues to sin, God in judgment takes his life (cf. 1 Cor 11:30). In either case, "sin not leading to death" is of a less serious nature.

5:18–20 *We know.* The letter ends with three striking statements, affirming the truths that "we know" and summarizing some of the letter's major themes.

5:18 *He who was born of God.* Jesus, the Son of God.

5:20 *Him who is true.* God the Father. *This is the true God.* Could refer to either God the Father or God the Son. *eternal life.* The letter began with this theme (1:1–2) and now ends with it.

5:21 *idols.* False gods, as opposed to the one true God (v. 20).

2 John

INTRODUCTION

Author

The author is John the apostle. Obvious similarities to 1 John and the Gospel of John suggest that the same person wrote all three books. Compare the following:

2 John 5	1 John 2:7	John 13:34–35
2 John 6	1 John 5:3	John 14:23
2 John 7	1 John 4:2–3	
2 John 12	1 John 1:4	John 15:11; 16:24

See Introductions to 1 John and the Gospel of John: Author.

Date

The letter was probably written about the same time as 1 John (A.D. 85–95), as the above comparisons suggest (see Introduction to 1 John: Date).

Occasion and Purpose

During the first two centuries the gospel was taken from place to place by traveling evangelists and teachers. Believers customarily took these missionaries into their homes and gave them provisions for their journey when they left. Since Gnostic teachers also relied on this practice (see note on 3 John 5), 2 John was written to urge discernment in supporting traveling teachers; otherwise, someone might unintentionally contribute to the propagation of heresy rather than truth.

Outline

I. Salutation (1–3)
II. Commendation (4)
III. Exhortation and Warning (5–11)
IV. Conclusion (12–13)

Walk According to His Commandments

1 [a]The elder to the [b]chosen [c]lady and her
children, whom I [d]love in truth; and not
only I, but also all who [e]know the truth,
2 for [a]the sake of the truth which abides
[b]in us and will be [c]with us forever:
3 [a]Grace, mercy *and* peace will be with
us, from God the Father and from Jesus
Christ, the Son of the Father, in truth and
love.
4 [a]I was very glad to find *some* of your
children walking in truth, just as we have
received commandment *to do* from the
Father.
5 Now I ask you, lady, [a]not as though *I*
were writing to you a new commandment,
but the one which we have had [a]from the
beginning, that we [b]love one another.
6 And [a]this is love, that we walk according to His commandments. This is the commandment, [b]just as you have heard [c]from
the beginning, that you should walk in it.
7 For [a]many deceivers have [b]gone out
into the world, those who [c]do not acknowledge Jesus Christ *as* coming in the flesh.
This is [a]the deceiver and the [d]antichrist.
8 [a]Watch yourselves, [b]that you do not
lose what we have accomplished, but that
you may receive a full reward.
9 [1]Anyone who [2]goes too far and [a]does
not abide in the teaching of Christ, does not
have God; the one who abides in the teaching, he has both the Father and the Son.
10 If anyone comes to you and does not
bring this teaching, [a]do not receive him into
your house, and do not give him a greeting;
11 for the one who gives him a greeting
[a]participates in his evil deeds.
12 [a]Though I have many things to write to
you, I do not want to *do so* with paper and
ink; but I hope to come to you and speak
face to face, so that [1]your [b]joy may be made
full.
13 The children of your [a]chosen sister
greet you.

1:1 [a]Acts 11:30; 1 Pet 5:1; 3 John 1 [b]Rom 16:13; 1 Pet 5:13; 2 John 13 [c]2 John 5 [d]1 John 3:18; 2 John 3; 3 John 1 [e]John 8:32; 1 Tim 2:4 **2** [a]2 Pet 1:12 [b]1 John 1:8 [c]John 14:16 **3** [a]Rom 1:7; 1 Tim 1:2 **4** [a]3 John 3f **5** [a]1 John 2:7 [b]John 13:34, 35; 15:12, 17; 1 John 3:11; 4:7, 11 **6** [a]1 John 2:5; 5:3 [b]1 John 2:24 [c]1 John 2:7 **7** [a]1 John 2:26 [b]1 John 2:19; 4:1 [c]1 John 4:2f

7 [d]1 John 2:18 **8** [a]Mark 13:9 [b]1 Cor 3:8; Heb 10:35 **9** [1]Lit *Everyone* [2]Lit *goes on ahead* [a]John 7:16; 8:31; 1 John 2:23 **10** [a]1 Kin 13:16f; Rom 16:17; 2 Thess 3:6, 14; Titus 3:10 **11** [a]Eph 5:11; 1 Tim 5:22; Jude 23 **12** [1]One early ms reads *our* [a]3 John 13, 14 [b]John 3:29; 1 John 1:4 **13** [a]2 John 1

1 *elder.* See note on 1 Tim 3:1. In his later years, John functioned as an elder, perhaps of the Ephesian church. The apostle Peter held a similar position (1 Pet 5:1). *chosen lady.* Either an unknown Christian woman in the province of Asia or a figurative designation of a local church there. *her children.* Children of that Christian lady or members of that local church. *truth.* See note on John 1:14.

3 *Grace . . . peace.* See notes on Gal 1:3; Eph 1:2. *mercy.* See note on Rom 9:23.

5 *new commandment.* See note on 1 John 2:7.

6 *from the beginning.* See note on 1 John 2:7.

7–11 This section deals with the basic Gnostic heresy attacked in 1 John, namely, that the Son of God did not become flesh (John 1:14), but that He temporarily came upon the man Jesus between his baptism and crucifixion (see Introduction to 1 John: Gnosticism).

7 *Jesus Christ as coming in the flesh.* See 1 John 4:2–3 and note. *antichrist.* See note on 1 John 2:18.

8 *accomplished . . . full reward.* Work faithfully accomplished on earth brings future reward (see Mark 9:41; 10:29–30; Luke 19:16–19; Heb 11:26).

9 *goes too far.* A reference to the Gnostics, who believed that they had advanced beyond the teaching of the apostles. *teaching of Christ.* The similarity of this letter to 1 John, the nature of the heresy combated, and the immediate context suggest that John is not referring to teaching given by Christ, but to true teaching about Christ as the incarnate God-man.

10 *receive him into your house.* A reference to the housing and feeding of traveling teachers (see Introduction: Occasion and Purpose). The instruction does not prohibit greeting or even inviting a person into one's home for conversation. John was warning against providing food and shelter, since this would be an investment in the "evil deeds" of false teachers and would give public approval (see v. 11).

12 *paper and ink.* Paper was made from papyrus reeds, which were readily available and cheap. The ink (the Greek for this word comes from a word that means "black") was made by mixing carbon, water and gum or oil. *that your joy may be made full.* See 1 John 1:4.

13 *chosen sister.* May be taken literally to designate another Christian woman or figuratively to refer to another local church (see note on v. 1).

3 John

INTRODUCTION

Author

The author is John the apostle. In the first verses of both 2 John and 3 John the author identifies himself as "the elder." Note other similarities: "love in truth" (v. 1 of both letters), "walking in the truth" (v. 4 of both letters) and the similar conclusions. See Introductions to 1 John and the Gospel of John: Author.

Date

The letter was probably written about the same time as 1 and 2 John (A.D. 85–95). See Introduction to 1 John: Date.

Occasion and Purpose

See Introduction to 2 John: Occasion and Purpose. Itinerant teachers sent out by John were rejected in one of the churches in the province of Asia by a dictatorial leader, Diotrephes, who even excommunicated members who showed hospitality to John's messengers. John wrote this letter to commend Gaius for supporting the teachers and, indirectly, to warn Diotrephes.

Outline

I. Salutation (1–2)
II. Commendation of Gaius (3–8)
III. Condemnation of Diotrephes (9–10)
IV. Exhortation to Gaius (11)
V. Example of Demetrius (12)
VI. Conclusion (13–14)

You Walk in the Truth

1 [a]The elder to the beloved [b]Gaius, whom I [c]love in truth.

2 Beloved, I pray that in all respects you may prosper and be in good health, just as your soul prospers.

3 For I [a]was very glad when [b]brethren came and testified to your truth, *that is,* how you [a]are walking in truth.

4 I have no greater joy than [1]this, to hear of [a]my children [b]walking in the truth.

5 Beloved, you are acting faithfully in whatever you accomplish for the [a]brethren, and [1]especially *when they are* [b]strangers;

6 and they have testified to your love before the church. You will do well to [a]send them on their way in a manner [b]worthy of God.

7 For they went out for the sake of [a]the Name, [b]accepting nothing from the Gentiles.

8 Therefore we ought to [1]support such men, so that we may [2]be fellow workers [3]with the truth.

9 I wrote something to the church; but Diotrephes, who loves to [a]be first among them, does not accept [1]what we say.

10 For this reason, [a]if I come, I will call attention to his deeds which he does, unjustly accusing us with wicked words; and not satisfied with this, he himself does not [b]receive the [c]brethren, either, and he forbids those who desire *to do so* and [d]puts *them* out of the church.

11 Beloved, [a]do not imitate what is evil, but what is good. [b]The one who does good is of God; [c]the one who does evil has not seen God.

12 Demetrius [a]has received a *good* testimony from everyone, and from the truth itself; and we add our testimony, and [b]you know that our testimony is true.

13 [a]I had many things to write to you, but I am not willing to write *them* to you with pen and ink;

14 but I hope to see you shortly, and we will speak face to face.

15 [a]Peace *be* to you. The friends greet you. Greet the friends [b]by name.

1:1 [a]2 John 1 [b]Acts 19:29; 20:4; Rom 16:23; 1 Cor 1:14 [c]1 John 3:18; 2 John 1
3 [a]2 John 4 [b]Acts 1:15; Gal 6:10; 3 John 5, 10
4 [1]Lit *these things, that I hear* [a]1 Cor 4:14f; 2 Cor 6:13; Gal 4:19; 1 Thess 2:11; 1 Tim 1:2; 2 Tim 1:2; Philem 10; 1 John 2:1 [b]2 John 4
5 [1]Lit *this* [a]Acts 1:15; Gal 6:10; 3 John 3, 10 [b]Rom 12:13; Heb 13:2
6 [a]Acts 15:3; Titus 3:13 [b]Col 1:10; 1 Thess 2:12
7 [a]John 15:21; Acts 5:41; Phil 2:9 [b]Acts 20:33, 35
8 [1]Or *receive such men as guests* [2]Or *prove ourselves to be* [3]Or *for*
9 [1]Lit *us* [a]2 John 9
10 [a]2 John 12 [b]2 John 10; 3 John 5 [c]Acts 1:15; Gal 6:10; 3 John 3, 5 [d]John 9:34
11 [a]Ps 34:14; 37:27 [b]1 John 2:29; 3:10 [c]1 John 3:6
12 [a]Acts 6:3; 1 Tim 3:7 [b]John 19:35; 21:24
13 [a]2 John 12
15 [a]John 20:19, 21, 26; Eph 6:23; 1 Pet 5:14 [b]John 10:3

1 *The elder.* See note on 2 John 1. *beloved.* A favorite term of John (see note on 1 John 2:7). *Gaius.* A Christian in one of the churches of the province of Asia. Gaius was a common Roman name. *truth.* See note on John 1:14.

4 *my children.* Perhaps John's converts, or believers currently under his spiritual guidance.

5 *accomplish for the brethren.* The early church provided hospitality and support for missionaries. See Introduction to 2 John: Occasion and Purpose; see also note on 2 John 10.

7 *Name.* See note on Acts 4:12. Today Orthodox Jews often address God by the title *Ha-Shem* ("The Name").

9 *I wrote.* There may have been a previous letter of the apostle that is now lost. *church.* Some identify this church with the chosen lady of 2 John 1. *Diotrephes.* A church leader who was exercising dictatorial power in the church. He must have had considerable influence since he was able to exclude people from the church fellowship (v. 10).

11 *does good.* The continual practice of good, not merely doing occasional good deeds.

13–14 See 2 John 12–13 for a similar conclusion.

14 *Peace be to you.* Not a prayer or wish but a benedictory pronouncement (see notes on John 14:27; 20:19; Gal 1:3; Eph 1:2).

Jude

INTRODUCTION

Author

The author identifies himself as Jude (v. 1), which is another form of the Hebrew name Judah (Greek "Judas"), a common name among the Jews. Of those so named in the NT, the ones most likely to be author of this letter are: (1) Judas the apostle (Luke 6:16; Acts 1:13)—not Judas Iscariot—and (2) Judas the brother of the Lord (Matt 13:55; Mark 6:3). The latter is more likely. For example, the author does not claim to be an apostle and even seems to separate himself from the apostles (see v. 17). Furthermore, he describes himself as a "brother of James" (v. 1). Ordinarily a person in Jude's day would describe himself as someone's son rather than as someone's brother. The reason for the exception here may have been James's prominence in the church at Jerusalem (see Introduction to James: Author).

Although neither Jude nor James describes himself as a brother of the Lord, others did not hesitate to speak of them in this way (see Matt 13:55; John 7:3–10; Acts 1:14; 1 Cor 9:5; Gal 1:19). Apparently they themselves did not ask to be heard because of the special privilege they had as members of the household of Joseph and Mary.

Possible references to the letter of Jude or quotations from it are found at a very early date: e.g., in Clement of Rome (c. A.D. 96). Clement of Alexandria (155–215), Tertullian (150–222) and Origen (185–253) accepted it; it was included in the Muratorian Canon (c. 170) and was accepted by Athanasius (298–373) and by the Council of Carthage (397). Eusebius (265–340) listed the letter among the questioned books, though he recognized that many considered it as from Jude.

According to Jerome and Didymus, some did not accept the letter as canonical because of its use of uninspired literature (see notes on vv. 9,14). But sound judgment has recognized that an inspired author may legitimately make use of uninspired literature—whether for illustrative purposes or for appropriation of historically reliable or otherwise acceptable material—and such use does not necessarily endorse that literature as inspired. Under the influence of the Spirit, the church came to the conviction that the authority of God stands behind the letter of Jude. The fact that the letter was questioned and tested but nonetheless was finally accepted by the churches indicates the strength of its claims to authenticity.

Date

There is nothing in the letter that requires a date beyond the lifetime of Jude the brother of the Lord. The error the author is combating, like that in 2 Peter, is not the heretical teaching of the second century, but that which could and did develop at an early date (cf. Acts 20:29–30; Rom 6:1; 1 Cor 5:1–11; 2 Cor 12:21; Gal 5:13; Eph 5:3–17; 1 Thess 4:6). (See also Introduction to 2 Peter: Date.) There is, moreover, nothing in the letter that requires a date after the time of the apostles, as some have argued. It may even be that Jude's readers had heard some of the apostles speak (see vv. 17–18). Likewise, the use of the word "faith" in the objective sense of the body of truth believed (v. 3) does not require a late dating of the letter. It was used in such a sense as early as Gal 1:23.

The question of the relationship between Jude and 2 Peter has a bearing on the date of Jude. If 2 Peter makes use of Jude—a commonly accepted view (see Introduction to 2 Peter: 2 Peter and Jude)—then Jude is to be dated prior to 2 Peter, probably c. A.D. 65. Otherwise, a date as late as c. 80 would be possible.

Recipients

The description of those to whom Jude addressed his letter is very general (see v. 1). It could apply to Jewish Christians, Gentile Christians, or both. Their location is not indicated. It should not be assumed that,

since 2 Pet 2 and Jude 4–18 appear to describe similar situations, they were both written to the same people. The kind of heresy depicted in these two passages was widespread (see Date).

Occasion and Purpose

Although Jude was very eager to write to his readers about salvation, he felt that he must instead warn them about certain immoral men circulating among them who were perverting the grace of God (v. 4). Apparently these false teachers were trying to convince believers that being saved by grace gave them license to sin since their sins would no longer be held against them. Jude thought it imperative that his readers be on guard against such men and be prepared to oppose their perverted teaching with the truth about God's saving grace.

It has generally been assumed that these false teachers were Gnostics. Although this identification is no doubt correct, they must have been forerunners of fully developed, second-century Gnosticism (see Introduction to 2 Peter: Date).

Outline

- I. Salutation (1–2)
- II. Occasion for the Letter (3–4)
  - A. The Change of Subject (3)
  - B. The Reason for the Change: The Presence of Godless Apostates (4)
- III. Warning against the False Teachers (5–16)
  - A. Historical Examples of the Judgment of Apostates (5–7)
    1. Unbelieving Israel (5)
    2. Angels who fell (6)
    3. Sodom and Gomorrah (7)
  - B. Description of the Apostates of Jude's Day (8–16)
    1. Their slanderous speech deplored (8–10)
    2. Their character graphically portrayed (11–13)
    3. Their destruction prophesied (14–16)
- IV. Exhortation to Believers (17–23)
- V. Concluding Doxology (24–25)

The Warnings of History to the Ungodly

1 [1][a]Jude, a [b]bond-servant of Jesus Christ,
and brother of [2]James,
To [c]those who are the called, beloved in
God the Father, and [d]kept for Jesus Christ:
2 [a]May mercy and peace and love [b]be
multiplied to you.
3 [a]Beloved, while I was making every
effort to write you about our [b]common salvation, I felt the necessity to write to you
appealing that you [c]contend earnestly for
[d]the faith which was once for all [e]handed
down to [f]the [1]saints.
4 For certain persons have [a]crept in
unnoticed, those who were long beforehand
[1][b]marked out for this condemnation, ungodly persons who turn [c]the grace of our God
into [d]licentiousness and [e]deny our only Master and Lord, Jesus Christ.
5 Now I desire to [a]remind you, though
[b]you know all things once for all, that [1]the
Lord, [c]after saving a people out of the land of
Egypt, [2]subsequently destroyed those who
did not believe.
6 And [a]angels who did not keep their
own domain, but abandoned their proper
abode, He has [b]kept in eternal bonds under
darkness for the judgment of the great day,
7 just as [a]Sodom and Gomorrah and the
[b]cities around them, since they in the same
way as these indulged in gross immorality
and [c]went after [1]strange flesh, are exhibited
as an [2][d]example in undergoing the [e]punish-
ment of eternal fire.
8 Yet in the same way these men, also by
dreaming, [a]defile the flesh, and reject
authority, and revile [1]angelic majesties.
9 But [a]Michael [b]the archangel, when he
disputed with the devil and argued about
[c]the body of Moses, did not dare pronounce
against him a railing judgment, but said,
"[d]The Lord rebuke you!"
10 But [a]these men revile the things which
they do not understand; and [b]the things
which they know by instinct, [a]like unrea-

1:1 [1]Gr *Judas* [2]Or *Jacob* [a]Matt 13:55; Mark 6:3; [Luke 6:16; John 14:22; Acts 1:13] [b]Rom 1:1 [c]Rom 1:6f [d]John 17:11f; 1 Pet 1:5; Jude 21
2 [a]Gal 6:16; 1 Tim 1:2 [b]1 Pet 1:2; 2 Pet 1:2
3 [1]Or *holy ones* [a]Heb 6:9; Jude 1, 17, 20 [b]Titus 1:4 [c]1 Tim 6:12 [d]Acts 6:7; Jude 20 [e]2 Pet 2:21 [f]Acts 9:13
4 [1]Or *written about...long ago* [a]Gal 2:4; 2 Tim 3:6 [b]1 Pet 2:8 [c]Acts 11:23 [d]2 Pet 2:7 [e]2 Tim 2:12; Titus 1:16; 2 Pet 2:1; 1 John 2:22
5 [1]Two early mss read *Jesus* [2]Lit *the second time* [a]2 Pet 1:12f; 3:1f [b]1 John 2:20 [c]Ex 12:51; 1 Cor 10:5-10; Heb 3:16f
6 [a]2 Pet 2:4 [b]2 Pet 2:9
7 [1]Lit *different* or *other flesh* [2]Or *example of eternal fire, in undergoing punishment* [a]Gen 19:24f; 2 Pet 2:6 [b]Deut 29:23; Hos 11:8 [c]2 Pet 2:2 [d]2 Pet 2:6 [e]Matt 25:41; 2 Thess 1:8f; 2 Pet 3:7
8 [1]Lit *glories* [a]2 Pet 2:10
9 [a]Dan 10:13, 21; 12:1; Rev 12:7 [b]1 Thess 4:16; 2 Pet 2:11 [c]Deut 34:6 [d]Zech 3:2
10 [a]2 Pet 2:12 [b]Phil 3:19

1 *bond-servant.* See note on Rom 1:1. *brother of James.* See Introduction: Author. *called.* See note on Rom 8:28. *beloved in God.* See John 3:16; Rom 8:28–39. *kept for Jesus Christ.* He who holds the whole universe together (see Col 1:17; Heb 1:3) will see that God's children are kept in the faith and that they reach their eternal inheritance (see John 6:37–40; 17:11–12; 1 Pet 1:3–5).

2 *peace.* The profound well-being of soul that flows from the experience of God's grace (see notes on John 14:27; 20:19; Gal 1:3; Eph 1:2).

3 *Beloved.* See vv. 17,20; see also note on 2 Pet 3:1. *our common salvation.* Jude's original intention was to write a general treatment of the doctrine of salvation, probably dealing with such subjects as man's sin and guilt, God's love and grace, the forgiveness of sins and the changed life-style that follows new birth. *the faith.* Here used of the body of truth held by believers everywhere—the gospel and all its implications (see Introduction: Date; see also 1 Tim 4:6). This truth was under attack and had to be defended. *once for all handed down.* The truth has finality and is not subject to change.

4 *For.* Introduces the reason Jude felt impelled to change the subject of his letter (see Introduction: Occasion and Purpose). *long beforehand marked out for this condemnation.* The reference may be to OT denunciations of ungodly men or to Enoch's prophecy (vv. 14–15). Or Jude may mean that judgment has long been about to fall on them because of their sin (see 2 Pet 2:3, which may be a clarification of this clause). *ungodly persons.* See vv. 15,18. *turn the grace of our God into licentiousness.* They assume that salvation by grace gives them the right to sin without restraint, either because God in His grace will freely forgive all their sins, or because sin, by contrast, magnifies the grace of God (cf. Rom 5:20; 6:1). *deny our only Master and Lord.* The Greek term translated "Master" describes power without limit, or absolute domination. The Greek construction indicates that both "Master" and "Lord" refer to the same person, and this verse, as well as the parallel passage (2 Pe 2:1), clearly states that that person is Christ.

5–7 Three examples of divine judgment.

5 *destroyed those who did not believe.* They did not believe that God would give them the land of Canaan; consequently all unbelieving adults died in the desert without entering the promised land.

6 *angels.* See note on 2 Pet 2:4. *domain.* See note on 2 Pet 2:4. God had assigned differing areas of responsibility and authority to each of the angels (see Dan 10:20–21, where the various princes may be angels assigned to various nations). Some of these angels refused to maintain their assignments and thus became the devil and his angels (cf. Matt 25:41). *their proper abode.* Angels apparently were assigned specific locations as well as responsibilities. Some assume that they left the heavenly realm and came to earth (see note on 2 Pet 2:4). *kept . . . bonds . . . judgment.* See note on 2 Pet 2:4. *the great day.* The final judgment.

7 *just as.* Does not mean that the sin of Sodom and Gomorrah was the same as that of the angels or vice versa. This phrase is used to introduce the third illustration of the fact that God will see to it that the unrighteous will be consigned to eternal punishment on judgment day. *gross immorality and . . . strange flesh.* More specifically, homosexuality (see Gen 19:5 and note; see also note on 2 Pet 2:10). *exhibited as an example in undergoing . . . eternal fire.* God destroyed Sodom and Gomorrah by pouring out "brimstone and fire" (Gen 19:24)—a foretaste of the eternal fire that is to come.

8 *men . . . by dreaming.* The reference to "dreaming" is either (1) because they claimed to receive revelations or, more likely, (2) because in their passion they were out of touch with truth and reality. *defile the flesh.* Probably a reference to the homosexuality in Sodom and Gomorrah (see vv. 4,7; 1 Cor 6:18). *reject authority.* See note on 2 Pet 2:10. *revile angelic majesties.* See note on 2 Pet 2:10.

9 According to several church fathers, this verse is based on a work called The Assumption of Moses. Other NT quotations from, or allusions to, non-Biblical works include Paul's quotations of Aratus (Acts 17:28), Menander (1 Cor 15:33) and Epimenides (Titus 1:12). Such usage in no way suggests that the quotations, or the books from which they were taken, are divinely inspired. It only means that the Biblical author found the quotations to be a helpful confirmation, clarification or illustration.

10 *things which they do not understand.* See note on 2 Pet 2:12; cf. 1 Cor 2:14. *like unreasoning animals.* See note on 2 Pet 2:12.

soning animals, by these things they are
[1]destroyed.
11 Woe to them! For they have gone [a]the
way of Cain, and for pay [1]they have rushed
headlong into [b]the error of Balaam, and [c]per-
ished in the rebellion of Korah.
12 These are the men who are [1]hidden
reefs [a]in your love feasts when they feast
with you [b]without fear, caring for themselves; [c]clouds without water, [d]carried along
by winds; autumn trees without fruit, [2]dou-
bly dead, [e]uprooted;
13 [a]wild waves of the sea, casting up
[b]their own [1]shame like foam; wandering
stars, [c]for whom the [2]black darkness has
been reserved forever.
14 *It was* also about these men *that*
[a]Enoch, *in* the seventh *generation* from
Adam, prophesied, saying, "[b]Behold, the
Lord came with [1]many thousands of His holy
ones,
15 [a]to execute judgment upon all, and to
convict all the ungodly of all their ungodly
deeds which they have done in an ungodly
way, and of all the harsh things which
[b]ungodly sinners have spoken against Him."
16 These are [a]grumblers, finding fault,
[b]following after their *own* lusts; [1]they speak
[c]arrogantly, flattering people [d]for the sake of
gaining an advantage.

Keep Yourselves in the Love of God

17 But you, [a]beloved, [b]ought to remember
the words that were spoken beforehand by
[c]the apostles of our Lord Jesus Christ,
18 that they were saying to you, "[a]In the
last time there will be mockers, [b]following
after their own ungodly lusts."
19 These are the ones who cause divisions,
[1][a]worldly-minded, [2]devoid of the Spirit.
20 But you, [a]beloved, [b]building yourselves up on your most holy [a]faith, [c]praying
in the Holy Spirit,
21 keep yourselves in the love of God,
[a]waiting anxiously for the mercy of our Lord
Jesus Christ to eternal life.
22 And have mercy on some, who are
doubting;
23 save others, [a]snatching them out of the

10 [1]Lit *corrupted*
11 [1]Lit *they have poured themselves out* [a]Gen 4:3-8; Heb 11:4; 1 John 3:12 [b]Num 31:16; 2 Pet 2:15; Rev 2:14 [c]Num 16:1-3, 31-35
12 [1]Or *stains* [2]Lit *twice* [a]1 Cor 11:20ff; 2 Pet 2:13 and mg [b]Ezek 34:2, 8, 10 [c]Prov 25:14; 2 Pet 2:17 [d]Eph 4:14 [e]Matt 15:13
13 [1]Or *shameless deeds* [2]Lit *blackness of darkness;* or *netherworld gloom* [a]Is 57:20 [b]Phil 3:19 [c]2 Pet 2:17; Jude 6
14 [1]Lit *His holy ten thousands* [a]Gen 5:18, 21ff [b]Deut 33:2; Dan 7:10; Matt 16:27; Heb 12:22
15 [a]2 Pet 2:6ff [b]1 Tim 1:9
16 [a]Num 16:11, 41; 1 Cor 10:10 [1]Lit *their mouth speaks* [b]2 Pet 2:10; Jude 18 [c]2 Pet 2:18 [d]2 Pet 2:3
17 [a]Jude 3 [b]2 Pet 3:2 [c]Heb 2:3
18 [a]Acts 20:29; 1 Tim 4:1; 2 Tim 3:1f; 4:3; 2 Pet 3:3 [b]Jude 4, 16
19 [1]Or *merely natural* [2]Lit *not having* [a]1 Cor 2:14f; James 3:15
20 [a]Jude 3 [b]Col 2:7; 1 Thess 5:11 [c]Eph 6:18
21 [a]Titus 2:13; Heb 9:28; 2 Pet 3:12
23 [a]Amos 4:11; Zech 3:2; 1 Cor 3:15

11 Three OT examples of the kind of persons Jude warns his readers about. *Woe to them!* A warning that judgment is coming (see Matt 23:13,15–16,23,25,27,29). *way of Cain.* The way of selfishness and greed (see note on Gen 4:3–4) and the way of hatred and murder (see 1John 3:12). *error of Balaam.* The error of consuming greed (see note on 2 Pet 2:15). *rebellion of Korah.* Korah rose up against God's appointed leadership (see Num 16). Jude may be suggesting that the false teachers of his day were rebelling against church leadership (cf. 3 John 9–10).
12–13 These verses contain six graphic metaphors: 1. *hidden reefs in your love feasts.* See note on 2 Pet 2:13. 2. *they feast . . . caring for themselves.* Instead of feeding the sheep for whom they are responsible (see Ezek 34:8–10). 3. *clouds without water.* Like clouds promising moisture for the parched land, the false teachers promise soul-satisfying truth, but in reality they have nothing to offer. 4. *autumn trees without fruit, doubly dead, uprooted.* Though the trees ought to be heavy with fruit. 5. *wild waves of the sea.* As wind-tossed waves constantly churn up rubbish, so these apostates continually stir up moral filth (see Is 57:20). 6. *wandering stars.* As shooting stars appear in the sky only to fly off into eternal oblivion, so these false teachers are destined for the darkness of eternal hell.
14 *Enoch, in the seventh generation from Adam.* Not the Enoch in the line of Cain (Gen 4:17) but the one in the line of Seth (Gen 5:18–24; 1 Chr 1:1–3). He was seventh if Adam is counted as the first. The quotation is from the book of Enoch, which purports to have been written by the Enoch of Gen 5, but actually did not appear until the first century B.C. The book of Enoch was a well-respected writing in NT times. That it was not canonical does not mean that it contained no truth; nor does Jude's quotation of the book mean that he considered it inspired (see Introduction: Author; see also note on v. 9). *prophesied.* Not in the sense of supernaturally revealing new truth, but merely in the sense of speaking things about the future that were already known (see Dan 7:9–14; Zech 14:1–5). *the Lord came.* Jude uses the quotation to refer to Christ's second coming and to His judgment of the wicked (see 2 Thess 1:6–10). *holy ones.* Probably angels (see Dan 4:13–17; 2 Thess 1:7). However, some think they are raptured saints who are returning with the Lord (see 1 Thess 3:13).
15 *ungodly . . . ungodly . . . ungodly . . . ungodly.* This thunderous repetition and the awesome judgment scene that is depicted emphasize the condemnation of the false teachers in v. 4.
16 *These.* The ungodly men first mentioned in v. 4 and subsequently referred to repeatedly as "these men" (vv. 10,12,14,19; cf. v. 8). They are the libertine false teachers who pervert the grace of God.
17 *remember the words . . . spoken beforehand by the apostles.* The coming of these godless men should not take believers by surprise, for it had been predicted by the apostles (Acts 20:29; 1 Tim 4:1; 2 Tim 3:1–5).
18 *they were saying.* The Greek for this phrase indicates that the apostles continually or repeatedly warned that such godless apostates would come. *last time.* See note on 2 Pet 3:3. *mockers.* In both 2 Pet 3:3 and Jude the mockers are said to be characterized by selfish lusts.
19 *the ones who cause divisions.* At the very least this phrase means that they were divisive, creating factions in the church—the usual practice of heretics. Or Jude may refer to the later Gnostics' division of men into the spiritual (the Gnostics) and the sensual (those for whom there is no hope). *worldly-minded.* An ironic description of the false teachers, who labeled others as "sensual." *devoid of the Spirit.* Rather than being the spiritual ones—the privileged elite class the Gnostics claimed to be—Jude denies that they even possess the Spirit. A person who does not have the Spirit is clearly not saved (see Rom 8:9).
20 *But you, beloved.* In contrast to the ungodly false teachers, about whom this letter speaks at length. *most holy faith.* See note on v. 3. *in the Holy Spirit.* According to the Spirit's promptings and with the power of the Spirit (see Rom 8:26–27; Gal 4:6; Eph 6:18).
21 *keep yourselves in the love of God.* God keeps believers in His love (see Rom 8:35–39), and enables them to keep themselves in His love.
22–23 *who are doubting . . . others.* Perhaps those who have come under the influence of the apostates.

fire; and on some have mercy with fear, [b]hating even the garment polluted by the flesh.
24 [a]Now to Him who is able to keep you from stumbling, and to [b]make you stand in the presence of His glory blameless with [c]great joy,
25 to the [a]only [b]God our Savior, through Jesus Christ our Lord, [c]*be* glory, majesty, dominion and authority, [d]before all time and now and [1]forever. Amen.

23 [b]Zech 3:3f; Rev 3:4 24 [a]Rom 16:25 [b]2 Cor 4:14 [c]1 Pet 4:13

25 [1]Lit *to all the ages* [a]John 5:44; 1 Tim 1:17 [b]Luke 1:47 [c]Rom 11:36 [d]Heb 13:8

23 *snatching them out of the fire.* Rescuing them from the verge of destruction. *mercy with fear.* Even in showing mercy one may be trapped by the allurement of sin. *garment polluted by the flesh.* The wicked are pictured as so corrupt that even their garments are polluted by their sinful nature.

24–25 After all the attention necessarily given in this letter to the ungodly and their works of darkness, Jude concludes his letter by focusing attention on God, who is fully able to keep those who put their trust in Him.

Revelation

INTRODUCTION

Author

Four times the author identifies himself as John (1:1,4,9; 22:8). From as early as Justin Martyr in the second century A.D. it has been held that this John was the apostle, the son of Zebedee (see Matt 10:2). The book itself reveals that the author was a Jew, well versed in Scripture, a church leader who was well known to the seven churches of Asia Minor, and a deeply religious person fully convinced that the Christian faith would soon triumph over the demonic forces at work in the world.

In the third century, however, an African bishop named Dionysius compared the language, style and thought of the Apocalypse (Revelation) with that of the other writings of John and decided that the book could not have been written by the apostle John. He suggested that the author was a certain John the Presbyter, whose name appears elsewhere in ancient writings. Although many today follow Dionysius in his view of authorship, the external evidence seems overwhelmingly supportive of the traditional view.

Date

Revelation was written when Christians were entering a time of persecution. The two periods most often mentioned are the latter part of Nero's reign (A.D. 54–68) and the latter part of Domitian's reign (81–96). Most scholars date the book c. 95. (A few suggest a date during the reign of Vespasian: 69–79.)

Occasion

Since Roman authorities at this time were beginning to enforce the cult of emperor worship, Christians—who held that Christ, not Caesar, was Lord—were facing increasing hostility. The believers at Smyrna are warned against coming opposition (2:10), and the church at Philadelphia is told of an hour of trial coming on the world (3:10). Antipas has already given his life (2:13) along with others (6:9). John has been exiled to the island of Patmos (probably the site of a Roman penal colony) for his activities as a Christian missionary (1:9). Some within the church are advocating a policy of compromise (2:14–15,20), which has to be corrected before its subtle influence can undermine the determination of believers to stand fast in the perilous days that lie ahead.

Purpose

John writes to encourage the faithful to resist staunchly the demands of emperor worship. He informs his readers that the final showdown between God and Satan is imminent. Satan will increase his persecution of believers, but they must stand fast, even to death. They are sealed against any spiritual harm and will soon be vindicated when Christ returns, when the wicked are forever destroyed, and when God's people enter an eternity of glory and blessedness.

Literary Form

For an adequate understanding of Revelation, the reader must recognize that it is a distinct kind of literature. Revelation is apocalyptic, a kind of writing that is highly symbolic. Although its visions often seem bizarre to the Western reader, fortunately the book provides a number of clues for its own interpretation (e.g., stars are angels, lampstands are churches, 1:20; "the great harlot," 17:1, is "Babylon" [Rome?], 17:5,18; and the heavenly Jerusalem is the wife of the Lamb, 21:9–10).

Distinctive Feature

A distinctive feature is the frequent use of the number seven (52 times). There are seven beatitudes (see note on 1:3), seven churches (1:4,11), seven spirits (1:4), seven golden lampstands (1:12), seven stars (1:16), seven seals (5:1), seven horns and seven eyes (5:6), seven trumpets (8:2), seven thunders (10:3), seven signs (12:1,3; 13:13–14; 15:1; 16:14; 19:20), seven crowns (12:3), seven plagues (15:6), seven golden bowls (15:7), seven hills (17:9) and seven kings (17:10), as well as other sevens. Symbolically, the number seven stands for completeness.

Interpretation

Interpreters of Revelation normally fall into four groups:

1. *Preterists* understand the book exclusively in terms of its first-century setting, claiming that most of its events have already taken place.
2. *Historicists* take it as describing the long chain of events from Patmos to the end of history.
3. *Futurists* place the book primarily in the end times.
4. *Idealists* view it as symbolic pictures of such timeless truths as the victory of good over evil.

Fortunately, the fundamental truths of Revelation do not depend on adopting a particular point of view. They are available to anyone who will read the book for its overall message and resist the temptation to become overly enamored with the details.

Outline

- I. Introduction (1:1–8)
  - A. Prologue (1:1–3)
  - B. Greetings and Doxology (1:4–8)
- II. Jesus among the Seven Churches (1:9–20)
- III. The Letters to the Seven Churches (chs. 2—3)
  - A. Ephesus (2:1–7)
  - B. Smyrna (2:8–11)
  - C. Pergamum (2:12–17)
  - D. Thyatira (2:18–29)
  - E. Sardis (3:1–6)
  - F. Philadelphia (3:7–13)
  - G. Laodicea (3:14–22)
- IV. The Throne, the Scroll and the Lamb (chs. 4—5)
  - A. The Throne in Heaven (ch. 4)
  - B. The Seven-Sealed Scroll (5:1–5)
  - C. The Lamb Slain (5:6–14)
- V. The Seven Seals (6:1—8:1)
  - A. First Seal: The White Horse (6:1–2)
  - B. Second Seal: The Red Horse (6:3–4)
  - C. Third Seal: The Black Horse (6:5–6)
  - D. Fourth Seal: The Pale Horse (6:7–8)
  - E. Fifth Seal: The Souls under the Altar (6:9–11)
  - F. Sixth Seal: The Great Earthquake (6:12–17)
  - G. The Sealing of the 144,000 (7:1–8)
  - H. The Great Multitude (7:9–17)
  - I. Seventh Seal: Silence in Heaven (8:1)
- VI. The Seven Trumpets (8:2—11:19)
  - A. Introduction (8:2–5)
  - B. First Trumpet: Hail and Fire Mixed with Blood (8:6–7)
  - C. Second Trumpet: A Mountain Thrown into the Sea (8:8–9)
  - D. Third Trumpet: The Star Wormwood (8:10–11)

E. Fourth Trumpet: A Third of the Sun, Moon and Stars Struck (8:12–13)
F. Fifth Trumpet: The Plague of Locusts (9:1–12)
G. Sixth Trumpet: Release of the Four Angels (9:13–21)
H. The Angel and the Little Scroll (ch. 10)
I. The Two Witnesses (11:1–14)
J. Seventh Trumpet: Judgments and Rewards (11:15–19)

VII. Various Personages and Events (chs. 12—14)
A. The Woman and the Dragon (ch. 12)
B. The Two Beasts (ch. 13)
C. The Lamb and the 144,000 (14:1–5)
D. The Harvest of the Earth (14:6–20)

VIII. The Seven Bowls (chs. 15—16)
A. Introduction: The Song of Moses and the Seven Angels with the Seven Plagues (ch. 15)
B. First Bowl: Ugly and Painful Sores (16:1–2)
C. Second Bowl: Sea Turns to Blood (16:3)
D. Third Bowl: Rivers and Springs of Water Become Blood (16:4–7)
E. Fourth Bowl: Sun Scorches People with Fire (16:8–9)
F. Fifth Bowl: Darkness (16:10–11)
G. Sixth Bowl: Euphrates River Dries Up (16:12–16)
H. Seventh Bowl: Tremendous Earthquake (16:17–21)

IX. Babylon: The Great Prostitute (17:1—19:5)
A. Babylon Described (ch. 17)
B. The Fall of Babylon (ch. 18)
C. Praise for Babylon's Fall (19:1–5)

X. Praise for the Wedding of the Lamb (19:6–10)

XI. The Return of Christ (19:11–21)

XII. The Thousand Years (20:1–6)

XIII. Satan's Doom (20:7–10)

XIV. Great White Throne Judgment (20:11–15)

XV. New Heaven, New Earth, New Jerusalem (21:1—22:5)

XVI. Conclusion (22:6–21)

The Revelation of Jesus Christ

1 The Revelation of Jesus Christ, which
[a]God gave Him to [b]show to His bond-servants, [c]the things which must soon take
place; and He sent and [1]communicated *it*
[d]by His angel to His bond-servant [e]John,
2 who testified to [a]the word of God and
to [b]the testimony of Jesus Christ, *even* to all
that he saw.
3 [a]Blessed is he who reads and those
who hear the words of the prophecy, and
[1]heed the things which are written in it; [b]for
the time is near.

Message to the Seven Churches

4 [a]John to [b]the seven churches that are
in [c]Asia: [d]Grace to you and peace, from [e]Him
who is and who was and who [1]is to come,
and from [f]the seven Spirits who are before
His throne,
5 and from Jesus Christ, [a]the faithful
witness, the [b]firstborn of the dead, and the
[c]ruler of the kings of the earth. To Him who
[d]loves us and released us from our sins [1]by
His blood—
6 and He has made us *to be* a [a]kingdom,
[a]priests to [1b]His God and Father—[c]to Him *be*
the glory and the dominion forever and ever.
Amen.
7 [a]BEHOLD, HE IS COMING WITH THE CLOUDS,
and [b]every eye will see Him, even those who
pierced Him; and all the tribes of the earth
will [c]mourn over Him. So it is to be. Amen.
8 "I am [a]the Alpha and the Omega," says
the [b]Lord God, "[c]who is and who was and
who [1]is to come, the Almighty."

The Patmos Vision

9 [a]I, John, your [b]brother and [c]fellow partaker in the tribulation and [d]kingdom and
[1e]perseverance *which are* in Jesus, was on
the island called Patmos [f]because of the
word of God and the testimony of Jesus.
10 I was [1a]in the Spirit on [b]the Lord's day,
and I heard behind me a loud voice [c]like *the
sound* of a trumpet,
11 saying, "[a]Write in a [1]book what you
see, and send *it* to the [b]seven churches: to
[c]Ephesus and to [d]Smyrna and to [e]Pergamum
and to [f]Thyatira and to [g]Sardis and to [h]Phil-
adelphia and to [i]Laodicea."
12 Then I turned to see the voice that was
speaking with me. And having turned I saw
[a]seven golden lampstands;
13 and [a]in the middle of the lampstands *I
saw* one [b]like [1]a son of man, [c]clothed in a
robe reaching to the feet, and [d]girded across
His chest with a golden sash.
14 His head and His [a]hair were white like
white wool, like snow; and [b]His eyes were
like a flame of fire.

1:1 [1]Or *signified* [a]John 17:8; Rev 5:7 [b]Rev 22:6 [c]Dan 2:28f; Rev 1:19 [d]Rev 17:1; 19:9f; 21:9; 22:16 [e]Rev 1:4, 9; 22:8
2 [a]Rev 1:9; 6:9; 12:17; 20:4 [b]1 Cor 1:6; Rev 12:17
3 [1]Or *keep* [a]Luke 11:28; Rev 22:7 [b]Rom 13:11; Rev 3:11; 22:7, 10, 12
4 [1]Or *is coming* [a]Rev 1:1, 9; 22:8 [b]Rev 1:11, 20 [c]Acts 2:9 [d]Rom 1:7 [e]Rev 1:8, 17; 4:8; 16:5 [f]Is 11:2; Rev 3:1; 4:5; 5:6; 8:2
5 [1]Or *in* [a]Rev 3:14; 19:11 [b]1 Cor 15:20; Col 1:18 [c]Rev 17:14; 19:16 [d]Rom 8:37
6 [1]Or *God and His Father* [a]Rev 5:10; 20:6 [b]Rom 15:6 [c]Rom 11:36
7 [a]Dan 7:13; 1 Thess 4:17 [b]Zech 12:10-14; John 19:37 [c]Luke 23:28
8 [a]Is 41:4; Rev 21:6; 22:13
8 [1]Or *is coming* [b]Rev 4:8; 11:17 [c]Rev 1:4

9 [1]Or *steadfastness* [a]Rev 1:1 [b]Acts 1:15 [c]Matt 20:23; Acts 14:22; 2 Cor 1:7; Phil 4:14 [d]2 Tim 2:12; Rev 1:6 [e]2 Thess 3:5; Rev 3:10 [f]Rev 1:2 **10** [1]Or *in spirit* [a]Matt 22:43; Rev 4:2; 17:3; 21:10 [b]Acts 20:7 [c]Rev 4:1 **11** [1]Or *scroll* [a]Rev 1:2, 19 [b]Rev 1:4, 20 [c]Rev 2:1 [d]Rev 2:8 [e]Rev 2:12 [f]Acts 16:14; Rev 2:18, 24 [g]Rev 3:1, 4 [h]Rev 3:7 [i]Col 2:1; Rev 3:14 **12** [a]Ex 25:37; 37:23; Zech 4:2; Rev 1:20; 2:1 **13** [1]Or *the Son of Man* [a]Rev 2:1 [b]Ezek 1:26; Dan 7:13; 10:16; Rev 14:14 [c]Dan 10:5 [d]Rev 15:6 **14** [a]Dan 7:9 [b]Dan 7:9; 10:6; Rev 2:18; 19:12

1:1 *Revelation.* Apocalypse ("unveiling" or "disclosure"). *of Jesus Christ.* Can mean (1) by or from Jesus Christ, (2) about Jesus Christ or (3) both. *bond-servants.* All believers. *soon take place.* See v. 3; 22:6–7,10,20. *His angel.* A mediating angel. The word "angel" (including its plural form) occurs over 70 times in Revelation. *John.* See Introduction: Author.

1:3 *Blessed.* The first of seven beatitudes in the book (see 14:13; 16:15; 19:9; 20:6; 22:7,14). "Blessed" means much more than "happy." It describes the favorable circumstance God has put a person in (see notes on Ps 1:1; Matt 5:3). *prophecy.* Includes not only foretelling the future but also proclaiming any word from God—whether command, instruction, history or prediction. *time is near.* See note on James 5:9.

1:4 *seven churches.* Located about 50 miles apart, forming a circle in Asia moving clockwise north from Ephesus and coming around full circle from Laodicea (east of Ephesus). They were perhaps postal centers serving seven geographic regions. Apparently the entire book of Revelation (including the seven letters) was sent to each church (see v. 11). *Asia.* A Roman province lying in modern western Turkey. *Grace . . . and peace.* See notes on Jon 4:2; John 14:27; 20:19; Gal 1:3; Eph 1:2. "Grace" is used only twice in Revelation (here and in 22:21) but over 100 times by Paul. *who is . . . was . . . is to come.* A paraphrase of the divine name from Ex 3:14–15. Cf. Heb 13:8. *seven Spirits.* The sevenfold Spirit (see Zech 4:2 and note; cf. Zech 4:10).

1:6 *a kingdom, priests.* This OT designation of Israel (see notes on Ex 19:6; Zech 3) is applied in the NT to the church (1 Pet 2:5,9).

1:7 *pierced.* See Ps 22:16; Is 53:5; Zech 12:10; John 19:34,37. *So it is to be. Amen.* A double affirmation.

1:8 *the Alpha and the Omega.* The first and last letters of the Greek alphabet. God is the beginning and the end (see 21:6). He sovereignly rules over all human history. In 22:13 Jesus applies the same title to Himself. *Almighty.* Nine of the ten occurrences of this term in the NT are in Revelation (here; 4:8; 11:17; 15:3; 16:7,14; 19:6,15; 21:22). The tenth occurrence is in 2 Cor 6:18.

1:9 *tribulation . . . kingdom . . . perseverance.* Three pivotal themes in Revelation: (1) "tribulation" (2:9–10,22; 7:14), (2) "kingdom" (11:15; 12:10; 16:10; 17:12,17–18), (3) "perseverance" (2:2–3,19; 3:10; 13:10; 14:12). *Patmos.* A small (four by eight miles), rocky island in the Aegean Sea some 50 miles southwest of Ephesus, off the coast of modern Turkey. It probably served as a Roman penal settlement. Eusebius, the "father of church history" (A.D. 265–340), reports that John was released from Patmos under the emperor Nerva (96–98).

1:10 *in the Spirit.* In a state of spiritual exaltation—not a dream, but a vision like Peter's in Acts 10:10. *the Lord's day.* A technical term for the first day of the week—so named because Jesus rose from the dead on that day. It was also the day on which the Christians met (see Acts 20:7) and took up collections (see 1 Cor 16:2).

1:11 *book.* Pieces of papyrus or parchment sewn together and rolled on a spindle (see note on Ex 17:14). The book form was not invented until about the second century A.D. *seven churches.* See note on v. 4.

1:12 *seven.* See Introduction: Distinctive Feature. *golden lampstands.* The seven churches (see v. 20).

1:13 *son of man.* See notes on Dan 7:13; Mark 8:31. *robe . . . to the feet.* The high priest wore a full-length robe (Ex 28:4; 29:5). Reference to Christ as high priest is supported by the reference to the golden sash around His chest.

1:14 *white like white wool.* Cf. Dan 7:9; Is 1:18. The hoary head

15 His [a]feet *were* like burnished bronze,
when it has been made to glow in a furnace,
and His [b]voice *was* like the sound of many
waters.
16 In His right hand He held [a]seven stars,
and out of His mouth came a [b]sharp two-
edged sword; and His [c]face was like [d]the sun
[1]shining in its strength.
17 When I saw Him, I [a]fell at His feet like
a dead man. And He [b]placed His right hand
on me, saying, "[c]Do not be afraid; [d]I am the
first and the last,
18 and the [a]living One; and I [1b]was dead,
and behold, I am alive forevermore, and I
have [c]the keys of death and of Hades.
19 "Therefore [a]write [b]the things which you
have seen, and the things which are, and the
things which will take place [c]after these
things.
20 "As for the [a]mystery of the [b]seven stars
which you saw in My right hand, and the
[c]seven golden lampstands: the [b]seven stars
are the angels of [d]the seven churches, and
the seven [e]lampstands are the seven
churches.

Message to Ephesus

2 "To the angel of the church in [a]Ephesus
write:
The One who holds [b]the seven stars in His
right hand, the One who walks [1c]among the
seven golden lampstands, says this:

15 [a]Ezek 1:7; Dan 10:6; Rev 2:18 [b]Ezek 1:24; 43:2; Rev 14:2; 19:6
16 [1]Lit *shines* [a]Rev 1:20; 2:1; 3:1 [b]Is 49:2; Heb 4:12; Rev 2:12, 16; 19:15 [c]Matt 17:2; Rev 10:1 [d]Judg 5:31
17 [a]Dan 8:17; 10:9, 10, 15 [b]Dan 8:18; 10:10, 12 [c]Matt 14:27; 17:7 [d]Is 41:4; 44:6; 48:12; Rev 2:8; 22:13
18 [1]Lit *became* [a]Luke 24:5; Rev 4:9f [b]Rom 6:9; Rev 2:8; 10:6; 15:7 [c]Job 38:17; Matt 11:23; 16:19; Rev 9:1; 20:1
19 [a]Rev 1:11 [b]Rev 1:12-16 [c]Rev 4:1
20 [a]Rom 11:25 [b]Rev 1:16; 2:1; 3:1 [c]Ex 25:37; 37:23; Zech 4:2; Rev 1:12; 2:1 [d]Rev 1:4, 11 [e]Matt 5:14f
2:1 [1]Lit *in the middle of* [a]Rev 1:11 [b]Rev 1:16 [c]Rev 1:12f
2 [1]Or *steadfastness* [a]Rev 2:19; 3:1, 8, 15 [b]John 6:6; 1 John 4:1

2 '[a]I know your deeds and your toil and
[1]perseverance, and that you cannot tolerate
evil men, and you [b]put to the test those who
call themselves [c]apostles, and they are not,
and you found them *to be* false;
3 and you have [1]perseverance and have
endured [a]for My name's sake, and have not
grown weary.
4 'But I have *this* against you, that you
have [a]left your first love.
5 'Therefore remember from where you
have fallen, and [a]repent and [b]do the [1]deeds
you did at first; or else I am coming to you
and will remove your [c]lampstand out of its
place—unless you repent.
6 'Yet this you do have, that you hate the
deeds of the [a]Nicolaitans, which I also hate.
7 '[a]He who has an ear, let him hear what
the Spirit says to the churches. [b]To him who
overcomes, I will grant to eat of [c]the tree of
life which is in the [d]Paradise of God.'

Message to Smyrna

8 "And to the angel of the church in
[a]Smyrna write:
[b]The first and the last, who [1c]was dead,
and has come to life, says this:

[c]2 Cor 11:13 **3** [1]V 2, note 1 [a]John 15:21 **4** [a]Jer 2:2; Matt 24:12 **5** [1]Lit *first deeds* [a]Rev 2:16, 22; 3:3, 19 [b]Heb 10:32; Rev 2:2 [c]Matt 5:14ff; Phil 2:15; Rev 1:20 **6** [a]Rev 2:15 **7** [a]Matt 11:15; Rev 2:11, 17; 3:6, 13, 22; 13:9 [b]Rev 2:11, 17, 26; 3:5, 12, 21; 21:7 [c]Gen 2:9; 3:22; Prov 3:18; 11:30; 13:12; 15:4; Rev 22:2, 14 [d]Ezek 28:13; 31:8f; Luke 23:43 **8** [1]Lit *became* [a]Rev 1:11 [b]Is 44:6; 48:12; Rev 1:17; 22:13 [c]Rev 1:18

suggests wisdom and dignity (Lev 19:32; Prov 16:31). *eyes . . . like a flame of fire.* Penetrating insight (see 4:6).

1:16 *sharp two-edged sword.* Like a long Thracian sword (also in 2:12,16; 6:8; 19:15,21). The sword in 6:4; 13:10,14 was a small sword or dagger. The sword symbolizes divine judgment (see Is 49:2; Heb 4:12).

1:17 *fell at His feet.* A sign of great respect and awe (4:10; 5:8; 7:11; 19:10; 22:8). *I am.* See note on John 6:35. *the first and the last.* Essentially the same as "the Alpha and the Omega" (v. 8; cf. Is 44:6; 48:12).

1:18 *living One.* Based on OT references to the "living God" (e.g., Josh 3:10; Ps 42:2; 84:2). In contrast to the dead gods of paganism, Christ possesses life in His essential nature. *keys of death and of Hades.* Absolute control over their domain (see Matt 16:18 and note).

1:19 Many take the threefold division of this verse as a clue to the entire structure of the book. "The things which you have seen" would be the inaugural vision of ch. 1; "the things which are" would be the letters to the seven churches (chs. 2–3); "the things which will take place after these things" would be everything from ch. 4 on. An alternative interpretation sees the initial clause as the essential unit (it parallels v. 11), followed by two explanatory clauses. The sense would be: "Write, therefore, what you are about to see, i.e., both what is now and what will take place later." Some who hold the latter view make no attempt to outline the book on this basis, maintaining that there is a mixture of "now" and "later" throughout.

1:20 The first of several places where the symbols are interpreted (see also 17:15,18). *angels.* Either (1) heavenly messengers, (2) earthly messengers/ministers or (3) personifications of the prevailing spirit of each church.

2:1–3:22 Some take the seven letters as a preview of church history in its downward course toward Laodicean lukewarmness. Others interpret them as characteristic of various kinds of Christian congregations that have existed from John's day until the present time. In either case, they were historical churches in Asia Minor (see map No. 11 at the end of the Study Bible). The general pattern in the letters is commendation, complaint and correction.

2:1 *angel.* See note on 1:20. *Ephesus.* See Introduction to Ephesians: The City of Ephesus. *holds the seven stars.* See 1:16,20. *seven golden lampstands.* See 1:12,20.

2:2 *put to the test.* The necessity of testing for correct doctrine and dependable advice was widely recognized in the early church (see 1 Cor 14:29; 1 Thess 5:21; 1 John 4:1).

2:4 *first love.* The love they had at first for one another and/or for Christ.

2:5 *remove your lampstand.* Immediate judgment.

2:6 *Nicolaitans.* A heretical sect within the church that had worked out a compromise with the pagan society. They apparently taught that spiritual liberty gave them sufficient leeway to practice idolatry and immorality. Tradition identifies them with Nicolas, the proselyte of Antioch who was one of the first seven deacons in the Jerusalem church (Acts 6:5), though the evidence is merely circumstantial. A similar group at Pergamum held the teaching of Balaam (vv. 14–15), and some at Thyatira were followers of the woman Jezebel (v. 20). From their heretical tendencies it would appear that all three groups were Nicolaitans.

2:7 *overcomes.* The challenge to overcome occurs in each letter (here; vv. 11,17,26; 3:5,12,21). *Paradise.* Originally a Persian word for a pleasure garden (see note on Luke 23:43). In Revelation it symbolizes the eschatological state in which God and man are restored to the perfect fellowship that existed before sin entered the world.

2:8 *Smyrna.* A proud and beautiful Asian city (modern Izmir)

9 'I know your [a]tribulation and your
[b]poverty (but you are [b]rich), and the blasphemy by those who [c]say they are Jews and
are not, but are a synagogue of [d]Satan.

10 'Do not fear what you are about to suffer. Behold, the devil is about to cast some of
you into prison, so that you will be [a]tested,
and you will have tribulation [b]for ten days.
[1]Be [c]faithful until death, and I will give you
[d]the crown of life.

11 '[a]He who has an ear, let him hear what
the Spirit says to the churches. [b]He who
overcomes will not be hurt by the [c]second
death.'

Message to Pergamum

12 "And to the angel of the church in [a]Per-
gamum write:

The One who has [b]the sharp two-edged
sword says this:

13 'I know where you dwell, where
[a]Satan's throne is; and you hold fast My
name, and did not deny [b]My faith even in
the days of Antipas, My [c]witness, My [d]faith-
ful one, who was killed among you, [e]where
Satan dwells.

14 'But [a]I have a few things against you,
because you have there some who hold the
[b]teaching of Balaam, who kept teaching
Balak to put a stumbling block before the
sons of Israel, [c]to eat things sacrificed to
idols and to commit *acts of* immorality.

15 'So you also have some who in the
same way hold the teaching of the [a]Nicolai-
tans.

16 'Therefore [a]repent; or else [b]I am coming

9 [a]Rev 1:9 [b]2 Cor 6:10; 8:9; James 2:5 [c]Rev 3:9 [d]Matt 4:10; Rev 2:13, 24 **10** [1]Or *Prove yourself faithful* [a]Rev 3:10; 13:14ff [b]Dan 1:12, 14 [c]Rev 2:13; 12:11; 17:14 [d]1 Cor 9:25; Rev 3:11 **11** [a]Matt 11:15; Rev 2:7, 17, 29; 3:6, 13, 22; 13:9 [b]Rev 2:7, 17, 26; 3:5, 12, 21; 21:7 [c]Rev 20:6, 14; 21:8 **12** [a]Rev 1:11 [b]Rev 1:16; 2:16 **13** [a]Matt 4:10; Rev 2:24 [b]1 Tim 5:8; Rev 14:12 [c]Acts 22:20; Rev 1:5; 11:3; 17:6 [d]Rev 2:10; 12:11; 17:14 [e]Rev 2:9 **14** [a]Rev 2:20 [b]Num 31:16; 2 Pet 2:15 [c]Num 25:1f; Acts 15:29; 1 Cor 10:20; Rev 2:20 **15** [a]Rev 2:6 **16** [a]Rev 2:5 [b]Rev 22:7, 20

closely aligned with Rome and eager to meet its demands for emperor worship. This plus a large and actively hostile Jewish population made it extremely difficult to live there as a Christian. Polycarp, the most famous of the early martyrs, was bishop of Smyrna. *The first and the last.* See note on 1:17.
2:9 *who say they are Jews.* See Rom 2:28–29. *Satan.* Hebrew for "accuser" (see Zech 3:1; cf. Job 1:6–12; 2:1–7).
2:10 *devil.* Greek *diabolos,* meaning "accuser." *tribulation.* See the warnings by Jesus (John 15:20) and Paul (2 Tim 3:12). *crown of life.* The crown that is eternal life. "Crown" does not refer to a royal crown (12:3; 13:1; 19:12) but to the garland or wreath awarded to the winner in athletic contests (3:11; 4:4,10; 6:2; 9:7; 12:1; 14:14).
2:11 *He who overcomes.* See note on v. 7. *second death.* The lake of fire (20:14; see 20:6; 21:8).
2:12 *Pergamum.* Modern Bergama; the ancient capital of Asia, built on a cone-shaped hill rising 1,000 feet above the surrounding valley. Its name in Greek means "citadel" and is the origin of our word "parchment" (lit. "from Pergamum" because of a legend that parchment was first manufactured there). *two-edged sword.* See note on 1:16.
2:13 *where Satan's throne is.* Satan "ruled" from Pergamum in that it was the official center of emperor worship in Asia. *Antipas.* First martyr of Asia. According to tradition he was slowly roasted to death in a bronze kettle during the reign of Domitian. *faithful one.* The Lord's title in 1:5.
2:14 *teaching of Balaam.* Balaam advised the Midianite women how to lead the Israelites astray (Num 25:1–2; 31:16; cf. Jude 11). He is a fitting prototype of corrupt teachers who deceive believers into compromise with worldliness. *things sacrificed to idols . . . immorality.* See Acts 15:20,29.
2:15 *Nicolaitans.* See note on v. 6.

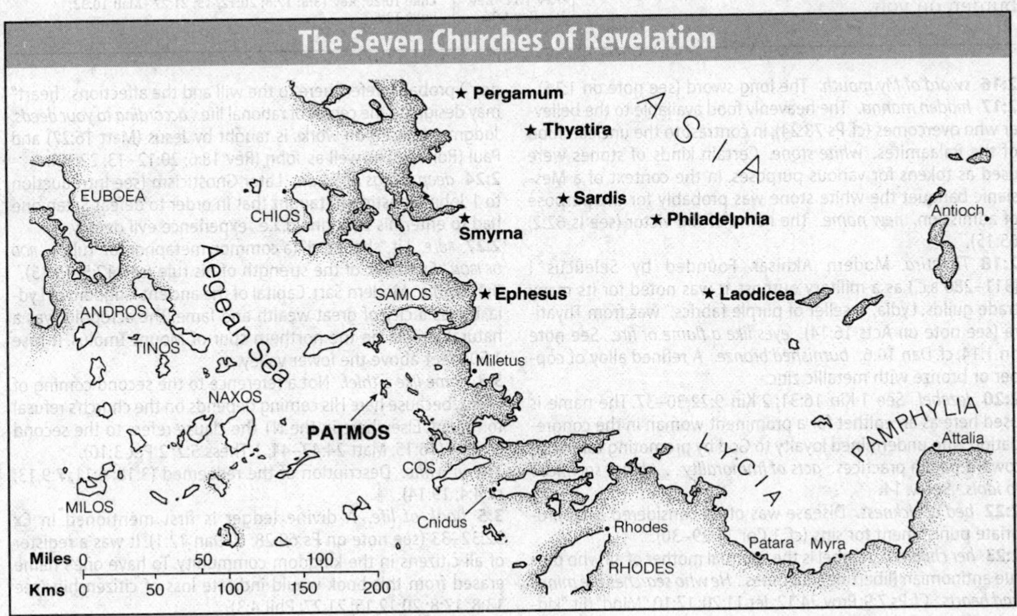

to you quickly, and I will make war against them with [c]the sword of My mouth.

17 ‘[a]He who has an ear, let him hear what the Spirit says to the churches. [a]To him who overcomes, to him I will give *some* of the hidden [b]manna, and I will give him a white stone, and a [c]new name written on the stone [d]which no one knows but he who receives it.’

Message to Thyatira

18 “And to the angel of the church in [a]Thyatira write:

[b]The Son of God, [c]who has [1]eyes like a flame of fire, and His feet are like burnished bronze, says this:

19 ‘[a]I know your deeds, and your love and faith and service and [1]perseverance, and that your [2]deeds of late are greater than [3]at first.

20 ‘But [a]I have *this* against you, that you tolerate the woman [b]Jezebel, who calls herself a prophetess, and she teaches and leads My bond-servants astray so that they [c]commit *acts of* immorality and eat things sacrificed to idols.

21 ‘[a]I gave her time to repent, and she [b]does not want to repent of her immorality.

22 ‘Behold, I will throw her [1]on a bed *of sickness,* and those who [a]commit adultery with her into great tribulation, unless they repent of [2]her deeds.

23 ‘And I will kill her children with [1]pestilence, and all the churches will know that I am He who [a]searches the [2]minds and hearts; and [b]I will give to each one of you according to your deeds.

24 ‘But I say to you, the rest who are in [a]Thyatira, who do not hold this teaching, who have not known the [b]deep things of Satan, as they call them—I [c]place no other burden on you.

25 ‘Nevertheless [a]what you have, hold fast [b]until I come.

26 ‘[a]He who overcomes, and he who keeps My deeds [b]until the end, [c]TO HIM I WILL GIVE AUTHORITY OVER THE [1]NATIONS;

27 AND HE SHALL [1a]RULE THEM WITH A ROD OF IRON, [b]AS THE VESSELS OF THE POTTER ARE BROKEN TO PIECES, as I also have received *authority* from My Father;

28 and I will give him [a]the morning star.

29 ‘[a]He who has an ear, let him hear what the Spirit says to the churches.’

Message to Sardis

3 “To the angel of the church in [a]Sardis write:

He who has [b]the seven Spirits of God and [c]the seven stars, says this: ‘[d]I know your deeds, that you have a name that you are alive, [1]but you are [e]dead.

2 ‘Wake up, and strengthen the things that remain, which were about to die; for I have not found your deeds completed in the sight of My God.

3 ‘So [a]remember [1]what you have received and heard; and keep *it,* and [a]repent. Therefore if you do not wake up, [a]I will come [b]like a thief, and you will not know at [c]what hour I will come to you.

4 ‘But you have a few [1a]people in [b]Sardis who have not [c]soiled their garments; and they will walk with Me [d]in white, for they are worthy.

5 ‘[a]He who overcomes will thus be clothed in [b]white garments; and I will not [c]erase his name from the book of life, and [d]I

16 [c]2 Thess 2:8; Rev 1:16
17 [a]Rev 2:7 [b]Ex 16:33; John 6:49f [c]Is 56:5; 62:2; 65:15 [d]Rev 14:3; 19:12
18 [1]Lit *His eyes* [a]Rev 1:11; 2:24 [b]Matt 4:3 [c]Rev 1:14f
19 [1]Or *steadfastness* [2]Lit *last deeds* [3]Lit *the first* [a]Rev 2:2
20 [a]Rev 2:14 [b]1 Kin 16:31; 21:25; 2 Kin 9:7, 22, 30 [c]Acts 15:29; 1 Cor 10:20; Rev 2:14
21 [a]Rom 2:4; 2 Pet 3:9 [b]Rom 2:5; Rev 9:20f; 16:9, 11
22 [1]Lit *into* [2]One early ms reads *their* [a]Rev 17:2; 18:9
23 [1]Lit *death* [2]Lit *kidneys,* i.e. inner man [a]Ps 7:9; 26:2; 139:1; Jer 11:20; 17:10; Matt 16:27; Luke 16:15; Acts 1:24; Rom 8:27 [b]Ps 62:12
24 [a]Rev 2:18 [b]1 Cor 2:10 [c]Acts 15:28
25 [a]Rev 3:11 [b]John 21:22
26 [1]Or *Gentiles* [a]Rev 2:7 [b]Matt 10:22; Heb 3:6 [c]Ps 2:8; Rev 3:21; 20:4
27 [1]Lit *shepherd* [a]Ps 2:9; Rev 12:5; 19:15 [b]Is 30:14; Jer 19:11
28 [a]1 John 3:2; Rev 22:16
29 [a]Rev 2:7
3:1 [1]Lit *and* [a]Rev 1:11 [b]Rev 1:4 [c]Rev 1:16 [d]Rev 2:2; 3:8, 15 [e]1 Tim 5:6
3 [1]Lit *how* [a]Rev 2:5 [b]1 Thess 5:2; 2 Pet 3:10; Rev 16:15 [c]Matt 24:43; Luke 12:39f
4 [1]Lit *names* [a]Rev 11:13 [b]Rev 1:11 [c]Jude 23 [d]Eccl 9:8; Rev 3:5, 18; 4:4; 6:11; 7:9, 13f; 19:8, 14
5 [a]Rev 2:7 [b]Rev 3:4 [c]Ex 32:32f; Ps 69:28; Luke 10:20; Rev 13:8; 17:8; 20:12, 15; 21:27 [d]Matt 10:32; Luke 12:8

2:16 *sword of My mouth.* The long sword (see note on 1:16).
2:17 *hidden manna.* The heavenly food available to the believer who overcomes (cf. Ps 78:24), in contrast to the unclean food of the Balaamites. *white stone.* Certain kinds of stones were used as tokens for various purposes. In the context of a Messianic banquet the white stone was probably for the purpose of admission. *new name.* The name of the victor (see Is 62:2; 65:15).
2:18 *Thyatira.* Modern Akhisar. Founded by Seleucus I (311–280 B.C.) as a military outpost, it was noted for its many trade guilds. Lydia, "a seller of purple fabrics," was from Thyatira (see note on Acts 16:14). *eyes like a flame of fire.* See note on 1:14; cf. Dan 10:6. *burnished bronze.* A refined alloy of copper or bronze with metallic zinc.
2:20 *Jezebel.* See 1 Kin 16:31; 2 Kin 9:22,30–37. The name is used here as an epithet for a prominent woman in the congregation who undermined loyalty to God by promoting tolerance toward pagan practices. *acts of immorality . . . things sacrificed to idols.* See v. 14.
2:22 *bed of sickness.* Disease was often considered as appropriate punishment for sins (cf. 1 Cor 11:29–30).
2:23 *her children.* Jezebel is the spiritual mother of all who pursue antinomian (libertine) doctrines. *He who searches the minds and hearts.* Cf. Ps 7:9; Prov 24:12; Jer 11:20; 17:10. "Mind" (lit. "kidney") probably refers here to the will and the affections; "heart" may designate the center of rational life. *according to your deeds.* Judgment based on works is taught by Jesus (Matt 16:27) and Paul (Rom 2:6) as well as John (Rev 18:6; 20:12–13; 22:12).
2:24 *deep things of Satan.* Later Gnosticism (see Introduction to 1 John: Gnosticism) taught that in order to defeat Satan one had to enter his stronghold, i.e., experience evil deeply.
2:27 *RULE.* Lit. "shepherd" (a common metaphor for "rule"). *ROD OF IRON.* Symbolic of the strength of his rule (see 12:5; 19:15).
3:1 *Sardis.* Modern Sart. Capital of the ancient kingdom of Lydia, it was a city of great wealth and fame. The acropolis was a natural citadel on the northern spur of Mount Tmolus. It rose 1,500 feet above the lower valley.
3:3 *come like a thief.* Not a reference to the second coming of Christ, because here His coming depends on the church's refusal to repent. Elsewhere in the NT the clause refers to the second advent (16:15; Matt 24:42–44; 1 Thess 5:2; 2 Pet 3:10).
3:4 *in white.* Description of the redeemed (3:18; 6:11; 7:9,13; cf. 4:4; 19:14).
3:5 *book of life.* A divine ledger is first mentioned in Ex 32:32–33 (see note on Ps 69:28; cf. Dan 12:1). It was a register of all citizens in the kingdom community. To have one's name erased from this book would indicate loss of citizenship (see 13:8; 17:8; 20:12,15; 21:27; Phil 4:3).

will confess his name before My Father and
before His angels.
6 '[a]He who has an ear, let him hear what
the Spirit says to the churches.'

Message to Philadelphia

7 "And to the angel of the church in [a]Phil-
adelphia write:
[b]He who is holy, [c]who is true, who has
[d]the key of David, who opens and no one
will shut, and who shuts and no one opens,
says this:
8 '[a]I know your [1]deeds. Behold, I have
put before you [b]an open door which no one
can shut, because you have a little power,
and have kept My word, and [c]have not
denied My name.
9 'Behold, I [1]will cause *those* of [a]the synagogue of Satan, who say that they are Jews
and are not, but lie—I will make them [b]come
and bow down [2]at your feet, and *make them*
know that [c]I have loved you.
10 'Because you have [a]kept the word of
[b]My [1]perseverance, [c]I also will keep you
from the hour of [2][d]testing, that *hour* which is
about to come upon the whole [3][e]world, to
[4]test [f]those who dwell on the earth.
11 '[a]I am coming quickly; [b]hold fast what
you have, so that no one will take your
[c]crown.
12 '[a]He who overcomes, I will make him a
[b]pillar in the temple of My God, and he will
not go out from it anymore; and I will write
on him the [c]name of My God, and [d]the name
of the city of My God, [e]the new Jerusalem,
which comes down out of heaven from My
God, and My [f]new name.

6 [a]Rev 2:7 **7** [a]Rev 1:11 [b]Rev 6:10 [c]1 John 5:20; Rev 3:14; 19:11 [d]Job 12:14; Is 22:22; Matt 16:19; Rev 1:18 **8** [1]Or *deeds (behold...shut), that you have* [a]Rev 3:1 [b]Acts 14:27 [c]Rev 2:13 **9** [1]Lit *give* [2]Lit *before* [a]Rev 2:9 [b]Is 45:14; 49:23; 60:14 [c]Is 43:4; John 17:23 **10** [1]Or *steadfastness* [2]Or *temptation* [3]Lit *inhabited earth* [4]Or *tempt* [a]John 17:6; Rev 3:8 [b]Rev 1:9 [c]2 Tim 2:12; 2 Pet 2:9 [d]Rev 2:10 [e]Matt 24:14; Rev 16:14 [f]Rev 6:10; 8:13; 11:10; 13:8, 14; 17:8 **11** [a]Rev 1:3; 22:7, 12, 20 [b]Rev 2:25 [c]Rev 2:10 **12** [a]Rev 3:5 [b]1 Kin 7:21; Jer 1:18; Gal 2:9 [c]Rev 14:1; 22:4 [d]Ezek 48:35; Rev 21:2 [e]Gal 4:26; Heb 13:14; Rev 21:2, 10 [f]Is 62:2; Rev 2:17

13 [a]Rev 3:6 **14** [1]I.e. Origin or Source [a]Rev 1:11 [b]2 Cor 1:20 [c]Rev 1:5; 3:7 [d]Gen 49:3; Deut 21:17; Prov 8:22; John 1:3; Col 1:18; Rev 21:6; 22:13

13 '[a]He who has an ear, let him hear what
the Spirit says to the churches.'

Message to Laodicea

14 "To the angel of the church in [a]Laodicea
write:
[b]The Amen, [c]the faithful and true Witness, [d]the [1]Beginning of the creation of God,
says this:
15 '[a]I know your deeds, that you are neither cold nor hot; [b]I wish that you were cold
or hot.
16 'So because you are lukewarm, and neither hot nor cold, I will [1]spit you out of My
mouth.
17 'Because you say, "[a]I am rich, and have
become wealthy, and have need of nothing,"
and you do not know that you are wretched
and miserable and poor and blind and naked,
18 I advise you to [a]buy from Me [b]gold
refined by fire so that you may become rich,
and [c]white garments so that you may clothe
yourself, and *that* [d]the shame of your nakedness will not be revealed; and eye salve to
anoint your eyes so that you may see.
19 '[a]Those whom I love, I reprove and discipline; therefore be zealous and [b]repent.
20 'Behold, I stand [a]at the door and
[b]knock; if anyone hears My voice and opens
the door, [c]I will come in to him and will dine
with him, and he with Me.
21 '[a]He who overcomes, I will grant to him
[b]to sit down with Me on My throne, as [c]I also

15 [a]Rev 3:1 [b]Rom 12:11 **16** [1]Lit *vomit* **17** [a]Hos 12:8; Zech 11:5; Matt 5:3; 1 Cor 4:8 **18** [a]Is 55:1; Matt 13:44 [b]1 Pet 1:7 [c]Rev 3:4 [d]Rev 16:15 **19** [a]Prov 3:12; 1 Cor 11:32; Heb 12:6 [b]Rev 2:5 **20** [a]Matt 24:33; James 5:9 [b]Luke 12:36; John 10:3 [c]John 14:23 **21** [a]Rev 2:7 [b]Matt 19:28; 2 Tim 2:12; Rev 2:26; 20:4 [c]John 16:33; Rev 5:5; 6:2; 17:14

3:7 *Philadelphia.* Modern Alashehir; a city of commercial importance conveniently located as the gateway to the high central plateau of the province of Asia in Asia Minor. The name means "brotherly love" and commemorates the loyalty and devotion of Attalus II (220–130 B.C.) to his brother Eumenes II. *holy . . . true.* See 6:10. For God as the Holy One see Is 40:25; Hab 3:2–3; Mark 1:24. *key of David.* Christ is the Davidic Messiah with authority to control entrance to the kingdom (see Is 22:22; Matt 16:19).
3:8 *open door.* Either the door of opportunity or the door to the kingdom. The context favors the latter.
3:9 *synagogue of Satan.* A bold metaphor directed against unbelieving and hostile Jews. Cf. Jesus' scathing rebuke in John 8:44; see also 2 Cor 11:14–15. The Jewish synagogue was a gathering place for worship, study and communal activities. *say that they are Jews.* See Rom 2:28–29. *bow down at your feet.* An appropriate act of worship in the Near East (see Is 45:14; 60:14; cf. Acts 10:25; Phil 2:10; see also note on Rev 1:17).
3:10 *keep you from.* The Greek for this phrase can mean either "keep you from undergoing" or "keep you through." *hour of testing.* The period of testing that precedes the consummation of the kingdom (see 13:5–10; Matt 24:4–28; cf. Dan 12:1; Mark 13:19; 2 Thess 2:1–12).
3:11 *I am coming quickly.* Cf. 1:1; 22:7,12,20 (see note on James 5:9).
3:12 *He who overcomes.* See note on 2:7. *temple.* See note on 7:15. *name of My God.* See 14:1; 22:4. *new Jerusalem.* See 21:2,10. *write on him . . . My new name.* Names revealed character. Christ's new name symbolizes all that He is by virtue of His redemptive work for mankind. This awaits the second advent.
3:14 *Laodicea.* Near modern Denizli. The wealthiest city in Phrygia during Roman times, it was widely known for its banking establishments, medical school and textile industry. Its major weakness was lack of an adequate water supply. Each of these characteristics is reflected in the letter. *The Amen.* Is 65:16 speaks of "the God of the Amen," i.e., "the God of truth." As a personal designation it describes one who is perfectly trustworthy or faithful. *faithful and true Witness.* See 1:5; 19:11. *Beginning.* The Greek word can mean first in point of time ("beginning") or first in rank ("ruler").
3:16 *lukewarm, and neither hot nor cold.* "Hot" may refer to the hot, medicinal waters of nearby Hierapolis. The church in Laodicea supplied neither healing for the spiritually sick nor refreshment for the spiritually weary. *spit.* Lit. "vomit."
3:18 Refers to three items in which Laodicea took great pride: financial wealth, an extensive textile industry and a famous eye salve.
3:19 *whom I love, I . . . discipline.* See Job 5:17; Ps 94:12; Prov 3:11–12; 1 Cor 11:32; Heb 12:5–11.
3:20 *I stand at the door and knock.* Usually taken as a picture of Christ's knocking on the door of the individual unbeliever's heart. In context, however, the self-deluded members of the congregation are being addressed.
3:21 *overcomes.* See note on 2:7. *sit down with Me on My throne.* See 20:4,6; Matt 19:28; 2 Tim 2:12.

overcame and sat down with My Father on His throne.

22 '[a]He who has an ear, let him hear what the Spirit says to the churches.' "

Scene in Heaven

4 After [a]these things I looked, and behold, [b]a door *standing* open in heaven, and the first voice which I had heard, [c]like *the sound* of a trumpet speaking with me, said, "[d]Come up here, and I will [e]show you what must take place after these things."

2 Immediately I was [1][a]in the Spirit; and behold, [b]a throne was standing in heaven, and [c]One sitting on the throne.

3 And He who was sitting *was* like a [a]jasper stone and a [b]sardius in appearance; and *there was* a [1][c]rainbow around the throne, like an [d]emerald in appearance.

4 [a]Around the throne *were* [b]twenty-four thrones; and upon the thrones *I saw* [c]twenty-four elders [d]sitting, clothed in [e]white garments, and [f]golden crowns on their heads.

The Throne and Worship of the Creator

5 Out from the throne come [a]flashes of lightning and sounds and peals of thunder. And *there were* [b]seven lamps of fire burning before the throne, which are [c]the seven Spirits of God;

6 and before the throne *there was something* like a [a]sea of glass, like crystal; and in the [1]center and [b]around the throne, [c]four living creatures [d]full of eyes in front and behind.

7 [a]The first creature *was* like a lion, and the second creature like a calf, and the third creature had a face like that of a man, and the fourth creature *was* like a flying eagle.

8 And the [a]four living creatures, each one of them having [b]six wings, are [c]full of eyes around and within; and [d]day and night [1]they do not cease to say,

"[e]HOLY, HOLY, HOLY *is* THE [f]LORD GOD, THE ALMIGHTY, [g]WHO WAS AND WHO IS AND WHO [2]IS TO COME."

9 And when the living creatures give glory and honor and thanks to Him who [a]sits on the throne, to [b]Him who lives forever and ever,

10 the [a]twenty-four elders will [b]fall down before Him who [c]sits on the throne, and will worship [d]Him who lives forever and ever, and will cast their [e]crowns before the throne, saying,

11 "[a]Worthy are You, our Lord and our God, to receive glory and honor and power; for You [b]created all things, and because of Your will they [1]existed, and were created."

The Book with Seven Seals

5 I saw [1]in the right hand of Him who [a]sat on the throne a [2][b]book written inside and on the back, [c]sealed up with seven seals.

22 [a]Rev 2:7 **4:1** [a]Rev 1:12ff, 19 [b]Ezek 1:1; Rev 19:11 [c]Rev 1:10 [d]Rev 11:12 [e]Rev 1:19; 22:6 **2** [1]Or *in spirit* [a]Rev 1:10 [b]1 Kin 22:19; Is 6:1; Ezek 1:26; Dan 7:9; Rev 4:9f [c]Rev 4:9 **3** [1]Or *halo* [a]Rev 21:11 [b]Rev 21:20 [c]Ezek 1:28; Rev 10:1 [d]Rev 21:19 **4** [a]Rev 4:6; 5:11; 7:11 [b]Rev 11:16 [c]Rev 4:10; 5:6, 8, 14; 19:4 [d]Matt 19:28; Rev 20:4 [e]Rev 3:18 [f]Rev 4:10 **5** [a]Ex 19:16; Rev 8:5; 11:19; 16:18 [b]Ex 25:37; Zech 4:2 [c]Rev 1:4 **6** [1]Lit *middle of the throne and around* [a]Ezek 1:22; Rev 15:2; 21:18, 21 [b]Rev 4:4 [c]Ezek 1:5; Rev 4:8f; 5:6; 6:1, 6; 7:11; 14:3; 15:7; 19:4 [d]Ezek 1:18; 10:12 **7** [a]Ezek 1:10; 10:14 **8** [1]Lit *they have no rest, saying,* [2]Or *is coming* [a]Ezek 1:5; Rev 4:6, 9; 5:6; 6:1, 6; 7:11; 14:3; 15:7; 19:4 [b]Is 6:2 [c]Ezek 1:18; 10:12 [d]Rev 14:11 [e]Is 6:3 [f]Rev 1:8 [g]Rev 1:4 **9** [a]Ps 47:8; Is 6:1; Rev 4:2 [b]Deut 32:40; Dan 4:34; 12:7; Rev 10:6; 15:7 **10** [a]Rev 4:4 [b]Rev 5:8, 14; 7:11; 11:16; 19:4 [c]Ps 47:8; Is 6:1; Rev 4:2 [d]Deut 32:40; Dan 4:34; 12:7 [e]Rev 4:4; 10:6; 15:7 **11** [1]Lit *were* [a]Rev 1:6; 5:12 [b]Acts 14:15; Rev 10:6; 14:7 **5:1** [1]Lit *upon* [2]Or *scroll* [a]Rev 4:9; 5:7, 13 [b]Ezek 2:9, 10 [c]Is 29:11; Dan 12:4

4:1–5:14 These two chapters constitute an introduction to chs. 6–20. In the throne room of heaven, the Lamb assumes the responsibility of initiating the great final conflict with the forces of evil, the end of which will see the Lamb triumphant and the devil consigned to the lake of fire.

4:1 *Come up here.* Similarly, Moses was called up on Mount Sinai to receive divine direction (Ex 19:20,24). Cf. also the heavenly ascent of the two witnesses (11:12). Some interpreters find the rapture of the church in this verse. *what must take place after these things.* See 1:1,19; Dan 2:28–29,45.

4:2 *in the Spirit.* In a state of heightened spiritual awareness (see note on 1:10; see also 17:3; 21:10). *throne . . . in heaven.* The depiction of God ruling from His throne in heaven is a regular feature of the OT (e.g., Ps 47:8).

4:3 *jasper . . . sardius . . . emerald.* Since God dwells in "unapproachable light" and is one "whom no man has seen or can see" (1 Tim 6:16), He is described in terms of the reflected brilliance of precious stones—an emerald rainbow around the throne (cf. Ezek 1:26–28).

4:4 *twenty-four elders.* Representative of either the whole company of believers in heaven or an exalted angelic order worshiping and serving God there (see vv. 9–11; 5:5–14; 7:11–17; 11:16–18; 14:3; 19:4). The number 24 is often understood to reflect the 12 Israelite tribes of the OT and the 12 apostles of the NT.

4:5 *flashes of lightning . . . thunder . . . burning.* Symbolic of the awesome majesty and power of God (cf. the manifestation of God at Sinai, Ex 19:16–19; cf. also the conventional OT depiction of God's coming in mighty power to deliver His people, Ps 18:12–15; 77:18). In Revelation, thunder and lightning always mark an important event connected with the heavenly temple (8:5; 11:19; 16:18). *seven Spirits.* See note on 1:4; "seven" symbolizes fullness, completeness or perfection.

4:6 *sea of glass.* See 15:2. The source of the imagery may be Ezek 1:22 (cf. Ex 24:10), but it is also possible that it is the basin in the heavenly temple (cf. 11:19; 14:15,17; 15:5–6,8; 16:1,17), whose counterpart in the earthly temple was referred to as the Sea (1 Kin 7:23–25; 2 Kin 16:17; 2 Chr 4:2,4,10,15; Jer 27:19). Other features of the temple in heaven are: the lamps (v. 5), the altar (6:9), the altar of incense (8:3) and the ark of the covenant (11:19). *four living creatures.* An exalted order of angelic beings whose task is to guard the heavenly throne and lead in worship and adoration of God. *full of eyes.* Nothing escapes their attention.

4:7 Ezekiel in a vision also saw four living creatures, each of which had four faces—human in front, lion on the right, ox on the left, and eagle behind (Ezek 1:6,10). In John's vision the creatures were in the form of a lion, an ox, and a flying eagle, and one had a face like that of a man.

4:8 *Holy, holy, holy.* See note on Is 6:3. *WAS . . . IS . . . IS TO COME.* An expansion of the divine name in Ex 3:14–15 (see note on Rev 1:4). God's power and holiness extend from eternity past to eternity yet to come (cf. Is 41:4).

4:10 *cast their crowns.* Acknowledgment that God alone is worthy of ultimate praise and worship.

4:11 *You created all things.* See Gen 1.

5:1 *book.* See note on 1:11; cf. the little scroll of 10:2,8–10. *written inside and on the back.* Like the stone tablets of the OT covenant law (Ex 32:15; see Ezek 2:9–10). The fibers of a papyrus scroll run horizontally on the inside, which makes writing

2 And I saw a [a]strong angel proclaiming
with a loud voice, "Who is worthy to open
the [1]book and to break its seals?"
3 And no one [a]in heaven or on the earth
or under the earth was able to open the
[1]book or to look into it.
4 Then I *began* to weep greatly because
no one was found worthy to open the [1]book
or to look into it;
5 and one of the elders *said to me,
"Stop weeping; behold, the [a]Lion that is
[b]from the tribe of Judah, the [c]Root of David,
has overcome so as to open the [1]book and its
seven seals."
6 And I saw [1]between the throne (with
the four living creatures) and [a]the elders a
[b]Lamb standing, as if [c]slain, having seven
[d]horns and [e]seven eyes, which are [f]the sev-
en Spirits of God, sent out into all the earth.
7 And He came and took [a]the book out
of the right hand of Him who [a]sat on the
throne.
8 When He had taken the [1]book, the
[a]four living creatures and the [b]twenty-four
elders [c]fell down before the [d]Lamb, each one
holding a [e]harp and [f]golden bowls full of
incense, which are the [g]prayers of the [2]saints.
9 And they *sang a [a]new song, saying,
"[b]Worthy are You to take the [1]book and
to break its seals; for You were [c]slain,
and [d]purchased for God with Your
blood *men* from [e]every tribe and
tongue and people and nation.
10 "You have made them *to be* a [a]kingdom
and [a]priests to our God; and they will
[b]reign upon the earth."

2 [1]Or *scroll* [a]Rev 10:1; 18:21 **3** [1]Or *scroll* [a]Phil 2:10; Rev 5:13 **4** [1]Or *scroll* **5** [1]Or *scroll* [a]Gen 49:9 [b]Heb 7:14 [c]Is 11:1, 10; Rom 15:12; Rev 22:16 **6** [1]Lit *in the middle of the throne and of the four living creatures, and in the middle of the elders* [a]Rev 4:4; 5:8, 14 [b]John 1:29; Rev 5:8, 12f; 13:8 [c]Rev 5:9, 12; 13:8 [d]Dan 8:3f [e]Zech 3:9; 4:10 [f]Rev 1:4 **7** [a]Rev 5:1 **8** [1]Or *scroll* [2]Or *holy ones* [a]Rev 4:6; 5:6, 11, 14 [b]Rev 4:4; 5:14 [c]Rev 4:10 [d]John 1:29; Rev 5:6, 12f; 13:8 [e]Rev 14:2; 15:2 [f]Rev 15:7 [g]Ps 141:2; Rev 8:3f **9** [1]Or *scroll* [a]Ps 33:3; 40:3; 98:1; 149:1; Is 42:10; Rev 14:3; 15:3 [b]Rev 4:11 [c]Rev 5:6, 12; 13:8 [d]1 Cor 6:20; Rev 14:3f [e]Dan 3:4; 5:19; Rev 7:9; 10:11; 11:9; 13:7; 14:6; 17:15 **10** [a]Rev 1:6 [b]Rev 3:21; 20:4 **11** [a]Rev 4:4 [b]Rev 4:6; 5:6, 8, 14 [c]Rev 4:4; 5:6, 14 [d]Dan 7:10;

Angels Exalt the Lamb

11 Then I looked, and I heard the voice of
many angels [a]around the throne and the
[b]living creatures and the [c]elders; and the
number of them was [d]myriads of myriads,
and thousands of thousands,
12 saying with a loud voice,
"[a]Worthy is the [b]Lamb that was [b]slain to
receive power and riches and wisdom
and might and honor and glory and
blessing."
13 And [a]every created thing which is in
heaven and on the earth and under the earth
and on the sea, and all things in them, I
heard saying,
"To Him who [b]sits on the throne, and to
the [c]Lamb, [d]*be* blessing and honor and
glory and dominion forever and ever."
14 And the [a]four living creatures kept saying, "[b]Amen." And the [c]elders [d]fell down
and worshiped.

The Book Opened; The First Seal—The False Christ

6 Then I saw when the [a]Lamb broke one of
the [b]seven seals, and I heard one of the
[c]four living creatures saying as with a [d]voice
of thunder, "Come[1]."
2 I looked, and behold, a [a]white horse,
and he who sat on it had a bow; and [b]a
crown was given to him, and he went out
[c]conquering and to conquer.

Heb 12:22; Jude 14; Rev 9:16 **12** [a]Rev 1:6; 4:11; 5:9 [b]John 1:29; Rev 5:6, 13; 13:8 **13** [a]Phil 2:10; Rev 5:3 [b]Rev 5:1 [c]John 1:29; Rev 5:6, 12f; 13:8 [d]Rom 11:36; Rev 1:6 **14** [a]Rev 4:6; 5:6, 8, 11 [b]1 Cor 14:16; Rev 7:12; 19:4 [c]Rev 4:4; 5:6, 8 [d]Rev 4:10 **6:1** [1]One early ms reads *and see* [a]John 1:29; Rev 5:6, 12f; 13:8 [b]Rev 5:1 [c]Rev 4:6; 5:6, 8, 11, 14 [d]Rev 14:2; 19:6 **2** [a]Zech 1:8; 6:3f; Rev 19:11 [b]Zech 6:11; Rev 9:7; 14:14; 19:12 [c]Rev 3:21

easier than on the reverse side (where the fibers are vertical). *sealed up with seven seals.* Indicating absolute inviolability (cf. Is 29:11; Dan 12:4).

5:2 *strong angel.* See 18:21.

5:3 *heaven . . . earth . . . under the earth.* A conventional phrase used to express the universality of the proclamation—no creature was worthy. It is not intended to teach a threefold division of the universe (cf. Ex 20:4; Phil 2:10).

5:5 *Lion that is from the tribe of Judah.* A Messianic title taken from Gen 49:8–10, where Judah is named a "lion's whelp" and promised the right to rule "Until Shiloh comes" (see also Ezek 21:27). *Root of David.* See Is 11:1,10, which looks forward to the ideal king in the line of David. The title is interpreted Messianically in Rom 15:12.

5:6 *Lamb.* Pictured as the sacrifice for sin ("slain"; cf. Is 53:7; John 1:29) and as the mighty conqueror (17:14). Revelation uses a special word for "lamb" (29 times in Revelation and only once elsewhere in the NT—John 21:15). The idea of the lamb as a victorious military leader seems to come from the apocalyptic tradition (1 Enoch 90:9; Testament of Joseph 19:8). *as if slain.* Bearing the marks of its slaughter—He has come to power through His death. *seven horns.* The horn is an ancient Jewish symbol for power or strength (cf. Deut 33:17). The fourth beast of Dan 7:7,20 had ten horns (cf. Dan 8:3,5). Seven horns would symbolize full strength. *seven Spirits.* See note on 4:5.

5:8 *harp.* An ancient stringed instrument (not the large modern harp) used especially to accompany songs (Ps 33:2). *bowls full of incense.* The bowl was a flat, shallow cup. Incense was a normal feature of Hebrew ritual (see Deut 33:10; cf. Ps 141:2; Rev 8:3–4). *prayers of the saints.* In later Jewish thought, angels often present the prayers of saints to God (Tobit 12:15; 3 Baruch 11).

5:9 *new song.* Cf. 14:3; Ps 33:3; 96:1; 144:9; Is 42:10. In the OT a new song celebrated a new act of divine deliverance or blessing. That is also its sense here; notice the theme of the song. *purchased . . . with Your blood men.* The sacrificial death of Christ is central to NT teaching (see Mark 10:45; 1 Cor 6:20).

5:10 *kingdom and priests.* See note on 1:6. *reign upon the earth.* See 2:26–27; 20:4,6; 22:5.

5:11 *thousands of thousands.* A rhetorical phrase for an indefinitely large number (see Dan 7:10; cf. Heb 12:22).

5:12 *power . . . blessing.* See David's farewell prayer in 1 Chr 29:10–19. The attributes increase from three in 4:11 to four in 5:13 to seven in 5:12; 7:12.

5:13 *heaven . . . earth . . . under the earth.* See note on v. 3.

6:1 *seven seals.* The first of three sevenfold numbered series of judgments (cf. the seven trumpets in chs. 8–9 and the seven bowls in ch. 16).

6:2 *white horse.* The imagery of the four horsemen comes from Zech 1:8–17; 6:1–8 (see note on Zech 6:2–3). The colors in Revelation correspond to the character of the rider; white symbolizes conquest. Major interpretations of the rider on the white horse are: (1) Christ (cf. 19:11), (2) the antichrist and (3) the spirit of conquest. The latter establishes a more natural sequence with the other three riders (which symbolize bloodshed, famine and death). *bow.* A battle weapon. *crown.* See note on 2:10.

The Second Seal—War

3 When He broke the second seal, I heard the [a]second living creature saying, "Come[1]."

4 And another, [a]a red horse, went out; and to him who sat on it, it was granted to [b]take peace from the earth, and that *men* would slay one another; and a great sword was given to him.

The Third Seal—Famine

5 When He broke the third seal, I heard the [a]third living creature saying, "Come[1]." I looked, and behold, a [b]black horse; and he who sat on it had a [c]pair of scales in his hand.

6 And I heard *something* like a voice in the center of the [a]four living creatures saying, "A [1]quart of wheat for a [2]denarius, and three [1]quarts of barley for a [2]denarius; and [b]do not damage the oil and the wine."

The Fourth Seal—Death

7 When the Lamb broke the fourth seal, I heard the voice of the [a]fourth living creature saying, "Come[1]."

8 I looked, and behold, an [1a]ashen horse; and he who sat on it had the name [b]Death; and [b]Hades was following with him. Authority was given to them over a fourth of the earth, [c]to kill with sword and with famine and with [2]pestilence and by the wild beasts of the earth.

The Fifth Seal—Martyrs

9 When the Lamb broke the fifth seal, I saw [a]underneath the [b]altar the [c]souls of those who had been slain [d]because of the word of God, and because of the [e]testimony which they had maintained;

10 and they cried out with a loud voice, saying, "[a]How long, O [1b]Lord, [c]holy and true, [2]will You refrain from [d]judging and avenging our blood on [e]those who dwell on the earth?"

11 And [a]there was given to each of them a white robe; and they were told that they should [b]rest for a little while longer, [c]until *the number of* their fellow servants and their brethren who were to be killed even as they had been, would be [d]completed also.

The Sixth Seal—Terror

12 I looked when He broke the sixth seal, and there was a great [a]earthquake; and the [b]sun became black as [c]sackcloth *made* of hair, and the whole moon became like blood;

13 and [a]the stars of the sky fell to the earth, [b]as a fig tree casts its unripe figs when shaken by a great wind.

14 [a]The sky was split apart like a scroll when it is rolled up, and [b]every mountain and island were moved out of their places.

15 Then [a]the kings of the earth and the great men and the [1]commanders and the rich and the strong and every slave and free man hid themselves in the caves and among the rocks of the mountains;

16 and they *[a]said to the mountains and to the rocks, "Fall on us and hide us from the [1]presence of Him [b]who sits on the throne, and from the [c]wrath of the Lamb;

17 for [a]the great day of their wrath has come, and [b]who is able to stand?"

3 [1]One early ms reads *and see* [a]Rev 4:7
4 [a]Zech 1:8; 6:2 [b]Matt 10:34
5 [1]One early ms reads *and see* [a]Rev 4:7 [b]Zech 6:2, 6 [c]Ezek 4:16
6 [1]Gr *choenix;* i.e. a dry measure almost equal to a qt [2]The denarius was equivalent to a day's wages [a]Rev 4:6f [b]Rev 7:3; 9:4
7 [1]One early ms reads *and see* [a]Rev 4:7
8 [1]Or *sickly pale* [2]Or *death* [a]Zech 6:3 [b]Prov 5:5; Hos 13:14; Matt 11:23; Rev 1:18; 20:13f [c]Jer 14:12; 15:2f; 24:10; 29:17f; Ezek 5:12, 17; 14:21; 29:5
9 [a]Ex 29:12; Lev 4:7; John 16:2 [b]Rev 14:18; 16:7 [c]Rev 20:4 [d]Rev 1:2, 9 [e]Rev 12:17
10 [1]Or *Master* [2]Lit *do You not judge and avenge* [a]Zech 1:12 [b]Luke 2:29; 2 Pet 2:1 [c]Rev 3:7 [d]Deut 32:43; Ps 79:10; Luke 18:7; Rev 19:2 [e]Rev 3:10
11 [a]Rev 3:4, 5; 7:9 [b]2 Thess 1:7; Heb 4:10; Rev 14:13 [c]Heb 11:40 [d]Acts 20:24; 2 Tim 4:7
12 [a]Matt 24:7; Rev 8:5; 11:13; 16:18 [b]Is 13:10; Joel 2:10, 31; 3:15; Matt 24:29; Mark 13:24 [c]Is 50:3; Matt 11:21
13 [a]Matt 24:29; Mark 13:25; Rev 8:10; 9:1 [b]Is 34:4
14 [a]Is 34:4; 2 Pet 3:10; Rev 20:11; 21:1 [b]Is 54:10; Jer 4:24; Ezek 38:20; Nah 1:5; Rev 16:20
15 [1]I.e. chiliarchs, in command of one thousand troops [a]Is 2:10f, 19, 21; 24:21; Rev 19:18
16 [1]Lit *face* [a]Hos 10:8; Luke 23:30; Rev 9:6 [b]Rev 4:9; 5:1 [c]Mark 3:5
17 [a]Is 63:4; Jer 30:7; Joel 1:15; 2:1f, 11, 31; Zeph 1:14f; Rev 16:14 [b]Ps 76:7; Nah 1:6; Mal 3:2; Luke 21:36

6:4 *another, a red horse.* Symbolizing bloodshed and war (cf. Zech 1:8; 6:2). *men would slay one another.* If the white horse is conquest from without, the red horse may be internal revolution. *sword.* See note on 1:16.

6:5 *black horse.* Symbolizing famine (cf. Zech 6:2,6). The sequence is thus conquest, bloodshed, famine. *pair of scales.* A balance beam with scales hung from either end. Weights were originally stones.

6:6 *wheat . . . barley.* One quart of wheat would be enough for only one person. Three quarts of the less nutritious barley would be barely enough for a small family. Famine had inflated prices to at least ten times their normal level. *oil and the wine.* Sets limits on the destruction by the rider of the black horse. The roots of the olive and vine go deeper and would not be immediately affected by a limited drought.

6:8 *ashen horse.* Describes the ashen appearance of the dead; it symbolizes death. *Hades.* Equivalent to Hebrew *Sheol* (see 1:18; 20:13–14; see also note on Matt 16:18).

6:9 *underneath the altar.* In OT ritual the blood of the slaughtered animal was poured out at the base of the altar (Ex 29:12; Lev 4:7).

6:10 *those who dwell on the earth.* A regular designation in Revelation for mankind in its hostility to God (see 3:10; 8:13; 11:10; 13:8,12; 17:2,8).

6:11 *white robe.* Symbol of blessedness and purity (see 3:5,18; 4:4; 7:9,13; 19:14). *until the number . . . would be completed.* Jewish thought held that God rules the world according to a predetermined time schedule (see 2 Esdras 4:35–37) and that the end awaits the death of a certain number of the righteous (1 Enoch 47:4).

6:12 *earthquake.* A regular feature of divine visitation (see Ex 19:18; Is 2:19; Hag 2:6). *moon became like blood.* See Joel 2:31, quoted by Peter in his Pentecost sermon (Acts 2:20).

6:13 *stars . . . fell.* One of the signs immediately preceding the coming of the Son of Man (Mark 13:25–26). *unripe figs.* Green figs appearing in the winter and easily blown from the tree, which at that season has no leaves.

6:14 *sky was split apart like a scroll.* See Is 34:4. *every mountain and island were moved.* Perhaps suggested by Jer 4:24 or Nah 1:5; see 16:20; 20:11.

6:15 *commanders.* A general was a Roman officer who commanded a cohort, i.e., about 1,000 men. *hid . . . in the caves.* See Jer 4:29.

6:16 *wrath of the Lamb.* God's wrath is a theme that permeates NT theology. It is both present (see Rom 1:18 and note) and future (see 19:15). It is prophesied in the OT (Zeph 1:14–18; Nah 1:6; Mal 3:2). *Lamb.* See note on 5:6.

An Interlude

7 After this I saw [a]four angels standing at the [b]four corners of the earth, holding back [c]the four winds of the earth, [d]so that no wind would blow on the earth or on the sea or on any tree.

2 And I saw another angel ascending [a]from the rising of the sun, having the [b]seal of [c]the living God; and he cried out with a loud voice to the [d]four angels to whom it was granted to harm the earth and the sea,

3 saying, "[a]Do not harm the earth or the sea or the trees until we have [b]sealed the bond-servants of our God on their [c]foreheads."

A Remnant of Israel—144,000

4 And I heard the [a]number of those who were sealed, [b]one hundred and forty-four thousand sealed from every tribe of the sons of Israel:

5 from the tribe of Judah, twelve thousand *were* sealed, from the tribe of Reuben twelve thousand, from the tribe of Gad twelve thousand,

6 from the tribe of Asher twelve thousand, from the tribe of Naphtali twelve thousand, from the tribe of Manasseh twelve thousand,

7 from the tribe of Simeon twelve thousand, from the tribe of Levi twelve thousand, from the tribe of Issachar twelve thousand,

8 from the tribe of Zebulun twelve thousand, from the tribe of Joseph twelve thousand, from the tribe of Benjamin, twelve thousand *were* sealed.

A Multitude from the Tribulation

9 After these things I looked, and behold, a great multitude which no one could count, from [a]every nation and *all* tribes and peoples and tongues, standing [b]before the throne and [c]before the Lamb, clothed in [d]white robes, and [e]palm branches *were* in their hands;

10 and they cry out with a loud voice, saying,

"[a]Salvation to our God [b]who sits on the throne, and to the Lamb."

11 And all the angels were standing [a]around the throne and *around* [a]the elders and the [b]four living creatures; and they [c]fell on their faces before the throne and worshiped God,

12 saying,

"[a]Amen, [b]blessing and glory and wisdom and thanksgiving and honor and power and might, *be* to our God forever and ever. [a]Amen."

13 Then one of the elders [a]answered, saying to me, "These who are clothed in the [b]white robes, who are they, and where have they come from?"

14 I [1]said to him, "My lord, you know." And he said to me, "These are the ones who come out of the [a]great tribulation, and they have [b]washed their robes and made them [c]white in the [d]blood of the Lamb.

15 "For this reason, they are [a]before the throne of God; and they [b]serve Him day and night in His [1c]temple; and [d]He who sits on the throne will spread His [e]tabernacle over them.

16 "[a]They will hunger no longer, nor thirst anymore; nor will the sun [1]beat down on them, nor any heat;

17 for the Lamb in the center of the throne will be their [a]shepherd, and will guide them to springs of the [1b]water of life; and [c]God will wipe every tear from their eyes."

7:1 [a]Rev 9:14 [b]Is 11:12; Ezek 7:2; Rev 20:8 [c]Jer 49:36; Dan 7:2; Zech 6:5; Matt 24:31 [d]Rev 7:3; 8:7; 9:4
2 [a]Is 41:2 [b]Rev 7:3; 9:4 [c]Matt 16:16 [d]Rev 9:14
3 [a]Rev 6:6 [b]John 3:33; Rev 7:3-8 [c]Ezek 9:4, 6; Rev 13:16; 14:1, 9; 20:4; 22:4
4 [a]Rev 9:16 [b]Rev 14:1, 3
9 [a]Rev 5:9 [b]Rev 7:15 [c]Rev 22:3 [d]Rev 6:11; 7:14 [e]Lev 23:40
10 [a]Ps 3:8; Rev 12:10; 19:1 [b]Rev 22:3
11 [a]Rev 4:4 [b]Rev 4:6 [c]Rev 4:10
12 [a]Rev 5:14 [b]Rev 5:12
13 [a]Acts 3:12 [b]Rev 7:9
14 [1]Lit *have said* [a]Dan 12:1; Matt 24:21; Mark 13:19 [b]Zech 3:3-5; Rev 22:14 [c]Rev 6:11; 7:9 [d]Heb 9:14; 1 John 1:7
15 [1]Or *sanctuary* [a]Rev 7:9 [b]Rev 4:8f; 22:3 [c]Rev 11:19; 21:22 [d]Rev 4:9 [e]Lev 26:11; Ezek 37:27; John 1:14; Rev 21:3
16 [1]Lit *fall* [a]Ps 121:5f; Is 49:10
17 [1]Lit *waters* [a]Ps 23:1f; Matt 2:6; John 10:11 [b]John 4:14; Rev 21:6; 22:1 [c]Is 25:8; Matt 5:4; Rev 21:4

7:1–17 A parenthesis separating the final seal from the preceding six (the same feature is found in the trumpet sequence; see 10:1–11:13). It contains two visions: (1) the sealing of the 144,000 (vv. 1–8) and (2) the innumerable multitude (vv. 9–17).
7:1 *four winds.* Destructive agents of God (see Jer 49:36).
7:2 *seal of the living God.* Ancient documents were folded and tied, and a lump of clay was pressed over the knot. The sender would then stamp the hardening clay with his signet ring or roll it with a cylinder seal, which authenticated and protected the contents. The sealing in ch. 7 results in the name of the Lord being stamped on the forehead of His followers (see 9:4; 14:1; cf. 22:4). Its primary purpose is to protect the people of God in the coming judgments. For the background see Ezek 9:4, where the mark was the Hebrew letter *Taw,* made like an *X* or +.
7:4 *one hundred and forty-four thousand.* Some find here a reference to members of actual Jewish tribes, the faithful Jewish remnant of the "great tribulation" (v. 14). Others take the passage as symbolic of all the faithful believers who live during the period of tribulation.
7:5 *Judah.* Perhaps listed before Reuben, his older brother, because the Messiah belonged to the tribe of Judah (but see note on Gen 37:21).
7:6 *Manasseh.* One of the two Joseph tribes (Ephraim and Manasseh), yet mentioned separately, probably to make up 12 tribes since Dan is omitted. This omission is due perhaps to Dan's early connection with idolatry (Judg 18:30), or to a tradition that the antichrist was to come from that tribe.
7:9 *great multitude.* Identified in v. 14 as those who have come out of the great tribulation. *every nation and all tribes and peoples and tongues.* All four are mentioned together also in 5:9; 11:9; 13:7; 14:6. Cf. 10:11; 17:15, in which one of the four is changed. *palm branches.* Used for festive occasions (see Lev 23:40; John 12:13).
7:10 *Salvation to our God.* See Gen 49:18 ("deliverance"); Jon 2:9.
7:11 *elders.* See note on 4:4. *four living creatures.* See note on 4:6.
7:12 *blessing . . . might.* The sevenfold list of attributes expresses complete or perfect praise (see note on 5:12).
7:13 *white robes.* See note on 6:11.
7:14 *the great tribulation.* The period of final hostility prior to Christ's return. Some hold that the beginning of this hostility was already being experienced by the church of John's day.
7:15 *temple.* All 16 references to the temple in Revelation use the word that designates the inner shrine rather than the larger precincts. It is the place where God's presence dwells. *spread His tabernacle.* The imagery would evoke memories of the tabernacle in the wilderness (Lev 26:11–13).
7:17 *shepherd.* Ancient kings often referred to themselves as the shepherds of their people.

The Seventh Seal—the Trumpets

8 When the Lamb broke the [a]seventh seal, there was silence in heaven for about half an hour.

2 And I saw [a]the seven angels who stand before God, and seven [b]trumpets were given to them.

3 [a]Another angel came and stood at the [b]altar, holding a [c]golden censer; and much [d]incense was given to him, so that he might [1]add it to the [d]prayers of all the [2]saints on the [e]golden altar which was before the throne.

4 And [a]the smoke of the incense, [1]with the prayers of the [2]saints, went up before God out of the angel's hand.

5 Then the angel [1]took the censer and [a]filled it with the fire of the altar, and [b]threw it to the earth; and there followed [c]peals of thunder and sounds and flashes of lightning and an [d]earthquake.

6 [a]And the seven angels who had the seven trumpets prepared themselves to sound them.

7 The first sounded, and there came [a]hail and fire, mixed with blood, and they were thrown to the earth; and [b]a third of the earth was burned up, and [b]a third of the [c]trees were burned up, and all the green [c]grass was burned up.

8 The second angel sounded, and *something* like a great [a]mountain burning with fire was thrown into the sea; and [b]a third of the [c]sea became blood,

9 and [a]a third of the creatures which were in the sea [1]and had life, died; and a third of the [b]ships were destroyed.

8:1 [a]Rev 5:1; 6:1, 3, 5, 7, 9, 12 **2** [a]Rev 1:4; 8:6-13; 9:1, 13; 11:15 [b]1 Cor 15:52; 1 Thess 4:16 **3** [1]Lit *give* [2]Or *holy ones* [a]Rev 7:2 [b]Amos 9:1; Rev 6:9 [c]Heb 9:4 [d]Ex 30:1; Rev 5:8 [e]Ex 30:3; Num 4:11; Rev 8:5; 9:13 **4** [1]Or *for* [2]V 3, note 2 [a]Ps 141:2 **5** [1]Lit *has taken* [a]Lev 16:12 [b]Ezek 10:2 [c]Ex 19:16; Rev 4:5; 11:19; 16:18 [d]Rev 6:12 **6** [a]Rev 8:2 **7** [a]Ex 9:23ff; Is 28:2; Ezek 38:22; Joel 2:30 [b]Zech 13:8, 9; Rev 8:7-12; 9:15, 18; 12:4 [c]Rev 9:4 **8** [a]Jer 51:25 [b]Zech 13:8, 9; Rev 8:7-12; 9:15, 18; 12:4 [c]Ex 7:17ff; Rev 11:6; 16:3 **9** [1]Lit *the ones having* [a]Zech 13:8, 9; Rev 8:7-12; 9:15, 18; 12:4 [b]Is 2:16

10 [a]Is 14:12; Rev 6:13; 9:1 [b]Zech 13:8, 9; Rev 8:7-12; 9:15, 18; 12:4 [c]Rev 14:7; 16:4 **11** [a]Zech 13:8, 9; Rev 8:7-12; 9:15, 18; 12:4 [b]Jer 9:15; 23:15

10 The third angel sounded, and a great star [a]fell from heaven, burning like a torch, and it fell on a [b]third of the rivers and on the [c]springs of waters.

11 The name of the star is called Wormwood; and a [a]third of the waters became [b]wormwood, and many men died from the waters, because they were made bitter.

12 The fourth angel sounded, and a [a]third of the [b]sun and a third of the [b]moon and a [a]third of the [b]stars were struck, so that a [a]third of them would be darkened and the day would not shine for a [a]third of it, and the night in the same way.

13 Then I looked, and I heard [1]an eagle flying in [a]midheaven, saying with a loud voice, "[b]Woe, woe, woe to [c]those who dwell on the earth, because of the remaining blasts of the trumpet of the [d]three angels who are about to sound!"

The Fifth Trumpet—the Bottomless Pit

9 Then the [a]fifth angel sounded, and I saw a [b]star from heaven which had fallen to the earth; and the [c]key of the [1][d]bottomless pit was given to him.

2 He opened the [1]bottomless pit, and [a]smoke went up out of the pit, like the smoke of a great furnace; and [b]the sun and the air were darkened by the smoke of the pit.

3 Then out of the smoke came [a]locusts

12 [a]Zech 13:8, 9; Rev 8:7-12; 9:15, 18; 12:4 [b]Ex 10:21ff; Is 13:10; Ezek 32:7; Joel 2:10, 31; 3:15; Rev 6:12f **13** [1]Lit *one eagle* [a]Rev 14:6; 19:17 [b]Rev 9:12; 11:14; 12:12 [c]Rev 3:10 [d]Rev 8:2 **9:1** [1]Lit *shaft of the abyss* [a]Rev 8:2 [b]Rev 8:10 [c]Rev 1:18 [d]Luke 8:31; Rev 9:2, 11 **2** [1]V 1, note 1 [a]Gen 19:28; Ex 19:18 [b]Joel 2:2, 10 **3** [a]Ex 10:12-15; Rev 9:7

8:1 *silence in heaven.* A dramatic pause before the next series of plagues—the final act of the drama is left undisclosed here, reserved to be presented later.
8:2 *seven trumpets.* In OT times the trumpet served to announce important events and give signals in time of war. The seven trumpets of Rev 8–9; 11:15–19 announce a series of plagues more severe than the seals but not as completely devastating as the bowls (ch. 16).
8:3 *censer.* A firepan used to hold live charcoal for the burning of incense (cf. Ex 27:3; 1 Kin 7:50). *to the prayers.* Most translations consider the incense to be mingled "with" prayers. The Greek for this phrase also allows a translation that takes the incense "to be" the prayers ("incense ... consisting of the prayers").
8:4 Although the angel is involved in presenting the prayers of the saints to God, he does not make them acceptable. The Jewish apocalyptic concept of angels as mediators finds no place in the NT.
8:5 *thunder . . . earthquake.* See note on 4:5.
8:7 *hail and fire, mixed with blood.* Cf. the imagery of the seventh plague on Egypt (Ex 9:13–25; cf. Ezek 38:22). *a third of the earth was burned up.* This fraction indicates that the punishment announced by the trumpets is not yet complete and final (the same fraction appears in each of the next three plagues: vv. 8–9, 10–11, 12). A smaller fraction (a fourth) of devastation accompanied the opening of the fourth seal (6:8).
8:8 *sea became blood.* Reminiscent of the first plague on Egypt (Ex 7:20–21). This is an eschatological judgment rather than natural pollution resulting from widespread volcanic upheavals.
8:10 *great star fell.* See notes on 6:13; 9:1.
8:11 *Wormwood.* A plant with a strong, bitter taste (Wormwood means "Bitterness"). It is used here as a metaphor for calamity and sorrow (see Prov 5:3–4; Jer 9:15; Lam 3:19). It is not poisonous, but its bitterness suggests death. *waters became wormwood.* The reverse of the miracle at Marah, where bitter waters were made sweet (Ex 15:25).
8:12 *a third of the sun . . . struck.* In the ninth plague on Egypt, thick darkness covered the land for three days (Ex 10:21–23). References to the Egyptian plagues suggest that in Revelation we have the final exodus of God's people from the bondage of a world controlled by hostile powers.
8:13 *Woe, woe, woe . . .* These three woes correspond to the three final trumpet plagues (see 9:12; 11:14 [10:1–11:13 is a parenthesis]; the seven bowl judgments of chs. 15–16 apparently constitute the third woe). The woes fall on the unbelieving world (the phrase "those who dwell on the earth" refers to the wicked; see note on 6:10), not on the righteous (see 9:4).
9:1 *star . . . which had fallen.* The star in 8:10 was part of a cosmic disturbance; here the star is a divine agent, probably an angel (cf. 20:1). *bottomless pit.* Conceived of as the subterranean abode of demonic hordes (see 20:1; Luke 8:31). The Greek word means "very deep" or "bottomless," and is used in the Septuagint (the Greek translation of the OT) to translate the Hebrew word for the primeval deep (see Gen 1:2; 7:11; Prov 8:28). Seven of the eight NT occurrences of the Greek words for *Abyss* are in Revelation.

[1]upon the earth, and power was given them,
as the [b]scorpions of the earth have power.
4 They were told not to [a]hurt the [b]grass
of the earth, nor any green thing, nor any
tree, but only the men who do not have the
[c]seal of God on their foreheads.
5 And [1]they were not permitted to kill
[2]anyone, but to torment for [a]five months;
and their torment was like the torment of a
[b]scorpion when it [3]stings a man.
6 And in those days [a]men will seek death
and will not find it; they will long to die, and
death flees from them.
7 The [1a]appearance of the locusts was
like horses prepared for battle; and on their
heads appeared to be crowns like gold, and
their faces were like the faces of men.
8 They had hair like the hair of women,
and their [a]teeth were like *the teeth* of lions.
9 They had breastplates like breastplates
of iron; and the [a]sound of their wings was
like the sound of chariots, of many horses
rushing to battle.
10 They have tails like [a]scorpions, and
stings; and in their [b]tails is their power to
hurt men for [c]five months.
11 They have as king over them, the angel
of the [a]abyss; his name in [b]Hebrew is
[1c]Abaddon, and in the Greek he has the
name [2]Apollyon.
12 [a]The first woe is past; behold, two
woes are still coming after these things.

The Sixth Trumpet—Army from the East

13 Then the sixth angel sounded, and I
heard [1]a voice from the [2]four [a]horns of the
[b]golden altar which is before God,
14 one saying to the sixth angel who had
the trumpet, "Release the [a]four angels who
are bound at the [b]great river Euphrates."
15 And the four angels, who had been prepared for the hour and day and month and
year, were [a]released, so that they would kill
a [b]third of [1]mankind.
16 The number of the armies of the horsemen was [a]two hundred million; [b]I heard the
number of them.
17 And [1]this is how I saw [a]in the vision
the horses and those who sat on them: *the
riders* had breastplates *the color* of fire and of
hyacinth and of [2b]brimstone; and the heads
of the horses are like the heads of lions; and
[c]out of their mouths proceed fire and smoke
and [2b]brimstone.
18 A [a]third of [1]mankind was killed by
these three plagues, by the [b]fire and the
smoke and the [2]brimstone which proceeded
out of their mouths.
19 For the power of the horses is in their
mouths and in their tails; for their tails are
like serpents and have heads, and with them
they do harm.
20 The rest of [1]mankind, who were not
killed by these plagues, [a]did not repent of
[b]the works of their hands, so as not to [c]wor-
ship demons, and [d]the idols of gold and of
silver and of brass and of stone and of wood,
which can neither see nor hear nor walk;
21 and they [a]did not repent of their murders nor of their [b]sorceries nor of their
[c]immorality nor of their thefts.

3 [1]Lit *into* [b]2 Chr 10:11, 14; Ezek 2:6; Rev 9:5, 10
4 [a]Rev 6:6 [b]Rev 8:7 [c]Ezek 9:4; Rev 7:2, 3
5 [1]Lit *it was given to them* [2]Lit *them* [3]Lit *strikes* [a]Rev 9:10 [b]2 Chr 10:11, 14; Ezek 2:6; Rev 9:3, 10
6 [a]Job 3:21; 7:15; Jer 8:3; Rev 6:16
7 [1]Lit *likenesses* [a]Joel 2:4
8 [a]Joel 1:6
9 [a]Jer 47:3; Joel 2:5
10 [a]2 Chr 10:11, 14; Ezek 2:6; Rev 9:3, 5 [b]Rev 9:19 [c]Rev 9:5
11 [1]I.e. destruction [2]I.e. destroyer [a]Luke 8:31; Rev 9:1, 2 [b]John 5:2; Rev 16:16 [c]Job 26:6; 28:22; 31:12; Ps 88:11 mg; Prov 15:11
12 [a]Rev 8:13; 11:14
13 [1]Lit *one voice* [2]Two early mss do not contain *four* [a]Ex 30:2f, 10 [b]Rev 8:3
14 [a]Rev 7:1 [b]Gen 15:18; Deut 1:7; Josh 1:4; Rev 16:12
15 [1]Gr *anthropoi* [a]Rev 20:7 [b]Rev 8:7; 9:18
16 [a]Rev 5:11 [b]Rev 7:4
17 [1]Lit *thus I saw* [2]I.e. burning sulphur [a]Dan 8:2; 9:21 [b]Rev 9:18; 14:10; 19:20; 20:10; 21:8 [c]Rev 11:5
18 [1]Gr *anthropoi* [2]I.e. burning sulphur [a]Rev 8:7; 9:15 [b]Rev 9:17
20 [1]Gr *anthropoi* [a]Rev 2:21 [b]Deut 4:28; Jer 1:16; Mic 5:13; Acts 7:41 [c]1 Cor 10:20 [d]Ps 115:4-7; 135:15-17; Dan 5:23
21 [a]Rev 9:20 [b]Is 47:9, 12; Rev 18:23 [c]Rev 17:2, 4, 5

9:3 *locusts.* For background see the plague of locusts in Ex 10:1–20. Joel 1:2–2:11 interprets the locust plague as a foreshadowing of the devastations that accompany the day of the Lord. Locusts traveled in enormous swarms and could strip a land of all vegetation. In 1866, 200,000 people died in a famine in Algiers following a locust plague. *scorpions.* Large spider-like organisms that injure or kill by means of a poisonous barb in the tail.

9:4 *men who do not have the seal of God.* The first woe does not affect the "bond-servants of God" (see 7:3). Cf. the Israelites, who were protected from the Egyptian plagues (Ex 8:22; 9:4,26; 10:23; 11:7).

9:5 *five months.* A limited period of time suggested by the life cycle of the locust or the dry season (spring through late summer, about five months), in which the danger of a locust invasion is always present.

9:6 *seek death and will not find it.* Cf. Hos 10:8 (quoted in Luke 23:30). Cornelius Gallus, a Roman poet living in the first century B.C., wrote: "Worse than any wound is the wish to die and yet not be able to do so." Cf. Paul's attitude toward death in Phil 1:23–24.

9:7 *faces of men.* The locusts appear to have the cunning of intelligent beings. They do not simply use brute force.

9:8 *hair of women.* Perhaps a reference to long antennae. *teeth of lions.* Cruel, inhumane.

9:9 *breastplates.* The breastplate was a coat of mail that protected the front. *like breastplates of iron.* Probably thin iron pieces riveted to a leather base.

9:10 *five months.* See note on v. 5.

9:11 *Abaddon.* A personification of destruction (cf. Prov 15:11).

9:12 *first woe.* See note on 8:13.

9:13 *horns of the golden altar.* See 8:3–5. The horns were projections at the four corners of the altar (Ex 27:2). Those fleeing judgment could seek mercy by taking hold of the horns (1 Kin 1:50–51; 2:28; see note on Amos 3:14).

9:14 *four angels.* Apparently in charge of the demonic horsemen (vv. 15–19). *Euphrates.* The longest river in western Asia (about 1,700 miles). It marked the boundary between Israel and her historic enemies (Assyria and Babylon) to the east (cf. Is 8:5–8).

9:15 *hour . . . day . . . month . . . year.* Apocalyptic thought views God as acting according to an exact timetable.

9:16 *two hundred million.* The reference is most likely general, intending an incalculable host rather than a specific number (cf. Ps 68:17; Dan 7:10; Rev 5:11).

9:17 *breastplates.* See note on v. 9. *out of their mouths proceed fire.* Cf. the two witnesses in 11:5.

9:19 *tails are like serpents and have heads.* Emphasizes the demonic origin of the horses (cf. 12:9).

9:20 *demons.* Spiritual beings in league with Satan and exerting an evil influence on human affairs (cf. Deut 4:28; Ps 115:5–7; 1 Cor 10:20).

9:21 *they did not repent.* See 16:9,11. Even physical pain will not change the rebellious heart. *sorceries.* Involved the mixing

The Angel and the Little Book

10 I saw another [a]strong angel [b]coming
down out of heaven, clothed with a
cloud; and the [c]rainbow was upon his head,
and [d]his face was like the sun, and his [e]feet
like pillars of fire;
2 and he had in his hand a [a]little book
which was open. He placed [b]his right foot on
the sea and his left on the land;
3 and he cried out with a loud voice, [a]as
when a lion roars; and when he had cried
out, the [b]seven peals of thunder [1]uttered
their voices.
4 When the seven peals of thunder had
spoken, [a]I was about to write; and I [b]heard a
voice from heaven saying, "[c]Seal up the
things which the seven peals of thunder have
spoken and do not write them."
5 Then the angel whom I saw standing
on the sea and on the land [a]lifted up his
right hand to heaven,
6 [a]and swore by [b]Him who lives forever
and ever, [c]WHO CREATED HEAVEN AND THE THINGS
IN IT, AND THE EARTH AND THE THINGS IN IT, AND
THE SEA AND THE THINGS IN IT, that [d]there will
be delay no longer,
7 but in the days of the voice of the [a]sev-
enth angel, when he is about to sound, then
[b]the mystery of God is finished, as He
[1]preached to His servants the prophets.
8 Then [a]the voice which I heard from
heaven, *I heard* again speaking with me, and
saying, "Go, take [b]the [1]book which is open
in the hand of the angel who [b]stands on the
sea and on the land."
9 So I went to the angel, telling him to give
me the little book. And he *said to me, "[a]Take
it and eat it; it will make your stomach bitter,
but in your mouth it will be sweet as honey."
10 I took the little book out of the angel's
hand and ate it, and in my mouth it was
sweet as honey; and when I had eaten it, my
stomach was made bitter.
11 And [a]they *said to me, "You must
[b]prophesy again concerning [c]many peoples
and nations and tongues and [d]kings."

The Two Witnesses

11 Then there was given me a [1][a]measur-
ing rod like a staff; [2]and [b]someone said,
"Get up and measure the [3]temple of God and
the altar, and those who worship in it.
2 "[1]Leave out the [a]court which is outside
the [2]temple and do not measure it, for [b]it has
been given to the nations; and they will
[b]tread under foot [c]the holy city for [d]forty-two
months.
3 "And I will grant *authority* to my two
[a]witnesses, and they will prophesy for
[b]twelve hundred and sixty days, clothed in
[c]sackcloth."

10:1 [a]Rev 5:2 [b]Rev 18:1; 20:1 [c]Rev 4:3 [d]Matt 17:2; Rev 1:16 [e]Rev 1:15
2 [a]Rev 5:1; 10:8-10 [b]Rev 10:5, 8
3 [1]Or *spoke* [a]Is 31:4; Hos 11:10 [b]Ps 29:3-9; Rev 4:5
4 [a]Rev 1:11, 19 [b]Rev 10:8 [c]Dan 8:26; 12:4, 9; Rev 22:10
5 [a]Deut 32:40; Dan 12:7
6 [a]Gen 14:22; Ex 6:8; Num 14:30; Ezek 20:5 [b]Rev 4:9 [c]Ex 20:11; Rev 4:11 [d]Rev 6:11; 12:12; 16:17; 21:6
7 [1]Lit *preached the gospel* [a]Rev 11:15 [b]Amos 3:7; Rom 16:25
8 [a]Rev 10:4
8 [1]Or *scroll* [b]Rev 10:2
9 [a]Jer 15:16; Ezek 2:8; 3:1-3
11 [a]Rev 11:1 [b]Ezek 37:4, 9 [c]Rev 5:9 [d]Rev 17:10, 12
11:1 [1]Lit *reed* [2]Lit *saying* [3]Or *sanctuary* [a]Ezek 40:3-42:20; Zech 2:1; Rev 21:15f [b]Rev 10:11
2 [1]Lit *throw out* [2]Or *sanctuary* [a]Ezek 40:17, 20 [b]Luke 21:24 [c]Is 52:1; Matt 4:5; 27:53; Rev 21:2, 10; 22:19 [d]Dan 7:25; 12:7; Rev 12:6; 13:5
3 [a]Rev 1:5; 2:13 [b]Dan 7:25; 12:7; Rev 12:6; 13:5 [c]Gen 37:34; 2 Sam 3:31; 1 Kin 21:27; 2 Kin 19:1f; Neh 9:1; Esth 4:1; Ps 69:11; Joel 1:13; Jon 3:5f, 8

of various ingredients (the Greek for this phrase is *pharmakon,* from which comes the English "pharmacy") for magical purposes. Believers at Ephesus publicly burned their books of magic, valued at 50,000 drachmas (Acts 19:19). (A drachma was a silver coin worth about a day's wages.)

10:1 *strong angel.* Perhaps the angel of 5:2. *rainbow.* Cf. Ezek 1:26–28. The rainbow became a sign of God's pledge never to destroy the earth again by a flood (Gen 9:8–17). *feet like pillars of fire.* Since the exodus supplies background for this central part of Revelation (see note on 8:12), this feature may recall the pillars of fire and cloud that guided (Ex 13:21–22) and protected (Ex 14:19,24) the Israelites during their wilderness journey.

10:2 *little book.* Not the same as the book of destiny in ch. 5, since that book was intended to reveal its contents and this book was to be eaten. Furthermore, the term "little book" sets this particular book off from all others. *right foot on the sea . . . left on the land.* Indicates his tremendous size and symbolizes that his coming has to do with the destiny of all creation (cf. v. 6).

10:3 *seven peals of thunder.* In 8:5; 11:19; 16:18 thunder is connected with divine punishment. Here, too, it anticipates the judgment to fall on those who refuse God's love and grace.

10:4 *Seal up.* In Dan 8:26; 12:4,9 the prophecies are sealed until the last times, when they will be opened. What the seven thunders said will not be revealed until their proper time. Cf. the angel's instructions in 22:10 not to seal the prophecies of Revelation.

10:5 *lifted up his right hand.* A part of oath taking (see Gen 14:22–23; Deut 32:40).

10:6 *Him who lives forever and ever.* Of special encouragement in a context of impending martyrdom (cf. 1:18; 4:9–10; 15:7). *delay no longer.* The martyrs in 6:9–11 were told to rest for a while, but now the end has come (cf. Dan 12:1; Mark 13:19).

10:7 *mystery of God.* In apocalyptic thought mysteries were secrets preserved in heaven and revealed to the apocalyptist. Here the mystery is that God has won the victory over the forces of evil and will reign for ever and ever (cf. 11:15).

10:9 *Take it and eat it.* Grasp and digest fully the contents of the scroll (cf. Ps 119:103). *make your stomach bitter.* The message of the little scroll (11:1–13) will involve suffering—the "bad news." *in your mouth . . . sweet as honey.* God's eternal purposes will experience no further delay—the "good news."

10:11 *prophesy again.* The prophecies following the sounding of the seventh trumpet in 11:15. *peoples . . . kings.* See note on 7:9.

11:1 *measuring rod.* A bamboo-like cane that often reached a height of 20 feet and grew in abundance in the waters along the banks of the Jordan. Straight and light, the reed was a convenient measuring rod (see Ezek 40:3; Zech 2:1–2). *temple.* See note on 7:15. *altar.* The context of worship suggests that this is the great altar.

11:2 *court which is outside.* The court of the Gentiles, approximately 26 acres. *tread under foot the holy city.* Cf. Ps 79:1; Is 63:18; Luke 21:24. *forty-two months.* Three and a half years. Some find the background for this period in the time of Jewish suffering under the Syrian tyrant, Antiochus Epiphanes (168–165 B.C.). Others point out that, whereas the temple was desolated for three years under Antiochus, the figure used in Revelation is three and a half years, which no doubt looks back to the dividing of the 70th "seven" (Dan 9:27) into two equal parts. The same time period is also designated as 1,260 days (v. 3; 12:6) and as "a time and times and half a time" (12:14; cf. Dan 7:25; 12:7). This period of time evidently became a conventional symbol for a limited period of unrestrained wickedness.

11:3 *two witnesses.* Modeled after Moses and Elijah (see notes

4 These are the [a]two olive trees and the
two lampstands that stand before the Lord of
the earth.
5 And if anyone wants to harm them,
[a]fire flows out of their mouth and devours
their enemies; so if anyone wants to harm
them, [b]he must be killed in this way.
6 These have the power to [a]shut up the
sky, so that rain will not fall during [b]the days
of their prophesying; and they have power
over the waters to [c]turn them into blood, and
[d]to strike the earth with every plague, as
often as they desire.
7 When they have finished their testimony, [a]the beast that comes up out of the
[b]abyss will [c]make war with them, and overcome them and kill them.
8 And their dead bodies *will lie* in the
street of the [a]great city which [1]mystically is
called [b]Sodom and [c]Egypt, where also their
Lord was crucified.
9 Those from [a]the peoples and tribes and
tongues and nations *will* look at their dead
[1]bodies for three and a half days, and [2b]will
not permit their dead bodies to be laid in a
tomb.
10 And [a]those who dwell on the earth *will*
rejoice over them and celebrate; and they
will [b]send gifts to one another, because these
two prophets tormented [a]those who dwell
on the earth.
11 But after the three and a half days, [a]the
breath of life from God came into them, and
they stood on their feet; and great fear fell
upon those who were watching them.
12 And they heard a loud voice from
heaven saying to them, "[a]Come up here."
Then they [b]went up into heaven in the
cloud, and their enemies watched them.
13 And in that hour there was a great
[a]earthquake, and a tenth of the city fell;
[1]seven thousand people were killed in the
earthquake, and the rest were terrified and
[b]gave glory to the [c]God of heaven.
14 The second [a]woe is past; behold, the
third woe is coming quickly.

The Seventh Trumpet—Christ's Reign Foreseen

15 Then the [a]seventh angel sounded; and
there were [b]loud voices in heaven, saying,
"[c]The kingdom of the world has become
the kingdom of our Lord and of [d]His [1]Christ;
and [e]He will reign forever and ever."
16 And the twenty-four elders, who [a]sit on
their thrones before God, [b]fell on their faces
and worshiped God,
17 saying,
"We give You thanks, [a]O Lord God, the
Almighty, who are and who were, because
You have taken Your great power and have
begun to [b]reign.
18 "And [a]the nations were enraged, and
[b]Your wrath came, and [c]the time *came* for
the dead to be judged, and *the time* to
[1]reward Your [d]bond-servants the prophets
and the [2]saints and those who fear Your
name, [e]the small and the great, and to
destroy those who destroy the earth."
19 And [a]the [1]temple of God which is in
heaven was opened; and [b]the ark of His cov-

4 [a]Ps 52:8; Jer 11:16; Zech 4:3, 11, 14 **5** [a]2 Kin 1:10-12; Jer 5:14; Rev 9:17f [b]Num 16:29, 35 **6** [a]1 Kin 17:1; Luke 4:25 [b]Rev 11:3 [c]Ex 7:17ff; Rev 8:8 [d]1 Sam 4:8 **7** [a]Rev 13:1ff; 17:8 [b]Rev 9:1 [c]Dan 7:21; Rev 13:7 **8** [1]Lit *spiritually* [a]Rev 14:8; 16:19; 17:18; 18:2, 10, 16, 18, 19, 21 [b]Is 1:9, 10; 3:9; Jer 23:14; Ezek 16:46, 49 [c]Ezek 23:3, 8, 19, 27 **9** [1]Lit *body* [2]Lit *do not permit* [a]Rev 5:9; 10:11 [b]1 Kin 13:22; Ps 79:2f **10** [a]Rev 3:10 [b]Neh 8:10, 12; Esth 9:19, 22 **11** [a]Ezek 37:5, 9, 10, 14 **12** [a]Rev 4:1

12 [b]2 Kin 2:11; Acts 1:9 **13** [1]Lit *names of people, seven thousand* [a]Rev 6:12; 8:5; 11:19; 16:18 [b]John 9:24; Rev 14:7; 16:9; 19:7 [c]Rev 16:11 **14** [a]Rev 8:13; 9:12 **15** [1]I.e. Messiah [a]Rev 8:2; 10:7 [b]Rev 16:17; 19:1 [c]Rev 12:10 [d]Ps 2:2; Acts 4:26 [e]Ex 15:18; Dan 2:44; 7:14, 27; Luke 1:33 **16** [a]Matt 19:28; Rev 4:4 [b]Rev 4:10 **17** [a]Rev 1:8 [b]Rev 19:6 **18** [1]Lit *give the reward to* [2]Or *holy ones* [a]Ps 2:1 [b]Ps 2:5; 110:5 [c]Dan 7:10; Rev 20:12 [d]Rev 10:7; 16:6 [e]Ps 115:13; Rev 13:16; 19:5 **19** [1]Or *sanctuary* [a]Rev 4:1; 15:5 [b]Heb 9:4

on vv. 5–6). They may symbolize testifying believers in the final period before Christ returns. Or they may be two actual individuals who will be martyred for the proclamation of the truth. *twelve hundred and sixty days.* See note on v. 2. These are months of 30 days (42 months x 30 days = 1,260 days). *sackcloth.* A coarse, dark cloth woven from the hair of goats or camels. It was worn as a sign of mourning and penitence (Joel 1:13; Jon 3:5–6; Matt 11:21).

11:4 The imagery emphasizes that the power for effective testimony is supplied by the Spirit of God (see notes on Zech 4).

11:5 *fire flows . . . and devours.* Cf. Elijah's encounters with the messengers of Ahaziah (2 Kin 1:10,12).

11:6 *power to shut up the sky.* Cf. the drought in the days of Elijah (1 Kin 17:1; see also Luke 4:25; James 5:17). *waters . . . into blood.* God used Moses to bring the same plague on the Egyptians (Ex 7:17–21).

11:7 *the beast.* First mention of the major opponent of God's people in the final days (see chs. 13; 17). That he comes up from the abyss (see note on 9:1) indicates his demonic character. *kill them.* They will suffer the same fate as their Lord (see v. 8).

11:8 *their dead bodies will lie in the street.* In the Near East the denial of burial was a flagrant violation of decency. *great city.* Possibly Jerusalem, though some say Rome, Babylon or some other city. It may be symbolic of the world opposed to God (see 16:19; 17:18; 18:10,16,18–19,21). Sodom (see similarly Is 1:10) refers to its low level of morality (cf. Gen 19:4–11), and Egypt emphasizes oppression and slavery. Some say that Jesus could have been crucified in Rome in the sense that her power extended throughout the known world and was immediately responsible for Christ's execution.

11:9 *three and a half days.* A short time when compared with the three and a half years of their ministry. *not permit . . . tomb.* See note on v. 8.

11:11 *the breath of life from God came into them.* A dramatic validation of the true faith (cf. Ezek 37:5,10).

11:12 *went up into heaven in the cloud.* Cf. 1 Thess 4:17. *enemies watched them.* Cf. 1:7.

11:13 *earthquake.* See notes on 6:12; Ezek 38:19. *gave glory to the God of heaven.* Not an act of repentance but the terrified realization that Christ, not the antichrist, is the true Lord of all.

11:14 *second woe.* Cf. 9:12.

11:15 *seventh angel sounded.* The series of trumpet blasts is now continued (see 9:13) and completed. *kingdom of our Lord.* Cf. Ex 15:18; Ps 10:16; Zech 14:9. *of our Lord and of His Christ.* Cf. Ps 2:2.

11:16 *twenty-four elders.* See note on 4:4.

11:17 *who are and who were.* In 1:4,8; 4:8 He is also the one "who is to come." This is now omitted because His reign is here pictured as having begun.

11:18 *nations were enraged.* See Ps 48:4. *Your wrath.* See note on 6:16. God's wrath triumphs in 14:10–11; 16:15–21; 20:8–9. *dead to be judged.* Anticipated in 6:10, carried out in 20:11–15. *Your bond-servants the prophets.* See Dan 9:6,10; Amos 3:7; Zech 1:6.

11:19 *ark of His covenant.* The OT ark was a chest of acacia wood (Deut 10:1–2). It symbolized the throne or presence of

enant appeared in His [1]temple, and there were flashes of [c]lightning and sounds and peals of thunder and an earthquake and a [d]great [2]hailstorm.

The Woman, Israel

12 A great [a]sign appeared [b]in heaven: [c]a woman [d]clothed with the sun, and the moon under her feet, and on her head a crown of twelve stars;

2 and she was with child; and she *[a]cried out, being in labor and in pain to give birth.

The Red Dragon, Satan

3 Then [a]another sign appeared in heaven: and behold, a great red [b]dragon having [c]seven heads and [d]ten horns, and on his heads *were* [e]seven diadems.

4 And his tail *swept away a [a]third of the stars of heaven and [b]threw them to the earth. And the [c]dragon stood before the woman who was about to give birth, so that when she gave birth [d]he might devour her child.

The Male Child, Christ

5 And [a]she gave birth to a son, a male *child,* who is to [1b]rule all the [2]nations with a rod of iron; and her child was [c]caught up to God and to His throne.

6 Then the woman fled into the wilderness where she *had a place prepared by God, so that there [1]she would be nourished for [a]one thousand two hundred and sixty days.

The Angel, Michael

7 And there was war in heaven, [a]Michael and his angels waging war with the [b]dragon. The dragon and [c]his angels waged war,

8 and they were not strong enough, and there was no longer a place found for them in heaven.

9 And the great [a]dragon was thrown down, the [b]serpent of old who is called the devil and [c]Satan, who [d]deceives the whole [1]world; he was [e]thrown down to the earth, and his angels were thrown down with him.

10 Then I heard [a]a loud voice in heaven, saying,

"Now the [b]salvation, and the power, and the [a]kingdom of our God and the authority of His Christ have come, for the [c]accuser of our brethren has been thrown down, he who accuses them before our God day and night.

11 "And they [a]overcame him because of [b]the blood of the Lamb and because of [c]the word of their testimony, and they [d]did not love their life even [1]when faced with death.

12 "For this reason, [a]rejoice, O heavens and [b]you who [1]dwell in them. [c]Woe to the earth and the sea, because [d]the devil has come down to you, having great wrath, knowing that he has *only* [e]a short time."

13 And when the [a]dragon saw that he was thrown down to the earth, he persecuted [b]the woman who gave birth to the male *child.*

14 But the [a]two wings of the great eagle were given to the woman, so that she could fly [b]into the wilderness to her place, where she *was nourished for [c]a time and times and half a time, from the [1]presence of the serpent.

15 And the [a]serpent [1]poured water like a river out of his mouth after the woman, so that he might cause her to be swept away with the flood.

16 [1]But the earth helped the woman, and the earth opened its mouth and drank up the river which the dragon [2]poured out of his mouth.

19 [1]Or *sanctuary* [2]Lit *hail* [c]Rev 4:5; 8:5; 16:18 [d]Rev 16:21
12:1 [a]Matt 24:30; Rev 12:3 [b]Rev 11:19 [c]Gal 4:26 [d]Ps 104:2; Song 6:10
2 [a]Is 26:17; 66:6-9; Mic 4:9f
3 [a]Rev 12:1; 15:1 [b]Is 27:1; Rev 12:4, 7, 9, 13, 16f; 13:2, 4, 11; 16:13; 20:2 [c]Rev 13:1; 17:3, 7, 9ff [d]Dan 7:7, 20, 24; Rev 13:1; 17:12, 16 [e]Rev 13:1; 19:12
4 [a]Rev 8:7, 12 [b]Dan 8:10 [c]Is 27:1; Rev 12:3, 7, 9, 13, 16f; 13:2, 4, 11; 16:13; 20:2 [d]Matt 2:16
5 [1]Or *shepherd* [2]Or *Gentiles* [a]Is 66:7 [b]Ps 2:9; Rev 2:27 [c]2 Cor 12:2ff
6 [1]Lit *they would nourish her for* [a]Rev 11:3; 13:5
7 [a]Dan 10:13, 21; 12:1; Jude 9 [b]Rev 12:3 [c]Matt 25:41
9 [1]Lit *inhabited earth* [a]Rev 12:3 [b]Gen 3:1; 2 Cor 11:3; Rev 12:15; 20:2 [c]Matt 4:10; 25:41 [d]Rev 13:14; 20:3, 8, 10 [e]Luke 10:18; John 12:31
10 [a]Rev 11:15 [b]Rev 7:10 [c]Job 1:11; 2:5; Zech 3:1; Luke 22:31; 1 Pet 5:8
11 [1]Lit *to death* [a]John 16:33; 1 John 2:13; Rev 15:2 [b]Rev 7:14 [c]Rev 6:9 [d]Luke 14:26; Rev 2:10
12 [1]Or *tabernacle* [a]Ps 96:11; Is 44:23; Rev 18:20 [b]Rev 13:6 [c]Rev 8:13 [d]Rev 12:9 [e]Rev 10:6 **13** [a]Rev 12:3 [b]Rev 12:5 **14** [1]Lit *face* [a]Ex 19:4; Deut 32:11; Is 40:31 [b]Rev 12:6 [c]Dan 7:25; 12:7
15 [1]Lit *threw* [a]Gen 3:1; 2 Cor 11:3; Rev 12:9; 20:2 **16** [1]Lit *And* [2]Lit *threw*

God among His people. It was probably destroyed when Nebuzaradan destroyed the temple in Jerusalem (2 Kin 25:8–10). In the NT it symbolizes God's faithfulness in keeping covenant with His people. *lightning . . . hailstorm.* See note on 4:5.

12:1 *sign.* An extraordinary spectacle or event that points beyond itself (cf. Luke 21:11,25; Acts 2:19). *a woman clothed with the sun.* Probably a symbolic reference to the believing Messianic community (see v. 5). *twelve stars.* Cf. the 12 tribes of Israel.

12:2 *cried out . . . in pain.* Cf. the similar language describing the rebirth of Jerusalem in Is 66:7 (see Mic 4:10).

12:3 *red dragon.* Identified in v. 9 (cf. 20:2). Dragons abound in the mythology of ancient peoples (Leviathan in Canaanite lore and Set-Typhon, the red crocodile, in Egypt). In the OT they are normally used metaphorically to depict the enemies of God and of Israel (see Ps 74:14; Is 27:1; Ezek 29:3). *seven heads.* Symbolizing universal wisdom (cf. 13:1). *ten horns.* Symbolizing great power.

12:5 *a son, a male child.* The Messiah. *rod of iron.* See note on 2:27. *caught up to God.* The ascension of Christ.

12:6 *wilderness.* Not a wasteland but a place of spiritual refuge (cf. Hos 2:14). *one thousand two hundred and sixty days.* The time of spiritual protection corresponds to the time of persecution (see note on 11:2; cf. 13:5).

12:7 *Michael.* An archangel who defeats Satan in heavenly warfare. In Dan 12:1 he is the protector of Israel who will deliver her from tribulation in the last days.

12:9 *dragon was thrown down . . . to the earth.* Not the original casting of Satan out of heaven, but his final exclusion—an explanation of his intense hostility against God's people in the last days (vv. 12–17). *devil and Satan.* See notes on 2:9–10. *deceives.* Cf. 2 Cor 11:3; see also Luke 22:31; John 13:2.

12:10 *accuser.* See Job 1:9–11; Zech 3:1. Satan in Hebrew means "accuser."

12:11 *blood of the Lamb.* See note on 5:9; see also 1:5; 7:14.

12:12 *he has only a short time.* The period of final, intense hostility of Satan toward the people of God.

12:13–16 Cf. the similarity to the exodus.

12:14 *wilderness.* See note on v. 6. *a time and times and half a time.* One year plus two years plus half a year (see note on 11:2).

12:16 *earth opened its mouth.* In Num 16:30–33 the earth opened and swallowed Korah's men.

17 So the dragon was enraged with the
woman, and went off to [a]make war with the
rest of her [1b]children, who [c]keep the commandments of God and [d]hold to the testimony of Jesus.

The Beast from the Sea

13 And the dragon stood on the sand of
the [1]seashore.
Then I saw a [a]beast coming up out of the
sea, having [b]ten horns and [b]seven heads,
and on his horns *were* [c]ten diadems, and on
his heads *were* [d]blasphemous names.
2 And the beast which I saw was [a]like a
leopard, and his feet were like *those* of [b]a
bear, and his mouth like the mouth of [c]a
lion. And the [d]dragon gave him his power
and his [e]throne and great authority.
3 *I saw* one of his heads as if it had been
[1]slain, and his [a]fatal wound was healed. And
the whole earth [b]was amazed *and followed*
after the beast;
4 they worshiped the [a]dragon because he
[a]gave his authority to the beast; and they
worshiped the beast, saying, "[b]Who is like
the beast, and who is able to wage war with
him?"
5 There was given to him a mouth
[a]speaking [1]arrogant words and blasphemies,
and authority to act for [b]forty-two months
was given to him.
6 And he opened his mouth in blasphemies against God, to blaspheme His name
and His tabernacle, *that is*, [a]those who
[1]dwell in heaven.
7 It was also given to him to [a]make war
with the [1]saints and to overcome them, and
authority over [b]every tribe and people and
tongue and nation was given to him.
8 All who [a]dwell on the earth will worship him, *everyone* [b]whose name has not
been [1]written [c]from the foundation of the
world in the [d]book of life of [e]the Lamb who
has been slain.
9 [a]If anyone has an ear, let him hear.
10 [a]If anyone [1]*is destined* for captivity, to
captivity he goes; [b]if anyone kills with the
sword, with the sword he must be killed.
Here is [c]the [2]perseverance and the faith of
the [3]saints.

The Beast from the Earth

11 Then [a]I saw another beast coming up
out of the earth; and he had [b]two horns like
a lamb and he spoke as a [c]dragon.
12 He [a]exercises all the authority of the
first beast [1b]in his presence. And he makes
[c]the earth and those who dwell in it to [d]wor-
ship the first beast, whose [e]fatal wound was
healed.
13 He [a]performs great signs, so that he
even makes [b]fire come down out of heaven
to the earth in the presence of men.
14 And he [a]deceives [b]those who dwell on
the earth because of [c]the signs which it was
given him to perform [1d]in the presence of the
beast, telling those who dwell on the earth to
make an image to the beast who *had the
[e]wound of the sword and has come to life.
15 And it was given to him to give breath
to the image of the beast, so that the image
of the beast would even [1]speak and cause
[a]as many as do not [b]worship the image of
the beast to be killed.
16 And he causes all, [a]the small and the
great, and the rich and the poor, and the free

17 [1]Lit *seed* [a]Rev 11:7; 13:7 [b]Gen 3:15 [c]1 John 2:3; Rev 14:12 [d]Rev 1:2; 6:9; 14:12; 19:10
13:1 [1]Lit *sea* [a]Dan 7:3; Rev 11:7; 13:14, 15; 15:2; 16:13; 17:8 [b]Rev 12:3 [c]Rev 12:3; 17:12 [d]Dan 7:8; 11:36; Rev 17:3
2 [a]Dan 7:6; Hos 13:7f [b]Dan 7:5 [c]Dan 7:4 [d]Rev 12:3; 13:4, 12 [e]Rev 2:13; 16:10
3 [1]Lit *slaughtered to death* [a]Rev 13:12, 14 [b]Rev 17:8
4 [a]Rev 12:3; 13:2, 12 [b]Ex 15:11; Is 46:5; Rev 18:18
5 [1]Lit *great things* [a]Dan 7:8, 11, 20, 25; 11:36; 2 Thess 2:3f [b]Rev 11:2
6 [1]Or *tabernacle* [a]Rev 7:15; 12:12
7 [1]Or *holy ones* [a]Dan 7:21; Rev 11:7 [b]Rev 5:9
8 [a]Rev 3:10; 13:12, 14 [b]Rev 3:5
8 [1]Or *written in the book...slain from the foundation of the world* [c]Matt 25:34; Rev 17:8 [d]Ps 69:28 [e]Rev 5:6
9 [a]Rev 2:7
10 [1]Or *leads into captivity* [2]Or *steadfastness* [3]Or *holy ones* [a]Is 33:1; Jer 15:2; 43:11 [b]Gen 9:6; Matt 26:52; Rev 11:18 [c]Heb 6:12; Rev 14:12

11 [a]Rev 13:1; 16:13 [b]Dan 8:3 [c]Rev 13:4 12 [1]Or *by his authority* [a]Rev 13:4 [b]Rev 13:14; 19:20 [c]Rev 13:8 [d]Rev 13:15; 14:9, 11; 16:2; 19:20; 20:4 [e]Rev 13:3 13 [a]Matt 24:24; Rev 16:14; 19:20 [b]1 Kin 18:38; Luke 9:54; Rev 11:5; 20:9 14 [1]Or *by the authority of* [a]Rev 12:9 [b]Rev 13:8 [c]2 Thess 2:9f [d]Rev 13:12; 19:20 [e]Rev 13:3 15 [1]One early ms reads *speak, and he will cause* [a]Dan 3:3ff [b]Rev 13:12; 14:9, 11; 16:2; 19:20; 20:4
16 [a]Rev 11:18; 19:5, 18

12:17 *rest of her children.* Believers in general as contrasted with Christ, the male child of vv. 5,13. *testimony of Jesus.* The testimony that Jesus bore (cf. 1:2,9; 19:10).

13:1 *beast coming up out of the sea.* First mentioned in 11:7. According to some, the beast symbolizes the Roman empire, the deification of secular authority. According to others, he is the final, personal antichrist. The background seems to be Daniel's vision of the four great beasts (Dan 7:2–7). See 17:8–11 for the interpreting angel's explanation of the beast. *ten horns.* See 17:12. *blasphemous name.* Roman emperors tended to assume titles of deity. Domitian, e.g., was addressed as *Dominus et Deus noster* ("Our Lord and God").

13:2 *leopard . . . bear . . . lion.* John's beast combined characteristics of Daniel's four beasts (Dan 7:4–6). *dragon.* See note on 12:3.

13:3 *fatal wound . . . healed.* Emphasizes the tremendous recuperative power of the beast. *whole earth was amazed.* See 17:8 for the same reaction.

13:5 *was given.* Four times in the Greek text of vv. 5–7 the passive "was given" occurs, emphasizing the subordinate role of the beast (see vv. 2,4). *forty-two months.* See note on 11:2.

13:7 *make war.* See 12:17; see also Dan 7:7.

13:8 *book of life of the Lamb.* See note on 3:5. *Lamb who has been slain.* Cf. Is 53:7; John 1:29,36.

13:11 *another beast coming up out of the earth.* According to some, he symbolizes religious power in the service of secular authorities. According to others, he is the personal false prophet (see 16:13; 19:20; 20:10). *two horns like a lamb.* He attempts to appear gentle and harmless. *spoke as a dragon.* See Jesus' warning in Matt 7:15 about ravenous wolves who come in sheep's clothing.

13:12 *exercises all the authority of the first beast.* The trinity of evil is now complete. The beast from the earth is under the authority of the beast from the sea. The latter is subject to the dragon. Satan, secular power and religious compromise (or Satan, the antichrist and the false prophet) join against the cause of God: Father, Son and Holy Spirit.

13:13 *great signs.* See the warning in Deut 13:1–3; see also Matt 24:24; 2 Thess 2:9; cf. Rev 19:20. *fire . . . out of heaven.* See 1 Kin 18:24–39.

13:14 *make an image.* Cf. Dan 3:1–11; 2 Thess 2:4.

13:15 *would even speak.* Belief in statues that could speak is widely attested in ancient literature. Ventriloquism and other forms of deception were common.

men and the slaves, [1]to be given a [b]mark on
their right hand or on their forehead,
17 and *he provides* that no one will be able
to buy or to sell, except the one who has the
[a]mark, *either* [b]the name of the beast or [c]the
number of his name.
18 [a]Here is wisdom. Let him who has
understanding calculate the number of the
beast, for the number is that [b]of a man; and
his number is [1]six hundred and sixty-six.

The Lamb and the 144,000 on Mount Zion

14 Then I looked, and behold, [a]the Lamb
was standing on [b]Mount Zion, and
with Him [c]one hundred and forty-four thousand, having [d]His name and the [d]name of
His Father written [e]on their foreheads.
2 And I heard a voice from heaven, like
[a]the sound of many waters and like the
[b]sound of loud thunder, and the voice which
I heard *was* like *the sound* of [c]harpists playing on their harps.
3 And they *[1]sang [a]a new song before
the throne and before the [b]four living creatures and the [c]elders; and [d]no one could
learn the song except the [e]one hundred and
forty-four thousand who had been [a]pur-
chased from the earth.
4 [a]These are the ones who have not been
defiled with women, for they [1]have kept
themselves chaste. These *are* the ones who
[b]follow the Lamb wherever He goes. These
have been [c]purchased from among men [d]as
first fruits to God and to the Lamb.
5 And [a]no lie was found in their mouth;
they are [b]blameless.

16 [1]Lit *causes all,...that they give them a mark* [b]Gal 6:17; Rev 7:3; 14:9; 20:4
17 [a]Gal 6:17; Rev 7:3; 14:9; 20:4 [b]Rev 14:11 [c]Rev 15:2
18 [1]One early ms reads 616 [a]Rev 17:9 [b]Rev 21:17
14:1 [a]Rev 5:6 [b]Ps 2:6; Heb 12:22 [c]Rev 7:4; 14:3 [d]Rev 3:12 [e]Ezek 9:4; Rev 7:3
2 [a]Rev 1:15 [b]Rev 6:1 [c]Rev 5:8
3 [1]Two early mss read *sing* something *like a new song* [a]Rev 5:9 [b]Rev 4:6 [c]Rev 4:4 [d]Rev 2:17 [e]Rev 7:4; 14:1
4 [1]Lit *are chaste men* [a]Matt 19:12; 2 Cor 11:2; Eph 5:27; Rev 3:4 [b]Rev 3:4; 7:17; 17:14 [c]Rev 5:9 [d]Heb 12:23; James 1:18
5 [a]Ps 32:2; Zeph 3:13; Mal 2:6; John 1:47; 1 Pet 2:22 [b]Heb 9:14; 1 Pet 1:19; Jude 24

Vision of the Angel with the Gospel

6 And I saw another angel flying in [a]mid-
heaven, having [b]an eternal gospel to preach
to [c]those who [1]live on the earth, and to
[d]every nation and tribe and tongue and people;
7 and he said with a loud voice, "[a]Fear
God, and [b]give Him glory, because the hour
of His judgment has come; worship Him
who [c]made the heaven and the earth and sea
and [d]springs of waters."
8 And another angel, a second one, followed, saying, "[1a]Fallen, fallen is [b]Babylon
the great, she who has [c]made all the nations
drink of the [d]wine of the [2]passion of her
immorality."

Doom for Worshipers of the Beast

9 Then another angel, a third one, followed them, saying with a loud voice, "If
anyone [a]worships the beast and his [b]image,
and receives a [c]mark on his forehead or on
his hand,
10 he also will drink of the [a]wine of the
wrath of God, which is mixed [1]in full
strength [b]in the cup of His anger; and he will
be tormented with [c]fire and [2]brimstone in
the presence of the [d]holy angels and in the
presence of the Lamb.

6 [1]Lit *sit* [a]Rev 8:13 [b]1 Pet 1:25; Rev 10:7 [c]Rev 3:10 [d]Rev 5:9
7 [a]Rev 15:4 [b]Rev 11:13 [c]Rev 4:11 [d]Rev 8:10
8 [1]Lit *Babylon...fell, fell, she who* [2]Or *wrath* [a]Is 21:9; Jer 51:8; Rev 18:2 [b]Dan 4:30; Rev 16:19; 17:5; 18:10 [c]Jer 51:7 [d]Rev 17:2, 4; 18:3
9 [a]Rev 13:12; 14:11 [b]Rev 13:14f; 14:11 [c]Rev 13:16
10 [1]Lit *unmixed;* in ancient times wine was usually diluted with water [2]I.e. burning sulphur [a]Is 51:17; Jer 25:15f, 27; Rev 16:19; 19:15 [b]Ps 75:8; Rev 18:6 [c]Gen 19:24; Ezek 38:22; 2 Thess 1:7; Rev 19:20; 20:10, 14f; 21:8 [d]Mark 8:38

13:16 *mark.* Whatever its origin—possibly the branding of slaves or enemy soldiers, the sealing and stamping of official documents, or the sign of the cross on the forehead of a new Christian—the mark of the beast apparently symbolized allegiance to the demands of the imperial cult. In the final days of the antichrist it will be the ultimate test of loyalty (cf. v. 17; 14:9,11; 15:2; 16:2; 19:20; 20:4). It imitates the sealing of the servants of God in ch. 7.

13:17 *buy or to sell.* Economic boycott against all faithful believers. *number of his name.* In ancient times the letters of the alphabet served for numbers. Riddles using numerical equivalents for names were popular.

13:18 *six hundred and sixty-six.* Various schemes for decoding these numbers result in such names as Euanthas, Lateinos, and Nero Caesar. Others take 666 as a symbol for the trinity of evil and imperfection—each digit falls short of the perfect number 7.

14:1 *Lamb.* See note on 5:6. *Mount Zion.* In the OT it was first the fortress of the pre-Israelite city of Jerusalem (2 Sam 5:7), captured by David and established as his capital. Later it became a virtual synonym for Jerusalem. In Revelation, as in Heb 12:22–24, it is the heavenly Jerusalem, the eternal dwelling place of God and His people (cf. Gal 4:26). It comes down to the new earth in 21:2–3. *one hundred and forty-four thousand.* See note on 7:4. *name.* Contrast 13:16–18.

14:2 *harps.* See note on 5:8.

14:3 *new song.* See note on 5:9. The theme is deliverance.

14:4 *not been defiled with women.* Probably a symbolic description of believers who kept themselves from defiling relationships with the pagan world system. *follow the Lamb.* As His disciples (see Matt 19:21; Mark 8:34). *first fruits.* See Lev 23:9–14. The word is used figuratively in the NT for the first converts in an area (Rom 16:5) and the first to rise from the dead (1 Cor 15:20). In Revelation believers are considered as a choice offering to God and the Lamb.

14:5 *no lie.* Contrast Rom 1:25; see Is 53:9.

14:6 *eternal gospel.* The content of this "good news" is perhaps found in v. 7.

14:7 *Him who made the heaven.* See Ex 20:11; Ps 146:6.

14:8 *Babylon the great.* Ancient Babylon in Mesopotamia was the political, commercial and religious center of a world empire. It was noted for its luxury and moral decadence. The title "Babylon the Great" is taken from Dan 4:30. According to some, it is used in Revelation (e.g., here and in 16:19; 17:5; 18:2,10,21) for Rome as the center of opposition to God and His people. According to others, it represents the whole political and religious system of the world in general. According to still others, it is to be understood as literal Babylon—rebuilt and restored. Babylon's fall is proclaimed in Is 21:9; Jer 51:8. *wine of the passion of her immorality.* Here Babylon (Rome?) is pictured as a prostitute whose illicit relations are achieved by intoxication.

14:10 *cup of His anger.* In the OT God's wrath is commonly pictured as a cup of wine to be drunk (Ps 75:8; Is 51:17; Jer 25:15). It is not the outworking of impersonal laws of retribution, but the response of a righteous God to those who refuse His love and grace. *fire and brimstone.* Sodom and Gomorrah were destroyed by a rain of fire and brimstone (Gen 19:24). Ps 11:6 speaks of a similar fate for the wicked. The figure occurs else-

11 "And the [a]smoke of their torment goes
up forever and ever; [b]they have no rest day
and night, those who [c]worship the beast and
his [c]image, and [1]whoever receives the [d]mark
of his name."
12 Here is [a]the [1]perseverance of the
[2]saints who [b]keep the commandments of
God and [3c]their faith in Jesus.
13 And I heard a voice from heaven, saying, "Write, '[a]Blessed are the dead who [b]die
in the Lord from now on!'" "Yes," [c]says the
Spirit, "so that they may [d]rest from their
labors, for their [e]deeds follow with them."

The Reapers

14 Then I looked, and behold, a [a]white
cloud, and sitting on the cloud *was* one [b]like
[1]a son of man, having a golden [c]crown on
His head and a sharp sickle in His hand.
15 And another angel [a]came out of the
[1]temple, crying out with a loud voice to Him
who sat on the cloud, "[2b]Put in your sickle
and reap, for the hour to reap has come,
because the [c]harvest of the earth [3]is ripe."
16 Then He who sat on the cloud [1]swung
His sickle over the earth, and the earth was
reaped.
17 And another angel [a]came out of the
[1]temple which is in heaven, and he also had
a sharp sickle.
18 Then another angel, [a]the one who has
power over fire, came out from [b]the altar; and
he called with a loud voice to him who had
the sharp sickle, saying, "[1c]Put in your sharp
sickle and gather the clusters [2]from the vine
of the earth, [d]because her grapes are ripe."
19 So the angel [1]swung his sickle to the
earth and gathered *the clusters from* the vine
of the earth, and threw them into [a]the great
wine press of the wrath of God.

11 [1]Lit *if anyone* [a]Is 34:8-10; Rev 18:9, 18; 19:3 [b]Rev 4:8 [c]Rev 13:12; 14:9 [d]Rev 13:17
12 [1]Or *steadfastness* [2]Or *holy ones* [3]Lit *the faith of* [a]Rev 13:10 [b]Rev 12:17 [c]Rev 2:13
13 [a]Rev 20:6 [b]1 Cor 15:18; 1 Thess 4:16 [c]Rev 2:7; 22:17 [d]Heb 4:9ff; Rev 6:11 [e]1 Tim 5:25
14 [1]Or *the Son of Man* [a]Matt 17:5 [b]Dan 7:13; Rev 1:13 [c]Ps 21:3; Rev 6:2
15 [1]Or *sanctuary* [2]Lit *Send forth* [3]Lit *has become dry* [a]Rev 11:19; 14:17; 15:6; 16:17 [b]Joel 3:13; Mark 4:29; Rev 14:18 [c]Jer 51:33; Matt 13:39-41
16 [1]Lit *cast*
17 [1]Or *sanctuary* [a]Rev 11:19; 14:15; 15:6; 16:17
18 [1]Lit *Send forth* [2]Lit *of* [a]Rev 16:8 [b]Rev 6:9; 8:3 [c]Joel 3:13; Mark 4:29; Rev 14:15 [d]Joel 3:13
19 [1]Lit *cast* [a]Is 63:2f; Rev 19:15
20 [1]Lit *from* [2]Lit *sixteen hundred stadia;* a stadion was approx 600 ft [a]Is 63:3; Lam 1:15; Rev 19:15 [b]Heb 13:12; Rev 11:8 [c]Gen 49:11; Deut 32:14
15:1 [a]Rev 12:1, 3 [b]Rev 15:6-8; 16:1; 17:1; 21:9 [c]Lev 26:21 [d]Rev 9:20

20 And [a]the wine press was trodden [b]out-
side the city, and [c]blood came out from the
wine press, up to the horses' bridles, [1]for a
distance of [2]two hundred miles.

A Scene of Heaven

15 Then I saw [a]another sign in heaven,
great and marvelous, [b]seven angels
who had [c]seven plagues, *which are* [d]the last,
because in them the wrath of God is finished.
2 And I saw something like a [a]sea of
glass mixed with fire, and those who had
[b]been victorious [1]over the [c]beast and [d]his
image and the [e]number of his name, standing on the [a]sea of glass, holding [f]harps of
God.
3 And they *sang the [a]song of Moses,
[b]the bond-servant of God, and the [c]song of
the Lamb, saying,

"[d]Great and marvelous are Your
works,
[e]O Lord God, the Almighty;
Righteous and true are Your ways,
[f]King of the [1]nations!
4 "[a]Who will not fear, O Lord, and glorify
Your name?
For You alone are holy;
For [b]ALL THE NATIONS WILL COME AND
WORSHIP BEFORE YOU,
FOR YOUR [1c]RIGHTEOUS ACTS HAVE BEEN
REVEALED."

5 After these things I looked, and [a]the
[1]temple of the [b]tabernacle of testimony in
heaven was opened,

2 [1]Lit *from* [a]Rev 4:6 [b]Rev 12:11 [c]Rev 13:1 [d]Rev 13:14f [e]Rev 13:17 [f]Rev 5:8 **3** [1]Two early mss read *ages* [a]Ex 15:1ff [b]Josh 22:5; Heb 3:5 [c]Rev 5:9f, 12f [d]Deut 32:3f; Ps 111:2; 139:14 [e]Hos 14:9; Rev 1:8 [f]1 Tim 1:17
4 [1]Or *judgments* [a]Jer 10:7; Rev 14:7 [b]Ps 86:9; Is 66:23 [c]Rev 19:8
5 [1]Or *sanctuary* [a]Rev 11:19 [b]Ex 38:21; Num 1:50; Heb 8:5; Rev 13:6

---

where in the OT and the Apocrypha. It is used several times in the final chapters of Revelation (19:20; 20:10; 21:8).

14:11 *torment . . . forever and ever.* Revelation offers no support for the doctrine of the annihilation of the wicked (also compare 19:20 with 20:10).

14:13 *Blessed.* The second beatitude (see note on 1:3).

14:14 *son of man.* See 1:13 and notes on Dan 7:13; Mark 8:31. *golden crown.* A victory wreath of gold. See note on 2:10 for the comparison between the victory crown and the royal crown. *sickle.* The Israelite sickle used for cutting grain was normally a flint or iron blade attached to a curved shaft of wood or bone.

14:15 *harvest of the earth.* Symbolizes in a general way the coming judgment (see Matt 13:30,40–42). Some interpreters think it refers to the ingathering of the righteous at the return of Christ.

14:18 *another angel, the one who has power over fire.* The angel of 8:3–5. Fire is commonly associated with judgment (see Matt 18:8; Luke 9:54; 2 Thess 1:7). *sharp sickle.* The context suggests (in contrast to the sickle of v. 14) the smaller grape-knife with which the farmer cut the clusters of grapes from the vine.

14:19 *wine press.* A rock-hewn trough about eight feet square with a channel leading to a lower and smaller trough. Grapes were thrown into the upper vat and tramped with bare feet. The juice was collected in the lower vat. At times mechanical pressure was added. The treading of grapes was a common OT figure for the execution of divine wrath (see Is 63:3; Lam 1:15; Joel 3:13).

14:20 *outside the city.* Bloodshed would defile the city (see Joel 3:12–14; Zech 14:1–4; cf. Heb 13:12). *two hundred miles.* It is approximately the length of the Holy Land from north to south.

15:1–8 Introduces the last of the three sevenfold series of judgments—the bowls of wrath (see note on 8:2).

15:1 *wrath of God.* See note on 6:16.

15:2 *sea of glass.* See note on 4:6. *victorious over the beast.* Cf. the saints' victory over the devil in 12:11. *number of his name.* See notes on 13:16–18. *harps.* See note on 5:8.

15:3 *song of Moses.* See Ex 15; Deut 32. Ex 15:1–18 was sung on Sabbath evenings in the synagogue to celebrate Israel's great deliverance from Egypt. *song of the Lamb.* The risen Lord triumphed over His enemies in securing spiritual deliverance for His followers (cf. Ps 22). *Great and marvelous are Your works.* See Ex 15:11; Ps 92:5; 111:2. *Almighty.* See note on 1:8. *King of the nations!* See Jer 10:10; cf. 1 Tim 1:17.

15:4 Universal recognition of God is taught in both the OT (Ps 86:9; Is 45:22–23; Mal 1:11) and the NT (Phil 2:9–11).

15:5 *tabernacle of testimony.* The dwelling place of God during the wilderness wandering of the Israelites (see Ex 40:34–35).

6 and the [a]seven angels who had the seven plagues [b]came out of the [1]temple, clothed in [2]linen, clean *and* bright, and [c]girded around their chests with golden sashes.

7 Then one of the [a]four living creatures gave to the [b]seven angels seven [c]golden bowls full of the [d]wrath of God, who [e]lives forever and ever.

8 And the [1]temple was filled with [a]smoke from the glory of God and from His power; and no one was able to enter the [1]temple until the seven plagues of the seven angels were finished.

Six Bowls of Wrath

16 Then I heard a loud voice from [a]the [1]temple, saying to the [b]seven angels, "Go and [c]pour out [2]on the earth the seven bowls of the wrath of God."

2 So the first *angel* went and poured out his bowl [1a]on the earth; and it became a loathsome and malignant [b]sore on the [2]people [c]who had the mark of the beast and who worshiped his image.

3 The second *angel* poured out his bowl [a]into the sea, and it became blood like *that* of a dead man; and every living [1]thing in the sea died.

4 Then the third *angel* poured out his bowl into the [a]rivers and the springs of waters; and they [b]became blood.

5 And I heard the angel of the waters saying, "[a]Righteous are You, [b]who are and who were, O [c]Holy One, because You [d]judged these things;

6 for they poured out [a]the blood of saints and prophets, and You have given them [b]blood to drink. They [1]deserve it."

7 And I heard [a]the altar saying, "Yes, O [b]Lord God, the Almighty, [c]true and righteous are Your judgments."

8 The fourth *angel* poured out his bowl upon [a]the sun, [b]and it was given to it to scorch men with fire.

9 Men were scorched with [1]fierce heat; and they [a]blasphemed the name of God who has the power over these plagues, and they [b]did not repent so as to [c]give Him glory.

10 Then the fifth *angel* poured out his bowl on the [a]throne of the beast, and his kingdom became [b]darkened; and they gnawed their tongues because of pain,

11 and they [a]blasphemed the [b]God of heaven because of their pains and their [c]sores; and they [d]did not repent of their deeds.

12 The sixth *angel* poured out his bowl on the [a]great river, the Euphrates; and [b]its water was dried up, so that [c]the way would be prepared for the kings [d]from the [1]east.

Armageddon

13 And I saw *coming* out of the mouth of the [a]dragon and out of the mouth of the [b]beast and out of the mouth of the [c]false prophet, three [d]unclean spirits like [e]frogs;

14 for they are [a]spirits of demons, [b]performing signs, which go out to the kings of the [c]whole [1]world, to [d]gather them together for the war of the [e]great day of God, the Almighty.

15 ("Behold, [a]I am coming like a thief. [b]Blessed is the one who stays awake and keeps his clothes, [c]so that he will not walk about naked and men will not see his shame.")

16 And they [a]gathered them together to the place which [b]in Hebrew is called [1c]Har-Magedon.

6 [1]Or *sanctuary* [2]One early ms reads *stone* [a]Rev 15:1 [b]Rev 14:15 [c]Rev 1:13 **7** [a]Rev 4:6 [b]Rev 15:1 [c]Rev 5:8 [d]Rev 14:10; 15:1 [e]Rev 4:9 **8** [1]Or *sanctuary* [a]Ex 19:18; 40:34f; Lev 16:2; 1 Kin 8:10f; 2 Chr 5:13f; Is 6:4 **16:1** [1]Or *sanctuary* [2]Lit *into* [a]Rev 11:19 [b]Rev 15:1 [c]Ps 79:6; Jer 10:25; Ezek 22:31; Zeph 3:8; Rev 16:2ff **2** [1]Lit *into* [2]Gr *anthropoi* [a]Rev 8:7 [b]Ex 9:9-11; Deut 28:35; Rev 16:11 [c]Rev 13:15-17; 14:9 **3** [1]Lit *soul* [a]Ex 7:17-21; Rev 8:8f; 11:6 **4** [a]Rev 8:10 [b]Ex 7:17-20; Ps 78:44; Rev 11:6 **5** [a]John 17:25 [b]Rev 11:17 [c]Rev 15:4 [d]Rev 6:10 **6** [1]Lit *are worthy* [a]Rev 17:6; 18:24 [b]Is 49:26; Luke 11:49-51 **7** [a]Rev 6:9; 14:18 [b]Rev 1:8 [c]Rev 15:3; 19:2 **8** [a]Rev 6:12 [b]Rev 14:18 **9** [1]Lit *great* [a]Rev 16:11, 21 [b]Rev 2:21 [c]Rev 11:13 **10** [a]Rev 13:2 [b]Ex 10:21f; Is 8:22; Rev 8:12; 9:2 **11** [a]Rev 16:9, 21 [b]Rev 11:13 [c]Rev 16:2 [d]Rev 2:21 **12** [1]Lit *rising of the sun* [a]Rev 9:14 [b]Is 11:15f; 44:27; Jer 51:36 [c]Is 41:2, 25; 46:11 [d]Rev 7:2 **13** [a]Rev 12:3 [b]Rev 13:1 [c]Rev 13:11, 14; 19:20; 20:10 [d]Rev 18:2 [e]Ex 8:6 **14** [1]Lit *inhabited earth* [a]1 Tim 4:1 [b]Rev 13:13 [c]Rev 3:10 [d]1 Kin 22:21-23; Rev 17:14; 19:19; 20:8 [e]Rev 6:17 **15** [a]Matt 24:43f; Luke 12:39f; Rev 3:3, 11 [b]Luke 12:37 [c]Rev 3:18 **16** [1]Two early mss read *Armageddon* [a]Rev 19:19 [b]Rev 9:11 [c]Judg 5:19; 2 Kin 23:29f; 2 Chr 35:22; Zech 12:11

It was so named because the ancient tent contained the two tablets of the Testimony brought down from Mount Sinai (Ex 32:15; 38:21; Deut 10:5).

15:6 *seven plagues.* The last series of plagues (see v. 1). *golden sashes.* Symbolic of royal and priestly functions.

15:7 *wrath of God.* Cf. 2 Thess 1:7–9.

15:8 *filled with smoke.* Cf. Ex 40:34; 1 Kin 8:10–11; Ezek 44:4. Smoke symbolizes the power and glory of God.

16:2 *earth.* Compare the first four bowls (vv. 2–9) with the first four trumpets (8:7–12). *loathsome and malignant sore.* Cf. the boils and abscesses of the sixth Egyptian plague (Ex 9:9–11; see also Job 2:7–8,13). *mark of the beast.* See 13:16 and note.

16:4 *rivers and the springs of waters.* Cf. 8:10–11; see also Ps 78:44.

16:5 *You, who are and who were.* See note on 11:17; cf. Ex 3:14.

16:6 *given them blood to drink.* Punishment is tailored to fit the crime (see Is 49:26).

16:7 *altar.* Personified.

16:8 *fire.* Often connected with judgment in Scripture (see Deut 28:22; 1 Cor 3:13; 2 Pet 3:7).

16:9 *did not repent.* In 11:13 the nations were dazzled into homage by the great earthquake. Here they curse the name of God.

16:10 *throne of the beast.* Cf. Satan's throne in 2:13. "Throne" occurs 42 times in Revelation. The other 40 references are to the throne of God. *gnawed their tongues.* Cf. the scene in 6:15–17.

16:11 *God of heaven.* Used in Dan 2:44 of the sovereign God, who destroys the kingdoms of the world and establishes His universal and eternal reign.

16:12 *Euphrates.* See note on 9:14. *kings from the east.* Evidently Parthian rulers (17:15–18:24), to be distinguished from the "kings of the whole world" (v. 14), who wage the final war against Christ and the armies of heaven (19:11–21).

16:13 *frogs.* Lev 11:10 classifies the frog as an unclean animal. The imagery suggests the deceptive propaganda that will, in the last days, lead people to accept and support the cause of evil.

16:14 *signs.* Cf. 13:13. *kings of the whole world.* See 6:15. *great day of God.* See 19:11–21 for this battle.

16:15 *Blessed.* The third beatitude (see note on 1:3).

16:16 *Har-Magedon.* Or "Armageddon"; probably stands for Har Mageddon, "the mountain of Megiddo" (see note on Judg 5:19). Many see no specific geographical reference in the designation and take it to be a symbol of the final overthrow of evil by God.

Seventh Bowl of Wrath

17 Then the seventh *angel* poured out his bowl upon [a]the air, and a [b]loud voice came out of the [1c]temple from the throne, saying, "[d]It is done."

18 And there were flashes of [a]lightning and sounds and peals of thunder; and there was [b]a great earthquake, [c]such as there had not been since man came to be upon the earth, so great an earthquake *was it, and* so mighty.

19 [a]The great city was split into three parts, and the cities of the [1]nations fell. [b]Babylon the great was [c]remembered before God, to give her [d]the cup of the wine of [2]His fierce wrath.

20 And [a]every island fled away, and the mountains were not found.

21 And [a]huge [1]hailstones, about [2]one hundred pounds each, *came down from heaven upon men; and men [b]blasphemed God because of the [c]plague of the hail, because its plague *was extremely [3]severe.

The Doom of Babylon

17 [a]Then one of the [b]seven angels who had the [c]seven bowls came and spoke with me, saying, "Come here, I will show you [d]the judgment of the [e]great harlot who [f]sits on many waters,

2 with whom [a]the kings of the earth committed *acts of* immorality, and [b]those who dwell on the earth were [c]made drunk with the wine of her immorality."

3 And [a]he carried me away [1b]in the Spirit [c]into a wilderness; and I saw a woman sitting on a [d]scarlet beast, full of [e]blasphemous names, having [f]seven heads and ten horns.

4 The woman [a]was clothed in purple and scarlet, and [1]adorned with gold and precious [2]stones and pearls, having in her hand [b]a gold cup full of abominations and of the unclean things of her immorality,

5 and on her forehead a name *was* written, a [a]mystery, "[b]BABYLON THE GREAT, THE MOTHER OF HARLOTS AND OF [c]THE ABOMINATIONS OF THE EARTH."

6 And I saw the woman drunk with [a]the blood of the [1]saints, and with the blood of the witnesses of Jesus. When I saw her, I wondered [2]greatly.

7 And the angel said to me, "Why [1]do you wonder? I will tell you the [a]mystery of the woman and of the beast that carries her, which has the [b]seven heads and the ten horns.

8 "[a]The beast that you saw [b]was, and is not, and is about to [c]come up out of the [d]abyss and [1e]go to destruction. And [f]those who dwell on the earth, [g]whose name has not been written in the book of life [h]from the foundation of the world, will [i]wonder when they see the beast, that he was and is not and will come.

9 "[a]Here is the mind which has wisdom. The [b]seven heads are seven mountains on which the woman sits,

10 and they are seven [a]kings; five have fallen, one is, the other has not yet come; and when he comes, he must remain a little while.

11 "The beast which [a]was and is not, is himself also an eighth and is *one* of the seven, and he [b]goes to destruction.

12 "The [a]ten horns which you saw are ten kings who have not yet received a kingdom, but they receive authority as kings with the beast [b]for one hour.

13 "These have [a]one [1]purpose, and they give their power and authority to the beast.

Victory for the Lamb

14 "These will wage [a]war against the Lamb, and the Lamb will [b]overcome them, because He is [c]Lord of lords and [c]King of kings, and [d]those who are with Him *are the* [e]called and chosen and faithful."

17 [1]Or *sanctuary* [a]Eph 2:2 [b]Rev 11:15 [c]Rev 14:15 [d]Rev 10:6; 21:6
18 [a]Rev 4:5 [b]Rev 6:12 [c]Dan 12:1; Matt 24:21
19 [1]Or *Gentiles* [2]Lit *wrath of His anger* [a]Rev 11:8; 17:18; 18:10, 18f, 21 [b]Rev 14:8 [c]Rev 18:5 [d]Rev 14:10
20 [a]Rev 6:14; 20:11
21 [1]Lit *hail* [2]Lit *the weight of a talent* [3]Lit *great* [a]Rev 8:7; 11:19 [b]Rev 16:9, 11 [c]Ex 9:18-25
17:1 [a]Rev 1:1; 21:9 [b]Rev 15:1 [c]Rev 15:7 [d]Rev 16:19 [e]Is 1:21; Jer 2:20; Nah 3:4; Rev 17:5, 15f; 19:2 [f]Jer 51:13; Rev 17:15
2 [a]Rev 2:22; 18:3, 9 [b]Rev 3:10; 17:8 [c]Rev 14:8
3 [1]Or *in spirit* [a]Rev 21:10 [b]Rev 1:10 [c]Rev 12:6, 14; 21:10 [d]Matt 27:28; Rev 18:12, 16 [e]Rev 13:1 [f]Rev 12:3; 17:7, 9, 12, 16
4 [1]Lit *gilded* [2]Lit *stone* [a]Ezek 28:13; Rev 18:12, 16 [b]Jer 51:7; Rev 18:6
5 [a]2 Thess 2:7; Rev 1:20; 17:7 [b]Rev 14:8; 16:19

5 [c]Rev 17:2
6 [1]Or *holy ones* [2]Lit *with great wonder* [a]Rev 16:6
7 [1]Lit *have you wondered* [a]2 Thess 2:7; Rev 1:20; 17:5 [b]Rev 17:3
8 [1]One early ms reads *is going* [a]Dan 7:7 [b]Rev 13:3, 12, 14; 17:11 [c]Rev 11:7; 13:1 [d]Rev 9:1; 13:1 [e]Rev 13:10; 17:11 [f]Rev 3:10 [g]Ps 69:28; Rev 3:5 [h]Matt 25:34; Rev 13:8 [i]Rev 13:3
9 [a]Rev 13:18 [b]Rev 17:3
10 [a]Rev 10:11
11 [a]Rev 13:3, 12, 14; 17:8 [b]Rev 13:10; 17:8
12 [a]Dan 7:24; Rev 12:3; 13:1; 17:16 [b]Rev 18:10, 17, 19
13 [1]Or *mind* [a]Rev 17:17
14 [a]Rev 16:14 [b]Rev 3:21 [c]1 Tim 6:15; Rev 19:16 [d]Rev 2:10f [e]Matt 22:14

17:1 *seven angels.* Cf. 15:1; 16. *great harlot.* See v. 18 for the angel's own identification of this symbol. In 17:5 the harlot is named "Babylon the Great." *sits on many waters.* See Ps 137:1; Jer 51:13.

17:2 *wine of her immorality.* See note on 14:8; cf. 18:3; Is 23:17; Jer 51:7.

17:3 *in the Spirit.* In a state of spiritual ecstasy (see notes on 1:10; 4:2; see also 21:10). *scarlet beast.* The beast that rose out of the sea in ch. 13. *blasphemous names.* See note on 13:1.

17:5 *mystery.* See note on 14:8.

17:6 *saints . . . the witnesses.* See 6:9.

17:7 *mystery.* See note on 10:7.

17:8 *was, and is not, and is about to come.* An obvious imitation of the description of the Lamb (1:18; 2:8). Cf. the description of God in 1:4,8; 4:8. Here the phrase seems to mean that the beast appeared once, is not presently evident, but will in the future again make his presence known. Evil is persistent. *abyss.* See note on 9:1. *go to destruction.* Although evil is real and persistent, there is no uncertainty about its ultimate fate. *book of life.* See note on 3:5.

17:9 *seven mountains.* It is perhaps significant that Rome began as a network of seven hill settlements on the left bank of the Tiber. Her designation as the city on seven hills is commonplace among Roman writers (e.g., Virgil, Martial, Cicero).

17:10 *seven kings.* That seven heads symbolize both seven hills and seven kings illustrates the fluidity of apocalyptic symbolism, unless the hills are figurative for royal (or political) power. *five . . . one . . . the other.* Taken (1) as seven actual Roman emperors, (2) as seven secular empires or (3) symbolically as the power of the Roman empire as a whole.

17:11 *and is not.* Cf. 13:3. *an eighth.* The antichrist, who plays the role of a king ("is one of the seven") but is in reality part of the cosmic struggle between God and Satan.

17:12 *one hour.* A short time.

17:14 *Lord of lords and King of kings.* Emphasizes the supreme sovereignty of the Lamb (cf. Deut 10:17; Ps 136:2–3; Dan 2:47; 1 Tim 6:15).

15 And he *said to me, "The [a]waters which you saw where the harlot sits, are [b]peoples and multitudes and nations and tongues.

16 "And the [a]ten horns which you saw, and the beast, these will hate the harlot and will make her [b]desolate and [c]naked, and will [d]eat her flesh and will [e]burn her up with fire.

17 "For [a]God has put it in their hearts to execute His [1]purpose [2]by [b]having a common purpose, and by giving their kingdom to the beast, until the [c]words of God will be fulfilled.

18 "The woman whom you saw is [a]the great city, which [1]reigns over the kings of the earth."

Babylon Is Fallen

18 After these things I saw another [a]angel [b]coming down from heaven, having great authority, and the earth was [c]illumined with his glory.

2 And he cried out with a mighty voice, saying, "[1][a]Fallen, fallen is Babylon the great! She [b]has become a dwelling place of demons and a [2]prison of every [c]unclean spirit, and a [2]prison of every unclean and hateful bird.

3 "For all the nations [1]have drunk of the [a]wine of the [2]passion of her immorality, and [b]the kings of the earth have committed *acts of* immorality with her, and the [c]merchants of the earth have become rich by the [3]wealth of her [4][d]sensuality."

4 I heard another voice from heaven, saying, "[a]Come out of her, my people, so that you will not participate in her sins and receive of her plagues;

5 for her sins have [1][a]piled up as high as heaven, and God has [b]remembered her iniquities.

6 "[a]Pay her back even as she has paid, and [1]give back *to her* double according to her deeds; in the [b]cup which she has mixed, mix twice as much for her.

7 "[a]To the degree that she glorified herself and [b]lived [1]sensuously, to the same degree give her torment and mourning; for she says in her heart, '[c]I SIT *as* A QUEEN AND I AM NOT A WIDOW, and will never see mourning.'

8 "For this reason [a]in one day her plagues will come, [1]pestilence and mourning and famine, and she will be [b]burned up with fire; for the Lord God who judges her [c]is strong.

Lament for Babylon

9 "And [a]the kings of the earth, who committed *acts of* immorality and [b]lived [1]sensuously with her, will [c]weep and lament over her when they [d]see the smoke of her burning,

10 [a]standing at a distance because of the fear of her torment, saying, '[b]Woe, woe, [c]the great city, Babylon, the strong city! For in [d]one hour your judgment has come.'

11 "And the [a]merchants of the earth [b]weep and mourn over her, because no one buys their cargoes any more—

12 cargoes of [a]gold and silver and precious [1]stones and pearls and fine linen and purple and silk and scarlet, and every *kind of* citron wood and every article of ivory and every article *made* from very costly wood and [2]bronze and iron and marble,

13 and cinnamon and [1]spice and incense and perfume and frankincense and wine and olive oil and fine flour and wheat and cattle and sheep, and *cargoes* of horses and chariots and [2]slaves and [3][a]human lives.

14 "The fruit [1]you long for has gone from you, and all things that were luxurious and splendid have passed away from you and *men* will no longer find them.

15 "The [a]merchants of [b]these things, who became rich from her, will [c]stand at a distance because of the fear of her torment, weeping and mourning,

16 saying, '[a]Woe, woe, [b]the great city, she who [c]was clothed in fine linen and purple and scarlet, and [1]adorned with gold and precious [2]stones and pearls;

17 for in [a]one hour such great wealth has been laid [b]waste!' And [c]every shipmaster and every [1]passenger and sailor, and as many as make their living by the sea, [a]stood at a distance,

15 [a]Is 8:7; Jer 47:2; Rev 17:1 [b]Rev 5:9
16 [a]Rev 17:12 [b]Rev 18:17, 19 [c]Ezek 16:37, 39 [d]Rev 19:18 [e]Rev 18:8
17 [1]Or *mind* [2]Lit *even to do one mind and to give* [a]2 Cor 8:16 [b]Rev 17:13 [c]Rev 10:7
18 [1]Lit *has a kingdom* [a]Rev 11:8; 16:19
18:1 [a]Rev 17:1, 7 [b]Rev 10:1 [c]Ezek 43:2
2 [1]Lit *Babylon...fell, fell* [2]Or *haunt* [a]Is 21:9; Jer 51:8; Rev 14:8 [b]Is 13:21f; 34:11, 13-15; Jer 50:39; 51:37; Zeph 2:14f [c]Rev 16:13
3 [1]Two early ancient mss read *have fallen by* [2]Lit *wrath* [3]Lit *power* [4]Or *luxury* [a]Jer 51:7; Rev 14:8 [b]Rev 17:2; 18:9 [c]Ezek 27:9-25; Rev 18:11, 15, 19, 23 [d]1 Tim 5:11; Rev 18:7, 9
4 [a]Is 52:11; Jer 50:8; 51:6, 9, 45; 2 Cor 6:17
5 [1]Lit *joined together* [a]Jer 51:9 [b]Rev 16:19
6 [1]Lit *double* to her [a]Ps 137:8; Jer 50:15, 29 [b]Rev 17:4
7 [1]Or *luxuriously* [a]Ezek 28:2-8 [b]1 Tim 5:11; Rev 18:3, 9 [c]Is 47:7f; Zeph 2:15
8 [1]Lit *death* [a]Is 47:9; Jer 50:31f; Rev 18:10

8 [b]Rev 17:16 [c]Jer 50:34; Rev 11:17f
9 [1]Or *luxuriously* [a]Rev 17:2; 18:3 [b]1 Tim 5:11; Rev 18:3, 7 [c]Ezek 26:16f; 27:35 [d]Rev 14:11; 18:18; 19:3
10 [a]Rev 18:15, 17 [b]Rev 18:16, 19 [c]Rev 11:8; 16:19; 18:16, 18, 19, 21 [d]Rev 17:12; 18:8, 17, 19
11 [a]Ezek 27:9-25; Rev 18:3, 15, 19, 23 [b]Ezek 27:27-34 **12** [1]Lit *stone* [2]Or *brass* [a]Ezek 27:12-22; Rev 17:4 **13** [1]Gr *amomon* [2]Lit *bodies* [3]Lit *souls of people* (Gr *anthropoi*) [a]1 Chr 5:21; Ezek 27:13; 1 Tim 1:10 **14** [1]Lit *of your soul's desire* **15** [a]Rev 18:3 [b]Rev 18:12, 13 [c]Rev 18:10 **16** [1]Lit *gilded* [2]Lit *stone and pearl* [a]Rev 18:10, 19 [b]Rev 18:10, 18, 19, 21 [c]Rev 17:4 **17** [1]Lit *one who sails to a place* [a]Rev 18:10 [b]Rev 17:16; 18:19 [c]Ezek 27:28f

---

17:18 *great city.* Cf. 17:1; see notes on 11:8; 14:8.
18:1 *earth was illumined with his glory.* Cf. Ex 34:29–35; Ps 104:2; Ezek 43:1–5; 1 Tim 6:16.
18:2 *fallen is Babylon.* Cf. Is 21:9; Jer 51:8; see notes on 11:8; 14:8.
18:3 *wine of the passion of her immorality.* See note on 14:8.
18:4 *Come out of her.* A common prophetic warning (cf. Is 52:11; Jer 51:45; 2 Cor 6:17).
18:6 *double.* In full, sufficiently (see note on Is 40:2). *cup which she has mixed.* See 17:4.
18:7 *I AM NOT A WIDOW.* A claim that the men of Babylon have not died on battlefields.
18:9–20 Three groups lament: (1) kings (v. 9), (2) merchants (v. 11) and (3) seamen (v. 17). The passage is modeled after Ezekiel's lament over Tyre (Ezek 27). Fifteen of the 29 commodities in vv. 12–13 are also listed in Ezek 27:12–22.
18:9 *kings . . . weep and lament over her.* Probably because of their own great financial loss (see v. 11).
18:12 *purple.* An expensive dye since it must be extracted a drop at a time from the murex shellfish. *citron wood.* An expensive dark wood from north Africa—used for inlay work in costly furniture. *marble.* Used to decorate public buildings and the homes of the very rich.
18:13 *perfume and frankincense.* Brought by the magi as gifts for the infant Jesus (Matt 2:11). *slaves and human lives.* Slave trade.
18:17 *shipmaster.* The pilot of the ship rather than the owner. Both are mentioned in Acts 27:11.

18 and were [a]crying out as they [b]saw the smoke of her burning, saying, '[c]What *city* is like [d]the great city?'

19 "And they threw [a]dust on their heads and were crying out, weeping and mourning, saying, '[b]Woe, woe, the great city, in which all who had ships at sea [c]became rich by her [1]wealth, for in [b]one hour she has been laid [d]waste!'

20 "[a]Rejoice over her, O heaven, and you [1]saints and [b]apostles and prophets, because [c]God has [2]pronounced judgment for you against her."

21 Then [1]a [a]strong angel [b]took up a stone like a great millstone and threw it into the sea, saying, "So will Babylon, [c]the great city, be thrown down with violence, and [d]will not be found any longer.

22 "And [a]the sound of harpists and musicians and flute-players and trumpeters will not be heard in you any longer; and no craftsman of any craft will be found in you any longer; and the [b]sound of a mill will not be heard in you any longer;

23 and the light of a lamp will not shine in you any longer; and the [a]voice of the bridegroom and bride will not be heard in you any longer; for your [b]merchants were the great men of the earth, because all the nations were deceived [c]by your sorcery.

24 "And in her was found the [a]blood of prophets and of [1]saints and of [b]all who have been slain on the earth."

The Fourfold Hallelujah

19 After these things I heard something like a [a]loud voice of a great multitude in heaven, saying,

"[b]**H**allelujah! [c]Salvation and [d]glory and power belong to our God;

2 [a]BECAUSE HIS [b]JUDGMENTS ARE [c]TRUE AND RIGHTEOUS; for He has judged the [d]great harlot who was corrupting the earth with her immorality, and HE HAS [e]AVENGED THE BLOOD OF HIS BOND-SERVANTS [1]ON HER."

3 And a second time they said, "[a]Hallelujah! [b]HER SMOKE RISES UP FOREVER AND EVER."

4 And the [a]twenty-four elders and the [b]four living creatures [c]fell down and worshiped God who sits on the throne saying, "[d]Amen. [e]Hallelujah!"

5 And a voice came from the throne, saying,

"[a]**G**ive praise to our God, all you His bond-servants, [b]you who fear Him, the small and the great."

6 Then I heard *something* like [a]the voice of a great multitude and like [b]the sound of many waters and like the [c]sound of mighty peals of thunder, saying,

"[a]**H**allelujah! For the [d]Lord our God, the Almighty, reigns.

Marriage of the Lamb

7 "Let us rejoice and be glad and [a]give the glory to Him, for [b]the marriage of the Lamb has come and His [1c]bride has made herself ready."

8 It was given to her to clothe herself in [a]fine linen, bright *and* clean; for the fine linen is the [b]righteous acts of the [1]saints.

9 Then [a]he *said to me, "[b]Write, '[c]Blessed are those who are invited to the marriage supper of the Lamb.'" And he *said to me, "[d]These are true words of God."

10 Then [a]I fell at his feet to worship him. [b]But he *said to me, "Do not do that; I am a [c]fellow servant of yours and your brethren who [d]hold the testimony of Jesus; worship God. For the testimony of Jesus is the spirit of prophecy."

The Coming of Christ

11 And I saw [a]heaven opened, and behold, a [b]white horse, and He who sat on it *is* called [c]Faithful and True, and in [d]righteousness He judges and wages war.

12 His [a]eyes *are* a flame of fire, and on His head *are* many [b]diadems; and He has a [c]name written *on Him* which no one knows except Himself.

13 *He is* clothed with a [a]robe dipped in blood, and His name is called [b]The Word of God.

18 [a]Ezek 27:30 [b]Rev 18:9 [c]Ezek 27:32; Rev 13:4 [d]Rev 18:10
19 [1]Lit *costliness* [a]Josh 7:6; Job 2:12; Lam 2:10 [b]Rev 18:10 [c]Rev 18:3, 15 [d]Rev 17:16; 18:17
20 [1]Or *holy ones* [2]Lit *judged your judgment of her* [a]Jer 51:48; Rev 12:12 [b]Luke 11:49f [c]Rev 6:10; 18:6ff; 19:2
21 [1]Lit *one* [a]Rev 5:2; 10:1 [b]Jer 51:63f [c]Rev 18:10 [d]Ezek 26:21
22 [a]Is 24:8; Ezek 26:13; Matt 9:23 [b]Eccl 12:4; Jer 25:10
23 [a]Jer 7:34; 16:9 [b]Is 23:8; Rev 6:15; 18:3 [c]Nah 3:4; Rev 9:21
24 [1]Or *holy ones* [a]Rev 16:6; 17:6 [b]Matt 23:35
19:1 [a]Jer 51:48; Rev 11:15; 19:6 [b]Ps 104:35; Rev 19:3, 4, 6 [c]Rev 7:10 [d]Rev 4:11
2 [1]Lit *from her hand* [a]Ps 19:9 [b]Rev 6:10 [c]Rev 16:7 [d]Rev 17:1 [e]Deut 32:43; 2 Kin 9:7; Rev 16:6; 18:20
3 [a]Ps 104:35; Rev 19:1, 4, 6 [b]Is 34:10; Rev 14:11
4 [a]Rev 4:4, 10 [b]Rev 4:6 [c]Rev 4:10
4 [d]Ps 106:48; Rev 5:14 [e]Ps 104:35; Rev 19:3, 6
5 [a]Ps 22:23; 115:13; 134:1; 135:1 [b]Rev 11:18
6 [a]Jer 51:48; Rev 11:15; 19:1 [b]Ezek 1:24; Rev 1:15 [c]Rev 6:1 [d]Ps 93:1; 97:1; 99:1; Rev 1:8
7 [1]Lit *wife* [a]Rev 11:13 [b]Matt 22:2; 25:10; Luke 12:36; John 3:29; Eph 5:23, 32; Rev 19:9 [c]Matt 1:20; Rev 21:2, 9
8 [1]Or *holy ones* [a]Rev 15:6; 19:14 [b]Rev 15:4 **9** [a]Rev 17:1; 19:10 [b]Rev 1:19 [c]Matt 22:2f; Luke 14:15 [d]Rev 17:17; 21:5; 22:6
10 [a]Rev 22:8 [b]Acts 10:26; Rev 22:9 [c]Rev 1:1f [d]Rev 12:17
11 [a]Ezek 1:1; John 1:51; Rev 4:1 [b]Rev 6:2; 19:19, 21 [c]Rev 3:14 [d]Ps 96:13; Is 11:4 **12** [a]Dan 10:6; Rev 1:14 [b]Rev 6:2; 12:3 [c]Rev 2:17; 19:16 **13** [a]Is 63:3 [b]John 1:1

18:19 *threw dust on their heads.* An act of sorrow and dismay (see Ezek 27:30). *in one hour.* See vv. 10,17.

18:21 *great millstone.* Similar to the large millstone of Mark 9:42, which was actually a "donkey millstone" (one large enough to require a donkey to turn it).

18:24 *blood of prophets.* See 6:10; 17:6; 19:2; cf. Ezek 24:7.

19:1 *great multitude.* See note on 7:9. *Hallelujah!* Occurs four times in vv. 1–6 but nowhere else in the NT. It is derived from two Hebrew words meaning "Praise the LORD."

19:4 *twenty-four elders and the four living creatures.* See notes on 4:4,6.

19:7 *marriage of the Lamb.* The imagery of a wedding to express the intimate relationship between God and His people has its roots in the prophetic literature of the OT (e.g., Is 54:5–7; Hos 2:19). Cf. the NT usage (Matt 22:2–14; Eph 5:32).

19:9 *Blessed.* The fourth beatitude (see note on 1:3).

19:10 *fell at his feet.* See note on 1:17; cf. Acts 10:25. *spirit.* Essence.

19:11 *white horse.* Probably not the white horse of 6:2. The context here indicates that the rider is Christ returning as Warrior-Messiah-King.

19:12 *name written.* A secret name whose meaning is veiled from all created beings.

19:13 *robe dipped in blood.* Either the blood of the enemy shed in conflict (cf. 14:14–20; Is 63:1–3), or the blood of Christ shed to atone for sin.

14 And the armies which are in heaven, clothed in [a]fine linen, [b]white *and* clean, were following Him on white horses.

15 [a]From His mouth comes a sharp sword, so that [b]with it He may strike down the nations, and He will [1][c]rule them with a rod of iron; and [d]He treads the [2]wine press of the fierce wrath of God, the Almighty.

16 And on His robe and on His thigh He has [a]a name written, "[b]KING OF KINGS, AND LORD OF LORDS."

17 Then I saw [1]an angel standing in the sun, and he cried out with a loud voice, saying to [a]all the birds which fly in [b]midheaven, "[c]Come, assemble for the great supper of God,

18 so that you may [a]eat the flesh of kings and the flesh of [1]commanders and the flesh of mighty men and the flesh of horses and of those who sit on them and the flesh of all men, [b]both free men and slaves, and [c]small and great."

19 And I saw [a]the beast and [b]the kings of the earth and their armies assembled to make war against Him who [c]sat on the horse and against His army.

Doom of the Beast and False Prophet

20 And the beast was seized, and with him the [a]false prophet who [b]performed the signs [1][c]in his presence, by which he [d]deceived those who had received the [e]mark of the beast and those who [f]worshiped his image; these two were thrown alive into the [g]lake of [h]fire which burns with [2]brimstone.

21 And the rest were killed with the sword which [a]came from the mouth of Him who [b]sat on the horse, and [c]all the birds were filled with their flesh.

14 [a]Rev 19:8 [b]Rev 3:4; 19:8 **15** [1]Or *shepherd* [2]Lit *wine press of the wine of the wrath of God's anger* [a]Rev 1:16; 19:21 [b]Is 11:4; 2 Thess 2:8 [c]Ps 2:9; Rev 2:27 [d]Is 63:3; Joel 3:13; Rev 14:19, 20 **16** [a]Rev 2:17; 19:12 [b]Rev 17:14 **17** [1]Lit *one* [a]Rev 19:21 [b]Rev 8:13 [c]1 Sam 17:44; Jer 12:9; Ezek 39:17 **18** [1]I.e. chiliarchs, in command of one thousand troops [a]Ezek 39:18-20 [b]Rev 6:15 [c]Rev 11:18; 13:16; 19:5 **19** [a]Rev 11:7; 13:1 [b]Rev 16:14, 16 [c]Rev 19:11, 21 **20** [1]Or *by his authority* [2]I.e. burning sulphur [a]Rev 16:13 [b]Rev 13:13 [c]Rev 13:12 [d]Rev 13:14 [e]Rev 13:16f [f]Rev 13:12, 15 [g]Rev 20:10, 14f; 21:8 [h]Is 30:33; Dan 7:11; Rev 14:10 **21** [a]Rev 19:15 [b]Rev 19:11, 19 [c]Rev 19:17

Satan Bound

20 Then I saw [a]an angel coming down from heaven, holding the [b]key of the abyss and a great chain [1]in his hand.

2 And he laid hold of the [a]dragon, the serpent of old, who is the devil and Satan, and [b]bound him for a thousand years;

3 and he threw him into the [a]abyss, and shut *it* and [b]sealed *it* over him, so that he would [c]not deceive the nations any longer, until the thousand years were completed; after these things he must be released for a short time.

4 Then I saw [a]thrones, and [b]they sat on them, and [c]judgment was given to them. And I *saw* [d]the souls of those who had been beheaded because of [1]their [e]testimony of Jesus and because of the word of God, and those who had not [f]worshiped the beast or his image, and had not received the [g]mark on their forehead and on their hand; and they [h]came to life and [i]reigned with Christ for a thousand years.

5 The rest of the dead did not come to life until the thousand years were completed. [a]This is the first resurrection.

6 [a]Blessed and holy is the one who has a part in the first resurrection; over these the [b]second death has no power, but they will be [c]priests of God and of Christ and will [d]reign with Him for a thousand years.

20:1 [1]Lit *upon* [a]Rev 10:1 [b]Rev 1:18; 9:1 **2** [a]Gen 3:1; Rev 12:9 [b]Is 24:22; 2 Pet 2:4; Jude 6 **3** [a]Rev 20:1 [b]Dan 6:17; Matt 27:66 [c]Rev 12:9; 20:8, 10 **4** [1]Lit *the* [a]Dan 7:9 [b]Matt 19:28; Rev 3:21 [c]Dan 7:22; 1 Cor 6:2 [d]Rev 6:9 [e]Rev 1:9 [f]Rev 13:12, 15 [g]Rev 13:16f [h]John 14:19 [i]Rev 3:21; 5:10; 20:6; 22:5 **5** [a]Luke 14:14; Phil 3:11; 1 Thess 4:16 **6** [a]Rev 14:13 [b]Rev 2:11; 20:14 [c]Rev 1:6 [d]Rev 3:21; 5:10; 20:4; 22:5

19:14 *armies . . . in heaven.* Angelic beings (cf. Deut 33:2; Ps 68:17); possibly also believers (cf. 17:14).
19:15 *sharp sword.* See note on 1:16. *rod of iron.* See note on 2:27. *wine press.* See note on 14:19.
19:16 *KING OF KINGS.* See note on 17:14.
19:17 *great supper of God.* A grim contrast to the "marriage supper of the Lamb" (v. 9; cf. Ezek 39:17–20).
19:20 *beast . . . false prophet.* See notes on 13:1,11. *lake of fire which burns with brimstone.* See 20:10,14–15; 21:8. Punishment by fire is prominent in both Biblical and non-Biblical Jewish writings (e.g., 1 Enoch 54:1). Although the designation *gehenna* is not used here, this is what John refers to (see note on Matt 5:22). Originally the site of a cultic shrine where human sacrifices were offered (2 Kin 16:3; 23:10; Jer 7:31), it came to be equated with the "hell" of final judgment in apocalyptic literature.
19:21 *birds were filled with their flesh.* The "great supper of God" of vv. 17–18.
20:1–22:21 These last three chapters reflect many of the subjects and themes of the first three chapters of Genesis.
20:1 *abyss.* See note on 9:1.
20:2 *dragon.* See note on 12:3. *serpent of old.* See 12:15; Gen 3:1–5. *thousand years.* The millennium (from the Latin *mille,* "thousand," and *annus,* "year"). It is taken literally by some as 1,000 actual years, while others interpret it metaphorically as a long but undetermined period of time. There are three basic approaches to the subject of the millennium: 1. Amillennialism: The millennium describes the present reign of the souls of deceased believers with Christ in heaven. The present form of God's kingdom will be followed by Christ's return, the general resurrection, the final judgment and Christ's continuing reign over the perfect kingdom on the new earth in the eternal state. 2. Premillennialism: The present form of God's kingdom is moving toward a grand climax when Christ will return, the first resurrection will occur and His kingdom will find expression in a literal, visible reign of peace and righteousness on the earth in space-time history. After the final resurrection, the last judgment and the renewal of the heavens and the earth, this future, temporal kingdom will merge into the eternal kingdom, and the Lord will reign forever on the new earth. 3. Postmillennialism: The world will eventually be Christianized, resulting in a long period of peace and prosperity called the millennium. This future period will close with Christ's second coming, the resurrection of the dead, the final judgment and the eternal state.
20:3 *released for a short time.* See vv. 7–10.
20:4 *souls of those who had been beheaded.* See 6:9–11. *the mark.* See note on 13:16. *came to life.* The "first resurrection" (v. 5).
20:5 *rest of the dead.* Either the wicked or everyone except the martyrs (see v. 4).
20:6 *Blessed.* The fifth beatitude (see note on 1:3). *second death.* Defined in v. 14 as the "lake of fire" (cf. 21:8).

Satan Freed, Doomed

7 When the thousand years are completed, Satan will be [a]released from his prison,

8 and will come out to [a]deceive the nations which are in the [b]four corners of the earth, [c]Gog and Magog, to [d]gather them together for the war; the number of them is like the [e]sand of the [1]seashore.

9 And they [a]came up on the [1]broad plain of the earth and surrounded the [b]camp of the [2]saints and the [c]beloved city, and [d]fire came down from heaven and devoured them.

10 And [a]the devil who [a]deceived them was thrown into the [b]lake of fire and [1]brimstone, where the [c]beast and the [c]false prophet are also; and they will be [d]tormented day and night forever and ever.

Judgment at the Throne of God

11 Then I saw a great white [a]throne and Him who sat upon it, from whose [1]presence [b]earth and heaven fled away, and [c]no place was found for them.

12 And I saw the dead, the [a]great and the small, standing before the throne, and [1b]books were opened; and another [2]book was opened, which is [c]*the book* of life; and the dead [a]were judged from the things which were written in the [1]books, [d]according to their deeds.

13 And the sea gave up the dead which were in it, and [a]death and Hades [b]gave up the dead which were in them; and they were judged, every one *of them* [c]according to their deeds.

14 Then [a]death and Hades were thrown into [b]the lake of fire. This is the [c]second death, the lake of fire.

15 And if [1]anyone's name was not found written in [a]the book of life, he was thrown into the lake of fire.

The New Heaven and Earth

21 Then I saw [a]a new heaven and a new earth; for [b]the first heaven and the first earth passed away, and there is no longer *any* sea.

2 And I saw [a]the holy city, [b]new Jerusalem, [c]coming down out of heaven from God, [d]made ready as a bride adorned for her husband.

3 And I heard a loud voice from the throne, saying, "Behold, [a]the tabernacle of God is among men, and He will [1b]dwell among them, and they shall be His people, and God Himself will be among them[2],

4 and He will [a]wipe away every tear from their eyes; and [b]there will no longer be *any* death; [c]there will no longer be *any* mourning, or crying, or pain; [d]the first things have passed away."

5 And [a]He who sits on the throne said, "Behold, I am [b]making all things new." And He *said, "Write, for [c]these words are faithful and true."

6 Then He said to me, "[1a]It is done. I am the [b]Alpha and the Omega, the beginning and the end. [c]I will give to the one who thirsts from the spring of the [d]water of life without cost.

7 "[a]He who overcomes will inherit these things, and [b]I will be his God and he will be My son.

8 "[a]But for the cowardly and [1]unbelieving and abominable and murderers and immoral persons and sorcerers and idolaters and all liars, their part *will be* in [b]the lake that burns with fire and [2]brimstone, which is the [c]second death."

9 [a]Then one of the seven angels who had the [b]seven bowls [1]full of the [c]seven last plagues came and spoke with me, saying, "[a]Come here, I will show you the [d]bride, the wife of the Lamb."

The New Jerusalem

10 And [a]he carried me away [1b]in the Spirit to a great and high mountain, and showed me [c]the holy city, Jerusalem, coming down out of heaven from God,

11 having [a]the glory of God. Her [1]brilliance was like a very costly stone, as a [b]stone of [c]crystal-clear jasper.

12 [1]It had a great and high wall, [1a]with twelve [b]gates, and at the gates twelve angels;

7 [a]Rev 20:2f **8** [1]Lit *sea* [a]Rev 12:9; 20:3, 10 [b]Ezek 7:2; Rev 7:1 [c]Ezek 38:2; 39:1, 6 [d]Rev 16:14 [e]Heb 11:12 **9** [1]Lit *breadth of the earth* [2]Or *holy ones* [a]Ezek 38:9, 16 [b]Deut 23:14 [c]Ps 87:2 [d]Ezek 38:22; 39:6; Rev 13:13 **10** [1]I.e. burning sulphur [a]Rev 20:2f [b]Rev 19:20; 20:14, 15 [c]Rev 16:13 [d]Rev 14:10f **11** [1]Lit *face* [a]Rev 4:2 [b]Rev 6:14; 21:1 [c]Dan 2:35; Rev 12:8 **12** [1]Or *scrolls* [2]Or *scroll* [a]Rev 11:18 [b]Dan 7:10 [c]Rev 3:5; 20:15 [d]Matt 16:27; Rev 2:23; 20:13 **13** [a]1 Cor 15:26; Rev 1:18; 6:8; 21:4 [b]Is 26:19 [c]Matt 16:27; Rev 2:23; 20:12 **14** [a]1 Cor 15:26; Rev 1:18; 6:8; 21:4 [b]Rev 19:20; 20:10, 15 [c]Rev 20:6 **15** [1]Lit *anyone was* [a]Rev 3:5; 20:12 **21:1** [a]Is 65:17; 66:22; 2 Pet 3:13 [b]2 Pet 3:10; Rev 20:11 **2** [a]Is 52:1; Rev 11:2; 21:10; 22:19 [b]Rev 3:12; 21:10 [c]Heb 11:10, 16; Rev 21:10 [d]Is 61:10; Rev 19:7; 21:9; 22:17

3 [1]Or *tabernacle* [2]One early ms reads, and be *their God* [a]Lev 26:11f; Ezek 37:27; 48:35; Heb 8:2; Rev 7:15 [b]John 14:23; 2 Cor 6:16 **4** [a]Is 25:8; Rev 7:17 [b]1 Cor 15:26; Rev 20:14 [c]Is 35:10; 51:11; 65:19 [d]2 Cor 5:17; Heb 12:27 **5** [a]Rev 4:9; 20:11 [b]2 Cor 5:17; Heb 12:27 [c]Rev 19:9; 22:6 **6** [1]Lit *They are* [a]Rev 10:6; 16:17 [b]Rev 1:8; 22:13 [c]Is 55:1; John 4:10; Rev 7:17; 22:17 [d]Rev 7:17 **7** [a]Rev 2:7 [b]2 Sam 7:14; Ps 89:26f; 2 Cor 6:16, 18; Rev 21:3 **8** [1]Or *untrustworthy* [2]I.e. burning sulphur [a]1 Cor 6:9; Gal 5:19-21; Rev 9:21; 21:27; 22:15 [b]Rev 19:20 [c]Rev 2:11 **9** [1]Lit *who were full* [a]Rev 17:1 [b]Rev 15:7 [c]Rev 15:1 [d]Rev 19:7; 21:2 **10** [1]Or *in spirit* [a]Ezek 40:2; Rev 17:3 [b]Rev 1:10 [c]Rev 21:2 **11** [1]Lit *luminary* [a]Is 60:1f; Ezek 43:2; Rev 15:8; 21:23; 22:5 [b]Rev 4:3; 21:18, 19 [c]Rev 4:6 **12** [1]Lit *having* [a]Ezek 48:31-34 [b]Rev 21:15, 21, 25; 22:14

20:7 *thousand years.* See note on v. 2.
20:8 *Gog and Magog.* Symbolize the nations of the world as they band together for a final assault on God. The OT background is Ezek 38–39.
20:10 *tormented day and night.* See note on 14:11; cf. 14:10.
20:12 *book of life.* See note on 3:5. *judged . . . according to their deeds.* The principle of judgment on the basis of works is taught in Ps 62:12; Jer 17:10; Rom 2:6; 1 Pet 1:17 and elsewhere.
20:13 *death and Hades.* See 6:8 and note.
20:14–15 *lake of fire.* See note on 19:20.
21:2–22:5 The "holy city" combines elements of Jerusalem, the temple and the Garden of Eden.
21:2 *bride.* See note on 19:7.
21:3 *tabernacle of God.* See Lev 26:11–12; Ezek 37:27; 2 Cor 6:16.
21:4 *wipe away every tear.* See 7:17; Is 25:8.
21:6 *the Alpha and the Omega.* See note on 1:8. *water of life.* Cf. Ps 36:9.
21:7 *He who overcomes.* Cf. the emphasis on overcoming in the seven letters (2:7,11,17,26; 3:5,12,21).
21:8 *sorcerers.* Cf. Acts 19:19. The magical tradition in ancient times called for the mixing of various herbs to ward off evil. *lake that burns with fire and brimstone.* See note on 19:20.
21:9 *seven last plagues.* See 15:1.
21:10 *in the Spirit.* See notes on 1:10; 4:2; 17:3.
21:12 *twelve gates.* See Ezek 48:30–35. The number 12 probably emphasizes the continuity of the NT church and the OT

and names *were* written on them, which are
the names of the twelve tribes of the sons of
Israel.
13 *There were* three gates on the east and
three gates on the north and three gates on
the south and three gates on the west.
14 And the wall of the city had [a]twelve
foundation stones, and on them *were* the
twelve names of the [b]twelve apostles of the
Lamb.
15 The one who spoke with me had a
[1]gold measuring [a]rod to measure the city,
and its [b]gates and its wall.
16 The city is laid out as a square, and its
length is as great as the width; and he measured the city with the [1]rod, [2]fifteen hundred
miles; its length and width and height are
equal.
17 And he measured its wall, [1]seventy-
two yards, *according to* [a]human [2]measure-
ments, which are *also* [b]angelic *measurements.*
18 The material of the wall was [a]jasper;
and the city was [b]pure gold, like [1]clear
[c]glass.
19 [a]The foundation stones of the city wall
were adorned with every kind of precious
stone. The first foundation stone was
[b]jasper; the second, sapphire; the third, chal-
cedony; the fourth, [c]emerald;
20 the fifth, sardonyx; the sixth, [a]sardius;
the seventh, chrysolite; the eighth, beryl; the
ninth, topaz; the tenth, chrysoprase; the
eleventh, jacinth; the twelfth, amethyst.
21 And the twelve [a]gates were twelve
[b]pearls; each one of the gates was a single
pearl. And the street of the city was [c]pure
gold, like transparent [d]glass.
22 I saw [a]no [1]temple in it, for the [b]Lord
God the Almighty and the [c]Lamb are its
[1]temple.
23 And the city [a]has no need of the sun or
of the moon to shine on it, for [b]the glory of
God has illumined it, and its lamp *is* the
[c]Lamb.
24 [a]The nations will walk by its light, and
the [b]kings of the earth [1]will bring their glory
into it.
25 In the daytime (for [a]there will be no
night there) [b]its gates [c]will never be closed;
26 and [a]they will bring the glory and the
honor of the nations into it;
27 and [a]nothing unclean, and no one who
practices abomination and lying, shall ever
come into it, but only those [1]whose names
are [b]written in the Lamb's book of life.

The River and the Tree of Life

22 Then [a]he showed me a [b]river of the
[c]water of life, [1]clear [d]as crystal, coming
from the throne of God and of [2]the Lamb,
2 in the middle of [a]its street. [b]On either
side of the river was [c]the tree of life, bearing
twelve [1]*kinds of* fruit, yielding its fruit every
month; and the leaves of the tree were for
the healing of the nations.
3 [a]There will no longer be any curse; and
[b]the throne of God and of the Lamb will be
in it, and His bond-servants will [c]serve Him;
4 they will [a]see His face, and His [b]name
will be on their [c]foreheads.
5 And [a]there will no longer be *any* night;
and they [1]will not have need [b]of the light of
a lamp nor the light of the sun, because the
Lord God will illumine them; and they will
[c]reign forever and ever.
6 And [a]he said to me, "[b]These words are
faithful and true"; and the Lord, the [c]God of
the spirits of the prophets, [d]sent His angel to
show to His bond-servants the things which
must soon take place.
7 "And behold, [a]I am coming quickly.
[b]Blessed is he who [1]heeds [c]the words of the
prophecy of this book."
8 [a]I, John, am the one who heard and
saw these things. And when I heard and saw,
[b]I fell down to worship at the feet of the
angel who showed me these things.
9 But [a]he *said to me, "Do not do that. I
am a [b]fellow servant of yours and of your
brethren the prophets and of those who
[1]heed the words of [c]this book. Worship
God."

The Final Message

10 And he *said to me, "[a]Do not seal up
[b]the words of the prophecy of this book, [c]for
the time is near.
11 "[a]Let the one who does wrong, still do
wrong; and the one who is filthy, still be

14 [a]Heb 11:10 [b]Acts 1:26 **15** [1]Lit *measure, a gold reed* [a]Ezek 40:3; Rev 11:1 [b]Rev 21:12, 21, 25 **16** [1]Lit *reed* [2]Lit *twelve thousand stadia;* a stadion was approx 600 ft **17** [1]Lit *one hundred forty-four cubits* [2]Lit *measure* [a]Deut 3:11; Rev 13:18 [b]Rev 21:9 **18** [1]Lit *pure* [a]Rev 21:11 [b]Rev 21:21 [c]Rev 4:6 **19** [a]Ex 28:17-20; Is 54:11f; Ezek 28:13 [b]Rev 21:11 [c]Rev 4:3 **20** [a]Rev 4:3 **21** [a]Rev 21:12, 15, 25 [b]Rev 17:4 [c]Rev 21:18 [d]Rev 4:6 **22** [1]Or *sanctuary* [a]Matt 24:2; John 4:21 [b]Rev 1:8 [c]Rev 5:6; 7:17; 14:4 **23** [a]Is 24:23; 60:19, 20; Rev 21:25; 22:5 [b]Rev 21:11 [c]Rev 5:6; 7:17; 14:4 **24** [1]Lit *bring* [a]Is 60:3, 5 [b]Ps 72:10f; Is 49:23; 60:16; Rev 21:26 **25** [a]Zech 14:7; Rev 21:23; 22:5 [b]Rev 21:12, 15 [c]Is 60:11 **26** [a]Ps 72:10f; Is 49:23; 60:16 **27** [a]Is 52:1; Ezek 44:9; Zech 14:21; Rev 22:14f

27 [1]Lit *who have been* [b]Rev 3:5 **22:1** [1]Lit *bright* [2]Or *the Lamb. In the middle of its street, and on either side of the river, was* [a]Rev 1:1; 21:9; 22:6 [b]Ps 46:4; Ezek 47:1 [c]Zech 14:8; Rev 7:17; 22:17 [d]Rev 4:6 **2** [1]Or *crops of fruit* [a]Rev 21:21 [b]Ezek 47:12 [c]Gen 2:9; Rev 2:7; 22:14, 19 **3** [a]Zech 14:11 [b]Rev 21:3 [c]Rev 7:15 **4** [a]Ps 17:15; 42:2; Matt 5:8 [b]Rev 14:1 [c]Rev 7:3 **5** [1]Lit *do not have* [a]Zech 14:7; Rev 21:25 [b]Is 60:19; Rev 21:23 [c]Dan 7:18, 27; Matt 19:28; Rom 5:17; Rev 20:4 **6** [a]Rev 1:1; 21:9 [b]Rev 19:9; 21:5 [c]1 Cor 14:32; Heb 12:9 [d]Rev 1:1; 22:16 **7** [1]Lit *keeps* [a]Rev 1:3; 3:3, 11; 16:15; 22:12, 20 [b]Rev 1:3; 16:15 [c]Rev 1:11; 22:9, 10, 18f **8** [a]Rev 1:1 [b]Rev 19:10 **9** [1]Lit *keep* [a]Rev 19:10 [b]Rev 1:1 [c]Rev 1:11; 22:10, 18f **10** [a]Dan 8:26; Rev 10:4 [b]Rev 1:11; 22:9, 18f [c]Rev 1:3 **11** [a]Ezek 3:27; Dan 12:10

people of God. See v. 14, where the 12 foundations bear the names of the 12 apostles.

21:15 *measure the city.* Cf. Ezek 40–41. In Rev 11 the measuring was to ensure protection; here it serves to show the size and symmetry of the eternal dwelling place of the faithful.

21:16 *length and wide and height.* Thus a perfect cube, as was the most holy place of the tabernacle and the temple.

21:20 The precise identification of some of these precious stones is uncertain.

21:27 *Lamb's book of life.* See note on 3:5.

22:2 *tree of life.* See Gen 2:9; 3:22; Ezek 47:12.

22:4 *they will see His face.* In ancient times criminals were banished from the presence of the king (Esth 7:8; cf. 2 Sam 14:24). One blessing of eternity will be to see the Lord face to face (cf. 1 Cor 13:12). *His name.* See note on 3:12.

22:5 *they will reign.* See 5:10; 20:6; Dan 7:18,27.

22:6 *His bond-servants.* See v. 3. *things which must soon take place.* See 1:1,19.

22:7 *I am coming quickly.* See vv. 12,20; 2:16; 3:11. *Blessed.* The sixth beatitude (see note on 1:3).

22:8 *fell down to worship.* See note on 1:17.

22:10 *Do not seal up the words.* Contrast Dan 12:4.

filthy; and let the one who is righteous, still
practice righteousness; and the one who is
holy, still keep himself holy."
12"Behold, [a]I am coming quickly, and My
[b]reward *is* with Me, [c]to render to every man
[1]according to what he has done.
13"I am the [a]Alpha and the Omega, [b]the
first and the last, [c]the beginning and the
end."
14 Blessed are those who [a]wash their
robes, so that they may have the right to [b]the
tree of life, and may [c]enter by the [d]gates into
the city.
15 [a]Outside are the [b]dogs and the sorcerers and the immoral persons and the murderers and the idolaters, and everyone who
loves and practices lying.
16"[a]I, Jesus, have sent [b]My angel to testify to you these things [1c]for the churches. I
am [d]the root and the [e]descendant of David,
the bright [f]morning star."
17 The [a]Spirit and the [b]bride say, "Come."
And let the one who hears say, "Come." And
[c]let the one who is thirsty come; let the one
who wishes take the [d]water of life without
cost.
18 I testify to everyone who hears [a]the
words of the prophecy of this book: if anyone [b]adds to them, God will add to him [c]the
plagues which are written in [d]this book;
19 and if anyone [a]takes away from the
[b]words of the book of this prophecy, God
will take away his part from [c]the tree of life
and [1]from the holy city, [d]which are written
in this book.
20 He who [a]testifies to these things says,
"Yes, [b]I am coming quickly." Amen. [c]Come,
Lord Jesus.
21 [a]The grace of the Lord Jesus be with
[1]all. Amen.

12 [1]Lit *as his work is* [a]Rev 22:7 [b]Is 40:10; 62:11 [c]Ps 28:4; Jer 17:10; Matt 16:27; Rev 2:23
13 [a]Rev 1:8 [b]Is 44:6; 48:12; Rev 1:17; 2:8 [c]Rev 21:6
14 [a]Rev 7:14 [b]Gen 2:9; 3:22; Rev 22:2 [c]Rev 21:27 [d]Rev 21:12
15 [a]Matt 8:12; 1 Cor 6:9f; Gal 5:19ff; Rev 21:8 [b]Deut 23:18; Matt 7:6; Phil 3:2
16 [1]Or *concerning* [a]Rev 1:1 [b]Rev 1:1; 22:6 [c]Rev 1:4, 11; 3:22 [d]Rev 5:5 [e]Matt 1:1 [f]Matt 2:2; Rev 2:28
17 [a]Rev 2:7; 14:13 [b]Rev 21:2, 9
17 [c]Is 55:1; Rev 21:6 [d]Rev 7:17; 22:1 **18** [a]Rev 22:7 [b]Deut 4:2; 12:32; Prov 30:6 [c]Rev 15:6-16:21 [d]Rev 22:7 **19** [1]Lit *out of* [a]Deut 4:2; 12:32; Prov 30:6 [b]Rev 22:7 [c]Rev 22:2 [d]Rev 21:10-22:5 **20** [a]Rev 1:2 [b]Rev 22:7 [c]1 Cor 16:22 **21** [1]One early ms reads *the saints* [a]Rom 16:20

22:12 *I am coming quickly.* See vv. 7,20; 2:16; 3:11. *according to what he has done.* See notes on 2:23; 20:12.
22:13 *the Alpha and the Omega.* See note on 1:8.
22:14 *Blessed.* The last of the seven beatitudes (see note on 1:3).
22:15 *dogs.* A term applied to all types of ceremonially impure persons. In Deut 23:18 it designates a male prostitute.
22:16 *My angel.* Cf. 1:1. *the root and the descendant of David.* See note on 5:5; cf. Is 11:1,10; Rom 1:3. *bright morning star.* See Num 24:17.
22:18–19 Cf. the commands in Deut 4:2; 12:32. The warning relates specifically to the book of Revelation.
22:20 *I am coming quickly.* See vv. 7,12; 2:16; 3:11. *Come, Lord Jesus.* See note on 1 Cor 16:22.

Study Helps

Index to Subjects

The Index to Subjects will lead you to key texts on a variety of subjects covered in the *Zondervan NASB Study Bible.*

A

B

C

Children (importance) Gen 19:31–32; Ex 21:22–23; Deut 25:11–12; Ruth 4:14–15; 1 Chr 2:32; Job 42:12–13; Ps 127:3–5; Jer 16:2; Mark 10:13; Luke 18:15

Choice Deut 31:16–21; 1 Kin 8:58; 12:15; 2 Chr 18:22; Job 14:5; Ps 25:12; 32:9; 103:19; 139:16; Is 54:15; 63:17; Jer 4:10; 29:13; Ezek 14:9; Matt 23:37; Luke 15:11–32; Acts 13:48; Rom 9:8–33; Eph 1:4–5

Christian fellowship Rom 16:1–16; 1 Cor 11:20–22; 2 Cor 1:5; Gal 6:10

Christian freedom 1 Cor 6:12; Rev 2:20

Church Matt 16:18; Acts 1:8; 5:5,10; Eph 2:22; 1 Pet 1:23; 2 John v. 1; Rev 11:12; 12:1

Discipline Ezek 40:5—42:20; 1 Cor 5:4; 5:11; 5:12; 2 Thess 3:14; 1 Tim 1:20; 5:20

Fighting 1 Cor 3:16–17; 3:21; 2 Cor 10:10–11; Phil 1:15–18; 1 Tim 5:17; 2 Tim 2:24–25; Titus 3:9; 3 John v. 1–14; Jude v. 3

Leaders Acts 14:23; 1 Thess 5:12; 1 Tim 3:2–7; Titus 1:6; 3 John v. 3,7

Structure Titus 1:5

Unity 1 Cor 1:10; 12:22; Col 3:11

Circumcision Gen 17:10; 34:24; Ex 4:24; 4:25; Josh 5:3; Acts 15:1; 16:3; 15:10–12; Rom 2:25–27; 1 Cor 7:18; Gal 5:2

Inner Deut 10:16; Jer 4:4; Rom 2:28–29; Col 2:11

Cleanness Lev 11—15; Ps 51:1–9; Heb 10:19–22; 1 John 1:5–10

Comfort Job 4:1; Ps 23:4; 2 Cor 1:5

Commitment Gen 15:6; Deut 33:9; Ruth 1:16–18; Ps 31:15; 40:6; 86:11; Prov 23:15; Is 58:6–7; Jer 9:2; 26:10–16; Ezek 20:3; Zech 13:3; Luke 14:26; John 6:51,53–58; 2 Tim 3:7; Rev 3:16

Compassion Prov 24:11; Is 21:3–4; Jer 4:19–26; 48:31–32,36; Mark 2:4; Luke 5:19; Gal 6:2,5

Competition Eccl 4:4–6

Complaining Ex 16:7; 17:2; Num 21:5–6; Job 6:5; Ps 3:1; Eccl 5:19–20; Is 45:9; Jer 45:3; 2 Cor 1:8

Confession Josh 7:19; 2 Sam 12:13; Neh 1:6; Job 16:17; Prov 14:9; 28:13; John 9:41; 1 John 1:9

Conscience Gen 39:9; Deut 28:65; Josh 1:1; Job 13:25; Ps 19:13; Prov 20:27; Ezek 38:22–23; Acts 24:25; Rom 14:13; 14:22–23; 1 Cor 8:10–11

Consecration Ex 13:1–2; 19:14,22; Lev 8:10; 11:44–47; Num 7:1; Josh 3:5

Contentment Ps 23:1; Eccl 1:6–8; 1 Cor 7:17,20,26; 1 Tim 6:6–8

Conversion Jer 31:3–14; John 4:1–30,39–42; Acts 8:26–40; 9:1–25; 16:11–15; 16:22–34; 2 Cor 5:17–19; Eph 2:1–10

Courage Josh 1; 1 Sam 17:26–50; Dan 3; Acts 4; 5:17–42

Covenant

Abraham's Ps 111:5–9; Jer 16:15

David's Ps 89:3

Everlasting Ezek 16:60

Israel's Deut 28:16–19; Josh 24:25; Judg 2:20–21; 2 Kin 21:9; Neh 9:5–38

New Is 65:17; Ezek 37:26–28; 39:29; Matt 17:3; Mark 14:22–24; Luke 9:30; Acts 15:19–21; Rom 2:25–27; Heb 8:6–7; 8:10–11; Rev 21:1

New Testament Ps 25:10; Is 59:21; Jer 31:31

Of nations Gen 35:11

Coveting Ex 20:17; Josh 7; 1 Kin 21:1–14; James 4:1–10

Creation Gen 1:5–31; 1—2; Job 37:14–16; 39:1–30; 39:17; Ps 19:1–6; 48:10; 74:13–14; 96:11–13; 104:6–9; 104:16–30; Prov 8:22–31; Rom 1:19–20; Col 1:15,18; 1 Tim 4:3–4

Criticism Job 6:15–17; Ps 64:3–6; Prov 12:1; 27:6; 29:19; Eccl 10:20; Jer 18:19–23; Rom 14:4; 2 Cor 5:13

Cross Matt 16:24; Mark 8:31—9:1; Luke 9:23; 23:26–49; John 3:14; Gal 3:1–14; 5:11; Eph 2:11–18; 1 Cor 1:18—2:5; 1 Pet 2:24

Crown

As a symbol Ps 8:5; 103:4; 149:4; Prov 10:6; 12:4; 16:31; 17:6; 1 Thess 2:19; Phil 4:1

Worn by leaders Lev 8:9; 2 Sam 12:30; Esth 1:11; 2:17; Song 3:11; Zech 6:9–11; Matt 27:29; John 19:2,5; Rev 14:14; 19:12

Cults Gen 9:25; 38:16; Ex 22:18–20; 2 Kin 1:2; Ps 77:12; Jer 2:8,27; Matt 6:23; 2 Cor 11:20; 1 John 3:2; Rev 2:24

D

David 1 Sam 16; 17; 2 Sam 7; 11—12; Ps 51; Matt 1:1–18; 21:41–45; Luke 1:26–33

Day of the Lord Is 13:6; 34:4; Jer 25:33; Joel 1:15; Amos 5:18; Zeph 1:7; Zech 14:1; 2 Cor 1:14; 1 Thess 5:2

Deacon Acts 6:1–4; 1 Tim 3:8–13

Death 2 Sam 22:6; Ps 116:15; Eccl 3:18; Is 25:7; Matt 9:24; Mark 5:39; Luke 8:52; 1 Thess 4:14,16

Inevitable Job 21:23–26; Eccl 1:18; 2:13–16; 9:1–3; Luke 13:3–5

Spiritual Eph 2:1

Death penalty Gen 4:15; 9:6; Num 25:7–8; Deut 17:7; 19:13; Josh 20:3; Judg 8:17; 1 Sam 15:33; 1 Kin 2:32; Ps 78:34; Acts 7:57–59

Debts Ex 21:2; Deut 15:1; Neh 5:5; Prov 22:7; Matt 18:24–28; 18:34

Deception 2 Sam 13:6; 16:4; 2 Chr 18:29; Jer 41:6

Decision making Gen 4:7; Ex 10:1; 9:34; 1 Chr 19:3–5; 2 Chr 32:31; Prov 15:22; 16:1–9; 1 Cor 2:15; 10:27–30

Dedication Lev 27:2; 27:26–28; Neh 12:27–43

Demon possession Matt 8:28–34; Mark 1:23; 5:1–10; Luke 4:33; Acts 16:16–19; 1 Tim 4:1–10

Denial Ps 32:3; Ezek 33:32; Mark 16:7

Depending on God Josh 24:19; Ps 62:3–6; 86:1; 104:16–30; Prov 27:1; Zech 10:1; Matt 10:9–10; Mark 6:8; Luke 6:24–26; John 15:4; 2 Cor 9:11; 1 Tim 6:6–8; 1 John 2:24

Depression Job 17:15; Ps 61:2; 69:1–3; Prov 25:20; Eccl 4:1–3

Despair 1 Kin 11:10–12; Job 7:8–10; 7:15–16; 9:22–24; Ps 10:1; 142:6; Eccl 1:15; Is 33:7–9; Jer 8:20; Ezek 37:11; Hab 3:17–18

Disabilities Ex 4:10; 4:11; Lev 21:17–23; Deut 27:18; 2 Sam 19:24; Ps 6:2–7; Luke 13:11

Discipleship Matt 4:20; 8:20; 16:24; 28:19; Mark 1:16–17; 8:34; 10:21; Luke 6:13; 9:23; 9:57–62; 14:25–34; John 1:40–42; 8:51; 15:1–17; 21:15–19; Rom 12:1; Phil 3:10

Discipline Ps 6:1; 66:10; 94:12–13; 141:5; Prov 3:11–12; 19:18; 29:19; Jer 16:15; 30:11; 1 Cor 9:27; 1 Thess 4:6; Heb 12:5

Discouragement 1 Kin 19:3; Neh 4:10; Hag 1—2; 2 Tim 4:9–11

Discrimination Gen 43:32; 1 Chr 1:5; Gal 3:28; Col 3:11; Philem v. 16; James 2:1–7

Disobedience

God's response Gen 2:17; Lev 10:1; Num 14:40–41; 20:12; Deut 1:37; 28:46; 1 Kin 20:36; 2 Chr 18:28; Ps 81:11; Prov 28:14; Jer 42:20; Ezek 7:27

Leaders' response 2 Sam 18:14

Disrespect 2 Kin 2:23–24

Divorce Deut 21:14; 24:1; 1 Chr 8:8; Ezra 10:17; Is 50:1; Mal 2:14; Matt 1:19; 19:1–9; Mark 10:1–12; John 4:18; 1 Cor 7:15

Doubts 1 Kin 17:24; Job 40:2; Ps 69:1–3; 73:3–5; Eccl 9:4–6; Jer 15:18; Mal 3:14–15; Luke 7:19–23; John 21:15–17; James 1:6–8

Dreams (visions) Gen 28:12–15; 31:11; Judg 7:14; 7:15; 1 Kin 3:15; 1 Chr 17:2; Job 42:5; Is 1:1; 6:1; Ezek 1:1; 3:14; Zech 1:8; Rev 1:19–20; 4:2

E

Education Judg 5:1; 2 Chr 17:7; Prov 19:18

Religious Judg 2:10; 2 Kin 22:2; 2 Chr 29:3; 32:7–8; Neh 8:7; Job 3:3; Ps 22:9–10; 103:17–18

Elder Acts 5:17–42; 14:21–25; 20:13–38; Titus 1:5–9; 1 Tim 3:1–7

Elderly Ps 92:14–15; Prov 16:31; Eccl 12:3–5

Election Gen 12:1–9; Ex 19:1–6; Deut 10:12–22; Is 41:8–16; John 15:9–17; Rom 9:6–13; Eph 1:3–14; 1 Pet 2:1–10; 2 Pe 1:3–10

Elijah 1 Kin 17–19,21; 2 Kin 2; Luke 9:28–36

Elisha 1 Kin 19:16–21; 2 Kin 2—13

Emotions (expressing) Ps 13:1–5; 88:5; 140:1–11; Prov 14:29; Lam 1:12

Encouragement 1 Sam 23:16; Job 4:1; Prov 25:20; Is 12:1–6

Enemies Ps 27:2; 31:6; 35:11–16; Prov 25:21–22; Luke 6:27–36; Rom 12:19–21

Envy Gen 37; Mark 7:20–23; James 3:13—4:10

Eternal life Matt 19:16–30; John 3:1–21; 6:46,57; Rom 2:7; 6:15–23; 1 John 5:1–13; Rev 21:22–27

Eternity Job 20:5–9; Ps 21:4; 30:9; Eccl 3:11

Eve Gen 1:26—5:2; 1 Cor 11:2–16; 1 Tim 2:8–15

Evil

Destroyed Mal 4:1; 1 Cor 15:24; Col 2:15

Fighting Ps 94:16; Matt 5:39; 18:10; Luke 6:29–30; James 4:7; 1 John 5:4; Rev 16:16

Source Gen 2:9; Ex 11:3; Deut 31:16–21; Judg 9:23; 1 Chr 21:1; Job 19:8–12; Ps 71:20; Eccl 7:13–14; Lam 3:38; Amos 9:4; John 9:2

Spirits 1 Sam 16:14; 18:10; Matt 8:31–32; Mark 1:23; 5:13; 9:18; Luke 4:33; 9:39; 11:19; Acts 16:17–18; 19:13; 1 John 4:1; Rev 16:13

Used by God 1 Kin 22:20–22; Amos 9:4; Hab 1:6,13; John 14:30; Acts 2:23

Example John 13:1–17; 1 Cor 10:1–13; Phil 2:1–11; 2:14–15; 1 Thess 1; Heb 11:4–40; James 5:10–11; 5:16–18; 1 Pet 2:11–12

Exile Is 5:13; 2 Kin 17,25; 2 Chr 36

Exodus

God's deliverance Ex 4:1–9; 5:1–5; 7:10—10:29; 11:1—12:39; 14:5–29

God's motive Gen 15:13–16; Deut 7:8–9; Hos 11:1

F

Failures Judg 14:4; Ps 106:7–43; Matt 26:75; Mark 14:72; Luke 22:61–62

Faith

Abraham's Gen 15:6; Rom 4:1–3

Asking for proof Matt 12:39; Luke 11:29

Beginning Josh 9:9; 9:25; 2 Kin 5:17; Matt 17:20; Luke 17:6

Childlike Ps 22:9–10; Matt 19:14; Mark 10:14–15

Cost of Matt 10:35–37; Luke 12:51–53; 2 Tim 3:12

Defending Jude v. 3

Defined Heb 11:1

During crisis Ps 116:10; Is 10:24; Jer 12:5–6; Lam 3:21–24; Hab 2:3; Zeph 3:15; Matt 11:3; 1 Pet 1:7

In action Josh 2:4–5; Matt 25:35–36; Luke 17:6; Acts 3:6; 2 Tim 2:15; Heb 11:7; James 2:14–24

Power of John 14:12

Results of 1 Chr 11:11; 2 Chr 27:6; Ps 106:31; Mark 11:22–24

Rewarded Job 22:21–25; Jer 39:18; Matt 5:19; 9:22; Mark 5:34–36; Luke 8:48; 2 Cor 5:10; Eph 1:3; 2 John v. 8

Signs of Matt 3:6; Luke 3:3

Ups and downs Gen 26:7; Num 21:5–6; 1 Kin 9:20–21; 2 Kin 13:18–19; 2 Chr 16:12; 24:18; Ps 13:1–5; Is 54:1–17; Matt 8:10; Mark 6:51–52; Luke 8:13; 17:5

Faithfulness Gen 17:10; Job 36:7; Ps 78; 111; Lam 3:22–32; Luke 8:18; Gal 5:16–26; Heb 3; Rev 2:8–11

False accusations Job 19:29; 31:35

False gods Acts 17:23

Fame Job 29:20; Matt 23:9

Family Gen 2:24; Lev 20:9; Ps 127:3–5; Mal 4:6; Matt 10:35–37; Mark 10:29; Luke 8:20–21; 12:51–53; 14:26; Acts 16:15

Blessings Gen 24:60; 27:38; 28:4; 48:20; Deut 33:1; Ruth 4:12; 1 Chr 5:1; 16:43; 26:10

Model Ps 103:17–18; 1 Cor 7:14

Name Gen 15:2; 19:31–32; 38:14; Deut 25:5–9; Job 30:8

Of God Eph 1:5; 1:13

Christ's 2 Sam 7:16; 1 Kin 11:36; Ps 132:12; Matt 1:1–17; Luke 2:48; 3:23–38; John 7:5

Famine Ruth 1:1; 1 Kin 17; 2 Kin 6:25—8:2

Fasting Lev 16:30; 23:27; Deut 9:18; 1 Kin 21:9; Is 58:3; Joel 1:14; Zech 8:19; Matt 6:18; 9:14–15; Mark 2:18–20; Luke 5:35; Acts 13:2–3

Fear Ps 140:1–11; Matt 8:26; Mark 4:40; 5:17; Luke 8:37

Consequences Job 31:23

Of death Is 38:10–14

Of God Ex 3:6; Num 17:12; Deut 5:5; 2 Chr 26:5; Job 9:9; 28:28; Ps 14:5; 19:7–9; 25:14; 103:11; Prov 1:7

Of the unknown Ex 14:12

Fellowship Acts 2:42–47; 4:24–35; 2 Cor 13:14; Eph 4:17—5:21; 1 John 1

Fights

Disputes 2 Sam 19:26–27

Feuds Esth 3:2–5; Is 11:13; Ezek 35:5; Luke 9:53; Acts 23:9

Quarrels Gen 45:24; Neh 5:1–5

Financial planning Prov 11:25–28; Eccl 11:2; Luke 12:33–34; 16:8–11

Flood Gen 7:19–20

Forgiveness

Human Gen 33:4; 50:15–21; Matt 18:35; Luke 11:4; 15:17–24; 23:34; Acts 7:60; Eph 4:32; Col 3:13; 2 Tim 4:16

God's Ex 34:6–7; Ps 32:5; 51:1–2,7,9; 103:8,12; Is 38:17; 43:25; 44:22; 55:7; Jer 31:34; Mark 2:1–11; Luke 24:47; Acts 2:38; 3:19; 10:43; 13:38; 1 John 1:9

Freedom John 8:31–36; Rom 6; 8:1–17; Gal 3:8–25; 4:21—5:26

Friendship 1 Sam 23:16; 2 Sam 1:26; Prov 17:17; 24:26; 27:10,17; Eccl 4:9–12

With God Ex 33:11; 33:12,17; Job 42:2; Ps 25:14; 119:57; 2 Cor 5:19

Fruit of the Spirit Luke 8:15; John 15:4; 1 Cor 13:1–3; Gal 5:16–26

G

Generosity Gen 13:9; Deut 23:24–25; Prov 11:25–28; Mal 3:10; Luke 16:9; 2 Cor 8:1,7

Gifts of the spirit Ex 31:1–5; Acts 10:46; 12:10,28–29; 19:6; Rom 12:6–8; 1 Cor 2:10,28–29; 7:7–8; 12:8–30; 14:3–28; Eph 4:11; 1 Pet 4:1

Glory Ex 40:34–38; 2 Chr 7:1–4; Ps 29,93,96; John 1:14–18; 12:20–33; 2 Cor 3; Rom 3:10–23

God Gen 27:35; 45:8; Ex 4:11; 11:3; 1 Chr 1:1; Job 16:6; Ps 118:18; Jer 51:24; Ezek 6:14; Hag 1:6,9; Rev 10:7

God as creator Ps 108:7–9

God as father Is 64:8; Hos 11:1,4; Mark 14:36; Rom 8:23

God as teacher Job 38:21; 40:7; 42:4; Jon 4:6–7

God's anger Deut 1:34; Ezra 10:14; Job 16:9; Ps 2:12; 76:10; 79:5; Is 6:5; 6:9–13; 12:1; 24:14–16; 47:6; Jer 17:4; 30:22–24; Lam 2:4–5; Ezek 5:13; Obad v. 10–11; Zech 1:2,15; Matt 21:12; Rev 14:19–20; 15:1; 16:1

God's appearance Ps 23:3

In human form Gen 18:10; 32:24,28; 32:30; 48:16; Josh 5:14; Judg 2:1,4; 6:11,14; Job 36:26; Ps 13:1; 32:7; 34:9–10; 67:1; Jer 18:17; Dan 3:25; Zech 4:10; Luke 1:46–55; 22:70–71; John 1:1; Heb 2:17

Invisible spirit Gen 3:8; Deut 5:4

Signs 2 Chr 5:13–14; Job 38:1; 42:5; Ps 18:2; 27:1; 35:2; 61:2; 71:3; 84:11; 100:3; Is 40:10–11; Ezek 34:11; Mic 7:14; John 10:1–15

God's call Jer 1:5; 20:7–9; Ezek 3:18; Amos 1:1; Jon 1:10; Luke 1:15; 2 Cor 10:12; Gal 1:1,12; 1:15–20; 1 Tim 1:18; 2 Tim 1:6

God's care Ex 16:31; Num 2:17; 33:49; Deut 14:23; Ezra 5:5; Job 10:13–14; 29:2; 39:1–30; Ps 23:3; 127:2; 131:2; 139:5; 145:14–16; Is 49:16; Zech 11:7

Physical needs Ex 16:8; Judg 15:19; Neh 3:1–32; Luke 6:35; Phil 4:19

God's character Ex 34:6–7; 1 Sam 15:29; 2 Sam 7:15; 22:27; 1 Chr 21:15; Neh 8:9–11; Job 23:13–17; Ps 7:11; 18:25–26; 33:14–15; 90:11–14; 95:10; 102:25–26; 150:2; Is 1:1; 43:25; 54:7; Jer 14:7; 14:21; 30:22–24; Ezek 10:12; 45:13–25; Dan 7:9; Nah 1:7; Zech 4:10

God's chosen people Deut 4:33; Esth 4:14; Ps 16:3; 78:67–68; 108:7–9; Ezek 36:35–38; Zech 2:8; Rom 11:22–32; 2 Thess 2:13; 1 Pet 1:1

God's compassion Gen 15:16; John 11:35

God's control Deut 17:15; Josh 1:4; Neh 11:3–19; Esth 4:16; 9:3–4; Job 9:13; Ps 46:8; 82:6; 103:19; 113:5; Is 40:23; 55:11; Jer 29:13; Ezek 1:5–6; Da; Hab 2:20; Zech 5:9; Rom 9:22–23

Over evil Deut 31:16–21; Josh 6:21; Judg 9:23; 1 Kin 15:34; Job 1:12; 2:3; 6:4; 16:10–11; 19:8–12; Hab 1:6,13; Matt 6:10; John 14:30; Acts 13:48; 2:23; Rom 8:28

Over man Gen 25:23; 50:20; Ex 11:3; Num 23:11,25; Judg 14:4; 1 Sam 2:25; 19:20; 2 Chr 10:15; 33:13; Job 3:23; 13:15; 40:8–14; Ps 33:10; 93:1–5; 118:6; Prov 16:1–9; Eccl 3:14; 7:13–14; Is 28:11; 53:10; Lam 5:21; Ezek 22:30; 38:16; Jon 1:10; Rom 4:17; 8:29–30; 9:8–33; Eph 1:4–5; 1 Tim 2:4

Over nations Gen 36:31; Deut 9:4; Josh 8:3–19; 1 Sam 8:21–22; 2 Kin 19:25; 1 Chr 17:9; 2 Chr 20:22–23; 28:5; Job 25:3; Ps 60:8; 108:7–9; Is 10:5–6; 33:17–19; Jer 21:5; 51:24; Matt 23:37

Over rulers Gen 41:16; Ex 10:1; 2 Kin 18:25; 1 Chr 5:26; Ezra 7:12–15; Job 34:29–30; Ps 82:6; Is 37:7; 44:28; Jer 27:6; Ezek 29:20; Dan 5:18

God's emotions

Hate Mal 1:2–3

Jealousy Hos 2:13–14; Joel 2:18; Nah 1:2; Zech 8:2

Joy Zeph 3:17

Pain Is 5:1; 63:10; Ezek 7:22; John 11:35; Eph 4:30

God's faithfulness Ex 16:34; Ps 18:31; 71:9–18; Lam 2:6

God's glory Ex 24:9–11; Lev 9:23; 1 Kin 8:10–13; 2 Chr 5:13–14; Job 37:21; Ps 26:8; Ezek 9:3; John 9:3; 17:1,5; 1 Cor 11:7; 2 Pet 1:17

God's guidance Ex 14:1–4; Ps 23:4; 25:12; 100:3; Zech 1:8; John 16:13; Acts 16:6–10

God's holiness Ex 13:13; 30:20–21; Num 1:51–53; 4:20; 17:12; 20:12–13; Deut 4:24; 9:4; Ezek 25:3–7; 28:25; 40:22,26,34,37

God's honor Num 14:13–16; Judg 11:23–24; 2 Sam 12:14; 2 Chr 2:1; Neh 2:17; Job 1:8; Ps 74:20–23; Is 5:15–16; 63:12,14; Jer 32:20–33; Ezek 36:20

God's house Ex 35:4—37:29; 1 Kin 8:27,29; 2 Chr 3:3–17; Ps 114:2; Is 57:15; Lam 2:1; Ezek 43:9; Mic 1:3; Eph 2:22

God's image Gen 1:27; 9:6; Deut 19:13; Job 33:16–17; Ps 51:4; 103:14; Prov 19:17; Eccl 7:29; 1 Cor 11:7

God's judgment Num 33:52–53; Deut 2:34; 3:2; Josh 6:21; 2 Kin 24:4; Job 20:23–29; Ps 98:9; Is 24:1–6; 26:9–10; 66:15–16; Jer 9:25–26; Ezek 7:2; Mal 4:1; Matt 11:22; Luke 10:14; Rev 6:12–17

God's law 2 Kin 11:12; 22:8; Neh 8:3; Ps 78:5–7; 93:5; 119:1–176; Is 13:9–11; Matt 23:23; Rom 5:20; 6:14; 7:10

After Christ Deut 12:32; Matt 8:3; Luke 16:16–17; Rom 10:4; 1 Cor 10:3–4; Eph 2:15

Keeping Matt 5:17–18; Gal 2:19

Misuse of Is 29:13

Reason for Lev 19:18–28; Deut 30:11; Ps 11:3; 19:7–9; 107:11; 2 Cor 3:6; Gal 3:1–25; 1 Tim 1:9

God's love Ex 34:14; Deut 4:24; 1 Chr 21:15; Ezra 2:2–61; Job 19:11; 23:14–15; 25:6; Ps 5:5; 33:5;

107:33–43; Is 59:2; Jer 12:7–8; Matt 18:12; Luke 15:3–7

God's name Gen 4:26; 17:1; Ex 3:14; Num 6:27; Deut 12:5; Josh 22:22; Ps 20:1; 25:11; Jer 14:7; Luke 1:31; 2 Pet 1:17

God's patience Is 54:7; Jer 22:2–5; Ezek 6:14; 14:20; Mic 3:4

God's presence

Everywhere Lev 15:31; 1 Sam 16:18; Job 26:6; Ps 22:1–2; 100:4; Ezek 11:16

Hidden Job 9:13; 23:8–9; Ps 10:1; 32:6; Is 45:15; Jer 14:8–9; Lam 2:1; Dan 1:2; Hos 5:6; Mic 5:2; John 12:36

Signs Gen 15:17; Ex 13:21–22; Lev 6:12–13; Num 9:15–16; 1 Chr 13:10,14; Ps 18:7–15; Is 33:14; Jer 3:16; Amos 4:13; Matt 27:51; Mark 9:2–3; 15:38

Within people Ps 26:8; Ezek 43:9; Matt 28:20; Col 1:27; Heb 1:3

God's promises Gen 22:16–17; Deut 4:40; Josh 1:8; 1:9; 2 Chr 7:14; 7:18; Neh 9:15; Ps 25:6; 89:39; Is 54:1–17; 59:21; Jer 14:21; 2 Cor 1:20

Fulfilled Josh 14—21; Ps 138:2; Is 40:3–5,9; Jer 31:33–34; Hab 2:3

God's protection Deut 2:7; Ps 20:1; 37:3–25; 54:7; 57:1; 91:10; 97:10; Mark 16:18; Luke 21:18; John 17:11–12; Rev 7:2; 11:7

Using angels Gen 32:1–2; 2 Kin 6:17; Ezek 9:1–2

God's record keeping Ps 56:8; 130:3–4; Dan 7:10; 10:21; Mal 3:16; Rev 3:5; 13:8; 20:12

God's silence 1 Sam 14:37; Job 19:7; 34:29; 42:2; Ps 10:1; 22:1–2; 74:9; 83:1; Is 42:14

God's timing Gen 40:23; Ex 12:40; Deut 4:33; 2 Chr 33:1–2; 34:27–28; Ps 70:1,5; Hag 2:6; Luke 21:32; John 2:4; Gal 4:4; Eph 1:10

God's will

Accepting 2 Kin 20:16–19; Job 1:20; 10:2; 23:2; 41:11; Ps 37:4; 88:10–12; Is 39:5–8

Asking for signs Gen 24:14; 44:5,15; Judg 6:37–40; 1 Sam 14:10–12; 2 Kin 20:8–11; Is 7:11; 38:7–8

Changing Ex 32:14; Num 23:19; Deut 9:19; 1 Sam 15:29; 2 Kin 20:5–6; Ps 106:23; Is 38:1–5; Jer 26:3; Dan 9:3; Hos 11:8; Amos 7:3,6; Matt 6:8

Resisting Ex 10:1; Deut 2:30; Eccl 3:14; Is 22:14; Jer 13:23; Luke 8:13; John 12:39; Rom 1:24,26,28; 2 Thess 2:11

Ways to know Gen 24:14; Num 34:13; Judg 7:15; 1 Sam 6:9; 1 Chr 14:10,14; Ps 95:7; Jer 21:1–2; Ezek 1:1; Acts 10:10–20; Rom 12:2; 1 Tim 4:1

God's word 1 Chr 28:19

Direction Ps 95:7; 119:11; 119:105; Prov 14:12; Acts 10:10–20; Eph 3:5; 5:26

Love for Ps 119:1–176

Recognize Ex 29:42–43; 2 Sam 2:1; 21:1; 1 Chr 28:12,19; 2 Chr 33:10; Dan 1:17; Jon 1:1; John 1:1; Acts 10:10–20; 1 Thess 2:13; Heb 2:3–4

Good works Neh 13:10; Matt 25:35–36; Luke 14:12–14; 16:9; Phil 2:12–13; 3:6–8; Col 1:29; 2 Tim 2:15; Heb 4:11; 2 Pet 1:5; 3 John v. 11

Gospel Acts 8:1–4; Rom 1:16–17; 15:14–16; Gal 1:6–9; Eph 2:1–10; Col 1:3–23

Gossip Ps 94:20–23; 122:5; 125:3; Prov 10:18–21; 29:18; Eccl 8:2–6; 10:6; Acts 4:19; Rom 13:1–7; Titus 3:1–2

Grace Gen 48:20; Ex 6:14–27; 1 Kin 8:58; Is 26:9–10; Jer 12:14–16; Ezek 36:26; Luke 17:7–10; Acts 4:12; Rom 6:14; 2 Cor 8:1,7; 9:8; Eph 4:7; Titus 2:11

Overcomes sin Gen 4:7; Ex 33:12; 2 Sam 12:13; Is 65:1; Amos 4:11; Rom 3:8; 5:18–19

Greed Num 11:33; 2 Sam 12:8; 1 Kin 20:34; Mic 2:1–2; Hab 2:5

Grief Lev 10:6; Deut 34:8; Josh 7:6–10; 2 Sam 13:19; Esth 4:1–2; Ezek 27:30

Grudges 2 Sam 14:24; Ps 95:10

Guilt Gen 44:16; Ex 20:24; Lev 4:2; 16:20–22; Deut 28:65; Job 25:4; Is 6:6–7

H

Happiness Ps 100:2; Eccl 7:3; Acts 17:18

Hate Ps 31:6; 139:21–22

Healing

By God (faith) Num 21:8; Matt 9:22; Mark 5:34–36; 6:13; Luke 4:39; 8:48; Acts 5:15; James 5:15–16

Relationships Gen 42:7; Mark 9:12

Heart 1 Sam 16:1–13; Ps 51; Prov 4:23; Jer 17:9–10; Matt 12:33–37

Heaven Job 36:7; Matt 22:30; Mark 12:25; John 14:2; Eph 2:6; 4:10; 1 Thess 4:14,16; Heb 1:3; Rev 4:1; 21:16

Hell Is 66:24; Matt 5:22; Phil 2:10; 1 Thess 4:14,16; 2 Pet 2:4; Rev 14:10–11; 19:20

Herod Matt 2; 14:1–12; Acts 12:1–23

Holiness (reasons for) Lev 19:2; Job 12:4; John 17:17,19; Rom 1:4; 3:8; 1 Thess 4:3–12; 2 Tim 1:9; Heb 12:14; 1 Pet 1:15

Personal Lev 5:2; 11:4–41; 2 Cor 7:1

Priestly Lev 22:32

Holy Spirit Gen 1:2; Matt 7:7–8; Mark 1:8; 3:29; John 14:16,26; 16:13; 16:8; Acts 19:2; Rom 1:4; 1 Cor 2:13; Eph 4:30; 1 Thess 5:19; 1 Pet 1:15

Filling Eph 5:18

Fruit of Luke 8:15; Gal 5:22–26; Heb 12:14

Gifts of Acts 21:9; Rom 12:6; 1 Cor 12:1–31; 14:2–4; 14:20–25

Praying Rom 8:27; Eph 6:18; Jude v. 20

Honesty Prov 24:26

Hope Job 17:15; Is 8:9–10; 40:31; Lam 3:21–24; Mic 7:8; Zech 9:12; 1 Pet 1:3–9

Hospitality Gen 18:4–5; 19:2; 19:8; 24:20; Lev 3:1; Judg 19:5–10; 1 Sam 25:8; 2 Sam 9:7; Ps 23:5; Luke 7:44–46; 10:38–41; Heb 13:2

Human nature Gen 8:21; Josh 4:14; Ps 53:3; Eccl 1:9–10; Is 64:6; Jer 24:7; 43:2; Zech 10:2; Mark 9:33–37; Luke 9:48; Acts 15:39

Corrupt Job 25:4; Ps 146:3–4; Rom 7:5–8; Eph 4:22; Col 3:5

Human sacrifice Gen 22:2; Lev 18:21; Deut 12:31; 2 Kin 3:27; 16:3; 21:16; Jer 19:5; Hos 13:2

Humility 1 Sam 15:22; 2 Kin 17:14; Ps 25:9; 131:1–2; Prov 30:2–3; Mark 9:33–37; Luke 2:9–12; 9:48; 14:11; John 13:14–15

Hunger and thirst (spiritual) Deut 8:3; Amos 8:11–12; Is 55:1–3; Matt 4:4; 5:6; John 4:13–14; 6:35,48–58; 7:37–38; 1 Cor 10:16

Hypocrisy Ps 26:4–5; 66:18; Prov 15:8; Is 5:18–19; Jer 17:10; 42:20; Amos

5:21–23; Matt 23:15; 23:33; Mark 7:11; Luke 12:1; John 8:7; Acts 5:5,10

I

Idolatry Deut 32:17; Judg 16:23; 2 Kin 8:18; Is 44:16–17; Jer 23:9–14
 Destruction 2 Chr 15:16; Ps 115:4–7
 God's power over Judg 18:17; 1 Sam 5:6; 2 Chr 25:14; Is 41:7; 43:10; 46:1
 Modern Ps 97:7; Hos 4:12
 Political reasons 2 Kin 10:29; Jer 44:8
 Punished 1 Kin 11:10–12; 2 Chr 10:14–16; Lam 1:8
 Results 2 Chr 27:2; Ps 115:8; Is 65:5; Jer 17:1; Amos 2:4; 9:4
Illness 2 Kin 5:1; 7:3; 2 Chr 16:12; 21:15; Job 2:7–8; Ps 38:3; 103:3
Image of God Gen 1:26–28; 5:1; 9:6; Ex 20:4; Ps 8:6–8; John 1:18; 12:45; 14:9; Acts 17:29; 1 Cor 11:7; 2 Cor 4:4; Col 1:15; Heb 1:3; James 3:9
Incarnation Matt 1:18–25; Luke 1—2; John 1:1–18
Incest Gen 4:17; 19:31–32; 35:22; Lev 20:17; Deut 27:22; 2 Sam 13:13; Amos 2:7
Infertility Gen 16:2; 25:2; 29:31; Num 5:28; 1 Sam 1:5; Ps 113:7–9
Injustice Job 24:1–12; Ps 140:12; Eccl 8:14; Amos 1—9; Obad v. 1–21
In-laws Gen 26:35; 31:2
Integrity Ex 8:28–32; Lev 19:36; Deut 25:15; 1 Kin 9:4–5; Ps 25:21; Prov 2:7; 10:9; 11:3; 16:11–13; 20:7; 28:6; Titus 2:7
Intercession Gen 18:23–32; 1 Kin 8:33–51; Ezra 9:5–15; Dan 9:3–19; John 17; Rom 8:26–27,31–34; 1 Tim 2:1–2; James 5:16; Heb 7:24–25; 1 John 2:1;
Isaac Gen 18:1–15; 22:1–19; 24; 27; 35:16–29; Rom 9:6–9; Gal 4:21–31
Israel Num 26:51; Jer 31:36,40; Ezek 36:35–38; 47:15–20; Amos 9:15; Rom 11:22–32

J

Jacob Gen 25:19–34; 27; 28:10–22; 29–30; 32
Jealousy Gen 43:34; Num 12:1; 16:3; 1 Sam 18:12; Ps 73:22; Eccl 4:4–6; Luke 15:25–32
Jerusalem
 Importance of 2 Sam 5:9; 2 Chr 1:4; Neh 11:1–2; Ps 3:4; 46:4; 48:8; 76:2; 137:5–6; Is 35:8; 58:12; Ezek 16:8; 48:35; Joel 3:17; Mic 1:13; 4:2; 7:8
 New Rev 21:2; 21:22–27
Jesus Christ
 Divinity John 5:18; 6:46,57; 8:58–59; 10:33; 14:9–28; Acts 1:9; Rom 1:4; 1 Cor 15:28; Col 1:19; Heb 1:3
 Enemies Luke 5:17; Heb 10:13
 Glory Matt 17:2; Mark 9:2–3; John 17:1,5; 17:5,24; 2 Cor 4:17
 Humanity Matt 4:3–11; 26:38–39; Mark 13:32; 14:33–35; Luke 4:3–13; 22:42–44; Rom 8:29; Heb 2:6–8; 4:15; 1 John 5:6; 2 John v. 7
 Humility Phil 2:6–7
 Power Matt 14:25; Mark 3:22; 5:11–13; 5:25–29; 6:48; Luke 5:17; 8:46; John 6:19; 1 Cor 15:28; Rev 9:17–19
 Prayers Matt 14:23; Mark 6:46; Heb 8:2
 Purpose Luke 13:32; Heb 5:5,10
 Reign Zech 14:9; Eph 1:10; 1:20; 4:10; Phil 2:10; Rev 5:11–14
 Second coming Is 35:1–2; Jer 23:5–8; Hos 14:5–7; Matt 24:29; Mark 13:24; Luke 17:22–37; Acts 1:11; Rom 13:11–12; 1 Thess 4:15; 2 Thess 2:3–12; 2 Pet 3:12; Rev 22:6,10
Jobs (attitude toward) Prov 18:9; 24:30–34; 28:19; 2 Thess 3:10
Joy Ps 100:2; Is 12; 35; Matt 5:1–12; Luke 15; John 13:1–17; Gal 5:16–26; Phil 4:4–9; Col 1:24; James 1:2–18; 1 Pet 1:1–9; 4:12–19
Judah Deut 33:7; Num 1:27; 26:22; Josh 15; Judg 1:1–20; 2 Sam 2:1–4; 1 Kin 12:21–22; 14:21–22; 2 Kin 24:1–16; 1 Chr 28:2–4; Ezra 1:1–5; Ezek 48:7; Matt 1:2–6; Rev 7:5
Judging others Luke 13:3–5; John 5:22; 8:7; Acts 10:4; Rom 14:1; 1 Cor 4:3; James 2:13
Judgment
 Attitude about Matt 7:1–5; 19:28; Luke 22:30; Rom 14:1–4,13; 1 Cor 4:5; 10:29; Gal 6:1–4; James 4:11–12
 God's Gen 18:26; Deut 32:4; Job 34:10; Ps 94:2; John 5:22; Acts 10:42; 2 Thess 1:5; 2 Tim 4:1
Judgment day Is 13:10; Joel 2:30–32; Rom 14:10; Heb 10:25
Justice Lev 24:20; 2 Chr 19:4–5; Job 24:18; Ps 122:5; Ezek 38:22–23
 Delayed Job 27:1–2; 34:19; 36:6; 36:9–11; Is 11:4–5
 God's Num 14:20–35; Deut 28:58–59; 28:63; Job 1:13–19; Ps 78:34; Eccl 3:17; Jer 12:1; Ezek 14:22–23; Nah 2:13; Zeph 3:5
Justification Luke 18:13–14; Acts 13:39; Rom 3:22–28; 5:1–21; 9:31–32; 1 Cor 1:30; Gal 2:21; 3:11; James 2:14–26; 1 Pet 2:22

K

Kindness Gen 32:10; 39:21; Ruth 2:20; 1 Kin 3:6; Ezra 9:9; Job 10:12; Is 54:8; Gal 5:16–26; Hos 11:4; Acts 14:17; Titus 3:4
King 1 Sam 8; 12; Ps 47; 99; Luke 1:26–38; Eph 1:15–34; 1 Tim 1:15–17; Heb 1:1–12
Kingdom of God 1 Chr 17:9; Jer 3:14–16; Matt 4:17; 5:3–10; 13:24; Luke 3:4–6; 16:16; 17:20–21
Kings Deut 17:15; 1 Sam 8:5–9; 10:24; 1 Kin 12:16; 2 Kin 11:12; 23:34; 25:30; 2 Chr 25:2; Ezek 28:2; Dan 3:13–14

L

Last days Is 2:2; 24:18–20; Joel 2:30–32; Mic 4:1; Acts 2:19–20; 1 Cor 7:29; 2 Thess 2:2; 2 Tim 3:1; Heb 9:26; 1 Pet 4:7
Lazarus John 11:1–44; Luke 16:19–31
Laziness Prov 6:6–11; 2 Thess 3:6–13
Leaders
 Ability Judg 6:25; 12:8,11,13; 13:25; 14:6; 1 Sam 10:9–11; 11:6; 2 Kin 2:9; Is 45:1
 Choosing Gen 49:10–12; Ex 6:14–27; Deut 16:18; 31:3; Judg 11:4–6; 1 Chr 5:2; 12:2; Is 3:6; Hos 8:4; 1 Tim 3:2–7; 5:24–25
 Preparation Ex 17:9; Deut 34:9; 1 Kin 3:7; 19:19; Prov 30:21–23
 Responsibility Jer 23:1; Ezek 44:20–23; Mal 2:3; James 3:1
 Spiritual Num 27:18; 2 Kin 4:13; 6:21; 13:14; 16:15–16; 2 Chr 24:16;

Neh 12:1; 13:28; Is 29:9–10; 32:5–6; 56:10; Jer 29:21–23; Hos 6:9; Zeph 3:4; Mal 2:3; Matt 20:26–28; 23:33; Luke 11:44; John 21:15–17; 1 Cor 4:16

Wicked Job 34:29–30; Ezek 11:3

Life

After death (Old Testament) Num 20:24; 1 Sam 28:19; 2 Sam 12:23; Ps 6:5; 17:15; 30:9; 49:15; Prov 2:18; Eccl 9:10; 12:7

Principles Prov 3:1–4

Source Gen 2:7; Job 27:3; Ps 104:30; Eccl 12:7

Unfair Gen 18:25; 2 Sam 21:6,9,14; Job 1:13–19; 34:19; Ps 73:3–5; Eccl 2:26; 4:13–16

Value of 2 Kin 11:1–2; Job 3:10–16; Eccl 12:6

Without God Eccl 1:2; 6:12

Light Gen 1:14–16; Ps 13:3; 112:4; 119:105; Is 42:6; 58:8,10; 60:3; 1 John 1:5

Loneliness Ps 42:3–4; 102:6–7; 102:16–18

Lord's Supper Matt 6:29; 26:26,28; Luke 22:17–20; John 6:51–56; 21:13; Acts 1:4; 2:42,46–47; 20:7,11; 1 Cor 10:16–17; 11:20–26 24:30,35,41–43

Love

For God Num 30:2; Ps 37:4; 69:9; 112:2–8; 130:5–6; Luke 14:26; John 21:15–17; Rom 13:10; Heb 10:6,8; Rev 2:4

For others Matt 5:48; John 13:34–35; 15:12–14,17; Rom 12:18; 12:20; 13:10; 1 Cor 1:7; 3:2; 13:1–3; 1 John 4:16

Loyalty 1 Kin 11:17–19; 2 Chr 11:13–14; 11:16; Ps 16:4; 84:11; Prov 17:17

Lying Ex 1:19–20; 1 Sam 21:2; 27:8–10; 2 Kin 8:10; 10:19; 2 Chr 18:22; Ps 62:4; Jer 38:27; Acts 5:5,10

M

Magic, witchcraft, and sorcery Ex 22:18; Lev 19:26,31; 20:6,27; Deut 18:10–12,20–21; Is 2:6; 47:10–14; Jer 27:9; Mic 5:12; Mal 3:5; Acts 8:9–24; 13:6–12; 16:16–18; 19:13–19; Gal 5:20

Marriage

Choosing a spouse Ruth 3:10; 2 Chr 21:6; Prov 21:9

Customs Gen 24:50–51; 24:67; 29:18; 29:23–25; 29:27; 31:15; 34:4; Ruth 3:7–8,13–14; 1 Chr 2:21; 2:34–35

Interfaith Gen 38:2; Deut 7:3–4; Judg 12:9; 1 Kin 7:8; 11:1–4; 16:31; 2 Chr 8:11; 21:6; Neh 13:26; 13:28; 1 Cor 7:14

Interracial Lev 24:10; Ruth 1:4; Jer 31:8

Political Gen 20:2; 41:45; 1 Kin 3:1; 2 Chr 18:1

Relationship Gen 2:24; 3:16; Prov 31:23; Jer 16:2; Mark 10:8

Remarriage Deut 24:4; Matt 19:9

Martyrs 1 Kin 18:4,13; 2 Kin 21:16; Ps 37:3–25; Is 57:1–2; Dan 6:22–23; Luke 21:18; Phil 3:10; 1 Pet 1:6; Rev 6:9; 11:7; 20:4–5

Materialism Matt 5:3–12; Luke 6:20–22 1 Cor 3:3; Eph 4:13

Meaning of life Ps 73:13; 90:17; 102:9–10; Prov 1:7; Eccl 1:2; 2:3–11; 2:13–16; 8:16–17; 11:8; 2 Cor 5:10

Mercy Ps 7:11; 25:11; 39:13; 51:1; 78:39; 139:19; 143:1–2; Is 30:18; Jer 3:1; 22:2–5; 24:7; Ezek 3:7; 39:25; Hos 11:8; Nah 2:13; James 2:13

Messiah Ps 110:4; Is 16:5; 32:3; Jer 33:16; Nah 1:15; Zech 11:7; Matt 16:20; 17:2; 20:30; Mark 8:30; 10:47; 11:8; Luke 2:32; 18:34; 20:41–44; John 1:46

Other names for Ps 2:2; 110:1; Zech 3:8; 10:4; Luke 2:25; John 10:1–15; Rev 5:5–6

Prophecy about Is 7:14–16; 9:4–6; 32:1; 53:2; Ezek 34:11; Dan 9:24–27; Zech 6:13; 12:10; Luke 3:4–6

Son of David Ps 72:5; 132:12; Is 11:1; Ezek 17:22–24; 34:23–24; Hag 2:23; Mark 12:35–37; Luke 18:38

Miracles Ex 4:1–9; 14:21; 16:31; Josh 3:16; 10:13–14; 2 Kin 20:11; Jon 1:17; Mark 8:12; Luke 11:29

Moderation Prov 25:16; Eccl 10:16–17

Money Deut 8; Ps 24; 62:10; Matt 6:19–34; 1 Tim 6:3–19 James 5:1–5

Moses Ex 2—40; Num 1—36; Deut 1—34; Matt 17:1–13; Heb 11:24–28

Murder Gen 9:6; Ex 2:12; Num 35:24–25; Deut 19:13; 21:1–9; 2 Sam 20:10; 2 Kin 11:1–2; 2 Chr 22:10

Mystery 1 Cor 15:50–58; Eph 3; Col 1:24—2:5; 1 Tim 3:16

N

Natural disasters Gen 7:11; 19:24; Is 24:1–6; Jer 27:8–15; 36:3; Amos 4:6–11

God's control Gen 9:13; Deut 3:22; 4:26; Josh 10:11; 2 Kin 3:20; 20:11; Ps 148:1–10; Is 38:7–8; Jon 1:10; Zech 10:1; Luke 4:39; 24:31

Lessons from Ps 29:10; Prov 30:24–28

Needs (spiritual) Ps 40:17; 63:1; 70:5; 86:1; Matt 5:20

Neighbor Lev 19:18; Matt 22:37–40; Luke 10:25–37; Rom 13:8–10

O

Obedience

To God Ex 4:13; Num 15:3; Deut 6:3; Judg 2:22; 1 Sam 15:22; 1 Kin 17:3; Prov 1:7; 10:27; Jer 36:8–9; Mic 6:8; Hag 1—2; John 13:34–35; Heb 5:8

To the law Deut 30:11; Mark 2:27; Acts 16:21; Titus 3:1–2

To leaders 2 Kin 4:2–7; Jer 38:2–3; Dan 3:13–14; Acts 4:19; Titus 3:1–2; 1 Pet 2:13–17

To parents Gen 22:9; Jer 35:8–16; Eph 6:1

Rewards of Gen 22:2; Ex 33:12; Lev 26:3–39; Josh 6:3; 1 Kin 11:4–8; 2 Kin 24:4; 2 Chr 25:2; Matt 6:10

Occult 1 Sam 28:12; Job 31:24–28; Dan 5:11; Mic 5:12; Matt 2:2; Acts 16:17–18; 19:18–19

Astrology 2 Kin 17:16; Is 47:9,12–13; Jer 10:1–2; Matt 2:1

Black magic Gen 41:8; Ex 7:11–12,22; 8:7; Ezek 13:18; Rev 9:21

Fortune telling (divination) Gen 30:27; 44:5,15; Num 22:7; Deut 18:14–15; 2 Kin 16:15; Ezek 13:17; 21:21

Sorcery Ex 22:18; 2 Kin 9:22; Job 3:8; Is 8:19; Acts 8:9–11; 19:13

Offerings Ex 23:15; 35:21; Lev 1:14; 3:3–5; 3:16; Deut 26:2; 1 Chr 21:26; Ezra 1:4–6; Ps 96:8; Prov 3:9–10; Ezek 45:13–25; Mal 1:10; Matt 26:10; 2 Cor 8:1,7

Oil Lev 8:10; Deut 33:24; 1 Kin 1:39; Ps 45:7; 133:2; Is 21:5; Mark 6:13; James 5:14

Ordination Lev 8:22; 1 Kin 19:19; 2 Tim 1:6

P

Pain Job 16:6; 33:19; Jer 15:15–21; Hab 1—3; Rom 5:1–5; 8:28–39; Rev 21:1–4

Parables 2 Sam 14:2–3; 1 Kin 22:19–20; 2 Chr 18:18–21; 25:18–19; Matt 13:11–13; Mark 4:10–12,21–25; Luke 8:4–10

Parenting Judg 13:8; 2 Sam 18:33; Prov 19:18; 22:6; 31:1; Luke 2:44; Eph 6:4

Passover Matt 26:26–29; Mark 14:22–24; Luke 22:19–20

Patience Gen 40:23; 1 Sam 13:11; Ps 27:14; Prov 14:29; 21:12; James 5:7–11

Paul Acts 9:1–31; 13:1—14:28; 15:36—19:41; 27:1—28:31; Rom 1

Peace Ps 85:10–11; 147:14; Eccl 11:10; Is 11:6–9; Nah 1:15; Rom 12:18

Persecution Ps 118:6; Dan 11:35; Matt 5:11–12; Luke 6:29–30; 10:3; Acts 7:51–53; 14:22; 28:22; Phil 3:10; 2 Thess 1:4–5; 1 Pet 1:6; Rev 7:14; 13:17

Forms of Ps 119:86; Luke 21:18; Gal 6:17; Phil 1:29; 2 Tim 3:12

Perseverance John 10:27–30; Rom 8:31–39; Eph 6:10–20; Phil 1:1–11; Heb 6:1–6; 10:26–39; James 1:1–12; Rev 2—3

Perspective

God's Ps 90:5–6; Hag 2:6; Acts 5:38–39; Rom 8:37; 1 Cor 1:2

Human Prov 21:17; Eccl 6:12; 9:11–12; Zech 4:10; Matt 6:22; Acts 2:12–13

Pessimism Eccl 1:2

Peter Matt 4:18–22; 26:31–75; John 21; Acts 2:1—5:42; 10:1—11:18

Pharisees Matt 16:1–4; 22:15–45; 23; Mark 7:1–23; Luke 11:37–54; 18:9–14; Acts 23:6–11; Phil 3:2–7

Plagues Ex 7:20–21; 8:18–19; 9:8–9; 9:19; 11:9–10; Num 11:33; Josh 22:17; 2 Kin 19:35; Is 37:36; Rev 16:2–4

Pleasure Eccl 2:1–2; Is 5:8

Politicians Ex 7:7; 2 Sam 19:13; 2 Chr 10:8–11; Ezra 1:1–2; Ps 26:4–5; 39:1; 82:1; Jer 10:21; 22:24; Hos 5:10; Rom 13:1–7

Ambition 2 Kin 10:16; 25:25; 1 Chr 14:1–2; 2 Chr 21:4; 22:10; Ezra 4:1–2; Hos 7:6; 8:4

Polygamy Judg 8:30; 2 Sam 5:13; 1 Kin 11:1–4; 1 Chr 14:3; 2 Chr 24:3; Prov 5:18–19; 31:3

Poor (people)

God's love for Ps 113:7–9; Prov 19:17

Helping Lev 25:36–37; Deut 15:1–11; Ruth 2:2; 1 Sam 25:8; Neh 5:7; Ps 10:18; Mark 10:21; 14:7; Luke 16:19–31; John 12:8; 1 Cor 16:1–4

Mistreated Jer 5:27; Ezek 24:7

Power

Abuse of 1 Sam 13:14; Dan 4:27; Mic 2:9

God's Ex 10:7; 17:11–12; Num 24:1; Deut 2:25; Judg 16:29–30; 1 Kin 18:46; 2 Kin 2:11; 1 Chr 4:9–10; 13:10,14; 2 Chr 14:14–15; Job 26:7–14; 41:10; Ps 46:8; 77:10; 93:1–5; Is 41:7; 52:10; 64:1–3; Jer 46:25; 49:38; Mark 11:22–24; Acts 5:15; 8:39–40; 1 Cor 2:4

Man's Ps 82:1; Dan 4:35

Of words Ps 64:3–6; Prov 10:18–21; 25:11; Eccl 6:10–11; Matt 5:22; 12:36–37; James 3:8

Over others Ps 101:4; Hag 2:13–14; Matt 16:11–12; Mark 8:15; Luke 11:44; Acts 27:36

Spiritual Ex 15:6; 2 Kin 2:9; 2:23–24; Job 1:6; Matt 21:21; 1 Thess 1:5

Struggle Neh 2:10,19; 6:17–18

Praise (of God) Ps 3:1; 54:6–7; 63:4; 76:10; 96:1–3; 96:7–8; 150:12; Prov 27:2; 27:21

Nature Ps 148:1–10; 150:6; Is 55:13

People Ps 22:30–31; 111:1; 112:2–8; 145:10; Is 24:14–16; Hos 14:2; Hag 1:8; Rev 4:9–10

Prayer Gen 4:26; Judg 3:15; 2 Kin 20:5–6; Neh 1:5–11; Ps 83:1; Is 38:1–5; Jer 11:11; Matt 6:8; John 15:7; Acts 7:60; Rom 15:31

Attitude 1 Sam 12:23; 2 Chr 6:13; 30:27; Neh 4:4–5; Job 16:17; 27:7; Jer 10:23–24; Matt 6:7; John 15:7; James 4:3; 1 Pet 3:7

Confession Ps 19:12

Delayed answers Job 13:20–22; 30:20; Ps 10:1; 27:14; 102:1–2; Is 62:7; 64:4; Hab 1:2; 3 John v. 2

Effects Ex 32:14; Deut 9:19; 1 Sam 30:6; Ps 106:23; Is 37:21; Jer 15:1; Amos 7:3,6; Matt 7:7–8; 21:21–22; 26:41; Mark 14:38; Luke 11:9–13; 22:40; Rev 8:3

For others Gen 18:17–19; 18:27–32; Esth 4:16; Job 1:5; 42:8; Ps 20:9; Jer 29:7; 37:3; Ezek 14:14; Rom 8:27;

Group Matt 18:19–20

Honest 1 Sam 1:13; Job 13:3; 34:12; 35:12–13; Ps 6:8; 83:13–16; 88:5,10–12; 88:14; Is 45:9; Hab 2:1

Ignored by God Job 35:12–13; Ps 66:18; 102:1–2; Is 59:2; Jer 11:11; 11:14; Lam 3:8; Mic 3:4; Zech 7:13; James 1:7–8; 4:3; 1 John 5:14

Need for Luke 5:16; Rom 8:27; 15:31; Col 4:18

Proper form 2 Chr 6:13; Matt 6:7; Acts 13:3; 1 Tim 2:8

Public 2 Chr 20:5–12; Ezra 9:6; Neh 9:5–38

Thanks Jon 2:2

Preaching Ps 119:43; Ezek 3:1; Jon 3:5; Matt 13:3–23; 16:19; Mark 4:13–20; Luke 4:15–20; Acts 16:6–10; 1 Thess 2:13; 2 Tim 4:3; Titus 2:1

False Ezek 11:1; 12:24; Amos 5:18; Mic 2:11; Zeph 3:4; 2 Cor 6:14–15,17; 1 Tim 1:3–4; 2 Pet 1—3

Preachers Matt 3:4; Mark 1:6; Acts 18:3; 1 Cor 9:15; Gal 2:2; Phil 1:18; 1 Tim 5:17

Prejudice Gen 43:32; 46:34; Esth 2:10; Amos 1:13; Jon 4:3; Matt 2:23; Luke 9:53; 20:16; John 4:9; Acts 6:1; 1 Thess 2:16

Pride (boasting) 2 Kin 17:14; 20:13; 2 Chr 32:25–26; Job 18:2; Ps 18:44–45; 25:9; Prov 21:4; Is 16:6; Obad v. 10–11; Luke 17:7–10; 1 Cor 5:2; 14:18; Gal 6:4

Examples of 2 Kin 5:10–12; 20:13; 2 Chr 12:14; 26:18; Prov 27:2; Luke 14:11; 15:25–32; John 5:16; Gal 6:1

Priests

Believers as Is 66:21; Jer 33:18; Ezek 44:20–25

Role of Ex 28:12; 1 Chr 16:2; Heb 5:5,10

Salaries Num 5:10; 18:8; 2 Kin 12:6–8; 2 Chr 31:4; Ezek 44:28

Priorities 1 Kin 7:1; Neh 10:36; Job 37:7; Ps 1:3–4; Matt 19:21; Luke

10:38–41; 14:18–20; 18:22–30; John 12:8; 1 Cor 7:29; Col 3:2; 1 Tim 6:9–11

Promises Gen 42:37; Lev 5:4; Josh 9:19; Job 31; Is 48:1; Jer 22:5; Matt 5:34–37; 23:16–22; Acts 23:14; Heb 6:13; James 5:12

Oaths and vows Gen 28:20–22; Num 6:2; 30:2; Josh 24:19; Judg 11:29–31; 11:39; 13:5; 16:20; Ps 22:25; 116:14–18; Eccl 5:4–6

Prophecy Ezra 1:1; Is 42:1; Mark 2:10

About Christ Matt 17:10; 21:7; 1 Pet 1:10–11

About Christ's birth Is 9:2; 40:3–5,9; Mic 5:2

About Christ's death Ps 22:16; 50:4–6; Is 52:14; 53:1–12

Examples of 1 Chr 12:18; 25:1,6–7; 2 Chr 18:9; Is 12:1–6; Jer 13:1–11; 28:10; 29:26; Hos 1:2; Mic 1:8

Fulfilled Is 49:22; Jer 31:8; 31:15; Ezek 17:22–24; Dan 2:31–45; 11:2–45; Obad v. 18–20; Matt 1:1; Luke 3:4–6; 19:41–44

Future 2 Chr 7:14; Is 41:18; Jer 7:30–34; Ezek 3:25; 4:3–6; 38:2–6; Dan 7:24

Purpose today Is 15:1–9; 21:1; Dan 12:9–10; Hos 1:11; Amos 9:11; Zech 1:8; Acts 11:27–30; 1 Cor 14:1

Understanding Jer 23:5–8; Dan 7:1; 8:27; Zeph 1:2; Zech 6:6; Matt 24:15; Mark 13:5–25; Luke 18:34; 24:45; Rev 1:19–20; 17:9–14

Warning Jer 25:15–17; Jon 3:4; Acts 21:4,11–12

Prophets 1 Sam 10:5; 1 Cor 12:28

Mistreated Jer 11:21; 20:1–2; 26:20–23; 32:3; 36:5; 37:16; Hos 9:7

Reliable Deut 18:21; 2 Chr 18:5–6

Role 2 Sam 12:1; 1 Kin 1:9–10; 12:24; 2 Kin 4:13; Jer 1:10; John 1:6

Test 1 Kin 12:24; 22:6–7; Jer 23:18; 26:8–9; 28:8–9; 28:15–16; Dan 1:17; Matt 7:15–16; 1 Thess 5:20–21

Prostitutes Gen 19:4–5; 38:15; 38:21; 1 Kin 14:24; 2 Kin 23:7; Prov 7:4–5; 23:28; James 2:25

Providence of God Ps 104; Matt 10:29–30; Acts 14:14–17

Punishment Gen 20:16; Ex 34:6–7; Num 14:20–35; Matt 12:31–32; Acts 13:46; Rom 11:8; 2 Thess 1:8

Delayed Num 33:52–53; 2 Kin 23:24–26; 2 Chr 34:27–28; Ps 140:12

Limits Deut 25:3; Zech 1:15; 9:1–6

Physical Prov 26:3

Substitute Is 53:5; 53:10; Rom 9:3; Gal 3:13

Purity Lev 6:10; Josh 5:15; Mal 3:2; 1 John 3:3

Q

Quiet time Ps 1:2; 16:7; 77:12; 119:11; 119:15; Matt 6:23

R

Racism Ex 1:9–10; Esth 2:10; Amos 1:13

Rape Gen 19:8; 34:26; Deut 22:19,29; Judg 19:24; 2 Sam 13:13

Rebellion (against God) Num 15:30; Ps 85:4; 107:11; Is 1:24; 57:17; Hos 4:4; Nah 3:1–4; Acts 26:14; Rev 16:6; 17:3

Reconciliation Matt 5:23–26; Phil 4:2–3; 2 Cor 5:11—6:2; Eph 2:11–22; Col 1:15–23

Redemption Ex 12:29; Num 35:19; Ruth 2:20; 3:12; 4:3–6; Job 19:25; Ps 54:7; 90:11–14; 130:7–8; Is 35:10; Jer 17:9; Hos 13:14; Col 1:17

Rejection Ps 88:14; John 9:22

Relationship (to God) Ps 5:5; 50:16; Eccl 12:13–14; Ezek 43:10; Acts 17:30; Rom 5:1

National Is 43:3; 59:18; Jer 18:7–10

Personal Ps 32:9; 107:33–43; Is 37:14; 64:8; Jer 22:16; Hag 1:8; Luke 18:22–30; Matt 19:21

Repentance Lev 26:41; 1 Kin 21:27; 2 Kin 6:30; 2 Chr 33:1–2; Ps 79:8; Joel 2:12–14

National Judg 3:15; 1 Sam 7:6; Neh 8:9–11; Lam 5:21; Dan 9:3; Hos 6:1–3

Personal Ps 38:4; 39:13; 143:1–2; Ezek 11:19; Zech 1:3; Matt 3:11; Luke 7:29–30; John 1:6; Philem v. 12; Rev 22:11

Respect

Elderly Job 33:2–7

God Ex 3:5; 30:20–21; Lev 16:2; 1 Chr 13:9–10; 15:29; 2 Chr 27:2; Job 9:9; 28:28; Ps 103:11; Eccl 5:1; Is 6:1–8; 54:5; Zech 2:13; Mal 2:17; John 12:3; 2 Cor 7:1

Leaders 1 Sam 26:9; 2 Sam 1:6–10; 2 Chr 24:15–16; Eccl 10:20; Rom 13:4; 1 Thess 5:12

Parents Ex 21:17; Prov 13:1; Jer 9:13–16; Matt 8:22; 12:46–50; Mark 3:31–35; John 2:4; Eph 6:1

Responsibility 2 Kin 21:9; 1 Tim 4:14

Accepting 2 Kin 6:5; Ps 104:14–15; 139:16; Is 4:4; 2 Thess 3:6–13

Resurrection Ezek 37:10; Dan 12:2,13; Matt 28:17; Luke 24:5–6; 24:31,37–39; Acts 10:41; 23:9; Rom 1:4; 1 Cor 15:2

Last days Is 26:19; John 20:17; 1 Cor 15:35–57; Heb 11:35; Rev 20:4–5

Revelation Ps 19:1–6; John 1:1–18; Acts 14:14–1; Rom 1:18–23; Heb 1; 2 Tim 3:14–17; 2 Pet 1:19–21

Revenge Ex 21:23–25; Lev 24:20; 2 Sam 19:22; 1 Kin 2:6; Ps 58:6–8; 94:1–3; 149:6–9; Jer 46:10; Ezek 25:3–7; Matt 5:39; 2 Tim 4:14

Revival 2 Kin 23:24–26; 2 Chr 15:12; 19:4–5; Neh 1:6; Ps 19:7; 80:18; Is 19:19–25; Ezek 37:10

The rich and the poor Ex 35:4–9; Deut 8:18; 1 Chr 29:3,12; Ps 62:10; 82:3–4; Hos 2:8; Mal 3:8–10; Matt 6:19–25; 19:16–21; Eph 4:28; 5:3; Col 3:5; 1 Tim 6:17–18; 1 Pet 5:2

Righteousness Ps 7; Jer 23:1–6; Matt 6:25–34; Rom 4:6–8; Gal 2:15–21; Phil 3:7–11; 1 Tim 6:11–16; 1 Pet 2:24–25

Role models Esth 4:16; Job 15:4; 2 Cor 8:8; Eph 5:1; Phil 4:9; Heb 12:1

S

Sacrifices Ex 20:24; 29:11–21; Lev 1:1; 17:11; Num 7:41–80; Ps 40:6; 50:5; 50:8–15; 50:23; 51:19; 1 Pet 2:5

Sadducees Matt 16:1–12; Mark 12:18–23; Acts 4:1–22; 5:17–42; 23:1–11

Salvation

Belief in Christ John 3:16–18; 6:29; 8:37,40; 8:51; 13:8; 17:2,6,9; Acts 13:48; 2 Cor 13:5; 2 Tim 2:19

By faith Gen 15:6; Ps 106:31; 127:1–2; Is 26:2; Ezek 33:13; Matt 5:20; 25:35–36; Luke 19:9; Acts 15:20; Rom 10:3–7; Heb 4:11; James 2:14–24

For all people Gen 35:11; Deut 4:33;

Ruth 4:22; 2 Chr 6:33; Esth 13:1–3; Ps 22:27; 86:9; Is 42:6; Jer 31:31; 48:47; Amos 9:12; Jon 2:7–9; Zeph 2:11; Zech 9:7; Matt 2:2; 15:23–26; Luke 2:32; John 10:16; Acts 10:45; 1 Tim 2:4

God's promise to Abraham Gen 12:3; Deut 26:18; 1 Kin 8:43; Ps 47:9; Is 19:19–25; Eph 3:3–4,6,9

Losing Rom 11:21–22; 1 Cor 9:27; Heb 6:6; 2 Pet 2:20–22

Understanding Ps 67:2; 87:4; 98:2–3; Prov 10:16; Is 52:15; Jer 22:16; Matt 10:5; 19:17; Acts 4:12; Rom 1:16; Phil 2:12–13

Sanctify John 17:17,19; 1 Cor 1:2; Phil 1:6; 1 Thess 4:3–12

Satan

Limited by God Job 1:12; 19:8–12; Luke 10:18; Rom 16:20; Col 2:15; 1 John 5:18

Names for 2 Sam 24:1; 2 Kin 1:2; Job 31:35; Zech 3:1; Matt 4:1; 4:1; 4:3–4; 10:25; Mark 1:12–13; 8:33; Luke 4:3; John 12:31; Col 1:13; James 4:7; Rev 12:11

Power of Job 1:13–19; Matt 4:8–9; 7:22–23; Luke 4:6; 22:3; John 13:27; Acts 19:19; 2 Cor 2:11; Eph 2:2; 6:12; 1 Thess 2:18; 1 Pet 5:8; 1 John 1:8; Rev 6:1–17

Scapegoat Lev 16:20–22; 2 Kin 6:32–33; 1 Pet 1:6

Second chances Lam 5:22

Second coming Matt 24—25; John 14:1–4; Acts 1:6–8; 1 Cor 15:12–28; 1 Thess 4:13—5:11; 2 Thess 2; 2 Pet 3; Rev 19—20

Self

Confidence 1 Sam 10:22; Ps 22:6–7; Prov 12:9; Rom 12:3; 1 Cor 2:3; Gal 6:4

Control Prov 6:6–11; 25:28; Titus 2:2

Defense Ex 22:3; 2 Sam 20:10

Denial Matt 7:13–14

Esteem Ex 30:15; 1 Chr 4:9–10; Ezra 2:2–61; Job 25:6; Ps 8:5; 103:14; 139:13–16; Prov 22:2; Is 41:14; 1 Pet 2:18–21

Reliance 2 Chr 12:14; Is 2:7–8; 26:18; 50:10–11

Will Judg 16:17

Service (to God and others) Num 35:2; 1 Chr 23:7–23; Matt 25:26–27; John 13:14–15; 1 Tim 3:13

Servant Is 49:1–6; 50:4–9; 52:13—53:12; Mark 10:35–45; John 13:1–17; 1 Cor 9:19–23; Gal 5:13–26; Phil 2:6–11; 1 Pet 2:18–25

Sex

Homosexuality Gen 13:13; 19:4–5; Lev 18:22; Judg 19:24; 2 Kin 23:7; Rom 1:26–27

In marriage 1 Cor 6:20

Pleasure Prov 5:18–19

Religious rituals Num 25:1; Josh 22:17; 1 Kin 14:24; 16:32; Hos 4:12; 4:14

Rules about Ex 19:15; 2 Sam 11:11

Temptation 2 Sam 11:2–3; Prov 5:3–10; 9:17; 23:28; 1 Cor 6:18

Shame Ezra 9:6–15; Ps 25; 34:1–7; Rom 1:16–17; 2 Tim 1:8–14

Sin

Acceptance Lev 26:41; Ps 38:4; John 9:41

Communal Josh 7:11; 2 Sam 24:15; Ezra 9:6; Is 59:12; Ezek 21:4; Dan 9:3; 9:5; Mal 4:6

Defeating Rom 6:2–14; 7:14–25

Development 2 Kin 18:4

Hated by God Ps 5:5

Individual Lev 20:9; Num 14:18; Deut 5:9; 23:2; Ezek 18:2

Punished 1 Chr 21:14; 1 Thess 4:6

Secret 2 Kin 17:9; Ps 90:8

Unforgivable Matt 12:31–32; Mark 3:29

Unintentional Ps 19:12; Acts 3:14–15,17; James 4:17

Sin's effects Gen 12:17; 1 Sam 2:31–33; 2 Sam 12:9–10; 21:6,9,14; 1 Chr 21:14; Job 5:7; 15:20; Ps 7:13,16; 51:4; 103:10; Jer 17:9; Ezek 7:27; 18:24; Matt 5:29–30; Rom 1:24,26,28; 5:13–14; 6:1; 2 Cor 7:9

Church 1 Cor 5:7; 8:12

Creation Gen 9:2; Ps 107:33–34; Jer 7:20; John 9:2; 9:3; Rom 8:20–21; Rev 8:7–11

Families Ps 79:8; Jer 2:9; 31:29; 32:18; Lam 2:11–12; Ezek 18:19–20; 18:19–20; Hos 2:4–5

God Job 35:6; Jer 12:7–8; Ezek 33:11; John 11:35

Health Gen 3:16; John 5:14

Nations Neh 1:6; Ps 51:18; Jer 9:3–8; 18:7–10; 29:21–23; Lam 2:11–12; Ezek 21:4; 22:30; Dan 9:5

Removed Rev 22:2

Slander Ps 12:5; Prov 10:18–21; James 4:11

Slavery Ex 10:27–28; Lev 22:6,11; 25:44–46; Josh 16:10; Judg 1:28; 1 Kin 12:18; 1 Chr 5:21; Matt 20:26–28; Mark 10:43–45; 1 Cor 7:21–24; 1 Pet 2:18–21

Son of God Matt 16:18; Luke 22:70–71; John 1:18; Heb 7:11

Son of man Ps 80:17; Ezek 2:1; Dan 7:13; 8:17; Mark 2:10; Heb 2:6–8; Rev 1:13; 14:14

Sorrow Ex 3:1–9; Matt 26:36–46

Soul Deut 6:1–5; 30:6; Ps 25:1; 42; 103; 130; Eccl 12:7; 1 Thess 5:23; Heb 4:12; Rev 6:9–10

Spirit of God Gen 6:3; Ex 24:2; 31:3; Judg 13:25; 1 Sam 11:6; 16:14; 2 Sam 23:2; 1 Chr 12:18; 28:12,19; 2 Chr 20:14; Ps 104:30; Prov 20:27; Joel 2:28; Zech 4:6; Mark 1:10

Stealing Ex 20:15; 22:1–15; Lev 19:11–13; Mal 3:8–10; Eph 4:28

Stewardship Matt 25:14–30; Luke 12:35–48; 16:10–12; Eph 5:15–16

Stubbornness Prov 29:1

Submission

In marriage Eph 5:24–33; 1 Pet 3:5–6

To God Is 18:7; 19:18; Jer 27:8–15; 29:7

To authority Col 3:18–4:1; 1 Pet 2:13–17

To others Eph 5:21

Success Deut 28:2–6; 2 Chr 26:5; Job 22:21–25; Ps 1:3–4; 90:17; Prov 6:6–11

Suffering Job 5:7; 6:24; 11:16; 34:37; Ps 88:3; Mark 8:34; 15:23; Acts 5:41; Rev 13:10

Alone Job 19:13–20; Ps 10:1; 12:1; 22:1; 88:6; 102:3–5; Lam 3:3; Matt 26:41; 27:46; Mark 14:38; 14:51–52; 15:34; Luke 22:40; 2 Tim 1:15

God's role 2 Sam 12:14–15; 2 Kin 5:1; Ps 34:17; 71:20; 97:10; Rev 13:8

Purpose of Job 32:14; 33:19; Ps 22:30–31; 102:9–10; Prov 22:4; Is 45:7; 48:10; Lam 3:38; Ezek 24:16–18; John 9:3; 1 Thess 3:3

Results Job 3:10–16; 23:10; Ps

119:67–75; Prov 17:3; Eccl 11:8; Lam 3:38; John 11:4; Rom 5:3; 2 Cor 4:12; Rev 9:20–21

Understanding Job 5:27; 9:22–24; 17:7–8; 23:10; 42:8; Is 13:16; 53:9; Rom 8:17; 2 Cor 1:5; 1 Pet 4:1

Suicide 1 Sam 31:5; 2 Sam 17:23; Is 57:1–2; Acts 1:18–19; 16:22–36

Talents 1 Chr 22:8; Matt 25:26–27; 1 Tim 4:14

Talking (with God) Gen 12:1; 18:10; Num 1:1; 7:89; Josh 1:1; 1 Sam 3:21; 30:6; Job 38:1; Ps 95:7; Hab 2:1; Mal 2:17

Temple 2 Chr 3:1; 3:3–17; Matt 24:2–3

Employees 1 Chr 23:26,28–32; 2 Chr 4:6–16; 23:8; Neh 12:29; Ps 134:1; Ezek 44:16

Finances Lev 27:2; 27:13; Num 5:10; 18:31; Josh 13:33; 2 Kin 12:6–8; 2 Chr 24:5; 31:4; Ezra 6:4

Temptation Deut 13:3; 1 Chr 21:1; Job 29:2; 31:1; Ps 81:7; Matt 4:1; 4:3–4; Mark 1:12–13; Luke 4:3; 1 Cor 10:13; Eph 6:14–17; Heb 4:15; James 1:13; 1 John 5:4

Ten Commandments Ex 3:1; 20:1–17; 31:18; Lev 16:13; Deut 5:1; 9:10; Josh 8:32; Mark 2:27; Rom 10:4

Terrorism 2 Kin 25:7–9; Jer 39:7

Testing

By God Deut 8:2; 13:3; 1 Chr 29:17; 2 Chr 32:31; Job 1:8; 7:18; 16:9; 23:10; Ps 66:10; 81:7; Matt 4:1; 15:23–26; Mark 7:26–27; Rom 16:10; 1 Thess 3:3; James 1:13; 1 Pet 1:7

Of God Ps 78:18

Thanksgiving Ex 23:15; 1 Sam 31:12; Ps 116:13; 116:17; Eph 5:20

Time Eccl 3:1–8; Eph 5:15; Col 4:5

Tithes Gen 14:20; 28:22; Lev 27:30; Deut 12:17; 26:12; 1 Chr 6:54; 2 Chr 31:5; Prov 3:9–10; Mal 3:9–10; 2 Cor 9:7

Tongues Acts 2:1–13; 10:44–48; 19:1–7; 1 Cor 12—14

Trinity Gen 1:26; 11:7; Deut 6:4; Matt 28:16–20; John 14:9–28; 2 Cor 13:14; Titus 3:3–8; Jude 20—21

Trust Deut 28:65; Ps 77:2; Eccl 11:10; Matt 6:25; Luke 12:22

In God Gen 22:2; Ex 30:12; Josh 11:6; Judg 7:5–6; 2 Kin 4:2–7; 18:14; 1 Chr 18:4; 2 Chr 28:5; Neh 6:13; Job 2:10; 12:15–16,22–23; 19:25; 23:14–15; Ps 11:1; 91:16; 112:6–7; 116:10; 142:6; Is 30:18; Mic 7:7; Hab 3:17; James 1:2; 1:7–8

In Idols 2 Chr 25:14; Is 27:10–11

In military power Josh 11:6; 1 Sam 12:12; 2 Sam 24:3,10; 1 Chr 21:1,6–7; Is 20:5–6; 22:8–11; 30:1–2; 31:1; 34:1–3; Jer 2:36; Ezek 16:26–29; 29:6–7; Hos 7:11; Hab 1:16

In money Job 36:19; Ps 12:8; 97:7; Is 2:7–8; 39:1–2

In people Ps 146:3–4

Learning to Ex 16:4; Ps 78:5–7; Is 43:2

Truth Prov 22:17; 23:23; Is 45:23; Jer 22:5; 38:2–3; Matt 5:34–37; Acts 16:18; 2 Tim 3:7; James 5:12; 2 John v. 1; Rev 1:19–20

Unbelief Num 20:12; Deut 1:34; Ps 78:32; 95:11; 115:2; Is 29:9–10; Matt 12:39; Mark 6:5–6; Luke 11:29; John 6:29; 10:26

Understanding God Gen 14:18; 41:37–39; Ex 5:1–3; Deut 10:17; 29:4; 1 Kin 5:7; 10:1; 2 Chr 32:16–19; Ezra 6:10; Job 10:2; 41:11; Ps 65:8; 97:2–5; Prov 25:2; 30:2–3; Eccl 11:5; Ezek 20:9; Jon 2:7–9; Luke 15:25–32; John 6:46,57

Unity Ps 133; John 17; Acts 2:42–47; 1 Cor 1–4; 10:16–17; 11:17–34; Gal 3:26–28; Eph 4:1–16

Unity of believers Ps 133:1; John 17:21–23; Acts 15:20; Rom 15:5–7; Eph 4:13; 5:21; Phil 2:2–5

Values (spiritual) Matt 5:3–10; 5:19

Virgin birth Matt 1:23

Wait (for God) Is 64:4; Amos 5:13; Hab 2:1

Wars Gen 49:24; Josh 11:23; Judg 20:8–43

Atrocities Josh 10:24–26; 1 Sam 27:9; 2 Kin 15:16; Ps 137:8–9; Is 21:3–4

Destruction 2 Kin 3:25

Spiritual Job 1:13–19; Ps 70:2; 83:2,6–8; Is 24:21–22; Dan 10:12; Matt 11:12; 2 Cor 10:4; Eph 6:14–17; 6:12; 2 Tim 2:3

Warning (others) Ezek 3:17; 33:6–9

Water John 4:10–14; 7:37–38; Rev 22:1–2

Wealth Num 7:26–80; Ps 12:8; Prov 8:10–11; 11:25–28; 19:10; 22:2; Eccl 5:11; 10:19; Amos 3:12; Luke 6:24–26; 16:19–31; 18:25; 1 Tim 6:9–11; James 5:1–6

Widows Deut 25:5–9; Is 4:1; 54:1–6; Mic 2:9; 1 Tim 5:9

Will of God Matt 26:36–46; John 4:34; 6:38; Rom 12:1–8; Eph 1:3–14; Phil 2:5–11; 1 Thess 4:1–8; James 4:13–15 1 Pet 4:12–19

Wisdom Num 27:18; Prov 1:2; 8:10–11; 21:5; 24:27; Eccl 1:18; James 4:13–15

God's 1 Kin 4:29–34; Job 2:10; 28:1–23; 1 Cor 2:13; 4:6; James 1:5

Using 1 Kin 11:4–8; Prov 21:22

Worldly 1 Kin 4:29–34

Witchcraft Lev 20:6–7; Deut 18:10–12; 1 Sam 28; Is 8:19–22; 47:10–14; Acts 8:9–24; 13:6–12; 19:13–19; Gal 5:19–21

Women

As property Gen 19:8; 30:3; 31:15; 38:14; Ex 21:7–11; Deut 20:14; Judg 19:24; 2 Sam 3:7; 20:3; 1 Kin 2:22–23; Is 13:16

Godly Esth 2:8; Prov 31:1; 31:10–31; 1 Tim 2:11

Leadership Ex 15:20; Judg 4:4; 2 Kin 22:14; 1 Chr 7:24; 2 Chr 22:10; Acts 18:26; Rom 16:1–2

Roles of Judg 1:12–13; 2 Sam 20:16,22; Neh 3:12

Status Gen 2:18–22; Ex 22:16–17; Num 30:3–16; Ruth 2:9; 2 Sam 11:4; Jer 44:19; John 4:7

Word of God Gen 1; Ps 33:6–9; Matt 4:1–11; John 1:1–18; Eph 6:10–17; Heb 4:12–13; 11:1–3; James 1:18; 1 Pet 1:22–25; Rev 9:13–16

Work

Daily Neh 4:6–9; Ps 90:17; 127:1–2; Is 26:12; 1 Cor 10:31; 15:58; Col 3:17; 2 Thess 3:10

Nature of Gen 1:28; 2:15,19–20; 3:17–19; Ex 20:9; Eccl 1:14; 2:11,17; 3:9–10; Eph 4:28; 1 Thess 4:11

God's relationship to Deut 5:13; Ps 104:23; Prov 6:6–11; 10:4–5; 14:23; 27:23–27

Worship Ex 39:2–7; Num 7:12–83; 2 Chr 16:1; 29:30; Ps 96:8; 150:3–5; Jon 3:7–9

Attitude 2 Chr 12:10; Neh 12:27–43; Ps 40:6; 51:19; 73:17; 99:5; Is 29:13; 58:6–7; 66:3; Jer 6:20; Hos 6:6; 14:2; Amos 5:21–23; Zech 7:5–6; Mal 1:10; Rom 15:17; Heb 10:6,8

Idols Judg 17:1–4; 18:30–31; 1 Kin 3:3; 16:31; 2 Kin 12:3; 16:15–16; 17:41; 2 Chr 33:17; Ezra 4:3; 6:10; Ps 65:8; Ezek 8:3; 20:3; Dan 2:47; 6:26; 2 Cor 11:4

Jerusalem 1 Kin 8:5; 2 Kin 18:22; 2 Chr 1:4; Ps 99:9; Acts 8:27

Many gods (polytheism) Gen 35:2; Josh 24:14,23; Judg 6:25; 17:1–4; 1 Kin 11:5–8; 16:31; 2 Kin 12:3; 16:15–16; 17:41; 2 Chr 33:17; Ezra 1:1–2; 4:3; 6:10; Ps 65:8; 78:32; Jer 11:13; 12:2; 40:2; Ezek 20:3; Dan 2:47; 6:26;

Music 2 Kin 3:15; 1 Chr 6:31; Ps 33:3; 90:9–10; 118:1–4

Place Ex 20:24; Lev 17:3–4; Deut 26:2; Josh 18:1; 22:10–12; 1 Sam 1:3; 1 Kin 8:5; 2 Kin 18:22; 1 Chr 16:39; 2 Chr 1:4; 3:3–17; 6:5–6; 11:16; 32:12; Ps 99:9; Amos 4:4

Preparing for Num 8:7; Jer 7:1–2; Ezek 44:7–9

Style 2 Sam 6:14; Ps 63:4; 68:24–25; 95:11; 96:1–3; 118:1–4; 133:1; 143:6; 149:3; Mic 6:6–7

Youth Eccl 11:7–12:7; Joel 2:28–32; Acts 2:13–36; 1 Tim 4:11–16

Z

Zion 2 Sam 5:6–7; 2 Kin 19:31; 2 Chr 5:2; Ps 2:6; 9:7,11; 20:2; 48:1–2; 74:2; 78:68; 110:2; Is 18:7; 28:16; 33:20; 51:16; 59:20; Joel 3:17,21; Amos 1:2; Mic 4:7; Heb 12:22; Rev 14:1

Index to Notes

All entries are words or concepts in the study notes, *not* in the NASB text. For references to key words in the text, consult either the Index to Subjects or the Concordance. For location of geographical names, check both the Index to Maps and the Index to Color Maps.

A

AMMON
2 Sam 12:30; Amos 1:13
AMMONITES
Gen 19:36-38; 1 Sam 11:1; 2 Sam 10:2; Zeph 1:5
AMNON
2 Sam 3:2-5,3; 12:10; 13:13,15,21
AMON
2 Kin 21:20,24; 23:5,12; 2 Chr 33:21-25; Ezra 4:10
AMORITES
Gen 10:16; 15:16; Josh 5:1; 10:5; Judg 1:34; 6:10; 2 Sam 21:2; 1 Kin 21:26; Amos 2:9
AMOS
1 Kin 13:1; Ezek 7:7; Hos 1:1; Amos 1:1; Introduction to Hosea: Author and Date—p. 1250; Introduction to Amos: Author—p. 1274
AMOZ
Is 1:1
AMPHIPOLIS
Acts 16:12; 17:1
AMPLIATUS
Rom 16:8-10
AMRAM
Ex 6:20; Num 3:27
AMUNHOTEP II
1 Kin 16:1; Introduction to Exodus: Chronology—p. 75
ANAKITES
Num 13:22; Deut 1:28; Josh 11:21; 2 Sam 21:16
ANAMMELECH
Is 36:19
ANANIAH
Neh 11:32
ANANIAS (high priest)
Acts 22:5,12; 23:2; 24:1
ANANIAS (husband of Sapphira)
Acts 5:1,13
ANANIAS (of Tarsus)
Acts 9:10
ANATA
Jer 1:1
ANATH
Judg 3:31; Jer 1:1
ANATHEMA
Gal 1:8
ANATHOTH
Is 10:30; Jer 1:1
ANCIENT OF DAYS
Dan 7:9
ANDREW
Mark 1:29,36; Luke 21:7; John 1:35
ANDRONICUS
Mark 6:30
ANGEL OF THE LORD
Gen 16:7; 2 Kin 1:3; Zech 1:8
ANGELS
as agents of God
Gen 32:1,24; Ex 12:23; Job 1:6; Ps 78:25; 1 Cor 11:10; 2 Thess 1:7; Heb 1:4; 2:2,5
elect
1 Tim 5:21
fallen, theories about
1 Pet 3:19-20
guardian
Matt 18:10; Acts 12:15; Heb 1:14
as mediators
Rev 1:1; 8:4
place of
Heb 1:4,5-14,6,7; 2:5; 12:23
of the seven churches
Rev 1:20
worship of
Col 1:16; 2:18; Introduction to Colossians: The Colossian Heresy—p. 1738
ANGER
Jon 4:1,2; Eph 4:26
ANGER, GOD'S
Rev 6:16
as eternal judgment
Rom 5:9; 9:3; 1 Thess 2:16
just
Num 16:24; Ps 2:5; John 3:36; Rom 1:18; Col 3:6; Rev 14:10
and kindness
Rom 11:22
nature of
Ex 4:14
against his people
Ex 4:14; Num 11:10; 2 Sam 24:1; Zech 1:2; Heb 3:16-19; Introduction to Numbers: Theological Teaching—p. 173
satisfaction of
Rom 3:25; Eph 2:8; Heb 2:17; 1 John 2:2
ANNA
Luke 2:36,37
ANNAS
Matt 26:3; Mark 8:31; 14:53-72; 15:1-15; Luke 3:2; John 18:13,19; Acts 4:6; 5:17
ANOINTING
Ex 29:7; Num 3:3; 1 Sam 2:10; 9:16; Mark 14:3; John 1:25; James 5:14
ANTI-LEBANON MOUNTAINS
Ezek 27:5
ANTICHRIST
as beast
Rev 13:1,12,16
characteristics of
1 John 2:18; 4:4
images of
Dan 7:8; 9:27; Zech 11:17; Rev 6:2; 17:11
as "man of lawlessness"
2 Thess 2:3
origin of
Rev 7:6
predicted in Daniel
Matt 24:15
ANTINOMIANISM
Rom 3:31; 6:1; Phil 3:19; Rev 2:23
ANTIOCH
Dan 11:7; Acts 6:5; 11:19; Gal 2:11; 2 Tim 3:11; Rev 2:6
of Pisidia
Acts 13:14
ANTIOCHUS II (Theos)
Dan 11:6
ANTIOCHUS III (the Great)
Ezra 7:22,24; Dan 11:10,11,12,13,16,18,19,20; Joel 3:4; Acts 13:14
ANTIOCHUS IV (Epiphanes)
Ex 25:23; 1 Sam 2:35; Ps 30:1; Dan 8:9-12,23-25; 11:21,28; 12:11-12; Matt 24:15; John 10:22; Rev 11:2; "The Time between the Testaments"—p. 1356
ANTIPAS
Rev 2:13
ANTIPATRIS
Acts 23:31
ANTONIA, TOWER OF
Acts 12:9
ANXIETY
Phil 2:28; 4:6
APELLES
Rom 16:8-10
APHEK
1 Sam 4:1; 29:1; 1 Kin 20:26,30; 2 Kin 13:17
APHRODITE
1 Cor 6:18; 7:2; 10:14
APIRU
Gen 14:13; "The Exodus"—p. 97
APIS
Josh 24:14; Jer 46:15
APOCALYPTIC LITERATURE
Introduction to Daniel: Literary Form—p. 1226; Introduction to Zechariah: Literary Form and Themes—p. 1332; Introduction to Revelation: Literary Form—p. 1846
APOCRYPHAL BOOKS
Ezra 1:8; 6:2; Jude 1:9,14; "The Time between the Testaments"—p. 1356
APOLLO
1 Cor 10:14

APOLLOS
Acts 18:25; 19:1; 1 Cor 1:1; 2:1; 3:6,9; 16:12; Titus 3:13; Introduction to Hebrews: Author—p. 1781

APOSTASY
Heb 10:26

APOSTLE
authority of
1 Cor 1:1; 13:3
distinguished from disciple
Luke 6:13
foundation of church
Eph 2:20; 4:11
Paul as
1 Cor 1:1; 9:1; Gal 2:7
word, meaning of
Mark 6:30; Acts 14:4; Rom 1:1; 16:7; 1 Cor 12:28; Phil 2:25; Heb 3:1

APPHIA
Philem 1:2

APRIES (Hophra)
2 Kin 24:20; Ezek 17:7; 30:21

AQABA, GULF OF
1 Kin 9:26; 2 Chr 20:35-37; Acts 7:29

AQUILA
Acts 18:18; 1 Cor 16:19; Col 4:15

ARABAH
Deut 1:1; 2 Kin 14:25; Is 33:9; Ezek 47:8; Amos 6:14

ARABIA
Acts 9:23; Gal 1:17,18

ARABS
Gen 17:12; 25:13,16

ARAH
Ezra 2:5

ARAM
Gen 10:22; Is 7:1,2,4

ARAM MAACAH
1 Chr 19:6

ARAM NAHARAIM
Gen 24:10; 28:2; 1 Chr 19:6

ARAMAIC
2 Kin 18:26; Ezra 4:8,18; Dan 2:4; Mark 5:41; Introduction to Ezra: Languages—p. 633

ARAMEAN
Gen 22:23-24; "The Divided Kingdom"—p. 471

ARARAT
Gen 8:4; Is 37:38

ARAUNAH
2 Sam 24:16; 2 Chr 7:1-3

ARCHAEOLOGY
"Solomon's Temple"—p. 459; "Major Archaeological Finds Relating to the New Testament"—p. 1561

ARCHELAUS
Matt 2:22; Luke 3:1; 19:14

ARCHIPPUS
Col 4:9-17

AREOPAGUS
Acts 17:19,33,34

ARETAS IV
Luke 3:19; Acts 9:23; 2 Cor 11:32

ARIEL (chief of the Jews)
Ezra 8:16

ARIEL (Jerusalem)
Is 29:1,2,7

ARIMATHEA
Matt 27:57

ARIOCH
Dan 2:14

ARISTARCHUS
Acts 19:29; Col 4:9-17

ARISTIDES
1 Cor 1:19

ARISTOBULUS
Acts 12:1; Rom 16:10

ARK. *See also* ARK NARRATIVES; ARK OF THE COVENANT
Gen 6:14; Ex 2:3

ARK NARRATIVES
Introduction to 1 Samuel: Contents and Theme—p. 353

ARK OF THE COVENANT (ARK OF THE TESTIMONY)
Ex 25:10,22; Josh 3:3; 1 Sam 4:3,11,21; 5:3,8,11; 6:19,20; 14:18; 2 Sam 15:25; 1 Kin 6:19; 1 Chr 13:1-4,10; 2 Chr 5:2,10; 35:3; Heb 9:4,5; "Tabernacle Furnishings"—p. 115; "Temple Furnishings"—p. 460

ARKITES
2 Sam 15:32

ARMAGEDDON
Dan 11:40-45; Rev 16:16

ARMENIA
Ezek 27:14

ARNON GORGE
Josh 12:1

ARNON RIVER
Josh 12:1; 13:9,15; 2 Kin 3:25

AROER
Josh 13:9; Is 17:2

ARPAD
2 Kin 18:34; Is 10:9

ARSAMES
Neh 2:7

ARTAXERXES I
Ezra 4:7,21-23; 6:14; 7:1,11; 9:9; Neh 1:3; 2:6; 11:23

ARTAXERXES II
Ezra 4:7

ARTAXERXES III
Ezra 4:7; Is 60:10

ARTEMIS
Acts 19:24,25; 1 Cor 16:9

ARVAD
Ezek 27:8

ASA
1 Kin 15:13,14,15,19,22; 2 Chr 14:1,5; 16:1,2-9

ASAHEL
2 Sam 3:27; 1 Chr 2:10-17

ASAPH (descendant of Kohath)
1 Chr 26:1

ASAPH (father of Joah)
2 Chr 29:13-14

ASAPH (Levite)
1 Chr 9:15-16

ASAPH (son of Berekiah)
1 Chr 6:31-48

ASCENSION OF CHRIST. *See* CHRIST: ASCENSION OF

ASCENSION OF ISAIAH, THE
Introduction to Isaiah: Author—p. 957

ASCLEPIUS
1 Cor 10:14

ASHDOD
1 Sam 5:1; Neh 4:7; Is 20:1; "Five Cities of the Philistines"—p. 312

ASHER
Ex 1:2-4; Josh 19:24,32; Ezek 48:2

ASHERAH
Ex 34:13; Judg 2:13; Job 9:8; Ezek 8:3

ASHERAH POLES
Ex 34:13; Deut 7:5

ASHKELON
Judg 1:18; 2 Sam 1:20; Amos 1:8; "Five Cities of the Philistines"—p. 312

ASHTORETH
Judg 2:13; 1 Sam 7:3

ASHUR-UBALLIT
2 Kin 23:29

ASHURBANIPAL
2 Chr 33:11; Ezra 4:9,10; Nah 1:11; 3:10

ASHURNASIRPAL I
2 Kin 10:8

ASHURNASIRPAL II
Neh 5:17

ASIA MINOR
Ezek 27:14; Obad 1:20; 2 Cor 1:8; Gal 1:2,21; 1 Pet 1:1; Rev 3:7

ASIARCHON
Acts 19:31

ASSARIUS
Luke 12:6

ASSEMBLY
Deut 16:8; Joel 2:16

ASSHUR
Ezek 27:23
ASSIR
1 Chr 6:22-23
ASSOS
Acts 20:13; 27:2
ASSYRIA
Gen 10:22; 2 Kin 15:29; 16:7; 18:7; 2 Chr 33:11; "Assyrian Campaigns against Israel and Judah"—p. 522; "Exile of the Northern Kingdom"—p. 529
ASSYRIAN KING LIST
1 Chr 1:4
ASWAN
Ezek 29:10; Acts 8:27
ATER
Ezra 2:16
ATHALIAH
1 Kin 12:24; 2 Kin 8:18; 2 Chr 18:1; 22:10-12; 24:4; Ezra 8:7; Neh 3:28
ATHEISM
Ps 14:1; Introduction to Genesis: Theme and Message—p. 2
ATHENS
Acts 17:14,15; Phil 4:15; 1 Thess 3:1-2
ATONEMENT. *See also* DEATH, CHRIST'S: AS ATONEMENT
Ex 25:17; Lev 4:4; 16:20-22; 17:11; Josh 2:18; Rom 3:25; Heb 2:17; 9:5,7; 1 Pet 2:24; 1 John 2:2
ATRAHASIS
Introduction to Genesis: Background—p. 1
ATRAHASIS EPIC
"Ancient Texts Relating to the Old Testament"—p. xix
ATTALIA
Acts 14:25
ATTRIBUTES OF GOD. *See* GOD: ATTRIBUTES/CHARACTER OF
AUGUSTINE
John 7:17; "The Book of the Twelve, or the Minor Prophets"—p. 1249
AVENGER
Josh 20:3; Ps 8:2
AVVA
2 Kin 17:24
AVVIM
Josh 18:23
AVVITES
Deut 2:23
AZARIAH (Abednego)
Dan 1:4
AZARIAH (Uzziah)
2 Chr 26:1,11; Is 6:1
AZARIAH (son of Amaziah)
2 Kin 14:21,22; 15:1
AZARIAH (son of Hilkiah)
Ezra 7:1
AZARIAH (son of Zadok)
1 Sam 2:35; 1 Kin 4:2,4
AZEKAH
1 Sam 17:1; Jer 34:7
AZEL
Zech 14:5
AZGAD
Ezra 2:12
AZIZUS
Acts 24:24
AZOTUS
Acts 8:40

B

BAAL
Josh 24:14; Judg 2:13; 1 Sam 5:2; 2 Sam 2:8; 1 Kin 16:31,32; 17:1; 18:24; Ezek 43:7; Hos 2:5,8
BAAL GAD
Josh 11:17
BAAL HAMON
Song 8:11
BAAL MEON
Ezek 25:9
BAAL PEOR
Num 31:1-24; Hos 9:10; 1 Cor 10:8
BAAL PERAZIM
2 Sam 5:20
BAAL TAMAR
Judg 20:33
BAAL ZEPHON
Ex 14:2
BAAL-BERITH
Judg 8:33
BAAL-ZEBUB
Judg 10:6; Matt 10:25
BAAL-ZEBUL
Judg 10:6; Matt 10:25
BAALAH OF JUDAH
1 Chr 13:6
BAALATH
1 Kin 9:18
BAANA (son of Ahilud)
1 Kin 4:12
BAANA (son of Hushai)
1 Kin 4:16
BAANAH
2 Sam 4:8
BAASHA
1 Kin 12:24; 15:19,28; 2 Chr 16:1,2-9
BABEL
Gen 11:4,9
BABEL, TOWER OF
Gen 11:4
BABYLON
Gen 11:4,9; Is 13:1-22; 13:19; 14:1-27; 14:22-23; 21:9; Jer 50:1-46; 51:1-64; Dan 4:30; Hab 1:6,11
BABYLONIAN CHRONICLES
Nah 2:6,10
BABYLONIAN THEODICY
"Ancient Texts Relating to the Old Testament"—p. xix
BACKSLIDING
Jer 2:19; 3:22
BAGOHI
Neh 2:10; 13:7
BAHURIM
2 Sam 3:16; 16:5
BAKBUK
Ezra 2:51
BALAAM
Num 22:5,8,9,23; 23:19; Josh 13:22; 24:10; Job 3:8; Rev 2:14,17; Introduction to Numbers: Theological Teaching—p. 173
BALAK
Num 22:1; 23:2
BALIKH RIVER
Is 37:12
BALM
Gen 37:25; Ezek 27:17
BANIAS
Matt 16:13
BAPTISM
and circumcision
Col 2:11-12
for the dead
1 Cor 15:29
different kinds of
Heb 6:1-2
figurative
Mark 10:38; Luke 12:50; 1 Cor 10:2
of households
1 Cor 1:16
meaning of
Acts 22:16; Rom 6:3-4; Eph 4:5; Titus 3:5; 1 Pet 3:21
Paul and
1 Cor 1:17
of repentance
Mark 1:4; Acts 2:14-40; 19:4
significance of Christ's
Matt 3:15
spiritual
1 Cor 12:13
BAR MITZVAH
Rom 7:9
BAR-JESUS
Acts 13:6
BARABBAS
Mark 15:7; Luke 23:18; John 18:40
BARADA RIVER
2 Kin 5:12

BARAK
Judg 4:6
BARBARIANS
Rom 1:14
BARKOS
Ezra 2:53
BARLEY
Ex 9:18; Judg 7:13; Ruth 1:22
BARNABAS
Is 49:6; Mark 6:30; Acts 4:36; 12:1; 13:1,5,9; 14:1,4,12,23; 15:12,39; 1 Cor 9:4; 2 Cor 8:18; Gal 2:1; Col 4:10; 2 Tim 4:11; Introduction to Hebrews: Author—p. 1781
BARRENNESS
Gen 30:23; Num 5:21; 2 Sam 6:23; Ps 113:9; Luke 1:25
BARSABBAS
Acts 1:23
BARTHOLOMEW
Luke 6:14; Acts 1:13
BARTIMAEUS
Luke 18:35; 19:37
BARUCH
Ezra 7:6; Jer 32:12
BARZILLAI
2 Sam 17:27; 21:8; Ezra 2:61
BASHAN
Num 21:33; Is 2:13; Ezek 39:18; Amos 4:1; Nah 1:4; Zech 11:2
BATH RABBIM
Song 7:4
BATHSHEBA
2 Sam 5:14; 11:4,5,27; 23:34; 1 Kin 1:11; Song 3:11
BAY OF NAPLES
Acts 28:13
BEALOTH
1 Kin 9:18
BEAR
Job 9:9
BEAST, THE
Rev 11:7; 13:1,3,5,11,12,16
BEATITUDES, THE
Matt 5:1-48; 6:1-34; 7:1-29; Luke 6:20-23
BEELIADA
1 Chr 14:7
BEELZEBUB. *See also* SATAN
Matt 10:25; Luke 11:22
BEER
Judg 9:21
BEER ELIM
Is 15:8
BEEROTH
2 Sam 4:2
BEERSHEBA
Gen 21:31; 1 Kin 19:3; Amos 5:5
BEHISTUN INSCRIPTION
Ezra 4:24; 6:12; Neh 6:6; Esth 2:23; Hag 1:1
BEIT JIBRIN
Neh 11:29
BEKER
2 Sam 20:1
BEL
Is 46:1; Dan 1:7; 4:8
BELA
1 Chr 7:6-12
BELIAL. *See also* SATAN
Deut 13:13; 2 Cor 6:15
BELSHAZZAR
Dan 5:1,22-23; 7:1
BELTESHAZZAR
Dan 1:7
BEN-ABINADAB
1 Kin 4:11
BENAIAH
2 Sam 23:20; 1 Kin 2:46; 4:4
BENEDICTION
Num 6:24-26; 2 Cor 13:14; Heb 13:20-21
BENEDICTUS
1 Sam 2:1; Luke 1:68-79
BEN-HADAD I
1 Kin 15:20; 20:1,4,9,22,32,42; 22:1; 2 Kin 15:29
BEN-HADAD II
1 Kin 20:1; 2 Kin 5:6,7; 8:9
BEN-HADAD III
2 Kin 13:3; Amos 1:4
BEN-HUR
1 Kin 4:8
BENJAMIN (son of Jacob)
Gen 35:18; 42:4
BENJAMIN (tribe of Israel)
Judg 3:15; 1 Kin 12:21; 1 Chr 8:1-40
BEQAA VALLEY
2 Sam 8:3
BEREA
Acts 17:10; Phil 4:15; 1 Thess 3:1-2
BEREKIAH
Neh 2:10
BERENICE
Dan 11:6,7
BERGAMA
Rev 2:12
BERNICE
Acts 25:13
BEROSSUS
Ezra 4:15
BEROTHAH
Ezek 47:16
BETH ANATH
Judg 1:33
BETH ARBEL
Hos 10:14
BETH AVEN
Josh 7:2; Hos 4:15; 10:5
BETH BAAL PEOR
Hos 9:10
BETH BARAH
Judg 7:24
BETH DIBLATHAIM
Ezek 6:14
BETH EDEN
Amos 1:5
BETH GILGAL
Neh 12:29
BETH HAKKEREM
Neh 3:14
BETH HORON
Josh 10:11; 1 Kin 9:17,18; 2 Chr 8:5
BETH JESHIMOTH
Ezek 25:9
BETH MILLO
Judg 9:6; 2 Kin 12:20
BETH PELET
Neh 11:26
BETH REHOB
1 Chr 18:5; 19:6
BETH SHAN
Josh 17:11; John 3:23
BETH SHEMESH
Judg 1:33; 1 Sam 6:9,14-15,19; 2 Kin 14:11
BETH TOGARMAH
Ezek 27:14
BETH ZUR
Neh 3:16
BETHANY
Neh 11:32; Matt 21:17; Mark 11:11; John 1:28
BETHEL
Gen 12:8; Josh 8:17; Judg 20:18; 1 Kin 12:29; 2 Kin 2:23; 17:28; Ezra 2:28; Hos 4:15; 8:5; 10:5; 12:3,4; Amos 3:14; 4:4; 5:6; 7:15; 9:1; Zech 7:3; Introduction to Amos: Author—p. 1275
BETHESDA, POOL OF
John 5:2
BETHLEHEM
Judg 12:8; 17:7; Ruth 1:1; 1 Sam 16:1; Mic 5:2; Matt 2:1,16; Luke 2:4,8,22
BETHPHAGE
Matt 21:1
BETHSAIDA
Matt 11:21; Mark 6:32,44; John 6:5
BEZALEL
Ex 31:2; 37:1; 1 Chr 2:18-24; 2 Chr 1:5; 27:1-9; Introduction to 2 Chron-

icles: The Building of the Temple in Chronicles—p. 589

BEZEK
Judg 1:4; 1 Sam 11:8

BEZER
Deut 4:43

BIBLE. *See* SCRIPTURE

BICRI
2 Sam 20:1

BIGTHANA
Esth 2:23

BIGVAI
Neh 2:10; 13:7

BILDAD
Job 2:11; 8:5-6,20; 18:1-4,17; 19:6; 26:5-14; 32:15-16

BILHAH
Ex 1:2-4; 1 Chr 7:13

BIRTHRIGHT
Gen 25:31; 27:36

BISHOP
Titus 1:7

BISITUN INSCRIPTION. *See* BEHISTUN INSCRIPTION

BIT ADINI
Is 37:12

BITHYNIA
Acts 16:7; 1 Pet 1:1

BLACK OBELISK
2 Kin 10:34; "Ancient Texts Relating to the Old Testament"—p. xix

BLASPHEMY
Mark 2:7; 14:64; Luke 5:21; John 8:59; 10:31,33; 19:7; Acts 6:11; 14:5; 26:11; 1 Tim 1:20

BLASTUS
Acts 12:20

BLESSED
Ps 1:1; Prov 31:28; Matt 5:3; Rev 1:3

BLESSING
Gen 12:2-3; 27:33,36; 33:11; 35:11-12; 49:2-27; Lev 26:3; Ezek 34:26; Eph 1:3

BLESSINGS AND CURSES
Deut 4:25; 28:1-14

BLOOD
Gen 9:4; Lev 4:5; 17:11; Mark 14:24; Heb 9:18; 12:24

BLOOD REVENGE
Gen 27:45; Num 35:6-15; Josh 20:1-9; 2 Sam 14:7; "Cities of Refuge"—p. 226

BOASTING. *See also* PRIDE
Rom 15:17; 2 Cor 11:30

BOAZ
Ruth 2:1; 3:1; 4:1

BOOK
of the Covenant
Ex 20:22-26; 21:1-36; 22:1-31; 23:1-19; 24:7; 2 Kin 23:2
of the Dead
Ezek 29:5
of Jashar
Josh 10:13; Introduction to 1 Samuel: Literary Features, Authorship and Date—p. 353
of the Law
Josh 1:8; 23:6; 2 Kin 22:8; 2 Chr 34:3-7; Neh 8:1
of Life
Ps 69:28; Rev 3:5
of Moses
Ezra 6:18
of Truth
Dan 10:21
of the Twelve
"The Book of the Twelve, or the Minor Prophets"—p. 1249
of the Wars of the Lord
Num 21:14; Ps 60:6-8

BOOTHS, FEAST OF. *See also* FEAST: OF INGATHERING; OF TABERNACLES
Ex 23:16; Lev 23:42

BOUNDARY STONE
Deut 19:14

BOZKATH
2 Kin 22:1

BOZRAH
Is 34:6; Jer 49:13; Amos 1:12

BRANCH
Is 4:2; Jer 23:5; Zech 3:8

BREAD OF LIFE
Jesus as
John 6:35

BREAD OF THE PRESENCE
Ex 25:30; Lev 24:8; 1 Sam 21:4

BREASTPLATE
Rev 9:9

BRIDEGROOM. *See* CHRIST: AS BRIDEGROOM

BROAD WALL
Neh 3:8; 11:9

BRONZE PILLARS
1 Kin 7:15

BRONZE SEA
1 Kin 7:23,24

BROOM TREE
1 Kin 19:4; Ps 120:4

BUBASTIS
Ezek 30:17

BUBONIC PLAGUE
1 Sam 6:4

BUCKTHORN
Judg 9:14

BURIAL CUSTOMS, JEWISH
Mark 14:8; Luke 23:56

BURNT OFFERING
Lev 1:3; 3:5; Neh 8:10; Ezek 40:39; "Tabernacle Furnishings"—p. 115; "Old Testament Sacrifices"—p. 139

BUSYBODIES
2 Thess 3:11

BUZITE
Job 32:2

BYBLOS
Josh 13:5; Ezek 27:9

C

CAESAR (Augustus)
Matt 11:21; Luke 2:1; 20:22; John 19:12; Acts 10:1; 17:7

CAESAR (Claudius)
Acts 12:21

CAESAREA
Mark 15:1; Acts 8:40; 10:1; 12:19; 19:6; 21:8; 23:33

CAESAREA PHILIPPI
Matt 16:13; Luke 23:1

CAIAPHAS
Matt 26:3; Mark 14:53-72; 15:1-15; Luke 3:2; John 11:50,51; Acts 4:6; 5:17; James 5:12

CAIN
Gen 4:3-4,5,11,13,17; 1 Sam 20:11; Heb 11:4

CALAH
Jon 1:2; 3:3

CALAMUS
Song 4:14; Is 43:24; Jer 6:20; Ezek 27:19

CALCOL
1 Chr 2:6

CALEB
Num 14:24; Judg 1:12; 1 Sam 25:3

CALENDAR, HEBREW
Ex 12:2; Lev 23:5,24; "Hebrew Calendar and Selected Events"—p. 92

CALF WORSHIP
Ex 32:4,5,6; 1 Kin 12:28

CALIGULA
2 Cor 11:32

CALNEH
Amos 6:2

CALNO
Is 10:9

CALVARY
Mark 15:22; John 19:17

CAMBYSES
Ezra 6:8,9; 9:9; Dan 11:2,8

CAMELS
Gen 12:16; Judg 6:5

CANA
John 2:1

CANAAN
Gen 10:6; Josh 1:4
people of
Gen 9:25; 34:9; Ex 3:8; Josh 2:2; 5:1
promised land
Gen 23:19; 37:1; Ex 3:8; Josh 3:10
religious practices
Gen 15:16; Deut 18:9; Judg 2:13; 1 Kin 14:24; 2 Kin 16:4; Zech 14:21

CANDACE
Acts 8:27

CANNEH
Ezek 27:23

CANNIBALISM
Deut 28:53; Is 49:26; Jer 19:9; Ezek 5:10

CANON
"The Time between the Testaments"—p. 1356

CAPERNAUM
Matt 4:13; Mark 3:8,21; Luke 10:15; "Capernaum Synagogue"—p. 1469

CAPHTOR
Gen 10:14

CAPITAL PUNISHMENT
Gen 9:6

CAPPADOCIA
Acts 2:9

CARCHEMISH
2 Chr 35:21; Is 10:9,19; Joel 1:15; Introduction to Habakkuk: Date—p. 1314

CARIA/CARITES
2 Kin 11:4; 2 Chr 23:1

CARMEL
1 Sam 15:12; Is 33:9; 35:2; Nah 1:4

CARMEL, MOUNT. *See* MOUNT: CARMEL

CARTHAGE
Is 23:7

CASIPHIA
Ezra 8:17

CASSANDER
Dan 7:4-7

CASSIA
Ex 25:6; Ezek 27:19

CASTOR
Acts 28:11

CAUDA
Acts 27:16

CEDARS OF LEBANON
Judg 9:15; 1 Kin 5:6; 7:2; Song 5:15; Is 9:10; 14:8; 37:24

CENCHREA
Acts 18:1; 20:3; Rom 16:1

CENSER
Num 16:37; Rev 8:3

CENSUS
Ex 30:12; Num 1:2; 26:1-51; 2 Sam 24:1

CENTURION
Matt 8:5; Luke 7:2; Acts 10:1

CHALDEANS
Ezra 5:12; Job 1:17; Ezek 23:23; Hab 1:6; Acts 7:4; "Nebuchadnezzar's Campaign against Judah"—p. 544

CHEMOSH
Judg 11:24; Ruth 1:15; Neh 13:26; Is 44:19; Amos 2:2

CHERUBIM
Gen 3:24; Ex 25:18; 1 Sam 4:4; 2 Sam 22:11; 1 Kin 6:23; Ps 18:10; Ezek 1:5; 41:18; Heb 9:5

CHILDREN. *See also* FAMILY, PARENTS
the blessing of. See also BARRENNESS
Ps 112:2; 127:3,5
disciplining. See DISCIPLINE: OF CHILDREN
their responsibility to parents
Is 51:18; Mark 7:11; John 19:27
teaching/influencing
Prov 27:11; 1 Cor 7:14; 2 Tim 3:15

CHILD SACRIFICE
Judg 11:30; 2 Kin 3:27; 16:3; 23:10; Jer 7:31; Ezek 16:20

CHRIST. *See also* SON: OF THE BLESSED ONE, OF DAVID, OF MAN, OF THE MOST HIGH
"The Life of Christ"—p. 1408; "Jesus in Judea and Samaria"—p. 1522; "Jesus in Galilee"—p. 1528
ascension of
Luke 24:53; John 16:10; Acts 1:2,12; 2:38; Eph 4:9; Phil 3:21; Heb 1:14; 4:14; 1 Pet 3:22; Rev 12:5
baptism of
Matt 3:15; Luke 3:21; John 5:37; 1 John 5:6; "Jesus' Baptism and Temptation"—p. 1370
believer in
Eph 1:3
as bread of life
Ex 16:4; John 6:35
as bridegroom
2 Cor 11:2
as cornerstone
1 Pet 2:6
death of. See DEATH, CHRIST'S
deity of
John 1:1; Rom 9:5; 10:9; Heb 1:2-3,6,8
exaltation of
Is 52:13; Eph 1:3; Phil 2:9
as example
Phil 2:5; 1 Pet 3:18
fullness of
Eph 4:13,15
glory of
John 12:41
humanity of
Mark 4:38; John 1:14
humility of
Phil 2:8
incarnation of
John 1:9; 8:56; Rom 8:3; 11:25; 2 Cor 8:9; Eph 4:9; Phil 2:6; 1 Tim 3:16; Heb 1:2-3; 2:10; 1 John 2:18
and Israel
Matt 2:15; John 1:51
judgment of
John 12:47; 2 Cor 5:10
law of
1 Cor 9:21
as Lord
Matt 2:2; Luke 2:11; John 1:18; Rom 9:5; 10:9; 14:9; 1 Cor 12:3; 2 Cor 10:5; Phil 2:10-11; 2 Tim 2:8; Titus 2:13; Heb 2:9; Rev 17:14
his natural family
Luke 8:19,21
obedience of
Phil 2:8; Heb 5:8; 7:28
priesthood of
Ex 20:19; Lev 4:3; 16:3; Heb 2:17; 4:14,16; 5:5; 7:25,27; 8:2,5
resurrection of. See RESURRECTION, CHRIST'S
as Savior
Luke 2:11; John 4:42
second coming of. See SECOND COMING
suffering of
Is 52:14; 53:1-12; Luke 2:35; 17:25; Heb 5:7; 1 Pet 1:11; 2:21; 3:18; 4:13
temptation of
Matt 4:1-11,1; Luke 4:2,3,7,9,13; 22:43; "Jesus' Baptism and Temptation"—p. 1370
transfiguration of
Matt 16:28; 17:1-9,1,2; Luke 9:28; 1 Pet 5:1
trial of
Mark 14:53-72; 15:1-15
triumphal entry of
Is 64:1; Mark 11:1-11; Luke 19:28-44; "Passion Week"—p. 1446
virgin birth and conception of
Is 7:14; Luke 1:26-35; 2:33; 3:23-28; John 8:41

CHRISTIANS
characteristics of
Luke 18:17; John 15:11; Acts 2:46; 4:13
demands of. See DISCIPLESHIP
the name
Acts 11:26
treatment of each other
Neh 5:9; Mark 9:50; Luke 6:37; John 13:14,34,35; 16:2; Acts 11:1; Phil 2:1,3; James 2:1
unity of. See UNITY, CHRISTIAN
and the world
John 15:21

CHRISTOPHANY
Josh 5:13

CHURCH
description of
Matt 16:18; 18:17; Acts 5:11; 9:31; 1 Cor 1:2; 2 Cor 1:1; Gal 1:13; Eph 2:22; 3:10; 2 Tim 2:19
discipline. *See* CHURCH DISCIPLINE
foundation of
Matt 16:18
growth of
Acts 6:1
opposition to
Acts 8:1; 1 Cor 15:9; Phil 1:28
unity of
1 Cor 10:17; 12:12

CHURCH DISCIPLINE
Matt 18:17; 1 Cor 5:5; 2 Cor 2:5-11; 2 Thess 3:15; 1 Tim 1:20

CHURCH OF THE HOLY SEPULCHRE
Mark 15:46

CICERO
1 Cor 5:1

CILICIA
Ezek 27:11; Acts 6:9; 15:23; 27:5; Gal 1:21

CILICIAN GATES
Acts 22:3

CINNAMON
Ex 25:6; Song 4:14

CIRCUMCISION
Ex 4:25; Ezek 28:10
and the covenant
Gen 17:10,11; Is 56:4,6; Col 2:11-12
and legalism
Acts 15:1; Rom 2:25; Gal 2:12; 6:12
meaning of
Gen 17:10,11,12; John 7:22; Rom 2:25; 4:11
and the passover
Josh 5:2
spiritual
Rom 2:29; Phil 3:3

CITADEL
Neh 2:8

CITIES
five, of the Philistines
Judg 3:3; Amos 1:6,8; "Five Cities of the Philistines"—p. 312
of refuge
Num 35:6-15,22,24,32; Josh 20:7; "Cities of Refuge"—p. 226

CITRON WOOD
Rev 18:12

CITY
of David
1 Kin 2:10; 3:1; Neh 3:26
of destruction
Is 19:18

CIVIL AUTHORITY
Rom 13:1,3,4; Titus 3:1; 1 Pet 2:13

CLAUDIUS (emperor)
Acts 23:34; 28:17

CLAUDIUS (Lysias)
Acts 21:31

CLEAN/UNCLEAN
Lev 4:12; Num 5:3; 9:10; Mark 7:20; Acts 10:14,15

CLEMENT
Phil 4:3; Introduction to 1 Corinthians: Author and Date—p. 1660

CLEOPAS
Luke 24:13

CLEOPATRA I
Dan 11:17

CNIDUS
Acts 27:7

COELE-SYRIA
Luke 1:5

COLOSSE
1 Cor 16:19; Introduction to Colossians: Colosse—p. 1738

COMFORT
2 Cor 1:3; Phil 2:1

COMMANDMENTS. *See* TEN COMMANDMENTS

CONCUBINE
Gen 25:1,6; 30:4,5-12; Judg 8:31; Eccl 2:8

CONFUSION OF LANGUAGES
Gen 11:9

CONIAH
Jer 22:24-30

CONVERSION
Acts 15:5; 1 Thess 1:9-10

COPPER
Deut 8:9

CORBAN
Lev 1:2; Mark 7:11,13

CORINTH
Rom 16:23; Introduction to 1 Corinthians: The City of Corinth—p. 1660; "Corinth in the Time of Paul"—p. 1661

CORNELIUS
Acts 10:1,2,3,26,30,34; 1 Cor 1:16

CORNER GATE
2 Kin 14:13; 2 Chr 25:23; 26:9; Zech 14:10

CORNERSTONE. *See* CHRIST: AS CORNERSTONE

CORPORATE SOLIDARITY
Josh 7:24

COUNCIL OF JAMNIA
"The Time between the Testaments"—p. 1356

COUNCIL OF TRENT
"The Time between the Testaments"—p. 1356

COUNSELOR
John 14:16

COURT OF THE GENTILES
Matt 21:12; Mark 11:15,17; Luke 19:45; Acts 3:2

COVENANT
Gen 9:9-18; 17:7; "Major Covenants in the Old Testament"—p. 16; "Major Social Concerns in the Covenant"—p. 255
Abrahamic
Gen 15:17,18; 17:1-23
blessings and/or curses
Ex 1:7; Lev 26:14; Num 1:46; Deut 5:2; 1 Kin 2:4; 8:33; 9:4-5; 14:15; 2 Kin 2:24; 17:7-23; Introduction to Numbers: Theological Teaching—p. 173
Davidic
2 Sam 7:1-29,11; 1 Kin 8:53; 2 Kin 11:1; 16:5; Ps 89:30-37; Is 42:6; 54:10
demands of
Gen 22:2; 26:5; Ex 24:6; Deut 30:12,14; 1 Sam 12:14; 1 Kin 17:13; Introduction to 1 Samuel: Contents and Theme—p. 353
document
Ex 31:18; Deut 1:5; 1 Sam 10:25; Introduction to Deuteronomy: Structure and Outline—p. 228
everlasting
2 Sam 23:5; Is 24:5; 55:3
God's faithfulness to
1 Sam 12:7; 1 Kin 2:4; Jer 33:17-26; Introduction to Judges: Theme and Theology—p. 307; Introduction to Jeremiah: Themes and Message—p. 1050
Levitical
Num 25:11
of love
Deut 7:8
messenger of
Mal 3:1
Mosaic
Ex 19:5; 20:2; Deut 5:2; 2 Kin 11:17; 17:17,35; Jer 31:32
new
Is 42:6; Jer 31:31-34; Ezek 34:25; Heb 8:8-12
Noahic
Gen 9:9
and oaths
Deut 4:31
of peace
Ezek 34:25
of salt
Num 18:19
sign of
Gen 9:12,13; 17:10,11; Ex 20:10
types of (in ancient Near East)
"Major Types of Royal Covenants/Treaties in the Ancient Near East"—p. 16

D

Zephaniah: Purpose and Theme—p. 1320

DEACON
Neh 13:13; Acts 6:6; 1 Cor 12:5,14; 1 Tim 3:8,11; "Qualifications for Elders/Overseers and Deacons"—p. 1765

DEAD, RAISING OF
1 Kin 17:22; Luke 7:14; Acts 9:40

DEAD SEA
Gen 14:3,10; Ezek 47:8; Mark 1:4; Luke 3:20

DEAD SEA SCROLLS
Gen 12:11; Ex 7:11; Deut 32:43; Josh 6:5; 1 Sam 1:23; Ezra 8:15; Jer 6:23; Dan 2:18; Joel 2:23; Luke 9:35; John 3:25; 5:2; Heb 1:4; "The Time between the Testaments"—p. 1356; "Ancient Texts Relating to the Old Testament"—p. xix

DEATH
Gen 5:5; Ps 6:5; John 11:11; 1 Cor 15:56; Phil 1:23-24,23; 1 Thess 4:13

DEATH, CHRIST'S
John 2:4; 1 Cor 15:44-49; 2 Cor 4:10; 2 Tim 2:11; 1 Pet 3:19-20
as atonement
Josh 2:18; Rom 5:6,9; 6:10; 2 Cor 8:9; Eph 2:13; Col 1:24; 1 Pet 3:18
baptism as symbol of
1 Pet 3:21
meaning of
2 Cor 5:14,21; Col 1:20; 1 Pet 1:18; 1 John 5:6
as mystery
Rom 11:25
predictions of
Is 52:13-15; 53:1-12; Zech 13:7
substitutionary character of
Eph 2:13; Col 1:2,14; 1 Pet 1:18,19; 2:24; Rev 5:9

DEATH PENALTY
Josh 1:18; 2 Sam 4:11; 11:5; 12:13

DEBIR
Josh 10:38

DEBORAH
Judg 4:1-24; 5:1-31; Luke 2:36

DECAPOLIS
Matt 4:25; Mark 8:1; "The Decapolis and the Lands Beyond the Jordan"—p. 1428; "The Territories of Tyre and Sidon"—p. 1433

DEDICATION, FEAST OF
John 10:22

DEITY OF CHRIST. *See* CHRIST: DEITY OF

DEMAS
Col 4:9-17,14

DEMETRIUS
Acts 19:24

DEMETRIUS I
Dan 11:21

DEMON POSSESSION
Mark 1:23; John 7:20

DEMONS
Luke 4:33; Rev 9:20

DENARIUS
Matt 20:2; 22:19; 26:15; Luke 12:6

DEPOSIT
2 Cor 1:22; Rom 8:23

DEPRAVITY, TOTAL
Gen 6:5; 8:21

DERBE
Acts 14:6,20

DESERT
of Edom
2 Kin 3:8
of Paran
Gen 21:21; Num 12:16; 1 Kin 11:18
of Shur
Ex 15:22
of Sin
Ex 16:1
of Sinai
Ex 19:2; Num 1:1
of Zin
Num 13:21

DEVIL. *See* SATAN

DIADOCHI
"Ptolemies and Seleucids"—p. 1246

DIANA
Acts 19:24

DIASPORA
Neh 1:8; "The Time between the Testaments"—p. 1356

DIBON
Is 15:2,9

DIDYMUS
John 11:16

DIMON
Is 15:9

DIONYSIUS
Acts 17:34

DIOTREPHES
3 John 1:9

DISCIPLESHIP
Matt 8:22; 10:38; 11:12; Mark 1:17; 9:39,50; 10:30,43; Luke 9:23; 14:28,33

DISCIPLINE
of believers
Job 5:17-26; Prov 3:11-12; Hos 5:2; 1 Cor 11:32; Heb 12:5,7,11
of children
2 Sam 13:21; 1 Kin 1:6; Prov 13:24
church
2 Cor 2:5-11; 2 Thess 3:15; 1 Tim 1:20
self
1 Cor 9:27; Titus 1:8

DIVINATION
Gen 30:27; Num 22:40; Deut 18:9

DIVINE ELECTION. *See* ELECTION, DIVINE

DIVORCE
Deut 22:19; 24:1-4; Ezra 10:3; Is 50:1; Jer 3:1; Matt 1:18,19; 19:3; Mark 10:2,5,9,11; Luke 16:18; John 4:18; 1 Cor 7:12,15

DOME OF THE ROCK
Gen 22:2

DOMITIAN
Rev 13:1

DOTHAN
2 Kin 6:13

DOUBT
Gen 3:1; Luke 7:19,23; John 20:25; 1 Cor 8:1

DOVE
Gen 8:11; Mark 1:10

DOXOLOGY
Eph 1:3-14; Introduction to Psalms: Collection, Arrangement and Date—p. 735

DRACHMA
Ezra 2:69; Luke 15:8; 19:13

DRAGON, THE
Rev 12:3

DREAM
Gen 20:3; 40:5; Judg 7:13-14; Job 4:12-21; Dan 1:17; Matt 1:20

DRINK OFFERING
Is 57:6; Joel 1:9; Phil 2:17; 2 Tim 4:6

DROPSY
Luke 14:2

DRUNKENNESS
Gen 9:21; 19:33; 1 Sam 1:13; Prov 23:20; Is 5:11-13; Joel 1:5; Eph 5:18

DRUSILLA
Acts 23:34; 24:24

DUNG GATE
Neh 2:13

DURA
Dan 3:1

DUST
Gen 13:16; Job 30:19; Jon 3:5-6

E

EARTHQUAKE
Ezek 38:19; Amos 1:1; Rev 6:12

EAST GATE
1 Chr 26:14; Neh 3:29

EBED
Ezra 8:6

EBENEZER
1 Sam 4:1

F

Introduction to Ecclesiastes: Purpose and Method—p. 986
Abraham's
Gen 12:4; 15:6; 17:1,11; 22:2,5,12; Rom 4:19; Heb 11:8,19
Daniel's
Dan 6:23
dead
James 2:14-26
defense of
1 Pet 3:15; 1 John 5:1
God's response to
Gen 15:6
and healing
John 5:9
Noah's
Heb 11:7
saving
John 14:11; Rom 3:28; 4:22; 6:3-4; 8:24; Gal 5:6
strong
Rom 14:2; 1 Cor 12:9; 13:2

FALSE WITNESS
Prov 6:19

FAMILY. *See also* CHILDREN, FATHER, MOTHER, PARENTS
Gen 6:18; Ex 20:5; Ezra 1:5; Ps 109:12; Luke 8:21; 1 John 5:1

FAMINE
Gen 41:27; 47:13; Neh 5:3; Hag 1:6

FASTING
Lev 16:29,31; Neh 1:4; Esth 4:16; 9:31; Joel 1:14; Matt 6:1; Mark 2:18; Luke 5:33; 18:12; Acts 13:3; 27:9; James 1:26

FAT OF RAMS
1 Sam 15:22

FATHER. *See also* CHILDREN, FAMILY, PARENTS
Judg 14:2; 17:10; Prov 27:11; Eph 6:4; 1 John 5:1
David as a
2 Sam 13:21; 18:33; 1 Kin 1:6
Eli as a
1 Sam 4:18

FAVORITISM
Gen 27:6; James 2:1,5-13

FEAR
1 Sam 17:11; 2 Sam 6:9

FEAR OF GOD. *See* GOD: FEAR (REVERENCE) OF

FEAST
of Booths **See of Tabernacles (Booths or Ingathering)**
Day of Atonement. *See* DAY OF ATONEMENT
"OT Feasts and Other Sacred Days"—p. 164
of Dedication
John 10:22
of Firstfruits
Ex 23:19; 1 Cor 16:8
of Harvest **See of Weeks (Pentecost or Harvest)**
Acts 2:1
of Ingathering **See of Tabernacles (Booths or Ingathering)**
of Passover
Ex 1:14; 12:11,26,48; Num 9:1-14; Josh 5:10; 2 Kin 23:21,22; 2 Chr 30:2,5; 30:8; 35:1; Esth 3:7; Matt 26:17; Mark 14:1,2,5,12,14; Luke 2:41; 21:37; 22:1,7,13,16; 23:7; John 1:29; 2:13; 5:1; 7:1; 12:12; 13:2; 19:14,31; Acts 20:6; 1 Cor 5:6,7,8; 10:16; 11:25; 16:8
of Pentecost **See of Weeks (Pentecost or Harvest)**
Purim. *See* PURIM
of Tabernacles (Booths or Ingathering)
Ex 23:16; Lev 23:34,42; Judg 21:19; 1 Sam 1:3; 1 Kin 8:2,65; 9:25; 12:32; 2 Chr 5:3; 7:9; 31:7; Neh 8:15,16,17; Ps 47:1-9; 81:3; Ezek 45:25; Zech 14:16; John 7:2; Acts 27:9
of Trumpets
Num 29:1-6; Neh 8:2
of Unleavened Bread
Ex 12:17; 23:15; Lev 23:6; 1 Kin 9:25; Ezra 6:9; Matt 26:17; Mark 14:1,2,12; Acts 20:6; 1 Cor 5:8
of Weeks (Pentecost or Harvest)
Ex 23:16; Lev 23:16; Num 28:26-31; 1 Kin 9:25; 2 Chr 15:10; 31:7; Luke 2:41; Acts 2:1; "Old Testament Feasts and Other Sacred Days"—p. 164

FELIX ANTONIUS
Acts 23:34; 24:2-3,22,24,25,26,27

FELLOWSHIP
Mark 10:30; 1 John 1:3,6

FELLOWSHIP OFFERING
Lev 3:1,5; Prov 7:14; Ezek 43:27; "Old Testament Sacrifices"—p. 139

FESTUS
Acts 24:27; 25:1,9,26; 26:1,3,8

FIELD OF BLOOD
Matt 27:8

FINGER OF GOD
Ex 8:19; 31:18

FIRST GATE
Zech 14:10

FIRSTBORN
Gen 4:3-4; Ex 4:22; 11:5; 13:2; Deut 21:17; Col 1:15,18; Heb 12:23

FIRSTFRUITS. *See also* FEAST: OF FIRSTFRUITS
Num 15:20; Deut 26:2; Neh 10:35; Prov 3:9; Jer 2:3; Acts 2:1; Rom 8:23; 11:16; 1 Cor 15:20,23; James 1:18; Rev 14:4

FISH GATE
Neh 3:3

FIVE PHILISTINE CITIES
Judg 3:3; Amos 1:6,8

FLESH
Ezek 36:26; Phil 3:3

FLOOD, THE
Gen 6:17; 2 Pet 3:6

FOOL
Prov 1:7; Eccl 5:4; 10:15

FOREKNOWLEDGE
Rom 8:29; 1 Pet 2:8

FORGIVENESS
Ps 32:1-11; Prov 16:6; Matt 18:35; Mark 2:5,7; Luke 3:3; 11:4; 17:4; 24:47; John 20:23; Acts 2:38; 3:19; 13:39; 19:4; Rom 11:27; Eph 4:32; 5:1; Phil 2:1; Heb 8:5,8-12; 12:24; 1 Pet 1:18; 1 John 1:9

FORMER PROPHETS
Introduction to Joshua: Title and Theme—p. 272

FORNICATION. *See* ADULTERY

FORTRESS OF ANTONIA
Acts 21:31,37

FORTY
Gen 7:4

FORUM OF APPIUS
Acts 28:15

FOUNTAIN GATE
Neh 2:14

FRANKINCENSE
Ex 30:34

FREE WILL
John 12:39; 1 Tim 2:4

FREEDOM
1 Cor 7:21; Gal 2:4; 5:1,13; James 1:25; 1 Pet 2:16

FUTURIST
Introduction to Revelation: Interpretation—p. 1847

G

GABRIEL
Luke 1:19; 1 Thess 4:16

GAD (David's seer)
1 Sam 22:5

GAD (Jacob's seventh son and tribe of)
Ex 1:2-4; Josh 13:24; 1 Chr 5:11-22; Ezek 48:27

GADARA
Matt 8:28

GADATES INSCRIPTION
Ezra 7:24

GAIUS (of Derbe)
Acts 20:4

GAIUS (friend of John)
3 John 1:1

GAIUS (of Macedonia)
Acts 14:6

GAIUS (Titius Justus)
Rom 16:23; 3 John 1:1

GALATIA
Acts 16:6; 18:23; 2 Tim 4:10

GALBANUM
Ex 25:6

GALEED
Gen 31:51

GALILEE
Is 9:1; Matt 2:22; Mark 2:14; 5:43; 7:24; Luke 4:23; 19:37; 22:59; John 4:45; 7:52

GALILEE, SEA OF
Mark 1:16; 4:37; Luke 5:1; John 6:1

GALL
Ps 69:21; Prov 5:4; Matt 27:34

GALLIO
Acts 18:12

GAMALIEL
Acts 5:34; 9:1; 22:3

GAMMAD
Ezek 27:11

GATE
Benjamin
Neh 3:1; Zech 14:10
city
Gen 19:1-2; 22:17; 23:10; Ruth 4:1
of Ephraim
Neh 3:6
of the guard
Neh 12:31

GATH
1 Sam 21:10; 2 Sam 1:20; 1 Kin 2:39; 1 Chr 7:20-29; Amos 1:8; Mic 1:10; "Five Cities of the Philistines"—p. 312

GATH HEPHER
2 Kin 14:25; Jon 1:2

GATH RIMMON
2 Sam 6:10

GAUMATA
Dan 11:2

GAZA
Josh 10:41; Judg 1:18; 16:1,21; 1 Kin 4:24; Is 20:1; Amos 1:6; Acts 8:26,36,40; "Five Cities of the Philistines"—p. 312

GAZELLE
Song 2:9,16; 6:2

GEBA
1 Sam 13:3; 1 Kin 15:22; 2 Kin 23:8; Zech 14:10

GEBALITES
Josh 13:5; Ezek 27:9

GEDALIAH
2 Kin 22:12; 25:22,24,25; Jer 26:24; Zech 8:19

GEHAZI
2 Kin 4:12,30; 5:22,26

GEHENNA
Is 66:24; Matt 5:22; Luke 12:5

GELILOTH
Josh 22:10

GEMARIAH
Jer 36:10

GENEALOGIES
Gen 4:17-18; 5:5; 11:10-26; Ruth 4:18-22; 1 Chr 1:5-23; Introduction to 1 Chronicles: Genealogies—p. 552

GENERATION
Gen 15:16

GENEROSITY. *See also* GIVING
Prov 11:24; 14:21

GENESIS
Introduction to Genesis: Title—p. 1

GENESIS APOCRYPHON
Gen 12:11

GENNESARET
plain of
Matt 14:34
sea of (lake of)
Mark 1:16; Luke 5:1

GENTILES
Num 15:14; Ruth 1:17; 2 Kin 5:14; Ps 117:1; Matt 2:2; 21:41; Luke 2:31; 4:26-27; John 12:32; Acts 9:43; 10:23,28,45,47; Rom 11:17; 15:19; Introduction to Jonah: Literary Characteristics—p. 1293

GERA
2 Sam 16:5; 1 Kin 2:8

GERAR
Gen 20:1

GERASA
Mark 5:1; Luke 8:26

GERSHOM (family of Phinehas)
Ezra 8:2

GERSHOM (father of Jonathan the Levite)
Judg 18:30

GERSHOM (son of Moses)
Ex 4:20; Acts 7:29

GERSHONITES
Josh 21:27; Zech 12:13

GESHEM
Neh 2:19

GESHURITES
Deut 3:14; 1 Sam 27:8; 2 Sam 3:3

GETHSEMANE
Matt 26:36; Mark 14:32; Luke 22:39; Heb 5:7

GEZER
Josh 10:33; 16:1,10; 1 Kin 3:1

GEZER CALENDAR
"Ancient Texts Relating to the Old Testament"—p. xix

GIBBETHON
1 Kin 15:27; 16:9

GIBEAH
in Benjamin
Judg 9:32; 19:14; 1 Sam 10:5; 26:1; Ezra 2:28; Hos 10:9
near Shiloh
Josh 24:33

GIBEON
Josh 10:2; 1 Sam 7:1; 2 Sam 2:12; 1 Chr 16:39; 2 Chr 7:12; Hab 3:11

GIBEONITES
Josh 9:1-27; 10:2; 2 Sam 21:1,4,6; 1 Kin 3:4

GIDEON
Judg 2:16; 6:1-40; 7:1-25; 8:1-35; 9:1-57; Is 9:4; "Gideon's Battles"—p. 323

GIFTS
of administration
1 Cor 12:28
spiritual
Ex 31:3; Num 11:29; 12:1,2; Rom 12:6; 1 Cor 1:7; 12:1,4-6,6,7,8,9,11,12,14,21-26,28,31; 14:1-5,20,26-27,32; Eph 4:11,12; 2 Tim 1:6; Heb 2:4

GIHON (city)
1 Kin 1:41

GIHON (spring)
2 Kin 20:20; Neh 3:26

GILBOA
1 Sam 28:4; 2 Sam 1:21

GILEADITES
Gen 31:21; Judg 10:18; 11:8; Hos 12:11

GILGAL
Josh 4:19; 10:9; Judg 1:1; 2:1; 1 Sam 11:14; 15:12; Neh 12:29; Hos 4:15; Amos 4:4

GILGAMESH
Introduction to Genesis: Background—p. 1

GILGAMESH EPIC
"Ancient Texts Relating to the Old Testament"—p. xix

GILONITE
2 Sam 15:12

GITTITE
2 Sam 6:10; 15:18

GIVING. *See also* GENEROSITY
2 Cor 8:5,6,8,12; 9:12,15

GLEANING
Judg 8:2; Ruth 1:22; 2:2

GLORY OF ISRAEL
1 Sam 15:29

GLORY OF THE LORD. *See* GOD: GLORY OF

GLUTTONY
1 Cor 11:20

GNOSTICISM
Col 1:19,28; 2:3,10-15,18; 1 Tim 1:3-11; 4:3; 6:20; 2 Tim 2:14-18; 2 Pet 2:12; 1 John 1:10; 2:3,18,27; 4:1,2; 5:6,16; 2 John 1:7-11,9; Jude 1:19; Rev 2:24; Introduction to 1 John: Gnosticism—p. 1829

GOAT
Song 4:1

GOBLET
Song 7:2

GOD
anger/wrath of. *See* ANGER, GOD'S
attributes/character of
Num 14:17-19; 23:19; 1 Sam 15:29; Jon 4:2,11; Rom 9:17; Introduction to Amos: Theme and Message—p. 1274
call of
Rom 11:29
as Creator
Gen 1:1,2,3,4,11,16,22,26; 2:4; Ps 29:1-11; Is 40:21; 43:1
faithfulness of
Ps 3:1-8; Rom 3:3; 1 Cor 1:9; 1 John 1:9; Introduction to Judges: Theme and Theology—p. 307
as Father
2 Sam 7:14; John 5:18; 8:44; Rom 8:14; Eph 1:3; Heb 1:5
fear (reverence) of
Gen 20:11; Josh 4:24; 2 Chr 19:7; Ps 34:8-14; 111:10; Prov 1:7; 3:2; Eccl 2:24-25; 7:18; 12:13; Luke 12:5; Rom 3:18; 2 Cor 5:11; 1 Pet 1:17; 3:14; 1 John 4:18
fellowship with
Mark 7:20; 1 John 1:3
glory of
Ex 29:43; 40:34; Ps 26:8; Ezek 1:28; 43:2; Hag 2:7; John 12:41; Rom 1:23; 3:23; 2 Cor 3:7,18
guidance of
Deut 31:6; 1 Sam 2:4-5; 1 Cor 10:1
jealousy of
Ex 20:5
as judge
Gen 18:25; Ex 2:14; Judg 11:27
judgment of. *See* JUDGMENT, GOD'S
love of
Deut 4:37; 7:8; 2 Sam 7:15; John 3:16; 5:42; Rom 8:37,39; 11:32; 2 Thess 3:5; Titus 3:4; 1 John 2:5; 3:17; 4:8,17; Introduction to Ruth: Theme and Theology—p. 345
mercy of
Ex 25:17; Num 18:1-7; Luke 15:28; Rom 11:25,27; 12:1; James 2:13
name of. *See* NAMES OF GOD
patience of
Rom 2:4; 9:22; 2 Pet 3:8,9; Introduction to Judges: Theme and Theology—p. 307
power of
Gen 18:14; Ex 14:14; Num 11:23; 14:9; Deut 3:22; Ps 97:1-6; 2 Cor 12:9
presence of
Num 14:9; Deut 1:43; 4:7; 1 Sam 4:3,4; 1 Kin 6:13; Jer 23:23; Luke 11:25
righteousness of
Ps 4:1; Rom 3:5
as shepherd
John 10:1-42; Zech 10:2
sovereignty of
Gen 25:23; Num 3:38; Josh 11:20; 1 Sam 2:6-8; 2 Sam 24:1; 1 Kin 12:15; 18:1; 2 Kin 20:5; Esth 4:12-16; Ps 9:1; Eccl 3:1-22; Jer 18:7-10; Jon 1:4; Rom 9:21; 1 Tim 2:4; Introduction to Ezekiel: Themes—p. 1157; Introduction to Daniel: Theme—p. 1226; Introduction to Zechariah: Theological Teaching—p. 1332
voice of
2 Sam 22:14
will of
John 7:6,17; 17:24; Rom 12:2; 1 Cor 12:10; Phil 2:7,14,15; Heb 5:7; 6:3; 8:8-12; 10:5,7; 1 Pet 2:19; 4:1

GOD OF HEAVEN
Ezra 1:2

GODLINESS
Zech 8:23; 1 Tim 2:2; 4:7; 2 Pet 1:6

GOG
Ezek 38:2; Rev 20:8

GOLDEN CALF
Ex 32:4,5,6; 2 Kin 23:15

GOLDEN GATE
Neh 3:29; Ezek 44:2

GOLDEN LAMPSTAND
Ex 25:37; 1 Sam 3:3; Heb 9:2

GOLDEN RULE
Matt 7:12; Luke 6:27

GOLGOTHA
John 19:17

GOLIATH
1 Sam 17:54; 2 Sam 9:8

GOMER (son of Japheth)
Gen 10:2; Ezek 38:6

GOMER (wife of Hosea)
Hos 3:1,2; Introduction to Hosea: Special Problems—p. 1251

GOMORRAH
Gen 13:10; Amos 4:11; Zeph 2:9

GOOD SHEPHERD
Zech 11:8,9,11,17; John 10:1-42

GOSHEN
Gen 45:10; Josh 10:41

GOSPEL
Mark 1:1; 2 Cor 2:16; 11:9; Phil 1:27; 1 John 2:8

GOSSIP
Prov 18:8

GOVERNMENT. *See* CIVIL AUTHORITY

GOZAN
2 Kin 17:6; Is 37:12

GRACE
Gen 3:16,17-19; 17:21; Is 26:10; Ezek 36:22; Dan 9:18; Matt 25:34-40; Mark 10:27; John 1:12; Rom 3:24; 6:14; 11:5; 2 Cor 2:14; 8:5; 9:14; 12:9; Gal 1:3; Eph 2:8; 3:8; Titus 2:11-14,11

GRAIN OFFERING
Lev 2:1; Joel 1:9; Acts 10:4; "Old Testament Sacrifices"—p. 139

GRANDCHILDREN
Prov 17:6

GRAVE
Gen 37:35; Jon 2:2

GREAT HALLEL
Ps 120:1

GREAT TRIBULATION
Matt 24:16,21,22; 25:31-46; Rev 7:4,9,14

GREAT WHITE THRONE JUDGMENT
1 Cor 15:26

GREECE
Dan 2:32-43; 7:4-7; 8:5; 1 Cor 16:6; "The Neo-Babylonian Empire"—p. 1234; "From Malachi to Christ"—p. 1355

GREED
Job 31:24-28; Luke 12:13; Acts 5:1; Eph 5:3,5; 2 Pet 2:3

GRIEF. *See also* MOURNING
2 Sam 1:12,17; 13:31; Ezra 9:3; John 11:31,33

GUBARU
Dan 5:31

GUILT OFFERING
Lev 5:15; 1 Sam 6:3; Is 53:10; "Old Testament Sacrifices"—p. 139

GYGES
Ezek 38:2

H

HABAKKUK
Introduction to Habakkuk: Author—p. 1314

HABIRU
Gen 14:13; "The Exodus"—p. 97

HACALIAH
Neh 1:1

HACMONITE
2 Sam 23:8

HADAD
1 Kin 11:14,21,22

HADAD RIMMON
Zech 12:11

HADADEZER
2 Sam 8:3; 10:19; 1 Kin 11:24; 22:1

HADES
Matt 16:18; Luke 12:5; 16:23; 1 Cor 15:26; Rev 1:18; 6:8

HADID
Neh 11:34

HAGAR
Gen 16:1; 1 Chr 5:10; Ezra 10:3

HAGGAI
Ezra 4:24; 5:1; 6:13-14; Neh 10:39; Introduction to Haggai: Author—p. 1326

HAGRITES
1 Chr 5:10; Ps 83:6

HAKKATAN
Ezra 8:12

HALLEL PSALMS
Ps 120:1; Matt 26:30; Mark 11:9

HALLELUJAH
Ps 111:1-10; 146:1-10; Rev 19:1

HAM
Gen 10:6

HAMAN
Esth 3:1,2-6,9,13; 5:9,11; 7:8; 8:2

HAMATH
2 Sam 8:9; Is 10:9; Ezek 47:15,16; Amos 6:2; Zech 9:1,2

HAMATH ZOBAH
1 Kin 11:24

HAMMEDATHA
Esth 3:1

HAMMURAPI
Gen 14:1; 16:2; 39:7; Lev 24:20; Ezra 8:34; 10:3; Job 13:27; "Ancient Texts Relating to the Old Testament"—p. xix

HAMOR
Judg 9:28

HANAN
Ezra 2:46

HANANI (brother of Nehemiah)
Neh 1:2; 13:7

HANANI (father of Jehu)
1 Kin 15:19; 2 Chr 19:2

HANANIAH (false prophet)
Jer 28:1,2,3,16

HANANIAH (priest)
Neh 1:2

HANANIAH (Shadrach)
Dan 1:6

HANANIAH (son of Zerubbabel)
1 Chr 3:20

HANES
Is 30:4

HANNAH
1 Sam 1:3; 2:1,4-5,6-8

HANUKKAH
Ezra 6:16; Ps 30:title; Dan 8:9-12; John 10:22

HANUN
2 Sam 17:27

HARAM ESH-SHARIF
Ezek 44:2

HARAN
Gen 11:31; 2 Kin 19:12; Is 37:12; Ezek 27:23; Acts 7:2,4

HAREM
Eccl 2:8

HAROD
Judg 7:1

HARP
Gen 31:27

HARVEST
Josh 3:15; Ruth 1:22; 3:3

HARVEST, FEAST OF. *See* FEAST: OF WEEKS (PENTECOST OR HARVEST)

HASIDIM
Mark 2:16

HATHACH
Esth 4:4-12

HATSHEPSUT, QUEEN
Ex 2:5

HAURAN
Neh 2:10

HAVILAH
Gen 2:11; 1 Sam 15:7

HAWK
Job 39:26

HAZAEL
2 Kin 8:12,13; Amos 1:4; 6:13

HAZAR SHUAL
Neh 11:27

HAZAZON TAMAR
Ezek 47:18

HAZER HATTICON
Ezek 47:16

HAZOR
Josh 11:1,10; Judg 4:2; 1 Kin 9:15

HEAD
1 Cor 11:3,4

HEALING
1 Cor 12:9; James 5:14

HEART
1 Sam 16:7; Ps 7:9
definition of
Ps 4:7; Matt 5:8; Rom 10:9
hardness of
Job 36:13-15; Mark 6:52

HEAVEN
Mark 11:30; Gal 4:26; Heb 3:2; 11:13

HEBER THE KENITE
Judg 4:11

HEBREW
Gen 10:21; 14:13; 2 Kin 18:26; Is 36:11

HEBRON
Gen 23:2; Num 13:22; Josh 14:12; 15:19; 21:11; Acts 7:16

HELAM
2 Sam 10:16

HELBON
Ezek 27:18

HELECH
Ezek 27:11

HELIODORUS
Dan 11:20

HELIOPOLIS
Gen 41:45; Is 19:18; Ezek 30:17

HELL. *See also* ABADDON; GEHENNA; HADES
Jer 7:31; Matt 5:22

HEMAN
1 Chr 2:6; 6:31-48; 2 Chr 29:13-14

HENA
2 Kin 18:34

HENNA
Song 1:14

HEQT
Ex 8:2

HERESIES
Eph 4:14; Col 1:16; 2:3,8,17,19,21,23; 1 Tim 1:3-11; 6:20; 2 Pet 2:1,12

HERMES
Acts 14:12

HERMON, MOUNT. *See* MOUNT: HERMON

HEROD (Agrippa I)
Acts 9:15; 12:1,19,21,23; 15:2; 24:24; 25:22,26; 26:1,3,8,27; Rom 16:10

HEROD (Antipas)
Neh 11:1; Matt 14:1; Mark 8:15; 10:2; Luke 3:19; Acts 12:1; 23:31; 25:22; Rom 16:10

HEROD (of Chalcis)
Acts 25:13

HEROD (the Great)
Matt 2:1,15; Luke 1:5; Acts 12:1; 23:31,35; Rom 16:10; "House of Herod"—p. 1367; "Herod's Temple"—p. 1372; "The Holy Land under Herod the Great"—p. 1465

HEROD (Philip)
Matt 14:3

HERODIANS
Matt 22:15-17; Mark 3:6

HERODIAS
Matt 14:3,6; Luke 3:19
HERODOTUS
Ezra 4:8; 6:11; 7:14; Esth 1:1,13-14; 3:9; 4:11; 5:11; 8:1; Is 37:36
HESHBON
Song 7:4
HEZEKIAH
2 Kin 16:20; 20:3,5,6; 23:6; 2 Chr 15:12; 29:5-11; 30:2; 32:27-29; Ezra 6:17; Neh 2:14; Is 10:20-22; 20:5; 29:15; 33:8; Hos 1:1; Zeph 1:1; "Jerusalem during the Time of the Prophets"—p. 1249
HEZIR
1 Chr 24:15
HEZRON
1 Chr 2:3-9
HIEL
1 Kin 16:34
HIEROPOLIS
1 Cor 16:19; Col 1:7; 4:13; Rev 3:16
HIGH PLACES
1 Sam 9:12; 1 Kin 3:2; 15:14; 2 Kin 12:3
HILKIAH
2 Kin 22:4; 25:18; 1 Chr 6:13; Ezra 7:1; Jer 1:1; 29:3
HILLEL, SCHOOL OF
Lev 24:20; Matt 19:3; Acts 5:34
HINNOM VALLEY.
2 Kin 23:10; 2 Chr 28:3; Is 66:24; Jer 7:31; Zeph 1:5; Matt 5:22
HIRAM
2 Sam 5:11; 1 Kin 5:1,9,11; 9:11; 10:11; 1 Chr 14:1; 2 Chr 2:3-10; 8:1-2
HISTORICIST
Introduction to Revelation: Interpretation—p. 1847
HITTITES
Gen 10:15; 23:9; Judg 1:26; 1 Sam 26:6; Ezek 16:3
HIVITES
Josh 9:7; Judg 3:3; 2 Sam 21:2
HOBAB
Num 10:29
HOLINESS
Ex 3:5; Lev 11:44; Rom 6:22; 1 Cor 5:6; Eph 1:4; 5:26; Phil 1:10; 1 Pet 1:16; Introduction to Leviticus: Themes—p. 134
HOLOCAUST OFFERING
Lev 1:3
HOLY CITY
Is 64:10
HOLY KISS
Rom 16:16; 1 Cor 16:20; 2 Cor 13:12; 1 Thess 5:26
HOLY LAND
Zech 2:12; 5:11
HOLY ONE OF GOD
Mark 1:24
HOLY ONE OF ISRAEL
2 Kin 19:22; Is 1:4
HOLY PLACE
Ex 26:31-35; 1 Sam 3:3; Ezra 6:15
HOLY SPIRIT
Gen 1:2; Judg 11:29; Ps 51:11
and God
Acts 5:3; Rom 8:27; Phil 1:19
and Pentecost
Matt 3:11; Acts 2:2,4; 1 Pet 1:12
baptism of
Acts 2:14; 19:2,6; 1 Cor 12:13
coming of
John 14:16,18,26; 16:7; 20:22; Acts 5:32
description of
Mark 1:10; John 14:17
fruit of
Rom 8:23; 14:17; Gal 5:22-23
gifts of
Ex 31:3; Rom 15:13; 1 Cor 1:7; 12:4,10; 2 Cor 3:6,8-9; 1 Thess 5:19; 2 Tim 1:6
grieving of
Eph 4:30,31
indwelling of
Acts 2:38; 8:16; 1 Cor 3:16; 6:18; Eph 2:22; 5:18; Phil 1:11; 2:1
and Jesus
Matt 3:16; 2 Cor 3:17; Phil 1:19
need of
1 Cor 2:14,15
power of
Ex 31:3; Zech 4:7; Rom 8:2,4; Gal 5:16; 1 Thess 1:5
as a seal
Hag 2:23; Eph 1:13
sovereignty of
John 3:8; 1 Cor 12:11
work of
John 7:39; 14:26; 16:13,14; Acts 1:2; 2:34; 9:31; 15:28; Rom 2:29; 12:11; 1 Cor 7:40; 12:3; Eph 6:17-18; 1 Pet 1:2; 1 John 2:27
HOLY TO THE LORD
Zech 14:20
HOLY WEEK
"Passion Week"—p. 1446
HOMOSEXUALITY
Gen 19:5; Deut 22:5; Judg 19:22,23; Rom 1:27; 1 Cor 6:9; 2 Pet 2:10; Jude 1:8
HONEY
Gen 43:11; Deut 32:13
HONOR
Ex 20:12
HOPE
Rom 4:18; 5:2,5; 8:24; 12:12; 15:13; Eph 1:18; 4:4; Col 1:5; 1 Thess 1:3; Heb 6:19; 7:19; 1 Pet 1:3
HOPHNI
1 Sam 4:4,11
HOREB, MOUNT. *See* MOUNT: HOREB
HORITES
Gen 14:6; Josh 9:7
HORMAH
Num 21:3
HORNS
Ex 27:2; Lev 4:7; 1 Kin 1:50
HORONITE
Neh 2:10
HORSE GATE
Neh 3:28
HORSEMEN, FOUR
Rev 6:2,4,5,6,8; 9:14
HOSANNA
Jer 31:7; Matt 21:9
HOSEA
2 Kin 15:19; Mic 1:1; Introduction to Hosea: Author and Date—p. 1250
HOSHEA
2 Kin 17:3; Hos 7:11; 8:9
HOSPITALITY
Gen 18:2; 19:8; Judg 4:21; 13:15; 19:21; 3 John 1:5
HOUSE OF JOSEPH
2 Sam 19:20
HOUSE OF THE HEROES
Neh 3:16
HOUSEHOLD GODS
Gen 31:19; Judg 17:5; Ezek 21:21
HOUSES, PALESTINIAN
Judg 3:10; Mark 2:4; Luke 15:8
HULDAH
2 Kin 22:14; Is 57:1
HUMILITY
Judg 6:15; 1 Sam 9:21; 23:17; Zeph 2:3; Mark 9:34; Luke 5:8; 14:11; John 13:5,8; Phil 2:3,5; Col 2:18; 1 Pet 5:5
HUR
Ex 17:10
HURAM-ABI
1 Kin 7:13,14; 1 Chr 2:18-24; 2 Chr 2:7,13
HURRIANS
Gen 14:6; Josh 9:7
HUSBAND
1 Cor 14:34-35; Eph 5:22,23,25,28-29; Titus 1:6,4; 1 Pet 3:1
HUSHAI
2 Sam 15:32,37; 17:12,16; 1 Kin 4:16
HYMENAEUS
2 Tim 2:14-18

HYMN TO THE ATEN
"Ancient Texts Relating to the Old Testament"—p. xix
HYPOCRISY
Matt 23:23; Luke 13:15; Acts 5:9
HYSSOP
Ex 12:22; Lev 14:4; John 19:29

I

I AM WHO I AM. *See* NAMES OF GOD: "I AMOS WHO I AM"
ICONIUM
Acts 13:51; 14:6; 16:6; 2 Tim 3:11
IDDO
Introduction to Zechariah: Author and Unity—p. 1331
IDEALIST
Introduction to Revelation: Interpretation—p. 1847
IDOL
Ezek 6:4; 21:21
IDOLATRY
Ex 20:4; Lev 26:1; 2 Kin 9:22; 17:16; Job 31:24-28; Is 44:9-20; Ezek 21:21; Hab 2:18,20; 1 Cor 8:5,7,9,10,12,13; 10:7,14,18,22; Eph 5:5
IDUMEANS
Neh 11:25,26; Mark 3:8
ILLYRICUM
Rom 15:19; 2 Tim 4:10
IMAGE OF GOD
Gen 1:26; Col 1:15
IMITATORS OF CHRIST
1 Thess 1:6
IMMANUEL
Is 7:14; 8:8
IMMEDIATE RETRIBUTION, THEORY OF
Introduction to 1 Chronicles: Purpose and Themes—p. 549
IMMORALITY
Prov 2:18; Acts 15:20; 1 Cor 6:9,13,16,19; 7:2,5; 10:8; 1 Thess 4:3,6,8
IMMORTALITY
Prov 12:28; Rom 2:6-7
INCARNATION. *See* CHRIST: INCARNATION OF
INCENSE
Ex 30:1; Lev 2:1; Rev 5:8
INCEST
Gen 19:33; Lev 18:6; 1 Cor 5:1
INDIVIDUAL RESPONSIBILITY
Jer 31:30; Ezek 3:16; 14:20; 18:4; Matt 22:13; Introduction to Jeremiah: Themes and Message—p. 1050
INGATHERING, FEAST OF. *See* FEAST: OF TABERNACLES (BOOTHS OR INGATHERING)
INHERITANCE
Gen 25:5; Ps 127:3; Jer 2:7; 3:19; Rom 8:17,23; Eph 1:18; 1 Pet 1:4
INSPIRATION (OF SCRIPTURE)
2 Tim 3:16
INTEREST
Ex 22:25-27; Lev 25:36; Deut 23:20; Neh 5:10
INTERMARRIAGE
Gen 26:35; Deut 7:4; Josh 23:12; Judg 14:1; Ruth 1:4; 1 Kin 11:1; Ezra 9:1; 2 Cor 6:14
IRON
Deut 8:9
ISAAC
burial of
Acts 7:16
chosen by God
Gen 17:21; Rom 9:15
and law of primogeniture
Gen 25:5
meaning of name
Gen 17:17
offered as sacrifice
Gen 22:2; Heb 11:19; James 2:21
as patriarch
Rom 9:5
promise of birth
Gen 18:10; Rom 4:17
ISAIAH
2 Kin 18:17; 19:2,20; Ezra 9:9; Job 18:14; Ezek 5:1; 12:2; 15:4; Hos 1:1; 7:5; Joel 2:11; Mic 1:1; Zeph 1:1; Zech 1:4; Matt 27:9; Mark 1:2-3; 7:6; 10:45; Luke 1:17; 5:8; Introduction to Isaiah: Author—p. 957
ISH-BOSHETH
1 Sam 31:2; 2 Sam 2:8,11; 3:14; 4:4; 1 Chr 10:6
ISHMAEL
Gen 37:25; Judg 13:3; 2 Kin 25:23; 1 Chr 5:10; Is 60:7
ISHTAR
Esth 2:7; Jer 7:18; 44:18,19
ISHTAR'S DESCENT
"Ancient Texts Relating to the Old Testament"—p. xix
ISRAEL
Gen 32:28; 34:9; Ex 40:38; 1 Kin 1:35; 18:31; Rom 9:4; "The Divided Kingdom"—p. 471; "Rulers of the Divided Kingdom of Israel and Judah"—p. 478; "Assyrian Campaigns against Israel and Judah"—p. 522; "Exile of Northern Kingdom"—p. 529
and aliens
Ex 22:21-27; Num 15:14; Josh 8:33; 20:9; Ruth 1:22
as a chosen people
Ex 19:5; 2 Sam 7:23; Rom 1:16; 1 Pet 2:9
corporate unity of
Josh 7:1-26,11,24
disobedience/unfaithfulness of
Num 14:1-11,34; 16:41; 20:2; 21:4-5; 25:1; Deut 1:43; 4:25
faithfulness of
Josh 24:31
as a theocracy
Judg 8:23; 1 Sam 8:7; 11:14; 12:12; 13:13; 15:23; 17:11; 2 Kin 1:10; Ps 93:1-5; Introduction to Judges: Theme and Theology—p. 307; Introduction to 1 Samuel: Contents and Theme—p. 353; Introduction to 2 Samuel: Contents and Theme—p. 401
ITHAMAR
1 Chr 6:1-3; Ezra 8:2

J

JAAZANIAH (Jewish captain)
2 Kin 25:23; Neh 5:18
JAAZANIAH (Recabite)
Jer 35:3
JAAZANIAH (son of Shaphan)
Ezek 8:11
JABBOK RIVER
Gen 32:22
JABESH GILEAD
Judg 21:11; 1 Sam 11:1
JABIN
Josh 11:1; Judg 4:2
JACKAL WELL
Neh 2:13
JACOB
Gen 25:26; 29:25; 30:2; 31:26; 32:24,26,28; 33:20; 35:11-12; 47:9; Heb 11:22; "Jacob's Journeys"—p. 47; "The Tribes of Israel"—p. 72
JAEL
Judg 4:18,21; 5:28
JAFFA
Acts 9:36
JAHAZ
Is 15:4
JAIR (judge of Israel)
Judg 10:3
JAIRUS
Matt 9:18; Acts 9:40
JAKIN
2 Kin 11:14; Ezek 40:49
JAMBRES
Ex 7:11; 2 Tim 3:8

JAMES (brother of Christ)
Mark 6:30; Luke 8:19; Acts 1:14; 9:26; 12:17; 15:13,14; 21:18; Gal 1:19; 2:2; Titus 1:1; Introduction to James: Author—p. 1803

JAMES (son of Alphaeus)
Luke 6:15; Acts 1:13

JAMES (son of Zebedee)
Mark 5:37; Luke 9:28,54; Acts 3:1; 12:2,17; 1 Cor 15:7

JANNES
Ex 7:11; 2 Tim 3:8

JAPHETHITES
Gen 10:2

JARMUTH
Neh 11:29

JASHAR, BOOK OF
Josh 10:13

JASON
Acts 17:5,9; Rom 16:21

JEBEL DRUZE
Ps 68:14

JEBUSITES
Gen 10:16; Josh 15:63; 2 Sam 5:6,8; Zech 9:7; "The City of the Jebusites/David's Jerusalem"—p. 409

JECONIAH
Matt 1:11

JEDIDIAH
2 Sam 12:25

JEDUTHUN
1 Chr 9:15-16; 2 Chr 29:13-14; Ps 39:1

JEHEZKEL
Ezek 1:3

JEHOAHAZ
2 Kin 23:30,33; 1 Chr 3:15-16; 2 Chr 36:4; Jer 22:11; Ezek 19:3

JEHOASH. *See also* JOASH
2 Kin 13:5,19; 14:8,13; 2 Chr 26:9; Amos 6:13

JEHOHANAN
Neh 2:10; 6:17-18

JEHOIACHIN
2 Kin 24:8,17; 1 Chr 3:15-16; 2 Chr 36:9-10; Ezra 1:8; 5:2; Ezek 1:2; 7:27; 17:4,5; 19:5; Matt 1:11

JEHOIACHIN'S RATION DOCKETS
"Ancient Texts Relating to the Old Testament"—p. xix

JEHOIADA (high priest)
2 Kin 11:2,14; 12:20; 2 Chr 15:12; 24:5,14,15-22

JEHOIAKIM
2 Kin 23:30,37; 24:1,5; 1 Chr 3:15-16; 2 Chr 36:4,5-8; Ezra 1:1; Ezek 17:5; Matt 1:11

JEHOIARIB
1 Chr 24:7

JEHONADAB
2 Kin 10:15,16; Jer 35:6

JEHORAM. *See also* JORAM
1 Kin 12:24; 22:50; 2 Kin 1:17; 8:16,17,18; 11:2; 2 Chr 21:5,8-10,12-15; 22:1; Matt 1:8

JEHOSHAPHAT
1 Kin 4:3,12; 22:2,4,5,7,15,41,44,48; 2 Kin 1:17; 3:7,9,11,14; 8:28; 2 Chr 17:6; 18:1; 19:4,5; 20:5-12,35-37

JEHOSHEBA
2 Kin 11:2

JEHOVAH ***See*** **NAMES OF GOD: LORD (YAHWEH/JEHOVAH)**

JEHOZADAK
2 Kin 25:18; 1 Chr 6:14; Ezra 2:2; Hag 1:1

JEHU (king of Judah)
1 Kin 1:39; 19:16; 2 Kin 9:27,31; 10:1,7,30

JEHU (prophet)
1 Kin 16:1; 2 Chr 22:6

JEHUCAL
Jer 37:3

JEPHTHAH
Judg 11:1,30

JERAHMEELITES
1 Sam 27:10; 1 Chr 2:25-33

JEREMIAH
2 Kin 22:11,12; 2 Chr 35:25; 36:5-8,22-23; Is 10:30; Matt 27:9; Luke 22:20; Gal 3:19; Heb 13:20; Introduction to Jeremiah: Author and Date—p. 1049

JERICHO
Josh 6:1; 1 Kin 16:34; Mark 10:46; Luke 10:30; Heb 11:30

JEROBOAM I
1 Kin 11:40; 12:28,30,32; 13:7,24; 14:1,2,7-8,9,12,13; 15:26; 16:7; 2 Kin 14:23; 16:3; 17:6; 2 Chr 30:2; Hos 8:5,6; 13:10

JEROBOAM II
1 Kin 13:1; 2 Kin 13:5,19,25; 14:25; 2 Chr 26:6-8; Hos 1:1,4; 4:2; 8:4; 10:1; Amos 6:2,13

JEROME
Introduction to Ezra: Ezra and Nehemiah—p. 632

JERUB-BAAL/JERUB-BESHETH
Judg 6:32; 2 Sam 11:21

JERUSALEM
conquest/destruction of
"Nebuchadnezzar's Campaign against Judah"—p. 544
geographical/physical aspects of
Judg 1:8; 2 Sam 5:6; Neh 3:1-32; Ps 48:2; "The City of the Jebusites/David's Jerusalem"—p. 409; "Solomon's Jerusalem"—p. 450; "Jerusalem of the Returning Exiles"—p. 657; "Jerusalem during the Time of the Prophets"—p. 1249; "Jerusalem during the Ministry of Jesus"—p. 1425
names of
Gen 14:18; 2 Sam 5:7; Is 1:26; Jer 33:16; Ezek 48:35
religious significance of
1 Kin 11:13; Ps 9:11; 24:7-10; 48:1-14; 76:1-12; 87:1-7; Ezek 38:12; Gal 4:25,26; Introduction to Psalms: Theology—p. 738

JESHANAH GATE
Neh 3:6

JESHUA
1 Chr 6:14; Ezra 1:8; 2:2; 3:2; 6:13-14

JESHURUN
Is 44:2

JESSE
1 Sam 16:1; 2 Sam 17:25; 1 Chr 2:10-17

JESUS. *See* CHRIST

JETHRO
Ex 2:16

JEZEBEL
1 Kin 16:25,31; 18:13; 21:9,19; 2 Kin 9:31; Mark 9:13; Rev 2:20,23

JEZREEL (son of Hosea)
Hos 1:4,11; 2:22

JEZREEL (city)
1 Sam 25:43; 2 Kin 8:28; 9:16

JOAB
1 Sam 26:6; 2 Sam 2:13; 3:25,29; 5:8; 14:2; 19:5; 20:10,23; 1 Kin 1:7; 1 Chr 21:6; 27:24

JOANNA
Luke 24:10

JOASH
2 Kin 12:2,6,17; 2 Chr 24:5,15-22; Ezra 3:10; Neh 10:32

JOB
James 5:11; Introduction to Job: Author—p. 690

JOCHEBED
Ex 6:20

JOEL
Acts 2:4,17; Introduction to Joel: Author—p. 1267

JOHANAN
1 Chr 3:15-16; Ezra 2:46; Neh 12:11

JOHANAN BEN ZACCAI
Acts 4:6

JOHN (the apostle)
Matt 20:20; Mark 5:37; 15:40; Luke 9:54; Acts 3:1; 4:13; 8:14; 10:37; 12:2,17; Gal 2:2; Rev 1:9; Introduction to John: Author—p. 1513

JOHN (the Baptist)
baptism of
Matt 3:11; Mark 1:4; Acts 2:38; 18:25; 19:4
beheading of
Acts 12:1,2
birthdate and childhood of
Matt 3:1; Luke 1:80
and Christ's baptism
Matt 3:15
compared to Jesus
Matt 4:17; 17:12; Luke 5:33; John 1:15
compared to others
Mal 4:5; Matt 11:11
disciples of
Mark 2:18; Acts 19:1
imprisonment of
Matt 4:12; Mark 6:17
lifestyle of
Matt 3:4; Luke 1:15; 5:33
ministry of
Mal 3:1; 4:1,6; Matt 3:3; 4:17; Luke 16:16; John 1:7,23; 3:30
name, meaning of
Mark 1:4

JOHN (Hyrcanus)
Mark 2:16; "The Time between the Testaments"—p. 1356

JOHN MARK. *See* MARK, JOHN

JONADAB
Jer 35:6

JONAH
Nah 1:8; Luke 11:30,31-32; Introduction to Jonah: Author—p. 1293; "The Book of Jonah"—p. 1295

JONATHAN (son of Annas)
Acts 4:6

JONATHAN (son of Gershom)
Judg 18:30

JONATHAN (son of Saul)
1 Sam 13:2; 14:24-26; 15:23; 18:3,4; 19:4; 20:11,15,16; Ezra 8:6

JOPPA
Josh 19:40; Acts 9:32,36

JORAM
1 Kin 16:30,31; 2 Kin 6:30,33; 2 Chr 22:6,7

JORDAN RIVER
Josh 1:2; 2 Sam 19:41; 1 Kin 20:26; 2 Kin 5:10; 1 Chr 12:8-15; Is 33:9; Zech 11:3; Mark 1:5,16

JORDAN VALLEY
Gen 13:10; 1 Kin 20:26

JOSEPH (of Arimathea)
Is 53:9; Luke 23:50; John 19:38

JOSEPH (Barsabbas)
Acts 1:23; 15:22

JOSEPH (brother of Christ)
Luke 8:19

JOSEPH (husband of Mary)
Matt 1:16,18,20; 13:55; Luke 1:32; 3:23-38

JOSEPH (son of Jacob)
and covenant of God
Gen 37:2
and Daniel
Dan 1:9
death of
Gen 50:25,26
faith of
Heb 11:22
and his brothers
Gen 43:30; 50:17; Is 42:14; Acts 7:9
interpreter of dreams
Judg 7:13-14
name of
Gen 41:45
as representative of Israel
Gen 39:1,6; 40:8
as ruler over Egypt
Gen 41:40; Neh 5:5
tribe of
1 Chr 2:1-2; 5:1-10; Is 9:21; Ezek 47:13; 48:31; Amos 5:6

JOSEPHUS
Matt 24:21; Introduction to Ezra: Ezra and Nehemiah—p. 632; "The Book of the Twelve, or the Minor Prophets"—p. 1249; "The Time between the Testaments"—p. 1356

JOSHUA (Moses' aide)
Ex 17:9; Josh 1:1-18,10; 3:7; 24:1-33; Neh 8:17; 1 Cor 10:5; Heb 4:1,6-8; 11:30; Introduction to Joshua: The Life of Joshua—p. 273; "Conquest of Canaan"—p. 292

JOSHUA (priest)
Zech 3:1,7; 4:1-14,3

JOSIAH
1 Kin 13:2; 2 Kin 22:3,20; 23:22,34; 2 Chr 28:3; 36:2; Is 57:1; Zeph 1:4-6; Matt 1:11

JOTBAH
2 Kin 21:19

JOTHAM (king of Judah)
2 Kin 15:5,33; 16:2; Introduction to Micah: Date—p. 1299

JOY
in the Lord
Deut 12:12; 1 Sam 11:15; Ps 45:7; John 3:29; Phil 1:21,26; 2:17-18; 1 Thess 5:16; 1 John 1:4
in suffering
Rom 5:3; Phil 4:4; James 1:2

JUBILEE, YEAR OF. *See* YEAR OF JUBILEE

JUDAH
Gen 43:3,9; 49:8-11; Num 2:3-7; Judg 1:2; "The Divided Kingdom"—p. 471; "Rulers of the Divided Kingdom of Israel and Judah"—p. 478; "Assyrian Campaigns against Israel and Judah"—p. 522; "Nebuchadnezzar's Campaign against Judah"—p. 544; "Exile of the Southern Kingdom"—p. 547

JUDAISM
Gal 1:13; 4:15,25; 5:9; "The Time between the Testaments"—p. 1356

JUDAIZERS
Rom 14:1; Gal 2:4,11,12; 4:30; 5:7; 6:12; Introduction to Galatians: Occasion and Purpose—p. 1706

JUDAS (Barsabbas)
Acts 1:23; 15:22

JUDAS (brother of Christ)
Luke 8:19

JUDAS (the Galilean)
Acts 5:37

JUDAS (Iscariot)
Matt 26:23; 28:16; Luke 24:9; John 6:71; 13:26,27; Acts 1:11,18,19,20; 1 Cor 15:2,5; 2 Thess 2:3

JUDAS (son of James)
Luke 6:16; Acts 1:13

JUDAS MACCABEUS
Dan 8:9-12,14; 11:34; John 10:22; "The Time between the Testaments"—p. 1356

JUDEANS
Mark 10:1; Luke 23:5; Acts 1:8; 8:1; 15:1; Rom 15:31

JUDGING OTHERS
Matt 7:1; Rom 2:1; 14:1,10; 1 Cor 5:4,12

JUDGMENT, GOD'S. *See also* GOD: AS JUDGE
as act of purification
Zeph 3:9-20; John 15:2; 1 Pet 4:17
agents of
Jer 1:16
of all people
Gen 3:14; Gal 6:5; 2 Tim 4:1
of believers
Jer 1:16; Rom 14:10; 2 Cor 5:10; Gal 6:5; James 2:12
disciplinary
Ezek 5:13; 1 Cor 11:29
eternal
Mic 7:4; 1 Cor 3:13; 1 Thess 1:10; 5:2; Heb 6:1-2; James 2:13; Jude 1:12
imagery of
Ezek 13:11; Rev 14:15
on Israel and Judah
Amos 1:2-15; 2:1-16; Introduction to Jeremiah: Themes and Message—p. 1050; Introduction to Amos: Theme and Message—p. 1274

K

L

LAMENTS
2 Sam 1:17; Amos 5:1,16-17; Introduction to Lamentations—p. 1145

LAMP
Ex 25:37; 2 Sam 22:29; 1 Kin 11:36; Ps 18:28

LAMPSTAND
Ex 25:37; Zech 4:2; Heb 9:2; "Tabernacle Furnishings"—p. 115; "Temple Furnishings"—p. 460

LAODICEA
1 Cor 16:19; Col 2:1; Rev 3:14,16,18

LASEA
Acts 27:8

LAST DAYS (LATER TIMES, ETC.)
Num 24:14; Is 2:2; Joel 2:28; Acts 2:17; 1 Tim 4:1; 2 Tim 3:1; Heb 1:1; James 5:9; 2 Pet 3:3; 1 John 2:18

LAST SUPPER. *See* LORD'S SUPPER: AND THE PASSOVER

LAW
Ex 18:16; Lev 18:5; Is 8:16; Matt 5:17; Acts 28:23; Rom 3:21; 7:4,5,6,7,12; 8:2; 1 Cor 9:20,21; Gal 4:25; 5:14; Heb 7:18,19
case, in Israel
Num 27:5; Josh 20:1-9; 1 Kin 3:16
of love
James 2:8
of retaliation
Ex 21:23-25

LAW OF MOSES. *See also* MOSES: LAW OF
applications/interpretations of
Matt 15:2; Luke 11:46; John 5:10; 7:49

LAYING ON OF HANDS
Ex 29:10; Acts 6:6; 2 Tim 1:6; Heb 6:1-2

LAZARUS
Ezra 7:5; John 11:1,4,17,22

LEAH
Gen 29:31-35; Mal 1:3

LEAVEN
1 Cor 5:6

LEBANON
Song 4:8,15; 5:15; Ezek 26:2; 31:3; Mark 7:24; Acts 11:19

LEBO HAMATH
2 Kin 14:25; Ezek 47:15; Amos 6:14

LEGALISM
1 Sam 21:4; Eccl 7:18; Matt 5:18-20; Mark 2:16,25; 7:11,13; 10:20; Luke 5:33; 11:46; Acts 15:1; 21:24; Rom 9:31; 14:1; Gal 2:16; 4:9,15; Phil 3:6

LEGION
Mark 5:9

LEHI
Judg 15:9

LENTIL
Gen 25:34

LEPROSY
Lev 13:2; 2 Kin 5:11; 2 Chr 26:23; Matt 8:2; Mark 1:44; Luke 5:12,14; 17:16

LEPTON
Luke 12:59

LEVI. *See also* MATTHEW
tribe of
1 Chr 2:6; 6:1-3; 15:4-10; "The Tribes of Israel"—p. 72; Introduction to Leviticus: Title—p. 134

LEVIATHAN
Job 3:8; 26:13; 41:1; Ps 104:26; Is 27:1; Jon 1:17; Rev 12:3

LEVIRATE LAW. *See* MARRIAGE: LEVIRATE

LEVIRATE MARRIAGE. *See* MARRIAGE: LEVIRATE

LEVITES
Introduction to Leviticus: Title—p. 134
and the ark
1 Chr 13:10
census of
1 Chr 23:3
cities of
Num 3:1-5,6-15
cleansing of
Num 8:5-26; Mal 3:3
duties of
Num 8:24,26; 1 Chr 9:28-34; 2 Chr 30:17; Neh 12:30; 13:30; John 1:19
set apart
Ex 32:29

LEVITICAL PRIESTHOOD. *See* PRIESTHOOD, LEVITICAL

LIBERTINISM
Eccl 7:18; Gal 5:22-23; Phil 3:19; Rev 2:23

LIBNAH
2 Kin 8:22; 2 Chr 21:10

LIBYA
Ezek 27:10; Acts 6:9

LIFE
the blessing/sacredness of
Gen 9:4,6; Lev 17:11; 1 Kin 17:22; Ps 69:32; John 5:21,25,26
descriptive of the Lord
Deut 30:20; John 1:4; 11:25
God's purpose for humanity
Gen 2:9; 50:20; Deut 30:20; Ezek 16:6
identified with light
Ps 27:1; 36:9; 2 Cor 4:6
resurrection
Rom 6:8; 1 Cor 4:11,16

LIGHT
Gen 1:3; Ps 27:1; John 1:4; 8:12; 2 Cor 4:6; Col 1:12; 1 John 1:5,6-7

LILY
Song 2:1

LION
Gen 49:9; Rev 5:5

LO DEBAR
2 Sam 9:4; Amos 6:13

LO-AMMI
Hos 1:9

LOCUSTS
and day of the Lord
Rev 9:3
destruction by
Joel 1:5,9
as food
Matt 3:4
plague of
Ex 10:4; Joel 1:6; Introduction to Joel: Message—p. 1267

LOIS
2 Tim 1:5

LONGEVITY
Gen 5:5,27; Is 65:20

LO-RUHAMAH
Hos 1:6; 2:19

LORD. *See* NAMES OF GOD: LORD (YAHWEH/JEHOVAH)

LORD ALMIGHTY. *See* NAMES OF GOD: LORD ALMIGHTY (*YAHWEH SABAOTH*)

LORD'S ANOINTED
1 Sam 2:10; 9:16; 24:6; Ps 2:1-12

LORD'S DAY
Rev 1:10

LORD'S PRAYER
Luke 11:1,4

LORD'S SUPPER
desecration of
Num 9:13; 1 Cor 11:20,21,27
explanation of
Mark 14:22
and faith
John 6:53-58; 1 Cor 11:28
foreshadowed
Ex 24:11
frequency of
1 Cor 11:26
and Messianic banquet
1 Chr 12:38-40
and the Passover
Ex 12:48; Luke 22:16
symbol of
1 Cor 10:16; 11:24,25
and the worship service
Acts 20:7; 28:14

LOT
Gen 13:12,14; 14:12; 19:1,14; 2 Sam 8:2; Is 15:5

LOTS, CASTING OF
Ex 28:30; Josh 7:14; 14:1; Judg 20:9; Neh 11:1; Prov 16:33; Ezek 21:21; Jon 1:7; Acts 1:26

LOT'S WIFE
Gen 19:26
LOVE
brotherly
1 Thess 4:9
as a debt
Rom 13:8
for enemies
Ex 23:4-5; Lev 19:18; Luke 6:27; 10:31-33; Rom 12:20
and forgiveness
Prov 10:12
God's
Deut 4:37; Josh 2:12; Luke 15:31; 1 Cor 13:13; 2 Cor 5:14; 1 Thess 1:4; 2 Thess 2:13; 3:5; Titus 3:4; 1 John 2:7-8; 4:12
and the great commandment
Luke 10:27; Rom 13:9; 1 Pet 1:22
marital
Ex 20:5; Song 8:6-7; Titus 2:4; Introduction to Song of Songs: Theme and Theology—p. 947
meaning of
Ex 20:5,6; Josh 22:5; Matt 22:37,39; John 21:15-17; 1 Cor 13:1
sincere
Rom 12:9; 2 Cor 8:8; 2 Pet 1:7
and spiritual gifts
1 Cor 14:1
LOVE FEAST. *See* AGAPE
LOWER POOL
Neh 3:15; Is 22:9
LUCIFER
Is 14:12
LUCIUS (of Cyrene)
Acts 13:1
LUKE
Acts 1:1; 2 Cor 8:18; Col 4:14; Introduction to Luke: Author—p. 1456; Introduction to Acts: Author—p. 1568
LUST
Prov 6:25; Eph 5:3
LUTHER, MARTIN
Ps 46:1-11; Rom 3:28; Philem 1:17,19
LYCAONIA
Acts 14:6
LYDDA
Ezra 2:33; Acts 9:32
LYDIA (woman)
Acts 16:14; 1 Cor 1:16; Rev 2:18
LYDIA (territory)
Dan 7:4-7; Rev 3:1
LYSANIAS
Luke 3:1
LYSTRA
Acts 14:6,12; 2 Tim 3:11

M

MAACAH (daughter of Absalom)
2 Sam 14:27; 1 Kin 15:2,13; 2 Chr 11:20
MAACAH (wife of David)
2 Sam 3:3; 13:1
MAACATHITES
Deut 3:14
MACCABEES
Dan 11:34; Mark 2:16; Heb 11:35; "The Neo-Babylonian Empire"—p. 1234; "The Time between the Testaments"—p. 1356
MACEDON
Dan 7:4-7
MACEDONIA
Acts 16:9; 1 Cor 16:5,10; Phil 4:15; 1 Thess 1:7
MACHAERUS
Mark 6:17
MACHPELAH
Gen 23:9
MAGADAN
Matt 15:39; Mark 8:10
MAGDALA
Mark 8:10
MAGI
Matt 2:1,2,11
MAGICIANS
Gen 41:8; Deut 18:9; Acts 19:19; Rev 9:21
MAGNIFICAT
Hannah's
1 Sam 2:1
Mary's
Luke 1:46-55
MAGOG
Gen 10:2; Ezek 38:2; Rev 20:8
MAHANAIM
Gen 32:2; 2 Sam 2:8,11; 17:24
MAHER-SHALAL-HASH-BAZ
Is 5:19; 7:14; 8:1-2,3
MAHLON
Ruth 1:5; 4:5
MAKIR
Gen 50:23; Josh 13:29; Judg 5:13-18; 2 Sam 9:4
MAKKEDAH
Josh 10:16
MALCHUS
Mark 14:47; Luke 22:51,59
MALKIJAH
Jer 35:6
MALTA
Acts 28:1
MALTHACE
Matt 14:3; "House of Herod"—p. 1367
MAN
creation of
Gen 1:26; 2:7; 9:5,6; Ps 139:14
his dominion over the earth
Gen 1:26,28; 2:15; 9:2; Ps 8:6-8; Heb 2:6-8; 8:1; 9:1-28
fall of
Gen 3:1,7,14; Rom 5:12-21,14; 16:17-20; 1 Cor 15:22,56
MANAEN
Acts 13:1
MANASSEH (grandfather of Jonathan)
Judg 18:30
MANASSEH (son of Hezekiah)
2 Kin 20:18; 21:1,3,15,16,20; 23:6; 2 Chr 33:11-17,20; Ezra 4:10; Is 9:21; 39:6; Nah 1:11; Zeph 1:5; Matt 5:22
MANASSEH (son of Joseph)
Gen 48:5-7,13; Josh 13:29; 14:4; Judg 10:3; 2 Kin 17:16; Acts 7:14; Rev 7:6
MANDRAKE
Gen 30:14
MANNA
Num 11:7; 21:5; Josh 5:12; 2 Chr 5:10; Matt 4:4; John 6:31,58; 1 Cor 10:3-4; Rev 2:17
MARAH
Ex 15:23; Rev 8:11
MARDIKH
Introduction to Genesis: Background—p. 1
MARDUK
Esth 2:5; Is 45:4; 46:1; Dan 1:7; 4:8; Introduction to Genesis: Background—p. 1
MARI
Gen 24:10; Introduction to Genesis: Background—p. 1
MARI TABLETS
"Ancient Texts Relating to the Old Testament"—p. xix
MARIAMNE
Matt 14:3; "House of Herod"—p. 1367
MARK, JOHN
Mark 14:51; Acts 1:13; 10:37; 12:25; 13:5,13; 15:38,39; Col 4:10; 2 Tim 4:11; 1 Pet 5:13; Introduction to Mark: John Mark in the NT—p. 1416
MARKET DISTRICT
Neh 11:9
MARRIAGE. *See also* DIVORCE
Mal 2:14; 1 Cor 6:16,17,18; 7:1,3,5,6,10,11,14,15,36,37,39; 11:5-6; Eph 5:22,23,25; 1 Tim 3:2; Titus 1:6

customs of ancient Near East
Gen 21:21; 29:22; Ex 22:16; Judg 14:2,10; Ruth 3:4,9; 1 Sam 18:25; Song 8:8; Matt 1:18; 22:11; Mark 2:19; John 2:1
levirate
Gen 38:8; Ruth 1:11; 4:5; 1 Chr 3:19; Matt 22:24

MARTHA
Luke 19:29; John 11:22,27,37

MARTYRDOM
1 Cor 13:3; Heb 12:1; Rev 10:6

MARY (of Bethany)
Luke 19:29; John 11:20,21,31; 12:3

MARY (Magdalene)
Mark 15:40; Luke 8:2; John 20:1,16,17

MARY (mother of Jesus)
Matt 1:16,18,20; 2:11; Luke 1:32; 2:5,35; 8:19; 24:10; Acts 1:14

MARY (mother of Mark)
Acts 1:13; 12:12; Col 4:15

MARY (wife of Clopas)
Matt 28:1

MASORETIC TEXT
1 Chr 14:12; 2 Chr 2:18

MASSAH
Ex 17:7; Num 20:13

MATERIALISM
Judg 17:10; 2 Kin 1:8; 5:26; Mark 10:22; Luke 12:13

MATTANIAH
2 Kin 24:17; 2 Chr 36:4

MATTATHIAS
1 Chr 24:7; Dan 11:34; "The Time between the Testaments"—p. 1356

MATTHEW
Hos 11:1; Mark 2:14; Luke 5:27,28,29; 6:15; Introduction to Matthew: Author—p. 1363

MATTHIAS
Acts 2:1

MATURITY
1 Cor 2:14-23; 3:1-4; Heb 5:14; 13:22

MEANINGLESSNESS
Eccl 1:2

MEDEBA
2 Kin 1:1; 1 Chr 19:7; Is 15:2

MEDES
Ezra 6:2; Is 13:17; Nah 1:14; Acts 2:9

MEDIATOR
Gen 28:12; Ex 20:19; 32:30; Job 5:1; Gal 3:20; Heb 8:6

MEDIUM (at Endor)
1 Sam 28:7,12,21

MEDIUMS
Lev 20:6; Deut 18:9

MEDO-PERSIA
Dan 2:32-43; 7:4-7; 8:3

MEEKNESS
Ps 37:11; Matt 5:5

MEGIDDO
Josh 17:11; Judg 5:19; 1 Kin 9:15; 22:39; Rev 16:16

MELCHIZEDEK
Gen 14:18-20; Ps 110:4; Eccl 1:16; Heb 5:5; 7:1,3,4,11,16; 8:7; 13:10

MELITA
Acts 28:1

MELQART
1 Kin 16:31

MEMPHIS
Is 19:13; Ezek 30:13; Hos 9:6

MENAHEM
2 Kin 15:12,14; Hos 5:13; 7:11; 8:9

MENANDER
1 Cor 15:33

MENELAUS
1 Sam 2:35

MENSTRUATION
Gen 31:35; Lev 15:24; Deut 22:14

MEPHIBOSHETH
Judg 6:32; 2 Sam 9:2,7; 19:27

MERARI
Ex 6:16; 1 Chr 15:4-10

MERATHAIM
Jer 50:21

MERCY
Gen 19:16; Hos 6:6; Rom 9:18; 12:8; Titus 3:5; Introduction to Jeremiah: Themes and Message—p. 1050

MERIB-BAAL
Judg 6:32; 2 Sam 4:4

MERIBAH
Ex 17:7; Num 20:13

MERIBAH KADESH
Ezek 47:19

MERODACH-BALADAN
2 Kin 20:1,12

MEROM
Josh 11:5

MEROZ
Judg 5:23

MESHA
2 Kin 3:27; Is 16:1

MESHA (MOABITE) STONE (INSCRIPTION)
Gen 49:19; 2 Kin 1:1

MESHACH
Dan 1:7

MESHECH (son of Japheth)
Gen 10:2

MESHECH (son of Shem)
Ezek 32:26; 38:2

MESHULLAM (leader in return from exile)
Ezra 8:16; 10:15

MESHULLAM (son of Berekiah)
Neh 2:10; 3:4; 6:17-18

MESOPOTAMIA
Gen 24:10; 1 Kin 4:30; Ezra 2:59,69; Acts 2:9

MESSIAH. *See also* CHRIST
Num 3:3; Ps 2:2; Is 9:6; 45:1; Dan 9:25-27; Amos 9:12; Mic 5:3,4; Mark 14:61; John 1:25

MESSIANIC REFERENCES
Gen 49:10; Deut 18:15; 2 Sam 7:16; Ps 110:1-7; Is 42:1-4; Jer 23:5; Dan 7:18; Introduction to Zechariah: Theological Teaching—p. 1332

MESSIANIC AGE
Is 2:2; 11:6-9; Luke 4:19; Heb 1:1

MESSIANIC BANQUET
1 Chr 12:38-40

MESSIANIC SECRET
Matt 8:4; 16:20; Mark 3:12; 5:19,43; Luke 9:21

MEUNITES
Judg 10:12; 2 Chr 20:1

MEZUZOT
Deut 6:8-9

MICAH (Ephraimite)
Judg 16:5; 17:2; 18:24

MICAH (prophet)
Job 30:29; Matt 2:6; Introduction to Micah: Author—p. 1299

MICAIAH
1 Kin 22:15,16,17

MICHAEL
Ezra 8:8; Dan 10:13; Luke 1:19; 1 Thess 4:16; Heb 1:4; Rev 12:7

MICHAL
1 Sam 15:23; 18:28; 19:24; 2 Sam 3:13; 6:23

MICMASH
1 Sam 13:2; Is 10:28

MIDIAN
Ex 2:15; Acts 7:29; Heb 11:27

MIDIANITES
Gen 37:25; Judg 6:1; 7:24; 1 Kin 11:18; "Gideon's Battles"—p. 323

MIDRASH
Zech 6:12

MIGDOL
Ex 14:2; Ezek 29:10

MILCOM
1 Kin 11:5

MILDEW
Lev 13:47

MILETUS
Acts 20:15; 2 Tim 4:20

MILK AND HONEY
Ex 3:8; Song 4:11

MILLENNIUM, THE
1 Cor 15:25; Rev 20:2

MILLO
Judg 9:6

MILLSTONES
Deut 24:6; Mark 9:42

MINA
Ezra 2:69; Dan 5:26-28; Luke 19:13

MINISTERS
"manual" for
1 Thess 2:1-12
payment of
Num 18:12; Neh 5:14; 1 Cor 9:4,11,18,19; 2 Cor 2:17; 11:7,12; 1 Thess 2:6
a warning to
Num 3:4

MINNITH
Ezek 27:17

MIRACLES OF JESUS. *See also* MIRACLES OF OTHERS
feeding of the 5,000
Matt 15:37; Mark 6:42,43,44
feeding of the 4,000
Matt 15:37; Mark 8:4
healing of lame man
John 7:21
list of "Miracles of Jesus"
purpose of
Mark 2:10; John 2:11

MIRACLES OF OTHERS. *See also* MIRACLES OF JESUS
Ex 4:8; 8:19; 1 Cor 12:12
of Elijah
1 Kin 17:4,16; 18:38; 2 Kin 1:10; 2:8
of Elisha
2 Kin 2:14,21,24; 4:4,33; 5:10,14; 6:6,18; 13:21
of Joshua
Josh 3:1-17,7,10,13; 4:1-24; 6:1; 10:13
of Moses
Ex 7:12,17; 14:21; 15:25; 17:6; Num 20:11; 21:8-9
of Samuel
1 Sam 12:19

MIRIAM
Ex 15:20; Luke 2:36

MISHAEL
Dan 1:6

MISHNAH
Neh 10:34; Jer 35:19; Matt 15:2; Mark 2:24; 11:15

MISHNEH
Neh 3:6

MITHREDATH
Ezra 1:8

MITYLENE
Acts 20:14

MIZPAH
Gen 31:49; Judg 10:17; 1 Sam 7:5; 1 Kin 15:22; 2 Kin 25:23; Hos 5:1; "Jacob's Journeys"—p. 47

MNASON
Acts 21:16

MOAB
Gen 19:36-38; Ruth 1:15; 2 Kin 3:23; Is 15:1,9; 16:3; "The Book of Ruth"—p. 347

MOABITE STONE
Introduction to 1 Kings: Theme—p. 442;; "Ancient Texts Relating to the Old Testament"—p. xix

MOABITES
Ruth 1:4; 2 Sam 8:2; 2 Kin 3:23; Is 15:9; 16:3; "The Book of Ruth"—p. 347

MOLECH
Lev 18:21; Judg 10:6; 1 Kin 11:5; Is 44:19; 57:9; Zeph 1:5; 3:10

MONEY
blessings of
Prov 3:2,10; 10:15,22; Eccl 10:19; Luke 16:9
dangers of
1 Kin 9:4-5; Mark 4:19; 10:21; Luke 12:33
love of
Prov 23:4; Eccl 5:10; Acts 5:1
true wealth
Luke 16:11; 2 Cor 6:10
using religion for
2 Kin 5:26; Ezek 13:19; 2 Cor 2:17; 11:7
and the wicked
Ps 49:1-20; 73:18-20; Is 53:9

MONOGAMY
Gen 2:24; 4:19; 1 Tim 3:2; Titus 1:6

MONOTHEISM
Deut 4:35; Introduction to Genesis: Theme and Message—p. 1

MOON
Gen 1:16

MORDECAI
Ezra 2:2; Esth 2:5,19; 3:2-6; 5:9; 6:1; 7:8,9; 8:2,3-6,15; 9:1,20

MORESHETH
Introduction to Micah: Author—p. 1299

MORIAH, MOUNT. *See* MOUNT: MORIAH

MOSES. *See also* MIRACLES: OF MOSES
birth of
Ex 2:2,10
call of
Acts 7:22,23,29,37; Heb 3:2
and Christ
Deut 18:15; 34:12; Matt 17:3; 22:24; John 6:31,32; Acts 7:35; Heb 3:2,5-6
death of
Josh 1:1; Heb 11:29
and fasting
Ezra 10:6
and the Holy Spirit
Hag 2:5
and John the Baptist
Matt 4:2
law of
1 Kin 14:23,24; 18:27; 21:10; 2 Kin 4:1; 1 Chr 23:3; Job 31:29-32; Is 47:6; John 5:10,45; 7:22; Heb 7:11; 10:5-6; Introduction to Genesis: Author and Date of Writing—p. 2
leadership of
Num 11:29; 16:1-7; 27:20; Introduction to Deuteronomy: Historical Setting—p. 228
as mediator
Ex 20:19; 24:2; 32:30; 33:11; Num 7:89; 11:12; Deut 9:19; Acts 7:38
obedience of
Num 3:16; 8:20
as prophet
Num 1:1; 9:23; 11:29; 12:6-8,8; Deut 18:15; Acts 3:22-26
punishment of
Num 20:11; 27:12-23
song of
Deut 32:4; Is 44:8; Introduction to Numbers: Author and Date—p. 173

MOST HIGH. *See* NAMES OF GOD

MOST HOLY PLACE
Ex 26:31-35; 27:12-13; 1 Kin 6:2,16,23; 2 Chr 3:8; Ezra 6:15; Ps 28:2; Ezek 41:22; Matt 27:51; Luke 1:9; Heb 4:14; 8:2; 9:4,28; 10:19,20

MOT
Judg 10:6; Job 18:14

MOTHER. *See also* BARRENNESS; CHILDREN; PARENTS
Ps 113:9; Prov 31:1,26

MOUNT
Carmel
1 Kin 18:19; Song 7:5; Amos 1:2
Ebal
Josh 8:30; John 4:20
Gerizim
John 4:20
Gilboa
Judg 7:3; 2 Sam 1:21
Gilead
Judg 7:3; Song 4:1
Hermon
Deut 3:8; Josh 12:1; Luke 9:28
Horeb
Ex 3:1; Deut 1:2; 1 Kin 19:7; 2 Kin 8:7
Mizar
Ps 42:6
Moriah
Gen 22:2; 2 Chr 3:1

O

PEKOD
Jer 50:21; Ezek 23:23

PELATIAH
1 Chr 3:21; Ezek 11:1

PELETHITES
2 Sam 8:18; 1 Chr 18:17

PELUSIUM
Ezek 30:15

PENIEL
Judg 8:8; 1 Kin 12:25

PENINNAH
1 Sam 2:3

PENTATEUCH
1 Sam 8:7; 1 Kin 1:50; 22:8; Neh 10:34; Matt 22:24; John 4:25; 10:34; Rom 8:2; Introduction to Genesis: Author and Date of Writing—p. 2

PENTECOST. *See also* FEAST: OF WEEKS (PENTECOST OR HARVEST)
Joel 2:28-32; Matt 3:11; 16:19,28; John 1:33; Acts 1:5; 2:1,2,3,15; 4:4; 8:16; 1 Cor 12:10; 16:8; Col 1:6; 1 Pet 1:12; "Countries of People Mentioned at Pentecost"—p. 1574

PEOR
Num 31:1-24; Josh 22:17

PERATH
Jer 13:4

PERAZIM
1 Chr 14:11

PEREA
Luke 13:31

PEREZ
Gen 38:29; Ruth 4:12; 1 Chr 9:4-6

PERFUME
Song 1:3,12; Mark 14:3,8; Luke 7:38; John 12:3

PERGA
Acts 13:13

PERGAMUM
Rev 2:12,13

PERIZZITES
Gen 13:7; Josh 17:15

PERJURY
Ex 20:7; Zech 5:3

PERSECUTION
John 15:21; Acts 9:4; 1 Cor 16:1; 2 Cor 5:13; Phil 1:28; Col 1:24; 2 Tim 3:12; Heb 10:32; 12:4,5; Rev 2:10

PERSEPOLIS
Ezra 5:6-7; 6:1,2

PERSEVERANCE
1 Cor 15:2; Phil 2:12; Heb 3:6,14; 6:11; 11:35; 12:1; James 5:11; 1 Pet 1:5

PERSIA
Ezra 5:28; 7:4-7; 8:3; 9:9; 10:13; Is 41:2; Dan 7:4-7; Hag 1:1; 2:6; Zech 1:20; Matt 2:1; Introduction to Esther: Author and Date—p. 677
Gulf of
Is 21:1; 43:14; Acts 2:9

PERSIANS
Ezra 1:1; 4:14; 6:2; Neh 5:4; Esth 2:23; 5:11; Is 43:3; 47:11; Dan 7:4-7; "From Malachi to Christ"—p. 1355

PETER
Introduction to 1 Peter: Author and Date—p. 1810
call of
Mark 1:17
and Christ's forgiveness
John 21:7,15-17,15
and Christ's resurrection
Luke 24:12; 1 Cor 15:5
in garden of Gethsemane
Mark 14:47,66,70; John 18:10,15
and his concept of Christ
Matt 16:18; Mark 8:32,33; Luke 9:20; John 6:68; 13:37
and his denial of Christ
Matt 26:31,73; Mark 14:37; 16:7; Luke 22:61; John 13:38; 18:17,18
and his ministry
Acts 8:14; 11:17; 15:7; 1 Cor 1:12; "Philip's and Peter's Missionary Journeys"—p. 1586
and his vision from God
Acts 10:10,14,23,26,28
house of
Matt 4:13; Mark 1:29; 9:33
marriage of
Mark 1:30; 1 Cor 9:5
and Pentecost
Acts 2:4,14,17,34
and the transfiguration
Mark 9:5; Luke 9:28
and the washing of feet
John 13:8,9

PETHUEL
Introduction to Joel: Author—p. 1267

PETRA
2 Kin 14:7; Acts 2:11

PHARAOH
Amunhotep II
1 Kin 6:1; Introduction to Exodus: Chronology—p. 75
Apries (Hophra)
2 Kin 24:20; Ezek 17:7; 30:21
Neco II
Judg 5:19; 2 Kin 22:20; 23:29,33,34,35; 2 Chr 36:2,4; Is 36:10; Ezek 31:3
Osorkon I
2 Chr 14:9
Psammeticus II
Ezek 17:7
Psusennes II
1 Kin 3:1
Rameses II
1 Kin 6:1; Lam 4:20; Heb 11:27; Introduction to Exodus: Chronology—p. 75
Seti I
Introduction to Exodus: Chronology—p. 75
Shabako
Is 18:1; 30:1
Shebitku
Is 37:9
Shishak
1 Kin 3:1; 11:40; 14:25; 2 Chr 12:2; "Ancient Texts Relating to the Old Testament"—p. xix
Siamun
1 Kin 3:1
Thutmose III
Ex 1:11; 2:15; Judg 4:3; 5:19; Introduction to Exodus: Chronology—p. 75

PHARISEES
Matt 3:7,11; 10:14; 22:15-17; 23:24; Mark 2:16,18; 3:4,6; 7:1; 8:15; 10:2; 12:18; Luke 5:17,21,30; 6:11; 11:39; 13:31; 15:28; 18:12; John 1:24; 4:1; 7:47,49,50-51,52; 8:15; 9:40,41; 11:47; 17:8; Acts 5:34; 15:1,5; 22:30; 24:21; Gal 4:10; "The Time between the Testaments"—p. 1356; "Jewish Sects"—p. 1401

PHICOL
Gen 21:22

PHILADELPHIA
Rev 3:7

PHILEMON
Col 3:22-25; 4:1,10; Introduction to Philemon: Recipient, Background and Purpose—p. 1779

PHILETUS
2 Tim 2:14-18

PHILIP (the apostle)
John 12:21

PHILIP (the evangelist)
Acts 8:5,14,34,40; 21:8; "Philip's and Peter's Missionary Journeys"—p. 1586

PHILIP (Herod I)
Matt 14:3

PHILIP (the tetrarch)
Matt 11:21; 14:6; Acts 12:1

PHILIPPI
Acts 16:11,12,13; Introduction to Philippians: Recipients—p. 1728; "Philippi in the Time of Paul"—p. 1729

PHILISTINES
Gen 10:14; Judg 4:1-2; 10:6; 14:3; 16:5; 1 Sam 4:7,8; 5:2,3,6,8; 14:24; 17:32,51; 21:11; 28:4; 29:1; 31:4; 2 Sam 1:20; 2:9; 5:17,21; 2 Kin

12:17; 16:6; Is 14:29; Ezek 25:15,16; Joel 3:4

PHILISTINES, FIVE CITIES OF
Judg 3:3; Amos 1:6,8; "Five Cities of the Philistines"—p. 312

PHINEHAS (son of Eleazar)
Ex 32:28; Num 25:11; 31:6; Judg 20:18,28; 1 Chr 9:17-21; Mal 2:5; "Major Covenants in the Old Testament"—p. 16

PHINEHAS (son of Eli)
1 Sam 4:4,11; 1 Chr 9:17-21; Mal 2:5

PHOEBE
Rom 16:1

PHOENICIANS
Gen 10:6; Ezek 28:10; Mark 7:24; Acts 11:19

PHOENIX
Acts 27:12

PHRYGIA
Acts 16:6; 18:23

PHYLACTERIES
Ex 13:9; Deut 6:8-9; Matt 23:5

PILATE
Matt 8:5; 27:2,65; Mark 15:1; Luke 23:1,7,16,18,25,38,44; John 18:29,33,34; 19:6,10,22; 1 Cor 2:8

PILLAR
Gen 28:18

PISIDIA
Acts 14:24

PISTACHIO
Gen 43:11

PLAGUES
Ex 7:14-25; 8:1-32; 9:1-35; 10:1-29; Ps 105:28-36; Rev 8:2,7,8,12; 9:3,4

PLAINS
of Aram
Gen 28:1
of Megiddo
Judg 5:19
of Moab
Num 22:1

PLEIADES
Job 9:9; Amos 5:8

PLUMB LINE
Amos 7:8; Zech 4:10

POLEMON
Acts 25:13

POLLUX
Acts 28:11

POLYBIUS
Dan 11:12

POLYCARP
Rev 2:8

POLYGAMY
Gen 4:19; 25:6; 2 Sam 3:2-5; 1 Kin 11:1; 1 Tim 3:2

POLYTHEISM
1 Kin 5:7; Introduction to Genesis: Theme and Message—p. 2

PONTUS
Acts 18:2; 1 Pet 1:1

POOR
Ex 22:21-27; Lev 25:4,13; Deut 15:4,11; Ps 14:6; 34:6; Amos 2:7; Zech 7:10; Mark 14:7; James 2:5-13

PORTION OF JACOB
Jer 10:16

POSTMILLENNIALISM
Rev 20:2

POTSHERD GATE
Jer 19:2

POZZUOLI
Acts 28:13

PRAETORIUM
Matt 27:27; Mark 15:16

PRAISE
Ps 8:1-9; 9:1; 26:6; 29:1-11; 33:1-22; 34:1; 150:3-5

PRAYER
Deut 4:7
and faith
John 15:7
faithfulness in
Neh 2:4; Luke 11:1; Rom 12:12; 1 Thess 3:10
and fasting
Acts 13:3
for forgiveness
Ps 51:1-19; Luke 11:4
and God's will
1 John 5:14
John 14:13
hindrances to
1 Pet 3:7
importance of
Mark 9:29; John 15:16; Acts 2:42; Eph 6:17-18
instruction in
Luke 11:1,4
intercessory
2 Kin 19:4; Job 42:10
in Jesus' name
John 14:13
and praise
Ps 7:17; 66:1-20
stated time for
Luke 18:10; Acts 3:1
and thanksgiving
Phil 1:3-4; 4:6; Introduction to Psalms: Theology—p. 738; Introduction to Psalms: Psalm Types—p. 736

PREDESTINATION
Rom 8:29,30; Eph 1:4

PREMILLENNIALISM
Rev 20:2

PRETERIST
Introduction to Revelation: Interpretation—p. 1847

PRIDE
Ps 31:23; 101:5; 123:4; 131:1; Prov 11:2; 1 Cor 4:8; 8:1; Introduction to Psalms: Theology—p. 738

PRIEST
garments of
Ex 28:2,6,8,35; Lev 16:1-34
role of
Ex 20:19; 28:1,12; Lev 4:5; 6:6; 16:1-34; 21:17; Num 3:4; 18:7; Deut 20:2; 31:11; 1 Sam 2:28; 1 Kin 1:39

PRIESTHOOD
Ex 19:22
Aaronic
Num 17:10; 18:1-7
Levitical
Ezek 1:1; Heb 7:27; 8:7; 10:1,11-14

PRIMOGENITURE, LAW OF
Gen 25:5,23; Deut 21:17

PRINCE OF THIS WORLD. *See* SATAN

PRISCA. *See* PRISCILLA

PRISCILLA
Acts 18:2,18,19; 1 Cor 16:19

PRISON LETTERS
Introduction to Colossians: Author, Date and Place of Writing—p. 1738

PRISONERS. *See* WAR: PRISONERS OF

PROMISED LAND
Josh 1:1-18; Ps 95:11; Introduction to Joshua: Title and Theme—p. 272

PROPHECY
definition of
Luke 1:67; John 11:51; Acts 11:27; 1 Cor 12:10; Rev 1:3
end of
1 Cor 13:8
false
Deut 13:1-5; 18:21-22; 1 Kin 13:20; Ezek 13:6; 1 John 4:1,4; Rev 13:11,12
gift of
1 Cor 13:1-3; 14:1-5
purpose of
Num 11:25; 1 Cor 14:3,5,24,30; 1 Tim 1:18

PROPHESY
1 Sam 10:5; 18:10; Matt 7:22; 1 Cor 14:24

PROPHET
Ex 3:4; 7:1-2; Num 12:8; Deut 18:15; 1 Sam 9:9; 10:5; 1 Kin 1:39; 22:19; 2 Kin 19:4; Ezek 3:16; 22:30; Amos 2:11; Jon 3:2; Eph 2:20; 4:11; 1 Thess 2:15

PROPHETESS
Ex 15:20; Judg 4:4; Luke 2:36

PROPHETS, THE
Matt 5:17; Rom 1:2; Heb 1:1; 1 Pet 1:10

PROPITIATION
Rom 3:25; 1 John 2:2

PROSTITUTE, SHRINE
Gen 38:21; Jer 2:20; Hos 4:13,14

PROSTITUTION. *See also* PROSTITUTE, SHRINE
Deut 23:18; Judg 2:17; 1 Kin 14:24; Prov 6:26; Ezek 16:15,24; 23:5; 43:7; Luke 7:37; 1 Cor 6:9,18; 7:2; Rev 14:8; 22:15

PROVERB
Introduction to Proverbs: The Nature of a Proverb—p. 890

PRUDENCE
Prov 1:4

PSAMMETICUS II
Ezek 17:7

PSEUDEPIGRAPHA
"The Time between the Testaments"—p. 1356

PTAHHOTEP
1 Kin 4:30

PTOLEMAIS
Acts 21:7

PTOLEMIES
Dan 11:5,6,7,11,14,22; "Ptolemies and Seleucids"—p. 1246; "The Time between the Testaments"—p. 1356

PUAH
Ex 1:15; Judg 10:1

PUBLICANS
Matt 5:46

PUBLIUS
Acts 28:7

PUL
2 Kin 15:19; 1 Chr 5:26; Neh 9:32

PURIM
Esth 2:9; 3:7; 9:18-19; "Old Testament Feasts and Other Sacred Days"—p. 164; Introduction to Esther: Author and Date—p. 677; Introduction to Esther: Purpose, Themes and Literary Features—p. 677

PURPLE
Ex 25:4; Acts 16:14

PUT
Gen 10:6; Ezek 27:10; Nah 3:9

PUTEOLI
Acts 28:13

Q

Q (Quelle)
"The Synoptic Gospels"—p. 1361

QARQAR, BATTLE OF
1 Kin 4:26; 2 Kin 5:1; 13:7; "The Divided Kingdom"—p. 471

QOS
Ezra 2:53

QUALIFICATIONS FOR ELDERS AND DEACONS
1 Tim 3:2; Titus 1:6-9; "Qualifications for Elders/Overseers and Deacons"—p. 1765

QUEEN
of Heaven
Jer 7:18
of Sheba
1 Kin 10:1,9; 2 Chr 9:1-12; Matt 12:42; Luke 11:31-32

QUIRINIUS
Luke 2:2; Acts 5:37

QUMRAN
Ezra 7:2; 8:15; Neh 8:16; 10:34; 12:9; Jer 32:14; Ezek 44:15; Joel 2:23; Zech 6:13; John 1:23; 3:25; "The Time between the Testaments"—p. 1356

R

RABBAH
Deut 3:11; 2 Sam 12:26

RABBI
Matt 26:49

RACA
Matt 5:22

RACHEL
Gen 29:30; 31:19; Ruth 4:11; Jer 31:15

RAHAB
Josh 2:1-24,1,8-11,12; 7:1-26; Ruth 1:4; Is 30:7; Matt 1:5; Heb 11:31; James 2:25

RAINBOW
Gen 9:13

RAM
Lev 5:15; Ezra 10:19
horn. See TRUMPET

RAMAH
1 Sam 1:1; 15:34; 1 Kin 15:17; Is 10:29; Jer 31:15

RAMATHAIM
1 Sam 1:1

RAMESES
Gen 47:11; Ezek 30:14; Introduction to Exodus: Chronology—p. 75

RAMESES II
1 Kin 6:1; Lam 4:20; Heb 11:27; Introduction to Exodus: Chronology—p. 75

RAMOTH-GILEAD
1 Kin 22:3; 2 Kin 5:2; 8:28; 2 Chr 22:5,6

RAMPARTS
Is 26:1

RANSOM
Ex 13:13; Matt 20:28; Mark 10:45; Heb 9:15

RAPHA
2 Sam 21:16

RAPTURE, THE
1 Cor 15:52; 2 Cor 12:2-4; 1 Thess 4:17; Rev 4:1

RAS SHAMRA TABLETS
Gen 15:16; "Ancient Texts Relating to the Old Testament"—p. xix

REBEKAH
Gen 27:6,8

RECABITES
2 Sam 4:8; 2 Kin 10:15; Jer 35:1-19

RECONCILIATION
Rom 5:10,11; 2 Cor 5:18,21; Eph 2:11-22; Col 1:20; Heb 12:24

RED SEA
Ex 13:18; 14:2; Deut 2:1; 1 Kin 9:26

REDEMPTION
Gen 18:17,21; Ex 6:7-8; 13:13; Ps 65:6-7; Rom 3:24; 2 Cor 5:17,18; Eph 1:7; Col 1:14; 1 Pet 1:2,18; Introduction to Exodus: Themes and Theology—p. 76

REHOBOAM
1 Kin 2:24; 12:8,14,15; 2 Chr 11:5-10,18-22,23; 13:7

REHOBOTH IR
Jon 1:2; 3:3

REHUM
Ezra 4:8; Neh 1:3

REMEMBER
Gen 8:1; 1 Sam 1:11; Neh 1:8; 13:31

REMNANT
2 Kin 19:4,30-31; 21:14; Is 1:9; 6:13; 10:20-22; 24:14; Amos 5:15; Mic 4:7; Rom 9:27-29; 11:5,7; Rev 7:4

REPENTANCE
Matt 3:2; 4:17; Mark 1:4; Luke 24:47; Acts 2:38; 3:19; 11:18; 19:4; Rom 2:4; 1 Cor 5:5; 2 Cor 2:5-11; 7:8-9,10; 2 Thess 3:14; Heb 6:1-2; James 5:1; Introduction to Jeremiah: Themes and Message—p. 1050; Introduction to Hosea: Theme and Message—p. 1520

REPHAITES
Deut 2:11; Josh 17:15; 2 Sam 21:16; 1 Chr 20:4

RESEN
Jon 1:2; 3:3

RESHEPH
Job 5:7
REST
Deut 3:20; Josh 1:13; 1 Kin 5:4; 8:56; Ps 95:11; Heb 4:1,3,10,11
RESURRECTION
Ps 6:5; Is 53:11; Dan 12:2; Mark 9:10; 1 Cor 15:42-44,44-49,51,52,57; 1 Thess 4:13; Heb 6:1-2; 1 Pet 3:18
RESURRECTION, CHRIST'S
appearances after
Acts 1:2,3; 1 Cor 15:3-5,5,6; "Resurrection Appearances"—p. 1511
evidence for
1 Cor 15:3-5,12,20,34
meaning of
Rom 10:9; 1 Cor 15:21,57,58; Gal 1:1; 2 Tim 2:8; 1 Pet 3:21
Paul and
Acts 26:8; Rom 4:17; Eph 4:9
prediction of
Is 53:11
and that of believers
Rom 8:11; 1 Cor 15:22,23,44-49; Phil 3:10,21; 1 Pet 1:3
theories about
1 Pet 3:19-20
timing of
1 Cor 15:4
RETALIATION
Ex 21:23-25; Lev 24:20; Job 31:1-40; Luke 6:29; "Cities of Refuge"—p. 226
REUBEN
Gen 35:22; 37:21; 42:37; 48:5; 1 Chr 5:1-10,23-26
REUEL
Ex 2:16
REVELATION
1 Cor 14:30
REWARDS (CROWNS)
2 Tim 4:8
REZIN
2 Kin 16:5; 2 Chr 28:5; Is 8:6
REZON
1 Kin 11:24
RHEGIUM
Acts 28:13
RHODA
Acts 12:13
RHODES
Gen 10:4; Ezek 27:15; Acts 21:2
RICH YOUNG RULER
Mark 10:17,18,19,20,21,22; Luke 10:25,27,29
RICHES. *See* MONEY
RIGHTEOUS, THE
Ps 1:5
RIGHTEOUSNESS
Gen 7:1; 15:6; Deut 6:25; 2 Sam 22:21; Ps 1:1-6; 89:14; Prov 12:28; 14:34; Is 45:8; 46:13; Matt 1:19; 6:1; John 16:10; Rom 1:17; 4:1; 9:31; 10:3,4,5,6-7,8; 14:17; 1 Cor 1:30; 2 Cor 3:8-9; Gal 5:5; Phil 1:11; 2 Tim 4:8; Heb 11:7; 12:11; 2 Pet 1:1
RIMMON
Judg 10:6; 2 Kin 5:18; Zech 14:10
RIVER
Abana
2 Kin 5:12
Arnon
Josh 13:9,15; 2 Kin 3:25
Balikh
Is 37:12
Barada
2 Kin 5:12
of Egypt
Gen 15:18
Euphrates
Gen 2:14; 2 Sam 8:3; Ezra 4:10; Rev 9:14
Jabbok
Gen 32:22
Jordan
Josh 1:2; 2 Sam 19:41; 1 Kin 20:26; 2 Kin 5:10; 1 Chr 12:8-15; Is 33:9; Zech 11:3; Mark 1:5,16
Kebar
Ezra 2:59; Ezek 1:1
Khoser
Nah 2:6
Nile
Ex 7:17,20,24; Amos 8:8
Shihor
Josh 13:3; 1 Chr 13:15; Is 23:3
RIZPAH
1 Sam 14:50; 2 Sam 12:8
ROCK
Gen 49:24; 1 Sam 2:2; 2 Sam 22:2; Ps 18:2
ROME
"The Neo-Babylonian Empire"—p. 1234; "From Malachi to Christ"—p. 1355; "Paul's Journey to Rome"—p. 1627; "Rome in the Time of Paul"—p. 1631; Introduction to Romans: Recipients—p. 1632
ROOT OF JESSE
Is 11:10
ROSH HASHANAH
Num 29:1-6; Ezek 40:1; "Old Testament Feasts and Other Sacred Days"—p. 164
RUFUS
Mark 15:21; Luke 23:26
RUTH
Ruth 1:4,16; "The Book of Ruth"—p. 347

S

SABBATH
Gen 2:3; Ex 16:23; 20:9-10; 31:13,16-17; Num 15:32; Neh 9:14; 10:31; 13:15; Is 56:2,4,6; Ezek 20:12; Amos 8:5; Matt 4:23; 12:10; 24:20; 27:62; Mark 2:25,27; Luke 4:40; 6:9; 14:1; John 5:17; 7:22; Acts 1:12; Rom 14:5; "Old Testament Feasts and Other Sacred Days"—p. 164
SABEANS
Job 1:15; Ezek 23:42; Joel 3:8
SACKCLOTH
Gen 37:34; 2 Kin 6:30; Is 20:2; Jon 3:5-6; Rev 11:3
SACRED
1 Cor 3:17
SACRIFICES
Num 28:1-31; 29:1-40; 1 Sam 15:22; Ps 50:8-13; 51:17; Is 53:11; Introduction to Leviticus: Themes—p. 134; "Old Testament Sacrifices"—p. 139
SADDUCEES
Ezra 7:2; Matt 2:4; 3:7; 3:11; 22:24; Mark 12:18; Luke 20:27; Acts 4:1; "The Time between the Testaments"—p. 1356; "Jewish Sects"—p. 1401
SAFFRON
Song 4:14
SAHRA
Ezek 27:18
SAINTS
1 Sam 2:9; Rom 1:7; 15:25; 1 Cor 6:1; 2 Cor 1:1; Eph 1:18; Phil 1:1
SALEM
Gen 14:18
SALOME
Ezra 8:10; Matt 14:6; Mark 15:40
SALT
Gen 19:26; Mark 9:50
SALT OF THE COVENANT
Lev 2:13; Num 18:19
SALVATION
at the last day
Rom 10:9
available to all
Rom 5:18
based on faith
Rom 11:26; 2 Tim 1:9; Titus 2:11; Heb 3:14
day of
Is 49:8; Rom 13:11; Phil 1:6
freely offered
Acts 16:30,31; 1 Tim 4:10
meaning of
Mark 5:34; Eph 2:8; Phil 2:1,12; 2 Thess 1:9; 1 Tim 4:16; Titus 2:14; 1 Pet 1:5

work of God
Mark 10:27; 1 Cor 1:26-31; 2 Thess 2:13; 1 Tim 2:4; Titus 3:5; Introduction to Exodus: Themes and Theology—p. 76

SAMARIA (city)
1 Kin 16:24; 1 Kin 21:1,19; 2 Kin 5:3; 6:8,25; 17:5,6; Is 28:1; Amos 3:12,13,15; 8:5

SAMARIA (territory)
1 Kin 13:32; 21:1; 2 Kin 17:29; 23:18; Ezra 4:10; Neh 2:10,19; Is 10:10; Hos 7:1; Nah 1:9; John 4:4; Acts 1:8; 12:1

SAMARIA OSTRACA
1 Chr 7:14-19

SAMARITAN
2 Kin 17:29; Matt 10:5; Luke 9:52; 10:31-33; John 4:20,25; 8:48

SAMOS
Acts 20:15

SAMOTHRACE
Acts 16:11

SAMSON
Judg 13:1-25,24; 14:1-20,10; 15:1-20,2; 16:1-31,1,7,13,20,21,30

SAMUEL
Introduction to 1 Samuel: Title—p. 353
and David
1 Sam 16:7,13; 2 Sam 2:4
death of
1 Sam 25:1
and Eli
1 Sam 3:1,11-14
as intercessor
1 Sam 7:5
and Israel
1 Sam 10:25; 12:15,24
as prophet
1 Sam 3:19; 10:5
and Saul
1 Sam 9:6; 11:15; 12:6; 15:21,31,35; Introduction to Judges: Title—p. 307; Introduction to 1 Samuel: Contents and Theme—p. 353; Introduction to 1 Samuel: Literary Features, Authorship and Date—p. 353

SANBALLAT
Neh 2:10; 6:5; 13:28

SANCTIFICATION
John 17:17,20; Rom 8:29; 1 Cor 1:2; 2 Cor 3:8-9,18; Eph 2:9; 1 Thess 3:13; 4:8; Heb 10:10; 1 Pet 1:5; 2:24; 4:1

SANHEDRIN
Matt 27:1,2; Mark 14:52-72,55; 15:1-15; Luke 23:1; Acts 5:21; 22:20,30; 24:1

SAPPHIRA
Acts 5:1

SARAH. *See also* SARAI
Rom 4:19; Gal 4:30

SARAI. *See also* SARAH
Gen 12:11; 17:15

SARDIS
Obad 1:20; Rev 3:1

SARGON II
2 Kin 17:6,24; 20:12; Ezra 4:7; Neh 2:19; Is 20:1

SARGON LEGEND
"Ancient Texts Relating to the Old Testament"—p. xix

SARGON'S DISPLAY INSCRIPTION
"Ancient Texts Relating to the Old Testament"—p. xix

SATAN
and Ananias
Acts 5:3
and believers, unbelievers
Job 1:12; 1 John 3:8
and David
2 Sam 24:1
and Eve
Gen 3:1
fall of
Luke 8:31; 10:18; John 12:31; Rom 16:20; 1 Thess 3:5; Rev 12:7
and Jesus
Matt 4:1-11; Mark 8:33; Luke 4:2,13; John 14:30
and Job
Job 1:6,8
and Judas
Luke 22:3
names for
Deut 13:13; Matt 10:25; 1 John 3:8; Rev 2:9
and the unpardonable sin
Matt 12:31

SAUL (king)
and the ark
1 Sam 14:18
called by God
1 Sam 11:5,13
and David
1 Sam 16:19; 17:37,55; 19:24; 2 Sam 3:13,14
death of
2 Sam 1:10
disobedience of
1 Sam 13:9,13; 14:24-26; 15:12,23; 17:33
origins of
1 Sam 9:21; 10:5
and Samuel
1 Sam 9:6; 10:8; 11:15; 15:13,31,35
and Spirit of God
1 Sam 16:14; 19:24

SAUL (of Tarsus). *See* PAUL

SCAPEGOAT
Lev 16:5; Is 53:6

SCEVA
Acts 19:14

SCRIBES, THE
Ezra 7:6; Jer 8:8; Luke 20:19

SCRIPTURE. *See also* WORD OF GOD
1 Tim 5:18; 2 Tim 3:16
divine origin of
Matt 1:22; 2 Pet 1:21
purpose of
Rom 15:4

SCROLL
Ex 17:14; 2 Tim 4:13

SCYTHIANS
Nah 1:14; 2:1; Col 3:11

SEA
Adriatic
Acts 27:27
Aegean
Acts 16:11; Rev 1:9
of the Arabah
2 Kin 14:25
Bronze
1 Kin 7:23,24
Dead
Gen 14:3,10; Ezek 47:8; Mark 1:4; Luke 3:20
of Galilee
Mark 1:16; 4:37; Luke 5:1; John 6:1
of Gennesaret
Mark 1:16; Luke 5:1
of Kinnereth
Mark 1:16
Mediterranean
Gen 28:12; Heb 8:6
Red
Ex 13:18; 14:2; Deut 2:1; 1 Kin 9:26
of Tiberias
Mark 1:16; Luke 5:1; John 6:1

SEA PEOPLES
"The Exodus"—p. 97; "Conquest of Canaan"—p. 292

SEAL
Gen 38:18; Hag 2:23

SECOND COMING
John 14:3,18; 21:22; 2 Cor 1:14; Phil 1:6; Col 3:4; 2 Thess 2:1; 2 Tim 4:8; Titus 2:13; Heb 10:25
judgment at
1 Thess 5:2; James 5:9
and "last days"
1 Tim 4:1; 2 Tim 3:1; 1 John 2:18
literary treatment of
Matt 3:12
manner of
Mark 13:26
outcome of
Is 52:7; Rom 13:11; 1 Cor 13:10; 15:23,24,26,44-49,58; 2 Cor 4:4; Phil 1:6,10; Rev 14:15
participants in
Luke 21:35; 1 Thess 4:15; 2 Thess 1:7

predictions of
Luke 21:27
signs of
Is 66:19; Mark 13:29; Luke 18:8; Heb 12:27
timing of
Luke 12:40; 17:23; 21:32; John 16:16; 1 Thess 5:2; 1 Tim 4:1; 6:15; 2 Tim 3:1; James 5:9; 1 Pet 4:7; Rev 22:12
waiting for
1 Thess 1:9-10; 1 John 2:18

SECOND DISTRICT
Neh 11:9

SECULARISM
Eccl 4:13-16

SEIR
Gen 36:8; Judg 5:4; Is 21:11; Ezek 25:8

SELA
2 Kin 14:7; Is 16:1; Obad 1:3

SELAH
Introduction to Psalms: Authorship and Titles—p. 736

SELEUCIA
Acts 13:4

SELEUCIDS
Dan 11:5,7,10,20,21; Rev 2:18; "Ptolemies and Seleucids"—p. 1246; "The Time between the Testaments"—p. 1356

SELF-CONTROL
Prov 16:32; 2 Pet 1:6

SELF-DENIAL
Luke 9:23,48; Rom 14:7; 15:1; 1 Cor 9:12,19

SEMITES
Gen 10:21; Neh 12:31

SENAAH
Ezra 2:35

SENIR
Song 4:8; Ezek 27:5

SENNACHERIB
2 Kin 18:13,14; 19:4,29,37; 2 Chr 32:21; Neh 11:27; Is 8:8; 36:1; 1 Cor 1:19

SENNACHERIB'S PRISM
"Ancient Texts Relating to the Old Testament"—p. xix

SEPHARVAIM
Is 36:19; Ezek 47:16

SEPTUAGINT
Eccl 1:1; Amos 5:26; Introduction to Leviticus: Title—p. 134; Introduction to Numbers: Title—p. 173; Introduction to 1 Samuel: Title—p. 353; Introduction to Ezra: Ezra and Nehemiah—p. 632; Introduction to Psalms: Name—p. 735; "The Book of the Twelve, or the Minor Prophets"—p. 1249; "The Time between the Testaments"—p. 1356

SERAIAH
2 Kin 25:18; 1 Chr 6:14; Ezra 7:1

SERAPH
Is 6:2

SERIAH
2 Sam 8:17

SERMON ON THE MOUNT/PLAIN
Matt 5:1-48; 6:1-34; 7:1-29; Luke 6:20-49; 11:1

SERPENT
Gen 3:1,14,15; Amos 9:3

SERVANT OF THE LORD
Ex 14:31; Deut 34:5; Judg 2:8; Ps 18:1; Is 41:8-9; 42:1-4; Rom 1:1; 6:18; 16:1; 2 Cor 11:23; Gal 1:10; 6:17; Phil 1:1; 2:7

SERVANTHOOD
Mark 10:35-36,45; Luke 22:26; John 13:5

SETI I
Introduction to Exodus: Chronology—p. 75

SEVEN
Gen 4:17-18; Lev 4:6; Josh 6:4; Ruth 4:15; Ps 12:6; Prov 9:1; Introduction to Genesis: Literary Features—p. 2; Introduction to Revelation: Distinctive Feature—p. 1847

SEVEN, THE
Acts 6:6; 8:5; 14:23

SEVEN LEAN YEARS TRADITON
"Ancient Texts Relating to the Old Testament"—p. xix

SEVENTY
Gen 10:2; 46:27

SEXUAL SIN. *See* ADULTERY; HOMOSEXUALITY

SHABAKO
Is 18:1; 30:1

SHABBETHAI
Ezra 10:15; Neh 13:15

SHADDAI. *See* NAMES OF GOD: GOD ALMIGHTY (*EL SHADDAI*)

SHADRACH
Dan 1:7

SHALLUM
2 Kin 15:27; 22:14; 23:30; 1 Chr 3:15-16; Jer 22:11; Hos 7:7

SHALMANESER III
1 Kin 18:5; 22:1; 2 Kin 8:7; 10:8,34; 13:7; 19:12; Nah 3:3

SHALMANESER IV
2 Kin 14:25

SHALMANESER V
2 Kin 17:3,6; Is 10:10

SHALMANESER'S BLACK OBELISK
"Ancient Texts Relating to the Old Testament"—p. xix

SHAMASH
Ezra 1:8

SHAMASH-SHUM-UKIN
2 Chr 33:11; Ezra 4:9

SHAMGAR
Judg 3:31

SHAMMAH
1 Sam 16:9; 2 Sam 13:3; 21:21

SHAMMAI, SCHOOL OF
Lev 19:18; 24:20; Matt 19:3

SHAPHAN
2 Kin 22:3; Ezra 7:6; Jer 29:3; 36:10

SHAPHAT
1 Kin 19:16; 2 Kin 3:11

SHAREZER
2 Kin 19:37

SHARON
Song 2:1; Is 33:9; Acts 9:35

SHEALTIEL
1 Chr 3:19; Ezra 5:2; Neh 12:1; Hag 1:1; Matt 1:12

SHEAR-JASHUB
Is 7:3

SHEBA (son of Bicri)
2 Sam 20:1,14,21; 1 Chr 18:17

SHEBA (son of Joktan)
Gen 10:28

SHEBA (Arabian home of queen)
1 Kin 10:1; Is 60:6; Jer 6:20; Ezek 38:13; Matt 12:42; "Hebrew Calendar and Selected Events"—p. 92

SHEBITKU
Is 37:9

SHEBNA
Is 22:15,16,21

SHECANIAH (head of Davidic family)
1 Chr 3:21,22

SHECANIAH (son of Jehiel)
Ezra 10:2

SHECHEM
Gen 33:18; Josh 8:30-35; Judg 9:1; Acts 7:16

SHEEP GATE
Neh 3:1,32

SHEKEL
Gen 20:16; Ezra 2:69

SHELAH
1 Chr 2:3-9; 9:4-6

SHELANITES
1 Chr 9:4-6

SHELOMITH
Ezra 8:10

SHEM
Gen 10:2,21; 1 Chr 1:5-23

SHEMA
Deut 4:1; 6:4-9; Mark 12:29,31; James 2:19

SHEMAIAH (prophet)
1 Kin 12:22; Jer 29:24

SHEMAIAH (son of Delaiah)
Neh 6:10,12

SHEMAIAH (son of Shechaniah)
1 Chr 3:22

SHENAZZAR
1 Chr 3:18; Ezra 1:8

SHEOL
Gen 37:35; Matt 16:18; Rev 6:8

SHEPHELAH
Josh 15:33; Mic 1:10-15; "Five Cities of the Philistines"—p. 312

SHEPHERD
Gen 48:15; Ps 23:1; 119:176; Ezek 34:2; Zech 10:2; Mark 6:42; John 10:1-30; 1 Pet 2:25; 5:2

SHESHACH
Jer 25:26

SHESHBAZZAR
1 Chr 3:18; Ezra 1:8,11; 2:63; Neh 5:15

SHIBBOLETH
Judg 12:6

SHIELD
Gen 15:1; Ps 3:3

SHIHOR RIVER
Josh 13:3; 1 Chr 13:5; Is 23:3

SHILOAH
Is 8:6

SHILOH
Josh 18:1; Judg 21:19; 1 Sam 1:3; 2:32; 9:12

SHILONITES
1 Chr 9:4-6

SHIMEI (Benjamite)
2 Sam 16:8,10; 19:17,23; 1 Kin 2:8,36,46

SHIMEI (son of Kish)
Esth 2:5

SHIMEON
Ezra 10:31

SHIMSHAI
Ezra 4:8; Neh 1:3

SHIPHRAH
Ex 1:15

SHIPS OF TARSHISH
1 Kin 10:22

SHISHAK
1 Kin 3:1; 11:40; 14:25; 2 Chr 12:2 "Ancient Texts Relating to the Old Testament"—p. xix

SHISHAK'S GEOGRAPHICAL LIST
"Ancient Texts Relating to the Old Testament"—p. xix

SHITTIM
Num 25:1

SHOBI
2 Sam 17:27

SHRINE PROSTITUTE. *See* PROSTITUTE, SHRINE

SHUAH
Job 2:11

SHUHAM
Judg 18:19

SHULAMMITE
Song 6:13

SHUNAMMITE
2 Kin 4:13; Song 6:13

SHUNEM
1 Sam 28:4; 1 Kin 1:3

SHUR, DESERT OF
Ex 15:22; 1 Sam 15:7

SIAMUN
1 Kin 3:1

SIBMAH
Is 16:8

SIDON
Judg 3:3; 10:6; 18:7; Ezek 27:8; Dan 11:15; Joel 3:4; Luke 4:26; Acts 12:20; 27:3; "The Territories of Tyre and Sidon"—p. 1433

SIGN
Ex 3:12; 4:8; Matt 12:38; Luke 1:18; 11:29,33; John 2:11

SIGNET RING
Hag 2:23

SIHON
Num 21:21-26; Song 7:4; Is 15:4

SILAS
Acts 15:22,40; 16:6,32,37; 17:10; 18:5; 1 Thess 1:1,5; 3:1-2; 1 Pet 5:12

SILLA
2 Kin 12:20

SILOAM, POOL OF
Neh 2:13,14; 3:15; Job 28:10; John 9:7

SILOAM, TOWER OF
Luke 13:4

SILOAM, TUNNEL OF
Neh 2:14; "Jerusalem during the Ministry of Jesus"—p. 1425

SILOAM INSCRIPTION
2 Kin 20:20; "Ancient Texts Relating to the Old Testament"—p. xix

SILVER
Deut 14:25

SILVERSMITH
Judg 17:4; Acts 19:24

SIMEON (high priest)
Luke 1:6; 2:25,29-32

SIMEON (Niger)
Acts 13:1

SIMEON (son of Jacob)
1 Chr 4:24-43; 2 Chr 34:6; Ezra 10:31

SIMEON (tribe)
Gen 49:7; Judg 1:3

SIMEON BAR KOSIBA (Kokhba)
Zech 11:17

SIMON (of Cyrene)
Mark 15:21; Luke 23:26; John 19:17

SIMON (the Zealot)
Matt 10:4

SIMON MAGUS (sorcerer)
Acts 8:9,10,13,18

SIMON PETER. *See* PETER

SIMON THE LEPER
Matt 26:6

SIN
freed from
Rom 6:6,7,22
inherited by all
Gen 6:5; 8:21
offering
Ex 29:10; Lev 4:3,20; 2 Kin 12:16; Neh 8:10; Ezek 43:19; "Old Testament Sacrifices"—p. 139
power of
Gen 4:7,13,23; John 8:34; Rom 3:10-18; 6:14; 1 Cor 15:56
universality of
Rom 3:9,22-23
unpardonable
Matt 12:31
victory over
Matt 4:1-11; 1 Cor 15:57; 1 John 1:7,9; 3:6
wages of
Gen 2:17; 3:22; 5:5; Lev 15:31; Num 15:2; Rom 5:12; 6:23; 7:9; 1 Cor 7:10

SIN, DESERT OF
Ex 16:1

SIN-SHAR-ISHKUN
Nah 3:18

SINAI, DESERT OF
Ex 19:2; Num 1:1

SINAI, MOUNT. *See* MOUNT: SINAI

SINUHE
Neh 9:25; Introduction to Genesis: Background—p. 1; "Ancient Texts Relating to the Old Testament"—p. xix

SINUHE'S STORY
"Ancient Texts Relating to the Old Testament"—p. xix

SIROCCO
Gen 41:6; Job 15:2

SISERA
Judg 4:7,18,22; 1 Sam 13:5

SLANDER
Prov 15:4; 2 Cor 8:21; 2 Pet 2:10

SLAVERY
Ex 1:11; 5:6; 6:7-8; 21:2,32; Lev 25:55; 1 Kin 9:15; 4:1; Neh 5:5; 1 Cor 7:21,22,23; Gal 5:1; Eph 6:5; Col 3:22-25; 4:1; Titus 2:9-10; 1 Pet 2:18
to God
Gal 1:10; 1 Pet 1:18

SLEDGE
Amos 1:3

SLINGSTONE
Judg 20:16; 1 Sam 17:40

SLUGGARD
Prov 6:6

SMYRNA
Rev 2:8

SNARE
Ex 4:3; Num 21:8-9; 2 Kin 18:4

SOCIAL JUSTICE
Introduction to Amos: Theme and Message—p. 1274

SOCIAL RESPONSIBILITY
Zech 7:10; Rom 12:13

SOCOH
1 Sam 17:1

SODOM
Gen 13:10,12; 18:20; 19:13; Ezek 16:47; Zeph 2:9; Luke 10:12; Rev 11:8; 14:10

SODOMY
Gen 19:5

SOLOMON
"Solomon's Jerusalem"—p. 450
anointed by Zadok
1 Kin 1:39
birth of
1 Kin 3:7
failures of
1 Kin 3:3,14; 11:11
idealized by Chronicler
Introduction to 1 Chronicles: Portrait of David and Solomon—p. 551
marriages of
1 Kin 3:1; 11:1,4; 2 Chr 9:28; 21:6
and queen of Sheba
1 Kin 10:1,9,13; 2 Chr 9:1-12
receives wisdom from God
2 Chr 1:5
son of Bathsheba
2 Sam 5:14; 1 Kin 1:11
successor to David
1 Kin 1:13; 2:4; 1 Chr 22:5
temple of
1 Kin 6:2; 8:27; "Solomon's Temple"—p. 458; Introduction to 2 Chronicles: The Building of the Temple in Chronicles—p. 589
wealth of
1 Kin 4:26

SOLOMON'S COLONNADE
John 10:23; Acts 3:11

SON
of the Blessed One
Mark 14:61
of David
Matt 1:1,16,20; 2:1; 9:27; Mark 10:47; 12:35
of man
Ezek 2:1; Dan 7:13; Mark 8:31; Luke 19:10; John 12:34; Acts 7:56; Eph 1:22; Rev 6:13
of the Most High
Luke 1:32; 8:28

SONG
of David
2 Sam 22:1
of Deborah
Judg 5:1-31
of Hannah
1 Sam 2:1
of Mary
Luke 1:46-55
of Moses
Ex 15:1-18; Deut 31:30; 32:1-43,4; Rev 15:3
of the Vineyard
Is 5:7
of Zechariah
Luke 1:68-79

SONS
of God
Gen 6:2; Job 5:1; Rom 8:14,15,19,23; Gal 4:5; Heb 2:10; 12:7
of thunder
Mark 3:17; Luke 9:54

SOOTHSAYER'S TREE
Judg 9:37

SOPATER
Acts 20:4; Rom 16:21

SOREK VALLEY
Judg 14:5

SOSIPATER
Acts 20:4; Rom 16:21

SOSTHENES
Acts 18:17; 1 Cor 1:1

SOUND DOCTRINE
Titus 1:9; 2:2-10; "The Pastoral Letters"—p. 1758

SOUTH GALATIAN THEORY, THE
Introduction to Galatians: Date and Destination—p. 1706

SOUTH GATE
1 Chr 26:15

SOVEREIGNTY OF GOD. *See* GOD: SOVEREIGNTY OF

SPAIN
Rom 15:24; 2 Cor 10:16

SPELT
Ex 9:32

SPICE
Song 4:10

SPIES
Num 13:2; Josh 2:1-24

SPIRIT OF BONDAGE
2 Cor 11:4

SPIRIT OF THE LORD
Judg 3:10; 6:34; 11:29; 1 Sam 11:6; 16:14; 19:24; 2 Sam 23:2; 1 Kin 18:12; Introduction to Judges: Theme and Theology—p. 307

SPIRITS, EVIL. *See* EVIL SPIRITS

SPIRITUAL GIFTS. *See* GIFTS: SPIRITUAL

STEPHANUS
1 Cor 16:15

STEPHEN
Acts 6:5,8,9,11,13; 7:9,14,16,23,35,43,44-50,49

STOICISM
Acts 17:18

STRAIGHT STREET
Acts 9:11; "Roman Damascus"—p. 1589

SUBMISSION
Ex 20:2; Ps 2:12; Rom 13:1; Eph 5:21,22; Heb 13:17; 1 Pet 3:1; 5:5

SUBSTITUTION
Gen 22:13; Ex 29:10; Lev 1:5; 16:20-22; Num 8:10; Matt 20:28; Mark 10:45

SUCCOTH
Ex 12:37; Judg 7:24; 1 Kin 7:46

SUFFERING
Rev 1:9; Introduction to Job: Theme and Message—p. 690; Introduction to Psalms: Theology—p. 738; Introduction to 1 Peter: Themes—p. 1810
for Christ
1 Cor 7:28; 13:3; 2 Cor 1:8; Phil 1:13,20,29; 1 Thess 3:3; 2 Tim 2:11-13,12; 3:11; 1 Pet 3:14; 4:1,4,13
of Christ
Is 52:14; Heb 2:10; 5:8; 12:2; 1 Pet 2:21
rejoicing in
Rom 5:3,4
of the righteous
Job 10:3; Ps 22:1-31; 73:1-28; Luke 13:2,4; Rom 8:36; 2 Cor 4:17; James 1:9-10
and spiritual gain
Job 2:10; Heb 12:5; 1 Pet 4:17

SUKKITES
2 Chr 12:3

SUN
Gen 1:16; Ex 10:21; Ps 19:4-6; 104:19-23

SUN OF RIGHTEOUSNESS
Mal 4:2

SUSA
Ezra 4:9; 6:2; Neh 5:4; Esth 1:2,5-6; 2:5

SWEARING
James 5:12

SYCAMORE (FIG) TREE
Amos 7:14; Luke 19:4

SYCHAR
John 4:5

SYNAGOGUE
description of
Ezek 8:1; Mark 1:21; Luke 21:12; Acts 13:14; "The Time between the Testaments"—p. 1356; "Capernaum Synagogue"—p. 1469
ruler of
Mark 5:22

SYNOPTIC GOSPELS
Matt 3:3; 13:3; 19:16; 20:30; 21:12-17; Luke 5:12-16; 9:12; 19:45; John 6:68; 18:11; "The Synoptic Gospels"—p. 1361; "Dating the Synoptic Gospels"—p. 1361; "Parables of Jesus"—p. 1493

SYNTYCHE
Phil 4:2-3

SYRACUSE
Acts 28:12

SYRIA
Is 30:1; Dan 7:4-7; 11:6; Gal 1:17,21; "The Time between the Testaments"—p. 1356

SYRO-EPHRAIMITE WAR
Is 7:1

T

TAANACH
Judg 5:19

TABEEL
Is 7:6

TABERNACLE
Ex 25:9; 26:1; 1 Sam 1:9; Rev 15:5; "The Tabernacle"—p. 114; "Tabernacle Furnishings"—p. 115

TABERNACLES, FEAST OF. *See* FEAST: OF TABERNACLES

TABITHA
Acts 9:40

TABLE OF NATIONS
Gen 10:2; 1 Chr 1:5-23; "Table of Nations"—p. 19

TABLETS
Ex 31:18; 2 Cor 3:3,6

TABRIMMON
1 Kin 15:19

TAHPANHES
Jer 2:16; Ezek 30:18

TALE OF TWO BROTHERS
"Ancient Texts Relating to the Old Testament"—p. xix

TALENT, THE
1 Kin 20:39; Matt 25:15; Luke 19:13

TALMAI
2 Sam 3:3; 13:37

TALMANUTHA
Mark 8:10

TALMUD
Zech 6:12; Mark 5:26; 15:23; Luke 16:22; Introduction to Ezra: Ezra and Nehemiah—p. 632

TAMAR
Gen 38:11; Ruth 1:4; 3:4; 2 Sam 3:2,3; 13:1,13,15,21; 14:27; 1 Kin 15:2; 2 Chr 11:20; Ezek 47:18

TAMARISK
Gen 21:33

TAMMUZ
Ezek 8:14

TANIS
Is 19:11; Ezek 30:14

TAPPUAH
2 Kin 15:16

TARGUM
Neh 8:8; Zech 6:12; 10:4; Introduction to Job: Date—p. 690

TARSHISH
Ps 72:10; Is 23:6; Ezek 27:12; Jon 1:3

TARSUS
Acts 6:9; 9:30; 22:3; Gal 1:21

TARTARUS
2 Pet 2:4

TARTESSUS
Is 23:6; Jon 1:3

TAWILAN
Obad 1:9

TAX COLLECTOR
Matt 5:46; Mark 2:16; Luke 3:12; 18:13; 19:2

TAXES
1 Chr 27:25-31; Neh 5:4; Matt 17:24; Mark 12:14; Rom 13:6

TEACHER OF RIGHTEOUSNESS
Joel 2:23

TEACHERS OF THE LAW
Matt 2:4; Mark 2:16; 12:40; Luke 5:17

TEACHING
1 Cor 12:28; Eph 4:11,14
false
2 Cor 2:17; 3:1; 4:2,5; 5:11; 6:14; 7:2,3; 10:4,7,12,13; 11:1,2,6,11,13,19,22; 12:12,16; 13:5; Phil 3:2; 1 Tim 1:3-11; 4:1; Titus 1:9; 2 Pet 2:15; Rev 2:14

TEBAH
1 Chr 18:8

TEKOA
2 Sam 14:1; Neh 3:5,27; Introduction to Amos: Author—p. 1274

TEL ABIB
Ezek 3:15; Acts 9:36

TEL MELAH
Ezra 2:59

TELL (mound)
Josh 11:13; Jer 30:18

TELL BEIT MIRSIM
Josh 10:38; 2 Chr 26:10

TELL ED-DUWEIR
2 Kin 14:19

TELL EL-MASKHUTAH
Ex 12:37; Neh 2:19

TEMA
Job 1:15; Is 21:14

TEMAN
Job 2:11; 4:1; Jer 49:7; Ezek 25:13; Amos 1:12; Obad 1:9; Hab 3:3

TEMPLE
curtain of
Ex 26:31; Num 3:25-26; Mark 15:38; Luke 23:45
early
1 Sam 1:9; Ps 24:2
Ezekiel's
Neh 8:16; "Ezekiel's Temple"—p. 1212
Herod's
Matt 2:1; 4:5; Luke 4:9; 21:5; John 2:20; Acts 3:2; "Herod's Temple"—p. 1372
Solomon's
1 Kin 6:1-38; 7:1-51; 8:2; Ezra 5:11; 6:15; Hag 2:3; Jon 2:4; "Solomon's Temple"—p. 458; "Temple Furnishings"—p. 460; Introduction to 2 Chronicles: The Building of the Temple in Chronicles—p. 589
Zerubbabel's
Ezra 4:24; 6:3,15; Hag 1:2; 2:3; Zech 4:1-14,6,10; "Zerubbabel's Temple"—p. 640
Scroll
Ezra 8:15; Neh 8:16,34

TEMPTATION
Gen 3:6; 22:1; Matt 4:1-11,1; 1 Cor 10:13; 1 Thess 3:5; Heb 4:15,16; James 1:13

TEN COMMANDMENTS
Ex 20:1-17,1; 31:18; Deut 5:6-21

TENDON
Gen 32:32

TENT OF MEETING
Ex 27:21; Lev 1:1; 16:16; Num 2:17; Josh 18:1; 1 Sam 7:1; 1 Kin 8:4; John 1:14

TENT-MAKING
Acts 18:3; 1 Cor 4:12

TERAH
Gen 11:31; Josh 24:14; Acts 7:4

TERAPHIM. *See* HOUSEHOLD GODS

TERTIUS
Acts 24:1; Rom 16:22

TERTULLUS
Acts 24:1,10

TESTING
Gen 22:1-2; Ex 15:25; Num 11:10; Deut 4:20; Ps 66:10; Matt 4:1; Rev 3:10

TETRARCH
Matt 14:1

THADDAEUS
Mark 3:18; Luke 6:16; Acts 1:13

THANKSGIVING
Rom 1:8,21; Eph 5:4; Phil 1:3-4; 4:6,18; Col 1:3; 3:16; 1 Thess 3:9; 5:18; Introduction to Psalms: Psalm Types—p. 736

THEBES. *See* KARNAK

THEOCRACY. *See also* ISRAEL: AS A THEOCRACY
Gen 9:5,6

THEOPHANY
Num 12:5; 14:10; Josh 5:13

THEOPHILUS
Acts 1:1; Introduction to Luke: Recipient and Purpose—p. 1456

THESSALONICA
Acts 16:12; Phil 4:15,16; Introduction to 1 Thessalonians: Thessalonica—p. 1746

THIRTY, THE
2 Sam 23:24; 1 Chr 27:9-15

THOMAS
John 11:16; 14:5

THREE, THE
2 Sam 23:8

THREE TAVERNS
Acts 28:15

THRESHING
Gen 50:10; Ruth 1:22; 2:17; Amos 1:3

THUCYDIDES
Neh 1:3

THUTMOSE III
Ex 1:11; 2:15; Judg 4:3; 5:19; Neh 5:18; Introduction to Exodus: Chronology—p. 75

THYATIRA
Acts 16:14; Rev 2:18

TIBERIAS (city)
Neh 11:1; Luke 23:7,8; John 6:1

TIBERIAS, SEA OF
Mark 1:16; Luke 5:1; John 6:1

TIBERIUS, EMPEROR
Matt 22:19; Luke 3:1; Rom 16:11

TIBNI
1 Kin 16:22,23

TIGLATH-PILESER III
1 Kin 15:20; 16:27; 2 Kin 15:19,30; 16:9; 1 Chr 5:6,26; 26:11; 28:20; Is 17:3; Hos 5:13; 7:9; "Assyrian Campaigns against Israel and Judah"—p. 522

TIKVAH
Ezra 10:15

TIMNA
1 Chr 1:36

TIMNAH
Judg 14:1,5

TIMNATH SERAH
Josh 19:50

TIMOTHY
Acts 14:6,20; 16:1,6; 17:10; 18:5; 19:22; 20:4; 21:24; 1 Cor 16:10; 2 Cor 1:1; Phil 1:1; 2:19-23; Col 1:1; 1 Thess 1:1; 2 Tim 1:5,7; 3:15; Titus 1:6-9; Heb 13:23; Introduction to 1 Timothy: Recipient—p. 1759

TIPHSAH
1 Kin 4:24; 2 Kin 15:16

TIRATHITES
1 Chr 2:55

TIRHAKAH
Is 37:9

TIRZAH
1 Kin 14:17; 2 Kin 15:14; Song 6:4

TISHRI
2 Chr 5:3; Ezra 3:1; Neh 8:1; "Hebrew Calendar and Selected Events"—p. 92

TITHE
Gen 14:20; 28:22; Lev 27:30; Num 18:26-32; Deut 14:22-29; Amos 4:4; Luke 18:12

TITIUS JUSTUS
Acts 18:7

TITUS
Acts 16:3; 2 Cor 2:12; 7:5-6; 8:6,16; 12:13; Gal 2:1; Introduction to Titus: Recipient—p. 1774

TOB
Judg 11:3; 1 Chr 19:6

TOBIAH
Neh 2:10; 3:4; 6:17-18; 13:5; Ezek 44:9

TOLA
Judg 10:1

TONGUE
Ps 5:9; 10:7; 120:4; Prov 13:3

TONGUES
of fire
Acts 2:3
languages and/or spiritual gift
Acts 2:4,6; 10:47; 1 Cor 12:10,28; 13:1-3,8; 14:1-5,2,5,6,9,10,14,15-17,19,20,23,27-28,29,32,34; Heb 2:4

TOPHETH
2 Kin 23:10; Is 30:33; Jer 7:31

TORAH
Neh 9:13; Ps 119:1; "The Time between the Testaments"—p. 1356

TOTAL DEPRAVITY. *See* DEPRAVITY, TOTAL

TOWER
of Babel
Gen 11:4
of Hananel
Neh 3:1; Zech 14:10
of the hundred
Neh 3:1
of the ovens
Neh 3:11

TRANSFIGURATION
Matt 16:28; 17:1-9,1,2; Mark 9:2; Luke 9:28; 1 Pet 5:1

TRANSFIGURATION, MOUNT OF. *See* MOUNT: OF TRANSFIGURATION

TRANSGRESSION
Rom 4:15

TRANSJORDAN
1 Chr 12:8-15; Neh 2:19; Matt 19:1

TRANSVESTISM
Deut 22:5

TREE OF LIFE
Gen 2:9

TRINITY, THE
Matt 3:16-17; Mark 1:10-11; John 14:17; 1 Cor 12:4-6; 15:28; 2 Cor 3:17; 4:4; 13:14; 1 Thess 1:1; 2 Thess 2:13; Heb 1:2-3; 1 Pet 1:2

TRIUMPHAL ENTRY
"Passion Week"—p. 1446

TROAS
Acts 16:8; 20:1,5; 2 Cor 2:12; 7:5-6

TROPHIMUS
Acts 20:4; 21:29

TRUMPET
Num 10:10; 29:1-6; Judg 7:16,22; Joel 2:1,15

TRUMPETS, FEAST OF
Num 29:1-6; Neh 8:2

TRUST
Ps 16:1-11; 31:1-24; Prov 3:5; Dan 6:23; John 14:1,11; Heb 2:13; 10:22; 11:7; Introduction to Psalms: Psalm Types—p. 736

TRUTH
1 Kin 17:24; Ps 51:6; Mark 3:28; John 1:14; Acts 5:9

TUBAL
Gen 10:2; Is 66:19; Ezek 32:26; 38:2

V

X

Y

Z

ZANOAH
Neh 11:30

ZAREPHATH
1 Kin 17:9; 2 Kin 4:37

ZEALOTS
Matt 10:4; Acts 5:37; "Jewish Sects"—p. 1401

ZEBEDEE
Matt 20:20

ZEBOIIM
Hos 11:8

ZEBULUN
Josh 19:10; Judg 5:13-18; 12:8,11; Matt 4:15-16

ZECHARIAH (prophet)
Hos 1:3; 7:7; Introduction to Zechariah: Author and Unity—p. 1331

ZECHARIAH (son of Hosah)
Ezra 5:1; 6:13-14; 8:3

ZECHARIAH (son of Jehoiada)
2 Kin 12:17,20; 14:29; 1 Chr 25:1; 2 Chr 24:25; 26:5; Heb 11:37

ZEDEKIAH (king of Judah)
Gen 49:10; 2 Kin 24:17,19,20; 25:7; 1 Chr 3:15-16; 2 Chr 36:4,9-10,11-14; Ezra 7:1; Ezek 7:27; 17:5,7; 19:5; 32:3; Mic 5:1

ZEDEKIAH (son of Kenaanah)
1 Kin 22:11,24

ZELOPHEHAD
Num 36:1-13; 1 Chr 7:14-19

ZENAS
Titus 3:13

ZEPHANIAH
2 Kin 22:2,14; Introduction to Zephaniah: Author—p. 1320

ZERAH (Ethiopian king)
2 Chr 14:1,9; 15:10

ZERAH (twin born to Judah)
1 Chr 9:4-6; Ps 88:1

ZERUBBABEL
1 Chr 3:18,19,20,21; 2 Chr 19:11; Ezra 1:8; 3:2; 5:2; 6:13-14; Hag 2:3,8; Zech 4:1-14,6,10; Matt 1:12; "Zerubbabel's Temple"—p. 640

ZERUIAH
1 Sam 26:6; 2 Sam 2:13

ZEUS
Dan 11:31; Acts 14:12

ZEUS OLYMPIUS
Dan 11:31

ZIBA
2 Sam 9:2,3; 16:2; 19:27

ZIGGURAT
Gen 11:4; 28:12,13,17; Introduction to Psalms: Literary Features—p. 737

ZIKLAG
1 Sam 27:6,7; Neh 11:28

ZILPAH
Ex 1:2-4; Ezek 48:2

ZIMRI
1 Kin 16:12; 2 Kin 9:31; Jer 25:25

ZIN, DESERT OF. *See* DESERT: OF ZIN

ZION. *See also* JERUSALEM
2 Sam 5:7; Ps 9:11; 87:1-7; Joel 2:1; Amos 1:2

ZION, MOUNT. *See* MOUNT: ZION

ZIPPORAH
Ex 4:25; 18:2; Ezra 8:2

ZOAN
Is 19:11; 30:4; Ezek 30:14

ZOAR
Is 15:5

ZOBAH
2 Sam 8:3; 1 Chr 18:5; 19:6; 2 Chr 8:3-4

ZOPHAR
Job 11:2-3,4,5,6,8-9,11-12; 17:10-16; 20:2-3,4-11,29

ZORAH
Judg 13:2

ZURIEL
Num 3:35

Index to Maps

All entries are place-names found on the maps within the study Bible. References are to the page on which the map is located. For additional information on place-names, see Index to Notes.

The New American Standard Concordance

A collection of the principal common words with their most widely used examples in text and lesser usages in reference. Related words, or synonyms follow the key word. The key word is abbreviated in the text to its first letter, e.g., "abide" is "a." Variants add suffixes or prefixes, e.g., "abiding" appears as "a-ing."

A

AARON
brother of Moses Ex 4:14
spokesman for Moses Ex 4:28; 7:1-2
as priest Ex 28:1; 29:44
rod of Num 17:8; Heb 9:4
critical of Moses Num 12:1
death Deut 10:6

ABADDON
1 *region of dead* Job 26:6; Prov 15:11
2 *angel of bottomless pit* Rev 9:11

ABANDON *leave*
LORD has **a-ed** us Judg 6:13
not **a** His people 1 Sam 12:22
a the remnant 2 Kin 21:14
not **a** my soul to Ps 16:10
not **a** His people Ps 94:14
a-ed My inheritance Jer 12:7
a my soul to Hades Acts 2:27

ABASE *humble*
man will be **a-d** Is 2:11
lofty will be **a-d** Is 10:33
a the haughtiness Is 13:11
a-d before all Mal 2:9

ABATED *decreased*
water was **a** Gen 8:8
his vigor **a** Deut 34:7

ABBA *father*
A! Father Mark 14:36
we cry out, **A!** Rom 8:15

ABED-NEGO
Hebrew name Azariah Dan 1:6,7
friend of Daniel
faithful to God Dan 3:16,17
cast into furnace Dan 3:20

ABEL
son of Adam Gen 4:2
shepherd Gen 4:2
favored by God Gen 4:4
slain by Cain Gen 4:8
called righteous Matt 23:35

ABHOR *despise, detest*
associates **a** me Job 19:19
greatly **a-red** Israel Ps 78:59
nations will **a** him Prov 24:24
To the One **a-red** Is 49:7
A what is evil Rom 12:9

ABIB
early name of first month of Hebrew calendar Ex 34:18
month of Passover and Unleavened Bread Deut 16:1

ABIDE *remain, stay*
LORD **a-s** forever Ps 9:7
a in Your tent Ps 15:1
a in the shadow Ps 91:1
wrath of God **a-s** John 3:36
If you **a** in Me John 15:7
a in My love John 15:9
now faith...**a** 1 Cor 13:13
love of God **a** 1 John 3:17
God **a-s** in us 1 John 4:12

ABIGAIL
1 *wife of Nabal* 1 Sam 25:3
kind to David 1 Sam 25:18ff
wife of David 1 Sam 25:42
2 *daughter of Nahash* 2 Sam 17:25

ABIHU
son of Aaron Ex 6:23
priest Ex 28:1
disobeyed God Lev 10:1
judged by God Lev 10:2

ABIJAH
1 *son of Samuel* 1 Sam 8:2
2 *son of Jeroboam* 1 Kin 14:1
3 *son of Becher* 1 Chr 7:8
4 *line of Eleazar* 1 Chr 24:10
5 *king of Judah* 2 Chr 12:16
6 *Hezekiah's mother* 2 Chr 29:1
7 *priest* Neh 10:7; 12:4

ABILITY *power, strength*
According to their **a** Ezra 2:69
a for serving Dan 1:4
a to conceive Heb 11:11

ABIMELECH
1 *king of Gerar* Gen 20:1-18
2 *king of Gerar* Gen 26:1ff
3 *king of Shechem* Judg 9:1ff
4 *priest* 1 Chr 18:16
5 *Psalm title* Ps 34

ABIRAM
opposed Moses Num 16:1ff
judged by God Num 16:25ff

ABISHAI
brother of Joab 1 Sam 26:6
warrior of David 1 Chr 18:12
aided Abner's assassination 2 Sam 3:30

ABLE *qualified*
a to judge 1 Kin 3:9
from these stones God...**a** Matt 3:9
I am **a** to do Matt 9:28
Him who is **a** Matt 10:28
a to separate us Rom 8:39
what you are **a** 1 Cor 10:13
a to comprehend Eph 3:18
be **a** to teach 2 Tim 2:2
a to save Him Heb 5:7
One who is **a** James 4:12
a to open Rev 5:3

ABNER
Saul's commander 1 Sam 17:55
loyal to David 2 Sam 3:12ff
killed by Joab 2 Sam 3:27
mourned by David 2 Sam 3:32

ABODE *habitation*
a of righteousness Jer 31:23
Our **a** with him John 14:23
their proper **a** Jude 6

ABOLISH
not come to **a** Matt 5:17
a-ing in His flesh Eph 2:15
who **a-ed** death 2 Tim 1:10

ABOMINABLE *detestable*
committed **a** deeds Ps 14:1
your beauty **a** Ezek 16:25
a idolatries 1 Pet 4:3
unbelieving and **a** Rev 21:8

ABOMINATION *hated thing*
a to the Egyptians Ex 8:26
a into your house Deut 7:26
seen their **a-s** Deut 29:17
a to the LORD Prov 3:32
all their **a-s** Ezek 33:29
a of desolation Matt 24:15
a-s of the earth Rev 17:5

ABOUND *excel, plentiful*
faithful man will **a** Prov 28:20
May your peace **a** Dan 4:1
a in hope Rom 15:13
a-ing in the work 1 Cor 15:58
affection **a-s** 2 Cor 7:15
all grace **a** 2 Cor 9:8

ABOVE *over*
exalted **a** the heavens Ps 57:5
disciple is not **a** Matt 10:24
I am from **a** John 8:23
a every name Phil 2:9
exalts himself **a** 2 Thess 2:4
gift is from **a** James 1:17

ABRAHAM
covenant Gen 17:1-8
promise of Isaac Gen 17:19
asked the Lord Gen 18:22ff
offers Isaac Gen 22:9,10
death Gen 25:8
righteousness of Rom 4:3-9

ABRAHAM'S BOSOM
rabbinic terminology for Paradise Luke 16:22

ABRAM
called of God Gen 12:1-3
rescued Lot Gen 14:14-16
covenant with God Gen 15:18
name changed Gen 17:5

ABSALOM
son of David 2 Sam 13:1
his revolt 2 Sam 15:1,2
popular 2 Sam 15:6
slain by Joab 2 Sam 18:15

ABSENT *being away*
we are **a** one from Gen 31:49

a in body 1 Cor 5:3
a from the Lord 2 Cor 5:6
a from the body 2 Cor 5:8

ABSTAIN ***refrain from***
a from wine Num 6:3
a-ing from foods 1 Tim 4:3
a from wickedness 2 Tim 2:19
a from fleshly lusts 1 Pet 2:11

ABUNDANCE ***plenty, surplus***
seven years of **a** Gen 41:34
a of all things Deut 28:47
a of Your house Ps 36:8
a of peace Ps 72:7
a of counselors Prov 24:6
he who loves **a** Eccl 5:10
delight yourself in **a** Is 55:2
one has an **a** Luke 12:15
the **a** of grace Rom 5:17

ABUNDANT ***enough, plenteous***
come...find **a** water 2 Chr 32:4
a righteousness Job 37:23
a in lovingkindness Ps 86:5
comfort is **a** 2 Cor 1:5

ABUNDANTLY
they may breed **a** Gen 8:17
Populate the earth **a** Gen 9:7
will prosper you **a** Deut 30:9
drip upon man **a** Job 36:28

ABUSE (n) ***insulting speech***
hurling **a** at Him Matt 27:39
was hurling **a** Luke 23:39

ABUSE (v) ***hurt, molest***
a-d her all night Judg 19:25
uncircumcised...**a** me 1 Chr 10:4

ABUSIVE ***filthy, vulgar***
a speech from your Col 3:8
strife, **a** language 1 Tim 6:4

ABYSS ***deep, depth***
go away into the **a** Luke 8:31
descend into the **a** Rom 10:7
angel of the **a** Rev 9:11
key of the **a** Rev 20:1

ACCEPT ***receive***
a the work of Deut 33:11
a good from God Job 2:10
the LORD **a-ed** Job Job 42:9
a-ed no chastening Jer 2:30
hear the word and **a** Mark 4:20
God has **a-ed** him Rom 14:3
a one another Rom 15:7

ACCEPTABLE ***pleasing***
my heart Be **a** Ps 19:14
sacrifice, **a** to God Rom 12:1
a to the saints Rom 15:31
now is the **a** time 2 Cor 6:2
to God an **a** service Heb 12:28
sacrifices **a** to God 1 Pet 2:5

ACCESS ***approach, entry***
grant you free **a** Zech 3:7
our **a** in one Spirit Eph 2:18

ACCOMPANY ***attach to, follow***
who **a** my lord 1 Sam 25:27
a-ied the king 2 Sam 19:40
a-ied by trumpets 2 Chr 5:13
allowed no one to **a** Mark 5:37
that **a** salvation Heb 6:9

ACCOMPLISH ***perform, realize***
a-ed deliverance 1 Sam 11:13
shall **a** my desire 1 Kin 5:9
God...**a-es** *all things* Ps 57:2
has **a-ed** His wrath Lam 4:11
a-ed redemption Luke 1:68
a His work John 4:34
I am **a-ing** a work Acts 13:41

when sin is **a-ed** James 1:15
man can **a** much James 5:16

ACCORD ***agreement, union***
one **a** to fight Josh 9:2
voices...with one **a** Acts 4:24
one **a** in Solomon's Acts 5:12
crowds with one **a** Acts 8:6
one **a** they came Acts 12:20

ACCORDING
a to your word Gen 30:34
Moses did; **a** to all Ex 40:16
a to our sins Ps 103:10
a to his deeds Matt 16:27
a to the revelation Rom 16:25
heirs **a** to promise Gal 3:29
a to His riches Phil 4:19

ACCOUNT (n) ***reckoning***
the **a** of the heavens Gen 2:4
On whose **a** *has* this Jon 1:8
settled **a-s** with Matt 25:19
who will give an **a** Heb 13:17

ACCOUNT (v) ***reckon***
do not **a** *this* sin Num 12:11
I am **a-ed** wicked Job 9:29
You have taken **a** of Ps 56:8
are **a-ed** as nothing Dan 4:35

ACCURATELY ***correctly***
teaching **a**...things Acts 18:25
a handling...word 2 Tim 2:15

ACCURSED ***damned***
camp of Israel **a** Josh 6:18
be *thought* **a** Is 65:20
Depart...**a** ones Matt 25:41
he is to be **a** Gal 1:8
in greed, **a** children 2 Pet 2:14

ACCUSATION ***charge of wrong***
wrote an **a** against Ezra 4:6
find a ground of **a** Dan 6:4
What **a** do you John 18:29
a against my nation Acts 28:19
Do not receive an **a** 1 Tim 5:19

ACCUSE ***testify against***
a-d his brother Deut 19:18
a-s you in judgment Is 54:17
He was being **a-d** Matt 27:12
a-ing...vehemently Luke 23:10
a you before the John 5:45
alternately **a-ing** Rom 2:15
not **a-d** of dissipation Titus 1:6
unjustly **a-ing** us 3 John 10

ACCUSER ***complainant***
they act as my **a-s** Ps 109:4
instructing his **a-s** Acts 23:30
when the **a-s** stood Acts 25:18
a of our brethren Rev 12:10

ACHAIA
province of Greece Acts 18:12; Rom 15:26; 1 Cor 16:15

ACHAN
stole from Jericho Josh 7:1
executed by people Josh 7:25

ACKNOWLEDGE ***confess***
I **a-d** my sin Ps 32:5
all your ways **a** Him Prov 3:6
Pharisees **a** them all Acts 23:8
see fit to **a** God Rom 1:28

ACQUAINTED ***become familiar***
a with all my ways Ps 139:3
a with grief Is 53:3

ACQUAINTANCE ***friend***
a-s are...estranged Job 19:13
dread to my **a-s** Ps 31:11
removed my **a-s** far Ps 88:8

relatives and **a-s** Luke 2:44
And all His **a-s** Luke 23:49

ACQUIRE ***get, purchase***
a property in it Gen 34:10
have **a-d** Ruth Ruth 4:10
a wise counsel Prov 1:5
You have **a-d** riches Ezek 28:4
Do not **a** gold Matt 10:9

ACQUIT ***declare innocent***
not **a** me of my guilt Job 10:14
A me of hidden *faults* Ps 19:12
You will not be **a-ted** Jer 49:12

ACT (n) ***deed, work***
a detestable **a** Lev 20:13
mighty **a-s** as Yours Deut 3:24
every abominable **a** Deut 12:31
the **a-s** of Solomon 1 Kin 11:41
over the rebellious **a** Mic 7:18

ACT (v) ***behave***
they refuse to **a** Prov 21:7
I **a-ed** ignorantly 1 Tim 1:13
So speak and so **a** James 2:12
are **a-ing** faithfully 3 John 5

ACTION ***behavior, work***
a-s are weighed 1 Sam 2:3
a-s of a...harlot Ezek 16:30
plan or **a** is Acts 5:38
prepare your minds for **a** 1 Pet 1:13

ADAM
1 *first man* Gen 2:20
fall of man Gen 3:6,7
type of Christ Rom 5:14
compared to Jesus 1 Cor 15:22
2 *site in Jordan Valley* Josh 3:16

ADAR
twelfth month of Hebrew calendar Ezra 6:15
Purim observed Esth 3:7; 9:19ff

ADD
a to your yoke 1 Kin 12:11
a-ing to the wrath Neh 13:18
not **a** to His words Prov 30:6
if anyone **a-s** to them Rev 22:18

ADJURE ***charge solemnly***
many times...I **a** 1 Kin 22:16
I **a** you, O daughters Song 3:5
I **a** you by Jesus Acts 19:13

ADMINISTRATION
a of the province Dan 3:12
healings, helps, **a-s** 1 Cor 12:28
in our **a** of this 2 Cor 8:20
a of the mystery Eph 3:9

ADMONISH ***warn***
prophets...had **a-ed** Neh 9:26
How shall I **a** you Lam 2:13
not cease to **a** each Acts 20:31
able also to **a** one Rom 15:14
a-ing one another Col 3:16
a the unruly 1 Thess 5:14
a him as a brother 2 Thess 3:15

ADONIJAH
1 *son of David* 2 Sam 3:4
aspired to throne 1 Kin 1:5ff
pardoned 1 Kin 1:52ff
executed 1 Kin 2:25
2 *Levite* 2 Chr 17:8
3 *of the restoration* Neh 10:16

ADOPTION ***acceptance***
spirit of **a** as sons Rom 8:15
to whom belongs...**a** Rom 9:4
receive the **a** as sons Gal 4:5
predestined us to **a** Eph 1:5

ADORN ***array, clothe***
A yourself with Job 40:10

as a bride **a-s** herself Is 61:10
a-ed with beautiful Luke 21:5
women to **a** 1 Tim 2:9
a the doctrine of God Titus 2:10
a-ed with gold Rev 17:4
as a bride **a-ed** Rev 21:2

ADULTERER
a and the adulteress Lev 20:10
eye of the **a** waits Job 24:15
associate with **a-s** Ps 50:18
a-s, nor effeminate 1 Cor 6:9
a-s God will judge Heb 13:4

ADULTERESS
a shall surely be Lev 20:10
a who flatters with Prov 2:16
mouth of an **a** Prov 22:14
You **a** wife, who Ezek 16:32
they are **a-es** Ezek 23:45
shall be called an **a** Rom 7:3

ADULTERY
shall not commit **a** Ex 20:14
man who commits **a** Lev 20:10
a-ies of faithless Jer 3:8
worn out by **a-ies** Ezek 23:43
committed **a** with her Matt 5:28
woman commits **a** Matt 5:32
Do not commit **a** Luke 18:20
eyes full of **a** 2 Pet 2:14

ADVANCE *ahead, beyond*
old, **a-d** in age Gen 24:1
a-d *in years* 1 Sam 17:12
have told you in **a** Matt 24:25
both **a-d** in years Luke 1:7
a-ing in Judaism Gal 1:14

ADVANTAGE *benefit, profit*
lead surely to **a** Prov 21:5
What **a** does man Eccl 1:3
Wisdom has the **a** Eccl 10:10
a that I go away John 16:7
what **a** has the Jew Rom 3:1
no **a** would be taken of us 2 Cor 2:11
sake of *gaining an* **a** Jude 16

ADVERSARY *foe, opponent*
an **a** to your **a-ies** Ex 23:22
an **a** to Solomon 1 Kin 11:14
And my **a-ies** will rejoice Ps 13:4
a-ies and my enemies Ps 27:2
redeemed...from the **a** Ps 78:42
crush his **a-ies** Ps 89:23
there are many **a-ies** 1 Cor 16:9
consume the **a-ies** Heb 10:27
Your **a,** the devil 1 Pet 5:8

ADVERSITY *distress, misfortune*
death and **a** Deut 30:15
not accept **a** Job 2:10
relief from...**a** Ps 94:13
falls into **a** Prov 13:17
A pursues sinners Prov 13:21

ADVICE *counsel*
forsook the **a** 1 Kin 12:13
a of the young 2 Chr 10:14
a of the cunning Job 5:13
they took his **a** Acts 5:40
have followed my **a** Acts 27:21

ADVISER *counselor*
with his **a** Ahuzzath Gen 26:26
Pharaoh's wisest **a-s** Is 19:11

ADVOCATE *defender, witness*
my **a** is on high Job 16:19
A with the Father 1 John 2:1

AFFECTION *devotion, love*
set His **a** to love Deut 10:15
in your own **a-s** 2 Cor 6:12
a of Christ Jesus Phil 1:8
fond an **a** for you 1 Thess 2:8

AFFLICT (v) *oppress, trouble*
a them with hard labor Ex 1:11
not **a** any widow Ex 22:22
Egyptians...**a-ed** us Deut 26:6
bind him to **a** him Judg 16:5
the wicked **a** them 2 Sam 7:10
They **a-ed** his feet Ps 105:18
He was **a-ed** Is 63:9
will **a** you no longer Nah 1:12
were sick or **a-ed** Acts 5:16
are **a-ed** in every 2 Cor 4:8
those who **a** you 2 Thess 1:6
a-ed, ill-treated Heb 11:37

AFFLICTED (n) *troubled*
save an **a** people 2 Sam 22:28
to catch the **a** Ps 10:9
justice to the **a** Ps 82:3
LORD supports the **a** Ps 147:6
days of the **a** Prov 15:15
O **a** one Is 54:11
good news to the **a** Is 61:1

AFFLICTION *oppression*
my **a** and the toil Gen 31:42
the land of my **a** Gen 41:52
the bread of **a** Deut 16:3
LORD saw the **a** 2 Kin 14:26
You saw the **a** Neh 9:9
afflicted in their **a** Job 36:15
Look upon my **a** Ps 25:18
a severe **a** Eccl 6:2
a or persecution Mark 4:17
healed of her **a** Mark 5:29
a-s await me Acts 20:23
out of much **a** 2 Cor 2:4
great ordeal of **a** 2 Cor 8:2
to suffer **a** 1 Thess 3:4

AFRAID *dreading, fearful*
a because...naked Gen 3:10
a to look at God Ex 3:6
a and fainthearted Deut 20:8
Whoever is **a** Judg 7:3
a of the terror Ps 91:5
not **a** of the snow Prov 31:21
a to swear Eccl 9:2
a of man who dies Is 51:12
a to take Mary Matt 1:20
were **a** of Him Mark 11:18
Do not be **a,** Mary Luke 1:30
a of those who kill Luke 12:4
a of the people Luke 22:2
a that, as the serpent 2 Cor 11:3
Do not be **a** Rev 1:17

AGABUS
prophet Acts 11:28; 21:10

AGE *period, year*
David reached old **a** 1 Chr 23:1
a should speak Job 32:7
either in this **a** Matt 12:32
the end of the **a** Matt 13:40
sons of this **a** are Luke 16:8
in the **a-s** to come Eph 2:7
hidden...*past* **a-s** Col 1:26
in the present **a** Titus 2:12

AGED *old*
Wisdom is...**a** men Job 12:12
a are among us Job 15:10
refined, **a** wine Is 25:6
Paul, the **a** Philem 9

AGONY *anguish*
a has seized me 2 Sam 1:9
A like...childbirth Jer 50:43
in **a** in this flame Luke 16:24
in **a** He was praying Luke 22:44
the **a** of death Acts 2:24

AGREE *consent*
if two of you **a** Matt 18:19
did you not **a** Matt 20:13
Jews had already **a-d** John 9:22

have **a-d** together Acts 5:9
words...Prophets **a** Acts 15:15
a with sound words 1 Tim 6:3

AGREEMENT *accord*
an **a** in writing Neh 9:38
Saul was in hearty **a** Acts 8:1
a has the temple 2 Cor 6:16
three are in **a** 1 John 5:8

AGRIPPA
1 **Herod Agrippa I *see* HEROD**
2 **Herod Agrippa II *see* HEROD**

AHAB
1 *king of Israel* 1 Kin 16:28
son of Omri 1 Kin 16:29
married Jezebel 1 Kin 16:31
idolater 1 Kin 16:33
2 *false prophet* Jer 29:21,22

AHASUERUS
1 *Persian king, Xerxes I* Ezra 4:6; Book of Esther
2 *father of Darius the Mede* Dan 9:1

AHAZ
1 *son of Jotham* 2 Kin 15:38
king of Judah 2 Kin 16:2
2 *line of Jonathan* 1 Chr 8:35

AHIJAH / AHIAH
1 *prophet of Shiloh* 1 Kin 14:2
2 *of Issachar* 1 Kin 15:27
3 *son of Jerahmeel* 1 Chr 2:25
4 *the Pelonite* 1 Chr 11:36
5 *under Nehemiah* Neh 10:26

AHIMELECH
1 *high priest* 1 Sam 22:16
gave bread and sword to David 1 Sam 21:1-9
2 *Hittite* 1 Sam 26:6,7

AHITHOPHEL
counselor of David 2 Sam 15:12; 1 Chr 27:33

AI
place near Bethel Gen 12:8
defeat of Israelites Josh 7:5
captured Josh 8:23, 29

AIJALON
1 *city of refuge* Josh 10:12
Levitical city Josh 21:24
2 *valley* Josh 19:42
3 *Zebulunite town* Judg 12:12

AIR *breeze, sky*
no **a** can come Job 41:16
They pant for **a** Jer 14:6
birds of the **a** Matt 6:26
not beating the **a** 1 Cor 9:26
speaking into the **a** 1 Cor 14:9
power of the **a** Eph 2:2
the Lord in the **a** 1 Thess 4:17

ALABASTER *whitish stone*
stones and **a** 1 Chr 29:2
pillars of **a** Song 5:15
brought an **a** vial Luke 7:37

ALARM (n) *danger, warning*
when you blow an **a** Num 10:5
The **a** of war Jer 4:19
shout of **a** at noon Jer 20:16
a on My...mountain Joel 2:1

ALARM (v) *frighten, warn*
he is not **a-ed** Job 40:23
interpretation **a** you Dan 4:19
thoughts **a-ed** him Dan 5:6
being much **a-ed** Acts 10:4
in no way **a-ed** by Phil 1:28

ALERT (n) *watch*
be on the **a** Matt 24:42
be **a** and sober 1 Thess 5:6

ALERT (v) ***be watchful***
keeping **a** in it Col 4:2
let us be **a** 1 Thess 5:6

ALEXANDER
1 *son of Simon of Cyrene* Mark 15:21
2 *of priestly family* Acts 4:6
3 *Ephesian Jew* Acts 19:33
4 *apostate teacher* 1 Tim 1:20
5 *enemy of Paul* 2 Tim 4:14

ALEXANDRIAN
1 *of Alexandria* Acts 6:9
2 *ship* Acts 27:6; 28:11
3 *Apollos* Acts 18:24

ALIEN ***foreigner, stranger***
love for the **a** Deut 10:19
give it to the **a** Deut 14:21
Our houses to **a-s** Lam 5:2
a-s in a foreign land Acts 7:6
no longer...**a-s** Eph 2:19
he lived as an **a** Heb 11:9
I urge you as **a-s** 1 Pet 2:11

ALIENATE ***estrange***
Or I shall be **a-d** Jer 6:8
a this choice *portion* Ezek 48:14
were formerly **a-d** Col 1:21

ALIVE
Is your father still **a** Gen 43:7
down **a** to Sheol Num 16:33
go down **a** to Sheol Ps 55:15
may keep **a** a heifer Is 7:21
when He was...**a** Matt 27:63
heard...He was **a** Mark 16:11
presented Himself **a** Acts 1:3
yet the spirit is **a** Rom 8:10
all will be made **a** 1 Cor 15:22
made us **a** together Eph 2:5
a in the spirit 1 Pet 3:18
I am **a** forevermore Rev 1:18

ALLEGIANCE ***loyalty***
pledged **a** to King 1 Chr 29:24
he pledged his **a** Ezek 17:18

ALLIANCE ***agreement***
formed a marriage **a** 1 Kin 3:1
after an **a** is made Dan 11:23

ALLIED ***joined***
a...by marriage 2 Chr 18:1
throne of...**a** Ps 94:20

ALLOT ***apportion, divide***
only **a** it to Israel Josh 13:6
a Him a portion Is 53:12
a-ted to each...faith Rom 12:3

ALLOTMENT ***portion***
an **a** from Pharaoh Gen 47:22
as a perpetual **a** Num 18:19
Jacob is the **a** Deut 32:9
set apart the...**a** Ezek 48:20

ALLOW ***permit***
not **a** the destroyer Ex 12:23
whether his body **a-s** Lev 15:3
a Your Holy One Ps 16:10
Nor **a** Your Holy One Acts 2:27
not be **a-ed** to live Acts 22:22
a you to be tempted 1 Cor 10:13
not **a** a woman 1 Tim 2:12

ALMIGHTY ***all-powerful***
I am God **A** Gen 17:1
vision of the **A** Num 24:4
A has afflicted me Ruth 1:21
limits of the **A** Job 11:7
A was yet with me Job 29:5
destruction from...**A** Joel 1:15
Lord God, the **A** Rev 4:8
the **A**, reigns Rev 19:6

ALMOND
a and plane trees Gen 30:37
shaped like **a** *blossoms* Ex 37:19
and it bore ripe **a-s** Num 17:8

ALMS ***charity***
a to the *Jewish* Acts 10:2
bring **a** to my nation Acts 24:17

ALONE
So He let him **a** Ex 4:26
Leave me **a**, for my Job 7:16
not live on bread **a** Matt 4:4
He was praying **a** Luke 9:18
I am not **a** *in it* John 8:16
receiving but you **a** Phil 4:15
and not by faith **a** James 2:24

ALOUD ***joyful, piercing***
crying **a** as she 2 Sam 13:19
read **a** from the book Neh 13:1
I will cry **a** Ps 77:1
Sing **a** with gladness Jer 31:7
The king called **a** Dan 5:7
began to weep **a** Acts 20:37

ALPHA
first letter of Gr. alphabet Rev 1:8
title of Jesus Christ Rev 21:6
expresses eternalness of God Rev 22:13

ALTAR ***place of sacrifice***
offerings on the **a** Gen 8:20
Moses built an **a** Ex 17:15
fire on the **a** Lev 6:9
Gideon built an **a** Judg 6:24
erect an **a** to 2 Sam 24:18
go to the **a** of God Ps 43:4
a-s may become waste Ezek 6:6
offering at the **a** Matt 5:23
a that sanctifies Matt 23:19
golden **a** of incense Heb 9:4
we have an **a** Heb 13:10
horns of the golden **a** Rev 9:13

ALWAYS ***ever, forever***
fear the LORD...**a** Deut 14:23
He will not **a** strive Ps 103:9
fear of the LORD **a** Prov 23:17
a loses his temper Prov 29:11
will I **a** be angry Is 57:16
I am with you **a** Matt 28:20
you **a** have...poor Mark 14:7
Rejoice in the Lord **a** Phil 4:4
a be with...Lord 1 Thess 4:17
I will **a** be ready 2 Pet 1:12

AMALEKITES
descendants of Esau Gen 36:12
tribe in Negev and Sinai Ex 17:8,9; Num 14:25; 1 Sam 15:7; 1 Chr 4:43

AMASA
1 *son of Abigail* 1 Chr 2:17
Absalom's commander 2 Sam 17:25
pardoned 2 Sam 19:13
2 *an Ephraimite* 2 Chr 28:12

AMAZED ***astonished, astounded***
are **a** at His rebuke Job 26:11
a at His teaching Mark 1:22
heard Him were **a** Luke 2:47
Do not be **a** that I said John 3:7
were **a** and astonished Acts 2:7
whole earth was **a** Rev 13:3

AMAZEMENT ***astonishment***
a came upon them Luke 4:36
with wonder and **a** Acts 3:10

AMAZIAH
1 *king of Judah* 2 Kin 12:21
son of Joash 2 Kin 14:1
2 *a Simeonite* 1 Chr 4:34
3 *son of Hilkiah* 1 Chr 6:45
4 *a priest of Bethel* Amos 7:10

AMBASSADOR ***envoy***
a-s of peace weep Is 33:7
a-s for Christ 2 Cor 5:20
an **a** in chains Eph 6:20

AMBITION ***design, intention***
out of selfish **a** Phil 1:17
a to lead a quiet 1 Thess 4:11
jealousy...selfish **a** James 3:14

AMBUSH (n) ***cover, hiding place***
a for the city Josh 8:2
rise from *your* **a** Josh 8:7
Israel set men in **a** Judg 20:29
a...behind them 2 Chr 13:13
Place men in **a** Jer 51:12

AMBUSH (v) ***lie in wait***
going to **a** the city Josh 8:4
a the innocent Prov 1:11
a their own lives Prov 1:18

AMEN ***so be it***
people shall say, **A** Deut 27:16
the LORD forever! **A** Ps 89:52
glory forever...**A** Phil 4:20
the **A**, the faithful Rev 3:14
A. Come, Lord Jesus Rev 22:20

AMMONITES
tribes E of Jordan Gen 19:38
defeated Israel Judg 3:13
hired Arameans 2 Sam 10:6
fought against Judah 2 Kin 24:2

AMNON
1 *eldest son of David* 2 Sam 3:2
raped his sister 2 Sam 13:2ff
ordered killed 2 Sam 13:28
2 *line of Judah* 1 Chr 4:20

AMON
1 *Ahab's governor* 1 Kin 22:26
2 *king of Judah* 2 Kin 21:18-26
3 *of the Nethinims* Neh 7:59
4 *Egyptian deity* Jer 46:25

AMORITES
tribe on both sides of Jordan Gen 15:16; Ex 34:11; Deut 1:27; Judg 11:23; Amos 2:9

AMOS
prophet to Israel Book of Amos

AMOUNT ***measure***
daily **a** of bricks Ex 5:19
a of your valuation Lev 27:23
large **a** of bronze 1 Chr 18:8

AMRAM
1 *father of Moses* Ex 6:18-20; 1 Chr 23:13
2 *son of Bani* Ezra 10:34

ANAK / ANAKIM
pre-Israelite tribe of Palestine Num 13:22-33
giants Deut 2:10; Josh 14:15

ANANIAS
1 *deceived Jerusalem church* Acts 5:1-5
2 *Damascus Christian* Acts 9:10,17
3 *high priest* Acts 23:2

ANCESTORS ***forefathers***
blessings of my **a** Gen 49:26
the **a** have set Deut 19:14
iniquities of their **a** Jer 11:10

ANCHOR
they weighed **a** Acts 27:13
they cast four **a-s** Acts 27:29
an **a** of the soul Heb 6:19

ANCIENT ***aged, old***
of the **a** mountains Deut 33:15
the records are **a** 1 Chr 4:22
keep to the **a** path Job 22:15
O **a** doors Ps 24:9
A of Days Dan 7:9

the **a-s** were told Matt 5:21
from **a** generations Acts 15:21
not spare the **a** world 2 Pet 2:5

ANDREW
fisherman Matt 4:18
brother of Peter Matt 4:18
receives Jesus John 1:40-42
apostle Luke 6:14

ANGEL ***divine messenger***
send His **a** before Gen 24:7
a-s...were ascending Gen 28:12
an **a** to Jerusalem 1 Chr 21:15
bread of **a-s** Ps 78:25
Praise Him, all His **a-s** Ps 148:2
a of His presence Is 63:9
a who was speaking Zech 4:4
command His **a-s** Matt 4:6
a Gabriel was sent Luke 1:26
they are like **a-s** Luke 20:36
two **a-s** in white John 20:12
like the face of an **a** Acts 6:15
as an **a** of light 2 Cor 11:14
worship of the **a-s** Col 2:18
entertained **a-s** Heb 13:2
God did not spare **a-s** 2 Pet 2:4
a of the church Rev 2:1

ANGEL OF THE LORD
a called to Abraham Gen 22:15
a took his stand Num 22:22
I have seen the **a** Judg 6:22
a said to Elijah 2 Kin 1:3
a destroying 1 Chr 21:12
a encamps around those Ps 34:7
a admonished Joshua Zech 3:6
a commanded him Matt 1:24
a appeared to Joseph Matt 2:13
a...opened the gates Acts 5:19

ANGER ***indignation, wrath***
My **a** will be kindled Ex 22:24
Moses' **a** burned Ex 32:19
from His burning **a** Deut 13:17
a with their idols 1 Kin 16:13
not turn back His **a** Job 9:13
not rebuke me in Your **a** Ps 6:1
a is but for a moment Ps 30:5
He who is slow to **a** Prov 14:29
a man *given* to **a** Prov 22:24
a of the LORD Is 5:25
sun go down...**a** Eph 4:26
put...aside: **a** Col 3:8
slow to **a** James 1:19

ANGRY ***enraged, indignant***
Why are you **a** Gen 4:6
king became very **a** Esth 1:12
that He not become **a** Ps 2:12
a man stirs up strife Prov 29:22
a beyond measure Is 64:9
and **a** no more Ezek 16:42
a with his brother Matt 5:22
Be **a**...do not sin Eph 4:26
a with this generation Heb 3:10

ANGUISH ***distress, pain***
writhed in great **a** Esth 4:4
My heart is in **a** Ps 55:4
land of distress and **a** Is 30:6
A has seized us Jer 6:24
and **a** of heart 2 Cor 2:4

ANIMAL ***beast, creature***
from man to **a-s** Gen 6:7
lies with an **a** Ex 22:19
the fat of the **a** Lev 7:25
wild **a-s** of the field Jer 27:6
a blemished **a** Mal 1:14
four-footed **a-s** Acts 10:12
like unreasoning **a-s** 2 Pet 2:12

ANNA
prophetess Luke 2:36

ANNAS
high priest Luke 3:2; John 18:13ff

ANNIHILATE ***destroy***
to **a** all the Jews Esth 3:13
My enemy **a-d** them Lam 2:22
to destroy and **a** Dan 11:44
let it be **a-d** Zech 11:9

ANNOUNCE ***proclaim***
Who **a-s** peace Is 52:7
I will **a** My words Jer 18:2
a-ing to...disciples John 20:18
a-d...the Righteous Acts 7:52

ANNUL ***dismiss, make void***
he shall **a** her vow Num 30:8
husband has **a-led** Num 30:12
not **a** Your covenant Jer 14:21
a-s one of the least Matt 5:19

ANOINT (v) ***sprinkle oil upon***
a them and ordain Ex 28:41
a Aaron and his sons Ex 30:30
LORD **a-ed** you king 1 Sam 15:17
a-ed my head with oil Ps 23:5
a the most holy *place* Dan 9:24
has **a-ed** My body Mark 14:8
did not **a** My head Luke 7:46
and **a-ed** my eyes John 9:11
a-ed...feet of Jesus John 12:3
a-ed Him...Holy Spirit Acts 10:38
a-ing him with oil James 5:14

ANOINTED (adj) ***consecrated***
if the **a** priest sins Lev 4:3
not touch My **a** 1 Chr 16:22
a cherub who Ezek 28:14
the two **a** ones Zech 4:14

ANOINTED (n) ***consecrated one***
walk before My **a** 1 Sam 2:35
he is the LORD's **a** 1 Sam 24:10
against His **A** Ps 2:2

ANOINTING (adj) ***consecration***
spices for the **a** oil Ex 25:6
shall be a holy **a** oil Ex 30:31
for the LORD's **a** oil Lev 10:7

ANOINTING (n) ***consecration***
a will qualify them Ex 40:15
a from the Holy 1 John 2:20
His **a** teaches you 1 John 2:27

ANSWER (n) ***response***
consider what **a** I 1 Chr 21:12
the king sent an **a** Ezra 4:17
Who gives a right **a** Prov 24:26
amazed at...His **a-s** Luke 2:47

ANSWER (v) ***respond***
anyone who will **a** you Job 5:1
The LORD **a-ed** me Ps 118:5
Jesus **a-ing** said Matt 3:15
who **a-s** back to God Rom 9:20

ANT ***insect***
to the **a**, O sluggard Prov 6:6
a-s are not a strong Prov 30:25

ANTELOPE ***animal***
Like an **a** in a net Is 51:20

ANTICHRIST ***foe of Christ***
a-s have appeared 1 John 2:18
This is the **a** 1 John 2:22
the *spirit* of the **a** 1 John 4:3
deceiver and the **a** 2 John 7

ANTIOCH
1 *city in Syria* Acts 6:5; 11:19,26
2 *city in Galatia* Acts 13:14; 14:19

ANTIPAS
1 *Pergamum martyr* Rev 2:13
2 *Herod Antipas see* **HEROD**

ANXIETY ***sorrow***
a because of my sin Ps 38:18
There is **a** by the sea Jer 49:23
casting all your **a** 1 Pet 5:7

ANXIOUS ***concern, worry***
and will become **a** for us 1 Sam 9:5
not be **a** in...drought Jer 17:8
my spirit is **a** to Dan 2:3
Be **a** for nothing Phil 4:6

APART ***separate***
So they set **a** Kedesh Josh 20:7
tear their fetters **a** Ps 2:3
a from your Father Matt 10:29
a from Him nothing John 1:3
a from Me you can John 15:5
faith **a** from works Rom 3:28

APOLLOS
Alexandrian Jew Acts 18:24
taught at Ephesus Acts 18:24
taught at Corinth 1 Cor 3:4,6

APOSTASY ***faithlessness***
a-ies are numerous Jer 5:6
Turned away in...**a** Jer 8:5
I will heal their **a** Hos 14:4
unless the **a** comes 2 Thess 2:3

APOSTLE ***sent with authority***
the twelve **a-s** Matt 10:2
named as **a-s** Luke 6:13
called *as* an **a** Rom 1:1
an **a** of Gentiles Rom 11:13
not fit to be called an **a** 1 Cor 15:9
men are false **a-s** 2 Cor 11:13
He gave some *as* **a-s** Eph 4:11
Jesus, the **A** and Heb 3:1
a-s of the Lamb Rev 21:14

APOSTLESHIP ***office of apostle***
received grace and **a** Rom 1:5
seal of my **a** 1 Cor 9:2
Peter in *his* **a** to Gal 2:8

APPAREL ***clothing, garment***
of gold on your **a** 2 Sam 1:24
majestic in His **a** Is 63:1
put on his royal **a** Acts 12:21

APPEAL ***ask, entreat***
standing and **a-ing** Acts 16:9
I **a** to Caesar Acts 25:11
Paul **a-ed** to be held Acts 25:21
a-ed to...Emperor Acts 25:25
a to *him* as a father 1 Tim 5:1
love's sake I...**a** Philem 9

APPEAR ***become visible***
LORD **a-ed** to Abram Gen 12:7
glory of the LORD **a-ed** Ex 16:10
a-ed on the wings 2 Sam 22:11
and **a-ed** to many Matt 27:53
first **a-ed** to Mary Mark 16:9
who, **a-ing** in glory Luke 9:31
a-ed to them tongues Acts 2:3
we must all **a** before 2 Cor 5:10
a-ing of the glory Titus 2:13
will **a** a second time Heb 9:28
Chief Shepherd **a-s** 1 Pet 5:4
not **a-ed** as yet 1 John 3:2

APPEARANCE ***countenance***
handsome in...**a** Gen 39:6
the **a** of the angel Judg 13:6
at the outward **a** 1 Sam 16:7
a is blacker than soot Lam 4:8
lapis lazuli in **a** Ezek 1:26
they neglect their **a** Matt 6:16
judge according to **a** John 7:24
a of His coming 2 Thess 2:8
a of the locusts Rev 9:7

APPEASE ***moderate, mollify***
I will **a** him Gen 32:20
wise man will **a** it Prov 16:14

have **a-d** My wrath Zech 6:8

APPETITE *desire, hunger*
our **a** is gone Num 11:6
a of the young lions Job 38:39
man of *great* **a** Prov 23:2
a is not satisfied Eccl 6:7
enlarges his **a** like Hab 2:5
whose god is *their* **a** Phil 3:19

APPLE *fruit*
as the **a** of the eye Ps 17:8
Like **a-s** of gold Prov 25:11
Refresh me with **a-s** Song 2:5
touches the **a** of His Zech 2:8

APPOINT *assign, commission*
shall **a** *as a penalty* Ex 21:23
I will **a** over you Lev 26:16
who **a-ed** Moses 1 Sam 12:6
to **a** their relatives 1 Chr 15:16
a magistrates and Ezra 7:25
there is a harvest **a-ed** Hos 6:11
a-ed elders for them Acts 14:23
a-ed a preacher and 1 Tim 2:7
For the Law **a-s** men Heb 7:28

APPORTION *distribute*
a the inheritance Num 34:29
a this land Josh 13:7
He **a-s** our fields Mic 2:4

APPROPRIATE *suitable*
blessing **a** to him Gen 49:28
eat at the **a** time Eccl 10:17
a to repentance Acts 26:20

APPROVAL *consent*
loved the **a** of men John 12:43
give hearty **a** to Rom 1:32
men of old gained **a** Heb 11:2

APPROVE *accept, attest*
the Lord does not **a** Lam 3:36
too pure to **a** evil Hab 1:13
standing by **a-ing** Acts 22:20
and **a-d** by men Rom 14:18
present yourself **a-d** 2 Tim 2:15

AQUILA
a native of Pontus Acts 18:2
Corinthian Christian Acts 18:18
co-worker with Paul Rom 16:3

ARAB
1 *town in Judah* Josh 15:52
2 *ethnic identity* 1 Kin 10:15; Neh 2:19; Is 13:20

ARABAH
1 *desert steppe* Is 35:1,6; Jer 52:7
2 *Jordan rift valley* Deut 1:1; Josh 3:17
3 *Dead Sea* Josh 3:16; 2 Kin 14:25

ARABIA
land SE of Israel / Judah Is 21:13; Ezek 30:5; Gal 1:17; 4:25

ARAM
1 *son of Shem* Gen 10:22,23
2 *line of Asher* 1 Chr 7:34
3 *ancestor of Jesus, shortened to Ram* Ruth 4:19; Matt 1:3; Luke 3:33
4 *Syria and N Mesopotamia* Num 23:7; 1 Kin 11:25; 2 Kin 13:19; Is 7:8

ARAMAIC
Semitic language 2 Kin 18:26; Ezra 4:7; Is 36:11; Dan 2:4

ARAMEANS
tribes of Aram 2 Sam 8:5; 1 Kin 20:20; 2 Kin 24:2

ARARAT
kingdom and mountain range in Armenia Gen 8:4; 2 Kin 19:37; Jer 51:27

ARAUNAH
Jebusite owner of threshing floor on Mt. Moriah 2 Sam 24:16,18
David purchases threshing floor for altar and later temple 2 Sam 24:23,24
see also **ORNAN**

ARCHANGEL
voice of *the* **a** 1 Thess 4:16
But Michael the **a** Jude 9

ARCHELAUS *see* **HEROD**

ARCHER *bowman*
the **a-s** hit him 1 Sam 31:3
a-s shot King Josiah 2 Chr 35:23
a-s equipped with bows Ps 78:9
an **a** who wounds Prov 26:10

ARCHIPPUS
Colossian Christian Col 4:17
co-worker with Paul Philem 2

AREOPAGUS
hill and council in Athens Acts 17:19,22

ARGUE *dispute, question*
I will **a** my ways Job 13:15
hastily to **a** *your case* Prov 25:8
Pharisees...**a** with Mark 8:11
scribes **a-ing** with Mark 9:14
a-ing with the...*Jews* Acts 9:29

ARGUMENT *disagreement*
Please hear my **a** Job 13:6
mouth are no **a-s** Ps 38:14
a started among them Luke 9:46

ARIEL
1 *a Moabite* 2 Sam 23:20; 1 Chr 11:22
2 *applied to Jerusalem* Is 29:1ff
3 *sent by Ezra* Ezra 8:16

ARISE *rise, stand*
A, walk about the Gen 13:17
Abraham **arose** early Gen 19:27
will **a** and play Deut 31:16
you have **a-n** early 1 Sam 29:10
arose and tore his robe Job 1:20
when God **a-s** Job 31:14
A, O LORD; save me Ps 3:7
Though war **a** Ps 27:3
A, my darling Song 2:13
a-n *anyone* greater Matt 11:11
false prophets will **a** Matt 24:11
arose from the dead Acts 10:41
a from the dead Eph 5:14

ARISTARCHUS
Thessalonian Christian Acts 20:4; 27:2
co-worker with Paul Col 4:10; Philem 24

ARK *chest, vessel*
a of gopher wood Gen 6:14
into the **a** to Noah Gen 7:9
a of acacia wood Ex 37:1
a of the covenant Josh 4:7
Noah entered the **a** Matt 24:38
a of His covenant Rev 11:19

ARM (n) *part of body*
the everlasting **a-s** Deut 33:27
a without strength Job 26:2
a-s of the wicked Ps 37:17
His holy **a** have gained Ps 98:1
a seal on your **a** Song 8:6
be carried in the **a-s** Is 60:4
took...in His **a-s** Mark 10:16
with an uplifted **a** Acts 13:17

ARM (v) *mobilize*
A men from among Num 31:3
a-ed for battle Num 32:29
a-ed with iron 2 Sam 23:7
a yourselves also 1 Pet 4:1

ARMAGEDDON
see **HAR-MAGEDON**

ARMED (adj) *mobilized*
the **a** men went Josh 6:13
their **a** camps 1 Sam 28:1
So the **a** men left 2 Chr 28:14
like an **a** man Prov 6:11

ARMOR *protective device*
a joint of the **a** 1 Kin 22:34
strip off his outer **a** Job 41:13
all his **a** on which Luke 11:22
put on...**a** of light Rom 13:12
full **a** of God Eph 6:11

ARMY *host, war*
not go out with the **a** Deut 24:5
like the **a** of God 1 Chr 12:22
a ready for battle 2 Chr 26:11
officers of the **a** Neh 2:9
forth with our **a-ies** Ps 60:10
exceedingly great **a** Ezek 37:10
a-ies...in heaven Rev 19:14
and against His **a** Rev 19:19

ARNON
river and border Num 21:13
valley in Moab Deut 2:24

AROMA *odor*
the soothing **a** Gen 8:21
his **a** has not changed Jer 48:11
through us...sweet **a** 2 Cor 2:14
a from life to life 2 Cor 2:16
as a fragrant **a** Eph 5:2

AROUSE *raise, stir*
A Yourself to help me Ps 59:4
a-s for you the spirits Is 14:9
a-d one from the north Is 41:25
He will **a** *His* zeal Is 42:13
LORD has **a-d** the spirit Jer 51:11

ARRANGE *set in order*
a what belongs on it Ex 40:4
shall **a** the pieces Lev 1:8
he **a-d** the wood 1 Kin 18:33
for so he had **a-d** it Acts 20:13

ARRAY (n) *arrangement, order*
went up in martial **a** Ex 13:18
in battle **a** Josh 4:12
Worship...in holy **a** 1 Chr 16:29
holy **a,** from the womb Ps 110:3

ARRAY (v) *adorn, clothe*
Israel **a-ed** for battle Judg 20:20
let them **a** the man Esth 6:9
A yourselves before Job 33:5

ARREST *restrain*
he **a-ed** Jeremiah Jer 37:13
Herod had John **a-ed** Matt 14:3
and clubs to **a** Me Matt 26:55
proceeded to **a** Peter Acts 12:3

ARROGANCE *pride*
your **a** has come 2 Kin 19:28
Pride and **a** and Prov 8:13
a of the proud Is 13:11
a, pride, and fury Is 16:6
a of your heart Jer 49:16
you boast in your **a** James 4:16

ARROGANT *proud*
a men have risen up Ps 86:14
But a fool is **a** Prov 14:16
a toward the LORD Jer 48:26
Knowledge makes **a** 1 Cor 8:1
boastful, **a,** revilers 2 Tim 3:2
speaking...**a** *words* 2 Pet 2:18

ARROW *dart, missile*
shot an **a** past him 1 Sam 20:36
a-s of the Almighty Job 6:4
a cannot make him Job 41:28

make ready their **a** Ps 11:2
broke the flaming **a-s** Ps 76:3
sword and a sharp **a** Prov 25:18
tongue is a deadly **a** Jer 9:8
target for the **a** Lam 3:12
deadly **a-s** of famine Ezek 5:16
a-s of the evil *one* Eph 6:16

ART *craft*
with their secret **a-s** Ex 7:22
the perfumers' **a** 2 Chr 16:14

ARTAXERXES
Persian king Ezra 4:7,8; 7:1,12; Neh 2:1; 5:14

ARTEMIS
Greek goddess Acts 19:24ff

ARTICLE *object, vessel*
a-s of silver Gen 24:53
any wooden **a** Lev 11:32
of every precious **a** Hos 13:15
every **a** of ivory Rev 18:12

ASA
1 *king of Judah* 1 Kin 15:8-24; 2 Chr 14:8-15
2 *a Levite* 1 Chr 9:16

ASCEND *go up*
a into the hill Ps 24:3
If I **a** to heaven Ps 139:8
Who has **a-ed** into Prov 30:4
breath of man **a-s** Eccl 3:21
has **a-ed** into heaven John 3:13
Son of Man **a-ing** John 6:62
a-ed to the Father John 20:17
who **a-ed** far above Eph 4:10

ASCENT *hill, rise*
by the **a** of Heres Judg 8:13
a of the...Olives 2 Sam 15:30
Song of **A-s** Ps 120-134

ASCRIBE *attribute*
have **a-d** to David 1 Sam 18:8
A to the LORD 1 Chr 16:28
a righteousness to Job 36:3

ASH
but dust and **a-es** Gen 18:27
from the **a** heap 1 Sam 2:8
a-es on her head 2 Sam 13:19
a-es were poured 1 Kin 13:5
proverbs of **a-es** Job 13:12
repent in dust and **a-es** Job 42:6
garland instead of **a-es** Is 61:3
roll in **a-es** Jer 6:26
sackcloth and **a-es** Luke 10:13
a-es of a heifer Heb 9:13

ASHAMED *embarrassed*
naked and were not **a** Gen 2:25
Let me never be **a** Ps 71:1
a of Me...My words Mark 8:38
a...when He comes Luke 9:26
not **a** of the gospel Rom 1:16
a of the testimony 2 Tim 1:8
God is not **a** Heb 11:16
he is not to be **a** 1 Pet 4:16

ASHDOD
Philistine city Josh 15:47; 1 Sam 5:1,6; Amos 1:8

ASHER
1 *eighth son of Jacob* Gen 35:26; 49:20
2 *tribe of Israel* Num 1:41; 13:13; Rev 7:6
3 *town in hill country* Josh 17:7

ASHERAH
Canaanite goddess and symbol Deut 16:21; Judg 6:25
Asherim *(pl)* 1 Kin 14:15; Mic 5:14
Asheroth *(pl)* Judg 3:7; 2 Chr 19:3

ASHKELON
Philistine city Judg 1:18; 2 Sam 1:20; Jer 47:5; Zeph 2:4

ASHTORETH
1 *Near Eastern goddess* 1 Kin 11:5,33; 2 Kin 23:13
Ashtaroth *(pl)* Judg 2:13; 1 Sam 7:4; 31:10
2 *town of Bashan in E Manasseh* Deut 1:4; Josh 13:12

ASIA
Roman province of Asia Minor Acts 6:9; Rom 16:5; Rev 1:4

ASK *appeal, beg, inquire*
whatever you **a** Ruth 3:11
Two things I **a-ed** Prov 30:7
A a sign for yourself Is 7:11
a for the ancient paths Jer 6:16
A rain from the LORD Zech 10:1
Give to him who **a-s** Matt 5:42
A, and it will be Matt 7:7
a...believing Matt 21:22
pray and **a**, believe Mark 11:24
Jews **a** for signs 1 Cor 1:22
let him **a** of God James 1:5

ASLEEP *death, rest*
sound **a**...exhausted Judg 4:21
they fall **a** Ps 90:5
not died, but is **a** Matt 9:24
in the stern, **a** Mark 4:38
Lazarus...fallen **a** John 11:11
said this, he fell **a** Acts 7:60
fallen **a** in Jesus 1 Thess 4:14

ASSAIL *attack*
will you **a** a man Ps 62:3
Whoever **a-s** you Is 54:15
storm was **a-ing** *us* Acts 27:20

ASSEMBLE *gather*
a all the congregation Lev 8:3
A the people to Me Deut 4:10
David **a-d** all Israel 1 Chr 13:5
peoples may be **a-d** Is 43:9
A...on the mountains Amos 3:9
I will...**a** all of you Mic 2:12
whole city **a-d** to Acts 13:44
a-d to make war Rev 19:19

ASSEMBLY *congregation*
holy **a** on the seventh Ex 12:16
the people of the **a** Lev 16:33
a before the rock Num 20:10
Or calls an **a** Job 11:10
a of the righteous Ps 1:5
hate the **a** of evildoers Ps 26:5
proclaim a solemn **a** Joel 2:15
I delight in...**a-ies** Amos 5:21
the **a** was divided Acts 23:7
general **a** and church Heb 12:23
comes into your **a** James 2:2

ASSOCIATE (n) *colleague*
All my **a-s** abhor me Job 19:19
high priest and...**a-s** Acts 5:21

ASSOCIATE (v) *identify with*
shall they **a** with 1 Kin 11:2
a with adulterers Ps 50:18
not **a** with a man Prov 22:24
dared to **a** with them Acts 5:13
but **a** with the lowly Rom 12:16
not **a** with him 2 Thess 3:14

ASSURANCE *confirmation*
no one has **a** of life Job 24:22
a of understanding Col 2:2
full **a** of hope Heb 6:11
full **a** of faith Heb 10:22
a of *things* hoped for Heb 11:1

ASSURE *confirm*
kingdom will be **a-d** Dan 4:26
I **a** you before God Gal 1:20
will **a** our heart 1 John 3:19

ASSYRIA
kingdom name from Asshur Gen 10:22; 1 Chr 1:17
empire in upper Mesopotamia 2 Kin 19:17; Is 19:24; Jer 2:36

ASTONISHED *amazed*
will be **a** and hiss 1 Kin 9:8
a at His teaching Matt 22:33
listeners were **a** Mark 6:2
were utterly **a** Mark 7:37
they were all **a** Luke 1:63

ASTOUNDED *astonished*
prophets will be **a** Jer 4:9
a at the vision Dan 8:27
were completely **a** Mark 5:42

ASTRAY *erring, wandering*
a like a lost sheep Ps 119:176
leading *them* **a** Is 9:16
like sheep have gone **a** Is 53:6
led My people **a** Jer 23:32
lead **a**...the elect Mark 13:22
a from the faith 1 Tim 6:21
go **a** in their heart Heb 3:10
My bond-servants **a** Rev 2:20

ATHALIAH
1 *wicked* 2 Kin 11:1
daughter of Ahab 2 Chr 21:6
wife of Jehoram
2 *a Benjamite* 1 Chr 8:26
3 *returned exile* Ezra 8:7

ATHENS
leading Greek city Acts 17:15ff

ATONEMENT *expiation*
by which **a** was made Ex 29:33
shall make **a** for him Lev 4:35
a before the LORD Lev 14:31
how can I make **a** 2 Sam 21:3
make **a** for iniquity Dan 9:24

ATONEMENT, DAY OF
see **DAY OF ATONEMENT**

ATTACK (n) *assault*
at the first **a** 2 Sam 17:9
king ready for the **a** Job 15:24
joined in the **a** Acts 24:9

ATTACK (v) *assault, fall upon*
that he will come and **a** Gen 32:11
adversary who **a-s** Num 10:9
and **a-ed** the camp Judg 8:11
a the Philistines 1 Sam 23:2
it **a-ed** the plant Jon 4:7
no man will **a** you Acts 18:10

ATTAIN *acquire*
I cannot **a** to it Ps 139:6
woman **a-s** honor Prov 11:16
worthy to **a** to that Luke 20:35
a-ed righteousness Rom 9:30
a to the resurrection Phil 3:11

ATTEND *pay attention to*
a to your priesthood Num 18:7
thousands were **a-ing** Dan 7:10
who **a** regularly 1 Cor 9:13
a to...business 1 Thess 4:11
ears **a** to their prayer 1 Pet 3:12

ATTENDANT *helper, servant*
the **a** of Moses Num 11:28
king's **a-s**, who served Esth 2:2
a-s of...bridegroom Mark 2:19

ATTENTION *heed, regard*
no **a** to false words Ex 5:9
gives **a** to the word Prov 16:20
pays **a** to falsehood Prov 29:12
they do not pay **a** Is 5:12
pay **a** to myths 1 Tim 1:4
a to the...reading 1 Tim 4:13

ATTIRE *covering, dress*
in his military **a** 2 Sam 20:8

cupbearers...**a** 2 Chr 9:4
Him in holy **a** 2 Chr 20:21

ATTITUDE *frame of mind*
see your father's **a** Gen 31:5
a of the righteous Luke 1:17
Have this **a** in Phil 2:5
have a different **a** Phil 3:15

AUGUSTUS
name of Caesar Octavianus Luke 2:1
see **CAESAR**

AUTHOR *source*
a of their salvation Heb 2:10
a...perfecter of faith Heb 12:2

AUTHORITY *power, right*
submit...to her **a** Gen 16:9
put...your **a** on him Num 27:20
Who gave Him **a** Job 34:13
a over...day of death Eccl 8:8
entrust him with your **a** Is 22:21
as *one* having **a** Matt 7:29
a on earth to forgive Matt 9:6
a over unclean spirits Matt 10:1
All **a**...given to Me Matt 28:18
Son of Man has **a** Luke 5:24
no **a** except from God Rom 13:1
majesty, dominion...**a** Jude 25
give **a** over...nations Rev 2:26

AVENGE *revenge*
He will **a** the blood Deut 32:43
the LORD **a** me 1 Sam 24:12
Shall I not **a** Myself Jer 5:9
I will **a** their blood Joel 3:21
a-ing our blood Rev 6:10

AVENGER *revenger*
The blood **a** himself Num 35:19
otherwise the **a** of blood Deut 19:6
a of their *evil* deeds Ps 99:8
God, an **a** who brings Rom 13:4
Lord is *the* **a** 1 Thess 4:6

AVOID *refuse*
A it, do not pass by Prov 4:15
a-ing...empty chatter 1 Tim 6:20

AWAIT *wait*
afflictions **a** me Acts 20:23
a-ing...the revelation 1 Cor 1:7
who eagerly **a** Him Heb 9:28

AWAKE *be attentive, watch*
awoke from his sleep Gen 28:16
A, a, Deborah Judg 5:12
Your likeness when I **a** Ps 17:15
dream when one **a-s** Ps 73:20
arouse or **a-n** *my* love Song 2:7
He **a-ns** My ear Is 50:4
A, a, put on strength Is 51:9
A, drunkards...weep Joel 1:5
that I may **a-n** him John 11:11
hour for you to **a-n** Rom 13:11

AWARE *know, understand*
the lad was not **a** 1 Sam 20:39
Will you not be **a** Is 43:19
But Jesus, **a** of *this* Matt 12:15
I was **a** that power Luke 8:46

AWE *fear, reverence*
stand in **a** of Him Ps 33:8
in **a** of Your words Ps 119:161
in **a** of My name Mal 2:5
feeling a sense of **a** Acts 2:43

AWESOME *fearful*
How **a** is this place Gen 28:17
angel of God, very **a** Judg 13:6
great and **a** God Neh 1:5
God is **a** majesty Job 37:22
As **a** as an army Song 6:4
a day of the LORD Joel 2:31

AXE *cutting tool*
his **a,** and his hoe 1 Sam 13:20
hammer nor **a** 1 Kin 6:7
a head fell into 2 Kin 6:5
a is already laid Luke 3:9

AZARIAH
1 *ancestor of Samuel* 1 Chr 6:36
2 *official of Solomon* 1 Kin 4:2
3 *son of Nathan* 1 Kin 4:5
4 *prophet* 2 Chr 15:1-8
5 *two sons of king Jehoshaphat* 2 Chr 21:2
6 *king of Judah, also* **Uzziah** 2 Kin 15:1; 2 Chr 26:1
7 *high priest* 1 Chr 6:10
8 *family of Merari* 2 Chr 29:12
9 *son of Hilkiah* 1 Chr 6:13,14
10 *original name of Abed-nego* Dan 1:7
the name of twelve other individuals in the OT

B

BAAL
1 *Canaanite god(s)* Num 22:41; Judg 6:25; 1 Kin 18:40
2 *line of Reuben* 1 Chr 5:5
3 *personal name* 1 Chr 8:30
4 *place name* 1 Chr 4:33

BAAL-HANAN
1 *king of Edom* Gen 36:38
2 *servant of David* 1 Chr 27:28

BAAL-HAZOR
mountain in central Palestine 2 Sam 13:23

BAAL-HERMON
part of Mt. Hermon Judg 3:3; 1 Chr 5:23

BAAL-ZEBUB
god of Ekron 2 Kin 1:2,16
see also **BEELZEBUL**

BAASHA
king of Israel 1 Kin 15:16,32

BABEL *a city*
founded by Nimrod Gen 10:10; 11:9
later called Babylon

BABES *infants*
From the mouth of...**b** Ps 8:2
abundance to their **b** Ps 17:14

BABY *infant*
woe...who are nursing **b-ies** Matt 24:19
b leaped...her womb Luke 1:41
b wrapped in cloths Luke 2:12
b as He lay Luke 2:16
like newborn **b-ies** 1 Pet 2:2

BABYLON *city*
1 *on the Euphrates* 2 Kin 17:24; Jer 20:4; Ezek 29:18; Dan 4:29
2 *symbolic of godlessness* Rev 14:8; 17:5

BACK *part of body*
you shall see My **b** Ex 33:23
turned his **b** to leave 1 Sam 10:9
law behind their **b-s** Neh 9:26
my sins behind Your **b** Is 38:17

BAD *evil, wrong*
b report of the land Num 13:32
basket had very **b** figs Jer 24:2
if your eye is **b** Matt 6:23
b tree bears **b** fruit Matt 7:17
B company corrupts 1 Cor 15:33

BAG *sack*
fill their **b-s** Gen 42:25
in the shepherd's **b** 1 Sam 17:40
silver in two **b-s** 2 Kin 5:23
carrying *his* **b** of seed Ps 126:6
b of...weights Mic 6:11
b for *your* journey Matt 10:10
Carry no money belt, no **b** Luke 10:4

BAGGAGE *bags, supplies*
stayed with the **b** 1 Sam 25:13
prepare...yourself **b** Ezek 12:3

BAKE *cook*
b-d unleavened bread Gen 19:3
b-d food for Pharaoh Gen 40:17
they **b-d** the dough Ex 12:39
B what you will **b** Ex 16:23
grain offering **b-d** Lev 2:4
b twelve cakes Lev 24:5
taste of cakes **b-d** Num 11:8
fire to **b** bread Is 44:15

BAKER *cook*
b for the king Gen 40:1
cooks and **b-s** 1 Sam 8:13
from the **b-s'** street Jer 37:21
oven heated by the **b** Hos 7:4

BALAAM
diviner Num 22:5-31; 23:5; Josh 13:22; Rev 2:14

BALAK
king of Moab Num 22:4; Mic 6:5

BALANCE *scale*
shall have just **b-s** Lev 19:36
b-s...with my calamity Job 6:2
False **b** is an Prov 11:1
mountains in a **b** Is 40:12

BALD *hairless*
If...head becomes **b** Lev 13:41
every head is **b** Jer 48:37
head was made **b** Ezek 29:18

BALDHEAD *hairless*
mocked him...you **b** 2 Kin 2:23

BALM *aromatic ointment*
b and myrrh Gen 37:25
a present, a little **b** Gen 43:11
no **b** in Gilead Jer 8:22
Gilead and obtain **b** Jer 46:11
Bring **b** for her pain Jer 51:8
honey, oil and **b** Ezek 27:17

BALSAM *aromatic gum*
tops of the **b** trees 2 Sam 5:24
like a bed of **b** Song 5:13

BAN *set apart to God*
city...under the **b** Josh 6:17
destroy...under the **b** Josh 7:12
who violated the **b** 1 Chr 2:7
consign Jacob to the **b** Is 43:28

BAND *bond* **or** *group*
b-s *shall be* of silver Ex 27:10
skillfully woven **b** Ex 28:8
saw a marauding **b** 2 Kin 13:21
b of destroying angels Ps 78:49
b-s of the yoke Is 58:6

BANISH *exile*
b-ed one will not 2 Sam 14:14
assemble the **b-ed** Is 11:12
gaiety...is **b-ed** Is 24:11
where I will **b** them Ezek 4:13

BANK *slope*
b of the Nile Gen 41:3
reeds by the **b** Ex 2:3
b of the river Ezek 47:7
herd rushed down...**b** Luke 8:33

BANNER *flag, standard*
set up our **b-s** Ps 20:5
b to those who fear Ps 60:4
b over me is love Song 2:4
as an army with **b-s** Song 6:4

BANQUET *dinner, feast*
b lasting seven days Esth 1:5
brought me to *his* **b** Song 2:4
lavish **b** for all Is 25:6
place of honor at **b-s** Matt 23:6

Herod...gave a **b** Mark 6:21

BAPTISM ***symbolic washing***
Saddducees coming...**b** Matt 3:7
b of repentance Mark 1:4
b with which I am Mark 10:38
with the **b** of John Luke 7:29
a **b** to undergo Luke 12:50
through **b** into death Rom 6:4
one faith, one **b** Eph 4:5
buried with Him in **b** Col 2:12

BAPTIZE ***symbolic washing***
b...Holy Spirit Matt 3:11
tax collectors...**b-d** Luke 3:12
Jesus was also **b-d** Luke 3:21
sent me to **b** in water John 1:33
b-ing more disciples John 4:1
b-d with the Holy Acts 1:5
each of you be **b-d** Acts 2:38
he got up and was **b-d** Acts 9:18
household...been **b-d** Acts 16:15
John **b-d** with the Acts 19:4
b-d into Christ Jesus Rom 6:3
b-d into Moses 1 Cor 10:2
b-d into one body 1 Cor 12:13
b-d for the dead 1 Cor 15:29

BAR ***metal*** **or** ***block***
b-s of your yoke Lev 26:13
a **b** of gold Josh 7:21
like **b-s** of iron Job 40:18
earth with its **b-s** Jon 2:6

BARABBAS
robber Matt 27:16; Luke 23:18
released by Pilate Matt 27:26

BARAK
Deborah's commander Judg 4:6

BARBARIAN ***non-Hellenic***
obligation...to **b-s** Rom 1:14
who speaks a **b** 1 Cor 14:11
b, Scythian, slave Col 3:11

BARE (adj) ***barren, uncovered***
to cover *their* **b** flesh Ex 28:42
he went to a **b** hill Num 23:3
strips the forests **b** Ps 29:9
were naked and **b** Ezek 16:7

BARE (v) ***expose, uncover***
foundations...laid **b** Ps 18:15
b-d His holy arm Is 52:10
foundation is laid **b** Ezek 13:14
open and laid **b** Heb 4:13

BAREFOOT ***without sandals***
priests walk **b** Job 12:19
gone naked and **b** Is 20:3

BAR-JESUS
magician Acts 13:6
see also **ELYMAS**

BARLEY ***grain***
land of wheat and **b** Deut 8:8
beginning...**b** harvest Ruth 1:22
stinkweed instead...**b** Job 31:40
has five **b** loaves John 6:9

BARN ***farm building***
b-s are torn down Joel 1:17
seed still in the **b** Hag 2:19
wheat into the **b** Matt 3:12
nor gather into **b-s** Matt 6:26
tear down my **b-s** Luke 12:18

BARNABAS
Cyprian by birth Acts 4:36
introduced Paul Acts 9:27
co-worker with Paul Acts 13:2,7
separated from Paul Acts 15:39

BARREN ***childless, sterile***
Sarai was **b** Gen 11:30
but Rachel was **b** Gen 29:31
wrongs the **b** woman Job 24:21
Shout...O **b** one Is 54:1
Blessed are the **b** Luke 23:29

BARSABBAS
1 *Apostolic candidate, also called Joseph and Justus* Acts 1:23
2 *colleague of Paul, also called Judas* Acts 15:22

BARTHOLOMEW
apostle Matt 10:3; Luke 6:14; Acts 1:13

BARTIMAEUS
healed by Jesus Mark 10:46

BARUCH
1 *scribe* Jer 36:26; 43:6
2 *priest* Neh 3:20
3 *a Judean* Neh 11:5

BASE ***dishonorable***
no **b** thought Deut 15:9
b things of...world 1 Cor 1:28

BASEMATH
1 *Esau's wife* Gen 26:34
2 *daughter of Solomon* 1 Kin 4:15

BASHAN
land E of Jordan Num 21:33; Josh 13:11; Is 2:13

BASIN ***bowl, vessel***
blood...in the **b** Ex 12:22
b-s...of pure gold 1 Chr 28:17
a *sacrificial* **b** Zech 9:15
water into the **b** John 13:5

BASKET ***container***
got him a wicker **b** Ex 2:3
b among the reeds Ex 2:5
b of summer fruit Amos 8:1
lamp...under a **b** Matt 5:15
not...put under a **b** Mark 4:21
seven large **b-s** full Mark 8:8
twelve **b-s** *full* Luke 9:17
let down in a **b** 2 Cor 11:33

BATH ***measure of capacity***
two thousand **b-s** 1 Kin 7:26
100 **b-s** of oil Ezra 7:22
only one **b** *of wine* Is 5:10
a tenth of a **b** from Ezek 45:14

BATHE ***wash***
wash his clothes and **b** Lev 15:5
b his body in water Num 19:7
saw a woman **b-ing** 2 Sam 11:2
B-d in milk Song 5:12

BATHSHEBA
wife of Uriah 2 Sam 11:3
taken by David 2 Sam 11:4
wife of David 2 Sam 11:27
mother of Solomon 2 Sam 12:24

BATTLE (n) ***conflict, war***
b is the LORD'S 1 Sam 17:47
b is...God's 2 Chr 20:15
scents the **b** from afar Job 39:25
with strength for **b** Ps 18:39
noise of **b** is in Jer 50:22
another king in **b** Luke 14:31
horses prepared for **b** Rev 9:7

BATTLE (v) ***fight***
b against the sons Judg 20:14
drew near to **b** 1 Sam 7:10
about to go to **b** 1 Chr 12:19
nations...to **b** Zech 14:2

BEACH ***coast***
crowd...on the **b** Matt 13:2
Jesus stood on the **b** John 21:4
down on the **b** Acts 21:5

BEAM ***log***
like a weaver's **b** 2 Sam 21:19
one was felling a **b** 2 Kin 6:5
b-s, the thresholds 2 Chr 3:7
b-s of His...chambers Ps 104:3

BEAR (n) ***animal***
b came and took 1 Sam 17:34
b robbed of...cubs Prov 17:12
the **b** will graze Is 11:7
resembling a **b** Dan 7:5

BEAR (v) ***sustain***
too great to **b** Gen 4:13
bore you on eagles' Ex 19:4
not **b** false witness Ex 20:16
Lord...**b-s** our burden Ps 68:19
b their iniquities Is 53:11
b the penalty Ezek 23:49
she will **b** a Son Matt 1:21
it **b-s** much fruit John 12:24
b-ing His own cross John 19:17
b fruit for God Rom 7:4
b the image of 1 Cor 15:49
B...another's burdens Gal 6:2
b the sins of many Heb 9:28
bore our sins 1 Pet 2:24

BEARD ***whiskers***
infection...on the **b** Lev 13:29
seized *him* by...**b** 1 Sam 17:35
shaved...their **b-s** 2 Sam 10:4
until your **b-s** grow 1 Chr 19:5

BEARER ***carrier***
the **b-s** of the ark 2 Sam 6:13
strength of...**b-s** Neh 4:10
b of good news Is 40:9

BEAST ***animal, creature***
God formed every **b** Gen 2:19
Noah and all the **b-s** Gen 8:1
eliminate harmful **b-s** Lev 26:6
b-s of the field Lev 26:22
But now ask the **b-s** Job 12:7
b of the forest Ps 50:10
b also had four heads Dan 7:6
they worshiped the **b** Rev 13:4
mark of the **b** Rev 16:2

BEAT ***hit, strike***
b-ing a Hebrew Ex 2:11
b out what she Ruth 2:17
b-ing tambourines Ps 68:25
B your plowshares Joel 3:10
b Him with their Matt 26:67
b-ing His head with Mark 15:19
b-ing his breast Luke 18:13
b-en us in public Acts 16:37
stopped **b-ing** Paul Acts 21:32
b-en with rods 2 Cor 11:25

BEAUTIFUL ***lovely, pleasing***
daughters...were **b** Gen 6:2
Rachel was **b** Gen 29:17
foliage of **b** trees Lev 23:40
Most **b** among women Song 1:8
Branch...will be **b** Is 4:2
Your **b** sheep Jer 13:20
enter the **B** Land Dan 11:41
How **b** are the feet Rom 10:15

BEAUTIFUL GATE *see* **GATES OF JERUSALEM**

BEAUTY
Your **b**...is slain 2 Sam 1:19
behold the **b** of the LORD Ps 27:4
Zion...perfection of **b** Ps 50:2
b is vain Prov 31:30
see the King in His **b** Is 33:17

BED ***pallet***
My **b** will comfort me Job 7:13
make my **b** swim Ps 6:6
remember...on my **b** Ps 63:6
in **b** with a fever Matt 8:14
pick up your **b** Matt 9:6
lamp...under a **b** Mark 4:21

BEDROOM ***sleeping area***
and into your **b** Ex 8:3
you speak in your **b** 2 Kin 6:12
his nurse in the **b** 2 Chr 22:11

BEELZEBUL
NT prince of the demons Matt 12:27; Luke 11:15
see also **BAAL-ZEBUB**

BEERSHEBA
well / town in Negev Gen 21:31; Judg 20:1
home of Abraham Gen 22:19
home of Isaac Gen 26:23

BEFOREHAND ***prior***
do not worry **b** Mark 13:11
anointed My body **b** Mark 14:8
God announced **b** Acts 3:18
prepared **b** for glory Rom 9:23

BEG ***appeal, ask***
children wander...**b** Ps 109:10
b-s during...harvest Prov 20:4
b You to look at Luke 9:38
I am ashamed to **b** Luke 16:3
who used to sit and **b** John 9:8
b-ging them to leave Acts 16:39

BEGET ***bring into being, sire***
Rock who **begot** Deut 32:18
whom you will **b** 2 Kin 20:18
begotten the...dew Job 38:28
I have **begotten** You Ps 2:7
have **begotten** You Acts 13:33

BEGINNING ***origin, starting***
In the **b** God created Gen 1:1
from **b** to end 1 Sam 3:12
b was insignificant Job 8:7
fear of the LORD...**b** Ps 111:10
The **b** of the gospel Mark 1:1
In the **b** was the Word John 1:1
This **b** of *His* signs John 2:11
He is the **b** Col 1:18
the **b** and the end Rev 21:6

BEGOTTEN (adj) ***born one***
b from the Father John 1:14
the only **b** God John 1:18
gave His only **b** Son John 3:16
only **b** Son of God John 3:18
offering...only **b** Heb 11:17
sent His only **b** Son 1 John 4:9

BEHALF ***sake of***
atonement on his **b** Lev 5:6
the Father on your **b** John 16:26
I ask on their **b** John 17:9
one man to die on **b** John 18:14
be sin on our **b** 2 Cor 5:21

BEHAVE ***act***
David **b-d** himself 1 Sam 18:30
b-ing as a madman 1 Sam 21:14
b properly as in Rom 13:13
blamelessly we **b-d** 1 Thess 2:10

BEHAVIOR ***conduct***
instruction in wise **b** Prov 1:3
reverent in their **b** Titus 2:3
holy...in all *your* **b** 1 Pet 1:15
the **b** of their wives 1 Pet 3:1

BEHEADED ***cut off***
killed him and **b** him 2 Sam 4:7
John **b** in the prison Matt 14:10
John, whom I **b** Mark 6:16
b because of their Rev 20:4

BEHEMOTH
hippopotamus Job 40:15

BEHOLD ***look, see***
upright will **b** His face Ps 11:7
b the works of the LORD Ps 46:8
b-ing as in a mirror 2 Cor 3:18
B, I stand at the door Rev 3:20

BEING ***existence, life***
man became a living **b** Gen 2:7
a...**b** coming up 1 Sam 28:13
wisdom in the...**b** Job 38:36
truth in the...**b** Ps 51:6
four living **b-s** Ezek 1:5
resembled a...**b** Dan 10:16

BEL
Babylonian god, related to Baal Jer 50:2; 51:44

BELA
1 *king of Edom* Gen 36:32
2 *son of Bejamin* Gen 46:21; 1 Chr 8:1
3 *a Reubenite* 1 Chr 5:8
4 *city of the plain near the Dead Sea* Gen 14:2,8
see also **ZOAR**

BELIEVE ***have faith, trust***
he **b-d** in the LORD Gen 15:6
did not **b** in God Ps 78:22
naive **b-s** everything Prov 14:15
you **b** that I am able Matt 9:28
ask in prayer, **b-ing** Matt 21:22
repent and **b** Mark 1:15
they **b-d**...Scripture John 2:22
whoever **b-s** in Him John 3:16
will you **b** My words John 5:47
who **b-s** has eternal John 6:47
men will **b** in Him John 11:48
b in the Light John 12:36
not see, and *yet* **b-d** John 20:29
b-d were of one heart Acts 4:32
B in the Lord Jesus Acts 16:31
Abraham **b-d** God Rom 4:3
How will they **b** Rom 10:14
love...**b-s** all 1 Cor 13:7
whom I have **b-d** 2 Tim 1:12
comes to God must **b** Heb 11:6
demons also **b** James 2:19
do not **b** every spirit 1 John 4:1

BELIEVERS ***faithful ones***
all the circumcised **b** Acts 10:45
example to all the **b** 1 Thess 1:7
toward you **b** 1 Thess 2:10

BELL
a **b**...a pomegranate Ex 39:26
b-s of the horses Zech 14:20

BELLY ***stomach***
On your **b**...you go Gen 3:14
crawls on its **b** Lev 11:42
b of the sea monster Matt 12:40

BELOVED ***dearly loved***
b of the LORD dwell Deut 33:12
gives to His **b** *even* Ps 127:2
b is like a gazelle Song 2:9
This is My **b** Son Matt 3:17
your upbuilding, **b** 2 Cor 12:19
stand firm...my **b** Phil 4:1
faithful and **b** brother Col 4:9
Luke, the **b** physician Col 4:14
slave, a **b** brother Philem 16
This is My **b** Son 2 Pet 1:17
the called, **b** in God Jude 1

BELSHAZZAR
ruler of Babylon Dan 5:1; 7:1

BELT ***waistband***
the **b** of the strong Job 12:21
leather **b** around his Matt 3:4
no money in their **b** Mark 6:8
Paul's **b** and bound Acts 21:11

BELTESHAZZAR
Daniel's Babylonian name Dan 1:7; 2:26; 5:12; 10:1

BENAIAH
1 *son of Jehoiada* 2 Sam 8:18
captain of David 2 Sam 23:23
2 *Levitical singer* 1 Chr 15:18,20
3 *a priest* 1 Chr 15:24; 16:5
the name of nine other individuals in the OT

BENEFIT ***blessing, profit***
no return for the **b** 2 Chr 32:25
forget none of His **b-s** Ps 103:2
His **b-s** toward me Ps 116:12
the **b** of circumcision Rom 3:1

BEN-HADAD
1 *Ben-hadad I* 1 Kin 15:18-21
2 *Ben-hadad II* 1 Kin 20,22
3 *Ben-hadad III* 2 Kin 8:7-15; 13:22

BEN-HINNOM, VALLEY OF
see **HINNOM VALLEY**

BENJAMIN
1 *son of Jacob* Gen 35:18
2 *tribe* Num 2:22
3 *of clan of Jediael* 1 Chr 7:10
4 *of the restoration* Neh 3:23

BENJAMIN GATE *see* **GATES OF JERUSALEM**

BEREA
city in Macedonia visited by Paul Acts 17:10,13

BEREAVE ***deprive, make sad***
be **b-d** of you both Gen 27:45
b...of your children Lev 26:22
I will **b** *them* Jer 15:7
longer **b** your nation Ezek 36:14

BERNICE
daughter of Herod Agrippa I Acts 25:13,23

BERODACH-BALADAN
king of Babylon 2 Kin 20:12
see also **MERODACH-BALADAN**

BESEECH ***ask earnestly***
LORD, I **b** You Ps 116:4
do save, we **b** You Ps 118:25
leper came...**b-ing** Mark 1:40
b the Lord of the Luke 10:2

BESIEGE ***assail, surround***
When you **b** a city Deut 20:19
enemies **b** them 2 Chr 6:28
was **b-ing** Jerusalem Jer 32:2
b-d...with bitterness Lam 3:5

BESTOWED ***granted***
b...royal majesty 1 Chr 29:25
that the Spirit was **b** Acts 8:18
which He freely **b** Eph 1:6
b on Him the name Phil 2:9
love the Father has **b** 1 John 3:1

BETHANY
1 *E of Jerusalem* Matt 21:17
home of Mary, Martha and Lazarus John 11:1,18
2 *where John baptized* John 1:28

BETHEL
town in Benjamin Gen 12:8
N of Jerusalem Josh 8:17

BETHESDA
pool in Jerusalem John 5:2

BETH-HORON
1 *famous battle site*
pass NW of Jerusalem Josh 10:10,11
2 *two towns at both ends of mountain pass* Josh 16:3,5

BETHLEHEM
1 *town S of Jerusalem* Gen 35:19
home of Ruth and Boaz Ruth 4:11
birthplace of Jesus Matt 2:1
2 *Zebulunite village* Josh 19:15

BETH-PEOR
Moabite city Deut 4:46; 34:6

BETHPHAGE
village on the Mount of Olives Matt 21:1; Mark 11:1

BETHSAIDA
village on Sea of Galilee Mark 8:22; Luke 9:10
home of Philip, Andrew and Peter John 1:44

BETH-SHAN/BETH-SHEAN
city at junction of Jezreel and Jordan valleys Josh 17:11; 1 Kin 4:12; 1 Chr 7:29

BETH-SHEMESH
1 *city of Judah* Josh 15:10
2 *Issachar border city* Josh 19:22
3 *city of Naphtali* Josh 19:38

BETRAY *break faith, disloyal*
do not **b** the fugitive Is 16:3
wine **b-s** the haughty Hab 2:5
b Him to you Matt 26:15
how to **b** Him Mark 14:11
one...will **b** Me Mark 14:18
Judas, are you **b-ing** Luke 22:48

BETROTH *promise to wed*
You shall **b** a wife Deut 28:30
I will **b** you to Me Hos 2:19
Mary had been **b-ed** Matt 1:18
I **b-ed** you to one 2 Cor 11:2

BEWARE *be careful, watch*
B of practicing Matt 6:1
B of the scribes Mark 12:38
B of the leaven Luke 12:1
b...false circumcision Phil 3:2

BEYOND *over and above*
it was **b** measure Gen 41:49
remove...**b** Babylon Acts 7:43
tempted **b** what 1 Cor 10:13
b their ability 2 Cor 8:3
b all that we ask Eph 3:20
and **b** reproach Col 1:22

BEZALEL
1 *architect of tabernacle* Ex 31:1ff
2 *Israelite* Ezra 10:30

BEZER
1 *son of Zophah* 1 Chr 7:37
2 *city of refuge* Josh 20:8

BIG *large*
on the **b** toes Ex 29:20
Pharaoh...a **b** noise Jer 46:17
gave a **b** reception Luke 5:29

BILDAD
one of Job's friends Job 2:11; 18:1; 42:9

BILHAH
1 *Rachel's servant* Gen 29:29
Jacob's concubine Gen 30:3,4
2 *Simeonite town* 1 Chr 4:29

BIND *fasten, secure*
bound his son Isaac Gen 22:9
were **b-ing** sheaves Gen 37:7
b them as a sign Deut 6:8
b-s up their wounds Ps 147:3
B up the testimony Is 8:16
b up the brokenhearted Is 61:1
b on earth Matt 16:19
and **bound** Him John 18:12
bound...a thousand Rev 20:2

BIRD *fowl*
let **b-s** fly above Gen 1:20
eat any clean **b** Deut 14:20
b-s of the heavens Ps 8:8
Flee *as* a **b** to Ps 11:1
snare of a **b** catcher Hos 9:8
b-s...*have* nests Luke 9:58

BIRTH *act of being born*
A time to give **b** Eccl 3:2
You gave me **b** Jer 2:27
b of Jesus Christ Matt 1:18
rejoice at his **b** Luke 1:14
gave **b** to a son Luke 1:57
a man blind from **b** John 9:1
in pain to give **b** Rev 12:2

BIRTHDAY *day of birth*
was Pharaoh's **b** Gen 40:20
Herod's **b** came Matt 14:6
his **b**...banquet Mark 6:21

BIRTHRIGHT *first-born rights*
First sell me your **b** Gen 25:31
He took away my **b** Gen 27:36
sold his own **b** Heb 12:16

BITE
serpent **bit** any man Num 21:9
it **b-s** like a serpent Prov 23:32
if you **b**...one another Gal 5:15

BITHYNIA
territory on the Bosporus in Asia Minor Acts 16:7; 1 Pet 1:1

BITTER *painful, unpleasant*
b with hard labor Ex 1:14
waters of Marah...**b** Ex 15:23
b speech *as* their arrow Ps 64:3
substitute **b** for sweet Is 5:20
Strong drink is **b** Is 24:9
fresh and **b** *water* James 3:11

BITTERNESS *unpleasantness*
in the **b** of my soul Job 10:1
because of the **b** Is 38:15
full of cursing and **b** Rom 3:14
all **b**...be put away Eph 4:31
no root of **b** Heb 12:15

BLACK *dark*
sky grew **b** with 1 Kin 18:45
darkness and **b** gloom Job 3:5
I am **b** but lovely Song 1:5
behold, a **b** horse Rev 6:5
sun became **b** Rev 6:12

BLAME *fault, responsibility*
let me bear the **b** Gen 43:9
bear the **b**...forever Gen 44:32

BLAMELESS *faultless*
show Yourself **b** 2 Sam 22:26
just *and* **b** *man* is a Job 12:4
His way is **b** Ps 18:30
b will inherit good Prov 28:10
a **b** conscience Acts 24:16
holy and **b** before Him Eph 1:4
in the Law, found **b** Phil 3:6
spotless and **b** 2 Pet 3:14
b with great joy Jude 24

BLASPHEME *curse*
enemies...to **b** 2 Sam 12:14
name is continually **b-d** Is 52:5
This *fellow* **b-s** Matt 9:3
b-s...Holy Spirit Mark 3:29
force them to **b** Acts 26:11
name of God is **b-d** Rom 2:24
taught not to **b** 1 Tim 1:20
b-d the God of Rev 16:11

BLASPHEMY *cursing, profanity*
b against the Spirit Matt 12:31
b-ies they utter Mark 3:28
You...heard the **b** Mark 14:64
man...speaks **b-ies** Luke 5:21
stone You...for **b** John 10:33
words and **b-ies** Rev 13:5

BLAST *burst*
the **b** of Your nostrils Ex 15:8
b with the ram's horn Josh 6:5
a trumpet **b** of war Jer 49:2

BLAZING *burning*
LORD...a **b** fire Ex 3:2
furnace of **b** fire Dan 3:6
and to a **b** fire Heb 12:18

BLEMISH *imperfection, spot*
there is no **b** in you Song 4:7
six lambs without **b** Ezek 46:4
Himself without **b** Heb 9:14
stains and **b-es** 2 Pet 2:13

BLESS (v) *bestow favor or praise*
God **b-ed** the...day Gen 2:3
I will greatly **b** you Gen 22:17
LORD **b-ed** the sabbath Ex 20:11
and **b** Your inheritance Ps 28:9
LORD will **b** His people Ps 29:11
B the LORD Ps 103:2
generous will be **b-ed** Prov 22:9
who **b-es** his friend Prov 27:14
rise up and **b** her Prov 31:28
b-ed of My Father Matt 25:34
He **b-ed** *the food* Mark 6:41
b...who curse you Luke 6:28
while He was **b-ing** Luke 24:51
you are **b-ed** if you John 13:17
B...who persecute Rom 12:14
we **b** *our* Lord James 3:9

BLESSED (adj) *favored, happy*
b be God Most High Gen 14:20
B are you, O Israel Deut 33:29
B be the name of Job 1:21
How **b** is the man Ps 127:5
b...who finds wisdom Prov 3:13
nations will call you **b** Mal 3:12
B are the poor in Matt 5:3
B are the gentle Matt 5:5
B *is* the...kingdom Mark 11:10
B *are* you among women Luke 1:42
more **b** to give Acts 20:35
looking for...**b** hope Titus 2:13

BLESSING (n) *God's favor*
you shall be a **b** Gen 12:2
taken away your **b** Gen 27:35
a **b** and a curse Deut 11:26
curse into a **b** Neh 13:2
b of the LORD be upon Ps 129:8
showers of **b** Ezek 34:26
pour out for you a **b** Mal 3:10
fullness of the **b** Rom 15:29
cup of **b** which we 1 Cor 10:16
inherit a **b** 1 Pet 3:9
honor and glory and **b** Rev 5:12

BLIND (adj) *sightless*
misleads a **b** *person* Deut 27:18
To open **b** eyes Is 42:7
b...guides a **b** man Matt 15:14
b beggar *named* Mark 10:46
b man was sitting Luke 18:35
I was **b**, now I see John 9:25

BLIND (n) *without sight*
block before the **b** Lev 19:14
I was eyes to the **b** Job 29:15
the **b** receive sight Matt 11:5
a guide to the **b** Rom 2:19

BLIND (v) *make sightless*
b-s the clear-sighted Ex 23:8
bribe to **b** my eyes 1 Sam 12:3
has **b-ed** the minds 2 Cor 4:4
darkness has **b-ed** 1 John 2:11

BLINDNESS *sightlessness*
madness and with **b** Deut 28:28
struck them with **b** 2 Kin 6:18
every horse...with **b** Zech 12:4

BLOOD
Whoever sheds man's **b** Gen 9:6
bridegroom of **b** Ex 4:25
b shall be a sign Ex 12:13
not eat...any **b** Lev 3:17
land is filled with **b** Ezek 9:9
b did not reveal Matt 16:17
covenant in My **b** Luke 22:20
sweat...drops of **b** Luke 22:44
drinks My **b** abides John 6:56

Field of **B** Acts 1:19
the moon into **b** Acts 2:20
justified by His **b** Rom 5:9
sharing in the **b** 1 Cor 10:16
redemption...His **b** Eph 1:7
cleansed with **b** Heb 9:22
b, as of a lamb 1 Pet 1:19
the sea became **b** Rev 8:8
b of the saints Rev 17:6

BLOODGUILTINESS
no **b** on his account Ex 22:2
b is upon them Lev 20:11
b shall be forgiven Deut 21:8
Deliver me from **b** Ps 51:14

BLOODSHED ***killing, murder***
abhors the man of **b** Ps 5:6
Men of **b** hate Prov 29:10
the **b** of Jerusalem Is 4:4
give you over to **b** Ezek 35:6
b follows **b** Hos 4:2

BLOSSOM ***bloom***
the almond tree **b-s** Eccl 12:5
Israel will **b** and sprout Is 27:6
arrogance has **b-ed** Ezek 7:10
fig tree should not **b** Hab 3:17

BLOT ***erase***
I will **b** out man Gen 6:7
b me...from Your book Ex 32:32
b out their name Deut 9:14
sin be **b-ted** out Neh 4:5
b out all my iniquities Ps 51:9
works...be **b-ted** out Ezek 6:6

BLUE ***color***
tent of **b** and purple Ex 26:36
ephod all of **b** Ex 28:31
royal robes of **b** Esth 8:15

BOANERGES
name of James and John Mark 3:17

BOAST (n) ***bragging***
soul will make its **b** Ps 34:2
the **b** of our hope Heb 3:6

BOAST (v) ***brag, glory***
B no more so 1 Sam 2:3
who **b-s** of his gifts Prov 25:14
not **b** about tomorrow Prov 27:1
let not a rich man **b** Jer 9:23
b in God Rom 2:17
who **b** in the Law Rom 2:23
b...my weaknesses 2 Cor 12:9
it **b-s** of great things James 3:5

BOASTFUL ***proud***
b shall not stand Ps 5:5
insolent, arrogant, **b** Rom 1:30
b pride of life 1 John 2:16

BOASTING ***bragging***
Where is your **b** Judg 9:38
Where then is **b** Rom 3:27
our **b** about you 2 Cor 9:3
all such **b** is evil James 4:16

BOAT ***watercraft***
slip by like reed **b-s** Job 9:26
left the **b** and their Matt 4:22
Peter got out of...**b** Matt 14:29
filled both of the **b-s** Luke 5:7
disciples into the **b** John 6:22

BOAZ
1 *husband of Ruth* Ruth 4:13
grandfather of David Ruth 4:17ff
2 *temple pillar* 2 Chr 3:17

BODY ***corpse, flesh***
b cleaves to the earth Ps 44:25
lamp of the **b** Matt 6:22
perfume on My **b** Matt 26:12
this is My **b** Mark 14:22
did not find His **b** Luke 24:23
b of sin...done away Rom 6:6
redemption of our **b** Rom 8:23
present your **b-ies** Rom 12:1
b-ies are members 1 Cor 6:15
b is a temple 1 Cor 6:19
you are Christ's **b** 1 Cor 12:27
b to be burned 1 Cor 13:3
absent from the **b** 2 Cor 5:8
one **b** and one Spirit Eph 4:4
building up of the **b** Eph 4:12
wives as...own **b-ies** Eph 5:28
transform the **b** Phil 3:21
b be preserved 1 Thess 5:23
bore...sins in His **b** 1 Pet 2:24

BODYGUARD ***guard, protector***
captain of the **b** put Gen 40:4
you my **b** for life 1 Sam 28:2

BOIL (n) ***sore, swelling***
When...has a **b** Lev 13:18
b-s of Egypt Deut 28:27
smote Job with sore **b-s** Job 2:7

BOIL (v) ***cook, heat***
not **b** a young goat in its Ex 34:26
we **b-ed** my son 2 Kin 6:29
fire causes water to **b** Is 64:2
b the guilt offering Ezek 46:20

BOISTEROUS ***clamorous, loud***
woman of folly is **b** Prov 9:13
of noise, You **b** town Is 22:2
will drink *and* be **b** Zech 9:15

BOLD ***brave, fearless***
wicked man...**b** face Prov 21:29
righteous are **b** as Prov 28:1
I *need* not be **b** 2 Cor 10:2

BOLDNESS ***confidence***
word of God with **b** Acts 4:31
b and...access Eph 3:12
with **b** the mystery Eph 6:19

BOND ***band, restraint***
neither **b** nor free 2 Kin 14:26
b of the covenant Ezek 20:37
with **b-s** of love Hos 11:4
he would break his **b-s** Luke 8:29
in the **b** of peace Eph 4:3
eternal **b-s** under Jude 6

BONDAGE ***servitude, slavery***
Israel sighed...**b** Ex 2:23
the **b** of iniquity Acts 8:23
sold into **b** to sin Rom 7:14

BOND-SERVANT ***servant, slave***
b-s of...Most High Acts 16:17
Paul, a **b** of Christ Rom 1:1
ourselves as your **b-s** 2 Cor 4:5
b...be quarrelsome 2 Tim 2:24
b of God...apostle Titus 1:1
His **b-s**...serve Him Rev 22:3

BONDSLAVE ***servant, slave***
state of His **b** Luke 1:48
a **b** of Jesus Christ Col 4:12
Urge **b-s** to be subject Titus 2:9
use it as **b-s** of God 1 Pet 2:16

BONE
now **b** of my **b-s** Gen 2:23
the **b-s** of Joseph Josh 24:32
my **b-s** are dismayed Ps 6:2
rottenness in his **b-s** Prov 12:4
tongue breaks the **b** Prov 25:15
can these **b-s** live Ezek 37:3
dead men's **b-s** Matt 23:27
Not a **b**...be broken John 19:36

BOOK ***scroll***
in a **b** as a memorial Ex 17:14
blot me...from Your **b** Ex 32:32
found the **b** of the 2 Kin 22:8
seal up the **b** Dan 12:4
not contain the **b-s** John 21:25
names are in the **b** Phil 4:3
worthy to open the **b** Rev 5:2
Lamb's **b** of life Rev 21:27

BOOK OF LIFE
God's book with names of righteous Ps 69:28; Phil 4:3; Rev 13:8; 17:8; 20:15

BOOTH ***shelters***
b-s for his livestock Gen 33:17
live in **b-s** for seven Lev 23:42
in **b-s** during the feast Neh 8:14
sitting in the tax **b** Luke 5:27

BOOTHS, FEAST OF
see **FEASTS**

BOOTY ***loot, plunder***
b that remained Num 31:32
Swift is the **b** Is 8:1
divide the **b** with Is 53:12
have his *own* life as **b** Jer 38:2

BORDER ***boundary***
enlarge your **b-s** Ex 34:24
b of...city of refuge Num 35:26
the Jordan as *a* **b** Deut 3:17
God extends your **b** Deut 12:20
peace in your **b-s** Ps 147:14

BORN ***brought into life***
man is **b** for trouble Job 5:7
mountains were **b** Ps 90:2
child will be **b** to us Is 9:6
land be **b** in one day Is 66:8
b King of the Jews Matt 2:2
those **b** of women Luke 7:28
b not of blood John 1:13
unless one is **b** again John 3:3
b of the Spirit John 3:6
to one untimely **b** 1 Cor 15:8
b...to a living hope 1 Pet 1:3
loves is **b** of God 1 John 4:7

BORROW ***use temporarily***
if a man **b-s** *anything* Ex 22:14
you shall not **b** Deut 28:12
b-s and does not pay Ps 37:21
wants to **b** from you Matt 5:42

BOSOM ***breast***
iniquity in my **b** Job 31:33
take fire in his **b** Prov 6:27
to Abraham's **b** Luke 16:22
the **b** of the Father John 1:18
reclining on Jesus' **b** John 13:23

BOTHER ***pester***
conscience **b-ed** 1 Sam 24:5
you **b** the woman Matt 26:10
worried and **b-ed** Luke 10:41
this widow **b-s** me Luke 18:5

BOTTOMLESS ***without bottom***
key of the **b** pit Rev 9:1
he opened the **b** pit Rev 9:2

BOUGH ***branch***
Joseph is a fruitful **b** Gen 49:22
b-s of leafy trees Lev 23:40
cedars...with its **b-s** Ps 80:10
nested in its **b-s** Ezek 31:6

BOUND (adj) ***fastened, tied***
Foolishness is **b** up Prov 22:15
cast **b** into the...fire Dan 3:24
A wife is **b** as long 1 Cor 7:39

BOUND (n) ***boundary, limit***
utmost **b** of...hills Gen 49:26
set **b-s** for the people Ex 19:12
b-s...the mountain Ex 19:23

BOUNDARY ***border, limit***
b-ies of the peoples Deut 32:8

b of light and Job 26:10
the **b-ies** of the earth Ps 74:17
set for the sea its **b** Prov 8:29
the **b** of the widow Prov 15:25

BOUNTY *generous gift*
to his royal **b** 1 Kin 10:13
crowned...with Your **b** Ps 65:11
over the **b** of the LORD Jer 31:12

BOW (n) *rainbow*
set My **b** in the cloud Gen 9:13

BOW (n) *shooting device*
his **b** remained firm Gen 49:24
a **b** of bronze 2 Sam 22:35
not trust in my **b** Ps 44:6
b-s are shattered Jer 51:56

BOW (v) *bend, worship*
nations **b** down to Gen 27:29
Israel **b-ed** *in* Gen 47:31
to Him you shall **b** 2 Kin 17:36
My soul is **b-ed** down Ps 57:6
B Your heavens, O LORD Ps 144:5
nations will **b** down Zeph 2:11
He **b-ed** His head John 19:30
every knee shall **b** Rom 14:11

BOWELS *entrails, innards*
a disease of your **b** 2 Chr 21:15
smote him in his **b** 2 Chr 21:18

BOWL *dish, jug*
golden **b** is crushed Eccl 12:6
from sacrificial **b-s** Amos 6:6
dips with Me in...**b** Mark 14:20
b-s full of the wrath Rev 15:7

BOX *container*
b with the golden 1 Sam 6:11
sashes, perfume **b-es** Is 3:20
Judas had the...**b** John 13:29

BOX *type of tree*
b tree and the cypress Is 41:19

BOY *child, lad*
she left the **b** Gen 21:15
let the **b-s** live Ex 1:17
b will lead them Is 11:6
Traded a **b** for a harlot Joel 3:3
b was cured at once Matt 17:18

BRACELETS *armlets*
two **b** for her wrists Gen 24:22
armlets and **b** Num 31:50
earrings, **b**, veils Is 3:19

BRAMBLE *briar*
trees said to the **b** Judg 9:14
fire...from the **b** Judg 9:15

BRANCH *bough*
David a righteous **B** Jer 23:5
b-es *fit* for scepters Ezek 19:11
beautiful **b-es** and Ezek 31:3
birds...in its **b-es** Luke 13:19
b-es of the palm John 12:13
b...not bear fruit John 15:2
you are the **b-es** John 15:5
is holy, the **b-es** Rom 11:16

BREACH *break*
For every **b** of trust Ex 22:9
LORD had made a **b** Judg 21:15
closed up the **b** 1 Kin 11:27
that no **b** remained Neh 6:1
Heal its **b-es** Ps 60:2

BREAD *food*
eat unleavened **b** Ex 12:20
rain **b** from heaven Ex 16:4
He will bless your **b** Ex 23:25
b of the Presence Ex 25:30
not live by **b** alone Deut 8:3
ravens brought...**b** 1 Kin 17:6

b of heaven Ps 105:40
satisfy...with **b** Ps 132:15
b *eaten* in secret Prov 9:17
eat the **b** of idleness Prov 31:27
Cast your **b**...waters Eccl 11:1
not live on **b** alone Matt 4:4
Give us...daily **b** Matt 6:11
gives you the true **b** John 6:32
I am the **b** of life John 6:35

BREAK *divide, shatter*
b down your pride Lev 26:19
never **b** My covenant Judg 2:1
broke the pitchers Judg 7:20
soft tongue **b-s** the Prov 25:15
reed He will not **b** Is 42:3
I **broke** your yoke Jer 2:20
B...fallow ground Hos 10:12
disciples **b** the Matt 15:2
waves were **b-ing** Mark 4:37
she **broke** the vial Mark 14:3
their nets *began* to **b** Luke 5:6
b his bonds Luke 8:29
b-ing the Sabbath John 5:18
did not **b** His legs John 19:33
your **b-ing** the Law Rom 2:23

BREAST *bosom*
orphan from the **b** Job 24:9
upon my mother's **b-s** Ps 22:9
b-s are like...fawns Song 7:3
b-s...never nursed Luke 23:29

BREASTPIECE *breast covering*
a **b** and an ephod Ex 28:4
make a **b** of judgment Ex 28:15
they bound the **b** Ex 39:21

BREASTPLATE *breast armor*
righteousness like a **b** Is 59:17
b of faith and love 1 Thess 5:8
like **b-s** of iron Rev 9:9

BREATH *air, spirit, wind*
the **b** of life Gen 2:7
days are *but* a **b** Job 7:16
man is a mere **b** Ps 39:11
b came into them Ezek 37:10
give **b** to the image Rev 13:15

BREATHE *inhale and exhale*
Abraham **b-d** his last Gen 25:8
such as **b** out violence Ps 27:12
garden **b**...*fragrance* Song 4:16
b on these slain Ezek 37:9
He **b-d** His last Mark 15:39
He **b-d** on them John 20:22

BRETHREN *brothers*
beating...his **b** Ex 2:11
b from all the nations Is 66:20
His **b** Will return Mic 5:3
b, why do you injure Acts 7:26
sinning against...**b** 1 Cor 8:12
dangers...false **b** 2 Cor 11:26
Peace be to the **b** Eph 6:23
faithful **b** in Christ Col 1:2
the love of the **b** 1 Thess 4:9
b...not grow weary 2 Thess 3:13
my **b**, do not swear James 5:12
our lives for the **b** 1 John 3:16
accuser of our **b** Rev 12:10

BRIAR *thistle, thorn*
b-s and thorns will come Is 5:6
land will be **b-s** Is 7:24
grapes from a **b** bush Luke 6:44

BRIBE *illegal gift*
b blinds...clear-sighted Ex 23:8
nor take a **b** Deut 10:17
who hates **b-s** will Prov 15:27
b corrupts the heart Eccl 7:7
Everyone loves a **b** Is 1:23

BRICK *clay block*
they used **b** for stone Gen 11:3

straw to make **b** as Ex 5:7
deliver...quota of **b-s** Ex 5:18
burning incense on **b-s** Is 65:3

BRIDE *newlywed*
as a **b** adorns herself Is 61:10
the voice of the **b** Jer 7:34
b out of her *bridal* Joel 2:16
He who has the **b** John 3:29
b...of the Lamb Rev 21:9

BRIDEGROOM *newlywed*
a **b** of blood to me Ex 4:25
As a **b** decks himself Is 61:10
voice of the **b** Jer 7:34
attendants of the **b** Matt 9:15
out to meet the **b** Matt 25:1

BRIDLE (n) *head harness*
My **b** in your lips 2 Kin 19:28
a **b** for the donkey Prov 26:3
up to the horses' **b-s** Rev 14:20

BRIDLE (v) *control*
not **b** his tongue James 1:26
man, able to **b** James 3:2

BRIGHT *shining*
b in the skies Job 37:21
night is as **b** as Ps 139:12
B eyes gladden Prov 15:30
b cloud...them Matt 17:5
b light...flashed Acts 22:6
the **b** morning star Rev 22:16

BRIMSTONE *sulfur*
b and fire from Gen 19:24
b and burning wind Ps 11:6
rained fire and **b** Luke 17:29
tormented with...**b** Rev 14:10
lake of fire and **b** Rev 20:10

BRING *carry, lead*
will **b** forth children Gen 3:16
Cain **brought**...offering Gen 4:3
b two of every *kind* Gen 6:19
B the ark of God 1 Sam 14:18
Kings will **b** gifts Ps 68:29
B water for the thirsty Is 21:14
B the whole tithe Mal 3:10
brought...a paralytic Matt 9:2
not...to **b** peace Matt 10:34
I **b** you good news Luke 2:10
Law **b-s** about wrath Rom 4:15
b-ing salvation Titus 2:11

BROAD *wide*
into a **b** place 2 Sam 22:20
land was **b** and 1 Chr 4:40
the sea, great and **b** Ps 104:25
dark in **b** daylight Amos 8:9
way is **b** that leads to Matt 7:13

BROKEN *crushed, separated*
My spirit is **b** Job 17:1
A **b** and a contrite heart Ps 51:17
they have **b** Your law Ps 119:126
deeps were **b** up Prov 3:20
silver cord is **b** Eccl 12:6
bind up the **b** Ezek 34:16
Scripture...be **b** John 10:35
Not a bone...**b** John 19:36
Branches were **b** off Rom 11:19

BROKENHEARTED *grieving*
LORD is near to the **b** Ps 34:18
He heals the **b** Ps 147:3
sent me to bind...**b** Is 61:1

BRONZE *metal*
implements of **b** Gen 4:22
made a **b** serpent Num 21:9
bend a bow of **b** 2 Sam 22:35
as walls of **b** Jer 1:18
third kingdom of **b** Dan 2:39
costly wood and **b** Rev 18:12

BROOD *group, offspring*
b of sinful men Num 32:14
You **b** of vipers Matt 3:7
hen *gathers* her **b** Luke 13:34

BROOK *stream, wadi*
stones from the **b** 1 Sam 17:40
by the **b** Cherith 1 Kin 17:5
deer pants for...**b-s** Ps 42:1
wisdom...bubbling **b** Prov 18:4

BROTHER *male relative*
Am I my **b-'s** Gen 4:9
b-s were jealous Gen 37:11
b-s may redeem Lev 25:48
b-s to dwell together Ps 133:1
b is born for Prov 17:17
closer than a **b** Prov 18:24
b-s of a poor man Prov 19:7
reconciled to your **b** Matt 5:24
B will betray **b** Matt 10:21
behold, His...**b-s** Matt 12:46
not forgive his **b** Matt 18:35
My **b** and sister Mark 3:35
b of yours was dead Luke 15:32
left...wife or **b-s** Luke 18:29
not even His **b-s** John 7:5
b will rise again John 11:23
b goes to law with **b** 1 Cor 6:6
my **b** to stumble 1 Cor 8:13
yet hates his **b** 1 John 2:9

BROTHERHOOD
the covenant of **b** Amos 1:9
love the **b**, fear God 1 Pet 2:17

BRUISE (n) *wound*
for wound, **b** for **b** Ex 21:25
Only **b-s**, welts and raw Is 1:6
the **b** He has inflicted Is 30:26

BRUISE (v) *batter, crush*
b him on the heel Gen 3:15
b-s me with a tempest Job 9:17

BRUTAL *fierce, vicious*
hand of **b** men Ezek 21:31
b, haters of good 2 Tim 3:3

BUD *blossom, a sprout*
flax was in **b** Ex 9:31
put forth **b-s** Num 17:8
the **b** blossoms Is 18:5

BUILD *construct, form*
Noah **built** an altar Gen 8:20
let us **b**...a city Gen 11:4
b for Me a house 1 Chr 17:12
b-ing...house of God 2 Chr 3:3
built high places 2 Chr 33:19
has **built** up Zion Ps 102:16
Unless the LORD **b-s** Ps 127:1
a time to **b** up Eccl 3:3
built his house on Matt 7:24
I will **b** My church Matt 16:18
able to **b** *you* up Acts 20:32
being **built** together Eph 2:22
stones...being **built** 1 Pet 2:5

BUILDER *fashioner, maker*
Solomon's **b-s** 1 Kin 5:18
b-s had laid the Ezra 3:10
the **b-s** rejected Matt 21:42
like a wise master **b** 1 Cor 3:10
architect and **b** is Heb 11:10

BUILDING *structure*
reconstructing this **b** Ezra 5:4
b that *was* in front Ezek 41:12
what wonderful **b-s** Mark 13:1
you are...God's **b** 1 Cor 3:9
have a **b** from God 2 Cor 5:1
whole **b**, being fitted Eph 2:21

BULB *part of plant*
a **b** and a flower Ex 25:33
b-s and their branches Ex 25:36

BULL *animal*
b of the sin offering Lev 4:20
b without blemish Ezek 45:18
blood of **b-s** and Heb 10:4

BULRUSH *marsh plant*
b in a single day Is 9:14
b-es by the Nile Is 19:7
palm branch or **b** Is 19:15

BUNDLE *package*
b...*was* in his sack Gen 42:35
the **b** of the living 1 Sam 25:29
in **b-s** to burn Matt 13:30

BURDEN (n) *load, weight*
b-s of the Egyptians Ex 6:6
the **b** of the people Num 11:17
I am a **b** to myself Job 7:20
who daily bears our **b** Ps 68:19
My **b** is light Matt 11:30
b-s hard to bear Luke 11:46
Bear one another's **b-s** Gal 6:2

BURDEN (v) *weigh down*
b-ed Me with your sins Is 43:24
were **b-ed** excessively 2 Cor 1:8
not **b** you myself 2 Cor 12:16
the church must not be **b-ed** 1 Tim 5:16

BURIAL *interment*
give me a **b** site Gen 23:4
even have a *proper* **b** Eccl 6:3
to prepare Me for **b** Matt 26:12
b custom of the Jews John 19:40

BURN (v) *consume, kindle*
Jacob's anger **b-ed** Gen 30:2
bush was **b-ing** Ex 3:2
Your anger **b** against Ex 32:11
Moses' anger **b-ed** Ex 32:19
did not **b** any cities Josh 11:13
jealousy **b** like fire Ps 79:5
to **b** their sons Jer 7:31
not to **b** the scroll Jer 36:25
will **b** up the chaff Luke 3:17
b-ed in their desire Rom 1:27
my body to be **b-ed** 1 Cor 13:3
works will be **b-ed** 2 Pet 3:10
lake of fire...**b-s** Rev 19:20

BURNING (adj)
Your **b** anger Ex 15:7
shall bewail the **b** Lev 10:6
b lips and a wicked Prov 26:23
b heat of famine Lam 5:10
b anger of the LORD Zeph 2:2

BURNISHED *polished*
gleamed like **b** bronze Ezek 1:7
feet...like **b** bronze Rev 1:15

BURNT OFFERINGS
see **OFFERINGS**

BURST *break*
great deep **b** open Gen 7:11
wine will **b** the skins Luke 5:37
he **b** open Acts 1:18

BURY *place in earth*
b-ied at...old age Gen 15:15
that I may **b** my dead Gen 23:4
b-ied the bones of Josh 24:32
go and **b** my father Matt 8:21
dead to **b** their own Matt 8:22
devout...**b-ied** Stephen Acts 8:2
that He was **b-ied** 1 Cor 15:4
b-ied...in baptism Col 2:12

BUSH *shrub*
boy under...the **b-es** Gen 21:15
the **b** was burning Ex 3:2
who dwelt in the **b** Deut 33:16
like a **b** in the desert Jer 17:6

BUSINESS *occupation, work*
until I...told my **b** Gen 24:33
carry on the *king's* **b** Esth 3:9
another to his **b** Matt 22:5
a place of **b** John 2:16
attend to your...**b** 1 Thess 4:11
engage in **b** James 4:13

BUSYBODIES *meddlers*
no work...like **b** 2 Thess 3:11
gossips and **b** 1 Tim 5:13

BUTTER
steps...bathed in **b** Job 29:6
smoother than **b** Ps 55:21
milk produces **b** Prov 30:33

BUYER *purchaser*
Bad, bad, says the **b** Prov 20:14
the **b** like the seller Is 24:2
Let not the **b** rejoice Ezek 7:12

BYSTANDERS *unlookers*
b...said to Peter Matt 26:73
the **b** heard it Mark 15:35

BYWORD *contemptible*
b among all peoples 1 Kin 9:7
a proverb and a **b** 2 Chr 7:20
He has made me a **b** Job 17:6
b among the nations Ps 44:14

C

CAESAR
1 *Roman emperor* Matt 22:17,21; Mark 12:14; John 19:12
2 *Augustus* Luke 2:1
3 *Tiberius* Luke 3:1; John 19:12
4 *Claudius* Acts 11:28; 17:7; 18:2
5 *Nero* Acts 25:12; 26:32; Phil 4:22

CAESAREA
Roman coastal city Acts 8:40; 10:1; 21:16; 25:4

CAESAREA PHILIPPI
city at base of Mt. Hermon Matt 16:13; Mark 8:27

CAIAPHAS
high priest Matt 26:57; Luke 3:2; John 11:49ff; Acts 4:6

CAIN
son of Adam Gen 4:1
tiller of the ground Gen 4:2
killed his brother Gen 4:8
marked by sign Gen 4:15

CAKE *type of bread*
and make bread **c-s** Gen 18:6
took one unleavened **c** Lev 8:26
make me a...**c** 1 Kin 17:13

CALAMITY *adversity, trouble*
day of my **c** 2 Sam 22:19
sorry over the **c** 1 Chr 21:15
palate discern **c-ies** Job 6:30
c from God is Job 31:23
stumble in *time of* **c** Prov 24:16
beginning to work **c** Jer 25:29
relents concerning **c** Jon 4:2

CALCULATE *count*
shall **c** from the year Lev 25:50
c the cost Luke 14:28
c the...beast Rev 13:18

CALEB
1 *aide to Moses* Num 13:30
son of Jephunneh Num 32:12
received Hebron Josh 14:13
2 *son of Hezron* 1 Chr 2:18

CALF *animal*
tender and choice **c** Gen 18:7
into a molten **c** Ex 32:4
c and the young lion Is 11:6
skip about like **c-ves** Mal 4:2

bring the fattened **c** Luke 15:23
blood of...**c-ves** Heb 9:12

CALL *address, summon, name*
God **c-ed** the light day Gen 1:5
c upon the name Gen 4:26
c-s up the dead Deut 18:11
LORD was **c-ing**...boy 1 Sam 3:8
c-ed fine gold my trust Job 31:24
c upon the LORD Ps 18:3
those who **c** evil good Is 5:20
c His name Immanuel Is 7:14
You shall **c** Me Jer 3:19
who is **c-ed** the Messiah Matt 1:16
to **c** the righteous Matt 9:13
c-s his own sheep John 10:3
c Me Teacher and John 13:13
God has not **c-ed** 1 Thess 4:7
c-s...a prophetess Rev 2:20

CALLING *summoning*
the **c** of assemblies Is 1:13
the **c** of God Rom 11:29
For consider your **c** 1 Cor 1:26
with a holy **c** 2 Tim 1:9
His **c** and choosing 2 Pet 1:10

CALM *still*
be **c**, have no fear Is 7:4
sea may become **c** Jon 1:11
it became perfectly **c** Matt 8:26
you ought to keep **c** Acts 19:36

CAMEL *animal*
dismounted...the **c** Gen 24:64
his wives upon **c-s** Gen 31:17
a garment of **c-'s** hair Matt 3:4
c...eye of a needle Matt 19:24
clothed with **c-'s** hair Mark 1:6

CAMP (n) *lodging area*
This is God's **c** Gen 32:2
people out of the **c** Ex 19:17
outside the **c** seven Num 31:19
pitch **c-s**, and place Ezek 4:2
the **c** of the saints Rev 20:9

CAMP (v) *settle*
you shall **c** in front Ex 14:2
they shall also **c** Num 1:50
Israel **c-ed** at Gilgal Josh 5:10
I will **c** against you Is 29:3
c around My house Zech 9:8

CANA
Galilean town John 2:1,11; 4:46

CANAAN
1 *son of Ham* Gen 9:18,25
2 *Syro-Palestine* Gen 13:12; 42:5; Ex 16:35; Ps 105:11
3 *language (Hebrew)* Is 19:18
see also **HEBREW**
see also **JUDEAN**

CANAL *water way*
c-s will emit a stench Is 19:6
rivers *and* wide **c-s** Is 33:21
the Nile **c-s** dry Ezek 30:12
in front of the **c** Dan 8:3

CAPERNAUM
city on Sea of Galilee Matt 4:13; Luke 4:23; John 6:24,59

CAPHTOR
Crete Deut 2:23; Jer 47:4; Amos 9:7
see also **CRETE**

CAPITAL *top part of column*
height of the other **c** 1 Kin 7:16
c on the top of each 2 Chr 3:15
c-s...were on top 2 Chr 4:12

CAPPADOCIA
province in Asia Minor Acts 2:9; 1 Pet 1:1

CAPTAIN *leader*
c of the bodyguard Gen 39:1
the **c-s** of hundreds Num 31:14
c of the host of Josh 5:14
the **c** of the ship Acts 27:11

CAPTIVE *prisoner*
firstborn of the **c** Ex 12:29
slain and the **c-s** Deut 32:42
restores his **c** people Ps 14:7
have led **c** *Your* **c-s** Ps 68:18
release to the **c-s** Luke 4:18
every thought **c** 2 Cor 10:5
having been held **c** 2 Tim 2:26

CAPTIVITY *imprisonment*
restore you from **c** Deut 30:3
land of their **c** 2 Chr 6:37
had come from the **c** Ezra 8:35
had survived the **c** Neh 1:2
destined for **c** Rev 13:10

CAPTURE *seize, take*
they **c-d** and looted Gen 34:29
c-d all his cities Deut 2:34
Can anyone **c** him Job 40:24
c...with her eyelids Prov 6:25
it **c-s** nothing at all Amos 3:5

CARAVAN *expedition*
a **c** of Ishmaelites Gen 37:25
The **c-s** of Tema Job 6:19
O **c-s** of Dedanites Is 21:13

CARCASS *corpse*
down upon the **c-es** Gen 15:11
one who touches...**c** Lev 11:39
c-es will be food Deut 28:26
c of the lion Judg 14:8
c-es of their...idols Jer 16:18

CARE (n) *concern*
into the **c** of...sons Gen 30:35
put him in my **c** Gen 42:37
friends and receive **c** Acts 27:3
c for one another 1 Cor 12:25

CARE (v) *have concern for*
He **c-d** for him Deut 32:10
No one **c-s** for...soul Ps 142:4
c for My sheep Ezek 34:12
and took **c** of him Luke 10:34
take **c** of the church 1 Tim 3:5
he **c-s** for you 1 Pet 5:7

CAREFUL *watchful, on guard*
I not be **c** to speak Num 23:12
c to observe all Deut 6:25
you shall be **c** to do Deut 8:1
be **c** not to drink Judg 13:4
be **c** how you walk Eph 5:15

CARELESS *thoughtless*
a fool is...**c** Prov 14:16
food, and **c** ease Ezek 16:49
that every **c** word Matt 12:36

CARGO *merchandise*
and they threw the **c** Jon 1:5
to unload its **c** Acts 21:3
no one buys...**c-es** Rev 18:11

CARMEL
1 *range of hills* 1 Kin 18:42; 2 Kin 4:25; Jer 46:18
2 *town in Judah* 1 Sam 15:12; 25:5,40

CARPENTER *craftsman*
c-s and stonemasons 2 Sam 5:11
to the masons and **c-s** Ezra 3:7
this the **c-'s** son Matt 13:55
c, the son of Mary Mark 6:3

CARRY *bear*
LORD...**c-ied** you Deut 1:31
c an ephod before 1 Sam 2:28
Spirit...will **c** you 1 Kin 18:12
c *them* in His bosom Is 40:11

our sorrows He **c-ied** Is 53:4
c-ied away...diseases Matt 8:17
C no money belt, no bag Luke 10:4
the cross to **c** Luke 23:26
c out the desire of Gal 5:16

CART *wagon*
So Moses took the **c-s** Num 7:6
the cows to the **c** 1 Sam 6:7
sin as if with **c** ropes Is 5:18
his **c** and his horses Is 28:28

CARVE (v) *cut, fashion*
he **c-d** all the walls 1 Kin 6:29
who **c** a resting place Is 22:16
c-d with cherubim Ezek 41:18
its maker has **c-d** it Hab 2:18

CARVED (adj) *cut, etched*
with **c** engravings 1 Kin 6:29
c image of the idol 2 Chr 33:7
abdomen is **c** ivory Song 5:14

CAST *throw*
one who **c-s** a spell Deut 18:11
Joshua **c** lots for Josh 18:10
c Your law behind Neh 9:26
c *lots* for the orphans Job 6:27
c My words behind Ps 50:17
Do not **c** me away Ps 51:11
c you out of My sight Jer 7:15
will **c** out demons Mark 16:17
c fire upon...earth Luke 12:49
clothing they **c** lots John 19:24
c-ing all your anxiety 1 Pet 5:7
but **c** them into hell 2 Pet 2:4
c their crowns before Rev 4:10

CATCH *seize, trap*
shall **c** his wife Judg 21:21
to **c** the afflicted Ps 10:9
C the foxes for us Song 2:15
caught in My snare Ezek 12:13
will be **c-ing** men Luke 5:10
unable to **c** Him Luke 20:26
caught in adultery John 8:3
who **c-es** the wise 1 Cor 3:19
if anyone is **caught** Gal 6:1
child was **caught** up Rev 12:5

CATTLE *domestic animals*
c and creeping things Gen 1:24
the firstborn of **c** Ex 12:29
defect from the **c** Lev 22:19
c on a thousand hills Ps 50:10
no **c** in the stalls Hab 3:17

CAUSE (n) *purpose, reason*
the **c** of the just Ex 23:8
to death without a **c** 1 Sam 19:5
place my **c** before God Job 5:8
hate me without a **c** Ps 69:4
wounds without **c** Prov 23:29
hated...without a **c** John 15:25

CAUSE (v) *make*
I **c** My name to be Ex 20:24
c Israel to inherit Deut 1:38
has **c-d** His name Ezra 6:12
c His face to shine Ps 67:1
speech **c** you to sin Eccl 5:6
who **c** dissensions Rom 16:17
was **c-ing** the growth 1 Cor 3:6

CAVE *shelter*
buried him in the **c** Gen 25:9
escaped to the **c** 1 Sam 22:1
by fifties in a **c** 1 Kin 18:4
mountains and **c-s** Heb 11:38
hid...in the **c-s** Rev 6:15

CEASE *stop*
you shall **c** *from labor* Ex 23:12
poor will never **c** Deut 15:11
He makes wars to **c** Ps 46:9
C...consideration Prov 23:4
make this proverb **c** Ezek 12:23

c-d to kiss My feet Luke 7:45
tongues, they will **c** 1 Cor 13:8
pray without **c-ing** 1 Thess 5:17

CEDAR *tree, wood*
with the **c** wood Lev 14:6
c-s beside the waters Num 24:6
all the **c-s** of Lebanon Is 2:13
the height of **c-s** Amos 2:9

CELEBRATE *rejoice*
may **c** a feast to Me Ex 5:1
you shall **c** it in Lev 23:41
C the Passover 2 Kin 23:21
all Israel were **c-ing** 1 Chr 13:8
to **c** *the feast* 2 Chr 30:23
David...**c-ing** 1 Chr 15:29
c with my friends Luke 15:29

CENSER *incense container*
c-s for yourselves Num 16:6
his **c** in his hand Ezek 8:11
holding a golden **c** Rev 8:3
angel took the **c** Rev 8:5

CENSUS *population roll*
c of...congregation Num 1:2
number of the **c** 1 Chr 21:5
c which...David 2 Chr 2:17
the first **c** taken Luke 2:2
in the days of the **c** Acts 5:37

CENT *money*
paid up the last **c** Matt 5:26
sparrows...for a **c** Matt 10:29
amount to a **c** Mark 12:42

CENTURION *captain*
Jesus said to the **c** Matt 8:13
summoning the **c** Mark 15:44
soldiers and **c-s** Acts 21:32
gave orders to the **c** Acts 24:23

CEPHAS
apostle Peter John 1:42; 1 Cor 1:12; 15:5; Gal 2:11

CERTAINTY *sureness*
know with **c** that Josh 23:13
c of the words Prov 22:21
you know with **c** Eph 5:5

CERTIFICATE *permit, record*
a **c** of divorce Deut 24:1
a **c** of divorce Matt 5:31
c of debt Col 2:14

CHAFF *husk*
consumes them as **c** Ex 15:7
c which the wind drives Ps 1:4
make the hills like **c** Is 41:15
c from the summer Dan 2:35
burn up the **c** Matt 3:12

CHAIN *band*
bound...bronze **c-s** Judg 16:21
he drew **c-s** of gold 1 Kin 6:21
whose hands are **c-s** Eccl 7:26
was bound with **c-s** Luke 8:29
c-s fell off his hands Acts 12:7
great **c** in his hand Rev 20:1

CHALDEA
S Babylonia Jer 50:10; 51:24; Ezek 23:15

CHALDEANS
inhabitants of Chaldea Gen 11:28; 2 Kin 24:2; Job 1:17; Jer 24:5; Dan 5:11; Hab 1:6

CHAMBER *room*
entered his **c** Gen 43:30
in his cool roof **c** Judg 3:20
c-s of the storehouse Neh 10:38
bridegroom...his **c** Ps 19:5
to the **c-s** of death Prov 7:27
out of her *bridal* **c** Joel 2:16
c-s in the heavens Amos 9:6

CHAMPION *fighter*
c, the Philistine 1 Sam 17:23
a Savior and a **C** Is 19:20
like a dread **c** Jer 20:11

CHANGE (n) *alteration*
gave **c-s** of garments Gen 45:22
had a **c** of heart Ex 14:5
two **c-s** of clothes 2 Kin 5:23
Until my **c** comes Job 14:14
a **c** of law Heb 7:12

CHANGE (v) *alter, transform*
and **c-d** my wages Gen 31:7
He **c-s** a wilderness Ps 107:35
c-d their glory Jer 2:11
Ethiopian **c** his skin Jer 13:23
He who **c-s** the times Dan 2:21
LORD **c-d** His mind Amos 7:6
I, the LORD, do not **c** Mal 3:6
will all be **c-d** 1 Cor 15:51

CHANNEL *furrow*
Who has cleft a **c** Job 38:25
c-s of water appeared Ps 18:15
heart is *like* **c-s** Prov 21:1
sent out its **c-s** Ezek 31:4

CHANT *sing*
David **c-ed**...this 2 Sam 1:17
Jeremiah **c-ed** a 2 Chr 35:25
daughters...shall **c** Ezek 32:16

CHARACTER
and proven **c**, hope Rom 5:4
Make sure...your **c** is free Heb 13:5

CHARGE (n) *responsibility*
under Joseph's **c** Gen 39:23
keep the **c** of the LORD Lev 8:35
c of his household Matt 24:45
allotted to your **c** 1 Pet 5:3

CHARGE (n) *accusation*
far from a false **c** Ex 23:7
bring **c-s** against Acts 19:38
c against God's elect Rom 8:33

CHARGE (n) *cost*
gospel without **c** 1 Cor 9:18

CHARGE (v) *command*
Abimelech **c-d** all Gen 26:11
I **c-d** your judges Deut 1:16
Moses **c-d** us with a Deut 33:4
I solemnly **c** you 1 Tim 5:21

CHARGE (v) *exact a price*
not **c** him interest Ex 22:25
c that to my account Philem 18

CHARIOT *wagon*
Joseph prepared...**c** Gen 46:29
appeared a **c** of fire 2 Kin 2:11
Some *boast* in **c-s** Ps 20:7
c-s of God are myriads Ps 68:17
Your **c-s** of salvation Hab 3:8
I will cut off the **c** Zech 9:10
and sitting in his **c** Acts 8:28

CHARIOTEERS *warriors*
David killed 700 **c** 2 Sam 10:18
7,000 **c** and 40,000 1 Chr 19:18
with horses and **c** Ezek 39:20

CHARITY *alms*
give that...as **c** Luke 11:41
and give to **c** Luke 12:33
deeds of...**c** Acts 9:36

CHARM *beauty*
A bribe is a **c** Prov 17:8
C is deceitful Prov 31:30
with *all* your **c-s** Song 7:6

CHASE *drive, pursue*
Egyptians **c-d** after Ex 14:9
will **c** your enemies Lev 26:7

one **c** a thousand Deut 32:30
c-ing...Philistines 1 Sam 17:53
be **c-d** like chaff Is 17:13

CHASTE *pure*
c...behavior 1 Pet 3:2
kept themselves **c** Rev 14:4

CHASTEN *discipline*
Man is also **c-ed** Job 33:19
Nor **c** me in Your wrath Ps 6:1
c-ed every morning Ps 73:14
who **c-s** the nations Ps 94:10

CHASTISE *punish*
You have **c-d** me Jer 31:18
I will **c** all of them Hos 5:2

CHATTER *babbling*
worldly...empty **c** 1 Tim 6:20
avoid...empty **c** 2 Tim 2:16

CHEAT *deceive*
your father has **c-ed** Gen 31:7
c with...scales Amos 8:5

CHEBAR
river in Babylonia Ezek 3:15; 10:15

CHEDORLAOMER
king of Elam Gen 14:9,17

CHEEK *part of face*
slapped me on the **c** Job 16:10
Your **c-s** are lovely Song 1:10
tears are on her **c-s** Lam 1:2
hits you on the **c** Luke 6:29

CHEERFUL
countenance and be **c** Job 9:27
joyful heart...a **c** Prov 15:13
c heart...feast Prov 15:15
God loves a **c** giver 2 Cor 9:7
Is anyone **c** James 5:13

CHEMOSH
god of Moab Judg 11:24; 1 Kin 11:7; Jer 48:13

CHERETHITES
1 *tribe on Philistine plain* 1 Sam 30:14; Ezek 25:16; Zeph 2:5
2 *David's bodyguards* 2 Sam 8:18; 15:18; 1 Kin 1:38; 1 Chr 18:17

CHERISH *love*
or the wife you **c** Deut 13:6
the wife he **c-es** Deut 28:54
men **c** themselves Acts 24:15
c-es it, just as Christ Eph 5:29

CHERUB *celestial being*
He rode on a **c** 2 Sam 22:11
one **c**...ten cubits 1 Kin 6:26
c stretched out his Ezek 10:7

CHERUBIM *plural of cherub*
He stationed the **c** Gen 3:24
c had *their* wings Ex 37:9
enthroned *above*...**c** 2 Sam 6:2
c appeared to have Ezek 10:8

CHEST *box*
the priest took a **c** 2 Kin 12:9
money in the **c** 2 Kin 12:10
levies...into the **c** 2 Chr 24:10

CHEW *eat*
which **c** the cud Lev 11:4
before it was **c-ed** Num 11:33

CHIEF *head, prominent*
c-s of the sons of Gen 36:15
the **c-s** of Edom Gen 36:43
of the thirty **c** men 2 Sam 23:13
c of the magicians Dan 4:9
C Shepherd appears 1 Pet 5:4

CHILD
c grew...weaned Gen 21:8
Train up a **c** in Prov 22:6
discipline from the **c** Prov 23:13
c will be born to us Is 9:6
with **c** by the Holy Matt 1:18
take the **C** and His Matt 2:13
He called a **c** to Matt 18:2
saying, **C**, arise Luke 8:54
a woman with **c** 1 Thess 5:3

CHILDBIRTH
multiply...pain in **c** Gen 3:16
as of a woman in **c** Ps 48:6
pains of **c** come Hos 13:13
suffers the pains of **c** Rom 8:22

CHILDLESS
I am **c**, and the heir Gen 15:2
They will die **c** Lev 20:20
c among women 1 Sam 15:33
and died **c** Luke 20:29

CHILDREN
pain...bring forth **c** Gen 3:16
Are these all the **c** 1 Sam 16:11
compassion on *his* **c** Ps 103:13
c are a gift Ps 127:3
c rise up and bless Prov 31:28
c were dashed to Nah 3:10
slew all the male **c** Matt 2:16
stones...to raise up **c** Matt 3:9
c...against parents Matt 10:21
and become like **c** Matt 18:3
bringing **c** to Him Mark 10:13
Being...the **c** of God Acts 17:29
if **c**, heirs Rom 8:17
C, obey your parents Eph 6:1
My little **c** 1 John 2:1
kill her **c** with Rev 2:23

CHINNERETH / CHINNEROTH
1 *lake* Num 34:11; Josh 12:3
also **Sea of Galilee**
also **Lake of Gennesaret**
also **Sea of Tiberias**
2 *city of Naphtali* Deut 3:17; Josh 19:35
3 *plain near Galilee* Josh 11:2; 1 Kin 15:20

CHISLEV
ninth month of Hebrew calendar Neh 1:1; Zech 7:1

CHOICE *option* **or** *best*
Saul, a **c**...*man* 1 Sam 9:2
c men of Israel 2 Sam 10:9
And eat its **c** fruits Song 4:16
God made a **c** among Acts 15:7
God's gracious **c** Rom 11:5
His **c** of you 1 Thess 1:4

CHOIR *chorus*
c proceeded to the Neh 12:38
two **c-s** took their Neh 12:40

CHOKE *stifle*
wealth **c** the word Matt 13:22
began to **c** *him* Matt 18:28
thorns...**c-d** it Mark 4:7
c-d with worries Luke 8:14

CHOOSE *select, take*
C men for us Ex 17:9
whom the LORD **c-s** Num 16:7
C wise...discerning Deut 1:13
He **c-s** our inheritance Ps 47:4
refuse evil and **c** good Is 7:15
not God **c** the poor James 2:5

CHOP *cut*
who **c-s** your wood Deut 29:11
c-ped down...altars 2 Chr 34:7
C down the tree Dan 4:14

CHOSE *selected*
Lot **c** for himself Gen 13:11
God has **c-n** you Deut 7:6
I **c** David to be 1 Kin 8:16
when I **c** Israel Ezek 20:5
c twelve of them Luke 6:13
has **c-n** the weak 1 Cor 1:27
He **c** us in Him Eph 1:4

CHOSEN *elected, selected*
Moses His **c** one Ps 106:23
My **c** *one in whom* Is 42:1
Israel My **c** *one* Is 45:4
c ones shall inherit Is 65:9
My Son, *My* **C** One Luke 9:35
c of God, holy and Col 3:12
of *His* **c** angels 1 Tim 5:21
you are a **c** race 1 Pet 2:9

CHRIST *Messiah*
birth of Jesus **C** was Matt 1:18
C would suffer and Luke 24:46
both Lord and **C** Acts 2:36
fellow heirs with **C** Rom 8:17
are one body in **C** Rom 12:5
preach **C** crucified 1 Cor 1:23
judgment seat of **C** 2 Cor 5:10
ambassadors for **C** 2 Cor 5:20
faith in **C** Jesus Gal 2:16
as sons through Jesus **C** Eph 1:5
to live is **C** Phil 1:21
C, who is our life Col 3:4
dead in **C** will 1 Thess 4:16
coming of...**C** 2 Thess 2:1
C...high priest Heb 9:11
Advocate...Jesus **C** 1 John 2:1
with **C** for a thousand Rev 20:4

CHRISTIAN *follower of Christ*
first called **C-s** in Acts 11:26
me to become a **C** Acts 26:28
suffers as a **C** 1 Pet 4:16

CHRONICLES *book of register*
1 *of kings of Israel* 1 Kin 14:19; 15:31; 2 Kin 14:28; 15:26
2 *of kings of Judah* 1 Kin 14:29; 15:23; 2 Kin 15:36; 24:5
3 *of kings of Media / Persia* Esth 10:2

CHURCH *a called out assembly*
I will build my **c** Matt 16:18
tell it to the **c** Matt 18:17
shepherd the **c** Acts 20:28
c-es of the Gentiles Rom 16:4
together as a **c** 1 Cor 11:18
woman...speak in **c** 1 Cor 14:35
to the **c-es** of Judea Gal 1:22
Christ...head of the **c** Eph 5:23
persecutor of the **c** Phil 3:6
c of the living God 1 Tim 3:15
Spirit says to the **c-es** Rev 2:11

CILICIA
region in SE Asia Minor Acts 15:41; 21:39; 27:5

CINNAMON *spice*
and of fragrant **c** Ex 30:23
myrrh, aloes and **c** Prov 7:17
and **c** and spice Rev 18:13

CIRCLE *area*
sleeping inside...**c** 1 Sam 26:7
He has inscribed a **c** Job 26:10
did not sit in the **c** Jer 15:17

CIRCUIT *course*
on **c** to Bethel 1 Sam 7:16
its **c** to the other end Ps 19:6

CIRCULATE *spread*
proclamation was **c-d** Ex 36:6
LORD's people **c-ing** 1 Sam 2:24
to **c** a proclamation 2 Chr 30:5

CIRCUMCISE *be pure* **or** *cut off*
every male...be **c-d** Gen 17:10
Abraham **c-d** his son Gen 21:4
So **c** your heart Deut 10:16
God will **c**...heart Deut 30:6
C yourselves...LORD Jer 4:4
came to **c** the child Luke 1:59
c-d the eighth day Phil 3:5

CIRCUMCISION *act of purity*
because of the **c** Ex 4:26
c is...of the heart Rom 2:29
if you receive **c** Gal 5:2
if I still preach **c** Gal 5:11
we are the *true* **c** Phil 3:3
c made without hands Col 2:11
those of the **c** Titus 1:10

CIRCUMSTANCE *condition*
spoken in right **c-s** Prov 25:11
may know...my **c-s** Eph 6:21
peace in every **c** 2 Thess 3:16
of humble **c-s** James 1:9

CISTERN *reservoir*
a **c** collecting water Lev 11:36
water from your...**c** Prov 5:15
wheel at the **c** is Eccl 12:6
prophet from the **c** Jer 38:10

CITADEL *fortress*
c of the king's 1 Kin 16:18
c of Susa Esth 2:3
in the **c** of Susa Dan 8:2
c-s of Jerusalem Amos 2:5
Proclaim on the **c-s** Amos 3:9
tramples on our **c-s** Mic 5:5

CITIES OF REFUGE
1 *Kedesh in Naphtali* Josh 20:7
2 *Shechem in Ephraim* Josh 20:7
3 *Hebron (Kiriath-arba)* Josh 20:7
4 *Bezer in Reuben* Josh 20:8
5 *Ramoth-gilead in Gad* Josh 20:8
6 *Golan in Manasseh* Josh 20:8

CITIZEN *resident*
your fellow **c-s** Ezek 33:12
fellow **c-s** who talk Ezek 33:30
c-s hated him Luke 19:14
c of no insignificant Acts 21:39
fellow **c-s** with the Eph 2:19

CITY
build...a **c** Gen 11:4
burned...their **c-ies** Num 31:10
die in my own **c** 2 Sam 19:37
glad the **c** of God Ps 46:4
LORD guards the **c** Ps 127:1
the **C** of Destruction Is 19:18
the **C** of Truth Zech 8:3
a **c** called Nazareth Matt 2:23
into the holy **c** Matt 4:5
the **c** was stirred Matt 21:10
c, shake the dust off Luke 9:5
He has prepared a **c** Heb 11:16
I saw the holy **c** Rev 21:2

CLAIM *demand*
Let darkness...**c** it Job 3:5
Do not **c** honor in Prov 25:6
c-ing to be someone Acts 8:9

CLAN *family, tribe*
c of the household Judg 9:1
and by your **c-s** 1 Sam 10:19
among...**c-s** of Judah Mic 5:2
I will make the **c-s** Zech 12:6

CLAP *applaud*
c-ped their hands 2 Kin 11:12
c-s his hands among Job 34:37
rivers **c** their hands Ps 98:8
trees...will **c** Is 55:12

CLAUDIA
Roman Christian 2 Tim 4:21

CLAUDIUS
Roman Emperor Acts 11:28; 18:2
see **CAESAR**

CLAUDIUS LYSIAS
Roman tribune Acts 23:26

CLAY
dwell in houses of **c** Job 4:19
Father, We are the **c** Is 64:8
c in the potter's hand Jer 18:6
the **c** to his eyes John 9:6

CLEAN *cleansed, washed*
animals that are not **c** Gen 7:2
eat in a **c** place Lev 10:14
pronounce him **c** Lev 13:28
Create in me a **c** heart Ps 51:10
make yourselves **c** Is 1:16
You can make me **c** Matt 8:2
things are **c** for you Luke 11:41
c because of the word John 15:3

CLEANSE *purify, wash*
To **c** the house then Lev 14:49
c the house of the 2 Chr 29:15
I have **c-d** my heart Prov 20:9
I am willing; be **c-d** Matt 8:3
the lepers are **c-d** Matt 11:5
not eat unless they **c** Mark 7:4
let us **c** ourselves 2 Cor 7:1
C...you sinners James 4:8
blood...**c-s** us 1 John 1:7

CLEAR *make free* **or** *plain*
c-s away many nations Deut 7:1
C the way for the LORD Is 40:3
c His threshing floor Matt 3:12
Christ has made **c** 2 Pet 1:14
river...**c** as crystal Rev 22:1

CLEFT *crevice*
in the **c** of the rock Judg 15:8
the **c-s** of the cliffs Is 2:21
who live in the **c-s** Obad 3

CLEOPAS
disciple of Christ Luke 24:18

CLEVER *smart*
c in their own sight Is 5:21
cleverness of the **c** 1 Cor 1:19

CLIFF *crag*
nest is set in the **c** Num 24:21
On the **c** he dwells Job 39:28
c-s are a refuge Ps 104:18

CLIMB *ascend*
I will **c** the palm tree Song 7:8
the one who **c-s** Jer 48:44
c-ed...a sycamore Luke 19:4
c-s up...other way John 10:1

CLING *cleave*
and **c** to Him Deut 13:4
c to the LORD Josh 23:8
My soul **c-s** to You Ps 63:8
c to Your testimonies Ps 119:31
Stop **c-ing** to Me John 20:17
c to what is good Rom 12:9

CLOAK *coat, mantle*
Give me the **c** Ruth 3:15
neither bread nor **c** Is 3:7
fringe of His **c** Matt 9:20
Wrap your **c** around Acts 12:8

CLOSE *shut, stop*
and the LORD **c-d** Gen 7:16
floodgates...were **c-d** Gen 8:2
earth **c-d** over them Num 16:33
c your door...pray Matt 6:6
have **c-d** their eyes Acts 28:27
every mouth...**c-d** Rom 3:19
c-s his heart 1 John 3:17

CLOTH *fabric*
spread over *it* a **c** Num 4:6
is wrapped in a **c** 1 Sam 21:9
with embroidered **c** Ezek 16:10
in the linen **c** Mark 15:46

CLOTHE *array, dress*
C me with skin Job 10:11
meadows are **c-d** with Ps 65:13
O Zion; **C** yourself Is 52:1
God so **c-s** the grass Matt 6:30
naked...you **c-d** Me Matt 25:36
are splendidly **c-d** Luke 7:25
c-d with power Luke 24:49
c...with humility 1 Pet 5:5
c-d in the white robes Rev 7:13

CLOTHES *garments*
c of her captivity Deut 21:13
your **c** have not worn Deut 29:5
and worn-out **c** on Josh 9:5
and changed his **c** 2 Sam 12:20
without wedding **c** Matt 22:12
Tearing his **c** Mark 14:63

CLOTHING *clothes, raiment*
reduce...her **c** Ex 21:10
c did not wear out Deut 8:4
purple are their **c** Jer 10:9
and the body more than **c** Matt 6:25
in sheep's **c** Matt 7:15
c as white as snow Matt 28:3
His **c** *became* white Luke 9:29
men...in dazzling **c** Luke 24:4
sister is without **c** James 2:15

CLOUD *mist*
set My bow in the **c** Gen 9:13
in a pillar of **c** Ex 13:21
c where God *was* Ex 20:21
c covered...mountain Ex 24:15
c for a covering Ps 105:39
voice came out...**c** Mark 9:7
Son...coming in **c-s** Mark 13:26
in a **c** with power Luke 21:27
and a **c** received Him Acts 1:9

CLUB *weapon*
went...with a **c** 2 Sam 23:21
C-s are...as stubble Job 41:29
Like a **c** and a Prov 25:18
with swords and **c-s** Matt 26:47

CLUSTER *collection*
c-s produced ripe Gen 40:10
c-s of raisins 1 Sam 25:18
breasts are...**c-s** Song 7:7
gather the **c-s** Rev 14:18

COAL *charcoal*
breath kindles **c-s** Job 41:21
man walk on hot **c-s** Prov 6:28
burning **c** in his hand Is 6:6
heap burning **c-s** Rom 12:20

COAST
c of the Great Sea Josh 9:1
along the **c** of Asia Acts 27:2

COASTLAND
inhabitants of this **c** Is 20:6
to the **c-s** of Kittim Jer 2:10
c-s shake at the Ezek 26:15
c-s of the nations Zeph 2:11

COAT *cloak*
opening...**c** of mail Ex 28:32
with his **c** torn 2 Sam 15:32
have your **c** also Matt 5:40
or even two **c-s** Matt 10:10
spread their **c-s** Mark 11:8

COBRA *snake*
deadly poison of **c-s** Deut 32:33
To the venom of **c-s** Job 20:14
tread upon the...**c** Ps 91:13

COFFIN *bier*
in a **c** in Egypt Gen 50:26
and touched the **c** Luke 7:14

COHORT *military unit*
the whole *Roman* **c** Matt 27:27
called the Italian **c** Acts 10:1
of the Augustan **c** Acts 27:1

COIN *money*
Show Me the **c** Matt 22:19
woman...loses one **c** Luke 15:8
He poured out...**c-s** John 2:15

COLD *cool*
covering against the **c** Job 24:7
Like the **c** of snow Prov 25:13
cup of **c** water Matt 10:42
love will grow **c** Matt 24:12
neither **c** nor hot Rev 3:15

COLLAPSE *fall*
grass **c-s** into the flame Is 5:24
pathways will **c** Ezek 38:20
ancient hills **c-d** Hab 3:6

COLLEAGUES *co-workers*
the rest of his **c** Ezra 4:7
and your **c** Ezra 6:6

COLLECT *exact, take*
c-ed his strength Gen 48:2
cistern **c-ing** water Lev 11:36
c captives like sand Hab 1:9
C no more than Luke 3:13
c-ed a tenth from Heb 7:6

COLLECTION *acquisition*
let your **c** *of idols* Is 57:13
no **c-s** be made 1 Cor 16:2

COLOSSAE
city in Asia Minor Col 1:2

COLT *foal*
camels and their **c-s** Gen 32:15
Even on a **c** Zech 9:9
and a **c** with her Matt 21:2
on a donkey's **c** John 12:15

COLUMN *pillar, text*
in a **c** of smoke Judg 20:40
and marble **c-s** Esth 1:6
read three...**c-s** Jer 36:23

COME
C, let us build Gen 11:4
C, let us worship Ps 95:6
All **came** from...dust Eccl 3:20
your king is **c-ing** Zech 9:9
Your kingdom **c** Matt 6:10
C to Me, all who Matt 11:28
children to **c** to Me Mark 10:14
not **c**...temptation Mark 14:38
Son of Man **c-ing** Luke 21:27
Father...hour has **c** John 17:1
His judgment has **c** Rev 14:7
I am **c-ing** quickly Rev 22:20

COMFORT (n) *consolation*
mourning without **c** Job 30:28
c in my affliction Ps 119:50
he will give you **c** Prov 29:17
c of the Holy Spirit Acts 9:31
and God of all **c** 2 Cor 1:3
your **c** and salvation 2 Cor 1:6

COMFORT (v) *console, cheer*
relatives came to **c** 1 Chr 7:22
Your rod...they **c** me Ps 23:4
I, am He who **c-s** you Is 51:12
To **c** all who mourn Is 61:2
he is being **c-ed** Luke 16:25
c one another 1 Thess 4:18

COMFORTER *consoler*
Sorry **c-s** are you all Job 16:2
c-s, but I found none Ps 69:20
She has no **c** Lam 1:9
Where will I seek **c-s** Nah 3:7

COMING (n) *arrival*
Joseph's **c** at noon Gen 43:25
the day of His **c** Mal 3:2
be the sign of Your **c** Matt 24:3
c of the Son of Man Matt 24:37
Christ's at His **c** 1 Cor 15:23
c of the Lord is James 5:8
the promise of His **c** 2 Pet 3:4

COMMAND (n) *order*
the **c** of the LORD Lev 24:12
disobeyed the **c** 1 Kin 13:21
to the king's **c** 2 Chr 35:10
no **c** of the Lord 1 Cor 7:25
could not bear the **c** Heb 12:20

COMMAND (v) *declare, order*
I **c-ed** you not to eat Gen 3:11
may **c** his children Gen 18:19
speak all that I **c** you Ex 7:2
bring all that I **c** Deut 12:11
the angel...**c-ed** Matt 1:24
c that these stones Matt 4:3
c-s even the winds Luke 8:25
c-ing the jailer Acts 16:23

COMMANDER *captain, general*
the **c-s** of Israel Judg 5:9
c of Saul's army 2 Sam 2:8
his chariot **c-s** 1 Kin 9:22
and Joab was the **c** 1 Chr 27:34
c for the peoples Is 55:4
the **C** of the host Dan 8:11
and the flesh of **c-s** Rev 19:18

COMMANDMENT *instruction*
and keep My **c-s** Ex 20:6
the Ten **C-s** Ex 34:28
and keep His **c-s** Josh 22:5
c of the LORD is pure Ps 19:8
the **c** of your father Prov 6:20
which is the great **c** Matt 22:36
A new **c** I give John 13:34
will keep My **c-s** John 14:15
I have kept...**c-s** John 15:10
not writing a new **c** 1 John 2:7
keep the **c-s** of God Rev 14:12

COMMEND *praise, present*
So I **c-ed** pleasure Eccl 8:15
I **c** you to God Acts 20:32
food will not **c** us 1 Cor 8:8
to **c** ourselves again 2 Cor 3:1

COMMISSION *appoint*
c him in their sight Num 27:19
He **c-ed** Joshua Deut 31:23
king has **c-ed** me 1 Sam 21:2
c it against the people Is 10:6

COMMISSIONERS *supervisors*
and over them three **c** Dan 6:2
Then the **c** and satraps Dan 6:4

COMMIT *entrust, practice*
c-ted to Joseph's Gen 39:22
shall not **c** adultery Ex 20:14
have **c-ted** incest Lev 20:12
I **c** my spirit Ps 31:5
C your way to the LORD Ps 37:5
weary...**c-ting** iniquity Jer 9:5
Do not **c** adultery Luke 18:20
I **c** My spirit Luke 23:46
everyone who **c-s** sin John 8:34
who **c-ted** no sin 1 Pet 2:22

COMMON *ordinary, shared*
anyone of...**c** people Lev 4:27
place of the **c** people Jer 26:23
iron...with **c** clay Dan 2:41
had all things in **c** Acts 2:44
about our **c** salvation Jude 3

COMMONWEALTH *nation*
from the **c** of Israel Eph 2:12

COMMOTION *disturbance*
the noise of this **c** 1 Sam 4:14
great **c** out of the Jer 10:22
Why make a **c** and Mark 5:39

COMPANION *comrade, friend*
are you striking your **c** Ex 2:13
brought thirty **c-s** Judg 14:11
And a **c** of ostriches Job 30:29
c of fools will suffer Prov 13:20
your **c** and your wife Mal 2:14
Paul and his **c-s** Acts 13:13

COMPANY *assembly, group*
into three **c-ies** Judg 9:43
c of the godless Job 15:34
c will stone them Ezek 23:47
Bad **c** corrupts 1 Cor 15:33

COMPARE *contrast, like*
none to **c** with You Ps 40:5
to what shall I **c** Matt 11:16
c the kingdom of Luke 13:20
be **c-d** with the glory Rom 8:18

COMPASS
outlines it with a **c** Is 44:13
four points of the **c** Dan 11:4

COMPASSION *concern, love*
God...grant you **c** Gen 43:14
whom I will show **c** Ex 33:19
in Your great **c** Neh 9:19
have **c** on the poor Ps 72:13
have **c** on Zion Ps 102:13
His **c-s** never fail Lam 3:22
He felt **c** for them Matt 9:36
his father...felt **c** Luke 15:20
put on a heart of **c** Col 3:12
Lord is full of **c** James 5:11

COMPASSIONATE *loving*
your God is a **c** God Deut 4:31
c, Slow to anger Neh 9:17
He is gracious and **c** Joel 2:13
a gracious and **c** God Jon 4:2

COMPEL *force, press*
Egyptians **c-led** the Ex 1:13
c *them* to come in Luke 14:23
c...to be circumcised Gal 6:12

COMPETE *strive*
can you **c** with horses Jer 12:5
everyone who **c-s** 1 Cor 9:25
c-s as an athlete 2 Tim 2:5

COMPLAIN *murmur*
c-ed to Abimelech Gen 21:25
c in the bitterness Job 7:11
I will **c** and murmur Ps 55:17
Do not **c**, brethren James 5:9

COMPLAINT *grumbling*
c-s of...Israel Num 14:27
couch will ease my **c** Job 7:13
today my **c** is rebellion Job 23:2
hospitable...without **c** 1 Pet 4:9

COMPLETE (adj) *full, total*
a sabbath of **c** rest Ex 35:2
be seven **c** sabbaths Lev 23:15
not...a **c** destruction Jer 5:10
you have been made **c** Col 2:10
be perfect and **c** James 1:4
joy may be made **c** 1 John 1:4

COMPLETE (v) *finish, fulfill*
God **c-d** His work Gen 2:2
C the week of this Gen 29:27
C your work quota Ex 5:13
your days are **c** 2 Sam 7:12
house...was **c-d** 2 Chr 8:16
thousand years are **c-d** Rev 20:7

COMPOSE *write*
c words against you Job 16:4
have **c-d** songs for Amos 6:5
The first account I **c-d** Acts 1:1

COMPOSE *make calm*
c-d and quieted my Ps 131:2
I **c-d** *my soul* Is 38:13

COMPREHEND *understand*
which we cannot **c** Job 37:5
speech...no one **c-s** Is 33:19
and they did not **c** Luke 18:34
darkness did not **c** John 1:5

COMPULSION *coercion*
under **c**...let them go Ex 6:1
in effect, by **c** Philem 14
not under **c**, but 1 Pet 5:2

CONCEAL *cover, hide*
man **c-s** knowledge Prov 12:23
They do not *even* **c** *it* Is 3:9
Do not **c** *it but* Jer 50:2
was **c-ed** from them Luke 9:45

CONCEIT *pride*
selfishness or empty **c** Phil 2:3
he is **c-ed** 1 Tim 6:4
c-ed, lovers of 2 Tim 3:4

CONCEIVE *become pregnant*
Sarah **c-d** and bore a Gen 21:2
c-d all this people Num 11:12
sin my mother **c-d** me Ps 51:5
she **c-d** and gave birth Is 8:3
when lust has **c-d** James 1:15

CONCERN *have care*
master does not **c** Gen 39:8
the LORD was **c-ed** Ex 4:31
You are **c-ed** about Job 7:17
c-ed about the poor John 12:6
is married is **c-ed** 1 Cor 7:33
not **c-ed** about oxen 1 Cor 9:9

CONCUBINE *secondary wife*
Ephraim...took a **c** Judg 19:1
Now Saul had a **c** 2 Sam 3:7
king left ten **c-s** 2 Sam 15:16
three hundred **c-s** 1 Kin 11:3
in charge of the **c-s** Esth 2:14

CONDEMN *discredit, judge*
c-ing the wicked 1 Kin 8:32
my mouth will **c** me Job 9:20
he who **c-s** Me Is 50:9
will **c** Him to death Mark 10:33
do not **c**, and you Luke 6:37
you **c** yourself Rom 2:1
he stood **c-ed** Gal 2:11
our heart **c-s** us 1 John 3:20

CONDEMNATION *judgment*
receive greater **c** Mark 12:40
same sentence of **c** Luke 23:40
Their **c** is just Rom 3:8
no **c**...in Christ Rom 8:1
c upon themselves Rom 13:2
c...by the devil 1 Tim 3:6

CONDITION *state, stipulation*
with you on this **c** 1 Sam 11:2
c-s were good in 2 Chr 12:12
c in which...called 1 Cor 7:20
or adds **c-s** to it Gal 3:15

CONDUCT (n) *behavior*
queen's **c**...known Esth 1:17
turn...*from his* **c** Job 33:17
who are upright in **c** Ps 37:14
sensual **c** of...men 2 Pet 2:7
holy **c** and godliness 2 Pet 3:11

CONDUCT (v) *behave*
c-s himself arrogantly Job 15:25
c...same spirit 2 Cor 12:18
C...with wisdom Col 4:5
c yourselves in fear 1 Pet 1:17

CONDUIT *channel*
c of the upper pool 2 Kin 18:17
at the end of the **c** Is 7:3

CONFESS *acknowledge*
that he shall **c** Lev 5:5
c-ing the sins of Neh 1:6
c my transgressions Ps 32:5
c-es Me before men Matt 10:32
c-ing their sins Mark 1:5
c with your mouth Rom 10:9
If we **c** our sins 1 John 1:9
I will **c** his name Rev 3:5

CONFESSION *admission*
praying and making **c** Ezra 10:1
your **c** of the gospel 2 Cor 9:13
testified the good **c** 1 Tim 6:13
the **c** of our hope Heb 10:23

CONFIDENCE *boldness, trust*
What is this **c** 2 Kin 18:19
they lost their **c** Neh 6:16
LORD will be your **c** Prov 3:26
proud **c** is this 2 Cor 1:12
c in me may abound Phil 1:26
no **c** in the flesh Phil 3:3

CONFINE *imprison, limit*
who were **c-d** in jail Gen 40:5
he does not **c** it Ex 21:29
be **c-d** in prison Is 24:22
c-d in the court Jer 33:1

CONFINEMENT *imprisonment*
c in his master's Gen 40:7
he put me in **c** Gen 41:10

CONFIRM *establish, strengthen*
LORD **c** His word 1 Sam 1:23
c-ed Your inheritance Ps 68:9
c the work of our Ps 90:17
C-ing the word of His Is 44:26
c-ed...by the signs Mark 16:20
who will also **c** you 1 Cor 1:8

CONFIRMATION *verification*
and **c** of the gospel Phil 1:7
an oath *given* as **c** Heb 6:16

CONFLICT *contention*
one of great **c** Dan 10:1
in **c** with the LORD Jer 50:24
experiencing...**c** Phil 1:30
source of...**c-s** James 4:1

CONFORMED *being like*
c...image of His Son Rom 8:29
not be **c** to...world Rom 12:2
being **c** to His death Phil 3:10

CONFOUND *confuse*
LORD **c-ed** them Josh 10:10
c their strategy Is 19:3
c-ing the Jews Acts 9:22

CONFRONT *challenge, face*
snares of death **c-ed** 2 Sam 22:6
Days of affliction **c** Job 30:27
Arise, O LORD, **c** him Ps 17:13
the elders **c-ed** *Him* Luke 20:1

CONFUSE *perplex*
c their language Gen 11:7
Send...and **c** them Ps 144:6
They are **c-d** by wine Is 28:7

CONFUSION *disorder*
into great **c** Deut 7:23
Jerusalem was in **c** Acts 21:31
not *a God* of **c** 1 Cor 14:33

CONGREGATION *assembly*
all the **c** of Israel Ex 12:3
c shall stone him Num 15:35
strife of the **c** Num 27:14
Bless God in the **c-s** Ps 68:26

c of the godly ones Ps 149:1
the **c** of the disciples Acts 6:2
In the midst of the **c** Heb 2:12

CONJURER *magician*
magician, **c** or Dan 2:10
wise men *and* the **c-s** Dan 5:15

CONQUER *be victorious*
c-ed all the country Gen 14:7
but could not **c** it Is 7:1
c through Him Rom 8:37
out **c-ing**, and to **c** Rev 6:2

CONSCIENCE *moral obligation*
David's **c** bothered 1 Sam 24:5
always a blameless **c** Acts 24:16
also for **c'** sake Rom 13:5
their **c** being weak is 1 Cor 8:7
faith with a clear **c** 1 Tim 3:9
seared in their own **c** 1 Tim 4:2
keep a good **c** 1 Pet 3:16

CONSECRATE (v) *sanctify*
sons of Israel **c** Ex 28:38
garments shall be **c-d** Ex 29:21
c it and all its Ex 40:9
C yourselves Lev 11:44
c the fiftieth year Lev 25:10
c-s his house as holy Lev 27:14
he shall **c** his head Num 6:11
C yourselves Josh 3:5
have **c-d** this house 1 Kin 9:3

CONSECRATED (adj) *sanctified*
touch any **c** thing Lev 12:4
c people...LORD Deut 26:19
there is **c** bread 1 Sam 21:4
c ones were purer Lam 4:7
ate the **c** bread Matt 12:4

CONSENT *agree*
Do not listen or **c** 1 Kin 20:8
entice you, Do not **c** Prov 1:10
If you **c** and obey Is 1:19
c-s to live with him 1 Cor 7:12

CONSIDER *observe, think*
were **c-ed** unclean Neh 7:64
C my groaning Ps 5:1
he who **c-s** the helpless Ps 41:1
We are **c-ed** as sheep Ps 44:22
day of adversity **c** Eccl 7:14
c the work of His hands Is 5:12
C the ravens, for Luke 12:24
c your calling 1 Cor 1:26
He **c-ed** me faithful 1 Tim 1:12
c how to stimulate Heb 10:24
c-ed...God is able Heb 11:19

CONSIST *composed of*
reverence for Me **c-s** Is 29:13
life **c** of his Luke 12:15
does not **c** in words 1 Cor 4:20
c-ing of decrees Col 2:14

CONSOLATION *comfort*
c-s of God too small Job 15:11
Your **c-s** delight my Ps 94:19
is any **c** of love Phil 2:1

CONSOLE *soothe*
Esau is **c-ing** himself Gen 27:42
servants to **c** him 2 Sam 10:2
c-d...comforted Job 42:11
c them concerning John 11:19

CONSPIRACY *plot, scheme*
the **c** was strong 2 Sam 15:12
found **c** in Hoshea 2 Kin 17:4
from the **c-ies** of man Ps 31:20

CONSPIRE *plot against*
have **c-d** against me 1 Sam 22:8
c-d against my 2 Kin 10:9
c together against Ps 83:3
Amos...**c-d** against Amos 7:10

CONSTELLATION *stars*
a **c** in its season Job 38:32
c-s Will not flash Is 13:10

CONSTRUCT *build*
c a sanctuary for Me Ex 25:8
c siegeworks Deut 20:20

CONSTRUCTION *structure*
c of the sanctuary Ex 36:3
it has been under **c** Ezra 5:16
the **c** of the ark 1 Pet 3:20

CONSULT *confer*
c-ed with the elders 1 Kin 12:6
C the mediums Is 8:19
Without **c-ing** Me Is 30:2
people **c** their wooden Hos 4:12
not...**c** with flesh Gal 1:16

CONSUME *destroy, devour*
c-d...purchase price Gen 31:15
the bush was not **c-d** Ex 3:2
c-d the burnt offering Lev 9:24
great fire will **c** us Deut 5:25
c the cedars Judg 9:15
You **c** as a moth Ps 39:11
c-d by Your anger Ps 90:7
c-s his own flesh Eccl 4:5
fire **c-ing** the stubble Joel 2:5
Zeal...will **c** John 2:17
c your flesh like fire James 5:3

CONSUMING (adj) *destroying*
glory...like a **c** fire Ex 24:17
the flame of a **c** fire Is 29:6
our God is a **c** fire Heb 12:29

CONTAIN *hold*
cannot **c** You 1 Kin 8:27
c the burnt offering 2 Chr 7:7
c-ing twenty...gallons John 2:6
not **c** the books John 21:25
is **c-ed** in Scripture 1 Pet 2:6

CONTEMPT *scorn*
He pours **c** on nobles Job 12:21
With pride and **c** Ps 31:18
treating Him with **c** Luke 23:11
your brother with **c** Rom 14:10

CONTEND *strive*
c with him in battle Deut 2:24
c-ed...vigorously Judg 8:1
c with the Almighty Job 40:2
not **c**...without cause Prov 3:30
Who will **c** with me Is 50:8
I will not **c** forever Is 57:16
he **c-ed** with God Hos 12:3
c...for the faith Jude 3

CONTENT *satisfied*
c with your wages Luke 3:14
c with weaknesses 2 Cor 12:10
have learned to be **c** Phil 4:11
c with what you have Heb 13:5

CONTENTION *strife*
object of **c** to our Ps 80:6
the **c-s** of a wife Prov 19:13
Strife exists and **c** Hab 1:3

CONTENTIOUS *quarrelsome*
a **c**...woman Prov 21:19
with a **c** woman Prov 25:24
inclined to be **c** 1 Cor 11:16

CONTINUE *persevere, persist*
My covenant may **c** Mal 2:4
c in My word John 8:31
c in the grace of Acts 13:43
Are we to **c** in sin Rom 6:1
you **c** in the faith Col 1:23
love of the brethren **c** Heb 13:1

CONTRARY *against*
c to the command Num 24:13

for the wind was **c** Matt 14:24
grafted **c** to nature Rom 11:24
c to the teaching Rom 16:17
a gospel **c** to what Gal 1:8
c to sound teaching 1 Tim 1:10

CONTRIBUTE *give*
Josiah **c-d** to the 2 Chr 35:7
c yearly one third Neh 10:32
c-ing to their support Luke 8:3
c-ing to...the saints Rom 12:13

CONTRIBUTION *gift, offering*
to raise a **c** for Me Ex 25:2
as a **c** to the LORD Lev 7:14
c-s, the first fruits Neh 12:44
a **c** for the poor Rom 15:26
liberality of your **c** 2 Cor 9:13

CONTRITE *sorrowful*
broken and a **c** heart Ps 51:17
humble and **c** of spirit Is 66:2

CONTROL (n) *order, rule*
people were out of **c** Ex 32:25
was it not under...**c** Acts 5:4
children under **c** 1 Tim 3:4

CONTROL (v) *rule, subdue*
he **c-led** himself and Gen 43:31
Joseph could not **c** Gen 45:1
Haman **c-led** himself Esth 5:10

CONTROVERSY *dispute*
wise man has a **c** Prov 29:9
LORD has a **c** with the Jer 25:31
avoid foolish **c-ies** Titus 3:9

CONVERSE *discuss*
Stoic...were **c-ing** Acts 17:18
and **c** with him Acts 24:26

CONVERSION *change*
c of the Gentiles Acts 15:3

CONVERTED *changed*
sinners will be **c** Ps 51:13
unless you are **c** Matt 18:3
perceive...and be **c** John 12:40

CONVICT *condemn, judge*
one of you **c-s** Me John 8:46
c...concerning sin John 16:8
he is **c-ed** by all 1 Cor 14:24
to **c** all the ungodly Jude 15

CONVINCED *persuaded*
c that John was a Luke 20:6
c that neither death Rom 8:38
c in the Lord Jesus Rom 14:14
c of better things Heb 6:9

CONVOCATION *conclave*
sabbath...a holy **c** Lev 23:3
shall have a holy **c** Num 29:7

CONVULSION *paroxysm*
threw him into a **c** Mark 9:20
a **c** with foaming Luke 9:39

COOK *prepare food*
Jacob had **c-ed** stew Gen 25:29
you shall **c** and eat Deut 16:7

COOL *cold*
in the **c** of the day Gen 3:8
in his **c** roof chamber Judg 3:20
who has a **c** spirit Prov 17:27

COPPER *metal*
you can dig **c** Deut 8:9
not acquire...**c** Matt 10:9
widow...**c** coins Luke 21:2

COPY *facsimile*
c of this law on a Deut 17:18
c of...law of Moses Josh 8:32
c of the edict Esth 8:13

mere **c** of the true Heb 9:24

CORBAN *offering*
C (that is...) Mark 7:11

CORD *band, rope*
c-s of Sheol 2 Sam 22:6
c-s of affliction Job 36:8
c-s of death Ps 18:4
silver **c** is broken Eccl 12:6
the **c-s** of falsehood Is 5:18
a scourge of **c-s** John 2:15

CORINTH
city in Greece Acts 18:1
NT church site 1 Cor 1:1,2

CORNELIUS
centurion, believer Acts 10:1ff

CORNER *angle, intersection*
the chief **c** *stone* Ps 118:22
lurks by every **c** Prov 7:12
on the street **c-s** Matt 6:5
the chief **c** *stone* Mark 12:10
four **c-s** of the earth Rev 7:1

CORNER GATE *see* **GATES OF JERUSALEM**

CORNERSTONE *support stone*
who laid its **c** Job 38:6
the **c** of her tribes Is 19:13
costly **c** *for* the Is 28:16
From them...the **c** Zech 10:4

CORPSE *dead body*
made unclean by a **c** Lev 22:4
Their **c-s** will rise Is 26:19
a mass of **c-s** Nah 3:3
boy...like a **c** Mark 9:26

CORRECT *reprove*
c him with the rod 2 Sam 7:14
He who **c-s** a scoffer Prov 9:7
C your son, and he Prov 29:17
C me, O LORD Jer 10:24
gentleness **c-ing** 2 Tim 2:25

CORRECTION *improvement*
Whether for **c**, or Job 37:13
refused to take **c** Jer 5:3
for reproof, for **c** 2 Tim 3:16

CORRUPT (adj) *evil, rotten*
the earth was **c** Gen 6:11
detestable and **c** Job 15:16
They are **c** Ps 14:1
all of them, are **c** Jer 6:28

CORRUPT (v) *make evil*
a bribe **c-s** the heart Eccl 7:7
c-ed your wisdom Ezek 28:17
have **c-ed** the covenant Mal 2:8
Bad company **c-s** 1 Cor 15:33
harlot who was **c-ing** Rev 19:2

CORRUPTION *decay, evil*
their **c** is in them Lev 22:25
no negligence or **c** Dan 6:4
from the flesh reap **c** Gal 6:8
c that is in the world 2 Pet 1:4
slaves of **c** 2 Pet 2:19

COSMETICS *beautifying aids*
provided her with...**c** Esth 2:9
the **c** for women Esth 2:12

COST *expense, price*
c of their lives Num 16:38
let the **c** be paid Ezra 6:4
calculate the **c** Luke 14:28
water...without **c** Rev 21:6

COSTLY *expensive*
redemption...is **c** Ps 49:8
gold, silver, **c** stones Dan 11:38
vial of...**c** perfume Mark 14:3
pearls or **c** garments 1 Tim 2:9

COUCH *bed, pallet*
he went up to my **c** Gen 49:4
falling on the **c** Esth 7:8
dissolve my **c** with my Ps 6:6
sprawl on their **c-es** Amos 6:4

COUNCIL *assembly*
not enter into their **c** Gen 49:6
the **c** of the holy ones Ps 89:7
the **c** of My people Ezek 13:9
to their **c** *chamber* Luke 22:66
conferred with his **c** Acts 25:12

COUNCIL
Sanhedrin Matt 26:59
Jewish governing body Mark 15:1,43; Luke 23:50

COUNSEL (n) *advice, opinion*
I will give you **c** Ex 18:19
Take **c** and speak up Judg 19:30
To Him belong **c** Job 12:13
not walk in the **c** Ps 1:1
Listen to **c** and Prov 19:20
the **c** of His will Eph 1:11

COUNSEL (v) *advise*
he has **c-ed** rebellion Deut 13:5
I **c** that all Israel 2 Sam 17:11
How do you **c** *me* 1 Kin 12:6
c you with My eye Ps 32:8

COUNSELOR *adviser*
the king and his **c-s** Ezra 7:15
c-s walk barefoot Job 12:17
abundance of **c-s** Prov 11:14
Wonderful **C**, Mighty Is 9:6
who became His **c** Rom 11:34

COUNT *consider, number*
c the stars, if you Gen 15:5
could not be **c-ed** 1 Kin 8:5
If I should **c** them Ps 139:18
my prayer be **c-ed** Ps 141:2
was **c-ed** among us Acts 1:17
I **c** all...loss Phil 3:8
as some **c** slowness 2 Pet 3:9

COUNTENANCE *appearance*
why has your **c** fallen Gen 4:6
LORD lift up His **c** Num 6:26
light of Your **c** Ps 4:6
an angry **c** Prov 25:23

COUNTRY *land, region*
Go forth from your **c** Gen 12:1
up into the hill **c** Deut 1:24
go out into the **c** Song 7:11
them from the **c-ies** Ezek 34:13
they are seeking a **c** Heb 11:14

COUNTRYMAN
not hate...fellow **c** Lev 19:17
among your **c-men** Deut 17:15
a man and his **c** Deut 25:11
my fellow **c-men** and Rom 11:14

COURAGE *heart, valor*
he lost **c** 2 Sam 4:1
and do not lose **c** 2 Chr 15:7
let your heart take **c** Ps 27:14
with justice and **c** Mic 3:8
Take **c**, son Matt 9:2
Take **c**, it is I Matt 14:27
c; I have overcome John 16:33
we are of good **c** 2 Cor 5:8

COURAGEOUS *brave*
Be strong and **c** Deut 31:6
be strong and very **c** Josh 1:7
I propose to be **c** 2 Cor 10:2

COURIER *messenger*
c-s went throughout 2 Chr 30:6
Letters...by **c-s** Esth 3:13
One **c** runs to meet Jer 51:31

COURSE *area, extent, way*
strong man to run his **c** Ps 19:5
on its circular **c-s** Eccl 1:6
I have finished the **c** 2 Tim 4:7
the **c** of *our* life James 3:6

COURT *area, hall, tribunal*
c of the tabernacle Ex 27:9
c of the harem Esth 2:11
a day in Your **c-s** Ps 84:10
c of the LORD's house Jer 26:2
c of the guardhouse Jer 39:15
if you have law **c-s** 1 Cor 6:4
drag you into **c** James 2:6

COURTYARD *compound*
a well in his **c** 2 Sam 17:18
c of the high priest Matt 26:58
Peter...in the **c** Mark 14:66

COVENANT *agreement*
establish My **c** Gen 6:18
for a sign of a **c** Gen 9:13
for an everlasting **c** Gen 17:13
ark of the **c** Num 10:33
My **c** of peace Num 25:12
book of the **c** 2 Kin 23:2
Remember His **c** 1 Chr 16:15
who keep His **c** Ps 103:18
I will make a new **c** Jer 31:31
forsake the holy **c** Dan 11:30
a **c** with Assyria Hos 12:1
the blood of *My* **c** Zech 9:11
cup...is the new **c** Luke 22:20
c which God made Acts 3:25
this is My **c** with Rom 11:27
servants of a new **c** 2 Cor 3:6
strangers to the **c-s** Eph 2:12
guarantee...better **c** Heb 7:22
blood of the...**c** Heb 13:20
ark of His **c** Rev 11:19

COVER (n)
c of porpoise skin Num 4:14
the **c** of a couch Amos 3:12

COVER (v) *hide, protest*
and **c** up his blood Gen 37:26
basket and **c-ed** it Ex 2:3
Whose sin is **c-ed** Ps 32:1
He will **c** you with Ps 91:4
love **c-s** all Prov 10:12
not **c** My face Is 50:6
c-ed...with sackcloth Jon 3:6
to the hills, **C** us Luke 23:30
c a multitude of sins James 5:20
love **c-s** a multitude 1 Pet 4:8

COVERING *canopy*
made...loin **c-s** Gen 3:7
spread a cloud for a **c** Ps 105:39
she makes **c-s** for Prov 31:22
sackcloth their **c** Is 50:3
given to her for a **c** 1 Cor 11:15
freedom as a **c** 1 Pet 2:16

COVET *crave, desire*
not **c** your neighbor's Ex 20:17
You shall not **c** Deut 5:21
I **c-ed** them and took Josh 7:21
They **c** fields and then Mic 2:2
c-ed no one's silver Acts 20:33

COVETOUS *desirous*
the **c** and swindlers 1 Cor 5:10
c, nor drunkards 1 Cor 6:10

COW *animal*
came up seven **c-s** Gen 41:2
c calves and does not Job 21:10
c and the bear will Is 11:7
you **c-s** of Bashan Amos 4:1

CRAFTINESS *shrewdness*
the wise in their **c** 1 Cor 3:19
not walking in **c** 2 Cor 4:2
by **c** in deceitful Eph 4:14

CRAFTSMAN *artisan*
the hands of the **c** Deut 27:15
all the **c-men** and 2 Kin 24:14
idol, a **c** casts it Is 40:19
business to...**c-men** Acts 19:24
c of any craft will Rev 18:22

CRAG *protrusion, rock*
sharp **c** on the one 1 Sam 14:4
Upon the rocky **c** Job 39:28
clefts of the **c-s** Is 57:5

CRAVE *covet, desire*
day long he is **c-ing** Prov 21:26
fig *which* I **c** Mic 7:1
generation **c-s** for Matt 12:39
would not **c** evil 1 Cor 10:6

CRAWLING *creeping*
venom of **c** things Deut 32:24
beasts and the **c** Acts 11:6
and **c** creatures Rom 1:23

CREATE *form, make*
c-d the heavens Gen 1:1
c-d man in His Gen 1:27
C in me a clean Ps 51:10
C-ing the praise of Is 57:19
c new heavens Is 65:17
one God **c-d** us Mal 2:10
c-d...for good works Eph 2:10
c-d in righteousness Eph 4:24
You **c-d** all Rev 4:11

CREATION
beginning of **c** Mark 10:6
preach...to all **c** Mark 16:15
whole **c** groans Rom 8:22
beginning of **c** 2 Pet 3:4

CREATOR *Maker*
Remember...your **C** Eccl 12:1
The **C** of Israel Is 43:15
rather than the **C** Rom 1:25
to a faithful **C** 1 Pet 4:19

CREATURE *created being*
every living **c** that Gen 1:21
winged **c** will make Eccl 10:20
and crawling **c-s** Rom 1:23
in Christ...new **c** 2 Cor 5:17
as **c-s** of instinct 2 Pet 2:12

CREDITOR *lender*
not to act as a **c** to Ex 22:25
every **c** shall release Deut 15:2
Let the **c** seize all Ps 109:11
My **c-s** did I sell you Is 50:1

CREEP *crawl*
everything that **c-s** Gen 1:25
that **c** on the earth Ezek 38:20

CREEPING *crawling*
cattle and **c** things Gen 1:24
c things and fish 1 Kin 4:33
c locust has eaten Joel 1:4
c locust strips and Nah 3:16

CRETANS
inhabitants of Crete Acts 2:11; Titus 1:12

CRETE
Mediterranean island Acts 27:7,21; Titus 1:5
see also **CAPHTOR**

CRIME *vice*
be a lustful **c** Job 31:11
committed no **c** Dan 6:22
full of bloody **c-s** Ezek 7:23
not of such **c-s** Acts 25:18

CRIMINAL *lawbreaker*
crucified...the **c-s** Luke 23:33
imprisonment as a **c** 2 Tim 2:9

CRIMSON *deep red*
purple, **c** and violet 2 Chr 2:7
like **c**...be like wool Is 1:18

CRIPPLED *lame*
a son **c** in his feet 2 Sam 4:4
enter life **c** or lame Matt 18:8
bring...**c** and blind Luke 14:21

CRISPUS
Corinthian Christian Acts 18:8; 1 Cor 1:14

CROOKED *evil, twisted*
and **c** generation Deut 32:5
to their **c** ways Ps 125:5
What is **c** cannot be Eccl 1:15
make **c** the straight Acts 13:10
c and perverse Phil 2:15

CROP *yield of produce*
old things from the **c** Lev 25:22
c-s to the grasshopper Ps 78:46
c began to sprout Amos 7:1
share of the **c-s** 2 Tim 2:6

CROSS (n) *execution device*
take his **c** and Matt 10:38
down from the **c** Matt 27:40
to bear His **c** Mark 15:21
take up his **c** daily Luke 9:23
standing by the **c** John 19:25
hanging Him on a **c** Acts 5:30
c of Christ would 1 Cor 1:17
word of the **c** is 1 Cor 1:18
boast, except in the **c** Gal 6:14
even death on a **c** Phil 2:8
enemies of the **c** Phil 3:18
blood of His **c** Col 1:20
endured the **c** Heb 12:2

CROSS (v) *pass over*
you **c** the Jordan Deut 12:10
c-ed opposite Jericho Josh 3:16
kept **c-ing** the ford 2 Sam 19:18
Jesus had **c-ed** over Mark 5:21
c-ing over to Acts 21:2

CROUCH *bow, stoop*
sin is **c-ing** at the Gen 4:7
Beneath Him **c** the Job 9:13
Nothing...but to **c** Is 10:4

CROWD *multitude*
send the **c-s** away Matt 14:15
because of the **c** Mark 2:4
He summoned the **c** Mark 8:34
c of tax collectors Luke 5:29
Him...a large **c** Luke 23:27
they stirred up the **c** Acts 17:8

CROWN (n) *royal emblem* **or** *top*
on the **c** of the head Gen 49:26
the **c** of their king 2 Sam 12:30
he set the royal **c** Esth 2:17
wife is the **c** of Prov 12:4
gray head is a **c** Prov 16:31
c of the drunkards Is 28:3
a **c** of thorns Matt 27:29
receive the **c** of life James 1:12
c-s before the throne Rev 4:10
golden **c** on His head Rev 14:14

CROWN (v) *to place crown on*
c him with glory Ps 8:5
Who **c-s** you with Ps 103:4
head **c-s** you like Song 7:5
c-ed him with glory Heb 2:7

CRUCIFY *to execute on a cross*
scourge and **c** *Him* Matt 20:19
C Him Matt 27:22
Jesus...been **c-ied** Matt 28:5
c your King John 19:15
Paul was not **c-ied** 1 Cor 1:13
preach Christ **c-ied** 1 Cor 1:23
not have **c-ied** the 1 Cor 2:8
c-ied with Christ Gal 2:20

world...**c-ied** to me — Gal 6:14
their Lord was **c-ied** — Rev 11:8

CRUEL *fierce, harsh*
their...**c** bondage — Ex 6:9
c man does...harm — Prov 11:17
compassion...is **c** — Prov 12:10
c and have no mercy — Jer 6:23
people has become **c** — Lam 4:3

CRUMBS *morsels*
dogs feed on the **c** — Matt 15:27
on the children's **c** — Mark 7:28

CRUSH *demolish, destroy*
a foot may **c** them — Job 39:15
saves...**c-ed** in spirit — Ps 34:18
lying tongue...**c-es** — Prov 26:28
by **c-ing** My people — Is 3:15
c-ed for our iniquities — Is 53:5
LORD was pleased To **c** — Is 53:10
who **c** the needy — Amos 4:1
c Satan under...feet — Rom 16:20

CRY (n) *scream, sob*
great and bitter **c** — Gen 27:34
the **c** of triumph — Ex 32:18
c has come to Me — 1 Sam 9:16
Hear my **c,** O God — Ps 61:1
the **c** of Jerusalem — Jer 14:2
Jesus uttered a...**c** — Mark 15:37

CRY (v)
do not **c** for help — Job 36:13
c aloud in the night — Lam 2:19
His elect, who **c** — Luke 18:7
stones will **c** out — Luke 19:40
Jesus stood and **c-ied** — John 7:37

CRYSTAL *glass*
awesome gleam of **c** — Ezek 1:22
sea of glass, like **c** — Rev 4:6
water...clear as **c** — Rev 22:1

CUB *whelp, young*
robbed of her **c-s** — 2 Sam 17:8
She reared her **c-s** — Ezek 19:2
lioness, and lion's **c** — Nah 2:11

CUBIT *linear measure*
ark three hundred **c-s** — Gen 6:15
length was nine **c-s** — Deut 3:11
gallows fifty **c-s** high — Esth 5:14
the altar by **c-s** — Ezek 43:13

CUD *previously swallowed food*
chews the **c** — Lev 11:3
not chew **c,** it is — Lev 11:7
chews the **c** — Deut 14:6

CULT *religious ritual*
be a **c** prostitute — Deut 23:17
male **c** prostitutes — 1 Kin 14:24
male **c** prostitutes — 2 Kin 23:7

CULTIVATE *till*
no man to **c** the — Gen 2:5
Eden to **c** it — Gen 2:15
and **c** vineyards — Deut 28:39
servants shall **c** — 2 Sam 9:10
and **c** faithfulness — Ps 37:3

CUMMIN *plant for seasoning*
driven over **c** — Is 28:27
mint and dill and **c** — Matt 23:23

CUNNING *crafty*
he is very **c** — 1 Sam 23:22
advice of the **c** — Job 5:13
harlot and **c** of heart — Prov 7:10

CUP *container*
into Pharaoh's **c** — Gen 40:11
My **c** overflows — Ps 23:5
the **c** of salvation — Ps 116:13
a **c** of consolation — Jer 16:7
c of cold water — Matt 10:42

let this **c** pass — Matt 26:39
washing of **c-s** and — Mark 7:4
gives you a **c** of — Mark 9:41
c...new covenant — Luke 22:20
c of blessing — 1 Cor 10:16
eat...drink the **c** — 1 Cor 11:26
c full of abominations — Rev 17:4

CUPBEARER *royal official*
c spoke to Pharaoh — Gen 41:9
his **c-s**, and his — 1 Kin 10:5
c-s and their attire — 2 Chr 9:4
c to the king — Neh 1:11

CURDS *butter, cheese*
he took **c** and milk — Gen 18:8
she brought him **c** — Judg 5:25
with honey and **c** — Job 20:17

CURE *heal*
c him of his leprosy — 2 Kin 5:3
c you of your wound — Hos 5:13
they could not **c** him — Matt 17:16
that...time He **c-d** — Luke 7:21

CURSE (n) *condemning oath*
upon myself a **c** — Gen 27:12
c on Mount Ebal — Deut 11:29
c to My chosen ones — Is 65:15
they will become a **c** — Jer 44:12
will no longer be a **c** — Zech 14:11
become a **c** for us — Gal 3:13

CURSE (v) *verbally condemn*
who **c-s** you I will **c** — Gen 12:3
You shall not **c** God — Ex 22:28
not **c** a deaf man — Lev 19:14
c-d the...anointed — 2 Sam 19:21
c-d the day of his *birth* — Job 3:1
began to **c** and — Mark 14:71
bless and do not **c** — Rom 12:14
with it we **c** men — James 3:9

CURSED (adj) *under a curse*
C is the ground — Gen 3:17
C be Canaan — Gen 9:25
C is the man who — Deut 27:15
C...who trusts — Jer 17:5
C...who hangs — Gal 3:13

CURTAIN *covering, drape*
on the edge of the **c** — Ex 26:4
heaven like a *tent* **c** — Ps 104:2
c-s of your dwellings — Is 54:2
c-s of the land of — Hab 3:7

CUSH
1 *area of W Asia* — Gen 2:13
2 *patriarch* — Gen 10:6,8
3 *region S of Egypt* — 2 Kin 19:9; Is 20:3
4 *a Benjamite* — Ps 7:title

CUSTODY *prison, protection*
they put him in **c** — Num 15:34
into the **c** of Hegai — Esth 2:3
John...taken into **c** — Matt 4:12
holding Jesus in **c** — Luke 22:63

CUSTOM *manner* or *tax*
it became a **c** in — Judg 11:39
not pay tribute, **c** — Ezra 4:13
c, He entered the — Luke 4:16
burial **c** of the Jews — John 19:40
c-s...not lawful — Acts 16:21
c-s of our fathers — Acts 28:17
whom tax *is due;* **c** — Rom 13:7

CUT *destroy, divide*
did not **c** the birds — Gen 15:10
c off from the earth — Ex 9:15
c down their Asherim — Ex 34:13
LORD **c** off...lips — Ps 12:3
tongue will be **c** — Prov 10:31
C off your hair and — Jer 7:29
were **c-ting** branches — Matt 21:8
and **c** off his ear — Matt 26:51
were **c** to the quick — Acts 7:54

you...will be **c** off — Rom 11:22

CYMBAL *musical instrument*
castanets and **c-s** — 2 Sam 6:5
loud-sounding **c-s** — 1 Chr 15:16
with loud **c-s** — Ps 150:5
or a clanging **c** — 1 Cor 13:1

CYPRESS *tree*
cedar and **c** timber — 1 Kin 5:10
c and algum timber — 2 Chr 2:8
Our rafters, **c-es** — Song 1:17
Wail, O **c,** for the — Zech 11:2

CYPRUS
Mediterranean island — Is 23:1; Acts 11:19; 15:39; 21:16
see also **KITTIM**

CYRENE
NW African port — Mark 15:21; Luke 23:26; Acts 2:10; 11:20

CYRUS
king of Persia — 2 Chr 36:22; Is 45:1
decreed to rebuild Temple — Ezra 1:1; 5:13

D

DAGON
god of Philistines — Judg 16:23; 1 Sam 5:4; 1 Chr 10:10

DAMAGE (n) *destruction*
any **d** may be found — 2 Kin 12:5
the **d-s** of the house — 2 Kin 12:6
d and great loss — Acts 27:10
incurred this **d** and — Acts 27:21

DAMAGE (v) *destroy, hurt*
it will **d** the revenue — Ezra 4:13
and **d-ing** to kings — Ezra 4:15
enemy has **d-d** — Ps 74:3
So that no one...**d** it — Is 27:3

DAMASCUS
city of Aram (Syria) — Gen 14:15; 2 Kin 5:12; Acts 9:3,27; 26:20

DAN
1 *son of Jacob* — Gen 30:6; 49:16
2 *tribal area* — Josh 19:40; Judg 18:2
3 *city in N Palestine* — Josh 19:47

DANCE (n) *rhythmic movement*
timbrels...with **d-ing** — Ex 15:20
they sing in the **d-s** — 1 Sam 29:5
will rejoice in the **d** — Jer 31:13
music and **d-ing** — Luke 15:25

DANCE (v) *move rhythmically*
from those who **d-d** — Judg 21:23
David was **d-ing** — 2 Sam 6:14
and a time to **d** — Eccl 3:4
Herodias **d-d** before — Matt 14:6

DANGER *peril*
not only is there **d** — Acts 19:27
often in **d** of death — 2 Cor 11:23
d-s from...Gentiles — 2 Cor 11:26

DANIEL
1 *son of David and Abigail* — 1 Chr 3:1
2 *priest* — Ezra 8:2
3 *prophet* — Ezek 14:14; Dan 1:6
see also **BELTESHAZZAR**

DARE *presume, risk*
who **d-s** rouse him up — Gen 49:9
who would **d** to risk — Jer 30:21
d from that day — Matt 22:46
did not **d** pronounce — Jude 9

DARIUS
1 *Darius the Mede* — Dan 5:31
2 *Darius I* — Ezra 4:5; Hag 1:1
3 *Darius II* — Neh 12:22

DARK *dim, shadow*
not in **d** sayings Num 12:8
d places of the land Ps 74:20
live in a **d** land Is 9:2
it was still **d** John 20:1
shining in a **d** place 2 Pet 1:19

DARKEN *obscure*
the land was **d-ed** Ex 10:15
this that **d-s** counsel Job 38:2
the stars are **d-ed** Eccl 12:2
sun will be **d-ed** Mark 13:24
their eyes be **d-ed** Rom 11:10

DARKNESS *gloom, shadow*
blind...gropes in **d** Deut 28:29
are silenced in **d** 1 Sam 2:9
illumines my **d** 2 Sam 22:29
that stalks in **d** Ps 91:6
those who dwelt in **d** Ps 107:10
as light excels **d** Eccl 2:13
people who walk in **d** Is 9:2
light will rise in **d** Is 58:10
into the outer **d** Matt 22:13
those who sit in **d** Luke 1:79
men loved the **d** John 3:19
turn from **d** to light Acts 26:18
has light with **d** 2 Cor 6:14
unfruitful deeds of **d** Eph 5:11
in Him there is no **d** 1 John 1:5
brother is in the **d** 1 John 2:9

DARLING *love*
you are, my **d** Song 1:15
Arise, my **d** Song 2:13
my **d**, My dove Song 5:2

DATHAN
rebelled against Moses Num 16:12; Ps 106:17

DAUGHTER
d-s were born to them Gen 6:1
if a man sells his **d** Ex 21:7
inheritance to his **d** Num 27:8
Kings' **d-s** are among Ps 45:9
d-s of song Eccl 12:4
destruction of the **d** Is 22:4
the **d** of my people Jer 9:1
D rises up against Mic 7:6
mother against **d** Luke 12:53

DAUGHTER-IN-LAW
said to his **d** Tamar Gen 38:11
nakedness of your **d** Lev 18:15
said to Ruth her **d** Ruth 2:22
D against her Mic 7:6

DAVID
anointed 1 Sam 16:13
killed Goliath 1 Sam 17:50
fled from Saul 1 Sam 19:18
spared Saul 1 Sam 26:9
king of Judah and Israel 2 Sam 2:4; 5:3
covenant with God 2 Sam 7:8
death 1 Kin 2:10

DAWN (n) *daylight*
at the approach of **d** Judg 19:25
caused the **d** to know Job 38:12
rise before **d** and Ps 119:147
wings of the **d** Ps 139:9
As the **d** is spread Joel 2:2

DAWN (v) *become light*
the day began to **d** Judg 19:26
when morning **d-s** Ps 46:5
a Light **d-ed** Matt 4:16
d toward the first Matt 28:1
until the day **d-s** 2 Pet 1:19

DAY *light*
God called the light **d** Gen 1:5
come on a festive **d** 1 Sam 25:8
d...LORD has made Ps 118:24
what a **d** may bring Prov 27:1
d-s of your youth Eccl 12:1
a **d** of reckoning Is 2:12
d of the LORD is near Is 13:6
has despised the **d** Zech 4:10
the **d** of His coming Mal 3:2
Give us this **d** Matt 6:11
raise...the last **d** John 6:39
judge...the last **d** John 12:48
the **d** of salvation 2 Cor 6:2
perfect it until the **d** Phil 1:6
d of the Lord 1 Thess 5:2
d is like a thousand 2 Pet 3:8
tormented **d**...night Rev 20:10

DAY OF ATONEMENT
month is the **d** Lev 23:27
for it is a **d** Lev 23:28

DAZZLING *blinding, bright*
My beloved is **d** Song 5:10
Like **d** heat Is 18:4
near...in **d** clothing Luke 24:4

DEACONS *officer, server*
overseers and **d** Phil 1:1
D likewise *must be* 1 Tim 3:8
let them serve as **d** 1 Tim 3:10
D must be husbands 1 Tim 3:12
served well as **d** 1 Tim 3:13

DEAD *without life*
you are a **d** man Gen 20:3
near to a **d** person Num 6:6
dealt with the **d** Ruth 1:8
forgotten as a **d** man Ps 31:12
d do not praise Ps 115:17
better than a **d** lion Eccl 9:4
Your **d** will live Is 26:19
not weep for the **d** Jer 22:10
rising from the **d** Mark 9:10
d will hear the John 5:25
resurrection of the **d** Acts 23:6
d in your trespasses Eph 2:1
firstborn from the **d** Col 1:18
living and the **d** 2 Tim 4:1
repentance...**d** works Heb 6:1
to those who are **d** 1 Pet 4:6
I was **d**...I am alive Rev 1:18
Hades gave up the **d** Rev 20:13

DEAF *without hearing*
makes *him* mute or **d** Ex 4:11
not curse a **d** man Lev 19:14
Like a **d** cobra Ps 58:4
the **d** will hear Is 29:18
and *the* **d** hear Matt 11:5
the **d** to hear Mark 7:37
d and mute spirit Mark 9:25

DEAL *allot, barter, treat*
let us **d** wisely Ex 1:10
have you **d-t** with us Ex 14:11
nor **d** falsely Lev 19:11
d-t with mediums 2 Kin 21:6
who **d** treacherously Ps 25:3
has **d-t** bountifully Ps 116:7
who **d** faithfully Prov 12:22
Everyone **d-s** falsely Jer 6:13
when I have **d-t** Ezek 20:44
has **d-t** with me Luke 1:25

DEALINGS *actions, relations*
no **d** with anyone Judg 18:7
no **d** with Samaritans John 4:9
of the Lord's **d** James 5:11

DEAR *beloved*
Is Ephraim My **d** son Jer 31:20
my life...as **d** to Acts 20:24
had become very **d** 1 Thess 2:8

DEATH *cessation of life*
d of the upright Num 23:10
d encompassed me 2 Sam 22:5
d for his own sin 2 Chr 25:4
D rather than my pains Job 7:15
no mention of You in **d** Ps 6:5
cords of **d** encompassed Ps 18:4
the shadow of **d** Ps 23:4
escapes from **d** Ps 68:20
doomed to **d** Ps 102:20
d of His godly ones Ps 116:15
who hate me love **d** Prov 8:36
love is as strong as **d** Song 8:6
He will swallow up **d** Is 25:8
D cannot praise You Is 38:18
no pleasure in the **d** Ezek 18:32
d is better to me Jon 4:3
is to be put to **d** Matt 15:4
will not taste **d** Matt 16:28
to the point of **d** Mark 14:34
passed out of **d** John 5:24
he will never see **d** John 8:51
sickness is not to end in **d** John 11:4
the agony of **d** Acts 2:24
d by hanging Him Acts 10:39
d reigned from Adam Rom 5:14
wages of sin is **d** Rom 6:23
the law of sin and of **d** Rom 8:2
proclaim...Lord's **d** 1 Cor 11:26
d, where...victory 1 Cor 15:55
even **d** on a cross Phil 2:8
He might taste **d** Heb 2:9
it brings forth **d** James 1:15
passed out of **d** 1 John 3:14
Be faithful until **d** Rev 2:10
had the name **D** Rev 6:8
second **d**...no power Rev 20:6

DEBATE *dispute*
d-d...themselves Mark 1:27
dissension and **d** Acts 15:2
had been much **d** Acts 15:7

DEBORAH
1 *nurse of Rebekah* Gen 35:8
2 *prophetess, judge* Judg 4:4ff

DEBT *obligation*
and pay your **d** 2 Kin 4:7
exaction of every **d** Neh 10:31
guarantors for **d-s** Prov 22:26
forgive us our **d-s** Matt 6:12

DEBTOR *borrower*
restores to the **d** Ezek 18:7
forgiven our **d-s** Matt 6:12
had two **d-s** Luke 7:41
his master's **d-s** Luke 16:5

DECAY *corruption*
own eyes see his **d** Job 21:20
Holy One to...**d** Acts 2:27
did not undergo **d** Acts 13:37

DECEASED *dead*
wife of the **d** shall Deut 25:5
the widow of the **d** Ruth 4:5
the name of the **d** Ruth 4:10
the sister of the **d** John 11:39

DECEIT *deception, falsehood, guile*
full of curses and **d** Ps 10:7
in whose spirit...no **d** Ps 32:2
your tongue frames **d** Ps 50:19
D is in the heart Prov 12:20
he lays up **d** Prov 26:24
Offspring of **d** Is 57:4
houses are full of **d** Jer 5:27
house of Israel...**d** Hos 11:12
d, sensuality, envy Mark 7:22
in whom...is no **d** John 1:47
full of envy...**d** Rom 1:29
the lusts of **d** Eph 4:22
all malice and all **d** 1 Pet 2:1
nor was any **d** found 1 Pet 2:22
lips from speaking **d** 1 Pet 3:10

DECEITFUL *false*
From a **d** tongue Ps 120:2
the wicked are **d** Prov 12:5
d are the kisses of Prov 27:6
Charm is **d** and Prov 31:30

The heart is more **d** Jer 17:9
false apostles, **d** 2 Cor 11:13

DECEIVE *cheat, mislead*
have you **d-d** me Gen 29:25
Jacob **d-d** Laban Gen 31:20
d-s his companion Lev 6:2
both stolen and **d-d** Josh 7:11
Do not **d** me 2 Kin 4:28
who **d-s** his neighbor Prov 26:19
Do not **d** yourselves Jer 37:9
your heart has **d-d** you Obad 3
they keep **d-ing** Rom 3:13
Let no one **d** you Eph 5:6
d-ing and being **d-d** 2 Tim 3:13

DECEIVER *liar*
as a **d** in his sight Gen 27:12
as **d-s** and yet true 2 Cor 6:8
d and the antichrist 2 John 7

DECEPTION *falsehood*
their mind prepares **d** Job 15:35
the hills are a **d** Jer 3:23
last **d** will be worse Matt 27:64
philosophy and empty **d** Col 2:8
reveling in their **d-s** 2 Pet 2:13

DECEPTIVE *misleading*
wicked...**d** wages Prov 11:18
Do not trust in **d** words Jer 7:4
d *stream* With water Jer 15:18

DECISION *judgment, resolution*
d is from the LORD Prov 16:33
in the valley of **d** Joel 3:14
My **d** is to gather Zeph 3:8
majority reached a **d** Acts 27:12

DECLARE *explain, proclaim*
Moses **d-d** to...sons Lev 23:44
d to Him the number Job 31:37
d Your faithfulness Ps 30:9
mouth...**d** Your praise Ps 51:15
d Your lovingkindness Ps 92:2
Who has **d-d** *this* Is 41:26
d-s the LORD Amos 4:11
He will **d** all things John 4:25
d-d the Son of God Rom 1:4

DECLINE *decrease*
for the shadow to **d** 2 Kin 20:10
our days have **d-d** Ps 90:9
for the day **d-s** Jer 6:4

DECREASE *abate, subside*
the water **d-d** steadily Gen 8:5
not let their cattle **d** Ps 107:38
increase...I must **d** John 3:30

DECREE (n) *judgment, order*
issued a **d** to rebuild Ezra 5:13
and **d** of the king Esth 2:8
devises mischief by **d** Ps 94:20
only one **d** for you Dan 2:9
delivering the **d-s** Acts 16:4
to the **d-s** of Caesar Acts 17:7

DECREE (v) *decide, determine*
been **d-d** against her Esth 2:1
will also **d** a thing Job 22:28
And rulers **d** justice Prov 8:15
Seventy weeks...**d-d** Dan 9:24

DEDICATE *consecrate, devote*
D yourselves today Ex 32:29
I wholly **d** the silver Judg 17:3
d-d by...David 1 Kin 7:51
David...**d-d** these 1 Chr 18:11
d-d part...the spoil 1 Chr 26:27
d-ing it to Him 2 Chr 2:4

DEDICATION *consecration*
the **d** of the altar 2 Chr 7:9
celebrated the **d** of Ezra 6:16
d of the wall Neh 12:27
d of the image Dan 3:2
assembled for the **d** Dan 3:3

DEDICATION, FEAST OF
see **FEASTS**

DEED *action or document*
What is this **d** Gen 44:15
for our evil **d-s** Ezra 9:13
blot out...loyal **d-s** Neh 13:14
abominable **d-s** Ps 14:1
I...sealed the **d** Jer 32:10
prophet mighty in **d** Luke 24:19
their **d-s** were evil John 3:19
d-s of the flesh are Gal 5:19
for every good **d** Titus 3:1
I know your **d-s** Rev 2:2

DEEP (adj) *far ranging*
d sleep falls on men Job 4:13
Your judgments are...**d** Ps 36:6
casts into a **d** sleep Prov 19:15
into **d** darkness Jer 13:16
the well is **d** John 4:11

DEEP (n) *abyss, depth*
fountains of the...**d** Gen 7:11
the **d** lying beneath Deut 33:13
surface of the **d** is Job 38:30
D calls to **d** Ps 42:7
The **d-s** also trembled Ps 77:16
His wonders in the **d** Ps 107:24
the springs of the **d** Prov 8:28

DEER *animal*
besides **d**, gazelles 1 Kin 4:23
d pants for the water Ps 42:1
lame will leap like a **d** Is 35:6

DEFEAT *conquer, overthrow*
d-ed...and pursued Gen 14:15
able to **d** them Num 22:6
sons of Israel **d-ed** Josh 12:7
d the Arameans 2 Kin 13:17
d-ed the Philistines 1 Chr 18:1
d-ed the entire army Jer 37:10

DEFECT (n) *blemish, spot*
No one who has a **d** Lev 21:18
one ram without **d** Num 6:14
if it has any **d** Deut 15:21
no **d** in him 2 Sam 14:25
in whom was no **d** Dan 1:4

DEFECT (v) *rebel, disobey*
d to his master 1 Chr 12:19
many **d-ed** to him 2 Chr 15:9
you have deeply **d-ed** Is 31:6

DEFEND *protect*
LORD of hosts will **d** Zech 9:15
d-ed him and took Acts 7:24
or else **d-ing** them Rom 2:15
are **d-ing** ourselves 2 Cor 12:19

DEFENSE *protection*
d-s are **d-s** of clay Job 13:12
the **d** of my life Ps 27:1
You have been a **d** Is 25:4
the **d**...of the gospel Phil 1:7

DEFILE *pollute, profane*
astray...**d-s** herself Num 5:29
d-d the high places 2 Kin 23:8
d-d the priesthood Neh 13:29
d-d Your holy temple Ps 79:1
your hands are **d-d** Is 59:3
those **d** the man Matt 15:18
is what **d-s** the man Mark 7:20
conscience...is **d-d** 1 Cor 8:7
d-s the entire body James 3:6

DEFILEMENT *filth*
her *interest,* for **d** Ezek 22:3
from all **d** of flesh 2 Cor 7:1

DEFRAUD *deprive, wrong*
whom have I **d-ed** 1 Sam 12:3
To **d** a man Lam 3:36
Do not **d** Mark 10:19
no one keep **d-ing** Col 2:18

DEITY *God, gods*
of strange **d-ies** Acts 17:18
fullness of **D** dwells Col 2:9

DELAY *hinder, linger, stall*
Do not **d** me Gen 24:56
Moses **d-ed** to come Ex 32:1
shall not **d** to pay Deut 23:21
bridegroom...**d-ing** Matt 25:5
Do not **d** in coming Acts 9:38
now why do you **d** Acts 22:16
in case I am **d-ed** 1 Tim 3:15

DELICACIES *fancy foods*
eat of their **d** Ps 141:4
Do not desire his **d** Prov 23:3
Those who ate **d** Lam 4:5

DELIGHT (n) *pleasure*
I have no **d** in you 2 Sam 15:26
Will he take **d** Job 27:10
his **d** is in the law Ps 1:2
commandments...**d** Ps 119:143
my **d** in the sons of Prov 8:31
a just weight is His **d** Prov 11:1
the **d** of kings Prov 16:13
I took great **d** Song 2:3
call the sabbath a **d** Is 58:13
My **d** is in her Is 62:4

DELIGHT (v) *desire*
LORD **d-ed** over you Deut 28:63
d in...offerings 1 Sam 15:22
d to revere Your name Neh 1:11
d in the Almighty Job 22:26
D yourself in the LORD Ps 37:4
not **d** in sacrifice Ps 51:16
Who **d** in doing evil Prov 2:14
d in my ways Prov 23:26
takes no **d** in fools Eccl 5:4
I **d** in loyalty Hos 6:6
d-s...unchanging love Mic 7:18
d-ing...self-abasement Col 2:18

DELIGHTFUL *pleasant*
d is a timely word Prov 15:23
to find **d** words Eccl 12:10
and how **d** you are Song 7:6
Is he a **d** child Jer 31:20

DELILAH
Philistine woman Judg 16:4
enticed Samson Judg 16:6-20

DELIVER *give, rescue, save*
come down to **d** them Ex 3:8
d the manslayer Num 35:25
My...power has **d-ed** Judg 7:2
can this one **d** 1 Sam 10:27
He will **d** you Job 5:19
d-ed my soul from Ps 56:13
none who can **d** Is 43:13
mind on **d-ing** Daniel Dan 6:14
d us from evil Matt 6:13
d-ed over to death 2 Cor 4:11

DELIVERANCE *salvation*
by a great **d** Gen 45:7
given this great **d** Judg 15:18
with songs of **d** Ps 32:7
a God of **d-s** Ps 68:20
d through...prayers Phil 1:19

DELIVERER *savior*
the LORD raised up a **d** Judg 3:9
gave them **d-s** Neh 9:27
my fortress and my **d** Ps 18:2
d-s...ascend Mount Obad 21
D...come from Zion Rom 11:26

DELUDE *lead astray*
they have **d-d** you Is 47:10
no one will **d** you Col 2:4

who **d** themselves James 1:22

DEMAND *order, require*
husband may **d** of him Ex 21:22
but I **d** one thing 2 Sam 3:13
captors **d-ed** of us Ps 137:3
do not **d** it back Luke 6:30
d-ing of Him a sign Luke 11:16

DEMETRIUS
1 *Ephesian smith* Acts 19:24,38
2 *a Christian* 3 John 12

DEMOLISH *destroy*
d all...high places Num 33:52
he **d-ed** its stones 2 Kin 23:15
to **d** its strongholds Is 23:11

DEMON *devil*
sacrificed to **d-s** Deut 32:17
daughters to the **d-s** Ps 106:37
after the **d** was cast Matt 9:33
sacrifice to **d-s** 1 Cor 10:20
d-s also believe James 2:19
not to worship **d-s** Rev 9:20

DEMONIACS *possessed ones*
d, epileptics Matt 4:24
what had happened to the **d** Matt 8:33

DEMON-POSSESSED
many who were **d** Matt 8:16
a mute, **d** man Matt 9:32
to the **d** man Mark 5:16
sayings of one **d** John 10:21

DEMONSTRATE *show*
God **d-s** His own love Rom 5:8
to **d** His wrath Rom 9:22
d-d yourselves to be 2 Cor 7:11
d His...patience 1 Tim 1:16

DEMONSTRATION *a showing*
for the **d**, *I say* Rom 3:26
in **d** of the Spirit 1 Cor 2:4

DEN *abode*
remains in its **d** Job 37:8
From the **d-s** of lions Song 4:8
the viper's **d** Is 11:8
cast into the lions' **d** Dan 6:7
it a robbers' **d** Mark 11:17

DENARIUS
Roman silver coin Matt 20:2,9
a day's wage Luke 20:24
Denarii *(pl)* John 6:7; 12:5

DENOUNCE *accuse, slander*
And come, **d** Israel Num 23:7
the LORD has not **d-d** Num 23:8
let us **d** him Jer 20:10
He...to **d** the cities Matt 11:20

DENY *conceal, refuse*
Sarah **d-ied** *it* Gen 18:15
so that you do not **d** your God Josh 24:27
not **d-ied** the words Job 6:10
and **d-ing** the LORD Is 59:13
whoever **d-ies** Me Matt 10:33
has **d-ied** the faith 1 Tim 5:8
deeds they **d** *Him* Titus 1:16
us to **d** ungodliness Titus 2:12
d-ies the Son 1 John 2:23

DEPART *leave*
scepter shall not **d** Gen 49:10
sword...never **d** 2 Sam 12:10
to **d** from evil is Job 28:28
His spirit **d-s** Ps 146:4
his foolishness will not **d** Prov 27:22
turned aside and **d-ed** Jer 5:23
I never knew you; **d** Matt 7:23
d from Me, all you Luke 13:27
d and be with Christ Phil 1:23

DEPARTURE *death or leaving*
after their **d** from Ex 16:1
speaking of His **d** Luke 9:31
time of my **d** has 2 Tim 4:6
any time after my **d** 2 Pet 1:15

DEPEND *rely, rest*
d-ed on the weapons Is 22:8
you did not **d** on Him Is 22:11
d the whole Law Matt 22:40

DEPORTATION *exile*
after the **d** to Matt 1:12
to the **d** to Babylon Matt 1:17

DEPORTED *exiled*
d...to Babylon Ezra 5:12
d...entire population Amos 1:6

DEPOSE *release*
d you from your office Is 22:19
d-d from his royal Dan 5:20

DEPOSIT (n) *security*
in regard to a **d** Lev 6:2
d which was entrusted Lev 6:4

DEPOSIT (v) *place, put*
d them in the tent Num 17:4
d *it* in your town Deut 14:28
d...in the temple Ezra 5:15
had **d-ed** the scroll Jer 36:20

DEPRAVED *degenerate*
over to a **d** mind Rom 1:28
men of **d** mind 2 Tim 3:8

DEPRIVE *take away*
d the needy of justice Is 10:2
d-d of...my years Is 38:10
d-ing one another 1 Cor 7:5
d-d of the truth 1 Tim 6:5

DEPTH *abyss, deep*
d-s boil like a pot Job 41:31
hand are the **d-s** Ps 95:4
went down to the **d-s** Ps 107:26
sins Into the **d-s** Mic 7:19
drowned in the **d** Matt 18:6
it had no **d** of soil Mark 4:5
nor height, nor **d** Rom 8:39
the **d** of the riches Rom 11:33
even the **d-s** of God 1 Cor 2:10

DEPUTY *proconsul*
he was the only **d** 1 Kin 4:19
Solomon's...**d-ies** 1 Kin 5:16
a **d** was king 1 Kin 22:47

DERISION *laughingstock*
d among...enemies Ex 32:25
d to those around us Ps 44:13
reproach and **d** all Jer 20:8
d to the rest of the Ezek 36:4

DESCEND *go down*
angels of God...**d-ing** Gen 28:12
His glory will not **d** Ps 49:17
breath of...**d-s** Eccl 3:21
will **d** to Hades Matt 11:23
Spirit **d-ing**...dove John 1:32
d into the abyss Rom 10:7
who **d-ed**...ascended Eph 4:10

DESCENDANT *seed, offering*
your **d-s** I will give Gen 12:7
will raise up your **d** 2 Sam 7:12
His **d-s** shall endure Ps 89:36
So shall your **d-s** be Rom 4:18
you are Abraham's **d-s** Gal 3:29
to the **d** of Abraham Heb 2:16
and the **d** of David Rev 22:16

DESCENT *hill or heritage*
of Median **d** Dan 9:1
the **d** of the Mount Luke 19:37
were of high-priestly **d** Acts 4:6

DESCRIBE *explain*
you shall **d** the land Josh 18:6
man, **d** the temple Ezek 43:10
who had seen it **d-d** Mark 5:16

DESECRATE *defile*
d the sanctuary Dan 11:31
tried to **d** the temple Acts 24:6

DESERT (n) *wilderness*
d plains of Jericho Josh 5:10
grieved Him in the **d** Ps 78:40
better to live in a **d** Prov 21:19
in the **d** a highway Is 40:3
Rivers in the **d** Is 43:19
like a bush in the **d** Jer 17:6
he lived in the **d-s** Luke 1:80

DESERT (v) *abandon, forsake*
d-ed to the king 2 Kin 25:11
who had **d-ed** them Acts 15:38
so quickly **d-ing** Him Gal 1:6
but all **d-ed** me 2 Tim 4:16
I will never **d** you Heb 13:5

DESERTERS *changers of loyalty*
d who had deserted 2 Kin 25:11
d who had gone over Jer 39:9

DESERVE *earn, merit*
with him as he **d-d** Judg 9:16
done this **d-s** to die 2 Sam 12:5
He **d-s** death Matt 26:66
receiving what we **d** Luke 23:41

DESIGN *creation, plan*
d-s for work in gold Ex 31:4
makers of **d-s** Ex 35:35
execute any **d** which 2 Chr 2:14
All their deadly **d-s** Jer 18:23

DESIGNATE *appoint*
if he **d-s** her for Ex 21:9
one whom I **d** to 1 Sam 16:3
were **d-d** by name 1 Chr 16:41
being **d-d** by God Heb 5:10

DESIRABLE *attractive*
the tree was **d** Gen 3:6
d in your eyes 1 Kin 20:6
more **d** than gold Ps 19:10
What is **d** in a man Prov 19:22
every kind of **d** object Nah 2:9

DESIRE (n) *appetite, craving*
d...for your husband Gen 3:16
poor from *their* **d** Job 31:16
the **d-s** of your heart Ps 37:4
d of the wicked will Ps 112:10
d of the righteous Prov 10:24
d of your eyes Ezek 24:16
great man speaks the **d** Mic 7:3
d and my prayer Rom 10:1
d-s of the flesh Eph 2:3
d to depart and be Phil 1:23
evil **d**, and greed Col 3:5

DESIRE (v) *crave, wish*
your heart **d-s** Deut 14:26
as much as you **d** 1 Sam 2:16
I **d** to argue with God Job 13:3
You **d** truth Ps 51:6
not **d** his delicacies Prov 23:3
all that my eyes **d-d** Eccl 2:10
righteous men **d-d** Matt 13:17
d the greater gifts 1 Cor 12:31
d...a good showing Gal 6:12
d a better *country* Heb 11:16

DESOLATE *lonely, waste*
your sanctuaries **d** Lev 26:31
sons of the **d** one Is 54:1
high places will be **d** Ezek 6:6
d wilderness behind Joel 2:3
loaves in *this* **d** place Matt 15:33
homestead be made **d** Acts 1:20
children of the **d** Gal 4:27

DESOLATION *ruin, waste*
a **d** and a curse 2 Kin 22:19
a heap forever, a **d** Josh 8:28
D is left in the city Is 24:12
d-s of many generations Is 61:4
an everlasting **d** Ezek 35:9
the abomination of **d** Dan 11:31
day of...**d** Zeph 1:15
her **d** is near Luke 21:20

DESPAIR (n) *grief*
words of one in **d** Job 6:26
my soul is in **d** Ps 42:6
Why are you in **d** Ps 43:5

DESPAIR (v) *grieve*
Saul then will **d** 1 Sam 27:1
I...**d-ed** of all Eccl 2:20
we **d-ed** even of life 2 Cor 1:8
but not **d-ing** 2 Cor 4:8

DESPISE *reject, scorn*
d-d his birthright Gen 25:34
those who **d** Me 1 Sam 2:30
d-d...in her heart 2 Sam 6:16
not **d** the discipline Job 5:17
hate and **d** falsehood Ps 119:163
Fools **d** wisdom and Prov 1:7
wisdom...is **d-d** Eccl 9:16
has **d-d** the day of Zech 4:10
have we **d-d** Your name Mal 1:6
not **d** one of these Matt 18:10
be devoted to one and **d** Luke 16:13
do you **d**...church 1 Cor 11:22

DESPOIL *injure, lay waste*
d-ed all the cities 2 Chr 14:14
the wicked who **d** me Ps 17:9
plundered and **d-ed** Is 42:22

DESTINE *appoint*
is **d-d** for the sword Job 15:22
d you for the sword Is 65:12
things **d-d** to perish Col 2:22
not **d-d** us for wrath 1 Thess 5:9

DESTITUTE *deprived, in need*
prayer of the **d** Ps 102:17
the land is **d** Ezek 32:15
being **d,** afflicted Heb 11:37

DESTROY *abolish, ruin, waste*
to **d** all flesh Gen 6:17
so that I do not **d** you 1 Sam 15:6
would You **d** me Job 10:8
seek my life to **d** it Ps 40:14
the wicked, He will **d** Ps 145:20
that which **d-s** kings Prov 31:3
one sinner **d-s** much Eccl 9:18
stronghold is **d-ed** Is 23:14
shepherds...are **d-ing** Jer 23:1
He will **d** mighty men Dan 8:24
moth and rust **d** Matt 6:19
who is able to **d** Matt 10:28
You come to **d** us Mark 1:24
seeking...to **d** Him Mark 11:18
d the temple and Mark 15:29
flood...**d-ed** them Luke 17:27
D this temple, and John 2:19
not for **d-ing** you 2 Cor 10:8
to save and to **d** James 4:12
heavens will be **d-ed** 2 Pet 3:12
d the works of the 1 John 3:8

DESTROYER *devastator*
d of our country Judg 16:24
of the **d-s** prosper Job 12:6
d comes upon him Job 15:21
d-s and devastators Is 49:17
I will set apart **d-s** Jer 22:7

DESTRUCTION *calamity, ruin*
the **d** of my kindred Esth 8:6
God apportion **d** Job 21:17
Your tongue devises **d** Ps 52:2
Pride *goes* before **d** Prov 16:18
foolish son is **d** to Prov 19:13
called the City of **D** Is 19:18
d of the daughter of Lam 2:11
broad that leads to **d** Matt 7:13
whose end is **d** Phil 3:19
d will come 1 Thess 5:3
penalty of eternal **d** 2 Thess 1:9
bringing swift **d** upon 2 Pet 2:1

DETERMINE *decide*
to **d** whether he laid Ex 22:8
his days are **d-d** Job 14:5
d-d *their* appointed Acts 17:26
but rather **d** this Rom 14:13
d-d to know nothing 1 Cor 2:2

DETEST *despise, loathe*
carcasses you shall **d** Lev 11:11
not **d** an Egyptian Deut 23:7
d his citadels Amos 6:8

DETESTABLE *abominable*
not eat any **d** thing Deut 14:3
who is **d** and corrupt Job 15:16
swine's flesh, **d** Is 66:17
their **d** idols Jer 16:18
remove all its **d** Ezek 11:18
d...sight of God Luke 16:15

DEVASTATE *destroy, lay waste*
d-d the nations 2 Kin 19:17
Until cities are **d-d** Is 6:11
the LORD...**d-s** it Is 24:1
my tents are **d-d** Jer 4:20
d...pride of Egypt Ezek 32:12

DEVASTATION *destruction*
d of the afflicted Ps 12:5
Nor **d** or destruction Is 60:18
raise up the former **d-s** Is 61:4
d in their citadels Amos 3:10

DEVICE *plan, scheme*
By their own **d-s** Ps 5:10
not promote his *evil* **d** Ps 140:8
a man of evil **d-s** Prov 14:17
in their **d-s** you walk Mic 6:16

DEVIL *demon, Satan*
tempted by the **d** Matt 4:1
one of you is a **d** John 6:70
you son of the **d** Acts 13:10
firm against...the **d** Eph 6:11
render powerless...**d** Heb 2:14
serpent...the **d** Rev 12:9
d...into the lake Rev 20:10

DEVISE *design, scheme, plot*
d-d against the Jews Esth 9:25
d-ing a vain thing Ps 2:1
d-s mischief by decree Ps 94:20
continually **d-s** evil Prov 6:14
man who **d-s** evil Prov 12:2
He **d-s** wicked schemes Is 32:7
do not **d** evil in Zech 7:10
d futile things Acts 4:25

DEVOTE *commit, dedicate*
shall **d** to the LORD Ex 13:12
d...to the law 2 Chr 31:4
d-d to one and despise Matt 6:24
d-ing...to prayer Acts 1:14
d-d to one another Rom 12:10
D yourselves to prayer Col 4:2

DEVOTED *set apart (to God)*
d to destruction Lev 27:28
Every **d** thing in Num 18:14
d to destruction 1 Sam 15:21
d thing in Israel Ezek 44:29

DEVOTION *consecration*
his deeds of **d** 2 Chr 32:32
excessive **d** *to books* Eccl 12:12
the **d** of your youth Jer 2:2

DEVOUR *consume, swallow*
wild beast **d-ed** him Gen 37:20
the sword **d** forever 2 Sam 2:26
is **d-ed** by disease Job 18:13
fire from...**d-ed** Ps 18:8
love all words that **d** Ps 52:4
To **d** the afflicted Prov 30:14
has **d-ed** your prophets Jer 2:30
caterpillar was **d-ing** Amos 4:9
d widows' houses Mark 12:40
bite...**d** one another Gal 5:15

DEVOUT *God-fearing*
d men are taken away Is 57:1
was righteous and **d** Luke 2:25
d men, from every Acts 2:5
the **d** women Acts 13:50

DEW *drops of moisture*
God give...the **d** Gen 27:28
d fell on the camp Num 11:9
d on the fleece only Judg 6:37
on him as the **d** 2 Sam 17:12
neither **d** nor rain 1 Kin 17:1
the **d** of Hermon Ps 133:3
skies drip with **d** Prov 3:20
Like a cloud of **d** Is 18:4
drenched with the **d** Dan 4:15
sky has withheld its **d** Hag 1:10

DIALECT *language*
in the Hebrew **d** Acts 21:40
the Hebrew **d** Acts 22:2

DIAMOND *jewel*
a sapphire and a **d** Ex 28:18
With a **d** point Jer 17:1

DICTATION *spoken words*
at the **d** of Jeremiah Jer 36:4
written at the **d** of Jer 36:27
book at Jeremiah's **d** Jer 45:1

DIE *decease, expire*
you will surely **d** Gen 2:17
not eat...which **d-s** Deut 14:21
Where you **d,** I will **d** Ruth 1:17
Curse God and **d** Job 2:9
even wise men **d** Ps 49:10
fools **d** for lack of Prov 10:21
and the fool alike **d** Eccl 2:16
soul who sins will **d** Ezek 18:4
to **d** with You Matt 26:35
child has not **d-d** Mark 5:39
live even if he **d-s** John 11:25
grain of wheat...**d-s** John 12:24
she fell sick and **d-d** Acts 9:37
d-d for the ungodly Rom 5:6
we who **d-d** to sin Rom 6:2
for whom Christ **d-d** Rom 14:15
I **d** daily 1 Cor 15:31
I **d-d** to the Law Gal 2:19
to **d** is gain Phil 1:21
Jesus **d-d** and rose 1 Thess 4:14
to **d** once and after Heb 9:27
these **d-d** in faith Heb 11:13
who **d** in the Lord Rev 14:13

DIFFICULT *hard*
too **d** for the LORD Gen 18:14
test Solomon with **d** 2 Chr 9:1
anything too **d** for Me Jer 32:27
speech or **d** language Ezek 3:5
solving of **d** problems Dan 5:12
last days **d** times 2 Tim 3:1

DIG *excavate, till*
opens a pit, or **d-s** Ex 21:33
you can **d** copper Deut 8:9
they **d** into houses Job 24:16
He has **dug** a pit Ps 7:15
dug through the wall Ezek 8:8
dug a wine press Matt 21:33
until I **d** around it Luke 13:8

DIGNITY *majesty*
Preeminent in **d** Gen 49:3
What honor or **d** has Esth 6:3
all godliness and **d** 1 Tim 2:2
must be men of **d** 1 Tim 3:8

DILIGENCE *effort*
carried out with all **d** Ezra 6:12
Watch...with all **d** Prov 4:23
lagging behind in **d** Rom 12:11
show the same **d** Heb 6:11

DILIGENT *persistent*
hand of the **d** makes Prov 10:4
plans of the **d** *lead* Prov 21:5
d to present 2 Tim 2:15
d to enter that rest Heb 4:11
I will also be **d** 2 Pet 1:15

DIM *cloudy, dark*
eye was not **d** Deut 34:7
eyesight...to grow **d** 1 Sam 3:2
d because of grief Job 17:7
windows grow **d** Eccl 12:3

DIMINISH *dwindle, reduce*
you shall **d** its price Lev 25:16
d their inheritance Num 26:54
are **d-ed** and bowed Ps 107:39

DINAH
daughter of Jacob Gen 34:1,3
raped by Shechem Gen 34:2,5

DINE *eat*
men are to **d** with Gen 43:16
to **d** with a ruler Prov 23:1
came and were **d-ing** Matt 9:10

DINNER *meal*
I have prepared...**d** Matt 22:4
because of...**d** guests Mark 6:26
was giving a big **d** Luke 14:16

DIP *plunge*
d-ped the tunic in Gen 37:31
priest shall **d** his Lev 4:6
d your piece of bread Ruth 2:14
d-ped...seven times 2 Kin 5:14
d-ped...with Me Matt 26:23
who **d-s** with Me Mark 14:20
robe **d-ped** in blood Rev 19:13

DIRECT *arrange, guide, order*
LORD **d-s** his steps Prov 16:9
d your heart in the Prov 23:19
has **d-ed** the Spirit Is 40:13
walks to **d** his steps Jer 10:23
I **d-ed** the churches 1 Cor 16:1
d their entire body James 3:3

DIRECTION *path or order*
which turned every **d** Gen 3:24
It changes **d** Job 37:12
d of the daughter Jer 4:11
of their four **d-s** Ezek 1:17

DIRGE *lament*
for you as a **d** Amos 5:1
we sang a **d** Luke 7:32

DISAPPEAR *vanish*
For the faithful **d** Ps 12:1
When the grass **d-s** Prov 27:25
old is ready to **d** Heb 8:13

DISAPPOINT *frustrate*
and were not **d-ed** Ps 22:5
hope does not **d** Rom 5:5

DISASTER *calamity*
d was close to them Judg 20:34
d on this people Jer 6:19
because of all its **d-s** Jer 19:8
In the day of their **d** Obad 13

DISBELIEVE *doubt*
Jews who **d-d** stirred Acts 14:2

for those who **d** 1 Pet 2:7

DISCERN *understand, recognize*
would **d**...future Deut 32:29
king to **d** good 2 Sam 14:17
not **d** its appearance Job 4:16
d-ed...the youths Prov 7:7
d the...sky Matt 16:3

DISCERNMENT *judgment*
blessed be your **d** 1 Sam 25:33
asked for yourself **d** 1 Kin 3:11
not a people of **d** Is 27:11
knowledge and all **d** Phil 1:9

DISCHARGE *emission*
a **d** from his body Lev 15:2
leper or who has a **d** Lev 22:4
everyone having a **d** Num 5:2
d, or who is a leper 2 Sam 3:29
the **d** of your blood Ezek 32:6

DISCIPLE *student, learner*
to listen as a **d** Is 50:4
His twelve **d-s** Matt 10:1
d is not above his Matt 10:24
d-s rebuked them Matt 19:13
d-s left Him...fled Matt 26:56
make **d-s** of all Matt 28:19
Your **d-s** do not fast Mark 2:18
Passover...My **d-s** Mark 14:14
gaze toward His **d-s** Luke 6:20
he cannot be My **d** Luke 14:26
d-s believed in Him John 2:11
His **d-s** withdrew John 6:66
wash the **d-s'** feet John 13:5
d whom He loved John 19:26
d-s were first called Acts 11:26

DISCIPLINE (n) *chastisement*
the **d** of the LORD Deut 11:2
d of the Almighty Job 5:17
The rod of **d** Prov 22:15
to see your good **d** Col 2:5
d...of little profit 1 Tim 4:8

DISCIPLINE (v) *chastise*
as a man **d-s** his son Deut 8:5
d-d you with whips 1 Kin 12:11
D your son while Prov 19:18
I **d** my body 1 Cor 9:27
d-d by the Lord 1 Cor 11:32
father does not **d** Heb 12:7

DISCLOSE *reveal*
without **d-ing** it to 1 Sam 20:2
Esther had **d-d** what Esth 8:1
will **d** Myself to him John 14:21
d the motives of 1 Cor 4:5
secrets...are **d-d** 1 Cor 14:25

DISCOURAGE *dishearten*
d-ing the sons of Num 32:7
people of the land **d-d** Ezra 4:4
d-d with the work Neh 6:9

DISCOVER *find, uncover*
strength was not **d-ed** Judg 16:9
d the depths of God Job 11:7
man will not **d** Eccl 7:14
shamed...he is **d-ed** Jer 2:26

DISCRETION *understanding*
LORD give you **d** 1 Chr 22:12
sound wisdom and **d** Prov 3:21
woman who lacks **d** Prov 11:22
Daniel replied with **d** Dan 2:14

DISCUSS *converse, reason*
d matters of justice Jer 12:1
d...among themselves Matt 16:7
What were you **d-ing** Mark 9:33
d-ed together what Luke 6:11

DISEASE *sickness*
none of the **d-s** on you Ex 15:26
harmful **d-s** of Egypt Deut 7:15

d-d in his feet 2 Chr 16:12
d-d...not healed Ezek 34:4
heals all your **d-s** Ps 103:3
various **d-s** and pains Matt 4:24
power...to heal **d-s** Luke 9:1

DISGRACE *reproach, shame*
a **d** to us Gen 34:14
nakedness, it is a **d** Lev 20:17
sin is a **d** to Prov 14:34
not **d** the throne Jer 14:21
and bear your **d** Ezek 16:52

DISGRACEFUL *shameful*
d thing in Israel Gen 34:7
shameful and **d** son Prov 19:26
d for a woman to 1 Cor 11:6

DISGUISE *pretend*
d-d his sanity 1 Sam 21:13
Arise now, and **d** 1 Kin 14:2
king of Israel **d-d** 1 Kin 22:30
he **d-s** his face Job 24:15
d-ing...as apostles 2 Cor 11:13

DISH *bowl, plate*
prepare a savory **d** Gen 27:7
was one silver **d** Num 7:43
as one wipes a **d** 2 Kin 21:13
30 gold **d-es** Ezra 1:9

DISHEARTENED *discouraged*
not be **d** or crushed Is 42:4
you **d** the righteous Ezek 13:22

DISHONEST *untruthful*
those who hate **d** gain Ex 18:21
order to get **d** gain Ezek 22:27
cheat with **d** scales Amos 8:5

DISHONOR (n) *disgrace, shame*
to see the king's **d** Ezra 4:14
Fill their faces with **d** Ps 83:16
man conceals **d** Prov 12:16

DISHONOR (v) *disgrace, shame*
who **d-s** his father Deut 27:16
be ashamed and **d-ed** Ps 35:4
and you **d** Me John 8:49
bodies would be **d-ed** Rom 1:24
do you **d** God Rom 2:23

DISMAY *be troubled, fear*
d-ed at his presence Gen 45:3
not tremble or be **d-ed** Josh 1:9
d-ed and...afraid 1 Sam 17:11
or I will **d** you Jer 1:17
are **d-ed** and caught Jer 8:9
mighty men...be **d-ed** Obad 9

DISMISS *release, send away*
d-ed the people Josh 24:28
Solomon **d-ed** 1 Kin 2:27
priest did not **d** *any* 2 Chr 23:8
he **d-ed** the assembly Acts 19:41

DISOBEDIENCE *rebellion*
the one man's **d** Rom 5:19
in the sons of **d** Eph 2:2
d received a just Heb 2:2
same example of **d** Heb 4:11

DISOBEDIENT *rebellious*
d and rebelled Neh 9:26
hardened and **d** Acts 19:9
d to parents Rom 1:30
d...obstinate people Rom 10:21

DISPERSE *spread*
d them in Jacob Gen 49:7
d-d...the peoples Esth 3:8
d them among the Ezek 20:23
who are **d-d** abroad James 1:1

DISPLAY *declare, show*
to **d** her beauty Esth 1:11
d-ed Your splendor Ps 8:1

d their sin like Is 3:9
works of God...**d-ed** John 9:3

DISPLEASE *annoy, trouble*
if it is **d-ing** to you Num 22:34
d-ing in the sight 1 Sam 8:6
may not **d** the lords 1 Sam 29:7
d-ing in His sight Is 59:15
it greatly **d-d** Jonah Jon 4:1

DISPOSSESS *remove*
d-ed the Amorites Num 21:32
Esau **d-ed** them Deut 2:12
He will assuredly **d** Josh 3:10
d-ing the nations Acts 7:45

DISPUTE (n) *controversy*
When they have a **d** Ex 18:16
bring the **d-s** to God Ex 18:19
d in your courts Deut 17:8
a great **d** among Acts 28:29

DISPUTE (v) *contend, debate*
wished to **d** with Him Job 9:3
with Israel he will **d** Mic 6:2
without...**d-ing** Phil 2:14
He **d-d** with the devil Jude 9

DISSENSION *division*
great **d** and debate Acts 15:2
d between the Acts 23:7
those who cause **d-s** Rom 16:17
without wrath and **d** 1 Tim 2:8

DISSIPATION *intemperance*
weighted...with **d** Luke 21:34
wine, for that is **d** Eph 5:18
not accused of **d** Titus 1:6

DISSOLVE *melt*
d me in a storm Job 30:22
I **d** my couch with Ps 6:6
d-d in tears Is 15:3
And the hills **d** Nah 1:5

DISTANCE *far away*
sister stood at a **d** Ex 2:4
some **d** from the Judg 18:22
following...at a **d** Matt 26:58
welcomed...from a **d** Heb 11:13

DISTINCTION *difference*
the Lord makes a **d** Ex 11:7
d between the holy Lev 10:10
have made no **d** Ezek 22:26
He made no **d** Acts 15:9
for there is no **d** Rom 3:22
d-s among yourselves James 2:4

DISTINGUISH (v) *discern*
I **d** between good 2 Sam 19:35
not **d** the sound Ezra 3:13
d...the righteous Mal 3:18
d-ing of spirits 1 Cor 12:10

DISTINGUISHING (adj)
became your **d** mark Ezek 27:7
this is a **d** mark 2 Thess 3:17

DISTORT *pervert*
who **d-s** the justice Deut 27:19
my garment is **d-ed** Job 30:18
they **d** my words Ps 56:5
d the gospel of Christ Gal 1:7

DISTRESS *adversity, trouble*
day of my **d** Gen 35:3
When you are in **d** Deut 4:30
deliver me...**d** 1 Sam 26:24
I am in great **d** 2 Sam 24:14
cry to You in our **d** 2 Chr 20:9
refuge in the day of **d** Jer 16:19
I am in **d** Lam 1:20
d upon the land Luke 21:23
d for every soul Rom 2:9
assisted those in **d** 1 Tim 5:10
widows in their **d** James 1:27

DISTRIBUTE *apportion*
d-d by lot in Shiloh Josh 19:51
to **d** to their kinsmen Neh 13:13
d it to the poor Luke 18:22
d-ing to each one 1 Cor 12:11

DISTRICT *area, province*
the **d** of Jerusalem Neh 3:12
d around the Jordan Matt 3:5
d of Galilee Mark 1:28
the **d-s** of Libya Acts 2:10

DISTURB *annoy, bother*
Why...**d-ed** me 1 Sam 28:15
no one **d** his bones 2 Kin 23:18
d them and destroy Esth 9:24
being greatly **d-ed** Acts 4:2
one who is **d-ing** you Gal 5:10

DISTURBANCE *turmoil*
to cause a **d** in it Neh 4:8
hear of wars and **d-s** Luke 21:9
d among the soldiers Acts 12:18
arrogance, **d-s** 2 Cor 12:20

DIVIDE *apportion, separate*
that **d-s** the hoof Deut 14:6
D the living child 1 Kin 3:25
d my garments among Ps 22:18
He will **d** the booty Is 53:12
d-d up His garments Matt 27:35
d-d his wealth Luke 15:12

DIVINATION *witchcraft*
nor practice **d** or Lev 19:26
witchcraft, used **d** 2 Chr 33:6
false vision, **d** Jer 14:14
falsehood and lying **d** Ezek 13:6
a spirit of **d** met us Acts 16:16

DIVINE (adj) *pertaining to deity*
in whom...**d** spirit Gen 41:38
I see a **d** being 1 Sam 28:13
D Nature...gold Acts 17:29
power and **d** nature Rom 1:20
is the **d** response Rom 11:4

DIVINE (v) *practice divination*
d-d that the Lord Gen 30:27
they **d** lies for you Ezek 21:29
d-ing lies for them Ezek 22:28
prophets **d** for money Mic 3:11

DIVINER *seer*
called for the...**d-s** 1 Sam 6:2
The **d** and the elder Is 3:2
your **d-s** deceive you Jer 29:8
d-s will be embarrassed Mic 3:7
d-s see lying visions Zech 10:2

DIVISION *dissension, segment*
d between My people Ex 8:23
divided...into **d-s** 1 Chr 23:6
d...in the crowd John 7:43
no **d-s** among you 1 Cor 1:10
d of soul and spirit Heb 4:12

DIVORCE (n) *separation*
a certificate of **d** Deut 24:1
given her a writ of **d** Jer 3:8
For I hate **d** Mal 2:16

DIVORCE (v) *separate*
he cannot **d** her Deut 22:19
husband **d-s** his wife Jer 3:1
man to **d** his wife Matt 19:3
Whoever **d-s** his Mark 10:11

DIVORCED (adj) *separated*
woman **d** from her Lev 21:7
or of a **d** woman Num 30:9
marries a **d** woman Matt 5:32
marries...who is **d** Luke 16:18

DOCTRINE *teaching*
Teaching as **d-s** the Matt 15:9
every wind of **d** Eph 4:14

to teach strange **d-s** 1 Tim 1:3
to exhort in sound **d** Titus 1:9

DOCUMENT *manuscript*
the **d** which you sent Ezra 4:18
And on the sealed **d** Neh 9:38
Darius signed the **d** Dan 6:9

DOER *workman*
recompenses the...**d** Ps 31:23
d-s of the Law will Rom 2:13
d-s of the word James 1:22
not a **d** of the law James 4:11

DOG *animal, scavenger*
Am I a **d** 1 Sam 17:43
d-s have surrounded Ps 22:16
they howl like a **d** Ps 59:6
live **d** is better than Eccl 9:4
Beware of the **d-s** Phil 3:2
d-s and the sorcerers Rev 22:15

DOMAIN *estate*
give You all this **d** Luke 4:6
the **d** of darkness Col 1:13
keep their own **d** Jude 6

DOMINION *authority, rule*
Yours is the **d** 1 Chr 29:11
places of His **d** Ps 103:22
d will be from sea Zech 9:10
and power and **d** Eph 1:21
thrones or **d-s** or Col 1:16
glory and the **d** forever Rev 1:6

DONKEY *ass*
a wild **d** of a man Gen 16:12
Balaam...to the **d** Num 22:29
the foal of a **d** Zech 9:9
you will find a **d** Matt 21:2
and mounted on a **d** Matt 21:5
a mute **d**, speaking 2 Pet 2:16

DOOR *entrance, opening*
crouching at the **d** Gen 4:7
set the **d** of the ark Gen 6:16
Uriah slept at the **d** 2 Sam 11:9
over the **d** of my lips Ps 141:3
d turns on its Prov 26:14
each had a double **d** Ezek 41:23
close your **d**...pray Matt 6:6
I am the **d** John 10:9
right at the **d** James 5:9
before you an open **d** Rev 3:8
I stand at the **d** Rev 3:20

DOORKEEPER *guard*
d-s have gathered 2 Kin 22:4
the Levites, the **d-s** 2 Chr 34:9
eunuchs who were **d-s** Esth 6:2
commanded the **d** Mark 13:34
To him the **d** opens John 10:3

DOORPOST
put it on the two **d-s** Ex 12:7
write them on the **d-s** Deut 6:9
on the seat by the **d** 1 Sam 1:9
Waiting at my **d-s** Prov 8:34

DOORWAY *entrance, opening*
the **d** of the tent Judg 4:20
d-s and doorposts 1 Kin 7:5
at my neighbor's **d** Job 31:9
chamber with its **d** Ezek 40:38

DORCAS
Tabitha, a Joppa Christian Acts 9:36-43

DOUBT (n) *unbelief*
life shall hang in **d** Deut 28:66
why do **d-s** arise Luke 24:38

DOUBT (v) *disbelieve*
why did you **d** Matt 14:31
not **d** in his heart Mark 11:23
d-s is condemned Rom 14:23
who **d-s** is like the James 1:6

DOUGH *flour mixture*
people took their **d** Ex 12:34
the first of your **d** Num 15:20
took **d**, kneaded *it* 2 Sam 13:8
knead **d** to make cakes Jer 7:18

DOVE *bird*
he sent out a **d** Gen 8:8
had wings like a **d** Ps 55:6
eyes are *like* **d-s** Song 1:15
descending as a **d** Matt 3:16
descending as a **d** John 1:32
selling the **d-s** John 2:16

DOWNFALL *collapse*
became the **d** of 2 Chr 28:23
noise of their **d** Jer 49:21

DOWNPOUR *rain*
the **d** and the rain Job 37:6
d of waters swept Hab 3:10

DOWRY *bequest*
must pay a **d** for her Ex 22:16
to the **d** for virgins Ex 22:17
d to his daughter 1 Kin 9:16

DRACHMA
Greek silver coin Neh 7:70-72; Matt 17:24

DRAG *draw, pull*
grasshopper **d-s** Eccl 12:5
D them off like sheep Jer 12:3
the dogs to **d** off Jer 15:3
Paul and **d-ged** Acts 14:19
d you into court James 2:6

DRAGON *monster, serpent*
d who *lives* in the sea Is 27:1
Who pierced the **d** Is 51:9
d stood before the Rev 12:4
he laid hold of the **d** Rev 20:2

DRAIN *empty*
blood is to be **d-ed** Lev 1:15
he **d-ed** the dew Judg 6:38
must **d** *and* drink down Ps 75:8
drink it and **d** it Ezek 23:34

DRAW *haul, pull*
out to **d** water Gen 24:13
drew him out of the Ex 2:10
but are **d-n** away Deut 30:17
He **d-s** up the drops Job 36:27
d near to my soul Ps 69:18
They are **d-ing** back Jer 46:5
redemption is **d-ing** Luke 21:28
d all men to Myself John 12:32
D near to God James 4:8

DRAWERS *servants*
wood and **d** of water Josh 9:21

DREAD (n) *fear*
in **d**...of Israel Ex 1:12
in **d** night and day Deut 28:66
d of the Jews Esth 8:17
they are in great **d** Ps 14:5
d comes like a storm Prov 1:27

DREAD (v) *fear*
what I **d** befalls me Job 3:25
Whom shall I **d** Ps 27:1
whose two kings you **d** Is 7:16
are **d-ed** and feared Hab 1:7

DREAM (n) *vision*
had a **d,** and behold Gen 28:12
man was relating a **d** Judg 7:13
flies away like a **d** Job 20:8
like a **d,** a vision Is 29:7
visions and **d-s** Dan 1:17
to Joseph in a **d** Matt 2:13

DREAM (v) *see a vision*
asleep and **d-ed** Gen 41:5
like those who **d** Ps 126:1

when a hungry man **d-s** Is 29:8
Your old men will **d** Joel 2:28

DREAMER *visionary*
Here comes this **d** Gen 37:19
If a prophet or a **d** Deut 13:1
your diviners, your **d-s** Jer 27:9

DRENCH *soak, wet*
d you with my tears Is 16:9
head is **d-ed** with dew Song 5:2
d-ed with the dew Dan 4:33

DRESS (n) *clothing*
have taken off my **d** Song 5:3
d was of fine linen Ezek 16:13
or putting on **d-es** 1 Pet 3:3

DRESS (v) *array, clothe*
d-ed in his military 2 Sam 20:8
D-ed as a harlot Prov 7:10
you **d** in scarlet Jer 4:30
d-ed Him...purple Mark 15:17

DRINK (n) *refreshment*
gave the lad a **d** Gen 21:19
or wine, or strong **d** Deut 14:26
to desire strong **d** Prov 31:4
gave Me *something* to **d** Matt 25:35
My blood is true **d** John 6:55
thirsty, give him a **d** Rom 12:20

DRINK (v)
he **drank** of the wine Gen 9:21
Do not **d** wine Lev 10:9
d from the brook 1 Kin 17:6
they all **drank** from Mark 14:23
after **d-ing** old *wine* Luke 5:39
who eats and **d-s** 1 Cor 11:29
ground that **d-s** the Heb 6:7

DRIP *drop*
clouds...They **d** Job 36:28
lips...**d** honey Song 4:11
d-ped with myrrh Song 5:5
D down, O heavens Is 45:8

DRIVE *chase, defeat*
You have **d-n** me Gen 4:14
and **drove** them away Ex 2:17
angel...**d-ing** *them* on Ps 35:5
d hard all your workers Is 58:3
drove Him out of...city Luke 4:29
drove *them* all out John 2:15
to **d** the ship Acts 27:39

DROP (n) *drip*
the **d-s** of water Job 36:27
a **d** from a bucket Is 40:15
like **d-s** of blood Luke 22:44

DROP (v) *fall*
olives will **d** off Deut 28:40
his bonds **d-ped** Judg 15:14
d off his unripe grape Job 15:33
d-ped their wings Ezek 1:24

DROSS *metallic waste*
of the earth *like* **d** Ps 119:119
Take away the **d** Prov 25:4
silver has become **d** Is 1:22
Israel has become **d** Ezek 22:18

DROUGHT *dryness*
Like heat in **d** Is 25:5
in regard to the **d** Jer 14:1
I called for a **d** Hag 1:11

DROWNED *suffocated*
d in the Red Sea Ex 15:4
to be **d** in the depth Matt 18:6
were **d** in the sea Mark 5:13

DRUNK *intoxicated*
arrows **d** with blood Deut 32:42
d, but not with wine Is 29:9
made...**d** in My wrath Is 63:6

not get **d** with wine Eph 5:18
I saw the woman **d** Rev 17:6

DRUNKARD *intoxicated person*
a glutton and a **d** Deut 21:20
song of the **d-s** Ps 69:12
Awake, **d-s,** and weep Joel 1:5
a reviler, or a **d** 1 Cor 5:11

DRUNKEN *intoxicated*
stagger like a **d** man Job 12:25
become like a **d** man Jer 23:9

DRUNKENNESS *intoxicated*
and not for **d** Eccl 10:17
weighted down...**d** Luke 21:34
in carousing and **d** Rom 13:13
envying, **d,** carousing Gal 5:21

DRY (adj) *parched, scorched*
let the **d** land appear Gen 1:9
In a **d** and weary land Ps 63:1
Better is a **d** morsel Prov 17:1
O **d** bones, hear Ezek 37:4

DRY (v) *scorch, wither*
My strength is **dried** Ps 22:15
dried up...streams Ps 74:15
I **d** up the sea Is 50:2
new wine **dries** up Joel 1:10
dries up...rivers Nah 1:4

DUE (adj) *proper, right*
In **d** time their foot Deut 32:35
food in **d** season Ps 104:27
d penalty of their Rom 1:27

DUE (n) *what is owed*
as *their* **d** forever Lev 7:34
be the priests' **d** Deut 18:3
Indeed it is Your **d** Jer 10:7

DULL *heavy, stupid*
eyes are **d** from wine Gen 49:12
Their ears **d** Is 6:10
people...become **d** Matt 13:15
become **d** of hearing Heb 5:11

DUNG *waste*
sweeps away **d** 1 Kin 14:10
dove's **d** for five 2 Kin 6:25
give you cow's **d** Ezek 4:15
their flesh like **d** Zeph 1:17

DUNGEON *prison*
put me into the **d** Gen 40:15
captive...in the **d** Ex 12:29
prisoners from the **d** Is 42:7
Jeremiah...into the **d** Jer 37:16

DUST *dirt, earth*
God formed man of **d** Gen 2:7
And **d** you will eat Gen 3:14
the poor from the **d** 1 Sam 2:8
repent in **d** and ashes Job 42:6
d before the wind Ps 18:42
Will the **d** praise You Ps 30:9
You who lie in the **d** Is 26:19
shake the **d** off Matt 10:14
the **d** of your city Luke 10:11
d on their heads Rev 18:19

DUTY *responsibility*
perform your **d** Gen 38:8
charged with any **d** Deut 24:5
the **d** of a husband's Deut 25:7
his **d** to his wife 1 Cor 7:3

DWELL *abide, live*
father of those who **d** Gen 4:20
Behold, I am **d-ing** 1 Chr 17:1
No evil **d-s** with You Ps 5:4
d on Your holy hill Ps 15:1
I will **d** in the house Ps 23:6
d among the wise Prov 15:31
have **d-t** in Jerusalem Jer 35:11
flesh, and **d-t** among John 1:14

His Spirit who **d-s** in you Rom 8:11
of God **d-s** in you 1 Cor 3:16
Christ may **d** in your Eph 3:17
d on these things Phil 4:8

DWELLING *habitation*
earth shall be your **d** Gen 27:39
name there for His **d** Deut 12:5
place for Your **d** 1 Kin 8:13
into the eternal **d-s** Luke 16:9
might find a **d** place Acts 7:46

DYED *colored*
rams' skins **d** red Ex 25:5
A spoil of **d** work Judg 5:30

E

EAGLE *bird*
bore you on **e-s'** wings Ex 19:4
the **e** swoops down Deut 28:49
swifter than **e-s** 2 Sam 1:23
with wings like **e-s** Is 40:31
the face of an **e** Ezek 1:10
was like a flying **e** Rev 4:7

EAR *hearing*
heard with our **e-s** 2 Sam 7:22
the **e** test words Job 12:11
And His **e-s** are *open* Ps 34:15
and incline your **e** Ps 45:10
He whose **e** listens Prov 15:31
e of the wise seeks Prov 18:15
e has not been open Is 48:8
let your **e** receive Jer 9:20
He who has **e-s** to Matt 11:15
and cut off his **e** Matt 26:51
fingers into his **e-s** Mark 7:33
if the **e** says 1 Cor 12:16
their **e-s** tickled 2 Tim 4:3
He who has an **e** Rev 2:7

EARLY *beforetime, soon*
they arose **e** and Gen 26:31
Let us rise **e** Song 7:12
dew which goes away **e** Hos 6:4
e on the first day Mark 16:2
at the tomb **e** Luke 24:22
the **e** and late rains James 5:7

EARNINGS *gain, wages*
her **e** she plants Prov 31:16
the **e** of a harlot Mic 1:7

EARRING *ornament*
brought...**e-s** Ex 35:22
e-s and necklaces Num 31:50
Like an **e** of gold Prov 25:12
her **e-s** and jewelry Hos 2:13

EARTH *land, world*
God created the...**e** Gen 1:1
Judge of all the **e** Gen 18:25
the **e** is the LORD'S Ex 9:29
way of all the **e** Josh 23:14
His stand on the **e** Job 19:25
foundation of the **e** Job 38:4
saints...in the **e** Ps 16:3
the shields of the **e** Ps 47:9
gave birth to the **e** Ps 90:2
He established the **e** Ps 104:5
wisdom founded...**e** Prov 3:19
the **e** remains forever Eccl 1:4
made the **e** tremble Is 14:16
the circle of the **e** Is 40:22
the ends of the **e** Is 45:22
the **e** is My footstool Is 66:1
e shone with His Ezek 43:2
make the **e** dark Amos 8:9
e will be devoured Zeph 3:8
shall inherit the **e** Matt 5:5
you bind on **e** Matt 16:19
on **e** peace among Luke 2:14
glorified...on the **e** John 17:4
man is from the **e** 1 Cor 15:47
heavens and a new **e** 2 Pet 3:13
e and heaven fled Rev 20:11

EARTHENWARE *pottery*
bird in an **e** vessel Lev 14:5
holy water in an **e** Num 5:17
shatter them like **e** Ps 2:9
buy a potter's **e** jar Jer 19:1
vessels of...**e** 2 Tim 2:20

EARTHQUAKE *temblor*
LORD *was* not...**e** 1 Kin 19:11
punished with...**e** Is 29:6
be famines and **e-s** Matt 24:7
will be great **e-s** Luke 21:11
there was a great **e** Rev 6:12
killed in the **e** Rev 11:13

EARTHY *mortal*
man is...**e** 1 Cor 15:47
those who are **e** 1 Cor 15:48

EASE *free from difficulty, pain*
He who is at **e** Job 12:5
at **e** and satisfied Job 21:23
women who are at **e** Is 32:9
Woe to those...at **e** Amos 6:1
nations who are at **e** Zech 1:15

EAST *direction of compass*
spread out...to the **e** Gen 28:14
directed an **e** wind Ex 10:13
sons of the **e** were Judg 7:12
men of the **e** Job 1:3
With the **e** wind You Ps 48:7
offspring from the **e** Is 43:5
faces toward the **e** Ezek 8:16
Jerusalem on the **e** Zech 14:4
saw His star in the **e** Matt 2:2
lightning...the **e** Matt 24:27
kings from the **e** Rev 16:12

EAST GATE *see* **GATES OF JERUSALEM**

EASY *without difficulty*
knowledge is **e** to one Prov 14:6
My yoke is **e** and Matt 11:30

EAT *consume, dine, feast*
shall not **e** from it Gen 3:17
they **ate** every plant Ex 10:15
not **e**...blood Lev 19:26
that we may **e** him 2 Kin 6:28
e and be satisfied Ps 22:26
not **e** the bread of Prov 31:27
will **e** curds and honey Is 7:15
words...I **ate** them Jer 15:16
e this scroll Ezek 3:1
e-ing grass like cattle Dan 4:33
what you will **e** Matt 6:25
e with unwashed Matt 15:20
Take, **e**; this is My Matt 26:26
sinners and **e-s** with Luke 15:2
e...at My table Luke 22:30
He took it and **ate** Luke 24:43
e the flesh of...Son John 6:53
Peter, kill and **e** Acts 10:13
kingdom...not **e-ing** Rom 14:17
ate...spiritual food 1 Cor 10:3
e-s...judgment 1 Cor 11:29

EBAL
1 *son of Shobal* Gen 36:23
2 *son of Joktan* 1 Chr 1:22
also Obal Gen 10:28
3 *mountain near Shechem* Deut 11:29

EBENEZER
a memorial stone 1 Sam 7:12

EBER
1 *line of Shem* Gen 10:21-24
progenitor of Jocktanide Arabs Gen 10:25-30
progenitor of Hebrews Gen 11:16ff
2 *a Gadite* 1 Chr 5:13
3 *son of Elpaal* 1 Chr 8:12
4 *son of Shashak* 1 Chr 8:22
5 *priest* Neh 12:20
see also **HEBER**

EDEN
1 *garden of God* Gen 2:15; Is 51:3
2 *city area* 2 Kin 19:12; Ezek 27:23
3 *son of Joah* 2 Chr 29:12

EDICT *decree*
the king's **e-s** Ezra 8:36
a royal **e** be issued Esth 1:19
king's command and **e** Esth 9:1
afraid of the king's **e** Heb 11:23

EDIFICATION *building up*
his good, to his **e** Rom 15:2
speaks to men for **e** 1 Cor 14:3
all things...for **e** 1 Cor 14:26

EDIFY *build up*
but love **e-ies** 1 Cor 8:1
not all things **e** 1 Cor 10:23
person is not **e-ied** 1 Cor 14:17

EDOM
1 *name of Esau* Gen 25:30
2 *Edomites* Num 20:18,20
3 *region or country* Gen 32:3; Judg 11:17
see also **SEIR**

EDUCATED *taught*
be **e** three years Dan 1:5
Moses was **e** in all Acts 7:22
e under Gamaliel Acts 22:3

EFFEMINATE *womanlike*
e, nor homosexuals 1 Cor 6:9

EGG
in the white of an **e** Job 6:6
gathers abandoned **e-s** Is 10:14
hatch adders' **e-s** and Is 59:5
is asked for an **e** Luke 11:12

EGLON
1 *town in Judah* Josh 10:34-37; 15:39
2 *Moabite king* Judg 3:12-30

EGYPT
country in NE Africa Gen 12:10; 37:25
source of food Gen 42:1,2
on the Nile Ex 4:19; 7:5
conflict with Moses Ex 7:8ff
scene of Passover Ex 12:1-36

EHUD
1 *left-handed Benjamite judge of Israel* Judg 3:15,21
2 *son of Bilhan* 1 Chr 7:10
3 *progenitor of clan* 1 Chr 8:6

EKRON
Philistine city Josh 13:3; 1 Sam 5:10; Jer 25:20

ELAH
1 *Edomite* Gen 36:41
2 *valley SW of Jerusalem* 1 Sam 17:2
3 *father of Shimei* 1 Kin 4:18
4 *king of Israel* 1 Kin 16:8-10
5 *father of Hoshea* 2 Kin 15:30
6 *son of Caleb* 1 Chr 4:15
7 *son of Uzzi* 1 Chr 9:8

ELAM
1 *son of Shem* Gen 10:22
2 *son of Shashak* 1 Chr 8:24
3 *Korahite Levite* 1 Chr 26:3
4 *head of restoration family* Ezra 2:7; Neh 7:12
5 *head of restoration family* Ezra 2:31; Neh 7:34
6 *chief of people* Neh 10:14
7 *priest* Neh 12:42
8 *region E of Babylonia* Is 21:2; Dan 8:2

ELATH / ELOTH *city*
at Gulf of Aqabah 2 Kin 14:22
near Ezion-geber

EL-BETHEL
altar Gen 35:7

ELDER *aged, older*
words of her **e** son Gen 27:42
the **e-s** of Israel Ex 17:6
sits among the **e-s** Prov 31:23
Assemble the **e-s** Joel 2:16
tradition of the **e-s** Matt 15:2
chief priests and **e-s** Matt 27:12
scribes...**e-s** came Mark 11:27
Council of **e-s** of Luke 22:66
e-s of the church Acts 20:17
I saw twenty-four **e-s** Rev 4:4

ELEAZAR
1 *son of Aaron*
high priest Ex 6:23
Num 20:25-28
2 *son of Abinadab* 1 Sam 7:1
3 *son of Dodo* 2 Sam 23:9
4 *a Levite* 1 Chr 23:22
5 *son of Phinehas* Ezra 8:33
6 *son of Parosh* Ezra 10:18-25
7 *priest* Neh 12:27
8 *ancestor of Jesus* Matt 1:15

ELECT *chosen*
sake of the **e** Matt 24:22
to lead astray...the **e** Mark 13:22
justice for His **e** Luke 18:7
against God's **e** Rom 8:33

ELEMENTARY *basic*
e principles of the Col 2:8
e principles of the Heb 5:12
e teaching about the Heb 6:1

ELEMENTS *physical matter*
e will be destroyed 2 Pet 3:10
the **e** will melt with 2 Pet 3:12

ELI
high priest 1 Sam 1:9; 2:12; 3:6; 4:18

ELIAKIM
1 *son of Hilkiah* 2 Kin 18:18; 19:2
2 *son of Josiah* 2 Kin 23:34
3 *priest* Neh 12:41
4 *ancestor of Jesus* Matt 1:13
5 *ancestor of Jesus* Luke 3:30,31

ELIEZER
1 *Abraham's servant* Gen 15:2
2 *son of Moses* 1 Chr 23:15
3 *son of Becher* 1 Chr 7:8
4 *priest* 1 Chr 15:24
5 *son of Zichri* 1 Chr 27:16
6 *a prophet* 2 Chr 20:37
7 *served under Ezra* Ezra 8:16
8 *son of Jeshua* Ezra 10:18
9 *Levite* Ezra 10:10,23
10 *son Harim* Ezra 10:10,31
11 *ancestor of Jesus* Luke 3:29

ELIHU
1 *son of Tohu* 1 Sam 1:1
2 *Manassite captain* 1 Chr 12:20
3 *temple gatekeeper* 1 Chr 26:1
4 *officer of Judah* 1 Chr 27:18
5 *one of Job's friends* Job 32:17

ELIJAH
1 *prophet* 1 Kin 17:1
aided by widow 1 Kin 17:8ff
revived child 1 Kin 17:23
defeats prophets 1 Kin 18:20ff
flees Jezebel 1 Kin 19:4-8
chooses Elisha 1 Kin 19:19-21
taken up 2 Kin 2:1-11
2 *Benjamite* 1 Chr 8:27
3 *son of Harim* Ezra 10:21
4 *son of Elam* Ezra 10:26

ELIMINATE *remove*
e harmful beasts Lev 26:6
I am going to **e** Jer 16:9
stomach, and is **e-d** Mark 7:19

ELIPHAZ
1 *son of Esau* Gen 36:4
2 *one of Job's friends* Job 2:11; 4:1; 42:7,9

ELISHA
prophet 2 Kin 6:12
called 1 Kin 19:19-21
Elijah's successor 2 Kin 2:1ff
miracle of oil 2 Kin 4:1-7
revived child 2 Kin 4:8-37
death 2 Kin 13:20

ELIZABETH
mother of John the Baptist Luke 1:7,13,41,57

ELOQUENT *persuasive*
I have never been **e** Ex 4:10
Apollos...an **e** man Acts 18:24

ELUL
sixth month of Hebrew calendar Neh 6:15

ELYMAS
magician Acts 13:8
see also **BAR-JESUS**

EMBALM *preserve*
to **e** his father Gen 50:2
he was **e-ed** and Gen 50:26

EMBARRASSED *ashamed*
e to lift up my face Ezra 9:6
e at the gardens Is 1:29
diviners will be **e** Mic 3:7

EMBITTERED *resentful*
the people were **e** 1 Sam 30:6
e them against the Acts 14:2

EMBRACE *clasp, hug*
Esau ran...and **e-d** Gen 33:4
e...a foreigner Prov 5:20
A time to **e** Eccl 3:5
ran and **e-d** him Luke 15:20

EMBROIDERED *woven*
spoil of dyed work **e** Judg 5:30
be led...in **e** work Ps 45:14
silk, and **e** cloth Ezek 16:13
purple, **e** work Ezek 27:16

EMERALD *precious stone*
ruby, topaz and **e** Ex 28:17
throne, like an **e** Rev 4:3

EMINENT *renowned*
nor anything **e** Ezek 7:11
the most **e** apostles 2 Cor 11:5
inferior to...**e** 2 Cor 12:11

EMISSION *issuance*
man has a seminal **e** Lev 15:16
nocturnal **e** Deut 23:10

EMMAUS
village by Jerusalem Luke 24:13

EMPOWERED *authorized*
e him to eat from Eccl 5:19
God has not **e** him Eccl 6:2

EMPTY (adj) *containing nothing*
Now the pit was **e** Gen 37:24
did not return **e** 2 Sam 1:22
sent widows away **e** Job 22:9
deceive you with **e** Eph 5:6
avoid...**e** chatter 2 Tim 2:16

EMPTY (v) *remove contents*
e-ing their sacks Gen 42:35
they **e** the house Lev 14:36
I **e-ied** them out as Ps 18:42
therefore **e** their net Hab 1:17
e the golden *oil* Zech 4:12
but **e-ied** Himself Phil 2:7

ENCAMP *abide, lodge*
the tabernacle **e-s** Num 1:51
and **e-ed** together Josh 11:5
a host **e** against me Ps 27:3
angel of the LORD **e-s** Ps 34:7

ENCIRCLE *go around*
entirely **e-ing** the sea 2 Chr 4:3
he **e-d** the Ophel 2 Chr 33:14
cords...have **e-d** me Ps 119:61
Who **e** yourselves with Is 50:11

ENCOMPASS *surround*
waves of death **e** 2 Sam 22:5
e-ing the walls of 1 Kin 6:5
e-ed...with bitterness Lam 3:5
Water **e-ed** me to the Jon 2:5

ENCOURAGE *strengthen*
charge Joshua and **e** Deut 3:28
e-d him in God 1 Sam 23:16
e them in the work Ezra 6:22
Paul was **e-ing** them Acts 27:33
e one another 1 Thess 5:11
e the young women Titus 2:4

ENCOURAGEMENT *support*
I arose to be an **e** Dan 11:1
God who gives...**e** Rom 15:5
is any **e** in Christ Phil 2:1
we...would have strong **e** Heb 6:18

END (n) *extremity, goal, result*
e of all flesh has Gen 6:13
one **e** of the heavens Deut 4:32
from beginning to **e** 1 Sam 3:12
what is my **e** Job 6:11
very **e-s** of the earth Ps 2:8
wicked come to an **e** Ps 7:9
e is the way of death Prov 14:12
no **e** to all his labor Eccl 4:8
summer is **e-ed** Jer 8:20
The **e** is coming Ezek 7:2
who endures to...**e** Matt 24:13
to the **e** of the age Matt 28:20
kingdom...no **e** Luke 1:33
He loved...to the **e** John 13:1
Christ...**e** of the law Rom 10:4
beginning and the **e** Rev 21:6

END (v) *complete, stop*
border **e-ed** at the sea Josh 15:4
words of Job are **e-ed** Job 31:40
days there were **e-ed** Acts 21:5
it **e-s** up being burned Heb 6:8

ENDLESS *limitless*
writing...is **e** Eccl 12:12
and **e** genealogies 1 Tim 1:4

ENDOW *provide a gift*
God has **e-ed** me Gen 30:20
e-ed with discretion 2 Chr 2:12
to **e** those who love Prov 8:21
e-ed with salvation Zech 9:9

ENDURANCE *patience*
in much **e**, in 2 Cor 6:4
you have need of **e** Heb 10:36
let us run with **e** Heb 12:1
of the **e** of Job James 5:11

ENDURE *persevere*
will be able to **e** Ex 18:23
that I should **e** Job 6:11
while the sun **e-s** Ps 72:5
May his name **e** Ps 72:17
and your name will **e** Is 66:22
Can your heart **e** Ezek 22:14
the one who has **e-d** Matt 10:22
who **e-s** to the end Mark 13:13
e-s all things 1 Cor 13:7
discipline that you **e** Heb 12:7
blessed who **e-d** James 5:11
word...LORD **e-s** 1 Pet 1:25

ENEMY *foe*
delivered your **e-ies** Gen 14:20
Your **e-ies** perish Judg 5:31
a man finds his **e** 1 Sam 24:19
consider me Your **e** Job 13:24

make the **e**...cease Ps 8:2
presence of my **e-ies** Ps 23:5
e has persecuted my Ps 143:3
If your **e** is hungry Prov 25:21
kisses of an **e** Prov 27:6
love your **e-ies,** and Matt 5:44
e-ies with each other Luke 23:12
e of all righteousness Acts 13:10
e is hungry, feed Rom 12:20
e...be abolished 1 Cor 15:26
an **e** of God James 4:4

ENGAGE *be involved, betroth*
virgin who is not **e-d** Ex 22:16
the girl who is **e-d** Deut 22:25
e-d in their work 1 Chr 9:33
e-d to...Joseph Luke 1:27
to **e** in good deeds Titus 3:8

ENGEDI
spring and town near Dead Sea 1 Sam 23:29; 24:1; Song 1:14

ENGRAVE *inscribe*
shall **e** the two stones Ex 28:11
e-d on the tablets Ex 32:16
e an inscription Zech 3:9
letters **e-d** on stones 2 Cor 3:7

ENGRAVINGS *carvings*
like the **e** of a seal Ex 28:36
the **e** of a signet Ex 39:30
carved **e** of cherubim 1 Kin 6:29

ENGULF *overwhelm, swallow*
water...to **e** them Deut 11:4
sea **e-ed** their enemies Ps 78:53
She has been **e-ed** Jer 51:42
great deep **e-ed** me Jon 2:5

ENLARGE *extend, increase*
May God **e** Japheth Gen 9:27
You will **e** my heart Ps 119:32
Sheol has **e-d** its Is 5:14
He **e-s** his appetite Hab 2:5

ENLIGHTEN *illumine*
e-ing the eyes Ps 19:8
eyes...may be **e-ed** Eph 1:18
who have...been **e-ed** Heb 6:4

ENMITY *hostility*
e Between you and Gen 3:15
had everlasting **e** Ezek 35:5
sorcery, **e-ies,** strife Gal 5:20
abolishing...the **e** Eph 2:15

ENOCH
1 *son of Cain* Gen 4:17
2 *city* Gen 4:17
3 *Methuselah's father* Gen 5:22
walked with God Gen 5:24

ENRAGE *anger*
e-d and curse their Is 8:21
jealousy **e-s** a man Prov 6:34
he became very **e-d** Matt 2:16
dragon was **e-d** with Rev 12:17

ENRICH *make wealthy*
king will **e** the 1 Sam 17:25
You greatly **e** Ps 65:9
You **e-ed** the kings Ezek 27:33

ENROLLED *recorded*
were **e** by genealogy 1 Chr 7:9
people to be **e** by Neh 7:5
e in heaven Heb 12:23

ENSLAVE *subjugate*
you have been **e-d** Is 14:3
e-d and mistreated Acts 7:6
anyone **e-s** you 2 Cor 11:20
e-d to various lusts Titus 3:3

ENSNARE *catch*
An evil man is **e-d** Prov 12:13

e him who adjudicates Is 29:21

ENTANGLE *ensnare*
camel **e-ing** her ways Jer 2:23
No soldier...**e-s** 2 Tim 2:4
sin which...**e-s** us Heb 12:1

ENTER *go in*
you shall **e** the ark Gen 6:18
He **e-s** into judgment Job 22:4
E His gates with Ps 100:4
E the rock and hide Is 2:10
He **e-s** into peace Is 57:2
Spirit **e-ed** me and Ezek 2:2
not **e** the kingdom Matt 5:20
E through the narrow gate Matt 7:13
to **e** life crippled Matt 18:8
afraid as they **e-ed** Luke 9:34
e into the kingdom John 3:5
not **e** by the door John 10:1
shall not **e** My rest Heb 3:11

ENTHRONED *exalt, make king*
e *above* the cherubim 2 Sam 6:2
LORD who is **e** *above* 1 Chr 13:6
e upon the praises of Ps 22:3
who sits **e** from of old Ps 55:19
Who is **e** on high Ps 113:5

ENTICE *deceive, seduce*
E your husband Judg 14:15
Who will **e** Ahab 2 Chr 18:19
if sinners **e** you Prov 1:10
e-d by his own lust James 1:14
e-ing unstable souls 2 Pet 2:14

ENTRAILS *inner organs*
fat that covers the **e** Ex 29:13
e and the lobe Lev 8:16
also washed the **e** Lev 9:14

ENTRANCE *doorway*
cloud...at the **e** Ex 33:10
mark well the **e** of Ezek 44:5
stone against the **e** Matt 27:60
e into the eternal 2 Pet 1:11

ENTREAT *appeal, ask*
E the LORD that he Ex 8:8
Moses **e-ed** the LORD Ex 32:11
Please **e** the LORD 1 Kin 13:6
gain if we **e** Him Job 21:15
demons *began* to **e** Matt 8:31

ENTRUST *assign, commit*
security **e-ed** *to him* Lev 6:2
He **e-ed** the vineyard Song 8:11
to whom they **e-ed** Luke 12:48
not **e-ing** Himself to John 2:24

ENVIOUS *covetous*
e of the arrogant Ps 73:3
not be **e** of evil men Prov 24:1
is your eye **e** Matt 20:15
You are **e** James 4:2

ENVIRONS *outskirts, suburbs*
the **e** of Jerusalem Jer 32:44
devour all his **e** Jer 50:32

ENVOY *agent, messenger*
e-s of the rulers 2 Chr 32:31
faithful **e** *brings* Prov 13:17
sent your **e-s** a great Is 57:9
his **e-s** to Egypt Ezek 17:15

ENVY (n) *jealousy*
full of **e,** murder Rom 1:29
preaching...from **e** Phil 1:15
out of which arise **e** 1 Tim 6:4
life in malice and **e** Titus 3:3
e and all slander 1 Pet 2:1

ENVY (v) *be discontent, jealous*
Philistines **e-ied** him Gen 26:14
e a man of violence Prov 3:31
not let your heart **e** Prov 23:17

e-ing one another Gal 5:26

EPAPHRAS
Colossian Christian Col 1:7; 4:12
colleague of Paul Philem 23

EPAPHRODITUS
Philippian Christian Phil 2:25
colleague of Paul Phil 4:18

EPHAH
1 *bushel, measure of capacity* Lev 5:11; Num 5:15
2 *son of Midian* Gen 25:4; 1 Chr 1:33
3 *Caleb's concubine* 1 Chr 2:46
4 *son of Jahdai* 1 Chr 2:47

EPHESUS
city of Asia Minor Acts 18:19; 1 Cor 16:8; Rev 1:11; 2:1

EPHOD
1 *priestly garment* Ex 28:6; 1 Sam 23:9; 2 Sam 6:14
2 *father of Hanniel* Num 34:23

EPHRAIM
1 *son of Joseph* Gen 41:52; 48:17
2 *tribe* Josh 16:5; Judg 7:24
3 *northern kingdom* Is 7:2-17; Hos 4:17; 9:3-17
4 *city* 2 Sam 13:23; John 11:54

EPHRAIM GATE *see* **GATES OF JERUSALEM**

EPHRATH(AH)
1 *Bethlehem* Gen 35:19; 48:7; Ruth 4:11; Mic 5:2
2 *wife of Caleb* 1 Chr 2:19,50
3 *territory* Ps 132:6

EPHRON
1 *a Hittite* Gen 23:8; 50:13
2 *mountain ridge* Josh 15:9
3 *city* 2 Chr 13:19

EPICUREAN
a Greek philosophy Acts 17:18

EPOCHS *ages, seasons*
the times and the **e** Dan 2:21
to know times or **e** Acts 1:7

EQUAL *same*
shall eat **e** portions Deut 18:8
a man my **e** Ps 55:13
That I would be *his* **e** Is 40:25
have made them **e** Matt 20:12
Himself **e** with God John 5:18

EQUIP *furnish, provide*
e-ped for war Josh 4:13
e-ped for...work 2 Tim 3:17
e you in every good Heb 13:21

EQUIPMENT *implements*
the **e** for the service Ex 39:40
e for his chariots 1 Sam 8:12
e of a foolish Zech 11:15

EQUITY *equality, fairness*
eyes look with **e** Ps 17:2
have established **e** Ps 99:4
justice and **e** Prov 1:3
e *and* every good Prov 2:9

ERASTUS
Corinthian Christian Acts 19:22; Rom 16:23; 2 Tim 4:20

ERROR *mistake, sin*
can discern *his* **e-s** Ps 19:12
like an **e** which goes Eccl 10:5
e against the LORD Is 32:6
e of unprincipled 2 Pet 3:17
the spirit of **e** 1 John 4:6
rushed...into the **e** Jude 11

ESARHADDON
Assyrian king 2 Kin 19:37; Ezra 4:2; Is 37:38

ESAU
son of Isaac Gen 25:25
twin of Jacob Gen 25:26
skillful hunter Gen 25:27
sold birthright Gen 25:34
despised Jacob Gen 27:41
reconciled with Jacob Gen 33:4

ESCAPE (n) ***deliverance, refuge***
there will be no **e** Job 11:20
is no **e** for me Ps 142:4
Let there be no **e** Jer 50:29
provide...**e** 1 Cor 10:13

ESCAPE (v) ***elude***
slave who has **e-d** Deut 23:15
let no one **e** *or* 2 Kin 9:15
Our soul has **e-d** Ps 124:7
tells lies will not **e** Prov 19:5
how shall we **e** Is 20:6
nothing at all **e-s** Joel 2:3
had not **e-d** notice Luke 8:47
how will we **e** if Heb 2:3
it **e-s** their notice 2 Pet 3:5

ESTABLISH ***confirm, found***
I will **e** My covenant Gen 17:19
how God **e-es** them Job 37:15
e-es the mountains Ps 65:6
my ways may be **e-ed** Ps 119:5
e-ed in lovingkindness Is 16:5
to **e** the heavens Is 51:16
we **e** the Law Rom 3:31
may **e** your hearts 1 Thess 3:13
e-ed in the truth 2 Pet 1:12

ESTATE ***domain*** **or** ***standard***
restore your...**e** Job 8:6
us in our low **e** Ps 136:23
squandered his **e** Luke 15:13

ESTEEM (n) ***honor***
man of high **e** Dan 10:11
held them in high **e** Acts 5:13

ESTEEM (v) ***have high regard***
I **e** right all *Your* Ps 119:128
e-ed Him stricken Is 53:4
e-ed among men Luke 16:15
e them...in love 1 Thess 5:13

ESTHER
Hebrew name Hadassah
cousin of Mordecai Esth 2:7
Persian queen Esth 2:16-18

ESTRANGED ***separated***
completely **e** from me Job 19:13
e from my brothers Ps 69:8

ETERNAL ***everlasting***
e God is a dwelling Deut 33:27
E Father, Prince of Is 9:6
An **e** decree Jer 5:22
cast into the **e** fire Matt 18:8
guilty of an **e** sin Mark 3:29
to inherit **e** life Luke 10:25
He may give **e** life John 17:2
gift of God is **e** life Rom 6:23
e weight of glory 2 Cor 4:17
with the **e** purpose Eph 3:11
Now to the King **e** 1 Tim 1:17
source of **e** salvation Heb 5:9
through the **e** Spirit Heb 9:14
kept in **e** bonds Jude 6
an **e** gospel to preach Rev 14:6

ETERNITY ***perpetuity***
set **e** in their heart Eccl 3:11
from **e** I am He Is 43:13
Jesus from all **e** 2 Tim 1:9
to the day of **e** 2 Pet 3:18

ETHIOPIA
NE African country Esth 1:1; Ps 68:31; Nah 3:9; Zeph 3:10

EUNICE
mother of Timothy 2 Tim 1:5

EUNUCH ***chamberlain official***
seven **e-s** who served Esth 1:10
Nor let the **e** say Is 56:3
children, and *the* **e-s** Jer 41:16
made **e-s** by men Matt 19:12
an Ethiopian **e** Acts 8:27

EUPHRATES
river of Mesopotamia Gen 2:14; Jer 13:5; 46:10; Rev 9:14; 16:12

EVANGELIST ***proclaimer***
house of Philip the **e** Acts 21:8
and some *as* **e-s** Eph 4:11
do the work of an **e** 2 Tim 4:5

EVE
first woman Gen 2:22
wife of Adam Gen 2:23
deceived by serpent Gen 3:1-7
named by Adam Gen 3:20

EVENING ***dusk, darkness***
cloud...from **e** Num 9:21
eats food before **e** 1 Sam 14:24
as the **e** offering Ps 141:2
not be idle in the **e** Eccl 11:6
When **e** came Matt 8:16

EVENT ***happening***
the **e-s** of the war 2 Sam 11:18
e became sin to the 1 Kin 13:34
recorded these **e-s** Esth 9:20
time for every **e** Eccl 3:1

EVERLASTING ***eternal***
e covenant between Gen 9:16
the LORD, the **E** God Gen 21:33
are the **e** arms Deut 33:27
e to **e**, You are God Ps 90:2
lovingkindness is **e** Ps 106:1
From **e** I was Prov 8:23
The **E** God, the LORD Is 40:28
e name which will Is 56:5
LORD for an **e** light Is 60:20
loved you with an **e** Jer 31:3

EVIDENCE ***facts, testimony***
the **e** of witnesses Num 35:30
on the **e** of two Deut 19:15
not able to give **e** Ezra 2:59
and giving **e** Acts 17:3

EVIDENT ***obvious, plain***
the tares became **e** Matt 13:26
for God made it **e** Rom 1:19
work will become **e** 1 Cor 3:13
Law before God is **e** Gal 3:11
it is **e** that our Lord Heb 7:14

EVIL ***bad, wicked, wrong***
man's heart is **e** Gen 8:21
keep...from every **e** Deut 23:9
discern good and **e** 2 Sam 14:17
rebellious and **e** city Ezra 4:12
I fear no **e** Ps 23:4
repay me **e** for good Ps 35:12
turn away from **e** Prov 3:7
run rapidly to **e** Prov 6:18
returns **e** for good Prov 17:13
taken away from **e** Is 57:1
committed two **e-s** Jer 2:13
deliver us from **e** Matt 6:13
what **e** has He Matt 27:23
If you then, being **e** Luke 11:13
who does **e** hates the John 3:20
Never...**e** for **e** Rom 12:17
love of money is...**e** 1 Tim 6:10
tongue...restless **e** James 3:8

EVILDOER ***wicked one***
LORD repay the **e** 2 Sam 3:39
e-s will be cut off Ps 37:9
e listens to wicked Prov 17:4

Offspring of **e-s** Is 1:4
is godless and an **e** Is 9:17
depart...you **e-s** Luke 13:27
punishment of **e-s** 1 Pet 2:14

EVIL-MERODACH
king of Babylon 2 Kin 25:27; Jer 52:31

EWE ***female sheep***
seven **e** lambs Gen 21:28
e lamb without Lev 14:10
poor man's **e** lamb 2 Sam 12:4
e-s with suckling Ps 78:71
like a flock of **e-s** Song 6:6

EXACT (adj) ***certain, correct***
e amount of money Esth 4:7
e meaning of all this Dan 7:16
know the **e** truth Luke 1:4
a more **e** knowledge Acts 24:22

EXACT (v) ***collect***
let him **e** a fifth Gen 41:34
He shall not **e** it Deut 15:2
He **e-ed** the silver 2 Kin 23:35
You are **e-ing** usury Neh 5:7
e a tribute of grain Amos 5:11

EXALT ***extol, honor, lift***
He is highly **e-ed** Ex 15:1
e-ed be God 2 Sam 22:47
He is **e-ed** in power Job 37:23
let us **e** His name Ps 34:3
e-ed far above all gods Ps 97:9
city is **e-ed** Prov 11:11
my God; I will **e** You Is 25:1
E that which is low Ezek 21:26
humbles...be **e-ed** Matt 23:12
e-ed to...right hand Acts 2:33
be **e-ed** in my body Phil 1:20
He will **e** you James 4:10

EXAMINE ***investigate, search***
That You **e** him every Job 7:18
E me, O LORD, and try Ps 26:2
e my heart's *attitude* Jer 12:3
e-ing the Scriptures Acts 17:11
e-d by scourging Acts 22:24
a man must **e** himself 1 Cor 11:28

EXAMPLE ***model, pattern***
the **e** of his father 2 Chr 17:3
I gave you an **e** John 13:15
e of those who 1 Tim 4:12
e of disobedience Heb 4:11
be **e-s** to the flock 1 Pet 5:3
made them an **e** 2 Pet 2:6

EXCEL ***be superior***
e in...wickedness Jer 5:28
wisdom **e-s** folly Eccl 2:13
you **e**...more 1 Thess 4:1

EXCELLENCE ***perfection***
greatness of Your **e** Ex 15:7
are a woman of **e** Ruth 3:11
if there is any **e** Phil 4:8
proclaim the **e-ies** of 1 Pet 2:9

EXCELLENT ***outstanding***
e wife is the crown Prov 12:4
E speech is not Prov 17:7
He has done **e** things Is 12:5
e governor Felix Acts 23:26
a still more **e** way 1 Cor 12:31
a more **e** name Heb 1:4

EXCESS ***too much***
he...had no **e** Ex 16:18
are in **e** among them Num 3:48
same **e-es** of dissipation 1 Pet 4:4

EXCHANGE ***trade, transfer***
shall **e** *it* for money Deut 14:25
they **e-d** their glory Ps 106:20
shall not sell or **e** Ezek 48:14
e-d the truth of God Rom 1:25

EXCLUDE *refuse to admit*
e-d from...assembly Ezra 10:8
e-d all foreigners Neh 13:3
e you for My name's Is 66:5
e-d from the life of Eph 4:18

EXCUSE *justification*
began to make **e-s** Luke 14:18
no **e** for their sin John 15:22
they are without **e** Rom 1:20

EXECUTE *carry out*
e-d the justice of Deut 33:21
He has **e-d** judgment Ps 9:16
e vengeance on the Ps 149:7
Lord will **e** His word Rom 9:28
e judgment upon all Jude 15

EXERCISE *perform*
man has **e-d** authority Eccl 8:9
e-s lovingkindness Jer 9:24
e authority over Matt 20:25
e-s self-control in all 1 Cor 9:25

EXHAUSTED *used up, wearied*
sound asleep and **e** Judg 4:21
too **e** to follow 1 Sam 30:21
of flour was not **e** 1 Kin 17:16
Their strength is **e** Jer 51:30

EXHORT *admonish, urge*
and kept on **e-ing** Acts 2:40
e, with...patience 2 Tim 4:2
e in sound doctrine Titus 1:9
e and reprove Titus 2:15
e-ing and testifying 1 Pet 5:12

EXHORTATION *urging*
with many other **e-s** Luke 3:18
given them much **e** Acts 20:2
who exhorts, in his **e** Rom 12:8
this word of **e** Heb 13:22

EXILE *banishment* **or** *capture*
Israel away into **e** 2 Kin 17:6
people of the **e** were Ezra 4:1
captivity of the **e-s** Neh 7:6
into **e** from Jerusalem Esth 2:6
e will soon be set free Is 51:14
Israel went into **e** Ezek 39:23

EXIST *be, live, occur*
they had never **e-ed** Obad 16
Strife **e-s** and Hab 1:3
live and move and **e** Acts 17:28
authority...which **e** Rom 13:1

EXODUS *departure*
e of...Israel Heb 11:22

EXPANSE *firmament, vastness*
e of the heavens Gen 1:20
e of the waters Job 37:10
in His mighty **e** Ps 150:1
from above the **e** Ezek 1:25

EXPECT *await*
never **e-ed** to see Gen 48:11
e-ed good, then evil Job 30:26
which we did not **e** Is 64:3
lend, **e-ing** nothing Luke 6:35

EXPECTATION *anticipation*
your **e** is false Job 41:9
e of the wicked Prov 10:28
to my earnest **e** Phil 1:20
e of judgment Heb 10:27

EXPECTED *awaited*
Are You the **E** One Matt 11:3
Are You the **E** One Luke 7:20

EXPERIENCE *undergo*
all who had not **e-d** Judg 3:1
Your people **e** hardship Ps 60:3
e-s Your judgments Is 26:9
e-d mockings and Heb 11:36

EXPERT *very skillful*
an **e** in warfare 2 Sam 17:8
be like an **e** warrior Jer 50:9
an **e** in all customs Acts 26:3

EXPLAIN *make clear*
no one who could **e** Gen 41:24
he did not **e** to her 2 Chr 9:2
e its interpretation Dan 5:7
E the parable to us Matt 15:15
e-ing the Scriptures Luke 24:32
e-ed to him the way Acts 18:26

EXPOSE *disclose, reveal*
shame...be **e-d** Is 47:3
He will **e** your sins Lam 4:22
deeds will be **e-d** John 3:20
would **e** their infants Acts 7:19
are **e-d** by the light Eph 5:13

EXTEND *enlarge, stretch out*
God **e-s**...border Deut 12:20
e-ed lovingkindness Ezra 7:28
e-s her hand to the Prov 31:20
I **e** peace to her Is 66:12
boundary shall **e** Ezek 47:17

EXTENT *amount* **or** *degree*
the **e** of my days Ps 39:4
e that you did it to Matt 25:40
such an **e** that Jesus Mark 1:45

EXTERMINATE *destroy*
planned to **e** us 2 Sam 21:5
He will **e** its sinners Is 13:9

EXTERNAL *outward*
not with **e** service Col 3:22
adornment must not be...**e** 1 Pet 3:3

EXTINGUISH *put out*
they will **e** my coal 2 Sam 14:7
not **e** the lamp of 2 Sam 21:17
my days are **e-ed** Job 17:1
when *I* **e** you Ezek 32:7
e all the flaming Eph 6:16

EXTOL *praise*
God, and I will **e** Him Ex 15:2
I will **e** You, O LORD Ps 30:1
I will **e** You, my God Ps 145:1
We will **e** your love Song 1:4

EXTORTION *stealing*
practicing...**e** Jer 22:17
practiced **e,** robbed Ezek 18:18

EXTRAORDINARY *exceptional*
will bring **e** plagues Deut 28:59
His **e** work Is 28:21
insight, and **e** wisdom Dan 5:14
e miracles by Acts 19:11
showed us **e** kindness Acts 28:2

EXULT *rejoice*
heart **e-s** in the LORD 1 Sam 2:1
Let the field **e** 1 Chr 16:32
e-ed when evil befell Job 31:29
let them **e** before God Ps 68:3
I will **e** in the LORD Hab 3:18
e in our tribulations Rom 5:3

EXULTATION *jubilation*
e like the nations Hos 9:1
joy or crown of **e** 1 Thess 2:19
may rejoice with **e** 1 Pet 4:13

EYE *sight*
e-s are dull from Gen 49:12
e for **e,** tooth for Ex 21:24
be as **e-s** for us Num 10:31
his **e** was not dim Deut 34:7
right in his own **e-s** Judg 17:6
open his **e-s** that he 2 Kin 6:17
e-s of the LORD 2 Chr 16:9
was **e-s** to the blind Job 29:15
e-s...look to You Ps 145:15
Haughty **e-s,** a lying Prov 6:17
e...mocks a father Prov 30:17
e is not satisfied Eccl 1:8
To open blind **e-s** Is 42:7
e-s will bitterly weep Jer 13:17
have **e-s** to see but Ezek 12:2
I lifted my **e-s** and Dan 8:3
Your **e-s**...too pure Hab 1:13
e for an **e,** and a Matt 5:38
e...you to stumble Matt 18:9
e is the lamp Luke 11:34
the clay to his **e-s** John 9:6
which **e** has not seen 1 Cor 2:9
e-s of your heart may Eph 1:18
e-s full of adultery 2 Pet 2:14
the lust of the **e-s** 1 John 2:16
God, who has **e-s** like Rev 2:18
His **e-s** *are* a flame Rev 19:12

EYEWITNESSES *observers*
e...of the word Luke 1:2
e of His majesty 2 Pet 1:16

EZEKIEL
Hebrew prophet Ezek 1:1
called by God Ezek 1:1,3
spoke to Israel Ezek 14:1ff
taken captive Ezek 33:21
spoke to false prophets Ezek 34:2ff
spoke to nations Ezek 35:2ff
restored temple Ezek 40:1ff

EZION-GEBER
on gulf of Aqabah 1 Kin 9:26; 22:48
near Elath / Eloth Deut 2:8; 2 Chr 8:17

EZRA
priest Ezra 7:1-5
scribe Ezra 7:6
sent by king Ezra 7:14,21
brought exiles Ezra 8:1-14
Nehemiah's colleague Neh 8:2-6

F

FACE *countenance*
sweat of your **f** You Gen 3:19
Abram fell on his **f** Gen 17:3
speak to Moses **f** to **f** Ex 33:11
skin of his **f** shone Ex 34:30
make His **f** shine Num 6:25
hide Your **f** from me Ps 13:1
Who seek Your **f** Ps 24:6
His **f** to shine upon us Ps 67:1
f of Your anointed Ps 84:9
makes a cheerful **f** Prov 15:13
set My **f** against you Jer 44:11
had the **f** of an eagle Ezek 1:10
Each...had four **f-s** Ezek 10:21
fast...wash your **f** Matt 6:17
they spat in His **f** Matt 26:67
like the **f** of an angel Acts 6:15
natural **f** in a mirror James 1:23
His **f** was like the sun Rev 1:16

FACT *truth*
f may be confirmed Matt 18:16
are undeniable **f-s** Acts 19:36
f is to be confirmed 2 Cor 13:1

FACTIONS *divisions*
be **f** among you 1 Cor 11:19
dissensions, **f** Gal 5:20

FADE *wither*
it **f-s,** and withers Ps 90:6
people...**f** away Is 24:4
rich man...will **f** James 1:11
will not **f** away 1 Pet 1:4

FAIL *be spent* **or** *fall short*
He will not **f** you Deut 4:31
none of his words **f** 1 Sam 3:19
no man's heart **f** 1 Sam 17:32
not one word...**f-ed** 1 Kin 8:56
my strength **f-s** me Ps 38:10

the olive should **f** Hab 3:17
faith may not **f** Luke 22:32
Love never **f-s** 1 Cor 13:8

FAINT ***languish, swoon***
has made my heart **f** Job 23:16
soul **f-ed** within Ps 107:5
grow **f** before Me Is 57:16
I was **f-ing** away Jon 2:7
men **f-ing** from fear Luke 21:26
f when...reproved Heb 12:5

FAINTHEARTED ***weak***
Do not be **f** Deut 20:3
encourage the **f** 1 Thess 5:14

FAIR HAVENS
harbor in Crete Acts 27:8

FAITH ***believe, trust***
because you broke **f** Deut 32:51
Will you have **f** Job 39:12
Who keeps **f** forever Ps 146:6
will live by his **f** Hab 2:4
Seeing their **f**, Jesus Matt 9:2
f the size of a mustard seed Matt 17:20
Your **f** has saved you Luke 7:50
Increase our **f** Luke 17:5
your **f** may not fail Luke 22:32
man full of **f** Acts 6:5
of **f** to the Gentiles Acts 14:27
sanctified by **f** in Me Acts 26:18
justified by **f** Rom 5:1
f...from hearing Rom 10:17
if I have all **f** 1 Cor 13:2
your **f** also is vain 1 Cor 15:14
we walk by **f** 2 Cor 5:7
live by **f** in the Son Gal 2:20
saved through **f** Eph 2:8
one Lord, one **f** Eph 4:5
joy in the **f** Phil 1:25
stability of your **f** Col 2:5
breastplate of **f** 1 Thess 5:8
for not all have **f** 2 Thess 3:2
fall away from the **f** 1 Tim 4:1
conduct, love, **f** 1 Tim 4:12
they upset the **f** 2 Tim 2:18
sound in the **f** Titus 1:13
showing all good **f** Titus 2:10
full assurance of **f** Heb 10:22
By **f** Enoch was taken Heb 11:5
perfecter of **f** Heb 12:2
ask in **f** James 1:6
prayer offered in **f** James 5:15
power of God...**f** 1 Pet 1:5
the **f** of the saints Rev 13:10

FAITHFUL ***loyal, trustworthy***
the **f** God, who keeps Deut 7:9
raise...a **f** priest 1 Sam 2:35
heart **f** before You Neh 9:8
LORD preserves the **f** Ps 31:23
commandments...**f** Ps 119:86
the LORD who is **f** Is 49:7
Well done...**f** Matt 25:23
God is **f** 1 Cor 1:9
F is He who calls 1 Thess 5:24
He considered me **f** 1 Tim 1:12
entrust...to **f** men 2 Tim 2:2
souls to a **f** Creator 1 Pet 4:19
He is **f**...to forgive 1 John 1:9
Be **f** until death Rev 2:10
called **F** and True Rev 19:11

FAITHFULNESS ***loyalty***
kindness and **f** Gen 47:29
A God of **f** Deut 32:4
make known Your **f** Ps 89:1
f to all generations Ps 100:5
and mercy and **f** Matt 23:23
nullify the **f** of God Rom 3:3
kindness, goodness, **f** Gal 5:22

FAITHLESS ***unbelieving***
what **f** Israel did Jer 3:6
O **f** daughter Jer 31:22

Their heart is **f** Hos 10:2
If we are **f** 2 Tim 2:13

FALL ***descend*** **or** ***fail***
deep sleep to **f** upon Gen 2:21
devices let them **f** Ps 5:10
I am ready to **f** Ps 38:17
dread...had **f-en** Ps 105:38
wicked will **f** Prov 11:5
a righteous man **f-s** Prov 24:16
whether a tree **f-s** Eccl 11:3
Assyrian will **f** Is 31:8
Babylon has **f-en** Jer 51:8
f down and worship Dan 3:5
will **f** into a pit Matt 15:14
f-ing on his knees Mark 1:40
all may **f**...I will Mark 14:29
appointed for the **f** Luke 2:34
watching Satan **f** Luke 10:18
house *divided*...**f-s** Luke 11:17
f-ing headlong Acts 1:18
sinned and **f** short Rom 3:23
have **f-en** asleep 1 Cor 15:6
f-en from grace Gal 5:4
rich **f** into temptation 1 Tim 6:9
rocks, **F** on us Rev 6:16

FALLOW ***unproductive***
rest and lie **f** Ex 23:11
f ground of the poor Prov 13:23

FALSE ***deceitful, dishonest***
not bear a **f** report Ex 23:1
I hate every **f** way Ps 119:104
But a **f** witness Prov 12:17
f witness will not go Prov 19:5
f scale is not good Prov 20:23
F and foolish *visions* Lam 2:14
And tell **f** dreams Zech 10:2
not bear **f** witness Matt 19:18
f Christs and **f** Matt 24:24
men are **f** apostles 2 Cor 11:13
the **f** circumcision Phil 3:2
and the **f** prophet Rev 20:10

FALSEHOOD ***deception***
lifted up his soul to **f** Ps 24:4
delight in **f** Ps 62:4
I hate and despise **f** Ps 119:163
Bread obtained by **f** Prov 20:17
trusted in **f** Jer 13:25
prophesying **f** in My Jer 14:14
laying aside **f** Eph 4:25

FAME ***greatness***
heard of Your **f** Num 14:15
Joshua, and his **f** Josh 6:27
the **f** of Solomon 1 Kin 10:1
heard My **f** Is 66:19
f in *the things of* 2 Cor 8:18

FAMILY ***household, relatives***
f-ies from the ark Gen 8:19
all the **f-ies** of Gen 12:3
f may redeem him Lev 25:49
f-ies of the Levites Num 3:20
my **f** is the least Judg 6:15
f-ies like a flock Ps 107:41
God of all the **f-ies** Jer 31:1
f-ies of the earth Amos 3:2
every **f** in heaven Eph 3:15
upsetting whole **f-ies** Titus 1:11

FAMINE ***shortage of food***
a **f** in the land Gen 12:10
seven years of **f** Gen 41:27
If there is **f** 2 Chr 6:28
In **f** He will redeem Job 5:20
keep them alive in **f** Ps 33:19
f and pestilence Jer 14:12
f and wild beasts Ezek 5:17
f-s and earthquakes Matt 24:7
plagues and **f-s** Luke 21:11
Now a **f** came Acts 7:11
mourning and **f** Rev 18:8

FAMISHED ***hungry, parched***
for I am **f** Gen 25:30
strength is **f** Job 18:12
honorable men are **f** Is 5:13

FAMOUS ***well-known***
f in Bethlehem Ruth 4:11
men of valor, **f** men 1 Chr 5:24

FAR ***distant***
f from a false charge Ex 23:7
come from a **f** country Josh 9:6
Be not **f** from me Ps 22:11
f above all gods Ps 97:9
As **f** as the east Ps 103:12
LORD is **f** from the Prov 15:29
a God **f** off Jer 23:23
heart is **f** away from Matt 15:8
f from the kingdom Mark 12:34
glory **f** beyond all 2 Cor 4:17
f above all rule Eph 1:21

FARM ***agricultural land***
consume the **f** land Amos 7:4
one to his own **f** Matt 22:5
or **f-s**, for My sake Mark 10:29

FARMER ***husbandman***
Does the **f** plow Is 28:24
will be your **f-s** Is 61:5
f-s...put to shame Jer 14:4
the **f** to mourning Amos 5:16

FASHION ***create, form***
f-ed into a woman Gen 2:22
f us in the womb Job 31:15
He who **f-s** the hearts Ps 33:15
f a graven image Is 44:9
I am **f-ing** calamity Jer 18:11

FAST (n) ***food abstinence***
Proclaim a **f** 1 Kin 21:9
you call this a **f** Is 58:5
Consecrate a **f** Joel 1:14
f was already over Acts 27:9

FAST (v) ***abstain from food***
and David **f-ed** 2 Sam 12:16
maidens also will **f** Esth 4:16
you **f** for contention Is 58:4
had **f-ed** forty days Matt 4:2
whenever you **f** Matt 6:16
disciples do not **f** Mark 2:18
I **f** twice a week Luke 18:12
had **f-ed** and prayed Acts 13:3

FASTING ***food abstinence***
times of **f** Esth 9:31
weak from **f** Ps 109:24
noticed...when they are **f** Matt 6:16
by prayer and **f** Matt 17:21
Pharisees were **f** Mark 2:18

FAT ***animal fat*** **or** ***obese***
f of the land Gen 45:18
shall not eat any **f** Lev 7:23
Go, eat of the **f** Neh 8:10
their body is **f** Ps 73:4
Good news puts **f** Prov 15:30

FATE ***destiny***
appalled at his **f** Job 18:20
one **f** befalls them Eccl 2:14
f for the righteous Eccl 9:2
one **f** for all men Eccl 9:3

FATHER ***God*** **or** ***parent***
leave his **f**...mother Gen 2:24
f of a multitude Gen 17:4
Honor your **f** Ex 20:12
who strikes his **f** Ex 21:15
iniquity of the **f-s** Deut 5:9
Is not He your **F** Deut 32:6
your **f-'s** instruction Prov 1:8
son makes a **f** glad Prov 10:1
Eternal **F**, Prince of Is 9:6
all have one **f** Mal 2:10

F who sees...in secret Matt 6:4
Our **F** who is in Matt 6:9
does the will of My **F** Matt 7:21
in My **F-'s** kingdom Matt 26:29
in the glory of His **F** Mark 8:38
be in my **F-'s** *house* Luke 2:49
F, hallowed be Your Luke 11:2
F, forgive them Luke 23:34
begotten from the **F** John 1:14
my **F-'s** house a John 2:16
F...testifies John 8:18
the **f** of lies John 8:44
I and the **F** are one John 10:30
In my **F-'s** house are John 14:2
F is the vinedresser John 15:1
ask the **F** for John 16:23
I ascend to My **F** John 20:17
one God and **F** of all Eph 4:6

FATHER-IN-LAW
she sent to her **f** Gen 38:25
returned to Jethro his **f** Ex 4:18
his **f,** the girl's Judg 19:4
f of Caiaphas John 18:13

FATHERLESS *orphan*
father of the **f** Ps 68:5
He supports the **f** Ps 146:9
fields of the **f** Prov 23:10
f and the widow Ezek 22:7

FATLING *young lamb* **or** *kid*
sacrificed...a **f** 2 Sam 6:13
f-s...in abundance 1 Kin 1:19
f-s of Bashan Ezek 39:18

FATNESS *abundance*
f of the earth Gen 27:28
Shall I leave my **f** Judg 9:9
satisfied as with...**f** Ps 63:5
eye bulges from **f** Ps 73:7

FAULT *error, offense*
found no **f** in him 1 Sam 29:3
let no one find **f** Hos 4:4
does He still find **f** Rom 9:19
grumblers, finding **f** Jude 16

FAVOR *kind regard*
Noah found **f** Gen 6:8
I will grant...**f** Ex 3:21
show no **f** to them Deut 7:2
Why have I found **f** Ruth 2:10
surround him with **f** Ps 5:12
showed **f** to Your land Ps 85:1
obtains **f**...LORD Prov 8:35
f is like a cloud Prov 16:15
found **f** with God Luke 1:30
in **f** with God and Luke 2:52
seeking the **f** of men Gal 1:10

FEAR (n) *awe, dread, reverence*
no **f** of God in Gen 20:11
f of the LORD is clean Ps 19:9
f...is the beginning Ps 111:10
afraid of sudden **f** Prov 3:25
f...prolongs life Prov 10:27
f of man brings a Prov 29:25
they cried out in **f** Matt 14:26
guards shook for **f** Matt 28:4
men fainting from **f** Luke 21:26
for **f** of the Jews John 7:13
no **f** of God before Rom 3:18
in weakness and in **f** 1 Cor 2:3
knowing the **f** of the 2 Cor 5:11
with **f** and trembling Eph 6:5
through **f** of death Heb 2:15
love casts out **f** 1 John 4:18

FEAR (v) *be afraid, revere*
the midwives **f-ed** God Ex 1:21
Moses said...Do not **f** Ex 14:13
may learn to **f** Me Deut 4:10
not **f** other gods 2 Kin 17:37
I **f** no evil Ps 23:4
Whom shall I **f** Ps 27:1
not **f** evil tidings Ps 112:7
who **f-s** the LORD Prov 31:30
Rather, **f** God Eccl 5:7
Take courage, **f** not Is 35:4
Do not **f**, for I am Is 41:10
will **f** and tremble Jer 33:9
do not **f** them Matt 10:26
f-ed the crowd Matt 14:5
who did not **f** God Luke 18:2
slavery leading to **f** Rom 8:15
I **f** for you Gal 4:11
let us **f** if Heb 4:1

FEARFUL *terrifying*
it is a **f** thing Ex 34:10
were **f** and amazed Luke 8:25
will be **f** *of sinning* 1 Tim 5:20

FEAST *celebration*
a **f** to the LORD Ex 12:14
godless jesters at a **f** Ps 35:16
hate...appointed **f-s** Is 1:14
and cheerful **f-s** Zech 8:19
refuse of your **f-s** Mal 2:3
a wedding **f** Matt 22:2
seeking Him at the **f** John 7:11
celebrate the **f** 1 Cor 5:8
f with you without Jude 12

FEASTS
1 **Feast of Booths** Lev 23:24; Deut 16:16; 2 Chr 8:13
also **Feast of Ingathering**
2 **Feast of Dedication** John 10:22
3 **Feast of Harvest** Ex 23:16
also **Feast of Weeks**
also **Feast of Pentecost**
4 **Feast of Ingathering** Ex 23:16
also **Feast of Booths**
5 **Feast of Passover** Ex 34:25; Luke 2:41
6 **Feast of Unleavened Bread** Ex 23:15; Luke 22:1
7 **Feast of Weeks** Ex 34:22; Deut 16:10,16
also **Feast of Harvest**
also **Feast of Pentecost**
8 **Feast of Pentecost** Acts 2:1; 20:16; 1 Cor 16:8
also **Feast of Harvest**
also **Feast of Weeks**

FEEBLE *weak*
when the flock was **f** Gen 30:42
What are these **f** Jews Neh 4:2
strengthen the **f** Is 35:3
knees that are **f** Heb 12:12

FEED *eat, supply*
fed you with manna Deut 8:3
f him sparingly 1 Kin 22:27
F me with the food Prov 30:8
He **f-s** on ashes Is 44:20
f you on knowledge Jer 3:15
He **fed** me this scroll Ezek 3:2
I will **f** My flock Ezek 34:15
dogs **f** on the Matt 15:27
hungry, and **f** You Matt 25:37
fed...the *crumbs* Luke 16:21
enemy is hungry, **f** Rom 12:20

FEEL *sense, touch*
I may **f** you, my son Gen 27:21
Isaac...**felt** him and Gen 27:22
Let me **f** the pillars Judg 16:26
He **felt** compassion Matt 9:36
she **felt**...was healed Mark 5:29
Jesus **felt** a love for Mark 10:21
f-ing a sense of awe Acts 2:43
f sensual desires 1 Tim 5:11

FELIX
Roman procurator Acts 23:26; 24:25; 25:14

FELL *collapse, come upon*
wall **f** down flat Josh 6:20
fire of the LORD **f** 1 Kin 18:38
the lot **f** on Jonah Jon 1:7
seeds **f** beside the Matt 13:4
He **f** asleep Luke 8:23
he **f** to the ground Acts 9:4
Holy Spirit **f** upon Acts 10:44
star **f** from heaven Rev 8:10

FELLOW *companion*
oil of joy above Your **f-s** Ps 45:7
your **f** exiles Ezek 11:15
beat his **f** slaves Matt 24:49
f heirs with Christ Rom 8:17
f citizens with the Eph 2:19
Gentiles are **f** heirs Eph 3:6
brother and **f** worker Phil 2:25
f worker in the 1 Thess 3:2
I am a **f** servant of Rev 22:9

FELLOWSHIP *companionship*
had sweet **f** together Ps 55:14
f...Holy Spirit 2 Cor 13:14
right hand of **f** Gal 2:9
f of His sufferings Phil 3:10
f is with the Father 1 John 1:3
f with one another 1 John 1:7

FEMALE *girl, woman*
and **f** He created Gen 1:27
a **f** slave Ex 21:7
f from the flock Lev 5:6
likeness of male or **f** Deut 4:16
neither male nor **f** Gal 3:28

FERTILE *productive*
a **f** land Neh 9:25
the **f** valley Is 28:4
in **f** soil Ezek 17:5

FERVENT *ardent*
being **f** in spirit Acts 18:25
f in spirit, serving Rom 12:11
keep **f** in your love 1 Pet 4:8

FESTIVAL *celebration*
celebrate a great **f** Neh 8:12
I reject your **f-s** Amos 5:21
turn your **f-s** into Amos 8:10
during the **f,** otherwise Matt 26:5

FESTUS, PORCIUS
Roman procurator of Judea Acts 24:27; 25:14,23; 26:25

FETTERS *chains*
your feet put in **f** 2 Sam 3:34
they are bound in **f** Job 36:8
tear their **f** apart Ps 2:3
with **f** of iron Ps 149:8

FEVER *inflammation*
bones burn with **f** Job 30:30
in bed with a **f** Matt 8:14
from a high **f** Luke 4:38
He rebuked the **f** Luke 4:39
the **f** left him John 4:52

FIELD *productive land*
hail struck...the **f** Ex 9:25
let me go to the **f** Ruth 2:2
glean in another **f** Ruth 2:8
f of the sluggard Prov 24:30
Zion...plowed *as* a **f** Jer 26:18
the lilies of the **f** Matt 6:28
the **f** is the world Matt 13:38
shepherds...in the **f-s** Luke 2:8
Two men...in the **f** Luke 17:36
f-s...white for John 4:35
F of Blood Acts 1:19

FIERCE *violent*
anger, for it is **f** Gen 49:7
Wrath is **f** Prov 27:4
see a **f** people Is 33:19
a **f** gale of wind Mark 4:37
scorched with **f** heat Rev 16:9
f wrath of God Rev 19:15

FIERCENESS *intensity*
f of His anger Josh 7:26

the **f** of battle Is 42:25

FIERY *burning*
LORD sent **f** serpents Num 21:6
with **f** heat Deut 28:22
His arrows **f** shafts Ps 7:13
f ordeal among you 1 Pet 4:12

FIG *fruit*
they sewed **f** leaves Gen 3:7
But the **f** tree said Judg 9:11
a piece of **f** cake 1 Sam 30:12
nor **f-s** from thistles Matt 7:16
the **f** tree withered Matt 21:19
f-s from thorns Luke 6:44
under the **f** tree John 1:48
Can a **f** tree James 3:12

FIGHT *struggle*
Hebrews were **f-ing** Ex 2:13
LORD will **f** for you Ex 14:14
fought for Israel Josh 10:14
stars **fought** from Judg 5:20
and **f** our battles 1 Sam 8:20
f for your brothers Neh 4:14
f-ing against God Acts 5:39
fought the good **f** 2 Tim 4:7
so you **f** and quarrel James 4:2

FIGURATIVE *metaphorical*
in **f** language John 16:25

FIGURE *shape, type*
f-s resembling four Ezek 1:5
f...of a man Ezek 1:26
using a **f** of speech John 16:29

FILIGREE *ornamental work*
f *settings* of gold Ex 28:13
cords on the two **f** Ex 28:25

FILL (n) *satisfaction*
eat your **f** Lev 25:19
They drink their **f** Ps 36:8
drink our **f** of love Prov 7:18
its **f** of their blood Jer 46:10

FILL (v) *make full*
and **f** the earth Gen 1:28
f-ed with violence Gen 6:11
Can you **f** his skin Job 41:7
was **f-ing** with smoke Is 6:4
I am **f-ed** with power Mic 3:8
hall was **f-ed** Matt 22:10
God of hope **f** you Rom 15:13

FILTHY *offensive*
are full of **f** vomit Is 28:8
like a **f** garment Is 64:6
clothed...**f** garments Zech 3:3
Let...the one who is **f** Rev 22:11

FILTHINESS *disgustingly foul*
not washed...his **f** Prov 30:12
your **f** is lewdness Ezek 24:13
no **f** and silly talk Eph 5:4
putting aside all **f** James 1:21

FIND *discover, uncover*
not **found** a helper Gen 2:20
But Noah **found** favor Gen 6:8
sin will **f** you out Num 32:23
that you may **f** rest Ruth 1:9
he who **f-s** me **f-s** life Prov 8:35
who **f-s** a wife **f-s** Prov 18:22
f gladness and joy Is 35:10
few who **f** it Matt 7:14
has **found** his life Matt 10:39
f rest for your souls Matt 11:29
f-ing one pearl Matt 13:46
f a colt tied Mark 11:2
found...sleeping Mark 14:40
seek, and you will **f** Luke 11:9
found the Messiah John 1:41
was **found** worthy Rev 5:4

FINGER *part of hand*
the **f** of God Ex 8:19
dip his **f** in the blood Lev 4:6
six **f-s** on each 2 Sam 21:20
twenty-four **f-s** and 1 Chr 20:6
tip of his **f** in water Luke 16:24
with His **f** wrote John 8:6
Reach here with your **f** John 20:27

FINISH *complete*
Moses **f-ed** the work Ex 40:33
Solomon **f-ed** the 2 Chr 7:11
It is **f-ed** John 19:30
I may **f** my course Acts 20:24
f doing it also 2 Cor 8:11
wrath of God is **f-ed** Rev 15:1

FINS *part of fish*
that have **f** and scales Lev 11:9
anything that has **f** Deut 14:9

FIR *tree, wood*
instruments...of **f** 2 Sam 6:5
He plants a **f** Is 44:14

FIRE *burning or flame*
the **f** and the knife Gen 22:6
bush...burning with **f** Ex 3:2
pillar of **f** by night Ex 13:21
offered strange **f** Num 3:4
f of the LORD fell 1 Kin 18:38
a chariot of **f** 2 Kin 2:11
jealousy burn like **f** Ps 79:5
Israel will become a **f** Is 10:17
Is not My word like **f** Jer 23:29
the Holy Spirit and **f** Matt 3:11
with unquenchable **f** Matt 3:12
tongues as of **f** Acts 2:3
lake that burns with **f** Rev 21:8

FIREBRAND *burning wood*
who throws **F-s** Prov 26:18
you were like a **f** Amos 4:11

FIREPAN *used in worship*
a **f** full of coals Lev 16:12
the **f-s** of pure gold 2 Chr 4:22

FIRM *establish, steadfast*
his bow remained **f** Gen 49:24
stood **f** on dry ground Josh 3:17
making my footsteps **f** Ps 40:2
He made **f** the skies Prov 8:28
stand **f** in the faith 1 Cor 16:13
f foundation of God 2 Tim 2:19
hope **f** until the end Heb 3:6

FIRST *number*
f fruits of your labors Ex 23:16
f of all your produce Prov 3:9
seek **f** His kingdom Matt 6:33
f take the log out Matt 7:5
f will be last Matt 19:30
f called Christians Acts 11:26
to the Jew **f** Rom 2:10
f fruits of the Spirit Rom 8:23
He **f** loved us 1 John 4:19
I am the **f** and the Rev 1:17
left your **f** love Rev 2:4
f things have passed Rev 21:4

FIRSTBORN *oldest*
Sidon, his **f** Gen 10:15
the **f** bore a son Gen 19:37
I am Esau your **f** Gen 27:19
LORD killed every **f** Ex 13:15
birth to her **f** son Luke 2:7
church of the **f** Heb 12:23
f of the dead Rev 1:5

FIRST GATE *see* **GATES OF JERUSALEM**

FISH
rule over the **f** Gen 1:26
Their **f** stink Is 50:2
a great **f** to swallow Jon 1:17
loaves and two **f** Matt 14:17
snake instead of a **f** Luke 11:11
net *full* of **f** John 21:8

FISH GATE *see* **GATES OF JERUSALEM**

FISHERMEN *fishers*
f will lament Is 19:8
for they were **f** Matt 4:18
the **f** had gotten out Luke 5:2

FISHERS *fishermen*
make you **f** of men Matt 4:19
become **f** of men Mark 1:17

FIT *be suitable, worthy*
f to remove His Matt 3:11
f for the kingdom Luke 9:62
not **f** to be...apostle 1 Cor 15:9
body, being **f-ted** Eph 4:16
f-ting in the Lord Col 3:18

FIX *make firm, secure*
I will **f** your boundary Ex 23:31
f-ed her hope on God 1 Tim 5:5
f-ing...eyes on Jesus Heb 12:2
f your hope 1 Pet 1:13

FIXED *established*
the **f** festivals 1 Chr 23:31
f order of the moon Jer 31:35
is a great chasm **f** Luke 16:26

FLAME *fire*
ascended in the **f** Judg 13:20
f...the wicked Ps 106:18
f of the LORD Song 8:6
his Holy One a **f** Is 10:17
crackling of a **f** Joel 2:5
f of a burning thorn Acts 7:30
eyes *are* a **f** of fire Rev 19:12

FLAMING *burning*
the **f** sword Gen 3:24
f fire by night Is 4:5
eyes were like **f** Dan 10:6
angels in **f** fire 2 Thess 1:7

FLASH *reflect, sparkle*
why do your eyes **f** Job 15:12
lightning was **f-ing** Ezek 1:13
Polished to **f** like Ezek 21:10
He who **f-es** forth Amos 5:9
light suddenly **f-ed** Acts 22:6

FLASK *utensil*
take this **f** of oil 2 Kin 9:1
took oil in **f-s** Matt 25:4

FLATTER
Nor **f** *any* man Job 32:21
f with their tongue Ps 5:9
adulteress who **f-s** Prov 2:16
who **f-s** his neighbor Prov 29:5

FLAX *plant*
the **f** was in bud Ex 9:31
looks for wool and **f** Prov 31:13
made from combed **f** Is 19:9

FLEE *escape, run away*
arise, **f** to Haran Gen 27:43
F *as* a bird Ps 11:1
f from Your presence Ps 139:7
rulers have **fled** Is 22:3
f to Egypt Matt 2:13
left Him and **fled** Matt 26:56
fled from the tomb Mark 16:8
f from idolatry 1 Cor 10:14
f from youthful lusts 2 Tim 2:22
and heaven **fled** Rev 20:11

FLEECE *wool*
put a **f** of wool Judg 6:37
dry only on the **f** Judg 6:39
warmed with the **f** Job 31:20

FLEET *group of ships*
Solomon...built a **f** 1 Kin 9:26

sent...with the **f** 1 Kin 9:27

FLESH *body, meat*
f of my **f** Gen 2:23
shall become one **f** Gen 2:24
from my **f** I shall see Job 19:26
heart and my **f** sing Ps 84:2
All **f** is grass Is 40:6
the **f** is weak Matt 26:41
spirit...not have **f** Luke 24:39
the Word became **f** John 1:14
born of the **f** is **f** John 3:6
who eats My **f** John 6:56
children of the **f** Rom 9:8
thorn in the **f** 2 Cor 12:7
desires of the **f** Eph 2:3
polluted by the **f** Jude 23
filled with their **f** Rev 19:21

FLESHLY *carnal*
not in **f** wisdom 2 Cor 1:12
His **f** body Col 1:22
abstain from **f** lusts 1 Pet 2:11

FLIES *insects*
sent...swarms of **f** Ps 78:45
swarm of **f** *And* gnats Ps 105:31
Dead **f** make a Eccl 10:1

FLIGHT *departure*
F will perish from Amos 2:14
f will not be in Matt 24:20
foreign armies to **f** Heb 11:34

FLINT *stone*
Zipporah took a **f** Ex 4:25
f into a fountain Ps 114:8
hoofs...seem like **f** Is 5:28
emery harder than **f** Ezek 3:9
hearts *like* **f** Zech 7:12

FLOCK *goats, sheep*
a keeper of **f-s** Gen 4:2
water their father's **f** Ex 2:16
Your people like a **f** Ps 77:20
He will tend His **f** Is 40:11
scattered My **f** Jer 23:2
over their **f** by night Luke 2:8
will become one **f** John 10:16
f of God among you 1 Pet 5:2

FLOOD *overflowing of water*
I am bringing the **f** Gen 6:17
f came upon the earth Gen 7:17
end...with a **f** Dan 9:26
the **f-s** came Matt 7:25
f...destroyed Luke 17:27

FLOOR *ground, level*
threshing **f** of Atad Gen 50:11
go down to the...**f** Ruth 3:3
the **f**...with gold 1 Kin 6:30
f-s...full of grain Joel 2:24
His threshing **f** Matt 3:12
fell...from the third **f** Acts 20:9

FLOUR *ground grain*
measures of fine **f** Gen 18:6
only a handful of **f** 1 Kin 17:12
f...not exhausted 1 Kin 17:16

FLOURISH *blossom, thrive*
may the righteous **f** Ps 72:7
who did iniquity **f-ed** Ps 92:7
your bones will **f** Is 66:14
make the dry tree **f** Ezek 17:24

FLOW *pour forth*
river **f-ed** out of Eden Gen 2:10
f-ing with milk and Ex 3:8
eyelids **f** with water Jer 9:18
hills will **f** with milk Joel 3:18
f of her blood Mark 5:29
f...living water John 7:38

FLOWER *blossom*
As a **f** of the field Ps 103:15
f-s have *already* Song 2:12
to the fading **f** Is 28:1
glory like the **f** 1 Pet 1:24

FLUTE *musical instrument*
tambourine, **f,** and 1 Sam 10:5
playing on **f-s** 1 Kin 1:40
the **f** or on the harp 1 Cor 14:7
musicians...**f-players** Rev 18:22

FLY *soar*
let birds **f** above Gen 1:20
a raven, and it **flew** Gen 8:7
As sparks **f** upward Job 5:7
f-ies away like a dream Job 20:8
glory will **f** away Hos 9:11
heard an eagle **f-ing** Rev 8:13
the birds which **f** Rev 19:17

FOAL *colt*
ties *his* **f** to the vine Gen 49:11
f of a wild donkey Job 11:12
f of a beast of burden Matt 21:5

FODDER *animal food*
give his donkey **f** Gen 42:27
eat salted **f** Is 30:24

FOE *enemy*
before your **f-s** 1 Chr 21:12
A **f** and an enemy Esth 7:6
iniquity of my **f-s** Ps 49:5
the evil to my **f-s** Ps 54:5
avenge...His **f-s** Jer 46:10

FOLD *animal pen*
goats out of your **f-s** Ps 50:9
the peaceful **f-s** Jer 25:37
cut off from the **f** Hab 3:17
not of this **f** John 10:16

FOLLOW *imitate, pursue*
not **f** other gods Deut 6:14
turn back from **f-ing** Ruth 1:16
f the LORD your God 1 Sam 12:14
who **f**...wickedness Ps 119:150
bloodshed **f-s** Hos 4:2
He said to them, **F** Matt 4:19
left...and **f-ed** Matt 4:20
his cross, and **f** Me Matt 16:24
crowd was **f-ing** Mark 5:24
and they **f** Me John 10:27
Peter...**f-ing** Jesus John 18:15
f-ing after...lusts Jude 16
ones who **f** the Lamb Rev 14:4

FOLLOWERS *disciples*
His **f**...*began* asking Mark 4:10

FOLLY *foolishness*
this act of **f** Judg 19:23
of fools spouts **f** Prov 15:2
F is joy to him Prov 15:21
devising of **f** is sin Prov 24:9

FOOD *bread, meat*
shall be **f** for you Gen 1:29
tree was good for **f** Gen 3:6
in giving them **f** Ruth 1:6
tears have been my **f** Ps 42:3
it is deceptive **f** Prov 23:3
his **f** was locusts Matt 3:4
life more than **f** Matt 6:25
f is to do the will John 4:34
My flesh is true **f** John 6:55
milk...not solid **f** 1 Cor 3:2

FOOL *unwise person*
The **f** has said in his Ps 14:1
F-s despise wisdom Prov 1:7
too exalted for a **f** Prov 24:7
f multiplies words Eccl 10:14
The prophet is a **f** Hos 9:7
says, You **f** Matt 5:22
f-s and blind men Matt 23:17
wise, they became **f-s** Rom 1:22
f-s for Christ's sake 1 Cor 4:10

FOOLISH *silly, unwise*
O **f** and unwise Deut 32:6
a **f** son is a grief Prov 10:1
False and **f** *visions* Lam 2:14
Woe to the **f** Ezek 13:3
f took their lamps Matt 25:3
O **f** men and slow Luke 24:25
he must become **f** 1 Cor 3:18
You **f** Galatians Gal 3:1
do not be **f** Eph 5:17

FOOLISHNESS *folly*
The naive inherit **f** Prov 14:18
folly of fools is **f** Prov 14:24
mouth is speaking **f** Is 9:17
f of God is wiser 1 Cor 1:25
is **f** before God 1 Cor 3:19

FOOT *part of body*
she lay at his **feet** Ruth 3:14
six toes on each **f** 2 Sam 21:20
pierced...my **feet** Ps 22:16
the **f** of pride Ps 36:11
lamp to my **feet** Ps 119:105
their **feet** run to evil Prov 1:16
signals with his **feet** Prov 6:13
beautiful...your **feet** Song 7:1
feet of the afflicted Is 26:6
feet...polished bronze Dan 10:6
dust off your **feet** Matt 10:14
Bind...hand and **f** Matt 22:13
f causes you to Mark 9:45
kissing His **feet** Luke 7:38
anointed the **feet** John 12:3
the disciples' **feet** John 13:5
beautiful...the **feet** Rom 10:15
Satan under...**feet** Rom 16:20
worship at the **feet** Rev 22:8

FOOTSTEPS *path*
make His **f** into a way Ps 85:13
f of Your anointed Ps 89:51
my **f** in Your word Ps 119:133

FOOTSTOOL *foot support*
the **f** of our God 1 Chr 28:2
worship at His **f** Ps 99:5
Your enemies a **f** Ps 110:1
the earth is My **f** Is 66:1
sit down by my **f** James 2:3

FORBEARANCE *restraint*
By **f**...be persuaded Prov 25:15
in the **f** of God Rom 3:25

FORBID *prohibit*
if her father should **f** Num 30:5
f-ding to pay taxes Luke 23:2
do not **f** to speak 1 Cor 14:39
men who **f** marriage 1 Tim 4:3
he **f-s** those who 3 John 10

FORCE (n) *power, strength*
with a heavy **f** Num 20:20
captains of the **f-s** 2 Kin 25:23
use **f** against you Neh 13:21
commanders of the **f-s** Jer 43:5
with **f** and with Ezek 34:4

FORCE (v) *compel*
are **f-d** into bondage Neh 5:5
man **f-d** to labor Job 7:1
f-s you to go one mile Matt 5:41
not take...by **f** Luke 3:14
f them to blaspheme Acts 26:11
f-d to appeal to Acts 28:19

FORCED LABOR *work as tax*
Canaanites to **f** Josh 17:13
was over the **f** 2 Sam 20:24
will be put to **f** Prov 12:24

FORCED LABORERS
Solomon levied **f** 1 Kin 5:13
Solomon raised as **f** 2 Chr 8:8
men will become **f** Is 31:8

FORD *shallow place*
the **f** of the Jabbok Gen 32:22
the **f-s** of the Jordan Judg 12:5
f-s...been seized Jer 51:32

FOREFATHER *ancestor*
iniquity of their **f-s** Lev 26:40
Your first **f** sinned Is 43:27
I swore to your **f-s** Jer 11:5
Abraham, our **f** Rom 4:1
the way my **f-s** did 2 Tim 1:3

FOREHEAD *brow*
on his bald **f** Lev 13:42
stone...into his **f** 1 Sam 17:49
put a mark on the **f-s** Ezek 9:4
seal of God on their **f-s** Rev 9:4
on her **f** a name Rev 17:5

FOREIGN *alien, strange*
Put away the **f** gods Gen 35:2
sojourner in a **f** land Ex 2:22
sell her to a **f** people Ex 21:8
drank **f** waters 2 Kin 19:24
married **f** women Ezra 10:2
f armies to flight Heb 11:34

FOREIGNER *alien, stranger*
no **f** is to eat of it Ex 12:43
sell it to a **f** Deut 14:21
charge...a **f** Deut 23:20
since I am a **f** Ruth 2:10
a **f** in their sight Job 19:15
f-s entered his gate Obad 11

FOREKNEW *know beforehand*
whom He **f**, He also Rom 8:29
people whom he **f** Rom 11:2
He was **foreknown** 1 Pet 1:20

FOREKNOWLEDGE
plan and **f** of God Acts 2:23
f of God the Father 1 Pet 1:2

FOREMOST *first*
f commandment Matt 22:38
among whom I am **f** 1 Tim 1:15

FORERUNNER *goes before*
Jesus...as a **f** for Heb 6:20

FORESKIN
the flesh of your **f** Gen 17:11
cut off her son's **f** Ex 4:25
a hundred **f-s** 1 Sam 18:25
the **f-s** of your heart Jer 4:4

FOREST *woods*
f devoured more 2 Sam 18:8
the **f** of Lebanon 1 Kin 7:2
f will sing for joy 1 Chr 16:33
every beast of the **f** Ps 50:10
the glory of his **f** Is 10:18
beasts in the **f**, Come Is 56:9
a **f** is set aflame James 3:5

FORETOLD *predicted*
the Holy Spirit **f** Acts 1:16
just as Isaiah **f** Rom 9:29

FOREVER *always, eternal*
eat, and live **f** Gen 3:22
not strive with man **f** Gen 6:3
throne shall be...**f** 1 Chr 17:14
the LORD abides **f** Ps 9:7
LORD sits as King **f** Ps 29:10
glorify Your name **f** Ps 86:12
riches are not **f** Prov 27:24
One Who lives **f** Is 57:15
Christ is to remain **f** John 12:34
He...with you **f** John 14:16
He is able...to save **f** Heb 7:25
Son, made perfect **f** Heb 7:28
they will reign **f** Rev 22:5

FORFEIT *lose*
possessions...**f-ed** Ezra 10:8
f-s his own life Prov 20:2
f my head to the king Dan 1:10
and **f-s** his soul Matt 16:26

FORGET *forsake, neglect*
God has made me **f** Gen 41:51
that you do not **f** the LORD Deut 6:12
f-got the God who Deut 32:18
God **f-s**...iniquity Job 11:6
nations who **f** God Ps 9:17
needy...be **f-gotten** Ps 9:18
Do not **f** the afflicted Ps 10:12
They **f-got** His deeds Ps 78:11
do not **f** my teaching Prov 3:1
you will **f** the shame Is 54:4
My people **f** My name Jer 23:27
f-ting what *lies* behind Phil 3:13
f your work and Heb 6:10

FORGIVE *pardon*
f the transgression Gen 50:17
f their sin Ex 32:32
f our sins Ps 79:9
not **f** their iniquity Jer 18:23
f us our debts Matt 6:12
authority...to **f** sins Matt 9:6
f-gave him the debt Matt 18:27
can **f** sins but God Mark 2:7
he who is **f-n** little Luke 7:47
Father, **f** them Luke 23:34
whom you **f** 2 Cor 2:10
f-ing each other Eph 4:32
f-n us all our Col 2:13
righteous to **f** us 1 John 1:9

FORGIVENESS *pardon*
a God of **f** Neh 9:17
there is **f** with You Ps 130:4
poured out...for **f** Matt 26:28
repentance for **f** Luke 24:47
receives **f** of sins Acts 10:43
f of our trespasses Eph 1:7
the **f** of sins Col 1:14
there is no **f** Heb 9:22

FORK *instrument*
a three-pronged **f** 1 Sam 2:13
His winnowing **f** Matt 3:12

FORM (n) *appearance, shape*
beautiful of **f** and Gen 29:17
the **f** of the LORD Num 12:8
image in the **f** Deut 4:23
like the **f** of a man Is 44:13
in a different **f** Mark 16:12
bodily **f** like a dove Luke 3:22
f of corruptible man Rom 1:23
existed in the **f** of God Phil 2:6

FORM (v) *fashion, shape*
f-ed man of dust Gen 2:7
f-ed the dry land Ps 95:5
f-ed my inward parts Ps 139:13
One **f-ing** light Is 45:7
who **f-s** mountains Amos 4:13
f-s the spirit of man Zech 12:1
plot was **f-ed** against Acts 20:3
Christ is **f-ed** in you Gal 4:19

FORMATION *rank*
in **f** against 1 Chr 19:17
battle **f** in the 2 Chr 14:10

FORMLESS *without form*
earth was **f** and void Gen 1:2
behold, *it was* **f** Jer 4:23

FORNICATION
f-s, thefts, false Matt 15:19
were not born of **f** John 8:41
strangled and from **f** Acts 15:29

FORNICATORS
neither **f**, nor 1 Cor 6:9
f...God will judge Heb 13:4

FORSAKE
Then he **f-sook** God Deut 32:15
not fail you or **f** you Josh 1:5
f-sook the law of the 2 Chr 12:1
f Him, He will **f** you 2 Chr 15:2
God has not **f-n** us Ezra 9:9
why have You **f-n** me Ps 22:1
not **f** your mother's Prov 1:8
wicked **f** his way Is 55:7
Your sons have **f-n** Me Jer 5:7
f the idols of Egypt Ezek 20:8
have You **f-n** Me Matt 27:46
persecuted...not **f-n** 2 Cor 4:9
f-ing...assembling Heb 10:25
nor will I ever **f** you Heb 13:5

FORTIFICATIONS *stronghold*
the unassailable **f** Is 25:12
your **f** are fig trees Nah 3:12

FORTIFIED *walled*
live in the **f** cities Num 32:17
f with high walls Deut 3:5
strike every **f** city 2 Kin 3:19
f cities into Is 37:26

FORTRESS *stronghold*
God is my strong **f** 2 Sam 22:33
my rock and my **f** Ps 18:2
My refuge and my **f** Ps 91:2
wealth is his **f** Prov 10:15
f-es will be destroyed Hos 10:14

FORTUNE *one's lot*
and the **f-s** of Israel Jer 33:7
f-s of My people Hos 6:11
restore their **f** Zeph 2:7

FORTY *number*
f days and **f** nights Gen 7:4
flood...for **f** days Gen 7:17
ate the manna **f** years Ex 16:35
with the LORD **f** days Ex 34:28
fasted **f** days and **f** Matt 4:2
f days being tempted Mark 1:13

FOUL *putrid, rotten*
Nile will become **f** Ex 7:18
My wounds grow **f** Ps 38:5
f with your feet Ezek 34:19

FOUNDATION *establishment*
f-s of heaven were 2 Sam 22:8
I laid the **f** of the Job 38:4
the **f** of His throne Ps 97:2
the earth upon its **f-s** Ps 104:5
an everlasting **f** Prov 10:25
cornerstone *for* the **f** Is 28:16
a **f** on the rock Luke 6:48
the firm **f** of God 2 Tim 2:19
laid the **f** Heb 1:10
a **f** of repentance Heb 6:1

FOUNDATION GATE *see* **GATES OF JERUSALEM**

FOUNDED *established*
the day it was **f** Ex 9:18
f it upon the seas Ps 24:2
by wisdom **f** the earth Prov 3:19
f His vaulted dome Amos 9:6
f on the rock Matt 7:25

FOUNTAIN *spring, well*
f-s of the great deep Gen 7:11
is the **f** of life Ps 36:9
The **f** of wisdom Prov 18:4
f of living waters Jer 2:13

FOUNTAIN GATE *see* **GATES OF JERUSALEM**

FOWL *bird*
and fattened **f** 1 Kin 4:23
things and winged **f** Ps 148:10

FOX *small animal*
three hundred **f-es** Judg 15:4
f-es that are ruining Song 2:15

like **f-es** among ruins Ezek 13:4
The **f-es** have holes Matt 8:20
Go and tell that **f** Luke 13:32

FRAGMENTS *pieces*
forth His ice as **f** Ps 147:17
Gather up the...**f** John 6:12
twelve baskets with **f** John 6:13

FRAGRANCE *pleasant aroma*
oils have a pleasing **f** Song 1:3
given forth *their* **f** Song 2:13
f like *the cedars* Hos 14:6
we are a **f** of Christ 2 Cor 2:15

FRAME *structure*
f-s of the tabernacle Num 3:36
with *artistic* **f-s** 1 Kin 6:4
He...knows our **f** Ps 103:14
My **f** was not hidden Ps 139:15

FRANKINCENSE *spice*
spices with pure **f** Ex 30:34
f and the spices 1 Chr 9:29
trees of **f** Song 4:14
gold, **f**, and myrrh Matt 2:11

FREE *at liberty*
she is not to go **f** Ex 21:7
be **f** from the oath Josh 2:20
let the oppressed go **f** Is 58:6
will make you **f** John 8:32
who has died is **f-d** Rom 6:7
the **f** gift of God Rom 6:23
f from the law Rom 8:2
Christ set us **f** Gal 5:1
whether slave or **f** Eph 6:8

FREEDOM *liberty*
proclaim...**f** to Is 61:1
f of the glory Rom 8:21
you were called to **f** Gal 5:13
do not use your **f** as 1 Pet 2:16

FREEWILL OFFERINGS *see* **OFFERINGS**

FRESH *new, recently prepared*
found a **f** jawbone Judg 15:15
anointed with **f** oil Ps 92:10
f water from your Prov 5:15
new wine into **f** Mark 2:22
f and bitter *water* James 3:11

FRIEND *companion, comrade*
man speaks to his **f** Ex 33:11
f-s are my scoffers Job 16:20
loved ones and my **f-s** Ps 38:11
my familiar **f** Ps 55:13
A **f** loves at all Prov 17:17
Wealth adds...**f-s** Prov 19:4
who blesses his **f** Prov 27:14
confidence in a **f** Mic 7:5
f of tax collectors Matt 11:19
F, your sins are Luke 5:20
f of the bridegroom John 3:29
his life for his **f-s** John 15:13
You are My **f-s**, if John 15:14

FRIENDSHIP
the **f** of God Job 29:4
f with the world James 4:4

FRIGHTEN *terrify*
to **f** *them* away Deut 28:26
You **f** me Job 7:14
I was **f-ed** and fell Dan 8:17
wars, do not be **f-ed** Mark 13:7

FRINGE *edge*
the **f-s** of His ways Job 26:14
touched the **f** of His Matt 9:20

FROGS
smite...with **f** Ex 8:2
f which destroyed Ps 78:45
land swarmed with **f** Ps 105:30
unclean spirits like **f** Rev 16:13

FRONTALS *prayer bands*
they shall be as **f** Deut 6:8
f on your forehead Deut 11:18
see also **PHYLACTERIES**

FROST *freezing*
and the **f** by night Gen 31:40
fine as the **f** Ex 16:14
sycamore trees with **f** Ps 78:47

FRUIT *growth, produce*
f trees...bearing **f** Gen 1:11
she took from its **f** Gen 3:6
the **f** of the womb Gen 30:2
offering of first **f-s** Lev 2:12
its **f** in its season Ps 1:3
yield **f** in old age Ps 92:14
eat its choice **f-s** Song 4:16
eaten the **f** of lies Hos 10:13
know...by their **f-s** Matt 7:16
bad tree bears bad **f** Matt 7:17
f for life eternal John 4:36
the **f** of the Spirit Gal 5:22
f in every good work Col 1:10

FRUITFUL *productive*
be **f** and multiply Gen 9:7
were **f** and increased Ex 1:7
gather a **f** harvest Ps 107:37
into the **f** land Jer 2:7
f labor for me Phil 1:22

FRUSTRATE *counteract*
to **f** their counsel Ezra 4:5
He **f-s** the plotting Job 5:12
plans are **f-d** Prov 15:22

FUEL *that which burns*
people are like **f** Is 9:19
You will be **f** Ezek 21:32

FUGITIVE *one who flees*
do not betray the **f** Is 16:3
Meet the **f** with bread Is 21:14
gather the **f-s** Jer 49:5

FULFILL *complete*
to **f** the word 2 Chr 36:21
May the LORD **f** all Ps 20:5
f-ing His word Ps 148:8
to **f** the vision Dan 11:14
the prophet was **f-ed** Matt 2:17
to abolish, but to **f** Matt 5:17
The time is **f-ed** Mark 1:15
f-ed in the kingdom Luke 22:16
Scripture...be **f-ed** John 13:18
husband must **f** his duty 1 Cor 7:3
f the law of Christ Gal 6:2
f your ministry 2 Tim 4:5

FULFILLMENT *completion*
the **f** of every vision Ezek 12:23
f of what had been Luke 1:45
f of *the* law Rom 13:10

FULL *complete, whole*
I went out **f** Ruth 1:21
The earth is **f** of Ps 33:5
until the **f** day Prov 4:18
twelve **f** baskets Matt 14:20
f of dead...bones Matt 23:27
f of the Holy Spirit Luke 4:1
also is **f** of light Luke 11:34
f of grace and truth John 1:14
f of the Spirit Acts 6:3
f armor of God Eph 6:11
f of compassion James 5:11

FULLER *one who bleaches cloth*
of the **f-'s** field 2 Kin 18:17
like **f-s'** soap Mal 3:2

FULLNESS *completeness*
Your presence is **f** of Ps 16:11
His **f** we...received John 1:16
the **f** of the Gentiles Rom 11:25
f of the time came Gal 4:4
all the **f** of God Eph 3:19
f to dwell in Him Col 1:19
the **f** of Deity dwells Col 2:9

FURIOUS *angry*
Pharaoh was **f** Gen 41:10
became **f** and very Neh 4:1
king became...**f** Dan 2:12

FURNACE *oven*
As silver tried in a **f** Ps 12:6
the **f** of affliction Is 48:10
into the midst of a **f** Dan 3:6
throw them into the **f** Matt 13:42
to glow in a **f** Rev 1:15

FURNISH *supply*
f-ed with silver bands Ex 38:17
shall **f** him liberally Deut 15:14
f-ing every kind Ps 144:13
upper room **f-ed** Mark 14:15

FURROWS *trench*
its **f** weep together Job 31:38
water its **f** Ps 65:10
weeds in the **f** Hos 10:4

FURY *anger*
brother's **f** subsides Gen 27:44
terrify them in His **f** Ps 2:5
plucked up in **f** Ezek 19:12
the **f** of a fire Heb 10:27

FUTILE *useless, vain*
go after **f** things 1 Sam 12:21
devise **f** things Acts 4:25
f in...speculations Rom 1:21

FUTURE *that which is ahead*
discern their **f** Deut 32:29
no **f** for the evil Prov 24:20
is hope for your **f** Jer 31:17
foundation for the **f** 1 Tim 6:19

G

GABRIEL
angel of high rank Dan 8:16; 9:21; Luke 1:19,26

GAD
1 *son of Jacob* Gen 30:11; 35:26
2 *tribe of* Num 1:25; 2:14
3 *valley* 2 Sam 24:5
4 *seer, prophet* 2 Sam 24:11,18

GAIETY *cheerfulness*
g...is banished Is 24:11
an end to all her **g** Hos 2:11

GAIN (n) *profit, increase*
hate dishonest **g** Ex 18:21
Ill-gotten **g-s** do not Prov 10:2
who rejects unjust **g** Is 33:15
greedy for **g** Jer 6:13
to die is **g** Phil 1:21
fond of sordid **g** 1 Tim 3:8

GAIN (v) *acquire*
they might **g** insight Neh 8:13
have **g-ed** the victory Ps 98:1
he will **g** knowledge Prov 19:25
will **g** ascendancy Dan 11:5
g-s the whole world Matt 16:26
that I may **g** Christ Phil 3:8
may **g** the glory 2 Thess 2:14

GAIUS
1 *Macedonian* Acts 19:29
2 *companion of Paul* Acts 20:4
3 *Corinthian believer* 1 Cor 1:14
4 *addressee of 3 John* 3 John 1

GALATIA
Roman province in Asia Minor 1 Cor 16:1; 2 Tim 4:10

GALE *storm*
dust before a **g** Is 17:13

a fierce **g** of wind Mark 4:37

GALILEE
1 *district in N Palestine* Josh 21:32; 1 Kin 9:11; Matt 2:22; Acts 10:37
2 *Sea of* Matt 4:18; Mark 7:31
also **Sea of Chinnereth**
also **Lake of Gennesaret**
also **Sea of Tiberias**

GALL ***bitter herb, bitterness***
gave me **g** for my food Ps 69:21
drink...with **g** Matt 27:34
the **g** of bitterness Acts 8:23

GALLIO
governor of Achaia Acts 18:12,17

GALLOWS ***for hanging***
Have a **g**...made Esth 5:14
hanged...on the **g** Esth 7:10
his sons...on the **g** Esth 9:25

GAMALIEL
1 *head of tribe* Num 2:20; 7:54
2 *Pharisee* Acts 5:34; 22:3

GARDEN ***planted area***
God walking in the **g** Gen 3:8
from the **g** of Eden Gen 3:23
Make my **g** breathe Song 4:16
plant **g-s,** and eat Jer 29:5
tabernacle like a **g** Lam 2:6
in the **g** with Him John 18:26
the **g** a new tomb John 19:41

GARLAND ***ornament***
a **g** instead of ashes Is 61:3
brought...**g-s** to the Acts 14:13

GARMENT ***clothing, dress***
God made **g-s** of skin Gen 3:21
caught him by his **g** Gen 39:12
in **g-s** of fine linen Gen 41:42
holy **g-s** for Aaron Ex 28:2
divide my **g-s** among Ps 22:18
on **g-s** of vengeance Is 59:17
g-s of glowing colors Is 63:1
g of camel's hair Matt 3:4
I just touch His **g-s** Mark 5:28
dividing up His **g-s** Luke 23:34
put his outer **g** on John 21:7
become old like a **g** Heb 1:11
clothed in white **g-s** Rev 3:5

GARRISON ***defense***
g of the Philistines 1 Sam 13:4
the **g**...trembled 1 Sam 14:15
set **g-s** in the land 2 Chr 17:2

GATE ***entry way***
is the **g** of heaven Gen 28:17
oppressed in the **g** Job 5:4
g-s with thanksgiving Ps 100:4
enter the **g-s** of Sheol Is 38:10
justice in the **g** Amos 5:15
Enter...narrow **g** Matt 7:13
g-s of Hades will Matt 16:18
did not open the **g** Acts 12:14

GATEKEEPERS ***guards***
g for the camp 1 Chr 9:18
divisions of the **g** 1 Chr 26:12
The sons of the **g** Ezra 2:42
g, and the singers Neh 10:39

GATES OF JERUSALEM
alternate names in italics
1 **Beautiful Gate** Acts 3:10
East Gate
2 **Benjamin Gate** Jer 20:2; Zech 14:10
Gate of the Guard
Inspection Gate
Sheep Gate
3 **Corner Gate** 2 Kin 14:13; 2 Chr 26:9
4 **East Gate** Neh 3:29; Ezek 10:19; 44:1
Beautiful Gate
5 **Ephraim Gate** 2 Kin 14:13; Neh 8:16
Middle Gate
Old Gate
6 **First Gate** Zech 14:10
7 **Fish Gate** 2 Chr 33:14; Neh 3:3
8 **Foundation Gate** 2 Chr 23:5
Gate of Sur
9 **Fountain Gate** Neh 2:14; 12:37
gate between two walls 2 Kin 25:4; Jer 39:4
10 **Guard, Gate of the** Neh 12:39
Benjamin Gate
Inspection Gate
Sheep Gate
11 **Horse Gate** 2 Chr 23:15; Neh 3:28
12 **Inspection Gate** Neh 3:31
Benjamin Gate
Gate of the Guard
Sheep Gate
13 **Middle Gate** Jer 39:3
Ephraim Gate
Old Gate
14 **Old Gate** Neh 3:6; 12:39
Ephraim Gate
Middle Gate
15 **Refuse Gate** Neh 2:13; 12:31
16 **Sheep Gate** Neh 3:1
Benjamin Gate
Gate of the Guard
Inspection Gate
17 **Sur, Gate of** 2 Kin 11:6
Foundation Gate
18 **Valley Gate** 2 Chr 26:9; Neh 3:13
19 **Water Gate** Neh 3:26; 8:1,3,16

GATEWAY ***entrance***
the **g** of the court Ex 40:8
the **g** of the peoples Ezek 26:2

GATH
Philistine city Josh 11:22; 1 Sam 17:23; 1 Chr 20:8

GATHER ***assemble, collect***
g-ed to his people Gen 25:8
g stubble for straw Ex 5:12
He **g-s** the waters Ps 33:7
G My godly ones Ps 50:5
g all nations and Is 66:18
hen **g-s** her chicks Matt 23:37
elders...were **g-ed** Matt 26:3
g...His elect Mark 13:27
G up the leftover John 6:12

GAZA
Philistine city Gen 10:19; Judg 16:1; Jer 47:5

GAZE (n) ***view, glance***
Turn Your **g** away from Ps 39:13
let your **g** be fixed Prov 4:25
turning His **g** toward His Luke 6:20

GAZE (v) ***look, stare***
man...**g-ing** at her Gen 24:21
and **g** after Moses Ex 33:8
eye **g-s** on their Job 17:2
LORD **g-d** upon the Ps 102:19
g-ing...into the sky Acts 1:10

GAZELLE ***animal***
swift as the **g-s** 1 Chr 12:8
a **g** Or a young stag Song 2:17
like a hunted **g** Is 13:14

GEDERAH
1 *town of Judah* Josh 15:36
2 *town of Benjamin* 1 Chr 12:4

GEHAZI
servant of Elisha 2 Kin 4:12; 5:20; 8:4

GENEALOGY ***family record***
found the book of...**g** Neh 7:5
g of Jesus the Messiah Matt 1:1
and endless **g-ies** 1 Tim 1:4
whose **g** is not traced Heb 7:6

GENERATION ***age, period***
this evil **g** Deut 1:35
the righteous **g** Ps 14:5
faithfulness to all **g-s** Ps 100:5
salvation to all **g-s** Is 51:8
this **g** seek for a sign Mark 8:12
g-s...not made known Eph 3:5
and perverse **g** Phil 2:15

GENEROUS ***bountiful***
g will be blessed Prov 22:9
because I am **g** Matt 20:15
g...ready to share 1 Tim 6:18

GENNESARET
1 *lake* Luke 5:1
also **Sea of Chinnereth**
also **Sea of Galilee**
also **Sea of Tiberias**
2 *land or district* Matt 14:34; Mark 6:53

GENTILES ***foreigners, non-Jews***
Galilee of the **G** Matt 4:15
hand Him over to the **G** Matt 20:19
revelation to the **G** Luke 2:32
Why did the **G** rage Acts 4:25
salvation...to the **G** Rom 11:11
preach...among the **G** Gal 1:16

GENTLE ***compassionate, mild***
g answer turns away Prov 15:1
I was like a **g** lamb Jer 11:19
Blessed are the **g** Matt 5:5
G, and mounted on Matt 21:5
a **g** and quiet spirit 1 Pet 3:4

GENTLENESS ***kindness***
and a spirit of **g** 1 Cor 4:21
and **g** of Christ 2 Cor 10:1
g, self-control Gal 5:23
humility and **g,** with Eph 4:2

GERAR
Philistine city Gen 20:2; 26:6

GERIZIM
mountain near Shechem Deut 11:29; Josh 8:33

GERSHOM
1 *son of Moses* Ex 2:22; 18:3
2 *son of Levi* 1 Chr 6:16,43
3 *line of Phinehas* Ezra 8:2

GERSHON
son of Levi Gen 46:11; Ex 6:16

GETHSEMANE
garden on Mount of Olives Matt 26:36; Mark 14:32

GEZER
Canaanite city of Ephraim Josh 10:33; 1 Kin 9:17

GHOST ***spirit***
resort to idols and **g-s** Is 19:3
and said, It is a **g** Matt 14:26
it was a **g** Mark 6:49

GIANT
were born to the **g** 2 Sam 21:22
from the **g-s** 1 Chr 20:6

GIBEAH
1 *village in Judah* Josh 15:57
2 *in Ephraim* Josh 24:33
3 *town of Benjamin* 1 Sam 10:26; 13:2; 2 Sam 23:29

GIBEON
town in Benjamin Josh 9:3,17; 1 Kin 3:5; 1 Chr 8:29

GIDEON
son of Joash Judg 6:11,36
judge Judg 8:4-21

GIFT ***present***
the sacred **g-s** Num 18:32
children are a **g** Ps 127:3
to Him **g-s** Matt 2:11
g of the Holy Spirit Acts 2:38
impart...spiritual **g** Rom 1:11

g of God is eternal Rom 6:23
desire...greater **g-s** 1 Cor 12:31
perfect **g** is from James 1:17

GIHON
1 *river of Eden* Gen 2:13
2 *Jerusalem spring* 2 Chr 32:30

GILBOA
mountain 2 Sam 1:6
where Saul died 2 Sam 21:12

GILEAD
1 *son of Machir* Num 36:1
2 *descendant of Gad* 1 Chr 5:14
3 *father of Jephthah* Judg 11:1
4 *land E of Jordan* Num 32:29
5 *mountain* Judg 7:3
6 *city* Hos 6:8

GILGAL
1 *in Arabah* Deut 11:30
2 *encampment in Jordan Valley* Josh 5:9; 1 Sam 7:16
near Jericho Josh 5:8,10
3 *in N Judah* Josh 15:7
4 *in Galilee* Josh 12:23
5 *village near Bethel* 2 Kin 2:1

GIRD *bind*
g him with the...band Ex 29:5
g up your loins like Job 38:3
g-ed me with gladness Ps 30:11
g-s herself with Prov 31:17
g-ed...with truth Eph 6:14
g-ed across His chest Rev 1:13

GIRDLE *belt, waistband*
man with a leather **g** 2 Kin 1:8
binds...with a **g** Job 12:18

GIRGASHITE(S)
Canaanite tribe Gen 10:16; Deut 7:1; Josh 24:11; Neh 9:8

GIRL *maiden*
the **g** and consult Gen 24:57
sold a **g** for wine Joel 3:3
boys and **g-s** playing Zech 8:5
the **g** has not died Matt 9:24

GIVE *bestow, yield*
g light on the earth Gen 1:17
g-n you every plant Gen 1:29
gave me from...tree Gen 3:12
in the land...God **g-s** Ex 20:12
I will **g** you rest Ex 33:14
g him to the LORD 1 Sam 1:11
G ear to my prayer Ps 17:1
gave me vinegar Ps 69:21
G me neither poverty Prov 30:8
a son will be **g-n** Is 9:6
gave birth to a Son Matt 1:25
G us this day Matt 6:11
g-ing thanks, He Matt 15:36
g you the keys Matt 16:19
authority...been **g-n** Matt 28:18
what will a man **g** Mark 8:37
body which is **g-n** Luke 22:19
gave His only...Son John 3:16
not as the world **g-s** John 14:27
gave up His spirit John 19:30
what I do have I **g** Acts 3:6
g-n among men Acts 4:12
more blessed to **g** Acts 20:35
was **g-n** me a thorn 2 Cor 12:7
always **g-ing** thanks Eph 5:20
who **gave** Himself 1 Tim 2:6
Every good thing **g-n** James 1:17
g-s a greater grace James 4:6
g-n us eternal life 1 John 5:11
to be **g-n** a mark Rev 13:16

GLAD *pleased*
g in his heart Ex 4:14
joy and a **g** heart Deut 28:47
righteous see...are **g** Job 22:19
Be **g** in the LORD Ps 32:11
g when they said Ps 122:1
son makes a father **g** Prov 10:1
Rejoice, and be **g** Matt 5:12
Be **g** in that day Luke 6:23

GLADNESS *joy*
celebrate...with **g** Neh 12:27
g...for the Jews Esth 8:17
Serve the LORD with **g** Ps 100:2
g and sincerity of Acts 2:46
With the oil of **g** Heb 1:9

GLASS *crystal*
or **g** cannot equal Job 28:17
sea of **g**, like crystal Rev 4:6

GLEAM *brilliance*
awesome **g** of crystal Ezek 1:22
g of a Tarshish stone Ezek 10:9
g of polished bronze Dan 10:6

GLEAN *gather, pick*
Nor shall you **g** Lev 19:10
Do not go to **g** Ruth 2:8
she **g-ed** in the field Ruth 2:17
g the vineyard Job 24:6
g-ing ears of grain Is 17:5

GLOOM *darkness*
cloud and thick **g** Deut 4:11
The land of utter **g** Job 10:22
darkness and **g** and Heb 12:18
and your joy to **g** James 4:9

GLORIFY *honor, worship*
g Your name forever Ps 86:12
Let the LORD be **g-ied** Is 66:5
g your Father Matt 5:16
shepherds...**g-ing** Luke 2:20
Jesus...not yet **g-ied** John 7:39
Father, **g** Your name John 12:28
God is **g-ied** in Him John 13:31
were all **g-ing** God Acts 4:21
Gentiles to **g** God Rom 15:9
g God in your body 1 Cor 6:20
did not **g** Himself Heb 5:5

GLORIOUS *exalted, great*
g name be blessed Neh 9:5
G things are spoken Ps 87:3
resting place will be **g** Is 11:10
the law great and **g** Is 42:21
g gospel of...God 1 Tim 1:11

GLORY (n) *honor, splendor*
show me Your **g** Ex 33:18
while My **g** is passing Ex 33:22
Tell of His **g** 1 Chr 16:24
King of **g** may come Ps 24:7
exchanged their **g** Ps 106:20
earth is full of His **g** Is 6:3
their **g** into shame Hos 4:7
Solomon in all his **g** Matt 6:29
g of the Lord shone Luke 2:9
G...in the highest Luke 2:14
He comes in His **g** Luke 9:26
do not seek My **g** John 8:50
short of the **g** of God Rom 3:23
all to the **g** of God 1 Cor 10:31
eternal weight of **g** 2 Cor 4:17
body of His **g** Phil 3:21
crowned Him with **g** Heb 2:7
unfading crown of **g** 1 Pet 5:4

GLORY (v) *exalt*
And **g** in Your praise 1 Chr 16:35
G in His holy name Ps 105:3
in Him they will **g** Jer 4:2
I...have reason to **g** Phil 2:16

GLUTTON *excessive eater*
g...come to poverty Prov 23:21
a companion of **g-s** Prov 28:7
evil beasts, lazy **g-s** Titus 1:12

GNASH *grind*
They **g-ed** at me Ps 35:16
He will **g** his teeth Ps 112:10
They hiss and **g** Lam 2:16
g-ing their teeth Acts 7:54

GNAT *insect*
dust...became **g-s** Ex 8:17
swarm of flies...**g-s** Ps 105:31
strain out a **g** and Matt 23:24

GO *move, proceed*
Let My people **g** Ex 7:16
God who **g-es** before Deut 1:30
where you **g**, I will **g** Ruth 1:16
the way he should **g** Prov 22:6
g one mile, **g**...two Matt 5:41
G into all...world Mark 16:15
I **g** to prepare a John 14:2
night is almost **gone** Rom 13:12

GOADS *inducements*
wise men are like **g** Eccl 12:11
kick against the **g** Acts 26:14

GOAL *end, object*
press on toward the **g** Phil 3:14
g...is love 1 Tim 1:5

GOAT *animal*
a young **g** from the flock Gen 38:17
curtains of **g-s'** *hair* Ex 26:7
not boil a young **g**...milk Ex 34:26
g for a sin offering Num 15:27
prepare a young **g** for you Judg 13:15
quilt of **g-s'** *hair* 1 Sam 19:13
g *had* a...horn Dan 8:5
shaggy **g** *represents* Dan 8:21
sheep from the **g-s** Matt 25:32
never given me a young **g** Luke 15:29
blood of **g-s**...bulls Heb 9:13

GOD *Deity, Eternal One*
In the beginning **G** Gen 1:1
G formed man of dust Gen 2:7
G sent him out Gen 3:23
G gave to Abraham Gen 28:4
tablets were **G-'s** work Ex 32:16
G is my...fortress 2 Sam 22:33
G of my salvation Ps 18:46
In **G**...put my trust Ps 56:4
Search me, O **G** Ps 139:23
word of **G** is tested Prov 30:5
servant of the living **G** Dan 6:20
I am **G** and not man Hos 11:9
Will a man rob **G** Mal 3:8
G descending...dove Matt 3:16
they shall see **G** Matt 5:8
What...**G** has joined Matt 19:6
kingdom of **G** is at Mark 1:15
My **G**, why have Mark 15:34
You the Son of **G** Luke 22:70
the Word was **G** John 1:1
No one has seen **G** John 1:18
the Lamb of **G** John 1:29
G so loved the world John 3:16
G is spirit John 4:24
voice of...Son of **G** John 5:25
obey **G** rather than Acts 5:29
judgment of **G** Rom 2:2
bear fruit for **G** Rom 7:4
we are children of **G** Rom 8:16
are a temple of **G** 1 Cor 3:16
full armor of **G** Eph 6:11
one **G**...one mediator 1 Tim 2:5
is inspired by **G** 2 Tim 3:16
word of **G** is...sharper Heb 4:12
impossible...**G** to lie Heb 6:18
G is love 1 John 4:8
great supper of **G** Rev 19:17

GOD *false deity, idols*
no other **g-s** before Me Ex 20:3
New **g-s** were chosen Judg 5:8
cast their **g-s** into Is 37:19
bowed...to other **g-s** Jer 22:9

no other **g** who is Dan 3:29
The voice of a **g** Acts 12:22
g-s...become like Acts 14:11
the **g** of this world 2 Cor 4:4

GOD, SON OF *see* **SON OF GOD**

GODDESS *female deity*
Ashtoreth the **g** of 1 Kin 11:5
great **g** Artemis Acts 19:27
blasphemers of...**g** Acts 19:37

GODLESS *pagan, without God*
hope of the **g** will Job 8:13
joy of...**g** momentary Job 20:5
g man destroys his Prov 11:9
hands of **g** men Acts 2:23
become of the **g** 1 Pet 4:18

GODLINESS *holiness*
in all **g** and dignity 1 Tim 2:2
the mystery of **g** 1 Tim 3:16
g is profitable 1 Tim 4:8
to a form of **g** 2 Tim 3:5
g, brotherly kindness 2 Pet 1:7

GODLY *holy*
keeps...His **g** ones 1 Sam 2:9
g man ceases to be Ps 12:1
not forsake His **g** ones Ps 37:28
and **g** sincerity 2 Cor 1:12
to live **g** in Christ 2 Tim 3:12
rescue the **g** from 2 Pet 2:9

GOG
1 *a Reubenite* 1 Chr 5:4
2 *prince of Meshech and Tubal* Ezek 38:2
3 *symbol of godless nations* Rev 20:8
see also **MAGOG**

GOLAN
city of refuge Josh 21:27
a Levitical city 1 Chr 6:71

GOLD *precious metal*
g of that land is good Gen 2:12
mercy seat of pure **g** Ex 25:17
Almighty...be your **g** Job 22:25
more desirable than **g** Ps 19:10
refine them like **g** Mal 3:3
to Him gifts of **g** Matt 2:11
Do not acquire **g** Matt 10:9
Divine Nature...**g** Acts 17:29
coveted no...**g** Acts 20:33
city was pure **g** Rev 21:18

GOLDSMITH *gold craftsman*
g-s and...merchants Neh 3:32
g, and he makes it Is 46:6

GOLGOTHA
site of Crucifixion Matt 27:33; Mark 15:22; John 19:17

GOLIATH
Philistine giant 1 Sam 17:4,23; 21:9; 1 Chr 20:5

GOMER
1 *son of Japheth* Gen 10:2
2 *group of people* Ezek 38:6
3 *wife of Hosea* Hos 1:3

GOMORRAH
city of Jordan plain Gen 10:19; 14:10; 19:24
probably S of Dead Sea Is 13:19; 2 Pet 2:6

GOOD *complete, right*
God saw that it was **g** Gen 1:18
knowledge of **g** and Gen 2:9
Proclaim **g** tidings 1 Chr 16:23
Do not withhold **g** Prov 3:27
joyful heart is **g** Prov 17:22
planted in **g** soil Ezek 17:8
feed in...**g** pasture Ezek 34:18
Seek **g** and not evil Amos 5:14
how to give **g** gifts Matt 7:11
Well done, **g** and Matt 25:23
sown on the **g** soil Mark 4:20
Salt is **g** Mark 9:50
No one is **g** except Luke 18:19
I am the **g** shepherd John 10:11
men of **g** reputation Acts 6:3
perseverance in...**g** Rom 2:7
nothing **g**...in me Rom 7:18
work together for **g** Rom 8:28
who bring **g** news Rom 10:15
overcome evil...**g** Rom 12:21
is of **g** repute Phil 4:8
g hope by grace 2 Thess 2:16
Fight the **g** fight 1 Tim 6:12
tasted the **g** word Heb 6:5

GOODNESS *excellence, value*
My **g** pass before you Ex 33:19
Surely **g**...will follow Ps 23:6
How great is Your **g** Ps 31:19
kindness, **g** Gal 5:22
every desire for **g** 2 Thess 1:11

GOODS *possessions, supplies*
the **g** for yourself Gen 14:21
have acquired...**g** Ezek 38:12

GORE *stab*
if an ox **g-s** a man Ex 21:28
g the Arameans 1 Kin 22:11

GOSHEN
1 *district of Egypt in Nile Delta* Gen 45:10; 47:6,27
2 *S Judah region* Josh 10:41
3 *town in Judah* Josh 15:51

GOSPEL *good news*
proclaiming the **g** of Matt 4:23
preach the **g** to all Mark 16:15
not ashamed of the **g** Rom 1:16
if our **g** is veiled 2 Cor 4:3
or a different **g** 2 Cor 11:4
distort the **g** of Christ Gal 1:7
g of your salvation Eph 1:13
g of peace Eph 6:15
defense of the **g** Phil 1:16
the hope of the **g** Col 1:23
eternal **g** to preach Rev 14:6

GOSSIP *babbler*
associate with a **g** Prov 20:19
malice; *they are* **g-s** Rom 1:29
g-s and busybodies 1 Tim 5:13

GOVERN *rule*
light to **g** the day Gen 1:16
light to **g** the night Gen 1:16
when the judges **g-ed** Ruth 1:1

GOVERNMENT *authority, rule*
g...on His shoulders Is 9:6
be no end to...*His* **g** Is 9:7

GOVERNOR *ruler*
not offer it to your **g** Mal 1:8
brought before **g-s** Matt 10:18
g was quite amazed Matt 27:14
Pilate was **g** of Judea Luke 3:1
g over Egypt Acts 7:10

GRACE *benevolence, favor*
G is poured upon Your Ps 45:2
g to the afflicted Prov 3:34
g of God was upon Luke 2:40
full of **g** and truth John 1:14
g abounded...more Rom 5:20
g of our Lord Jesus Rom 16:20
My **g** is sufficient 2 Cor 12:9
by **g** you have been Eph 2:8
justified by His **g** Titus 3:7
to the throne of **g** Heb 4:16
g to the humble James 4:6

GRACIOUS *kind*
God be **g** to you Gen 43:29
g to whom I will be Ex 33:19
a **g** and...God Neh 9:31
Be **g** to me, O LORD Ps 6:2
and **g**, Slow to anger Ps 86:15
g to a poor man Prov 19:17
be **g** to...remnant Amos 5:15

GRAFT *insert, join*
I might be **g-ed** in Rom 11:19
God is able to **g** Rom 11:23
g-ed into their own Rom 11:24

GRAIN
Joseph stored up **g** Gen 41:49
glean among the...**g** Ruth 2:2
g...for your enemies Is 62:8
then the mature **g** Mark 4:28
g of wheat falls John 12:24

GRAIN OFFERING *see* **OFFERINGS**

GRANDCHILDREN
G are the crown of Prov 17:6
widow has...or **g** 1 Tim 5:4

GRANDDAUGHTER
g-s, and all his Gen 46:7
g of Omri king of 2 Kin 8:26

GRANDSON
g might fear the LORD Deut 6:2
sons and thirty **g-s** Judg 12:14
master's **g** shall eat 2 Sam 9:10

GRANT *give, provide*
g this people favor Ex 3:21
have **g-ed** me life Job 10:12
g us Your salvation Ps 85:7
G that we may sit Mark 10:37
Father has **g-ed** Me Luke 22:29
g repentance to Acts 5:31
g-ing...deliverance Acts 7:25

GRAPE *fruit*
nor eat...dried **g-s** Num 6:3
of **g-s** you drank Deut 32:14
when the **g** harvest is Is 24:13
G-s are not gathered Matt 7:16
g-s from a briar Luke 6:44

GRASP *hold, seize*
hands **g** the spindle Prov 31:19
He who **g-s** the bow Amos 2:15
a thing to be **g-ed** Phil 2:6

GRASS *vegetation*
g *springs* out 2 Sam 23:4
his days are like **g** Ps 103:15
dry **g** collapses into Is 5:24
g withers, the flower Is 40:7
was given **g** to eat Dan 5:21
if God so clothes...**g** Matt 6:30
All flesh is like **g** 1 Pet 1:24
not to hurt the **g** Rev 9:4

GRASSHOPPER *insect*
the **g** in its kinds Lev 11:22
we became like **g-s** Num 13:33
inhabitants are like **g-s** Is 40:22

GRATITUDE *thankfulness*
overflowing with **g** Col 2:7
is received with **g** 1 Tim 4:4
let us show **g** Heb 12:28

GRAVE *sepulchre, tomb*
pillar of Rachel's **g** Gen 35:20
throat is an open **g** Ps 5:9
I will open your **g-s** Ezek 37:12
I will prepare your **g** Nah 1:14
made the **g** secure Matt 27:66

GRAVEN *sculptured*
make...a **g** image Deut 4:23
ashamed who serve **g** Ps 97:7
praise to **g** images Is 42:8

GRAY *color*
g hair...in sorrow Gen 42:38
with the man of **g** Deut 32:25
Both the **g-haired** Job 15:10

when *I am* old and **g** Ps 71:18
g head is a crown Prov 16:31

GRAZE *feed*
cattle...**g-ing** in 1 Chr 27:29
wolf...shall **g** Is 65:25
he will **g** on Carmel Jer 50:19

GREAT *big, excellent, grand*
made...two **g** lights Gen 1:16
make you a **g** nation Gen 12:2
lovingkindness is **g** Ps 57:10
your iniquity is **g** Jer 30:15
g day of the LORD Zeph 1:14
rejoiced...with **g** joy Matt 2:10
woman...faith is **g** Matt 15:28
good news of **g** joy Luke 2:10
reward is **g** in Luke 6:23
because of His **g** love Eph 2:4
so **g** a salvation Heb 2:3
we have a **g**...priest Heb 4:14
so **g** a cloud of Heb 12:1
g supper of God Rev 19:17
a **g** white throne Rev 20:11

GREATEST *most important*
who is the **g** among Luke 22:26
g of these is love 1 Cor 13:13
least to the **g** Heb 8:11

GREATNESS *magnitude*
Yours...is the **g** 1 Chr 29:11
g...lovingkindness Neh 13:22
g of Your compassion Ps 51:1
the **g** of His strength Is 63:1
amazed at the **g** of Luke 9:43
surpassing **g** of His Eph 1:19

GREECE
country in SE Europe Dan 8:21; 10:20; 11:2; Zech 9:13; Acts 20:2

GREED *excessive desire*
caught by *their*...**g** Prov 11:6
every form of **g** Luke 12:15
wickedness, **g**, evil Rom 1:29
a pretext for **g** 1 Thess 2:5
a heart trained in **g** 2 Pet 2:14

GREEDY *craving*
had **g** desires Num 11:4
g man curses Ps 10:3
Everyone is **g** for Jer 6:13

GREEKS
people of Greece Joel 3:6; Acts 16:1,3; Rom 1:16; 1 Cor 12:13

GREEN *fertile, fruitful*
every **g** plant for Gen 1:30
lie down in **g** pastures Ps 23:2
dry up the **g** tree Ezek 17:24
nor any **g** thing Rev 9:4

GREET *hail, welcome*
g no one on the way Luke 10:4
G one another with 1 Pet 5:14

GRIEF *heartache, sorrow*
weeps because of **g** Ps 119:28
foolish son is a **g** Prov 17:25
acquainted with **g** Is 53:3
our **g-s** He Himself Is 53:4
g...turned into joy John 16:20
joy and not with **g** Heb 13:17

GRIEVE *distress, sorrow*
was **g-d** in His heart Gen 6:6
Do not be **g-d** Neh 8:10
g-d Him in the desert Ps 78:40
g-d His Holy Spirit Is 63:10
g-d at their hardness Mark 3:5
Peter was **g-d** John 21:17
not **g** the Holy Spirit Eph 4:30

GRIND *crush, press*
my wife **g** for another Job 31:10
g-ing...the poor Is 3:15
millstones and **g** meal Is 47:2
women...*be* **g-ing** Matt 24:41
and **g-s** his teeth Mark 9:18

GROAN *cry, moan*
From the city men **g** Job 24:12
man rules, people **g** Prov 29:2
wounded will **g** Jer 51:52
whole creation **g-s** Rom 8:22

GROANING *crying*
God heard their **g** Ex 2:24
O LORD, Consider my **g** Ps 5:1
g of the prisoner Ps 79:11
g-s of a wounded Ezek 30:24
g-s too deep for Rom 8:26

GROPE *move about blindly*
you will **g** at noon Deut 28:29
They **g** in darkness Job 12:25
g...like blind men Is 59:10
g for Him and find Acts 17:27

GROUND *earth, land, soil*
man of dust from...**g** Gen 2:7
Cursed is the **g** Gen 3:17
crossed on dry **g** Josh 3:17
a spirit from the **g** Is 29:4
talent in the **g** Matt 25:25
finger wrote on the **g** John 8:6
standing is holy **g** Acts 7:33
g that drinks the rain Heb 6:7

GROUNDED *established*
hope...is firmly **g** 2 Cor 1:7
rooted and **g** in love Eph 3:17

GROW *develop, increase*
Moses had **g-n** up Ex 2:11
You are **g-n** fat Deut 32:15
my spirit **g-s** faint Ps 77:3
youths **g** weary Is 40:30
sun and moon **g** dark Joel 3:15
lilies of the field **g** Matt 6:28
love will **g** cold Matt 24:12
Child continued to **g** Luke 2:40
grew strong in faith Rom 4:20
as your faith **g-s** 2 Cor 10:15
not **g** weary of 2 Thess 3:13
g in the grace 2 Pet 3:18

GROWTH *increase*
new **g** is seen Prov 27:25
God who causes the **g** 1 Cor 3:7

GRUDGE *hostile feeling*
Esau bore a **g** Gen 27:41
nor bear any **g** Lev 19:18
Herodias had a **g** Mark 6:19

GRUMBLE *complain*
they **g-d** against Moses Ex 17:3
the congregation **g** Num 14:36
g-d in their tents Ps 106:25
scribes *began* to **g** Luke 15:2
g among yourselves John 6:43

GRUMBLING *complaint*
for He hears your **g-s** Ex 16:7
g-s against Me Num 17:10
Do all...without **g** Phil 2:14

GUARD (n) *keeper*
set a **g** over me Job 7:12
be a **g** for them Ezek 38:7
g-s shook for fear Matt 28:4
Him away under **g** Mark 14:44

GUARD (v) *keep watch*
g the way to the tree Gen 3:24
g-ed the threshold 2 Kin 12:9
G-ing...justice Prov 2:8
Discretion will **g** you Prov 2:11
soldier...was **g-ing** Acts 28:16
will **g** your hearts Phil 4:7
g...from idols 1 John 5:21

GUARDHOUSE *prison*
the court of the **g** Jer 37:21
the court of the **g** Jer 38:28

GUARDIAN *overseer*
g-s of *the children* 2 Kin 10:1
under **g-s** and Gal 4:2
G of your souls 1 Pet 2:25

GUEST *visitor*
Herod and his...**g-s** Mark 6:22
Where...My **g** room Mark 14:14
to the invited **g-s** Luke 14:7
g of a...sinner Luke 19:7

GUIDANCE *counsel*
no **g**, the people fall Prov 11:14
make war by wise **g** Prov 20:18

GUIDE (n) *advisor, director*
The righteous is a **g** Prov 12:26
Woe to...blind **g-s** Matt 23:16
You blind **g-s**, who Matt 23:24
are a **g** to the blind Rom 2:19

GUIDE (v) *direct, lead*
LORD alone **g-d** him Deut 32:12
He **g-s** me in the paths Ps 23:3
g us until death Ps 48:14
my mind was **g-ing** *me* Eccl 2:3
blind...**g-s** a blind Matt 15:14
g you into...truth John 16:13
unless someone **g-s** Acts 8:31

GUILT *offence*
be free from **g** Num 5:31
according to his **g** Deut 25:2
charge me with a **g** 2 Sam 3:8
our **g** has grown Ezra 9:6
land is full of **g** Jer 51:5
must bear their **g** Hos 10:2
I find no **g** in Him John 18:38

GUILT OFFERING *see* **OFFERINGS**

GUILTY *charged* or *condemned*
he sins and becomes **g** Lev 6:4
murderer...**g** of Num 35:31
as one who is **g** 2 Sam 14:13
g by the blood Ezek 22:4
g of an eternal sin Mark 3:29
has become **g** of all James 2:10

GUSHED *burst, flowed*
so that waters **g** out Ps 78:20
the rock...water **g** Is 48:21
all his intestines **g** out Acts 1:18

H

HABAKKUK
prophet Hab 1:1; 3:1

HABITATION *abode, dwelling*
from Your holy **h** Deut 26:15
a rock of **h** Ps 71:3
h-s of violence Ps 74:20
live in a peaceful **h** Is 32:18
holy and glorious **h** Is 63:15
laid waste his **h** Jer 10:25
a **h** of shepherds Jer 33:12

HABOR
river in Mesopotamia 2 Kin 17:6; 18:11; 1 Chr 5:26

HADAD
1 *son of Ishmael* Gen 25:15; 1 Chr 1:30
2 *king of Edom, son of Bedad* Gen 36:35,36; 1 Chr 1:46,47
3 *king of Edom* Gen 36:39; 1 Chr 1:50,51
4 *Edomite prince* 1 Kin 11:14ff

HADASSAH
Esther's Hebrew name Esth 2:7

HADES *hell, place of dead*
will descend to **H** Matt 11:23
in **H** he lifted up Luke 16:23

abandoned to **H** Acts 2:31
see also **HELL** *and* SHEOL

HAGAR
Sarah's handmaiden Gen 16:1
Abraham's slave wife Gen 16:3
mother of Ishmael Gen 16:15

HAGGAI
prophet Ezra 5:1; Hag 1:1

HAGGITH
David's wife 2 Sam 3:4
mother of Adonijah 1 Kin 1:11

HAIL (n) *pieces of ice*
rained **h** on the land Ex 9:23
storehouses of the **h** Job 38:22
gave them **h** for rain Ps 105:32
plague of the **h** Rev 16:21

HAIL (v) *greeting*
H, Rabbi Matt 26:49
H, King of...Jews Matt 27:29

HAILSTONES *pieces of ice*
who died from the **h** Josh 10:11
H and coals of fire Ps 18:13
you, O **h,** will fall Ezek 13:11
h...one hundred Rev 16:21

HAIR
gray **h**...to Sheol Gen 42:38
locks of his **h** and Judg 16:14
h...bristled Job 4:15
h...like pure wool Dan 7:9
garment of camel's **h** Matt 3:4
make one **h** white Matt 5:36
h-s...all numbered Matt 10:30
His feet with her **h** John 11:2
not with braided **h** 1 Tim 2:9

HALL *corridor*
h of pillars 1 Kin 7:6
h of judgment 1 Kin 7:7
wedding **h** was Matt 22:10

HALLELUJAH *praise Yahweh*
H! Salvation and Rev 19:1
H! Her smoke rises Rev 19:3
Amen. **H** Rev 19:4
H! For the Lord our Rev 19:6

HALLOWED *consecrated, holy*
H be Your name Matt 6:9

HAM
1 *son of Noah* Gen 5:32; 9:18
2 *city* Gen 14:5
3 *poetic name for Egypt* Ps 105:27; 106:22

HAMAN
Persian prime minister
son of Hammedatha Esth 3:1

HAMATH
city in Aram 2 Kin 23:33; 25:21

HAMMER *mallet, tool*
and seized a **h** Judg 4:21
neither **h** nor axe 1 Kin 6:7
smash with...**h-s** Ps 74:6
like a **h** which Jer 23:29

HAMON-GOG
valley where army of Gog is defeated Ezek 39:11,15

HANANIAH
1 *son of Zerubbabel* 1 Chr 3:19
2 *son of Shishak* 1 Chr 8:24
3 *musician* 1 Chr 25:4,23
4 *in Uzziah's army* 2 Chr 26:11
5 *repaired wall* Neh 3:30
6 *overseer of palace* Neh 7:2
7 *false prophet* Jer 28:15
8 *Shadrach* Dan 1:6,7
name of six other individuals

HAND *part of body*
cover you with My **h** Ex 33:22
for tooth, **h** for **h** Deut 19:21
sling was in his **h** 1 Sam 17:40
They pierced my **h-s** Ps 22:16
buries his **h** Prov 19:24
the hollow of His **h** Is 40:12
clay in the potter's **h** Jer 18:6
not let your left **h** Matt 6:3
laying His **h-s** on Mark 10:16
the right **h** of God Mark 16:19
into the **h-s** of men Luke 9:44
into Your **h-s** I Luke 23:46
reach here your **h** John 20:27
not made with **h-s** 2 Cor 5:1
lifting up holy **h-s** 1 Tim 2:8
h-s of...God Heb 10:31

HANDMAID *servant, slave*
save the son of Your **h** Ps 86:16
the son of Your **h** Ps 116:16
her **h-s** are moaning Nah 2:7

HANDSOME *attractive*
a choice and **h** *man* 1 Sam 9:2
ruddy, with a **h** 1 Sam 17:42

HANG *attach, suspend*
h you on a tree Gen 40:19
h up the veil Ex 40:8
h-ed is accursed of Deut 21:23
h-ing in an oak 2 Sam 18:10
they **h-ed** Haman Esth 7:10
he...**h-ed** himself Matt 27:5
millstone were **hung** Luke 17:2
h-ing Him on a cross Acts 5:30
who **h-s** on a tree Gal 3:13

HANNAH
mother of Samuel 1 Sam 2:21

HAPPINESS *joy*
give **h** to his wife Deut 24:5
eat your bread in **h** Eccl 9:7
I have forgotten **h** Lam 3:17

HAPPY *blessed, joyful*
Leah said, **H** am I Gen 30:13
h...man whom God Job 5:17
h...who keeps the Prov 29:18

HARAN
1 *brother of Abraham* Gen 11:27
father of Lot Gen 11:31
2 *Gershonite Levite* 1 Chr 23:9
3 *Mesopotamian city* Gen 11:32; 27:43

HARD *difficult, firm*
bitter with **h** labor Ex 1:14
case that is too **h** Deut 1:17
made our yoke **h** 2 Chr 10:4
Water becomes **h** Job 38:30
h for a rich man Matt 19:23
h it is to enter Mark 10:24
worked **h** all night Luke 5:5

HARDEN *make hard, callous*
h Pharaoh's heart Ex 7:3
dust **h-s** into a mass Job 38:38
who **h-s** *his* neck Prov 29:1
h-s whom He Rom 9:18
minds were **h-ed** 2 Cor 3:14
Do not **h** your hearts Heb 3:15

HARDNESS *callousness*
give them **h** of heart Lam 3:65
Because of your **h** Matt 19:8
grieved at their **h** Mark 3:5
unbelief and **h** of Mark 16:14

HARDSHIP *difficulty*
H after **h** is with me Job 10:17
people experience **h** Ps 60:3
afflictions, in **h-s** 2 Cor 6:4
our labor and **h** 1 Thess 2:9
Suffer **h** with *me* 2 Tim 2:3

HAREM *royal wives' quarters*
best place in the **h** Esth 2:9
the court of the **h** Esth 2:11
from the **h** to the Esth 2:13
to the second **h** Esth 2:14

HARLOT *prostitute*
thought she *was* a **h** Gen 38:15
the hire of a **h** Deut 23:18
h whose name was Josh 2:1
Dressed as a **h** Prov 7:10
city has become a **h** Is 1:21
also played the **h** Ezek 16:26
Traded a boy for a **h** Joel 3:3
Mother of **H-s** Rev 17:5

HARLOTRY *prostitution*
with child by **h** Gen 38:24
profaned by **h** Lev 21:7
uncovered her **h-ies** Ezek 23:18
children of **h** Hos 1:2
spirit of **h** Hos 5:4

HARM (n) *evil, hurt*
pillar to me, for **h** Gen 31:52
h to this people Ex 5:22
keep *me* from **h** 1 Chr 4:10
Do not devise **h** Prov 3:29
great **h** to yourselves Jer 44:7
the fire without **h** Dan 3:25
did me much **h** 2 Tim 4:14

HARM (v) *damage, hurt*
David seeks to **h** 1 Sam 24:9
planning to **h** me Neh 6:2
have not **h-ed** me Dan 6:22
in order to **h** you Acts 18:10
is there to **h** you 1 Pet 3:13

HAR-MAGEDON
hill of Megiddo Rev 16:16
see also **MEGIDDO**

HARMONY *agreement*
what **h** has Christ 2 Cor 6:15
live in **h** in the Phil 4:2

HARP *musical instrument*
my **h** is turned to Job 30:31
praises...with a **h** Ps 33:2
Awake, **h** and lyre Ps 57:8
gaiety of the **h** ceases Is 24:8
each one holding a **h** Rev 5:8
holding **h-s** of God Rev 15:2

HARSH *difficult, hard*
man was **h** and evil 1 Sam 25:3
h word stirs up anger Prov 15:1
A **h** vision Is 21:2
under **h** servitude Lam 1:3

HARVEST *reap and gather*
Seedtime and **h** Gen 8:22
fruits of the wheat **h** Ex 34:22
you reap your **h** Deut 24:19
he who sleeps in **h** Prov 10:5
snow...time of **h** Prov 25:13
like rain in **h** Prov 26:1
the gladness of **h** Is 9:3
time of **h** will come Jer 51:33
Lord of the **h** Matt 9:38
h is the end of the Matt 13:39
fields...white for **h** John 4:35
h of the earth is Rev 14:15

HARVEST, FEAST OF *see* **FEASTS**

HASHUM
1 *family of exiles* Ezra 2:19
2 *was with Ezra* Neh 8:4

HASTEN *accelerate*
h-ed after deceit Job 31:5
H to me, O God Ps 70:5
they **h** to shed blood Prov 1:16
bird **h-s** to the snare Prov 7:23
eye **h-s** after wealth Prov 28:22

h-ing...day of God 2 Pet 3:12

HATE ***despise, loathe***
you **h** discipline Ps 50:17
who **h** the LORD Ps 81:15
I **h** every false way Ps 119:104
fools **h** knowledge Prov 1:22
withholds his rod **h-s** Prov 13:24
a time to **h** Eccl 3:8
H evil, love good Amos 5:15
For I **h** divorce Mal 2:16
good to those who **h** Luke 6:27
you will be **h-d** Luke 21:17
he who **h-s** his life John 12:25
the very thing I **h** Rom 7:15
Esau I **h-d** Rom 9:13
h-ing one another Titus 3:3
yet **h-s** his brother 1 John 2:9

HATERS ***those who hate***
slanderers, **h** of God Rom 1:30
brutal, **h** of good 2 Tim 3:3

HATRED ***hate, ill will***
h for my love Ps 109:5
H stirs up strife Prov 10:12
who conceals **h** *has* Prov 10:18

HAUGHTY ***proud***
nor my eyes **h** Ps 131:1
H eyes, a lying Prov 6:17
h spirit before Prov 16:18
Proud, **H,** Scoffer Prov 21:24
wine betrays the **h** Hab 2:5
do not be **h** in mind Rom 12:16

HAVEN ***harbor, shelter***
be a **h** for ships Gen 49:13
to their desired **h** Ps 107:30

HAVILAH
1 *second son of Cush* Gen 10:7
2 *son of Joktan* Gen 10:29; 1 Chr 1:23
3 *region encompassed by one of Eden's rivers* Gen 2:11
4 *area in W Arabia* Gen 25:18

HAWK ***bird***
sea gull, and the **h** Deut 14:15
h-s will be gathered Is 34:15

HAZAEL
anointed by Elijah 1 Kin 19:15
killed Ben Hadad 2 Kin 8:15
Aramaic king 2 Kin 8:15; 9:14
defeated Israel 2 Kin 10:32

HAZOR
1 *Canaanite city in N Palestine* Josh 11:11
2 *town of the Negev* Josh 15:23
3 *Benjamite city* Neh 11:33
4 *desert kingdom* Jer 49:33

HEAD ***chief*** **or** ***part of body***
bruise you on the **h** Gen 3:15
anointed my **h** with oil Ps 23:5
h a garland of grace Prov 4:9
gray **h** is a crown Prov 16:31
coals on his **h** Prov 25:22
h was made bald Ezek 29:18
had four **h-s** Dan 7:6
an oath by your **h** Matt 5:36
nowhere to lay His **h** Matt 8:20
h of John the Baptist Matt 14:8
not a hair of your **h** Luke 21:18
crown...on His **h** John 19:2
God is the **h** of 1 Cor 11:3
husband is the **h** Eph 5:23

HEADLONG ***headfirst***
He rushes **h** at Him Job 15:26
falling **h,** he burst Acts 1:18
h into the error Jude 11

HEAL ***make well, restore***
will **h** their land 2 Chr 7:14
h-s the brokenhearted Ps 147:3
a time to **h** Eccl 3:3
H me, O LORD Jer 17:14
will **h** their apostasy Hos 14:4
h-ed all who were Matt 8:16
H *the* sick, raise Matt 10:8
h him on...Sabbath Mark 3:2
Physician, **h** yourself Luke 4:23
you may be **h-ed** James 5:16
fatal wound was **h-ed** Rev 13:3

HEALING ***health, wholeness***
be **h** to your body Prov 3:8
h to the bones Prov 16:24
sorrow is beyond **h** Jer 8:18
There is no **h** for Jer 46:11
their leaves for **h** Ezek 47:12
h every kind of Matt 4:23
gifts of **h** 1 Cor 12:9
h of the nations Rev 22:2

HEALTH ***soundness, wholeness***
no **h** in my bones Ps 38:3
restore you to **h** Jer 30:17
and be in good **h** 3 John 2

HEAP (n) ***mound, pile***
stones and made a **h** Gen 31:46
waters stood...like a **h** Ex 15:8
made a refuse **h** Ezra 6:11
needy from the ash **h** Ps 113:7
Jerusalem a **h** of ruins Jer 9:11
altars are...**h-s** Hos 12:11

HEAP (v) ***pile up, place***
h misfortunes on Deut 32:23
will **h** burning coals Prov 25:22
H on the wood Ezek 24:10
h up rubble to Hab 1:10

HEAR ***listen***
h-d the sound of Gen 3:10
God **h-d** their groaning Ex 2:24
H, O Israel Deut 6:4
h the wisdom of 1 Kin 4:34
h in heaven 1 Kin 8:30
Will God **h** his cry Job 27:9
who **h** prayer Ps 65:2
h Your lovingkindness Ps 143:8
poor **h-s** no rebuke Prov 13:8
deaf will **h** words Is 29:18
bones, **h** the word Ezek 37:4
ears to **h,** let him **h** Matt 11:15
h of wars and Mark 13:7
he who **h-s** My word John 5:24
does not **h** sinners John 9:31
sheep **h** My voice John 10:27
we **h-d** of your faith Col 1:4
anyone **h-s** My voice Rev 3:20

HEARING ***listening***
in the LORD's **h** 1 Sam 8:21
in the **h** of a fool Prov 23:9
fulfilled in your **h** Luke 4:21
I will give you a **h** Acts 23:35
become dull of **h** Heb 5:11

HEART ***mind*** **or** ***seat of emotions***
intent of man's **h** is Gen 8:21
I will harden his **h** Ex 4:21
great searchings of **h** Judg 5:16
LORD looks at the **h** 1 Sam 16:7
fool has said in his **h** Ps 14:1
meditation of my **h** Ps 19:14
My **h** is like wax Ps 22:14
in me a clean **h** Ps 51:10
and a contrite **h** Ps 51:17
Your word...in my **h** Ps 119:11
Deceit is in the **h** Prov 12:20
A joyful **h** is good Prov 17:22
to a troubled **h** Prov 25:20
bribe corrupts the **h** Eccl 7:7
a new **h** and a new Ezek 18:31
uncircumcised in **h** Ezek 44:7
are the pure in **h** Matt 5:8
adultery...in his **h** Matt 5:28
and humble in **h** Matt 11:29
h is far...from Me Matt 15:8
pondering...in her **h** Luke 2:19
pierced to the **h** Acts 2:37
cleansing their **h-s** Acts 15:9
who searches the **h-s** Rom 8:27
tablets of human **h-s** 2 Cor 3:3
not lose **h** in doing Gal 6:9
melody with your **h** Eph 5:19
intentions of the **h** Heb 4:12
deceives his *own* **h** James 1:26

HEAT ***hotness, warmth***
the **h** of the day Gen 18:1
and **h** consume Job 24:19
hidden from its **h** Ps 19:6
a shade from the **h** Is 25:4
burning **h** of famine Lam 5:10
scorching **h** of the Matt 20:12
with intense **h** 2 Pet 3:10
scorched with fierce **h** Rev 16:9

HEAVE OFFERING ***see*** **OFFERINGS**

HEAVEN ***place of God*** **or** ***sky***
God created the **h-s** Gen 1:1
rain bread from **h** Ex 16:4
shut up the **h-s** Deut 11:17
thunder in the **h-s** 1 Sam 2:10
fire came...from **h** 2 Kin 1:14
make windows in **h** 2 Kin 7:2
walks...vault of **h** Job 22:14
I consider Your **h-s** Ps 8:3
h and earth praise Ps 69:34
fixed patterns of **h** Jer 33:25
lights in the **h-s** Ezek 32:8
open...windows of **h** Mal 3:10
kingdom of **h** is at Matt 3:2
voice out of the **h-s** Matt 3:17
reward in **h** is great Matt 5:12
Father who is in **h** Matt 6:9
shall have been loosed in **h** Matt 16:19
great signs from **h** Luke 21:11
Him go into **h** Acts 1:11
no...name under **h** Acts 4:12
up to the third **h** 2 Cor 12:2
citizenship is in **h** Phil 3:20
there was war in **h** Rev 12:7
new **h** and a new Rev 21:1

HEAVENLY ***related to God***
h Father is perfect Matt 5:48
h Father knows that Matt 6:32
h host praising God Luke 2:13
I tell you **h** things John 3:12
Him in the **h** *places* Eph 2:6
partakers of a **h** Heb 3:1
shadow of the **h** Heb 8:5

HEAVY ***burdensome, hard to lift***
Moses' hands were **h** Ex 17:12
servitude was **h** on Neh 5:18
h drinkers of wine Prov 23:20
A stone is **h** Prov 27:3
Jerusalem a **h** stone Zech 12:3
eyes were very **h** Mark 14:40

HEBER
1 *son of Beriah* Gen 46:17
2 *husband of Jael* Judg 4:17
3 *son of Mered* 1 Chr 4:18
4 *son of Elpaal* 1 Chr 8:17
see also **EBER**

HEBREW(S)
1 *people* Gen 14:13; Ex 1:15; 9:13; Jon 1:9
2 *language* John 19:17; Acts 22:2; 26:14
see also **JUDEAN**
see also **CANAAN**

HEBRON
1 *site of Sarah's death* Gen 23:2
visited by spies Num 13:22
destroyed Josh 10:37
city of refuge Josh 20:7
residence of David 2 Sam 2:1
2 *son of Kohath* Ex 6:18

3 *son of Mareshah* 1 Chr 2:42

HEDGE ***border* or *protection***
You not made a **h** Job 1:10
as a **h** of thorns Prov 15:19
along the **h-s,** and Luke 14:23

HEEL ***back of foot***
bruise him on the **h** Gen 3:15
on to Esau's **h** Gen 25:26
his **h** against Me John 13:18

HEIFER ***young cow***
unblemished red **h** Num 19:2
plowed with my **h** Judg 14:18
Egypt is a pretty **h** Jer 46:20
Like a stubborn **h** Hos 4:16

HEIGHT ***elevation, heaven, sky***
in the **h** of heaven Job 22:12
from His holy **h** Ps 102:19
Praise Him in the **h-s** Ps 148:1
As the heavens for **h** Prov 25:3
ascend above the **h-s** Is 14:14
nor **h,** nor depth Rom 8:39

HEIR ***person who inherits***
in my house is my **h** Gen 15:3
has he no **h-s** Jer 49:1
h-s also, **h-s** of God Rom 8:17
an **h** through God Gal 4:7
h-s of the kingdom James 2:5

HELIOPOLIS
ancient Egyptian city Jer 43:13
see also **ON**

HELL ***place of dead***
go into the fiery **h** Matt 5:22
soul and body in **h** Matt 10:28
to be cast into **h** Mark 9:47
set on fire by **h** James 3:6
cast them into **h** 2 Pet 2:4
see also **HADES** *and* **SHEOL**

HELLENISTIC JEWS
Greek speaking Jews Acts 6:1; 9:29

HELMET ***headpiece***
bronze **h** on his 1 Sam 17:5
h of salvation Is 59:17
take the **h** of Eph 6:17

HELP (n) ***assistance, relief***
h is not within me Job 6:13
He is our **h** and our Ps 33:20
present **h** in trouble Ps 46:1
I cried for **h** Jon 2:2
gifts of...**h-s** 1 Cor 12:28

HELP (v) ***aid, assist***
h-ing the Hebrew Ex 1:16
the LORD **h-ed** David 2 Sam 8:6
whence shall my **h** Ps 121:1
I will **h** you Is 41:13
Lord, **h** me Matt 15:25
h my unbelief Mark 9:24
must **h** the weak Acts 20:35
Spirit also **h-s** our Rom 8:26
earth **h-ed** the Rev 12:16

HELPER ***one who assists***
h of the orphan Ps 10:14
be my **h** Ps 30:10
Behold, God is my **h** Ps 54:4
give you another **H** John 14:16
H, the Holy Spirit John 14:26

HELPLESS ***weak***
the **h** has hope Job 5:16
who considers the **h** Ps 41:1
while we were still **h** Rom 5:6

HEMAN
1 *sage of Solomon* 1 Kin 4:31
2 *line of Samuel* 1 Chr 15:19

HEMORRHAGE ***bleeding***
suffering from a **h** Matt 9:20
a **h** for twelve years Mark 5:25
her **h** stopped Luke 8:44

HEN ***fowl***
h gathers her Matt 23:37
as a **h** *gathers* her Luke 13:34

HEPHZIBAH
Manasseh's mother 2 Kin 21:1
Hezekiah's wife 2 Kin 21:3

HERB ***dried plant***
bread and bitter **h-s** Ex 12:8
fade like the green **h** Ps 37:2
h-s of...mountains Prov 27:25
sweet-scented **h-s** Song 5:13

HERD ***cattle, flock***
firstborn of your **h** Deut 12:6
h, or flock taste a Jon 3:7
h of many swine Matt 8:30

HERDSMEN ***keepers of flocks***
h of Abram's livestock Gen 13:7
between my **h** and Gen 13:8
the **h** ran away Matt 8:33

HERITAGE ***what is inherited***
the **h** decreed to him Job 20:29
my **h** is beautiful Ps 16:6
their land as a **h** Ps 136:21
inherit the desolate **h-s** Is 49:8
you who pillage My **h** Jer 50:11

HERMES
1 *Greek god* Acts 14:12
2 *Roman Christian* Rom 16:14

HERMOGENES
Asian Christian who failed to support Paul 2 Tim 1:15

HERMON
mountain region in N Palestine Josh 11:17; Ps 42:6; 133:3
N boundary of Promised Land Deut 3:8

HEROD
1 **Herod the Great**
king of Judea, Samaria, Ituraea and Traconitis Matt 2:1
ruled during Jesus' birth Matt 2:1ff
2 **Herod Archelaus**
son of Herod the Great Matt 2:22
governor of Ituraea and Traconitis
3 **Herod Antipas**
son of Herod the Great Matt 14:1
tetrarch of Galilee and Perea Luke 3:1
ruled during Jesus' ministry Luke 13:31; 23:7,8,11
executed John the Baptist Matt 14:10; Mark 6:27
4 **Herod Philip I**
son of Herod the Great Mark 6:17
5 **Herod Philip II**
son of Herod the Great Luke 3:1
tetrarch of Ituraea and Traconitis
6 **Herod Agrippa I**
grandson of Herod the Great Acts 12:1
king of Judea and Samaria
persecuted the early church Acts 12:2-23
7 **Herod Agrippa II**
son of Agrippa I Acts 25:13
tetrarch of Tiberias, Abila and Traconitis
heard Paul's testimony Acts 25:23ff; 26:1ff

HERODIANS
influential Jews favoring Herod Matt 22:16; Mark 3:6

HERODIAS
wife of Herod Antipas Matt 14:3; Mark 6:17
requested head of John the Baptist Matt 14:8; Mark 6:24

HETH
1 *son of Canaan* Gen 10:15
2 *Hebrew eponym for Hittites* Gen 23:10

HEW ***chop, cut***
h down their Asherim Deut 7:5
H-n cisterns, vineyards Neh 9:25
h-n out in the rock Mark 15:46

HEZEKIAH
king of Judah 2 Kin 18:1
reformer 2 Kin 18:4
warrior 2 Kin 18:7,8
builder 2 Kin 20:20

HIDE ***conceal, cover***
man and his wife **hid** Gen 3:8
I **h** from Abraham Gen 18:17
Moses **hid** his face Ex 3:6
h me in Sheol Job 14:13
h-ing my iniquity Job 31:33
H me in the shadow Ps 17:8
Do not **h** Your face Ps 27:9
wrongs are not **h-den** Ps 69:5
sees evil *and* **h-s** Prov 27:12
hid your talent Matt 25:25
nothing is **h-den** Mark 4:22
Jesus **hid** Himself John 8:59
h us from...Him Rev 6:16

HIDDEN (adj) ***concealed***
Acquit me of **h** *faults* Ps 19:12
h wealth of secret Is 45:3
h snares for my feet Jer 18:22
profound and **h** Dan 2:22
some of the **h** manna Rev 2:17

HIDING PLACE
Clouds are a **h** Job 22:14
He lurks in a **h** Ps 10:9
You are my **h** Ps 32:7
uncovered his **h-s** Jer 49:10

HIERAPOLIS
city in Asia Minor Col 4:13

HIGH ***elevated* or *heavenly***
it is still **h** day Gen 29:7
the **h** places of Baal Num 22:41
h above all nations Deut 26:19
h as the heavens Job 11:8
my advocate is on **h** Job 16:19
set him *securely* on **h** Ps 91:14
or **h** as heaven Is 7:11
to a very **h** mountain Matt 4:8
the **h** priest Matt 26:57
Son of the Most **H** Mark 5:7
from a **h** fever Luke 4:38
He ascended on **h** Eph 4:8

HIGH PLACE
worship place of God or idols Num 22:41; 1 Sam 9:12-14

HIGH PRIEST
first in hierarchy Ex 27:21
under Aaron Ex 28:1,2
enters Holy of Holies Ex 28:29,30; Heb 9:7
head of Sanhedrin Matt 26:57; Acts 5:21
Jesus as High Priest Heb 3:1; 5:5-9

HIGHWAY ***road***
along the king's **h** Num 20:17
h from Egypt to Is 19:23
the **H** of Holiness Is 35:8
a **h** for our God Is 40:3
Go out into the **h-s** Luke 14:23

HILKIAH
1 *father of Eliakim* 2 Kin 18:18
2 *high priest* 2 Kin 22:4-14
3 *Merarite Levite* 1 Chr 6:45
4 *son of Hosah* 1 Chr 26:11
5 *was with Ezra* Neh 8:4
6 *returned from exile* Neh 12:7

HILL ***mountain***
the everlasting **h-s** Gen 49:26
the **h** of God 1 Sam 10:5

dwell on Your holy **h** Ps 15:1
to Your holy **h** Ps 43:3
cattle...thousand **h-s** Ps 50:10
h-s, Fall on us Hos 10:8
city set on a **h** Matt 5:14
h...brought low Luke 3:5
the brow of the **h** Luke 4:29
h-s, Cover us Luke 23:30

HINDER *delay, impede, restrain*
h meditation before Job 15:4
do not **h** them Matt 19:14
do not **h** them Luke 18:16
h-ed you from obeying Gal 5:7
prayers...not be **h-ed** 1 Pet 3:7

HINNOM
1 *valley SW of Jerusalem* Josh 15:8; Neh 11:30
2 *person for whom valley named* 2 Kin 23:10; Jer 7:31

HIP *part of body*
the sinew of the **h** Gen 32:32
curves of your **h-s** are Song 7:1
h joints went slack Dan 5:6

HIRAM / HURAM
1 *king of Tyre* 1 Kin 5:1ff; 2 Chr 2:3,11
2 *skilled craftsman* 1 Kin 7:14; 2 Chr 4:11

HIRE (n) *wages*
it came for its **h** Ex 22:15
the **h** of a harlot Deut 23:18

HIRE (v) *engage for labor*
h...for bread 1 Sam 2:5
and **h-d** the Arameans 2 Sam 10:6
to **h**...chariots 1 Chr 19:6
he who **h-s** a fool Prov 26:10
to **h** laborers for Matt 20:1

HIRED (adj) *employed*
as a **h** man, as if Lev 25:40
oppress a **h** servant Deut 24:14
as one of your **h** Luke 15:19
h hand...not a shepherd John 10:12
because he is a **h** hand John 10:13

HISS *to show dislike*
h him from his place Job 27:23
*object of...***h-ing** Jer 18:16
They **h** and shake Lam 2:15
h *And* wave his hand Zeph 2:15

HITTITES
1 *people in Palestine in patriarchal age* Gen 15:20; 49:29
2 *inhabitants of Aram during Israelite monarchy* 2 Kin 7:6; 2 Chr 8:7

HIVITES
people dispossessed by the Israelites Ex 23:28; Josh 3:10; 2 Sam 24:7

HOGLAH
daughter of Zelophehad Num 26:33; 27:1; Josh 17:3

HOLD *grasp, retain*
Moses **held** his hand Ex 17:11
h fast to Him Deut 11:22
h fast...evil purpose Ps 64:5
heart **h** fast my words Prov 4:4
Take **h** of instruction Prov 4:13
h fast My covenant Is 56:4
h to the tradition Mark 7:8
h fast the word 1 Cor 15:2
h-ing to the mystery 1 Tim 3:9
h of the eternal 1 Tim 6:12
He **held** seven stars Rev 1:16

HOLE *opening*
the **h** of the cobra Is 11:8
a **h** in the wall Ezek 8:7
a purse with **h-s** Hag 1:6
foxes have **h-s** Matt 8:20

HOLIDAY *period of leisure*
a feast and a **h** Esth 8:17
a **h** for rejoicing Esth 9:19
mourning into a **h** Esth 9:22

HOLINESS *sacredness*
majestic in **h** Ex 15:11
H befits Your house Ps 93:5
the Highway of **H** Is 35:8
without blame in **h** 1 Thess 3:13
we may share His **h** Heb 12:10

HOLLOW *empty space*
the **h** of a sling 1 Sam 25:29
in the **h** of His hand Is 40:12

HOLY *sacred, sanctified*
standing is **h** ground Ex 3:5
sabbath...keep it **h** Ex 20:8
you are a **h** people Deut 7:6
ten thousand **h** ones Deut 33:2
h like the LORD 1 Sam 2:2
Worship...**h** array 1 Chr 16:29
His **h** dwelling 2 Chr 30:27
Jerusalem, the **h** city Neh 11:1
Zion, My **h** mountain Ps 2:6
to His **h** land Ps 78:54
bless His **h** name Ps 145:21
H, H, H, is the LORD Is 6:3
the **H** One of Israel Is 30:15
what is **h** to dogs Matt 7:6
righteous and **h** man Mark 6:20
the **H** One of God Luke 4:34
in the **h** Scriptures Rom 1:2
and **h** sacrifice Rom 12:1
with a **h** kiss Rom 16:16
h both in body 1 Cor 7:34
lifting up **h** hands 1 Tim 2:8
with a **h** calling 2 Tim 1:9
I saw the **h** city Rev 21:2

HOLY OF HOLIES
most holy place in the Tabernacle / Temple Ex 26:33,34; 2 Chr 3:8

HOLY SPIRIT
Third Person of the Godhead Matt 28:19; 2 Cor 13:14
Helper John 14:16,26
Giver of gifts Rom 12:6-8; 1 Cor 12:8-11
fruit of the Spirit Gal 5:22

HOMAGE *act of reverence*
my people shall do **h** Gen 41:40
did **h** to the LORD 1 Chr 29:20
and paid **h** to Haman Esth 3:2
did **h** to Daniel Dan 2:46

HOME *place of dwelling*
free at **h** one year Deut 24:5
God makes a **h** Ps 68:6
husband is not at **h** Prov 7:19
to his eternal **h** Eccl 12:5
Go **h** to your people Mark 5:19
let him eat at **h** 1 Cor 11:34
at **h** in the body 2 Cor 5:6
at **h** with the Lord 2 Cor 5:8

HOMER *measure of capacity*
a **h** of barley Lev 27:16
a **h** of seed Is 5:10
from a **h** of wheat Ezek 45:13

HOMESTEAD *family dwelling*
h forlorn and forsaken Is 27:10
h be made desolate Acts 1:20

HOMOSEXUALS
effeminate, nor **h** 1 Cor 6:9
immoral men and **h** 1 Tim 1:10

HONEST *respectable, truthful*
we are **h** men Gen 42:11
painful are **h** words Job 6:25
an **h** and good heart Luke 8:15

HONEY *sweetness*
with milk and **h** Ex 3:8
swarm of bees and **h** Judg 14:8
is sweeter than **h** Judg 14:18
sweet as **h** in my Ezek 3:3
locusts and wild **h** Matt 3:4

HONEYCOMB *honey storage*
drippings of the **h** Ps 19:10
Pleasant words...a **h** Prov 16:24

HONOR (n) *glory, great respect*
both riches and **h** 1 Kin 3:13
stripped my **h** from Job 19:9
wise will inherit **h** Prov 3:35
is not without **h** Matt 13:57
glory and **h** and Rom 2:10
Marriage...*be held* in **h** Heb 13:4
blessing and **h** and Rev 5:13

HONOR (v) *show respect*
H your father Ex 20:12
h the aged Lev 19:32
who **h** Me I will **h** 1 Sam 2:30
am **h-ed** in the sight Is 49:5
A son **h-s** *his* father Mal 1:6
may be **h-ed** by men Matt 6:2
h-s Me with...lips Matt 15:8
does not **h** the Son John 5:23
fear God, **h** the king 1 Pet 2:17

HONORABLE *respectable*
the elder and **h** man Is 9:15
one vessel for **h** use Rom 9:21
whatever is **h** Phil 4:8

HOOF *part of animal foot*
which divide the **h** Lev 11:4
with horns and **h-s** Ps 69:31
h-s of beasts will Ezek 32:13
tear off their **h-s** Zech 11:16

HOOK *fastener*
into pruning **h-s** Is 2:4
My **h** in your nose Is 37:29
h-s into your jaws Ezek 38:4

HOPE (n) *expectation*
Where now is my **h** Job 17:15
h of the afflicted Ps 9:18
My **h** is in You Ps 39:7
You are my **h** Ps 71:5
while there is **h** Prov 19:18
the **h** of Israel Jer 17:13
our **h** has perished Ezek 37:11
on trial for the **h** Acts 23:6
h does not disappoint Rom 5:5
rejoicing in **h** Rom 12:12
may the God of **h** Rom 15:13
ought to plow in **h** 1 Cor 9:10
now faith, **h,** love, abide 1 Cor 13:13
h of righteousness Gal 5:5
the **h** of His calling Eph 1:18
the **h** of the gospel Col 1:23
the **h** of glory Col 1:27
the **h** of salvation 1 Thess 5:8
h of eternal life Titus 3:7
to a living **h** 1 Pet 1:3
h that is in you 1 Pet 3:15

HOPE (v) *expect with confidence*
I will **h** in Him Job 13:15
For I **h** in You Ps 38:15
We **h** for justice Is 59:11
are **h-ing** for light Jer 13:16
Gentiles will **h** Matt 12:21
h-s all things 1 Cor 13:7
first to **h** in Christ Eph 1:12
I **h** in the Lord Jesus Phil 2:19
of *things* **h-d** for Heb 11:1
I **h** to come to you 2 John 12

HOPHNI
son of Eli 1 Sam 1:3; 4:11

HOPHRA *see* **PHARAOH**

HOR
mountain Num 20:22,23
place of Aaron's death Num 20:28; Deut 32:50

HORDE *throng*
against Babylon A **h** Jer 50:9
h-s of grasshoppers Nah 3:17

HOREB
another name for Mount Sinai Ex 3:1; Deut 4:10; Ps 106:19

HORITES
inhabitants of Mount Seir in Edom Gen 14:6; 36:29

HORN
caught...by his **h-s** Gen 22:13
h-s of the altar Ex 29:12
you shall sound a **h** Lev 25:9
with the ram's **h** Josh 6:5
h of my salvation 2 Sam 22:3
the **h,** flute, lyre Dan 3:5
it had ten **h-s** Dan 7:7

HORROR *terror*
h overwhelms me Is 21:4
object of **h** Jer 49:13
clothed with **h** Ezek 7:27
cup of **h** Ezek 23:33

HORSE *animal*
bites the **h-'s** heels Gen 49:17
h-s and chariots of 2 Kin 6:17
A **h** is a false hope Ps 33:17
whip is for the **h** Prov 26:3
slaves *riding* on **h-s** Eccl 10:7
behold, a black **h** Rev 6:5

HORSE GATE *see* **GATES OF JERUSALEM**

HORSEMEN *cavalry, horse rider*
Pharaoh, his **h** and Ex 14:9
chariots and **h** 1 Kin 10:26
h riding on Ezek 23:12
H charging, Swords Nah 3:3
armies of the **h** Rev 9:16

HOSANNA *acclamation of praise*
H to the Son of Matt 21:9
H in the highest Mark 11:10
H! Blessed is He John 12:13

HOSEA
prophet Hos 1:1,2

HOSHEA
1 *name of Joshua* Num 13:8,16
2 *king of Israel* 2 Kin 15:30; 17:6
3 *Ephraim's officer* 1 Chr 27:20
4 *signer of covenant* Neh 10:23

HOSPITABLE *friendly*
h, able to teach 1 Tim 3:2
h, loving what is Titus 1:8
h to one another 1 Pet 4:9

HOSPITALITY *open to guests*
practicing **h** Rom 12:13
show **h** to strangers Heb 13:2

HOST *army, multitude*
all the **h** of heaven Deut 4:19
captain...LORD's **h** Josh 5:15
LORD of **h-s,** He is Ps 24:10
of the heavenly **h** Luke 2:13

HOSTILE *antagonistic*
h to...Jesus Acts 26:9
set on the flesh is **h** Rom 8:7
h to all men 1 Thess 2:15

HOT *very warm, violent*
when the sun grew **h** Ex 16:21
and **h** displeasure Deut 9:19
My heart was **h** within Ps 39:3
man walk on **h** coals Prov 6:28
neither cold nor **h** Rev 3:15

HOUR *time*
add a *single* **h** to Matt 6:27
watch...for one **h** Matt 26:40
the **h** is at hand Matt 26:45
ninth **h** Jesus cried Mark 15:34
save Me from this **h** John 12:27
the **h** has come John 17:1
the **h** of testing Rev 3:10

HOUSE *home* **or** *temple*
born in my **h** is my Gen 15:3
passed over the **h-s** Ex 12:27
the **h** of slavery Ex 20:2
consecrates his **h** Lev 27:14
as for me and my **h** Josh 24:15
Set your **h** in order 2 Kin 20:1
h of God forsaken Neh 13:11
h like the spider's Job 27:18
Holiness befits Your **h** Ps 93:5
LORD builds the **h** Ps 127:1
Wisdom...built her **h** Prov 9:1
in My **h** of prayer Is 56:7
O **h** of Israel Jer 18:6
his **h** on the rock Matt 7:24
My **h**...a **h** of Matt 21:13
devour widows' **h-s** Mark 12:40
guards his own **h** Luke 11:21
left **h** or wife or Luke 18:29
In My Father's **h** John 14:2
h not made...hands 2 Cor 5:1
h for a holy 1 Pet 2:5

HOUSE OF GOD / LORD *see* **TEMPLE**

HOUSE OF THE LORD *see* **TABERNACLE**

HOUSEHOLD *family, home*
herds and a great **h** Gen 26:14
stole the **h** idols Gen 31:19
each one with his **h** Ex 1:1
to the ways of her **h** Prov 31:27
like a head of a **h** Matt 13:52
are of God's **h** Eph 2:19
manages his own **h** 1 Tim 3:4
in the **h** of God 1 Tim 3:15

HOUSETOP *roof*
As grass on the **h-s** 2 Kin 19:26
lonely bird on a **h** Ps 102:7
upon the **h-s** Matt 10:27
Peter went...the **h** Acts 10:9

HULDAH
a Hebrew prophetess 2 Kin 22:14; 2 Chr 34:22

HUMAN *mankind, person*
the life of any **h** Lev 24:17
guilt of **h** blood Prov 28:17
they had **h** form Ezek 1:5
tablets of **h** hearts 2 Cor 3:3

HUMBLE (adj) *gentle, modest*
Moses was very **h** Num 12:3
h will inherit Ps 37:11
with the **h** is wisdom Prov 11:2
H, and mounted on Zech 9:9
gentle and **h** in Matt 11:29
along with **h** means Phil 4:12
grace to the **h** James 4:6

HUMBLE (v) *modest*
refuse to **h** yourself Ex 10:3
He might **h** you Deut 8:2
h...and pray 2 Chr 7:14
h-s...as this child Matt 18:4
H yourselves 1 Pet 5:6

HUMILIATE *embarrass*
h-d who seek my hurt Ps 71:24
do not feel **h-d** Is 54:4
His opponents...**h-d** Luke 13:17

HUMILIATION *embarrassment*
h has overwhelmed me Ps 44:15
go away together in **h** Is 45:16
let our **h** cover us Jer 3:25
In **h** His judgment Acts 8:33

HUMILITY *self-abasement*
before honor...**h** Prov 15:33
with **h** of mind Phil 2:3
clothe...with **h** 1 Pet 5:5

HUNDRED *number* **or** *many*
Adam had lived one **h** Gen 5:3
h of you will chase Lev 26:8
captains of **h-s** Num 31:14
h pieces of money Josh 24:32
went out by **h-s** 2 Sam 18:4
in groups of **h-s** Mark 6:40

HUNGER (n) *craving, starvation*
in **h,** in thirst Deut 28:48
lions...suffer **h** Ps 34:10
man will suffer **h** Prov 19:15
h is not satisfied Is 29:8
faint because of **h** Lam 2:19
sleeplessness, in **h** 2 Cor 6:5

HUNGER (v) *crave, need food*
the righteous to **h** Prov 10:3
are those who **h** Matt 5:6
to Me will not **h** John 6:35
They will **h** no longer Rev 7:16

HUNGRY *empty, needing food*
let you be **h** Deut 8:3
people are **h** and 2 Sam 17:29
h soul He has filled Ps 107:9
If your enemy is **h** Prov 25:21
when a **h** man dreams Is 29:8
He then became **h** Matt 4:2
disciples became **h** Matt 12:1
For I was **h** Matt 25:35
if your enemy is **h** Rom 12:20

HUNT *pursue, seek*
to **h** for game Gen 27:5
h-s a partridge 1 Sam 26:20
evil **h** the violent Ps 140:11
H-ed me down like Lam 3:52

HUNTER *seeker of game*
Nimrod a mighty **h** Gen 10:9
became a skillful **h** Gen 25:27

HUR
1 *helped Moses and Aaron* Ex 17:12; 24:14
2 *Bezalel's grandfather* Ex 31:2
3 *king of Midian* Num 31:8
4 *father of Rephaiah* Neh 3:9

HURAM
a Benjamite 1 Chr 8:5
see also **HIRAM / HURAM**

HURT (n) *damage, harm, wound*
Who delight in my **h** Ps 70:2
hoarded...to his **h** Eccl 5:13
your brother is **h** Rom 14:15

HURT (v) *cause pain, wound*
not allow him to **h** Gen 31:7
may be **h** by them Eccl 10:9
will not **h** or destroy Is 11:9
their power to **h** men Rev 9:10

HUSBAND *family head, spouse*
desire...your **h** Gen 3:16
honor to their **h-s** Esth 1:20
crown of her **h** Prov 12:4
is loved by *her* **h** Hos 3:1
divorces her **h** and Mark 10:12
have had five **h-s** John 4:18
if her **h** dies Rom 7:2
have her own **h** 1 Cor 7:2
unbelieving **h** is 1 Cor 7:14
h is the head of Eph 5:23
H-s, love your wives Eph 5:25
h-s of...one wife 1 Tim 3:12
adorned for her **h** Rev 21:2

HUSHAI
servant of David 2 Sam 15:32; 16:17

HYMENAEUS
heretical teacher at Ephesus 1 Tim 1:20; 2 Tim 2:17

HYMN *song of praise*
h-s of thanksgiving Neh 12:46
after singing a **h** Matt 26:30
singing **h-s** of praise Acts 16:25
psalms and **h-s** and Eph 5:19

HYPOCRISY *pretense*
full of **h** and Matt 23:28
love be without **h** Rom 12:9
without **h** James 3:17

HYPOCRITE *a pretender*
as the **h-s** do Matt 6:2
and Pharisees, **h-s** Matt 23:13
You **h**, first take Luke 6:42

HYSSOP *fragrant plant*
bunch of **h** and dip it Ex 12:22
scarlet string and **h** Lev 14:4
Purify me with **h** Ps 51:7
upon *a branch of* **h** John 19:29

I

I AM
related to name of God in Hebrew
I WHO **I** Ex 3:14
I has sent me Ex 3:14
I the LORD Ex 6:2
I the LORD your God Lev 19:3
I the first Is 44:6
I the Son of God Matt 27:43
Jesus said, **I** Mark 14:62
believe that **I** *He* John 8:24
will know that **I** *He* John 8:28
before Abraham...**I** John 8:58
believe that **I** *He* John 13:19
I the Alpha and Rev 1:8
I the first and Rev 1:17

ICE *frost*
turbid because of **i** Job 6:16
womb has come...**i** Job 38:29
casts forth His **i** Ps 147:17

ICHABOD
1 *son of Phinehas* 1 Sam 4:19,20
grandson of Eli 1 Sam 14:3
2 *name commemorates departed glory from Israel* 1 Sam 4:21,22

ICONIUM
city of Asia Minor Acts 14:1,19; 16:2; 2 Tim 3:11

IDLE *unemployed, uninvolved*
i man will suffer Prov 19:15
been standing here **i** Matt 20:6
this **i** babbler Acts 17:18

IDOL *false deity, image*
not make...an **i** Ex 20:4
Do not turn to **i-s** Lev 19:4
who makes an **i** or Deut 27:15
the gods...are **i-s** Ps 96:5
who blesses an **i** Is 66:3
abstain from...**i-s** Acts 15:20
guard...from **i-s** 1 John 5:21

IDOLATER *idol worshiper*
covetous, or an **i** 1 Cor 5:11
Do not be **i-s** 1 Cor 10:7
sorcerers and **i-s** Rev 21:8

IDOLATRY *idol worship*
flee from **i** 1 Cor 10:14
i, sorcery, enmities Gal 5:20
and abominable **i-ies** 1 Pet 4:3

IGNORANCE *lack of knowledge*
you worship in **i** Acts 17:23
i that is in them Eph 4:18
silence the **i** of 1 Pet 2:15

IGNORANT *without knowledge*
I was senseless and **i** Ps 73:22
not **i** of his schemes 2 Cor 2:11
and **i** speculations 2 Tim 2:23

ILL *unhealthy, sick*
woman who is **i** Lev 15:33
became mortally **i** Is 38:1
lunatic and is...**i** Matt 17:15
healed many...**i** Mark 1:34

ILLEGITIMATE *bastard*
No one of **i** birth Deut 23:2
borne **i** children Hos 5:7
you are **i** children Heb 12:8

ILLNESS *infirmity, sickness*
sick with the **i** 2 Kin 13:14
after his **i** and Is 38:9
because of a bodily **i** Gal 4:13

ILLUMINE *light up*
God **i-s** my darkness Ps 18:28
fire to **i** by night Ps 105:39
glory of God has **i-d** Rev 21:23
God will **i** them Rev 22:5

IMAGE *copy, likeness*
make man in Our **i** Gen 1:26
i of God He made Gen 9:6
burn their graven **i-s** Deut 7:5
worshiped a molten **i** Ps 106:19
made an **i** of gold Dan 3:1
i and glory of God 1 Cor 11:7
i of the invisible Col 1:15
the **i** of the beast Rev 13:15

IMITATORS *followers*
be **i** of me 1 Cor 4:16
be **i** of God Eph 5:1
i of the churches 1 Thess 2:14

IMMANUEL
1 *son born to a virgin* Is 7:14
a sign to King Ahaz Is 8:8
2 *title of Jesus* Matt 1:23

IMMORAL *lewd, unchaste*
with **i** people 1 Cor 5:9
the **i** man sins 1 Cor 6:18
i men...liars 1 Tim 1:10
i or godless person Heb 12:16
and **i** persons Rev 21:8

IMMORALITY *immoral acts*
no **i** in your midst Lev 20:14
except for **i** Matt 19:9
Flee **i** 1 Cor 6:18
abstain from...**i** 1 Thess 4:3
the wine of her **i** Rev 17:2

IMMORTALITY *everlasting life*
must put on **i** 1 Cor 15:53
alone possesses **i** 1 Tim 6:16
life and **i** to light 2 Tim 1:10

IMPATIENT *restless*
the people became **i** Num 21:4
should I not be **i** Job 21:4
my soul was **i** with Zech 11:8

IMPERISHABLE *indestructible*
wreath, but we an **i** 1 Cor 9:25
will be raised **i** 1 Cor 15:52
inheritance...*is* **i** 1 Pet 1:4

IMPLEMENTS *tools, utensils*
forger of all **i** of Gen 4:22
the **i** of the oxen 1 Kin 19:21

IMPLORE *ask, beseech, entreat*
I **i** you, give glory Josh 7:19
i-d him to avert Esth 8:3
i the compassion of Job 8:5
centurion...**i-ing** Him Matt 8:5
I **i** You by God Mark 5:7
They were **i-ing** Him Luke 8:31

I **i-d** the Lord 2 Cor 12:8
i you to walk in a Eph 4:1

IMPORTED *brought in*
chariot was **i** from 1 Kin 10:29
horses were **i** 2 Chr 1:16

IMPOSE *force upon*
i-d hard labor on us Deut 26:6
whatever you **i** on 2 Kin 18:14
you **i** heavy rent Amos 5:11
i-d until a time of Heb 9:10

IMPOSSIBLE *cannot be done*
nothing...will be **i** Gen 11:6
With people this is **i** Matt 19:26
i for God to lie Heb 6:18
without faith it is **i** Heb 11:6

IMPRISON *jail, restrict*
i-ed him at Riblah 2 Kin 23:33
i his princes at will Ps 105:22
not **i** their survivors Obad 14
I used to **i** and beat Acts 22:19

IMPRISONMENT *confinement*
in **i-s**, in tumults 2 Cor 6:5
Remember my **i** Col 4:18
even to **i** as a 2 Tim 2:9

IMPURE *unclean*
her **i** discharge Lev 15:25
eating...with **i** hands Mark 7:2
no immoral or **i** person Eph 5:5

IMPURITY *uncleanness*
menstrual **i** for seven Lev 15:19
i-ies of the sons of Lev 16:19
the **i** of the nations Ezra 6:21
as slaves to **i** Rom 6:19
of **i** with greediness Eph 4:19

INCENSE *fragrant substance*
burn fragrant **i** on Ex 30:7
i as an offering Lev 2:16
gold pans, full of **i** Num 7:86
My altar, to burn **i** 1 Sam 2:28
i on the high places 2 Kin 14:4
i before the LORD 1 Chr 23:13
golden altar of **i** Heb 9:4
the smoke of the **i** Rev 8:4

INCEST *illicit sexual relations*
they...committed **i** Lev 20:12

INCITE *stir up*
i-d David against 2 Sam 24:1
Jezebel...**i-d** him 1 Kin 21:25
I will **i** Egyptians Is 19:2
who **i-s** the people Luke 23:14
Jews **i-d** the devout Acts 13:50

INCLINE *bend, lean*
i your hearts to Josh 24:23
I my heart to Your Ps 119:36
i-s toward wickedness Is 32:6
I Your ear, O LORD Is 37:17
have not **i-d** your ear Jer 35:15

INCOME *wages*
i of the wicked Prov 10:16
i with injustice Prov 16:8
abundance *with its* **i** Eccl 5:10

INCORRUPTIBLE *not impure*
glory of the **i** God Rom 1:23
Christ with **i** *love* Eph 6:24

INCREASE (n) *multiplication*
the **i** of your herd Deut 7:13
the **i** of your house 1 Sam 2:33
the LORD give you **i** Ps 115:14
i of *His* government Is 9:7

INCREASE (v) *multiply*
If riches **i**, do not Ps 62:10
the righteous **i** Prov 28:28
i-ing in wisdom Luke 2:52

i-ing in...knowledge Col 1:10
Lord cause...to **i** 1 Thess 3:12

INCURABLE *fatal, without cure*
with an **i** sickness 2 Chr 21:18
sickliness and **i** pain Is 17:11
Your wound is **i** Jer 30:12

INDIA
lower Indus valley in S Asia Esth 1:1; 8:9

INDIGNANT *be angry*
i toward His enemies Is 66:14
the ten became **i** Matt 20:24
Jesus...was **i** Mark 10:14
i because Jesus had Luke 13:14

INDIGNATION *anger*
God who has **i** Ps 7:11
Pour out Your **i** Ps 69:24
lips are filled with **i** Is 30:27
filled me with **i** Jer 15:17
stand before His **i** Nah 1:6

INFANT *child*
carries a nursing **i** Num 11:12
an **i** *who lives* Is 65:20
tongue of the **i** Lam 4:4
the mouth of **i-s** Matt 21:16
as to **i-s** in Christ 1 Cor 3:1

INFECTION *disease*
an **i** of leprosy Lev 13:2
with the scaly **i** Lev 13:31
against an **i** of Deut 24:8

INFERIOR *lower in status*
I am not **i** to you Job 12:3
i against the honorable Is 3:5
i to...apostles 2 Cor 12:11

INFINITE *unlimited*
His understanding is **i** Ps 147:5

INFLICT *strike, impose*
frogs...He had **i-ed** Ex 8:12
i all these curses Deut 30:7
i-s pain, and gives Job 5:18

INGATHERING, FEAST OF *see* **FEASTS**

INHABIT *dwell*
no one would **i** Job 15:28
She shall be **i-ed** Is 44:26
build houses and **i** Is 65:21
those **i-ing** the desert Jer 9:26
who **i** the coastlands Ezek 39:6
but not **i** *them* Zeph 1:13

INHABITANT *resident*
i-s of the cities Gen 19:25
cities...without **i** Is 6:11
ruins Without **i** Jer 4:7
i-s of the seacoast Zeph 2:5
i-s of Jerusalem Zech 12:10

INHERIT *receive a legacy*
shall **i** *it* forever Ex 32:13
humble will **i** the land Ps 37:11
wise will **i** honor Prov 3:35
The naive **i** foolishness Prov 14:18
gentle...**i** the earth Matt 5:5
do to **i** eternal life Luke 10:25
not **i** the kingdom 1 Cor 6:9
might **i** a blessing 1 Pet 3:9
who overcomes will **i** Rev 21:7

INHERITANCE *bequest, legacy*
Levites for an **i** Num 18:24
the LORD is his **i** Deut 10:9
the nations as Your **i** Ps 2:8
will He forsake His **i** Ps 94:14
man leaves an **i** Prov 13:22
I...abandoned My **i** Jer 12:7
Your **i** a reproach Joel 2:17
A man and his **i** Mic 2:2
the **i** will be ours Mark 12:7

we...obtained an **i** Eph 1:11
the **i** of the saints Col 1:12
i...imperishable 1 Pet 1:4

INIQUITY *injustice, wickedness*
bear...their **i-ies** Lev 16:22
the **i** of the fathers Deut 5:9
those who plow **i** Job 4:8
O LORD, Pardon my **i** Ps 25:11
my **i** I did not hide Ps 32:5
blot out all my **i-ies** Ps 51:9
sows **i** will reap Prov 22:8
weighed down with **i** Is 1:4
the workers of **i** Is 31:2
die for his own **i** Jer 31:30
Repent...so that **i** Ezek 18:30
the bondage of **i** Acts 8:23
the *very* world of **i** James 3:6
remembered her **i-ies** Rev 18:5

INJUNCTION *decree*
establish the **i** Dan 6:8
that no **i** or statute Dan 6:15

INJURE *harm, wrong*
who seek to **i** me Ps 38:12
i-d your neighbors Ezek 22:12
nothing will **i** you Luke 10:19
do you **i** one another Acts 7:26

INJURY *wound*
there is no *further* **i** Ex 21:22
because of my **i** Jer 10:19
no **i**...was found Dan 6:23

INJUSTICE *inequity, unfairness*
do no **i** in judgment Lev 19:15
A God...without **i** Deut 32:4
there **i** on my tongue Job 6:30
They devise **i-s** Ps 64:6
is no **i** with God Rom 9:14

INK *writing liquid*
I wrote them with **i** Jer 36:18
with pen and **i** 3 John 13

INN *lodge for travelers*
no room...in the **i** Luke 2:7
brought him to...**i** Luke 10:34

INNKEEPER *traveler's host*
gave them to the **i** Luke 10:35

INNOCENCE *blamelessness*
wash my hands in **i** Ps 26:6
be incapable of **i** Hos 8:5

INNOCENT *blameless*
do not kill the **i** Ex 23:7
the blood of the **i** Deut 19:13
i before the LORD 2 Sam 3:28
the **i** mock them Job 22:19
that shed **i** blood Prov 6:17
and **i** as doves Matt 10:16
betraying **i** blood Matt 27:4
i of this Man's Matt 27:24
holy, **i**, undefiled Heb 7:26

INQUIRE *ask, seek*
to **i** of the LORD Gen 25:22
I of God, please Judg 18:5
David **i-d** of...LORD 1 Sam 23:2
you come to **i** of Me Ezek 20:3
i-d...where the Messiah Matt 2:4
i-d of them the hour John 4:52

INSANE *mad*
a demon and is **i** John 10:20
I speak as if **i** 2 Cor 11:23

INSCRIBE *carve, write*
were **i-d** in a book Job 19:23
i it on a scroll Is 30:8
and **i** a city on it Ezek 4:1
i *it* on tablets Hab 2:2

INSCRIPTION *writing*
could not read the **i** Dan 5:8
I will engrave an **i** Zech 3:9
Pilate...wrote an **i** John 19:19
i, To An Unknown Acts 17:23

INSECTS
swarms of **i** on you Ex 8:21
all other winged **i** Lev 11:23

INSIGHT *discernment*
a counselor with **i** 1 Chr 26:14
according to his **i** Prov 12:8
i with understanding Dan 9:22
not gained any **i** Mark 6:52
In all wisdom and **i** Eph 1:8

INSIGNIFICANT *unimportant*
was **i** in Your eyes 2 Sam 7:19
your beginning was **i** Job 8:7
citizen of no **i** city Acts 21:39

INSOLENT *arrogant*
acts with **i** pride Prov 21:24
haters of God, **i** Rom 1:30

INSPECTION GATE *see* **GATES OF JERUSALEM**

INSPIRED *stimulated*
the love we **i** in you 2 Cor 8:7
All Scripture is **i** 2 Tim 3:16

INSTINCT *natural tendency*
as creatures of **i** 2 Pet 2:12
they know by **i** Jude 10

INSTRUCT *teach*
Your good Spirit to **i** Neh 9:20
I will **i** you Ps 32:8
the wise is **i-ed** Prov 21:11
i-ed out of the Law Rom 2:18
just as you were **i-ed** Col 2:7
may **i** certain men 1 Tim 1:3

INSTRUCTION *teaching*
will walk in My **i** Ex 16:4
Heed **i** and be wise Prov 8:33
Get wisdom and **i** Prov 23:23
i-s to His twelve Matt 11:1
written for our **i** Rom 15:4
i of the Lord Eph 6:4
goal of our **i** is love 1 Tim 1:5
i about washings Heb 6:2

INSTRUMENT *object, vessel*
cut...with sharp **i-s** 1 Chr 20:3
and **i-s** of music 2 Chr 5:13
with stringed **i-s** Ps 150:4
he is a chosen **i** Acts 9:15
i-s of unrighteousness Rom 6:13

INSULT (n) *affront, indignity*
i-s of the nations Ezek 34:29
evil, or **i** for **i** 1 Pet 3:9

INSULT (v) *treat with scorn*
and do not **i** her Ruth 2:15
to **i** the LORD 2 Chr 32:17
times you have **i-ed** Job 19:3
i-ing...with the same words Matt 27:44
and **i** you Luke 6:22
i-ed the Spirit of Heb 10:29

INTEGRITY *honesty*
In the **i** of my heart Gen 20:5
dealt in truth and **i** Judg 9:19
holds fast his **i** Job 2:3
He who walks with **i** Ps 15:2
have walked in my **i** Ps 26:1
The **i** of the upright Prov 11:3

INTELLIGENCE *mental ability*
He deprives of **i** Job 12:24
gave them...**i** Dan 1:17
Paulus, a man of **i** Acts 13:7

INTELLIGENT *bright, smart*
was **i** and beautiful 1 Sam 25:3

mind of the **i** seeks Prov 15:14
from *the* wise and **i** Matt 11:25

INTEND *purpose*
Are you **i-ing** to kill Ex 2:14
I **i** to build a house 1 Kin 5:5
i to make My people Jer 23:27
i-ing to betray Him John 12:4
i-ing...to take Paul Acts 20:13

INTENTION *aim, goal*
the **i-s** of the heart 1 Chr 29:18
i of your heart Acts 8:22
kind **i** of His will Eph 1:5

INTERCEDE *plead, mediate*
i-d for the people Num 21:7
who can **i** for him 1 Sam 2:25
And **i-d** for the Is 53:12
do not **i** with Me Jer 7:16
Spirit Himself **i-s** Rom 8:26

INTERCOURSE *copulation*
not have **i** with Lev 18:20
not have **i**...animal Lev 18:23
husband has had **i** Num 5:20

INTEREST *concern* **or** *usury*
not charge him **i** Ex 22:25
not take usurious **i** Lev 25:36
i to a foreigner Deut 23:20
his money at **i** Ps 15:5
mind on God's **i-s** Matt 16:23
money...with **i** Matt 25:27
he has a morbid **i** 1 Tim 6:4

INTERMARRY
I with us Gen 34:9
shall not **i** with Deut 7:3
i with the peoples Ezra 9:14

INTERPRET *explain, translate*
no one who could **i** Gen 41:8
one who **i-s** omens Deut 18:10
He **i** the message Is 28:9
unless he **i-s** 1 Cor 14:5
pray that he may **i** 1 Cor 14:13

INTERPRETATION *explain*
i-s belong to God Gen 40:8
the dream and its **i** Judg 7:15
make its **i** known Dan 5:16
the **i** of tongues 1 Cor 12:10
of one's own **i** 2 Pet 1:20

INTIMATE *close*
my **i** friends have Job 19:14
i with the upright Prov 3:32
separates **i** friends Prov 16:28

INVADE *attack*
king of Assyria **i-d** 2 Kin 17:5
nation has **i-d** my land Joel 1:6
Assyrian **i-s** our land Mic 5:5

INVALIDATE *nullify*
i-d the word of God Matt 15:6
i-ing the word of Mark 7:13
does not **i** a covenant Gal 3:17

INVESTIGATE *examine*
the judges shall **i** Deut 19:18
the plot was **i-d** Esth 2:23
i, and to seek wisdom Eccl 7:25
having **i-d** everything Luke 1:3

INVISIBLE *unseen*
His **i** attributes Rom 1:20
image of the **i** God Col 1:15
visible and **i** Col 1:16
eternal, immortal, **i** 1 Tim 1:17

INVITE *request*
i-d us to impoverish Judg 14:15
you shall **i** Jesse 1 Sam 16:3
i-d all the king's 2 Sam 13:23
I am **i-d** by her Esth 5:12

did not **i** Me in Matt 25:43
i *the* poor Luke 14:13

IRON *metal*
was an **i** bedstead Deut 3:11
whose stones are **i** Deut 8:9
had **i** chariots Judg 1:19
made the **i** float 2 Kin 6:6
break them...rod of **i** Ps 2:9
from the **i** furnace Jer 11:4
as strong as **i** Dan 2:40
rule...rod of **i** Rev 19:15

ISAAC
birth, son of Abraham Gen 21:3
offered for sacrifice Gen 22:2
took Rebekah as wife Gen 24
father of twins Gen 25:26
blessed Jacob Gen 27:1-40

ISAIAH
prophet of Judah Is 1:1
son of Amoz 2 Kin 19:2
called Is 6:8ff
under four kings Is 1:1

ISCARIOT
geographical identity of Judas Mark 3:19; John 12:4; 13:26

ISH-BOSHETH
son of Saul 2 Sam 2:8; 3:8; 4:8

ISHMAEL
1 *son of Abraham* Gen 16:11; 17:18; 25:17
2 *son of Nethaniah* 2 Kin 25:23
3 *line of Jonathan* 1 Chr 8:38; 9:44
4 *Zebadiah's father* 2 Chr 19:11
5 *son of Jehohanan* 2 Chr 23:1
6 *son of Pashhur* Ezra 10:22

ISLAND *surrounded by water*
the many **i-s** be glad Ps 97:1
He lifts up the **i-s** Is 40:15
i was called Malta Acts 28:1
every **i** fled away Rev 16:20

ISOLATE *set apart*
priest shall **i** *him* Lev 13:4
i him for seven days Lev 13:21
fortified city is **i-d** Is 27:10

ISRAEL
1 *Jacob* Gen 32:28-32; 35:10; 37:3
2 *line of Jacob* Gen 34:7
tribal nation Ex 1:7; 4:22; Num 10:29
3 *united kingdom* 1 Sam 15:35; 1 Kin 4:1
4 *northern kingdom* 1 Kin 14:19; 15:9; 2 Kin 10:29
5 *under Roman rule* Luke 2:32; John 1:49; Rom 9:6

ISSACHAR
1 *son of Jacob* Gen 30:18; 49:14
2 *tribe* Num 1:29; Josh 21:28; Rev 7:7
3 *Levite* 1 Chr 26:5

ISSUE (n) *outflow, out go*
first **i** of the womb Num 3:12
offspring and **i** Is 22:24
like the **i** of horses Ezek 23:20
concerning this **i** Acts 15:2

ISSUE (v) *go forth, put forth*
Moses **i-d** a command Ex 36:6
shall **i** from you 2 Kin 20:18
decree was **i-d** at Esth 3:15
i-d a proclamation Dan 5:29

ITALY
S European country Acts 18:2; 27:1,6; Heb 13:24

ITURAEA
region N of Palestine Luke 3:1
tetrarchy of Herod Philip II

IVORY *elephant tusk*
a great throne of **i** 1 Kin 10:18
silver, **i** and apes 2 Chr 9:21
Out of **i** palaces Ps 45:8

every article of **i** Rev 18:12

J

JABAL
son of Lamech Gen 4:20
father of herders

JABBOK
tributary of Jordan Gen 32:22; Num 21:24; Josh 12:2; Judg 11:13,22

JABESH-GILEAD
town of Gilead Judg 21:8ff
E of Jordan River 1 Sam 11:1,9; 2 Sam 2:4,5

JACINTH *precious stone*
a **j**, an agate Ex 28:19
the eleventh, **j** Rev 21:20

JACKALS *wild dogs*
j in their...palaces Is 13:22
ruins, A haunt of **j** Jer 9:11
a lament like the **j** Mic 1:8

JACOB
1 *son of Isaac* Gen 25:26
brother of Esau Gen 25:27
obtained birthright Gen 25:33
fled to Aram Gen 28:5,6
marriage Gen 29:1ff
wrestled angel Gen 32:24ff
name changed Gen 35:9,10
went down to Egypt Gen 46:4ff
death and burial Gen 49:28ff
2 *father of Joseph* Matt 1:15,16

JAEL
wife of Heber Judg 4:17
slayer of Sisera Judg 4:21
described as blessed Judg 5:24

JAIL *place of confinement*
put him into the **j** Gen 39:20
in **j** in the house Jer 37:15
put them in...**j** Acts 5:18

JAILER *warden*
sight of the chief **j** Gen 39:21
chief **j** did not Gen 39:23
the **j** to guard them Acts 16:23

JAIR
1 *judge of Israel* Judg 10:3
2 *son of Segub* 1 Chr 2:22
3 *father of Elhanan* 1 Chr 20:5
4 *Mordecai's father* Esth 2:5

JAIRUS
ruler of synagogue Mark 5:22; Luke 8:41

JAMES
1 *son of Zebedee* Matt 4:21
brother of John Matt 10:2
called as apostle Matt 10:2ff
martyred Acts 12:2
2 *son of Alphaeus* Matt 10:3
called as apostle Matt 10:3ff
3 *brother of Jesus* Matt 13:55; Mark 6:3
church leader Acts 12:17; 15:13
4 *Judas's father* Luke 6:16

JAPHETH
son of Noah Gen 7:13; 9:23,27

JAPHIA
1 *king of Lachish* Josh 10:3
2 *son of David* 2 Sam 5:15
3 *town of Zebulun* Josh 19:12

JAR *container, jug*
and a **j** of honey 1 Kin 14:3
Bring me a new **j** 2 Kin 2:20
potter's earthenware **j** Jer 19:1
j full of sour wine John 19:29

JASHAR
book quoted in Bible Josh 10:13; 2 Sam 1:18

JASON
Christian of Thessalonica Acts 17:5-9; Rom 16:21

JASPER ***precious stone***
fourth row...a **j** Ex 28:20
the onyx, and the **j** Ezek 28:13
was like a **j** stone Rev 4:3
of crystal-clear **j** Rev 21:11

JAVAN
Hebrew word for Greeks or Greece Gen 10:2,4; 1 Chr 1:5,7; Is 66:19; Ezek 27:13,19

JAVELIN ***spear***
Stretch out the **j** Josh 8:18
j *slung* between his 1 Sam 17:6
flashing spear and **j** Job 39:23
seize *their*...**j** Jer 50:42

JAW ***part of face***
j-s of the wicked Job 29:17
cleaves to my **j-s** Ps 22:15
j teeth *like* knives Prov 30:14
hooks into your **j-s** Ezek 38:4

JAWBONE
j of a donkey Judg 15:15
threw the **j** from Judg 15:17

JEALOUS ***envious, zealous***
brothers were **j** of Gen 37:11
your God, am a **j** God Ex 20:5
whose name is **J**, is Ex 34:14
j with My jealousy Num 25:11
He is a **j** God Josh 24:19
j and avenging God Nah 1:2
j for Jerusalem Zech 1:14
Jews, becoming **j** Acts 17:5
I will make you **j** Rom 10:19
love is kind...not **j** 1 Cor 13:4

JEBUS
Jerusalem Judg 19:10,11; 1 Chr 11:4,5

JEBUSITES
clan or tribe Gen 10:16
inhabitants of Jebus Ex 3:8,17; Josh 15:63; 2 Sam 24:16,18; Ezra 9:1; Zech 9:7

JECONIAH
variant of Jehoiachin's name 1 Chr 3:16,17; Esth 2:6

JEHAZIEL
1 *Benjamite warrior* 1 Chr 12:4
2 *priest* 1 Chr 16:6
3 *son of Hebron* 1 Chr 23:19
4 *son of Zechariah* 2 Chr 20:14

JEHOAHAZ
1 *son of Jehu* 2 Kin 10:35
king of Israel 2 Kin 13:1ff
2 *son of Josiah* 2 Kin 23:30-34
king of Judah 2 Kin 23:30
see also **SHALLUM** 1 Chr 3:15
3 *son of Jehoram* 2 Chr 21:17
also **Ahaziah** 2 Chr 22:1ff

JEHOASH
1 *king of Judah* 2 Kin 11:21
son of Ahaziah 2 Kin 12:1-18
2 *king of Israel* 2 Kin 13:10
son of Jehoahaz 2 Kin 13:25; 14:13

JEHOIACHIN
son of Jehoiakim 2 Kin 24:6
king of Judah 2 Kin 24:8-15; 2 Chr 36:8,9; Jer 52:31,33

JEHOIADA
1 *father of Benaiah* 2 Sam 8:18
priest 1 Chr 27:5
2 *son of Benaiah* 1 Chr 27:34
3 *high priest* 2 Kin 11:4,9
4 *priest* Jer 29:26

JEHOIAKIM
son of King Josiah 2 Kin 23:34; 2 Chr 36:4
king of Judah 2 Kin 23:36; 2 Chr 36:5; Jer 22:18; Dan 1:2
father of Jehoiachin 2 Kin 24:6

JEHORAM
1 *son of Ahab* 2 Kin 3:1
king of Israel 2 Kin 3:6
2 *priest* 2 Chr 17:8
3 *Jehoshaphat's son* 2 Kin 8:16
king of Judah 2 Kin 8:25,29
see also **JORAM**

JEHOSHAPHAT
1 *son of Ahilud* 2 Sam 8:16
2 *son of Paruah* 1 Kin 4:17
3 *son of Asa* 1 Kin 15:24
king of Judah 1 Kin 22:2-51; 2 Chr 17:1-12
4 *father of Jehu* 2 Kin 9:2,14
5 *wadi E of Jerusalem* Joel 3:2,12

JEHU
1 *prophet, son of Hanani* 1 Kin 16:1,7,12; 2 Chr 19:2
2 *king of Israel* 1 Kin 19:16; 2 Kin 9:14,30; 2 Chr 22:7
3 *man of Judah* 1 Chr 2:38
4 *Simeonite* 1 Chr 4:35
5 *Benjamite* 1 Chr 12:3

JEMIMAH
daughter of Job Job 42:14

JEPHTHAH
a Gileadite Judg 11:1
judge of Israel Judg 11:2-40

JEREMIAH
1 *lived in Libnah* 2 Kin 23:31
2 *man of Manasseh* 1 Chr 5:24
3 *three individuals who joined David* 1 Chr 12:4,10,13
4 *prophet* Jer 1:1
called Jer 1:2-10
put in stocks Jer 20:2,3
life threatened Jer 26
put in prison Jer 32:2; 37:13ff
taken to Egypt Jer 43:1-6
5 *son of Habazziniah* Jer 35:3
6 *priest* Neh 10:2
7 *priest from Babylon* Neh 12:1

JERICHO
city in Jordan Valley Josh 3:16
N of Dead Sea Josh 6:1; 1 Kin 16:34; Luke 18:35

JEROBOAM
1 *Solomon's warrior* 1 Kin 11:28
first king of N Kingdom 1 Kin 12:26,27; 2 Chr 10:13
made golden calves 1 Kin 12:28
2 *son of Joash* 2 Kin 14:27
king of Israel 2 Kin 14:28,29

JERUBBAAL
name of Gideon Judg 6:32
judge of Israel Judg 7:1

JERUSALEM
city called Salem Gen 14:18
city called Jebus Judg 1:21; 19:10
David's capital 2 Sam 5:5,6
capital of united kingdom 1 Kin 2:36; 11:42
site of temple 1 Kin 6:2; 8:6,12
destroyed by Babylonians Jer 52:12-14
rebuilt by remnant Neh 2:11-20; 12:27
city of Roman period Matt 2:1,3; 21:1,10; Luke 13:34; Acts 11:2,22
new Jerusalem Rev 3:12; 21:2,10

JESHUA
1 *line of Aaron* 1 Chr 24:11
2 *under Kore* 2 Chr 31:15
3 *high priest* Ezra 3:2; Neh 7:7
4 *of Pahath-moab* Ezra 2:6; Neh 7:11
5 *part of remnant* Ezra 2:40; Neh 7:43
6 *aided Ezra* Neh 8:7
7 *village in Judah* Neh 11:26
see also **JOSHUA**

JESHURUN
poetic name for Israel Deut 32:15; 33:5,26; Is 44:2

JESSE
father of David 1 Sam 16:1,8; 2 Sam 20:1; 1 Kin 12:16; 1 Chr 2:12,13

JEST ***joke, mock***
appeared...be **j-ing** Gen 19:14
Against whom do you **j** Is 57:4

JESUS
1 *name of the Lord* Matt 1:21; Luke 1:31
birth in Bethlehem Matt 1:18-25; Luke 2:1-7
youth in Nazareth Matt 2:19ff
baptized Matt 3:13ff; Mark 1:9ff; Luke 3:21; John 1:31ff
tempted Matt 4:1-11; Mark 1:12; Luke 4:1ff
called disciples Matt 4:18ff; Mark 1:16ff; Luke 5:1ff
transfigured Matt 17:1ff; Mark 9:2ff; Luke 9:28ff
triumphal entry to Jerusalem Matt 21:1ff; Mark 11:1ff; Luke 19:29ff
crucified Matt 27:31ff; Mark 15:20ff; Luke 23:26ff; John 19:16ff
resurrected Christ Matt 28:1ff; Mark 16:1ff; Luke 24:13ff; John 20:11ff
ascended to the Father Mark 16:19; Luke 24:50ff; Acts 1:9ff
2 *Jewish Christian called Justus* Col 4:11

JETHRO
priest of Midian Ex 3:1
Moses' father-in-law Ex 4:18; 18:1-12

JEW(S)
originally an inhabitant of Judah, a Judean 2 Kin 16:6
Judean shortened to Jew during exile 2 Kin 25:25
synonym for Hebrew Ezra 4:12,23; Neh 4:1,2; Esth 4:3,7; Jer 34:9
later term for all Israelites in the land and in Diaspora Matt 27:11; Mark 7:3; Luke 23:51; John 4:9; Acts 22:3; Rom 3:1; Gal 3:28; Rev 2:9

JEWEL ***precious stone***
precious than **j-s** Prov 3:15
better than **j-s** Prov 8:11
adorns...her **j-s** Is 61:10
the **J** of *his* kingdom Dan 11:20

JEWISH
pertaining to Jews Neh 5:1; Esth 6:13; John 2:6; Acts 13:6

JEZEBEL
1 *wife of Ahab* 1 Kin 21:5ff; 2 Kin 9:7ff
2 *woman at Thyatira* Rev 2:20

JEZREEL
1 *valley and plain* Josh 17:16; Judg 6:33; Hos 1:5
2 *fortified town* Josh 19:18; 1 Kin 18:45; 2 Kin 8:29; 9:30
3 *descendant of Etam* 1 Chr 4:3
4 *son of Hosea* Hos 1:4

JOAB
1 *son of Zeruiah* 2 Sam 8:16
David's nephew 2 Sam 17:25
David's commander 2 Sam 20:23; 1 Chr 11:6
2 *son of Seraiah* 1 Chr 4:14
3 *father of those returning from captivity* Ezra 2:6; 8:9; Neh 7:11

JOANNA
wife of Chuza Luke 8:3
ministered to Jesus Luke 24:10

JOASH
1 *father of Gideon* Judg 6:11,31
2 *son of Ahab* 1 Kin 22:26; 2 Chr 18:25
3 *son of Ahaziah* 2 Kin 11:2
king of Judah 2 Chr 24:1-4
4 *son of Jehoahaz* 2 Kin 13:9
king of Israel 2 Kin 13:25
5 *line of Shelah* 1 Chr 4:22
6 *son of Becher* 1 Chr 7:8

7 *a Benjamite* 1 Chr 12:3
8 *official of David* 1 Chr 27:28

JOB
pious man from Uz Job 1:1
experienced tragedy Job 2:7,8
showed great endurance Job 2:9,10; James 5:11

JOB *occupation*
workmen...**j** to **j** 2 Chr 34:13

JOCHEBED
mother of Moses Ex 6:20; Num 26:59

JOEL
1 *son of Samuel* 1 Sam 8:2
2 *line of Simeon* 1 Chr 4:35
3 *line of Reuben* 1 Chr 5:4
4 *chief of Gadites* 1 Chr 5:12
5 *ancestor of Samuel* 1 Chr 6:36
6 *son of Izrahiah* 1 Chr 7:3
7 *brother of Nathan* 1 Chr 11:38
8 *Gershonite Levite* 1 Chr 15:7; 26:22
9 *son of Pedaiah* 1 Chr 27:20
10 *Kohathite Levite* 2 Chr 29:12
11 *son of Nebo* Ezra 10:43
12 *son of Zichri* Neh 11:9
13 *prophet* Joel 1:1; Acts 2:16

JOHN
1 *father of Peter* John 1:42
2 *the Baptist* Matt 3:1
baptizing Matt 3:13
beheaded Mark 6:25
birth foretold Luke 1:13
son of Zacharias Luke 1:57ff
praised by Jesus Luke 7:28
preached John 1:15
3 *the apostle* Matt 10:2
called by Jesus Matt 4:21
Sons of Thunder Mark 3:17
inner circle Matt 17:1
request refused Mark 10:35ff
assigned the care of Mary John 19:26,27
with Peter Acts 3:1,3
4 *Jewish leader* Acts 4:6
5 *Mark, evangelist* Acts 12:12,25

JOIN *bring together, couple*
j-ed to his wife Gen 2:24
do not **j** your hand Ex 23:1
j field to field Is 5:8
j...in hypocrisy Dan 11:34
God...**j-ed** together Matt 19:6
j-ed him...believed Acts 17:34
shall be **j-ed** to his wife Eph 5:31
j...me in suffering 2 Tim 1:8

JOINT *juncture*
bones are out of **j** Ps 22:14
together by the **j-s** Col 2:19
both **j-s** and marrow Heb 4:12

JOKTAN
person and tribe descended from Shem Gen 10:25,26,29; 1 Chr 1:19,20,23

JONAH
prophet of Israel Jon 1:1
son of Amittai 2 Kin 14:25
disobedient Jon 1:3
preached to Nineveh Jon 3:4

JONATHAN
1 *son of Gershom* Judg 18:30
2 *son of King Saul* 1 Sam 13:16; 14:49
friend of David 1 Sam 18:1
3 *son of Abiathar* 2 Sam 15:36
4 *son of Shimei* 2 Sam 21:21
5 *son of Jada* 1 Chr 2:32
6 *son of Shagee* 1 Chr 11:34
7 *official of David* 1 Chr 27:25
8 *David's uncle* 1 Chr 27:32

JOPPA
seaport W of Jerusalem 2 Chr 2:16; Ezra 3:7; Jon 1:3; Acts 9:36

JORAM
1 *son of Toi* 2 Sam 8:10
2 *son of Ahab* 2 Kin 8:16
king of Israel 2 Kin 8:25
3 *line of Eliezer* 1 Chr 26:25
4 *son of Jehoshaphat* Matt 1:8
king of Judah
see also **JEHORAM**

JORDAN
1 *river in Palestine* Gen 32:10; Josh 3:17; Judg 8:4; 2 Kin 5:10; Matt 3:6
2 *valley* Gen 13:10,11

JOSEPH
1 *son of Jacob* Gen 30:23,24
sold by brothers Gen 37:28
put in prison Gen 40:3
prime minister Gen 41:41
revealed himself Gen 45:4
death Gen 50:26
2 *father of spy* Num 13:7ff
3 *son of Asaph* 1 Chr 25:9
4 *son of Bani* Ezra 10:42
5 *son of Shebaniah* Neh 12:14
6 *husband of Mary* Matt 1:18; 2:13; Luke 2:16; John 6:42
7 *brother of Jesus* Matt 13:55
see also **JOSES**
8 *brother of James the Less* Matt 27:56
see also **JOSES**
9 *of Arimathea* Matt 27:57ff
in Sanhedrin (Council) Mark 15:43
disciple of Jesus John 19:38
provided tomb Matt 27:57
10 *ancestor of Jesus* Luke 3:24
11 *ancestor of Jesus* Luke 3:30
12 *surname Barsabbas* Acts 1:23
13 *Barnabas* Acts 4:36

JOSES
1 *brother of James the Less* Mark 15:40
see also **JOSEPH**
2 *brother of Jesus* Mark 6:3
see also **JOSEPH**

JOSHUA
1 *Moses' successor* Deut 31:23
attended Moses Num 11:28
chosen by God Num 27:18
encouraged by God Josh 1:1-9
charged Israel Josh 23:1ff
death Josh 24:29
2 *of Beth-shemesh* 1 Sam 6:14
3 *governor* 2 Kin 23:8
4 *high priest* Hag 1:1,12; Zech 3:1ff
see also **JESHUA**

JOSIAH
1 *son of Amon* 2 Kin 21:24
king of Judah 2 Kin 21:26
removed false worship 2 Kin 23:19,24; 2 Chr 34:33
responded to the Law 2 Chr 34:15-28
2 *son of Zephaniah* Zech 6:10

JOTHAM
1 *son of Gideon* Judg 9:5ff
2 *king of Judah* 2 Kin 15:5
son of Uzziah 2 Chr 27:2
3 *line of Caleb* 1 Chr 2:47

JOURNEY *traveling, trip*
Let us take our **j** Gen 33:12
day's **j** on the other Num 11:31
seek...a safe **j** Ezra 8:21
a bag for *your* **j** Matt 10:10
nothing for *your* **j** Luke 9:3
Sabbath day's **j** away Acts 1:12
on frequent **j-s** 2 Cor 11:26

JOURNEYED *traveled*
about as they **j** east Gen 11:2
Jacob **j** to Succoth Gen 33:17
the sons of Israel **j** Num 22:1
j from the river Ezra 8:31

JOY *delight, happiness*
raise sounds of **j** 1 Chr 15:16
shouted aloud for **j** Ezra 3:12
see His face with **j** Job 33:26
Restore to me the **j** Ps 51:12
j at Your name Ps 89:12
godly ones sing for **j** Ps 132:9
Everlasting **j** will be Is 61:7
their mourning into **j** Jer 31:13
with great **j** Matt 2:10
enter into the **j** Matt 25:21
j in heaven over one Luke 15:7
j in the Holy Spirit Rom 14:17
love, **j**, peace Gal 5:22
make my **j** complete Phil 2:2

JOYFUL *feeling gladness*
be altogether **j** Deut 16:15
j with gladness Ps 21:6
shall reap with **j** Ps 126:5
j heart is good Prov 17:22

JOYFULLY *full of joy, happy*
go **j** with the king Esth 5:14
Shout **j** to God, all Ps 66:1
They shout **j** together Is 52:8
to praise God **j** Luke 19:37

JUBAL
inventor of lyre and pipe Gen 4:21

JUBILANT *elated*
no...**j** shouting Is 16:10
Is this your **j** *city* Is 23:7
because you are **j** Jer 50:11
they may become **j** Jer 51:39

JUBILEE, YEAR OF
return of ancestral possessions every fiftieth year
year of liberty Lev 25:8ff

JUDAH
1 *son of Jacob* Gen 29:35; 37:26; 44:14; 49:8,10
2 *tribe* Num 1:27; Judg 1:8; 2 Sam 2:4; 1 Kin 12:20
3 *border city* Josh 19:34
4 *S kingdom* 1 Kin 14:21; 1 Chr 9:1; Ps 60:7; Jer 20:4
5 *relative of Kadmiel* Ezra 2:40
6 *urged by Ezra to put away foreign wife* Ezra 10:23
7 *Benjamite* Neh 11:9
8 *Levite who returned from captivity* Neh 12:8
9 *participant in wall dedication* Neh 12:34
10 *musician* Neh 12:36

JUDAISM *Jewish way of life*
manner of life in **J** Gal 1:13
advancing in **J** Gal 1:14

JUDAS
1 *Iscariot* Matt 10:4
used by Satan Luke 22:3
son of Simon John 6:71
treasurer John 13:29
betrayed Jesus John 18:2
2 *Jesus' brother* Matt 13:55; Mark 6:3
3 *apostle* Luke 6:16; Acts 1:13
4 *Judas of Galilee* Acts 5:37
5 *of Damascus* Acts 9:11
6 *Barsabbas* Acts 15:22,27

JUDE
brother of Jesus Matt 13:55; Mark 6:3
brother of James Jude 1

JUDEA
Roman province in Palestine based on earlier Judah Matt 2:1; Mark 1:5; Luke 2:4; John 11:7

JUDEAN
language (Hebrew) 2 Kin 18:26,28; Is 36:11,13
see also **CANAAN**
see also **HEBREW**

JUDGE (n) *leader*
J of all the earth Gen 18:25
prince or a **j** over us Ex 2:14
LORD was with the **j** Judg 2:18
For God Himself is **j** Ps 50:6
unrighteous **j** said Luke 18:6
one Lawgiver and **J** James 4:12

JUDGE (v) *pass judgment*
LORD **j** between you Gen 16:5
Moses sat to **j** the Ex 18:13
LORD will **j**...earth 1 Sam 2:10
coming to **j** the earth Ps 98:9
He will **j** the poor Is 11:4
Do not **j**...will not be **j-d** Matt 7:1
Son...world to **j** John 3:17
Law...not **j** a man John 7:51
not come to **j** the John 12:47
able to **j**...thoughts Heb 4:12
adulterers God will **j** Heb 13:4

JUDGMENT *condemnation*
I will execute **j-s** Ex 12:12
partiality in **j** Deut 1:17
let **j** be executed Ezra 7:26
will not stand in the **j** Ps 1:5
in the day of **j** Matt 10:15
j, that the light John 3:19
resurrection of **j** John 5:29
My **j** is just John 5:30
after this *comes* **j** Heb 9:27
incur a stricter **j** James 3:1
not fall under **j** James 5:12
kept for the day of **j** 2 Pet 3:7
j of the great day Jude 6
to execute **j** upon all Jude 15
His **j-s** are true Rev 19:2

JUMP *leap*
legs with which to **j** Lev 11:21
if a fox should **j** Neh 4:3
j-ed up, and came Mark 10:50

JUNIPER *tree*
slept under a **j** tree 1 Kin 19:5
The **j**, the box tree Is 60:13
like a **j** in the Jer 48:6

JUST *fair, right*
shall have **j** balances Lev 19:36
a man be **j** with God Job 25:4
Hear a **j** cause, O LORD Ps 17:1
He is **j** and endowed Zech 9:9
My judgment is **j** John 5:30
the **j** for the unjust 1 Pet 3:18

JUSTICE *fairness, righteousness*
shall not distort **j** Deut 16:19
Does God pervert **j** Job 8:3
j to the afflicted Job 36:6
Righteousness and **j** Ps 89:14
do not understand **j** Prov 28:5
j is turned back Is 59:14
let **j** roll down Amos 5:24
j and mercy and Matt 23:23
acknowledged...**j** Luke 7:29
grant to your slaves **j** Col 4:1

JUSTIFICATION *vindication*
because of our **j** Rom 4:25
j of life to all men Rom 5:18

JUSTIFY *declare guiltless*
how...**j** ourselves Gen 44:16
they **j** the righteous Deut 25:1
he **j-ied** himself Job 32:2
wishing to **j** himself Luke 10:29
these...He also **j-ied** Rom 8:30
God...**j-ies** Rom 8:33
seeking to be **j-ied** Gal 2:17

JUSTUS
1 *Joseph, apostolic candidate also called Barsabbas* Acts 1:23
2 *Titus, Corinthian disciple* Acts 18:7
3 *Jewish Christian* Col 4:11

JUTTAH
Levitical city in Judah Josh 15:55; 21:16

K

KADESH / KADESH-BARNEA
desert oasis in Negev Gen 14:7
Israelite encampment Num 13:26; 33:37

KEDAR
1 *son of Ishmael* Gen 25:13
2 *tribal descendants* Is 42:11

KEDEMAH
1 *son of Ishmael* Gen 25:15
2 *tribal descendants* 1 Chr 1:31

KEDESH
1 *city in S Judah* Josh 15:23
2 *city of Issachar* 1 Chr 6:72
3 *city of Naphtali* Josh 12:22
4 *city of refuge, in Galilee* Josh 20:7

KEEP *hold, guide, preserve*
k the way of the LORD Gen 18:19
love Me and **k** My Ex 20:6
shall **k** your sabbath Lev 23:32
LORD bless you, and **k** Num 6:24
to **k** the Passover Matt 26:18
if anyone **k-s** My John 8:51
he will **k** My word John 14:23
k-ing faith and a 1 Tim 1:19
k yourself free from 1 Tim 5:22
k his tongue...evil 1 Pet 3:10

KEEPER *guard, protector*
Am I my brother's **k** Gen 4:9
been **k-s** of livestock Gen 46:32
The LORD is your **k** Ps 121:5
I, the LORD, am its **k** Is 27:3

KEILAH
1 *town of Judah* Josh 15:44; 1 Sam 23:1ff; Neh 3:17,18
2 *line of Caleb* 1 Chr 4:19

KENAZ
1 *Esau's grandson* Gen 36:10,11
2 *father of Othniel* Josh 15:17
3 *line of Caleb* 1 Chr 4:15

KENITE(S)
Canaanite tribe Gen 15:19; Num 24:21
tribe of metal-workers Judg 4:11; 1 Sam 15:6

KENIZZITE
Canaanite tribe in S Palestine and Edom Gen 15:19; Num 32:12; Josh 14:14

KEREN-HAPPUCH
daughter of Job Job 42:14

KERIOTH
1 *town of Judah* Josh 15:25
2 *town in Moab* Jer 48:41; Amos 2:2

KETURAH
second wife of Abraham Gen 25:1,4; 1 Chr 1:32,33

KEY *unlocking tool*
k-s of the kingdom Matt 16:19
the **k** of knowledge Luke 11:52
k-s of death and of Rev 1:18
k of the bottomless pit Rev 9:1

KEZIAH
daughter of Job Job 42:14

KIDNEYS *innards*
two **k** and the fat Ex 29:13
remove with the **k** Lev 3:15
He splits my **k** open Job 16:13

KIDRON
brook and valley between Jerusalem and Mount of Olives 2 Sam 15:23; 2 Kin 23:6; 2 Chr 29:16; John 18:1

KILL *take life*
for Cain **k-ed** him Gen 4:25
k-ed every firstborn Ex 13:15
who **k-s** a man shall Lev 24:21
LORD **k-s** and makes 1 Sam 2:6
Am I God, to **k** 2 Kin 5:7
jealousy **k-s** the simple Job 5:2
he **k-s** the innocent Ps 10:8
A time to **k** Eccl 3:3
unable to **k** the Matt 10:28
k-ed, and be raised Luke 9:22
do you seek to **k** Me John 7:19
Get up, Peter, **k** and Acts 10:13
the letter **k-s**, but 2 Cor 3:6
who **k** their father 1 Tim 1:9
k a third of mankind Rev 9:15

KIND (adj) *good, tender*
be **k** to this people 2 Chr 10:7
He Himself is **k** Luke 6:35
love is **k** 1 Cor 13:4
be **k** to one another Eph 4:32

KIND (n) *group, variety*
fruit after their **k** Gen 1:11
plant all **k-s** of trees Lev 19:23
all **k-s** of evil Matt 5:11
k-s of tongues 1 Cor 12:28
every **k** of impurity Eph 4:19

KINDLE *cause to burn*
anger...was **k-d** Num 11:10
His breath **k-s** coals Job 41:21
man to **k** strife Prov 26:21
all you who **k** a fire Is 50:11
k-d a fire in Zion Lam 4:11

KINDNESS *tenderness*
teaching of **k** is on Prov 31:26
to love **k**, And to Mic 6:8
with deeds of **k** Acts 9:36
k and...of God Rom 11:22
joy, peace, patience, **k** Gal 5:22
compassion, **k** Col 3:12
tasted the **k** of the 1 Pet 2:3
godliness, brotherly **k** 2 Pet 1:7

KINDRED *relative*
her people or her **k** Esth 2:10
destruction of my **k** Esth 8:6
no one...of **k** spirit Phil 2:20

KING *monarch, regent*
the **k-'s** highway Num 20:17
no **k** in Israel Judg 17:6
appoint a **k** for us 1 Sam 8:5
anointed David **k** 2 Sam 5:3
my **K** and my God Ps 5:2
The LORD is **K** forever Ps 10:16
Who is the **k** of glory Ps 24:8
will shatter **k-s** Ps 110:5
By me **k-s** reign Prov 8:15
He will...before **k-s** Prov 22:29
The Creator...your **K** Is 43:15
O **K** of the nations Jer 10:7
born **K** of the Jews Matt 2:2
Are You the **K** of Matt 27:11
your **K** is coming John 12:15
no **k** but Caesar John 19:15
K of **k-s** and Lord 1 Tim 6:15
God, honor the **k** 1 Pet 2:17

KINGDOM *domain, monarchy*
his **k** was Babel Gen 10:10
to Me a **k** of priests Ex 19:6
tear the **k** from 1 Kin 11:11
will establish his **k** 1 Chr 28:7
the **k** is the LORD'S Ps 22:28
Sing to God, O **k-s** Ps 68:32
an everlasting **k** Ps 145:13
k against **k** Is 19:2
k of heaven is at Matt 3:2
showed Him...**k-s** Matt 4:8
Your **k** come Matt 6:10
sons of the **k** Matt 13:38
keys of the **k** Matt 16:19

in My Father's **k** Matt 26:29
enter the **k** of God Mark 10:24
to give you the **k** Luke 12:32
cannot see the **k** of John 3:3
preaching the **k** Acts 28:31
k of His beloved Son Col 1:13
to His heavenly **k** 2 Tim 4:18
faith conquered **k-s** Heb 11:33
heirs of the **k** James 2:5

KINSMAN *relative*
of my master's **k** Gen 24:48
he took his **k-men** Gen 31:23
a man has no **k** Lev 25:26
Naomi had a **k** of her Ruth 2:1
k-men stand afar off Ps 38:11
Herodion, my **k** Rom 16:11

KIRIATHAIM
1 *Reubenite city* Num 32:37; Josh 13:19
2 *Levitical city* 1 Chr 6:76

KIRIATH-ARBA
old name of Hebron Gen 23:2; Josh 14:15; 15:13,54; Judg 1:10
city of refuge Josh 20:7

KIRIATH-JEARIM
Gibeonite town Josh 9:17; Judg 18:12; Jer 26:20
location of ark of covenant 1 Sam 6:21; 7:1,2; 2 Chr 1:4

KISH
1 *father of Saul* 1 Sam 9:3; 10:21
2 *son of Jeiel* 1 Chr 8:30
3 *son of Mahli* 1 Chr 23:21
4 *son of Abdi* 2 Chr 29:12
5 *a Benjamite* Esth 2:5

KISHON
battle scene Judg 4:7
river Judg 4:13; 5:21
priests of Baal slain on its bank 1 Kin 18:40

KISS (n) *expression of affection*
threw a **k** from my Job 31:27
the **k-es** of his mouth Song 1:2
You gave Me no **k** Luke 7:45
betraying...with a **k** Luke 22:48
with a holy **k** Rom 16:16
with a **k** of love 1 Pet 5:14

KISS (v) *expression of affection*
come close and **k** Gen 27:26
let me **k** my father 1 Kin 19:20
I would **k** you Song 8:1
Whomever I **k** Mark 14:44
not...to **k** My feet Luke 7:45

KITTIM
1 *grandson of Japheth* Gen 10:4; 1 Chr 1:7
2 *island of Cyprus* Num 24:24; Jer 2:10; Dan 11:30

KNEAD *work dough, clay*
took flour, **k-ed** it 1 Sam 28:24
the women **k** dough Jer 7:18

KNEE *part of body*
strengthened feeble **k-s** Job 4:4
k-s began knocking Dan 5:6
every **k** shall bow Rom 14:11
every **k** will bow Phil 2:10

KNEEL *bend, rest on knee*
made the camels **k** Gen 24:11
people **k-ed** to drink Judg 7:6
k before the LORD Ps 95:6
knelt...before Him Matt 27:29
man ran...**knelt** Mark 10:17
He **knelt** down Luke 22:41

KNIFE *cutting instrument*
k to slay his son Gen 22:10
jaw teeth *like* **k-ves** Prov 30:14
with a scribe's **k** Jer 36:23

KNIT *joined together*
Jonathan was **k** to 1 Sam 18:1
k me together with Job 10:11
his thighs are **k** Job 40:17
His hand they are **k** Lam 1:14
k together in love Col 2:2

KNOCK *smite, strike*
his knees began **k-ing** Dan 5:6
k, and it will be Matt 7:7
stand outside and **k** Luke 13:25
he **k-ed** at the door Acts 12:13
at the door and **k** Rev 3:20

KNOW *experience, understand*
like one of Us, **k-ing** Gen 3:22
make **k-n** the statutes Ex 18:16
k that my Redeemer Job 19:25
Make me **k** Your ways Ps 25:4
He **k-s** the secrets Ps 44:21
k that I am God Ps 46:10
made **k-n** His salvation Ps 98:2
Try me and **k** my Ps 139:23
You **k** me Jer 12:3
left hand **k** what Matt 6:3
k...by their fruits Matt 7:20
I never **knew** you Matt 7:23
God **k-s** your hearts Luke 16:15
you will **k** the truth John 8:32
I **k** My own John 10:14
k-ing that His hour John 13:1
k that I love You John 21:15
and **k** all mysteries 1 Cor 13:2
who **knew** no sin 2 Cor 5:21
k the love of Christ Eph 3:19
value of **k-ing** Christ Phil 3:8
k...I have believed 2 Tim 1:12
k...eternal life 1 John 5:13
I **k** your deeds Rev 2:2

KNOWLEDGE *information*
tree of the **k** of good Gen 2:9
LORD is a God of **k** 1 Sam 2:3
anyone teach God **k** Job 21:22
k is too wonderful Ps 139:6
the beginning of **k** Prov 1:7
fools hate **k** Prov 1:22
Wise...store up **k** Prov 10:14
k increases power Prov 24:5
would He teach **k** Is 28:9
in accordance with **k** Rom 10:2
K makes arrogant 1 Cor 8:1
k, it will be done 1 Cor 13:8
have no **k** of God 1 Cor 15:34
love...surpasses **k** Eph 3:19
treasures of...**k** Col 2:3
grow in...grace and **k** 2 Pet 3:18

KOHATH
son of Levi Gen 46:11; Num 3:17; Josh 21:5

KOHATHITES
line of Kohath Num 3:30; 4:34; Josh 21:4

KOR *measure of capacity*
k-s of fine flour 1 Kin 4:22
20,000 **k-s** of barley 2 Chr 2:10
100 **k-s** of wheat Ezra 7:22
a bath from *each* **k** Ezek 45:14

KORAH
1 *son of Esau* Gen 36:5
2 *opposed Moses* Num 16:8,16
3 *son of Hebron* 1 Chr 2:43
4 *a Kohathite* 1 Chr 6:37

L

LABAN
1 *Abraham's kinsman* Gen 24:29
Rachel's father Gen 29:10,16
2 *place in the desert* Deut 1:1

LABOR (n) *work, childbirth*
fruits of your **l-s** Ex 23:16
their **l** to the locust Ps 78:46
bread of painful **l-s** Ps 127:2
return for their **l** Eccl 4:9
in **l** and hardship 2 Cor 11:27
fruitful **l** for me Phil 1:22
faith and **l** of love 1 Thess 1:3
cried out, being in **l** Rev 12:2

LABOR (v) *toil, work*
Six days you shall **l** Ex 20:9
l in vain who build Ps 127:1
for whom am I **l-ing** Eccl 4:8
l-ed over you in vain Gal 4:11

LABORER *workman*
l-s for his vineyard Matt 20:1
Call the **l-s** and pay Matt 20:8
l-s into His harvest Luke 10:2
l is worthy of his Luke 10:7

LACHISH
city in Judah Josh 10:3; 2 Kin 14:19; 2 Chr 32:9

LACK (n) *deficiency, need*
where there is no **l** Judg 18:10
for **l** of instruction Prov 5:23
for **l** of a shepherd Ezek 34:5
l of self-control 1 Cor 7:5

LACK (v) *be deficient, need*
will not **l** anything Deut 8:9
l-ing in counsel Deut 32:28
man **l-ing** sense Prov 7:7
am I still **l-ing** Matt 19:20
One thing you **l** Mark 10:21
not **l-ing** in any gift 1 Cor 1:7
if any...**l-s** wisdom James 1:5

LAD *boy*
God heard the **l** Gen 21:17
the **l** is not *with us* Gen 44:31
the **l** was dead 2 Kin 4:32
a **l** here who has five John 6:9

LADDER *steps*
l...set on the earth Gen 28:12

LADY *woman*
Your noble **l-ies** Ps 45:9
elder to the chosen **l** 2 John 1

LAISH
1 *a Benjamite* 1 Sam 25:44; 2 Sam 3:15
2 *place in N Palestine later called Dan* Judg 18:27,29

LAKE *pool, water*
standing by the **l** Luke 5:1
wind...on the **l** Luke 8:23
into the **l** and was Luke 8:33
into the **l** of fire Rev 20:10

LAMB *young sheep*
l for the burnt Gen 22:7
shall redeem with a **l** Ex 34:20
l without defect Lev 14:10
will dwell with the **l** Is 11:6
l...led to slaughter Is 53:7
wolf and the **l** will Is 65:25
send you out as **l-s** Luke 10:3
Behold, the **L** of God John 1:29
Tend My **l-s** John 21:15
l before its shearer Acts 8:32
Worthy is the **L** Rev 5:12
blood of the **L** Rev 12:11

LAME *crippled, disabled*
was **l** in both feet 2 Sam 9:13
feet to the **l** Job 29:15
Then the **l** will leap Is 35:6
the **l** walk Matt 11:5
l from his mother's Acts 14:8

LAMECH
1 *in linage of Cain* Gen 4:17,18
2 *father of Noah* Gen 5:28,29

LAMENT (n) *dirge, wail*
this **l** over Saul 2 Sam 1:17
chanted a **l** 2 Chr 35:25
I must make a **l** Mic 1:8

LAMENT (v) *mourn, wail*
house of Israel **l-ed** 1 Sam 7:2
her gates will **l** Is 3:26
fishermen will **l** Is 19:8
And **l** over you Ezek 27:32
weep and **l** over her Rev 18:9

LAMENTATION *weeping*
great...sorrowful **l** Gen 50:10
in Ramah, **L** *and* Jer 31:15
your songs into **l** Amos 8:10
made loud **l** over him Acts 8:2

LAMP *light*
You are my **l** 2 Sam 22:29
l-s of pure gold 2 Chr 4:20
his **l** goes out Job 18:6
Your word is a **l** Ps 119:105
commandment is a **l** Prov 6:23
l of the body Matt 6:22
l-s are going out Matt 25:8
l-s in the upper room Acts 20:8
l shining in a dark 2 Pet 1:19
seven **l-s** of fire Rev 4:5

LAMPSTAND *candlestick*
l of pure gold Ex 25:31
and a chair and a **l** 2 Kin 4:10
puts it on a **l** Luke 8:16
will remove your **l** Rev 2:5

LAND *country, earth*
let the dry **l** appear Gen 1:9
famine in the **l** Gen 12:10
I have given this **l** Gen 15:18
out of the **l** of Egypt Ex 6:13
l flowing with milk Deut 6:3
in to possess the **l** Josh 1:11
l of their captivity 2 Chr 6:38
will heal their **l** 2 Chr 7:14
the **l** of the living Job 28:13
will inherit the **l** Ps 37:11
In a dry and weary **l** Ps 63:1
l be born in one day Is 66:8
again to this **l** Jer 24:6
l is filled with blood Ezek 9:9
smite the **l** with a Mal 4:6
darkness...all the **l** Matt 27:45
owned a tract of **l** Acts 4:37

LANDOWNER *landlord*
slaves of the **l** Matt 13:27
kingdom...like a **l** Matt 20:1
l who planted a Matt 21:33

LANGUAGE *speech, word*
according to his **l** Gen 10:5
earth used the same **l** Gen 11:1
speech or difficult **l** Ezek 3:5
in figurative **l** John 16:25
speak in his own **l** Acts 2:6
many kinds of **l-s** 1 Cor 14:10

LANGUISH *faint*
l-ed because of the Gen 47:13
My soul **l-es** for Ps 119:81
never **l** again Jer 31:12
refresh...who **l-es** Jer 31:25

LAODICEA
city in Asia Minor Col 2:1
location of early church Col 4:15; Rev 1:11; 3:14

LAODICEANS
people of Laodicea Col 4:16

LAPIS LAZULI *precious stone*
polishing *was* like **l** Lam 4:7
like **l** in appearance Ezek 1:26
the jasper; The **l** Ezek 28:13

LARGE *big, great, huge*
tears in **l** measure Ps 80:5
a **l** upper room Mark 14:15
a **l** crowd Luke 7:11
what **l** letters Gal 6:11

LAST *final, utmost*
breathed his **l** Gen 25:8
In the **l** days Is 2:2
first will be **l** Matt 19:30
The **l** Adam 1 Cor 15:45
at the **l** trumpet 1 Cor 15:52
in these **l** days Heb 1:2
it is the **l** hour 1 John 2:18
the first and the **l** Rev 1:17

LATIN
language of the Roman Empire
one of three languages written on Jesus' cross John 19:20

LATTICE *trellis*
fell through the **l** 2 Kin 1:2
looked out...my **l** Prov 7:6
peering through...**l** Song 2:9

LAUGH *be amused, mock*
Why did Sarah **l** Gen 18:13
will **l** at violence Job 5:22
l at your calamity Prov 1:26
weep, and a time to **l** Eccl 3:4
began **l-ing** at Him Matt 9:24

LAUGHINGSTOCK *derision*
l among the peoples Ps 44:14
was not Israel a **l** Jer 48:27
I have become a **l** Lam 3:14

LAUGHTER *amusement*
God has made **l** for Gen 21:6
Even in **l** the heart Prov 14:13
Sorrow is better than **l** Eccl 7:3

LAVER *wash basin*
make a **l** of bronze Ex 30:18
set the **l** between Ex 40:7
anoint the **l** Ex 40:11

LAW *scripture, statute*
tablets with the **l** Ex 24:12
Moses wrote this **l** Deut 31:9
found the...**l** 2 Kin 22:8
walk in My **l** 2 Chr 6:16
l...is perfect Ps 19:7
I delight in Your **l** Ps 119:70
abolish the **L** or the Matt 5:17
Our **L**...not judge John 7:51
by that **l** He ought John 19:7
by a **l** of faith Rom 3:27
L brings...wrath Rom 4:15
not under **l** Rom 6:14
Is the **L** sin Rom 7:7
the **L** is holy Rom 7:12
L...become our tutor Gal 3:24
thereby fulfill the **l** Gal 6:2
L...nothing perfect Heb 7:19

LAWFUL *legal, right*
not **l** for him to eat Matt 12:4
Is it **l** to heal Matt 12:10
l...man to divorce Mark 10:2
All things are **l** 1 Cor 6:12

LAWGIVER *lawmaker*
The LORD is our **l** Is 33:22
one **L** and Judge James 4:12

LAWLESS *illegal, without law*
l one will be 2 Thess 2:8
are **l** and rebellious 1 Tim 1:9
from every **l** deed Titus 2:14

LAWYER *interpreter of law*
a **l**, asked Him *a* Matt 22:35
One of the **l-s** said Luke 11:45
Woe to you **l-s** Luke 11:52

LAY *place, put*
laid him on the altar Gen 22:9
l My hand on Egypt Ex 7:4
laid its cornerstone Job 38:6
l my glory in the dust Ps 7:5
he **l-s** up deceit Prov 26:24
laid Him in a tomb Mark 15:46
l-s down His life John 10:11
l l down My life John 10:15
have you **laid** Him John 11:34
l L in Zion a stone Rom 9:33
l-ing aside falsehood Eph 4:25

LAYMAN *non-ecclesiastic*
l shall not eat *them* Ex 29:33
married to a **l** Lev 22:12
l who comes near Num 3:10

LAZARUS
1 *beggar* Luke 16:20-25
2 *brother of Mary and Martha* John 11:1,2,5,11,43

LAZY *idle, slothful*
Because they are **l** Ex 5:8
You are **l**, *very* **l** Ex 5:17
You wicked, **l** slave Matt 25:26
beasts, **l** gluttons Titus 1:12

LEAD (n) *metal*
They sank like **l** Ex 15:10
an iron stylus and **l** Job 19:24
l is consumed by Jer 6:29
l in the furnace Ezek 22:18

LEAD (v) *direct, guide*
God **led** the people Ex 13:18
cloud by day to **l** Ex 13:21
l-s me beside quiet Ps 23:2
L me in Your truth Ps 25:5
led captive *Your* Ps 68:18
little boy will **l** Is 11:6
lamb that is **led** to Is 53:7
not **l** us into Matt 6:13
l astray...the elect Mark 13:22
led Him...crucify Mark 15:20
and **l-s** them out John 10:3
led by the Spirit Rom 8:14
led captive a host Eph 4:8
that **l-s** to salvation 2 Tim 3:15

LEADER *director, guide*
Let us appoint a **l** Num 14:4
one **l** of every tribe Num 34:18
l over My people 1 Kin 14:7
the **l** like the servant Luke 22:26
Obey your **l-s** Heb 13:17

LEADING (adj) *chief, noted*
gathered **l** men Ezra 7:28
number...**l** women Acts 17:4
l men of the Jews Acts 28:17

LEAF *foliage*
sewed fig **l-ves** Gen 3:7
sound of a driven **l** Lev 26:36
its **l** does not wither Ps 1:3
puts forth its **l-ves** Matt 24:32

LEAH
wife of Jacob Gen 29:23,30
mother of Reuben, Simeon, Levi and Judah Gen 29:32-35

LEAN (adj) *thin*
seven **l**...ugly cows Gen 41:27
my flesh has grown **l** Ps 109:24
and the **l** sheep Ezek 34:20

LEAN (v) *incline, rest*
may **l** against them Judg 16:26
l...own understanding Prov 3:5
l on the God of Israel Is 48:2

LEAP *jump, spring*
l-ing and dancing 2 Sam 6:16
I can **l** over a wall Ps 18:29
baby **l-ed** in her Luke 1:41

and **l** *for joy* Luke 6:23
l-ed up and *began* Acts 14:10

LEARN *get knowledge*
l to fear the LORD Deut 31:13
I may **l** Your statutes Ps 119:71
have I **l-ed** wisdom Prov 30:3
will they **l** war Is 2:4
l from Me Matt 11:29
l-ed to be content Phil 4:11
He **l-ed** obedience Heb 5:8

LEARNING (n) *knowledge*
increase *his* **l** Prov 9:9
l of the Egyptians Acts 7:22
great **l** is driving Acts 26:24

LEAST *insignificant*
l of my master's 2 Kin 18:24
greatest to the **l** 2 Chr 34:30
l in the kingdom Matt 5:19
the one who is **l**...is Matt 11:11
l of the apostles 1 Cor 15:9
very **l** of all saints Eph 3:8

LEATHER *animal skin*
man with a **l** girdle 2 Kin 1:8
a **l** belt around his Matt 3:4
and *wore* a **l** belt Mark 1:6

LEAVE *abandon, depart, forsake*
shall **l** his father Gen 2:24
arise, **l** this land Gen 31:13
not **l** me defenseless Ps 141:8
kindness and truth **l** Prov 3:3
l the ninety-nine Matt 18:12
Peace I **l** with you John 14:27
I am **l-ing**...world John 16:28
L your country Acts 7:3

LEAVEN *yeast*
no **l** found in your Ex 12:19
not be baked with **l** Lev 6:17
seven days no **l** shall Deut 16:4
heaven is like **l** Matt 13:33
little **l** leavens the 1 Cor 5:6

LEAVENED *raised by yeast*
whoever eats what is **l** Ex 12:19
with cakes of **l** bread Lev 7:13
not eat **l** bread Deut 16:3
until it was all **l** Matt 13:33

LEBANON
mountain range N of Israel Josh 9:1; Judg 3:3; 1 Kin 5:6
showing God's greatness Ps 29:6
symbol of prosperity Ps 92:12

LEG *part of body*
l-s are pillars of Song 5:15
Uncover the **l** Is 47:2
not break His **l-s** John 19:33

LEGAL *lawful*
has a **l** matter Ex 24:14
Give me **l** protection Luke 18:3

LEGION *division, group*
twelve **l-s** of angels Matt 26:53
My name is **L** Mark 5:9
man who had...**l** Mark 5:15
L; for many demons Luke 8:30

LEMUEL
royal author of section of Proverbs Prov 31:1,4

LEND *loan*
l-ing them money Neh 5:10
l-s...on interest Ezek 18:13
l, expecting nothing Luke 6:35
l me three loaves Luke 11:5

LENDER *loaner*
becomes the **l-'s** slave Prov 22:7
l like the borrower Is 24:2

LENGTH
the **l** of the ark Gen 6:15
l of days and years Prov 3:2
breadth and **l** and Eph 3:18
l and width...equal Rev 21:16

LEOPARD *animal*
l will lie down with Is 11:6
Or the **l** his spots Jer 13:23
Like a **l** I will lie Hos 13:7
beast...was like a **l** Rev 13:2

LEPER *one having leprosy*
As for the **l** Lev 13:45
King Uzziah...a **l** 2 Chr 26:21
a **l** came to Him Matt 8:2
cleanse *the* **l-s** Matt 10:8
home of Simon the **l** Mark 14:3

LEPROSY *infectious disease*
of **l** on the skin Lev 13:2
mark of **l** on a Lev 14:34
an infection of **l** Deut 24:8
cure him of his **l** 2 Kin 5:3
his **l** was cleansed Matt 8:3

LEPROUS *having leprosy*
hand was **l** like snow Ex 4:6
is a **l** malignancy Lev 13:51
ten **l**...met Him Luke 17:12

LET *allow, permit*
L there be light Gen 1:3
L My people go Ex 5:1
L the children alone Matt 19:14
l this cup pass from Matt 26:39
Do not **l** your heart be John 14:1

LETTER *epistle* or *symbol*
a **l** sent to Solomon 2 Chr 2:11
smallest **l** or stroke Matt 5:18
You are our **l** 2 Cor 3:2
l caused you sorrow 2 Cor 7:8
large **l-s** I am writing Gal 6:11

LEVEL *flat, plain*
lead me in a **l** path Ps 27:11
path of the righteous **l** Is 26:7
stood on a **l** place Luke 6:17

LEVI
1 *son of Jacob* Gen 34:25
2 *tribe* Num 1:49; Rev 7:7
3 *two ancestors of Jesus* Luke 3:24,29
4 *apostle* Mark 2:14; Luke 5:27,29

LEVIATHAN
symbolic monster of the deep Job 3:8; Ps 104:26; Is 27:1

LEVITES
descendants of Levi Ex 6:19,25
charged with the care of the sanctuary Num 1:50; 3:41

LEVY (n) *payment, tax*
the LORD's **l** Num 31:38
l *fixed by* Moses 2 Chr 24:6

LEVY (v) *impose a tax*
l a tax for the LORD Num 31:28
l-ied forced laborers 1 Kin 9:21

LEWDNESS *lascivious, lust*
land...full of **l** Lev 19:29
not commit this **l** Ezek 16:43
I will uncover her **l** Hos 2:10

LIAR *one telling lies*
who...prove me a **l** Job 24:25
a poor man than a **l** Prov 19:22
I will be a **l** like John 8:55
hypocrisy of **l-s** 1 Tim 4:2
we make Him a **l** 1 John 1:10

LIBATION *see* **OFFERINGS**

LIBERTY *freedom*
I will walk at **l** Ps 119:45
proclaim **l** to captives Is 61:1
spy out our **l** Gal 2:4
the *law* of **l** James 1:25

LIBNAH
1 *place in wilderness* Num 33:21
2 *Canaanite city* Josh 10:29; 2 Kin 23:31
a Levitical city 1 Chr 6:57

LIBYA
country in N Africa Ezek 30:5; Acts 2:10

LICK *lap up*
dogs will **l** up your 1 Kin 21:19
his enemies **l** the dust Ps 72:9
dogs were...**l-ing** Luke 16:21

LIE (n) *false statement*
speak **l-s** go astray Ps 58:3
tells **l-s** will perish Prov 19:9
prophesy a **l** to you Jer 27:10
the father of **l-s** John 8:44
truth of God for a **l** Rom 1:25
no **l** is of the truth 1 John 2:21

LIE (v) *make false statement*
nor **l** to one another Lev 19:11
l-d to Him with their Ps 78:36
l-d about the LORD Jer 5:12
l to the Holy Spirit Acts 5:3
not **l** to one another Col 3:9
impossible...God to **l** Heb 6:18

LIE (v) *recline*
when you **l** down Deut 11:19
she **lay** at his feet Ruth 3:14
Saul **lay** sleeping 1 Sam 26:7
makes me **l** down Ps 23:2
lying in a manger Luke 2:12

LIFE *living* or *salvation*
the breath of **l** Gen 2:7
l for **l** Ex 21:23
l...is in the blood Lev 17:11
Our **l** for yours Josh 2:14
my **l** is *but* breath Job 7:7
Who redeems your **l** Ps 103:4
the springs of **l** Prov 4:23
way of **l** and...death Jer 21:8
to everlasting **l** Dan 12:2
take my **l** from me Jon 4:3
worried about your **l** Matt 6:25
loses his **l** for My Matt 16:25
His **l** a ransom for Matt 20:28
to inherit eternal **l** Mark 10:17
l is more than food Luke 12:23
but have eternal **l** John 3:16
out of death into **l** John 5:24
I am the bread of **l** John 6:35
lays down his **l** John 10:11
resurrection and...**l** John 11:25
truth, and the **l** John 14:6
lay down his **l** for John 15:13
walk in newness of **l** Rom 6:4
the Spirit gives **l** 2 Cor 3:6
Christ, who is our **l** Col 3:4
an undisciplined **l** 2 Thess 3:11
receive...crown of **l** James 1:12
lay down our **l-ves** 1 John 3:16
book of **l** of the lamb Rev 13:8

LIFEBLOOD
I will require your **l** Gen 9:5
poured out their **l** Is 63:6
l of the innocent Jer 2:34

LIFETIME *length of life*
Throughout his **l** 2 Chr 34:33
His favor is for a **l** Ps 30:5
my **l** of futility Eccl 7:15
as the **l** of a tree Is 65:22

LIFT *exalt, raise*
l up your eyes and Gen 13:14
l up your staff and Ex 14:16
l up your voice Job 38:34
One who **l-s** my head Ps 3:3
I Will **l** up my eyes Ps 121:1
will not **l** up sword Is 2:4
Spirit **l-ed** me up Ezek 3:14
Son of Man be **l-ed** John 3:14
He was **l-ed** up Acts 1:9
l-ing up holy hands 1 Tim 2:8

LIGHT *brightness, lamp*
Let there be **l** Gen 1:3
Israel had **l** in Ex 10:23
l of the wicked Job 18:5
LORD is my **l** Ps 27:1
And a **l** to my path Ps 119:105
like the **l** of dawn Prov 4:18
walk in the **l** of the Is 2:5
your **l** has come Is 60:1
stars for **l** by night Jer 31:35
the **l** of the world Matt 5:14
body will be full of **l** Matt 6:22
L of revelation to Luke 2:32
There was the true **l** John 1:9
I am the **L** John 8:12
while you have...**L** John 12:35
l of the gospel 2 Cor 4:4
walk as children of **L** Eph 5:8
Father of **l-s** James 1:17
if we walk in the **L** 1 John 1:7

LIGHTNING *flash of light in sky*
thunder and **l** flashes Ex 19:16
He spreads His **l** Job 36:30
makes **l** for the rain Jer 10:13
l...from the east Matt 24:27
appearance...like **l** Matt 28:3

LIKENESS *similarity*
according to Our **l** Gen 1:26
an idol, or any **l** Ex 20:4
the **l** of sinful flesh Rom 8:3
made in the **l** of men Phil 2:7

LILY *flower*
The **l** of the valleys Song 2:1
blossom like the **l** Hos 14:5
l-ies of the field Matt 6:28

LIMIT *end, extent*
there is no **l** 1 Chr 22:16
no **l** to windy words Job 16:3
set a **l** for the rain Job 28:26
no **l** to the treasure Nah 2:9

LINE *boundary* or *cord*
draw your *border* **l** Num 34:7
ran from...battle **l** 1 Sam 4:12
a **l** into the Nile Is 19:8
plumb **l** in the hand Zech 4:10

LINEN *type of cloth*
makes **l** garments Prov 31:24
buy...a **l** waistband Jer 13:1
pulled free of the **l** sheet Mark 14:52
wrapped Him...**l** Mark 15:46
saw the **l** wrappings John 20:5
clothed in fine **l** Rev 19:14

LINTEL *horizontal crosspiece*
blood on the **l** Ex 12:23
l *and* five-sided 1 Kin 6:31

LION *wild animal*
Judah is a **l-'s** whelp Gen 49:9
a **l** or a bear 1 Sam 17:34
hunt me like a **l** Job 10:16
tear my soul like a **l** Ps 7:2
are bold as a **l** Prov 28:1
cast into the **l-s'** Dan 6:16
like a roaring **l** 1 Pet 5:8

LIPS *part of mouth*
My **l** will praise Ps 63:3
With her flattering **l** Prov 7:21
Your **l**, *my* bride Song 4:11
a man of unclean **l** Is 6:5
honors Me with...**l** Matt 15:8

LIQUOR *alcoholic drink*
concerning wine and **l** Mic 2:11
drink no wine or **l** Luke 1:15

LISTEN *hear, heed*
Pharaoh does not **l** Ex 7:4
l to His voice Deut 4:30
l...commandments Deut 11:27
scoffer does not **l** Prov 13:1
L to your father Prov 23:22
draw near to **l** Eccl 5:1
L to Me, O Jacob Is 48:12
L...another parable Matt 21:33
care what you **l** to Mark 4:24
l-ing to the word Luke 5:1
My Son...**l** to Him Luke 9:35

LITERATURE *writings*
teach them the **l** Dan 1:4
every *branch of* **l** Dan 1:17

LITTLE *small quantity*
a **l** lower than God Ps 8:5
a **l** boy will lead Is 11:6
You of **l** faith Matt 6:30
forgiven **l**, loves **l** Luke 7:47
a **l** leaven leavens 1 Cor 5:6
l children, abide 1 John 2:28

LIVE (v) *reside* or *be alive*
eat, and **l** forever Gen 3:22
does not **l** by bread Deut 8:3
my Redeemer **l-s** Job 19:25
Let my soul **l** Ps 119:175
Listen, that you may **l** Is 55:3
can these bones **l** Ezek 37:3
righteous will **l** by Hab 2:4
l-d in...Nazareth Matt 2:23
not **l** on bread alone Matt 4:4
l even if he dies John 11:25
because **I l** John 14:19
shall **l** by faith Rom 1:17
Christ died and **l-d** Rom 14:9
no longer I who **l** Gal 2:20
to **l** is Christ Phil 1:21
worship Him who **l-s** Rev 4:10

LIVER *internal organ*
the lobe of the **l** Ex 29:13
l of the sin offering Lev 9:10
pierces through his **l** Prov 7:23
he looks at the **l** Ezek 21:21

LIVESTOCK *domestic animals*
was very rich in **l** Gen 13:2
their **l** to Joseph Gen 47:17
l of Egypt died Ex 9:6
large number of **l** Num 32:1

LIVING (adj) *alive*
man became a **l** being Gen 2:7
voice of the **l** god Deut 5:26
Divide the **l** child 1 Kin 3:25
Son of the **l** God Matt 16:16
given you **l** water John 4:10
I am the **l** bread John 6:51
l and holy sacrifice Rom 12:1
became a **l** soul 1 Cor 15:45
temple of the **l** God 2 Cor 6:16
word of God is **l** Heb 4:12

LIVING (n) *what is alive*
mother of all *the* **l** Gen 3:20
land of the **l** Job 28:13
that the **l** may know Dan 4:17
God...of the **l** Matt 22:32
judge the **l** and the 1 Pet 4:5

LOAD *burden*
in all their **l-s** Num 4:27
l alone bear the **l** Deut 1:12

LOAF *portion of bread*
gave him a **l** of bread Jer 37:21
asks for a **l** Matt 7:9
five **l-ves** and two Matt 14:17

LO-AMMI
second son of Hosea Hos 1:9

LOAN *something lent*
your neighbor a **l** Deut 24:10
rich with **l-s** Hab 2:6

LOATHE *despise, detest*
l l-d *that* generation Ps 95:10
sated man **l-s** honey Prov 27:7
l l the arrogance of Amos 6:8

LOATHSOME *detestable*
l to the Egyptians Gen 46:34
like **l** food to me Job 6:7
l and malignant sore Rev 16:2

LOCK (n) *tuft of hair*
seven **l-s** of my hair Judg 16:13
flowing **l-s** of...head Song 7:5
a **l** of my head Ezek 8:3

LOCK (v) *secure, shut*
l the door behind 2 Sam 13:17
l-ed quite securely Acts 5:23
l up...the saints Acts 26:10

LOCUST *grasshopper*
wind brought the **l-s** Ex 10:13
you may eat: the **l** Lev 11:22
come in like **l-s** Judg 6:5
leap like the **l** Job 39:20
l-s have no king Prov 30:27
like the swarming **l** Nah 3:17
food was **l-s** and wild Matt 3:4

LOD / LYDDA
town of Benjamin SE of coastal Jaffa 1 Chr 8:12; Neh 11:35; Acts 9:32-38

LODGE *dwell, spend the night*
where you **l**, I will **l** Ruth 1:16
drank and **l-d** there Judg 19:4
In his neck **l-s** Job 41:22
l in the wilderness Ps 55:7

LODGING (adj) *dwelling*
fodder at the **l** place Gen 42:27
about at the **l** place Ex 4:24
A wayfarers' **l** place Jer 9:2

LOFTINESS *elevated, haughty*
l of man will be Is 2:11
l of your dwelling Obad 3

LOFTY *grand, high*
built You a **l** house 1 Kin 8:13
high and **l** mountain Is 57:7

LOG *beam, wood*
he who splits **l-s** Eccl 10:9
l out of your own eye Matt 7:5

LOINS *lower back*
with your **l** girded Ex 12:11
Gird up your **l** 2 Kin 4:29
l are full of anguish Is 21:3
having girded your **l** Eph 6:14

LOIS
grandmother of Timothy 2 Tim 1:5

LONELY *alone, isolated*
I am **l** and afflicted Ps 25:16
makes a home for the **l** Ps 68:6
How **l** sits the city Lam 1:1

LONG (adj) *extended*
there was a **l** war 2 Sam 3:1
L life is in her Prov 3:16
you make **l** prayers Matt 23:14
if a man has **l** hair 1 Cor 11:14

LONG (v) ***desire, want***
Who **l** for death Job 3:21
my soul **l-s** for You Is 26:9
l-ing to be fed Luke 16:21
I l to see you Rom 1:11
angels **l** to look 1 Pet 1:12
l for the pure milk 1 Pet 2:2

LOOK ***see, stare***
Do not **l** behind you Gen 19:17
afraid to **l** at God Ex 3:6
Lord **l-s** at...heart 1 Sam 16:7
L upon my affliction Ps 25:18
The sea **l-ed** and fled Ps 114:3
not **l** on the wine Prov 23:31
l eagerly for Him Is 8:17
l to the Holy One Is 17:7
l on Me...pierced Zech 12:10
L at the birds of Matt 6:26
l-ing up...heaven Matt 14:19
plow and **l-ing** back Luke 9:62
l on the fields John 4:35
l on Him...pierced John 19:37
l-ing for the blessed Titus 2:13
l-ing for...heavens 2 Pet 3:13

LOOSE ***release***
l the cords of Orion Job 38:31
have **l-d** my bonds Ps 116:16
l on earth shall have been Matt 16:19
you **l** on earth Matt 18:18

LORD ***personal name of God***
Old Testament
Different Hebrew words are translated as Lord
Lord ***(Yahweh)*** Gen 4:1; Ex 3:2,15; Ps 23:1; Is 40:31; Ezek 11:23
Lord God ***(Adonai Yahweh)*** Gen 15:2; 2 Sam 7:18,19; Is 1:24; Ezek 28:6; Hab 3:19
Lord God ***(Yahweh Elohim)*** Gen 2:4; Ps 59:5; 68:18; Jer 15:16; Jon 1:9
Lord ***(Adonai)*** Gen 18:27; Ex 4:10; Josh 3:11; Ps 68:19; Mic 4:13
Lord God ***(Yah Yahweh)*** Is 12:2
New Testament
Different Greek words are translated as Lord
Lord ***(Kyrios, refers to either the Father or the Son)*** Matt 1:20; John 11:2; Acts 5:19; 2 Cor 5:6; 1 Thess 4:16
Lord ***(Despotes, refers to the Father)*** Luke 2:29; Acts 4:24; Rev 6:10
Lord God ***(Kyrios Theos, refers to either the Father or the Son)*** Luke 1:32; Rev 1:8; 11:17; 16:7; 18:8
Lord Jesus ***(Kyrios Iesous)*** Mark 16:19; Luke 24:3; Acts 4:33; 7:59
Lord Jesus Christ ***(Kyrios Iesous Christos)*** Acts 15:26; Rom 1:7; 5:1; 1 Cor 1:10; Eph 1:2,3; 1 Thess 5:9; James 2:1

LORD ***human master, ruler***
Hear us, my **l** Gen 23:6
not my **l** be angry Gen 31:35
Moses, my **l** Num 11:28
l-s of...Philistines Judg 16:27
counsel of my **l** Ezra 10:3
l-s of the nations Is 16:8
his **l** commanded Matt 18:25
write to my **l** Acts 25:26

LO-RUHAMAH
daughter of Hosea Hos 1:6,8

LOSE ***mislay, suffer loss***
do not **l** courage 2 Chr 15:7
lost their confidence Neh 6:16
stars **l** their Joel 2:10
his life will **l** it Matt 10:39
that which was **lost** Matt 18:11
not **l** his reward Mark 9:41
whoever **l-s** his life Luke 9:24

LOSS ***damage, what is lost***
might not suffer **l** Dan 6:2
damage and great **l** Acts 27:10
might not suffer **l** 2 Cor 7:9
all things to be **l** Phil 3:8

LOST (adj) ***missing, ruined***
like a **l** sheep Ps 119:176
have become **l** sheep Jer 50:6
l sheep...of Israel Matt 10:6
the wine is **l** Mark 2:22

LOST (n) ***without God***
I will seek the **l** Ezek 34:16
sent only to the **l** Matt 15:24

LOT
nephew of Abraham Gen 12:5; 19:15,36

LOT ***portion or decision process***
one **l** for the Lord Lev 16:8
clothing they cast **l-s** Ps 22:18
your **l** with us Prov 1:14
let us cast **l-s** Jon 1:7
tear it, but cast **l-s** John 19:24
l fell to Matthias Acts 1:26

LOUD ***great, noisy***
very **l** trumpet sound Ex 19:16
with a **l** shout Ezra 3:13
Jesus cried...**l** voice Matt 27:50
heard...a **l** voice Rev 1:10

LOVE (n) ***compassion, devotion***
l covers all Prov 10:12
in unchanging **l** Mic 7:18
l will grow cold Matt 24:12
abide in My **l** John 15:10
Greater **l** has no one John 15:13
demonstrates His...**l** Rom 5:8
separate us from...**l** Rom 8:39
l edifies 1 Cor 8:1
l is kind 1 Cor 13:4
Pursue **l** 1 Cor 14:1
l of Christ controls 2 Cor 5:14
through **l** serve one Gal 5:13
fruit...is **l** Gal 5:22
speaking...truth in **l** Eph 4:15
l of money is a root 1 Tim 6:10
for **l** is from God 1 John 4:7
God is **l** 1 John 4:16
l casts out fear 1 John 4:18
have left your first **l** Rev 2:4

LOVE (v)
who **l** Me and keep My Ex 20:6
l your neighbor as Lev 19:18
l the Lord your God Deut 6:5
the Lord **l-d** Israel 1 Kin 10:9
I l Your testimonies Ps 119:119
Lord **l-s** He reproves Prov 3:12
friend **l-s** at all Prov 17:17
Do not **l** sleep Prov 20:13
A time to **l** Eccl 3:8
Hate evil, **l** good Amos 5:15
do not **l** perjury Zech 8:17
l your enemies Matt 5:44
l to stand and pray Matt 6:5
God so **l-d** the world John 3:16
you **l** one another John 13:34
l-s a cheerful giver 2 Cor 9:7
Husbands, **l**...wives Eph 5:25
Do not **l** the world 1 John 2:15
whom I **l**, I reprove Rev 3:19

LOVERS ***one who desires, loves***
l have been crushed Jer 22:20
I called to my **l** Lam 1:19
the hands of your **l** Ezek 16:39
I will go after my **l** Hos 2:5
l of pleasure...**l** of 2 Tim 3:4

LOVINGKINDNESS ***compassion***
His **l** is upon Israel Ezra 3:11
abundant in **l** and Ps 86:15
sing of the **l** of the Ps 89:1
By **l** and truth Prov 16:6
with everlasting **l** Is 54:8

LOWLAND ***low hills***
country and in the **l** Deut 1:7
the Negev and the **l** Josh 10:40
sycamores in the **l** 2 Chr 1:15
the cities of the **l** Jer 32:44
see also **SHEPHELAH**

LOWLY ***humble, little***
He sets on high...**l** Job 5:11
He regards the **l** Ps 138:6
associate with the **l** Rom 12:16

LOYALTY ***faithfulness***
Is this your **l** 2 Sam 16:17
proclaims his own **l** Prov 20:6
I delight in **l** Hos 6:6

LUKE
associate of Paul 2 Tim 4:11; Philem 24
author of Luke and Acts Luke 1:1; Acts 1:1
physician Col 4:14

LUKEWARM ***tepid***
because you are **l** Rev 3:16

LUST ***sexual desire***
looks at...woman with **l** Matt 5:28
from youthful **l-s** 2 Tim 2:22
You **l** and do not James 4:2
l of the eyes 1 John 2:16

LUXURIANT ***lush, productive***
beneath...**l** tree 1 Kin 14:23
Israel is a **l** vine Hos 10:1

LUXURY ***extravagance***
L is not fitting for Prov 19:10
clothed and live in **l** Luke 7:25

LUZ
1 *ancient name of Bethel* Gen 28:19; 48:3
2 *town in Aram* Judg 1:26

LYCAONIA
Roman province in Asia Minor Acts 14:6

LYDDA ***see*** **LOD**

LYDIA
1 *seller of purple dyes and goods* Acts 16:14,40
2 *region on the W coast of Asia Minor* Jer 46:9

LYING (adj) ***false***
with a **l** tongue Ps 109:2
hatred *has* **l** lips Prov 10:18
l pen of the scribes Jer 8:8
and **l** divination Ezek 13:6

LYRE ***stringed instrument***
play the **l** and pipe Gen 4:21
prophesy with **l-s** 1 Chr 25:1
Awake, harp and **l** Ps 57:8

LYSTRA
a Lycaonian town Acts 14:6; 16:1,2

M

MACEDONIA
Roman province Acts 16:9,12
N Greece Phil 4:15; 1 Tim 1:3
visited by Paul Acts 16:10; 2 Cor 2:13

MACHIR
1 *grandson of Joseph* Josh 17:1
2 *son of Ammiel* 2 Sam 9:4,5

MACHPELAH
cave near Hebron Gen 23:17,19
Sarah's burial place Gen 23:19
Abraham buried there Gen 25:9
burial place of Jacob, Isaac, Rebekah, and Leah Gen 49:29ff; 50:13

MAD ***insane***
makes a wise man **m** Eccl 7:7
nations are going **m** Jer 51:7

MADMAN ***insane person***
behaving as a **m** 1 Sam 21:14

m who prophesies Jer 29:26

MADNESS *lunacy*
laughter, It is **m** Eccl 2:2
consider...**m** and folly Eccl 2:12

MAGADAN
village on the Sea of Galilee Matt 15:39

MAGDALENE
Mary Matt 27:56,61
from village of Magdala Mark 15:40,47; John 20:1,18

MAGI
wise men from Persia who visited Jesus, Mary, and Joseph Matt 2:1,7,16

MAGIC *sorcery*
practicing **m** Acts 8:9
who practiced **m** Acts 19:19

MAGICIAN *sorcerer, wizard*
called for...**m-s** Gen 41:8
the **m-s** of Egypt Ex 7:11
of any **m,** conjurer or Dan 2:10
found a **m** Acts 13:6

MAGISTRATE
appear before the **m** Luke 12:58
to the chief **m-s** Acts 16:20

MAGNIFY *extol, praise*
name...be **m-ied** 2 Sam 7:26
You **m** him Job 7:17
O **m** the LORD with me Ps 34:3
have **m-ied** Your word Ps 138:2
Jesus was...**m-ied** Acts 19:17
I **m** my ministry Rom 11:13

MAGOG
1 *son of Japheth* 1 Chr 1:5
2 *region in Asia Minor or further N ruled by Gog* Ezek 38:2; 39:6
see also **GOG**

MAHANAIM
city in Trans-Jordan Josh 13:26,30
city of refuge Josh 21:38
Levitical city 1 Chr 6:80

MAHER-SHALAL-HASH-BAZ
symbolic name of one of Isaiah's sons Is 8:3

MAHLAH
1 *daughter of Zelophehad* Num 26:33; 27:1; Josh 17:3
2 *a Manassite* 1 Chr 7:18

MAHLON
husband of Ruth Ruth 1:5; 4:10

MAID
Hagar, Sarai's **m** Gen 16:8
gave my **m** to my Gen 30:18
I am Ruth your **m** Ruth 3:9
way of a man...a **m** Prov 30:19

MAIDENS *young woman*
at the Nile...her **m** Ex 2:5
m...tambourines Ps 68:25

MAIDSERVANT *female slave*
do...to your **m** Deut 15:17
give Your **m** a son 1 Sam 1:11
let your **m** speak 2 Sam 14:12
while your **m** slept 1 Kin 3:20

MAJESTIC *dignified, grand*
Who is like You, **m** Ex 15:11
with His **m** voice Job 37:4
How **m** is Your name Ps 8:1
They are the **m** ones Ps 16:3
m is His work Ps 111:3
by the **M** Glory 2 Pet 1:17

MAJESTY *grandeur*
Around God is...**m** Job 37:22
He is clothed with **m** Ps 93:1
The **m** of our God Is 35:2
right hand of the **M** Heb 1:3
revile angelic **m-ies** Jude 8

MAKE *cause, create, do*
Let Us **m** man in Gen 1:26
not **m** for...an idol Ex 20:4
M me know Your ways Ps 25:4
M ready the way of Matt 3:3
m you fishers of men Matt 4:19

MAKER *creator*
Where is God my **M** Job 35:10
kneel before...our **M** Ps 95:6
M of heaven and Ps 115:15
I, the LORD, am the **m** Is 44:24

MAKKEDAH
Canaanite city in Judah Josh 10:21; 15:41

MALACHI
prophet Mal 1:1

MALCHUS
servant whose ear was cut off by Peter John 18:10

MALE
m and female He Gen 1:27
lamb...unblemished **m** Ex 12:5
likeness of **m** or Deut 4:16
slew...**m** children Matt 2:16
made...**m** and female Matt 19:4
neither **m** nor female Gal 3:28

MALICE *evil, mischief*
perceived their **m** Matt 22:18
leaven of **m** and 1 Cor 5:8
wrath, **m,** slander Col 3:8
putting aside all **m** 1 Pet 2:1

MALICIOUS *harmful, spiteful*
to be a **m** witness Ex 23:1
m gossips, without 2 Tim 3:3

MALTA
island S of Sicily where Paul was shipwrecked Acts 28:1

MAMRE
1 *Abraham's dwelling place near Hebron* Gen 13:18
2 *Amorite chieftain* Gen 14:24

MAN *male*
make **m** in Our image Gen 1:26
God formed **m** of dust Gen 2:7
Elisha the **m** of God 2 Kin 5:8
m is born for trouble Job 5:7
blessed is the **m** Ps 1:1
m is a mere breath Ps 39:11
righteous **m** hates Prov 13:5
Will a **m** rob God Mal 3:8
light...before **men** Matt 5:16
fishers of **men** Mark 1:17
Sabbath...for **m** Mark 2:27
rich **m** to enter Mark 10:25
what is a **m** profited Luke 9:25
a **m,** sent from God John 1:6
How can a **m** be born John 3:4
a **m** of Macedonia Acts 16:9
through one **m** sin Rom 5:12
as is common to **m** 1 Cor 10:13
when I became a **m** 1 Cor 13:11
m...leave his father Eph 5:31

MAN, SON OF *see* **SON OF MAN**

MANASSEH
1 *son of Joseph* Gen 41:51; 46:20
2 *tribe and area* Num 13:11; Josh 17:1
3 *king of Judah* 2 Kin 21:1,11
4 *Pahath-moab's son* Ezra 10:30
5 *son of Hashum* Ezra 10:33

MANDRAKES *love fruit*
found **m** in the field Gen 30:14
m...fragrance Song 7:13

MANGER *feeding trough*
spend...at your **m** Job 39:9
the **m** is clean Prov 14:4
laid Him in a **m** Luke 2:7

MANIFEST *reveal*
I have **m-ed** Your name John 17:6
became **m** to those Rom 10:20
made **m** to God 2 Cor 5:11
m-ed to His saints Col 1:26

MANIFOLD *many and varied*
the **m** wisdom of God Eph 3:10
stewards...**m** grace 1 Pet 4:10

MANKIND *the human race*
God...dwell with **m** 2 Chr 6:18
All **m** is stupid Jer 51:17
His love for **m** Titus 3:4
kill a third of **m** Rev 9:15

MANNA *food of the desert*
Israel named it **m** Ex 16:31
m was like coriander Num 11:7
m ceased on the day Josh 5:12
He rained down **m** Ps 78:24
Our fathers ate the **m** John 6:31

MANNER *way*
Your **m** with those Ps 119:132
spoke in such a **m** Acts 14:1
m worthy of...saints Rom 16:2
walk in a **m** worthy Eph 4:1

MANOAH
father of Samson Judg 13:2ff

MANSLAYER
for the **m** to flee to Num 35:6
m might flee there Deut 4:42
the **m** who kills any Josh 20:3

MANTLE *cloak, garment*
threw his **m** on him 1 Kin 19:19
the **m** of Elijah 2 Kin 2:13
like a **m** You will roll Heb 1:12

MARAH
spring of bitter water Ex 15:23

MARCH *pace, walk*
m around...seven times Josh 6:4
m everyone in his path Joel 2:8

MARDUK
chief Babylonian god Jer 50:2

MARESHAH
1 *father of Hebron* 1 Chr 2:42
2 *son of Laadah* 1 Chr 4:21
3 *town in Judah* 2 Chr 11:5-8

MARK *sign, spot*
make any tattoo **m-s** Lev 19:28
m on the foreheads Ezek 9:4
m on his forehead Rev 14:9
m of the beast Rev 19:20

MARK, JOHN
author of Gospel of Mark
accompanied Paul and Barnabas Acts 13:5; 15:37
cousin of Barnabas Col 4:10

MARKET *selling or trading place*
was the **m** of nations Is 23:3
coastlands were...**m** Ezek 27:15
idle in the **m** place Matt 20:3
sold in the meat **m** 1 Cor 10:25

MARRIAGE *wedlock*
a **m** alliance with 1 Kin 3:1
nor are given in **m** Matt 22:30
M *is to be held* in honor Heb 13:4
m supper of the Lamb Rev 19:9

MARRY *join in wedlock*
m-ied foreign wives Ezra 10:10
m-ies a divorced Matt 5:32

better not to **m** Matt 19:10
neither **m** nor are Mark 12:25
m-ied woman is bound Rom 7:2
better to **m** than to 1 Cor 7:9

MARTHA
sister of Lazarus and Mary John 11:1,5

MARVEL *be amazed, wonder*
Jesus heard...**m-ed** Matt 8:10
the crowd **m-ed** Matt 15:31
m-ed at the sight Acts 7:31

MARVELOUS *extraordinary*
and see this **m** sight Ex 3:3
It is **m** in our eyes Ps 118:23
into His **m** light 1 Pet 2:9
m are Your works Rev 15:3

MARY
1 *mother of Jesus* Matt 1:16
2 *Mary Magdalene* Matt 27:56; Mark 15:40
3 *mother of James and Joseph* Matt 27:56; Mark 16:1
4 *sister of Martha and Lazarus* John 11:1
5 *mother of Mark* Acts 12:12
6 *wife of Clopas* John 19:25
7 *Roman believer* Rom 16:6

MASTER *lord, ruler*
God of...**m** Abraham Gen 24:12
m shall pierce his ear Ex 21:6
can serve two **m-s** Matt 6:24
death no longer is **m** Rom 6:9
sin shall not be **m** Rom 6:14
obedient to...your **m-s** Eph 6:5
a **M** in heaven Col 4:1

MATTHEW
tax-gatherer Matt 9:9; 10:3
apostle Matt 10:3; Luke 6:15; Acts 1:13

MATTHIAS
replaced Judas Acts 1:23,26

MATURE *full grown* **or** *stable*
then the **m** grain Mark 4:28
those who are **m** 1 Cor 2:6
your thinking be **m** 1 Cor 14:20
food is for the **m** Heb 5:14

MATURITY *ripeness, adulthood*
bring no fruit to **m** Luke 8:14
let us press on to **m** Heb 6:1

MEAL *prepared food*
a **m** for enjoyment Eccl 10:19
not even eat a **m** Mark 3:20
washed before...**m** Luke 11:38
m-s together with Acts 2:46
for a *single* **m** Heb 12:16

MEAL OFFERING
see **OFFERINGS**

MEANINGLESS *senseless*
with **m** arguments Is 29:21
not use **m** repetition Matt 6:7

MEASURE (n) *amount*
a full and just **m** Deut 25:15
good **m**—pressed Luke 6:38
to each a **m** of faith Rom 12:3
m of Christ's gift Eph 4:7

MEASURE (v) *determine extent*
he stopped **m-ing** *it* Gen 41:49
m their former work Is 65:7
He **m-d** the gate Ezek 40:13
will be **m-d** to you Mark 4:24
rod to **m** the city Rev 21:15

MEASURING *standard*
justice the **m** line Is 28:17
was given me a **m** rod Rev 11:1

MEAT *flesh, food*
Who will give us **m** Num 11:4
LORD...you **m** Num 11:18
you may eat **m** Deut 12:20
rained **m** upon them Ps 78:27
from **m** sacrificed Acts 21:25
good not to eat **m** Rom 14:21
I will never eat **m** 1 Cor 8:13
m sacrificed...idols 1 Cor 10:28

MEDE(S)
ancient Indo-Europeans of NW Iran Dan 5:31; 11:1

MEDEBA
Moabite town E of Dead Sea Josh 13:9; 1 Chr 19:7

MEDIA
country of the Medes Ezra 6:2; Esth 1:18; Is 21:2

MEDIATOR *intermediary*
by the agency of a **m** Gal 3:19
one **m**...between God 1 Tim 2:5
Jesus...**m** of a new Heb 12:24

MEDITATE *ponder*
Isaac went out to **m** Gen 24:63
His law he **m-s** day Ps 1:2
M in your heart Ps 4:4
I **m** on You in the Ps 63:6

MEDITATION *deep reflection*
m...Be acceptable Ps 19:14
m be pleasing to Him Ps 104:34
my **m** all the day Ps 119:97

MEDIUM *summons spirits*
not turn to **m-s** or Lev 19:31
m...be put to death Lev 20:27
a **m**, or a spiritist Deut 18:11
woman who is a **m** 1 Sam 28:7
will resort to...**m-s** Is 19:3

MEEKNESS *gentleness*
cause of truth and **m** Ps 45:4
m and...of Christ 2 Cor 10:1

MEET *encounter*
Esau ran to **m** him Gen 33:4
people out...to **m** God Ex 19:17
God...will **m** me Ps 59:10
Prepare to **m**...God Amos 4:12
to **m** the bridegroom Matt 25:1
m-s his accusers Acts 25:16
m...in the air 1 Thess 4:17

MEETING *assembly*
house of **m** for all Job 30:23
midst of Your **m** place Ps 74:4

MEETING, TENT OF
see **TABERNACLE**

MEGIDDO
strategic city between Manasseh and Issachar Josh 12:21; 2 Kin 9:27
plain in Jezreel Valley 2 Chr 35:22; Zech 12:11
see also **HAR-MAGEDON**

MELCHIZEDEK
1 *king of Salem* Gen 14:18,19
priest Ps 110:4
2 *type of undying priesthood* Heb 5:6,10; 6:20; 7:1ff

MELODY *tune*
lyre...the sound of **m** Ps 98:5
singing...making **m** Eph 5:19

MELT *dissolve*
people **m** with fear Josh 14:8
His voice...earth **m-ed** Ps 46:6
mountains **m-ed** like Ps 97:5
As silver is **m-ed** Ezek 22:22

MEMBER *part of the whole*
m-s of...household Matt 10:25
m-s one of another Rom 12:5
if one **m** suffers 1 Cor 12:26
m-s of His body Eph 5:30

MEMORIAL *commemoration*
this is My **m-name** Ex 3:15
in a book as a **m** Ex 17:14
stones...become a **m** Josh 4:7
ascended as a **m** Acts 10:4

MEMORY *remembrance*
M of him perishes Job 18:17
cut off their **m** Ps 109:15
m of the righteous Prov 10:7
spoken of in **m** of Mark 14:9

MEMPHIS
city in Egypt Is 19:13; Jer 46:19; Ezek 30:13

MENAHEM
king of Israel 2 Kin 15:14,17

MENSTRUAL
m impurity for seven Lev 15:19
a woman during...**m** Ezek 18:6

MENSTRUATION
in the days of her **m** Lev 12:2
like her bed at **m** Lev 15:26

MEPHIBOSHETH
1 *son of Jonathan* 2 Sam 4:4
also **Merib-baal** 1 Chr 8:34
2 *son of Saul* 2 Sam 21:8

MERAB
Saul's daughter 1 Sam 18:17,19

MERARI
son of Levi Gen 46:11
head of a Levitical family Ex 6:19; 2 Chr 34:12

MERCHANT *buyer / seller*
m-s procured *them* 1 Kin 10:28
m of the peoples Ezek 27:3
A **m**, in whose hands Hos 12:7
m seeking...pearls Matt 13:45
m-s of the earth Rev 18:3

MERCIFUL *compassionate*
God **m** and gracious Ps 86:15
The LORD is...and **m** Ps 145:8
The **m** man...good Prov 11:17
Blessed are the **m** Matt 5:7
as your Father is **m** Luke 6:36
m to me, the sinner Luke 18:13

MERCY *compassion*
Great are Your **m-ies** Ps 119:156
in His **m** He redeemed Is 63:9
m to *the* poor Dan 4:27
the orphan finds **m** Hos 14:3
they shall receive **m** Matt 5:7
tender **m** of our God Luke 1:78
m on whom I have **m** Rom 9:15
by the **m-ies** of God Rom 12:1
God, being rich in **m** Eph 2:4

MERCY SEAT *covering over ark*
a **m** of pure gold Ex 25:17
put the **m** on the ark Ex 26:34
in front of the **m** Ex 30:6
sprinkle it on the **m** Lev 16:15
overshadowing the **m** Heb 9:5

MERIBAH
1 *fountain of Rephidim* Ex 17:7
2 *fountain of Kadesh-Barnea* Num 27:14

MERODACH-BALADAN
king of Babylon Is 39:1
see also **BERODACH-BALADAN**

MERRY *joyful, lively*
wine makes life **m** Eccl 10:19
eat, drink *and* be **m** Luke 12:19

MESHA
1 *territorial boundary in Arabia* Gen 10:30
2 *Moabite king* 2 Kin 3:4
3 *man of Judah* 1 Chr 2:42
4 *a Benjamite* 1 Chr 8:9

MESHACH
one of three Jews thrown into furnace Dan 3:19ff
see also **MISHAEL** Dan 1:7

MESHECH
1 *son of Japheth* Gen 10:2
2 *descendants and nation* Is 66:19; Ezek 27:13

MESOPOTAMIA
land of Tigris and Euphrates Rivers Deut 23:4; Judg 3:8; 1 Chr 19:6; Acts 7:2

MESSAGE *communication*
m from God for you Judg 3:20
m...with authority Luke 4:32
m and my preaching 1 Cor 2:4
the **m** of truth Eph 1:13
m we have heard 1 John 1:5

MESSENGER *one sent*
My **m** whom I send Is 42:19
m of the LORD of hosts Mal 2:7
I send My **m** ahead Matt 11:10
m-s of the churches 2 Cor 8:23
m of Satan 2 Cor 12:7

MESSIAH
anointed one Dan 9:25,26; John 1:41; 4:25
Greek: Christ

METAL
like glowing **m** Ezek 1:4
their **m** images Dan 11:8

METHUSELAH
son of Enoch Gen 5:21
grandfather of Noah Gen 5:25ff

MICAH
1 *an Ephraimite* Judg 17:1
2 *line of Reuben* 1 Chr 5:5
3 *father of Abdon* 2 Chr 34:20
4 *prophet* Jer 26:18; Mic 1:1
name of several other people

MICAIAH
1 *prophet* 1 Kin 22:8-26
2 *father of Achbor* 2 Kin 22:12
3 *wife of Rehoboam* 2 Chr 13:2
4 *under Jehoshaphat* 2 Chr 17:7
5 *line of Asaph* Neh 12:35
6 *under Nehemiah* Neh 12:41
7 *son of Gemariah* Jer 36:11

MICHAEL
1 *an archangel* Dan 10:21; 12:1; Jude 9; Rev 12:7
2 *Jehoshaphat's son* 2 Chr 21:2
prince of Judah
3 *army captain* 1 Chr 12:20
4 *line of Gershom* 1 Chr 6:40
name of seven other people

MICHAL
daughter of Saul 1 Sam 18:20
David's wife 1 Sam 19:11

MIDDLE *midst*
the **m** of the garden Gen 3:3
sun stopped in the **m** Josh 10:13
m of the lampstands Rev 1:13

MIDDLE GATE
see **GATES OF JERUSALEM**

MIDHEAVEN *directly overhead*
eagle flying in **m** Rev 8:13
angel flying in **m** Rev 14:6
birds which fly in **m** Rev 19:17

MIDIAN
1 *a son of Abraham* Gen 25:1,2
2 *land SE of Canaan in desert* Ex 2:15; Num 31:8; Judg 8:28

MIDIANITES
people of Midian Gen 37:36; Num 31:2; Judg 7:7

MIDST *middle, within*
God is in the **m** Ps 46:5
in the **m** of the fire Dan 3:25
Holy One in your **m** Hos 11:9
I am...in their **m** Matt 18:20

MIDWIFE *aids childbirth*
m...tied a scarlet Gen 38:28
before the **m** can get Ex 1:19

MIGDOL
1 *Israelite camp near Red Sea* Ex 14:2; Num 33:7
2 *town in Egypt* Jer 44:1

MIGHT *strength*
my firstborn; My **m** Gen 49:3
and with all your **m** Deut 6:5
With Him are...**m** Job 12:13
Not by **m** nor by Zech 4:6
strength of His **m** Eph 1:19

MIGHTY *powerful*
a **m** hunter before Gen 10:9
m...awesome God Deut 10:17
m men of valor 1 Chr 12:8
The LORD **m** in battle Ps 24:8
a **m** king will rule Is 19:4
m in the Scriptures Acts 18:24
the **m** hand of God 1 Pet 5:6

MILCAH
1 *daughter of Haran* Gen 11:29
2 *daughter of Zelophehad* Num 26:33; 27:1; Josh 17:3

MILCOM
god of Ammonites 1 Kin 11:5,33; 2 Kin 23:13; Zeph 1:5
see also **MOLECH**

MILE *distance, measurement*
one **m**, go with him Matt 5:41
m-s from Jerusalem Luke 24:13

MILETUS
town in Asia Minor Acts 20:15,17; 2 Tim 4:20

MILK
land flowing with **m** Ex 3:8
pour me out like **m** Job 10:10
m produces butter Prov 30:33
m to drink, not 1 Cor 3:2
pure **m** of the word 1 Pet 2:2

MILL *grinding stones*
sound of the...**m** Eccl 12:4
at the grinding **m** Lam 5:13
women...at the **m** Matt 24:41

MILLO
1 *fort near Shechem* Judg 9:6,20
Beth-millo
2 *fortress in Jerusalem* 2 Sam 5:9; 1 Kin 9:15,24; 1 Chr 11:8; 2 Chr 32:5

MILLSTONE *grinding stone*
upper **m** in pledge Deut 24:6
woman threw...**m** Judg 9:53
m hung around Matt 18:6
stone like a great **m** Rev 18:21

MINA
measure of gold or silver coin 1 Kin 10:17; Ezra 2:69; Neh 7:71; Luke 19:13ff

MIND *memory, thought*
God tries the...**m-s** Ps 7:9
Recall it to **m** Is 46:8
I test the **m** Jer 17:10
Let his **m** be changed Dan 4:16
He opened...**m-s** Luke 24:45
with one **m** in the Acts 2:46
to a depraved **m** Rom 1:28
m set on the flesh Rom 8:7
the **m** of Christ 1 Cor 2:16
m-s were hardened 2 Cor 3:14
with humility of **m** Phil 2:3

MINDFUL *aware*
Lord be **m** of me Ps 40:17
He is **m** that we are Ps 103:14
LORD has been **m** Ps 115:12
m of the...faith 2 Tim 1:5

MINISTER (n) *one who serves*
m-s before the ark 1 Chr 16:4
spoken of *as* **m-s** Is 61:6
a **m** and a witness Acts 26:16
a **m** of Christ Jesus Rom 15:16
is Christ then a **m** Gal 2:17
I was made a **m** Eph 3:7
faithful **m** in the Eph 6:21
His **m-s** a flame of Heb 1:7
a **m** in the sanctuary Heb 8:2

MINISTER (v) *give help, serve*
to **m** as priest to Me Ex 28:1
the boy **m-ed** to 1 Sam 2:11
not stand to **m** 1 Kin 8:11
to the LORD, To **m** Is 56:6
angels were **m-ing** Mark 1:13
follow Him and **m** Mark 15:41

MINISTRY *service*
He began His **m** Luke 3:23
to the **m** of the word Acts 6:4
m of the Spirit 2 Cor 3:8
m of reconciliation 2 Cor 5:18
fulfill your **m** 2 Tim 4:5
a more excellent **m** Heb 8:6

MIRACLE *supernatural event*
Work a **m** Ex 7:9
I will perform **m-s** Ex 34:10
m-s had occurred Matt 11:21
He could do no **m** Mark 6:5
perform a **m** in My Mark 9:39
this **m** of healing Acts 4:22
works **m-s** among you Gal 3:5
wonders and...**m-s** Heb 2:4

MIRE *mud*
cast me into the **m** Job 30:19
Deliver me from the **m** Ps 69:14
wallowing in the **m** 2 Pet 2:22

MIRIAM
1 *sister of Moses and Aaron* Ex 15:20; Num 12:4,10; 20:1
2 *line of Ezrah* 1 Chr 4:17

MIRROR *image reflector*
see in a **m** dimly 1 Cor 13:12
natural face in a **m** James 1:23

MISCARRIAGE *aborted fetus*
so that she has a **m** Ex 21:22
m-s of a woman Ps 58:8

MISERABLE *bad, unhappy*
loathe this **m** food Num 21:5
m and chronic Deut 28:59
Be **m** and mourn James 4:9
m and poor and blind Rev 3:17

MISERY *sorrow, suffering*
conscious of my **m** Job 10:15
Destruction and **m** Rom 3:16

MISFORTUNE *adversity*
M will not come Jer 5:12
m which He has Jer 26:13
The day of his **m** Obad 12

MISHAEL
1 *of family of Kohath* Ex 6:22; Lev 10:4
2 *associate of Ezra* Neh 8:4
3 *Daniel's friend* Dan 1:6,7,11,19; 2:17
see also **MESHACH**

MISLEAD *lead astray*
m-s a blind *person* Deut 27:18
m-led My people Ezek 13:10
that no one **m-s** you Mark 13:5
m-ing our nation Luke 23:2

MISTREAT ***treat badly, wrong***
not **m**...the stranger Jer 22:3
slaves...**m-ed** them Matt 22:6
pray for...who **m** Luke 6:28
mocked and **m-ed** Luke 18:32
m and to stone them Acts 14:5

MISTRESS ***woman in charge***
her **m** was despised Gen 16:4
m of the house 1 Kin 17:17
the maid like her **m** Is 24:2
the **m** of sorceries Nah 3:4

MIZPAH / MIZPEH
1 *heap of stones* Gen 31:49
2 *near Mt. Hermon* Josh 11:3
3 *village in Judah* Josh 15:38
4 *Benjamite town* Josh 18:26
5 *town in Gilead* Judg 10:17
6 *Moabite town* 1 Sam 22:3

MIZRAIM
1 *son of Ham* Gen 10:6
father of nations Gen 10:13
2 *Heb. for Egypt* 1 Chr 1:8,11

MOAB
1 *son of Lot* Gen 19:37
2 *country E of the Dead Sea* Ex 15:15; Josh 24:9; Ruth 1:2; 2 Kin 3:7; Ps 60:8; Jer 48:1

MOCK ***ridicule, scorn***
lads...**m-ed** him 2 Kin 2:23
Fools **m** at sin Prov 14:9
who **m-s** the poor Prov 17:5
soldiers also **m-ed** Luke 23:36
God is not **m-ed** Gal 6:7

MOCKERY ***object of ridicule***
a **m** of the Egyptians Ex 10:2
made a **m** of me Num 22:29
a **m** of justice Prov 19:28
m *and* insinuations Hab 2:6

MOLECH
god of the Ammonites Lev 18:21; 1 Kin 11:7; Jer 32:35
see also **MILCOM**

MOLTEN ***cast metal***
made it into a **m** calf Ex 32:4
make...no **m** gods Ex 34:17
destroy...**m** images Num 33:52
capitals of **m** bronze 1 Kin 7:16
his **m** images are Jer 10:14

MONEY ***currency***
take double *the* **m** Gen 43:12
not sell her for **m** Deut 21:14
time to receive **m** 2 Kin 5:26
loves **m** will not be Eccl 5:10
no **m** in their belt Mark 6:8
m in the bank Luke 19:23
love of **m** is a root 1 Tim 6:10

MONEYCHANGERS
the tables of the **m** Matt 21:12
coins of the **m** John 2:15

MONSTER ***enormous animal***
created...sea **m-s** Gen 1:21
sea, or the sea **m** Job 7:12
sea **m-s** in the waters Ps 74:13
belly of the sea **m** Matt 12:40

MOON
m and...were bowing Gen 37:9
the **m** stopped Josh 10:13
m and stars to rule Ps 136:9
beautiful as...**m** Song 6:10
the **m** into blood Joel 2:31
m will not...light Matt 24:29
signs in...and **m** Luke 21:25

MORALS ***principles***
Bad...good **m** 1 Cor 15:33

MORDECAI
1 *returned from exile with Zerubbabel* Ezra 2:2
2 *Esther's cousin* Esth 2:7; 3:2; 9:20; 10:3

MORIAH
land / mountain where Abraham offered Isaac Gen 22:2
threshing floor of Araunah (Ornan) 2 Sam 24:18
site of Temple 2 Chr 3:1

MORNING ***dawn***
was **m,** a fifth day Gen 1:23
Rise early in the **m** Ex 8:20
the **m** stars sang Job 38:7
m or evening sowing Eccl 11:6
the bright **m** star Rev 22:16

MORSEL ***piece of bread***
have eaten my **m** Job 31:17
Better is a dry **m** Prov 17:1
After the **m,** Satan John 13:27

MORTAL ***what eventually dies***
not trust...In **m** man Ps 146:3
life to your **m** bodies Rom 8:11
m...immortality 1 Cor 15:53
in our **m** flesh 2 Cor 4:11

MOSES
birth Ex 2:1-3
in Pharaoh's care Ex 2:5-10
killed an Egyptian Ex 2:11,12
exiled Ex 2:15
called by God Ex 3:1-22
opposed Pharaoh Ex 5:11
crossed Red Sea Ex 14
Ten Commandments Ex 20:1-18
saw Canaan Deut 3:23ff; 34:1ff
death Deut 31:14; 34:5

MOTH ***insect***
crushed before the **m** Job 4:19
The **m** will eat them Is 50:9
like a **m** to Ephraim Hos 5:12
m and rust destroy Matt 6:19

MOTHER
leave...and his **m** Gen 2:24
m of all *the* living Gen 3:20
Honor...and your **m** Ex 20:12
a grief to his **m** Prov 10:1
Contend with your **m** Hos 2:2
When His **m** Mary Matt 1:18
Take...and His **m** Matt 2:13
Who is My **m** Matt 12:48
Honor your...**m** Matt 19:19
Behold, your **m** John 19:27

MOTHER-IN-LAW
who lies with his **m** Deut 27:23
Orpah kissed her **m** Ruth 1:14
m lying sick in bed Matt 8:14

MOTIVES ***attitudes, intentions***
LORD weighs the **m** Prov 16:2
disclose the **m** of 1 Cor 4:5
than from pure **m** Phil 1:17
judges with evil **m** James 2:4
ask with wrong **m** James 4:3

MOUNT (n) ***hill, mountain***
In the **m** of the LORD Gen 22:14
Moses on **M** Sinai Num 3:1
Israel at **M** Carmel 1 Kin 18:19
M Zion which He Ps 78:68
M of Olives...split Zech 14:4

MOUNT (v) ***climb up***
to **m** his chariot 2 Chr 10:18
m up *with* wings Is 40:31
My fury will **m** up Ezek 38:18
m-ed on a donkey Zech 9:9
m-ed on a donkey Matt 21:5

MOUNT OF OLIVES
see **OLIVES, MOUNT OF**

MOUNT ZION
see **ZION**

MOUNTAIN
sacrifice on the **m** Gen 31:54
from His holy **m** Ps 3:4
lift up...to the **m-s** Ps 121:1
lovely on the **m-s** Is 52:7
eat at the **m** shrines Ezek 18:6
m-s will melt Mic 1:4
the **m** will move Zech 14:4
m-s, Fall on us Luke 23:30
withdrew...to the **m** John 6:15
faith...remove **m-s** 1 Cor 13:2

MOURN ***grieve, lament***
m her father and Deut 21:13
David **m-ed**...son 2 Sam 13:37
A time to **m** Eccl 3:4
earth **m-s** *and* withers Is 24:4
comfort all who **m** Is 61:2
Blessed...who **m** Matt 5:4
shall **m** and weep Luke 6:25
Be miserable and **m** James 4:9

MOUSE ***rodent***
the mole, and the **m** Lev 11:29
five golden **mice** 1 Sam 6:4
mice that ravage 1 Sam 6:5

MOUTH
has made man's **m** Ex 4:11
m condemns you Job 15:6
From the **m** of infants Ps 8:2
Let the words of my **m** Ps 19:14
fool's **m** is his ruin Prov 18:7
your **m** is lovely Song 4:3
out of the **m** of God Matt 4:4
confess with your **m** Rom 10:9

MOVE ***change position, stir***
Spirit of God...**m-ing** Gen 1:2
pillar of cloud **m-d** Ex 14:19
I will not be **m-d** Ps 10:6
all the hills **m-d** Jer 4:24
m-d with compassion Mark 1:41
He was deeply **m-d** John 11:33
in Him we live...**m** Acts 17:28
m-d by the...Spirit 2 Pet 1:21

MULE ***animal***
mounted his **m** 2 Sam 13:29
Absalom...on *his* **m** 2 Sam 18:9
ride on the king's **m** 1 Kin 1:44
war horses and **m-s** Ezek 27:14

MULTIPLY ***increase***
Be fruitful and **m** Gen 1:22
the fool **m-ies** words Eccl 10:14
He **m-ies** lies and Hos 12:1
and peace be **m-ied** 2 Pet 1:2

MULTITUDE ***crowd, number***
father of a **m** of Gen 17:4
cover a **m** of sins James 5:20
love covers a **m** of 1 Pet 4:8

MURDER ***premeditated killing***
You shall not **m** Ex 20:13
Whoever commits **m** Matt 5:21
m-ed the prophets Matt 23:31
full of envy, **m** Rom 1:29

MURDERER ***killer***
m shall be put to Num 35:30
m from...beginning John 8:44
this man is a **m** Acts 28:4
no **m** has eternal 1 John 3:15

MUSIC ***harmony, melody***
instruments of **m** 1 Chr 15:16
m to the LORD 2 Chr 7:6
m upon the lyre Ps 92:3
heard **m** and Luke 15:25

MUSICIAN ***skilled in music***
m, a mighty man 1 Sam 16:18

the **m-s** after *them* Ps 68:25
harpists and **m-s** Rev 18:22

MUSTARD *type of plant*
kingdom...like a **m** Matt 13:31
faith the size of a **m** seed Matt 17:20
It is like a **m** seed Luke 13:19

MUTE *silent*
who makes *him* **m** Ex 4:11
I was **m** and silent Ps 39:2
a **m**...man Matt 9:32
and the **m** to speak Mark 7:37
astray to the **m** idols 1 Cor 12:2

MUZZLE *gag*
shall not **m** the ox Deut 25:4
guard...as with a **m** Ps 39:1

MYRIADS *countless*
chariots...are **m** Ps 68:17
m of angels Heb 12:22
number...was **m** Rev 5:11

MYRRH *spice*
aromatic gum...**m** Gen 43:11
Dripping with...**m** Song 5:13
frankincense and **m** Matt 2:11
mixture of **m** and John 19:39

MYRTLE *type of plant*
the **m**, and the olive Is 41:19
among the **m** trees Zech 1:11

MYSTERY *hidden truth, secret*
no **m** baffles you Dan 4:9
God's wisdom in a **m** 1 Cor 2:7
know all **m-ies** 1 Cor 13:2
into the **m** of Christ Eph 3:4
the **m** of the gospel Eph 6:19
the **m** of the faith 1 Tim 3:9

MYTHS *fables*
to pay attention to **m** 1 Tim 1:4
will turn aside to **m** 2 Tim 4:4
attention to Jewish **m** Titus 1:14

N

NAAMAH
1 *daughter of Lamech* Gen 4:22
2 *wife of Solomon* 1 Kin 14:21
3 *town in Judah* Josh 15:41

NAAMAN
1 *son, grandson, and great grandson of Benjamin* Gen 46:21; Num 26:40; 1 Chr 8:7
2 *Ben-hadad's commander* 2 Kin 5:1ff

NABAL
husband of Abigail 1 Sam 25:3ff
refused to help David

NABOTH
owner of a vineyard taken by Ahab 1 Kin 21:1-19

NADAB
1 *son of Aaron* Ex 6:23
2 *king of Israel* 1 Kin 14:20
3 *son of Shammai* 1 Chr 2:28
4 *son of Jehiel* 1 Chr 8:29,30

NAHOR
1 *Abram's grandfather* Gen 11:24ff
2 *brother of Abram* Gen 11:27; 22:23
3 *city in N Mesopotamia* Gen 24:10

NAHUM
1 *prophet* Nah 1:1
2 *ancestor of Christ* Luke 3:25

NAILED (v) *attached*
you **n** to a cross Acts 2:23
n it to the cross Col 2:14

NAILS (n) *finger ends* **or** *pins*
and trim her **n** Deut 21:12
fasten it with **n** Jer 10:4

imprint of the **n** John 20:25

NAIVE *simple, not suspicious*
prudence to the **n** Prov 1:4
n believes everything Prov 14:15
the **n** becomes wise Prov 21:11
goes astray or is **n** Ezek 45:20

NAKED *unclothed*
n and...not ashamed Gen 2:25
n I shall return there Job 1:21
n...you clothed Me Matt 25:36

NAKEDNESS *unclothed*
the **n** of his father Gen 9:22
n of...father's sister Lev 18:12
Your **n**...be uncovered Is 47:3
shame of your **n** Rev 3:18

NAME *designation, title*
man gave **n-s** to all Gen 2:20
takes His **n** in vain Ex 20:7
blot out his **n** Deut 29:20
How majestic is Your **n** Ps 8:1
sing praises to Your **n** Ps 18:49
good **n**...desired Prov 22:1
LORD, that is My **n** Is 42:8
Hallowed be Your **n** Matt 6:9
n-s of the twelve Matt 10:2
such child in My **n** Matt 18:5
n-s are recorded Luke 10:20
will come in My **n** Luke 21:8
baptized in the **n** Acts 2:38
of faith in His **n** Acts 3:16
other **n** under heaven Acts 4:12
n-s are in the book Phil 4:3

NAOMI
woman of Bethlehem Ruth 1:1
Ruth's mother-in-law Ruth 1:4,6

NAPHTALI
1 *son of Jacob* Gen 30:8
2 *tribe / district* Num 13:14; 1 Chr 2:2; Rev 7:6

NARD *fragrant ointment*
henna with **n** plants Song 4:13
perfume of pure **n** John 12:3

NARROW *limited*
stood in a **n** path Num 22:24
Enter through the **n** gate Matt 7:13
the way is **n** Matt 7:14

NATHAN
1 *a son of David* 2 Sam 5:14; Luke 3:31
2 *prophet* 2 Sam 7:2; 12:1ff
3 *son of Attai* 1 Chr 2:36
4 *helped Ezra* Ezra 8:16,17
name of several other individuals

NATHANAEL
disciple of Jesus John 1:49

NATION *government, people*
make you a great **n** Gen 12:2
priests and a holy **n** Ex 19:6
scatter...the **n-s** Lev 26:33
the **n-s** in an uproar Ps 2:1
n-s...fear the name Ps 102:15
N will not lift up sword Is 2:4
sprinkle many **n-s** Is 52:15
glory among the **n-s** Is 66:19
n...rise against **n** Matt 24:7
n not perish John 11:50
men, from every **n** Acts 2:5
tongue...people and **n** Rev 5:9

NATIVE *indigenous*
or a **n** of the land Ex 12:19
Or see his **n** land Jer 22:10
the **n-s** showed us Acts 28:2
n-s saw the creature Acts 28:4

NATURAL *normal*
died a **n** death Ezek 44:31
n man...not accept 1 Cor 2:14

is sown a **n** body 1 Cor 15:44

NATURE *essence*
of the same **n** as you Acts 14:15
n itself teach you 1 Cor 11:14
We are Jews by **n** Gal 2:15
of the divine **n** 2 Pet 1:4

NAZARENE
1 *of Nazareth* John 18:7
2 *follower of Jesus* Acts 24:5

NAZARETH
town of Galilee Matt 2:23
home of Joseph, Mary, and Jesus Luke 4:16; John 1:45

NAZIRITE
1 *one consecrated to God* Num 6:2,19,20
2 *religious vow* Judg 13:5,7; Amos 2:11,12

NEBO
1 *Moabite town* Num 32:38
2 *mountain where Moses viewed promised land* Deut 32:49; 34:1
3 *Babylonian god* Is 46:1
4 *town W of Jordan* Ezra 2:29; Neh 7:33
5 *Jew whose sons married foreign wives* Ezra 10:43

NEBUCHADNEZZAR
king of Babylon 2 Kin 24:1,10
captured Judah 1 Chr 6:15; Ezra 2:1

NEBUZARADAN
Babylonian commander responsible for destruction of Jerusalem and the Temple 2 Kin 25:8ff; Jer 39:9,10

NECK *part of body*
you shall break its **n** Ex 13:13
yoke on your **n** Deut 28:48
stiffened their **n-s** Jer 17:23
risked their own **n-s** Rom 16:4

NECKLACE *neck ornament*
n around his neck Gen 41:42
earrings and **n-s** Num 31:50
pride is their **n** Ps 73:6

NECO *see* **PHARAOH**

NEED *necessity, obligation*
sufficient for his **n** Deut 15:8
ministered to...**n-s** Acts 20:34
n-s of the saints 2 Cor 9:12
supply all your **n-s** Phil 4:19

NEEDLE
the eye of a **n** Matt 19:24
n than for a rich Mark 10:25

NEEDY *destitute, poor*
to your **n** and poor Deut 15:11
a father to the **n** Job 29:16
n will not always be Ps 9:18
the LORD hears the **n** Ps 69:33
n will lie down in Is 14:30

NEGEV
S desert region Gen 12:9; Judg 1:9; Jer 32:44; Zech 7:7

NEGLECT *disregard, ignore*
You **n-ed** the Rock Deut 32:18
who **n-s** discipline Prov 15:32
n so great a salvation Heb 2:3
n to show hospitality Heb 13:2
do not **n** doing good Heb 13:16

NEHEMIAH
1 *Jewish exile* Ezra 2:2; Neh 7:7
2 *son of Azbuk* Neh 3:16
3 *son of Hacaliah* Neh 1:1
rebuilt walls Neh 3:1ff
governor of Jerusalem Neh 8:9

NEIGHBOR *one living nearby*
not covet...**n-'s** wife Ex 20:17

shall love your **n** Lev 19:18
make your **n-s** drink Hab 2:15
love your **n** and Matt 5:43
And who is my **n** Luke 10:29
love your **n** as Gal 5:14

NEPHEW
and Lot his **n** Gen 12:5
Lot, Abram's **n** Gen 14:12

NEPHILIM *people of great stature* Gen 6:4; Num 13:33

NEST
n is set in the cliff Num 24:21
n among the stars Obad 4
birds...*have* **n-s** Matt 8:20

NET *snare*
a **n** for my steps Ps 57:6
an antelope in a **n** Is 51:20
casting a **n** into Matt 4:18
left their **n-s** and Mark 1:18
n *full* of fish John 21:8

NETHINIM *temple servants* Ezra 7:24

NEW *fresh, recent*
nothing **n** under the Eccl 1:9
Will gain **n** strength Is 40:31
a **n** spirit within Ezek 11:19
n wine into old Mark 2:22
A **n** commandment John 13:34
he is a **n** creature 2 Cor 5:17
a **n** and living way Heb 10:20
making all things **n** Rev 21:5

NEWBORN *just born*
like **n** babies, long 1 Pet 2:2

NEWNESS *freshness*
walk in **n** of life Rom 6:4
in **n** of the Spirit Rom 7:6

NEWS *report, tidings*
a day of good **n** 2 Kin 7:9
Good **n** puts fat on Prov 15:30
the **n** about Jesus Matt 14:1
n about Him spread Mark 1:28
n of great joy Luke 2:10
bring good **n** of good Rom 10:15
n of your faith 1 Thess 3:6

NICODEMUS
Pharisee John 3:1,4,9
in Sanhedrin John 7:50; 19:39

NICOLAITANS *sect in Ephesian and Pergamum church* Rev 2:6,15

NICOLAS
deacon, servant Acts 6:1-6
proselyte from Antioch Acts 6:5

NIGHT *darkness*
darkness He called **n** Gen 1:5
pillar of fire by **n** Ex 13:21
meditate...day and **n** Josh 1:8
make **n** into day Job 17:12
The terror by **n** Ps 91:5
At **n** my soul longs Is 26:9
over their flock by **n** Luke 2:8
a thief in the **n** 1 Thess 5:2
tormented day and **n** Rev 20:10

NILE *river of Egypt* Gen 41:1; Ex 1:22; 7:20; Is 23:10

NIMROD
son of Cush Gen 10:8
a mighty hunter Gen 10:9
ruler of Shinar Gen 10:10

NINEVEH
capital of Assyria 2 Kin 19:36
visited by Jonah Jon 1:1ff

NISAN *first month of the Hebrew calendar* Neh 2:1; Esth 3:7

NOAH
1 *son of Lamech* Gen 5:28,29
father of Shem, Ham, Japheth Gen 5:32
built an ark Gen 6:14-22
saved from Flood Gen 6:9; 7:15; 8:1; 8:13
promised by God Gen 9:9-17
2 *daughter of Zelophehad* Num 26:33; 27:1; 36:11

NO-AMON *Egyptian city of Thebes* Nah 3:8

NOBLE *lofty or renowned one*
king's most **n** princes Esth 6:9
speak **n** things Prov 8:6
all the **n-s** of Judah Jer 39:6

NOBLEMAN *of high rank*
the house of the **n** Job 21:28
A **n** went to Luke 19:12

NOISE *loud sound*
You who were full of **n** Is 22:2
Egypt *is but* a big **n** Jer 46:17
from heaven a **n** Acts 2:2

NOMADS *desert wanderers*
n of the desert bow Ps 72:9

NONSENSE *foolishness*
a fool speaks **n** Is 32:6
appeared...as **n** Luke 24:11

NORTH *direction of compass*
stretches out the **n** Job 26:7
Zion *in* the far **n** Ps 48:2
king of the **N** will Dan 11:13
three gates on the **n** Rev 21:13

NOSE *part of face*
the ring on her **n** Gen 24:47
n-s...cannot smell Ps 115:6
My hook in your **n** Is 37:29

NOSTRILS *nose*
breathed into his **n** Gen 2:7
breath of His **n** 2 Sam 22:16
breath of God...my **n** Job 27:3

NOTICE *attention, seen*
take **n** of me Ruth 2:10
not **n** the log Matt 7:3
deeds to be **n-d** by Matt 23:5

NOURISH *feed, sustain*
n-es and cherishes it Eph 5:29
constantly **n-ed** on 1 Tim 4:6
she would be **n-ed** Rev 12:6

NULLIFY *annul, make void*
LORD **n-ies** the counsel Ps 33:10
unbelief will not **n** Rom 3:3
the promise is **n-ied** Rom 4:14
n the grace of God Gal 2:21

NUMBER (n) *group, total*
their **n** according to Num 29:21
the **n** of the stars Ps 147:4
increasing in **n** daily Acts 16:5
his **n** is six hundred Rev 13:18

NUMBER (v) *count, enumerate*
n...by their armies Num 1:3
You **n** my steps Job 14:16
hairs...all **n-ed** Matt 10:30

NUN *father of Joshua* Ex 33:11; Num 14:6; Josh 1:1

NURSE (n) *attendant*
Deborah, Rebekah's **n** Gen 35:8
and call a **n** for you Ex 2:7
n carries a nursing Num 11:12
n in the bedroom 2 Kin 11:2

NURSE (v) *suckle an infant*
Sarah...**n** children Gen 21:7
the child and **n-d** him Ex 2:9
morning to **n** my son 1 Kin 3:21
who are **n-ing** babies in Mark 13:17
breasts...never **n-d** Luke 23:29

O

OAK *type of tree*
by the **o-s** of Mamre Gen 13:18
the diviners' **o** Judg 9:37
o-s of righteousness Is 61:3
strong as the **o-s** Amos 2:9

OAR *pole used in rowing*
no boat with **o-s** will Is 33:21
All who handle...**o** Ezek 27:29
straining at the **o-s** Mark 6:48

OATH *declaration, vow*
confirm the **o** which Deut 9:5
free from the **o** Josh 2:20
make no **o** at all Matt 5:34
priests without an **o** Heb 7:21

OBADIAH
1 *in Ahab's court* 1 Kin 18:3ff
2 *Gadite warrior* 1 Chr 12:8,9
3 *sent to teach* 2 Chr 17:7
4 *Levite, of Merari* 2 Chr 34:12
5 *son of Jehiel* Ezra 8:9
6 *signer of covenant* Neh 10:1,5
7 *prophet* Obad 1
name of five other Old Testament people

OBED
1 *son of Ruth / Boaz* Ruth 4:17
ancestor of Jesus Matt 1:5; Luke 3:32
2 *son of Ephlal* 1 Chr 2:37
3 *warrior* 1 Chr 11:26,47
4 *temple gatekeeper* 1 Chr 26:1,7
5 *father of Azariah* 2 Chr 23:1

OBED-EDOM
1 *a Gittite* 2 Sam 6:10-12
2 *temple musician* 1 Chr 15:21
3 *in charge of Temple vessels* 2 Chr 25:24

OBEDIENCE *submission*
the **o** of the peoples Gen 49:10
pretend **o** to me 2 Sam 22:45
the **o** of the One Rom 5:19
leading to **o** of faith Rom 16:26
in **o** to the truth 1 Pet 1:22

OBEDIENT *willing to obey*
we will be **o** Ex 24:7
o from the heart Rom 6:17
o to the...death Phil 2:8
Children, be **o** to Col 3:20

OBEY *follow commands, orders*
have **o-ed** My voice Gen 22:18
o My voice and keep Ex 19:5
o the LORD your God Deut 27:10
to **o** is better than 1 Sam 15:22
O-ing...His word Ps 103:20
and the sea **o** Him Matt 8:27
o God rather than Acts 5:29
o your parents Eph 6:1
O your leaders Heb 13:17
to **o** Jesus Christ 1 Pet 1:2

OBJECT *implement or goal*
struck...an iron **o** Num 35:16
an **o** of loathing to Ps 88:8
o like a great sheet Acts 10:11
god or **o** of worship 2 Thess 2:4

OBLIGATION *duty*
o toward the LORD Num 32:22
for his daily **o-s** 2 Chr 31:16
under **o**, not to the Rom 8:12
o to keep the...Law Gal 5:3

OBSERVE ***keep or notice***
surely **o** My sabbaths Ex 31:13
o all My statutes Lev 19:37
you may **o** discretion Prov 5:2
the ant...**O** her ways Prov 6:6
O how the lilies Matt 6:28
o-ing the traditions Mark 7:3
the word...**o** it Luke 11:28
o days and months Gal 4:10

OBSTACLE ***hindrance***
Remove *every* **o** out of Is 57:14
an **o** or a stumbling Rom 14:13

OBSTINATE ***stubborn***
you are an **o** people Ex 33:3
made his heart **o** Deut 2:30
Israel is...**o** Ezek 3:7
disobedient and **o** Rom 10:21

OBTAIN ***get possession of***
o children through Gen 16:2
finds a wife...**o-s** Prov 18:22
may **o** eternal life Matt 19:16
o the gift of God Acts 8:20
o-ed an inheritance Eph 1:11
for **o-ing** salvation 1 Thess 5:9

OCCUR ***happen, take place***
this sign will **o** Ex 8:23
will **o** at the final Dan 8:19
otherwise a riot might **o** Matt 26:5
predestined to **o** Acts 4:28

ODED
1 *father of Azariah* 2 Chr 15:1,8
2 *prophet* 2 Chr 28:9

ODIOUS ***offensive***
o in Pharaoh's sight Ex 5:21
o to the Philistines 1 Sam 13:4

OFFEND ***insult or violate***
I will not **o** *anymore* Job 34:31
A brother **o-ed** *is* Prov 18:19
Pharisees were **o-ed** Matt 15:12

OFFENSE ***anger or transgression***
of my *own* **o-s** Gen 41:9
they took **o** at Him Matt 13:57
of the **o** of Adam Rom 5:14
and a rock of **o** 1 Pet 2:8

OFFER (v) ***give, present***
o him...as a burnt Gen 22:2
O to God a sacrifice Ps 50:14
my mouth **o-s** praises Ps 63:5
o both gifts and Heb 5:1
o-ed Himself Heb 9:14
prayer **o-ed** in faith James 5:15
o...spiritual sacrifices 1 Pet 2:5

OFFERING (n) ***contribution***
freewill **o** to the LORD Ex 35:29
o of first fruits Lev 2:12
your worthless **o-s** Is 1:13
presenting your **o** Matt 5:23
any **o** for sin Heb 10:18

OFFERINGS
1 **Burnt Offering** Gen 22:13; Lev 1:17
2 **Drink Offering** Phil 2:17; 2 Tim 4:6
also **Libation**
3 **Freewill Offering** Ex 35:29; Lev 7:16
4 **Grain Offering** Lev 9:4; Josh 22:29
also **Meal Offering**
5 **Guilt Offering** Lev 5:6; Num 6:12
6 **Heave Offering** Ex 29:27,28
7 **Libation Offering** Num 6:15,17; 28:9,10
also **Drink Offering**
8 **Meal Offering** 2 Kin 16:15; Ps 40:6
also **Grain Offering**
9 **Ordination Offering** Lev 8:28,31
10 **Peace Offering** Lev 4:31; Num 6:14
11 **Sin Offering** Ex 29:14; Ezek 46:20
12 **Thank Offering** 2 Chr 33:16; Jer 33:11
13 **Votive Offering** Deut 12:26; 23:18
14 **Wave Offering** Lev 14:12; Num 18:18

OFFICE ***function or position***
wield the staff of **o** Judg 5:14
priests in their **o-s** 2 Chr 35:2
to the **o** of overseer 1 Tim 3:1

OFFICIAL ***one in authority***
o-s in the palace 2 Kin 20:18
o of the synagogue Luke 8:41

OFFSPRING ***descendants***
o in place of Abel Gen 4:25
bring forth **o** from Is 65:9

OG
Amorite king Num 21:33; Deut 3:4; Josh 12:4

OHOLAH
symbolic for Samaria Ezek 23:4

OHOLIBAH
symbolic for Jerusalem Ezek 23:4

OHOLIBAMAH
1 *wife of Esau* Gen 36:2-25
2 *descendant of Esau* Gen 36:41

OIL
o for lighting Ex 25:6
anointed my head...**o** Ps 23:5
the **o** of joy Ps 45:7
words...softer than **o** Ps 55:21
prudent took **o** in Matt 25:4
not anoint...with **o** Luke 7:46

OINTMENT ***salve***
a jar of **o** Job 41:31
anointed...with **o** John 11:2

OLD ***aged, obsolete***
buried at a...**o** age Gen 15:15
too **o** to have a Ruth 1:12
honor of **o** men Prov 20:29
o men will dream Joel 2:28
wine into **o** wineskins Matt 9:17
be born when he is **o** John 3:4
o self was crucified Rom 6:6
o things passed away 2 Cor 5:17
men of **o** gained Heb 11:2
serpent of **o**...devil Rev 12:9

OLD GATE *see* **GATES OF JERUSALEM**

OLIVE ***tree or fruit***
freshly picked **o** leaf Gen 8:11
land of **o** oil and Deut 8:8
cherubim of **o** wood 1 Kin 6:23
children like **o** plants Ps 128:3

OLIVES, MOUNT OF
mountain E of Jerusalem 2 Sam 15:30; Zech 14:4; Matt 24:3; Mark 11:1
place where Jesus prayed Matt 26:30; Luke 22:39-41

OMEGA
last letter of Gr. alphabet Rev 1:8
title of Jesus Christ Rev 21:6
expresses eternalness of God Rev 22:13

OMEN ***foretells a future event***
who interprets **o-s** Deut 18:10
took this as an **o** 1 Kin 20:33

OMER ***dry measure***
take an **o** apiece Ex 16:16
o is a tenth of an Ex 16:36

OMRI
1 *king of Israel* 1 Kin 16:22ff
2 *a Benjamite* 1 Chr 7:8
3 *line of Perez* 1 Chr 9:4
4 *son of Michael* 1 Chr 27:18

ON
1 *Egyptian city* Gen 41:45,50; 46:20
see also **HELIOPOLIS**
2 *son of Peleth* Num 16:1

ONE ***single unit***
shall become **o** flesh Gen 2:24
God, the LORD is **o** Deut 6:4
Holy **O** of Israel Ps 71:22
His chosen **o-s** Ps 105:6
Are You the...**O** Matt 11:3
joy...over **o** sinner Luke 15:7
I...Father are **o** John 10:30
they may all be **o** John 17:21
o body in Christ Rom 12:5
o died for all 2 Cor 5:14
o Lord, **o** faith Eph 4:5
o God...**o** mediator 1 Tim 2:5
husband of **o** wife 1 Tim 3:2

ONESIMUS
Christian slave of Philemon Col 4:9; Philem 10

ONESIPHORUS
Ephesian Christian 2 Tim 1:16; 4:19

ONYX ***precious stone***
bdellium and the **o** Gen 2:12
o, and the jasper Ezek 28:13

OPEN (adj) ***not shut, exposed***
throat is an **o** grave Ps 5:9
Better is **o** rebuke Prov 27:5
before you an **o** door Rev 3:8

OPEN (v) ***expose, free, unfasten***
eyes will be **o-ed** Gen 3:5
Ezra **o-ed** the book Neh 8:5
He **o-s** their ear Job 36:10
O Lord, **o** my lips Ps 51:15
O my eyes, that I Ps 119:18
To **o** blind eyes Is 42:7
o...windows of heaven Mal 3:10
knock...will be **o-ed** Matt 7:7
o-ed a door of faith Acts 14:27
and **o-s** the door Rev 3:20
worthy to **o** the book Rev 5:2

OPHEL
citadel on S slope of Temple Mount in Jerusalem 2 Chr 27:3; 33:14; Neh 3:27
home of temple servants (Nethinim) Neh 3:26; 11:21

OPHIR
1 *son of Joktan* Gen 10:29
2 *gold producing region of SW Arabia* 1 Kin 10:11; Job 22:24

OPPONENT ***adversary***
friends...with your **o** Matt 5:25
protection from my **o** Luke 18:3

OPPORTUNITY ***occasion***
o to betray Jesus Matt 26:16
o for your testimony Luke 21:13
an **o** for the flesh Gal 5:13
not give...devil an **o** Eph 4:27

OPPOSE ***contend, resist***
o the Prince of Dan 8:25
o-d the ordinance of Rom 13:2
men also **o** the truth 2 Tim 3:8
God is **o-d** to the James 4:6

OPPOSITION ***hostility***
you...know My **o** Num 14:34
these are in **o** Gal 5:17
gospel...much **o** 1 Thess 2:2

OPPRESS (v) ***trouble, tyrannize***
enslaved and **o-ed** Gen 15:13
Egyptians are **o-ing** Ex 3:9
not **o** your neighbor Lev 19:13
woman **o-ed** in 1 Sam 1:15
do not **o** the widow Zech 7:10
healing all...**o-ed** Acts 10:38
the rich who **o** you James 2:6

OPPRESSED (n) ***afflicted***
stronghold for the **o** Ps 9:9

justice for the **o** Ps 146:7
let the **o** go free Is 58:6
devour...**o** in secret Hab 3:14
vengeance for the **o** Acts 7:24

OPPRESSION *affliction*
Do not trust in **o** Ps 62:10
o makes a...man mad Eccl 7:7
and water of **o** Is 30:20
o of My people Acts 7:34

OPPRESSOR *one who afflicts*
And crush the **o** Ps 72:4
a great **o** lacks Prov 28:16
punish all their **o-s** Jer 30:20

ORACLE *revelation*
The **o** of Balaam Num 24:3
o concerning Babylon Is 13:1
the **o** of the LORD Jer 23:33
and misleading **o-s** Lam 2:14
entrusted with the **o-s** Rom 3:2

ORDAIN *invest, set apart*
anoint...and **o** them Ex 28:41
o Aaron and his sons Ex 29:9
o-ed His covenant Ps 111:9
law as **o-ed** by angels Acts 7:53

ORDEAL *difficulty, trial*
great **o** of affliction 2 Cor 8:2
at the fiery **o** 1 Pet 4:12

ORDER (n) *arrangement*
Set your house in **o** 2 Kin 20:1
fixed **o** of the moon Jer 31:35
the **o** of Melchizedek Heb 5:6

ORDER (v) *command or request*
I will **o** *my prayer* Ps 5:3
o-ed him to tell no Luke 5:14
confidence...to **o** you Philem 8

ORDINANCE *statute*
o of the Passover Ex 12:43
they rejected My **o-s** Lev 26:43
o-s of the heavens Job 38:33
opposed the **o** of God Rom 13:2

ORDINATION
Aaron's ram of **o** Ex 29:26
and the **o** offering Lev 7:37
period of your **o** Lev 8:33

ORDINATION OFFERING
see **OFFERINGS**

ORIGIN *beginning, source*
of Jewish **o** Esth 6:13
o is from antiquity Is 23:7
Your **o** and your Ezek 16:3

ORIGINATE *bring into being*
not **o** from woman 1 Cor 11:8
all things **o**...God 1 Cor 11:12

ORION
constellation of stars Job 9:9; 38:31; Amos 5:8

ORNAMENT *decoration*
put off your **o-s** Ex 33:5
o of fine gold Prov 25:12
beauty of His **o-s** Ezek 7:20

ORNAN
Jebusite owner of threshing floor on Mount Moriah 1 Chr 21:15,18
sells threshing floor to David for altar and temple 1 Chr 21:25,28
see also **ARAUNAH**

ORPAH
daughter-in-law of Naomi Ruth 1:4,14

ORPHAN *fatherless child*
not afflict any...**o** Ex 22:22
justice for the **o** Deut 10:18
helper of the **o** Ps 10:14
may plunder the **o-s** Is 10:2
Leave...**o-s** behind Jer 49:11
visit **o-s** and widows James 1:27

OSTRICH *bird*
the **o** and the owl Lev 11:16
a companion of **o-es** Job 30:29
cruel Like **o-es** Lam 4:3
mourning like the **o-es** Mic 1:8

OTHNIEL
son of Kenaz Josh 15:17
brother or nephew of Caleb Judg 1:13; 3:11

OUTBURST *sudden release*
great **o** of anger Deut 29:24
o of anger I hid My Is 54:8
jealousy, **o-s** of anger Gal 5:20

OUTCAST *rejected*
the **o-s** of Israel Ps 147:2
Hide the **o-s** Is 16:3
called you an **o** Jer 30:17
o-s from...synagogue John 16:2

OUTCRY *strong cry or protest*
no **o** in our streets Ps 144:14
o is heard among the Jer 50:46
a *single* **o** arose Acts 19:34

OUTSIDER *stranger*
o may not come near Num 18:4
toward **o-s** 1 Thess 4:12

OUTSTRETCHED *extended*
redeem...with an **o** arm Ex 6:6
war...with an **o** hand Jer 21:5

OUTWARD *external*
at the **o** appearance 1 Sam 16:7
is **o** in the flesh Rom 2:28

OVEN *baking, cooking vessel*
appeared a...**o** Gen 15:17
make them as a fiery **o** Ps 21:9

OVERCOME *conquer, master*
a man **o** with wine Jer 23:9
I have **o** the world John 16:33
but **o** evil with good Rom 12:21
have **o** the evil one 1 John 2:13
who **o-s** will inherit Rev 21:7

OVERFLOW *flood, inundate*
My cup **o-s** Ps 23:5
waters will **o** the Is 28:17
I am **o-ing** with joy 2 Cor 7:4
o-ing with gratitude Col 2:7

OVERLAID *decorate, spread*
o...with gold 1 Kin 6:28
vessel **o** with silver Prov 26:23
o with gold...silver Hab 2:19

OVERLOOK *ignore or view*
o a transgression Prov 19:11
widows were...**o-ed** Acts 6:1

OVERPOWER *subdue*
deceive you and **o** you Obad 7
Hades will not **o** Matt 16:18
attacks him and **o-s** Luke 11:22

OVERSEER *director, leader*
o in the house of Jer 29:26
the **o-s** and deacons Phil 1:1
the office of **o** 1 Tim 3:1
o...above reproach Titus 1:7

OVERSHADOW *engulf, obscure*
Most High...**o** you Luke 1:35
o-ing the mercy seat Heb 9:5

OVERSIGHT *supervision*
o of the house of 2 Kin 12:11
having **o** at...gates Ezek 44:11
exercising **o** not 1 Pet 5:2

OVERWHELM *crush, overcome*
humiliation has **o-ed** Ps 44:15
darkness will **o** me Ps 139:11
my spirit was **o-ed** Ps 142:3
o-ed by...sorrow 2 Cor 2:7

OWE *be indebted*
Pay...what you **o** Matt 18:28
O nothing to anyone Rom 13:8
that you **o** to me Philem 19

OWL *bird*
the **o,** the sea gull Deut 14:15
o of the waste places Ps 102:6
houses...full of **o-s** Is 13:21

OWN (adj) *belonging to*
man in His **o** image Gen 1:27
led...His **o** people Ps 78:52
calls his **o** sheep John 10:3
in his **o** language Acts 2:6

OWN (n) *belonging to*
He came to His **o** John 1:11
provide for his **o** 1 Tim 5:8

OWNER *possessor*
restitution to its **o** Ex 22:12
when the **o**...comes Matt 21:40
who were **o-s** of land Acts 4:34

OX *bull used as draft animal*
oxen and donkeys Gen 12:16
servant or his **o** Ex 20:17
horns of the wild **oxen** Ps 22:21
An **o** knows its owner Is 1:3
not muzzle the **o** 1 Tim 5:18

P

PACE *step, stride*
the **p** of the cattle Gen 33:14
not slow down the **p** 2 Kin 4:24

PACT *agreement*
Sheol we...made a **p** Is 28:15
p with Sheol will Is 28:18

PADDAN-ARAM
NW Mesopotamia Gen 25:20
home of Laban Gen 28:5
birthplace of most of Jacob's sons Gen 35:22-26

PAHATH-MOAB
1 *head of Jewish clan* Ezra 2:6
2 *Jewish clan* Neh 3:11

PAIN *discomfort, hurt*
multiply Your **p** Gen 3:16
p-s came upon her 1 Sam 4:19
rejoice in unsparing **p** Job 6:10
rest from your **p** Is 14:3
Your **p** is incurable Jer 30:15
bring **p** to my soul Lam 3:51
no longer be...**p** Rev 21:4

PAINFUL *hurting*
p are honest words Job 6:25
the bread of **p** labors Ps 127:2

PALACE *royal residence*
build...royal **p** 2 Chr 2:12
to the king's **p** Esth 2:8
Out of ivory **p-s** Ps 45:8
A **p** of strangers Is 25:2
luxury...royal **p-s** Luke 7:25

PALLET *bed, mat*
they let down the **p** Mark 2:4
pick up your **p** and Mark 2:9

PALM *type of tree*
the city of **p** trees Deut 34:3
flourish like the **p** Ps 92:12
branches of the **p** John 12:13

PALTI
1 *son of Raphu* Num 13:9

spy for Israel Num 13:2
2 *Michal's husband* 1 Sam 25:44

PAMPHYLIA
Roman province in Asia Minor Acts 2:10; 13:13; 14:24

PANIC ***fear***
P seized them there Ps 48:6
P and pitfall have Lam 3:47
great **p**...will fall Zech 14:13

PANT ***breathe rapidly***
deer **p-s** for the water Ps 42:1
my soul **p-s** for You Ps 42:1
I will both gasp and **p** Is 42:14
beasts...**p** for You Joel 1:20

PAPHOS
city on Cyprus Acts 13:6,13

PAPYRUS ***reed plant***
p...without a marsh Job 8:11
Even in **p** vessels Is 18:2

PARABLE ***story for illustration***
speak a **p** to Ezek 17:2
p of the sower Matt 13:18
heard His **p-s** Matt 21:45
p from the fig tree Mark 13:28
spoke by way of a **p** Luke 8:4

PARADISE
abode of the righteous dead Luke 23:43; 2 Cor 12:4; Rev 2:7
see also **ABRAHAM'S BOSOM**

PARALYTIC
said to the **p**, Get up Matt 9:6
p, carried by four Mark 2:3

PARAN
wilderness area in Sinai Gen 21:21; Num 13:3
place of Israelite wanderings and encampments Num 12:16
mountain in Sinai Deut 33:2

PARDON ***forgive, release***
he will not **p** your Ex 23:21
May the...LORD **p** 2 Chr 30:18
O LORD, **P** my iniquity Ps 25:11
He will abundantly **p** Is 55:7
p, and you will be Luke 6:37

PARENTS ***father and mother***
rise up against **p** Matt 10:21
left house or...**p** Luke 18:29
evil, disobedient to **p** Rom 1:30
Children, obey your **p** Eph 6:1
disobedient to **p** 2 Tim 3:2

PART ***portion***
God...have no **p** in 2 Chr 19:7
formed my inward **p-s** Ps 139:13
have no **p** with Me John 13:8
no **p** or portion in Acts 8:21
prophesy in **p** 1 Cor 13:9
now I know in **p** 1 Cor 13:12
tongue is a small **p** James 3:5

PARTAKERS ***participators***
do not be **p** with Eph 5:7
become **p** of Christ Heb 3:14
p of the Holy Spirit Heb 6:4
p of *the* divine nature 2 Pet 1:4

PARTIAL ***favoring***
not be **p** to the poor Lev 19:15
you shall not be **p** Deut 16:19
now be **p** to no one Job 32:21
You are not **p** Matt 22:16

PARTIALITY ***favoritism***
show **p** in judgment Deut 1:17
p is not good Prov 28:21
God shows no **p** Gal 2:6

PARTICIPATE ***take part***
not **p**...deeds of Eph 5:11
p-s in his evil deeds 2 John 11
will not **p** in her sins Rev 18:4

PARTNER ***comrade***
is a **p** with a thief Prov 29:24
been **p-s** with them Matt 23:30
regard me a **p** Philem 17

PASS ***proceed***
LORD will **p** over the Ex 12:23
My glory is **p-ing** by Ex 33:22
heaven and earth **p** Matt 5:18
words will not **p** Matt 24:35
this cup **p** from Me Matt 26:39
p-ed out of death John 5:24
old things **p-ed** away 2 Cor 5:17
first earth **p-ed** away Rev 21:1

PASSION ***desire, lust***
p is rottenness to Prov 14:30
over to degrading **p-s** Rom 1:26
flesh with its **p-s** Gal 5:24
dead to...**p** Col 3:5
not in lustful **p** 1 Thess 4:5

PASSOVER
Israel's firstborn protected from the plague of death prior to the exodus from Egypt Ex 12:1-30
Feast commemorating Israelite exodus and protection from death Ex 12:42,43; Lev 23:5; Num 9:2,12,14; Matt 26:2,18; John 19:14; Acts 12:4
see also **FEASTS**

PASTORS ***shepherds of people***
and some *as* **p** Eph 4:11

PASTURE (n) ***grazing field***
lie down in green **p-s** Ps 23:2
sheep of Your **p** Ps 79:13

PASTURE (v) ***feed, graze***
Moses...**p-ing** the flock Ex 3:1
They will **p** on it Zeph 2:7
So I **p-d** the flock Zech 11:7

PATCH ***mending cloth***
p of unshrunk cloth Matt 9:16
p pulls away from it Mark 2:21

PATH ***way***
snake in the **p** Gen 49:17
the **p** of life Ps 16:11
a light to my **p** Ps 119:105
p of the upright is Prov 15:19
Make His **p-s** straight Matt 3:3

PATHROS
upper Egypt Is 11:11; Jer 44:1,15; Ezek 29:14; 30:14

PATIENCE ***endurance***
try the **p** of men Is 7:13
in **p**, in kindness 2 Cor 6:6
love, joy, peace, **p** Gal 5:22
exhort, with great **p** 2 Tim 4:2
endure it with **p** 1 Pet 2:20

PATIENT ***bearing, enduring***
Love is **p**, love is 1 Cor 13:4
p when wronged 2 Tim 2:24
Lord...is **p** toward 2 Pet 3:9

PATMOS
Aegean island, site of John's exile Rev 1:9

PATRIARCH ***father of clan***
regarding the **p** David Acts 2:29
the twelve **p-s** Acts 7:8
Abraham, the **p**, gave Heb 7:4

PATTERN ***model, plan***
fixed **p-s** of heaven Jer 33:25
walk according to...**p** Phil 3:17

PAUL
heritage Acts 21:39; 22:3; Phil 3:5
persecuted believers Acts 7:58; 8:1,3; 9:1,2; 1 Cor 15:9
conversion and call Acts 9:1-19
name changed Acts 13:9
Jerusalem council Acts 15:2-6
missionary journeys Acts 13:1ff; 15:36ff; 18:23ff
apostolic defense Acts 11:5ff; Gal 1:13ff
arrest and imprisonment Acts 21:33; 22:24-28:31
defense Acts 22:1ff; 24:10ff; 25:10,11; 26:2ff
final journey to Rome Acts 27,28
see also **SAUL**

PAULUS, SERGIUS
proconsul of Cyprus Acts 13:7

PAVEMENT ***paved road***
on a **p** of stone 2 Kin 16:17
mosaic **p** of porphyry Esth 1:6
place called The **P** John 19:13

PAY ***give what is due***
thief...**p** double Ex 22:7
P You my vows Ps 66:13
P back what you Matt 18:28
Never **p** back evil Rom 12:17
p the penalty 2 Thess 1:9

PEACE ***calmness, tranquility***
grant **p** in the land Lev 26:6
made **p** with David 1 Chr 19:19
Seek **p**, and pursue Ps 34:14
for the **p** of Jerusalem Ps 122:6
all her paths are **p** Prov 3:17
a time for **p** Eccl 3:8
Prince of **P** Is 9:6
p...like a river Is 66:12
have withdrawn My **p** Jer 16:5
not come to bring **p** Matt 10:34
on earth **p** among Luke 2:14
P I leave with you John 14:27
we have **p** with God Rom 5:1
love, joy, **p** Gal 5:22
He Himself is our **p** Eph 2:14
gospel of **p** Eph 6:15
p of God...surpasses Phil 4:7
p through the blood Col 1:20
take **p** from the earth Rev 6:4

PEACEABLE
gentle, **p**, free from 1 Tim 3:3
be **p**, gentle Titus 3:2

PEACEMAKERS
Blessed are the **p** Matt 5:9

PEACE OFFERING *see* **OFFERINGS**

PEARL ***precious gem***
wisdom is above...**p-s** Job 28:18
p-s before swine Matt 7:6
one **p** of great value Matt 13:46

PEKAH
king of Israel 2 Kin 15:25ff

PEKAHIAH
king of Israel 2 Kin 15:22,23

PELEG
son of Eber Gen 10:25
descendant of Shem Gen 11:18

PENALTY ***punishment***
you will bear the **p** Ezek 23:49
pay the **p** of eternal 2 Thess 1:9
received a just **p** Heb 2:2

PENIEL
where Jacob wrestled with God Gen 32:30
see also **PENUEL**

PENTECOST
Jewish feast held 50 days after Passover Acts 20:16; 1 Cor 16:8

coming of the Holy Spirit Acts 2:1
see also **FEASTS**

PENUEL
1 *tower destroyed* Judg 8:17
rebuilt 1 Kin 12:25
see also **PENIEL**
2 *father of Gedor* 1 Chr 4:4
3 *son of Shashak* 1 Chr 8:25

PEOPLE *group, nation*
they are one **p** Gen 11:6
Let My **p** go Ex 5:1
You are an obstinate **p** Ex 33:5
blessed above all **p-s** Deut 7:14
Forgive Your **p** Israel Deut 21:8
LORD loves His **p** 2 Chr 2:11
p who are called by 2 Chr 7:14
restores His captive **p** Ps 14:7
We are His **p** Ps 100:3
LORD will judge His **p** Ps 135:14
p are unrestrained Prov 29:18
p whom I formed Is 43:21
do **p** say that I am Mark 8:27
they feared the **p** Luke 20:19
die for the **p** John 11:50
not rejected His **p** Rom 11:2
every tribe and **p** Rev 13:7

PEOR
1 *mountain in Moab* Num 23:28
2 *Moabite deity* Num 25:3

PERCEIVE *be aware, discern*
p-d all the wisdom 1 Kin 10:4
listening, but do not **p** Is 6:9
p-ing in Himself Mark 5:30
p with their heart John 12:40

PERDITION *damnation*
the son of **p** John 17:12

PEREZ
son of Judah Gen 38:29

PERFECT (adj) *flawless*
His work is **p** Deut 32:4
law of the LORD is **p** Ps 19:7
heavenly Father is **p** Matt 5:48
p bond of unity Col 3:14
be **p** and complete James 1:4
p love casts out 1 John 4:18

PERFECTED *completed*
is **p** in weakness 2 Cor 12:9
love is **p** with us 1 John 4:17

PERFORM *carry out*
I will **p** miracles Ex 34:10
p My judgments Lev 18:4
p-s righteous deeds Ps 103:6
p a miracle in My Mark 9:39
John **p-ed** no sign John 10:41
p-ing great wonders Acts 6:8

PERFUME *fragrant oil*
and **p** make the heart Prov 27:9
instead of sweet **p** Is 3:24
p on My body Matt 26:12
anointed...with **p** Luke 7:46
prepared...**p-s** Luke 23:56

PERGA
city in Asia Minor Acts 13:13

PERGAMUM
city in Asia Minor Rev 1:11
early church Rev 2:12

PERISH *be destroyed*
we **p**, we are dying Num 17:12
weapons...**p-ed** 2 Sam 1:27
if I **p**, I **p** Esth 4:16
hope...will **p** Job 8:13
the wicked will **p** Ps 1:6
rod of his fury will **p** Prov 22:8
our hope has **p-ed** Ezek 37:11
little ones **p** Matt 18:14
p by the sword Matt 26:52
p, but have eternal John 3:16
for any to **p** 2 Pet 3:9

PERIZZITES
early Canaanite tribe Gen 34:30; Ex 23:23; Deut 7:1

PERMANENT *lasting*
it is a **p** ordinance Lev 6:18
p right of redemption Lev 25:32
use them as **p** slaves Lev 25:46
p home for the ark 1 Chr 28:2

PERMISSION *consent*
p they had from Cyrus Ezra 3:7
Jesus gave them **p** Mark 5:13
he had given him **p** Acts 21:40

PERMIT *allow*
not **p-ting**...demons Mark 1:34
p the children Mark 10:14
Spirit...did not **p** Acts 16:7
if the Lord **p-s** 1 Cor 16:7

PERPETUAL *lasting*
p incense before the Ex 30:8
as a **p** covenant Ex 31:16
for a **p** priesthood Ex 40:15
may sleep a **p** sleep Jer 51:39

PERSECUTE *afflict, oppress*
Why do you **p** me Job 19:22
has **p-d** my soul Ps 143:3
pray for those who **p** Matt 5:44
p you in one city Matt 10:23
why are you **p-ing** Me Acts 9:4
used to **p** the church Gal 1:13

PERSECUTION *oppression*
p arises because of Mark 4:17
p began against the Acts 8:1
a **p** against Paul Acts 13:50
distress, or **p**, or Rom 8:35

PERSEVERANCE *persistence*
by **p** in doing good Rom 2:7
tribulation brings...**p** Rom 5:3
for your **p** and faith 2 Thess 1:4
p of the saints Rev 14:12

PERSIA
ancient Near Eastern empire 2 Chr 36:20; Ezra 1:1; Esth 1:3; Ezek 27:10; Dan 8:20

PERSON *human being*
If a **p** sins Lev 4:2
hungry **p** unsatisfied Is 32:6
p...be in subjection Rom 13:1
hidden **p** of the heart 1 Pet 3:4

PERSUADE *convince, prevail on*
a ruler may be **p-d** Prov 25:15
trying to **p** Jews and Acts 18:4
p-s men to worship Acts 18:13
you will **p** me Acts 26:28

PERSUASIVE *convincing*
p words of wisdom 1 Cor 2:4
delude you with **p** Col 2:4

PERVERSE *corrupt*
a **p** and crooked Deut 32:5
A **p** heart shall depart Ps 101:4
mind will utter **p** Prov 23:33
and **p** generation Phil 2:15

PERVERT *distort, misdirect*
not **p** the justice Ex 23:6
Does God **p** justice Job 8:3
have **p-ed** their way Jer 3:21

PESTILENCE *epidemic, plague*
LORD sent a **p** 2 Sam 24:15
sword, famine, and **p** Jer 27:13
p and mourning and Rev 18:8

PETER
heritage and occupation Matt 4:18; John 1:42,44
called by Jesus Matt 1:17; Mark 3:16; Luke 5:1ff
names: Cephas, Simon Matt 4:18; Mark 3:16; John 1:42; Acts 15:14
walked on water Matt 14:28ff
confessed Jesus as Messiah Matt 16:16; Luke 9:20
on mount of Transfiguration Matt 17:1ff; Mark 9:2ff
denied Jesus Matt 26:70; Mark 14:70; Luke 22:58
at Pentecost Acts 2
apostle of Christ Gal 2:8; 1 Pet 1:1; 2 Pet 1:1

PETITION *request, supplication*
God...grant your **p** 1 Sam 1:17
p to any god or man Dan 6:7
p-s...be made 1 Tim 2:1

PHARAOH *title of Egyptian kings*
1 **Pharaoh,** time of Abraham Gen 12:15ff
2 **Pharaoh,** time of Joseph Gen 37:36; 39:1-50:26
3 **Pharaoh,** during oppression Ex 1:8-2:23
4 **Pharaoh,** during the Exodus Ex 5:1-12:41
5 **Pharaoh,** father of Bithiah 1 Chr 4:17
6 **Pharaoh,** time of David 1 Kin 11:14ff
7 **Pharaoh,** whose daughter married Solomon 1 Kin 3:1; 7:8; 9:16
8 **Shishak,** time of Rehoboam 1 Kin 14:25,26
9 **So,** time of Hoshea 2 Kin 17:4
10 **Tirhakah,** time of Hezekiah 2 Kin 19:9; Is 37:9
11 **Neco,** slew Josiah 2 Kin 23:29,33,34
12 **Hophra,** subject of prophecy Jer 44:30

PHARISEES
Jewish religious party Matt 3:7; 23:13; Mark 2:18; 7:3; Luke 11:42; 16:14; John 3:1; 11:47

PHARPAR
river of Damascus 2 Kin 5:12

PHILADELPHIA
city in Asia Minor Rev 1:11
early church Rev 3:7

PHILEMON
owner of Onesimus Philem 1
friend of Paul

PHILIP
1 *Herod Philip I, son of Herod the Great* Mark 6:17
see also **HEROD**
2 *Herod Philip II, son of Herod the Great* Luke 3:1
see also **HEROD**
3 *Philip the apostle* Matt 10:3; Mark 3:18; Luke 6:14; John 1:43ff; Acts 1:13
4 *Philip the evangelist* Acts 6:5; 8:5,29; 21:8

PHILIPPI
Macedonian city Acts 16:12; 20:6

PHILIPPIANS
people of Philippi Phil 4:15

PHILISTIA
coastal area of SW Palestine Ex 15:14; Ps 60:8; 83:7; Joel 3:4

PHILISTINES
people of Philistia Gen 10:14; Josh 13:2; Judg 13:1; 1 Sam 4:2

PHINEHAS
1 *grandson of Aaron* Num 25:7; 31:6; Judg 20:28
2 *son of Eli* 1 Sam 1:3; 4:4,11
3 *father of a priest* Ezra 8:33

PHOEBE
Cenchrea (Corinth) deaconess commended by Paul Rom 16:1

PHOENICIA
coastal land N of land of Israel Acts 11:19; 21:2
visited by Paul Acts 15:3

PHRYGIA
Asia Minor province Acts 2:10
visited by Paul Acts 16:6; 18:23

PHYGELUS
Asian Christian, deserted Paul 2 Tim 1:15

PHYLACTERIES ***prayer bands***
as **p** on your forehead Ex 13:16
they broaden their **p** Matt 23:5
see also **FRONTALS**

PHYSICIAN
all worthless **p-s** Job 13:4
healthy who need a **p** Matt 9:12
P, heal yourself Luke 4:23
Luke, the beloved **p** Col 4:14

PIECE ***part, portion***
dip your **p** of bread Ruth 2:14
thirty **p-s** of silver Matt 27:3
gave Him a **p**...fish Luke 24:42
woven in one **p** John 19:23

PIERCE ***penetrate***
master shall **p** his ear Ex 21:6
They **p-d** my hands Ps 22:16
He was **p-d** through Is 53:5
whom they have **p-d** Zech 12:10
sword will **p**...soul Luke 2:35
p-d His side John 19:34
p-d to the heart Acts 2:37

PIETY ***reverence***
learn to practice **p** 1 Tim 5:4
because of His **p** Heb 5:7

PILATE, PONTIUS
Roman governor of Judea Matt 27:2; Luke 3:1
presided at Jesus' trial Matt 27:11ff; Mark 15:2ff; Luke 23:1ff; John 18:28-38
warned by his wife Matt 27:19
orders Jesus' crucifixion Matt 27:24ff; Mark 15:15; Luke 23:24,25; John 19:15,16

PILLAR ***column*** **or** ***memorial***
became a **p** of salt Gen 19:26
p of fire by night Ex 13:21
set up...a **p** 2 Sam 18:18
hewn...her seven **p-s** Prov 9:1
feet like **p-s** of fire Rev 10:1

PILOT ***steersman***
sailors, and your **p-s** Ezek 27:27
the **p** and...captain Acts 27:11
inclination of the **p** James 3:4

PINION ***wing***
p and plumage of Job 39:13
cover you with His **p-s** Ps 91:4

PINNACLE ***highest point***
had Him...on the **p** Matt 4:5
p of the temple Luke 4:9

PISGAH
mountain height in Moab Num 21:20; Josh 13:20

PISHON
river of Eden Gen 2:11

PISIDIA / PISIDIAN
district of Asia Minor Acts 13:14; 14:24

PIT ***deep hole, dungeon***
full of tar **p-s** Gen 14:10
Joseph...not in the **p** Gen 37:29
redeems...from the **p** Ps 103:4
harlot is a deep **p** Prov 23:27
silenced me in the **p** Lam 3:53
to **p-s** of darkness 2 Pet 2:4
the bottomless **p** Rev 9:1

PITCH (n) ***tar***
inside and out with **p** Gen 6:14
covered it over...**p** Ex 2:3

PITCH (v) ***set up***
p-ed his tent in the Gen 31:25
he will **p** the tents Dan 11:45
tabernacle...Lord **p-ed** Heb 8:2

PITCHER ***container***
torches inside the **p-s** Judg 7:16
Fill four **p-s** 1 Kin 18:33
carrying a **p** of Mark 14:13

PITHOM
Egyptian storage city built by Hebrew slaves Ex 1:11

PITY (n) ***sympathy***
shall not show **p** Deut 19:21
I will not show **p** Jer 13:14
No eye looked with **p** Ezek 16:5

PITY (v) ***have compassion***
she had **p** on him Ex 2:6
eye shall not **p** them Deut 7:16
P me, **p** me, O you Job 19:21
take **p** on us Mark 9:22
most to be **p-ied** 1 Cor 15:19

PLACE ***area, space***
waters...into one **p** Gen 1:9
he enters the holy **p** Ex 28:29
God is a dwelling **p** Deut 33:27
a **p** for My people 1 Chr 17:9
earth out of its **p** Job 9:6
You are my hiding **p** Ps 32:7
love the **p** of honor Matt 23:6
a **p** called Golgotha Matt 27:33
I go to prepare a **p** John 14:2

PLAGUE ***contagious disease***
no **p** will befall you Ex 12:13
Remove Your **p** from Ps 39:10
p of the hail Rev 16:21
the seven last **p-s** Rev 21:9

PLAIN ***flat area***
p in...Shinar Gen 11:2
desert **p-s** of Jericho Josh 4:13
the **p** of Megiddo 2 Chr 35:22
broad **p** of the earth Rev 20:9

PLAN ***design, scheme***
tabernacle...its **p** Ex 26:30
P-s *formed* long ago Is 25:1
follow our own **p-s** Jer 18:12
p and foreknowledge Acts 2:23

PLANT (n) ***growth from soil***
every **p** yielding seed Gen 1:29
eat the **p-s** of the Gen 3:18
hail...struck every **p** Ex 9:25
God appointed a **p** Jon 4:6

PLANT (v) ***put into soil***
God **p-ed** a garden Gen 2:8
p...trees for food Lev 19:23
shall **p** a vineyard Deut 28:30
A time to **p** Eccl 3:2
her earnings she **p-s** Prov 31:16
p-ed a vineyard Mark 12:1
I **p-ed**, Apollos 1 Cor 3:6

PLATTER ***shallow dish***
on a **p** the head of Matt 14:8
his head on a **p** Mark 6:28

PLAY ***take part***
who **p** the lyre Gen 4:21
man who can **p** 1 Sam 16:17
p-ed the fool 1 Sam 26:21
P skillfully with a Ps 33:3
nursing child will **p** Is 11:8
not **p** the harlot Hos 3:3
We **p-ed** the flute Matt 11:17

PLEAD ***appeal, beseech***
p-ed with the LORD Deut 3:23
man...**p** with God Job 16:21
LORD...**p** their case Prov 22:23
P for the widow Is 1:17
Elijah...**p-s** with God Rom 11:2

PLEASANT ***pleasing***
despised the **p** land Ps 106:24
P words are a Prov 16:24
sleep...is **p** Eccl 5:12
Speak to us **p** words Is 30:10

PLEASE ***satisfy***
it **p** You to bless 2 Sam 7:29
You are **p-d** with me Ps 41:11
sacrifices...not **p** Him Hos 9:4
how he may **p** his 1 Cor 7:33
p all men in all 1 Cor 10:33
striving to **p** men Gal 1:10
to walk and **p** God 1 Thess 4:1
impossible to **p** Heb 11:6

PLEASING ***agreeable, gratifying***
tree that is **p** Gen 2:9
meditation be **p** Ps 104:34
not as **p** men but 1 Thess 2:4
p in His sight 1 John 3:22

PLEASURE ***gratification***
old, shall I have **p** Gen 18:12
p in His people Ps 149:4
He who loves **p** *will* Prov 21:17
work for *His* good **p** Phil 2:13
lovers of **p** rather 2 Tim 3:4
passing **p-s** of sin Heb 11:25

PLEDGE ***promise***
cloak as a **p** Ex 22:26
those who give **p-s** Prov 22:26
the Spirit as a **p** 2 Cor 5:5
p of our inheritance Eph 1:14

PLEIADES
constellation of stars Job 9:9; 38:31; Amos 5:8

PLENTIFUL ***abundant***
shed abroad a **p** rain Ps 68:9
harvest is **p** Matt 9:37

PLOT ***plan, scheme***
wicked **p-s** against Ps 37:12
you have **p-ted** *evil* Prov 30:32
Jews **p-ted** together Acts 9:23

PLOW ***dig the soil***
not **p** with an ox Deut 22:10
those who **p** iniquity Job 4:8
sluggard does not **p** Prov 20:4
his hand to the **p** Luke 9:62
ought to **p** in hope 1 Cor 9:10

PLOWSHARES ***blade of plow***
their swords into **p** Is 2:4
your **p** into swords Joel 3:10

PLUMB LINE ***vertical line***
the **p** of emptiness Is 34:11
p In the midst of My Amos 7:8
when they see the **p** Zech 4:10

PLUNDER (n) ***booty, loot***
took no **p** in silver Judg 5:19
You will become **p** Hab 2:7
wealth will become **p** Zeph 1:13

PLUNDER (v) ***rob***
will **p** the Egyptians Ex 3:22
stouthearted were **p-ed** Ps 76:5
he will **p** his house Matt 12:29

POINT ***particular time***
grieved, to the **p** of Matt 26:38
obedient to the **p** of Phil 2:8
to the **p** of shedding Heb 12:4

POISON ***lethal substance***
P...under their lips Ps 140:3
given us **p-ed** water Jer 8:14
turned justice into **p** Amos 6:12

POLL-TAX ***income and head tax***
collect customs or **p** Matt 17:25
give a **p** to Caesar Matt 22:17

POLLUTE ***contaminate***
blood **p-s** the land Num 35:33
earth is also **p-d** Is 24:5

POMEGRANATE *fruit*
golden bell and a **p** — Ex 28:34
p-s of blue and purple — Ex 39:24
juice of my **p-s** — Song 8:2
the fig tree, the **p** — Hag 2:19

PONDER *think deeply*
not **p** the path of life — Prov 5:6
Or **p** things...past — Is 43:18

PONTUS
region in N Asia Minor — Acts 2:9; 1 Pet 1:1
homeland of Aquila — Acts 18:2

POOL *pond*
of the upper **p** — 2 Kin 18:17
rock into a **p** — Ps 114:8
land will become a **p** — Is 35:7
in the **p** of Siloam — John 9:7

POOR *impoverished, needy*
p will never cease — Deut 15:11
raises the **p** from the — 1 Sam 2:8
or you will become **p** — Prov 20:13
not rob the **p** — Prov 22:22
are the **p** in spirit — Matt 5:3
a **p** widow came — Mark 12:42
you always have the **p** — Mark 14:7
sake He became **p** — 2 Cor 8:9
not God choose the **p** — James 2:5

POPULATE *increase number*
P the earth abundantly — Gen 9:7
whole earth was **p-d** — Gen 9:19

POPULATION *people*
with all *his* great **p** — Is 16:14
deported an entire **p** — Amos 1:6

PORPOISE SKIN
covering of **p-s** above — Ex 26:14
put sandals of **p** on — Ezek 16:10

PORTICO *porch*
in the **p** of Solomon — John 10:23
one accord in...**p** — Acts 5:12

PORTION *part, share*
gather a day's **p** — Ex 16:4
LORD's **p** is...people — Deut 32:9
double **p** of...spirit — 2 Kin 2:9
The LORD is my **p** — Ps 119:57
joy over their **p** — Is 61:7

POSSESS *control, take*
give...this land to **p** — Gen 15:7
are to **p** their land — Lev 20:24
go in and **p** the land — Deut 1:8
p-es all the nations — Ps 82:8
p-ed by Beelzebul — Mark 3:22
sell all you **p** — Mark 10:21
p-ed with demons — Luke 8:27
do not **p** silver and — Acts 3:6

POSSESSION *ownership*
for an everlasting **p** — Gen 17:8
you shall be My own **p** — Ex 19:5
people for His own **p** — Deut 4:20
full of Your **p-s** — Ps 104:24
charge of all his **p-s** — Matt 24:47
selling their...**p-s** — Acts 2:45

POSSIBLE *can be done*
all things are **p** — Matt 19:26
p with God — Luke 18:27

POSTERITY *descendants*
P will serve Him — Ps 22:30
p of the wicked — Ps 37:38

POT *container, vessel*
death in the **p** — 2 Kin 4:40
refining **p** is for — Prov 17:3
I see a boiling **p** — Jer 1:13

POTIPHAR
Egyptian official who purchased Joseph — Gen 39:1

POTIPHERA
Joseph's father-in-law — Gen 41:45,50; 46:20

POTSHERD *piece of pottery*
p to scrape himself — Job 2:8
is dried up like a **p** — Ps 22:15

POTTER *one who molds clay*
clay say to the **p** — Is 45:9
and You our **p** — Is 64:8
as it pleased the **p** — Jer 18:4
Throw it to the **p** — Zech 11:13

POTTER'S FIELD
burial place bought with Judas' money — Matt 27:3ff
also called **Field of Blood**

POUR *cause to flow*
p me out like milk — Job 10:10
I **p** out my soul — Ps 42:4
P out your heart — Ps 62:8
I will **p** out My Spirit — Is 44:3
P out Your wrath — Jer 10:25
p out...a blessing — Mal 3:10
p-ed it on His — Matt 26:7
p forth of My Spirit — Acts 2:17

POVERTY *destitution, want*
glutton...come to **p** — Prov 23:21
neither **p** nor riches — Prov 30:8
through His **p** might — 2 Cor 8:9

POWER *authority, strength*
to show you My **p** — Ex 9:16
from the **p** of Sheol — Ps 49:15
the **p** of His works — Ps 111:6
p of the tongue — Prov 18:21
the **p** of the sword — Jer 18:21
Not by might nor...**p** — Zech 4:6
Yours is...the **p** — Matt 6:13
the right hand of **p** — Mark 14:62
clothed with **p** from — Luke 24:49
you will receive **p** — Acts 1:8
gospel...**p** of God — Rom 1:16
the **p** of our Lord — 1 Cor 5:4
p of sin is the law — 1 Cor 15:56
p of Christ...dwell — 2 Cor 12:9
prince of the **p** of — Eph 2:2
p of His resurrection — Phil 3:10
timidity, but of **p** — 2 Tim 1:7
by the word of His **p** — Heb 1:3
quenched the **p** of — Heb 11:34
p-s...been subjected — 1 Pet 3:22

POWERLESS *without strength*
p before this great — 2 Chr 20:12
He might render **p** — Heb 2:14

PRACTICE (n) *custom, habit*
evil of their **p-s** — Ps 28:4
disclosing their **p-s** — Acts 19:18
laid aside...*evil* **p-s** — Col 3:9

PRACTICE (v) *engage in*
keep...statutes and **p** — Lev 20:8
He who **p-s** deceit — Ps 101:7
Who **p** righteousness — Ps 106:3
p-ing hospitality — Rom 12:13
learn to **p** piety — 1 Tim 5:4
the one who **p-s** sin — 1 John 3:8

PRAETORIAN / PRAETORIUM *guard or palace*
1 *Imperial palace guards in Rome* — Phil 1:13
2 *Pontius Pilate's palace in Jerusalem* — Matt 27:27; Mark 15:16; John 18:28,33
3 *Herod's palace at Caesarea* — Acts 23:35

PRAISE (n) *acclamation, honor*
offering of **p** — Lev 19:24
sing **p-s** to Him — 1 Chr 16:9
songs of **p**...hymns — Neh 12:46
From You...my **p** — Ps 22:25
sound His **p** abroad — Ps 66:8
makes Jerusalem a **p** — Is 62:7
his **p** is not from men — Rom 2:29
anything worthy of **p** — Phil 4:8
a sacrifice of **p** — Heb 13:15
Give **p** to our God — Rev 19:5

PRAISE (v) *extol, glorify*
I will **p** Him — Ex 15:2
greatly to be **p-d** — 1 Chr 16:25
Will the dust **p** You — Ps 30:9
My lips will **p** You — Ps 63:3
heavens will **p** Your — Ps 89:5
P Him, sun and moon — Ps 148:3
P Him with trumpet — Ps 150:3
Death cannot **p** You — Is 38:18
I **p** You, Father — Matt 11:25
heavenly host **p-ing** — Luke 2:13
disciples began to **p** — Luke 19:37
leaping and **p-ing** God — Acts 3:8

PRAY *ask, worship*
Abraham **p-ed** to — Gen 20:17
For this boy I **p-ed** — 1 Sam 1:27
found *courage* to **p** — 1 Chr 17:25
For to You I **p** — Ps 5:2
P for...Jerusalem — Ps 122:6
p to a god who cannot — Is 45:20
We earnestly **p** — Jon 1:14
p for...persecute — Matt 5:44
by Himself to **p** — Matt 14:23
p and ask, believe — Mark 11:24
until I have **p-ed** — Mark 14:32
Lord, teach us to **p** — Luke 11:1
they ought to **p** — Luke 18:1
I have **p-ed** for you — Luke 22:32
p-ed with fasting — Acts 14:23
if I **p** in a tongue — 1 Cor 14:14
p without ceasing — 1 Thess 5:17
p for one another — James 5:16
p-ing in the...Spirit — Jude 20

PRAYER
I have heard your **p** — 2 Chr 7:12
And my **p** is pure — Job 16:17
LORD receives my **p** — Ps 6:9
Give ear to my **p** — Ps 55:1
p of the righteous — Prov 15:29
joyful in My house of **p** — Is 56:7
ask in **p**, believing — Matt 21:22
you make long **p-s** — Matt 23:14
whole night in **p** — Luke 6:12
My house...of **p** — Luke 19:46
devoting...to **p** — Acts 1:14
offering **p** with joy — Phil 1:4
but in everything by **p** — Phil 4:6
p-s...not be hindered — 1 Pet 3:7
p-s of the saints — Rev 5:8

PREACH *exhort, proclaim*
Jesus began to **p** — Matt 4:17
as you go, **p** — Matt 10:7
teach and **p** in their — Matt 11:1
p-ing...repentance — Mark 1:4
p the gospel to all — Mark 16:15
p the kingdom of — Luke 4:43
he **p-ed** Jesus to him — Acts 8:35
p...the good news — Acts 13:32
How will they **p** — Rom 10:15
we **p** Christ crucified — 1 Cor 1:23
He...**p-ed** peace — Eph 2:17
p the word — 2 Tim 4:2

PREACHER *one who proclaims*
hear without a **p** — Rom 10:14
appointed a **p** and an — 1 Tim 2:7
Noah, a **p** of — 2 Pet 2:5

PRECEPTS *commandments*
All His **p** are sure — Ps 111:7
meditate on Your **p** — Ps 119:15
as doctrines the **p** of — Matt 15:9

PRECIOUS *beloved or costly*
P in the sight of — Ps 116:15
like the **p** oil upon the — Ps 133:2
more **p** than jewels — Prov 3:15
p things...no profit — Is 44:9
more **p** than gold — 1 Pet 1:7
with **p** blood — 1 Pet 1:19

PREDESTINED *foreordained*
purpose **p** to occur Acts 4:28
foreknew, He also **p** Rom 8:29
God **p** before the ages 1 Cor 2:7
p us to adoption Eph 1:5
p according to His Eph 1:11

PREDETERMINED
p plan...of God Acts 2:23

PREEMINENT *foremost*
P in dignity Gen 49:3

PREFECTS *Persian officials*
shatter governors...**p** Jer 51:23
the satraps, the **p** Dan 3:3

PREGNANT *with child*
womb of...**p** woman Eccl 11:5
And her womb ever **p** Jer 20:17
ripped open...**p** Amos 1:13
Elizabeth...became **p** Luke 1:24

PREPARATION *readiness*
distracted with...**p-s** Luke 10:40
Jewish day of **p** John 19:42
making **p-s**, he fell Acts 10:10
p of the gospel of Eph 6:15

PREPARE *make ready*
p a savory dish Gen 27:4
mind **p-s** deception Job 15:35
p a table before me Ps 23:5
P to meet your God Amos 4:12
will **p** Your way Matt 11:10
kingdom **p-d** for Matt 25:34
to **p** Me for burial Matt 26:12
p-d spices and Luke 23:56
I go to **p** a place John 14:2
worlds were **p-d** by Heb 11:3
p your minds for 1 Pet 1:13

PRESENCE *appearance*
My **p** shall go *with* Ex 33:14
in the **p** of my enemies Ps 23:5
the light of Your **p** Ps 44:3
tremble at Your **p** Is 64:2
the **p** of His glory Jude 24
the **p** of the Lamb Rev 14:10

PRESENT (n) *gift*
a **p** for his brother Gen 32:13
sent a **p** to the king 2 Kin 16:8
and a **p** to Hezekiah Is 39:1

PRESENT (v) *give, offer*
p you with a crown of Prov 4:9
you **p** the blind for Mal 1:8
p Him to the Lord Luke 2:22
p yourselves to God Rom 6:13
p your bodies a Rom 12:1
p you before Him holy Col 1:22

PRESERVE *protect*
no son to **p** my 2 Sam 18:18
P me, O God Ps 16:1
P my soul Ps 86:2
LORD **p-s** the simple Ps 116:6
p-d ones of Israel Is 49:6
p the unity of the Eph 4:3
be **p-d** complete 1 Thess 5:23

PRESS *compel, force*
measure, **p-ed** down Luke 6:38
I **p** on toward...goal Phil 3:14

PRETEND *deceive, feign*
p to be a mourner 2 Sam 14:2
p to be another 1 Kin 14:5
p-s to be poor Prov 13:7
spies who **p-ed** to Luke 20:20

PREVAIL *exist or triumph*
water **p-ed**...increased Gen 7:18
not by might...man **p** 1 Sam 2:9
Iniquities **p** against me Ps 65:3
overcome me and **p-ed** Jer 20:7

PREY *what is hunted*
birds of **p** came Gen 15:11
lion tearing the **p** Ezek 22:25
no longer be a **p** to Ezek 34:28

PRICE *cost, value*
shall increase its **p** Lev 25:16
their redemption **p** Num 18:16
p of the pardoning of Is 27:9
it is the **p** of blood Matt 27:6
p of his wickedness Acts 1:18
kept back *some*...**p** Acts 5:2
bought with a **p** 1 Cor 7:23

PRIDE *exaggerated self-esteem*
P *goes* before Prov 16:18
you an everlasting **p** Is 60:15
p of Israel testifies Hos 5:5
envy, slander, **p** Mark 7:22
boastful **p** of life 1 John 2:16

PRIEST *intermediary*
a **p** of God Most Gen 14:18
a kingdom of **p-s** Ex 19:6
Aaron's sons, the **p-s** Lev 1:5
if the anointed **p** sins Lev 4:3
p...make atonement Lev 4:31
without a teaching **p** 2 Chr 15:3
You are a **p** forever Ps 110:4
all the chief **p-s** Matt 2:4
show yourself to the **p** Matt 8:4
faithful high **p** Heb 2:17
have a great high **p** Heb 4:14
You are a **p** forever Heb 5:6

PRIESTHOOD *office of priest*
for a perpetual **p** Ex 40:15
have defiled the **p** Neh 13:29
His **p** permanently Heb 7:24
royal **p**, a holy nation 1 Pet 2:9

PRIME *fully mature period*
die in the **p** of life 1 Sam 2:33
p of life...fleeting Eccl 11:10

PRINCE *ruler*
Who made you a **p** Ex 2:14
p-s of the tribes 1 Chr 29:6
contempt upon **p-s** Ps 107:40
Do not trust in **p-s** Ps 146:3
Father, **P** of Peace Is 9:6
p-s will rule justly Is 32:1
to death the **P** of life Acts 3:15
p of...the air Eph 2:2

PRISCA / PRISCILLA
wife of Aquila Rom 16:3
co-worker with Paul Acts 18:2,18,26; 1 Cor 16:19

PRISON *jail*
Put this man in **p** 1 Kin 22:27
my soul out of **p** Ps 142:7
beheaded in the **p** Matt 14:10
I was in **p**, and Matt 25:36
opened...the **p** Acts 5:19
spirits *now* in **p** 1 Pet 3:19

PRISONER *one who is confined*
sets the **p-s** free Ps 146:7
a notorious **p** Matt 27:16
p of the law of sin Rom 7:23
Paul, a **p** of Christ Philem 1

PRIVATE *not public*
show him his fault in **p** Matt 18:15
but *I did so* in **p** Gal 2:2

PRIZE *reward*
one receives the **p** 1 Cor 9:24
p of the upward call Phil 3:14

PROCEED *go forth*
p from evil to evil Jer 9:3
p-s out of the mouth Matt 4:4
p-s from...Father John 15:26

PROCLAIM *announce, declare*
p...name of the LORD Ex 33:19
P good tidings 1 Chr 16:23
appointed...to **p** Neh 6:7
p liberty to captives Is 61:1
p justice to the Matt 12:18
he *began* to **p** Jesus Acts 9:20
first to **p** light Acts 26:23
faith is being **p-ed** Rom 1:8
p...eternal life 1 John 1:2

PROCLAMATION *declaration*
a **p** was circulated Ex 36:6
made **p** to the spirits 1 Pet 3:19

PROCONSUL *Roman governor*
the **p**, Sergius Paulus Acts 13:7
p-s are *available* Acts 19:38

PRODUCE (n) *yield of the soil*
land will yield its **p** Lev 25:19
tithe all the **p** Deut 14:22
earth has yielded its **p** Ps 67:6
precious **p** of...soil James 5:7

PRODUCE (v) *bring forth*
milk **p-s** butter Prov 30:33
cannot **p** bad fruit Matt 7:18
they **p** quarrels 2 Tim 2:23
faith **p-s** endurance James 1:3

PROFANE *defile, desecrate*
p My holy name Lev 20:3
is **p-d** by harlotry Lev 21:7
and **p-d** My sabbaths Ezek 22:8
p-d your sanctuaries Ezek 28:18
to **p** the covenant Mal 2:10

PROFESS *confess, declare*
P-ing to be wise Rom 1:22
They **p** to know God Titus 1:16

PROFIT (n) *benefit, gain*
labor there is **p** Prov 14:23
no **p** for the charmer Eccl 10:11
not seeking my...**p** 1 Cor 10:33
business...make a **p** James 4:13

PROFIT (v) *reap an advantage*
p...my destruction Job 30:13
what does it **p** a Mark 8:36
the flesh **p-s** nothing John 6:63
it **p-s** me nothing 1 Cor 13:3

PROFITABLE *useful*
not all things are **p** 1 Cor 6:12
godliness is **p** 1 Tim 4:8
p for teaching 2 Tim 3:16

PROMINENT *well-known*
a **p** member of the Mark 15:43
of **p** Greek women Acts 17:12
p men of the city Acts 25:23

PROMISE (n) *agreement, pledge*
p of the Holy Spirit Acts 2:33
the **p** made by God Acts 26:6
the **p** is nullified Rom 4:14
children of the **p** Rom 9:8
commandment...a **p** Eph 6:2
heirs of the **p** Heb 6:17
precious...**p-s** 2 Pet 1:4
the **p** of His coming 2 Pet 3:4

PROMISED *made an agreement*
land which He had **p** Deut 9:28
p to keep Your words Ps 119:57
p long ages ago Titus 1:2
He who **p** is faithful Heb 10:23

PRONOUNCE *declare officially*
shall **p** him clean Lev 13:23
I will **p** My judgments Jer 1:16
Pilate **p-d** sentence Luke 23:24
God...**p-d** judgment Rev 18:20

PROOF *evidence*
- furnished **p** to all Acts 17:31
- **p** of your love 2 Cor 8:24
- **p** of the Christ 2 Cor 13:3

PROPER *suitable*
- fulfilled...**p** time Luke 1:20
- is it **p** for a woman 1 Cor 11:13
- as is **p** among saints Eph 5:3

PROPERTY *goods* **or** *land*
- acquire **p** in it Gen 34:10
- **p**...too great Gen 36:7
- buys a slave as *his* **p** Lev 22:11
- who owned much **p** Matt 19:22
- selling their **p** and Acts 2:45
- things...common **p** Acts 4:32

PROPHECY *proclamation*
- seal up vision and **p** Dan 9:24
- **p**...fulfilled Matt 13:14
- have *the gift of* **p** 1 Cor 13:2
- no **p**...of human will 2 Pet 1:21
- the spirit of **p** Rev 19:10

PROPHESY *predict, proclaim*
- to **p** with lyres 1 Chr 25:1
- he never **p-ies** good 2 Chr 18:7
- **p-ing**...false vision Jer 14:14
- **P** over these bones Ezek 37:4
- sons and...will **p** Joel 2:28
- did we...**p** in Your Matt 7:22
- **P** to us...Christ Matt 26:68
- speaking...**p-ing** Acts 19:6
- who **p-ies** edifies 1 Cor 14:4

PROPHET *spokesman for God*
- Aaron shall be your **p** Ex 7:1
- a **p** or a dreamer Deut 13:1
- I will raise up a **p** Deut 18:18
- **p** in your place 1 Kin 19:16
- summon all...**p-s** 2 Kin 10:19
- vision of...the **p** 2 Chr 32:32
- Woe...foolish **p-s** Ezek 13:3
- written by the **p** Matt 2:5
- persecuted the **p-s** Matt 5:12
- Beware...false **p-s** Matt 7:15
- He...receives a **p** Matt 10:41
- the **p** Jesus Matt 21:11
- false **p-s**...arise Mark 13:22
- **p** of the Most High Luke 1:76
- great **p** has arisen Luke 7:16
- Are you the **P** John 1:21
- reading Isaiah the **p** Acts 8:30
- a Jewish false **p** Acts 13:6
- All are not **p-s** 1 Cor 12:29
- and some *as* **p-s** Eph 4:11
- beast and...false **p** Rev 20:10

PROPHETESS *speaker for God*
- Miriam the **p** Ex 15:20
- Deborah, a **p** Judg 4:4
- there was a **p**, Anna Luke 2:36
- calls herself a **p** Rev 2:20

PROPHETIC *predictive*
- not...**p** utterances 1 Thess 5:20
- **p** word...sure 2 Pet 1:19

PROPITIATION *atonement*
- a **p** in His blood Rom 3:25
- **p** for the sins Heb 2:17
- He himself is the **p** 1 John 2:2
- **p** for our sins 1 John 4:10

PROSELYTE *convert*
- both Jews and **p-s** Acts 2:10
- a **p** from Antioch Acts 6:5
- God-fearing **p-s** Acts 13:43

PROSPER *flourish, succeed*
- I will surely **p** you Gen 32:12
- David was **p-ing** 1 Sam 18:14
- they built and **p-ed** 2 Chr 14:7
- His ways **p** at all Ps 10:5
- they **p** who love you Ps 122:6

PROSPERITY *success, wealth*
- my **p** has passed away Job 30:15
- soul will abide in **p** Ps 25:13
- saw the **p** of the wicked Ps 73:3
- know how to live in **p** Phil 4:12

PROSPEROUS *successful*
- exceedingly **p** Gen 30:43
- make your way **p** Josh 1:8
- generous man...be **p** Prov 11:25

PROSTITUTE *harlot*
- Where...temple **p** Gen 38:21
- male cult **p-s** in the 1 Kin 14:24
- an adulterer and a **p** Is 57:3
- to a **p** is one body 1 Cor 6:16

PROSTRATE *fall down flat*
- **p-d** himself before 2 Sam 18:28
- man dies and lies **p** Job 14:10
- fell...**p-d** Matt 18:26

PROTECT *guard, shield*
- The LORD will **p** him Ps 41:2
- LORD **p-s** the strangers Ps 146:9
- LORD...**p** Jerusalem Is 31:5
- He will...**p** you 2 Thess 3:3
- **p-ed** by the power of 1 Pet 1:5

PROTECTION *safe-keeping*
- **p** has been removed Num 14:9
- For wisdom is **p** Eccl 7:12
- **p** from the storm Is 4:6
- let him rely on My **p** Is 27:5

PROUD *exaggerated self-esteem*
- heart will become **p** Deut 8:14
- recompense to the **p** Ps 94:2
- eyes and a **p** heart Prov 21:4
- daughters of Zion are **p** Is 3:16
- opposed to the **p** James 4:6

PROVE *establish, test*
- you will be **p-d** a liar Prov 30:6
- will **p** Myself holy Ezek 20:41
- **p** to be My disciples John 15:8
- **p**...the will of God Rom 12:2
- **p** yourselves doers James 1:22

PROVERB *adage, short saying*
- become...a **p** Deut 28:37
- spoke 3,000 **p-s** 1 Kin 4:32
- Israel...become a **p** 1 Kin 9:7
- To understand a **p** Prov 1:6
- quote this **p** to Me Luke 4:23
- to the true **p** 2 Pet 2:22

PROVIDE *furnish, supply*
- **p** for Himself...lamb Gen 22:8
- **p** for...redemption Lev 25:24
- **p-d** bread from heaven Neh 9:15
- Who **p-s** rain for the Ps 147:8
- **p**...way of escape 1 Cor 10:13
- not **p** for his own 1 Tim 5:8
- God had **p-d** Heb 11:40

PROVINCE *district* **or** *territory*
- rulers of the **p-s** 1 Kin 20:17
- holiday for the **p-s** Esth 2:18
- whole **p** of Babylon Dan 2:48
- arrived in the **p** Acts 25:1

PROVISION *supply, requirement*
- bread of their **p** was Josh 9:5
- bless her **p** Ps 132:15
- **p-s** of the law Matt 23:23
- no **p** for the flesh Rom 13:14

PROVOKE *evoke, excite*
- images to **p** Me 1 Kin 14:9
- who **p** God are secure Job 12:6
- love...is not **p-d** 1 Cor 13:4,5
- not **p** your children Eph 6:4

PROWL *roam in search*
- beasts...**p** about Ps 104:20
- devil, **p-s** around like 1 Pet 5:8

PRUDENT *careful, wise*
- a **p** man conceals Prov 12:16
- **p** wife is from the Prov 19:14
- the **p** took oil in Matt 25:4
- you are **p** in Christ 1 Cor 4:10

PRUNING *cutting*
- spears into **p** hooks Is 2:4

PSALMS *sacred songs*
- shout...with **p** Ps 95:2
- **P** must be fulfilled Luke 24:44
- speaking...in **p** Eph 5:19

PUBLIC *open*
- of his **p** appearance Luke 1:80
- beaten us in **p** Acts 16:37
- refuted...Jews in **p** Acts 18:28
- made a **p** display Col 2:15
- made a **p** spectacle Heb 10:33

PUL
- *Tiglath-pileser III, king of Assyria* 2 Kin 15:19; 1 Chr 5:26

PUNISH *chastise, penalize*
- **p** them for their sin Ex 32:34
- and are **p-ed** for it Prov 22:3
- **p** the world for its Is 13:11
- will **p** your iniquity Lam 4:22
- **p** Him and release Luke 23:16
- I **p-ed** them often Acts 26:11
- **p** all disobedience 2 Cor 10:6

PUNISHMENT *penalty*
- My **p** is too great Gen 4:13
- **p** of the sword Job 19:29
- fear involves **p** 1 John 4:18
- the **p** of eternal fire Jude 7

PUPIL *part of eye or student*
- as the **p** of His eye Deut 32:10
- **p** is not above his Luke 6:40

PURCHASE *buy*
- **p-d** with His...blood Acts 20:28
- **p-d** for God with Your Rev 5:9

PURE *genuine, undefiled*
- mercy seat of **p** gold Ex 25:17
- be **p** before his Maker Job 4:17
- My teaching is **p** Job 11:4
- commandment...is **p** Ps 19:8
- pleasant words are **p** Prov 15:26
- As **p** as the sun Song 6:10
- hair...like **p** wool Dan 7:9
- Blessed are the **p** in Matt 5:8
- whatever is **p** Phil 4:8
- love from a **p** heart 1 Tim 1:5
- **p** milk of the word 1 Pet 2:2
- the city was **p** gold Rev 21:18

PURGE *remove*
- **p**...evil from among Deut 13:5
- Many will be **p-d** Dan 12:10

PURIFICATION *cleansing*
- Jewish custom of **p** John 2:6
- He...made **p** of sins Heb 1:3

PURIFY *make clean*
- **p-ied** these waters 2 Kin 2:21
- **P** me with hyssop Ps 51:7
- **p**...a people Titus 2:14
- **p** your hearts James 4:8
- **p-ied** your souls 1 Pet 1:22

PURIM
- *Jewish festival* Esth 9:26ff

PURITY *not corrupted*
- who loves **p** of heart Prov 22:11
- love, faith *and* **p** 1 Tim 4:12
- *with* **p** in doctrine Titus 2:7

PURPLE *color*
- a veil of blue and **p** Ex 26:31
- Those reared in **p** Lam 4:5

clothed Daniel with **p** Dan 5:29
dressed Him...**p** Mark 15:17
a seller of **p** fabrics Acts 16:14
clothed in **p** and Rev 17:4

PURPOSE *intention, reason*
p of shedding blood Ezek 22:9
rejected God's **p** Luke 7:30
for this **p** I have Acts 26:16
according to *His* **p** Rom 8:28

PURSUE *chase, follow*
p the manslayer Deut 19:6
They **p** my honor Job 30:15
the enemy **p** my soul Ps 7:5
Seek peace, and **p** it Ps 34:14
Adversity **p-s** Prov 13:21
p-s righteousness Prov 21:21
may **p** strong drink Is 5:11
p righteousness 2 Tim 2:22
P peace with...men Heb 12:14

PUT *place*
p enmity Between Gen 3:15
He **p** a new song Ps 40:3
p a purple robe on Him John 19:2
p on the Lord Jesus Rom 13:14
p on the new self Eph 4:24
P on the full armor Eph 6:11

PUT
1 *son of Ham* Gen 10:6; 1 Chr 1:8
2 *African country* Jer 46:9; Ezek 27:10; 30:5; Nah 3:9

Q

QUAIL *type of bird*
q-s came up and Ex 16:13
q from the sea Num 11:31

QUAKE *shake, tremble*
The mountains **q-d** Judg 5:5
made the land **q** Ps 60:2
The earth **q-d** Ps 68:8
q at Your presence Is 64:1

QUALITY *character*
test the **q** of each 1 Cor 3:13
imperishable **q** of a 1 Pet 3:4

QUANTITY *amount*
large **q-ies** of cedar 1 Chr 22:4
a great **q** of fish Luke 5:6

QUARANTINE *isolate*
shall **q** the article Lev 13:50
q the house for Lev 14:38

QUARREL (n) *altercation*
if men have a **q** Ex 21:18
So abandon the **q** Prov 17:14
are **q-s** among you 1 Cor 1:11
the source of **q-s** James 4:1

QUARREL (v) *contend, fight*
did not **q** over it Gen 26:22
Why do you **q** with me Ex 17:2
any fool will **q** Prov 20:3
those who **q** with you Is 41:12

QUART *measure*
A **q** of wheat for a Rev 6:6

QUEEN *female sovereign*
when the **q** of Sheba 1 Kin 10:1
king saw Esther the **q** Esth 5:2
The **q** of kingdoms Is 47:5
The **Q** *of the* South Matt 12:42
Candace, **q** of the Acts 8:27

QUENCH *extinguish*
donkeys **q** their thirst Ps 104:11
waters cannot **q** love Song 8:7
not **q** the Spirit 1 Thess 5:19
q-ed...power of fire Heb 11:34

QUESTION (n) *inquiry, problem*
Was it not just a **q** 1 Sam 17:29
answered all her **q-s** 2 Chr 9:2
Jesus asked...a **q** Matt 22:41
in controversial **q-s** 1 Tim 6:4

QUESTION (v) *ask*
q-ed the priests 2 Chr 31:9
Jeremiah and **q-ed** Jer 38:27
He *began* to **q** them Mark 9:33
to **q** Him closely on Luke 11:53
Q those who have John 18:21

QUICK (adj) *rapid*
is **q**-tempered exalts Prov 14:29
q to hear, slow to James 1:19

QUICK (n) *deepest feelings*
cut to the **q** and Acts 5:33
were cut to the **q** Acts 7:54

QUIET (adj) *calm, still*
he knew no **q** within Job 20:20
me beside **q** waters Ps 23:2
lead a...**q** life 1 Tim 2:2
gentle and **q** spirit 1 Pet 3:4

QUIET (v) *become calm, still*
God, do not remain **q** Ps 83:1
and **q-ed** my soul Ps 131:2
will be **q** in His love Zeph 3:17
Be **q**, and come out Mark 1:25

QUIRINIUS
Roman governor at time of Judean census Luke 2:2

QUIVER *case for holding arrows*
your **q** and your bow Gen 27:3
man whose **q** is full Ps 127:5
hidden Me in His **q** Is 49:2
q is like an open grave Jer 5:16
fill the **q-s** Jer 51:11

QUOTA *portion assigned*
complete your work **q** Ex 5:13
deliver the **q** of bricks Ex 5:18

QUOTE *repeat a passage*
who **q-s** proverbs Ezek 16:44
will **q** this proverb Luke 4:23

R

RAAMSES / RAMESES
where Joseph settled Gen 47:11
Egyptian storage city built by Hebrew slaves Ex 1:11
origin of exodus Ex 12:37; Num 33:3,5

RABBI / RABBONI
respectful form of address Matt 23:7; 26:25; Mark 10:51
master, teacher John 1:49; 6:25; 11:8; 20:16

RAB-MAG
title of Babylonian official Jer 39:3,13

RAB-SARIS
title of Assyrian official 2 Kin 18:17; Jer 39:3,13

RABSHAKEH
title of Assyrian official 2 Kin 18:17ff; Is 36:2,4,11

RACE (n) *nation, people*
r has intermingled Ezra 9:2
mongrel **r** will dwell Zech 9:6
advantage of our **r** Acts 7:19
you are a chosen **r** 1 Pet 2:9

RACE (n) *competition of speed*
r is not to...swift Eccl 9:11
in a **r** all run, but 1 Cor 9:24
r...set before us Heb 12:1

RACHEL
Jacob's wife Gen 29:18,28
mother of Joseph and Benjamin Gen 30:25; 35:24; 46:19

RADIANCE *brightness*
a **r** around Him Ezek 1:27
His **r** is like Hab 3:4
r of His glory Heb 1:3

RADIANT *shining brightly*
looked to Him...were **r** Ps 34:5
you will see and be **r** Is 60:5
His garments...**r** Mark 9:3

RAFTS *boats*
r *to go* by sea 1 Kin 5:9
bring it to you on **r** 2 Chr 2:16

RAGE (n) *violent anger*
Haman was filled...**r** Esth 3:5
with **r** as they heard Luke 4:28

RAGE (v) *be very angry*
r-s against the LORD Prov 19:3
foolish man...**r-s** Prov 29:9
Why...Gentiles **r** Acts 4:25

RAHAB
1 *harlot in Jericho* Josh 2:1
assisted spies Josh 2:4-7
family spared Josh 2:13,14; 6:22,23
ancestor of Jesus Matt 1:5
example of faith Heb 11:31; James 2:25
2 *symbolic for sea monster* Job 9:13; 26:12; Ps 89:10
3 *symbolic for Egypt* Ps 87:4; Is 30:7

RAID (n) *robbery*
a **r** on the land 1 Sam 23:27
a **r** on the camels Job 1:17

RAID (v) *make a sudden attack*
r *at* their heels Gen 49:19
Bandits **r** outside Hos 7:1

RAIN (n)
God had not sent **r** Gen 2:5
r fell upon the earth Gen 7:12
I shall give you **r-s** Lev 26:4
LORD sent...**r** 1 Sam 12:18
no **r** in the land 1 Kin 17:7
the mountain **r-s** Job 24:8
shed...a plentiful **r** Ps 68:9
r is over *and* gone Song 2:11
anger a flooding **r** Ezek 13:13
r on *the* righteous Matt 5:45
ground...drinks the **r** Heb 6:7

RAIN (v) *fall down, pour*
r bread from heaven Ex 16:4
the LORD **r-ed** hail Ex 9:23
it **r-ed** fire and Luke 17:29
not **r**...for three James 5:17

RAINBOW *colored arc in sky*
appearance of the **r** Ezek 1:28
a **r** around the throne Rev 4:3
r was upon his head Rev 10:1

RAISE *elevate, lift*
will **r** up a prophet Deut 18:18
LORD **r-d** up judges Judg 2:16
r-s the poor from 1 Sam 2:8
eyelids are **r-d** *in* Prov 30:13
r up shepherds over Jer 23:4
He will **r** us up Hos 6:2
Heal...**r** *the* dead Matt 10:8
He will be **r-d** up Matt 20:19
three days I will **r** John 2:19
Jesus God **r-d** up Acts 2:32
r-d a spiritual 1 Cor 15:44
r-d us up with Him Eph 2:6
God is able to **r** *people* Heb 11:19

RAISIN *dried grapes*
clusters of **r-s** 2 Sam 16:1
Sustain me with **r** Song 2:5
and love **r** cakes Hos 3:1

RAM *male sheep*
Abraham...took the **r** Gen 22:13

a **r** without defect Lev 5:15
the **r** of atonement Num 5:8
r which had two horns Dan 8:3

RAMAH
1 *city of Naphtali* Josh 19:36
2 *town of Asher* Josh 19:29
3 *town of Benjamin* Josh 18:25; Judg 4:5; 19:13
4 *town in the Negev* Josh 19:8
5 *town in Gilead* 2 Kin 8:28,29; 2 Chr 22:5,6

RAMOTH
1 *city in Gilead* Deut 4:43; Josh 20:8
see **RAMOTH-GILEAD**
2 *city in the Negev* 1 Sam 30:27
also **Ramah of the Negev**
3 *Gershonite city* 1 Chr 6:73

RAMOTH-GILEAD
Gadite city E of the Jordan Deut 4:43
city of refuge Josh 20:8
Ahab killed 1 Kin 22:29-37

RAMPART *bulwark, siege*
and **r-s** for security Is 26:1
Whose **r** *was* the sea Nah 3:8
station myself on the **r** Hab 2:1

RANK *position*
men of **r** are a lie Ps 62:9
He...has a higher **r** John 1:15
a Man...higher **r** John 1:30

RANSOM (n) *payment*
give a **r** for himself Ex 30:12
not take **r** for Num 35:31
wicked is a **r** for Prov 21:18
His life a **r** for Matt 20:28
gave Himself as a **r** 1 Tim 2:6

RANSOM (v) *redeem*
You have **r-ed** me Ps 31:5
R me because of my Ps 69:18
LORD has **r-ed** Jacob Jer 31:11
Shall I **r** them from Hos 13:14

RAVAGE *devastate*
famine will **r** the Gen 41:30
mice that **r** the land 1 Sam 6:5
r-ing the church Acts 8:3

RAVEN *type of bird*
he sent out a **r** Gen 8:7
young **r-s** which cry Ps 147:9
Consider the **r-s** Luke 12:24

RAVENOUS *wildly hungry*
Benjamin is a **r** wolf Gen 49:27
inwardly are **r** wolves Matt 7:15

RAVINE *gorge*
settle on the steep **r-s** Is 7:19
smooth *stones* of the **r** Is 57:6
Every **r** will be filled Luke 3:5

RAVISH *seize and take*
you may **r** them Judg 19:24
And their wives **r-ed** Is 13:16
r-ed...women in Zion Lam 5:11

RAZOR *instrument for shaving*
no **r** shall pass over Num 6:5
no **r** shall come upon Judg 13:5
A **r** has never come Judg 16:17
Like a sharp **r** Ps 52:2

READ
you shall **r** this Deut 31:11
r from the scroll Jer 36:6
who **r-s** it may run Hab 2:2
r-ing...Isaiah Acts 8:28
prophets...are **read** Acts 13:27
Moses is **read** 2 Cor 3:15
Blessed is he who **r-s** Rev 1:3

READY *equipped, prepared*
and **r** to forgive Ps 86:5
Let Your hand be **r** Ps 119:173
Make **r** the way Matt 3:3
you also must be **r** Matt 24:44
be **r** in season 2 Tim 4:2
r to make a defense 1 Pet 3:15

REALIZE *achieve or understand*
Desire **r-d** is sweet Prov 13:19
r-d through Jesus John 1:17
to **r**...assurance Heb 6:11

REALM *area, kingdom*
ruler over the **r** of Dan 4:17
kingdom is not...**r** John 18:36

REAP *cut, gather*
when you **r**...harvest Lev 19:9
iniquity will **r** vanity Prov 22:8
they **r** the whirlwind Hos 8:7
nor **r** Matt 6:26
neither sow nor **r** Luke 12:24
sows...another **r-s** John 4:37
r eternal life Gal 6:8
your sickle and **r** Rev 14:15

REAPER *harvester*
after the **r-s** Ruth 2:3
will overtake the **r** Amos 9:13
the **r-s** are angels Matt 13:39

REASON (n) *explanation*
r a man shall leave Matt 19:5
this **r** the Father John 10:17
this **r** I found mercy 1 Tim 1:16
For this **r**, rejoice Rev 12:12

REASON (v) *analyze, argue*
upright would **r** with Job 23:7
let us **r** together Is 1:18
Pharisees began to **r** Luke 5:21
r-ing in...synagogue Acts 17:17
like a child, **r** like a 1 Cor 13:11

REBEKAH
wife of Isaac Gen 24:67; 26:8
mother of Esau and Jacob Gen 25:21ff

REBEL (n) *rebellious one*
Your rulers are **r-s** Is 1:23
called a **r** from birth Is 48:8
their princes are **r-s** Hos 9:15

REBEL (v) *revolt*
not **r** against the Num 14:9
r-led against...words Ps 107:11
r-led against Me Ezek 20:21

REBELLION *insurrection*
he has counseled **r** Deut 13:5
I know your **r** Deut 31:27
r is as the sin of 1 Sam 15:23
my **r** and my sin Job 13:23
children of **r** Is 57:4

REBELLIOUS *defiant*
r against the LORD Deut 9:7
r generation Ps 78:8
A **r** man seeks only Prov 17:11
stubborn and **r** heart Jer 5:23
there are many **r** Titus 1:10

REBUILD *restore*
r the house of the Ezra 1:3
let us **r** the wall Neh 2:17
r the ancient ruins Is 58:12
r it in three days Matt 26:61
r the tabernacle Acts 15:16

REBUKE (n) *reprimand*
amazed at His **r** Job 26:11
At Your **r** they fled Ps 104:7
the poor hears no **r** Prov 13:8

REBUKE (v) *scold*
r me not in Your wrath Ps 38:1
r the arrogant Ps 119:21
LORD **r** you, Satan Zech 3:2
r-d the winds Matt 8:26
Jesus **r-d** him Matt 17:18
He **r-d** the fever Luke 4:39
Do not sharply **r** 1 Tim 5:1
reprove, **r**, exhort 2 Tim 4:2

RECEIVE *encounter, take*
The LORD **r-s** my prayer Ps 6:9
r me to glory Ps 73:24
man **r-s** a bribe Prov 17:23
Freely you **r-d** Matt 10:8
who **r-s** you **r-s** Me Matt 10:40
the blind **r** sight Matt 11:5
ask...you will **r** Matt 21:22
r-d up into heaven Mark 16:19
This man **r-s** sinners Luke 15:2
as many as **r-d** Him John 1:12
r you to Myself John 14:3
R the Holy Spirit John 20:22
you will **r** power Acts 1:8
to give than to **r** Acts 20:35
one **r-s** the prize 1 Cor 9:24
r the crown of life James 1:12
whatever...ask we **r** 1 John 3:22
r-d the mark of Rev 19:20

RECHABITES
line of Jonadab Jer 35:6
strict life style Jer 35:1-18

RECKONED *accounted for*
r it to him as Gen 15:6
r among the nations Num 23:9
r...as righteousness James 2:23

RECLINE *lean, lie down*
r on beds of ivory Amos 6:4
r *at the table* in Luke 13:29
r-ing on Jesus' John 13:23

RECOGNIZE *be aware, know*
he did not **r** him Gen 27:23
Saul **r-d** David's 1 Sam 26:17
r that He is near Matt 24:33
I did not **r** Him John 1:31

RECOMPENSE (n) *reward*
the **r** of the wicked Ps 91:8
r to the proud Ps 94:2
r of God will come Is 35:4

RECOMPENSE (v) *compensate*
LORD has **r-d** me 2 Sam 22:25
He will **r** the evil Ps 54:5
But if you do **r** Me Joel 3:4

RECONCILE *bring together*
r-d to your brother Matt 5:24
be **r-d** to God 2 Cor 5:20
r them both in one Eph 2:16
r all...to Himself Col 1:20

RECONCILIATION
now received the **r** Rom 5:11
the **r** of the world Rom 11:15
the ministry of **r** 2 Cor 5:18
the word of **r** 2 Cor 5:19

RECORD (n) *document, register*
the **r-s** are ancient 1 Chr 4:22
r-s of the kings 2 Chr 33:18
discover in...**r** books Ezra 4:15
I found the...**r** Neh 7:5

RECORD (v) *register, write*
r-ed their starting Num 33:2
R the vision Hab 2:2
are **r-ed** in heaven Luke 10:20

RECOVER *reclaim, become well*
did you not **r** them Judg 11:26
Will I **r** from this 2 Kin 8:8
and they will **r** Mark 16:18

RED *color*
first came forth **r** Gen 25:25
water...**r** as blood 2 Kin 3:22
they are **r** like crimson Is 1:18

the sky is **r** Matt 16:2
a great **r** dragon Rev 12:3

RED SEA
Hebrew: Sea of Reeds Ex 10:19
body of water between Egypt and Sinai Ex 13:18; Ps 106:9; Jer 49:21

REDEEM *buy back*
I will also **r** you Ex 6:6
family may **r** him Lev 25:49
wish to **r** the field Lev 27:19
I will **r** *it* Ruth 4:4
God will **r** my soul Ps 49:15
He will **r** Israel Ps 130:8
Christ **r-ed** us Gal 3:13
He might **r** those Gal 4:5

REDEEMER *one who buys back*
left you without a **r** Ruth 4:14
know that my **R** lives Job 19:25
my rock and my **R** Ps 19:14
your **R** is the Holy Is 41:14
our Father, Our **R** Is 63:16
Their **R** is strong Jer 50:34

REDEMPTION *deliverance*
r of the land Lev 25:24
have my right of **r** Ruth 4:6
r of his soul is Ps 49:8
r is drawing near Luke 21:28
r...in Christ Jesus Rom 3:24
r of our body Rom 8:23
r through His blood Eph 1:7
in whom we have **r** Col 1:14
obtained eternal **r** Heb 9:12

REED *tall marsh grass*
set *it* among the **r-s** Ex 2:3
bruised **r** He will Is 42:3
the **r**...to beat Him Matt 27:30
and put it on a **r** Matt 27:48

REEL *stagger, sway*
earth **r-s** to and fro Is 24:20
r with strong drink Is 28:7

REFINE *purify*
r-d seven times Ps 12:6
in order to **r** Dan 11:35
R them as silver Zech 13:9
r them like gold Mal 3:3
gold **r-d** by fire Rev 3:18

REFRAIN *abstain*
not **r** from spitting Job 30:10
to **r** from working 1 Cor 9:6
r from judging Rev 6:10

REFRESH *renew, replenish*
you may **r** yourselves Gen 18:5
R me with apples Song 2:5
times of **r-ing** may Acts 3:19
r my heart in Christ Philem 20

REFUGE *protection, shelter*
in whom I take **r** 2 Sam 22:3
God is our **r** Ps 46:1
r in the LORD Ps 118:8
the **r** of lies Is 28:17
r in...distress Jer 16:19
who have taken **r** Heb 6:18

REFUGE, CITIES OF *see* **CITIES OF REFUGE**

REFUSE (n) *waste*
be made a **r** heap Ezra 6:11
corpses lay like **r** Is 5:25
its waters toss up **r** Is 57:20
sell...**r** of the wheat Amos 8:6

REFUSE (v) *decline*
r you his grave Gen 23:6
r to let My people go Ex 10:4
his hands **r** to work Prov 21:25
ey **r** to know Me Jer 9:6
o be comforted Matt 2:18

can **r** the water Acts 10:47
not **r** Him who is Heb 12:25

REFUSE GATE *see* **GATES OF JERUSALEM**

REFUTE *prove wrong*
R me if you can Job 33:5
he...**r-d** the Jews Acts 18:28
to **r** those who Titus 1:9

REGAIN *recover*
r-ed their sight Matt 20:34
want to **r** my sight Mark 10:51
he might **r** his sight Acts 9:12

REGARD (n) *respect*
LORD had **r** for Abel Gen 4:4
r to the prayer 1 Kin 8:28
have **r** for his Maker Is 17:7
r for the humble Luke 1:48

REGARD (v) *esteem, respect*
If I **r** wickedness Ps 66:18
Yet He **r-s** the lowly Ps 138:6
who **r-s** reproof Prov 15:5
highly **r-ed** by him Luke 7:2
r one another Phil 2:3
did not **r** equality Phil 2:6

REGENERATION *renewal*
r when the Son Matt 19:28
the washing of **r** Titus 3:5

REGION *area*
r of the Jordan Josh 22:10
the **r-s** of Galilee Matt 2:22
to the **r** of Judea Mark 10:1
same **r**...shepherds Luke 2:8

REGISTER *enroll, record*
r...people of Israel 2 Sam 24:4
to **r** for the census Luke 2:3

REHOBOAM
son of Solomon 1 Kin 11:43
king of Judah 1 Kin 12:16ff; 2 Chr 11:1ff

REIGN *rule*
LORD shall **r** forever Ex 15:18
Shall Saul **r** over 1 Sam 11:12
David **r-ed** over all 2 Sam 8:15
The LORD **r-s** Ps 93:1
By me kings **r** Prov 8:15
will **r** righteously Is 32:1
death **r-ed**...Adam Rom 5:14
He must **r** until 1 Cor 15:25
also **r** with Him 2 Tim 2:12
He will **r** forever Rev 11:15
will **r** with Him Rev 20:6

REJECT *decline, refuse*
have **r-ed** the LORD Num 11:20
will **r** you forever 1 Chr 28:9
not **r** the discipline Prov 3:11
A fool **r-s** his Prov 15:5
have **r-ed** this word Is 30:12
He who **r-s** unjust gain Is 33:15
r-ed My ordinances Ezek 20:13
have **r-ed** knowledge Hos 4:6
they **r-ed** the law Amos 2:4
the builders **r-ed** Matt 21:42
who **r-s** you **r-s** Me Luke 10:16
He who **r-s** Me John 12:48

REJOICE *be glad*
r before the LORD Lev 23:40
R, O nations Deut 32:43
I **r** in Your salvation 1 Sam 2:1
let the earth **r** 1 Chr 16:31
my soul shall **r** Ps 35:9
king will **r** in God Ps 63:11
Let us **r** and be glad Ps 118:24
I **r** at Your word Ps 119:162
R, young man Eccl 11:9
God will **r** over you Is 62:5
r-d exceedingly Matt 2:10
r at his birth Luke 1:14
crowd was **r-ing** Luke 13:17
you would have **r-d** John 14:28
r-ing in hope Rom 12:12
yet always **r-ing** 2 Cor 6:10
R in the Lord Phil 4:4
I **r** in my sufferings Col 1:24
r, O heavens Rev 12:12

REJOICING (n) *delight*
a holiday for **r** Esth 9:19
hills gird...with **r** Ps 65:12
Jerusalem *for* **r** Is 65:18

RELATIONS *sexual intercourse*
r with his wife Eve Gen 4:1
had no **r** with a man Judg 11:39
we may have **r** with Judg 19:22
had **r** with Hannah 1 Sam 1:19

RELATIVE *kinsman*
and to my **r-s** Gen 24:4
The man is our **r** Ruth 2:20
My **r-s** have failed Job 19:14
among his *own* **r-s** Mark 6:4
your **r** Elizabeth has Luke 1:36

RELEASE (n) *liberation*
a **r** through the land Lev 25:10
r for you the King Mark 15:9
r to the captives Luke 4:18

RELEASE (v) *set free*
he **r-d** Barabbas Matt 27:26
wanting to **r** Jesus Luke 23:20
efforts to **r** Him John 19:12
you **r-d** from a wife 1 Cor 7:27
r-d us from our sins Rev 1:5
R the four angels Rev 9:14

RELENT *yield*
I am tired of **r-ing** Jer 15:6
r...the calamity Jer 18:8
whether He will...**r** Joel 2:14
God may turn and **r** Jon 3:9

RELIEF *lessening of burden*
r and deliverance Esth 4:14
my *prayer for* **r** Lam 3:56
r of the brethren Acts 11:29

RELIGION *system of belief*
about their own **r** Acts 25:19
sect of our **r** Acts 26:5
pure and undefiled **r** James 1:27

RELIGIOUS *devout, pious*
r in all respects Acts 17:22
thinks...to be **r** James 1:26

RELY *depend, trust*
r-ied on the LORD 2 Chr 16:8
who...**r** on horses Is 31:1
r on his God Is 50:10
You **r** on your sword Ezek 33:26
r upon the Law Rom 2:17

REMAIN *abide, be left*
While the earth **r-s** Gen 8:22
R...in his place Ex 16:29
ark...not **r** with us 1 Sam 5:7
r-s yet...youngest 1 Sam 16:11
flee to Egypt, and **r** Matt 2:13
dove...**r-ed** upon John 1:32
not **r** in darkness John 12:46
not **r** on the cross John 19:31
she must **r** unmarried 1 Cor 7:11
gospel would **r** Gal 2:5
He **r-s** faithful 2 Tim 2:13

REMEMBER *recall, recollect*
God **r-ed** Noah Gen 8:1
I will **r** My covenant Gen 9:15
R the sabbath day Ex 20:8
not **r** the sins of my Ps 25:7
R also your Creator Eccl 12:1
O LORD, **R** me Jer 15:15
sin I will **r** no more Jer 31:34

Peter **r-ed** the word Matt 26:75
R Lot's wife Luke 17:32
r the words of Acts 20:35
to **r** the poor Gal 2:10

REMEMBRANCE ***memory***
Your **r**, O LORD Ps 135:13
Put Me in **r** Is 43:26
a book of **r** was Mal 3:16
do this in **r** of Me Luke 22:19
in **r** of Me 1 Cor 11:25

REMNANT ***remaining part***
preserve for you a **r** Gen 45:7
prayer for the **r** 2 Kin 19:4
an escaped **r** Ezra 9:8
A **r** will return Is 10:21
the **r** of Israel Jer 6:9
a **r** of the Spirit Mal 2:15
r that will be saved Rom 9:27

REMOVE ***take away*** **or** ***off***
r your sandals Ex 3:5
r-d all the idols 1 Kin 15:12
He **r-d** the high 2 Kin 18:4
r the heart of stone Ezek 36:26
not fit to **r** His Matt 3:11
r this cup from Me Luke 22:42
R the stone John 11:39
as to **r** mountains 1 Cor 13:2

REND ***tear***
r the heavens Is 64:1
r their garments Jer 36:24
r your heart and not Joel 2:13

RENDER ***inflict, repay***
I will **r** vengeance Deut 32:41
R recompense to the Ps 94:2
r to Caesar the Matt 22:21
R to all what is due Rom 13:7

RENEW ***make new, revive***
r a steadfast spirit Ps 51:10
r-ed like the eagle Ps 103:5
R our days as of old Lam 5:21
inner man...**r-ed** 2 Cor 4:16

RENOWN ***fame***
men of **r** Gen 6:4
a people, for **r** Jer 13:11
shame into...and **r** Zeph 3:19

REPAIR ***restore***
r the house of 1 Chr 26:27
r-ing...foundations Ezra 4:12
r of the walls Neh 4:7

REPAY ***pay back***
you thus **r** the LORD Deut 32:6
so God has **repaid** Judg 1:7
LORD **r** the evildoer 2 Sam 3:39
repaid me evil for Ps 109:5
r their iniquity Jer 16:18
He will fully **r** Jer 51:56
is Mine, I will **r** Rom 12:19
no one **r-s**...evil 1 Thess 5:15

REPENT ***change mind***
that He should **r** Num 23:19
r in dust and ashes Job 42:6
have refused to **r** Jer 5:3
R, for the kingdom Matt 3:2
r-ed long ago in Matt 11:21
r and believe Mark 1:15
one sinner who **r-s** Luke 15:7
R...be baptized Acts 2:38
all...should **r** Acts 17:30
r and turn to God Acts 26:20

REPENTANCE ***penitence***
with water for **r** Matt 3:11
baptism of **r** Mark 1:4
r for forgiveness Luke 24:47
appropriate to **r** Acts 26:20
r without regret 2 Cor 7:10
r from dead works Heb 6:1

to come to **r** 2 Pet 3:9

REPHAIM
1 *pre-Israelite people of Palestine* Gen 14:5; 15:20
people of large stature
2 *valley near Jerusalem* Josh 15:8; 2 Sam 23:13

REPHIDIM
Israelite campsite in Sinai Ex 17:1,8; Num 33:14,15

REPORT ***account, statement***
not bear a false **r** Ex 23:1
r concerning Him Luke 7:17
has believed our **r** John 12:38

REPRESENTATION ***likeness***
exact **r** of His nature Heb 1:3

REPRESENTATIVE ***substitute***
people's **r** before God Ex 18:19
the king's **r** Neh 11:24

REPROACH (n) ***dishonor***
taken away my **r** Gen 30:23
a **r** on all Israel 1 Sam 11:2
I have become a **r** Ps 31:11
with dishonor...**r** Prov 18:3
not fear the **r** of Is 51:7
the **r** of Christ Heb 11:26

REPROACH (v) ***accuse, rebuke***
to **r** the living God 2 Kin 19:4
My heart does not **r** Job 27:6
foolish man **r-es** You Ps 74:22
enemies have **r-ed** me Ps 102:8
He **r-ed** them for Mark 16:14

REPROOF ***correction, rebuke***
spurned all my **r** Prov 1:30
regards **r** is sensible Prov 15:5
who hates **r** will Prov 15:10
and **r** give wisdom Prov 29:15
for teaching, for **r** 2 Tim 3:16

REPROVE ***correct, rebuke***
r your neighbor Lev 19:17
LORD loves He **r-s** Prov 3:12
Do not **r** a scoffer Prov 9:8
R the ruthless Is 1:17
r, rebuke, exhort 2 Tim 4:2
whom I love, I **r** Rev 3:19

REPTILE ***snake***
and the sand **r** Lev 11:30
r-s of the earth Mic 7:17
r-s and creatures James 3:7

REPUTATION ***character***
seven men of good **r** Acts 6:3
a **r** for good works 1 Tim 5:10

REQUEST ***desire, petition***
my people as my **r** Esth 7:3
the **r** of his lips Ps 21:2
He gave them their **r** Ps 106:15
r-s be made known to Phil 4:6

REQUIRE ***demand, insist***
r your lifeblood Gen 9:5
God **r** from you Deut 10:12
as each day **r-d** Ezra 3:4
your soul is **r-d** Luke 12:20
r-d of stewards 1 Cor 4:2

REQUIREMENT ***necessity***
r-s of the Lord Luke 1:6
r of the Law Rom 8:4
law of physical **r** Heb 7:16

RESCUE ***deliver, redeem***
O LORD, **r** my soul Ps 6:4
R the weak and needy Ps 82:4
He delivers and **r-s** Dan 6:27
The Lord will **r** me 2 Tim 4:18
r the godly from 2 Pet 2:9

RESERVE ***retain, store up***
r-d a blessing for Gen 27:36

darkness...in **r** Job 20:26
lips may **r** knowledge Prov 5:2
r-s wrath for Nah 1:2
r-d in heaven 1 Pet 1:4
r-d for fire 2 Pet 3:7

RESIDE ***dwell, live***
stranger who **r-s** Lev 19:34
a son of man **r** in it Jer 49:18
those who **r** as aliens 1 Pet 1:1

RESIST ***oppose, withstand***
not **r** an evil person Matt 5:39
none...able to **r** Luke 21:15
r-ing the Holy Spirit Acts 7:51
whoever **r-s** authority Rom 13:2
R the devil James 4:7

RESPECT (n) ***regard***
no **r** for the old Deut 28:50
where is My **r** Mal 1:6
please *Him* in all **r-s** Col 1:10
to your masters...**r** 1 Pet 2:18

RESPECT (v) ***esteem***
They will **r** my son Matt 21:37
not fear God nor **r** Luke 18:4
R what is right Rom 12:17
wife...**r-s** her husband Eph 5:33

RESPOND ***answer, reply***
He will **r** to them Is 19:22
r to the heavens Hos 2:21
how you should **r** Col 4:6
Peter **r-ed** to her Acts 5:8

REST (n) ***remainder***
r turned and fled Judg 20:45
the **r** of the exiles Ezra 6:16
the **r** of your days Prov 19:20
I will slay the **r** Amos 9:1
to the **r**...parables Luke 8:10

REST (n) ***tranquility***
r from our work Gen 5:29
sabbath of solemn **r** Lev 16:31
God gives you **r** Josh 1:13
the weary are at **r** Job 3:17
Return to your **r** Ps 116:7
whole earth is at **r** Is 14:7
there is no **r** Lam 5:5
I will give you **r** Matt 11:28
no **r** for my spirit 2 Cor 2:13
not enter My **r** Heb 3:11
no **r** day and night Rev 14:11

REST (v) ***settled, refresh***
the ark **r-ed** upon Gen 8:4
glory...LORD **r-ed** Ex 24:16
Spirit **r-ed** upon Num 11:25
R in the LORD Ps 37:7
Wisdom **r-s** in Prov 14:33
government will **r** on Is 9:6
iniquity **r-ed** on Ezek 32:27
r-ed on the seventh Heb 4:4
r from their labors Rev 14:13

RESTING PLACE
dove found no **r** Gen 8:9
This is My **r** forever Ps 132:14
Do not destroy his **r** Prov 24:15
r will be glorious Is 11:10

RESTITUTION ***reparation***
owner...make **r** Ex 21:34
make **r** in full Num 5:7
r for the lamb 2 Sam 12:6

RESTORE ***reestablish, replace***
son he had **r-d** to 2 Kin 8:1
they **r-d** Jerusalem Neh 3:8
r His righteousness Job 33:26
He **r-s** my soul Ps 23:3
R to me the joy Ps 51:12
O God, **r** us Ps 80:3
the LORD **r-s** Zion Is 52:8
R us to You Lam 5:21

his hand was **r-d** Mark 3:5
r-ing the kingdom Acts 1:6

RESTRAIN ***hold back***
the rain...was **r-ed** Gen 8:2
who can **r** Him Job 11:10
He **r-ed** His anger Ps 78:38
who **r-s** his lips Prov 10:19
Will You **r** Yourself Is 64:12
R your voice from Jer 31:16
r-ed the crowds Acts 14:18

RESULT (n) ***consequence, effect***
a **r** of the anguish Is 53:11
not as a **r** of works Eph 2:9
have *its* perfect **r** James 1:4
as a **r** of the works James 2:22

RESULT (v) ***follow, happen***
r-ed In reproach Jer 20:8
sin **r-ing** in death Rom 6:16
proved to **r** in death Rom 7:10
r-ing in salvation Rom 10:10

RESURRECTION
who say...no **r** Matt 22:23
r of the righteous Luke 14:14
being sons of the **r** Luke 20:36
r of judgment John 5:29
the **r** and the life John 11:25
r of the dead Acts 24:21
if there is no **r** 1 Cor 15:13
power of His **r** Phil 3:10
hope through the **r** 1 Pet 1:3
This is the first **r** Rev 20:5

RETRIBUTION ***punishment***
days of **r** have come Hos 9:7
stumbling block...**r** Rom 11:9
dealing out **r** to 2 Thess 1:8

RETURN ***go back*** **or** ***repay***
to dust you shall **r** Gen 3:19
r-ed me evil for 1 Sam 25:21
clouds **r** after the Eccl 12:2
a remnant...will **r** Is 10:22
ransomed...will **r** Is 51:11
r-ed to Galilee Luke 4:14
repent and **r** Acts 3:19
not **r-ing** evil for 1 Pet 3:9

REUBEN
1 *son of Jacob / Leah* Gen 29:32
2 *tribe* Ex 6:14; Num 1:21

REVEAL ***expose, make known***
God had **r-ed** Himself Gen 35:7
He **r-s** mysteries Job 12:22
will **r** his iniquity Job 20:27
do not **r** the secret Prov 25:9
glory...will be **r-ed** Is 40:5
r this mystery Dan 2:47
r-ed them to infants Matt 11:25
blood did not **r** *this* Matt 16:17
Son of Man is **r-ed** Luke 17:30
glory...to be **r-ed** Rom 8:18
r-ed with fire 1 Cor 3:13
to **r** His Son in me Gal 1:16
lawlessness is **r-ed** 2 Thess 2:3
r-ed in the flesh 1 Tim 3:16

REVELATION ***divine disclosure***
a **r** to Your servant 2 Sam 7:27
the **r** ended Dan 7:28
r to the Gentiles Luke 2:32
r of...judgment Rom 2:5
the **r** of the mystery Rom 16:25
awaiting...the **r** 1 Cor 1:7
through a **r** of Jesus Gal 1:12
by **r**...made known Eph 3:3
The **R** of Jesus Rev 1:1

REVENGE ***vengeance***
take our **r** on him Jer 20:10
Never take...**r** Rom 12:19

REVERE ***adore, venerate***
r My sanctuary Lev 19:30
nations will **r** You Is 25:3

REVERENCE ***respect, awe***
you do away with **r** Job 15:4
Worship...with **r** Ps 2:11
bow in **r** for You Ps 5:7
in **r** prepared an ark Heb 11:7
service with **r** and Heb 12:28

REVILE ***use abusive language***
Do you **r** God's high Acts 23:4
are **r-d**, we bless 1 Cor 4:12
r-d for the name of 1 Pet 4:14
r angelic majesties Jude 8

REVIVE ***bring back to life***
they **r** the stones Neh 4:2
let your heart **r** Ps 69:32
r us again Ps 85:6
r me in Your ways Ps 119:37
r-d your concern Phil 4:10

REVOLT ***rebellion***
incited **r** within it Ezra 4:15
Speaking...and **r** Is 59:13
stirred up a **r** Acts 21:38

REWARD ***prize***
emptiness...his **r** Job 15:31
r for the righteous Ps 58:11
The **r** of humility Prov 22:4
chases after **r-s** Is 1:23
His **r** is with Him Is 62:11
your **r** in heaven Matt 5:12
not lose his **r** Matt 10:42
looking to the **r** Heb 11:26
receive a full **r** 2 John 8

RHODA
Christian servant girl Acts 12:13

RHODES
Mediterranean isle Acts 21:1

RIB ***bone***
took one of his **r-s** Gen 2:21
r-s *were* in its mouth Dan 7:5

RICH (adj) ***wealthy***
Abram was very **r** Gen 13:2
LORD makes poor...**r** 1 Sam 2:7
not a **r** man boast Jer 9:23
woe to you who are **r** Luke 6:24
a **r** man Luke 16:1
being **r** in mercy Eph 2:4
r in good works 1 Tim 6:18

RICH (n) ***wealthy***
r shall not pay more Ex 30:15
the **r** above the poor Job 34:19
r among the people Ps 45:12
The **r** and the poor Prov 22:2

RICHES ***wealth***
R do not profit Prov 11:4
who trusts in his **r** Prov 11:28
neither poverty nor **r** Prov 30:8
choked with...**r** Luke 8:14
abounding in **r** Rom 10:12
r of His grace Eph 1:7
r of Christ Eph 3:8
His **r** in glory Phil 4:19
uncertainty of **r** 1 Tim 6:17
Your **r** have rotted James 5:2

RIDDLE ***puzzle***
propound a **r** Judg 14:12
my **r** on the harp Ps 49:4
wise and their **r-s** Prov 1:6
propound a **r** Ezek 17:2

RIGHT (adj) ***correct*** **or** ***direction***
r in the sight of Deut 12:25
r in his own eyes Judg 17:6
precepts...are **r** Ps 19:8
r eye makes you Matt 5:29
what your **r** hand is Matt 6:3
Sit at My **r** hand Matt 22:44
the **r** hand of God Mark 16:19
at the **r** time Christ Rom 5:6
r hand of fellowship Gal 2:9
whatever is **r** Phil 4:8
forsaking the **r** way 2 Pet 2:15

RIGHT (n) ***due, prerogative***
her conjugal **r-s** Ex 21:10
r of redemption Lev 25:32
r of the firstborn Deut 21:17
the **r-s** of the poor Prov 29:7
r-s of the afflicted Prov 31:9
my **r** in the gospel 1 Cor 9:18

RIGHTEOUS (adj) ***virtuous***
Noah was a **r** man Gen 6:9
LORD is the **r** one Ex 9:27
You are more **r** 1 Sam 24:17
God is a **r** judge Ps 7:11
A **r** man hates Prov 13:5
for David a **r** Branch Jer 23:5
LORD our God is **r** Dan 9:14
ninety-nine **r** Luke 15:7
coming of the **R** One Acts 7:52
r *man* shall live by Rom 1:17
none **r**, not even one Rom 3:10
many will be made **r** Rom 5:19
prayer of a **r** man James 5:16

RIGHTEOUS (n) ***moral one***
assembly of the **r** Ps 1:5
LORD tests the **r** Ps 11:5
LORD loves the **r** Ps 146:8
the paths of the **r** Prov 2:20
the **r** will flourish Prov 11:28
joy for the **r** Prov 21:15
way of the **r** is Is 26:7
they sell the **r** for Amos 2:6
sends rain on *the* **r** Matt 5:45
r into eternal life Matt 25:46

RIGHTEOUSNESS
reckoned it...as **r** Gen 15:6
will repay...his **r** 1 Sam 26:23
I put on **r** Job 29:14
in the paths of **r** Ps 23:3
judge the world in **r** Ps 96:13
declare His **r** Ps 97:6
His **r** endures forever Ps 111:3
R exalts a nation Prov 14:34
clouds pour down **r** Is 45:8
wrapped me with...**r** Is 61:10
The LORD our **r** Jer 23:6
to rain **r** on you Hos 10:12
to fulfill all **r** Matt 3:15
and thirst for **r** Matt 5:6
kingdom and His **r** Matt 6:33
you enemy of all **r** Acts 13:10
through one act of **r** Rom 5:18
breastplate of **r** Eph 6:14
pursue **r**, faith 2 Tim 2:22
the crown of **r** 2 Tim 4:8
peaceful fruit of **r** Heb 12:11
not achieve the **r** James 1:20
suffer for...**r** 1 Pet 3:14

RIMMON
1 *a Benjamite* 2 Sam 4:2
2 *Aramean deity* 2 Kin 5:18
3 *town in Simeon* Josh 19:1,7
4 *city of Zebulun* Josh 19:13
5 *rock of* Judg 20:45; 21:13

RING ***jewelry, ornament***
make four gold **r-s** Ex 25:26
took his signet **r** Esth 3:10
As a **r** of gold Prov 11:22
finger **r-s**, nose **r-s** Is 3:21

RIOT ***tumult, uprising***
otherwise a **r** might occur Matt 26:5
a **r** was starting Matt 27:24
accused of a **r** Acts 19:40

RIPE *fully developed*
old man of **r** age Gen 35:29
produced **r** grapes Gen 40:10
the harvest is **r** Joel 3:13
harvest...is **r** Rev 14:15

RISE *go up, issue forth*
mist used to **r** from Gen 2:6
Cain **rose** up against Gen 4:8
scepter shall **r** Num 24:17
witnesses **r** up Ps 35:11
children **r** up Prov 31:28
nation will **r** Matt 24:7
r-n, just as He said Matt 28:6
children will **r** up Mark 13:12
Lord has really **r-n** Luke 24:34

RIVER
r flowed out of Eden Gen 2:10
the **r** Euphrates Josh 1:4
r of Your delights Ps 36:8
He changes **r-s** into Ps 107:33
the **r-s** of Babylon Ps 137:1
A place of **r-s** and Is 33:21
r-s in the desert Is 43:20
peace...like a **r** Is 66:12
tears...like a **r** Lam 2:18
baptized...Jordan **R** Mark 1:5
r-s of living water John 7:38
r of the water of life Rev 22:1

RIZPAH
concubine of Saul 2 Sam 3:7

ROAD *path, way*
a lion in the **r** Prov 26:13
the rough **r-s** smooth Luke 3:5
coats on the **r** Luke 19:36
the Lord on the **r** Acts 9:27

ROAR (n) *loud deep sound*
the sound of the **r** 1 Kin 18:41
young lions' **r** Zech 11:3
pass away with a **r** 2 Pet 3:10

ROAR (v) *utter a deep sound*
a voice **r-s** Job 37:4
Let the sea **r** Ps 96:11
LORD will **r** from Jer 25:30
a lion **r** in the Amos 3:4

ROAST *cook*
grain **r-ed** in the fire Lev 2:14
r-ed the...*animals* 2 Chr 35:13
lazy man...**r** Prov 12:27

ROB *steal*
bear **r-bed** of her Prov 17:12
Do not **r** the poor Prov 22:22
Will a man **r** God Mal 3:8
do you **r** temples Rom 2:22
I **r-bed**...churches 2 Cor 11:8

ROBBER *thief*
she lurks as a **r** Prov 23:28
become a den of **r-s** Jer 7:11
crucified two **r-s** Mark 15:27
fell among **r-s** Luke 10:30
a thief and a **r** John 10:1
r-s of temples Acts 19:37

ROBBERY *theft*
not vainly hope in **r** Ps 62:10
I hate **r** in the Is 61:8
they are full of **r** Matt 23:25
you are full of **r** Luke 11:39

ROBE *cloak, garment*
cut off...Saul's **r** 1 Sam 24:4
justice was like a **r** Job 29:14
r of righteousness Is 61:10
put a scarlet **r** on Matt 27:28
walk...in long **r-s** Mark 12:38
wearing a white **r** Mark 16:5
bring...the best **r** Luke 15:22
washed their **r-s** Rev 7:14
a **r** dipped in blood Rev 19:13

ROCK *stone*
the cleft of the **r** Ex 33:22
struck the **r** twice Num 20:11
R of his salvation Deut 32:15
LORD is my **r** 2 Sam 22:2
engraved in the **r** Job 19:24
my **r** and my fortress Ps 18:2
r and my Redeemer Ps 19:14
set my feet upon a **r** Ps 40:2
a **r** to stumble over Is 8:14
an everlasting **R** Is 26:4
his house on the **r** Matt 7:24
upon this **r** I will Matt 16:18
the **r-s** were split Matt 27:51
hewn out in the **r** Mark 15:46
a **r** of offense Rom 9:33

ROD *staff, stick*
fresh **r-s** of poplar Gen 30:37
r of Aaron Num 17:8
break them with a **r** Ps 2:9
Your **r** and Your staff Ps 23:4
who withholds his **r** Prov 13:24
The **r** of discipline Prov 22:15
r of My anger Is 10:5
rule them with a **r** Rev 19:15

ROLL *move*
sky will be **r-ed** up Is 34:4
let justice **r** down Amos 5:24
r-ed away the stone Matt 28:2
Who will **r** away the Mark 16:3

ROMANS
citizens of Roman Empire John 11:48; Acts 16:21,37

ROME
Italian city Acts 2:10
Roman Empire capital Acts 18:2
Paul held there Acts 28:14,16

ROOF
brought...to the **r** Josh 2:6
r...woman bathing 2 Sam 11:2
removed the **r** above Mark 2:4
r and let him down Luke 5:19

ROOM *chamber*
the ark with **r-s** Gen 6:14
go into your inner **r** Matt 6:6
a large upper **r** Mark 14:15
no **r** for them in Luke 2:7
r for the wrath Rom 12:19

ROOSTER *bird*
The strutting **r** Prov 30:31
before a **r** crows Matt 26:34
r will not crow John 13:38

ROOT (n) *source*
the **r** of Jesse Is 11:10
no **r**, it withered Mark 4:6
if the **r** is holy Rom 11:16
of money is a **r** 1 Tim 6:10
no **r** of bitterness Heb 12:15
the **R** of David Rev 5:5

ROOT (v) *establish or tear out*
r out your Asherim Mic 5:14
r-ed and grounded in Eph 3:17

ROPE *cord*
them down by a **r** Josh 2:15
bound...two new **r-s** Judg 15:13
he snapped the **r-s** Judg 16:12
Instead of a belt, a **r** Is 3:24

ROSE (n) *flower*
I am the **r** of Sharon Song 2:1

ROSH
1 *son of Benjamin* Gen 46:21
2 *place of God* Ezek 38:2,3; 39:1

ROT *decay*
their flesh will **r** Zech 14:12
riches have **r-ted** James 5:2

ROTTENNESS *decay*
passion is **r** to Prov 14:30
r to the house of Hos 5:12

ROUGH *jagged, uneven*
r ground become a Is 40:4
the **r** places smooth Is 45:2

ROYAL *kingly*
captured the **r** city 2 Sam 12:26
his **r** bounty 1 Kin 10:13
all the **r** offspring 2 Kin 11:1
put on her **r** robes Esth 5:1
And a **r** diadem Is 62:3
roof of the **r** palace Dan 4:29
a **r** official John 4:46
fulfilling the **r** law James 2:8
a **r** priesthood 1 Pet 2:9

RUDDY *reddish in complexion*
he was **r** 1 Sam 16:12
a youth, and **r** 1 Sam 17:42
beloved is...and **r** Song 5:10

RUHAMAH
symbolic for Israel Hos 2:1

RUIN (n) *destruction*
shall be a **r** forever Deut 13:16
become a heap of **r-s** 1 Kin 9:8
the perpetual **r-s** Ps 74:3
Jerusalem in **r-s** Ps 79:1
r of the poor is Prov 10:15
fool's mouth is his **r** Prov 18:7
rebuild its **r-s** Acts 15:16

RUIN (v) *destroy*
to **r** him without Job 2:3
the grain is **r-ed** Joel 1:10
skins will be **r-ed** Luke 5:37

RULE (n) *authority, government*
to establish his **r** 1 Chr 18:3
against the **r** of 2 Chr 21:8
will walk by this **r** Gal 6:16
above all **r** and Eph 1:21
according to the **r-s** 2 Tim 2:5

RULE (v) *govern*
r over the fish Gen 1:26
Gideon, **R** over us Judg 8:22
godless men...not **r** Job 34:30
r-s over the nations Ps 22:28
The sun to **r** by day Ps 136:8
By me princes **r** Prov 8:16
women **r** over them Is 3:12
r over the Gentiles Rom 15:12
peace of Christ **r** Col 3:15
r them with a rod Rev 2:27

RULER *king, monarch*
Joseph was the **r** Gen 42:6
nor curse a **r** Ex 22:28
no chief...or **r** Prov 6:7
your **r-s** have fled Is 22:3
Most High is **r** Dan 4:32
come forth a **R** Matt 2:6
r of the demons Matt 9:34
r-s of the Gentiles Mark 10:42
the **r** of this world John 12:31
Who made you a **r** Acts 7:27
be subject to **r-s** Titus 3:1

RUMOR *gossip, hearsay*
r will be *added* to **r** Ezek 7:26
wars and **r-s** of wars Matt 24:6

RUN *move rapidly*
to **r** his course Ps 19:5
their feet **r** to evil Prov 1:16
streams **r-ning** with Is 30:25
r and not get tired Is 40:31
rivers to **r** like oil Ezek 32:14
Peter got up and **ran** Luke 24:12
disciple **ran** ahead John 20:4
who **r** in a race 1 Cor 9:24

RUSH *move quickly*
and **r** upon the city Judg 9:33
r-es headlong at Him Job 15:26
herd **r-ed** down the Matt 8:32
horses **r-ing** to battle Rev 9:9

RUSHES *marshy plant*
Can the **r** grow Job 8:11
reeds and **r** will rot Is 19:6

RUST *corrosion*
in which there is **r** Ezek 24:6
moth and **r** destroy Matt 6:19
r will be a witness James 5:3

RUTH
Moabitess Ruth 1:4
Naomi's daughter-in-law Ruth 1:14ff
married Boaz Ruth 4:13
in Messianic line Matt 1:5

RUTHLESS *cruel*
r men attain riches Prov 11:16
Reprove the **r** Is 1:17
song of the **r** is Is 25:5
most **r** of the Ezek 28:7

S

SABAOTH
Lord of Sabaoth is same as Lord of Hosts Rom 9:29; James 5:4
see also **HOST**

SABBATH *day of rest*
Remember the **s** day Ex 20:8
LORD blessed the **s** day Ex 20:11
keep My **s-s** and Lev 26:2
Observe the **s** day Deut 5:12
new moon nor **s** 2 Kin 4:23
call the **s** a delight Is 58:13
My **s-s** to be a sign Ezek 20:12
is Lord of the **S** Matt 12:8
S was made for man Mark 2:27
to do good...on the **S** Mark 3:4
the cross on the **S** John 19:31
a **S** day's journey Acts 1:12
are read every **S** Acts 13:27
S rest for the people Heb 4:9

SABBATICAL YEAR
seventh year of rest Lev 25:5

SABEANS
people of Sheba in SW Arabia Job 1:15; Is 45:14; Joel 3:8

SACKCLOTH *coarse cloth*
put **s** on his loins Gen 37:34
gird on **s** and lament 2 Sam 3:31
put on **s** and ashes Esth 4:1
sewed **s** over my skin Job 16:15
with fasting, **s**, and Dan 9:3
sun became black as **s** Rev 6:12

SACRED *consecrated, holy*
took all the **s** things 2 Kin 12:18
perform **s** services 1 Cor 9:13
known...**s** writings 2 Tim 3:15
table and the **s** bread Heb 9:2

SACRIFICE (n) *offering of a life*
Jacob offered a **s** Gen 31:54
a Passover **s** to Ex 12:27
s-s of righteousness Ps 4:5
The **s** of the wicked Prov 15:8
loyalty rather than **s** Hos 6:6
compassion...not **s** Matt 9:13
a **s** to the idol Acts 7:41
a living and holy **s** Rom 12:1
an acceptable **s** Phil 4:18
by the **s** of Himself Heb 9:26
s-s God is pleased Heb 13:16
offer up spiritual **s-s** 1 Pet 2:5

SACRIFICE (v) *offer a life*
we may **s** to the Lord Ex 5:3
s on it your burnt Ex 20:24
when you **s** a sacrifice Lev 22:29
they **s-d** to the LORD Judg 2:5
even **s-d** their sons Ps 106:37
s-ing to the Baals Hos 11:2
lamb had to be **s-d** Luke 22:7
they **s** to demons 1 Cor 10:20

SAD *sorrowful, unhappy*
people heard...**s** word Ex 33:4
Why is your face **s** Neh 2:2
heart is **s**, the Prov 15:13

SADDUCEES
Jewish religious party Matt 3:7; 16:11,12; Mark 12:18; Acts 5:17; 23:6-8

SAFE *free from danger*
houses are **s** from fear Job 21:9
runs into it and is **s** Prov 18:10
back **s** and sound Luke 15:27

SAIL (n) *canvas for wind*
Nor spread out the **s** Is 33:23
s was...embroidered Ezek 27:7

SAIL (v) *proceed by boat*
they **s-ed** to Cyprus Acts 13:4
to **s** past Ephesus Acts 20:16
set **s** from Crete Acts 27:21

SAILOR *mariner, seaman*
s-s...knew the sea 1 Kin 9:27
s-s and your pilots Ezek 27:27
every passenger and **s** Rev 18:17

SAINTS *ones faithful to God*
s...in the earth Ps 16:3
the **s** of the Highest Dan 7:22
s...fallen asleep Matt 27:52
lock up...**s** in prisons Acts 26:10
intercedes for the **s** Rom 8:27
s will judge the 1 Cor 6:2
citizens with the **s** Eph 2:19
perseverance of the **s** Rev 14:12

SALAMIS
city on Cyprus Acts 13:5

SALEM
Jerusalem Gen 14:18; Ps 76:2; Heb 7:1,2

SALOME
1 *wife of Zebedee* Mark 15:40
mother of James and John at open tomb Mark 16:1
2 *daughter of Herodias* Matt 14:6ff; Mark 6:22-26

SALT *preservative*
became a pillar of **s** Gen 19:26
and sowed it with **s** Judg 9:45
be eaten without **s** Job 6:6
the **s** of the earth Matt 5:13
seasoned with **s** Col 4:6
can **s** water produce James 3:12

SALT SEA
the Dead Sea Gen 14:3; Num 34:3; Deut 3:17; Josh 15:2

SALT, VALLEY OF
S of Dead Sea 2 Sam 8:13; 2 Chr 25:11

SALVATION *deliverance*
For Your **s** I wait Gen 49:18
He has become my **s** Ex 15:2
scorned...his **s** Deut 32:15
S belongs to the LORD Ps 3:8
my light and my **s** Ps 27:1
lift up the cup of **s** Ps 116:13
My **s** will be forever Is 51:6
helmet of **s** on His Is 59:17
S is from the LORD Jon 2:9
eyes have seen Your **s** Luke 2:30
s in no one else Acts 4:12
power of God for **s** Rom 1:16
now is the day of **s** 2 Cor 6:2
take the helmet of **s** Eph 6:17
work out your **s** with Phil 2:12
s through our Lord 1 Thess 5:9
that leads to **s** 2 Tim 3:15
who will inherit **s** Heb 1:14
neglect so great a **s** Heb 2:3
S to our God who Rev 7:10

SAMARIA
1 *capital of N kingdom* 1 Kin 16:24; 2 Chr 18:9
2 *another name for N kingdom* 1 Kin 13:32; 2 Kin 17:24; Hos 8:5; Amos 3:9; Obad 19
3 *region of central hill country* John 4:4-7; Acts 8:1ff

SAMOTHRACE
N Aegean island Acts 16:11

SAMSON
a Hebrew judge Judg 13:24
weak in character Judg 14:1ff
slave of passion Judg 16:1ff
great strength Judg 16:5,12

SAMUEL
son of Elkanah and Hannah 1 Sam 1:20
dedicated to God 1 Sam 1:21ff
called by God 1 Sam 3:1-18
judge 1 Sam 7:15-17
opposed monarchy 1 Sam 8:6
anointed Saul 1 Sam 10:1
anointed David 1 Sam 16:12
death 1 Sam 25:1

SANBALLAT
man of Beth-horon Neh 2:10
against Nehemiah Neh 6:1ff

SANCTIFICATION *holiness*
resulting in **s** Rom 6:22
righteousness and **s** 1 Cor 1:30
will of God, your **s** 1 Thess 4:3
s by the Spirit 2 Thess 2:13
s without which no Heb 12:14

SANCTIFY *set apart to God*
S to Me every Ex 13:2
the LORD who **s-ies** Lev 22:32
They will **s** My name Is 29:23
will **s** the Holy One Is 29:23
S My sabbaths Ezek 20:20
S them in the truth John 17:17
s-ied by the...Spirit Rom 15:16
husband is **s-ied** 1 Cor 7:14
s Christ as Lord 1 Pet 3:15

SANCTUARY *place of worship*
construct a **s** for Me Ex 25:8
revere My **s** Lev 19:30
utensils of the **s** 1 Chr 9:29
into the **s** of God Ps 73:17
Praise God in His **s** Ps 150:1
beautify...My **s** Is 60:13
a minister in the **s** Heb 8:2

SAND
descendants as the **s** Gen 32:12
treasures of the **s** Deut 33:19
built...on the **s** Matt 7:26
innumerable as the **s** Heb 11:12

SANDAL *footwear*
s has not worn out Deut 29:5
fit to remove His **s-s** Matt 3:11
two coats, or **s-s** Matt 10:10

SANHEDRIN *see* **COUNCIL**

SAPPHIRA
wife of Ananias Acts 5:1-10
struck dead for lying

SAPPHIRE *precious stone*
a **s** and a diamond Ex 28:18
Inlaid with **s-s** Song 5:14
foundations...in **s-s** Is 54:11

SARAH / SARAI
wife of Abraham Gen 11:29
barren Gen 11:30
beautiful Gen 12:11
gave birth to Isaac Gen 21:2,3
death Gen 23:2

SARDIS
city in Asia Minor Rev 1:11; 3:1,4

SARGON
son of Tiglath-pileser III Is 20:1
king of Assyria

SATAN
Titles:
Abaddon Rev 9:11
accuser Ps 109:6; Rev 12:10
adversary 1 Pet 5:8
Apollyon Rev 9:11
Beelzebul Matt 10:25; Mark 3:22
Belial 2 Cor 6:15
deceiver of the world Rev 12:9
devil Matt 4:1,5; 25:41; John 6:70; 13:2; Eph 4:27; 6:11; 1 Tim 3:6,7; Heb 2:14; 1 Pet 5:8; Rev 2:10; 20:2,10
dragon Rev 12:9
enemy Matt 13:28,39
evil one Matt 13:19,38; John 17:15; Eph 6:16; 1 John 2:13,14; 5:18,19
father of lies John 8:44
god of this world 2 Cor 4:4
liar John 8:44
murderer John 8:44
prince of the power of the air Eph 2:2
ruler of the demons Matt 9:34; Mark 3:22
ruler of this world John 12:31; 14:30; 16:11
serpent of old Rev 12:9

SATISFY *be content*
eat and not be **s-ied** Lev 26:26
s-ied their desire Ps 78:30
steals To **s** himself Prov 6:30
Nor will he be **s-ied** Prov 6:35
hunger is not **s-ied** Is 29:8
to **s** the crowd Mark 15:15

SATRAPS *Persian officials*
to the king's **s** Ezra 8:36
the **s**, the governors Esth 8:9
commissioners and **s** Dan 6:4

SAUL
1 *son of Kish* 1 Sam 9:1,2
anointed 1 Sam 10:1ff
first king 1 Sam 11:15
rejected as king 1 Sam 15:11ff
jealous of David 1 Sam 18:6ff
death 1 Sam 31:4ff
2 *apostle Paul, see* **PAUL**

SAVE *deliver, rescue*
s-d by the LORD Deut 33:29
S with Your right hand Ps 60:5
He will **s** you Prov 20:22
Turn to Me, and be **s-d** Is 45:22
s you from afar Jer 30:10
he will **s** his life Ezek 18:27
will **s** His people Matt 1:21
wishes to **s** his life Matt 16:25
Son...has come to **s** Matt 18:11
faith has **s-d** you Luke 7:50
world might be **s-d** John 3:17
Father, **s** Me from John 12:27
by which we...be **s-d** Acts 4:12
be **s-d** by His life Rom 5:10
will **s** your husband 1 Cor 7:16
Jesus came...to **s** 1 Tim 1:15
One who is able to **s** James 4:12
the righteous is **s-d** 1 Pet 4:18

SAVIOR *one who saves*
My **s**, You 2 Sam 22:3
forgot God their **S** Ps 106:21
send them a **S** and a Is 19:20
no **s** besides Me Is 43:11
righteous God and a **S** Is 45:21
S, who is Christ Luke 2:11
the **S** of the world John 4:42
as a Prince and a **S** Acts 5:31
S of all men 1 Tim 4:10
appearing of our **S** 2 Tim 1:10
our great God and **S** Titus 2:13
kingdom of our...**S** 2 Pet 1:11

SAVORY *appetizing*
prepare a **s** dish for Gen 27:4
mother made **s** food Gen 27:14

SAWS *cutting tools*
set *them* under **s** 2 Sam 12:31
cut *them* with **s** 1 Chr 20:3

SAY *pronounce, speak*
God blessed...**s-ing** Gen 1:22
not **s** in your heart Deut 9:4
to the wicked God **s-s** Ps 50:16
Do not **s** to your Prov 3:28
s-s the Preacher Eccl 1:2
He will **s**, Here I am Is 58:9
Many will **s** to Me Matt 7:22
If we **s**...no sin 1 John 1:8

SAYINGS *statements*
utter dark **s** of old Ps 78:2
s of understanding Prov 1:2
s of the wise Prov 24:23
anyone hears my **s** John 12:47

SCALE *for measuring weight*
with accurate **s-s** Job 31:6
false **s** is not good Prov 20:23
been weighed on the **s-s** Dan 5:27
with dishonest **s-s** Amos 8:5
justify wicked **s-s** Mic 6:11
a pair of **s-s** in his Rev 6:5

SCAPEGOAT *for removal of sin*
lot for the **s** fell Lev 16:10
released the goat...**s** Lev 16:26

SCARLET *bright red*
tied a **s** *thread* Gen 38:28
s thread...window Josh 2:18
lips are like a **s** Song 4:3
sins are as **s** Is 1:18
put a **s** robe on Him Matt 27:28

SCATTER *spread, sprinkle*
s among the nations Lev 26:33
Brimstone is **s-ed** on Job 18:15
storm will **s** them Is 41:16
s-ing the sheep of my Jer 23:1
s him like dust Matt 21:44
sheep...shall be **s-ed** Matt 26:31

SCEPTER *symbol of authority*
s shall not depart Gen 49:10
s...rise from Israel Num 24:17
A **s** of uprightness Ps 45:6
The **s** of rulers Is 14:5
s of His kingdom Heb 1:8

SCHEME *plan, plot*
s...he had devised Esth 9:25
s brings him down Job 18:7
carries out wicked **s-s** Ps 37:7
ignorant of his **s-s** 2 Cor 2:11
the **s-s** of the devil Eph 6:11

SCOFF *mock, sneer*
s-ed...His prophets 2 Chr 36:16
The Lord **s-s** at them Ps 2:4
s at all the nations Ps 59:8
were **s-ing** at Him Luke 16:14

SCOFFER *mocker*
My friends are my **s-s** Job 16:20
sit in the seat of **s-s** Ps 1:1
He who corrects a **s** Prov 9:7
Behold, you **s-s** Acts 13:41

SCORCHING *burning*
words are like **s** fire Prov 16:27
s heat or sun strike Is 49:10
appointed a **s** east wind Jon 4:8
s heat of the day Matt 20:12

SCORN *treat with contempt*
s-ed...his salvation Deut 32:15
and **s-s** a mother Prov 30:17

SCORPION *poisonous spider*
serpents and **s-s** Deut 8:15
discipline...with **s-s** 1 Kin 12:11
tread on...**s-s** Luke 10:19
not give him a **s** Luke 11:12
s-s...have power Rev 9:3

SCOURGE (n) *whip*
the **s** of the tongue Job 5:21
arouse a **s** against Is 10:26
He made a **s** of cords John 2:15

SCOURGE (v) *flog, whip*
s and crucify *Him* Matt 20:19
having Jesus **s-d** Matt 27:26
lawful for you to **s** Acts 22:25
He **s-s** every son Heb 12:6

SCRAPE *rub, scratch*
plaster that they **s** Lev 14:41
s-d the honey into Judg 14:9
potsherd to **s** himself Job 2:8

SCREEN *conceal, separate*
s the ark with the veil Ex 40:3
s-ed off the ark Ex 40:21

SCRIBE *copier, writer*
and Sheva was **s** 2 Sam 20:25
then the king's **s** 2 Chr 24:11
Ezra the **s** stood Neh 8:4
lying pen of the **s-s** Jer 8:8
chief priests and **s-s** Matt 2:4
and not as the **s-s** Mark 1:22
Where is the **s** 1 Cor 1:20

SCRIPTURE
understanding...**S-s** Matt 22:29
fulfill...**S-s** Mark 14:49
S has been fulfilled Luke 4:21
You search the **S-s** John 5:39
S cannot be broken John 10:35
mighty in the **S-s** Acts 18:24
what does the **S** say Rom 4:3
S is inspired by God 2 Tim 3:16

SCROLL *parchment*
these curses on a **s** Num 5:23
Take a **s** and write Jer 36:2
eat this **s**, and go Ezek 3:1
like a **s**...rolled Rev 6:14

SEA *body of salt water*
waters He called **s-s** Gen 1:10
s, or the **s** monster Job 7:12
founded it upon the **s-s** Ps 24:2
to the **s** in ships Ps 107:23
the waters cover the **s** Is 11:9
rebukes the **s** and Nah 1:4
walking on the **s** Matt 14:26
s *began* to be stirred John 6:18
dangers on the **s** 2 Cor 11:26
s of glass, like crystal Rev 4:6

SEA OF GALILEE *see* **GALILEE, SEA OF**

SEACOAST *seashore*
remnant of the **s** Ezek 25:16
inhabitants of the **s** Zeph 2:5
s will be pastures Zeph 2:6

SEAL (n) *mark, stamp*
Your **s** and your cord Gen 38:18
the engravings of a **s** Ex 28:21
the **s** of perfection Ezek 28:12
testimony has set his **s** John 3:33
s of God on their Rev 9:4

SEAL (v) *mark, secure*
s-ed...his seal 1 Kin 21:8
s *it*...king's signet Esth 8:8
a spring **s-ed** up Song 4:12
to **s** up vision Dan 9:24
s up the book until Dan 12:4

SEARCH *examine, inquire*
LORD **s-es** all hearts 1 Chr 28:9
S me, O God, and Ps 139:23
LORD, **s** the heart Jer 17:10
s for the Child Matt 2:13
companions **s-ed** for Mark 1:36
You **s** the Scriptures John 5:39

SEASHORE *sea coast*
sand that is on the **s** Josh 11:4
the **s** in abundance 1 Kin 4:20
the dragon stood on...**s** Rev 13:1

SEASON *time of the year*
rains in their **s** Lev 26:4
grain in its **s** Job 5:26
its fruit in its **s** Ps 1:3
in **s** *and* out of **s** 2 Tim 4:2

SEAT (n) *chair, stool*
mercy **s** of pure gold Ex 25:17
sit in the **s** of scoffers Ps 1:1
sit in the **s** of gods Ezek 28:2
s-s in the synagogues Matt 23:6
before...judgment **s** Rom 14:10

SEAT (v) *sit*
s-ed at the Lord's feet Luke 10:39
coming, **s-ed**...colt John 12:15
s-ed at the right hand Col 3:1

SECRET *what is hidden*
sets *it* up in **s** Deut 27:15
the **s-s** of wisdom Job 11:6
the **s-s** of the heart Ps 44:21
bread *eaten* in **s** Prov 9:17
A gift in **s** subdues Prov 21:14
have not spoken in **s** Is 45:19
giving will be in **s** Matt 6:4
Father who sees...in **s** Matt 6:4
God will judge the **s-s** Rom 2:16

SECT *faction, party*
s of the Sadducees Acts 5:17
s of the Pharisees Acts 15:5
s of the Nazarenes Acts 24:5

SECURE *safe, stable*
overthrows the **s** Job 12:19
be **s** on their land Ezek 34:27
s in the mountain Amos 6:1
made the grave **s** Matt 27:66

SECURITY *certainty, safety*
Israel dwells in **s** Deut 33:28
in it living in **s** Judg 18:7
provides them with **s** Job 24:23
will lie down in **s** Is 14:30
will dwell in **s** Zech 14:11

SEDUCE *entice, persuade*
if a man **s-s** a virgin Ex 22:16
s you from...LORD Deut 13:10
s-d them to do evil 2 Kin 21:9
lips she **s-s** him Prov 7:21

SEE *look, perceive*
I have **s-n** God face Gen 32:30
No eye will **s** me Job 24:15
s the works of God Ps 66:5
the blind will **s** Is 29:18
s the glory of the LORD Is 35:2
to **s** but do not **s** Ezek 12:2
s your good works Matt 5:16
and the blind **s-ing** Matt 15:31
s the Son of Man Matt 16:28
s-ing their faith Mark 2:5
s-n Your salvation Luke 2:30
we **saw** His glory John 1:14
No one has **s-n** God John 1:18
s the Son of Man John 6:62
you will **s** Me John 16:16
may **s** My glory John 17:24
s in a mirror dimly 1 Cor 13:12
of things not **s-n** Heb 11:1
No one has **s-n** 1 John 4:12

SEED *descendant* **or** *plant*
sow your **s** uselessly Lev 26:16
establish your **s** Ps 89:4
O **s** of Abraham Ps 105:6
s to the sower Is 55:10
like a mustard **s** Matt 13:31
went out to sow his **s** Luke 8:5
s is the word of God Luke 8:11
s which is perishable 1 Pet 1:23
His **s** abides in him 1 John 3:9

SEEK *pursue, search for*
s the LORD your God Deut 4:29
pray, and **s** My face 2 Chr 7:14
S peace, and pursue it Ps 34:14
s me will find me Prov 8:17
man **s-s** only evil Prov 17:11
s wisdom and an Eccl 7:25
I will **s** the lost Ezek 34:16
time to **s** the LORD Hos 10:12
S good and not evil Amos 5:14
s first His kingdom Matt 6:33
s, and you will find Matt 7:7
s for a sign Mark 8:12
he who **s-s**, finds Luke 11:10
I do not **s** My glory John 8:50
s-ing the favor of men Gal 1:10
s-ing the things above Col 3:1

SEER *prophet*
prophets...every **s** 2 Kin 17:13
Who say to the **s-s** Is 30:10
Go, you **s**, flee away Amos 7:12
s-s will be ashamed Mic 3:7

SEIR
1 *land of Edom* Gen 32:3; 36:8,9; Num 24:18; Ezek 25:8
2 *mountain range within Edom* Gen 14:6; Deut 1:2; 2:4
3 *on boundary of Judah* Josh 11:17; 15:10

SEIZE *grasp, take*
mother shall **s** him Deut 21:19
Babylon has been **s-d** Jer 50:46
and **s** her plunder Ezek 29:19
fields and then **s** *them* Mic 2:2
seeking to **s** Him John 7:30

SELA
rock city in Edom Judg 1:36; Is 16:1; 42:11
also **Joktheel** 2 Kin 14:7
later known as Petra

SELAH
musical or liturgical sign Ps 3:2,4,8; 20:3; 60:4; 81:7; Hab 3:3,9,13

SELEUCIA
port in N Syria Acts 13:4

SELF-CONTROL
s and the judgment Acts 24:25
your lack of **s** 1 Cor 7:5
gentleness, **s** Gal 5:23
without **s**, brutal 2 Tim 3:3
in *your* knowledge, **s** 2 Pet 1:6

SELFISH *self-centered*
the bread of a **s** man Prov 23:6
s ambition in your James 3:14

SELL *barter, trade*
s me your birthright Gen 25:31
s me food for money Deut 2:28
s the oil and pay 2 Kin 4:7
sold a girl for wine Joel 3:3
sold all that he had Matt 13:46
s-ing their property Acts 2:45
sold into bondage Rom 7:14

SELLER *merchant, trader*
the buyer like the **s** Is 24:2
a **s** of purple Acts 16:14

SENATE
Sanhedrin Acts 5:21
see also **COUNCIL**

SEND *convey, dispatch*
s rain on the earth Gen 7:4
he **sent** out a raven Gen 8:7
Whom shall I **s** Is 6:8
Lord God has **sent** Me Is 48:16
s-s rain on *the* Matt 5:45
He has **sent** Me Luke 4:18
s-ing His own Son Rom 8:3
not **s** her husband 1 Cor 7:13
s him...in peace 1 Cor 16:11
God **sent** forth His Son Gal 4:4

SENNACHERIB
king of Assyria 2 Kin 18:13; 19:16,20; 2 Chr 32:1-22; Is 36:1; 37:17

SENSUALITY
deceit, **s**, envy Mark 7:22
promiscuity and **s** Rom 13:13
themselves over to **s** Eph 4:19
the wealth of her **s** Rev 18:3

SENTENCE *judgment*
s is by the decree Dan 4:17
escape the **s** of hell Matt 23:33
Pilate pronounced **s** Luke 23:24
to the **s** of death Luke 24:20

SEPARATE *divide, set apart*
God **s-d** the light Gen 1:4
They **s** with the lip Ps 22:7
s-s intimate friends Prov 16:28
let no man **s** Matt 19:6
Who will **s** us from Rom 8:35

SEPARATION *division, isolation*
of his **s** to the LORD Num 6:6
his **s** he is holy Num 6:8
his **s** was defiled Num 6:12
have made a **s** Is 59:2

SEPHARAD
place in Assyria for Jerusalem exiles Obad 20

SEPHARVAIM
place in Aram; people relocated to Samaria 2 Kin 17:31; 18:34; Is 36:19; 37:13

SERAPHIM
celestial beings Is 6:2,6

SERGIUS PAULUS *see* **PAULUS, SERGIUS**

SERPENT *snake*
s was more crafty Gen 3:1
they turned into **s-s** Ex 7:12
viper and flying **s** Is 30:6
be shrewd as **s-s** Matt 10:16
will pick up **s-s** Mark 16:18
Moses lifted up the **s** John 3:14

SERVANT *helper, slave*
s of **s-s** He shall be Gen 9:25
Your **s** is listening 1 Sam 3:9
to shine upon Your **s** Ps 31:16
s-s of a new covenant 2 Cor 3:6
they **s-s** of Christ 2 Cor 11:23
s of Christ Jesus 1 Tim 4:6

SERVE *help, work for*
shall **s** the LORD Ex 23:25
s Him with...heart Josh 22:5
s-d as priests 1 Chr 24:2
you will **s** strangers Jer 5:19
God whom we **s** is Dan 3:17
s God and wealth Matt 6:24
If anyone **s-s** Me John 12:26
s-ing the Lord Rom 12:11
through love **s** one Gal 5:13

SERVICE *ministry, work*
s of righteous Is 32:17
spiritual **s** of worship Rom 12:1
for the work of **s** Eph 4:12
s with reverence Heb 12:28

SETH
son of Adam Gen 4:25,26; 5:3-8; 1 Chr 1:1
line of Jesus Luke 3:38

SETTLED *arranged or inhabited*
Lot **s** in the cities Gen 13:12
cloud **s** over the Num 9:18
assault shall be **s** Deut 21:5
word is **s** in heaven Ps 119:89
mountains were **s** Prov 8:25
s in the lawful Acts 19:39

SEVEN *number*
Jacob served **s** years Gen 29:20
For **s** women...one man Is 4:1
will be **s** weeks Dan 9:25
s other spirits more Matt 12:45
forgive...**s** times Matt 18:21
John to the **s** churches Rev 1:4
s golden lampstands Rev 1:12

SEVERE *difficult, hard*
famine was **s** Gen 12:10
a very **s** pestilence Ex 9:3
s and lasting plagues Deut 28:59
s judgments against Ezek 14:21
a **s** earthquake had Matt 28:2

SEW *fasten, join*
s-ed fig leaves together Gen 3:7
s-ed sackcloth over Job 16:15
a time to **s** together Eccl 3:7
women who **s** *magic* Ezek 13:18

SEXUAL
not in **s** promiscuity Rom 13:13
from **s** immorality 1 Thess 4:3

SHACKLES *fetters*
will tear off your **s** Nah 1:13
s broken in pieces Mark 5:4
with chains and **s** Luke 8:29

SHADE *protection*
cover him with **s** Job 40:22
The LORD is your **s** Ps 121:5
lived under its **s** Ezek 31:6
over Jonah to be a **s** Jon 4:6
nest under its **s** Mark 4:32

SHADOW *image of shade*
days...like a **s** 1 Chr 29:15
the **s** of Your wings Ps 17:8
in the **s**...Almighty Ps 91:1
the **s-s** flee away Song 2:17
his **s** might fall on Acts 5:15
s of the heavenly Heb 8:5

SHADRACH
Hebrew: Hananiah Dan 1:7
friend of Daniel Dan 2:49; 3:12-30

SHAKE *quiver, tremble*
made all my bones **s** Job 4:14
s my head at you Job 16:4
peace will not be **s-n** Is 54:10
s the dust off Matt 10:14
A reed **s-n** by the Matt 11:7
heavens will be **s-n** Luke 21:26
he **shook** the creature Acts 28:5
voice **shook** the earth Heb 12:26

SHALLUM
1 *king of Israel* 2 Kin 15:8-15
2 *Huldah's husband* 2 Kin 22:14
3 *son of Josiah* 1 Chr 3:15
king of Judah 2 Kin 23:31-33
called **JEHOAHAZ** 2 Kin 23:30
4 *gatekeeper* 1 Chr 9:17
5 *son of Zadok* 1 Chr 6:12
6 *time of Nehemiah* Neh 3:12
name of nine other men

SHALMANESER
king of Assyria 2 Kin 17:3; 18:9

SHAME *disgrace, dishonor*
wicked be put to **s** Ps 31:17
my reproach and my **s** Ps 69:19
s to his mother Prov 29:15
wise men are put to **s** Jer 8:9
unjust knows no **s** Zeph 3:5
worthy to suffer **s** Acts 5:41
glory is in their **s** Phil 3:19
put Him to open **s** Heb 6:6

SHAMGAR
judge of Israel Judg 3:31; 5:6

SHARE (n) *portion*
them take their **s** Gen 14:24
s from My offerings Lev 6:17
give me the **s** Luke 15:12
I do my **s** Col 1:24

SHARE (v) *partake, participate*
stranger does not **s** Prov 14:10
s in the inheritance Prov 17:2
s it...yourselves Luke 22:17
s all good things Gal 6:6
may **s** His holiness Heb 12:10
s the sufferings of 1 Pet 4:13

SHARON
coastal plain in central Israel Is 33:9; 65:10

SHARP *cutting*
their tongue a **s** sword Ps 57:4
S...two-edged sword Prov 5:4
Put in your **s** sickle Rev 14:18

SHATTER *break, burst*
s-ed every tree of the Ex 9:25
the mighty are **s-ed** 1 Sam 2:4
s them like earthenware Ps 2:9
s the doors of bronze Is 45:2
iron crushes and **s-s** Dan 2:40

SHAUL
1 *king of Edom* Gen 36:37,38
2 *son of Simeon* Gen 46:10
3 *Kohathite Levite* 1 Chr 6:24

SHAVE *cut or scrape*
he shall **s** his head Lev 14:9
s off the seven Judg 16:19
s-d off half of 2 Sam 10:4
will **s** with a razor Is 7:20

SHEAF *bundle of grain stalks*
s-ves in the field Gen 37:7
s of the first fruits Lev 23:10
among the **s-ves** Ruth 2:15

SHEARER *wool cutter*
silent before its **s-s** Is 53:7
lamb before its **s** Acts 8:32

SHEAR-JASHUB
son of Isaiah Is 7:3
name symbolizes prophecy

SHEBA
1 *son of Raamah* Gen 10:7
2 *son of Joktan* Gen 10:28
3 *grandson of Abraham* Gen 25:3
4 *Simeonite town* Josh 19:2
5 *a Benjamite* 2 Sam 20:1-7
6 *a Gadite* 1 Chr 5:13
7 *kingdom* Job 6:19; Ps 72:10,15; Jer 6:20
8 *Queen of* 2 Chr 9:1ff

SHEBAT
eleventh month of Hebrew calendar Zech 1:7

SHECHEM
1 *city in Ephraim hill country* Gen 12:6; 33:18; 1 Chr 7:28
city of refuge Josh 20:7
2 *son of Hamor* Gen 34:2
3 *line of Manasseh* Num 26:31
4 *son of Shemida* 1 Chr 7:19

SHED *pour out*
Whoever **s-s** man's Gen 9:6
s streams of water Ps 119:136
hasten to **s** blood Prov 1:16
will not **s** its light Is 13:10
bribes to **s** blood Ezek 22:12
swift to **s** blood Rom 3:15
s-ding of blood Heb 9:22

SHEEP *animal*
Rachel came with...**s** Gen 29:9
not be like **s** Num 27:17
the fleece of my **s** Job 31:20
s of His pasture Ps 100:3
All of us like **s** Is 53:6
a **s** that is silent Is 53:7
will care for My **s** Ezek 34:12
lost **s** of...Israel Matt 10:6
s from the goats Matt 25:32
my **s** which was lost Luke 15:6
His life for the **s** John 10:11
s hear My voice John 10:27
Tend My **s** John 21:17
Shepherd of the **s** Heb 13:20

SHEEP GATE *see* **GATES OF JERUSALEM**

SHEEPFOLDS *enclosure*
s for the flocks 2 Chr 32:28
lie down among the **s** Ps 68:13
took him from the **s** Ps 78:70

SHEEPSKINS *coverings*
they went about in **s** Heb 11:37

SHEET
hammered out gold **s-s** Ex 39:3
s over *his* naked Mark 14:51
object like a great **s** Acts 10:11

SHELTER *cover, refuge*
under the **s** of my Gen 19:8
in the **s** of Your wings Ps 61:4
a **s** to *give* shade Is 4:6
a **s** from the storm Is 32:2
made a **s** for himself Jon 4:5

SHEM
son of Noah Gen 5:32; 6:10; 9:27; 11:11

SHEOL
place of the dead Gen 37:35; Job 7:9; Ps 49:15; Prov 15:11; Is 38:10; Ezek 32:27; Hab 2:5
see also **HADES** *and* **HELL**

SHEPHELAH
low hill country 1 Chr 27:28; Obad 19
see also **LOWLAND**

SHEPHERD (n)
sheep...have no **s** Num 27:17
The LORD is my **s** Ps 23:1
Like a **s** He Is 40:11
s-s after My own heart Jer 3:15
for lack of a **s** Ezek 34:5
raise up a **s** Zech 11:16
sheep without a **s** Matt 9:36
strike down the **s** Matt 26:31
s-s...in the fields Luke 2:8
I am the good **s** John 10:11
the great **S** Heb 13:20
the Chief **S** 1 Pet 5:4

SHEPHERD (v)
s My people 2 Sam 5:2
s My people Matt 2:6
S My sheep John 21:16
to **s** the church Acts 20:28
s the flock of God 1 Pet 5:2

SHESHBAZZAR
governor of Judah under Cyprus Ezra 5:14,16

SHIBBOLETH
test word for identification Judg 12:6

SHIELD ***protection***
Abram, I am a **s** Gen 15:1
He is a **s** to all 2 Sam 22:31
My **s** is with God Ps 7:10
faithfulness is a **s** Ps 91:4
the **s** of faith Eph 6:16

SHILOH
1 *Messianic title* Gen 49:10
2 *town N of Bethel* Josh 18:1
site of tabernacle Judg 18:31

SHINAR
Babylonian plain Gen 10:10; 11:2; Josh 7:21; Dan 1:2

SHINE ***be radiant, glow***
his face **shone** Ex 34:29
His face **s** on you Num 6:25
Your face to **s** *upon us* Ps 80:3
light **s** before men Matt 5:16
s-s in the darkness John 1:5
lamp **s-ing** in a dark 2 Pet 1:19
Light is...**s-ing** 1 John 2:8

SHIP ***boat***
a haven for **s-s** Gen 49:13
to the sea in **s-s** Ps 107:23
like merchant **s-s** Prov 31:14
escape from the **s** Acts 27:30

SHISHAK ***see*** **PHARAOH**

SHOOT ***new growth***
s will spring from Is 11:1
like a tender **s** Is 53:2
His **s-s** will sprout Hos 14:6

SHORT ***lacking***
Is My hand so **s** Is 50:2
days will be cut **s** Matt 24:22
s of the grace Heb 12:15

SHOULDER ***part of body***
He bowed his **s** Gen 49:15
turned a stubborn **s** Neh 9:29
relieved his **s** Ps 81:6
government...on His **s-s** Is 9:6

SHOUT ***cry out loudly***
s with a great **s** Josh 6:5
the people **s-ed** with Ezra 3:11
s for joy Ps 35:27
S joyfully to God Ps 66:1

SHOW ***manifest, reveal***
land...I will **s** you Gen 12:1
s me Your glory Ex 33:18
s you the secrets Job 11:6
s Your lovingkindness Ps 17:7
s him his fault in private Matt 18:15
S us the Father John 14:9
God **s-s** no partiality Gal 2:6
s hospitality Heb 13:2
if you **s** partiality James 2:9

SHOWBREAD
tables of **s** 1 Chr 28:16
s is *set*...table 2 Chr 13:11

SHOWER ***abundant flow***
roar of a *heavy* **s** 1 Kin 18:41
Like **s-s** that water Ps 72:6
be **s-s** of blessing Ezek 34:26
A **s** is coming Luke 12:54

SHREWD ***cunning***
frustrates...the **s** Job 5:12
be **s** as serpents Matt 10:16

SHRINE ***object of worship***
built yourself a **s** Ezek 16:24
tear down your **s-s** Ezek 16:39
who made silver **s-s** Acts 19:24

SHULAMMITE
title of young woman Song 6:13

SHUNAMMITE ***from Shunem***
1 *David's nurse* 1 Kin 1:3,15; 2:17,21,22
2 *hostess of Elisha* 2 Kin 4:12ff

SHUR
wilderness in NW Sinai Gen 16:7; 20:1; Ex 15:22; 1 Sam 15:7

SHUT ***close***
wilderness has **s** them Ex 14:3
s the lions' mouths Dan 6:22
power to **s** up the sky Rev 11:6

SIBBOLETH
test word for identification Judg 12:6

SICK ***unwell***
strengthen the **s** Ezek 34:16
lying **s** with a fever Mark 1:30
Lazarus was **s** John 11:2
anyone among you **s** James 5:14

SICKLE ***cutting tool***
who wields the **s** Jer 50:16
sharp **s** in His hand Rev 14:14
Put in your **s** Rev 14:15

SICKNESS ***illness***
remove from you...**s** Deut 7:15
every kind of **s** Matt 4:23
authority over...**s** Matt 10:1
s is not to end in death John 11:4

SIDON
1 *son of Canaan* Gen 10:15; 1 Chr 1:13
2 *Phoenician port* Gen 10:19; Is 23:4; Ezek 28:22

SIEGE ***encirclement***
throw up a **s** ramp 2 Kin 19:32
city came under **s** 2 Kin 24:10
their **s** towers Is 23:13
s against Jerusalem Jer 6:6
build a **s** wall Ezek 4:2

SIGHT ***perception, vision***
pleasing to the **s** Gen 2:9
acceptable in Your **s** Ps 19:14
precious in My **s** Is 43:4
blind receive **s** Matt 11:5
three days without **s** Acts 9:9
by faith, not by **s** 2 Cor 5:7

SIGN ***indication*** **or** ***wonder***
a **s** for Cain Gen 4:15
s of the covenant Gen 9:12
this shall be the **s** Ex 3:12
blood shall be a **s** Ex 12:13
His **s-s** in Egypt Ps 78:43
Ask a **s** for yourself Is 7:11
an everlasting **s** Is 55:13
a **s** from You Matt 12:38
s of Your coming Matt 24:3
show **s-s** and Mark 13:22
s-s in sun and moon Luke 21:25
beginning of *His* **s-s** John 2:11
s of circumcision Rom 4:11
Jews ask for **s-s** 1 Cor 1:22
tongues are for a **s** 1 Cor 14:22
s-s...false wonders 2 Thess 2:9

SIGNET ***seal***
examine...whose **s** Gen 38:25
engravings of a **s** Ex 39:14
s rings of his nobles Dan 6:17

SILAS
co-worker with Paul Acts 15:22,32,40; 16:19,25; 17:4,10,14
also **Silvanus**

SILENCE ***quietness***
My soul *waits* in **s** Ps 62:1
war will be **s-d** Jer 50:30
s the ignorance 1 Pet 2:15

s in heaven Rev 8:1

SILENT ***quiet***
LORD, do not keep **s** Ps 35:22
A time to be **s** Eccl 3:7
But Jesus kept **s** Matt 26:63
women...keep **s** 1 Cor 14:34

SILOAM
1 *tower in Jerusalem* Luke 13:4
2 *water pool in Jerusalem* John 9:7,11

SILVANUS ***see*** **SILAS**

SILVER ***precious metal***
rich in...**s** Gen 13:2
took no plunder in **s** Judg 5:19
as **s** is refined Ps 66:10
in settings of **s** Prov 25:11
s has become dross Is 1:22
The **s** is Mine Hag 2:8
not acquire...**s** Matt 10:9
thirty pieces of **s** Matt 26:15

SIMEON
1 *son of Jacob* Gen 29:33
2 *tribe* Num 1:23; Rev 7:7
3 *devout Jew* Luke 2:25
4 *ancestor of Jesus* Luke 3:30
5 *Christian prophet* Acts 13:1
6 *Simon Peter* Acts 15:14

SIMON
1 *apostle* Matt 4:18; Mark 1:16
see also **PETER**
2 *the Zealot* Matt 10:4; Mark 3:18; Luke 6:15
3 *brother of Jesus* Matt 13:55; Mark 6:3
4 *leper* Matt 26:6; Mark 14:3
5 *a Pharisee* Luke 7:40,43
6 *of Cyrene* Matt 27:32
carried Jesus' cross Mark 15:21; Luke 23:26
7 *father of Judas* John 6:71; 13:2
8 *Magus* Acts 8:9,13,18
sorcerer
9 *the tanner* Acts 9:43; 10:6,32

SIMPLE ***innocent*** **or** ***humble***
making wise the **s** Ps 19:7
LORD preserves the **s** Ps 116:6

SIN (n) ***transgression***
please forgive my **s** Ex 10:17
atonement for your **s** Ex 32:30
purification from **s** Num 19:9
s will find you out Num 32:23
s of divination 1 Sam 15:23
the **s-s** of my youth Ps 25:7
s my mother conceived Ps 51:5
Fools mock at **s** Prov 14:9
bore the **s** of many Is 53:12
s-s of her prophets Lam 4:13
an eternal **s** Mark 3:29
forgive us our **s-s** Luke 11:4
takes away the **s** John 1:29
wash away your **s-s** Acts 22:16
wages of **s** is death Rom 6:23
died for our **s-s** 1 Cor 15:3
Him who knew no **s** 2 Cor 5:21
pleasures of **s** Heb 11:25
confess your **s-s** James 5:16
a multitude of **s-s** James 5:20
confess our **s-s** 1 John 1:9
s is lawlessness 1 John 3:4

SIN (v) ***transgress***
When a leader **s-s** Lev 4:22
s against the LORD 1 Sam 14:34
Job did not **s** Job 1:22
s against You Ps 119:11
Father, I have **s-ned** Luke 15:18
s no more John 8:11
all have **s-ned** Rom 3:23
that you may not **s** 1 John 2:1

SIN
1 *wilderness in Sinai* Ex 16:1; Num 33:11,12
2 *Egyptian city* Ezek 30:15,16

SIN OFFERING
see **OFFERINGS**

SINAI
1 *mountain* Ex 19:11; Lev 26:46; Num 28:6
where Law received Ex 31:18; 34:29
see also **HOREB**
2 *desert wilderness* Ex 16:1; 19:1; Num 1:19; 9:5

SINCERE *without deceit*
be **s** and blameless Phil 1:10
mindful of the **s** faith 2 Tim 1:5
s love...brethren 1 Pet 1:22

SINEW *strength* **or** *tendon*
with bones and **s-s** Job 10:11
neck is an iron **s** Is 48:4
will put **s-s** on you Ezek 37:6

SINFUL *wicked*
a brood of **s** men Num 32:14
s generation Mark 8:38
I am a **s** man Luke 5:8
likeness of **s** flesh Rom 8:3

SING
s to the LORD Ex 15:1
s-ing and dancing 1 Sam 18:6
I will **s** praises 2 Sam 22:50
morning stars **sang** Job 38:7
S to Him a new song Ps 33:3
the righteous **s-s** Prov 29:6
birds will **s** Zeph 2:14
after **s-ing** a hymn Mark 14:26
s-ing...thankfulness Col 3:16
sang a new song Rev 5:9

SINGERS
these are the **s** 1 Chr 9:33
male and female **s** Eccl 2:8

SINK *descend, fall*
do not let me **s** Ps 69:14
so shall Babylon **s** Jer 51:64

SINNER *wrongdoer*
He instructs **s-s** Ps 25:8
if **s-s** entice you Prov 1:10
Adversity...**s-s** Prov 13:21
one **s** destroys much Eccl 9:18
a friend of...**s-s** Matt 11:19
one **s** who repents Luke 15:7
merciful to me...**s** Luke 18:13
God...not hear **s-s** John 9:31
while we were yet **s-s** Rom 5:8
came...to save **s-s** 1 Tim 1:15

SISERA
1 *Canaanite warrior* Judg 4:2ff
2 *class of Nethinim* Ezra 2:53; Neh 7:55

SISTER
She is my **s** Gen 12:19
We have a little **s** Song 8:8
a **s** called Mary Luke 10:39
commend...our **s** Rom 16:1
younger women...**s-s** 1 Tim 5:2

SIT *recline, rest*
Moses **sat** to judge Ex 18:13
Nor **s** in the seat Ps 1:1
S at My right hand Ps 110:1
lonely **s-s** the city Lam 1:1
s down on the grass Matt 14:19
who **s** in darkness Luke 1:79
dead man **sat** up Luke 7:15
where the harlot **s-s** Rev 17:15

SIVAN
third month of Hebrew calendar Esth 8:9

SKILL *proficiency*
filled them with **s** Ex 35:35
the heavens with **s** Ps 136:5
work of **s-ed** men Jer 10:9
s-ed in destruction Ezek 21:31

SKILLFUL *accomplished*
became a **s** hunter Gen 25:27
s player on...harp 1 Sam 16:16
praises with a **s** psalm Ps 47:7

SKIN *covering*
garments of **s** Gen 3:21
s of his face shone Ex 34:29
Clothe me with **s** Job 10:11
My **s** turns black Job 30:30
will burst the **s-s** Mark 2:22

SKIP *hop, leap*
children **s** about Job 21:11
Lebanon **s** like a calf Ps 29:6
go forth and **s** Mal 4:2

SKULL *bony framework of head*
head, crushing his **s** Judg 9:53
the **s** and the feet 2 Kin 9:35
Place of a **S** Matt 27:33

SKY *heavens*
sun stopped in...**s** Josh 10:13
the **s** grew black 1 Kin 18:45
witness in the **s** Ps 89:37
s will be rolled up Is 34:4
for the **s** is red Matt 16:2
will appear in the **s** Matt 24:30
s was shut up Luke 4:25
gazing...into the **s** Acts 1:10
s was split apart Rev 6:14

SLANDER (n) *defamation*
spreads **s** is a fool Prov 10:18
s-s, gossip 2 Cor 12:20
and **s** be put away Eph 4:31

SLANDER (v) *defame*
He does not **s** Ps 15:3
Whoever secretly **s-s** Ps 101:5
Do not **s** a slave Prov 30:10

SLANDERER *defamer*
s separates...friends Prov 16:28
s-s, haters of God Rom 1:30

SLAUGHTER (n) *brutal killing*
great **s** at Gibeon Josh 10:10
lamb led to the **s** Jer 11:19
as a sheep to **s** Acts 8:32
in a day of **s** James 5:5

SLAUGHTER (v) *kill*
shall **s** the bull Ex 29:11
shall **s** the lamb Lev 14:25
Who **s** the children Is 57:5
s-ed My children Ezek 16:21

SLAVE *bondservant*
The Hebrew **s** Gen 39:17
s at forced labor Gen 49:15
sold *in* a **s** sale Lev 25:42
Is Israel a **s** Jer 2:14
S-s rule over us Lam 5:8
s above his master Matt 10:24
good and faithful **s** Matt 25:21
shall be **s** of all Mark 10:44
is the **s** of sin John 8:34
neither **s** nor free Gal 3:28
as **s-s** of Christ Eph 6:6

SLAVERY *servitude*
from the house of **s** Ex 13:3
ransomed you from...**s** Mic 6:4
received a spirit of **s** Rom 8:15
to a yoke of **s** Gal 5:1

SLAY *destroy, kill*
knife to **s** his son Gen 22:10
s-s the foolish Job 5:2
Though He **s** me Job 13:15
Evil...**s** the wicked Ps 34:21
s her with thirst Hos 2:3
Lamb that was **slain** Rev 5:12

SLEEP (n) *rest*
caused a deep **s** Gen 2:21
Do not love **s** Prov 20:13
a spirit of deep **s** Is 29:10
s fled from him Dan 6:18
overcome by **s** Acts 20:9

SLEEP (v) *slumber*
why do You **s** Ps 44:23
neither slumber nor **s** Ps 121:4
who **s-s** in harvest Prov 10:5
found them **s-ing** Matt 26:43
we will not all **s** 1 Cor 15:51

SLOW *not quick*
I am **s** of speech Ex 4:10
gracious, **S** to anger Ps 103:8
to hear, **s** to speak James 1:19
Lord is not **s** 2 Pet 3:9

SLUGGARD *lazy one*
to the ant, O **s** Prov 6:6
the **s** craves Prov 13:4
s buries his hand Prov 26:15

SLUMBER *sleep*
s in their beds Job 33:15
He...will not **s** Ps 121:3
None **s-s** or sleeps Is 5:27
Dreamers...love to **s** Is 56:10

SMALL *little*
both **s** and great 2 Kin 25:26
s among the nations Jer 49:15
day of **s** things Zech 4:10
For the gate is **s** Matt 7:14
a few **s** fish Mark 8:7
he was **s** in stature Luke 19:3
tongue is a **s** part James 3:5

SMILE *grin*
I **s-d** on them Job 29:24
that I may **s** *again* Ps 39:13
she **s-s** at the future Prov 31:25

SMITE *hit, strike*
s...with frogs Ex 8:2
smote Job with sore Job 2:7
sun will not **s** you Ps 121:6
righteous **s** me Ps 141:5

SMITH *worker of metal*
a vessel for the **s** Prov 25:4
created the **s** who Is 54:16
s-s from Jerusalem Jer 24:1

SMOKE *mist, vapor*
s...ascended Gen 19:28
Sinai *was* all in **s** Ex 19:18
like **s** they vanish Ps 37:20
temple was filling with **s** Is 6:4
s rises up forever Rev 19:3

SMOOTH *no roughness*
I am a **s** man Gen 27:11
five **s** stones 1 Sam 17:40
Make **s**...a highway Is 40:3
the rough roads **s** Luke 3:5
s...flattering speech Rom 16:18

SMYRNA
city in Asia Minor Rev 1:11; 2:8

SNAKE *serpent*
horned **s** in the path Gen 49:17
a **s** bites him Amos 5:19
s instead of a fish Luke 11:11

SNARE *trap*
gods will be a **s** Judg 2:3
s-s of death 2 Sam 22:6
laid a **s** for me Ps 119:110
his lips are the **s** Prov 18:7
caught in My **s** Ezek 12:13
table become a **s** Rom 11:9
s of the devil 1 Tim 3:7

SNOW *ice flakes*
storehouses of the **s** Job 38:22
be whiter than **s** Ps 51:7
He gives **s** like wool Ps 147:16
Like **s** in summer Prov 26:1
as white as **s** Matt 28:3

SOBER *serious, temperate*
words of **s** truth Acts 26:25
be alert and **s** 1 Thess 5:6
Be of **s** *spirit* 1 Pet 5:8

SODOM
city S of Dead Sea Gen 10:19
home of Lot Gen 19:1,4
destroyed by God Gen 19:24

SODOMITE
one guilty of unnatural sexual practices 1 Kin 22:46

SOFT *kind*
speak to you **s** words Job 41:3
s tongue breaks the Prov 25:15

SOIL *earth, ground*
first fruits of your **s** Ex 23:19
he loved the **s** 2 Chr 26:10
fell into the good **s** Mark 4:8
produce of the **s** James 5:7

SOJOURN *visit temporarily*
S in this land Gen 26:3
stranger **s-s** with you Ex 12:48
s...land of Moab Ruth 1:1

SOJOURNER
s in a foreign land Ex 2:22
are **s-s** before You 1 Chr 29:15
oppressed the **s** Ezek 22:29

SOLDIER *military man*
s-s took Him away Mark 15:16
s-s also mocked Luke 23:36
s-s pierced His side John 19:34
a devout **s** Acts 10:7
good **s** of Christ 2 Tim 2:3

SOLEMN *deeply earnest, serious*
sabbath of **s** rest Lev 16:31
have a **s** assembly Num 29:35
sworn **s** oaths Ezek 21:23
bound...a **s** oath Acts 23:14

SOLOMON
1 *son of David* 2 Sam 12:24
king of Israel 1 Kin 1:43
ruled wisely 1 Kin 4:29,34
built the Temple 1 Kin 6:2; 9:1
international fame 1 Kin 10:1
ruled foolishly 1 Kin 11:6
death 1 Kin 11:43
2 *Song of Solomon*
also **Song of Songs**

SON *male descendant*
the **s-s** of Noah Gen 9:18
Take...your only **s** Gen 22:2
O Absalom, my **s** 2 Sam 18:33
to be a **s** to Me 1 Chr 28:6
s-s of God shouted Job 38:7
You are My **S** Ps 2:7
wise **s** makes a Prov 10:1
Discipline your **s** Prov 19:18
bear a **s**...Immanuel Is 7:14
Egypt I called My **s** Hos 11:1
she gave birth to a **S** Matt 1:25
This is My beloved **S** Matt 3:17
the carpenter's **s** Matt 13:55
I am the **S** of God Matt 27:43
S of Man...suffer Mark 8:31
her firstborn **s** Luke 2:7
If You are the **S** Luke 4:3
man had two **s-s** Luke 15:11
only begotten **S** John 3:16
S also gives life John 5:21
become **s-s** of Light John 12:36
sending His own **S** Rom 8:3
image of His **S** Rom 8:29
not spare His own **S** Rom 8:32
fellowship with His **S** 1 Cor 1:9
if a **s**, then an heir Gal 4:7
shall be a **S** to Me Heb 1:5
abide in the **S** 1 John 2:24
He who has the **S** 1 John 5:12

SON-IN-LAW
the **s** of the Timnite Judg 15:6
be the king's **s** 1 Sam 18:18
s of Sanballat Neh 13:28

SON OF GOD
Messianic title indicating deity of Jesus Christ
Matt 4:3; 8:29; 16:16; Mark 1:20; 3:11; 14:61;
Luke 1:35; John 3:13; 11:27; Acts 8:37

SON OF MAN
Messianic title of Jesus Christ Matt 8:20; 9:6;
Mark 2:10; 10:33; Luke 12:10;
18:31; John 6:27; 13:31

SONG *melody, music*
LORD is my...**s** Ex 15:2
ministered with **s** 1 Chr 6:32
gives **s-s** in the night Job 35:10
s-s of deliverance Ps 32:7
Sing to Him a new **s** Ps 33:3
A **s** of my beloved Is 5:1
Praise the LORD in **s** Is 12:5
not drink wine with **s** Is 24:9
hymns...spiritual **s-s** Eph 5:19

SORCERER *witch*
interprets...or a **s** Deut 18:10
witness against the **s-s** Mal 3:5
immoral persons...**s-s** Rev 21:8

SORCERY *witchcraft*
practiced **s** 2 Chr 33:6
idolatry, **s**, enmities Gal 5:20
deceived by your **s** Rev 18:23

SORDID *filthy*
fond of **s** gain 1 Tim 3:8
the sake of **s** gain Titus 1:11
not for **s** gain 1 Pet 5:2

SOREK
valley SW of Jerusalem Judg 16:4

SORROW *grief, sadness*
down to Sheol in **s** Gen 42:38
life is spent with **s** Ps 31:10
man of **s-s** Is 53:3
s is beyond healing Jer 8:18
if I cause you **s** 2 Cor 2:2

SOSTHENES
1 *synagogue leader* Acts 18:17
2 *Corinthian believer* 1 Cor 1:27

SOUL *life, spirit*
her **s** was departing Gen 35:18
humble your **s-s** Lev 16:29
poured out my **s** 1 Sam 1:15
not abandon my **s** Ps 16:10
He restores my **s** Ps 23:3
my **s** pants for You Ps 42:1
Bless...LORD, O my **s** Ps 103:1
who is wise wins **s-s** Prov 11:30
s who sins will die Ezek 18:4
unable to kill the **s** Matt 10:28
exchange for his **s** Matt 16:26
My **s** is...grieved Matt 26:38
and forfeit his **s** Mark 8:36
My **s** exalts the Lord Luke 1:46
your **s** is required Luke 12:20
one heart and **s** Acts 4:32
an anchor of the **s** Heb 6:19
able to save your **s-s** James 1:21
save his **s** from James 5:20
war against the **s** 1 Pet 2:11

SOUND (adj) *accurate, stable*
s wisdom...two sides Job 11:6
I give you **s** teaching Prov 4:2
the **s** doctrine 1 Tim 4:6

SOUND (n) *noise*
s of You in...garden Gen 3:10
s of war in the camp Ex 32:17
s of a great army 2 Kin 7:6
s of many waters Ezek 43:2

SOUND (v) *express*
s His praise abroad Ps 66:8
s an alarm Joel 2:1
trumpet will **s** 1 Cor 15:52

SOUR *distasteful, tart*
eaten **s** grapes Jer 31:29
offering...**s** wine Luke 23:36

SOURCE *origin*
the **s** of sapphires Job 28:6
s of eternal salvation Heb 5:9
s of quarrels James 4:1

SOVEREIGNTY *authority*
His **s** rules over all Ps 103:19
s from Damascus Is 17:3
s will be uprooted Dan 11:4

SOW *plant, spread*
you may **s** the land Gen 47:23
s your seed uselessly Lev 26:16
who **s** in tears Ps 126:5
who **s-s** iniquity will Prov 22:8
they **s** the wind Hos 8:7
birds...do not **s** Matt 6:26
s good seed Matt 13:27
s-ed spiritual things 1 Cor 9:11
whatever a man **s-s** Gal 6:7

SOWER *planter*
seed to the **s** Is 55:10
s went out to sow Matt 13:3
s sows the word Mark 4:14

SPAIN
S European land Rom 15:24,28

SPARE *save or be lenient*
did not **s** their soul Ps 78:50
No man **s-s** his brother Is 9:19
not **s** His own Son Rom 8:32
I will not **s** *anyone* 2 Cor 13:2
God did not **s** angels 2 Pet 2:4

SPEAK *proclaim, tell*
God **spoke** to Noah Gen 8:15
God **s-s** with man Deut 5:24
S of all His wonders 1 Chr 16:9
He who **s-s** falsehood Ps 101:7
and a time to **s** Eccl 3:7
the mute to **s** Mark 7:37
s of what we know John 3:11
Never has a man **spoken** John 7:46
s with other tongues Acts 2:4
we **s** God's wisdom 1 Cor 2:7
If I **s** with...tongues 1 Cor 13:1

SPEAR *weapon*
leaning on his **s** 2 Sam 1:6
s-s into pruning hooks Is 2:4
pruning hooks into **s-s** Joel 3:10
pierced...with a **s** John 19:34

SPECK *particle*
regarded as a **s** of Is 40:15
s out of your eye Matt 7:4

SPEECH *message, word*
I am slow of **s** Ex 4:10
His **s** was smoother Ps 55:21
in cleverness of **s** 1 Cor 1:17
I am unskilled in **s** 2 Cor 11:6

SPELL *incantation*
one who casts a **s** Deut 18:11
skillful caster of **s-s** Ps 58:5
power of your **s-s** Is 47:9

SPICE
s and the oil Ex 35:28
mix in the s-s Ezek 24:10
prepared s-s and Luke 23:56
wrappings with...s-s John 19:40

SPIES (n) ***clandestine persons***
we are not s Gen 42:31
two men as s Josh 2:1
David sent out s 1 Sam 26:4
welcomed the s Heb 11:31

SPIN ***make thread***
nor do they s Matt 6:28
neither toil nor s Luke 12:27

SPIRIT
S rested upon them Num 11:26
God sent an evil s Judg 9:23
My s is broken Job 17:1
renew a steadfast s Ps 51:10
my s grows faint Ps 77:3
a haughty s before Prov 16:18
the S lifted me up Ezek 3:14
his s was troubled Dan 2:1
four s-s of heaven Zech 6:5
are the poor in s Matt 5:3
authority over...s-s Matt 10:1
put My S upon Him Matt 12:18
blasphemy...the S Matt 12:31
yielded up *His* s Matt 27:50
S like a dove Mark 1:10
s...not have flesh Luke 24:39
born of...the S John 3:5
worship in s and John 4:24
gave up His s John 19:30
pour forth of My S Acts 2:17
Jesus, receive my s Acts 7:59
power of the S Rom 15:19
taught by the s 1 Cor 2:13
pray with the s 1 Cor 14:15
walk by the S Gal 5:16
fruit of the S is love Gal 5:22
one body and one S Eph 4:4
be filled with the S Eph 5:18
sword of the S Eph 6:17
not quench the S 1 Thess 5:19
division of soul and s Heb 4:12
the s-s *now* in prison 1 Pet 3:19
S who testifies 1 John 5:6
see also **HOLY SPIRIT**

SPIRIT OF GOD
the S was moving Gen 1:2
S came upon him 1 Sam 10:10
a vision by the S Ezek 11:24
S descending as a Matt 3:16
being led by the S Rom 8:14
S dwells in you 1 Cor 3:16
worship in the S Phil 3:3
see also **HOLY SPIRIT**

SPIRIT OF THE LORD
S came upon him Judg 3:10
S departed from 1 Sam 16:14
S gave them rest Is 63:14
filled with...the S Mic 3:8
S is upon Me Luke 4:18
see also **HOLY SPIRIT**

SPIRITIST ***medium***
not turn to...s-s Lev 19:31
s...be put to death Lev 20:27
removed...the s-s 2 Kin 23:24

SPIRITUAL ***of the spirit***
the Law is s Rom 7:14
s service of worship Rom 12:1
raised a s body 1 Cor 15:44
with every s blessing Eph 1:3
hymns and s songs Eph 5:19
offer up s sacrifices 1 Pet 2:5

SPIT
began to s at Him Mark 14:65
and s upon Luke 18:32
He **spat** on...ground John 9:6
I will s you out Rev 3:16

SPLENDOR ***magnificence***
the moon going in s Job 31:26
displayed Your s Ps 8:1
Your s and Your majesty Ps 45:3
clothed with s Ps 104:1
s covers the heavens Hab 3:3

SPLIT ***divide***
He s the rock Is 48:21
valleys will be s Mic 1:4
Mount...will be s Zech 14:4
sky was s apart Rev 6:14

SPOIL ***booty, pillage***
he divides the s Gen 49:27
the s of the cities Deut 2:35
divide the s with Prov 16:19
widows may be their s Is 10:2
for s to the nations Ezek 25:7

SPONGE ***absorbent matter***
taking a s, he filled Matt 27:48
a s with sour wine Mark 15:36

SPOT ***speck***
Or the leopard his s-s Jer 13:23
no s or wrinkle Eph 5:27

SPOTLESS ***no defects***
unblemished and s 1 Pet 1:19
s and blameless 2 Pet 3:14

SPREAD ***stretch out***
He s His wings Deut 32:11
I s My skirt over Ezek 16:8
death s to all men Rom 5:12

SPRING (adj) ***period, season***
has been no s rain Jer 3:3
Like the s rain Hos 6:3
s crop began to sprout Amos 7:1

SPRING (n) ***water source***
went down to the s Gen 24:16
twelve s-s of water Ex 15:27
stop all s-s of water 2 Kin 3:19
s-s of the deep...fixed Prov 8:28
the s-s of salvation Is 12:3
s of the water of life Rev 21:6

SPRING (v) ***jump, leap***
S up, O well Num 21:17
Truth s-s from the Ps 85:11
s-ing up to eternal John 4:14

SPRINKLE ***scatter***
take its blood and s Ex 29:16
s some of the blood Lev 4:6
s *it* seven times Lev 4:17
s some of the oil Lev 14:16

SPY (v) ***investigate***
Moses sent...to s Num 13:17
to s out Jericho Josh 6:25
spied out Bethel Judg 1:23
s out our liberty Gal 2:4

SQUARE ***area or shape***
altar shall be s Ex 27:1
voice in the s Prov 1:20
city is...a s Rev 21:16

STAFF ***rod***
s of God in his hand Ex 4:20
Your s, they comfort Ps 23:4
or sandals, or a s Matt 10:10
a mere s; no bread Mark 6:8

STAIN ***blemish***
s of your iniquity Jer 2:22
without s...reproach 1 Tim 6:14

STAND ***maintain position***
s before the LORD Deut 10:8
O sun, s still Josh 10:12
s before kings Prov 22:29
word of our God s-s Is 40:8
will s on the Mount Zech 14:4
love to s and pray Matt 6:5
s-ing by the cross John 19:25
why do you s looking Acts 1:11
s by your faith Rom 11:20
s before...judgment Rom 14:10
s firm in the faith 1 Cor 16:13
foundation...s-s 2 Tim 2:19
I s at the door Rev 3:20

STANDARD ***banner or rule***
set up their own s-s Ps 74:4
set up My s Is 49:22
s of the Law Acts 22:12
s of sound words 2 Tim 1:13

STAR ***heavenly body***
He made the s-s Gen 1:16
s shall come forth Num 24:17
morning s-s sang Job 38:7
s of the morning Is 14:12
s-s for light by night Jer 31:35
His s in the east Matt 2:2
morning s arises 2 Pet 1:19
wandering s-s Jude 13
s fell from heaven Rev 8:10
the bright morning s Rev 22:16

STATE ***position***
s of expectation Luke 3:15
of our humble s Phil 3:21
s has become worse 2 Pet 2:20

STATEMENT ***assertion***
let your s be Matt 5:37
trap Him in a s Mark 12:13
catch Him in...s Luke 20:20
This is a difficult s John 6:60

STATURE ***height***
was growing in s 1 Sam 2:26
in wisdom and s Luke 2:52
he was small in s Luke 19:3
measure of the s Eph 4:13

STATUTE ***law, rule***
My s-s and My laws Gen 26:5
a perpetual s Ex 29:9
keep My s-s Lev 18:5
Teach me Your s-s Ps 119:26
not walked in My s-s Ezek 5:7

STEADFAST ***established, firm***
be s and not fear Job 11:15
renew a s spirit Ps 51:10
My heart is s Ps 57:7
s in righteousness Prov 11:19
be s, immovable 1 Cor 15:58

STEAL ***rob, take***
You shall not s Ex 20:15
be in want and s Prov 30:9
thieves break in...s Matt 6:19
Do not s Mark 10:19

STEPHANAS
Corinthian Christian 1 Cor 1:16; 16:15,17

STEPHEN
deacon Acts 6:5,8
martyred Acts 7:59; 8:2

STEPS ***distance or movements***
number my s Job 14:16
s...bathed in butter Job 29:6
His s do not slip Ps 37:31
s take hold of Sheol Prov 5:5
in the s of the faith Rom 4:12
follow in His s 1 Pet 2:21

STEWARD ***supervisor***
and sensible s Luke 12:42
s-s of the mysteries 1 Cor 4:1
above reproach...s Titus 1:7

STEWARDSHIP *responsibility*
a **s** entrusted to me 1 Cor 9:17
s of God's grace Eph 3:2

STIFFEN *make rigid*
s your neck no longer Deut 10:16
do not **s** your neck 2 Chr 30:8
have **s-ed** their necks Jer 19:15

STILL *motionless* or *quiet*
O sun, stand **s** Josh 10:12
the storm to be **s** Ps 107:29
Why are we sitting **s** Jer 8:14
sea, Hush, be **s** Mark 4:39

STIMULATE *excite*
how to **s** my body Eccl 2:3
s one another to Heb 10:24

STING *pain*
where is your **s** 1 Cor 15:55
s of death is sin 1 Cor 15:56

STIR *agitate*
S up Yourself Ps 35:23
word **s-s** up anger Prov 15:1
man **s-s** up strife Prov 29:22
s-red up the water John 5:4

STOCKS *confinement*
put my feet in the **s** Job 13:27
Jeremiah from the **s** Jer 20:3
their feet in the **s** Acts 16:24

STOMACH *part of body*
s will be satisfied Prov 18:20
s of the fish Jon 1:17
Food is for the **s** 1 Cor 6:13
s was made bitter Rev 10:10

STONE (n) *rock*
they used brick for **s** Gen 11:3
two **s** tablets Ex 34:1
do these **s-s** mean Josh 4:6
five smooth **s-s** 1 Sam 17:40
there was no **s** seen 1 Kin 6:18
Water wears...**s-s** Job 14:19
foot against a **s** Ps 91:12
in Zion a **s** Is 28:16
take the heart of **s** Ezek 11:19
serving wood and **s** Ezek 20:32
foot against a **s** Matt 4:6
will give him a **s** Matt 7:9
rolled away the **s** Matt 28:2
s-s will cry out Luke 19:40
six **s** waterpots John 2:6
first to throw a **s** John 8:7
Remove the **s** John 11:39
s-s, wood, hay 1 Cor 3:12
as to a living **s** 1 Pet 2:4
A **s** of stumbling 1 Pet 2:8

STONE (v) *throw stones*
people will **s** us Luke 20:6
seeking to **s** You John 11:8
went on **s-ing** Stephen Acts 7:59
they **s-d** Paul Acts 14:19

STOP *cease*
the sun **s-ped** Josh 10:13
And the oil **s-ped** 2 Kin 4:6
put a **s** to sacrifice Dan 9:27
s weeping for Me Luke 23:28
s sinning 1 Cor 15:34

STORE *accumulate*
s up the grain Gen 41:35
His sin is **s-d** up Hos 13:12
s up...treasures Matt 6:20
place to **s** my crops Luke 12:17
s-d up your treasure James 5:3

TOREHOUSE *storage place*
of the snow Job 38:22
from His **s-s** Jer 10:13
nto the **s** Mal 3:10

STORK *bird*
the **s**, the heron Lev 11:19
the **s** in the sky Jer 8:7
wings of a **s** Zech 5:9

STORM *tempest, whirlwind*
A refuge from the **s** Is 25:4
will come like a **s** Ezek 38:9
a great **s** on the sea Jon 1:4
mists driven by a **s** 2 Pet 2:17

STRAIGHT *direct*
Make Your way **s** Ps 5:8
make your paths **s** Prov 3:6
Make His paths **s** Matt 3:3
Make **s** the way John 1:23

STRANGE *foreign*
offered **s** fire Lev 10:1
no **s** god among you Ps 81:9
to teach **s** doctrines 1 Tim 1:3
went after **s** flesh Jude 7

STRANGER *alien, sojourner*
s-s in a land Gen 15:13
a **s** and a sojourner Gen 23:4
shall not wrong a **s** Ex 22:21
a **s** in the earth Ps 119:19
LORD protects the **s-s** Ps 146:9
violence to the **s** Jer 22:3
I was a **s** Matt 25:35
hospitality to **s-s** Heb 13:2

STRAW *stalk of grain*
s to make brick Ex 5:7
s for the horses 1 Kin 4:28
as **s** before the wind Job 21:18
wood, hay, **s** 1 Cor 3:12

STRAY *wander*
not **s** into her paths Prov 7:25
no longer **s** from Me Ezek 14:11
s-s from the truth James 5:19
s-ing like sheep 1 Pet 2:25

STREAM *current, flow*
planted by **s-s** of water Ps 1:3
The **s** of God Ps 65:9
like a rushing **s** Is 59:19

STREET *road, way*
Wisdom shouts in...**s** Prov 1:20
race madly in the **s-s** Nah 2:4
on the **s** corners Matt 6:5
s of the city...gold Rev 21:21

STRENGTH *force, power*
no longer yield its **s** Gen 4:12
The LORD is my **s** Ex 15:2
was no **s** in him 1 Sam 28:20
My **s** is dried up Ps 22:15
The LORD is my **s** Ps 28:7
s in time of trouble Ps 37:39
God is our refuge...**s** Ps 46:1
s of my salvation Ps 140:7
your **s** to women Prov 31:3
s to the weary Is 40:29
Strangers devour his **s** Hos 7:9
with all your **s** Mark 12:30
s which God supplies 1 Pet 4:11
sun shining in its **s** Rev 1:16

STRENGTHEN *make strong*
please **s** me Judg 16:28
David **s-ed** himself 1 Sam 30:6
s-ed weak hands Job 4:3
s the feeble Is 35:3
s the sick Ezek 34:16
s your brothers Luke 22:32
s-ed in the faith Acts 16:5
Him who **s-s** me Phil 4:13
s-ed with all power Col 1:11
s your hearts 2 Thess 2:17
who has **s-ed** me 1 Tim 1:12

STRETCH *extend*
I will **s** out My hand Ex 3:20

He **s-es** out the north Job 26:7
S-ing out heaven Ps 104:2
I **s-ed** out the heavens Is 45:12

STRIFE *discord, quarrel*
s between...herdsmen Gen 13:7
the **s** of tongues Ps 31:20
Hatred stirs up **s** Prov 10:12
fool's lips bring **s** Prov 18:6
puts an end to **s** Prov 18:18
of envy, murder, **s** Rom 1:29
and **s** among you 1 Cor 3:3
enmities, **s**, jealousy Gal 5:20

STRIKE *hit*
I will **s** the water Ex 7:17
you shall **s** the rock Ex 17:6
He who **s-s** a man Ex 21:12
s the timbrel Ps 81:2
you do not **s** your foot Ps 91:12
S a scoffer Prov 19:25
He will **s** the earth Is 11:4
let us **s** at him Jer 18:18
S the Shepherd Zech 13:7
s...the shepherd Matt 26:31
struck Jesus John 18:22
struck them with many blows Acts 16:23
s the earth Rev 11:6

STRIVE *contend, struggle*
not **s** with man forever Gen 6:3
He will not always **s** Ps 103:9
and **s-ing** after wind Eccl 1:14
s together with me Rom 15:30
s-ing to please men Gal 1:10
we labor and **s** 1 Tim 4:10
s-ing against sin Heb 12:4

STRONG *powerful, steadfast*
a very **s** west wind Ex 10:19
not drink...**s** drink Lev 10:9
Be **s** and courageous Deut 31:6
Israel became **s** Judg 1:28
God is...**s** fortress 2 Sam 22:33
The LORD **s** and mighty Ps 24:8
s drink a brawler Prov 20:1
their Redeemer is **s** Prov 23:11
ants are not a **s** people Prov 30:25
love is as **s** as death Song 8:6
Their Redeemer is **s** Jer 50:34
grew **s** in faith Rom 4:20
act like men, be **s** 1 Cor 16:13
be **s** in the Lord Eph 6:10
weakness...made **s** Heb 11:34
I saw a **s** angel Rev 5:2

STRONGHOLD *fortress, refuge*
David lived in the **s** 2 Sam 5:9
s and my refuge 2 Sam 22:3
s for the oppressed Ps 9:9
For God is my **s** Ps 59:9
my salvation, My **s** Ps 62:2
a **s** to the upright Prov 10:29

STRUGGLE (n) *conflict*
the days of my **s** Job 14:14
our **s** is not against Eph 6:12
have shared my **s** Phil 4:3

STRUGGLE (v) *contend*
children **s-d** together Gen 25:22
men **s**...each other Ex 21:22

STUBBLE *short stumps*
gather **s** for straw Ex 5:12
fire consumes **s** Is 5:24
give birth to **s** Is 33:11
house of Esau...**s** Obad 18

STUBBORN *obstinate*
Pharaoh's heart is **s** Ex 7:14
you are a **s** people Deut 9:6
s...generation Ps 78:8
house of Israel is **s** Ezek 3:7

STUBBORNNESS *intractable*
I know your...**s** Deut 31:27

s of their heart Ps 81:12
s...unrepentant heart Rom 2:5

STUMBLE ***fall, trip***
your foot will not **s** Prov 3:23
a rock to **s** over Is 8:14
arrogant one will **s** Jer 50:32
eye makes you **s** Matt 5:29
a stone of **s-ing** Rom 9:33
all **s** in many *ways* James 3:2

STUMBLING BLOCK ***obstacle***
s before the blind Lev 19:14
s of iniquity Ezek 44:12
You are a **s** to Me Matt 16:23
to Jews a **s** 1 Cor 1:23
s of the cross Gal 5:11

STUMP ***part of plant***
s dies in the dry soil Job 14:8
The holy seed is its **s** Is 6:13
the **s** with the roots Dan 4:26

STUPID ***foolish, senseless***
s and the senseless Ps 49:10
I am more **s** than Prov 30:2
they are altogether **s** Jer 10:8

STYLUS ***marking / writing device***
an iron **s** and lead Job 19:24
with an iron **s** Jer 17:1

SUBDUE ***conquer, overcome***
fill the earth, and **s** Gen 1:28
the land was **s-d** Josh 18:1
us completely **s** them Ps 74:8
s nations before him Is 45:1

SUBJECT (adj) ***under authority***
s to forced labor Judg 1:30
demons are **s** to us Luke 10:17
church is **s** to Christ Eph 5:24
s to...husbands Titus 2:5
be **s** to the Father Heb 12:9

SUBJECT (v)
s him to a slave's Lev 25:39
creation was **s-ed** Rom 8:20
s themselves 1 Cor 14:34
all things are **s-ed** 1 Cor 15:28

SUBJECTION ***under authority***
kingdom...in **s** Ezek 17:14
He continued in **s** Luke 2:51
s to the governing Rom 13:1
all things in **s** 1 Cor 15:27

SUBMISSIVE ***yielding***
Servants, be **s** 1 Pet 2:18
s to...husbands 1 Pet 3:5

SUBMIT ***yield to***
Foreigners **s** to me Ps 18:44
s yourself to decrees Col 2:20
S therefore to God James 4:7

SUBSTITUTE
s shall become holy Lev 27:10
s darkness for light Is 5:20
s bitter for sweet Is 5:20

SUCCESS ***accomplishment***
grant me **s** today Gen 24:12
hands cannot attain **s** Job 5:12
Daniel enjoyed **s** Dan 6:28

SUCCESSFUL ***having achieved***
make your journey **s** Gen 24:40
make Your servant **s** Neh 1:11
make his ways **s** Is 48:15

SUCCOTH
1 *Israelite camping place* Ex 12:37; 13:20
2 *Gadite town in Jordan Valley* Josh 13:27; Ps 60:6

SUDDENLY ***abruptly***
in case he should come **s** Mark 13:36
s...from heaven Acts 2:2

SUFFER ***experience pain***
s the fate of all Num 16:29
Son of Man must **s** Mark 8:31
s and rise again Luke 24:46
worthy to **s** shame Acts 5:41
we **s** with *Him* Rom 8:17
creation...**s-s** Rom 8:22
if one member **s-s** 1 Cor 12:26
s-ing for the gospel 2 Tim 1:8
Christ also **s-ed** 1 Pet 2:21

SUFFERINGS ***distress***
s of this present Rom 8:18
sharers of our **s** 2 Cor 1:7
fellowship of His **s** Phil 3:10
rejoice in my **s** Col 1:24
share the **s** of Christ 1 Pet 4:13

SUFFICIENT ***enough***
s for its redemption Lev 25:26
bread is not **s** John 6:7
My grace is **s** 2 Cor 12:9

SUMMER ***season***
fever heat of **s** Ps 32:4
You have made **s** Ps 74:17
Like snow in **s** Prov 26:1
know that **s** is near Matt 24:32

SUMMIT ***peak, top***
Like the **s** of Lebanon Jer 22:6
hide on the **s** Amos 9:3

SUMMON ***call, gather***
s-ed all Israel Deut 5:1
s all the prophets 2 Kin 10:19
He **s-s** the heavens Ps 50:4
He **s-ed** the twelve Mark 6:7

SUN ***heavenly body***
when the **s** grew hot Ex 16:21
the **s** stood still Josh 10:13
chariots of the **s** 2 Kin 23:11
God is a **s** Ps 84:11
s will not smite Ps 121:6
s to rule by day Ps 136:8
new under the **s** Eccl 1:9
s go down at noon Amos 8:9
shine forth as the **s** Matt 13:43
signs in **s** Luke 21:25
not let the **s** go down Eph 4:26
clothed with the **s** Rev 12:1

SUNRISE ***appearance of sun***
toward the **s** Num 3:38
Jordan toward the **s** Josh 1:15

SUNSET
Passover...at **s** Deut 16:6
dawn and the **s** shout Ps 65:8

SUNSHINE
Through **s** after rain 2 Sam 23:4
dazzling heat in the **s** Is 18:4

SUPPER ***meal***
made Him a **s** John 12:2
eat the Lord's **S** 1 Cor 11:20
marriage **s** of the Rev 19:9
the great **s** of God Rev 19:17

SUPPLICATION ***petition***
Make **s** to the LORD Ex 9:28
s of Your people 1 Kin 8:52
LORD has heard my **s** Ps 6:9
poor man utters **s-s** Prov 18:23
seek *Him by*...**s-s** Dan 9:3
by prayer and **s** Phil 4:6

SUPPLY ***provide***
He who **s-ies** seed 2 Cor 9:10
my God will **s** Phil 4:19
s moral excellence 2 Pet 1:5

SUPPORT (n) ***strength***
the LORD was my **s** 2 Sam 22:19
gave him strong **s** 1 Chr 11:10

Both supply and **s** Is 3:1
worthy of his **s** Matt 10:10

SUPPORT (v) ***uphold***
Hur **s-ed** his hands Ex 17:12
will He **s**...evildoers Job 8:20
He **s-s** the fatherless Ps 146:9
ought to **s** such men 3 John 8

SUR ***see*** **GATES OF JERUSALEM**

SURE ***secure, true***
testimony...is **s** Ps 19:7
His precepts are **s** Ps 111:7
His water will be **s** Is 33:16

SURFACE ***exterior***
s of the deep Gen 1:2
ark floated on the **s** Gen 7:18
water was on the **s** Gen 8:9

SURPASS ***excel***
you **s** in beauty Ezek 32:19
s-ing riches of His Eph 2:7
which **s-es** knowledge Eph 3:19

SURRENDER ***yield***
s me into his hand 1 Sam 23:11
How can I **s** you Hos 11:8

SURROUND ***encircle***
s him with favor Ps 5:12
Sheol **s-ed** me Ps 18:5
s me with songs Ps 32:7
witnesses **s-ing** us Heb 12:1

SURVIVE ***outlive***
your household will **s** Jer 38:17
how...can we **s** Ezek 33:10

SURVIVORS ***continued to live***
inheritance for...**s** Judg 21:17
out of...Zion **s** 2 Kin 19:31
left us a few **s** Is 1:9
imprison their **s** Obad 14

SUSA
a Persian capital city Neh 1:1; Esth 1:2,5; 3:15; 9:15

SUSTAIN ***provide for***
land could not **s** Gen 13:6
LORD **s-s** the righteous Ps 37:17
He will **s** you Ps 55:22
S...with raisin cakes Song 2:5

SWALLOW (n) ***bird***
the **s** a nest Ps 84:3
like a **s** in *its* Prov 26:2

SWALLOW (v) ***take in***
earth may **s** us up Num 16:34
He will **s** up death Is 25:8
great fish to **s** Jonah Jon 1:17
s-ed up in victory 1 Cor 15:54

SWARM ***collect, gather***
Nile will **s** with frogs Ex 8:3
which **s** on the earth Lev 11:29
land **s-ed** with frogs Ps 105:30

SWEAR ***take oath, vow***
s by the LORD Gen 24:3
oath which I **swore** Gen 26:3
person **s-s** thoughtlessly Lev 5:4
not **s** falsely Lev 19:12
sworn by My holiness Ps 89:35
s by My name Jer 12:16
whoever **s-s** by heaven Matt 23:22
began to...**s** Matt 26:74
brethren do not **s** James 5:12

SWEAT ***perspiration***
By the **s** of your face Gen 3:19
s...like drops of Luke 22:44

SWEET ***fresh, pleasant***
waters became **s** Ex 15:25
s psalmist of Israel 2 Sam 23:1

who had **s** fellowship Ps 55:14
s are Your words Ps 119:103
your sleep will be **s** Prov 3:24
Stolen water is **s** Prov 9:17
it was **s** as honey Ezek 3:3

SWIFT *fast, rapid*
horses and **s** steeds 1 Kin 4:28
s as the gazelles 1 Chr 12:8
race is not to the **s** Eccl 9:11
riding on a **s** cloud Is 19:1
s to shed blood Rom 3:15

SWINDLER *cheater*
cursed be the **s** Mal 1:14
a drunkard, or a **s** 1 Cor 5:11
revilers, nor **s-s** 1 Cor 6:10

SWINE *pig*
gold in a **s-'s** snout Prov 11:22
Who eat **s-'s** flesh Is 65:4
your pearls before **s** Matt 7:6
Send us into the **s** Mark 5:12

SWORD *weapon with blade*
flaming **s**...turned Gen 3:24
by your **s** you shall Gen 27:40
the **s** will bereave Deut 32:25
A **s** for the LORD Judg 7:20
s devour forever 2 Sam 2:26
fell on his **s** 1 Chr 10:5
tongue a sharp **s** Ps 57:4
as a two-edged **s** Prov 5:4
teeth are *like* **s-s** Prov 30:14
s against nation Is 2:4
the power of the **s** Jer 18:21
abolish...the **s** Hos 2:18
s-s into plowshares Mic 4:3
perish by the **s** Matt 26:52
s of the Spirit Eph 6:17
than any two-edged **s** Heb 4:12
s of My mouth Rev 2:16

SYCAMORE *tree*
olive and **s** trees 1 Chr 27:28
plentiful as **s-s** 2 Chr 1:15
grower of **s** figs Amos 7:14
climbed up into a **s** Luke 19:4

SYCHAR
town in Samaria John 4:5
also **Shechem**

SYMPATHY *mutual feeling*
I looked for **s** Ps 69:20
s to the prisoners Heb 10:34

SYNAGOGUE *assembly*
pray in the **s-s** Matt 6:5
He went into their **s** Matt 12:9
flogged in *the* **s-s** Mark 13:9
chief seats in...**s-s** Luke 20:46
outcasts from the **s** John 16:2
taught in **s-s** John 18:20
reasoning in the **s** Acts 17:17
but are a **s** of Satan Rev 2:9

SYRIA
NE of Israel Matt 4:24; Acts 15:23,41; 20:3
see also **ARAM**

T

TAANACH
Canaanite royal city Josh 12:21; 21:25; Judg 5:19

TABERNACLE *assembly and area for sacrificial worship*
dwelling place of God among the Israelites Ex 25:8
construction directed by God Ex 25:9
contained Ark of the Covenant Ex 25:10
other descriptive names of the tabernacle:
house of the LORD Ex 23:19; 34:26; Deut 23:18
abernacle of the house of God 1 Chr 6:48
ernacle of the tent of meeting Ex 39:40; 40:6,29
rnacle of the testimony Ex 38:21; Num 1:50,53
tent of meeting Ex 29:32; 30:26; 38:30; 38:43; 40:2,6,7

TABITHA *see* **DORCAS**

TABLE *furniture*
gold **t** before the LORD Lev 24:6
You prepare a **t** Ps 23:5
crumbs...masters' **t** Matt 15:27
t-s...moneychangers Matt 21:12
dogs under the **t** Mark 7:28
drink at My **t** Luke 22:30
in order to serve **t-s** Acts 6:2
t of the Lord 1 Cor 10:21

TABLET *writing surface*
give you the stone **t-s** Ex 24:12
t-s of the testimony Ex 31:18
the **t** of their heart Jer 17:1
t-s of human hearts 2 Cor 3:3

TABOR
1 *mountain* Judg 4:6,12
2 *city in Zebulun* 1 Chr 6:77
3 *oak in Benjamin* 1 Sam 10:3

TAHPANHES
Egyptian city Jer 2:16
place where Jeremiah escaped Jer 43:7-9; 44:1

TAHPENES
queen of Egypt 1 Kin 11:19,20

TAIL
grasp *it* by its **t** Ex 4:4
the foxes **t** to **t** Judg 15:4
cuts off head and **t** Is 9:14
t-s like scorpions Rev 9:10

TAKE *get, grasp*
t...the tree of life Gen 3:22
T My yoke upon Matt 11:29
T, eat; this is My Matt 26:26
t-s away the sin John 1:29
day that He was **t-n** Acts 1:22
to **t** hold of...hope Heb 6:18

TALENT
measure of weight Ex 38:27; 2 Sam 12:30; 1 Chr 20:2
measure of money 1 Kin 20:39; Matt 18:24; 25:15,25

TALK (n) *conversation, speech*
argue with useless **t** Job 15:3
no...silly **t** Eph 5:4
their **t** will spread 2 Tim 2:17

TALK (v) *converse, speak*
God **t-ed** with him Gen 17:3
lips **t** of trouble Prov 24:2
who **t** about you Ezek 33:30
they were **t-ing** Luke 24:15
Paul kept on **t-ing** Acts 20:9

TALL *high*
cut...its **t** cedars 2 Kin 19:23
a nation **t** and smooth Is 18:2
grew up, became **t** Ezek 16:7

TAMAR
1 *Judah's daughter-in-law* Gen 38:6ff
2 *daughter of David* 2 Sam 13:1
3 *daughter of Absalom* 2 Sam 14:27
4 *town near the Dead Sea* 1 Kin 9:18; Ezek 47:19; 48:28

TAMARISK *tree*
a **t** tree at Beersheba Gen 21:33
under the **t** tree 1 Sam 22:6

TAMBOURINE
accompanied by...**t** Is 5:12
gaiety of **t-s** ceases Is 24:8

TAMMUZ
Mesopotamian god Ezek 8:14

TARES *weeds*
t among the wheat Matt 13:25
gather up the **t** Matt 13:30
parable of the **t** Matt 13:36

TARSHISH
1 *lineage of Japheth* Gen 10:4
2 *ships of* 1 Kin 10:22; 22:48; 2 Chr 9:21; Ps 48:7
3 *line of Benjamin* 1 Chr 7:6-10
4 *Persian official* Esth 1:14
5 *city* Is 66:19; Jon 1:3

TARSUS
birthplace of Paul Acts 21:39
capital of Cilicia Acts 22:3

TASKMASTERS *overseers*
appointed **t** over them Ex 1:11
Pharaoh commanded...**t** Ex 5:6

TASTE *test flavor*
As the palate **t-s** Job 34:3
O **t** and see Ps 34:8
will not **t** death Matt 16:28
t death for everyone Heb 2:9
t-d...heavenly gift Heb 6:4

TASTELESS *without taste*
Can something **t** be Job 6:6
salt has become **t** Matt 5:13

TAUNT *object of ridicule*
a **t** among all Deut 28:37
I have become their **t** Job 30:9

TAX *charge, tribute*
a **t** for the LORD Num 31:28
money for the king's **t** Neh 5:4
sitting in the **t** collector's booth Matt 9:9
pay **t-es** to Caesar Luke 20:22
t to whom **t** *is due* Rom 13:7

TAX COLLECTOR *tax gatherer*
t-s do the same Matt 5:46
many **t-s** and sinners Matt 9:10
Matthew the **t** Matt 10:3
a friend of **t-s** Matt 11:19
he was a chief **t** Luke 19:2

TEACH *instruct*
t you what...to say Ex 4:12
t them the good way 1 Kin 8:36
Can anyone **t** God Job 21:22
T me Your paths Ps 25:4
T me to do Your will Ps 143:10
would He **t** knowledge Is 28:9
He...*began* to **t** them Matt 5:2
t-ing...in parables Mark 4:2
Lord, **t** us to pray Luke 11:1
Spirit will **t** you Luke 12:12
He will **t** you all John 14:26
t strange doctrines 1 Tim 1:3
allow a woman to **t** 1 Tim 2:12
she **t-es** and leads Rev 2:20

TEACHER *instructor*
will behold your **T** Is 30:20
T, I will follow You Matt 8:19
not above his **t** Matt 10:24
why trouble the **T** Mark 5:35
the **t** of Israel John 3:10
call Me **T** and Lord John 13:13
t of the immature Rom 2:20
as pastors and **t-s** Eph 4:11
t of the Gentiles 1 Tim 2:7
false **t-s** among you 2 Pet 2:1

TEACHING (n) *instruction*
t drop as the rain Deut 32:2
your mother's **t** Prov 1:8
amazed at His **t** Matt 7:28
My **t** is not Mine John 7:16
contrary to sound **t** 1 Tim 1:10

TEAR *crying*
have seen your **t-s** 2 Kin 20:5
my **t-s** in Your bottle Ps 56:8

sow in **t-s** shall reap Ps 126:5
drench you with my **t-s** Is 16:9
eyes a fountain of **t-s** Jer 9:1
His feet with her **t-s** Luke 7:38
God...wipe every **t** Rev 7:17

TEBETH
name of the tenth month in Hebrew calendar Esth 2:16

TEL-ABIB
place in Babylonia Jewish exiles located there Ezek 3:15

TELL *relate, speak*
not **t** the riddle Judg 14:14
T of His glory 1 Chr 16:24
t of Your righteousness Ps 71:15
t-s lies will perish Prov 19:9
t you great and mighty Jer 33:3
See that you **t** no one Matt 8:4
t you about Me John 18:34
t you the mystery Rev 17:7

TEMA
1 *son of Ishmael* Gen 25:15
2 *town in Arabia* Job 6:19; Is 21:14

TEMPER *anger*
always loses his **t** Prov 29:11
the ruler's **t** rises Eccl 10:4

TEMPEST *storm*
bruises me with a **t** Job 9:17
stormy wind *and* **t** Ps 55:8
t of destruction Is 28:2
on the day of **t** Amos 1:14

TEMPLE *structure for worship*
doorpost of the **t** 1 Sam 1:9
t is not for man 1 Chr 29:1
LORD is in His holy **t** Ps 11:4
meditate in His **t** Ps 27:4
t of the LORD Jer 7:4
pinnacle of the **t** Matt 4:5
will destroy this **t** Mark 14:58
veil of the **t** Luke 23:45
Destroy this **t**, and John 2:19
you are a **t** of God 1 Cor 3:16
t of the Holy Spirit 1 Cor 6:19
his seat in the **t** 2 Thess 2:4
the Lamb, are its **t** Rev 21:22

TEMPT *test, try*
And **t-ed** God in the Ps 106:14
being **t-ed** by Satan Mark 1:13
so that Satan will not **t** you 1 Cor 7:5
t-ed beyond what 1 Cor 10:13
Himself does not **t** James 1:13

TEMPTATION *testing, trial*
not lead us into **t** Matt 6:13
not enter into **t** Matt 26:41
time of **t** fall away Luke 8:13
t has overtaken you 1 Cor 10:13
the godly from **t** 2 Pet 2:9

TEN *number*
T Commandments Deut 10:4
it had **t** horns Dan 7:7
has the **t** talents Matt 25:28

TEND *take care of*
t his father's flock 1 Sam 17:15
He will **t** His flock Is 40:11
T My lambs John 21:15
T My sheep John 21:17

TENDER *gentle, young*
t and choice calf Gen 18:7
your heart was **t** 2 Kin 22:19
like a **t** shoot Is 53:2
t mercy of our God Luke 1:78

TENT *mobile shelter*
Abram moved his **t** Gen 13:18
man, living in **t-s** Gen 25:27
your **t-s**, O Israel 1 Kin 12:16
t-s of the destroyers Job 12:6
dwell in Your **t** forever Ps 61:4
grumbled in their **t-s** Ps 106:25
Like a shepherd's **t** Is 38:12

TENT OF MEETING
perhaps the same as the Tabernacle or at certain periods a separate meeting place Ex 33:7; Lev 1:1; Num 7:5; Josh 18:1
see also **TABERNACLE**

TENT OF TESTIMONY *see* **TABERNACLE**

TERAH
father of Abraham Gen 11:24; Num 33:27; Luke 3:34

TERAPHIM
household gods, idols 2 Kin 23:24; Zech 10:2

TERRIBLE *dreadful*
and **t** wilderness Deut 8:15
t day of the LORD Mal 4:5
into **t** convulsions Mark 9:26

TERRIFY *frighten*
t-ied by the sword 1 Chr 21:30
t me by visions Job 7:14
t them with Your storm Ps 83:15
Him and were **t-ied** Mark 6:50
t you by my letters 2 Cor 10:9

TERRITORY *country, land*
smite your whole **t** Ex 8:2
God enlarges your **t** Deut 19:8
t of...inheritance Josh 19:10
possess the **t** Obad 19

TERROR *intense fear*
Sounds of **t** are in Job 15:21
t-s of thick darkness Job 24:17
t-s of Sheol came Ps 116:3
meditate on **t** Is 33:18
t-s and great signs Luke 21:11

TERTIUS
Paul's scribe Rom 16:22

TEST (n) *trial*
put God to the **t** Ps 78:18
put Him to the **t** Luke 10:25
you fail the **t** 2 Cor 13:5

TEST (v) *try*
God **t-ed** Abraham Gen 22:1
Why do you **t** the LORD Ex 17:2
she came to **t** him 1 Kin 10:1
T my mind and my Ps 26:2
word of God is **t-ed** Prov 30:5
Spirit...to the **t** Acts 5:9
fire itself will **t** 1 Cor 3:13
t the spirits to see 1 John 4:1

TESTIFY *give witness*
nor shall you **t** Ex 23:2
them **t** against him 1 Kin 21:10
I will **t** against you Ps 50:7
our sins **t** against us Is 59:12
John **t-ied** John 1:15
John **t-ied** John 1:32
Jesus Himself **t-ied** John 4:44
If I *alone* **t** John 5:31
t about Me John 15:26
you *will* **t** John 15:27
Spirit...**t-ies** Rom 8:16
three that **t** 1 John 5:7

TESTIMONY *witness*
into the ark the **t** Ex 25:16
two tablets of the **t** Ex 31:18
t of the LORD is sure Ps 19:7
t-ies are righteous Ps 119:144
Bind up the **t** Is 8:16
t to all the nations Matt 24:14
t against Jesus Matt 26:59
My **t** is true John 8:14
t of two men is true John 8:17
t concerning Christ 1 Cor 1:6
ashamed of the **t** 2 Tim 1:8
This **t** is true Titus 1:13
t of God is greater 1 John 5:9

TETRARCH
governor of a region Matt 14:1; Luke 3:1,19; Acts 13:1

THADDAEUS
apostle Matt 10:3; Mark 3:18

THANK (v) *express gratitude*
my song I shall **t** Him Ps 28:7
God, I **t** You Luke 18:11
I **t** my God always 1 Cor 1:4

THANKS (n) *gratitude*
give **t** to the LORD 1 Chr 16:7
It is good to give **t** Ps 92:1
giving **t**, He broke Matt 15:36
a cup and given **t** Matt 26:27
But **t** be to God Rom 6:17
not cease giving **t** Eph 1:16
always to give **t** 2 Thess 1:3

THANKSGIVING *gratitude*
the sacrifice of **t** Lev 7:12
with the voice of **t** Ps 26:7
His presence with **t** Ps 95:2
supplication with **t** Phil 4:6
t and honor and Rev 7:12

THEBES
Egyptian city Jer 46:25; Ezek 30:14-16

THEFT *robbery*
be sold for his **t** Ex 22:3
t-s, murders Mark 7:21

THEOPHILUS
addressee of Luke's gospel and Acts Luke 1:3; Acts 1:1

THESSALONICA
Macedonian city visited by Paul Acts 27:2; Phil 4:16; Acts 17:1,11,13

THICKET *underbrush*
ram caught in the **t** Gen 22:13
the **t** of the Jordan Jer 50:44

THIEF *robber*
that **t** shall die Deut 24:7
partner with a **t** Prov 29:24
companions of **t-ves** Is 1:23
enter...like a **t** Joel 2:9
t comes...to steal John 10:10
a **t** in the night 1 Thess 5:2

THIGH *part of leg*
hand under my **t** Gen 24:2
socket of Jacob's **t** Gen 32:25
Your sword on *Your* **t** Ps 45:3
on His **t**...a name Rev 19:16

THIN *lean*
t ears scorched Gen 41:27
t yellowish hair Lev 13:30
streams...will **t** out Is 19:6

THINK *ponder, reflect*
as he **t-s**...so he is Prov 23:7
not **t**...to abolish Matt 5:17
not to **t** more highly Rom 12:3
t like a child 1 Cor 13:11
t-s he is something Gal 6:3
beyond all that we...**t** Eph 3:20

THIRD *number*
morning, a **t** day Gen 1:13
raised...the **t** day Matt 16:21
raised on the **t** day 1 Cor 15:4
to the **t** heaven 2 Cor 12:2

THIRST (n) *craving, dryness*
for my **t**...vinegar Ps 69:21

donkeys quench...**t** Ps 104:11
not hunger or **t** Is 49:10
in Me will never **t** John 6:35
no longer...nor **t** Rev 7:16

THIRST (v) *have a craving*
My soul **t-s** for God Ps 42:2
Every one who **t-s**, come Is 55:1
t for righteousness Matt 5:6

THIRSTY *lacking water*
satisfied the **t** soul Ps 107:9
In a dry and **t** land Ezek 19:13
I was **t**, and you Matt 25:35
If anyone is **t** John 7:37
one who is **t** come Rev 22:17

THOMAS
apostle Matt 10:3; Mark 3:18; Luke 6:15
doubted Jesus' resurrection John 20:24-28

THORN *sharp point*
Both **t-s** and thistles Gen 3:18
as **t-s** in your sides Num 33:55
as a hedge of **t-s** Prov 15:19
lily among the **t-s** Song 2:2
have reaped **t-s** Jer 12:13
fell among the **t-s** Matt 13:7
a crown of **t-s** Matt 27:29
a burning **t** bush Acts 7:30
t in the flesh 2 Cor 12:7

THOUGHT *concept, idea*
t-s of his heart Gen 6:5
knows the **t-s** of man Ps 94:11
My **t-s** are not your **t-s** Is 55:8
Jesus knowing...**t-s** Matt 9:4
heart come evil **t-s** Matt 15:19
every **t** captive 2 Cor 10:5

THREAD *string*
cord of scarlet **t** Josh 2:18
lips...a scarlet **t** Song 4:3

THREE *number*
Job's **t** friends Job 2:11
or **t** have gathered Matt 18:20
deny Me **t** times Matt 26:34
t days I will raise John 2:19

THRESH *beat out*
ox while he is **t-ing** Deut 25:4
like the dust at **t-ing** 2 Kin 13:7
will **t** the mountains Is 41:15
Arise and **t** Mic 4:13

THRESHING FLOOR
winnows...at the **t** Ruth 3:2
David bought...**t** 2 Sam 24:24
clear His **t** Matt 3:12

THROAT *part of neck*
t is an open grave Ps 5:9
my **t** is parched Ps 69:3
has enlarged its **t** Is 5:14
t is an open grave Rom 3:13

THRONE *seat of sovereign*
sitting on His **t** 1 Kin 22:19
LORD's **t** is in heaven Ps 11:4
Your **t** is established Ps 93:2
it is the **t** of God Matt 5:34
sit upon twelve **t-s** Matt 19:28
Your **t**...is forever Heb 1:8
to the **t** of grace Heb 4:16
a great white **t** Rev 20:11

THRUST *cast, push*
He will **t** them out Josh 23:5
t away like thorns 2 Sam 23:6
Nor to **t** aside Prov 18:5
LORD has **t**...down Jer 46:15

THUMMIM
obj in high priest's breastplate for determining will of God Ex 28:30; Lev 8:8; Deut 33:8; Ezra 2:63; Neh 7:65

THUNDER (n)
LORD sent **t** Ex 9:23
But His mighty **t** Job 26:14
the hiding place of **t** Ps 81:7
be punished with **t** Is 29:6
sound of loud **t** Rev 14:2

THUNDER (v)
t in the heavens 1 Sam 2:10
you **t** with a voice Job 40:9
LORD also **t-ed** Ps 18:13

THYATIRA
city in Asia minor
home of Lydia Acts 16:14
early church Rev 1:11; 2:18,24

TIBERIAS
city on W shore of Sea of Galilee John 6:23
Sea of Tiberias John 6:1; 21:1
also **Sea of Chinnereth**
also **Sea of Galilee**
also **Lake of Gennesaret**

TIBERIUS
Roman emperor Luke 3:1
see also **CAESAR**

TIDINGS *information, news*
t of His salvation 1 Chr 16:23
not fear evil **t** Ps 112:7

TIGLATH-PILESER
Assyrian king 2 Kin 15:29; 16:7,10
see also **PUL**
see also **TILGATH-PILNESER**

TIGRIS
Mesopotamian river Gen 2:14; Dan 10:4

TILGATH-PILNESER
Assyrian king 1 Chr 5:6,26; 2 Chr 28:20
see also **PUL**
see also **TIGLATH-PILESER**

TILLER *cultivator*
Cain was a **t** Gen 4:2
a **t** of the ground Zech 13:5

TIMBER *wood*
cedar and cypress **t** 1 Kin 9:11
whatever **t** you need 2 Chr 2:16
t of Lebanon Song 3:9

TIMBREL *musical instrument*
with songs, with **t** Gen 31:27
strike the **t** Ps 81:2
Praise Him with **t** Ps 150:4

TIME *day, period, season*
in **t-s** of trouble Ps 9:9
t-s are in Your hand Ps 31:15
for a **t**, **t-s**, and half Dan 12:7
t to seek the LORD Hos 10:12
signs of the **t-s** Matt 16:3
My **t** is near Matt 26:18
deny Me three **t-s** Luke 22:61
My **t** is not yet John 7:6
not...you to know **t-s** Acts 1:7
is the acceptable **t** 2 Cor 6:2
grace...in **t** of need Heb 4:16
for the **t** is near Rev 1:3

TIMOTHY
companion of Paul Acts 17:15; 18:5; Phil 1:1; Col 1:1; Heb 13:23

TIRED *weary*
I am **t** of living Gen 27:46
run and not get **t** Is 40:31

TIRZAH
1 *daughter of Zelophehad* Num 26:33; 27:1; 36:11
2 *royal Canaanite city* 1 Kin 14:17; 2 Kin 15:14

TISHBITE
town identity of Elijah 1 Kin 17:1; 21:17; 2 Kin 1:3,8

TITHE (n) *tenth*
all the **t** of the land Lev 27:30
a **t** of the **t** Num 18:26
the **t** of your grain Deut 12:17
t into the storehouse Mal 3:10
t-s of all that I get Luke 18:12
mortal men receive **t-s** Heb 7:8

TITHE (v) *pay a tithe*
shall surely **t** all Deut 14:22
you **t** mint and dill Matt 23:23

TITUS
co-worker with Paul 2 Cor 2:13; 8:23; Gal 2:1

TODAY *present time*
t you...be with Me Luke 23:43
same yesterday and **t** Heb 13:8

TOGARMAH
grandson of Japheth Gen 10:1-3; 1 Chr 1:6

TOIL (n) *labor, work*
the **t** of our hands Gen 5:29
t is not *in* vain 1 Cor 15:58

TOIL (v) *work hard*
I have **t-ed** in vain Is 49:4
they do not **t** nor Matt 6:28

TOMB *grave, sepulchre*
from womb to **t** Job 10:19
you have hewn a **t** Is 22:16
like whitewashed **t-s** Matt 23:27
laid Him in a **t** Mark 15:46
Lazarus out of the **t** John 12:17
outside the **t** John 20:11

TOMORROW *future time*
not boast about **t** Prov 27:1
for **t** we may die Is 22:13
not worry about **t** Matt 6:34

TONGUE *speech, talk*
speech and slow of **t** Ex 4:10
flatter with their **t** Ps 5:9
their **t** a sharp sword Ps 57:4
a lying **t** Prov 6:17
t of the wise Prov 12:18
soft **t** breaks...bone Prov 25:15
His **t** is like...fire Is 30:27
t is a deadly arrow Jer 9:8
impediment of his **t** Mark 7:35
and his **t** *loosed* Luke 1:64
no one...tame the **t** James 3:8

TONGUE *language*
speak with new **t-s** Mark 16:17
speak with other **t-s** Acts 2:4
t-s of men...angels 1 Cor 13:1
if I pray in a **t** 1 Cor 14:14
every tribe and **t** Rev 5:9

TOOL *work instrument*
among your **t-s** Deut 23:13
nor any iron **t** 1 Kin 6:7
iron into a cutting **t** Is 44:12

TOOTH
teeth white from Gen 49:12
eye for eye, **t** for **t** Ex 21:24
and a **t** for a **t** Matt 5:38

TOPAZ *precious stone*
ruby, **t**, and emerald Ex 39:10
t of Ethiopia Job 28:19
the ninth, **t** Rev 21:20

TOPHETH
site of Baal worship in Hinnom Valley 2 Kin 23:10; Jer 7:31,32; 19:6,12,14

TORMENT (n) *pain, torture*
this place of **t** Luke 16:28
their **t** was like Rev 9:5
the fear of her **t** Rev 18:15

TORMENT (v) *annoy, harass*
- long will you **t** me — Job 19:2
- **t** us before the time — Matt 8:29
- do not **t** me — Luke 8:28
- Satan to **t** me — 2 Cor 12:7

TORRENT *flood*
- The ancient **t** — Judg 5:21
- **t-s** of destruction — 2 Sam 22:5
- **t-s** of ungodliness — Ps 18:4
- like an overflowing **t** — Is 30:28

TOUCH *feel, handle*
- not eat...or **t** it — Gen 3:3
- an angel **t-ing** him — 1 Kin 19:5
- evil will not **t** you — Job 5:19
- not **t** My anointed — Ps 105:15
- **T** nothing unclean — Is 52:11
- **t** the fringe of His — Matt 14:36
- not to **t** a woman — 1 Cor 7:1

TOWER *fortress structure*
- **t** whose top *will reach* — Gen 11:4
- Count her **t-s** — Ps 48:12
- name...strong **t** — Prov 18:10
- and built a **t** — Matt 21:33

TOWN *city, village*
- many unwalled **t-s** — Deut 3:5
- founds a **t** with — Hab 2:12
- except in his home **t** — Matt 13:57

TRADE (n) *business, occupation*
- abundance of your **t** — Ezek 28:16
- of the same **t** — Acts 18:3

TRADE (v) *buy or sell*
- may **t** in the land — Gen 42:34
- **t-d** with them — Matt 25:16

TRADERS *merchants*
- Midianite **t** passed — Gen 37:28
- king's **t** procured — 2 Chr 1:16
- in a city of **t** — Ezek 17:4
- increased your **t** — Nah 3:16

TRADITION *custom*
- sake of your **t** — Matt 15:3
- hold to the **t** of men — Mark 7:8
- hold...to the **t-s** — 1 Cor 11:2
- my ancestral **t-s** — Gal 1:14

TRAIN *guide, instruct*
- **T** up a child — Prov 22:6
- will they **t** for war — Mic 4:3
- **t-ed** to discern good — Heb 5:14
- heart **t-ed** in greed — 2 Pet 2:14

TRAMPLE *crush, hurt*
- **t-s** down the waves — Job 9:8
- let him **t** my life — Ps 7:5
- **t-d** the nations — Hab 3:12
- Jerusalem...**t-d** — Luke 21:24

TRANCE *daze, dream*
- he fell into a **t** — Acts 10:10
- in a **t** I saw a vision — Acts 11:5
- fell into a **t** — Acts 22:17

TRANSFIGURED *changed*
- He was **t** before them — Matt 17:2

TRANSFORM *change*
- **t-ed** by the renewing — Rom 12:2
- **t-ed** into the same — 2 Cor 3:18
- who will **t** the body — Phil 3:21

TRANSGRESS *break, overstep*
- you **t** the covenant — Josh 23:16
- rulers also **t-ed** — Jer 2:8
- they **t-ed** laws — Is 24:5

TRANSGRESSION *trespass, sin*
- forgives iniquity, **t** — Ex 34:7
- I am pure, without **t** — Job 33:9
- I know my **t-s** — Ps 51:3
- removed our **t-s** from — Ps 103:12
- love covers all **t-s** — Prov 10:12
- pierced...for our **t-s** — Is 53:5
- not forgive your **t-s** — Matt 6:15
- dead in our **t-s** — Eph 2:5

TRANSGRESSOR *sinner*
- teach **t-s** Your ways — Ps 51:13
- numbered with the **t-s** — Is 53:12
- a **t** of the law — James 2:11

TRANSLATED
- **t** and read before me — Ezra 4:18
- Immanuel...**t** means — Matt 1:23
- Golgotha, which is **t** — Mark 15:22
- Messiah...**t** means — John 1:41

TRAP (n) *snare*
- a snare and a **t** — Josh 23:13
- hidden a **t** for me — Ps 142:3
- table become...a **t** — Rom 11:9

TRAP (v) *catch*
- they might **t** Him — Matt 22:15
- in order to **t** Him — Mark 12:13

TRAVAIL *intense pain*
- **t-ed** nor given birth — Is 23:4

TRAVEL *journey*
- **t** by day and by night — Ex 13:21
- who **t** on the road — Judg 5:10
- Jesus...*began* **t-ing** — Luke 24:15

TREACHEROUS *traitorous*
- I behold the **t** — Ps 119:158
- **t** will be uprooted — Prov 2:22
- way of the **t** is hard — Prov 13:15

TREAD *walk on*
- They **t** wine presses — Job 24:11
- as the potter **t-s** clay — Is 41:25
- **t** on serpents — Luke 10:19
- **t-s** the wine press — Rev 19:15

TREASURE (n) *valuable thing*
- **t-s** of the sand — Deut 33:19
- the LORD is his **t** — Is 33:6
- opening their **t-s** — Matt 2:11
- for where your **t** is — Matt 6:21
- have **t** in heaven — Matt 19:21
- **t** in earthen vessels — 2 Cor 4:7
- stored up your **t** — James 5:3

TREASURE (v) *value greatly*
- I have **t-d** the words — Job 23:12
- Your word I have **t-d** — Ps 119:11
- **t** my commandments — Prov 7:1

TREASURY *place of valuables*
- **t** of the LORD — Josh 6:19
- paid from the royal **t** — Ezra 6:4
- fill their **t-ies** — Prov 8:21
- into the temple **t** — Matt 27:6

TREATY *agreement, contract*
- *Let there be* a **t** — 1 Kin 15:19
- go, break your **t** — 2 Chr 16:3

TREE *woody plant*
- fruit **t-s**...bearing — Gen 1:11
- **t** of life — Gen 2:9
- gave me from the **t** — Gen 3:12
- hang him on a **t** — Deut 21:22
- said to the olive **t** — Judg 9:8
- **t** *firmly* planted — Ps 1:3
- she is a **t** of life — Prov 3:18
- Beneath the apple **t** — Song 8:5
- like a **t** planted by — Jer 17:8
- under his fig **t** — Mic 4:4
- good **t** bears good — Matt 7:17
- the fig **t** withered — Matt 21:19
- a sycamore **t** — Luke 19:4
- autumn **t-s** without — Jude 12
- eat of the **t** of life — Rev 2:7

TREMBLE *shake*
- **T** before Him — 1 Chr 16:30
- pillars of heaven **t** — Job 26:11
- **T**, and do not sin — Ps 4:4
- make the heavens **t** — Is 13:13
- His soul **t-s** — Is 15:4
- my inward parts **t-d** — Hab 3:16

TREMBLING (n) *fear, reverence*
- rejoice with **t** — Ps 2:11
- eat...with **t** — Ezek 12:18
- with fear and **t** — Phil 2:12

TRESPASS *fault, sin*
- Saul died for his **t** — 1 Chr 10:13
- caught in any **t** — Gal 6:1
- dead in your **t-es** — Eph 2:1

TRIAL *testing*
- if we are on **t** today — Acts 4:9
- which was a **t** to you — Gal 4:14
- perseveres under **t** — James 1:12

TRIBE *common ancestry*
- twelve **t-s** of Israel — Gen 49:28
- a man of each **t** — Num 1:4
- **t-s** of the LORD — Ps 122:4
- judging...twelve **t-s** — Luke 22:30
- *men* from every **t** — Rev 5:9

TRIBULATION *affliction*
- will be a great **t** — Matt 24:21
- world you have **t** — John 16:33
- exult in our **t-s** — Rom 5:3
- my **t-s** on your behalf — Eph 3:13
- out of the great **t** — Rev 7:14

TRIBUNAL *court*
- before Caesar's **t** — Acts 25:10

TRIBUTE *tax*
- sons of Israel sent **t** — Judg 3:15
- impose...**t** or toll — Ezra 7:24
- exact a **t** of grain — Amos 5:11

TRIGON *musical instrument*
- sound of...lyre, **t** — Dan 3:5

TRIUMPH *victory*
- the righteous **t** — Prov 28:12
- **t** in Christ — 2 Cor 2:14
- mercy **t-s** over — James 2:13

TROAS
- *city in Asia Minor* — Acts 16:8,11
- *visited by Paul* — Acts 20:5; 2 Cor 2:12

TROPHIMUS
- *companion of Paul* — Acts 20:4; 2 Tim 4:20
- *Ephesian Christian* — Acts 21:29

TROUBLE (n) *affliction*
- forget all my **t** — Gen 41:51
- man is born for **t** — Job 5:7
- Look upon...my **t** — Ps 25:18
- very present help in **t** — Ps 46:1
- remember his **t** no — Prov 31:7
- **t** is heavy upon him — Eccl 8:6
- day has enough **t** — Matt 6:34

TROUBLE (v) *bother, disturb*
- **t** you in the land — Num 33:55
- **t-s** his own house — Prov 11:29
- also **t** the hearts — Ezek 32:9
- Herod...was **t-d** — Matt 2:3
- why **t** the Teacher — Mark 5:35
- your heart be **t-d** — John 14:1

TROUBLED (adj) *disturbed*
- songs to a **t** heart — Prov 25:20
- soul has become **t** — John 12:27

TRUE *actual, real, reliable*
- *gets* a **t** reward — Prov 11:18
- There was the **t** light — John 1:9
- gives you...**t** bread — John 6:32
- let God be found **t** — Rom 3:4
- signs of a **t** apostle — 2 Cor 12:12
- This testimony is **t** — Titus 1:13
- **t** grace of God — 1 Pet 5:12
- faithful and **t** Witness — Rev 3:14

TRUMPET ***wind instrument***
t-s of rams' horns Josh 6:6
t-s...empty pitchers Judg 7:16
Praise Him with **t** Ps 150:3
do not sound a **t** Matt 6:2
at the last **t** 1 Cor 15:52
voice like...a **t** Rev 1:10

TRUST (n) ***confidence, hope***
whose **t** a spider's web Job 8:14
In God...put my **t** Ps 56:11
put My **t** in Him Heb 2:13

TRUST (v) ***commit to***
t in the LORD Ps 4:5
Than to **t** in man Ps 118:8
t-s in his riches Prov 11:28
not **t** in a neighbor Mic 7:5
not **t** in ourselves 2 Cor 1:9

TRUSTWORTHY ***reliable***
t witness will not lie Prov 14:5
who can find a **t** Prov 20:6
It is a **t** statement 1 Tim 3:1

TRUTH ***genuineness, honesty***
walk before Me in **t** 1 Kin 2:4
speaks **t** in his heart Ps 15:2
Your word is **t** Ps 119:160
Buy **t**, and do not Prov 23:23
judge with **t** Zech 8:16
full of grace and **t** John 1:14
worship in...**t** John 4:24
t will make you free John 8:32
the way, and the **t** John 14:6
exchanged the **t** of Rom 1:25
t of the gospel Gal 2:5
speaking the **t** in love Eph 4:15
the word of **t** 2 Tim 2:15
the **t** is not in us 1 John 1:8

TUBAL
1 *son of Japheth* Gen 10:2
2 *land ruled by Gog* Ezek 38:3; 39:1

TUBAL-CAIN
son of Zillah Gen 4:22
inventor of cutting tools

TUMULT ***disturbance***
t of the peoples Ps 65:7
A sound of **t** Is 13:4
t of waters Jer 51:16

TUNIC ***cloak, garment***
a varicolored **t** Gen 37:3
the holy linen **t** Lev 16:4

TURBAN ***headdress***
a **t** of fine linen Ex 28:39
justice was like...a **t** Job 29:14
Remove the **t** Ezek 21:26

TURMOIL ***tumult***
treasure and **t** with Prov 15:16
rest from your...**t** Is 14:3
ill repute, full of **t** Ezek 22:5

TURN ***change*** **or** ***move***
not **t** to mediums Lev 19:31
leave you *or* **t** back Ruth 1:16
T from your evil 2 Kin 17:13
forget, nor **t** away Prov 4:5
T to Me, and be saved Is 45:22
t-ed to his own way Is 53:6
t their mourning into Jer 31:13
t...shame into praise Zeph 3:19
t from darkness to Acts 26:18
he who **t-s** a sinner James 5:20
t away from evil 1 Pet 3:11

TURTLEDOVE ***bird***
t for a sin offering Lev 12:6
the voice of the **t** Song 2:12

TUTOR ***teacher***
in Christ 1 Cor 4:15
Law...become our **t** Gal 3:24

TWELVE ***number***
t tribes of Israel Gen 49:28
summoned His **t** Matt 10:1
t legions of angels Matt 26:53
when He became **t** Luke 2:42
a crown of **t** stars Rev 12:1

TWILIGHT ***darkness, dusk***
lamb...offer at **t** Ex 29:39
waits for the **t** Job 24:15
midday as in the **t** Is 59:10

TWINKLING ***flicker***
in the **t** of an eye 1 Cor 15:52

TWINS ***pair, two***
t in her womb Gen 25:24
T of a gazelle Song 4:5

TWO-EDGED ***with two edges***
than any **t** sword Heb 4:12
His mouth...**t** sword Rev 1:16

TYRE
Phoenician seaport Josh 19:29; Ezek 27:3; Matt 15:21; Acts 21:3

U

UGLY ***unsightly***
u and gaunt cows Gen 41:4
seven lean...**u** cows Gen 41:27

UNBELIEF ***lack of faith***
wondered at their **u** Mark 6:6
help my **u** Mark 9:24
continue in their **u** Rom 11:23

UNBELIEVER ***non-believer***
a place with the **u-s** Luke 12:46
wife who is an **u** 1 Cor 7:12
ungifted men or **u-s** 1 Cor 14:23
bound...with **u-s** 2 Cor 6:14
worse than an **u** 1 Tim 5:8

UNBELIEVING ***doubting***
O **u** generation Mark 9:19
u husband is 1 Cor 7:14
blinded the...**u** 2 Cor 4:4
evil, **u** heart Heb 3:12

UNBLEMISHED ***without defect***
shall be an **u** male Ex 12:5
u and spotless 1 Pet 1:19

UNCEASING ***continuous***
u complaint in his Job 33:19
sorrow and **u** grief Rom 9:2

UNCHANGEABLENESS
the **u** of His purpose Heb 6:17

UNCIRCUMCISED
But an **u** male Gen 17:14
u heart...humbled Lev 26:41
the nations are **u** Jer 9:26
who is physically **u** Rom 2:27
the gospel to the **u** Gal 2:7

UNCIRCUMCISION
has become **u** Rom 2:25
who are called **U** Eph 2:11
the **u** of your flesh Col 2:13

UNCLEAN ***not clean*** **or** ***not holy***
touches any **u** thing Lev 5:2
u in their practices Ps 106:39
man of **u** lips Is 6:5
authority over **u** Matt 10:1
u spirits entered Mark 5:13
eaten anything...**u** Acts 10:14
nothing is **u** in itself Rom 14:14

UNCOVER ***expose***
to **u** her nakedness Lev 18:7
u his feet and Ruth 3:4
head **u-ed** while 1 Cor 11:5

UNDEFILED ***uncorrupted***
holy, innocent, **u** Heb 7:26
marriage bed...*be* **u** Heb 13:4
pure and **u** religion James 1:27
imperishable and **u** 1 Pet 1:4

UNDERGARMENTS
u next to his flesh Lev 6:10
linen **u** shall be on Ezek 44:18

UNDERGO ***experience***
Holy One to **u** decay Ps 16:10
should not **u** decay Ps 49:9
did not **u** decay Acts 13:37

UNDERSTAND ***comprehend***
u-s every intent 1 Chr 28:9
To **u** a proverb Prov 1:6
O fools, **u** wisdom Prov 8:5
do not **u** justice Prov 28:5
Who can **u** it Jer 17:9
u that the vision Dan 8:17
Hear, and **u** Matt 15:10
to **u** the Scriptures Luke 24:45
Why do you not **u** John 8:43
none who **u-s** Rom 3:11
things hard to **u** 2 Pet 3:16

UNDERSTANDING
a wise and **u** people Deut 4:6
servant an **u** heart 1 Kin 3:9
Holy One is **u** Prov 9:10

UNDISCIPLINED
in an **u** manner 2 Thess 3:7
leading an **u** life 2 Thess 3:11

UNDISTURBED ***peaceful***
land was **u** for forty Judg 8:28
an **u** habitation Is 33:20

UNFADING ***lasting***
u crown of glory 1 Pet 5:4

UNFAITHFUL
u to her husband Num 5:27
very **u** to the LORD 2 Chr 28:19
u to our God Ezra 10:2

UNFAITHFULNESS ***faithless***
u...they committed Lev 26:40
to Babylon for their **u** 1 Chr 9:1
the **u** of the exiles Ezra 9:4

UNFATHOMABLE
How...**u** His ways Rom 11:33
u riches of Christ Eph 3:8

UNFRUITFUL ***not productive***
the land is **u** 2 Kin 2:19
my mind is **u** 1 Cor 14:14
u deeds of darkness Eph 5:11

UNGODLINESS ***sinfulness***
torrents of **u** terrified Ps 18:4
remove **u**...Jacob Rom 11:26
lead to further **u** 2 Tim 2:16

UNGODLY ***sinful, wicked***
who justifies the **u** Rom 4:5
Christ died for the **u** Rom 5:6
destruction of **u** men 2 Pet 3:7
their own **u** lusts Jude 18

UNHOLY ***not holy***
no *longer* consider **u** Acts 10:15
for the **u** and profane 1 Tim 1:9

UNINTENTIONALLY
If a person sins **u** Lev 4:2
who kills a person **u** Num 35:15

UNITED ***joined, union***
u as one man Judg 20:11
become **u** with *Him* Rom 6:5
love, **u** in spirit Phil 2:2

not **u** by faith Heb 4:2

UNITY ***united, union***
dwell together in **u** Ps 133:1
perfected in **u** John 17:23
all attain to the **u** Eph 4:13
perfect bond of **u** Col 3:14

UNJUST ***unfair***
u man is abominable Prov 29:27
For God is not **u** Heb 6:10
the just for *the* **u** 1 Pet 3:18

UNKNOWN ***not known***
To An **U** God Acts 17:23
as **u** yet well-known 2 Cor 6:9

UNLEAVENED ***non-fermented***
and baked **u** bread Gen 19:3
you shall eat **u** bread Ex 12:15
first day of **U** Bread Matt 26:17
you are *in fact* **u** 1 Cor 5:7

UNLEAVENED BREAD, FEAST OF ***see*** **FEASTS**

UNLOVED ***not loved***
that Leah was **u** Gen 29:31
loved and the **u** Deut 21:15
Under an **u** woman Prov 30:23

UNMARRIED ***single***
I say to the **u** 1 Cor 7:8
she must remain **u** 1 Cor 7:11

UNPRINCIPLED ***unscrupulous***
conduct of **u** men 2 Pet 2:7
error of **u** men 2 Pet 3:17

UNPROFITABLE ***without value***
u and worthless Titus 3:9
grief...**u** for you Heb 13:17

UNPUNISHED ***not punished***
not leave him **u** Ex 20:7
shall go **u** Ex 21:19
not let him go **u** 1 Kin 2:9

UNQUENCHABLE
burn...with **u** fire Matt 3:12
into the **u** fire Mark 9:43

UNRESTRAINED ***uncontrolled***
the people are **u** Prov 29:18
with **u** persecution Is 14:6

UNRIGHTEOUS ***evil, wicked***
u man his thoughts Is 55:7
rain on...*the* **u** Matt 5:45
u in a...little thing Luke 16:10
God...is not **u** Rom 3:5
u will not inherit 1 Cor 6:9
u under punishment 2 Pet 2:9

UNRIGHTEOUSNESS ***evil***
have no part in **u** 2 Chr 19:7
no **u** in Him Ps 92:15
not rejoice in **u** 1 Cor 13:6
cleanse us from all **u** 1 John 1:9
All **u** is sin 1 John 5:17

UNRULY ***disorderly***
admonish the **u** 1 Thess 5:14
who leads an **u** life 2 Thess 3:6

UNSEARCHABLE ***inscrutable***
His greatness is **u** Ps 145:3
u are His judgments Rom 11:33

UNSKILLED ***lack of training***
I am **u** in speech Ex 6:12
u in speech, yet I 2 Cor 11:6

UNSTABLE ***unreliable***
Her ways are **u** Prov 5:6
u in all his ways James 1:8
enticing **u** souls 2 Pet 2:14

UNWILLING ***reluctant***
u to move the ark 2 Sam 6:10
they were **u** to come Matt 22:3
He was **u** to drink Matt 27:34
u to be obedient Acts 7:39

UNWISE ***foolish***
foolish and **u** people Deut 32:6
walk, not as **u** men Eph 5:15

UNWORTHY ***not deserving***
u of...lovingkindness Gen 32:10
We are **u** slaves Luke 17:10
u of eternal life Acts 13:46

UPRIGHT ***honest, just***
the death of the **u** Num 23:10
blameless and **u** man Job 1:8
u will behold His face Ps 11:7
led you in **u** paths Prov 4:11
God made men **u** Eccl 7:29
no **u**...among men Mic 7:2
Stand **u** on your feet Acts 14:10

UPROAR ***loud noise***
Why...such an **u** 1 Kin 1:41
nations in an **u** Ps 2:1
there occurred a great **u** Acts 23:9

UPROOT ***tear out***
He will **u** Israel 1 Kin 14:15
He has **u-ed** my hope Job 19:10
u-ed and be planted Luke 17:6

UR
1 *city in S Mesopotamia* Gen 11:31; 15:7
original home of Abraham Gen 11:28; Neh 9:7
2 *father of Eliphal* 1 Chr 11:35

URBANUS
Roman Christian Rom 16:9

URGE ***entreat***
Do not **u** me to leave Ruth 1:16
hunger **u-s** him *on* Prov 16:26
Therefore I **u** you Rom 12:1

URIAH
1 *husband of Bathsheba* 2 Sam 11:3; 12:9
2 *priest under Ezra* Neh 8:4
3 *priest under Ahaz* Is 8:2
also **Urijah** 2 Kin 16:10ff
4 *time of Jeremiah* Jer 26:20

URIM
kept in high priest's breastplate for determining the will of God Ex 28:30; Lev 8:8; Num 27:21

USE ***utilization***
be of **u** to God Job 22:2
for common **u** Ezek 48:15
for honorable **u** Rom 9:21
not make full **u** of 1 Cor 7:31

USEFUL ***beneficial***
man be **u** to himself Job 22:2
u to me for service 2 Tim 4:11

USELESS ***worthless***
they have become **u** Rom 3:12
without works is **u** James 2:20

USURY ***interest***
leave off this **u** Neh 5:10
by interest and **u** Prov 28:8

UTENSILS ***vessels***
table also and its **u** Ex 31:8
u of the sanctuary 1 Chr 9:29

UTTER ***express***
righteous **u-s** wisdom Ps 37:30
Let my lips **u** praise Ps 119:171
He **u-s** His voice Jer 10:13
u words of...truth Acts 26:25

UTTERANCE ***expression***
was giving them **u** Acts 2:4
in faith and **u** 2 Cor 8:7
u may be given Eph 6:19
through prophetic **u** 1 Tim 4:14

UZ
1 *grandson of Shem* Gen 10:23
2 *son of Nahor* Gen 22:21
3 *son of Dishan* Gen 36:28
4 *home of Job* Job 1:1
land of Uz Jer 25:20; Lam 4:21

V

VAIN ***empty*** **or** ***profane***
name of...God in **v** Ex 20:7
devising a **v** thing Ps 2:1
labor in **v** who build Ps 127:1
our preaching is **v** 1 Cor 15:14

VALIANT ***brave, strong***
these...**v** warriors Judg 20:46
be a **v** man for me 1 Sam 18:17
even all the **v** men 1 Chr 28:1
He drags off the **v** Job 24:22

VALLEY ***ravine***
v of the Jordan Gen 13:10
the **v** of Aijalon Josh 10:12
v of the shadow of Ps 23:4
The lily of the **v-s** Song 2:1
v of the dead bodies Jer 31:40
v...full of bones Ezek 37:1
the **v** of decision Joel 3:14

VALLEY GATE ***see*** **GATES OF JERUSALEM**

VALOR ***bravery***
mighty man of **v** 1 Sam 16:18
mighty men of **v** 1 Chr 12:8

VALUE ***worth***
one pearl of great **v** Matt 13:46
v of knowing Christ Phil 3:8

VANISH ***disappear***
When a cloud **v-es** Job 7:9
sky will **v** like smoke Is 51:6
v-ed from...sight Luke 24:31

VANITY ***futility, pride***
will reap **v** Prov 22:8
V of **v-ies!** All is **v** Eccl 1:2
arrogant *words* of **v** 2 Pet 2:18

VAPOR ***smoke***
causes the **v-s** to Ps 135:7
Is a fleeting **v** Prov 21:6
You are *just* a **v** James 4:14

VARICOLORED ***multicolored***
made him a **v** tunic Gen 37:3

VARIOUS ***different***
v diseases and pains Matt 4:24
led on by **v** impulses 2 Tim 3:6
encounter **v** trials James 1:2
distressed by **v** trials 1 Pet 1:6

VASHTI
deposed queen of Ahasuerus Esth 1:19; 2:4

VEGETABLE ***plant***
like a **v** garden Deut 11:10
Better...dish of **v-s** Prov 15:17
weak eats **v-s** *only* Rom 14:2

VEGETATION ***plant life***
earth brought forth **v** Gen 1:12
ate up all **v** Ps 105:35
wither all their **v** Is 42:15

VEIL ***cover, curtain***
a **v** over his face Ex 34:33
v of the sanctuary Lev 4:6
Remove your **v** Is 47:2
v of the temple Matt 27:51

enters within the **v** Heb 6:19

VENGEANCE *revenge*
not take **v** Lev 19:18
V is Mine Deut 32:35
God...executes **v** 2 Sam 22:48
LORD takes **v** on His Nah 1:2
V is Mine, I will Heb 10:30

VESSEL *utensil*
Go, borrow **v-s** 2 Kin 4:3
I am like a broken **v** Ps 31:12
v-s of wrath Rom 9:22
treasure in...**v-s** 2 Cor 4:7
be a **v** for honor 2 Tim 2:21
v-s of the potter Rev 2:27

VESTURE *apparel*
v *was* like...snow Dan 7:9

VIAL *small container*
alabaster **v** of Matt 26:7
she broke the **v** Mark 14:3

VICTORIOUS *triumphant*
A **v** warrior Zeph 3:17
v over the beast Rev 15:2

VICTORY *triumph*
LORD brought...**v** 2 Sam 23:10
had given **v** to Aram 2 Kin 5:1
the glory and the **v** 1 Chr 29:11
gained the **v** for Him Ps 98:1
v belongs to...LORD Prov 21:31
He leads justice to **v** Matt 12:20
swallowed up in **v** 1 Cor 15:54
v that has overcome 1 John 5:4

VIGOR *vitality*
nor his **v** abated Deut 34:7
grave in full **v** Job 5:26
his youthful **v** Job 20:11

VILLAGE *small town*
land of unwalled **v-s** Ezek 38:11
Go into the **v** Matt 21:2
entered a **v** Luke 10:38

VINDICATE *justify*
will **v** His people Deut 32:36
V the weak Ps 82:3
wisdom is **v-d** by Matt 11:19

VINE *stem of plant*
trees said to the **v** Judg 9:12
every man...his **v** 1 Kin 4:25
like a fruitful **v** Ps 128:3
the **v-s** in blossom Song 2:13
mother was like a **v** Ezek 19:10
Israel is a luxuriant **v** Hos 10:1
The **v** dries up Joel 1:12
fruit of the **v** Matt 26:29
I am the true **v** John 15:1

VINEDRESSER *gardener*
v-s and plowmen 2 Kin 25:12
My Father is the **v** John 15:1

VINEGAR *sour liquid*
he shall drink no **v** Num 6:3
bread in the **v** Ruth 2:14
gave me **v** to drink Ps 69:21
Like **v** to the teeth Prov 10:26

VINE-GROWERS
rented it out to **v** Matt 21:33
and destroy the **v** Mark 12:9

VINEYARD *grapevines*
Noah...planted a **v** Gen 9:20
Nor...glean your **v** Lev 19:10
Hewn cisterns, **v-s** Neh 9:25
shelter in a **v** Is 1:8
ruined My **v** Jer 12:10
laborers for his **v** Matt 20:1
Who plants a **v** 1 Cor 9:7

VIOLATE *assault* or *break*
shall not **v** his word Num 30:2
do not **v** me 2 Sam 13:12
who **v-d** the ban 1 Chr 2:7
If they **v** My statutes Ps 89:31

VIOLENCE *destructive action*
earth was filled with **v** Gen 6:11
implements of **v** Gen 49:5
such as breathe out **v** Ps 27:12
drink the wine of **v** Prov 4:17
He had done no **v** Is 53:9
not mistreat *or* do **v** Jer 22:3

VIOLENT *destructive*
a wicked, **v** man Ps 37:35
a **v**, rushing wind Acts 2:2

VIPER *snake*
v-'s tongue slays him Job 20:16
hand on the **v-'s** den Is 11:8
v and flying serpent Is 30:6
You brood of **v-s** Matt 3:7

VIRGIN *unmarried maiden*
very beautiful, a **v** Gen 24:16
if a man seduces a **v** Ex 22:16
could I gaze at a **v** Job 31:1
the **v** will rejoice Jer 31:13
v shall be with child Matt 1:23
kept her a **v** Matt 1:25
comparable to ten **v-s** Matt 25:1
v-'s name was Mary Luke 1:27
if a **v** marries 1 Cor 7:28

VISIBLE *manifest, seen*
He become **v** Acts 10:40
becomes **v** is light Eph 5:13
things which are **v** Heb 11:3

VISION *dream, foresight*
to Abram in a **v** Gen 15:1
v-s were infrequent 1 Sam 3:1
Where there is no **v** Prov 29:18
prophets find No **v** Lam 2:9
I saw **v-s** of God Ezek 1:1
in a night **v** Dan 2:19
young men...see **v-s** Joel 2:28
Tell the **v** to no one Matt 17:9
young men...see **v-s** Acts 2:17

VISIT *come or go to see*
v-ing the iniquity of Ex 20:5
You **v** the earth Ps 65:9
you did not **v** Me Matt 25:43
For He has **v-ed** us Luke 1:68
v orphans...widows James 1:27

VOICE *sound, speech*
have obeyed My **v** Gen 22:18
listen to His **v** Deut 4:30
v of singing men 2 Sam 19:35
You will hear my **v** Ps 5:3
the **v** of my teachers Prov 5:13
v of the turtledove Song 2:12
Give ear...hear my **v** Is 28:23
A **v** is calling Is 40:3
v came from heaven Dan 4:31
v...heard in Ramah Matt 2:18
v...out of the cloud Mark 9:7
v of one crying in Luke 3:4
v of the Son of God John 5:25
v has gone out Rom 10:18
v of *the* archangel 1 Thess 4:16
His **v** shook...earth Heb 12:26
if anyone hears My **v** Rev 3:20
with a **v** of thunder Rev 6:1

VOID *empty, invalid*
was formless and **v** Gen 1:2
make **v** the counsel Jer 19:7
faith is made **v** Rom 4:14
cross...be made **v** 1 Cor 1:17

VOMIT *throw up*
will **v** them up Job 20:15
returns to its **v** Prov 26:11
staggers in his **v** Is 19:14
and it **v-ed** Jonah Jon 2:10
returns to its own **v** 2 Pet 2:22

VOTIVE *dedicated*
his offering is a **v** Lev 7:16
choice **v** offerings Deut 12:11

VOW *solemn promise*
Jacob made a **v** Gen 28:20
v of a Nazirite Num 6:2
I shall pay my **v-s** Ps 22:25
not make false **v-s** Matt 5:33
he was keeping a **v** Acts 18:18

VOYAGE *journey*
v was now dangerous Acts 27:9

VULTURE *bird*
not eat...the **v** Deut 14:12
the **v-s** will gather Matt 24:28
the **v-s** will be gathered Luke 17:37

W

WAFER *thin cake of bread*
w-s with honey Ex 16:31
one unleavened **w** Num 6:19

WAGE *salary*
God has given...**w-s** Gen 30:18
w-s of the righteous Prov 10:16
w is not credited Rom 4:4
the **w-s** of sin Rom 6:23
worthy of his **w-s** 1 Tim 5:18

WAIL *lament, mourn*
w with a broken spirit Is 65:14
w, son of man Ezek 21:12
I must lament and **w** Mic 1:8
W, O inhabitants of Zeph 1:11
weeping and **w-ing** Mark 5:38

WAIT *expect*
For You I **w** Ps 25:5
I **w** for Your word Ps 119:81
who **w** for the LORD Is 40:31
creation **w-s** eagerly Rom 8:19
w-ing for the hope Gal 5:5

WALK *follow, go along*
w-ing in the garden Gen 3:8
W before Me Gen 17:1
w in My instruction Ex 16:4
w in My statutes Lev 26:3
w-ed forty years Josh 5:6
w before Me in truth 1 Kin 2:4
W about Zion Ps 48:12
I will **w** at liberty Ps 119:45
fool **w-s** in darkness Eccl 2:14
w in the light Is 2:5
w and not...weary Is 40:31
w-ed with Me in peace Mal 2:6
Get up, and **w** Matt 9:5
w-ed on the water Matt 14:29
w in newness of life Rom 6:4
we **w** by faith 2 Cor 5:7
w by the Spirit Gal 5:16
w in love Eph 5:2
w as children of Light Eph 5:8
if we **w** in the Light 1 John 1:7
w by its light Rev 21:24

WALL *structure*
living on the **w** Josh 2:15
So we built the **w** Neh 4:6
I can leap over a **w** Ps 18:29
w-s of Jerusalem Jer 39:8
built a siege **w** Jer 52:4
you whitewashed **w** Acts 23:3
w-s of Jericho fell Heb 11:30
a great and high **w** Rev 21:12

WANDER *roam*
w in the wilderness Num 32:13
I would **w** far away Ps 55:7

w...Your statutes Ps 119:118
people **w** like sheep Zech 10:2
w-ed...the faith 1 Tim 6:10
w-ing stars, for whom Jude 13

WANDERER ***roamer***
a **w** on the earth Gen 4:12
an exile and a **w** Is 49:21
w-s among...nations Hos 9:17

WAR ***battle, conflict***
when they see **w** Ex 13:17
sound of **w** in...camp Ex 32:17
land...rest from **w** Josh 11:23
He makes **w-s** to cease Ps 46:9
the weapons of **w** Ps 76:3
A time for **w** Eccl 3:8
will they learn **w** Is 2:4
w-s...rumors of **w-s** Matt 24:6
w against the law Rom 7:23
w in your members James 4:1
w against the soul 1 Pet 2:11
judges and wages **w** Rev 19:11

WARS OF THE LORD, BOOK OF
ancient Hebrew literature Num 21:14

WARM ***heat***
could not keep **w** 1 Kin 1:1
the child became **w** 2 Kin 4:34
can one be **w** *alone* Eccl 4:11
no one is **w** *enough* Hag 1:6

WARN ***give notice***
w the people Ex 19:21
not...**w** the wicked Ezek 33:8
w-ed...in a dream Matt 2:12
w you whom to fear Luke 12:5
Moses was **w-ed** Heb 8:5

WARRIOR ***soldier***
The LORD is a **w** Ex 15:3
O valiant **w** Judg 6:12
w from his youth 1 Sam 17:33
w-s will flee naked Amos 2:16

WASH ***bathe, clean***
w your feet, and rest Gen 18:4
w in the Jordan 2 Kin 5:10
w...in innocence Ps 26:6
W...from my iniquity Ps 51:2
w-ed off your blood Ezek 16:9
do not **w** their hands Matt 15:2
ceremonially **w-ed** Luke 11:38
w in the pool of John 9:7
w the disciples' feet John 13:5
w away your sins Acts 22:16
w-ed...saints' feet 1 Tim 5:10
w-ed with pure Heb 10:22
who **w** their robes Rev 22:14

WASTE (n) ***wilderness***
land was laid **w** Ex 8:24
land into a salt **w** Ps 107:34
lay **w** the mountains Is 42:15
laid **w** like a desert Jer 9:12
altars may become **w** Ezek 6:6
Egypt...become a **w** Joel 3:19

WASTE (v) ***destroy, use up***
he **w-d** his seed Gen 38:9
w away the eyes Lev 26:16
sick man **w-s** away Is 10:18
perfume been **w-d** Mark 14:4

WASTE PLACE ***barren***
w-s of the wealthy Is 5:17
Seek Me in a **w** Is 45:19
like the ancient **w-s** Ezek 26:20
w-s will be rebuilt Ezek 36:10

WATCH (n) ***guard***
at the morning **w** Ex 14:24
in the night **w-es** Ps 63:6
His eyes keep **w** Ps 66:7
keep **w** with Me Matt 26:38
w over their flock Luke 2:8
w over your souls Heb 13:17

WATCH (v) ***observe***
LORD **w** between you Gen 31:49
w all my paths Job 13:27
W over your heart Prov 4:23
who **w-es** the wind Eccl 11:4
w...for the LORD Mic 7:7

WATCHMAN ***one who guards***
w keeps awake in vain Ps 127:1
w-men for...morning Ps 130:6
W, how far gone is Is 21:11
I set **w-men** over you Jer 6:17
Ephraim *was* a **w** Hos 9:8

WATER (n) ***flood, liquid***
moving over...the **w-s** Gen 1:2
flood of **w** came Gen 7:6
w-s *were like* a wall Ex 14:22
w of bitterness Num 5:18
the clouds dripped **w** Judg 5:4
W wears away stones Job 14:19
poured out like **w** Ps 22:14
beside quiet **w-s** Ps 23:2
Stolen **w** is sweet Prov 9:17
bread on the...**w-s** Eccl 11:1
come to the **w-s** Is 55:1
fountain of living **w-s** Jer 2:13
eyes run...with **w** Lam 1:16
knees...*like* **w** Ezek 7:17
baptize you with **w** Matt 3:11
a cup of cold **w** Matt 10:42
walked on the **w** Matt 14:29
no **w** for My feet Luke 7:44
one is born of **w** John 3:5
given you living **w** John 4:10
John baptized with **w** Acts 1:5
of **w** with the word Eph 5:26
formed out of **w** 2 Pet 3:5
by **w** and blood 1 John 5:6
sound of many **w-s** Rev 19:6

WATER (v) ***make moist***
to **w** the garden Gen 2:10
I will **w** your camels Gen 24:46
w their father's flock Ex 2:16
that **w** the earth Ps 72:6
Apollos **w-ed** 1 Cor 3:6

WAVES ***billows***
w of death 2 Sam 22:5
tramples down the **w** Job 9:8
Your **w** have rolled Ps 42:7
w were breaking Mark 4:37
wild **w** of the sea Jude 13

WAX ***paraffin***
My heart is like **w** Ps 22:14
Like **w** before the fire Mic 1:4

WAY ***manner*** **or** ***path***
guard the **w** Gen 3:24
all His **w-s** are just Deut 32:4
blameless...His **w** 2 Sam 22:33
from your evil **w-s** 2 Kin 17:13
joy of His **w** Job 8:19
w of the righteous Ps 1:6
Commit your **w** to Ps 37:5
your **w-s** acknowledge Prov 3:6
is the **w** of death Prov 14:12
Clear the **w** Is 40:3
w of the wicked Jer 12:1
Make ready the **w** Matt 3:3
Pray...in this **w** Matt 6:9
w is broad that leads Matt 7:13
teach...**w** of God Mark 12:14
into the **w** of peace Luke 1:79
I am the **w** John 14:6
belonging to the **W** Acts 9:2
the **w** of salvation Acts 16:17
unfathomable...**w-s** Rom 11:33
the **w** of escape 1 Cor 10:13
new and living **w** Heb 10:20
the **w** of the truth 2 Pet 2:2

WEAK ***feeble***
I will become **w** Judg 16:17
Rescue the **w** Ps 82:4
but the flesh is **w** Matt 26:41
must help the **w** Acts 20:35
who is **w** in faith Rom 14:1
God...chosen the **w** 1 Cor 1:27

WEAKNESS ***fault***
Spirit...helps our **w** Rom 8:26
bear the **w-es** Rom 15:1
w of God is stronger 1 Cor 1:25
it is sown in **w** 1 Cor 15:43
perfected in **w** 2 Cor 12:9

WEALTH ***riches***
power to make **w** Deut 8:18
a man of great **w** Ruth 2:1
who trust in their **w** Ps 49:6
Honor...from your **w** Prov 3:9
W adds many friends Prov 19:4
A **w** of salvation Is 33:6
the **w** of all nations Hag 2:7
serve God and **w** Matt 6:24
deceitfulness of **w** Matt 13:22
w of their liberality 2 Cor 8:2
rich by her **w** Rev 18:19

WEAPON ***armament***
girded on his **w-s** Deut 1:41
flee from the iron **w** Job 20:24
turn back the **w-s** Jer 21:4
w-s of righteousness 2 Cor 6:7

WEARY ***tired***
the people were **w** 1 Sam 14:28
the **w** are at rest Job 3:17
w with my crying Ps 69:3
water to a **w** soul Prov 25:25
and not become **w** Is 40:31
sustain the **w** one Is 50:4
all who are **w** Matt 11:28
w of doing good 2 Thess 3:13

WEAVE ***interlace***
You **wove** me Ps 139:13
w the spider's web Is 59:5

WEB ***woven work***
loom and the **w** Judg 16:14
trust a spider's **w** Job 8:14

WEDDING ***marriage***
had no **w** songs Ps 78:63
day of his **w** Song 3:11
come to the **w** feast Matt 22:4
a **w** in Cana John 2:1

WEEK ***period of time***
Complete the **w** of Gen 29:27
Seventy **w-s** Dan 9:24
first *day* of the **w** Matt 28:1
I fast twice a **w** Luke 18:12

WEEKS, FEAST OF *see* **FEASTS**

WEEP ***cry, sorrow***
sought *a place* to **w** Gen 43:30
do not mourn or **w** Neh 8:9
My eye **w-s** to God Job 16:20
widows could not **w** Ps 78:64
Let me **w** bitterly Is 22:4
w day and night Jer 9:1
Rachel **w-ing** for her Matt 2:18
w-ing and gnashing Matt 13:42
he...**wept** bitterly Matt 26:75
saw the city...**wept** Luke 19:41
w for yourselves Luke 23:28
Jesus **wept** John 11:35
why are you **w-ing** John 20:13
w with...who **w** Rom 12:15

WEIGH ***measure out***
actions are **w-ed** 1 Sam 2:3
LORD **w-s** the motives Prov 16

WEIGHT *heaviness*
a full and just **w** Deut 25:15
w to the wind Job 28:25
bag of deceptive **w-s** Mic 6:11
eternal **w** of glory 2 Cor 4:17

WELCOME *gladly receive*
no prophet is **w** Luke 4:24
people **w-d** Him Luke 8:40
who fears Him...**w** Acts 10:35
she...**w-d** the spies Heb 11:31

WELL *water shaft*
sat down by a **w** Ex 2:15
w of Bethlehem 1 Chr 11:17
Like...a polluted **w** Prov 25:26
A **w** of fresh water Song 4:15
Jacob's **w** was there John 4:6

WELL-PLEASED *satisfied*
in whom I am **w** Matt 3:17
in You I am **w** Luke 3:22
God was not **w** 1 Cor 10:5

WEST *direction*
very strong **w** wind Ex 10:19
east is from the **w** Ps 103:12
gather you from the **w** Is 43:5

WHEAT *grain*
days of **w** harvest Gen 30:14
first fruits of the **w** Ex 34:22
plant **w** in rows Is 28:25
gather His **w** into Matt 3:12
to sift you like **w** Luke 22:31
unless a grain of **w** John 12:24

WHEEL *circular disk*
the **w**...is crushed Eccl 12:6
w-s like a whirlwind Is 5:28
one **w** were within Ezek 1:16
rattling of the **w** Nah 3:2

WHIRLWIND
take...Elijah by a **w** 2 Kin 2:1
comes like a **w** Prov 1:27
chariots like the **w** Jer 4:13
they reap the **w** Hos 8:7

WHISPER *talk quietly*
who hate me **w** Ps 41:7
w a prayer Is 26:16
your speech will **w** Is 29:4

WHISTLE *shrill sound*
And will **w** for it Is 5:26
LORD will **w** for the fly Is 7:18
I will **w** for them Zech 10:8

WHITE *color*
teeth **w** from milk Gen 49:12
w of an egg Job 6:6
be as **w** as snow Is 1:18
make one hair **w** Matt 5:36
clothing *became* **w** Luke 9:29
fields...**w** for harvest John 4:35
clothed in **w** robes Rev 7:9

WHITEWASHED *wall covering*
like **w** tombs Matt 23:27
you **w** wall Acts 23:3

WHOLE *entire*
water the **w** surface Gen 2:6
w earth...populated Gen 9:19
leavens the **w** lump 1 Cor 5:6
keeps the **w** law James 2:10

WICK *candle thread*
extinguished like a **w** Is 43:17
a smoldering **w** Matt 12:20

ICKED *evil, ungodly*
demn the **w** Deut 25:1
es are silenced 1 Sam 2:9
of the **w** Ps 1:1
urned God Ps 10:13

The **w** strut about Ps 12:8
devises **w** plans Prov 6:18
When a **w** man dies Prov 11:7
no peace for the **w** Is 48:22
turn from his **w** way Jon 3:8
taking...some **w** men Acts 17:5
righteous and the **w** Acts 24:15

WICKEDNESS *evil*
w of man was great Gen 6:5
If I regard **w** Ps 66:18
eat the bread of **w** Prov 4:17
inclines toward **w** Is 32:6
w of My people Jer 7:12
You have plowed **w** Hos 10:13
repent of this **w** Acts 8:22
spiritual *forces* of **w** Eph 6:12

WIDOW *husband dead*
Remain a **w** Gen 38:11
not afflict any **w** Ex 22:22
sent **w-s** away empty Job 22:9
judge for the **w-s** Ps 68:5
Plead for the **w** Is 1:17
devour **w-s'** houses Matt 23:14
w put in more Mark 12:43
Honor **w-s** 1 Tim 5:3
visit orphans...**w-s** James 1:27

WIFE *married woman*
joined to his **w** Gen 2:24
man and his **w** hid Gen 3:8
shall not covet...**w** Ex 20:17
w of your youth Prov 5:18
An excellent **w** Prov 31:10
who divorces his **w** Matt 5:32
Remember Lot's **w** Luke 17:32
have his own **w** 1 Cor 7:2
head of the **w** Eph 5:23
husband of one **w** 1 Tim 3:2
w-ves, be submissive 1 Pet 3:1
w of the Lamb Rev 21:9

WILD *untamed*
w donkey of a man Gen 16:12
horns of the **w** ox Num 23:22
locusts and **w** honey Mark 1:6
being a **w** olive Rom 11:17

WILDERNESS *barren area*
water in the **w** Gen 16:7
journey into the **w** Ex 5:3
to die in the **w** Ex 14:11
forty years in the **w** Deut 29:5
pastures of the **w** Ps 65:12
roadway in the **w** Is 43:19
Have I been a **w** Jer 2:31
preaching in the **w** Matt 3:1
into the **w**...tempted Matt 4:1
crying in the **w** Mark 1:3
manna in the **w** John 6:31

WILL *attitude, purpose*
delight to do Your **w** Ps 40:8
Your **w** be done Matt 6:10
the **w** of My Father Matt 7:21
not My **w**, but Luke 22:42
nor of the **w** of man John 1:13
who resists His **w** Rom 9:19
what the **w** of God Rom 12:2
knowledge of His **w** Col 1:9
come to do Your **w** Heb 10:9
an act of human **w** 2 Pet 1:21

WIN *succeed*
wise **w-s** souls Prov 11:30
we will **w** him over Matt 28:14
that I might **w** Jews 1 Cor 9:20
won without a word 1 Pet 3:1

WIND
caused a **w** to pass Gen 8:1
scorched by...**w** Gen 41:27
will inherit **w** Prov 11:29
prophets are *as* **w** Jer 5:13
they sow the **w** Hos 8:7

reed shaken by...**w** Matt 11:7
w and the sea obey Mark 4:41
He...rebuked the **w** Luke 8:24
violent, rushing **w** Acts 2:2
every **w** of doctrine Eph 4:14
driven by strong **w-s** James 3:4

WINDOW *opening*
enter through the **w-s** Joel 2:9
open...**w-s** of heaven Mal 3:10
sitting on the **w** sill Acts 20:9
basket through a **w** 2 Cor 11:33

WINE *strong drink*
eyes...dull from **w** Gen 49:12
Do not drink **w** Lev 10:9
overflow with new **w** Prov 3:10
W is a mocker Prov 20:1
love is better than **w** Song 1:2
new **w** into old Matt 9:17
gave Him **w** to Matt 27:34
made the water **w** John 4:46
full of sweet **w** Acts 2:13
not get drunk with **w** Eph 5:18
not addicted to **w** 1 Tim 3:3

WINESKINS *animal skin bag*
These **w**...were new Josh 9:13
Like new **w** Job 32:19
wine into fresh **w** Matt 9:17

WINGS
bore you on eagles' **w** Ex 19:4
He spread His **w** Deut 32:11
under whose **w** Ruth 2:12
under His **w**...refuge Ps 91:4
with **w** like eagles Is 40:31
healing in its **w** Mal 4:2
chicks under her **w** Matt 23:37

WINK *blink*
w maliciously Ps 35:19
w-s with his eyes Prov 6:13

WINNOW *scatter*
king **w-s** the wicked Prov 20:26
You will **w** them Is 41:16
His **w-ing** fork Matt 3:12

WINTER *season*
And summer and **w** Gen 8:22
the **w** is past Song 2:11
even spend the **w** 1 Cor 16:6

WIPE *pass over, rub*
GOD will **w** tears Is 25:8
w-d His feet John 11:2
sins...**w-d** away Acts 3:19
w away every tear Rev 21:4

WISDOM *discernment*
the spirit of **w** Ex 28:3
w has two sides Job 11:6
the beginning of **w** Ps 111:10
Fools despise **w** Prov 1:7
w to fear Your name Mic 6:9
w given to Him Mark 6:2
kept increasing in **w** Luke 2:52
made foolish the **w** 1 Cor 1:20
any of you lacks **w** James 1:5

WISE *judicious, prudent*
not find a **w** man Job 17:10
making **w** the simple Ps 19:7
w in your own eyes Prov 3:7
the words of the **w** Prov 22:17
He is not a **w** son Hos 13:13
Who...you is **w** James 3:13

WITCHCRAFT *magic, sorcery*
who practices **w** Deut 18:10
practiced **w** and 2 Kin 21:6

WITHER *dry up*
its leaf does not **w** Ps 1:3
w...like the grass Ps 37:2
earth mourns *and* **w-s** Is 24:4

the leaf will **w** Jer 8:13
whose hand was **w-ed** Mark 3:1
the fig tree **w-ed** Mark 11:20

WITNESS (n) *testimony*
This heap is a **w** Gen 31:48
is **w** between us Judg 11:10
my **w** is in heaven Job 16:19
a **w** to the LORD Is 19:20
He came as a **w** John 1:7
you shall be My **w-es** Acts 1:8
For God is my **w** Phil 1:8
Christ, the faithful **w** Rev 1:5

WITNESS (v) *testify*
not bear false **w** Ex 20:16
w against you today Deut 4:26

WOLF *animal*
w will dwell with Is 11:6
the midst of **w-ves** Matt 10:16
w snatches them John 10:12

WOMAN *female, lady*
She shall be called **W** Gen 2:23
w...not wear man's Deut 22:5
a **w** of excellence Ruth 3:11
Man...born of **w** Job 14:1
gracious **w** attains Prov 11:16
a contentious **w** Prov 25:24
like a **w** in labor Is 42:14
looks at a **w** with lust Matt 5:28
w-en...grinding Matt 24:41
Blessed...among **w-en** Luke 1:42
W, behold, your son John 19:26
not to touch a **w** 1 Cor 7:1
w is the glory of 1 Cor 11:7
w to speak in 1 Cor 14:35
His Son, born of a **w** Gal 4:4
w clothed with...sun Rev 12:1

WOMB
nations...in your **w** Gen 25:23
LORD...closed her **w** 1 Sam 1:5
from **w** to tomb Job 10:19
formed you from the **w** Is 44:2
baby leaped in...**w** Luke 1:41

WONDER *marvel, sign*
consider the **w-s** of Job 37:14
tell of all Your **w-s** Ps 9:1
His **w-s** in the deep Ps 107:24
w-s in the sky Joel 2:30
were filled with **w** Acts 3:10

WONDERFUL *marvelous*
His **w** deeds 1 Chr 16:12
name will be called **W** Is 9:6

WOOD *cut tree*
ark of gopher **w** Gen 6:14
other gods, **w** and Deut 28:36
children gather **w** Jer 7:18
stones, **w**, hay 1 Cor 3:12

WOOL *cloth or hair*
of **w** and linen Deut 22:11
put a fleece of **w** on Judg 6:37
They will be like **w** Is 1:18
hair...like pure **w** Dan 7:9
white like white **w** Rev 1:14

WORD *message, speech*
to the **w** of Moses Lev 10:7
declare to you the **w** Deut 5:5
Joshua wrote...**w-s** Josh 24:26
proclaim the **w** of 1 Sam 9:27
Your **w**...confirmed 2 Chr 6:17
no limit to windy **w-s** Job 16:3
w-s of my mouth Ps 19:14
Your **w** is a lamp Ps 119:105
harsh **w** stirs up Prov 15:1
w of God is tested Prov 30:5
despised the **w** Is 5:24
w-s of a sealed book Is 29:11
speak My **w** in truth Jer 23:28
conceal these **w-s** Dan 12:4
every **w** that proceeds Matt 4:4
these **w-s** of Mine Matt 7:24
sower sows the **w** Mark 4:14
the **W** was God John 1:1
the **W** became flesh John 1:14
w-s of eternal life John 6:68
continue in My **w** John 8:31
glorifying the **w** Acts 13:48
too deep for **w-s** Rom 8:26
hearing by the **w** Rom 10:17
the **w** of the cross 1 Cor 1:18
fulfilled in one **w** Gal 5:14
no unwholesome **w** Eph 4:29
sanctified by...**w** 1 Tim 4:5
the **w** of truth 2 Tim 2:15
the faithful **w** Titus 1:9
w of God is living Heb 4:12
doers of the **w** James 1:22
pure milk of the **w** 1 Pet 2:2
the **W** of Life 1 John 1:1
The **W** of God Rev 19:13

WORK (n) *act, deed, labor*
God completed His **w** Gen 2:2
You shall **w** six days Ex 34:21
His **w** is perfect Deut 32:4
the **w** of His hands Ps 19:1
see the **w-s** of God Ps 66:5
Commit your **w-s** to Prov 16:3
let Him hasten His **w** Is 5:19
His **w** on Mount Zion Is 10:12
see your good **w-s** Matt 5:16
the **w-s** of Christ Matt 11:2
the **w** of the Law Rom 2:15
faith apart from **w-s** Rom 3:28
not...a result of **w-s** Eph 2:9
for the **w** of service Eph 4:12
began a good **w** Phil 1:6
fruit in...good **w** Col 1:10
rich in good **w-s** 1 Tim 6:18
faith without **w-s** James 2:20

WORK (v) *perform, produce*
has **w-ed** with God 1 Sam 14:45
those who **w** iniquity Ps 28:3
Who...**w-s** wonders Ps 72:18
not **w** for the food John 6:27
w together for good Rom 8:28
So death **w-s** in us 2 Cor 4:12
w out your salvation Phil 2:12
anyone is not willing to **w** 2 Thess 3:10

WORKER *laborer*
O **w** of deceit Ps 52:2
w-s of iniquity Prov 10:29
w is worthy of his Matt 10:10
God's fellow **w-s** 1 Cor 3:9
beware...evil **w-s** Phil 3:2
pure, **w-s** at home Titus 2:5

WORKMAN *craftsman*
a skillful **w** Ex 38:23
approved...as a **w** 2 Tim 2:15

WORKMANSHIP *craftsmanship*
we are His **w** Eph 2:10

WORLD *earth, humanity*
foundations of...**w** 2 Sam 22:16
He will judge the **w** Ps 9:8
first dust of the **w** Prov 8:26
the light of the **w** Matt 5:14
the field is the **w** Matt 13:38
Go into all the **w** Mark 16:15
gains the whole **w** Luke 9:25
God so loved the **w** John 3:16
Savior of the **w** John 4:42
w cannot hate you John 7:7
the Light of the **w** John 8:12
overcome the **w** John 16:33
have upset the **w** Acts 17:6
sin entered...the **w** Rom 5:12
reconciling the **w** 2 Cor 5:19
unstained by the **w** James 1:27
flood upon the **w** 2 Pet 2:5
Do not love the **w** 1 John 2:15

WORLDLY *earthly*
w fables fit only 1 Tim 4:7
avoid **w**...chatter 2 Tim 2:16

WORM *creeping animal*
But I am a **w** Ps 22:6
w-s are your covering Is 14:11
God appointed a **w** Jon 4:7
their **w** does not die Mark 9:48
he was eaten by **w-s** Acts 12:23

WORMWOOD
1 *a bitter plant* Deut 29:18
2 *used figuratively* Prov 5:4; Amos 6:12; Rev 8:11

WORRY *anxious*
not be **w-ied** about your life Matt 6:25
not **w** about tomorrow Matt 6:34
do not **w** beforehand Mark 13:11
w-ing can add a *single* Luke 12:25

WORSHIP *bow, revere*
not **w** any other god Ex 34:14
you shall **w** Him Deut 6:13
W the LORD Ps 2:11
earth will **w** You Ps 66:4
in vain do they **w** Matt 15:9
w in spirit and truth John 4:24
w in the Spirit Phil 3:3
w Him who lives Rev 4:10
who **w** the beast Rev 14:11

WORTHLESS *useless*
all **w** physicians Job 13:4
w man digs up evil Prov 16:27
your **w** offerings Is 1:13
your faith is **w** 1 Cor 15:17
w for any good Titus 1:16
man's religion is **w** James 1:26

WORTHY *having merit*
sin **w** of death Deut 21:22
w of his support Matt 10:10
is not **w** of Me Matt 10:37
is **w** of his wages Luke 10:7
manner **w** of the Rom 16:2
w of the gospel Phil 1:27
world was not **w** Heb 11:38
W is the Lamb Rev 5:12

WOUND *injury*
My **w** is incurable Job 34:6
binds up their **w-s** Ps 147:3
Your **w** is incurable Jer 30:12
bandaged...his **w-s** Luke 10:34
by His **w-s** you were 1 Pet 2:24
fatal **w** was healed Rev 13:3

WRAPPINGS *cloth coverings*
bound...with **w** John 11:44
linen **w** lying *there* John 20:5

WRATH *anger, indignation*
and in great **w** Deut 29:28
Nor chasten...in Your **w** Ps 6:1
Pour out Your **w** Ps 79:6
turns away **w** Prov 15:1
Or else My **w** will go forth Jer 4:4
spent My **w** upon Ezek 5:13
from the **w** to come Matt 3:7
w of God abides on John 3:36
God who inflicts **w** Rom 3:5
children of **w** Eph 2:3
w of God will come Col 3:6
the **w** of the Lamb Rev 6:16

WRETCHED *miserable*
in to this **w** place Num 20:5
W man that I am Rom 7:24

WRITE *enscribe*
Moses, **W** this in a Ex 17:14
W them on the tablet Prov 3:3
he **wrote** the dream Dan 7:1
w a certificate Mark 10:4
with His finger **wrote** John 8:6
w...King of the Jews John 19:21

W in a book Rev 1:11

WRITINGS *literary work*
not believe his **w** John 5:47
known the sacred **w** 2 Tim 3:15

WRITTEN *enscribed*
w by...God Ex 31:18
w in the law 2 Chr 23:18
remembrance was **w** Mal 3:16
w by the prophet Matt 2:5
about whom it is **w** Matt 11:10
Law **w** in...hearts Rom 2:15
name has not been **w** Rev 13:8
w in the Lamb's Rev 21:27

WRONG *do evil, harm*
not **w** a stranger Ex 22:21
not **w** one another Lev 25:14
I...have done **w** 2 Sam 24:17
Love does no **w** Rom 13:10

WROUGHT *accomplished*
He **w** wonders Ps 78:12
been **w** in God John 3:21

Y

YAHWEH *see* **YHWH** *and* **LORD**

YEAR *period, time*
atonement...every **y** Lev 16:34
fiftieth **y**...jubilee Lev 25:11
the **y** of remission Deut 15:9
crowned the **y** with Ps 65:11
length of...**y-s** Prov 3:2
favorable **y** of the LORD Is 61:2
thirty **y-s** of age Luke 3:23
y of the LORD Luke 4:19
priest *enters,* once a **y** Heb 9:7
sacrifices...**y** by **y** Heb 10:1
y-s like one day 2 Pet 3:8
reign...thousand **y-s** Rev 20:6

YEARLING *one year old*
a **y** ewe lamb Lev 14:10
With **y** calves Mic 6:6

YEARNS *deeply moved*
my flesh **y** for You Ps 63:1
My heart **y** for him Jer 31:20

YESTERDAY *past*
we are *only* of **y** Job 8:9
thousand years...**y** Ps 90:4
same **y** and today Heb 13:8

YHWH
Hebrew tetragrammaton for name of God, probably pronounced Yahweh
Derived from Hebrew verb meaning "to be"
Translated usually as LORD
see also **LORD**
see also introductory material to NASB

YIELD *produce*
no longer **y** its Gen 4:12
land...**y** its produce Lev 25:19
Which **y-s** its fruit Ps 1:3
y-ed up *His* spirit Matt 27:50
not **y** in subjection Gal 2:5
y-s the peaceful Heb 12:11

YOKE *wooden bar*
break his **y** from Gen 27:40
iron **y** on...neck Deut 28:48
made our **y** hard 1 Kin 12:4
the **y** of their burden Is 9:4
Take My **y** upon Matt 11:29
to a **y** of slavery Gal 5:1

YOUNG *early age, youth*
he sent **y** men Ex 24:5
or two **y** pigeons Lev 15:29
glory of **y** men is Prov 20:29
y men stumble Is 40:30
like a **y** lion Hos 5:14
finding a **y** donkey John 12:14
y men...visions Acts 2:17
urge the **y** men Titus 2:6

YOUTH *young*
evil from his **y** Gen 8:21
fresher than in **y** Job 33:25
the sins of my **y** Ps 25:7
confidence from my **y** Ps 71:5
your **y** is renewed Ps 103:5
the wife of your **y** Prov 5:18
y-s grow weary Is 40:30
the reproach of my **y** Jer 31:19
life from my **y** up Acts 26:4

Z

ZACCHEUS
tax collector who followed Jesus Luke 19:2,5,8

ZACHARIAS
father of John the Baptist Luke 1:5,12,18; 3:2

ZAREPHATH
scene of miracle by Elijah 1 Kin 17:9,10
Phoenician town Obad 20; Luke 4:26

ZEAL *fervor, passion*
kill them in his **z** 2 Sam 21:2
my **z** for the LORD 2 Kin 10:16
z has consumed me Ps 119:139
Your **z** for the people Is 26:11
have a **z** for God Rom 10:2
your **z** for me 2 Cor 7:7

ZEALOT
member of radical Jewish nationalist party Matt 10:4; Mark 3:18; Luke 6:15; Acts 1:13

ZEALOUS *fervent*
z for the LORD 1 Kin 19:10
all **z** for the Law Acts 21:20
z of...*gifts* 1 Cor 14:12
z for good deeds Titus 2:14
be **z** and repent Rev 3:19

ZEBEDEE
father of James and John Matt 4:21; 27:56; Mark 1:19; 10:35; Luke 5:10; John 21:2

ZEBULUN
1 *son of Jacob* Gen 30:20
2 *tribe* Num 34:25; Josh 21:34
3 *territory of the tribe, located in N Palestine* Josh 19:27; Judg 12:12; Is 9:1; Ezek 48:27

ZECHARIAH
1 *son of Jeiel* 1 Chr 9:35-37
2 *priest with ark* 1 Chr 15:24
3 *son of Isshiah* 1 Chr 24:25
4 *father of Iddo* 1 Chr 27:21
5 *son of Benaiah* 2 Chr 20:14
6 *son of Jehoshaphat* 2 Chr 21:2
7 *son of Jehoida* 2 Chr 24:20
8 *prophet* 2 Chr 26:5
9 *priest under Ezra* Neh 12:41
10 *minor prophet* Zech 1:1

ZELOPHEHAD
Manassite, son of Hepher Num 26:33
daughters became his heirs Num 27:1; 36:2

ZEPHANIAH
1 *priest* 2 Kin 25:18
2 *Kohathite Levite* 1 Chr 6:36
3 *minor prophet* Zeph 1:1
4 *father of Josiah* Zech 6:10

ZERUBBABEL
line of David 1 Chr 3:1-19
helped rebuild temple Ezra 3:8

ZERUIAH
mother of Joab, Abishai, and Asahel 2 Sam 2:18
David's half-sister 1 Chr 2:16

ZIKLAG
town in S Judah Josh 15:31; 1 Sam 27:6; 1 Chr 12:1

ZILPAH
concubine of Jacob Gen 29:24; 30:10; 46:18

ZIN
wilderness in Negev Num 13:21; Deut 32:51; Josh 15:1,3

ZION
1 *hill / City of David which is Jerusalem* 2 Sam 5:7; 1 Chr 11:5
2 *after Temple built, name extended to top of hill, Mount Zion* Is 8:18; 18:7; Mic 4:7
3 *applied to all of Jerusalem as city spreads* 2 Kin 19:21; Ps 69:35; Is 1:8
4 *used in the corporate sense for the people and land* Ps 97:8; 149:2; Is 3:16; 8:14; 59:20; Joel 2:23; Zech 9:9; Rom 9:33; 1 Pet 2:3
5 *used eschatologically for heavenly Jerusalem* Is 60:14; Heb 12:22; Rev 14:1

ZIPPORAH
wife of Moses Ex 2:21; 4:25

ZIV
name of the second month in Hebrew calendar 1 Kin 6:1,37

ZOAN
Egyptian delta city Num 13:22; Ps 78:12; Is 19:11; Ezek 30:14

ZOAR
city of the plain near the Dead Sea Gen 13:10; 14:2; 19:23,30; Deut 34:3; Jer 48:34
see also **BELA**

ZOPHAR
one of Job's friends Job 2:11; 11:1; 20:1; 42:9

ZUZIM
pre-Israelite tribe in Palestine Gen 14:5

Index to Color Maps

The Index to Color Maps will lead you to place-names found on the color maps in the back of this Bible. References are to the map number and the margin markings.

Jarmuth **3** C3
Jazer **4** C4
Jericho **2** E3; **3** D3; **4** C4; **6** C4; **9** C5
Jerusalem **2** D3; **3** D3; **4** B4; **5** B4; **6** B4; **7a** B2; **7b** B5; **9** B6; **10** B6; **11** H5; **13** E4
Jezreel **4** B3; **6** C3
Joppa **2** D3; **4** B4; **5** A4; **6** B4; **10** A5
Jordan **12** h6
Jordan River **2** E2; **3** D2; **4** C3; **5** B4; **6** C3; **7a** B2; **7b** B5; **9** C4; **10** B5; **11** H5
Judah **4** B5; **6** B5
Judea **9** B6; **10** B6; **11** H5; **13** E4
Judean Mts. **2** D3

Kadesh **5** B2
Kadesh Barnea **1** C3; **3** C4; **5** A5
Kazakhstan **12** F1
Kedesh **3** D2; **4** C2; **5** B3
Kenya **12** E3
Kerith Ravine **6** C3
Khersa **9** C3
Kidron Valley **8** D1, D5
Kinnereth, Sea of **2** E1; **3** D2; **4** C2; **5** B3; **6** C2
Kios **11** E3
Kir Hareseth **5** B5; **6** C5
Kiriath Jearim **4** B4
Kishon River **2** D2; **4** B3; **6** B2
Kittim **1** C2; **5** A2
Knossos **1** A2
Korazin **9** C2
Kuwait **12** h6
Kyrgyzstan **12** F2

Lachish **3** C3; **4** B4
Laodicea **11** F3
Laos **12** G2
Lasea **11** E4
Latvia **12** g5
Lebanon **12** h6
Lesotho **12** E4
Liberia **12** D3
Libnah **3** C3
Libya **12** E2
Liechtenstein **12** g5
Litani River **2** D1; **4** C1; **5** B3; **10** B4
Lithuania **12** g5
Little Bitter Lake **2** A5
Loire River **13** B2
London **13** B1
Lower City **8** C5
Luxembourg **12** f5
Lycaonia **11** G3
Lycia **11** F3
Lydda **10** A5
Lydia **11** F3
Lyons **13** B2
Lystra **11** G3

Macedonia **11** D2; **12** g5; **13** D3
Machaerus **9** C6
Madagascar **12** E4
Magdala **9** C3
Mahanaim **4** C3; **5** B4
Mainz **13** B1
Makkedah **3** C3
Malawi **12** E3
Malaysia **12** G3
Maldives **12** F3
Mali **12** D2
Malta **11** C4; **12** g6
Manasseh **4** B3
Manasseh, East **4** C2
Marah **3** B4
Mari **1** D2
Mariamne, Tower of **8** A4
Martinique **12** c6
Mauretania **13** A3
Mauritania **12** D2
Mauritius **12** F3
Medeba **5** B4
Media **7a** D2; **7b** D5
Mediterranean Sea **2** B2; **13** C4
Megiddo **1** C3; **4** B3; **5** B4
Memphis **1** B3; **3** A4; **7a** A3; **7b** A6; **13** E4
Men, Court of **8** C3
Menzaleh, Lake **3** A3
Merom **3** D2; **4** C2
Mesopotamia **13** F3
Mexico **12** B2
Midian **3** C5
Miletus **11** F3
Mitylene **11** F3
Mizpah **4** B4; **6** B4; **7b** B5
Moab **3** D3; **4** C5; **5** B5; **6** C5
Moesia **11** E1; **13** D2
Moldova **12** g5
Monaco **12** f5
Mongolia **12** G2
Montserrat **12** c5
Moreh, Mt. **2** D2; **4** C3
Moresheth Gath **6** B4
Morocco **12** D2
Mozambique **12** E3
Mycenae **1** A1
Myra **11** F4
Mysia **11** F3; **13** D3

Nabatea **13** E4
Nain **9** C3
Namibia **12** E3
Naphtali **4** C2
Nazareth **2** D2; **9** B3
Neapolis **11** E2
Nebo, Mt. **2** E3; **3** D3; **4** C4
Negev **2** D4
Nepal **12** F2
Netherlands **12** f5
Netherlands Antilles **12** b6
New Caledonia **12** H4
New Zealand **12** H4
Nicaragua **12** a6
Niger **12** E2
Nigeria **12** D3
Nile River **1** B4; **3** A5; **11** G6; **13** E4
Nineveh **1** E2; **7a** C2; **7b** C5
Nippur **1** E3; **7a** C2; **7b** C5
Noph **1** B3; **3** A4
North Korea **12** G2
Norway **12** D1
Numidia **11** A4
Nuzi **1** E2

Oboth **3** D3
Olives, Mt. of **2** D3; **8** D3; **9** B5
Olympus, Mt. **11** E2
Oman **12** F2
On **1** B3; **3** A4
Orontes River **5** B1; **7a** B2; **7b** B5; **10** C3

Paddan Aram **1** D2
Pakistan **12** F2
Pamphylia **11** G3
Panama **12** b6
Paphos **11** G4
Papua New Guinea **12** H3
Paraguay **12** C4
Paran, Desert of **2** C6; **3** C4
Parthia **13** F3
Patara **11** F4
Patmos **11** F3
Pella **13** E4
Perea **9** C5
Perga **11** G3
Pergamum **11** F3; **13** D3
Persian Gulf **1** F4; **7a** D3; **7b** D6; **13** F4
Peru **12** B3
Pharpar River **4** D1; **6** D1
Phasael, Tower of **8** A4
Philadelphia **11** F3
Philippi **11** E2; **13** D3
Philippines **12** G2
Philistia **3** C3; **5** A4; **6** A5
Phoenicia **5** B3; **6** C1; **9** C1; **11** H4
Phoenix **11** E4
Phrygia **11** F3; **13** D3
Pinnacle of the Temple **8** D4
Pisidia **11** G3
Pisidian Antioch **11** G3
Pithom **3** A4
Po River **13** B2
Poland **12** g5
Portugal **12** f6
Ptolemais **9** B2; **10** B5; **11** H5
Puerto Rico **12** c5
Punon **3** D4
Puteoli **11** C2; **13** C3

Qatar **12** F2
Qatna **5** C2

Rabbah **2** E3; **4** C4; **5** B4
Ramah **6** B4
Rameses **3** A3
Ramoth Gilead **4** D3; **5** B4; **6** D3

NOTES

NOTES

NOTES

NOTES

NOTES

NOTES

NOTES

NOTES

NOTES

NOTES

NOTES

NOTES

NOTES

NOTES

Map 1: **WORLD OF THE PATRIARCHS**

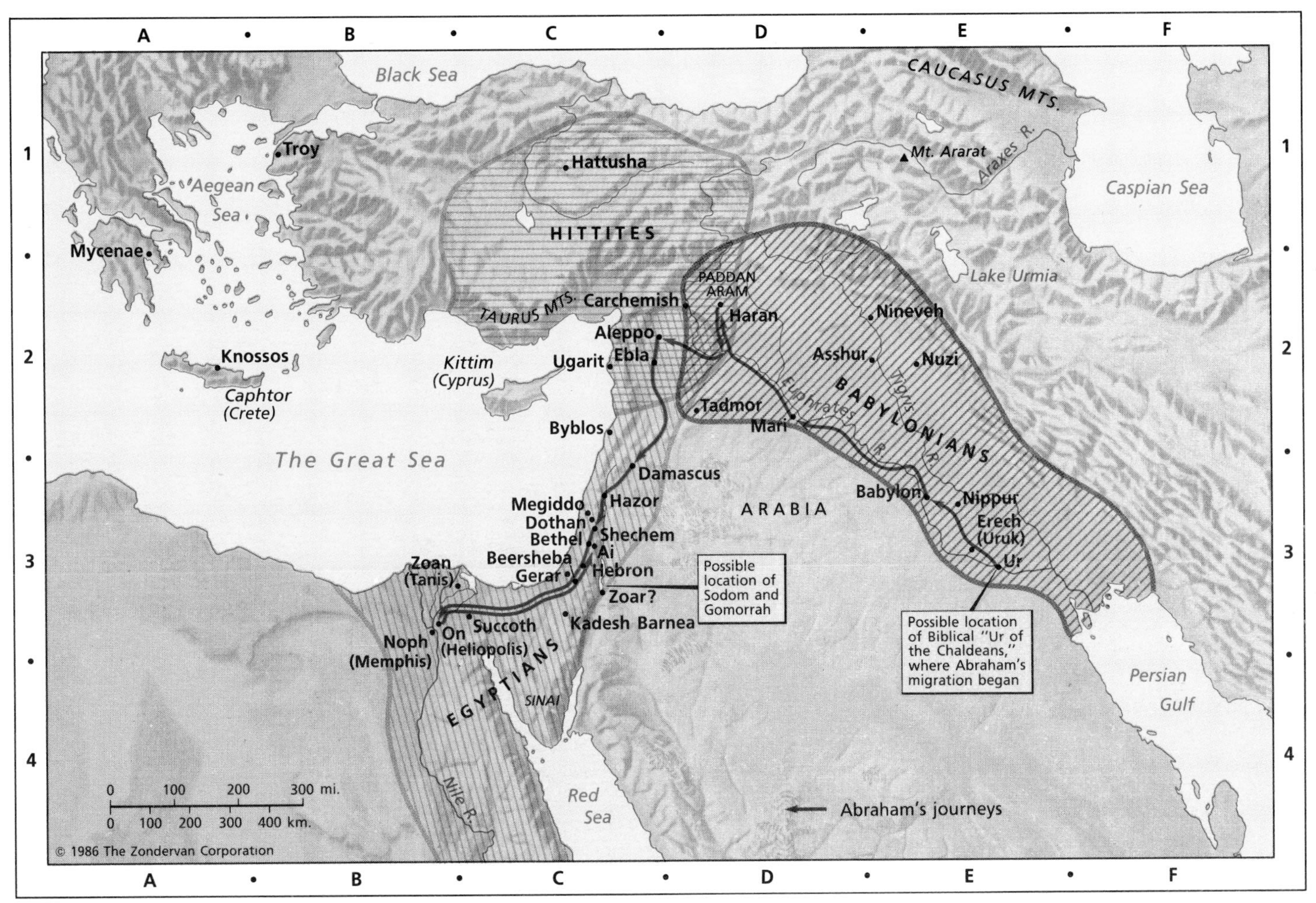

Map 2: **PALESTINE AND SINAI**

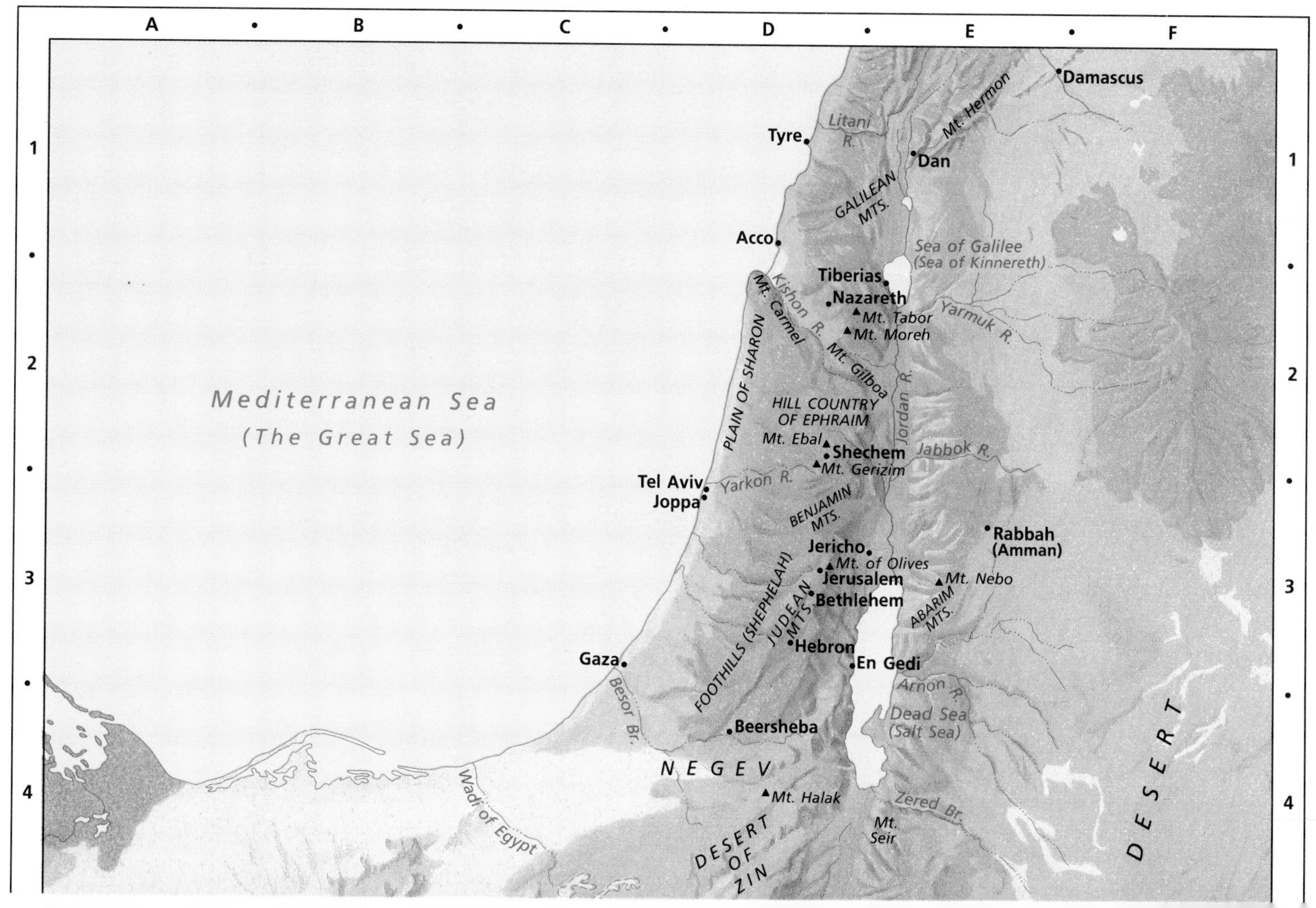

A
B
C
D
E
F
1
2
3
4
Damascus
Mt. Hermon
Litani R.
Tyre
Dan
GALILEAN MTS.
Acco
Sea of Galilee
(Sea of Kinnereth)
Tiberias
Nazareth
Mt. Tabor
Mt. Moreh
Yarmuk R.
Mt. Carmel
Kishon R.
Mt. Gilboa
PLAIN OF SHARON
Jordan R.
Mediterranean Sea
(The Great Sea)
HILL COUNTRY
OF EPHRAIM
Mt. Ebal
Shechem
Mt. Gerizim
Jabbok R.
Tel Aviv
Joppa
Yarkon R.
BENJAMIN MTS.
Rabbah
(Amman)
Jericho
Mt. of Olives
Jerusalem
Mt. Nebo
Bethlehem
ABARIM MTS.
JUDEAN MTS.
FOOTHILLS (SHEPHELAH)
Hebron
Gaza
En Gedi
Arnon R.
Besor Br.
Dead Sea
(Salt Sea)
Beersheba
NEGEV
Mt. Halak
Zered Br.
Wadi of Egypt
Mt.
Seir
DESERT
OF
ZIN
DESERT

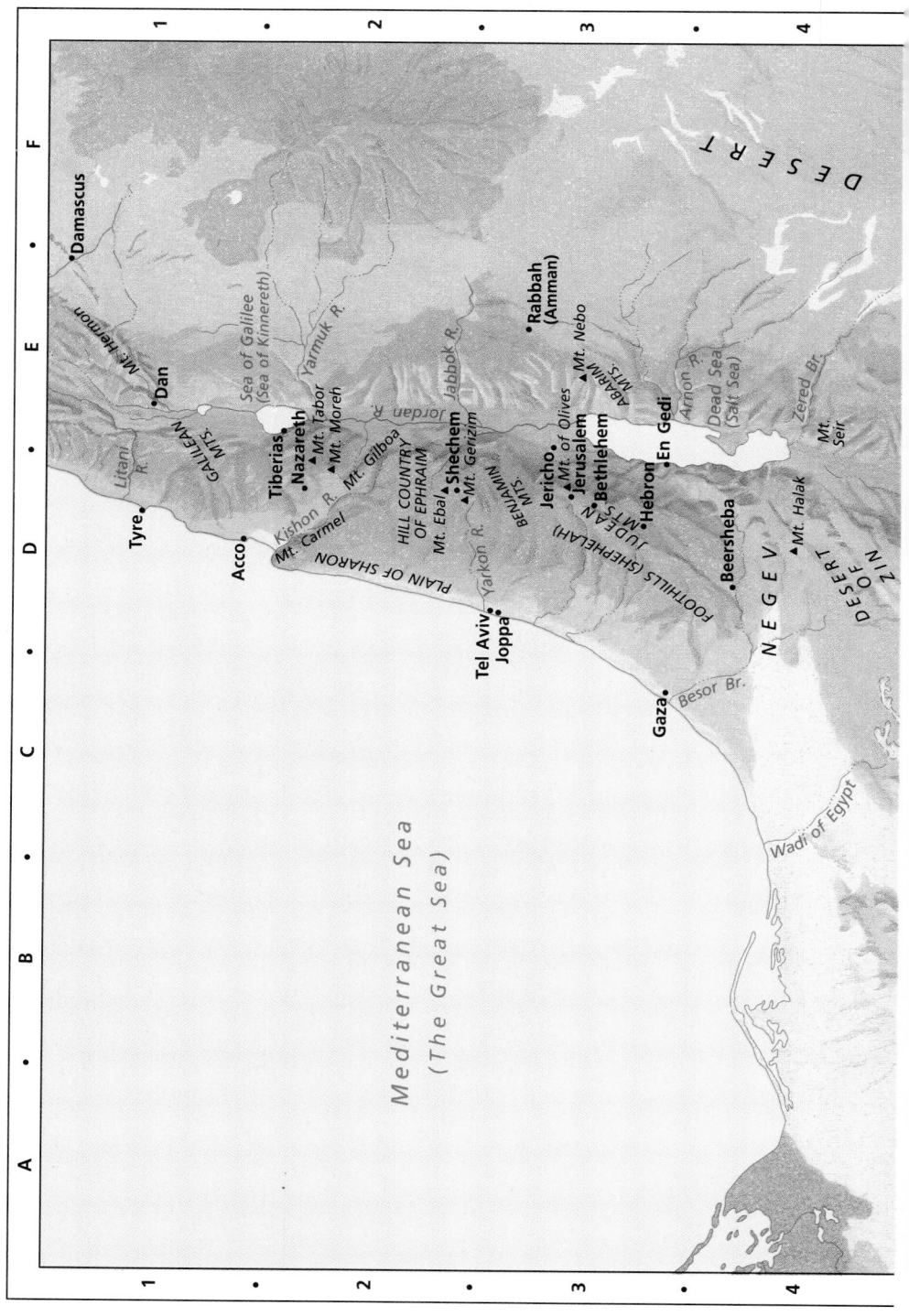

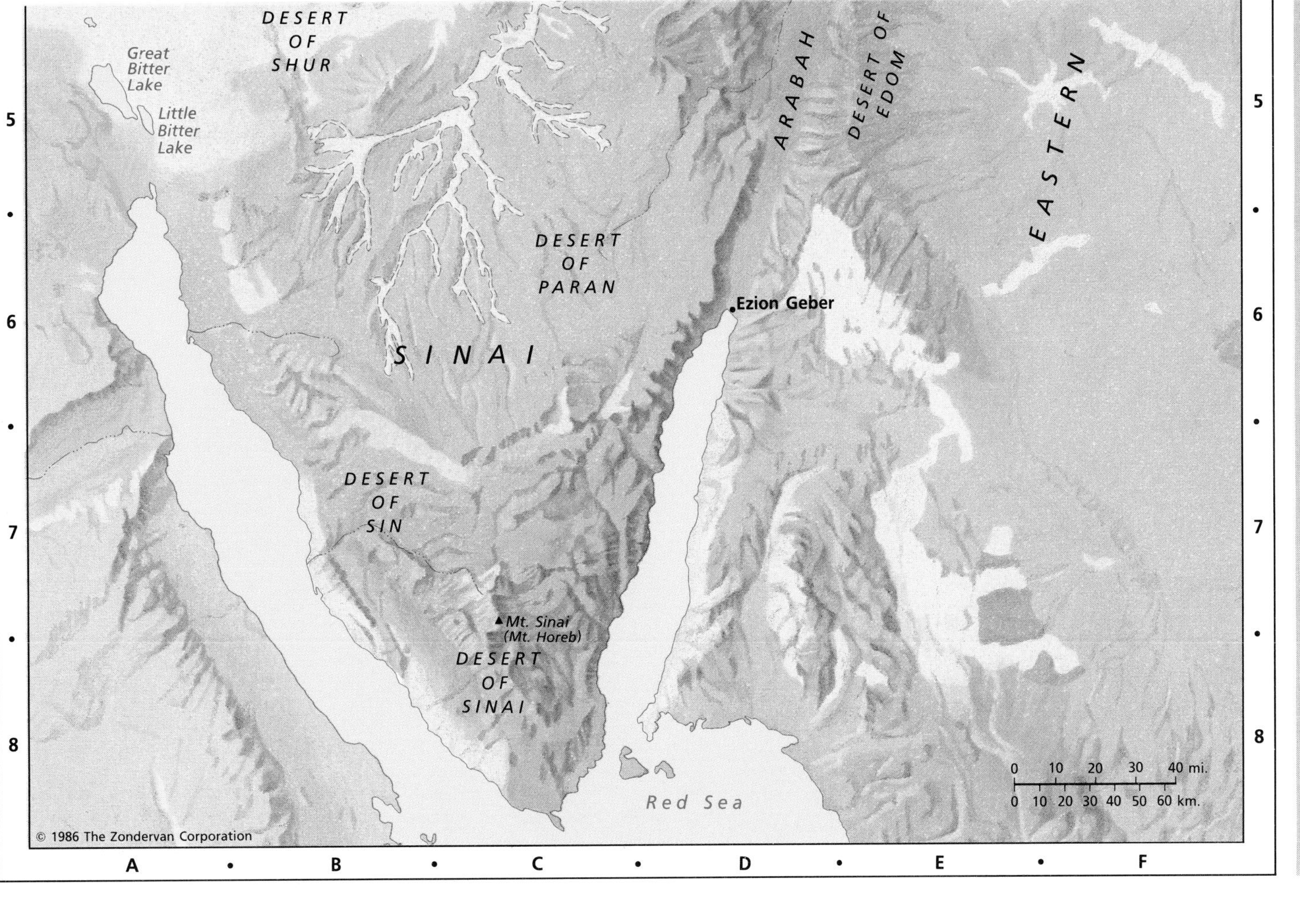
DESERT OF SHUR
Great Bitter Lake
Little Bitter Lake
ARABAH
DESERT OF EDOM
EASTERN
DESERT OF PARAN
Ezion Geber
SINAI
DESERT OF SIN
Mt. Sinai (Mt. Horeb)
DESERT OF SINAI
Red Sea
0 10 20 30 40 mi.
0 10 20 30 40 50 60 km.
A B C D E F
5 6 7 8
© 1986 The Zondervan Corporation

Map 3: EXODUS AND CONQUEST OF CANAAN

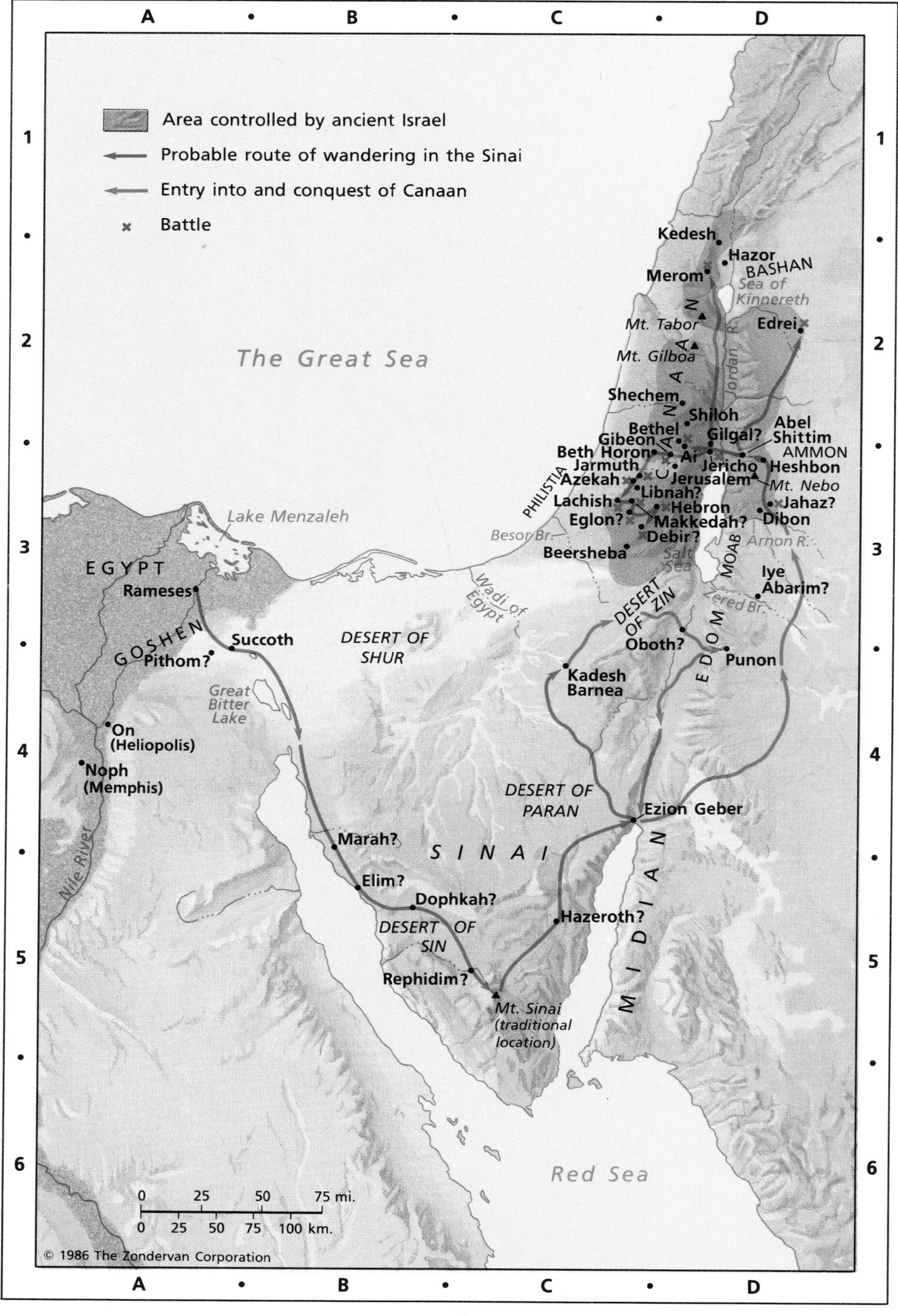

A
B
C
D
1
2
3
4
5
6
Area controlled by ancient Israel
Probable route of wandering in the Sinai
Entry into and conquest of Canaan
Battle
The Great Sea
Kedesh
Hazor
BASHAN
Merom
Sea of Kinnereth
Mt. Tabor
Edrei
Mt. Gilboa
CANAAN
Jordan R.
Shechem
Shiloh
Bethel
Abel Shittim
Gilgal?
Gibeon
Beth Horon
Ai
AMMON
Jarmuth
Jericho
Heshbon
Azekah
Jerusalem
Mt. Nebo
PHILISTIA
Libnah?
Lachish
Hebron
Jahaz?
Eglon?
Makkedah?
Dibon
Debir?
Arnon R.
Besor Br.
Beersheba
Salt Sea
MOAB
Lake Menzaleh
EGYPT
Rameses
Iye Abarim?
Wadi of Egypt
DESERT OF ZIN
Zered Br.
GOSHEN
Succoth
DESERT OF SHUR
Oboth?
EDOM
Pithom?
Punon
Kadesh Barnea
Great Bitter Lake
On (Heliopolis)
Noph (Memphis)
DESERT OF PARAN
Ezion Geber
Marah?
SINAI
MIDIAN
Nile River
Elim?
Dophkah?
DESERT OF SIN
Hazeroth?
Rephidim?
Mt. Sinai (traditional location)
Red Sea
0 25 50 75 mi.
0 25 50 75 100 km.

© 1986 The Zondervan Corporation

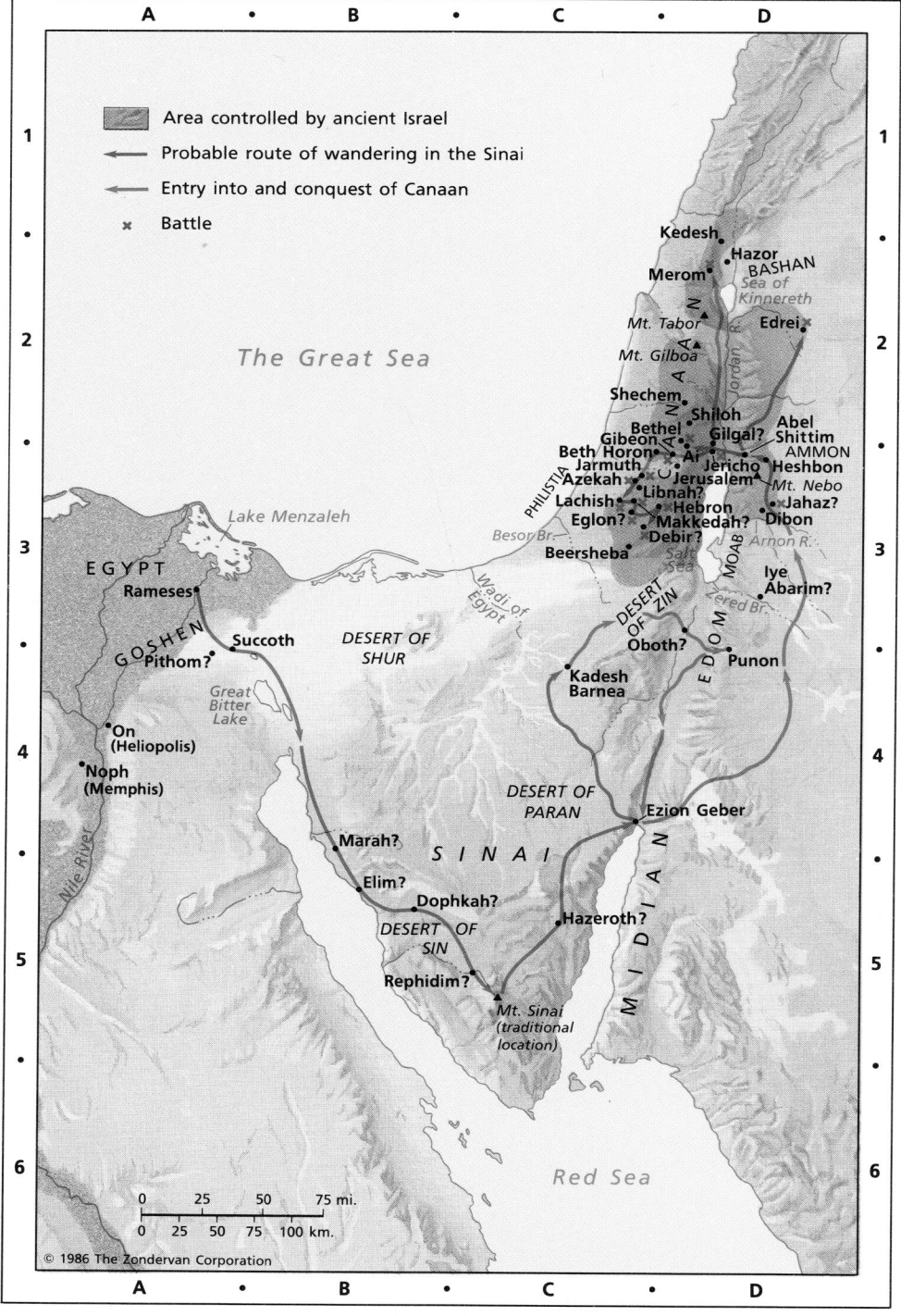

Map 4: **LAND OF THE TWELVE TRIBES**

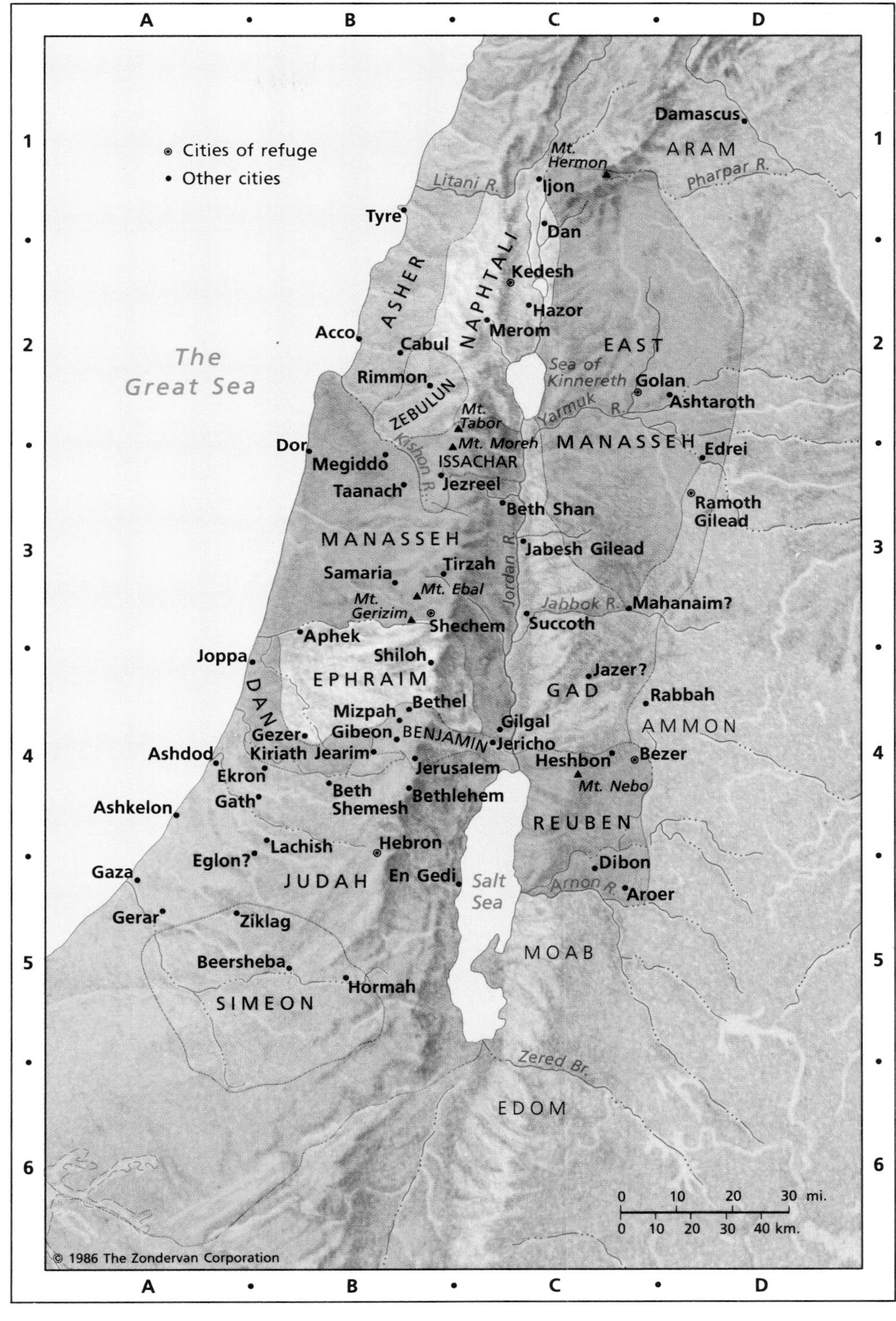

A
B
C
D
1
2
3
4
5
6
Cities of refuge
Other cities
Damascus
ARAM
Mt. Hermon
Pharpar R.
Litani R.
Ijon
Tyre
Dan
ASHER
NAPHTALI
Kedesh
Hazor
Acco
Merom
Cabul
EAST
The Great Sea
Sea of Kinnereth
Rimmon
Golan
ZEBULUN
Ashtaroth
Yarmuk R.
Mt. Tabor
Mt. Moreh
MANASSEH
Dor
Edrei
Megiddo
ISSACHAR
Kishon R.
Taanach
Jezreel
Ramoth Gilead
Beth Shan
MANASSEH
Jordan R.
Jabesh Gilead
Tirzah
Samaria
Mt. Ebal
Mt. Gerizim
Jabbok R.
Mahanaim?
Shechem
Succoth
Aphek
Joppa
Shiloh
Jazer?
EPHRAIM
DAN
GAD
Rabbah
Bethel
Mizpah
AMMON
Gilgal
Gezer
Gibeon
BENJAMIN
Jericho
Ashdod
Kiriath Jearim
Heshbon
Bezer
Jerusalem
Ekron
Mt. Nebo
Beth Shemesh
Bethlehem
Gath
Ashkelon
REUBEN
Lachish
Hebron
Eglon?
Dibon
Gaza
JUDAH
En Gedi
Salt Sea
Arnon R.
Aroer
Gerar
Ziklag
MOAB
Beersheba
Hormah
SIMEON
Zered Br.
EDOM
0 10 20 30 mi.
0 10 20 30 40 km.
© 1986 The Zondervan Corporation

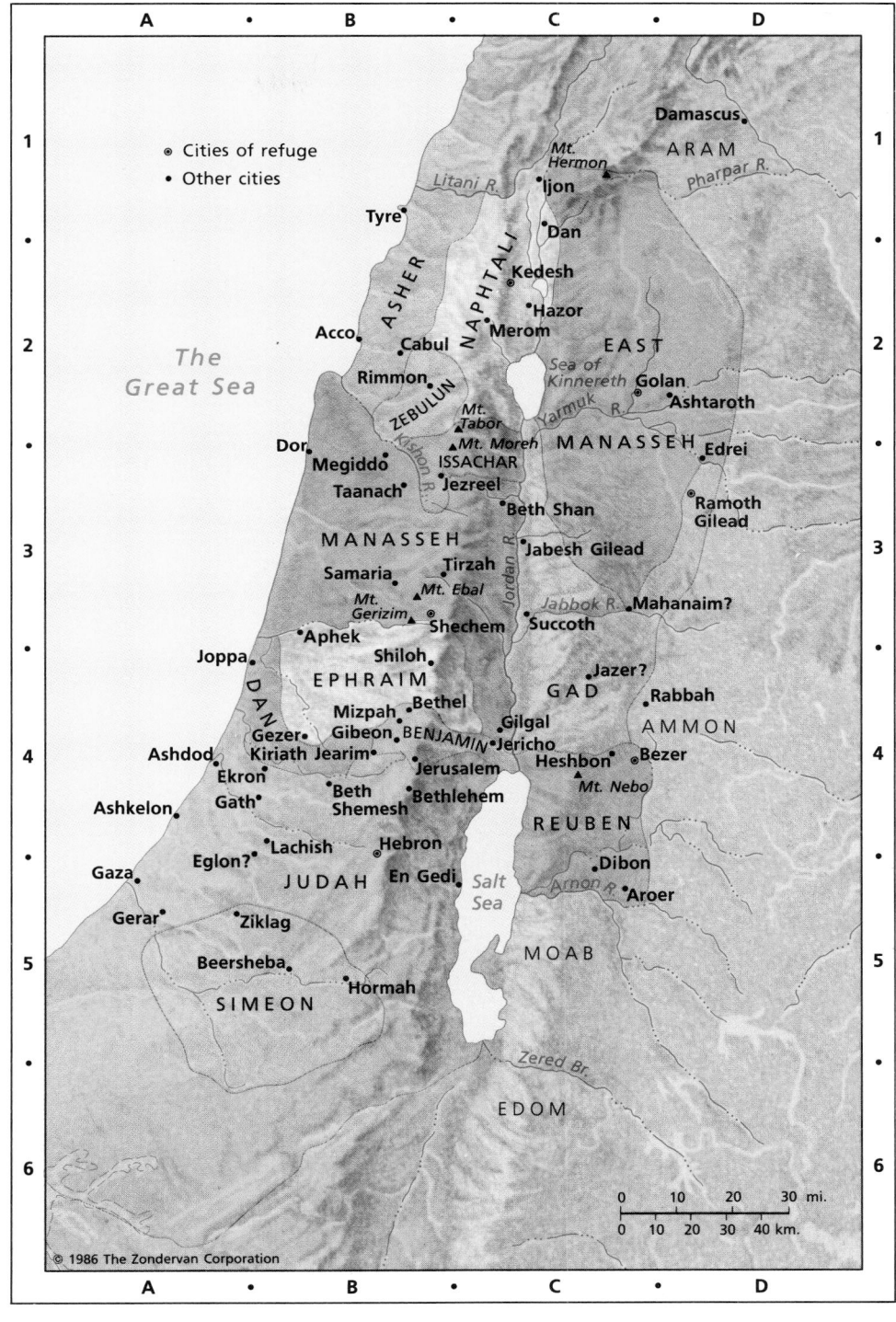

Map 5: KINGDOM OF DAVID AND SOLOMON

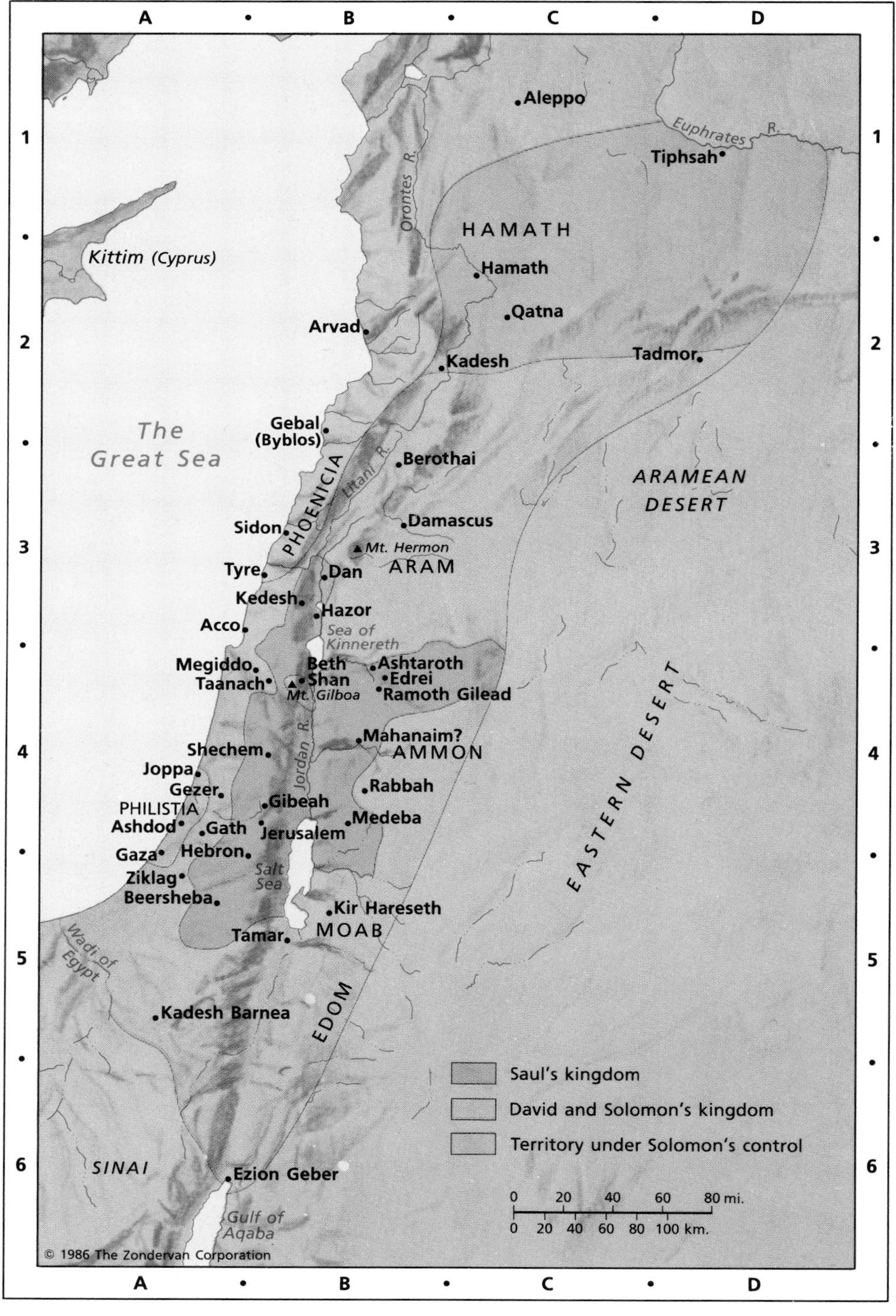

A
B
C
D
1
2
3
4
5
6
Aleppo
Euphrates R.
Tiphsah
Orontes R.
HAMATH
Hamath
Kittim (Cyprus)
Qatna
Arvad
Kadesh
Tadmor
The Great Sea
Gebal (Byblos)
Berothai
Litani R.
PHOENICIA
ARAMEAN DESERT
Damascus
Sidon
Mt. Hermon
Tyre
Dan
ARAM
Kedesh
Hazor
Acco
Sea of Kinnereth
Megiddo
Beth Shan
Ashtaroth
Taanach
Edrei
Mt. Gilboa
Ramoth Gilead
Jordan R.
Mahanaim?
Shechem
AMMON
Joppa
Gezer
Rabbah
PHILISTIA
Gibeah
Ashdod
Gath
Jerusalem
Medeba
Gaza
Hebron
Salt Sea
Ziklag
Beersheba
Kir Hareseth
EASTERN DESERT
Tamar
MOAB
Wadi of Egypt
Kadesh Barnea
EDOM
Saul's kingdom
David and Solomon's kingdom
Territory under Solomon's control
SINAI
Ezion Geber
Gulf of Aqaba
0 20 40 60 80 mi.
0 20 40 60 80 100 km.

© 1986 The Zondervan Corporation

Map 6: **PROPHETS IN ISRAEL AND JUDAH**

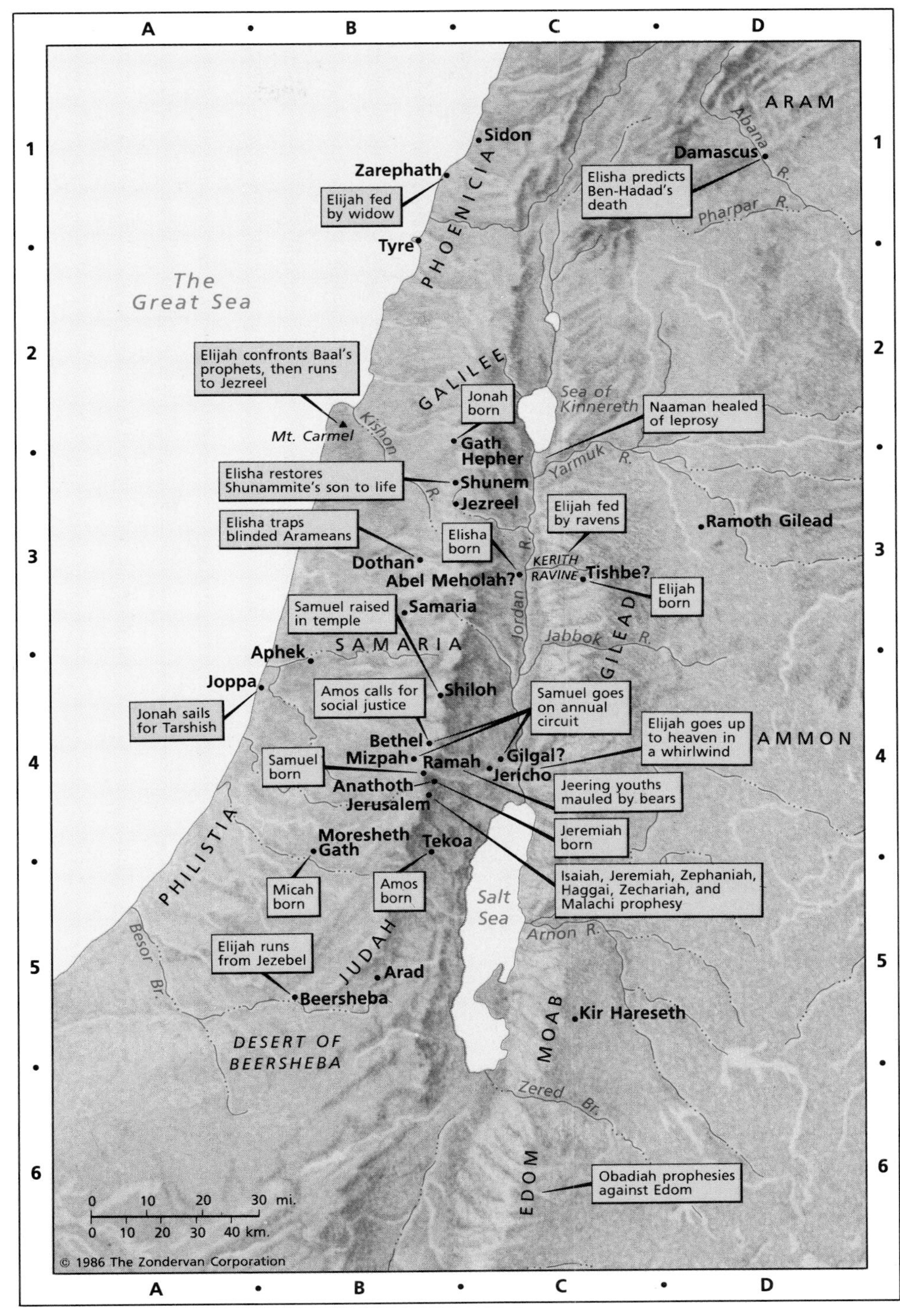

ARAM
Abana R.
Damascus
Elisha predicts Ben-Hadad's death
Pharpar R.
Sidon
Zarephath
Elijah fed by widow
Tyre
PHOENICIA
The Great Sea
Elijah confronts Baal's prophets, then runs to Jezreel
Mt. Carmel
Kishon R.
GALILEE
Jonah born
Sea of Kinnereth
Naaman healed of leprosy
Yarmuk R.
Gath Hepher
Elisha restores Shunammite's son to life
Shunem
Jezreel
Elijah fed by ravens
Ramoth Gilead
Elisha traps blinded Arameans
Elisha born
Dothan
Abel Meholah?
KERITH RAVINE
Tishbe?
Elijah born
Jordan R.
Samuel raised in temple
Samaria
SAMARIA
Jabbok R.
GILEAD
Aphek
Joppa
Jonah sails for Tarshish
Amos calls for social justice
Shiloh
Samuel goes on annual circuit
Elijah goes up to heaven in a whirlwind
AMMON
Bethel
Samuel born
Mizpah
Ramah
Gilgal?
Jericho
Jeering youths mauled by bears
Anathoth
Jerusalem
Jeremiah born
PHILISTIA
Moresheth Gath
Tekoa
Micah born
Amos born
Isaiah, Jeremiah, Zephaniah, Haggai, Zechariah, and Malachi prophesy
Salt Sea
Arnon R.
Besor Br.
Elijah runs from Jezebel
JUDAH
Arad
Beersheba
MOAB
Kir Hareseth
DESERT OF BEERSHEBA
Zered Br.
EDOM
Obadiah prophesies against Edom
0 10 20 30 mi.
0 10 20 30 40 km.
A B C D
1 2 3 4 5 6

© 1986 The Zondervan Corporation

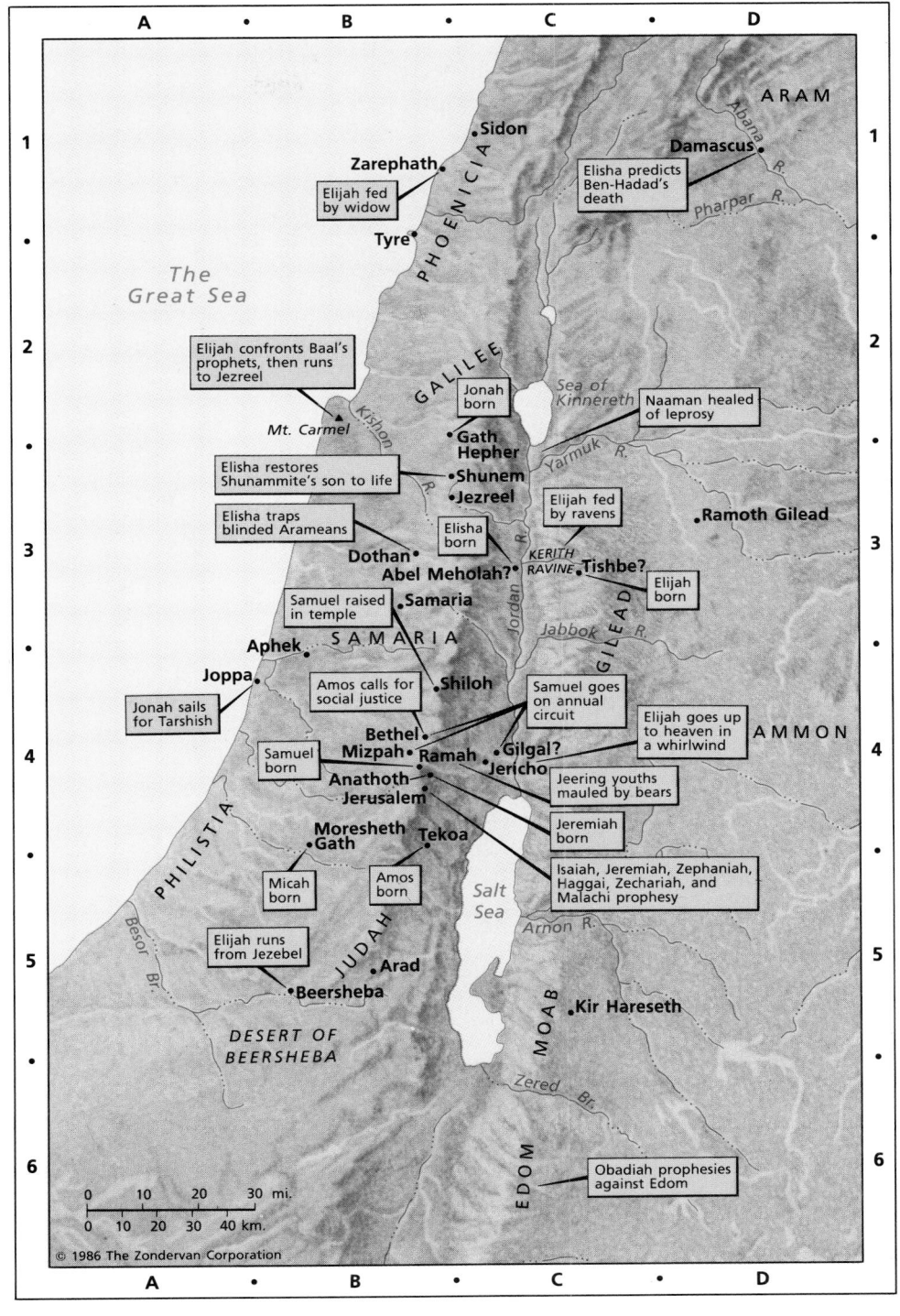

Map 7: ASSYRIAN AND BABYLONIAN EMPIRES

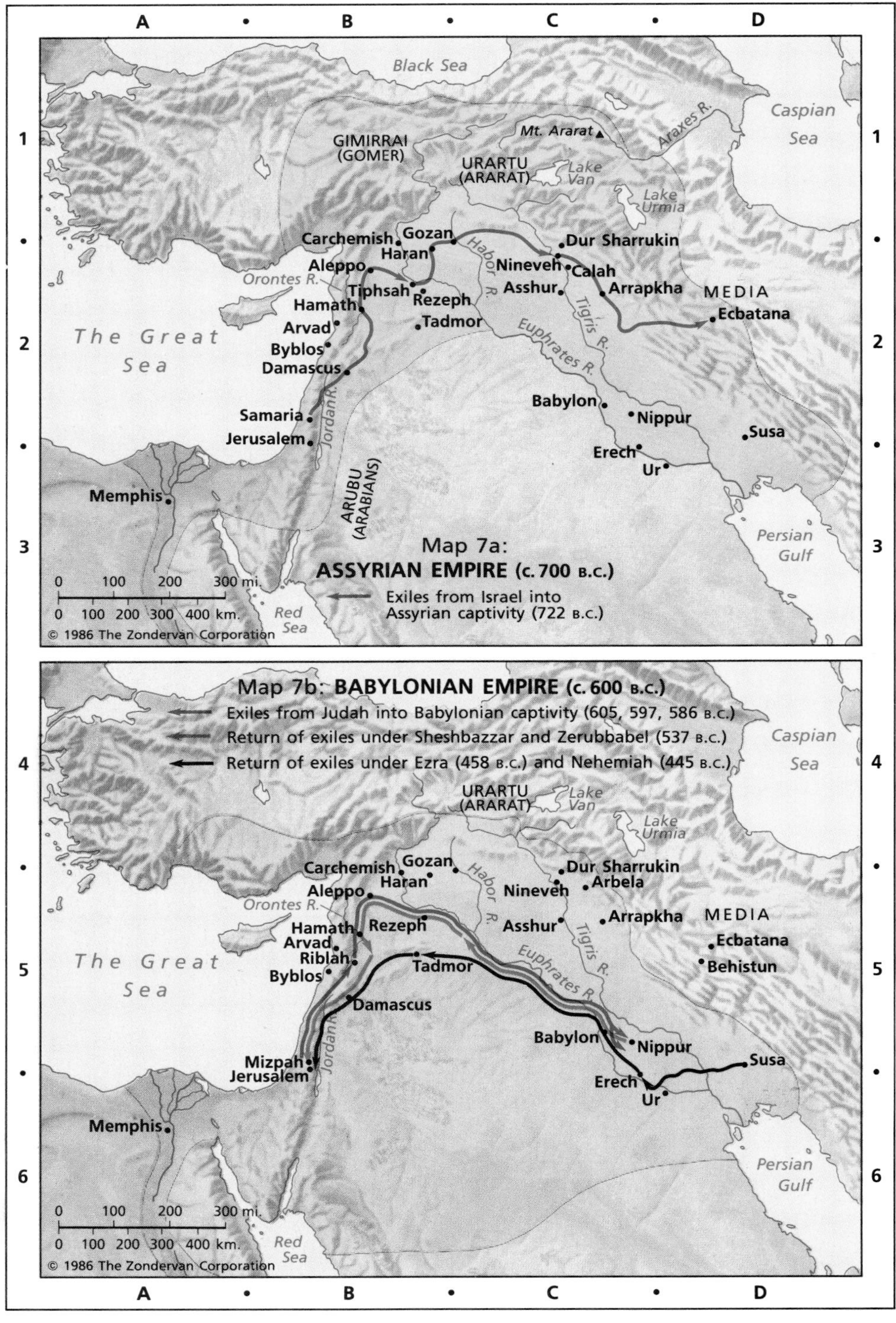

A
B
C
D
1
2
3
4
5
6
Black Sea
Caspian Sea
GIMIRRAI (GOMER)
Mt. Ararat
Araxes R.
URARTU (ARARAT)
Lake Van
Lake Urmia
Carchemish
Gozan
Haran
Dur Sharrukin
Aleppo
Habor R.
Nineveh
Calah
Orontes R.
Tiphsah
Rezeph
Asshur
Arrapkha
MEDIA
Hamath
Ecbatana
Arvad
Tadmor
Tigris R.
The Great Sea
Byblos
Euphrates R.
Damascus
Babylon
Samaria
Jordan R.
Nippur
Jerusalem
Susa
Erech
Ur
Memphis
ARUBU (ARABIANS)
Persian Gulf
Map 7a:
ASSYRIAN EMPIRE (c. 700 B.C.)
Exiles from Israel into Assyrian captivity (722 B.C.)
0 100 200 300 mi.
0 100 200 300 400 km.
Red Sea
© 1986 The Zondervan Corporation
Map 7b: BABYLONIAN EMPIRE (c. 600 B.C.)
Exiles from Judah into Babylonian captivity (605, 597, 586 B.C.)
Return of exiles under Sheshbazzar and Zerubbabel (537 B.C.)
Return of exiles under Ezra (458 B.C.) and Nehemiah (445 B.C.)
Caspian Sea
URARTU (ARARAT)
Lake Van
Lake Urmia
Carchemish
Gozan
Haran
Habor R.
Dur Sharrukin
Nineveh
Arbela
Aleppo
Orontes R.
Asshur
Arrapkha
MEDIA
Hamath
Rezeph
Tigris R.
Arvad
Ecbatana
Riblah
Tadmor
Euphrates R.
Behistun
The Great Sea
Byblos
Damascus
Babylon
Nippur
Mizpah
Jordan R.
Jerusalem
Susa
Erech
Ur
Memphis
Persian Gulf
0 100 200 300 mi.
0 100 200 300 400 km.
Red Sea
© 1986 The Zondervan Corporation

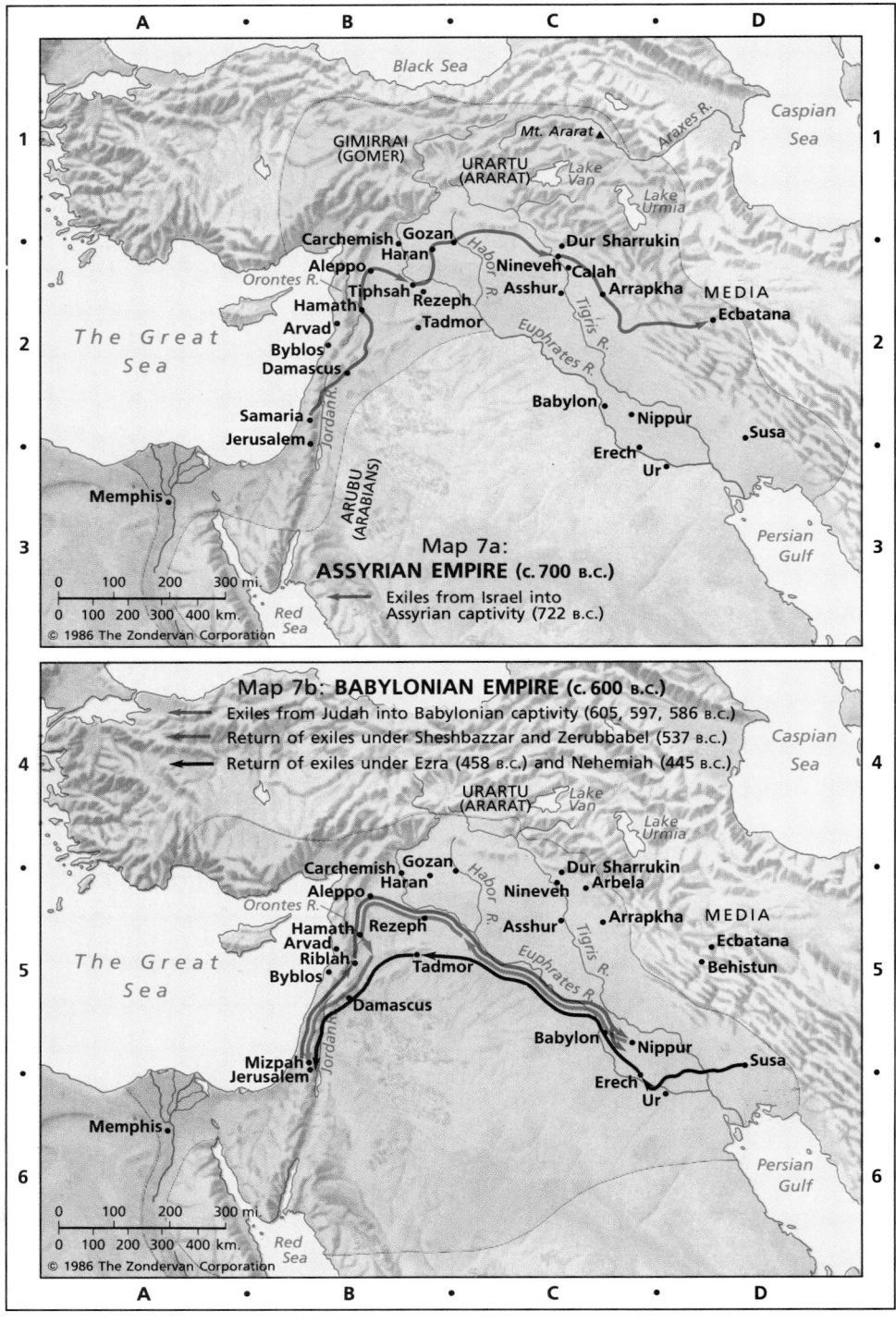

Map 8: **JERUSALEM IN JESUS' TIME**

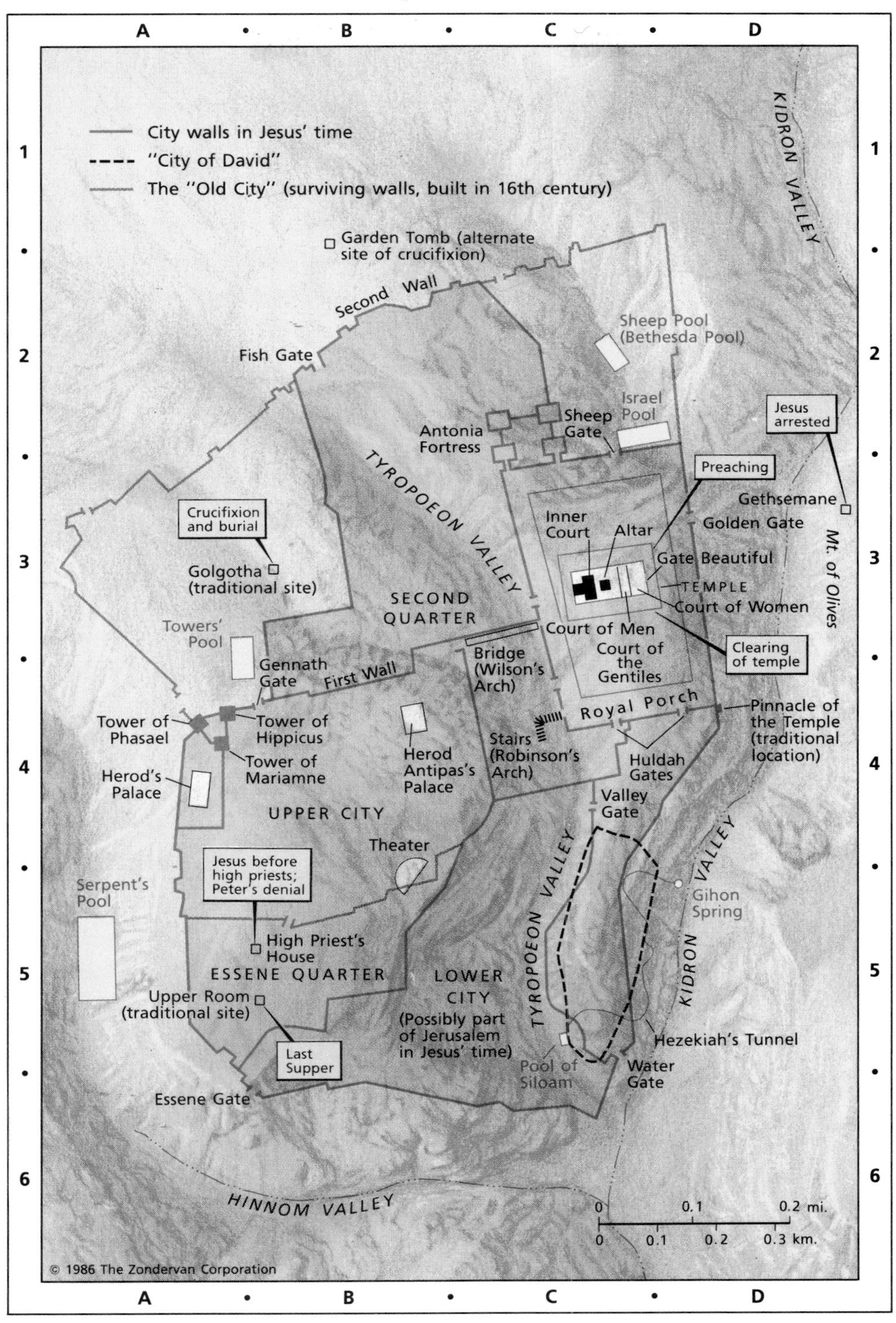

A
B
C
D
1
2
3
4
5
6
City walls in Jesus' time
"City of David"
The "Old City" (surviving walls, built in 16th century)
Garden Tomb (alternate site of crucifixion)
Second Wall
Fish Gate
Sheep Pool (Bethesda Pool)
Israel Pool
Sheep Gate
Antonia Fortress
KIDRON VALLEY
Jesus arrested
Preaching
Gethsemane
Golden Gate
Mt. of Olives
TYROPOEON VALLEY
Crucifixion and burial
Golgotha (traditional site)
Inner Court
Altar
Gate Beautiful
TEMPLE
Court of Women
SECOND QUARTER
Court of Men
Court of the Gentiles
Clearing of temple
Towers' Pool
Gennath Gate
First Wall
Bridge (Wilson's Arch)
Royal Porch
Pinnacle of the Temple (traditional location)
Tower of Phasael
Tower of Hippicus
Tower of Mariamne
Herod Antipas's Palace
Stairs (Robinson's Arch)
Huldah Gates
Herod's Palace
Valley Gate
UPPER CITY
Theater
Jesus before high priests; Peter's denial
Serpent's Pool
Gihon Spring
High Priest's House
ESSENE QUARTER
LOWER CITY (Possibly part of Jerusalem in Jesus' time)
TYROPOEON VALLEY
KIDRON VALLEY
Upper Room (traditional site)
Last Supper
Hezekiah's Tunnel
Pool of Siloam
Water Gate
Essene Gate
HINNOM VALLEY
0 0.1 0.2 mi.
0 0.1 0.2 0.3 km.

© 1986 The Zondervan Corporation

Map 9: **JESUS' MINISTRY**

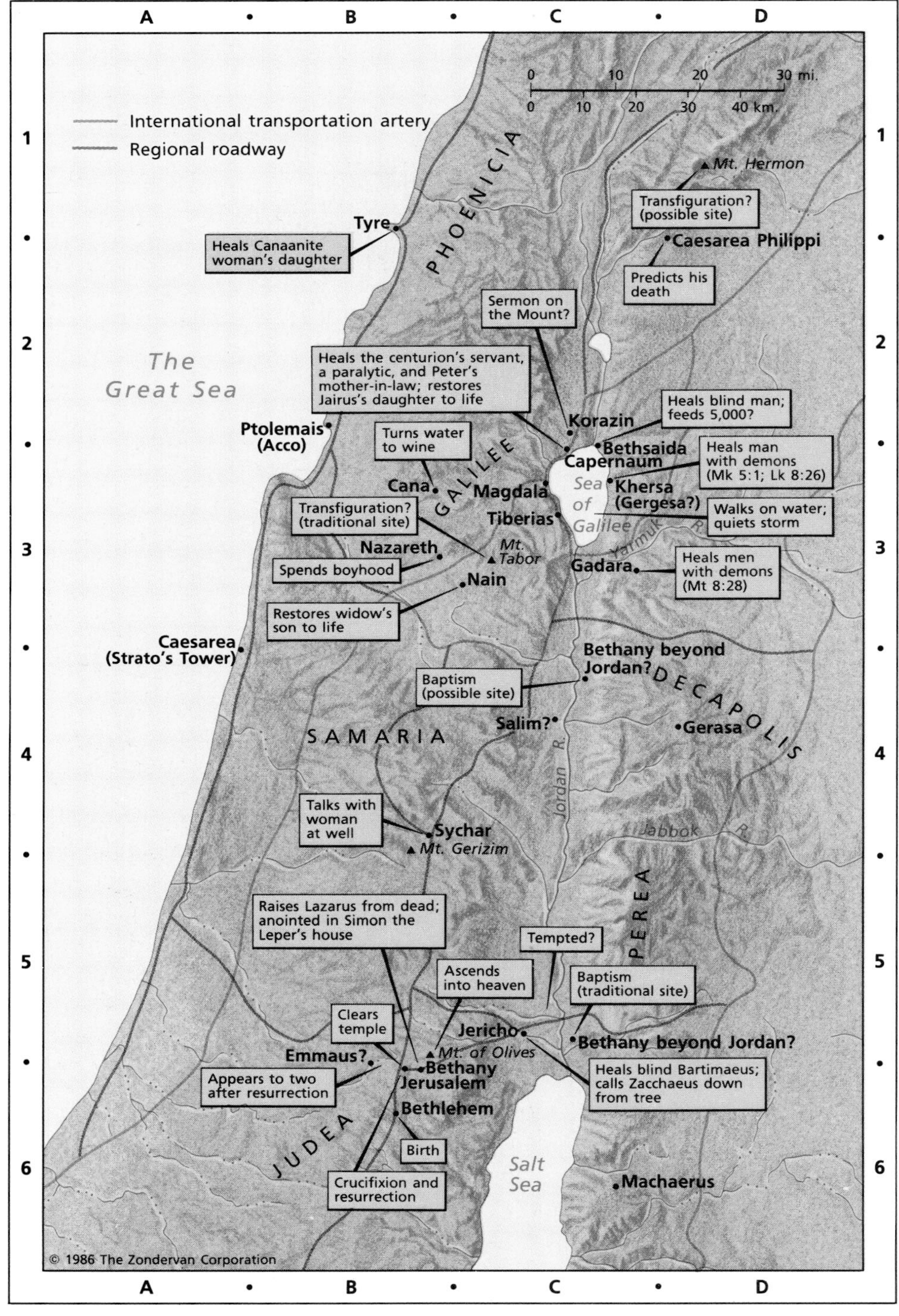

A
B
C
D
1
2
3
4
5
6
0
10
20
30 mi.
0
10
20
30
40 km.
International transportation artery
Regional roadway
The Great Sea
PHOENICIA
Mt. Hermon
Transfiguration? (possible site)
Caesarea Philippi
Predicts his death
Tyre
Heals Canaanite woman's daughter
Sermon on the Mount?
Heals the centurion's servant, a paralytic, and Peter's mother-in-law; restores Jairus's daughter to life
Heals blind man; feeds 5,000?
Korazin
Bethsaida
Capernaum
Ptolemais (Acco)
Turns water to wine
Heals man with demons (Mk 5:1; Lk 8:26)
GALILEE
Cana
Magdala
Sea of Galilee
Khersa (Gergesa?)
Transfiguration? (traditional site)
Tiberias
Walks on water; quiets storm
Yarmuk R.
Nazareth
Mt. Tabor
Spends boyhood
Gadara
Heals men with demons (Mt 8:28)
Nain
Restores widow's son to life
Caesarea (Strato's Tower)
Bethany beyond Jordan?
DECAPOLIS
Baptism (possible site)
Salim?
Gerasa
SAMARIA
Jordan R.
Talks with woman at well
Sychar
Mt. Gerizim
Jabbok R.
PEREA
Raises Lazarus from dead; anointed in Simon the Leper's house
Tempted?
Ascends into heaven
Baptism (traditional site)
Clears temple
Jericho
Bethany beyond Jordan?
Mt. of Olives
Emmaus?
Bethany
Jerusalem
Appears to two after resurrection
Heals blind Bartimaeus; calls Zacchaeus down from tree
Bethlehem
JUDEA
Birth
Salt Sea
Machaerus
Crucifixion and resurrection

© 1986 The Zondervan Corporation

Map 10: **APOSTLES' EARLY TRAVELS**

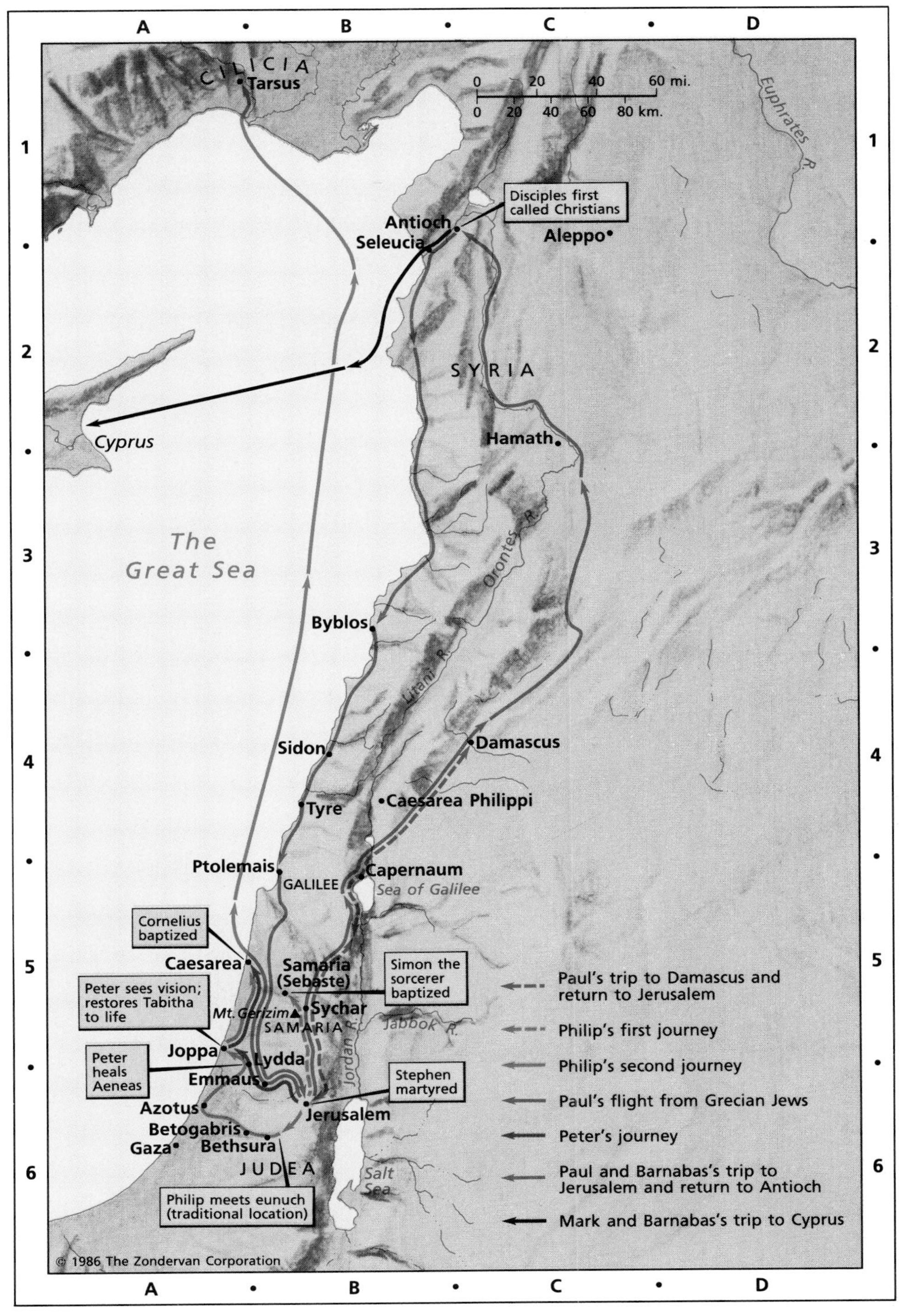

A
B
C
D
1
2
3
4
5
6
CILICIA
Tarsus
0 20 40 60 mi.
0 20 40 60 80 km.
Euphrates R.
Disciples first called Christians
Antioch
Seleucia
Aleppo
SYRIA
Cyprus
Hamath
The Great Sea
Orontes R.
Byblos
Litani R.
Damascus
Sidon
Tyre
Caesarea Philippi
Ptolemais
GALILEE
Capernaum
Sea of Galilee
Cornelius baptized
Caesarea
Samaria (Sebaste)
Simon the sorcerer baptized
Peter sees vision; restores Tabitha to life
Mt. Gerizim
Sychar
SAMARIA
Jabbok R.
Joppa
Lydda
Peter heals Aeneas
Emmaus
Jordan R.
Stephen martyred
Azotus
Jerusalem
Betogabris
Gaza
Bethsura
JUDEA
Salt Sea
Philip meets eunuch (traditional location)
Paul's trip to Damascus and return to Jerusalem
Philip's first journey
Philip's second journey
Paul's flight from Grecian Jews
Peter's journey
Paul and Barnabas's trip to Jerusalem and return to Antioch
Mark and Barnabas's trip to Cyprus

© 1986 The Zondervan Corporation

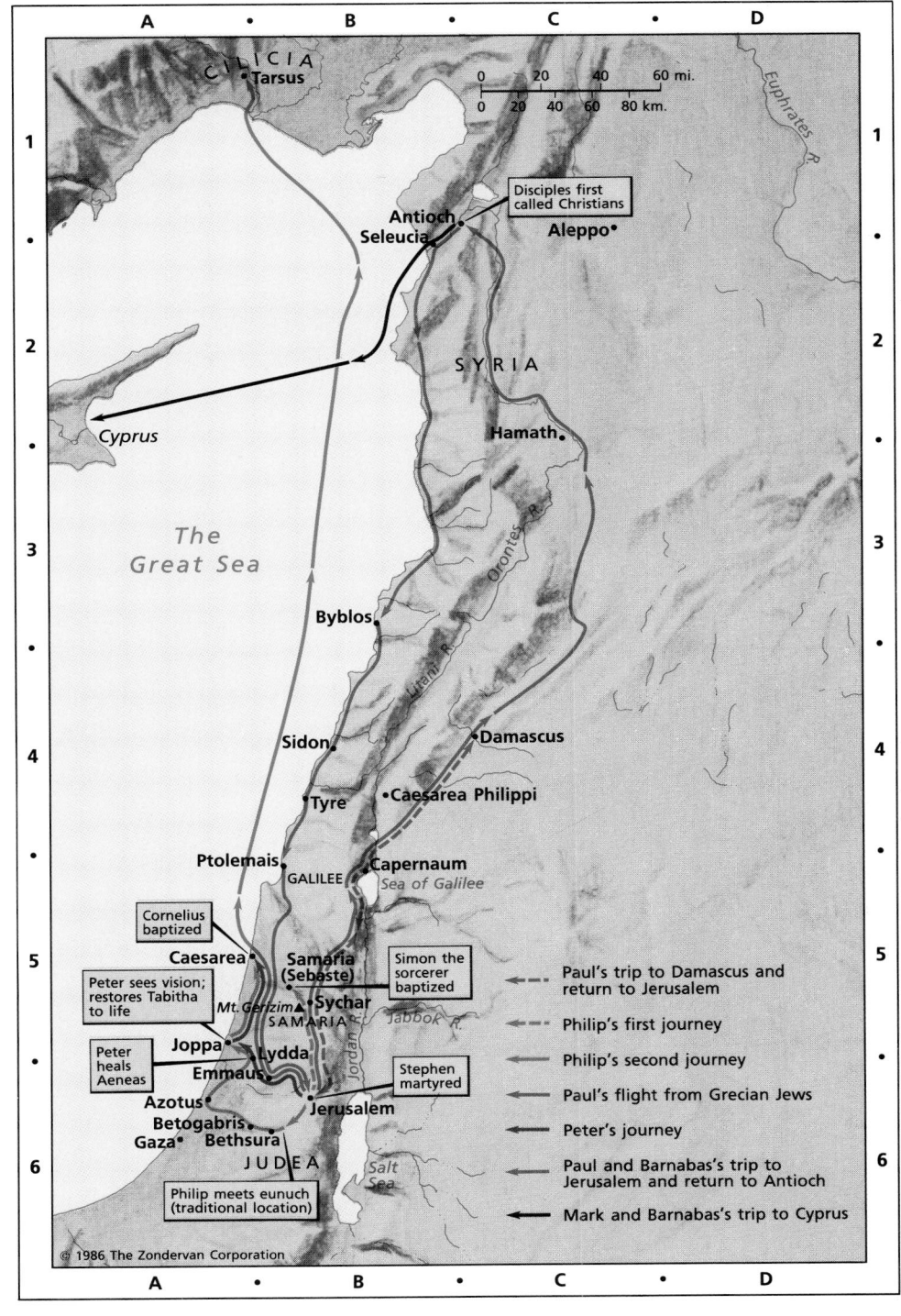

Map 11: **PAUL'S MISSIONARY JOURNEYS**

A
B
C
D
1
2
3
4
5
6
GALLIA
GERMANIA
DALMATIA
ITALY
Adriatic Sea
Corsica
Sardinia
Rome
Forum of Appius
Three Taverns
Puteoli
MACED
Berea
EPIRUS
Tyrrhenian Sea
Rhegium
Ionian Sea
Sicily
Syracuse
ACH
NUMIDIA
Malta
AFRICA
The
TRIPOLITANIA
First Missionary Journey (A.D. 46–48)
Second Missionary Journey (A.D. 49–52)
Third Missionary Journey (A.D. 53–57)
Trip to Rome (A.D. 59–60)

© 1986 The Zondervan Corporation

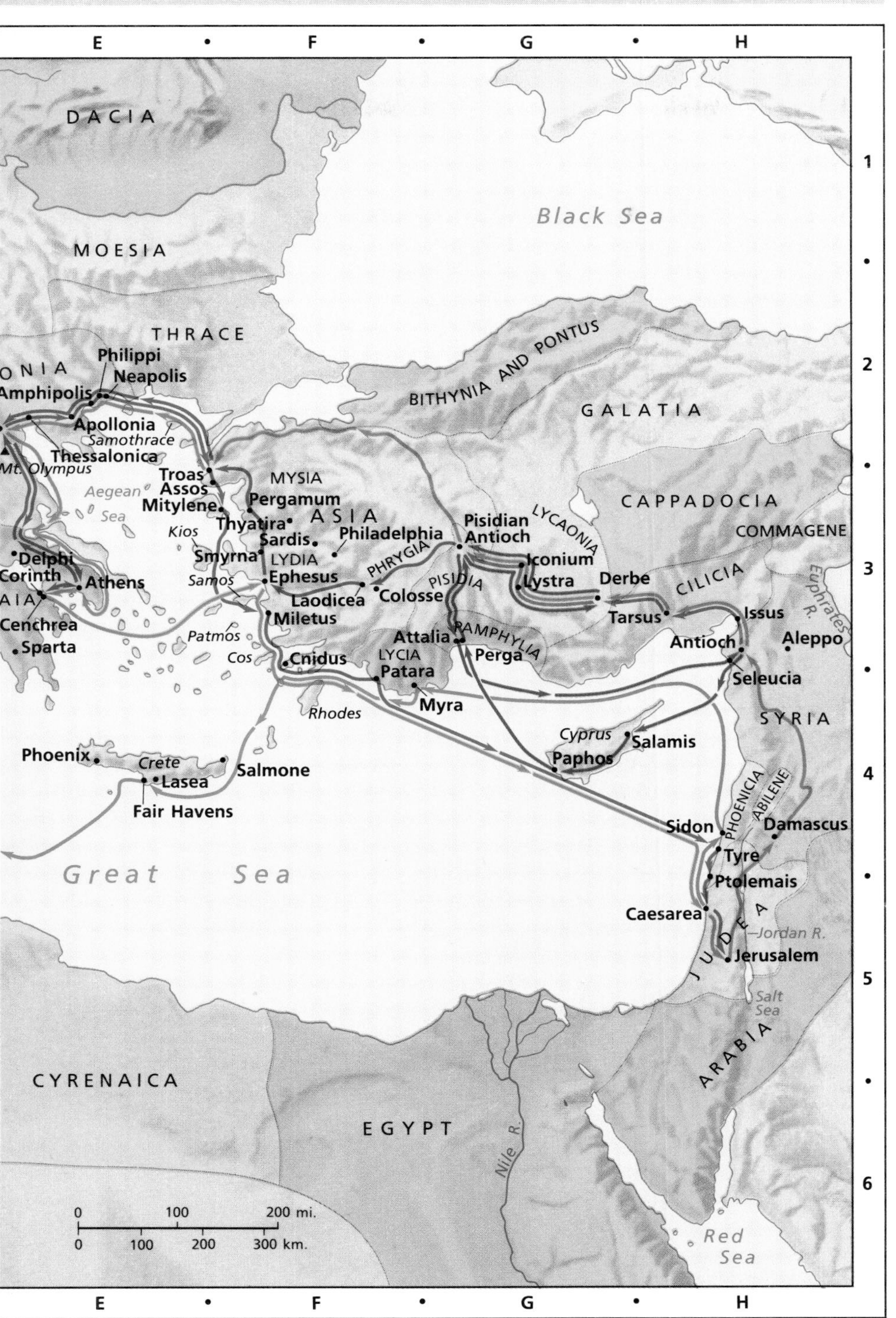
E
F
G
H
1
2
3
4
5
6
DACIA
MOESIA
THRACE
ONIA
Black Sea
BITHYNIA AND PONTUS
GALATIA
CAPPADOCIA
COMMAGENE
Philippi
Neapolis
Amphipolis
Apollonia
Samothrace
Thessalonica
Mt. Olympus
Troas
Assos
Mitylene
Aegean Sea
MYSIA
Pergamum
ASIA
Thyatira
Sardis
Philadelphia
Kios
Smyrna
LYDIA
Delphi
Corinth
Athens
AIA
Cenchrea
Sparta
Samos
Ephesus
Laodicea
Colosse
PHRYGIA
PISIDIA
Pisidian Antioch
LYCAONIA
Iconium
Lystra
Derbe
CILICIA
Tarsus
Issus
Euphrates R.
Aleppo
Antioch
Seleucia
Miletus
Patmos
Cos
Cnidus
LYCIA
Patara
Myra
Attalia
PAMPHYLIA
Perga
Rhodes
Cyprus
Salamis
Paphos
SYRIA
Phoenix
Crete
Lasea
Fair Havens
Salmone
PHOENICIA
ABILENE
Sidon
Damascus
Tyre
Ptolemais
Caesarea
JUDEA
Jordan R.
Jerusalem
Salt Sea
Great Sea
ARABIA
CYRENAICA
EGYPT
Nile R.
Red Sea
0 100 200 mi.
0 100 200 300 km.

Map 12: **THE WORLD TODAY**

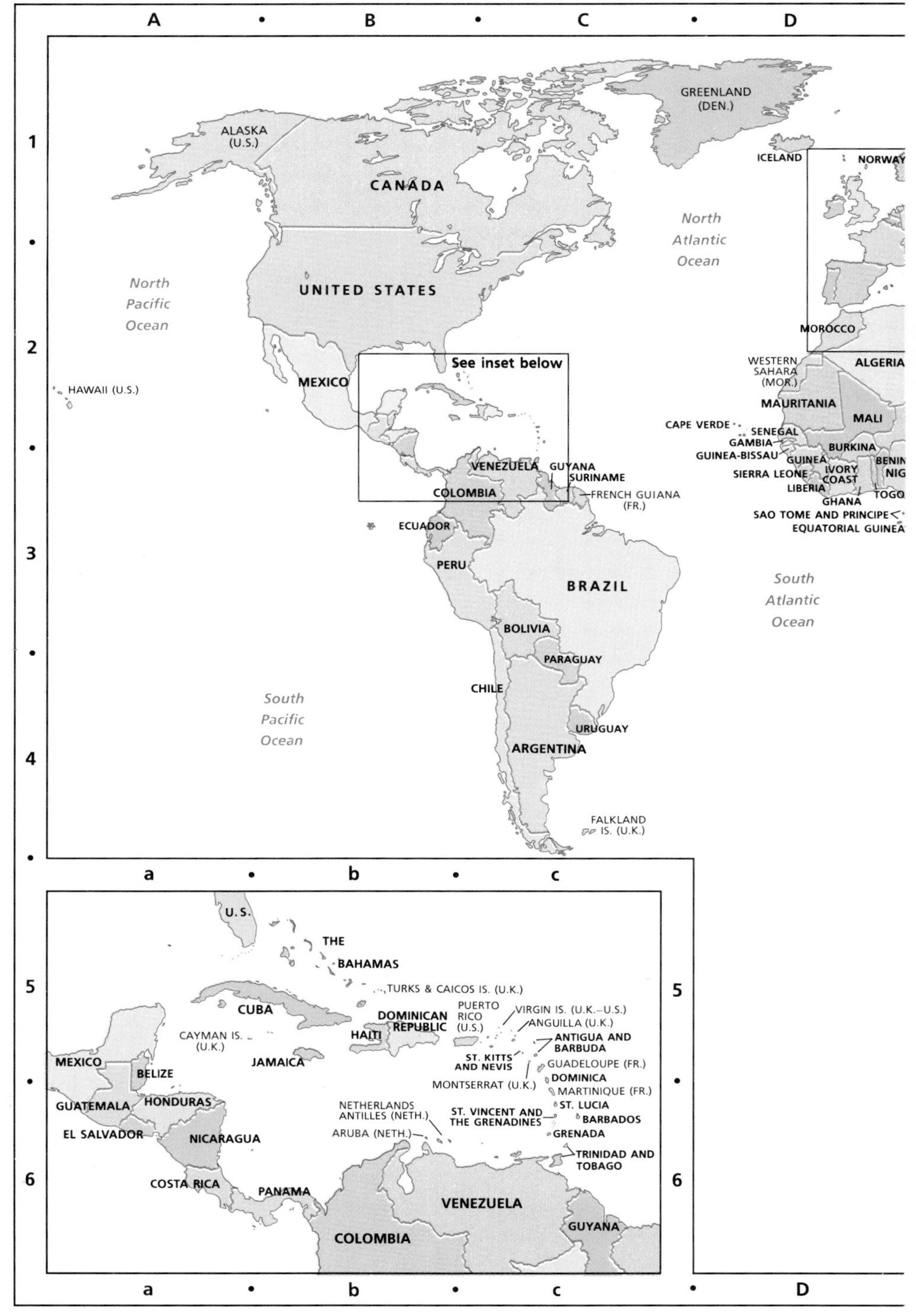
A
B
C
D
1
2
3
4
5
6
a
b
c
GREENLAND
(DEN.)
ALASKA
(U.S.)
CANADA
ICELAND
NORWAY
North
Atlantic
Ocean
North
Pacific
Ocean
UNITED STATES
MOROCCO
See inset below
HAWAII (U.S.)
MEXICO
WESTERN
SAHARA
(MOR.)
ALGERIA
MAURITANIA
MALI
CAPE VERDE
SENEGAL
GAMBIA
GUINEA-BISSAU
BURKINA
GUINEA
BENIN
SIERRA LEONE
IVORY
COAST
LIBERIA
GHANA
TOGO
SAO TOME AND PRINCIPE
EQUATORIAL GUINEA
VENEZUELA
GUYANA
SURINAME
COLOMBIA
FRENCH GUIANA
(FR.)
ECUADOR
PERU
BRAZIL
South
Atlantic
Ocean
BOLIVIA
PARAGUAY
CHILE
South
Pacific
Ocean
URUGUAY
ARGENTINA
FALKLAND
IS. (U.K.)
U.S.
THE
BAHAMAS
TURKS & CAICOS IS. (U.K.)
CUBA
DOMINICAN
REPUBLIC
HAITI
PUERTO
RICO
(U.S.)
VIRGIN IS. (U.K.–U.S.)
ANGUILLA (U.K.)
ANTIGUA AND
BARBUDA
CAYMAN IS.
(U.K.)
JAMAICA
ST. KITTS
AND NEVIS
GUADELOUPE (FR.)
MONTSERRAT (U.K.)
DOMINICA
MARTINIQUE (FR.)
MEXICO
BELIZE
GUATEMALA
HONDURAS
EL SALVADOR
NICARAGUA
NETHERLANDS
ANTILLES (NETH.)
ARUBA (NETH.)
ST. VINCENT AND
THE GRENADINES
ST. LUCIA
BARBADOS
GRENADA
TRINIDAD AND
TOBAGO
COSTA RICA
PANAMA
VENEZUELA
GUYANA
COLOMBIA

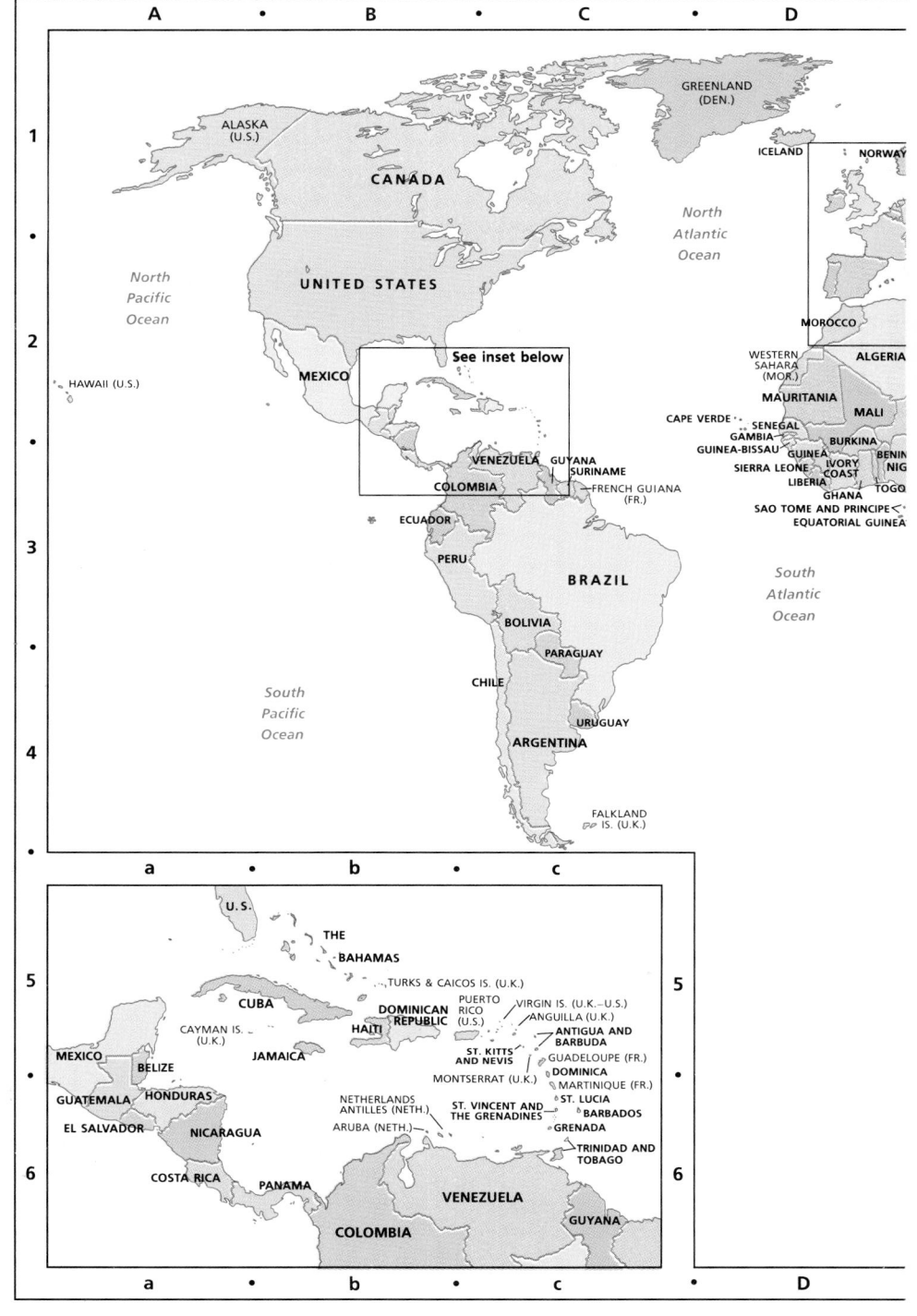

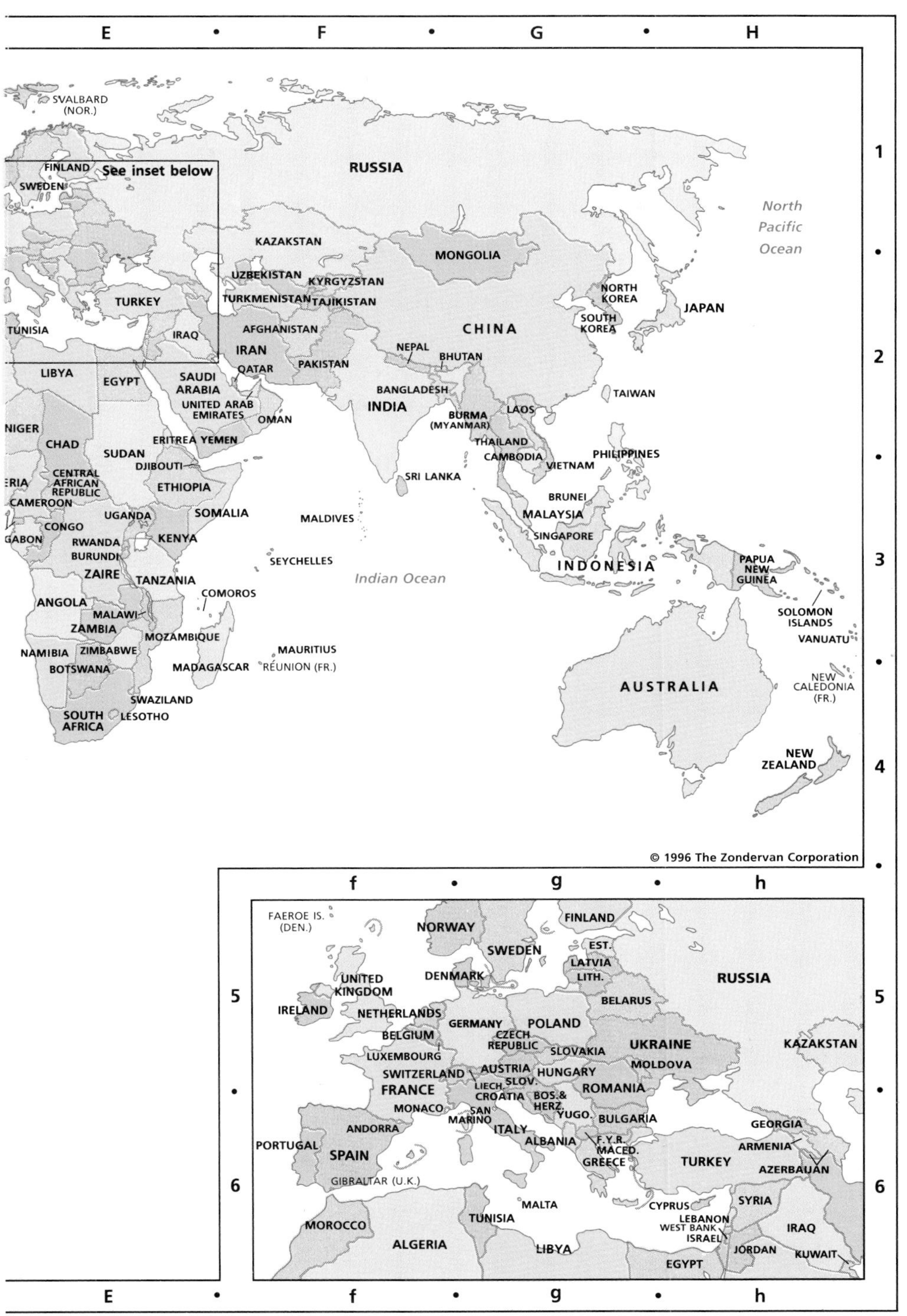
E
F
G
H
1
2
3
4
5
6
f
g
h
SVALBARD
(NOR.)
FINLAND
SWEDEN
See inset below
RUSSIA
North
Pacific
Ocean
KAZAKSTAN
MONGOLIA
UZBEKISTAN
KYRGYZSTAN
TURKMENISTAN
TAJIKISTAN
TURKEY
NORTH
KOREA
JAPAN
SOUTH
KOREA
TUNISIA
IRAQ
AFGHANISTAN
CHINA
IRAN
NEPAL
BHUTAN
LIBYA
EGYPT
QATAR
PAKISTAN
SAUDI
ARABIA
BANGLADESH
TAIWAN
UNITED ARAB
EMIRATES
INDIA
OMAN
BURMA
(MYANMAR)
LAOS
NIGER
ERITREA
YEMEN
CHAD
THAILAND
SUDAN
CAMBODIA
PHILIPPINES
DJIBOUTI
VIETNAM
CENTRAL
AFRICAN
REPUBLIC
ETHIOPIA
SRI LANKA
CAMEROON
BRUNEI
UGANDA
SOMALIA
MALAYSIA
CONGO
MALDIVES
GABON
RWANDA
KENYA
SINGAPORE
BURUNDI
SEYCHELLES
ZAIRE
INDONESIA
PAPUA
NEW
GUINEA
TANZANIA
Indian Ocean
ANGOLA
COMOROS
MALAWI
SOLOMON
ISLANDS
ZAMBIA
MOZAMBIQUE
VANUATU
NAMIBIA
ZIMBABWE
MAURITIUS
BOTSWANA
MADAGASCAR
RÉUNION (FR.)
NEW
CALEDONIA
(FR.)
AUSTRALIA
SWAZILAND
SOUTH
AFRICA
LESOTHO
NEW
ZEALAND
© 1996 The Zondervan Corporation
FAEROE IS.
(DEN.)
NORWAY
FINLAND
SWEDEN
EST.
LATVIA
LITH.
UNITED
KINGDOM
DENMARK
RUSSIA
IRELAND
BELARUS
NETHERLANDS
GERMANY
POLAND
BELGIUM
CZECH
REPUBLIC
UKRAINE
KAZAKSTAN
LUXEMBOURG
SLOVAKIA
MOLDOVA
AUSTRIA
HUNGARY
SWITZERLAND
LIECH.
SLOV.
FRANCE
CROATIA
BOS.&
HERZ.
ROMANIA
MONACO
YUGO.
SAN
MARINO
BULGARIA
GEORGIA
ANDORRA
ITALY
ALBANIA
F.Y.R.
MACED.
ARMENIA
PORTUGAL
SPAIN
GREECE
TURKEY
AZERBAIJAN
GIBRALTAR (U.K.)
MALTA
CYPRUS
SYRIA
TUNISIA
LEBANON
WEST BANK
ISRAEL
IRAQ
MOROCCO
ALGERIA
LIBYA
JORDAN
KUWAIT
EGYPT

Map 13: **ROMAN EMPIRE**

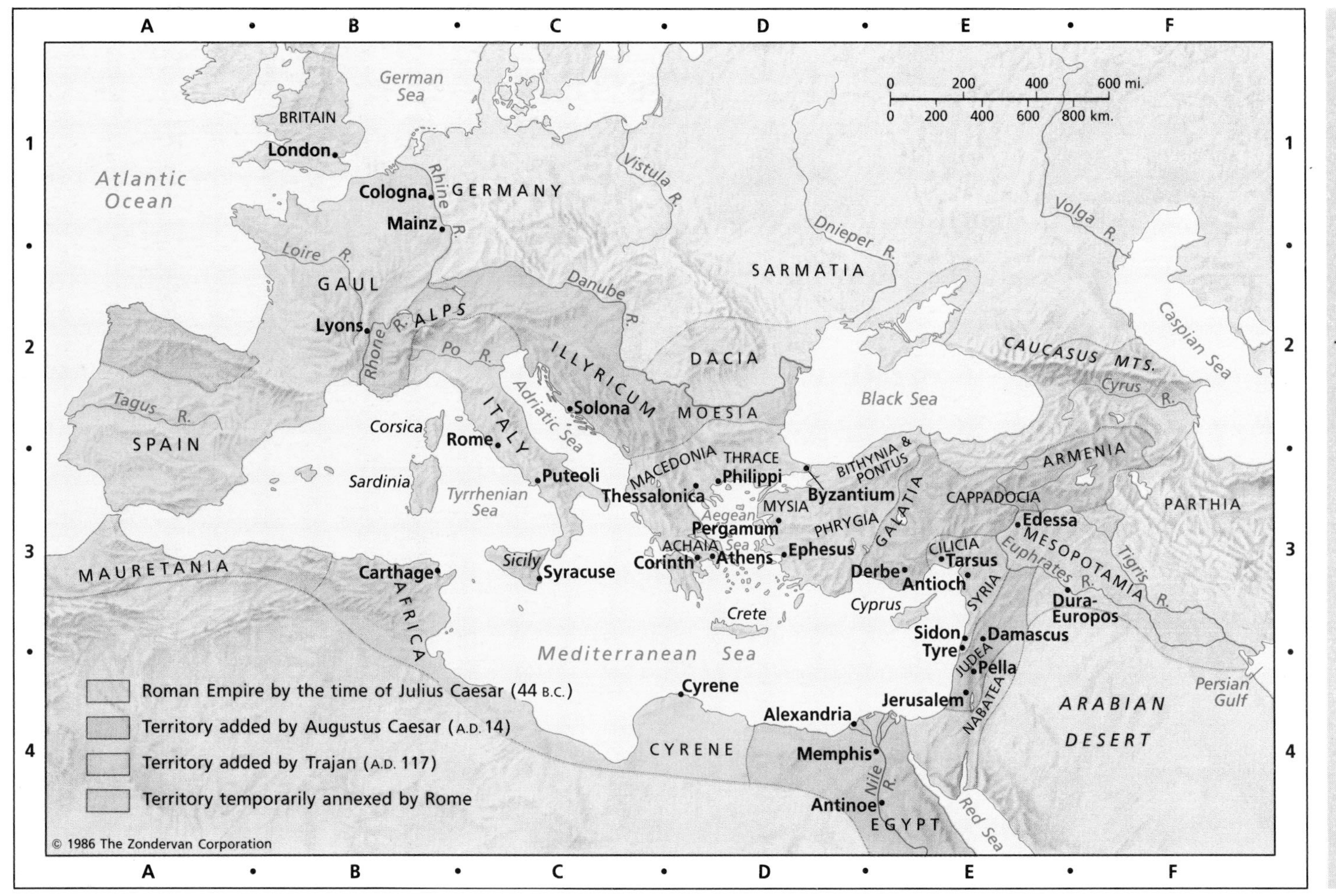

© 1986 The Zondervan Corporation